Olympics 84
USA 40c
Airmail

Olympics 84
USA 13c

Olympics 84
USA

Olympics 84
USA

Olympics 84
USA

Olympics 84
USA

Olympics 84
USA

Olympics 84
USA 28c
Airmail

Olympics 84
USA 28c
Airmail

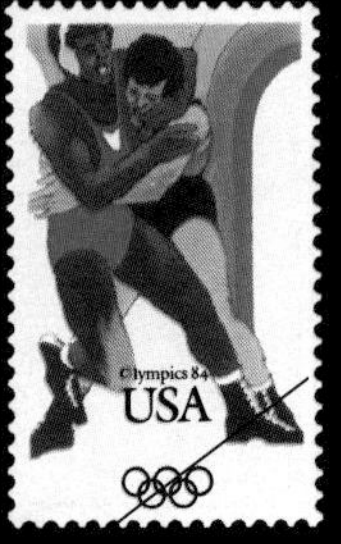

Olympics 84
USA

Olympics 84
USA

Olympics 84
USA 20c

Olympics 84
USA 20c

Olympics 84
USA 20c

Olympics 84
USA 20c

SCOTT®

STANDARD POSTAGE STAMP CATALOGUE

1984

One Hundred and Fortieth Edition
in Four Volumes

VOLUME II

EUROPEAN COUNTRIES and COLONIES
INDEPENDENT NATIONS of
AFRICA, ASIA, LATIN AMERICA
A—F

SCOTT PUBLISHING CO.

3 East 57th St., New York, N.Y. 10022

Publisher—BERT TAUB
Vice-President—ESTELLE DENARO

Catalogue Editor Emeritus—JAMES B. HATCHER

Executive Editor—WILLIAM W. CUMMINGS

Editor—ELAINE MILANO

New Issues Editor—BARBARA A. WEINFIELD

Staff Editors—STEPHEN W. BRAHAM, MARTIN FRANKEVICZ, RICHARD GORDON

Associate Editors—IRVING KOSLOW, GEORGE A. McNAMARA, WILLIAM N. SALOMON, BERT TAUB

Production Coordinator—GAIL D. ISRAEL

Director of Advertising—BRIAN KOSLOW

Advertising Sales—ELEANOR KASMIR

ACKNOWLEDGMENT

The Editor thanks all those many good friends of Scott who have helped this year or in previous years in the task of revising the Standard Catalogue. They have generously shared their stamp knowledge with others through this medium.

No list of aides can be complete, and several helpers prefer anonymity. The following men are chiefly those who have undertaken to assist on one or more specific countries:

Bruce W. Ball
John K. Bash
Brian M. Bleckwenn
Herbert J. Bloch
William G. Bogg
John R. Boker, Jr.
Paul Brenner
George W. Brett

Alex A. Cohen
Herbert E. Conway

Ellery Denison
Pandelis J. Drossos

Daniel S. Franklin

Frank P. Geiger
Brian M. Green
David Gronbeck-Jones

Mihran B. Hagopian
Calvet M. Hahn
J. Hannaney
Leo John Harris
Clifford O. Herrick
Juan J. Holler
Robert L. Huggins
J. R. Hughes

Lewis S. Kaufman
Ernest A. Kehr

Joseph E. Landry, Jr.
Andrew Levitt

David MacDonnell
Robert L. Markovits

Robert P. Odenweller

Souren Panirian
Frank E. Patterson III
Gilbert N. Plass
Henrik Pollak

Alex Rendon
Stanley J. Richmond
Col. Milo D. Rowell

Otto G. Schaffling
Richard Schwartz
Alfredo M. Seiferheld
F. Burton Sellers
Michael Shamilzadeh
Sherwood Springer
Willard F. Stanley

Carlos Vieiro

Richard A. Washburn
John M. Wilson
Paul B. Woodward
Edmund H. Wright

Among the organizations that have helped are:

AMERICAN AIR MAIL SOCIETY
102 Arbor Road, Cinnaminson, NJ 08077

AMERICAN PHILATELIC SOCIETY
P.O. Box 8000, State College, Pa. 16801

AMERICAN REVENUE ASSOCIATION
Bruce Miller, Sec'y, 1010 S. Fifth Ave., Arcadia, CA 91006

AMERICAN STAMP DEALERS' ASSOCIATION
840 Willis Ave., Albertson, N.Y. 11507

ARABIAN PHILATELIC ASSOCIATION
Aramco Box 1929, Dhahran, Saudi Arabia

BRAZIL PHILATELIC ASSOCIATION
Tony DeBellis, 30 W. 60th St., New York, NY 10023

BUREAU ISSUES ASSOCIATION
59 West Germantown Pike, Norristown, PA 19401

CANADIAN STAMP DEALERS' ASSOCIATION
John H. Talman, 35 Victoria St., Toronto, Canada M5C 2A1

CANAL ZONE STUDY GROUP
Alfred R. Bew, Sec'y., 29 S. South Carolina Ave., Atlantic City, N.J. 08401

CHINA STAMP SOCIETY
J. Lewis Blackburn, Pres., 21816 8th Place W., Bothell, WA 98011

CONFEDERATE STAMP ALLIANCE
Jack Solomon, 612 East Park Avenue, Long Beach, New York 11561

COSTA RICA COLLECTORS, Society of
Rt. 4, Box 472, Marble Falls, TX 78654

CROATIAN PHILATELIC SOCIETY
260 Vancouver St., London, Ontario, Canada N5W 4R8

CZECHOSLOVAK PHILATELY, Society for
87 Carmita Ave., Rutherford, N.J. 07070

EIRE PHILATELIC ASSOCIATION
Joseph E. Foley, Sec'y., Box 2352, Denver, CO 80201

ESTONIAN PHILATELIC SOCIETY
Rudolf Hamar, Pres., 243 E. 34th St., New York, N.Y. 10016

FRANCE & COLONIES PHILATELIC SOCIETY
Walter Parshall, Sec'y., 103 Spruce St., Bloomfield, N.J. 07003

FRIEDL EXPERT COMMITTEE
10 East 40th St., New York, N.Y. 10016

GERMANY PHILATELIC SOCIETY
c/o Fred Behrendt, Sec'y., P.O. Box 2034, Westminster, Maryland 21157

GUATEMALA COLLECTORS, International Society of
Henry B. Madden, Pres., 4003 N. St. Charles St., Baltimore, MD 21218

HELLENIC PHILATELIC Society of America
Dr. Nicholas Asimakopulos, Sec'y, 541 Cedar Hill Ave., Wyckoff, N.J. 07481

JAPANESE PHILATELY, International Society for
Lois M. Evans, Sec'y., P.O. Box 752, Quincy, MA 02169

KOREA STAMP SOCIETY, INC.
Forrest W. Calkins, Sec'y., P.O. Box 1057, Grand Junction, Colo. 81502

MEXICO-ELMHURST PHILATELIC SOCIETY INTERNATIONAL
Mrs. Judith Saks, 2310 Veteran, West Los Angeles, CA 90064

OCEANIA PHILATELIC SOCIETY
William Hagan, Pres., 1523 East Meadowbrook Drive, Loveland, OH 45140

PHILATELIC FOUNDATION
270 Madison Ave., New York, N.Y. 10016

POLONUS PHILATELIC SOCIETY
864 N. Ashland Ave., Chicago, Ill. 60622

PORTUGUESE PHILATELY, International Society for
Nancy M. Gaylord, 1116 Marineway West, North Palm Beach, FL 33408

ROSSICA, Society of Russian Philately
Norman Epstein, Treas., 33 Crooke Ave., Brooklyn, N.Y. 11226

EL SALVADOR, Associated Collectors of
Robert Fisher, Box 306, Oaks, Pa. 19456

SCANDINAVIAN COLLECTORS CLUB
Robert B. Brandeberry, 58 W. Salisbury Dr., Wilmington, DE 19809

SOCIETY OF PHILATELIC AMERICANS
Grant C. Ricksecker, Sec'y, 6693 Parma Blvd, Parma Heights,OH 44130

TURKEY & OTTOMAN PHILATELIC SOCIETY
Gary F. Paiste, Sec'y, 4249 Berritt St., Fairfax, VA 22030

UNITED POSTAL STATIONERY SOCIETY
P.O. Box 48, Redlands, CA 92373

ISBN 0-89487-054-8

Library of Congress Card No. 2-3301

CONTENTS OF VOLUME II

See Index at back of book for page numbers

Nations of Europe, Africa, Asia and their colonies, and Latin America appear alphabetically in Vols. II, III and IV.

Vol. II runs from A to F (Territory of the Afars and Issas through Funchal).

Vol. III covers G to O (Gabon through Oltre Giuba).

Vol. IV covers P to Z (Panama through Zambezia).

See Vol. I for United States and Affiliated Territories, United Nations, and British Commonwealth of Nations.

SPECIAL NOTICES

This Catalogue lists adhesive postage stamps of the various countries, except for the United States where additional listings cover revenue stamps and postal stationery.

To facilitate identification, the following style of listing is used:

Cuba

13	A1	1r p gray green	5.00	60
		a. 1r p pale yellow green	7.00	1.50

The number (13) in the first column is the index or identification number; the letter and number combination (A1) indicates the design and refers to the illustration having this (A1) designation; next comes the denomination (1r p) followed by the color (gray green); the prices are in two columns at the right, the first (3.00) being that of an unused stamp and the last (60) of a canceled one. This is known as a major listing or variety.

Variations from so-called "normal" stamps are listed in small type and designated by lowercase letters of the alphabet. These are called minor varieties. When they immediately follow the major listing in the catalogue the original index and design numbers are understood to be the same. In the preceding example, the minor variety, No. 13a, differs from the major variety, No. 13, only in shade; its design, perforation, etc., remain unchanged.

When year, perforation, watermark or printing method is mentioned, the description applies to all succeeding listings until a change is noted. The heading note "Without Gum" applies only to the set it precedes.

When a stamp is printed in black on colored paper, the color of the paper alone is given in italics.

With stamps printed in two or more colors, the color given first is that of the frame or outer parts of the design starting at upper left corner. The colors that follow are those of the vignette or inner parts of the design.

For some sets which include both vertical and horizontal format stamps, a single illustration is used, with the various designs and formats described beneath the illustration.

ABBREVIATIONS

The most frequently used abbreviations are:

Imperf. = Imperforate. Perf. = Perforated. Wmk. = Watermark. Unwmkd. = Unwatermarked. Litho. = Lithographed. Photo. = Photogravure. Engr. = Engraved. Typo. = Typographed.

When no color is given for an overprint or surcharge, it is understood to be in black. Abbreviations are sometimes used, as (B) or (Bk) Black, (Bl) Blue, (R) Red, (G) Green, etc.

NEW ISSUE LISTINGS

Scott's Chronicle of New Issues appears regularly in the Scott's Monthly Stamp Journal and reports new listings.

CONDITION

Condition is the all-important factor of price. Prices quoted are for stamps in fine condition. Extra fine copies often bring higher prices, while unused stamps without gum or with partial gum usually sell for less than copies with full original gum. Prices given in this Catalogue for unused stamps are for specimens which have the major part of the original gum on the back, except, of course, those varieties which were issued without gum. In certain countries, such as Brunswick, a note indicates that prices are for specimens without gum. **Slightly defective stamps which are off-center, heavily canceled, faded or stained are usually sold at large discounts. Damaged stamps which are torn or mutilated or have serious defects seldom bring more than a small fraction of the price of a fine specimen.**

Standards of condition vary greatly in the stamps of different countries. Early United States, Great Britain, Victoria and Japan stamps, for example, were poorly perforated and as a rule heavily canceled. They cannot be obtained in as fine condition as stamps from countries where more care was taken in perforating and lighter cancellations applied.

PRICES

The prices appearing in this Catalogue were estimated after careful study of available wholesale and retail offerings together with recommendations and information submitted by many of the leading philatelic societies. These and other factors were considered in determining the figures which the editors consider represent the proper or present price basis for a fine specimen when offered by an informed dealer to an informed buyer. Sales are frequently made at lower figures occasioned by individual bargaining, changes in popularity, temporary over-supply, local custom, the "vest pocket dealer," or the many other reasons which cause deviations from any accepted standard. Sales at higher prices are usually because of exceptionally fine condition, unusual postal markings, unexpected political changes or newly discovered information. While the minimum price of a stamp is fixed at 3c to cover the dealer's labor and service cost of sorting, cataloguing and filling orders individually, the sum of these list prices does not properly represent the "value" of a packet of unsorted or unmounted stamps sold in bulk which generally consists of only the cheaper stamps.

Prices in italics indicate infrequent sales, lack of pricing information, or that the market value is fluctuating excessively. The condition of early issues of many countries varies greatly. In some instances very fine to superb copies are rarely obtainable. Many of these older issues are priced in italics because the actual value is determined by the condition of each individual stamp.

The absence of price does not necessarily indicate that the stamp is scarce or rare. In the United States listings, a dash in the price column means that the stamp is known in a stated form or variety, but that information is lacking or insufficient for pricing.

Unused prices are for stamps that have been hinged, through 1960, unhinged thereafter. Where used are considerably higher than unused, the price applies to a stamp showing a distinct contemporary postmark of origin.

Beginning around 1900, sometimes earlier, prices for sets are given for most issues of five or more stamps. Unless otherwise noted, the set price excludes minor varieties. The parenthetical number in the set-price line tells the number of stamps in the priced total. Set prices are the sum of the individual prices.

Many countries sell canceled-to-order stamps at a marked reduction of face value. (Exceptions include Australia, Netherlands, France and Switzerland, which sell or have sold CTO stamps at full face value.) It is almost impossible to identify such stamps, if the gum has been removed, as the official government canceling devices are used. Examples on cover and used in the proper period are worth more.

Price changes affecting this Catalogue are published regularly in the Scott Chronicle of New Issues, which is a part of the Scott Stamp Monthly. Subscribe today.

HOW TO ORDER FROM YOUR DEALER

It is not necessary to write the full description of a stamp as listed in this Catalogue. All that is needed is the name of the country, the index number and whether unused or used. For example, "Japan No. 422 unused" is sufficient to identify the stamp of Japan listed as: "422 A206 5y brown."

ADDENDA and NUMBER CHANGES

Stamps received too late to be included in the body of the Catalogue are listed in the Addenda at the back of this volume.

A list of stamps whose catalogue numbers have been changed from those of the preceding edition appears at the back of this volume.

EXAMINATION

Scott Publishing Co. cannot undertake to pass upon genuineness or condition of stamps, due to the time and responsibility involved, but refers collectors to the several expert committees which undertake this work. Neither can Scott Publishing Co. undertake to appraise or identify. The Company cannot take responsibility for unsolicited stamps or covers.

The 1981 edition of the *Scott Standard Postage Stamp Catalogue* was the first to be produced by computer typesetting procedures. For each of the preceding one-hundred thirty-six editions, the *Scott Catalogue* was prepared by "hot-metal" technology. Hot-metal typesetting (using Linotype, Monotype and copper engravings for most of the illustrations) was the state of the art in the early 1900's when the *Catalogue* took its present form. Today, however, hot-metal is a dying art, and it is both slow and expensive.

In order to prepare the *Scott Catalogue* for computer typesetting, several years of systems design, data entry and proofreading were required. Due to the literally millions of characters that have been processed, there will undoubtedly be errors. The editors hope that readers will point out any corrections to the *Catalogue* text.

The advantages of the computer approach are severalfold: the timeliness of price changes in future editions will be improved; the quality of the illustrations will remain constant rather than deteriorating each year: and finally, all of the *Catalogue* information will eventually be incorporated into a "data base" of prices from which new publishing products can be derived for collectors and investors.

COLOR ABBREVIATIONS

amb	amber	chnt	chestnut	ind	indigo	redsh	reddish
anil	aniline	choc	chocolate	int	intense	res	reseda
ap	apple	chr	chrome	lav	lavender	ros	rosine
aqua	aquamarine	cit	citron	lem	lemon	ryl	royal
az	azure	cl	claret	lil	lilac	sal	salmon
bis	bister	cob	cobalt	lt	light	saph	sapphire
bl	blue	cop	copper	mag	magenta	scar	scarlet
bld	blood	crim	crimson	man	manila	sep	sepia
blk	black	cr	cream	mar	maroon	sien	sienna
bril	brilliant	dk	dark	mv	mauve	sil	silver
brn	brown	dl	dull	multi	multicolored	sl	slate
brnsh	brownish	dp	deep	mlky	milky	stl	steel
brnz	bronze	db	drab	myr	myrtle	turq	turquoise
brt	bright	emer	emerald	ol	olive	ultra	ultramarine
brnt	burnt	gldn	golden	olvn	olivine	ven	venetian
car	carmine	grysh	grayish	org	orange	ver	vermilion
cer	cerise	grn	green	pck	peacock	vio	violet
chlky	chalky	grnsh	greenish	pnksh	pinkish	yel	yellow
cham	chamois	hel	heliotrope	Prus	Prussian	yelsh	yellowish
		hn	henna	pur	purple		

INFORMATION FOR COLLECTORS

The anatomy of a stamp can be divided into the following parts: paper, watermark, separation, impression, design and gum.

PAPER

Paper is a material composed of a compacted web of cellulose fibers formed into sheets. The fibers most often used for the paper on which stamps are printed are mulberry bark, wood, straw and certain grasses, with linen or cotton rags added for greater strength. These fibers are ground, bleached and boiled until they are reduced to a slushy pulp known as "stuff." Sizing, or weak glue, and coloring matter may be added to the pulp. Thin coatings of pulp are poured on sieve-like frames which allow the water to run off while retaining the matted pulp. When it is almost dry, the appearance of the pulp is converted by mechanical processes. It may be passed through smooth or engraved rollers (dandy rolls) or placed between cloth in a press that flattens and dries the product under pressure, thus forming a sheet of paper.

Stamp paper falls broadly into two divisions–"wove" and "laid." The differences in appearance are caused by the surface of the frame onto which the pulp is first fed. If the surface is smooth and even, the paper will be of uniform texture throughout, showing no light and dark areas when held up to a light. This is called **Wove Paper.** Early paper making machines poured the pulp on to continuously circulating webs of felt, but modern machines feed the pulp on to a cloth-like screen made of closely interwoven fine wires. This paper, when held up to a light, will show little dots or points, very close together. Technically, it is called "wire wove," but because it is the most common form, it is generally known as "wove paper." Any United States or British stamp printed after 1880 will furnish an example of wire wove paper.

The frames utilized for **Laid Paper** are made of closely spaced parallel wires, with cross wires at wider intervals. Obviously a greater thickness of the pulp will settle between the wires, and the paper, when held up to a light, will show alternate light and dark lines. The spacing and the thickness of the lines may vary, but on any one sheet of paper, they are all alike. (Russia Nos. 31-38.)

If the lines are spaced quite far apart, like the ruling on a writing tablet, the paper is called **Batonné** from the French word meaning a staff. Batonné paper may be either wove or laid. If it is laid, fine laid lines can be seen between the batons. The laid lines, which are actually a form of watermark, may be geometrical figures such as squares, diamonds, rectangles, or wavy lines.

When the lines form little squares, the paper is called **Quadrille.** When they form rectangles instead of squares, the paper is called **Oblong Quadrille.** (Mexico–Guadalajara Nos. 38-41.)

Paper is also classified as thick or thin, hard or soft, and by color if dye was added during production, such as yellowish, greenish, bluish and reddish.

Pelure Paper is an extremely thin, hard and often brittle paper. It is sometimes bluish or grayish. (Serbia No. 170.)

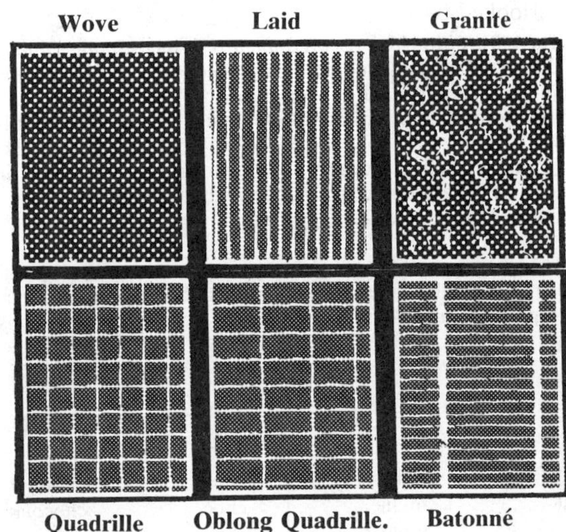

Native Paper is a term applied to the handmade papers on which some of the early stamps of the Indian States were printed. Japanese paper, originally made of mulberry fibers and rice flour, is part of this group. (Japan Nos. 1-18.)

Manila Paper, often used to make stamped envelopes and wrappers, is a coarse textured stock, usually smooth on one side and rough on the other. It is made in a variety of colors.

Silk Paper, introduced by the British in 1847 as a safeguard against counterfeiting, has scattered bits of colored silk thread in it. Silk-thread paper has continuous threads of colored silk arranged so that one or more threads run through the stamp or postal stationery. (Great Britain Nos. 5-8.)

Granite Paper, not to be confused with either of the silk papers, is filled with minute fibers of various colors and lengths in the paper substance. (Austria Nos. 172-175.)

Chalky Paper is coated with a chalk-like substance to discourage the cleaning and reuse of canceled stamps. As the design is imprinted on the water-soluble coating of the stamp, any attempts to remove a cancellation will destroy the stamp. **Collectors are warned not to soak these stamps in any fluid.** If one is to be removed from envelope paper, a good way is to wet the paper from underneath until the gum dissolves enough to slip the stamp off it. (St. Kitts-Nevis Nos. 89-90.)

India Paper, originally introduced from China about 1750, is sometimes referred to as China Paper. It is a thin, opaque paper often used for plate and die proofs by many countries.

Double Paper in philately has two distinct meanings. The first, used experimentally as a means to discourage re-use,is two-ply paper, usually of a thick and thin sheet, joined together during the process of manufacture. Any attempt to remove a cancellation would destroy the design which is printed on the thin paper. The second occurs on the rotary press when the printer glues the end of one paper roll onto the next roll to save time in feeding the paper through the press. Stamp designs are printed over the joined paper and if overlooked by inspectors, may get into post-office stocks.

Goldbeater's Skin, used for the 1886 issue of Prussia, was made of a tough translucent paper. The design was printed in reverse on the back of the stamp, and the gum applied on top of the printing. It is impossible to remove them from the paper to which they are affixed without destroying the design.

Ribbed Paper has an uneven, corrugated surface made by passing it through ridged rollers. (Exists on some copies of U.S. No. 163.)

Various other substances that have been used for stamp manufacture include aluminum, copper, silver and gold foil, plastic, silk and cotton fabrics. Most of these are considered novelties designed for sale to novice collectors.

WATERMARKS

Watermarks are an integral part of the paper as they are formed in the process of manufacture. They consist of small designs such as crowns, stars, anchors, letters, etc. formed of wire or cut from metal that are soldered to the surface of the dandy roll or mold. These pieces of metal (referred to as "bits") impress a design into the paper which may be seen by holding the stamp up to the light. They are more easily seen in a watermark detector, a small black tray. The stamp is placed face down in the tray and dampened with carbon tetrachloride or lighter fluid, which brings up the watermark in dark lines against a lighter background.

WARNING. Some inks used in the photogravure process dissolve in watermark fluids. (See SOLUBLE PRINTING INKS.) There are also electric watermark detectors that come with plastic discs of various colors. When the light is turned on the watermark can be seen through the disc that neutralizes the color of the stamp.

Watermarks may be found reversed, inverted, sideways or diagonal, as seen from the back of the stamp, depending on the position of the printing plates or the manner in which paper was fed through the press. On machine-made paper they normally read from right to left. In a "multiple watermark" the design is repeated closely throughout the sheet. In a "sheet watermark" the design appears only once on the sheet, but extends over many stamps. Individual stamps may carry only a small fraction or none of the watermark.

"Marginal watermarks" occur in the margins of sheets or panes of stamps. Outside the border of some papers a large

Multiple Watermarks of Crown Agents and Burma

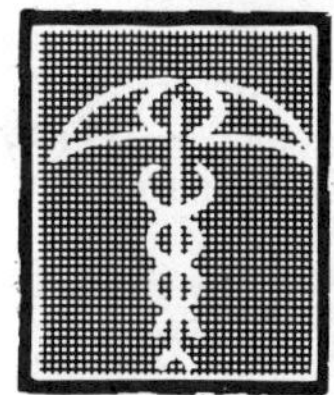

Watermarks of Uruguay, Vatican and Jamaica

row of letters may spell the name of the country or of the manufacturer of the paper. Careless press feeding may cause parts of these letters to show on stamps of the outer rows. **For easier reference watermarks are numbered in the Scott Catalogue. See numerical index of Watermarks at back of this volume.**

SEPARATION

Separation is the general term used to describe methods of separating stamps. The earliest issues, such as the 1840 Penny Blacks, did not have any means provided for separating and were intended to be cut apart with scissors. These are called imperforate stamps. As many stamps that were first issued imperforate were later issued perforated, care must be observed in buying imperforate stamps to be sure they are really imperforate and not perforated copies that have been trimmed. Although sometimes priced as singles, it is recommended that imperforate varieties of normally perforated stamps be collected in pairs or larger pieces as indisputable evidence of their imperforate character.

Separation is effected by two general methods, rouletting and perforating. In rouletting the paper is cut partly or wholly through, but no paper is removed. In perforating a part of the paper is removed. Rouletting derives its name from the French roulette, a spur-like wheel. As the wheel is rolled over the paper, each point makes a small cut. The number of cuts made in two centimeters determines the gauge of the roulette. This is fully explained under "Perforation."

ROULETTING: The shape and arrangement of the teeth on the wheels varies. French names are usually used to describe the various roulettes:

Percé en lignes: rouletted in lines. The paper receives short, straight cuts in lines. (Mexico No. 500.)

Percé en points: pin-perforated. Round, equidistant holes are pricked through the paper, but no paper is removed, which distinguishes it from a small perforation. (Mexico Nos. 242-256.)

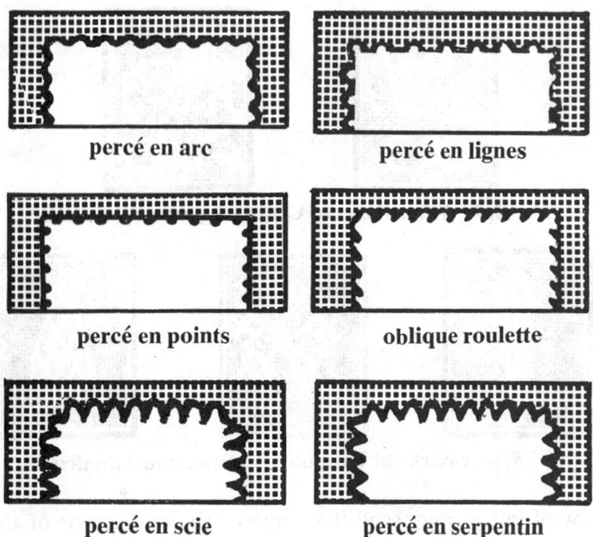

Percé en arc and percé en scie: pierced in an arc or saw-toothed rouletted, forming half circles or small triangles. (Hanover Nos. 25-29.)

Percé en serpentin: serpentine roulette. The cuts form a serpentine or wavy line. (Brunswick Nos. 13-22.)

PERFORATION: The second chief style of separation of stamps, and the one which is in universal use today, is called perforating. By this process the paper between the stamps is cut away in a line of holes, usually round, leaving little bridges of paper between the stamps to hold them together. These little bridges, which project from the stamp when it is torn from the sheet are called the teeth of the perforation. As the size of the perforation is sometimes the only way to differentiate between two otherwise identical stamps, it is necessary to be able to measure and describe them. This is done with a perforation gauge, a ruler-like device that has dots to show how many perforations can be counted in the space of 2 centimeters, the space universally adopted as the length in which perforations are measured. Run your stamp along the gauge until the dots on it fit exactly into the perforations. If the number alongside the dots into which it fits is 11, this means that 11 perforations fit between two centimeters and the stamp is described as "perf. 11." If the gauge of the perforations on the top and bottom of a stamp differs from that on the sides, it is called a "compound perforation." In measuring compound perforations the gauge at the top and bottom is always given first, then the sides. Thus a stamp that measures 10½ at top and bottom and 11 at the sides is described as "10½ x 11." (U.S. No. 1526.)

A perforation with small holes and teeth close together is called a "fine perforation." One with large holes and teeth far apart is a "coarse perforation." If the holes are jagged rather than clean cut, it is called "rough perforation." Blind perforations are the slight impressions left by the perforating pins if they fail to puncture the paper. Multiples showing blind perfs may command a slight premium over normally perforated stamps.

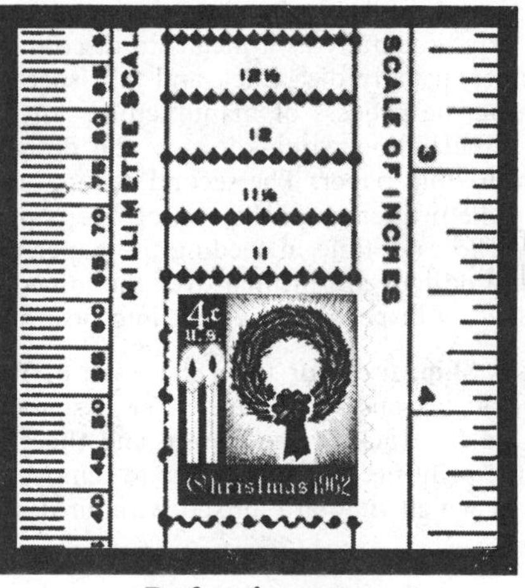

Perforation gauge

PRINTING PROCESSES

ENGRAVING (Intaglio): Master Die—The initial operation in the engraving process is the making of the master die. The die is a small flat block of soft steel on which the stamp design is recess engraved in reverse.

The original art is reduced photographically to the appropriate size, and serves as a tracing guide for the initial outline of the design. After the engraving is completed, the die is hardened to withstand the stress and pressures of subsequent transfer operations.

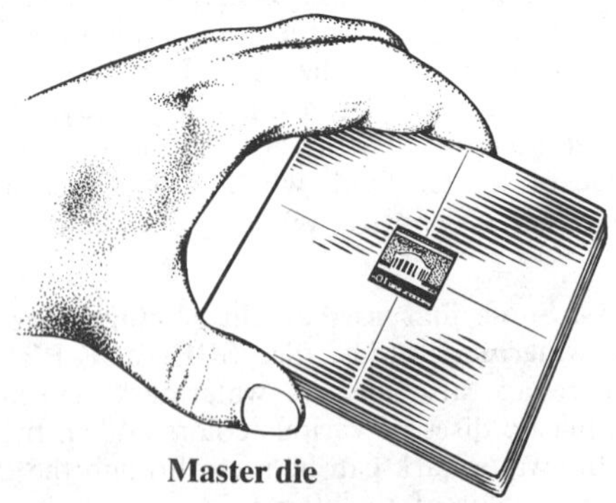

Master die

Transfer Roll—The next operation is the making of the transfer roll which, as the name implies, is the medium used to transfer the subject from the die to the plate. A blank roll of soft steel, mounted on a mandrel, is placed under the bearers of a transfer press, so as to allow it to roll freely on its axis. The hardened die is placed on the bed of the press and the face of the transfer roll is brought to bear on the die under pressure. The bed is then rocked back and forth under increasing pressure until the soft steel of the roll is forced into every engraved line of the die. The resulting impression on the roll is known as a "relief" or a "relief transfer." When the required number of reliefs are "rocked in," the soft steel transfer roll is also hardened.

A "relief" is the normal reproduction of the design on the die in reverse. A "defective relief" may occur during the "rocking in" process due to a minute piece of foreign material lodging on the die, or other causes. Imperfections in the steel of the transfer roll may result in a breaking away of parts of the design. If the damaged relief is continued in use, it will transfer a repeating defect to the plate. Sometimes reliefs are deliberately altered. "Broken relief" and "altered relief" are terms used to designate these changed conditions.

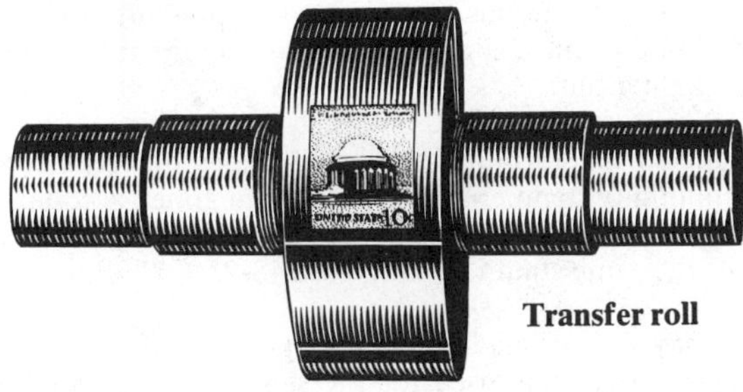

Transfer roll

Plate–The final step in the procedure is the making of the printing plate. A flat piece of soft steel replaces the die on the bed of the transfer press and one of the reliefs on the transfer roll is brought to bear on it. The position on the plate is determined by position dots, which have been lightly marked on the plate in advance. After the position of the relief is determined, pressure is brought to bear and, by following the same method used in making the transfer roll, a transfer is entered, This transfer reproduces in reverse and in detail the design of the relief. As many transfers are entered on the plate as there are to be subjects.

After the required transfers have been entered, the position dots, layout dots and lines, scratches, etc. are generally burnished out. Any required *guide lines, plate numbers* or other *marginal markings* are added. A proof impression is then taken and if "certified" (approved), the plate is machined for fitting to the press, hardened and sent to the plate vault ready for use.

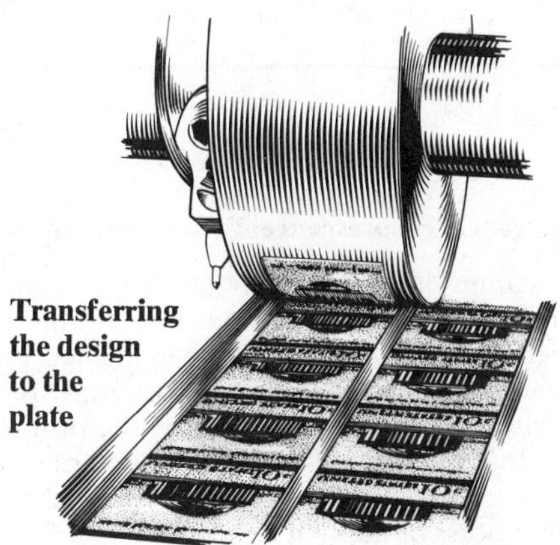

Transferring the design to the plate

On press, the plate is inked and the surface automatically wiped clean, leaving the ink only in the depressed lines. Damp paper under pressure is forced down into the engraved depressed lines, thereby receiving the ink. Consequently, the lines on engraved stamps are slightly raised; and, conversely, slight depressions occur on the back of the stamp.

The expressions *taille douce,* engraved, line engraved and steel plate all designate substantially the same processes for producing engraved stamps.

Rotary Press–Engraved stamps were printed only with flat plates until 1915, when rotary press printing was introduced. *Rotary press plates,* after being certified, require additional machining. They are curved to fit the press cylinder and "gripper slots" are cut into the back of each plate to receive the "grippers," which hold the plate securely on the press, after which the plate is hardened. Stamps printed from rotary press plates are usually longer or wider than the same stamps printed from flat press plates. The stretching of the plate during the curving process causes this enlargement.

Re-entry–In order to execute a re-entry the transfer roll is reapplied to the plate, usually at some time after it has been put to press. Thus worn-out designs can be resharpened by carefully re-entering the transfer roll. If the transfer roll is not precisely in line with the impression on the plate, the registration will not be true and a double transfer will result. After a plate has been curved for the rotary press, it is impossible to make a re-entry.

Double Transfer–A description of the condition of a transfer on a plate that shows evidence of a duplication of all, or a portion of the design. It is usually the result of the changing of the registration between the transfer roll and the plate during the rocking-in of the original entry.

It is sometimes necessary to remove the original transfer from a plate and repeat the process a second time. If the finished re-transfer shows indications of the original impression due to incomplete erasure, the result is also a double transfer.

Re-engraved–Either the die that has been used to make a plate or the plate itself may have its "temper" drawn (softened) and be re-cut. The resulting impressions from such a re-engraved die or plate may differ slightly from the original issue, and are known as "re-engraved."

Short Transfer–It sometimes happens that the transfer roll is not rocked its entire length in entering a transfer on a plate, with the result that the finished transfer fails to show the complete design. This is known as a "short transfer." (U.S. No. 8, type III of 1851-56 1c.)

TYPOGRAPHY (Letterpress, Surface Printing)–As related to the printing of postage stamps, typography is the reverse of engraving. It includes all printing wherein the design is raised above the surface area, whether it is wood, metal, or in some instances hard rubber.

The master die is made in much the same manner as the engraved die. However, in this instance the area not being utilized as a printing surface is cut away, leaving the surface area raised. The original die is then reproduced by stereotyping or electrotyping. The resulting electrotypes are assembled in the required number and format of the desired sheet of stamps. The plate used in printing the stamps is an electroplate of these assembled electrotypes.

Ink is applied to the raised surface and the pressure of the press transfers the ink impression to the paper. Again, as opposed to engraving, the fine lines of typography are impressed on the surface of the stamp. When viewed from the back (as on a typewritten page) the corresponding linework will be raised slightly above the surface.

PHOTOGRAVURE (Rotogravure, Heliogravure)—In this process the basic principles of photography are applied to a sensitized metal plate, as opposed to photographic paper. The design is photographically transferred to the plate through a halftone screen, breaking the reproduction into tiny dots. The plate is treated chemically and the dots form depressions of varying depths, depending on the degrees of shade in the design. The depressions in the plate hold the ink, which is lifted out when the paper is pressed against the plate, in a manner similar to that of engraved printing.

LITHOGRAPHY—This process is based on the principle that oil and water will not mix. The design is drawn by hand or transferred from an engraving to the surface of a lithographic stone or metal plate in a greasy (oily) ink. The stone (or plate) is wet with an acid fluid, causing it to repel the printing ink in all areas not covered by the greasy ink.

Transfers are made from the original stone or plate by means of transfer paper. A series of duplicate transfers are grouped and these in turn are transferred to the final printing plate.

Photolithography—The application of photographic processes to lithography. This process allows greater flexibility of design, relating to use of halftone screens combined with linework.

Offset—A development of the lithographic process. A rubber-covered blanket cylinder takes up the impression from the inked lithographic plate. From the "blanket" the impression is *offset* or transferred to the paper. Because of its greater flexibility and speed, offset printing has largely displaced lithography. Since the processes and results are almost identical, stamps printed by either method are designated as lithographed.

Sometimes two or even three printing methods are combined in producing stamps.

EMBOSSED (RELIEF) PRINTING—A method in which the design is sunk in the metal of the die and the printing is done against a yielding platen, such as leather or linoleum, which is forced up into the depression of the die, thus forming the design on the paper in relief.

Embossing may be done without color (Sardinia Nos. 4-6); with color printed around the embossed area (Great Britain No. 5 and most U.S. envelopes); and with color in exact registration with the embossed subject (Canada Nos. 656-657).

INK COLORS: Pigments or dyes, usually of mineral origin, are used in the manufacture of inks or colored papers on which stamps are printed. The tone of any given color may be affected by numerous factors: heavier pressure will cause a more intense color; slight interruptions in the ink feed will cause a lighter tint.

Hand-mixed ink formulas produced under different conditions (humidity, temperature) at different times account for notable color variations in early printings, mostly 19th century, of the same stamp (U.S. Nos. 248-250, 279B, etc.).

Colors may vary in shade because papers of different quality and consistency were used for the same printing. Most pelure papers, for example, show a richer color when compared to wove or laid papers. (Russia No. 181a.)

The very nature of the printing processes can cause a variety of differences in shades or hues of the same stamp. Some of these shades are scarcer than others, and are of particular interest to the advanced collector.

SOLUBLE PRINTING INKS. WARNING. Most stamp colors are permanent. That is, they are not seriously affected by light or water. Some colors may fade from excessive exposure to light. Other stamps are printed in inks which dissolve easily in water or in benzine, carbon tetrachloride or other fluids used to detect watermarks. These inks were often used intentionally to prevent the removal of cancellations.

Benzine affects most photogravure printings. Water affects all aniline prints, those on safety paper, and some photogravure printings. All the above are called *fugitive colors.*

TAGGED STAMPS

(Luminescence, Fluorescence, Phosphorescence)

Some tagged stamps have bars (Great Britain, Canada), frames (South Africa), or an overall coating of luminescent material applied after the stamps have been printed (United States). Another tagging method is to incorporate the luminescent material into some or all colors of the printing ink (Australia No. 366, Netherlands No. 478). A third is to mix the luminescent material with the pulp during the paper manufacturing process or apply it as a surface coating afterwards. These are called "fluorescent" papers. (Switzerland Nos. 510-514, Germany No. 848.)

The treated stamps show up in specific colors when exposed to ultraviolet light. The wave length of the luminescent material determines the colors and activates the triggering mechanism of the electronic machinery for sorting, facing or canceling letters.

Various fluorescent substances have been used as paper whiteners, but the resulting "hi-brite papers" show up differently under ultraviolet light and do not trigger the machines. They are not noted in the Catalogue.

Introduced in Great Britain in 1959 on an experimental basis, tagging in its various forms is now used by many countries to expedite the handling of mail. Following Great Britain were Germany ('61); Canada and Denmark ('62); United States, Australia, Netherlands and Switzerland ('63); Belgium and Japan ('66); Sweden and Norway ('67); Italy ('68); Russia ('69), and so forth.

Certain stamps were issued both with and without the luminescent factor. In these instances, the "tagged" variety is listed in the United States, Canada, Great Britain and Switzerland, and is noted in some of the other countries.

GUM

The gum on a stamp's back may be smooth, crinkly, dark, white, colored or tinted, and either obvious or virtually invisible as on Canada No. 453 or Rwanda Nos. 287-294. Most stamp gumming has been carried out with adhesives using gum arabic or dextrine as a base, but certain polymers such as polyvinyl alcohol (PVA) have been used extensively since World War II. The PVA gum which Harrison & Sons of Great Britain introduced in 1968 is dull, slightly yellowish and almost invisible.

Stamps having full **original gum** sell for more than those from which the gum has been removed. Reprints may have gum differing from the originals.

REPRINTS AND REISSUES

Reprints are impressions of stamps (usually obsolete) made from the original plates or stones. If valid for postage and from obsolete issues, they are called reissues. If they are from current issues, they are *second, third,* etc. *printings.* If designated for a particular purpose, they are called *special printings.*

When reprints are not valid for postage, but made from original dies and plates by authorized persons they are *official reprints*—to distinguish them from *private reprints* made from original plates and dies by private hands. *Official reproductions* or imitations are made from new dies and plates by government authorization.

For the 1876 Centennial, the U.S. government made official imitations of its first postage stamps, which are listed as Nos. 3-4; official reprints of the demonetized pre-1861 issues; reissued the 1869 stamps and made special printings of the current 1875 denominations. An example of the private reprint is that of the New Haven postmaster's provisional.

Most reprints differ slightly from the original stamp in some characteristic such as gum, paper, perforation, color, watermark (or lack thereof). Sometimes the details have been followed so meticulously that only a student of that stamp can tell the reprint from the original.

REMAINDERS AND CANCELED TO ORDER

Some countries sell their stock of old stamps when a new issue replaces them. The **remainders** are usually canceled with a punch hole, a heavy line or bar, or a more or less regular cancellation to avoid postal use. The most famous merchant of remainders was Nicholas F. Seebeck, who arranged printing contracts between the Hamilton Bank Note Co., of which he was a director, and several Central and Latin American countries in the 1880's and 1890's. The contracts provided that the plates and all remainders of the yearly issues became the property of Hamilton, and Seebeck saw to it that ample stock remained. The "Seebecks," both remainders and reprints, were standard packet fillers for decades.

Some countries also issue stamps **canceled to order** (CTO), either in sheets with original gum or stuck onto pieces of paper or envelopes and canceled. Such CTO items generally are worth less than postally used stamps. Most can be detected by the presence of gum. However, as the CTO practice goes back at least to 1885, the gum inevitably has been washed off some stamps so they could pass for postally used. The normally applied postmarks usually differ slightly and specialists can tell the difference. When applied individually to envelopes by philatelically minded persons, CTO material is known as *favor canceled* and generally sells at large discounts.

CINDERELLAS AND FACSIMILES

Cinderella is a catchall term used by collectors of phantoms, fantasies, bogus items, municipal issues, exhibition seals, local revenues, transportation stamps, labels, poster stamps, etc. Cinderellas are not issued by any national government for postal purposes. Some cinderella collectors include local postage issues, telegraph stamps, essays and proofs, forgeries and counterfeits.

A fantasy is an adhesive created for a nonexisting stamp issuing authority. Fantasy items range from imaginary countries (Kingdom of Sedang or Principality of Trinidad) to nonexisting locals (Winans City Post), or nonexisting transportation lines (McRobish & Co.'s Acapulco-San Francisco Line). On the other hand, if the entity exists and might have issued stamps or did issue other stamps, the items are *bogus* stamps. These would include the Mormon postage stamps of Utah, S. Allan Taylor's Guatemala and Paraguay inventions, the propaganda issues for the South Moluccas and the adhesives of the Page & Keyes local post of Boston.

Both fantasies and bogus issues are sometimes called *phantoms.*

Facsimiles are copies or imitations made to represent original stamps, but which do not pretend to be originals. A catalogue illustration is such a facsimile. Illustrations from the Moëns catalogue of the last century were occasionally colored and passed as stamps. Since the beginning of stamp collecting, facsimiles have been made for collectors as space fillers or for reference. They often carry the words "facsimile," "falsch" (German), "sanko" or "mozo" (Japanese), or "faux" (French) overprinted on the face or stamped on the back. Naturally, they have only curio value.

COUNTERFEITS OR FORGERIES

Postal counterfeits or **postal forgeries** are unauthorized imitations of stamps intended to deprive the post of revenue. They often command higher prices than the genuine stamps they imitate. Sales are illegal and governments can, and do, prosecute.

The first postal forgery was of Spain's 4-cuartos carmine of 1854, No. 25. The forgers lithographed it, though the original was typographed. Apparently they were not satisfied and soon made an engraved forgery which is fairly common, unlike the scarce lithographed counterfeit. Postal forgeries quickly followed in Spain, Austria, Naples, Sardinia and the Roman States.

An infamous counterfeit to defraud the government is the 1-shilling Great Britain "Stock Exchange" forgery of 1872 used on telegrams at the exchange that year. It escaped detection until a stamp dealer noticed it in 1898. Recent postal counterfeits include the U.S. 4c Lincoln and the 8c Eisenhower as well as Canada's 6c orange of 1968 (which was later faked in turn).

Because the governments concerned did not issue them, the *wartime propaganda* stamps of both World Wars may be classed as postal counterfeits. They were put out by other governments or resistance groups.

Philatelic forgeries or *counterfeits* are unauthorized imitations of stamps designed to deceive and defraud collectors. Such spurious items first appeared on the market around 1860 and most old-time collections contain one or more. Many are crude and easily spotted even by the non-specialist, but some can deceive the better-than-average collector.

An important supplier of these early philatelic forgeries was the Hamburg printer, Gebrüder Spiro. Many others indulged in this craft including S. Allan Taylor, George Hussey, James Chute, Georges Foure, Benjamin & Sarpy, Julius Goldner, E. Oneglia and L. H. Mercier. Among the noted 20th century forgers are Francois Fournier, Jean Sperati and the prolific Raoul DeThuin.

Most classic rarities, many medium priced stamps and, in this century, cheap stamps on a wholesale basis destined for beginners' packets, have been fraudulently produced. However, few new philatelic forgeries have appeared in recent decades and virtually no new frauds of valuable classics. Successful imitation of engraved work is virtually impossible. It has proven far easier to produce a fake by altering a genuine stamp than to duplicate a stamp completely.

REPAIRS AND FAKES

Most collectors will not object to restoration of a stamp or cover, although they will not accept repairs on the same basis. *Restoration* in this sense includes cleaning with a soft eraser or soap and water. It may include the ironing out of a crease or removal of a cellophane tape stain. Removal of old hinges is acceptable. Some collectors believe that freshening of a stamp is valid restoration, whether done by the removal of oxides, "toning," or the effect of wax paper left on stamps shipped to the tropics between such sheets. Regumming may have been acceptable restoration half a century ago, but today it is considered faking. Restored stamps or covers do not normally sell at a discount, and may even change hands at a premium.

Repairs include filling in thin spots, mending tears by reweaving, adding a missing corner or perforation "tooth." Repaired stamps sell at substantial discounts.

Fakes are genuine stamps altered in some way to make them more desirable and sold without revealing the alterations. According to one major student, 30,000 varieties of fakes were known in the 1950's. The number has grown. The widespread existence of fakes makes it important for collectors to study their philatelic holdings and relevant literature. For the same reason they should buy from reputable dealers who will guarantee their stamps and make full prompt refund should a purchase be declared not genuine by some mutually agreed-upon authority. Because fakes always have some genuine characteristics, it is not always possible to obtain unanimity among expert students regarding specific items. These students may change their opinions as philatelic knowledge increases. More than 80 per cent of all fakes on the market today are regummed, reperforated or altered in regard to overprints, surcharges or cancellations.

Stamps can be chemically treated to alter or eliminate colors. For example a pale rose can be recolored into a blue of a higher value, or a "missing color" variety created. Designs may be changed by "painting," or a stroke or dot added or bleached out to turn an ordinary variety into a scarce stamp. Part of a stamp can be bleached and reprinted in a different version, achieving an inverted center or frame. Margins can be added or repairs done so deceptively that the stamp moves from the repaired to the fake category.

The fakers have not left the backs of stamps untouched. They may create false watermarks or add fake grills (or press out genuine ones). A thin India paper proof may be glued onto a thicker backing to "create" an issued stamp, or a cardboard proof may be shaved down. Silk threads have been impressed in and stamps have been split so that a rare paper variety, from a cheap stamp, can be applied as a back to falsely identify the stamp. However, the most common back treatment is regumming.

Some operators openly advertise "foolproof" application of "original gum" to stamps that lack it. This is faking, not counterfeiting. As few early stamps have survived without being hinged, the large number of never-hinged examples now offered for sale suggests the extent of regumming that has been and is being done. Regumming may be used to hide repairs and thin spots, but dipping in watermark fluid will often reveal these flaws.

The fakers also tamper with separations. Ingenious ways to add margins are known, and perforated wide-margin stamps may be falsely represented as imperforate when trimmed. Reperforating is commonly done to create scarce coil or perforation varieties and to eliminate the straight-edge stamps found in sheet margin positions of many earlier issues. Custom has made straight edges less desirable and the fakers have obliged by reperforating them so extensively that many are now uncommon if not rare.

Another main field of the faker is that of the overprint, surcharge and cancellation. The forging of rare surcharges or overprints began in the 1880's or 1890's. These forgeries are sometimes difficult to detect, but the better experts have probably identified almost all of them. Only occasionally are the overprints or cancellations removed to create unoverprinted stamps or unused items. The SPECIMEN overprints are sometimes removed–scraping and repainting is one way –to create unoverprinted varieties. Cheap revenues or pen-canceled stamps are used to generate "unused" stamps for further faking by adding other markings. The quartz lamp and a high-powered magnifying glass help in detecting cancellation removals.

The big problem, however, is the addition of overprints, surcharges or cancellations–many quite dangerous. Plating of the stamps or the overprint can be an important detecting method.

Fake postmarks can range from numerous spurious fancy cancellations, to the host of markings applied to transatlantic covers to create rare uses. With the advance of cover collecting and the wide interest in postal history, a fertile new field for fakers arose. Some have tried to create entire covers. Others specialize in adding stamps, tied by fake cancellations, to genuine stampless covers, or replacing cheaper or damaged stamps with more valuable ones. Detailed study of rates and postmarks (including the analysis of "breaks" in each handstamp over a period), ink analysis, etc. will usually unmask the fraud.

TERMINOLOGY

BOOKLETS: Many countries have issued stamps in small booklets for the convenience of users. They are usually sold by the post office at a small premium. Booklets have been issued in all sizes and forms, often with advertising on the covers, on the panes of stamps or on the interleaving. The panes may be printed from special plates or made from regular sheets. All panes from booklets issued by the United States and many from those of other countries are straight edged on the bottom and both sides, but perforated between the stamps. Any unit in the pane, either printed or blank, which is not a postage stamp, is called a *label* in the catalogue listings.

CANCELLATIONS: The marks or obliterations put on a stamp by the postal authorities to show that it has done service and is no longer valid for postage. If it is made with a pen, it is called a pen cancellation. When the location of the post office appears in the cancellation, it is called a town cancellation. When it calls attention to a cause or celebration, it is a slogan cancellation. Many other types and styles of cancellations exist, such as duplex, numerals, targets, etc.

COIL STAMPS–Stamps issued in rolls for use in affixing and vending machines. Those of the United States, Canada, etc., are perforated horizontally or vertically only, with the outer edges imperforate. Coil stamps of some countries (Great Britain) are perforated on all four sides.

COVERS: Envelopes, with or without adhesive postage stamps, which have passed through the mail and bear postal or other markings of philatelic interest. Before the introduction of envelopes (1840), people folded letters and wrote the address on the outside. Many people covered their letters with an extra sheet of paper on the outside for the address. Hence the word "cover." Used air letter sheets, stamped envelopes, and other items of postal stationery are also referred to as "covers."

ERRORS: Stamps having some unintentional deviation from the normal. Errors include, but are not limited to, mistakes in color, paper or watermark; inverted centers (or frames), surcharges or overprints, and double impressions. A factually wrong or misspelled inscription, if it appears on all examples of a stamp, is not classified as a philatelic error. (Panama No. J1).

OVERPRINTED AND SURCHARGED STAMPS: Overprinting is wording placed on stamps to alter the place of use ("Canal Zone" on U.S. issues); to adapt them for a special purpose ("Porto" on Denmark's 1913-20 regular issues for use as postage dues, Nos. J1-J7); or for a special occasion (Guatemala Nos. 374-378).

The term **surcharge** is used when the overprint changes or restates the value (1923 "Inflation Issues" of Germany; Australia No. 580).

Surcharges and overprints may be handstamped, typeset or, occasionally, lithographed or engraved.

PRECANCELS: Stamps canceled by the issuing government before they are sold at the post office. Precanceling is done to expedite the handling of large mailings.

In the United States precancellations generally identify the point of origin. That is, the city and state names (or initials) appear, usually centered by an arrangement of parallel lines.

In France the abbreviation **Affranchts** in a semicircle together with the word **Postes** is the general form. Belgian precancellations are usually a square box in which the name of the city appears. Netherlands' precancellations have the name of the city enclosed between a large and small circle, sometimes called a "life-saver."

Precancellations of other countries usually follow these patterns, but may be any arrangement of bars, boxes and city names.

PROOFS AND ESSAYS: Proofs are impressions taken from an approved die, plate or stone in which the design and color are the same as the stamp issued to the public. Trial color proofs are impressions taken from approved dies, plates or stones in varying colors. An essay is the impression of a design that differs in some way from the stamp as issued.

PROVISIONALS: Stamps issued on short notice and intended for temporary use pending the arrival of regular (definitive) issues. They are usually issued to meet contingencies: changes in government or currency; shortage of necessary postage values, or military occupation.

In the 1840's, postmasters in certain American cities issued stamps that were valid only at specific post offices. Postmasters of the Confederate States also issued stamps with limited validity. These are known as Postmasters' Provisionals.

SE-TENANT: Joined together, referring to an unsevered pair, strip or block of stamps differing in design, denomination or overprint (U.S. Nos. 1530-1537).

TETE BECHE: A pair of stamps in which one is upside down in relation to the other. Some of these are the result of intentional sheet arrangement (Morocco Nos. B10-B11). Others occurred when one or more electrotypes were accidentally placed upside down on the plate (Colombia No. 57a). Separation of course destroys the tête bêche variety.

SPECIMENS: One of the regulations of the Universal Postal Union requires member nations to send samples of all stamps they put into service to the International Bureau in Switzerland. These are then sent to all other member nations as samples of what stamps are valid for postage. Many are overprinted, handstamped or initial-perforated "Specimen," "Canceled" or "Muestra." Some are marked with bars across the denominations (China), punched holes (Czechoslovakia) or back inscriptions (Mongolia).

Stamps distributed to government officials or for publicity purposes, and stamps submitted by private security printers for official approval may also receive such defacements.

These markings prevent postal use, and all such items are generally known as "specimens."

CLASSIFICATION OF STAMPS

The various functions of stamps are classified by their names. Postage stamps; air post stamps; postage due stamps for unpaid postage, collected at time of delivery; late fee stamps, a special fee for forwarding a letter after regular mail delivery; registration stamps, fee for keeping special record of letter and ensuring its delivery; special delivery and express stamps, for delivery of letter in advance of regular delivery. With the exception of regular postage, all numbers in the catalogue include a prefix letter denoting the class to which the stamp belongs. (B=Semi-Postal; C=Air Post; E=Special Delivery; J=Postage Due; O=Official; CO=Air Post Official; etc.).

COMMON DESIGN TYPES

Pictured in this section are issues where one illustration has been used for a number of countries in the Catalogue. Not included in this section are overprinted stamps or those issues which are illustrated in each country.

EUROPA

Europa Issue, 1956

The design symbolizing the cooperation among the six countries comprising the Coal and Steel Community is illustrated in each country.

Country	Nos.
Belgium	444–445
France	805–806
Germany	748–749
Italy	715–716
Luxembourg	318–320
Netherlands	368–369

Europa Issue, 1958

"E" and Dove
CD1

European Postal Union at the service of European integration.

1958, Sept. 13	
Belgium	478–479
France	889–890
Germany	790–791
Italy	750–751
Luxembourg	341–343
Netherlands	375–376
Saar	317–318

Europa Issue, 1959

6-Link Endless Chain
CD2

1959, Sept. 19	
Belgium	479–498
France	929–930
Germany	805–806
Italy	791–792
Luxembourg	354–355
Netherlands	379–380

Europa Issue, 1960

19-Spoke Wheel
CD3

First anniversary of the establishment of C.E.P.T. (Conférence Européenne des Administrations des Postes et des Télécommunications.)

The spokes symbolize the 19 founding members of the Conference.

1960, Sept.	
Belgium	518–519
Denmark	379
Finland	376–377
France	970–971
Germany	818–820
Great Britain	377–378
Greece	688
Iceland	327–328
Ireland	175–176
Italy	809–810
Luxembourg	374–375
Netherlands	385–386
Norway	387
Portugal	866–867
Spain	941–942
Sweden	562–563
Switzerland	400–401
Turkey	1493–1494

Europa Issue, 1961

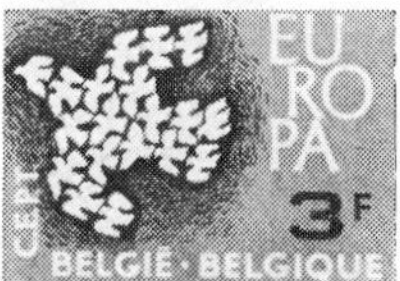

19 Doves Flying as One
CD4

The 19 doves represent the 19 members of the Conference of European Postal and Telecommunications Administrations, C.E.P.T.

1961–62	
Belgium	536–537
Cyprus	201–203
France	1005–1006
Germany	844–845
Great Britain	383–384
Greece	718–719
Iceland	340–341
Italy	845–846
Luxembourg	382–383
Netherlands	387–388
Spain	1010–1011
Switzerland	410–411
Turkey	1518–1520

Europa Issue 1962

Young Tree with 19 Leaves
CD5

The 19 leaves represent the 19 original members of C.E.P.T.

1962–63	
Belgium	546–547
Cyprus	219–221
France	1045–1046
Germany	852–853
Greece	739–740
Iceland	348–349
Ireland	184–185
Italy	860–861
Luxembourg	386–387
Netherlands	394–395
Norway	414–415
Switzerland	416–417
Turkey	1553–1555

Europa Issue, 1963

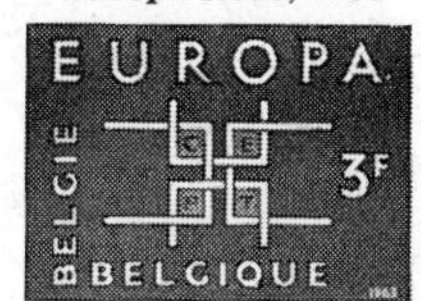

Stylized Links, Symbolizing Unity
CD6

1963, Sept.	
Belgium	562–563
Cyprus	229–231
Finland	419
France	1074–1075
Germany	867–868
Greece	768–769
Iceland	357–358
Ireland	188–189
Italy	880–881
Luxembourg	403–404
Netherlands	416–417
Norway	441–442
Switzerland	429
Turkey	1602–1603

Europa Issue, 1964

Symbolic Daisy
CD7

5th anniversary of the establishment of C.E.P.T. The 22 petals of the flower symbolize the 22 members of the Conference.

1964, Sept.	
Austria	738
Belgium	578–579
Cyprus	244–246
France	1109–1110
Germany	897–898
Greece	801–802
Iceland	367–368
Ireland	196–197
Italy	894–895
Luxembourg	411–412
Monaco	590–591
Netherlands	428–429
Norway	458
Portugal	931–933
Spain	1262–1263
Switzerland	438–439
Turkey	1628–1629

Europa Issue, 1965

Leaves and "Fruit"
CD8

1965	
Belgium	600–601
Cyprus	262–264
Finland	437
France	1131–1132
Germany	934–935
Greece	833–834
Iceland	375–376
Ireland	204–205
Italy	915–916
Luxembourg	432–433
Monaco	616–617
Netherlands	438–439
Norway	475–476
Portugal	958–960
Switzerland	469
Turkey	1665–1666

Europa Issue, 1966

Symbolic Sailboat
CD9

1966, Sept.	
Andorra, French	172
Belgium	622–628
Cyprus	275–277
France	1163–1164
Germany	963–964
Greece	862–863
Iceland	384–385
Ireland	216–217
Italy	942–943
Liechtenstein	415
Luxembourg	440–441
Monaco	639–640
Netherlands	441–442
Norway	496–497
Portugal	980–982
Switzerland	477–478
Turkey	1718–1719

Europa Issue, 1967

Cogwheels
CD10

1967

Andorra, French 174–175
Belgium 641–642
Cyprus 297–299
France 1178–1179
Greece 891–892
Germany 969–970
Iceland 389–390
Ireland 232–233
Italy 951–952
Liechtenstein 420
Luxembourg 449–450
Monaco 669–670
Netherlands 444–447
Norway 504–505
Portugal 994–996
Spain 1465–1466
Switzerland 482
Turkey B120–B121

Europa Issue, 1968

Golden Key with C.E.P.T. Emblem
CD11

1968

Andorra, French 182–183
Belgium 664–665
Cyprus 314–316
France 1209–1210
Germany 983–984
Greece 916–917
Iceland 395–396
Ireland 242–243
Italy 979–980
Liechtenstein 442
Luxembourg 466–467
Monaco 689–691
Netherlands 452–453
Portugal 1019–1021
San Marino 687
Spain 1526
Turkey 1775–1776

Europa Issue, 1969

"EUROPA" and "CEPT"
CD12

Tenth anniversary of C.E.P.T.

1969

Andorra, French 188–189
Austria 837
Belgium 683–684
Cyprus 326–328
Denmark 458
Finland 483
France 1245–1246
Germany 996–997
Great Britain 585
Greece 947–948
Iceland 406–407
Ireland 270–271
Italy 1000–1001
Jugoslavia 1003–1004
Liechtenstein 453
Luxembourg 474–475
Monaco 722–724
Netherlands 475–476
Norway 533–534
Portugal 1038–1040
San Marino 701–702
Spain 1567
Sweden 814–816
Switzerland 500–501
Turkey 1799–1800
Vatican 470–472

Europa Issue, 1970

Interwoven Threads
CD13

1970

Andorra, French 196–197
Belgium 708–709
Cyprus 340–342
France 1271–1272
Germany 1018–1019
Greece 985, 987
Iceland 420–421
Ireland 279–281
Italy 1013–1014
Jugoslavia 1024–1025
Liechtenstein 470
Luxembourg 489–490
Monaco 768–770
Netherlands 483–484
Portugal 1060–1062
San Marino 729–730
Spain 1607
Switzerland 515–516
Turkey 1848–1849

Europa Issue, 1971

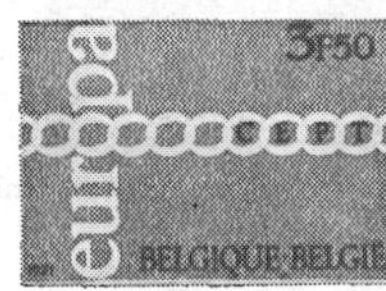

"Fraternity, Cooperation, Common Effort"—CD14

1971

Andorra, French 205–206
Belgium 742–743
Cyprus 365–367
Finland 504
France 1304
Germany 1064–1065
Greece 1029–1030
Iceland 429–430
Ireland 305–306
Italy 1038–1039
Jugoslavia 1052–1053
Liechtenstein 485
Luxembourg 500–501
Malta 425–427
Monaco 797–799
Netherlands 488–489
Portugal 1094–1096
San Marino 749–750
Spain 1675–1676
Switzerland 531–532
Turkey 1876–1877

Europa Issue, 1972

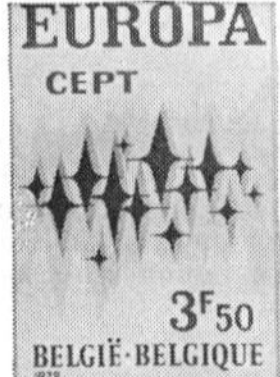

Sparkles, Symbolic of Communications
CD15

1972

Andorra, French 210–211
Andorra, Spanish 62
Belgium 768–769
Cyprus 380–382
Finland 512–513
France 1341
Germany 1089–1090
Greece 1049–1050
Iceland 439–440
Ireland 316–317
Italy 1065–1066
Jugoslavia 1100–1101
Liechtenstein 504
Luxembourg 512–513
Malta 450–453
Monaco 831–832
Netherlands 494–495
Portugal 1141–1143
San Marino 771–772
Spain 1718
Switzerland 544–545
Turkey 1907–1908

Europa Issue, 1973

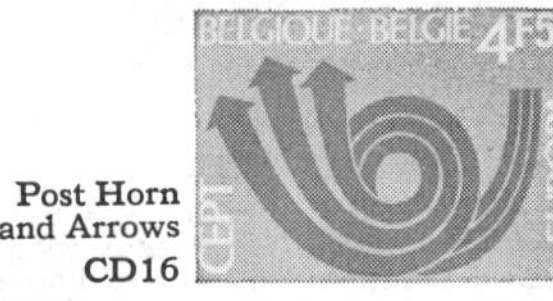

Post Horn and Arrows
CD16

1973

Andorra, French 319–320
Andorra, Spanish 76
Belgium 782–783
Cyprus 396–398
Finland 526
France 1367
Germany 1114–1115
Greece 1090–1092
Iceland 447–448
Ireland 329–330
Italy 1108–1109
Jugoslavia 1138–1139
Liechtenstein 528–529
Luxembourg 523–524
Malta 469–471
Monaco 866–867
Netherlands 504–505
Norway 604–605
Portugal 1170–1172
San Marino 802–803
Spain 1753
Switzerland 580–581
Turkey 1935–1936

PORTUGAL & COLONIES

Vasco da Gama Issue

Fleet Departing—CD20

Fleet Arriving at Calicut
CD21

Embarking at Rastello—CD22

Muse of History
CD23

Flagship San Gabriel, da Gama and Camoens
CD24

Archangel Gabriel, the Patron Saint
CD25

Flagship San Gabriel
CD26

Vasco da Gama
CD27

Fourth centenary of Vasco da Gama's discovery of the route to India.

1898

Azores 93–100
Macao 67–74
Madeira 37–44
Portugal 147–154
Port. Africa 1–8
Port. India 189–196
Timor 45–52

Pombal Issue

POSTAL TAX

Marquis de Pombal
CD28

Planning Reconstruction of Lisbon, 1755
CD29

Pombal Monument, Lisbon
CD30

Sebastiao José de Carvalho e Mello, Marquis de Pombal (1699–1782), statesman, rebuilt Lisbon after earthquake of 1755. Tax was for the erection of Pombal monument. Obligatory on all mail on certain days throughout the year.

1925

Angola RA1–RA3
Azores RA9–RA11
Cape Verde RA1–RA3
Macao RA1–RA3
Madeira RA1–RA3
Mozambique RA1–RA3
Portugal RA11–RA13
Port. Guinea RA1–RA3
Port. India RA1–RA3
St. Thomas & Prince Islands RA1–RA3
Timor RA1–RA3

Pombal Issue

POSTAL TAX DUES

Marquis de Pombal
CD31

Planning Reconstruction of Lisbon, 1755
CD32

Pombal Monument, Lisbon
CD33

1925

Angola	RAJ1–RAJ3
Azores	RAJ2–RAJ4
Cape Verde	RAJ1–RAJ3
Macao	RAJ1–RAJ3
Madeira	RAJ1–RAJ3
Mozambique	RAJ1–RAJ3
Portugal	RAJ2–RAJ4
Port. Guinea	RAJ1–RAJ3
Port. India	RAJ1–RAJ3
St. Thomas & Prince Islands	RAJ1–RAJ3
Timor	RAJ1–RAJ3

Vasco da Gama
CD34

Mousinho de Albuquerque
CD35

Dam
CD36

Prince Henry the Navigator
CD37

Affonso de Albuquerque
CD38

1938–39

Angola	274–291
Cape Verde	234–251
Macao	289–305
Mozambique	270–287
Port. Guinea	233–250
Port. India	439–453
St. Thomas & Prince Islands	302–319, 323–340
Timor	223–239

Plane over Globe
CD39

1938–39

Angola	C1–C9
Cape Verde	C1–C9
Macao	C7–C15
Mozambique	C1–C9
Port. Guinea	C1–C9
Port. India	C1–C8
St. Thomas & Prince Islands	C1–C18
Timor	C1–C9

Lady of Fatima Issue

Our Lady of the Rosary, Fatima, Portugal
CD40

1948–49

Angola	315–318
Cape Verde	266
Macao	336
Mozambique	325–328
Port. Guinea	271
Port. India	480
St. Thomas & Prince Islands	351
Timor	254

A souvenir sheet of 9 stamps was issued in 1951 to mark the extension of the 1950 Holy Year. The sheet contains: Angola No. 316, Cape Verde No. 266, Macao No. 336, Mozambique No. 325, Portuguese Guinea No. 271, Portuguese India Nos. 480, 485, St. Thomas & Prince Islands No. 351, Timor No. 254.

The sheet also contains a portrait of Pope Pius XII and is inscribed "Encerramento do Ano Santo, Fatima 1951." It was sold for 11 escudos.

Holy Year Issue

Church Bells and Dove
CD41

Angel Holding Candelabra
CD42

Holy Year, 1950.

1950–51

Angola	331–332
Cape Verde	268–269
Macao	339–340
Mozambique	330–331
Port. Guinea	273–274
Port. India	490–491, 496–503
St. Thomas & Prince Islands	353–354
Timor	258–259

A souvenir sheet of 8 stamps was issued in 1951 to mark the extension of the Holy Year. The sheet contains: Angola No. 331, Cape Verde No. 269, Macao No. 340, Mozambique No. 331, Portuguese Guinea No. 275, Portuguese India No. 490, St. Thomas & Prince Islands No. 354, Timor No. 258, some with colors changed. The sheet contains doves and is inscribed "Encerramento do Ano Santo, Fatima 1951." It was sold for 17 escudos.

Holy Year Conclusion Issue

Our Lady of Fatima
CD43

Conclusion of Holy Year. Sheets contain alternate vertical rows of stamps and labels bearing quotation from Pope Pius XII, different for each colony.

1951

Angola	357
Cape Verde	270
Macao	352
Mozambique	356
Port. Guinea	275
Port. India	506
St. Thomas & Prince Islands	355
Timor	270

Medical Congress Issue

Medical Examination
CD44

First National Congress of Tropical Medicine, Lisbon, 1952.
Each stamp has a different design.

1952

Angola	358
Cape Verde	287
Macao	364
Mozambique	359
Port. Guinea	276
Port. India	516
St. Thomas & Prince Islands	356
Timor	271

POSTAGE DUE STAMPS

CD45

1952

Angola	J37–J42
Cape Verde	J31–J36
Macao	J53–J58
Mozambique	J51–J56
Port. Guinea	J40–J45
Port. India	J47–J52
St. Thomas & Prince Islands	J52–J57
Timor	J31–J36

Sao Paulo Issue

Father Manuel da Nobrega and View of Sao Paulo
CD46

400th anniversary of the founding of Sao Paulo, Brazil.

1954

Angola	385
Cape Verde	297
Macao	382
Mozambique	395
Port. Guinea	291
Port. India	530
St. Thomas & Prince Islands	369
Timor	279

Tropical Medicine Congress Issue

Securidaca Longipedunculata
CD47

Sixth International Congress for Tropical Medicine and Malaria, Lisbon, Sept. 1958.
Each stamp shows a different plant.

1958

Angola	409
Cape Verde	303
Macao	392
Mozambique	404
Port. Guinea	295
Port. India	569
St. Thomas & Prince Islands	371
Timor	289

Sports Issue

Flying
CD48

Each stamp shows a different sport.

1962

Angola	433–438
Cape Verde	320–325
Macao	394–399
Mozambique	424–429
Port. Guinea	299–304
St. Thomas & Prince Islands	374–379
Timor	313–318

Anti-Malaria Issue

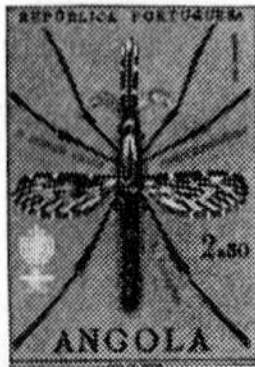

Anopheles Funestus and Malaria Eradication Symbol

CD49

World Health Organization drive to eradicate malaria.

1962

Angola	439
Cape Verde	326
Macao	400
Mozambique	430
Port. Guinea	305
St. Thomas & Prince Islands	380
Timor	319

Airline Anniversary Issue

Map of Africa, Super Constellation and Jet Liner

CD50

Tenth anniversary of Transportes Aéreos Portugueses (TAP).

1963

Angola	490
Cape Verde	327
Mozambique	434
Port. Guinea	318
St. Thomas & Prince Islands	381

National Overseas Bank Issue

Antonio Teixeira de Sousa

CD51

Centenary of the National Overseas Bank of Portugal.

1964, May 16

Angola	509
Cape Verde	328
Port. Guinea	319
St. Thomas & Prince Islands	382
Timor	320

ITU Issue

ITU Emblem and St. Gabriel

CD52

Centenary of the International Communications Union.

1965, May 17

Angola	511
Cape Verde	329
Macao	402
Mozambique	464
Port. Guinea	320
St. Thomas & Prince Islands	383
Timor	321

National Revolution Issue

St. Pauls's Hospital, and Commercial and Industrial School

CD53

40th anniversary of the National Revolution.
Different buildings on each stamp.

1966, May 28

Angola	525
Cape Verde	338
Macao	403
Mozambique	465
Port. Guinea	329
St. Thomas & Prince Islands	392
Timor	322

Navy Club Issue

Mendes Barata and Cruiser Dom Carlos I

CD54

Centenary of Portugal's Navy Club.
Each stamp has a different design.

1967, Jan. 31

Angola	527–528
Cape Verde	339–340
Macao	412–413
Mozambique	478–479
Port. Guinea	330–331
St. Thomas & Prince Islands	393–394
Timor	323–324

Admiral Coutinho Issue

Admiral Gago Coutinho and his First Ship

CD55

Centenary of the birth of Admiral Carlos Viegas Gago Coutinho (1869–1959), explorer and aviation pioneer.
Each stamp has a different design.

1969, Feb. 17

Angola	547
Cape Verde	355
Macao	417
Mozambique	484
Port. Guinea	335
St. Thomas & Prince Islands	397
Timor	335

Administration Reform Issue

Luiz Augusto Rebello da Silva

CD56

Centenary of the administration reforms of the overseas territories.

1969, Sept. 25

Angola	549
Cape Verde	357
Macao	419
Mozambique	491
Port. Guinea	337
St. Thomas & Prince Islands	399
Timor	338

Marshal Carmona Issue

Marshal A. O. Carmona

CD57

Birth centenary of Marshal Antonio Oscar Carmona de Fragoso (1869–1951), President of Portugal.
Each stamp has a different design.

1970, Nov. 15

Angola	563
Cape Verde	359
Macao	422
Mozambique	493
Port. Guinea	340
St. Thomas & Prince Islands	403
Timor	341

Olympic Games Issue

Racing Yachts and Olympic Emblem

CD59

20th Olympic Games, Munich, Aug. 26–Sept. 11.
Each stamp shows a different sport.

1972, June 20

Angola	569
Cape Verde	361
Macao	426
Mozambique	504
Port. Guinea	342
St. Thomas & Prince Islands	408
Timor	343

Lisbon-Rio de Janeiro Flight Issue

"Santa Cruz" over Fernando de Noronha

CD60

50th anniversary of the Lisbon to Rio de Janeiro flight by Arturo de Sacadura and Coutinho, March 30–June 5, 1922.
Each stamp shows a different stage of the flight.

1972, Sept. 20

Angola	570
Cape Verde	362
Macao	427
Mozambique	505
Port. Guinea	343
St. Thomas & Prince Islands	409
Timor	344

WMO Centenary Issue

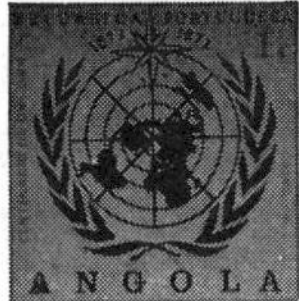

WMO Emblem

CD61

Centenary of international meteorological cooperation.

1973, Dec. 15

Angola	571
Cape Verde	363
Macao	429
Mozambique	509
Port. Guinea	344
St. Thomas & Prince Islands	410
Timor	345

FRENCH COMMUNITY

Colonial Exposition Issue

People of French Empire

CD70

Women's Heads

CD71

France Showing Way to Civilization

CD72

"Colonial Commerce"

CD73

International Colonial Exposition, Paris 1931.

1931

Cameroun 213–216
Chad 60–63
Dahomey 97–100
Fr. Guiana 152–155
Fr. Guinea 116–119
Fr. India 100–103
Fr. Polynesia 76–79
Fr. Sudan 102–105
Gabon 120–123
Guadeloupe 138–141
Indo-China 140–142
Ivory Coast 92–95
Madagascar 169–172
Martinique 129–132
Mauritania 65–68
Middle Congo 61–64
New Caledonia 176–179
Niger 73–76
Reunion 122–125
St. Pierre & Miquelon 132–135
Senegal 138–141
Somali Coast 135–138
Togo 254–257
Ubangi-Shari 82–85
Upper Volta 66–69
Wallis & Futuna Isls. 85–88

Paris International Exposition Issue

Colonial Arts Exposition Issue

"Colonial Resources"

CD74 CD77

Overseas Commerce

CD75

Exposition Buildings and Women

CD76

"France and the Empire"

CD78

Cultural Treasures of the Colonies

CD79

Souvenir sheets contain one imperf. stamp.

1937

Cameroun 217–222A
Dahomey 101–107
Fr. Equatorial Africa 27–32, 73
Fr. Guiana 162–168
Fr. Guinea 120–126
Fr. India 104–110
Fr. Polynesia 117–123
Fr. Sudan 106–112
Guadeloupe 148–154
Indo-China 193–199
Inini 41
Ivory Coast 152–158
Kwangchowan 132
Madagascar 191–197
Martinique 179–185
Mauritania 69–75
New Caledonia 208–214
Niger 72–83
Reunion 167–173
St. Pierre & Miquelon 165–171
Senegal 172–178
Somali Coast 139–145
Togo 258–264
Wallis & Futuna Isls. 89

Curie Issue

Pierre and Marie Curie

CD80

40th anniversary of the discovery of radium. The surtax was for the benefit of the International Union for the Control of Cancer.

1938

Cameroun B1
Dahomey B2
France B76
Fr. Equatorial Africa B1
Fr. Guiana B3
Fr. Guinea B2
Fr. India B6
Fr. Polynesia B5
Fr. Sudan B1
Guadeloupe B3
Indo-China B14
Ivory Coast B2
Madagascar B2
Martinique B2
Mauritania B3
New Caledonia B4
Niger B1
Reunion B4
St. Pierre & Miquelon B3
Senegal B3
Somali Coast B2
Togo B1

Caillié Issue

René Caillié and Map of Northwestern Africa

CD81

Death centenary of René Caillié (1799–1838), French explorer.

All three denominations exist with colony name omitted.

1939

Dahomey 108–110
Fr. Guinea 161–163
Fr. Sudan 113–115
Ivory Coast 160–162
Mauritania 109–111
Niger 84–86
Senegal 188–190
Togo 265–267

New York World's Fair Issue

Natives and New York Skyline

CD82

1939

Cameroun 223–224
Dahomey 111–112
Fr. Equatorial Africa 78–79
Fr. Guiana 169–170
Fr. Guinea 164–165
Fr. India 111–112
Fr. Polynesia 124–125
Fr. Sudan 116–117
Guadeloupe 155–156
Indo-China 203–204
Inini 42–43
Ivory Coast 163–164
Kwangchowan 121–122
Madagascar 209–210
Martinque 186–187
Mauritania 112–113
New Caledonia 215–216
Niger 87–88
Reunion 174–175
St. Pierre & Miquelon 205–206
Senegal 191–192
Somali Coast 179–180
Togo 268–269
Wallis & Futuna Isls. 90–91

French Revolution Issue

Storming of the Bastille

CD83

150th anniversary of the French Revolution. The surtax was for the defense of the colonies.

1939

Cameroun B2–B6
Dahomey B3–B7
Fr. Equatorial Africa B4–B8, CB1
Fr. Guiana B4–B8, CB1
Fr. Guinea B3–B7
Fr. India B7–B11
Fr. Polynesia B6–B10, CB1
Fr. Sudan B2–B6
Guadeloupe B4–B8
Indo-China B15–B19, CB1
Inini B1–B5
Ivory Coast B3–B7
Kwangchowan B1–B5
Madagascar B3–B7, CB1
Martinique B3–B7
Mauritania B4–B8
New Caledonia B5–B9, CB1
Niger B2–B6
Reunion B5–B9, CB1
St. Pierre & Miquelon B4–B8
Senegal B4–B8, CB1
Somali Coast B3–B7
Togo B2–B6
Wallis & Futuna Isls. B1–B5

Plane over Coastal Area

CD85

All five denominations exist with colony name omitted.

1940

Dahomey C1–C5
Fr. Guinea C1–C5
Fr. Sudan C1–C5
Ivory Coast C1–C5
Mauritania C1–C5
Niger C1–C5
Senegal C12–C16
Togo C1–C5

Colonial Infantryman

CD86

1941

Cameroun B13B
Dahomey B13
Fr. Equatorial Africa B8B
Fr. Guiana B10
Fr. Guinea B13
Fr. India B13
Fr. Polynesia B12
Fr. Sudan B12
Guadeloupe B10
Indo-China B19B
Inini B7
Ivory Coast B13
Kwangchowan B7
Madagascar B9
Martinique B9
Mauritania B14
New Caledonia B11
Niger B12
Reunion B11
St. Pierre & Miquelon B8B
Senegal B14
Somali Coast B9
Togo B10B
Wallis & Futuna Isls. B7

Cross of Lorraine and Four-motor Plane

CD87

1941–5

Cameroun C1–C7
Fr. Equatorial Africa C17–C23
Fr. Guiana C9–C10
Fr. India C1–C6
Fr. Polynesia C3–C9
Fr. West Africa C1–C3
Guadeloupe C1–C2
Madagascar C37–C43
Martinique C1–C2
New Caledonia C7–C13
Reunion C18–C24
St. Pierre & Miquelon C1–C7
Somali Coast C1–C7

Transport Plane

CD88

Caravan and Plane—CD89

1942

Dahomey	C6–C13
Fr. Guinea	C6–C13
Fr. Sudan	C6–C13
Ivory Coast	C6–C13
Mauritania	C6–C13
Niger	C6–C13
Senegal	C17–C25
Togo	C6–C13

Red Cross Issue

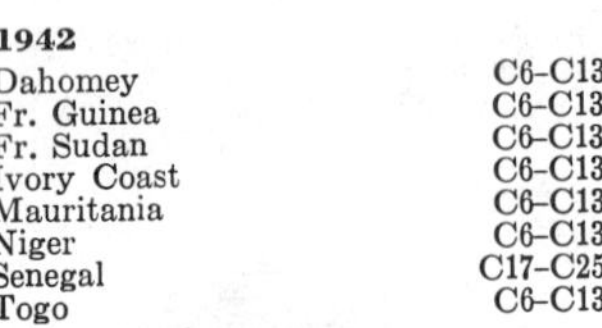

Marianne
CD90

The surtax was for the French Red Cross and national relief.

1944

Cameroun	B28
Fr. Equatorial Africa	B38
Fr. Guiana	B12
Fr. India	B14
Fr. Polynesia	B13
Fr. West Africa	B1
Guadeloupe	B12
Madagascar	B15
Martinique	B11
New Caledonia	B13
Reunion	B15
St. Pierre & Miquelon	B13
Somali Coast	B13
Wallis & Futuna Isls.	B9

Eboué Issue

Félix Eboué
CD91

Félix Eboué, first French colonial administrator to proclaim resistance to Germany after French surrender in World War II.

1945

Cameroun	296–297
Fr. Equatorial Africa	156–157
Fr. Guiana	171–172
Fr. India	210–211
Fr. Polynesia	150–151
Fr. West Africa	15–16
Guadeloupe	187–188
Madagascar	259–260
Martinique	196–197
New Caledonia	274–275
Reunion	238–239
St. Pierre & Miquelon	322–323
Somali Coast	238–239

Victory Issue

Victory
CD92

European victory of the Allied Nations in World War II.

1946, May 8

Cameroun	C8
Fr. Equatorial Africa	C24
Fr. Guiana	C11
Fr. India	C7
Fr. Polynesia	C10
Fr. West Africa	C4
Guadeloupe	C3
Indo-China	C19
Madagascar	C44
Martinique	C3
New Caledonia	C14
Reunion	C25
St. Pierre & Miquelon	C8
Somali Coast	C8
Wallis & Futuna Isls.	C1

Chad to Rhine Issue

Leclerc's Departure from Chad
CD93

Battle at Cufra Oasis
CD94

Tanks in Action, Mareth
CD95

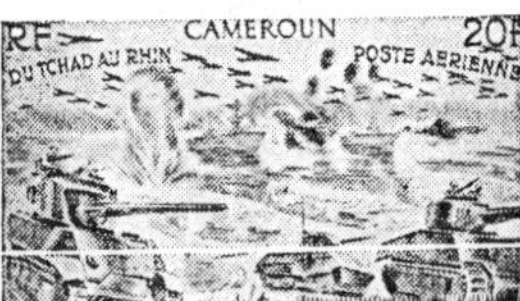

Normandy Invasion
CD96

Entering Paris
CD97

Liberation of Strasbourg
CD98

"Chad to the Rhine" march, 1942–44, by Gen. Jacques Leclerc's column, later French 2nd Armored Division.

1946, June 6

Cameroun	C9–C14
Fr. Equatorial Africa	C25–C30
Fr. Guiana	C12–C17
Fr. India	C8–C13
Fr. Polynesia	C11–C16
Fr. West Africa	C5–C10
Guadeloupe	C4–C9
Indo-China	C20–C25
Madagascar	C45–C50
Martinique	C4–C9
New Caledonia	C15–C20
Reunion	C26–C31
St. Pierre & Miquelon	C9–C14
Somali Coast	C9–C14
Wallis & Futuna Isls.	C2–C7

UPU Issue

French Colonials, Globe and Plane
CD99

75th anniversary of the Universal Postal Union.

1949, July 4

Cameroun	C29
Fr. Equatorial Africa	C34
Fr. India	C17
Fr. Polynesia	C20
Fr. West Africa	C15
Indo-China	C26
Madagascar	C55
New Caledonia	C24
St. Pierre & Miquelon	C18
Somali Coast	C18
Togo	C18
Wallis & Futuna Isls.	C10

Tropical Medicine Issue

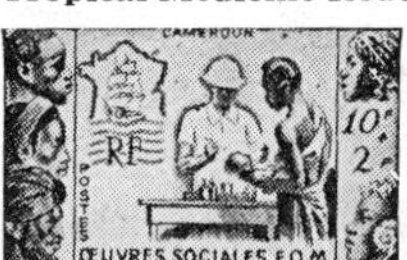

Doctor Treating Infant
CD100

The surtax was for charitable work.

1950

Cameroun	B29
Fr. Equatorial Africa	B39
Fr. India	B15
Fr. Polynesia	B14
Fr. West Africa	B3
Madagascar	B17
New Caledonia	B14
St. Pierre & Miquelon	B14
Somali Coast	B14
Togo	B11

Military Medal Issue

Medal, Early Marine and Colonial Soldier
CD101

Centenary of the creation of the French Military Medal.

1952

Cameroun	332
Comoro Isls.	39
Fr. Equatorial Africa	186
Fr. India	233
Fr. Polynesia	179
Fr. West Africa	57
Madagascar	286
New Caledonia	295
St. Pierre & Miquelon	345
Somali Coast	267
Togo	327
Wallis & Futuna Isls.	149

Liberation Issue

Allied Landing, Victory Sign and Cross of Lorraine
CD102

10th anniversary of the liberation of France.

1954, June 6

Cameroun	C32
Comoro Isls.	C4
Fr. Equatorial Africa	C38
Fr. India	C18
Fr. Polynesia	C23
Fr. West Africa	C17
Madagascar	C57
New Caledonia	C25
St. Pierre & Miquelon	C19
Somali Coast	C19
Togo	C19
Wallis & Futuna Isls.	C11

FIDES Issue

Plowmen
CD103

Efforts of FIDES, the Economic and Social Development Fund for Overseas Possessions (Fonds d' Investissement pour le Developpement Economique et Social.)

Each stamp has a different design.

1956

Cameroun	326–329
Comoro Isls.	43
Fr. Polynesia	181
Madagascar	292–295
New Caledonia	303
Somali Coast	268
Togo	331

Flower Issue

Euadania
CD104

Each stamp shows a different flower.

1958–9

Cameroun	333
Comoro Isls.	45
Fr. Equatorial Africa	200–201
Fr. Polynesia	192
Fr. So. & Antarctic Terr.	11
Fr. West Africa	79–83
Madagascar	301–302
New Caledonia	304–305
St. Pierre & Miquelon	357

Somali Coast	270
Togo	348–349
Wallis & Futuna Isls.	152

Human Rights Issue

Sun, Dove and U. N. Emblem

CD105

10th anniversary of the signing of the Universal Declaration of Human Rights.

1958

Comoro Isls.	44
Fr. Equatorial Africa	202
Fr. Polynesia	191
Fr. West Africa	85
Madagascar	300
New Caledonia	306
St. Pierre & Miquelon	356
Somali Coast	274
Wallis & Futuna Isls.	153

C.C.T.A. Issue

Map of Africa and Cogwheels

CD106

10th anniversary of the Commission for Technical Cooperation in Africa south of the Sahara.

1960

Cameroun	335
Cent. African Rep.	3
Chad	66
Congo, P.R.	90
Dahomey	138
Gabon	150
Ivory Coast	180
Madagascar	9
Mali	117
Mauritania	104
Niger	89
Upper Volta	89

Air Afrique Issue, 1961

Modern and Ancient Africa, Map and Planes

CD107

Founding of Air Afrique (African Airlines).

1961–62

Cameroun	C37
Cent. African Rep.	C5
Chad	C7
Congo, P.R.	C5
Dahomey	C17
Gabon	C5
Ivory Coast	C18
Mauritania	C17
Niger	C22
Senegal	C31
Upper Volta	C4

Anti-Malaria Issue

Malaria Eradication Emblem

CD108

World Health Organization drive to eradicate malaria.

1962, Apr. 7

Cameroun	B36
Cent. African Rep.	B1
Chad	B1
Comoro Isls.	B1
Congo, P.R.	B3
Dahomey	B15
Gabon	B4
Ivory Coast	B15
Madagascar	B19
Mali	B1
Mauritania	B16
Niger	B14
Senegal	B16
Somali Coast	B15
Upper Volta	B1

Abidjan Games Issue

Relay Race

CD109

Abidjan Games, Ivory Coast, Dec. 24–31, 1961.

Each stamp shows a different sport.

1962

Chad	83–84
Cent. African Rep.	19–20
Congo, P.R.	103–104
Gabon	163–164
Niger	109–111
Upper Volta	103–105

African and Malagasy Union Issue

Flag of African and Malagasy Union

CD110

First anniversary of the Union.

1962, Sept. 8

Cameroun	373
Cent. African Rep.	21
Chad	85
Congo, P.R.	105
Dahomey	155
Gabon	165
Ivory Coast	198
Madagascar	332
Mauritania	170
Niger	112
Senegal	211
Upper Volta	106

Telstar Issue

Telstar and Globe Showing Andover and Pleumeur-Bodou

CD111

First television connection of the United States and Europe through the Telstar satellite, July 11–12, 1962.

1962–63

Andorra, French	154
Comoro Isls.	C7
Fr. Polynesia	C29
Fr. So. & Antarctic Terr.	C5
New Caledonia	C33
Somali Coast	C31
St. Pierre & Miquelon	C26
Wallis & Futuna Isls.	C17

Freedom From Hunger Issue

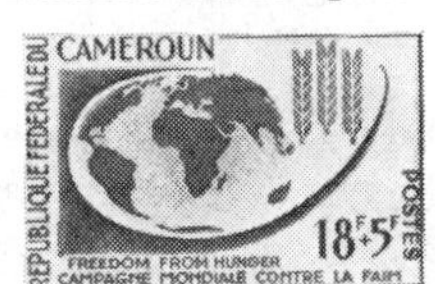

World Map and Wheat Emblem

CD112

United Nations Food and Agriculture Organization's "Freedom from Hunger" campaign.

1963, Mar. 21

Cameroun	B37–B38
Cent. African Rep.	B2
Chad	B2
Congo, P.R.	B4
Dahomey	B16
Gabon	B5
Ivory Coast	B16
Madagascar	B21
Mauritania	B17
Niger	B15
Senegal	B17
Upper Volta	B2

Red Cross Centenary Issue

Centenary Emblem

CD113

Centenary of the International Red Cross.

1963, Sept. 2

Comoro Isls.	55
Fr. Polynesia	205
New Caledonia	328
St. Pierre & Miquelon	367
Somali Coast	297
Wallis & Futuna Isls.	165

African Postal Union Issue

UAMPT Emblem, Radio Masts, Plane and Mail

CD114

Establishment of the African and Malagasy Posts and Telecommunications Union, UAMPT.

1963, Sept. 8

Cameroun	C47
Cent. African Rep.	C10
Chad	C9
Congo, P.R.	C13
Dahomey	C19
Gabon	C13
Ivory Coast	C25
Madagascar	C75
Mauritania	C22
Niger	C27
Rwanda	36
Senegal	C32
Upper Volta	C9

Air Afrique Issue, 1963

Symbols of Flight

CD115

First anniversary of Air Afrique and inauguration of DC-8 service.

1963, Nov. 19

Cameroun	C48
Chad	C10
Congo, P.R.	C14
Gabon	C18
Ivory Coast	C26
Mauritania	C26
Niger	C35
Senegal	C33

Europafrica Issue

Europe and Africa Linked Together

CD116

Signing of an economic agreement between the European Economic Community and the African and Malagasy Union, Yaoundé, Cameroun, July 20, 1963.

1963–64

Cameroun	402
Chad	C11
Cent. African Rep.	C12
Congo, P.R.	C16

Gabon	C19
Ivory Coast	217
Niger	C43
Upper Volta	C11

Human Rights Issue

Scales of Justice and Globe

CD117

15th anniversary of the Universal Declaration of Human Rights.

1963, Dec. 10

Comoro Isls.	58
Fr. Polynesia	206
New Caledonia	329
St. Pierre & Miquelon	368
Somali Coast	300
Wallis & Futuna Isls.	166

PHILATEC Issue

Stamp Album, Champs Elysées Palace and Horses of Marly

CD118

"PHILATEC," International Philatelic and Postal Techniques Exhibition, Paris, June 5-21, 1964.

1963–64

Comoro Isls.	60
France	1078
Fr. Polynesia	207
New Caledonia	341
St. Pierre & Miquelon	369
Somali Coast	301
Wallis & Futuna Isls.	167

Cooperation Issue

Maps of France and Africa and Clasped Hands

CD119

Cooperation between France and the French-speaking countries of Africa and Madagascar.

1964

Cameroun	409-410
Cent. African Rep.	39
Chad	103
Congo, P.R.	121
Dahomey	193
France	1111
Gabon	175
Ivory Coast	221
Madagascar	360
Mauritania	181
Niger	143
Senegal	236
Togo	495

ITU Issue

Telegraph, Syncom Satellite and ITU Emblem

CD120

Centenary of the International Telecommunication Union.

1965, May 17

Comoro Isls.	C14
Fr. Polynesia	C33
Fr. So. & Antarctic Terr.	C8
New Caledonia	C40
New Hebrides	124-125
St. Pierre & Miquelon	C29
Somali Coast	C36
Wallis & Futuna Isls.	C20

French Satellite A-1 Issue

Diamant Rocket and Launching Installations

CD121

Launching of France's first satellite, Nov. 26, 1965.

1965–66

Comoro Isls.	C15-C16
France	1137-1138
Fr. Polynesia	C40-C41
Fr. So. & Antarctic Terr.	C9-C10
New Caledonia	C44-C45
St. Pierre & Miquelon	C30-C31
Somali Coast	C39-C40
Wallis & Futuna Isls.	C22-C23

French Satellite D-1 Issue

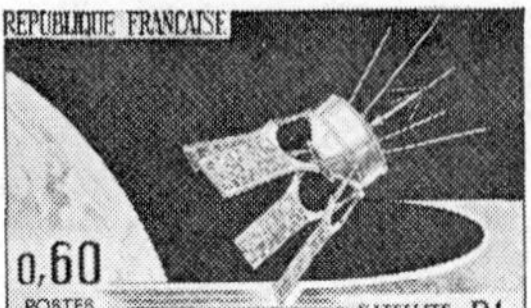

D-1 Satellite in Orbit

CD122

Launching of the D-1 satellite at Hammaguir, Algeria, Feb. 17, 1966.

1966

Comoro Isls.	C17
France	1148
Fr. Polynesia	C42
Fr. So. & Antarctic Terr.	C11
New Caledonia	C46
St. Pierre & Miquelon	C32
Somali Coast	C49
Wallis & Futuna Isls.	C24

Air Afrique Issue, 1966

Planes and Air Afrique Emblem

CD123

Introduction of DC-8F planes by Air Afrique.

1966

Cameroun	C79
Cent. African Rep.	C35
Chad	C26
Congo, P.R.	C42
Dahomey	C42
Gabon	C47
Ivory Coast	C32
Mauritania	C57
Niger	C63
Senegal	C47
Togo	C54
Upper Volta	C31

African Postal Union Issue, 1967

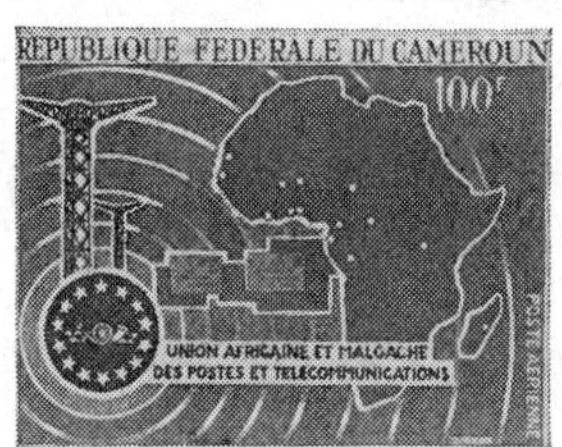

Telecommunications Symbols and Map of Africa

CD124

Fifth anniversary of the establishment of the African and Malagasy Union of Posts and Telecommunications, UAMPT.

1967

Cameroun	C90
Cent. African Rep.	C46
Chad	C37
Congo, P.R.	C57
Dahomey	C61
Gabon	C58
Ivory Coast	C34
Madagascar	C85
Mauritania	C65
Niger	C75
Rwanda	C1-C3
Senegal	C60
Togo	C81
Upper Volta	C50

Monetary Union Issue

Gold Token of the Ashantis, 17–18th Centuries

CD125

Fifth anniversary of the West African Monetary Union.

1967, Nov. 4

Dahomey	244
Ivory Coast	259
Mauritania	238
Niger	204
Senegal	294
Togo	623
Upper Volta	181

WHO Anniversary Issue

Sun, Flowers and WHO Emblem

CD126

20th anniversary of the World Health Organization.

1968, May 4

Afars & Issas	317
Comoro Isls.	73
Fr. Polynesia	241-242
Fr. So. & Antarctic Terr.	31
New Caledonia	367
St. Pierre & Miquelon	377
Wallis & Futuna Isls.	169

Human Rights Year Issue

Human Rights Flame

CD127

International Human Rights Year.

1968, Aug. 10

Afars & Issas	322-323
Comoro Isls.	76
Fr. Polynesia	243-244
Fr. So. & Antarctic Terr.	32
New Caledonia	369
St. Pierre & Miquelon	382
Wallis & Futuna Isls.	170

2nd PHILEXAFRIQUE Issue

Gabon No. 131 and Industrial Plant

CD128

Opening of PHILEXAFRIQUE, Abidjan, Feb. 14.

Each stamp shows a local scene and stamp.

1969, Feb. 14

Cameroun	C118
Cent. African Rep.	C65
Chad	C48
Congo, P.R.	C77
Dahomey	C94
Gabon	C82
Ivory Coast	C38-C40
Madagascar	C92
Mali	C65
Mauritania	C80
Niger	C104
Senegal	C68
Togo	C104
Upper Volta	C62

Concorde Issue

Concorde in Flight
CD129

First flight of the prototype Concorde super-sonic plane at Toulouse, Mar. 1, 1969.

1969

Afars & Issas	C56
Comoro Isls.	C29
France	C42
Fr. Polynesia	C50
Fr. So. & Antarctic Terr.	C18
New Caledonia	C63
St. Pierre & Miquelon	C40
Wallis & Futuna Isls.	C30

Development Bank Issue

Bank Emblem—CD130

Fifth anniversary of the African Development Bank.

1969

Cameroun	499
Chad	217
Congo, P.R.	181–182
Ivory Coast	281
Mali	127–128
Mauritania	267
Niger	220
Senegal	317–318
Upper Volta	201

ILO Issue

ILO Headquarters, Geneva, and Emblem
CD131

50th anniversary of the International Labor Organization.

1969–70

Afars & Issas	337
Comoro Isls.	83
Fr. Polynesia	251–252
Fr. So. & Antarctic Terr.	35
New Caledonia	379
St. Pierre & Miquelon	396
Wallis & Futuna Isls.	172

ASECNA Issue

Map of Africa, Plane and Airport
CD132

10th anniversary of the Agency for the Security of Aerial Navigation in Africa and Madagascar (ASECNA, Agence pour la Sécurité de la Navigation Aérienne en Afrique et à Madagascar).

1969–70

Cameroun	500
Cent. African Rep.	119
Chad	222
Congo, P.R.	197
Dahomey	269
Gabon	260
Ivory Coast	287
Mali	130
Niger	221
Senegal	321
Upper Volta	204

U.P.U. Headquarters Issue

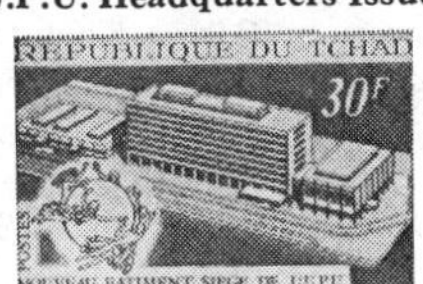

U.P.U. Headquarters and Emblem
CD133

New Universal Postal Union headquarters, Bern, Switzerland.

1970

Afars & Issas	342
Algeria	443
Cameroun	503–504
Cent. African Rep.	125
Chad	225
Comoro Isls.	84
Congo, P.R.	216
Fr. Polynesia	261–262
Fr. So. & Antarctic Terr.	36
Gabon	258
Ivory Coast	295
Madagascar	444
Mali	134–135
Mauritania	283
New Caledonia	382
Niger	231–232
St. Pierre & Miquelon	397–398
Senegal	328–329
Tunisia	535
Wallis & Futuna Isls.	173

De Gaulle Issue

General de Gaulle, 1940
CD134

First anniversary of the death of Charles de Gaulle, (1890–1970), President of France.

1971–72

Afars & Issas	356–357
Comoro Isls.	104–105
France	1322–1325
Fr. Polynesia	270–271
Fr. So. & Antarctic Terr.	52–53
New Caledonia	393–394
Reunion	377, 380
St. Pierre & Miquelon	417–418
Wallis & Futuna Isls.	177–178

African Postal Union Issue, 1971

Carved Stool, UAMPT Building, Brazzaville, Congo
CD135

10th anniversary of the establishment of the African and Malagasy Posts and Telecommunications Union, UAMPT.

Each stamp has a different native design.

1971, Nov. 13

Cameroun	C177
Cent. African Rep.	C89
Chad	C94
Congo, P.R.	C136
Dahomey	C146
Gabon	C120
Ivory Coast	C47
Mauritania	C113
Niger	C164
Rwanda	C8
Senegal	C105
Togo	C166
Upper Volta	C97

West African Monetary Union Issue

African Couple, City, Village and Commemorative Coin
CD136

10th anniversary of the West African Monetary Union.

1972, Nov. 2

Dahomey	300
Ivory Coast	331
Mauritania	299
Niger	258
Senegal	374
Togo	825
Upper Volta	280

African Postal Union Issue, 1973

Telecommunications Symbols and Map of Africa
CD137

11th anniversary of the African and Malagasy Posts and Telecommunications Union (UAMPT).

1973, Sept. 12

Cameroun	574
Cent. African Rep.	194
Chad	272
Congo, P.R.	289
Dahomey	311
Gabon	320
Ivory Coast	361
Madagascar	500
Mauritania	304
Niger	287
Rwanda	540
Senegal	393
Togo	849
Upper Volta	285

Philexafrique II—Essen Issue

Buffalo and Dahomey No. C33
CD138

Wild Ducks and Baden No. 1
CD139

Designs: Indigenous fauna, local and German stamps.

Types CD138–CD139 printed horizontally and vertically se-tenant in sheets of 10 (2x5). Label between horizontal pairs alternately commemorates Philexafrique II, Libreville, Gabon, June 1978, and 2nd International Stamp Fair, Essen, Germany, Nov. 1–5.

HISTORICAL FOOTNOTES

Scouting Year: 75th anniversary of scouting and 125th birth anniversary of its founder, Lord Baden-Powell (1857-1941).

Robert Koch: Centenary of tuberculosis bacillus discovery by Robert Koch (1843-1910), German physician. Awarded 1905 Nobel Prize for physiology and medicine; also discovered cholera bacillus, 1883.

George Washington: 250th birth anniversary of George Washington (1732-1799), first U.S. president.

Charles Darwin: Death centenary of Charles Darwin (1809-1882), British naturalist. Traveled through South America and Australasia, 1831-1836, aboard the Beagle developing his theory of evolution. Published findings in *On the Origin of Species,* 1859.

Norman Rockwell (1894-1978): American illustrator who is best known for his paintings of people in everyday situations. Many of his works have been on the covers of *The Saturday Evening Post, Boy's Life, American Boy* and *St. Nicholas.*

Lewis B. Carroll (1832-1898): English author of the childhood classics *Alice in Wonderland* and *Through the Looking Glass.* He also wrote many works on mathematics under his real name, Charles Lutwidge Dodgson.

World Cup Soccer: The 12th World Cup Soccer Championship was held in Spain from June 13th to July 11th. The series, held every 4 years, opened in Barcelona with Belgium over Argentina before a crowd of 95,000. The 52 games were held in 17 stadiums in 14 cities with 24 participating teams. The final game was played in Madrid with Italy defeating Germany by a score of 3 to 1.

SCOTT'S STANDARD POSTAGE STAMP CATALOGUE

ABYSSINIA

(See Ethiopia.)

AFARS AND ISSAS, French Territory of the

(ä-färz′ and ī-säz′)

LOCATION—East Africa.
GOVT.—French Overseas Territory.
AREA—8,880 sq. mi.
POP.—150,000 (est. 1974).
CAPITAL—Djibouti (Jibuti).

The French overseas territory of Somali Coast was renamed the French Territory of the Afars and Issas in 1967. It became the Djibouti Republic (which see) on June 27, 1977.

100 Centimes = 1 Franc

Imperforates

Most stamps of Afars and Issas exist imperforate in issued and trial colors, and also in small presentation sheets in issued colors.

Gray-headed Kingfisher
A48

Designs: 15fr, Oystercatcher. 50fr, Greenshanks. 55fr, Abyssinian roller. 60fr, Ground squirrel (vert.).

Unwmkd.

1967 Engraved *Perf. 13*

310	A48	10fr brt bl, gray grn & blk	1.35	1.35
311	A48	15fr dk brn, bl, ol & ocher	2.25	1.75
312	A48	50fr blk, sl grn & brn	5.00	3.50
313	A48	55fr vio, brt bl & gray grn	7.00	5.50
314	A48	60fr ocher, brt grn & sl grn	9.00	6.00
		Nos. 310-314 (5)	24.60	18.10

Dates of Issue: 10fr, 55fr, Aug. 21; 15fr, 50fr, 60fr, Sept. 25. See No. C50.

Soccer
A49

Design: 30fr, Basketball.

1967, Dec. 18 Engraved *Perf. 13*

315	A49	25fr bl, brn & emer	2.00	1.50
316	A49	30fr red lil, Prus bl & brn	2.50	2.10

WHO Anniversary Issue

Common Design Type

1968, May 4 Engraved *Perf. 13*

317	CD126	15fr multi	1.20	90

Issued to commemorate the 20th anniversary of the World Health Organization.

Common Design Types pictured in section at front of book.

Damerdjog Fortress
A50

Administration Buildings: 25fr, Ali Addé. 30fr, Dorra. 40fr, Assamo.

1968, May 17 Engraved *Perf. 13*

318	A50	20fr sl, brn & emer	80	55
319	A50	25fr brt grn, bl & brn	90	55
320	A50	30fr brn ol, brn org & sl	1.00	75
321	A50	40fr brn ol, sl & brt grn	2.25	1.35

Human Rights Year Issue

Common Design Type

1968, Aug. 10 Engraved *Perf. 13*

322	CD127	10fr pur, ver & org	90	75
323	CD127	70fr grn, pur & org	2.25	1.65

International Human Rights Year.

Radio-television Station, Djibouti
A52

High Commission Palace, Djibouti
A53

Designs: 2fr, Justice Building. 5fr, Chamber of Deputies. 8fr, Great Mosque. 15fr, Monument of Free French Forces (vert.). 40fr, Djibouti Post Office. 70fr, Residence of Gov. Léonce Lagarde at Obock. No. 332, Djibouti Harbormaster's Building. No. 333, Control tower, Djibouti Airport.

1968–70 Engraved *Perf. 13*

324	A52	1fr dk red, sky bl & ind ('69)	18	12
325	A52	2fr grn, bl & ind ('69)	18	12
326	A52	5fr brn, sky bl & grn ('69)	28	18
327	A52	8fr choc, emer & gray ('69)	35	22
328	A52	15fr grn, sky bl & yel brn ('69)	1.60	1.20
329	A52	40fr grn, brn & sl ('70)	1.50	1.10
330	A53	60fr multi	2.10	1.50
331	A53	70fr dl grn, gray & ol bis ('69)	2.50	1.85
332	A53	85fr multi ('69)	3.00	1.75
333	A52	85fr dk grn, bl & gray ('70)	3.00	2.25
		Nos. 324-333 (10)	14.69	10.29

Locust
A54

Designs: 50fr, Pest control by helicopter. 55fr, Pest control by plane.

1969, Oct. 6 Engraved *Perf. 13*

334	A54	15fr brn, grn & sl	90	55
335	A54	50fr dk grn, bl & ol brn	1.60	1.25
336	A54	55fr red brn, bl & brn	2.00	1.35

Campaign against locusts.

ILO Issue

Common Design Type

1969, Nov. 24 Engraved *Perf. 13*

337	CD131	30fr org, gray & lil	1.50	1.10

Afar Daggar in Ornamental Scabbard
A56

1970, Apr. 3 Engraved *Perf. 13*

338	A56	10fr yel grn, dk grn & org brn	45	32
339	A56	15fr yel grn, bl & org brn	55	32
340	A56	20fr yel grn, red & org brn	65	50
341	A56	25fr yel grn, plum & org brn	1.10	50

See No. 364.

U.P.U. Headquarters Issue

Common Design Type

1970, May 20 Engr. *Perf. 13*

342	CD133	25fr brn, brt grn & choc	90	65

Trap-shooting
A57

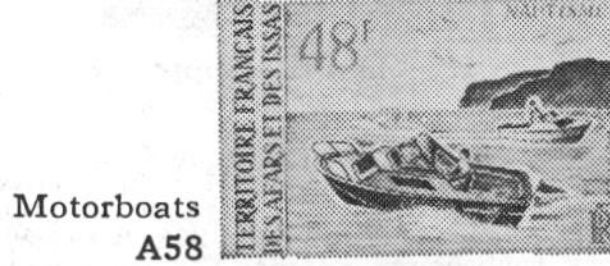

Motorboats
A58

Designs: 50fr, Steeplechase. 55fr, Sailboat (vert.). 60fr, Equestrians.

1970 Engraved *Perf. 13*

343	A57	30fr dp brn, yel grn & brt bl	1.10	75
344	A58	48fr bl & multi	1.50	90
345	A58	50fr cop red, bl & pur	1.75	1.00
346	A58	55fr red brn, bl & ol	1.60	1.20
347	A58	60fr ol, blk & red brn	2.25	1.35
		Nos. 343-347 (5)	8.20	5.20

Issue dates: 30fr, June 5; 48fr, Oct. 9; 50fr, 60fr, Nov. 6.

Automatic Ferry, Tadjourah
A59

1970, Nov. 25

348	A59	48fr bl, brn & grn	1.50	90

Volcanic Geode
A60

Diabase and Chrysolite
A61

Designs: 10fr, Doleritic basalt. 15fr, Olivine basalt.

1971 Photogravure *Perf. 13*

349	A61	10fr blk & multi	40	30
350	A61	15fr blk & multi	50	35
351	A60	25fr blk, crim & brn	90	60
352	A61	40fr blk & multi	1.50	90

Issue dates: 10fr, Nov. 22; 15fr, Oct. 8; 25fr, Apr. 26; 40fr, Jan. 25.

Manta Ray
A62

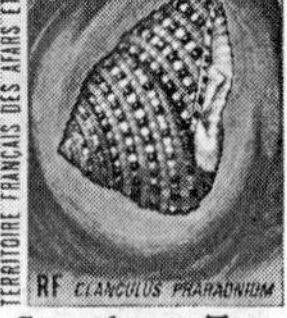

Strawberry Top
A63

Fishes: 5fr, Dolphinfish. 9fr, Smalltooth sawfish.

1971, July 1 Photo. *Perf. 12x12½*

353	A62	4fr grn & multi	55	45
354	A62	5fr bl & multi	55	45
355	A62	9fr red & multi	1.10	90

See No. C60.

De Gaulle Issue

Common Design Type

Designs: 60fr, Gen. Charles de Gaulle, 1940. 85fr, Pres. de Gaulle, 1970.

1971, Nov. 9 Engraved *Perf. 13*

356	CD134	60fr dk vio bl & blk	2.00	1.50
357	CD134	85fr dk vio bl & blk	2.50	2.10

1972, Mar. 8 Photo. *Perf. 12½x13*

Shells: 9fr, Cypraea pantherina. 20fr, Bull-mouth helmet. 50fr, Ethiopian volute.

358	A63	4fr ol & multi	35	22
359	A63	9fr dk bl & multi	55	30
360	A63	20fr dp grn & multi	90	45
361	A63	50fr dp cl & multi	1.75	90

Shepherd—A64

Design: 10fr, Dromedary breeding.

1973, Apr. 11 Photo. *Perf. 13*

362	A64	9fr bl & multi	40	22
363	A64	10fr bl & multi	50	22

Afar Dagger A65

1974, Jan. 29 Engraved *Perf. 13*

364	A65	30fr sl grn & dk brn	1.10	75

Flamingos, Lake Abbé—A66

Designs: Flamingos and different views of Lake Abbé.

1974, Feb. 22 Photogravure *Perf. 13*

370	A60	5fr multi	22	18
371	A60	15fr multi	45	25
372	A60	50fr multi	1.60	90

Soccer Ball—A67

1974, May 24 Engr. *Perf. 13*

373	A67	25fr blk & emer	1.35	90

World Cup Soccer Championship, Munich, June 13–July 7.

Letters Around UPU Emblem A68 — Oleo Chrysophylla A69

1974, Oct. 9 Engraved *Perf. 13*

374	A68	20fr multi	1.10	55
375	A68	100fr multi	3.00	2.50

Centenary of Universal Postal Union.

1974, Nov. 22 Photogravure
Multicolored

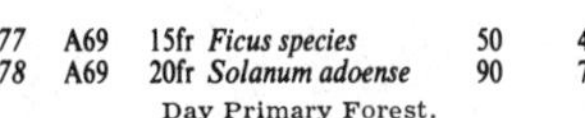

376	A69	10fr *shown*	40	30
377	A69	15fr *Ficus species*	50	40
378	A69	20fr *Solanum adoense*	90	70

Day Primary Forest.

No. 364 Surcharged with New Value and Two Bars in Red

1975, Jan. 1 Engr. *Perf. 13*

379	A65	40fr on 30fr multi	1.25	90

Treasury—A70

Design: 25fr, Government buildings.

1975, Jan. 7 Engr. *Perf. 13*

380	A70	8fr bl, gray & red	38	22
381	A70	25fr red, bl & ind	70	50

Ranella Spinosa—A71

Sea Shells: No. 382, Darioconus textile. No. 383, Murex palmarosa. 10fr, Conus sumatrensis. 15fr, Cypraea pulchra. No. 386, 45fr, Murex scolopax. No. 387, Cypraea exhusta. 55fr, Cypraea erythraensis. 60fr, Conus taeniatus.

1975–76 Engraved *Perf. 13*

382	A71	5fr bl grn & brn	32	22
383	A71	5fr bl & multi ('76)	22	12
384	A71	10fr lil, blk & brn	45	30
385	A71	15fr bl, ind & brn	60	40
386	A71	20fr pur & lt brn	90	55
387	A71	20fr brt grn & multi ('76)	45	30
388	A71	40fr grn & brn	1.50	1.00
389	A71	45fr grn, bl & bis	1.35	90
390	A71	55fr turq & multi ('76)	1.20	90
391	A71	60fr buff & sep ('76)	1.50	1.00
		Nos. 382-391 (10)	8.49	5.69

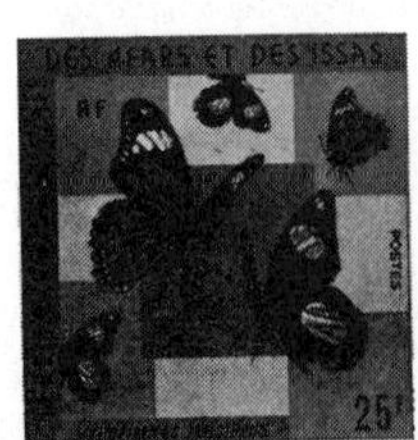

Hypolimnas Misippus A72

Butterflies: 40fr, Papilio nireus. 50fr, Acraea anemosa. 65fr, Holocerina smilax menieri. 70fr, Papilio demodocus. No. 397, Papilio dardanus. No. 398, Balachowsky gonimbrasca. 150fr, Vanessa cardui.

1975–76 Photogravure *Perf. 13*

392	A72	25fr emer & multi	75	55
393	A72	40fr yel & multi	90	60
394	A72	50fr ultra & multi ('76)	1.10	70
395	A72	65fr ol & multi ('76)	1.35	90
396	A72	70fr vio & multi	2.25	1.60
397	A72	100fr bl & multi	2.50	2.10
398	A72	100fr Prus bl & multi ('76)	2.25	1.75
399	A72	150fr grn & multi ('76)	2.50	1.80
		Nos. 392-399 (8)	13.60	10.00

Mongoose—A73

Animals: 10fr, Hyena. No. 401, Catarrhine monkeys (vert.). No. 402, Wild ass (vert.). 30fr, Antelope. 60fr, Porcupines (vert.). 70fr, Skunks. 200fr, Aardvarks.

Perf. 13x12½, 12½x13

1975–76 Photogravure

400	A73	10fr lt vio & multi ('76)	30	22
401	A73	15fr yel grn & multi	50	35
402	A73	15fr grn & multi ('76)	38	30
403	A73	30fr bl & multi ('76)	75	50
404	A73	50fr dp org & multi	1.50	1.00
405	A73	60fr yel brn & multi	2.10	1.20
406	A73	70fr blk & brn	2.75	1.60
407	A73	200fr bl gray & multi	4.50	3.25
		Nos. 400-407 (8)	12.78	8.42

Pin-tailed Whydah A74 — Palms A75

Birds: 25fr, Rose-ringed parakeet. 50fr, Variable sunbird. 60fr, Purple heron. No. 417, Hammerhead. No. 418, Turtle dove. 300fr, African spoonbill.

1975–76 Photo. *Perf. 12½x13*

413	A74	20fr lil, blk & org	50	30
414	A74	25fr car rose & multi ('76)	55	30
415	A74	50fr bl & multi	1.00	60
416	A74	60fr multi	1.50	1.10
417	A74	100fr lt grn & multi	1.80	1.50
418	A74	100fr lt yel & multi ('76)	1.75	1.40
419	A74	300fr multi ('76)	5.00	3.25
		Nos. 413-419 (7)	12.10	8.45

1975, Dec. 19 Engr. *Perf. 13*

421	A75	20fr brt bl & multi	45	30

Satellite and Alexander Graham Bell A76

1976, Mar. 10 Engr. *Perf. 13*

422	A76	200fr dp bl, org & sl grn	3.25	2.25

Centenary of the first telephone call by Alexander Graham Bell, Mar. 10, 1876.

Basketball A77

Designs: 15fr, Bicycling. 40fr, Soccer. 60fr, Running.

1976, July 7 Litho. *Perf. 12½*

423	A77	10fr lt bl & multi	22	18
424	A77	15fr yel & multi	30	25
425	A77	40fr org red & multi	80	60
426	A77	60fr lt grn & multi	1.20	1.00

21st Olympic Games, Montreal, Canada, July 17–Aug. 1.

Turkeyfish—A78

1976, Aug. 10 Photo. *Perf. 13x13½*

428	A78	45fr bl & multi	1.10	80

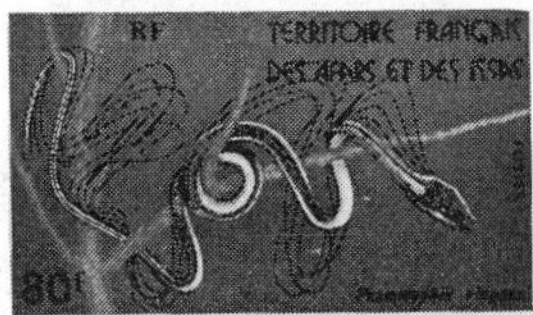

Psammophis Elegans—A79

Design: 70fr, Naja nigricollis (vert.).

Perf. 13x13½, 13½x13

1976, Sept. 27 Photogravure

430	A79	70fr ocher & multi	1.40	1.10
431	A79	80fr emer & multi	1.60	1.40

Motorcyclist A80

1977, Jan. 27 Litho. *Perf. 12x12½*

432	A80	200fr multi	3.75	2.75

Moto-Cross motorcycle race.

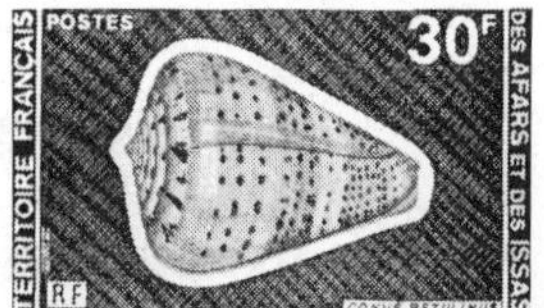

Conus Betulinus—A81

Sea Shells: 5fr, Cyprea tigris. 70fr, Conus striatus. 85fr, Cyprea mauritiana.

1977 Engr. *Perf. 13*

433	A81	5fr multi	45	30
434	A81	30fr multi	55	40

435	A81	70fr multi	1.60	1.25
436	A81	85fr multi	2.75	1.75

Gaterin Gaterinus
A82

Design: 65fr, Barracudas.

1977, Apr. 15 Photo. *Perf. 13x12½*

437	A82	15fr multi	45	30
438	A82	65fr multi	1.20	85

Stamps of the French Territory of the Afars and Issas were replaced in 1977 by those of the Republic of Djibouti.

AIR POST STAMPS

Tawny Eagles AP16 — Parachutists AP17

1967, Aug. 21 Engraved *Perf. 13*

C50	AP16	200fr multi	9.00	4.25

1968 Engraved *Perf. 13*

Design: 85fr, Water skier and skin diver.

C51	AP17	48fr brn ol, Prus bl & brn	2.50	1.50
C52	AP17	85fr dk brn, ol & Prus bl	3.75	3.00

Issue dates: 48fr. Jan. 5; 85fr, Mar. 15.

Aerial Map of the Territory
AP18

1968, Nov. 15 Engraved *Perf. 13*

C53	AP18	500fr bl, dk brn & ocher	13.50	6.75

Buildings Type of Regular Issue

Designs: 100fr, Cathedral (vert.). 200fr, Sayed Hassan Mosque (vert.).

1969 Engraved *Perf. 13*

C54	A53	100fr grn, sky bl & bis brn	2.75	1.35
C55	A53	200fr lil, bl, brn & blk	5.50	3.25

Issue dates: 100fr, Apr. 4; 200fr, May 8.

Concorde Issue

Common Design Type

1969, Apr. 17

C56	CD129	100fr org red & ol	15.00	12.00

Arta Ionospheric Station—AP19 — Japanese Sword Guard, Fish Design—AP20

1970, May 8 Engraved *Perf. 13*

C57	AP19	70fr multi	2.75	2.00

Gold Embossed

1970, Sept. 29 *Perf. 12½*

Design: 200fr, Japanese sword guard, horse design.

C58	AP20	100fr gold, yel grn, ultra & brn	4.75	3.75
C59	AP20	200fr gold, car, yel grn & brn	7.50	5.50

EXPO '70 International Exposition, Osaka, Japan, Mar. 15–Sept. 13.

Parrot-fish
AP21

1971, July 1 Photo. *Perf. 12½*

C60	AP21	30fr blk & multi	1.60	1.35

Djibouti Harbor—AP22

1971, Nov. 26

C61	AP22	100fr bl & multi	2.75	1.80

New Djibouti harbor.

Lichtenstein's Sandgrouse AP23 — Running, Olympic Rings AP24

Birds: 49fr, Hoopoe. 66fr, Great snipe. 500fr, Tawny-breasted francolin.

1972 Photogravure *Perf. 12½x13*

C62	AP23	30fr multi	1.35	85
C63	AP23	49fr multi	2.25	1.40
C64	AP23	66fr bl & multi	2.75	2.00
C65	AP23	500fr multi	12.50	6.25

Issue dates: No. C65, Nov. 3, others Apr. 21.

1972, June 8 Engr. *Perf. 13*

Designs (Olympic Rings and): 10fr, Basketball. 55fr, Swimming (horiz.). 60fr, Olympic torch and Greek frieze (horiz.).

C66	AP24	5fr pur, bl grn & dk brn	40	30
C67	AP24	10fr dk red, sl grn & dk brn	50	40
C68	AP24	55fr grn, brn & bl	1.80	1.10
C69	AP24	60fr bl grn, dk red & pur	2.40	1.25

20th Olympic Games, Munich, Aug. 26–Sept. 11.

Louis Pasteur—AP25

Design: 100fr, Albert Calmette and C. Guérin.

1972, Oct. 5 Engraved *Perf. 13*

C70	AP25	20fr rose car, ol bis & brt grn	1.00	55
C71	AP25	100fr dk brn, brt grn & dl red	2.75	2.25

Pasteur, Calmette, Guérin, chemists and bacteriologists, benefactors of mankind.

Map and Views of Territory—AP26

Design: 200fr, Woman and Mosque of Djibouti (vert.).

1973, Jan. 15 Photo. *Perf. 13*

C72	AP26	30fr brn & multi	2.50	2.00
C73	AP26	200fr multi	8.00	6.25

Visit of Pres. Georges Pompidou of France, Jan. 15–17.

Oryx—AP27

Animals: 50fr, Dik-dik. 66fr, Caracal.

1973, Feb. 26 Photo. *Perf. 13x12½*

C74	AP27	30fr grn & multi	1.30	90
C75	AP27	50fr rose & multi	2.25	1.20
C76	AP27	66fr lil & multi	2.50	2.00

See also Nos. C94–C96.

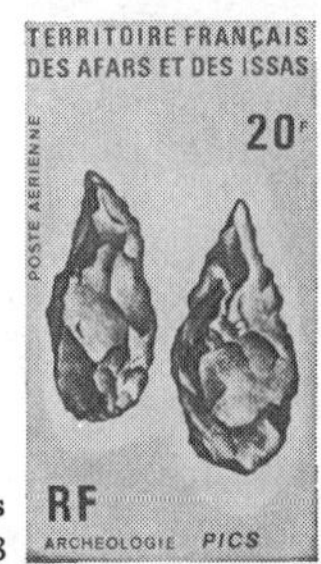

Celts
AP28

Designs: Various pre-historic flint tools. 40fr, 60fr, horizontal.

1973 Photographed *Perf. 13*

C77	AP28	20fr yel grn, blk & brn	1.25	75
C78	AP28	40fr yel & multi	1.25	90
C79	AP28	49fr lil & multi	2.00	1.50
C80	AP28	60fr bl & multi	2.25	1.40

Issue dates: 20fr, 49fr, Mar. 16; 40fr, 60fr, Sept. 7.

Octopus—AP29

Design: 60fr, Dugong.

1973, Mar. 16

C81	AP29	40fr multi	1.20	90
C82	AP29	60fr brn & multi	2.10	1.25

Copernicus AP30

Baboons AP31

Designs: 8fr, Nicolaus Copernicus (1473–1534), Polish astronomer. 9fr, William C. Roentgen (1845–1923), physicist, X-ray discoverer. C85, Edward Jenner (1749–1823), physician, discoverer of vaccination. No. C86, Marie Curie (1867–1934), discoverer of radium and polonium. 49fr, Robert Koch (1843–1910), physician and bacteriologist. 50fr, Clément Ader (1841–1925), French aviation pioneer. 55fr, Guglielmo Marconi (1874–1937), Italian electrical engineer, inventor. 85fr, Molière (1622–1673), French playwright. 100fr, Henri Farman (1874–1937), French aviation pioneer. 150fr, André-Marie Ampère (1775–1836), French physicist. 250fr, Michelangelo Buonarroti (1475–1564), Italian sculptor, painter and architect.

1973–75 Engraved *Perf. 13*

C83	AP30	8fr blk, dk bis & mar	45	30
C84	AP30	9fr brn, ocher & vio brn	45	30
C85	AP30	10fr car, brn & vio brn	45	38
C86	AP30	10fr red lil, dp cl & bl	45	38
C87	AP30	49fr sl grn, yel grn & vio brn	2.25	1.50
C88	AP30	50fr ol brn, sl grn & bl	1.75	1.00
C89	AP30	55fr multi ('74)	1.75	1.40
C90	AP30	85fr bl, vio & ind	2.75	2.00
C91	AP30	100fr yel grn, vio brn & bl ('74)	3.25	2.75
C92	AP30	150fr multi	3.25	2.25
C93	AP30	250fr blk, grn & brn	5.00	4.00
		Nos. C83-C93 (11)	21.80	16.26

Issue dates: 8fr, 85fr, May 9, 1973. 9fr, C85, 49fr, Oct. 12, 1973. 100fr, Jan. 29, 1974. 55fr, Mar. 22, 1974. C86, Aug. 23, 1974. 150fr, July 24, 1975. 250fr, June 26, 1975. 50fr, Sept. 25, 1975.

Perf. 12½x13, 13x12½

1973, Dec. 12 Photogravure

Designs: 50fr, Genets (horiz.). 66fr, Hares.

C94	AP31	20fr org & multi	75	60
C95	AP31	50fr multi	1.50	1.10
C96	AP31	66fr bl & multi	2.75	2.25

Spearfishing—AP32

1974, Apr. 14 Engr. *Perf. 13*

C97	AP32	200fr multi	5.50	4.50

No. C97 was prepared for release in Nov. 1972, to commemorate the 3rd Underwater Spearfishing Contest in the Red Sea. Dates have been obliterated with a rectangle and the stamp was not issued without this obliteration.

Rock Carvings, Balho—AP33

1974, Apr. 26

C98	AP33	200fr car & sl	5.00	4.00

Lake Assal—AP34

Designs (Lake Assal): 50fr, Rock formations on shore. 85fr, Crystallized wood.

1974, Oct. 25 Photogravure *Perf. 13*

C99	AP34	49fr multi	1.20	1.00
C100	AP34	50fr multi	1.50	1.20
C101	AP34	85fr multi	2.40	1.80

Guinea Dove AP35

1975, May 23 Photo. *Perf. 13*

C102	AP35	500fr multi	10.00	5.50

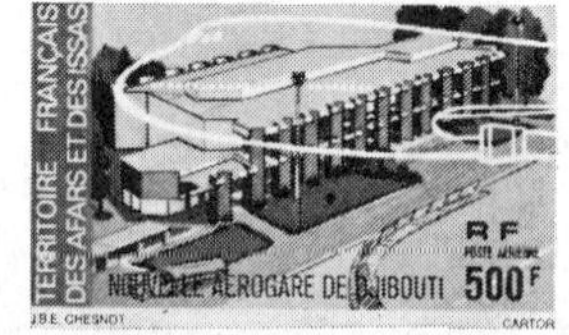

Djibouti Airport—AP36

1977, Mar. 1 Litho. *Perf. 12*

C103	AP36	500fr multi	9.00	7.50

Opening of new Djibouti Airport.

Thomas A. Edison and Phonograph—AP37

Design: 75fr, Alexander Volta, electric train, lines and light bulb.

1977, May 5 Engr. *Perf. 13*

C104	AP37	55fr multi	1.50	1.20
C105	AP37	75fr multi	2.50	2.25

Famous inventors: Thomas Alva Edison (1847–1931) and Alexander Volta (1745–1827).

POSTAGE DUE STAMPS

Nomad's Milk Jug D3

Unwmkd.

1969, Dec. 15 Engr. *Perf. 14x13*

J49	D3	1fr red brn, red lil & sl	10	10
J50	D3	2fr red brn, emer & sl	12	12
J51	D3	5fr red brn, bl & sl	22	22
J52	D3	10fr red brn, brn & sl	40	40

AFGHANISTAN

(ăf·găn'ĭ·stăn ; ăf·găn'ĭs·tăn')

LOCATION—Central Asia, bounded by Persia, Russian Turkestan, Pakistan, Baluchistan and China.

GOVT.—Republic.

AREA—253,861 sq. mi.

POP.—19,800,000 (est. 1976).

CAPITAL—Kabul.

Afghanistan changed from a constitutional monarchy to a republic in July, 1973.

12 Shahi = 6 Sanar = 3 Abasi =

2 Krans = 1 Rupee Kabuli

60 Paisas = 1 Rupee (1921)

100 Pouls = 1 Rupee Afghani (1927)

CHARACTERS OF VALUE.

Shahi.

1871-78 A7 A8

Sanar. Abasi. 6 Shahi.

1871–78 1871 1872

1 Rupee. ½ Rupee.

1874 1876(A8) 1876 (A7)

1 Rupee.

Rupee.

1872 1874 1876 (A8) 1877-78

From 1871 to 1892 and 1898 the Moslem year date appears on the stamp. Numerals as follows:

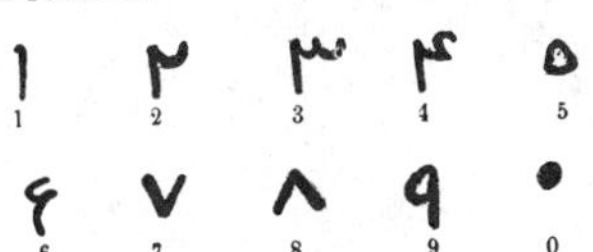

Until 1891 cancellation consisted of cutting or tearing a piece from the stamps. Such copies should not be considered as damaged.

Prices are for cut square examples of good color. Cut to shape or faded copies sell for much less, particularly Nos. 2–10.

Nos. 2–108 are on laid paper of varying thickness except where wove is noted.

Until 1907 all stamps were issued ungummed.

The tiger's head on types A2 to A11 symbolizes the name of the contemporary amir, Sher (Tiger) Ali.

Kingdom of Kabul

Tiger's Head—A2
(Both circles dotted.)

Dated "1288".
Lithographed

1871 *Imperf.* **Unwmkd.**

2	A2	1sh black	150.00	25.00
3	A2	1sa black	90.00	22.50
4	A2	1ab black	50.00	22.50

Thirty varieties of the shahi, 10 of the sanar and 5 of the abasi.

Similar designs without the tiger's head in the center are revenues.

A3
(Outer circle dotted.)

Dated "1288".

5	A3	1sh black	210.00	45.00
6	A3	1sa black	90.00	30.00
7	A3	1ab black	50.00	32.50

Five varieties of each.

A4

Dated "1289".
Toned Wove Paper

1872

8	A4	6sh violet	*700.00*	*450.00*
9	A4	1rup violet	850.00	525.00

Two varieties of each. Date varies in location. Printed in sheets of 4 (2x2) containing two of each denomination.

Most used copies are smeared with a greasy ink cancel.

A4a

Dated "1290"

1873 White Laid Paper

10	A4a	1sh black	12.00	6.00
	a.	Corner ornament missing	*550.00*	*450.00*
	b.	Corner ornament retouched	*85.00*	*35.00*

15 varieties. Nos. 10a, 10b are the sixth stamp on the sheet.

A5

1873

11	A5	1sh black	3.00	2.50
11A	A5	1sh violet	*600.00*	

Sixty varieties of each.

1874 Dated "1291".

12	A5	1ab black	50.00	35.00
13	A5	½rup black	27.50	25.00
14	A5	1rup black	32.50	27.50

Five varieties of each.

Nos. 12–14 were printed on the same sheet. Se-tenant varieties exist.

A6 A7

1875 Dated "1292".

15	A6	1sa black	210.00	150.00
	a.	Wide outer circle	*750.00*	
16	A6	1ab black	300.00	210.00
17	A6	1sa brn vio	32.50	32.50
	a.	Wide outer circle	150.00	
18	A6	1ab brn vio	55.00	35.00

Ten varieties of the sanar, five of the abasi.

Nos. 15–16 and 17–18 were printed in the same sheets. Se-tenant pairs exist.

1876 Dated "1293"

19	A7	1sh black	350.00	190.00
20	A7	1sa black	450.00	250.00
21	A7	1ab black	625.00	250.00
22	A7	½rup black	450.00	250.00
23	A7	1rup black	625.00	250.00
24	A7	1sh violet	450.00	250.00
25	A7	1sa violet	425.00	250.00
26	A7	1ab violet	550.00	250.00
27	A7	½rup violet	110.00	67.50
28	A7	1rup violet	110.00	85.00

12 varieties of the shahi and 3 each of the other values.

A8

1876 Dated "1293".

29	A8	1sh gray	7.00	5.50
30	A8	1sa gray	10.00	5.50
31	A8	1ab gray	20.00	10.00
32	A8	½rup gray	22.50	14.00
33	A8	1rup gray	30.00	14.00
34	A8	1sh ol blk	160.00	
35	A8	1sa ol blk	200.00	
36	A8	1ab ol blk	425.00	
37	A8	½rup ol blk	285.00	
38	A8	1rup ol blk	350.00	
39	A8	1sh green	30.00	5.00
40	A8	1sa green	45.00	21.00
41	A8	1ab green	62.50	45.00
42	A8	½rup green	125.00	50.00
43	A8	1rup green	125.00	95.00
44	A8	1sh ocher	30.00	10.00
45	A8	1sa ocher	45.00	20.00
46	A8	1ab ocher	75.00	35.00
47	A8	½rup ocher	90.00	75.00
48	A8	1rup ocher	160.00	140.00
49	A8	1sh violet	30.00	7.00
50	A8	1sa violet	30.00	10.00
51	A8	1ab violet	45.00	14.00
52	A8	½rup violet	75.00	30.00
53	A8	1rup violet	90.00	40.00

24 varieties of the shahi, 4 of which show denomination written

12 varieties of the sanar, 6 of the abasi and 3 each of the ½ rupee and rupee.

A9

1877 Dated "1294".

54	A9	1sh gray	4.75	3.00
55	A9	1sa gray	7.50	3.75
56	A9	1ab gray	12.50	7.50
57	A9	½rup gray	16.50	16.50
58	A9	1rup gray	16.50	16.50
59	A9	1sh black	12.50	
60	A9	1sa black	24.00	
61	A9	1ab black	55.00	
62	A9	½rup black	60.00	
63	A9	1rup black	60.00	
64	A9	1sh green	6.00	4.50
	a.	Wove paper	16.50	
65	A9	1sa green	10.00	4.50
	a.	Wove paper	22.50	16.50
66	A9	1ab green	12.50	12.50
	a.	Wove paper	35.00	
67	A9	½rup green	18.50	18.50
	a.	Wove paper	40.00	40.00
68	A9	1rup green	18.50	18.50
	a.	Wove paper	40.00	40.00
69	A9	1sh ocher	4.50	2.75
70	A9	1sa ocher	12.50	4.50
71	A9	1ab ocher	24.00	20.00
72	A9	½rup ocher	40.00	40.00
73	A9	1rup ocher	40.00	40.00
74	A9	1sh violet	5.00	2.75
75	A9	1sa violet	10.00	3.50
76	A9	1ab violet	15.00	10.00
77	A9	½rup violet	24.00	18.50
78	A9	1rup violet	24.00	18.50

25 varieties of the shahi, 8 of the sanar, 3 of the abasi and 2 each of the ½ rupee and rupee.

A10 A11

1878 Dated "1295"

79	A10	1sh gray	2.00	2.00
80	A10	1sa gray	2.50	2.50
81	A10	1ab gray	5.00	5.00
82	A10	½rup gray	12.50	10.00
83	A10	1rup gray	12.50	10.00
84	A10	1sh black	4.00	
85	A10	1sa black	4.00	
86	A10	1ab black	14.00	
87	A10	½rup black	27.50	
88	A10	1rup black	27.50	
89	A10	1sh green	30.00	27.50
90	A10	1sa green	4.00	4.00
91	A10	1ab green	15.00	12.50
92	A10	½rup green	30.00	25.00
93	A10	1rup green	30.00	25.00
94	A10	1sh ocher	12.50	4.00
95	A10	1sa ocher	4.00	3.25
96	A10	1ab ocher	15.00	12.50
97	A10	½rup ocher	30.00	22.50
98	A10	1rup ocher	30.00	22.50
99	A10	1sh violet	2.25	2.25
100	A10	1sa violet	2.25	2.25
101	A10	1ab violet	7.00	7.00
102	A10	½rup violet	30.00	24.00
103	A10	1rup violet	30.00	24.00
104	A11	1sh gray	2.75	2.50
105	A11	1sh black	*110.00*	
106	A11	1sh green	2.25	2.25
107	A11	1sh ocher	1.75	1.75
108	A11	1sh violet	2.75	2.50

40 varieties of the shahi, 30 of the sanar, 6 of the abasi and 2 each of the ½ rupee and 1 rupee.

The 1876, 1877 and 1878 issues were printed in separate colors for each main post office on the Peshawar-Kabul-Khulm (Tashkurghan) postal route. Some specialists consider the black printings to be proofs or trial colors.

There are many shades of these colors.

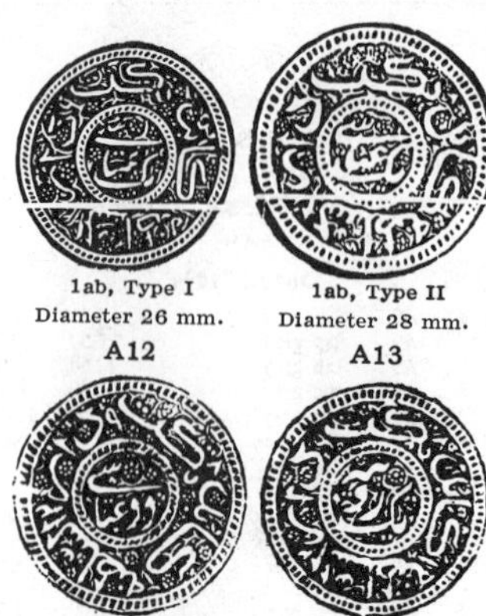

1ab, Type I
Diameter 26 mm.
A12

1ab, Type II
Diameter 28 mm.
A13

A14 A15

1881–90

Handstamped, in watercolor.
Dated "1298", numerals scattered through design.

Thin White Laid Batonné Paper

No.	Type	Denom. / Color	Unused	Used
109	A12	1ab violet	2.50	1.75
109A	A13	1ab violet	5.00	3.75
110	A12	1ab blk brn	5.00	2.75
111	A12	1ab rose	3.00	3.00
b.		Se-tenant with 111A	20.00	
111A	A13	1ab rose	3.75	3.00
112	A14	2ab violet	2.75	2.25
113	A14	2ab blk brn	7.50	6.00
114	A14	2ab rose	4.50	4.50
115	A15	1rup violet	3.75	2.25
116	A15	1rup blk brn	10.00	10.00
117	A15	1rup rose	4.50	4.50

Thin White Wove Batonné Paper

No.	Type	Denom. / Color	Unused	Used
118	A12	1ab violet	10.00	6.00
119	A12	1ab vermilion	6.25	
120	A12	1ab rose		
121	A14	2ab violet		
122	A14	2ab vermilion	7.50	
122A	A14	2ab blk brn		
123	A15	1rup violet	12.50	
124	A15	1rup vermilion	10.00	
125	A15	1rup blk brn	12.50	

Thin White Laid Batonné Paper

No.	Type	Denom. / Color	Unused	Used
126	A12	1ab brn org	3.75	3.75
126A	A13	1ab brn org (II)	5.00	5.00
127	A12	1ab car lake	3.75	3.75
a.		Laid paper		
128	A14	2ab brn org	3.75	3.75
129	A14	2ab car lake	4.50	4.50
130	A15	1rup brn org	15.00	15.00
131	A15	1rup car lake	6.25	6.25

Yellowish Laid Batonné Paper

No.	Type	Denom. / Color	Unused	Used
132	A12	1ab purple		5.00
133	A12	1ab red	10.00	5.00

1884

Colored Wove Paper

No.	Type	Denom. / Color	Unused	Used
133A	A13	1ab pur, *yel*(II)	25.00	25.00
134	A12	1ab pur, *grn*	27.50	
135	A12	1ab pur, *bl*	42.50	30.00
136	A12	1ab red, *grn*	50.00	
137	A12	1ab red, *yel*	2.50	
139	A12	1ab red, *rose*	8.75	
140	A14	2ab red, *yel*	8.75	
142	A14	2ab red, *rose*	8.00	
143	A15	1rup red, *yel*	10.00	10.00
145	A15	1rup red, *rose*	11.00	11.00

Thin Colored Ribbed Paper

No.	Type	Denom. / Color	Unused	Used
146	A14	2ab red, *yel*	4.50	
147	A15	1rup red, *yel*	12.50	
148	A12	1ab lake, *lil*	6.00	
149	A14	2ab lake, *lil*	7.25	
150	A15	1rup lake, *lil*	6.00	
151	A12	1ab lake, *grn*	3.00	
152	A14	2ab lake, *grn*	6.00	
153	A15	1rup lake, *grn*	6.00	

1886–88

Colored Wove Paper.

No.	Type	Denom. / Color	Unused	Used
155	A12	1ab *magenta*	37.50	
156	A12	1ab cl brn, *org*	27.50	
156A	A12	1ab red, *org*	3.00	
156B	A14	2ab red, *org*	7.00	
156C	A15	1rup red, *org*	5.00	

Laid Batonné Paper.

No.	Type	Denom. / Color	Unused	Used
157	A12	1ab *lavender*	4.00	
158	A12	1ab cl brn, *grn*	10.00	
159	A12	1ab *pink*	25.00	
160	A14	2ab *pink*	45.00	
161	A15	1rup *pink*	27.50	

Laid Paper.

No.	Type	Denom. / Color	Unused	Used
162	A12	1ab *pink*	42.50	
163	A14	2ab *pink*	42.50	
164	A15	1rup *pink*	42.50	
165	A12	1ab brn, *yel*	42.50	
166	A14	2ab brn, *yel*	42.50	
167	A15	1rup brn, *yel*	42.50	
168	A12	1ab bl, *grn*	42.50	
169	A14	2ab bl, *grn*	42.50	
170	A15	1rup bl, *grn*	42.50	

1891

Colored Wove Paper.

No.	Type	Denom. / Color	Unused	Used
175	A12	1ab grn, *rose*	30.00	
176	A15	1rup pur, *grn batonne'*	30.00	

Nos. 109–176 fall into three categories:

1. Those regularly issued and in normal postal use from 1881 on, handstamped on thin white laid or wove paper in strip sheets containing 12 or more impressions of the same denomination arranged in two irregular rows, with the impressions often touching or overlappng.

2. The 1884 postal issues provisionally printed on smooth or ribbed colored wove paper as needed to supplement low stocks of the normal white paper stamps.

3. The "special" printings made in a range of colors on several types of laid or wove colored papers, most of which were never used for normal printings. These were produced periodically from 1886 to 1891 to meet philatelic demands. Although nominally valid for postage, most of the special printings were exported directly to fill dealers' orders, and few were ever postally used. Many of the sheets contained all three denominations with impressions separated by ruled lines. Sometimes different colors were used, so se-tenant multiples of denomination or color exist. Many combinations of stamp and paper colors exist besides those listed.

Various shades of each color exist.

Type A12 is known dated "1297".

Counterfeits, lithographed or typographed, are plentiful.

Kingdom of Afghanistan

A16

A17

A18

Dated "1309".

1891 Pelure Paper Lithographed

No.	Type	Denom. / Color	Unused	Used
177	A16	1ab sl bl	1.25	1.25
a.		Tête bêche pair	12.50	
178	A17	2ab sl bl	8.75	7.50
179	A18	1rup sl bl	18.50	15.00

Revenue stamps of similar design exist in various colors.

Nos. 177–179 were printed in panes on the same sheet, so se-tenant gutter pairs exist. Examples in black or red are proofs.

A Mosque Gate and Crossed Cannons (National Seal)
A19

Dated "1310" in Upper Right Corner.

1892 Flimsy Wove Paper

No.	Type	Denom. / Color	Unused	Used
180	A19	1ab *green*	3.00	2.50
181	A19	1ab *orange*	3.75	3.75
182	A19	1ab *yellow*	3.00	2.50
183	A19	1ab *pink*	3.75	2.50
184	A19	1ab *lil rose*	3.75	3.75
185	A19	1ab *blue*	6.25	5.00
186	A19	1ab *salmon*	3.75	3.00
187	A19	1ab *magenta*	3.75	3.75
188	A19	1ab *violet*	3.75	3.75
188A	A19	1ab *scarlet*	3.75	2.50

Many shades exist.

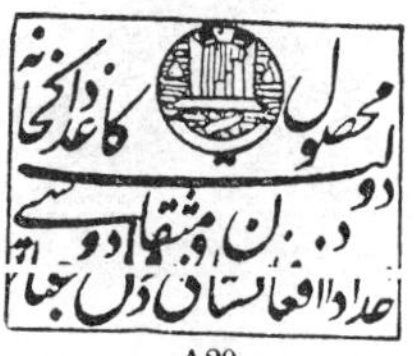

A20

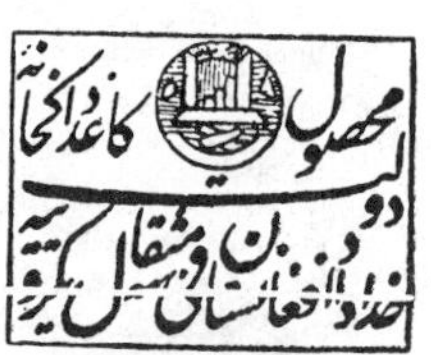

A21

Undated

1894 Flimsy Wove Paper

No.	Type	Denom. / Color	Unused	Used
189	A20	2ab *green*	8.75	7.50
190	A21	1rup *green*	12.50	8.75

24 varieties of the 2 abasi and 12 varieties of the rupee.

Nos. 189–190 and F3 were printed se-tenant in the same sheet. Pairs exist.

A21a

Dated "1316"

1898 Flimsy Wove Paper

No.	Type	Denom. / Color	Unused	Used
191	A21a	2ab *pink*	3.75	
192	A21a	2ab *magenta*	3.75	
193	A21a	2ab *yellow*	1.75	
193A	A21a	2ab *salmon*	4.50	
194	A21a	2ab *green*	2.00	
195	A21a	2ab *purple*	2.50	
195A	A21a	2ab *blue*	42.50	

Nos. 191–195A were not regularly issued. Genuinely used copies are scarce. No. 195A was found in remainder stocks and probably was never released.

National Coat of Arms
A22 A23

A24

1907 Engraved *Imperf.*

Medium Wove Paper

No.	Type	Denom. / Color	Unused	Used
196	A22	1ab bl grn	3.75	2.50
a.		emerald	8.50	5.00
197	A22	1ab brt bl	7.50	6.25
198	A23	2ab dp bl	1.85	1.25
199	A24	1rup green	3.00	2.50
a.		bl grn	6.00	6.00

Zigzag Roulette 10

No.	Type	Denom. / Color	Unused	Used
200	A22	1ab green	35.00	25.00
201	A23	2ab blue	50.00	45.00
201A	A24	1rup bl grn	*70.00*	*60.00*

1908 *Perf. 12*

No.	Type	Denom. / Color	Unused	Used
202	A22	1ab green	6.25	6.25
203	A23	2ab dp bl	1.25	1.25
204	A24	1rup bl grn	3.00	3.00

Twelve varieties of the 1 abasi, 6 of the 2 abasi, 4 of the 1 rupee.

Nos. 196–204 were issued in small sheets containing 3 or 4 panes. Gutter pairs, normal and tête bêche, exist.

A25

A26

A27

1909–19 Typo. *Perf. 12*

No.	Type	Denom. / Color	Unused	Used
205	A25	1ab ultra	50	35
a.		Imperf., pair	3.00	
206	A25	1ab red ('16)	35	25
a.		Imperf.		
207	A25	1ab rose ('18)	35	25
208	A26	2ab green	75	75
a.		Imperf., pair	7.00	
b.		Horizontal pair, imperf. between		
208C	A26	2ab yel ('16)	1.25	1.25
209	A26	2ab bis ('18-'19)	90	90
210	A27	1rup lil brn	1.50	1.50
a.		red brn	1.50	1.50
211	A27	1rup ol bis ('16)	1.50	1.50
		Nos. 205-211 (8)	7.10	6.75

A28

1913

No.	Type	Denom. / Color	Unused	Used
212	A28	2pa db brn	1.25	1.25
a.		red brn	1.25	1.25

No. 212 is inscribed "Tiket waraq dak" (Postal card stamps). It was usable only on postcards and not accepted for postage on letters.

Nos. 196–212 sometimes show letters of a papermaker's watermark, "Howard & Jones, London."

Royal Star
A29

1920, Aug. 24 ***Perf. 12***

Size: 39x47mm.

214	A29	10pa rose	18.50	16.00
215	A29	20pa red brn	42.50	25.00
216	A29	30pa green	87.50	87.50

Issued in sheets of two.

1921, Mar.

Size: 22½x28¼mm.

217	A29	10pa rose	50	25
a.		Perf. 11 ('27)	1.00	1.50
218	A29	20pa red brn	75	50
219	A29	30pa yel grn	75	50
a.		Tête bêche pair	4.50	4.50
b.		30pa grn	75	50
c.		As "b," Tête bêche pair	4.50	4.50

Two types of the 10pa, three of the 20pa.

Crest of King Amanullah
A30

1924, Feb. 26 ***Perf. 12***

220	A30	10pa chocolate	16.00	10.00
a.		Tête bêche pair	35.00	30.00

Issued to commemorate the 6th Independence Day.

Printed in sheets of four consisting of two tête bêche pairs, and in sheets of two. Two types exist.

Some authorities believe that Nos. Q15–Q16 were issued as regular postage stamps.

Crest of King Amanullah
A32

1925, Feb. 26 ***Perf. 12***

Size: 29x37mm.

222	A32	10pa lt brn	15.00	8.75

Issued to commemorate the 7th Independence Day.

Printed in sheets of 8 (two panes of 4).

1926, Feb. 28 **Wove Paper**

Size: 26x33mm.

224	A32	10pa dk bl	1.50	1.50
a.		Imperf., pair	12.50	12.50
b.		Horizontal pair, imperf. between	15.00	
c.		Vertical pair, imperf. between	12.50	
d.		Laid paper	10.00	7.50

Issued for the 7th anniversary of Independence. Printed in sheets of 4, and in sheets of 8 (two panes of 4). Tête bêche gutter pairs exist.

Tughra and Crest of Amanullah—A33

1927, Feb.

225	A33	10pa magenta	5.00	3.75
a.		Vertical pair, imperf. between	20.00	

Dotted Background.

226	A33	10pa magenta	4.50	3.75
a.		Horizontal pair, imperf. between	15.00	

The surface of No. 226 is covered by a net of fine dots.

Nos. 225 and 226 were issued to commemorate the eighth anniversary of Independence. Printed in sheets of 8 (two panes of 4). Tête bêche gutter pairs exist.

National Seal
A34

A35

A35a

A36

1927, Oct. ***Imperf.***

227	A34	15p pink	35	35
228	A35	30p Prus grn	80	40
229	A36	60p lt bl	1.50	1.50
a.		Tête bêche pair	4.50	5.00

1927–30 ***Perf. 11, 12***

230	A34	15p pink	35	25
231	A34	15p ultra ('29)	50	35
232	A35	30p Prus grn	50	50
233	A35a	30p dp grn ('30)	75	75
234	A36	60p brt bl	1.50	1.50
a.		Tête bêche pair	4.50	4.50
235	A36	60p blk ('29)	1.35	1.00
		Nos. 230-235 (6)	4.95	4.35

Nos. 230, 232 and 234 are usually imperforate on one or two sides.

No. 233 has been redrawn. A narrow border of pearls has been added and "30", in European and Arabic numerals, inserted in the upper spandrels.

Tughra and Crest of Amanullah
A37

1928, Feb. 27

236	A37	15p pink	1.50	1.25
a.		Tête bêche pair	4.50	3.75
b.		Imperf. vertically, pair	5.00	
c.		Same as "a", imperf. vertically		

Issued to commemorate the ninth anniversary of Independence. This stamp is always imperforate on one or two sides.

A 15p blue of somewhat similar design was prepared for the 10th anniversary, but was not issued due to Amanullah's dethronement. Price, $5.

National Seal—A38

A39

A40

A41

A42

1928–30 ***Perf. 11, 12***

237	A38	2p dl bl	3.75	2.50
a.		Vertical pair, imperf. between		
238	A38	2p lt rose ('30)	25	25
239	A39	10p gray grn	25	15
a.		Tête bêche pair	7.50	7.50
b.		Imperf. horizontally, pair	1.00	
c.		Vertical pair, imperf. between	75	
240		10p choc ('30)	40	35
a.		10p brn pur ('29)	2.50	1.50
241	A40	25p car rose	35	25
242	A40	25p Prus grn ('29)	75	60
243	A41	40p ultra	40	35
a.		Tête bêche pair	7.50	7.50
244	A41	40p rose ('29)	75	75
a.		Tête bêche pair	7.50	7.50
b.		Imperf. horizontally, pair	2.50	
245	A42	50p red	40	40
246	A42	50p dk bl ('29)	1.25	1.00
		Nos. 237-246 (10)	8.55	6.60

The sheets of these stamps are often imperforate at the outer margins.

Nos. 237–238 are newspaper stamps.

Revolutionary Gov't. Issue

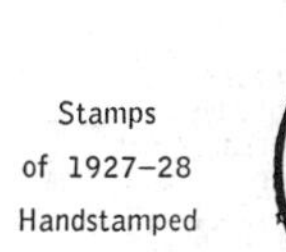

Stamps of 1927–28 Handstamped

On Stamps of 1927.

1929 ***Imperf.***

252	A34	15p pink	4.50
253	A35	30p Prus grn	5.00
253A	A36	60p lt bl	8.75

Perf. 11

254	A34	15p pink	4.50
255	A35	30p Prus grn	5.00
256	A36	60p brt bl	8.75

On Stamps of 1928.

257	A38	2p dl bl	3.75
258	A39	10p gray grn	3.75
a.		Vertical pair, imperf. between	
259	A40	25p car rose	5.00
260	A41	40p ultra	6.50
a.		Tête bêche pair	75.00
261	A42	50p red	10.00
		Nos. 257-261 (5)	29.00

Impressions of the overprint vary greatly. It reads: "Khadim Din Mohammed Rasul Ullah Amir Habib Ullah, 1347." (The Servant of the Faith of Mohammed, Prophet of God, Amir Habibullah). Genuinely used copies are extremely rare. Counterfeit overprints and bogus cancellations are plentiful.

Independence Monument
A46

Lithographed.

Wmkd. Large Seal in the Sheet.

1931, Aug. **Laid Paper** ***Perf. 12***

262	A46	20p red	85	50

Issued to commemorate the 13th Independence Day. Issued without gum.

National Assembly Chamber
A47

National Assembly Chamber
A48 A50

National Assembly Building
A49

National Assembly Chamber
A51

National Assembly Building
A52

Typographed

Wove Paper

1932 ***Perf. 12*** **Unwmkd.**

263	A47	40p olive	60	40
264	A48	60p violet	1.00	75
265	A49	80p dk red	1.50	1.25
266	A50	1af black	12.50	6.25
267	A51	2af ultra	5.00	4.00
268	A52	3af gray grn	6.50	5.00
		Nos. 263-268 (6)	27.10	17.65

Issued to commemorate the formation of the National Council. Imperforate or perforated examples of Nos. 263–268 on ungummed chalky paper are proofs.

See also Nos. 304–305.

Mosque at Balkh A53 — Kabul Fortress A54

Parliament House, Darul Funun
A55

Parliament House, Darul Funun A56 — Arch of Qalai Bist A57

Memorial Pillar of Knowledge and Ignorance
A58

Independence Monument
A59

Minaret at Herat
A60

Arch of Paghman
A61

Ruins at Balkh
A62

Minarets of Herat
A63

Great Buddha at Bamian
A64

1932 Typographed *Perf. 12*

No.	Type	Description	Unused	Used
269	A53	10p brown	18	15
270	A54	15p dk brn	30	15
271	A55	20p red	40	25
272	A56	25p dk grn	40	20
273	A57	30p red	40	25
274	A58	40p orange	50	35
275	A59	50p blue	1.25	40
a.		Tête bêche pair	8.00	
276	A60	60p blue	85	50
277	A61	80p violet	1.75	1.50
278	A62	1af dk bl	4.00	85
279	A63	2af dk red vio	4.50	3.00
280	A64	3af claret	6.50	3.75
		Nos. 269-280 (12)	21.03	11.35

Counterfeits of types A53—A65 exist.
See also Nos. 290–295, 298–299, 302–303.

Entwined 2's
A65

Two types:
Type I. Numerals shaded. Size about 21x29mm.
Type II. Numerals unshaded. Size about 21¾x30mm.

1931–38 *Perf. 12, 11x12*

No.	Type	Description	Unused	Used
281	A65	2p red brn (I)	8	8
282	A65	2p ol blk (I) ('34)	8	8
283	A65	2p grnsh gray (I) ('34)	8	8
283A	A65	2p blk (II) ('36)	8	8
284	A65	2p sal (II) ('38)	8	8
284A	A65	2p rose (I) ('38)	10	10
b.		Imperf., pair	75	

Imperf.

No.	Type	Description	Unused	Used
285	A65	2p blk (II) ('37)	10	10
286	A65	2p sal (II) ('38)	10	10
		Nos. 281-286 (8)	70	70

The newspaper rate was 2 pouls.

Independence Monument
A66

1932, Aug. *Perf. 12*

No.	Type	Description	Unused	Used
287	A66	1af dp rose	2.75	2.25

Issued to commemorate the 14th Independence Day.

1929 Liberation Monument, Kabul
A67

1932, Oct. Typographed

No.	Type	Description	Unused	Used
288	A67	80p red brn	1.25	75

Arch of Paghman
A68

1933, Aug.

No.	Type	Description	Unused	Used
289	A68	50p lt ultra	1.50	1.50

Issued to commemorate the 15th Independence Day.

Types of 1932 and

Royal Palace, Kabul
A69

Darrah-Shikari Pass, Hindu Kush
A70

1934–38 Typographed *Perf. 12*

No.	Type	Description	Unused	Used
290	A53	10p dp vio	15	12
291	A54	15p turq grn	18	15
292	A55	20p magenta	25	15
293	A56	25p dp rose	30	25
294	A57	30p orange	35	30
295	A58	40p bl blk	50	40
296	A69	45p dk bl	1.50	1.50
297	A69	45p red ('38)	25	25
298	A59	50p orange	35	25
299	A60	60p purple	50	50
300	A70	75p red	2.25	2.25
301	A70	75p dk bl ('38)	75	60
302	A61	80p brn vio	1.10	75
303	A62	1af red vio	1.50	1.50
304	A51	2af gray blk	3.75	3.00
305	A52	3af ultra	5.00	4.50
		Nos. 290-305 (16)	18.68	16.47

Independence Monument
A71

1934, Aug. Litho. Without Gum

No.	Type	Description	Unused	Used
306	A71	50p pale grn	1.50	1.50
a.		Tête bêche pair	4.50	4.50

Issued to commemorate the 16th year of Independence. Each sheet of 40 (4x10) included 4 tête bêche pairs as lower half of sheet was inverted.

Independence Monument
A74

Fireworks Display
A75

1935, Aug. Laid Paper

No.	Type	Description	Unused	Used
309	A74	50p dk bl	1.50	1.50

Issued in commemoration of the 17th year of Independence.

Wove Paper

1936, Aug. *Perf. 12*

No.	Type	Description	Unused	Used
310	A75	50p red vio	1.50	1.50

Issued in commemoration of the 18th year of Independence.

Independence Monument and Nadir Shah—A76

No.	Type	Description	Unused	Used
311	A76	50p vio & bis brn	1.25	75
a.		Imperf., pair	2.75	

Issued in commemoration of the 19th year of Independence.

Mohammed Nadir Shah
A77

A78

1938 *Perf. 11x12*

No.	Type	Description	Unused	Used
315	A77	50p brt bl & sep	75	75
a.		Imperf. pair	6.25	3.75

Issued in commemoration of the 20th year of Independence. Issued without gum.

1939 *Perf. 11*

No.	Type	Description	Unused	Used
317	A78	50p dp sal	1.10	60

Issued in commemoration of the 21st year of Independence.

National Arms
A79

Parliament House, Darul Funun
A80

Royal Palace, Kabul
A81

Independence Monument
A82

Independence Monument and Nadir Shah
A83

Mohammed Zahir Shah
A84

Mohammed Zahir Shah
A85

Perf. 11, 11x12, 12x11, 12

1939–61 Typographed

318	A79	2p int blk	10	10
318A	A79	2p brt pink ('61)	7	7
319	A80	10p brt pur	10	10
320	A80	15p brt grn	12	10
321	A80	20p red lil	15	10
322	A81	25p rose red	30	15
322A	A81	25p grn ('41)	12	8
323	A81	30p orange	20	15
324	A81	40p dk gray	20	15
325	A82	45p brt car	20	15
326	A82	50p dp org	30	20
327	A82	60p violet	30	20
328	A83	75p ultra	2.00	75
328A	A83	75p red vio ('41)	50	30
328C	A83	75p brt red ('44)	1.35	1.35
328D	A83	75p chnt brn ('49)	1.65	1.65
329	A83	80p chocolate	50	50
a.		80p dl red vio (error)		
330	A84	1af brt red vio	1.50	75
330A	A85	1af brt red vio ('44)	1.50	1.50
331	A85	2af dp rose red	2.50	1.35
a.		2af cop red	1.75	50
332	A84	3af dp bl	3.75	1.60
		Nos. 318-332 (21)	17.41	11.30

On No. 332 the King faces slightly left.
No. 318A is without gum.
See Nos. 795A–795B.

Mohammed Nadir Shah
A86

1940, Aug. 23 ***Perf. 11***

333	A86	50p gray grn	1.00	85

Issued in commemoration of the 22nd year of Independence.

Independence Monument
A87

Arch of Paghman
A88

1941, Aug. 23 ***Perf. 12***

334	A87	15p gray grn	5.00	2.75
335	A88	50p red brn	1.00	85

Issued in commemoration of the 23rd year of Independence.

Sugar Factory, Baghlan
A89

1942, April ***Perf. 12***

336	A89	1.25af ultra	2.50	1.75
a.		1.25af bl (shades)	1.50	50

In 1949, a 1.50af brown, type A89, was sold for 3af by the Philatelic Office, Kabul. It was not valid for postage. Price $3.50.

Independence Monument
A90

Mohammed Nadir Shah and Arch of Paghman
A91

1942, Aug. 23 ***Perf. 12***

337	A90	35p brt grn	3.50	3.00
338	A91	125p chlky bl	1.75	1.75

Issued in commemoration of the 24th year of Independence.

Independence Monument and Nadir Shah
A92

Mohammed Nadir Shah
A93

Perf. 11x12, 12x11

1943, Aug. 25 Typo. **Unwmkd.**

339	A92	35p carmine	12.00	9.00
340	A93	1.25af dk bl	2.10	1.75

Issued to commemorate the 24th year of Independence.

Tomb of Gohar Shad, Herat
A94

Ruins of Qalai Bist
A95

1944, May 1 ***Perf. 12, 11x12***

341	A94	35p orange	60	40
342	A95	70p violet	1.20	75
a.		70p rose lil	2.50	1.00

Arch of Paghman
A96

Independence Monument and Mohammed Nadir Shah
A97

1944, Aug. ***Perf. 12***

343	A96	35p crimson	1.00	75
344	A97	1.25af ultra	1.75	1.50

Issued to commemorate the 26th year of Independence.

Independence Monument
A98

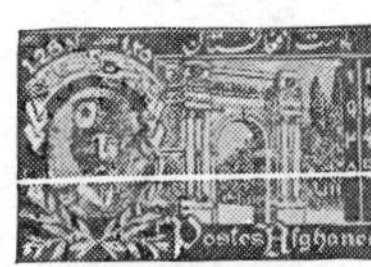

Mohammed Nadir Shah and Arch of Paghman
A99

1945, July

345	A98	35p dp red lil	1.00	90
346	A99	1.25af blue	2.50	2.00

Issued to commemorate the 27th year of Independence.

Mohammed Zahir Shah
A100

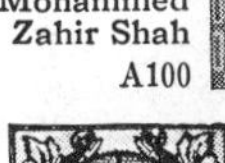

Independence Monument
A101

Mohammed Nadir Shah
A102

1946, July

347	A100	15p emerald	60	45
348	A101	20p dp red lil	90	70
349	A102	125p blue	2.25	2.25

Issued to commemorate the 28th year of Independence.

Zahir Shah and Ruins of Qalai Bist—A103

Arch of Paghman
A104

Nadir Shah and Independence Monument
A105

1947, Aug.

350	A103	15p yel grn	40	20
351	A104	35p plum	50	30
352	A105	125p dp bl	1.85	1.85

Issued to commemorate the 29th year of Independence.

Begging Child
A106

A107

Typographed.

1948, May ***Perf. 12*** **Unwmkd.**

353	A106	35p yel grn	4.00	2.75
354	A107	125p gray bl	4.00	3.25

Issued to commemorate Children's Day, May 29, 1948, and valid only on that day. Proceeds were used for Child Welfare.

Arch of Paghman
A108

Independence Monument
A109

Mohammed Nadir Shah
A110

1948, Aug.

355	A108	15p green	30	20
356	A109	20p magenta	50	25
357	A110	125p dk bl	1.10	90

Issued to commemorate the 30th year of Independence.

United Nations Emblem
A111

1948, Oct. 24

358	A111	125p dk vio bl	10.00	8.50

Issued to commemorate the third anniversary of the formation of the United Nations. Valid one day only. Sheets of 9.

Maiwand Victory Column, Kandahar
A112

Zahir Shah and Ruins of Qalai Bist
A113

Independence Monument and Nadir Shah
A114

1949, Aug. Typo. *Perf. 12*

359	A112	25p green	35	25
360	A113	35p magenta	50	35
361	A114	1.25af blue	1.25	1.00

Issued to commemorate the 31st year of Independence.

Nadir Shah
A117

1950, Aug.

364	A117	35p red brn	40	40
365	A117	125p blue	1.00	75

Issued to commemorate the 32nd year of Independence.

Medical School and Nadir Shah
A119

1950, Dec. 22 Typo. *Perf. 12*

Size: 38x25mm.

367	A119	35p emerald	75	75

Size: 46x30mm.

368	A119	1.25af dp bl	2.50	2.00
a.		1.25af blk (error)	6.00	

Issued to commemorate the 19th anniversary of the founding of Afghanistan's Faculty of Medicine. On sale and valid for use on Dec. 22-23, 1950.

Minaret, Herat
A120

Zahir Shah
A121

Mosque of Khodja Abu Parsar, Balkh
A122

Zahir Shah
A123 A124

Designs: 20p, Buddha at Bamian. 40p, Ruined arch. 45p, Maiwand Victory Monument. 50p, View of Kandahar. 60p, Ancient tower. 70p, Afghanistan flag. 80p, 1af, Profile of Zahir Shah in uniform.

Photogravure, Engraved, Engraved and Lithographed.

Perf. 12, 12½, 13x12½, 13½.

1951, Mar. 21 Unwmkd.

Imprint:
"Waterlow & Sons Limited, London."

369	A120	10p yel & brn	10	8
370	A120	15p bl & brn	15	8
371	A120	20p black	7.00	3.50
372	A121	25p green	18	10
373	A122	30p cerise	25	12
374	A121	35p violet	25	12
375	A122	40p chnt brn	30	12
376	A120	45p dp bl	25	15
377	A122	50p ol blk	60	18
378	A120	60p black	60	20
379	A122	70p dk grn, blk, red & grn	35	20
380	A123	75p cerise	80	25
381	A123	80p car & blk	85	50
382	A123	1af dp grn & vio	60	50
383	A124	1.25af rose lil & blk	75	50
384	A124	2af ultra	1.40	50
385	A124	3af ultra & blk	3.25	1.25
		Nos. 369-385 (17)	17.68	8.35

Nos. 372, 374 and 381 to 385 are engraved, No. 379 is engraved and lithographed.

See also Nos. 445-451, 453, 552A-552D.

Arch of Paghman
A125

Nadir Shah and Independence Monument
A126

Overprint in Violet سال ۳۳ استقلال

Perf. 13½x13, 13

1951, Aug. 25 Engraved

386	A125	35p dk grn & blk	85	50
387	A126	1.25af dp bl	2.10	1.25

Overprint reads "Sol 33 Istiqlal" or "33rd Year of Independence." Overprint measures about 11 mm. wide.

See also Nos. 398-399B, 441-442.

Proposed Flag of Pashtunistan
A127

Design: 1.25af, Flag and Pashtunistan warrior.

1951, Sept. 2 Litho. *Perf. 11½*

388	A127	35p dl choc	1.25	1.00
389	A127	125p blue	3.00	2.75

Issued to publicize "Free Pashtunistan" Day.

Imperforates

From 1951 to 1958, quantities of nearly all locally-printed stamps were left imperforate and sold by the government at double face. From 1959 until March, 1964, many of the imperforates were sold for more than face value.

Avicenna—A128

1951, Nov. 4 Typo. *Perf. 11½*

390	A128	35p dp cl	75	50
391	A128	125p blue	2.10	1.65

Issued to commemorate the 20th anniversary of the founding of the national Graduate School of Medicine.

A129

Dove and U. N. Symbols
A130

1951, Oct. 24

392	A129	35p magenta	2.00	1.50
393	A130	125p blue	5.00	4.00

Issued to commemorate the 7th anniversary of the formation of the United Nations.

Amir Sher Ali Khan and Tiger Head Stamp
A131

Design: Nos. 395 and 397, Zahir Shah and stamp.

1951, Dec. 23 Lithographed

394	A131	35p chocolate	50	50
395	A131	35p rose lil	50	50
396	A131	125p ultra	1.00	90
a.		Cliche of 35p in plate of 125p	125.00	125.00
397	A131	125p aqua	1.00	90

Issued to commemorate the 76th anniversary of the formation of the Universal Postal Union.

Types of 1951
Without Overprint.

Perf. 13½x13, 13

1952, Aug. 24 Engraved

398	A125	35p dk grn & blk	2.50	2.50
399	A126	1.25af dp bl	2.50	2.50

Same Overprinted in Violet

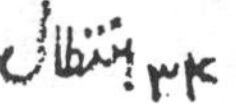

399A	A125	35p dk grn & blk	90	60
399B	A126	1.25af dp bl	2.50	1.50

Nos. 398-399B were issued to commemorate the 34th Independence Day.

Globe—A132

Lithographed

1952, Oct. 25 *Perf. 11½* Unwmkd.

400	A132	35p rose	80	70
401	A132	125p aqua	1.75	1.50

Issued to honor the United Nations.

Symbol of Medicine
A134

Tribal Warrior and National Flag
A135

1952, Nov. *Perf. 11½*

403	A134	35p chocolate	60	50
404	A134	125p vio bl	1.75	1.75

Issued to commemorate the 21st anniversary of the national Graduate School of Medicine.

No. 404 is inscribed in French with white letters on a colored background.

1952, Sept. 1 *Perf. 11*

405	A135	35p red	40	40
406	A135	125p dk bl	85	85

No. 406 is inscribed in French "Pashtunistan Day, 1952."

Flags of Afghanistan and Pashtunistan
A139

Badge of Pashtunistan
A140

Perf. 10½x11, 11

1953, Sept. 1 Unwmkd.

411	A139	35p vermilion	30	25
412	A140	125p blue	85	65

Issued to publicize "Free Pashtunistan" Day.

Nadir Shah and Flag Bearer
A141

Nadir Shah and Independence Monument
A142

1953, Aug. 24 *Perf. 11*

413	A141	35p green	25	20
414	A142	125p violet	1.00	75

Issued to commemorate the 35th anniversary of Independence.

United Nations Emblem
A143

1953, Oct. 24

415	A143	35p lilac	75	75
416	A143	125p vio bl	1.85	1.50

Issued to publicize United Nations Day, 1953.

Nadir Shah
A144 A145

1953, Nov. 29

417	A144	35p orange	1.00	1.00
418	A145	125p chlky bl	2.25	2.25

Issued to commemorate the 22nd anniversary of the founding of the national Graduate School of Medicine.

Redrawn.

35p. Original - Right character in second line of Persian inscription: ٣

Redrawn - Persian character: ٢

125p. Original - Inscribed "XXIII," "MADECINE" and "ANNIVERAIRE"
Redrawn - Inscribed "XXII," "MEDECINE" and "ANNIVERSAIRE"

1953

419	A144	35p dp org	5.00
420	A145	125p chlky bl	6.50

Nadir Shah and Symbols of Independence
A146

1954, Aug. Typo. *Perf. 11*

421	A146	35p car rose	50	40
422	A146	125p vio bl	1.50	1.25

Issued to commemorate the 36th year of Independence.

Raising Flag of Pashtunistan
A147

1954, Sept. *Perf. 11½*

423	A147	35p chocolate	50	40
424	A147	125p blue	1.50	1.25

Issued to publicize "Free Pashtunistan" Day.

U.N. Flag and Map
A148

1954, Oct. 24 *Perf. 11*

425	A148	35p car rose	1.00	1.00
426	A148	125p dk vio bl	3.00	3.00

Issued to commemorate the 9th anniversary of the United Nations.

U. N. Symbols
A149

Design: 125p, U. N. emblem & flags.

1955, June 26 Litho. *Perf. 11*

Size: 26½x36mm.

427	A149	35p dk grn	60	50

Size: 28½x36mm.

428	A149	125p aqua	1.50	1.25

Issued to commemorate the 10th anniversary of the signing of the United Nations charter.

Nadir Shah (center) and Brothers
A150

1929 Civil War Scene and Zahir Shah
A151

Tribal Elders' Council and Pashtun Flag
A152

1955, Aug. *Perf. 11* **Unwmkd.**

429	A150	35p brt pink	40	40
430	A150	35p vio bl	40	40
431	A151	125p rose lil	1.25	1.00
432	A151	125p lt vio	1.25	1.00

Issued to commemorate the 37th anniversary of Independence.

1955, Sept. 5

433	A152	35p org brn	35	35
434	A152	125p yel grn	1.25	1.00

Issued for "Free Pashtunistan" Day.

United Nations Flag
A153

Nadir Shah and Independence Monument
A154

1955, Oct. 24 *Perf. 11* **Unwmkd.**

435	A153	35p org brn	90	75
436	A153	125p brt ultra	1.85	1.50

Issued to commemorate the tenth anniversary of the United Nations, Oct. 24, 1955.

1956, Aug. Lithographed

437	A154	35p lt grn	35	30
438	A154	140p lt vio bl	1.35	1.10

Issued to commemorate the 38th year of Independence.

Jesh'n Exhibition Hall
A155

1956, Aug. 25

439	A155	50p chocolate	45	30
440	A155	50p lt vio bl	45	30

International Exposition at Kabul.

Of the 50p face value, only 35p paid postage. The remaining 15p went to the Exposition.

Nos. 398-399 Handstamped in Violet

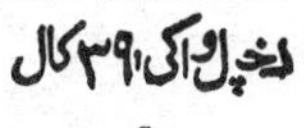

a

39 em Anv

b

Perf. 13½x13, 13

1957, Aug. Engraved

441	A125 (a)	35p dk grn & blk	60	30
442	A126 (b)	1.25af dp bl	90	75

Arabic overprint on No. 441 measures 19mm. No. 442 overprinted: "39 em Anv". Issued to commemorate the 39th year of independence.

Pashtunistan Flag
A156

1957, Sept. 1 Litho. *Perf. 11*

443	A156	50p pale lil rose	75	50
444	A156	155p lt vio	1.25	1.00

Issued for "Free Pashtunistan" Day. French inscription on No. 444.

Types of 1951 and

Game of Buzkashi—A157

Photogravure, Engraved, Engraved and Lithographed.

Perf. 12, 12½, 12½x13, 13, 13x12, 13x12½, 13½x14

1957, Nov. 23 **Unwmkd.**

Imprint: " Waterlow & Sons Limited, London."

445	A122	30p brown	15	6
446	A122	40p rose red	22	6
447	A122	50p yellow	32	8
448	A120	60p ultra	38	10
449	A123	75p brt vio	45	10
450	A123	80p vio & brn	50	10
451	A123	1af car & ultra	75	20
452	A157	140p ol & dp cl	1.50	75
453	A124	3af org & blk	1.85	75
		Nos. 445-453 (9)	6.12	2.20

No. 452 lacks imprint.

Nadir Shah and Flag-bearer
A158

1958, Aug. 25 *Perf. 13½x14*

454	A158	35p dp yel grn	25	20
455	A158	140p brown	60	50

Issued to commemorate the 40th year of Independence.

Exposition Buildings
A159

1958, Aug. 23 Litho. *Perf. 11*

456	A159	35p brt bl grn	25	20
457	A159	140p vermilion	70	60

Issued for the International Exposition at Kabul.

Pres. Celal Bayar of Turkey
A160

Flags of U.N. and Afghanistan
A161

1958, Sept. 13 **Unwmkd.**

458	A160	50p lt bl	30	20
459	A160	100p brown	50	40

Issued to commemorate the visit of President Celal Bayar of Turkey.

Perf. 14x13½

1958, Oct. 24 Photogravure

Flags in Original Colors.

460	A161	50p dk gray	75	75
461	A161	100p green	1.50	1.25

Issued for United Nations Day, Oct. 24.

Atomic Energy Encircling the Hemispheres—A162

1958, Oct. 20 *Perf. 13½x14*

462	A162	50p blue	50	50
463	A162	100p dp red lil	85	85

Issued to promote Atoms for Peace.

UNESCO Building, Paris
A163

1958, Nov. 3

464	A163	50p dp yel grn	75	60
465	A163	100p brn ol	1.10	90

Issued to commemorate the opening of UNESCO (U.N. Educational, Scientific and Cultural Organization) Headquarters in Paris, Nov. 3.

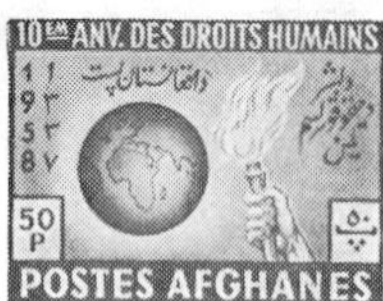

Globe and Torch
A164

Perf. 13½x14

1958, Dec. 10 **Unwmkd.**

466	A164	50p lil rose	50	50
467	A164	100p maroon	1.00	1.00

Issued to commemorate the tenth anniversary of the signing of the Universal Declaration of Human Rights.

Nadir Shah and Flags
A165

1959, Aug. Litho. *Perf. 11 Rough*

468	A165	35p lt ver	30	30
469	A165	165p lt vio	1.00	60

Issued to commemorate the 41st year of Independence.

Uprooted Oak Emblem
A166

1960, Apr. 7 *Perf. 11*

470	A166	50p dp org	20	15
471	A166	165p blue	50	40

Issued to publicize World Refugee Year, July 1, 1959–June 30, 1960.

Two imperf. souvenir sheets exist. Both contain a 50p and a 165p, type A166, with marginal inscriptions and WRY emblem in maroon. On one sheet the stamps are in the colors of Nos. 470–471 (size 108x81 mm.). On the other, the 50p is blue and the 165p is deep orange (size 107x80 mm.). Price $6 each.

Buzkashi—A167

1960, May 4 *Perf. 11, Imperf.*

472	A167	25p rose red	35	20
473	A167	50p bluish grn	75	50
a.		Cliché of 25p in plate of 50p	20.00	20.00

See also Nos. 549–550A.

Independence Monument
A168

1960, Aug.

474	A168	50p lt bl	15	15
475	A168	175p brt pink	50	50

Issued to commemorate the 42nd Independence Day.

Globe and Flags
A169

1960, Oct. 24 Litho. *Perf. 11*

476	A169	50p rose lil	30	25
477	A169	175p ultra	1.00	85

Issued to commemorate United Nations Day.

An imperf. souvenir sheet contains one each of Nos. 476–477 with marginal inscriptions ("La Journée des Nations Unies 1960" in French and Persian) and UN emblem in light blue. Size: 127x85½mm. Price $5.

This sheet was surcharged "+20ps" in 1962. Price $8.50.

Teacher Pointing to Globe
A170

1960, Oct. 23 *Perf. 11*

478	A170	50p brt pink	25	18
479	A170	100p brt grn	90	60

Issued to publicize Teacher's Day.

Mohammed Zahir Shah
A171

1960, Oct. 15

480	A171	50p red brn	40	20
481	A171	150p dk car rose	1.25	40

Issued to honor the King on his 46th birthday.

Buzkashi
A172

1960, Nov. 9 *Perf. 11*

482	A172	175p lt red brn	1.50	60

See also Nos. 551–552.

No. 482 Overprinted "1960" and Olympic Rings in Bright Green.

1960, Dec. 24

483	A172	175p red brn	3.25	3.00
a.		Souvenir sheet	12.00	

Issued to commemorate the 17th Olympic Games, Rome, Aug. 25–Sept. 11.

No. 483a contains one of No. 483, imperf. Bright green marginal inscription. Size: 86x61mm.

Mir Wais
A173

1961, Jan. 5 *Perf. 10½* **Unwmkd.**

484	A173	50p brt rose lil	30	20
485	A173	175p ultra	75	50
a.		Souv. sheet of 2	2.25	2.25

Issued to honor Mir Wais (1665–1708), national leader.

No. 485a contains one each of Nos. 484–485, imperf. Emerald marginal inscription. Size: 108x78mm.

No Postal Need

existed for the 1p to 15p denominations released with commemorative or semipostal sets of 1961–63 (between Nos. 486 and 649, B37 and B65). The lowest denomination actually used for non-philatelic postage in that period was 25p (except for the 2p newspaper rate for which separate stamps were provided).

Horse, Sheep and Camel
A174

Designs: No. 487, 175p, Rock partridge. 10p, 100p, Afghan hound. 15p, 150p, Grain and grasshopper (vert.).

1961, Mar. 29 Photo. *Perf. 13½x14*

486	A174	2p mar & buff		
487	A174	2p ultra & org		
488	A174	5p brn & yel		
489	A174	10p blk & sal		
490	A174	15p bl grn & yel		
491	A174	25p blk & pink		
492	A174	50p blk & cit		
493	A174	100p blk & pink		
494	A174	150p grn & yel		
495	A174	175p ultra & pink		
		Nos. 486-495 (10)		3.00

Two souvenir sheets, perf. and imperf., contain two stamps, one each of Nos. 492–493. Black marginal inscriptions, "Journee d'Agriculture 1961" in Persian and French. Size: 111x64mm. Price $2 each.

Afghan Fencing
A175

Designs: No. 497, 5p, 25p, 50p, Wrestlers. 10p, 100p, Man with Indian clubs. 15p, 150p, Afghan fencing. 175p, Children skating.

1961, July 6 *Perf. 13½x14*

496	A175	2p grn & rose lil		
497	A175	2p brn & cit		
498	A175	5p gray & rose		
499	A175	10p bl & bis		
500	A175	15p sl bl & dl lil		
501	A175	25p blk & dl bl		
502	A175	50p sl grn & bis brn		
503	A175	100p brn & bl grn		
504	A175	150p brn & org yel		
505	A175	175p blk & bl		
		Nos. 496-505 (10)		1.75

Issued for Children's Day.

A souvenir sheet exists containing one each of Nos. 502–503, with slate green marginal inscription and black control number. Size: 111x65mm. Price $3.50.

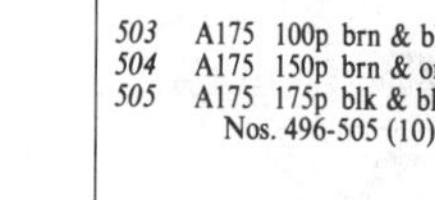

Bandé Amir Lakes
A176

1961, Aug. 7 Photo. *Perf. 13½x14*

506	A176	3af brt bl	50	40
507	A176	10af rose cl	1.75	1.50

Nadir Shah
A177

Girl Scout
A178

1961, Aug. 23 *Perf. 14x13½*

508	A177	50p rose red & blk	50	40
509	A177	175p brt grn & org brn	1.00	80

Issued to commemorate the 43rd Independence Day.

Two souvenir sheets, perf. and imperf., contain one each of Nos. 508–509. Black marginal inscription and control number, flag in black, red & green. Size: 104x74mm. Price, each $2.50.

Perf. 14x13½

1961, July 23 **Unwmkd.**

510	A178	50p dp car & dk gray	40	20
511	A178	175p dp grn & rose brn	90	60

Issued for Women's Day.

Two souvenir sheets exist, perf. and imperf., containing one each of Nos. 510–511. Black marginal inscription. Size: 105x75mm. Price $4 each.

Exhibition Hall, Kabul
A179

1961, Aug. 23 *Perf. 13½x14*

512	A179	50p yel brn & yel grn	25	20
513	A179	175p bl & brn	60	40

International Exhibition at Kabul.

Pathan with Pashtunistan Flag
A180

Photogravure

1961, Aug. 31 *Perf. 14x13½*

514	A180	50p blk, lil & red	20	18
515	A180	175p brn, grnsh bl & red	50	40

Issued for "Free Pashtunistan Day."
Souvenir sheets exist perf. and imperf. containing one each of Nos. 514–515 with black marginal inscription and flag in red and black. Size: 104x75mm. Price $2 each.

Assembly Building—A181

1961, Sept. 10 *Perf. 12*

516	A181	50p dk gray & brt grn	25	18
517	A181	175p ultra & brn	65	45

Issued to commemorate the anniversary of the founding of the National Assembly.
Souvenir sheets exist, perf. and imperf., containing one each of Nos. 516–517 with black marginal inscription and flower in ultramarine and green. Size: 106x70mm. Price $1 each.

Exterminating Anopheles Mosquito
A182

1961, Oct. 5 *Perf. 13½x14*

518	A182	50p blk & brn lil	70	40
519	A182	175p mar & brt grn	1.50	75

Issued to publicize the Anti-Malaria campaign. Souvenir sheets exist, perf. and imperf., containing one each of Nos. 518–519 with black marginal inscription and mosquito. Size: 110x65mm. Price $5 each.

Zahir Shah
A183

1961, Oct. 15 *Perf. 13½*

520	A183	50p lil & bl	25	20
521	A183	175p emer & red brn	60	50

Issued to honor King Mohammed Zahir Shah on his 47th birthday.
See also Nos. 609–612.

Pomegranates—A184

Fruit: No. 523, 5p, 25p, 50p, Grapes. 10p, 150p, Apples. 15p, 175p, Pomegranates. 100p, Melons.

1961, Oct. 16 *Perf. 13½x14*

Fruit in Natural Colors.

522	A184	2p black		
523	A184	2p green		
524	A184	5p lil rose		
525	A184	10p lilac		
526	A184	15p dk bl		
527	A184	25p dl red		
528	A184	50p purple		
529	A184	100p brt bl		
530	A184	150p brown		
531	A184	175p ol gray		
		Nos. 522-531 (10)	2.00	

For Afghan Red Crescent Society.
Souvenir sheets exist, perf. and imperf., containing one each of Nos. 528–529 with black marginal inscription and red crescent. Size: 110x65mm. Price $1.75 each.

U.N. Headquarters, N.Y.—A185

1961, Oct. 24 *Perf. 13½x14*

Vertical Borders in Emerald, Red and Black.

532	A185	1p rose lil		
533	A185	2p slate		
534	A185	3p brown		
535	A185	4p ultra		
536	A185	50p rose red		
537	A185	75p gray		
538	A185	175p brt grn		
		Nos. 532-538 (7)	1.25	

Issued to commemorate the 16th anniversary of the United Nations. Souvenir sheets exist, perf. and imperf., containing one each of Nos. 536–538. Black marginal inscription with U.N. emblem and control number. Size: 114x95mm. Price $2.25 each.

Children Giving Flowers to Teacher
A186

People Raising UNESCO Symbol
A187

Designs: No. 540, 5p, 25p, 50p, Tulips. 10p, 100p, Narcissus. 15p, 150p, Children giving flowers to teacher. 175p, Teacher with children in front of school.

1961, Oct. 26 Photo. *Perf. 12*

539	A186	2p multi		
540	A186	2p multi		
541	A186	5p multi		
542	A186	10p multi		
543	A186	15p multi		
544	A186	25p multi		
545	A186	50p multi		
546	A186	100p multi		
547	A186	150p multi		
548	A186	175p multi		
		Nos. 539-548 (10)	2.00	

Issued for Teacher's Day.
Souvenir sheets exist, perf. and imperf. containing one each of Nos. 545–546. Gray marginal inscription and black control number. Size: 104x78mm. Price, 2 sheets, $3.

Buzkashi Types of 1960.

1961–72 Lithographed *Perf. 10½*

549	A167	25p violet	10	5
b.		25p brt vio, typo. ('72)	5	5
549A	A167	25p cit ('63)	15	5
550	A167	50p blue	30	5
550A	A167	50p yel org ('69)	10	5
551	A172	100p citron	40	10
551A	A172	150p org ('64)	30	15
552	A172	2af lt grn	1.00	60
		Nos. 549-552 (7)	2.35	1.05

Zahir Shah Types of 1951

Imprint: "Thomas De La Rue & Co. Ltd."

Photo., Engr., Engr. & Litho.

1962 *Perf. 13x12, 13*

552A	A123	75p brt pur	1.50	35
552B	A123	1af car & ultra	1.85	42
552C	A124	2af blue	2.25	95
552D	A124	3af org & blk	5.25	1.40

1962, July 2 Photo. *Perf. 14x13½*

553	A187	2p rose lil & brn		
554	A187	2p ol bis & brn		
555	A187	5p dp org & dk grn		
556	A187	10p gray & mag		
557	A187	15p bl & brn		
558	A187	25p org yel & pur		
559	A187	50p lt grn & pur		
560	A187	75p brt cit & brn		
561	A187	100p dp org & brn		
		Nos. 553-561 (9)	1.40	

Issued to commemorate the 15th anniversary of UNESCO (U.N. Educational, Scientific and Cultural Organization). Souvenir sheets exist, perf. and imperf. One contains Nos. 558–559 with purple marginal inscription; the other contains one each of Nos. 560–561 with brown marginal inscription and black control numbers. Size: 99x80mm. Price, $4 each.

Ahmad Shah
A188

Afghan Hound
A189

1962, Feb. 24 Photo. *Perf. 13½*

562	A188	50p red brn & gray	15	10
563	A188	75p grn & sal	25	20
564	A188	100p cl & bis	40	30

Issued to honor Ahmad Shah (1724–1773), who founded the Afghan kingdom in 1747 and ruled until 1773.

1962, Apr. 21 *Perf. 14x13½*

Designs: 5p, 75p, Afghan cock. 10p, 100p, Kondjid plant. 15p, 125p, Astrakhan skins.

565	A189	2p rose & brn		
566	A189	2p lt grn & brn		
567	A189	5p dp rose & cl		
568	A189	10p lt grn & sl grn		
569	A189	15p bl grn & blk		
570	A189	25p bl & brn		
571	A189	50p gray & brn		
572	A189	75p rose lil & lil		
573	A189	100p gray & dl grn		
574	A189	125p rose brn & blk		
		Nos. 565-574 (10)	2.00	

Issued for Agriculture Day. Perf. and imperf. souvenir sheets exist. Set of 4 sheets, price $4.

Athletes with Flag and Nadir Shah
A190

Woman in National Costume
A191

1962, Aug. 23 *Perf. 12*

575	A190	25p multi	12	4
576	A190	50p multi	18	6
577	A190	150p multi	25	8

44th Independence Day.

1962, Aug. 30 *Perf. 11½x12*

578	A191	25p lil & brn	12	6
579	A191	50p grn & brn	25	15

Issued for Women's Day. For souvenir sheet see note after No. C16.

Man and Woman with Flag
A192

Malaria Eradication Emblem and Swamp
A193

1962, Aug. 31 Photogravure

580	A192	25p blk, pale bl & red	12	6
581	A192	50p blk, grn & red	25	12
582	A192	150p blk, pink & red	60	20

Issued for "Free Pashtunistan Day."

1962, Sept. 5 *Perf. 14x13½*

583	A193	2p dk grn & ol gray		
584	A193	2p dk grn & sal		
585	A193	5p red brn & ol		
586	A193	10p red brn & brt grn		
587	A193	15p red brn & gray		
588	A193	25p brt bl & bluish grn		
589	A193	50p brt bl & rose lil		
590	A193	75p blk & bl		
591	A193	100p blk & brt pink		
592	A193	150p blk & bis brn		
593	A193	175p blk & org		
		Nos. 583-593 (11)	2.25	

Issued for the World Health Organization drive to eradicate malaria. Perf. and imperf. souvenir sheets exist. Set of 4 sheets, price $6.50.

National Assembly Building
A194

Lithographed

1962, Sept. 10 *Perf. 10½* **Unwmkd.**

594	A194	25p lt grn	8	6
595	A194	50p blue	12	8
596	A194	75p rose	15	12
597	A194	100p violet	25	20
598	A194	125p ultra	28	25
		Nos. 594-598 (5)	88	71

Establishment of the National Assembly.

Stamps not listed in this Catalogue or mentioned in "For the Record" (unless recent issues) usually are revenues, locals or labels.

Horse Racing
A195

Designs: 3p, Wrestling. 4p, Weight lifting. 5p, Soccer.

1962, Sept. 22 Photo. *Perf. 12*

Black Inscriptions

599	A195	1p lt ol & red brn		
600	A195	2p lt grn & red brn		
601	A195	3p yel & dk pur		
602	A195	4p pale bl & grn		
603	A195	5p bluish grn & dk brn		
		Nos. 599-603,C17-C22 (11)	2.50	

Issued to commemorate the 4th Asian Games, Djakarta, Indonesia. Two souvenir sheets exist. A perforated one contains a 125p blue, dark blue and brown stamp in horse racing design. An imperf. one contains a 2af buff, purple and black stamp in soccer design. Both sheets have black control number. Size: 64x90mm. Price, $4.50 each.

Runners
A196

Designs: 1p, 2p, Diver (vert.). 4p, Peaches. 5p, Iris (vert.).

Perf. 11½x12, 12x11½

1962, Oct. 2 Unwmkd.

604	A196	1p rose lil & brn		
605	A196	2p bl & brn		
606	A196	3p brt bl & lil		
607	A196	4p ol gray & multi		
608	A196	5p gray & multi		
		Nos. 604-608, C23-C25 (8)	2.00	

Issued for Children's Day.

King Type of 1961, Dated "1962"

Various Frames

1962, Oct. 15 *Perf. 13½*

609	A183	25p lil rose & brn	8	8
610	A183	50p org brn & grn	15	15
611	A183	75p bl & lake	22	22
612	A183	100p grn & red brn	30	30

Issued to honor King Mohammed Zahir Shah on his 48th birthday.

Grapes
A197

Designs: 3p, Pears. 4p, Wistaria. 5p, Blossoms.

1962, Oct. 16 *Perf. 12*

Fruit and Flowers in Natural Colors; Carmine Crescent

613	A197	1p dp rose		
614	A197	2p blue		
615	A197	3p lilac		
616	A197	4p gray brn		
617	A197	5p gray		
		Nos. 613-617, C26-C28 (8)	1.20	

For the Afghan Red Crescent Society.

U.N. Headquarters, N.Y. and Flags of U.N. and Afghanistan
A198

1962, Oct. 24 Unwmkd.

Flags in Original Colors, Black Inscriptions

618	A198	1p ol bis		
619	A198	2p lil rose		
620	A198	3p dl vio		
621	A198	4p green		
622	A198	5p redsh brn		
		Nos. 618-622, C29-C31 (8)	1.50	

Issued for United Nations Day. Souvenir sheets exist. One contains a single 4af ultramarine stamp, perforated; the other, a 4af ocher stamp, imperf. Both sheets have a black marginal inscription and control number. Size: 89x65mm. Price, 2 sheets, $6.50.

Boy Scout
A199

Pole Vault
A200

1962, Oct. 18 Photo. *Perf. 12*

623	A199	1p yel, dk grn & sal		
624	A199	2p dl yel, sl & sal		
625	A199	3p rose, blk & sal		
626	A199	4p multi		
		Nos. 623-626, C32-C35 (8)	1.75	

Issued to honor the Boy Scouts.

1962, Oct. 25 *Perf. 12* Unwmkd.

Designs: 3p, High jump. 4p, 5p, Different blossoms.

627	A200	1p lil & dk grn		
628	A200	2p yel grn & brn		
629	A200	3p bis & vio		
630	A200	4p sal pink, grn & ultra		
631	A200	5p yel, grn & bl		
		Nos. 627-631, C36-C37 (7)	1.40	

Issued for Teacher's Day.

Rockets—A201

1962, Nov. 29

632	A201	50p pale lil & dk bl	60	
633	A201	100p lt bl & red brn	1.25	

Issued to commemorate the United Nations World Meteorological Day. A souvenir sheet contains one 5af pink and green stamp, green marginal inscription and black control number. Size: 89x65mm. Price $8.

Ansari Mausoleum, Herat
A202

Photogravure

1963, Jan. 3 *Perf. 13½* Unwmkd.

634	A202	50p pur & grn	12	12
635	A202	75p gray & mag	18	18
636	A202	100p org brn & brn	30	30

Issued to honor Khwaja Abdullah Ansari, Sufi, religious leader and poet, on the 900th anniversary of his death.

Sheep—A203

Silkworm, Cocoons, Moth and Mulberry Branch
A204

1963, March 1 *Perf. 12*

637	A203	1p grnsh bl & blk		
638	A203	2p yel grn & blk		
639	A203	3p lil rose & blk		
640	A204	4p gray, grn & brn		
641	A204	5p red lil, grn & brn		
		Nos. 637-641, C42-C44 (8)	1.75	

Issued for the Day of Agriculture.

Rice—A205

Designs: 3p, Corn. 300p, Wheat emblem.

1963, March 27 *Perf. 14* Unwmkd.

642	A205	2p gray, cl & grn	8	8
643	A205	3p grn, yel & ocher	12	12
644	A205	300p dk bl & yel	45	45

Issued for the "Freedom from Hunger" campaign of the U.N. Food and Agriculture Organization.

Meteorological Measuring Instrument
A206

Designs: 3p, 10p, Weather station. 4p, 5p, Rockets in space.

1963, May 23 Photo. *Perf. 13½x14*

645	A206	1p dp mag & brn		
646	A206	2p brt bl & brn		
647	A206	3p red & brn		
648	A206	4p org & lil		
649	A206	5p grn & dl vio		

Imperf.

650	A206	10p red brn & grn		
		Nos. 645-650, C46-C50 (11)	9.50	

Issued to commemorate the United Nations Third World Meteorological Day, Mar. 23.

Independence Monument
A207

1963, Aug. 23 Litho. *Perf. 10½*

651	A207	25p lt grn	10	6
652	A207	50p orange	20	15
653	A207	150p rose car	50	35

Issued to commemorate the 45th Independence Day.

Pathans in Forest
A208

1963, Aug. 31 *Perf. 10½* Unwmkd.

654	A208	25p pale vio	10	6
655	A208	50p sky bl	20	18
656	A208	150p dl red brn	60	50

Issued for "Free Pashtunistan Day."

National Assembly Building
A209

1963, Sept. 10 Litho.

657	A209	25p gray	6	6
658	A209	50p dl red	12	8
659	A209	75p brown	20	15
660	A209	100p olive	30	15
661	A209	125p lilac	40	20
		Nos. 657-661 (5)	1.08	64

Issued to honor the National Assembly.

Balkh Gate
A210

1963, Oct. 8

662	A210	3af choc (screened margins)	60	40
a.		white margins	1.50	50

In the original printing (No. 662), a halftone screen extended across the plate, covering the space between the stamps. A retouch removed the screen between the stamps (No. 662a).

Zahir Shah
A211

Kemal Ataturk
A212

1963, Oct. 15 *Perf. 10½*

663	A211	25p green	10	4
664	A211	50p gray	20	8
665	A211	75p car rose	30	15
666	A211	100p dl redsh brn	40	18

Issued to honor King Mohammed Zahir Shah on his 49th birthday.

1963, Oct. 10 *Perf. 10½*

667	A212	1af blue	15	12
668	A212	3af rose lil	60	50

Issued to commemorate the 25th anniversary of the death of Kemal Ataturk, president of Turkey.

"Tiger's Head" of 1878—A214

1964, March 22 Photo. *Perf. 12*

675	A214	1.25af gold, grn & blk	20	10
676	A214	5af gold, rose car & blk	50	35

Issued to honor philately.

Unisphere and Flags—A215

1964, May 3 *Perf. 13½x14*

677	A215	6af crim, gray & grn	40	30

New York World's Fair, 1964-65.

Hand Holding Torch
A216
Photogravure

1964, May 12 *Perf. 14x13½*

678	A216	3.75af brt bl, org, yel & blk	25	25

Issued to commemorate the first United Nations Seminar on Human Rights in Kabul, May 1964. The denomination in Persian at right erroneously reads "3.25" but the stamp was sold and used as 3.75af.

Kandahar Airport
A217

1964 Lithographed *Perf. 10½*

679	A217	7.75af dk red brn	60	30
680	A217	9.25af lt grn	75	35
681	A217	10.50af lt grn	75	40
682	A217	13.75af car rose	90	50

Inauguration of Kandahar Airport.

Snow Leopard
A218

Designs: 50p, Ibex (vert.). 75p, Head of argali. 5af, Yak.

1964, June 25 Photogravure *Perf. 12*

683	A218	25p yel & bl	8	8
684	A218	50p dl red & grn	8	8
685	A218	75p Prus bl & lil	8	8
686	A218	5af brt grn & dk brn	30	30

View of Herat
A219

Flag and Map of Afghanistan
A220

Design: 75p, Tomb of Queen Gowhar Shad (vert.).

Perf. 13½x14, 14x13½

1964, July 12

687	A219	25p sep & bl	5	5
688	A219	75p dp bl & buff	5	5
689	A220	3af red, blk & grn	30	10

Issued for tourist publicity.

Wrestling
A221

Designs: 25p, Hurdling (vert.). 1af, Diving (vert.). 5af, Soccer.

1964, July 26 *Perf. 12*

690	A221	25p ol bis, blk & car	5	5
691	A221	1af bl grn, blk & car	8	8
692	A221	3.75af yel grn, blk & car	35	35
693	A221	5af brn, blk & car	45	45
a.		Souv. sheet of 4	1.10	1.10

Issued to commemorate the 18th Olympic Games, Tokyo, Oct. 10-25, 1964. No. 693a contains 4 imperf. stamps similar to Nos. 690-693, black inscription. Size: 95x95mm. Sold for 15af. The additional 5af went to the Afghanistan Olympic Committee.

Flag and Outline of Nadir Shah's Tomb
A222

1964, Aug. 24 Photogravure

695	A222	25p gold, bl, blk, red & grn	7	7
696	A222	75p gold, bl, blk, red & grn	10	10

Issued to commemorate Independence Day. The stamps were printed with an erroneous inscription in upper left corner: "33rd year of independence." This was locally obliterated with a typographed gold bar.

Pashtunistan Flag
A223

Zahir Shah
A225

1964, Sept. 1 Unwmkd.

697	A223	100p gold, blk, red, bl & grn	7	7

Issued for "Free Pashtunistan Day."

1964, Oct. 17 *Perf. 14x13½*

699	A225	1.25af gold & yel grn	10	5
700	A225	3.75af gold & rose	20	15
701	A225	50af gold & gray	3.00	2.50

Issued to honor King Mohammed Zahir Shah on his 50th birthday.

Coat of Arms of Afghanistan and U.N. Emblem
A226

1964, Oct. 24 *Perf. 13½x14*

702	A226	5af gold, blk & dl bl	30	20

Issued for United Nations Day.

Emblem of Afghanistan Women's Association
A227

1964, Nov. 9 Photo. Unwmkd.

703	A227	25p pink, dk bl & emer	5	3
704	A227	75p aqua, dk bl & emer	5	4
705	A227	1af sil, dk bl & emer	10	5

Issued for Women's Day.

Abdul Rahman Jami
A228
Lithographed

1964, Nov. 23 *Perf. 11 Rough*

706	A228	1.50af blk, emer & yel	1.25

Issued to commemorate the 550th anniversary of the birth of the poet Mowlana Nooruddin Abdul Rahman Jami (1414-1492).

Woodpecker
A229

Birds: 3.75af, Black-throated jay (vert.). 5af, Impeyan pheasant (vert.).

Perf. 13½x14, 14x13½

1965, Apr. 20 Photo. Unwmkd.

707	A229	1.25af multi	12	6
708	A229	3.75af multi	30	20
709	A229	5af multi	40	20

ITU Emblem, Old and New Communication Equipment
A230

1965, May 17 *Perf. 13½x14*

710	A230	5af lt bl, blk & red	35	35

Issued to commemorate the centenary of the International Telecommunication Union.

"Red City," Bamian
A231

Designs: 3.75af, Ruins of ancient Bamian city. 5af, Bandé Amir, mountain lakes.

1965, May 30 *Perf. 13x13½*

711	A231	1.25af pink & multi	10	10
712	A231	3.75af lt bl & multi	25	25
713	A231	5af yel & multi	40	40

Issued for tourist publicity.

ICY Emblem
A232

1965, June 25 ***Perf. 13½x13***

714	A232	5af grn, yel, blk, red & vio bl	25	25

International Cooperation Year, 1965.

ARIANA Air Lines Emblem and DC-3
A233

Designs: 5af, DC-6 at right. 10af, DC-3 on top.

Perf. 13½x14

1965, July 15 Photo. **Unwmkd.**

715	A233	1.25af brt bl, gray & blk	10	10
716	A233	5af red lil, blk & bl	30	30
717	A233	10af bis, blk, bl gray & grn	75	75
a.		Souv. sheet of 3	1.25	1.25

Issued to commemorate the 10th anniversary of Afghan Air Lines, ARIANA. No. 717a contains 3 imperf. stamps similar to Nos. 715–717; blue marginal inscription, black control number. Size: 90x90mm.

Nadir Shah
A234

1965, Aug. 23 ***Perf. 14x13½***

718	A234	1af dl grn, blk & red brn	12	12

For the 47th Independence Day.

Flag of Pashtunistan
A235

Perf. 13½x14

1965, Aug. 31 Photo. **Unwmkd.**

719	A235	1af ultra, blk, gold, car & grn	10	10

Issued for "Free Pashtunistan Day."

Zahir Shah Signing Constitution
A236

1965, Sept. 11 ***Perf. 13x13½***

720	A236	1.50af brt grn & blk	25	25

Promulgation of the new Constitution.

Zahir Shah and Oak Leaves
A237

1965, Oct. 14 ***Perf. 14x13½***

721	A237	1.25af blk, ultra & sal	20	15
722	A237	6af blk, lt bl & rose lil	60	50

Issued to honor King Mohammed Zahir Shah on his 51st birthday.

Flags of UN and Afghanistan
A238

1965, Oct. 24 ***Perf. 13½x14***

723	A238	5af multi	30	30

Issued for United Nations Day.

Dappled Ground Gecko
A239

Designs: 4af, Caucasian agamid (lizard). 8af, Horsfield's tortoise.

Perf. 13½x14

1966, May 10 Photo. **Unwmkd.**

724	A239	3af tan & multi	30	30
725	A239	4af brt grn & multi	30	30
726	A239	8af vio & multi	50	50

Soccer Player and Globe
A240

1966, July 31 Litho. ***Perf. 14x13½***

727	A240	2af rose red & blk	30	25
728	A240	6af vio bl & blk	60	35
729	A240	12af bis brn & blk	1.20	75

Issued to commemorate the World Cup Soccer Championship, Wembley, England, July 11–30.

Cotton Flower and Boll
A241

Designs: 5af, Silkworm. 7af, Farmer plowing with oxen.

1966, July 31 ***Perf. 13½x14***

730	A241	1af multi	15	10
731	A241	5af multi	40	30
732	A241	7af multi	60	40

Issued for the Day of Agriculture.

Independence Monument
A242

1966, Aug. 23 Photo. ***Perf. 13½x14***

733	A242	1af multi	10	10
734	A242	3af multi	35	25

Issued to commemorate Independence Day.

Flag of Pashtunistan
A243

1966, Aug. 31 Litho. ***Perf. 11 rough***

735	A243	1af brt bl	25	10

Issued for "Free Pashtunistan Day."

Bagh-i-Bala Park Casino
A244

Designs: 2af, Map of Afghanistan. 8af, Tomb of Abd-er-Rahman. The casino on 4af is the former summer palace of Abd-er-Rahman near Kabul.

1966, Oct. 3 Photo. ***Perf. 13½x14***

736	A244	2af red & multi	18	15
737	A244	4af multi	40	30
738	A244	8af multi	65	60
a.		Souvenir sheet of 3	1.50	1.50

Issued for tourist publicity. No. 738a contains 3 imperf. stamps similar to Nos. 736–738: light yellow margin with black inscription and control number. Size: 110x80mm.

Zahir Shah
A245

UNESCO Emblem
A246

1966, Oct. 14 ***Perf. 14x13½***

739	A245	1af dk sl grn	20	10
740	A245	5af red brn	50	25

Issued to honor King Mohammed Zahir Shah on his 52nd birthday. See Nos. 760–761.

1967 Litho. ***Perf. 12***

741	A246	2af multi	30	20
742	A246	6af multi	50	20
743	A246	12af multi	1.00	40

Issued to commemorate the 20th anniversary of UNESCO (United Nations Educational, Scientific and Cultural Organization).

Zahir Shah and U.N. Emblem
A247

1967 Photogravure

744	A247	5af multi	50	20
745	A247	10af multi	1.00	40

Issued to commemorate the 20th anniversary of the U.N. International Organization for Refugees.

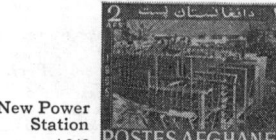

New Power Station
A248

Designs: 5af, Carpet (vert.). 8af, Cement factory.

1967, Jan. 7 Photo. ***Perf. 13½x14***

746	A248	2af red lil & ol grn	12	8
747	A248	5af multi	30	25
748	A248	8af blk, dk bl & tan	50	35

Issued to publicize industrial development.

International Tourist Year Emblem
A249

Designs: 6af, International Tourist Year emblem and map of Afghanistan.

1967, May 11 Photo. ***Perf. 12***

749	A249	2af yel, blk & lt bl	15	10
750	A249	6af bis brn, blk & lt bl	50	30
a.		Souv. sheet of 3	1.00	1.00

Issued for International Tourist Year, 1967. No. 750a contains 2 imperf. stamps similar to Nos. 749–750 with black marginal inscription. Size: 110x70mm. Sold for 10af.

Power Dam, Doruta
A250

Macaque
A251

Designs: 6af, Sirobi Dam (vert.). 8af, Reservoir at Jalalabad.

1967, July 2 Photo. ***Perf. 12***

751	A250	1af dk grn & lil	6	6
752	A250	6af red brn & grnsh bl	35	35
753	A250	8af plum & dk bl	50	50

Issued to publicize progress in agriculture through electricity.

1967, July 28 Photo. ***Perf. 12***

Designs: 6af, Striped hyena (horiz.). 12af, Persian gazelles (horiz.).

754	A251	2af dl yel & ind	12	12
755	A251	6af lt grn & sep	35	35
756	A251	12af lt bl & red brn	75	75

Pashtun Dancers
A252

1967, Sept. 1 Photo. ***Perf. 12***

757	A252	2af mag & vio	12	12

Issued for "Free Pashtunistan Day."

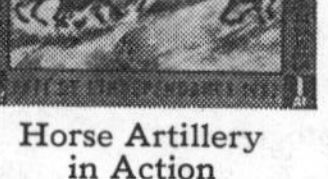

Horse Artillery in Action
A253

Fireworks and U.N. Emblem
A254

1967, Aug. 24

758	A253	1af dk brn & org ver	7	7
759	A253	2af dk brn & brt pink	12	12

Issued to commemorate Independence Day.

King Type of 1966.

1967, Oct. 15 Photo. ***Perf. 14x13½***

760 A245 2af brn red 12 10
761 A245 8af dk bl 50 25

Issued to honor King Mohammed Zahir Shah on his 53rd birthday.

1967, Oct. 24 Litho. ***Perf. 12***

762 A254 10af vio bl & multi 65 35

Issued for United Nations Day.

Greco-Roman Wrestlers
A255

Said Jamalluddin Afghan
A256

Design: 6af, Wrestlers (free style).

1967, Nov. 20 Photogravure

763 A255 4af ol grn & rose lil 25 12
764 A255 6af dp car & brn 40 20
a. Souv. sheet of 2 1.10 1.10

Issued to publicize the 1968 Olympic Games. No. 764a contains 2 imperf. stamps similar to Nos. 763-764. Rose lilac marginal inscription and black control number. Size: 100x65mm.

1967, Nov. 27

765 A256 1af magenta 7 7
766 A256 5af brown 35 20

Issued to honor Said Jamalluddin Afghan, politician (1839-1897).

Bronze Vase, 11th-12th Centuries
A257

WHO Emblem
A258

Design: 7af, Bronze vase, Ghasnavide era, 11th-12th centuries.

1967, Dec. 23 Photo. ***Perf. 12***

767 A257 3af lt grn & brn 18 15
768 A257 7af yel & sl grn 42 30
a. Souv. sheet of 2 1.25 1.25

No. 768a contains 2 imperf. stamps similar to Nos. 767-768. Slate green marginal inscription and black control number. Size: 65x100mm.

1968, Apr. 7 Photo. ***Perf. 12***

769 A258 2af cit & brt bl 8 8
770 A258 7af rose & brt bl 28 22

Issued to commemorate the 20th anniversary of the World Health Organization.

Karakul
A259

1968, May 20 Photo. ***Perf. 12***

771 A259 1af yel & blk 6 3
772 A259 6af lt bl & blk 35 20
773 A259 12af lt ultra & dk brn 70 40

Issued for the Day of Agriculture.

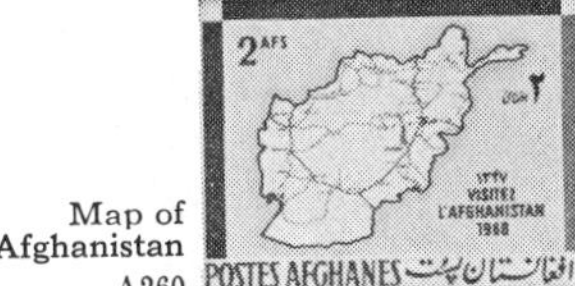

Map of Afghanistan
A260

Victory Tower, Ghazni
A261

Cinereous Vulture
A262

Design: 16af, Mausoleum, Ghazni.

1968, June 3 ***Perf. 13½x14, 12***

774 A260 2af red, blk, lt bl & grn 12 8
775 A261 3af yel, dk brn & lt bl 18 10
776 A261 16af pink & multi 95 50

Issued for tourist publicity.

1968, July 3 ***Perf. 12***

Birds: 6af, Eagle owl. 7af, Greater flamingoes.

777 A262 1af sky bl & multi 7 3
778 A262 6af yel & multi 45 20
779 A262 7af multi 50 30

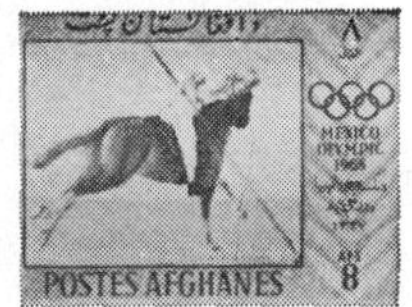

Game of "Peg-sticking"
A263

Designs: 2af, Olympic flame and rings (vert.). 12af, Buzkashi.

1968, July 20 Photo. ***Perf. 12***

780 A263 2af multi 12 7
781 A263 8af org & multi 50 30
782 A263 12af multi 75 45

19th Olympic Games, Mexico City, Oct. 12-27.

Flower-decked Armored Car
A264

1968, Aug. 23

783 A264 6af multi 40 20

Issued to commemorate Independence Day.

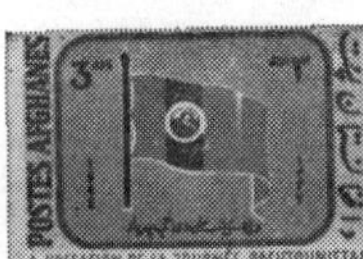

Flag of Pashtunistan
A265

1968, Aug. 31 Photo. ***Perf. 12***

784 A265 3af multi 25 10

Issued for "Free Pashtunistan Day."

Zahir Shah
A266

Human Rights Flame
A267

1968, Oct. 14 Photo. ***Perf. 12***

785 A266 2af ultra 12 6
786 A266 8af brown 45 28

Issued to honor King Mohammed Zahir Shah on his 54th birthday.

1968, Oct. 24

787 A267 1af multi 10 3
788 A267 2af vio, bis & blk 25 6
789 A267 6af vio blk, bis & vio 50 20

Souvenir Sheet
Imperf.

790 A267 10af plum, bis & red org 1.00 1.00

Issued for International Human Rights Year. No. 790 contains one stamp. Bister margin with plum inscription and black control number. Size: 100x65mm.

Maolana Djalalodine Balkhi
A268

Kushan Mural
A269

1968, Nov. 26 Photo. ***Perf. 12***

791 A268 4af dk grn & mag 27 12

Maolana Djalalodine Balkhi (1207-1273), historian.

1969, Jan. 2 ***Perf. 12***

Design: 3af, Jug shaped like female torso.

792 A269 1af dk grn, mar & yel 10 4
793 A269 3af vio, gray & mar 25 10
a. Souv. sheet of 2 40 40

Issued to publicize the archaeological finds at Bagram, 1st century B.C. to 2nd century A.D.

No. 793a contains 2 imperf. stamps similar to Nos. 792-793. Maroon marginal inscription and black control number. Size: 100x65mm.

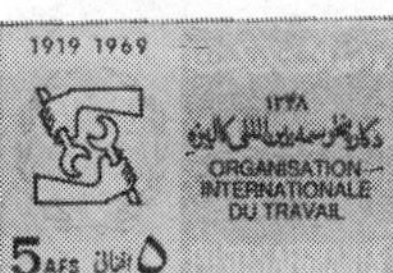

ILO Emblem
A270

1969, Mar. 23 Photo. ***Perf. 12***

794 A270 5af lt yel, lem & blk 30 18
795 A270 8af lt bl, grnsh bl & blk 50 30

Issued for the 50th anniversary of the International Labor Organization.

Arms Type of 1939

1969, May (?) Typographed

795A A79 100p dk grn 8 4
795B A79 150p dp brn 10 6

Nos. 795A-795B were normally used as newspaper stamps.

Badakhshan Scene
A271

Designs: 2af, Map of Afghanistan. 7af, Three men on mules ascending the Pamir Mountains.

1969, July 6 Photo. ***Perf. 13½x14***

796 A271 2af ocher & multi 15 6
797 A271 4af multi 25 12
798 A271 7af multi 55 22
a. Souv. sheet of 3 1.10 1.10

Issued for tourist publicity. No. 798a contains 3 imperf. stamps similar to Nos. 796-798. Black marginal inscription and control number. Size: 136x90½mm. Sold for 15af.

Bust, from Hadda Treasure, 3rd-5th Centuries
A272

Zahir Shah and Queen Humeira
A273

Designs: 5af, Vase and jug. 10af, Statue of crowned woman. 5af and 10af from Bagram treasure, 1st-2nd centuries.

1969, Aug. 3 Photo. ***Perf. 14x13½***

799 A272 1af ol grn & gold 4 3
800 A272 5af pur & gold 20 16
801 A272 10af dp bl & gold 40 32

1969, Aug. 23 ***Perf. 12***

802 A273 5af gold, dk bl & red brn 35 20
803 A273 10af gold, dp lil & bl grn 65 35

Issued to commemorate Independence Day.

Map of Pashtunistan and Rising Sun
A274

1969, Aug. 31 Typo. ***Perf. 10½***

804 A274 2af lt bl & red 12 6

Issued for "Free Pashtunistan Day."

Zahir Shah
A275

1969, Oct. 14 Photo. ***Perf. 12***

Portrait in Natural Colors

805 A275 2af dk brn & gold 15 6
806 A275 6af brn & gold 45 20

Issued to honor King Mohammed Zahir Shah on his 55th birthday.

U.N. Emblem and Flag of Afghanistan—A276

1969, Oct. 24 **Litho.** ***Perf. 13½***

807 A276 5af bl & multi 27 16

Issued for United Nations Day.

ITU Emblem A277 — Wild Boar A278

1969, Nov. 12

808 A277 6af ultra & multi 30 20
809 A277 12af rose & multi 60 35

Issued for World Telecommunications Day.

1969, Dec. 7 **Photo.** ***Perf. 12***

Designs: 1af, Long-tailed porcupine. 8af, Red deer.

810 A278 1af yel & multi 6 3
811 A278 3af bl & multi 18 10
812 A278 8af pink & multi 50 25

Man's First Footprints on Moon, and Earth A279

1969, Dec. 28 ***Perf. 13½x14***

813 A279 1af yel grn & multi 6 3
814 A279 3af yel & multi 17 10
815 A279 6af bl & multi 30 20
816 A279 10af rose & multi 50 32

Moon landing. See note after Algeria No. 427.

Anti-cancer Symbol A280 — Mirza Abdul Quader Bedel A281

1970, Apr. 7 **Photogravure** ***Perf. 14***

817 A280 2af dk grn & rose car 15 6
818 A280 6af dk bl & rose cl 40 20

Issued to publicize the fight against cancer.

1970, May 6 ***Perf. 14x13½***

819 A281 5af multi 27 15

Issued for the 250th anniversary of the death of Mirza Abdul Quader Bedel (1643–1720), poet.

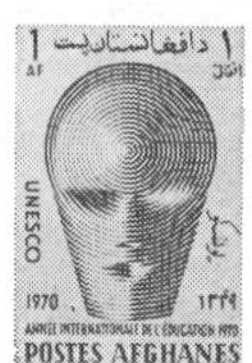

Education Year Emblem A282 — Mother and Child A283

1970, June 7 **Photo.** ***Perf. 12***

820 A282 1af black 6 3
821 A282 6af dp rose 35 20
822 A282 12af green 75 35

International Education Year 1970.

1970, June 15 ***Perf. 13½***

823 A283 6af yel & multi 27 20

Issued for Mother's Day.

U.N. Emblem, Scales of Justice, Spacecraft A284

1970, June 26

824 A284 4af yel, dk bl & dp bl 20 12
825 A284 6af sal pink, dk bl & brt bl 35 20

25th anniversary of United Nations.

Mosque of the Amir of the two Swords, Kabul—A285

Designs: 2af, Map of Afghanistan. 7af, Arch of Paghman.

1970, July 6 ***Perf. 12***

Size: 30½x30½mm.

826 A285 2af lt bl, blk & cit 12 6

Size: 36x26mm.

827 A285 3af pink & multi 18 10
828 A285 7af yel & multi 42 22

Issued for tourist publicity.

Zahir Shah Reviewing Troops A286

1970, Aug. 23 **Photo.** ***Perf. 13½***

829 A286 8af multi 60 25

Issued to commemorate Independence Day.

Pathans A287

1970, Aug. 31 **Typo.** ***Perf. 10½***

830 A287 2af ultra & red 12 6

Issued for "Free Pashtunistan Day."

Quail A288

Dsigns: 4af, Golden eagle. 6af, Ring-necked pheasant.

1970, Sept. **Photo.** ***Perf. 12***

831 A288 2af multi 8 6
832 A288 4af multi 16 12
833 A288 6af multi 24 20

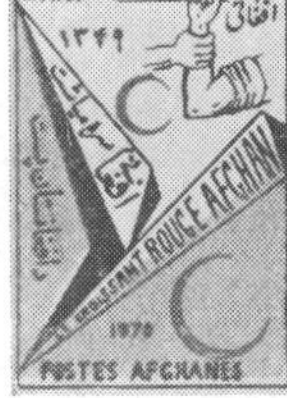

Zahir Shah A289 — Red Crescents A290

1970, Oct. 14 **Photo.** ***Perf. 14x13½***

834 A289 3af grn & vio 20 10
835 A289 7af dk bl & vio brn 60 22

Issued to honor King Mohammed Zahir Shah on his 56th birthday.

1970, Oct. 16 **Typo.** ***Perf. 10½***

836 A290 2af blk, gold & red 12 6

Issued for the Red Crescent Society.

U. N. Emblem and Charter A291

1970, Oct. 24 **Photo.** ***Perf. 14***

837 A291 1af gold & multi 10 5
838 A291 5af gold & multi 20 16

United Nations Day.

Tiger Heads of 1871 A292

1970, Nov. 10 ***Perf. 12***

839 A292 1af sal, lt grnsh bl & blk 4 3
840 A292 4af lt ultra, yel & blk 16 12
841 A292 12af lil, lt bl & blk 48 35

Issued to commemorate the centenary of the first Afghan postage stamps. The postal service was established in 1870, but the first stamps were issued in May, 1871.

Globe and Waves A293

1971, May 17 **Photo.** ***Perf. 13½***

842 A293 12af grn, blk & bl 60 35

3rd World Telecommunications Day.

Callimorpha Principalis A294

Designs: 3af, Epizygaenella species. 5af, Parnassius autocrator.

1971, May 30 ***Perf. 13½x14***

843 A294 1af ver & multi 4 3
844 A294 3af yel & multi 12 10
845 A294 5af ultra & multi 20 15

"UNESCO" and Half of Ancient Kushan Statue A295

1971, June 26 **Photo.** ***Perf. 13½***

846 A295 6af ocher & vio 40 20
847 A295 10af lt bl & mar 65 30

UNESCO-sponsored International Kushani Seminar.

Tughra and Independence Monument A296

1971, Aug. 23

848 A296 7af rose red & multi 40 22
849 A296 9af red org & multi 65 28

Independence Day.

Pashtunistan Square, Kabul A297

1971, Aug. 31 **Typo.** ***Perf. 10½***

850 A297 5af dp rose lil 27 15

"Free Pashtunistan Day."

Zahir Shah
A298

1971, Oct. 14 Photo. *Perf. 12½x12*

851 A298 9af lt grn & multi 40 28
852 A298 17af yel & multi 75 55

57th birthday of King Mohammed Zahir Shah.

Map of Afghanistan, Red Crescent, Various Activities
A299

1971, Oct. 16 *Perf. 14x13½*

853 A299 8af lt bl, red, grn & blk 45 25

For Afghan Red Crescent Society.

Equality Year Emblem
A300

1971, Oct. 24 *Perf. 12*

854 A300 24af brt bl 1.25 70

International Year Against Racial Discrimination and United Nations Day.

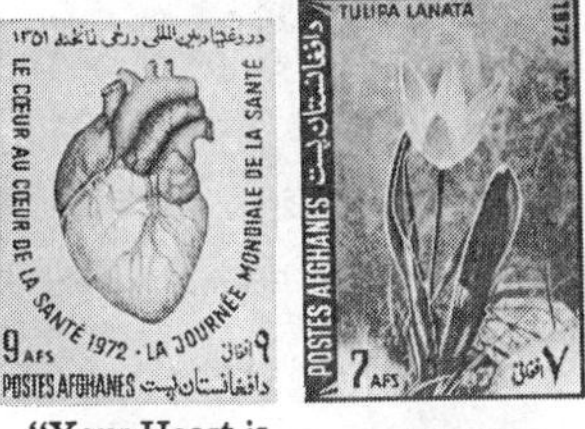

"Your Heart is your Health"
A301

Tulip
A302

1972, Apr. 7 Photo. *Perf. 14*

855 A301 9af pale yel & multi 36 28
856 A301 12af gray & multi 48 35

World Health Day.

1972, June 5 Photo. *Perf. 14*

Designs: 10af, Rock partridge (horiz.). 12af, Lynx (horiz.). 18af, Allium stipitatum (flower).

857 A302 7af grn & multi 28 22
858 A302 10af bl & multi 40 32
859 A302 12af lt grn & multi 48 35
860 A302 18af bl grn & multi 72 60

Buddhist Shrine, Hadda
A302a

Designs: 7af, Greco-Bactrian animal seal, 250 B.C. 9af, Greco-Oriental temple, Ai-Khanoum, 3rd–2nd centuries B.C.

1972, July 16 Photo. *Perf. 12*

861 A302a 3af brn & dl bl 12 9
862 A302a 7af rose cl & dl grn 28 22
863 A302a 9af grn & lil 36 30

Tourist publicity.

King and Queen Reviewing Parade
A303

1972, Aug. 23 Photo. *Perf. 13½*

864 A303 25af gold & multi 1.35 85

Independence Day.

Wrestling
A304

Designs: 8af, Like 4af. 10af, 19af, 21af, Wrestling, different hold.

1972, Aug. 26

865 A304 4af ol bis & multi 20 12
866 A304 8af lt bl & multi 40 25
867 A304 10af yel grn & multi 50 32
868 A304 19af multi 90 40
869 A304 21af lil & multi 1.00 45
a. Souv. sheet of 5 3.25 3.25
Nos. 865-869 (5) 3.00 1.54

20th Olympic Games, Munich, Aug. 26–Sept. 11. No. 869a contains 5 imperf. stamps similar to Nos. 865–869. Olive bister marginal inscription and ornament, black control number. Size: 159x110mm. Sold for 60af.

Pathan and View of Tribal Territory
A305

Zahir Shah
A306

1972, Aug. 31 *Perf. 12½x12*

870 A305 5af ultra & multi 27 15

Pashtunistan day.

1972, Oct. 14 Photo. *Perf. 14x13½*

871 A306 7af gold, blk & Prus bl 50 22
872 A306 14af gold, blk & lt brn 1.00 45

58th birthday of King Mohammed Zahir Shah.

City Destroyed by Earthquake, Refugees—A307

1972, Oct. 16 *Perf. 13½*

873 A307 7af lt bl, red & blk 40 22

For Afghan Red Crescent Society.

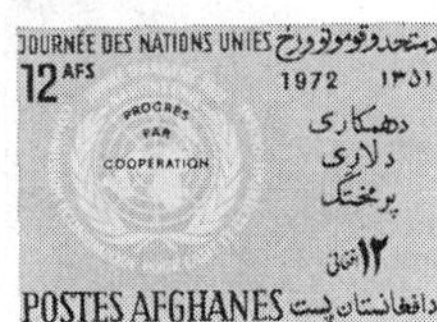

U.N. Emblem
A308

1972, Oct. 24

874 A308 12af lt ultra & blk 65 35

United Nations Economic Commission for Asia and the Far East (ECAFE), 25th anniversary.

Ceramics
A309

Designs: 9af, Leather coat (vert.). 12af, Metal ware (vert.). 16af, Inlaid artifacts.

1972, Dec. 10 Photo. *Perf. 12*

875 A309 7af gold & multi 42 22
876 A309 9af gold & multi 55 28
877 A309 12af gold & multi 70 35
878 A309 16af gold & multi 1.00 50
a. Souvenir sheet of 4 2.75 2.75

Handicraft industries. No. 878a contains 4 imperf. stamps similar to Nos. 875–878. Gold marginal inscription and black control number. Size: 109x109mm. Sold for 45af.

WMO and National Emblems—A310

1973, Apr. 3 Photo. *Perf. 14*

879 A310 7af lt lil & dk grn 42 22
880 A310 14af lt bl & dp cl 85 45

Centenary of international meteorological cooperation.

abu-al-Rayhan al-Biruni
A311

Family
A312

1973, June 16 Photo. *Perf. 13½*

881 A311 10af multi 55 32

Millennium of the birth of abu-al-Rayhan al-Biruni (973–1048), philosopher and mathematician.

1973, June 30 Photo. *Perf. 13½*

882 A312 9af org & red lil 50 30

International Family Planning Federation, 21st anniversary.

Republic

Impeyan Pheasant
A313

Birds: 9af, Great crested grebe. 12af, Himalayan snow cock.

1973, July 29 Photo. *Perf. 12x12½*

883 A313 8af yel & multi 32 25
884 A313 9af bl & multi 36 30
885 A313 12af multi 48 35

Stylized Buzkashi Horseman
A314

1973, Aug. *Perf. 13½*

886 A314 8af black 32 25

Tourist publicity.

Fireworks
A315

1973, Aug. 23 Photo. *Perf. 12*

887 A315 12af multi 48 35

55th Independence Day.

Lake Abassine, Pashtunistan Flag
A316

1973, Aug. 31 *Perf. 14x13½*

888 A316 9af multi 50 30

Pashtunistan Day.

Red Crescent
A317

1973, Oct. 16 *Perf. 13½*

889 A317 10af red, blk & gold 60 32

Red Crescent Society.

Kemal Ataturk
A318

1973, Oct. 28 Litho. Perf. 10½

890	A318	1af blue	6	3
891	A318	7af redsh brn	42	22

50th anniversary of the Turkish Republic.

Human Rights Flame, Arms of Afghanistan
A319

1973, Dec. 10 Photo. Perf. 12

892	A319	12af sil, blk & lt bl	45	35

25th anniversary of the Universal Declaration of Human Rights.

Asiatic Black Bears
A320

1974, Mar. 26 Lithographed Perf. 12
Multicolored

893	A320	5af *shown*	15	12
894	A320	7af *Afghan hound*	22	20
895	A320	10af *Persian goat*	30	25
896	A320	12af *Leopard*	40	30
a.		Souvenir sheet of 4	1.25	1.25

No. 896a contains 4 imperf. stamps similar to Nos. 893–896. Magenta border and black marginal inscription. Size: 120x100mm.

Worker and Farmer
A321

1974, May 1 Photo. Perf. 13½x12½

897	A321	9af rose red & multi	40	25

International Labor Day, May 1.

Independence Monument and Arch
A322

1974, May 27 Photo. Perf. 12

898	A322	4af bl & multi	12	10
899	A322	11af gold & multi	35	30

56th Independence Day.

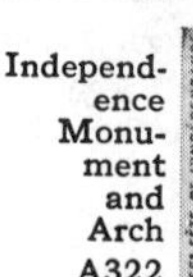

Arms of Afghanistan and Symbol of Cooperation—A323

Pres. Mohammad Daoud Khan
A324

Designs: 5af, Flag of Republic of Afghanistan. 15af, Soldiers and coat of arms of the Republic.

1974, July 25 Perf. 13½x12½, 14

Sizes: 4af, 15af, 36x22mm.; 5af, 7af, 36x26, 26x36mm.

900	A323	4af multi	18	10
901	A323	5af multi	22	12
902	A324	7af grn, brn & blk	32	18
a.		Souvenir sheet of 2	70	70
903	A323	15af multi	65	40
a.		Souvenir sheet of 2	1.00	1.00

First anniversary of the Republic of Afghanistan. No. 902a contains 2 imperf. stamps similar to Nos. 901–902, No. 903a contains 2 imperf. stamps similar to Nos. 900 and 903. Both sheets have yellow margins, black inscriptions and control numbers. Sizes: No. 902a, 99x99mm., No. 903a, 120x80mm.

Lesser Spotted Eagle
A325

Birds: 6af, White-fronted goose, ruddy shelduck and gray-lag goose. 11af, European coots and European crane.

1974, Aug. 6 Photo. Perf. 13½x13

904	A325	1af car rose & multi	6	3
905	A325	6af bl & multi	35	15
906	A325	11af yel & multi	70	30

Nos. 904–906 printed se-tenant.

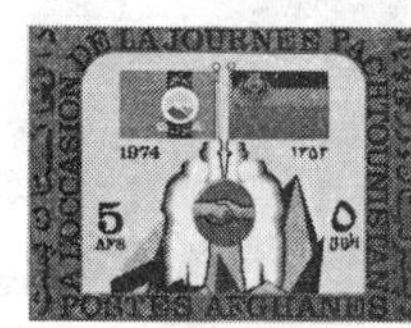

Flags of Pashtunistan and Afghanistan—A326

1974, Aug. 31 Photo. Perf. 14

907	A326	5af multi	27	12

Pashtunistan Day.

Coat of Arms
A327

1974, Oct. 9

908	A327	7af gold, grn & blk	22	18

Centenary of Universal Postal Union.

"UN" and UN Emblem
A328

1974, Oct. 24 Photo. Perf. 14

909	A328	5af lt ultra & dk bl	27	12

United Nations Day.

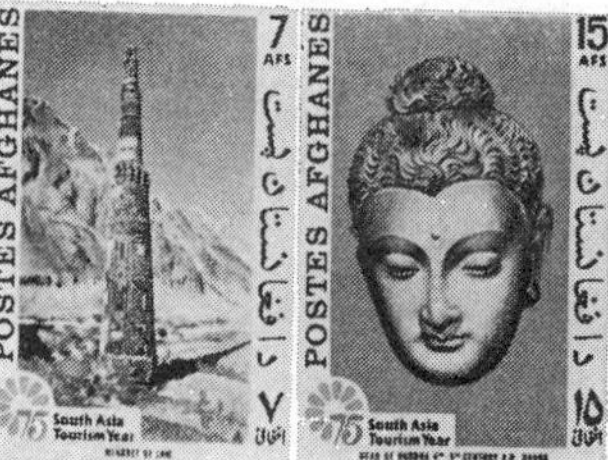

Minaret of Jam A329 — Buddha, Hadda A330

Design: 14af, Lady riding griffin, 2nd century, Bagram.

1975, May 5 Photo. Perf. 13½

910	A329	7af multi	22	15
911	A330	14af multi	44	30
912	A330	15af multi	48	30
a.		Souvenir sheet of 3	1.50	1.50

South Asia Tourism Year 1975.

No. 912a contains 3 imperf. stamps similar to Nos. 910–912. Tourism Year emblem in margin and black control number. Size: 130x90mm.

New Flag of Afghanistan
A331

1975, May 27 Photo. Perf. 12

913	A331	16af multi	75	35

57th Independence Day.

Celebrating Crowd
A332

1975, July 17 Photo. Perf. 13½

914	A332	9af bl & multi	42	20
915	A332	12af car & multi	55	28

Second anniversary of the Republic.

Women's Year Emblems
A333

1975, Aug. 24 Photo. Perf. 12

916	A333	9af car, lt bl & blk	28	22

International Women's Year 1975.

Pashtunistan Flag, Sun Rising Over Mountains
A334

Mohammed Akbar Khan
A335

1975, Aug. 31 Perf. 13½

917	A334	10af multi	30	25

Pashtunistan Day.

1976, Feb. 4 Photo. Perf. 14

918	A335	15af lt brn & multi	45	35

Mohammed Akbar Khan (1816–1846), warrior son of Amir Dost Mohammed Khan.

Pres. Mohammad Daoud Khan
A336 A337

1975–78 Photo. Perf. 14

919	A336	10af multi ('76)	45	25
920	A336	16af multi ('78)	70	
921	A336	19af multi ('76)	85	48
922	A336	21af multi ('76)	90	50
923	A336	22af multi ('78)	1.00	
924	A336	30af multi ('78)	1.35	
925	A337	50af multi	2.25	1.25
926	A337	100af multi	4.50	2.50
		Nos. 919-926 (8)	12.00	

Arms of Republic, Independence Monument
A338

1976, June 1 Photo. Perf. 14

927	A338	22af bl & multi	65	45

58th Independence Day.

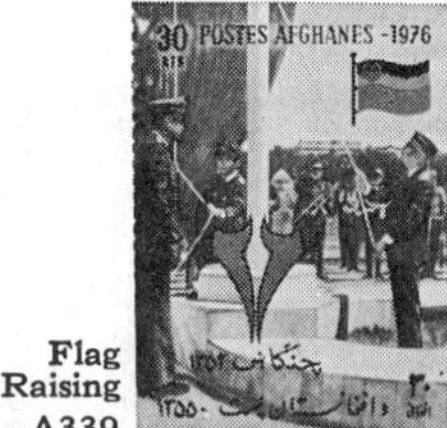

Flag Raising
A339

1976, July 17 Photo. Perf. 14

928	A339	30af multi	90	75

Republic Day.

Mountain Peaks and Flag of Pashtunistan
A340

1976, Aug. 31 Photo. Perf. 14

929	A340	16af multi	48	38

Pashtunistan Day.

Coat of Arms—A340a

1977 Litho. *Roulette 11, Rough*

929A A340a 25p salmon
930 A340a 50p lt grn 3 3
931 A340a 1af ultra 3 3

Flag and Views on Open Book
A341

1977, May 27 Photo. *Perf. 14*

937 A341 20af grn & multi 60 50

59th Independence Day.

Pres. Daoud and National Assembly
A342

President Taking Oath of Office
A343

Designs: 10af, Inaugural address. 18af, Promulgation of Constitution.

1977, June 22

938 A342 7af multi 22 16
939 A343 8af multi 24 20
940 A343 10af multi 30 25
941 A342 18af multi 55 45
a. Souvenir sheet of 4 1.50 1.50

Election of first President and promulgation of Constitution. No. 941a contains 4 imperf. stamps similar to Nos. 938–941. Black marginal inscription and control number. Size: 135x105mm.

Jamalluddin Medal
A344

1977, July 6 Photo. *Perf. 14*

942 A344 12af bl, blk & gold 35 30

Sajo Jamalluddin Afghani, reformer, 80th death anniversary.

Afghanistan Flag over Crowd
A345

1977, July 17

943 A345 22af multi 65 55

Republic Day.

Dancers, Fountain, Pashtunistan Flag
A346

1977, Aug. 31

944 A346 30af multi 90 75

Pashtunistan Day.

Members of Parliament Congratulating Pres. Daoud—A347

1978, Feb. 5 Litho. *Perf. 14*

945 A347 20af multi 60

Election of first president, first anniversary.

Map of Afghanistan, UPU Emblem
A348

1978, Apr. 1 Photo. *Perf. 14*

946 A348 10af grn, blk & gold 30 25

50th anniversary of Afghanistan's membership in Universal Postal Union.

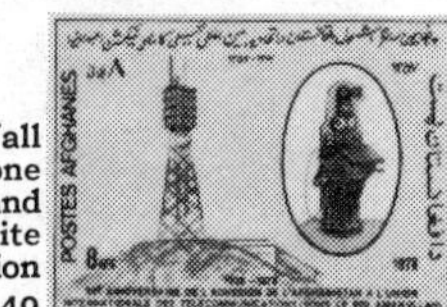

Wall Telephone and Satellite Station
A349

1978, Apr. 12

947 A349 8af multi 24 20

50th anniversary of Afghanistan's membership in International Telecommunications Union.

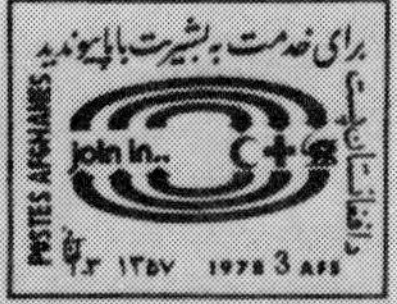

Arrows Pointing to Crescent, Cross and Lion
A350

1978, July 6 Litho. *Perf. 11 Rough*

948 A350 3af black 10 6

50th anniversary of Afghani Red Crescent Society.

Arch of Qalai Bist
A351

1978, Aug. 19 *Perf. 14*

949 A351 16af
949A A351 22af sil & multi 65 55
949B A351 30af

Men with Pashtunistan Flag
A352

Coat of Arms and Emblems
A353

1978, Aug. 31 *Perf. 11 Rough*

950 A352 7af ultra & red 22 16

Pashtunistan Day.

1978, Sept. 8 *Perf. 11*

951 A353 20af rose red 60 50

World Literacy Day.

Abdul Qadir
A354

1978 Litho. *Perf. 11½ Rough*

952 A354 18af lt grn 55 45

Hero of the Khalq Revolution.

New Afghan Flag
A355

1978 Photogravure *Perf. 11½*

953 A355 8af blk, red & gold 24 20
954 A355 9af blk, red & gold 30 22

"The mail serving the people."

Nour Mohammad Taraki
A356

1979, Jan. 1 Litho. *Perf. 12*

955 A356 12af multi 35 10

Nour Mohammad Taraki, founder of People's Democratic Party of Afghanistan, installation as president.

Woman Breaking Chain
A357

1979, Mar. 8 Litho. *Perf. 11*

956 A357 14af red & ultra 60

Women's Day. Inscribed "POSSTES."

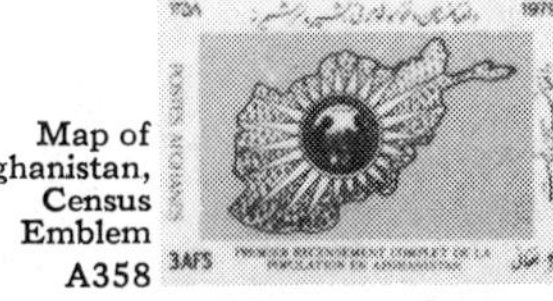
Map of Afghanistan, Census Emblem
A358

1979, Mar. 25 Litho. *Perf. 12*

957 A358 3af multi 10 8

First comprehensive population census.

Farmers
A359

1979, Mar. 21

958 A359 1af multi 3 3

Agriculture Day.

Pres. Taraki Reading First Issue of Khalq—A360

1979, Apr. 11 *Perf. 12½x12*

959 A360 2af multi 10 8

Khalq, newspaper of People's Democratic Republic of Afghanistan.

Pres. Noor Mohammad Taraki
A361

Plaza with Tank Monument and Fountain—A362

House where Revolution Started
A363

Design: 12af, House where 1st Khalq Party Congress was held.

Perf. 12, 12½x12 (A362)

1979, Apr. 27 Lithographed

960 A361 4af multi 12 10

961	A362	5af multi	15	12
962	A363	6af multi	18	15
963	A363	12af multi	35	30

1st anniversary of revolution.

Carpenter and Blacksmith A364

1979, May 1 *Perf. 12*

964 A364 10af multi 30 25

Int'l Labor Day.

Children, Flag and Map of Afghanistan—A366

1979, June 1 **Litho.** *Perf. 12½x12*

966 A366 16af multi 48 40

International Year of the Child.

Armed Afghans, Kabul Memorial and Arch A367

Pashtunistan Citizens, Flag A368

1979, Aug. 19 **Litho.** *Perf. 12*

967 A367 30af multi 90 75

60th anniv. of independence.

1979, Aug. 31

968 A368 9 af multi 28 22

Pashtunistan Day.

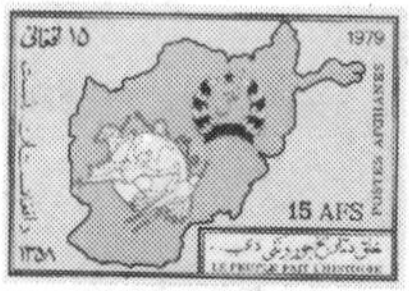

UPU Day—A369

1979, Oct. **Litho.** *Perf. 12*

969 A369 15af multi 45 38

International Women's Day—A370

1980, Mar. 8 **Litho.** *Perf. 12*

970 A370 8af multi *1.00*

Farmers' Day—A371

1980, Mar. 21 **Litho.** *Perf. 11½x12*

971 A371 2af multi 10 8

Non-smoker and Smoker—A372

1980, Apr. 7 *Perf. 11½*

972 A372 5af multi 15 12

Anti-smoking campaign; World Health Day.

Lenin, 110th Birth Anniversary—A373

1980, Apr. 22 *Perf. 12x12½*

973 A373 12af multi 35 30

People and Fist on Map of Afghanistan—A374

1980, Apr. 27 **Litho.** *Perf. 12½x12*

974 A374 1af multi 3 3

Saur Revolution, 2nd anniversary.

International Workers' Solidarity Day—A375

1980, May 1

975 A375 9af multi 28 22

Wrestling, Moscow '80 Emblem—A376

1980, July 19 *Perf. 12x12½, 12½x12*

976	A376	3af *Soccer*, vert.	20	8
977	A376	6af *shown*	35	15
978	A376	9af *Buzkashi*	55	22
979	A376	10af *Pigsticking*	60	25

22nd Summer Olympic Games, Moscow, July 19-Aug. 3.

61st Anniversary of Independence—A377

1980, Aug. 19 **Litho.** *Perf. 12½x12*

980 A377 3af multi 10 8

Pashtunistan Day—A378

1980, Aug. 30

981 A378 25af multi 80 65

International U.P.U. Day—A379

1980, Oct. 19 **Litho.** *Perf. 12½x12*

982 A379 20af multi 60 50

Hegira (Pilgrimage Year)—A380

1981, Jan. 17 **Litho.** *Perf. 12½x12*

983 A380 15af (13+2af) multi 45 38

International Women's Day—A381

1981, Mar. 9 **Litho.** *Perf. 12½x12*

984 A381 15af multi 45 38

Farmers' Day—A382

1981, Mar. 20 **Litho.** *Perf. 12½x12*

985 A382 1af multi 3 3

Bighorn Mountain Sheep (Protected Species)—A383

1981, Apr. 4 *Perf. 12x12½*

986 A383 12af multi 36 30

Saur Revolution, 3rd Anniversary A384

International Workers' Solidarity Day A385

1981, Apr. 27 *Perf. 11*

987 A384 50p brown 3 3

1981, May 1 *Perf. 12½x12*

988 A385 10af multi 30 25

International Red Cross Day—A386

1981, May 8 *Perf. 12x12½*

989 A386 5af (1+4af) multi 15 12

13th World Telecommunications Day A387

Intl. Children's Day A388

1981, May 17 **Litho.** *Perf. 12½x12*

990 A387 9af multi 28 22

1981, June 1 *Perf. 12x12½*

991 A388 15af multi 45 38

62nd Anniv. of Independence—A389

1981, Aug. 19
992 A389 4af multi 12 10

Pashtunistan Day—A389a

1981, Aug. Litho. *Perf. 12*
992A A389a 2af multi 6 3

Intl. Tourism Day A390 — Intl. Year of the Disabled A391

1981, Sept. 27 *Perf. 12½x12*
993 A390 5af multi 15 12

1981, Oct. 12 *Perf. 12x12½*
994 A391 7af (6+1af) multi 22 15

World Food Day—A392

1981, Oct. 16
995 A392 7af multi 22 15

Asia—Africa Solidarity Meeting—A393

1981, Nov. 18 Litho. *Perf. 11*
996 A393 8af blue 24 20

Struggle Against Apartheid A394 — 1300th Anniv. of Bulgaria A395

1981, Dec. 1 *Perf. 12½x12*
997 A394 4af multi 12 10

1981, Dec. 9 *Perf. 12x12½*
998 A395 20af multi 60 50

Intl. Women's Day—A396

1982, Mar. 8 Litho. *Perf. 12*
999 A396 6af multi 18 15

Farmers' Day A397

1982, Mar. 21
1000 A397 4af multi 12 10

Rhubarb Plant A398 — Saur Revolution, 4th Anniv. A399

Designs: Various local plants.

1982, Apr. 9 Litho. *Perf. 12*
1001 A398 3af multi 10 8
1002 A398 4af multi 12 10
1003 A398 16af multi 50 40

1982, Apr. 27
1004 A399 1af multi 3 3

George Dimitrov (1882-1947), First Prime Minister of Bulgaria A400

Intl. Workers' Solidarity Day A401

1982, Apr. 30
1005 A400 30af multi 90 75

1982, May 1
1006 A401 10af multi 30 25

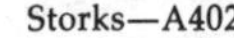

Storks—A402

1982, May 31
1007 A402 6af shown 20 15
1008 A402 11af Nightingales 35 28

Hedgehogs—A403

1982, July 6 Litho. *Perf. 12*
1009 A403 3af shown 10 8
1010 A403 14af Cobra 45 35

63rd Anniv. of Independence—A404

1982, Aug. 19
1011 A404 20af Triumphal Arch, Kabul 60 50

Pashtunistan Day—A405

1982, Aug. 31
1012 A405 32af multi 1.00 80

World Tourism Day—A406

1982, Sept. 27 Litho. *Perf. 12*
1013 A406 9af multi 30 22

UPU Day—A407

1982, Oct. 9
1014 A407 4af multi 12 10

World Food Day—A408

1982, Oct. 16
1015 A408 9af multi 30 22

37th Anniv. of UN—A409

1982, Oct. 24
1016 A409 15af multi 45 38

ITU Plenipotentiaries Conference, Nairobi, Sept.—A410

1982, Oct. 26
1017 A410 8af multi 25 20

SEMI-POSTAL STAMPS.

No. 373 Surcharged in Violet

a

MILLIEME ANNIVERSAIRE
DE BOALI SINAI BALKI
125 POULS

b

1952, July 12 ***Perf. 12½*** **Unwmkd.**

B1	A122(a)	40p +30p cer	1.85	1.85
B2	A122(b)	125p +30p cer	3.00	2.50

Issued to commemorate the 1000th anniversary of the birth of Avicenna.

Children at Play
SP1

1955, July 3 **Typo.** ***Perf. 11***

B3	SP1	35p +15p dk grn	60	40
B4	SP1	125p +25p pur	1.25	1.00

The surtax was for child welfare.

Amir Sher Ali Khan, Tiger Head Stamp and Zahir Shah
SP2

Children at Play
SP3

1955, July 2 **Lithographed**

B5	SP2	35p +15p car	60	40
B6	SP2	125p +25p pale vio bl	1.25	80

Issued to commemorate the 85th anniversary of the Afghan post.

1956, June 20 **Typographed**

B7	SP3	35p +15p brt vio bl	40	40
B8	SP3	140p +15p dk org brn	1.00	1.00

Issued for Children's Day. The surtax was for child welfare. No. B8 inscribed in French.

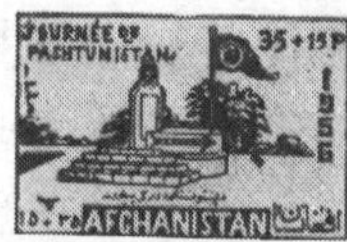

Pashtunistan Monument, Kabul
SP4

1956, Sept. 1 **Lithographed**

B9	SP4	35p +15p dp vio	25	25
B10	SP4	140p +15p dk brn	75	75

Issued for "Free Pashtunistan" Day. The surtax aided the "Free Pashtunistan" movement.

No. B9 measures 30½x19½mm.; No. B10, 29x19mm. On sale and valid for use only on Sept. 1–2.

Globe and Sun SP5 — Children on Seesaw SP6

1956, Oct. 24 *Perf. 11*

B11	SP5	35p +15p ultra	1.00	85
B12	SP5	140p +15p red brn	1.85	1.50

Issued for the tenth anniversary of Afghanistan's admission to the United Nations.

1957, June 20 **Unwmkd.**

B13	SP6	35p +15p brt rose	50	30
B14	SP6	140p +15p ultra	1.25	90

Issued for Children's Day. The surtax was for child welfare.

U. N. Headquarters and Emblems
SP7

1957, Oct. 24 *Perf. 11 Rough*

B15	SP7	35p +15p red brn	50	30
B16	SP7	140p +15p lt ultra	1.00	90

Issued for United Nations Day.

Swimming Pool and Children
SP8

1958, June 22 *Perf. 11*

B17	SP8	35p +15p rose	40	30
B18	SP8	140p +15p dl red brn	1.00	75

Issued for Children's Day. The surtax was for child welfare.

Pashtunistan Flag
SP9

1958, Aug. 31

B19	SP9	35p +15p lt bl	25	25
B20	SP9	140p +15p red brn	75	75

Issued for "Free Pashtunistan Day."

Children Playing Tug of War
SP10

1959, June 23 **Litho.** *Perf. 11*

B21	SP10	35p +15p brn vio	35	25
B22	SP10	165p +15p brt pink	1.10	75

Issued for Children's Day. The surtax was for child welfare.

Pathans in Tribal Dance—SP11

Perf. 11 Rough

1959, Sept. **Unwmkd.**

B23	SP11	35p +15p grn	20	20
B24	SP11	165p +15p org	75	75

Issued for "Free Pashtunistan Day."

Afghan Cavalryman with U.N. Flag
SP12

1959, Oct. 24 *Perf. 11 Rough*

B25	SP12	35p +15p org	30	25
B26	SP12	165p +15p lt bl grn	65	60

Issued for United Nations Day.

Children
SP13

1960, Oct. 23 **Lithographed**

B27	SP13	75p +25p lt ultra	35	30
B28	SP13	175p +25p lt grn	60	45

Issued for Children's Day. The surtax was for child welfare.

Man with Spray Gun—SP14

1960, Sept. 6 *Perf. 11 Rough*

B29	SP14	50p +50p org	1.25	1.00
B30	SP14	175p +50p red brn	3.00	2.00

11th anniversary of the WHO malaria control program in Afghanistan.

SP15

1960, Sept. 1 **Unwmkd.**

B31	SP15	50p +50p rose	35	30
B32	SP15	175p +50p dk bl	85	60

Issued for "Free Pashtunistan Day."

Ambulance—SP16

Crescent in Red

1960, Oct. 16 *Perf. 11*

B33	SP16	50p +50p vio	50	25
B34	SP16	175p +50p bl	1.10	90

Issued for the Red Crescent Society.

Nos. 470–471 Surcharged in Blue or Orange.

1960, Dec. 31 **Litho.** *Perf. 11*

B35	A166	50p +25p dp org (Bl)	3.00	3.00
B36	A166	165p +25p bl (O)	3.00	3.00

The imperf. souvenir sheet with 50p in blue and 1.65af in deep orange, described in note below Nos. 470–471, was surcharged in carmine like Nos. B35–B36 ("+25 Ps" on each stamp). Price $5.
See note after No. 485.

Nos. 496–500 Surcharged UNICEF یونیسف +25PS

Photogravure

1961 *Perf. 13½x14* **Unwmkd.**

B37	A175	2p +25p grn & rose lil		
B38	A175	2p +25p brn & cit		
B39	A175	5p +25p gray & rose		
B40	A175	10p +25p bl & bis		
B41	A175	15p +25p sl bl & dl lil		
		Nos. B37-B41 (5)	2.25	

Issued for the United Nations Children's Fund, UNICEF. The same surcharge was applied to an imperf. souvenir sheet like that noted after No. 505. Price $4.50.

Nos. 522–526 Surcharged "+25PS" and Crescent in Red.

1961, Oct. 16 *Perf. 13½x14*

B42	A184	2p +25p blk		
B43	A184	2p +25p grn		
B44	A184	5p +25p lil rose		
B45	A184	10p +25p lil		
B46	A184	15p +25p dk bl		
		Nos. B42-B46 (5)	2.50	

Issued for the Red Crescent Society.

Nos. 539–543 Surcharged in Red: "UNESCO + 25PS"

1962 *Perf. 12*

B47	A186	2p +25p multi		
B48	A186	2p +25p multi		
B49	A186	5p +25p multi		
B50	A186	10p +25p multi		
B51	A186	15p +25p multi		
		Nos. B47-B51 (5)	1.50	

Issued for the United Nations Educational, Scientific and Cultural Organization. The same surcharge was also applied to the souvenir sheets mentioned after No. 548. Price, 2 sheets, $3.50.

Nos. 553–561 Surcharged: "Dag Hammarskjöld +20PS"

1962, Sept. 17 *Perf. 14x13½*

B52	A187	2p +20p rose lil & brn		
B53	A187	2p +20p ol bis & brn		
B54	A187	5p +20p dp org & dk grn		
B55	A187	10p +20p gray & mag		
B56	A187	15p +20p bl & brn		
B57	A187	25p +20p org yel & pur		
B58	A187	50p +20p lt grn & pur		
B59	A187	75p +20p brt cit & brn		
B60	A187	100p +20p dp org & brn		
		Nos. B52-B60 (9)	2.25	

Issued in memory of Dag Hammarskjold, Secretary General of the United Nations, 1953–61. Perf. and imperf. souvenir sheets exist. Price, 2 sheets, $3.

Nos. 583–593 Surcharged "+15PS"

1963, Mar. 15 *Perf. 14x13½*

B61	A193	2p +15p dk grn & ol gray		
B62	A193	2p +15p dk grn & sal		
B63	A193	5p +15p red brn & ol		
B64	A193	10p +15p red brn & brt grn		
B65	A193	15p +15p red brn & gray		
B66	A193	25p +15p brt bl & bluish grn		
B67	A193	50p +15p brt bl & rose lil		
B68	A193	75p +15p blk & bl		
B69	A193	100p +15p blk & brt pink		
B70	A193	150p +15p blk & bis brn		
B71	A193	175p +15p blk & org		
		Nos. B61-B71 (11)	10.00	

Issued for the World Health Organization drive to eradicate malaria.
Postally used copies of Nos. B35–B71 are uncommon and command a considerable premium over the prices for unused copies.

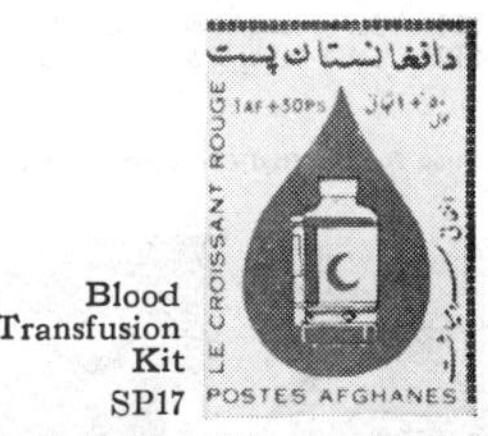

Blood Transfusion Kit
SP17

1964, Oct. 18 **Litho.** *Perf. 10½*

B72	SP17	1af +50p blk & rose	15	10

Issued for the Red Crescent Society and Red Crescent Week, Oct. 18–24.

First Aid Station
SP18

1965, Oct. **Photo.** *Perf. 13½x14*

B73	SP18	1.50af +50p grn, choc & red	25	10

Issued for the Red Crescent Society.

Children Playing
SP19

1966, Nov. 28 **Photo.** *Perf. 13½x14*

B74	SP19	1af +1af yel grn & cl	18	12
B75	SP19	3af +2af yel & brn	40	30
B76	SP19	7af +3af rose lil & grn	85	60

Children's Day.

Nadir Shah Presenting Society Charter—SP20

1967 Photogravure *Perf. 13x14*

B77 SP20 2af + 1af red & dk grn 25 15
B78 SP20 5af + 1af lil rose & brn 50 25

Issued for the Red Crescent Society.

Vaccination SP21 — Red Crescent SP22

1967, June 6 Photo. *Perf. 12*

B79 SP21 2af + 1af yel & blk 25 10
B80 SP21 5af + 2af pink & brn 50 25

The surtax was for anti-tuberculosis work.

1967, Oct. 18 Photo. *Perf. 12*

Crescent in Red

B81 SP22 3af + 1af gray ol & blk 25 15
B82 SP22 5af + 1af dl bl & blk 35 20

Issued for the Red Crescent Society.

Queen Humeira SP23 — Red Crescent SP24

1968, June 14 Photo. *Perf. 12*

B83 SP23 2af + 2af red brn 25 20
B84 SP23 7af + 2af dl grn 75 50

Issued for Mother's Day.

1968, Oct. 16 Photo. *Perf. 12*

B85 SP24 4af + 1af yel, blk & red 45 27

Issued for the Red Crescent Society.

Red Cross, Crescent, Lion and Sun Emblems SP25 — Mother and Child SP26

1969, May 5 Litho. *Perf. 14x13½*

B86 SP25 3af + 1af multi 30 18
B87 SP25 5af + 1af multi 50 30

Issued to commemorate the 50th anniversary of the League of Red Cross Societies.

1969, June 14 Photo. *Perf. 12*

B88 SP26 1af + 1af yel org & brn 18 12
B89 SP26 4af + 1af rose lil & pur 40 27
a. Souv. sheet of 2 1.10 1.10

Issued for Mother's Day. No. B89a contains 2 imperf. stamps similar to Nos. B88–B89. Brown marginal inscription and black control number. Size: 120x80mm. Sold for 10af.

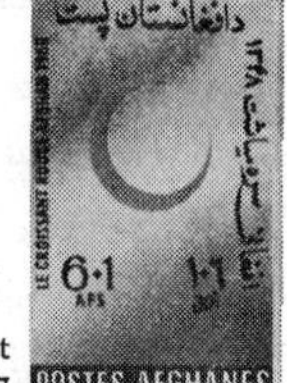

Red Crescent SP27

1969, Oct. 16 Photo. *Perf. 12*

B90 SP27 6af + 1af multi 55 30

Issued for the Red Crescent Society.

UN and FAO Emblems, Farmer SP28

1973, May 24 Photo. *Perf. 13½*

B91 SP28 14af + 7af grnsh bl & lil 1.10 75

World Food Program, 10th anniversary.

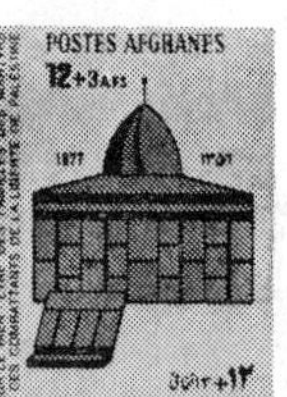

Dome of the Rock, Jerusalem SP29

1977, Sept. 11 Photo. *Perf. 14*

B92 SP29 12af + 3af multi 45 36

The surtax was for Palestinian families and soldiers.

AIR POST STAMPS

Plane over Kabul—AP1

Perf. 12, 12x11, 11

1939, Oct. 1 Typographed. Unwmkd.

C1 AP1 5af orange 3.00 3.00
a. Imperf. pair ('47) 35.00 35.00
b. Imperf. vertically, pair 30.00
C2 AP1 10af blue 3.00 2.50
a. lt bl 4.00 4.00
b. Imperf. pair ('47) 35.00
c. Imperf. vertically, pair 30.00
C3 AP1 20af emerald 7.00 7.00
a. Imperf. pair ('47) 35.00
b. Imperf. vertically, pair 30.00
c. Imperf. horiz., pair 35.00

These stamps come with clean-cut or rough perforations. Counterfeits exist.

1948, June 14 *Perf. 12x11½.*

C4 AP1 5af emerald 22.50 22.50
C5 AP1 10af red org 22.50 22.50
C6 AP1 20af blue 22.50 22.50

Imperforates exist.

Plane over Palace Grounds, Kabul—AP2

Imprint: "Waterlow & Sons, Limited, London"

1951-54 Engraved. *Perf. 13½.*

C7 AP2 5af hn brn 2.00 80
C8 AP2 5af dp grn ('54) 1.50 70
C9 AP2 10af gray 6.00 2.00
C10 AP2 20af dk bl 10.00 3.50

1957

C11 AP2 5af ultra 1.25 75
C12 AP2 10af dk vio 2.50 1.50

See also No. C38.

Ariana DC-3 Plane over Hindu Kush AP3

Perf. 11, Imperf.

1960–63 Lithographed Unwmkd.

C13 AP3 75p lt vio 30 30
C14 AP3 125p blue 40 45

Perf. 10½

C14A AP3 5af cit ('63) 1.10 1.10

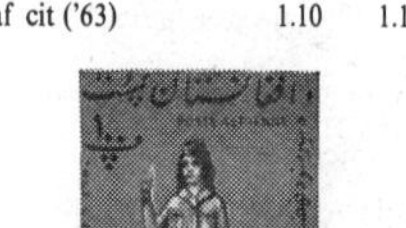

Girl Scout AP4

1962, Aug. 30 Photo. *Perf. 11½x12*

C15 AP4 100p ocher & brn 60 60
C16 AP4 175p brt yel grn & brn 85 85

Issued for Women's Day. A souvenir sheet exists containing one each of Nos. 578–579 and C15–C16. Brown inscription. Size: 109x105mm. Price $3.

Sports Type of Regular Issue, 1962

Designs: 25p, 50p, Horse racing. 75p, 100p, Wrestling. 150p, Weight lifting. 175p, Soccer.

1962, Sept. 25 *Perf. 12* Unwmkd.

Black Inscriptions.

C17 A195 25p rose & red brn
C18 A195 50p gray & red brn
C19 A195 75p pale vio & dk grn
C20 A195 100p gray ol & dk pur
C21 A195 150p rose lil & grn
C22 A195 175p sal & brn
Nos. C17-C22 (6) 2.25

4th Asian Games, Djakarta, Indonesia.

Children's Day Type of Regular Issue

Designs: 75p, Runners. 150p, Peaches. 200p, Iris (vert.).

Perf. 11½x12, 12x11½

1962, Oct. 14 Unwmkd.

C23 A196 75p lt grn & lil
C24 A196 150p bl & multi
C25 A196 200p ol & multi

Issued for Children's Day. A souvenir sheet contains one each of Nos. C23–C25. Lilac marginal inscription and black control number. Size: 119x90mm. Price $2.50.

Red Crescent Type of Regular Issue

Designs: 25p, Grapes. 50p, Pears. 100p, Wistaria.

1962, Oct. 16 *Perf. 12*

Fruit and Flowers in Natural Colors; Carmine Crescent

C26 A197 25p brown
C27 A197 50p dl grn
C28 A197 100p dk bl gray

Issued for the Afghan Red Crescent Society. Two souvenir sheets exist. One contains a 150p gray brown stamp in blossom design, the other a 200p gray stamp in wistaria design, imperf. Each sheet has marginal inscriptions in color of stamp, and black control number. Size: 89x65mm. Price, each $5.

U.N. Type of Regular Issue

1962, Oct. 24 Photogravure

Flags in Original Colors, Black Inscriptions

C29 A198 75p blue
C30 A198 100p lt brn

C31	A198	125p brt grn		

Issued for United Nations Day.

Boy Scout Type of Regular Issue

1962, Oct. 25 ***Perf. 12*** **Unwmkd.**

C32	A199	25p gray, blk, dl grn & sal		
C33	A199	50p grn, brn & sal		
C34	A199	75p bl grn, red brn & sal		
C35	A199	100p bl, sl & sal		

Issued to honor the Boy Scouts.

Teacher's Day Type of Regular Issue

Designs: 100p, Pole vault. 150p, High jump.

1962, Oct. 25

C36	A200	100p yel & blk		
C37	A200	150p bluish grn & brn		

Issued for Teacher's Day. A souvenir sheet contains one 250p pink and slate green stamp in design of 150p. Slate green marginal inscription and black control number. Size: 65x89mm. Price $2.50.

Type of 1951–54

1962 **Engraved** ***Perf. 13½***

Imprint: "Thomas De La Rue & Co. Ltd."

C38	AP2	5af ultra	9.00	1.00

Agriculture Types of Regular Issue

Photogravure

1963, March 1 ***Perf. 12*** **Unwmkd.**

C42	A204	100p dk car, grn & brn		
C43	A203	150p ocher & blk		
C44	A204	200p ultra, grn & brn		

Issued for the Day of Agriculture.

Hands Holding Wheat Emblem
AP5

1963, Mar. 27 **Photo.** ***Perf. 14***

C45	AP5	500p lil, lt brn & brn	85	85

Issued for the "Freedom from Hunger" campaign of the U.N. Food and Agriculture Organization.

Two souvenir sheets exist. One contains a 1000p blue green, light brown and brown, type AP5, imperf. Claret marginal inscription. Size: 76x100mm. The other contains a 200p brown and green and 300p ultramarine, yellow and ocher in rice and corn designs, type A205. Green marginal inscription. Size: 100x75mm. Both sheets have black control number. Prices $6 and $2.50.

Meteorological Day Type of Regular Issue

Designs: 100p, 500p, Meteorological measuring instrument. 200p, 400p, Weather station. 300p, Rockets in space.

1963, May 23 ***Imperf.***

C46	A206	100p brn & bl		

Perf. 13½x14

C47	A206	200p brt grn & lil		
C48	A206	300p dk bl & rose		
C49	A206	400p bl & dl red brn		
C50	A206	500p car rose & gray grn		

Issued to commemorate the United Nations Third World Meteorological Day, March 23. Nos. C47 and C50 printed se-tenant.

Two souvenir sheets exist. One contains a 125p red and brown stamp in rocket design. Red marginal inscription. The other contains a 100p blue and dull red brown in "rockets in space" design. Blue marginal inscription. Both sheets have black control number, and measure 100x75mm. Prices $5 and $7.50.

Kabul International Airport
AP8
Photogravure

1964, Apr. ***Perf. 12x11*** **Unwmkd.**

C57	AP8	10af red lil & grn	80	35
C58	AP8	20af dk grn & red lil	1.20	60
C59	AP8	50af dk bl & grnsh bl	3.25	1.50

Inauguration of Kabul Airport Terminal.

Nos. C58-C59 are 36mm. wide. They were reissued in 1968, 35½mm. wide.

Zahir Shah and Ariana Plane—AP9

Design: 50af, Zahir Shah and Kabul Airport.

1971 **Photo.** ***Perf. 12½x13½***

C60	AP9	50af multi	4.00	
C61	AP9	100af blk, red & grn	6.00	

No. C60 was used in 1978 with king's portrait removed.

REGISTRATION STAMPS.

R1
Lithographed
Dated "1309"

1891 ***Imperf.*** **Unwmkd.**

Pelure Paper.

F1	R1	1r sl bl	1.60	
a.		Tête bêche pair	15.00	

R2
Thin Wove Paper.

1893 **Dated "1311".**

F2	R2	1r *grn*	1.60	

Genuinely used copies of Nos. F1–F2 are rare. Counterfeit cancellations exist.

R3

1894 **Undated.**

F3	R3	2ab *green*	11.00	14.00

12 varieties. See note below Nos. 189–190.

R4

1898–1900 **Undated**

F4	R4	2ab *dp rose*	6.25	7.50
F5	R4	2ab *lil rose*	6.25	7.50
F6	R4	2ab *magenta*	6.25	7.50
F7	R4	2ab *salmon*	6.25	7.50
F8	R4	2ab *orange*	6.25	7.50
F9	R4	2ab *yellow*	6.25	7.50
F10	R4	2ab *green*	6.25	7.50
		Nos. F4-F10 (7)	43.75	52.50

Many shades of paper.

Nos. F4–F10 come in two sizes, measured between outer frame lines: 52x36 mm., first printing; 46x33mm., second printing. The outer frame line (not pictured) is 3–6mm. from inner frame line.

OFFICIAL STAMPS.

(Used only on interior mail.)

Coat of Arms
O1
Typographed

1909 ***Perf. 12*** **Unwmkd.**

Wove Paper.

O1	O1	red	1.00	1.00
a.		car ('19?)	1.25	1.25

Later printings of No. O1 in scarlet, vermilion, claret, etc., on various types of paper, were issued until 1927.

Official Stamp of 1909 Handstamped like Regular Issues of 1929.

1929

O2	O1	red	12.50	

See note after No. 261.

Coat of Arms
O2

1939–68? **Typo.** ***Perf. 11, 12***

O3	O2	15p emerald	25	15
O4	O2	30p ocher ('40)	50	50
O5	O2	45p dk car	35	25
O6	O2	50p brt car ('68?)	25	25
a.		car rose ('55)	50	40
O7	O2	1af brt red vio	75	50
		Nos. O3-O7 (5)	2.10	1.65

Size of 50p, 24x31mm. Others 22½x28mm.

1964-65 **Lithographed** ***Perf. 11***

O8	O2	50p rose	50	50
a.		sal ('65)	1.00	1.00

Stamps of this type are revenues.

PARCEL POST STAMPS.

Coat of Arms
PP1

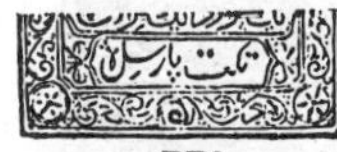

PP2

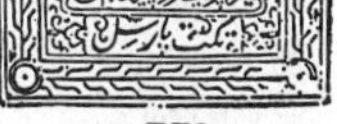

PP3

PP4
Typographed.

1909 ***Perf. 12.*** **Unwmkd.**

Q1	PP1	3sh bister	50	60
a.		Imperf., pair	1.25	
Q2	PP2	1kr ol gray	75	1.00
a.		Imperf., pair	2.00	
Q3	PP3	1r orange	3.00	2.25
Q4	PP3	1r ol grn	1.25	2.75
Q5	PP4	2r red	3.75	2.50
		Nos. Q1-Q5 (5)	9.25	9.10

1916–18

Q6	PP1	3sh green	1.00	75
Q7	PP2	1kr pale red	1.50	1.25
a.		rose red ('18)	2.00	2.00
Q8	PP3	1r brn org	1.50	1.25
a.		dp brn ('18)	2.50	2.50
Q9	PP4	2r blue	3.00	3.00

Nos. Q1–Q9 sometimes show letters of the papermaker's watermark "HOWARD & JONES LONDON."

Ungummed copies are remainders. They sell for one-third the price of mint examples.

The indexes in each volume of the Scott Catalogue contain many listings which help to identify stamps.

Old Habibia College, near Kabul

PP5

1921 Wove Paper.

Q10	PP5	10pa chocolate	1.75	1.75
a.		Tête bêche pair	6.25	8.75
Q11	PP5	15pa lt brn	2.50	2.50
a.		Tête bêche pair	6.25	7.50
Q12	PP5	30pa red vio	3.50	2.75
a.		Tête bêche pair	8.75	10.00
b.		Laid paper	*7.50*	*7.50*
Q13	PP5	1r brt bl	5.50	5.50
a.		Tête bêche pair	18.50	18.50

Stamps of this issue are usually perforated on one or two sides only.

The laid paper of No. Q12b has a papermaker's watermark in the sheet.

PP6

1924–26 Wove Paper

Q15	PP6	5kr ultra ('26)	15.00	15.00
Q16	PP6	5r lilac	8.75	8.75

A 15r rose exists, but is not known to have been placed in use.

PP7

PP8

1928–29 *Perf. 11, 11xImperf.*

Q17	PP7	2r yel org	3.00	2.50
Q18	PP7	2r grn ('29)	2.75	2.50
Q19	PP8	3r dp grn	5.50	5.00
Q20	PP8	3r brn ('29)	5.50	5.00

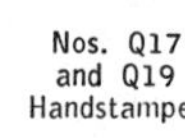

Nos. Q17 and Q19 Handstamped

1929

Q21	PP7	2r yel org	*15.00*
Q22	PP7	3r dp grn	18.50

See note after No. 261.

POSTAL TAX STAMPS.

Aliabad Hospital near Kabul

PT1

Pierre and Marie Curie

PT2

Perf. 12x11½, 12

1938, Dec. 22 Typo. Unwmkd.

RA1	PT1	10p pck grn	2.75	2.75
RA2	PT2	15p dl bl	2.75	2.75

Obligatory on all mail Dec. 22-28, 1938. The money was used for the Allabad Hospital. See note with CD80.

Begging Child

PT3 PT4

1949, May 28 Typo. *Perf. 12*

RA3	PT3	35p red org	2.00	2.00
RA4	PT4	125p ultra	3.00	2.00

United Nations Children's Day, May 28. Obligatory on all foreign mail on that date. Proceeds were used for child welfare.

Paghman Arch and U. N. Emblem

PT5

1949, Oct. 24

RA5	PT5	125p dk bl grn	12.50	11.00

Issued to commemorate the fourth anniversary of the formation of the United Nations. Valid one day only. Issued in sheets of 9 (3x3).

Zahir Shah and Map of Afghanistan

PT6

1950, Mar. 30 Typographed

RA6	PT6	125p bl grn	2.50	1.25

Issued to celebrate the return of Zahir Shah from a trip to Europe for his health. Valid for two weeks. The tax was used for public health purposes.

Hazara Youth

PT7

1950, May 28 Typo. *Perf. 11½*

RA7	PT7	125p dk bl grn	3.00	2.00

The tax was for Child Welfare. Obligatory and valid only on May 28, 1950, on foreign mail.

Ruins of Qalai Bist and Globe

PT8

1950, Oct. 24

RA8	PT8	1.25af ultra	6.50	5.00

Issued to commemorate the 5th anniversary of the formation of the United Nations. Proceeds went to Afghanistan's U.N. Projects Committee.

Zahir Shah and Medical Center

PT9

Typographed.

1950, Dec. 22 *Perf. 11½*

Size: 38x25mm.

RA9	PT9	35p carmine	50	50
RA10	PT9	1.25af black	6.00	3.00

The tax was for the national Graduate School of Medicine.

Koochi Girl with Lamb

PT10

Kohistani Boy and Sheep

PT11

1951, May 28

RA11	PT10	35p emerald	1.25	1.00
RA12	PT11	1.25af ultra	1.25	1.00

The tax was for Child Welfare.

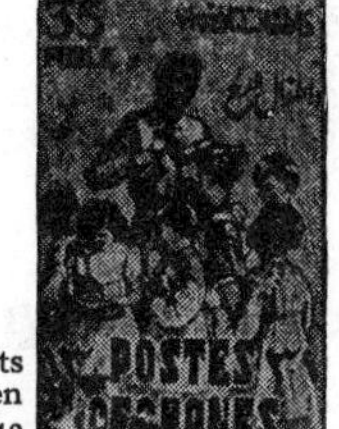

Distributing Gifts to Children

PT12

Qandahari Boys Dancing the 'Attan'

PT13

1952, May 28 Lithographed

RA13	PT12	35p chocolate	40	40
RA14	PT13	125p violet	1.10	1.10

The tax was for Child Welfare.

Soldier Receiving First Aid

PT14

1952, Oct.

RA15	PT14	10p lt grn	50	45

Stretcher-bearers and Wounded
PT15

Soldier Assisting Wounded
PT16

1953, Oct.

RA16	PT15	10p yel grn & org red	60	50
RA17	PT16	10p vio brn & org red	60	50

Prince Mohammed Nadir
PT17

Map and Young Musicians
PT18

1953, May 28

RA18	PT17	35p org yel	25	20
RA19	PT17	125p chlky bl	75	75

No. RA19 is inscribed in French "Children's Day." The tax was for child welfare.

1954, May 28 ***Perf. 11*** **Unwmkd.**

RA20	PT18	35p purple	40	20
RA21	PT18	125p ultra	1.50	1.50

No. RA21 is inscribed in French. The tax was for child welfare.

Red Crescent
PT19 PT20

1954, Oct. 17 ***Perf. 11½***

RA22	PT19	20p bl & red	35	30

1955, Oct. 18 ***Perf. 11***

RA23	PT20	20p dl grn & car	30	25

Zahir Shah and Red Crescent
PT21

1956, Oct. 18

RA24	PT21	20p lt grn & rose car	35	25

Red Crescent Headquarters, Kabul
PT22

1957, Oct. 17

RA25	PT22	20p lt ultra & car	35	25

Map and Crescent
PT23

1958, Oct. ***Perf. 11*** **Unwmkd.**

RA26	PT23	25p yel grn & red	25	20

PT24

1959, Oct. 17 Lithographed ***Perf. 11***

RA27	PT24	25p lt vio & red	25	15

The tax on Nos. RA15–RA17, RA22–RA27 was for the Red Crescent Society. Use of these stamps was required for one week.

AGUERA, LA

(ä·gwä'rä)

LOCATION—An administrative district in southern Rio de Oro on the northwest coast of Africa.

GOVT.—Spanish possession.

AREA—Because of indefinite political boundaries, figures for area and population are not available.

See Spanish Sahara.

100 Centimos = 1 Peseta

Type of 1920 Issue of Rio de Oro Overprinted **LA AGÜERA**

1920 ***Perf. 13*** **Unwmkd.**

1	A8	1c bl grn	2.25	2.25
2	A8	2c ol brn	2.25	2.25
3	A8	5c dp grn	2.25	2.25
4	A8	10c lt red	2.25	2.25
5	A8	15c yellow	2.25	2.25
6	A8	20c lilac	2.25	2.25
7	A8	25c dp bl	2.25	2.25
8	A8	30c dk brn	2.25	2.25
9	A8	40c pink	2.25	2.25
10	A8	50c brt bl	6.50	5.50
11	A8	1p red brn	11.00	9.00
12	A8	4p dk vio	35.00	27.50
13	A8	10p orange	72.50	65.00
		Nos. 1-13 (13)	145.25	127.25

King Alfonso XIII
A2

1922 **Typographed**

14	A2	1c turq bl	1.10	1.10
15	A2	2c dk grn	1.10	1.10
16	A2	5c bl grn	1.10	1.10
17	A2	10c red	1.10	1.10
18	A2	15c red brn	1.10	1.10
19	A2	20c yellow	1.10	1.10
20	A2	25c dp bl	1.10	1.10
21	A2	30c dk brn	1.10	1.10
22	A2	40c rose red	1.40	1.40
23	A2	50c red vio	4.50	4.00
24	A2	1p rose	8.50	7.50
25	A2	4p violet	20.00	16.50
26	A2	10p orange	35.00	32.00
		Nos. 14-26 (13)	78.20	70.20

For later issues see Spanish Sahara in Vol. IV.

ALAOUITES

(à·lȧ'wēt')

LOCATION—A division of Syria, in Western Asia.

GOVT.—Under French Mandate.

AREA—2,500 sq. mi.

POP.—278,000 (approx. 1930).

CAPITAL—Latakia.

This territory became an independent state in 1924, although still administered under the French Mandate. In 1930 it was renamed Latakia and Syrian stamps overprinted "Lattaquie" superseded the stamps of Alaouites. For these and subsequent issues see Latakia and Syria.

100 Centimes = 1 Piastre

Issued under French Mandate.

Stamps of France Surcharged:

ALAOUITES
0 P. 25
العلويين
١/٤ الغرش
a

ALAOUITES
2 PIASTRES
العلويين
غروش ٢
b

1925 ***Perf. 14x13½*** **Unwmkd.**

1	A16 (a)	10c on 2c vio brn	1.25	1.25
2	A22 (a)	25c on 5c org	70	70
3	A20 (a)	75c on 15c gray grn	1.35	1.35
4	A22 (a)	1p on 20c red brn	1.10	1.10
5	A22 (a)	1.25p on 25c bl	1.50	1.50
6	A22 (a)	1.50p on 30c red	3.75	3.75
7	A22 (b)	2p on 35c vio	1.10	1.10
8	A18 (b)	2p on 40c red & pale bl	1.65	1.65
9	A18 (b)	2p on 45c grn & bl	4.00	4.00
10	A18 (b)	3p on 60c vio & ultra	2.00	2.00
11	A20 (b)	3p on 60c lt vio	4.00	4.00
12	A20 (b)	4p on 85c ver	60	60
13	A18 (b)	5p on 1fr cl & ol grn	2.10	2.10
14	A18 (b)	10p on 2fr org & pale bl	2.75	2.75
15	A18 (b)	25p on 5fr Bl & buff	4.00	4.00
		Nos. 1-15 (15)	31.85	31.85

Same Surcharges on Stamps of France, 1923-24 (Pasteur)

16	A23 (a)	50c on 10c grn	70	70
17	A23 (a)	75c on 15c grn	70	70
18	A23 (a)	1.50p on 30c red	80	80
19	A23 (b)	2p on 45c red	90	90
20	A23 (b)	2.50p on 50c bl	1.25	1.25
21	A23 (b)	4p on 75c bl	1.40	1.40
		Nos. 16-21 (6)	5.75	5.75

Stamps of Syria, 1925, Overprinted in Red, Black or Blue:

ALAOUITES
العلويين
c

ALAOUITES
العلويين
d

1925, Mar. 1 ***Perf. 12½, 13½***

25	A3 (c)	10c dk vio (R)	35	35
a.		Dbl. ovpt.	11.00	11.00
26	A4 (d)	25c ol blk (R)	60	60
a.		Inverted overprint	6.00	6.00
b.		Blue ovpt.	11.00	11.00
27	A4 (d)	50c yel grn	45	45
a.		Inverted overprint	6.00	6.00
b.		Blue ovpt.	11.00	11.00
c.		Red ovpt.	11.00	11.00
28	A4 (d)	75c brn org	45	45
a.		Inverted overprint	6.00	6.00
29	A5 (c)	1p magenta	75	75
30	A4 (d)	1.25p dp grn	60	60
a.		Red ovpt.	9.00	9.00
31	A4 (d)	1.50p rose red (Bl)	55	55
a.		Inverted overprint	6.00	6.00
b.		Black ovpt.	10.00	10.00
32	A4 (d)	2p dk brn (R)	55	55
a.		Blue ovpt.	2.00	2.00
33	A4 (d)	2.50p pck bl (R)	75	75
a.		Black ovpt.	4.00	4.00
34	A4 (d)	3p org brn	60	60
a.		Inverted overprint	6.50	6.50
b.		Blue ovpt.	12.00	12.00
35	A4 (d)	5p violet	60	60
a.		Red ovpt.	12.00	12.00
36	A4 (d)	10p vio brn	90	90
37	A4 (d)	25p ultra (R)	2.10	2.10
		Nos. 25-37 (13)	9.25	9.25

Stamps of Syria, 1925, Surcharged in Black or Red:

1926

38	A4 (e)	3.50p on 75c brn org	70	65
a.		Surcharged on face and back	5.50	5.50
39	A4 (e)	4p on 25c ol blk (R)	80	65
40	A4 (e)	6p on 2.50p pck bl (R)	75	65
41	A4 (e)	12p on 1.25p dp grn	75	65
a.		Inverted surch.	8.00	8.00
42	A4 (e)	20p on 1.25p dp grn	1.15	80
43	A4 (f)	4.50p on 75c brn org	1.60	1.50
a.		Invtd. surch.	6.00	
44	A4 (f)	7.50p on 2.50p pck bl	1.20	1.15
45	A4 (f)	15p on 25p ultra	2.75	2.50
		Nos. 38-45 (8)	9.70	8.55

Syria No. 199 Overprinted Type "c" in Red.

1928

46	A3 (c)	5c on 10c dk vio	35	35
a.		Double surcharge	8.50	

Syria Nos. 178 and 174
Surcharged in Red.

47	A4 (f)	2p on 1.25p dp grn	5.00	3.25
48	A4 (f)	4p on 25c ol blk	3.00	2.75

= 4P ٤ق =
ALAOUITES
العلويين
g

49	A4 (g)	4p on 25c ol blk	23.50	22.50
a.		Double impression		

AIR POST STAMPS.

Nos. 8, 10, 13 & 14 with
Additional Overprint in Black

Perf. 14 x 13½.

1925, Jan. 1 **Unwmkd.**

C1	A18	2p red & pale bl	3.25	3.25
a.		Overprint reversed	35.00	
C2	A18	3p on 60c vio & ultra	4.50	4.50
a.		Overprint reversed	35.00	35.00
C3	A18	5p on 1fr cl & ol grn	3.25	3.25
C4	A18	10p on 2fr org & pale bl	3.25	3.25

Nos. 32, 34, 35 & 36
With Additional Overprint in Green

AVION

1925, Mar. 1 ***Perf. 13½***

C5	A4	2p dk brn	1.10	1.10
C6	A4	3p org brn	90	90
C7	A4	5p violet	90	90
C8	A4	10p vio brn	1.10	1.10

Nos. 32, 34, 35 & 36
With Additional Overprint in Red

k

1926, May 1

C9	A4	2p dk brn	1.20	1.20
C10	A4	3p org brn	1.20	1.20
C11	A4	5p violet	1.20	1.20
C12	A4	10p vio brn	1.20	1.20

No. C9 has the type "d" overprint in black.

Double or inverted overprints, types "d" or "k," are known on most of Nos. C9–C12. Price, $8–$10.

The red plane overprint, "k," was also applied to Nos. C5–C8. These are believed to have been essays, and were not regularly issued.

Nos. 27, 29, and 37
With Additional Overprint of Airplane
(k) in Red or Black.

1929, June-July

C17	A4	50c yel grn (R)	75	75
a.		Red overprint (k) double	10.00	
b.		Red overprint (k) on face and back	10.00	
c.		Pair with overprint (k) tête bêche	30.00	
C18	A5	1p mag (Bk)	2.75	2.75
C19	A4	25p ultra (R)	15.00	13.50
a.		Overprint (k) inverted	40.00	40.00

Nos. 47 and 45
With Additional Overprint of
Airplane (k) in Red.

1929-30

C20	A4	2p on 1.25p dp grn ('30)	1.20	1.10
a.		Surcharge inverted	6.00	
b.		Double surch.	5.00	
C21	A4	15p on 25p ultra (Bk + R)	20.00	13.50
a.		Overprint (k) inverted	35.00	35.00

POSTAGE DUE STAMPS.

Postage Due Stamps of France,
1893-1920, Surcharged in Black.

1925 ***Perf. 14 x 13½.*** **Unwmkd.**

J1	D2 (a)	50c on 10c choc	1.60	1.60
J2	D2 (a)	1p on 20c ol grn	1.60	1.60
J3	D2 (b)	2p on 30c red	1.60	1.60
J4	D2 (b)	3p on 50c vio brn	1.60	1.60
J5	D2 (b)	5p on 1 fr red brn, *straw*	1.60	1.60
		Nos. J1-J5 (5)	8.00	8.00

Postage Due Stamps of Syria, 1925,
Overprinted in Black, Blue or Red.

1925 ***Perf. 13½***

J6	D5 (d)	50c brn, *yel*	55	55
J7	D6 (c)	1p vio *rose* (Bl)	55	55
a.		Blk. overprint	10.00	10.00
b.		Double overprint (Bk + Bl)	16.00	16.00
J8	D5 (d)	2p *blue*	75	75
J9	D5 (d)	3p *red org*	1.35	1.35
J10	D5 (d)	5p *bl grn*	1.80	1.80
		Nos. J6-J10 (5)	5.00	5.00

The stamps of Alaouites were superseded in 1930 by those of Latakia.

ALBANIA

(ăl·bā'nĭ·ȧ)

LOCATION—Southeastern Europe.

GOVT.—Republic.

AREA—11,100 sq. mi.

POP.—2,550,000 (estimated 1976).

CAPITAL—Tirana.

After the outbreak of World War I, the country fell into a state of anarchy when the Prince and all members of the International Commission left Albania. Subsequently General Ferrero in command of Italian troops declared Albania an independent country. A constitution was adopted and a republican form of government was instituted which continued until 1928 when, by constitutional amendment, Albania was declared to be a monarchy. The President of the republic, Ahmed Zogu, became king of the new state. Many unlisted varieties of surcharges and lithographed labels are said to have done postal duty in Albania and Epirus during this unsettled period.

In March 1939, Italy invaded Albania. King Zog fled but did not abdicate. The King of Italy acquired the crown.

Germany occupied Albania from September, 1943, until late 1944 when it became an independent state. The People's Republic began in January, 1946.

40 Paras = 1 Piastre = 1 Grossion
100 Centimes = 1 Franc (1917)
100 Qintar = 1 Franc
100 Qintar (Qindarka) = 1 Lek (1947)

Stamps of Turkey
Handstamped

1913, June **Unwmkd.**
Perf. 12, 13½ and Compound.

Handstamped on Issue of 1908.

1	A19	2½pi vio brn	275.00	225.00

With Additional Overprint
in Carmine ب

2	A19	10pa bl grn	250.00	225.00

The eagle handstamp was applied to other Turkish stamps of 1908: 25pi green and 50 pi red brown. The 5pa ocher, Albania #4, was surcharged "2 paras". These three stamps were retained by officials.

Prices, $2500, $6000, $500.

Handstamped on Issue of 1909.

4	A21	5pa ocher	125.00	100.00
5	A21	10pa bl grn	100.00	90.00
6	A21	20pa car rose	75.00	60.00
7	A21	1pi ultra	85.00	75.00
8	A21	2pi bl blk	130.00	110.00
10	A21	5pi dk vio	400.00	325.00
11	A21	10pi dl red	1,400.	1,200.

With Additional Overprint
in Blue or Carmine ب

14	A21	20pa car rose (Bl)	225.00	175.00
15	A21	1pi brt bl (C)	575.00	525.00

Handstamped on Newspaper Stamp of 1911

17	A21	2pa ol grn	130.00	120.00

Handstamped on
Postage Due Stamp of 1908.

18	A19	1pi *dp rose*	775.00	575.00

No. 18 was used for regular postage.

No. 6 Surcharged With New Value.

19	A21	10pa on 20pa car rose	300.00	275.00

The overprint on Nos. 1 to 19 was handstamped and, as usual, is found inverted, double, etc.

Nos. 6, 7 and 8 exist with the handstamp in red, blue or violet, but these varieties are not known to have been regularly issued.

Excellent counterfeits exist of Nos. 1 to 19.

A1

1913, July ***Imperf.***

Handstamped on White Laid Paper Without Eagle or Value.

20	A1	(1pi) black	125.00	110.00
		Cut to shape	60.00	60.00
a.		Sewing machine perf.	200.00	200.00

1913, Aug. **With Eagle.**

Value Typewritten in Violet

21	A1	10pa violet	5.50	3.00
22	A1	20pa red & blk	5.50	3.75
23	A1	1gr black	5.50	3.50
24	A1	2gr bl & vio	6.50	5.00
25	A1	5gr vio & bl	8.75	7.00
26	A1	10gr blue	9.00	7.00
		Nos. 21-26 (6)	40.75	29.25

Nos. 21-26 exist with the eagle inverted or omitted and with numerous errors in the figures of value and the spelling of the word "grosh".

A2

Skanderbeg
(George Castriota)

A3

1913, Nov. ***Perf. 11½***

Handstamped on White Laid Paper Eagle and Value in Black.

27	A2	10pa green	2.00	1.00
a.		Imperf.	10.00	
b.		Eagle and value in grn	20.00	
c.		10pa red (error)	15.00	15.00
d.		10pa vio (error)	15.00	15.00
29	A2	20pa red	2.00	1.00
a.		Imperf.	10.00	
b.		20pa grn (error)	15.00	15.00
30	A2	30pa violet	2.00	1.00
a.		30pa ultra (error)	15.00	15.00
b.		30pa red (error)	15.00	15.00
31	A2	1gr ultra	3.00	1.75
a.		1gr grn (error)	15.00	15.00
b.		1gr blk (error)	15.00	15.00
c.		1gr vio (error)	15.00	15.00
33	A2	2gr black	5.00	3.75
a.		2gr vio (error)	15.00	15.00
b.		2gr bl (error)	15.00	15.00
		Nos. 27-33 (5)	14.00	8.50

The stamps of this issue are known with eagle or value inverted or omitted.

The stamps were issued in commemoration of the first anniversary of Albanian independence.

1913, Dec. **Typographed** ***Perf. 14***

35	A3	2q org brn & buff	65	50
36	A3	5q grn & bl grn	65	50
37	A3	10q rose red	60	40
38	A3	25q dk bl	80	60
39	A3	50q vio & red	1.25	1.00
40	A3	1fr dp brn	6.00	6.00
		Nos. 35-40 (6)	9.95	9.00

Nos. 35–40
Handstamped in
Black or Violet

7. Mars
1467. RROFTË MBRETI. 1914

1914, Mar. 7

41	A3	2q org brn & buff	12.50	10.00
42	A3	5q grn & bl grn (V)	12.50	10.00
43	A3	10q rose red	12.50	10.00
44	A3	25q dk bl (V)	12.50	10.00
45	A3	50q vio & red	12.50	10.00
46	A3	1fr dp brn	12.50	10.00
		Nos. 41-46 (6)	75.00	60.00

Issued to celebrate the arrival of Prince Wilhelm zu Wied on Mar. 7, 1914.

Nos. 35–40 Surcharged in Black:

5 PARA (a) **1 GROSH** (b)

1914, Apr. 2

47	A3 (a)	5pa on 2q org brn & buff	60	60
a.		Inverted surcharge	2.50	2.50
48	A3 (a)	10pa on 5q grn & bl grn	60	60
a.		Inverted surcharge	2.50	2.50
49	A3 (a)	20pa on 10q rose red	90	70
a.		Inverted surcharge	2.50	2.50
50	A3 (b)	1gr on 25q bl	90	90
a.		Inverted surcharge	3.25	3.25
51	A3 (b)	2gr on 50q vio & red	1.25	1.10
a.		Inverted surcharge	5.25	5.25
52	A3 (b)	5gr on 1fr dp brn	7.50	7.50
b.		Invtd. surch.		
		Nos. 47-52 (6)	11.75	11.40

Korce (Korytsa) Issues

A4

1914 Handstamped ***Imperf.***

No.	Type	Description	Unused	Used
52A	A4	10pa vio & red	60.00	50.00
c.		10pa blk & red	75.00	60.00
53	A4	25pa vio & red	60.00	50.00
a.		25pa blk & red	100.00	95.00

Nos. 52A-53a originally were handstamped directly on the cover, so the paper varies. Later they were also produced in sheets; these are rarely found. Nos. 52A-53a were issued by Albanian military authorities.

A5

A6

1917 Typo. & Litho. ***Perf. 11½***

No.	Type	Description	Unused	Used
54	A5	1c dk brn & grn	11.00	8.00
55	A5	2c red & grn	11.00	8.00
56	A5	3c gray grn & grn	11.00	8.00
57	A5	5c grn & blk	8.00	4.50
58	A5	10c rose red & blk	8.00	4.50
59	A5	25c bl & blk	8.00	4.50
60	A5	50c vio & blk	8.00	4.50
61	A5	1fr brn & blk	11.00	8.00
		Nos. 54-61 (8)	76.00	50.00

1917-18

No.	Type	Description	Unused	Used
62	A6	1c dk brn & grn	3.00	2.25
63	A6	2c red brn & grn	3.00	2.25
a.		"CTM" for "CTS"	17.50	17.50
64	A6	3c blk & grn	3.00	2.25
a.		"CTM" for "CTS"	17.50	17.50
65	A6	5c grn & blk	3.50	3.50
66	A6	10c dl red & blk	3.50	3.50
67	A6	50c vio & blk	7.00	7.00
68	A6	1fr red brn & blk	15.00	9.00
		Nos. 62-68 (7)	38.00	29.75

Counterfeits exist of Nos. 54-68, 80-81.

No. 65 Surcharged in Red

QARKU
I
KORÇËS
25 CTS

1918

No.	Type	Description	Unused	Used
80	A6	25c on 5c grn & blk	50.00	40.00

A7

1918

No.	Type	Description	Unused	Used
81	A7	25c bl & blk	27.50	25.00

General Issue

A8

A9

Handstamped in Rose or Blue

XV I MCMXIX

1919 ***Perf. 12½***

No.	Type	Description	Unused	Used
84	A8	(2)q on 2h brn	4.00	3.50
85	A8	5q on 16h grn	4.00	3.50
86	A8	10q on 8h rose (Bl)	4.00	3.50
87	A8	25q on 64h bl	4.00	3.50
88	A9	25q on 64h bl	*200.00*	*175.00*
89	A8	50q on 32h vio	4.00	3.50
90	A8	1fr on 1.28k org, *bl*	4.00	3.50
		Nos. 84-90 (7)	*224.00*	*196.00*

Handstamped in Rose or Blue

1919, Jan. 16

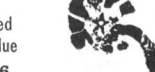

No.	Type	Description	Unused	Used
91	A8	(2)q on 2h brn	5.00	5.00
92	A8	5q on 16h grn	5.00	5.00
93	A8	10q on 8h rose (Bl)	5.00	5.00
94	A8	25q on 64h bl	32.50	32.50
95	A9	25q on 64h bl	27.50	27.50
96	A8	50q on 32h vio	5.00	5.00
97	A8	1fr on 1.28k org, *bl*	5.00	5.00
		Nos. 91-97 (7)	85.00	85.00

Handstamped in Violet

1919

No.	Type	Description	Unused	Used
98	A8	(2)q on 2h brn	7.00	7.00
99	A8	5q on 16h grn	7.00	7.00
100	A8	10q on 8h rose	7.00	7.00
101	A8	25q on 64h bl	7.00	7.00
102	A9	25q on 64h bl	25.00	25.00
103	A8	50q on 32h vio	7.00	7.00
104	A8	1fr on 1.28k org, *bl*	7.00	7.00
		Nos. 98-104 (7)	67.00	67.00

No. 50 Overprinted in Violet

1919 ***Perf. 14***

No.	Type	Description	Unused	Used
105	A3	1gr on 25q bl	2.50	3.00

A10

A11

1919, June 5 ***Perf. 11½, 12½***

No.	Type	Description	Unused	Used
106	A10	10q on 2h brn	3.50	3.50
107	A11	15q on 8h rose	3.50	3.50
108	A11	20q on 16h grn	3.50	3.50
109	A10	25q on 64h bl	3.50	3.50
110	A11	50q on 32h vio	3.50	3.50
111	A11	1fr on 96h org	3.50	3.50
112	A10	2fr on 1.60k vio, *buff*	7.00	7.00
		Nos. 106-112 (7)	28.00	28.00

Nos. 106-108, 110 exist with inverted surcharge.

A12 A13

Black or Violet Surcharge

1919

No.	Type	Description	Unused	Used
113	A12	10q on 8h car	3.50	3.50
114	A12	15q on 8h car (V)	3.50	3.50
115	A13	20q on 16h grn	3.50	3.50
116	A13	25q on 32h vio	2.50	2.50
117	A13	50q on 64h bl	8.00	8.00
118	A13	1fr on 96h org	4.50	4.50
119	A12	2fr on 1.60k vio, *buff*	4.50	4.50
		Nos. 113-119 (7)	30.00	30.00

A14

A15

Overprinted in Blue or Black, Without New Value.

1920 ***Perf. 12½.***

No.	Type	Description	Unused	Used
120	A14	1q gray (Bl)	30.00	35.00
121	A14	10q rose (Bk)	3.50	4.00
a.		Double overprint	30.00	35.00
122	A14	20q brn (Bl)	15.00	17.50
123	A14	25q bl (Bk)	150.00	*175.00*
124	A14	50q brn vio (Bk)	22.50	25.00
		Nos. 120-124 (5)	221.00	*256.50*

Counterfeit overprints exist.

Surcharged with New Value.

No.	Type	Description	Unused	Used
125	A14	2q on 10q rose (R)	4.00	5.00
126	A14	5q on 10q rose (G)	4.00	5.00
127	A14	25q on 10q rose (Bl)	4.00	5.00
128	A14	50q on 10q rose (Br)	4.00	5.00

Stamps of type A14 (Portrait of the Prince zu Wied) were not placed in use without overprint or surcharge.

Post Horn Overprinted in Black.

1920 ***Perf. 14x13***

No.	Type	Description	Unused	Used
129	A15	2q orange	1.50	1.50
130	A15	5q dp grn	3.00	2.00
131	A15	10q red	6.00	4.00
132	A15	25q lt bl	10.00	5.00
133	A15	50q gray grn	1.75	1.75
134	A15	1fr claret	1.75	1.75
		Nos. 129-134 (6)	24.00	16.00

Type A15 was never placed in use without post horn or "Besa" overprint.

Stamps of Type A15 (No Post Horn) Overprinted

BESA

1921

No.	Type	Description	Unused	Used
135	A15	2q orange	1.25	1.25
136	A15	5q dp grn	1.25	1.25
137	A15	10q red	2.50	2.50
138	A15	25q lt bl	6.00	3.50
139	A15	50q gray grn	1.75	1.75
140	A15	1fr claret	1.75	1.75
		No. 135-140 (6)	14.50	12.00

Stamps of these types, and with "TAKSE" overprint, were unauthorized and never placed in use.

Gjinokaster
A18

Korcha
A19

Designs: 5q, Kanina. 10q, Berati. 25q, Bridge at Vezirit. 50q, Rozafat. 2fr, Dursit.

1922 Typographed. ***Perf. 12½.***

No.	Type	Description	Unused	Used
147	A18	2q orange	60	50
148	A18	5q yel grn	30	20
149	A18	10q carmine	30	20
150	A18	25q dk bl	30	20
151	A18	50q dk grn	30	20
152	A19	1fr dk vio	60	60
153	A19	2fr ol grn	1.50	1.50
		Nos. 147-153 (7)	3.90	3.40

No. 135 Surcharged

Q 1

1922 ***Perf. 14x13***

No.	Type	Description	Unused	Used
154	A15	1q on 2q org	1.25	1.25

Stamps of Type A15 (No Post Horn) Overprinted

BESA

1922

No.	Type	Description	Unused	Used
156	A15	5q dp grn	1.75	1.75
157	A15	10q red	1.75	1.75

Nos. 147-151 Overprinted (top line in Black; diamond in Violet)

Mbledhje Kushtetuese
TIRANE
KALLNUER
1924

1924, Jan ***Perf. 12½***

No.	Type	Description	Unused	Used
158	A18	2q red org	2.50	3.00
159	A18	5q yel grn	2.50	3.00
160	A18	10q carmine	2.50	3.00
161	A18	25q dk bl	2.50	3.00
162	A18	50q dk grn	2.50	3.00
		Nos. 158-162 (5)	12.50	15.00

The words "Mbledhje Kushtetuese" are in taller letters on the 25q than on the other values. This issue was to commemorate the opening of the Constituent Assembly.

No. 147 Surcharged

= 1 =

1924

No.	Type	Description	Unused	Used
163	A18	1q on 2q red org	60	60

Nos. 163, 147-152 Overprinted

Triumf' i legalitetit
24 Dhetuer 1924

1924

No.	Type	Description	Unused	Used
164	A18	1q on 2q org	1.00	1.00
165	A18	2q orange	1.00	1.00
166	A18	5q yel grn	1.00	1.00
167	A18	10q carmine	1.00	1.00
168	A18	25q dk bl	1.00	1.00
169	A18	50q dk grn	1.00	1.00
170	A19	1fr dk vio	1.00	1.00
		Nos. 164-170 (7)	7.00	7.00

Issued to celebrate the return of the Government to the Capital after a revolution.

Nos. 163, 147–152 Overprinted

Republika Shqiptare

21 Kallnduer 1925

1925

No.	Type	Description	Unused	Used
171	A18	1q on 2q org	1.25	1.25
172	A18	2q orange	1.25	1.25
173	A18	5q yel grn	1.25	1.25
174	A18	10q carmine	1.25	1.25
175	A18	25q dk bl	1.25	1.25
176	A18	50q dk grn	1.25	1.25
177	A19	1fr dk vio	1.25	1.25
		Nos. 171-177 (7)	8.75	8.75

Issued in honor of the proclamation of the Republic, Jan. 21, 1925. The date "1921" instead of "1925" occurs once in each sheet of 50.

Nos. 163, 147–153 Overprinted

1925

No.	Type	Description	Unused	Used
178	A18	1q on 2q org	50	50
a.		Inverted overprint	7.50	7.50
179	A18	2q orange	50	50
180	A18	5q yel grn	50	50
a.		Inverted overprint	7.50	7.50
181	A18	10q carmine	50	50
182	A18	25q dk bl	50	50
183	A18	50q dk grn	50	50
184	A19	1fr dk vio	65	65
185	A19	2fr ol grn	65	65
		Nos. 178-185 (8)	4.30	4.30

President Ahmed Zogu

A25 A26

1925 *Perf. 13½, 13½x13*

No.	Type	Description	Unused	Used
186	A25	1q orange	10	10
187	A25	2q red brn	10	10
188	A25	5q green	10	10
189	A25	10q rose red	10	10
190	A25	15q gray brn	1.25	1.25
191	A25	25q dk bl	10	10
192	A25	50q bl grn	50	50
193	A26	1fr red & ultra	75	75
194	A26	2fr grn & org	75	75
195	A26	3fr brn & vio	1.00	1.00
196	A26	5fr vio & blk	3.75	3.75
		Nos. 186-196 (11)	8.50	8.50

No. 193 in ultramarine and brown, and No. 194 in gray and brown were not regularly issued.

Price, both $12

Nos. 186–196 Overprinted in Various Colors

1927 *Perf. 11½, 13½, 13½x13*

No.	Type	Description	Unused	Used
197	A25	1q org (V)	30	30
198	A25	2q red brn (G)	15	15
199	A25	5q grn (R)	80	10
200	A25	10q rose red (Bl)	10	5
201	A25	15q gray brn (G)	8.00	8.00
202	A25	25q dk bl (R)	10	6
203	A25	50q bl grn (Bl)	10	8
204	A26	1fr red & ultra (Bk)	10	10
205	A26	2fr grn & org (Bk)	15	15
206	A26	3fr brn & vio (Bk)	60	60
207	A26	5fr vio & blk (Bk)	85	85
		Nos. 197-207 (11)	11.25	10.44

The letters "A. Z." are the initials of the President's name, Ahmed Zogu.

Nos. 200, 202

Surcharged = 5 =

in Black or Red.

1928

No.	Type	Description	Unused	Used
208	A25	1q on 10q rose red	30	20
a.		Inverted surcharge	3.50	3.50
b.		Double surcharge, one inverted		
209	A25	5q on 25q dk bl (R)	30	20
a.		Inverted surcharge	3.50	3.50
b.		Double surcharge, one inverted		

King Zog I

A27 A28

Black Overprint.

1928 *Perf. 14x13½.*

No.	Type	Description	Unused	Used
210	A27	1q org brn	2.00	2.00
211	A27	2q slate	2.00	2.00
212	A27	5q bl grn	2.00	2.00
213	A27	10q rose red	2.00	2.00
214	A27	15q bister	13.50	13.50
215	A27	25q dp bl	1.50	1.50
216	A27	50q lil rose	2.00	2.00

Red Overprint.

Perf. 13½x14.

No.	Type	Description	Unused	Used
217	A28	1fr bl & sl	2.25	2.25
		Nos. 210-217 (8)	27.25	27.25

A29 A30

Black or Red Overprint.

1928 *Perf. 14x13½.*

No.	Type	Description	Unused	Used
218	A29	1q org brn	7.50	7.50
219	A29	2q sl (R)	7.50	7.50
220	A29	5q bl grn	6.00	6.00
221	A29	10q rose red	4.00	4.00
222	A29	15q bister	4.25	4.25
223	A29	25q dp bl (R)	4.25	4.25
224	A29	50q lil rose	4.50	4.50

Perf. 13½x14.

No.	Type	Description	Unused	Used
225	A30	1fr bl & sl (R)	7.50	7.50
226	A30	2fr grn & sl (R)	9.00	9.00
		Nos. 218-226 (9)	54.50	54.50

Issued in commemoration of the proclamation of Ahmed Zogu as King of Albania.

A31 A32

Black Overprint.

1928 *Perf. 14x13½.*

No.	Type	Description	Unused	Used
227	A31	1q org brn	30	30
228	A31	2q slate	15	15
229	A31	5q bl grn	1.25	15
230	A31	10q rose red	15	10
231	A31	15q bister	9.00	7.50
232	A31	25q dp bl	15	10
233	A31	50q lil rose	15	10

Perf. 13½x14.

No.	Type	Description	Unused	Used
234	A32	1fr bl & sl	30	60
235	A32	2fr grn & sl	40	70
236	A32	3fr dk red & ol bis	75	1.00
237	A32	5fr dl vio & gray	1.50	1.50
		Nos. 227-237 (11)	14.10	12.20

The overprint reads "Kingdom of Albania".

Mbr. Shqiptare

Nos. 203, 202, 200

Surcharged in Black

■ 5 ■

1929 *Perf. 13½x13, 11½*

No.	Type	Description	Unused	Used
238	A25	1q on 50q bl grn	30	30
239	A25	5q on 25q dk bl	30	30
240	A25	15q on 10q rose red	60	30

RROFT-MBRETI

Nos. 186–189, 191–194 Overprinted in Black or Red

8X1929.

1929 *Perf. 11½, 13½.*

No.	Type	Description	Unused	Used
241	A25	1q orange	3.50	3.50
242	A25	2q red brn	3.50	3.50
243	A25	5q green	3.50	3.50
244	A25	10q rose red	3.50	3.50
245	A25	25q dk bl	3.50	3.50
246	A25	50q bl grn (R)	4.50	4.50
247	A26	1fr red & ultra	6.00	6.00
248	A26	2fr grn & org	7.50	7.50
		Nos. 241-248 (8)	35.50	35.50

Issued to commemorate the 34th birthday of King Zog. The overprint reads "Long live the King."

Lake Butrinto

A33

King Zog I

A34

Zog Bridge

A35

Ruin at Zog Manor

A36

Wmk. 220

Wmkd.

Double Headed Eagle. (220)

1930, Sept. 1 Photo. *Perf. 14, 14½*

No.	Type	Description	Unused	Used
250	A33	1q slate	15	8
251	A33	2q org red	15	8
252	A34	5q yel grn	15	8
253	A34	10q carmine	20	8
254	A34	15q dk brn	24	16
255	A34	25q dk ultra	24	20
256	A33	50q sl grn	40	24
257	A35	1fr violet	95	95
258	A35	2fr indigo	95	95
259	A36	3fr gray grn	2.25	2.25
260	A36	5fr org brn	3.50	3.50
		Nos. 250-260 (11)	9.18	8.57

2nd anniversary of accession of King Zog I.

Nos. 250–259 Overprinted in Black

1 1
9 9
2 3
4-24Dhetuer-4

1934, Dec. 24

No.	Type	Description	Unused	Used
261	A33	1q slate	1.75	1.75
262	A33	2q org red	1.75	1.75
263	A34	5q yel grn	1.75	1.75
264	A34	10q carmine	1.75	1.75
265	A34	15q dk brn	1.75	1.75
266	A34	25q dk ultra	1.75	1.75
267	A33	50q sl grn	1.75	1.75
268	A35	1fr violet	5.00	5.00
269	A35	2fr indigo	10.00	10.00
270	A36	3fr gray grn	15.00	15.00
		Nos. 261-270 (10)	42.25	42.25

Tenth anniversary of the Constitution.

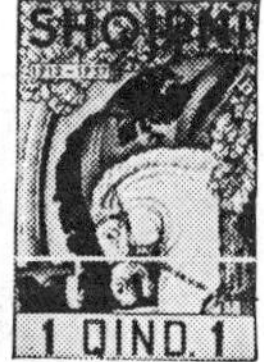

Allegory of Death of Skanderbeg

A37

Albanian Eagle in Turkish Shackles

A38

Designs: 5q, 25q, 40q, 2fr, Eagle with wings spread.

1937 *Perf. 14* **Unwmkd.**

No.	Type	Description	Unused	Used
271	A37	1q brn vio	20	20
272	A38	2q brown	20	20
273	A38	5q lt grn	35	35
274	A37	10q ol brn	45	45
275	A38	15q rose red	55	55
276	A38	25q blue	1.00	1.00
277	A37	50q dp grn	1.65	1.65
278	A38	1fr violet	3.00	3.00
279	A38	2fr org brn	6.00	6.00
		Nos. 271-279 (9)	13.40	13.40

Souvenir Sheet.

No.	Type	Description	Unused	Used
280		Sheet of three	12.00	15.00
a.		A37 20q red vio	2.50	3.00
b.		A38 30q ol brn	2.50	3.00
c.		A38 40q red	2.50	3.00

Nos. 271–280 commemorate the 25th anniversary of independence from Turkey, proclaimed Nov. 26, 1912. No. 280 measures 138x140mm.

Queen Geraldine and King Zog

A40

1938 *Perf. 14*

No.	Type	Description	Unused	Used
281	A40	1q sl vio	18	18
282	A40	2q red brn	18	18
283	A40	5q green	18	18
284	A40	10q ol brn	27	33
285	A40	15q rose red	40	60
286	A40	25q blue	75	1.00
287	A40	50q Prus grn	2.00	2.25
288	A40	1fr purple	4.50	5.00
		Nos. 281-288 (8)	8.46	9.72

Souvenir Sheet.

No.	Type	Description	Unused	Used
289	A40	Sheet of four	15.00	17.50
a.		20q dk red vio	1.50	1.50
b.		30q brn ol	1.50	1.50

Nos. 281–289 were issued to commemorate the wedding of King Zog and Countess Geraldine Apponyi, April 27, 1938. Souvenir sheet measures 110½x139mm.

Queen Geraldine
A42

National Emblems
A43

King Zog I
A44

1938

No.	Type	Description	Unused	Used
290	A42	1q dp red vio	30	40
291	A43	2q red org	30	40
292	A42	5q dp grn	40	40
293	A44	10q red brn	60	65
294	A42	15q dp rose	80	80
295	A44	25q dp bl	85	1.00
296	A43	50q gray blk	1.65	2.00
297	A44	1fr sl grn	5.00	5.50
		Nos. 290-297 (8)	9.90	11.15

Souvenir Sheet.

No.	Type	Description	Unused	Used
298		Sheet of three	15.00	17.50
b.	A43	20q Prus grn	2.25	2.25
c.	A44	30q dp vio	2.25	2.25

Nos. 290–298 were issued to commemorate the 10th anniversary of royal rule. They were on sale for three days (Aug. 30–31, Sept. 1) only, during which their use was required on all mail.

No. 298 has marginal inscriptions in Prussian green. Size: 110x65mm. The 15q deep rose (type A42) is identical with No. 294.

Issued under Italian Dominion.

Nos. 250–260 Overprinted in Black

Mbledhja Kushtetuëse 12-IV-1939 XVII

1939 *Perf. 14* **Wmk 220**

No.	Type	Description	Unused	Used
299	A33	1q slate	10	10
300	A33	2q org red	14	7
301	A34	5q yel grn	14	12
302	A34	10q carmine	12	6
303	A34	15q dk brn	20	20
304	A34	25q dk ultra	24	22
305	A33	50q sl grn	35	30
306	A35	1fr violet	70	70
307	A35	2fr indigo	1.00	1.00
308	A36	3fr gray grn	3.00	3.00
309	A36	5fr org brn	4.00	4.00
		Nos. 299-309 (11)	9.99	9.77

Issued in commemoration of the resolution adopted by the National Assembly, April 12, 1939, offering the Albanian Crown to Italy.

Native Costumes
A46 A47 A48

King Victor Emmanuel III
A49 A50

Native Costume
A51

Monastery
A52

Designs: 2fr, Bridge at Vezirit. 3fr, Ancient Columns. 5fr, Amphitheater.

Photogravure

1939 *Perf. 14* **Unwmkd.**

No.	Type	Description	Unused	Used
310	A46	1q bl gray	10	10
311	A47	2q ol grn	8	8
312	A48	3q gldn brn	8	8
313	A49	5q green	15	3
314	A50	10q brown	15	5
315	A50	15q crimson	25	6
316	A50	25q sapphire	30	10
317	A50	30q brt vio	40	10
318	A51	50q dl pur	50	10
319	A49	65q red brn	85	75
320	A52	1fr myr grn	1.00	1.00
321	A52	2fr brn lake	2.00	2.00
322	A52	3fr brn blk	4.50	4.50
323	A52	5fr gray vio	8.50	8.50
		Nos. 310-323 (14)	18.86	17.45

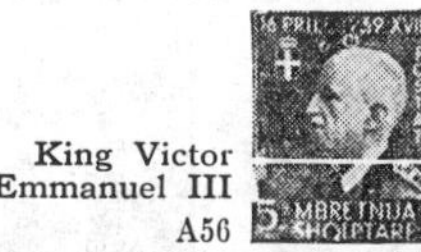

King Victor Emmanuel III
A56

1942 **Photogravure**

No.	Type	Description	Unused	Used
324	A56	5q green	9	9
325	A56	10q brown	12	12
326	A56	15q rose red	12	12
327	A56	25q blue	20	20
328	A56	65q red brn	30	30
329	A56	1fr myr grn	60	60
330	A56	2fr gray vio	1.50	1.50
		Nos. 324-330 (7)	2.93	2.93

Issued to commemorate the third anniversary of the conquest of Albania by Italy.

No. 311 Surcharged in Black **1 QIND**

No.	Type	Description	Unused	Used
331	A47	1q on 2q ol grn	30	30

Issued under German Administration

Stamps of 1939 Overprinted in Carmine or Brown

14 Shtator 1943

1943

No.	Type	Description	Unused	Used
332	A47	2q ol grn	1.25	2.00
333	A48	3q gldn brn	1.25	2.00
334	A49	5q green	1.25	2.00
335	A50	10q brown	1.25	2.00
336	A50	15q crim (Br)	1.25	2.00
337	A50	25q sapphire	1.25	2.00
338	A50	30q brt vio	1.25	2.00
339	A49	65q red brn	1.50	3.50
340	A52	1fr myr grn	9.00	15.00
341	A52	2fr brn lake	12.00	*30.00*
342	A52	3fr brn blk	52.50	*80.00*

Surcharged with New Values.

No.	Type	Description	Unused	Used
343	A48	1q on 3q gldn brn	1.25	2.00
344	A49	50q on 65q red brn	1.50	3.50
		Nos. 332-344 (13)	86.50	*148.00*

Proclamation of Albanian independence. The overprint "14 Shtator 1943" on Nos. 324 to 328 is private and fraudulent.

Independent State

Nos. 312 to 317 and 319 to 321 Surcharged with New Value and Bars in Black or Carmine, and

QEVERIJA DEMOKRAT. E SHQIPERISE 22-X-1944

1945

No.	Type	Description	Unused	Used
345	A48	30q on 3q gldn brn	2.00	2.00
346	A49	40q on 5q grn	2.00	2.00
347	A50	50q on 10q brn	2.00	2.00
348	A50	60q on 15q crim	2.00	2.00
349	A50	80q on 25q saph (C)	2.00	2.00
350	A50	1fr on 30q brt vio	2.00	2.00
351	A49	2fr on 65q red brn	2.00	2.00
352	A52	3fr on 1fr myr grn	2.00	2.00
353	A52	5fr on 2fr brn lake	2.00	2.00
		Nos. 345-353 (9)	18.00	18.00

"DEMOKRATIKE" is not abbreviated on Nos. 352 and 353.

Nos. 250, 251, 256 and 258 Surcharged in Black or Carmine, and

1943 U.N.ÇL.SHQ. 1945
10 [illegible]RRIK.
FR.SHQ. 5

1945 **Wmk. 220**

No.	Type	Description	Unused	Used
354	A33	30q on 1q sl	22	22
355	A33	60q on 1q sl	22	25
356	A33	80q on 1q sl	30	35
357	A33	1fr on 1q sl	45	45
358	A33	2fr on 2q org red	90	1.00
359	A33	3fr on 50q sl grn	3.25	3.75
360	A35	5fr on 2fr ind	4.75	5.50
		Nos. 354-360 (7)	10.09	11.52

Albanian National Army of Liberation, second anniversary.

The surcharge on No. 360 is condensed to fit the size of the stamp.

Country House, Labinot
A57

Designs: 40q, 60q, Bridge at Berat. 1fr, 3fr, Permet.

Typographed.

1945, Nov. 28 *Perf. 11* **Unwmkd.**

No.	Type	Description	Unused	Used
361	A57	20q bluish grn	15	15
362	A57	30q dp org	30	30
363	A57	40q brown	30	30
364	A57	60q red vio	45	45
365	A57	1fr rose red	1.75	1.75
366	A57	3fr dk bl	7.50	7.50
		Nos. 361-366 (6)	10.45	10.45

Counterfeits exist. See note after No. B33.

Nos. 361 to 366 Overprinted in Black

ASAMBLEJA KUSHTETUESE
10 KALLHUER 1946

1946

No.	Type	Description	Unused	Used
367	A57	20q bluish grn	30	30
368	A57	30q dp org	35	35
369	A57	40q brown	45	45
370	A57	60q red vio	80	80
371	A57	1fr rose red	6.00	6.00
372	A57	3fr dk bl	9.50	9.50
		Nos. 367-372 (6)	17.40	17.40

Issued to commemorate the convocation of the Constitutional Assembly, January 10, 1946.

People's Republic

Nos. 361 to 366 Overprinted in Black

REPUBLIKA POPULLORE E SHQIPERISE

1946

No.	Type	Description	Unused	Used
373	A57	20q bluish grn	35	35
374	A57	30q dp org	60	60
375	A57	40q brown	60	60
376	A57	60q red vio	1.25	1.25
377	A57	1fr rose red	6.00	6.00
378	A57	3fr dk bl	10.50	10.50
		Nos. 373-378 (6)	19.30	19.30

Issued to commemorate the proclamation of the Albanian People's Republic.

Globe, Dove and Olive Branch
A60

Typographed

1946, Mar. 8 *Perf. 11½, Imperf.*

Denomination in Black.

No.	Type	Description	Unused	Used
379	A60	20q lil & dl red	10	10
380	A60	40q dp lil & dl red	20	20
381	A60	50q vio & dl red	30	30
382	A60	1fr lt bl & red	60	60
383	A60	2fr dk bl & red	1.25	1.25
		Nos. 379-383 (5)	2.45	2.45

International Women's Congress.

Athletes with Shot and Indian Club
A61

Perf. 11½

1946, Oct. 6 **Litho.** **Unwmkd.**

No.	Type	Description	Unused	Used
384	A61	1q grnsh blk	7.00	6.00
385	A61	2q green	7.00	6.00
386	A61	5q brown	7.00	6.00
387	A61	10q crimson	7.00	6.00
388	A61	20q ultra	7.00	6.00
389	A61	40q rose vio	7.00	6.00
390	A61	1fr dp org	12.50	11.00
		Nos. 384-390 (7)	54.50	47.00

Balkan Games, Tirana, Oct. 6–13.

Qemal Stafa
A62

1947, May 5 *Perf. 12½x11½*

No.	Type	Description	Unused	Used
391	A62	20q brn & yel brn	1.20	1.20
392	A62	28q dk bl & bl	1.60	1.60
393	A62	40q brn blk & gray brn	2.75	2.75
a.		Souvenir sheet	6.50	6.50

Nos. 391 to 393a commemorate the 5th anniversary of the death of Qemal Stafa, May 5, 1942. No. 393a contains one each of Nos. 391-393 imperf. with illustrations above and below the stamps.

Young Railway Laborers
A64

1947, May 16 *Perf. 11½*

No.	Type	Description	Unused	Used
395	A64	1q brn blk & gray brn	1.00	40
396	A64	4q dk grn & grn	1.00	40
397	A64	10q blk brn & bis brn	1.00	40
398	A64	15q dk red & red	1.00	40

399	A64	20q ind & bl gray	1.50	60
400	A64	28q dk bl & bl	2.50	90
401	A64	40q brn vio & rose vio	5.00	2.00
402	A64	68q dk brn & org brn	8.00	4.50
		Nos. 395-402 (8)	21.00	9.60

Issued to publicize the construction of the Durrës Elbasan Railway by Albanian youths.

Citizens Led by Hasim Zeneli
A65

Enver Hoxha and Vasil Shanto
A66

Vojo Kushi
A68

Inauguration of Vithkuq Brigade
A67

1947, July 10 **Lithographed**

403	A65	16q brn org & red brn	1.50	1.25
404	A66	20q org brn & dk brn	1.50	1.25
405	A67	28q bl & dk bl	2.00	1.75
406	A68	40q lil & dk brn	3.25	3.00

Issued to commemorate the 4th anniversary of the formation of Albania's army, July 10, 1943.

Conference Building Ruins, Peza
A69

Disabled Soldiers
A70

1947, Sept. 16

407	A69	2 l red vio	2.25	1.50
408	A69	2.50 l dp bl	2.25	1.50

Issued to commemorate the 5th anniversary of the Peza Conference, September 16, 1942.

1947, Nov. 17 ***Perf. 12½x11½***

408A	A70	1 l red	3.50	2.75

Issued to publicize the Disabled War Veterans Congress, November 14–20, 1947.

A71

A73

Designs: 2 l, Banquet. 2.50 l, Peasants rejoicing.

Perf. 11½x12½, 12½x11½

1947, Nov. 17 **Unwmkd.**

409	A71	1.50 l dl vio	3.00	2.00
410	A71	2 l brown	3.00	2.00
411	A71	2.50 l blue	3.00	2.00
412	A73	3 l rose red	3.00	2.00

Issued to commemorate the 1st anniversary of the agrarian reform law of November 17, 1946.

Burning Farm Buildings
A74

Designs: 2.50 l, Trench scene. 5 l, Firing line. 8 l, Winter advance. 12 l, Infantry column.

1947, Nov. 29 ***Perf. 11½x12½***

Inscribed: "29-XI-1944-1947 Pervjetori I IIIte Iclirimit."

413	A74	1.50 l red	1.50	1.50
414	A74	2.50 l rose brn	2.00	2.00
415	A74	5 l blue	3.00	3.00
416	A74	8 l purple	5.00	5.00
417	A74	12 l brown	7.50	7.50
		Nos. 413-417 (5)	19.00	19.00

Issued to commemorate the third anniversary of Albania's liberation.

Nos. 373 to 378 Surcharged with New Value and Bars in Black.

1948, Feb. 22 ***Perf. 11***

418	A57	50q on 30q dp org	50	50
419	A57	1 l on 20q bluish grn	50	50
420	A57	2.50 l on 60q red vio	1.25	1.25
421	A57	3 l on 1fr rose red	2.00	2.00
422	A57	5 l on 3fr dk bl	3.00	3.00
423	A57	12 l on 40q brn	7.50	7.50
		Nos. 418-423 (6)	14.75	14.75

The two bars consist of four type squares each set close together.

Map, Train and Construction Workers
A75

1948, June 1 **Litho.** ***Perf. 11½***

424	A75	50q dk car rose	75	50
425	A75	1 l lt grn & blk	75	50
426	A75	1.50 l dp rose	75	50
427	A75	2.50 l org brn & dk brn	1.25	75
428	A75	5 l dl bl	1.75	1.00
429	A75	8 l sal & dk brn	4.00	1.50
430	A75	12 l red vio & dk vio	5.00	1.50
431	A75	20 l ol gray	9.00	4.50
		Nos. 424-431 (8)	23.25	10.75

Issued to publicize the construction of the Durrës-Tirana Railway.

Marching Soldiers
A76

Design: 8 l, Battle scene.

1948, July 10

432	A76	2.50 l yel brn	75	60
433	A76	5 l dk bl	1.50	1.25
434	A76	8 l vio gray	2.25	2.25

Issued to commemorate the 5th anniversary of the formation of Albania's army.

Bricklayer, Flag, Globe and "Industry"
A77

Map and Soldier
A78

1949, May 1 **Photo.** ***Perf. 12½x12***

435	A77	2.50 l ol brn	45	35
436	A77	5 l blue	60	60
437	A77	8 l vio brn	1.50	1.25

Issued to publicize Labor Day, May 1, 1949.

1949, July 10 **Unwmkd.**

438	A78	2.50 l brown	45	35
439	A78	5 l lt ultra	60	50
440	A78	8 l brn org	1.50	1.25

Issued to commemorate the 6th anniversary of the formation of Albania's army.

Enver Hoxha
A79

Albanian Citizen and Spasski Tower, Kremlin
A80

1949, Oct. 16 **Engr.** ***Perf. 12½***

441	A79	50q purple	7	3
442	A79	1 l dl grn	7	3
443	A79	1.50 l car lake	15	3
444	A79	2.50 l brown	30	3
445	A79	5 l vio bl	60	20
446	A79	8 l sepia	1.00	75
447	A79	12 l rose lil	2.25	1.25
448	A79	20 l gray bl	4.50	2.00
		Nos. 441-448 (8)	8.94	4.32

Photogravure.

1949, Sept. 10 ***Perf. 12½x12***

449	A80	2.50 l org brn	35	35
450	A80	5 l dp ultra	90	90

Albanian-Soviet friendship.

Albanian Soldier and Flag
A81

Battle Scene
A82

1949, Nov. 29 ***Perf. 12*** **Unwmkd.**

451	A81	2.50 l brown	20	20
452	A82	3 l dk red	30	40
453	A81	5 l violet	45	55
454	A82	8 l black	1.50	1.50

Fifth anniversary of Albania's liberation.

Joseph V Stalin
A83

Symbols of UPU and Postal Transport
A84

1949, Dec. 21

455	A83	2.50 l dk brn	25	30
456	A83	5 l vio bl	65	75
457	A83	8 l rose brn	1.10	1.25

Issued to commemorate the 70th anniversary of the birth of Joseph V. Stalin.

Canceled to Order

Beginning in 1950, Albania sold some issues in sheets canceled to order. Prices in second column when much less than unused are for "CTO" copies. Postally used stamps are valued at slightly less than, or the same as, unused.

1950, July 1 **Photo.** ***Perf. 12x12½***

458	A84	5 l blue	1.00	1.00
459	A84	8 l rose brn	1.50	1.50
460	A84	12 l sepia	2.00	2.00

Issued to commemorate the 75th anniversary (in 1949) of the formation of the Universal Postal Union.

Sami Frasheri
A85

Arms and Albanian Flags
A86

Authors: 2.50 l, Andon Zako. 3 l, Naim Frasheri. 5 l, Kostandin Kristoforidhi.

1950, Nov. 5 ***Perf. 14***

461	A85	2 l dk grn	20	15
462	A85	2.50 l red brn	30	20
463	A85	3 l brn car	36	25
464	A85	5 l dp bl	75	60

Issued to commemorate the "Jubilee of the Writers of the Renaissance."

1951, Jan. 11 **Engr.** ***Perf. 14x13½***

465	A86	2.50 l brn car	40	25
466	A86	5 l dp bl	85	50
467	A86	8 l sepia	1.50	1.00

Issued to commemorate the 5th anniversary of the formation of the Albanian People's Republic.

Skanderbeg A87

Enver Hoxha and Congress of Permet A88

1951, Mar. 1

468	A87	2.50 l	brown	40	25
469	A87	5 l	violet	85	50
470	A87	8 l	ol bis	1.50	1.00

Issued to commemorate the 483rd anniversary of the death of George Castriota (Skanderbeg).

1951, May 24 Photo. ***Perf. 12***

471	A88	2.50 l	dk brn	30	20
472	A88	3 l	rose brn	45	30
473	A88	5 l	vio bl	75	50
474	A88	8 l	rose lil	1.25	80

Congress of Permet, 7th anniversary.

Child and Globe A89

Weighing Baby A90

1951, July 16

475	A89	2 l	green	45	30
476	A90	2.50 l	brown	60	40
477	A90	3 l	red	85	50
478	A89	5 l	blue	1.25	80

Issued to publicize International Children's Day, June 1, 1951.

Enver Hoxha and Birthplace of Albanian Communist Party

A91

1951, Nov. 8 Photo. ***Perf. 14***

479	A91	2.50 l	ol brn	25	25
480	A91	3 l	rose brn	35	35
481	A91	5 l	dk sl bl	60	60
482	A91	8 l	black	85	85

Issued to commemorate the 10th anniversary of the founding of Albania's Communist Party.

Battle Scene

A92

Designs: 5 l, Schoolgirl, "Agriculture and Industry." 8 l, Four portraits.

1951, Nov. 28 ***Perf. 12x12½***

483	A92	2.50 l	brown	30	15
484	A92	5 l	blue	50	40
485	A92	8 l	brn car	1.00	75

Issued to commemorate the 10th anniversary of the formation of the Albanian Communist Youth Organization.

Albanian Heroes (Haxhija, Lezhe, Giyebegej, Mezi and Dedej)

A93

1950, Dec. 25 ***Perf. 14*** **Unwmkd.**

Various Portraits

486	A93	2 l	dk grn	30	20
487	A93	2.50 l	purple	35	25
488	A93	3 l	scarlet	45	35
489	A93	5 l	brt bl	75	50
490	A93	8 l	ol brn	2.00	1.50
			Nos. 486-490 (5)	3.85	2.80

Isssued to commemorate the 6th anniversary of Albania's liberation. Nos. 486-489 each show five "Heroes of the People"; No. 490 shows two (Stafa and Shanto).

Tobacco Factory, Shkoder A94

Composite, Lenin Hydro-electric Plant A95

Designs: 1 l, Canal. 2.50 l, Textile factory. 3 l, "8 November" Cannery. 5 l, Motion Picture Studio, Tirana. 8 l, Stalin Textile Mill, Tirana. 20 l, Central Hydroelectric Dam.

Perf. 12x12½, 12½x12

1953, Aug. 1

491	A94	50q	red brn	5	3
492	A94	1 l	dl grn	10	3
493	A94	2.50 l	brown	30	4
494	A94	3 l	rose brn	45	10
495	A94	5 l	blue	65	12
496	A94	8 l	brn ol	1.00	25
497	A95	12 l	dp plum	1.75	50
498	A94	20 l	sl bl	3.00	75
			Nos. 491-498 (8)	7.30	1.82

Liberation Scene

A96

1954, Nov. 29 ***Perf. 12x12½***

499	A96	50q	brn vio	5	3
500	A96	1 l	ol grn	15	3
501	A96	2.50 l	yel brn	35	8
502	A96	3 l	car rose	60	17
503	A96	5 l	gray bl	90	17
504	A96	8 l	rose brn	2.25	75
			Nos. 499-504 (6)	4.30	1.23

10th anniversary of Albania's liberation.

School A97

Pandeli Sotiri, Petro Nini Luarasi, Nuci Naci

A98

1956, Feb. 23 **Unwmkd.**

505	A97	2 l	rose vio	20	6
506	A98	2.50 l	lt grn	30	12
507	A98	5 l	ultra	75	30
508	A97	10 l	brt grnsh bl	1.50	50

Issued to commemorate the 70th anniversary of the opening of the first Albanian school.

Flags

A99

Designs: 5 l, Labor Party headquarters, Tirana. 8 l, Marx and Lenin.

1957, June 1 Engr. ***Perf. 11½x11***

509	A99	2.50 l	brown	30	8
510	A99	5 l	lt vio bl	60	20
511	A99	8 l	rose lil	1.50	30

Issued to commemorate the 15th anniversary of the founding of Albania's Labor Party.

Congress Emblem

A100

1957, Oct. 4 ***Perf. 11½*** **Unwmkd.**

512	A100	2.50 l	gray brn	15	8
513	A100	3 l	rose red	15	10
514	A100	5 l	dk bl	40	15
515	A100	8 l	green	1.25	30

Issued to publicize the fourth International Trade Union Congress, Leipzig, Oct. 4-15.

Lenin and Cruiser "Aurora"

A101

1957, Nov. 7 Litho. ***Perf. 10½***

516	A101	2.50 l	vio brn	25	12
517	A101	5 l	vio bl	50	22
518	A101	8 l	gray	1.00	40

Issued to commemorate the 40th anniversary of the Russian Revolution.

Albanian Fighter Holding Flag A102

Naum Veqilharxhj A103

1957, Nov. 28 ***Perf. 10½***

519	A102	1.50 l	magenta	10	6
520	A102	2.50 l	brown	30	10
521	A102	5 l	blue	60	25
522	A102	8 l	green	1.25	40

Issued to commemorate the 45th anniversary of the proclamation of independence.

1958, Feb. 1 **Unwmkd.**

523	A103	2.50 l	dk brn	20	12
524	A103	5 l	vio bl	50	20
525	A103	8 l	rose lil	75	40

Issued to commemorate the 160th anniversary of the birth of Naum Veqilharxhj, patriot and writer.

Luigi Gurakuqi A104

Soldiers A105

1958, Apr. 15 Photo. ***Perf. 10½***

526	A104	1.50 l	dk grn	15	5
527	A104	2.50 l	brown	30	10
528	A104	5 l	blue	1.00	20
529	A104	8 l	sepia	1.25	30

Issued to commemorate the transfer of the ashes of Luigi Gurakuqi.

1958, July 10 **Lithographed**

Design: 2.50 l, 11 l, Airman, sailor, soldier and tank.

530	A105	1.50 l	bl grn	8	5
531	A105	2.50 l	dk red brn	12	6
532	A105	8 l	rose red	50	20
533	A105	11 l	brt bl	80	30

15th anniversary of Albanian army.

Cerciz Topulli and Mihal Grameno A106

Buildings and Tree A107

1958, July 1

534	A106	2.50 l	dk ol bis	20	8
535	A107	3 l	green	25	10
536	A106	5 l	blue	45	18
537	A107	8 l	red brn	90	30

50th anniversary, Battle of Mashkullore.

Ancient Amphitheater and Goddess of Butrinto

A108

1959, Jan. 25 Litho. ***Perf. 10½***

538	A108	2.50 l	redsh brn	15	6
539	A108	6.50 l	lt bl grn	70	25
540	A108	11 l	dk bl	1.25	50

Cultural Monuments Week.

Frederic Joliot-Curie and World Peace Congress Emblem A109

Basketball A110

1959, July 1 **Unwmkd.**

541	A109	1.50 l	car rose	75	20
542	A109	2.50 l	rose vio	1.50	30
543	A109	11 l	blue	3.50	1.50

Issued to commemorate the 10th anniversary of the World Peace Movement.

1959, Nov. 20 ***Perf. 10½***

Sports: 2.50 l, Soccer. 5 l, Runner. 11 l, Man and woman runners with torch and flags.

544	A110	1.50 l	brt vio	20	8

545	A110	2.50 l emerald	30	15
546	A110	5 l car rose	60	25
547	A110	11 l ultra	2.25	75

Issued to publicize the first Albanian Spartacist Games.

Fighter and Flags
A111

Mother and Child, U.N. Emblem
A112

1959, Nov. 29

Designs: 2.50 l, Miner with drill standing guard. 3 l, Farm woman with sheaf of grain. 6.50 l, Man and woman in laboratory.

548	A111	1.50 l brt car	35	3
549	A111	2.50 l red brn	55	5
550	A111	3 l brt bl grn	60	10
551	A111	6.50 l brt red	1.25	30
a.		Souvenir sheet	6.00	6.00

15th anniversary of Albania's liberation.

No. 551a contains one each of Nos. 548–551, imperf. and all in bright carmine. Inscribed ribbon frame of sheet and frame lines for each stamp are blue green. Size: 144x97mm.

1959, Dec. 5 **Unwmkd.**

552	A112	5 l lt grnsh bl	1.50	60
a.		Miniature sheet	3.25	3.25

Issued to commemorate the 10th anniversary (in 1958) of the signing of the Universal Declaration of Human Rights.

No. 552a contains one imperf. stamp similar to No. 552; ornamental border. Size: 74½x66mm.

Woman with Olive Branch
A113

Alexander Moissi
A114

1960, Mar. 8 Litho. ***Perf. 10½***

553	A113	2.50 l chocolate	30	12
554	A113	11 l rose car	1.25	40

Issued to commemorate the 50th anniversary of International Women's Day, March 8.

1960, Apr. 20

555	A114	3 l dp brn	30	8
556	A114	11 l Prus grn	1.25	25

80th anniversary of the birth of Alexander Moissi (Moisiu) (1880–1935), German actor.

Lenin
A115

School Building
A116

1960, Apr. 22

557	A115	4 l Prus bl	35	8
558	A115	11 l lake	1.10	20

90th anniversary of birth of Lenin.

1960, May 30 Litho. ***Perf. 10½***

559	A116	5 l green	45	15
560	A116	6.50 l plum	75	30

Issued to commemorate the 50th anniversary of the first Albanian secondary school.

Soldier on Guard Duty
A117

Liberation Monument, Tirana, Family and Policeman
A118

1960, May 12 ***Perf. 10½*** **Unwmkd.**

561	A117	1.50 l car rose	20	8
562	A117	11 l Prus bl	1.10	30

15th anniversary of the Frontier Guards.

1960, May 14

563	A118	1.50 l green	20	5
564	A118	8.50 l brown	1.00	30

15th anniversary of the People's Police.

Congress Site
A119

Pashko Vasa
A120

1960, Mar. 25

565	A119	2.50 l sepia	20	10
566	A119	7.50 l dl bl	90	25

40th anniversary, Congress of Louchnia.

1960, May 5

Designs: 1.50 l, Jani Vreto. 6.50 l, Sami Frasheri. 11 l, Page of statutes of association.

567	A120	1 l gray ol	5	3
568	A120	1.50 l brown	15	3
569	A120	6.50 l blue	65	12
570	A120	11 l rose red	1.10	25

Issued to commemorate the 80th anniversary (in 1959) of the Association of Albanian Authors.

Albanian Fighter and Cannon
A121

TU-104 Plane, Clock Tower, Tirana, and Kremlin, Moscow
A122

1960, Aug. 2 Litho. ***Perf. 10½***

571	A121	1.50 l ol brn	15	5
572	A121	2.50 l maroon	20	10
573	A121	5 l dk bl	65	20

Issued to commemorate the 40th anniversary of the Battle of Viona (against Italian troops.)

1960, Aug. 18

574	A122	1 l redsh brn	15	6
575	A122	7.50 l brt grnsh bl	1.00	18
576	A122	11.50 l gray	1.50	50

Issued to commemorate the 2nd anniversary of TU-104 flights, Moscow-Tirana.

Rising Sun and Federation Emblem
A123

Ali Kelmendi
A124

1960, Nov. 10 ***Perf. 10½*** **Unwmkd.**

577	A123	1.50 l ultra	15	6
578	A123	8.50 l red	75	20

Issued to commemorate the 15th anniversary of the International Youth Federation.

1960, Dec. 5 Litho. ***Perf. 10½***

579	A124	1.50 l pale gray grn	10	6
580	A124	11 l dl rose lake	80	20

Issued to honor Ali Kelmendi, communist leader, on his 60th birthday.

Flags of Russia and Albania and Clasped Hands
A125

Marx and Lenin
A126

1961, Jan. 10 ***Perf. 10½*** **Unwmkd.**

581	A125	2 l violet	15	6
582	A125	8 l dl red brn	80	20

Issued to commemorate the 15th anniversary of the Albanian-Soviet Friendship Society.

1961, Feb. 13 **Lithographed**

583	A126	2 l rose red	15	6
584	A126	8 l vio bl	90	20

Fourth Communist Party Congress.

Man from Shkoder
A127

Otter
A128

1961, Apr. 28 ***Perf. 10½***

Costumes: 1.50 l, Woman from Shkoder. 6.50 l, Man from Lume. 11 l, Woman from Mirdite.

585	A127	1 l slate	20	5
586	A127	1.50 l dl cl	40	6
587	A127	6.50 l ultra	1.25	25
588	A127	11 l red	2.25	50

1961, June 25 ***Perf. 10½*** **Unwmkd.**

Designs: 6.50 l, Badger. 11 l, Brown bear.

589	A128	2.50 l grysh bl	75	18
590	A128	6.50 l bl grn	1.75	45
591	A128	11 l dk red brn	3.00	75

Dalmatian Pelicans
A129

Cyclamen
A130

Birds: 7.50 l, Gray herons. 11 l, Little egret.

1961, Sept. 30 ***Perf. 14***

592	A129	1.50 l rose car, *pnksh*	60	20
593	A129	7.50 l vio, *bluish*	1.25	40
594	A129	11 l red brn, *pnksh*	3.25	60

1961, Oct. 27 **Lithographed**

Designs: 8 l, Forsythia. 11 l, Lily.

595	A130	1.50 l brt bl & lil rose	50	10
596	A130	8 l red lil & org	1.10	35
597	A130	11 l brt grn & car rose	2.25	60

Milosh G. Nikolla
A131

Flag with Marx and Lenin
A132

1961, Oct. 30 ***Perf. 14***

598	A131	50q vio brn	15	6
599	A131	8.50 l Prus grn	75	25

Issued to commemorate the 50th anniversary of the birth of Milosh Gjergj Nikolla, poet.

1961, Nov. 8

600	A132	2.50 l vermilion	20	10
601	A132	7.50 l dl red brn	75	30

Issued to commemorate the 20th anniversary of the founding of Albania's Communist Party.

Worker, Farm Woman and Emblem
A133

Yuri Gagarin and Vostok 1
A134

1961, Nov. 23 ***Perf. 14*** **Unwmkd.**

602	A133	2.50 l vio bl	20	12
603	A133	7.50 l rose cl	90	35

Issued to commemorate the 20th anniversary of the Albanian Workers' Party.

1962, Feb. 15 ***Perf. 14*** **Unwmkd.**

604	A134	50q blue	35	7
605	A134	4 l red lil	1.50	20
606	A134	11 l dk sl grn	3.00	90

Issued to commemorate the first manned space flight, made by Yuri A. Gagarin, Soviet astronaut, Apr. 12, 1961.

Nos. 604–606 were overprinted with an over-all yellow tint and with "POSTA AJRORE" (Air Mail) in maroon in 1962.

Price, set $50.

Petro Nini Luarasi
A135

Malaria Eradication Emblem
A136

1962, Feb. 28 **Lithographed**

607	A135	50q Prus bl	30	4
608	A135	8.50 l ol gray	1.25	20

Issued to commemorate the 50th anniversary (in 1961) of the death of Petro Nini Luarasi, Albanian patriot.

1962, Apr. 30 ***Perf. 14*** **Unwmkd.**

609	A136	1.50 l brt grn	10	6
610	A136	2.50 l brn red	15	8
611	A136	10 l red lil	60	30
612	A136	11 l blue	90	40

Issued for the World Health Organization drive to eradicate malaria.

A souvenir sheet, issued both perf. and imperf., contains one each of Nos. 609-612, with blue marginal inscription and U.N. emblem. Size: 88x106½mm.

Price $10 each.
Nos. 609-612 imperf., price, set $12.50.

Camomile
A137

Woman Diver
A138

1962, May 10

Medicinal Plants: 8 l, Linden. 11.50 l, Garden sage.

613	A137	50q gray vio, yel & grn	15	7
614	A137	8 l gray, yel & grn	75	25
615	A137	11.50 l bis, grn & pur	2.25	40

Price, imperf. set $15.

1962, May 31 ***Perf. 14***

Designs: 2.50 l, Pole vault. 3 l, Mt. Fuji and torch (horiz.). 9 l, Woman javelin thrower. 10 l, Shot putting.

616	A138	50q brt grnsh bl & blk	15	3
617	A138	2.50 l gldn brn & sep	20	7
618	A138	3 l bl & gray	45	8
619	A138	9 l rose car & dk brn	1.25	20
620	A138	10 l ol & blk	1.35	25
		Nos. 616-620 (5)	3.40	63

1964 Olympic Games, Tokyo.
Price, imperf. set $15.

Globe and Orbits
A139

Dog Laika and Sputnik 2
A140

Designs: 1.50 l, Rocket to the sun. 20 l, Lunik 3 photographing far side of the moon.

1962, June ***Perf. 14*** **Unwmkd.**

621	A139	50q vio & org	20	3
622	A140	1 l bl grn & brn	30	6
623	A140	1.50 l yel & ver	50	15
624	A139	20 l mag & bl	3.00	65

Russian space explorations.

Nos. 621-624 exist imperforate in changed colors.

Two miniature sheets exist (101x77mm.), each containing one 14-lek picturing Sputnik 1. The perforated 14-lek is yellow and brown; the imperf. red and brown. Marginal design in blue and black.

Soccer Game, Map of South America
A141

Design: 2.50 l, 15 l, Soccer game and globe as ball.

1962, July **Lithographed**

625	A141	1 l org & dk pur	15	3
626	A141	2.50 l emer & bluish grn	20	5
627	A141	6.50 l lt brn & pink	75	15
628	A141	15 l bluish grn & mar	1.50	50

Issued to commemorate the World Soccer Championships, Chile, May 30–June 17.

Nos. 625-628 exist imperforate in changed colors.

Two miniature sheets exist (67x49mm.), each containing a single 20-lek in design similar to A141. The perforated sheet is brown and green; the imperforate sheet, brown and orange.

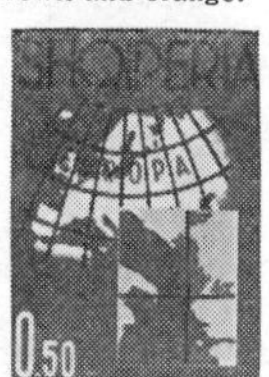

Map of Europe and Albania
A142

Woman of Dardhë
A143

Designs: 1 l, 2.50 l, Map of Adriatic Sea and Albania and Roman statue.

1962, Aug.

630	A142	50q multi	15	15
631	A142	1 l ultra & red	35	35
632	A142	2.50 l bl & red	1.50	1.50
633	A142	11 l multi	3.00	3.00

Issued for tourist propaganda. Imperforates in changed colors exist.

Miniature sheets containing a 7 l and 8 l stamp, perf. and imperf., exist.

1962, Sept.

Regional Costumes: 1 l, Man from Devoll. 2.50 l, Woman from Lunxheri. 14 l, Man from Gjirokastër.

635	A143	50q car, bl & pur	7	3
636	A143	1 l red brn & ocher	15	4
637	A143	2.50 l vio, yel grn & blk	30	12
638	A143	14 l red brn & pale grn	1.35	35

Price, imperf. set $10.

Chamois
A144

Ismail Qemali
A145

Animals: 1 l, Lynx (horiz.). 1.50 l, Wild boar (horiz.). 15 l, 20 l, Roe deer.

1962, Oct. 24 ***Perf. 14*** **Unwmkd.**

639	A144	50q sl grn & dk pur	25	5
640	A144	1 l org & blk	50	8
641	A144	1.50 l red brn & blk	75	12
642	A144	15 l yel ol & red brn	3.00	1.25

Miniature Sheet

643	A144	20 l yel ol & red brn	12.50	12.50

No. 643 measures 71½x89mm.

Imperfs. in changed colors, price #639-642 $10, #643 $17.50.

1962, Dec. 28 **Lithographed**

Designs: 1 l, Albanian eagle. 16 l, Eagle over fortress formed by "RPSH."

644	A145	1 l red & red brn	20	5
645	A145	3 l org brn & blk	35	10
646	A145	16 l dk car rose & blk	1.75	60

50th anniv. of independence

Imperfs. in changed colors, price, set $10.

Monument of October Revolution
A146

Henri Dunant, Cross, Globe and Nurse
A147

Design: 10 l, Lenin statue.

1963, Jan. 5 ***Perf. 14*** **Unwmkd.**

647	A146	5 l yel & dl vio	30	10
648	A146	10 l red org & blk	80	25

Issued to commemorate the 45th anniversary of the October Revolution (Russia, 1917).

1963, Jan 25 ***Perf. 14*** **Unwmkd.**

649	A147	1.50 l rose lake, red & blk	15	5
650	A147	2.50 l lt bl, red & blk	35	8
651	A147	6 l emer, red & blk	75	25
652	A147	10 l dl yel, red & blk	1.25	60

Issued to commemorate the centenary of the Geneva Conference, which led to the establishment of the International Red Cross in 1864.

Imperfs. in changed colors, price, set $10.

Stalin and Battle of Stalingrad
A148

Andrian G. Nikolayev
A149

1963, Feb. 2

653	A148	8 l dk grn & sl	1.00	25

Issued to commemorate the 20th anniversary of the Battle of Stalingrad. See No. C67.

1963, Feb. 28 **Lithographed**

Designs: 7.50 l, Vostoks 3 and 4 and globe (horiz.). 20 l, Pavel R. Popovich. 25 l, Nikolayev, Popovich and globe with trajectories.

654	A149	2.50 l vio bl & sep	25	5
655	A149	7.50 l lt bl & blk	65	15
656	A149	20 l vio & sep	2.25	60

Miniature Sheet

657	A149	25 l vio bl & sep	12.00	12.00

Issued to commemorate the first group space flight of Vostoks 3 and 4, Aug. 11–15, 1962. No. 657 measures 88x73mm.

Imperfs. in changed colors, price #654-656 $8, #657 $13.50.

"Albania" Decorating Police Officer
A150

Polyphylla Fullo
A151

1963, Mar. 20 ***Perf. 14*** **Unwmkd.**

658	A150	2.50 l crim, mag & blk	30	15
659	A150	7.50 l org ver, dk red & blk	1.00	22

20th anniversary of the security police.

1963, Mar. 20

Beetles: 1.50 l, Lucanus cervus. 8 l, Procerus gigas. 10 l, Cicindela Albanica.

660	A151	50q ol grn & brn	15	3
661	A151	1.50 l bl & brn	30	10
662	A151	8 l dl rose & blk vio	1.50	50
663	A151	10 l brt cit & blk	2.00	85

1913 Stamp and Postmark
A152

Design: 10 l, Stamps of 1913, 1937 and 1962.

1963, May 5

664	A152	5 l yel, buff, bl & blk	75	20
665	A152	10 l car rose, grn & blk	1.35	30

50th anniversary of Albanian stamps.

Boxer
A153

Crested Grebe
A154

Designs: 3 l, Basketball baskets. 5 l, Athletes and umpire. 6 l, Bicyclists. 9 l, Gymnast. 15 l, Hands holding torch, and map of Japan.

1963, May 25 ***Perf. 13½***

666	A153	2 l yel, blk & red brn	20	3
667	A153	3 l ocher, brn & bl	20	5
668	A153	5 l gray bl, red brn & brn	50	12
669	A153	6 l gray, dk gray & grn	80	30
670	A153	9 l rose, red brn & bl	1.25	40
		Nos. 666-670 (5)	2.95	90

Miniature Sheet

671	A153	15 l lt bl, car, blk & brn	6.00	6.00

Issued to publicize the 1964 Olympic Games in Tokyo. No. 671 contains one stamp (31x49mm.) with ocher border. Size: 60x80mm.

Price, imperfs. #666-670 $5, #671 $6.

1963, Apr. 20 Litho. *Perf. 14*

Birds: 3 l, Golden eagle. 6.50 l, Gray partridges. 11 l, Capercaillie.

672	A154	50q multi	15	7
673	A154	3 l multi	60	15
674	A154	6.50 l multi	1.25	45
675	A154	11 l multi	2.25	1.00

Soldier and Building

A155

Designs: 2.50 l, Soldier with pack, ship and plane. 5 l, Soldier in battle. 6 l, Soldier and bulldozer.

1963, July 10 *Perf. 12* Unwmkd.

676	A155	1.50 l brick red, yel & blk	15	3
677	A155	2.50 l bl, ocher & brn	20	6
678	A155	5 l bluish grn, gray & blk	45	15
679	A155	6 l red brn, buff & bl	65	20

Albanian army, 20th anniversary.

Maj. Yuri A. Gagarin

A156

Designs: 5 l, Maj. Gherman Titov. 7 l, Maj. Andrian G. Nikolayev. 11 l, Lt. Col. Pavel R. Popovich. 14 l, Lt. Col. Valeri Bykovski. 20 l, Lt. Valentina Tereshkova.

1963, July 30

Portraits in Yellow and Black

680	A156	3 l brt pur	30	10
681	A156	5 l dl bl	45	15
682	A156	7 l gray	70	20
683	A156	11 l dp cl	1.00	30
684	A156	14 l bl grn	1.50	60
685	A156	20 l ultra	2.25	1.00
		Nos. 680-685 (6)	6.20	2.35

Man's conquest of space.
Price, imperf. set $12.50.

Volleyball

A157

Sports: 3 l, Weight lifting. 5 l, Soccer. 7 l, Boxing. 8 l, Rowing.

1963, Aug. 31 *Perf. 12x12½*

686	A157	2 l cit, red & blk	15	5
687	A157	3 l dk red, bis & blk	25	8
688	A157	5 l emer, org & blk	50	20
689	A157	7 l dp pink, emer & blk	1.10	30
690	A157	8 l dp bl, dp pink & blk	1.25	35
		Nos. 686-690 (5)	3.25	98

European championships.

Imperfs. in changed colors, price set $12.50.

Papilio Podalirius

A158

Various Butterflies and Moths in Natural Colors

1963, Sept. 29 Lithographed

691	A158	1 l red	20	3
692	A158	2 l blue	30	10
693	A158	4 l dl lil	40	15
694	A158	5 l pale grn	65	20
695	A158	8 l bister	1.35	35
696	A158	10 l lt bl	1.75	45
		Nos. 691-696 (6)	4.65	1.28

Oil Refinery, Cerrik A159 — Flag and Shield A160

Designs: 2.50 l, Food processing plant, Tirana (horiz.). 30 l, Fruit canning plant. 50 l, Tannery (horiz.).

1963, Nov. 15 *Perf. 14* Unwmkd.

697	A159	2.50 l rose red, *pnksh*	35	8
698	A159	20 l sl grn, *grnsh*	1.10	35
699	A159	30 l dl pur, *grysh*	2.50	65
700	A159	50 l ocher, *yel*	3.00	1.25

Industrial development in Albania.

1963, Nov. 24 *Perf. 12½x12*

701	A160	2 l grnsh bl, blk, ocher & red	35	6
702	A160	8 l bl, blk, ocher & red	1.00	60

1st Congress of Army Aid Assn.

Chinese, Caucasian and Negro Men

A161

1963, Dec. 10 *Perf. 12x11½*

703	A161	3 l bis & blk	35	15
704	A161	5 l bis & ultra	60	20
705	A161	7 l bis & vio	90	45

Issued to commemorate the 15th anniversary of the Universal Declaration of Human Rights.

Slalom Ascent

A162

Lenin

A163

Designs: 50q, Bobsled (horiz.). 6.50 l, Ice hockey (horiz.). 12.50 l, Women's figure skating. No. 709A, Ski jumper.

1963, Dec. 25 *Perf. 14*

706	A162	50q grnsh bl & blk	10	3
707	A162	2.50 l red, gray & blk	15	6
708	A162	6.50 l yel, blk & gray	65	15
709	A162	12.50 l red, blk & yel grn	1.25	45

Miniature Sheet

709A	A162	12.50 l multi	4.50	4.50

Issued to publicize the 9th Winter Olympic Games, Innsbruck, Jan. 29–Feb. 9, 1964. Size of No. 709A: 56x75mm.

Imperfs. in changed colors, price #706-709 $15, #709A $17.50.

1964, Jan. 21 *Perf. 12½x12*

710	A163	5 l gray & bis	30	12
711	A163	10 l gray & ocher	90	30

40th anniversary, death of Lenin.

Hurdling A164 — Sturgeon A165

Designs: 3 l, Track (horiz.). 6.50 l, Rifle shooting (horiz.). 8 l, Basketball.

Perf. 12½x12, 12x12½

1964, Jan. 30 Lithographed

712	A164	2.50 l pale vio & ultra	15	6
713	A164	3 l lt grn & red brn	30	15
714	A164	6.50 l bl & cl	45	20
715	A164	8 l lt bl & ocher	90	35

Issued to commemorate the 1st Games of the New Emerging Forces, GANEFO, Jakarta, Indonesia, Nov. 10–22, 1963.

1964, Feb. 26 *Perf. 14* Unwmkd.

Designs: Various fish.

Multicolored

716	A165	50q *shown*	10	3
717	A165	1 l *Gilthead*	15	3
718	A165	1.50 l *Striped mullet*	25	10
719	A165	2.50 l *Carp*	40	15
720	A165	6.50 l *Mackerel*	1.00	30
721	A165	10 l *Lake Ohrid trout*	1.75	60
		Nos. 716-721 (6)	3.65	1.21

Red Squirrel

A166

Designs: Wild animals.

1964, March 28 *Perf. 12½x12*

Multicolored

722	A166	1 l *shown*	10	3
723	A166	1.50 l *Beech marten*	20	4
724	A166	2 l *Red fox*	30	5
725	A166	2.50 l *Hedgehog*	40	6
726	A166	3 l *Hare*	45	15
727	A166	5 l *Jackal*	80	20
728	A166	7 l *Wildcat*	1.00	35
729	A166	8 l *Wolf*	1.75	50
		Nos. 722-729 (8)	5.00	1.38

Lighting Olympic Torch

A167

Designs: 5 l, Torch and globes. 7 l, 15 l, Olympic flag and Mt. Fuji. 10 l, National Stadium, Tokyo.

1964, May 18 *Perf. 12x12½*

730	A167	3 l lt yel grn, yel & buff	20	6
731	A167	5 l red & vio bl	30	10
732	A167	7 l lt bl, ultra & yel	50	15
733	A167	10 l org, bl & vio	90	45

Miniature Sheet

734	A167	15 l lt bl, ultra & org	7.50	7.50

Issued to publicize the 18th Olympic Games, Tokyo, October 10–25, 1964. No. 734 contains one stamp (49x62mm.) with orange border. Size: 80x90mm.

Imperfs. in changed colors, price #730-733 $7.50, #734 $10.

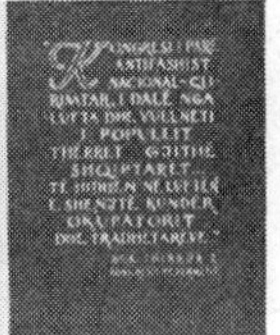

Partisans—A168

Designs: 5 l, Arms of Albania. 8 l, Enver Hoxha.

Perf. 12½x12

1964, May 24 Litho. Unwmkd.

735	A168	2 l org, red & blk	15	6
736	A168	5 l multi	30	18
737	A168	8 l red brn, blk & red	75	35

Issued to commemorate the 20th anniversary of the National Anti-Fascist Congress of Liberation, Permet, May 24, 1944. The label attached to each stamp, without perforations between, carries a quotation from the 1944 Congress.

Albanian Flag and Revolutionists

A169

Full Moon

A170

Perf. 12½x12

1964, June 10 Litho. Unwmkd.

738	A169	2.50 l red & gray	15	10
739	A169	7.50 l lil rose & gray	60	35

Issued to commemorate the 40th anniversary of the Albanian revolution of 1924.

1964, June 27 *Perf. 12x12½*

Designs: 5 l, New moon. 8 l, Half moon. 11 l, Waning moon. 15 l, Far side of moon.

740	A170	1 l pur & yel	20	3
741	A170	5 l vio & yel	50	15
742	A170	8 l bl & yel	85	35
743	A170	11 l grn & yel	1.10	60

Miniature Sheet
Perf. 12 on 2 sides

744	A170	15 l ultra & yel	7.00	7.00

No. 744 contains one stamp (35x36mm.) with bister border, perforated at top and bottom. Size: 66½x79mm.

Imperfs. in changed colors, price #740-743 $6, #744 $9.

No. 733 with Added Inscription: "Rimini 25-VI-64"

1964 ***Perf. 12x12½***

745	A167	10 l org, bl & vio	2.25	2.00

Issued to commemorate the "Toward Tokyo 1964" Philatelic Exhibition at Rimini, Italy, June 25-July 6.

Wren
A171

Birds: 1 l, Penduline titmouse. 2.50 l, Green woodpecker. 3 l, Tree creeper. 4 l, Nuthatch. 5 l, Great titmouse. 6 l, Goldfinch. 18 l, Oriole.

1964, July 31 ***Perf. 12x12½***

746	A171	50q multi	10	3
747	A171	1 l org & multi	15	3
748	A171	2.50 l multi	20	4
749	A171	3 l bl & multi	30	7
750	A171	4 l yel & multi	45	7
751	A171	5 l bl & multi	75	15
752	A171	6 l lt vio & multi	1.10	30
753	A171	18 l pink & multi	2.25	1.00
		Nos. 746-753 (8)	5.30	1.69

Running and Gymnastics
A172

Sport: 2 l, Weight lifting—judo. 3 l, Equestrian—bicycling. 4 l, Soccer—water polo. 5 l, Wrestling—boxing. 6 l, Pentathlon—hockey. 7 l, Swimming—sailing. 8 l, Basketball—netball. 9 l, Rowing—canoeing. 10 l, Fencing—pistol shooting. 20 l, Three winners.

Perf. 12x12½

1964, Sept. 25 Litho. Unwmkd.

754	A172	1 l lt bl, rose & emer	10	3
755	A172	2 l bis brn, bluish grn & vio	15	3
756	A172	3 l vio, red org & ol bis	20	5
757	A172	4 l grnsh bl, ol & ultra	30	7
758	A172	5 l grnsh bl, car & pale lil	45	25
759	A172	6 l dk bl, org & lt bl	60	30
760	A172	7 l dk bl, lt ol & org	75	45
761	A172	8 l emer, gray & yel	90	45
762	A172	9 l bl, yel & lil rose	1.25	60
763	A172	10 l brt grn, org brn & yel grn	2.25	90
		Nos. 754-763 (10)	6.95	3.13

Miniature Sheet
Perf. 12

764	A172	20 l vio & lem	6.50	6.50

Issued to commemorate the 18th Olympic Games, Tokyo, Oct. 10-25. No. 764 contains one stamp (41x68mm.) with violet border. Size: 55x82mm.

Imperfs. in changed colors, price #754-763 $10, #764 $11.50.

Arms of Republic of China
A173

Mao Tse-tung and Flag
A174

Perf. 11½x12, 12x11½

1964, Oct. 1

765	A173	7 l blk, red & yel	65	30
766	A174	8 l blk, red & yel	85	40

Issued to commemorate the 15th anniversary of the People's Republic of China.

Karl Marx
A175

Jeronim de Rada
A176

Designs: 5 l, St. Martin's Hall, London. 8 l, Friedrich Engels.

1964, Nov. 5 ***Perf. 12x11½***

767	A175	2 l red, lt vio & blk	45	10
768	A175	5 l gray bl	1.00	30
769	A175	8 l ocher, blk & red	1.75	50

Centenary of First Socialist International.

1964, Nov. 15 ***Perf. 12½x11½***

770	A176	7 l sl grn	75	25
771	A176	8 l dl vio	1.00	45

Issued to commemorate the 150th anniversary of the birth of Jeronim de Rada, poet.

Arms of Albania
A177

Factories
A178

Designs: 3 l, Combine harvester. 4 l, Woman chemist. 10 l, Hands holding Constitution, hammer and sickle.

Perf. 11½x12, 12x11½

1964, Nov. 29

772	A177	1 l multi	5	3
773	A178	2 l red, yel & vio bl	12	6
774	A178	3 l red, yel & brn	25	8
775	A178	4 l red, yel & gray grn	35	15
776	A177	10 l red, bl & blk	1.10	45
		Nos. 772-776 (5)	1.87	77

20th anniversary of liberation.

Planet Mercury
A179

Planets: 2 l, Venus and rocket. 3 l, Earth, moon and rocket. 4 l, Mars and rocket. 5 l, Jupiter. 6 l, Saturn. 7 l, Uranus. 8 l, Neptune. 9 l, Pluto. 15 l, Solar system and rocket.

1964, Dec. 15 ***Perf. 12x12½***

777	A179	1 l yel & pur	15	3
778	A179	2 l multi	15	3
779	A179	3 l multi	25	3
780	A179	4 l multi	35	10
781	A179	5 l yel, dk pur & brn	45	10
782	A179	6 l lt grn, vio brn & yel	60	20
783	A179	7 l yel & grn	70	30
784	A179	8 l yel & vio	90	35
785	A179	9 l lt grn, yel & blk	1.10	35
		Nos. 777-785 (9)	4.65	1.49

Miniature Sheet
Perf. 12 on 2 sides

786	A179	15 l car, bl, yel & grn	8.00	8.00

No. 786 contains one stamp (62x51mm.) with yellow marginal inscription, perforated at top and bottom. Size: 87x72mm.

Imperfs. in changed colors, price #777-785 $7.50, #786 $9.

European Chestnut
A180

Symbols of Industry
A181

1965, Jan. 25 ***Perf. 11½x12***

Multicolored

787	A180	1 l *shown*	5	3
788	A180	2 l *Medlars*	15	4
789	A180	3 l *Persimmon*	30	15
790	A180	4 l *Pomegranate*	35	15
791	A180	5 l *Quince*	50	25
792	A180	10 l *Orange*	1.25	45
		Nos. 787-792 (6)	2.60	1.07

1965, Feb. 20

Designs: 5 l, Books, triangle and compass. 8 l, Beach, trees and hotel.

793	A181	2 l blk, car rose & pink	40	35
794	A181	5 l yel, gray & blk	1.25	90
795	A181	8 l blk, vio bl & lt bl	1.75	1.50

Issued to commemorate the 20th anniversary of professional trade associations.

Water Buffalo
A182

Various designs: Water buffalo.

1965, Mar. ***Perf. 12x11½***

796	A182	1 l lt yel grn, yel & brn blk	5	3
797	A182	2 l lt bl, dk gray & blk	35	10
798	A182	3 l yel, brn & grn	60	20
799	A182	7 l brt grn, yel & brn blk	1.40	50
800	A182	12 l pale lil, dk brn & ind	2.00	85
		Nos. 796-800 (5)	4.40	1.68

Mountain View, Valbona
A183

Views: 1.50 l, Seashore. 3 l, Glacier and peak (vert.). 4 l, Gorge (vert.). 5 l, Mountain peaks. 9 l, Lake and hills.

1965, Mar. Lithographed ***Perf. 12***

801	A183	1.50 l multi	35	15
802	A183	2.50 l multi	50	25
803	A183	3 l multi	65	30
804	A183	4 l multi	75	40
805	A183	5 l multi	1.00	50
806	A183	9 l multi	1.75	85
		Nos. 801-806 (6)	5.00	2.45

Frontier Guard
A184

Small-bore Rifle Shooting, Prone
A185

1965, Apr. 25 **Unwmkd.**

807	A184	2.50 l lt bl & multi	45	20
808	A184	12.50 l ultra & multi	2.00	90

20th anniversary of the Frontier Guards.

1965, May 10

Designs: 2 l, Rifle shooting, standing. 3 l, Target over map of Europe, showing Bucharest. 4 l, Pistol shooting. 15 l, Rifle shooting, kneeling.

809	A185	1 l lil, car rose, blk & brn	5	3
810	A185	2 l bl, blk, brn & vio bl	15	5
811	A185	3 l pink & car rose	25	6
812	A185	4 l bis, blk & vio brn	35	15
813	A185	15 l brt grn, brn & vio brn	1.75	75
		Nos. 809-813 (5)	2.55	1.04

Issued to commemorate the European Shooting Championships, Bucharest.

ITU Emblem, Old and New Communications Equipment
A186

Col. Pavel Belyayev
A187

1965, May 17 *Perf. 12½x12*

814	A186	2.50 l brt grn, blk & lil rose	45	10
815	A186	12.50 l vio, blk & brt bl	2.25	60

Issued to commemorate the centenary of the International Telecommunication Union.

1965, June 15 *Perf. 12*

Designs: 2 l, Voskhod II. 6.50 l, Lt. Col. Alexei Leonov. 20 l, Leonov floating in space.

816	A187	1.50 l lt bl & brn	15	3
817	A187	2 l dk bl, lt vio & lt ultra	20	3
818	A187	6.50 l lil & brn	50	20
819	A187	20 l chlky bl, yel & blk	1.50	60

Miniature Sheet
Perf. 12 on 2 sides

820	A187	20 l brt bl, org & blk	7.00	7.00

Issued to commemorate the space flight of Voskhod II and the first man walking in space, Lt. Col. Alexei Leonov. No. 820 contains one stamp (size: 51x59½mm.), orange border, perforated at top and bottom; size: 72x85mm.

Imperf., brt grn background, price $6.

Marx and Lenin
A188

1965, June 21 *Perf. 12*

821	A188	2.50 l dk brn, red & yel	40	5
822	A188	7.50 l sl grn, org ver & buff	1.25	30

Issued to commemorate the 6th Conference of Postal Ministers of Communist Countries, Peking, June 21–July 15.

Mother and Child
A189

Designs: 2 l, Pioneers. 3 l, Boy and girl at play (horiz.). 4 l, Child on beach. 15 l, Girl with book.

Perf. 12½x12, 12x12½

1965, June 29 Litho. Unwmkd.

823	A189	1 l brt bl, rose lil & blk	4	3
824	A189	2 l sal, vio & blk	15	10
825	A189	3 l grn, org & vio	25	12
826	A189	4 l multi	35	15
827	A189	15 l lil rose, brn & ocher	1.75	60
		Nos. 823-827 (5)	2.54	1.00

Issued for International Children's Day.

Statue of Magistrate
A190

Fuchsia
A191

1965, July 20 *Perf. 12*

Designs: 1 l, Amphora. 2 l, Illyrian armor. 3 l, Mosaic (horiz.). 15 l, Torso, Apollo statue.

828	A190	1 l lt ol, org & brn	10	3
829	A190	2 l gray grn, grn & brn	25	4
830	A190	3 l tan, brn, car & lil	30	15
831	A190	4 l grn, bis & brn	50	20
832	A190	15 l gray & pale cl	1.75	90
		Nos. 828-832 (5)	2.90	1.32

1965, Aug. 11 *Perf. 12½x12*

Flowers: 2 l, Cyclamen. 3 l, Tiger lily. 3.50 l, Iris. 4 l, Dahlia. 4.50 l, Hydrangea. 5 l, Rose. 7 l, Tulips.

833	A191	1 l multi	4	3
834	A191	2 l multi	15	3
835	A191	3 l multi	30	4
836	A191	3.50 l multi	45	5
837	A191	4 l multi	45	8
838	A191	4.50 l multi	50	15
839	A191	5 l multi	60	30
840	A191	7 l multi	90	45
		Nos. 833-840 (8)	3.39	1.13

Nos. 698–700 Surcharged New Value and Two Bars

1965, Aug. 16 *Perf. 14*

841	A159	5q on 30 l dl pur, *grysh*	7	3
842	A159	15q on 30 l dl pur, *grysh*	15	3
843	A159	25q on 50 l ocher, *yel*	30	10
844	A159	80q on 50 l ocher, *yel*	90	35
845	A159	1.10 l on 20 l sl grn, *grnsh*	1.75	60
846	A159	2 l on 20 l sl grn, *grnsh*	2.50	1.00
		Nos. 841-846 (6)	5.67	2.11

White Stork
A192

"Homecoming," by Bukurosh Sejdini
A193

Migratory Birds: 20q, Cuckoo. 30q, Hoopoe. 40q, European bee-eater. 50q, European nightjar. 1.50 l, Quail.

1965, Aug. 31 *Perf. 12*

847	A192	10q yel, blk & gray	5	3
848	A192	20q brt pink, blk & dk bl	20	4
849	A192	30q vio, blk & bis	30	7
850	A192	40q emer, blk yel & org	40	15
851	A192	50q ultra, brn & red brn	75	30
852	A192	1.50 l bis, red brn & dp org	2.25	90
		Nos. 847-852 (6)	3.95	1.49

1965, Sept. 26 Litho. *Perf. 12x12½*

853	A193	25q ol blk	50	15
854	A193	65q bl blk	1.25	40
855	A193	1.10 l black	2.25	70

Second war veterans' meeting.

Hunter and Capercaillie
A194

Oleander
A195

Hunting: 20q, Deer. 30q, Pheasant. 40q, Mallards. 50q, Boar. 1 l, Rabbit.

1965, Oct. 6 Litho. Unwmkd.

856	A194	10q gray & multi	6	3
857	A194	20q lt grn, red brn & dk brn	20	3
858	A194	30q bl & multi	30	10
859	A194	40q rose lil & grn	40	15
860	A194	50q lt vio bl, blk & brn	75	20
861	A194	1 l cit, ol & brn	1.25	60
		Nos. 856-861 (6)	2.96	1.11

1965, Oct. 26 *Perf. 12½x12*

Flowers: 20q, Forget-me-nots. 30q, Pink. 40q, White water lily. 50q, Bird's foot. 1 l, Corn poppy.

862	A195	10q brt bl, grn & car rose	4	3
863	A195	20q org red, bl, brn & grn	20	5
864	A195	30q vio, car rose & grn	30	10
865	A195	40q emer, yel & blk	40	10
866	A195	50q org brn, yel & grn	75	20
867	A195	1 l yel grn, blk & rose red	1.25	60
		Nos. 862-867 (6)	2.94	1.08

Hotel Turizmi, Fier
A196

Freighter "Teuta"
A197

Buildings: 10q, Hotel, Peshkopi. 15q, Sanatorium, Tirana. 25q, Rest home, Pogradec. 65q, Partisan Sports Arena, Tirana. 80q, Rest home, Mali Dajt. 1.10 l, Culture House, Tirana. 1.60 l, Hotel Adriatik, Durrës. 2 l, Migjeni Theater, Shkoder. 3 l, Alexander Moissi House of Culture, Durrës.

1965, Oct. *Perf. 12x12½*

868	A196	5q bl & blk	3	3
869	A196	10q ocher & blk	4	3
870	A196	15q dl grn & blk	15	3
871	A196	25q vio & blk	30	10
872	A196	65q lt brn & blk	75	20
873	A196	80q yel grn & blk	95	30
874	A196	1.10 l lil & blk	1.25	45
875	A196	1.60 l lt vio bl & blk	1.75	60
876	A196	2 l dl rose & blk	2.25	80
877	A196	3 l gray & blk	3.25	1.25
		Nos. 868-877 (10)	10.72	3.79

1965, Nov. 16

Ships: 20q, Raft. 30q, Sailing ship, 19th century. 40q, Sailing ship, 18th century. 50q, Freighter "Vlora." 1 l, Illyric galleys.

878	A197	10q brt grn & dk grn	5	3
879	A197	20q ol bis & dk grn	20	3
880	A197	30q lt & dp ultra	30	6
881	A197	40q vio & dp vio	40	8
882	A197	50q pink & dk red	75	30
883	A197	1 l bis & brn	1.25	60
		Nos. 878-883 (6)	2.95	1.10

Brown Bear
A198

Basketball and Players
A199

Designs: Various Albanian bears. 50q, 55q, 60q, horizontal.

1965, Dec. 7 *Perf. 11½x12*

884	A198	10q bis & dk brn	10	3
885	A198	20q pale brn & dk brn	25	3
886	A198	30q bis, dk brn & car	30	10
887	A198	35q pale brn & dk brn	40	15
888	A198	40q bis & dk brn	60	15
889	A198	50q bis & dk brn	75	20
890	A198	55q bis & dk brn	90	25
891	A198	60q pale brn, dk brn & car	1.10	35
		Nos. 884-891 (8)	4.40	1.26

1965, Dec. 15 Litho. *Perf. 12½x12*

Designs: 10q, Games' emblem (map of Albania and basket). 30q, 50q, Players with ball (diff. designs). 1.40 l, Basketball medal on ribbon.

892	A199	10q bl, yel & car	5	3
893	A199	20q rose lil, lt brn & blk	20	3
894	A199	30q bis, lt brn, red & blk	30	10
895	A199	50q lt grn, lt brn & blk	75	20
896	A199	1.40 l rose, blk, brn & yel	1.75	45
		Nos. 892-896 (5)	3.05	81

Issued to commemorate the Seventh Balkan Basketball Championships, Tirana, Dec. 15–19.

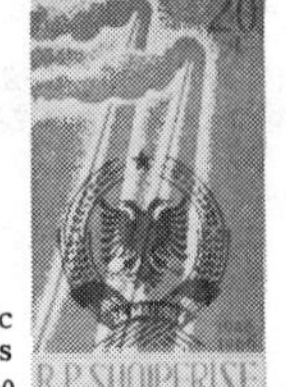

Arms of Republic and Smokestacks
A200

Designs (Arms and): 10q, Book. 30q, Wheat. 60q, Book, hammer and sickle. 80q, Factories.

1966, Jan. 11 Litho. *Perf. 11½x12*

Coat of Arms in Gold

897	A200	10q crim & brn	5	3
898	A200	20q bl & vio bl	10	3
899	A200	30q org yel & brn	20	7
900	A200	60q yel grn & brt grn	40	20
901	A200	80q crim & brn	1.00	30
		Nos. 897-901 (5)	1.75	63

Issued to commemorate the 20th anniversary of the Albanian People's Republic.

Cow
A201

Perf. 12½x12, 12x12½

1966, Feb. 25

Multicolored

902 A201 10q *shown* 10 3
903 A201 20q *Pig* 20 3
904 A201 30q *Ewe & lamb* 30 10
905 A201 35q *Ram* 35 10
906 A201 40q *Dog* 40 10
907 A201 50q *Cat*, vert. 50 20
908 A201 55q *Horse*, vert. 75 30
909 A201 60q *Ass*, vert. 90 35
Nos. 902-909 (8) 3.50 1.21

Soccer Player and Map of Uruguay
A202

Andon Zako Cajupi
A203

Designs: 5q, Globe in form of soccer ball. 15q, Player and map of Italy. 20q, Goalkeeper and map of France. 25q, Player and map of Brazil. 30q, Player and map of Switzerland. 35q, Player and map of Sweden. 40q, Player and map of Chile. 50q, Player and map of Great Britain. 70q, World Championship cup and ball.

1966, March 20 Litho. *Perf. 12*

910 A202 5q gray & dp org 3 3
911 A202 10q lt brn, bl & vio 10 3
912 A202 15q cit, dk bl & brt bl 12 3
913 A202 20q org, vio bl & brt bl 15 3
914 A202 25q sal & sep 20 3
915 A202 30q lt yel grn & brn 25 10
916 A202 35q lt ultra & emer 30 15
917 A202 40q pink & brn 35 15
918 A202 50q pale grn, mag & rose red 60 30
919 A202 70q gray, brn, yel & blk 90 45
Nos. 910-919 (10) 3.00 1.30

Issued to publicize the World Cup Soccer Championship, Wembley, England, July 11–30.

1966, March 27 Unwmkd.

920 A203 40q bluish blk 25 7
921 A203 1.10 l dk grn 75 25

Issued to commemorate the centenary of the birth of the poet Andon Zako Cajupi.

Painted Lady

A204

WHO Headquarters, Geneva, and Emblem

A205

Designs: 20q, Blue dragonfly. 30q, Cloudless sulphur butterfly. 35q, 40q, Splendid dragonfly. 50q, Machaon swallowtail. 55q, Sulphur butterfly. 60q, White-marbled butterfly.

1966, Apr. 21 Litho. *Perf. 11½x12*

922 A204 10q multi 10 3
923 A204 20q yel & multi 15 3
924 A204 30q yel & multi 25 5
925 A204 35q sky bl & multi 30 10
926 A204 40q multi 35 10
927 A204 50q rose & multi 45 20
928 A204 55q multi 65 20
929 A204 60q multi 75 30
Nos. 922-929 (8) 3.00 1.01

Perf. 12x12½, 12½x12

1966, May 3 Lithographed

Designs (WHO Emblem and): 35q, Ambulance and stretcher bearers (vert.). 60q, Albanian mother and nurse weighing infant (vert.). 80q, X-ray machine and hospital.

930 A205 25q lt bl & blk 25 4
931 A205 35q sal & ultra 35 6
932 A205 60q lt grn, bl & red 65 15
933 A205 80q yel, bl, grn & lt brn 1.10 35

Issued to commemorate the inauguration of the World Health Organization Headquarters, Geneva.

Bird's Foot Starfish
A206

Designs: 25q, Starfish. 35q, Brittle star. 45q, But-thorn starfish. 50q, Starfish. 60q, Sea cucumber. 70q, Sea urchin.

1966, May 10 *Perf. 12x12½*

934 A206 15q multi 15 3
935 A206 25q multi 25 4
936 A206 35q multi 30 10
937 A206 45q multi 35 10
938 A206 50q multi 45 15
939 A206 60q multi 75 20
940 A206 70q multi 90 30
Nos. 934-940 (7) 3.15 92

Luna 10
A207

Designs: 30q, 80q, Trajectory of Luna 10, earth and moon.

1966, June 10 *Perf. 12x12½*

941 A207 20q bl, yel & blk 30 4
942 A207 30q yel grn, blk & bl 45 15
943 A207 70q vio, yel & blk 75 25
944 A207 80q yel, vio, grn & blk 1.25 25

Issued to commemorate the launching of the first artificial moon satellite, Luna 10, April 3, 1966.

Jules Rimet Cup and Soccer
A208

Designs: Various scenes of soccer play.

1966, July 12 Litho. *Perf. 12x12½*

Black Inscriptions

945 A208 10q ocher & lil 5 3
946 A208 20q lt bl & cit 15 3
947 A208 30q brick red & Prus bl 25 4
948 A208 35q lt ultra & rose 30 10
949 A208 40q yel grn & lt red brn 35 15
950 A208 50q lt red brn & yel grn 45 15
951 A208 55q rose lil & yel grn 60 15
952 A208 60q dp rose & ocher 90 20
Nos. 945-952 (8) 3.05 85

Issued to commemorate the World Cup Soccer Championship, Wembley, England, July 11–30.

Water Level Map of Albania
A209

Designs: 30q, Water measure and fields. 70q, Turbine and pylon. 80q, Hydrological decade emblem.

1966, July *Perf. 12½x12*

953 A209 20q brick red, blk & org 15 8
954 A209 30q emer, blk & lt brn 25 15
955 A209 70q brt vio & blk 75 35
956 A209 80q brt bl, org, yel & blk 90 40

Issued to publicize the Hydrological Decade (UNESCO), 1965–74.

Greek Turtle—A210

Designs: 15q, Grass snake. 25q, European pond turtle. 30q, Wall lizard. 35q, Wall gecko. 45q, Emerald lizard. 50q, Slowworm. 90q, Horned viper (or sand viper).

1966, Aug. 10 Litho. *Perf. 12½x12*

957 A210 10q gray & multi 10 3
958 A210 15q yel & multi 20 3
959 A210 25q ultra & multi 30 3
960 A210 30q multi 35 5
961 A210 35q multi 45 10
962 A210 45q multi 50 15
963 A210 50q org & multi 65 15
964 A210 90q lil & multi 1.75 65
Nos. 957-964 (8) 4.30 1.19

Persian Cat
A211

Cats: 10q, Siamese (vert.). 15q, European tabby (vert.). 25q, Black kitten. 60q, 65q, 80q, Various Persians.

Perf. 12x12½, 12½x12

1966, Sept. 20 Lithographed

965 A211 10q multi 10 3
966 A211 15q blk, sep & car 15 3
967 A211 25q blk, dk & lt brn 20 4
968 A211 45q blk, org & yel 35 10
969 A211 60q blk, brn & yel 60 30
970 A211 65q multi 75 30
971 A211 80q blk, gray & yel 1.00 45
Nos. 965-971 (7) 3.15 1.25

Pjeter Budi
A212

1966, Oct. 5 *Perf. 12x12½*

972 A212 25q buff & sl grn 15 6
973 A212 1.75 l gray & dl cl 1.25 60

Issued to honor Pjeter Budi, writer.

UNESCO Emblem
A213

Designs (UNESCO Emblem and): 15q, Open book, rose and school. 25q, Male folk dancers. 1.55 l, Jug, column and old building.

1966, Oct. 20 Litho. *Perf. 12*

974 A213 5q lt gray & multi 10 3
975 A213 15q dp bl & multi 20 10
976 A213 25q gray & multi 30 10
977 A213 1.55 l multi 2.25 55

Issued to commemorate the 20th anniversary of UNESCO (United Nations Educational, Scientific and Cultural Organization).

Hand Holding Book with Pictures of Marx, Engels, Lenin and Stalin
A214

Hammer and Sickle, Party Emblem in Sunburst
A215

Designs: 25q, Map of Albania, hammer and sickle, symbols of agriculture and industry. 65q, Symbolic grain and factories. 95q, Fists holding rifle, spade, axe, sickle and book.

1966, Nov. 1 Litho. *Perf. 11½x12*

978 A214 15q ver & gold 15 3
979 A214 25q multi 20 4
980 A214 65q brn, brn org & gold 50 20
981 A214 95q yel & multi 1.00 45

Issued to commemorate the 5th Congress of the Albanian Communist Party.

1966, Nov. 8

Designs: 25q, Partisan and sunburst. 65q, Steel worker and blast furnace. 95q, Combine harvester, factories, and pylon.

982 A215 15q org & multi 15 3
983 A215 25q red & multi 20 3
984 A215 65q multi 50 20
985 A215 95q bl & multi 1.00 45

Issued to commemorate the 25th anniversary of the founding of the Albanian Workers Party.

Russian Wolfhound—A216

Dogs: 15q, Sheep dog. 25q, English setter. 45q, English springer spaniel. 60q, Bulldog. 65q, Saint Bernard. 80q, Dachshund.

1966 Litho. *Perf. 12½x12*

986	A216	10q grn & multi	15	3
987	A216	15q multi	20	3
988	A216	25q lil & multi	35	15
989	A216	45q rose & multi	60	15
990	A216	60q brn & multi	85	20
991	A216	65q ultra & multi	90	50
992	A216	80q bl grn & multi	1.50	60
		Nos. 986-992 (7)	4.55	1.66

Ndre Mjeda
A217

Proclamation
A218

1966 *Perf. 12½x12*

993	A217	25q brt bl & dk brn	20	10
994	A217	1.75 l brt grn & dk brn	1.50	45

Birth Centenary of the priest Ndre Mjeda.

1966 *Perf. 11½x12, 12x11½*

Designs: 10q, Banner, man and woman holding gun and axe (horiz.). 1.85 l, man with axe and banner and partisan with gun.

995	A218	5q lt brn, red & blk	5	3
996	A218	10q red, blk, gray & bl	15	4
997	A218	1.85 l red, blk & sal	1.25	35

Issued to commemorate the 25th anniversary of the Albanian Communist Party.

Golden Eagle
A219

Birds of Prey: 15q, European sea eagle. 25q, Griffon vulture. 40q, Common sparrowhawk. 50q, Osprey. 70q, Egyptian vulture. 90q, Kestrel.

1966, Dec. 20 Litho. *Perf. 11½x12*

998	A219	10q gray & multi	10	3
999	A219	15q multi	15	3
1000	A219	25q cit & multi	20	10
1001	A219	40q multi	45	15
1002	A219	50q multi	50	30
1003	A219	70q yel & multi	1.00	45
1004	A219	90q multi	1.50	55
		Nos. 998-1004 (7)	3.90	1.61

Hake
A220

Fish: 15q, Red mullet. 25q, Opah. 40q, Atlantic wolf fish. 65q, Lumpfish. 80q, Swordfish. 1.15 l, Shorthorn sculpin.

1967, Jan. Photo. *Perf. 12x11½*

Fish in Natural Colors

1005	A220	10q blue	4	3
1006	A220	15q lt yel grn	10	3
1007	A220	25q Prus bl	20	4
1008	A220	40q emerald	30	15
1009	A220	65q brt bl grn	50	25
1010	A220	80q blue	90	45
1011	A220	1.15 l brt grn	1.35	65
		Nos. 1005-1011 (7)	3.39	1.60

White Pelican
A221

Designs: Various groups of pelicans.

1967, Feb. 22 Litho. *Perf. 12*

1012	A221	10q pink & multi	15	3
1013	A221	15q pink & multi	15	6
1014	A221	25q pink & multi	22	8
1015	A221	50q pink & multi	65	30
1016	A221	2 l pink & multi	3.00	1.25
		Nos. 1012-1016 (5)	4.17	1.72

Camellia
A222

Flowers: 10q, Chrysanthemum. 15q, Hollyhock. 25q, Flowering Maple. 35q, Peony. 65q, Gladiolus. 80q, Freesia. 1.15 l, Carnation.

Lithographed

1967, Apr. 12 *Perf. 12* Unwmkd.

Flowers in Natural Colors

1017	A222	5q pale brn	10	3
1018	A222	10q lt lil	10	3
1019	A222	15q gray	10	3
1020	A222	25q ultra	20	10
1021	A222	35q lt bl	30	10
1022	A222	65q lt bl grn	45	20
1023	A222	80q lt bluish gray	75	30
1024	A222	1.15 l dl yel	1.50	45
		Nos. 1017-1024 (8)	3.50	1.24

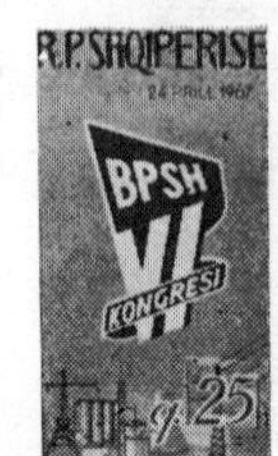

Congress Emblem and Power Station
A223

1967, Apr. 24 Litho. *Perf. 12*

1025	A223	25q gray lil, sep & brt rose	30	10
1026	A223	1.75 l gray, blk & brt rose	2.25	60

Issued to commemorate the Congress of the Union of Professional Workers, Tirana, Apr. 24.

Rose
A224

Various Roses in Natural Colors

1967, May 15 *Perf. 12x12½*

1027	A224	5q bl gray	3	3
1028	A224	10q brt bl	7	3
1029	A224	15q rose vio	8	3
1030	A224	25q lemon	15	4
1031	A224	35q brt grnsh bl	20	6
1032	A224	65q gray	60	20
1033	A224	80q brown	75	30
1034	A224	1.65 l gray grn	1.75	45
		Nos. 1027-1034 (8)	3.63	1.14

Seashore, Bregdet Borsh
A225

Views: 15q, Buthrotum (vert.). 25q, Shore, Fshati Piqeras. 45q, Shore, Bregdet. 50q, Shore, Bregdet Himare. 65q, Ship, Sarande (Santi Quaranta). 80q, Shore, Dhermi. 1 l, Sunset, Bregdet (vert.).

Perf. 12x12½, 12½x12

1967, June 10

1035	A225	15q multi	15	3
1036	A225	20q multi	20	3
1037	A225	25q multi	30	4
1038	A225	45q multi	50	15
1039	A225	50q multi	60	20
1040	A225	65q multi	80	25
1041	A225	80q multi	95	30
1042	A225	1 l multi	1.25	60
		Nos. 1035-1042 (8)	4.75	1.60

Fawn
A226

Roe Deer: 20q, Stag (vert.). 25q, Doe (vert.). 30q, Young stag and doe. 35q, Doe and fawn. 40q, Young stag (vert.). 65q, Stag and doe (vert.). 70q, Running stag and does.

Perf. 12½x12, 12x12½

1967, July 20 Lithographed

1043	A226	15q yel grn, gldn brn & blk	20	3
1044	A226	20q lt bl, org brn & blk	20	3
1045	A226	25q yel, org brn & blk	35	10
1046	A226	30q vio bl, ol bis & blk	35	15
1047	A226	35q pink, dk red brn & blk	35	15
1048	A226	40q lt vio, bis brn & blk	50	15
1049	A226	65q yel, org brn & blk	80	35
1050	A226	70q grnsh bl, org brn & blk	90	35
		Nos. 1043-1050 (8)	3.65	1.31

Man and Woman from Madhe
A227

Fighters and Newspaper
A228

Regional Costumes: 20q, Woman from Zadrimës. 25q, Dancer and drummer, Kukesit. 45q, Woman spinner, Dardhës. 50q, Farm couple, Myseqesë. 65q, Dancer with tambourine, Tirana. 80q, Man and woman, Dropullit. 1 l, Piper, Labërisë.

1967, Aug. 25 *Perf. 12*

1051	A227	15q tan & multi	10	3
1052	A227	20q lt yel grn	20	3
1053	A227	25q multi	30	4
1054	A227	45q sky bl & multi	50	20
1055	A227	50q lem & multi	60	25
1056	A227	65q pink & multi	75	30
1057	A227	80q multi	95	40
1058	A227	1 l gray & multi	1.25	50
		Nos. 1051-1058 (8)	4.65	1.75

1967, Aug. 25 *Perf. 12½x12*

Designs: 75q, Printing plant, newspapers and microphone. 2 l, People holding newspaper.

1059	A228	25q multi	20	4
1060	A228	75q pink & multi	60	14
1061	A228	2 l multi	1.75	45

Issued for the Day of the Press.

Street Scene, by Kolé Idromeno
A229

Hakmarrja Battalion, by Sali Shijaku
A230

Designs: 20q, David, fresco by Onufri, 16th century (vert.). 45q, Woman's head, ancient mosaic (vert.). 50q, Men on horseback from 16th century icon (vert.). 65q, Farm Women, by Zef Shoshi. 80q, Street Scene, by Vangjush Mio. 1 l, Bride, by Kolé Idromeno (vert.).

Perf. 12, 12x12½, (A230)

1967, Oct. 25 Lithographed

1062	A229	15q multi	20	3
1063	A229	20q multi	30	5
1064	A230	25q multi	35	6
1065	A229	45q multi	65	8
1066	A229	50q multi	75	8
1067	A230	65q multi	95	14
1068	A230	80q multi	1.25	15
1069	A230	1 l multi	1.50	30
		Nos. 1062-1069 (8)	5.95	89

Lenin at Storming of Winter Palace
A231

Rabbit
A232

Designs: 15q, Lenin and Stalin (horiz.). 50q, Lenin and Stalin addressing meeting. 1.10 l, Storming of the Winter Palace (horiz.).

1967, Nov. 7 *Perf. 12*

1070	A231	15q red & multi	10	3
1071	A231	25q sl grn & blk	20	4
1072	A231	50q brn, blk & brn vio	30	10
1073	A231	1.10 l lil, gray & blk	1.25	35

Issued to commemorate the 50th anniversary of the Russian October Revolution.

1967, Nov. 25

Designs: Various hares and rabbits. The 15q, 25q, 35q, 40q and 1 l are horizontal.

1074	A232	15q org & multi	15	3
1075	A232	20q brt yel & multi	15	3
1076	A232	25q lt brn & multi	15	4
1077	A232	35q multi	20	10
1078	A232	40q yel & multi	30	10
1079	A232	50q pink & multi	35	15
1080	A232	65q multi	75	25
1081	A232	1 l lil & multi	1.10	35
		Nos. 1074-1081 (8)	3.15	1.05

University, Torch and Book
A233

1967 Lithographed *Perf. 12*

1082	A233	25q multi	20	4
1083	A233	1.75 l multi	1.50	35

Issued to commemorate the 10th anniversary of the founding of the State University, Tirana.

Coat of Arms and Soldiers
A234

Designs: 65q, Arms, Factory, grain, flag, gun and radio tower. 1.20 l, Arms and hand holding torch.

1967 *Perf. 12x11½*

1084	A234	15q multi	15	3
1085	A234	65q multi	45	15
1086	A234	1.20 l multi	90	20

25th anniversary of the Democratic Front.

Turkey
A235

Designs: 20q, Duck. 25q, Hen. 45q, Rooster. 50q, Guinea fowl. 65q, Goose (horiz.). 80q, Mallard (horiz.). 1 l, Chicks (horiz.).

Perf. 12x12½, 12½x12

1967, Nov. 25 Photogravure

1087	A235	15q gold & multi	15	3
1088	A235	20q gold & multi	15	5
1089	A235	25q gold & multi	15	5
1090	A235	45q gold & multi	30	10
1091	A235	50q gold & multi	35	10
1092	A235	65q gold & multi	45	15
1093	A235	80q gold & multi	70	25
1094	A235	1 l gold & multi	1.00	35
		Nos. 1087-1094 (8)	3.25	1.08

Skanderbeg
A236

Designs: 10q, Arms of Skanderbeg. 25q, Helmet and sword. 30q, Kruje Castle. 35q, Petreles Castle. 65q, Berati Castle. 80q, Skanderbeg addressing national chiefs. 90q, Battle of Albulenes.

1967, Dec. 10 Litho. *Perf. 12x12½*

Medallion in Bister and Dark Brown

1095	A236	10q gold & vio	6	3
1096	A236	15q gold & rose car	8	3
1097	A236	25q gold & vio bl	13	6
1098	A236	30q gold & dk bl	15	9
1099	A236	35q gold & mar	20	9
1100	A236	65q gold & grn	35	15
1101	A236	80q gold & gray brn	60	18
1102	A236	90q gold & ultra	1.00	30
		Nos. 1095-1102 (8)	2.57	93

Issued to commemorate the 500th anniversary of the death of Skanderbeg (George Castriota), national hero.

Ice Hockey
A237

Designs: 15q, 2 l, Winter Olympics emblem. 30q, Women's figure skating. 50q, Slalom. 80q, Downhill skiing. 1 l, Ski jump.

1967-68

1103	A237	15q multi	6	3
1104	A237	25q multi	10	4
1105	A237	30q multi	15	5
1106	A237	50q multi	30	10
1107	A237	80q multi	60	15
1108	A237	1 l multi	95	30
		Nos. 1103-1108 (6)	2.16	67

Miniature Sheet

Imperf.

1109	A237	2 l red, gray & brt bl ('68)	5.50	5.50

Issued to publicize the 10th Winter Olympic Games, Grenoble, France, Feb. 6-18. Size of No. 1109: 55x66mm. Nos. 1103-1108 issued Dec. 29, 1967.

Skanderbeg Monument, Kruje
A238

Designs: 10q, Skanderbeg monument, Tirana. 15q, Skanderbeg portrait, Uffizi Galleries, Florence. 25q, Engraved portrait of Gen. Tanush Topia. 35q, Portrait of Gen. Gjergj Arianti (horiz.). 65q, Portrait bust of Skanderbeg by O. Paskali. 80q, Title page of "The Life of Skanderbeg." 90q, Skanderbeg battling the Turks, painting by S. Rrota (horiz.).

Perf. 12x12½, 12½x12

1968, Jan 17 Lithographed

1110	A238	10q multi	6	3
1111	A238	15q multi	15	3
1112	A238	25q blk, yel & lt bl	30	5
1113	A238	30q multi	35	5
1114	A238	35q lt vio, pink & blk	50	10
1115	A238	65q multi	65	15
1116	A238	80q pink, blk & yel	90	15
1117	A238	90q beige & multi	1.00	20
		Nos. 1110-1117 (8)	3.91	76

Issued to commemorate the 500th anniversary of the death of Skanderbeg (George Castriota), national hero.

Carnation
A239

1968, Feb. 15 *Perf. 12*

Various Carnations in Natural Colors

1118	A239	15q green	8	3
1119	A239	20q dk brn	10	3
1120	A239	25q brt bl	12	4
1121	A239	50q gray ol	25	8
1122	A239	80q bluish gray	50	20
1123	A239	1.10 l vio gray	75	30
		Nos. 1118-1123 (6)	1.80	68

"Electrification"
A240

Designs: 65q, Farm tractor (horiz.). 1.10 l, Cow and herd.

1968, Mar. 5 Litho. *Perf. 12*

1124	A240	25q multi	30	4
1125	A240	65q multi	65	15
1126	A240	1.10 l multi	90	35

Fifth Farm Cooperatives Congress.

Goat
A241

Designs: Various goats. 15q, 20q and 25q are vertical.

Perf. 12x12½, 12½x12

1968, Mar. 25

1127	A241	15q multi	15	3
1128	A241	20q multi	15	3
1129	A241	25q multi	20	4
1130	A241	30q multi	20	5
1131	A241	40q multi	30	10
1132	A241	50q multi	30	15
1133	A241	80q multi	60	30
1134	A241	1.40 l multi	1.25	30
		Nos. 1127-1134 (8)	3.15	1.00

Zee N. Jubani
A242

Physician and Hospital
A243

1968, Mar. 30 *Perf. 12*

1135	A242	25q yel & choc	20	10
1136	A242	1.75 l lt vio & blk	1.10	35

Issued to commemorate the sesquicentennial of the birth of Zee N. Jubani, writer and scholar.

Perf. 12½x12, 12x12½

1968, Apr. 7 Lithographed

Designs (World Health Organization Emblem and): 65q, Hospital and microscope (horiz.). 1.10 l, Mother feeding child.

1137	A243	25q grn & cl	30	6
1138	A243	65q blk, yel & bl	65	15
1139	A243	1.10 l blk & dp org	1.00	30

Issued to commemorate the 20th anniversary of the World Health Organization.

Scientist
A244

Women: 15q, Militia member. 60q, Farm worker. 1 l, Factory worker.

1968, Apr. 14 *Perf. 12*

1140	A244	15q ver & dk red	15	3
1141	A244	25q bl grn & grn	20	10
1142	A244	60q dl yel & brn	45	20
1143	A244	1 l lt vio & vio	90	35

Issued to commemorate the 25th anniversary of the Albanian Women's Organization.

Karl Marx
A245

Designs: 25q, Marx lecturing to students. 65q, "Das Kapital," "Communist Manifesto" and marching crowd. 95q, Full-face portrait.

1968, May 5 Litho. *Perf. 12*

No.	Type	Description	Unused	Used
1144	A245	15q gray, dk bl & bis	20	3
1145	A245	25q brn vio, dk brn & dl yel	35	10
1146	A245	65q gray, blk, brn & car	80	35
1147	A245	95q gray, ocher & blk	1.25	60

Karl Marx, 150th birth anniversary.

Heliopsis
A246

Flowers: 20q, Red flax. 25q, Orchid. 30q, Gloxinia. 40q, Turk's-cap lily. 80q, Amaryllis. 1.40 l, Red magnolia.

1968, May 10 *Perf. 12x12½*

No.	Type	Description	Unused	Used
1148	A246	15q gold & multi	6	3
1149	A246	20q gold & multi	8	3
1150	A246	25q gold & multi	10	4
1151	A246	30q gold & multi	12	5
1152	A246	40q gold & multi	50	10
1153	A246	80q gold & multi	65	15
1154	A246	1.40 l gold & multi	95	35
		Nos. 1148-1154 (7)	2.46	75

Proclamation of Prizren
A247

Designs: 25q, Abdyl Frasheri. 40q, House in Prizren.

1968, June 10 Litho. *Perf. 12*

No.	Type	Description	Unused	Used
1155	A247	25q emer & blk	15	4
1156	A247	40q multi	45	15
1157	A247	85q yel & multi	75	35

Issued to commemorate the 90th anniversary of the League of Prizren against the Turks.

Shepherd, by A. Kushi
A248

Paintings from Tirana Art Gallery: 20q, View of Tirana, by V. Mio (horiz.). 25q, Mountaineer, by G. Madhi. 40q, Refugees, by A. Buza. 80q, Guerrillas of Shahin Matrakut, by S. Xega. 1.50 l, Portrait of an Old Man, by S. Papadhimitri. 1.70 l, View of Scutari, by S. Rrota. 2.50 l, Woman in Scutari Costume, by Z. Colombi.

1968, June 20 *Perf. 12x12½*

No.	Type	Description	Unused	Used
1158	A248	15q gold & multi	10	3
1159	A248	20q gold & multi	12	3
1160	A248	25q gold & multi	15	4
1161	A248	40q gold & multi	35	7
1162	A248	80q gold & multi	50	18
1163	A248	1.50 l gold & multi	95	30
1164	A248	1.70 l gold & multi	1.10	35
		Nos. 1158-1164 (7)	3.27	1.00

Miniature Sheet

Perf. 12½xImperf.

No.	Type	Description	Unused	Used
1165	A248	2.50 l multi	2.25	1.00

No. 1165 contains one stamp with picture frame in margin. Size of stamp: 50x71mm.; size of sheet: 89x113mm.

Soldier and Guns—A249

Designs: 25q, Sailor and warships. 65q, Aviator and planes (vert.). 95q, Militiamen and woman.

1968, July 10 Litho. *Perf. 12*

No.	Type	Description	Unused	Used
1166	A249	15q multi	15	3
1167	A249	25q multi	30	10
1168	A249	65q multi	65	15
1169	A249	95q multi	1.10	30

25th anniversary of the People's Army.

Squid
A250

Designs: 20q, Crayfish. 25q, Whelk. 50q, Crab. 70q, Spiny lobster. 80q, Shore crab. 90q, Norway lobster.

1968, Aug. 20

No.	Type	Description	Unused	Used
1170	A250	15q multi	15	3
1171	A250	20q multi	15	4
1172	A250	25q multi	20	4
1173	A250	50q multi	30	8
1174	A250	70q multi	50	12
1175	A250	80q multi	65	30
1176	A250	90q multi	95	35
		Nos. 1170-1176 (7)	2.90	96

Women's Relay Race
A251

Sport: 20q, Running. 25q, Women's discus. 30q, Equestrian. 40q, High jump. 50q, Women's hurdling. 80q, Soccer. 1.40 l, Woman diver. 2 l, Olympic stadium.

1968, Sept. 23 Photo. *Perf. 12*

No.	Type	Description	Unused	Used
1177	A251	15q multi	8	3
1178	A251	20q multi	10	3
1179	A251	25q multi	15	4
1180	A251	30q multi	30	5
1181	A251	40q multi	30	10
1182	A251	50q multi	45	15
1183	A251	80q multi	90	30
1184	A251	1.40 l multi	1.35	50
		Nos. 1177-1184 (8)	3.63	1.20

Souvenir Sheet

Perf. 12½ Horizontally

No.	Type	Description	Unused	Used
1185	A251	2 l multi	2.25	75

Issued to publicize the 19th Olympic Games, Mexico City, Oct. 12-27. No. 1185 contains one rectangular stamp, size: 64x54mm. Sheet has ocher marginal inscription. Size: 90x82mm.

Price of imperfs., #1177-1184 $6, #1185 $4.

Enver Hoxha
A252

1968, Oct. 16 Litho. *Perf. 12*

No.	Type	Description	Unused	Used
1186	A252	25q bl gray	18	12
1187	A252	35q rose brn	35	14
1188	A252	80q violet	80	30
1189	A252	1.10 l brown	1.10	65

Souvenir Sheet

Imperf.

No.	Type	Description	Unused	Used
1190	A252	1.50 l rose red, bl vio & gold	*45.00*	*45.00*

Issued for the 60th birthday of Enver Hoxha, First Secretary of the Central Committee of the Communist Party of Albania. No. 1190 contains portrait (size: 45x55mm.) with name of country, denomination and commemorative inscription in margin. Size: 79x90mm.

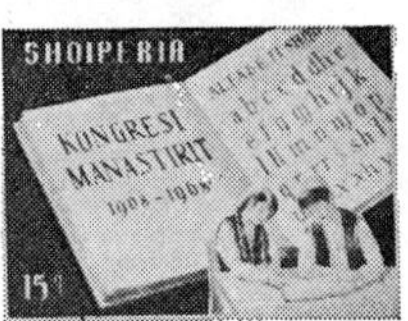

Book and Pupils
A253

1968, Nov. 14 Photogravure

No.	Type	Description	Unused	Used
1191	A253	15q mar & sl grn	30	10
1192	A253	85q gray ol & sep	1.50	30

Issued to commemorate the 60th anniversary of the Congress of Monastir, Nov. 14-22, 1908, which adopted a unified Albanian alphabet.

Waxwing
A254

Birds: 20q, Rose-colored starling. 25q, Kingfishers. 50q, Long-tailed tits. 80q, Wallcreeper. 1.10 l, Bearded tit.

1968, Nov. 15 Lithographed

Birds in Natural Colors

No.	Type	Description	Unused	Used
1193	A254	15q lt bl & blk	15	3
1194	A254	20q bis & blk	15	3
1195	A254	25q pink & blk	30	10
1196	A254	50q lt yel grn & blk	35	20
1197	A254	80q bis brn & blk	80	30
1198	A254	1.10 l pale grn & blk	1.10	35
		Nos. 1193-1198 (6)	2.85	1.01

Mao Tse-tung—A255

1968, Dec. 26 Litho. *Perf. 12½x12*

No.	Type	Description	Unused	Used
1199	A255	25q gold, red & blk	30	20
1200	A255	1.75 l gold, red & blk	1.50	45

Issued to commemorate the 75th birthday of Mao Tse-tung, Chairman of the Communist Party of the People's Republic of China.

Adem Reka and Crane
A256

Portraits: 10q, Pjeter Lleshi and power lines. 15q, Mohammed Shehu and Myrteza Kepi. 25q, Shkurte Vata and women railroad workers. 65q, Agron Elezi, frontier guard. 80q, Ismet Bruçaj and mountain road. 1.30 l, Fuat Cela, blind revolutionary.

1969, Feb. 10 Litho. *Perf. 12x12½*

No.	Type	Description	Unused	Used
1201	A256	5q multi	3	3
1202	A256	10q multi	6	3
1203	A256	15q multi	10	3
1204	A256	25q multi	15	6
1205	A256	65q multi	50	10
1206	A256	80q multi	65	15
1207	A256	1.30 l multi	95	35
		Nos. 1201-1207 (7)	2.44	75

Issued to honor a contemporary heroine and heroes.

Meteorological Instruments
A257

Designs: 25q, Water gauge. 1.60 l, Radar, balloon and isobars.

1969, Feb. 25 *Perf. 12*

No.	Type	Description	Unused	Used
1208	A257	15q multi	9	5
1209	A257	25q ultra, org & blk	20	10
1210	A257	1.60 l rose vio, yel & blk	1.50	50

Issued to commemorate the 20th anniversary of Albanian hydrometeorology.

Partisans, 1944, by F. Haxmiu
A258

Paintings: 5q, Student Revolutionists, by P. Mele (vert.). 65q, Steel Mill, by C. Ceka. 80q, Reconstruction, by V. Kilica. 1.10 l, Harvest, by N. Jonuzi. 1.15 l, Terraced Landscape, by S. Kaceli. 2 l, Partisans' Meeting.

Perf. 12x12½, 12½x12

1969, Apr. 25 Lithographed

Size: 31½x41½mm.

No.	Type	Description	Unused	Used
1211	A258	5q buff & multi	3	3

Size: 51½x30½mm.

No.	Type	Description	Unused	Used
1212	A258	25q buff & multi	10	4

Size: 40½x32mm.

No.	Type	Description	Unused	Used
1213	A258	65q buff & multi	28	10

Size: 51½x30½mm.

1214 A258 80q buff & multi 35 12
1215 A258 1.10 l buff & multi 60 18
1216 A258 1.15 l buff & multi 80 20
Nos. 1211-1216 (6) 2.16 67

Miniature Sheet

Imperf.

Size: 111x90mm.

1217 A258 2 l ocher & multi 1.50 90

Leonardo da Vinci, Self-portrait
A259

Designs (after Leonardo da Vinci): 35q, Lilies. 40q, Design for a flying machine (horiz.). 1 l, Portrait of Beatrice. No. 1222, Portrait of a Noblewoman. No. 1223, Mona Lisa.

Perf. 12x12½, 12½x12

1969, May 2 Lithographed

1218 A259 25q gold & sep 15 4
1219 A259 35q gold & sep 30 15
1220 A259 40q gold & sep 35 15
1221 A259 1 l gold & multi 95 30
1222 A259 2 l gold & sep 1.75 80
Nos. 1218-1222 (5) 3.50 1.44

Miniature Sheet

Imperf.

1223 A259 2 l gold & multi 3.00 3.00

Issued to commemorate the 450th anniversary of the death of Leonardo da Vinci (1452–1519), painter, sculptor, architect and engineer. Size of No. 1223: 64x95 mm.

First Congress Meeting Place
A260

Designs: 1 l, Albanian coat of arms. 2.25 l, Two partisans with guns and flag.

1969, May 24 *Perf. 12*

1224 A260 25q lt grn, blk & red 35 20
1225 A260 2.25 l multi 2.25 1.25

Souvenir Sheet

1226 A260 1 l gold, bl, blk & red *15.00* *10.00*

25th anniversary of the First Anti-Fascist Congress of Permet, May 24, 1944.

No. 1226 contains one stamp; blue, black and red decorative margin. Size: 94½x100mm.

Albanian Violet
A261

Designs: Violets and Pansies.

1969, June 30 Litho. *Perf. 12x12½*

1227 A261 5q gold & multi 3 3
1228 A261 10q gold & multi 10 3
1229 A261 15q gold & multi 10 3
1230 A261 20q gold & multi 20 10
1231 A261 25q gold & multi 35 15
1232 A261 80q gold & multi 60 25
1233 A261 1.95 l gold & multi 1.10 65
Nos. 1227-1233 (7) 2.48 1.24

Plum, Fruit and Blossoms
A262

Designs: Blossoms and Fruits.

1969, Aug. 10 Litho. *Perf. 12*

Multicolored

1234 A262 10q *shown* 4 3
1235 A262 15q *Lemon* 8 3
1236 A262 25q Pomegranate 14 3
1237 A262 50q *Cherry* 28 10
1238 A262 80q *Peach* 50 20
1239 A262 1.20 l *Apple* 1.00 35
Nos. 1234-1239 (6) 2.04 74

Basketball
A263

Designs: 10q, 80q, 2.20 l, Various views of basketball game. 25q, Hand aiming ball at basket and map of Europe (horiz.).

1969, Sept. 15 Litho. *Perf. 12*

1240 A263 10q multi 7 3
1241 A263 15q buff & multi 9 3
1242 A263 25q bl & multi 14 7
1243 A263 80q multi 50 15
1244 A263 2.20 l multi 1.75 50
Nos. 1240-1244 (5) 2.55 78

Issued to publicize the 16th European Basketball Championships, Naples, Italy, Sept. 27–Oct. 5.

Runner
A264

Designs: 5q, Games' emblem. 10q, Woman gymnast. 20q, Pistol shooting. 25q, Swimmer at start. 80q, Bicyclist. 95q, Soccer.

1969, Sept. 30

1245 A264 5q multi 3 3
1246 A264 10q multi 8 3
1247 A264 15q multi 10 3
1248 A264 20q multi 12 6
1249 A264 25q multi 14 8
1250 A264 80q multi 50 20
1251 A264 95q multi 75 25
Nos. 1245-1251 (7) 1.72 68

Second National Spartakiad.

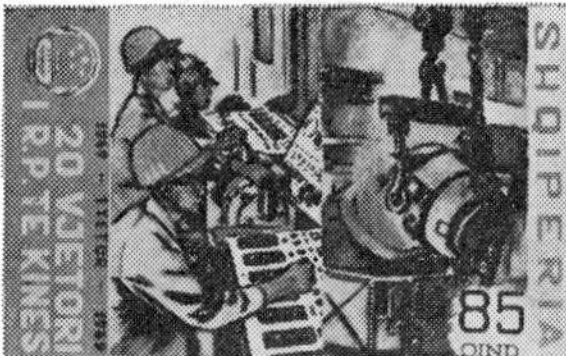

Electronic Technicians, Steel Ladle
A265

Designs: 25q, Mao Tse-tung with microphones (vert.). 1.40 l, Children holding Mao's red book (vert.).

1969, Oct. 1 Litho. *Perf. 12*

1252 A265 25q multi 15 3
1253 A265 85q multi 38 20
1254 A265 1.40 l multi 90 45

Issued to commemorate the 20th anniversary of the People's Republic of China.

Enver Hoxha
A266

Designs: 80q, Pages from Berat resolution. 1.45 l, Partisans with flag.

1969, Oct. 20 Litho. *Perf. 12*

1255 A266 25q multi 20 4
1256 A266 80q gray & multi 45 12
1257 A266 1.45 l ocher & multi 80 27

Issued to commemorate the 25th anniversary of the second reunion of the National Antifascist Liberation Council, Berat.

Soldiers—A267

Designs: 30q, Oil refinery. 35q, Combine harvester. 45q, Hydroelectric station and dam. 55q, Militia woman, man and soldier. 1.10 l, Dancers and musicians.

1969, Nov. 29

1258 A267 25q multi 13 3
1259 A267 30q multi 17 3
1260 A267 35q multi 20 4
1261 A267 45q multi 23 7
1262 A267 55q multi 30 11
1263 A267 1.10 l multi 95 25
Nos. 1258-1263 (6) 1.98 53

Issued to commemorate the 25th anniversary of the socialist republic.

Joseph V. Stalin
A268

1969, Dec. 21 Litho. *Perf. 12*

1264 A268 15q lilac 6 3
1265 A268 25q sl bl 10 4
1266 A268 1 l brown 55 20
1267 A268 1.10 l vio bl 60 25

Issued to commemorate the 90th anniversary of the birth of Joseph V. Stalin (1879–1953), Russian political leader.

Head of Woman
A269

1969, Dec. 25 *Perf. 12½x12*

Greco-Roman Mosaics: 25q, Geometrical floor design (horiz.). 80q, Bird and tree (horiz.). 1.10 l, Floor with birds and grapes (horiz.). 1.20 l, Fragment with corn within oval design.

1268 A269 15q gold & multi 10 3
1269 A269 25q gold & multi 15 3
1270 A269 80q gold & multi 45 15
1271 A269 1.10 l gold & multi 60 20
1272 A269 1.20 l gold & multi 90 30
Nos. 1268-1272 (5) 2.20 71

Cancellation of 1920
A270

Design: 25q, Proclamation and congress site.

1970, Jan. 21 Litho. *Perf. 12*

1273 A270 25q red, gray & blk 20 6
1274 A270 1.25 l dk grn, yel & blk 1.00 25

Congress of Louchnia, 50th anniversary.

Worker, Student and Flag
A271

1970, Feb. 11 *Perf. 12½x12*

1275 A271 25q red & multi 20 4
1276 A271 1.75 l red & multi 1.05 45

Issued to commemorate the 25th anniversary of vocational organizations in Albania.

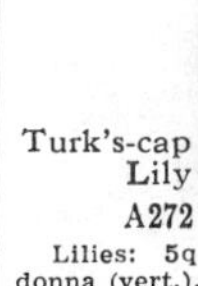

Turk's-cap Lily
A272

Lilies: 5q, Cernum (vert.). 15q, Madonna (vert.). 25q, Royal (vert.). 1.10 l, Tiger. 1.15 l, Albanian.

Perf. 11½x12, 12x11½

1970, Mar. 10 Lithographed

1277 A272 5q multi 5 3

1278	A272	15q	multi	8	3
1279	A272	25q	multi	15	4
1280	A272	80q	multi	45	12
1281	A272	1.10 l	multi	65	25
1282	A272	1.15 l	multi	95	28
		Nos. 1277-1282 (6)		2.33	75

Lenin
A273

Designs (Lenin): 5q, Portrait (vert.). 25q, As volunteer construction worker. 95q, Addressing crowd. 1.10 l, Saluting (vert.).

1970, Apr. 22 Litho. *Perf. 12*
Red, Black & Silver

1283	A273	5q	3	3
1284	A273	15q	7	3
1285	A273	25q	14	4
1286	A273	95q	55	10
1287	A273	1.10 l	65	25
		Nos. 1283-1287 (5)	1.44	45

Centenary of birth of Lenin (1870–1924).

Frontier Guard
A274

1970, Apr. 25

1288	A274	25q	multi	20	4
1289	A274	1.25 l	multi	80	30

25th anniversary of Frontier Guards.

Soccer Players
A275

Designs: 5q, Jules Rimet Cup and globes. 10q, Aztec Stadium, Mexico City. 25q, Defending goal. 65q, 80q, No. 1296, Two soccer players in various plays. No. 1297, Mexican horseman and volcano Popocatepetl.

1970, May 15 Litho. *Perf. 12½x12*

1290	A275	5q	multi	3	3
1291	A275	10q	multi	3	3
1292	A275	15q	multi	3	3
1293	A275	25q	lt grn & multi	15	6
1294	A275	65q	pink & multi	32	13
1295	A275	80q	lt bl & multi	60	18
1296	A275	2 l	yel & multi	1.25	28
		Nos. 1290-1296 (7)		2.41	74

Souvenir Sheet
Perf. 12x Imperf.

1297	A275	2 l	multi	2.25	1.10

Issued to publicize the World Soccer Championships for the Jules Rimet Cup, Mexico City, May 31–June 21, 1970. No. 1297 contains one large horizontal stamp, decorative border and inscription. Size: 81x74mm.

U.P.U. Headquarters and Monument, Bern
A276

1970, May 30 Litho. *Perf. 12½x12*

1298	A276	25q	ultra, gray & blk	15	3
1299	A276	1.10 l	org, buff & blk	75	20
1300	A276	1.15 l	grn, gray & blk	90	35

Issued to commemorate the inauguration of the new Universal Postal Union Headquarters in Bern.

Bird and Grapes Mosaic
A277

Mosaics, 5th–6th centuries, excavated near Pogradec: 10q, Waterfowl and grapes. 20q, Bird and tree stump. 25q, Bird and leaves. 65q, Fish. 2.25 l, Peacock (vert.).

Perf. 12½x12, 12x12½
1970, July 10

1301	A277	5q	multi	3	3
1302	A277	10q	multi	10	3
1303	A277	20q	multi	15	3
1304	A277	25q	multi	20	8
1305	A277	65q	multi	45	20
1306	A277	2.25 l	multi	1.50	45
		Nos. 1301-1306 (6)		2.43	82

Fruit Harvest and Dancers
A278

Designs: 25q, Contour-plowed fields and conference table. 80q, Cattle and newspapers. 1.30 l, Wheat harvest.

1970, Aug. 28 Litho. *Perf. 12x11½*

1307	A278	15q	brt vio & blk	10	3
1308	A278	25q	dp bl & blk	15	4
1309	A278	80q	dp brn & blk	40	8
1310	A278	1.30 l	org brn & blk	75	30

Issued to commemorate the 25th anniversary of the agrarian reform law.

Attacking Partisans
A279

Designs: 25q, Partisans with horses and flag. 1.60 l, Partisans.

1970, Sept. 3 *Perf. 12*

1311	A279	15q	org brn & blk	10	3
1312	A279	25q	brn, yel & blk	13	3
1313	A279	1.60 l	dp grn & blk	1.00	50

50th anniversary of liberation of Vlona.

Miners, by Nexhmedin Zajmi
A280

Paintings from the National Gallery, Tirana: 5q, Bringing in the Harvest, by Isuf Sulovari (vert.). 15q, The Activists, by Dhimitraq Trebicka (vert.). 65q, Instruction of Partisans, by Hasan Nallbani. 95q, Architectural Planning, by Vilson Kilica. No. 1319, Woman Machinist, by Zef Shoshi (vert.). No. 1320, Partisan Destroying Tank, by Sali Shijaku (vert.).

Perf. 12½x12, 12x12½
1970, Sept. 25 Lithographed

1314	A280	5q	multi	3	3
1315	A280	15q	multi	4	3
1316	A280	25q	multi	15	4
1317	A280	65q	multi	26	8
1318	A280	95q	multi	40	15
1319	A280	2 l	multi	1.20	45
		Nos. 1314-1319 (6)		2.08	78

Miniature Sheet
Imperf.

1320	A280	2 l	multi	1.75	1.50

Size of No. 1320: 66x93½mm.

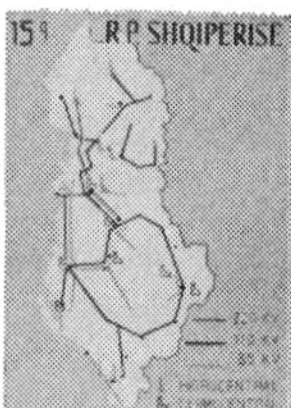

Electrification Map of Albania
A281

Designs: 25q, Light bulb, hammer and sickle emblem, map of Albania and power graph. 80q, Linemen at work. 1.10 l, Use of electricity on the farm, in home and business.

1970, Oct. 25 Litho. *Perf. 12*

1321	A281	15q	multi	10	3
1322	A281	25q	multi	15	4
1323	A281	80q	multi	50	15
1324	A281	1.10 l	multi	75	25

Issued to publicize the completion of Albanian village electrification.

Friedrich Engels
A282

Designs: 1.10 l, Engels as young man. 1.15 l, Engels addressing crowd.

1970, Nov. 28 Litho. *Perf. 12x12½*

1325	A282	25q	bis & dk bl	13	4
1326	A282	1.10 l	bis & dp cl	60	20
1327	A282	1.15 l	bis & dk ol grn	80	30

Issued to commemorate the 150th anniversary of the birth of Friedrich Engels (1820–1895), German socialist, collaborator with Karl Marx.

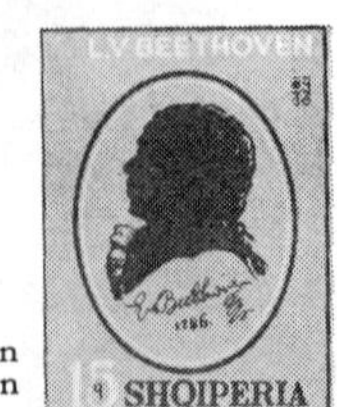

Ludwig van Beethoven
A283

Designs: 5q, Birthplace, Bonn. 25q, 65q, 1.10 l, various portraits. 1.80 l, Scene from Fidelio (horiz.).

1970, Dec. 16 Litho. *Perf. 12*

1328	A283	5q	dp plum & gold	3	3
1329	A283	15q	brt rose lil & sil	4	3
1330	A283	25q	grn & gold	15	4
1331	A283	65q	mag & sil	30	10
1332	A283	1.10 l	dk bl & gold	65	22
1333	A283	1.80 l	blk & sil	1.25	45
		Nos. 1328-1333 (6)		2.42	87

Bicentenary of the birth of Ludwig van Beethoven (1770–1827), composer.

Coat of Arms
A284

Designs: 25q, Proclamation. 80q, Enver Hoxha reading proclamation. 1.30 l, Young people and proclamation.

1971, Jan. 11 Litho. *Perf. 12*

1334	A284	15q	lt bl, gold, blk & red	10	3
1335	A284	25q	rose lil, blk, gold & gray	15	4
1336	A284	80q	emer, blk & gold	45	12
1337	A284	1.30 l	yel org, blk & gold	75	35

Declaration of the Republic, 25th anniversary.

"Liberty" A285 — Black Men A286

Designs: 50q, Women's brigade. 65q, Street battle (horiz.). 1.10 l, Execution (horiz.).

Perf. 12x11½, 11½x12
1971, March 18 Lithographed

1338	A285	25q	dk bl & bl	13	4
1339	A285	50q	sl grn	22	7
1340	A285	65q	dk brn & chnt	35	15
1341	A285	1.10 l	purple	65	20

Centenary of the Paris Commune.

1971, March 21 *Perf. 12x12½*

Designs: 1.10 l, Men of 3 races. 1.15 l, Black protest.

1342	A286	25q	blk & bis brn	12	4
1343	A286	1.10 l	blk & rose car	60	20
1344	A286	1.15 l	blk & ver	65	30

International year against racial discrimination.

Tulip
A287

Horseman, by Dürer
A288

Designs: Various tulips.

1971, March 25

1345	A287	5q multi	3	3
1346	A287	10q yel & multi	4	3
1347	A287	15q pink & multi	6	3
1348	A287	20q lt bl & multi	8	3
1349	A287	25q multi	12	6
1350	A287	80q multi	35	12
1351	A287	1 l multi	45	14
1352	A287	1.45 l cit & multi	1.00	30
		Nos. 1345-1352 (8)	2.13	74

Perf. 11½x12, 12x11½

1971, May 15 Lithographed

Art Works by Dürer: 15q, Three peasants. 25q, Dancing peasant couple. 45q, The bagpiper. 65q, View of Kalkreut (horiz.). 2.40 l, View of Trent (horiz.). 2.50 l, Self-portrait.

1353	A288	10q blk & pale grn	4	3
1354	A288	15q blk & pale lil	10	3
1355	A288	25q blk & pale bl	15	4
1356	A288	45q blk & pale rose	20	7
1357	A288	65q blk & multi	35	15
1358	A288	2.40 l blk & multi	1.40	45
		Nos. 1353-1358 (6)	2.24	77

Miniature Sheet

Imperf.

1359	A288	2.50 l multi	1.75	1.50

500th anniversary of the birth of Albrecht Dürer (1471–1528), German painter and engraver. Size of No. 1359: 93x90 mm.

Satellite Orbiting Globe—289

Designs: 1.20 l, Government Building, Tirana, and Red Star emblem. 2.20 l, like 60q, 2.50 l, Flag of People's Republic of China forming trajectory around globe.

1971, June 10 Litho. ***Perf. 12x12½***

1360	A289	60q pur & multi	32	8
1361	A289	1.20 l ver & multi	75	20
1362	A289	2.20 l grn & multi	1.40	50

Imperf.

1363	A289	2.50 l vio blk & multi	2.00	90

Space developments of People's Republic of China. Size of No. 1363: 64x112mm.

Mao Tse-tung A290

Designs: 1.05 l, House where Communist Party was founded (horiz.). 1.20 l, Peking crowd with placards (horiz.).

Perf. 12x12½, 12½x12

1971, July 1

1364	A290	25q sil & multi	18	4
1365	A290	1.05 l sil & multi	70	14
1366	A290	1.20 l sil & multi	80	30

50th anniversary of Chinese Communist Party.

Crested Titmouse—A291

1971, Aug. 15 Litho. ***Perf. 12½x12***

Multicolored

1367	A291	5q *shown*	3	3
1368	A291	10q *European serin*	6	3
1369	A291	15q *Linnet*	8	3
1370	A291	25q *Firecrest*	15	4
1371	A291	45q *Rock thrush*	30	7
1372	A291	60q *Blue tit*	45	20
1373	A291	2.40 l *Chaffinch*	1.75	65
		Nos. 1367-1373 (7)	2.82	1.05

Printed se-tenant in blocks of 8 (2x4) including a label showing bird's nest. The label is se-tenant horizontally with the 5q, and vertically with the 10q.

Olympic Rings and Running—A292

Designs (Olympic Rings and): 10q, Hurdles. 15q, Canoeing. 25q, Gymnastics. 80q, Fencing. 1.05 l, Soccer. 2 l, Runner at finish line. 3.60 l, Diving, women's.

1971, Sept. 15

1374	A292	5q grn & multi	3	3
1375	A292	10q multi	6	3
1376	A292	15q bl & multi	8	3
1377	A292	25q vio & multi	12	4
1378	A292	80q lil & multi	35	8
1379	A292	1.05 l multi	60	12
1380	A292	3.60 l multi	2.00	65
		Nos. 1374-1380 (7)	3.24	98

Souvenir Sheet

Imperf.

1381	A292	2 l brt bl & multi	1.75	1.25

20th Olympic Games, Munich, Aug. 26–Sept. 10, 1972. No. 1381 contains one stamp, gray margin with brown inscription. Olympic rings and deep orange and silver flame emblem. Size: 68x82mm.

Workers with Flags A293

Designs: 1.05 l, Party Headquarters, Tirana, and Red Star. 1.20 l, Rifle, star, flag and "VI" (vert.).

1971, Nov. 1 ***Perf. 12***

1382	A293	25q gold, sil, red & bl	15	3
1383	A293	1.05 l gold, sil, red & bl	60	14
1384	A293	1.20 l gold, sil, red & blk	75	30

6th Congress of Workers' Party.

Factories and Workers A294

Designs: 80q, "XXX" and flag (vert.). 1.55 l, Enver Hoxha and flags.

1971, Nov. 8

1385	A294	15q gold, sil, lil & yel	6	3
1386	A294	80q gold, sil & red	50	10
1387	A294	1.55 l gold, sil, red & brn	1.00	35

30th anniversary of Workers' Party.

Construction Work, by M. Fushekati A295

Albanian Paintings: 5q, Young Man, by R. Kuci (vert.). 25q, Partisan, by D. Jukniu (vert.). 80q, Fliers, by S. Kristo. 1.20 l, Girl in Forest, by A. Sadikaj. 1.55 l, Warriors with Spears and Shields, by S. Kamberi. 2 l, Freedom Fighter, by I. Lulani.

Perf. 12x12½, 12½x12

1971, Nov. 20

1388	A295	5q gold & multi	3	3
1389	A295	15q gold & multi	7	3
1390	A295	25q gold & multi	11	5
1391	A295	80q gold & multi	35	10
1392	A295	1.20 l gold & multi	55	15
1393	A295	1.55 l gold & multi	1.00	28
		Nos. 1388-1393 (6)	2.11	64

Miniature Sheet

Imperf.

1394	A295	2 l gold & multi	1.75	90

Contemporary Albanian paintings. Size of No. 1394: 87x67½mm.

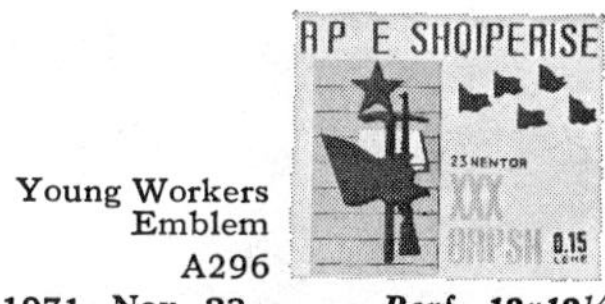

Young Workers Emblem A296

1971, Nov. 23 ***Perf. 12x12½***

1395	A296	15q lt bl & multi	15	3
1396	A296	1.35 l grnsh gray & multi	85	25

30th anniversary of the Albanian Young Workers' Union.

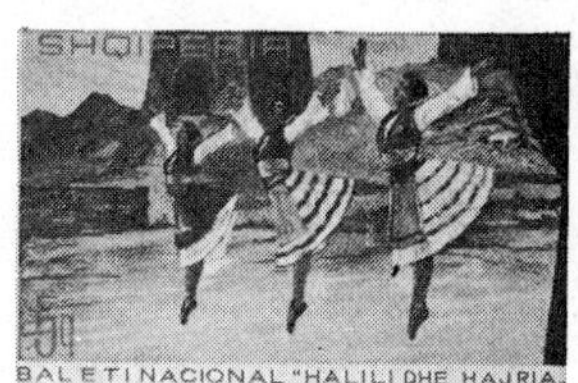

"Halili and Hajria" Ballet—A297

Scenes from "Halili and Hajria" Ballet: 10q, Brother and sister. 15q, Hajria before Sultan Suleiman. 50q, Hajria and husband. 80q, Execution of Halili. 1.40 l, Hajria killing her husband.

1971, Dec. 27 ***Perf. 12½x12***

1397	A297	5q sil & multi	4	3
1398	A297	10q sil & multi	6	3
1399	A297	15q sil & multi	7	3
1400	A297	50q sil & multi	27	10
1401	A297	80q sil & multi	45	12
1402	A297	1.40 l sil & multi	75	35
		Nos. 1397-1402 (6)	1.64	66

Albanian ballet Halili and Hajria after drama by Kol Jakova.

Biathlon and Olympic Rings—A298

Designs (Olympic Rings and): 10q, Sledding. 15q, Ice hockey. 20q, Bobsledding. 50q, Speed skating. 1 l, Slalom. 2 l, Ski jump. 2.50 l, Figure skating, pairs.

1972, Feb. 10

1403	A298	5q lt ol & multi	3	3
1404	A298	10q lt vio & multi	6	3
1405	A298	15q multi	7	3
1406	A298	20q pink & multi	12	3
1407	A298	50q lt bl & multi	25	15
1408	A298	1 l ocher & multi	60	30
1409	A298	2 l lil & multi	1.40	60
		Nos. 1403-1409 (7)	2.53	1.17

Souvenir Sheet

Imperf.

1410	A298	2.50 l bl & multi	1.75	75

11th Winter Olympic Games, Sapporo, Japan, Feb. 3–13. No. 1410 contains one stamp. Blue, ultramarine and silver margin with inscription. Size: 71x90mm.

Wild Strawberries A299

Wild Fruits and Nuts: 10q, Blackberries. 15q, Hazelnuts. 20q, Walnuts. 25q, Strawberry-tree fruit. 30q, Dogwood berries. 2.40 l, Rowan berries.

1972, Mar. 20 Litho. ***Perf. 12***

1411	A299	5q lt grn & multi	3	3
1412	A299	10q yel & multi	6	3
1413	A299	15q lt vio & multi	10	3
1414	A299	20q pink & multi	15	3
1415	A299	25q multi	20	15
1416	A299	30q multi	35	15
1417	A299	2.40 l multi	1.50	70
		Nos. 1411-1417 (7)	2.39	1.12

"Your Heart is your Health" A300

Worker and Student A301

Design: 1.20 l, Cardiac patient and electrocardiogram.

1972, Apr. 7 ***Perf. 12x12½***

1418	A300	1.10 l multi	65	30
1419	A300	1.20 l rose & multi	1.10	45

World Health Day 1972.

1972, Apr. 24 Litho. *Perf. 11½x12½*

Design: 2.05 l, Assembly Hall, dancers and emblem.

1420	A301	25q multi	20	5
1421	A301	2.05 l bl & multi	1.25	45

7th Trade Union Congress, May 8.

Qemal Stafa A302

Designs: 15q, Memorial flame. 25q, Monument "Spirit of Defiance" (vert.).

Perf. 12½x12, 12x12½

1972, May 5

1422	A302	15q gray & multi	7	3
1423	A302	25q sal rose, blk & gray	15	5
1424	A302	1.90 l dl yel & blk	1.25	40

30th anniversary of the murder of Qemal Stafa and of Martyrs' Day.

Camellia A303

Designs: Various camellias.

1972, May 10 *Perf. 12x12½*

Flowers in Natural Colors

1425	A303	5q lt bl & blk	3	3
1426	A303	10q cit & blk	6	3
1427	A303	15q grnsh gray & blk	7	3
1428	A303	25q pale sal & blk	15	5
1429	A303	45q gray & blk	30	10
1430	A303	50q sal pink & blk	45	15
1431	A303	2.50 l bluish gray & blk	1.50	75
		Nos. 1425-1431 (7)	2.56	1.14

High Jump—A304

Designs (Olympic and Motion Emblems and): 10q, Running. 15q, Shot put. 20q, Bicycling. 25q, Pole vault. 50q, Hurdles, women's. 75q, Hockey. 2 l, Swimming. 2.50 l, Diving, women's.

1972, June 30 Litho. *Perf. 12½x12*

1432	A304	5q multi	3	3
1433	A304	10q lt brn & multi	5	3
1434	A304	15q lt lil & multi	7	3
1435	A304	20q multi	12	3
1436	A304	25q lt vio & multi	14	3
1437	A304	50q lt grn & multi	30	15
1438	A304	75q multi	60	20
1439	A304	2 l multi	1.40	40
		Nos. 1432-1439 (8)	2.71	90

Miniature Sheet

Imperf.

1440	A304	2.50 l multi	2.00	1.10

20th Olympic Games, Munich, Aug. 26–Sept. 11. Nos. 1432–1439 each issued in sheets of 8 stamps and one label (3x3) showing Olympic rings in gold. Size of No. 1440: 70x87mm.

Autobus A305

Designs: 25q, Electric train. 80q, Ocean liner Tirana. 1.05 l, Automobile. 1.20 l, Trailer truck.

1972, July 25 Litho. *Perf. 12*

1441	A305	15q org brn & multi	10	3
1442	A305	25q gray & multi	11	5
1443	A305	80q dp grn & multi	40	8
1444	A305	1.05 l multi	65	20
1445	A305	1.20 l multi	80	25
		Nos. 1441-1445 (5)	2.06	61

Arm Wrestling A306

Folk Games: 10q, Piggyback ball game. 15q, Women's jumping. 25q, Rope game (srum). 90q, Leapfrog. 2 l, Women throwing pitchers.

1972, Aug. 18

1446	A306	5q multi	3	3
1447	A306	10q lt bl & multi	5	3
1448	A306	15q rose & multi	10	3
1449	A306	25q lt bl & multi	15	5
1450	A306	90q ocher & multi	60	15
1451	A306	2 l lt grn & multi	1.25	35
		Nos. 1446-1451 (6)	2.18	64

1st National Festival of People's Games.

Mastheads—A307

Designs: 25q, Printing press. 1.90 l, Workers reading paper.

1972, Aug. 25

1452	A307	15q lt bl & blk	7	3
1453	A307	25q red, grn & blk	15	5
1454	A307	1.90 l lt vio & blk	1.05	35

30th Press Day.

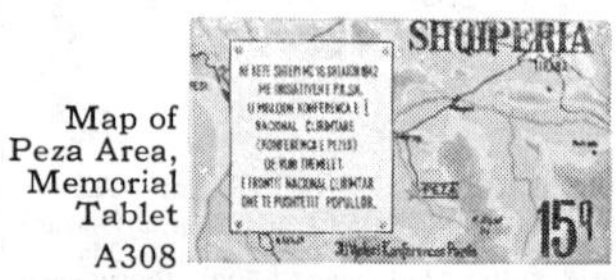

Map of Peza Area, Memorial Tablet A308

1972, Sept. 16 Multicolored

1455	A308	15q *shown*	15	3
1456	A308	25q *Guerrillas with flag*	20	5
1457	A308	1.90 l *Peza Conference memorial*	1.10	45

30th anniversary, Conference of Peza.

Partisans, by Sotir Capo—A309

Paintings: 10q, Woman, by Ismail Lulani (vert.). 15q, "Communists," by Lec Shkreli (vert.). 20q, View of Nendorit, 1941, by Sali Shijaku (vert.). 50q, Woman with Sheaf, by Zef Shoshi (vert.). 1 l, Landscape with Children, by Dhimitraq Trebicka. 2 l, Women on Bicycles, by Vilson Kilica. 2.30 l, Folk Dance, by Abdurrahim Buza.

Perf. 12½x12, 12x12½

1972, Sept. 25 Lithographed

1458	A309	5q gold & multi	3	3
1459	A309	10q gold & multi	5	3
1460	A309	15q gold & multi	7	3
1461	A309	20q gold & multi	12	4
1462	A309	50q gold & multi	27	15
1463	A309	1 l gold & multi	65	20
1464	A309	2 l gold & multi	1.25	45
		Nos. 1458-1464 (7)	2.44	93

Miniature Sheet

Imperf.

1465	A309	2.30 l gold & multi	1.50	1.00

No. 1465 contains one stamp (41x68 mm.); silver margin. Size: 55x82mm.

Congress Emblem A310

Design: 2.05 l, Young worker with banner.

1972, Oct. 23 Litho. *Perf. 12*

1466	A310	25q sil, red & gold	15	5
1467	A310	2.05 l sil & multi	1.10	45

Union of Working Youth, 6th Congress.

Hammer and Sickle A311

Ismail Qemali A312

Design: 1.20 l, Lenin as orator.

1972, Nov. 7 Litho. *Perf. 11½x12*

1468	A311	1.10 l multi	55	20
1469	A311	1.20 l multi	65	30

55th anniversary of the Russian October Revolution.

Perf. 12x11½, 11½x12

1972, Nov. 29

Designs: 15q, Albanian fighters (horiz.). 65q, Rally (horiz.). 1.25 l, Coat of arms.

1470	A312	15q red, brt bl & blk	7	3
1471	A312	25q yel, blk & red	15	5
1472	A312	65q red, sal & blk	35	15
1473	A312	1.25 l dl red & blk	65	20

60th anniversary of independence.

Cock, Mosaic A313

Mosaics, 2nd–5th centuries, excavated near Buthrotium and Apollonia: 10q, Bird (vert.). 15q, Partridges (vert.). 25q, Warrior's legs. 45q, Nymph riding dolphin (vert.). 50q, Fish (vert.). 2.50 l, Warrior with helmet.

1972, Dec. 10 *Perf. 12½x12, 12x12½*

1474	A313	5q sil & multi	3	3
1475	A313	10q sil & multi	5	3
1476	A313	15q sil & multi	10	6
1477	A313	25q sil & multi	14	8
1478	A313	45q sil & multi	25	9
1479	A313	50q sil & multi	27	10
1480	A313	2.50 l sil & multi	1.50	60
		Nos. 1474-1480 (7)	2.34	99

Nicolaus Copernicus A314

Designs: 10q, 25q, 80q, 1.20 l, Various portraits of Copernicus. 1.60 l, Heliocentric solar system.

1973, Feb. 19 Litho. *Perf. 12x12½*

1481	A314	5q lil rose & multi	4	3
1482	A314	10q dl ol & multi	5	3
1483	A314	25q multi	15	5
1484	A314	80q lt vio & multi	42	14
1485	A314	1.20 l bl & multi	80	30
1486	A314	1.60 l gray & multi	1.00	35
		Nos. 1481-1486 (6)	2.46	90

500th anniversary of the birth of Nicolaus Copernicus (1473–1543), Polish astronomer.

Flowering Cactus—A315

Designs: Various flowering cacti.

1973, Mar. 25 Litho. *Perf. 12*

1487	A315	10q multi	5	3
1488	A315	15q multi	7	3
1489	A315	20q beige & multi	10	4
1490	A315	25q gray & multi	15	5
1491	A315	30q beige & multi	20	6
1492	A315	65q gray & multi	40	12
1493	A315	80q multi	50	20
1494	A315	2 l multi	1.25	45
		Nos. 1487-1494 (8)	2.72	98

Nos. 1487–1494 printed se-tenant.

Guard and Factories A316

Design: 1.80 l, Guard and guards with prisoner.

1973, Mar. 20 Litho. *Perf. 12½x12*

1495	A316	25q ultra & blk	14	10
1496	A316	1.80 l dk red & multi	95	75

30th anniversary of the State Security Branch.

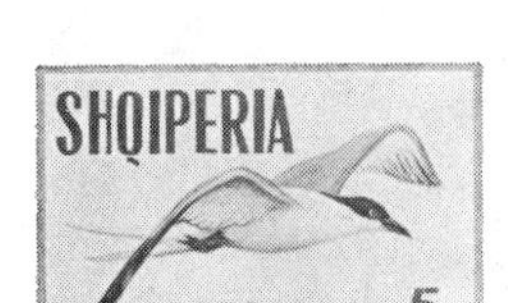

Common Tern A317

Sea Birds: 15q, White-winged black terns (vert.). 25q, Black-headed gull (vert.). 45q, Great black-headed gull. 80q, Slender-billed gull (vert.). 2.40 l, Sandwich terns.

Perf. 12½x12, 12x12½

1973, Apr. 30

1497	A317	5q gold & multi	3	3
1498	A317	15q gold & multi	8	3
1499	A317	25q gold & multi	14	5
1500	A317	45q gold & multi	25	9
1501	A317	80q gold & multi	45	30
1502	A317	2.40 l gold & multi	1.75	70
		Nos. 1497-1502 (6)	2.70	1.20

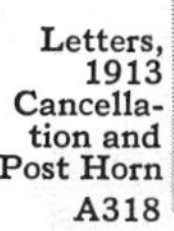
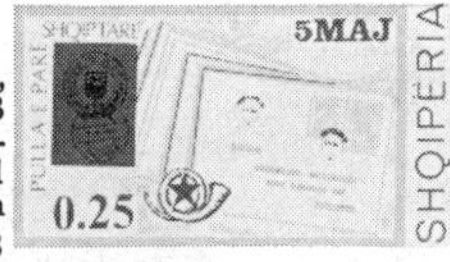

Letters, 1913 Cancellation and Post Horn A318

Design: 1.80 l, Mailman and 1913 cancelation.

1973, May. 5 Litho. *Perf. 12x11½*

1503	A318	25q red & multi	20	10
1504	A318	1.80 l red & multi	1.25	75

60th anniversary of Albanian stamps.

Farmer, Worker, Soldier A319

Design: 25q, Woman and factory (vert.).

1973, June 4 *Perf.12*

1505	A319	25q car rose	20	10
1506	A319	1.80 l yel, dp org & blk	1.00	60

7th Congress of Albanian Women's Union.

Creation of General Staff, by G. Madhi—A320

Designs: 40q, "August 1949," sculpture by Sh. Haderi (vert.). 60q, "Generation after Generation," sculpture by H. Dule (vert.). 80q, "Defend Revolutionary Victories," by M. Fushekati.

1973, July 10 Litho. *Perf. 12½x12*

1507	A320	25q gold & multi	20	5
1508	A320	40q gold & multi	45	8
1509	A320	60q gold & multi	50	12
1510	A320	80q gold & multi	80	30

30th anniversary of the People's Army.

"Electrification," by S. Hysa—A321

Albanian Paintings: 10q, Woman Textile Worker, by N. Nallbani. 15q, Gymnasts, by M. Fushekati. 50q, Aviator, by F. Stamo. 80q, Fascist Prisoner, by A. Lakuriqi. 1.20 l, Workers with Banner, by P. Mele. 1.30 l, Farm Woman, by Zef Shoshi. 2.05 l, Battle of Tenda, by F. Haxhiu. 10q, 50q, 80q, 1.20 l, 1.30 l, vertical.

Perf. 12½x12, 12x12½

1973, Aug. 10

1511	A321	5q gold & multi	3	3
1512	A321	10q gold & multi	5	3
1513	A321	15q gold & multi	13	3
1514	A321	50q gold & multi	30	10
1515	A321	80q gold & multi	55	17
1516	A321	1.20 l gold & multi	75	25
1517	A321	1.30 l gold & multi	95	27
		Nos. 1511-1517 (7)	2.76	88

Souvenir Sheet

Imperf.

1518	A321	2.05 l multi	1.50	75

No. 1518 contains one stamp; light yellow margin. Size: 98x62mm.

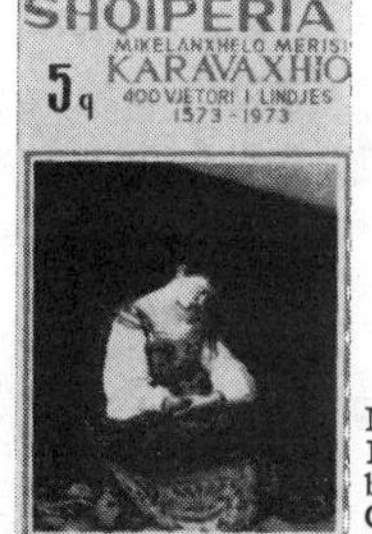

Mary Magdalene, by Caravaggio A322

Paintings by Michelangelo da Caravaggio: 10q, The Lute Player (horiz.). 15q, Self-portrait. 50q, Boy Carrying Fruit and Flowers. 80q, Still Life (horiz.). 1.20 l, Narcissus. 1.30 l, Boy Peeling Apple. 2.05 l, Man with Feathered Hat.

Perf. 12x12½, 12½x12

1973, Sept. 28

1519	A322	5q gold & multi	3	3
1520	A322	10q gold & multi	5	3
1521	A322	15q gold, blk & gray	7	3
1522	A322	50q gold & multi	25	10
1523	A322	80q gold & multi	40	17
1524	A322	1.20 l gold & multi	65	25
1525	A322	1.30 l gold & multi	75	27
		Nos. 1519-1525 (7)	2.20	88

Souvenir Sheet

Imperf.

1526	A322	2.05 l multi	1.25	75

400th anniversary of the birth of Michelangelo da Caravaggio (Merisi; 1573?–1609), Italian painter. No. 1526 contains one stamp (63x73mm.); gray marginal inscription. Size: 81x99mm.

Soccer—A323

Designs: 5q–1.25 l, Various soccer scenes. 2.05 l, Ball in goal and list of cities where championships were held.

1973, Oct. 30 Litho. *Perf. 12½x12*

1527	A323	5q multi	3	3
1528	A323	10q multi	5	3
1529	A323	15q multi	7	3
1530	A323	20q multi	10	3
1531	A323	25q multi	15	5
1532	A323	90q multi	50	18
1533	A323	1.20 l multi	75	25
1534	A323	1.25 l multi	90	25
		Nos. 1527-1534 (8)	2.55	85

Minature Sheet

Imperf.

1535	A323	2.05 l multi	1.75	90

World Soccer Cup, Munich 1974. Size of No. 1535: 82x54mm.

Weight Lifter A324

Designs: Various stages of weight lifting. 1.20 l, 1.60 l, horizontal.

1973, Oct. 30 Litho. *Perf. 12*

1536	A324	5q multi	3	3
1537	A324	10q multi	5	3
1538	A324	25q multi	11	5
1539	A324	90q multi	40	18
1540	A324	1.20 l multi	60	25
1541	A324	1.60 l multi	80	33
		Nos. 1536-1541 (6)	1.99	87

Weight Lifting Championships, Havana, Cuba.

Ballet A325 Harvester Combine A326

Perf. 12½x12, 12x12½

1973–74 Lithographed

Designs: 5q, Cement factory, Kavaje. 10q, Ali Kelmendi truck factory and tank cars (horiz.). 25q, "Communication." 35q, Skiers and hotel (horiz.). 60q, Resort (horiz.). 80q, Mountain lake. 1 l, Mao Tse-tung textile mill. 1.20 l, Steel workers. 2.40 l, Welder and pipe. 3 l, Skanderbeg Monument, Tirana. 5 l, Roman arches, Durrës.

1543	A325	5q gold & multi	3	3
1544	A325	10q gold & multi	5	3
1545	A325	15q gold & multi	7	3
1545A	A326	20q gold & multi	10	3
1546	A326	25q gold & multi	15	5
1547	A326	35q gold & multi	16	7
1548	A326	60q gold & multi	30	12
1549	A326	80q gold & multi	36	17
1549A	A326	1 l gold & multi	45	20
1549B	A326	1.20 l gold & multi	54	25
1549C	A326	2.40 l gold & multi	1.10	50
1550	A326	3 l gold & multi	1.50	60
1551	A326	5 l gold & multi	2.50	1.00
		Nos. 1543-1551 (13)	7.31	3.08

Issue dates: Nos. 1545–1546, 1549–1550, Dec. 5, 1973; others in 1974.

Mao Tse-tung A327

Design: 1.20 l, Mao Tse-tung addressing crowd.

1973, Dec. 26 *Perf. 12*

1552	A327	85q gold, red & sep	38	17
1553	A327	1.20 l gold, red & sep	54	25

80th birthday of Mao Tse-tung.

Old Man and Dog, by Gericault A328

Paintings by Jean Louis André Theodore Gericault: 10q, Horse's Head. 15q, Male Model. 25q, Head of Black Man. 1.20 l, Self-portrait. 2.05 l, Raft of the Medusa (horiz.). 2.20 l, Battle of the Giants.

Perf. 12x12½, 12½x12

1974, Jan. 18 Lithographed

1554	A328	10q gold & multi	5	3
1555	A328	15q gold & multi	7	3
1556	A328	20q gold & multi	10	3
1557	A328	25q gold & blk	11	5
1558	A328	1.20 l gold & multi	60	25
1559	A328	2.20 l gold & multi	1.25	45
		Nos. 1554-1559 (6)	2.18	84

Souvenir Sheet

Imperf.

1560	A328	2.05 l gold & multi	1.25	75

No. 1560 contains one stamp (87x78 mm.). Sheet has gold margin and inscription. Size: 100x78mm.

Lenin, by Pandi Mele A329

Designs: 25q, Lenin with Sailors on Cruiser Aurora, by Dhimitraq Trebicka (horiz.). 1.20 l, Lenin, by Vilson Kilica.

Perf. 12½x12, 12x12½

1974, Jan. 21

1561	A329	25q gold & multi	15	5
1562	A329	60q gold & multi	35	15
1563	A329	1.20 l gold & multi	90	30

50th anniversary of the death of Lenin (1870–1924).

Swimming Duck, Mosaic—A330

Designs: Mosaics from the 5th–6th Centuries A.D., excavated near Buthrotium, Pogradec and Apollonia.

1974, Feb. 20 Litho. *Perf. 12½x12*

Multicolored

1564	A330	5q	*shown*	3	3
1565	A330	10q	*Bird and flower*	5	3
1566	A330	15q	*Vase and grapes*	7	3
1567	A330	25q	*Duck*	15	5
1568	A330	40q	*Donkey and bird*	20	6
1569	A330	2.50 l	*Sea horse*	1.25	50
			Nos. 1564-1569 (6)	1.75	70

Soccer—A331

Designs: Various scenes from soccer. 2.05 l, World Soccer Cup and names of participating countries.

1974, Apr. 25 Litho. *Perf. 12½x12*

1570	A331	10q	gold & multi	5	3
1571	A331	15q	gold & multi	7	3
1572	A331	20q	gold & multi	10	3
1573	A331	25q	gold & multi	11	5
1574	A331	40q	gold & multi	20	6
1575	A331	80q	gold & multi	45	20
1576	A331	1 l	gold & multi	75	20
1577	A331	1.20 l	gold & multi	80	50
			Nos. 1570-1577 (8)	2.53	1.10

Souvenir Sheet

Imperf.

1578	A331	2.05 l	gold & multi	1.75	75

World Cup Soccer Championship, Munich, June 13–July 7. No. 1578 contains one stamp (60x60mm.) with simulated perforations. Size: 72x75mm.

Arms of Albania, Soldier
A332

Design: 1.80 l, Soldier and front page of 1944 Congress Book.

1974, May 24 Litho. *Perf. 12*

1579	A332	25q	multi	11	5
1580	A332	1.80 l	multi	90	35

30th anniversary of the First Anti-Fascist Liberation Congress of Permet.

Bittersweet
A333

Designs: Medicinal Plants. 40q, 80q, 2.20 l, horizontal.

1974, May 5 *Perf. 12x12½*

Multicolored

1581	A333	10q	*shown*	5	3
1582	A333	15q	*Arbutus*	7	3
1583	A333	20q	*Lilies of the valley*	10	3
1584	A333	25q	*Autumn crocus*	11	5
1585	A333	40q	*Borage*	20	6
1586	A333	80q	*Soapwort*	45	15
1587	A333	2.20 l	*Gentian*	95	60
			Nos. 1581-1587 (7)	1.93	95

Revolutionaries with Albanian Flag
A334

Design: 1.80 l, Portraits of 5 revolutionaries (vert.).

Perf. 12½x12, 12x12½

1974, June 10

1588	A334	25q	red, blk & lil	11	5
1589	A334	1.80 l	yel, red & blk	90	35

50th anniversary Albanian Bourgeois Democratic Revolution.

European Redwing—A335

Designs: Songbirds; Nos. 1597–1600 vertical.

Perf. 12½x12, 12x12½

1974, July 15 Lithographed

Multicolored

1594	A335	10q	*shown*	5	3
1595	A335	15q	*European robin*	7	3
1596	A335	20q	*Greenfinch*	10	3
1597	A335	25q	*Bullfinch*	11	5
1598	A335	40q	*Hawfinch*	20	6
1599	A335	80q	*Blackcap*	60	20
1600	A335	2.20 l	*Nightingale*	1.25	60
			Nos. 1594-1600 (7)	2.38	1.00

Globe
A336

Designs: 1.20 l, UPU emblem. 2.05 l, Jet over globe.

1974, Aug. 25 Litho. *Perf. 12x12½*

1601	A336	85q	grn & multi	50	20
1602	A336	1.20 l	vio & ol grn	75	30

Miniature Sheet

Imperf.

1603	A336	2.05 l	bl & multi	9.00	9.00

Centenary of Universal Postal Union. No. 1603 contains one stamp, gold margin. Size: 77x78mm.

Widows, by Sali Shijaku—A337

Albanian Paintings: 15q, Drillers, by Danish Jukniu (vert.). 20q, Workers with Blueprints, by Clirim Ceka. 25q, Call to Action, by Spiro Kristo (vert.). 40q, Winter Battle, by Sabaudin Xhaferi. 80q, Comrades, by Clirim Ceka (vert.). 1 l, Aiding the Partisans, by Guri Madhi. 1.20 l, Teacher with Pupils, by Kleo Nini Brezat. 2.05 l, Comrades in Arms, by Guri Madhi.

Perf. 12½x12, 12x12½

1974, Sept. 25

1604	A337	10q	sil & multi	5	3
1605	A337	15q	sil & multi	7	3
1606	A337	20q	sil & multi	10	5
1607	A337	25q	sil & multi	11	5
1608	A337	40q	sil & multi	20	6
1609	A337	80q	sil & multi	40	12
1610	A337	1 l	sil & multi	50	20
1611	A337	1.20 l	sil & multi	65	25
			Nos. 1604-1611 (8)	2.08	79

Miniature Sheet

Imperf.

1612	A337	2.05 l	sil & multi	1.25	75

No. 1612 contains one stamp. Size: 86x77mm.

Crowd on Tien An Men Square
A338

Design: 1.20 l, Mao Tse-tung (vert.).

1974, Oct. 1 *Perf. 12*

1613	A338	85q	gold & multi	42	12
1614	A338	1.20 l	gold & multi	54	25

25th anniversary of the proclamation of the People's Republic of China.

Women's Volleyball
A339

Designs (Spartakiad Medal and): 15q, Women hurdlers. 20q, Women gymnasts. 25q, Mass exercises in Stadium. 40q, Weight lifter. 80q, Wrestlers. 1 l, Military rifle drill. 1.20 l, Soccer.

1974, Oct. 9 *Perf. 12x12½*

1615	A339	10q	multi	5	3
1616	A339	15q	multi	7	3
1617	A339	20q	multi	10	3
1618	A339	25q	gray & multi	11	5
1619	A339	40q	multi	20	6
1620	A339	80q	multi	40	12
1621	A339	1 l	multi	45	20
1622	A339	1.20 l	tan & multi	54	25
			Nos. 1615-1622 (8)	1.92	77

National Spartakiad, Oct. 9–17.

View of Berat
A340

Designs: 80q, Enver Hoxha addressing Congress, bas-relief (horiz.). 1 l, Hoxha and leaders leaving Congress Hall.

Perf. 12x12½, 12½x12

1974, Oct. 20 Lithographed

1623	A340	25q	rose car & blk	11	5
1624	A340	80q	yel, brn & blk	40	12
1625	A340	1 l	dp lil & blk	45	20

30th anniversary of 2nd Congress of Berat.

Anniversary Emblem, Factory Guards
A341

Designs (Anniversary Emblem and): 35q, Chemical industry. 50q, Agriculture. 80q, Arts. 1 l, Atomic diagram and computer. 1.20 l, Youth education. 2.05 l, Anniversary emblem: Crowd and History Book.

1974, Nov. 29 Litho. *Perf. 12½x12*

1626	A341	25q	grn & multi	11	5
1627	A341	35q	ultra & multi	16	7
1628	A341	50q	brn & multi	22	10
1629	A341	80q	multi	40	12
1630	A341	1 l	vio & multi	45	20
1631	A341	1.20 l	multi	54	25
			Nos. 1626-1631 (6)	1.88	79

Miniature Sheet

Imperf.

1632	A341	2.05 l	gold & multi	1.25	75

30th anniversary of liberation from Fascism. No. 1632 contains one stamp. Size: 80x69mm.

Artemis, from Apolloni
A342

1974, Dec. 25 Photo. *Perf. 12x12½*

Silver & Multicolored

1633	A342	10q	*shown*	5	3
1634	A342	15q	*Zeus statue*	7	3
1635	A342	20q	*Poseidon statue*	10	3
1636	A342	25q	*Illyrian helmet*	11	5
1637	A342	40q	*Amphora*	20	6
1638	A342	80q	*Agrippa*	40	12
1639	A342	1 l	*Demosthenes*	45	20
1640	A342	1.20 l	*Head of Bilia*	54	25
			Nos. 1633-1640 (8)	1.92	77

Miniature Sheet

Imperf.

1641	A342	2.05 l	*Artemis and amphora*	95	65

Archaeological discoveries in Albania. No. 1641 contains one stamp. Size: 95x95 mm.

Workers and Factories
A343

Design: 25q, Handshake, tools and book (vert.).

1975, Feb. 11 Litho. *Perf. 12*

1642	A343	25q	brn & multi	11	5
1643	A343	1.80 l	yel & multi	85	32

Albanian Trade Unions, 30th anniversary.

Chicory
A344

1975, Feb. 15

Gray and Multicolored

1644	A344	5q *shown*	3	3
1645	A344	10q *Houseleek*	5	3
1646	A344	15q *Columbine*	7	3
1647	A344	20q *Anemone*	10	3
1648	A344	25q *Hibiscus*	11	5
1649	A344	30q *Gentian*	14	6
1650	A344	35q *Hollyhock*	17	6
1651	A344	2.70 l *Iris*	1.20	50
		Nos. 1644-1651 (8)	1.87	79

Protected flowers.

Jesus, from Doni Madonna
A345

Works by Michelangelo: 10q, Slave, sculpture. 15q, Head of Dawn, sculpture. 20q, Awakening Giant, sculpture. 25q, Cumaenian Sybil, Sistine Chapel. 30q, Lorenzo di Medici, sculpture. 1.20 l, David, sculpture. 2.05 l, Self-portrait. 3.90 l, Delphic Sybil, Sistine Chapel.

1975, Mar. 20 Litho. ***Perf. 12x12½***

1652	A345	5q gold & multi	3	3
1653	A345	10q gold & multi	5	3
1654	A345	15q gold & multi	7	3
1655	A345	20q gold & multi	10	3
1656	A345	25q gold & multi	11	5
1657	A345	30q gold & multi	14	6
1658	A345	1.20 l gold & multi	54	25
1659	A345	3.90 l gold & multi	2.00	80
		Nos. 1652-1659 (8)	3.04	1.28

Miniature Sheet

Imperf.

1660	A345	2.05 l gold & multi	1.10	75

500th birth anniversary of Michelangelo Buonarroti (1475–1564), Italian sculptor, painter and architect. Size of No. 1660: 76x85mm.

Two-wheeled Cart—A346

Albanian Transportation of the Past: 5q, Horseback rider. 15q, Lake ferry. 20q, Coastal three-master. 25q, Phaeton. 3.35 l, Early automobile on bridge.

1975, Apr. 15 Litho. ***Perf. 12½x12***

1661	A346	5q bl grn & multi	3	3
1662	A346	10q ol & multi	5	3
1663	A346	15q lil & multi	7	3
1664	A346	20q multi	10	3
1665	A346	25q multi	11	5
1666	A346	3.35 l ocher & multi	1.75	65
		Nos. 1661-1666 (6)	2.11	82

Guard at Frontier Stone
A347

Guardsman and Militia
A348

1975, Apr. 25 ***Perf. 12***

1667	A347	25q multi	11	5
1668	A348	1.80 l multi	86	32

30th anniversary of Frontier Guards.

Posting Illegal Poster—A349

Designs: 60q, Partisans in battle. 1.20 l, Partisan killing German soldier, and Albanian coat of arms.

1975, May 9 ***Perf. 12½x12***

1669	A349	25q multi	11	5
1670	A349	60q multi	30	12
1671	A349	1.20 l red & multi	60	30

30th anniversary of victory over Fascism.

European Widgeons
A350

Waterfowl: 10q, Red-crested pochards. 15q, White-fronted goose. 20q, Northern pintails. 25q, Red-breasted merganser. 30q, Eider ducks. 35q, Whooper swan. 2.70 l, Shovelers.

1975, June 15 Litho. ***Perf. 12***

1672	A350	5q brt bl & multi	3	3
1673	A350	10q yel grn & multi	5	3
1674	A350	15q brt rose lil & multi	7	3
1675	A350	20q bl grn & multi	10	3
1676	A350	25q multi	12	5
1677	A350	30q multi	14	6
1678	A350	35q org & multi	18	6
1679	A350	2.70 l multi	1.20	50
		Nos. 1672-1679 (8)	1.89	79

Shyqyri Kanapari, by Musa Qarri
A351

Albanian Paintings: 10q, Woman Saving Children in Sea, by Agim Faja. 15q, "November 28, 1912" (revolution), by Petrit Ceno (horiz.). 20q, "Workers Unite," by Sali Shijaku. 25q, The Partisan Shota Galica, by Ismail Lulani. 30q, Victorious Resistance Fighters, 1943, by Nestor Jonuzi. 80q, Partisan Couple in Front of Red Flag, by Vilson Halimi. 2.05 l, Dancing Procession, by Abdurahim Buza. 2.25 l, Republic Day Celebration, by Fatmir Haxhiu (horiz.).

Perf. 12x12½, 12½x12

1975, July 15 Lithographed

1680	A351	5q gold & multi	3	3
1681	A351	10q gold & multi	5	3
1682	A351	15q gold & multi	7	3
1683	A351	20q gold & multi	12	4
1684	A351	25q gold & multi	14	5
1685	A351	30q gold & multi	17	6
1686	A351	80q gold & multi	50	12
1687	A351	2.25 l gold & multi	1.15	45
		Nos. 1680-1687 (8)	2.23	81

Miniature Sheet

Imperf.

1688	A351	2.05 l gold & multi	1.10	75

No. 1688 contains one stamp. Size: 67x98mm. Nos. 1680–1687 issued in sheets of 8 stamps and gold center label showing palette and easel.

Farmer Holding Reform Law
A352

Design: 2 l, Produce and farm machinery.

1975, Aug. 28 ***Perf. 12***

1689	A352	15q multi	7	3
1690	A352	2 l multi	90	40

Agrarian reform, 30th anniversary.

Alcynonium Palmatum
A353

Corals: 10q, Paramuricea chamaeleon. 20q, Coralium rubrum. 25q, Eunicella covalini. 3.70 l, Cladocora cespitosa.

1975, Sept. 25 Litho. ***Perf. 12***

1691	A353	5q bl, ol & blk	3	3
1692	A353	10q bl & multi	5	3
1693	A353	20q bl & multi	10	4
1694	A353	25q bl & blk	11	5
1695	A353	3.70 l bl & blk	1.65	70
		Nos. 1691-1695 (5)	1.94	85

Bicycling
A354

Designs (Montreal Olympic Games Emblem and): 10q, Canoeing. 15q, Fieldball. 20q, Basketball. 25q, Water polo. 30q, Hockey. 1.20 l, Pole vault. 2.05 l, Fencing. 2.15 l, Montreal Olympic Games emblem and various sports.

1975, Oct. 20 Litho. ***Perf. 12½***

1696	A354	5q multi	3	3
1697	A354	10q multi	5	3
1698	A354	15q multi	7	3
1699	A354	20q multi	10	4
1700	A354	25q multi	11	5
1701	A354	30q multi	14	6
1702	A354	1.20 l multi	54	25
1703	A354	2.05 l multi	95	50
		Nos. 1696-1703 (8)	1.99	99

Miniature Sheet

Imperf.

1704	A354	2.15 l org & multi	3.25	2.50

21st Olympic Games, Montreal, July 18–Aug. 8, 1976. Size of No. 1704: 72x76mm.

Power Lines Leading to Village
A355

Designs: 25q, Transformers and insulators. 80q, Dam and power station. 85q, Television set, power lines, grain and cogwheel.

1975, Oct. 25 ***Perf. 12x12½***

1705	A355	15q ultra & yel	7	3
1706	A355	25q brt vio & pink	11	5
1707	A355	80q lt grn & gray	45	12
1708	A355	85q ocher & brn	45	15

General electrification, 5th anniversary.

Child, Rabbit and Teddy Bear Planting Tree—A356

Fairy Tales: 10q, Mother fox. 15q, Ducks in school. 20q, Little pigs building house. 25q, Animals watching television. 30q, Rabbit and bear at work. 35q, Working and playing ants. 2.70 l, Wolf in sheep's clothes.

1975, Dec. 25 Litho. ***Perf. 12½x12***

1709	A356	5q blk & multi	3	3
1710	A356	10q blk & multi	5	3
1711	A356	15q blk & multi	7	3
1712	A356	20q blk & multi	12	4
1713	A356	25q blk & multi	14	5
1714	A356	30q blk & multi	16	6
1715	A356	35q blk & multi	20	6
1716	A356	2.70 l blk & multi	1.40	50
		Nos. 1709-1716 (8)	2.17	80

Arms, People, Factories
A357

Design: 1.90 l, Arms, government building, celebrating crowd.

1976, Jan. 11 Litho. *Perf. 12*

1717	A357	25q gold & multi	12	5
1718	A357	1.90 l gold & multi	88	34

30th anniversary of proclamation of Albanian People's Republic.

Ice Hockey, Olympic Games' Emblem
A358

Designs: 10q, Speed skating. 15q, Biathlon. 50q, Ski jump. 1.20 l, Slalom. 2.15 l, Figure skating, pairs. 2.30 l, One-man bobsled.

1976, Feb. 4

1719	A358	5q sil & multi	3	3
1720	A358	10q sil & multi	5	3
1721	A358	15q sil & multi	7	3
1722	A358	50q sil & multi	22	10
1723	A358	1.20 l sil & multi	54	25
1724	A358	2.30 l sil & multi	1.05	48
		Nos. 1719-1724 (6)	1.96	92

Miniature Sheet

Perf. 12 on 2 sides x imperf.

1725	A358	2.15 l sil & multi	1.10	90

12th Winter Olympic Games, Innsbruck, Austria, Feb. 4–15. Size of No. 1725 66x79mm.

Meadow Saffron
A359

Medicinal Plants: 10q, Deadly nightshade. 15q, Yellow gentian. 20q, Horse chestnut. 70q, Shield fern. 80q, Marsh mallow. 2.30 l, Thorn apple.

1976, Apr. 10 Litho. *Perf. 12x12½*

1726	A359	5q blk & multi	3	3
1727	A359	10q blk & multi	5	3
1728	A359	15q blk & multi	7	3
1729	A359	20q blk & multi	10	4
1730	A359	70q blk & multi	32	12
1731	A359	80q blk & multi	40	12
1732	A359	2.30 l blk & multi	1.00	55
		Nos. 1726-1732 (7)	1.97	92

Bowl and Spoon—A360

Designs: 15q, Flask (vert.). 20q, Carved handles (vert.). 25q, Pistol and dagger. 80q, Wall hanging (vert.). 1.20 l, Earrings and belt buckle. 1.40 l, Jugs (vert.).

1976 Litho. *Perf. 12½x12, 12x12½*

1733	A360	10q lil & multi	5	3
1734	A360	15q gray & multi	7	3
1735	A360	20q multi	10	4
1736	A360	25q car & multi	11	5
1737	A360	80q yel & multi	40	12
1738	A360	1.20 l multi	54	25
1739	A360	1.40 l tan & multi	75	35
		Nos. 1733-1739 (7)	2.02	87

National Ethnographic Conference, Tirana, June 28.

Founding of Cooperatives, by Zef Shoshi
A361

Paintings: 10q, Going to Work, by Agim Zajmi (vert.). 25q, Crowd Listening to Loudspeaker, by Vilson Kilica. 40q, Woman Welder, by Sabaudin Xhaferi (vert.). 50q, Factory, by Isuf Sulovari (vert.). 1.20 l, 1942 Revolt, by Lec Shkreli (vert.). 1.60 l, Coming Home from Work, by Agron Dine. 2.05 l, Honoring a Young Pioneer, by Andon Lakuriqi.

Perf. 12½x12, 12x12½

1976, Aug. 8 Lithographed

1740	A361	5q gold & multi	3	3
1741	A361	10q gold & multi	5	3
1742	A361	25q gold & multi	11	5
1743	A361	40q gold & multi	20	8
1744	A361	50q gold & multi	22	10
1745	A361	1.20 l gold & multi	54	25
1746	A361	1.60 l gold & multi	80	30
		Nos. 1740-1746 (7)	1.95	84

Miniature Sheet

Perf. 12 on 2 sides x imperf.

1747	A361	2.05 l gold & multi	1.10	75

Size of No. 1747: 92x79mm.

Red Flag, Agricultural Symbols
A362

Enver Hoxha, Partisans and Albanian Flag
A363

Design: 1.20 l, Red flag and raised pickax.

1976, Nov. 1

1748	A362	25q multi	12	5
1749	A362	1.20 l multi	60	25

7th Workers Party Congress.

1976, Oct. 28 *Perf. 12x12½*

Design: 1.90 l, Demonstrators with Albanian flag.

1750	A363	25q multi	12	5
1751	A363	1.90 l multi	95	34

35th anniversary of anti-Fascist demonstrations.

Attacking Partisans, Meeting House
A364

Designs (Red Flag and): 25q, Partisans, pickax and gun. 80q, Workers, soldiers, pickax and gun. 1.20 l, Agriculture and industry. 1.70 l, Dancers, symbols of science and art.

1976, Nov. 8 Litho. *Perf. 12x12½*

1752	A364	15q gold & multi	8	3
1753	A364	25q gold & multi	12	5
1754	A364	80q gold & multi	40	12
1755	A364	1.20 l gold & multi	60	25
1756	A364	1.70 l gold & multi	85	28
		Nos. 1752-1756 (5)	2.05	73

35th anniversary of 1st Workers Party Congress.

Young Workers and Track
A365

Design: 1.25 l, Young soldiers and Albanian flag.

1976, Nov. 23 *Perf. 12*

1757	A365	80q yel & multi	40	12
1758	A365	1.25 l car & multi	65	30

Union of Young Communists, 35th anniversary.

"Cuca e Maleve" Ballet
A366

Designs: Scenes from ballet "Mountain Girl."

1976, Dec. 14 *Perf. 12*

1759	A366	10q gold & multi	5	3
1760	A366	15q gold & multi	8	3
1761	A366	20q gold & multi	10	4
1762	A366	25q gold & multi	12	5
1763	A366	80q gold & multi	40	12
1764	A366	1.20 l gold & multi	60	25
1765	A366	1.40 l gold & multi	70	30
		Nos. 1759-1765 (7)	2.05	82

Miniature Sheet

Perf. 12 on 2 sides x imperf.

1766	A366	2.05 l gold & multi	1.10	75

Size of No. 1766: 77x68mm.

Bashtoves Castle
A367

Albanian Castles: 15q, Gjirokastres. 20q, Ali Pash Tepelenes. 25q, Petreles. 80q, Beratit. 1.20 l, Durresit. 1.40 l, Krujes.

1976, Dec. 30 Litho. *Perf. 12*

1767	A367	10q blk & dl bl	5	3
1768	A367	15q blk & grn	8	3
1769	A367	20q blk & gray	10	4
1770	A367	25q blk & brn	12	5
1771	A367	80q blk & rose	40	12
1772	A367	1.20 l blk & vio	60	25
1773	A367	1.40 l blk & brn red	70	30
		Nos. 1767-1773 (7)	2.05	82

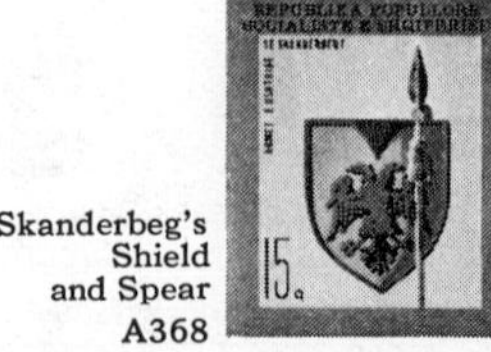

Skanderbeg's Shield and Spear
A368

Skanderbeg's Weapons: 80q, Helmet, sword and scabbard. 1 l, Halberd, quiver with arrows, crossbow and spear.

1977, Jan. 28 Litho. *Perf. 12*

1774	A368	15q sil & multi	15	3
1775	A368	80q sil & multi	60	30
1776	A368	1 l sil & multi	1.10	50

Skanderbeg (1403–1468), national hero.

Ilia Oiqi, Messenger in Storm
A369

Polyvinylchloride Plant, Vlore
A370

Modern Heroes: 10q, Ilia Dashi, sailor in battle. 25q, Fran Ndue Ivanaj, fisherman in storm. 80q, Zeliha Allmetaj, woman rescuing child. 1 l, Ylli Zaimi, rescuing goats from flood. 1.90 l, Isuf Plloci, fighting forest fire.

1977, Feb. 28 Litho. *Perf. 12x12½*

1777	A369	5q brn & multi	3	3
1778	A369	10q ultra & multi	5	3
1779	A369	25q bl & multi	12	5
1780	A369	80q ocher & multi	40	12
1781	A369	1 l brn & multi	45	20
1782	A369	1.90 l brn & multi	85	38
		Nos. 1777-1782 (6)	1.90	81

1977, Mar. 29 Litho. *Perf. 12½x12*

Designs: 25q, Naphtha fractioning plant, Ballsh. 65q, Hydroelectric station and dam, Fjerzes. 1 l, Metallurgical plant and blast furance, Elbasan.

1783	A370	15q sil & multi	8	3
1784	A370	25q sil & multi	12	5
1785	A370	65q sil & multi	32	12
1786	A370	1 l sil & multi	45	20

6th Five-year plan.

Qerime Halil Galica
A371

Victory Monument, Tirana
A372

Design: 1.25 l, Qerime Halil Galica "Shota" and father Azem Galica.

1977, Apr. 20 Litho. *Perf. 12*

1787	A371	80q dk red	40	12
1788	A371	1.25 l gray bl	60	25

"Shota" Galica, communist fighter.

1977, May 5 Litho. *Perf. 12*

Designs (Red Star and): 80q, Clenched fist, Albanian flag. 1.20 l, Bust of Qemal Stafa and poppies.

1789	A372	25q multi	12	5
1790	A372	80q multi	40	12
1791	A372	1.20 l multi	60	25

35th anniversary of Martyrs' Day.

Physician Visiting Farm, Mobile Clinic
A373

Designs: 10q, Cowherd and cattle ranch. 20q, Militia woman helping with harvest, rifle and combine. 80q, Modern village, highway and power lines. 2.95 l, Tractor and greenhouses.

1977, June 18

1792	A373	5q multi	3	3
1793	A373	10q multi	5	3
1794	A373	20q multi	10	4
1795	A373	80q multi	40	12
1796	A373	2.95 l multi	1.50	58
		Nos. 1792-1796 (5)	2.08	80

"Socialist transformation of the villages."

Armed Workers, Flag and Factory A374

Design: 1.80 l, Workers with proclamation and flags.

1977, June 20

1797	A374	25q multi	12	5
1798	A374	1.80 l multi	85	30

9th Labor Unions Congress.

Kerchief Dance A375

Designs: Various folk dances.

1977, Aug. 20 Litho. *Perf. 12*

1799	A375	5q multi	3	3
1800	A375	10q multi	5	3
1801	A375	15q multi	8	3
1802	A375	25q multi	12	5
1803	A375	80q multi	40	12
1804	A375	1.20 l multi	60	25
1805	A375	1.55 l multi	75	35
		Nos. 1799-1805 (7)	2.03	86

Miniature Sheet

Perf. 12 on 2 sides x imperf.

1806	A375	2.05 l multi	1.10	75

Size of No. 1806: 56x74mm.
See Nos. 1836-1840, 1884-1888.

Attack A376

Designs: 25q, Enver Hoxha addressing Army. 80q, Volunteers and riflemen. 1 l, Volunteers, hydrofoil patrolboat and MiG planes. 1.90 l, Volunteers and Albanian flag.

1977, July 10 Litho. *Perf. 12*

1807	A376	15q gold & multi	8	3
1808	A376	25q gold & multi	12	5
1809	A376	80q gold & multi	40	12
1810	A376	1 l gold & multi	45	20
1811	A376	1.90 l gold & multi	85	38
		Nos. 1807-1811 (5)	1.90	78

"One People—One Army."

Armed Workers, Article 3 of Constitution A377

Design: 1.20 l, Symbols of farming and fertilizer industry, Article 25 of Constitution.

1977, Oct.

1812	A377	25q red, gold & blk	12	5
1813	A377	1.20 l red, gold & blk	60	25

New Constitution.

Picnic A378

Film Frames: 15q, Telephone lineman in winter. 25q, Two men and a woman. 80q, Workers. 1.20 l, Boys playing in street. 1.60 l, Harvest.

1977, Oct. 25 Litho. *Perf. 12½x12*

1814	A378	10q bl grn	5	3
1815	A378	15q multi	8	3
1816	A378	25q black	12	5
1817	A378	80q multi	40	12
1818	A378	1.20 l dp cl	60	25
1819	A378	1.60 l multi	80	30
		Nos. 1814-1819 (6)	2.05	78

Albanian films.

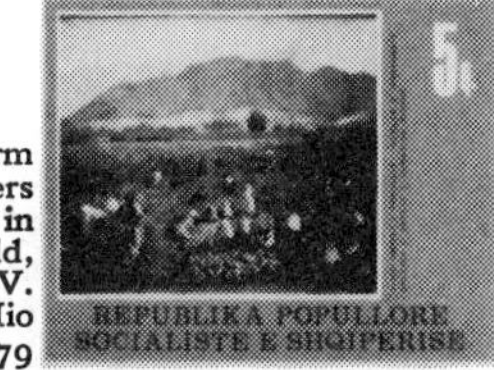

Farm Workers in Field, by V. Mio A379

Paintings by V. Mio: 10q, Landscape in Snow. 15q, Grazing Sheep under Walnut Tree in Spring. 25q, Street in Korce. 80q, Horseback Riders on Mountain Pass. 1 l, Boats on Shore. 1.75 l, Tractors Plowing Fields. 2.05 l, Self-portrait.

1977, Dec. 25 Litho. *Perf. 12½x12*

1820	A379	5q gold & multi	3	3
1821	A379	10q gold & multi	5	3
1822	A379	15q gold & multi	8	3
1823	A379	25q gold & multi	12	5
1824	A379	80q gold & multi	40	12
1825	A379	1 l gold & multi	50	20
1826	A379	1.75 l gold & multi	85	35
		Nos. 1820-1826 (7)	2.03	81

Miniature Sheet

Imperf.; Perf. 12 Horiz. between Vignette and Value Panel.

1827	A379	2.05 l gold & multi	1.00	60

Size of No. 1827: 66x101mm.

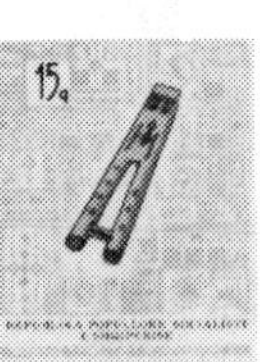

Pan Flute A380

Albanian Flag, Monument and People A381

Folk Musical Instruments: 25q, Single-string goat's-head fiddle. 80q, Woodwind. 1.20 l, Drum. 1.70 l, Bagpipe. Background shows various woven folk patterns.

1978, Jan. 20 *Perf. 12x12½*

1828	A380	15q multi	8	3
1829	A380	25q multi	12	5
1830	A380	80q multi	40	12
1831	A380	1.20 l multi	60	25
1832	A380	1.70 l multi	85	32
		Nos. 1828-1832 (5)	2.05	77

1978 *Perf. 12½x12, 12x12½*

Designs: 25q, Ismail Qemali and fighters (horiz.). 1.65 l, People dancing around Albanian flag (horiz.).

1833	A381	15q multi	8	3
1834	A381	25q multi	12	5
1835	A381	1.65 l multi	82	35

65th anniversary of independence.

Folk Dancing Type of 1977

Designs: Various dances.

1978, Feb. 15 Litho. *Perf. 12*

1836	A375	5q multi	3	3
1837	A375	25q multi	12	5
1838	A375	80q multi	40	12
1839	A375	1 l multi	50	20
1840	A375	2.30 l multi	1.10	45
		Nos. 1836-1840 (5)	2.15	85

Nos. 1836–1840 have white background around dancers, Nos. 1799–1805 have pinkish shadows.

Tractor Drivers, by Dhimitraq Trebicka A382

Working Class Paintings: 80q, Steeplejack, by Spiro Kristo. 85q, "A Point in the Discussion," by Skender Milori. 90q, Oil rig crew, by Anesti Cini (vert.). 1.60 l, Metal workers, by Ramadan Karanxha. 2.20 l, Political discussion, by Sotiraq Sholla.

1978, Mar. 25 Litho. *Perf. 12*

1841	A382	25q multi	12	5
1842	A382	80q multi	40	12
1843	A382	85q multi	42	14
1844	A382	90q multi	45	16
1845	A382	1.60 l multi	80	25
		Nos. 1841-1845 (5)	2.19	72

Miniature Sheet

Perf. 12 on 2 sides x imperf.

1846	A382	2.20 l multi	1.50	75

Size of No. 1846: 72x98mm.

Woman with Rifle and Pickax—A383

Design: 1.95 l, Farm and Militia women, industrial plant.

1978, June 1 Litho. *Perf. 12*

1847	A383	25q gold & red	12	5
1848	A383	1.95 l gold & red	95	38

8th Congress of Women's Union.

Children and Flowers A384

Designs: 10q, Children with rifle, ax, book and flags. 25q, Dancing children in folk costume. 1.80 l, Children in school.

1978, June 1 Lithographed

1849	A384	5q multi	3	3
1850	A384	10q multi	5	3
1851	A384	25q multi	12	5
1852	A384	1.80 l multi	90	35

International Children's Day.

Spirit of Skanderbeg as Conqueror A385

Designs: 10q, Battle at Mostar Bridge. 80q, Marchers and Albanian flag. 1.20 l, Riflemen in winter battle. 1.65 l, Abdyl Frasheri (1839–1892). 2.20 l, Rifles, scrol, and pen, League building. 2.60 l, League headquarters, Prizren.

1978, June 10 Litho. *Perf. 12*

1853	A385	10q multi	5	3
1854	A385	25q multi	12	5
1855	A385	80q multi	40	12
1856	A385	1.20 l multi	60	25
1857	A385	1.65 l multi	82	25
1858	A385	2.60 l multi	1.25	45
		Nos. 1853-1858 (6)	3.24	1.15

Miniature Sheet

Perf. 12 on 2 sides x imperf.

1859	A385	2.20 l multi	1.20	60

Centenary of League of Prizren. Size of No. 1859: 74x69mm.

Guerrillas and Flag, 1943 A386

Designs: 25q, Soldier, sailor, airman, militiaman (horiz.). 1.90 l, Members of armed forces, civil guards, and Young Pioneers.

1978, July 10 *Perf. 11½x12½*

1860	A386	5q multi	3	3
1861	A386	25q multi	12	5
1862	A386	1.90 l multi	95	38

35th anniversary of People's Army.

Woman with Machine Carbine A387

Kerchief Dance A388

Designs: 25q, Man with target rifle (horiz.). 95q, Man shooting with telescopic sights (horiz.). 2.40 l, Woman target shooting with pistol.

Perf. 12½x12, 12x12½

1978, Sept. 20 Lithographed

1863	A387	25q blk & yel	12	5
1864	A387	80q org & blk	40	12
1865	A387	95q red & blk	42	14
1866	A387	2.40 l car & blk	1.15	45

32nd National Rifle-shooting Championships, Sept. 20.

1978, Oct. 6 *Perf. 12*

Designs: 15q, Musicians. 25q, Fiddler with single-stringed instrument. 80q, Dancers, men. 1.20 l, Saber dance. 1.90 l, Singers, women.

1867	A388	10q multi	5	3
1868	A388	15q multi	8	3
1869	A388	25q multi	12	5
1870	A388	80q multi	40	12
1871	A388	1.20 l multi	60	25
1872	A388	1.90 l multi	90	38
		Nos. 1867-1872 (6)	2.15	86

National Folklore Festival.

No. 1736 Surcharged with New Value, 2 Bars and "RICCIONE 78"

1978 Litho. *Perf. 12½x12*

1873	A360	3.30 l on 25q multi	3.50	3.50

Riccione 78 Philatelic Exhibition.

Enver Hoxha
A389

1978, Oct. 16 Litho. *Perf. 12x12½*

1874 A389 80q red & multi 40 12
1875 A389 1.20 l red & multi 60 25
1876 A389 3.40 l red & multi 1.20 50

Miniature Sheet

Perf. 12½ on 2 sides x imperf.

1877 A389 2.20 l red & multi 1.20 1.20

70th birthday of Enver Hoxha, First Secretary of Central Committee of the Communist Party of Albania. Size of No. 1877: 67x88½mm.

Woman and Wheat
A390

Designs: 25q, Woman with egg crates. 80q, Shepherd and sheep. 2.60 l, Milkmaid and cows.

1978, Dec. 15 *Perf. 12x12½*

1878 A390 15q multi 8 3
1879 A390 25q multi 12 5
1880 A390 80q multi 40 12
1881 A390 2.60 l multi 1.25 45

Dora d'Istria
A391

Tower House
A392

Design: 1.10 l, Full portrait of Dora d'Istria, author; birth sesquicentennial.

1979, Jan. 22 Litho. *Perf. 12*

1882 A391 80q lt grn & blk 40 12
1883 A391 1.10 l vio brn & blk 55 22

Costume Type of 1977

Designs: Various folk dances.

1979, Feb. 25

1884 A375 15q multi 8 3
1885 A375 25q multi 12 5
1886 A375 80q multi 40 12
1887 A375 1.20 l multi 60 25
1888 A375 1.40 l multi 70 30
Nos. 1884-1888 (5) 1.90 75

Nos. 1884–1888 have white background. Denomination in upper left on No. 1885, in upper right on No. 1802; lower left on No. 1886, upper left on No. 1803.

1979, Mar. 20

Traditional Houses: 15q, Stone gallery house (horiz.). 80q, House with wooden galleries (horiz.). 1.20 l, Galleried tower house. 1.40 l, 1.90 l, Tower houses (diff.).

1889 A392 15q multi 8 3
1890 A392 25q multi 12 5
1891 A392 80q multi 40 12
1892 A392 1.20 l multi 60 25
1893 A392 1.40 l multi 70 30
Nos. 1889-1893 (5) 1.90 75

Miniature Sheet

Perf. 12 on 2 sides x imperf.

1894 A392 1.90 l multi 1.00 1.00

Size of No. 1894: 62x75mm.

Soldier, Factories, Wheat
A393

Design: 1.65 l, Soldiers, workers and coat of arms.

1979, May 14 Litho. *Perf. 12*

1895 A393 25q multi 12 5
1896 A393 1.65 l multi 82 25

Congress of Permet, 35th anniversary.

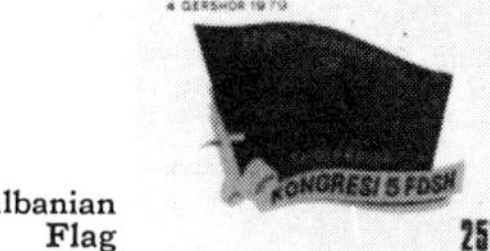

Albanian Flag
A394 RPS E SHQIPERISE

1979, June 4

1897 A394 24q multi 12 5
1898 A394 1.65 l multi 82 25

5th Congress of Albanian Democratic Front.

Vasil Shanto
A395

Alexander Moissi
A396

1979

1899 A395 15q multi 8 3
1900 A395 25q multi 12 8
1901 A395 60q multi 32 10
1902 A396 80q multi 40 12
1903 A396 90q multi 48 15
1904 A396 1.10 l multi 58 18
Nos. 1899-1904 (6) 1.98 66

Vasil Shanto (1913–1944) and Qemal Stafa (1921–1942), Anti-Fascist fighters; Alexander Moissi (1880–1935), actor.

Winter Campaign, by Arben Basha
A397

Paintings of Military Scenes by: 25q, Ismail Lulani. 80q, Myrteza Fushekati. 1.20 l, Muhamet Deliu. 1.40 l, Jorgji Gjikopulli. 1.90 l, Fatmir Haxhiu.

1979, Oct. Litho. *Perf. 12½×12*

1905 A397 15q multi 8 3
1906 A397 25q multi 12 8
1907 A397 80q multi 40 12
1908 A397 1.20 l multi 60 25
1909 A397 1.40 l multi 70 30
Nos.1905-1909 (5) 1.90 78

Miniature Sheet

Perf. 12 on 2 sides x imperf.

1910 A397 1.90 l multi 1.00 1.00

Size of No. 1910: 78×103mm.

Athletes Surrounding Flag-A398

Literary Society Headquarters-A399

1979, Oct. 1 Litho. *Perf. 12*

1911 A398 15q *shown* 8 3
1912 A398 25q *Shooting* 12 5
1913 A398 80q *Dancing* 40 18
1914 A398 1.20 l *Soccer* 60 25
1915 A398 1.40 l *High jump* 70 30
Nos. 1911-1915 (5) 1.90 81

Liberation Spartakiad, 35th anniversary.

1979, Oct. 12

Albanian Literary Society Centenary: 25q, Seal and charter. 80q, Founder. 1.55 l, 1879 Headquarters. 1.90 l, Founders.

1916 A399 25q multi 12 5
1917 A399 80q multi 40 18
1918 A399 1.20 l multi 60 25
1919 A399 1.55 l multi 75 35

Miniature Sheet

Perf. 12½ on 2 sides × imperf.

1920 A399 1.90 l multi 1.25 60

Size of No. 1920: 78½×66mm.

Congress Statute, Coat of Arms—A400

1979, Oct. 20 Photo. *Perf. 12×12½*

1921 A400 25q multi 12 5
1922 A400 1.65 l multi 82 25

2nd Congress of Berat, 35th anniversary.

Children Entering School, Books—A401

1979 Litho. *Perf. 12½x12*

1923 A401 5q shown 3 3
1924 A401 10q Communications 5 3
1925 A401 15q Steel workers 8 3
1926 A401 20q Dancers, instruments 10 4
1927 A401 25q Newspapers, radio, television 12 5
1928 A401 60q Textile worker 30 10
1929 A401 80q Armed forces 40 18
1930 A401 1.20 l Industry 60 25
1931 A401 1.60 l transportation 80 32
1932 A401 2.40 l Agriculture 1.20 50
1932A A401 3 l Medicine 1.50 60
Nos. 1923-1932A (11) 5.18 2.13

Workers and Factory—A402

Worker, Red Flag and: 80q, Hand holding sickle and rifle. 1.20l, Red star and open book. 1.55l, Open book and cogwheel.

1979, Nov. 29

1933 A402 25q multi 12 5
1934 A402 80q multi 40 18
1935 A402 1.20 l multi 60 25
1936 A402 1.55 l multi 75 35

35th anniversary of independence.

Joseph Stalin—A403

Design: 1.10l, Stalin on dais (horiz.).

1979, Dec. 21 Litho. *Perf. 12*

1937 A403 80q red & dk bl 40 18
1938 A403 1.10 l red & dk bl 58 22

Joseph Stalin (1879-1953), birth centenary.

Fireplace and Pottery, Korcar—A404

Home Furnishings: 80q, Cupboard bed, dagger, pistol, ammunition pouch, Shkodar. 1.20 l, Stool, pot, chair, Mirdit. 1.35 l, Chimney, dagger, jacket, Gjirokastro.

1980, Feb. 27 Litho. *Perf. 12*

1939 A404 25q multi 12 5
1940 A404 80q multi 40 18
1941 A404 1.20 l multi 60 25
1942 A404 1.35 l multi 68 28

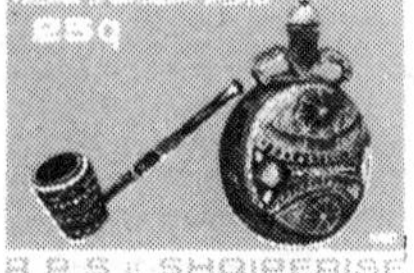

Pipe, Painted Flask—A405

1980, Mar. 4

1943 A405 25q *shown* 12 5
1944 A405 80q *Leather handbags* 40 18
1945 A405 1.20 l *Carved eagle, embroidered rug* 60 25
1946 A405 1.35 l *Lace* 68 28

Prof. Aleksander Xhuvanit Birth Centenary—A406

1980, Mar. 14

1947	A406	80q	multi	40	18
1948	A406	1 l	multi	50	20

Revolutionaries on Horseback—A407

Insurrection at Kosove, 70th Anniversary: 1 l, Battle scene.

1980, Apr. 4

1949	A407	80q	red & blk	40	18
1950	A407	1 l	red & blk	50	20

Soldiers and Workers Laboring to Aid the Stricken Populations, by D. Jukinui and I. Lulani—A408

1980, Apr. 15 **Litho.** ***Perf. 12½***

1951	A408	80q	lt bl & multi	40	18
1952	A408	1 l	lt bl grn & multi	50	20

Lenin, 110th Birth Anniversary—A409

1980, Apr. 22

1953	A409	80q	multi	40	18
1954	A409	1 l	multi	50	20

Misto Mame and Ali Demi, War Martyrs—A410

War Martyrs: 80q, Sadik Staveleci, Vojo Kusji, Hoxhi Martini. 1.20 l, Bule Naipi, Persefoni Kokedhima. 1.35 l, Ndoc Deda, Hydajet Lezha, Naim Gjylbegu, Ndoc Mazi, Ahmed Haxha.

1980, May 5

1955	A410	25q	multi	12	5
1956	A410	80q	multi	40	18
1957	A410	1.20 l	multi	60	25
1958	A410	1.35 l	multi	68	28

Scene from "Mirela"—A411

1980, June 7

1959	A411	15q	*shown*	8	3
1960	A411	25q	*The Scribbler*	12	5
1961	A411	80q	*Circus Bears*	40	18
1962	A411	2.40 l	*Waterdrops*	1.20	50

Carrying Iron Castings in the Enver Hoxha Tractor Combine, by S. Shijaku and M. Fushekati—A412

Paintings (Gallery of Figurative Paintings, Tirana): 80q, The Welder, by Harilla Dhima. 1.20 l, Steel Erectors, by Petro Kokushta. 1.35 l, 1.80 l, Communists, by Vilson Kilica.

1980, July 22

1963	A412	25q	multi	12	5
1964	A412	80q	multi	40	18
1965	A412	1.20 l	multi	60	25
1966	A412	1.35 l	multi	68	28

Souvenir Sheet

1967	A412	1.80 l	multi	1.00	40

Gate, Parchment Miniature, 11th Cent.—A413

Bas reliefs of the Middle Ages: 80q, Eagle, 13th cent. 1.20 l, Heraldic lion, 14th cent. 1.35 l, Pheasant, 14th cent.

1980, Sept. 27 **Litho.** ***Perf. 12***

1968	A413	25q	gold & blk	12	5
1969	A413	80q	gold & blk	40	18
1970	A413	1.20 l	gold & blk	60	25
1971	A413	1.35 l	gold & blk	68	28

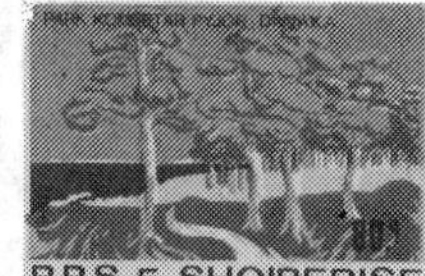

Divjaka National Park—A414

1980, Nov. 6 **Photo.**

1972	A414	80q	shown	40	18
1973	A414	1.20 l	Lura	60	25
1974	A414	1.60 l	Thethi	80	35

Park Type of 1980
Souvenir Sheet

1980, Nov. 6 **Photo.** ***Perf. 12½***

1975	A414	1.80 l	Llogara Park	1.00	50

No. 1975 has multicolored decorative margin. Size: 90x90mm.

Citizens, Flag and Arms of Albania—A415

1981, Jan. 11 **Litho.** ***Perf. 12***

1976	A415	80q	shown	40	18
1977	A415	1 l	People's Party Headquarters, Tirana	50	20

35th anniversary of the Republic.

Child's Bed—A416

1981, Mar. 20 **Litho.** ***Perf. 12***

1978	A416	25q	shown	12	5
1979	A416	80q	Wooden bucket, brass bottle	40	18
1980	A416	1.20 l	Shoes	60	25
1981	A416	1.35 l	Jugs	68	28

Soldiers Fighting with Rifles—A417

1981, Apr. 20

1982	A417	80q	shown	40	18
1983	A417	1 l	Sword combat	50	20

Souvenir Sheet
Perf. 12½ Vert.

1984	A417	1.80 l	Soldier with pistol	1.00	50

Battle of Shtimje centenary. No. 1984 contains one stamp; purple margin shows battle scene. Size: 85x68mm.

House Interior, Labara—A418

1981, Feb. 25 **Litho.** ***Perf. 12***

1985	A418	25q	shown	12	5
1986	A418	80q	Labara, diff.	40	18
1987	A418	1.20 l	Mat	60	25
1988	A418	1.35 l	Dibres	68	28

Boys Riding Unicycles—A419

Designs: Children's circus.

1981, June ***Perf. 12***

1989	A419	15q	multi	8	3
1990	A419	25q	multi	12	5
1991	A419	80q	multi	40	18
1992	A419	2.40 l	multi	1.20	50

Soccer Players A420

1982 World Cup Soccer Elimination Games: Various soccer players.

1981, Mar. 31 **Litho.** ***Perf. 12***

1993	A420	25q	multi	12	5
1994	A420	80q	multi	40	18
1995	A420	1.20 l	multi	60	25
1996	A420	1.35 l	multi	68	28

Allies, by S. Hysa—A421

Paintings: 80q, Warriors, by A. Buza. 1.20 l, Rallying to the Flag, Dec. 1911, by A. Zajmi (vert.). 1.35 l, My Flag is My Heart, by L. Cefa (vert.). 1.80 l, Circling the Flag in a Common Cause, by N. Vasia.

1981, July 10 ***Perf. 12½x12***

1997	A421	25q	multi	12	5
1998	A421	80q	multi	40	18
1999	A421	1.20 l	multi	60	25
2000	A421	1.35 l	multi	68	28

Souvenir Sheet

2001	A421	1.80 l	multi	1.00	50

No. 2001 contains one stamp (55x55mm.); multicolored margin. Size: 82x109mm.

Rifleman—A422

1981, Aug. 30 ***Perf. 12***

2002	A422	25q	shown	12	5
2003	A422	80q	Weight lifting	40	18
2004	A422	1.20 l	Volleyball	60	25
2005	A422	1.35 l	Soccer	68	28

Albanian Workers' Party, 8th Congress—A423

1981, Nov. 1

2006	A423	80q	Flag, star	40	18
2007	A423	1 l	Flag, hammer and sickle	50	20

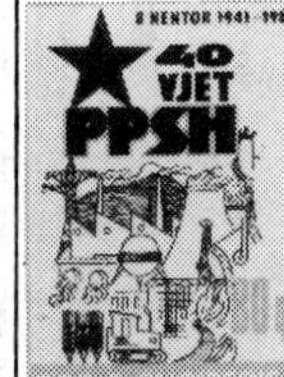

Albanian Workers' Party, 40th Anniv. A424

Communist Youth Org., 40th Anniv. A425

1981, Nov. 8

2008	A424	80q	Symbols of industrialization	40	18
2009	A424	2.80 l	Fist, emblem	1.40	60

Souvenir Sheet

2010	A424	1.80 l	Enver Hoxha, Memoirs	1.00	50

Size of No. 2010: 79x99mm.

1981, Nov. 23

2011	A425	80q	Star, ax, map	40	18
2012	A425	1 l	Flags, star	50	20

Fan S. Noli, Writer, Birth Centenary
A426

Traditional House, Bulqize
A427

1982, Jan. 6 **Litho.** *Perf. 12*

2013	A426	80q	lt ol grn & gold	40	18
2014	A426	1.10 l	lt red brn & gold	55	22

1982, Feb. *Perf. 12½x12*

2015	A427	25q	shown	12	5
2016	A427	80q	Lebush	40	18
2017	A427	1.20 l	Bicaj	60	25
2018	A427	1.55 l	Klos	80	35

TB Bacillus Centenary—A428

1982, Mar. 24 *Perf. 12*

2019	A428	80q	Globe	40	18
2020	A428	1.10 l	Koch	55	22

Albanian League House, Prizren, by K. Buza—A429

Kosova Landscapes: 25q, Castle at Prizrenit, by G. Madhi. 1.20 l, Mountain Gorge at Rogove, by K. Buza. 1.55 l, Street of the Hadhji at Zekes, by G. Madhi. 25q, 1.20 l, 1.55 l vert.

Perf. 12x12½, 12½x 12

1982, Apr. 15 **Litho.**

2021	A429	25q	multi	12	5
2022	A429	80q	multi	40	18
2023	A429	1.20 l	multi	60	25
2024	A429	1.55 l	multi	80	35

War Martyr Type of 1980

Designs: 25q, Hibe Palikuqi, Liri Gero. 80q, Mihal Duri, Kajo Karafili. 1.20 l, Fato Dudumi, Margarita Tutulani, Shejnaze Juka. 1.55 l, Memo Meto, Gjok Doci.

1982, May *Perf. 12*

2025	A410	25q	multi	12	5
2026	A410	80q	multi	40	18
2027	A410	1.20 l	multi	60	25
2028	A410	1.55 l	multi	80	35

Loading Freighter—A430

Children's Paintings.

1982, June 15 *Perf. 12½x12*

2029	A430	15q	shown	8	3
2030	A430	80q	Forest	40	18
2031	A430	1.20 l	City	60	25
2032	A430	1.65 l	Park	85	36

Handkerchief Dancers—A438

Folkdancers.

1983, Feb. 20 **Litho.** *Perf. 12*

2056	A438	25q	shown	12	5
2057	A438	80q	With kerchief, drum	40	18
2058	A438	1.20 l	With guitar, flute, tambourine	60	25
2059	A438	1.55 l	Women	80	35

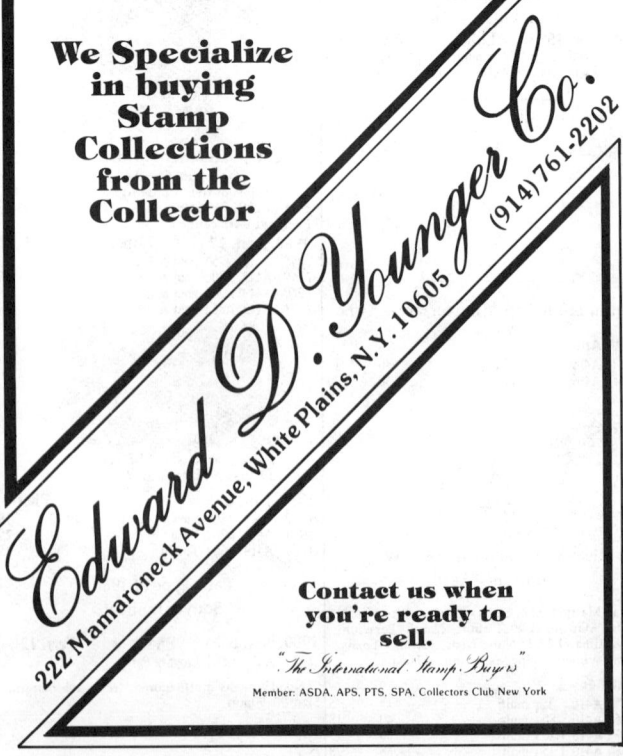

SEMI-POSTAL STAMPS.

Nos. 148-151 Surcharged in Red and Black

5 qind.

1924 *Perf. 12½, 12* **Unwmkd.**

B1	A18	5q +5q yel grn	3.50	3.50
B2	A18	10q +5q car	3.50	3.50
B3	A18	25q +5q dk bl	3.50	3.50
B4	A18	50q +5q dk grn	3.50	3.50

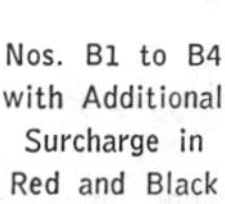

Nos. B1 to B4 with Additional Surcharge in Red and Black

+ 5 qind.

1924 *Perf. 12½x11½, 12½.*

B5	A18	5q +5q+5q yel grn	3.50	3.50
B6	A18	10q +5q+5q car	3.50	3.50
B7	A18	25q +5q+5q dk bl	3.50	3.50
B8	A18	50q +5q+5q dk grn	3.50	3.50

Issued under Italian Dominion.

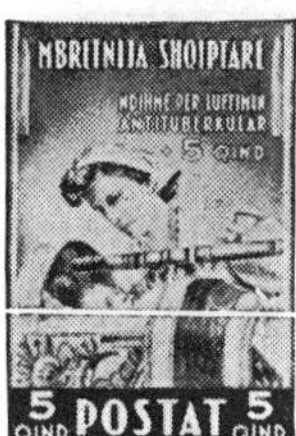

Nurse and Child
SP1

Photogravure

1943 *Perf. 14* **Unwmkd.**

B9	SP1	5q +5q dk grn	10	15
B10	SP1	10q +10q ol brn	10	15
B11	SP1	15q +10q rose red	15	20
B12	SP1	25q +15q saph	20	25
B13	SP1	30q +20q vio	25	30
B14	SP1	50q +25q dk org	30	35
B15	SP1	65q +30q grnsh blk	45	50
B16	SP1	1fr +40q chnt	80	90
		Nos. B9-B16 (8)	2.35	2.80

The surtax was for the control of tuberculosis.

Issued under German Administration.

War Victims
SP2

1944

B17	SP2	5q +5(q) dp grn	3.00	4.00
B18	SP2	10q +5(q) dp brn	3.00	4.00
B19	SP2	15q +5(q) car lake	3.00	4.00
B20	SP2	25q +10(q) dp bl	3.00	4.00
B21	SP2	1fr +50q dk ol	3.00	4.00
B22	SP2	2fr +1(fr) pur	3.00	4.00
B23	SP2	3fr +1.50(fr) dk org	3.00	4.00
		Nos. B17-B23 (7)	21.00	28.00

The surtax was for victims of World War II.

Independent State

Nos. B9 to B12 Surcharged in Carmine

1945 *Perf. 14.* **Unwmkd.**

B24	SP1	30q +15q on 5q+5q dk grn	1.50	1.50
B25	SP1	50q +25q on 10q+10q ol brn	1.50	1.50
B26	SP1	1fr +50q on 15q+10q rose red	5.00	5.00
B27	SP1	2fr +1fr on 25q+15q saph	9.00	9.00

The surtax was for the Albanian Red Cross.

People's Republic

Nos. 361 to 366 Overprinted in Red (cross) and Surcharged in Black

KONGRESI
K.K.SH.
24-25-11-46
+0.10

1946 **Lithographed** *Perf. 11*

B28	A57	20q +10q bluish grn	7.00	7.00
B29	A57	30q +15q dp org	7.00	7.00
B30	A57	40q +20q brn	7.00	7.00
B31	A57	60q +30q red vio	7.00	7.00
B32	A57	1fr +50q rose red	7.00	7.00
B33	A57	3fr +1.50fr dk bl	7.00	7.00
		Nos. B28-B33 (6)	42.00	42.00

To honor and benefit the Congress of the Albanian Red Cross.

Counterfeits: lithographed, dull gum. Genuine: typographed, shiny gum.

First Aid and Red Cross
SP3

Designs: 25q+5q, Nurse carrying child on stretcher. 65q+25q, Symbolic blood transfusion. 80q+40q, Mother and child.

1967, Dec. 1 **Litho.** *Perf. 11½x12*

B34	SP3	15q +5q blk, red & brn	90	70
B35	SP3	25q +5q multi	1.00	90
B36	SP3	65q +25q blk, gray & red	3.00	1.00
B37	SP3	80q +40q multi	5.00	2.25

6th congress of the Albanian Red Cross.

AIR POST STAMPS.

Airplane Crossing Mountains
AP1

Wmk. 125

Wmkd. Lozenges. (125)

1925, May 30 **Typo.** *Perf. 14*

C1	AP1	5q green	60	60
C2	AP1	10q rose red	60	60
C3	AP1	25q dp bl	75	75
C4	AP1	50q dk grn	1.50	1.50
C5	AP1	1fr dk vio & blk	2.50	2.50
C6	AP1	2fr ol grn & vio	3.50	3.50
C7	AP1	3fr brn org & dk grn	6.00	6.00
		Nos. C1-C7 (7)	15.45	15.45

Nos. C1-C7 exist imperforate but are not known to have been regularly issued in that condition.

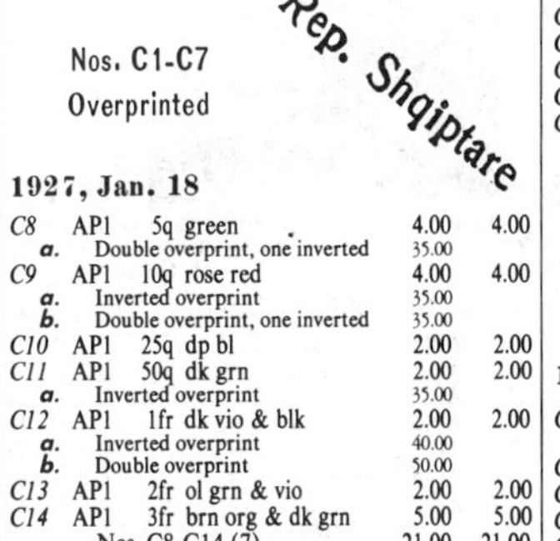

Nos. C1-C7 Overprinted

Rep. Shqiptare

1927, Jan. 18

C8	AP1	5q green	4.00	4.00
a.		Double overprint, one inverted	35.00	
C9	AP1	10q rose red	4.00	4.00
a.		Inverted overprint	35.00	
b.		Double overprint, one inverted	35.00	
C10	AP1	25q dp bl	2.00	2.00
C11	AP1	50q dk grn	2.00	2.00
a.		Inverted overprint	35.00	
C12	AP1	1fr dk vio & blk	2.00	2.00
a.		Inverted overprint	40.00	
b.		Double overprint	50.00	
C13	AP1	2fr ol grn & vio	2.00	2.00
C14	AP1	3fr brn org & dk grn	5.00	5.00
		Nos. C8-C14 (7)	21.00	21.00

Nos. C1-C7 Overprinted

REP. SHQYPTARE
Fluturim' i I-ar
Vlonë--Brindisi
21. IV. 1928

1928, Apr. 21

C15	AP1	5q green	1.50	1.50
a.		Inverted overprint	20.00	
C16	AP1	10q rose red	1.50	1.50
C17	AP1	25q dp bl	1.50	1.50
C18	AP1	50q dk grn	1.50	1.50
C19	AP1	1fr dk vio & blk	25.00	25.00
C20	AP1	2fr ol grn & vio	25.00	25.00
C21	AP1	3fr brn org & dk grn	25.00	25.00
		Nos. C15-C21 (7)	81.00	81.00

First flight across the Adriatic, Valona to Brindisi, Apr. 21, 1928.

The variety "SHQYRTARE" occurs once in the sheet for each value. Price 3 times normal.

Nos. C1-C7 Overprinted in Red Brown

Mbr. Shqiptare

1929, Dec. 1

C22	AP1	5q green	4.00	4.00
C23	AP1	10q rose red	4.00	4.00
C24	AP1	25q dp bl	4.00	4.00
C25	AP1	50q dk grn	15.00	15.00
C26	AP1	1fr dk vio & blk	175.00	175.00
C27	AP1	2fr ol grn	175.00	175.00
C28	AP1	3fr brn org & dk grn	175.00	175.00
		Nos. C22-C28 (7)	552.00	552.00

Excellent counterfeits exist of Nos. C22 to C28.

King Zog and Airplane over Tirana
AP2

AP3

1930, Oct. 8 **Photo.** **Unwmkd.**

C29	AP2	5q yel grn	20	20
C30	AP2	15q rose red	45	45
C31	AP2	20q sl bl	65	65
C32	AP2	50q ol grn	80	80
C33	AP3	1fr dk bl	2.00	2.00
C34	AP3	2fr ol brn	6.50	6.50
C35	AP3	3fr purple	8.00	8.00
		Nos. C29-C35 (7)	18.60	18.60

Nos. C29-C35 Overprinted

TIRANE-ROME
6 KORRIK 1931

1931, July 6

C36	AP2	5q yel grn	2.00	2.00
a.		Double overprint		
C37	AP2	15q rose red	2.00	2.00
C38	AP2	20q sl bl	2.00	2.00
C39	AP2	50q ol grn	2.00	2.00
C40	AP3	1fr dk bl	17.50	17.50
C41	AP3	2fr ol brn	17.50	17.50
C42	AP3	3fr purple	17.50	17.50
a.		Inverted overprint		
		Nos. C36-C42 (7)	60.50	60.50

Issued in connection with the first air post flight from Tirana to Rome.

Only a very small part of this issue was sold to the public. Most of the stamps were given to the Aviation Company to help provide funds for conducting the service.

Issued under Italian Dominion.

Nos. C29-C30 Overprinted in Black

Mbledhja
Kushtetuëse
12-IV-1939
XVII

1939, Apr. 19 *Perf. 14.* **Unwmkd.**

C43	AP2	5q yel grn	75	75
C44	AP2	15q rose red	75	75

No. C32 With Additional Surcharge of New Value

C45	AP2	20q on 50q ol grn	1.25	1.25
a.		Inverted ovpt.		

See note after No. 309.

King Victor Emmanuel III and Plane over Mountains
AP4

1939, Aug. 4 **Photogravure.**

C46	AP4	20q brown	7.00	3.00

Shepherds
AP5

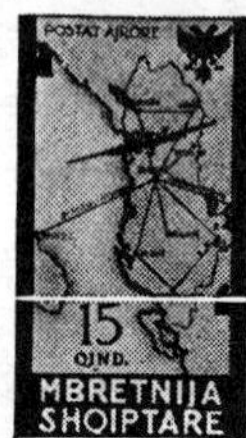

Map of Albania Showing Air Routes
AP6

Designs: 20q, Victor Emmanuel III and harbor view. 50q, Woman and river valley. 1fr, Bridge at Vezirit. 2fr, Ruins. 3fr, Women waving to plane.

1940, Mar. Unwmkd.

C47	AP5	5q green	20	15
C48	AP6	15q rose red	20	15
C49	AP5	20q dp bl	20	12
C50	AP6	50q brown	35	35
C51	AP5	1fr myr grn	75	85
C52	AP6	2fr brn blk	3.00	3.50
C53	AP6	3fr rose vio	9.00	10.00
		Nos.C47-C53 (7)	13.70	15.12

People's Republic

Vuno-Himare
AP12

Designs (Albanian towns): 1 l and 10 l, Rozafat-Shkoder. 2 l and 20 l, Keshtjelle-Butrinto.

1950, Dec. 15 Engr. *Perf. 12½x12*

C54	AP12	50q gray blk	10	5
C55	AP12	1 l red brn	15	7
C56	AP12	2 l ultra	35	12
C57	AP12	5 l dp grn	90	35
C58	AP12	10 l dp bl	1.75	90
C59	AP12	20 l purple	5.00	2.00
		Nos. C54-C59 (6)	8.25	3.49

Nos. C56-C58 Surcharged with New Value and Bars in Red or Black

1952–53

C60	AP12	50q on 2 l (R)	60.00	60.00
C61	AP12	50q on 5 l ('53)	10.00	6.00
C62	AP12	2.50 l on 5 l (R)	100.00	100.00
C63	AP12	2.50 l on 10 l ('53)	12.00	6.00

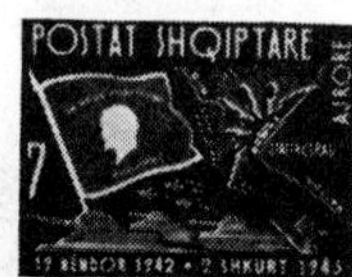

Banner with Lenin, Map of Stalingrad and Tanks
AP13

1963, Feb. 2 Litho. *Perf. 14*

C67	AP13	7 l grn & dp car	3.00	75

20th anniversary, Battle of Stalingrad.

Sputnik and Sun
AP14

Designs: 3 l, Lunik 4. 5 l, Lunik 3 photographing far side of the Moon. 8 l, Venus space probe. 12 l, Mars 1.

1963, Oct. 31 *Perf. 12* Unwmkd.

C68	AP14	2 l org, yel & blk	20	3
C69	AP14	3 l multi	50	4
C70	AP14	5 l rose lil, yel & blk	90	25
C71	AP14	8 l dl vio, yel & dp car	1.25	35
C72	AP14	12 l bl & org	2.25	1.10
		Nos. C68-72 (5)	5.10	1.77

Russian interplanetary explorations.

Nos. C68 and C71 Overprinted: "Riccione 23-8-1964"

1964, Aug. 23

C73	AP14	2 l org, yel & blk	3.00	3.00
C74	AP14	8 l dl vio, yel & dp car	6.00	6.00

Issued to commemorate the International Space Exhibition in Riccione, Italy.

Plane over Berat
AP15

Designs (Plane over): 40q, Gjirokaster. 60q, Sarande. 90q, Dürres. 1.20 l, Kruje. 2.40 l, Boga. 4.05 l, Tirana.

1975, Nov. 25 Litho. *Perf. 12*

C75	AP15	20q multi	10	4
C76	AP15	40q multi	20	8
C77	AP15	60q multi	28	12
C78	AP15	90q multi	42	18
C79	AP15	1.20 l multi	60	24
C80	AP15	2.40 l multi	1.25	48
C81	AP15	4.05 l multi	1.90	1.00
		Nos. C75-C81 (7)	4.75	2.14

SPECIAL DELIVERY STAMPS.

Issued under Italian Dominion.

King Victor Emmanuel III
SD1

Photogravure.

1940 *Perf. 14.* Unwmkd.

E1	SD1	25q brt vio	35	35
E2	SD1	50q red org	1.35	1.60

Issued under German Administration.

No. E1 Overprinted in Carmine

14 Shtator 1943

1943

E3	SD1	25q brt vio	15.00	17.50

Proclamation of Albanian independence.

POSTAGE DUE STAMPS.

Nos. 35–39 Handstamped in Various Colors

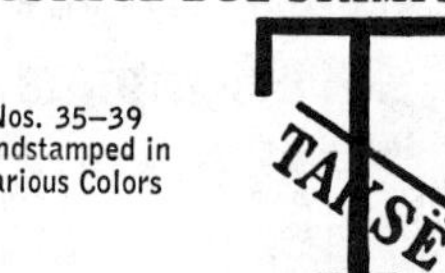

1914 *Perf. 14.* Unwmkd.

J1	A3	2q org brn & buff	1.75	1.20
J2	A3	5q green	1.75	1.50
J3	A3	10q rose red	2.50	1.50
J4	A3	25q dk bl	3.00	2.25
J5	A3	50q vio & red	3.50	3.00
		Nos. J1-J5 (5)	12.50	9.45

The two parts of the overprint are handstamped separately. Stamps exist with one or both handstamps inverted, double, omitted or in wrong color.

Nos. 48–51 Overprinted in Black **TAKSË**

1914

J6	A3 (a)	10pa on 5q grn	2.00	2.00
J7	A3 (a)	20pa on 10q rose red	2.00	2.00
J8	A3 (b)	1gr on 25q bl	2.00	2.00
J9	A3 (b)	2gr on 50q vio & red	2.00	2.00

Same Design as Regular Issue of 1919, Overprinted

1919 *Perf. 11½, 12½*

J10	A8	(4)q on 4h rose	5.00	6.00
J11	A8	(10)q on 10k red, *grn*	5.00	6.00
J12	A8	20q on 2k org, *gray*	5.00	6.00
J13	A8	50q on 5k brn, *yel*	5.00	6.00

Fortress at Scutari
D3

D5

Post Horn Overprinted in Black.

1920 *Perf. 14x13.*

J14	D3	4q ol grn	40	50
J15	D3	10q rose red	40	50
J16	D3	20q bis brn	40	50
J17	D3	50q black	70	80

1922 *Perf. 12½.*

Background of Red Wavy Lines.

J23	D5	4q *red*	75	1.00
J24	D5	10q *red*	75	1.00
J25	D5	20q *red*	75	1.00
J26	D5	50q *red*	75	1.00

Same Overprinted in White **Republika Shqiptare**

1925

J27	D5	4q *red*	75	1.00
J28	D5	10q *red*	75	1.00
J29	D5	20q *red*	75	1.00
J30	D5	50q *red*	75	1.00

The 10q with overprint in gold was a trial printing. It was not put in use.

D7

Coat of Arms
D8

Overprinted "QINDAR" in Red.

1926 *Perf. 13½x13*

J31	D7	10q dk bl	15	25
J32	D7	20q green	30	50
J33	D7	30q red brn	50	75
a.		Double overprint		
J34	D7	50q dk brn	75	1.25

Wmkd. Double Headed Eagle. (220)

1930 Photogravure *Perf. 14, 14½*

J35	D8	10q dk bl	5.00	5.00
J36	D8	20q rose red	1.25	1.25
J37	D8	30q violet	1.25	1.25
J38	D8	50q dk grn	1.50	1.50

Nos. J36–J38 exist with overprint "14 Shtator 1943" (see Nos. 332–344) which is private and fraudulent on these stamps.

No. 253 Overprinted **Taksë**

1936 *Perf. 14*

J39	A34	10q carmine	6.00	8.00

Issued under Italian Dominion.

Coat of Arms
D9

Photogravure.

1940 *Perf. 14.* Unwmkd.

J40	D9	4q red org	8.00	8.00
J41	D9	10q brt vio	2.50	2.50
J42	D9	20q brown	2.50	2.50
J43	D9	30q dk bl	3.00	3.00
J44	D9	50q car rose	6.00	6.00
		Nos. J40-J44 (5)	22.00	22.00

ALEXANDRETTA

(ăl′ĕg-zăn-drĕt′ȧ)

LOCATION—A political territory in northern Syria, bordering on Turkey.

GOVT.—A former French mandate.

AREA—10,000 sq. mi. (approx.).

POP.—270,000 (approx.).

Included in the Syrian territory mandated to France under the Versailles Treaty, the name was changed to Hatay in 1938. The following year France returned the territory to Turkey in exchange for certain concessions. See Hatay.

100 Centimes = 1 Piastre

Stamps of Syria, 1930–36, Overprinted or Surcharged in Black or Red:

Sandjak d'Alexandrette
a

SANDJAK D'ALEXANDRETTE
b

Sandjak d'Alexandrette
c

d

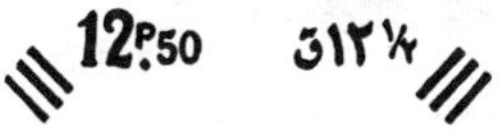
e

1938 *Perf. 12x12½, 13½.* Unwmkd.

1	A6 (a)	10c vio brn	35	35
2	A7 (a)	20c brn org	35	35
3	A9 (b)	50c vio (R)	35	35
4	A10 (b)	1p bis brn	50	50
5	A12 (b)	2p dk vio (R)	60	60
6	A13 (b)	3p yel grn (R)	1.35	1.35
7	A14 (b)	4p yel org	1.50	1.50
8	A16 (b)	6p grnsh blk (R)	1.60	1.60
9	A20 (b)	25p vio brn	5.25	5.25

Perf. 13½

10	A15 (c)	75c org red	50	50
11	A14 (d)	2.50p on 4p yel org	1.00	1.00
12	AP2 (e)	12.50p on 15p org red	2.85	2.85
		Nos. 1-12 (12)	16.20	16.20

Nos. 4, 7, 10–12 Overprinted in Black

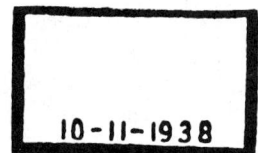

1938, Dec.

13	A15	75c org red	27.50	22.50
14	A10	1p bis brn	20.00	16.50
15	A14	2.50p on 4p yel org	11.00	10.00
16	A14	4p yel org	16.50	11.50
17	AP2	12.50p on 15p org red	30.00	27.50
		Nos. 13-17 (5)	105.00	88.00

Death of Kemal Atatürk, president of Turkey.

AIR POST STAMPS.

Air Post Stamps of Syria, 1937, Overprinted Type "b" in Red or Black

1938 *Perf. 13.* Unwmkd.

C1	AP14	½p dk vio (R)	45	45
C2	AP15	1p blk (R)	45	45
C3	AP14	2p bl grn (R)	1.50	1.50
C4	AP15	3p dp ultra	2.25	2.25
C5	AP14	5p rose lake	5.00	5.00
C6	AP15	10p red brn	5.00	5.00
C7	AP14	15p lake brn	5.50	5.50
C8	AP15	25p dk bl (R)	7.25	7.25
		Nos. C1-C8 (8)	27.40	27.40

POSTAGE DUE STAMPS.

Postage Due Stamps of Syria, 1925–31, Overprinted Type "b" in Black or Red

1938 *Perf. 13½.* Unwmkd.

J1	D5	50c brn, *yel*	1.10	1.10
J2	D6	1p vio, *rose*	1.50	1.50
J3	D5	2p *bl* (R)	2.00	2.00
J4	D5	3p *red org*	3.00	3.00
J5	D5	5p *bl grn* (R)	5.25	5.25
J6	D7	8p *gray bl* (R)	5.25	5.25
		Nos. J1-J6 (6)	18.10	18.10

On No. J2, the overprint is vertical, reading up. On the other denominations, it is horizontal.

Stamps of Alexandretta were discontinued in 1938 and replaced by those of Hatay.

ALGERIA

(ăl-jĕr′ĭ-ȧ)

LOCATION—North Africa.

GOVT.—Republic.

AREA—919,591 sq. mi.

POP.—17,300,000 (est. 1976).

CAPITAL—Algiers.

The former French colony of Algeria became an integral part of France on Sept. 1, 1958, when French stamps replaced Algerian stamps. Algeria became an independent country July 3, 1962.

100 Centimes = 1 Franc
100 Centimes = 1 Dinar (1964)

Stamps of France Overprinted in Red, Blue or Black:

ALGÉRIE *a* — ALGÉRIE *b* — ALGÉRIE *c* — ALGÉRIE *d*

1924-26 *Perf. 14x13½* Unwmkd.

1	A16 (a)	1c dk gray (R)	5	5
2	A16 (a)	2c vio brn	5	5
3	A16 (a)	3c orange	5	5
4	A16 (a)	4c yel brn (Bl)	5	5
5	A22 (a)	5c org (Bl)	7	5
6	A16 (a)	5c grn ('25)	12	12
7	A23 (a)	10c green	8	6
a.		Double ovpt.		
b.		Booklet pane of 10	2.50	
8	A22 (a)	10c grn ('25)	12	12
a.		Double ovpt.		
9	A20 (a)	15c sl grn	8	6
10	A23 (a)	15c grn ('25)	12	12
11	A22 (a)	15c red brn (Bl) ('26)	8	5
12	A22 (a)	20c red brn (Bl)	6	5
13	A22 (a)	25c bl (R)	6	4
a.		Booklet pane of 10	5.00	
14	A23 (a)	30c red (Bl)	18	12
15	A22 (a)	30c cer ('25)	40	22
16	A22 (a)	30c lt bl (R) ('25)	6	5
a.		Booklet pane of 10	3.50	
17	A22 (a)	35c violet	15	8
18	A18 (b)	40c red & pale bl	22	12
a.		Inverted overprint		
19	A22 (a)	40c ol brn (R) ('25)	32	28
20	A18 (b)	45c grn & bl (R)	22	18
a.		Inverted overprint		
21	A23 (a)	45c red (Bl) ('25)	15	12
22	A23 (a)	50c bl (R)	12	6
23	A20 (a)	60c lt vio	22	12
a.		Inverted overprint	325.00	
24	A20 (a)	65c rose (Bl)	18	13
25	A23 (a)	75c bl (R)	30	15
a.		Double overprint	55.00	
26	A20 (a)	80c ver ('26)	50	22
27	A20 (a)	85c ver (Bl)	30	15
28	A18 (b)	1fr cl & ol grn	65	22
29	A22 (a)	1.05fr ver ('26)	60	32
30	A18 (c)	2fr org & pale bl	55	40
31	A18 (b)	3fr vio & bl ('26)	1.90	60
32	A18 (d)	5fr bl & buff (R)	7.25	5.50
		Nos. 1-32 (32)	15.26	9.91

No. 15 was issued precanceled only. Prices for precanceled stamps in first column are for those which have not been through the post and have original gum. Prices in second column are for postally used, gumless stamps.

Street in Kasbah, Algiers
A1

Mosque of Sidi Abd-er-Rahman
A2

La Pêcherie Mosque
A3

Marabout of Sidi Yacoub
A4

1926-39 Typo. *Perf. 14x13½*

33	A1	1c olive	12	12
34	A1	2c red brn	6	5
35	A1	3c orange	12	12
36	A1	5c bl grn	5	3
37	A1	10c brt vio	5	3
a.		Booklet pane of 10	4.00	
38	A2	15c org brn	8	6
39	A2	20c green	5	5
40	A2	20c dp rose	12	5
41	A2	25c bl grn	12	12
42	A2	25c bl ('27)	30	6
43	A2	25c vio bl ('39)	5	3
44	A2	30c blue	28	15
45	A2	30c bl grn ('27)	65	38
46	A2	35c dp vio	85	65
47	A2	40c ol grn	5	3
a.		Booklet pane of 10	3.50	
48	A3	45c vio brn	28	22
49	A3	50c blue	18	13
a.		Booklet pane of 10	3.50	
50	A3	50c dk red ('30)	5	3
a.		Booklet pane of 10	5.00	
51	A3	60c yel grn	12	5
52	A3	65c blk brn ('27)	1.50	1.20
53	A1	65c ultra ('38)	12	3
a.		Booklet pane of 10	1.50	
54	A3	75c carmine	40	35
55	A3	75c bl ('29)	2.25	18
56	A3	80c org red	40	35
57	A3	90c red ('27)	5.50	2.25
58	A4	1fr gray grn & red brn	60	22
59	A3	1.05fr lt brn	40	30
60	A3	1.10fr mag ('27)	4.75	1.25
61	A4	1.25fr dk bl & ultra	60	60
62	A4	1.50fr dk bl & ultra ('27)	1.85	12
63	A4	2fr Prus bl & blk brn	1.85	20
64	A4	3fr vio & org	3.00	1.00
65	A4	5fr red & vio	7.00	2.50
66	A4	10fr ol brn & rose ('27)	37.50	25.00
67	A4	20fr vio & grn ('27)	3.25	3.25
		Nos. 33-67 (35)	74.55	41.16

Type A4, 50c blue and rose red, inscribed "CENTENAIRE-ALGERIE" is France No. 255.

Stamps of 1926 Surcharged with New Values.

1927

68	A2	10c on 35c dp vio	10	10
69	A2	25c on 30c bl	7	6
70	A2	30c on 25c bl grn	15	8
71	A3	65c on 60c yel grn	75	60
72	A3	90c on 80c org red	32	30
73	A3	1.10fr on 1.05fr lt brn	30	18
74	A4	1.50fr on 1.25fr dk bl & ultra	1.60	70
		Nos. 68-74 (7)	3.29	2.02

Bars cancel the old value on Nos. 68, 69, 73 and 74.

No. 4 Surcharged 5c

1927

75	A16	5c on 4c yel brn	8	8

Bay of Algiers
A5

1930, May 4 Engr. *Perf. 11, 12½*

78	A5	10fr red brn	11.00	11.00
a.		Imperf. (pair)	37.50	

Centenary of Algeria and for International Philatelic Exhibition of North Africa, May, 1930.

One copy of No. 78 was sold with each 10fr admission.

Travel across the Sahara
A6

Arch of Triumph, Lambese
A7

Admiralty Building, Algiers
A8

Kings' Tombs near Touggourt
A9

El-Kebir Mosque, Algiers
A10

Oued River at Colomb-Béchar
A11

Sidi Bon Medine Cemetery at Tlemcen
A13

View of Ghardaia
A12

1936–41 Engraved *Perf. 13*

79	A6	1c ultra	5	5
80	A11	2c dk vio	5	5
81	A7	3c dk bl grn	6	6
82	A12	5c red vio	6	6
83	A8	10c emerald	6	5
84	A9	15c red	6	5
85	A13	20c dk bl grn	6	5
86	A10	25c rose vio	45	7
87	A12	30c yel grn	35	8
88	A9	40c brn vio	6	6
89	A13	45c dp ultra	80	60
90	A8	50c red	55	5
91	A6	65c red brn	2.75	2.00
92	A6	65c rose car ('37)	30	5
93	A6	70c red brn ('39)	8	7
94	A11	75c sl bl	28	12
95	A7	90c hn brn	75	70
96	A10	1fr brown	28	5
97	A8	1.25fr lt vio	40	32
98	A8	1.25fr car rose ('39)	15	12
99	A11	1.50fr turq bl	1.20	32
99A	A11	1.50fr rose ('40)	30	18
100	A12	1.75fr hn brn	12	6
101	A7	2fr dk brn	12	8
102	A6	2.25fr yel grn	10.00	7.00

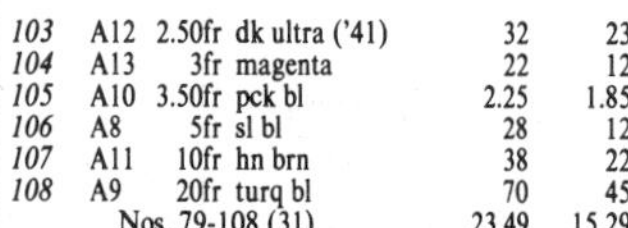

103	A12	2.50fr dk ultra ('41)	32	23
104	A13	3fr magenta	22	12
105	A10	3.50fr pck bl	2.25	1.85
106	A8	5fr sl bl	28	12
107	A11	10fr hn brn	38	22
108	A9	20fr turq bl	70	45
		Nos. 79-108 (31)	23.49	15.29

See also Nos. 124–125, 162.

Nos. 82 and 100 with surcharge "E. F. M. 30frs" (Emergency Field Message) were used in 1943 to pay cable tolls for U. S. and Canadian servicemen.

Algerian Pavilion
A14

1937 *Perf. 13*

109	A14	40c brt grn	50	38
110	A14	50c rose car	28	12
111	A14	1.50fr blue	65	35
112	A14	1.75fr brn blk	80	70

Paris International Exposition.

Constantine in 1837
A15

1937

113	A15	65c dp rose	40	8
114	A15	1fr brown	4.00	45
115	A15	1.75fr bl grn	22	22
116	A15	2.15fr red vio	18	15

Issued in commemoration of the centenary of the taking of Constantine by the French.

Ruins of a Roman Villa
A16

1938

117	A16	30c green	60	40
118	A16	65c ultra	5	5
119	A16	75c rose vio	60	50
120	A16	3fr car rose	2.00	2.00
121	A16	5fr yel brn	2.85	2.50
		Nos. 117-121 (5)	6.10	5.45

Centenary of Philippeville.

No. 90 Surcharged in Black

0,25

1938

122	A8	25c on 50c red	6	4
a.		Dbl. surch.	28.50	22.50
b.		Invtd. surch.	21.00	15.00

1939 Types of 1936.
Numerals of Value on Colorless Background.

124	A7	90c hn brn	10	5
125	A10	2.25fr bl grn	22	18

American Export Liner Unloading Cargo
A17

1939

126	A17	20c green	70	55
127	A17	40c red vio	70	55
128	A17	90c brn blk	38	22
129	A17	1.25fr rose	3.00	90
130	A17	2.25fr ultra	70	65
		Nos. 126-130 (5)	5.48	2.87

New York World's Fair.

Type of 1926, Surcharged in Black **1F**

Two types of surcharge:
I. Bars 6mm.
II. Bars 7mm.

1939–40 *Perf. 14x13½*

131	A1	1fr on 90c crim (I)	5	5
a.		Booklet pane of 10		
b.		Dbl. surcharge (I)	37.50	
c.		Invtd. surcharge (I)	22.50	
d.		Pair, one without surch. (I)	800.00	
e.		Type II ('40)	1.50	12
f.		Invtd. surcharge (II)	32.50	
g.		Pair, one without surch. (II)	800.00	

View of Algiers
A18

1941 Typographed

132	A18	30c ultra	6	5
133	A18	70c sepia	6	5
134	A18	1fr car rose	8	5

See also No. 163.

Marshal Pétain
A19 A20

1941 Engraved *Perf. 13*

135	A19	1fr dk bl	12	8

No. 53 Surcharged in Black with New Value and Bars.

1941 *Perf. 14x13½*

136	A1	50c on 65c ultra	28	6
a.		Booklet pane of 10		
b.		Inverted surch.	22.50	
c.		Pair, one without surch.	55.00	

1942 *Perf. 14x13*

137	A20	1.50fr org red	7	7

Four other denominations of type A20 exist (4fr, 5fr, 10fr, 20fr), but were not placed in use.

Constantine A21 — Arms of Oran A22 — Algiers A23

Engraver's Name at Lower Left.

1942-43 Photogravure. *Perf. 12.*

138	A21	40c dk vio ('43)	12	12
139	A22	60c rose ('43)	6	6
140	A21	1.20fr yel grn ('43)	10	8
141	A23	1.50fr car rose	6	6
142	A22	2fr sapphire	12	6
143	A21	2.40fr rose ('43)	8	7
144	A23	3fr sapphire	12	6
145	A21	4fr bl ('43)	12	12
146	A22	5fr yel grn ('43)	8	8
		Nos. 138-146 (9)	86	71

Imperforates

Nearly all of Algeria Nos. 138–285, B39–B96, C1–C12 and CB1–CB3 exist imperforate. See note after France No. 395.

Without Engraver's Name.

1942–45 Typo. *Perf. 14x13½*

147	A23	10c dl brn vio ('45)	5	5
148	A22	30c dp bl grn ('45)	7	7
149	A21	40c dl brn vio ('45)	5	4
150	A22	60c rose ('45)	6	6
151	A21	70c dp bl ('45)	6	5
152	A23	80c dk bl grn ('43)	18	18
153	A21	1.20fr dp bl grn ('45)	6	6
154	A23	1.50fr brt rose ('43)	5	4
155	A22	2fr dp bl ('45)	6	4
156	A21	2.40fr rose ('45)	15	15
157	A23	3fr dp bl ('45)	8	7
158	A22	4.50fr brn vio	15	15
		Nos. 147-158 (12)	1.02	96

La Pêcherie Mosque
A24

1942 Typographed

159	A24	50c dl red	4	4
a.		Booklet pane of 10	3.50	

1942 Photogravure *Perf. 12*

160	A24	40c gray grn	8	8
161	A24	50c red	7	7

Types of 1936–41, Without "RF"

1942 Engraved *Perf. 13*

162	A11	1.50fr rose	6	4

Typographed.
Perf. 14x13½.

163	A18	30c ultra	6	6

"One Aim Alone—Victory"
A25 A26

1943 Lithographed *Perf. 12*

164	A25	1.50fr dp rose	5	5
165	A26	1.50fr dk bl	5	5

Type of 1942–3
Surcharged with New Value in Black.

1943 Photogravure

166	A22	2fr on 5fr red org	8	8
a.		Surcharge omitted	135.00	

Summer Palace, Algiers
A27

1944, Dec. 1 **Lithographed**

No.	Type	Description	Unused	Used
167	A27	15fr slate	1.00	90
168	A27	20fr lt bl grn	70	35
169	A27	50fr dk car	50	40
170	A27	100fr dp bl	1.40	1.15
171	A27	200fr dl bis brn	2.50	1.25
		Nos. 167-171 (5)	6.10	4.05

Marianne A28 — Gallic Cock A29

1944-45

No.	Type	Description	Unused	Used
172	A28	10c gray	5	5
173	A28	30c red vio	4	4
174	A29	40c rose car ('45)	12	12
175	A28	50c red	6	5
176	A28	80c emerald	6	6
177	A29	1fr grn ('45)	6	5
178	A28	1.20fr rose lil	8	6
179	A28	1.50fr dk bl	5	5
a.		Dbl impression	22.50	
180	A29	2fr red	6	5
a.		Double impression	27.50	
181	A29	2fr dk brn ('45)	6	5
182	A28	2.40fr rose red	7	6
183	A28	3fr purple	8	5
184	A29	4fr ultra ('45)	7	6
185	A28	4.50fr ol blk	18	18
186	A29	10fr grnsh blk ('45)	40	32
		Nos. 172-186 (15)	1.44	1.25

No. 38 Surcharged in Black **0f.30**

1944 ***Perf. 14x13½.***

No.	Type	Description	Unused	Used
187	A2	30c on 15c org brn	12	4
a.		Inverted surch.	9.00	5.00

This stamp exists precanceled only. See note below No. 32.

No. 154 Surcharged "RF" and New Value.

1945

No.	Type	Description	Unused	Used
190	A23	50c on 1.50fr brt rose	6	5
a.		Inverted surch.	16.50	

Stamps of France, 1944, Overprinted in Black **ALGÉRIE** *a*

1945-46

No.	Type	Description	Unused	Used
191	A99	80c yel grn	5	4
192	A99	1fr grnsh bl	7	4
193	A99	1.20fr violet	12	12
194	A99	2fr vio brn	18	7
195	A99	2.40fr car rose	18	12
196	A99	3fr orange	18	12
		Nos. 191-196 (6)	78	51

Same Overprint on Stamps of France, 1945-47, in Black, Red or Carmine.

1945-47

No.	Type	Description	Unused	Used
197	A145	40c lil rose	6	4
198	A145	50c vio bl (R)	6	4
199	A146	60c brt ultra (R)	22	12
200	A146	1fr rose red ('47)	6	5
201	A146	1.50fr rose lil ('47)	6	5
202	A147	2fr myr grn (R) ('46)	6	4
203	A147	3fr dp rose	5	4
204	A147	4.50fr ultra (C) ('47)	45	12
205	A147	5fr lt grn ('46)	6	5
206	A147	10fr ultra	35	30
		Nos. 197-206 (10)	1.43	85

Same Overprint on France No. 383 and New Value Surcharged in Black

1946

No.	Type	Description	Unused	Used
207	A99	2fr on 1.50fr hn brn	6	3
a.		Without "2F"	120.00	

Same Overprint on France Nos. 562 and 564, in Carmine or Blue.

1947

No.	Type	Description	Unused	Used
208	A153	10c dp ultra & blk (C)	5	5
209	A155	50c brn, yel & red (Bl)	30	30

Arms of: Constantine A30 — Algiers A31 — Oran A32

Typographed

1947-49 ***Perf. 14x13½*** **Unwmkd.**

No.	Type	Description	Unused	Used
210	A30	10c dk grn & brt red	3	3
211	A31	50c blk & org	4	3
212	A32	1fr ultra & yel	5	3
213	A30	1.30fr blk & grnsh bl	55	38
214	A31	1.50fr pur & org yel	5	3
215	A32	2fr blk & brt grn	6	3
216	A30	2.50fr blk & brt red	35	30
217	A31	3fr vio brn & grn	12	5
218	A32	3.50fr lt grn & rose lil	12	10
219	A30	4fr dk brn & brt grn	12	12
220	A31	4.50fr ultra & scar	6	4
221	A31	5fr blk & grnsh bl	5	4
222	A32	6fr brn & scar	15	10
223	A32	8fr choc & ultra ('48)	12	6
224	A30	10fr car & choc ('48)	38	5
225	A31	15fr blk & red ('49)	40	3
		Nos. 210-225 (16)	2.65	1.42

See also Nos. 274-280, 285.

Peoples of the World A33

1949, Oct. 24 **Engr.** ***Perf. 13***

No.	Type	Description	Unused	Used
226	A33	5fr green	1.10	90
227	A33	15fr scarlet	1.10	90
228	A33	25fr ultra	3.25	2.25

Issued to commemorate the 75th anniversary of the formation of the Universal Postal Union.

Grapes A34 — Apollo of Cherchell A35

Designs: 25fr, Dates. 40fr, Oranges and lemons.

1950, Feb. 25

No.	Type	Description	Unused	Used
229	A34	20fr vio brn, grn & cl	90	28
230	A34	25fr dk brn, dk grn & brn org	1.10	35
231	A34	40fr brn, grn, red org & org	2.50	55

1952 ***Perf. 13*** **Unwmkd.**

Designs: 12fr, 18fr, Isis statue, Cherchell. 15fr, 20fr, Child with eagle.

No.	Type	Description	Unused	Used
240	A35	10fr gray blk	30	5
241	A35	12fr org brn	40	8
242	A35	15fr dp bl	28	4
243	A35	18fr rose red	40	28
244	A35	20fr dp grn	35	5
245	A35	30fr dp bl	70	35
		Nos. 240-245 (6)	2.43	85

War Memorial, Algiers A38 — Fossilized Nautilus A39

Phonolite Dike A40

1952, Apr. 11

No.	Type	Description	Unused	Used
246	A38	12fr dk grn	40	38

Issued to honor the French Africa Army.

1952, Aug. 11

No.	Type	Description	Unused	Used
247	A39	15fr brt crim	75	55
248	A40	30fr dp ultra	85	65

Issued to publicize the 19th International Geological Congress, Algiers, Sept. 8-15, 1952.

French and Algerian Soldiers and Camel A41

1952, Nov. 30

No.	Type	Description	Unused	Used
249	A41	12fr chnt brn	75	45

Issued to commemorate the 50th anniversary of the establishment of the Sahara Companies.

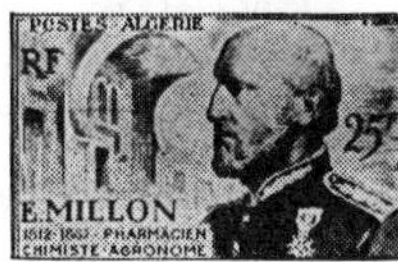

Eugène Millon A42

François C. Maillot A43 — Oranges A44

Portrait: 50fr, Alphonse Laveran.

Engraved.

1954, Jan. 4 ***Perf. 13*** **Unwmkd.**

No.	Type	Description	Unused	Used
250	A42	25fr dk grn & choc	90	18
251	A43	40fr org brn & brn car	1.35	50
252	A42	50fr ultra & ind	1.35	18

Military Health Service.

1954, May 8

No.	Type	Description	Unused	Used
253	A44	15fr ind & bl	55	40

Issued to publicize the third International Congress on Agronomy, Algiers, 1954.

Type of France, 1954 Overprinted type "a" in Black.

Engraved.

1954, June 6 ***Perf. 13*** **Unwmkd.**

No.	Type	Description	Unused	Used
254	A240	15fr rose car	40	40

Liberation of France, 10th anniversary.

Darguinah Hydroelectric Works A45 — Patio of Bardo Museum A46

1954, June 19

No.	Type	Description	Unused	Used
255	A45	15fr lil rose	55	40

Issued to commemorate the opening of Darguinah hydroelectric works.

1954 **Typographed** ***Perf. 14x13½***

No.	Type	Description	Unused	Used
257	A46	12fr red brn & brn org	22	12
258	A46	15fr dk bl & bl	28	5

See also Nos. 267-271.

Type of France, 1954, Overprinted type "a" in Carmine.

1954 **Engraved** ***Perf. 13***

No.	Type	Description	Unused	Used
260	A247	12fr dk grn	50	45

Issued to commemorate the 150th anniversary of the first Legion of Honor awards at Camp de Boulogne.

St. Augustine—A47

1954, Nov. 11

No.	Type	Description	Unused	Used
261	A47	15fr chocolate	45	45

Issued to commemorate the 1600th anniversary of the birth of St. Augustine.

Aesculapius Statue and El Kattar Hospital, Algiers

A48

1955, Apr. 3 ***Perf. 13*** **Unwmkd.**

262	A48	15fr red	40	35

Issued to publicize the 30th French Congress of Medicine, Algiers, April 3-6, 1955.

Chenua Mountain and View of Tipasa

A49

1955, May 31

263	A49	50fr brn car	65	12

Issued to commemorate the 2000th anniversary of the founding of Tipasa.

Type of France, 1955 Overprinted type "a" in Red

1955, June 13

264	A251	30fr dp ultra	75	55

Issued to commemorate the 50th anniversary of the founding of Rotary International.

Marianne A50 Great Kabylia Mountains A51

Perf. 14x13½

1955, Oct. 3 **Typo.** **Unwmkd.**

265	A50	15fr carmine	22	5

See also No. 284.

1955, Dec. 17 **Engraved** ***Perf. 13***

266	A51	100fr ind & ultra	2.00	22

Bardo Type of 1954, "Postes" and "Algerie" in White. Typographed.

1955-57 ***Perf. 14x13½*** **Unwmkd.**

267	A46	10fr dk brn & lt brn	15	5
268	A46	12fr red brn & brn org ('56)	12	5
269	A46	18fr crim & ver ('57)	45	18
270	A46	20fr grn & yel grn ('57)	30	28
271	A46	25fr pur & brt pur	45	8
		Nos. 267-271 (5)	1.47	64

Marshal Franchet d'Esperey

A52

1956, May 25 **Engraved** ***Perf. 13***

272	A52	15fr saph & ind	60	60

Birth centenary of Marshal Franchet d'Esperey.

Marshal Jacques Leclerc

A53

1956, Nov. 29

273	A53	15fr red brn & sep	45	45

Issued to commemorate the death of Marshal Leclerc.

Type of 1947-49 and

Arms of Bône

A54

Designs: 2fr, Arms of Tizi-Ouzou. 3fr, Arms of Mostaganem. 5fr, Arms of Tlemcen. 10fr, Arms of Setif. 12fr, Arms of Orleansville.

1956-58 Typographed. ***Perf. 14x13½***

274	A54	1fr grn & ver	5	5
275	A54	2fr ver & ultra ('58)	35	30
276	A54	3fr ultra & emer ('58)	40	12
277	A54	5fr ultra & yel	18	5
278	A31	6fr red & grn ('57)	40	32
279	A54	10fr dp cl & emer ('58)	40	32
280	A54	12fr ultra & red ('58)	45	40
		Nos. 274-280 (7)	2.23	1.56

Nos. 275 and 279 are inscribed "Republique Francaise." See also No. 285.

View of Oran

A55

1956-58 **Engraved.** ***Perf. 13.***

281	A55	30fr dl pur	45	15
282	A55	35fr car rose ('58)	75	50

Electric Train Crossing Bridge

A56

1957, Mar. 25

283	A56	40fr dk bl grn & emer	45	22

Marianne Type of 1955 Inscribed "Algerie" Vertically.

Perf. 14x13½

1957, Dec. 2 **Typo.** **Unwmkd.**

284	A50	20fr ultra	30	7

Arms Type of 1947-49 Inscribed "Republique Francaise"

1958, July

285	A31	6fr red & grn	10.00	10.00

Independent State

France Nos. 939, 968, 945-946 and 1013 Overprinted "EA" and Bars, Handstamped or Typographed, in Black or Red

1962, July 2

286	A336	10c brt grn	28	22
	a.	Typographed ovpt.	40	32
287	A349	25c lake & gray	35	18
	a.	Handstamped ovpt.	35	22
288	A339	45c brt vio & ol gray	3.50	3.25
	a.	Handstamped ovpt.	16.50	12.00
289	A339	50c sl grn & lt cl	3.50	3.25
	a.	Handstamped ovpt.	16.50	12.00
290	A372	1fr dk bl, sl & bis	2.50	1.50
	a.	Handstamped ovpt.	2.10	1.40
		Nos. 286-290 (5)	10.13	8.40

Post offices were authorized to overprint their stock of these 5 French stamps. The size of the letters was specified as 3x6mm. each, but various sizes were used. The post offices had permission to make their own rubber stamps. Typography, pen or pencil were also used. Many types exist. Colors of handstamped overprints include black, red, blue, violet. "EA" stands for Etat Algérien.

Mosque, Tlemcen

A57

Roman Gates of Lodi, Médéa

A58

Designs: 5c, Kerrata Gorge. 10c, Dam at Foum el Gherza. 95c, Oil field, Hassi Messaoud.

1962, Nov. 1 **Engr.** ***Perf. 13***

291	A57	5c Prus grn, grn & choc	15	8
292	A58	10c ol blk & dk bl	18	8
293	A57	25c sl grn, brn & ver	55	7
294	A57	95c dk bl, blk & bis	1.85	60
295	A58	1fr grn & blk	1.90	1.50
		Nos. 291-295 (5)	4.63	2.33

The designs of Nos. 291–295 are similar to French issues of 1959–61 with "Republique Algeriénne" replacing "Republique Francaise."

Flag, Rifle, Olive Branch

A59

Design: Nos. 300–303, Broken chain and rifle added to design A59.

1963, Jan. 6 **Litho.** ***Perf. 12½***

Flag in Green and Red

296	A59	5c bis brn	18	12
297	A59	10c blue	25	12
298	A59	25c vermilion	1.65	5
299	A59	95c violet	1.40	75
300	A59	1fr green	1.25	22
301	A59	2fr brown	3.00	80
302	A59	5fr lilac	4.50	2.25
303	A59	10fr gray	18.50	12.50
		Nos. 296-303 (8)	30.73	16.81

Nos. 296–299 commemorate the successful revolution and Nos. 300–303 commemorate the return of peace.

Men of Various Races, Wheat Emblem and Globe

A60

1963, Mar. 21 **Engraved** ***Perf. 13***

304	A60	25c mar, dl grn & yel	35	28

Issued for the "Freedom from Hunger" campaign of the U.N. Food and Agriculture Organization.

Map of Algeria and Emblems A61 Physicians from 13th Century Manuscript A62

1963, July 5 ***Perf. 13*** **Unwmkd.**

305	A61	25c bl, dk brn, grn & red	55	35

Issued to commemorate the first anniversary of Algeria's independence.

1963, July 29 **Engraved**

306	A62	25c brn red, grn & bis	1.15	35

Issued to commemorate the Second Congress of the Union of Arab physicians.

Orange and Blossom A63 Scales and Scroll A64

1963 ***Perf. 14x13***

307	A63	8c gray grn & org	15	12
308	A63	20c sl & org red	20	18
309	A63	40c grnsh bl & org	45	35
310	A63	55c ol grn & org red	60	55

Nos. 307–310 issued precanceled only. See note below No. 32.

1963, Oct. 13 ***Perf. 13*** **Unwmkd.**

311	A64	25c blk, grn & rose red	70	40

Issued to honor the new constitution.

Guerrilla Fighters A65 Centenary Emblem A66

1963, Nov. 1

312	A65	25c dk brn, yel grn & car	70	35

9th anniversary of Algerian revolution.

1963, Dec. 8 Photo. ***Perf. 12***

313	A66	25c lt vio bl, yel & dk red	70	40

Centenary of International Red Cross.

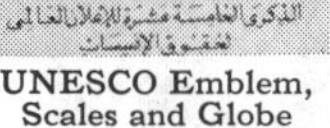

UNESCO Emblem, Scales and Globe — A67

Workers — A68

1963, Dec. 16 ***Perf. 12*** **Unwmkd.**

314	A67	25c lt bl & blk	65	28

Issued to commemorate the 15th anniversary of the Universal Declaration of Human Rights.

1964, May 1 **Engraved** ***Perf. 13***

315	A68	50c dl red, red org & bl	1.10	40

Issued for the Labor Festival.

Map of Africa and Flags
A69

1964, May 25 ***Perf. 13*** **Unwmkd.**

316	A69	45c bl, org & car	75	35

Issued for Africa Day on the first anniversary of the Addis Ababa charter on African unity.

Ramses II Battling the Hittites (from Abu Simbel)—A70

Design: 30c, Two statues of Ramses II.

1964, June 28 **Engraved** ***Perf. 13***

317	A70	20c choc, red & vio bl	60	40
318	A70	30c brn, red & grnsh bl	80	50

Issued to publicize the UNESCO world campaign to save historic monuments in Nubia.

Tractors — A71

Communications Tower — A72

Designs: 5c, 25c, 85c, Tractors. 10c, 30c, 65c, Men working with lathe. 12c, 15c, 45c, Electronics center and atom symbol. 20c, 50c, 95c, Draftsman and bricklayer.

1964-65 Typographed ***Perf. 14x13½***

319	A71	5c red lil	5	3
320	A71	10c brown	8	3
321	A71	12c emer ('65)	32	8
322	A71	15c dk bl ('65)	18	12
323	A71	20c yellow	22	12
324	A71	25c red	42	3
325	A71	30c pur ('65)	32	3
326	A71	45c rose car	35	20
327	A71	50c ultra	50	10
328	A71	65c orange	70	20
329	A71	85c green	1.10	22
330	A71	95c car rose	1.25	30
		Nos. 319-330 (12)	5.49	1.46

1964, Aug. 30 **Engraved** ***Perf. 13***

331	A72	85c bl, blk & red brn	1.60	70

Inauguration of the Hertzian cable telephone line Algiers-Annaba.

Industrial and Agricultural Symbols — A73

Gas Flames and Pipes — A74

1964, Sept. 26 **Typo.** ***Perf. 13½x14***

332	A73	25c lt ultra, yel & red	32	22

Issued to publicize the first International Fair at Algiers, Sept. 26–Oct. 11.

1964, Sept. 27

333	A74	30c vio, bl & yel	50	40

Issued to commemorate the opening of the Arzew natural gas liquification plant.

Planting Trees — A75

Children and UNICEF Emblem — A76

1964, Nov. 29 **Unwmkd.**

334	A75	25c sl grn, yel & car	38	28

National reforestation campaign.

1964, Dec. 13 ***Perf. 13½x14***

335	A76	15c pink, vio bl & lt grn	35	28

Issued for Children's Day.

Decorated Camel Saddle
A77

1965, May 29 **Typo.** ***Perf. 13½x14***

336	A77	20c blk, red, emer & brn	28	20

Handicrafts of Sahara.

ICY Emblem
A78

1965, Aug. 29 **Engraved** ***Perf. 13***

337	A78	30c blk, mar & bl grn	75	45
338	A78	60c blk, brt bl & bl grn	1.25	55

International Cooperation Year, 1965.

ITU Emblem
A79

1965, Sept. 19

339	A79	60c pur, emer & buff	75	50
340	A79	95c dk brn, mar & buff	1.10	60

Issued to commemorate the centenary of the International Telecommunication Union.

Musicians
A80

Miniatures by Mohammed Racim: 60c, Two female musicians. 5d, Algerian princess and antelope.

1965, Dec. 27 Photo. ***Perf. 11½***

341	A80	30c multi	75	55
342	A80	60c multi	1.10	70
343	A80	5d multi	8.50	4.50

Bulls, Painted in 6000 B.C.
A81

Wall Paintings from Tassili-N-Ajjer, c. 6000 B.C.: No. 345, Shepherd (vert.). 2d, Fleeing ostriches. 3d, Two girls (vert.).

1966, Jan. 29 Photo. ***Perf. 11½***

344	A81	1d brn, bis & red brn	3.25	2.25
345	A81	1d gray, blk, ocher & dk brn	3.25	2.25
346	A81	2d brn, ocher & red brn	6.25	3.75
347	A81	3d buff, blk, ocher & brn red	8.00	5.25

See also Nos. 365-368.

Pottery
A82

Handicrafts from Great Kabylia: 50c, Weaving, woman at loom (horiz.). 70c, Jewelry.

1966, Feb. 26 **Engraved** ***Perf. 13***

348	A82	40c Prus bl, brn red & blk	40	32
349	A82	50c dk red, ol & ocher	50	40
350	A82	70c vio bl, blk & red	90	55

Weather Balloon, Compass Rose and Anemometer
A83

1966, Mar. 23 **Engr.** **Unwmkd.**

351	A83	1d cl, brt bl & grn	1.10	45

World Meteorological Day.

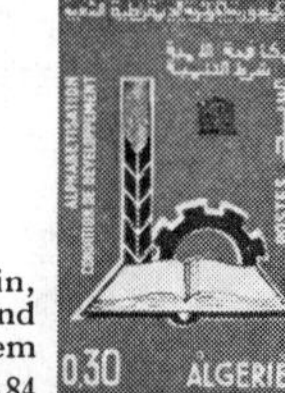

Book, Grain, Cogwheel and UNESCO Emblem
A84

Design: 60c, Grain, cogwheel, book and UNESCO emblem.

1966, May 2 **Typo.** ***Perf. 13x14***

352	A84	30c yel bis & blk	32	28
353	A84	60c dk red, gray & blk	50	28

Literacy as basis for development.

WHO Headquarters, Geneva
A85

1966, May 30 **Engraved** ***Perf. 13***

354	A85	30c multi	38	28
355	A85	60c multi	75	35

Issued to commemorate the inauguration of the World Health Organization Headquarters, Geneva.

Algerian Scout Emblem — A86

Arab Jamboree Emblem — A87

1966, July 23 Photo. ***Perf. 12x12½***

356	A86	30c multi	35	32
357	A87	1d multi	1.10	55

No. 356 commemorates the 30th anniversary of the Algerian Mohammedan Boy Scouts. No. 357, the 7th Arab Boy Scout Jamboree, held at Good Daim, Libya, Aug. 12.

Map of Palestine and Victims
A88

Abd-el-Kader
A89

1966, Sept. 26 Typo. ***Perf. 10½***

358	A88	30c red & blk	30	18

Deir Yassin Massacre, Apr. 9, 1948.

1966, Nov. 2 Photo. ***Perf. 11½***

359	A89	30c multi	25	12
360	A89	95c multi	90	35

Issued to commemorate the transfer from Damascus to Algiers of the ashes of Abd-el-Kader (1807?–1883), Emir of Mascara. See also Nos. 382–387.

UNESCO Emblem
A90

1966, Nov. 19 Typo. ***Perf. 10½***

361	A90	1d multi	1.00	50

Issued to commemorate the 20th anniversary of UNESCO (United Nations Educational, Scientific and Cultural Organization).

Horseman
A91

Miniatures by Mohammed Racim: 1.50d, Woman at her toilette. 2d, The pirate Barbarossa in front of the Admiralty.

1966, Dec. 17 Photo. ***Perf. 11½***
Granite Paper

362	A91	1d multi	2.50	1.50
363	A91	1.50d multi	4.25	2.25
364	A91	2d multi	6.00	3.75

Wall Paintings Type of 1966

Wall Paintings from Tassili-N-Ajjer, c.6000 B.C.: 1d, Cow. No. 366, Antelope. No. 367, Archers. 3d, Warrior (vert.).

1967, Jan. 28 Photo. ***Perf. 11½***

365	A81	1d brn, bis & dl vio	3.25	1.85
366	A81	2d brn, ocher & red brn	4.50	3.25
367	A81	2d brn, yel & red brn	4.50	3.25
368	A81	3d blk, gray, yel & red brn	7.50	5.00

Bardo Museum
A92

La Kalaa Minaret
A93

Design: 1.30d, Ruins at Sedrata.

1967, Feb. 27 Photo. ***Perf. 13***

369	A92	35c multi	32	28
370	A93	95c multi	80	55
371	A92	1.30d multi	1.20	75

Moretti and International Tourist Year Emblem
A94

Design: 70c, Tuareg riding camel, Tassili, and Tourist Year Emblem (vert.).

1967, Apr. 29 Litho. ***Perf. 14***

372	A94	40c multi	50	35
373	A94	70c multi	90	45

International Tourist Year, 1967.

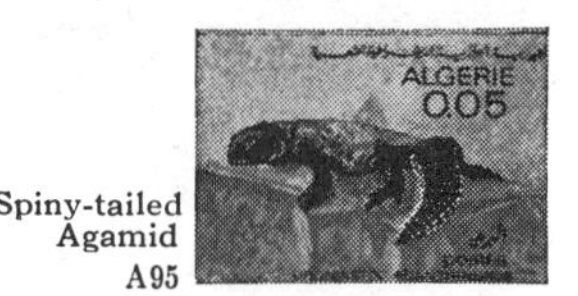

Spiny-tailed Agamid
A95

Designs: 20c, Ostrich (vert.). 40c, Slender-horned gazelle (vert.). 70c, Fennec.

1967, June 24 Photo. ***Perf. 11½***

374	A95	5c bis & blk	22	18
375	A95	20c ocher, blk & pink	45	32
376	A95	40c ol bis, blk & red brn	70	45
377	A95	70c gray, blk & dp org	1.30	80

Dancers
A96

Typographed and Engraved

1967, July 4 ***Perf. 10½***

378	A96	50c gray vio, yel & blk	65	45

National Youth Festival.

Map of the Mediterranean and Sport Scenes—A97

1967, Sept. 2 Typo. ***Perf. 10½***

379	A97	30c blk, red & bl	35	28

Issued to publicize the 5th Mediterranean Games, Tunis, Sept. 8–17.

Skiers
A98

Olympic Emblem and Sports
A99

1967, Oct. 21 Engraved ***Perf. 13***

380	A98	30c brt bl & ultra	55	35
381	A99	95c brn org, pur & brt grn	1.40	90

Issued to publicize the 10th Winter Olympic Games, Grenoble, Feb. 6–18, 1968.

Abd-el-Kader Type of 1966
Lithographed, Photogravure

1967–71 ***Perf. 13½, 11½***

382	A89	5c dl pur ('68)	5	5
383	A89	10c green	8	8
383A	A89	10c sl grn (litho.,'69)	12	5
383B	A89	25c org ('71)	22	10
384	A89	30c blk ('68)	22	6
385	A89	30c lt vio ('68)	28	15
386	A89	50c rose cl	55	25
387	A89	70c vio bl	65	35
		Nos. 382-387 (8)	2.17	1.09

The 10c (No. 383), 50c and 70c are on granite paper, photogravure, and were issued Nov. 13, 1967. The 5c, 10c (No. 383A), 25c and both 30c are lithographed and perf. 13½; others, perf. 11½.

The three 1967 stamps (No. 383, 50c, 70c) have numerals thin, narrow and close together; the Arabic inscription at lower right is 2mm. high. The five lithographed stamps are redrawn, with numerals thicker and spaced more widely; Arabic at lower right 3mm. high.

Boy Scouts Holding Jamboree Emblem
A100

1967, Dec. 23 Engraved ***Perf. 13***

388	A100	1d multi	1.20	70

Issued to commemorate the 12th Boy Scout World Jamboree, Farragut State Park, Idaho, Aug. 1–9.

No. 324 Surcharged

1967 Typographed ***Perf. 14x13½***

389	A71	30c on 25c red	32	22

Mandolin
A101

Musical Instruments: 40c, Lute. 1.30d, Rebec.

1968, Feb. 17 Photo. ***Perf. 12½x13***

390	A101	30c dk brn, ocher & lt bl	45	32
391	A101	40c multi	55	35
392	A101	1.30d multi	1.50	90

Nememcha Rug
A102

Algerian Rugs: 70c, Guergour. 95c, Djebel-Amour. 1.30d, Kalaa.

1968, Apr. 13 Photo. ***Perf. 11½***

393	A102	30c multi	60	35
394	A102	70c multi	1.10	45
395	A102	95c multi	1.65	90
396	A102	1.30d multi	2.00	1.20

Human Rights Flame
A103

1968, May 18 Typo. ***Perf. 10½***

397	A103	40c bl, red & yel	45	35

International Human Rights Year, 1968.

WHO Emblem
A104

1968, May 18

398	A104	70c blk, lt bl & yel	60	35

Issued for the 20th anniversary of the World Health Organization.

Welder

A105

Athletes, Olympic Flame and Rings

A106

1968, June 15 Engr. *Perf. 13*

399 A105 30c gray, brn & ultra 32 25

Algerian emigration to Europe.

Perf. 12½x13, 13x12½

1968, July 4 Photogravure

Designs: 50c, Soccer player. 1d, Mexican pyramid, emblem, Olympic flame, rings and athletes (horiz.).

400 A106 30c grn, red & yel 45 40
401 A106 50c rose car & multi 70 45
402 A106 1d dk grn, org, brn & red 1.35 90

Issued to publicize the 19th Olympic Games, Mexico City, Oct. 12–27.

Scouts and Emblem

A107

Barbary Sheep

A108

1968, July 4 ***Perf. 13***

403 A107 30c multi 35 25

Issued to publicize the 8th Arab Boy Scout Jamboree, Algiers, 1968.

1968, Oct. 19 Photo. ***Perf. 11½***

Design: 1d, Red deer.

404 A108 40c red brn, bis & blk 60 35
405 A108 1d lt & dk ol grn & brn 1.50 70

Hunting Scenes, Djemila

A109

"Industry"

A110

Design: 95c, Neptune's chariot, Timgad (horiz.). Both designs are from Roman mosaics.

Perf. 12½x13, 13x12½

1968, Nov. 23 Photogravure

406 A109 40c gray & multi 35 30
407 A109 95c gray & multi 1.00 55

1968, Dec. 14 ***Perf. 11½***

Designs: No. 409, Miner with drill. 95c, "Energy" (circle and rays).

408 A110 30c dp org & sil 35 25
409 A110 30c brn & multi 35 25
410 A110 95c sil, red & blk 1.10 35

Issued to publicize industrial development.

Opuntia Ficus Indica

A111

Flowers: 40c, Carnations. 70c, Roses. 95c, Bird-of-paradise flower.

1969, Jan. Photo. ***Perf. 11½***

Flowers in Natural Colors

411 A111 25c pink & blk 35 28
412 A111 40c yel & blk 55 40
413 A111 70c gray & blk 90 45
414 A111 95c brt bl & blk 1.35 80

See also Nos. 496–499.

Irrigation Dam at Djorf Torba-Oued Guir

A112

Design: 1.50d, Truck on Highway No. 51 and camel caravan.

1969, Feb. 22 Photo. ***Perf. 11½***

415 A112 30c multi 32 25
416 A112 1.50d multi 1.60 80

Public works in the Sahara.

Mail Coach

A113

1969, Mar. 22 Photo. ***Perf. 11½***

417 A113 1d multi 1.50 70

Issued for Stamp Day, 1969.

Capitol, Timgad

A114

Design: 1d, Septimius Temple, Djemila (horiz.).

1969, Apr. 5 Photo. ***Perf. 13x12½***

418 A114 30c gray & multi 35 28
419 A114 1d gray & multi 90 32

Second Timgad Festival, Apr. 4–8.

ILO Emblem

A115

Arabian Saddle

A116

1969, May 24 Photo. ***Perf. 11½***

420 A115 95c dp car, yel & blk 1.20 45

50th anniversary of the International Labor Organization.

1969, June 28 Photo. ***Perf. 12x12½***

Algerian Handicrafts: 30c, Bookcase. 60c, Decorated copper plate.

Granite Paper

421 A116 30c multi 40 32
422 A116 60c multi 60 35
423 A116 1d multi 1.20 45

No. 321 Surcharged

0,20

1969 Typographed ***Perf. 14x13½***

424 A71 20c on 12c emer 22 18

Pan-African Culture Festival Emblem

A117

African Development Bank Emblem

A118

1969, July 19 Photo. ***Perf. 12½***

425 A117 30c multi 32 28

Issued to commemorate the First Pan-African Culture Festival, Algiers, July 21–Aug. 1.

1969, Aug. 23 Typo. ***Perf. 10½***

426 A118 30c dl bl, yel & blk 32 32

Issued to commemorate the 5th anniversary of the African Development Bank.

Astronauts and Landing Module on Moon

A119

Photogravure

1969, Aug. 23 ***Perf. 12½x11½***

427 A119 50c gold & multi 70 45

Issued to commemorate man's first landing on the moon, July 20, 1969. U.S. astronauts Neil A. Armstrong and Col. Edwin E. Aldrin, Jr., with Lieut. Col. Michael Collins piloting Apollo 11.

Algerian Women, by Dinet

A120

Design: 1.50d, The Watchmen, by Etienne Dinet.

1969, Nov. 29 Photo. ***Perf. 14½***

428 A120 1d multi 1.15 80
429 A120 1.50d multi 1.85 1.10

Mother and Child

A121

1969, Dec. 27 Photo. ***Perf. 11½***

430 A121 30c multi 55 40

Issued to promote mother and child protection.

Agricultural Growth Chart, Tractor and Dam

A122

Designs: 30c, Transportation and development. 50c, Abstract symbols of industrialization.

1970, Jan. 31 Photo. ***Perf. 12½***

Size: 37x23mm.

431 A122 25c dk brn, yel & org 25 20

Lithographed *Perf. 14*

Size: 49x23mm.

432 A122 30c bl & multi 35 25

Photogravure *Perf. 12½*

Size: 37x23mm.

433 A122 50c rose lil & blk 40 30

Issued to publicize the Four-Year Development Plan.

Old and New Mail Delivery

A123

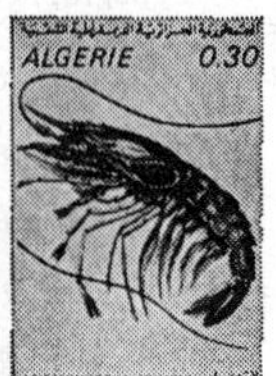

Spiny Lobster

A124

1970, Feb. 28 Photo. ***Perf. 11½***

Granite Paper

434 A123 30c multi 35 28

Issued for Stamp Day.

1970, Mar. 28

Designs: 40c, Mollusks. 75c, Retepora cellulosa. 1d, Red coral.

435 A124 30c ocher & multi 35 28
436 A124 40c multi 45 32
437 A124 75c ultra & multi 85 40
438 A124 1d lt bl & multi 1.10 55

Oranges, EXPO '70 Emblem

A125

Designs (EXPO '70 Emblem and): 60c, Algerian pavilion. 70c, Grapes.

1970, Apr. 25 Photo. ***Perf. 12½x12***

439 A125 30c lt bl, grn & org 35 20
440 A125 60c multi 50 25

441 A125 70c multi 65 50

EXPO '70 International Exhibition, Osaka, Japan, Mar. 15–Sept. 13, 1970.

Olives, Oil Bottle A126 — Saber A127

1970, May 16 Photo. *Perf. 12½x12*

442 A126 1d yel & multi 80 55

Olive Year, 1969–1970.

U.P.U. Headquarters Issue
Common Design Type

1970, May 30 *Perf. 13*
Size: 36x26mm.

443 CD133 75c multi 70 45

1970, June 27 Photo. *Perf. 12½*

Designs: 40c, Guns, 18th century (horiz.). 1d, Pistol, 18th century (horiz.).

444 A127 40c yel & multi 55 28
445 A127 75c red & multi 80 50
446 A127 1d multi 1.10 60

Map of Arab Countries and Arab League Flag A128

Typographed and Engraved

1970, July 25 *Perf. 10½*

447 A128 30c grn, ocher & lt bl 30 20

25th anniversary of the Arab League.

Lenin A129

1970, Aug. 29 Litho. *Perf. 11½x12*

448 A129 30c brn & buff 25 18

Issued to commemorate the centenary of the birth of Lenin (1870–1924), Russian communist leader.

Exhibition Hall and Algiers Fair Emblem—A130

1970, Sept. 11 Engr. *Perf. 14x13½*

449 A130 60c lt ol grn 50 30

New Exhibition Hall for Algiers International Fair.

Common Design Types
pictured in section at front of book.

Education Year Emblem, Blackboard, Atom Symbol—A131

Koran Page A132

1970, Oct. 24 Photo. *Perf. 14*

450 A131 30c pink, blk, gold & lt bl 25 20
451 A132 3d multi 2.75 1.85

Issued for International Education Year.

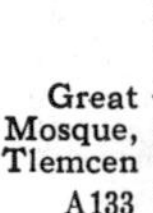

Great Mosque, Tlemcen A133

Design: 40c, Ketchaoua Mosque, Algiers (vert.). 1d, Mosque, Sidi-Okba (vert.).

1970–71 Lithographed *Perf. 14*

456 A133 30c multi 28 22
457 A133 40c sep & lem ('71) 32 18
458 A133 1d multi 75 42

Symbols of the Arts A134

1970, Dec. 26 Photo. *Perf. 13x12½*

459 A134 1d grn, lt grn & org 80 45

Main Post Office, Algiers A135

1971, Jan. 23 *Perf. 11½*

460 A135 30c multi 45 32

Stamp Day, 1971.

Hurdling A136

Designs: 40c, Vaulting (vert.). 75c, Basketball (vert.).

1971, Mar. 7 Photo. *Perf. 11½*

461 A136 20c lt bl & sl 32 22
462 A136 40c lt ol grn & sl 50 35
463 A136 75c sal pink & sl 75 50

Mediterranean Games, Izmir, Turkey, Oct. 1971.

Symbolic Head A137

1971, March 27 *Perf. 12½*

464 A137 60c car rose, blk & sil 50 28

International year against racial discrimination.

Emblem and Technicians A138

1971, Apr. 24 Photo. *Perf. 12½x12*

465 A138 70c cl, org & bluish blk 55 35

Founding of the Institute of Technology.

Woman from Aurès A139

Regional Costumes: 70c, Man from Oran. 80c, Man from Algiers. 90c, Woman from Amour Mountains.

1971, Oct. 16 *Perf. 11½*

466 A139 50c gold & multi 60 45
467 A139 70c gold & multi 70 60
468 A139 80c gold & multi 1.10 75
469 A139 90c gold & multi 1.15 90

See Nos. 485–488, 534–537.

UNICEF Emblem, Birds and Plants A140

1971, Dec. 6 *Perf. 11½*

470 A140 60c multi 60 45

25th anniversary of United Nations International Children's Fund (UNICEF).

Lion of St. Mark—A141

Design: 1.15d, Bridge of Sighs, Venice (vert.).

1972, Jan. 24 Litho. *Perf. 12*

471 A141 80c multi 85 60
472 A141 1.15d multi 1.35 90

UNESCO campaign to save Venice.

Javelin A142 — Book and Book Year Emblem A143

Designs: 25c, Bicycling (horiz.). 60c, Wrestling. 1d, Gymnast on rings.

1972, Mar. 25 Photo. *Perf. 11½*

473 A142 25c mar & multi 32 22
474 A142 40c ocher & multi 40 28
475 A142 60c ultra & multi 60 40
476 A142 1d rose & multi 90 55

20th Olympic Games, Munich, Aug. 26–Sept. 11.

1972, Apr. 15

477 A143 1.15d bis, brn & red 80 60

International Book Year 1972.

Mailmen A144 — Jasmine A145

1972, Apr. 22

478 A144 40c gray & multi 32 22

Stamp Day 1972.

1972, May 27

Flowers: 60c, Violets. 1.15d, Tuberose.

Flowers in Natural Colors

479 A145 50c brn & pale sal 50 35
480 A145 60c vio & gray 60 40
481 A145 1.15d lt bl & Prus bl 1.10 55

Olympic Stadium, Chéraga A146

1972, June 10

482 A146 50c gray, choc & grn 45 35

New Day, Algerian Flag A147

1972, July 5

483 A147 1d grn & multi 90 60

10th anniversary of independence.

Festival Emblem A148 — Mailing a Letter A149

1972, July 5 Litho. *Perf. 10½*

484 A148 40c grn, dk brn & org 28 15

First Arab Youth Festival, Algiers, July 5–11.

Costume Type of 1971

Regional Costumes: 50c, Woman from Hoggar. 60c, Kabyle woman. 70c, Man from Mzab. 90c, Woman from Tlemcen.

1972, Nov. 18 Photo. *Perf. 11½*

485 A139 50c gold & multi 80 45
486 A139 60c gold & multi 80 50
487 A139 70c gold & multi 90 55
488 A139 90c gold & multi 1.10 70

1973, Jan. 20 Photo. *Perf. 11*

489 A149 40c org & multi 32 22

Stamp Day.

Ho Chi Minh, Map of Viet Nam A150

1973, Feb. 17 Photo. *Perf. 11½*

490 A150 40c multi 32 15

To honor the people of Viet Nam.

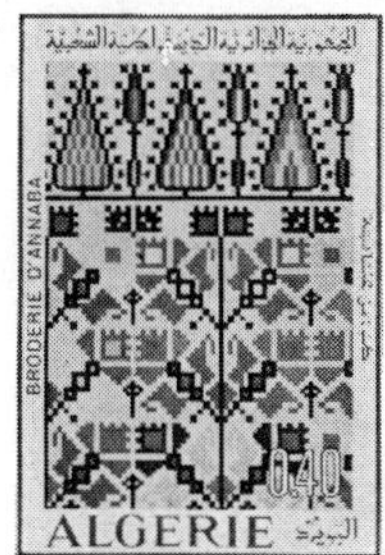

Embroidery from Annaba A151

Designs: 60c, Tree of Life pattern from Algiers. 80c, Constantine embroidery.

1973, Feb. 24

491 A151 40c gray & multi 55 35
492 A151 60c bl and multi 70 45
493 A151 80c dk red, gold & blk 90 50

Scott's editorial staff cannot undertake to identify, authenticate or appraise stamps and postal markings.

Stylized Globe and Wheat A152

1973, Mar. 26 Photo. *Perf. 11½*

494 A152 1.15d brt rose lil, org & grn 70 38

World Food Program, 10th anniversary.

Soldier and Flag—A153

1973, Apr. 23 Photo. *Perf. 14x13½*

495 A153 40c multi 30 22

Honoring the National Service.

Flower Type of 1969

Flowers: 30c, Opuntia ficus indica. 40c, Roses. 1d, Carnations. 1.15d, Bird-of-paradise flower.

1973, May 21 Photo. *Perf. 11½*

Flowers in Natural Colors

496 A111 30c pink & blk 32 28
497 A111 40c gray & blk 40 32
498 A111 1d yel & multi 90 60
499 A111 1.15d multi 1.10 70

OAU Emblem A154

1973, May 28 Photo. *Perf. 12½x13*

500 A154 40c multi 35 28

Organization for African Unity, 10th anniversary.

Desert and Fruitful Land, Farmer and Family—A155

1973, June 18 *Perf. 11½*

501 A155 40c gold & multi 45 32

Agricultural revolution.

Map of Africa, Scout Emblem A156

1973, July 16 Litho. *Perf. 10½*

502 A156 80c purple 60 40

24th Boy Scout World Conference (1st in Africa), Nairobi, Kenya, July 16–21.

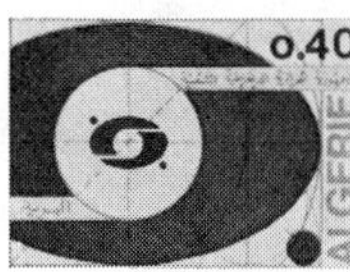

Algerian PTT Emblem A157

1973, Aug. 6 *Perf. 14*

503 A157 40c bl & org 32 22

Adoption of new emblem for Post, Telegraph and Telephone System.

Conference Emblem A158

1973, Sept. 5 Photo. *Perf. 13½x12½*

504 A158 40c dp rose & multi 32 25
505 A158 80c bl grn & multi 60 35

4th Summit Conference of Non-aligned Nations, Algiers, Sept. 5–9.

Port of Skikda A159

1973, Sept. 29 Photo. *Perf. 11½*

506 A159 80c ocher, blk & ultra 70 40

New port of Skikda.

Young Workers A160

1973, Oct. 22 Photo. *Perf. 13*

507 A160 40c multi 30 18

Voluntary work service.

Arms of Algiers A161

1973, Dec. 22 Photo. *Perf. 13*

508 A161 2d gold & multi 2.00 1.20

Millennium of Algiers.

Infant A162

1974, Jan. 7 Litho. *Perf. 10½x11*

509 A162 80c org & multi 65 45

Fight against tuberculosis.

Man and Woman, Industry and Transportation A163

1974, Feb. 18 Photo. *Perf. 11½*

510 A163 80c multi 60 30

Four-year plan.

A164

1974, Feb. 25 Photo. *Perf. 11½*

511 A164 1.50d multi 1.10 65

Millennium of the birth of abu-al-Rayhan al-Biruni (973–1048), philosopher and mathematician.

Map and Colors of Algeria, Tunisia, Morocco A165

1974, Mar. 4 Photo. *Perf. 13*

512 A165 40c gold & multi 32 28

Maghreb Committee for Coordination of Posts and Telecommunications.

Hand Holding Rifle A166 — Mother and Children A167

1974, Mar. 25 *Perf. 11½*

513 A166 80c red & blk 40 32

Solidarity with the struggle of the people of South Africa.

1974, Apr. 8 *Perf. 13½*

514 A167 85c multi 55 35

Honoring Algerian mothers.

Village—A168

Designs: 80c, Harvest. 90c, Tractor and sun. Designs after children's drawings.

1974, June 15 Size: 45x26mm.

515	A168	70c multi	55	22

Size: 48x33mm.

516	A168	80c multi	65	45
517	A168	90c multi	75	60

Nos. 498–499 Overprinted "FLORALIES/1974"

1974, June 22 Photo. ***Perf. 11½***

518	A111	1d multi	70	40
519	A111	1.15d multi	90	50

1974 Flower Show.

Stamp Vending Machine
A169

1974, Oct. 7 Photogravure ***Perf. 13***

520	A169	80c multi	55	32

Stamp Day 1974.

UPU Emblem and Globe
A170

1974, Oct. 14 ***Perf. 14***

521	A170	80c multi	60	40

Centenary of Universal Postal Union.

"Revolution"
A171

Soldiers and Mountains
A172

Raising New Flag
A173

Design: 1d, Algerian struggle for independence (people, sun and fields).

1974, Nov. 4 Photogravure ***Perf. 14***

522	A171	40c multi	32	28
523	A172	70c multi	45	32
524	A173	95c multi	60	32
525	A171	1d multi	60	40

20th anniversary of the start of the revolution.

"Horizon 1980"
A174

Ewer and Basin
A175

1974, Nov. 23 Photo. ***Perf. 13***

526	A174	95c ocher, dk red & blk	60	40

10-year development plan, 1971–1980.

1974, Dec. 21 ***Perf. 11½***

Designs: 60c, Coffee pot. 95c, Sugar bowl. 1d, Bath tub.

527	A175	50c pink & multi	35	28
528	A175	60c pale yel & multi	40	32
529	A175	95c cit & multi	60	40
530	A175	1d ultra & multi	85	45

17th century Algerian copperware.

No. 497 Surcharged with New Value and Heavy Bar

1975, Jan. 4

531	A111	50c on 40c multi	35	20

Mediterranean Games' Emblem—A176

1975, Jan. 27 ***Perf. 13½***

532	A176	50c pur, yel & grn	35	28
533	A176	1d org, bl & mar	60	32

Mediterranean Games, Algiers, 1975.

Costume Type of 1971

Regional Costumes: No. 534, Woman from Hoggar. No. 535, Woman from Algiers. No. 536, Woman from Oran. No. 537, Man from Tlemcen.

1975, Feb. 22 Photo. ***Perf. 11½***

534	A139	1d gold & multi	90	55
535	A139	1d gold & multi	90	55
536	A139	1d gold & multi	90	55
537	A139	1d gold & multi	95	55

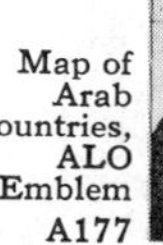

Map of Arab Countries, ALO Emblem
A177

1975, Mar. 10 Litho. ***Perf. 10½x11***

538	A177	50c red brn	30	18

Arab Labor Organization, 10th anniversary.

Blood Transfusion
A178

1975, Mar. 15 ***Perf. 14***

539	A178	50c car rose & multi	35	28

Blood donations and transfusions.

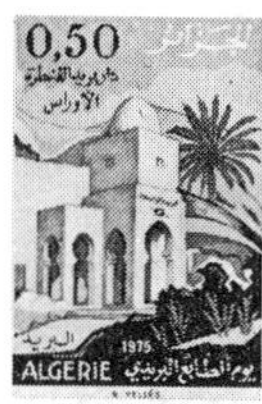

Post Office, Al-Kantara
A179

Policeman and Map of Algeria
A180

1975, May 10 Photo. ***Perf. 11½***

Granite Paper

540	A179	50c multi	35	15

Stamp Day 1975.

1975, June 1 Photo. ***Perf. 13***

541	A180	50c multi	35	22

National Security and 10th National Police Day.

Ground Receiving Station
A181

Designs: 1d, Map of Algeria with locations of radar sites, transmission mast and satellite. 1.20d, Main and subsidiary stations.

1975, June 28 Photo. ***Perf. 13***

542	181	50c bl & multi	35	22
543	181	1d bl & multi	65	32
544	181	1.20d bl & multi	70	38

National satellite telecommunications network.

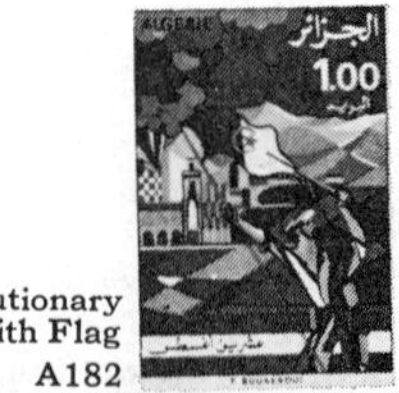

Revolutionary with Flag
A182

1975, Aug. 20 Photo. ***Perf. 11½***

545	A182	1d multi	60	35

August 20th Revolutionary Movement (Skikda), 20th anniversary.

Swimming and Games' Emblem
A183

Perf. 13x13½, 13½x13

1975, Aug. 23 Photogravure

Multicolored

546	A183	25c *shown*	22	18
547	A183	50c *Wrestling and map*	32	28
548	A183	70c *Soccer* (vert.)	55	32
549	A183	1d *Running* (vert.)	60	40
550	A183	1.20d *Handball* (vert.)	85	55
a.		Souvenir sheet of 5	6.50	6.50
		Nos. 546-550 (5)	2.54	1.73

7th Mediterranean Games, Algiers, Aug. 23–Sept. 6.

No. 550a contains one each of Nos. 546–550, perf. 13, buff margin with marginal inscription and ornament in blue and maroon. Size: 135x135mm. Sold for 4.50d. Exists imperf.; same price.

Setif, Guelma, Kherrata
A184

1975 Litho. ***Perf. 13½x14***

551	A184	5c org & blk	12	3
552	A184	10c emer & brn	5	5
553	A184	25c dl bl & blk	12	6
554	A184	30c lem & blk	18	8
555	A184	50c brt grn & blk	28	8
556	A184	70c fawn & blk	35	18
557	A184	1d ver & blk	50	30
		Nos. 551-557 (7)	1.60	78

30th anniversary of victory in World War II.

Issue dates: 50c, 1d, Nov. 3; others, Dec. 17.

Map of Maghreb and APU Emblem
A185

1975 Nov. 20 Photo. ***Perf. 11½***

558	A185	1d multi	60	35

10th Congress of Arab Postal Union, Algiers.

Mosaic, Bey Constantine's Palace
A186

Dey-Alger Palace—A187

Design: 2d, Prayer niche, Medersa Sidi—Boumediene, Tlemcen.

1975, Dec. 22

559	A186	1d lt bl & multi	70	32
560	A186	2d buff & multi	1.20	75
561	A186	2.50d buff & blk	1.85	1.10

Famous buildings.

Al-Azhar University
A188

Lithographed

1975, Dec. 29 *Perf. 11½x12½*

562 A188 2d multi 1.35 70

Millennium of Al-Azhar University.

Red-billed Firefinch
A189

Birds: 1.40d, Black-headed bush shrike (horiz.). 2d, Blue tit. 2.50d, Black-bellied sandgrouse (horiz.).

1976, Jan. 24 Photo. *Perf. 11½*

563	A189	50c multi	40	22
564	A189	1.40d multi	80	60
565	A189	2d multi	1.25	80
566	A189	2.50d multi	1.50	1.20

See Nos. 595–598.

Telephones 1876 and 1976
A190

Map of Africa with Angola and its Flag
A191

1976, Feb. 23 Photo. *Perf. 13½x13*

567 A190 1.40d rose, dk & lt bl 80 60

Centenary of first telephone call by Alexander Graham Bell, Mar. 10, 1876.

1976, Feb. 23 *Perf. 11½*

568 A191 50c brn & multi 35 20

Algeria's solidarity with the People's Republic of Angola.

Sahraoui Flag and Child, Map of former Spanish Sahara
A192

1976, Mar. 15 Photo. *Perf. 11½*

569 A192 50c multi 35 20

Algeria's solidarity with Sahraoui Arab Democratic Republic, former Spanish Sahara.

Mailman
A193

1976, Mar. 22

570 A193 1.40d multi 80 50

Stamp Day 1976.

Microscope, Slide with TB Bacilli, Patients
A194

1976, Apr. 26 *Perf. 13x13½*

571 A194 50c multi 35 18

Fight against tuberculosis.

"Setif, Guelma, Kherrata"
A195

1976, May 24 Photo. *Perf. 13½x13*

572 A195 50c bl & yel 28 6
a. Booklet pane of 6 1.75
b. Booklet pane of 10 3.00

No. 572 was issued in booklets only.

Ram's Head over Landscape
A196

1976, June 17 Photo. *Perf. 11½*

573 A196 50c multi 35 28

Livestock breeding.

People Holding Torch, Map of Algeria
A197

Palestine Map and Flag
A198

1976, June 29 Photo. *Perf. 14x13½*

574 A197 50c multi 35 18

National Charter.

1976, July 12 *Perf. 11½*

Granite Paper

575 A198 50c multi 32 18

Solidarity with the Palestinians.

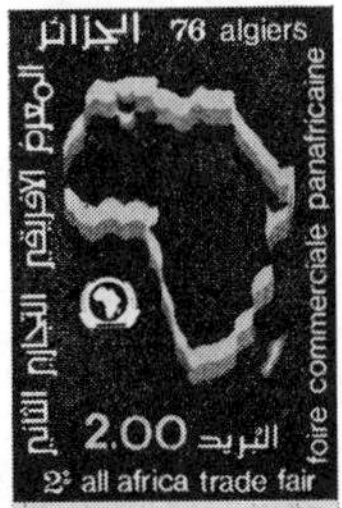

Map of Africa
A199

1976, Oct. 3 Litho. *Perf. 10½x11*

576 A199 2d dk bl & multi 1.20 70

2nd Pan-African Commercial Fair, Algiers.

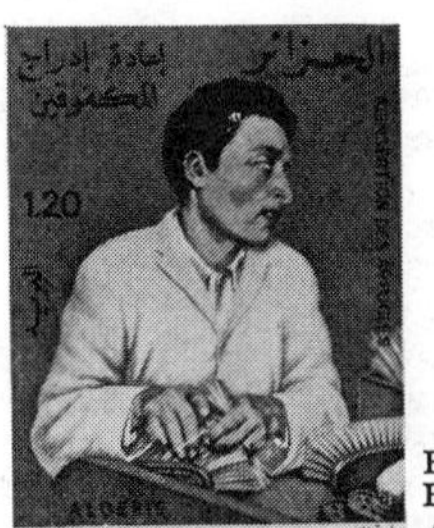

Blind Brushmaker
A200

The Blind, by Dinet
A201

1976, Oct. 23 Photo. *Perf. 14½*

577 A200 1.20d bl & multi 70 45
578 A201 1.40d gold & multi 90 60

Rehabilitation of the blind.

"Constitution 1976"—A202

1976, Nov. 19 Photo. *Perf. 11½*

579 A202 2d multi 1.10 60

New Constitution.

Soldiers Planting Seedlings
A203

1976, Nov. 25 Litho. *Perf. 12*

580 A203 1.40d multi 90 45

Green barrier against the Sahara.

Ornamental Border and Inscription
A204

1976, Dec. 18 Photo. *Perf. 11½*

Granite Paper

581 A204 2d multi 1.10 60

Re-election of Pres. Houari Boumediene.

Map with Charge Zones and Dials
A205

People and Buildings
A206

1977, Jan. 22 *Perf. 13*

582 A205 40c sil & multi 28 22

Inauguration of automatic national and international telephone service.

1977, Jan. 29 Photo. *Perf. 11½*

583 A206 60c on 50c multi 35 28

2nd General Population and Buildings Census. No. 583 was not issued without the typographed red brown surcharge, date, and bars.

Sahara Museum, Uargla
A207

1977, Feb. 12 Litho. *Perf. 14*

584 A207 60c multi 32 22

El-Kantara Gorge
A208

1977, Feb. 19 Photo. *Perf. 12½x13½*

585 A208 20c grn & yel 8 6
a. Booklet pane of 7 (3 #585, 4 #586 + label) 1.75
b. Booklet pane of 7 (5 #585, 2 #587 + label) 2.10
586 A208 60c brt lil & yel 25 12
587 A208 1d brn & yel 50 18

Nos. 585–587 issued only in booklets.

National Assembly—A209

1977, Feb. 27 *Perf. 11½*

588 A209 2d multi 1.10 60

People and Flag
A210

Soldier and Flag
A211

Perf. 13½, 11½ (3d)

1977, Mar. 12 Photogravure

589 A210 2d multi 1.00 65
590 A211 3d multi 1.50 90

Solidarity with the peoples of Zimbabwe (Rhodesia), 2d; Namibia, 3d.

Winter, Roman Mosaic
A212

The Seasons from Roman Villa, 2nd century A.D.: 1.40d, Fall. 2d, Summer. 3d, Spring.

1977, Apr. 21 Photo. *Perf. 11½*

Granite Paper

591 A212 1.20d multi 70 35
592 A212 1.40d multi 90 35
593 A212 2d multi 1.20 70
594 A212 3d multi 1.85 1.10
a. Souv. sheet of 4, perf. imperf. 5.00 5.00

No. 594a contains one each of Nos. 591-594; gray marginal inscription. Size: 101x145mm. Sold for 8d.

Bird Type of 1976

Birds: 60c, Tristram's warbler. 1.40d, Moussier's redstart (horiz.). 2d, Temminck's horned lark (horiz.). 3d, Eurasian hoopoe.

1977, May 21 Photo. *Perf. 11½*

595 A189 60c multi 45 32
596 A189 1.40d multi 80 60
597 A189 2d multi 1.25 80
598 A189 3d multi 2.00 1.25

Horseman
A213

Design: 5d, Attacking horsemen (horiz.).

1977, June 25 Photo. *Perf. 11½*

599 A213 2d multi 1.50 1.00
600 A213 5d multi 3.00 2.00

Helpful notes abound in the "Information for Collectors" section at the front of this volume.

Flag Colors, Games Emblem
A214

Wall Painting, Games Emblem
A215

1977, Sept. 24 Photo. *Perf. 11½*

601 A214 60c multi 35 32
602 A215 1.40d multi 85 60

3rd African Games, Algiers 1978.

Village and Tractor
A216

1977, Nov. 12 *Perf. 14x13*

603 A216 1.40d multi 90 50

Socialist agricultural village.

Almohades Dirham, 12th Century—A217

Ancient Coins: 1.40d, Almohades coin, 12th century. 2d, Almoravides dinar, 11th century.

1977, Dec. 17 Photo. *Perf. 11½*

604 A217 60c ultra, sil & blk 35 28
605 A217 1.40d grn, gold & brn 85 50
606 A217 2d red brn, gold & brn 1.20 75

Cherry Blossoms
A218

Flowering Trees: 1.20d, Peach. 1.30d, Almond. 1.40d, Apple.

1978, Feb. 11 Photo. *Perf. 11½*

607 A218 60c multi 30 18
608 A218 1.20d multi 55 40
609 A218 1.30d multi 65 40
610 A218 1.40d multi 70 45

No. 555 Surcharged with New Value and Bar

1978, Feb. 11 Litho. *Perf. 13½x14*

611 A184 60c on 50c 30 6

Children with Traffic Signs and Car
A219

1978, Apr. 29 Photo. *Perf. 11½*

612 A219 60c multi 30 18

Road safety and protection of children.

Sports and Games Emblems
A220

Designs (Games Emblem and): 60c, Rower (vert.). 1.20d, Flag colors. 1.30d, Fireworks (vert.). 1.40d, Map of Africa and dancers (vert.).

1978, July 13 Photo. *Perf. 11½*

613 A220 40c multi 18 18
614 A220 60c multi 30 25
615 A220 1.20d multi 50 35
616 A220 1.30d multi 65 40
617 A220 1.40d multi 70 40
Nos. 613-617 (5) 2.33 1.58

3rd African Games, Algiers, July 13–28.

TB Patient Returning to Family
A221

1978, Oct. 5 Photo. *Perf. 13½x14*

618 A221 60c multi 30 15

Anti-tuberculosis campaign.

Holy Kaaba
A222

1978, Oct. 28 Photo. *Perf. 11½*

619 A222 60c multi 30 15

Pilgrimage to Mecca.

National Servicemen Building Road
A223

1978, Nov. 4

620 A223 60c multi 30 20

African Unity Road from El Goleah to In Salah, inauguration.

Fibula
A224

Jewelry: 1.35d, Pendant. 1.40d, Ankle ring.

1978, Dec. 21 Photo. *Perf. 12x11½*

621 A224 1.20d multi 60 30
622 A224 1.35d multi 68 30
623 A224 1.40d multi 70 40

Pres. Boumediène—A225

1979, Jan. 7 Photo. *Perf. 12x11½*

624 A225 60c grn, red & brn 30 15

Houari Boumediène, president of Algeria 1965–1978.

Torch and Books
A226

1979, Jan. 27 Photo. *Perf. 11½*

625 A226 60c multi 30 22

National Front of Liberation Party Congress.

Pres. Boumediène—A227

1979, Feb. 4 Photo. *Perf. 11½*

626 A227 1.40d multi 70 30

40 days after death of Pres. Houari Boumediène.

Proclamation of New President
A228

1979, Feb. 10

627	A228	2d multi		1.00	30

Election of Pres. Chadli Bendjedid.

Sheik Abdul-Hamid Ben Badis (1889–1940)
A229

1979, Apr. 18 Photo. *Perf. 11½*

628	A229	60c multi		30	18

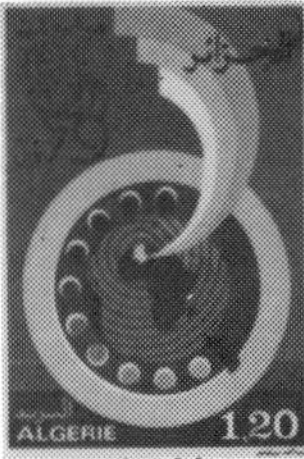

Telephone Dial, Map of Africa
A230

1979, May 19 Photo. *Perf. 13½x14*

Design: 1.40d, Symbolic Morse key and waves.

629	A230	1.20d multi		60	30
630	A230	1.40d multi		70	30

Telecom '79 Exhibition, Geneva, Sept. 20–26.

Harvest, IYC Emblem
A231

Design: 1.40d, Dancers and IYC emblem (vert.).

Perf. 11½x11, 11x11½

1979, June 21

631	A231	60c multi		30	18
632	A231	1.40d multi		70	35

International Year of the Child.

Nuthatch—A232

1979, Oct. 20 Photo. *Perf. 11½*

633	A232	1.40d multi		60	22

Flag, Soldiers and Workers—A233

Design: 3rd, Revolutionaries and emblem.

1979, Nov. 1 Photo. *Perf. 12½*

634	A233	1.40d multi		60	28

Size: 37×48mm. ***Perf. 11½***

635	A233	3d multi		1.40	55

November 1 revolution, 25th anniversary.

Hegira (Pilgrimage Year)—A234

1979, Dec. 2 Photo. *Perf. 11½*

636	A234	3d multi		1.40	75

Camels, Lion, Men and Slave—A235

Dionysian Procession (Setif Mosaic): 1.35d, Elephants, tigers and women. Men in tiger-drawn cart. Nos. 637-639 se-tenant in continuous design.

1980, Feb. 16 Photo. *Perf. 11½*

Granite Paper

637	A235	1.20d multi		50	30
638	A235	1.35d multi		60	40
639	A235	1.40d multi		70	50

Science Day—A236

1980, Apr. 19 Photo. *Perf. 12*

640	A236	60c multi		30	15

Dam and Workers—A237

1980, June 17 Photo. *Perf. 11½*

641	A237	60c multi		30	15

Extraordinary Congress of the National Liberation Front Party.

Olympic Sports, Moscow '80 Emblem—A238

1980, June 28

642	A238	50c	Flame, rings, vert.	25	12
643	A238	1.40d	*shown*	70	35

22nd Summer Olympic Games, Moscow, July 19-Aug. 3.

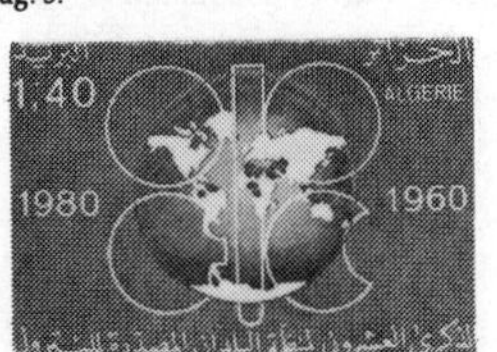

20th Anniversary of OPEC—A239

Engr.

1980, Sept. 15 *Perf. 11x10½, 10½x11*

644	A239	60c	*Men holding OPEC emblem*, vert.	30	15
645	A239	1.40d	*shown*	70	35

Aures Valley—A240

1980, Sept. 25 Litho. *Perf. 13½x14*

646	A240	50c	*shown*	15	8
647	A240	1d	*El Oued Oasis*	50	18
648	A240	1.40d	*Tassili Rocks*	70	28
649	A240	2d	*View of Algiers*	1.00	50

World Tourism Conference, Manila, Sept. 27.

Avicenna (980-1037), Philosopher and Physician—A241

1980, Oct. 25 Photo. *Perf. 12*

650	A241	2d multi		1.00	50

Ruins of El Asnam—A242

1980, Nov. 13 Photo. *Perf. 12*

651	A242	3d multi		1.50	60

Earthquake relief.

Crown—A243

1980, Dec. 20 Photo. *Perf. 12*

Granite Paper

652	A243	60c	*Necklace*, vert.	30	18
653	A243	1.40d	*Earrings, bracelet*, vert.	70	35
654	A243	2d	*shown*	1.00	50

1980-1984 Five-Year Plan—A244

1981, Jan. 29 Litho. *Perf. 14*

655	A244	60c multi		30	15

Basket Weaving—A245

1981, Feb. 19 Photo. *Perf. 12½*

Granite Paper

656	A245	40c	shown	20	10
657	A245	60c	Rug weaving	30	15
658	A245	1d	Coppersmith	50	25
659	A245	1.40d	Jeweler	70	35

Cedar Tree—A246

Arbor Day: 1.40d, Cypress tree (vert.).

1981, Mar. 19 Photo. *Perf. 12*
Granite Paper

660	A246	60c multi	30	15
661	A246	1.40d multi	70	35

Mohamed Bachir el Ibrahimi (1869-1965) A247

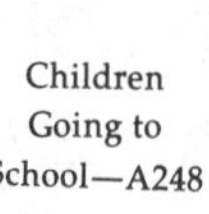

Children Going to School—A248

1981, Apr. 16 Granite Paper

662	A247	60c multi	30	15
663	A248	60c multi	30	15

Science Day.

12th International Hydatidological Congress, Algiers—A249

1981, Apr. 23 *Perf. 14x13½*

664	A249	2d multi	1.00	50

13th World Telecommunications Day—A250

1981, May 14 Photo. *Perf. 14x13½*

665	A250	1.40d multi	70	35

Disabled People and Hand Offering Flower—A251

1981, June 20 Litho. *Perf. 12½x13, 13x12½*

666	A251	1.20d Symbolic globe, vert.	60	30
667	A251	1.40d shown	70	35

Intl. Year of the Disabled.

Papilio Machaon—A252

1981, Aug. 20 Photo. *Perf. 11½*
Granite Paper

668	A252	60c shown	30	15
669	A252	1.20d Rhodocera rhamni	60	30
670	A252	1.40d Charaxes jasius	70	35
671	A252	2d Papilio podalirius	1.00	50

Monk Seal—A253

1981, Sept. 17 *Perf. 14x13½*

672	A253	60c shown	30	15
673	A253	1.40d Macaque	70	35

World Food Day A254

Cave Drawings of Tassili A255

1981, Oct. 16 Photo. *Perf. 14x14½*

674	A254	2d multi	1.00	50

1981, Nov. 21 *Perf. 11½*

Designs: Various cave drawings. 1.60d, 2d horiz.

675	A255	60c multi	30	15
676	A255	1d multi	50	25
677	A255	1.60d multi	80	40
678	A255	2d multi	1.00	50

Galley, 17-18th Cent.—A256

1981, Dec. 17 Photo. *Perf. 11½*

679	A256	60c shown	30	15
680	A256	1.60d Ship, diff.	80	40

1982 World Cup Soccer—A257

Designs: Various soccer players.

1982, Feb. 25 Litho. *Perf. 13x12½x 12½x13*

681	A257	80c multi, vert.	40	20
682	A257	2.80fr multi	1.40	70

TB Bacillus Centenary—A258

1982, Mar. 20 Photo. *Perf. 14½x14*

683	A258	80c multi	40	20

Painted Stand—A259

1982, Apr. 24 Photo. *Perf. 11½*
Granite Paper

684	A259	80c Mirror, vert.	40	20
685	A259	2d shown	1.00	50

Size: 48x33mm.

686	A259	2.40d Chest	1.20	60

Djamaael Djadid Mosque, Algiers—A260

1982, May 15 Litho. *Perf. 14*

687	A260	80c shown	40	20
688	A260	2.40d Sidi Boumediene Mosque, Tlemcen	1.20	60
689	A260	3d Garden of Dey, Algiers	1.50	75

Callitris Articulata A261

Independence, 20th Anniv. A262

Designs: Medicinal plants.

1982, May 27 Photo. *Perf. 11½*
Granite Paper

690	A261	50c shown	25	12
691	A261	80c Artemisia herba-alba	40	20
692	A261	1d Ricinus communis	50	25
693	A261	2.40d Thymus fontanesii	1.25	60

1982, July 5 Granite Paper

694	A262	50c Riflemen	25	12
695	A262	80c Soldiers, horiz.	40	20
696	A262	2d Symbols, citizens, horiz.	1.00	50

Souvenir Sheet

697	A262	5d Emblem	2.50	1.25

No. 697 contains one stamp (32x39mm.); green and red decorative margin. Size: 75x83mm.

Soummam Congress—A263

1982, Aug. 20 Litho.

698	A263	80c Congress building	40	20

Scouting Year—A264

1982, Oct. 21 Photo.

699	A264	2.80d multi	1.40	70

Palestinian Child A265

Chlamydotis Undulata A266

1982, Nov. 25 Litho. *Perf. 10½*

700	A265	1.60d multi	80	40

1982, Dec. 23 Photo. Perf 15x14, 14x15

Protected birds. 50c, 2d horiz.

701	A266	50c Geronticus eremita	25	12
702	A266	80c shown	40	20
703	A266	2d Aguila rapax	1.00	50
704	A266	2.40d Gypaetus barbatus	1.20	60

Jewelry Type of 1980

1983, Feb. 10

705	A243	50c Picture frame	25	12
706	A243	1d Flasks	50	25
707	A243	2d Brooch, horiz.	1.00	50

Intl. Arbor Day—A267

1983, Mar. 17 Photo. *Perf. 11½*
Granite Paper

708	A267	80c Abies numidica, vert.	40	20
709	A267	2.80d Acacia raddiana	1.40	70

SEMI-POSTAL STAMPS.

Regular Issue of 1926 Surcharged in Black or Red

+10c ☪

1927 *Perf. 14x13½.* **Unwmkd.**

B1	A1	5c +5c bl grn	35	35
B2	A1	10c +10c lil	35	35
B3	A2	15c +15c org brn	35	35
B4	A2	20c +20c car rose	35	35
B5	A2	25c +25c bl grn	35	35
B6	A2	30c +30c lt bl	35	35
B7	A2	35c +35c dp vio	35	35
B8	A2	40c +40c ol grn	35	35
B9	A3	50c +50c dp bl (R)	35	35
a.		Dbl. surch.	120.00	120.00
B10	A3	80c +80c red org	35	35
B11	A4	1fr +1fr gray grn & red brn	40	40
B12	A4	2fr +2fr Prus bl & blk brn	14.00	14.00
B13	A4	5fr +5fr red & vio	16.50	16.50
		Nos. B1-B13 (13)	34.40	34.40

The surtax was for the benefit of wounded soldiers. Government officials speculated in this issue.

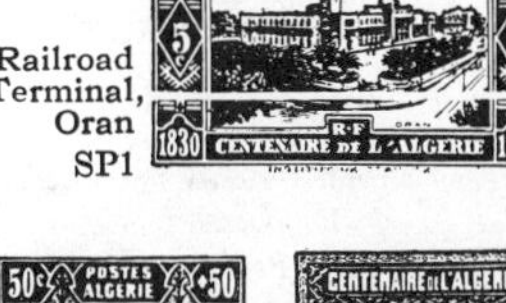

Railroad Terminal, Oran
SP1

Ruins at Djemila
SP2

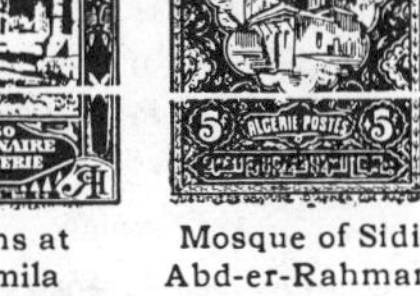

Mosque of Sidi Abd-er-Rahman
SP3

Designs: 10c+10c, Rummel Gorge, Constantine. 15c+15c, Admiralty Buildings, Algiers. 25c+25c, View of Algiers. 30c+30c, Trajan's Arch, Timgad. 40c+40c, Temple of the North, Djemila. 75c+75c Mansourah Minaret, Tlemcen. 1f+1f, View of Ghardaia. 1.50f+1.50f, View of Tolga. 2f+2f, Tuareg warriors. 3f+3f, Kasbah, Algiers.

1930 **Engraved.** *Perf. 12½.*

B14	SP1	5c +5c org	5.00	5.00
B15	SP1	10c +10c ol grn	5.00	5.00
B16	SP1	15c +15c dk brn	5.00	5.00
B17	SP1	25c +25c blk	5.00	5.00
B18	SP1	30c +30c dk red	5.00	5.00
B19	SP1	40c +40c ap grn	5.00	5.00
B20	SP2	50c +50c ultra	5.00	5.00
B21	SP2	75c +75c red pur	5.00	5.00
B22	SP2	1fr +1fr org red	5.00	5.00
B23	SP2	1.50fr +1.50fr dp ultra	5.00	5.00
B24	SP2	2fr +2fr dk car	5.00	5.00
B25	SP2	3fr +3fr dk grn	5.00	5.00
B26	SP3	5fr +5fr grn & car	10.00	10.00
a.		Center inverted	325.00	
		Nos. B14-B26 (13)	70.00	70.00

Issued in connection with the celebration of the centenary of the French occupation of Algeria. The surtax on the stamps was given to the funds for the celebration.

Nos. B14–B26 exist imperf. Price, set in pairs, $250.

No. 102 Surcharged in Red

1918-11 Nov.-1938
0.65 + 0.35
= =

1938 *Perf. 13.*

B27	A6	65c +35c on 2.25fr yel grn	40	40

20th anniversary of Armistice.

René Caillié, Charles Lavigerie and Henri Duveyrier—SP14

1939 **Engraved.**

B28	SP14	30c +20c dk bl grn	70	70
B29	SP14	90c +60c car rose	70	70
B30	SP14	2.25fr +75c ultra	6.75	6.75
B31	SP14	5fr +5fr brn blk	15.00	15.00

Pioneers of the Sahara.

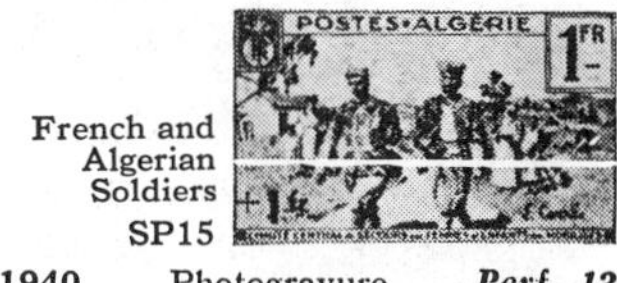

French and Algerian Soldiers
SP15

1940 **Photogravure** *Perf. 12*

B32	SP15	1fr +1fr bl & car	50	50
B33	SP15	1fr +2fr brn rose & blk	50	50
B34	SP15	1fr +4fr dp grn & red	60	60
B35	SP15	1fr +9fr brn & car	1.15	1.15

The surtax was used to assist the families of mobilized men.

Type of Regular Issue, 1941 Surcharged in Carmine

+4f

1941 **Engraved.** *Perf. 13.*

B36	A19	1fr +4fr blk	15	15

No. 135 Surcharged in Carmine

SECOURS NATIONAL +4f

B37	A19	1fr +4fr dk bl	15	15

The surtax was for National Relief.

No. 124 Surcharged in Black "+60c"

1942

B38	A7	90c +60c hn brn	6	6
a.		Double surch.	55.00	

The surtax was used for National Relief. The stamp could also be used as 1.50 francs for postage.

Mother and Child
SP16

1943, Dec. 1 **Litho.** *Perf. 12*

B39	SP16	50c +4.50fr brt pink	32	32
B40	SP16	1.50fr +8.50fr lt grn	32	32
B41	SP16	3fr +12fr dp bl	32	32
B42	SP16	5fr +15fr vio brn	32	32

The surtax was for the benefit of soldiers and prisoners of war.

Planes over Fields
SP17

Engraved.

1945, July 2 *Perf. 13* **Unwmkd.**

B43	SP17	1.50fr +3.50fr lt ultra, red org & blk	22	22

The surtax was for the benefit of Algerian airmen and their families.

France No. B192 Overprinted in Black

ALGÉRIE
a

1945

B44	SP146	4fr +6fr dk vio brn	30	30

The surtax was for war victims of the P. T. T.

Overprinted in Blue on Type of France, 1945.

1945, Oct. 15

B45	SP150	2fr +3fr dk brn	35	35

For Stamp Day.

Overprinted in Blue on Type of France, 1946.

1946, June 29

B46	SP160	3fr +2fr red	60	60

For Stamp Day.

Children Playing by Stream
SP18

Girl
SP19

Athlete
SP20

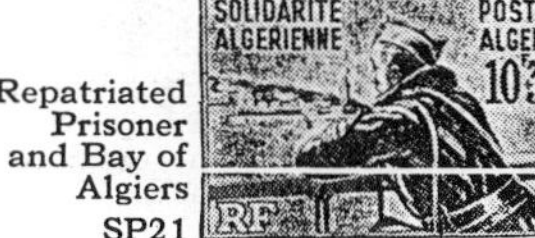

Repatriated Prisoner and Bay of Algiers
SP21

1946, Oct. 2 **Engraved** *Perf. 13*

B47	SP18	3fr +17fr dk grn	90	90
B48	SP19	4fr +21fr red	90	90
B49	SP20	8fr +27fr rose lil	2.75	2.75
B50	SP21	10fr +35fr dk bl	1.00	1.00

Type of France, 1947, Overprinted type "a" in Carmine.

1947, Mar. 15

B51	SP172	4.50fr +5.50fr dp ultra	45	45

For Stamp Day.

Same on Type of France, 1947, Surcharged Like No. B36 in Carmine.

1947, Nov. 13

B52	A173	5fr +10fr dk Prus grn	40	40

Type of France, 1948, Overprinted in Dark Green

ALGÉRIE
f

1948, Mar. 6

B53	SP176	6fr +4fr dk grn	50	50

For Stamp Day.

Type of France, 1948, Overprinted type "a" in Blue and New Value.

1948, May

B54	A176	6fr +4fr red	40	40

Battleship Richelieu and the Admiralty, Algiers
SP22

Aircraft Carrier Arromanches
SP23

Engraved.

1949, Jan. 15 *Perf. 13* **Unwmkd.**

B55	SP22	10fr +15fr dp bl	3.50	3.50
B56	SP23	18fr +22fr red	3.50	3.50

The surtax was for naval charities.

Type of France, 1949, Overprinted in Blue

ALGÉRIE
g

1949, Mar. 26

B57	SP180	15fr +5fr lil rose	90	90

For Stamp Day, Mar. 26–27.

Type of France, 1950, Overprinted type "f" in Green.

1950, Mar. 11

B58	SP183	12fr +3fr blk brn	1.00	1.00

For Stamp Day, Mar. 11–12.

Foreign Legionary
SP24

1950, Apr. 30

B59	SP24	15fr +5fr dk grn	1.00	1.00

Charles de Foucauld and Gen. J. F. H. Laperrine
SP25

1950, Aug. 21 *Perf. 13* **Unwmkd.**

B60	SP25	25fr +5fr brn ol & brn blk	3.25	3.25

50th anniversary of the presence of the French in the Sahara.

Emir Abd-el-Kader and Marshal T. R. Bugeaud
SP26

1950, Aug. 21

B61	SP26	40fr +10fr dk brn & blk brn	3.25	3.25

Unveiling of a monument to Emir Abd-el-Kader at Cacheron.

Col. Colonna d'Ornano and Fine Arts Museum, Algiers
SP27

1951, Jan. 11

B62	SP27	15fr +5fr blk brn, vio brn & red brn	60	60

Issued to commemorate the tenth anniversary of the death of Col. Colonna d'Ornano.

Type of France, 1951, Overprinted type "a" in Black.

1951, Mar. 10

B63	SP186	12fr +3fr brn	90	90

For Stamp Day.

Type of France, 1952, Overprinted type "g" in Dark Blue.

1952, Mar. 8 *Perf. 13* Unwmkd.

B64	SP190	12fr +3fr dk bl	1.50	1.50

For Stamp Day.

French Military Medal
SP28

Engraved.

1952, July 5 *Perf. 13* Unwmkd.

B65	SP28	15fr +5fr grn, yel & brn	1.35	1.35

Issued to commemorate the centenary of the creation of the French Military Medal.

Type of France 1952, Surcharged type "g" and Surtax in Black

1952, Sept. 15

B66	A222	30fr +5fr dp ultra	1.20	1.20

Issued to commemorate the 10th anniversary of the defense of Bir-Hakeim.

View of El Oued
SP29

Design: 12fr+3fr, View of Bou-Noura.

1952, Nov. 15 Engraved

B67	SP29	8fr +2fr ultra & red	1.25	1.25
B68	SP29	12fr +3fr red	1.65	1.65

The surtax was for the Red Cross.

Type of France, 1953, Overprinted type "a" in Black.

1953, Mar. 14 Engraved

B69	SP193	12fr +3fr pur	1.10	1.00

For Stamp Day. Surtax for Red Cross.

Victory of Cythera
SP30

Engraved.

1953, Dec. 18 *Perf. 13* Unwmkd.

B70	SP30	15fr +5fr blk brn & brn	60	60

The surtax was for army welfare work.

Type of France, 1954, Overprinted type "a" in Black.

1954, Mar. 20 *Perf. 13* Unwmkd.

B71	SP196	12fr +3fr scar	75	75

For Stamp Day.

Soldiers and Flags
SP31

Foreign Legionary
SP32

1954, Mar. 27

B72	SP31	15fr +5fr dk brn	38	38

The surtax was for old soldiers.

1954, Apr. 30

B73	SP32	15fr +5fr dk grn	80	80

The surtax was for the welfare fund of the Foreign Legion.

Nurses and Verdun Hospital, Algiers—SP33

Design: 15fr+5fr, J. H. Dunant & ruins at Djemila.

1954, Oct. 30

B74	SP33	12fr +3fr ind & red	2.00	2.00
B75	SP33	15fr +5fr pur & red	2.50	2.50

The surtax was for the Red Cross.

Earthquake Victims and Ruins
SP34

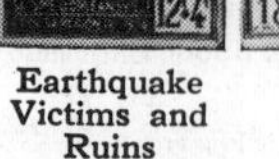

First Aid
SP35

Designs: 15fr+5fr, As No. B75. 20fr+7fr, As No. B77. 25fr+8fr & 30fr+10fr, Removing wounded.

1954, Dec. 5

B76	SP34	12fr +4fr dk vio brn	1.40	1.40
B77	SP34	15fr +5fr dp bl	1.40	1.40
B78	SP35	18fr +6fr lil rose	1.50	1.50
B79	SP35	20fr +7fr vio	1.50	1.50
B80	SP35	25fr +8fr rose brn	1.75	1.75
B81	SP35	30fr +10fr brt bl grn	1.75	1.75
		Nos. B76-B81 (6)	9.30	9.30

The surtax was for victims of the Orleansville earthquake disaster of September 1954.

Type of France, 1955, Overprinted type "a" in Black.

1955, Mar. 19

B82	SP199	12fr +3fr dp ultra	75	75

For Stamp Day, Mar. 19–20.

Women and Children
SP36

Cancer Victim
SP37

1955, Nov. 5

B83	SP36	15fr +5fr bl & ind	50	50

The tax was for war victims.

1956, Mar. 3 *Perf. 13* Unwmkd.

B84	SP37	15fr +5fr dk brn	50	50

The surtax was for the Algerian Cancer Society. The male figure in the design is Rodin's "Age of Bronze."

Type of France, 1956, Overprinted type "a" in Black.

1956, Mar.

B85	SP202	12fr +3fr red	50	50

For Stamp Day, Mar. 17–18.

Foreign Legion Rest Home
SP38

1956, Apr. 29

B86	SP38	15fr +5fr dk bl grn	90	90

Issued in honor of the French Foreign Legion.

Type of France, 1957, Overprinted type "f" in Black

1957, Mar. 16 Engraved *Perf. 13*

B87	SP204	12fr +3fr dl pur	75	75

For Stamp Day and to honor the Maritime Postal Service.

Fennec
SP39

Design: 15fr+5fr, Stork flying over roofs.

1957, Apr. 6

B88	SP39	12fr +3fr red brn & red	3.50	3.50
B89	SP39	15fr +5fr sep & red	3.50	3.50

The surtax was for the Red Cross.

Type of Regular Issue, 1956 Surcharged in Da k Blue

18 JUIN 1940
+ 5F

1957, June 18

B90	A53	15fr +5fr scar & rose red	55	55

Issued to commemorate the 17th anniversary of General de Gaulle's appeal for a Free France.

The Giaour, by Delacroix
SP40

On the Banks of the Oued, by Fromentin
SP41

Design: 35fr+10fr, Dancer, by Chasseriau.

Engraved.

1957, Nov. 30 *Perf. 13* Unwmkd.

B91	SP40	15fr +5fr dk car	3.25	3.25
B92	SP41	20fr +5fr grn	3.25	3.25
B93	SP40	35fr +10fr dk bl	3.25	3.25

The surtax was for army welfare organizations.

Type of France Overprinted type "f" in Blue.

1958, Mar. 15 *Perf. 13* Unwmkd.

B94	SP206	15fr 5fr org brn	75	75

For Stamp Day.

Bird-of-Paradise Flower
SP42

Arms and Marshal's Baton
SP43

1958, June 14 Engr. *Perf. 13*

B95	SP42	20fr +5fr grn, org & vio	2.00	2.00

The surtax was for Child Welfare.

1958, July 20

B96	SP43	20fr +5fr ultra, car & grn	90	90

Issued for the Marshal de Lattre Foundation.

Independent State

Clasped Hands, Wheat and Olive Branch SP44 — Burning Books SP45

1963, May 27 *Perf. 13* Unwmkd.

B97	SP44	50c +20c sl grn, brt grn & car	1.20	80

The surtax was for the National Solidarity Fund.

1965, June 7 Engraved *Perf. 13*

B98	SP45	20c +5c ol grn, red & blk	45	35

Issued to commemorate the burning of the Library of Algiers, June 7, 1962.

Soldiers and Woman Comforting Wounded Soldier SP46

1966, Aug. 20 Photo. *Perf. 11½*

B99	SP46	30c +10c multi	75	75
B100	SP46	95c +10c multi	1.60	1.40

Issued for the Day of the Moudjahid (Moslem volunteers).

Red Crescent, Boy and Girl SP47

1967, May 27 Litho. *Perf. 14*

B101	SP47	30c +10c brt grn, brn & car	55	40

Algerian Red Crescent Society.

Flood Victims SP48

Design: 95c+25c, Rescuing flood victims.

1969, Nov. 15 Typo. *Perf. 10½*

B102	SP48	30c +10c dl bl, sal & blk	45	40

Lithographed

B103	SP48	95c +25c multi	1.10	75

Red Crescent Flag SP49

1971, May 17 Engraved *Perf. 10½*

B104	SP49	30c +10c sl grn & car	40	35

Algerian Red Crescent Society.

AIR POST STAMPS.

Plane over Algiers Harbor AP1

Two types of 20fr:

Type I. Monogram "F" without serifs. "POSTE" indented 3mm.

Type II. Monogram "F" with serifs. "POSTE" indented 4½mm.

Engraved.

1946, June 20 *Perf. 13.* Unwmkd.

C1	AP1	5fr red	6	5
C2	AP1	10fr dp bl	8	5
C3	AP1	15fr dp grn	32	5
C4	AP1	20fr brn (II)	20	5
C4A	AP1	20fr brn (I)	80.00	57.50
C5	AP1	25fr violet	38	12
C6	AP1	40fr gray blk	60	12
		Nos. C1-C4, C5-C6 (6)	1.64	44

No. C1 Surcharged in Black — **—10 %**

1947, Jan. 18

C7	AP1(4.50fr)	on 5fr red	8	7

Storks over Mosque AP2

Plane over Village AP3

1949–53

C8	AP2	50fr green	2.25	30
C9	AP3	100fr brown	1.75	30
C10	AP2	200fr brt red	4.50	3.00
C11	AP3	500fr ultra ('53)	15.00	11.00

Beni Bahdel Dam AP4

1957, July 1 *Perf. 13* Unwmkd.

C12	AP4	200fr dk red	4.50	90

Caravelle over Ghardaia AP5

Designs: 2d, Caravelle over El Oued. 5d, Caravelle over Tipasa.

1967–68 Engraved *Perf. 13*

C13	AP5	1d lil, org brn & emer	1.20	65
C14	AP5	2d brt bl, org brn & emer	2.50	1.35
C15	AP5	5d brt bl, grn & org brn ('68)	5.50	3.00

Plane over Casbah, Algiers AP6

Designs: 3d, Plane over Oran. 4d, Plane over Rhumel Gorge.

1971–72 Photogravure *Perf. 12½*

C16	AP6	2d grysh blk & multi	1.35	85
C17	AP6	3d vio & blk ('72)	2.00	1.35
C18	AP6	4d blk & multi ('72)	2.75	1.75

Issue dates: 2d, June 12, 1971; 3d, 4d, Feb. 28, 1972.

AIR POST SEMI-POSTAL STAMPS.

No. C2 Surcharged in Carmine

‡ 18 Juin 1940 +10Fr.

1947, June 18 *Perf. 13.*

CB1	AP1	10fr +10fr dp bl	50	50

Issued to commemorate the 7th anniversary of Gen. Charles de Gaulle's speech in London, June 18, 1940.

No. C1 Surcharged in Blue

‡ 18 JUIN 1940 +10 Fr.

1948, June 18

CB2	AP1	5fr +10fr red	50	50

Issued to commemorate the 8th anniversary of Gen. Charles de Gaulle's speech in London, June 18, 1940.

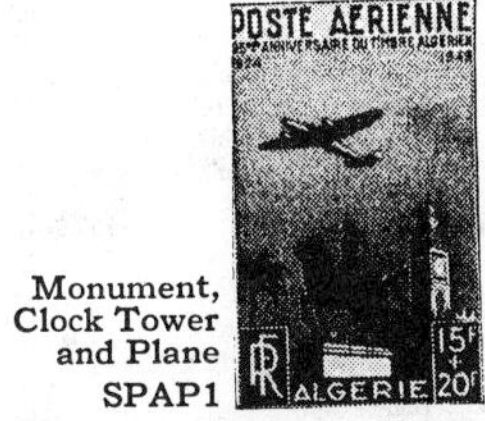

Monument, Clock Tower and Plane SPAP1

1949, Nov. 10 Engraved Unwmkd.

CB3	SPAP1	15fr +20fr dk brn	3.25	3.25

Issued to commemorate the 25th anniversary of Algeria's first postage stamps.

POSTAGE DUE STAMPS.

D1

D2

Perf. 14x13½.

1926-27 Typographed. Unwmkd.

J1	D1	5c lt bl	7	7
J2	D1	10c dk brn	7	7
J3	D1	20c ol grn	20	18
J4	D1	25c car rose	35	35
J5	D1	30c rose red	20	15
J6	D1	45c bl grn	40	40
J7	D1	50c brn vio	5	5
J8	D1	60c grn ('27)	1.40	40
J9	D1	1fr red brn, *straw*	15	15
J10	D1	2fr lil rose ('27)	20	20
J11	D1	3fr dp bl ('27)	20	15
		Nos. J1-J11 (11)	3.29	2.17

1926-27

J12	D2	1c ol grn	5	5
J13	D2	10c violet	45	22
J14	D2	30c bister	35	22
J15	D2	60c dl red	28	22
J16	D2	1fr brt vio ('27)	9.50	2.25
J17	D2	2fr lt bl ('27)	7.50	90
		Nos. J12-J17 (6)	18.13	3.86

See note below France No. J51.

Stamps of 1926 Surcharged with New Values.

1927

J18	D1	60c on 20c ol grn	70	28
J19	D1	2fr on 45c bl grn	1.10	80
J20	D1	3fr on 25c car rose	45	28

Recouvrement Stamps of 1926 Surcharged — **10c**

1927-32

J21	D2	10c on 30c bis ('32)	1.85	1.85
J22	D2	1fr on 1c ol grn	75	60
J23	D2	1fr on 60c dl red ('32)	12.00	28
J24	D2	2fr on 10c vio	6.25	6.25

Type of 1926, Without "R F".

1942 Typographed *Perf. 14x13½*

J25	D1	30c dk red	8	8
J26	D1	2fr magenta	18	18

Type of 1926 Surcharged in Red — **T 0.50**

1944 *Perf. 14x13½.*

J27	A2	50c on 20c yel grn	5	5
	a.	Inverted surch.	3.50	
	b.	Double surch.	10.00	

No. J27 was issued precanceled only. See note after No. 32.

Type of 1926.

1944 Lithographed. *Perf. 12.*

J28	D1	1.50fr brt rose lil	28	22
J29	D1	2fr grnsh bl	28	22
J30	D1	5fr rose car	28	22

Type of 1926.

1947 Typographed *Perf. 14x13½*

J32	D1	5fr green	65	55

France Nos. J80–J81 Overprinted in Carmine or Black — **ALGÉRIE**

1947

J33	D5	10c sep (C)	4	4
J34	D5	30c brt red vio	8	8

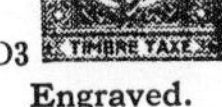
D3

Engraved.

1947–55 *Perf. 14x13* Unwmkd.

J35	D3	20c red	15	15
J36	D3	60c ultra	32	28
J37	D3	1fr dk org brn	5	5
J38	D3	1.50fr dl grn	50	40
J39	D3	2fr red	5	4

J40	D3	3fr violet	12	12
J41	D3	5fr ultra ('49)	12	12
J42	D3	6fr black	22	18
J43	D3	10fr lil rose	22	15
J44	D3	15fr ol grn ('55)	55	50
J45	D3	20fr brt grn	30	18
J46	D3	30fr red org ('55)	50	45
J47	D3	50fr ind ('51)	1.20	1.10
J48	D3	100fr brt bl ('53)	4.00	3.75
		Nos. J35-J48 (14)	8.30	7.47

Independent State

France Nos. J93–J97 Overprinted "EA" in Black like Nos. 286-290

Perf. 14x13½

1962, July 2 Typo. Unwmkd.

Handstamped Overprint

J49	D6	5c brt pink	2.00	1.75
J50	D6	10c red org	2.00	1.40
J51	D6	20c ol bis	2.00	1.20
J52	D6	50c dk grn	3.50	2.85
J53	D6	1fr dp grn	5.00	4.75

Typographed Overprint

J49a	D6	5c brt pink	5.00	5.00
J50a	D6	10c red org	5.00	5.00
J51a	D6	20c ol bis	4.50	4.50
J52a	D6	50c dk grn	12.50	12.50
J53a	D6	1fr dp grn	20.00	20.00

See note after No. 290.

Scales—D4

Grain—D5

1963, June 25 ***Perf. 14x13½***

J54	D4	5c car rose & blk	7	5
J55	D4	10c ol & car	15	12
J56	D4	20c ultra & blk	25	18
J57	D4	50c bis brn & grn	60	50
J58	D4	1fr lil & org	1.35	1.00
		Nos. J54-J58 (5)	2.42	1.85

No. J58 Surcharged with New Value and 3 Bars

1968, Mar. 28 Typo. ***Perf. 14x13½***

J59	D4	60c on 1fr lil & org	45	28

1972, Oct. 21 Litho. ***Perf. 13½x14***

J60	D5	10c bister	4	3
J61	D5	20c dp brn	12	6
J62	D5	40c orange	20	7
J63	D5	50c dk vio bl	25	12
J64	D5	80c dk ol gray	40	15
J65	D5	1d green	50	25
J66	D5	2d blue	1.00	45
		Nos. J60-J66 (7)	2.51	1.13

NEWSPAPER STAMPS.

No. 1 Surcharged in Red

1/2 centime

1924 ***Perf. 14x13½*** **Unwmkd.**

P1	A16	½c on 1c dk gray	5	5
a.		Triple surcharge	55.00	

1926

Same Surcharge in Red on No. 33

P2	A1	½c on 1c ol	5	5

ALLENSTEIN

(äl'ĕn·shtīn)

LOCATION—In East Prussia.

AREA—4,457 sq. mi.

POP.—540,000 (estimated 1920).

CAPITAL—Allenstein.

Allenstein, a district of East Prussia, held a plebiscite in 1920 under the Versailles Treaty, voting to join Germany rather than Poland. Later that year, Allenstein became part of the German Republic.

100 Pfennig = 1 Mark

Stamps of Germany, 1906-20, Overprinted

PLÉBISCITE
OLSZTYN
ALLENSTEIN

Perf. 14, 14½, 14x14½, 14½x14

1920 Wmkd. Lozenges. (125)

1	A16	5pf green	25	25
2	A16	10pf carmine	25	25
3	A22	15pf dk vio	25	25
4	A22	15pf vio brn	8.00	8.00
5	A16	20pf bl vio	25	25
6	A16	30pf org & blk, *buff*	38	38
7	A16	40pf lake & blk	28	28
8	A16	50pf pur & blk, *buff*	30	30
9	A16	75pf grn & blk	30	28
10	A17	1m car rose	1.00	1.00
a.		Double ovpt.	450.00	*750.00*
11	A17	1.25m green	85	85
a.		Double ovpt.	600.00	*1,250.*
12	A17	1.50m yel brn	85	85
13	A21	2.50m lil rose	1.00	1.00
14	A19	3m blk vio	2.00	2.00
a.		Double ovpt.	450.00	*1,250.*
b.		Inverted overprint	450.00	*750.00*
		Nos. 1-14 (14)	15.96	15.94

Overprinted

15	A16	5pf green	25	38
16	A16	10pf carmine	25	38
17	A22	15pf dk vio	25	25
18	A22	15pf vio brn	30.00	40.00
19	A16	20pf bl vio	25	25
20	A16	30pf org & blk, *buff*	38	38
21	A16	40pf lake & blk	38	38
22	A16	50pf pur & blk, *buff*	22	25
23	A16	75pf grn & blk	25	25
24	A17	1m car rose	85	85
a.		Inverted overprint	400.00	500.00
25	A17	1.25m green	85	85
26	A17	1.50m yel brn	85	85
27	A21	2.50m lil rose	1.25	1.25
28	A19	3m blk vio	1.50	1.50
a.		Inverted overprint	400.00	*750.00*
b.		Double ovpt.	375.00	*600.00*
		Nos 15-28 (14)	37.53	47.82

The 40pf carmine rose (Germany No. 124) exists with this oval overprint, but it is doubtful whether it was regularly issued. Price $400.

ANATOLIA

(ăn'ȧ·tō'lĭ·ȧ)

See Turkey in Asia, Vol. IV.

ANDORRA

(ăn·dŏr'ȧ)

LOCATION—On the southern slope of the Pyrenees Mountains between France and Spain.

GOVT.—Co-principality.

AREA—179 sq. mi.

POP.—26,500 (1976).

CAPITAL—Andorre-la-Vieille.

Andorra is subject to the joint control of France and the Spanish Bishop of Urgel and pays annual tribute to both. The country has no monetary unit of its own, the peseta and franc both being in general use.

100 Centimos = 1 Peseta
100 Centimes = 1 Franc

Spanish Administration.

Stamps of Spain, 1922-26, Overprinted in Red or Black

:-: CORREOS :-:
ANDORRA

Perf. 14, 13½x12½, 12½x11½.

1928 Unwmkd.

1	A49	2c ol grn	32	25

Control Numbers on Back

2	A49	5c car rose (Bk)	38	38
3	A49	10c green	38	38
4	A49	15c sl bl	2.25	2.50
5	A49	20c violet	2.25	2.50
6	A49	25c rose red (Bk)	2.25	2.50
7	A49	30c blk brn	12.50	7.00
8	A49	40c dp bl	12.50	5.00
9	A49	50c org (Bk)	12.50	7.25
10	A49a	1p bl blk	15.00	9.50
11	A49a	4p lake (Bk)	105.00	75.00
12	A49a	10p brn (Bk)	175.00	100.00
		Nos. 1-12 (12)	340.33	212.26

Counterfeit overprints exist.

La Vall
A1

St. Juan de Caselles
A2

St. Julia de Loria
A3

St. Coloma
A4

General Council
A5

1929 Engraved ***Perf. 14, 11½***

13	A1	2c ol grn	1.25	32

Control Numbers on Back

14	A2	5c car lake	2.75	42
a.		Perf. 11½	7.50	1.75
15	A3	10c yel grn	2.75	1.25
16	A4	15c sl grn	2.75	1.25
17	A3	20c violet	2.75	1.25
18	A4	25c car rose	7.00	2.00
19	A1	30c ol brn	105.00	42.50
a.		Perf. 11½	120.00	52.50
20	A2	40c dk bl	6.75	1.00
21	A3	50c dp org	6.75	1.25
a.		Perf. 11½	*450.00*	
22	A5	1p slate	9.00	4.25
23	A5	4p dp rose	72.50	26.00
a.		Perf. 11½	*450.00*	
24	A5	10p bis brn	85.00	37.50
		Nos. 13-24 (12)	304.25	118.99

Both perforations were used for all values through 4p. The 10p is perf. 14.

Nos. 13–24, 26, 28, 32 exist imperforate.

Without Control Numbers.

1936–43 ***Perf. 11½x11***

25	A1	2c red brn ('37)	1.75	75
26	A2	5c dk brn	1.75	75
27	A3	10c bl grn	8.25	1.75
a.		10c yel grn	100.00	20.00
28	A4	15c grn ('37)	5.50	1.75
29	A3	20c violet	5.50	1.75
30	A4	25c dp rose ('37)	2.00	1.75
31	A1	30c carmine	3.50	1.75
31A	A2	40c dk bl	*450.00*	20.00
32	A1	45c rose red ('37)	1.75	75
33	A3	50c dp org	8.00	2.50
34	A1	60c dp bl ('37)	5.50	1.75
34A	A5	1p slate	*2,750.*	
35	A5	4p dp rose ('43)	28.50	20.00
36	A5	10p bis brn ('43)	40.00	20.00
		Nos. 25-34, 35-36 (13)	*562.00*	75.25

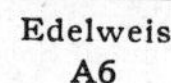

Edelweiss
A6

Provost
A7

Coat of Arms
A8

Plaza of Ordino
A9

Chapel of Meritxell
A10

Map
A11

Photogravure.

1948–53 ***Perf. 12½*** **Unwmkd.**

37	A6	2c dk ol grn ('51)	60	30
38	A6	5c dp org ('53)	60	30
39	A6	10c dp bl ('53)	60	30

Engraved

Perf. 9½x10

40	A7	20c brn vio	17.50	1.25
41	A7	25c org, perf. 12½ ('53)	11.00	65
42	A8	30c dk sl grn	17.50	1.75
43	A9	50c dp grn	21.00	2.25
44	A10	75c dk bl	27.50	2.25
45	A9	90c dp car rose	14.00	2.25
46	A10	1p brt org ver	21.00	2.25
47	A8	1.35p dk bl vio	14.00	2.50

Perf. 10.

48	A11	4p ultra ('53)	21.00	4.25
49	A11	10p dk vio brn ('51)	42.50	8.00
		Nos. 37-49 (13)	208.80	28.30

Bridge of St. Anthony

A12

Madonna of Meritxell, 8th Century

A13

Designs: 70c, Aynos pasture. 1p, View of Canillo. 2p, St. Coloma. 2.50p, Arms of Andorra. 3p, Old Andorra (horiz.). 5p, View of Ordino (horiz.).

Engraved

1963–64 ***Perf. 13*** **Unwmkd.**

50	A12	25c dk gray & sep	6	6
51	A12	70c dk sl grn & brn blk	6	6
52	A12	1p sl & dl pur	25	6
53	A12	2p vio & dl pur	25	6
54	A12	2.50p rose cl ('64)	1.00	60
55	A12	3p blk & grnsh gray ('64)	1.75	60
56	A12	5p dk brn & choc ('64)	3.25	1.10
57	A13	6p sep & car ('64)	4.25	1.10
		Nos. 50-57 (8)	10.87	3.64

Narcissus

A14

Encamp Valley

A15

Flowers: 1p, Pinks. 5p, Jonquils. 10p, Hellebore.

1966, June 10 **Engraved** ***Perf. 13***

58	A14	50c sl bl & vio bl	12	12
59	A14	1p brn & cl	25	12
60	A14	5p brt grn & sl bl	1.25	50
61	A14	10p dk vio & blk	3.00	60

Europa Issue 1972

Common Design Type

1972, May 2 **Photo.** ***Perf. 13***

Size: 25½x38mm.

62	CD15	8p dk grn & multi	*325.00*	*175.00*

1972, July 4 **Photo.** ***Perf. 13***

Designs: 1.50p, Massana (village). 2p, Skiing on De La Casa Pass. 5p, Pessons Lake (horiz.).

63	A15	1p multi	25	12
64	A15	1.50p multi	1.00	50
65	A15	2p multi	2.00	50
66	A15	5p multi	2.50	90

Tourist publicity.

Butterfly Stroke

A16

Design: 2p, Volleyball (vert.).

1972, Oct. **Photo.** ***Perf. 13***

67	A16	2p lt bl & multi	60	30
68	A16	5p multi	80	42

20th Olympic Games, Munich, Aug. 26–Sept. 11.

Common Design Types

pictured in section at front of book.

St. Anthony Singers

A17

1972, Dec. 5 **Photo.** ***Perf. 13***

Multicolored

69	A17	1p *shown*	12	6
70	A17	1.50p *Les Caramelles (boys' choir)*	12	6
71	A17	2p *Nativity scene*	18	10
72	A17	5p *Man holding giant cigar* (vert.)	85	18
73	A17	8p *Hermit of Meritxell* (vert.)	1.10	42
74	A17	15p *Marratxa dancers*	3.00	60
		Nos. 69-74 (6)	5.37	1.42

Andorran customs. No. 71 is for Christmas 1972.

Europa Issue 1973

Common Design Type and

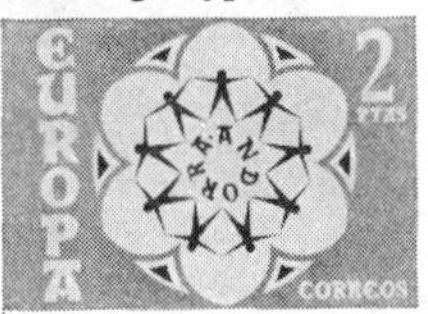

Symbol of Unity

A18

1973, Apr. 30 **Photo.** ***Perf. 13***

75	A18	2p ultra, red & blk	50	25

Size: 37x25mm.

76	CD16	8p tan, red & blk	2.00	70

Nativity

A19

Virgin of Ordino

A20

Design: 5p, Adoration of the Kings. Designs are from altar panels of Meritxell Parish Church.

1973, Dec. 14 **Photo.** ***Perf. 13***

77	A19	2p multi	18	18
78	A19	5p multi	90	30

Christmas 1973.

Europa Issue 1974

1974, Apr. 29 **Photo.** ***Perf. 13***

Design: 8p, Les Banyes Cross.

79	A20	2p multi	1.25	42
80	A20	8p sl & brt bl	2.75	1.10

Cupboard

A21

Crowns of Virgin and Child of Roser

A22

1974, July 30 **Photo.** ***Perf. 13***

81	A21	10p multi	1.25	42
82	A22	25p dk red & multi	2.75	1.10

UPU Monument, Bern

A23

1974, Oct. **Photogravure** ***Perf. 13***

83	A23	15p multi	1.75	60

Centenary of Universal Postal Union.

Nativity

A24

Design: 5p, Adoration of the Kings.

1974, Dec. 4 **Photo.** ***Perf. 13***

84	A24	2p multi	60	18
85	A24	5p multi	2.10	42

Christmas 1974.

Mail Delivery, Andorra, 19th Century

A25

12th Century Painting, Ordino Church

A26

1975, Apr. 4 **Photo.** ***Perf. 13***

86	A25	3p multi	50	18

España 75 International Philatelic Exhibition, Madrid, Apr. 4–13.

1975, Apr. 28 **Photo.** ***Perf. 13***

Design: 12p, Christ in Glory, 12th century Romanesque painting, Ordino church.

87	A26	3p multi	1.85	25
88	A26	12p multi	3.00	50

Urgel Cathedral and Document

A27

1975, Oct. 4 **Photo.** ***Perf. 13***

89	A27	7p multi	2.50	1.25

Millennium of consecration of Urgel Cathedral, and Literary Festival 1975.

Nativity, Ordino

A28

Design: 7p, Adoration of the Kings, Ordino.

1975, Dec. 3 **Photo.** ***Perf. 13***

90	A28	3p multi	50	25
91	A28	7p multi	75	38

Christmas 1975.

Caldron and CEPT Emblem

A29

Slalom and Montreal Olympic Emblem

A30

Europa Issue 1976

Design: 12p, Chest and CEPT emblem (horiz.).

1976, May 3 **Photo.** ***Perf. 13***

92	A29	3p bis & multi	50	12
93	A29	12p yel & multi	1.50	42

1976, July 9 **Photo.** ***Perf. 13***

Design: 15p, One-man canoe and Montreal Olympic emblem (horiz.).

94	A30	7p multi	42	18
95	A30	15p multi	1.00	42

21st Olympic Games, Montreal, Canada, July 17–Aug. 1.

Nativity

A31

Design: 25p, Adoration of the Kings. Wall paintings in La Massana Church.

1976, Dec. 7 **Photo.** ***Perf. 13***

96	A31	3p multi	25	12
97	A31	25p multi	1.00	50

Christmas 1976.

Europa Issue 1977

View of Ansalonge

A32

Design: 12p, Xuclar, valley and mountains.

1977, May 2 **Litho.** ***Perf. 13***

98	A32	3p multi	30	18
99	A32	12p multi	1.00	38

Cross of Terme

A33

Map of Post Offices

A34

Design: 12p, Church of St. Miguel d'Engolasters.

1977, Dec. 2 **Photo.** ***Perf. 13x12½***

100	A33	5p multi	50	30
101	A33	12p multi	1.25	75

Christmas 1977.

Souvenir Sheet

Designs: 10p, Mail delivery. 20p, Post Office, 1928. 25p, Andorran coat of arms.

1978, Mar. 31 Photo. ***Perf. 13x13½***

102	Sheet of 4	1.40	1.40
a.	A34 5p multi	12	6
b.	A34 10p multi	25	12
c.	A34 20p multi	38	30
d.	A34 25p multi	42	38

Spanish postal service in Andorra, 50th anniversary. No. 102 has black marginal inscription. Size: 105x149mm.

Europa Issue 1978

La Vall
A35

Design: 12p, St. Juan de Caselles.

1978, May 2 ***Perf. 13***

103	A35	5p multi	30	12
104	A35	12p multi	75	30

Crown, Bishop's Mitre and Staff
A36

1978, Sept. 24 Photo. ***Perf. 13***

105	A36	5p brn, car & yel	50	12

700th anniversary of the signing of treaty establishing Co-Principality of Andorra.

Holy Family
A37

Design: 25p, Adoration of the Kings. Both designs after frescoes in the Church of St. Mary d'Encamp.

1978, Dec. 5 Photo. ***Perf. 13***

106	A37	5p multi	18	12
107	A37	25p multi	75	42

Young Woman
A38

Designs: 5p, Young man. 12p, Bridegroom and bride riding mule.

1978, Feb. 14 Photo. ***Perf. 13***

108	A38	3p multi	12	6
109	A38	5p multi	18	6
110	A38	12p multi	38	18

Europa Issue 1979

Old Mail Truck
A39

Design: 12p, Stampless covers of 1846 and 1854.

1979, Apr. 30 Engr. ***Perf. 13***

111	A39	5p yel grn & dk bl	38	12
112	A39	12p dk red & vio	90	32

Children Holding Hands—A40

1979, Oct. 18 Photo. ***Perf. 13***

113	A40	19p multi	75	38

International Year of the Child.

St. Coloma's Church—A41

Design: 25p, Agnus Dei roundel, St. Coloma's Church.

1979, Nov. 28 Photo. ***Perf. 13½***

114	A41	8p multi	25	8
115	A41	25p multi	60	38

Christmas 1979.

Bishop Pere d'Arg—A42

Bishops of Urgel: 5p, Josep Caixal. 13p, Joan Benlloch.

1979, Dec. 27 **Engraved**

116	A42	1p dk bl & brn	3	3
117	A42	5p rose lake & pur	12	6
118	A42	13p brn & dk grn	25	8

Europa Issue 1980

Antoni Fiter I. Rosell, Magistrate—A43

Design: 19p, Francesc Cairat I. Freixes, magistrate.

1980, Apr Photo. ***Perf. 13x13½***

119	A43	8p bis, blk & brn	15	10
120	A43	19p lt grn & blk	38	18

Boxing, Moscow '80 Emblem—A44

1980 Photo. ***Perf. 13½x13***

121	A44	5p *Downhill skiing*	10	6
122	A44	8p *shown*	15	10
123	A44	50p *Target shooting*	90	50

12th Winter Olympic Games, Lake Placid, N.Y., Feb. 12-24 (5p); 22nd Summer Olympic Games, Moscow, July 19-Aug. 3.

Nativity—A45

1980 Litho. ***Perf. 13***

124	A45	10p *Nativity*, vert.	18	12
125	A45	22p *shown*	42	22

Christmas 1980.

Europa Issue 1981

Children Dancing at Santa Anna Feast—A46

Design: 30p, Going to church on Aplec de la Verge de Canolich Day.

1981, May 7 Photo. ***Perf. 13***

126	A46	12p multi	22	12
127	A46	30p multi	55	25

50th Anniv. of Police Force—A47

1981, July 2 Photo. ***Perf. 13½x13***

128	A47	30p multi	55	25

Intl. Year of the Disabled—A48

1981, Oct. 8 Photo. ***Perf. 13½***

129	A48	50p multi	90	38

Christmas 1981—A49

Designs: Encamp Church retable.

1981, Dec. 3 Photo. ***Perf. 13½***

130	A49	12p Nativity	22	12
131	A49	30p Adoration	55	25

Bishops of Urgel—A50

1981, Dec. 12 Engr. ***Perf. 13½***

132	A50	7p Salvador Casanas	12	6
133	A50	20p Josep de Boltas	38	15

Natl. Arms—A51

1982, Feb. 17 Photo. ***Perf. 13x13½***

134	A51	1p brt pink	3	3
135	A51	3p bis brn	10	6
136	A51	7p red org	22	15
137	A51	12p lake	36	24
138	A51	15p ultra	45	30
139	A51	20p bl grn	60	40
140	A51	30p crim rose	90	60
		Nos. 134-140 (7)	2.66	1.78

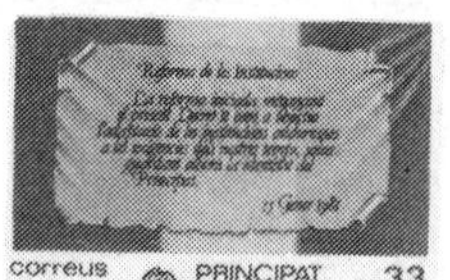

Europa 1982—A52

1982, May 12 Photo. ***Perf. 13***

141	A52	14p New Reforms, 1866, vert.	45	30
142	A52	33p Reform of Institutions, 1981	1.00	65

1982 World Cup—A53

Designs: Various soccer players.

1982, June 13 Photo. ***Perf. 13x13½***

143	A53	14p multi	45	30
144	A53	33p multi	1.00	65

Natl. Arms Type of 1982

1982, July Engr. ***Perf. 13x12½***

145	A51	50p dk grn	1.50	1.00
146	A51	100p dk bl	3.00	2.00

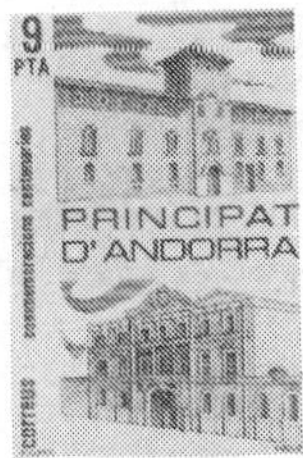

Centenary of Permanent Spanish and French Delegations—A54

Anniversaries: 14p, 50th anniv. of Andorran stamps. 23p, St. Francis of Assisi (1182-1226). 33p, Anyos Pro-Vicarial District membership centenary (Relacio sobre la Vall de Andorra titlepage).

1982, Sept. 7 Engr. *Perf. 13*

147	A54	9p dk bl & brn	28	18
148	A54	14p	45	30
149	A54	23p dk bl & brn	70	32
150	A54	33p blk & ol grn	1.00	65

Christmas 1982—A55

Designs: 14p, Madonna and Child, Andorra la Vella Church (vert.). 33p, El Tio de Nadal (children in traditional costumes striking hollow tree).

1982, Dec. 9 Photo. *Perf. 13x13½, 13½x13*

151	A55	14p multi	45	30
152	A55	33p multi	1.00	65

AIR POST STAMP

AP1

Engraved.

1951, June 27 ***Perf. 11.*** **Unwmkd.**

C1	AP1	1p	dk vio brn	35.00	3.00

SPECIAL DELIVERY STAMPS.

Special Delivery Stamp of Spain, 1905 Overprinted

CORREOS

ANDORRA

1928 ***Perf. 14.*** **Unwmkd.**

Without Control Number on Back.

E1	SD1	20c	red	67.50	37.50

With Control Number on Back.

E2	SD1	20c	pale red	35.00	16.00

Eagle over Mountain Pass

SD2

Arms and Squirrel

SD3

1929 ***Perf. 14***

With Control Number on Back.

E3	SD2	20c	scarlet	21.00	*6.25*
a.			Perf. 11½	*450.00*	

Without Control Number on Back.

1937 ***Perf. 11½x11.***

E4	SD2	20c	red	7.50	3.75

Engraved.

1949 ***Perf. 10x9½.*** **Unwmkd.**

E5	SD3	25c	red	9.00	3.00

French Administration.

Stamps and Types of France, 1900–1929, Overprinted **ANDORRE**

1931 ***Perf. 14x13½*** **Unwmkd.**

1	A16	1c	gray	75	75
a.			Double ovpt.	*1,000.*	*1,000.*
2	A16	2c	red brn	1.00	1.00
3	A16	3c	orange	1.00	1.00
4	A16	5c	green	1.50	1.50
5	A16	10c	lilac	2.50	2.50
6	A22	15c	red brn	5.50	5.50
7	A22	20c	red vio	7.50	7.50
8	A22	25c	yel brn	7.50	7.50
9	A22	30c	green	7.25	7.25
10	A22	40c	ultra	12.50	12.50
11	A20	45c	lt vio	14.00	14.00
12	A20	50c	vermilion	11.50	11.50
13	A20	65c	gray grn	20.00	20.00
14	A20	75c	rose lil	25.00	25.00
15	A22	90c	red	32.50	32.50
16	A20	1fr	dl bl	37.50	37.50
17	A22	1.50fr	lt bl	42.50	42.50

Overprinted **ANDORRE**

18	A18	2fr	org & pale bl	32.50	32.50
19	A18	3fr	brt vio & rose	115.00	115.00
20	A18	5fr	dk bl & buff	175.00	175.00
21	A18	10fr	grn & red	375.00	375.00
22	A18	20fr	mag & grn	450.00	450.00
			Nos. 1-22 (22)	1,377.50	1,377.50

See No. P1 for ½c on 1c gray.

Nos. 9, 15 and 17 were not issued in France without overprint.

Chapel of Meritxell

A50

Bridge of St. Anthony

A51

St. Miguel d'Engolasters

A52

Gorge of St. Julia

A53

Old Andorra

A54

1932–43 **Engraved** ***Perf. 13***

23	A50	1c	gray blk	45	38
24	A50	2c	violet	75	75
25	A50	3c	brown	45	38
26	A50	5c	bl grn	75	60
27	A51	10c	dl lil	1.25	1.00
28	A50	15c	dp red	1.60	1.60
29	A51	20c	lt rose	12.50	10.00
30	A52	25c	brown	5.00	5.00
31	A51	25c	brn car ('37)	10.00	10.00
32	A51	30c	emerald	3.00	2.75
33	A51	40c	ultra	11.50	10.00
34	A51	40c	brn blk ('39)	1.25	1.10
35	A51	45c	lt red	12.00	10.00
36	A51	45c	bl grn ('39)	6.00	5.00
37	A52	50c	lil rose	13.00	11.00
38	A51	50c	lt vio ('39)	6.00	5.00
38A	A51	50c	grn ('40)	2.50	1.75
39	A51	55c	lt vio ('38)	21.00	16.00
40	A51	60c	yel brn ('38)	1.00	85
41	A52	65c	bl grn	55.00	50.00
42	A51	65c	bl ('38)	14.00	11.00
43	A51	70c	red ('39)	2.50	1.75
44	A52	75c	violet	6.75	5.50
45	A51	75c	ultra ('39)	5.00	4.00
46	A51	80c	grn ('38)	25.00	20.00
46A	A53	80c	bl grn ('40)	45	50
47	A53	90c	dp rose	6.75	5.50
48	A53	90c	dk grn ('39)	4.00	2.00
49	A53	1fr	bl grn	20.00	11.50
50	A53	1fr	scar ('38)	25.00	20.00
51	A53	1fr	dp ultra ('39)	45	40
51A	A53	1.20fr	brt vio ('42)	45	40
52	A50	1.25fr	rose car ('33)	16.50	15.00
52A	A50	1.25fr	rose ('38)	6.25	2.50
52B	A53	1.30fr	sep ('40)	40	40
53	A54	1.50fr	ultra	19.00	17.50
53A	A53	1.50fr	crim ('40)	40	40
54	A53	1.75fr	vio ('33)	115.00	110.00
55	A53	1.75fr	dk bl ('38)	42.50	35.00
56	A53	2fr	red vio	8.00	6.50
56A	A50	2fr	rose red ('40)	1.75	1.25
56B	A50	2fr	dk bl grn ('42)	45	32
57	A50	2.15fr	dk vio ('38)	62.50	50.00
58	A50	2.25fr	ultra ('39)	8.00	6.50
58A	A50	2.40fr	red ('42)	45	38
59	A50	2.50fr	gray blk ('39)	8.50	6.75
59A	A50	2.50fr	dp ultra ('40)	2.25	2.00
60	A53	3fr	org brn	8.00	6.50
60A	A50	3fr	red brn ('40)	50	45
60B	A50	4fr	sl bl ('42)	50	45
60C	A50	4.50fr	dp vio ('42)	1.40	70
61	A54	5fr	brown	65	45
62	A54	10fr	violet	75	60
62B	A54	15fr	dp ultra ('42)	85	50
63	A54	20fr	rose lake	75	60
63A	A51	50fr	turq bl ('43)	1.75	85
			Nos. 23-63A (56)	582.45	491.31

A 20c ultra exists. Price $11,500.

No. 37 Surcharged with Bars and New Value in Black.

1935

64	A52	20c	on 50c lil rose	14.00	12.00
a.			Double surcharge	*750.00*	

Coat of Arms

A55 A56

1936–42 ***Perf. 14x13***

65	A55	1c	blk ('37)	12	12
66	A55	2c	blue	12	12
67	A55	3c	brown	12	12
68	A55	5c	rose lil	12	12
69	A55	10c	ultra ('37)	12	12
70	A55	15c	red vio	85	85
71	A55	20c	emer ('37)	12	12
72	A55	30c	cop red ('38)	38	38
72A	A55	30c	blk brn ('42)	22	22
73	A55	35c	Prus grn ('38)	52.50	52.50
74	A55	40c	cop red ('42)	22	22
75	A55	50c	Prus grn ('42)	22	22
76	A55	60c	turq bl ('42)	22	22
77	A55	70c	vio ('42)	22	22
			Nos. 65-77 (14)	55.55	55.55

1944

78	A56	10c	violet	4	4
79	A56	30c	dp mag	5	5
80	A56	40c	dl bl	5	5
81	A56	50c	org red	6	6
82	A56	60c	black	8	8
83	A56	70c	brt red vio	12	8
84	A56	80c	bl grn	12	6
			Nos. 78-84 (7)	52	42

See also No. 114.

St. Jean de Caselles

A57

La Maison des Vallees

A58

Old Andorra

A59

Provost

A60

1944–47 ***Perf. 13***

85	A57	1fr	brn vio	22	12
86	A57	1.20fr	blue	18	12
87	A57	1.50fr	red	22	12
88	A57	2fr	dk bl grn	18	12
89	A58	2.40fr	rose red	25	22
90	A58	2.50fr	rose red ('46)	45	35
91	A58	3fr	sepia	18	12
92	A58	4fr	ultra	22	15
93	A59	4.50fr	brn blk	22	18
94	A58	4.50fr	dk bl grn ('47)	2.50	2.25
95	A59	5fr	ultra	25	22
96	A59	5fr	Prus grn ('46)	42	32
97	A59	6fr	rose car ('45)	32	18
98	A59	10fr	Prus grn	18	12
99	A59	10fr	ultra ('46)	22	12
100	A60	15fr	rose lil	42	27
101	A60	20fr	dp bl	60	50
102	A60	25fr	lt rose red ('46)	1.35	1.00
103	A60	40fr	dk grn ('46)	1.35	1.25
104	A60	50fr	sepia	1.40	1.00
			Nos. 85-104 (20)	11.13	8.73

1948-49

105	A58	4fr	lt bl grn	80	80
106	A59	6fr	vio brn	40	40
107	A59	8fr	indigo	1.10	1.10
108	A59	12fr	brt red	85	85
109	A59	12fr	bl grn ('49)	1.00	85
110	A59	15fr	crim ('49)	50	50
111	A60	18fr	dp bl	2.75	1.75
112	A60	20fr	dk vio	2.00	1.80
113	A60	25fr	ultra ('49)	1.40	1.25
			Nos. 105-113 (9)	10.80	9.30

1949–51 ***Perf. 14x13, 13***

114	A56	1fr	dp bl	65	60
115	A57	3fr	red ('51)	5.00	3.75
116	A57	4fr	sepia	2.25	1.75
117	A58	5fr	emerald	2.50	1.75
118	A58	5fr	pur ('51)	2.25	1.40
119	A58	6fr	bl grn ('51)	2.25	1.50
120	A58	8fr	brown	65	65
121	A59	15fr	blk brn ('51)	2.25	1.75
122	A59	18fr	rose red ('51)	11.00	7.50
123	A60	30fr	ultra ('51)	14.00	8.50
			Nos. 114-123 (10)	42.80	29.15

Les Escaldres Spa

A61

St. Coloma Belfry

A62

Designs: 15fr, 18fr, 20fr, 25fr, Gothic cross. 30fr, 35fr, 40fr 50fr, 65fr, 70fr, 75fr, Village of Les Bons.

Engraved.

1955-58 ***Perf. 13*** **Unwmkd.**

124	A61	1fr dk gray bl	22	18
125	A61	2fr dp grn	22	18
126	A61	3fr red	22	18
127	A61	5fr chocolate	22	18
128	A62	6fr dk bl grn	50	38
129	A62	8fr rose brn	50	45
130	A62	10fr brt vio	80	60
131	A62	12fr indigo	85	60
132	A61	15fr red	1.10	95
133	A61	18fr bl grn	1.10	95
134	A61	20fr dp pur	1.85	1.60
135	A61	25fr sepia	2.10	1.60
136	A62	30fr dp bl	30.00	16.50
137	A62	35fr Prus bl ('57)	11.00	8.50
138	A62	40fr dk grn	32.50	22.50
139	A62	50fr cerise	3.50	2.50
140	A62	65fr pur ('58)	10.00	7.00
141	A62	70fr chnt ('57)	7.50	7.00
142	A62	75fr vio bl	47.50	37.50
		Nos. 124-142 (19)	151.68	109.35

Coat of Arms
A63

Gothic Cross, Meritxell
A64

Designs: 65c, 85c, 1fr, Pond of Engolasters. 30c, 45c, 50c, as 25c.

1961, June 19 **Typo.** ***Perf. 14x13***

143	A63	5c brt grn & blk	5	5
144	A63	10c red, pink & blk	5	5
145	A63	15c bl & blk	8	8
146	A63	20c yel & brn	12	12

Engraved ***Perf. 13***

147	A64	25c vio, bl & grn	25	25
148	A64	30c mar, ol grn & brn	38	38
149	A64	45c ind, bl & grn	14.00	8.50
150	A64	50c pur, lt brn & ol grn	1.50	1.50
151	A64	65c bl, ol & brn	15.00	11.00
152	A64	85c rose lil, vio bl & brn	15.00	11.00
153	A64	1fr grnsh bl, ind & brn	1.50	1.00
		Nos. 143-153 (11)	47.93	33.93

See also Nos. 161–166A.

Imperforates

Most stamps of Andorra, French Administration, from 1961 onward exist imperforate in issued and trial colors, and also in small presentation sheets in issued colors.

Telstar and Globe Showing Andover and Pleumeur-Bodou
A65

1962, Sept. 29 **Engraved**

154	A65	50c ultra & pur	2.00	2.00

Issued to commemorate the first television connection of the United States and Europe through the Telstar satellite, July 11–12.

"La Sardane"
A66

Charlemagne Crossing Andorra
A67

Design: 1fr, Louis le Debonnaire giving founding charter.

1963, June 22 ***Perf. 13*** **Unwmkd.**

155	A66	20c lil rose, cl & ol grn	4.00	4.00
156	A67	50c sl grn & dk car rose	6.75	6.75
157	A67	1fr red brn, ultra & dk grn	10.00	10.00

Old Andorra Church and Champs-Elysées Palace
A68

1964, Jan. 20 **Engraved**

158	A68	25c blk, grn & vio brn	1.60	1.00

Issued to publicize "PHILATEC," International Philatelic and Postal Techniques Exhibition, Paris, June 5–21, 1964.

Bishop of Urgel and Seigneur of Caboët Confirming Co-Principality, 1288
A69

Design: 60c, Napoleon re-establishing Co-principality, 1806.

1964, Apr. 25 **Engraved** ***Perf. 13***

159	A69	60c dk brn, red brn & sl grn	13.50	13.50
160	A69	1fr brt bl, org brn & blk	13.50	13.50

Arms Type of 1961

1964, May 16 **Typo.** ***Perf. 14x13***

161	A63	1c dk bl & gray	12	12
162	A63	2c blk & org	5	5
163	A63	12c pur, emer & yel	12	12
164	A63	18c blk, lil & pink	12	12

Scenic Type of 1961

Designs: 40c, 45c, Gothic Cross, Meritxell. 60c, 90c, Pond of Engolasters.

1965–71 **Engraved** ***Perf. 13***

165	A64	40c dk brn, org brn & sl grn	60	60
165A	A64	45c vio bl, ol bis & sl ('70)	1.10	85
166	A64	60c org brn & dk brn	65	65
166A	A64	90c ultra, bl grn & bis ('71)	60	60

Syncom Satellite over Pleumeur-Bodou Station
A70

Andorra House, Paris
A71

1965, May 17 **Unwmkd.**

167	A70	60c dp car, lil & bl	5.75	5.00

Issued to commemorate the centenary of the International Telecommunication Union.

1965, June 5

168	A71	25c dk bl, org brn & ol gray	1.00	75

Ski Lift
A72

Design: 25c, Chair lift (vert.).

1966, Apr. 2 **Engraved** ***Perf. 13***

169	A72	25c brt bl, grn & dk brn	1.00	75
170	A72	40c mag, brt ultra & sep	1.50	1.10

Winter sports in Andorra.

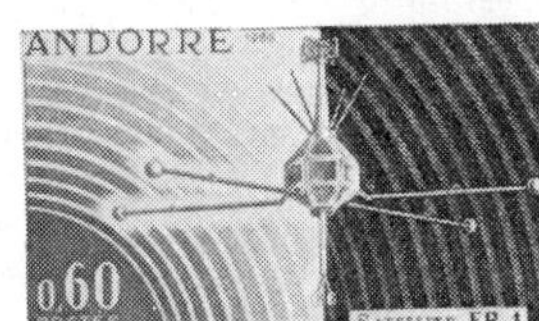

FR-1 Satellite
A73

1966, May 7 ***Perf. 13***

171	A73	60c brt bl, grn & dk grn	2.10	2.10

Issued to commemorate the launching of the scientific satellite FR-1, Dec. 6, 1965.

Europa Issue, 1966
Common Design Type

1966, Sept. 24 **Engraved** ***Perf. 13***
Size: 21½x35½mm.

172	CD9	60c brown	4.00	3.50

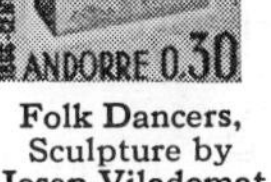

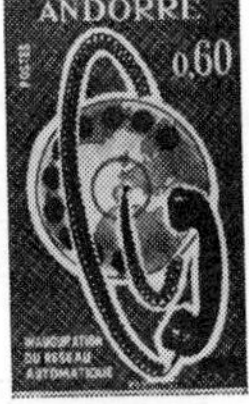

Folk Dancers, Sculpture by Josep Viladomat
A74

Telephone Encircling the Globe
A75

1967, Apr. 29 **Engraved** ***Perf. 13***

173	A74	30c ol grn, dp grn & sl	65	50

Issued to commemorate the centenary (in 1966) of the New Reform, which reaffirmed and strengthened political freedom in Andorra.

Europa Issue, 1967
Common Design Type

1967, Apr. 29
Size: 22x36mm.

174	CD10	30c bluish blk & lt bl	2.50	2.00
175	CD10	60c dk red & brt pink	4.00	2.75

1967, Apr. 29

176	A75	60c dk car, vio & blk	1.50	1.10

Automatic telephone service.

Injured Father at Home
A76

1967, Sept. 23 **Engraved** ***Perf. 13***

177	A76	2.30fr ocher, dk red brn & brn red	8.75	5.50

Introduction of Social Security System.

Jesus in Garden of Gethsemane
A77

Designs (from 16th century frescoes in La Maison des Vallees): 30c, The Kiss of Judas. 60c, The Descent from the Cross (Pieta).

1967, Sept. 23

178	A77	25c blk & red brn	75	60
179	A77	30c pur & red lil	1.10	75
180	A77	60c ind & Prus bl	1.85	1.00

See also Nos. 185–187.

Downhill Skier
A78

1968, Jan. 27 **Engraved** ***Perf. 13***

181	A78	40c org, ver & red lil	1.10	85

Issued to publicize the 10th Winter Olympic Games, Grenoble, France, Feb. 6–18.

Europa Issue, 1968
Common Design Type

1968, Apr. 27 **Engraved** ***Perf. 13***
Size: 36x22mm.

182	CD11	30c gray & brt bl	3.75	3.00
183	CD11	60c brn & lil	5.00	4.25

High Jump
A79

1968, Oct. 12 Engraved *Perf. 13*

184	A79	40c brt bl & brn	1.35	1.10

Issued to commemorate the 19th Olympic Games, Mexico City, Oct. 12–27.

Fresco Type of 1967

Designs (from 16th century frescoes in La Maison des Vallees): 25c, The Scourging of Christ. 30c, Christ Carrying the Cross. 60c, The Crucifixion. (All horizontal.)

1968, Oct. 12

185	A77	25c dk grn & gray grn	75	75
186	A77	30c dk brn & lil	1.10	1.10
187	A77	60c dk car & vio brn	1.75	1.75

Europa Issue, 1969
Common Design Type

1969, Apr. 26 Engraved *Perf. 13*

188	CD12	40c rose car, gray & dl bl	3.75	3.00
189	CD12	70c ind, dl red & ol	5.75	4.25

Issued to commemorate the 10th anniversary of the Conference of European Postal and Telecommunications Administrations.

Kayak on Isère River
A80

Drops of Water and Diamond
A80a

1969, Aug. 2 Engraved *Perf. 13*

190	A80	70c dk sl grn, ultra & ind	1.60	1.60

Issued to commemorate the International Canoe and Kayak Championships, Bourg-Saint-Maurice, Savoy, July 31–Aug. 6.

1969, Sept. 27 Engraved *Perf. 13*

191	A80a	70c blk, dp ultra & grnsh bl	2.10	2.10

European Water Charter.

St. John, the Woman and the Dragon
A81

The Revelation (From the Altar of St. John, Caselles): 40c, St. John Hearing Voice from Heaven on Patmos. 70c, St. John and the Seven Candlesticks.

1969, Oct. 18

192	A81	30c brn, dp pur & brn red	85	85
193	A81	40c gray, dk brn & brn ol	1.10	1.10
194	A81	70c dk red, mar & brt rose lil	1.85	1.85

See also Nos. 199–201, 207–209, 214–216.

Field Ball
A82

Shot Put
A83

1970, Feb. 21 Engraved *Perf. 13*

195	A82	80c multi	1.65	1.40

Issued to publicize the 7th International Field Ball Games, France, Feb. 26–Mar. 8.

Europa Issue, 1970
Common Design Type

1970, May 2 Engraved *Perf. 13*
Size: 36x22mm.

196	CD13	40c orange	1.85	1.50
197	CD13	80c vio bl	2.75	2.25

1970, Sept. 11 Engraved *Perf. 13*

198	A83	80c bl & dk brn	1.40	1.00

Issued to publicize the First European Junior Athletic Championships, Colombes, France, Sept. 11–13.

Altar Type of 1969

The Revelation (from the Altar of St. John, Caselles): 30c, St. John recording angel's message. 40c, Angel erecting column symbolizing faithful in heaven. 80c, St. John's trial in kettle of boiling oil.

1970, Oct. 24

199	A81	30c dp car, dk brn & brt pur	1.10	1.10
200	A81	40c vio & sl grn	1.20	1.20
201	A81	80c ol, dk bl & car rose	1.75	1.75

Ice Skating
A84

1971, Feb. 20 Engraved *Perf. 13*

202	A84	80c dk red, red lil & pur	2.10	1.85

World Figure Skating Championships, Lyons, France, Feb. 23–28.

Capercaillie
A85

Design: No. 204, Brown bear.

1971, Apr. 24 Photo. *Perf. 13*

203	A85	80c multi	2.25	1.65

Engraved

204	A85	80c bl grn & brn	2.25	1.65

Nature Protection.

Europa Issue, 1971
Common Design Type

1971, May 8 Engraved *Perf. 13*
Size: 35½x22mm.

205	CD14	50c rose red	2.50	1.85
206	CD14	80c lt bl grn	3.75	2.50

Altar Type of 1969

The Revelation (from the Altar of St. John, Caselles): 30c, St. John preaching, Rev. 1:3. 50c, "The Sign of the Beast . . ." Rev. 16:1–2. 90c, The Woman, Rev. 17:1.

1971, Sept. 18

207	A81	30c dl grn, ol & brt grn	85	85
208	A81	50c rose car, org & ol brn	1.10	1.10
209	A81	90c blk, dk pur & bl	1.85	1.85

Europa Issue 1972
Common Design Type

1972, Apr. 29 Photo. *Perf. 13*
Size: 21½x37mm.

210	CD15	50c brt mag & multi	2.75	2.25
211	CD15	90c multi	3.75	3.00

Golden Eagle
A86

1972, May 27 Engraved

212	A86	60c dk grn, ol & plum	1.65	1.35

Nature protection.

Shooting
A87

1972, July 8

213	A87	1fr dk pur	1.85	1.50

20th Olympic Games, Munich, Aug. 26–Sept. 11.

Altar Type of 1969

The Revelation (from the Altar of St. John, Caselles): 30c, St. John, bishop and servant. 50c, Resurrection of Lazarus. 90c, Angel with lance and nails.

1972, Sept. 16 Engraved *Perf. 13*

214	A81	30c dk ol, gray & red lil	85	85
215	A81	50c vio bl & sl	1.10	1.10
216	A81	90c dk Prus bl & sl grn	1.85	1.85

De Gaulle as Co-prince of Andorra
A88

Design: 90c, De Gaulle in front of Maison des Vallées.

1972, Oct. 23 Engr. *Perf. 13*

217	A88	50c vio bl	1.35	1.35
218	A88	90c dk car	2.25	2.25

5th anniversary of the visit of Charles de Gaulle to Andorra. Nos. 217–218 printed se-tenant in sheets of 10 stamps and 5 labels showing Andorran coat of arms and commemorative inscription.

Europa Issue 1973
Common Design Type

1973, Apr. 28 Photo. *Perf. 13*
Size: 36x22mm.

219	CD16	50c vio & multi	2.75	2.25
220	CD16	90c dk red & multi	3.75	2.75

Virgin of Canòlich
A89

1973, June 16 Engraved *Perf. 13*

221	A89	1fr ol, Prus bl & vio	1.85	1.85

Lily
A90

Designs: 45c, Iris. 50c, Columbine. 65c, Tobacco. No. 226, Pinks. No. 227, Narcissuses.

1973–74 Photo. *Perf. 13*

222	A90	30c car rose & multi	50	50
223	A90	45c yel grn & multi	28	28
224	A90	50c buff & multi	1.25	1.25
225	A90	65c gray & multi	45	45
226	A90	90c ultra & multi	1.25	1.25
227	A90	90c grnsh bl & multi	70	70
		Nos. 222-227 (6)	4.43	4.43

See Nos. 238–240.

Blue Titmouse
A91

Designs: 60c, Citril finch and mistletoe. 80c, Eurasian bullfinch. 1fr, Lesser spotted woodpecker.

1973–74 Photo. *Perf. 13*

228	A91	60c buff & multi	1.50	1.10
229	A91	80c gray & multi	1.50	1.10
230	A91	90c gray & multi	1.20	1.00
231	A91	1fr yel grn & multi	1.75	1.50

Nature protection.

Europa Issue 1974

Virgin of Pal
A92

Design: 90c, Virgin of Santa Coloma. Statues are polychrome 12th century carvings by rural artists.

1974, Apr. 27 Engr. *Perf. 13*

232	A92	50c multi	3.25	2.25
233	A92	90c multi	4.75	3.50

Arms of Andorra and Cahors Bridge
A93

Mail Box, Chutes and Globe
A94

1974, Aug. 24 Engr. *Perf. 13*
234 A93 1fr bl, vio & org 1.10 90

First anniversary of meeting of the co-princes of Andorra: Pres. Georges Pompidou of France and Msgr. Juan Marti Alanis, Bishop of Urgel.

1974, Oct. 5 Engraved *Perf. 13*
235 A94 1.20fr multi 1.75 1.25

Centenary of Universal Postal Union.

Europa Issue 1975

Coronation of St. Marti, 16th Century—A95

Design: 80c, Crucifixion, 16th century (vert.).

Perf. 11½x13, 13x11½

1975, Apr. 26 Photogravure
236 A95 80c gold & multi 2.75 2.25
237 A95 1.20fr gold & multi 3.50 2.75

Flower Type of 1973

Designs: 60c, Gentian. 80c, Anemone. 1.20fr, Autumn crocus.

1975, May 10 Photo. *Perf. 13*
238 A90 60c ol & multi 38 38
239 A90 80c brt rose & multi 70 60
240 A90 1.20fr grn & multi 90 80

Abstract Design—A96

1975, June 7 Engr. *Perf. 13*
241 A96 2fr bl, mag & emer 2.00 2.00

ARPHILA 75 International Philatelic Exhibition, Paris, June 6–16.

Pres. Georges Pompidou
A97

1975, Aug. 23 Engr. *Perf. 13*
242 A97 80c vio bl & blk 75 75

Georges Pompidou (1911–1974), president of France and co-prince of Andorra (1969–1974).

Costume and IWY Emblem
A98

1975, Nov. 8 Engr. *Perf. 13*
243 A98 1.20fr multi 1.10 1.00

International Women's Year.

Skier and Snowflake
A99

1976, Jan. 31 Engr. *Perf. 13*
244 A99 1.20fr multi 1.20 1.10

12th Winter Olympic Games, Innsbruck, Austria, Feb. 4–15.

Telephone and Satellite
A100

1976, Mar. 20 Engr. *Perf. 13*
245 A100 1fr multi 90 90

Centenary of first telephone call by Alexander Graham Bell, Mar. 10, 1976.

Europa Issue 1976

Catalan Forge
A101

Design: 1.20fr, Lacemaker.

1976, May 8 Engr. *Perf. 13*
246 A101 80c multi 90 75
247 A101 1.20fr multi 1.40 1.10

Thomas Jefferson
A102

Trapshooting
A103

1976, July 3 Engr. *Perf. 13*
248 A102 1.20fr multi 1.25 1.10

American Bicentennial.

1976, July 17 Engr. *Perf. 13*
249 A103 2fr multi 1.75 1.50

21st Olympic Games, Montreal, Canada, July 17–Aug. 1.

Meritxell Sanctuary and Old Chapel—A104

1976, Sept. 4 Engr. *Perf. 13*
250 A104 1fr multi 90 75

Dedication of rebuilt Meritxell Church, Sept. 8, 1976.

Apollo
A105

Ermine
A106

Design: 1.40fr, Morio butterfly.

1976, Oct. 16 Photo. *Perf. 13*
251 A105 80c blk & multi 85 70
252 A105 1.40fr sal & multi 1.25 1.00

Nature protection.

1977, Apr. 2 Photo. *Perf. 13*
253 A106 1fr vio bl, gray & blk 90 85

Nature protection.

St. Jean de Caselles
A107

Manual Digest, 1748, Arms of Andorra
A108

Europa Issue 1977

Design: 1.40fr, Sant Vicens Castle.

1977, Apr. 30 Engr. *Perf. 13*
254 A107 1fr multi 1.10 90
255 A107 1.40fr multi 1.50 1.10

1977, June 11 Engr. *Perf. 13*
256 A108 80c grn, bl & brn 65 65

Establishment of Institute of Andorran Studies.

St. Romanus of Caesarea
A109

1977, July 23 Engr. *Perf. 12½x13*
257 A109 2fr multi 1.25 1.25

Design from altarpiece in Church of St. Roma de les Bons.

General Council Chamber
A110

Guillem d'Arény Plandolit
A111

1977, Sept. 24 Engr. *Perf. 13*
258 A110 1.10fr multi 85 85
259 A111 2fr car & dk brn 1.25 1.25

Andorran heritage. Guillem d'Arény Plandolit started Andorran reform movement in 1866.

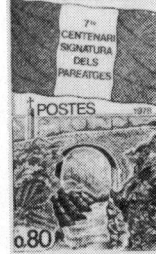

Squirrel
A112

Flag and Valira River Bridge
A113

1978, Mar. 18 Engr. *Perf. 13*
260 A112 1fr multi 65 55

1978, Apr. 8
261 A113 80c multi 50 50

700th anniversary of the signing of the treaty establishing the Co-Principality of Andorra.

Europa Issue 1978

Pal Church
A114

Design: 1.40fr, Charlemagne's Castle, Charlemagne on horseback (vert.).

1978, Apr. 29 Engr. *Perf. 13*
262 A114 1fr multi 90 75
263 A114 1.40fr multi 1.40 1.10

Virgin of Sispony
A115

1978, May 20 Engr. *Perf. 12x13*
264 A115 2fr multi 1.10 1.10

Visura Tribunal A116

1978, June 24 **Engr.** ***Perf. 13***

265 A116 1.20fr multi 75 75

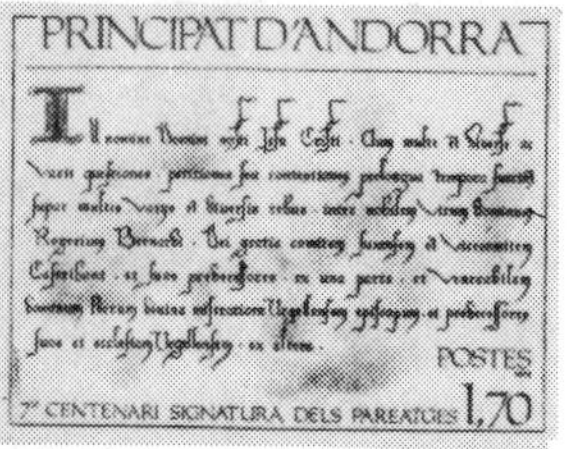

Preamble of 1278 Treaty—A117

1978, Sept. 2 **Engr.** ***Perf. 13x12½***

266 A117 1.70fr multi 85 70

700th anniversary of the signing of treaty establishing Co-Principality of Andorra.

Pyrenean Chamois A118 White Partridges A119

1979, Mar. 26 **Engr.** ***Perf. 13***

267 A118 1fr multi 35 35

1979, Apr. 9 **Photo.** ***Perf. 13***

268 A119 1.20fr multi 70 60

Nature protection. See Nos. 288-289.

Europa Issue 1979

French Mailman, 1900 A120

Design: 1.70fr, First French post office in Andorra.

1979, Apr. 28 **Engr.** ***Perf. 13***

269 A120 1.20fr multi 80 65
270 A120 1.70fr multi 1.20 1.00

Falcon, Pre-Roman Painting A121

1979, June 2 **Engr.** ***Perf. 12½x13***

271 A121 2fr multi 85 75

Child with Lambs, Church, IYC Emblem A122

1979, July 7 **Photo.** ***Perf. 13***

272 A122 1.70fr multi 85 75

International Year of the Child.

Bas-relief, Trobada Monument A123

1979, Sept. 29 **Engraved** ***Perf. 13***

273 A123 2fr multi 85 75

700th anniversary of Co-Principality of Andorra.

Judo Hold—A124

1979, Nov. 24 **Engr.** ***Perf. 13***

274 A124 1.30fr multi 60 50

World Judo Championships, Paris, Dec. 1979.

Farm House, Cortinada—A125

1980, Jan. 26 **Engraved** ***Perf. 13***

275 A125 1.10fr multi 42 40

Cross-Country Skiing—A126

1980, Feb. 9

276 A126 1.80fr ultra & lil rose 1.50 1.25

13th Winter Olympic Games, Lake Placid, N.Y., Feb. 12-24.

World Bicycling Championships—A128

1980, Aug. 30 **Engr.** ***Perf. 13***

278 A128 1.20fr multi 45 40

Europa Issue 1980

Charlemagne (742-814) —A129

Design: 1.80fr, Napoleon I (1769-1821).

1980, Apr. 26 **Engraved** ***Perf. 13***

279 A129 1.30fr multi 60 50
280 A129 1.80fr gray grn & brn 90 72

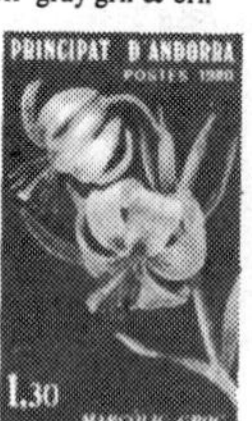

Pyrenees Lily—A130

1980 **Photo.**

281 A130 1.10fr *Dog-toothed violet* 38 32
282 A130 1.30fr *shown* 45 42

Nature protection. Issue dates: 1.10fr, June 21, 1.30fr, May 17.

De La Vall House, 400th Anniversary of Restoration—A131

1980, Sept. 6 **Engraved**

283 A131 1.40fr multi 45 42

Angel, Church of St. Cerni de Nagol, Pre-Romanesque Fresco—A132

1980, Oct. 27 ***Perf. 13x12½***

284 A132 2fr multi 65 60

Bordes de Mereig Mountain Village—A133

1981, Mar. 21 **Engr.** ***Perf. 13***

285 A133 1.40fr bl gray & dk brn 50 45

Europa Issue 1981

Ball de l'Ossa, Winter Game—A134

1981, May 16 **Engr.**

286 A134 1.40fr shown 50 42
287 A134 2fr El Contrapas dance 70 60

Bird Type of 1979

1981, June 20 **Photo.**

288 A119 1.20fr Phylloscopus bonelli 38 32
289 A119 1.40fr Tichodroma muraria 42 32

World Fencing Championship, Clermont-Ferrand, July 2-13—A135

1981, July 4 **Engr.**

290 A135 2fr bl & blk 65 50

St. Martin, 12th Cent. Tapestry A136

1981, Sept. 5 **Engr.** ***Perf. 12x13***

291 A136 3fr multi 1.50 90

Intl. Drinking Water Decade A137

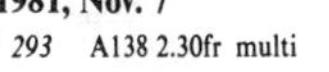

Intl. Year of the Disabled A138

1981, Oct. 17 *Perf. 13*

292	A137	1.60fr multi	80	55

1981, Nov. 7

293	A138	2.30fr multi	1.15	75

Europa 1982—A139

1982, May 8 **Engr.** ***Perf. 13***

294	A139	1.60fr Creation of Andorran govt., 1982	80	55
295	A139	2.30fr Land Council, 1419	1.15	75

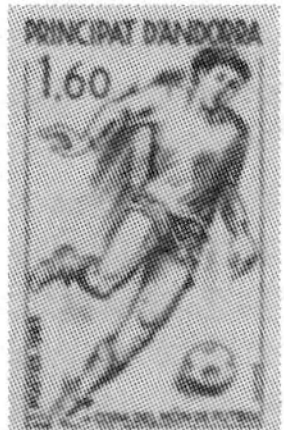

1982 World Cup—A140

Designs: Various soccer players. Nos. 296-297 se-tenant with label showing natl. arms.

1982, June 12 **Engr. *Perf. 13***

296	A140	1.60fr red & dk brn	80	55
297	A140	2.60fr red & dk brn	1.30	85

Souvenir Sheet

No. 52—A141

1982, Aug. 21 **Engr.**

298	A141	5fr blk & rose car	2.50	1.50

First Andorran Stamp Exhibition, Aug. 21-Sept. 19. Black marginal inscription. Size: 143x93mm.

Horse, Roman Wall Painting—A142

1982, Sept. 4 **Photo.** ***Perf. 13x12½***

299	A142	3fr multi	1.50	90

SEMI-POSTAL STAMP

Virgin of St. Coloma SP1

Engraved

1964, July 25 ***Perf. 13*** **Unwmkd.**

B1	SP1	25c +10c multi	27.50	27.50

The surtax was for the Red Cross.

AIR POST STAMPS.

Chamois—AP1

Engraved.

1950, Feb. 20 ***Perf. 13*** **Unwmkd.**

C1	AP1	100fr indigo	55.00	42.50

East Branch of Valira River AP2

1955–57

C2	AP2	100fr dk grn	8.50	6.75
C3	AP2	200fr cerise	18.00	13.00
C4	AP2	500fr dp bl ('57)	90.00	65.00

D'Inclès Valley AP3

1961, June 19 ***Perf. 13*** **Unwmkd.**

C5	AP3	2fr red, ol gray & cl	1.00	85
C6	AP3	3fr bl, mar & sl grn	1.75	1.75
C7	AP3	5fr rose lil & red org	2.50	2.25

1964, Apr. 25

C8	AP3	10fr bl grn & sl grn	5.00	4.50

POSTAGE DUE STAMPS.

Postage Due Stamps of France, 1893-1931, Overprinted **ANDORRE**

On Stamps of 1893-1926.

1931–33 ***Perf. 14x13½*** **Unwmkd.**

J1	D2	5c blue	1.75	1.75
J2	D2	10c brown	1.75	1.75
J3	D2	30c rose red	45	45
J4	D2	50c vio brn	1.75	1.75
J5	D2	60c green	11.50	11.50
J6	D2	1fr red brn, *straw*	75	75
J7	D2	2fr brt vio	10.00	10.00
J8	D2	3fr magenta	2.00	2.00
		Nos. J1-J8 (8)	29.95	29.95

On Stamps of 1927-31.

J9	D4	1c ol grn	1.85	1.85
J10	D4	10c rose	4.25	4.25
J11	D4	60c red	26.00	26.00
J12	D4	1fr Prus grn ('32)	85.00	85.00
J13	D4	1.20fr on 2fr bl	72.50	72.50
J14	D4	2fr ol brn ('33)	120.00	120.00
J15	D4	5fr on 1fr vio	75.00	75.00
		Nos. J9-J15 (7)	384.60	384.60

D5

D6

1935-41 **Typographed.**

J16	D5	1c gray grn	1.85	1.50
J17	D6	5c lt bl ('37)	7.50	6.75
J18	D6	10c brn ('41)	7.50	6.75
J19	D6	2fr vio ('41)	6.00	5.00
J20	D6	5fr red org ('41)	5.00	3.75
		Nos. J16-J20 (5)	27.85	23.75

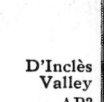

Wheat Sheaves D7

1943–46 ***Perf. 14x13½***

J21	D7	10c sepia	45	45
J22	D7	30c brt red vio	75	75
J23	D7	50c bl grn	1.00	1.00
J24	D7	1fr brt ultra	45	45
J25	D7	1.50fr rose red	3.00	3.00
J26	D7	2fr turq bl	75	75
J27	D7	3fr brn org	1.75	1.75
J28	D7	4fr dp vio ('45)	2.50	2.50
J29	D7	5fr brt pink	2.50	2.50
J30	D7	10fr red org ('45)	2.50	2.50
J31	D7	20fr ol brn ('46)	3.25	3.25
		Nos. J21-J31 (11)	18.90	18.90

Inscribed: "Timbre Taxe."

1946-53

J32	D7	10c sep ('46)	85	85
J33	D7	1fr ultra	45	45
J34	D7	2fr turq bl	60	60
J35	D7	3fr org brn	2.00	2.00
J36	D7	4fr violet	2.25	2.25
J37	D7	5fr brt pink	1.40	1.40
J38	D7	10fr red org	2.25	2.25
J39	D7	20fr ol brn	4.75	4.75
J40	D7	50fr dk grn ('50)	16.00	16.00
J41	D7	100fr dp grn ('53)	60.00	60.00
		Nos. J32-J41 (10)	90.55	90.55

Inscribed: "Timbre Taxe."

1961, June 19 ***Perf. 14x13½***

J42	D7	5c rose pink	3.00	3.00
J43	D7	10c red org	5.00	5.00
J44	D7	20c olive	7.00	7.00
J45	D7	50c dk sl grn	10.00	10.00

Flower Type of France, 1964.

Designs: 5c, Centaury. 10c, Gentian. 15c, Corn poppy. 20c, Violets. 30c, Forget-me-not. 40c, Columbine. 50c, Clover.

1964–71 **Typo.** ***Perf. 14x13½***

J46	D7	5c car rose, red & grn ('65)	5	5
J47	D7	10c car rose, brt bl & grn ('65)	8	8
J48	D7	15c brn, grn & red	8	8
J49	D7	20c dk grn, grn & vio ('71)	10	10
J50	D7	30c brn, ultra & grn	15	15
J51	D7	40c dk grn, scar & yel ('71)	18	18
J52	D7	50c vio bl, car & grn ('65)	30	30
		Nos. J46-J52 (7)	94	94

NEWSPAPER STAMP.

France No. P7 Overprinted **ANDORRE**

1931 ***Perf. 14x13½.*** **Unwmkd.**

P1	A16	½c on 1c gray	75	75

See "Special Notices" at the front of this volume for data on the listing methods of this Catalogue, abbreviations, condition, prices and examination.

ANGOLA

(ăng·gō'lȧ)

LOCATION—Southwestern Africa between Congo and South-West Africa.

GOVT.—Republic.

AREA—481,351 sq. mi.

POP.—5,800,000 (est. 1972).

CAPITAL—Luanda.

Angola was a Portuguese overseas territory until it became independent Nov. 11, 1975, as the People's Republic of Angola.

1000 Reis = 1 Milreis
100 Centavos = 1 Escudo (1913, 1954)
100 Centavos = 1 Angolar (1932)
10 Lweys = 1 Kwanza (1977)

Portuguese Crown
A1

Perf. 12½, 13½.

1870–77 Typographed Unwmkd.

No.	Type	Denomination	Unused	Used
1	A1	5r black	2.50	2.00
a.		Perf. 13½	10.00	5.00
2	A1	10r yellow	20.00	10.00
3	A1	20r bister	3.00	1.90
a.		Perf. 13½	80.00	60.00
4	A1	25r red	12.00	4.50
a.		25r rose	12.00	4.50
b.		Laid paper		
c.		25r rose, perf. 14	140.00	80.00
d.		Perf. 13½	24.00	12.00
5	A1	40r bl ('77)	135.00	70.00
6	A1	50r green	50.00	12.00
a.		Perf. 13½	240.00	80.00
7	A1	100r lilac	4.00	2.25
a.		Perf. 12½	15.00	8.00
8	A1	200r org ('77)	5.00	2.00
a.		Perf. 12½	7.00	3.00
9	A1	300r choc ('77)	5.00	4.00
a.		Perf. 12½	14.00	5.50

1881-85

No.	Type	Denomination	Unused	Used
10	A1	10r grn ('83)	5.00	2.25
a.		Perf. 12½	15.00	3.00
11	A1	20r car rose ('85)	9.00	7.00
a.		Cliche of 40r in plate of 20r		*750.00*
12	A1	25r vio ('85)	7.00	2.25
a.		Perf. 13½	8.00	4.00
13	A1	40r buff ('82)	5.50	3.00
a.		Perf. 12½	6.00	3.00
15	A1	50r blue	20.00	2.25
a.		Perf. 13½	30.00	2.25

Two types of numerals are found on No. 2 and Nos. 11 to 15.

The error, No. 11a, was discovered before the stamps were issued. All copies were cancelled by a blue pencil mark.

In perf. 12½, Nos. 1–4, 4a and 6, as well as 7a, were printed in 1870 on thicker paper and 1875 on normal paper. Stamps of the earlier printing sell for 2 to 15 times more than those of the 1875 printing.

Some reprints of the 1870–85 issues are on a smooth white chalky paper, ungummed and perf. 13½. Price each, 50 cents.

Other reprints of these issues are on thin white paper with shiny white gum and clear-cut perf. 13½. Price each, $2.50.

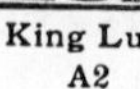

King Luiz
A2

King Carlos
A3

1886 Embossed *Perf. 12½*

No.	Type	Denomination	Unused	Used
16	A2	5r black	9.00	5.00
a.		Perf. 13½	16.00	12.00
17	A2	10r green	9.00	5.00
a.		Perf. 13½	19.00	10.00
18	A2	20r rose	14.00	11.00
a.		Perf. 13½	17.00	9.00
19	A2	25r red vio	10.00	2.25
20	A2	40r chocolate	11.00	5.50
21	A2	50r blue	14.00	3.25
22	A2	100r yel brn	20.00	7.50
23	A2	200r gray vio	24.00	10.00
24	A2	300r orange	24.00	10.00

Reprints of 5r, 20r and 100r have clean-cut perf. 13½. Price each $2.

Typographed.

1893-94 *Perf. 11½, 12½, 13½.*

No.	Type	Denomination	Unused	Used
25	A3	5r yellow	1.50	1.10
26	A3	10r redsh vio	3.25	1.40
27	A3	15r chocolate	4.00	2.10
28	A3	20r lavender	4.50	2.25
29	A3	25r green	2.00	1.25
a.		Perf. 12½	4.50	1.75
30	A3	50r lt bl	3.50	1.50
a.		Perf. 13½	7.50	4.50
31	A3	75r carmine	7.50	4.50
a.		Perf. 11½	9.50	7.50
32	A3	80r lt grn	10.00	5.50
33	A3	100r brn, *buff*	10.50	5.50
a.		Perf. 11½	65.00	45.00
34	A3	150r car, *rose*	17.00	11.00
35	A3	200r dk bl, *lt bl*	17.00	11.00
36	A3	300r dk bl, *sal*	17.00	11.00

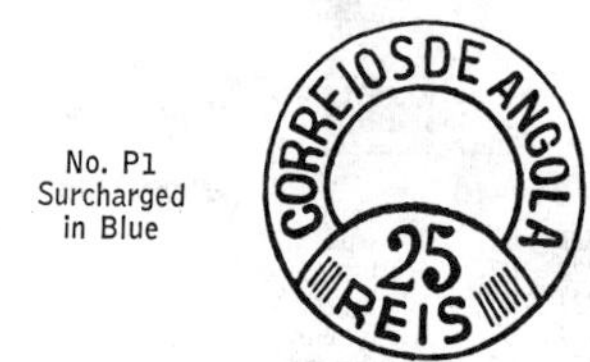

No. P1 Surcharged in Blue

1894, Aug.

No.	Type	Denomination	Unused	Used
37	N1	25r on 2½r brn	60.00	40.00

King Carlos
A5

1898–1903 *Perf. 11½*

Name and Value in Black except 500r

No.	Type	Denomination	Unused	Used
38	A5	2½r gray	20	15
39	A5	5r orange	20	15
40	A5	10r yel grn	20	15
41	A5	15r vio brn	2.25	1.25
42	A5	15r gray grn ('03)	1.00	60
43	A5	20r gray vio	40	30
44	A5	25r sea grn	1.50	60
45	A5	25r car ('03)	50	20
46	A5	50r blue	2.25	70
47	A5	50r brn ('03)	5.50	3.00
48	A5	65r dl bl ('03)	7.50	6.50
49	A5	75r rose	7.50	2.50
50	A5	75r red vio ('03)	2.00	1.50
51	A5	80r violet	7.50	2.75
52	A5	100r dk bl, *bl*	1.50	1.00
53	A5	115r org brn, *pink* ('03)	7.00	5.00
54	A5	130r brn, *straw* ('03)	7.00	5.00
55	A5	150r brn, *straw*	7.50	4.25
56	A5	200r red vio, *pink*	3.50	1.50
57	A5	300r dk bl, *rose*	4.25	4.00
58	A5	400r dl bl, *straw* ('03)	3.75	2.50
59	A5	500r blk & red, *bl* ('01)	5.00	4.00
60		Nos. 38-60 (23)	24.00	14.00
		Nos. 38-60 (23)	78.00	47.60

Stamps of 1886–94 Surcharged in Black or Red

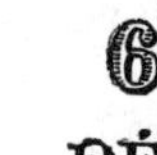

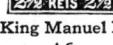

Two types of surcharge:
I. 3mm. between numeral and REIS.
II. 4½mm. spacing.

1902 *Perf. 12½*

No.	Type	Denomination	Unused	Used
61	A2	65r on 40r choc	8.00	4.00
62	A2	65r on 300r org, I	8.00	4.00
a.		Type II	45.00	25.00
63	A2	115r on 10r grn	6.50	4.00
a.		Inverted surcharge		
b.		Perf. 13½	25.00	22.00
64	A2	115r on 200r gray vio	6.00	3.50
65	A2	130r on 50r bl	8.75	6.50
66	A2	130r on 100r brn	5.50	3.25
67	A2	400r on 20r rose	45.00	30.00
a.		Perf. 13½	55.00	35.00
68	A2	400r on 25r vio	12.50	7.50
69	A2	400r on 5r blk (R)	12.00	9.00
a.		Double surcharge		
		Nos. 61-69 (9)	112.25	71.75

Perf. 11½, 12½, 13½.

No.	Type	Denomination	Unused	Used
70	A3	65r on 5r yel, I	6.00	4.00
a.		Type II	15.00	15.00
71	A3	65r on 10r red vio, I	5.00	3.50
a.		Type II	20.00	8.00
b.		Perf. 11½, type I	13.50	8.00
c.		Perf. 11½, type II	3.75	2.50
72	A3	65r on 20r lav	6.00	4.00
a.		Type II	10.00	9.00
73		65r on 25r grn	4.50	3.50
a.		Perf. 11½	14.00	11.00
74	A3	115r on 80r lt grn	8.50	6.25
75	A3	115r on 100r brn, *buff*	14.00	10.00
a.		Perf. 12½	8.50	5.00
76	A3	115r on 150r car, *rose*	15.00	9.00
a.		Perf. 11½	12.00	8.00
77	A3	130r on 15r choc	4.00	3.00
78	A3	130r on 75r car	5.50	3.50
a.		Perf. 13½	22.50	17.50
79	A3	130r on 300r dk bl, *sal*	13.50	8.50
80	A3	400r on 50r lt bl	4.50	4.00
81	A3	400r on 200r bl, *bl*	3.00	90
a.		Perf. 13½	32.50	13.50
82	N1	400r on 2½r brn	1.25	1.25
a.		Type II	3.75	3.50
		Nos. 70-82 (13)	90.75	61.40

Reprints of Nos. 65, 67, 68 and 69 have clean-cut perforation 13½. Price $2 each.

Stamps of 1898 Overprinted

PROVISORIO
a

1902 *Perf. 11½*

No.	Type	Denomination	Unused	Used
83	A5	15r brown	1.50	85
84	A5	25r sea grn	1.25	60
85	A5	50r blue	2.25	1.40
86	A5	75r rose	4.25	3.00

No. 48 Surcharged in Black

50
RÉIS

1905

No.	Type	Denomination	Unused	Used
87	A5	50r on 65r dl bl	3.50	2.25

Stamps of 1898-1903 Overprinted in Carmine or Green

REPUBLICA
b

1911

No.	Type	Denomination	Unused	Used
88	A5	2½r gray	30	20
89	A5	5r org yel	30	20
90	A5	10r lt grn	35	30
a.		Inverted overprint	5.75	5.75
91	A5	15r gray grn	50	30
92	A5	20r gray vio	50	30
93	A5	25r car (G)	50	25
a.		Inverted overprint	5.00	4.00
94	A5	50r brown	2.25	1.50
95	A5	75r lilac	4.00	4.00
96	A5	100r dk bl, *bl*	4.00	4.00
97	A5	115r org brn, *pink*	1.50	90
98	A5	130r brn, *straw*	1.50	90
99	A5	200r red lil, *pnksh*	1.50	90
100	A5	400r dl bl, *straw*	2.00	1.00
101	A5	500r blk & red, *bl*	2.00	1.00
102	A5	700r vio, *yelsh*	2.25	1.10
		Nos. 88-102 (15)	23.45	16.85

King Manuel II
A6

Ceres
A7

1912 *Perf. 11½ x12.*

Overprinted in Carmine or Green.

No.	Type	Denomination	Unused	Used
103	A6	2½r violet	35	*50*
104	A6	5r black	45	*60*
105	A6	10r gray grn	55	45
106	A6	20r car (G)	55	45
107	A6	25r vio brn	55	45
108	A6	50r dk bl	90	75
109	A6	75r bis brn	1.00	*1.50*
110	A6	100r brn, *lt grn*	2.50	1.25
111	A6	200r dk grn, *sal*	2.00	1.25
112	A6	300r *azure*	2.00	1.25
		Nos. 103-112 (10)	10.85	*8.45*

No. 91 Surcharged with New Values as **5** ■

1912, June *Perf. 11½*

No.	Type	Denomination	Unused	Used
113	A5	2½r on 15r gray grn	4.00	4.00
114	A5	5r on 15r gray grn	3.00	2.25
115	A5	10r on 15r gray grn	3.00	2.25

Inverted and double surcharges of Nos. 113-115 were made intentionally.

Nos. 86 and 50 Surcharged "25" in Black and Overprinted in Violet

c

1912

No.	Type	Denomination	Unused	Used
116	A5	25r on 75r rose	50.00	35.00
117	A5	25r on 75r red vio	4.00	2.50
a.		"REUPBLICA"	37.50	37.50
b.		"25" omitted	37.50	37.50
c.		"REPUBLICA" omitted	37.50	37.50

Typographed.

Name and Value in Black.

1914-26 *Perf. 12x11½, 15x14.*

No.	Type	Denomination	Unused	Used
118	A7	¼c ol brn	12	*25*
a.		Inscriptions inverted	3.00	
119	A7	½c black	12	*25*
120	A7	1c bl grn	12	*25*
121	A7	1c yel grn ('22)	12	12
122	A7	1½c lil brn	12	12
123	A7	2c carmine	12	12
124	A7	2c gray ('25)	40	*1.00*
125	A7	2½c lt vio	12	12
126	A7	3c org ('22)	12	*1.00*
127	A7	4c dl rose ('22)	12	12
128	A7	4½c gray ('22)	12	*1.00*
130	A7	5c blue	12	12
131	A7	6c lil ('22)	12	12
132	A7	7c ultra ('22)	12	12
133	A7	7½c yel brn	12	12
134	A7	8c slate	12	12
135	A7	10c org brn	40	12
136	A7	12c ol brn ('22)	65	35
137	A7	12c dp grn ('25)	35	15
138	A7	15c plum	65	35
139	A7	15c brn rose ('22)	17	15
140	A7	20c yel grn	15	10
141	A7	24c ultra ('25)	1.75	50
142	A7	25c choc ('25)	1.75	50
143	A7	30c brn, *grn*	2.00	*2.00*
144	A7	30c gray grn ('22)	1.00	10

145	A7	40c brn, *pink*	3.00	1.75
146	A7	40c turq bl ('22)	90	12
147	A7	50c org, *sal*	8.00	4.50
148	A7	50c lt vio ('25)	1.50	15
149	A7	60c dk bl ('22)	80	15
150	A7	60c dp rose ('26)	60.00	50.00
151	A7	80c pink ('22)	2.00	15
152	A7	1e grn, *bl*	4.50	3.50
153	A7	1e rose ('22)	2.25	15
154	A7	1e dp bl ('25)	2.00	1.50
155	A7	2e dk vio ('22)	2.25	80
156	A7	5e buff ('25)	6.50	3.00
157	A7	10e pink ('25)	14.00	10.00
158	A7	20e pale turq ('25)	65.00	35.00
		Nos. 118-158 (40)	183.77	*120.04*

Two kinds of chalky-surfaced paper, ordinary and coated, were used for Nos. 118–120, 122–123, 130, 133–135, 138 and 140. Those on coated paper sell unused for 10 to 40 times the prices listed; used for about 5 to 20 times.

Stamps of 1898–1903 Overprinted type "c" in Red or Green

On Stamps of 1898-1903.

1914 *Perf. 11½, 12.*

159	A5	10r yel grn (R)	4.25	3.25
160	A5	15r gray grn (R)	4.25	3.25
161	A5	20r gray vio (G)	75	50
163	A5	75r red vio (G)	85	45
164	A5	100r bl, *bl* (R)	1.00	75
165	A5	115r org brn, *pink* (R)	*40.00*	
167	A5	200r red vio, *pnksh* (G)	1.25	60
169	A5	400r dl bl, *straw* (R)	24.00	16.00
170	A5	500r blk & red, *bl* (R)	3.50	3.00
171	A5	700r vio, *yelsh* (G)	13.00	11.00

Inverted and double surcharges were made intentionally. No. 165 was not regularly issued.

On Provisional Stamps of 1902.

Perf. 11½, 12½, 13½.

172	A2	115r on 10r grn (R)	11.00	8.25
a.		Perf. 13½	12.50	12.50
173	A2	115r on 200r gray vio (R)	11.00	8.25
174	A2	130r on 50r bl (R)	14.00	12.00
175	A3	115r on 80r lt grn (R)	125.00	110.00
176	A3	115r on 100r brn, *buff* (R)	170.00	160.00
177	A3	115r on 150r car, *rose* (G)	140.00	130.00
178	A3	130r on 75r car (G)	3.00	2.75
179	A3	130r on 300r dk bl, *sal* (R)	5.50	3.50
a.		Perf. 12½	10.00	6.50
180	N1	400r on 2½r brn (R)	50	50
a.		Perf. 11½	2.50	2.00
		Nos. 172-180 (9)	480.00	435.25

On Stamps of 1902.

Overprinted PROVISORIO

Perf. 11½, 12.

181	A5	50r bl (R)	1.25	80
a.		"Republica" double		
182	A5	75r rose (G)	3.50	2.50
a.		"Republica" inverted		

On Stamp of 1905.

183	A5	50r on 65r dl bl (R)	3.50	2.75
a.		"Republica" inverted		
b.		"Republica" double		

Vasco da Gama Issue of Various Portuguese Colonies

Common Design Types CD20–CD27 Surcharged

REPUBLICA
ANGOLA
¼ C.

On Stamps of Macao.

1913 *Perf. 12½ to 16.*

184		¼c on ½a bl grn	2.00	2.00
185		½c on 1a red	1.65	1.65
186		1c on 2a red vio	1.65	1.65
187		2½c on 4a yel grn	1.40	1.40
188		5c on 8a dk bl	1.40	1.40
189		7½c on 12a vio brn	3.50	3.50
190		10c on 16a bis brn	1.90	1.90
191		15c on 24a bis	1.90	1.90
		Nos. 184-191 (8)	15.40	15.40

On Stamps of Portuguese Africa.

Perf. 14 to 15.

192	¼c on 2½r bl grn	1.00	1.00
193	½c on 5r red	1.00	1.00
194	1c on 10r red vio	1.00	1.00
195	2½c on 25r yel grn	1.00	1.00
196	5c on 50r dk bl	1.00	1.00
197	7½c on 75r vio brn	4.00	4.00
198	10c on 100r bis brn	1.40	1.40
199	15c on 150r bis	2.25	2.25
	Nos. 192-199 (8)	12.65	12.65

On Stamps of Timor

200	¼c on ½a bl grn	2.00	2.00
201	½c on 1a red	2.00	2.00
202	1c on 2a red vio	2.00	2.00
203	2½c on 4a yel grn	1.90	1.90
204	5c on 8a dk bl	1.90	1.90
205	7½c on 12a vio brn	3.25	3.25
206	10c on 16a bis brn	2.25	2.25
207	15c on 24a bis	2.25	2.25
	Nos. 200-207 (8)	17.55	17.55

Provisional Issue of 1902 Overprinted in Carmine

REPUBLICA

1915 *Perf. 11½, 12½, 13½.*

208	A2	115r on 10r grn	1.65	*2.00*
209	A2	115r on 200r gray vio	1.40	*1.75*
210	A2	130r on 100r brn	1.20	*1.75*
211	A3	115r on 80r lt grn	1.65	*2.00*
212	A3	115r on 100r brn, *buff*	1.40	*1.75*
a.		Perf. 11½	22.50	*22.50*
213	A3	115r on 150r car, *rose*	2.25	*3.00*
214	A3	130r on 15r choc	1.10	*1.75*
a.		Perf. 12½	6.00	4.50
215	A3	130r on 75r car	2.25	*2.75*
216	A3	130r on 300r dk bl, *sal*	1.75	*2.75*
		Nos. 208-216 (9)	14.65	*19.50*

Stamps of 1911-14 Surcharged in Black:

½ C.

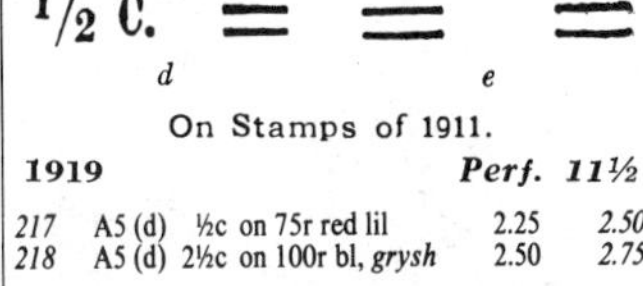

On Stamps of 1911.

1919 *Perf. 11½*

217	A5 (d)	½c on 75r red lil	2.25	*2.50*
218	A5 (d)	2½c on 100r bl, *grysh*	2.50	*2.75*

On Stamps of 1912.

Perf. 11½x12.

219	A6 (e)	½c on 75r bis brn	1.00	*1.00*
220	A6 (e)	2½c on 100r brn, *lt grn*	1.25	60

On Stamps of 1914.

221	A5 (d)	½c on 75r red lil	1.00	75
222	A5 (d)	2½c on 100r bl, *grysh*	1.25	80

Inverted and double surcharges were made for sale to collectors.

Nos. 163, 98 and Type of 1914 Surcharged with New Values and Bars in Black.

1921

223	A5 (c)	00.5c on 75c red vio	*90.00*	*90.00*
224	A5 (b)	4c on 130r brn, *straw* (#98)	1.25	*1.25*
225	A5 (c)	4c on 130r brn, *straw*	4.00	3.00
a.		Surch. omitted	100.00	

Nos. 109 and 108 Surcharged with New Values and Bars in Black.

226	A6	00.5c on 75c bis brn	1.25	80
227	A6	1c on 50r dk bl	1.25	80

Nos. 133 and 138 Surcharged with New Values and Bars in Black.

228	A7	00.5c on 7½c yel brn	1.25	80
229	A7	04c on 15c plum	1.25	80

Nos. 81–82 Surcharged

República
40 C.

1925 *Perf. 12½*

234	A3	40c on 400r on 200r bl, *bl*	85	55
a.		Perf. 13½	5.00	3.50
235	N1	40c on 400c on 2½r brn	55	45
a.		Perf. 13½	55	45

Nos. 150–151, 154–155 Surcharged

70 C.

1931 *Perf. 11½.*

236	A7	50c on 60c dp rose	1.40	1.20
237	A7	70c on 80c pink	2.75	1.50
238	A7	70c on 1e dp bl	2.25	1.75
239	A7	1.40e on 2e dk vio	1.65	1.25

Ceres
A14

Wmk. 232

Wmkd. Maltese Cross. (232)

1932–46 Typo. *Perf. 12x11½*

243	A14	1c bis brn	12	12
244	A14	5c dk brn	12	12
245	A14	10c dp vio	12	12
246	A14	15c black	12	12
247	A14	20c gray	12	12
248	A14	30c myr grn	12	12
249	A14	35c yel grn ('46)	3.00	1.25
250	A14	40c dp org	12	12
251	A14	45c lt bl	1.00	60
252	A14	50c lt brn	12	12
253	A14	60c ol grn	40	15
254	A14	70c org brn	40	15
255	A14	80c emerald	40	15
256	A14	85c rose	3.00	3.00
257	A14	1a claret	80	18
258	A14	1.40a dk bl	4.50	1.50
258A	A14	1.75a dk bl ('46)	6.00	1.50
259	A14	2a dl vio	2.50	30
260	A14	5a pale yel grn	4.00	60
261	A14	10a ol bis	11.00	1.50
262	A14	20a orange	30.00	2.50
		Nos. 243-262 (21)	67.96	14.34

Stamps of 1932

Surcharged with New Value and Bars.

5½mm. between bars and new value.

1934

263	A14	10c on 45c lt bl	2.00	1.25
264	A14	20c on 85c rose	1.50	1.00
265	A14	30c on 1.40a dk bl	1.50	1.00
266	A14	70c on 2a dl vio	2.25	1.75
267	A14	80c on 5a pale yel grn	3.50	1.60

See also Nos. 294A–300.

Nos. J26, J30 Surcharged in Black

CORREIOS
5
CENTAVOS

1935 *Perf. 11½* **Unwmkd.**

268	D2	5c on 6c lt brn	1.50	1.00
269	D2	30c on 50c gray	1.50	1.00
270	D2	40c on 50c gray	1.50	1.00

No. 255 Surcharged in Black

0,15 Cent.

1938 *Perf. 12x11½* **Wmk. 232**

271	A14	5c on 80c emer	60	*1.00*
272	A14	10c on 80c emer	80	*2.00*
273	A14	15c on 80c emer	1.25	*3.50*

Vasco da Gama Issue

Common Design Types

Engraved; Name and Value Typographed in Black.

Perf. 13½x13

1938, July 26 **Unwmkd.**

274	CD34	1c gray grn	12	12
275	CD34	5c org brn	12	12
276	CD34	10c dk car	12	12
277	CD34	15c dk vio brn	25	12
278	CD34	20c slate	28	12
279	CD35	30c rose vio	40	12
280	CD35	35c brt grn	55	30
281	CD35	40c brown	40	25
282	CD35	50c brt red vio	40	25
283	CD36	60c gray blk	50	25
284	CD36	70c brn vio	40	25
285	CD36	80c orange	40	25
286	CD36	1a red	40	25
287	CD37	1.75a blue	95	40
288	CD37	2a brn car	2.00	40
289	CD37	5a ol grn	6.00	40
290	CD38	10a bl vio	15.00	1.00
291	CD38	20a red brn	30.00	1.75
		Nos. 274-291 (18)	58.29	6.47

Common Design Types

pictured in section at front of book.

Marble Column and Portuguese Arms with Cross
A20

1938, July 29 *Perf. 12½*

292	A20	80c bl grn	2.10	1.90
293	A20	1.75a dp bl	20.00	4.00
294	A20	20a dk red brn	50.00	25.00

Issued to commemorate the visit of the President of Portugal to this colony in 1938.

Stamps of 1932 Surcharged with New Value and Bars.

8mm. between bars and new value.

1941-45 ***Perf. 12x11½.*** **Wmk. 232**

294A	A14	5c on 80c emer ('45)	40	33
295	A14	10c on 45c lt bl	1.00	75
296	A14	15c on 45c lt bl	1.50	50
297	A14	20c on 85c rose	60	50
298	A14	35c on 85c rose	60	50
299	A14	50c on 1.40a dk bl	60	50
300	A14	60c on 1a cl	5.50	3.00
		Nos. 294A-300 (7)	10.20	6.08

Nos. 285 to 287 Surcharged with New Values and Bars in Black or Red.

1945 ***Perf. 13½x13.*** **Unwmkd.**

301	CD36	5c on 80c org	40	33
302	CD36	50c on 1a red	60	33
303	CD37	50c on 1.75a bl (R)	40	33
304	CD37	50c on 1.75a bl	60	33

São Miguel Fort, Luanda
A21

John IV
A22

Designs: 10c, Our Lady of Nazareth Church, Luanda. 50c, Salvador Correia de Sa e Benevides. 1a, Surrender of Luanda. 1.75a, Diogo Cao. 2a, Manuel Cerveira Pereira. 5a, Stone Cliffs, Yelala. 10a, Paulo Dias de Novais. 20a, Massangano Fort.

Lithographed.

1948, May ***Perf. 14½*** **Unwmkd.**

305	A21	5c dk vio	12	12
306	A21	10c dk brn	60	35
307	A22	30c bl grn	30	25
308	A22	50c vio brn	25	12
309	A21	1a carmine	55	20
310	A22	1.75a sl bl	1.10	40
311	A22	2a green	1.10	30
312	A21	5a gray blk	3.75	65
313	A22	10a rose lil	6.00	65
314	A21	20a gray bl	16.00	1.90
a.		Sheet of ten	60.00	60.00
		Nos. 305-314 (10)	29.77	4.94

Issued to commemorate the 300th anniversary of the restoration of Angola to Portugal.

No. 314a measures 225x162mm. and contains one each of Nos. 305-314 with marginal inscriptions in gray. The sheet sold for 42.50 angolars.

Lady of Fatima Issue

Common Design Type

1948, Dec.

315	CD40	50c carmine	1.50	1.00
316	CD40	3a ultra	4.00	2.75
317	CD40	6a red org	22.50	8.50
318	CD40	9a dp cl	45.00	10.00

Issued to honor Our Lady of the Rosary at Fatima, Portugal.

Chiumbe River
A24

Black Rocks
A25

Designs: 50c, View of Luanda. 2.50a, Sa da Bandeira. 3.50a, Mocamedes. 15a, Cubal River. 50a, Duke of Bragança Falls.

1949 ***Perf. 13½*** **Unwmkd.**

319	A24	20c dk sl bl	40	20
320	A25	40c blk brn	45	15
321	A24	50c rose brn	45	20
322	A24	2.50a bl vio	1.90	30
323	A24	3.50a sl gray	2.25	55
323A	A24	15a dk grn	17.50	1.90
324	A24	50a dp grn	125.00	6.00
		Nos. 319-324 (7)	147.95	9.30

Sailing Vessel
A26

U.P.U. Symbols
A27

1949, Aug. ***Perf. 14***

325	A26	1a chocolate	6.00	50
326	A26	4a dk Prus grn	20.00	1.25

Centenary of founding of Mocamedes.

1949, Oct.

327	A27	4a dk grn & lt grn	7.00	2.00

Issued to commemorate the 75th anniversary of the formation of the Universal Postal Union.

Stamp of 1870
A28

1950, Apr. 2 ***Perf. 11½x12***

328	A28	50c yel grn	1.50	35
329	A28	1a fawn	1.25	40
330	A28	4a black	5.00	1.25
a.		Sheet of three, perf. 11½		15.00

Issued for Angola's first philatelic exhibition, marking the 80th anniversary of Angola's first stamps.

No. 330a contains one each of Nos. 328, 329 (inverted) and 330, and sold for 6.50 angolars. Size: 119x80 mm. All copies carry an oval exhibition cancellation.

Holy Year Issue

Common Design Types

1950, May ***Perf. 13x13½***

331	CD41	1a dl rose vio	1.20	20
332	CD42	4a black	5.00	60

Issued to commemorate the Holy Year, 1950.

Dark Chanting Goshawk
A31

European Bee Eater
A32

Designs: 10c, Racquet-tailed roller. 15c, Bataleur eagle. 50c, Giant kingfisher. 1a, Yellow-fronted barbet. 1.50a, Openbill (stork). 2a, Southern ground hornbill. 2.50a, African skimmer. 3a, Shikra. 3.50a, Denham's bustard. 4a, African golden oriole. 4.50a, Long-tailed shrike. 5a, Red-shouldered glossy starling. 6a, Sharp-tailed glossy starling. 7a, Red-shouldered widow bird. 10a, Half-colored kingfisher. 12.50a, White-crowned shrike. 15a, White-winged babbling starling. 20a, Yellow-billed hornbill. 25a, Amethyst starling. 30a, Orange-breasted shrike. 40a, Secretary bird. 50a, Rosy-faced lovebird.

Photogravure and Lithographed.

1951 ***Perf. 11½*** **Unwmkd.**

Birds in Natural Colors.

333	A31	5c lt bl	25	*1.00*
334	A32	10c aqua	25	20
335	A32	15c sal pink	40	*2.00*
336	A32	20c pale yel	55	45
337	A31	50c gray bl	45	20
338	A31	1a lilac	45	20
339	A31	1.50a gray buff	75	20
340	A31	2a cream	80	20
341	A32	2.50a gray	1.10	35
342	A32	3a lem yel	90	35
343	A31	3.50a lt gray	90	35
344	A31	4a rose buff	1.00	35
345	A32	4.50a rose lil	3.00	2.50
346	A31	5a green	4.50	60
347	A31	6a blue	5.50	1.20
348	A31	7a orange	5.50	1.50
349	A31	10a lil rose	40.00	2.75
350	A32	12.50a sl gray	7.25	4.50
351	A31	15a pale ol	7.25	4.50
352	A31	20a pale bis brn	75.00	15.00
353	A31	25a lil rose	20.00	8.25
354	A32	30a pale sal	22.50	10.00
355	A31	40a yellow	30.00	12.50
356	A31	50a turquoise	100.00	32.50
		Nos. 333-356 (24)	328.30	*101.65*

Holy Year Extension Issue.

Common Design Type

1951, Oct. **Litho.** ***Perf. 14***

357	CD43	4a orange	2.25	90

Issued to publicize the extension of the Holy Year into 1951.

Sheets contain alternate vertical rows of stamps and labels bearing quotations from Pope Pius XII or the Patriarch Cardinal of Lisbon.

Medical Congress Issue.

Common Design Type

Design: Medical examination

1952, June ***Perf. 13½***

358	CD44	1a vio bl & brn blk	50	20

Issued to publicize the first National Congress of Tropical Medicine, Lisbon, 1952.

Head of Christ
A35

1952, Oct. ***Perf. 13*** **Unwmkd.**

359	A35	10c dk bl & buff	15	5
360	A35	50c dk ol grn & ol gray	40	10
361	A35	2a rose vio & cr	2.00	20

Issued to commemorate the Exhibition of Sacred Missionary Art held at Lisbon in 1951.

Leopard
A36

Sable Antelope
A37

Animals: 20c, Elephant. 30c, Eland. 40c, African crocodile. 50c, Impala. 1a, Mountain zebra. 1.50a, Sitatunga. 2a, Black rhinoceros. 2.30a, Gemsbok. 2.50a, Lion. 3a, Buffalo. 3.50a, Springbok. 4a, Brindled gnu. 5a, Hartebeest. 7a, Wart hog. 10a, Defassa waterbuck. 12.50a, Hippopotamus. 15a, Greater kudu. 20a, Giraffe.

1953, Aug. 15 ***Perf. 12½***

362	A36	5c multi	10	10
363	A37	10c multi	10	10
364	A37	20c multi	10	10
365	A37	30c multi	10	10
366	A36	40c multi	10	10
367	A37	50c multi	10	10
368	A37	1a multi	35	10
369	A37	1.50a multi	25	10
370	A36	2a multi	30	15
371	A37	2.30a multi	40	15
372	A37	2.50a multi	1.00	12
373	A36	3a multi	1.20	12
374	A37	3.50a multi	30	12
375	A37	4a multi	16.00	60
376	A37	5a multi	55	20
377	A37	7a multi	1.90	55
378	A37	10a multi	3.00	35
379	A37	12.50a multi	6.50	*7.50*
380	A37	15a multi	6.50	*7.50*
381	A37	20a multi	7.50	1.00
		Nos. 362-381 (20)	46.35	*19.16*

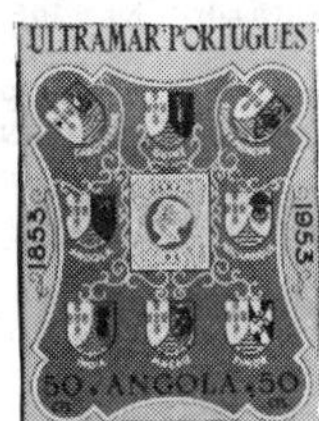

Stamp of Portugal and Arms of Colonies
A38

1953, Nov. **Photo.** ***Perf. 13***

Stamp and Arms Multicolored.

382	A38	50c gray & dk gray	85	55

Issued to commemorate the centenary of Portugal's first postage stamps.

Map and Plane
A39

Typographed and Lithographed.

1954, May 27 ***Perf. 13½***

383	A39	35c dk grn, ol, bl grn & red	15	15
384	A39	4.50e blk, dl vio, aqua & red	1.10	30

Issued to publicize the visit of Pres. Francisco H. C. Lopes.

Sao Paulo Issue

Common Design Type

1954 **Lithographed**

385	CD46	1e bis & gray	40	20

Issued to commemorate the 400th anniversary of the founding of Sao Paulo.

Map of Angola
A41

Artur de Paiva
A42

1955, Aug. ***Perf. 13½*** **Unwmkd.**

Blue Outline, Red Highways, Black Inscriptions

386	A41	5c gray & pale grn	6	6
387	A41	20c gray, lt bl & sal	7	6
388	A41	50c brn buff, pale grn & lt bl	15	6
389	A41	1e gray, lt bl grn, & org yel	25	6
390	A41	2.30e brn buff, aqua & yel	55	12
391	A41	4e bis, pale grn & lt bl	1.75	25
392	A41	10e lil, aqua & cit	1.65	30
393	A41	20e ol grn & pale grn	3.50	60
		Nos. 386-393 (8)	7.98	1.51

1956, Oct. 9 ***Perf. 13½x12½***

394	A42	1e blk, dk bl & ocher	40	20

Issued to commemorate the centenary of the birth of Col. Artur de Paiva.

Man of Malange
A43

José M. Antunes
A44

Various Costumes in Multicolor; Inscriptions in Black Brown.

1957, Jan. 1 Photo. ***Perf. 11½***

Granite Paper.

395	A43	5c gray	5	4
396	A43	10c org yel	7	6
397	A43	15c lt bl grn	12	8
398	A43	20c pale rose vio	12	8
399	A43	30c brt rose	12	8
400	A43	40c bl gray	12	8
401	A43	50c pale ol	12	8
402	A43	80c lt vio	30	30
403	A43	1.50e buff	2.50	20
404	A43	2.50e lt yel grn	3.00	18
405	A43	4e salmon	1.25	18
406	A43	10e sal pink	1.90	45
		Nos. 395-406 (12)	9.67	1.81

1957, April ***Perf. 13½***

407	A44	1e aqua & brn	1.00	60

Issued to commemorate the centenary of the birth of Father José Maria Antunes.

Fair Emblem, Globe and Arms
A45

1958, July Litho. ***Perf. 12x11½***

408	A45	1.50e multi	50	30

World's Fair, Brussels, Apr. 17–Oct. 19.

Tropical Medicine Congress Issue

Common Design Type

Design: Securidaca longipedunculata.

1958, Dec. 15 ***Perf. 13½***

409	CD47	2.50e multi	1.90	1.10

Issued to publicize the 6th International Congress for Tropical Medicine and Malaria, Lisbon, Sept. 1958.

Medicine Man
A47

Welwitschia Mirabilis
A48

Designs: 1.50e, Early government doctor. 2.50e, Modern medical team.

1958, Dec. 18 ***Perf. 11½x12***

410	A47	1e bl blk & brn	30	15
411	A47	1.50e gray, blk & brn	80	30
412	A47	2.50e multi	1.00	50

Issued to commemorate the 75th anniversary of the Maria Pia Hospital, Luanda.

1959, Oct. 1 Litho. ***Perf. 14½***

Various Views of Plant and Various Frames.

413	A48	1.50e lt brn, grn & blk	1.00	70
414	A48	2.50e multi	1.30	55
415	A48	5e multi	1.90	80
416	A48	10e multi	5.25	1.65

Centenary of discovery of Welwitschia mirabilis, desert plant.

Map of West Africa, c. 1540, by Jorge Reinel—A49

1960, June 25 ***Perf. 13½***

417	A49	2.50e multi	45	30

Issued to commemorate the 500th anniversary of the death of Prince Henry the Navigator.

Distributing Medicines
A50

Girl of Angola
A51

1960, Oct. Litho. ***Perf. 14½***

418	A50	2.50e multi	45	25

Issued to commemorate the 10th anniversary of the Commission for Technical Co-operation in Africa South of the Sahara (C.C.T.A.).

1961, Nov. 30 ***Perf. 13*** **Unwmkd.**

Portraits of Angolese Women in Natural Colors

419	A51	10c blk, yel grn & grn	8	4
420	A51	15c blk, gray bl & lil	8	8
421	A51	30c blk, yel & dk bl	10	10
422	A51	40c blk, gray & dk red	5	5
423	A51	60c blk, sal & ol	8	8
424	A51	1.50e blk, bl & red	18	5
425	A51	2e blk, lil & bis	1.00	12
426	A51	2.50e blk, yel & brn	1.25	12
427	A51	3e blk, pink & ol	3.00	30
428	A51	4e blk, gray grn & brn	1.85	40
429	A51	5e blk, lt bl & car	1.50	30
430	A51	7.50e blk, dl yel & brn	1.75	1.40
431	A51	10e blk, ocher & grn	1.65	60
432	A51	15e blk, beige & grn	1.75	1.50
432A	A51	25e blk, rose & red brn	3.25	1.80
432B	A51	50e blk, gray & vio bl	6.75	3.25
		Nos. 419-432B (16)	24.32	10.19

Sports Issue

Common Design Type

Sports: 50c, Flying. 1e, Rowing. 1.50e, Water polo. 2.50e, Hammer throwing. 4.50e, High jump. 15e, Weight lifting.

1962, Jan. 18 ***Perf. 13½***

Multicolored Design

433	CD48	50c lt bl	15	10
434	CD48	1e ol bis	95	35
435	CD48	1.50e salmon	50	15
436	CD48	2.50e lt brn	45	15
437	CD48	4.50e pale bl	60	60
438	CD48	15e yellow	2.00	1.75
		Nos. 433-438 (6)	4.65	3.10

Anti-Malaria Issue

Common Design Type

Design: Anopheles funestus.

1962, April Litho. ***Perf. 13½***

439	CD49	2.50e multi	1.00	40

Issued for the World Health Organization drive to eradicate malaria.

Gen. Norton de Matos
A54

1962, Aug. 8 ***Perf. 14½*** **Unwmkd.**

440	A54	2.50e multi	45	20

Issued to commemorate the 50th anniversary of the founding of Nova Lisboa.

Locusts
A56

1963, June 2 Litho. ***Perf. 14***

447	A56	2.50e multi	60	30

Issued to commemorate the 15th anniversary of the International Anti-Locust Organization.

Arms of Luanda
A57

Vila de Santo Antonio do Zaire
A58

Coats of Arms (Provinces and Cities): 10c, Massangano. 15c, Sanza-Pombo. 25c, Ambriz. 30c, Muxima. 40c, Ambrizete. 50c, Carmona. 60c, Catete. 70c, Quibaxe. No. 458, Maquelo do Zombo. 1e, Salazar. 1.20e, Bembe. No. 461, Caxito. 1.50e, Malanje. 1.80e, Dondo. No. 465, Damba. 2e, Henrique de Carvalho. 2.50e, Moçâmedes. 3e, Novo Redondo. 3.50e, S. Salvador do Congo. 4e, Cuimba. 5e, Luso. 6.50e, Negage. 7e, Quitexe. 7.50e, S. Filipe de Benguela. 8e, Mucaba. 9e, 31 de Janeiro. 10e, Lobito. 11e, Nova Cabemba. 12.50e, Gabela. 14e, Songo. 15e Sa' da Bandeira. 17e, Quimbele. 17.50e, Silva Porto. 20e, Nova Lisboa. 22.50e, Cabinda. 25e, Noqui. 30e, Serpa Pinto. 35e, Santa Cruz. 50e, General Freire.

1963 ***Perf. 13½***

Arms in Original Colors; Red and Violet Blue Inscriptions.

448	A57	5c tan	10	10
449	A57	10c lt bl	10	10
450	A58	15c salmon	10	10
451	A58	20c olive	10	10
452	A58	25c lt bl	12	10
453	A57	30c buff	10	10
454	A58	40c gray	12	10
455	A57	50c lt grn	10	10
456	A58	60c brt yel	18	12
457	A58	70c dl rose	18	12
458	A57	1e pale lil	25	10
459	A58	1e dl yel	30	10
460	A58	1.20e rose	12	10
461	A57	1.50e pale sal	50	10
462	A58	1.50e lt grn	55	12
463	A58	1.80e yel ol	30	18
464	A57	2e lt yel grn	45	10
465	A57	2.50e lt gray	1.50	15
466	A58	2.50e dl bl	1.50	18
467	A57	3e yel ol	65	12
468	A57	3.50e gray	75	15
469	A58	4e citron	55	35
470	A57	5e citron	60	35
471	A58	6.50e tan	70	45
472	A58	7e rose lil	65	45
473	A57	7.50e pale lil	85	55
474	A58	8e lt aqua	85	55
475	A58	9e yellow	90	55
476	A57	10e dp sal	1.10	55
477	A58	11e dl yel grn	1.10	85
478	A57	12.50e pale bl	1.40	85
479	A58	14e lt gray	1.40	85
480	A57	15e lt bl	1.65	85
481	A58	17e pale bl	1.65	1.10
482	A57	17.50e dl yel	2.25	1.25
483	A57	20e lt aqua	2.40	1.20
484	A57	22.50e gray	2.25	1.50
485	A58	25e citron	3.00	2.25
486	A57	30e yellow	3.25	2.75
487	A58	35e grysh bl	3.75	3.00
488	A58	50e dp yel	5.50	4.00
		Nos. 448-488 (41)	43.87	26.69

Pres. Américo Rodrigues Thomaz
A59

1963, Sept. 16 **Lithographed**

489	A59	2.50e multi	60	25

Visit of the President of Portugal.

Airline Anniversary Issue

Common Design Type

1963, Oct. 5 ***Perf. 14½*** **Unwmkd.**

490	CD50	1e lt bl & multi	40	20

Issued to commemorate the 10th anniversary of Transportes Aéreos Portugueses.

Cathedral of Sá da Bandeira
A61

Malange Cathedral
A62

Churches: 20c, Landana. 30c, Luanda Cathedral. 40c, Gabela. 50c, St. Martin's Chapel, Baia dos Tigres. 1.50e, St. Peter, Chibia. 2e, Church of Our Lady, Benguela. 2.50e, Church of Jesus, Luanda. 3e, Camabatela. 3.50e, Mission, Cabinda. 4e, Vila Folgares. 4.50e, Church of Our Lady, Lobito. 5e, Church of Cabinda. 7.50e, Cacuso Church, Malange. 10e, Lubango Mission. 12.50e, Huila Mission. 15e, Church of Our Lady, Luanda Island.

1963, Nov. 1 **Lithographed**
Multicolored Design and Inscription

491	A61	10c gray bl		10	10
492	A61	20c pink		10	10
493	A61	30c lt bl		10	10
494	A61	40c tan		10	10
495	A61	50c lt grn		10	10
496	A62	1e buff		12	10
497	A61	1.50e lt vio bl		15	10
498	A62	2e pale rose		18	10
499	A61	2.50e gray		25	10
500	A62	3e buff		28	10
501	A61	3.50e olive		33	12
502	A62	4e buff		35	30
503	A62	4.50e pale bl		42	35
504	A61	5e tan		45	35
505	A62	7.50e gray		70	60
506	A61	10e dl yel		90	75
507	A62	12.50e bister		1.20	90
508	A62	15e pale gray vio		2.00	1.10
		Nos. 491-508 (18)		7.83	5.47

National Overseas Bank Issue
Common Design Type

Design: Antonio Teixeira de Sousa.

1964, May 16 ***Perf. 13½***

509	CD51	2.50e multi	60	20

Issued to commemorate the centenary of the National Overseas Bank of Portugal.

Commerce Building and Arms of Chamber of Commerce—A64

1964, Nov. **Litho.** ***Perf. 12***

510	A64	1e multi	30	20

Luanda Chamber of Commerce centenary.

ITU Issue
Common Design Type

1965, May 17 ***Perf. 14½*** **Unwmkd.**

511	CD52	2.50e gray & multi	1.00	40

Issued to commemorate the centenary of the International Telecommunication Union.

Plane over Luanda Airport
A65

Harquebusier, 1539
A66

1965, Dec. 3 **Litho.** ***Perf. 13***

512	A65	2.50e multi	35	20

Issued to commemorate the 25th anniversary of DTA, Direccão dos Transportes Aéreos.

1966, Feb. 25 **Litho.** ***Perf. 14½***

Designs: 50c, Harquebusier, 1539. 1e, Harquebusier, 1640. 1.50e, Infantry officer, 1777. 2e, Standard bearer, infantry, 1777. 2.50e, Infantry soldier, 1777. 3e, Cavalry officer, 1783. 4e, Cavalry soldier, 1783. 4.50e, Infantry officer, 1807. 5e, Infantry soldier, 1807. 6e, Cavalry officer, 1807. 8e, Cavalry soldier, 1807. 9e, Infantry soldier, 1873.

513	A66	50c multi	15	15
514	A66	1e multi	18	18
515	A66	1.50e multi	15	15
516	A66	2e multi	18	18
517	A66	2.50e multi	50	30
518	A66	3e multi	55	12
519	A66	4e multi	75	40
520	A66	4.50e multi	85	30
521	A66	5e multi	1.00	40
522	A66	6e multi	1.00	45
523	A66	8e multi	1.50	55
524	A66	9e multi	1.50	55
		Nos. 513-524 (12)	8.31	3.73

National Revolution Issue
Common Design Type

Design: St. Paul's Hospital and Commercial and Industrial School.

1966, May 28 **Litho.** ***Perf. 12***

525	CD53	1e multi	30	15

40th anniversary, National Revolution.

Emblem of Holy Ghost Society
A68

1966 **Lithographed** ***Perf. 13***

526	A68	1e bl & multi	25	10

Centenary of the Holy Ghost Society.

Navy Club Issue
Common Design Type

Designs: 1e, Mendes Barata and cruiser Dom Carlos I. 2.50e, Capt. Augusto de Castilho and corvette Mindelo.

1967, Jan. 31 **Litho.** ***Perf. 13***

527	CD54	1e multi	40	15
528	CD54	2.50e multi	60	20

Centenary of Portugal's Navy Club.

Fatima Basilica
A70

Angola Map, Manuel Cerveira Pereira
A71

1967, May 13 **Litho.** ***Perf. 12½x13***

529	A70	50c multi	10	10

Issued to commemorate the 50th anniversary of the apparition of the Virgin Mary to three shepherd children at Fatima.

1967, Aug. 15 **Litho.** ***Perf. 12½x13***

530	A71	50c multi	18	15

Issued to commemorate the 350th anniversary of the founding of Benguela.

Administration Building, Carmona—A72

1967 **Lithographed** ***Perf. 12***

531	A72	1e multi	15	15

Issued to commemorate the 50th anniversary of the founding of Carmona.

Military Order of Valor
A73

Our Lady of Hope
A74

Designs: 50c, Ribbon of the Three Orders. 1.50e, Military Order of Avis. 2e, Military Order of Christ. 2.50e, Military Order of St. John of Espada. 3e, Order of the Empire. 4e, Order of Prince Henry. 5e, Order of Benemerencia. 10e, Order of Public Instruction. 20e, Order for Industrial and Agricultural Merit.

1967, Oct. 31 ***Perf. 14***

532	A73	50c lt gray & multi	10	6
533	A73	1e lt grn & multi	10	6
534	A73	1.50e yel & multi	12	6
535	A73	2e multi	18	6
536	A73	2.50e multi	25	15
537	A73	3e lt ol & multi	28	10
538	A73	4e gray & multi	35	15
539	A73	5e multi	55	30
540	A73	10e lil & multi	1.10	55
541	A73	20e lt bl & multi	1.85	1.10
		Nos. 532-541 (10)	4.88	2.59

Cabral Issue

Designs: 1e, Belmonte Castle (horiz.). 1.50e, St. Jerome's Convent. 2.50e, Cabral's Armada.

1968, Apr. 22 **Litho.** ***Perf. 14***

542	A74	50c yel & multi	10	10
543	A74	1e gray & multi	60	15
544	A74	1.50e lt bl & multi	70	20
545	A74	2.50e buff & multi	95	20

Issued to commemorate the 500th anniversary of the birth of Pedro Alvares Cabral, navigator who took possession of Brazil for Portugal.

Francisco Inocencio de Souza Coutinho
A75

1969, Jan. 7 **Litho.** ***Perf. 14***

546	A75	2e multi	50	40

Issued to commemorate the 200th anniversary of the founding of Novo Redondo.

Admiral Coutinho Issue
Common Design Type

Design: Adm. Gago Coutinho and his first ship.

1969, Feb. 17 **Litho.** ***Perf. 14***

547	CD55	2.50e multi	45	20

Compass Rose
A77

Portal of St. Jeronimo's Monastery
A79

1969, Aug. 29 **Litho.** ***Perf. 14***

548	A77	1e multi	20	20

Issued to commemorate the 500th anniversary of the birth of Vasco da Gama (1469–1524), navigator.

Administration Reform Issue
Common Design Type

1969, Sept. 25 **Litho.** ***Perf. 14***

549	CD56	1.50e multi	20	20

Issued to commemorate the centenary of the administration reforms of the overseas territories.

1969, Dec. 1 **Litho.** ***Perf. 14***

550	A79	3e multi	35	25

Issued to commemorate the 500th anniversary of the birth of King Manuel I.

Angolasaurus Bocagei
A80

Fossils and Minerals: 1e, Ferrometeorite. 1.50e, Dioptase crystals. 2e, Gondwanidium. 2.50e, Diamonds. 3e, Estromatolite. 3.50e, Procarcharodon megalodon. 4e, Microceratodus angolensis. 4.50e, Moscovite. 5e, Barite. 6e, Nostoceras. 10e, Rotula orbiculus angolensis.

1970, Oct. 31 **Litho.** ***Perf. 13***

551	A80	50c tan & multi	15	10
552	A80	1e multi	25	15
553	A80	1.50e multi	25	10
554	A80	2e multi	30	10
555	A80	2.50e lt gray & multi	40	15
556	A80	3e multi	45	25
557	A80	3.50e bl & multi	60	30
558	A80	4e lt gray & multi	65	30
559	A80	4.50e gray & multi	70	35
560	A80	5e gray & multi	70	40
561	A80	6e pink & multi	1.00	45
562	A80	10e lt bl & multi	1.50	90
		Nos. 551-562 (12)	6.95	3.55

Marshal Carmona Issue
Common Design Type

1970, Nov. 15 ***Perf. 14***

563	CD57	2.50e multi	30	10

Birth centenary of Marshal Antonio Oscar Carmona de Fragoso (1869–1951), President of Portugal.

Arms of Malanje, Cotton Boll and Field
A82

1970, Nov. 20 ***Perf. 13***

564	A82	2.50e multi	35	30

Centenary of the municipality of Malanje.

Mail Ships and Angola No. 1
A83

Designs: 4.50e, Steam locomotive and Angola No. 4.

1970, Dec. 1 ***Perf. 13½***

565	A83	1.50e multi	30	20
566	A83	4.50e multi	75	35

Centenary of stamps of Angola. See No. C36.

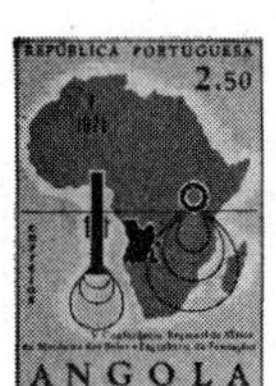

Map of Africa, Diagram of Seismic Tests
A84

Galleon on Congo River
A85

1971, Aug. 22 Litho. *Perf. 13*

567 A84 2.50e multi 35 20

5th Regional Conference of Soil and Foundation Engineers, Luanda, Aug. 22–Sept. 5.

1972, May 25 Litho. *Perf. 13*

568 A85 1e emer & multi 20 15

4th centenary of the publication of The Lusiads by Luiz Camoëns.

Olympic Games Issue
Common Design Type

1972, June 20 *Perf. 14x13½*

569 CD59 50c multi 20 15

20th Olympic Games, Munich, Aug. 26–Sept. 11.

Lisbon-Rio de Janeiro Flight Issue
Common Design Type

1972, Sept. 20 Litho. *Perf. 13½*

570 CD60 1e multi 25 15

WMO Centenary Issue
Common Design Type

1973, Dec. 15 Litho. *Perf. 13*

571 CD61 1e dk gray & multi 25 15

Centenary of international meteorological cooperation.

Radar Station
A89

1974, June 25 Litho. *Perf. 13*

572 A89 2e multi 35 20

Establishment of satellite communications network via Intelsat among Portugal, Angola and Mozambique.

Harpa Doris
A90

Designs: Sea shells.

1974, Oct. 25 Litho. *Perf. 12x12½*
Multicolored

573 A90 25c *shown* 12 12
574 A90 30c *Murex melanamathos* 12 12
575 A90 50c *Venus foliaceo lamellosa* 12 12
576 A90 70c *Lathyrus filosus* 12 12
577 A90 1e *Cymbium cisium* 12 12
578 A90 1.50e *Cassis tesselata* 20 15
579 A90 2e *Cypraea stercoraria* 25 12
580 A90 2.50e *Conus prometheus* 35 20
581 A90 3e *Strombus latus* 40 25
582 A90 3.50e *Tympanotonus fuscatus* 45 25
583 A90 4e *Cardium costatum* 50 35
584 A90 5e *Natica fulminea* 60 45
585 A90 6e Lyropecten nodosus 85 45
586 A90 7e *Tonna galea* 85 50
587 A90 10e *Donax rugosus* 1.20 75
588 A90 25e *Cymatium trigonum* 3.00 1.90
589 A90 30e *Olivancilaria acuminata* 3.75 2.25
590 A90 35e *Semifusus morio* 4.25 2.50
591 A90 40e *Clavatula lineata* 4.75 3.00
592 A90 50e *Solarium granulatum* 6.50 4.50
Nos. 573-592 (20) 28.50 18.22

No. 386 Overprinted in Blue: "1974 / FILATELIA / JUVENIL"

1974, Dec. 21 Litho. *Perf. 13½*

593 A41 5c multi 50 50

Youth philately.

Republic

Star and Hand Holding Rifle
A91

1975, Nov. 11 Litho. *Perf. 13x13½*

594 A91 1.50e red & multi 50 50

Independence in 1975.

Diquiche Mask
A92

Design: 3e, Bui ou Congolo mask.

1976, Feb. 6 *Perf. 13½*

595 A92 50c lt bl & multi 15 15
596 A92 3e multi 75 75

Workers
A93

President Agostinho Neto
A94

1976, May 1 Litho. *Perf. 12*

597 A93 1e red & multi 35 25

International Workers' Day.

No. 392 Overprinted Bar and: "DIA DO SELO / 15 Junho 1976 / REP. POPULAR / DE"

1976, June 15 Litho. *Perf. 13½*

598 A41 10e multi 85 85

Stamp Day.

1976, Nov. 11 Litho. *Perf. 13*

599 A94 50c yel & dk brn 10 10
600 A94 2e lt gray & plum 40 10
601 A94 3e gray & ind 50 15
602 A94 5e buff & brn 85 25
603 A94 10e tan & sep 1.50 60
a. Souvenir sheet 2.25 1.25
Nos. 599-603 (5) 3.35 1.20

First anniversary of independence. No. 603a contains one imperf. stamp. Gold margin with brown inscription. Size: 60x75mm.

Nos. 393, 588–589, 592 Overprinted with Bar over Republica Portuguesa and: "REPUBLICA POPULAR DE"

1977, Feb. 9 *Perf. 13½, 12x12½*

604 A41 20e multi 1.75 60
605 A90 25e multi 1.75 60
606 A90 30e multi 2.75 90
607 A90 50e multi 4.50 1.50

Overprint in 3 lines on No. 604, in 2 lines on others.

No. 438 Overprinted with Bar over Republica Portuguesa and: "S. Silvestre / 1976 / Rep. Popular / de"

1976, Dec. 31 *Perf. 13½*

608 CD48 15e multi 90 45

Child and WHO Emblem
A95

Map of Africa, Flag of Angola
A96

1977 Litho. *Perf. 10½*

609 A95 2.50k blk & lt bl 25 10

Campaign for vaccination against poliomyelitis.

1977 Photogravure

610 A96 6k blk, red & bl 60 40

First congress of Popular Movement for the Liberation of Angola.

Anti-Apartheid Emblem
A97

1979, July Litho. *Perf. 13½*

611 A97 1k multi 10 5

Anti-Apartheid Year.

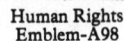

Human Rights Emblem-A98

Child Flowers, Globe, IYC Emblem—A99

1979 Litho. *Perf. 13½*

612 A98 2.50k multi 25 10

Declaration of Human Rights, 30th anniversary, in 1975.

1980, Aug. Litho. *Perf. 14x14½*

613 A99 3.50k multi 35 10

International Year of the Child (1979).

Running, Moscow '80 Emblem
A100

5th Anniv. of Independence
A101

1980 Litho. *Perf. 13½*

614 A100 9k shown 90 40
615 A100 12k Swimming, horiz. 1.20 60

22nd Summer Olympic Games, Moscow, July 19-Aug. 3.

1980

616 A101 5.50k multi 55 20

Nos. 577-580, 582-591 Overprinted with Black Bar over "Republica Portuguesa"

1981, Sept. Litho. *Perf. 12x12½*

617 A90 1e multi
618 A90 1.50e multi
619 A90 2e multi
620 A90 2.50e multi
621 A90 3.50e multi
622 A90 4e multi
623 A90 5e multi
624 A90 6e multi
625 A90 7e multi
626 A90 10e multi
627 A90 25e multi
628 A90 30e multi
629 A90 35e multi
630 A90 40e multi
Nos. 617-630 (14) *17.50 8.00*

Man Walking with Canes, Tchibinda Ilunga Statue—A102

1981, Sept. Litho. *Perf. 13½*

631 A102 9k multi 90 40

Turipex '81 tourism exhibition.

M.P.L.A. Workers' Party Congress—A103

1981 Litho. *Perf. 14*

632 A103 50l Millet 5
633 A103 5k Coffee 50
634 A103 7.50k Sunflowers 75
635 A103 13.50k Cotton 1.35
636 A103 14k Oil 1.40
637 A103 16k Diamonds 1.60
Nos. 632-637 (6) 5.65

People's Power

A104

Natl. Heros' Day

A105

1981

638	A104	40k lt bl & blk	4.00

1981 *Perf. 14x13½*

639	A105	4.50k Former Pres. Neto	45
640	A105	50k Neto, diff.	5.00

Soweto Uprising, 5th Anniv.—A106

1981

641	A106	4.50k multi	45

Souvenir Sheet

2nd Central African Games—A107

1981 **Litho.** *Imperf.*

646	A107	15k multi	*3.00*

Size: 112x130mm.

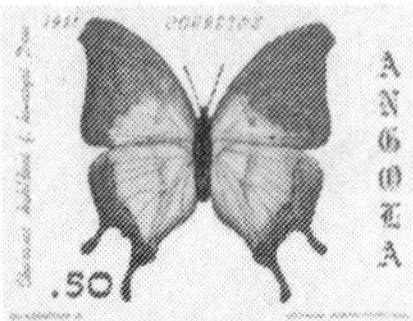

Charaxes Kahldeni—A108

1981, Nov. 30 **Litho.** *Perf. 13½*

647	A108	50 l shown	3
648	A108	1k Abantis zambesiaca	5
649	A108	5k Catacroptera cloanthe	25
650	A108	9k Myrina ficedula, vert.	45
651	A108	10k Colotis danae	50
652	A108	15k Acraea acrita	75
653	A108	100k Precis hierta	5.00
a.		30k Souvenir sheet	1.50
		Nos. 647-653 (7)	7.03

No. 653a contains Nos. 647-653 (imperf.); blue and black margin. Size: 155x105mm.

5th Anniv. of UN Membership—A109

Designs: 5.50k, The Silence of the Night, by Musseque Catambor. 7.50k, Cotton picking, Catete.

1982, Sept. 22 **Litho.**

654	A109	5.50k multi	28
655	A109	7.50k multi	38

20th Anniv. of Engineering Laboratory—A110

1982, Dec. 21 **Litho.** *Perf. 14*

656	A110	9k Lab	45
657	A110	13k Worker, vert.	65
658	A110	100k Equipment, vert.	5.00

Local Flowers—A111

1983, Feb. 18 *Perf. 13½*

659	A111	5k Dichrostachys glomerata	25
660	A111	12k Amblygonocarpus obtusangulus	60
661	A111	50k Albizzia versicolor	2.50

AIR POST STAMPS.

Common Design Type

Perf. 13½x13.

1938, July 26 **Engraved** **Unwmkd.**

Name and Value in Black.

C1	CD39	10c scarlet	40	35
C2	CD39	20c purple	50	35
C3	CD39	50c orange	55	35
C4	CD39	1a ultra	60	30
C5	CD39	2a lil brn	1.25	40
C6	CD39	3a dk grn	2.50	45
C7	CD39	5a red brn	3.75	55
C8	CD39	9a rose car	5.50	1.75
C9	CD39	10a magenta	7.50	1.75
		Nos. C1-C9 (9)	22.55	6.25

No. C7 exists with overprint "Exposicao Internacional de Nova York, 1939–1940" and Trylon and Perisphere.

AP2

1947, Aug. **Litho.** *Perf. 10½*

C10	AP2	1a red brn	7.50	2.50
C11	AP2	2a yel grn	7.50	2.50
C12	AP2	3a orange	9.00	1.50
C13	AP2	3.50a orange	15.00	5.00
C14	AP2	5a ol grn	100.00	7.50
C15	AP2	6a rose	100.00	10.00
C16	AP2	9a red	250.00	125.00
C17	AP2	10a green	200.00	45.00
C18	AP2	20a blue	200.00	45.00
C19	AP2	50a black	325.00	150.00
C20	AP2	100a yellow	550.00	450.00
		Nos. C10-C20 (11)	1,764.	844.00

Planes Circling Globe
AP3

1949, May 1 **Photo.** *Perf. 11½*

C21	AP3	1a hn brn	45	25
C22	AP3	2a red brn	90	25
C23	AP3	3a plum	1.65	30
C24	AP3	6a dl grn	3.75	85
C25	AP3	9a vio brn	5.75	1.90
		Nos. C21-C25 (5)	12.50	3.55

Cambambe Dam
AP4

Designs: 1.50e, Oil refinery (vert.). 3e, Salazar Dam. 4e, Capt. Teófilo Duarte Dam. 4.50e, Craveiro Lopes Dam. 5e, Cuango Dam. 6e, Quanza River Bridge. 7e, Capt. Teófilo Duarte Bridge. 8.50e, Oliveira Salazar Bridge. 12.50e, Capt. Silva Carvalho Bridge.

Perf. 11½x12, 12x11½

1965, July 12 **Litho.** **Unwmkd.**

C26	AP4	1.50e multi	2.50	15
C27	AP4	2.50e multi	1.25	20
C28	AP4	3e multi	1.50	30
C29	AP4	4e multi	1.00	30
C30	AP4	4.50e multi	1.00	35
C31	AP4	5e multi	1.40	40
C32	AP4	6e multi	1.40	55
C33	AP4	7e multi	1.90	55
C34	AP4	8.50e multi	2.75	85
C35	AP4	12.50e multi	3.00	85
		Nos. C26-C35 (10)	17.70	4.50

Stamp Centenary Type of Regular Issue

Design: 2.50e, Boeing 707 jet and Angola No. 2.

1970, Dec. 1 Litho. *Perf. 13½*

C36	A83	2.50e multi	55	40
a.		Souvenir sheet of 3	3.75	3.75

Centenary of stamps of Angola.

No. C36a contains one each of No. 565–566, C36. Margin shows Duke of Bragança Waterfall, with commemorative inscription. Size: 150x105mm. Sold for 15e.

POSTAGE DUE STAMPS.

D1 D2

Typographed.

1904 *Perf. 11½x12.* Unwmkd.

J1	D1	5r yel grn	40	30
J2	D1	10r slate	40	30
J3	D1	20r yel brn	45	45
J4	D1	30r orange	60	60
J5	D1	50r gray brn	60	60
J6	D1	60r red brn	6.00	3.00
J7	D1	100r lilac	3.00	2.75
J8	D1	130r dl bl	3.00	2.75
J9	D1	200r carmine	6.00	4.00
J10	D1	500r gray vio	6.00	3.75
		Nos.J1-J10 (10)	26.45	18.50

Postage Due Stamps of 1904 Overprinted in Carmine or Green

REPUBLICA

1911

J11	D1	5r yel grn	30	30
J12	D1	10r slate	30	30
J13	D1	20r yel brn	30	30
J14	D1	30r orange	45	45
J15	D1	50r gray brn	45	45
J16	D1	60r red brn	1.00	1.00
J17	D1	100r lilac	1.00	1.00
J18	D1	130r dl bl	1.00	1.00
J19	D1	200r car (G)	1.00	1.00
J20	D1	500r gray vio	1.25	1.25
		Nos. J11-J20 (10)	7.05	7.05

1921 *Perf. 11½.*

J21	D2	½c yel grn	12	12
J22	D2	1c slate	12	12
J23	D2	2c org brn	12	12
J24	D2	3c orange	12	12
J25	D2	5c gray brn	12	12
J26	D2	6c lt brn	12	12
J27	D2	10c red vio	12	12
J28	D2	13c dl bl	25	25
J29	D2	20c carmine	25	25
J30	D2	50c gray	25	25
		Nos. J21-J30 (10)	1.59	1.59

Stamps of 1932 Surcharged in Black

PORTEADO
10
Centavos

1948 *Perf. 12x11½.* Wmk. 232

J31	A14	10c on 20c gray	40	30
J32	A14	20c on 30c myr grn	40	30
J33	A14	30c on 50c lt brn	45	30
J34	A14	40c on 1a cl	45	30
J35	A14	50c on 2a dl vio	80	45
J36	A14	1a on 5a pale yel grn	1.10	90
		Nos. J31-J36 (6)	3.60	2.55

Common Design Type

Photogravure and Typographed.

1952 *Perf. 14.* Unwmkd.

Numeral in Red, Frame Multicolored.

J37	CD45	10c red brn	15	15
J38	CD45	30c ol grn	15	15
J39	CD45	50c chocolate	15	15
J40	CD45	1a dk vio bl	15	15
J41	CD45	2a red brn	30	30
J42	CD45	5a blk brn	70	70
		Nos. J37-J42 (6)	1.60	1.60

NEWSPAPER STAMP.

N1

Perf. 11½, 12½, 13½.

1893 Typographed Unwmkd.

P1	N1	2½r brown	1.75	1.10

No. P1 was also used for ordinary postage.

POSTAL TAX STAMPS.

Pombal Issue.

Common Design Types

1925 *Perf. 12½.* Unwmkd.

RA1	CD28	15c lil & blk	50	40
RA2	CD29	15c lil & blk	50	40
RA3	CD30	15c lil & blk	50	40

"Charity"
PT1

Coat of Arms
PT2

Without Gum

1929 Lithographed. *Perf. 11.*

RA4	PT1	50c dk bl	4.00	1.50

1939 Without Gum. *Perf. 10½.*

RA5	PT2	50c turq grn	3.25	20
RA6	PT2	1a red	5.50	4.50

A 1.50a, type PT2, was issued for fiscal use.

Old Man
PT3

Mother and Child
PT4

Designs: 1e, Boy. 1.50e, Girl.

Imprint: "Foto-Lito—E.G.A.—Luanda"

1955 *Perf. 13* Unwmkd.

Heads in dark brown.

RA7	PT3	50c dk ocher	20	15
RA8	PT3	1e org ver	90	30
RA9	PT3	1.50e brt yel grn	55	25

A 2.50e, type PT3 showing an old woman, was issued for revenue use.

See also Nos. RA16, RA19–RA21, RA25–RA27.

No. RA7 Surcharged with New Values and two Bars in Red or Black.

1957-58 Head in dark brown.

RA11	PT3	10c on 50c dk ocher (R)	40	25
RA12	PT3	10c on 50c dk ocher ('58)	30	20
RA13	PT3	30c on 50c dk ocher	35	25

1959 Lithographed. *Perf. 13*

Design: 30c, Boy and girl.

RA14	PT4	10c org & blk	15	15
RA15	PT4	30c sl & blk	15	15

Type of 1955 Redrawn

Design: 1e, Boy.

1961, Nov. *Perf. 13*

RA16	PT3	1e sal pink & dk brn	30	30

Denomination in italics.

Yellow, White and Black Men
PT5

1962 Typographed *Perf. 10½*

Without Gum

RA17	PT5	50c multi	50	50
RA18	PT5	1e multi	60	60

Issued for the Provincial Settlement Committee (Junta Provincial do Povoamento). The tax was used to promote Portuguese settlement in Angola, and to raise educational and living standards of recent immigrants.

See also No. RAJ4. Denominations higher than 2e were used for revenue purposes.

Head Type of 1955

Without Imprint

Designs: 50c, Old man. 1e, Boy. 1.50e, Girl.

1964–65 Litho. *Perf. 11½*

Heads in dark bown

RA19	PT3	50c orange	22	15
RA20	PT3	1e dl red org ('65)	30	15
RA21	PT3	1.50e yel grn ('65)	40	25

No. RA20 is second redrawing of 1e, with bolder lettering and denomination in gothic. Space between "Assistencia" and denomination on RA19–RA21 is ½mm.; on 1955 issue space is 2mm.

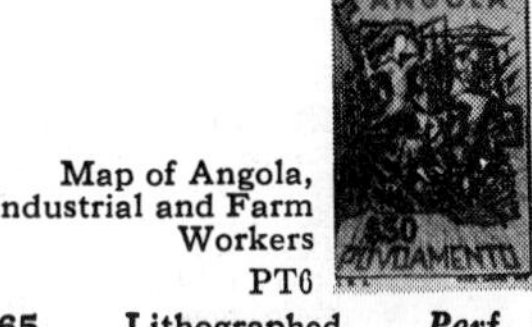

Map of Angola, Industrial and Farm Workers
PT6

1965 Lithographed *Perf. 13*

RA22	PT6	50c multi	30	30
RA23	PT6	1e multi	45	45

See also No. RAJ5.

Head Type of 1955

1966

Imprint: "I.N.A." or "INA" (1e)

Heads in dark brown

RA25	PT3	50c dl org	15	15
RA26	PT3	1e dl brick red	25	15
RA27	PT3	1.50e lt yel grn	25	20

Woman Planting Tree
PT7

Designs: 1e, Workers. 2e, Produce.

1972 Lithographed *Perf. 13*

RA28	PT7	50c gray & pink	10	10
RA29	PT7	1e grn & blk	20	20
RA30	PT7	2e brn & blk	30	30

POSTAL TAX DUE STAMPS.

Pombal Issue.

Common Design Types

1925 *Perf. 12½.* Unwmkd.

RAJ1	CD31	30c lil & blk	75	*1.25*
RAJ2	CD32	30c lil & blk	75	*1.25*
RAJ3	CD33	30c lil & blk	75	*1.25*

See note after Portugal No. RAJ4.

Three-Men Type of Postal Tax Stamps, 1962.

1962 Typographed *Perf. 10½*

Without Gum

RAJ4	PT5	2e multi	80	*1.00*

See note after Nos. RA17–RA18.

Type of Postal Tax Stamps, 1965

1965 Lithographed *Perf. 13*

RAJ5	PT6	2e multi	35	*1.00*

ANGRA

(äng'grȧ)

LOCATION — An administrative district of the Azores, consisting of the islands of Terceira, São Jorge and Graciosa.

GOVT.—A district of Portugal.

AREA—275 sq. mi.

POP.—70,000 (approx.).

CAPITAL—Angra do Heroismo.

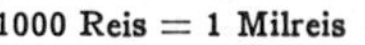

1000 Reis = 1 Milreis

King Carlos

A1 A2

Perf. 11½, 12½, 13½.

1892-93 Typographed. Unwmkd.

No.	Type	Description	Unused	Used
1	A1	5r yellow	2.00	1.25
a.		Perf. 11½	5.00	3.00
2	A1	10r redsh vio	2.75	1.75
3	A1	15r chocolate	3.25	2.25
4	A1	20r lavender	3.50	2.25
a.		Perf. 13½	6.75	2.50
5	A1	25r green	1.40	35
a.		Perf. 12½	6.00	75
7	A1	50r blue	4.50	1.75
a.		Perf. 13½	8.00	4.75
8	A1	75r carmine	8.50	4.00
9	A1	80r yel grn	9.50	6.00
10	A1	100r brn, *yel*, perf. 13½ ('93)	30.00	15.00
a.		Perf. 12½	110.00	90.00
11	A1	150r car, *rose* ('93)	35.00	27.50
12	A1	200r dk bl, *bl* ('93)	35.00	27.50
13	A1	300r dk bl, *sal* ('93)	35.00	27.50

Reprints of 50r, 150r, 200r and 300r, made in 1900, are perf. 11½ and ungummed. Price, each $7.50. Reprints of all values, made in 1905, have shiny white gum and clean-cut perf. 13½. Price, each $1.

1897–1905 ***Perf. 11½***

Name and Value in Black except Nos. 26 and 35.

No.	Type	Description	Unused	Used
14	A2	2½r gray	30	25
15	A2	5r orange	30	25
a.		Diagonal half used as 2½r on cover		10.00
16	A2	10r yel grn	30	25
17	A2	15r brown	6.00	2.50
18	A2	15r gray grn ('99)	1.25	70
19	A2	20r gray vio	1.25	45
20	A2	25r sea grn	1.50	50
a.		Imperf., pair	10.00	
21	A2	25r car rose ('99)	70	20
22	A2	50r dk bl	2.50	90
23	A2	50r ultra ('05)	8.00	7.00
24	A2	65r sl bl ('98)	45	30
25	A2	75r rose	1.25	75
26	A2	75r gray brn & car, *straw* ('05)	8.50	7.50
27	A2	80r violet	55	40
28	A2	100r dk bl, *bl*	1.30	55
29	A2	115r org brn, *pink* ('98)	1.10	80
30	A2	130r gray brn, *straw* ('98)	1.10	80
31	A2	150r lt brn, *straw*	1.00	75
32	A2	180r sl, *pnksh* ('98)	1.60	1.25
33	A2	200r red vio, *pnksh*	2.50	1.75
34	A2	300r bl, *rose*	4.75	3.75
35	A2	500r blk & red, *bl*	9.50	7.00
a.		Perf. 12½	20.00	12.50
		Nos. 14-35 (22)	55.70	38.60

Azores stamps were used in Angra from 1906 to 1931, when they were superseded by those of Portugal.

ANJOUAN

(än'jōō·än')

LOCATION—One of the Comoro Islands in the Mozambique Channel between Madagascar and Mozambique.

GOVT.—Former French colony.

AREA—89 sq. mi.

POP.—20,000 (approx. 1912).

CAPITAL—Mossamondu.

See Comoro Islands.

100 Centimes = 1 Franc

Navigation and Commerce

A1

Perf. 14x13½.

1892–1907 Typographed Unwmkd.

Name of Colony in Blue or Carmine.

No.	Type	Description	Unused	Used
1	A1	1c *blue*	70	70
2	A1	2c brn, *buff*	1.00	1.00
3	A1	4c cl, *lav*	1.75	1.50
4	A1	5c grn, *grnsh*	2.75	2.50
5	A1	10c *lavender*	3.25	3.00
6	A1	10c red ('00)	9.00	8.00
7	A1	15c bl, quadrille paper	3.75	3.50
8	A1	15c gray, *lt gray* ('00)	6.25	5.50
9	A1	20c red, *grn*	4.00	3.50
10	A1	25c *rose*	4.50	4.25
11	A1	25c bl ('00)	7.25	6.75
12	A1	30c brn, *bis*	9.00	7.25
13	A1	35c *yel* ('06)	4.50	4.00
14	A1	40c red, *straw*	15.00	12.50
15	A1	45c *gray grn* ('07)	65.00	55.00
16	A1	50c car, *rose*	16.00	13.50
17	A1	50c brn, *az* ('00)	11.50	9.00
18	A1	75c vio, *org*	15.00	13.00
19	A1	1fr brnz grn, *straw*	32.50	32.50
		Nos. 1-19 (19)	212.70	186.95

Issues of 1892-1907 Surcharged in Black or Carmine

05 10

1912

No.	Type	Description	Unused	Used
20	A1	5c on 2c brn, *buff*	25	25
21	A1	5c on 4c cl, *lav* (C)	25	25
22	A1	5c on 15c bl (C)	25	25
23	A1	5c on 20c red, *grn*	25	25
24	A1	5c on 25c *rose* (C)	25	25
25	A1	5c on 30c brn, *bis* (C)	35	35
26	A1	10c on 40c red, *straw*	45	45
27	A1	10c on 45c *gray grn* (C)	75	75
28	A1	10c on 50c car, *rose*	1.25	1.25
29	A1	10c on 75c vio, *org*	90	90
30	A1	10c on 1fr brnz grn, *straw*	1.00	1.00
		Nos. 20-30 (11)	5.95	5.95

Nos. 21-23, 30 exist in pairs, one without surcharge. Price, $225 each.

Two spacings between the surcharged numerals are found on Nos. 20 to 30.

Nos. 20 to 30 were available for use in Madagascar and the entire Comoro archipelago.

The stamps of Anjouan were superseded by those of Madagascar, and in 1950 by those of Comoro Islands.

ANNAM AND TONKIN

(ă·năm' & tŏn'kĭn')

LOCATION — In French Indo-China bordering on the China Sea on the east and Siam on the west.

GOVT.—French Protectorate.

AREA—97,503 sq. mi.

POP.—14,124,000 (approx. 1890).

CAPITALS—Annam: Hué.
Tonkin: Hanoi.

For administrative purposes, the Protectorates of Annam, Tonkin, Cambodia, Laos and the Colony of Cochin-China were grouped together and were known as French Indo-China.

100 Centimes = 1 Franc

Stamps of French Colonies, 1881-86 Surcharged in Black:

A&T 1 or **A&T 5**

1888 ***Perf. 14x13½.*** **Unwmkd.**

No.	Type	Description	Unused	Used
1	A9	1c on 2c brn, *buff*	15.00	13.50
a.		Inverted surch.	40.00	40.00
2	A9	1c on 4c cl, *lav*	12.50	11.00
a.		Inverted surch.	40.00	40.00
3	A9	5c on 10c *lav*	12.00	11.00
a.		Inverted surch.	40.00	40.00

A 5c on 2c was prepared but not issued.

Hyphen between "A" and "T"

No.	Type	Description	Unused	Used
7	A9	1c on 2c brn, *buff*	140.00	135.00
8	A9	1c on 4c cl, *lav*	200.00	165.00
9	A9	5c on 10c *lav*	115.00	110.00

In these surcharges there are different types of numerals and letters.

These stamps were superseded in 1892 by those of Indo-China.

ARABIA

See Saudi Arabia, Vol. IV.

ARGENTINA

(är'jĕn·tē'nȧ)

LOCATION—In South America.

GOVT.—Republic.

AREA—1,072,700 sq. mi.

POP.—26,060,000 (est. 1977).

CAPITAL—Buenos Aires.

100 Centavos = 1 Peso

Argentine Confederation.

Symbolical of the Argentine Confederation

A1 A2

Lithographed

1858, May 1 ***Imperf.*** **Unwmkd.**

No.	Type	Description	Unused	Used
1	A1	5c red	1.50	*12.00*
a.		Colon after '5'	1.50	*15.00*
b.		Colon after 'V'	1.50	*15.00*
2	A1	10c green	3.00	*75.00*
a.		Half used as 5c on cover		*275.00*
3	A1	15c blue	20.00	*200.00*
a.		One-third used as 5c on cover		*5,000.*

1860, Jan.

No.	Type	Description	Unused	Used
4	A2	5c red	3.00	*100.00*
4A	A2	10c green	7.50	
4B	A2	15c blue	35.00	

Nos. 4A and 4B were never placed in use. There are nine varieties of Nos. 1, 2 and 3, sixteen of No. 4 and eight of Nos. 4A and 4B. Forged cancellations are plentiful.

Prices for Unused

Unused prices for Nos. 5-15, 17-67 are for copies without gum. Copies with original gum command higher prices. From No. 68 onward, unused prices are for stamps with original gum.

Argentine Republic.

Seal of the Republic

A3

Broad "C" in "CENTAVOS", Accent on "U" of "REPUBLICA".

1862, Jan. 11

No.	Type	Description	Unused	Used
5	A3	5c rose	60.00	60.00
a.		rose lil	125.00	50.00
6	A3	10c green	250.00	110.00
b.		Diagonal half used as 5c on cover		*6,000.*
7	A3	15c blue	500.00	400.00
a.		Without accent on 'U'	*8,000.*	*4,000.*
b.		Tête bêche pair	*50,000.*	*30,000.*
i.		15c ultra	600.00	450.00

Broad "C" in "CENTAVOS", No Accent on "U"

1863

No.	Type	Description	Unused	Used
7C	A3	5c rose	30.00	35.00
d.		5c rose lil	150.00	165.00
e.		Worn plate	300.00	75.00
7F	A3	10c yel grn	500.00	250.00
g.		10c ol grn	*900.00*	350.00

Narrow "C" in "CENTAVOS", No Accent on "U"

1864

No.	Type	Description	Unused	Used
7H	A3	5c rose red	300.00	50.00

The so-called reprints of 10c and 15c are counterfeits. They have narrow "C" and straight lines in shield. Nos. 7C and 7H have been extensively counterfeited.

Rivadavia Issue.

Bernardino Rivadavia

A4 A5

Rivadavia

A6

Wmk. 84

Wmkd. RA in Italics (84)

1864-67 Engraved *Imperf.*

Clear Impressions.

No.	Type	Description	Unused	Used
8	A4	5c brn rose	2,500.	300.00
a.		5c org red, no gum ('67)	2,500.	300.00
9	A5	10c green	3,000.	2,250.
10	A6	15c blue	10,000.	6,000.

Perf. 11½.

Dull to Worn Impressions.

No.	Type	Description	Unused	Used
11	A4	5c brn rose ('65)	45.00	20.00
11B	A4	5c lake	125.00	30.00
12	A5	10c green	100.00	40.00
a.		Diagonal half used as 5c on cover		1,000.
13	A6	15c blue	250.00	150.00

1867-72 *Imperf.* Unwmkd.

No.	Type	Description	Unused	Used
14	A4	5c car ('72)	300.00	100.00
15	A4	5c rose	300.00	125.00
15A	A5	10c green	6,000.	6,000.
16	A6	15c blue	3,000.	3,000.

Nos. 15A-16 issued without gum.

1867 *Perf. 11½.*

No.	Type	Description	Unused	Used
17	A4	5c carmine	500.00	225.00

Nos. 14, 15 and 17 exist with part of papermaker's wmk. "LACROIX FRERES"

Rivadavia
A7

Manuel Belgrano
A8

José de San Martín
A9

Groundwork of Horizontal Lines.

1867-68 *Perf. 12.*

No.	Type	Description	Unused	Used
18	A7	5c vermilion	300.00	12.50
18A	A8	10c green	45.00	7.50
b.		Diagonal half used as 5c on cover		750.00
19	A9	15c blue	75.00	22.50

Groundwork of Crossed Lines.

No.	Type	Description	Unused	Used
20	A7	5c vermilion	15.00	1.00
21	A9	15c blue	150.00	17.50

See also Nos. 27, 33-34, 39 and types A19, A33, A34, A37.

Gen. Antonio G. Balcarce
A10

Mariano Moreno
A11

Carlos Maria de Alvear
A12

Gervasio Antonio Posadas
A13

Cornelio Saavedra
A14

1873

No.	Type	Description	Unused	Used
22	A10	1c purple	5.00	3.00
a.		1c gray vio	9.00	3.00
23	A11	4c brown	8.00	55
a.		4c red brn	25.00	3.00
24	A12	30c orange	150.00	24.00
25	A13	60c black	150.00	8.00
26	A14	90c blue	35.00	4.00

1873 Laid Paper.

No.	Type	Description	Unused	Used
27	A8	10c green	225.00	25.00

A15

A16

Surcharged in Black.

1877, Feb. Wove Paper

No.	Type	Description	Unused	Used
30	A15	1c on 5c ver	75.00	25.00
a.		Inverted surcharge	500.00	300.00
31	A15	2c on 5c ver	150.00	70.00
a.		Inverted surcharge	1,000.	750.00
32	A16	8c on 10c grn	175.00	50.00
b.		Inverted surcharge	750.00	600.00

Forgeries of these surcharges include the inverted and double varieties.

1876-77 *Rouletted*

No.	Type	Description	Unused	Used
33	A7	5c vermilion	225.00	100.00
34	A7	8c lake ('77)	35.00	50

Belgrano
A17

Dalmacio Vélez Sarsfield
A18

San Martín
A19

1878 *Rouletted*

No.	Type	Description	Unused	Used
35	A17	16c green	12.50	2.00
36	A18	20c blue	15.00	5.00
37	A19	24c blue	27.50	4.50

See also No. 56.

Vicente López
A20

Alvear
A21

1877-80 *Perf. 12.*

No.	Type	Description	Unused	Used
38	A20	2c yel grn	6.00	1.50
39	A7	8c lake ('80)	6.00	50
a.		8c brn lake	40.00	50
40	A21	25c lake ('78)	35.00	10.00

A22

A23

1882 Surcharged in Black.

No.	Type	Description	Unused	Used
41	A22	½c on 5c ver	1.35	1.00
a.		Double surcharge	35.00	20.00
b.		Inverted surcharge	15.00	12.50
c.		"PROVISORIO" omitted	22.50	20.00
d.		Fraction omitted	35.00	
e.		"PROVISOBIO"	12.50	12.50
f.		Pair, one without surcharge	65.00	

Perforated across Middle of Stamp.

No.	Type	Description	Unused	Used
42	A22	½c on 5c ver	1.75	1.35
a.		"PROVISORIQ"	15.00	12.50
b.		Inverted surch.	32.50	
c.		Pair, one without perforation across the stamp	20.00	

The "½ (PROVISORIO)" surcharge on Nos. 41-42 is found in two types: I. Small "P" and narrow "V." II. Large "P" and wider "V."

1882 Typographed *Perf. 12*

No.	Type	Description	Unused	Used
43	A23	½c brown	2.00	1.25
a.		Imperf., pair	35.00	35.00
44	A23	1c red, perf. 14	4.00	1.35
a.		Perf. 12	12.50	6.00
45	A23	12c ultra	90.00	15.00
a.		Perf. 14	65.00	15.00

Perf. 14

No.	Type	Description	Unused	Used
46	A23	12c grnsh bl	160.00	20.00

No. 21 Surcharged in Red:

1884
½
a

b

1884 Engr. *Perf. 12*

No.	Type	Description	Unused	Used
47	A9 (a)	½c on 15c bl	2.75	2.00
a.		Groundwork of horizontal lines	80.00	60.00
b.		Inverted surcharge	20.00	15.00
48	A9 (b)	1c on 15c bl	15.00	12.00
a.		Groundwork of horizontal lines	9.00	7.00
b.		Inverted surcharge	60.00	50.00
c.		Double surcharge	22.50	20.00
d.		Triple surch.	35.00	25.00

Nos. 20-21 Surcharged in Black

CUATRO
Centavos
1884
c

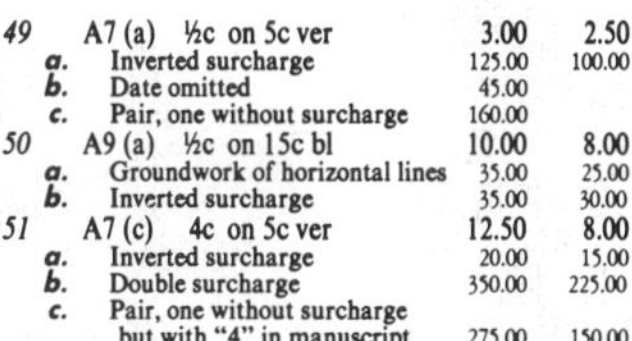

No.	Type	Description	Unused	Used
49	A7 (a)	½c on 5c ver	3.00	2.50
a.		Inverted surcharge	125.00	100.00
b.		Date omitted	45.00	
c.		Pair, one without surcharge	160.00	
50	A9 (a)	½c on 15c bl	10.00	8.00
a.		Groundwork of horizontal lines	35.00	25.00
b.		Inverted surcharge	35.00	30.00
51	A7 (c)	4c on 5c ver	12.50	8.00
a.		Inverted surcharge	20.00	15.00
b.		Double surcharge	350.00	225.00
c.		Pair, one without surcharge but with "4" in manuscript	275.00	150.00

A29

1884-85 Engraved *Perf. 12*

No.	Type	Description	Unused	Used
52	A29	½c red brn	1.35	60
a.		Imperf., pair	65.00	
53	A29	1c rose red	7.50	60
a.		Imperf., pair	65.00	
54	A29	12c grnsh bl ('85)	35.00	2.00
a.		12c dp bl	35.00	2.00
b.		Imperf., pair	65.00	

San Martin Type of 1878

1887 Engraved

No.	Type	Description	Unused	Used
56	A19	24c blue	25.00	2.00

Justo José de Urquiza
A30

López
A31

Miguel Juárez Celman
A32

Rivadavia (Large head)
A33

Rivadavia (Small head)
A34

Domingo F. Sarmiento
A35

Nicolás Avellaneda
A36

San Martin
A37

Julio A. Roca
A37a

Belgrano
A37b

Manuel Dorrego
A38

Moreno
A39

Bartolomé Mitre
A40

CINCO CENTAVOS.

Type I. A33. Shows collar on left side only.

Type II. A34. Shows collar on both sides. Lozenges in background larger and clearer than in type I.

1888–90 Lithographed *Perf. 11½*

57	A30	½c blue	75	60
a.		Imperf. pair	50.00	35.00
58	A31	2c yel grn	15.00	10.00
a.		Imperf., pair	40.00	
59	A32	3c bl grn	2.00	1.00
a.		Imperf., pair	25.00	17.50
b.		Imperf. vert., pair	35.00	
c.		Horizontal pair, imperf. between	40.00	
d.		Vertical pair, imperf. between	15.00	
60	A33	5c car, type I	17.50	3.00
61	A34	5c car, type II	12.50	1.00
a.		Imperf., pair		*75.00*
b.		Vertical pair, imperf. between	*50.00*	
62	A35	6c red	35.00	25.00
a.		Imperf., pair	*40.00*	
b.		Vertical pair, imperf. between	*50.00*	
c.		Perf. 12	75.00	60.00
63	A36	10c brown	25.00	1.75
a.		Imperf. pair	*40.00*	
64	A37	15c orange	25.00	2.75
c.		Imperf., pair		*150.00*
64A	A37a	20c green	20.00	2.00
64B	A37b	25c purple	25.00	2.75
65	A38	30c chocolate	35.00	4.00
a.		Imperf., pair	*200.00*	*150.00*
66	A39	40c sl, perf.12	35.00	5.00
a.		Perf. 11½	85.00	22.50
67	A40	50c blue	130.00	12.00
		Nos. 57-67 (13)	377.75	70.85

In this issue there are several varieties of each value, the difference between them being in the relative position of the head to the frame.

Urquiza
A41

Vélez Sarsfield
A42

Miguel Juárez Celman
A43

Rivadavia
(Large head)
A44

Sarmiento
A45

Juan Bautista Alberdi
A46

1888–89 Engr. *Perf. 11½, 11½x12*

68	A41	½c ultra	35	15
a.		Imperf. horiz., pair	25.00	15.00
b.		Imperf., pair	25.00	15.00
69	A42	1c brown	1.00	30
a.		Imperf. horiz., pair	25.00	
b.		Vertical pair, imperf. between	25.00	
c.		Imperf. pair	22.50	
70	A43	3c bl grn	2.00	60
71	A44	5c rose	3.00	20
a.		Imperf., pair	32.50	25.00
72	A45	6c bl blk	2.00	70
a.		Imperf., pair	62.50	62.50
b.		Perf. 11½x12	6.00	1.50
73	A46	12c blue	3.75	85
a.		Imperf., pair	20.00	
b.		bluish paper	4.50	1.25
c.		Perf. 11½	9.00	3.00
		Nos. 68-73 (6)	12.10	2.80

Nos. 69-70 exist with papermakers' watermarks.

See also Nos. 77 and 89.

José Maria Paz
A48

Santiago Derqui
A49

Rivadavia
(Small head)
A50

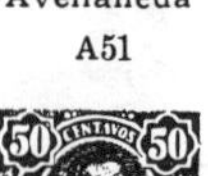

Avellaneda
A51

Moreno
A53

Mitre
A54

Posadas—A55

A56

1890 Engraved *Perf. 11½*

75	A48	¼c green	20	10
76	A49	2c violet	1.25	30
a.		2c pur	1.25	30
b.		2c sl	2.00	50
c.		Horizontal pair, imperf. between	22.50	
d.		Imperf., pair	27.50	
e.		Perf. 11½x12	2.50	40
77	A50	5c carmine	2.75	12
a.		Imperf., pair	37.50	30.00
b.		Perf. 11½x12	3.00	60
78	A51	10c brown	2.50	40
b.		Imperf., pair		125.00
80	A53	40c ol grn	5.00	1.25
a.		Imperf., pair	27.50	
81	A54	50c orange	5.00	1.25
a.		Imperf., pair	40.00	
b.		Perf. 11½x12	6.00	1.25
82	A55	60c black	20.00	4.00
a.		Imperf., pair	50.00	50.00
		Nos. 75-82 (7)	36.70	7.42

Type A50 differs from type A44 in having the head smaller, the letters of "Cinco Centavos" not as tall, and the curved ornaments at sides close to the first and last letters of "Republica Argentina".

1890 *Perf. 11½x12*

Black or Red Lithographed Surcharge.

83	A56	¼c on 12c bl (Blk)	50	50
a.		Perf. 11½	50.00	30.00
84	A56	¼c on 12c bl (R)	60	50
a.		Double surcharge	75.00	75.00
b.		Perf. 11½	10.00	3.00

Rivadavia
A57

José de San Martin
A58

Gregorio Araoz de Lamadrid
A59

Admiral Guillermo Brown
A60

1891 Engraved. *Perf. 11½*

85	A57	8c car rose	2.00	35
a.		Imperf., pair	85.00	
86	A58	1p dp bl	55.00	10.00
87	A59	5p ultra	275.00	35.00
88	A60	20p green	350.00	90.00

A 10p brown and a 50p red were prepared but not issued.

Prices $1,500 and $1,000.

Vélez Sarsfield
A61

1890 *Perf. 11½*

89	A61	1c brown	1.50	40

Type A61 is a re-engraving of A42. The figure "1" in each upper corner has a short horizontal serif instead of a long one pointing downward. In type A61 the first and last letters of "Correos y Telegrafos" are closer to the curved ornaments below than in type A42. Background is of horizontal lines (crosshatching on No. 69).

"Santa Maria," "Niña" and "Pinta"—A62

Wmk. 85

Wmk. 86

The Small Sun (85) is 4½mm. in diameter and the Large Sun (86) 6mm.

Wmkd. Small Sun. (85)

1892, Oct. 12 *Perf. 11½*

90	A62	2c lt bl	7.50	4.50
a.		Dbl. impression	250.00	
91	A62	5c dk bl	10.00	6.00

Discovery of America, 400th anniv. Counterfeits of Nos. 90-91 are litho.

Rivadavia
A63

Belgrano
A64

San Martín
A65

Perf. 11½, 12 and Compound.

1892–95 Wmk. 85

92	A63	½c dl bl	30	10
a.		½c brt ultra	35.00	10.00
b.		Imperf., pair	40.00	
93	A63	1c brown	60	8
a.		Imperf., pair	40.00	
94	A63	2c green	60	8
a.		Imperf., pair	17.50	
95	A63	3c org ('95)	1.50	10
96	A63	5c carmine	2.00	5
a.		Imperf., pair	17.50	17.50
b.		5c grn (error)	500.00	375.00
98	A64	10c car rose	9.00	12
a.		Imperf., pair	45.00	
99	A64	12c dp bl ('93)	9.00	40
a.		Imperf., pair	45.00	
100	A64	16c gray	16.50	1.00
a.		Imperf., pair	45.00	
101	A64	24c gray brn	16.50	1.00
a.		Imperf., pair	45.00	
b.		Perf. 12	35.00	10.00
102	A64	50c bl grn	24.00	1.00
a.		Imperf., pair	35.00	
b.		Perf. 12	35.00	4.00
103	A65	1p lake ('93)	12.50	1.35
a.		1p red brn	20.00	7.00
b.		Imperf., pair	40.00	
104	A65	2p dk grn	25.00	3.50
a.		Perf. 12	100.00	40.00
105	A65	5p dk bl	45.00	4.00
a.		Imperf., pair	95.00	
		Nos. 92-105 (13)	162.50	12.78

Part-perforate varieties of Nos. 92–98 include vert. or horiz. pairs imperf. between and pairs imperf. vert. or horiz. Price $6–$35.

The high values of this and succeeding issues are frequently punched with the word "INUTILIZADO," parts of the letters showing on each stamp. These punched stamps sell for only a small fraction of the catalogue prices.

Reprints of No. 96b have white gum. The original stamp has yellowish gum. *Price $125.*

1896–97 Wmkd. Large Sun. (86)

106	A63	½c slate	50	10
a.		½c gray bl	50	10
b.		½c ind	50	10
107	A63	1c brown	60	5
108	A63	2c yel grn	1.00	5
109	A63	3c orange	1.00	10
110	A63	5c carmine	1.00	5
a.		Imperf., pair	30.00	
111	A64	10c car rose	9.00	5
112	A64	12c dp bl	4.50	5
a.		Imperf., pair	*40.00*	
113	A64	16c gray	12.50	85
114	A64	24c gray brn	14.00	2.25
a.		Imperf., pair	22.50	
115	A64	30c org ('97)	14.00	85
116	A64	50c bl grn	14.00	85
117	A64	80c dl vio	20.00	1.10
118	A65	1p lake	30.00	1.10
119	A65	1p20c blk ('97)	15.50	4.00
120	A65	2p dk grn	20.00	10.00
121	A65	5p dk bl	100.00	10.00
a.		Perf. 12	275.00	70.00
		Nos. 106-121 (16)	257.60	31.45

Allegory, Liberty Seated
A66 A67

Perf. 11½, 12 and Compound

1899-1903

122 A66 ½c yel brn 12 5
a. Imperf., pair 22.50
123 A66 1c green 30 4
a. Imperf., pair 32.50
124 A66 2c slate 30 4
a. Imperf., pair 7.50 5.00
125 A66 3c org ('01) 1.00 30
a. Imperf., pair 125.00 85.00
126 A66 4c yel ('03) 2.00 35
127 A66 5c car rose 30 5
a. Imperf., pair 7.50 6.00
128 A66 6c blk ('03) 1.10 40
a. Imperf., pair 40.00
129 A66 10c dk grn 2.00 5
a. Imperf., pair 40.00
130 A66 12c dl bl 1.50 60
131 A66 12c ol grn ('01) 1.50 50
132 A66 15c sea grn ('01) 4.00 25
a. Imperf., pair 40.00
132B A66 15c dl bl ('01) 3.00 30
133 A66 16c orange 11.00 8.00
134 A66 20c claret 3.00 15
135 A66 24c violet 5.00 1.50
136 A66 30c rose 11.00 85
137 A66 30c ver ('01) 5.50 30
a. 30c scar 70.00 3.00
138 A66 50c brt bl 7.00 35
139 A67 1p bl & blk, perf. 11½ 17.50 1.00
a. Center inverted *2,000.* *700.00*
b. Perf. 12 250.00 75.00
140 A67 5p org & blk 70.00 15.00
Punch cancellation 1.25
a. Center inverted *2,000.*
141 A67 10p grn & blk 80.00 17.50
Punch cancellation 1.25
a. Center invtd. *4,500.*
Punch cancellation 1,000.
142 A67 20p red & blk 250.00 45.00
Punch cancellation 60
a. Center inverted (punch canc.) *2,250.*
Nos. 122-142 (22) 477.12 92.58

Part-perforate varieties of Nos. 122–129 include vert. or horiz. pairs imperf. between and pairs imperf. vert. or horiz. Price 50 cents to $10.

River Port of Rosario
A68

1902, Oct. 26 ***Perf. 11½, 11½x12***

143 A68 5c dp bl 7.00 3.00
a. Imperf., pair 110.00

Completion of port facilities at Rosario.

San Martín
A69 A70

Perf. 13½, 13½x12½.

1908-09 **Typographed.**

144 A69 ½c violet 20 10
145 A69 1c brnsh buff 30 10
146 A69 2c chocolate 90 10
147 A69 3c green 1.10 50
148 A69 4c redsh vio 2.25 50
149 A69 5c carmine 50 10
150 A69 6c ol bis 1.25 40
151 A69 10c gray grn 2.50 15
152 A69 12c yel buff 65 60
153 A69 12c dk bl ('09) 2.00 20
154 A69 15c ap grn 2.75 1.35
155 A69 20c ultra 2.00 15
156 A69 24c red brn 5.00 1.00
157 A69 30c dl rose 8.00 1.00
158 A69 50c black 7.50 70
159 A70 1p sl bl & pink 17.50 2.75
Nos. 144-159 (16) 54.40 9.70

The 1c in blue was not issued. Price $250.
Wmk. 86 appears on ½, 1, 6, 20, 24 and 50c. Other values have similar wmk. with wavy rays.
Stamps lacking wmk. are from outer rows printed on sheet margin.

Centenary of the Republic Issue.

Pyramid of May
A71

Nicolás Rodríguez Peña and Hipólito Vieytes
A72

Meeting at Peña's Home
A73

Designs: 3c, Miguel de Azcuénaga (1754–1833) and Father Manuel M. Alberti (1763–1811). 4c, Viceroy's house and Fort Buenos Aires. 5c, Cornelio Saavedra (1759–1829). 10c, Antonio Luis Beruti (1772–1842) and French distributing badges. 12c, Congress building. 20c, Juan José Castelli (1764–1812) and Domingo Matheu (1765–1831). 24c, First council. 30c, Manuel Belgrano (1770–1820) and Juan Larrea (1782–1847). 50c, First meeting of republican government, May 25, 1810. 1p, Mariano Moreno (1778–1811) and Juan José Paso (1758–1833). 5p, Oath of the Junta. 10p, Centenary Monument. 20p, José Francisco de San Martín (1778–1850).

Inscribed "1810 1910"
Various Frames

1910, May 1 **Engraved** ***Perf. 11½***

160 A71 ½c bl & gray bl 60 20
a. Center inverted *800.00*
161 A72 1c bl grn & blk 60 15
a. Center inverted *800.00*
b. Horiz. pair, imperf. between *80.00*
162 A73 2c ol & gray 45 10
a. Center inverted *950.00*
163 A72 3c green 1.25 25
164 A73 4c dk bl & grn 1.25 40
a. Center inverted *450.00*
165 A71 5c carmine 1.00 5
166 A73 10c yel brn & blk 3.00 35
167 A73 12c brt bl 2.50 40
a. Center inverted *800.00*
168 A72 20c gray brn & blk 4.00 60
169 A73 24c org brn & bl 3.00 1.50
170 A72 30c lil & blk 3.00 1.10
171 A71 50c car & blk 8.00 1.50
a. Center inverted *800.00*
172 A72 1p brt bl 16.00 6.00
173 A73 5p org & vio 125.00 50.00
Punch cancel 4.00
a. Center inverted *800.00*
174 A71 10p org & blk 200.00 110.00
Punch cancel 5.00
175 A71 20p dp bl & ind 300.00 150.00
Punch cancel 7.50
Nos. 160-175 (16) 669.65 322.60

Domingo F. Sarmiento — Agriculture
A87 A88

1911, May 15 **Typo.** ***Perf. 13½***

176 A87 5c gray brn & blk 1.00 60

Issued to commemorate the centenary of the birth of Domingo Faustino Sarmiento (1811-88), president of Argentina, 1868-74.

Wmkd. Large Sun. (86)

1911 **Engraved.** ***Perf. 12.***

Size: 19x25mm.

177 A88 5c vermilion 60 10
a. Booklet pane of 4
b. Booklet pane of 6
178 A88 12c dp bl 7.50 30

1911 Typographed *Perf. 13½x12½*

Size: 18x23mm.

179 A88 ½c violet 15 8
180 A88 1c brn ocher 20 8
181 A88 2c chocolate 30 6
a. Perf. 13½ 7.50 3.00
b. Imperf., pair *45.00*
182 A88 3c green 75 15
183 A88 4c brn vio 60 35
184 A88 10c gray grn 90 10
185 A88 20c ultra 7.50 1.50
186 A88 24c red brn 9.00 5.00
187 A88 30c claret 3.00 85
188 A88 50c black 15.00 1.50
Nos. 179-188 (10) 37.40 9.67

The 5c dull red is a proof.

Wmk. 87

Wmkd. Honeycomb. (87) (Horizontal or Vertical)

1912–14 ***Perf. 13½x12½***

189 A88 ½c violet 30 10
a. Perf. 13½ 1.50 50
190 A88 1c ocher 30 10
a. Perf. 13½ 1.50 50
191 A88 2c chocolate 60 6
a. Perf. 13½ 1.50 30
192 A88 3c green 1.10 30
a. perf. 13½ 65.00 30.00
193 A88 4c brn vio 1.10 30
a. Perf. 13½ 3.00 1.25
194 A88 5c red 30 5
a. Perf. 13½ 60 10
195 A88 10c dp grn 2.50 15
196 A88 12c dp bl 2.50 4
a. Perf. 13½ 6.00 1.50
197 A88 20c ultra 15.00 1.25
a. Perf. 13½ 9.00 1.25
198 A88 24c red brn 6.00 3.00
199 A88 30c claret 15.00 1.10
200 A88 50c black 9.00 1.10
Nos. 189-200 (12) 53.70 7.55

See also Nos. 208–212.

A89

1912-13 ***Perf. 13½.***

201 A89 1p dl bl & rose 11.00 1.75
Punch cancel 25
202 A89 5p sl & ol grn 30.00 10.00
Punch cancel 50
203 A89 10p vio & bl 125.00 16.50
Punch cancel 1.25
204 A89 20p bl & cl 300.00 100.00
Punch cancel 1.75

1915 ***Perf. 13½x12½.*** **Unwmkd.**

208 A88 1c ocher 75 12
209 A88 2c chocolate 75 8
212 A88 5c red 60 7

Only these denominations were printed on paper without watermark.
Other stamps of the series are known unwatermarked but they are from the outer rows of sheets the other parts of which are watermarked.

Francisco Narciso de Laprida — Declaration of Independence
A90 A91

José de San Martín
A92 A92a

Perf. 13½, 13½x12½.

1916, July 9 Lithographed Wmk. 87

215 A90 ½c violet 30 6
216 A90 1c buff 40 8

Perf. 13½x12½

217 A90 2c chocolate 30 10
218 A90 3c green 75 15
219 A90 4c red vio 1.10 15

Perf. 13½

220 A91 5c red 50 5
a. Imperf., pair *65.00*
221 A91 10c gray grn 2.00 15
222 A92 12c blue 1.10 20
223 A92 20c ultra 1.10 25
224 A92 24c red brn 3.00 1.25
225 A92 30c claret 3.00 60
226 A92 50c gray blk 6.00 75
227 A92a 1p sl bl & red 15.00 6.00
Punch cancel 60
a. Imperf., pair *400.00*
228 A92a 5p blk & gray grn 160.00 75.00
Punch cancel 6.00
229 A92a 10p vio & bl 250.00 135.00
Punch cancel 4.00
230 A92a 20p dl bl & cl 225.00 120.00
Punch cancel 1.50
a. Imperf., pair 600.00
Nos. 215-230 (16) 669.55 339.79

Issued to commemorate the centenary of Argentina's declaration of independence of Spain, July 9, 1816.
The watermark is either vertical or horizontal on Nos. 215–220, 222; only vertical on No. 221, and only horizontal on Nos. 223–230.

A93

A94

A94a

1917 ***Perf. 13½, 13½x12½***

231	A93	½c violet	30	6
232	A93	1c buff	30	6
233	A93	2c brown	30	4
234	A93	3c lt grn	1.00	10
235	A93	4c red vio	1.00	50
236	A93	5c red	30	3
a.		Imperf., pair	20.00	
237	A93	10c gray grn	2.00	10

Perf. 13½

238	A94	12c blue	1.25	10
239	A94	20c ultra	2.00	30
240	A94	24c red brn	6.50	3.00
241	A94	30c claret	6.50	85
242	A94	50c gray blk	6.00	90
243	A94a	1p sl bl & red	6.00	60
244	A94a	5p blk & gray grn	22.50	4.00
		Punch cancel		1.00
245	A94a	10p vio & bl	55.00	16.00
		Punch cancel		60
246	A94a	20p dl bl & cl	125.00	25.00
		Punch cancel		60
a.		Center inverted	1,500.	1,100.
		Nos. 231-246 (16)	235.95	51.64

The watermark is either vertical or horizontal on Nos. 231–236, 238; only vertical on No. 237, and only horizontal on Nos. 239–246.

Juan Gregorio Pujol

A95

1918, June 15 **Litho.** ***Perf. 13½***

247	A95	5c bis & gray	1.00	30

Issued to commemorate the centenary of the birth of Juan G. Pujol (1817–61), lawyer and legislator.

Perf. 13½, 13½x12½

1918–19 **Unwmkd.**

248	A93	½c violet	20	10
249	A93	1c buff	20	6
a.		Imperf., pair	25.00	
250	A93	2c brown	25	5
251	A93	3c lt grn	45	10
252	A93	4c red vio	45	15
253	A93	5c red	25	5
254	A93	10c gray grn	2.00	5

Perf. 13½

255	A94	12c blue	2.00	8
256	A94	20c ultra	3.00	8
257	A94	24c red brn	3.50	85
258	A94	30c claret	4.25	50
259	A94	50c gray blk	10.00	45
		Nos. 248-259 (12)	26.55	2.52

The stamps of this issue sometimes show letters of papermakers' watermarks.

There were two printings, in 1918 and 1923, using different ink and paper.

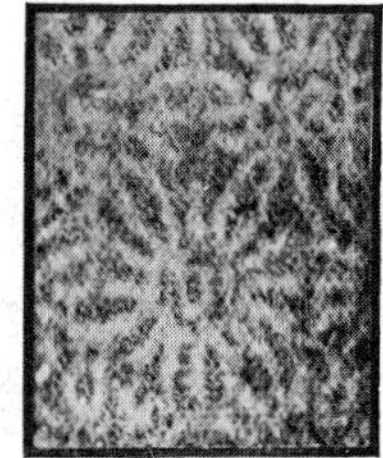

Wmk. 88

Wmkd. Multiple Suns. (88)

1920 ***Perf. 13½, 13½x12½***

264	A93	½c violet	30	10
265	A93	1c buff	40	6
266	A93	2c brown	40	8
267	A93	3c green	2.25	60
268	A93	4c red vio	3.00	1.50
269	A93	5c red	60	5
270	A93	10c gray grn	5.00	12

Perf. 13½

271	A94	12c blue	2.75	15
272	A94	20c ultra	4.00	15
274	A94	30c claret	9.00	1.10
275	A94	50c gray blk	7.50	1.75
		Nos. 264-275 (11)	35.20	5.66

See also Nos. 292–300, 304–307A, 310–314, 318, 322.

Belgrano's Mausoleum

A96

Gen. Manuel Belgrano

A98

Creation of Argentine Flag

A97

1920, June 18 ***Perf. 13½***

280	A96	2c red	75	25
a.		Perf. 13½x12½	75	25
281	A97	5c rose & bl	75	10
282	A98	12c grn & bl	1.50	1.10

Issued to commemorate the centenary of the death of Manuel Belgrano (1770–1820), Argentine general, patriot and diplomat.

Gen. Justo José de Urquiza

A99

Bartolomé Mitre

A100

1920, Nov. 11

283	A99	5c gray bl	45	20

Issued to honor Gen. Justo José de Urquiza (1801–1870), president of Argentina, 1854–1860. See also No. 303.

1921, June 26 **Unwmkd.**

284	A100	2c vio brn	50	25
285	A100	5c lt bl	50	20

Issued to commemorate the centenary of the birth of Bartolomé Mitre (1821–1906), president of Argentina, 1862–65.

Allegory, Pan-America

A101

1921, Aug. 25 ***Perf. 13½***

286	A101	3c violet	1.10	40
287	A101	5c blue	1.50	20
288	A101	10c vio brn	2.75	50
289	A101	12c rose	4.00	1.00

Inscribed "Buenos Aires—Agosto de 1921"

A102

Inscribed "Republica Argentina"

A103

1921, Oct. ***Perf. 13½x12½***

290	A102	5c rose	50	8
a.		Perf. 13½	2.25	8
291	A103	5c rose	2.75	6
a.		Perf. 13½	4.00	6

Issued to commemorate the first Pan-American Postal Congress, held at Buenos Aires, August, 1921.

See also Nos. 308–309, 319.

Wmk. 89

In this watermark the face of the sun is 7 mm. in diameter, the rays are heavier than in the large sun watermark of 1896-1911 and the watermarks are placed close together, so that parts of several frequently appear on one stamp. This paper was intended to be used for fiscal stamps and is usually referred to as "fiscal sun paper".

Wmkd. Large Sun. (89)

1920 ***Perf. 13½, 13½x12½***

292	A93	½c violet	2.50	1.00
293	A93	1c buff	5.50	1.00
294	A93	2c brown	4.00	1.00
297	A93	5c red	5.50	60
298	A93	10c gray grn	5.50	60

Perf. 13½

299	A94	12c blue	3,000.	125.00
300	A94	20c ultra	15.00	1.25
		Nos. 292-298, 300 (6)	38.00	5.45

1920

303	A99	5c gray bl	450.00	300.00

Wmk. 90

In 1928 the watermark R. A. in Sun (90) was slightly modified, making the diameter of the Sun 9 mm. instead of 10 mm. Several types of this watermark exist.

Wmkd. RA in Sun. (90)

1922–23 ***Perf. 13½, 13½x12½***

304	A93	½c violet	25	10
305	A93	1c buff	25	5
306	A93	2c brown	25	5
307	A93	3c green	75	50
307A	A93	4c red vio	6.00	1.50
308	A102	5c rose	3.75	20
309	A103	5c red	2.50	10
310	A93	10c gray grn	7.50	50

Perf. 13½

311	A94	12c blue	1.10	20
312	A94	20c ultra	2.00	10
313	A94	24c red brn	15.00	7.00
314	A94	30c claret	9.00	75
		Nos. 304-314 (12)	48.35	11.05

Paper with Gray Overprint RA in Sun.

Perf. 13½, 13½x12½

1922-23 **Unwmkd.**

318	A93	2c brown	4.00	1.25
319	A103	5c red	2.50	35

Perf. 13½

322	A94	20c ultra	25.00	1.75

San Martín

A104 A105

With Period after Value.

1923, May **Litho.** **Wmk. 90**

323	A104	½c red vio	40	30
324	A104	1c buff	60	15
325	A104	2c dk brn	60	6
326	A104	3c lt grn	60	35
327	A104	4c red brn	60	30
328	A104	5c red	60	5
329	A104	10c dl grn	5.00	15
330	A104	12c dp bl	75	15
331	A104	20c ultra	2.00	8
332	A104	24c lt brn	5.00	2.75
333	A104	30c claret	15.00	85
334	A104	50c black	7.50	60

Without Period after Value.

Wmkd. Honeycomb. (87) ***Perf. 13½***

335	A105	1p bl & red	7.50	20
336	A105	5p gray lil & grn	25.00	3.00
		Punch cancel		75
337	A105	10p cl & bl	90.00	17.50
		Punch cancel		1.25
338	A105	20p sl & brn lake	140.00	45.00
		Punch cancel		70
a.		Center inverted		
		Nos. 323-338 (16)	301.15	71.49

Nos. 335 to 338 and 353 to 356 cancelled with round or oval killers in purple (revenue cancellations) sell for one-fifth to one-half the price of postally used copies.

Design of 1923.

Without Period after Value.

Wmkd. RA in Sun. (90)

1923–31 ***Perf. 13½, 13½x12½***

340	A104	½c red vio	12	4
341	A104	1c buff	12	4
342	A104	2c dk brn	12	4
343	A104	3c green	20	4
a.		Imperf., pair	15.00	
b.		Typographed	2.00	40
344	A104	4c red brn	75	5
345	A104	5c red	12	3
a.		Typographed	3.75	75
346	A104	10c dl grn	50	3
a.		Typographed	6.00	30
347	A104	12c dp bl	90	10
a.		Typographed	12.50	2.25
348	A104	20c ultra	1.25	5
a.		Typographed	50.00	2.50
349	A104	24c lt brn	3.00	1.50
350	A104	25c purple	1.50	5
a.		Typographed	30.00	1.10
351	A104	30c claret	3.00	10
a.		Typographed	22.50	60
352	A104	50c black	3.00	10
353	A105	1p bl & red	3.75	10

No.	Type	Description	Unused	Used
354	A105	5p dk vio & grn	25.00	1.00
a.		Punch cancel		30
355	A105	10p cl & bl	50.00	4.50
		Punch cancel		35
356	A105	20p sl & lake	80.00	15.00
		Punch cancel		35
		Nos. 340-356 (17)	173.33	22.77

There were two printings of many of the stamps of type A104: lithographed (1923-24), clear impression, and typographed (1931-33), rough impression with heavy shading about the eyes and nose. The typographed stamps were issued only in coils. Nos. 343 and 346 are known without watermark.

The 1c through 5c and 12c through 30c may be found in pairs, one without period.

See note after No. 338. See also Nos. 362-368.

Rivadavia
A106

1926, Feb. 8 ***Perf. 13½***

No.	Type	Description	Unused	Used
357	A106	5c rose	75	20

Issued in commemoration of the centenary of the Presidency of Bernardino Rivadavia.

Rivadavia
A108

San Martín
A109

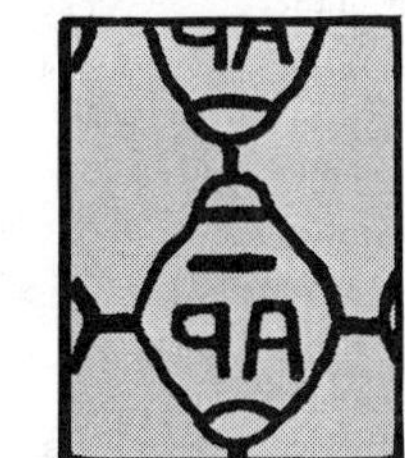

General Post Office, 1926
A110

General Post Office, 1826
A111

1926, July 1 ***Perf. 13½x12½***

No.	Type	Description	Unused	Used
358	A108	3c gray grn	25	10
359	A109	5c red	25	8

Perf. 13½

No.	Type	Description	Unused	Used
360	A110	12c dp bl	1.50	30
361	A111	25c chocolate	2.75	15
a.		"1326" for "1826"	5.00	60

Centenary of the Post Office.

Wmk. 205

The letters "A. P." in the watermark are the initials of "AHORRO POSTAL". This paper was formerly used exclusively for Postal Savings stamps.

Type of 1923-31 Issue.
Without Period after Value.
Wmk. AP in Oval. (205)

1927 ***Perf. 13½x12½***

No.	Type	Description	Unused	Used
362	A104	½c red vio	40	30
a.		Pelure paper	3.00	2.50
363	A104	1c buff	40	30
364	A104	2c dk brn	40	15
a.		Pelure paper	60	30
365	A104	5c red	50	15
a.		Period after value	6.00	3.00
b.		Pelure paper	75	35
366	A104	10c dl grn	7.50	3.00
367	A104	20c ultra	30.00	3.00

Perf. 13½

No.	Type	Description	Unused	Used
368	A105	1p bl & red	60.00	9.00
		Nos. 362-368 (7)	99.20	15.90

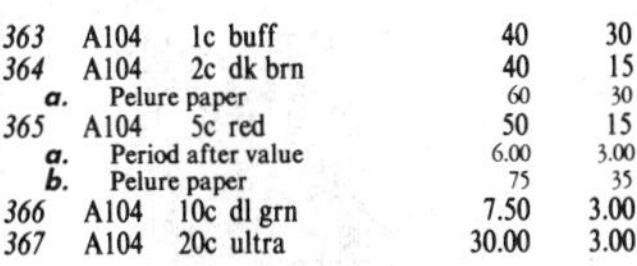

Arms of Argentina and Brazil
A112

Wmkd. RA in Sun. (90)

1928, Aug. 27 ***Perf. 12½x13***

No.	Type	Description	Unused	Used
369	A112	5c rose red	1.50	50
370	A112	12c dp bl	3.00	1.00

Commemorative of the centenary of peace between the Empire of Brazil and the United Provinces of the Rio de la Plata.

Allegory, Discovery of the New World
A113

"Spain" and "Argentina"
A114

"America" Offering Laurels to Columbus
A115

1929, Oct. 12 **Litho.** ***Perf. 13½***

No.	Type	Description	Unused	Used
371	A113	2c lil brn	1.25	30
372	A114	5c lt red	1.40	12
373	A115	12c dl bl	2.50	1.10

Issued to commemorate the 437th anniversary of the discovery of America by Columbus.

Spirit of Victory Attending Insurgents
A116

March of the Victorious Insurgents
A117

Perf. 13½x12½ **(A116),** ***12½x13*** **(A117)**

1930

No.	Type	Description	Unused	Used
374	A116	½c vio gray	30	20
375	A116	1c myr grn	40	20
376	A117	2c dl vio	50	10
377	A116	3c green	75	35
378	A116	4c violet	60	35
379	A116	5c rose red	30	10
380	A116	10c gray blk	1.75	50
381	A117	12c dl bl	1.25	35
382	A117	20c ocher	1.25	30
383	A117	24c red brn	5.00	2.25
384	A117	25c green	6.00	2.25
385	A117	30c dp vio	9.00	3.00
386	A117	50c black	13.50	4.00
387	A117	1p sl bl & red	25.00	15.00
388	A117	2p blk & org	45.00	15.00
389	A117	5p dl grn & blk	135.00	60.00
390	A117	10p dp red brn & dl bl	175.00	75.00
391	A117	20p yel grn & dl bl	500.00	175.00
392	A117	50p dk grn & vio	1,350.	1,000.
		Nos. 374-392 (19)	2,270.60	1,353.95

Issued to commemorate the Revolution of 1930.

Nos. 387 to 392 with oval (parcel post) cancellation sell for one-fifth of above prices.

1931 ***Perf. 12½x13***

No.	Type	Description	Unused	Used
393	A117	½c red vio	20	15
394	A117	1c gray blk	1.50	60
395	A117	3c green	75	35
396	A117	4c red brn	60	30
397	A117	5c red	20	5
a.		Plane omitted, top left corner	5.00	2.50
398	A117	10c dl grn	1.50	40
		Nos. 393-398 (6)	4.75	1.85

Issued to commemorate the Revolution of 1930.

Stamps of 1924-25 Overprinted in Red or Green

•6•
Septiembre
1930 - 1931

Perf. 13½, 13½x12½

1931, Sept. 6

No.	Type	Description	Unused	Used
399	A104	3c grn (R)	35	35
400	A104	10c dl grn (R)	1.00	1.00
401	A104	30c cl (G)	5.50	3.50
402	A104	50c blk (R)	5.50	3.50

Overprinted in Blue

1930
Septiembre
6
1931

No.	Type	Description	Unused	Used
403	A105	1p bl & red	6.50	3.50
404	A105	5p dk vio & grn	100.00	32.50

No. 388 Overprinted in Blue

6 Septiembre 1931

Perf. 12½x13

No.	Type	Description	Unused	Used
405	A117	2p blk & org	20.00	12.50
		Nos. 399-405 (7)	138.85	56.85

Issued in commemoration of the first anniversary of the Revolution of 1930.

Refrigeration Compressor
A118

Lithographed.

1932, Aug. 29 ***Perf. 13½x12½***

No.	Type	Description	Unused	Used
406	A118	3c green	75	40
407	A118	10c scarlet	2.50	25
408	A118	12c gray bl	6.00	1.50

Issued to commemorate the sixth International Refrigeration Congress.

Port of La Plata
A119

President Julio A. Roca
A120

Municipal Palace
A121

Cathedral of La Plata
A122

Dardo Rocha
A123

Perf. 13½x13, 13x13½ **(10c)**

1933, Jan.

No.	Type	Description	Unused	Used
409	A119	3c grn & dk brn	60	40
410	A120	10c org & dk vio	90	30
411	A121	15c dk bl & dp bl	6.00	3.00
412	A122	20c vio & yel brn	3.00	1.50
413	A123	30c dk grn & vio brn	22.50	8.50
		Nos. 409-413 (5)	33.00	13.70

Issued in commemoration of the 50th anniversary of the founding of the city of La Plata, November 19th, 1882.

Christ of the Andes
A124

Buenos Aires Cathedral
A125

Perf. 13x13½, 13½x13

1934, Oct. 1

No.	Type	Description	Unused	Used
414	A124	10c rose & brn	1.25	35
415	A125	15c dk bl	2.50	85

Issued to commemorate the 32nd International Eucharistic Congress, Oct. 10–14, 1934.

"Liberty" with Arms of Brazil and Argentina
A126

Symbolical of "Peace" and "Friendship"
A127

1935, May 15 ***Perf. 13x13½***

416	A126	10c red	1.25	30
417	A127	15c blue	2.50	70

Visit of Pres. Getulio Vargas of Brazil.

Belgrano
A128

Sarmiento
A129

Urquiza
A130

Louis Braille
A131

San Martin
A132

Brown
A133

Moreno
A134

Alberdi
A135

Nicolás Avellaneda
A136

Rivadavia
A137

Mitre
A138

Bull (Cattle Breeding)
A139

Martín Güemes
A140

Agriculture
A141

Oil Well (Petroleum)
A144

Merino Sheep (Wool)
A142

Sugar Cane
A143

Map of South America
A145 A146

Fruit
A147

Iguassú Falls (Scenic Wonders)
A148

Grapes (Vineyards)
A149

Cotton
A150

Two types of the 20c.
Type I—Inscribed Juan Martín Guemes.
Type II—Inscribed Martin Güemes.

Lithographed

Wmkd. RA in Sun. (90)

1935-51 ***Perf. 13, 13½x13, 13x13½***

418	A128	½c red vio	12	3
419	A129	1c buff	12	3
a.		Typographed	12	3
420	A130	2c dk brn	12	3
421	A131	2½c blk ('39)	12	6
422	A132	3c green	20	4
423	A132	3c lt gray ('39)	12	3
424	A134	3c lt gray ('46)	12	6
425	A133	4c lt gray	20	3
426	A133	4c sage grn ('39)	20	3
427	A134	5c yel brn	1.75	3
a.		Tête bêche pair, typo.	8.00	4.00
b.		Booklet pane of 8, typo.		
c.		Booklet pane of 4, typo.		
d.		Typographed	20	4
428	A135	6c ol grn	40	4
429	A136	8c org ('39)	20	8
430	A137	10c car, typo.	20	3
431	A137	10c brn ('42)	20	3
a.		Typographed	40	4
432	A138	12c brown	35	10
433	A138	12c red ('39)	15	5
434	A139	15c sl bl ('36)	60	5
435	A139	15c pale ultra ('39)	75	4
436	A140	15c lt gray bl (II) ('42)	55.00	2.25
437	A140	20c lt ultra (I)	60	6
438	A140	20c lt ultra (II) ('36)	60	4
439	A140	20c bl gray (II) ('39)	60	4
439A	A139	20c dk bl & pale bl, 22x33mm ('42)	1.50	3
440	A139	20c bl ('51)	20	3
a.		Typographed	20	3
441	A141	25c car ('36)	40	3
442	A142	30c org brn ('36)	90	4
443	A143	40c dk vio ('36)	75	5
444	A144	50c red & org ('36)	60	3
445	A145	1p brn blk & lt bl ('36)	27.50	60
446	A146	1p brn blk & lt bl ('37)	7.50	10
a.		Chalky paper	75.00	1.50
447	A147	2p brn lake & dk ultra ('36)	1.25	8
448	A148	5p ind & ol grn ('36)	9.00	20
449	A149	10p brn lake & blk	25.00	1.75
450	A150	20p bl grn & brn ('36)	50.00	5.00
		Nos. 418-450 (34)	187.32	11.12

See Nos. 485-500, 523-540, 659, 668.

No. 439A exists with attached label showing medallion.
Price $75 unused, $40 used.

Souvenir Sheet.

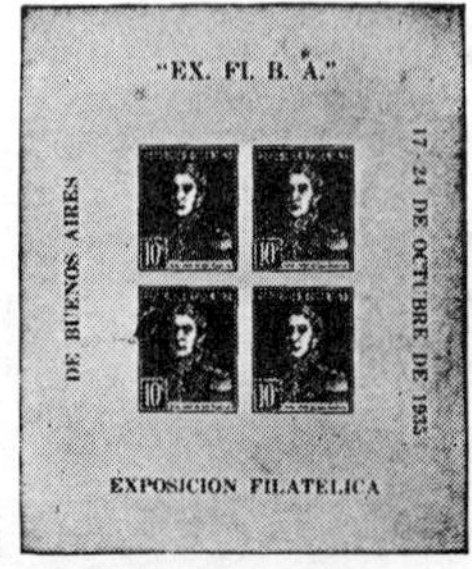

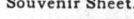

A151

Without Period after Value.

1935, Oct. 17 **Litho.** ***Imperf.***

452	A151	10c dl grn, sheet of four	80.00	40.00
a.		Single stamp	12.00	6.00

Issued in commemoration of the Philatelic Exhibition at Buenos Aires, October 17-24, 1935. The stamps were on sale during the eight days of the exhibition only. Sheets measure 83x101mm.

Plaque
A152

1936, Dec. 1 ***Perf. 13x13½***

453	A152	10c rose	75	25

Issued in commemoration of the Inter-American Conference for Peace.

Domingo Faustino Sarmiento
A153

"Presidente Sarmiento"
A154

1938, Sept. 5

454	A153	3c sage grn	25	10
455	A153	5c red	25	5
456	A153	15c dp bl	75	20
457	A153	50c orange	2.50	1.00

Issued in commemoration of the 50th anniversary of the death of Domingo Faustino Sarmiento, president, educator and author.

1939, Mar. 16

458	A154	5c grnsh bl	30	12

Issued in commemoration of the final voyage of the training ship "Presidente Sarmiento."

Allegory of the Universal Postal Union
A155

Coat of Arms
A157

Post Office, Buenos Aires
A156

Iguassú Falls
A158

Bonete Hill, Nahuel Huapi Park
A159

Allegory of Modern Communications
A160

Argentina, Land of Promise
A161

Lake Frias, Nahuel Huapi Park
A162

Perf. 13x13½, 13½x13

1939, Apr. 1 Photogravure

459	A155	5c rose car	25	5
460	A156	15c grnsh blk	60	35
461	A157	20c brt bl	60	15
462	A158	25c dp bl grn	1.25	50
463	A159	50c brown	2.50	85
464	A160	1p brn vio	3.00	1.10
465	A161	2p magenta	15.00	7.50
466	A162	5p purple	60.00	25.00
		Nos. 459-466 (8)	83.20	35.50

Universal Postal Union, 11th Congress.

Souvenir Sheets.

A163

A164

1939, May 12 *Imperf.* **Wmk. 90**

467	A163	Sheet of four	10.00	7.00
a.		5c rose car (A155)	1.75	1.25
b.		20c brt bl (A157)	1.75	1.25
c.		25c dp bl grn (A158)	1.75	1.25
d.		50c brn (A159)	1.75	1.25
468	A164	Sheet of four	10.00	7.00

Issued in four forms:

a.	Unsevered horizontal pair of sheets Type A163 at left Type A164 at right	25.00	25.00
b.	Unsevered vertical pair of sheets Type A163 at top Type A164 at bottom	25.00	25.00
c.	Unsevered block of four sheets Type A163 at left Type A164 at right	90.00	90.00
d.	Unsevered block of four sheets Type A163 at top Type A164 at bottom	90.00	90.00

Issued in commemoration of the 11th Congress of the Universal Postal Union and the Argentina International Philatelic Exposition (C.Y.T.R.A.).

No. 468 contains one each of Nos. 467a–467d.

Size: No. 468a, 190x95mm. No. 468b, 95x190mm.

Family and New House
A165

Perf. 13½x13

1939, Oct. 2 Litho. **Wmk. 90**

469 A165 5c bluish grn 30 6

Issued to commemorate the first Pan-American Housing Congress.

Bird Carrying Record
A166

Head of Liberty and Arms of Argentina
A167

Record and Winged Letter
A168

1939, Dec. 11 Photo. *Perf. 13*

470	A166	1.18p indigo	22.50	12.50
471	A167	1.32p brt bl	22.50	12.50
472	A168	1.50p dk brn	85.00	50.00

These stamps were issued for the recording and mailing of flexible phonograph records.

Map of the Americas
A169

1940, Apr. 14 *Perf. 13x13½*

473 A169 15c ultra 50 10

Issued to commemorate the 50th anniversary of the Pan American Union.

Souvenir Sheet.

Reproductions of Early Argentine Stamps
A170

Wmkd. RA in Sun. (90)

1940, May 25 Litho. *Imperf.*

474	A170	Sheet of five	15.00	9.00
a.		5c dk bl (*Corrientes*)	1.75	1.25
b.		5c red (*Argentine Republic*)	1.75	1.25
c.		5c dk bl (*Cordoba*)	1.75	1.25
d.		5c red (*Argentine Republic*)	1.75	1.25
e.		10c dk bl (*Buenos Aires*)	1.75	1.25

Issued in sheets measuring 111x116mm., in commemoration of the 100th anniversary of the first postage stamp.

General Domingo French and Colonel Antonio Beruti
A171

1941, Feb. 20 *Perf. 13½x13*

475 A171 5c dk gray bl & lt bl 40 6

Issued in honor of General French and Colonel Beruti, patriots.

Marco M. de Avellaneda
A172

Statue of Gen. Julio Roca
A173

1941, Oct. 3 *Perf. 13x13½*

476 A172 5c dl sl bl 40 5

Issued in commemoration of the centenary of the death of Marco M. de Avellaneda, (1814–41), Army leader and martyr.

1941, Oct. 19 Photo. **Wmk. 90**

477 A173 5c dk ol grn 40 6

Issued to commemorate the dedication of a monument to Lt. Gen. Julio Argentino Roca (1843–1914).

Carlos Pellegrini and Bank of the Nation
A174

1941, Oct. 26 *Perf. 13½x13*

478 A174 5c brn car 40 5

Issued to commemorate the 50th anniversary of the founding of the Bank of the Nation.

Gen. Juan Lavalle
A175

1941, Dec. 5 *Perf. 13x13½*

479 A175 5c brt bl 40 6

Issued to commemorate the centenary of the death of Gen. Juan Galo de Lavalle (1797–1841).

National Postal Savings Bank
A176

1942, Apr. 5 Litho. *Perf. 13½x13*

480 A176 1c pale ol 12 5

José Manuel Estrada
A177

1942, July 13 *Perf. 13x13½*

481 A177 5c brn vio 40 6

Issued to commemorate the centenary of the birth of José Estrada (1842–1894), writer and diplomat.

No. 481 exists with label, showing medallion, attached. The pair sells for 15 times the price of the single stamp.

Wmk. 288

Types of 1935-51.

Wmkd. RA in Sun with Straight Rays. (288)

Perf. 13, 13x13½, 13½x13.

1942-50 Lithographed.

485	A128	½c brn vio	7.50	1.25
486	A129	1c buff ('50)	12	4
487	A130	2c dk brn ('50)	12	4
488	A132	3c lt gray	25.00	1.50
489	A134	3c lt gray ('49)	25	5
490	A137	10c red brn ('49)	30	5
491	A138	12c red	30	10
492	A140	15c lt gray bl (II)	45	5
493	A139	20c dk sl bl & pale bl	2.00	5
494	A141	25c dl rose ('49)	90	10
495	A142	30c org brn ('49)	2.00	6
496	A143	40c vio ('49)	12.50	20
497	A144	50c red & org ('49)	12.50	30
498	A146	1p brn blk & lt bl	10.00	30
499	A147	2p brn lake & bl ('49)	20.00	1.00

500	A148	5p ind & ol grn ('49)	70.00	5.00
		Nos. 485-500 (16)	163.94	10.09

No. 493 measures 22x33mm.

Post Office, Buenos Aires
A178

Proposed Columbus Lighthouse
A179

Inscribed: "Correos y Telegrafos".

1942, Oct. 5 Litho. *Perf. 13*

503	A178	35c lt ultra	5.00	6

See also Nos. 541-543.

1942, Oct. 12 Wmk. 288

504	A179	15c dl bl	2.50	10

Wmk. 90

505	A179	15c dl bl	90.00	5.00

Nos. 504-505 were issued to commemorate the 450th anniversary of the discovery of America by Columbus.

José C. Paz
A180

Books and Argentine Flag
A181

1942, Dec. 15 Wmk. 288

506	A180	5c dk gray	60	5

Issued in commemoration of the centenary of the birth of José C. Paz, statesman and founder of the newspaper La Prensa.

1943, Apr. 1 Litho. *Perf. 13*

507	A181	5c dl bl	25	5

Issued to commemorate the first Book Fair of Argentina.

Arms of Argentina Inscribed "Honesty, Justice, Duty"
A182

1943-50 *Perf. 13* Wmk. 288

Size: 20x26mm.

508	A182	5c red ('50)	3.50	4

Wmk. 90

509	A182	5c red	30	4
a.		5c dl red, unsurfaced paper	5.00	8
510	A182	15c green	1.00	15

Perf. 13x13½

Size: 22x33mm.

511	A182	20c dk bl	1.50	15

Issued to commemorate the change of political organization on June 4, 1943.

Independence House, Tucuman
A183

Liberty Head and Savings Bank
A184

1943-51 *Perf. 13* Wmk. 90

512	A183	5c bl grn	1.20	8

Wmk. 288

513	A183	5c bl grn ('51)	50	8

Issued to commemorate the restoration of Independence House.

1943, Oct. 25 Wmk. 90

514	A184	5c vio brn	25	5

Wmk. 288

515	A184	5c vio brn	55.00	3.00

Issued to commemorate the first conference of National Postal Savings.

Port of Buenos Aires in 1800
A185

1943, Dec. 11 Wmk. 90

516	A185	5c gray blk	25	5

Day of Exports.

Warship, Merchant Ship and Sailboat
A186

Arms of Argentine Republic
A187

1944, Jan. 31 *Perf. 13*

517	A186	5c blue	25	6

Issued to commemorate Sea Week.

1944, June 4

518	A187	5c dl bl	15	6

Issued to commemorate the first anniversary of the change of political organization in Argentina.

St. Gabriel
A188

Cross at Palermo
A189

1944, Oct. 11

519	A188	3c yel grn	25	8
520	A189	5c dp rose	25	8

Fourth national Eucharistic Congress.

Allegory of Savings
A190

Reservists
A191

1944, Oct. 24

521	A190	5c gray	15	5

Issued to commemorate the 20th anniversary of the National Savings Bank.

1944, Dec. 1

522	A191	5c blue	15	5

Day of the Reservists.

Types of 1935-51.

Perf. 13x13½, 13½x13.

1945-47 Lithographed. Unwmkd.

523	A128	½c brn vio ('46)	12	3
524	A129	1c yel grn	12	3
525	A130	2c sepia	15	3
526	A132	3c lt gray (*San Martin*)	70	5
527	A134	3c lt gray (*Moreno*) ('46)	25	4
528	A135	6c ol grn ('47)	30	15
529	A137	10c brn ('46)	2.50	5
530	A140	15c lt gray bl (II)	1.25	5
531	A139	20c dk sl bl & pale bl	2.00	5
532	A141	25c dl rose	75	5
533	A142	30c org brn	60	5
534	A143	40c violet	2.50	12
535	A144	50c red & org	2.50	5
536	A146	1p brn blk & lt bl	3.75	10
537	A147	2p brn lake & bl	12.00	35
538	A148	5p ind & ol grn ('46)	90.00	3.00
539	A149	10p dp cl & int blk	12.00	1.50
540	A150	20p bl grn & brn ('46)	12.50	1.50
		Nos. 523-540 (18)	143.99	7.20

No. 531 measures 22x33mm.

Post Office Type

Inscribed: "Correos y Telecommunicaciones".

1945 *Perf. 13x13½* Unwmkd.

541	A178	35c lt ultra	2.00	5

Wmk. 90

542	A178	35c lt ultra	2.00	5

Wmk. 288

543	A178	35c lt ultra	60	5

Bernardino Rivadavia
A192 A193

Mausoleum of Rivadavia
A194

Perf. 13½x13.

1945, Sept. 1 Litho. Unwmkd.

544	A192	3c bl grn	20	6
545	A193	5c rose	20	5
546	A194	20c blue	50	6

Issued to commemorate the centenary of the death of Bernardino Rivadavia, Argentina's first president.

No. 546 exists with mute label attached. The pair sells for four times the price of the single stamp.

General José de San Martín
A195

Monument to Army of the Andes, Mendoza
A196

Lithographed or Typographed.

1945-46 Wmk. 90

547	A195	5c car, typo.	15	6
a.		Lithographed ('46)	20	6

Wmk. 288

548	A195	5c car, litho.	175.00	30.00

Unwmkd.

549	A195	5c car, typo. ('46)	75	5
a.		Lithographed ('46)	30	5

1946, Jan. 14 Litho. *Perf. 13½x13*

550	A196	5c vio brn	15	5

Issued to honor the Unknown Soldier of the War for Independence.

Franklin D. Roosevelt
A197

Liberty Administering Presidential Oath—A198

1946, Apr. 12

551	A197	5c sl blk	20	8

Issued in memory of Franklin D. Roosevelt.

1946, June 4 *Perf. 13x13½*

552	A198	5c blue	15	5

Issued to commemorate the inauguration of President Juan D. Perón, June 4, 1946.

Argentina Receiving Popular Acclaim
A199

1946, Oct. 17 *Perf. 13½x13*

553	A199	5c rose vio	30	10
554	A199	10c bl grn	45	15
555	A199	15c dk bl	90	20
556	A199	50c red brn	1.25	40
557	A199	1p car rose	2.50	1.10
		Nos. 553-557 (5)	5.40	1.95

First anniversary of the political organization change of Oct. 17, 1945.

Coin Bank and World Map
A200

1946, Oct. 31 Unwmkd.

558	A200	30c dk rose car & pink	1.00	15

Issued to commemorate the Universal Day of Savings, October 31, 1946.

Argentine Industry
A201

International Bridge Connecting Argentina and Brazil
A202

1946, Dec. 6 ***Perf. 13x13½***

559 A201 5c vio brn 15 5

Day of Argentine Industry, Dec. 6.

1947, May 21 Litho. ***Perf. 13½x13***

560 A202 5c green 15 5

Issued to commemorate the opening of the Argentina-Brazil International Bridge, May 21, 1947.

Map of Argentine Antarctic Claims A203

Justice A204

1947-49 ***Perf. 13x13½*** **Unwmkd.**

561 A203 5c vio & lil 20 6
562 A203 20c dk car rose & rose 40 10

Wmk. 90

563 A203 20c dk car rose & rose 2.50 10

Wmk. 288

564 A203 20c dk car rose & rose ('49) 2.50 10

Issued to note the 43rd anniversary of the first Argentine Antarctic mail.

1947, June 4 **Unwmkd.**

565 A204 5c brn vio & pale yel 15 5

Issued to commemorate the 1st anniversary of the Perón government.

Icarus Falling A205

1947, Sept. 25 ***Perf. 13½x13***

566 A205 15c red vio 25 8

Aviation Week.

Training Ship Presidente Sarmiento A206

1947, Oct. 5 ***Perf. 13x13½***

567 A206 5c blue 20 7

Issued to commemorate the 50th anniversary of the launching of the Argentine training frigate "Presidente Sarmiento".

Cervantes and Characters from Don Quixote—A207

Perf. 13½x13

1947, Oct. 12 Photo. Wmk. 90

568 A207 5c ol grn 20 5

Issued to commemorate the 400th anniversary of the birth of Miguel de Cervantes Saavedra, playwright and poet.

Gen. José de San Martin A208

Lithographed.

1947-49 ***Perf. 13½x13*** **Unwmkd.**

569 A208 5c dl grn 15 6

Wmk. 288

570 A208 5c dl grn ('49) 25 4

Issued to commemorate the transfer of the remains of Gen. José de San Martin's parents.

School Children A209

Statue of Araucanian Indian A210

1947-49 ***Perf. 13x13½*** **Unwmkd.**

571 A209 5c green 15 4

Wmk. 90

574 A209 20c brown 50 10

Wmk. 288

575 A209 5c green 50 5

Argentine School Crusade for World Peace.

1948, May 21 **Wmk. 90**

576 A210 25c yel brn 50 10

American Indian Day, Apr. 19.

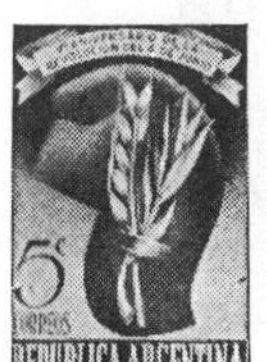

Cap of Liberty A211

Manual Stop Signal A212

1948, July 16

577 A211 5c ultra 15 5

Issued to commemorate the 5th anniversary of the Revolution of June 4, 1943.

1948, July 22

578 A212 5c choc & yel 15 5

Traffic Safety Day, June 10.

Post Horn and Oak Leaves A213

Argentine Farmers A214

1948, July 22 **Unwmkd.**

579 A213 5c lil rose 15 5

Issued to commemorate the 200th anniversary of the establishment of regular postal service on the Plata River.

Perf. 13x13½

1948, Sept. 20 **Wmk. 288**

580 A214 10c red brn 25 6

Agriculture Day, Sept. 8, 1948.

Liberty and Symbols of Progress A215

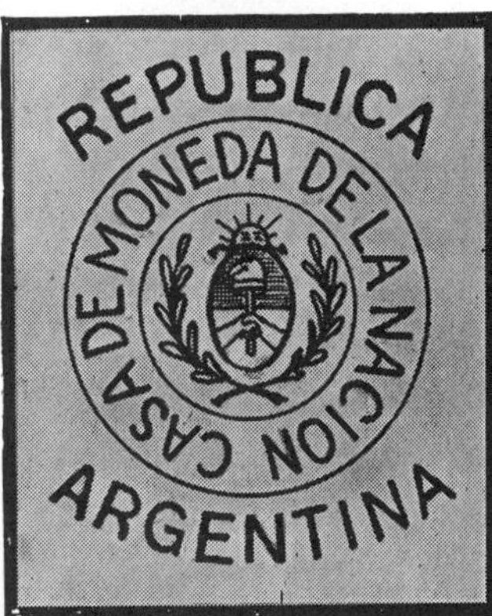

Wmk. 287

Wmkd. Double Circle and Letters in Sheet. (287)

1948, Nov. 23 Photo. ***Perf. 13x13½***

581 A215 25c red brn 30 6

Issued to commemorate the third anniversary of President Juan D. Peron's return to power, October 17, 1945.

Souvenir Sheets.

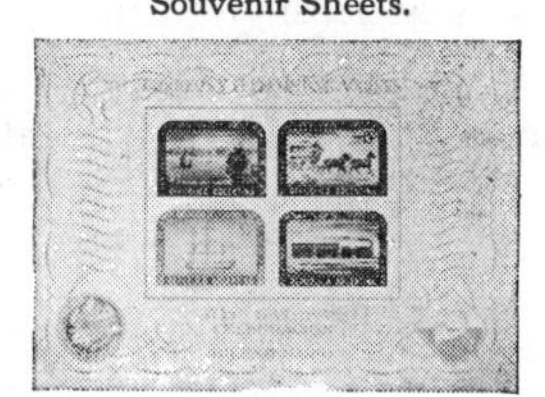

A216

Designs: 15c, Mail coach. 45c, Buenos Aires in 18th century. 55c, First train, 1857. 85c, Sailing ship, 1767.

1948, Dec. 21 ***Imperf.*** **Unwmkd.**

582 A216 Sheet of four 3.00 3.00
a. 15c dk grn 60 60
b. 45c org brn 60 60
c. 55c lil brn 60 60
d. 85c ultra 60 60

A217

Designs: 85c, Domingo de Basavilibaso (1709-75). 1.05p, Postrider. 1.20p, Sailing ship, 1798. 1.90p, Courier in the Andes, 1772.

583 A217 Sheet of four 18.00 14.00
a. 85c brn 4.00 3.00
b. 1.05p dk grn 4.00 3.00
c. 1.20p dk bl 4.00 3.00
d. 1.90p red brn 4.00 3.00

Issued in sheets measuring 143x101mm. (No. 582) and 101x143mm. (No. 583) to commemorate the 200th anniversary of the establishment of regular postal service on the Plata River.

Winged Wheel A218

Perf. 13½x13

1949, Mar. 1 **Wmk. 288**

584 A218 10c blue 25 5

Nationalization of the railroads, first anniversary.

Liberty A219

1949, June 20 Engraved Wmk. 90

585 A219 1p red & red vio 75 15

Ratification of the Constitution of 1949.

Allegory of the U.P.U. A220

1949, Nov. 19

586 A220 25c dk grn & yel grn 40 10

Issued to commemorate the 75th anniversary of the formation of the Universal Postal Union.

Gen. José de San Martín A221

Mausoleum of San Martín A223

San Martín at Boulogne sur Mer
A222

Designs: 20c, 50c, 75c, Different Portraits of San Martin. 1p, House where San Martin died.

Inscribed:

"Centenario de la Muerte del General Don José de San Martin 1850-1950."

Engraved, Photogravure (25c, 1p, 2p)

1950, Aug. 17 *Perf. 13½* Wmk. 90

587	A221	10c ind & dk pur	20	5
588	A221	20c red brn & dk brn	20	6
589	A222	25c brown	25	8
590	A221	50c dk grn & ind	75	12
591	A221	75c choc & dk grn	75	18
a.		Souv. sheet of 4	2.00	1.25
592	A222	1p dk grn	1.50	30
593	A223	2p dp red lil	1.25	50
		Nos. 587-593 (7)	4.90	1.29

Issued to commemorate the centenary of the death of General José de San Martin. No. 591a measures 120x150mm. and contains one each of Nos. 587, 588, 590 and 591, imperf., with marginal inscriptions and ornamental border in brown.

Map Showing Antarctic Claims
A224

1951, May 21 Litho. *Perf. 13x13½*

594	A224	1p choc & lt bl	60	5

Pegasus and Train
A225

Communications Symbols
A226

Design: 25c, Ship and dolphin.

1951, Oct. 17 Photo. *Perf. 13½*

595	A225	5c dk brn	20	5
596	A225	25c Prus grn	40	12
597	A226	40c rose brn	45	15

Close of Argentine Five Year Plan.

Woman Voter and "Argentina"
A227

1951, Dec. 14 *Perf. 13½x13*

598	A227	10c brn vio	15	6

Granting of women's suffrage.

Eva Perón

A228 A229

Lithographed or Engraved (#605).

1952, Aug. 26 *Perf. 13* Wmk. 90

599	A228	1c org brn	12	5
600	A228	5c gray	12	5
601	A228	10c rose lil	12	5
602	A228	20c rose pink	12	5
603	A228	25c dl grn	12	8
604	A228	40c dl vio	20	5
605	A228	45c dp bl	25	10
606	A228	50c dl brn	25	10

Photogravure

607	A229	1p dk brn	45	10
608	A229	1.50p dp grn	2.50	15
609	A229	2p brt car	75	15
610	A229	3p indigo	1.25	20
		Nos. 599-610 (12)	6.25	1.13

Inscribed: "Eva Perón."

1952–53 *Perf. 13x13½*

611	A229	1p dk brn	90	5
612	A229	1.50p dp grn	90	5
613	A229	2p brt car ('53)	2.00	15
614	A229	3p indigo	2.75	20

Engraved

Size: 30x40mm.

Perf. 13½x13.

615	A229	5p red brn	2.75	60
616	A228	10p red	7.50	2.50
617	A229	20p green	20.00	7.00
618	A228	50p ultra	30.00	17.50
		Nos. 611-618(8)	66.80	28.05

Indian Funeral Urn
A230

1953, Aug. 28 Photo. *Perf. 13x13½*

619	A230	50c bl grn	25	10

Issued to commemorate the 400th anniversary of the founding of Santiago del Estero.

Rescue Ship "Uruguay"
A231

1953, Oct. 8 *Perf. 13½*

620	A231	50c ultra	45	12

Issued to commemorate the 50th anniversary of the rescue of the Antarctic expedition of Otto C. Nordenskjold.

Planting Argentine Flag in the Antarctic
A232

Engraved

1954, Jan. 20 *Perf. 13½x13*

621	A232	1.45p blue	1.00	15

Issued to commemorate the 50th anniversary of Argentina's first antarctic post office and the establishing of the La Hoy radio post office in the South Orkneys.

Wired Communications
A233

Television
A234

Design: 3p, Radio.

Perf. 13x13½, 13½x13.

1954, Apr. Photo. Wmk. 90

622	A233	1.50p vio brn	60	25
623	A233	3p vio bl	2.00	50
624	A234	5p carmine	2.50	1.00

Issued to publicize the International Plenipotentiary Conference of Telecommunications, Buenos Aires, 1952.

Pediment, Buenos Aires Stock Exchange
A235

1954, July 13 *Perf. 13½x13*

625	A235	1p dk grn	50	10

Issued to commemorate the centenary of the establishment of the Buenos Aires Stock Exchange.

Eva Perón
A236

1954 Wmk. 90

626	A236	3p dp car rose	2.00	30

Wmk. 288

627	A236	3p dp car rose	250.00	50.00

Issued to commemorate the second anniversary of the death of Eva Perón.

José de San Martin A237 — Eva Perón Foundation Building A239

Wheat A238 — Industry A238a

Cliffs of Humahuaca
A240

Gen. José de San Martin
A241

Designs: 50c, Buenos Aires harbor. 1p, Cattle ranch (Ganaderia). 3p, Nihuil Dam. 5p, Iguassu Falls (vert.). 20p, Mt. Fitz Roy (vert.).

1954-59 Wmk. 90
Engr. (#632, 638-642), Photo. (#634-637)
Perf. 13½, 13x13½ (80c), 13½x13 (#639, 641-642)

No.	Type	Value	Description	Unused	Used
628	A237	20c	brt red, typo.	12	3
629	A237	20c	red, litho. ('55)	90	5
630	A237	40c	red, litho. ('56)	25	3
631	A237	40c	brt red, typo. ('55)	40	3
632	A239	50c	bl ('56)	15	3
633	A239	50c	bl, litho. ('59)	25	3
634	A238	80c	brown	35	4
635	A239	1p	brn ('58)	40	3
636	A238a	1.50p	ultra ('58)	30	7
637	A239	2p	dk rose lake	50	6
638	A239	3p	vio brn ('56)	50	6
639	A240	5p	gray grn ('55)	8.00	6
a.			Perf. 13½	10.00	6
640	A240	10p	yel grn ('55)	6.00	8
641	A240	20p	dl vio ('55)	12.00	15
a.			Perf. 13½	15.00	15
642	A241	50p	ultra & ind ('55)	12.00	15
a.			Perf. 13½	12.00	15
			Nos. 628-642 (15)	42.12	90

See Nos. 699–700. For similar designs inscribed "Republica Argentina" see Nos. 823–827, 890, 935, 937, 940, 990, 995, 1039, 1044, 1048.

Allegory
A242

1954, Aug. 26 Typo. *Perf. 13½*

643 A242 1.50p sl blk 1.00 10

Issued to commemorate the centenary of the establishment of the Buenos Aires Grain Exchange.

Clasped Hands and Congress Medal
A243

1955, Mar. 21 Photo. *Perf. 13½x13*

644 A243 3p red brn 1.25 15

Issued to publicize the National Productivity and Social Welfare Congress.

Allegory of Aviation
A244

Argentina Breaking Chains
A245

Perf. 13½.

1955, June 18 Wmk. 90

645 A244 1.50p ol gray 1.00 8

Issued to commemorate the 25th anniversary of commercial aviation in Argentina.

1955, Oct. 16 Lithographed

647 A245 1.50p ol grn 50 6

Liberation Revolution of Sept. 16, 1955.

Army Navy and Air Force Emblems—A246

Perf. 13½x13

1955, Dec. 31 Photo. Wmk. 90

648 A246 3p blue 75 10

"Brotherhood of the Armed Forces."

Justo José de Urquiza
A247

1956, Feb. 3 *Perf. 13½*

649 A247 1.50p green 50 6

Battle of Caseros, 104th anniversary.

Coin and Die
A248

Engraved.

1956, July 28 *Perf. 13½x13*

650 A248 2p gray brn & redsh brn 50 10

75th anniversary of the Argentine Mint.

1856 Stamp of Corrientes
A249

Juan G. Pujol
A250

Design: 2.40p, Stamp of 1860–78.

1956, Aug. 21

651 A249 40c dk grn & bl 25 10
652 A249 2.40p brn & lil rose 50 12

Photogravure.

653 A250 4.40p brt bl 1.10 30
a. Souvenir sheet 2.50 2.25

Centenary of Argentine postage stamps.

No. 653a commemorates both the Argentine stamp centenary and the Philatelic Exhibition for the Centenary of Corrientes Stamps, Oct. 12–21. It is imperf. and contains one each of Nos. 651–653, with the 4.40p in photogravure and the other two stamps and border lithographed. Colors of 40c and 2.40p differ slightly from engraved stamps. Marginal inscriptions, coats of arms and scroll work in dull purple. Size: 146x170mm.

Felling Trees, La Pampa
A251

Maté Herb and Gourd, Misiones
A252

Design: 1p, Cotton plant and harvest, Chaco.

1956, Sept. 1 *Perf. 13½*

654 A251 50c ultra 12 5
655 A251 1p magenta 30 6
656 A252 1.50p green 40 8

Issued to commemorate the elevation of the territories of La Pampa, Chaco and Misiones to provinces.

"Liberty"
A253

Florentino Ameghino
A254

Photogravure.

1956, Sept. 15 *Perf. 13½* Wmk. 90

657 A253 2.40p lil rose 50 10

Issued to commemorate the first anniversary of the Revolution of Liberation.

1956, Nov. 30

658 A254 2.40p brown 40 5

Issued to honor Florentino Ameghino (1854–1911), anthropologist.

Adm. Brown Type of 1935–51.

1956 Lithographed *Perf. 13*

Two types:
I. Bust touches upper frame line of name panel at bottom.
II. White line separates bust from frame line.

Size: 19½–20½x26–27mm.

659 A133 20c dl pur (I) 30 3
a. Type II 30 3
b. Size 19½x25¼ mm (I) 25 3

Benjamin Franklin
A255

1956, Dec. 22 Photo. *Perf. 13½*

660 A255 40c int bl 35 8

Issued to commemorate the 250th anniversary of the birth of Benjamin Franklin.

Frigate "Hercules"
A256

Guillermo Brown
A257

1957, Mar. 2

661 A256 40c brt bl 15 6
662 A257 2.40p gray blk 60 15

Issued to commemorate the centenary of the death of Admiral Guillermo (William) Brown (1777–1857), founder of the Argentine navy.

Roque Saenz Peña
A258

Church of Santo Domingo, 1807
A259

1957, Apr. 1

663 A258 4.40p grnsh gray 60 12

Issued to honor Roque Saenz Peña (1851–1914), president in 1910–1914.

1957, July 6 Wmk. 90

664 A259 40c brt bl grn 15 7

Issued to commemorate the 150th anniversary of the defense of Buenos Aires.

"La Portena"
A260

1957, Aug. 31 *Perf. 13½* Wmk. 90

665 A260 40c pale brn 15 7

Centenary of Argentine railroads.

Esteban Echeverria
A261

"Liberty"
A262

1957, Sept. 2 *Perf. 13x13½*

666 A261 2p claret 30 5

Esteban Echeverria (1805–1851), poet.

1957, Sept. 28 ***Perf. 13½***

667	A262	40c car rose	12	6

Constitutional reform convention.

Portrait Type of 1935–51.

Portrait: 5c, Jose Hernandez.

1957, Oct. 28 **Litho.** ***Perf. 13½***
Size: 16½x22mm.

668	A128	5c buff	15	6

Oil Derrick and Hands Holding Oil
A263

Photogravure.

1957, Dec. 21 ***Perf. 13½*** **Wmk. 90**

669	A263	40c brt bl	12	6

Issued to commemorate the 50th anniversary of the national oil industry.

Museum, La Plata
A264

1958, Jan. 11

670	A264	40c dk gray	12	6

City of La Plata, 75th anniversary.

Locomotive and Arms of Argentina and Bolivia
A265

Map of Argentine-Bolivian Boundary and Plane
A266

1958, Apr. 19 ***Perf. 13½*** **Wmk. 90**

671	A265	40c sl & dp car	20	8
672	A266	1p dk brn	20	8

Issued to celebrate Argentine-Bolivian friendship. No. 671 commemorates the opening of the Jacuiba-Santa Cruz railroad; No. 672, the exchange of presidential visits.

Symbols of the Republic
A267

Flag Monument
A268

Engraved and Photogravure

1958, Apr. 30 **Wmk. 90**

673	A267	40c multi	15	4
674	A267	1p multi	25	6
675	A267	2p multi	40	12

Transmission of Presidential power.

1958, June 21 **Litho.** **Wmk. 90**

676	A268	40c bl & vio bl	15	6

Issued to commemorate the first anniversary of the Flag Monument of Rosario.

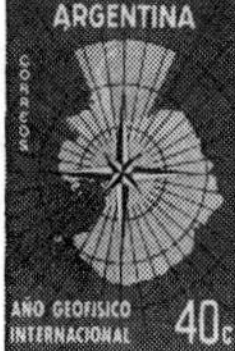

Map of Antarctica
A269

Stamp of Cordoba and Mail Coach
A270

1958, July 12 ***Perf. 13½***

677	A269	40c car rose & blk	20	6

International Geophysical Year, 1957–58.

1958, Oct. 18

678	A270	40c pale bl & sl	20	8

Centenary of Cordoba postage stamps.
See also Nos. C72–C73.

"Slave" by Michelangelo and U. N. Emblem
A271

Engraved and Lithographed

1959, Mar. 14 ***Perf. 13½*** **Wmk. 90**

679	A271	40c vio brn & gray	15	8

Issued to commemorate the tenth anniversary (in 1958) of the signing of the Universal Declaration of Human Rights.

Orchids and Globe
A272

1959, May 23 **Photo.** ***Perf. 13½***

680	A272	1p dl cl	20	6

1st International Horticulture Exposition.

Pope Pius XII
A273

William Harvey
A274

1959, June 20 **Engraved** ***Perf. 13½***

681	A273	1p yel & blk	20	6

Issued in memory of Pope Pius XII, 1876–1958.

1959, Aug. 8 **Litho.** **Wmk. 90**

Portraits: 1p, Claude Bernard. 1.50p, Ivan P. Pavlov.

682	A274	50c green	10	5
683	A274	1p dk red	15	6
684	A274	1.50p brown	25	8

Issued to publicize the 21st International Congress of Physiological Sciences, Buenos Aires.

Type of 1958 and

Domestic Horse
A275

José de San Martin
A276

Tierra del Fuego
A277

Inca Bridge, Mendoza
A278

Ski Jumper
A279

Mar del Plata
A280

Designs: 10c, Cayman. 20c, Llama. 50c, Puma. No. 690, Sunflower. 3p, Zapata Slope, Catamarca. 12p, 23p, 25p, Red quebracho tree. 20p, Nahuel Huapi Lake. 22p, "Industry" (cogwheel and factory).

Two overall paper sizes for 1p, 5p:
I. 27x37½mm. or 37½x27mm.
II. 27x39mm. or 39x27mm.

Perf. 13x13½

1959–70 **Lithographed** **Wmk. 90**

685	A275	10c sl grn	10	3
686	A275	20c dl red brn ('61)	10	3
687	A275	50c bis, litho. ('60)	10	3
688	A275	50c bis, typo. ('60)	30	3
689	A275	1p rose red	10	3

Perf. 13½

690	A278	1p brn, photogravure, paper I ('61)	10	3
a.		Paper II ('69)	30	3
690B	A278	1p brn, litho., paper I	1.00	3
691	A276	2p rose red, litho. ('61)	40	6
692	A276	2p red, typo. (19½x26mm) ('61)	50	3
a.		Redrawn (19½x25mm)	7.50	3
693	A277	3p dk bl, photo. ('60)	25	3
694	A276	4p red, typo ('62)	30	3
694A	A276	4p red, litho. ('62)	60	3
695	A277	5p gray brn, photo., paper I	60	4
e.		5p dk brn, paper II ('70)	10.00	4
695A	A276	8p ver, litho. ('65)	2.00	6
695B	A276	8p red, typo. ('65)	50	5
695C	A276	10p ver, litho. ('66)	1.00	8
695D	A276	10p red, typo. ('66?)	75	6

Photogravure

696	A278	10p lt red brn ('60)	75	9
697	A278	12p dk brn vio ('62)	1.25	5
697A	A278	12p dk brn, litho. ('64)	12.50	10
698	A278	20p Prus grn ('60)	3.50	8
698A	A276	20p red, typo. ('67)	40	5
699	A238a	22p ultra ('62)	2.50	8
700	A238a	22p ultra, litho. ('62)	37.50	10
701	A278	23p grn ('65)	7.50	6
702	A278	25p dp vio ('66)	2.00	6
703	A278	25p pur, litho. ('66?)	10.00	6
704	A279	100p bl ('61)	8.00	15
705	A280	300p dp vio ('62)	3.75	20
		Nos. 685-705 (29)	98.35	1.76

See Nos. 882–887, 889, 892, 923–925, 928–930, 938, 987–989, 991.

The 300p remained on sale as a 3p stamp after the 1970 currency exchange.

Symbolic Sailboat
A281

Child Playing with Doll
A282

1959, Oct. 3 **Litho.** ***Perf. 13½***

706	A281	1p blk, red & bl	12	5

Red Cross sanitary education campaign.

1959, Oct. 17

707	A282	1p red & blk	12	5

Issued for Mother's Day, 1959.

Buenos Aires 1p Stamp of 1859
A283

1959, Nov. 21 ***Perf. 13½*** **Wmk. 90**

708	A283	1p gray & dk bl	15	6

Issued for the Day of Philately.

Bartolomé Mitre and Justo José de Urquiza
A284

1959, Dec. 12 **Photo.** ***Perf. 13½***

709	A284	1p purple	12	5

Treaty of San Jose de Flores, centenary.

WRY Emblem A285 — Abraham Lincoln A286

1960, Apr. 7 Litho. Wmk. 90

710 A285 1p bis & car 12 6
711 A285 4.20p ap grn & dp cl 30 18

World Refugee Year, July 1, 1959–June 30, 1960. See also No. B25.

1960, Apr. 14 Photo. *Perf. 13½*

712 A286 5p ultra 40 15

Issued to commemorate the sesquicentennial (in 1959) of the birth of Abraham Lincoln.

Cornelio Saavedra and Cabildo, Buenos Aires—A287

"Cabildo" and: 2p, Juan José Paso. 4.20p, Manuel Alberti and Miguel Azcuénaga. 10.70p, Juan Larrea and Domingo Matheu.

Photogravure

1960, May 28 *Perf. 13½* Wmk. 90

713 A287 1p rose lil 12 5
714 A287 2p bluish grn 12 6
715 A287 4.20p gray & grn 30 12
716 A287 10.70p gray & ultra 60 25
Nos. 713-716, C75-C76 (6) 1.64 73

150th anniversary of the May Revolution. Souvenir sheets are Nos. C75a and C76a.

Luis Maria Drago A288 — Juan Bautista Alberdi A289

1960, July 8

717 A288 4.20p brown 20 8

Issued to commemorate the centenary of the birth of Dr. Luis Maria Drago, statesman and jurist.

1960, Sept. 10 *Perf. 13½* Wmk. 90

718 A289 1p green 12 6

Issued to commemorate the 150th anniversary of the birth of Juan Bautista Alberdi, statesman and philosopher.

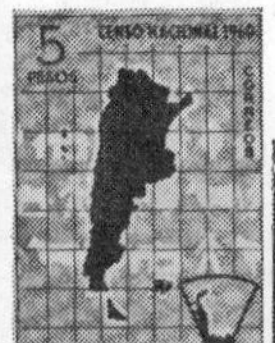

Map of Argentina and Antarctic Sector A290 — Caravel and Emblem A291

1960, Sept. 24 Litho. *Perf. 13½*

719 A290 5p violet 75 15

National census of 1960.

1960, Oct. 1 Photogravure

720 A291 1p dk ol grn 20 6
721 A291 5p brown 50 18

Issued to commemorate the 8th Congress of the Postal Union of the Americas and Spain. See also Nos. C78–C79.

Virgin of Luján, Patroness of Argentina—A292 — Argentine Boy Scout Emblem—A293

1960, Nov. 12 *Perf. 13½* Wmk. 90

722 A292 1p dk bl 15 8

First Inter-American Marian Congress.

1961, Jan. 17 Lithographed

723 A293 1p car rose & blk 20 8

International Patrol Encampment of the Boy Scouts, Buenos Aires.

"Shipment of Cereals," by Quinquela Martin—A294

Photogravure

1961, Feb. 11 *Perf. 13½* Wmk. 90

724 A294 1p red brn 25 8

Export drive: "To export is to advance."

Naval Battle of San Nicolás A295 — Mariano Moreno by Juan de Dios Rivera A296

1961, Mar. 2 *Perf. 13½*

725 A295 2p gray 20 8

Issued to commemorate the 150th anniversary of the naval battle of San Nicolás.

1961, Mar. 25 *Perf. 13½* Wmk. 90

726 A296 2p blue 20 6

Issued to commemorate the 150th anniversary of the death of Mariano Moreno (1778–1811), writer, politician, member of the 1810 Junta.

Emperor Trajan Statue A297

1961, Apr. 11

727 A297 2p sl grn 20 8

Issued to commemorate the visit of Pres. Giovanni Gronchi of Italy to Argentina, April 1961.

Rabindranath Tagore A298

1961, May 13 Photo. *Perf. 13½*

728 A298 2p pur, *grysh* 20 6

Issued to commemorate the centenary of the birth of Rabindranath Tagore, Indian poet.

San Martin Statue, Madrid—A299

1961, May 24 Wmk. 90

729 A299 1p ol gray 20 6

Issued to commemorate the unveiling of a statue of General José de San Martin in Madrid.

Manuel Belgrano A300

1961, June 17 *Perf. 13½*

730 A300 2p vio bl 20 6

Issued to commemorate the erection of a monument by Hector Rocha, to General Manuel Belgrano in Buenos Aires.

Explorers, Sledge and Dog Team A301

1961, Aug. 19 Photo. Wmk. 90

731 A301 2p black 50 10

Issued to commemorate the 10th anniversary of the General San Martin Base, Argentine Antarctic.

Spanish Conquistador and Sword A302 — Sarmiento Statue by Rodin, Buenos Aires A303

1961, Aug. 19 Lithographed

732 A302 2p red & blk 20 8

First city of Jujuy, 400th anniversary.

1961, Sept. 9 Photogravure

733 A303 2p violet 20 8

Issued to commemorate the 150th anniversary of the birth of Domingo Faustino Sarmiento (1811–1888), political leader and writer.

Symbol of World Town Planning A304

Lithographed

1961, Nov. 25 *Perf. 13½* Wmk. 90

734 A304 2p ultra & yel 20 8

World Town Planning Day, Nov. 8.

Manuel Belgrano Statue, Buenos Aires A305 — Grenadier, Flag and Regimental Emblem A306

1962, Feb. 24 Photogravure

735 A305 2p Prus bl 20 10

150th anniversary of the Argentine flag.

Perf. 13½

1962, March 31 Wmk. 90

736 A306 2p car rose 20 10

Issued to commemorate the 150th anniversary of the San Martin Grenadier Guards regiment.

Mosquito and Malaria Eradication Emblem A307

1962, Apr. 7 Lithographed

737 A307 2p ver & blk 20 10

Issued for the World Health Organization drive to eradicate malaria.

Church of the Virgin of Lujàn A308 — Bust of Juan Jufrè A309

1962, May 12 *Perf. 13½* Wmk. 90

738 A308 2p org brn & blk 20 8

Issued to commemorate the 75th anniversary of the pontifical coronation of the Virgin of Lujan.

1962, June 23 Photogravure

739 A309 2p Prus bl 20 8

Issued to commemorate the fourth centenary of the founding of San Juan.

"Soaring into Space"
A310

Juan Vucetich
A311

1962, Aug. 18 Litho. *Perf. 13½*

740 A310 2p mar, blk & bl 20 8

Argentine Air Force, 50th anniversary.

1962, Oct. 6 Photo. Wmk. 90

741 A311 2p green 20 8

Issued to honor Juan Vucetich (1864–1925), inventor of the Argentine system of fingerprinting.

Domingo F. Sarmiento
A312

February 20th Monument, Salta
A313

Design: 4p, José Hernandez.

1962–66 Photogravure *Perf. 13½*

742 A312 2p dp grn 90 5

Lithographed

742A A312 2p lt grn ('64) 75 4

Photogravure

742B A312 4p dl red ('65) 60 4

Lithographed

742C A312 4p rose red ('66) 60 4

See also No. 817–819.

1963, Feb. 23 Photo. Wmk. 90

743 A313 2p dk grn 20 8

Issued to commemorate the 150th anniversary of the Battle of Salta, War of Independence.

Gear Wheels
A314

1963, Mar. 16 Litho. *Perf. 13½*

744 A314 4p gray, blk & brt rose 20 8

Issued to commemorate the 75th anniversary of the Argentine Industrial Union.

National College, Buenos Aires
A315

Child Draining Cup
A316

1963, Mar. 16 Wmk. 90

745 A315 4p dl org & blk 25 8

Issued to commemorate the centenary of the National College of Buenos Aires.

1963, Apr. 6

746 A316 4p multi 20 8

Issued for the "Freedom from Hunger" campaign of the U.N. Food and Agriculture Organization.

Frigate "La Argentina," 1817, by Emilio Biggeri
A317

1963, May 18 Photogravure

747 A317 4p bluish grn 30 6

Issued for Navy Day, May 17.

Seat of 1813 Assembly and Official Seal
A318

Lithographed

1963, July 13 *Perf. 13½* Wmk. 90

748 A318 4p lt bl & blk 20 8

150th anniversary of the 1813 Assembly.

Battle of San Lorenzo, 1813
A319

1963, Aug. 24

749 A319 4p grn & blk, *grnsh* 25 8

Issued to commemorate the sesquicentennial of the Battle of San Lorenzo.

Queen Nefertari Offering Papyrus Flowers, Abu Simbel
A320

1963, Sept. 14 *Perf. 13½* Wmk. 90

750 A320 4p ocher, blk & bl grn 20 8

Campaign to save the historic monuments in Nubia.

Government House, Buenos Aires
A321

1963, Oct. 12 *Perf. 13½* Wmk. 90

751 A321 5p rose & brn 20 8

Inauguration of President Arturo Illia.

"Science"
A322

Francisco de las Carreras, Supreme Court Justice—A323

1963, Oct. 16 Lithographed

752 A322 4p org brn, bl & blk 20 8

Issued to publicize the 10th Latin-American Neurosurgery Congress.

Photogravure

1963, Nov. 23 *Perf. 13½* Wmk. 90

753 A323 5p bluish grn 20 8

Centenary of judicial power.

Blackboards
A324

1963, Nov. 23 Lithographed

754 A324 5p red, blk & bl 20 8

Issued to publicize "Teachers for America" through the Alliance for Progress program.

Kemal Atatürk
A325

"Payador" by Juan Carlos Castagnino
A326

1963, Dec. 28 Photo. *Perf. 13½*

755 A325 12p dk gray 40 15

Issued to commemorate the 25th anniversary of the death of Kemal Atatürk, president of Turkey.

1964, Jan. 25 Lithographed

756 A326 4p ultra, blk & lt bl 20 8

Fourth National Folklore Festival.

Maps of South Georgia, South Orkney and South Sandwich Islands
A327

Design: 4p, Map of Argentina and Antarctic claims (vert.).

1964, Feb. 22 *Perf. 13½* Wmk. 90

Size: 33x22mm.

757 A327 2p lt & dk bl & bis 85 20

Size: 30x40mm.

758 A327 4p lt & dk bl & ol grn 1.15 25

Issued to commemorate the 60th anniversary of Argentina's claim to Antarctic territories. See also No. C92.

Jorge Newbery in Cockpit
A328

1964, Feb. 23 Photogravure

759 A328 4p dp grn 20 8

Issued to commemorate the 50th anniversary of the death of Jorge Newbery, aviator.

John F. Kennedy
A329

José Brochero by José Cuello
A330

1964, Apr. 14 Engraved Wmk. 90

760 A329 4p cl & dk bl 35 10

Issued in memory of President John F. Kennedy (1917–63).

1964, May 9 Photo. *Perf. 13½*

761 A330 4p lt sep 20 8

Issued to commemorate the 50th anniversary of the death of Father José Gabriel Brochero.

Soldier of Patricios Regiment
A331

Pope John XXIII
A332

1964, May 29 Litho. Wmk. 90

762 A331 4p blk, ultra & red 50 12

Issued for Army Day. Later Army Day stamps, inscribed "Republica Argentina," are of type A340a.

1964, June 27 Engraved

763 A332 4p org & blk 20 10

Issued in memory of Pope John XXIII.

University of Cordoba Arms
A333

Pigeons and U.N. Building, N.Y.
A334

1964, Aug. 22 Litho. Wmk. 90

764 A333 4p blk, ultra & yel 20 10

Issued to commemorate the 350th anniversary of the University of Cordoba.

1964, Oct. 24 ***Perf. 13½***

765 A334 4p dk bl & lt bl 20 10

Issued for United Nations Day.

Joaquin V. Gonzalez
A335

Julio Argentino Roca
A336

1964, Nov. 14 Photogravure

766 A335 4p dk rose car 20 10

Issued to commemorate the centenary (in 1963) of the birth of Joaquin V. Gonzalez, writer.

1964, Dec. 12 ***Perf. 13½*** **Wmk. 90**

767 A336 4p vio bl 20 10

Issued to commemorate the 50th anniversary of the death of General Julio A. Roca, (1843–1914), president of Argentina, (1880–86, 1898–1904).

Market at Montserrat Square, by Carlos Morel
A337

1964, Dec. 19 Photogravure

768 A337 4p sepia 35 12

Issued to honor the 19th century Argentine painter Carlos Morel.

Icebreaker General San Martin
A338

Girl with Piggy Bank
A339

Design: 2p, General Belgrano Base, Antarctica.

1965 ***Perf. 13½*** **Wmk. 90**

769 A338 2p dl pur 30 10
770 A338 4p ultra 40 10

Issued to publicize the national territory of Tierra del Fuego, Antarctic and South Atlantic Isles.

Issue dates: 4p, Feb. 27; 2p, June 5.

1965, Apr. 3 Lithographed

771 A339 4p red org & blk 15 10

Issued to commemorate the 50th anniversary of the National Postal Savings Bank.

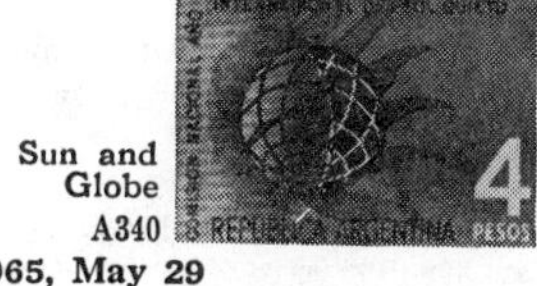

Sun and Globe
A340

1965, May 29

772 A340 4p blk, org & dl bl 30 10

Issued for the International Quiet Sun Year, 1964–65. See also Nos. C98–C99.

Hussar of Pueyrredon Regiment
A340a

Ricardo Rojas (1882–1957)
A341

1965, June 5 ***Perf. 13½*** **Wmk. 90**

773 A340a 8p dp ultra, blk & red 60 12

Issued for Army Day. See also Nos. 796, 838, 857, 893, 944, 958, 974, 1145.

1965, June 26 Photogravure

Portraits: No. 775, Ricardo Guiraldes (1886–1927). No. 776, Enrique Larreta (1873–1961). No. 777, Leopoldo Lugones (1874–1938). No. 778, Roberto J. Payro (1867–1928).

774 A341 8p brown 40 10
775 A341 8p brown 40 10
776 A341 8p brown 40 10
777 A341 8p brown 40 10
778 A341 8p brown 40 10
Nos. 774-778 (5) 2.00 50

Issued to honor Argentine writers. Printed se-tenant in sheets of 100 (10x10); 2 horizontal rows of each design with Guiraldes in top rows and Rojas in bottom rows.

Hipolito Yrigoyen
A342

1965, July 3 Lithographed

779 A342 8p pink & blk 25 10

Issued in memory of Hipolito Yrigoyen (1852–1933), president of Argentina 1916–22 and 1928–30.

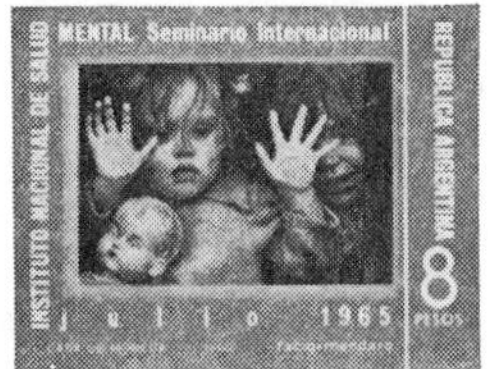

Children Looking Through Window
A343

1965, July 24 Photogravure

780 A343 8p sal & blk 30 10

International Seminar on Mental Health.

Child's Funerary Urn and 16th Century Map
A344

1965, Aug. 7 Lithographed

781 A344 8p lt grn, dk red, brn & ocher 30 10

City of San Miguel de Tucuman, 400th anniversary.

Cardinal Cagliero
A345

Dante Alighieri
A346

1965, Aug. 21 Photogravure

782 A345 8p violet 30 10

Issued to honor Juan Cardinal Cagliero (1839–1926), missionary to Argentina and Bishop of Magida.

1965, Sept. 16 ***Perf. 13½*** **Wmk. 90**

783 A346 8p lt ultra 30 10

Issued to commemorate the 700th anniversary of the birth of Dante Alighieri (1265–1321), Italian poet.

Clipper "Mimosa" and Map of Patagonia—A347

1965, Sept. 25 Lithographed

784 A347 8p red & blk 30 10

Issued to commemorate the centenary of Welsh colonization of Chubut, and the founding of the city of Rawson.

Map of Buenos Aires, Cock and Compass Emblem of Federal Police
A348

1965, Oct. 30 **Photo.** ***Perf. 13½***

785 A348 8p car rose 25 10

Issued for Federal Police Day.

Child's Drawing of Children
A349

1965, Nov. 6 **Litho.** **Wmk. 90**

786 A349 8p lt yel grn & blk 30 10

Public education law, 81st anniversary.

Church of St. Francis, Catamarca
A350

Ruben Dario
A351

1965, Dec. 8

787 A350 8p org yel & red brn 30 10

Issued to honor Brother Mamerto de la Asuncion Esquiu, preacher, teacher and official of 1885 Provincial Constitutional Convention.

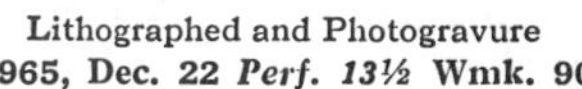

Lithographed and Photogravure

1965, Dec. 22 ***Perf. 13½*** **Wmk. 90**

788 A351 15p bl vio, *gray* 30 15

Issued to honor Ruben Dario (pen name of Felix Ruben Garcia Sarmiento, 1867–1916), Nicaraguan poet, newspaper correspondent and diplomat.

"The Orange Seller"
A352

Pueyrredon Paintings: No. 790, "Stop at the Grocery Store." No. 791, "Landscape at San Fernando" (sailboats). No. 792, "Bathing Horses at River Plata."

1966, Jan. 29 Photo. ***Perf. 13½***

789 A352 8p bluish grn 80 25
790 A352 8p bluish grn 80 25
791 A352 8p bluish grn 80 25
792 A352 8p bluish grn 80 25

Issued to honor Prilidiano Pueyrredon (1823–1870), painter. Nos. 789–792 are printed in one sheet of 40 stamps and 20 labels.

Sun Yat-sen, Flags of Argentina and China
A353

1966, March 12 ***Perf. 13½*** **Wmk. 90**

793 A353 8p dk red brn 1.00 8

Issued to commemorate the centenary of the birth of Dr. Sun Yat-sen (1866–1925), founder of the Republic of China.

Souvenir Sheet

Rivadavia Issue of 1864
A354

Lithographed

1966, Apr. 20 ***Imperf.*** **Wmk. 90**

794 A354 Sheet of three 75
a. 4p gray & red brn 15
b. 5p gray & grn 20
c. 8p gray & dk bl 25

Issued to commemorate the Second Rio de la Plata Stamp Show, Buenos Aires, March 16–24. No. 794 shows flags of Argentina and Uruguay in margin. Marginal inscriptions in gray and red brown, flags in blue and border in green. Size of stamps: 33x43mm. Size of sheet: 140x99mm.

People of Various Races and WHO Emblem
A355

1966, Apr. 23 ***Perf. 13½***

795	A355	8p brn & blk	30	9

Issued to commemorate the opening of the World Health Organization Headquarters, Geneva.

Soldier Type of 1965

Design: 8p, Cavalryman, Güemes Infernal Regiment.

1966, May 28 Lithographed

796	A340a	8p multi	60	12

Issued for Army Day.

Coat of Arms
A356

Designs (all 10p): Arms of Buenos Aires, Federal Capital, Catamarca, Cordoba, Corrientes, Chaco, Chubut, Entre Rios, Formosa, Jujuy, La Pampa, La Rioja, Mendoza, Misiones, Neuquen, Salta, San Juan, San Luis, Santa Cruz, Santa Fe, Santiago del Estero, Tucuman; maps of Rio Negro, and of Tierra del Fuego, Antarctica and South Atlantic Islands.

1966, July 30 ***Perf. 13½*** **Wmk. 90**

797	A356	10p blk & multi	90	40
a.		Sheet of 25	37.50	

Issued to commemorate the 150th anniversary of Argentina's Declaration of Independence.

Sheets of 25 (5x5) contain 25 different designs with commemorative inscription and border in sheet margin.

Three Crosses, Caritas Emblem
A357

1966, Sept. 10 **Litho.** ***Perf. 13½***

798	A357	10p ol grn, blk & lt bl	30	8

Caritas, charity organization.

Hilario Ascasubi (1807–75)
A358

Portraits: No. 800, Estanislao del Campo (1834–80). No. 801, Miguel Cane (1851–1905). No. 802, Lucio V. Lopez (1848–94). No. 803, Rafael Obligado (1851–1920). No. 804, Luis Agote (1868–1954), M.D. No. 805, Juan B. Ambrosetti (1865–1917), naturalist and archaeologist. No. 806, Miguel Lillo (1862–1931), botanist and chemist. No. 807, Francisco P. Moreno (1852–1919), naturalist and paleontologist. No. 808, Francisco J. Muñiz (1795–1871), physician.

1966 Photogravure **Wmk. 90**

799	A358	10p dk bl grn *(Ascasubi)*	60	15
800	A358	10p dk bl grn *(del Campo)*	60	15
801	A358	10p dk bl grn *(Cane)*	60	15
802	A358	10p dk bl grn *(Lopez)*	60	15
803	A358	10p dk bl grn *(Obligado)*	60	15
804	A358	10p dp vio *(Agote)*	60	15
805	A358	10p dp vio *(Ambrosetti)*	60	15
806	A358	10p dp vio *(Lillo)*	60	15
807	A358	10p dp vio *(Moreno)*	60	15
808	A358	10p dp vio *(Muniz)*	60	15
		Nos. 799-808 (10)	6.00	1.50

Nos. 799–803 issued Sept. 17 to honor Argentine writers. Printed se-tenant in sheets of 100 (10x10); 2 horizontal rows of each portrait with Ascasubi in top two rows and Obligado in bottom rows. Nos. 804–808 issued Oct. 22 to honor Argentine scientists; 2 horizontal rows of each portrait with Agote in top two rows and Muñiz in bottom rows. Scientists set has value at upper left, frame line with rounded corners.

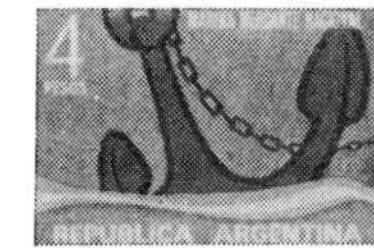

Anchor
A359

1966, Oct. 8 Lithographed

809	A359	4p multi	20	10

Argentine merchant marine.

Flags and Map of the Americas
A360

Argentine National Bank
A361

1966, Oct. 29 ***Perf. 13½*** **Wmk. 90**

810	A360	10p gray & multi	25	10

7th Conference of American Armies.

1966, Nov. 5 Photogravure

811	A361	10p brt bl grn	25	8

Issued to commemorate the 75th anniversary of the Argentine National Bank.

La Salle Monument and College, Buenos Aires
A362

1966, Nov. 26 **Litho.** ***Perf. 13½***

812	A362	10p brn org & blk	25	8

Issued to commemorate the 75th anniversary of the Colegio de la Salle, Buenos Aires, and to honor Saint Jean Baptiste de la Salle (1651–1719), educator.

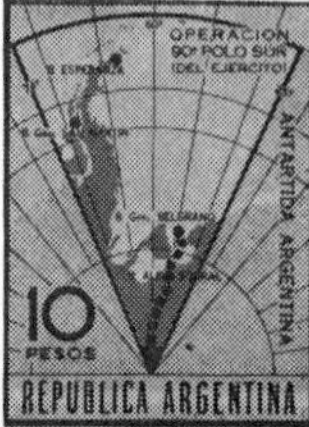

Map of Argentine Antarctica and Expedition Route
A363

1966, Dec. 10 **Wmk. 90**

813	A363	10p multi	50	15

Issued to commemorate the 1965 Argentine Antarctic expedition, which planted the Argentine flag on the South Pole. See also No. 851.

Juan Martin de Pueyrredon
A364

Gen. Juan de Las Heras
A365

1966, Dec. 17 **Photo.** ***Perf. 13½***

814	A364	10p dl red brn	25	10

Issued to honor Juan Martin de Pueyrredon (1777–1850), Governor of Cordoba and of the United Provinces of the River Plata.

1966, Dec. 17 Engraved

815	A365	10p black	25	10

Issued to honor Gen. Juan Gregorio de Las Heras (1780–1866), Peruvian field marshal and aide-de-camp to San Martin.

Inscribed "Republica Argentina" Types of 1955–61 and

Guillermo Brown
A366

Trout Leaping in National Park
A366a

Designs: 6p, José Hernandez. 50p, Gen. José de San Martin. 500p, Red deer in forest.

Two overall paper sizes for 6p, 50p (No. 827) and 90p:

I. 27x37½mm.
II. 27x39mm.

Photogravure

1965–68 ***Perf. 13½*** **Wmk. 90**

817	A366	6p rose red, litho, paper I ('67)	1.75	8
818	A366	6p rose red, photo. ('67)	3.25	8
819	A366	6p brn, 15x22mm ('68)	10	6
823	A238a	43p dk car rose	9.00	10
824	A238a	45p brn, photo ('66)	6.00	10
825	A238a	45p brn, litho ('67)	10.00	20
826	A241	50p dk bl, 29x40mm	10.00	18
827	A241	50p dk bl, 22x31½ mm,paper I ('67)	6.75	8
a.		Paper II	3.75	8
828	A366	90p ol bis, paper I ('67)	4.50	15
a.		Paper II	18.00	15

Engraved

829	A495	500p yel grn ('66)	1.50	25
829A	A366a	1,000p vio bl ('68)	7.00	1.25
		Nos. 817-829A (11)	59.85	2.53

The 500p and 1,000p remained on sale as 5p and 10p stamps after the 1970 currency exchange.

See also Nos. 888, 891, 939, 941, 992, 1031, 1040, 1045–1047.

Pre-Columbian Pottery
A367

1967, Feb. 18 **Litho.** ***Perf. 13½***

830	A367	10p multi	25	10

Issued to commemorate the 20th anniversary of UNESCO (United Nations Educational, Scientific and Cultural Organization).

"The Meal" by Fernando Fader
A368

1967, Feb. 25 **Photo.** **Wmk. 90**

831	A368	10p red brn	30	10

Issued in memory of the Argentine painter Fernando Fader (1882–1935).

Col. Juana Azurduy de Padilla (1781–1862), Soldier
A369

Schooner "Invencible," 1811
A370

Famous Women: No. 833, Juana Manuela Gorriti, writer. No. 834, Cecilia Grierson (1858–1934), physician. No. 835, Juana Paula Manso (1819–75), writer and educator. No. 836, Alfonsina Storni (1892–1938), writer and educator.

1967, May 13 **Photo.** ***Perf. 13½***

832	A369	6p dk brn	35	10
833	A369	6p dk brn	35	10
834	A369	6p dk brn	35	10
835	A369	6p dk brn	35	10
836	A369	6p dk brn	35	10
		Nos. 832-836 (5)	1.75	50

Issued to honor famous Argentine women. Printed se-tenant in sheets of 100 (10x10); 2 horizontal rows of each portrait with Azurduy in two top rows and Storni in bottom rows.

1967, May 20 Lithographed

837	A370	20p multi	1.00	10

Issued for Navy Day.

Soldier Type of 1965

Design: 20p, Highlander (Arribeños Corps).

1967, May 27

838	A340a	20p multi	75	10

Issued for Army Day.

Souvenir Sheet

Manuel Belgrano and José Artigas
A371

1967, June 22 *Imperf.*

839 A371 Souv. sheet of 2 45
a. 6p gray & brn 10
b. 22p brn & gray 30

Third Rio de la Plata Stamp Show, Montevideo, Uruguay, June 18–25. Gray marginal inscription. Size: 56x42mm.

Peace Dove and Valise
A372

PADELAI Emblem
A373

1967, Aug. 5 Litho. *Perf. 13½*

840 A372 20p multi 30 10

Issued for International Tourist Year 1967.

1967, Aug. 12 Lithographed

841 A373 20p multi 30 10

Issued to commemorate the 75th anniversary of the Children's Welfare Association (Patronato de la Infancia—PADELAI).

Stagecoach and Modern City
A374

1967, Sept. 23 *Perf. 13½* Wmk. 90

842 A374 20p rose, yel & blk 35 10

Centenary of Villa Maria, Córdoba.

San Martin by Ibarra
A375

"Battle of Chacabuco" by P. Subercaseaux
A376

1967, Sept. 30 Lithographed

843 A375 20p blk brn & pale yel 65 10

Engraved

844 A376 40p bl blk 1.00 24

Battle of Chacabuco, 150th anniversary.

Exhibition Rooms
A377

1967, Oct. 11 Photogravure

845 A377 20p bl gray 30 10

Issued to commemorate the 10th anniversary of the Government House Museum.

Pedro L. Zanni, Fokker and 1924 Flight Route
A378

1967, Oct. 21 Litho. *Perf. 13½*

846 A378 20p multi 30 10

Issued for Aviation Week and to commemorate the 1924 flight of the Fokker seaplane "Province of Buenos Aires" from Amsterdam, Netherlands, to Osaka, Japan.

Training Ship General Brown, by Emilio Biggeri
A379

1967, Oct. 28 Wmk. 90

847 A379 20p multi 1.00 10

Issued to honor the Military Naval School.

Ovidio Lagos and Front Page
A380

St. Barbara
A381

1967, Nov. 11 Photogravure

848 A380 20p sepia 20 10

Centenary of La Capital, Rosario newspaper.

1967, Dec. 2 *Perf. 13½* Wmk. 90

849 A381 20p rose red 30 10

Issued to honor St. Barbara, patron saint of artillerymen.

Portrait of his Wife, by Eduardo Sivori
A382

1968, Jan. 27 Photo. *Perf. 13½*

850 A382 20p bl grn 35 10

Issued to commemorate the 50th anniversary of the death of Eduardo Sivori (1847–1918), painter.

Antarctic Type of 1966 and

Admiral Brown Scientific Station
A383

Planes over Map of Antarctica
A384

Design: 6p, Map showing radio-postal stations 1966–67.

1968, Feb. 17 Litho. Wmk. 90

851 A363 6p multi 35 10
852 A383 20p multi 50 10
853 A384 40p multi 1.00 25

Issued to publicize Argentine research projects in Argentine Antarctica.

The Annunciation, by Leonardo da Vinci
A385

Man in Wheelchair and Factory
A386

1968, Mar. 23 Photo. *Perf. 13½*

854 A385 20p lil rose 30 10

Issued for the Day of the Army Communications System and its patron saint, Gabriel.

1968, Mar. 23 Lithographed

855 A386 20p grn & blk 30 10

Day of Rehabilitation of the Handicapped.

Children and WHO Emblem
A387

1968, May 11 *Perf. 13½* Wmk. 90

856 A387 20p dk vio bl & ver 30 10

Issued for the 20th anniversary of the World Health Organization.

Soldier Type of 1965

Design: 20p, Uniform of First Artillery Regiment "General Iriarte."

1968, June 8 Lithographed

857 A340a 20p multi 90 10

Issued for Army Day.

Frigate "Libertad," Painting by Emilio Biggeri
A388

1968, June 15 Wmk. 90

858 A388 20p multi 1.00 10

Issued for Navy Day.

Guillermo Rawson and Old Hospital
A389

1968, July 20 Photo. *Perf. 13½*

859 A389 6p ol bis 20 10

Issued to commemorate the centenary of Rawson Hospital, Buenos Aires.

Student Directing Traffic for Schoolmates
A390

1968, Aug. 10 Litho. *Perf. 13½*

860 A390 20p lt bl, blk, buff & car 20 10

Traffic safety and education.

O'Higgins Joining San Martin at Battle of Maipu, by P. Subercaseaux
A391

1968, Aug. 15 Engraved

861 A391 40p bluish blk 75 20

Sesquicentennial of the Battle of Maipu.

Osvaldo Magnasco
A392

1968, Sept. 7 Photo. *Perf. 13½*

862 A392 20p brown 30 10

Issued to honor Osvaldo Magnasco (1864–1920), lawyer, Professor of Law and Minister of Justice.

Grandmother's Birthday, by Patricia Lynch
A393

The Sea, by Edgardo Gomez
A394

1968, Sept. 21 Lithographed

863 A393 20p multi 30 10
864 A394 20p multi 30 10

The designs were chosen in a competition among kindergarten and elementary school children.

Mar del Plata at Night
A395

1968, Oct. 19 Litho. *Perf. 13½*

865 A395 20p blk, ocher & bl 35 10

Issued to publicize the 4th Plenary Assembly of the International Telegraph and Telephone Consultative Committee, Mar del Plata, Sept. 23–Oct. 25. See Nos. C113–C114.

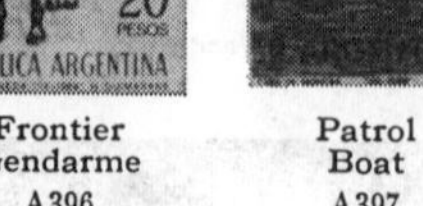

Frontier Gendarme
A396

Patrol Boat
A397

1968, Oct. 26

866 A396 20p multi 30 10
867 A397 20p bl, vio bl & blk 30 10

No. 866 honors the Gendarmery; No. 867 the Coast Guard.

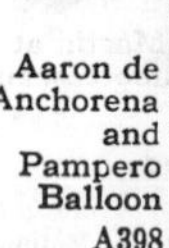

Aaron de Anchorena and Pampero Balloon
A398

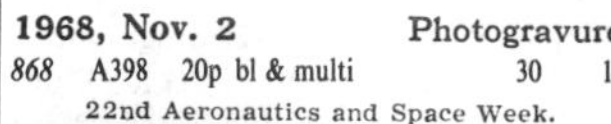

1968, Nov. 2 Photogravure

868 A398 20p bl & multi 30 10

22nd Aeronautics and Space Week.

St. Martin of Tours, by Alfredo Guido
A399

1968, Nov. 9 Lithographed

869 A399 20p lil & dk brn 30 10

Issued to honor St. Martin of Tours, patron saint of Buenos Aires.

Municipal Bank Emblem
A400

1968, Nov. 16

870 A400 20p multi 30 10

Issued to commemorate the 90th anniversary of the Buenos Aires Municipal Bank.

Anniversary Emblem
A401

1968, Dec. 14 *Perf. 13½* Wmk. 90

871 A401 20p car rose & dk grn 30 10

Issued to commemorate the 25th anniversary of ALPI (Fight Against Polio Association).

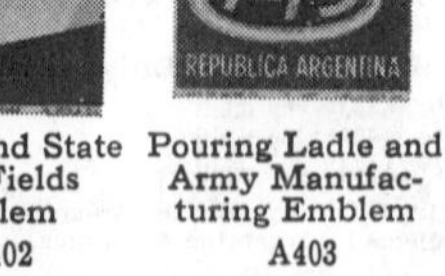

Shovel and State Coal Fields Emblem
A402

Pouring Ladle and Army Manufacturing Emblem
A403

1968, Dec. 21 Lithographed

872 A402 20p org, bl & blk 30 10
873 A403 20p dl vio, dl yel & blk 30 10

Issued to publicize the National Coal and Steel industry at the Rio Turbio coal fields and the Zapla blast furnaces.

Woman Potter, by Ramon Gomez Cornet
A404

1968, Dec. 21 Photo. *Perf. 13½*

874 A404 20p car rose 35 10

Centenary of the Witcomb Gallery.

View of Buenos Aires and Rio de la Plata by Ulrico Schmidl—A405

1969, Feb. 8 Litho. Wmk. 90

875 A405 20p yel, blk & ver 35 10

Issued to honor Ulrico Schmidl (c. 1462–1554) who wrote "Journey to the Rio de la Plata and Paraguay."

Types of 1955–67

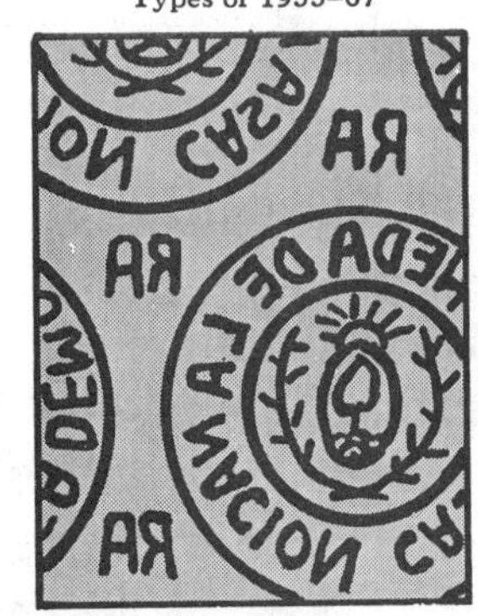

Wmk. 365

Designs: 50c, Puma. 1p, Sunflower. 3p, Zapata Slope, Catamarca. 5p, Tierra del Fuego. 6p, José Hernandez. 10p, Inca Bridge, Mendoza. 50p, José de San Martin. 90p, Guillermo Brown. 100p, Ski jumper.

Wmkd. Argentine Arms, 'Casa de Moneda de la Nacion' & 'RA' Mult. (365)

Photo.; Litho. (50c, 3p, 10p)

1969–70 *Perf. 13½*

882 A275 50c bis ('70) 90 8
883 A277 5p brown 1.25 12
884 A279 100p blue 37.50 1.00

Unwmkd.

885 A278 1p brn ('70) 90 8
886 A277 3p dk bl ('70) 90 8
a. Wmk. 90 7.50 50
887 A277 5p brn ('70) 1.10 8
888 A366 6p red brn, 15x22mm('70) 90 12
889 A278 10p dl red ('70) 75 18
a. Wmk. 90 500.00 40.00
890 A241 50p dk bl, 22x31½mm ('70) 2.50 15
891 A366 90p ol brn, 22x32mm ('70) 4.00 25
892 A279 100p bl ('70) 13.00 30
Nos. 882-892 (11) 63.70 2.44

Soldier Type of 1965

Design: 20p, Sapper (gastador) of Buenos Aires Province, 1856.

Lithographed

1969, May 31 *Perf. 13½* Wmk. 365

893 A340a 20p multi 1.10 12

Issued for Army Day.

Frigate Hercules, by Emilio Biggeri
A406

1969, May 31

894 A406 20p multi 1.10 12

Issued for Navy Day.

"All Men are Equal"
A407

ILO Emblem
A408

1969, June 28 Wmk. 90

895 A407 20p blk & ocher 30 10

International Human Rights Year.

1969, June 28 Litho. Wmk. 365

896 A408 20p lt grn & multi 30 10

Issued to commemorate the 50th anniversary of the International Labor Organization.

Pedro N. Arata (1849–1922), Chemist
A409

Radar Antenna, Balcarce Station and Satellite
A410

Portraits: No. 898, Miguel Fernandez (1883–1950), zoologist. No. 899, Angel P. Gallardo (1867–1934), biologist. No. 900, Cristobal M. Hicken (1875–1933), botanist. No. 901, Eduardo Ladislao Holmberg, M.D. (1852–1937), natural scientist.

1969, Aug. 9 *Perf. 13½* Wmk. 365

Red Brown Design on Orange Yellow Background

897 A409 6p (*Arata*) 60 10
898 A409 6p (*Fernandez*) 60 10
899 A409 6p (*Gallardo*) 60 10
900 A409 6p (*Hicken*) 60 10
901 A409 6p (*Holmberg*) 60 10
Nos. 897-901 (5) 3.00 50

Issued to honor Argentine scientists.

1969, Aug. 23 Wmk. 90

902 A410 20p yel & blk 35 10

Issued to publicize communications by satellite through International Telecommunications Satellite Consortium (INTELSAT). See No. C115.

Nieuport 28, Flight Route and Map of Buenos Aires Province
A411

1969, Sept. 13 Litho. Wmk. 90

903 A411 20p multi 35 10

Issued to commemorate the 50th anniversary of the first Argentine airmail service from El Palomar to Mar del Plata, flown Feb. 23–24, 1919, by Capt. Pedro L. Zanni.

Military College Gate and Emblem

A412

1969, Oct. 4 *Perf. 13½* Wmk. 365

904 A412 20p multi 35 10

Issued to commemorate the centenary of the National Military College, El Palomar (Greater Buenos Aires).

Gen. Angel Pacheco — A413

La Farola, Logotype of La Prensa — A414

1969, Nov. 8 Photo. Wmk. 365

905 A413 20p dp grn 30 10

Issued to commemorate the centenary of the death of Gen. Angel Pacheco (1795–1869).

1969, Nov. 8 Litho. *Perf. 13½*

Design: No. 907, Bartolomé Mitre and La Nacion logotype.

906 A414 20p org, yel & blk 90 12
907 A414 20p brt grn & blk 90 12

Centenary of newspapers La Prensa and La Nacion.

Julian Aguirre

A415

Musicians: No. 909, Felipe Boero. No. 910, Constantino Gaito. No. 911, Carlos Lopez Buchardo. No. 912, Alberto Williams.

Photogravure

1969, Dec. 6 *Perf. 13½* Wmk. 365

Dark Green Design on Light Blue Background

908	A415	6p *(Aguirre)*	70	15
909	A415	6p *(Boero)*	70	15
910	A415	6p *(Gaito)*	70	15
911	A415	6p *(Buchardo)*	70	15
912	A415	6p *(Williams)*	70	15
		Nos. 908-912 (5)	3.50	75

Issued to honor Argentine musicians.

Lt. Benjamin Matienzo and Nieuport Plane

A416

1969, Dec. 13 Lithographed

913 A416 20p multi 75 12

23rd Aeronautics and Space Week.

High Power Lines and Map

A417

Design: 20p, Map of Santa Fe Province and schematic view of tunnel.

1969, Dec. 13

914 A417 6p multi 60 10
915 A417 20p multi 1.25 20

Issued to publicize the completion of development projects. The 6p commemorates the hydroelectric dams on the Limay and Neuquen Rivers, the 20p the tunnel under the Rio Grande from Sante Fe to Parana.

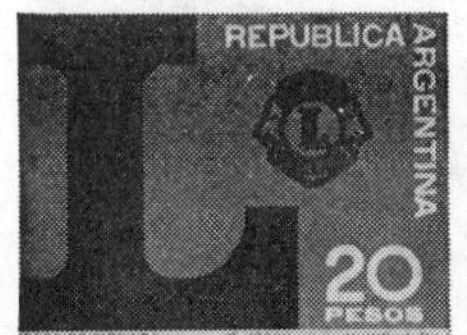

Lions Emblem

A418

1969, Dec. 20 *Perf. 13½* Wmk. 365

916 A418 20p blk, emer & org 90 12

Issued to commemorate the 50th anniversary of the Argentine Lions International Club.

Madonna and Child, by Raul Soldi

A419

1969, Dec. 27 Lithographed

917 A419 20p multi 90 12

Christmas 1969.

Manuel Belgrano, by Jean Gericault

A420

The Creation of the Flag, Bas-relief by José Fioravanti

A421

Photogravure

1970, July 4 *Perf. 13½* Unwmkd.

918 A420 20c dp brn 45 12

Lithographed

Perf. 12½

919 A421 50c bis, blk & bl 1.00 35

Issued to commemorate the sesquicentennial of the death of Gen. Manuel Belgrano (1770–1820), Argentine patriot.

San José Palace

A422

1970, Aug. 9 Litho. *Perf. 13½*

920 A422 20c yel grn & multi 30 10

Issued to commemorate the centenary of the death of Gen. Justo José de Urquiza (1801–1870), president of Argentina, 1854–60.

Schooner "Juliet"

A423

1970, Aug. 8 Unwmkd.

921 A423 20c multi 1.10 25

Issued for Navy Day.

Receiver of 1920 and Waves—A424

1970, Aug. 29

922 A424 20c lt bl & multi 20 10

Issued to commemorate the 50th anniversary of Argentine broadcasting.

Types of 1955–67 Inscribed "Republica Argentina" and Types A425, A426

Manuel Belgrano — A425

Lujan Basilica — A426

Designs: 1c, Sunflower. 3c, Zapata Slope, Catamarca. 5c, Tierra del Fuego. 8c, No. 931, Belgrano. 10c, Inca Bridge, Mendoza. 25c, 50c, 70c, Jose de San Martin. 65c, 90c, 1.20p, San Martin. 1p, Ski jumper. 1.15p, 1.80p, Adm. Brown.

Unwmkd.

1970–73 Photogravure *Perf. 13½*

923	A278	1c dk grn ('71)	10	4
924	A277	3c car rose ('71)	10	5
925	A277	5c bl ('71)	10	5
926	A425	6c dp bl	10	5
927	A425	8c grn ('72)	10	5
928	A278	10c dl red ('71)	30	6
929	A278	10c brn, litho. ('71)	50	6
930	A278	10c org brn ('72)	30	4
931	A425	10c brn ('73)	20	4
932	A426	18c yel & dk brn, litho ('73)	20	3
933	A425	25c brn ('71)	30	4
934	A425	50c scar ('72)	1.50	4
935	A241	65c brn, 22x31½mm, paper II ('71)	75	4
936	A425	70c dk bl ('73)	35	4
937	A241	90c emer, 22x31½mm('72)	3.75	4
938	A279	1p brn, 22½x29½ mm ('71)	2.50	4
939	A366	1.15p dk bl, 22½x32mm('71)	1.10	4
940	A241	1.20p org, 22x31½mm('73)	1.25	4
941	A366	1.80p brn ('73)	1.10	4
		Nos. 923-941 (19)	14.60	83

The imprint "Casa de Moneda de la Nacion" (in capitals) appears on 3c, 5c, Nos. 928–929; 65c, 90c, 1p, 1.20p.

On type A425 only the 6c is inscribed "Ley 18.188" below denomination.

Fluorescent paper was used in printing the 25c, 50c, and 70c. The 3c, 8c, No. 931 and 65c were issued on both ordinary and fluorescent paper.

See also Nos. 987-996, 1032-1038, 1042-1043, 1089-1107.

Soldier Type of 1965

Design: 20c, Galloping messenger of Field Army, 1879.

1970, Oct. 17 Litho. *Perf. 13½*

944 A340a 20c multi 1.10 25

Dome of Cathedral of Cordoba

A430

1970, Nov. 7 Unwmkd.

945 A430 50c gray & blk 1.25 20

Bishopric of Tucuman, 400th anniversary. See No. C131.

People Around U.N. Emblem

A431

1970, Nov. 7

946 A431 20c tan & multi 30 10

25th anniversary of the United Nations.

State Mint and Medal

A432

1970, Nov. 28 *Perf. 13½* Unwmkd.

947 A432 20c gold, grn & blk 30 10

Inauguration of the State Mint Building, 25th anniversary.

St. John Bosco and Dean Funes College
A433

1970, Dec. 19 Lithographed

948 A433 20c ol & blk 30 10

Honoring the work of the Salesian Order in Patagonia.

Nativity, by Horacio Gramajo Gutierrez—A434

1970, Dec. 19

949 A434 20c multi 60 15

Christmas 1970.

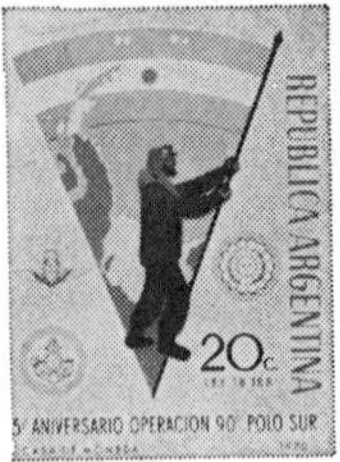

Argentine Flag, Map of Argentine Antarctica
A435

1971, Feb. 20 Litho. *Perf. 13½*

950 A435 20c multi 1.00 12

Fifth anniversary of Argentine South Pole Expedition.

Phosphorescent Sorting Code and Albert Einstein
A436

1971, Apr. 30 *Perf. 13½* Unwmkd.

951 A436 25c multi 30 10

Electronics in postal development.

Symbolic Road Crossing
A437

1971, May 29 Lithographed

952 A437 25c bl & blk 35 10

Inter-American Regional Meeting of the International Federation of Roads, Buenos Aires, March 28–31.

Elias Alippi
A438

Actors: No. 954, Juan Aurelio Casacuberta. No. 955, Angelina Pagano. No. 956, Roberto Casaux. No. 957, Florencio Parravicini.

1971, May 29 Lithographed

Black Design on Pale Rose Background

953 A438 15c (*Alippi*) 50 10
954 A438 15c (*Casacuberta*) 50 10
955 A438 15c (*Pagano*) 50 10
956 A438 15c (*Casaux*) 50 10
957 A438 15c (*Parravicini*) 50 10
Nos. 953-957 (5) 2.50 50

Soldier Type of 1965

Design: 25c, Artilleryman, 1826.

1971, July 3 *Perf. 13½* Unwmkd.

958 A340a 25c multi 1.50 20

Army Day, May 29.

Bilander "Carmen," by Emilio Biggeri
A439

1971, July 3

959 A439 25c multi 1.75 20

Navy Day

Peruvian Order of the Sun
A440

1971, Aug. 28

960 A440 31c multi 50 10

Sesquicentennial of Peru's independence.

Güemes in Battle, by Lorenzo Gigli
A441

Design: No. 962, Death of Güemes, by Antonio Alice.

1971, Aug. 28 Size: 39x29mm.

961 A441 25c multi 60 10

Size: 84x29mm.

962 A441 25c multi 60 10

Sesquicentennial of the death of Martin Miguel de Güemes, leader in Gaucho War, Governor and Captain General of Salta Province.

Stylized Tulip
A442

1971, Sept. 18

963 A442 25c tan & multi 35 10

3rd International and 8th National Horticultural Exhibition.

Father Antonio Saenz, by Juan Gut
A443

1971, Sept. 18

964 A443 25c gray & multi 35 10

Sesquicentennial of University of Buenos Aires, and to honor Father Antonio Saenz, first Chancellor and Rector.

Fabricaciones Militares Emblem
A444

1971, Oct. 16 *Perf. 13½* Unwmkd.

965 A444 25c brn, gold, bl & blk 35 10

30th anniversary of military armament works.

Cars and Trucks
A445

Design: 65c, Tree converted into paper.

1971, Oct. 16

966 A445 25c dl bl & multi 75 10
967 A445 65c grn & multi 1.75 30

Nationalized industries. See No. C134.

Luis C. Candelaria and his Plane, 1918
A446

1971, Nov. 27

968 A446 25c multi 35 10

25th Aeronautics and Space Week.

Observatory and Nebula of Magellan
A447

1971, Nov. 27

969 A447 25c multi 35 10

Centenary of Cordoba Astronomical Observatory.

Christ in Majesty
A448

1971, Dec. 18 Lithographed

970 A448 25c blk & multi 35 10

Christmas 1971. Design is from a tapestry by Horacio Butler in Basilica of St. Francis, Buenos Aires.

Mother and Child, by J. C. Castagnino
A449

1972, May 6 *Perf. 13½* Unwmkd.

971 A449 25c fawn & blk 35 10

25th anniversary (in 1971) of the International United Nations Children's Fund (UNICEF).

Mailman's Bag
A450

1972, Sept. 2 Litho. *Perf. 13½*

972 A450 25c lem & multi 20 8

Bicentenary of appointment of first Argentine mailman.

Adm. Brown Station, Map of Antarctica
A451

1972, Sept. 2

973 A451 25c bl & multi 50 10

10th anniversary (in 1971) of Antarctic Treaty.

Soldier Type of 1965

Design: 25c, Sergeant, Negro and Mulatto Corps, 1806–1807.

1972, Sept. 23

974 A340a 25c multi 1.00 25

Army Day, May 29.

Brigantine "Santisima Trinidad"
A452

1972, Sept. 23

975 A452 25c multi 1.00 25

Navy Day. See also No. 1006.

Oil Pump
A453

1972, Sept. 30 Litho. *Perf. 13½*

976	A453	45c blk & multi	1.50	15

50th anniversary of the organization of the state oil fields (Yacimientos Petroliferos Fiscales).

Sounding Balloon
A454

1972, Sept. 30

977	A454	25c blk, bl & ocher	35	10

Centenary of National Meteorological Service.

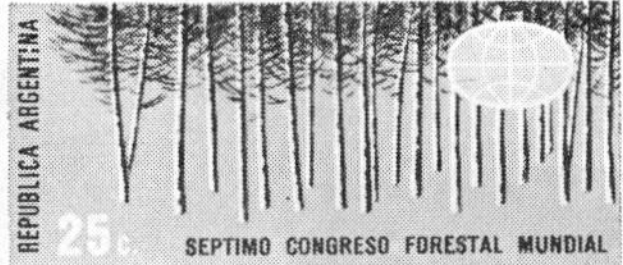

Trees and Globe—A455

1972, Oct. 14 *Perf. 13x13½*

978	A455	25c bl, blk & lt bl	1.10	15

7th World Forestry Congress, Buenos Aires, Oct. 4–18.

Arms of Naval School, Frigate "Presidente Sarmiento"—A456

1972, Oct. 14

979	A456	25c gold & multi	90	10

Centenary of Military Naval School.

Early Balloon and Plane, Antonio de Marchi—A457

Bartolomé Mitre A458

1972, Nov. 4 *Perf. 13½*

980	A457	25c multi	35	10

Aeronautics and Space Week, and in honor of Baron Antonio de Marchi (1875–1934), aviation pioneer.

1972, Nov. 4 Engraved

981	A458	25c dk bl	20	8

Pres. Bartolomé Mitre (1821–1906), writer, historian, soldier.

Flower and Heart
A459

1972, Dec. 2 Litho. *Perf. 13½*

982	A459	90c lt bl, ultra & blk	60	15

"Your heart is your health," World Health Day.

"Martin Fierro," by Juan C. Castignano
A460

"Spirit of the Gaucho," by Vicente Forte
A461

1972, Dec. 2 Litho. *Perf. 13½*

983	A460	50c multi	35	15
984	A461	90c multi	75	25

International Book Year 1972, and to commemorate the centenary of publication of the poem, Martin Fierro, by José Hernandez (1834–1886).

Iguassu Falls and Tourist Year Emblem—A462

1972, Dec. 16 *Perf. 13x13½*

985	A462	45c multi	45	12

Tourism Year of the Americas.

King, Wood Carving, 18th Century
A463

1972, Dec. 16 *Perf. 13½*

986	A463	50c multi	75	12

Christmas 1972.

Types of 1955–73 Inscribed "Republica Argentina" and

Moon Valley, San Juan Province
A463a

Designs: 1c, Sunflower. 5c, Tierra del Fuego. 10c, Inca Bridge, Mendoza. 50c, Lujan Basilica. 65c, 22.50p, San Martin. 1p, Ski jumper. 1.15p, 4.50p, Guillermo Brown. 1.80p, Manuel Belgrano.

Perf. 13½, 12½ (1.80p)
Litho.; Photo. (1c, 65c, 1p)

1972–75 **Wmk. 365**

987	A278	1c dk grn	20	3
988	A277	5c dk bl	20	3
989	A278	10c bis brn	20	3
989A	A426	50c dl pur ('75)	20	3
990	A241	65c gray brn	4.00	10
991	A279	1p brown	1.75	6
992	A366	1.15p dk gray bl	1.50	6
993	A425	1.80p bl ('75)	15	3
994	A366	4.50p grn ('75)	75	6
995	A241	22.50p vio bl ('75)	1.50	10
996	A463a	50p multi ('75)	3.00	50
		Nos. 987-996 (11)	13.45	1.03

Paper size of 1c is 27½x39mm.; others of 1972, 37x27, 27x37mm.
Size of 22.50p, 50p: 26½x38½mm.
See No. 1050.

Cock (Symbolic of Police)
A464

First Coin of Bank of Buenos Aires
A465

1973, Feb. 3 Litho. **Unwmkd.**

997	A464	50c lt grn & multi	30	10

Sesquicentennial of Federal Police of Argentina.

1973, Feb. 3 *Perf. 13½*

998	A465	50c pur, yel & brn	20	10

Sesquicentennial of the Bank of Buenos Aires Province.

DC-3 Planes Over Antarctica
A466

1973, Apr. 28 Litho. *Perf. 13½*

999	A466	50c lt bl & multi	90	15

10th anniversary of Argentina's first flight to the South Pole.

Rivadavia's Chair, Argentine Arms and Colors
A467

1973, May 19 Litho. *Perf. 13½*

1000	A467	50c multi	35	12

Inauguration of Pres. Hector J. Cámpora, May 25, 1973.

San Martin, by Gil de Castro
A468

San Martin and Bolívar
A469

1973, July 7 Litho. *Perf 13½*

1001	A468	50c lt grn & multi	45	10
1002	A469	50c yel & multi	45	10

Gen. San Martin's farewell to the people of Peru and his meeting with Simon Bolívar at Guayaquil July 26–27, 1822.

Eva Perón
A470

1973, July 26 Litho. *Perf. 13½*

1003	A470	70c blk, org & bl	30	10

Maria Eva Duarte de Perón (1919–1952), political leader.

House of Viceroy Sobremonte, by Hortensia de Virgilion—A471

1973, July 28 *Perf. 13x13½*

1004	A471	50c bl & multi	30	10

400th anniversary of the city of Córdoba.

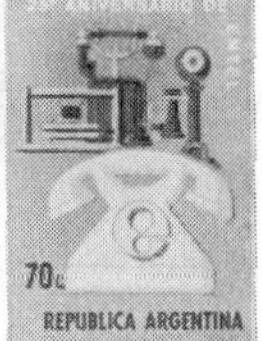

Woman, by Lino Spilimbergo
A472

New and Old Telephones
A473

1973, Aug. 28 Litho. *Perf. 13½*

1005	A472	70c multi	1.10	10

Philatelists' Day. See Nos. B60–B61.

Ship Type of 1972

Design: 70c, Frigate "La Argentina."

1973, Oct. 27 Litho. *Perf. 13½*

1006	A452	70c multi	75	15

Navy Day.

1973, Oct. 27

1007	A473	70c brt bl & multi	35	10

25th anniversary of national telecommunications system.

Plume Made of Flags of Participants
A474

1973, Nov. 3 *Perf. 13½*

1008 A474 70c yel bis & multi 35 10

12th Congress of Latin Notaries, Buenos Aires.

No. 940 Overprinted

TRANSMISION DEL MANDO PRESIDENCIAL
12 OCTUBRE 1973

1973, Nov. 30 Photogravure

1010 A241 1.20p orange 1.10 20

Assumption of presidency by Juan Peron, Oct. 12.

Virgin and Child, Window, La Plata Cathedral
A476

Design: 1.20p, Nativity, by Bruno Venier, b. 1914.

1973, Dec. 15 Litho. *Perf. 13½*

1011 A476 70c gray & multi 35 12
1012 A476 1.20p blk & multi 75 20

Christmas 1973.

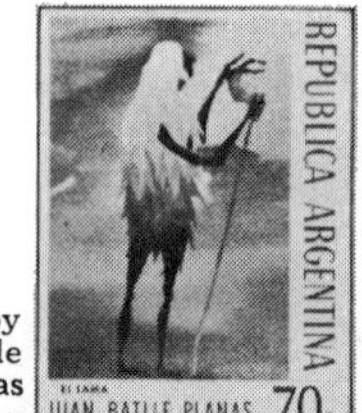

The Lama, by Juan Batlle Planas
A477

Paintings: 50c, Houses in Boca District, by Eugenio Daneri (horiz.). 90c, The Blue Grotto, by Emilio Pettoruti (horiz.).

1974, Feb. 9 Litho. *Perf. 13½*

1013 A477 50c multi 30 10
1014 A477 70c multi 35 15
1015 A477 90c multi 75 20

Argentine painters. See No. B64.

Mar del Plata
A478

1974, Feb. 9

1016 A478 70c multi 35 12

Centenary of Mar del Plata.

Weather Symbols
A479

Justo Santa Maria de Oro
A480

1974, Mar. 23 Litho. *Perf. 13½*

1017 A479 1.20p multi 45 15

Centenary of international meteorological cooperation.

1974, Mar. 23

1018 A480 70c multi 30 10

Bicentenary of the birth of Brother Justo Santa Maria de Oro (1772–1836), theologian, patriot, first Argentine bishop.

Belisario Roldan
A481

1974, June 29 Photo. **Unwmkd.**

1019 A481 70c bl & brn 20 10

Birth centenary of Belisario Roldan (1873–1922), writer.

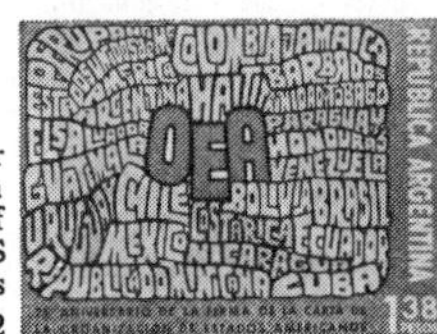

Poster with Names of OAS Members
A482

1974, June 29 Lithographed

1020 A482 1.38p multi 25 15

25th anniversary of the Organization of American States.

ENCOTEL Emblem—A483

1974, Aug. 10 Litho. *Perf. 13*

1021 A483 1.20p bl, gold & blk 60 15

ENCOTEL, National Post and Telegraph Press.

Flags of Argentina, Bolivia, Brazil, Paraguay, Uruguay
A484

1974, Aug. 16 *Perf. 13½*

1022 A484 1.38p multi 25 15

6th Meeting of Foreign Ministers of Rio de la Plata Basin Countries.

El Chocon Hydroelectric Complex, Limay River
A485

Somisa Steel Mill, San Nicolas
A486

Gen. Belgrano Bridge, Chaco-Corrientes—A487

Perf. 13½, 13x13½ (4.50p)

1974, Sept. 14

1023 A485 70c multi 35 10
1024 A486 1.20p multi 60 15
1025 A487 4.50p multi 2.75 30

Development projects.

Brigantine Belgrano, by Emilio Biggeri
A488

1974, Oct. 26 Litho. *Perf. 13½*

1026 A488 1.20p multi 80 15

Departure into exile in Chile of General San Martin, Sept. 22, 1822.

Alberto R. Mascias and Bleriot Plane
A489

1974, Oct. 26 **Unwmk.**

1027 A489 1.20p multi 60 15

Air Force Day, Aug. 10, and to honor Alberto Roque Garcias (1878–1951), aviation pioneer.

Exists with wmk. 365.

Hussar, 1812, by Eleodoro Marenco
A490

1974, Oct. 26

1028 A490 1.20p multi 60 15

Army Day.

Post Horn and Flags
A491

1974, Nov. 23 *Perf. 13½* **Unwmkd.**

1029 A491 2.65p multi 1.25 15

Centenary of Universal Postal Union. Exists with wmk. 365.

Franciscan Monastery
A492

1974, Nov. 23 Lithographed

1030 A492 1.20p multi 60 15

400th anniversary, city of Santa Fe.

Trout Type of 1968.

1974 Engraved **Unwmkd.**

1031 A366a 1000p vio bl 4.50 50

Due to a shortage of 10p stamps a quantity of this 1,000p was released for use as 10p.

Types of 1954–73
Inscribed "Republica Argentina" and

Red Deer in Forest
A495

Congress Building
A497

Designs: 30c, 60c, 1.80p, Manuel Belgrano. 50c, Lujan Basilica. No. 1036, 2p, 6p, San Martin (16x22½mm.). 2.70p, 7.50p, 22.50p, San Martin (22x31½mm.). 4.50p, 13.50p, Guillermo Brown. 10p, Leaping trout.

Photogravure

1974–75 *Perf. 13½* **Unwmkd.**

1032 A425 30c brn vio 15 3
1033 A426 50c blk & brn red ('75) 15 3
1034 A426 50c bis & bl ('75) 15 3
1035 A425 60c ocher ('75) 15 3
1036 A425 1.20p red 45 3
1037 A425 1.80p dp bl ('75) 20 3
1038 A425 2p dk pur ('75) 30 3
1039 A241 2.70p dk bl 22x31½mm 35 3
1040 A366 4.50p green 1.30 4
1041 A495 5p yel grn 60 4
1042 A425 6p red org ('75) 30 4
1043 A425 6p emer ('75) 30 4
1044 A241 7.50p grn, 22x31½mm('75) 1.25 6
1045 A366a 10p vio bl 1.50 6

1046 A366 13.50p scar, 16x22½mm ('75) 1.25 6
1047 A366 13.50p scar, 22x31½mm('75) 1.25 8
1048 A241 22.50p dp bl, 22x31½mm('75) 1.10 10
1049 A497 30p yel & dk red brn 1.75 12
1050 A463a 50p multi ('76) 2.25 15
Nos. 1032-1050 (19) 14.75 1.03

Fluorescent paper was used in printing No. 1036, 2p, Nos. 1044 and 1047. The 30p was issued on both ordinary and fluorescent paper.
See also No. 829.

Miniature Sheet

A498

1974, Dec. 7 Litho. *Perf. 13½*

1052 A498 Sheet of 6, multi 4.50 3.50
a. 1p *Mariano Necochea* 35
b. 1.20p *Jose de San Martin* 35
c. 1.70p *Manuel Isidoro Suarez* 50
d. 1.90p *Juan Pascual Pringles* 60
e. 2.70p *Latin American flags* 90
f. 4.50p *Jose Felix Bogado* 1.50

Sesquicentennial of Battles of Junin and Ayacucho. No. 1052 has black control number. Size: 140x132mm.

Dove, by Vito Campanella
A499

St. Anne, by Raul Soldi
A500

1974, Dec. 21 Litho. *Perf. 13½*

1053 A499 1.20p multi 60 8
1054 A500 2.65p multi 90 15

Christmas 1974.

Boy Looking at Stamp
A501

1974, Dec. 21

1055 A501 1.70p blk & yel 50 18

World Youth Philately Year.

Space Monsters, by Raquel Forner
A502

Design: 4.50p, Dream, by Emilio Centurion.

1975, Feb. 22 Litho. *Perf. 13½*

1056 A502 2.70p multi 1.10 25
1057 A502 4.50p multi 2.25 35

Argentine modern art.

Indian Woman and Cathedral, Catamarca—A503

Designs: No. 1059, Carved chancel and street scene. No. 1060, Grazing cattle and monastery yard. No. 1061, Painted pottery and power station. No. 1062, Farm cart and colonial mansion. No. 1063, Perito Moreno glacier and spinning mill. No. 1064, Lake Lapataia and scientific surveyor. No. 1065, Los Alerces National Park and oil derrick.

1975 Lithographed *Perf. 13½*
Unwmkd.; Wmk. 365 (6p)

1058 A503 1.20p *shown* 35 10
1059 A503 1.20p *Jujuy* 35 10
1060 A503 1.20p *Salta* 35 10
1061 A503 1.20p *Santiago del Estero* 35 10
1062 A503 1.20p *Tucuman* 35 10
1063 A503 6p *Santa Cruz* 35 10
1064 A503 6p *Tierra del Fuego* 35 10
1065 A503 6p *Chubut* 35 10
Nos. 1058-1065 (8) 2.80 80

Tourist publicity.
Issue dates: 1.20p, Mar. 8; 6p, Dec. 20.

"We Have Been Inoculated"
A504

1975, Apr. 26 Unwmkd. *Perf. 13½*

1066 A504 2p multi 60 24

Children's inoculation campaign (child's painting).

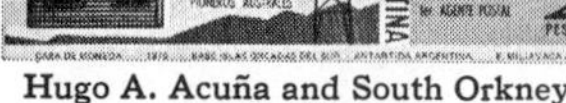

Hugo A. Acuña and South Orkney Station—A505

Designs: No. 1068, Francisco P. Moreno and Lake Nahuel Huapi. No. 1069, Lt. Col. Luis Piedra Buena and cutter, Luisito. No. 1070, Ensign José M. Sobral and Snow Hill House. No. 1071, Capt. Carlos M. Moyano and Cerro del Toro (mountain).

1975, June 28 Litho. *Perf. 13*

1067 A505 2p grnsh bl & multi 30 10
1068 A505 2p yel grn & multi 30 10
1069 A505 2p lt vio & multi 30 10
1070 A505 2p gray bl & multi 30 10
1071 A505 2p pale grn & multi 30 10
Nos. 1067-1071 (5) 1.50 50

Pioneers of Antarctica.

Frigate "25 de Mayo"
A506

1975, Sept. 27 *Perf. 13½* Unwmkd.

1072 A506 6p multi 45 12

Navy Day 1975.

Eduardo Bradley and Balloon
A507

1975, Sept. 27 Wmk. 365

1073 A507 6p multi 45 12

Air Force Day.

Declaration of Independence, by Juan M. Blanes
A508

1975, Oct. 25

1074 A508 6p multi 45 12

Sesquicentennial of Uruguay's declaration of independence.

Flame
A509

1975, Oct. 17 Unwmkd.

1075 A509 6p gray & multi 45 12

Loyalty Day, 30th anniversary of Pres. Peron's accession to power.

Nos. 886, 891 and 932 Surcharged

REVALORIZADO
6 c.
a

REVALORIZADO
30 c
b

REVALORIZADO
5 pesos
c

1975 Litho., Photo.

1076 A277 6c on 3p 15 5
1077 A366 30c on 90p 15 5
1078 A426 5p on 18c 50 20

Issue dates: 6c, Oct. 30; 30c, Nov. 20; 5p, Oct. 24. The 6c also exists on No. 886a.

International Bridge, Flags of Argentina and Uruguay
A510

1975, Oct. 25 Litho. Wmk. 365

1081 A510 6p multi 45 12

Opening of bridge connecting Colon, Argentina, and Paysandu, Uruguay.

Post Horn, Surcharged
A511

1975, Nov. 8

1082 A511 10p on 20c multi 75 20

Introduction of postal code. Not issued without surcharge.

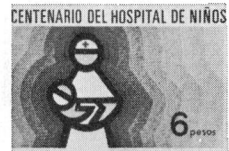

Nurse Holding Infant
A512

1975, Dec. 13 Litho. *Perf. 13½*

1083 A512 6p multi 75 20

Children's Hospital, centenary.

Nativity, Nueva Pompeya Church
A513

1975, Dec. 13 Litho. Unwmkd.

1084 A513 6p multi 35 10

Christmas 1975.

Types of 1970–75 and

Church of St. Francis, Salta
A515

Designs: 3p, No. 1099, 60p, 90p, Manuel Belgrano. 12p, 15p, 20p, 30p, No. 1100, 100p, 110p, 120p, 130p, San Martin. 15p, 70p, Guillermo Brown. 300p, Moon Valley (lower inscriptions italic). 500p, Adm. Brown Station, Antarctica.

Photo.; *Perf. 13½;* Unwmkd.
Litho.; *Perf. 12½x13;* Wmk. 365

1976–78

1089 A425 3p slate 5 3
1090 A425 12p rose red 20 6

1091	A425	12p rose red, litho.	20	6
1092	A425	12p emer, litho.	20	6
1093	A425	12p emer ('77)	20	6
1094	A425	15p rose red	20	8
1095	A425	15p vio bl ('77)	20	8
1097	A425	20p rose red ('77)	30	10
1098	A425	30p rose red ('77)	45	14
1099	A425	40p dp grn	60	20
1100	A425	40p rose red ('77)	35	15
1101	A425	60p dk bl ('77)	90	28
1102	A425	70p dk bl ('77)	1.00	30
1103	A425	90p emer ('77)	1.25	40
1104	A425	100p red	1.10	35
1105	A425	110p rose red ('78)	65	25
1106	A425	120p rose red ('78)	75	30
1107	A425	130p rose red ('78)	90	35

Litho.; *Perf. 13½*; Unwmkd.

1108	A463a	300p multi	4.50	2.25
1109	A515	500p multi ('77)	6.00	2.00
1110	A515	1000p multi ('77)	12.00	3.00
		Nos. 1089-1110 (21)	32.00	10.50

Fluorescent paper was used in printing both 12p rose red, 15p rose red, 20p, 30p, 40p rose red, 100p, 110p, 120p, 130p. No. 1099 and the 300p were issued on both ordinary and fluorescent paper.

300p and 500p exist with wmk. 365.

Numeral
A516

Photo.; *Perf. 13½*; Unwmkd.
Litho.; *Perf. 13x12½*; Wmk. 365

1976

1112	A516	12c gray & blk	5	3
1113	A516	50c gray & grn	10	3
1114	A516	1p red & blk	10	3
1115	A516	4p bl & blk	20	3
1116	A516	5p org & blk	20	3
1117	A516	5p org & blk, litho.	20	3
1118	A516	6p dp brn & blk	20	3
1119	A516	10p gray & vio bl	30	4
1120	A516	27p lt grn & blk	75	8
1121	A516	27p lt grn & blk, litho.	75	8
1122	A516	30p lt bl & blk	1.25	10
1123	A516	45p yel & blk	1.25	15
1124	A516	45p yel & blk, litho.	1.25	15
1125	A516	50p dl grn & blk	1.75	18
1126	A516	100p brt grn & red	2.25	35
		Nos. 1112-1126 (15)	10.60	1.34

Fluorescent paper was used in printing the 50p. The 1p, 6p, 10p and No. 1116 were issued on both ordinary and fluorescent paper.

Jet and Airlines Emblem—A517
Unwmkd.

1976, Apr. 24 Litho. *Perf. 13x13½*

1130	A517	30p bl, lt bl & dk bl	1.50	20

Argentine Airlines, 25th anniversary.

Frigate Heroina and Map of Falkland Islands—A518

1976, Apr. 26

1131	A518	6p multi	60	12

Argentina's claim to Falkland Islands.

Louis Braille—A519
Wmk. 365

1976, May 22 Engr. *Perf. 13½*

1132	A519	19.70 dp bl	45	15

Sesquicentennial of the invention of the Braille system of writing for the blind by Louis Braille (1809–1852).

Private, 7th Infantry Regiment
A520

1976, May 29 Litho. *Unwmkd.*

1133	A520	12p multi	45	10

Army Day.

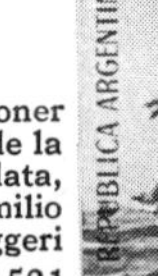

Schooner Rio de la Plata, by Emilio Biggeri
A521

1976, June 19

1134	A521	12p multi	45	10

Navy Day.

Dr. Bernardo Houssay
A522

Nobel Prize Winners: 15p, Luis F. Leloir, chemistry, 1970. 20p, Carlos Saavedra Lamas, peace, 1936. Bernardo Houssay, medicine and physiology, 1947.

1976, Aug. 14 Litho. *Perf. 13½*

1135	A522	10p org & blk	30	10
1136	A522	15p yel & blk	45	15
1137	A522	20p ocher & blk	60	20

Argentine Nobel Prize winners.

Rio de la Plata International Bridge—A523

1976, Sept. 18 Litho. *Perf. 13½*

1138	A523	12p multi	30	10

Inauguration of International Bridge connecting Puerte Unzue, Argentina, and Fray Bentos, Uruguay.

Pipelines and Cooling Tower, Gen. Mosconi Plant—A524

1976, Nov. 20 Litho. *Perf. 13½*

1139	A524	28p multi	45	20

Pablo Teodoro Fels and Bleriot Monoplane, 1910—A525

1976, Nov. 20

1140	A525	15p multi	30	10

Air Force Day.

Nativity
A526

1976, Dec. 18 Litho. *Perf. 13½*

1141	A526	20p multi	45	15

Christmas 1976. Painting by Edith Chiapetto.

Water Conference Emblem
A527

1977, Mar. 19 Litho. *Perf. 13½*

1142	A527	70p multi	1.00	35

U.N. Water Conference, Mar del Plata, Mar. 14–25.

Dalmacio Vélez Sarsfield
A528

1977, Mar. 19 Engraved

1143	A528	50p blk & red brn	75	25

Dalmacio Vélez Sarsfield (1800–1875), author of Argentine civil code.

Red Deer Type of 1974 Surcharged

100 PESOS
150°. ANIV. DEL CORREO NACIONAL DEL URUGUAY

1977, July 30 Photo. *Perf. 13½*

1144	A495	100p on 5p brn	1.50	30

Sesquicentennial of Uruguayan postal service. Not issued without surcharge.

Soldier, 16th Lancers
A529

1977, July 30

1145	A529	30p multi	45	15

Army Day.

Schooner Sarandi, by Emilio Biggeri
A530

1977, July 30

1146	A530	30p multi	45	15

Navy Day.

Soccer Games' Emblem
A531

Design: 70p, Argentina '78 emblem, flags and soccer field.

1977, May 14

1147	A531	30p multi	60	15
1148	A531	70p multi	1.25	35

11th World Cup Soccer Championship, Argentina, June 1–25, 1978.

The Visit, by Horacio Butler
A532

Consecration, by Miguel P. Caride
A533

1977, Mar. 26 **Lithographed**

1149	A532	50p multi	75	25
1150	A533	70p multi	1.00	35

Argentine artists.

Sierra de la Ventana—A534

Views: No. 1152, Civic Center, Santa Rosa. No. 1153, Skiers, San Martin de los Andes. No. 1154, Boat on Lake Fonck, Rio Negro.

1977, Oct. 8 Litho. *Perf. 13x13½*

1151	A534	30p multi	45	15
1152	A534	30p multi	45	15
1153	A534	30p multi	45	15
1154	A534	30p multi	45	15

Guillermo Brown, by R. del Villar
A535

1977, Oct. 8 ***Perf. 13½***

1155	A535	30p multi	45	15

Adm. Guillermo Brown (1777–1857), leader in fight for independence, bicentenary of birth.

Jet
A536

Double-decker, 1926
A537

1977 Litho. *Perf. 13½*

1156	A536	30p multi	35	15
1157	A537	40p multi	45	20

50th anniversary of military plane production (30p); Air Force Day (40p).
Issue dates: 30p, Dec. 3; 40p, Nov. 26.

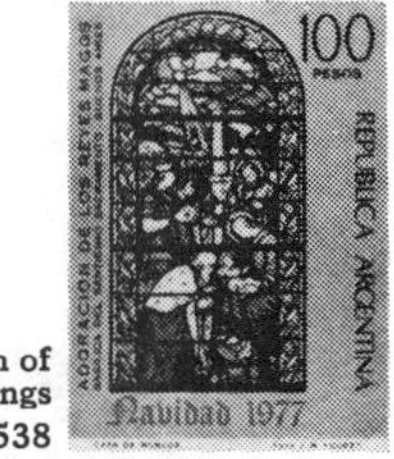

Adoration of the Kings
A538

1977, Dec. 17

1158	A538	100p multi	1.10	20

Christmas 1977.

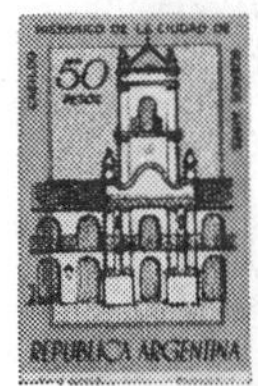

Historic City Hall, Buenos Aires
A539

Chapel of Rio Grande Museum, Tierra del Fuego
A540

Designs: 5p, 20p, La Plata Museum. 10p, Independence Hall, Tucuman. 40p, City Hall, Salta (vert.). No. 1165, City Hall, Buenos Aires. 100p, Columbus Theater, Buenos Aires. 200p, flag Monument, Rosario. 280p, 300p, Chapel of Rio Grande Museum, Tierra del Fuego. 480p, 520p, 800p, Ruins of Jesuit Mission Church of San ignacio, Misiones. 500p, Candonga Chapel, Cordoba. 1000p, G.P.O., Buenos Aires. 2000p, Civic Center, Bariloche, Rio Negro.

Three types of 10p: I. Nine vertical window bars; small imprint "E. MILIAVACA Dib." II. Nine bars; large imprint "E. MILIAVACA DIB." III. Redrawn; 5 bars; large imprint.

Unwmkd.

1977– Photogravure *Perf. 13½*

Size: 32x21mm., 21x32mm.

1159	A540	5p gray & blk ('78)	5	3
1160	A540	10p lt ultra & blk, I ('78)	5	3
a.		Type II ('78)	3	3
1161	A540	10p lt bl & blk, III ('79)	5	3
1162	A540	20p cit & blk, litho. ('78)	5	3
1163	A540	40p gray bl & blk ('78)	20	3
1164	A539	50p yel & blk	35	15
1165	A540	50p cit & blk ('79)	20	3
1166	A540	100p org & blk, litho. ('78)	45	10
a.		Wmk. 365	100.00	25.00
1167	A540	100p red org & blk, photo. ('79)	3	3
1168	A540	100p turq & blk ('81)	3	3
1169	A539	200p lt bl & blk ('79)	60	30
1170	A540	280p rose & blk	15.00	20
1171	A540	300p lem & blk ('78)	1.25	15
1172	A540	480p org & blk ('78)	2.25	30
1173	A540	500p yel grn & blk ('78)	2.25	25
1174	A540	520p org & blk ('78)	2.25	30
1175	A540	800p rose lil & blk ('79)	2.75	40
1176	A540	1000p lem bis & blk ('79)	3.00	50
1177	A540	1000p gold & blk, 40x29mm ('78)	5.00	50
1178	A540	2000p multi ('80)	2.80	50
		Nos. 1159-1178 (20)	38.61	3.89

Soccer Games' Emblem
A544

1978, Feb. 10 Photo. *Perf. 13½*

1179	A544	200p yel grn & bl	1.00	20

11th World Cup Soccer Championship, Argentina, June 1-25. Exists with wmk. 365.

View of El Rio, Rosario—A545

Designs (Argentina '78 Emblem and): 100p, Rio Tercero Dam, Cordoba. 150p, Cordillera Mountains, Mendoza. 200p, City Center, Mar del Plata. 300p, View of Buenos Aires.

1978, May 6 Litho. *Perf. 13*

1180	A545	50p multi	20	10
1181	A545	100p multi	45	10
1182	A545	150p multi	65	15
1183	A545	200p multi	60	20
1184	A545	300p multi	1.50	30
		Nos. 1180-1184 (5)	3.40	85

Sites of 11th World Cup Soccer Championship, June 1–25.

Children—A546

1978, May 20

1185	A546	100p multi	45	15

50th anniversary of Children's Institute.

Labor Day, by B. Quinquela Martin
A547

Design: No. 1187, Woman's torso, sculpture by Orlando Pierri.

1978, May 20 ***Perf. 13½***

1186	A547	100p multi	45	10
1187	A547	100p multi	45	10

Argentina, Hungary, France, Italy and Emblem—A548

Stadium
A549

Teams and Argentina '78 Emblem: 200p, Poland, Fed. Rep. of Germany, Tunisia, Mexico. 300p, Austria, Spain, Sweden, Brazil. 400p, Netherlands, Iran, Peru, Scotland.

1978 Litho. *Perf. 13*

1188	A548	100p multi	45	10
1189	A548	200p multi	90	10
1190	A548	300p multi	1.35	15
1191	A548	400p multi	1.75	25

Souvenir Sheet

Litho. and Engr. *Perf. 13½*

1192	A549	700p buff & blk	3.50	2.00

11th World Cup Soccer Championship, Argentina, June 1–25. No. 1192 contains one stamp; blue and black margin shows sports and communications emblems. Size: 89x60mm. Issue dates, Nos. 1188–1191, June 6, No. 1192, June 3.

Stadium Type of 1978 Inscribed in Red: "ARGENTINA / CAMPEON"

Lithographed and Engraved

1978, Sept. 2 ***Perf. 13½***

1193	A549	1000p buff, blk & red	5.00	2.00

Argentina's victory in 1978 Soccer Championship. No. 1193 has margin similar to No. 1192 with Rimet Cup emblem added in red. Size: 89x60mm.

Young Tree Nourished by Old Trunk, U.N. Emblem—A550

1978, Sept. 2 **Lithographed**

1194	A550	100p multi	45	15

Technical Cooperation among Developing Countries Conference, Buenos Aires, Sept. 1978.

Emblems of Buenos Aires and Bank
A551

1978, Sept. 16

1195	A551	100p multi	45	15

Bank of City of Buenos Aires, centenary.

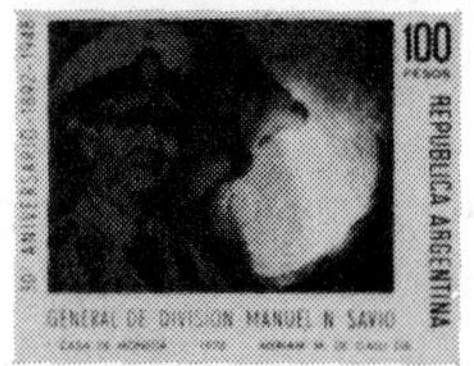

General Savio and Steel Production
A552

1978, Sept. 16

1196	A552	100p multi	45	15

Gen. Manuel N. Savio (1892–1948), general manager of military heavy industry, 30th death anniversary.

San Martin
A553

1978, Oct. **Engraved**

1197	A553	2000p grnsh blk	9.00	1.50
1198	A553	2000p grnsh blk, wmk. 365 ('79)	6.00	50

Gen Jose de San Martin (1778-1850), soldier and statesman. See No. 1292.

Globe and Argentine Flag
A554

Chessboard, Queen and Pawn
A555

1978, Oct. 7 Litho. *Perf. 13½*

1199 A554 200p multi 90 15

12th International Cancer Congress, Buenos Aires, Oct. 5–11.

1978, Oct. 7

1200 A555 200p multi 2.00 25

23rd National Chess Olympics, Buenos Aires, Oct. 25–Nov. 12.

Correct Positioning of Stamps
A557

Design: 50p, Use correct postal code number.

1978 Photogravure *Perf. 13½*

1201 A557 20p ultra 6 5
1203 A557 50p carmine 15 5

Numeral
A558

A559

1978 Photogravure *Perf. 13½*

1204 A558 150p bl & ultra 45 10
1205 A558 180p bl & ultra 55 15
1206 A558 200p bl & ultra 40 12
1207 A559 240p ol bis & bl ('79) 48 16
1208 A559 260p blk & lt bl ('79) 52 18
1209 A559 290p blk & lt bl ('79) 58 18
1210 A559 310p mag & bl ('79) 62 22
1211 A559 350p ver & bl ('79) 70 25
1212 A559 450p ultra & bl 65 22
1213 A559 600p grn & bl ('80) 85 30
1214 A559 700p blk & bl ('80) 85 30
1215 A559 800p red & bl ('81) 80 10
1216 A559 1100p gray & bl ('81) 1.10 10
1217 A559 1500p blk & bl ('81) 45 10
1218 A559 1700p grn & bl ('82) 55
Nos. 1204-1218 (15) 9.55

No. 1206 issued on fluorescent and ordinary paper.

See Nos. 1293-1294.

Balsa "24"
A561

Ships: 200p, Tug Legador. 300p, River Parana tug No. 34. 400p, Passenger ship Ciudad de Parana.

1978, Nov. 4 Litho. *Perf. 13½*

1220 A561 100p multi 30 5
1221 A561 200p multi 60 5
1222 A561 300p multi 90 10
1223 A561 400p multi 1.20 15

20th anniversary of national river fleet. Nos. 1220 and 1223, 1221–1222 printed se-tenant in sheets of 50. Issued on fluorescent paper.

View and Arms of Bahia Blanca
A562

1978, Nov. 25 Litho. *Perf. 13½*

1224 A562 20p multi 60 10

Sesquicentennial of Bahia Blanca.

"Spain," (Queen Isabella and Columbus) by Arturo Dresco—A563

1978, Nov. 25

1225 A563 300p multi 4.00 25

Visit of King Juan Carlos and Queen Sofia of Spain to Argentina, Nov. 26.

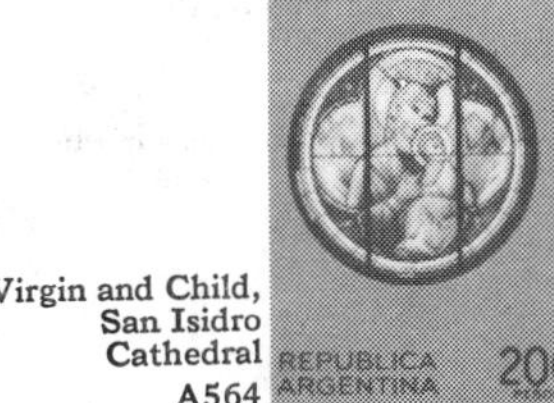

Virgin and Child, San Isidro Cathedral
A564

1978, Dec. 16

1226 A564 200p gold & multi 60 10

Christmas 1978.

Slope at Chacabuco, by Pedro Subercaseaux—A565

Painting: 1000p, The Embrace of Maipu (San Martin and O'Higgins), by Pedro Subercaseaux (vert.).

1978, Dec. 16 Litho. *Perf. 13½*

1227 A565 500p multi 1.00 20
1228 A565 1000p multi 2.00 30

José de San Martin, 200th birth anniversary.

Adolfo Alsina
A566

Design: No. 1230, Mariano Moreno.

1979, Jan. 20

1229 A566 200p lt bl & blk 40 14
1230 A566 200p yel red & blk 40 14

Aldolfo Alsina (1829–1877), political leader, vice-president; Mariano Moreno (1778–1811), lawyer, educator, political leader.

Argentina No. 37 and UPU Emblem—A567

1979, Jan. 20

1231 A567 200p multi 40 14

Centenary of Argentina's UPU membership.

Still-life, by Cárcova
A568

Painting: 300p, The Laundresses, by Faustino Brughetti.

1979, Mar. 3

1232 A568 200p multi 40 15
1233 A568 300p multi 60 25

Ernesto de la Cárcova (1866–1927) and Faustino Brughetti (1877–1956), Argentine painters.

Balcarce Earth Station
A569

1979, Mar. 3

1234 A569 200p multi 40 15

Third Inter-American Telecommunications Conference, Buenos Aires, March 5-9.

Stamp Collecting
A570

1979

1235 A570 30p brt grn 6 3

European Olive
A571

Laurel and Regimental Emblem
A572

Designs: 200p, Tea. 300p, Sorghum. 400p, Common flax.

1979, June 2 Litho. *Perf. 13½*

1236 A571 100p multi 20 10
1237 A571 200p multi 40 15
1238 A571 300p multi 60 20
1239 A571 400p multi 80 30

1979, June 9

1240 A572 200p gold & multi 40 14

Founding of Subteniente Berdina Village in memory of Sub-lieutenant Rodolfo Hernan Berdina, killed by terrorists in 1975.

"75" and Automobile Club Emblem
A573

1979, June 9

1241 A573 200p gold & multi 30 14

Argentine Automobile Club, 75th anniversary.

Exchange Building and Emblem
A574

1979, June 9

1242 A574 200p bl, blk & gold 40 14

Grain Exchange, 125th anniversary.

Cavalry Officer, 1817
A575

1979, July 7 Litho. *Perf. 13½*

1243 A575 200p multi 40 20

Army Day.

Corvette Uruguay and Navy Emblem
A576

Design: No. 1245, Hydrographic service ship and emblem.

1979 *Perf. 13*

1244 A576 250p multi 50 20
1245 A576 250p multi 50 20

Navy Day (No. 1244); Centenary of Naval Hydrographic Service (No. 1245). Issue dates: No. 1244, July 28; No. 1245, July 7.

See "Special Notices" at the front of this volume for data on the listing methods of this Catalogue, abbreviations, condition, prices and examination.

Tree and Man
A577

1979, July 28 *Perf. 13½*

1246 A577 250p multi 50 15

Protection of the Environment Day, June 5.

"Spad" Flying over Andes, and Vicente Almandos Almonacid—A578

1979, Aug. 4

1247 A578 250p multi 50 15

Air Force Day.

Gen. Julio A. Roca Occupying Rio Negro, by Juan M. Blanes—A579

1979, Aug. 4

1248 A579 250p multi 50 15

Conquest of Rio Negro Desert, centenary.

Rowland Hill—A580

1979, Sept. 29 **Litho.** *Perf. 13½*

1249 A580 300p gray, red & blk 60 15

Sir Rowland Hill (1795-1879), originator of penny postage.

Viedma y Navarez Monument—A581

1979, Sept. 29

1250 A581 300p multi 60 15

Viedma and Carmen de Patagones towns, bicentenary.

Pope Paul VI—A582

Design: No. 1252, Pope John Paul I.

1979, Oct. 27 **Engr.** *Perf. 13½*

1251 A582 500p black 1.00 15
1252 A582 500p sepia 1.00 15

No. 1164A Overprinted in Red: "75 ANNIV. / SOCIEDAD/ FILATELICA / DE ROSARIO"

1979, Nov. 10 **Photo.** *Perf. 13½*

1253 A539 200p lt bl & blk 28 15

Rosario Philatelic Society, 75th anniversary.

Frontier Resettlement—A583

1979, Nov. 10 **Litho.**

1254 A583 300p multi 42 15

Military Geographic Institute Centenary
A584

1979, Dec. 1 **Litho.** *Perf. 13½*

1255 A584 300p multi 42 20

Christmas 1979—A585

1979, Dec. 1

1256 A585 300p multi 42 15

General Mosconi Birth Centenary
A586

1979, Dec. 15 **Engr.** *Perf. 13½*

1257 A586 1000p blk & bl 1.40 25

Rotary Emblem and Globe—A587

1979, Dec. 29 **Litho.**

1258 A587 300p multi 60 20

Rotary International, 75th anniversary.

Child and IYC Emblem—A588

Family, by Pablo Menicucci—A589

1979, Dec. 29

1259 A588 500p lt bl & sep 1.00 20
1260 A589 1000p multi 2.00 30

International Year of the Child.

Microphone, Waves, ITU Emblem—A590

1980, Mar. 22 **Litho.** *Perf. 13x13½*

1261 A590 500p multi 70 15

Regional Administrative Conference on Broadcasting by Hectometric Waves for Area 2, Buenos Aires, Mar. 10-29.

Guillermo Brown—A591

1980 **Engraved** *Perf. 13½*

1262 A591 5000p black 7.00 15

Argentine Red Cross Centenary—A592

1980, Apr. 19 **Litho.** *Perf. 13½*

1263 A592 500p multi 70 15

OAS Emblem—A593

1980, Apr. 19

1264 A593 500p multi 70 20

Day of the Americas, Apr. 14.

Dish Antennae, Balcarce—A594

1980, Apr. 26 **Litho. & Engr.**

1265 A594 300p *shown* 42 12
1266 A594 300p *Hydroelectric Station, Salto Grande* 42 12
1267 A594 300p *Bridge, Zarate-Brazo Largo* 42 12

Capt. Hipolito Bouchard, Frigate "Argentina"—A595

1980, May 31 **Litho.** *Perf. 13x13½*

1268 A595 500p multi 70 20

Navy Day.

"Villarino," San Martin, by Theodore Gericault—A596

1980, May 31

1269 A596 500p multi 70 20

Return of the remains of Gen. José de San Martin to Argentina, centenary.

Buenos Aires Gazette, 1810, Signature—A597

1980, June 7 ***Perf. 13½***

1270 A597 500p multi 70 15

Journalism Day.

Coaches in Victoria Square—A598

1980, June 14

1271 Block of 14 multi 10.00 3.50
a. A598 500p, any single 70 25

Buenos Aires, 400th anniversary. No. 1271 shows ceramic mural of Victoria Square by Rodolfo Franco in continuous design.

See No. 1285.

Gen. Pedro Aramburu—A599

1980, July 12 **Litho.** ***Perf. 13½***

1272 A599 500p yel & blk 70 15

Gen. Pedro Eugenio Aramburu (1903-1970), provisional president, 1955.

Army Day—A600

1980, July 12

1273 A600 500p multi 70 15

Gen. Juan Gregorio de Las Heras (1780-1866), Hero of 1817 War of Independence—A601

Grandees of Argentina Bicentenary: No. 1275, Bernardino Rivadavia (1780-1845), stateman and president. No. 1276, Brig. Gen José Matias Zapiola (1780-1874), naval commander and statesman.

1980, Aug. 2 **Litho.** ***Perf. 13½***

1274 A601 500p tan & blk 70 15
1275 A601 500p multi 70 15
1276 A601 500p lt lil & blk 70 15

Avro "Gosport" Biplane, Maj. Francisco de Artega—A602

1980, Aug. 16 ***Perf. 13***

1277 A602 500p multi 70 15

Air Force Day. Artega (1882-1930) was first director of Military Aircraft Factory where Avro "Gosport" was built (1927).

University of La Plata, 75th Anniversary—A603

1980, Aug. 16 ***Perf. 13½***

1278 A603 500p multi 70 15

Souvenir Sheets

Emperor Penguin—A604

South Orkneys Argentine Base
A605 A606

1980, Sept. 20 **Litho.** ***Perf. 13½***

1279 Sheet of 12 8.50 5.00
a. A604 500p *shown* 70 30
b. A604 500p *Bearded penguin* 70 30
c. A604 500p *Adeli penguins* 70 30
d. A604 500p *Papua penguins* 70 30
e. A604 500p *Sea elephants* 70 30
f. A605 500p *shown* 70 30
g. A606 500p *shown* 70 30
h. A604 500p *Fur seals* 70 30
i. A604 500p *Giant petrels* 70 30
j. A604 500p *Blue-eyed cormorants* 70 30
k. A604 500p *Stormy petrel* 70 30
m. A604 500p *Antarctic doves* 70 30
1280 Sheet of 12 8.50 5.00
a. A605 500p *Puerto Soledad* 70 30
b. A606 500p *Different view* 70 30

75th anniversary of Argentina's presence in the South Orkneys and 150th anniversary of political and military command in the Falkland Islands. Nos. 1279-1280 each contain 12 stamps (4x3) with landscape designs in center of sheets. Silhouettes of Argentine exploration ships in margins. Size: 150x173mm. No. 1280 contains Nos. 1279a-1279e, 1279h-1279m, 1280a-1280b.

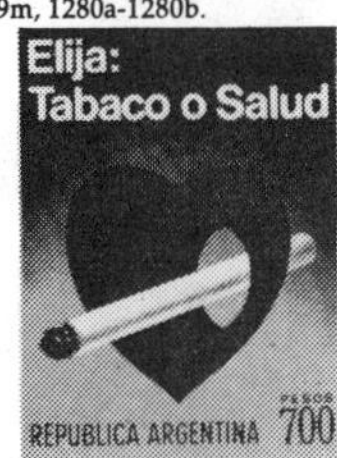

Anti-smoking Campaign—A608

1980, Oct. 11

1282 A608 700p multi 1.00 15

National Census—A609

1980, Sept.

1283 A609 500p blk & bl 70 10

Madonna and Child (Congress Emblem)—A610

1980, Oct. 1 **Litho.**

1284 A610 700p multi 1.00 15

National Marian Congress, Mendoza, Oct. 8-12

Mural Type of 1980

1980, Oct. 25

1285 Block of 14, multi 10.00 3.50
a. A598 500p, any single 70 25

Buenos Aires, 400th anniversary/Buenos Aires '80 Stamp Exhibition, Oct. 24-Nov. 2. No. 1285 shows ceramic mural Arte bajo la Cuidad by Alfredo Guido in continuous design.

Technical Military Academy, 50th Anniversary
A611

Amateur Radio Operation
A612

1980, Nov. 1

1286 A611 700p multi 1.00 15

1980, Nov. 1

1287 A612 700p multi 1.00 15

Medal
A613

Lujan Cathedral Floor Plan
A614

1980, Nov. 29 **Litho.** ***Perf. 13½***

1288 A613 700p multi 1.00 15
1289 A614 700p ol & brn 1.00 15

Christmas 1980. 150th anniversary of apparition of Holy Virgin to St. Catherine Laboure, Paris (No. 1288), 350th anniversary of apparition at Lujan.

150th Death Anniversary of Simon Bolivar—A615

1980, Dec. 13

1290 A615 700p multi 1.00 15

Soccer Gold Cup Championship, Montevideo, 1980—A616

1981, Jan. 3 **Litho.**

1291 A616 1000p multi 1.40 15

San Martin Type of 1978

1981, Jan. 20 **Engraved** ***Perf. 13½***

1292 A553 10,000p dk bl 10.00 20

Landscape in Lujan, by Marcos Tiglio—A617

Paintings: No. 1304, Expansion of Light along a Straight Line, by Miguel Angel Vidal (vert.).

1981, Apr. 11 **Litho.**

1303 A617 1000p multi 1.00 15
1304 A617 1000p multi 1.00 15

Intl. Sports Medicine Congress, June 7-12—A618

1981, June 6 **Litho.** ***Perf. 13½***

1305 A618 1000p bl & dk brn 1.00 15

Esperanza Base, Antarctica—A619

Cargo Plane, Map of Vice-Commodore Marambio Island—A620

1981, June 13
Perf. 13½,13x13½(No. 1308)

1306 A619 1000p shown 1.00 20
1307 A619 2000p Almirante Irizar 2.00 30
1308 A620 2000p shown 2.00 40

Antarctic Treaty 20th anniv.

Antique Pistols (Military Club Centenary) A621

1981, June 27 ***Perf. 13½***

1309 A621 1000p Club building 1.00 15
1310 A621 2000p shown 2.00 15

Gen. Juan A. Alvarez de Arenales (1770-1831)—A622

Famous Men: No. 1312, Felix G. Frias (1816-1881), writer. No. 1313, José E. Uriburu (1831-1914), statesman.

1311 A622 1000p multi 1.00 15
1312 A622 1000p multi 1.00 15
1313 A622 1000p multi 1.00 15

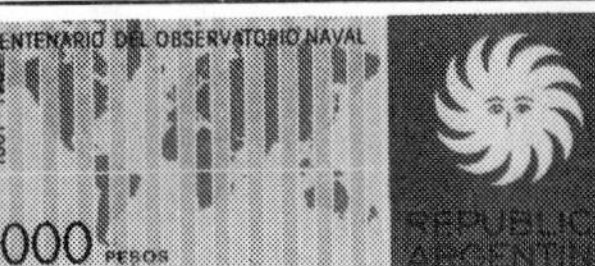

Naval Observatory Centenary—A623

1981, Aug. 15 **Litho.** ***Perf. 13x13½***

1314 A623 1000p multi 1.00 20

No. 1176 Overprinted in Red: "50° ANNIV. DE LA ASOCIACION / FILATELICA Y NUMISMATICA / DE BAHIA BLANCA"

1981, Aug. 15 **Photo.** ***Perf. 13½***

1315 A540 1000p lem & blk 1.20 30

50th anniv. of Bahia Blanca Philatelic and Numismatic Society.

St. Cayetano, Stained-glass Window, Buenos Aires—A624

1981, Sept. 5 **Litho.** ***Perf. 13½***

1316 A624 1000p multi 1.00 15

St. Cayetano, founder of Teatino Order, 500th birth anniv.

Pablo Castaibert (1883-1909) and his Monoplane (Air Force Day)—A625

1981, Sept. 5 ***Perf. 13x13½***

1317 A625 1000p multi 1.00 15

Intl. Year of the Disabled A626

1981, Sept. 10 ***Perf. 13½***

1318 A626 1000p multi 1.00 15

22nd Latin—American Steelmakers' Congress, Buenos Aires, Sept. 21-23—A627

1981, Sept. 19

1319 A627 1000p multi 1.00 15

Army Regiment No. 1 (Patricios), 175th Anniv.—A628

1981, Oct. 10 **Litho.** ***Perf. 13½***

1320 A628 1500p Natl. arms 45 15
1321 A628 1500p shown 45 15

Nos. 1320-1321 se-tenant.

Jose San Martin as Artillery Captain in Battle of Bailen, 1808—A629

1981, Oct. 5

1322 Sheet of 8 3.00 1.50
a.-d. A629 1000p multi 30 15
e.-h. A629 1500p multi 45 15

Espamer '81 Intl. Stamp Exhibition (Americas, Spain, Portugal), Buenos Aires, Nov. 13-22. No. 1322 has multicolored margin. Size 136x212mm.

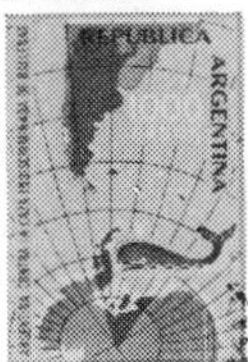

Anti-indiscriminate Whaling A630

Espamer '81 Emblem and Ship A631

1981, Oct. 5

1323 A630 1000p multi 30 10

1981

1324 A631 1300p multi 40 10

No. 1324 Overprinted in Blue: "CURSO SUPERIOR DE ORGANIZACION DE SERVICIOS FILATELICOS-UPAE-BUENOS AIRES-1981"

1981, Nov. 7 **Photo.** ***Perf. 13½***

1325 A631 1300p multi 40 15

Postal Administration philatelic training course.

Soccer Players—A632

Designs: Soccer players.

1981, Nov. 13 **Litho.**

1326 Sheet of 4 + 2 labels 10.00 6.00
a. A632 1000p multi 30 20
b. A632 3000p multi 90 30
c. A632 5000p multi 1.50 50
d. A632 15000p multi 4.50 1.50

Espamer '81. No. 1326 has black marginal inscription and control number. Size: 137x130mm.

"Peso" Coin Centenary—A633

1981, Nov. 21

1327 A633 2000p Patacon, 1881 60 15
1328 A633 3000p Argentine Oro, 1881 90 15

Christmas 1981 A634

1981, Dec. 12

1329 A634 1500p multi 45 15

Traffic Safety—A635

1981, Dec. 19 **Litho.**

1330 A635 1000p Observe traffic lights, vert. 30 15
1331 A635 2000p Drive carefully, vert. 60 15
1332 A635 3000p Cross at white lines 90 20
1333 A635 4000p Don't shine headlights 1.20 20

Francisco Luis Bernardez, Ciuda Laura—A636

Designs: Writers and title pages from their works.

1982, Mar. 20 **Litho.**

1334 A636 1000p shown 30
1335 A636 2000p Lucio V. Mansilla, Excursion a los indios ranqueles 60
1336 A636 3000p Conrado Nale Roxlo, El Grillo 90
1337 A636 4000p Victoria Ocampo, Sur 1.20

No. 1219A Overprinted: "LAS / MALVINAS / SON/ ARGENTINAS"

1982, Apr. 17 **Photo.** ***Perf. 13½***
1338 A559 1700p grn & bl 55

Argentina's claim on Falkland Islds.

Robert Koch A637

American Airforces Commanders' 22nd Conference A638

1982, Apr. 17 **Litho.**
1339 A637 2000p multi 60

TB bacillus centenary and 25th Intl. Tuberculosis Conference.

1982, Apr. 17
1340 A638 2000p multi 60

Stone Carving, City Founder's Signature (Don Hernando de Lerma)—A639

1982, Apr. 17
1341 A639 2000p multi 60

Souvenir Sheet

1342 A639 5000p multi 1.50

City of Salta, 400th anniv. No. 1342 contains one stamp (43x30mm.); multicolored margin shows map. Size: 89x60mm.

Naval Center Centenary—A640

1982, Apr. 24 ***Perf. 13x13½***
1343 A640 2000p multi 60

Chorisia Speciosa—A641

1982		**Photo.**	***Perf. 13½***
1344A A641	200p	Zinnia peruviana	4
1344B A641	300p	Ipomola purpurea	5
1344C A641	400p	Tillandsia aeranthos	5
1345 A641	500p	shown	8
1346 A641	800p	Oncidium bifolium	12
1347 A641	1000p	Erythrina crista-galli	15
1348 A641	2000p	Jacaranda mimosifolia	30
1349 A641	3000p	Bauhinia candicans	45
1351 A641	5000p	Tecoma stans	75
1356 A641	10,000p	Tabebuia ipe	1.50
1360 A641	20,000p	Passiflora coerulea	3.00
1361 A641	30,000p	Aristolochia elegans	4.50
1363 A641	50,000p	Oxalis enneaphylla	7.50

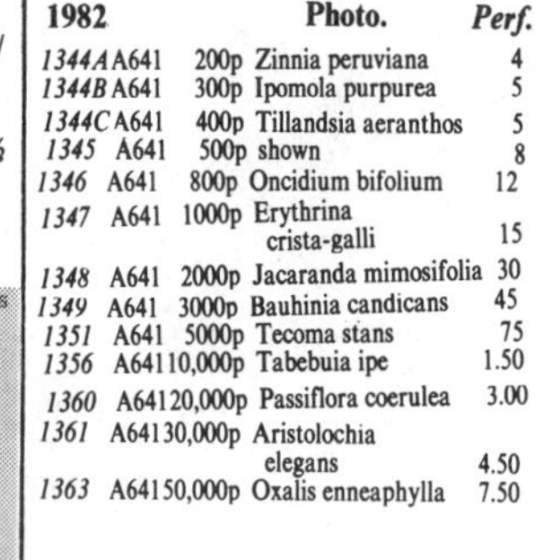

10th Death Anniv. of Gen. Juan C. Sanchez—A642

1982, May 29 **Litho.**
1364 A642 5000p grn & blk 75

153rd Anniv. of Malvinas Political and Military Command District—A643

1982, June 12
1365 A643 5000p Luis Venet, 1st commander 75

Size: 83x28mm.

1366 A643 5000p Map 75

Visit of Pope John-Paul II—A644

1982, June 12
1367 A644 5000p multi 75

Organ Grinder, by Aldo Severi (b. 1928)—A645

1982, July 3
1368 A645 2000p shown 30
1369 A645 3000p Still Life, by Santiago Cogorno (b. 1915) 45

Guillermo Brown Type of 1980 and:

Jose de San Martin—A646

1982 **Litho. & Engr.** ***Perf. 13½***
1372 A591 30000p blk & bl 4.50
1376 A656 50000p sep & car 7.50

Issue dates: 30,000, June; 50,000, July.

Scouting Year—A647

1982, Aug. 7 **Litho.** ***Perf. 13½***
1380 A647 2000p multi 30

Alconafta Fuel Campaign—A648

1982, Aug. 7
1381 A648 2000p multi 30

No. 1351 Overprinted: "50 ANIVERSARIO SOCIEDAD FILATELICA DE TUCUMAN"

1982, Aug. 7 **Photo.**
1382 A641 5000p multi 75

Rio III Central Nuclear Power Plant, Cordoba—A642

1982, Sept. 4 **Litho.** ***Perf. 13½***
1383 A642 2000p shown 30
1384 A642 2000p Control room 30

Namibia Day—A643

1982, Sept. 4
1385 A643 5000p Map 75

Churches and Cathedrals of the Northeast: 2000p, Our Lady of Itati, Corrientes (vert.). 3000p, Resistencia Cathedral, Chaco (vert.). 10,000p, St. Ignatius Church ruins, Misiones.

1982, Sept. 18 **Wmk. 365** **Engr.**
1386 A644 2000p dk grn & blk 30
1387 A644 3000p dk brn & brn 45
1388 A644 5000p dk bl & brn 75
1389 A644 10,000p dp org & blk 1.50

Tension Sideral, by Mario Alberto Agatiello—A645

Sculpture (Espamer '81 and Juvenex '82 Exhibitions): 3000p, Sugerencia II, by Eduardo Mac Entyre. 5000p, Storm, by Carlos Silva.

1982, Oct. 2 Litho. *Perf. 13½*

1390	A645	2000p multi	30
1391	A645	3000p multi	45
1392	A645	5000p multi	75

Sante Fe Bridge—A646

1982, Oct. 16 Litho. & Engr.

1393	A646	2000p bl & blk	30

2nd Southern Cross Games, Santa Fe and Rosario, Nov. 26-Dec. 5.

10th World Men's Volleyball Championship—A647

1982, Oct. 16 Litho.

1394	A647	2000p multi	30
1395	A647	5000p multi	75

Los Andes Newspaper Centenary—A648

Design: Army of the Andes Monument, Hill of Glory, Mendoza.

1982, Oct. 30

1396	A648	5000p multi	75

50th Anniv. of Natl. Roads, Administration—A649

1982, Oct. 30

1397	A649	5000p Signs	75

La Plata City Centenary—A650

1982, Nov. 20 Litho.

1398	A650	5000p Cathedral	75
1399	A650	5000p City Hall	75
1400		Sheet of 6	2.25
a.	A650	2500p Cathedral, diff.	35
b.	A650	2500p Head, top	35
c.	A650	2500p Observatory	35
d.	A650	2500p City Hall, diff.	35
e.	A650	2500p Head, bottom	35
f.	A650	2500p University	35

No. 1400 has black control number. Size: 120x115mm.

75th Anniv. of Oil Discovery, Comodoro Rivadavia—A651

1982, Nov. 20

1401	A651	5000p Well, Natl. Hydrocarbon Congress emblem	75

Jockey Club of Buenos Aires Centenary A652

Navidad 1982
$3000
Republica Argentina

Christmas 1982 A653

1982, Dec. 4 Litho.

1402	A652	5000p Emblem	75
1403	A652	5000p Carlos Pellegrini, 1st pres.	75

1982, Dec. 18 *Perf. 13½*

1404	A653	3000p St. Vincent de Paul	45

Size: 29x38mm.

1405	A653	5000p St. Francis Assisi	75

Pedro B. Palacios (1854-1917), Writer—A654

Writers: 2000p, Leopoldo Marechal (1900-1970). 3000p, Delfina Bunge de Galvez (1881-1952). 4000p, Manuel Galvez (1882-1962). 5000p, Evaristo Carriego (1883-1912). Se-tenant.

1983, Mar. 26 Litho. *Perf. 13½*

1406	A654	1000p multi	15
1407	A654	2000p multi	30
1408	A654	3000p multi	45
1409	A654	4000p multi	60
1410	A654	5000p multi	75
		Nos. 1406-1410 (5)	2.25

SEMI-POSTAL STAMPS.

Samuel F. B. Morse SP1

Globe SP2

Landing of Columbus SP5

Designs: 10c+5c, Alexander Graham Bell. 25c+15c, Rowland Hill.

Wmkd. RA in Sun. (90)

1944, Jan. 5 Lithographed *Perf. 13*

B1	SP1	3c +2c lt vio & sl bl	60	35
B2	SP2	5c +5c dl red & sl bl	1.25	30
B3	SP1	10c +5c org & sl bl	2.50	90
B4	SP1	25c +15c red brn & sl bl	3.25	1.50
B5	SP5	1p +50c lt grn & sl bl	16.00	12.00
		Nos. B1-B5 (5)	23.60	15.05

The surtax was for the Postal Employees Benefit Association.

Map of Argentina SP6

1944, Feb. 17 *Perf. 13* Wmk. 90

B6	SP6	5c +10c ol yel & sl	1.50	75
B7	SP6	5c +50c vio brn & sl	6.00	3.00
B8	SP6	5c +1p dl org & sl	17.50	12.50
B9	SP6	5c +20p dp bl & sl	45.00	25.00

The surtax was for the victims of the San Juan earthquake.

Souvenir Sheets

National Anthem and Flag SP7

1944, July 17 *Imperf.*

B10	SP7	5c +1p vio brn & lt bl	2.50	2.50
B11	SP7	5c +50p bl blk & lt bl	450.00	400.00

The sheets measure 75x110mm. The surtax was for the needy in the provinces of La Rioja and Catamarca.

Stamp Designing
SP8

1950, Aug. 26 Photo. *Perf. 13½*

B12	SP8	10c +10c vio	20	20

Issued to publicize the Argentine International Philatelic Exhibition, 1950.
See also Nos. CB1–CB5 and note after No. CB5.

Poliomyelitis Victim
SP9

1956, Apr. 14 *Perf. 13½x13*

B13	SP9	20c +30c sl	40	15

The surtax was for the poliomyelitis fund. Head in design is from Correggio's "Antiope," Louvre.

Stamp of 1858 and Mail Coach on Raft
SP10

Designs: 2.40p+1.20p, Album, magnifying glass and stamp of 1858. 4.40p+2.20p, Government seat of Confederation, Parana.

Lithographed

1958, Mar. 29 *Perf. 13½* Wmk. 90

B14	SP10	40c +20c brt grn & dl pur	50	35
B15	SP10	2.40p +1.20p ol gray & bl	60	40
B16	SP10	4.40p +2.20p lt bl & dp cl	90	60
		Nos. B14-B16, CB8-CB12 (8)	8.80	7.05

The surtax was for the International Centennial Philatelic Exhibition, Paraná, Entre Rios, April 19–27.

View of Flooded Land
SP11

1958, Oct. 4 Photo. *Perf. 13½*

B17	SP11	40c +20c brn	15	10

The surtax was for flood victims in the Buenos Aires district. See Nos. CB13–CB14.

Child Receiving Blood
SP12

Runner
SP13

1958, Dec. 20 Litho. Wmk. 90

B18	SP12	1p +50c blk & rose red	20	15

The surtax went to the Anti-Leukemia Foundation.

1959, Sept. 5 *Perf. 13½*

Designs: 50c+20c, Basketball players (vert.). 1p+50c, Boxers (vert.).

B19	SP13	20c +10c emer & blk	15	12
B20	SP13	50c +20c yel & blk	20	20
B21	SP13	1p +50c mar & blk	25	25
		Nos. B19-B21, CB15-CB16 (5)	2.10	1.72

Issued to commemorate the third Pan American Games, Chicago, Aug. 27-Sept. 7, 1959.

Condor
SP14

Birds: 50c+20c, Fork-tailed flycatchers. 1p+50c, Magellanic woodpecker.

1960, Feb. 6

B22	SP14	20c +10c dk bl	12	10
B23	SP14	50c +20c dp vio bl	20	12
B24	SP14	1p +50c brn & buff	30	15
		Nos. B22-B24, CB17-CB18(5)	1.62	1.12

The surtax was for child welfare work.
See also No. B30, CB29.

Souvenir Sheet

Uprooted Oak Emblem—SP15

1960, Apr. 7 *Imperf.* Wmk. 90

B25	SP15	Sheet of two	2.00	2.00
a.		1p+50c bis & car	85	85
b.		4.20p+2.10p ap grn & dp cl	85	85

Issued to publicize World Refugee Year, July 1, 1959—June 30, 1960. No. B25 measures 112x84mm. with deep claret marginal inscription.
The surtax was for aid to refugees.

Jacaranda
SP16

Flowers: 1p+1p, Passionflower. 3p+3p, Orchid. 5p+5p, Tabebuia.

1960, Dec. 3 Photo. *Perf. 13½*

B26	SP16	50c +50c dp bl	12	8
B27	SP16	1p +1p bluish grn	20	12
B28	SP16	3p +3p hn brn	45	30
B29	SP16	5p +5p dk brn	75	50

Issued to publicize "TEMEX 61" (International Thematic Exposition).

Type of 1960

Bird: 4.20p+2.10p, Blue-eyed shag.

1961, Feb. 25 *Perf. 13½* Wmk. 90

B30	SP14	4.20p +2.10p chnt brn	75	50

The surtax was for child welfare work. See also No. CB29.

Nos. B26-B29 Overprinted in Black, Brown, Blue or Red:
"14 DE ABRIL DIA DE LAS AMERICAS"

1961, Apr. 15

B31	SP16	50c +50c dp bl	12	12
B32	SP16	1p +1p bluish grn (Brn)	20	15
B33	SP16	3p +3p hn brn (Bl)	45	35
B34	SP16	5p +5p dk brn (R)	75	60

Day of the Americas, Apr. 14.

Cathedral, Cordoba
SP17

Stamp of 1862
SP18

Flight into Egypt, by Ana Maria Moncalvo
SP19

Design: 10p+10p, Cathedral, Buenos Aires.

Photogravure

1961, Oct. 21 *Perf. 13½* Wmk. 90

B35	SP17	2p +2p rose cl	30	20
B36	SP18	3p +3p grn	45	25
B37	SP17	10p +10p brt bl	1.25	75
a.		Souvenir sheet of 3	2.25	1.50

Issued to publicize the 1962 International Stamp Exhibition.
No. B37a contains three imperf. stamps similar to Nos. B35–B37 in dark blue. Violet brown marginal inscription. Size: 85x86mm.

1961, Dec. 16 Lithographed

B38	SP19	2p +1p lil & blk brn	20	12
B39	SP19	10p +5p lt cl & dp cl	75	20

The surtax was for child welfare.

Chalk-browed Mockingbird
SP20

Soccer
SP21

Design: 12p+6p, Rufous-collared sparrow.

1962, Dec. 29 *Perf. 13½* Wmk. 90

B40	SP20	4p +2p bis, brn & bl grn	75	60
B41	SP20	12p +6p gray, yel, grn & brn	1.25	1.00

The surtax was for child welfare. See also Nos. B44, B47, B48–B50, CB32, CB35–CB36.

1963, May 18 *Perf. 13½* Wmk. 90

Design: 12p+6p, Horsemanship.

B42	SP21	4p +2p brt pink, grn & blk	30	15
B43	SP21	12p +6p sal, dk car & blk	65	50
a.		Dark car (jacket) omitted		

Issued to commemorate the 4th Pan American Games, Sao Paulo. See also No. CB31.

Bird Type of 1962.

Design: Vermilion flycatcher.

1963, Dec. 21 Lithographed

B44	SP20	4p +2p blk, red, org & grn	60	35

The surtax was for child welfare. See also No. CB32.

Fencers
SP22

Design: 4p+2p, National Stadium, Tokyo (horiz.).

1964, July 18 *Perf. 13½* Wmk. 90

B45	SP22	4p +2p red, ocher & brn	25	20
B46	SP22	12p +6p bl grn & blk	60	50

Issued to publicize the 18th Olympic Games, Tokyo, Oct. 10–25, 1964. See also No. CB33.

Bird Type of 1962

Design: Red-crested cardinal.

1964, Dec. 23 Lithographed

B47	SP20	4p +2p dk bl, red & grn	60	35

The surtax was for child welfare. See also No. CB35.

Bird Type of 1962
Inscribed "R. ARGENTINA"

Designs: 8p+4p, Lapwing. 10p+5p, Scarlet-headed marshbird (horiz.). 20p+10p, Amazon kingfisher.

1966–67 *Perf. 13½* Wmk. 90

B48	SP20	8p +4p blk, ol, brt grn & red	60	35
B49	SP20	10p +5p blk, bl, org & grn ('67)	90	60
B50	SP20	20p +10p blk, yel, bl & pink ('67)	50	35

The surtax was for child welfare.
Issue dates: 8p+4p, Mar. 26, 1966. 10p+5p, Jan. 14, 1967. 20p+10p, Dec. 23, 1967.
See also Nos. CB36, CB38–CB39.

Grandmother's Birthday, by Patricia Lynch; Lions Emblem—SP23

Perf. 12½x13½

1968, Dec. 14 Litho. Wmk. 90

B51	SP23	40p +20p multi	60	50

Issued to publicize the First Lions International Benevolent Philatelic Exhibition. The surtax was for the Children's Hospital Benevolent Fund.

White-faced Tree Duck SP24

1969, Sept. 20 *Perf. 13½* Wmk. 365

B52	SP24	20p +10p multi	35	30

The surtax was for child welfare. See No. CB40.

Slender-tailed Woodstar (Hummingbird) SP25

1970, May 9 *Perf. 13½* Wmk. 365

B53	SP25	20c +10c multi	35	30

The surtax was for child welfare. See Nos. CB41, B56–B59, B62–B63.

Dolphinfish—SP26

1971, Feb. 20 *Perf. 12½* Unwmkd.

Size: 75x15mm.

B54	SP26	20c +10c multi	60	50

The surtax was for child welfare. See No. CB42.

Children with Stamps, by Mariette Lydis SP27

1971, Dec. 18 Litho. *Perf. 13½*

B55	SP27	1p +50p multi	75	50

2nd Lions International Solidarity Stamp Exhibition.

Bird Type of 1970

Birds: 25c+10c, Saffron finch. 65c+30c, Rufous-bellied thrush (horiz.).

1972, May 6 *Perf. 13½* Unwmkd.

B56	SP25	25c +10c multi	40	30
B57	SP25	65c +30c multi	60	50

Surtax was for child welfare.

Bird Type of 1970

Birds: 50c+25c, Southern screamer (chaja). 90c+45c, Saffron-cowled blackbird (horiz.).

1973, Apr. 28

B58	SP25	50c +25c multi	50	50
B59	SP25	90c +45c multi	75	75

Surtax was for child welfare.

Painting Type of Regular Issue

Designs: 15c+15c, Still Life, by Alfredo Guttero (horiz.). 90c+90c, Nude, by Miguel C. Victorica (horiz.).

1973, Aug. 28 Litho. *Perf. 13½*

B60	A472	15c +15c multi	30	25
B61	A472	90c +90c multi	1.25	1.00

Philatelists' Day.

Bird Type of 1970

Birds: 70c+30c, Blue seed-eater. 1.20p +60c, Hooded siskin.

1974, May 11 Litho. *Perf. 13½*

B62	AP25	70c +30c multi	60	50
B63	AP25	1.20p +60c multi	90	60

Surtax was for child welfare.

Painting Type of 1974

Design: 70c+30c, The Lama, by Juan Batlle Planas.

1974, May 11 Litho. *Perf. 13½*

B64	A477	70c +30c multi	25	20

PRENFIL-74 UPU, International Exhibition of Philatelic Periodicals, Buenos Aires, Oct. 1–12.

Plush-crested Jay SP28

Designs: 13p+6.50p, Golden-collared macaw. 20p+10p, Begonia. 40p+20p, Teasel.

1976, June 12 Litho. *Perf. 13½*

B65	SP28	7p +3.50p multi	25	20
B66	SP28	13p +6.50p multi	40	30
B67	SP28	20p +10p multi	60	50
B68	SP28	40p +20p multi	1.25	75

Argentine philately.

Telegraph, Communications Satellite SP29

Designs: 20p+10p, Old and new mail trucks. 60p+30p, Old, new packet boats. 70p+35p, Biplane and jet.

1977, July 16 Litho. *Perf. 13½*

B69	SP29	10p +5p multi	30	15
B70	SP29	20p +10p multi	50	30
B71	SP29	60p +30p multi	1.10	75
B72	SP29	70p +35p multi	1.25	75

Surtax was for Argentine philately.
No. B70 exists with wmk. 365.

Church of St. Francis Type, 1977, Inscribed: "EXPOSICION ARGENTINA '77"

1977, Aug. 27

B73	A515	160p +80p multi	3.00	1.75

Surtax was for Argentina '77 Philatelic Exhibition. Issued in sheets of 4.

No. B73 Overprinted with Soccer Cup Emblem

1978, Feb. 4 Litho. *Perf. 13½*

B74	A515	160p +80p multi	4.00	3.00
a.		Souvenir sheet of 4	15.00	12.00

11th World Cup Soccer Championship, Argentina, June 1–25.

No. B74a contains 4 No. B74, light blue margin with black inscription. Size: 103x133mm.

Spinus Magellanicus SP30

Birds: 100p+100p, Variable seedeater. 150p+150p, Yellow thrush. 200p+200p, Pyrocephalus rubineus. 500p+500p, Great kiskadee.

1978, Aug. 5 Litho. *Perf. 13½*

B75	SP30	50p +50p multi	75	35
B76	SP30	100p +100p multi	1.00	50
B77	SP30	150p +150p multi	1.25	60
B78	SP30	200p +200p multi	1.50	90
B79	SP30	500p +500p multi	7.50	4.00
		Nos. B75-B79 (5)	12.00	6.35

ARGENTINA '78, Inter-American Philatelic Exhibition, Buenos Aires, Oct. 27–Nov. 5. Nos. B75–B79 issued in sheets of 4 with marginal inscriptions commemorating Exhibition and 1978 Soccer Championship.

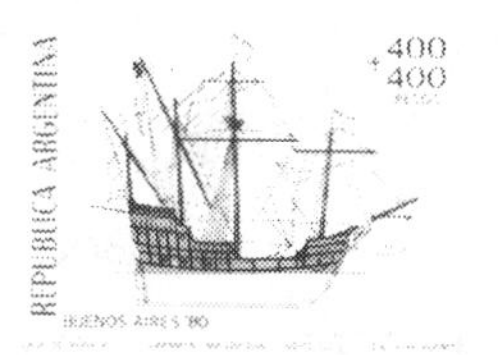

Caravel "Magdalena," 16th Century SP31

Sailing Ships: 500+500p, Three master "Rio de la Plata," 17th century. 600+600p, Corvette "Descubierta," 18th century. 1500+1500p, Naval Academy yacht "A.R.A. Fortuna," 1979.

1979, Sept. 8 Litho. *Perf. 13½*

B80	SP31	400p +400p multi	6.00	4.00
B81	SP31	500p +500p multi	7.50	5.00
B82	SP31	600p +600p multi	9.00	6.00
B83	SP31	1500p +1500p multi	22.50	15.00

Buenos Aires '80, International Philatelic Exhibition, Buenos Aires, Oct. 24–Nov. 2, 1980.

Purmamarca Church—SP32

Churches: 200p + 100p, Molinos. 300p + 150p, Animana. 400p + 200p, San Jose de Lules.

1979, Nov. 3 Litho. *Perf. 13½*

B84	SP32	100p +50p multi	22	15
B85	SP32	200p +100p multi	42	20
B86	SP32	300p +150p multi	65	30
B87	SP32	400p +200p multi	85	40

Buenos Aires No. 3, Exhibition and Society Emblems—SP33

Argentine Stamps: 750p+750p, type A580. 1000p+1000p, No. 91. 2000p+2000p, type A588.

1979, Dec. 15 Litho. *Perf. 13½*

B88	SP33	250p +250p multi	1.25	1.00
B89	SP33	750p +750p multi	3.25	2.50
B90	SP33	1000p +1000p multi	4.25	3.50
B91	SP33	2000p +2000p multi	8.50	7.00

PRENFIL '80, International Philatelic Literature and Publications Exhibition, Buenos Aires, Nov. 7-16, 1980. Multicolored margins show Exhibition and Society emblems. Size: 89×60mm.

Minuet, by Carlos E. Pellegrini—SP34

Paintings: 700p+350p, Media Cana, by Carlos Morel. 800p+400p, Cielito, by Pellegrini. 1000p+500p, El Gato, by Juan Leon Palliere.

1981, July 11 Litho. *Perf. 13½*

B92	SP34	500 + 250p multi	75	20
B93	SP34	700 + 350p multi	1.05	30
B94	SP34	800 + 400p multi	1.20	50
B95	SP34	1000 + 500p multi	1.50	70

Espamer '81 Intl. Stamp Exhibition (Americas, Spain, Portugal), Buenos Aires, Nov. 13-22.

Canal, by Beatriz Bongliani (b. 1933)—SP35

Tapestries: 1000p+500p, Shadows, by Silvia Sieburger (vert.). 2000p+1000p, Interpretation of a Rectangle, by Silke R. de Haupt (vert.). 4000p+2000p, Tilcara, by Tana Sachs.

1982, July 31 Litho. *Perf. 13½*

B96	SP35	1000 +500p multi	22
B97	SP35	2000 +1000p multi	45
B98	SP35	3000 +1500p multi	68
B99	SP35	4000 +2000p multi	90

AIR POST STAMPS.

Airplane Circles the Globe
AP1

Eagle
AP2

Wings Cross the Sea
AP3

Condor on Mountain Crag
AP4

Perforations of Nos. C1–C37 vary from clean-cut to rough and uneven, with many skipped perfs.

Lithographed

Wmkd. RA in Sun. (90)

1928, Mar. 1 *Perf. 13x13½, 13½x13*

C1	AP1	5c	lt red	2.00	75
C2	AP1	10c	Prus bl	4.00	1.25
C3	AP2	15c	lt brn	4.00	1.25
C4	AP1	18c	lil gray	5.50	5.00
a.			18c brn lil	5.50	5.00
b.			Double impression	*500.00*	
C5	AP2	20c	ultra	4.00	1.25
C6	AP2	24c	dp bl	6.50	4.00
C7	AP3	25c	brt vio	6.50	2.00
C8	AP3	30c	rose red	8.25	1.50
C9	AP4	35c	rose	6.50	1.50
C10	AP1	36c	bis brn	4.00	2.00
C11	AP4	50c	gray blk	6.50	75
C12	AP2	54c	chocolate	6.50	3.00
C13	AP2	72c	yel grn	7.50	3.00
a.			Double impression	*400.00*	
C14	AP3	90c	dk brn	15.00	2.75
C15	AP3	1p	sl bl & red	17.50	1.00
C16	AP3	1.08p	rose & dk bl	25.00	7.00
C17	AP4	1.26p	dl vio & grn	30.00	12.00
C18	AP4	1.80p	bl & lil rose	30.00	12.00
C19	AP4	3.60p	gray & bl	65.00	30.00
			Nos. C1-C19 (19)	254.25	92.00

The watermark on No. C4a is larger than on the other stamps of this set, measuring 10 mm. across Sun.

Zeppelin First Flight.

Air Post Stamps of 1928 Overprinted in Blue

1930, May

C20	AP2	20c	ultra	15.00	10.00
C21	AP4	50c	gray blk	30.00	20.00
a.			Invtd. ovpt.	*750.00*	
C22	AP3	1p	sl bl & red	32.50	20.00
a.			Invtd. ovpt.	*1,100.*	
C23	AP4	1.80p	bl & lil rose	80.00	50.00
C24	AP4	3.60p	gray & bl	220.00	150.00
			Nos. C20-C24 (5)	377.50	250.00

Overprinted in Green.

C25	AP2	20c	ultra	13.50	10.00
C26	AP4	50c	gray blk	17.50	12.50

C27	AP3	90c dk brn	13.50	10.00
C28	AP3	1p sl bl & red	30.00	20.00
C29	AP4	1.80p bl & lil rose	900.00	600.00
a.		Thick paper	*1,200.*	
		Nos. C25-C29 (5)	974.50	652.50

Air Post Stamps of 1928 Overprinted in Red

1930
6
Septiembre
-1931-

1931

C30	AP1	18c lil gray	3.00	1.50
C31	AP2	72c yel grn	22.50	16.00

Overprinted in Red or Blue

6 de Septiembre
1930 — 1931

C32	AP3	90c dk brn	22.50	16.00
C33	AP4	1.80p bl & lil rose (Bl)	45.00	30.00
C34	AP4	3.60p gray & bl	90.00	60.00
		Nos. C30-C34 (5)	183.00	123.50

Issued in commemoration of the first anniversary of the Revolution of 1930.

Zeppelin Issue.

Air Post Stamps of 1928 Overprinted in Blue or Red

GRAF
ZEPPELIN
1932

1932, Aug. 4

C35	AP1	5c lt red (Bl)	3.75	2.50
C36	AP1	18c lil gray (R)	17.50	11.00
a.		18c brn lil (R)	110.00	80.00

Overprinted

GRAF ZEPPELIN
1932

C37	AP3	90c dk brn (R)	50.00	30.00

Plane and Letter
AP5

Mercury
AP6

Plane in Flight
AP7

Photogravure
Wmkd. RA in Sun. (90)

1940, Oct. 23 ***Perf. 13½x13, 13x13½***

C38	AP5	30c dp org	11.00	15
C39	AP6	50c dk brn	17.50	25
C40	AP5	1p carmine	3.75	10
C41	AP7	1.25p dp grn	75	15
C42	AP5	2.50p brt bl	3.00	25
		Nos. C38-C42 (5)	36.00	90

Plane and Letter
AP8

Mercury and Plane
AP9

Perf. 13½x13, 13x13½

1942, Oct. 6 Lithographed Wmk. 90

C43	AP8	30c orange	30	5
C44	AP9	50c dl brn & buff	75	5

See also Nos. C49–C52, C57, C61.

Plane over Iguaçu Falls
AP10

Plane over the Andes
AP11

Perf. 13½x13

1946, June 10 **Unwmkd.**

C45	AP10	15c dl red brn	50	8
C46	AP11	25c gray grn	30	8

See also Nos. C53–C54.

Allegory of Flight
AP12

Astrolabe
AP13

Surface-Tinted Paper.

Perf. 13½x13, 13x13½.

1946, Sept. 25 Litho. Unwmkd.

C47	AP12	15c sl grn, *pale grn*	80	15
C48	AP13	60c vio brn, *ocher*	80	25

Types of 1942.

1946-48 ***Perf. 13½x13*** **Unwmkd.**

C49	AP8	30c orange	2.25	8
C50	AP9	50c dl brn & buff	3.75	20
C51	AP8	1p car ('47)	2.25	15
C52	AP8	2.50p brt bl ('48)	10.00	1.00

Types of 1946.

1948 **Wmk. 90**

C53	AP10	15c dl red brn	20	10
C54	AP11	25c gray grn	40	10

Atlas (National Museum, Naples)
AP14

Map of Argentine Republic, Globe and Caliper—AP15

Perf. 13½x13, 13x13½.

1948-49 Photogravure. **Wmk. 288**

C55	AP14	45c dk brn ('49)	50	20
C56	AP15	70c dk grn	60	20

Issued to commemorate the 4th Pan-American Reunion of Cartographers, Buenos Aires, October–November, 1948.

Mercury Type of 1942.

Lithographed

1949 ***Perf. 13x13½*** **Wmk. 288**

C57	AP9	50c dl brn & buff	75	18

Marksmanship Trophy
AP16

1949, Nov. 4 Photogravure.

C58	AP16	75c brown	1.25	30

World Rifle Championship, 1949.

Douglas DC-3 and Condor
AP17

Perf. 13x13½.

1951, June 20 **Wmk. 90**

C59	AP17	20c dk ol grn	20	8

10th anniversary of the State air lines.

Douglas DC-6 and Condor
AP18

1951, Oct. 17 ***Perf. 13½.***

C60	AP18	20c blue	20	9

End of Argentine 5-year Plan.

Plane-Letter Type of 1942.

Lithographed

1951 ***Perf. 13½x13*** **Wmk. 90**

C61	AP8	1p carmine	60	18

Jesus by Leonardo da Vinci (detail, "Virgin of the Rocks")
AP19

Perf. 13½x13

1956, Sept. 29 **Photo.** **Wmk. 90**

C62	AP19	1p dl pur	50	20

Issued to express the gratitude of the children of Argentina to the people of the world for their help against poliomyelitis.

Battle of Montevideo
AP20

Leonardo Rosales and Tomas Espora
AP21

Guillermo Brown
AP22

Map of Americas and Arms of Buenos Aires
AP23

1957, March 2 ***Perf. 13½***

C63	AP20	60c bl gray	20	10
C64	AP21	1p brt pink	20	10
C65	AP22	2p brown	35	15

Issued to commemorate the centenary of the death of Admiral Guillermo Brown, founder of the Argentine navy.

1957, Aug. 16

C66	AP23	2p rose vio	35	15

Issued to publicize the Inter-American Economic Conference in Buenos Aires.

Modern Locomotive
AP24

1957, Aug. 31 ***Perf. 13½*** **Wmk. 90**

C67	AP24	60c gray	15	8

Centenary of Argentine railroads.

Globe, Flag and Compass Rose
AP25

Design: 2p, Key.

1957, Sept. 14

C68	AP25	1p	redsh brn	25	10
C69	AP25	2p	Prus bl	40	12

Issued to publicize the 1957 International Congress for Tourism.

Birds Carrying Letters
AP26

1957, Nov. 6

C70	AP26	1p	brt bl	20	8

Issued for Letter Writing Week, Oct. 6–12.

Early Plane
AP27

1958, May 31 *Perf. 13½* Wmk. 90

C71	AP27	2p	maroon	25	18

Issued to commemorate the 50th anniversary of the Argentine Aviation Club.

Stamp of 1858 and "The Post of Santa Fe"
AP28

Design: 80c, Stamp of Buenos Aires and view of the Plaza de la Aduana.

1958 Lithographed *Perf. 13½*

C72	AP28	80c	pale bis & sl bl	25	10
C73	AP28	1p	red org & dk bl	30	18

Issued to commemorate the centenary of the first postage stamps of Buenos Aires and the Argentine Confederation.
Issue dates: 80c, Oct. 18; 1p, Aug. 23.

Comet Jet over World Map
AP29

1959, May 16 *Perf. 13½* Wmk. 90

C74	AP29	5p	blk & ol	40	10

Issued to commemorate the inauguration of jet flights by Argentine Airlines.

Type of Regular Issue, 1960.

"Cabildo" and: 1.80p, Mariano Moreno. 5p, Manuel Belgrano and Juan José Castelli.

Photogravure

1960, May 28 *Perf. 13½* Wmk. 90

C75	A287	1.80p	red brn	20	10
a.			Souvenir sheet of 3	90	60
C76	A287	5p	buff & pur	45	15
a.			Souvenir sheet of 3	2.00	1.25

Issued to commemorate the 150th anniversary of the May Revolution.

Souvenir sheets are imperf. No. C75a contains one No. C75 and 1p and 2p resembling Nos. 713–714; stamps in reddish brown, marginal inscriptions in green. No. C76a contains one No. C76 and 4.20p and 10.70p resembling Nos. 715–716; stamps are in green, marginal inscriptions in reddish brown. Sheet size: 152x106mm.

Symbolic of New Provinces
AP30

1960, July 8 Lithographed

C77	AP30	1.80p	dp car & bl	20	10

Issued to commemorate the elevation of the territories of Chubut, Formosa, Neuquen, Rio Negro and Santa Cruz to provinces.

Type of Regular Issue, 1960

Photogravure

1960, Oct. 1 *Perf. 13½* Wmk. 90

C78	A291	1.80p	rose lil	25	10
C79	A291	10.70p	brt grnsh bl	60	25

Issued to commemorate the 8th Congress of the Postal Union of the Americas and Spain.

UNESCO Emblem
AP31

1962, July 14 Lithographed

C80	AP31	13p	ocher & brn	60	40

Issued to commemorate the 15th anniversary of UNESCO (U.N. Educational, Scientific and Cultural Organization).

Mail Coach
AP32

1962, Oct. 6 *Perf. 13½* Wmk. 90

C81	AP32	5.60p	gray brn & blk	30	15

Mailman's Day, Sept. 14, 1962.

No. 695 and Type of 1959 Surcharged in Green

AEREO
5 60 PESOS

1962, Oct. 31 Photogravure

C82	A277	5.60p	on 5p brn	40	20
C83	A277	18p	on 5p brn, *grnsh*	1.50	30

UPAE Emblem
AP33

Skylark
AP34

Photogravure

1962, Nov. 24 *Perf. 13½* Wmk. 90

C84	AP33	5.60p	dk bl	25	15

Issued to commemorate the 50th anniversary of the founding of the Postal Union of the Americas and Spain, UPAE.

1963, Feb. 9 Lithographed

Design: 11p, Super Albatros.

C85	AP34	5.60p	bl & blk	25	15
C86	AP34	11p	bl, blk & red	45	20

9th World Gliding Championships.

Symbolic Plane
AP35

1963–65 *Perf. 13½* Wmk. 90

C87	AP35	5.60p	dk pur, car & brt grn	30	15
C88	AP35	7p	blk & bis ('64)	60	12
C88A	AP35	7p	blk & bis ('65)	5.00	50
C89	AP35	11p	blk, dk pur & grn	60	25
C90	AP35	18p	dk pur, red & vio bl	1.25	35
C91	AP35	21p	brn, red & gray	1.50	50
			Nos. C87-C91 (6)	9.25	1.87

"Argentina" reads down on No. C88, up on No. C88A. See also Nos. C101–C104, C108–C111, C123–C126, C135–C141.

Type of Regular Issue, 1964

Design: 18p, Map of Falkland Islands (Islas Malvinas).

1964, Feb. 22 *Perf. 13½* Wmk. 90

Size: 33x22mm.

C92	A327	18p	lt & dk bl & ol grn	90	50

Issued to commemorate the 60th anniversary of Argentina's claim to Antarctic territories.

U.P.U. Monument, Bern, and U.N. Emblem
AP36

Engraved

1964, May 23 *Perf. 13½* Wmk. 90

C93	AP36	18p	red & dk brn	75	30

Issued to commemorate the 15th Universal Postal Union Congress, Vienna, Austria, May–June 1964.

Discovery of America, Florentine Woodcut
AP37

1964, Oct. 10 Lithographed

C94	AP37	13p	tan & blk	45	25

Issued for the Day of the Race, Columbus Day.

Lt. Matienzo Base, Antarctica
AP38

1965, Feb. 27 Photo. *Perf. 13½*

C95	AP38	11p	sal pink	75	20

Issued to publicize the national territory of Tierra del Fuego, Antarctic and South Atlantic Isles.

No. C88A Overprinted in Silver: "PRIMERAS / JORNADAS FILATELICAS / RIOPLATENSES"

1965, Mar. 17 Lithographed

C96	AP35	7p	blk & bis	30	20

Issued to commemorate the First Rio de la Plata Stamp Show, sponsored jointly by the Argentine and Uruguayan Philatelic Associations, Montevideo, March 19–28.

ITU Emblem
AP39

Ascending Rocket
AP40

1965, May 11 *Perf. 13½* Wmk. 90

C97	AP39	18p	sl, blk & red	60	30

Issued to commemorate the centenary of the International Telecommunication Union.

1965, May 29 Photo. *Perf. 13½*

Design: 50p, Earth with trajectories and magnetic field (horiz.).

C98	AP40	18p	vermilion	60	30
C99	AP40	50p	dp vio bl	1.50	65

Issued to commemorate the 6th Symposium on Space Research, held in Buenos Aires, and to honor the National Commission of Space Research.

Type of 1963–65 Inscribed "Republica Argentina" Reading Down

1965, Oct. 13 Litho. Wmk. 90

C101	AP35	12p	dk car rose & brn	1.50	20
C102	AP35	15p	vio bl & dk red	90	25
C103	AP35	27.50p	dk bl grn & gray	1.50	40
C104	AP35	30.50p	dk brn & dk bl	2.25	50

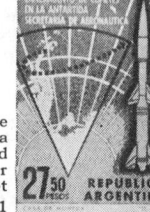

Argentine Antarctica Map and Centaur Rocket
AP41

1966, Feb. 19 *Perf. 13½* Wmk. 90

C105	AP41	27.50p	bl, blk & dp org	85	35

Issued to commemorate the launchings of sounding balloons and of a Gamma Centaur rocket in Antarctica during February, 1965.

Sea Gull and Southern Cross
AP42

1966, May 14 *Perf. 13½* **Wmk. 90**

C106	AP42	12p Prus bl, blk & red	25	15

Issued to commemorate the 50th anniversary of the Naval Aviation School.

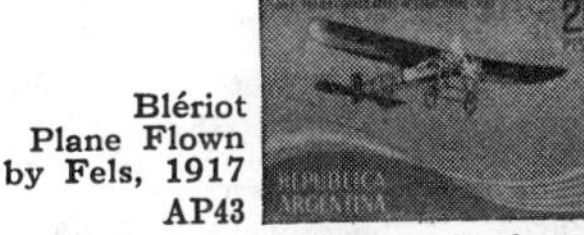

Blériot Plane Flown by Fels, 1917
AP43

1967, Sept. 2 Litho. *Perf. 13½*

C107	AP43	26p ol, bl & blk	40	15

Issued to commemorate the flight by Theodore Fels from Buenos Aires to Montevideo, Sept. 2, 1917, allegedly the first International airmail flight.

Type of 1963–65 Inscribed "Republica Argentina" Reading Down

1967, Dec. 20 *Perf. 13½* **Wmk. 90**

C108	AP35	26p brown	75	20
C109	AP35	40p violet	6.00	30
C110	AP35	68p bl grn	3.50	40
C111	AP35	78p ultra	1.25	50

Vito Dumas and Ketch "Legh II"
AP44

1968, July 27 Litho. **Wmk. 90**

C112	AP44	68p bl, blk, red & vio bl	60	30

Issued to commemorate Vito Dumas's one-man voyage around the world in 1943.

Type of Regular Issue and

Assembly Emblem
AP45

Design: 40p, Globe and map of South America.

1968, Oct. 19 Litho. *Perf. 13½*

C113	A395	40p brt pink, lt bl & blk	50	25
C114	AP45	68p bl, lt bl, gold & blk	75	40

Issued to publicize the 4th Plenary Assembly of the International Telegraph and Telephone Consultative Committee, Mar del Plata, Sept. 23–Oct. 25.

Radar Antenna, Balcarce Station
AP46

Photogravure

1969, Aug. 23 *Perf. 13½* **Wmk. 90**

C115	AP46	40p bl gray	60	25

Issued to publicize communications by satellite through International Telecommunications Consortium (INTELSAT).

Atucha Nuclear Center
AP47

1969, Dec. 13 Litho. **Wmk. 365**

C116	AP47	26p bl & multi	1.50	30

Completion of Atucha Nuclear Center.

Type of 1963–65 Inscribed "Republica Argentina" Reading Down

1969–71 *Perf. 13½* **Wmk. 365**

C123	AP35	40p violet	6.50	20
C124	AP35	68p dk bl grn ('70)	2.00	25

Unwmkd.

C125	AP35	26p yel brn ('71)	35	10
C126	AP35	40p vio ('71)	3.00	16

Old Fire Engine and Fire Brigade Emblem
AP48

1970, Aug. 8 Litho. **Unwmkd.**

C128	AP48	40c grn & multi	55	15

Centenary of the Fire Brigade.

Education Year Emblem
AP49

1970, Aug. 29 *Perf. 13½*

C129	AP49	68c bl & blk	60	25

Issued for International Education Year.

Fleet Leaving Valparaiso, by Antonio Abel
AP50

1970, Oct. 17 Litho. *Perf. 13½*

C130	AP50	26c multi	1.00	20

Issued to commemorate the 150th anniversary of the departure for Peru of the liberation fleet from Valparaiso, Chile.

Sumampa Chapel
AP51

1970, Nov. 7 Photogravure

C131	AP51	40c multi	1.25	25

Bishopric of Tucuman, 400th anniversary.

Buenos Aires Planetarium
AP52

1970, Nov. 28 Litho. *Perf. 13½*

C132	AP52	40c multi	75	25

Jorge Newbery and Morane Saulnier Plane
AP53

1970, Dec. 19

C133	AP53	26c bl, blk, yel & grn	40	15

24th Aeronautics and Space Week.

Industries Type of Regular Issue

Design: 31c, Refinery.

1971, Oct. 16 Litho. *Perf. 13½*

C134	A445	31c red, blk & yel	60	15

Nationalized industries.

Type of 1963–65 Inscribed "Republica Argentina" Reading Down

1971–74 **Unwmkd.**

C135	AP35	45c brown	4.00	6
C136	AP35	68c red	45	8
C137	AP35	70c vio bl ('73)	1.00	8
C138	AP35	90c emer ('73)	2.50	10
C139	AP35	1.70p bl ('74)	60	20
C140	AP35	1.95p emer ('74)	60	22
C141	AP35	2.65p dp cl ('74)	60	25
		Nos. 135-C141 (7)	9.75	99

Fluorescent paper was used for Nos. C135–C136, C138–C141. The 70c was issued on both ordinary and fluorescent paper.

Don Quixote, Drawing by Ignacio Zuloaga
AP54

1975, Apr. 26 Photo. *Perf. 13½*

C145	AP54	2.75p yel, blk & red	75	24

Day of the Race and for España 75 International Philatelic Exhibition, Madrid, Apr. 4–13.

No. C87 Surcharged

100 PESOS

1975, Sept. 15 Litho. **Wmk. 90**

C146	AP35	9.20p on 5.60p	90	15
C147	AP35	19.70p on 5.60p	1.25	30
C148	AP35	100p on 5.60p	6.00	2.00

REVALORIZADO

No. C87 Surcharged

920 PESOS

1975, Oct. 15

C149	AP35	9.20p on 5.60p	90	15
C150	AP35	19.70p on 5.60p	1.50	35

AIR POST SEMI-POSTAL STAMPS.

Stamp Engraving
SPAP1

Designs: 70c+70c, Proofing stamp die. 1p+1p, Sheet of stamps. 2.50p+2.50p, The letter. 5p+5p, Gen. San Martín.

Photogravure.

1950, Aug. 26 *Perf. 13½.* Wmk. 90

CB1 SPAP1 45c +45c vio bl 60 40
CB2 SPAP1 70c +70c dk brn 90 60
a. Souvenir sheet of 3 5.00 5.00
CB3 SPAP1 1p +1p cer 2.50 2.50
CB4 SPAP1 2.50p +2.50p ol gray 14.00 10.00
CB5 SPAP1 5p +5p dl grn 15.00 12.00
Nos. CB1-CB5 (5) 33.00 25.50

Issued to publicize the Argentine International Philatelic Exhibition, 1950.

No. CB2a measures 120x150mm., and contains one each of Nos. B12, CB1 and CB2, imperf., with marginal inscriptions and ornamental border in olive green.

Pieta by Michelangelo
SPAP2

1951, Dec. 22 *Perf. 13½x13.*

CB6 SPAP2 2.45p +7.55p grnsh blk 35.00 22.50

The surtax was for the Eva Perón Foundation.

Flower and Child's Head
SPAP3

Stamp of 1858
SPAP4

1958, Mar. 15 *Perf. 13½*

CB7 SPAP3 1p +50c dp cl 35 35

Surtax for National Council for Children.

1958, Mar. 29 Litho. Wmk. 90

CB8 SPAP4 1p +50c gray ol & bl 60 50
CB9 SPAP4 2p +1p rose lil & vio 80 65
CB10 SPAP4 3p +1.50p grn & brn 90 80
CB11 SPAP4 5p +2.50p gray ol & car rose 1.50 1.25
CB12 SPAP4 10p +5p gray ol & brn 3.00 2.50
Nos. CB8-CB12 (5) 6.80 5.70

The surtax was for the International Centennial Philatelic Exhibition, Buenos Aires, April 19–27.

Type of Semi-Postal Issue, 1958.

Designs: 1p+50c, Flooded area. 5p+2.50p, House and truck under water.

Photogravure.

1958, Oct. 4 *Perf. 13½* Wmk. 90

CB13 SP11 1p +50c dl pur 30 25
CB14 SP11 5p +2.50p grnsh bl 1.00 90

The surtax was for victims of a flood in the Buenos Aires district.

Type of Semi-Postal Issue, 1959.

Designs: 2p+1p, Rowing. 3p+1.50p, Woman diver.

1959, Sept. 5 Litho. *Perf. 13½*

CB15 SP13 2p +1p brt bl & blk 60 40
CB16 SP13 3p +1.50p ol & blk 90 75

Issued to commemorate the third Pan American Games, Chicago, Aug. 27–Sept. 7, 1959.

Type of Semi-Postal Issue, 1960.

Birds: 2p+1p, Rufous tinamou. 3p+1.50p, Rhea.

1960, Feb. 6 *Perf. 13½*

CB17 SP14 2p +1p rose car & sal 40 25
CB18 SP14 3p +1.50p sl grn 60 50

The surtax was for child welfare work. See also No. CB29.

Buenos Aires Market Place, 1810
SPAP5

Seibo, National Flower
SPAP6

Designs: 6p+3p, Oxcart water carrier. 10.70p+5.30p, Settlers landing. 20p+10p, The Fort.

1960, Aug. 20 Photo. Wmk. 90

CB19 SPAP5 2p +1p rose brn 25 12
CB20 SPAP5 6p +3p gray 50 35
CB21 SPAP5 10.70 +5.30p bl 90 50
CB22 SPAP5 20p +10p bluish grn 1.50 1.25

Issued to publicize the Inter-American Philatelic Exhibition EFIMAYO 1960, Buenos Aires, Oct. 12–24, held to commemorate the sesquicentennial of the May Revolution of 1910.

1960, Sept. 10 *Perf. 13½*

Design: 10.70p+5.30p, Copihue, Chile's national flower.

CB23 SPAP6 6p +3p lil rose 50 40
CB24 SPAP6 10.70p +5.30p ver 75 60

The surtax was for earthquake victims in Chile.

Nos. CB19–CB22 Overprinted:
"DIA DE LAS NACIONES UNIDAS
24 DE OCTUBRE"

1960, Oct. 8

CB25 SPAP5 2p +1p rose brn 35 25
CB26 SPAP5 6p +3p gray 60 50
CB27 SPAP5 10.70p +5.30p bl 80 75
CB28 SPAP5 20p +10p bluish grn 1.50 1.35

United Nations Day, Oct. 24, 1960.

Type of Semi-Postal Issue, 1960

Design: Emperor penguins.

1961, Feb. 25 Photo. Wmk. 90

CB29 SP14 1.80p +90c gray 40 30

The surtax was for child welfare work.

Stamp of 1862
SPAP7

Crutch, Olympic Torch and Rings
SPAP8

1962, May 19 Lithographed

CB30 SPAP7 6.50p +6.50p Prus bl & grnsh bl 90 80

Issued to publicize the opening of the "Argentina 62" Philatelic Exhibition, Buenos Aires, May 19–29.

Type of Semi-Postal Issue, 1963

Design: 11p+5p, Bicycling.

1963, May 18 *Perf. 13½* Wmk. 90

CB31 SP21 11p +5p grn, red & blk 70 60

Issued to commemorate the 4th Pan American Games, Sao Paulo, Brazil.

Type of Semi-Postal Issue, 1962.

Design: 11p+5p, Great kiskadee.

1963, Dec. 21 *Perf. 13½* Wmk. 90

CB32 SP20 11p +5p dk brn, brn, yel & grn 80 70

The surtax was for child welfare.

Type of Semi-Postal Issue, 1964.

Design: 11p+5p, Sailboat.

1964, July 18 Lithographed

CB33 SP22 11p +5p brt bl & blk 75 75

Issued to publicize the 18th Olympic Games, Tokyo, Oct. 10–25, 1964.

1964, Sept. 19 Litho. *Perf. 13½*

CB34 SPAP8 18p +9p bluish grn, blk, red & yel 80 80

Issued to publicize the 13th "Olympic" games for the handicapped, Tokyo, 1964.

Bird Type of Semi-Postal Issue, 1962

Design: Chilean swallow.

1964, Dec. 23 Litho. Wmk. 90

CB35 SP20 18p +9p brn, dk bl & grn 1.25 1.00

The surtax was for child welfare.

Bird Type of Semi-Postal Issue, 1962, Inscribed "R. ARGENTINA"

Design: Rufous ovenbird.

1966, Mar. 26 *Perf. 13½* Wmk. 90

CB36 SP20 27.50p +12.50p bl, ocher, yel & grn 75 60

The surtax was for child welfare.

Coat of Arms—SPAP9

1966, June 25 Litho. *Perf. 13½*

CB37 SPAP9 10p +10p yel & multi 2.25 1.75

Issued to publicize the ARGENTINA '66 Philatelic Exhibition held in connection with the sesquicentennial celebration of the Declaration of Independence, Buenos Aires, July 16–23. The surtax was for the Exhibition. Issued in sheets of 4.

Bird Type of Semi-Postal Issue, 1962, Inscribed "R. ARGENTINA"

Designs: 15p+7p, Blue and yellow tanager. 26p+13p, Toco toucan.

1967 Lithographed Wmk. 90

CB38 SP20 15p +7p blk, bl, grn & yel 60 50
CB39 SP20 26p +13p blk, org, yel & bl 60 50

The surtax was for child welfare.
Issue dates: 15p+7p, Jan. 14. 26p+13p, Dec. 23.

Bird Type of Semi-Postal Issue, 1969

Design: 26p+13p, Lineated woodpecker.

1969, Sept. 20 *Perf. 13½* Wmk. 365

CB40 SP24 26p +13p multi 40 30

The surtax was for child welfare.

Bird Type of Semi-Postal Issue, 1970

Design: 40c+20c, Chilean flamingo.

1970, May 9 Litho. Wmk. 365

CB41 SP25 40c +20c multi 60 50

The surtax was for child welfare.

Fish Type of Semi-Postal Issue, 1971

Design: Pejerrey (atherinidae family).

1971, Feb. 20 *Perf. 12½* Unwmkd.
Size: 75x15mm.

CB42 SP26 40c +20c lt bl & multi 50 40

The surtax was for child welfare.

OFFICIAL STAMPS.

Regular Issues Overprinted in Black

1884–87 *Perf. 12, 14.* Unwmkd.

O1 A29 ½c brown 9.00 6.00
a. Inverted overprint 9.00 6.00
O2 A23 1c red 5.50 4.00
a. Invtd. ovpt., perf.14 50.00 37.50
b. Perf. 12 55.00 40.00
c. As "a," perf. 12 35.00 35.00
O3 A29 1c red 60 40
a. Inverted overprint 1.25 85
b. Double overprint 30.00 30.00
O4 A20 2c green 60 40
a. Inverted overprint 55.00 27.50
b. Double overprint 30.00 30.00
O5 A11 4c brown 60 40
a. Inverted overprint 40.00 27.50
O6 A7 8c lake 60 40
a. Inverted overprint 55.00 55.00
O7 A8 10c green 55.00 27.50
O8 A23 12c ultra (#45) 4.00 3.00
a. Perf. 14 55.00 55.00
O9 A29 12c grnsh bl 90 75
a. Inverted overprint 110.00 80.00
O10 A19 24c blue 1.25 90
a. Inverted overprint 4.00 2.50
O11 A21 25c lake 11.00 7.00
O12 A12 30c orange 22.50 15.00
O13 A13 60c black 15.00 9.00
a. Inverted overprint 55.00 35.00
O14 A14 90c blue 11.00 6.50
a. Inverted overprint 45.00 35.00
b. Double overprint 45.00
Nos. O1-O14 (14) 137.55 81.25

1884 *Rouletted.*

O15 A17 16c green 2.00 1.00
a. Double overprint 15.00 15.00
b. Inverted overprint 110.00
O16 A18 20c blue 9.00 6.50
a. Inverted overprint 55.00 37.50
O17 A19 24c blue 1.25 1.10
a. Inverted overprint 4.00 3.50
b. Double ovpt., one inverted 27.50

Overprinted Diagonally in Red.

1885 ***Perf. 12.***

No.	Type	Description	Unused	Used
O18	A20	2c green	2.00	1.00
a.		Inverted overprint	45.00	27.50
O19	A11	4c brown	2.00	1.25
a.		Inverted overprint	45.00	27.50
b.		Double overprint	45.00	45.00
O20	A13	60c black	22.50	15.00
O21	A14	90c blue	250.00	175.00

1885 ***Rouletted***

No.	Type	Description	Unused	Used
O22	A19	24c blue	20.00	11.00

On all of these stamps, the overprint is found reading both upwards and downwards.

Counterfeits exist of No. O21 overprint and others.

Regular Issues Handstamped Horizontally in Black **OFICIAL**

1884 ***Perf. 12, 14.***

No.	Type	Description	Unused	Used
O23	A23	1c red	70.00	25.00
a.		Perf. 12	225.00	125.00
O24	A20	2c green	225.00	175.00
a.		Diagonal ovpt.	35.00	20.00
O25	A11	4c brown	15.00	11.00
O26	A7	8c lake	15.00	11.00
O27	A23	12c ultra	40.00	25.00

Overprinted Diagonally.

No.	Type	Description	Unused	Used
O28	A19	24c bl, rouletted	30.00	20.00
O29	A13	60c black	20.00	10.00

Counterfeit overprints exist.

Liberty Head
O1

1901, Dec. 1 **Engraved** ***Perf. 11½***

No.	Type	Description	Unused	Used
O31	O1	1c gray	30	20
O32	O1	2c org brn	45	25
O33	O1	5c red	60	25
O34	O1	10c dk grn	70	30
O35	O1	30c dk bl	4.50	1.10
O36	O1	50c orange	2.50	75
		Nos. O31-O36 (6)	9.05	2.85

Regular Stamps of 1935-51 Overprinted in Black

SERVICIO OFICIAL
c

Wmkd. RA in Sun. (90)

Perf. 13x13½, 13½x13, 13.

1938-54

No.	Type	Description	Unused	Used
O37	A129	1c buff ('40)	10	5
O38	A130	2c dk brn ('40)	10	5
O39	A132	3c grn ('39)	12	5
O40	A132	3c lt gray ('39)	10	5
O41	A134	5c yel brn	10	5
O42	A195	5c car ('53)	12	5
O43	A137	10c carmine	10	4
O44	A137	10c brn ('39)	10	3
O45	A140	15c lt gray bl, type II ('47)	12	5
O46	A139	15c sl bl	35	5
O47	A139	15c pale ultra ('39)	12	5
O48	A139	20c bl ('53)	30	3
O49	A141	25c carmine	12	3
a.		Overprint 11mm	20	4
O49B	A143	40c dk vio	75	8
O50	A144	50c red & org	10	5
a.		Overprint 11mm	25	5
O51	A146	1p brn blk & lt bl ('40)	20	5
a.		Overprint 11mm		
O52	A224	1p choc & lt bl ('51)	20	8
a.		Overprint 11mm	20	8
O53	A147	2p brn lake & dk ultra (ovpt. 11mm) ('54)	75	8
		Nos. O37-O53 (18)	3.85	92

Overprinted in Black on Stamps and Types of 1945-47

Perf. 13x13½, 13½x13.

1945-46 **Unwmkd.**

No.	Type	Description	Unused	Used
O54	A130	2c sepia	1.25	30
O55	A134	3c lt gray	1.25	20
O56	A134	5c yel brn	30	5
O57	A195	5c dp car	8	5
O58	A137	10c brown	8	5
a.		Double overprint		
O59	A140	15c lt gray bl, type II	12	5
O61	A141	25c dl rose	12	5
O62	A144	50c red & org	30	5
O63	A146	1p brn blk & lt bl	12	5
O64	A147	2p brn lake & bl	12	5
O65	A148	5p ind & ol grn	12	6
O66	A149	10p dp cl & int blk	25	8
O67	A150	20p bl grn & brn	50	20
		Nos. O54-O67 (13)	4.61	1.24

Overprinted in Black on Stamps and Types of 1942-50

Perf. 13, 13x13½.

1944-51 **Wmk. 288**

No.	Type	Description	Unused	Used
O73	A134	3c lt gray	1.50	40
O74	A134	5c yel brn	25	6
O75	A137	10c red brn	10	3
O76	A140	15c lt gray bl, type II	25	5
O77	A144	50c red & org (overprint 11 mm)	2.25	40
O78	A146	1p brn blk & lt bl (overprint 11mm)	2.25	30
		Nos. O73-O78 (6)	6.60	1.24

Regular Issue of 1952

Overprinted in Black SERVICIO OFICIAL
d

1953 ***Perf. 13.*** **Wmk. 90**

No.	Type	Description	Unused	Used
O79	A228	5c gray	8	3
O80	A228	10c rose lil	8	3
O81	A228	20c rose pink	8	3
O82	A228	25c dl grn	12	3
O83	A228	40c dl vio	8	3
O84	A228	45c dp bl	20	5
O85	A228	50c dl brn	12	5

Nos. 611-617 Overprinted Type "e" in Blue

SERVICIO OFICIAL
e

SERVICIO OFICIAL
f

Perf. 13x13½, 13½x13

No.	Type	Description	Unused	Used
O86	A229	1p dk brn	15	6
O87	A229	1.50p dp grn	30	8
O88	A229	2p brt car	20	10
O89	A229	3p indigo	60	20

Size: 30x40mm.

No.	Type	Description	Unused	Used
O90	A229	5p red brn	60	35
O91	A228	10p red	3.00	1.50
O92	A229	20p green	32.50	15.00
		Nos. O79-O92 (14)	38.11	17.54

No. 612 Overprinted Type "f" in Blue.

No.	Type	Description	Unused	Used
O93	A229	1.50p dp grn	1.00	15

Regular Issue of 1954-59 Variously Overprinted in Black or Blue

S. OFICIAL
g

SERVICIO OFICIAL
h

Perf. 13½, 13x13½, 13½x13

1955-61 **Lithographed** **Wmk. 90**

No.	Type	Description	Unused	Used
O94	A237 (c)	20c red (#629)	12	4
O95	A237 (d)	20c red (#629)	10	4
O96	A237 (d)	40c red, ovpt. 15mm (#630)	12	4

Engraved

No.	Type	Description	Unused	Used
O97	A239 (g)	50c bl (#632) ('58)	10	5

Photogravure

No.	Type	Description	Unused	Used
O98	A239 (h)	1p brn (#635) ('59)	10	5
O99	A239 (e)	1p brn (Bl) (#635) ('59)	10	5
O100	A239 (e)	1p brn (Bk) (#635) ('60)	10	5

Engraved

No.	Type	Description	Unused	Used
O101	A239 (h)	3p vio brn (#638) ('58)	12	5
O102	A240 (h)	5p gray grn (#639) ('57)	30	8
O103	A240 (e)	10p yel grn (#640) ('58)	50	15
O104	A240 (f)	20p dl vio (#641) ('59)	90	30
O105	A240 (h)	20p dl vio (#641) ('58)	90	25
O106	A241 (e)	50p ultra & ind (#642) ('61)	1.25	15
		Nos. O94-O106 (13)	4.71	1.30

The overprints on Nos. O99-O100 and O103-O104 are horizontal; that on No. O109 is vertical. On No. O106 overprint measures 23mm.

No. 659 Overprinted Type "d".

Lithographed.

1957 ***Perf. 13*** **Wmk. 90**

No.	Type	Description	Unused	Used
O108	A133	20c dl pur (ovpt. 15mm)	10	5

Nos. 666, 658 and 663 Variously Overprinted

1957 **Photo.** ***Perf. 13x13½, 13½***

No.	Type	Description	Unused	Used
O109	A261 (g)	2p claret	20	5
O110	A254(e)	2.40p brown	20	5
O111	A258(c)	4.40p grnsh gray	25	8

Nos. 668, 685-687, 690-691, 693-705, 742, 742C and Types of 1959-65 Overprinted in Black, Blue or Red Types "e," "g" or

S. OFICIAL
i

S. OFICIAL
j

S. OFICIAL
k

S. OFICIAL
m

S. OFICIAL
n

Lithographed; Photogravure

1960-68 ***Perf. 13x13½, 13½***

No.	Type	Description	Unused	Used
O112	A128 (g)	5c buff (vert. ovpt.) ('62)	10	3
O113	A275 (j)	10c sl grn ('62)	8	3
O114	A275 (j)	20c dl red brn ('62)	8	3
O115	A275 (i)	50c bister	8	3
O116	A278 (k)	1p brn ('62)	12	4
O117	A278 (j)	1p brn, photo. (vert. ovpt.) ('65)	20	5
O117A	A278 (j)	1p brn, litho., (vert. ovpt., down, '68)	20	7
O118	A276 (j)	2p rose red ('62)	12	5
O119	A312 (m)	2p dp grn (vert. ovpt., down) ('64)	25	8
O120	A312 (j)	2p brt grn (vert. ovpt., up) ('66)	12	5
O121	A312 (j)	2p grn litho. (vert. ovpt., down) ('67)	25	8
O122	A277 (e)	3p dk bl (horiz.) ('61)	20	7
O123	A277 (j)	3p dk bl ('67)	20	7
O124	A276 (j)	4p red, litho. ('63?)	20	5
O125	A312 (j)	4p rose red, litho. (vert. ovpt., down) ('65)	20	3
O126	A277 (e)	5p brn (Bl) (horiz.)	25	8
O127	A277 (e)	5p brn (Bk) (horiz.) ('61)	25	8
O128	A277 (j)	5p sep ('66)	15	3
O129	A277 (e)	5p sep (horiz. ovpt.) ('67)	15	4
O130	A276 (j)	8p red ('65)	20	8
O131	A278 (i)	10p lt red brn	50	10
O132	A276 (j)	10p ver ('66)	20	5
O133	A278 (j)	10p brn car (vert. ovpt., up) ('66)	20	5
O134	A278 (m)	12p dk brn vio ('64)	40	5
O135	A278 (k)	20p Prus grn ('61)	60	10
O136	A278 (j)	20p Prus grn (vert. ovpt., up) ('66)	45	6
O137	A276 (j)	20p red, litho. ('67)	40	6
O138	A276 (m)	20p red, litho. ('67)	25	5
O139	A278 (j)	23p grn (vert. ovpt.) ('65)	60	10
O140	A278 (j)	25p dp vio, photo. (R) (vert. ovpt., up) ('66)	60	6
O141	A278 (j)	25p pur, litho. (R) (vert. ovpt., down) ('67)	60	10
O142	A241 (n)	50p dk bl ('66)	1.25	10
O143	A279(m)	100p bl (horiz. ovpt.) ('64)	1.25	25
O144	A279(m)	100p bl (vert. ovpt., up) ('65)	1.25	25
O145	A280(m)	300p dp vio ('66)	2.50	50

The "m" overprint measures 15½mm. on 2p; 14½mm. on 12p, 100p and 300p; 13mm. on 20p.

Nos. 699, 818, 823-825, 827-829, and Type of 1962 Overprinted in Black or Red Types "j," "m" or "o"

SERVICIO OFICIAL
o

Inscribed: "Republica Argentina"

Litho., Photo., Engraved

1964-67 ***Perf. 13½*** **Wmk. 90**

No.	Type	Description	Unused	Used
O149	A312 (j)	6p rose red (vert. ovpt., down) ('67)	30	4
O153	A238a(m)	22p ultra ('64)	60	6
O154	A238a (j)	43p dk car rose (vert. ovpt., down)	85	6
O155	A238a (j)	45p brn, photo. (vert. ovpt., up) ('66)	85	6
O156	A238a (j)	45p brn, litho. (vert. ovpt., up) ('67)	1.25	15
O157	A241 (j)	50p dk bl (vert. ovpt., up) (R) ('67)	2.50	15
O158	A366 (j)	90p ol bis (vert. ovpt., up) ('67)	3.00	15
O162	A279 (o)	500p yel grn ('67)	4.00	75

Type of 1959-67 Overprinted Type "J"

Perf. 13½

1969 **Lithographed** **Wmk. 365**

No.	Type	Description	Unused	Used
O163	A276	20p vermilion	25	10

OFFICIAL DEPARTMENT STAMPS

Regular issues of 1911-37 Overprinted in Black

Ministry of Agriculture

M. A. (Type I) | **M. A.** (Type II)

1913-37 **On Stamp of 1911**

No.	Type	Description	Unused	Used
OD1	A88	2c #181	10	5

On Stamps of 1912-14

No.	Type	Description	Unused	Used
OD2	A88	1c #190	10	5
OD3	A88	2c #191	15	6
OD4	A88	5c #194	30	5
OD5	A88	12c #196	10	5

On Stamps of 1915-16

No.	Type	Description	Unused	Used
OD6	A88	1c #208	15	12
OD7	A88	2c #209	10	6
OD8	A88	5c #212	10	6
OD9	A91	5c #220	10	5

On Stamp of 1917

No.	Type	Description	Unused	Used
OD10	A94	12c #238	30	5

On Stamps of 1918-19

OD11	A93	1c #249	10	5
OD12	A93	2c #250	10	5
OD13	A93	5c #253	10	5
OD14	A94	12c #255	10	5
OD15	A94	20c #256	15	10

On Stamps of 1920

OD16	A93	1c #265	30	20
OD17	A93	2c #266	50	20
OD18	A93	5c #269	20	5

On Stamps of 1922-23

OD19	A94	12c #311	75	25
OD20	A94	20c #312	20.00	

On Stamps of 1923

OD21	A104	1c #324	5	5
OD22	A104	2c #325	25	10
OD23	A104	5c #328	5	5
OD24	A104	12c #330	5	5
OD25	A104	20c #331	5	5

On Stamps of 1923-31

OD26	A104	1c #341	5	5
OD27	A104	2c #342, I	5	5
a.		Type II	1.20	60
OD28	A104	3c #343	10	5
OD29	A104	5c #345, II	5	5
a.		Type I	10	5
OD30	A104	10c #346, II	5	5
a.		Type I	10	5
OD31	A104	12c #347	10	5
OD32	A104	20c #348, I	15	5
a.		Type II	15	5
OD33	A104	30c #351	15	5

On Stamp of 1926

OD34	A110	12c #360	5	5

On Stamps of 1935-37

OD35	A129	1c #419	5	5
OD36	A130	2c #420	5	5
OD37	A132	3c #422	5	5
OD38	A134	5c #427	5	5
OD39	A137	10c #430	5	5
OD40	A139	15c #434	30	5
OD41	A140	20c #437	20	6
OD42	A140	20c #438	10	5
OD43	A141	25c #441	20	5
OD44	A142	30c #442	15	5
OD45	A145	1p #445	2.00	1.00
OD46	A146	1p #446	25	10

Ministry of War

M. G. (Type I) | M. G. (Type II)

On Stamp of 1911

OD47	A88	2c #181	10	5

On Stamps of 1912-14

OD48	A88	1c #190	10	5
OD49	A88	2c #191	10	5
OD50	A88	5c #194	10	5
OD51	A88	12c #196	10	5

On Stamps of 1915-16

OD52	A88	1c #208	6.00	60
OD53	A88	2c #209	50	10
OD54	A88	5c #212	60	5
OD55	A91	5c #220	75	15
OD56	A92	12c #222	75	25

On Stamps of 1917

OD57	A93	1c #232	20	5
OD58	A93	2c #233	30	5
OD59	A93	5c #236	30	5
OD60	A94	12c #238	45	5

On Stamps of 1918-19

OD61	A93	1c #249	15	5
OD62	A93	2c #250	10	5
OD63	A93	5c #253	10	5
OD64	A94	12c #255	30	5
OD65	A94	20c #256	90	5

On Stamps of 1920

OD66	A93	2c #266	30	5
OD67	A93	5c #269	30	5
OD68	A94	12c #271	25	5

On Stamp of 1920

OD69	A94	12c #299	1.50	15

On Stamps of 1922-23

OD70	A93	1c #305	60	10
OD71	A93	2c #306	1.25	30
OD72	A103	5c #309	60	5
OD73	A94	20c #312	20	5

On Stamp of 1922-23

OD74	A93	2c #318	3.50	50

On Stamps of 1923

OD75	A104	1c #324	10	5
OD76	A104	2c #325	10	5
OD77	A104	5c #328	10	5
OD78	A104	10c #330	10	5
OD79	A104	20c #331	75	5

On Stamps of 1923-31

OD80	A104	1c #341	1.00	30
OD81	A104	2c #342	15	5
OD82	A104	3c #343, I	5	5
a.		Type II	30	5
OD83	A104	5c #345, I	5	5
a.		Type II	15	3
OD84	A104	10c #346, II	5	3
a.		Type I	45	5
OD85	A104	20c #348, I	10	5
a.		Type II	30	3
OD86	A104	30c #351, II	15	5
a.		Type I	90	10
OD87	A105	1p #353	1.25	20

On Stamp of 1926

OD88	A109	5c #359	45	5

On Stamps of 1935-37

OD89	A129	1c #419	5	5
OD90	A130	2c #420	5	5
OD91	A132	3c #422	5	5
OD92	A134	5c #427	6	5
OD93	A137	10c #430	10	5
OD94	A139	15c #434	15	5
OD95	A140	20c #437	75	5
OD96	A140	20c #438	15	5
OD97	A141	25c #441	10	5
OD98	A142	30c #442	10	5
OD99	A144	50c #444	15	5
OD100	A145	1p #445	80	20
OD101	A146	1p #446	25	10

Ministry of Finance

M. H. (Type I) | M. H. (Type II)

Type I

On Stamp of 1911

OD102	A88	2c #181	10	5

On Stamps of 1912-14

OD103	A88	1c #190	10	5
OD104	A88	2c #191	10	5
OD105	A88	5c #194	10	5
OD106	A88	12c #196	10	5

On Stamps of 1915-16

OD107	A88	2c #209	10	6
OD108	A88	5c #212	10	5
OD109	A91	5c #220	10	5

On Stamps of 1917

OD110	A93	2c #233	10	5
OD111	A93	5c #236	90	5
OD112	A94	12c #238	10	5

On Stamps of 1918-19

OD113	A93	2c #250		20.00
OD114	A93	5c #253	10	5
OD115	A94	12c #255	30	5
OD116	A94	20c #256	30	5

On Stamps of 1920

OD117	A93	1c #265	60	30
OD118	A93	2c #266	90	30
OD119	A93	5c #269	20	5
OD120	A94	12c #271	45	10

On Stamp of 1922-23

OD121	A94	20c #312	10.00	2.00

On Stamps of 1923

OD122	A104	1c #324	60	30
OD123	A104	2c #325	5	5
OD124	A104	5c #328	5	5
OD125	A105	10c #330	5	5
OD126	A104	20c #331	5	5

On Stamps of 1923-31

OD127	A104	3c #343	6.00	1.00
OD128	A104	5c #345	5	5
OD129	A104	10c #346	5	3
OD130	A104	12c #347	6.00	3.00
OD131	A104	20c #348, I	10	5
a.		Type II	25	3
OD132	A104	30c #351	15	3
OD133	A105	1p #353	30	15

On Stamp of 1926

OD134	A110	12c #360	10.00	10.00

On Stamps of 1935-37

OD135	A129	1c #419	5	5
OD136	A130	2c #420	5	5
OD137	A132	3c #422	5	5
OD138	A134	5c #427	5	5
OD139	A137	10c #430	10	5
OD140	A139	15c #434	30	5
OD141	A140	20c #437	15	5
OD142	A140	20c #438	10	5
OD143	A142	30c #442	10	5
OD144	A145	1p #445	1.20	40
OD145	A146	1p #446	25	5

Ministry of the Interior

M. I. (Type I) | M. I. (Type II)

Type I

On Stamp of 1911

OD146	A88	2c #181	25	5

On Stamps of 1912-14

OD147	A88	1c #190	10	5
OD148	A88	2c #191	10	5
OD149	A88	5c #194	10	5
OD150	A8	12c #196	10	5

On Stamps of 1915-17

OD151	A88	2c #209	75	30
OD152	A88	5c #212	60	10
OD153	A91	5c #220	45	10
OD154	A93	5c #236	1.20	10

On Stamps of 1918-19

OD155	A93	2c #250	10	5
OD156	A93	5c #253	10	5

On Stamps of 1920

OD157	A93	1c #265	3.00	75
OD158	A93	5c #269	60	25

On Stamps of 1922-23

OD159	A93	2c #306	10.00	10.00
OD160	A103	5c #309	2.50	75
OD161	A94	12c #311	75	25
OD162	A94	20c #312	75	25

On Stamps of 1923

OD163	A104	1c #324	5	5
OD164	A104	2c #325	5	5
OD165	A104	5c #328	5	5
OD166	A104	10c #330	1.50	1.50
OD167	A104	20c #331	50	5

On Stamps of 1923-31

OD168	A104	1c #341	5	5
OD169	A104	2c #342	5	5
OD170	A104	3c #343, II	5	5
a.		Type I	90	20
OD171	A104	5c #345, I	5	5
a.		Type II	5	5
OD172	A104	10c #346	5	5
OD173	A104	12c #347	30	5
OD174	A104	20c #348, II	5	5
a.		Type I	60	5
OD175	A104	30c #351	5	15

On Stamps of 1935-37

OD176	A129	1c #419	5	5
OD177	A130	2c #420	5	5
OD178	A132	3c #422	5	5
OD178A	A134	5c #427	5	5
OD179	A137	10c #430	5	5
OD180	A139	15c #434	20	5
OD181	A140	20c #437	60	5
OD182	A140	20c #438	10	5
OD183	A142	30c #442	10	5
OD184	A145	1p #445	1.20	50
OD185	A146	1p #446	25	10

Ministry of Foreign Affairs and Religion

M. J. I. (Type I) | M. J. I. (Type II)

Type I

On Stamp of 1911

OD183	A88	2c #181	90	5

On Stamps of 1912-14

OD184	A88	1c #190	1.20	5
OD185	A88	2c #191	75	15
OD186	A88	5c #194	30	5
OD187	A88	12c #196	30	5

On Stamps of 1915-17

OD188	A88	1c #208	20	5
OD189	A88	2c #209	20	5
OD190	A88	5c #212	75	10
OD191	A91	5c #220	15	5
OD192	A92	12c #222	50	5

On Stamps of 1917

OD193	A93	1c #232	20	5
OD194	A93	2c #233	60	5
OD195	A93	5c #236	20	5
OD196	A94	12c #238	17.50	5.00

On Stamps of 1918-19

OD197	A93	1c #249	10	5
OD198	A93	2c #250	10	5
OD199	A93	5c #253	10	5
OD200	A94	12c #255	20	5
OD201	A94	20c #256	40	5

On Stamps of 1920

OD202	A93	1c #265	15	5
OD203	A93	2c #266	10	5
OD204	A93	5c #269	10	5
OD205	A94	12c #271	25	5

On Stamps of 1922-23

OD206	A93	1c #305	15	5
OD207	A93	2c #306	1.20	30
OD208	A103	5c #309	15	5
OD209	A94	12c #311	7.50	1.20
OD210	A94	20c #312	1.20	20

On Stamp of 1922-23

OD211	A93	2c #318	2.00	2.00

On Stamps of 1923

OD212	A104	1c #324	10	5
OD213	A104	2c #325	5	5
OD214	A104	5c #328	10	5
OD215	A104	10c #330	10	5
OD216	A104	20c #331	30	5

On Stamps of 1923-31

OD217	A104	½c #340	1.50	50
OD218	A104	1c #341, I	5	5
a.		Type II	5	5
OD219	A104	2c #342	5	5
OD220	A104	3c #343, I	5	5
a.		Type II	5	5
OD221	A104	5c #345, I	5	5
a.		Type II	5	5
OD222	A104	10c #346, II	5	5
a.		Type I	20	5
OD223	A104	12c #347, I	5	5
a.		Type II	30	15
OD224	A104	20c #348, I	5	5
a.		Type II	5	5
OD225	A104	30c #351	5	5
OD226	A105	1p #353	30	50

On Stamps of 1926

OD227A109	5c #359	10	5
OD228A110	12c #360	15	5

On Stamps of 1935-37

OD229A129	1c #419	5	5
OD230A130	2c #420	5	5
OD231A132	3c #422	5	5
OD232A134	5c #427	6	5
OD233A137	10c #430	5	5
OD234A139	15c #434	30	5
OD235A140	20c #437	10	5
OD236A140	20c #438	15	5
OD237A141	25c #441	10	5
OD238A142	30c #442	10	5
OD239A145	1p #445	60	30
OD240A146	1p #446	15	10

Ministry of Marine

M. M. (Type I) | M. M. (Type II)

Type I

On Stamp of 1911

OD235A88	2c #181	20	5

On Stamps of 1912-14

OD236A88	1c #190	10	5
OD237A88	2c #191	10	5
OD238A88	5c #194	2.00	10
OD239A88	12c #196	15	5

On Stamps of 1915-16

OD240A88	2c #209	50	5
OD241A88	5c #212	30	5

On Stamps of 1917

OD242A93	1c #232	10	5
OD243A93	2c #233	10	5
OD244A93	5c #236	10	5

On Stamps of 1918-19

OD245A93	1c #249	10	5
OD246A93	2c #250	10	5
OD247A93	5c #253	20	5
OD248A94	12c #255	20	10
OD249A94	20c #256	2.50	25

On Stamps of 1920

OD250A93	1c #265	10	5
OD251A93	2c #266	15	5
OD252A93	5c #269	20	5

On Stamps of 1922-23

OD253A103	5c #309	60	10
OD254A94	12c #311	7.50	7.50
OD255A94	20c #312	6.00	1.00

On Stamps of 1923

OD256A104	1c #324	5	5
OD257A104	2c #325	10	5
OD258A104	5c #328	25	5
OD259A104	10c #330	50	15
OD260A104	20c #331	50	5

On Stamps of 1923-31

OD261A104	1c #341	60	15
OD262A104	2c #342	15	5
OD263A104	3c #343	45	15
OD264A104	5c #345, I	10	5
a.	Type II	45	3
OD265A104	10c #346	45	3
OD266A104	20c #348, II	45	5
a.	Type I	60	5
OD267A104	30c #351	90	5
OD268A105	1p #353	9.00	2.00

On Stamp of 1926

OD269A109	5c #359	50	5

On Stamps of 1935-37

OD270A129	1c #419	5	5
OD271A130	2c #420	5	5
OD272A132	3c #422	5	5
OD273A134	5c #427	5	3
OD274A137	10c #430	20	3
OD275A139	15c #434	20	5
OD276A140	20c #437	30	5
OD277A140	20c #438	20	3
OD278A142	30c #442	20	3
OD279A145	1p #445	2.50	60
OD280A146	1p #446	60	15

Ministry of Public Works

M. O. P. (Type I) | M. O. P. (Type II)

Type I

On Stamp of 1911

OD281A88	2c #181	30	5

On Stamps of 1912-14

OD282A88	1c #190	30	5
OD283A88	5c #194	15	5
OD284A88	12c #196	1.50	25

On Stamps of 1916-19

OD285A91	5c #220	12.00	75
OD286A94	12c #238	20.00	
OD287A94	20c #256	20.00	

On Stamps of 1920

OD288A93	2c #266	5.00	2.00
OD289A93	5c #269	1.50	10
OD290A94	12c #271	18.00	5.00

On Stamps of 1923

OD291A104	1c #324	30	10
OD292A104	2c #325	30	5
OD293A104	5c #328	30	5
OD294A104	10c #330	50	10
OD295A104	20c #331	75	10

On Stamps of 1923-31

OD296A104	1c #341	5	5
OD297A104	2c #342	5	5
OD298A104	3c #343	5	5
OD299A104	5c #345, I	5	5
a.	Type II	5	5
OD300A104	10c #346	5	5
OD301A104	12c #347	7.50	90
OD302A104	20c #348, I	5	5
a.	Type II	1.80	50
OD303A104	30c #351	30	5
OD304A105	1p #353	18.00	5.00

On Stamp of 1926

OD305A109	5c #359	50	5

On Stamps of 1935-37

OD306A129	1c #419	5	5
OD307A130	2c #420	5	5
OD308A132	3c #422	5	5
OD309A134	5c #427	5	5
OD310A137	10c #430	30	5
OD311A139	15c #434	45	5
OD312A140	20c #437	60	6
OD313A140	20c #438	10	5
OD314A142	30c #442	10	5
OD315A144	50c #444	10	5
OD316A145	1p #445	1.20	40
OD317A146	1p #446	25	10

Ministry of Foreign Affairs and Religion

M. R. C. (Type I) | M. R. C. (Type II)

Type I

On Stamp of 1911

OD318A88	2c #181	7.50	1.25

On Stamps of 1912-14

OD319A88	1c #190	10	5
OD320A88	2c #191	10	5
OD321A88	5c #194	30	5
OD322A88	12c #196	1.50	25

On Stamps of 1915-19

OD323A88	5c #212	30	5
OD324A91	5c #220	15	5
OD325A94	20c #256	1.50	50

On Stamps of 1920

OD326A93	1c #265	30	10
OD327A93	5c #269	10	5

On Stamps of 1922-23

OD328A93	2c #306	10.00	4.00
OD329A103	5c #309	25.00	
OD330A93	10c #311	20.00	

On Stamps of 1923

OD331A104	1c #324	5	5
OD332A104	2c #325	5	5
OD333A104	5c #328	5	5
OD334A104	10c #330	10	5
OD335A104	20c #331	15	5

On Stamps of 1923-31

OD336A104	½c #340	75	30
OD337A104	1c #341	6	5
OD338A104	2c #342	6	5
OD339A104	3c #343	5	5
OD340A104	5c #345	5	5
OD341A104	10c #346, II	5	5
a.	Type I	1.20	5
OD342A104	12c #347	5	5
OD343A104	20c #348, I	5	5
a.	Type II	15	5
OD344A104	30c #351, I	15	5
a.	Type II	15	5
OD345A105	1p #353	30	10

On Stamp of 1926

OD346A110	12c #360	10	5

On Stamps of 1935-37

OD347A129	1c #419	5	5
OD348A130	2c #420	5	5
OD349A132	3c #422	5	5
OD350A134	5c #427	5	5
OD351A137	10c #430	10	5
OD352A139	15c #434	10	5
OD353A140	20c #437	10	5
OD354A140	20c #438	10	5
OD355A142	30c #442	10	5
OD356A145	1p #445	1.50	60
OD357A146	1p #446	75	35

Buenos Aires

(bwā'nos ī'rās)

The central point of the Argentine struggle for independence. At intervals Buenos Aires maintained an independent government but after 1862 became a province of the Argentine Republic.

8 REALES=1 PESO

> Prices of Buenos Aires Nos. 1–8 vary according to condition. Quotations are for fine copies. Very fine to superb specimens sell at much higher prices, and inferior or poor copies sell at reduced prices, depending on the condition of the individual specimen.

Steamship

A1

Typographed.

1858 ***Imperf.*** **Unwmkd.**

1	A1	1 (in) pesos lt brn	250.00	150.00
2	A1	2 (dos) pesos bl	300.00	190.00
3	A1	3 (tres) pesos grn	1,500.	*1,000.*
a.		3p dk grn	1,750.	*1,250.*
4	A1	4 (cuato) pesos ver	5,000.	*3,000.*
5	A1	5 (cinco) pesos org	5,000.	*3,000.*
a.		5p ocher	5,000.	*3,000.*
b.		5p ol yel	5,000.	*3,000.*

Issue dates: Nos. 2–5, Apr. 29, 1858. No. 1, Oct. 26, 1858.

1858, Oct. 26

6	A1	4 (cuato) reales brn	350.00	300.00
a.		4r gray brn	350.00	300.00
b.		4r yel brn	350.00	300.00

1859, Jan. 1

7	A1	1 (in) pesos bl	225.00	150.00
a.		1p ind	300.00	175.00
b.		Impression on reverse of stamp in bl	*2,500.*	
c.		Double impression	300.00	225.00
d.		Tête bêche pair		*50,000.*
8	A1	1 (to) pesos bl	500.00	250.00

Nos. 1, 2, 3 and 7 have been reprinted on very thick, hand-made paper. The same four stamps and No. 8 have been reprinted on thin, hard, white wove paper.

Counterfeits of Nos. 1–8 are plentiful.

Liberty Head

A2

1859, Sept. 3

9	A2	4r grn, *bluish*	350.00	200.00
10	A2	1p blue	45.00	25.00
11	A2	2p vermilion	500.00	300.00
a.		2p red	500.00	300.00

Both clear and rough impressions of these stamps may be found. They have generally been called Paris and Local prints, respectively, but the opinion now obtains that the differences are due to the impression and that they do not represent separate issues.

Many shades exist of Nos. 1–11.

1862, Oct. 4

12	A2	1p rose	225.00	100.00
13	A2	2p blue	500.00	150.00

All three values have been reprinted in black, brownish black, blue and red brown on thin hard white paper. The 4r has also been reprinted in green on bluish paper.

Cordoba

(kôr'dô·bä)

A province in the central part of the Argentine Republic.

100 CENTAVOS=1 PESO

Arms of Cordoba

A1

Lithographed

Laid Paper.

1858, Oct. 28 ***Imperf.*** **Unwmkd.**

1	A1	5c blue	125.00	
2	A1	10c black	*2,500.*	

Cordoba stamps were printed on laid paper, but stamps from edges of the sheets sometimes do not show any laid lines and appear to be on wove paper. Counterfeits are plentiful.

Corrientes

(kŏr'rē·ĕn'tēs)

The northeast province of the Argentine Republic.

1 REAL M(ONEDA) C(ORRIENTE)=12½ CENTAVOS M. C.=50 CENTAVOS

100 CENTAVOS FUERTES=1 PESO FUERTE

Ceres

A1 A2

1856, Aug. 21 *Imperf.* **Unwmkd.**

1 A1 1r *blue* 125.00 400.00

1860, Feb. 8

Value Cancelled by Pen Stroke.

2 A1 (3c) *blue* 500.00 750.00

1860-78

3 A2 (3c) *blue* 12.50 40.00
4 A2 (2c) *yel grn* ('64) 50.00 60.00
a. (2c) *bl grn* 125.00 150.00
5 A2 (2c) *yel* ('67) 10.00 25.00
6 A2 (3c) *dk bl* ('71) 4.00 25.00
7 A2 (3c) *lil rose* ('75) 150.00 75.00
a. (3c) *rose red* ('76) 125.00 75.00
8 A2 (3c) *red vio* ('78) 150.00 125.00

Printed from settings of eight varieties, three or four impressions constituting a sheet. Some impressions were printed inverted and tête bêche pairs may be cut from adjacent impressions.

From Jan. 1st to Feb. 24th, 1864, No. 4 was used as a 5 centavos stamp but copies so used can only be distinguished when they bear dated cancellations.

The reprints show numerous spots and small defects which are not found on the originals. They are printed on gray blue, dull blue, gray green, dull orange and light magenta papers

ARMENIA

(är·mē'nĭ·ȧ)

LOCATION—In southern Russia bounded by Georgia, Azerbaijan, Persia and Turkey.

GOVT.—A Soviet Socialist Republic.

AREA—11,945 sq. mi.

POP.—1,214,391 (1923).

CAPITAL—Erevan.

With Azerbaijan and Georgia, Armenia made up the Transcaucasian Federation of Soviet Republics.

Stamps of Armenia were replaced in 1923 by those of Transcaucasian Federated Republics.

100 Kopecks = 1 Ruble

Counterfeits abound of all overprinted and surcharged stamps.

National Republic.

Russian Stamps of 1902–19 Handstamped

Thirteen types exist of both framed and unframed overprints. The device is the Armenian "H," initial of Hayasdan (Armenia). Inverted and double overprints are found.

Surcharged K 60 K

Type I. Without periods.
Type II. Periods after first "K" and "60".

Black Surcharge.

1919 *Perf.* **14, 14½x15.** **Unwmkd.**

1 A14 60k on 1k org (II) 35 40
a. Imperf. (I) 25 30
b. Imperf. (II) 25 30

Violet Surcharge.

2 A14 60k on 1k org (II) 45 50

Handstamped in Violet

a

Perf. **14, 14½x15, 13½.**

6 A15 4k carmine 75 75
7 A14 5k claret 3.50 4.00
a. Imperf. 2.25 2.50
9 A14 10k on 7k lt bl 1.75 2.00
10 A11 15k red brn & bl 40 40
11 A8 20k bl & car 1.25 1.50
13 A11 35k red brn & grn 75 75
14 A8 50k vio & grn 60 60
15 A14 60k on 1k org (II) 3.00 3.50
a. Imperf. (I) 2.50 2.75
b. Imperf. (II) 14.00 15.00

18 A13 5r dk bl, grn & pale bl 6.00 7.00
a. Imperf. 1.50 1.50
19 A12 7r dk grn & pink 2.00 2.25
20 A13 10r scar, yel & gray 2.00 2.25

Handstamped in Black.

Perf. **14, 14½x15, 13½.**

31 A14 2k green 6.00 7.00
a. Imperf. 25 25
32 A14 3k red 3.50 4.00
a. Imperf. 25 25
33 A15 4k carmine 15 20
34 A14 5k claret 25 30
a. Imperf. 2.00 2.00
36 A15 10k dk bl 1.00 1.00
37 A14 10k on 7k lt bl 10 15
38 A11 15k red brn & bl 10 15
a. Imperf. 2.00 2.00
39 A8 20k bl & car 15 20
40 A11 25k grn & gray vio 15 20
41 A11 35k red brn & grn 10 15
42 A8 50k vio & grn 10 15
43 A14 60k on 1k org (II) 3.00 3.00
43A A11 70k brn & org 30 35
b. Imperf. 25 30
44 A9 1r pale brn, dk brn & org 70 75
a. Imperf. 40 50
45 A12 3½r mar & lt grn 1.20 1.25
a. Imperf. 75 85
46 A13 5r dk bl, grn & pale bl 75 85
a. Imperf. 1.25 1.25
47 A12 7r dk grn & pink 1.75 1.75
48 A13 10r scar, yel & gray 1.50 1.50

Vertically Laid Paper.

Wmkd. Wavy Lines. (168)

1920 *Imperf.*

60 A13 5r dk bl, grn & pale bl 30.00

Handstamped in Violet

c

Unwmkd.

Perf. **14, 14½x15, 13½.**

Wove Paper.

62 A14 2k green 7.00 7.00
a. Imperf. 50 50
63 A14 3k red 4.50 4.50
a. Imperf. 25 25
64 A15 4k carmine 60 60
65 A14 5k claret 60 60
a. Imperf. 1.00 1.00
67 A15 10k dk bl 1.25 1.25
68 A14 10k on 7k lt bl 1.00 1.00
69 A11 15k red brn & bl 50 50
70 A8 20k bl & car 60 60
71 A11 25k grn & gray vio 50 50
72 A11 35k red brn & grn 40 40
73 A8 50k vio & grn 30 30
74 A14 60k on 1k org (II) 3.00 3.00
a. Imperf. (I) 2.50 2.50
b. Imperf. (II) 3.00 3.00
75 A9 1r pale brn, dk brn & org 1.00 1.00
a. Imperf. 75 75
76 A12 3½r mar & lt grn 1.50 1.50
a. Imperf. 1.00 1.00
77 A13 5r dk bl, grn & pale bl 3.00 3.00
a. Imperf. 1.50 1.50
78 A12 7r dk grn & pink 2.50 2.50
79 A13 10r scar, yel & gray 2.50 2.50

Imperf.

85 A11 70k brn & org 2.00 2.00

Handstamped in Black.

Perf. **14, 14½x15, 13½.**

90 A14 1k orange 6.50 6.50
a. Imperf. 9.00 9.00
91 A14 2k green 5.00 5.00
a. Imperf. 10 10
92 A14 3k red 5.00 5.00
a. Imperf. 25 25
93 A15 4k carmine 20 20
94 A14 5k claret 10 10
a. Imperf. 1.00 1.00
95 A14 7k lt bl 6.00 6.00
96 A15 10k dk bl 1.25 1.25
97 A15 10k on 7k lt bl 10 10
98 A11 15k red brn & bl 12 12
99 A8 20k bl & car 12 12
100 A11 25k grn & gray vio 25 25
101 A11 35k red brn & grn 15 15
102 A8 50k vio & grn 12 12
102A A14 60k on 1k org (II) 2.00 2.00
b. Imperf. (I) 40 40
c. Imperf. (II) 60 60
103 A9 1r pale brn, dk brn & org 50 50
a. Imperf. 35 35
104 A12 3½r mar & lt grn 75 75
a. Imperf. 50 50
105 A13 5r dk bl, grn & pale bl 1.00 1.00
a. Imperf. 1.25 1.25
106 A12 7r dk grn & pink 1.00 1.00
107 A13 10r scar, yel & gray 1.00 1.00

Imperf.

113 A11 70k brn & org 40 40

Handstamped in Violet or Black:

5r 10r

f g

Violet Surcharge.

1920 *Perf.* **14, 14½x15**

120 A14 (f) 3r on 3k red 3.00 3.00
a. Imperf. 1.25 1.25
121 A14 (f) 5r on 3k red 5.00 5.00
122 A15 (f) 5r on 4k car 3.50 3.50
123 A14 (f) 5r on 5k cl 3.00 3.00
a. Imperf. 2.50 2.50
124 A15 (f) 5r on 10k dk bl 3.50 3.50
125 A14 (f) 5r on 10k on 7k lt bl 3.00 3.00
126 A8 (f) 5r on 20k bl & car

Imperf.

127 A14 (f) 5r on 2k grn 12.50 12.50
128 A11 (f) 5r on 35k red brn & grn 12.50 12.50

Black Surcharge.

Perf. 14 to 15

and Compound, 13½

130 A14 (g) 1r on 1k org 15 15
a. Imperf. 25 25
131 A14 (f) 3r on 3k red 8 8
a. Imperf. 8 8
132 A15 (f) 3r on 4k car 5.00 5.00
133 A14 (f) 5r on 2k grn 1.00 1.00
a. Imperf. 12 12
134 A14 (f) 5r on 3k red 2.50 2.50
a. Imperf. 2.50 2.50
135 A15 (f) 5r on 4k car 60 60
a. Imperf. 7.50 7.50
136 A14 (f) 5r on 5k cl 12 12
a. Imperf. 25 25
137 A14 (f) 5r on 7k lt bl 1.00 1.00
138 A15 (f) 5r on 10k dk bl 12 12
139 A14 (f) 5r on 10k on 7k lt bl 12 12
140 A11 (f) 5r on 14k bl & rose 3.50 3.50
141 A11 (f) 5r on 15k red brn & bl 20 20
a. Imperf. 4.00 4.00
142 A8 (f) 5r on 20k bl & car 20 20
a. Imperf. 4.00 4.00
143 A11 (f) 5r on 20k on 14k bl & rose 5.00 5.00
144 A11 (f) 5r on 25k grn & gray vio 5.00 5.00
145 A14 (g) 10r on 1k org *175.00* *175.00*
a. Imperf. 1.25 1.25
146 A14 (g) 10r on 3k red *90.00* *90.00*
147 A14 (g) 10r on 5k cl 6.00 6.00
a. Imperf. 8.00
148 A8 (g) 10r on 20k bl & car 6.00 6.00
148A A11 (f) 10r on 25k grn & gray vio 2.50 2.50
149 A11 (g) 10r on 25k grn & gray vio 2.00 2.00
a. Imperf. 12.00 12.00
150 A11 (g) 10r on 35k red brn & grn 25 25
151 A8 (f) 10r on 50k brn vio & grn 2.50 2.50
152 A8 (g) 10r on 50k brn vio & grn 65 65
152A A11 (g) 10r on 70k brn & org *100.00* *100.00*
b. Imperf. 4.50 4.50
152C A8 (g) 25r on 20k bl & car 1.50 1.50
153 A11 (g) 25r on 25k grn & gray vio 1.25 1.25
154 A11 (g) 25r on 35k red brn & grn 1.25 1.25
a. Imperf. 6.00 6.00
155 A8 (g) 25r on 50k vio & grn 1.75 1.75
a. Imperf. 3.00 3.00
156 A11 (g) 25r on 70k brn & org 3.00 3.00
a. Imperf. 3.00 3.00
157 A9 (g) 50r on 1r pale brn, dk brn & org 2.00 2.00
a. Imperf. 50 50
158 A13 (g) 50r on 5r dk bl, grn & lt bl 4.00 4.00
a. Imperf. 4.00 4.00
159 A12 (g) 100r on 3½r mar & lt grn 3.50 3.50
a. Imperf. 3.50 3.50
160 A13 (g) 100r on 5r dk bl, grn & pale bl 3.50 3.50
a. Imperf. 3.50 3.50
161 A12 (g) 100r on 7r dk grn & pink 4.00 4.00
a. Imperf. 16.00 16.00
162 A13 (g) 100r on 10r scar, yel & gray 3.50 3.50

Wmkd. Wavy Lines. (168)

Perf. **11½.**

Vertically Laid Paper.

163 A12 (g) 100r on 3½r blk & gray 15.00 15.00
164 A12 (g) 100r on 7r blk & yel 12.50 12.50

1920 *Imperf.* **Unwmkd.**

Wove Paper.

No.	Type	Description	Unused	Used
166	A14 (g)	1r on 60k on 1k org (I)	4.00	4.00
168	A14 (f)	5r on 1k org	12.50	12.50
173	A11 (f)	5r on 35k red brn & grn	4.00	4.00
177	A11 (g)	50r on 70k brn & org	4.00	4.00
179	A12 (g)	50r on 3½r mar & lt grn	3.00	3.00
181	A9 (g)	100r on 1r pale brn, dk brn & org	6.00	6.00

Romanov Issues Surcharged Types "f" or "g".

On Stamps of 1913.

1920 *Perf. 13½*

No.	Type	Description	Unused	Used
184	A16 (g)	1r on 1k brn org	3.50	3.50
185	A18 (f)	3r on 3k rose red	3.00	3.00
186	A19 (f)	5r on 4k dl red	3.00	3.00
187	A22 (f)	5r on 14k bl grn	18.00	18.00
187A	A19 (g)	10r on 4k dl red	20.00	
187B	A26 (g)	10r on 35k gray vio & dk grn		
187C	A19 (g)	25r on 4k dl red	4.00	4.00
188	A26 (g)	25r on 35k gray vio & dk grn	4.00	4.00
189	A28 (g)	25r on 70k yel grn & brn	4.00	4.00
190	A31 (f)	50r on 3r dk vio	3.00	3.00
190A	A16 (g)	100r on 1k brn org	75.00	75.00
190B	A17 (g)	100r on 2k grn	75.00	75.00
191	A30 (g)	100r on 2r brn	16.00	16.00
192	A31 (g)	100r on 3r dk vio	16.00	16.00

On Stamps of 1915.

Thin Cardboard.

Inscriptions on Back.

Perf. 12.

No.	Type	Description	Unused	Used
193	A21 (g)	100r on 10k bl	4.00	
194	A23 (g)	100r on 15k brn	4.00	
195	A24 (g)	100r on 20k ol grn	4.00	

On Stamps of 1916.

Perf. 13½.

No.	Type	Description	Unused	Used
196	A20 (f)	5r on 10k on 7k brn	3.00	3.00
197	A22 (f)	5r on 20k on 14k bl grn	5.00	5.00

Surcharged

Type "f" or "g" over type "c",

Type "c" in Violet.

Perf. 14, 14½x15, 13½.

No.	Type	Description	Unused	Used
200	A15 (f)	5r on 4k car	1.75	1.75
201	A15 (f)	5r on 10k dk bl	1.75	1.75
202	A11 (f)	5r on 15k red brn & bl	3.00	3.00
203	A8 (f)	5r on 20k bl & car	2.50	2.50
204	A11 (g)	10r on 25k grn & gray vio	2.50	2.50
205	A11 (g)	10r on 35k red brn & grn	4.50	4.50
205A	A8 (g)	10r on 50k brn vio & grn	5.50	5.50
206	A8 (f)	25r on 50k brn vio & grn	*75.00*	*75.00*
207	A9 (g)	50r on 1r pale brn, dk brn & org	45.00	45.00
a.		Imperf.	5.00	5.00
207B	A12 (g)	100r on 3½r mar & lt grn	12.00	
207C	A12 (g)	100r on 7r dk grn & pink	12.00	

Imperf.

No.	Type	Description	Unused	Used
208	A14 (f)	5r on 2k grn	8.00	8.00
209	A14 (f)	5r on 5k cl	2.50	2.50
210	A11 (g)	25r on 70k brn & org	8.00	8.00
211	A13 (g)	100r on 5r dk bl, grn & pale bl	1.25	1.25

Type "c" in Black.

Perf. 14, 14½x15, 13½.

No.	Type	Description	Unused	Used
212	A14 (f)	5r on 7k lt bl	*100.00*	*100.00*
213	A14 (f)	5r on 10k on 7k lt bl	1.75	1.75
214	A11 (g)	5r on 15k red brn & bl	70	70
215	A8 (f)	5r on 20k bl & car	50	50
215A	A11 (g)	10r on 5r on 25k grn & gray vio	7.50	7.50
216	A11 (g)	10r on 35k red brn & grn	75	75
217	A8 (g)	10r on 50k brn vio & grn	1.25	1.25
217A	A9 (g)	50r on 1r pale brn, dk brn & org	1.50	1.50
217C	A12 (g)	100r on 3½r mar & lt grn	2.50	2.50
218	A13 (g)	100r on 5r dk bl, grn & pale bl	3.50	3.50
a.		Imperf.	3.00	3.00
219	A12 (f)	100r on 7r dk grn & pink	5.00	5.00
219A	A13 (f)	100r on 10r scar, yel & gray	5.00	5.00

Imperf.

No.	Type	Description	Unused	Used
220	A14 (g)	1r on 60k on 1k org (I)	7.00	7.00
221	A14 (f)	5r on 2k grn	1.00	1.00
222	A14 (f)	5r on 5k cl	4.00	4.00
223	A11 (g)	10r on 70k brn & org	3.00	3.00
224	A11 (g)	25r on 70k brn & org	2.50	2.50

Surcharged

Type "f" or "g" over type "a".

Type "a" in Violet.

Imperf.

No.	Type	Description	Unused	Used
231	A9 (g)	50r on 1r pale brn, dk brn & org	*60.00*	*60.00*
232	A13 (g)	100r on 5r dk bl, grn & pale bl	16.00	

Type "a" in Black.

Perf. 14, 14½x15, 13½.

No.	Type	Description	Unused	Used
233	A8 (f)	5r on 20k bl & car	1.00	1.00
233A	A11 (g)	10r on 25k grn & gray vio	*75.00*	*75.00*
234	A11 (g)	10r on 35k red brn & grn	1.25	1.25
235	A12 (g)	100r on 3½r mar & lt grn	2.00	2.00
a.		Imperf.	2.50	2.50

Imperf.

No.	Type	Description	Unused	Used
237	A14 (g)	5r on 2k grn	75.00	75.00
237A	A11 (g)	10r on 70k brn & org		

Surcharged Type "a" and New Value.

Type "a" in Violet.

Perf. 14, 14½x15.

No.	Type	Description	Unused	Used
238	A11	10r on 15k red brn & bl	1.00	1.00

Type "a" in Black.

No.	Type	Description	Unused	Used
239	A8	5r on 20k bl & car	1.75	1.75
239A	A8	10r on 20k bl & car	5.00	5.00
239B	A8	10r on 50k brn red & grn	10.00	

Imperf.

No.	Type	Description	Unused	Used
240	A12	100r on 3½r mar & lt grn	3.00	3.00

Surcharged Type "c" and New Value.

Type "c" in Black.

1920 ***Perf. 14, 14½x15, 13½***

No.	Type	Description	Unused	Used
241	A15	5r on 4k red	3.00	3.00
242	A11	5r on 15k red brn & bl	1.75	1.75
243	A8	10r on 20k bl & car	3.00	3.00
243A	A11	10r on 25k grn & gray vio	1.25	1.25
244	A11	10r on 35k red brn & grn	1.00	1.00
a.		With additional surcharge "5r"	2.00	2.00
245	A12	100r on 3½r mar & lt grn	2.00	2.00

Imperf.

No.	Type	Description	Unused	Used
247	A14	3r on 3k red	8.00	8.00
248	A14	5r on 2k grn	50	50
249	A9	50r on 1r pale brn, dk brn & org	1.50	1.50

Type "c" in Violet.

No.	Type	Description	Unused	Used
249A	A14	5r on 2k grn	10.00	

Postal Savings Stamps Surcharged.

A1 A2

A3 Wmk. 171

Wmkd. Diamonds. (171)

Perf. 14½x15.

No.	Type	Description	Unused	Used
250	A1	60k on 1k red & buff	15.00	15.00
251	A2	1r on 1k red & buff	8.00	8.00
252	A3	5r on 5k grn & buff	10.00	10.00
253	A3	5r on 10k brn & buff	10.00	10.00

Russian Semi-Postal Stamps of 1914-18 Surcharged with Armenian Monogram and New Values like Regular Issues.

Unwmkd.

Perf. 11½, 12½, 13½.

On Stamps of 1914.

No.	Type	Description	Unused	Used
255	SP5	25r on 1k red brn & dk grn *straw*	100.00	110.00
256	SP6	25r on 3k mar & gray grn, *pink*	80.00	90.00
257	SP7	50r on 7 dk brn & dk grn, *buff*	14.00	15.00
258	SP5	100r on 1k red brn & dk grn, *straw*	5.50	6.00
259	SP6	100r on 3k mar & gray grn, *pink*	5.50	6.00
260	SP7	100r on 7k dk brn & dk grn, *buff*	5.50	6.00

On Stamps of 1915-19.

No.	Type	Description	Unused	Used
261	SP5	25r on 1k org brn & gray	100.00	110.00
262	SP6	25r on 3k car & gray	65.00	70.00
263	SP8	50r on 10k dk bl & brn	17.50	20.00
264	SP5	100r on 1k org brn & gray	5.50	6.00
265	SP8	100r on 10k dk bl & brn	5.50	6.00

These surcharged semi-postal stamps were used for ordinary postage.

A set of 10 stamps in the above designs, and in a third design showing a woman quilling, was prepared in 1920, but not issued. Price of set, $2. Exist with "SPECIMEN" overprint and imperf. Counterfeits exist.

Soviet Socialist Republic.

Hammer and Sickle
A7

Mythological Monster
A8

Symbols of Soviet Republics on Designs from old Armenian Manuscripts
A9

Ruined City of Ani
A10

Mythological Monster
A11

Armenian Soldier
A12

Fisherman on River Aras
A16

Mythological Monster
A13

Soviet Symbols, Armenian Designs
A14

Mt. Alagöz and Plain of Shirak
A15

Post Office in Erevan and Mt. Ararat
A17

Ruin in City of Ani
A18

Street in Erevan
A19

Lake Gökcha and Sevan Monastery
A20

Mythological Subject from old Armenian Monument
A21

Mt. Ararat
A22

Perf. 11½, Imperf.

1921 **Unwmkd.**

No.	Type	Value	Color	Unused	Used
278	A7	1r	gray grn	10	
279	A8	2r	sl gray	10	
280	A9	3r	carmine	10	
281	A10	5r	dk brn	10	
282	A11	25r	gray	10	15
283	A12	50r	red	10	
284	A13	100r	orange	10	
285	A14	250r	dk bl	10	
286	A15	500r	brn vio	10	
287	A16	1000r	sea grn	15	
288	A17	2000r	bister	15	
289	A18	5000r	dk brn	15	
290	A19	10,000r	dl red	25	
291	A20	15,000r	sl bl	25	
292	A21	20,000r	lake	25	
293	A22	25,000r	gray bl	50	
294	A22	25,000r	brn ol	2.50	
		Nos. 278-294 (17)		5.10	

Except the 25r, Nos. 278–294 were not regulary issued and used. Counterfeits exist.

Russian Stamps of 1909-17 Surcharged

Wove Paper

Lozenges of Varnish on Face

1921, August ***Perf. 13½***

No.	Type	Surcharge	Unused
295	A9	5000r on 1r pale brn, dk brn & org	3.50
296	A12	5000r on 3½r mar & lt grn	3.50
297	A13	5000r on 5r dk bl, grn & pale bl	3.50
298	A12	5000r on 7r dk grn & pink	3.50
299	A13	5000r on 10r scar, yel & gray	3.50
		Nos. 295-299 (5)	17.50

Nos. 295–299 were not officially issued. Counterfeits abound.

Mt. Ararat and Soviet Star
A23 A24

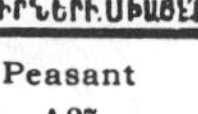

Soviet Symbols
A25

Crane
A26

Peasant
A27

Harpy
A28

Peasant Sowing
A29

Soviet Symbols
A30

Forging
A31

Plowing
A32

1922 ***Perf. 11½.***

No.	Type	Value	Color	Unused
300	A23	50r	grn & red	10
301	A24	300r	sl bl & buff	15
302	A25	400r	bl & pink	15
303	A26	500r	vio & pale lil	10
304	A27	1000r	dl bl & pale bl	10
305	A28	2000r	blk & gray	25
306	A29	3000r	blk & grn	15
307	A30	4000r	blk & lt brn	30
308	A31	5000r	blk & dl red	15
309	A32	10,000r	blk & pale rose	15
a.		Tête bêche pair		15.00
		Nos. 300-309 (10)		1.60

Nos. 300 to 309 were not placed in use without surcharge.

Stamps of types A23 to A32, printed in other colors than Nos. 300 to 309, are essays.

1922-23

Stamps of Preceding Issue with Handstamped Surcharge of New Values in Rose, Violet or Black

No.	Type	Surcharge	Unused	Used
310	A23	10,000 on 50r grn & red (R)	7.50	7.50
311	A23	10,000 on 50r grn & red (V)	2.00	2.00
312	A23	10,000 on 50r grn & red (Bk)	75	75
313	A24	15,000 on 300r sl bl & buff (R)	10.00	10.00
314	A24	15,000 on 300r sl bl & buff (V)	2.00	2.00
315	A24	15,000 on 300r sl bl & buff (Bk)	1.00	1.00
316	A25	25,000 on 400r bl & pink (V)	2.00	2.00
317	A25	25,000 on 400r bl & pink (Bk)	50	50
318	A26	30,000 on 500r vio & pale lil (R)	15.00	15.00
319	A26	30,000 on 500r vio & pale lil (V)	1.00	1.00
320	A26	30,000 on 500r vio & pale lil (Bk)	60	60
321	A27	50,000 on 1000r dl bl & pale bl (R)	10.00	10.00
322	A27	50,000 on 1000r dl bl & pale bl (V)	4.00	4.00
323	A27	50,000 on 1000r dl bl & pale bl (Bk)	1.00	1.00
324	A29	75,000 on 3000r blk & grn (Bk)	1.25	1.25
325	A28	100,000 on 2000r blk & gray (R)	15.00	15.00
326	A28	100,000 on 2000r blk & gray (V)	4.00	4.00
327	A28	100,000 on 2000r blk & gray (Bk)	1.00	1.00
328	A30	200,000 on 4000r blk & lt brn (V)	1.00	1.00
329	A30	200,000 on 4000r blk & lt brn (Bk)	1.00	1.00
330	A31	300,000 on 5000r blk & dl red (V)	8.00	8.00
331	A31	300,000 on 5000r blk & dl red (Bk)	75	75
332	A32	500,000 on 10,000r blk & pale rose (V)	4.00	4.00
333	A32	500,000 on 10,000r blk & pale rose (Bk)	75	75
		Nos. 310-333 (24)	94.10	94.10

Goose

A33

Armenian Woman at Well

A35

Armenian Village Scene

A34

Mt. Ararat

A36

Mt. Ararat

A37

New Values in Gold Kopecks, Handstamped Surcharge in Black.

1922 ***Imperf.***

334	A33	1(k) on 250r rose	2.50	2.50
335	A33	1(k) on 250r gray	5.00	5.00
336	A34	2(k) on 500r rose	2.00	2.00
337	A34	3(k) on 500r gray	1.50	1.50
338	A35	4(k) on 1000r rose	1.50	1.50
339	A35	4(k) on 1000r gray	3.00	3.00
340	A36	5(k) on 2000r gray	1.50	1.50
341	A36	10(k) on 2000r rose	1.50	1.50
342	A37	15(k) on 5000r rose	10.00	10.00
343	A37	20(k) on 5000r gray	1.75	1.75
		Nos. 334-343 (10)	30.25	30.25

Nos. 334–343 were issued for postal tax purposes.

Nos. 334 to 343 exist without surcharge but are not known to have been issued in that condition. Counterfeits exist of both sets.

Regular Issue of 1921 Handstamped with New Values in Black or Red.

Short, Thick Numerals.

1922-23 ***Imperf.***

347	A8	2(k) on 2r sl gray (R)	17.50	17.50
350	A11	4(k) on 25r gray (R)	6.00	6.00
353	A13	10(k) on 100r org (R)	12.50	12.50
354	A14	15(k) on 250r dk bl	1.00	1.00
355	A15	20(k) on 500r brn vio	1.50	1.50
a.		With "k" written in red	2.00	2.00
357	A22	50(k) on 25,000r bl (R)	20.00	20.00
358	A22	50(k) on 25,000r brn ol (R)	15.00	15.00
359	A22	50(k) on 25,000r brn ol	73.50	73.50
		Nos. 347-358 (7)		

Perf. 11½.

360	A7	1(k) on 1r gray grn	10.00	10.00
a.		Imperf.	3.00	3.00
361	A7	1(k) on 1r gray grn (R)	6.00	6.00
a.		Imperf.	10.00	10.00
362	A8	2(k) on 2r sl gray	15.00	15.00
a.		Imperf.	6.00	6.00
363	A15	2(k) on 500r brn vio	3.50	3.50
a.		Imperf.	3.00	3.00
364	A15	2(k) on 500r brn vio (R)	15.00	15.00
365	A11	4(k) on 25r gray	12.00	12.00
a.		Imperf.	6.00	6.00
366	A12	5(k) on 50r red	4.00	4.00
a.		Imperf.	3.00	3.00
367	A13	10(k) on 100r org	3.50	3.50
a.		Imperf.	3.50	3.50
368	A21	35(k) on 20,000r cl	15.00	15.00
a.		With "k" written in vio	15.00	15.00
b.		Imperf.	6.00	6.00
c.		As "a," imperf.	6.00	6.00
d.		With "kop" written in vio, imperf.		
		Nos. 360-368 (9)	84.00	84.00

Manuscript Surcharge in Red.

Perf. 11½.

371	A14	1k on 250r dk bl	4.00	4.00

Handstamped in Black or Red.

Tall, Thin Numerals.

Imperf.

377	A11	4(k) on 25r gray (R)	7.00	7.00
379	A13	10(k) on 100r org	4.00	4.00
380	A15	20(k) on 500r brn vio	10.00	10.00
381	A22	50k on 25,000r bl	1.50	1.50
a.		Surcharged "50" only	25.00	25.00
382	A22	50k on 25,000r bl (R)	20.00	20.00
382A	A22	50k on 25,000r brn ol	40.00	40.00
		Nos. 377-382A (6)	82.50	82.50

On Nos. 381, 382 and 382A the letter "k" forms part of the surcharge.

Perf. 11½.

383	A7	1(k) on 1r gray grn (R)	5.00	5.00
a.		Imperf.		
384	A14	1(k) on 250r dk bl	3.00	3.00
385	A15	2(k) on 500r brn vio	3.75	3.75
a.		Imperf.	4.00	4.00
386	A15	2(k) on 500r brn vio (R)	8.00	8.00
387	A9	3(k) on 3r rose	10.00	10.00
a.		Imperf.	10.00	10.00
388	A21	3(k) on 20,000r cl	30.00	30.00
a.		Imperf.	5.00	5.00
389	A11	4(k) on 25r gray	4.00	4.00
a.		Imperf.	7.00	7.00
390	A12	5(k) on 50r red	3.00	3.00
a.		Imperf.	2.00	2.00
		Nos. 383-390 (8)	66.75	66.75

Foreign postal stationery (stamped envelopes, postal cards and air letter sheets) lies beyond the scope of this Catalogue which is limited to adhesive postage stamps.

AUSTRIA

(ôs′trĭ·ȧ)

LOCATION—In Central Europe.
GOVT.—Republic.
AREA—32,376 sq. mi.
POP.—7,520,000 (est. 1977).
CAPITAL—Vienna.

Before 1867 Austria was an absolute monarchy which included Hungary and Lombardy-Venetia. In 1867 the Austro-Hungarian Monarchy was established, with Austria and Hungary as equal partners. After the first World War, in 1918, the different nationalities established their own states and only the German-speaking parts remained, forming a republic under the name "Deutschösterreich" (German Austria), which name was shortly again changed to Austria. In 1938 German forces occupied Austria, which became part of the German Reich. After the liberation by Allied troops in 1945, an independent republic was re-established.

60 Kreuzer = 1 Gulden
100 Neu-Kreuzer = 1 Gulden (1858)
100 Heller = 1 Krone (1899)
100 Groschen = 1 Schilling (1925)

Prices of early Austrian stamps vary according to condition. Quotations for Nos. 1–5, P1–P7 and PR1–PR4 are for fine copies. Very fine to superb specimens sell at much higher prices, and inferior or poor copies sell at reduced prices, depending on the condition of the individual specimen.

Prices for unused stamps of 1850–80 issues are for copies in fine condition with original gum. Specimens without gum sell for about one-third of the figures quoted.

Issues of the Austrian Monarchy

(including Hungary).

Coat of Arms

A1

Wmkd. K. K. H. M. in Sheet or Unwmkd.

1850 Typographed ***Imperf.***

Thin to Thick Paper.

The stamps of this issue were at first printed on a rough hand-made paper, varying in thickness and having a watermark in script letters K. K. H. M., the initials of Kaiserlich Königliches Handels-Ministerium (Imperial and Royal Ministry of Commerce), vertically in the gutter between the panes. Parts of these letters show on margin stamps in the sheet. From 1854 a thick, smooth machine-made paper without watermark was used.

NINE KREUZER.

Type I. The top of "9" is about on a level with "Kreuzer" and not near the top of the label.

Type IA. Similar to type I but with 1¾mm. instead of ½mm. space between "9" and "Kreuzer."

Type II. The top of "9" is much higher than the top of the word "Kreuzer" and nearly touches the top of the label.

1	A1	1kr yellow	850.00	80.00
a.		Printed on both sides	*1,500.*	140.00
b.		1kr org	1,350.	110.00
c.		1kr brn org	2,500.	450.00
2	A1	2kr black	900.00	67.50
a.		Ribbed paper		*1,650.*
b.		2kr gray blk	1,350.	90.00
3	A1	3kr red	400.00	3.00
a.		Ribbed paper	*2,000.*	72.50
b.		Laid paper		*10,000.*
c.		Printed on both sides		*8,500.*
4	A1	6kr brown	450.00	4.00
a.		Ribbed paper		*1,350.*
5	A1	9kr bl, type II	675.00	3.50
a.		9kr bl, type I	*1,350.*	9.00
b.		9kr bl, type IA		*1,300.*
c.		Laid paper, type II		*10,000.*
d.		Printed on both sides, type II		*8,500.*

In 1852–54, Nos. 1 to 5, rouletted 14, were used in Tokay. A 12kr blue exists, but was not issued.

The reprints are printed in brighter colors, some on paper watermarked "Briefmarken" in the sheet.

Emperor Franz Josef

A2 A3 A4

A5

A6

1858-59 Embossed. ***Perf. 14½.***

Two Types of Each Value.

Type I. Loops of the bow at the back of the head broken, except the 2kr. In the 2kr, the "2" has a flat foot, thinning to the right.

Type II. Loops complete. Wreath projects further at top of head. In the 2kr, the "2" has a more curved foot of uniform thickness, with a shading line in the upper and lower curves.

6	A2	2kr yel, type II	650.00	35.00
a.		2kr yel, type I	1,500.	300.00
b.		2kr org, type II	1,500.	300.00
7	A3	3kr blk, type II	2,250.	225.00
a.		3kr blk, type I	900.00	225.00
8	A3	3kr grn, type II ('59)	675.00	100.00
9	A4	5kr red, type II	210.00	1.00
a.		5kr red, type I	300.00	10.00
10	A5	10kr brn, type II	550.00	2.75
a.		10kr brn, type I	550.00	22.50
11	A6	15kr bl, type II	425.00	1.90
a.		Type I	900.00	13.50

The reprints are of type II and are perforated 10½, 11, 12, 12½ and 13. There are also imperforate reprints of Nos. 6 to 8.

Emperor Franz Josef

A7

Coat of Arms

A8

1860-61 Embossed ***Perf. 14***

12	A7	2kr yellow	350.00	25.00
13	A7	3kr green	325.00	19.00
14	A7	5kr red	200.00	85
15	A7	10kr brown	275.00	1.85
16	A7	15kr blue	210.00	95

The reprints are perforated 9, 9½, 10, 10½, 11, 11½, 12, 12½, 13 and 13½. There are also imperforate reprints of the 2 and 3kr.

1863

17	A8	2kr yellow	500.00	100.00
18	A8	3kr green	375.00	85.00
19	A8	5kr rose	210.00	5.50
20	A8	10kr blue	700.00	7.00
21	A8	15kr yel brn	850.00	10.00

Wmk. 91

Unwmkd. or, after June 1864, Wmkd. "BRIEF-MARKEN" in Double-lined Capitals Across the Middle of the Sheet (91).

1863-64 *Perf. 9½.*

22	A8	2kr yel ('64)	125.00	9.50
23	A8	3kr grn ('64)	125.00	8.50
24	A8	5kr rose	47.50	28
25	A8	10kr blue	110.00	2.00
26	A8	15kr yel brn	120.00	1.25

The reprints are perforated 10½, 11½, 13 and 13½. There are also imperforate reprints of the 2 and 3kr.

Issues of Austro-Hungarian Monarchy

From 1867 to 1871 the independent postal administrations of Austria and Hungary used the same stamps.

Emperor Franz Josef

A9 A10

5 kr:

Type I. In arabesques in lower left corner, the small ornament at left of the curve nearest the figure "5" is short and has three points at bottom.

Type II. The ornament is prolonged within the curve and has two points at bottom. The corresponding ornament at top of the lower left corner does not touch the curve (1872).

Type III. Similar to type II but the top ornament is joined to the curve (1881).

Two different printing methods were used for the 1867-74 issues. The first produced stamps on which the hair and whiskers were coarse and thick, from the second they were fine and clear.

Typographed

1867-72 *Perf. 9½* **Wmk. 91**

Coarse Print.

27	A9	2kr yellow	125.00	2.25
28	A9	3kr green	110.00	1.35
29	A9	5kr rose, type I	67.50	10
a.		5kr rose, type II	72.50	13
b.		Perf. 10½, type II	125.00	
c.		Cliché of 3kr in plate of 5kr		25,000.
30	A9	10kr blue	130.00	45
31	A9	15kr brown	140.00	4.50
32	A9	25kr lilac	20.00	16.00
a.		25kr gray lil	20.00	15.00
b.		25kr brn vio	110.00	35.00

Perf. 12.

33	A10	50kr lt brn	30.00	70.00
a.		50kr pale red brn	110.00	80.00
b.		50kr brnsh rose	375.00	160.00
c.		Pair, imperf. btwn., vert. or horizontal	500.00	1,000.

Issues for Austria only.

1874-80 *Perf. 9½*

Fine Print.

34	A9	2kr yel ('76)	11.00	85
a.		Perf. 9	175.00	22.50
b.		Perf. 10½	45.00	4.25
c.		Perf. 12	250.00	95.00
d.		Perf. 13	185.00	150.00
35	A9	3kr grn ('76)	32.50	55
a.		Perf. 9	160.00	20.00
b.		Perf. 10½	45.00	2.50
c.		Perf. 12	185.00	9.00
d.		Perf. 13	150.00	22.50
36	A9	5kr rose, type III	3.00	6
a.		Perf. 9	75.00	3.50
b.		Perf. 10½	11.00	75
c.		Perf. 12	60.00	2.50
d.		Perf. 13	90.00	10.00
37	A9	10kr bl ('75)	75.00	20
a.		Perf. 9	300.00	22.50
b.		Perf. 10½	80.00	2.50
c.		Perf. 12	375.00	100.00
d.		Perf. 13	185.00	80.00
38	A9	15kr brn ('77)	7.00	4.00
a.		Perf. 9	385.00	70.00
b.		Perf. 10½	185.00	20.00
c.		Perf. 12	600.00	110.00
d.		Perf. 13	350.00	200.00
39	A9	25kr gray lil ('78)	2.00	52.50
40	A10	50kr brn, perf. 12 ('80)	12.50	65.00
a.		Perf. 13	15.00	75.00
b.		Perf. 10½x12	300.00	

Various compound perforations exist.

A11

Inscriptions in Black

Perf. 9, 9½, 10, 10½, 11½, 12, 12½

1883

41	A11	2kr brown	5.00	20
42	A11	3kr green	5.50	10
43	A11	5kr rose	11.00	5
a.		Vertical pair, imperf. between	275.00	350.00
44	A11	10kr blue	5.50	8
45	A11	20kr gray	50.00	2.50
46	A11	50kr red lil	300.00	52.50

The last printings of Nos. 41 to 46 are watermarked "ZEITUNGS-MARKEN" instead of "BRIEF-MARKEN."

The 5kr has been reprinted in a dull red rose, perforated 10½.

Emperor Franz Josef

A12 A13

Granite Paper.

Perf. 9 to 13½, also Compound.

1890-96 **Unwmkd.**

Numerals in black, Nos. 51 to 61.

51	A12	1kr dk gray	2.50	10
a.		Pair, imperf. between	275.00	500.00
52	A12	2kr lt brn	40	5
53	A12	3kr gray grn	50	5
a.		Pair, imperf. between	325.00	475.00
54	A12	5kr rose	40	5
a.		Pair, imperf. between	275.00	385.00
55	A12	10kr ultra	70	4
a.		Pair, imperf. between	350.00	550.00
56	A12	12kr claret	2.75	25
57	A12	15kr lilac	1.75	25
a.		Pair, imperf. between	350.00	550.00
58	A12	20kr ol grn	35.00	2.50
59	A12	24kr gray bl	3.50	1.10
a.		Pair, imperf. between	385.00	550.00
60	A12	30kr dk brn	3.00	35
61	A12	50kr violet	12.50	10.00

Engraved

62	A13	1gld dk bl	2.25	2.75
63	A13	1gld pale lil ('96)	55.00	3.75
64	A13	2gld carmine	5.00	10.00
65	A13	2gld gray grn ('96)	30.00	30.00

Nearly all values of the 1890-1907 issues are found with numerals missing in one or more corners, some with numerals printed on the back.

A14

1891 Typographed.

Numerals in black.

Perf. 9 to 13½, also Compound.

66	A14	20kr ol grn	1.50	10
67	A14	24kr gray bl	3.00	60
68	A14	30kr brown	1.50	10
a.		Pair, imperf. between	425.00	600.00
b.		Perf. 9	175.00	35.00
69	A14	50kr violet	2.00	35

A15

A16

A17

A18

Perf. 10½ to 13½ and Compound.

Numerals in black, Nos. 70 to 82.

1899 Without Varnish Bars.

70	A15	1h lilac	1.10	7
b.		Imperf.	90.00	115.00
c.		Perf. 10½	21.00	5.50
d.		Numerals inverted	550.00	750.00
71	A15	2h dk gray	3.75	18
72	A15	3h bis brn	5.00	4
b.		"3" in lower right corner sideways		1,100.
73	A15	5h bl grn	12.50	5
c.		Perf. 10½	17.50	5.00
74	A15	6h orange	60	5
75	A16	10h rose	8.00	5
b.		Perf. 10½	400.00	100.00
76	A16	20h brown	1.00	10
77	A16	25h ultra	75.00	12
78	A16	30h red vio	27.50	2.75
b.		Horizontal pair, imperf. between	375.00	
80	A17	40h green	45.00	3.25
81	A17	50h gray bl	35.00	4.00
b.		All four "50's" parallel		1,500.
82	A17	60h brown	55.00	1.10
b.		Horizontal pair, imperf. between	375.00	
c.		Perf. 10½	65.00	1.35

Engraved

83	A18	1k car rose	3.00	13
a.		1k car	7.50	13
b.		Vertical pair, imperf. between	375.00	400.00
84	A18	2k gray lil	70.00	45
a.		Vertical pair, imperf. between	500.00	550.00
85	A18	4k gray grn	7.50	6.75

1901 With Varnish Bars.

70a	A15	1h lilac	1.75	30
71a	A15	2h dk gray	1.75	20
72a	A15	3h bis brn	60	5
73a	A15	5h bl grn	30	5
74a	A15	6h orange	30	5
75a	A16	10h rose	40	5
76a	A16	20h brown	1.25	4
77a	A16	25h ultra	1.50	15
78a	A16	30h red vio	1.50	1.00
79	A17	35h green	1.50	15
80a	A17	40h green	2.75	4.50
81a	A17	50h gray bl	7.00	7.25
82a	A17	60h brown	3.50	60
		Nos. 70a-78a, 79, 80a-82a (13)	24.10	14.39

The diagonal yellow bars of varnish were printed across the face to prevent cleaning.

A19

A20

A21

Perf. 12½ to 13½ and Compound.

Colored Numerals.

1904-07 Typographed.

Without Varnish Bars.

86	A19	1h lilac	18	15
87	A19	2h dk gray	25	10
88	A19	3h bis brn	28	7
89	A19	5h dk bl grn	12.50	7
90	A19	5h yel grn ('06)	50	5
91	A19	6h dp org	50	7
92	A20	10h car ('06)	75	5
93	A20	12h vio ('07)	1.50	50
94	A20	20h brn ('06)	2.75	10
95	A20	25h ultra ('06)	4.00	30
96	A20	30h red vio ('06)	6.75	25

Black Numerals.

97	A20	10h carmine	9.00	7
98	A20	20h brown	50.00	1.25
99	A20	25h ultra	50.00	3.00
100	A20	30h red vio	50.00	3.00

White Numerals.

101	A21	35h green	3.00	25
102	A21	40h dp vio	3.00	1.00
103	A21	50h dl bl	3.75	4.50
104	A21	60h yel brn	3.75	50
105	A21	72h rose	3.75	1.65
		Nos. 86-105 (20)	206.21	16.93

1905 With Varnish Bars.

86a	A19	1h lilac	75	50
87a	A19	2h dk gray	2.75	50
88a	A19	3h bis brn	2.75	6
89a	A19	5h dk bl grn	6.50	10
91a	A19	6h dp org	10.00	30
97a	A20	10h carmine	3.75	5
98a	A20	20h brown	52.50	65
99a	A20	25h ultra	60.00	65
100a	A20	30h red vio	65.00	1.35
101a	A21	35h green	55.00	50
102a	A21	40h dp vio	52.50	4.50
103a	A21	50h dl bl	50.00	7.25
104a	A21	60h yel brn	50.00	90
105a	A21	72h rose	1.50	85
		Nos. 86a-105a (14)	413.00	18.16

Stamps of the 1901, 1904 and 1905 issues perf. 9 or 10½, also compound with 12½, were not sold at any post office, but were supplied only to some high-ranking officials. This applies also to the contemporary issues of Austrian Offices Abroad.

Emperor Karl VI

A22

Emperor Franz Josef

A23

Schönbrunn Castle
A24

Emperor Franz Josef
A25

Designs: 2h, Empress Maria Theresa. 3h, Emperor Joseph II. 5h, 10h, 25h, Emperor Franz Josef. 6h, Emperor Leopold II. 12h, Emperor Franz I. 20h, Emperor Ferdinand I. 30h, Franz Josef as youth. 35h, Franz Josef in middle age. 60h, Franz Josef on horseback. 1k, Franz Josef in royal robes. 5k, Hofburg, Vienna.

1908-13 Typographed. *Perf. 12½.*

110	A22	1h gray blk	40	8
111	A22	2h bl vio ('13)	40	30
a.		2h vio	50	8
112	A22	3h magenta	25	10
113	A22	5h yel grn	25	5
a.		Booklet pane of 6	30.00	
114	A22	6h org brn ('13)	2.10	1.50
a.		6h ocher ('13)	2.10	1.50
b.		6h buff	1.00	90
115	A22	10h rose	25	5
a.		Booklet pane of 6	110.00	
116	A22	12h scarlet	2.00	60
117	A22	20h chocolate	4.00	18
118	A22	25h ultra ('13)	1.75	20
a.		25h dp bl	3.50	25
119	A22	30h ol grn	7.00	27
120	A22	35h slate	5.00	30

Engraved.

121	A23	50h dk grn	1.00	25
a.		Pair, imperf. btwn., vert. or horizontal	325.00	350.00
122	A23	60h dp car	55	10
a.		Pair, imperf. btwn., vert. or horizontal	450.00	500.00
123	A23	72h dk brn ('13)	3.00	25
124	A23	1k purple	20.00	20
a.		Pair, imperf. btwn., vert. or horizontal	325.00	350.00
125	A24	2k lake & ol grn	30.00	60
126	A24	5k bis & dk vio	55.00	6.25
127	A25	10k bl, bis & dp brn	290.00	80.00
		Nos. 110-127 (18)	422.95	91.28

Issued in commemoration of the 60th year of the reign of Emperor Franz Josef for permanent use.

The 1 to 35h inclusive exist on both ordinary and chalk-surfaced paper.

All values exist imperforate. They were not sold at any post office, but presented to a number of high government officials. This applies also to all imperforate stamps of later issues, including semi-postals, etc., and those of the Austrian Offices Abroad.

Forgeries of No. 127 exist.

Birthday Jubilee Issue.

Similar to 1908 Issue, but designs enlarged by labels at top and bottom bearing dates "1830" and "1910".

1910 Typographed.

128	A22	1h gray blk	6.00	6.50
129	A22	2h violet	7.50	8.50
130	A22	3h magenta	7.50	8.50
131	A22	5h yel grn	25	20
132	A22	6h buff	3.00	3.25
133	A22	10h rose	25	20
134	A22	12h scarlet	4.00	5.00
135	A22	20h chocolate	6.00	7.50
136	A22	25h dp bl	1.00	1.10
137	A22	30h ol grn	5.50	6.50
138	A22	35h slate	5.50	6.50

Engraved

139	A23	50h dk grn	6.00	8.50
140	A23	60h dp car	6.00	8.50
141	A23	1k purple	7.00	10.00
142	A24	2k lake & ol grn	180.00	250.00
143	A24	5k bis & dk vio	140.00	200.00
144	A25	10k bl, bis & dp brn	275.00	400.00
		Nos. 128-144 (17)	660.50	930.75

Issued in celebration of the eightieth birthday of Emperor Franz Josef.

All values exist imperforate.

Forgeries of Nos. 142 to 144 exist.

Austrian Crown
A37

Emperor Franz Josef
A38

Coat of Arms
A39 A40

1916-18 Typographed.

145	A37	3h brt vio	4	4
146	A37	5h lt grn	3	3
a.		Bklt. pane of 6	15.00	
b.		Booklet pane of 4+2 labels	30.00	
147	A37	6h dp org	30	75
148	A37	10h magenta	5	5
a.		Bklt. pane of 6	15.00	
149	A37	12h lt bl	50	1.25
150	A38	15h rose red	70	8
a.		Booklet pane of 6	21.00	
151	A38	20h chocolate	6.00	15
152	A38	25h blue	9.00	65
153	A38	30h slate	8.00	90
154	A39	40h ol grn	18	4
155	A39	50h bl grn	30	4
156	A39	60h dp bl	25	5
157	A39	80h org brn	20	5
158	A39	90h red vio	20	8
159	A39	1k car, *yel* ('18)	50	10

Engraved.

160	A40	2k dk bl	1.00	25
161	A40	3k claret	10.00	1.10
162	A40	4k dp grn	2.00	2.25
163	A40	10k dp vio	37.50	50.00
		Nos. 145-163 (19)	76.75	57.86

Stamps of type A38 have two varieties of the frame. Stamps of type A40 have various decorations about the shield.

Nos. 145-163 exist imperf. Price, set $425.

1917 Ordinary Paper

164	A40	2k lt bl	1.00	40
165	A40	3k car rose	12.50	90
166	A40	4k yel grn	1.50	1.40
167	A40	10k violet	150.00	75.00

Nos. 164-167 exist imperf. Price, set $325.

See Nos. 172-175 (granite paper).

Emperor Karl I
A42

1917-18 Typographed

168	A42	15h dl red	12	5
a.		Booklet pane of 6	15.00	
169	A42	20h dk grn ('18)	10	5
a.		20h grn ('17)	85	10
170	A42	25h blue	25	5
171	A42	30h dl vio	20	5

Nos. 168-171 exist imperf. Price, set $50.

Engraved.

1918-19 Granite Paper.

172	A40	2k lt bl	16	70
a.		Perf. 11½	625.00	500.00
173	A40	3k car rose	35	1.50
174	A40	4k yel grn ('19)	6.50	15.00
175	A40	10k dp vio ('19)	8.50	13.00

Issues of the Republic.

Austrian Stamps of 1916-18 Overprinted

1918-19 *Perf. 12½.* Unwmkd.

181	A37	3h brt vio	5	5
182	A37	5h lt grn	5	5
183	A37	6h dp org	15	45
184	A37	10h magenta	5	5
185	A37	12h lt bl	25	70
186	A42	15h dl red	15	70
187	A42	20h dp grn	8	5
188	A42	25h blue	20	10
189	A42	30h dl vio	14	10
190	A39	40h ol grn	13	15
191	A39	50h dp grn	70	90
192	A39	60h dp bl	60	75
193	A39	80h org brn	10	20
a.		Inverted overprint	325.00	325.00
194	A39	90h red vio	15	20
195	A39	1k car, *yel*	20	20

Granite Paper.

196	A40	2k lt bl	9	5
a.		Pair, imperf. between	400.00	400.00
b.		Perf. 11½	12.50	7.50
197	A40	3k car rose	30	85
198	A40	4k yel grn	1.50	2.75
a.		Perf. 11½	16.50	13.50
199	A40	10k dp vio	14.00	20.00
		Nos. 181-199 (19)	18.89	28.30

Nos. 181, 182, 184, 187 to 191, 194, 197 and 199 exist imperforate.

Post Horn
A43

Coat of Arms
A44

Allegory of New Republic
A45

Ordinary Paper.

1919-20 Typographed. *Perf. 12½.*

200	A43	3h gray	3	3
201	A44	5h yel grn	3	3
202	A44	5h gray ('20)	3	3
203	A43	6h orange	10	35
204	A44	10h dp rose	3	3
205	A44	10h red ('20)	3	3
a.		Thick grysh paper ('20)	5	5
206	A43	12h grnsh bl	6	45
207	A43	15h bis ('20)	25	75
a.		Thick grysh paper ('20)	5	5
208	A45	20h dk grn	3	3
a.		20h yel grn	3	3
b.		As "a," thick grysh paper ('20)	55	1.00
209	A44	25h blue	4	4
210	A43	25h vio ('20)	3	3
211	A45	30h dk brn	4	4
212	A45	40h violet	4	4
213	A45	40h lake ('20)	3	3
214	A44	45h ol grn	20	42
215	A45	50h dk bl	6	5
a.		Thick grysh paper ('20)	15	15
216	A43	60h ol grn ('20)	3	8
217	A44	1k car, *yel*	3	8
218	A44	1k lt bl ('20)	3	3
		Nos. 200-218 (19)	1.12	2.57

All values exist imperf. (For regularly issued imperfs, see Nos. 227-235).

Parliament Building
A46

Granite Paper.

1919-20 Engraved *Perf. 12½, 11½*

219	A46	2k ver & blk	30	50
a.		Center inverted	4,000.	
220	A46	2½k ol bis ('20)	10	22
221	A46	3k bl & blk brn	10	15
222	A46	4k car & blk	10	15
a.		Center invert.	2,250.	2,000.
223	A46	5k blk ('20)	10	12
a.		Perf. 11½x12½	50.00	60.00
224	A46	7½k plum	10	35
a.		Perf. 11½	110.00	150.00
b.		Perf. 11½x12½	110.00	150.00
225	A46	10k ol grn & blk brn	25	50
a.		Perf. 11½x12½	90.00	110.00
b.		Perf. 11½	22.50	30.00
226	A46	20k lil & red ('20)	10	65
a.		Center invert.	11,000.	9,000.
b.		Perf. 11½	55.00	75.00
		Nos. 219-226 (8)	1.15	2.64

A number of values exist in pairs, imperforate between. Price $350 to $450 a pair.

See also No. 248.

Ordinary Paper.

1920 Typographed. *Imperf.*

227	A44	5h yel grn	10	30
228	A44	5h gray	3	3
229	A44	10h dp rose	3	3
230	A44	10h red	3	3
231	A43	15h bister	7	10
232	A43	25h violet	3	3
233	A45	30h dk brn	7	10
234	A45	40h violet	5	7
235	A43	60h ol grn	3	12
		Nos. 227-235 (9)	44	81

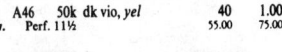

Arms
A47 A48

Ordinary Paper.

1920-21 Typo. *Perf. 12½*

238	A47	80h rose	5	8
239	A47	1k blk brn	5	3
241	A47	1½k grn ('21)	6	10
242	A47	2k blue	3	3
243	A48	3k yel grn & dk grn ('21)	5	3
244	A48	4k red & cl ('21)	6	5
245	A48	5k vio & cl ('21)	6	4
246	A48	7½k yel & brn ('21)	6	6
247	A48	10k ultra & bl ('21)	5	8
		Nos. 238-247 (9)	47	50

Nos. 238-245, 247 exist on white paper of good quality and on thick grayish paper of inferior quality; No. 246 only on white paper.

1921 Engraved

248	A46	50k dk vio, *yel*	40	1.00
a.		Perf. 11½	55.00	75.00

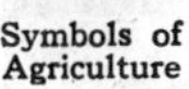

Symbols of Agriculture
A49

Symbols of Labor and Industry
A50

1922–24 Typographed *Perf. 12½*

No.	Type	Denomination / Color	Unused	Used
250	A49	½k ol bis	5	*75*
251	A50	1k brown	3	3
252	A50	2k cob bl	3	3
253	A49	2½k org brn	3	3
254	A50	4k dl vio	5	*90*
255	A50	5k gray grn	3	3
256	A49	7½k gray vio	3	3
257	A50	10k claret	3	3
258	A49	12½k gray grn	5	3
259	A49	15k bluish grn	3	3
260	A49	20k dk bl	3	3
261	A49	25k claret	3	3
262	A50	30k pale gray	3	3
263	A50	45k pale red	3	3
264	A50	50k org brn	3	3
265	A50	60k yel grn	3	3
266	A50	75k ultra	3	3
267	A50	80k yellow	3	3
268	A49	100k gray	3	3
269	A49	120k brown	5	3
270	A49	150k orange	3	3
271	A49	160k lt grn	3	3
272	A49	180k red	3	3
273	A49	200k pink	3	3
274	A49	240k dk vio	3	3
275	A49	300k lt bl	6	3
276	A49	400k dp grn	1.25	12
a.		400k gray grn	1.25	25
277	A49	500k yellow	3	3
278	A49	600k slate	3	3
279	A49	700k brn ('24)	45	3
280	A49	800k vio ('24)	90	*3.75*
281	A50	1000k vio ('23)	55	25
282	A50	1200k car rose ('23)	35	60
283	A50	1500k org ('24)	1.40	12
284	A50	1600k sl ('23)	1.75	3.25
285	A50	2000k dp bl ('23)	6.00	60
286	A50	3000k lt bl ('23)	15.00	1.25
287	A50	4000k dk bl, *bl* ('24)	6.75	3.00
		Nos. 250-287 (38)	35.35	*15.40*

Nos. 250–287 exist imperf. Price, set $750.

Symbols of Art and Science

A51

1922–24 Engraved *Perf. 12½*

No.	Type	Denomination / Color	Unused	Used
288	A51	20k dk brn	9	8
a.		Perf. 11½	1.40	1.40
289	A51	25k blue	9	6
a.		Perf. 11½	1.40	1.40
290	A51	50k brn red	6	7
a.		Perf. 11½	3.50	4.50
291	A51	100k dp grn	5	8
a.		Perf. 11½	7.25	8.00
292	A51	200k dk vio	15	10
a.		Perf. 11½	11.00	16.00
293	A51	500k dp org	15	90
294	A51	1000k blk vio, *yel*	5	6
a.		Perf. 11½	175.00	250.00
295	A51	2000k ol grn *yel*	15	10
296	A51	3000k cl brn ('23)	14.00	65
297	A51	5000k gray blk ('23)	2.25	1.90

Granite Paper.

No.	Type	Denomination / Color	Unused	Used
298	A51	10,000k red brn ('24)	3.75	4.75
		Nos. 288-298 (11)	20.79	8.75

On Nos. 281 to 287 and Nos. 291 to 298 "kronen" is abbreviated to "k" and transposed with the numerals.

Nos. 288–298 exist imperf. Price, set $425.

Numeral

A52

Fields Crossed by Telegraph Wires

A53

White-Shouldered Eagle

A54

Church of Minorite Friars

A55

1925–27 Typographed *Perf. 12*

No.	Type	Denomination / Color	Unused	Used
303	A52	1g dk gray	25	3
304	A52	2g claret	50	3
305	A52	3g scarlet	50	3
306	A52	4g grnsh bl ('27)	1.75	5
307	A52	5g brn org	3.00	3
308	A52	6g ultra	2.00	3
309	A52	7g chocolate	3.75	3
310	A52	8g yel grn	10.00	3
311	A53	10g orange	50	3
313	A53	15g red lil	50	3
314	A53	16g dk bl	50	3
315	A53	18g ol grn	1.50	40
316	A54	20g dk vio	50	3
317	A54	24g carmine	1.00	40
318	A54	30g dk brn	75	3
319	A54	40g ultra	1.75	8
320	A54	45g yel brn	2.00	7
321	A54	50g gray	2.50	18
322	A54	80g turq bl	6.00	4.50

Engraved.

Perf. 12½

No.	Type	Denomination / Color	Unused	Used
323	A55	1s dp grn	20.00	40
a.		1s lt grn	200.00	2.00
324	A55	2s brn rose	11.00	12.00
		Nos. 303-324 (21)	70.25	18.44

Nos. 303–305 and 307–324 exist imperf. Price, set $450.

Güssing

A56

National Library, Vienna

A57

Designs: 15g, Hochosterwitz. 16g, 20g, Durnstein. 18g, Traunsee. 24g, Salzburg. 30g, Seewiesen. 40g, Innsbruck. 50g, Worthersee. 60g, Hohenems. 2s, St. Stephen's Cathedral, Vienna.

1929–30 Typo. *Perf. 12½*

Size: 25½x21½mm

No.	Type	Denomination / Color	Unused	Used
326	A56	10g brn org	1.25	3
327	A56	10g bis ('30)	1.25	3
328	A56	15g vio brn	1.00	2.00
329	A56	16g dk gray	25	13
330	A56	18g bl grn	50	70
331	A56	20g dk gray ('30)	50	3
332	A56	24g maroon	6.00	9.00
333	A56	24g lake ('30)	12.50	75
334	A56	30g dk vio	7.50	15
335	A56	40g dk bl	12.50	20
336	A56	50g gray vio ('30)	45.00	25
337	A56	60g ol grn	35.00	35

Engraved.

Size: 21x26mm.

No.	Type	Denomination / Color	Unused	Used
338	A57	1s blk brn	9.00	30
339	A57	2s dk grn	15.00	10.00
		Nos. 326-339 (14)	147.25	23.92

Type of 1929–30 Issue.

Designs: 12g, Traunsee. 64g, Hohenems.

1932 *Perf. 12*

Size: 21 x 16½ mm.

No.	Type	Denomination / Color	Unused	Used
340	A56	10g ol brn	1.00	3
341	A56	12g bl grn	2.00	3
342	A56	18g bl grn	90	2.75
343	A56	20g dk gray	1.00	3
344	A56	24g car rose	7.50	3
345	A56	24g dl vio	6.00	3
346	A56	30g dk vio	25.00	8
347	A56	30g car rose	5.50	13
348	A56	40g dk bl	30.00	1.00
349	A56	40g dk vio	8.00	40
350	A56	50g gray vio	37.50	40
351	A56	50g dl bl	9.00	40
352	A56	60g gray grn	75.00	2.50
353	A56	64g gray grn	10.00	25
		Nos. 340-353 (14)	218.40	8.06

Burgenland

A67

Tyrol

A68

Designs (costumes of various districts): 3g, Burgenland. 4g, 5g, Carinthia. 6g, 8g, Lower Austria. 12g, 20g, Upper Austria. 24g, 25g, Salzburg. 30g, 35g, Styria. 45g, Tyrol. 60g, Vorarlberg bridal couple. 64g, Vorarlberg. 1s, Viennese family. 2s, Military.

1934–35 Typographed *Perf. 12*

No.	Type	Denomination / Color	Unused	Used
354	A67	1g dk vio	5	3
355	A67	3g scarlet	5	3
356	A67	4g ol grn	10	7
357	A67	5g red vio	10	3
358	A67	6g ultra	25	30
359	A67	8g green	12	3
360	A67	12g dk brn	12	3
361	A67	20g yel brn	15	3
362	A67	24g grnsh bl	15	3
363	A67	25g violet	25	18
364	A67	30g maroon	20	3
365	A67	35g rose car	40	50

Perf. 12½

No.	Type	Denomination / Color	Unused	Used
366	A68	40g sl gray	50	15
367	A68	45g brn red	40	15
368	A68	60g ultra	75	25
369	A68	64g brown	1.00	10
370	A68	1s dp vio	85	50
371	A68	2s dl grn	50.00	80.00

Designs Redrawn

Perf. 12 (6g), 12½ (2s)

No.	Type	Denomination / Color	Unused	Used
372	A67	6g ultra ('35)	20	15
373	A68	2s emer ('35)	4.50	7.50
		Nos. 354-373 (20)	60.14	90.09

The design of No. 358 looks as though the man's ears were on backwards, while No. 372 appears correctly.

On No. 373 there are seven feathers on each side of the eagle instead of five.

Nos. 354–373 exist imperf. Price, set $550.

Dollfuss Mourning Issue.

Engelbert Dollfuss

A85

1934 Engraved *Perf. 12½*

No.	Type	Denomination / Color	Unused	Used
374	A85	24g grnsh blk	75	50

1935

No.	Type	Denomination / Color	Unused	Used
375	A85	24g indigo	1.50	1.25

"Mother and Child" by Joseph Danhauser

A86

"Madonna and Child", after Painting by Albrecht Dürer

A87

1935, May 1

No.	Type	Denomination / Color	Unused	Used
376	A86	24g dk bl	75	30

Issued for Mother's Day.

Nos. 376–377 exist imperf. Price, each $200.

1936, May 5 Photogravure

No.	Type	Denomination / Color	Unused	Used
377	A87	24g vio bl	30	40

Issued for Mother's Day.

Farm Workers

A88

Design: 5s, Factory workers.

1936, June Engraved *Perf. 12½*

No.	Type	Denomination / Color	Unused	Used
378	A88	3s red org	17.50	22.50
379	A88	5s brn blk	40.00	55.00

Nos. 378–379 exist imperf. Price, set $350.

Engelbert Dollfuss

A90

Mother and Child

A91

1936, July 25

No.	Type	Denomination / Color	Unused	Used
380	A90	10s dk bl	900.00	1,400.

Second anniversary of death of Engelbert Dollfuss, chancellor. Exists imperf. Price, $2,500.

1937, May 5 Photo. *Perf. 12*

No.	Type	Denomination / Color	Unused	Used
381	A91	24g hn brn	38	30

Issued for Mother's Day. Exists imperf. Price, $225.

S. S. Maria Anna

A92

Steamships: 24g, Uranus, 64g, Oesterreich.

1937, June 9

No.	Type	Denomination / Color	Unused	Used
382	A92	12g red brn	1.00	35
383	A92	24g dp bl	1.00	35
384	A92	64g dk grn	1.00	1.10

Centenary of steamship service on Danube River.

Exist imperf. Price, set $175.

First Locomotive, "Austria"

A95

Designs: 25g, Modern steam locomotive. 35g, Modern electric train.

1937, Nov. 22

No.	Type	Denomination / Color	Unused	Used
385	A95	12g blk brn	13	10
386	A95	25g dk vio	65	1.00
387	A95	35g brn red	2.25	2.25

Centenary of Austrian railways. Exist imperf. Price, set $150.

Rose and Zodiac Signs
A98

1937 Engraved. *Perf. 13x12½.*

388	A98	12g dk grn	15	25
389	A98	24g dk car	15	25

For Use in Vienna, Lower Austria and Burgenland.

Germany Nos. 509-511 and 511B Overprinted in Black

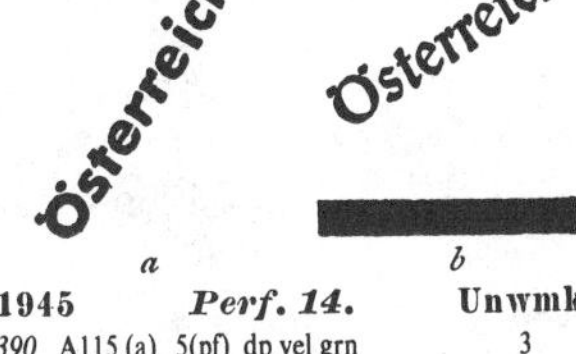

a *b*

1945 *Perf. 14.* Unwmkd.

390	A115 (a)	5(pf) dp yel grn	3	15
391	A115 (b)	6(pf) purple	10	35
392	A115 (a)	8(pf) red	5	15
393	A115 (b)	12(pf) carmine	10	35

Nos. 390–393 exist with overprint inverted or double.

Germany No. 507, the 3pf, with overprint "a" was prepared, not issued, but sold to collectors after the definitive Republic issue had been placed in use. Price $50.

German Semi-Postal Stamps, Nos. B207, B209, B210 and B283 Surcharged in Black

ÖSTERREICH
5 Pf.
c

ÖSTERREICH
8 Pf.

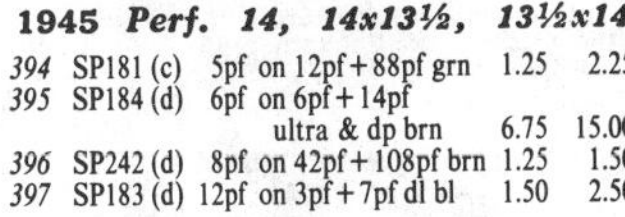

d

1945 *Perf. 14, 14x13½, 13½x14*

394	SP181 (c)	5pf on 12pf+88pf grn	1.25	2.25
395	SP184 (d)	6pf on 6pf+14pf ultra & dp brn	6.75	15.00
396	SP242 (d)	8pf on 42pf+108pf brn	1.25	1.50
397	SP183 (d)	12pf on 3pf+7pf dl bl	1.50	2.50

The surcharges are spaced to fit the stamps.

Stamps not listed in this Catalogue or mentioned in "For the Record" (unless recent issues) usually are revenues, locals or labels.

Stamps of Germany, Nos. 509 to 511, 511B, 519 and 529 Overprinted

e *f*

1945 Typo. *Perf. 14*

Size: 18½x22½mm.

398	A115 (e)	5(pf) dp yel grn	50	1.50
399	A115 (f)	5(pf) dp yel grn	9.00	*15.00*
400	A115 (e)	6(pf) purple	30	2.50
401	A115 (e)	8(pf) red	30	*1.40*
402	A115 (e)	12(pf) carmine	45	*3.50*

Engraved.

Size: 21½x26mm.

403	A115 (e)	30(pf) ol grn	9.00	*15.00*
a.		Thin bar at bottom	30.00	*35.00*
404	A118 (e)	42(pf) brt grn	30.00	*45.00*
a.		Thin bar at bottom	18.50	*30.00*
		Nos. 398-404 (7)	49.55	*83.90*

On Nos. 403a and 404a, the bottom bar of the overprint is 2½mm. wide, and, as the overprint was applied in two operations, "Osterreich" is usually not exactly centered in its diagonal slot. On Nos. 403 and 404, the bottom bar is 3mm. wide, and "Osterreich" is always well centered.

Germany Nos. 524–527 (the 1m, 2m, 3m and 5m), overprinted with vertical bars and "Osterreich" similar to "e" and "f", were prepared, not issued, but sold to collectors after the definitive Republic issue had been placed in use. Price for set $140.

For Use in Styria.

Stamps of Germany Nos. 506 to 511, 511A, 511B, 514 to 523 and 529 Overprinted in Black

Österreich

1945 Typographed ***Perf. 14*** **Unwmkd.**

Size: 18½x22½mm.

405	A115	1(pf) gray blk	2.50	5.75
406	A115	3(pf) lt brn	2.25	5.50
407	A115	4(pf) slate	9.50	20.00
408	A115	5(pf) dp yel grn	2.00	3.50
409	A115	6(pf) purple	35	55
410	A115	8(pf) red	1.40	2.75
411	A115	10(pf) dk brn	3.00	5.75
412	A115	12(pf) carmine	35	55

Engraved.

413	A115	15(pf) brn lake	1.40	2.75
414	A115	16(pf) pck grn	18.50	37.50
415	A115	20(pf) blue	4.75	9.50
416	A115	24(pf) org brn	18.50	37.50

Size: 22½x26mm.

417	A115	25(pf) brt ultra	2.00	4.50
418	A115	30(pf) ol grn	2.00	4.25
419	A115	40(pf) brt red vio	2.25	4.75
420	A118	42(pf) brt grn	3.50	7.00
421	A115	50(pf) myr grn	3.75	9.00
422	A115	60(pf) dk red brn	4.75	9.50
423	A115	80(pf) indigo	4.00	9.00
		Nos. 405-423 (19)	86.75	179.60

Overprinted on Nos. 524 to 527.
Perf. 12½, 14.

424	A116	1m dk sl grn	14.00	*37.50*
a.		Perf. 12½	225.00	
425	A116	2m violet	14.00	*32.50*
a.		Perf. 14	25.00	*75.00*
426	A116	3m cop red	27.50	*85.00*
a.		Perf. 14	275.00	
427	A116	5m dk bl	375.00	*900.00*
a.		Perf. 14	*800.00*	

On the preceding four stamps the innermost vertical lines are 10½ mm. apart; on the pfennig values 6½ mm. apart.

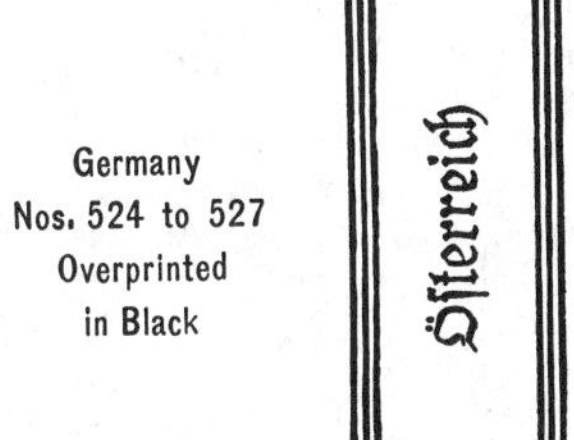

Germany Nos. 524 to 527 Overprinted in Black

Perf. 14

428	A116	1m dk sl grn	15.00	*32.50*
429	A116	2m violet	15.00	*35.00*

Perf. 12½

430	A116	3m cop red	30.00	*67.50*
431	A116	5m dk bl	250.00	*475.00*
a.		Perf. 14	*850.00*	

On the preceding four stamps, "Osterreich" is thinner, measuring 16 mm. On the previous set of 23 values it measures 18 mm.

Counterfeits exist of Nos. 424–431 overprints.

For Use in Vienna, Lower Austria and Burgenland.

Coat of Arms
A99 A100

Typographed or Lithographed.
Perf. 14x13½

1945, July 3 Unwmkd.

Size: 21x25mm.

432	A99	3(pf) brown	3	3
433	A99	4(pf) slate	4	4
434	A99	5(pf) dk grn	3	3
435	A99	6(pf) dp vio	3	3
436	A99	8(pf) org brn	3	3
437	A99	10(pf) dp brn	3	3
438	A99	12(pf) rose car	3	3
439	A99	15(pf) org red	3	3
440	A99	16(pf) dl bl grn	3	5

Perf. 14.

Size: 24x28½mm.

441	A99	20(pf) lt bl	5	4
442	A99	24(pf) orange	5	5
443	A99	25(pf) dk bl	5	3
444	A99	30(pf) dp gray grn	5	3
445	A99	38(pf) ultra	5	5
446	A99	40(pf) brt red vio	5	5
447	A99	42(pf) sage grn	5	5
448	A99	50(pf) bl grn	5	7
449	A99	60(pf) maroon	5	7
450	A99	80(pf) dl lil	6	12

Engraved
Perf. 14x13½

451	A100	1(m) dk grn	10	28
452	A100	2(m) dk pur	12	32
453	A100	3(m) dk vio	18	40
454	A100	5(m) brn red	30	65
		Nos. 432-454 (23)	1.49	2.51

Nos. 432, 433, 437, 439, 440, 443, 446, 448 and 449 are typographed. Nos. 434, 435, 441 and 442 are lithographed; the other values exist both ways.

For General Use.

Lermoos, Winter Scene
A101

The Prater Woods, Vienna
A105

Hochosterwitz, Carinthia
A106

Lake Constance
A110

Dürnstein, Lower Austria
A124

Designs: 4g, Eisenerz surface mine. 5g, Leopoldsberg, near Vienna. 6g, Hohensalzburg, Salzburg Province. 12g, Wolfgang See, near Salzburg. 15g, Forchtenstein Castle, Burgenland. 16g, Gesäuse Valley. 24g, Höldrichs Mill, Lower Austria. 25g, Oetz Valley Outlet, Tyrol. 30g, Neusiedler Lake, Burgenland. 35g, Belvedere Palace, Vienna. 38g, Langbath Lake. 40g, Mariazell, Styria. 42g, Traunkirchen. 45g, Hartenstein Castle. 50g, Silvretta Mountains, Vorarlberg. 60g, Railroad viaducts near Semmering. 70g, Waterfall of Bad-Gastein, Salzburg. 80g, Kaiser Mountains, Tyrol. 90g, Wayside Shrine, Tragöss, Styria. 2s, St. Christof am Arlberg, Tyrol. 3s, Heiligenblut, Carinthia. 5s, Schönbrunn, Vienna.

Perf. 14x13½

1945–46 Photogravure Unwmkd.

455	A101	3g sapphire	3	3
456	A101	4g dp org ('46)	3	3
457	A101	5g dk car rose	3	3
458	A101	6g dk sl grn	3	3
459	A105	8g gldn brn	3	3
460	A106	10g dk grn	3	3
461	A106	12g dk brn	3	3
462	A106	15g dk sl bl ('46)	3	3
463	A106	16g chnt brn ('46)	3	3

Perf. 13½x14

464	A110	20g dp ultra ('46)	3	3
465	A110	24g dp yel grn ('46)	3	3
466	A110	25g gray blk ('46)	3	3
467	A110	30g dk red	3	3
468	A110	35g brn red ('46)	3	3
469	A110	38g brn ol ('46)	5	5
470	A110	40g gray	3	3
471	A110	42g brn org ('46)	3	3
472	A110	45g dk bl ('46)	25	50
473	A110	50g dk bl	3	3
474	A110	60g dk vio	8	6
a.		Imperf. (pair)	50.00	80.00
475	A110	70g Prus bl ('46)	12	15
476	A110	80g brown	20	75
477	A110	90g Prus grn	75	1.25
478	A124	1s dk red brn ('46)	45	70
479	A124	2s bl gray ('46)	1.75	2.75
480	A124	3s dk sl grn ('46)	60	90
481	A124	5s dk red ('46)	1.10	1.75
		Nos. 455-481 (27)	5.86	9.37

See also Nos. 486–488, 496–515.

No. 461 Overprinted in Carmine

1946, Sept. 26

482	A106	12g dk brn	12	25

Issued to commemorate the meeting of the Society for Cultural and Economic Relations with the Soviet Union, Vienna, September 26 to 29, 1946.

City Hall Park, Vienna
A128

Hochosterwitz, Carinthia
A129

Perf. 14x13½

1946-47 Photogravure. Unwmkd.

483	A128	8g dp plum	3	3
484	A128	8g ol brn	7	8
a.		8g dk ol grn	3	3
485	A129	10g dk brn vio ('47)	6	5

Perf. 13½x14

486	A110	30g bl gray ('47)	5	20
487	A110	50g brn vio ('47)	27	45
488	A110	60g vio bl ('47)	1.85	1.50
		Nos. 483-488 (6)	2.33	2.31

See also No. 502.

Franz Grillparzer
A130

Franz Schubert
A131

1947 Engraved. *Perf. 14x13½.*

489	A130	18g chocolate	10	10

Photogravure.

490	A130	18g dk vio brn	12	12

Issued to commemorate the 75th anniversary of the death of Franz Grillparzer, dramatic poet.

A second printing of No. 490 on thicker paper has a darker frame and clearer delineation of the portrait.

1947, Mar. 31 Engraved

491	A131	12g dk grn	8	10

Issued to commemorate the 150th anniversary of the birth of Franz Schubert, musician and composer.

Nos. 469 and 463 Surcharged in Brown

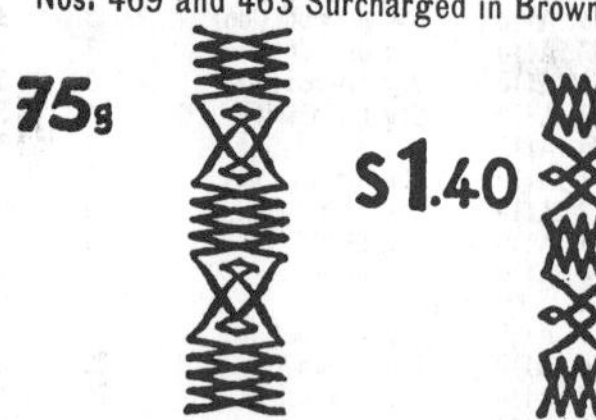

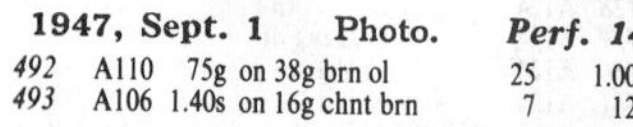

1947, Sept. 1 Photo. *Perf. 14*

492	A110	75g on 38g brn ol	25	1.00
493	A106	1.40s on 16g chnt brn	7	12

The surcharge on No. 493 varies from brown to black brown.

Symbols of Global Telegraphic Communication
A132

Engraved

1947, Nov. 5 *Perf. 14x13½*

495	A132	40g dk vio	6	20

Centenary of the telegraph in Austria.

Scenic Type of 1946.

1946, Aug. Photo. *Perf. 13½x14*

496	A124	1s dk brn	75	50
497	A124	2s dk bl	5.25	4.50
498	A124	3s dk sl grn	1.20	1.00
499	A124	5s dk red	30.00	12.50

On Nos. 478 to 481 the upper and lower panels show a screen effect. On Nos. 496 to 499 the panels appear to be solid color.

Scenic Types of 1945-46.

1947-48 Photo. *Perf. 14x13½*

500	A101	3g brt red	3	4
501	A101	5g brt red	4	3
502	A129	10g brt red	8	3
503	A106	15g brt red ('48)	1.10	1.00

Perf. 13½x14

504	A110	20g brt red	30	3
505	A110	30g brt red	55	22
506	A110	40g brt red	55	3
507	A110	50g brt red	75	4
508	A110	60g brt red ('48)	6.00	1.85
509	A110	70g brt red ('48)	3.50	6
510	A110	80g brt red ('48)	3.50	12
511	A110	90g brt red ('48)	3.75	50
512	A124	1s dk vio	55	4
513	A124	2s dk vio	80	20
514	A124	3s dk vio ('48)	9.00	1.40
515	A124	5s dk vio ('48)	10.50	1.40
		Nos. 500-515 (16)	41.00	6.99

Carl Michael Ziehrer
A133

Designs: No. 517, Adalbert Stifter. No. 518, Anton Bruckner. 60g, Friedrich von Amerling.

1948-49 Engraved

516	A133	20g dl grn	30	15
517	A133	40g chocolate	4.00	4.50
518	A133	40g dk grn ('49)	8.00	10.00
519	A133	60g rose brn	45	35

Issued to commemorate anniversaries of the death of Carl Michael Ziehrer (1843-1922), composer; Adalbert Stifter (1805-1868), novelist; Friedrich von Amerling (1803-1887), painter, and the birth of Anton Bruckner (1824-1896), composer.

Vorarlberg, Montafon Valley
A134

Costume of Vienna, 1850
A135

Designs (Austrian Costumes): 3g, Tyrol, Inn Valley. 5g, Salzburg, Pinzgau. 10g, Styria, Salzkammergut. 15g, Burgenland, Lutzmannsburg. 25g, Vienna, 1850. 30g, Salzburg, Pongau. 40g, Vienna, 1840. 45g, Carinthia, Lesach Valley. 50g, Vorarlberg, Bregenzer Forest. 60g, Carinthia, Lavant Valley. 70g, Lower Austria, Wachau. 75g, Styria, Salzkammergut. 80g, Styria, Enns Valley. 90g, Central Styria. 1s, Tyrol, Puster Valley. 1.20s, Lower Austria, Vienna Woods. 1.40s, Upper Austria, Inn District. 1.45s, Wilten. 1.50s, Vienna, 1853. 1.60s, Vienna, 1830. 1.70s, East Tyrol, Kals. 2s, Upper Austria. 2.20s, Ischl, 1820. 2.40s, Kitzbuhel. 2.50s, Upper Steiermark, 1850. 2.70s, Little Walser Valley. 3s, Burgenland. 3.50s, Lower Austria, 1850. 4.50s, Gail Valley. 5s, Ziller Valley. 7s, Steiermark, Sulm Valley.

Photogravure

1948-52 *Perf. 14x13½* Unwmkd.

520	A134	3g gray ('50)	45	65
521	A134	5g dk grn ('49)	7	3
522	A134	10g dp bl	7	3
523	A134	15g brown	45	3
524	A134	20g yel grn	10	3
525	A134	25g brn ('49)	10	4
526	A134	30g dk car rose	2.00	3
527	A134	30g dk vio ('50)	45	3
528	A134	40g violet	2.00	3
529	A134	40g grn ('49)	15	3
530	A134	45g vio bl	1.75	45
531	A134	50g org brn ('49)	45	3
532	A134	60g scarlet	15	3
533	A134	70g brt bl grn ('49)	15	3
534	A134	75g blue	3.00	45
535	A134	80g car rose ('49)	30	3
536	A134	90g brn vio ('49)	22.50	35
537	A134	1s ultra	4.50	4
538	A134	1s rose red ('50)	60.00	12
539	A134	1s dk grn ('51)	15	3
540	A134	1.20s vio ('49)	30	6
541	A134	1.40s brown	2.00	22
542	A134	1.45s dk car ('51)	90	10
543	A134	1.50s ultra ('51)	45	3
544	A134	1.60s org red ('49)	15	4
545	A134	1.70s vio bl ('50)	2.00	90
546	A134	2s bl grn	30	4
547	A134	2.20s sl ('52)	1.50	4
548	A134	2.40s bl ('51)	75	12
549	A134	2.50s brn ('52)	1.20	40
550	A134	2.70s dk brn ('51)	38	55
551	A134	3s brn car ('49)	1.40	3
552	A134	3.50s dl grn ('51)	6.00	4
553	A134	4.50s brn vio ('51)	45	55
554	A134	5s dk red vio	75	4
555	A134	7s ol ('52)	60	6

Engraved

556	A135	10s gray ('50)	27.50	5.50
		Nos. 520-556 (37)	145.42	11.21

In 1958-59, 21 denominations of this set were printed on white paper, differing from the previous grayish paper with yellowish gum.

Pres. Karl Renner
A136

1948, Nov. 12 *Perf. 14x13½*

557	A136	1sh dp bl	2.75	2.25

Issued to commemorate the 30th anniversary of the founding of the Austrian Republic. See also Nos. 573, 636.

Franz Gruber and Josef Mohr
A137

1948, Dec. 18 *Perf. 13½x14*

558	A137	60g red brn	6.00	9.00

Issued to commemorate the 130th anniversary of the hymn "Silent Night, Holy Night."

Symbolical of Child Welfare
A138

Johann Strauss, the Younger
A139

Photogravure

1949, May 14 *Perf. 14x13½*

559	A138	1s brt bl	18.00	2.10

Issued to commemorate the first year of activity of the United Nations International Children's Emergency Fund in Austria.

1949 Engraved

Designs: 30g, Johann Strauss, the elder. No. 561, Johann Strauss, the younger. No. 562, Karl Millöcker.

560	A139	30g vio brn	3.00	4.00
561	A139	1s dk bl	4.00	2.00
562	A139	1s dk bl	14.50	15.00

Issued to commemorate the centenary of the death of Johann Strauss, the elder (1804-1849), and the 50th anniversary of the deaths of Johann Strauss, the younger (1825-1899), and Karl Millöcker (1842-1899), composers. See also No. 574.

Esperanto Star, Olive Branches
A140

St. Gebhard
A141

1949, June 25 Photogravure

563	A140	20g bl grn	1.50	90

Austrian Esperanto Congress at Graz.

1949, Aug. 6 Engraved

564	A141	30g dk vio	2.50	2.75

Issued to commemorate the millenary of the birth of St. Gebhard (949-995), Bishop of Vorarlberg.

Letter, Roses and Post Horn
A142

Designs: 60g, Plaque. 1s, "Austria," wings and monogram.

1949, Oct. 8 *Perf. 13½x14*

565	A142	40g dk grn	4.00	3.75
566	A142	60g dk car	4.00	3.75
567	A142	1s dk vio bl	8.25	9.00

Issued to commemorate the 75th anniversary of the formation of the Universal Postal Union.

Moritz Michael Daffinger
A143

Andreas Hofer
A144

Designs: 30g, Alexander Girardi. No. 569, Daffinger. No. 570, Hofer. No. 571, Josef Madersperger.

1950 *Perf. 14x13½* **Unwmkd.**

568 A144 30g dk bl 2.00 1.10
569 A143 60g red brn 8.25 7.50
570 A144 60g dk vio 14.50 15.00
571 A144 60g purple 6.75 4.75

Issued to commemorate the centenary of the birth of Alexander Girardi (1850–1918), actor; the death centenary of Moritz Michael Daffinger (1790–1849), painter; the 140th anniversary of the death of Andreas Hofer (1767–1810), patriot, and the death centenary of Josef Madersperger (1768–1850), inventor.

Austrian Stamp of 1850
A146

1950, May 20 *Perf. 14½*

572 A146 1s *straw* 2.75 2.25

Centenary of Austrian postage stamps.

Renner Type of 1948, Frame and Inscriptions Altered.

1951, Mar. 3

573 A136 1s *straw* 2.25 30

Issued in memory of Pres. Karl Renner, 1870–1950.

Strauss Type of 1949.

Portrait: 60g, Joseph Lanner.

1951, Apr. 12

574 A139 60g dk bl grn 4.25 2.25

Issued to commemorate the 150th anniversary of the birth of Joseph Lanner, composer.

Martin Johann Schmidt
A147

Boy Scout Emblem
A148

Engraved.

1951, June 28 *Perf. 14x13½*

575 A147 1sh brn red 6.00 4.50

Issued to commemorate the 150th anniversary of the death of Martin Johann Schmidt, painter.

1951, Aug. 3 **Engr. & Litho.**

576 A148 1sh dk grn, ocher & pink 5.50 7.25

Issued in connection with the 7th World Scout Jamboree, Bad Ischl-St. Wolfgang, Aug. 3–13, 1951.

Wilhelm Kienzl
A149

Josef Schrammel
A150

Design: 1s, Karl von Ghega.

1951–52 **Engraved** **Unwmkd.**

577 A149 1s dp grn ('52) 7.50 2.25
578 A149 1.50s indigo 4.25 1.75
579 A150 1.50s vio bl ('52) 7.50 2.25

Issued to commemorate the 150th anniversary of the birth of Karl von Ghega (1802–1860), civil engineer; the 10th anniversary of the death of Wilhelm Kienzl (1857–1941), composer, and the birth centenary of Josef Schrammel (1852–1895), composer. See also No. 582.

Breakfast Pavilion, Schönbrunn
A151

1952, May 24 *Perf. 13½x14*

580 A151 1.50s dk grn 7.00 2.25

Issued to commemorate the 200th anniversary of the founding of the Vienna Zoological Gardens.

Globe as Dot Over "i"
A152

School Girl
A153

1952, July 1 *Perf. 14x13½*

581 A152 1.50s dk bl 7.50 1.35

Issued to publicize the formation of the International Union of Socialist Youth Camp, Vienna, July 1-10, 1952.

Type Similar to A150.

Portrait: 1s, Nikolaus Lenau.

1952, Aug. 13

582 A150 1s dp grn 8.00 2.25

Issued to commemorate the 150th anniversary of the birth of Nikolaus Lenau, pseudonym of Nikolaus Franz Niembsch von Strehlenau (1802–1850), poet.

1952, Sept. 6

583 A153 2.40s dp vio bl 13.00 4.50

Issued to stimulate letter-writing between Austrian and foreign school children.

Hugo Wolf
A154

Pres. Theodor Körner
A155

Engraved.

1953, Feb. 21 *Perf. 14x13½*

587 A154 1.50s dk bl 9.00 1.40

Issued to commemorate the 50th anniversary of the death of Hugo Wolf, composer.

1953, Apr. 24

588 A155 1.50s dk vio bl 8.00 1.40

Issued to commemorate the 80th birthday of Pres. Theodor Körner. See also Nos. 591, 614.

State Theater, Linz, and Masks
A156

1953, Oct. 17 *Perf. 13½x14*

589 A156 1.50s dk gray 16.00 2.50

Issued to commemorate the 150th anniversary of the founding of the State Theater at Linz.

Child and Christmas Tree
A157

Karl von Rokitansky
A158

1953, Nov. 30 *Perf. 14x13½*

590 A157 1s dk grn 2.00 35

See also No. 597.

Type Similar to A155.

Portrait: 1.50s, Moritz von Schwind.

1954, Jan. 21 *Perf. 14x13½*

591 A155 1.50s purple 12.50 2.50

Issued to commemorate the 150th anniversary of the birth of Moritz von Schwind, painter.

1954, Feb. 19

592 A158 1.50s purple 21.00 3.25

Issued to commemorate the 150th anniversary of the birth of Karl von Rokitansky, physician. See also No. 595.

Esperanto Star and Wreath
A159

Engraved and Photogravure

1954, June 5 *Perf. 13½14*

593 A159 1s dk brn & emer 6.00 35

Issued to commemorate the 50th anniversary of the Esperanto movement in Austria.

Johann Michael Rottmayr
A160

Engraved

1954, Aug. 4 *Perf. 14x13½*

594 A160 1s dk bl grn 13.00 3.50

300th birth anniversary of Johann Michael Rottmayr von Rosenbrunn, painter.

Type Similar to A158

Portrait: 1.50s, Carl Auer von Welsbach.

595 A158 1.50s vio bl 37.50 2.75

25th death anniversary of Carl Auer von Welsbach (1858–1929), chemist.

Organ, St. Florian Monastery and Cherub
A161

1954, Oct. 2 **Unwmkd.**

596 A161 1s brown 3.65 45

Issued to publicize the second International Congress for Catholic Church Music, Vienna, October 4-10, 1954.

Christmas Type of 1953

1954, Nov. 30

597 A157 1s dk bl 3.85 60

Arms of Austria and Official Publication
A162

1954, Dec. 18 **Engraved**

598 A162 1s sal & blk 3.00 35

Issued to commemorate the 150th anniversary of the founding of Austria's State Printing Plant and the 250th year of publication of the government newspaper, Wiener Zeitung.

Parliament Building
A163

Designs: 1s, Western railroad station, Vienna. 1.45s, Letters forming flag. 1.50s, Public housing, Vienna. 2.40s, Limberg dam.

1955, Apr. 27 *Perf. 13½x14*

599 A163 70g rose vio 1.50 30
600 A163 1s dp ultra 6.00 28
601 A163 1.45s scarlet 9.00 3.50
602 A163 1.50s brown 21.00 30
603 A163 2.40s dk bl grn 9.00 7.50
Nos. 599-603 (5) 46.50 11.88

Issued to commemorate the 10th anniversary of Austria's liberation.

Type of 1945 Overprinted in Blue

STAATSVERTRAG 1955

1955, May 15 *Perf. 14x13½*

604 A100 2(s) bl gray 2.75 55

Issued to commemorate the signing of the state treaty with the United States, France, Great Britain and Russia, May 15, 1955.

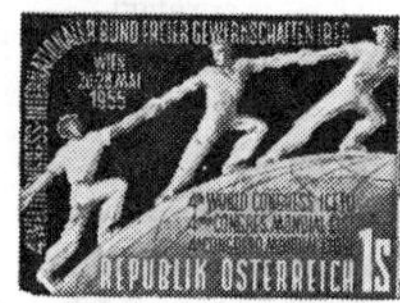

Workers of Three Races Climbing Globe
A164

1955, May 20 *Perf. 13½x14*

605 A164 1s indigo 2.75 3.25

Issued to publicize the 4th congress of the International Confederation of Free Trade Unions, Vienna, May 1955.

Burgtheater, Vienna
A165

Design: 2.40s, Opera House, Vienna.

1955, July 25

606 A165 1.50s lt sep 3.75 28
607 A165 2.40s dk bl 4.75 3.00

Issued to celebrate the re-opening of the Burgtheater and Opera House in Vienna.

Symbolic of Austria's Desire to Join the U. N.
A166

1955, Oct. 24 **Unwmkd.**

608 A166 2.40s green 18.50 3.25

Tenth anniversary of United Nations.

Wolfgang Amadeus Mozart
A167

Symbolic of Austria's Joining the U. N.
A168

1956, Jan. 21 *Perf. 14x13½*

609 A167 2.40s sl bl 3.75 1.35

Issued to commemorate the 200th anniversary of the birth of Wolfgang Amadeus Mozart, composer.

1956, Feb. 20

610 A168 2.40s chocolate 16.50 2.50

Issued to commemorate Austria's admission to the United Nations Organization.

Globe Showing Energy of the Earth
A169

1956, May 8 *Perf. 13½14*

611 A169 2.40s dp bl 15.00 4.00

Issued to publicize the Fifth International Power Conference, Vienna, June 17-23, 1956.

Map of Europe and City Maps
A170

J. B. Fischer von Erlach
A171

Photogravure and Typographed

1956, June 8 *Perf. 14x13½*

612 A170 1.45s lt grn blk & red 4.25 1.35

Issued to publicize the 23rd International Housing and Town Planning Congress, Vienna, July 22-28.

1956, July 20 **Engraved**

613 A171 1.50s brown 2.00 2.00

Issued to commemorate the 300th anniversary of the birth of Johann Bernhard Fischer von Erlach, architect.

Körner Type of 1953.

1957, Jan. 11

614 A155 1.50s gray blk 2.00 1.75

Issued to commemorate the death of Pres. Theodor Körner.

Dr. Julius Wagner-Jauregg
A172

Anton Wildgans
A173

1957, Mar. 7 *Perf. 14x13½*

615 A172 2.40s brn vio 4.25 3.25

Issued to commemorate the centenary of the birth of Dr. Julius Wagner-Jauregg, psychiatrist.

1957, May 3 **Unwmkd.**

616 A173 1s vio bl 60 28

Issued to commemorate the 25th anniversary of the death of Anton Wildgans, poet.

Old and New Postal Motor Coach
A174

1957, June 14 *Perf. 13½x14*

617 A174 1s *yellow* 60 28

Issued to commemorate the 50th anniversary of Austrian Postal Motor Coach Service.

Gasherbrum II and Glacier
A175

1957, July 27

618 A175 1.50s gray bl 60 25

Issued in honor of the Austrian Karakorum Expedition, which climbed Mount Gasherbrum II on July 7, 1956.

Mariazell
A176

Heidenreichstein Castle
A177

Designs: 20g, Farmhouse at Mörbisch. 50g, Heiligenstadt, Vienna. 1.40s, County seat, Klagenfurt. 1.50s, Rabenhof Building, Erdberg, Vienna. 1.80s, The Mint, Hall, Tyrol. 2s, Christkindl Church. 3.40s, Steiner Gate, Krems. 4s, Vienna Gate, Hainburg. 4.50s, Schwechat Airport, Vienna. 5.50s, Chur Gate, Feldkirch. 6s, County seat, Graz. 6.40s, "Golden Roof," Innsbruck.

1957-61 *Perf. 14x13½*

Lithographed.

Size: 20x25mm.

618A A176 20g vio blk ('61) 5 3
619 A176 50g bluish blk ('59) 10 3

Engraved.

620 A176 1s chocolate 2.50 6

Typographed.

621 A176 1s chocolate 2.50 3

Lithographed.

622 A176 1s choc ('59) 2.00 3
622A A176 1.40s brt grnsh bl ('60) 20 6
623 A176 1.50s rose lake ('58) 25 3
624 A176 1.80s brt ultra ('60) 25 5
625 A176 2s dl bl ('58) 12.50 3
626 A176 3.40s yel grn ('60) 45 45
627 A176 4s brt red lil ('60) 60 3
627A A176 4.50s dl grn ('60) 65 35
628 A176 5.50s grnsh gray ('60) 75 25
629 A176 6s brt vio ('60) 80 3
629A A176 6.40s brt bl ('60) 1.25 70

Engraved.

Size: 22x28mm.

630 A177 10s dk bl grn 1.50 20
Nos. 618A-630 (16) 26.35 2.36

Of the three 1s stamps above, Nos. 620 and 621 have two names in imprint (designer H. Strohofer, engraver G. Wimmer). No. 622 has only Strohofer's name.

Prices for Nos. 618A-624, 626-630 are for stamps on white paper. Most denominations also come on grayish paper with yellowish gum.

See also Nos. 688-702.

1960-65 Photogravure *Perf. 14½x14*

Size: 17x21mm.

630A A176 50g sl ('64) 6 3

Size: 18x21½ mm.

630B A176 1s chocolate 15 5

Size: 17x21mm.

630C A176 1.50s dk car ('65) 25 18

Nos. 630A-630C issued in sheets and coils.

Graukogel, Badgastein
A180

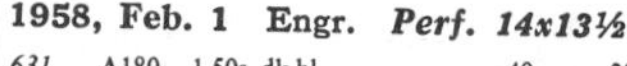

1958, Feb. 1 **Engr.** *Perf. 14x13½*

631 A180 1.50s dk bl 40 22

Alpine championships of the International Ski Federation, Badgastein, Feb. 2-7.

Plane over Map of Austria
A181

1958, Mar. 27 *Perf. 13½x14*

632 A181 4s red 85 35

Re-opening of Austrian Airlines.

Mother and Daughter
A182

Walther von der Vogelweide
A183

Perf. 14x13½

1958, May 8 **Unwmkd.**

633 A182 1.50s dk bl 40 35

Issued for Mother's Day, 1958.

1958, July 17 **Litho. & Engr.**

634 A183 1.50s multi 45 22

Issued to commemorate the 3rd Austrian Song Festival, Vienna, July 17-20.

Oswald Redlich
A184

Giant "E" on Map
A185

1958, Sept. 17 **Engraved**

635 A184 2.40s ultra 75 35

Issued to commemorate the centenary of the birth of Prof. Oswald Redlich (1858-1944), historian.

Renner Type of 1948.

1958, Nov. 12

636 A136 1.50s dp grn 45 45

Issued to commemorate the 40th anniversary of the founding of the Austrian Republic.

1959, Mar. 9

637 A185 2.40s emerald 55 50

Issued to promote the idea of a United Europe.

Cigarette Machine and Trademark of Tobacco Monopoly
A186

Archduke Johann
A187

1959, May 8 ***Perf. 13½*** **Unwmkd.**

638 A186 2.40s dk ol bis 45 32

Issued to commemorate the 175th anniversary of the establishment of the Austrian tobacco monopoly.

1959, May 11 ***Perf. 14x13½***

639 A187 1.50s dp grn 45 22

Issued to commemorate the centenary of the death of Archduke Johann of Austria, military leader and humanitarian.

Capercaillie A188 — Joseph Haydn A189

Animals: 1.50s, Roe buck. 2.40s, Wild boar. 3.50s, Red deer, doe and fawn.

1959, May 20 **Engraved**

640 A188 1s rose vio 42 25
641 A188 1.50s bl vio 90 17
642 A188 2.40s dk bl grn 65 65
643 A188 3.50s dk brn 45 40

Issued to publicize the Congress of the International Hunting Council, Vienna, May 20-24.

1959, May 30 **Unwmkd.**

644 A189 1.50s vio brn 75 20

Issued to commemorate the sesquicentennial of the death of Joseph Haydn, composer.

Coat of Arms, Tyrol A190 — Antenna, Zugspitze A191

1959, June 13 ***Perf. 14x13½***

645 A190 1.50s rose red 40 20

Issued to commemorate the 150th anniversary of the fight for the liberation of Tyrol.

1959, June 19 ***Perf. 13½***

646 A191 2.40s dk bl grn 40 25

Inauguration of Austria's relay system.

Field Ball Player A192 — Orchestral Instruments A193

Designs: 1s, Runner. 1.80s, Gymnast on vaulting horse. 2s, Woman hurdler. 2.20s, Hammer thrower.

1959–70 **Engr.** ***Perf. 14x13½***

647 A192 1s lilac 35 25
648 A192 1.50s bl grn 90 30
648A A192 1.80s car ('62) 55 45
648B A192 2s rose lake ('70) 30 20
648C A192 2.20s bluish blk ('67) 30 25
Nos. 647-648C (5) 2.40 1.45

Lithographed and Engraved

1959, Aug. 19 ***Perf. 14x13½***

649 A193 2.40s dl bl & blk 45 30

Issued to publicize the 1959 world tour of the Vienna Philharmonic Orchestra.

Family Fleeing over Mountains A194

Engraved

1960, Apr. 7 ***Perf. 13½x14***

650 A194 3s Prus grn 85 50

Issued to publicize World Refugee Year, July 1, 1959–June 30, 1960.

President Adolf Schärf A195

1960, Apr. 20 ***Perf. 14x13½***

651 A195 1.50s gray ol 85 35

Issued to honor President Adolf Schärf on his 70th birthday.

Young Hikers and Hostel A196

1960, May 20 ***Perf. 13½x14***

652 A196 1s car rose 30 25

Issued to publicize youth hiking and the youth hostel movement.

Anton Eiselsberg A197 — Gustav Mahler A198

Lithographed and Engraved

1960, June 20 ***Perf. 14x13½***

653 A197 1.50s buff & dk brn 85 30

Issued to commemorate the centenary of the birth of Dr. Anton Eiselsberg, surgeon.

1960, July 7 **Engraved**

654 A198 1.50s chocolate 85 30

Issued to commemorate the centenary of the birth of Gustav Mahler, composer.

Jakob Prandtauer, Melk Abbey A199 — Gross Glockner Mountain Road A200

1960, July 16 **Unwmkd.**

655 A199 1.50s red brn 85 30

Issued to commemorate the 300th anniversary of the birth of Jakob Prandtauer, architect.

1960, Aug. 3

656 A200 1.80s dk bl 85 65

Issued to commemorate the 25th anniversary of the opening of the Gross Glockner Mountain Road.

Europa Issue, 1960

Ionic Capital A201

1960, Aug. 29 ***Perf. 14x13½***

657 A201 3s black 1.75 1.10

Issued to promote the idea of a united Europe.

Griffen, Carinthia A202

Engraved

1960, Oct. 10 ***Perf. 13½x14***

658 A202 1.50s sl grn 50 25

Issued to commemorate the 40th anniversary of the plebiscite which kept Carinthia with Austria.

Flame and Broken Chain A203

Perf. 14x13½

1961, May 8 **Unwmkd.**

659 A203 1.50s scarlet 60 25

Issued to honor the victims in Austria's fight for freedom.

First Austrian Mail Plane, 1918 A204

1961, May 15 ***Perf. 13½x14***

660 A204 5s vio bl 1.50 60

Issued to publicize the Airmail Philatelic Exhibition, LUPOSTA 1961, Vienna, May, 1961.

Transportation by Road, Rail and Waterway A205 — Mountain Mower, by Albin Egger-Lienz A206

Engraved and Typographed

1961, May 29 ***Perf. 13½***

661 A205 3s rose red & ol 75 65

Issued to commemorate the 13th European Conference of Transportation ministers, Vienna, May 29–31.

Engraved

1961, June 12 ***Perf. 13½x14***

Designs: 1.50s, The Kiss, by August von Pettenkofen. 3s, Girl, by Anton Romako. 5s, Ariadne's Triumph, by Hans Makart.

Inscriptions in Red Brown

662 A206 1s rose lake 35 30
663 A206 1.50s dl vio 45 40
664 A206 3s ol grn 1.50 1.50
665 A206 5s bl vio 1.10 1.00

Issued to commemorate the centenary of the Society of Creative Artists, Künstlerhaus, Vienna.

Sonnblick Mountain and Observatory A207 — Mercury and Globe A208

1961, Sept. 1 ***Perf. 14x13½***

666 A207 1.80s vio bl 75 60

Issued to commemorate the 75th anniversary of the establishment of the Sonnblick meteorological observatory.

1961, Sept. 18

667 A208 3s black 1.25 90

Issued to publicize the International Banking Congress, Vienna, Sept. 1961. English inscription listing United Nations financial groups.

Coal Mine Shaft
A209

Designs: 1.50s, Generator. 1.80s, Iron blast furnace. 3s, Pouring steel. 5s, Oil refinery.

Engraved

1961, Sept. 15 ***Perf. 14x13½***

668	A209	1s black	30	25
669	A209	1.50s green	45	35
670	A209	1.80s dk car rose	1.00	95
671	A209	3s brt lil	1.25	1.10
672	A209	5s blue	1.75	1.75
		Nos. 668-672 (5)	4.75	4.40

15th anniversary of nationalized industry.

Arms of Burgenland
A210

Franz Liszt
A211

Engraved and Lithographed

1961, Oct. 9

673	A210	1.50s blk, yel & dk red	75	30

Issued to commemorate the 40th anniversary of Burgenland's joining the Austrian Republic.

1961, Oct. 20 **Engraved**

674	A211	3s dk brn	1.10	90

Issued to commemorate the 150th anniversary of the birth of Franz Liszt, composer.

Parliament
A212

1961, Dec. 18 ***Perf. 13½x14***

675	A212	1s brown	35	25

Issued to commemorate the 200th anniversary of the Austrian Bureau of Budget.

Kaprun-Mooserboden Reservoir
A213

Hydroelectric Power Plants: 1.50s, Ybbs-Persenbeug dam and locks. 1.80s, Lünersee dam and reservoir. 3s, Grossraming dam. 4s, Bisamberg transformer plant. 6.40s, St. Andrä power plant.

1962, March 26 **Unwmkd.**

676	A213	1s vio bl	35	25
677	A213	1.50s red lil	60	35
678	A213	1.80s green	90	90
679	A213	3s brown	80	70
680	A213	4s rose red	80	55
681	A213	6.40s gray	2.75	2.75
		Nos. 676-681 (6)	6.20	5.50

Issued to commemorate the 15th anniversary of the nationalization of the electric power industry.

Johann Nestroy
A214

Friedrich Gauermann
A215

1962, May 25 ***Perf. 14x13½***

682	A214	1s violet	40	25

Issued to commemorate the centenary of the death of Johann Nepomuk Nestroy, Viennese playwright, author and actor.

1962, July 6 **Engraved**

683	A214	1.50s int bl	40	25

Issued to commemorate the centenary of the death of Friedrich Gauermann (1807–1862), landscape painter.

Scout Emblem and Handshake
A216

1962, Oct. 5

684	A216	1.50s dk grn	60	35

Issued to commemorate the 50th anniversary of Austria's Boy Scouts.

Lowlands Forest
A217

Designs: 1.50s, Deciduous forest. 3s, Fir and larch forest.

1962, Oct. 12 ***Perf. 13½x14***

685	A217	1s grnsh gray	38	30
686	A217	1.50s redsh brn	60	45
687	A217	3s dk sl grn	1.50	1.50

Buildings Types of 1957–61

Designs: 30g, City Hall, Vienna. 40g, Porcia Castle, Spittal on the Drau. 60g, Tanners' Tower, Wels. 70g, Residenz Fountain, Salzburg. 80g, Old farmhouse, Pinzgau. 1s, Romanesque columns, Millstatt Abbey. 1.20s, Kornmesser House, Bruck on the Mur. 1.30s, Schatten Castle, Feldkirch, Vorarlberg. 2s, Dragon Fountain, Klagenfurt. 2.20s, Beethoven House, Vienna. 2.50s, Danube Bridge, Linz. 3s, Swiss Gate, Vienna. 3.50s, Esterhazy Palace, Eisenstadt. 8s, City Hall, Steyr. 20s, Melk Abbey

1962–70 **Litho.** ***Perf. 14x13½***

Size: 20x25mm.

688	A176	30g grnsh gray	8	3
689	A176	40g rose red	10	3
690	A176	60g vio brn	10	4
691	A176	70g dk bl	10	3
692	A176	80g yel brn	12	3
693	A176	1s brn ('70)	50	3
694	A176	1.20s red lil	15	3
695	A176	1.30s grn ('67)	18	3
696	A176	2s dk bl ('68)	25	3
697	A176	2.20s green	30	3
698	A176	2.50s violet	35	8
699	A176	3s brt bl	45	3
700	A176	3.50s rose car	50	8
701	A176	8s cl ('65)	1.75	15

Engraved

Perf. 13½

Size: 28x36½mm.

702	A177	20s rose cl ('63)	2.50	45
		Nos. 688-702 (15)	7.43	1.10

Prices for Nos. 688–702 are for stamps on white paper. Some denominations also come on grayish paper with yellowish gum.

Electric Locomotive and Train of 1837
A218

Lithographed and Engraved

1962, Nov. 9 ***Perf. 13½x14***

703	A218	3s buff & blk	1.40	95

125th anniversary of Austrian railroads.

Postilions and Postal Clerk, 1863
A219

Hermann Bahr
A220

1963, May 7 **Photo.** ***Perf. 14x13½***

704	A219	3s dk brn & cit	1.25	95

Issued to commemorate the centenary of the first International Postal Conference, Paris, 1863.

Lithographed and Engraved

1963, July 19 ***Perf. 14x13½***

705	A220	1.50s bl & blk	50	25

Centenary of birth of Hermann Bahr, poet.

St. Florian Statue, Kefermarkt, Contemporary and Old Fire Engines
A221

1963, Aug. 30 **Unwmkd.**

706	A221	1.50s brt rose & blk	55	25

Issued to commemorate the centenary of the Austrian volunteer fire brigades.

Factory, Flag and "ÖGB" on Map of Austria
A222

Lithographed

1963, Sept. 23 ***Perf. 13½x14***

707	A222	1.50s gray, red & dk brn	50	25

Issued to commemorate the 5th Congress of the Austrian Trade Union Federation (ÖGB), Sept. 23–28.

Arms of Austria and Tyrol
A223

1963, Sept. 27 **Unwmkd.**

708	A223	1.50s tan, blk, red & yel	50	25

Issued to commemorate the 600th anniversary of Tyrol's union with Austria.

Prince Eugene of Savoy
A224

Centenary Emblem
A225

Engraved

1963, Oct. 18 ***Perf. 14x13½***

709	A224	1.50s violet	50	25

Issued to commemorate the 300th anniversary of the birth of Prince Eugene of Savoy (1663–1736), Austrian general.

Engraved and Photogravure

1963, Oct. 25 **Unwmkd.**

710	A225	3s blk, sil & red	95	75

Issued to commemorate the centenary of the founding of the International Red Cross.

Slalom
A226

Sports: 1.20s, Biathlon (skier with rifle). 1.50s, Ski jump. 1.80s, Women's figure skating. 2.20s, Ice hockey. 3s, Tobogganing. 4s, Bobsledding.

Photogravure and Engraved

1963, Nov. 11 ***Perf. 13½x14***

Inscriptions in Gold; Athletes in Black

711	A226	1s lt gray	15	10
712	A226	1.20s lt bl	20	20
713	A226	1.50s gray	25	15
714	A226	1.80s pale lil	30	30
715	A226	2.20s lt grn	75	75
716	A226	3s gray	60	60

717	A226	4s grysh bl	1.40	1.40
	Nos. 711-717 (7)		3.65	3.50

Issued to publicize the 9th Winter Olympic Games, Innsbruck, Jan. 29–Feb. 9, 1964.

Baroque Crèche by Josef Thaddäus Stammel
A227

Engraved

1963, Nov. 29 *Perf. 14x13½*

718	A227	2s dk Prus grn	45	25

Nasturtium
A228

Flowers: 1.50s, Peony. 1.80s, Clematis. 2.20s, Dahlia. 3s, Morning glory. 4s, Hollyhock.

Lithographed

1964, Apr. 17 *Perf. 14* Unwmkd.

Gray Background

719	A228	1s yel, grn & dk red	15	15
720	A228	1.50s pink, grn & yel	25	25
721	A228	1.80s lil, grn & yel	50	50
722	A228	2.20s car, grn & yel	60	60
723	A228	3s bl, grn & yel	75	75
724	A228	4s grn, yel & pink	60	60
	Nos. 719-724 (6)		2.85	2.85

Issued to publicize the Vienna International Garden Show, Apr. 16–Oct. 11.

St. Mary Magdalene and Apostle
A229

Pallas Athena and National Council Chamber
A230

1964, May 21 Engraved *Perf. 13½*

725	A229	1.50s bluish blk	40	35

Issued to publicize Romanesque art in Austria. The 12th century stained-glass window is from the Weitensfeld Church, the bust of the Apostle from the portal of St. Stephen's Cathedral, Vienna.

Engraved and Lithographed

1964, May 25 *Perf. 14x13½*

726	A230	1.80s blk & emer	55	45

Issued to commemorate the second Parliamentary and Scientific Conference, Vienna.

The Kiss, by Gustav Klimt
A231

1964, June 5 Litho. *Perf. 13½*

727	A231	3s multi	1.00	85

Issued to commemorate the re-opening of the Vienna Secession, a museum devoted to early 20th century art (art nouveau).

Brother of Mercy and Patient
A232

Perf. 14x13½

1964, June 11 Engr. Unwmkd.

728	A232	1.50s dk bl	40	25

Issued to commemorate the 350th anniversary of the Brothers of Mercy in Austria.

"Bringing the News of Victory at Kunersdorf" by Bernardo Bellotto
A233

"The Post in Art": 1.20s, Changing Horses at Relay Station, by Julius Hörmann. 1.50s, The Honeymoon Trip, by Moritz von Schwind. 1.80s, After the Rain, by Ignaz Raffalt. 2.20s, Mailcoach in the Mountains, by Adam Klein. 3s, Changing Horses at Bavarian Border, by Friedrich Gauermann. 4s, Postal Sleigh (Truck) in the Mountains, by Adalbert Pilch. 6.40s, Saalbach Post Office, by Adalbert Pilch.

1964, June 15 *Perf. 13½x14*

729	A233	1s rose cl	15	10
730	A233	1.20s sepia	35	30
731	A233	1.50s vio bl	25	20
732	A233	1.80s brt vio	50	45
733	A233	2.20s black	40	35
734	A233	3s dl car rose	60	55
735	A233	4s sl grn	75	65
736	A233	6.40s dl cl	2.00	1.90
	Nos. 729-736 (8)		5.00	4.50

Issued to commemorate the 15th Universal Postal Union Congress, Vienna, May-June 1964.

Workers
A234

1964, Sept. 4 *Perf. 14x13½*

737	A234	1s black	30	25

Centenary of Austrian Labor Movement.

Europa Issue, 1964

Common Design Type

Lithographed

1964, Sept. 14 *Perf. 12* Unwmkd.

Size: 21x36mm.

738	CD7	3s dk bl	55	45

Emblem of Radio Austria and Transistor Radio Panel
A235

1964, Oct. 1 Photogravure *Perf. 13½*

739	A235	1s blk brn & red	30	25

Forty years of Radio Austria.

Old Printing Press
A236

Lithographed and Engraved

1964, Oct. 12 *Perf. 14x13½*

740	A236	1.50s tan & blk	30	25

Issued to publicize the 6th Congress of the International Graphic Federation, Vienna, Oct. 12–17.

Pres. Adolf Schärf and Schärf Student Center
A237

Ruins and New Buildings
A238

Typographed and Engraved

1965, Apr. 20 *Perf. 12*

741	A237	1.50s bluish blk	50	35

Issued in memory of Dr. Adolf Schärf (1890–1965), President of Austria (1957–65).

Engraved

1965, Apr. 27 *Perf. 14x13½*

742	A238	1.80s car lake	35	30

Twenty years of reconstruction.

Oldest Seal of Vienna University
A239

St. George, 16th Century Wood Sculpture
A240

Photogravure and Engraved

1965, May 10 *Perf. 14x13½*

743	A239	3s gold & red	60	45

Issued to commemorate the 600th anniversary of the founding of the University of Vienna.

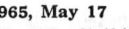

1965, May 17 Engraved

744	A240	1.80s bluish blk	45	40

Issued to publicize the art of the Danube Art School, 1490–1540, in connection with an art exhibition, May–Oct. 1965. The stamp background shows an engraving by Albrecht Altdorfer.

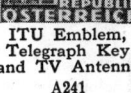

ITU Emblem, Telegraph Key and TV Antenna
A241

Ferdinand Raimund
A242

1965, May 17 Unwmkd.

745	A241	3s vio bl	50	38

Issued to commemorate the centenary of the International Telecommunication Union.

1965 Engraved *Perf. 14x13½*

Portraits: No. 746, Ignaz Philipp Semmelweis. No. 747, Bertha von Suttner. No. 749, Ferdinand Georg Waldmüller.

746	A242	1.50s violet	30	20
747	A242	1.50s bluish blk	25	18
748	A242	3s dk brn	50	35
749	A242	3s grnsh blk	50	35

No. 746 commemorates the centenary of the death of Dr. Ignaz Philipp Semmelweis (1818–65), who discovered the cause of puerperal fever and introduced antisepsis into obstetrics. No. 747, the 60th anniversary of the awarding of the Nobel Prize for Peace to Bertha von Suttner (1843–1914), pacifist and author. No. 748, the 175th anniversary of the birth of Ferdinand Raimund (1790–1836), actor and playwright. No. 749, the centenary of the death of Ferdinand Georg Waldmüller (1793–1865), painter.

Issue dates: No. 746, Aug. 13; No. 747, Dec. 1; No. 748, June 1; No. 749, Aug. 23.

Dancers with Tambourines
A243

Red Cross and Strip of Gauze
A244

Design: 1.50s, Male gymnasts with practice bars.

1965, July 20 Photo. and Engraved

750	A243	1.50s gray & blk	30	25
751	A243	3s bis & blk	60	55

Issued to commemorate the Fourth Gymnaestrada, international athletic meet, Vienna, July 20–24.

1965, Oct. 1 Litho. *Perf. 14x13½*

752	A244	3s blk & red	50	35

Issued to publicize the 20th International Red Cross Conference, Vienna.

Austrian Flag and Eagle with Mural Crown
A245

Austrian Flag, U.N. Headquarters and Emblem
A246

1965, Oct. 7 Photo. and Engraved

753 A245 1.50s gold, red & blk 25 22

Issued to commemorate the 50th anniversary of the Union of Austrian Towns.

Lithographed and Engraved

1965, Oct. 25 *Perf. 12* Unwmkd.

754 A246 3s blk, brt bl & red 1.00 35

Issued to commemorate the 10th anniversary of Austria's admission to the United Nations.

University of Technology, Vienna
A247

1965, Nov. 8 Engraved *Perf. 13½x14*

755 A247 1.50s violet 25 17

Issued to commemorate the 150th anniversary of the founding of the Vienna University of Technology.

Map of Austria with Postal Zone Numbers—A248

1966, Jan. 14 Photo. *Perf. 12*

756 A248 1.50s yel, red & blk 25 10

Issued to publicize the introduction of postal zone numbers, Jan. 1, 1966.

PTT Building, Emblem and Churches of Sts. Maria Rotunda and Barbara
A249

Maria von Ebner Eschenbach
A250

Lithographed and Engraved

1966, March 4 *Perf. 14x13½*

757 A249 1.50s *dl yel* 25 12

Issued to commemorate the centenary of the headquarters of the Post and Telegraph Administration.

1966, March 11 Engraved

758 A250 3s plum 50 30

Issued to commemorate the 50th anniversary of the death of Maria von Ebner Eschenbach (1830–1916), novelist and poet.

Ferris Wheel, Prater
A251

1966, Apr. 19 Engr. *Perf. 14x13½*

759 A251 1.50s sl grn 25 18

Issued to commemorate the 200th anniversary of the opening of the Prater (park), Vienna, to the public by Emperor Joseph II.

Josef Hoffmann
A252

Unwmkd.

1966, May 6 Engraved *Perf. 12*

760 A252 3s dk brn 50 25

Issued to commemorate the tenth anniversary of the death of Josef Hoffmann (1870–1956), architect.

Arms of Wiener Neustadt
A253

Photogravure and Engraved

1966, May 27 *Perf. 14*

761 A253 1.50s gray & multi 25 17

Issued to publicize the Wiener Neustadt Art Exhibition, centered around the time and person of Emperor Frederick III (1440–1493).

Austrian Eagle and Emblem of National Bank
A254

1966, May 27 *Perf. 14*

762 A254 3s gray grn, dk brn & dk grn 50 30

Issued to commemorate the 150th anniversary of the Austrian National Bank.

Puppy
A255

Lithographed and Engraved

1966, June 16 *Perf. 12*

763 A255 1.80s yel & blk 30 20

Issued to commemorate the 120th anniversary of the Vienna Humane Society.

Columbine
A256

Alpine Flowers: 1.80s, Turk's cap. 2.20s, Wulfenia carinthiaca. 3s, Globeflowers. 4s, Fire lily. 5s, Pasqueflower.

Lithographed

1966, Aug. 17 *Perf. 13½* Unwmkd.

Flowers in Natural Colors

764 A256 1.50s dk bl 25 25
765 A256 1.80s dk bl 25 25
766 A256 2.20s dk bl 50 50
767 A256 3s dk bl 70 70
768 A256 4s dk bl 80 80
769 A256 5s dk bl 80 80
Nos. 764-769 (6) 3.30 3.30

Fair Building
A257

1966, Aug. 26 Engr. *Perf. 13½x13*

770 A257 3s vio bl 50 30

First International Fair at Wels.

Peter Anich, Map, Globe and Books
A258

Sick Worker and Health Emblem
A259

1966, Sept. 1 *Perf. 14x13½*

771 A258 1.80s black 30 20

Issued to commemorate the 200th anniversary of the death of Peter Anich (1723–1766), Tirolean cartographer and farmer.

1966, Sept. 19 Engr. and Litho.

772 A259 3s blk & ver 50 30

Issued to publicize the 15th Occupational Medicine Congress, Vienna, Sept. 19–24.

Theater Collection: "Eunuchus" by Terence from a 1496 Edition
A260

Designs: 1.80s, Map Collection: Title page of Geographia Blavania (Cronus, Hercules and celestial sphere). 2.20s, Picture Archive and Portrait Collection: View of Old Vienna after a watercolor by Anton Stutzinger. 3s, Manuscript Collection: Illustration from the 15th century "Livre du Cuer d'Amours Espris" of the Duke René d'Anjou.

Photogravure and Engraved

1966, Sept. 28 *Perf. 13½x14*

773 A260 1.50s multi 20 20
774 A260 1.80s multi 25 25
775 A260 2.20s multi 35 32
776 A260 3s multi 40 40

Austrian National Library.

Young Girl
A261

Lithographed and Engraved

1966, Oct. 3 *Perf. 14x13½*

777 A261 3s lt bl & blk 45 30

Issued to commemorate the 10th anniversary of the "Save the Child" society.

Strawberries
A262

Coat of Arms of University of Linz
A263

Fruit: 1s, Grapes. 1.50s, Apple. 1.80s, Blackberries. 2.20s, Apricots. 3s, Cherries.

1966, Nov. 25 Photo. *Perf. 13½x13*

778 A262 50g multi 22 22
779 A262 1s multi 20 20
780 A262 1.50s multi 20 20
781 A262 1.80s multi 30 28
782 A262 2.20s multi 30 28
783 A262 3s multi 35 35
Nos. 778-783 (6) 1.57 1.53

Photogravure and Engraved

1966, Dec. 9 *Perf. 14x13½*

784 A263 3s gray, blk, red, sil & gold 50 30

Issued to commemorate the inauguration of the Universary of Linz, Oct. 8, 1966.

Ice Skater, 1866
A264

Ballet Dancer
A265

Photogravure and Engraved

1967, Feb. 3 *Perf. 14x13½*

785 A264 3s pale bl & dk bl 50 30

Centenary of Vienna Ice Skating Club.

1967, Feb. 15 Engr. *Perf. 11½x12*

786 A265 3s dp cl 50 35
a. Perf. 12 2.25 1.75

Issued to commemorate the centenary of the "Blue Danube" waltz by Johann Strauss.

Karl Schönherr
A266

1967, Feb. 24 Engr. *Perf. 14x13½*

787 A266 3s gray brn 50 30

Issued to commemorate the centenary of the birth of Dr. Karl Schönherr (1867–1943), poet, playwright and physician.

Ice Hockey Goalkeeper
A267

Photogravure and Engraved

1967, March 17 ***Perf. 13½x14***

788 A267 3s pale grn & dk bl 50 30

Issued to publicize the Ice Hockey Championships, Vienna, March 18–29.

Violin, Organ and Laurel
A268

1967, Mar. 28 **Engr.** ***Perf. 13½***

789 A268 3.50s indigo 55 35

Issued to commemorate the 125th anniversary of the Vienna Philharmonic Orchestra.

Motherhood, Watercolor by Peter Fendi
A269

Lithographed

1967, Apr. 28 ***Perf. 14*** **Unwmkd.**

790 A269 2s multi 35 25

Issued for Mother's Day, 1967.

Gothic Mantle Madonna
A270

1967, May 19 **Engr.** ***Perf. 13½x14***

791 A270 3s slate 45 30

Issued to publicize the art exhibition "Austrian Gothic," Krems, 1967. The Gothic wood carving is from Frauenstein in Upper Austria.

Medieval Gold Cross
A271

Swan, Tapestry by Oscar Kokoschka
A272

Lithographed and Engraved

1967, June 9 ***Perf. 13½***

792 A271 3.50s Prus grn & multi 55 40

Issued to publicize the Salzburg Treasure Chamber in connection with an exhibition at Salzburg Cathedral, June 12–Sept. 15.

1967, June 9 **Photogravure**

793 A272 2s multi 32 25

Issued to publicize the Nibelungen District Art Exhibition, Pöchlarn, celebrating the 700th anniversary of Pöchlarn as a city. The design is from the border of the Amor and Psyche tapestry at the Salzburg Festival Theater.

View and Arms of Vienna
A273

Engraved and Photogravure

1967, June 12 ***Perf. 13x13½***

794 A273 3s blk & red 50 30

Issued to publicize the 10th Europa Talks, "Science and Society in Europe," Vienna, June 13–17.

Prize Bull "Mucki"
A274

1967, Aug. 28 **Engr.** ***Perf. 13½***

795 A274 2s dp cl 35 25

Issued to commemorate the centenary of the Ried Festival and the Agricultural Fair.

Potato Beetle
A275

Engraved and Photogravure

1967, Aug. 29 ***Perf. 13½x14***

796 A275 3s blk & multi 30 30

Issued to publicize the 6th International Congress for Plant Protection, Vienna.

First Locomotive Used on Brenner Pass—A276

1967, Sept. 23 **Photo.** ***Perf. 12***

797 A276 3.50s tan & sl grn 35 40

Centenary of railroad over Brenner Pass.

Christ in Glory
A277

1967, Oct. 9 ***Perf. 13½***

798 A277 2s multi 35 30

Issued to commemorate the restoration of the Romanesque (11th century) frescoes in the Lambach monastery church.

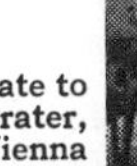

Main Gate to Fair, Prater, Vienna
A278

1967, Oct. 24 **Photo.** ***Perf. 13½x14***

799 A278 2s choc & buff 35 30

Issued to publicize the Congress of International Trade Fairs, Vienna, Oct., 1967.

Medal Showing Minerva and Art Symbols
A279

Frankfurt Medal for Reformation, 1717
A280

Lithographed and Engraved

1967, Oct. 25 ***Perf. 13½***

800 A279 2s dk brn, dk bl & yel 35 30

Issued to commemorate the 275th anniversary of the Vienna Academy of Fine Arts. The medal was designed by Georg Raphael Donner (1693–1741) and is awarded as an artist's prize.

1967, Oct. 31 **Engr.** ***Perf. 14x13½***

801 A280 3.50s bl blk 55 35

450th anniversary of the Reformation.

Mountain Range and Stone Pines
A281

1967, Nov. 7 ***Perf. 13½***

802 A281 3.50s green 55 35

Centenary of academic study of forestry.

Land Survey Monument, 1770
A282

St. Leopold, Window, Heiligenkreuz Abbey
A283

1967, Nov. 7 **Photogravure**

803 A282 2s ol blk 35 25

150th anniversary of official land records.

1967, Nov. 15 **Engr. & Photo.**

804 A283 1.80s multi 35 30

Issued in memory of Margrave Leopold III (1075–1136), patron saint of Austria.

Tragic Mask and Violin
A284

Nativity from 15th Century Altar
A285

1967, Nov. 17 ***Perf. 13½***

805 A284 3.50s bluish lil & blk 55 35

Issued to commemorate the 150th anniversary of the Academy of Music and Dramatic Art.

1967, Nov. 27 **Engr.** ***Perf. 14x13½***

806 A285 2s green 35 25

Christmas 1967.

The design shows the late Gothic carved center panel of the altar in St. John's Chapel in Nonnberg Convent, Salzburg.

Innsbruck Stadium, Alps and FISU Emblem
A286

Camillo Sitte
A287

1968, Jan. 22 **Engraved** ***Perf. 13½***

807 A286 2s dk bl 40 25

Issued to publicize the Winter University Games under the auspices of FISU (Fédération Internationale du Sport Universitaire), Innsbruck, Jan. 21–28.

1968, Apr. 17 ***Perf. 13½***

808 A287 2s blk brn 40 25

Issued to commemorate the 125th anniversary of the birth of Camillo Sitte (1843–1903), architect and city planner.

Mother and Child
A288

Cup and Serpent Emblem
A289

1968, May 7

809 A288 2s sl grn 40 25

Issued for Mother's Day, 1968.

1968, May 7 **Photogravure**

810 A289 3.50s dp plum, gray & gold 55 40

Bicentenary of the Veterinary College.

Bride with Lace Veil
A290

1968, May 24 Engraved *Perf. 12*

811 A290 3.50s bl blk 55 40

Issued to commemorate the centenary of the embroidery industry of Vorarlberg.

Horse Race
A291

1968, June 4 *Perf. 13½*

812 A291 3.50s sepia 60 50

Issued to commemorate the centenary of horse racing at Freudenau, Vienna.

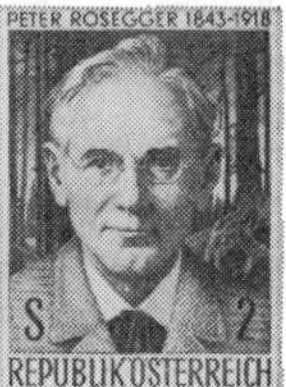

Dr. Karl Landsteiner A292 — Peter Rosegger A293

1968, June 14 *Perf. 14x13½*

813 A292 3.50s dk bl 60 50

Issued to commemorate the centenary of the birth of Dr. Karl Landsteiner (1868–1943), pathologist, discoverer of the four main human blood types.

1968, June 26

814 A293 2s sl grn 35 25

Issued to commemorate the 50th anniversary of the death of Peter Rosegger (1843–1918), poet and writer.

Angelica Kauffmann, Self-portrait A294 — Bronze Statue of Young Man, 1st Century B.C. A295

1968, July 15 Engr. *Perf. 14x13½*

815 A294 2s int blk 35 25

Issued to publicize the art exhibitions "Angelica Kauffmann and her Contemporaries," Bregenz, July 28–Oct. 13, 1968, and Vienna, Oct. 22, 1968–January 6, 1969.

1968, July 15 Litho. and Engr.

816 A295 2s grnsh gray & blk 35 25

Issued to publicize 20 years of excavations on Magdalene Mountain, Carinthia.

Bishop, Romanesque Bas-relief
A296

1968, Sept. 20 Engr. *Perf. 14x13½*

817 A296 2s bl gray 35 25

Issued to commemorate the 750th anniversary of the Graz-Seckau Bishopric.

Koloman Moser A297 — Human Rights Flame—A298

Engraved and Photogravure

1968, Oct. 18 *Perf. 12*

818 A297 2s blk brn & ver 35 25

Issued to commemorate the 50th anniversary of the death of Koloman Moser (1868–1918), stamp designer and painter.

1968, Oct. 18 Photo. *Perf. 14x13½*

819 A298 1.50s gray, dp car & dk grn 80 35

International Human Rights Year.

Pres. Karl Renner and States' Arms
A299

Designs: No. 821, Coats of arms of Austria and Austrian states. No. 822, Article I of Austrian Constitution and States' coats of arms.

Engraved and Photogravure

1968 Nov. 11 *Perf. 13½*

820 A299 2s blk & multi 65 60
821 A299 2s blk & multi 65 60
822 A299 2s blk & multi 65 60

50th anniversary of Republic of Austria.

Crèche, Memorial Chapel, Oberndorf-Salzburg
A300

Perf. 14x13½

1968, Nov. 29 Engraved

823 A300 2s sl grn 35 25

Christmas 1968. 150th anniversary of "Silent Night, Holy Night."

Angels, from Last Judgment by Troger (Röhrenbach-Greillenstein Chapel)—A301

Baroque Frescoes: No. 825, Vanquished Demons, by Paul Troger, Altenburg Abbey. No. 826, Sts. Peter and Paul, by Troger, Melk Abbey. No. 827, The Glorification of Mary, by Franz Anton Maulpertsch, Maria Treu Church, Vienna. No. 828, St. Leopold Carried into Heaven, by Maulpertsch, Ebenfurth Castle Chapel. No. 829, Symbolic figures from The Triumph of Apollo, by Maulpertsch, Halbthurn Castle.

Engraved and Photogravure

1968, Dec. 11 *Perf. 13½x14*

824 A301 2s multi 60 60
825 A301 2s multi 60 60
826 A301 2s multi 60 60
827 A301 2s multi 60 60
828 A301 2s multi 60 60
829 A301 2s multi 60 60
Nos. 824-829 (6) 3.60 3.60

St. Stephen
A302

Statues in St. Stephen's Cathedral, Vienna: No. 831, St. Paul. No. 832, Mantle Madonna. No. 833, St. Christopher. No. 834, St. George and the Dragon. No. 835, St. Sebastian.

1969, Jan. 28 Engraved *Perf. 13½*

830 A302 2s black 60 60
831 A302 2s rose cl 60 60
832 A302 2s gray vio 60 60
833 A302 2s sl bl 60 60
834 A302 2s sl grn 60 60
835 A302 2s dk red brn 60 60
Nos. 830-835 (6) 3.60 3.60

500th anniversary of Diocese of Vienna.

Parliament and Pallas Athena Fountain, Vienna
A303

1969, Apr. 8 Engraved *Perf. 13½*

836 A303 2s grnsh blk 35 25

Issued to publicize the Interparliamentary Union Conference, Vienna, Apr. 7–13.

Europa Issue, 1969
Common Design Type

1969, Apr. 28 Photo. *Perf. 12*

837 CD12 2s gray grn, brick red & bl 45 35

Council of Europe Emblem
A304

1969, May 5

838 A304 3.50s gray, ultra, blk & yel 90 60

20th anniversary of Council of Europe.

Frontier Guards
A305

Engraved and Photogravure

1969, May 14 *Perf. 12*

839 A305 2s sep & red 35 25

Honor to Austrian Federal Army.

Don Giovanni, by Mozart A306 — Gothic Armor of Maximilian I A307

1969, May 23 *Perf. 13½*

840 A306 Sheet of 8, gold, red & brn blk 6.50 6.50
- *a.* 2s *Don Giovanni, Mozart* 65 65
- *b.* 2s *Magic Flute, Mozart* 65 65
- *c.* 2s *Fidelio, Beethoven* 65 65
- *d.* 2s *Lohengrin, Wagner* 65 65
- *e.* 2s *Don Carlos, Verdi* 65 65
- *f.* 2s *Carmen, Bizet* 65 65
- *g.* 2s *Rosencavalier, Richard Strauss* 65 65
- *h.* 2s *Swan Lake, Ballet by Tchaikovsky* 65 65

Centenary of Vienna Opera House.

No. 840 contains 8 stamps arranged around gold and red center label showing Opera House. Printed in sheets containing 4 Nos. 840 with wide gutters between.

1969, June 4 Engraved

841 A307 2s bluish blk 35 25

Issued to publicize the Emperor Maximilian I Exhibition, Innsbruck, May 30–Oct. 5.

Oldest Municipal Seal of Vienna A308 — Girl's Head and Village House A309

1969, June 16 Photo. *Perf. 13½*

842 A308 2s tan, red & blk 35 25

Issued to publicize the 19th Congress of the International Organization of Municipalities, Vienna, June 1969.

Engraved and Photogravure

1969, June 16 *Perf. 13½x14*

843 A309 2s yel grn & sep 35 25

Issued to publicize the 20th anniversary of the Children's Village Movement in Austria (SOS Villages).

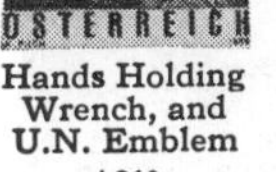
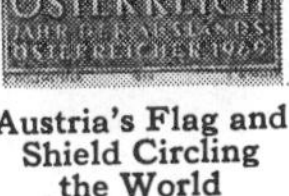

Hands Holding Wrench, and U.N. Emblem
A310

Austria's Flag and Shield Circling the World
A311

1969, Aug. 22 Photo. ***Perf. 13x13½***

844	A310	2s dp grn	35	25

Issued to commemorate the 50th anniversary of the International Labor Organization.

Engraved and Lithographed

1969, Aug. 22 ***Perf. 14x13½***

845	A311	3.50s sl & red	55	40

Issued to publicize 1969 as the Year of Austrians Living Abroad.

Young Hare, by Dürer
A312

Etchings: No. 847, El Cid Killing a Bull, by Francisco de Goya. No. 848, Madonna with the Pomegranate, by Raphael. No. 849, The Painter, by Peter Brueghel. No. 850, Rubens' Son Nicolas, by Rubens. No. 851, Self-portrait, by Rembrandt. No. 852, Lady Reading, by Francois Guerin. No. 853, Wife of the Artist, by Egon Schiele.

Engraved and Photogravure

1969, Sept. 26 ***Perf. 13½***

Gray Frame, Buff Background

846	A312	2s blk & brn	50	45
847	A312	2s black	50	45
848	A312	2s black	50	45
849	A312	2s black	50	45
850	A312	2s blk & sal	50	45
851	A312	2s black	50	45
852	A312	2s blk & sal	50	45
853	A312	2s black	50	45
		Nos. 846-853 (8)	4.00	3.60

Bicentenary of the etching collection in the Albertina, Vienna.

President Franz Jonas
A313

1969, Oct. 3

854	A313	2s gray & vio bl	35	25

Issued to commemorate the 70th birthday of Franz Jonas, president of Austria.

Post Horn, Globe and Lightning
A314

1969, Oct. 17 ***Perf. 13½x14***

855	A314	2s multi	35	25

Issued to commemorate the 50th anniversary of the Union of Postal and Telegraph employees.

Savings Box, about 1450
A315

Madonna, by Albin Egger-Lienz
A316

1969, Oct. 31 Photo. ***Perf. 13x13½***

856	A315	2s sil & sl grn	35	25

Issued to publicize the importance of savings.

Engraved and Photogravure

1969, Nov. 24 ***Perf. 12***

857	A316	2s dp cl & pale yel	35	25

Christmas 1969.

Josef Schöffel
A317

St. Klemens M. Hofbauer
A318

1970, Feb. 6 Engr. ***Perf. 14x13½***

858	A317	2s dl pur	35	25

Issued to commemorate the 60th anniversary of the death of Josef Schöffel, (1832–1910), who saved the Vienna Woods.

Engraved and Photogravure

1970, Mar. 13 ***Perf. 14x13½***

859	A318	2s dk brn & lt tan	35	25

Issued to commemorate the 150th anniversary of the death of St. Klemens Maria Hofbauer (1751–1820); Redemptorist preacher in Poland and Austria, canonized in 1909.

Chancellor Leopold Figl
A319

Belvedere Palace, Vienna
A320

1970, Apr. 27 Engraved ***Perf. 13½***

860	A319	2s dk ol gray	45	27
861	A320	2s dk rose brn	45	27

25th anniversary of Second Republic.

Krimml Waterfalls
A321

1970, May 19 Engraved ***Perf. 13½***

862	A321	2s sl grn	35	25

Issued for the European Nature Conservation Year, 1970.

St. Leopold on Oldest Seal of Innsbruck University
A322

Lithographed and Engraved

1970, June 5 ***Perf. 13½***

863	A322	2s red & blk	35	25

Issued to commemorate the 300th anniversary of the founding of the Leopold Franzens University in Innsbruck.

Organ, Great Hall, Music Academy
A323

Photogravure and Engraved

1970, June 5 ***Perf. 14***

864	A323	2s gold & dp cl	35	25

Issued to commemorate the centenary of the Vienna Music Academy Building.

Tower Clock, 1450–1550
A324

The Beggar Student, by Carl Millöcker
A325

Old Clocks from Vienna Horological Museum: No. 866, Lyre clock, 1790–1815. No. 867, Pendant clock 1600–1650. No. 868, Pendant watch, 1800–1830. No. 869, Bracket clock, 1720–1760. No. 870, French column clock, 1820–1850.

1970

865	A324	1.50s buff & sep	45	45
866	A324	1.50s grnsh & grn	45	45
867	A324	2s pale & dk bl	50	50
868	A324	2s pale rose & lake	50	50
869	A324	3.50s buff & brn	80	80
870	A324	3.50s pale lil & brn vio	80	80
		Nos. 865-870 (6)	3.50	3.50

Issue dates: Nos. 865, 867, 869, June 22. Others, Oct. 23.

1970 Photo. and Engr. ***Perf. 13½***

Operettas: No. 872, Fledermaus, by Johann Strauss. No. 873, The Dream Waltz, by Oscar Strauss. No. 874, The Bird Seller, by Carl Zeller. No. 875, The Merry Widow, by Franz Lehar. No. 876, Two Hearts in Three-quarter Time, by Robert Stolz.

871	A325	1.50s pale grn & grn	45	45
872	A325	1.50s yel & vio bl	45	45
873	A325	2s pale rose & vio brn	50	50
874	A325	2s pale grn & sep	50	50
875	A325	3.50s pale bl & ind	80	80
876	A325	3.50s beige & sl	80	80
		Nos. 871-876 (6)	3.50	3.50

Issue dates: Nos. 871, 873, 875, July 3. Others Sept. 11.

Bregenz Festival Stage
A326

1970, July 23 Photogravure

877	A326	3.50s dk bl & buff	60	50

25th anniversary of Bregenz Festival.

Salzburg Festival Emblem
A327

1970, July 27 ***Perf. 14***

878	A327	3.50s blk, red, gold & gray	60	50

50th anniversary of Salzburg Festival.

St. John, by Thomas Schwanthaler
A328

1970, Aug. 31 Engraved

879	A328	3.50s dk gray	60	45

Issued to publicize the 13th General Assembly of the World Veterans Federation, Aug. 28–Sept. 4. The head of St. John is from a sculpture showing the Agony in the Garden in the chapel of the Parish Church in Ried. It is attributed to Thomas Schwanthaler (1634–1702).

Thomas Koschat
A329

1970, Sept. 16 *Perf. 14x13½*

880 A329 2s chocolate 35 25

Issued to commemorate the 125th anniversary of the birth of Thomas Koschat (1845–1914), Carinthian composer of songs.

Mountain Scene
A330

1970, Sept. 16 Photo. *Perf. 14x13½*

881 A330 2s vio bl & pink 35 25

Issued to publicize hiking and mountaineering in Austria.

Alfred Cossmann
A331

Arms of Carinthia
A332

1970, Oct. 2 Engraved *Perf. 14x13½*

882 A331 2s dk brn 35 25

Issued to commemorate the centenary of the birth of Alfred Cossmann (1870–1951), engraver.

Photogravure and Engraved

1970, Oct. 2 *Perf. 14*

883 A332 2s ol, red, gold, blk & sil 35 25

Carinthian plebiscite, 50th anniversary.

U.N. Emblem
A333

1970, Oct. 23 Litho. *Perf. 14x13½*

884 A333 3.50s lt bl & blk 80 50

25th anniversary of the United Nations.

Adoration of the Shepherds, Carving from Garsten Vicarage
A334

1970, Nov. 27 Engr. *Perf. 13½x14*

885 A334 2s dk vio bl 35 25

Christmas 1970.

Karl Renner
A335

Beethoven, by Georg Waldmüller
A336

1970, Dec. 14 Engr. *Perf. 14x13½*

886 A335 2s dp cl 35 25

Centenary of the birth of Karl Renner (1870–1950), President of Austria.

Photogravure and Engraved

1970, Dec. 16 *Perf. 13½*

887 A336 3.50s blk & buff 60 50

Bicentenary of the birth of Ludwig van Beethoven (1770–1827), composer.

Enrica Handel-Mazzetti
A337

1971, Jan. 11 Engr. *Perf. 14x13½*

888 A337 2s sepia 35 25

Centenary of the birth of Enrica von Handel-Mazzetti (1871–1955), novelist and poet.

"Watch Out for Children!"
A338

1971, Feb. 18 Photo. *Perf. 13½*

889 A338 2s blk, red brn & brt grn 50 35

Traffic safety.

Saltcellar, by Benvenuto Cellini
A339

Art Treasures: 1.50s, Covered vessel, made of prase, gold and precious stones, Florentine, 1580. 2s, Emperor Joseph I, ivory statue by Matthias Steinle, 1693.

Photogravure and Engraved

1971, March 22 *Perf. 14*

890 A339 1.50s gray & sl grn 45 45
891 A339 2s gray & dp plum 50 50
892 A339 3.50s gray, blk & bis 80 80

Emblem of Austrian Wholesalers' Organization
A340

1971, Apr. 16 Photo. *Perf. 13½*

893 A340 3.50s multi 60 50

International Chamber of Commerce, 23rd Congress, Vienna, Apr. 17–23.

Jacopo de Strada, by Titian
A341

Seal of Paulus of Franchenfordia, 1380—A342

Paintings in Vienna Museum: 2s, Village Feast, by Peter Brueghel, the Elder. 3.50s, Young Venetian Woman, by Albrecht Dürer.

1971, May 6 Engraved *Perf. 13½*

894 A341 1.50s rose lake 45 45
895 A341 2s grnsh blk 50 50
896 A341 3.50s dp brn 80 80

Photogravure and Engraved

1971, May 6 *Perf. 13½x14*

897 A342 3.50s dk brn & bis 60 50

Congress commemorating the centenary of the Austrian Notaries' Statute, May 5–8.

St. Matthew
A343

August Neilreich
A344

1971, May 27 *Perf. 12½x13½*

898 A343 2s brt rose lil & brn 35 25

Exhibition of "1000 Years of Art in Krems." The statue of St. Matthew is from the Lentl Altar, created about 1520 by the Master of the Pulkau Altar.

1971, June 1 Engr. *Perf. 14x13½*

899 A344 2s brown 35 25

Centenary of the death of August Neilreich (1803–1871), botanist.

Singer with Lyre
A345

Photogravure and Engraved

1971, July 1 *Perf. 13½x14*

900 A345 4s lt bl, vio bl & gold 85 75

International Choir Festival, Vienna, July 1–4.

Coat of Arms of Kitzbuhel
A346

1971, Aug. 23 *Perf. 14*

901 A346 2.50s gold & multi 45 35

700th anniversary of the town of Kitzbuhel.

Vienna Stock Exchange—A347

1971, Sept. 1 Engr. *Perf. 13½x14*

902 A347 4s redsh brn 65 45

Bicentenary of the Vienna Stock Exchange.

First and Latest Exhibition Halls
A348

1971, Sept. 6 Photo. *Perf. 13½x13*

903 A348 2.50s dp rose lil 45 30

50th anniversary of Vienna International Fair.

Trade Union Emblem
A349

Arms of Burgenland
A350

1971, Sept. 20 *Perf. 14x13½*

904 A349 2s gray, buff & red 35 25

25th anniversary of Austrian Trade Union Association.

1971, Oct. 1

905 A350 2s dk bl, gold, red & blk 35 25

50th anniversary of Burgenland's joining Austria.

Marcus Car
A351

Photogravure and Engraved

1971, Oct. 1 *Perf. 14*

906 A351 4s pale grn & blk 65 50

75th anniversary of the Austrian Automobile, Motorcycle and Touring Club.

Europa Bridge
A352

1971, Oct. 8 Engr. *Perf. 14x13½*

907 A352 4s vio bl 65 50

Opening of highway over Brenner Pass.

Styria's Iron Mountain
A353

Designs: 2s, Austrian Nitrogen Products, Ltd., Linz. 4s, United Austrian Iron and Steel Works, Ltd. (VÖEST), Linz Harbor.

1971, Oct. 15 *Perf. 13½*

908 A353 1.50s redsh brn 30 30
909 A353 2s bluish blk 45 40
910 A353 4s dk sl grn 70 65

25 years of nationalized industry.

High-speed Train on Semmering Pass—A354

Trout Fisherman
A355

1971, Oct. 21 *Perf. 14*

911 A354 2s claret 35 25

Inter-city rapid train service.

1971, Nov. 15 *Perf. 13½*

912 A355 2s dk red brn 35 25

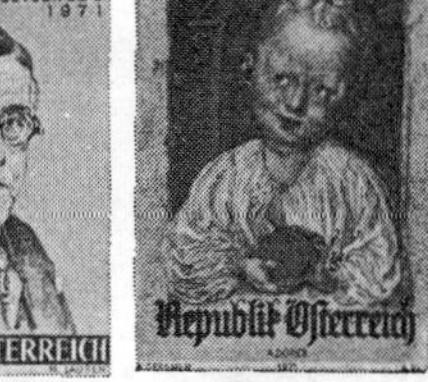

Erich Tschermak-Seysenegg
A356

Infant Jesus as Savior, by Dürer
A357

Photogravure and Engraved

1971, Nov. 15 *Perf. 14x13½*

913 A356 2s pale ol & dk pur 35 25

Centenary of the birth of Dr. Erich Tschermak-Seysenegg (1871–1962), botanist.

1971, Nov. 26 *Perf. 13½*

914 A357 2s gold & multi 35 25

Christmas 1971.

Franz Grillparzer, by Moritz Daffinger
A358

Fountain, Main Square, Friesach
A359

Lithographed and Engraved

1972, Jan. 21 *Perf. 14x13½*

915 A358 2s buff, gold & blk 35 25

Death centenary of Franz Grillparzer (1791–1872), dramatic poet.

1972, Feb. 23 Engr. *Perf. 14x13½*

Designs: 2s, Fountain, Heiligenkreuz Abbey. 2.50s, Leopold Fountain, Innsbruck.

916 A359 1.50s rose lil 30 25
917 A359 2s brown 40 35
918 A359 2.50s olive 60 60

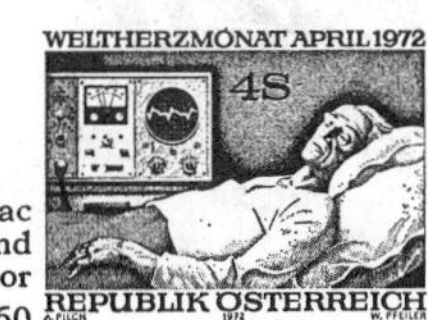

Cardiac Patient and Monitor
A360

1972, Apr. 11 *Perf. 13½x14*

919 A360 4s vio brn 65 35

World Health Day 1972.

St. Michael's Gate, Royal Palace, Vienna
A361

1972, Apr. 11 *Perf. 14x13½*

920 A361 4s vio bl 70 60

Conference of European Post and Telecommunications Ministers, Vienna, Apr. 11–14.

Sculpture, Gurk Cathedral
A362

Photogravure and Engraved

1972, May 5 *Perf. 14*

921 A362 2s gold & dk brn vio 35 25

900th anniversary of Gurk (Carinthia) Diocese. The design is after the central column supporting the sarcophagus of St. Hemma in Gurk Cathedral.

City Hall, Congress Emblem
A363

1972, May 23 Litho. and Engr.

922 A363 4s red, blk & yel 65 50

9th International Congress of Public and Cooperative Economy, Vienna, May 23–25.

Power Line in Carnic Alps
A364

Designs: 2.50s, Power Station, Simmering. 4s, Zemm Power Station (lake in Zillertaler Alps).

1972, June 28 *Perf. 13½x14*

923 A364 70g gray & vio 15 15
924 A364 2.50s gray & red brn 45 40
925 A364 4s gray & sl 60 55

25 years of nationalization of the power industry.

Runner with Olympic Torch
A365

St. Hermes, by Conrad Laib
A366

Engraved and Photogravure

1972, Aug. 21 *Perf. 14x13½*

926 A365 2s sep & red 35 25

Olympic torch relay from Olympia, Greece, to Munich, Germany, passing through Austria.

1972, Aug. 21 Engraved

927 A366 2s vio brn 35 25

Exhibition of Late Gothic Art, Salzburg.

Pears
A367

1972, Sept. *Perf. 14*

928 A367 2.50s dk bl & multi 45 35

World Congress of small plot Gardeners, Vienna, Sept. 7–10.

Souvenir Sheet

Spanish Walk
A368

1972, Sept. 12 *Perf. 13½*

929 A368 Sheet of 6, gold, car & dk brn 4.00 4.00
a. 2s *Spanish walk* 45 45
b. 2s *Piaffe* 45 45
c. 2.50s *Levade* 55 55
d. 2.50s *On long rein* 55 55
e. 4s *Capriole* 80 80
f. 4s *Courbette* 80 80

400th anniversary of the Spanish Riding School in Vienna. Gold and carmine margin. Size: 135x180mm.

Arms of University of Agriculture
A369

Church and Old University
A370

Photogravure and Engraved

1972, Oct. 17 *Perf. 14x13½*

930 A369 2s blk & multi 40 25

Centenary of the University of Agriculture, Vienna.

1972, Nov. 7 Engraved

931 A370 4s red brn 65 50

350th anniversary of the Paris Lodron University, Salzburg.

Carl Michael Ziehrer
A371

1972, Nov. 14

932 A371 2s rose cl 40 25

50th anniversary of the death of Carl Michael Ziehrer (1843–1922), composer.

Virgin and Child, Wood, 1420–30
A372

Photogravure and Engraved

1972, Dec. 1 *Perf. 13½*

933 A372 2s ol & choc 40 25

Christmas 1972.

Racing Sleigh, 1750
A373

Designs: 2s, Coronation landau, 1824. 2.50s, Imperial state coach, 1763.

1972, Dec. 12

934 A373 1.50s pale gray & brn 40 30
935 A373 2s pale gray & sl grn 45 45
936 A373 2.50s pale gray & plum 55 55

Collection of historic state coaches and carriages in Schönbrunn Palace.

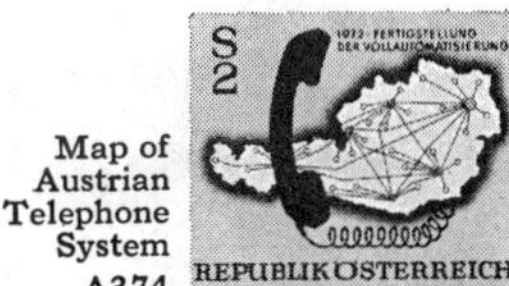

Map of Austrian Telephone System
A374

1972, Dec. 14 Photo. *Perf. 14*

937 A374 2s yel & blk 35 25

Completion of automation of Austrian telephone system.

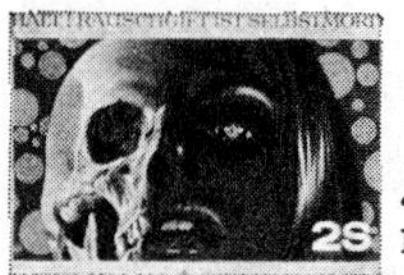

"Drugs are Death"
A375

1973, Jan. 26 Photo. *Perf. 13½x14*

938	A375	2s scar & multi	2.50	75

Fight against drug abuse.

Alfons Petzold A376 — Theodor Körner A377

1973, Jan. 26 Engr. *Perf. 14x13½*

939	A376	2s redsh brn	40	25

50th anniversary of the death of Alfons Petzold (1882–1923), poet.

Photogravure and Engraved

1973, Apr. 24 *Perf. 14x13½*

940	A377	2s gray & dp cl	40	25

Centenary of the birth of Theodor Körner (1873–1957), President of Austria.

Douglas DC-9
A378

1973, May 14 *Perf. 13½x14*

941	A378	2s vio bl & rose red	40	25

Austrian aviation anniversaries: First international airmail service Vienna to Kiev, Mar. 31, 1918, 55th anniversary; Austrian Aviation Corporation, 50th anniversary; Austrian Airlines, 15th anniversary.

Otto Loewi A379 — "Support" A380

1973, June 4 Engr. *Perf. 14x13½*

942	A379	4s dp vio	65	50

Centenary of the birth of Otto Loewi (1873–1961), pharmacologist, winner of 1936 Nobel prize.

1973, June 25

943	A380	2s dk bl	40	25

Federation of Austrian Social Insurance Institutes, 25th anniversary.

Europa Issue 1973

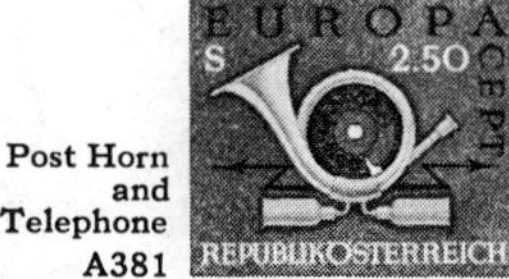

Post Horn and Telephone
A381

1973, July 9 Photo. *Perf. 14*

944	A381	2.50s ocher, blk & yel	45	35

Dornbirn Fair Emblem
A382

1973, July 27 *Perf. 13½x14*

945	A382	2s multi	40	25

Dornbirn Trade Fair, 25th anniversary.

Hurdles A383 — Leo Slezak A384

1973, Aug. 13 Engr. *Perf. 14x13½*

946	A383	4s gray ol	65	50

23rd International Military Pentathlon Championships, Wiener Neustadt, Aug. 13–18.

1973, Aug. 17 *Perf. 14*

947	A384	4s dk brn	65	50

Centenary of the birth of Leo Slezak (1873–1946), operatic tenor.

Gate, Vienna Hofburg, and ISI Emblem
A385

Photogravure and Engraved

1973, Aug. 20 *Perf. 14x13½*

948	A385	2s gray, dk brn & ver	40	25

39th Congress of International Statistical Institute, Vienna, Aug. 20–30.

Tegetthoff off Franz Josef Land, by Julius Prayer
A386

1973, Aug. 30 Engr. *Perf. 13½x14*

949	A386	2.50s Prus grn	45	35

Centenary of the discovery of Franz Josef Land by an Austrian North Pole expedition.

Academy of Science, by Canaletto
A387

1973, Sept. 4

950	A387	2.50s violet	45	35

Centenary of international meteorological cooperation.

Arms of Viennese Tanners A388 — Max Reinhardt A389

Photogravure and Engraved

1973, Sept. 4 *Perf. 14*

951	A388	4s red & multi	65	50

13th Congress of the International Union of Leather Chemists' Societies, Vienna, Sept. 1—7.

1973, Sept. 7 Engr. *Perf. 13x13½*

952	A389	2s rose mag	40	25

Centenary of the birth of Max Reinhardt (1873–1943), theatrical director and stage manager.

Trotter
A390

1973, Sept. 28 *Perf. 13½*

953	A390	2s green	40	25

Centenary of Vienna Trotting Association.

Ferdinand Hanusch
A391

1973, Sept. 28 *Perf. 14x13½*

954	A391	2s rose brn	40	25

50th anniversary of the death of Ferdinand Hanusch (1866–1923), secretary of state.

Police Radio Operator
A392

1973, Oct. 2 *Perf. 13½x14*

955	A392	4s vio bl	65	50

50th anniversary of International Criminal Police Organization (INTERPOL).

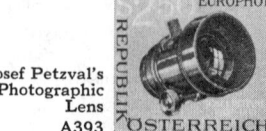

Josef Petzval's Photographic Lens
A393

Lithographed and Engraved

1973, Oct. 8 *Perf. 14*

956	A393	2.50s bl & multi	45	35

EUROPHOT Photographic Congress, Vienna.

Emperor's Spring, Hell Valley
A394

Photogravure and Engraved

1973, Oct. 23 *Perf. 13½x14*

957	A394	2s sep, bl & red	40	25

Centenary of Vienna's first mountain spring water supply system.

Almsee, Upper Austria A395 — Hofburg and Prince Eugene Statue, Vienna A395a

Designs: 50g, Farmhouses, Zillertal, Tirol. 1s, Kahlenbergerdorf. 1.50s, Bludenz, Vorarlberg. 2s, Inn Bridge, Alt Finstermunz. 2.50s, Murau, Styria. 3s, Bischofsmütze, Salzburg. 3.50s, Easter Church, Oberwart. 4.50s, Windmill, Retz. 5s, Aggstein Castle, Lower Austria. 6s, Lindauer Hut, Vorarlberg. 6.50s, Holy Cross Church, Villach, Carinthia. 7s, Falkenstein Castle, Carinthia. 7.50s, Hohensalzburg. 8s, Votive column, Reiteregg, Styria. 10s, Lake Neusiedl, Burgenland. 11s, Old Town, Enns. 16s, Open-air Museum, Bad Tatzmannsdorf. 20s, Myra waterfalls.

Photogravure and Engraved

1973–78 *Perf. 13½x14*

Size: 23x29mm.

958	A395	50g gray & sl grn ('75)	8	3
959	A395	1s brn & dk brn ('75)	12	3
960	A395	1.50s rose & brn ('74)	20	3
961	A395	2s gray bl & dk bl ('74)	25	3
962	A395	2.50s vio & dp vio ('74)	30	3
963	A395	3s lt ultra & vio bl ('74)	40	3
963A	A395	3.50s dl org & brn ('78)	45	15
964	A395	4s brt lil & pur	50	3
965	A395	4.50s brt grn & bl grn ('76)	60	15
966	A395	5s lil & vio	65	3
967	A395	6s dp rose & dk vio ('75)	75	10
968	A395	6.50s bl grn & ind ('77)	85	20
969	A395	7s sage grn & sl grn	90	10
970	A395	7.50s lil rose & cl ('77)	95	30
971	A395	8s dl red & dp brn ('76)	1.00	20
972	A395	10s gray grn & dk grn	1.25	20
973	A395	11s ver & dk car ('76)	1.40	15
974	A395	16s ocher & blk ('77)	2.00	25
975	A395	20s ol bis & ol grn ('77)	2.50	40
976	A395a	50s gray vio & vio bl ('75)	6.25	1.50
		Nos. 958-976 (20)	21.40	3.94

See Nos. 1100-1109.

Nativity A396 — Fritz Pregl A397

1973, Nov. 30 *Perf. 14*

977	A396	2s multi	40	25

Christmas 1973. Design from 14th century stained-glass window.

1973, Dec. 12 Engr. *Perf. 14x13½*

978 A397 4s dp bl 65 50

50th anniversary of the awarding of the Nobel prize for chemistry to Fritz Pregl (1869–1930).

Telex Machine A398 Hugo Hofmannsthal A399

1974, Jan. 14 Photo. *Perf. 14x13½*

979 A398 2.50s ultra 45 35

50th anniversary of Radio Austria.

1974, Feb. 1 Engraved *Perf. 14*

980 A399 4s vio bl 65 50

Centenary of the birth of Hugo Hofmannsthal (1874–1929), poet and playwright.

Anton Bruckner and Bruckner House—A400

1974, Mar. 22 Engraved *Perf. 14*

981 A400 4s brown 65 50

Founding of Anton Bruckner House (concert hall), Linz, and sesquicentennial of the birth of Anton Bruckner (1824–1896), composer.

Vegetables A401

Photogravure and Engraved

1974, Apr. 18 *Perf. 14*

Multicolored

982 A401 2s *shown* 35 25
983 A401 2.50s *Fruits* 45 28
984 A401 4s *Flowers* 65 60

International Garden Show, Vienna, Apr. 18–Oct. 14.

Seal of Judenburg A402 Karl Kraus A403

1974, Apr. 24 Photo. *Perf. 14x13½*

985 A402 2s plum & multi 40 25

750th anniversary of Judenburg.

1974, Apr. 6 Engraved

986 A403 4s dk red 65 50

Centenary of the birth of Karl Kraus (1874–1936), poet and satirist.

St. Michael, by Thomas Schwanthaler A404

King Arthur, from Tomb of Maximilian I A405

1974, May 3

987 A404 2.50s sl grn 45 35

Exhibition of the works by the Schwanthaler Family of sculptors, (1633–1848), Reichersberg am Inn, May 3–Oct. 13.

Europa Issue 1974

1974, May 8 *Perf. 13½*

988 A405 2.50s ocher & sl bl 45 35

De-Dion-Bouton Motor Tricycle A406

Photogravure and Engraved

1974, May 17 *Perf. 14x13½*

989 A406 2s gray & vio brn 40 25

75th anniversary of the Austrian Automobile Association.

Satyr's Head, Terracotta A407

1974, May 22 *Perf. 13½x14*

990 A407 2s org brn, gold & blk 40 25

Exhibition, "Renaissance in Austria," Schallaburg Castle, May 22–Nov. 14.

Road Transport Union Emblem A408

F. A. Maulbertsch, Self-portrait A409

1974, May 24 Photo. *Perf. 14x13½*

991 A408 4s dp org & blk 65 50

14th Congress of the International Road Transport Union, Innsbruck.

1974, June 7 Engr. *Perf. 14x13½*

992 A409 2s vio brn 40 25

250th anniversary of the birth of Franz Anton Maulbertsch (1724–1796), painter.

Gendarmes, 1824 and 1974 A410

1974, June 7 Photo. *Perf. 13½x14*

993 A410 2s red & multi 40 25

125th anniversary of Austrian gendarmery.

Fencing A411

Photogravure and Engraved

1974, June 14 *Perf. 13½*

994 A411 2.50s red org & blk 45 35

Transportation Symbols A412

St. Virgil, Sculpture from Nonntal Church A413

1974, June 18 Photo. *Perf. 14x13½*

995 A412 4s lt ultra & multi 65 50

European Conference of Transportation Ministers, Vienna, June 18–21.

1974, June 28 Engr. *Perf. 13½x14*

996 A413 2s vio bl 40 25

1200th anniversary of the consecration of the Cathedral of Salzburg by Scotch-Irish Bishop Feirgil (St. Virgil). Salzburg was a center of Christianization in the 8th century.

Franz Jonas and Austrian Eagle A414

1974, June 28

997 A414 2s black 40 25

Franz Jonas (1899–1974), President of Austria 1965–1974.

Franz Stelzhamer A415

Diver A416

1974, July 12 Engr. *Perf. 14x13½*

998 A415 2s indigo 40 25

Death centenary of Franz Stelzhamer (1802–1874), poet who wrote in Upper Austrian vernacular.

Perf. 13x13½

1974, Aug. 16 Photo. and Engr.

999 A416 4s bl & sep 65 50

13th European Swimming, Diving and Water Polo Championships, Vienna, Aug. 18–25.

Ferdinand Ritter von Hebra A417

1974, Sept. 10 Engr. *Perf. 14x13½*

1000 A417 4s brown 65 50

30th Meeting of the Association of German-speaking Dermatologists, Graz, Sept. 10–14. Dr. von Hebra (1816–1880) was a founder of modern dermatology.

Arnold Schönberg A418

1974, Sept. 13 *Perf. 13½x14*

1001 A418 2.50s purple 45 35

Centenary of the birth of Arnold Schönberg (1874–1951), composer.

Radio Station, Salzburg A419

1974, Oct. 1 Photo. *Perf. 13½x14*

1002 A419 2s multi 40 25

50th anniversary of Austrian broadcasting.

Edmund Eysler A420

1974, Oct. 4 Engr. *Perf. 14x13½*

1003 A420 2s dk ol 40 25

25th death anniversary of Edmund Eysler (1874–1949), composer.

Mailman, Mail Coach and Train, UPU Emblem—A421

Design: 4s, Mailman, jet, truck, 1974, and UPU emblem.

1974, Oct. 9 Photo. *Perf. 13½*

1004 A421 2s dp cl & lil 40 25
1005 A421 4s dk bl & gray 65 50

Centenary of Universal Postal Union.

Gauntlet Protecting Rose A422

1974, Oct. 23 Photo. ***Perf. 13½x14***

1006	A422	2s multi	40	25

Environment protection.

Austrian Sports Pool Emblem
A423

1974, Oct. 23 Photo. ***Perf. 13½x14***

1007	A423	70g multi	15	7

Austrian Sports Pool (lottery), 25th anniversary.

Carl Ditters von Dittersdorf
A424

Virgin and Child, Wood, c. 1600
A425

1974, Oct. 24 Engr. ***Perf. 14x13½***

1008	A424	2s Prus grn	40	25

175th death anniversary of Carl Ditters von Dittersdorf (1739–1799), composer.

1974, Nov. 29 Photo. & Engr.

1009	A425	2s brn & gold	40	25

Christmas 1974.

Franz Schmidt
A426

St. Christopher
A427

1974, Dec. 18

1010	A426	4s gray & blk	65	50

Birth centenary of Franz Schmidt (1874–1939), composer.

Photogravure and Engraved

1975, Jan. 24 ***Perf. 13½***

1011	A427	2.50s gray & brn	40	30

European Architectural Heritage Year. The design shows part of a wooden figure from central panel of the retable in the Kefermarkt Church, 1490–1497.

Safety Belt and Skeleton Arms
A428

Stained Glass Window, Vienna City Hall
A429

1975, Apr. 1 Photo. ***Perf. 14x13½***

1012	A428	70g vio & multi	15	6

Introduction of obligatory use of automobile safety belts.

1975, Apr. 2 ***Perf. 14***

1013	A429	2.50s multi	40	30

11th meeting of the Council of European Municipalities, Vienna, Apr. 2–5.

Austria as Mediator
A430

Forest
A431

1975, May 2 Litho. ***Perf. 14***

1014	A430	2s blk & bis	40	25

30th anniversary of the Second Republic of Austria.

1975, May 6 Engraved

1015	A431	2s green	40	25

National forests, 50th anniversary.

High Priest, by Michael Pacher
A432

Gosaukamm Funicular
A433

Europa Issue 1975

Photogravure and Engraved

1975, May 27 ***Perf. 14x13½***

1016	A432	2.50s blk & multi	40	30

Design is detail from painting "The Marriage of Joseph and Mary," by Michael Pacher (c. 1450–1500).

1975, June 23 ***Perf. 14x13½***

1017	A433	2s sl & red	40	25

4th International Funicular Congress, Vienna, June 23–27.

Josef Misson and Mühlbach am Manhartsberg
A434

1975, June 27 ***Perf. 13½x14***

1018	A434	2s choc & redsh brn	40	25

Death centenary of Josef Misson (1803–1875), poet who wrote in Lower Austrian vernacular.

Setting Sun and "P"
A435

1975, Aug. 27 Litho. ***Perf. 14x13½***

1019	A435	1.50s org, blk & bl	25	15

Austrian Association of Pensioners 25th anniversary meeting, Vienna, Aug. 1975.

Ferdinand Porsche
A436

Photogravure and Engraved

1975, Sept. 3 ***Perf. 13½x14***

1020	A436	1.50s gray & pur	25	15

Ferdinand Porsche (1875–1951), engineer, developer of Porsche and Volkswagen cars, birth centenary.

Leo Fall
A437

1975, Sept. 16 Engr. ***Perf. 14x13½***

1021	A437	2s violet	40	25

Leo Fall (1873–1925), composer, 50th death anniversary.

Judo Throw
A438

Heinrich Angeli
A439

1975, Oct. 20 Photo. ***Perf. 14x13½***

1022	A438	2.50s gold & multi	40	30

10th World Judo Championships, Vienna, Oct. 20–26.

1975, Oct. 21 Engr. ***Perf. 14x13½***

1023	A439	2s rose lake	40	25

Heinrich Angeli (1840–1925), painter, 50th death anniversary.

Johann Strauss and Dancers
A440

Photogravure and Engraved

1975, Oct. 24 ***Perf. 13½x14***

1024	A440	4s ocher & sep	65	50

Johann Strauss (1825–1899), composer, 150th birth anniversary.

Stylized Musician Playing a Viol
A441

Symbolic House
A442

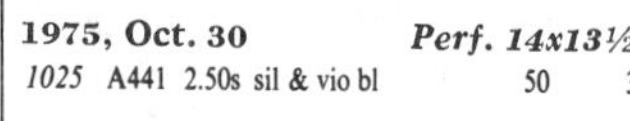

1975, Oct. 30 ***Perf. 14x13½***

1025	A441	2.50s sil & vio bl	50	30

Vienna Symphony Orchestra, 75th anniversary.

1975, Oct. 31 Photogravure

1026	A442	2s multi	40	25

Austrian building savings societies, 50th anniversary.

Fan with "Hanswurst" Scene, 18th Century
A443

1975, Nov. 14 Photo. ***Perf. 13½x14***

1027	A443	1.50s grn & multi	30	25

Salzburg Theater bicentenary.

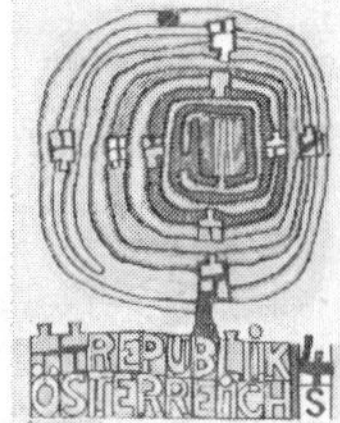

Virgin and Child, from 15th Century Altar
A444

"The Spiral Tree," by Hundertwasser
A445

Photogravure and Engraved

1975, Nov. 28 ***Perf. 13x13½***

1028	A444	2s gold & dl pur	40	25

Christmas 1975.

Photo., Engr. and Typo.

1975, Dec. 11 ***Perf. 13½x14***

1029	A445	4s multi	80	60

Austrian modern art. Friedensreich Hundertwasser is the pseudonym of Friedrich Stowasser (b. 1928).

Old Burgtheater—A446

Design: No. 1030b, Grand staircase, new Burgtheater.

Perf. 14 (pane), 13½x14 (stamps)

1976, Apr. 8 Engraved

1030	A446	Pane of 2 + label	1.40	1.40
a.		3s vio bl	55	55
b.		3s dp brn	55	55

Bicentenary of Vienna Burgtheater. Printed in sheets of 5 panes. Label (head of Pan) and commemorative inscription in vermilion. Size: 130x60mm.

Dr. Robert Barany
A447

Photogravure and Engraved

1976, Apr. 22 *Perf. 14x13½*

1031 A447 3s bl & brn 40 30

Robert Barany (1876–1936), winner of Nobel Prize for Medicine, 1914, birth centenary.

Ammonite
A448

1976, Apr. 30 Photo. *Perf. 13½x14*

1032 A448 3s red & multi 40 30

Vienna Museum of Natural History, Centenary Exhibition.

Carinthian Dukes' Coronation Chair
A449

Siege of Linz, 17th Century Etching
A450

Photogravure and Engraved

1976, May 6 *Perf. 14x13½*

1033 A449 3s grnsh blk & org 50 35

Millennium of Carinthia.

1976, May 14

1034 A450 4s blk & gray grn 65 50

Upper Austrian Peasants' War, 350th anniversary.

Skittles
A451

1976, May 14 *Perf. 13½x14*

1035 A451 4s blk & org 65 50

11th World Skittles Championships, Vienna.

Duke Heinrich II, Stained-glass Window
A452

1976, May 14 *Perf. 14*

1036 A452 3s multi 50 35

Babenberg Exhibition, Lilienfeld.

St. Wolfgang, from Pacher Altar
A453

1976, May 26 Engr. *Perf. 13½*

1037 A453 6s brt vio 1.00 75

International Art Exhibition at St. Wolfgang.

Europa Issue 1976

Tassilo Cup, Kremsmunster, 777
A454

Photogravure & Engraved

1976, Aug. 13 *Perf. 14x13½*

1038 A454 4s ULRA & multi 65 50

Timber Fair Emblem
A455

Constantin Economo, M.D.
A456

1976, Aug. 13 Photogravure

1039 A455 3s grn & multi 50 35

25 years of Austrian Timber Fair, Klagenfurt.

1976, Aug. 23 Engraved

1040 A456 3s dk red brn 50 35

Dr. Constantin Economo (1876–1931); neurologist.

Administrative Court, by Salomon Klein
A457

1976, Oct. 25 Engr. *Perf. 13½x14*

1041 A457 6s dp brn 1.00 75

Austrian Central Administrative Court, centenary.

Souvenir Sheet

Arms of Lower Austria
A458

Designs: Coats of Arms of Austrian Provinces.

Photogravure and Engraved

1976, Oct. 25 *Perf. 14*

1042	A458	Sheet of 9, multi	3.25	3.25
	a.	2s *shown*	30	30
	b.	2s *Upper Austria*	30	30
	c.	2s *Styria*	30	30
	d.	2s *Carinthia*	30	30
	e.	2s *Tyrol*	30	30
	f.	2s *Vorarlberg*	30	30
	g.	2s *Salzburg*	30	30
	h.	2s *Burgenland*	30	30
	i.	2s *Vienna*	30	30

Millennium of Austria. Austrian coat of arms, red border and black inscription in margin. Size: 135x180mm.

"Cancer"
A459

1976, Nov. 17 Photo. *Perf. 14x13½*

1043 A459 2.50s multi 65 25

Fight against cancer.

UN Emblem and Bridge
A460

1976, Nov. 17

1044 A460 3s bl & gold 1.00 35

UN Industrial Development Organization (UNIDO), 10th anniversary.

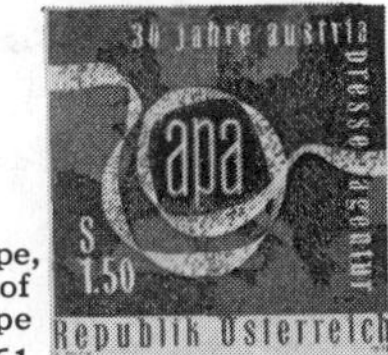

Punched Tape, Map of Europe
A461

1976, Nov. 17 *Perf. 14*

1045 A461 1.50s multi 20 15

Austrian Press Agency (APA), 30th anniversary.

Viktor Kaplan, Kaplan Turbine
A462

Photogravure and Engraved

1976, Nov. 26 *Perf. 13½x14*

1046 A462 2.50s multi 40 30

Viktor Kaplan (1876–1934), inventor of Kaplan turbine, birth centenary.

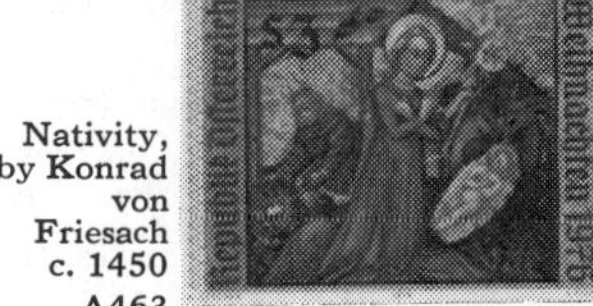

Nativity, by Konrad von Friesach c. 1450
A463

1976, Nov. 26 *Perf. 13½*

1047 A463 3s multi 40 30

Christmas 1976.

Augustin, the Piper
A464

Photogravure and Engraved

1976, Dec. 29 *Perf. 13½*

1048 A464 6s multi 80 50

Modern Austrian art.

Rainer Maria Rilke
A465

Vienna City Synagogue
A466

1976, Dec. 29 Engr. *Perf. 14x13½*

1049 A465 3s dp vio 40 25

Rainer Maria Rilke (1875–1926), poet.

1976, Dec. 29 Photo. *Perf. 13½*

1050 A466 1.50s multi 20 12

Sesquicentennial of Vienna City Synagogue.

Nikolaus Joseph Jacquin
A467

1977, Feb. 16 Engr. *Perf. 14x13½*

1051 A467 4s chocolate 50 40

Nikolaus Joseph von Jacquin (1727–1817), botanist.

Oswald von Wolkenstein
A468

Photogravure and Engraved

1977, Feb. 16 *Perf. 14*

1052 A468 3s multi 40 25

Oswald von Wolkenstein (1377–1445), poet, 600th birth anniversary.

Handball
A469

1977, Feb. 25 Photo. *Perf. 13½x14*

1053 A469 1.50s multi 20 12

World Indoor Handball Championships, Austria, Feb. 5–Mar. 6.

Alfred Kubin
A470

1977, Apr. 12 Engr. *Perf. 14x13½*

1054 A470 6s dk vio bl 85 50

Alfred Kubin (1877–1959), illustrator and writer, birth centenary.

Great Spire, St. Stephen's Cathedral A471

Designs: 3s, Heathen Tower and Frederick's Gable. 4s, Interior view with Albertinian Choir.

1977, Apr. 22 Engr. *Perf. 13½*

1055 A471 2.50s dk brn 35 25
1056 A471 3s dk bl 40 30
1057 A471 4s rose lake 60 40

Restoration and re-opening of St. Stephen's Cathedral, Vienna, 25th anniversary.

Fritz Hermanovsky-Orlando A472

Photogravure and Engraved

1977, Apr. 29 *Perf. 13½x14*

1058 A472 6s Prus grn & gold 85 50

Fritz Hermanovsky-Orlando (1877–1954), poet and artist, birth centenary.

IAEA Emblem A473

Arms of Schwanenstadt A474

1977, May 2 Photo. *Perf. 14*

1059 A473 3s brt bl, lt bl & gold 45 25

International Atomic Energy Agency (IAEA), 20th anniversary.

1977, June 10 Photo. *Perf. 14x13½*

1060 A474 3s dk brn & multi 45 25

350th anniversary of the town Schwanenstadt.

Europa Issue 1977

Attersee, Upper Austria—A475

1977, June 10 Engr. *Perf. 14*

1061 A475 6s ol grn 80 40

Globe, by Vincenzo Coronelli, 1688 A476

Photogravure and Engraved

1977, June 29 *Perf. 14*

1062 A476 3s blk & buff 40 20

5th International Symposium of the Coronelli World Federation of Friends of the Globe, Austria, June 29–July 3.

Kayak Race A477

1977, July 15 Photo. *Perf. 13½x14*

1063 A477 4s multi 50 20

3rd Kayak Slalom White Water Race on Lieser River, Spittal.

The Good Samaritan, by Francesco Bassano A478

Photogravure and Engraved

1977, Sept. 16

1064 A478 1.50s brn & red 20 12

Workers' Good Samaritan Organization, 50th anniversary.

Papermakers' Coat of Arms A479

Man with Austrian Flag Lifting Barbed Wire A480

1977, Oct. 10 *Perf. 14x13½*

1065 A479 3s multi 40 20

17th Conference of the European Committee of Pulp and Paper Technology (EUCEPA), Vienna.

1977, Nov. 3 *Perf. 14*

1066 A480 2.50s sl & red 40 20

Honoring the martyrs for Austria's freedom.

"Austria," First Steam Locomotive in Austria—A481

Designs: 2.50s, Steam locomotive 214. 3s, Electric locomotive 1044.

Photogravure and Engraved

1977, Nov. 17 *Perf. 13½*

1067 A481 1.50s multi 20 10
1068 A481 2.50s multi 35 15
1069 A481 3s multi 45 25

140th anniversary of Austrian railroads.

Virgin and Child, Wood Statue, Mariastein, Tyrol A482

1977, Nov. 25 *Perf. 14x13½*

1070 A482 3s multi 40 20

Christmas 1977.

The Danube Maiden, by Wolfgang Hutter A483

1977, Dec. 2 *Perf. 13½x14*

1071 A483 6s multi 80 35

Modern Austrian art.

Egon Friedell A484

Photogravure and Engraved

1978, Jan. 23

1072 A484 3s lt bl & blk 40 20

Egon Friedell (1878–1938), writer and historian.

Subway Train A485

1978, Feb. 24 Photo. *Perf. 13½x14*

1073 A485 3s multi 50 25

New Vienna subway system.

Biathlon Competition A486

1978, Feb. 28 Photo. & Engr.

1074 A486 4s multi 55 30

Biathlon World Championships, Hochfilzen, Tyrol, Feb. 28–Mar. 5.

Leopold Kunschak A487

1978, Mar. 13 Engr. *Perf. 14x13½*

1075 A487 3s vio bl 40 20

Leopold Kunschak (1871–1953), political leader, 25th death anniversary.

Coyote, Aztec Feather Shield A488

1978, Mar. 13 Photo. *Perf. 13½x14*

1076 A488 3s multi 40 20

Ethnographical Museum, 50th anniversary exhibition.

Alpine Farm, Woodcut by Suitbert Lobisser A489

1978, Mar. 23 Engr. *Perf. 13½*

1077 A489 3s dk brn, *buff* 40 20

Suitbert Lobisser (1878–1943), graphic artist, birth centenary.

Capercaillie, Hunting Bag, 1730, and Rifle, 1655 A490

Photogravure and Engraved

1978, Apr. 28 *Perf. 13½*

1078 A490 6s multi 90 45

International Hunting Exhibition, Marchegg.

Europa Issue 1978

Riegersburg, Styria—A491

1978, May 3 Engraved

1079 A491 6s dp rose lil 90 45

Parliament, Vienna, and Map of Europe
A492

Admont Pietà, c. 1410
A493

1978, May 3 Photo. *Perf. 14x13½*

1080 A492 4s multi 55 30

3rd Interparliamentary Conference for European Cooperation and Security, Vienna.

Photogravure and Engraved

1978, May 26

1081 A493 2.50s ocher & blk 35 20

Gothic Art in Styria Exhibition, St. Lambrecht, 1978.

Ort Castle, Gmunden
A494

1978, June 9

1082 A494 3s multi 40 20

700th anniversary of Gmunden City.

Child with Flowers and Fruit
A495

Lehar and his Home, Bad Ischl
A496

Photogravure and Engraved

1978, June 30 *Perf. 14x13½*

1083 A495 6s gold & multi 90 45

25 years of Social Tourism.

1978, July 14 Engr. *Perf. 14x13½*

1084 A496 6s slate 80 40

International Lehar Congress, Bad Ischl. Franz Lehar (1870–1948), operetta composer.

Congress Emblem
A497

1978, Aug. 21 Photo. *Perf. 13½x14*

1085 A497 1.50s blk, red & yel 25 15

Congress of International Federation of Building Construction and Wood Workers, Vienna, Aug. 20–24.

Ottokar of Bohemia and Rudolf of Hapsburg—A498

Photogravure and Engraved

1978, Aug. 25

1086 A498 3s multi 45 25

Battle of Durnkrut and Jedenspeigen (Marchfeld), which established Hapsburg rule in Austria, 700th anniversary.

First Documentary Reference to Villach, "ad pontem uillah"
A499

1978, Sept. 8 Litho. *Perf. 13½x14*

1087 A499 3c multi 45 25

1100th anniversary of Villach, Carinthia.

Seal of Graz, 1440
A500

Emperor Maximilian Fishing
A501

Photogravure and Engraved

1978, Sept. 13 *Perf. 14x13½*

1088 A500 4s multi 60 30

850th anniversary of Graz.

1978, Sept. 15 *Perf. 14x13½*

1089 A501 4s multi 60 30

World Fishing Championships, Vienna, Sept. 1978.

"Aid to the Handi-capped"
A502

1978, Oct. 2 Photo. *Perf. 13½x14*

1090 A502 6s org brn & blk 80 40

Symbolic Column
A503

1978, Oct. 9 Photo. *Perf. 13½*

1091 A503 2.50s org, blk & gray 40 20

9th International Congress of Concrete and Prefabrication Industries, Vienna, Oct. 8–13.

Grace, by Albin Egger-Lienz
A504

1978, Oct. 27 *Perf. 13½x14*

1092 A504 6s multi 80 40

European Family Congress, Vienna, Oct. 26–29.

Lise Meitner and Atom Symbol
A505

1978, Nov. 7 Engr. *Perf. 14x13½*

1093 A505 6s dk vio 80 40

Lise Meitner (1878–1968), physicist.

Viktor Adler, by Anton Hanak
A506

Photogravure and Engraved

1978, Nov. 10 *Perf. 13½x14*

1094 A506 3s ver & blk 45 25

Viktor Adler (1852–1918), leader of Social Democratic Party, 60th death anniversary.

Franz Schubert, by Josef Kriehuber
A507

Virgin and Child, Wilhering Church
A508

1978, Nov. 17 Engr. *Perf. 14*

1095 A507 6s redsh brn 90 45

Franz Schubert (1797–1828), composer.

Photogravure and Engraved

1978, Dec. 1 *Perf. 12½x13½*

1096 A508 3s multi 45 25

Christmas 1978.

Archduke Johann Shelter, Grossglockner—A509

1978, Dec. 6 *Perf. 13½x14*

1097 A509 1.50s gold & dk vio bl 25 15

Austrian Alpine Club, centenary.

Adam, by Rudolf Hausner
A510

Bound Hands
A511

1978, Dec. 6 Photo. *Perf. 13½x14*

1098 A510 6s multi 90 45

Modern Austrian art.

1978, Dec. 6 *Perf. 14x13½*

1099 A511 6s dp cl 80 45

30th anniversary of Universal Declaration of Human Rights.

Type of 1973

Designs: 20g, Freistadt, Upper Austria. 3s, Bishofsmutze, Salzburg. 4.20s, Hirschegg, Kleinwalsertal. 12s, Kufstein, Fortress. 14s Weiszsee, Salzburg.

Size: 20g, 27×33mm. 3s, 17x21mm. 4.20s, 12s, 14s, 23x29mm.

1978-80 Photo. and Engr. Perf. 13½x14

1100	A395	20g	vio bl & dk bl ('80)	5	5
1102	A395	3s	lt ultra & vio bl	45	10
1104	A395	4.20s	blk & grysh bl ('79)	55	5
1105	A395	5.50s	lil & pur	85	55
1106	A395	5.60s	yel grn & ol grn	90	55
1108	A395	12s	ocher & vio brn ('80)	1.60	50
1109	A395	14s	lt grn & grn ('82)	2.00	65

Child and IYC Emblem
A512

Photogravure and Engraved

1979, Jan. 16 *Perf. 14*

1110 A512 2.50s dk bl, blk & brn 35 15

International Year of the Child.

CCIR Emblem
A513

1979, Jan. 16 Photo. *Perf. 13½x14*

1111 A513 6s multi 80 40

International Radio Consultative Committee (CCIR) of the International Telecommunications Union, 50th anniversary.

Air Rifle, Air Pistol and Club Emblem—A514

Photogravure and Engraved

1979, Mar. 7 *Perf. 13½*

1112 A514 6s multi 80 40

Centenary of Austrian Shooting Club, and European Air Rifle and Air Pistol Championships, Graz.

Figure Skater
A515

1979, Mar. 7 Photo. *Perf. 14x13½*

1113	A515	4s multi	55	30

World Ice Skating Championships, Vienna.

Steamer Franz I
A516

Designs: 2.50s, Tugboat Linz. 3s, Passenger ship Theodor Körner.

1979, Mar. 13 Engr. *Perf. 13½*

1114	A516	1.50s vio bl	22	15
1115	A516	2.50s sepia	35	20
1116	A516	3s magenta	40	30

First Danube Steamship Company, 150th anniversary.

Fashion Design, by Theo Zasche, 1900
A517

Photogravure and Engraved

1979, Mar. 26 *Perf. 13x13½*

1117	A517	2.50s multi	38	20

50th International Fashion Week, Vienna.

Wiener Neustadt Cathedral
A518

1979, Mar. 27 Engr. *Perf. 13½*

1118	A518	4s vio bl	58	30

Cathedral of Wiener Neustadt, 700th anniversary.

Teacher and Pupils, by Franz A. Zauner
A519

Population Chart and Barock Angel
A520

Photogravure and Engraved

1979, Mar. 30 *Perf. 14x13½*

1119	A519	2.50s multi	38	20

Education of the deaf in Austria, 200th anniversary.

1979, Apr. 6

1120	A520	2.50s multi	38	20

Austrian Central Statistical Bureau, 150th anniversary.

Laurenz Koschier
A521

Diesel Motor
A522

Europa Issue, 1979

1979, May 4

1121	A521	6s ocher & pur	80	40

1979, May 4 Photogravure

1122	A522	4s multi	55	30

13th CIMAC Congress (International Organization for Internal Combustion Machines).

Arms of Ried, Schärding and Braunau
A523

Photogravure and Engraved

1979, June 1 *Perf. 14x13½*

1123	A523	3s multi	40	20

200th anniversary of Innviertel District.

Flood and City
A524

1979, June 1 *Perf. 13½x14*

1124	A524	2.50s multi	38	20

Control and eliminate water polution.

Arms of Rottenmann
A525

Jodok Fink
A526

Photogravure and Engraved

1979, June 22 *Perf. 14x13½*

1125	A525	3s multi	40	20

700th anniversary of Rottenmann.

1979, June 29 Engr. *Perf. 14*

1126	A526	3s brn car	40	20

Jodok Fink (1853–1929), governor of Vorarlberg.

Arms of Wels, Returnees' Emblem, "Europa Sail"
A527

1979, July 6 Photo. *Perf. 14x13½*

1127	A527	4s yel grn & blk	55	30

5th European Meeting of the International Confederation of Former Prisoners of War, Wels, July 6–8.

Symbolic Flower, Conference Emblem
A528

1979, Aug. 20 Litho. *Perf. 14x13½*

1128	A528	4s turq bl	55	30

U.N. Conference for Science and Technology, Vienna, Aug. 20-31.

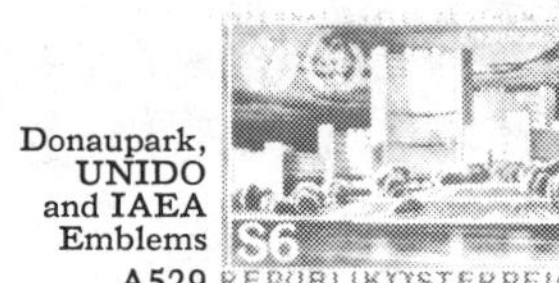

Donaupark, UNIDO and IAEA Emblems
A529

1979, Aug. 24 Engr. *Perf. 13½x14*

1129	A529	6s grysh bl	80	40

Opening of the Donaupark International Center in Vienna, seat of the United Nations Industrial Development Organization (UNIDO) and the International Atomic Energy Agency (IAEA).

Diseased Eye and Blood Vessels
A530

1979, Sept. 10 Photo. *Perf. 14*

1130	A530	2.50s multi	28	18

10th World Congress of International Diabetes Federation, Vienna, Sept. 9-14.

View of Stanz Valley through East Portal of Arlberg Tunnel—A531

1979, Sept. 14 Photo. & Engr.

1131	A531	4s multi	55	30

16th World Road Congress, Vienna, Sept. 16-21.

COLORS

Please refer to page v for a complete list of color abbreviations used in this book.

Steam Printing Press
A532

Photogravure and Engraved

1979, Sept. 18 *Perf. 13½x14*

1132	A532	3s multi	40	20

175th anniversary of Austrian Government Printing Office.

Richard Zsigmondy
A533

1979, Sept. 21 Engr. *Perf. 14x13½*

1133	A533	6s multi	80	40

Richard Zsigmondy (1865–1929), chemist.

"Save Energy"
A534

1979, Oct. 1 Photo. *Perf. 14x13½*

1134	A534	2.50s multi	32	20

Festival and Convention Center, Bregenz (Model)—A535

1979, Oct. 1 Engr. *Perf. 14*

1135	A535	2.50s purple	32	20

Lions International Emblem
A536

1979, Oct. 11 Photo. & Engr.

1136	A536	4s multi	55	30

25th Lions Europa Forum, Vienna, Oct. 11-13.

Wilhelm Exner
A537

Photogravure and Engraved

1979, Oct. 19 *Perf. 13½x14*

1137	A537	2.50s vio brn & blk	32	20

Centenary of Technological Handicraft Museum, founded by Wilhelm Exner.

The Compassionate Christ, by Hans Fronius A538

1979, Oct. 23 Litho. Perf. 13½x14

1138 A538 4s ol & ol blk 55 30
Modern Austrian art.

Locomotive and Arms A539

1979, Oct. 24 Photo. Perf. 13½x14

1139 A539 2.50s multi 32 20
Centenary of Raab-Odenburg-Ebenfurt railroad.

August Musger A540

Photo. & Engr.

1979, Oct. 30 Perf. 14x13½

1140 A540 2.50s bl gray & blk 32 20

August Musger (1868-1929), developer of slow-motion film technic.

Nativity, St. Barbara's Church—A541

Photogravure and Engraved

1979, Nov. 30 Perf. 13½×14

1141 A541 4s multi 55 30

Christmas 1979.

Arms of Baden—A542

Photogravure and Engraved

1980, Jan. 25 Perf. 14

1142 A542 4s multi 55 30

Baden, 500th anniversary.

Fight Rheumatism—A543

1980, Feb. 21 Perf. 13½

1143 A543 2.50s red & aqua 32 20

Austrian Exports A544

Rudolph Kirchschlager A546

Austrian Red Cross Centenary A545

1980, Feb. 21 Photo. Perf. 14×13½

1144 A544 4s dk bl & red 55 30

1980, Mar. 14 Photo. Perf. 13½×14

1145 A545 2.50s multi 32 20

Photo. & Engr.

1980, Mar. 20 Perf. 14×13½

1146 A546 4s sep & red 55 30

Robert Hamerling—A547

1980, Mar. 24 Engr. Perf. 13½×14

1147 A547 2.50s ol grn 35 20

Robert Hamerling (1830-1889), poet.

Seal of Hallein A548

Maria Theresa, by Andreas Moller A549

1980, Apr. 30 Photo. & Engr. Perf. 14x13½

1148 A548 4s red & blk 55 30

Hallein, 750th anniversary.

1980, May 13 Engraved Perf. 13½

Empress Maria Theresa (1717-1780) Paintings by: 4s, Martin van Meytens. 6s, Josef Ducreux.

1149 A549 2.50s vio brn 35 20
1150 A549 4s dk bl 55 35
1151 A549 6s rose lake 80 60

Flags of Austria and Four Powers A550

1980, May 14 Photo. Perf. 13½x14

1152 A550 4s multi 55 30
State Treaty, 25th anniversary.

St. Benedict, by Meinrad Guggenbichler A551

Hygeia by Gustav Klimt A552

1980, May 16 Engraved Perf. 14½

1153 A551 2.50s ol grn 35 20
Congress of Benedictine Order of Austria.

1980, May 20 Photo. Perf. 14

1154 A552 4s multi 55 30
175th anniversary of academic teaching of hygiene.

Aflenz Ground Satellite Receiving Station Inauguration—A553

1980, May 30 Photo. Perf. 14

1155 A553 6s multi 80 40

Steyr, Etching, 1693—A554

1980, June 4 Photo. & Engr. Perf. 13½

1156 A554 4s multi 55 30
Millennium of Steyr.

Worker, Oil Drill Head—A555

1980, June 12

1157 A555 2.50s multi 35 20
Austrian oil production, 25th anniversary.

Seal of Innsbruck, 1267—A556

1980, June 23 Perf. 13½x14½

1158 A556 2.50s multi 35 20
Innsbruck, 800th anniversary.

Duke's Hat A557

Bible Illustration, Book of Genesis A559

Leo Ascher (1880-1942), composer—A558

1980, June 23 Photo. Perf. 14½x13½

1159 A557 4s multi 55 30
800tn anniversary of Styria as a Duchy.

1980, Aug. 18 Engraved Perf. 14

1160 A558 3s dk pur 40 20

1980, Aug. 25 Perf. 13½

1161 A559 4s multi 55 30
10th International Congress of the Organization for Old Testament Studies.

Europa Issue 1980

Robert Stolz—A560

1980, Aug. 25 Engraved *Perf. 14x13½*
1162 A560 6s red brn 80 40

Robert Stolz (1880-1975), composer.

Old and Modern Bridges—A561

1980, Sept. 1 Photo. *Perf. 13½*
1163 A561 4s multi 55 30

11th Congress of the International Association for Bridge and Structural Engineering, Vienna.

Moon Figure, by Karl Brandstätter A562

Customs Service, Sesquicentennial A563

Photogravure and Engraved

1980, Oct. 10 *Perf. 14x13½*
1164 A562 4s multi 55 30

1980, Oct. 13 Photogravure
1165 A563 2.50s multi 35 20

Gazette Masthead, 1810—A564

1980, Oct. 23 Photo. *Perf. 13½*
1166 A564 2.50s multi 35 20

Official Gazette of Linz, 350th anniversary.

Waidhofen Town Book Title Page, 14th Century—A565

1980, Oct. 24 Photo. & Engr. *Perf. 14*
1167 A565 2.50s multi 35 20

Waidhofen on Thaya, 750th anniversary.

Federal Austrian Army, 25th Anniversary—A566

1980, Oct. 24 Photo. *Perf. 13½x14*
1168 A566 2.50s grnsh blk & red 35 20

Alfred Wegener—A567

1980, Oct. 31 Engraved
1169 A567 4s vio bl 55 30

Alfred Wegener (1880-1930), scientist, discovered theory of continental drift.

Robert Musil (1880-1942), Poet—A568

1980, Nov. 6 *Perf. 14x13½*
1170 A568 4s dk red brn 55 30

Nativity, Stained Glass Window, Klagenfurt—A569

1980, Nov. 28 Photo. & Engr. *Perf. 13½*
1171 A569 4s multi 55 30

Christmas 1980.

25th Anniversary of Social Security—A570

1981, Jan. 19 Litho. *Perf. 13½x14*
1172 A570 2.50s multi 35 20

Niebelungen Saga, 1926, by Wilhelm Dachauer A571

Machinist in Wheelchair A572

1981, Apr. 6 Engr. *Perf. 14x13½*
1173 A571 3s sepia 45 25

Wilhelm Dachauer (1881-1951), artist and engraver.

1981,Apr. 6 Photo & Engr.
1174 A572 6s multi 85 45

Rehabilitation International, 3rd European Regional Conference.

Sigmund Freud A573

UNICHAL Congress, Vienna A574

1981, May 6 Engr.
1175 A573 3s rose vio 45 25

Sigmund Freud (1856-1939), psychoanalyst.

1981, May 11 Photo.
1176 A574 4s multi 55 30

Azzo (Founder of House of Kuenringer) and his Followers, Bear-skin Manuscript—A575

1981, May 15 Photo. & Engr.
1177 A575 3s multi 45 25

Kuenringer Exhibition, Zwettl Monastery.

Europa Issue 1981

Maypole—A576

1981, May 22 Photo.
1178 A576 6s multi 85 45

Telephone Service Centenary—A577

1981, May 29 Photo. & Engr.
Perf. 13½x14
1179 A577 4s multi 55 30

Seibersdorf Research Center, 25th Anniv. A578

1981, June 29 Photo. *Perf. 13½*
1180 A578 4s multi 55 30

The Frog King (Child's Drawing) A579

1981, June 29 *Perf. 13½x14*
1181 A579 3s multi 45 25

Town Hall and Town Seal of 1250—A580

1981, July 17 Photo. & Engr. *Perf. 13½x14*
1182 A580 4s multi 55 30

St. Veit and der Glan, 800th anniv.

Johann Florian Heller (1813-1871), Pioneer of Urinalysis A581

1981, Aug. 31 *Perf. 14x13½*
1183 A581 6s red brn 85 45

11th Intl. Clinical Chemistry Congress.

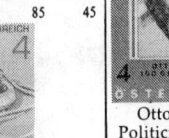

Ludwig Boltzmann (1844-1906), Physicist A582

Scale A583

1981, Sept. 4 Engr. *Perf. 14x13½*
1184 A582 3s dk grn 45 25

1981, Sept. 7 Photo. & Engr. *Perf. 14*
1185 A583 6s multi 85 45

Intl. Pharmaceutical Federation World Congress, Vienna, Sept. 6-11.,

Otto Bauer, Politician, Birth Centenary A584

Escher's Impossible Cube A585

1981, Sept. 7 **Photo.** *Perf. 14x13½*
1186 A584 4s multi 55 30

1981, Sept. 14
1187 A585 4s dk bl & brt bl 55 30

10th Intl. Mathematicians' Congress, Innsbruck.

Kneeling Virgin, Detail of Coronation of Mary Altarpiece, St. Wolfgang, 500th Anniv.—A586

1981, Sept. 25 **Engr.** *Perf. 14x13½*
1188 A586 3s dk bl 45 25

South-East Fair, Graz, 75th Anniv.—A587

1981, Sept. 25 **Photo.** *Perf. 13½x14*
1189 A587 4s multi 55 30

Holy Trinity, 12th Cent. Byzantine Miniature—A588

1981, Oct. 5
1190 A588 6s multi 85 45

16th Intl. Byzantine Congress.

Hans Kelsen (1881-1973), Co-author of Federal Constitution—A589

1981, Oct. 9 **Engr.**
1191 A589 3s dk car 45 25

Emperor Joseph II (Edict of Tolerance Bicentenary)—A590

1981, Oct. 9 **Photo. & Engr.** *Perf. 14*
1192 A590 4s multi 55 30

World Food Day—A591

1981, Oct. 16 **Photo.** *Perf. 13½*
1193 A591 6s multi 85 45

Between the Times, by Oscar Asboth—A592

1981, Oct. 22 **Litho.** *Perf. 13½x14*
1194 A592 4s multi 55 30

Intl. Catholic Workers' Day—A593

1981, Oct. 23 **Photo. & Engr.** *Perf. 14x13½*
1195 A593 3s multi 45 25

Baron Josef Hammer-Purgstall, Founder of Oriental Studies, 125th Death Anniv.—A594

1981, Nov. 23 **Photo. & Engr.** *Perf. 14*
1196 A594 3s multi 45 25

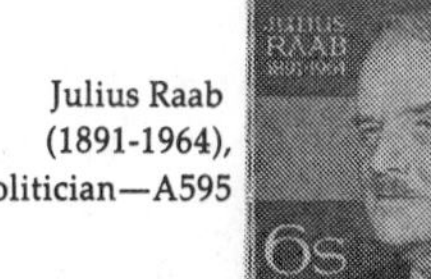

Julius Raab (1891-1964), Politician—A595

1981, Nov. 27 **Engr.** *Perf. 13½*
1197 A595 6s rose lake 85 45

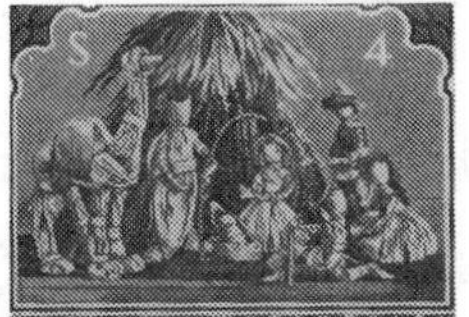

Nativity, Corn Straw Figures—A596

1981, Nov. 27 **Photo. & Engr.**
1198 A596 4s multi 55 30

Christmas 1981.

Stefan Zweig (1881-1942), Poet—A597

1981, Nov. 27 **Engr.** *Perf. 14x13½*
1199 A597 4s dl vio 55 30

800th Anniv. of St. Nikola on the Danube—A598

1981, Dec. 4
1200 A598 4s multi 55 30

Vienna Emergency Medical Service Centenary—A599

1981, Dec. 9 **Photo.** *Perf. 13½x14*
1201 A599 3s multi 45 25

Schladming-Haus Alpine World Skiing Championship—A600

1982, Jan. 27 *Perf. 14*
1202 A600 4s multi 55 30

Dorotheum (State Auction Gallery), 275th Anniv. A601

Water Rescue Service, 25th Anniv. A602

1982, Mar. 12 **Photo. & Engr.** *Perf. 14*
1203 A601 4s multi 60 40

1982, Mar. 19 **Photo.** *Perf. 14x13½*
1204 A602 5s multi 75 50

St. Severin A603

Intl. Kneipp Hydropathy Congress, Vienna A604

1982, Apr. 23 **Photo. & Engr.** *Perf. 14x13½*
1205 A603 3s multi 45 30

St. Severin and the End of the Roman Era exhibition.

1982, May 4 *Perf. 14*
1206 A604 4s multi 60 40

Arms of Printers' Guild A605

Urine Analysis, Canone di Avicenna Manuscript A606

1982, May 7
1207 A605 4s multi 60 40

Printing in Austria, 500th anniv.

1982, May 12 **Photo.**
1208 A606 6s multi 90 60

5th European Urology Society Congress, Vienna.

800th Birth Anniv. of St. Francis of Assisi A607

Haydn and His Time Exhibition, Rohrau A608

1982, May 14 **Photo. & Engr.**
1209 A607 3s multi 45 30

1982, May 19 **Engr.** *Perf. 13½*
1210 A608 3s ol grn 45 30

25th World Milk Day
A609

800th Anniv of Gfohl (Market Town)
A610

1982, May 25 Photo. *Perf. 14x13½*
1211 A609 7s multi 1.05 70

1982, May 28 Photo. & Engr. *Perf. 14*
1212 A610 4s multi 60 40

Tennis Player and Austrian Tennis Federation Emblem—A611

1982, June 11
1213 A611 3s multi 45 30

900th Anniv. of City of Langenlois—A612

1982, June 11 Photo. & Engr. *Perf. 13½x14*
1214 A612 4s multi 60 40

800th Anniv. of City of Weiz—A613

1982, June 18 Photo. *Perf. 14x13½*
1215 A613 4s Arms 60 40

Ignaz Seipel (1876-1932), Statesman—A614

1982, July 30 Engr. *Perf. 14x13½*
1216 A614 3s brn vio 45 30

Europa Issue 1982

Sesquicentennial of Linz-Freistadt-Budweis Horse-drawn Railroad—A615

1982, July 30 *Perf. 13½*
1217 A615 6s brown 90 60

Mail Bus Service, 75th Anniv.
A616

Rocket Lift-off
A617

1982, Aug. 6 Photo. *Perf. 14x13½*
1218 A616 4s multi 60 40

1982, Aug. 9 *Perf. 14*
1219 A617 4s multi 60 40

2nd UN Conference on Peaceful Uses of Outer Space, Vienna, Aug. 9-21.

Geodesists' Day—A618

1982, Sept. 1 Photo. & Engr. *Perf. 13½x14*
1220 A618 3s Tower, Office of Standards 45 30

Protection of Endangered Species—A619

1982, Sept. 9 *Perf. 14*
1221 A619 3s Bustard 45 30
1222 A619 4s Beaver 60 40
1223 A619 6s Capercaillie 90 60

10th Anniv. of Intl. Institute for Applied Systems Analysis, Vienna—A620

1982, Oct. 4 Photo. *Perf.*
1224 A620 3s Laxenburg Castle 45 30

St. Apollonia (Patron Saint of Dentists)—A621

1982, Oct. 11 Photo. & Engr.
1225 A621 4s multi 60 40

70th Annual World Congress of Dentists.

Emmerich Kalman (1882-1953), Composer—A622

1982, Oct. 22 Engr. *Perf. 13½*
1226 A622 3s dk bl 45 30

Max Mell (1882-19), Poet
A623

Christmas 1982
A624

1982, Nov. 10 Photo.
1227 A623 3s multi 45 30

1982, Nov. 25 Photo. & Engr.

Design: Christmas crib, Damuls Church, Vorarlberg, 1630.
1228 A624 4s multi 60 40

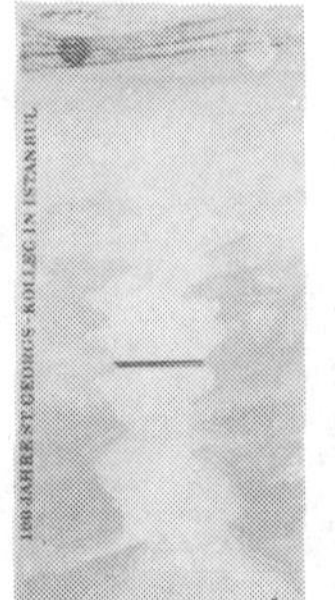

Centenary of St. George's College, Istanbul—A625

1982, Nov. 26 Litho.
1229 A625 4s Bosphorus 60 40

Portrait of a Girl, by Ernst Fuchs—A626

1982, Dec. 10 Photo & Engr.
1230 A626 4s multi 60 40

Postal Savings Bank Centenary—A627

1983, Jan. 12 Photo. & Engr. *Perf. 14*
1231 A627 4s Bank 60 40

Hildegard Burjan (1883-1933), Founder of Caritas Socialis—A628

1983, Jan. 28 Engr.
1232 A628 4s rose lake 60 40

World Communications Year
A629

75th Anniv. Children's Friends Org.
A630

1983, Feb. 18 Photo. *Perf. 13½x14*
1233 A629 7s multi 1.05 70

1983, Feb. 23 Photo. & Engr. *Perf. 14x13½*
1234 A630 4s multi 60 40

Josef Matthias Hauer (1883-1959), Composer—A631

1983, Mar. 18 Engr. *Perf. 14*
1235 A631 3s dp lil rose 45 30

SEMI-POSTAL STAMPS.
Issues of the Monarchy.

Emperor Franz Josef SP1

Perf. 12½

1914, Oct. 4 Typo. Unwmkd.

B1	SP1	5h green	12	10
B2	SP1	10h rose	20	18

Nos. B1-B2 were sold at an advance of 2h each over face value. Exist imperf.; price, set $100.

The Firing Step
SP2

Designs: 5h+2h, Cavalry. 10h+2h, Siege gun. 20h+3h, Battleship. 35h+3h, Airplane.

1915, May 1

B3	SP2	3h +1h vio brn	20	50
B4	SP2	5h +2h grn	3	3
B5	SP2	10h +2h dp rose	3	3
B6	SP2	20h +3h Prus bl	38	1.50
B7	SP2	35h +3h ultra	4.50	2.75
		Nos. B3-B7 (5)	5.14	4.81

Exist imperf. Price, set $160.

Issues of the Republic.

Types of Austria, 1919-20, Overprinted in Black

Kärnten
Abstimmung

1920, Sept. 16 *Perf. 12½*

B11	A44	5h gray, *yel*	45	70
B12	A44	10h red, *pink*	80	1.20
B13	A43	15h bis, *yel*	45	70
B14	A45	20h dk grn, *bl*	45	70
B15	A43	25h vio, *pink*	45	70
B16	A45	30h brn, *buff*	1.40	2.10
B17	A45	40h car, *yel*	70	1.00
B18	A45	50h dk bl, *bl*	70	1.00
B19	A43	60h ol grn, *az*	1.50	2.50
B20	A47	80h red	45	70
B21	A47	1k org brn	50	80
B22	A47	2k pale bl	35	70

Granite Paper.
Imperf.

B23	A46	2½k brn red	55	90
B24	A46	3k dk bl & grn	55	90
B25	A46	4k car & vio	80	1.40
B26	A46	5k blue	1.00	1.75
B27	A46	7½k yel grn	1.00	1.75
B28	A46	10k gray grn & red	1.00	1.75
B29	A46	20k lil & org	1.00	1.75
		Nos. B11-B29 (19)	14.10	23.00

Carinthia Plebiscite. Sold at three times face value for the benefit of the Plebiscite Propaganda Fund.
Nos. B11-B22 exist imperf. Price, set $175.

Types of Regular Issues of 1919-21 Overprinted

Hochwasser
1920

1921, Mar. 1 *Perf. 12½*

B30	A44	5h gray, *yel*	30	50
B31	A44	10h org brn	30	50
B32	A43	15h gray	30	50
B33	A45	20h grn, *yel*	30	50
B34	A43	25h bl, *yel*	30	50
B35	A45	30h vio, *bl*	30	50
B36	A45	40h org brn, *pink*	35	75
B37	A45	50h grn, *bl*	1.50	3.00
B38	A43	60h lil, *yel*	30	50
B39	A47	80h pale bl	30	50
B40	A47	1k red org, *bl*	75	1.75
B41	A47	1½k grn, *yel*	30	50
B42	A47	2k lil brn	30	50

Overprinted

Hochwasser
1920

B43	A46	2½k lt bl	30	50
B44	A46	3k ol grn & brn red	30	50
B45	A46	4k lil & org	1.00	2.25
B46	A46	5k ol grn	50	1.00
B47	A46	7½k brn red	50	1.00
B48	A46	10k bl & ol grn	60	1.50
B49	A46	20k car rose & vio	75	1.75
		Nos. B30-B49 (20)	9.55	19.00

Exists imperf. Price, set $325.

Nos. B30-B49 were sold at three times face value, the excess going to help flood victims. Set exists imperf. Price $250.

Franz Joseph Haydn
SP9

View of Bregenz
SP16

Musicians: 5k, Mozart. 7½k, Beethoven. 10k, Schubert. 25k, Anton Bruckner. 50k, Johann Strauss (son). 100k, Hugo Wolf.

Engraved

1922, Apr. 24 *Perf. 11½, 12½*

B50	SP9	2½k brown	10.00	7.50
B51	SP9	5k dk bl	2.00	2.50
B52	SP9	7½k black	2.50	4.00
a.		Perf. 11½	70.00	90.00
B53	SP9	10k dk vio	3.75	4.00
B54	SP9	25k dk grn	4.50	6.00
B55	SP9	50k claret	3.75	5.00
B56	SP9	100k brn ol	12.50	11.00
		Nos. B50-B56 (7)	39.00	40.00

These stamps were sold at 10 times face value, the excess being given to needy musicians.
All values exist imperf. on both regular and handmade papers. Price, set $500.
A 1969 souvenir sheet without postal validity contains reprints of the 5k in black, 7½k in claret and 50k in dark blue, each overprinted "NEUDRUCK" in black at top. It was issued for the Vienna State Opera Centenary Exhibition.

1923, May 22 *Perf. 12½*

Designs: 120k, Mirabelle Gardens, Salzburg. 160k, Church at Eisenstadt. 180k, Assembly House, Klagenfurt. 200k, "Golden Roof," Innsbruck. 240k, Main Square, Linz. 400k, Castle Hill, Graz. 600k, Abbey at Melk. 1000k, Upper Belvedere, Vienna.

Various Frames.

B57	SP16	100k dk grn	5.00	5.00
B58	SP16	120k dp bl	5.00	5.00
B59	SP16	160k dk vio	5.00	5.00
B60	SP16	180k red vio	5.00	5.00
B61	SP16	200k lake	5.00	5.00
B62	SP16	240k red brn	5.00	5.00
B63	SP16	400k dk brn	5.00	5.00
B64	SP16	600k ol brn	5.00	5.00
B65	SP16	1000k black	5.00	5.00
		Nos. B57-B65 (9)	45.00	45.00

Nos. B57-B65 were sold at five times face value, the excess going to needy artists.
All values exist imperf. on both regular and handmade papers. Price, set $400.

Feebleness
SP25

Siegfried Slays the Dragon
SP30

Designs: 300k+900k, Aid to industry. 500k+1500k, Orphans and widow. 600k+1800k, Indigent old man. 1000k+3000k, Alleviation of hunger.

1924, Sept. 6 Photogravure

B66	SP25	100k +300k yel grn	6.00	5.00
B67	SP25	300k +900k red brn	7.50	10.00
B68	SP25	500k +1500k brn vio	7.50	10.00
B69	SP25	600k +1800k pck bl	7.50	10.00
B70	SP25	1000k +3000k brn org	12.50	15.00
		Nos. B66-B70 (5)	41.00	50.00

The surtax was for child welfare and anti-tuberculosis work. Set exists imperf. Price, $375.

1926, Mar. 8 Engraved

Designs: 8g+2g, Gunther's voyage to Iceland. 15g+5g, Brunhild accusing Kriemhild. 20g+5g, Nymphs telling Hagen the future. 24g+6g, Rudiger von Bechelaren welcomes the Nibelungen. 40g+10g, Dietrich von Bern vanquishes Hagen.

B71	SP30	3g +2g ol blk	2.00	50
B72	SP30	8g +2g ind	50	50
B73	SP30	15g +5g dk cl	50	50
B74	SP30	20g +5g ol grn	75	1.00
B75	SP30	24g +6g dk vio	75	1.00
B76	SP30	40g +10g red brn	6.50	6.00
		Nos. B71-B76 (6)	11.00	9.50

Nibelungen issue.
The surtax was for child welfare. Set exists imperf. Price, $350.

President Michael Hainisch
SP36

President Wilhelm Miklas
SP37

1928, Nov. 5

B77	SP36	10g dk brn	7.50	10.00
B78	SP36	15g red brn	7.50	10.00
B79	SP36	30g black	7.50	10.00
B80	SP36	40g indigo	7.50	10.00

Tenth anniversary of Austrian Republic. Sold at double face value, the premium aiding war orphans and children of war invalids.
Set exists imperf. Price, $375.

1930, Oct. 4

B81	SP37	10(g) lt brn	15.00	16.50
B82	SP37	20(g) red	15.00	16.50
B83	SP37	30(g) brn vio	15.00	16.50
B84	SP37	40(g) indigo	15.00	16.50
B85	SP37	50(g) dk grn	15.00	16.50
B86	SP37	1s blk brn	15.00	16.50
		Nos. B81-B86 (6)	90.00	99.00

Nos. B81-B86 were sold at double face value. The excess aided the anti-tuberculosis campaign and the building of sanatoria in Carinthia.
Set exists imperf. Price, $450.

Regular Issue of 1929-30 Overprinted in Various Colors

CONVENTION
WIEN 1931

1931, June 20

B87	A56	10g bis (Bl)	55.00	60.00
B88	A56	20g dk gray (R)	55.00	60.00
B89	A56	30g dk vio (Gl)	55.00	60.00
B90	A56	40g dk bl (Gl)	55.00	60.00
B91	A56	50g gray vio (O)	55.00	60.00
B92	A57	1s blk brn (Bk)	55.00	60.00
		Nos. B87-B92 (6)	330.00	360.00

Rotary convention, Vienna.
Nos. B87 to B92 were sold at double their face values. The excess was added to the beneficent funds of Rotary International.
Exists imperf. Price, set $1000.

Ferdinand Raimund
SP38

Poets: 20g, Franz Grillparzer. 30g, Johann Nestroy. 40g, Adalbert Stifter. 50g, Ludwig Anzengruber. 1s, Peter Rosegger.

1931, Sept. 12

B93	SP38	10(g) dk vio	20.00	22.50
B94	SP38	20(g) gray blk	20.00	22.50
B95	SP38	30(g) org red	20.00	22.50
B96	SP38	40(g) dl bl	20.00	22.50
B97	SP38	50(g) gray grn	20.00	22.50
B98	SP38	1s yel brn	20.00	22.50
		Nos. B93-B98 (6)	120.00	135.00

Nos. B93-B98 were sold at double face value. The surtax aided unemployed young people.
Sets exists imperf. Price, $600.

Chancellor Ignaz Seipel
SP44

Ferdinand Georg Waldmüller
SP45

1932, Oct. 12 *Perf. 13*

B99	SP44	50g ultra	19.00	27.50

Msgr. Ignaz Seipel, Chancellor of Austria, 1922-29. Sold at double face value, the excess aiding wounded veterans of World War I.
Exists imperf. Price, $225.

1932, Nov. 21

Artists: 24g, Moritz von Schwind. 30g, Rudolf von Alt. 40g, Hans Makart. 64g, Gustav Klimt. 1s, Albin Egger-Lienz.

B100	SP45	12(g) sl grn	25.00	37.50
B101	SP45	24(g) dp vio	25.00	37.50
B102	SP45	30(g) dk red	25.00	37.50
B103	SP45	40(g) dk gray	25.00	37.50
B104	SP45	64(g) dk brn	25.00	37.50
B105	SP45	1s claret	25.00	37.50
		Nos. B100-B105 (6)	150.00	225.00

Nos. B100 to B105 were sold at double their face values. The surtax was for the assistance of charitable institutions.
Set exists imperf. Price, $750.

Mountain Climbing
SP51

Designs: 24g, Ski gliding. 30g, Walking on skis. 50g, Ski jumping.

1933, Jan. 9 Photo. *Perf. 12½*

B106	SP51	12(g) dk grn	12.50	17.50
B107	SP51	24(g) dk vio	110.00	135.00

B108	SP51	30(g) brn red	40.00	25.00
B109	SP51	50(g) dk bl	110.00	140.00

Issued in connection with a meeting of the International Ski Federation at Innsbruck, Feb. 8–13, 1933.

These stamps were sold at double their face value. The surtax was for the benefit of "Youth in Distress."

Nos. B106–B109 exist imperf. Price $1,500.

Vienna Philatelic Exhibition Issue.

Stagecoach, after Painting by Moritz von Schwind
SP55

Ordinary Paper.

1933, June 23 Engraved *Perf. 12½*

B110	SP55	50g dp ultra	190.00	285.00
a.		Granite paper	400.00	700.00

Sheets of 25.

Nos. B110 and B110a exist imperf. Prices four times those of perf. stamps.

Souvenir Sheet

SP55a

Perf. 12.

Granite Paper.

B111	SP55a	50g dp ultra, sheet of 4	3,250.	4,250.
a.		Single stamp	450.00	700.00

Issued in connection with the International Philatelic Exhibition at Vienna in 1933. In addition to the postal value of 50g the stamp was sold at a premium of 50g for charity and of 1s60g for the admission fee to the exhibition.

Size of No. B111: 126x103mm.

The 50g dark red in souvenir sheet, with dark blue overprint ("NEUDRUCK WIPA 1965"), had no postal validity.

St. Stephen's Cathedral in 1683
SP56

Marco d'Aviano, Papal Legate
SP57

Designs: 30g, Count Ernst Rudiger von Starhemberg. 40g, John III Sobieski, King of Poland. 50g, Karl V, Duke of Lorraine. 64g, Burgomaster Johann Andreas von Liebenberg.

1933, Sept. 6 Photo. *Perf. 12½*

B112	SP56	12(g) dk grn	35.00	45.00
B113	SP57	24(g) dk vio	30.00	37.50
B114	SP57	30(g) brn red	30.00	37.50
B115	SP57	40(g) bl blk	45.00	65.00
B116	SP57	50(g) dk bl	30.00	37.50
B117	SP57	64(g) ol brn	40.00	55.00
		Nos. B112-B117 (6)	210.00	277.50

Issued in commemoration of the 250th anniversary of the deliverance of Vienna from the Turks and in connection with the Pan-German Catholic Congress on September 6th, 1933.

The stamps were sold at double their face value, the excess being for the aid of Catholic works of charity.

Sets exists imperf. Price, $1,000.

Types of Regular Issue of 1925-30 Surcharged:

+2g Winterhilfe *a*

WINTERHILFE +6g *b*

+50g WINTERHILFE *c*

1933, Dec. 15

B118	A52 (a)	5g +2g ol grn	25	75
B119	A56 (b)	12g +3g lt bl	25	75
B120	A56 (b)	24g +6g brn org	25	75
B121	A57 (c)	1s +50g org red	45.00	65.00

Winterhelp. Exists imperf. Price, set $225.

Winterhelp. Set exists imperf. Price, $200.

Anton Pilgram
SP62

Architects: 24g, J. B. Fischer von Erlach. 30g, Jakob Prandtauer. 40g, A. von Siccardsburg & E. van der Null. 60g, Heinrich von Ferstel. 64g, Otto Wagner.

Thick Yellowish Paper.

1934, Dec. 2 Engr. *Perf. 12½*

B122	SP62	12gr (+12gr) blk	15.00	20.00
B123	SP62	24gr (+24gr) dl vio	15.00	20.00
B124	SP62	30gr (+30gr) car	15.00	20.00
B125	SP62	40gr (+40gr) brn	15.00	20.00
B126	SP62	60gr (+60gr) bl	15.00	20.00
B127	SP62	64gr (+64gr) dl grn	15.00	20.00
		Nos. B122-B127 (6)	90.00	120.00

Exist imperf. Price, set $750.

Nos. B124-B127 exist in horiz. pairs imperf. between. Price, each $325.

The surtax on this and the following issues was devoted to general charity.

Nos. B122–B127 exist imperf. Price, set $650.

Types of Regular Issue of 1934 Surcharged in Black:

+50g

Winterhilfe +2g *a*

WINTERHILFE *b*

1935, Nov. 11 *Perf. 12, 12½*

B128	A67 (a)	5S +2g emer	75	2.00
B129	A67 (a)	12g +3g bl	75	2.00
B130	A67 (a)	24g +6g lt brn	75	2.00
B131	A68 (b)	1s +50g ver	40.00	57.50

Winterhelp. Set exists imperf. Price, $180.

Prince Eugene of Savoy
SP68

Slalom Turn
SP74

Military Leaders: 24g, Field Marshal Laudon. 30g, Archduke Karl. 40g, Field Marshal Josef Radetzky. 60g, Admiral Wilhelm Tegetthoff. 64g, Field Marshal Franz Conrad Hotzendorff.

1935, Dec. 1 *Perf. 12½*

B132	SP68	12g (+12g) brn	14.00	20.00
B133	SP68	24g (+24g) dk grn	14.00	20.00
B134	SP68	30g (+30g) cl	14.00	20.00
B135	SP68	40g (+40g) sl	14.00	20.00
B136	SP68	60g (+60g) dp ultra	14.00	20.00
B137	SP68	64g (+64g) dk vio	14.00	20.00
		Nos. B132-B137 (6)	84.00	120.00

Set exists imperf. Price, $650.

1936, Feb. 20 Photogravure

Designs: 24g, Jumper taking off. 35g, Slalom turn. 60g, Innsbruck view.

B138	SP74	12g (+12g) Prus grn	3.75	4.00
B139	SP74	24g (+24g) dp vio	6.25	6.00
B140	SP74	35g (+35g) rose car	37.50	50.00
B141	SP74	60g (+60g) saph	37.50	55.00

Ski concourse issue. Set exists imperf. Price, $500.

St. Martin of Tours
SP78

Designs: 12g+3g, Medical clinic. 24g+6g, St. Elizabeth of Hungary. 1s+1s, "Flame of Charity."

1936, Nov. 2

B142	SP78	5g +2g dp grn	50	1.00
B143	SP78	12g +3g dp vio	50	1.00
B144	SP78	24g +6g dp bl	50	1.00
B145	SP78	1s +1s dk car	11.00	21.00

Winterhelp. Set exists imperf. Price, $175.

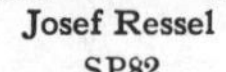

Josef Ressel
SP82

Nurse and Infant
SP88

Inventors: 24g, Karl von Ghega. 30g, Josef Werndl. 40g, Carl Auer von Welsbach. 60g, Robert von Lieben. 64g, Viktor Kaplan.

1936, Dec. 6 Engraved

B146	SP82	12g (+12g) dk brn	4.00	6.00
B147	SP82	24g (+24g) dk vio	4.00	6.00
B148	SP82	30g (+30g) dp cl	4.00	6.00

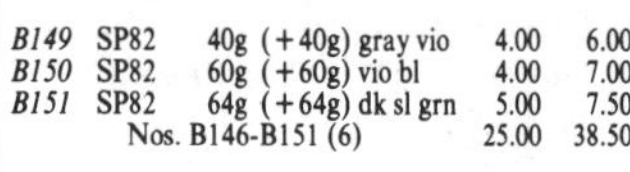

B149	SP82	40g (+40g) gray vio	4.00	6.00
B150	SP82	60g (+60g) vio bl	4.00	7.00
B151	SP82	64g (+64g) dk sl grn	5.00	7.50
		Nos. B146-B151 (6)	25.00	38.50

Set exists imperf. Price, $400.

1937, Oct. 18 Photogravure

Designs: 12g+3g, Mother and child. 24g+6g, Nursing the aged. 1s+1s, Sister of Mercy with patient.

B152	SP88	5g +2g dk grn	25	50
B153	SP88	12g +3g dk brn	25	50
B154	SP88	24g +6g dk bl	25	50
B155	SP88	1s +1s dk car	6.50	10.00

Winterhelp. Set exists imperf. Price, $175.

Gerhard van Swieten
SP92

The Dawn of Peace
SP101

Physicians: 8g, Leopold Auenbrugger von Auenbrugg. 12g, Karl von Rokitansky. 20g, Joseph Skoda. 24g, Ferdinand von Hebra. 30g, Ferdinand von Arlt. 40g, Joseph Hyrtl. 60g, Theodor Billroth. 64g, Theodor Meynert.

1937, Dec. 5 Engr. *Perf. 12½*

B156	SP92	5g +(5g) choc	3.50	5.00
B157	SP92	8g +(8g) dk red	3.50	5.00
B158	SP92	12g +(12g) brn blk	3.50	5.00
B159	SP92	20g +(20g) dk grn	3.50	5.00
B160	SP92	24g +(24g) dk vio	3.50	5.00
B161	SP92	30g +(30g) brn car	3.50	5.00
B162	SP92	40g +(40g) dp ol grn	3.50	5.00
B163	SP92	60g +(60g) ind	3.50	5.00
B164	SP92	64g +(64g) brn vio	3.50	5.00
		Nos. B156-B164 (9)	31.50	45.00

Set exists imperf. Price, $525.

Photogravure.

1945, Sept. 10 *Perf. 14* Unwmkd.

B165	SP101	1s +10s dk grn	90	1.50

No. 467 Surcharged in Black

1946, June 25

B166	A110	30g +20g dk red	3.25	6.00

First anniversary of United Nations.

Pres. Karl Renner
SP102

1946 Engraved. *Perf. 13½x14.*

B167	SP102	1s +1s dk sl grn	2.75	4.75

B168	SP102	2s +2s dk bl vio	2.75	4.75
B169	SP102	3s +3s dk pur	2.75	4.75
B170	SP102	5s +5s dk vio brn	2.75	4.75

See also Nos. B185-B188.

Nazi Sword Piercing Austria SP103

Sweeping Away Fascist Symbols SP104

Designs: 8g + 6g, St. Stephen's Cathedral in Flames. 12g+12g, Pleading hand in concentration camp. 30g + 30g, Hand choking Nazi serpent. 42g + 42g, Hammer breaking Nazi pillar. 1s + 1s, Oath of allegiance. 2s + 2s, Austrian eagle and burning swastika.

Photogravure

1946, Sept. 16 ***Perf. 14*** **Unwmkd.**

B171	SP103	5(g) +3(g) dk brn	55	1.00
B172	SP104	6(g) +4(g) dk sl grn	35	75
B173	SP104	8(g) +6(g) org red	35	75
B174	SP104	12(g) +12(g) sl blk	35	75
B175	SP104	30(g) +30(g) vio	35	75
B176	SP104	42(g) +42(g) dl brn	35	75
B177	SP104	1s +1s dk red	55	1.00
B178	SP104	2s +2s dk car rose	60	1.00
		Nos. B171-B178 (8)	3.45	6.75

Issued as anti-fascist propaganda.

Race Horse with Foal—SP111

Engraved.

1946, Oct. 20 ***Perf. 13½x14***

Various Race Horses.

B179	SP111	16g +16g rose brn	2.50	4.00
B180	SP111	24g +24g dk pur	2.50	4.00
B181	SP111	60g +60g dk grn	2.50	4.00
B182	SP111	1s +1s dk bl gray	2.50	4.00
B183	SP111	2s +2s yel brn	2.50	4.00
		Nos. B179-B183 (5)	12.50	20.00

Austria Prize race, Vienna.

St. Ruprecht's Church, Vienna SP116

1946, Oct. 30 ***Perf. 14x13½***

B184	SP116	30g +70g dk red	50	1.25

Issued to commemorate the 950th anniversary of the founding of Austria. The surtax aided the Stamp Day celebration.

Souvenir Sheets.

President Karl Renner SP117

1946, Sept. 5 ***Imperf.***

B185	SP117	1s +1s dk sl grn	600.00	1,100.
a.		Single stamp	65.00	120.00
B186	SP117	2s +2s dk bl vio	600.00	1,100.
a.		Single stamp	65.00	120.00
B187	SP117	3s +3s dk pur	600.00	1,100.
a.		Single stamp	65.00	120.00
B188	SP117	5s +5s dk vio brn	600.00	1,100.
a.		Single stamp	65.00	120.00

First anniversary of Austria's liberation. Sheets of 8. Size: 180x153mm.

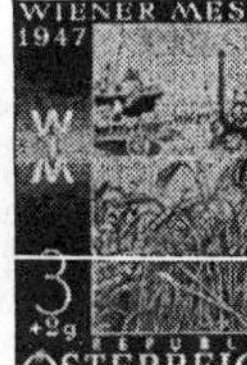

Statue of Rudolf IV the Founder SP118

Reaping Wheat SP128

Designs: 5g+20g, Tomb of Frederick III. 6g+24g, Main pulpit. 8g+32g, Statue of St. Stephen. 10g+40g, Madonna of the Domestics statue. 12g+48g, High altar. 30g+1.20s, Organ, destroyed in 1945. 50g+1.80s, Anton Pilgram statue. 1s+5s, Cathedral from northeast. 2s+10s, Southwest corner of cathedral.

Engraved.

1946, Dec. 12 ***Perf. 14x13½***

B189	SP118	3g +12g brn	22	45
B190	SP118	5g +20g dk vio brn	22	45
B191	SP118	6g +24g dk bl	22	45
B192	SP118	8g +32g dk grn	20	45
B193	SP118	10g +40g dp bl	38	60
B194	SP118	12g +48g dk vio	45	90
B195	SP118	30g +1.20s car	1.10	1.75
B196	SP118	50g +1.80s dk bl	1.50	2.75
B197	SP118	1s +5s brn vio	2.25	4.00
B198	SP118	2s +10s vio brn	4.50	7.25
		Nos. B189-B198 (10)	11.04	19.05

The surtax aided reconstruction of St. Stephen's Cathedral, Vienna.

1947, Mar. 23 ***Perf. 14x13½***

Designs: 8g+2g, Log raft. 10g+5g, Cement factory. 12g+8g, Coal mine. 18g+12g, Oil derricks. 30g+10g, Textile machinery. 35g+15g, Iron furnace. 60g+20g, Electric power lines.

B199	SP128	3g +2g yel brn	35	65
B200	SP128	8g +2g dk bl grn	35	65
B201	SP128	10g +5g sl blk	35	65
B202	SP128	12g +8g dk pur	35	65
B203	SP128	18g +12g ol grn	35	65
B204	SP128	30g +10g dp cl	35	65
B205	SP128	35g +15g crim	35	65
B206	SP128	60g +20g dk bl	35	65
		Nos. B199-B206 (8)	2.80	5.20

Vienna International Sample Fair, 1947.

Race Horse and Jockey SP136

1947, June 29 ***Perf. 13½x14***

B207	SP136	60g +20g dp bl, *pale pink*	12	30

Cup of Corvinus SP137

Prisoner of War SP147

Designs: 8g+2g, Statue of Providence, Vienna. 10g+5g, Abbey at Melk. 12g+8g, Picture of a Woman, by Kriehuber. 18g+12g, Children at the Window, by Waldmuller. 20g + 10g, Entrance, Upper Belvedere Palace. 30g+10g, Nymph Egeria, Schönbrunn Castle. 35g+15g, National Library, Vienna. 48g + 12g, "Workshop of a Printer of Engravings," by Schmutzer. 60g+20g, Girl with Straw Hat, by Amerling.

1947, June 20 ***Perf. 14x13½***

B208	SP137	3g +2g brn	30	50
B209	SP137	8g +2g dk bl grn	28	50
B210	SP137	10g +5g dp cl	28	50
B211	SP137	12g +8g dk pur	28	50
B212	SP137	18g +12g gldn brn	28	50
B213	SP137	20g +10g sep	28	50
B214	SP137	30g +10g dk yel grn	28	50
B215	SP137	35g +15g dp car	28	50
B216	SP137	48g +12g dk brn vio	28	50
B217	SP137	60g +20g dp bl	28	50
		Nos. B208-B217 (10)	2.82	5.00

1947, Aug. 30

Designs: 12g+8g, Prisoners' Mail. 18g+12g, Prison camp visitor. 35g + 15g, Family reunion. 60g+20g, "Industry" beckoning. 1s+40g, Sower.

B218	SP147	8g +2(g) dk grn	15	30
B219	SP147	12g +8(g) dk vio brn	15	30
B220	SP147	18g +12(g) blk brn	15	30
B221	SP147	35g +15(g) rose brn	15	30
B222	SP147	60g +20(g) dp bl	15	30
B223	SP147	1s +40(g) redsh brn	15	45
		Nos. B218-B223 (6)	90	1.95

Olympic Flame and Emblem SP153

Laabenbach Bridge Neulengbach SP154

1948, Jan. 16 **Engraved.**

B224	SP153	1s +50g dk bl	38	45

The surtax was used to help defray expenses of Austria's 1948 Olympics team.

1948, Feb. 18 ***Perf. 14x13½***

Designs: 20g+10g, Dam, Vermunt Lake. 30g+10g, Danube Port, Vienna. 40g+20g, Mining, Erzberg. 45g+20g, Tracks, Southern Railway Station, Vienna. 60g + 30g, Communal housing project, Vienna. 75g+35g, Gas Works, Vienna. 80g+40g, Oil refinery. 1s+50g, Gesäuse Highway, Styria. 1.40s+70g, Parliament Building, Vienna.

B225	SP154	10g +5g sl blk	22	30
B226	SP154	20g +10g lil	22	30
B227	SP154	30g +10g dl grn	50	75
B228	SP154	40g +20g ol brn	15	22
B229	SP154	45g +20g dk bl	6	9
B230	SP154	60g +30g dk red	8	12
B231	SP154	75g +35g dk vio brn	10	15
B232	SP154	80g +40g vio brn	10	15
B233	SP154	1s +50g dp bl	12	18
B234	SP154	1.40s +70g dp car	45	65
		Nos. B225-B234 (10)	2.00	2.91

The surtax was for the Reconstruction Fund.

Violet SP155

Designs: 20g+10g, Anemone. 30g+10g, Crocus. 40g+20g, Yellow primrose. 45g+20g, Pasqueflower. 60g + 30g, Rhododendron. 75g + 35g, Dogrose. 80g + 40g, Cyclamen. 1s + 50g, Alpine Gentian. 1.40s + 70g, Edelweiss.

Engraved and Typographed.

1948, May 14 **Unwmkd.**

B235	SP155	10g +5g multi	30	22
B236	SP155	20g +10g multi	16	12
B237	SP155	30g +10g multi	3.75	4.50
B238	SP155	40g +20g multi	45	50
B239	SP155	45g +20g multi	15	15
B240	SP155	60g +30g multi	15	18
B241	SP155	75g +35g multi	15	18
B242	SP155	80g +40g multi	30	35
B243	SP155	1s +50g multi	38	50
B244	SP155	1.40s +70g multi	90	1.00
		Nos. B235-B244 (10)	6.69	7.70

Hans Makart SP156

St. Rupert SP157

Designs: 20g+10g, Künstlerhaus, Vienna. 40g+20g, Carl Kundmann. 50g+25g, A. S. von Siccardsburg. 60g+30g, Hans Cannon. 1s+50g, William Unger. 1.40s+70g, Friedrich von Schmidt.

1948, June 15 **Engraved**

B245	SP156	20g +10g dp yel grn	7.00	10.00
B246	SP156	30g +15g dk brn	3.00	3.50
B247	SP156	40g +20g ind	3.00	3.50
B248	SP156	50g +25g dk vio	3.75	5.50
B249	SP156	60g +30g dk red	3.75	5.50
B250	SP156	1s +50g dk bl	7.00	11.00
B251	SP156	1.40s +70g red brn	11.00	16.00
		Nos. B245-B251 (7)	38.50	55.00

Issued to commemorate the 80th anniversary of the Kunstlerhaus, home of the leading Austrian Artists Association.

1948, Aug. 6 ***Perf. 14x13½***

Designs: 30g + 15g, Cathedral and Fountain. 40g+20g, Facade of Cathedral. 50g+25g, Cathedral from South. 60g+30g, Abbey of St. Peter. 80g + 40g, Inside Cathedral. 1s + 50g, Salzburg Cathedral and Castle. 1.40s + 70g, Madonna by Michael Pacher.

B252	SP157	20g +10g dp grn	7.00	8.00
B253	SP157	30g +15g red brn	2.75	4.00

B254	SP157	40g	+20g sl blk	2.00	2.75
B255	SP157	50g	+25g choc	45	65
B256	SP157	60g	+30g dk red	45	65
B257	SP157	80g	+40g dk brn vio	45	65
B258	SP157	1s	+50g dp bl	90	90
B259	SP157	1.40s	+70g dk grn	1.50	1.75
	Nos. B252-B259 (8)			15.50	19.35

The surtax was to aid in the reconstruction of Salzburg Cathedral.

Easter SP158 — Arms of Austria, 1230 SP159

Designs: 60g + 20g, St. Nicholas Day. 1s+25g, Birthday. 1.40s+35g, Christmas.

1949, Apr. 13 **Unwmkd.**

Inscribed: "Glückliche Kindheit".

B260	SP158	40g	+10g brn vio	18.50	25.00
B261	SP158	60g	+20g brn red	18.50	25.00
B262	SP158	1s	+25g dp ultra	18.50	25.00
B263	SP158	1.40s	+35g dk grn	18.50	25.00

The surtax was for Child Welfare.

1949, Aug. 17

Designs: 60g+15g, Arms, 1450. 1s+25g, Arms, 1600. 1.60s+40g, Arms, 1945.

Engraved and Photogravure.

B264	SP159	40g	+10g yel brn & yel	7.50	10.00

Engraved and Typographed.

B265	SP159	60g	+15g brn car & sal	7.50	10.00
B266	SP159	1s	+25g dp bl & ver	7.50	10.00
B267	SP159	1.60s	+40g dp grn & sal	7.50	10.00

The surtax was for returned prisoners of war.

Laurel Branch, Stamps and Magnifier
SP160

1949, Dec. 3 **Engraved**

B268	SP160	60g	+15g dk red	3.00	3.50

Stamp Day, Dec. 3-4.

Arms of Austria and Carinthia SP161 — Carinthian with Austrian Flag SP162

Design: 1.70s+40g, Casting ballot.

Photogravure.

1950, Oct. 10 ***Perf. 14x13½***

B269	SP161	60g	+15g bl grn & choc	30.00	35.00
B270	SP162	1s	+25g red org & red	45.00	40.00
B271	SP162	1.70s	+40g dp bl & grnsh bl	45.00	50.00

Issued to mark the 30th anniversary of the plebiscite in Carinthia.

Collector Examining Cover SP163 — Miner and Mine SP164

1950, Dec. 2 **Engraved**

B272	SP163	60g	+15g bl grn	9.00	9.50

Stamp Day.

1951, Mar. 10 **Unwmkd.**

Designs: 60g + 15g, Mason holding brick and trowel. 1s + 25g, Bridge builder with hook and chain. 1.70s+40g, Electrician, pole and insulators.

B273	SP164	40g	+10g dk brn	15.00	22.50
B274	SP164	60g	+15g dk grn	15.00	22.50
B275	SP164	1s	+25g red brn	15.00	22.50
B276	SP164	1.70s	+40g vio bl	15.00	22.50

Issued to publicize Austrian reconstruction.

Laurel Branch and Olympic Circles
SP165

1952, Jan. 26 ***Perf. 13½x14***

B277	SP165	2.40s	+60g grnsh blk	17.50	25.00

The surtax was used to help defray expenses of Austria's athletes in the 1952 Olympic Games.

Cupid as Postman
SP166

1952, Mar. 10 ***Perf. 14x13½***

B278	SP166	1.50s	+35g dk brn car	20.00	28.50

Stamp Day.

Sculpture, "Christ, The Almighty"
SP167

1952, Sept. 6 ***Perf. 13½x14***

B279	SP167	1s	+25g grnsh gray	12.00	17.50

Issued to publicize the Austrian Catholic Convention, Vienna, Sept. 11-14, 1952.

Type of 1945-46 Overprinted in Gold

1s+25g

1953, Aug. 29 **Unwmkd.**

B280	A124	1s	+25g on 5s dl bl	4.00	5.75

Issued to commemorate the 60th anniversary of labor unions in Austria.

Bummerlhaus Steyr SP168 — Globe and Philatelic Accessories SP169

Designs: 1s+25g, Johannes Kepler. 1.50s+40g, Lutheran Bible, 1st edition. 2.40s+60g, Theophil von Hansen. 3s+75g, Reconstructed Lutheran School, Vienna.

1953, Nov. 5 **Engr.** ***Perf. 14x13½***

B281	SP168	70g	+15g vio brn	30	35
B282	SP168	1s	+25g dk gray bl	30	55
B283	SP168	1.50s	+40g choc	1.10	45
B284	SP168	2.40s	+60g dk grn	3.00	3.50
B285	SP168	3s	+75g dk pur	8.25	12.00
	Nos. B281-B285 (5)			12.95	16.85

The surtax was used toward reconstruction of the Lutheran School, Vienna.

1953, Dec. 5

B286	SP169	1s	+25g choc	7.50	8.50

Stamp Day.

Type of 1945-46 with Denomination Replaced by Asterisks

Surcharged in Brown

LAWINENOPFER
1954
1s + 20g

1954, Feb. 19 ***Perf. 13½x14***

B287	A124	1s	+20g bl gray	25	15

The surtax was used for aid to avalanche victims.

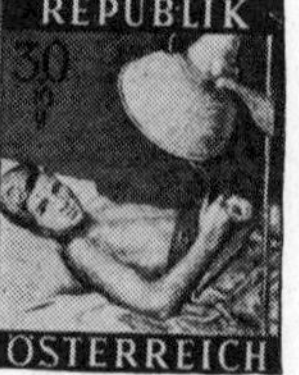

Patient Under Sun Lamp
SP170

Designs: 70g+15g, Physician using microscope. 1s+25g, Mother and children. 1.45s+35g, Operating room. 1.50s+35g, Baby on scale. 2.40s+60g, Nurse.

1954 **Engraved.** ***Perf. 14x13½.***

B288	SP170	30g	+10g pur	1.50	1.90
B289	SP170	70g	+15g dk brn	22	22
B290	SP170	1s	+25g dk bl	30	32
B291	SP170	1.45s	+35g dk bl grn	38	45
B292	SP170	1.50s	+35g dk red	6.00	7.25
B293	SP170	2.40s	+60g dk red brn	6.75	9.50
	Nos. B288-B293 (6)			15.15	19.64

The surtax was for social welfare.

Early Vienna-Ulm Ferryboat
SP171

1954, Dec. 4 ***Perf. 13½x14***

B294	SP171	1s	+25g dk gray grn	6.00	9.00

Stamp Day.

"Industry" Welcoming Returned Prisoner of War
SP172

1955, June 29

B295	SP172	1s	+25g red brn	2.75	3.25

The surtax was for returned prisoners of war and relatives of prisoners not yet released.

Collector Looking at Album SP173 — Ornamental Shield and Letter SP174

1955, Dec. 3 ***Perf. 14x13½***

B296	SP173	1s	+25g vio brn	4.00	5.75

Issued for the Day of the Stamp. The surtax was for the promotion of Austrian philately.

1956, Dec. 1 **Engraved**

B297	SP174	1s	+25g scar	3.50	5.00

Stamp Day. See note after No. B296.

Arms of Austria, 1945
SP175

Engraved and Typographed

1956, Dec. 21 ***Perf. 14x13½***

B298	SP175	1.50s	+50g on 1.60s +40g gray & red	40	55

The surtax was for Hungarian refugees.

New Post Office, Linz 2
SP176

1957, Nov. 30 Engr. *Perf. 13½x14*

B299 SP176 1s +25g dk sl grn 3.75 5.50

Stamp Day. See note after No. B296.

1958, Dec. 6

Design: 2.40s+60g, Post office, Kitzbuhel.

B300 SP176 2.40s +60g bl 1.00 1.50

Stamp Day. See note after B296. See also No. B303.

Roman Carriage from Tomb at Maria Saal
SP177

Lithographed and Engraved

1959, Dec. 5 *Perf. 13½x14*

B301 SP177 2.40s +60g pale lil & blk 75 1.10

Stamp Day.

Progressive Die Proof under Magnifying Glass
SP178

1960, Dec. 2 Engr. *Perf. 13½x14*

B302 SP178 3s +70g vio brn 1.75 1.75

Stamp Day.

P. O. Type of 1957

Design: 3s+70g, Post Office, Rust.

1961, Dec. 1 *Perf. 13½*

B303 SP176 3s +70g dk bl grn 1.75 1.75

Stamp Day. See note after No. B296.

Hands of Stamp Engraver at Work—SP179

1962, Nov. 30 *Perf. 13½x14*

B304 SP179 3s +70g dl pur 2.40 2.40

Stamp Day.

Railroad Exit, Post Office Vienna 101—SP180

Lithographed and Engraved

1963, Nov. 29 Unwmkd.

B305 SP180 3s +70g tan & blk 1.10 1.10

Stamp Day.

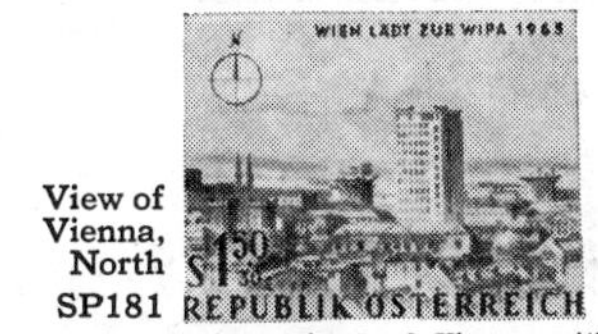

View of Vienna, North
SP181

Designs: Various views of Vienna with compass indicating direction.

1964, July 20 Litho. *Perf. 13½x14*

Multicolored

B306	SP181	1.50s +30g ("N")		25	25
B307	SP181	1.50s +30g ("NO")		25	25
B308	SP181	1.50s +30g ("O")		25	25
B309	SP181	1.50s +30g ("SO")		25	25
B310	SP181	1.50s +30g ("S")		25	25
B311	SP181	1.50s +30g ("SW")		25	25
B312	SP181	1.50s +30g ("W")		25	25
B313	SP181	1.50s +30g ("NW")		25	25
		Nos. B306-B313 (8)		2.00	2.00

Issued to publicize the Vienna International Philatelic Exhibition (WIPA 1965).

Post Bus Terminal, St. Gilgen, Wolfgangsee—SP182

1964, Dec. 4 *Perf. 13½* Unwmkd.

B314 SP182 3s +70g multi 65 65

Stamp Day.

Wall Painting, Tomb at Thebes
SP183

Development of Writing: 1.80s+50g, Cuneiform writing on stone tablet and man's head from Assyrian palace. 2.20s+60g, Wax tablet with Latin writing, Corinthian column. 3s+80g, Gothic writing on sealed letter, Gothic window from Munster Cathedral. 4s+1s, Letter with seal and postmark and upright desk. 5s+1.20s, Typewriter.

Lithographed and Engraved

1965, June 4 *Perf. 14x13½*

B315	SP183	1.50s +40g dp rose & blk	18	18
B316	SP183	1.80s +50g yel & blk	25	25
B317	SP183	2.20s +60g pale vio & blk	85	85
B318	SP183	3s +80g ap grn & blk	38	38
B319	SP183	4s +1s lt bl & blk	1.10	1.10
B320	SP183	5s +1.20s brt grn & blk	1.35	1.35
		Nos. B315-B320 (6)	4.11	4.11

Issued to commemorate the Vienna International Philatelic Exhibition, WIPA, June 4–13.

Mailman Distributing Mail
SP184

Perf. 13½x14

1965, Dec. 3 Engraved Unwmkd.

B321 SP184 3s +70g bl grn 55 55

Stamp Day.

Letter Carrier, 16th Century
SP185

Letter Carrier, 16th Century Playing Card
SP186

Lithographed and Engraved

1966, Dec. 2 *Perf. 13½* Unwmkd.

B322 SP185 3s +70g multi 55 50

Stamp Day. Design is from Ambras Heroes' Book, Austrian National Library.

Engraved and Photogravure

1967, Dec. 1 *Perf. 13x13½*

B323 SP186 3.50s +80g multi 75 75

Stamp Day.

Mercury, Bas-relief from Purkersdorf
SP187

Unken Post Station Sign, 1710
SP188

1968, Nov. 29 Engr. *Perf. 13½*

B324 SP187 3.50s +80g sl grn 70 70

Stamp Day.

Engraved and Photogravure

1969, Dec. 5 *Perf. 12*

B325 SP188 3.50s +80g tan, red & blk 65 65

Stamp Day. Design is from a watercolor by Friedrich Zeller.

Saddle, Bag, Harness and Post Horn
SP189

Engraved and Lithographed

1970, Dec. 4 *Perf. 13½x14*

B326 SP189 3.50s +80g gray blk & yel 70 65

Stamp Day.

"50 Years"
SP190

Engraved and Photogravure

1971, Dec. 3 *Perf. 13½*

B327 SP190 4s +1.50s gold & red brn 90 90

50th anniversary of the Federation of Austrian Philatelic Societies.

Local Post Carrier
SP191

Gabriel, by Lorenz Luchsperger, 15th Century
SP192

1972, Dec. 1 Engraved *Perf. 14x13½*

B328 SP191 4s +1s ol grn 80 80

Stamp Day.

1973, Nov. 30

B329 SP192 4s +1s mar 85 85

Stamp Day.

Mail Coach Leaving Old PTT Building
SP193

1974, Nov. 29 Engr. *Perf. 14x13½*

B330 SP193 4s +2s vio bl 90 90

Stamp Day.

Alpine Skiing, Women's
SP194

Designs (Innsbruck Winter Olympic Games Emblem and): 1.50s+70g, Ice hockey. 2s+90g, Ski jump. 4s+1.90s, Bobsledding.

1975, Mar. 14 Photo. *Perf. 13½x14*

B331	SP194	1s +50g multi	30	30
B332	SP194	1.50s +70g multi	40	40
B333	SP194	2s +90g multi	50	50
B334	SP194	4s +1.90s multi	1.00	1.00

1975, Nov. 14

Designs (Innsbruck Winter Olympic Games Emblem and): 70g+30g, Figure skating, pair. 2s+1s, Cross-country skiing. 2.50s+1s, Luge. 4s+2s, Biathlon.

B335	SP194	70g +30g multi	30	30
B336	SP194	2s +1s multi	40	40
B337	SP194	2.50s +1s multi	50	50
B338	SP194	4s +2s multi	1.00	1.00

12th Winter Olympic Games, Innsbruck, Feb. 4–15, 1976.

Austria Nos. 5, 250, 455
SP195

Photogravure and Engraved

1975, Nov. 28 *Perf. 14*

B339 SP195 4s +2s multi 1.10 1.10

Stamp Day and 125th anniversary of Austrian stamps.

Postilion's Gala Hat and Horn
SP196

1976, Dec. 3 ***Perf. 13½x14***

B340 SP196 6s +2s blk & lt vio 1.10 1.10

Stamp Day 1976.

Emanuel Herrmann
SP197

1977, Dec. 2 ***Perf. 14x13½***

B341 SP197 6s +2s multi 1.10 1.10

Stamp Day 1977. Emanuel Herrmann (1839–1902), economist, invented postal card. Austria issued first postal card in 1869.

Post Bus, 1913
SP198

1978, Dec. 1 Photo. ***Perf. 13½x14***

B342 SP198 10s +5s multi 2.10 2.10

Stamp Day 1978.

Heroes' Square, Vienna—SP199

Photo. & Engr.

1979, Nov. 30 ***Perf. 13½***

B343 SP199 16s +8s multi 3.25 3.25

No. B343 Inscribed "2. Phase"

1980, Nov. 21 Photo. & Engr. ***Perf. 13½***

B344 SP199 16s +8s multi 3.25 3.25

WIPA 1981 Philatelic Exhibition, Vienna, May 22-31, 1981.

Souvenir Sheet

1981, Feb. 20 Photo. & Engr. ***Perf. 13½***

B345 SP199 16s +8s multi 5.00 5.00

WIPA 1981 Philatelic Exhibition, Vienna, May 22-31. No. B345 contains one stamp (without inscription); black and red margin. Size: 90x72mm.

Stamp Day 1982—SP200

1982, Nov. 26 Photo. & Engr. ***Perf.***

B346 SP200 6 +3s Mainz-Weber mailbox, 1870 1.35 1.35

AIR POST STAMPS.
Issues of the Monarchy.

FLUGPOST

Types of Regular Issue of 1916 Surcharged

2·50 K 2·50

Perf. 12½.

1918, Mar. 30 **Unwmkd.**

C1	A40	1.50k on 2k lil	3.50	4.50
C2	A40	2.50k on 3k ocher	15.00	25.00
a.		Inverted surch.	1,650.	
b.		Perf. 11½	400.00	250.00
c.		Perf. 12½x11½	32.50	37.50

Overprinted FLUGPOST

C3	A40	4k gray	10.00	13.50

Set exists imperf. Price, $500.

Nos. C1-C3 also exist without surcharge or overprint. Price, set perf., $900; imperf., $750.

Nos. C1-C3 were printed on grayish and on white paper.

A 7k on 10k red brown was prepared but not regularly issued. Price, perf. or imperf., $600.

Issues of the Republic.

Hawk AP1 — Wilhelm Kress AP2

1922-24 Typographed *Perf. 12½*

C4	AP1	300k claret	30	1.35
C5	AP1	400k grn ('24)	7.50	11.50
C6	AP1	600k bister	15	65
C7	AP1	900k brn org	15	65

Engraved

C8	AP2	1200k brn vio	15	65
C9	AP2	2400k slate	15	65
C10	AP2	3000k dp brn ('23)	2.50	3.50
C11	AP2	4800k dk bl ('23)	2.50	4.00
		Nos. C4-C11 (8)	13.40	22.95

Set exists imperf. Price, $900.

Plane and Pilot's Head AP3 — Airplane Passing Crane AP4

1925-30 Typographed *Perf. 12½*

C12	AP3	2g gray brn	50	1.10
C13	AP3	5g red	30	30
a.		Horizontal pair, imperf. between	350.00	
C14	AP3	6g dk bl	1.25	2.00
C15	AP3	8g yel grn	1.50	2.25
C16	AP3	10g dp org ('26)	1.50	2.25
a.		Horiz. pair, imperf. between	375.00	
C17	AP3	15g red vio ('26)	60	1.00
a.		Horiz. pair, imperf. between	450.00	
C18	AP3	20g org brn ('30)	20.00	7.50
C19	AP3	25g blk vio ('30)	4.00	11.00
C20	AP3	30g bis ('26)	10.00	10.00
C21	AP3	50g bl gray ('26)	25.00	15.00
C22	AP3	80g dk grn ('30)	2.00	6.00

Photogravure

C23	AP4	10g org red	1.50	3.25
a.		Horiz. pair, imperf. btwn.	375.00	
C24	AP4	15g claret	1.00	1.50
C25	AP4	30g brn vio	1.50	3.25
C26	AP4	50g gray blk	1.50	3.75
C27	AP4	1s dp bl	3.50	6.00
C28	AP4	2s dk grn	2.50	6.00
a.		Vertical pair, imperf. between	350.00	
C29	AP4	3s red brn ('26)	75.00	55.00
C30	AP4	5s ind ('26)	22.50	32.50

Size: 25½x32mm.

C31	AP4	10s blk brn, *gray* ('26)	16.50	27.50
		Nos. C12-C31 (20)	192.15	197.15

Set exists imperf. Price, $1,250.

Airplane over Güssing Castle AP5 — Airplane over the Danube AP6

Designs (each includes plane): 10g, Maria-Worth. 15g, Durnstein. 20g, Hallstatt. 25g, Salzburg. 30g, Upper Dachstein and Schladminger Glacier. 40g, Lake Wetter. 50g, Arlberg. 60g, St. Stephen's Cathedral. 80g, Church of the Minorites. 2s, Railroad viaduct, Carinthia. 3s, Gross Glockner mountain. 5s, Aerial railway. 10s, Seaplane and yachts.

1935, Aug. 16 Engraved. *Perf. 12½.*

C32	AP5	5g rose vio	15	20
C33	AP5	10g red org	14	20
C34	AP5	15g yel grn	90	1.00
C35	AP5	20g gray bl	20	50
C36	AP5	25g vio brn	20	50
C37	AP5	30g brn org	22	50
C38	AP5	40g gray grn	22	55
C39	AP5	50g lt sl bl	25	60
C40	AP5	60g blk brn	45	1.00
C41	AP5	80g lt brn	45	1.00
C42	AP6	1s rose red	45	1.40
C43	AP6	2s ol grn	3.00	8.00
C44	AP6	3s yel brn	12.50	20.00
C45	AP6	5s dk grn	7.00	20.00
C46	AP6	10s sl bl	55.00	100.00
		Nos. C32-C46 (15)	81.13	155.45

Set exists imperf. Price, $425.

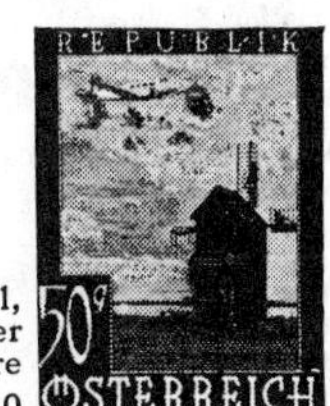

Windmill, Neusiedler Lake Shore AP20

Designs: 1s, Roman arch, Carnuntum. 2s, Town Hall, Gmund. 3s, Schieder Lake, Hinterstoder. 4s, Praegraten, Eastern Tyrol. 5s, Torsäule, Salzburg. 10s, St. Charles Church, Vienna.

1947 *Perf. 14x13½* **Unwmkd.**

C47	AP20	50g blk brn	15	38
C48	AP20	1s dk brn vio	28	55
C49	AP20	2s dk grn	40	85
C50	AP20	3s chocolate	2.00	4.00
C51	AP20	4s dk grn	1.40	2.75
C52	AP20	5s dk bl	1.40	2.75
C53	AP20	10s dk bl	55	1.35
		Nos. C47-C53 (7)	6.18	12.63

Rooks AP27

Birds: 1s, Barn swallows. 2s, Black-headed gulls. 3s, Great cormorants. 5s, Buzzard. 10s, Gray heron. 20s, Golden eagle.

1950-53 *Perf. 13½x14*

C54	AP27	60g dk bl vio	4.50	4.00
C55	AP27	1s dk vio bl ('53)	22.50	35.00
C56	AP27	2s dk bl	13.00	10.00
C57	AP27	3s dk sl grn ('53)	110.00	110.00
C58	AP27	5s red brn ('53)	100.00	110.00
C59	AP27	10s gray vio ('53)	52.50	52.50
C60	AP27	20s brn blk ('52)	9.50	5.50
		Nos C54-C60 (7)	312.00	327.00

Value at lower left on Nos. C59 and C60. No. C60 exists imperf.

Etrich "Dove" AP28

Designs: 3.50s, Twin-engine jet airliner. 5s, Four-engine jet airliner.

1968, May 31 Engr. *Perf. 13½x14*

C61	AP28	2s ol bis	38	55
C62	AP28	3.50s sl grn	55	85
C63	AP28	5s dk bl	80	1.20

Issued to publicize IFA WIEN 1968 (International Air Post Exhibition), Vienna, May 30-June 4.

POSTAGE DUE STAMPS.
Issues of the Monarchy.

D1 — D2

Wmkd.

ZEITUNGS-MARKEN. (91)

1894-95 Typo. *Perf. 10 to 13½*

J1	D1	1kr brown	3.50	2.00
a.		Perf. 13½	25.00	7.50
J2	D1	2kr brn ('95)	6.00	2.00
a.		Pair, imperf. btwn.	185.00	225.00
J3	D1	3kr brown	5.50	50
J4	D1	5kr brown	5.00	50
a.		Perf. 13½	17.50	7.50
b.		Pair, imperf. btwn.	165.00	200.00
J5	D1	6kr brn ('95)	5.00	4.50
J6	D1	7kr brn ('95)	1.50	2.50
a.		Pair, imperf. btwn.	210.00	250.00
J7	D1	10kr brown	8.50	50
J8	D1	20kr brown	1.50	3.50
J9	D1	50kr brown	65.00	45.00
		Nos. J1-J9 (9)	101.50	61.00

See also Nos. J204-J231.

1899-1900 *Imperf.*

J10	D2	1h brown	35	45
J11	D2	2h brown	35	45
J12	D2	3h brn ('00)	35	35
J13	D2	4h brown	4.50	1.25
J14	D2	5h brn ('00)	4.00	35
J15	D2	6h brown	50	1.50
J16	D2	10h brown	35	35
J17	D2	12h brown	60	3.25
J18	D2	15h brown	65	1.60
J19	D2	20h brown	30.00	85
J20	D2	40h brown	1.50	3.25
J21	D2	100h brown	7.00	2.50
		Nos. J10-J21 (12)	50.15	16.15

Perf. 10½, 12½, 13½ and Compound.

J22	D2	1h brown	90	30
J23	D2	2h brown	65	25
J24	D2	3h brn ('00)	55	15
J25	D2	4h brown	55	15
J26	D2	5h brn ('00)	40	15
J27	D2	6h brown	40	20
J28	D2	10h brown	60	12
J29	D2	12h brown	65	65
J30	D2	15h brown	1.00	45
J31	D2	20h brown	75	35
J32	D2	40h brown	1.10	1.00
J33	D2	100h brown	27.50	1.50
		Nos. J22-J33 (12)	35.05	5.27

Nos. J10 to J33 exist on unwatermarked paper.

D3

1908-13 *Perf. 12½* **Unwmkd.**

J34	D3	1h carmine	1.50	1.25
J35	D3	2h carmine	50	50
J36	D3	4h carmine	50	25
J37	D3	6h carmine	50	25
J38	D3	10h carmine	60	25
J39	D3	14h car ('13)	5.00	2.00
J40	D3	20h carmine	6.00	25
J41	D3	25h car ('10)	12.50	3.50
J42	D3	30h carmine	8.00	25
J43	D3	50h carmine	10.00	35
J44	D3	100h carmine	20.00	40
		Nos. J34-J44 (11)	65.10	9.25

All values exist on ordinary paper, Nos. J34 to J38, J40 and J42 to J44 on chalky paper and Nos. J34 to J38, J40 and J44 on thin ordinary paper. All values exist imperforate.

1911

J45	D3	5k violet	60.00	12.50
J46	D3	10k violet	325.00	7.50

Regular Issue of 1908 Overprinted or Surcharged in Carmine or Black:

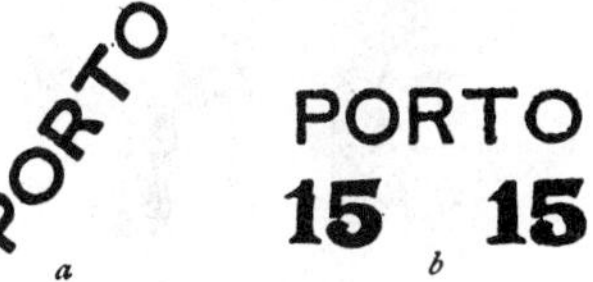

1916

J47	A22	1h gray (C)	20	12
a.		Pair, one without overprint	150.00	
J48	A22	15h on 2h vio (Bk)	50	38

D4 — D5

1916

J49	D4	5h rose red	15	10
J50	D4	10h rose red	15	10
J51	D4	15h rose red	15	10
J52	D4	20h rose red	15	10
J53	D4	25h rose red	60	50
J54	D4	30h rose red	25	15
J55	D4	40h rose red	30	15
J56	D4	50h rose red	1.50	1.50
J57	D5	1k ultra	50	15
a.		Horizontal pair, imperf. btwn.	500.00	500.00
J58	D5	5k ultra	2.50	2.50
J59	D5	10k ultra	2.50	1.50
		Nos. J49-J59 (11)	8.75	6.85

Set exists imperf. Price $135.

Type of Regular Issue of 1916 Surcharged

15 * 15

1917

J60	A38	10h on 24h bl	3.75	38
J61	A38	15h on 36h vio	60	25

J62	A38	20h on 54h org	60	38
J63	A38	50h on 42h choc	60	25

All values of this issue are known imperforate, also without surcharge, perforated and imperforate.

Issues of the Republic.

Postage Due Stamps of 1916 Overprinted

1919

J64	D4	5h rose red	20	25
a.		Inverted ovpt.	275.00	275.00
J65	D4	10h rose red	20	25
J66	D4	15h rose red	25	50
J67	D4	20h rose red	45	38
J68	D4	25h rose red	10.00	20.00
J69	D4	30h rose red	25	25
J70	D4	40h rose red	25	38
J71	D4	50h rose red	50	1.25
J72	D5	1k ultra	9.00	7.50
J73	D5	5k ultra	11.00	7.50
J74	D5	10k ultra	12.50	5.00
		Nos. J64-J74 (11)	44.60	43.26

Nos. J64, J65, J67 and J70 exist imperforate.

D6

D7

1920-21 *Perf. 12½.*

J75	D6	5h brt red	10	25
J76	D6	10h brt red	5	8
J77	D6	15h brt red	5	50
J78	D6	20h brt red	5	10
J79	D6	25h brt red	10	50
J80	D6	30h brt red	5	15
J81	D6	40h brt red	5	7
J82	D6	50h brt red	5	15
J83	D6	80h brt red	5	15
J84	D7	1k ultra	5	15
J85	D7	1½k ultra ('21)	5	15
J86	D7	2k ultra ('21)	5	12
J87	D7	3k ultra ('21)	5	25
J88	D7	4k ultra ('21)	5	25
J89	D7	5k ultra	5	15
J90	D7	8k ultra ('21)	5	25
J91	D7	10k ultra	5	15
J92	D7	20k ultra ('21)	25	75
		Nos. J75-J92 (18)	1.20	4.17

Nos. J84 to J92 exist on white paper and on grayish white paper. They also exist imperf.; price, set $80.

Imperf.

J93	D6	5h brt red	5	35
J94	D6	10h brt red	5	10
J95	D6	15h brt red	5	40
J96	D6	20h brt red	5	10
J97	D6	25h brt red	5	50
J98	D6	30h brt red	5	20
J99	D6	40h brt red	5	15
J100	D6	50h brt red	5	40
J101	D6	80h brt red	5	20
		Nos. J93-J101 (9)	45	2.40

Nachmarke

No. 207a Surcharged in Dark Blue

7½K

1921 *Perf. 12½*

J102	A43	7½k on 15h bis	5	20
a.		Inverted surch.	300.00	300.00

D8

1922

J103	D8	1k redsh buff	5	7
J104	D8	2k redsh buff	5	10
J105	D8	4k redsh buff	5	12
J106	D8	5k redsh buff	5	12
J107	D8	7½k redsh buff	5	12
J108	D8	10k bl grn	5	12
J109	D8	15k bl grn	6	12
J110	D8	20k bl grn	9	15
J111	D8	25k bl grn	7	12
J112	D8	40k bl grn	7	13
J113	D8	50k bl grn	7	17
		Nos. J103-J113 (11)	66	1.34

D9

D10

1922-24

J114	D9	10k cob bl	9	10
J115	D9	15k cob bl	7	9
J116	D9	20k cob bl	10	10
J117	D9	50k cob bl	6	9
J118	D10	100k plum	5	5
J119	D10	150k plum	5	5
J120	D10	200k plum	5	5
J121	D10	400k plum	6	6
J122	D10	600k plum ('23)	7	7
J123	D10	800k plum	6	5
J124	D10	1,000k plum ('23)	5	7
J125	D10	1,200k plum ('23)	50	*1.50*
J126	D10	1,500k plum ('24)	15	20
J127	D10	1,800k plum ('24)	2.00	*5.00*
J128	D10	2,000k plum ('23)	25	50
J129	D10	3,000k plum ('24)	7.00	10.00
J130	D10	4,000k plum ('24)	4.50	*12.50*
J131	D10	6,000k plum ('24)	4.50	*20.00*
		Nos. J114-J131 (18)	19.61	*50.48*

Price, #J103-J131 imperf, $350.

D11

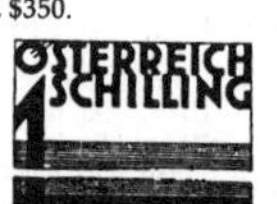

D12

1925-34 *Perf. 12½*

J132	D11	1g red	6	6
J133	D11	2g red	6	6
J134	D11	3g red	6	12
J135	D11	4g red	6	6
J136	D11	5g red ('27)	6	6
J137	D11	6g red	30	60
J138	D11	8g red	20	30
J139	D11	10g dk bl	6	6
J140	D11	12g dk bl	10	14
J141	D11	14g dk bl ('27)	25	14
J142	D11	15g dk bl	15	12
J143	D11	16g dk bl ('29)	45	20
J144	D11	18g dk bl ('34)	1.65	4.75
J145	D11	20g dk bl	15	10
J146	D11	23g dk bl	1.00	20
J147	D11	24g dk bl ('32)	2.00	12
J148	D11	28g dk bl ('27)	55	35
J149	D11	30g dk bl	38	15
J150	D11	31g dk bl ('29)	1.65	25
J151	D11	35g dk bl ('30)	85	20
J152	D11	39g dk bl ('32)	2.25	12
J153	D11	40g dk bl	1.25	2.25
J154	D11	60g dk bl	1.00	1.40
J155	D12	1s dk grn	7.25	1.40
J156	D12	2s dk grn	42.50	4.50
J157	D12	5s dk grn	135.00	40.00
J158	D12	10s dk grn	65.00	5.50
		Nos. J132-J158 (27)	264.29	63.21

Issues of 1925-27 (21 values) imperf, price, set $650.

Coat of Arms

D13 D14

1935

J159	D13	1g red	10	10
J160	D13	2g red	10	10
J161	D13	3g red	10	10
J162	D13	5g red	8	5
J163	D13	10g blue	8	5
J164	D13	12g blue	8	5
J165	D13	15g blue	30	70
J166	D13	20g blue	10	10
J167	D13	24g blue	15	5
J168	D13	30g blue	30	10
J169	D13	39g blue	50	6
J170	D13	60g blue	1.00	2.00
J171	D14	1s green	1.25	75
J172	D14	2s green	2.00	1.00
J173	D14	5s green	3.75	2.00
J174	D14	10s green	8.00	1.00
		Nos. J159-J174 (16)	17.89	8.21

On Nos. J163–J170, background lines are horizontal.

Nos. J159–J174 exist imperf. Price, set $125.

Coat of Arms

D15 D16

Typographed.

1945 *Perf. 10½* **Unwmkd.**

J175	D15	1g vermilion	3	3
J176	D15	2g vermilion	3	3
J177	D15	3g vermilion	3	3
J178	D15	5g vermilion	3	3
J179	D15	10g vermilion	3	3
J180	D15	12g vermilion	7	10
J181	D15	20g vermilion	3	7
J182	D15	24g vermilion	9	10
J183	D15	30g vermilion	4	7
J184	D15	60g vermilion	4	7
J185	D15	1s violet	5	7
J186	D15	2s violet	6	7
J187	D15	5s violet	8	14
J188	D15	10s violet	12	15
		Nos. J175-J188 (14)	73	99

Occupation Stamps of the Allied Military Government Overprinted in Black

PORTO

1946 *Perf. 11.*

J189	OS1	3g dp org	5	10
J190	OS1	5g brt grn	5	5
J191	OS1	6g red vio	8	8
J192	OS1	8g rose pink	5	5
J193	OS1	10g lt gray	5	25
J194	OS1	12g pale buff brn	5	5
J195	OS1	15g rose red	8	25
J196	OS1	20g cop brn	5	5
J197	OS1	25g dp bl	8	8
J198	OS1	30g brt vio	5	5
J199	OS1	40g lt ultra	7	7
J200	OS1	60g lt ol grn	5	5
J201	OS1	1s dk vio	10	20
J202	OS1	2s yellow	28	32
J203	OS1	5s dp ultra	28	32
		Nos. J189-J203 (15)	1.37	1.97

Nos. J189–J203 were issued by the Renner Government. Inverted overprints exist on about half of the denominations.

Type of 1894-95.

Inscribed "Republik Osterreich".

1947 Typographed *Perf. 14*

J204	D1	1g chocolate	3	5
J205	D1	2g chocolate	3	5
J206	D1	3g chocolate	3	5
J207	D1	5g chocolate	3	5
J208	D1	8g chocolate	3	5
J209	D1	10g chocolate	4	4
J210	D1	12g chocolate	3	3
J211	D1	15g chocolate	3	3
J212	D1	16g chocolate	18	45
J213	D1	17g chocolate	18	45
J214	D1	18g chocolate	18	45
J215	D1	20g chocolate	38	7
J216	D1	24g chocolate	25	32
J217	D1	30g chocolate	15	25
J218	D1	36g chocolate	38	65
J219	D1	40g chocolate	6	8
J220	D1	42g chocolate	35	65
J221	D1	48g chocolate	40	65
J222	D1	50g chocolate	50	12
J223	D1	60g chocolate	15	15
J224	D1	70g chocolate	7	15
J225	D1	80g chocolate	3.25	2.00
J226	D1	1s blue	15	12
J227	D1	1.15s blue	2.00	30
J228	D1	1.20s blue	2.75	1.10
J229	D1	2s blue	30	45
J230	D1	5s blue	30	45
J231	D1	10s blue	38	45
		Nos. J204-J231 (28)	12.61	9.66

1949-57

J232	D16	1g carmine	15	6
J233	D16	2g carmine	15	6
J234	D16	4g car ('51)	60	15
J235	D16	5g carmine	1.50	28
J236	D16	8g car ('51)	2.00	1.35
J237	D16	10g carmine	12	3
J238	D16	20g carmine	12	3
J239	D16	30g carmine	12	3
J240	D16	40g carmine	10	3
J241	D16	50g carmine	12	3
J242	D16	60g car ('50)	5.00	15
J243	D16	63g car ('57)	3.00	3.25
J244	D16	70g carmine	12	3
J245	D16	80g carmine	10	10
J246	D16	90g car ('50)	15	12
J247	D16	1s purple	15	3
J248	D16	1.20s purple	22	10
J249	D16	1.35s purple	18	7
J250	D16	1.40s pur ('51)	30	22
J251	D16	1.50s pur ('53)	15	3
J252	D16	1.65s pur ('50)	25	15
J253	D16	1.70s purple	25	15
J254	D16	2s purple	22	5
J255	D16	2.50s pur ('51)	30	8
J256	D16	3s pur ('51)	60	8
J257	D16	4s pur ('51)	60	45
J258	D16	5s purple	1.10	22
J259	D16	10s purple	1.85	22
		Nos. J232-J259 (28)	19.52	7.55

MILITARY STAMPS.

Issues of the Austro-Hungarian Military Authorities for the Occupied Territories in World War I.

Stamps of Bosnia of 1912-14 Overprinted

K.U.K. FELDPOST

1915 *Perf. 12½* **Unwmkd.**

M1	A23	1h ol grn	20	20
M2	A23	2h brt bl	20	20
M3	A23	3h claret	20	20
M4	A23	5h green	12	15
M5	A23	6h dk gray	20	20
M6	A23	10h rose car	12	15
M7	A23	12h dp ol grn	32	30
M8	A23	20h org brn	50	35
M9	A23	25h ultra	50	30
M10	A23	30h org red	4.00	4.25
M11	A24	35h myr grn	3.50	3.50
M12	A24	40h dk vio	3.50	3.50
M13	A24	45h ol brn	3.75	3.75
M14	A24	50h sl bl	3.50	3.50
M15	A24	60h brn vio	50	50
M16	A24	72h dk bl	3.50	3.50
M17	A25	1k brn vio, *straw*	4.00	4.25
M18	A25	2k dk gray, *bl*	4.00	3.50
M19	A26	3k car, *grn*	35.00	37.50
M20	A26	5k dk vio, *gray*	35.00	37.50

M21	A25	10k dk ultra, *gray*	225.00	225.00
		Nos. M1-M21 (21)	327.61	332.30

Set exists imperf. Price, $450.

Nos. M1–M21 also exist with overprint double, inverted and in red. These varieties were made by order of an official but were not regularly issued.

Emperor Franz Josef
M1 M2

1915-17 Engraved.

Perf. 11½, 12½ and Compound.

M22	M1	1h ol grn	11	9
M23	M1	2h dl bl	15	13
M24	M1	3h claret	11	9
M25	M1	5h green	11	9
a.		Perf. 11½	25.00	10.00
b.		Perf. 11½x12½	37.50	15.00
c.		Perf. 12½x11½	60.00	30.00
M26	M1	6h dk gray	11	9
M27	M1	10h rose car	15	9
M28	M1	10h gray bl ('17)	15	13
M29	M1	12h dp ol grn	15	18
M30	M1	15h car rose ('17)	8	8
a.		Perf. 11½	10.00	7.50
M31	M1	20h org brn	40	20
M32	M1	20h ol grn ('17)	40	20
M33	M1	25h ultra	20	15
M34	M1	30h vermilion	20	18
M35	M1	35h dk grn	38	40
M36	M1	40h dk vio	38	40
M37	M1	45h ol brn	35	40
M38	M1	50h myr grn	35	22
M39	M1	60h brn vio	35	35
M40	M1	72h dk bl	35	35
M41	M1	80h org brn ('17)	20	15
M42	M1	90h mag ('17)	1.00	1.00
M43	M2	1k brn vio, *straw*	2.00	1.50
M44	M2	2k dk gray, *bl*	1.50	70
M45	M2	3k car, *grn*	1.10	1.00
M46	M2	4k dk vio, *gray* ('17)	1.10	1.00
M47	M2	5k dk vio, *gray*	35.00	30.00
M48	M2	10k dk ultra, *gray*	3.50	5.00
		Nos. M22-M48 (27)	49.88	44.17

Nos. M22–M48 exist imperf. Price, set $80.

Emperor Karl I
M3 M4

1917–18 ***Perf. 12½***

M49	M3	1h grnsh bl ('18)	8	5
a.		Perf. 11½	4.00	3.00
M50	M3	2h red org ('18)	8	5
M51	M3	3h ol gray	8	5
a.		Perf. 11½, 11½x12½	12.50	11.00
M52	M3	5h ol grn	8	5
M53	M3	6h violet	10	5
M54	M3	10h org brn	8	5
M55	M3	12h blue	8	8
a.		Perf. 11½	3.50	3.00
M56	M3	15h brt rose	8	5
M57	M3	20h red brn	7	5
M58	M3	25h ultra	45	20
M59	M3	30h slate	12	5
M60	M3	40h ol bis	12	7
a.		Perf. 11½	2.00	1.60
M61	M3	50h dp grn	12	5
a.		Perf. 11½	6.00	5.00
M62	M3	60h car rose	12	12
M63	M3	80h dl bl	10	5
M64	M3	90h dk vio	50	35
M65	M4	2k rose, *straw*	12	5
a.		Perf. 11½	2.25	2.00
M66	M4	3k grn, *bl*	1.25	1.00
M67	M4	4k rose, *grn*	25.00	15.00
a.		Perf. 11½	42.50	35.00
M68	M4	10k dl vio, *gray*	3.25	3.50
a.		Perf. 11½	15.00	13.00
		Nos. M49-M68 (20)	35.38	23.92

Nos. M49–M68 exist imperf. Price, set $27.50.

Emperor Karl I
M5

1918 Typographed ***Perf. 12½***

M69	M5	1h grnsh bl	45.00
M70	M5	2h orange	20.00
M71	M5	3h ol gray	20.00
M72	M5	5h yel grn	25
M73	M5	10h dk brn	25
M74	M5	20h red	1.50
M75	M5	25h blue	1.50
M76	M5	30h bister	100.00
M77	M5	45h dk sl	150.00
M78	M5	50h dp grn	100.00
M79	M5	60h violet	150.00
M80	M5	80h rose	100.00
M81	M5	90h brn vio	3.00

Engraved.

M82	M4	1k ol bis, *bl*	25
		Nos. M69-M82 (14)	691.75

Nos. M69–M82 were on sale at the Vienna post office for a few days before the Armistice signing. They were never issued at the Army Post Offices. They exist imperf.; price, set $950.

MILITARY SEMI-POSTAL STAMPS.

Emperor Karl I MSP7 — Empress Zita MSP8

Typographed

1918 ***Perf. 12½x13*** **Unwmkd.**

MB1	MSP7	10h gray grn	50	30
MB2	MSP8	20h magenta	50	30
MB3	MSP7	45h blue	50	30

These stamps were sold at a premium of 10h each over face value. The surtax was for "Karl's Fund."

Nos. MB1–MB3 exist imperf. Price, set $11.

MILITARY NEWSPAPER STAMPS.

Mercury
MN1

Typographed

1916 ***Perf. 12½*** **Unwmkd.**

MP1	MN1	2h blue	5	5
a.		Perf. 11½	2.00	1.25
b.		Perf. 12½x11½	60.00	25.00
MP2	MN1	6h orange	1.00	50
MP3	MN1	10h carmine	1.25	50
MP4	MN1	20h brown	85	40
a.		Perf. 11½	2.50	1.50

Set exists imperf. Price, $42.50.

NEWSPAPER STAMPS.

From 1851 to 1866, the Austrian Newspaper Stamps were also used in Lombardy-Venetia.

Prices for unused stamps 1851–67 are for fine copies with original gum. Specimens without gum sell for about a third of the figures quoted.

Issues of the Monarchy.

Mercury
N1

Typographed.

Machine-made Paper.

Two Types.

Type I. The "G" of "Zeitungs" has no crossbar.
Type II. The "G" of "Zeitungs" has a crossbar.

1851–56 ***Imperf.*** **Unwmkd.**

P1	N1	(0.6kr) bl, type II	175.00	100.00
a.		bl, type I	200.00	150.00
b.		Ribbed paper	425.00	200.00
P2	N1	(6kr) yel, type I	*12,500.*	*7,500.*
P3	N1	(30kr) rose, type I	*17,500.*	*10,000.*
P4	N1	(6kr) scar, type II ('56)	*35,000.*	*37,500.*

From 1852 No. P3 and from 1856 No. P2 were used as 0.6 kreuzer values.

Pale shades of Nos. P2 and P3 sell at considerably lower prices.

Originals of Nos. P2 and P3 are usually in pale colors and poorly printed. Prices are for stamps clearly printed and in bright colors. Numerous reprints of Nos. P1 to P4 were made between 1866 and 1904. Those of Nos. P2 and P3 are always well printed and in much deeper colors. All reprints are in type I, but occasionally show faint traces of a crossbar on "G" of "ZEITUNGS."

N2 N3

Two Types of the 1858–59 Issue

Type I. Loops of the bow at the back of the head broken.

Type II. Loops complete. Wreath projects further at top of head.

1858–59 Embossed

P5	N2	(1kr) bl, type I	550.00	750.00
P6	N2	(1kr) lil, type II ('59)	800.00	325.00

1861

P7	N3	(1kr) gray	175.00	135.00
a.		(1kr) gray lil	450.00	190.00
b.		(1kr) dp lil	1,850.	575.00

The embossing on the reprints of the 1858–59 and 1861 issues is not as sharp as on the originals.

N4

1863

Unwmkd., or, after June 1864, Wmkd. "ZEITUNGS-MARKEN" in Double-lined Capitals across the Sheet. (91)

P8	N4	(1.05kr) gray	35.00	12.50
a.		Tête bêche pair	*20,000.*	
b.		(1.05kr) gray lil	65.00	25.00

The embossing of the reprints is not as sharp as on the originals.

Mercury
N5 N6

Typographed.

Wmkd. "ZEITUNGS-MARKEN" in Double-lined Capitals across the Sheet. (91)

Three Types.

Type I. Helmet not defined at back, more or less blurred. Two thick short lines in front of wing of helmet. Shadow on front of face not separated from hair.

Type II. Helmet distinctly defined. Four thin short lines in front of wing. Shadow on front of face clearly defined from hair.

Type III. Outer white circle around head is open at top (closed on types I and II). Greek border at top and bottom is wider than on types I and II.

1867-73 Coarse Print.

P9	N5	(1kr) vio, type I	60.00	2.00
a.		(1kr) vio, type II ('73)	235.00	17.50

1874-76 Fine Print.

P9B	N5	(1kr) vio, type III ('76)	40	25
c.		(1kr) gray lil, type I ('76)	175.00	25.00
d.		(1kr) vio, type II	45.00	5.00
e.		Double impression, type III		225.00

Stamps of this issue, except No. P9Bc, exist in many shades, from gray to lilac brown and deep violet. Stamps in type III exist also privately perforated or rouletted.

1880

P10	N6	½kr green	8.00	85

Nos. P9B and P10 also exist on thicker paper without sheet watermark and No. P10 exists with unofficial perforation.

N7

1899 ***Imperf.*** **Unwmkd.**

Without Varnish Bars.

P11	N7	2h dk bl	25	5
P12	N7	6h orange	3.25	1.35
P13	N7	10h brown	1.50	1.40
P14	N7	20h rose	2.00	2.00

1901 With Varnish Bars

P11a	N7	2h dk bl	1.00	30
P12a	N7	6h orange	14.00	15.00
P13a	N7	10h brown	12.50	12.50
P14a	N7	20h rose	25.00	30.00

Nos. P11 to P14 were re-issued in 1905.

Mercury
N8 N9

1908 ***Imperf.***

P15	N8	2h dk bl	1.75	8
a.		Tête bêche pair	375.00	375.00
P16	N8	6h orange	2.50	40
P17	N8	10h carmine	2.50	40
P18	N8	20h brown	2.50	25

All values are found on chalky, regular and thin ordinary paper. They exist privately perforated.

1916 ***Imperf.***

P19	N9	2h brown	5	5
P20	N9	4h green	22	50
P21	N9	6h dk bl	25	1.00
P22	N9	10h orange	25	50
P23	N9	30h claret	30	50
		Nos. P19-P23 (5)	1.07	2.55

Issues of the Republic.

Newspaper Stamps of 1916 Overprinted

1919

P24 N9 2h brown 5 5
P25 N9 4h green 10 *1.00*
P26 N9 6h dk bl 10 *1.50*
P27 N9 10h orange 25 *1.00*
P28 N9 30h claret 15 *1.50*
Nos. P24-P28 (5) 65 *5.05*

Mercury

N10 N11

1920–21 ***Imperf.***

P29 N10 2h violet 3 5
P30 N10 4h brown 3 6
P31 N10 5h slate 3 6
P32 N10 6h turq bl 3 6
P33 N10 8h green 3 7
P34 N10 9h yel ('21) 3 6
P35 N10 10h red 3 7
P36 N10 12h blue 3 12
P37 N10 15h lil ('21) 3 5
P38 N10 18h bl grn ('21) 5 12
P39 N10 20h orange 5 10
P40 N10 30h yel brn ('21) 5 12
P41 N10 45h grn ('21) 5 12
P42 N10 60h claret 5 10
P43 N10 72h choc ('21) 5 17
P44 N10 90h vio ('21) 8 20
P45 N10 1.20k red ('21) 5 20
P46 N10 2.40k yel grn ('21) 5 20
P47 N10 3k gray ('21) 8 23
Nos. P29-P47 (19) 83 2.16

Nos. P37–P40, P42, P44 and P47 exist also on thick gray paper.

1921-22

P48 N11 45h gray 8 12
P49 N11 75h brn org ('22) 8 20
P50 N11 1.50k ol bis ('22) 8 25
P51 N11 1.80k gray bl ('22) 8 25
P52 N11 2.25k lt brn 8 25
P53 N11 3k dl grn ('22) 8 50
P54 N11 6k cl ('22) 8 50
P55 N11 7.50k bister 25 50
Nos. P48-P55 (8) 81 2.57

Nos. P24-P55 exist privately perforated.

NEWSPAPER TAX STAMPS.

Prices for unused stamps 1853–59 are for copies in fine condition with gum. Specimens without gum sell for about one-third of the figures quoted.

Issues of the Monarchy.

NT1 NT2

Typographed

1853 ***Imperf.*** **Unwmkd.**

PR1 NT1 2kr green 1,900. 72.50

The reprints are in finer print than the more coarsely printed originals, and on a smooth toned paper.

Unwmkd. or, after June 1864, Wmkd. ZEITUNGS-MARKEN. (91)

1858-59

Two Types.

Type I. The banderol on the Crown of the left eagle touches the beak of the eagle.
Type II. The banderol does not touch the beak.

PR2 NT2 1kr bl, type II ('59) 35.00 7.50
a. 1kr bl, type I 675.00 150.00
b. Printed on both sides, type II
PR3 NT2 2kr brn, type II ('59) 25.00 7.50
a. 2kr red brn, type II 375.00 135.00
PR4 NT2 4kr brn, type I 450.00 *1,100.*

Nos. PR2a, PR3a, and PR4 were printed only on unwatermarked paper. Nos. PR2 and PR3 exist on unwatermarked and watermarked paper.

Nos. PR2 and PR3 exist in coarse and (after 1874) in fine print, like the contemporary postage stamps.

The reprints of the 4kr brown are of type II and on a smooth toned paper.

NT3 NT4

1877 **Redrawn.**

PR5 NT3 1kr blue 15.00 1.25
a. 1kr pale ultra *1,100.*
PR6 NT3 2kr brown 13.50 1.50

In the redrawn stamps the shield is larger and the vertical bar has eight lines above the white square and nine below, instead of five.

Nos. PR5 and PR6 exist also watermarked "WECHSEL" instead of "ZEITUNGS-MARKEN".

1890

PR7 NT4 1kr brown 12.50 75
PR8 NT4 2kr green 14.00 1.50

Nos. PR5 to PR8 exist with private perforation.

NT5

Wmkd. "STEMPEL-MARKEN" in Double-lined Capitals, across the Sheet. (91)

Perf. 13, 12½

PR9 NT5 25kr carmine 125.00 160.00

Nos. PR1 to PR9 did not pay postage, but were a fiscal tax, collected by the postal authorities on newspapers.

SPECIAL HANDLING STAMPS (For Printed Matter Only.)

Issues of the Monarchy.

Mercury

SH1

1916 ***Perf. 12½*** **Unwmkd.**

QE1 SH1 2h cl, *yel* 45 60
QE2 SH1 5h dp grn, *yel* 45 60

SH2

1917 ***Perf. 12½***

QE3 SH2 2h cl, *yel* 18 20
a. Pair, imperf. between 400.00 400.00
b. Perf. 11½x12½ 75.00 90.00
c. Perf. 12½x11½ 100.00 135.00
d. Perf. 11½ 1.75 2.50
QE4 SH2 5h dp grn, *yel* 18 20
a. Pair, imperf. between 375.00 375.00
b. Perf. 11½x12½ 75.00 90.00
c. Perf. 12½x11½ 100.00 135.00
d. Perf. 11½ 1.75 2.50

Nos. QE1–QE4 exist imperforate.

Issues of the Republic.

Nos. QE3 and QE4 Overprinted

Deutschösterreich

1919

QE5 SH2 2h cl, *yel* 5 30
a. Inverted overprint 325.00
b. Perf. 11½x12½ 7.50 11.00
c. Perf. 12½x11½ 90.00 120.00
QE6 SH2 5h dp grn, *yel* 5 40
a. Perf. 11½x12½ 3.00 5.00
b. Perf. 12½x11½ 35.00 50.00

Nos. QE5 and QE6 exist imperforate.

SH3

1921 Dark Blue Surcharge.

QE7 SH3 50h on 2h cl, *yel* 6 10

SH4

1922 ***Perf. 12½***

QE8 SH4 50h lil, *yel* 6 20

Nos. QE5 to QE8 exist in vertical pairs, imperforate between. No. QE8 exists imperforate.

OCCUPATION STAMPS.

Issued under Italian Occupation.

Issued in Trieste.

Austrian Stamps of 1916-18 Overprinted

Regno d'Italia
Venezia Giulia
3. XI. 18.

1918 ***Perf. 12½.*** **Unwmkd.**

N1 A37 3h brt vio 20 20
a. Double overprint 15.00 15.00
b. Inverted ovpt. 15.00 15.00
N2 A37 5h lt grn 20 20
a. Inverted ovpt. 15.00 15.00
b. "3.XI." omitted 12.00 12.00
c. Double overprint 15.00
N3 A37 6h dp org 40 40
N4 A37 10h magenta 20 20
a. Inverted overprint 9.00 9.00
N5 A37 12h lt bl 1.20 1.20
a. Double overprint 15.00 15.00
N6 A42 15h dl red 20 20
a. Inverted ovpt. 15.00 15.00
b. Double overprint 15.00 15.00
c. "3.XI." omitted 12.00 12.00
N7 A42 20h dk grn 20 20
a. Inverted ovpt. 9.00 9.00
b. "3.XI." omitted 12.00 12.00
c. Double overprint 40.00
N8 A42 25h dp bl 2.75 2.75
a. Inverted ovpt. 35.00 35.00
b. "3.XI." omitted 60.00 60.00
N9 A42 30h dl vio 60 60
N10 A39 40h ol grn 40.00 40.00
N11 A39 50h dk grn 1.35 1.35
N12 A39 60h dp bl 2.00 2.00
N13 A39 80h org brn 1.35 1.35
a. Inverted overprint
N14 A39 1k car, *yel* 1.35 1.35
a. Double ovpt. 25.00 25.00
N15 A40 2k lt bl 85.00 75.00
N16 A40 4k yel grn 150.00 140.00

Handstamped.

N17 A40 10k dp vio *13,000.* *13,000.*

Granite Paper.

N18 A40 2k lt bl
N19 A40 3k car rose 100.00 90.00

Some authorities question the authenticity of No. N18. Counterfeits of Nos. N10, N15–N19 are plentiful.

Italian Stamps of 1901-18 Overprinted

Venezia
Giulia

Wmkd. Crown. (140) ***Perf. 14.***

N20 A42 1c brown 18 18
a. Inverted overprint 2.50 2.50
N21 A43 2c org brn 18 18
a. Inverted overprint 1.50 1.50
N22 A48 5c green 15 15
a. Inverted overprint 3.00 3.00
b. Double overprint 15.00
N23 A48 10c claret 15 15
a. Inverted overprint 7.50 7.50
b. Double overprint 15.00
N24 A50 20c brn org 15 15
a. Inverted overprint 9.00 9.00
b. Double overprint 15.00 15.00
N25 A49 25c blue 15 15
a. Double overprint 50.00
b. Invtd. overprint 13.50 13.50
N26 A49 40c brown 1.35 80
a. Inverted overprint 40.00
N27 A45 45c ol grn 15 15
a. Inverted overprint 13.50 13.50
N28 A49 50c violet 45 22
N29 A49 60c brn car 5.50 4.75
N30 A46 1 l brn & grn 2.65 2.00
Nos. N20-N30 (11) 11.06 8.88

Italian Stamps of 1901-18 Surcharged

Venezia
Giulia
5 Heller

N31 A48 5h on 5c grn 15 15
a. "5" omitted 2.50 2.50
b. Inverted surch. 7.00 7.00
N32 A50 20h on 20c brn org 15 15
a. Double surcharge 7.00 7.00

Issued in the Trentino.

Austrian Stamps of 1916-18 Overprinted

Regno d Italia
Trentino
3 nov 1918

1918 ***Perf. 12½*** **Unwmkd.**

N33 A37 3h brt vio 1.50 1.65
a. Double ovpt. 25.00 25.00
b. Inverted ovpt. 27.50 17.50
N34 A37 5h lt grn 1.00 1.00
a. "8 nov. 1918" *250.00*
b. Inverted ovpt. 27.50 17.50
N35 A37 6h dp org 55.00 55.00
N36 A37 10h magenta 1.00 1.00
a. "8 nov. 1918" 30.00 25.00
N37 A37 12h lt bl 175.00 175.00
N38 A42 15h dl red 4.00 4.00
N39 A42 20h dk grn 35 35
a. "8 nov. 1918" 40.00 35.00
b. Double ovpt. 25.00 25.00
c. Inverted ovpt. 12.50 12.50
N40 A42 25h dp bl 30.00 30.00
N41 A42 30h dl vio 6.00 6.00
N42 A39 40h ol grn 55.00 55.00
N43 A39 50h dk grn 12.50 12.50
a. Inverted ovpt. 50.00 50.00
N44 A39 60h dp bl 35.00 35.00
a. Double ovpt. 60.00 60.00
N45 A39 80h org brn 55.00 55.00
N46 A39 90h red vio *750.00* *750.00*
N47 A39 1k car, *yel* 55.00 55.00
N48 A40 2k lt bl 275.00 275.00
N49 A40 4k yel grn *1,100.* *1,100.*
N50 A40 10k dp vio *35,000.*

Granite Paper.

N51	A40	2k lt bl	325.00	350.00

Counterfeits of Nos. N33–N51 are plentiful.

Italian Stamps of 1901-18 Overprinted

Venezia Tridentina

Wmkd. Crown. (140) *Perf. 14.*

N52	A42	1c brown	15	18
a.		Inverted overprint	6.00	6.00
N53	A43	2c org brn	15	18
a.		Inverted overprint	6.00	6.00
N54	A48	5c green	15	18
a.		Inverted overprint	6.00	6.00
b.		Double overprint	8.00	8.00
N55	A48	10c claret	15	18
a.		Inverted overprint	8.00	8.00
b.		Double overprint	8.00	8.00
N56	A50	20c brn org	15	18
a.		Inverted overprint	8.00	8.00
N57	A49	40c brown	8.00	9.00
N58	A45	45c ol grn	5.50	6.50
a.		Double overprint	25.00	25.00
N59	A49	50c violet	5.50	6.50
N60	A46	1 l brn & grn	6.00	7.00
a.		Double overprint	25.00	25.00
		Nos. N52-N60 (9)	25.75	29.90

Italian Stamps of 1906-18 Surcharged

Venezia Tridentina 5 Heller

N61	A48	5h on 5c grn	15	18
N62	A48	10h on 10c cl	15	18
a.		Inverted overprint	10.00	10.00
N63	A50	20h on 20c brn org	15	18
a.		Double surcharge	8.00	8.00

General Issue.

Italian Stamps of 1901-18 Surcharged

5 centesimi di corona

1919

N64	A42	1c on 1c brn	15	15
a.		Inverted surcharge	1.25	1.25
N65	A43	2c on 2c org brn	15	15
a.		Double surcharge	25.00	
b.		Inverted surcharge	25	25
N66	A48	5c on 5c grn	15	15
a.		Inverted surcharge	2.25	2.25
b.		Double surcharge	10.00	10.00
N67	A48	10c on 10c cl	15	15
a.		Inverted surcharge	2.25	2.25
b.		Double surcharge	10.00	10.00
N68	A50	20c on 20c brn org	15	15
a.		Double surcharge	15.00	15.00
N69	A49	25c on 25c bl	15	15
a.		Double surcharge	12.50	12.50
N70	A49	40c on 40c brn	15	15
a.		"ccrona"	4.00	4.00
N71	A45	45c on 45c ol grn	15	15
a.		Inverted surcharge	7.50	7.50
N72	A49	50c on 50c vio	15	15
N73	A49	60c on 60c brn car	15	15
a.		"00" for "60"	3.00	3.00

Surcharged:

1 corona

N74	A49	1 cor on 1 l brn & grn	15	15
		Nos. N64-N74 (11)	1.65	1.65

Surcharges similar to these but differing in style or arrangement of type were used in Dalmatia.

SPECIAL DELIVERY STAMPS.

Issued in Trieste.

Special Delivery Stamp of Italy of 1903 Overprinted

Venezia Giulia

Wmkd. Crown. (140)

1918 *Perf. 14.*

NE1	SD1	25c rose red	5.25	4.50
a.		Invtd. ovpt.	25.00	25.00

General Issue.

1919

Special Delivery Stamps of Italy of 1903-09 Surcharged

25 centesimi di corona

NE2	SD1	25c on 25c rose	15	15
a.		Double surcharge	6.00	6.00
NE3	SD2	30c on 30c bl & rose	15	15

POSTAGE DUE STAMPS.

Issued in Trieste.

Postage Due Stamps of Italy, 1870-94, Overprinted

Venezia Giulia

Wmkd. Crown. (140)

1918 *Perf. 14.*

NJ1	D3	5c buff & mag	15	15
a.		Inverted overprint	1.00	1.00
b.		Double overprint	30.00	
NJ2	D3	10c buff & mag	15	15
a.		Inverted overprint	6.00	5.00
NJ3	D3	20c buff & mag	15	15
a.		Double overprint	30.00	
b.		Inverted overprint	6.00	5.00
NJ4	D3	30c buff & mag	30	30
NJ5	D3	40c buff & mag	1.65	1.65
a.		Inverted overprint	30.00	30.00
NJ6	D3	50c buff & mag	12.50	12.50
a.		Inverted overprint	30.00	30.00
NJ7	D3	1 l bl & mag	47.50	47.50
		Nos. NJ1-NJ7 (7)	62.40	62.40

General Issue.

Postage Due Stamps of Italy, 1870–1903 Surcharged

5 centesimi di corona

1919

NJ8	D3	5c on 5c buff & mag	15	15
a.		Inverted overprint	65	65
NJ9	D3	10c on 10c buff & mag	15	15
a.		Center and surcharge invtd.	10.00	10.00
NJ10	D3	20c on 20c buff & mag	15	15
a.		Double overprint	16.50	16.50
NJ11	D3	30c on 30c buff & mag	15	15
NJ12	D3	40c on 40c buff & mag	15	15
NJ13	D3	50c on 50c buff & mag	15	15

Surcharged

una corona

NJ14	D3	1 cor on 1 l bl & mag	15	15
NJ15	D3	2 cor on 2 l bl & mag	13.50	16.50
NJ16	D3	5 cor on 5 l bl & mag	13.50	16.50
		Nos. NJ8-NJ16 (9)	28.05	34.05

A. M. G. Issue for Austria.

Issued jointly by the Allied Military Government of the United States and Great Britain, for civilian use in areas under American, British and French occupation. (Upper Austria, Salzburg, Tyrol, Vorarlberg, Styria and Carinthia).

OS1

Lithographed.

1945 *Perf. 11.* **Unwmkd.**

4N1	OS1	1g aqua	6	30
4N2	OS1	3g dp org	3	3
4N3	OS1	4g buff	3	3
4N4	OS1	5g brt grn	3	3
4N5	OS1	6g red vio	3	3
4N6	OS1	8g rose pink	3	3
4N7	OS1	10g lt gray	3	10
4N8	OS1	12g pale buff brn	3	3
4N9	OS1	15g rose red	3	5
4N10	OS1	20g cop brn	3	5
4N11	OS1	25g dp bl	3	6
4N12	OS1	30g brt vio	3	3
4N13	OS1	40g lt ultra	3	15
4N14	OS1	60g lt ol grn	3	30
4N15	OS1	1s dk vio	7	40
4N16	OS1	2s yellow	25	50
4N17	OS1	5s dp ultra	30	75
		Nos. 4N1-4N17 (17)	1.07	2.87

AUSTRIAN OFFICES ABROAD

Offices in Crete.

100 CENTIMES=1 FRANC

These stamps were on sale and usable at all Austrian post-offices in Crete and in the Turkish Empire.

> Used prices are italicized for stamps often found with false cancellations.

Stamps of Austria of 1899–1901 Issue, Surcharged in Black:

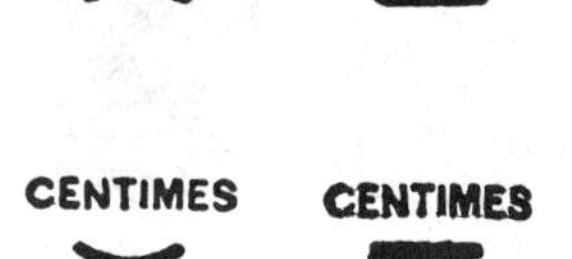

a *b*

c *d*

Granite Paper.

1903–04 *Perf. 12½, 13½* **Unwmkd.**

With Varnish Bars (On Nos. 73a, 75a, 77a, 81a)

1	A15 (a)	5c on 5h bl grn	2.50	3.50
2	A16 (b)	10c on 10h rose	1.25	*4.00*
3	A16 (b)	25c on 25h ultra	42.50	30.00
4	A17 (c)	50c on 50h gray bl	8.00	*60.00*

Without Varnish Bars (On Nos. 83, 83a, 84, 85)

5	A18 (d)	1fr on 1k car rose	3.75	*65.00*
a.		1fr on 1k car	6.25	
b.		Horiz. or vert. pair, imperf. between	250.00	
6	A18 (d)	2fr on 2k gray lil ('04)	14.00	*210.00*
7	A18 (d)	4fr on 4k gray grn ('04)	15.00	*325.00*

Surcharged on Austrian Stamps of 1904–05.

1905 Without Varnish Bars (On Nos. 89, 97)

8	A19 (a)	5c on 5h bl grn	55.00	27.50
9	A20 (b)	10c on 10h car	1.50	*7.50*

With Varnish Bars. (On Nos. 89a, 97a, 99a, 103a)

8a	A19 (a)	5c on 5h bl grn	6.25	6.00
9a	A20 (b)	10c on 10h car	30.00	20.00
10	A20 (b)	25c on 25h ultra	1.25	*60.00*
11	A21 (b)	50c on 50h dl bl	1.75	*250.00*

Surcharged on Austrian Stamps and Type of 1906-07.

1907 *Perf. 12½, 13½.*

Without Varnish Bars

12	A19 (a)	5c on 5h yel grn (#90)	1.50	5.00
13	A20 (b)	10c on 10h car (#92)	2.00	*15.00*
14	A20 (b)	15c on 15h vio	2.50	*22.50*

A5

A6

1908 Typographed *Perf. 12½*

15	A5	5c grn, *yel*	50	40
16	A5	10c scar, *rose*	60	60
17	A5	15c brn, *buff*	70	*4.00*
18	A5	25c dp bl, *bl*	17.50	4.00

Engraved.

19	A6	50c lake, *yel*	3.50	*25.00*
20	A6	1fr brn, *gray*	5.00	*37.50*
a.		Vertical pair, imperf. between	225.00	
		Nos. 15-20 (6)	27.80	*71.50*

Nos. 15 to 18 are on paper colored on the surface only. All values exist imperforate.

Issued to commemorate the sixtieth year of the reign of Emperor Franz Josef, for permanent use.

Paper Colored Through.

1914 Typographed.

21	A5	10c rose, *rose*	2.50	*900.00*
22	A5	25c ultra, *bl*	1.00	*100.00*

Nos. 21 and 22 exist imperforate.

Offices in the Turkish Empire.

From 1863 to 1867 the stamps of Lombardy-Venetia (Nos. 15 to 24) were used at the Austrian Offices in the Turkish Empire.

> Prices for unused stamps are for copies with gum. Specimens without gum sell for about one-third the figures quoted.
> Used prices are italicized for stamps often found with false cancellations.

100 SOLDI=1 FLORIN
40 PARAS=1 PIASTRE

A1

A2

Typographed

Wmkd. "BRIEF-MARKEN" in Double-lined Capitals, across the Sheet. (91)

Two different printing methods were used, as in the 1867-74 issues of Austria. They may be distinguished by the coarse or fine lines of the hair and whiskers.

1867 Coarse Print. *Perf. 9½.*

1	A1	2sld orange	1.50	*20.00*
a.		2sld yel	70.00	32.50
2	A1	3sld green	100.00	30.00
a.		3sld dk grn	120.00	40.00

3	A1	5sld red	100.00	14.00
a.		5sld car	110.00	20.00
4	A1	10sld blue	100.00	1.75
a.		10sld lt bl	110.00	3.00
b.		10sld dk bl	110.00	3.25
5	A1	15sld brown	15.00	6.00
a.		15sld dk brn	50.00	17.50
b.		15sld redsh brn	17.50	12.50
6	A1	25sld gray lil	12.50	*30.00*
a.		25sld brn vio	15.00	*35.00*
7	A2	50sld brn, perf. 10½	1.50	*50.00*
a.		Perf. 12	110.00	75.00
b.		Perf. 13	350.00	
k.		Perf. 9 or 10½x9	30.00	*60.00*
l.		50sld pale red brn, perf. 12	60.00	65.00
m.		Vertical pair, imperf. between	500.00	1,100.
n.		Horiz. pair, imperf. btwn.	425.00	*1,000.*

Fine Print.

Perf. 9, 9½, 10½ and Compound.

1876-83

7C	A1	2sld yel ('83)	25	*1,500.*
7D	A1	3sld grn ('78)	1.50	*22.50*
7E	A1	5sld red ('78)	50	*17.50*
7F	A1	10sld blue	75.00	1.40
7I	A1	15sld org brn ('81)	7.50	*125.00*
7J	A1	25sld gray lil ('83)	75	*225.00*

The 10 soldi has been reprinted in deep dull blue, perforated 10½.

A3

1883 ***Perf. 9½, 10, 10½.***

8	A3	2sld brown	25	*100.00*
9	A3	3sld green	1.25	*12.50*
10	A3	5sld rose	25	*7.50*
11	A3	10sld blue	1.00	50
12	A3	20sld gray	2.50	*5.00*
13	A3	50sld red lil	2.50	*12.50*

A4 A5

10 PARAS ON 3 SOLDI:

Type I. Surcharge 16⅓mm. across. "PARA" about ⅓mm. above bottom of "10". 2mm. space between "10" and "P"; 1½mm. between "A" and "10". Perf. 9½ only.

Type II. Surcharge 15¾ to 16mm. across. "PARA" on same line with figures or slightly higher or lower. 1½mm. space between "10" and "P"; 1mm. between "A" and "10". Perf. 9½ and 10.

1886 ***Perf. 9½ and 10***

14	A4	10pa on 3sld grn, type II	40	*5.00*
a.		10pa on 3sld grn, type I	325.00	400.00
b.		Inverted surcharge, type I		*2,500.*

1888

15	A5	10pa on 3kr grn	5.00	6.00
a.		"O1 PARA 1O"		*500.00*
16	A5	20pa on 5kr rose	1.00	*7.00*
17	A5	1pi on 10kr bl	65.00	1.50
a.		Perf. 13½		200.00
b.		Double surcharge		200.00
18	A5	2pi on 20kr gray	2.50	3.50
19	A5	5pi on 50kr vio	4.00	*17.50*

A6

Granite Paper.

1890-92 ***Perf. 9 to 13½*** **Unwmkd.**

20	A6	8pa on 2kr brn ('92)	25	30
a.		Perf. 9½	5.00	3.00
21	A6	10pa on 3kr grn	1.00	25
a.		Pair, imperf. between		100.00
22	A6	20pa on 5kr rose	25	25
23	A6	1pi on 10kr ultra	50	10
24	A6	2pi on 20kr ol grn	15.00	*25.00*
25	A6	5pi on 50kr vio	20.00	*60.00*

See note after Austria No. 65 on missing numerals, etc.

A7 A8

1891 ***Perf. 9 to 13½***

26	A7	2pi on 20kr ol grn	7.50	50
a.		Perf. 9½	125.00	20.00
27	A7	5pi on 50kr vio	5.00	2.50

There are two types of the surcharge on No. 26.

1892 ***Perf. 10½, 11½***

28	A8	10pi on 1gld bl	20.00	25.00
29	A8	20pi on 2gld car	20.00	*30.00*
a.		Double surcharge		

1896 ***Perf. 10½, 11½, 12½***

30	A8	10pi on 1gld pale lil	20.00	25.00
31	A8	20pi on 2gld gray grn	60.00	60.00

A9 A10

A11 A12

Perf. 10½, 12½, 13½ and Compound.

1900 **Without Varnish Bars**

32	A9	10pa on 5h bl grn	6.00	1.50
33	A10	20pa on 10h rose	6.00	1.50
b.		Perf. 12½x10½	350.00	45.00
34	A10	1pi on 25h ultra	6.00	25
35	A11	2pi on 50h gray bl	12.50	2.00
36	A12	5pi on 1k car rose	2.00	25
a.		5pi on 1k car	2.50	1.00
b.		Horiz. or vert. pair, imperf. between	165.00	
37	A12	10pi on 2k gray lil	5.00	3.00
a.		Horizontal pair, imperf. between		
38	A12	20pi on 4k gray grn	4.00	*7.00*
		Nos. 32-38 (7)	41.50	*15.50*

In the surcharge on Nos. 37 and 38 "plaster" is printed "PIAST."

1901 **With Varnish Bars.**

32a	A9	10pa on 5h bl grn	4.00	2.00
33a	A10	20pa on 10h rose	4.00	*100.00*
34a	A10	1pi on 25h ultra	3.00	50
35a	A11	2pi on 50h gray bl	6.00	2.00

A13 A14

A15

1906 ***Perf. 12½ to 13½***

Without Varnish Bars.

39	A13	10pa dk grn	20.00	1.50
40	A14	20pa rose	1.25	50
41	A14	1pi ultra	50	25

1903 **With Varnish Bars.**

39a	A13	10pa dk grn	8.00	1.25
40a	A14	20pa rose	4.00	50
41a	A14	1pi ultra	3.00	25
42	A15	2pi gray bl	1.50	75
42a	A15	2pi gray bl	175.00	1.50

1907 **Without Varnish Bars.**

43	A13	10pa yel grn	50	*2.00*
45	A14	30pa violet	90	*3.50*

A16 A17

1908 **Typographed.** ***Perf. 12½.***

46	A16	10pa grn, *yel*	25	15
47	A16	20pa scar, *rose*	40	20
48	A16	30pa brn, *buff*	60	75
49	A16	1pi dp bl, *bl*	22.50	6
50	A16	60pa vio, *bluish*	1.00	*4.00*

Engraved

51	A17	2pi lake, *yel*	60	15
52	A17	5pi brn, *gray*	90	75
53	A17	10pi grn, *yel*	1.50	2.00
54	A17	20pi bl, *gray*	2.75	4.00
		Nos. 46-54 (9)	30.50	*12.06*

Nos. 46 to 50 are on paper colored on the surface only. Issued in commemoration of the sixtieth year of the reign of Emperor Franz Josef I for permanent use. All values exist imperforate.

1913-14 **Typographed**

Paper Colored Through.

57	A16	20pa rose, *rose* ('14)	1.50	*300.00*
58	A16	1pi ultra, *bl*	65	50

Nos. 57 and 58 exist imperforate.

POSTAGE DUE STAMPS.

D1 D2

Black Surcharge.

1902 ***Perf. 12½, 13½*** **Unwmkd.**

J1	D1	10pa on 5h grn	2.00	*4.50*
J2	D1	20pa on 10h grn	2.00	*4.00*
J3	D1	1pi on 20h grn	3.50	6.00
J4	D1	2pi on 40h grn	3.50	4.50
J5	D1	5pi on 100h grn	5.00	2.50
		Nos. J1-J5 (5)	16.00	*21.50*

Shades of Nos. J1 to J5 exist, varying from yellowish green to dark green.

1908 **Typographed.** ***Perf. 12½.***

J6	D2	¼pi green	5.00	8.50
J7	D2	½pi green	2.50	5.50
J8	D2	1pi green	3.50	*8.50*
J9	D2	1½pi green	1.00	*10.00*
J10	D2	2pi green	4.00	*12.50*
J11	D2	5pi green	4.00	*8.50*
J12	D2	10pi green	30.00	*125.00*
J13	D2	20pi green	25.00	*150.00*
J14	D2	30pi green	20.00	12.00
		Nos. J6-J14 (9)	95.00	*340.50*

Nos. J6 to J14 exist in distinct shades of green and on thick chalky, regular and thin ordinary paper. All values exist imperforate.

LOMBARDY-VENETIA

(lŏm'bĕr-dĭ ; lŭm'-- ; vĕ-nĕ'shĭ-ȧ ;- shȧ)

Formerly a kingdom in the north of Italy forming part of the Austrian Empire. Milan and Venice were the two principal cities. Lombardy was annexed to Sardinia in 1859, and Venetia to the kingdom of Italy in 1866.

100 CENTESIMI = 1 LIRA

100 SOLDI = 1 FLORIN (1858)

> Prices of the earliest Lombardy-Venetia stamps vary according to condition. Quotations for Nos. 1-6, PR1-PR3 are for fine copies. Very fine to superb specimens sell at much higher prices, and inferior or poor copies sell at reduced prices, depending on the condition of the individual specimen.
>
> Prices for unused stamps are for fine copies with gum. Specimens without gum sell for about one-quarter of the prices quoted.

Coat of Arms A1

15 CENTESIMI:

Type I. "5" of "15" is on a level with the "1."

Type II. "5" is a trifle sideways and is higher than the "1."

45 CENTESIMI:

Type I. Lower part of "45" is lower than "Centes."

Type II. Lower part of "45" is on a level with lower part of "Centes."

Wmkd. K. K. H. M. in Sheet or Unwmkd.

1850 **Typographed** ***Imperf.***

Thick to Thin Paper.

1	A1	5c buff	900.00	90.00
a.		Printed on both sides	*7,000.*	140.00
b.		5c yel	*4,500.*	450.00
c.		5c org	1,000.	100.00
d.		5c lem yel		*1,000.*
3	A1	10c black	1,250.	67.50
a.		10c gray blk	1,500.	80.00
4	A1	15c pale red, type II	375.00	2.25
b.		15c red, type I	*1,500.*	13.50
c.		Ribbed paper, type II	*11,000.*	225.00
d.		Ribbed paper, type I	*6,500.*	67.50
e.		Laid paper, type II		*3,750.*
5	A1	30c brown	1,250.	4.75
a.		Ribbed paper	3,000.	35.00
6	A1	45c bl, type II	*3,250.*	12.00
a.		45c bl, type I	*5,500.*	22.50
b.		Ribbed paper, type I	*11,500.*	135.00

The note about the paper of the 1850 issue of Austria will also apply here. No. 1 and its minor varieties exist only on hand-made paper.

The reprints are in brighter colors.

A2 A3 A4

A5 A6

Two Types of Each Value.

Type I. Loops of the bow at the back of the head broken.

Type II. Loops complete. Wreath projects further at top of head.

1858-62 Embossed. *Perf. 14½.*

7	A2	2s yel, type II	325.00	62.50
a.		2s yel, type I	950.00	325.00
8	A3	3s blk, type II	1,450.	100.00
a.		3s blk, type I	700.00	190.00
b.		Perf. 16, type I		600.00
c.		Perf. 15x16 or 16x15, type I	*1,350.*	400.00
9	A3	3s grn, type II ('62)	275.00	55.00
10	A4	5s red, type II	140.00	3.75
a.		5s red, type I	225.00	9.50
b.		Printed on both sides, type II		*2,000.*
11	A5	10s brn, type II	625.00	10.00
a.		10s brn, type I	185.00	35.00
12	A6	15s bl, type II	550.00	14.00
a.		15s bl, type I	900.00	60.00

The reprints are of type II and are perforated 10½, 11, 11½, 12, 12½ and 13. There are also imperforate reprints of Nos. 7, 8 and 9.

A7

A8

1861-62 *Perf. 14.*

13	A7	5s red	800.00	2.50
14	A7	10s brn ('62)	750.00	20.00

The reprints are perforated 9, 9½, 10½, 11, 12, 12½ and 13. There are also imperforate reprints of the 2 and 3s.

The 2, 3 and 15s of this type exist only as reprints.

1863

15	A8	2s yellow	80.00	110.00
16	A8	3s green	600.00	70.00
17	A8	5s rose	600.00	11.00
18	A8	10s blue	1,500.	60.00
19	A8	15s yel brn	1,100.	100.00

Wmkd. "BRIEF-MARKEN" in Double-lined Capitals across the Sheet. (91)

1864-65 *Perf. 9½.*

20	A8	2s yel ('65)	80.00	*275.00*
21	A8	3s green	14.00	12.00
22	A8	5s rose	2.00	1.50
23	A8	10s blue	14.00	5.00
24	A8	15s yel brn	20.00	20.00

The reprints are perforated 10½ and 13. There are also imperforate reprints of the 2s and 3s.

NEWSPAPER TAX STAMPS.

From 1853 to 1858 the Austrian Newspaper Tax Stamp 2kr green (No. PR1) was also used in Lombardy-Venetia, at the value of 10 centesimi.

NT1

Type I. The banderol of the left eagle touches the beak of the eagle.

Type II. The banderol does not touch the beak.

Typographed

1858-59 *Imperf.* Unwmkd.

PR1	NT1	1kr blk, type I ('59)	1,150.	*3,250.*
PR2	NT1	2kr red, type II ('59)	175.00	52.50
PR3	NT1	4kr red, type I	*40,000.*	*3,000.*

No. PR2 exists also with watermark "ZEITUNGS-MARKEN" (91).

The reprints are on a smooth toned paper and are all of type II.

AZERBAIJAN

(ă'zĕr·bī'jan' ; ăz'ĕr-)

(Azerbaidjan)

LOCATION—Southernmost part of Russia in Eastern Europe. Bounded by Georgia, Dagestan, Caspian Sea, Persia and Armenia.

GOVT.—A Soviet Socialist Republic.

AREA—32,686 sq. mi.

POP.—2,096,973 (1923).

CAPITAL—Baku.

100 Kopecks = 1 Ruble

National Republic.

Standard Bearer A1

Farmer at Sunset A2

Baku A3

Temple of Eternal Fires A4

Lithographed

1919 *Imperf.* Unwmkd.

1	A1	10k multi	10	15
2	A1	20k multi	10	15
3	A2	40k grn, yel & blk	10	15
4	A2	60k red, yel & blk	10	15
5	A2	1r bl, yel & blk	15	25
6	A3	2r red, bis & blk	15	25
7	A3	5r bl, bis & blk	25	50
8	A3	10r ol grn, bis & blk	40	60
9	A4	25r bl, red & blk	75	1.00
10	A4	50r ol grn, red & blk	85	1.10
		Nos. 1-10 (10)	2.95	4.30

The two printings of Nos. 1–10 are distinguished by the grayish or thin white paper. Both have yellowish gum.

Soviet Socialist Republic.

Symbols of Labor A5

Oil Well A6

Bibi Eibatt Oil Field A7

Khan's Palace, Baku A8

Globe and Workers A9

Maiden's Tower, Baku A10

Blacksmiths A12

Goukasoff House A11

Hall of Judgment, Baku A13

1922

15	A5	1r gray grn	15	30
16	A6	2r ol blk	15	30
17	A7	5r gray brn	15	30
18	A8	10r gray	40	60
19	A9	25r org brn	15	35
20	A10	50r violet	15	35
21	A11	100r dl red	25	40
22	A12	150r blue	25	40
23	A9	250r vio & buff	25	40
24	A13	400r dk bl	25	40
25	A12	500r gray vio & blk	25	40
26	A13	1000r dk bl & rose	25	40
27	A8	2000r bl & blk	25	40
28	A7	3000r brn & bl	25	40
a.		Tête bêche pair	14.00	15.00
29	A11	5000r *ol grn*	50	60
		Nos. 15-29 (15)	3.65	6.00

Counterfeits exist of Nos. 1–29.

Stamps of 1922 Handstamped from Metal Dies in a Numbering Machine

15000

1922

32	A5	10.000r on 1r gray grn	6.50	7.00
33	A7	15.000r on 5r gray brn	8.50	9.00
34	A9	33.000r on 250r vio & buff	3.00	3.00
35	A7	50.000r on 3.000r brn & bl	4.00	4.00
36	A8	66.000r on 2.000r bl & blk	8.50	7.50
		Nos. 32-36 (5)	30.50	30.50

Same Surcharges on Regular Issue and Semi-Postal Stamps of 1922.

1922-23

36A	A7	500r on 5r gray brn	70.00	80.00
37	A6	1.000r on 2r ol blk	10.00	10.00
38	A8	2.000r on 10r gray	3.50	3.50
39	A8	5.000r on 2.000r bl & blk	2.00	2.00
40	A11	15.000r on 5.000r *ol grn*	7.50	7.50
41	A5	20.000r on 1r gray grn	8.00	8.00
42	SP1	25.000r on 500r bl & pale bl	27.50	
43	A7	50.000r on 5r gray brn	12.50	12.50
44	SP2	50.000r on 1.000r brn & bis	27.50	
45	A11	50.000r on 5.000r *ol grn*	4.00	3.00
45A	A8	60.000r on 2.000r bl & blk	12.50	15.00
46	A11	70.000r on 5.000r *ol grn*	20.00	20.00
47	A6	100.000r on 2r ol blk	12.50	10.00
48	A8	200.000r on 10r gray	4.00	4.00
49	A9	200.000r on 25r org brn	16.50	16.50
50	A7	300.000r on 3.000r brn & bl	4.00	4.00
51	A8	500.000r on 2.000r bl & blk	8.50	7.50

Revalued.

52	A7	500r on 15.000r on 5r gray brn	30.00	*60.00*
53	A11	15.000r on 70.000r on 5.000r *ol grn*	30.00	*60.00*
54	A7	300.000r on 50.000r on 3.000r brn & bl	50.00	*100.00*
55	A8	500.000r on 66.000r on 2.000r bl & blk	60.00	*120.00*

The surcharged semi-postal stamps were used for regular postage.

Same Surcharges on Stamps of 1919.

57	A1	25.000r on 10k grn, bl, red & blk	50	75
58	A1	50.000r on 20k bl, red, grn & blk	50	75
59	A2	75.000r on 40k grn, yel & blk	1.35	2.00
60	A2	100.000r on 60k red, yel & blk	50	75
61	A2	200.000r on 1r bl, yel & blk	50	75
62	A3	300.000r on 2r red, bis & blk	60	1.00
63	A3	500.000r on 5r bl, bis & blk	75	1.00
64	A2	750.000r on 40k grn, yel & blk	2.50	2.50
		Nos. 57-64 (8)	7.20	9.50

Handstamped from Settings of Rubber Type in Black or Violet

100000 *b* **200.000** *c*

On Stamps of 1922.

65	A6	(b) 100.000r on 2r ol blk	10.00	11.00
66	A8	(b) 200.000r on 10r gray	17.50	15.00
67	A8	(b) 200.000r on 10r gray (V)	12.00	13.00

68 A9 (b) 200,000r on 25r org brn (V) 10.00 11.00
a. blk surch. 30.00 32.50
69 A7 (c) 300.000r on 3.000r brn & bl (V) 25.00 27.50
70 A8 (c) 500.000r on 2.000r bl & blk (V) 20.00 22.50
a. Black surch. 30.00 32.50
71 A11 (b) 1.500.000r on 5.000r *ol grn* 15.00 15.00
72 A11 (b) 1.500.000r on 5.000r *ol grn* (V) 15.00 15.00

On Stamps of 1919.

75 A1 (b) 50.000r on 20k bl, red, grn & blk 50
76 A2 (b) 75.000r on 40k grn, yel & blk 25
77 A2 (b) 100.000r on 60k red, yel & blk 75
78 A2 (b) 200.000r on 1r bl, yel & blk 20 25
79 A3 (b) 300.000r on 2r red, bis & blk 50
80 A3 (b) 500,000r on 5r bl, bis & blk 75

Inverted and double surcharges of Nos. 32–80 sell for twice the normal price.
Counterfeits exist of Nos. 32–80.

Baku Province.

Regular Issue and Semi-Postal Stamps of 1922 Handstamped in Violet

БАКИНСКОИ П. К.

The overprint reads "Bakinskoi P(ochtovoy) K(ontory)," meaning Baku Post Office.

1922 *Imperf.* **Unwmkd.**

300 A5 1r gray grn 15.00
301 A7 5r gray brn 15.00
302 A12 150r blue 4.00
303 A9 250r vio & buff 7.00
304 A13 400r dk bl 6.00
305 SP1 500r bl & pale bl 7.00
306 SP2 1000r brn & bis 8.00
307 A8 2000r bl & blk 8.00
308 A7 3000r brn & bl 15.00
309 A11 5000r *ol grn* 15.00
Nos. 300-309 (10) 100.00

Stamps of 1922 Handstamped in Violet

БАКИНСКАГО Г-П-Т-О. №1

Overprint reads: Baku Post, Telegraph Office No. 1.

1924

Overprint 24x2mm.

312 A12 150r blue 7.00
313 A9 250r vio & buff 7.00
314 A13 400r dk bl 7.00
317 A8 2000r bl & blk 8.00
318 A7 3000r brn & bl 8.00
319 A11 5000r *ol grn* 8.00

Overprint 30x3½mm.

323 A12 150r blue 7.00
324 A9 250r vio & buff 7.00
325 A13 400r dk bl 7.00
328 A8 2000r bl & blk 7.00
329 A7 3000r brn & bl 8.00
330 A11 5000r *ol grn* 7.00

Overprinted on Nos. 32–33, 35.

331 A5 10,000r on 1r gray grn 27.50
332 A7 15,000r on 5r gray brn 27.50
333 A7 50,000r on 3000r brn & bl 32.50
Nos. 312-333 (15) 175.50

The overprinted semipostal stamps were used for regular postage.
This handstamp on Nos. 17, B1–B2 in size 24x2mm., and on Nos. 15, 17, B1–B2 in size 30x3½mm., was of private origin and not officially issued.

SEMI-POSTAL STAMPS.

Carrying Food to Sufferers
SP1

1922 *Imperf.* **Unwmkd.**

B1 SP1 500r bl & pale bl 50 75

Widow and Orphans
SP2

B2 SP2 1000r brn & bis 1.00 1.50

Counterfeits exist.

OCCUPATION AZIRBAYEDJAN

Russian stamps of 1909–18 were privately overprinted as above in red, blue or black by a group of Entente officers working with Russian soldiers returning from Persia. Azerbaijan was not occupied by the Allies. There is evidence that existing covers (some seemingly postmarked at Baku, dated Oct. 19, 1917, and at Tabriz, Russian Consulate, Apr. 25, 1917) are fakes.

AZORES

(ȧ-zōrz')

LOCATION—A group of islands in the North Atlantic Ocean, due west of Portugal.

GOVT.—Integral part of Portugal, former colony.

AREA—922 sq. mi.

POP.—253,935 (1930).

CAPITAL—Ponta Delgada.

Azores stamps were supplanted by those of Portugal in 1931.

1000 Reis = 1 Milreis
100 Centavos = 1 Escudo (1912)

Prices of early Azores stamps vary according to condition. Quotations for Nos. 1–37 are for fine copies. Very fine to superb specimens sell at much higher prices, and inferior or poor copies sell at reduced prices, depending on the condition of the individual specimen.

Stamps of Portugal Overprinted in Black or Carmine

AÇORES
a

A second type of this overprint has a broad "O" and open "S".

1868 *Imperf.* **Unwmkd.**

1 A14 5r black *1,750. 1,200.*
2 A14 10r yellow *4,000. 3,000.*
3 A14 20r bister 170.00 110.00
4 A14 50r green 175.00 125.00
5 A14 80r orange 175.00 125.00
6 A14 100r lilac 175.00 125.00

The reprints are on thick chalky white wove paper, ungummed, and on thin white paper with shiny white gum. Price $7.50 each.

1868-70 *Perf. 12½.*

5 REIS:

Type I. The "5" at the right is 1mm. from end of label.
Type II. The "5" is 1½mm. from end of label.

7 A14 5r blk (C) 45.00 30.00
8 A14 10r yellow 60.00 50.00
a. Inverted overprint *100.00 100.00*
9 A14 20r bister 50.00 35.00
10 A14 25r rose 45.00 4.50
a. Inverted overprint *75.00 75.00*
11 A14 50r green 110.00 80.00
12 A14 80r orange 140.00 110.00
13 A14 100r lilac 140.00 110.00
14 A14 120r blue 70.00 50.00
15 A14 240r violet 350.00 225.00

The reprints are on thick chalky white paper ungummed and perforated 13, and on thin white paper with shiny white gum and perforated 13½. Price $6 each.

1871-75 *Perf. 12½, 13½*

21 A15 5r blk (C) 8.00 5.50
a. Inverted overprint 40.00 40.00
23 A15 10r yellow 12.50 8.50
a. Inverted overprint 30.00 25.00
24 A15 20r bister 15.00 12.00
25 A15 25r rose 8.50 1.75
a. Inverted overprint 30.00 15.00
b. Double overprint 30.00
c. Perf. 14 140.00 40.00
d. Double impression of stamp
26 A15 50r green 30.00 15.00
27 A15 80r orange 45.00 15.00
28 A15 100r lilac 30.00 15.00
a. Perf. 14 150.00 90.00
29 A15 120r blue 75.00 45.00
a. Inverted overprint *125.00 110.00*
30 A15 240r violet 550.00 350.00

The reprints are of the second type. They are on thick chalky white paper ungummed and perforated 13, also on thin white paper with shiny white gum and perforated 13½. Price $4 each.

Overprinted in Black

AÇORES
b

1875-80

15 REIS:

Type I. The figures of value, 1 and 5, at the right in upper label are close together.
Type II. The figures of value at the right in upper label are spaced.

31 A15 10r bl grn 65.00 50.00
32 A15 10r yel grn 40.00 25.00
33 A15 15r lil brn 9.00 7.50
a. Inverted overprint 25.00 18.50
34 A15 50r blue 60.00 30.00
35 A15 150r blue 85.00 60.00
36 A15 150r yellow 90.00 75.00
37 A15 300r violet 32.50 25.00

The reprints have the same papers, gum and perforations as those of the preceding issue. Price $4 each.

1880 Black Overprint.

Perf. 11½, 12½ and 13½.

38 A17 25r gray 35.00 8.00
39 A18 25r red lil 11.00 3.75
a. 25r gray 11.00 3.75
b. Dbl. ovpt.

Overprinted in Carmine or Black

1881-82

40 A16 5r blk (C) 10.00 3.75
41 A23 25r brn ('82) 11.00 2.50
a. Double overprint
42 A19 50r blue 65.00 20.00

Reprints of Nos. 38, 39, 39a, 40 and 42 have the same papers, gum and perforations as those of preceding issues. Price $1.50 each.

Overprinted in Red or Black

AÇORES
c

1882-85

15, 20 REIS

Type I. The figures of value are some distance apart and close to the end of the label.
Type II. The figures are closer together and farther from the end of the label. On the 15 reis this is particularly apparent in the upper right figures.

43 A16 5r blk (R) 9.50 5.50
44 A21 5r slate 5.00 1.75
a. Dbl. ovpt.
c. Inverted overprint
45 A15 10r green 27.50 22.00
a. Inverted overprint
46 A22 10r green 9.00 4.00
a. Dbl. ovpt.
47 A15 15r lil brn 15.00 9.00
a. 15r red brn 15.00 9.00
b. Inverted overprint
48 A15 20r bister 22.50 15.00
a. Inverted overprint
49 A15 20r carmine 40.00 25.00
a. Double overprint
50 A23 25r brown 7.00 1.50
51 A15 50r blue 375.00 300.00
52 A24 50r blue 9.00 1.50
a. Double overprint
53 A15 80r orange 25.00 18.50
a. 80r yel 21.00 14.00
b. Double overprint
54 A15 100r lilac 15.00 10.00
55 A15 150r blue 375.00 300.00
56 A15 150r yellow 25.00 12.00
57 A15 300r violet 27.50 22.50

Reprints of the 1882-85 issues have the same papers, gum and perforations as those of preceding issues. Price $3 each.

Red Overprint.

58 A21 5r slate 3.00 1.25
59 A24a 500r black 100.00 75.00
60 A15 1000r black 40.00 30.00

1887 Black Overprint.

61 A25 20r pink 12.00 6.00
a. Inverted overprint
b. Dbl. ovpt.
62 A26 25r lil rose 12.00 90
a. Inverted overprint
b. Double overprint, one inverted
63 A26 25r red vio 12.00 90
a. Dbl. ovpt.
64 A24a 500r red vio 75.00 37.50
a. Perf. 13½ 100.00 85.00

Nos. 58 to 64 inclusive have been reprinted on thin white paper with shiny white gum and perforated 13½. Price $2 each.

Prince Henry the Navigator Issue.

Portugal Nos. 97–109 Overprinted

AÇORES

1894 *Perf. 14.*

65 A46 5r org yel 2.00 1.00
a. Inverted overprint 13.50 11.00
66 A46 10r vio rose 2.00 1.10
a. Dbl. ovpt. 18.50
b. Inverted overprint 15.00 11.00
67 A46 15r brown 3.00 1.25
68 A46 20r violet 3.00 1.75
a. Double overprint 16.50
69 A47 25r green 3.00 1.50
a. Double overprint 13.50 13.50
b. Inverted overprint 13.50 13.50
70 A47 50r blue 4.50 2.50
71 A47 75r dp car 10.00 6.50
72 A47 80r yel grn 12.00 6.50
73 A47 100r lt brn, *pale buff* 10.00 5.25
a. Dbl. ovpt. 22.50

74	A48	150r lt car, *pale rose*	15.00	12.00
75	A48	300r dk bl, *sal buff*	20.00	12.00
76	A48	500r brn vio, *pale lil*	35.00	17.50
77	A48	1000r gray blk, *yelsh*	80.00	35.00
a.		Double overprint		
		Nos. 65-77 (13)	210.00	113.10

St. Anthony of Padua Issue.

Portugal Nos. 132–146 Overprinted in Red or Black

AÇORES

1895 ***Perf. 12***

78	A50	2½r blk (R)	2.00	2.00
79	A51	5r brn yel	4.00	2.00
80	A51	10r red lil	4.00	3.25
81	A51	15r red brn	6.00	4.50
82	A51	20r gray lil	6.00	4.50
83	A51	25r grn & vio	4.00	2.75
84	A52	50r bl & brn	13.00	9.75
85	A52	75r rose & brn	22.50	20.00
86	A52	80r lt grn & brn	32.50	32.50
87	A52	100r choc & blk	25.00	20.00
88	A53	150r vio rose & bis	70.00	55.00
89	A53	200r bl & bis	80.00	60.00
90	A53	300r sl & bis	100.00	75.00
91	A53	500r vio brn & grn	150.00	100.00
92	A53	1000r vio & grn	275.00	200.00
		Nos. 78-92 (15)	794.00	591.25

Issued in commemoration of the seventh centenary of the birth of Saint Anthony of Padua.

Vasco da Gama Issue.

Common Design Types

1898 ***Perf. 14, 15.***

93	CD20	2½r bl grn	1.00	60
94	CD21	5r red	1.20	80
a.		Horizontal pair, imperf. between		
95	CD22	10r gray lil	2.75	1.50
96	CD23	25r yel grn	2.00	85
97	CD24	50r dk bl	5.00	3.00
98	CD25	75r vio brn	10.00	6.50
99	CD26	100r bis brn	10.00	6.00
100	CD27	150r bister	15.00	10.00
		Nos. 93-100 (8)	46.95	29.25

King Carlos A28

King Manuel II A29

1906 **Typographed** ***Perf. 11½x12***

101	A28	2½r gray	20	15
a.		Inverted overprint	13.50	13.50
102	A28	5r org yel	20	15
a.		Inverted overprint	13.50	13.50
103	A28	10r yel grn	20	15
104	A28	20r gray vio	50	25
105	A28	25r carmine	25	15
106	A28	50r ultra	3.00	2.50
107	A28	75r brn, *straw*	70	*1.00*
108	A28	100r dk bl, *bl*	60	*1.25*
109	A28	200r red lil, *pnksh*	1.00	*1.50*
110	A28	300r dk bl, *rose*	1.20	*1.75*
111	A28	500r blk, *bl*	2.25	1.50
		Nos. 101-111 (11)	10.10	*10.35*

"Acores" and letters and figures in the corners are in red on the 2½, 10, 20, 75 and 500r and in black on the other values.

1910 ***Perf. 14x15***

112	A29	2½r violet	25	20
113	A29	5r black	35	30
114	A29	10r dk grn	40	35
115	A29	15r lil brn	65	60
116	A29	20r carmine	65	60
117	A29	25r vio brn	35	20
a.		Perf. 11½	1.50	1.00
118	A29	50r blue	1.25	60
a.		Booklet pane of 6		
119	A29	75r bis brn	2.50	1.75
120	A29	80r slate	2.50	1.75
121	A29	100r brn, *lt grn*	3.00	2.50
122	A29	200r grn, *sal*	3.00	2.50
123	A29	300r *blue*	4.50	3.50
124	A29	500r ol & brn	6.50	5.00
125	A29	1000r bl & blk	11.00	11.00
		Nos. 112-125 (14)	36.90	30.85

The errors of color 10r black, 15r dark green, 25r black and 50r carmine were not regularly issued.

Stamps of 1910 Overprinted in Carmine or Green

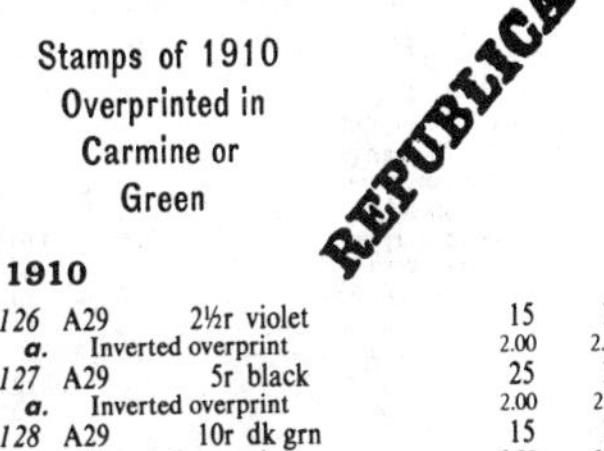

1910

126	A29	2½r violet	15	10
a.		Inverted overprint	2.00	2.00
127	A29	5r black	25	15
a.		Inverted overprint	2.00	2.00
128	A29	10r dk grn	15	12
a.		Inverted overprint	2.00	2.00
129	A29	15r lil brn	1.00	80
a.		Inverted overprint	2.00	2.00
130	A29	20r car (G)	1.25	1.00
a.		Inverted overprint	3.00	3.00
b.		Double overprint	3.00	3.00
131	A29	25r vio brn	20	15
a.		Perf. 11½	30.00	25.00
132	A29	50r blue	90	70
133	A29	75r bis brn	50	20
a.		Double overprint	2.00	2.00
134	A29	80r slate	65	30
135	A29	100r brn, *grn*	50	25
136	A29	200r grn, *sal*	50	*1.00*
137	A29	300r *blue*	1.50	1.50
138	A29	500r ol & brn	1.75	*2.50*
139	A29	1000r bl & blk	3.25	*4.00*
		Nos. 126-139 (14)	12.55	*12.77*

Vasco da Gama Issue Overprinted or Surcharged in Black:

REPUBLICA
d

REPUBLICA REPUBLICA

REIS 15 REIS
e

1$000
f

1911 ***Perf. 14, 15***

141	CD20 (d)	2½r bl grn	40	35
142	CD21 (e)	15r on 5r red	35	35
143	CD23 (d)	25r yel grn	50	30
144	CD24 (d)	50r dk bl	1.25	85
145	CD25 (d)	75r vio brn	90	90
146	CD27 (e)	80r on 150r bis	90	90
147	CD26 (d)	100r yel brn	90	90
a.		Dbl. surch.	8.00	8.00
148	CD22 (f)	1000r on 10r lil	10.00	10.00
		Nos. 141-148 (8)	15.20	14.55

Postage Due Stamps of Portugal Overprinted or Surcharged in Black "ACORES" and

REPUBLICA

REPUBLICA
g

Rs 300 Rs
h

1911 ***Perf. 12***

149	D1 (g)	5r black	60	50
a.		Half used as 2½r on cover		
150	D1 (g)	10r magenta	1.50	80
a.		"Acores" double	7.50	7.50
151	D1 (g)	20r orange	2.25	2.00
152	D1 (g)	200r brn, *buff*	8.00	5.50
a.		"Acores" inverted		
153	D1 (h)	300r on 50r sl	8.00	5.50
154	D1 (h)	500r on 100r car, *pink*	8.00	5.50
		Nos. 149-154 (6)	28.35	19.80

Ceres A30

Ceres Issue of Portugal Overprinted "ACORES" in Black or Carmine

With Imprint.

1912–31 ***Perf. 12x11½, 15x14***

155	A30	¼c ol brn	10	10
a.		Inverted overprint	2.00	
156	A30	½c blk (C)	10	10
157	A30	1c dp grn	70	40
a.		Inverted overprint	4.50	
158	A30	1c dp brn ('18)	12	5
a.		Inverted overprint		
159	A30	1½c choc ('13)	75	60
a.		Inverted overprint	3.00	
160	A30	1½c dp grn ('18)	25	15
a.		Inverted overprint		
161	A30	2c carmine	35	25
a.		Inverted overprint	4.50	
162	A30	2c org ('18)	20	10
a.		Inverted overprint	11.00	
163	A30	2½c violet	27	15
164	A30	3c rose ('18)	20	10
165	A30	3c dl ultra ('25)	20	15
166	A30	3½c lt grn ('18)	25	10
167	A30	4c lt grn ('19)	15	6
168	A30	4c org ('30)	40	30
169	A30	5c dp bl	40	12
170	A30	5c yel brn ('18)	35	25
171	A30	5c ol brn ('23)	12	8
172	A30	5c blk brn ('30)	3.50	3.00
173	A30	6c dl rose ('20)	25	15
174	A30	6c choc ('25)	25	15
175	A30	6c red brn ('31)	25	*1.00*
176	A30	7½c yel brn	4.00	1.50
177	A30	7½c dp bl ('18)	85	50
178	A30	8c sl ('13)	35	25
179	A30	8c bl grn ('22)	25	20
180	A30	8c org ('25)	65	35
181	A30	10c org brn	20	10
182	A30	12c bl gray ('20)	1.25	90
183	A30	12c dp grn ('22)	65	50
184	A30	13½c chlky bl ('20)	1.25	*3.00*
185	A30	14c dk bl, *yel*('20)	4.00	*5.00*
186	A30	15c plum ('13)	75	25
187	A30	15c blk (R) ('23)	50	50
188	A30	16c brt ultra ('24)	1.00	30
189	A30	16c dp bl ('30)	1.50	*2.00*
190	A30	20c vio brn, *grn* ('13)	9.00	4.00
191	A30	20c choc ('20)	75	25
192	A30	20c dp grn ('23)	1.00	1.00
a.		Double overprint		
193	A30	20c gray ('24)	75	25
194	A30	24c grnsh bl ('21)	75	25
195	A30	25c sal ('23)	35	20
196	A30	30c brn, *pink* ('13)	40.00	27.50
197	A30	30c brn, *yel* ('19)	2.75	2.75
198	A30	30c gray brn ('21)	1,00	60
199	A30	32c dp grn ('25)	1.75	1.25
200	A30	36c red ('21)	50	25
201	A30	40c dp bl ('23)	50	50
202	A30	40c blk brn ('24)	25	10
203	A30	40c brt grn ('30)	1.75	50
204	A30	48c brt rose ('24)	1.75	1.25
205	A30	48c dl pink ('31)	2.00	1.50
206	A30	50c org, *sal* ('13)	5.00	1.25
207	A30	50c yel ('23)	1.50	1.25
208	A30	50c bis ('30)	3.00	2.25
209	A30	50c red brn ('31)	2.50	1.75
210	A30	60c bl ('21)	1.10	90
211	A30	64c pale ultra ('24)	1.75	1.25
212	A30	64c brn rose ('31)	15.00	10.00
213	A30	75c dl rose ('23)	6.00	4.00
214	A30	75c car rose ('30)	2.00	1.50
215	A30	80c dl rose ('21)	1.50	85
216	A30	80c vio ('24)	1.50	1.00
217	A30	80c dk grn ('31)	2.00	1.50
218	A30	90c chlky bl ('21)	1.50	85
219	A30	96c dp rose ('26)	8.50	4.00
220	A30	1e dp grn, *bl*	6.00	2.50
221	A30	1e vio ('21)	1.50	85
222	A30	1e gray vio ('24)	2.00	1.25
223	A30	1e brn lake ('30)	32.50	22.50
224	A30	1.10e yel brn ('21)	1.50	1.50
225	A30	1.20e yel grn ('21)	1.75	1.00
226	A30	1.20e buff ('24)	4.50	2.25
227	A30	1.25e dk bl ('30)	1.75	85
228	A30	1.50e blk vio ('23)	3.25	2.00
229	A30	1.50e lil ('25)	3.50	2.00
230	A30	1.60e dp bl ('25)	3.50	2.00
231	A30	2e sl grn ('21)	5.00	2.00
232	A30	2.40e ap grn ('26)	37.50	19.00
233	A30	3e lil pink ('26)	37.50	19.00
234	A30	3.20e gray grn ('25)	10.00	5.00
235	A30	5e emer ('24)	12.50	6.00
236	A30	10e pink ('24)	25.00	10.00
237	A30	20e pale turq ('25)	85.00	55.00
		Nos. 155-237 (83)	418.31	*251.91*

Castello-Branco Issue.

Stamps of Portugal, 1925, Overprinted in Black or Red

AÇORES

1925 ***Perf. 12½.***

238	A73	2c orange	20	20
239	A73	3c green	20	20
240	A73	4c ultra (R)	20	20
241	A73	5c scarlet	20	20
242	A74	10c pale bl	20	20
243	A74	16c red org	30	30
244	A75	25c car rose	30	30
245	A74	32c green	50	50
246	A75	40c grn & blk (R)	30	30
247	A74	48c red brn	1.00	1.00
248	A76	50c bl grn	1.00	1.00
249	A76	64c org brn	1.00	1.00
250	A76	75c gray blk (R)	1.25	1.25
251	A75	80c brown	1.25	1.25
252	A76	96c car rose	1.50	1.50
253	A77	1.50e dk bl, *bl* (R)	1.50	1.10
254	A75	1.60e ind (R)	1.50	1.10
255	A77	2e dk grn, *grn* (R)	2.00	2.00
256	A77	2.40e red, *org*	2.50	2.25
257	A77	3.20e *grn* (R)	3.75	3.00
		Nos. 238-257 (20)	20.65	18.85

First Independence Issue.

Stamps of Portugal, 1926, Overprinted in Red

AÇÔRES

1926 ***Perf. 14, 14½***

Center in Black.

258	A79	2c orange	40	40
259	A80	3c ultra	40	40
260	A79	4c yel grn	40	40
261	A80	5c blk brn	40	40
262	A79	6c ocher	40	40
263	A80	15c dk grn	75	75
264	A81	20c dl vio	75	75
265	A82	25c scarlet	75	75
266	A81	32c dp grn	75	75
267	A82	40c yel brn	75	75
268	A82	50c ol bis	2.00	2.00
269	A82	75c red brn	2.00	2.00
270	A83	1e blk vio	2.50	2.50
271	A84	4.50e ol grn	6.00	6.00
		Nos. 258-271 (14)	18.25	18.25

The use of these stamps instead of those of the regular issue was obligatory on Aug. 13th and 14th Nov. 30th and Dec. 1st, 1926.

Second Independence Issue.

Stamps of Portugal, 1927, Overprinted in Red

AÇÔRES

1927 **Center in Black.**

272	A86	2c lt brn	30	30
273	A87	3c ultra	30	30
274	A86	4c orange	30	30
275	A88	5c dk brn	30	30
276	A89	6c org brn	30	30
277	A87	15c blk brn	30	30
278	A86	25c gray	1.25	1.25
279	A89	32c bl grn	1.25	1.25
280	A90	40c yel grn	1.25	1.25
281	A90	96c red	3.00	3.00
282	A88	1.60e myr grn	3.00	3.00
283	A91	4.50e bister	6.00	6.00
		Nos. 272-283 (12)	17.55	17.55

Third Independence Issue.

Stamps of Portugal, 1928, Overprinted in Red **AÇÔRES**

1928 **Center in Black.**

284	A93	2c lt bl	30	30
285	A94	3c lt grn	30	30
286	A95	4c lake	30	30
287	A96	5c ol grn	30	30
288	A97	6c org brn	30	30
289	A94	15c slate	50	50
290	A95	16c dk vio	85	85
291	A93	25c ultra	85	85
292	A97	32c dk grn	85	85
293	A96	40c ol brn	85	85
294	A95	50c red org	1.75	1.75
295	A94	80c lt gray	1.75	1.75
296	A97	96c carmine	2.25	2.25
297	A96	1e claret	2.25	2.25
298	A93	1.60e dk bl	2.25	2.25
299	A98	4.50e yellow	5.50	5.50
		Nos. 284-299 (16)	21.15	21.15

A31

A32

1929–30 ***Perf. 12x11½, 15x14***

300	A31	4c on 25c pink ('30)	50	50
301	A31	4c on 60c dp bl	50	50
302	A31	10c on 25c pink	60	50
303	A31	12c on 25c pink	60	50
304	A31	15c on 25c pink	75	60
305	A31	20c on 25c pink	1.00	85
306	A31	40c on 1.10e yel brn	3.25	2.75
		Nos. 300-306 (7)	7.20	6.20

Black or Red Overprint.

1930 ***Perf. 14.***

Without Imprint at Foot.

307	A32	4c orange	60	40
308	A32	5c dp brn	2.25	1.50
309	A32	10c vermilion	1.00	70
310	A32	15c blk (R)	1.00	70
311	A32	40c brt grn	1.00	70
312	A32	80c violet	12.50	10.00
313	A32	1.60e dk bl	2.25	1.25
		Nos. 307-313 (7)	20.60	15.25

POSTAGE DUE STAMPS.

D2

D3

Portugal Nos. J7–J13 Overprinted in Black

1904 ***Perf. 12*** **Unwmkd.**

J1	D2	5r brown	60	60
J2	D2	10r orange	60	60
J3	D2	20r lilac	1.00	1.00
J4	D2	30r gray grn	1.00	1.00
a.		Double overprint		
J5	D2	40r gray vio	1.75	1.75
J6	D2	50r carmine	2.00	2.00
J7	D2	100r dl bl	3.50	3.50
		Nos J1-J7 (7)	10.45	10.45

Same Overprinted in Carmine or Green (Portugal Nos. J14–J20) **REPUBLICA**

1911

J8	D2	5r brown	30	30
J9	D2	10r orange	30	30
J10	D2	20r lilac	30	30
J11	D2	30r gray grn	30	30
J12	D2	40r gray vio	50	50
J13	D2	50r car (G)	2.50	2.50
J14	D2	100r dl bl	1.50	1.50
		Nos. J8-J14 (7)	5.70	5.70

Portugal Nos. J21–J27 Overprinted in Black

1918

J15	D3	½c brown	15	15
a.		Inverted overprint	50	50
b.		Double overprint	50	50
J16	D3	1c orange	15	15
a.		Inverted overprint	50	50
b.		Double overprint	50	50
J17	D3	2c red lil	15	15
a.		Inverted overprint	1.00	1.00
b.		Double overprint	1.00	1.00
J18	D3	3c green	15	15
a.		Inverted overprint	1.00	1.00
b.		Double overprint	1.00	1.00
J19	D3	4c gray	15	15
a.		Inverted overprint	1.00	1.00
b.		Double overprint	1.00	1.00
J20	D3	5c rose	15	15
b.		Double overprint	1.00	1.00
J21	D3	10c dk bl	25	25
		Nos. J15-J21 (7)	1.15	1.15

Stamps and Type of Portugal Postage Dues, 1921–27, Overprinted in Black

1922-24 ***Perf. 11½x12.***

J30	D3	½c gray grn ('23)	15	15
J31	D3	1c gray grn ('23)	15	15
J32	D3	2c gray grn ('23)	15	15
J33	D3	3c gray grn ('24)	50	50
J34	D3	8c gray grn ('24)	25	25
J35	D3	10c gray grn ('24)	30	30
J36	D3	12c gray grn ('24)	25	25
J37	D3	16c gray grn ('24)	25	25
J38	D3	20c gray grn	60	60
J39	D3	24c gray grn	25	25
J40	D3	32c gray grn ('24)	25	25
J41	D3	36c gray grn	25	25
J42	D3	40c gray grn ('24)	60	60
J43	D3	48c gray grn ('24)	35	35
J44	D3	50c gray grn	60	60
J45	D3	60c gray grn	40	40
J46	D3	72c gray grn	40	40
J47	D3	80c gray grn ('24)	1.75	1.75
J48	D3	1.20e gray grn	1.75	1.75
		Nos. J30-J48 (19)	9.20	9.20

NEWSPAPER STAMPS.

N1

N2

N3

Newspaper Stamps of Portugal Overprinted in Black or Red

Perf. 11½, 12½ and 13½.

1876-88 **Unwmkd.**

P1	N1	2½r olive	4.50	1.50
a.		Inverted overprint		
P2	N2	2½r ol ('82)	3.00	1.25
a.		Inverted overprint		
b.		Double overprint		
P3	N3	2r blk ('85)	1.50	90
a.		Inverted overprint		
b.		Double overprint, one inverted		
P4	N2	2½r bis ('82)	3.00	75
a.		Double overprint		
P5	N3	2r blk (R) ('88)	7.00	3.00

Reprints of the newspaper stamps have the same papers, gum and perforations as reprints of the regular issues. Price $2 each.

PARCEL POST STAMPS.

Mercury and Commerce
PP1

Portugal Nos. Q1–Q17 Overprinted in Black or Red.

1921-22 ***Perf. 12.*** **Unwmkd.**

Q1	PP1	1c lil brn	20	18
a.		Inverted overprint	50	50
Q2	PP1	2c orange	20	18
a.		Inverted overprint	50	50
Q3	PP1	5c lt brn	20	18
a.		Inverted overprint	1.00	1.00
b.		Double overprint	1.00	1.00
Q4	PP1	10c red brn	40	30
a.		Inverted overprint	1.00	1.00
b.		Double overprint	1.00	1.00
Q5	PP1	20c gray bl	40	30
a.		Inverted overprint	1.00	1.00
b.		Double overprint	1.00	1.00
Q6	PP1	40c carmine	40	40
a.		Double overprint	1.50	1.50
Q7	PP1	50c blk (R)	70	70
Q8	PP1	60c dk bl (R)	70	70
Q9	PP1	70c gray brn	1.75	1.50
a.		Double overprint		
Q10	PP1	80c ultra	1.75	1.50
Q11	PP1	90c lt vio	1.75	1.50
Q12	PP1	1e lt grn	1.75	1.50
Q13	PP1	2e pale lil	2.50	2.50
Q14	PP1	3e olive	3.00	3.00
Q15	PP1	4e ultra	5.00	5.00
Q16	PP1	5e gray	5.00	5.00
Q17	PP1	10e chocolate	15.00	15.00
		Nos. Q1-Q17 (17)	40.70	39.44

POSTAL TAX STAMPS.

These stamps represent a special fee for the delivery of postal matter on certain days in the year. The money derived from their sale is applied to works of public charity.

Nos. 114 and 157 Overprinted in Carmine

ASSISTENCIA

1911–13 ***Perf. 14x15*** **Unwmkd.**

RA1	A29	10r dk grn	75	60

The 20r of this type was for use on telegrams.

Perf. 15x14

RA2	A30	1c dp grn	1.50	1.50

The 2c of this type was for use on telegrams.

Charity Sheltering Poor
PT1

Postal Tax Stamp of Portugal Overprinted in Black.

1915 ***Perf. 12.***

RA3	PT1	1c carmine	15	12

The 2c of this type was for use on telegrams.

Postal Tax Stamp of 1915 Surcharged **15 ctvs.**

1924

RA4	PT1	15c on 1c rose	50	*1.00*

Comrades of the Great War Issue.

Postal Tax Stamps of Portugal, 1925, Overprinted AÇORES

1925 ***Perf. 11.***

RA5	PT3	10c brown	40	40
RA6	PT3	10c green	40	40
RA7	PT3	10c rose	40	40
RA8	PT3	10c ultra	40	40

The use of Nos. RA5–RA11 in addition to the regular postage was compulsory on certain days. If the tax represented by these stamps was not prepaid, it was collected by means of Postal Tax Due Stamps.

Pombal Issue.

Common Design Types

1925 ***Perf. 12½.***

RA9	CD28	20c dp grn & blk	40	35
RA10	CD29	20c dp grn & blk	40	35
RA11	CD30	20c dp grn & blk	40	35

POSTAL TAX DUE STAMPS.

Postal Tax Due Stamp of Portugal Overprinted AÇORES

1925 ***Perf. 11x11½.*** **Unwmkd.**

RAJ1	PTD1	20c brn org	50	50

See note after No. RA8.

Pombal Issue.

Common Design Types

1925 ***Perf. 12½.***

RAJ2	CD31	40c dp grn & blk	75	*1.25*
RAJ3	CD32	40c dp grn & blk	75	*1.25*
RAJ4	CD33	40c dp grn & blk	75	*1.25*

See note after No. RA8.
See Portugal for later issues.

BADEN

See Vol. III, Early German States group preceding Germany.

BATUM

See Vol. I, British section.

BAVARIA

See Vol. III, Early German States group preceding Germany.

BELGIAN CONGO

LOCATION—Central Africa.
GOVT.—Belgian colony.
AREA—902,082 sq. mi. (estimated).
POP.—12,660,000 (1956).
CAPITAL—Léopoldville.

Congo was an independent state, founded by Leopold II of Belgium, until 1908 when it was annexed to Belgium as a colony. In 1960 it became the independent Republic of the Congo. See Congo Democratic Republic and Zaire.

100 Centimes = 1 Franc

Independent State

King Leopold II

A1 A2 A3

Typographed.

1886 ***Perf. 15.*** **Unwmkd.**

1	A1	5c green	12.50	17.50
2	A1	10c rose	4.50	4.50
3	A2	25c blue	50.00	40.00
4	A3	50c ol grn	5.00	4.50
5	A1	5fr lilac	375.00	250.00
a.		Perf. 14	600.00	

King Leopold II
A4

1887-94

6	A4	5c grn ('89)	65	65
7	A4	10c rose ('89)	1.25	1.10
8	A4	25c bl ('89)	75	90
9	A4	50c brown	57.50	19.00
10	A4	50c gray ('94)	2.50	9.00
11	A4	5fr violet	750.00	375.00
12	A4	5fr gray ('92)	125.00	90.00
13	A4	10fr buff ('91)	350.00	225.00

The 25fr and 50fr in gray were not issued. Prices $21, $20.

Port Matadi
A5

River Scene on the Congo, Stanley Falls
A6

Inkissi Falls
A7

Railroad Bridge on M'pozo River
A8

Hunting Elephants
A9

Bangala Chief and Wife
A10

Engraved.

1894-1901 ***Perf. 12½ to 15***

14	A5	5c pale bl & blk	12.50	11.50
15	A5	5c red brn & blk ('95)	3.50	1.40
16	A5	5c grn & blk ('00)	2.25	50
17	A6	10c red brn & blk	15.00	14.00
18	A6	10c grnsh bl & blk ('95)	1.10	1.10
a.		Center invtd.	1,350.	2,100.
19	A6	10c car & blk ('00)	2.75	50
20	A7	25c yel org & blk	4.00	2.25
21	A7	25c lt bl & blk ('00)	3.25	1.25
22	A8	50c grn & blk	1.40	1.20
23	A8	50c ol & blk ('00)	3.25	65
24	A9	1fr lil & blk	25.00	11.50
a.		1fr rose lil & blk	165.00	17.50
25	A9	1fr car & blk ('01)	150.00	2.00
26	A10	5fr lake & blk	37.50	14.00
		Nos. 14-26 (13)	261.50	61.85

Climbing Oil Palms
A11

Congo Canoe
A12

1896

27	A11	15c ocher & blk	3.75	55
28	A12	40c bluish grn & blk	4.00	2.75

Congo Village—A13

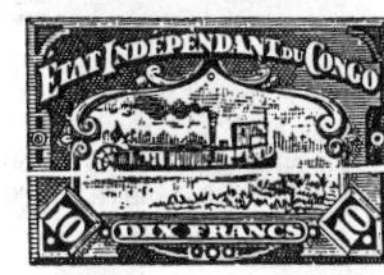

River Steamer on the Congo
A14

1898

29	A13	3.50fr red & blk	135.00	62.50
30	A14	10fr yel grn & blk	95.00	17.50
a.		Center invtd.	5,500.	
b.		Perf. 12	450.00	17.50
c.		Perf. 12x14	350.00	125.00

Belgian Congo

Overprinted **CONGO BELGE**

1908

31	A5	5c grn & blk	7.50	7.50
a.		Handstamped	2.25	1.65
32	A6	10c car & blk	12.50	12.50
a.		Handstamped	2.25	1.65
33	A11	15c ocher & blk	6.50	3.50
a.		Handstamped	5.00	2.75
34	A7	25c lt bl & blk	5.00	3.50
a.		Handstamped	7.50	3.25
35	A12	40c bluish grn & blk	2.25	2.25
a.		Handstamped	7.50	5.25
36	A8	50c ol & blk	4.25	2.50
a.		Handstamped	4.00	2.50
37	A9	1fr car & blk	21.00	2.50
a.		Handstamped	25.00	2.00
38	A13	3.50fr red & blk	20.00	12.50
a.		Handstamped	150.00	75.00
39	A10	5fr car & blk	32.50	17.50
a.		Handstamped	57.50	25.00
40	A14	10fr yel grn & blk	75.00	15.00
a.		Perf. 14	110.00	19.00
b.		Handstamped	110.00	27.50
c.		Handstamped, perf. 14	300.00	175.00
		Nos. 31-40 (10)	186.50	79.25

Most of the above handstamps are also found inverted and double.

Port Matadi—A15

River Scene on the Congo, Stanley Falls
A16

Climbing Oil Palms
A17

Railroad Bridge on M'pozo River
A18

1909 ***Perf. 14***

41	A15	5c grn & blk	75	75
42	A16	10c car & blk	65	50
43	A17	15c ocher & blk	21.00	12.00
44	A18	50c ol & blk	3.25	2.00

Port Matadi
A19

River Scene on the Congo, Stanley Falls
A20

Climbing Oil Palms
A21

Bangala Chief and Wife
A27

Inkissi Falls
A22

Congo Canoe
A23

Railroad Bridge on M'pozo River
A24

Hunting Elephants
A25

Congo Village
A26

River Steamer on the Congo
A28

1910-15 Engraved. *Perf. 14, 15.*

No.	Type	Description	Unused	Used
45	A19	5c grn & blk	1.25	28
46	A20	10c car & blk	70	22
47	A21	15c ocher & blk	70	22
48	A21	15c grn & blk ('15)	38	25
a.		Bklt pane of 10	11.00	
49	A22	25c bl & blk	1.50	28
50	A23	40c bluish grn & blk	2.00	1.75
51	A23	40c brn red & blk ('15)	4.50	2.25
52	A24	50c ol & blk	3.75	2.00
53	A24	50c brn lake & blk ('15)	7.00	2.00
54	A25	1fr car & blk	3.50	2.75
55	A25	1fr ol bis & blk ('15)	2.25	90
56	A26	3fr red & blk	17.50	13.00
57	A27	5fr car & blk	20.00	17.50
58	A27	5fr ocher & blk ('15)	1.90	90
59	A28	10fr grn & blk	23.50	20.00
		Nos. 45-59 (15)	90.43	64.30

Nos. 48, 51, 53, 55 and 58 exist imperforate.

Port Matadi
A29

Stanley Falls, Congo River
A30

Inkissi Falls—A31

TEN CENTIMES.

Type I. Large white space at top of picture and two small white spots at lower edge. Vignette does not fill frame.

Type II. Vignette completely fills frame.

1915

No.	Type	Description	Unused	Used
60	A29	5c grn & blk	25	20
a.		Booklet pane of 10	10.00	
61	A30	10c car & blk (II)	30	20
a.		10c car & blk (I)	30	20
b.		Vertical pair, Imperf. between	15.00	
d.		Booklet pane of 10 (II)	12.00	
62	A31	25c bl & blk	1.40	38
a.		Booklet pane of 10	45.00	

Nos. 60 to 62 exist imperforate.

Stamps of 1910 Issue Surcharged in Red or Black

10c 10c

1921

No.	Type	Description	Unused	Used
64	A23	5c on 40c bluish grn & blk (R)	30	30
65	A19	10c on 5c grn & blk (R)	30	30
66	A24	15c on 50c ol & blk (R)	30	30
67	A21	25c on 15c ocher & blk (R)	1.90	1.40
68	A20	30c on 10c car & blk	30	30
a.		Inverted surcharge	25.00	
69	A22	50c on 25c bl & blk (R)	1.75	1.40
		Nos. 64-69 (6)	4.85	4.00

The position of the new value and the bars varies on Nos. 64 to 69.

Overprinted **1921**

1921

No.	Type	Description	Unused	Used
70	A25	1fr car & blk	1.15	1.15
a.		Double overprint	17.50	
71	A26	3fr red & blk	3.25	3.25
72	A27	5fr car & blk	4.50	4.50
73	A28	10fr grn & blk (R)	6.25	3.75

Belgian Surcharges.

Stamps of 1915 Surcharged in Black or Red ·10c

1922

No.	Type	Description	Unused	Used
74	A24	5c on 50c brn lake & blk	50	45
75	A29	10c on 5c grn & blk (R)	50	38
76	A23	25c on 40c brn red & blk (R)	2.00	45
77	A30	30c on 10c car & blk (II)	28	25
a.		30c on 10c car & blk (I)	28	25
b.		Double surcharge	6.00	6.00
78	A31	50c on 25c bl & blk (R)	50	38
		Nos. 74-78 (5)	3.78	1.91

No. 74 has the surcharge at each side.

Nos. 74-78 were issued only in sheets of 50. Blocks of 10 (5x2), so-called "booklet panes," are believed to be from the sheets of 50.

Congo Surcharges.

Nos. 60, 51 Surcharged in Red or Black:

10 c.

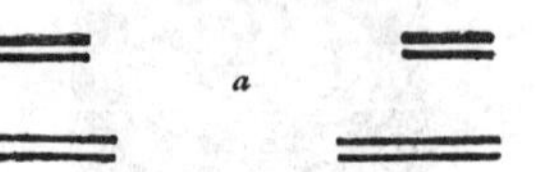

a

25 c.

b

1922

No.	Type	Description	Unused	Used
80	A29 (a)	10c on 5c grn & blk (R)	65	65
a.		Invtd. surch	20.00	20.00
b.		Double surcharge	6.00	
c.		Double surcharge, one inverted	40.00	
d.		Pair, one without surcharge	45.00	
e.		On No.45	150.00	150.00
81	A23 (b)	25c on 40c brn red & blk	75	38
a.		Inverted surcharge	20.00	20.00
b.		Double surcharge	7.00	
c.		"25c" double		
d.		25c on 5c, No. 60	135.00	135.00

Nos. 55, 58 Surcharged **10 c.** and vertical bars over original values.

1922

No.	Type	Description	Unused	Used
84	A25	10c on 1fr ol bis & blk (R)	65	65
a.		Double surcharge	15.00	
b.		Inverted surcharge	25.00	25.00
85	A27	25c on 5fr ocher & blk	1.90	1.90

Nos. 68, 77 Handstamped **0,25**

No.	Type	Description	Unused	Used
86	A20	25c on 30c on 10c car & blk	9.50	9.50
87	A30	25c on 30c on 10c car & blk (II)	9.50	9.50

Nos. 86-87 exist with handstamp surcharge inverted.

Ubangi Woman A32 Watusi Cattle A44

Designs: 10c, Baluba woman. 15c, Babuende woman. No. 91, 40c, 1.25fr, 1.50fr, 1.75fr, Ubangi man. 25c, Basket making. 30c, 35c, 75c, Carving wood. 50c, Archer. No. 92, 75c, Weaving. 1fr, Making pottery. 3fr, Working rubber. 5fr, Making palm oil. 10fr, African elephant.

1923-27 Engraved *Perf. 12*

No.	Type	Description	Unused	Used
88	A32	5c yellow	20	12
89	A32	10c green	20	12
90	A32	15c ol brn	20	12
91	A32	20c ol grn ('24)	18	12
92	A32	20c grn ('26)	20	15
93	A32	25c red brn	30	12
94	A32	30c rose red ('24)	50	50
95	A32	30c ol grn ('25)	20	15
96	A32	35c grn ('27)	50	50
97	A32	40c vio ('25)	20	15
98	A32	50c gray bl	30	22
99	A32	50c buff ('25)	35	8
100	A32	75c red org	42	42
101	A32	75c gray bl ('25)	45	28
102	A32	75c sal red ('26)	25	15
103	A32	1fr bis brn	55	22
104	A32	1fr dl bl ('25)	45	12
105	A32	1fr rose red ('27)	75	15
106	A32	1.25fr dl bl ('26)	38	28
107	A32	1.50fr dl bl ('26)	38	22
108	A32	1.75fr dl bl ('27)	3.75	2.85
109	A32	3fr gray brn ('24)	4.00	1.40
110	A32	5fr gray ('24)	8.50	4.00
111	A32	10fr gray blk ('24)	20.00	6.25
		Nos. 88-111 (24)	43.21	18.69

1925-26 *Perf. 12*

No.	Type	Description	Unused	Used
112	A44	45c dk vio ('26)	45	38
113	A44	60c car rose	45	22

No. 107 Surcharged **175**

1927, June 14

No.	Type	Description	Unused	Used
114	A32	1.75fr on 1.50fr dl bl	65	38

Sir Henry Morton Stanley
A45

1928, June 30 *Perf. 14*

No.	Type	Description	Unused	Used
115	A45	5c gray blk	8	8
116	A45	10c dp vio	10	10
117	A45	20c org red	22	22
118	A45	35c green	80	65
119	A45	40c red brn	32	20
120	A45	60c blk brn	32	20
121	A45	1fr carmine	32	10
122	A45	1.60fr dk gray	3.50	2.75
123	A45	1.75fr dp bl	1.50	90
124	A45	2fr dk brn	1.00	38
125	A45	2.75fr red vio	4.00	45
126	A45	3.50fr rose lake	1.25	75
127	A45	5fr sl grn	1.00	30
128	A45	10fr vio bl	1.50	75
129	A45	20fr claret	5.00	2.75
		Nos. 115-129 (15)	20.91	10.58

Issued in memory of Sir Henry M. Stanley (1841-1904), explorer.

Stamps of 1928 Surcharged in Red, Blue or Black **1F25**

1931, Jan. 15

No.	Type	Description	Unused	Used
130	A45	40c on 35c grn (R)	70	55
131	A45	1.25fr on 1fr car (Bl)	55	15
132	A45	2fr on 1.60fr dk gray (R)	1.10	38
133	A45	2fr on 1.75fr dp bl (R)	1.00	35
134	A45	3.25fr on 2.75fr red vio (Bk)	3.00	2.25
135	A45	3.25fr on 3.50fr rose lake (Bk)	3.75	2.50

Stamps of 1923-27 Surcharged in Red

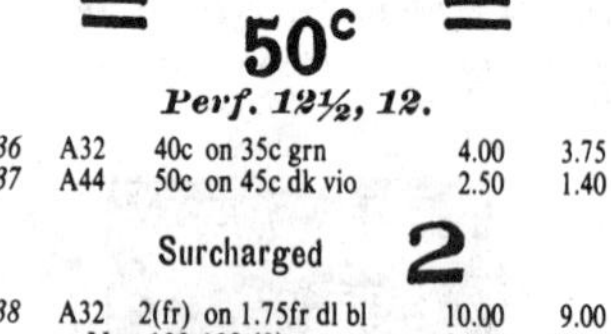

50c

Perf. 12½, 12.

No.	Type	Description	Unused	Used
136	A32	40c on 35c grn	4.00	3.75
137	A44	50c on 45c dk vio	2.50	1.40

Surcharged **2**

No.	Type	Description	Unused	Used
138	A32	2(fr) on 1.75fr dl bl	10.00	9.00
		Nos. 130-138 (9)	26.60	20.33

View of Sankuru River
A46

Flute Players
A50

Designs: 15c, Kivu Kraal. 20c, Sankuru River rapids. 25c, Uele hut. 50c, Musicians of Lake Leopold II. 60c, Batetelas drummers. 75c, Mangbetu woman. 1fr, Domesticated elephant of Api. 1.25fr, Mangbetu chief. 1.50fr, 2fr, Village of Mondimbi. 2.50fr, 3.25fr, Okapi. 4fr, Canoes at Stanleyville. 5fr, Woman preparing cassava. 10fr, Baluba chief. 20fr, Young woman of Irumu.

1931-37 Engraved. *Perf. 11½.*

No.	Type	Description	Unused	Used
139	A46	10c gray brn ('32)	8	8
140	A46	15c gray ('32)	8	8
141	A46	20c brn lil ('32)	8	8
142	A46	25c dp bl ('32)	8	8
143	A50	40c dp grn ('32)	25	25
144	A46	50c vio ('32)	8	8
a.		Imperf.	20.00	
b.		Booklet pane of 8	7.50	
145	A50	60c vio brn ('32)	15	12
146	A50	75c rose ('32)	12	8
a.		Imperf	20.00	
b.		Booklet pane of 8	1.65	
147	A50	1fr rose red ('32)	20	10
148	A50	1.25fr red brn	18	8
a.		Imperf.	20.00	
b.		Booklet pane of 8	1.65	
149	A46	1.50fr dk ol gray ('37)	20	15
a.		Imperf.	20.00	
b.		Booklet pane of 8	7.50	
150	A46	2fr ultra ('32)	25	15
151	A46	2.50fr dp bl ('37)	45	18
a.		Imperf., pair	50.00	
b.		Bklt pane of 8	11.00	
152	A46	3.25fr gray blk ('32)	70	40
153	A46	4fr dl vio ('32)	30	20
154	A50	5fr dp vio ('32)	70	30
155	A50	10fr red ('32)	75	50
156	A50	20fr blk brn ('32)	2.25	1.85
		Nos.139-156 (18)	6.90	4.76

No. 109 Surcharged in Red

3F25

= =

1932, Mar. 15 *Perf. 12*

No.	Type	Description	Unused	Used
157	A32	3.25fr on 3fr gray brn	3.50	2.50

King Albert Memorial Issue.

King Albert
A62

1934, May 7 Photo. *Perf. 11½*

No.	Type	Description	Unused	Used
158	A62	1.50fr black	90	25

Leopold I, Leopold II, Albert I, Leopold III
A63

1935, Aug. 15 Engr. *Perf. 12½x12*

No.	Type	Description	Unused	Used
159	A63	50c green	90	65
160	A63	1.25fr dk car	90	22
161	A63	1.50fr brn vio	90	15
162	A63	2.40fr brn org	3.00	2.50
163	A63	2.50fr lt bl	2.65	1.00
164	A63	4fr brt vio	3.00	1.50
165	A63	5fr blk brn	3.00	1.75
		Nos. 159-165 (7)	14.35	7.77

Issued to commemorate the 50th anniversary of the founding of Congo Free State.

Molindi River
A64

Bamboos
A65

Suza River
A66

Rutshuru River
A67

Karisimbi
A68

Mitumba Forest
A69

1937-38 Photo. *Perf. 11½*

No.	Type	Description	Unused	Used
166	A64	5c pur & blk	8	8
167	A65	90c car & brn	70	55
168	A66	1.50fr dp red brn & blk	18	12
169	A67	2.40fr ol blk & brn	30	20
170	A68	2.50fr dp ultra & blk	45	22
171	A69	4.50fr dk grn & brn	45	20
172	A69	4.50fr car & sep	35	35
		Nos. 166-172 (7)	2.51	1.72

National Parks.

No. 172 was issued in sheets of four measuring 140x111mm. It was sold by subscription, the subscription closing Oct. 20, 1937. Price, $1.60.

Nos. 166-171 were issued Mar. 1, 1938.

King Albert Memorial, Leopoldville
A70

1941, Feb. 7 Litho. *Perf. 11*

No.	Type	Description	Unused	Used
173	A70	10c lt gray	30	28
174	A70	15c brn vio	30	28
175	A70	25c lt bl	30	28
176	A70	50c lt vio	30	28
177	A70	75c rose pink	1.10	42
178	A70	1.25fr gray	30	28
179	A70	1.75fr orange	90	90
180	A70	2.50fr carmine	70	15
181	A70	2.75fr vio bl	1.00	1.00
182	A70	5fr lt ol grn	1.50	1.50
183	A70	10fr rose red	3.25	3.25
		Nos.173-183 (11)	9.95	8.62

Exist imperforate.

Stamps of 1938-41 Surcharged in Blue or Black

5 c.

75 c.

a b

1941-42 *Perf. 11½, 11.*

No.	Type	Description	Unused	Used
184	A66 (a)	5c on 1.50fr dp red brn & blk (Bl)	12	12
a.		Inverted surcharge	15.00	15.00
185	A70 (b)	75c on 1.75fr org (Bk) ('42)	50	50
a.		Inverted surcharge	15.00	15.00
186	A67 (a)	2.50(fr) on 2.40fr ol blk & brn (Bk) ('42)	1.25	1.00
a.		Double surcharge	30.00	30.00
b.		Inverted surcharge	15.00	15.00

Oil Palms
A71 A72

Congo Woman
A73

Askari
A75

Leopard
A74

Okapi
A76

1942, May 23 Engr. *Perf. 12½*

Inscribed "Congo Belge Belgisch Congo".

No.	Type	Description	Unused	Used
187	A71	5c red	6	6
188	A72	10c ol grn	8	6
189	A72	15c brn car	8	6
190	A72	20c dp ultra	8	6
191	A72	25c brn vio	8	6
192	A72	30c blue	8	8
193	A72	50c dp grn	8	8
194	A72	60c chestnut	10	10
195	A73	75c dl lil & blk	15	10
196	A73	1fr dk brn & blk	20	10
197	A73	1.25fr rose red & blk	20	15
198	A74	1.75fr dk gray brn	75	55
199	A74	2fr ocher	75	18
200	A74	2.50fr carmine	75	8
201	A75	3.50fr dk ol grn	30	12
202	A75	5fr orange	55	20
203	A75	6fr brt ultra	50	12
204	A75	7fr black	50	12
205	A75	10fr dp brn	65	12
206	A76	20fr plum & blk	3.50	95
		Nos. 187-206 (20)	9.44	3.35

Same

Inscribed "Belgisch Congo Congo Belge".

No.	Type	Description	Unused	Used
207	A72	10c ol grn	8	6
208	A72	15c brn car	8	6
209	A72	20c dp ultra	8	6
210	A72	25c brn vio	8	6
211	A72	30c blue	8	8
212	A72	50c dp grn	8	8
213	A72	60c chestnut	10	10
214	A73	75c dl lil & blk	15	10
215	A73	1fr dk brn & blk	20	10
216	A73	1.25fr rose red & blk	20	15
217	A74	1.75fr dk gray brn	75	55
218	A74	2fr ocher	75	18
219	A74	2.50fr carmine	75	8
220	A75	3.50fr dk ol grn	30	12
221	A75	5fr orange	55	20
222	A75	6fr brt ultra	50	12
223	A75	7fr black	50	12
224	A75	10fr dp brn	65	12
225	A76	20fr plum & blk	3.50	95
		Nos. 207-225 (19)	9.38	3.29

Miniature sheets of Nos. 193, 194, 197, 200, 211, 214, 217 and 219 were printed in 1944 by the Belgian Government in London and given to the Belgian political review, Message, which distributed them to its subscribers, one a month. Price per sheet, about $12.50.

Remainders of these eight miniature sheets received marginal overprints in various colors in 1950, specifying a surtax of 100fr per sheet and paying tribute to the Universal Postal Union. These sheets, together with four of Ruanda-Urundi, were sold by the Committee of Cultural Works (and not at post offices) in sets of 12 for 1,217.15 francs. Set price, about $150.

Nos. 187 to 227 exist imperforate but had no franking value.

Congo Woman
A77

Askari
A78

1943, Jan. 1

No.	Type	Description	Unused	Used
226	A77	50fr ultra & blk	3.25	65
227	A78	100fr car & blk	5.75	1.00

Slaves and Arab Guards
A79

Auguste Lambermont
A80

Design: 10fr, Leopold II.

Perf. 13x11½, 12½x12.

1947 Engraved. Unwmkd.

228	A79	1.25fr blk brn	25	10
229	A80	3.50fr dk bl	38	12
230	A80	10fr red org	75	12

Issued to commemorate the 50th anniversary of the abolition of slavery in Belgian Congo. See also Nos. 261–262.

Baluba Carving of Former King

A82

Carved Figures and Masks of Baluba Tribe: 10c, 50c, 2fr, "Ndoha," figure of tribal king. 15c, 70c, 1.20fr, 2.50fr, "Tshimanyi," an idol. 20c, 75c, 1.60fr, 3.50fr, "Buangakokoma," statue of kneeling beggar. 25c, 1fr, 2.40fr, 5fr, "Mbuta," sacred double cup, carved with two faces, Man and Woman. 40c, 1.25fr, 6fr, 8fr, "Ngadimuashi," female mask. 1.50fr, 3fr, 10fr, 50fr, "Buadi-Muadi," mask with squared features. 6.50fr, 20fr, 100fr, "Mbowa," executioner's mask with buffalo horns.

1947-50 ***Perf. 12½.***

231	A82	10c dp org ('48)	8	8
232	A82	15c ultra ('48)	8	8
233	A82	20c brt bl ('48)	12	12
234	A82	25c rose car ('48)	25	15
235	A82	40c vio ('48)	15	8
236	A82	50c ol brn	15	8
237	A82	70c yel grn ('48)	10	10
238	A82	75c mag ('48)	15	12
239	A82	1fr yel org & dk vio	1.10	8
240	A82	1.20fr gray & brn ('50)	15	15
241	A82	1.25fr lt bl grn & mag ('48)	25	22
242	A82	1.50fr ol & mag ('50)	6.00	1.50
243	A82	1.60fr bl gray & brt bl ('50)	20	20
244	A82	2fr org & mag ('48)	18	8
245	A82	2.40fr bl grn & dk grn ('50)	25	22
246	A82	2.50fr brn red & bl grn	15	8
247	A82	3fr lt ultra & ind ('49)	3.00	8
248	A82	3.50fr lt bl & blk ('48)	2.50	30
249	A82	5fr bis & mag ('48)	40	12
250	A82	6fr brn org & ind ('48)	55	10
251	A82	6.50fr red org & red brn ('49)	1.10	10
252	A82	8fr gray bl & dk grn ('50)	42	30
253	A82	10fr pale vio & red brn ('48)	1.75	15
254	A82	20fr red org & vio brn ('48)	90	12
255	A82	50fr dp org & blk ('48)	2.50	38
256	A82	100fr crim & blk brn ('48)	3.50	70
		Nos. 231-256 (26)	25.98	5.69

Railroad Train and Map

A83

1948, July 1 ***Perf. 13½*** **Unwmkd.**

257	A83	2.50fr dp bl & grn	65	18

50th anniversary of railway service in the Congo.

Globe and Ship—A84

1949, Nov. 21 ***Perf. 11½***

Granite Paper

258	A84	4fr vio bl	65	22

Issued to commemorate the 75th anniversary of the formation of the Universal Postal Union.

Allegorical Figure and Map

A85

1950, Aug. 12 ***Perf. 12x12½***

259	A85	3fr bl & ind	1.25	15
260	A85	6.50fr car rose & blk brn	1.50	22

Issued to commemorate the 50th anniversary of the establishment of Katanga Province.

Portrait Type of 1947.

Designs: 1.50fr, Cardinal Lavigerie. 3fr, Baron Dhanis.

Perf. 12½x12

1951, June 25 Unwmkd.

261	A80	1.50fr purple	2.00	28
262	A80	3fr blk brn	2.00	10

Littonia

A86

Flowers: 10c, Dissotis. 15c, Protea. 20c, Vellozia. 40c, Ipomoea. 50c, Angraecum. 60c, Euphorbia. 75c, Ochna. 1fr, Hibiscus. 1.25fr, Protea. 1.50fr, Schizoglossum. 2fr, Ansellia. 3fr, Costus. 4fr, Nymphaea. 5fr, Thunbergia. 6.50fr, Thonningia. 7fr, Gerbera. 8fr, Gloriosa. 10fr, Silene. 20fr, Aristolochia. 50fr, Eulophia. 100fr, Cryptosepalum.

Granite Paper.

1952-53 Photogravure. ***Perf. 11½.***

Flowers in Natural Colors.

Size: 21x25½mm.

263	A86	10c dp plum & ocher	5	5
264	A86	15c red & yel grn	5	5
265	A86	20c grn & gray	5	5
266	A86	25c dk grn & dl org	5	5
267	A86	40c grn & sal	8	5
268	A86	50c dk car & aqua	8	5
269	A86	60c bl grn & pink	8	5
270	A86	75c dp plum & gray	8	5
271	A86	1fr car & yel	12	5
272	A86	1.25fr dk grn & bl ('53)	65	50
273	A86	1.50fr vio & ap grn	15	5
274	A86	2fr ol grn & buff	25	5
275	A86	3fr ol grn & pink	25	5
276	A86	4fr choc & lil	30	5
277	A86	5fr dp plum & lt bl grn	45	8
278	A86	6.50fr dk car & lil	55	5
279	A86	7fr dk grn & fawn	55	10
280	A86	8fr grn & lt yel ('53)	90	18
281	A86	10fr dp plum & pale ol ('53)	1.75	5
282	A86	20fr vio bl & dl sal	1.40	8

Size: 22x32mm.

283	A86	50fr dp plum & gray bl ('53)	7.00	50
284	A86	100fr grn & buff ('53)	11.00	1.10
		Nos. 263-284 (22)	25.84	3.29

No. 264 surcharged "10c" is Congo Democratic Republic No. 324a.

St. Francis Xavier

A86a

1953, Jan. 5 Engr. ***Perf. 12½x13***

285	A86a	1.50fr ultra & gray blk	70	55

Issued to commemorate the 400th anniversary of the death of St. Francis Xavier.

Canoe on Lake Kivu

A87

1953, Jan. 5 ***Perf. 14***

286	A87	3fr car & blk	1.25	30
287	A87	7fr dp bl & brn org	1.50	45

Issued to publicize the Kivu Festival, 1953.

Royal Colonial Institute Jubilee Medal

A88

Design: 6.50fr, Same with altered background and transposed inscriptions.

1954, Dec. 27 Photo. ***Perf. 13½***

288	A88	4.50fr ind & gray	1.40	45
289	A88	6.50fr dk grn & brn	1.10	18

Issued to commemorate the 25th anniversary of the founding of the Belgian Royal Colonial Institute.

King Baudouin and Tropical Scene

A89

Designs: King and various views.

Engraved; Portrait Photogravure.

1955, Feb. 15 ***Perf. 11½*** **Unwmkd.**

Portrait in Black.

Inscribed "Congo Belge - Belgisch Congo."

290	A89	1.50fr rose car	90	38
291	A89	3fr green	32	8
292	A89	4.50fr ultra	42	15
293	A89	6.50fr dp cl	65	12

Inscribed "Belgisch Congo - Congo Belge."

294	A89	1.50fr rose car	42	28
295	A89	3fr green	32	8
296	A89	4.50fr ultra	42	15
297	A89	6.50fr dp cl	65	12
		Nos. 290-297 (8)	4.10	1.36

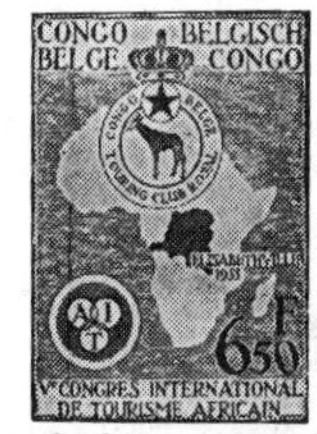

Map of Africa and Emblem of Royal Touring Club

A90

1955, July 26 Engr. ***Perf. 11½***

Inscription in French.

298	A90	6.50fr vio bl	3.25	38

Inscription in Flemish.

299	A90	6.50fr vio bl	3.25	38

5th International Congress of African Tourism, Elisabethville, July 26-Aug. 4. Nos. 298-299 printed in alternate rows.

Kings of Belgium—A91

1958, July 1 ***Perf. 12½*** **Unwmkd.**

300	A91	1fr rose vio	25	8
301	A91	1.50fr ultra	25	8
302	A91	3fr rose car	25	8
303	A91	5fr green	80	55
304	A91	6.50fr brn red	50	10
305	A91	10fr dl vio	70	15
		Nos. 300-305 (6)	2.75	1.04

Issued to commemorate the 50th anniversary of Belgium's annexation of Congo.

Roan Antelope

A92

Black Buffaloes

A93

Animals: 20c, White rhinoceros. 40c, Giraffe. 50c, Thick-tailed bushbaby. 1fr, Gorilla. 2fr, Black-and-white colobus (monkey). 3fr, Elephants. 5fr, Okapis. 6.50fr, Impala. 8fr, Giant pangolin. 10fr, Eland and zebras.

1959 Photogravure. ***Perf. 11½***

Granite Paper.

306	A92	10c bl & brn	4	3
307	A93	20c red org & sl	6	4
308	A92	40c brn & bl	8	8
309	A93	50c brt ultra, red & sep	8	8

310	A92	1fr brn, grn & blk	10	8
311	A93	1.50fr blk & org yel	12	8
312	A92	2fr crim, blk & brn	15	9
313	A93	3fr blk, gray & lil rose	25	10
314	A92	5fr brn, dk brn & brt grn	40	18
315	A93	6.50fr bl, brn & org yel	45	10
316	A92	8fr org brn, ol bis & lil	50	30
317	A93	10fr multi	60	15
		Nos. 306-317 (12)	2.83	1.31

Madonna and Child
A94

1959, Dec. 1 ***Perf. 11½*** **Unwmkd.**

318	A94	50c gldn brn, ocher & red brn	10	6
319	A94	1fr dk bl, pur & red brn	10	8
320	A94	2fr gray, brt bl & red brn	18	12

Map of Africa and Symbolic Honeycomb
A95

1960, Feb. 19 ***Perf. 11½*** **Unwmkd.**

Inscription in French.

321	A95	3fr gray & red	25	15

Inscription in Flemish.

322	A95	3fr gray & red	25	15

Issued to commemorate the 10th anniversary of the Commission for Technical Co-operation in Africa South of the Sahara. (C. C. T. A.)

Succeeding issues are listed under Congo Democratic Republic.

SEMI-POSTAL STAMPS.

Types of 1910-15 Issues

Surcharged in Red **+ 10c**

Perf. 14, 15

1918, May 15 **Unwmkd.**

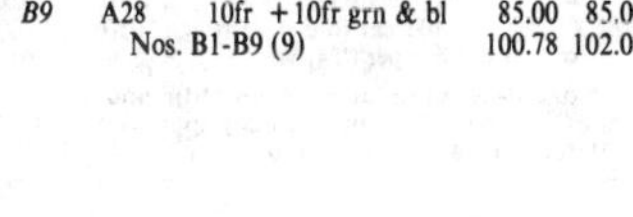

B1	A29	5c +10c grn & bl	30	38
B2	A30	10c +15c car & bl (I)	30	38
B3	A21	15c +20c bl grn & bl	30	38
B4	A31	25c +25c dp bl & pale bl	38	38
B5	A23	40c +40c brn red & bl	50	65
B6	A24	50c +50c brn lake & bl	50	65
B7	A25	1fr +1fr ol bis & bl	2.00	2.25
B8	A27	5fr +5fr ocher & bl	11.50	12.00
B9	A28	10fr +10fr grn & bl	85.00	85.00
		Nos. B1-B9 (9)	100.78	102.07

The position of the cross and the added value varies on the different stamps.

Nos. B1 to B9 exist imperforate.

SP1

Design: No. B11 inscribed "Belgisch Congo."

1925 ***Perf. 12½.***

B10	SP1	25c +25c car & blk	25	25
B11	SP1	25c +25c car & blk	25	25

Colonial campaigns in 1914–1918.

The stamps with French and Flemish inscriptions alternate in the sheet.

The surtax helped erect at Kinshasa a monument to those who died in World War I.

Nurse Weighing Child
SP3

First Aid Station
SP5

Designs: 20c+10c, Missionary and Child. 60c+30c, Congo hospital. 1fr+50c, Dispensary service. 1.75fr+75c, Convalescent area. 3.50fr+1.50fr, Instruction on bathing infant. 5fr+2.50fr, Operating room. 10fr+5fr, Students.

1930, Jan. 16 **Engr.** ***Perf. 11½***

B12	SP3	10c +5c ver	55	55
B13	SP3	20c +10c dp brn	70	70
B14	SP5	35c +15c dp grn	1.25	1.25
B15	SP5	60c +30c dl vio	1.50	1.50
B16	SP3	1fr +50c dk car	2.50	2.50
B17	SP5	1.75fr +75c dp bl	3.25	3.25
B18	SP5	3.50fr +1.50fr rose lake	6.25	6.25
B19	SP5	5fr +2.50fr red brn	6.00	6.00
B20	SP5	10fr +5fr gray blk	6.25	6.25
		Nos. B12-B20 (9)	28.25	28.25

The surtax on these stamps was intended to aid welfare work among the natives, especially the children.

Nos. 161, 163
Surcharged "+50c" in Blue or Red.

1936, May 15 ***Perf. 12½x12***

B21	A63	1.50fr +50c brn vio (Bl)	2.25	2.25
B22	A63	2.50fr +50c lt bl (R)	2.25	2.25

The surtax was for the benefit of the King Albert Memorial Fund.

Queen Astrid with Congolese Children
SP12

1936, Aug. 29 **Photo.** ***Perf. 12½***

B23	SP12	1.25fr +5c dk brn	75	65
B24	SP12	1.50fr +10c dl rose	75	65
B25	SP12	2.50fr +25c dk bl	90	90

Issued in memory of Queen Astrid. The surtax was for the aid of the National League for Protection of Native Children.

Souvenir Sheet.

SP13

1938, Oct. 3 ***Perf. 11½***

B26	SP13	Sheet of six	9.00	10.00
a.		5c ultra & lt brn (A64)	1.50	1.50
b.		90c ultra & lt brn (A65)	1.50	1.50
c.		1.50fr ultra & lt brn (A66)	1.50	1.50
d.		2.40fr ultra & lt brn (A67)	1.50	1.50
e.		2.50fr ultra & lt brn (A68)	1.50	1.50
f.		4.50fr ultra & lt brn (A69)	1.50	1.50

Issued in sheets measuring 139x122mm. The star is printed in yellow. Issued in commemoration of the International Tourist Congress. A surtax of 3.15fr was for the benefit of the Congo Tourist Service.

Marabou Storks and Vultures
SP14

Buffon's Kob
SP15

Designs: 1.50fr+1.50fr, Pygmy chimpanzees. 4.50fr+4.50fr, Dwarf crocodiles. 5fr+5fr, Lioness.

1939 **Photogravure** ***Perf. 14***

B27	SP14	1fr +1fr dp cl	4.75	4.75
B28	SP15	1.25fr +1.25fr car	4.75	4.75
B29	SP15	1.50fr +1.50fr brt pur	7.25	7.25
B30	SP14	4.50fr +4.50fr sl grn	4.75	4.75
B31	SP15	5fr +5fr brn	5.00	5.00
		Nos. B27-B31 (5)	26.50	26.50

The surtax was for the Leopoldville Zoological Gardens.

Nos. B27–B31 were sold in full sets by subscription.

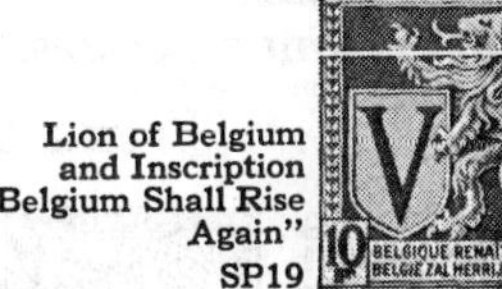

Lion of Belgium and Inscription "Belgium Shall Rise Again"
SP19

1942, Feb. 17 **Engr.** ***Perf. 12½***

B32	SP19	10fr +40fr brt grn	1.40	1.40
B33	SP19	10fr +40fr vio bl	1.40	1.40

Nos. 193, 216, 198 and 220
Surcharged in Red

Au profit de la Croix Rouge + 50 Fr. Ten voordeele van het Roode Kruis
a

Ten voordeele van het Roode Kruis + 100 Fr. Au profit de la Croix Rouge
b

Au profit de la Croix Rouge + 100 Fr. Ten voordeele van het Roode Kruis
c

1945

B34	A72 (a)	50c +50fr dp grn	2.50	2.50
B35	A73 (b)	1.25fr +100fr rose red & blk	2.50	2.50
B36	A74 (c)	1.75fr +100fr dk gray brn	2.50	2.75
B37	A75 (b)	3.50fr +100fr dk ol grn	2.50	2.75

The surtax was for the Red Cross.

Nos. B34–B37 were sold in full sets by subscription.

Mozart at Age 7
SP20

Queen Elisabeth and Sonata by Mozart
SP21

Engraved.

1956, Oct. 10 ***Perf. 11½*** **Unwmkd.**

B38	SP20	4.50fr +1.50fr brt lil	1.50	1.50
B39	SP21	6.50fr +2.50fr ultra	2.00	2.00

Issued to commemorate the 200th anniversary of the birth of Wolfgang Amadeus Mozart.

The surtax was for the Pro-Mozart Committee.

Nurse and Children
SP22

Designs: 4.50fr+50c, Patient receiving injection. 6.50fr+40c, Patient being bandaged.

1957, Dec. 10 Photo. *Perf. 13x10½*

Cross in Carmine.

No.	Design	Description	Unused	Used
B40	SP22	3fr +50c dk bl	1.10	1.10
B41	SP22	4.50fr +50c dk grn	1.00	1.00
B42	SP22	6.50fr +50c red brn	1.25	1.25

The surtax was for the Red Cross.

High Jumper
SP23

Sports: 1.50fr+50c, Hurdlers. 2fr+1fr, Soccer. 3fr+1.25fr, Javelin thrower. 6.50fr+3.50fr, Discus thrower.

1960, May 2 *Perf. 13½* Unwmkd.

No.	Design	Description	Unused	Used
B43	SP23	50c +25c ultra & red	12	12
B44	SP23	1.50fr +50c car & grn	22	22
B45	SP23	2fr +1fr grn & ver	22	22
B46	SP23	3fr +1.25fr rose cl & bl	95	95
B47	SP23	6.50fr +3.50fr red brn & car	1.25	1.25
		Nos. B43-B47 (5)	2.76	2.76

Issued to commemorate the 17th Olympic Games, Rome, Aug. 25–Sept. 11. The surtax was for the youth of Congo.

AIR POST STAMPS.

Wharf on Congo River
AP1

Congo "Country Store"
AP2

View of Congo River
AP3

Stronghold in the Interior
AP4

Engraved.

1920, July 1 *Perf. 12* Unwmkd.

No.	Design	Description	Unused	Used
C1	AP1	50c org & blk	25	15
a.		Booklet pane of 10		
C2	AP2	1fr dl vio & blk	25	12
a.		Booklet pane of 10		
C3	AP3	2fr bl & blk	80	30
C4	AP4	5fr grn & blk	1.50	70

Kraal
AP5

Porters on Safari
AP6

1930, Apr. 2

No.	Design	Description	Unused	Used
C5	AP5	15fr dk brn & blk	3.50	1.25
C6	AP6	30fr brn vio & blk	4.00	1.25

Fokker F VII over Congo
AP7

1934, Jan. 22 *Perf. 13½x14*

No.	Design	Description	Unused	Used
C7	AP7	50c gray blk	20	20
C8	AP7	1fr dk car	30	20
a.		Bklt pane of 8	8.50	8.50
C9	AP7	1.50fr green	20	15
C10	AP7	3fr brown	30	15
C11	AP7	4.50fr brt ultra	35	15
a.		Bklt pane of 8	16.50	16.50
C12	AP7	5fr red brn	35	15
C13	AP7	15fr brn vio	70	45
C14	AP7	30fr red org	1.25	1.10
C15	AP7	50fr violet	3.75	1.25
		Nos. C7-C15 (9)	7.40	3.80

The 1fr, 3fr, 4.50fr, 5fr and 15fr exist imperf.

No. C10 Surcharged in Blue with New Value and Bars.

1936, Mar. 25

No.	Design	Description	Unused	Used
C16	AP7	3.50fr on 3fr brn	25	15

No. C9 Surcharged in Black

50 c.

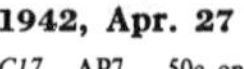

1942, Apr. 27

No.	Design	Description	Unused	Used
C17	AP7	50c on 1.50fr grn	30	30
a.		Inverted surcharge	6.25	6.25

POSTAGE DUE STAMPS.

In 1908–23 regular postage stamps handstamped "TAXES" or "TAXE," usually boxed, were used in lieu of postage due stamps.

D1

D2

Perf. 14, 14½.

1923-29 Typographed. Unwmkd.

No.	Design	Description	Unused	Used
J1	D1	5c blk brn	18	18
J2	D1	10c rose red	20	18
J3	D1	15c violet	25	20
J4	D1	30c green	40	38
J5	D1	50c ultra	55	50
J6	D1	50c bl ('29)	55	50
J7	D1	1fr gray	65	45
		Nos. J1-J7 (7)	2.78	2.39

1943 *Perf. 14x14½*

No.	Design	Description	Unused	Used
J8	D2	10c ol grn	6	6
J9	D2	20c dk ultra	6	6
J10	D2	50c green	15	15
J11	D2	1fr dk brn	18	18
J12	D2	2fr yel org	22	22
		Nos. J8-J12 (5)	67	67

1943 *Perf. 12½*

No.	Design	Description	Unused	Used
J8a	D2	10c ol grn	25	25
J9a	D2	20c dk ultra	25	25
J10a	D2	50c green	25	25
J11a	D2	1fr dk brn	38	38
J12a	D2	2fr yel org	38	38
		Nos. J8a-J12a (5)	1.51	1.51

D3

1957 Engraved. *Perf. 11½*

No.	Design	Description	Unused	Used
J13	D3	10c ol brn	6	6
J14	D3	20c claret	10	10
J15	D3	50c green	15	15
J16	D3	1fr lt bl	30	30
J17	D3	2fr vermilion	45	40
J18	D3	4fr purple	60	55
J19	D3	6fr vio bl	85	70
		Nos. J13-J19 (7)	2.51	2.26

PARCEL POST STAMPS.

PP1

PP2

PP3

Handstamped Surcharges on Nos. 5, 11–12

1887–1893 *Perf. 15* Unwmkd.

Blue-Black Surcharge

No.	Design	Description	Unused	Used
Q1	PP1	3.50fr on 5fr lil	550.00	450.00

Black Surcharge

No.	Design	Description	Unused	Used
Q3	PP2	3.50fr on 5fr vio	575.00	375.00
Q4	PP3	3.50fr on 5fr vio ('88)	500.00	300.00
a.		bl surcharge	500.00	300.00
Q6	PP3	3.50fr on 5fr gray ('93)	95.00	62.50

Nos. Q1, Q3–Q4, Q4a and Q6 are known with inverted surcharge, No. Q1 with double surcharge and No. Q6 in pair with unsurcharged stamp. Most of these handstamp varieties sell for more than the normal surcharges.

BELGIAN EAST AFRICA

(See Ruanda-Urundi in Vol. IV.)

BELGIUM

(bĕl′jĭ·ŭm)

LOCATION — In western Europe, bordering on the North Sea.

GOVT.—Constitutional Monarchy.

AREA—11,781 sq. mi.

POP.—9,830,000 (est. 1977).

CAPITAL—Brussels.

100 Centimes = 1 Franc

Prices of early Belgian stamps vary according to condition. Quotations for Nos. 1–12 are for fine copies. Very fine to superb specimens sell at much higher prices, and inferior or poor copies sell at reduced prices, depending on the condition of the individual specimen.

Prices for unused stamps of 1849–1863 issues are for copies with original gum. Copies without gum sell for one third of the figures quoted, or less.

King Leopold I
A1 A2

Wmk. 96

Wmkd. Two "L"s Framed. (96)

1849 Engraved. *Imperf.*

No.	Design	Description	Unused	Used
1	A1	10c brown	*2,250.*	100.00
a.		10c red brn	*3,500.*	325.00
2	A1	20c blue	*3,500.*	80.00
a.		20c mlky bl	*4,000.*	225.00

The reprints are on thick and thin wove and thick laid paper unwatermarked.

A souvenir sheet containing reproductions of the 10c, 20c and 40c of 1849–51 with black burelage on back was issued Oct. 17, 1949, for the centenary of the first Belgian stamps. It was sold at BEPITEC 1949, an international stamp exhibition at Brussels, and was not valid. Size: 139x90mm.

1849-50

No.	Design	Description	Unused	Used
3	A2	10c brn ('50)	*2,000.*	90.00
4	A2	20c bl ('50)	*2,250.*	72.50
5	A2	40c car rose	*2,500.*	325.00

Nos. 3–5 on thin paper are as priced. Copies on thick paper sell for 5 to 12 percent more.

Wmkd. Two "L"s Without Frame. (96)

1851–54

No.	Design	Description	Unused	Used
6	A2	10c brown	900.00	15.00
a.		Ribbed paper ('54)	1,100.	60.00
7	A2	20c blue	900.00	15.00
a.		Ribbed paper ('54)	1,100.	60.00
8	A2	40c car rose	*2,250.*	100.00
a.		Ribbed paper ('54)	*2,750.*	300.00

Nos. 6–8 were printed on thin and thick paper. Nos. 6–7 on thick paper, unused, sell for 7 to 10 percent more.

1858–61 Unwmkd.

No.	Design	Description	Unused	Used
9	A2	1c grn ('61)	275.00	225.00
a.		Laid paper		
10	A2	10c brown	500.00	15.00
11	A2	20c blue	500.00	15.00

12	A2	40c car rose	*2,500.*	100.00

Nos. 9 and 13 were valid for postage on newspapers and printed matter only.

Reprints of Nos. 9 to 12 are on thin wove paper. The colors are brighter than those of the originals. They were made from the dies and show lines outside the stamps.

1863

Perf. 12½, 12½x13, 12½x13½, 14½

13	A2	1c green	50.00	37.50
14	A2	10c brown	70.00	2.50
15	A2	20c blue	72.50	2.50
16	A2	40c car rose	450.00	22.50

King Leopold I

A3 A3a

A4 A4a

A5

London Print.

1865 Typographed ***Perf. 14***

17	A5	1fr pale vio	1,000.	120.00

Brussels Print.

Thick or Thin Paper.

1865–66 ***Perf. 15, 14½x14***

18	A3	10c sl ('66)	100.00	1.00
a.		Pair, imperf. between		175.00
19	A3a	20c bl ('66)	135.00	1.00
a.		20c lil bl	140.00	1.10
20	A4	30c brown	265.00	8.00
a.		Pair, imperf. between	900.00	
21	A4a	40c rose ('66)	375.00	17.50
22	A5	1fr violet	1,000.	135.00

Nos. 18 to 22 on thin paper are perf. 14½x14; on thick paper, perf. 15.

The reprints are on thin paper, imperforate and ungummed.

Coat of Arms

A6

1866–67 ***Imperf.***

23	A6	1c gray	250.00	200.00

Perf. 15, 14½x14

24	A6	1c gray	40.00	17.50
25	A6	2c bl ('67)	150.00	90.00
a.		2c ultra	165.00	100.00
26	A6	5c brown	150.00	100.00

Nos. 23-26 were valid for postage on newspapers and printed matter only.

Nos. 24 to 26 on thin paper are perf. 14½ x 14; on thick paper, perf. 15.

Reprints of Nos. 24 to 26 are on thin paper, imperforate and ungummed.

King Leopold II

A7 A8

A9 A10

A11 A12

1869–70 ***Perf. 15***

28	A7	1c green	9.50	22
a.		Imperf., pair	200.00	
29	A7	2c ultra ('70)	12.50	42
a.		Imperf., pair	225.00	
30	A7	5c buff ('70)	60.00	70
a.		Imperf., pair	300.00	
31	A7	8c lil ('70)	100.00	67.50
32	A8	10c green	32.50	22
a.		Imperf., pair	225.00	
33	A9	20c lt ultra ('70)	115.00	85
34	A10	30c buff ('70)	90.00	5.00
a.		Imperf., pair	600.00	
35	A11	40c brt rose ('70)	125.00	5.25
a.		Imperf., pair	2,500.	
36	A12	1fr dl lil ('70)	275.00	22.50
a.		1fr rose lil	300.00	25.00
b.		Imperf., pair	2,250.	

The frames and inscriptions of Nos. 30, 31 and 42 differ slightly from the illustration.

Minor "broken letter" varieties exist on several values.

Imperf. varieties of 1869–1912 (between Nos. 28–105) are without gum.

See also Nos. 40–43, 49–51, 55.

A13 A14 A15

1875–78

37	A13	25c ol bis	75.00	1.65
a.		25c ocher	75.00	1.65
b.		Imperf., pair	135.00	
38	A14	50c gray	250.00	8.50
a.		50c gray blk	500.00	57.50
39	A15	5fr pale brn ('78)	4,000.	1,000.
		Roller cancel		375.00
a.		5fr dp red brn	2,000.	1,000.

Printed in Aniline Colors.

1881 ***Perf. 14, 15***

40	A7	1c gray grn	9.50	70
41	A7	2c lt ultra	14.00	85
a.		Imperf., pair	225.00	
42	A7	5c org buff	57.50	1.00
a.		5c red org	57.50	1.00
b.		Imperf., pair	300.00	
43	A8	10c gray grn	35.00	75
a.		Imperf., pair	225.00	
44	A13	25c ol bis	62.50	1.75
a.		Imperf., pair	120.00	
		Nos. 40-44 (5)	178.50	5.05

King Leopold II

A16 A17

A18 A19

1883

45	A16	10c carmine	37.50	1.00
a.		Imperf., pair	100.00	
46	A17	20c gray	150.00	3.75
a.		Imperf., pair	100.00	
47	A18	25c blue	300.00	35.00
		Roller cancel		10.00
a.		Imperf., pair	100.00	
48	A19	50c violet	250.00	32.50
		Roller cancel		11.00
a.		Imperf., pair	100.00	

A20 A21

A22

1884–85 ***Perf. 14***

49	A7	1c ol grn	11.00	60
50	A7	1c gray	5.50	8
a.		Imperf., pair	75.00	
51	A7	5c green	16.50	15
a.		Imperf., pair	125.00	
52	A20	10c rose, *bluish*	8.25	10
a.		grysh paper	10.00	35
b.		Imperf., pair	100.00	
c.		yelsh paper	110.00	21.00
53	A21	25c bl, *pink* ('85)	13.50	50
a.		Imperf., pair	500.00	
54	A22	1fr brn, *grnsh*	800.00	10.00
a.		Imperf., pair	350.00	

The frame and inscription of No. 51 differ slightly from the illustration. See note after No. 36.

A23 A24

A25 A26

1886–91

55	A7	2c pur brn ('88)	12.00	50
56	A23	20c ol, *grnsh*	150.00	70
a.		Imperf., pair	525.00	
57	A24	35c vio brn, *brnsh* ('91)	25.00	2.75
a.		Imperf., pair	200.00	
58	A25	50c bis, *yelsh*	13.00	2.10
59	A26	2fr vio, *pale lil*	150.00	25.00
		Roller cancel		6.00

Coat of Arms King Leopold

A27 A28

1893-1900

60	A27	1c gray	1.40	10
61	A27	2c yellow	1.75	1.50
a.		Wmkd. coat of arms in sheet ('95)		
62	A27	2c vio brn ('94)	3.50	25
63	A27	2c red brn ('98)	3.50	25
64	A27	5c yel grn	5.00	15
65	A28	10c org brn	6.00	10
a.		Imperf., pair	250.00	
66	A28	10c brt rose ('00)	6.00	10
67	A28	20c ol grn	35.00	50
a.		Imperf., pair	250.00	
68	A28	25c ultra	32.50	50
a.		No ball to "5" in upper left corner	50.00	18.50
69	A28	35c vio brn	55.00	1.10
a.		35c brn	67.50	1.40
70	A28	50c bister	95.00	11.00
71	A28	50c gray ('97)	100.00	2.25
72	A28	1fr car, *lt grn*	100.00	16.50
73	A28	1fr org ('00)	175.00	6.00
a.		Imperf., pair	250.00	
74	A28	2fr lil, *rose*	150.00	120.00
75	A28	2fr lil ('00)	265.00	15.00

Prices quoted for Nos. 60–107, B1–B24 are for stamps with label attached. Stamps without label sell for about half.

Antwerp Exhibition Issue.

Arms of Antwerp

A29

1894

76	A29	5c grn, *rose*	11.00	4.00
77	A29	10c car, *bluish*	10.00	1.65
78	A29	25c bl, *rose*	60	50

Brussels Exhibition Issue.

St. Michael and Satan

A30 A31

1896–97 ***Perf. 14x14½.***

79	A30	5c dp vio	1.25	75
80	A31	10c org brn	19.00	4.25
81	A31	10c lil brn	85	60

Coat of Arms King Leopold II

A32 A33

King Leopold II

A34 A35

A36 A37

A38 A39

Two types of 1c:
I. Periods after "Dimanche" and "Zondag" in label.
II. No period after "Dimanche". Period often missing after "Zondag".

1905-07 ***Perf. 14.***

No.	Type	Description	Unused	Used
82	A32	1c gray (I) ('07)	2.50	18
a.		Type II ('08)	2.50	20
83	A32	2c red brn ('07)	11.00	2.25
84	A32	5c grn ('07)	11.00	18
a.		Booklet pane of 5		
b.		Booklet pane of 10		
85	A33	10c dl rose	4.50	15
a.		Imperf., pair	250.00	
b.		Booklet pane of 10		
c.		Booklet pane of 5		
86	A34	20c ol grn	30.00	75
a.		Imperf., pair	250.00	
87	A35	25c ultra	25.00	65
a.		25c dl bl	25.00	65
b.		Imperf., pair	125.00	
88	A36	35c pur brn	45.00	1.65
a.		Imperf., pair	500.00	
89	A37	50c bluish gray	120.00	1.90
90	A38	1fr yellow	150.00	8.50
a.		Imperf., pair	325.00	
91	A39	2fr violet	160.00	18.00
		Bar cancellation		4.00
		Nos. 82-91 (10)	559.00	34.21

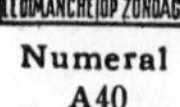

Numeral A40 Coat of Arms A41

Lion of Belgium A42 King Albert I A43

A44

1912

No.	Type	Description	Unused	Used
92	A40	1c orange	20	10
a.		Imperf., pair	4.25	
93	A41	2c org brn	32	32
94	A42	5c green	25	10
a.		Booklet pane of 10		
b.		Booklet pane of 5		
95	A43	10c red	2.50	28
a.		Booklet pane of 5		
b.		Booklet pane of 10		
96	A43	20c ol grn	24.00	1.50
97	A43	35c bis brn	3.00	85
98	A43	40c green	32.50	20.00
99	A43	50c gray	3.00	85
100	A43	1fr orange	15.00	5.00
101	A43	2fr violet	35.00	22.50
102	A44	5fr plum	225.00	27.50
		Nos. 92-102 (11)	340.77	79.00

A45

1912-13 Larger Head

No.	Type	Description	Unused	Used
103	A45	10c red	40	18
a.		Without engraver's name	15	15
b.		Imperf., pair	3.75	
c.		Booklet pane of 5		
d.		Booklet pane of 10		
e.		As "a", booklet pane of 5		
f.		As "a", booklet pane of 10		
104	A45	20c ol grn ('13)	65	35
a.		Without engraver's name	90	85
105	A45	25c ultra	6.00	1.50
a.		Without engraver's name	35	35
107	A45	40c grn ('13)	90	50

King Albert I A46 Cloth Hall of Ypres A47

Bridge of Dinant A48

Library of Louvain A49

Scheldt River at Antwerp A50

Anti-slavery Campaign in the Congo A51

King Albert I at Furnes A52

Kings of Belgium Leopold I, Albert I, Leopold II A53

1915-20 Typographed. ***Perf. 14, 14½***

No.	Type	Description	Unused	Used
108	A46	1c orange	6	5
109	A46	2c chocolate	6	5
110	A46	3c gray blk ('20)	25	6
111	A46	5c green	50	5
112	A46	10c carmine	1.00	5
113	A46	15c purple	1.20	6
114	A46	20c red vio	1.00	5
115	A46	25c blue	1.40	22
		Engraved.		
116	A47	35c brn org & blk	1.15	30
117	A48	40c grn & blk	1.65	30
a.		Vertical pair, imperf. between		
118	A49	50c car rose & blk	8.50	28
119	A50	1fr violet	47.50	50
120	A51	2fr slate	57.50	2.00
121	A52	5fr dp bl	450.00	150.00
		Telegraph or railroad cancel		100.00
122	A53	10fr brown	55.00	35.00
		Nos. 108-122 (15)	626.77	188.97

Two types each of the 1c, 10c and 20c; three of the 2c and 15c; four of the 5c, differing in the top left corner.

Nos. 108 to 120 and 122 exist imperforate. See also No. 138.

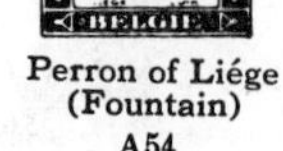

Perron of Liége (Fountain) A54 King Albert in Trench Helmet A55

1919 ***Perf. 11½***

No.	Type	Description	Unused	Used
123	A54	25c dp bl	4.25	18
a.		Sheet of ten	12,500.	12,500.

1919 ***Perf. 11, 11½, 11½x11, 11x11½.***

Size: 18½x22mm.

No.	Type	Description	Unused	Used
124	A55	1c lil brn	12	12
125	A55	2c olive	12	12
		Size: 23x26mm.		
126	A55	5c green	45	30
127	A55	10c carmine	20	25
128	A55	15c gray vio	25	25
129	A55	20c ol blk	1.00	1.65
130	A55	25c dp bl	1.10	1.85
131	A55	35c bis brn	1.75	3.25
132	A55	40c red	2.75	3.75
133	A55	50c red brn	6.25	9.00
134	A55	1fr lt org	45.00	55.00
135	A55	2fr violet	500.00	475.00
		Size: 28x33½mm.		
136	A55	5fr car lake	165.00	190.00
137	A55	10fr claret	225.00	225.00
		Nos. 124-137 (14)	948.99	965.54

Type of 1915 Inscribed: "FRANK" instead of "FRANKEN"

1919, Dec. ***Perf. 14, 15***

No.	Type	Description	Unused	Used
138	A52	5fr dp bl	5.00	2.00
a.		Vert. pair, imperf. between		

Town Hall at Termonde

A56 A57

1920 ***Perf. 11½***

No.	Type	Description	Unused	Used
139	A56	65c cl & blk	2.50	28
a.		Center inverted	5,000.	5,000.

Semi-Postal Stamps of 1920 Surcharged in Red or Black

20c X 20c X

1921 ***Perf. 12***

No.	Type	Description	Unused	Used
140	SP6	20c on 5c dp grn (R)	2.25	45
a.		Invtd. surcharge	250.00	250.00
141	SP7	20c on 10c car	1.40	45
a.		Surcharged on back instead of face		
b.		Invtd. surcharge	250.00	250.00
142	SP8	20c on 15c dk brn (R)	1.75	45
a.		Invtd. surcharge	250.00	250.00

Red Surcharge.

No.	Type	Description	Unused	Used
143	A57	55c on 65c cl & blk	1.50	55
a.		Pair, one without surcharge	2.50	1.50

A58 A59

1922-27 Typographed ***Perf. 14***

No.	Type	Description	Unused	Used
144	A58	1c orange	8	5
145	A58	2c ol ('26)	25	10
146	A58	3c fawn	12	3
147	A58	5c gray	20	3
a.		Booklet pane of 6	9.00	
148	A58	10c bl grn	25	3
149	A58	15c plum ('23)	30	7
a.		Booklet pane of 6	10.00	
150	A58	20c blk brn	45	7
151	A58	25c dl vio	55	8
152	A58	30c vermilion	1.00	10
153	A58	30c rose ('25)	90	7
154	A58	35c red brn	65	18
a.		Booklet pane of 6	7.50	
155	A58	35c bl grn ('27)	2.25	35

156	A58	40c rose	1.20	15
157	A58	50c bis ('25)	1.10	8
158	A58	60c ol brn ('27)	3.75	3
a.		Booklet pane of 6	40.00	
159	A58	1.25fr dp bl ('26)	1.25	85
160	A58	1.50fr brt bl ('26)	3.75	25
161	A58	1.75fr ultra ('27)	2.00	15
a.		Tête bêche pair	18.00	9.00
b.		Bklt pane of 6	47.50	
c.		Bklt. pane of 4 + 2 labels	57.50	
		Nos. 144-161 (18)	20.05	2.67

See also Nos. 185–190.

Perf. 11½, 11½x11, 11½x12, 11½x12½.

1921–25 Engraved

162	A59	50c dl bl	85	5
163	A59	75c scar ('22)	50	15
164	A59	75c ultra ('24)	85	15
165	A59	1fr blk brn ('22)	1.35	12
166	A59	1fr dk bl ('25)	85	12
167	A59	2fr dk grn ('22)	1.25	35
168	A59	5fr brn vio ('23)	20.00	27.50
169	A59	10fr mag ('22)	17.50	3.50
		Nos. 162-169 (8)	43.15	31.94

No. 162 measures 18x20¾mm. and was printed in sheets of 100.

Philatelic Exhibition Issue.

1921, May 26 ***Perf. 11½***

170	A59	50c dk bl	9.00	8.50
a.		Sheet of 25	425.00	350.00

No. 170 measures 17½x21¼mm., was printed in sheets of 25 and sold at the Philatelic Exhibition at Brussels.

Philatelic Exhibition Issue.
Souvenir Sheet.

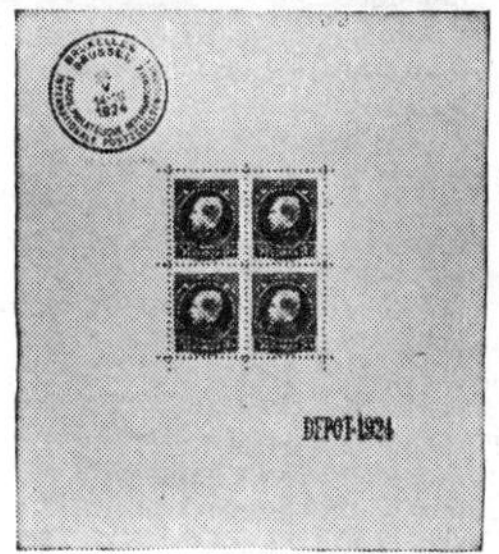

A59a

1924, May 24 ***Perf. 11½***

171	A59a	5fr red brn, sheet of 4	150.00	160.00
a.		Single stamp (A59)	27.50	30.00

Sold only at the International Philatelic Exhibition, Brussels. Sheet size: 130x145 mm.

Kings Leopold I and Albert I
A60

1925 ***Perf. 14***

172	A60	10c dp grn	11.00	13.00
173	A60	15c dl vio	7.50	9.50
174	A60	20c red brn	7.50	9.50
175	A60	25c grnsh blk	7.50	9.50
176	A60	30c vermilion	7.50	9.50
177	A60	35c lt bl	7.50	9.50
178	A60	40c brnsh blk	7.50	9.50
179	A60	50c yel brn	7.50	9.50
180	A60	75c dk bl	7.50	9.50
181	A60	1fr dk vio	11.00	14.00
182	A60	2fr ultra	8.00	9.50
183	A60	5fr bl blk	9.50	11.00
184	A60	10fr dp rose	17.50	20.00
		Nos. 172-184 (13)	117.00	143.50

75th anniversary of Belgian postage stamps.

Nos. 172–184 were sold only in sets and only by The Administration of Posts, not at post offices.

A61

1926-27 Typographed.

185	A61	75c dk vio	1.15	80
186	A61	1fr pale yel	1.00	25
187	A61	1fr rose red ('27)	1.75	15
a.		Tête bêche pair	10.00	6.00
b.		Bklt pane of 6	27.50	
c.		Bklt pane 4 + 2 labels	30.00	
188	A61	2fr Prus bl	4.50	12
189	A61	5fr emer ('27)	30.00	1.00
190	A61	10fr dk brn ('27)	60.00	2.50
		Nos. 185-190 (6)	98.40	4.82

Stamps of 1921-27 Surcharged in Carmine, Red or Blue

≡ 1F75 ≡

1927

191	A58	3c on 2c ol (C)	15	12
192	A58	10c on 15c plum (R)	25	10
193	A58	35c on 40c rose (Bl)	65	12
194	A58	1.75fr on 1.50fr brt bl (C)	2.50	1.00

Nos. 153, 185 and 159 Surcharged in Black

BRUXELLES
1929
BRUSSEL
=5c=

1929, Jan. 1

195	A58	5c on 30c rose	25	10
196	A61	5c on 75c dk vio	45	35
197	A58	5c on 1.25fr dp bl	20	15

The surcharge on Nos. 195 to 197 is a precancelation which alters the value of the stamp to which it is applied.

Prices for precanceled stamps in first column are for those which have not been through the post and have original gum. Prices in second column are for postally used, gumless stamps.

A63

A64

1929–32 Typographed ***Perf. 14***

198	A63	1c orange	20	12
199	A63	2c emer ('31)	45	45
200	A63	3c red brn	20	5
201	A63	5c slate	25	3
a.		Tête bêche pair	1.65	1.35
b.		Bklt pane of 6	11.50	
c.		Bklt pane of 4 + 2 labels	11.00	
202	A63	10c ol grn	25	3
a.		Tête bêche pair	75	60
b.		Bklt pane of 6	6.00	
c.		Bklt pane of 4 + 2 labels	6.00	
203	A63	20c brt vio	1.75	15
204	A63	25c rose red	1.00	5
a.		Tête bêche pair	4.25	3.25
b.		Bklt pane of 6	12.00	
c.		Bklt pane of 4 + 2 labels	11.00	
205	A63	35c green	1.50	15
a.		Tête bêche pair	6.25	5.00
b.		Bklt pane of 6	14.00	
c.		Bklt pane of 4 + 2 labels	13.00	
206	A63	40c red vio ('30)	1.40	5
a.		Tête bêche pair	6.00	4.25
b.		Bklt pane of 6	14.00	
c.		Bklt pane of 4 + 2 labels	13.00	
207	A63	50c dp bl	1.25	5
a.		Tête bêche pair	4.75	2.50
b.		Bklt. pane of 6	11.00	
c.		Bklt pane of 4 + 2 labels	11.00	
208	A63	60c rose ('30)	3.25	20
a.		Tête bêche pair	16.00	13.00
b.		Bklt pane of 6	40.00	
c.		Bklt pane of 4 + 2 labels	40.00	
209	A63	70c org brn ('30)	2.25	5
a.		Tête bêche pair	11.00	9.50
b.		Bklt pane of 6	30.00	
c.		Bklt pane of 4 + 2 labels	30.00	
210	A63	75c dk bl ('30)	4.00	10
a.		Tête bêche pair	16.50	15.00
211	A63	75c dp brn ('32)	18.50	5
a.		Tête bêche pair	60.00	40.00
b.		Bklt pane of 4 + 2 labels	135.00	
c.		Bklt pane of 6	185.00	
		Nos. 198-211 (14)	36.25	1.53

Nos. 198 and 199 exist se-tenant in booklets.

1929, Jan. 25 Engr. ***Perf. 14½, 14***

212	A64	10fr dk brn	27.50	9.00
213	A64	20fr dk grn	150.00	11.00
214	A64	50fr red vio	10.00	7.50
a.		Perf. 14½	35.00	32.50
215	A64	100fr rose lake	25.00	19.00
a.		Perf. 14½	37.50	32.50

Nos. 212 to 215 exist imperforate.

Peter Paul Rubens
A65

Zenobe Gramme
A66

1930, Apr. 26 Photo. ***Perf. 12½x12***

216	A65	35c bl grn	1.35	35
217	A66	35c bl grn	1.35	35

No. 216 issued for the Antwerp Exhibition, No. 217 the Liege Exhibition.

King Leopold I, by Jacques de Winne
A67

King Leopold II, by Joseph Lempoels
A68

Design: 1.75fr, King Albert I.

1930, July 1 Engraved ***Perf. 11½***

218	A67	60c brn vio	65	15
219	A68	1fr carmine	3.50	3.00
220	A68	1.75fr dk bl	7.25	2.25

Centenary of Belgian independence.

Antwerp Exhibition Issue.
Souvenir Sheet.

Arms of Antwerp
A70

1930, Aug. 9 ***Perf. 11½***

221	A70	Sheet of one	160.00	225.00
a.		4fr dk grn & gray grn	90.00	110.00

Issued in sheets of one stamp measuring 142x141 mm. Inscription in lower margin "ATELIER DU TIMBRE—1930—ZEGELFABRIEK." Each purchaser of a ticket to the Antwerp Philatelic Exhibition, August 9th to 15th, 1930, was allowed to purchase one of the exhibition stamps. The ticket cost 6 francs.

Nos. 218–220 Overprinted in Blue or Red

B.I.T.
OCT. 1930

1930, Oct.

222	A67	60c brn vio (Bl)	5.50	3.50
223	A68	1fr car (Bl)	12.00	14.00
224	A68	1.75fr dk bl (R)	25.00	25.00

Issued to commemorate the 50th meeting of the administrative council of the International Labor Bureau at Brussels.

The names of the painters and the initials of the engraver have been added at the foot of these stamps.

Stamps of 1929-30 Surcharged in Blue or Black:

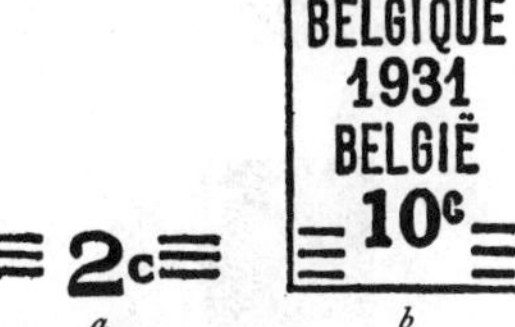

a *b*

1931, Feb. 20 ***Perf. 14***

225	A63 (a)	2c on 3c red brn (Bl)	22	10
226	A63 (b)	10c on 60c rose (Bk)	1.25	25

The surcharge on No. 226 is a precancelation which alters the denomination. See note after No. 197.

King Albert
A71 A71a

1931, June 15 **Photogravure**

227	A71	1fr brn car	1.60	12

1932, June 1

228	A71a	75c bis brn	75	4
a.		Tête bêche pair	22.50	18.50
b.		Booklet pane of 6	27.50	
c.		Bklt pane 4 + 2 labels	27.50	

See also No. 257.

A72

1931–32 Engraved

229	A72	1.25fr gray blk	2.00	35
230	A72	1.50fr brn vio	2.75	30
231	A72	1.75fr dp bl	2.25	12
232	A72	2fr red brn	2.75	12
233	A72	2.45fr dp vio	3.50	30
234	A72	2.50fr blk brn ('32)	32.50	35
235	A72	5fr dp grn	30.00	60
236	A72	10fr claret	65.00	10.00
		Nos. 229-236 (8)	140.75	12.14

Nos. 206 and 209 Surcharged as No. 226, but dated "1932."

1932, Jan. 1

240	A63	10c on 40c red vio	5.75	65
241	A63	10c on 70c org brn	3.75	30

The surcharge on Nos. 240 and 241 is a precancelation which alters the value of the stamps. See note after No. 197.

Gleaner A73 — Mercury A74

1932, June 1 Typo. *Perf. 13½x14*

245	A73	2c pale grn	45	60
246	A74	5c dp org	22	10
247	A73	10c ol grn	50	5
a.		Tête bêche pair	8.50	6.75
b.		Booklet pane of 6	15.00	
c.		Bklt pane 4 + 2 labels	15.00	
248	A74	20c brt vio	1.25	15
249	A73	25c dp red	1.10	5
a.		Tête bêche pair	7.00	6.00
b.		Bklt pane of 6	15.00	
c.		Bklt pane 4 + 2 labels	15.00	
250	A74	35c dp grn	7.50	10
		Nos. 245-250 (6)	11.02	1.05

Auguste Piccard's Balloon
A75

1932, Nov. 26 Engraved *Perf. 11½*

251	A75	75c red brn	8.00	20
252	A75	1.75fr dk bl	18.50	1.85
253	A75	2.50fr dk vio	24.00	15.00

Issued in commemoration of Prof. Auguste Piccard's two ascents to the stratosphere.
Nos. 251 to 253 are known imperforate.

Nos. 206 and 209 Surcharged as No. 226, but dated "1933."

1933, Nov. *Perf. 14*

254	A63	10c on 40c red vio	20.00	6.00
255	A63	10c on 70c org brn	15.00	2.50

No. 206 Surcharged as No. 226, but dated "1934."

1934, Feb.

256	A63	10c on 40c red vio	15.00	1.50

The surcharge on Nos. 254 to 256 is a precancelation which alters the value of the stamps. See note after No. 197.
Regummed copies of Nos. 254–256 abound.

King Albert Memorial Issue.

Type of 1932 with Black Margins.

1934, Mar. 10 Photogravure

257	A71a	75c black	90	7
a.		Imperf., pair	85.00	

Brussels International Exhibition of 1935.

Congo Pavilion
A76

Designs: 1fr, Brussels pavilion. 1.50fr, "Old Brussels." 1.75fr, Belgian pavilion.

1934, July 1 *Perf. 14x13½*

258	A76	35c green	1.85	10
259	A76	1fr dk car	2.50	25
260	A76	1.50fr brown	7.50	1.65
261	A76	1.75fr blue	15.00	20

King Leopold III
A80 — A81

1934-35 *Perf. 13½x14.*

262	A80	70c ol blk ('35)	65	5
a.		Tête bêche pair	2.75	1.10
b.		Booklet pane of 6	7.50	
c.		Bklt pane 4 + 2 labels	7.50	
263	A80	75c brown	1.65	15

Perf. 14x13½

264	A81	1fr rose car ('35)	11.50	50

Coat of Arms
A82

1935-46 Typographed. *Perf. 14.*

265	A82	2c grn ('37)	12	3
266	A82	5c orange	15	3
267	A82	10c ol bis	15	3
a.		Tête bêche pair	40	30
b.		Bklt pane 4 + 2 labels	6.00	
c.		Booklet pane of 6	6.00	
268	A82	15c dk vio	15	3
269	A82	20c lilac	20	5
270	A82	25c car rose	18	3
a.		Tête bêche pair	1.00	60
b.		Bklt pane of 6	11.00	
c.		Bklt pane 4 + 2 labels	6.00	
d.		Booklet pane of 6	6.00	
270B	A82	25c yel org ('46)	25	5
271	A82	30c brown	50	5
272	A82	35c green	18	3
a.		Tête bêche pair	40	30
b.		Booklet pane of 6	4.00	
c.		Bklt pane 4 + 2 labels	4.00	
273	A82	40c red vio ('38)	90	5
274	A82	50c blue	75	3
274A	A82	60c sl ('41)	55	5
274B	A82	70c lt bl grn ('45)	38	5
274C	A82	75c lil rose ('45)	85	5
274D	A82	1fr red brn ('45)	85	5
		Nos. 265-274D (15)	6.16	61

Several stamps of type A82 exist in various shades.
See also Nos. 352, 352A and 353.
Nos. 265 and 345 were privately overprinted, and surcharged "+10FR.", by the Association Belgo-Américaine for the dedication of the Bastogne Memorial, July 16, 1950. The overprint is in four types.

King Leopold III
A83 — A83a

1936-43 Photo. *Perf. 14, 14x13½*

Size: 17½x21¾ mm.

275	A83	70c brown	65	5
a.		Tête bêche pair	3.75	2.00
b.		Bklt pane of 6	11.00	
c.		Bklt pane 4 + 2 labels	10.00	

Size: 20¾x24 mm.

276	A83a	1fr rose car	1.10	8
277	A83a	1.50fr brt red vio ('43)	70	12
278	A83a	1.75fr dp ultra ('43)	35	18
279	A83a	2fr dk pur ('43)	1.25	75
280	A83a	2.25fr grnsh blk ('43)	60	8
281	A83a	3.25fr chnt ('43)	70	5
282	A83a	5fr dp grn ('43)	3.75	50
		Nos. 275-282 (8)	9.10	1.81

Nos. 278, 280 and 282 inscribed "Belgie-Belgique."
See also Nos. 400–402.

King Leopold III
A84 — A85

1936-41 Engraved *Perf. 14x13½*

283	A84	1.50fr rose lil	1.00	10
284	A84	1.75fr dl bl	65	5
285	A84	2fr dl vio	3.00	10
286	A84	2.25fr gray vio ('41)	1.10	12
287	A84	2.45fr black	62.50	45
288	A84	2.50fr ol blk ('40)	7.50	15
289	A84	3.25fr org brn ('41)	1.25	12
290	A84	5fr dl grn	4.00	15
291	A84	10fr dk vio brn	3.50	5
292	A84	20fr vermilion	3.50	15
		Nos. 283-292 (10)	88.00	1.44

See also Nos. 403–406A.

No. 206 Surcharged as No. 226, but dated "1937."

1937 *Perf. 14.* Unwmkd.

293	A63	10c on 40c red vio	50	50

The surcharge on No. 293 is a precancelation which alters the value of the stamp. See note after No. 197.

1938-41 Photo. *Perf. 13½x14*

294	A85	75c ol gray	1.00	5
a.		Tête bêche pair	3.00	1.65
b.		Booklet pane of 6	9.00	
c.		Bklt pane 4 + 2 labels	9.00	
295	A85	1fr rose pink ('41)	20	3
a.		Tête bêche pair	65	30
b.		Booklet pane of 6	3.00	
c.		Bklt pane 4 + 2 labels	3.00	

No. 287 Surcharged in Red ≡ 2F50

1938, Oct. 31 *Perf. 14*

296	A84	2.50fr on 2.45fr blk	40.00	30

Basilica and Bell Tower A86 — Water Exhibition Buildings A87

Designs: 1.50fr, Albert Canal and Park. 1.75fr, Eygenbilsen Cut in Albert Canal.

Perf. 14x13½, 13½x14

1938, Oct. 31

297	A86	35c dk bl grn	38	15
298	A87	1fr rose red	95	18
299	A87	1.50fr vio brn	2.75	1.10
300	A87	1.75fr ultra	3.50	23

Publicity for the International Water Exhibition, Liège, 1939.

See "Special Notices" at the front of this volume for data on the listing methods of this Catalogue, abbreviations, condition, prices and examination.

Nos. 271, 273, 275, 294 and 288 Surcharged in Blue, Black or Carmine:

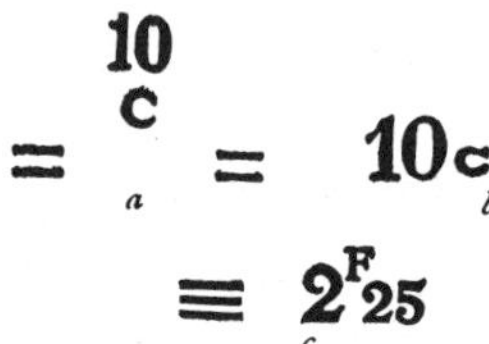

1941-42 *Perf. 14, 14x13½*

301	A82 (a)	10c on 30c brn (Bl)	30	12
302	A82 (a)	10c on 40c red vio (Bl)	30	12
303	A83 (b)	10c on 70c brn (Bk)	35	12
304	A85 (b)	50c on 75c ol gray (C)	70	28
305	A84 (c)	2.25fr on 2.50fr ol blk (C)	1.25	1.00
		Nos. 301-305 (5)	2.90	1.64

Lion Rampant A90 — King Leopold III with Crown and V A91

Photogravure.

1944 *Perf. 12½.* Unwmkd.

Inscribed: "Belgique-Belgie".

306	A90	5c chocolate	8	5
307	A90	10c green	12	5
308	A90	25c lt bl	15	5
309	A90	35c brown	18	5
310	A90	50c lt bl grn	22	5
310A	A90	75c purple	28	12
311	A90	1fr vermilion	18	3
312	A90	1.25fr chestnut	45	22
313	A90	1.50fr orange	90	60
314	A90	1.75fr brt ultra	30	5
314A	A90	2fr aqua	3.50	1.85
315	A90	2.75fr dp mag	60	15
316	A90	3fr claret	90	85
317	A90	3.50fr sl blk	1.50	85
318	A90	5fr dk ol	6.50	7.25
319	A90	10fr black	2.10	1.50
		Nos. 306-319 (16)	17.96	13.72

Inscribed: "Belgie-Belgique".

320	A90	5c chocolate	8	5
321	A90	10c green	12	5
322	A90	25c lt bl	15	5
323	A90	35c brown	18	5
324	A90	50c lt bl grn	22	5
324A	A90	75c purple	28	12
325	A90	1fr vermilion	18	3
326	A90	1.25fr chestnut	45	22
327	A90	1.50fr orange	90	60
328	A90	1.75fr brt ultra	30	5
329	A90	2fr aqua	3.50	1.25
329A	A90	2.75fr dp mag	60	15
330	A90	3fr claret	90	85
331	A90	3.50fr sl blk	1.50	85
332	A90	5fr dk ol	6.50	6.75
333	A90	10fr black	2.00	1.50
		Nos. 320-333 (16)	17.86	12.62

1944-57 *Perf. 14x13½*

334	A91	1fr brt rose red	45	6
335	A91	1.50fr magenta	75	6
336	A91	1.75fr dp ultra	75	55
337	A91	2fr dp vio	2.25	8
338	A91	2.25fr grnsh blk	80	35
339	A91	3.25fr chnt brn	1.25	5
340	A91	5fr dk bl grn	3.75	5
a.		Perf. 11½ ('57)	100.00	10
		Nos. 334-340 (7)	10.00	1.20

Nos. 335, 337 and 339 are inscribed "Belgique Belgie".

Stamps of 1935-41 Overprinted in Red **V**

1944 ***Perf. 14.***

345	A82	2c pale grn	10	5
346	A82	15c indigo	12	7
347	A82	20c brt vio	15	7
348	A82	60c slate	30	15

See note following No. 274D regarding Bastogne overprint on No. 345.

Nos. 335, 337 and 340 Surcharged Typographically in Black or Carmine **—10%**

1946 ***Perf. 14x13½.***

348A	A91	On 1.50fr mag	75	10
348B	A91	On 2fr dp vio (C)	3.50	65
348C	A91	On 5fr dk bl grn (C)	3.75	7

To provide denominations created by a reduction in postal rates, the Government produced Nos. 348A-348C by surcharging typographically. Also, each post office was authorized on May 20, 1946, to surcharge its stock of 1.50fr, 2fr and 5fr stamps "—10 percent." Hundreds of types and sizes of this surcharge exist, both handstamped and typographed. These include the "1,35", "1,80" and "4,50" applied at Ghislenghien.

M. S. Prince Baudouin
A92

Designs: 2.25fr, S. S. Marie Henriette. 3.15fr, S. S. Diamant.

Perf. 14x13½, 13½x14.

1946, June 15 Photo. Unwmkd.

349	A92	1.35fr brt bluish grn	25	7
350	A92	2.25fr sl grn	50	18
351	A92	3.15fr sl blk	65	28

Issued to commemorate the centenary of the steamship line between Ostend and Dover.

No. 349 exists in two sizes: 21¼ x 18¼ mm. and 21 x 17 mm. Nos. 350-351 measure 24¼ x 20 mm.

Arms Type of 1935-46.

1946-48 Typographed ***Perf. 14***

352	A82	65c red lil	85	5
352A	A82	80c grn ('48)	10.00	50
353	A82	90c dl vio	85	5

Capt. Adrien de Gerlache
A95

Belgica and Explorers
A96

1947, June ***Perf. 14x13½, 11½***

354	A95	1.35fr crim rose	38	7
355	A96	2.25fr gray blk	2.25	1.20

Issued to commemorate the 50th anniversary of Capt. Adrien de Gerlache's Antarctic Expedition.

Joseph A. F. Plateau
A97

1947, June ***Perf. 14x13½***

356	A97	3.15fr dp bl	75	15

Issued to mark the World Film and Fine Arts Festival, Brussels, June, 1947.

Sheets of thin cardboard, containing one each of Nos. 354 to 356, bearing commemorative inscriptions in French and Flemish, were also issued in 1947. Size: 180x150 mm.

Chemical Industry
A98

Industrial Arts
A99

Agriculture
A100

Communications Center
A101

Textile Industry
A102

Iron Manufacture
A103

Photogravure (#357-359, 361), Typographed (#360, 363), Engraved.

1948 ***Perf. 11½*** **Unwmkd.**

357	A98	60c bl grn	50	15
358	A98	1.20fr brown	2.50	10
359	A99	1.35fr red brn	50	5
360	A100	1.75fr brt red	1.25	7
361	A99	1.75fr dk gray grn	1.00	5
362	A101	2.25fr gray bl	1.75	90
363	A100	2.50fr dk car rose	9.00	12
364	A101	3fr brt red vio	11.50	18
365	A102	3.15fr dp bl	2.25	15
366	A102	4fr brt ultra	10.00	12
367	A103	6fr bl grn	15.00	12
368	A103	6.30fr brt red vio	4.00	4.00
		Nos. 357-368 (12)	59.25	6.01

King Leopold I
A104

Engraved

1949, July 1 ***Perf. 14x13½***

369	A104	90c dk grn	75	60
370	A104	1.75fr brown	65	15
371	A104	3fr red	4.25	5.00
372	A104	4fr dp bl	5.75	1.10

Issued to commemorate the centenary of Belgium's first postage stamps.

See note on souvenir sheet below No. 2.

Stamps of 1935-45 Precanceled and Surcharged in Black

1949 ***Perf. 14***

373	A82	5c on 15c dk vio	10	10
374	A82	5c on 30c brn	10	10
375	A82	5c on 40c red vio	10	10
376	A82	20c on 70c lt bl grn	22	25
377	A82	20c on 75c lil rose	15	10

Similar Surcharge and Precancelation in Black on Nos. B455-B458.

Perf. 14x13½.

378	SP251	10c on 65+35 rose red	5.75	7.00
379	SP251	40c on 90c+60c gray	1.75	1.85
380	SP251	80c on 1.35fr+1.15fr hn brn	1.25	85
381	SP251	1.20fr on 3.15+1.85 brt bl	4.00	3.25
		Nos. 373-381 (9)	13.42	13.60

The surcharges on Nos. 373 to 381 are combined with the precancelations. See note after No. 197.

St. Mary Magdalene, from Painting by Gerard David
A105

1949, July 15 Photo. ***Perf. 11***

382	A105	1.75fr dk brn	90	30

Issued to publicize the Gerard David Exhibition at Bruges, 1949.

Allegory of U.P.U.—A106

1949, Oct. 1 Engr. ***Perf. 11½***

383	A106	4fr dp bl	4.00	4.50

Issued to commemorate the 75th anniversary of the formation of the Universal Postal Union.

Symbolical of Pension Fund
A107

Lion Rampant
A108

Photogravure.

1950, May 1 ***Perf. 11½*** **Unwmkd.**

385	A107	1.75fr dk brn	70	20

Issued to commemorate the centenary of the foundation of the General Pension Fund.

1951, Feb. 15 Engr. ***Perf. 11½***

388	A108	20c blue	55	8

1951 Typographed ***Perf. 13½x14***

Size: 17½x21mm.

389	A108	5c pale vio	22	5
390	A108	10c red org	15	5
391	A108	20c claret	5	5
392	A108	25c green	2.00	18
393	A108	40c brn ol	75	5
394	A108	50c ultra	5	5
a.		50c lt bl	30	5
395	A108	60c lil rose	5	5
396	A108	65c vio brn	25.00	42
397	A108	80c emerald	1.50	5
398	A108	90c dp bl	2.00	12
399	A108	1fr rose	25	5
		Nos. 389-399 (11)	32.02	1.12

On every other denomination, the order of "Belgique Belgie" is changed. See also Nos. 462, 500-503, 612-614B, 680, 680D, 681b, 714A-716, 878-884, 923.

Counterfeits exist of No. 396.

Leopold Types of 1936.

Photogravure.

1950-51 ***Perf. 14x13½, 11½.***

400	A83a	1.20fr dk brn	4.00	5
401	A83a	1.75fr dk car ('50)	1.25	3
402	A83a	2.50fr org red	11.50	10

Engraved.

Perf. 11½.

403	A84	3fr yel brn	5.00	5
404	A84	4fr bl, *bluish* ('50)	11.50	10
a.		White paper	30.00	5
405	A84	6fr brt rose car	15.00	8
406	A84	10fr brn vio	2.50	4
406A	A84	20fr red	5.75	6
		Nos. 400-406A (8)	56.50	51

Nos. 401 and 402 are inscribed "Belgie-Belgique."

Francois de Tassis (Franz von Taxis)
A109

Portraits: 1.75fr, Jean-Baptiste of Thurn & Taxis. 2fr, Baron Leonard I. 2.50fr, Count Lamoral I. 3fr, Count Leonard II. 4fr, Count Lamoral II. 5fr, Prince Eugene Alexander. 5.75fr, Prince Anselme Francois. 8fr, Prince Alexander Ferdinand. 10fr, Prince Charles Anselme. 20fr, Prince Charles Alexander.

Laid Paper.

Inscribed: "Congres 1952 U.P.U." etc.

1952, May 14 Engraved

407	A109	80c ol grn	75	30
408	A109	1.75fr red org	75	10
409	A109	2fr vio brn	1.75	18
410	A109	2.50fr carmine	2.50	1.50
411	A109	3fr ol bis	2.25	25
412	A109	4fr ultra	3.25	15
413	A109	5fr red brn	5.00	1.10
414	A109	5.75fr bl vio	8.75	1.85
415	A109	8fr gray	14.00	2.10
416	A109	10fr rose vio	25.00	7.50
417	A109	20fr brown	60.00	45.00
		Nos. 407-417 (11)	124.00	60.03

Issued on the occasion of the 13th Universal Postal Union Congress, Brussels, 1952. See No. B514.

King Baudouin
A110 A111

1952 **Size: 21x24mm.**

418	A110	1.50fr gray	1.25	8
419	A110	2fr crimson	1.00	5
420	A110	4fr ultra	7.50	30

Size: 24½x35mm.

421	A110	50fr gray brn	3.50	30
a.		50fr vio brn	32.50	60

See also No. 489.

1953 **Photogravure.**
Size: 21x24mm.

422	A111	1.50fr gray	50	3
423	A111	2fr rose car	15.00	3
424	A111	4fr brt ultra	75	3

See also Nos. 463–464, 480–488, 615, 680A–681D, 738A–738C.

No. 422 was also issued in coils with black control number on back of every 5th stamp.

Luminescent Paper

Stamps issued on both luminescent and ordinary paper include: Nos. 406, 406A, 421, 422, 424, 463–464, 480–482, 482A, 483, 483B, 485, 488–489, 503, 613, 615, 629–630, 646–647, 680A, 780, Q385, Q410.

Stamps issued only on luminescent paper include: Nos. 463a, 616–622, 633–636, 641–643, 650–652, 655–656, 659–662, 664–665, 668–673, 675–680, 680c, 680G, 681, 681C, 682–693, 696–710, 713–714, 717–717A, 718–728, 730–732, 734, 736–738, 740–746, 748–754, 757–761, 763–777, 779, 781–791. See note after No. 793.

Nos. 396 and 398 Surcharged and Precanceled in Black

20c
I-I-54
31-XII-54

Perf. 13½x14

1954, Jan. 1 **Unwmkd.**

425	A108	20c on 65c vio brn	2.25	65
426	A108	20c on 90c dp bl	2.00	50

The surcharges on Nos. 425–426 are combined with the precancellations. See note after No. 197.

Map and Rotary Emblem
A112

Designs: 80c, Mermaid and Mercury holding emblem. 4fr, Rotary emblem and two globes.

1954, Sept. 10 **Engr.** ***Perf. 11½***

427	A112	20c red	25	15
428	A112	80c dk grn	75	45
429	A112	4fr ultra	1.75	75

Nos. 427–428 were issued to publicize the fifth regional conference of Rotary International at Ostend; No. 429 to commemorate the 50th anniversary (in 1955) of the founding of Rotary.

A souvenir sheet containing one each of Nos. 427–429, imperforate, together with typographed inscriptions in black was sold for 500 francs. It was not valid for postage.

The Rabot and Begonia
A113

Designs: 2.50fr, The Oudeburg and azalea. 4fr, "Three Towers" and orchid.

1955, Feb. 15 **Photogravure**

430	A113	80c brt car	75	30
431	A113	2.50fr blk brn	5.00	5.50
432	A113	4fr dk rose brn	4.25	1.65

Issued to publicize the Ghent International Flower Exhibition, 1955.

Homage to Charles V as a Child, by Albrecht de Vriendt
A114

Charles V, by Titian
A115

Design: 4fr, Abdication of Charles V, by Louis Gallait.

1955, Mar. 25 ***Perf. 11½*** **Unwmkd.**

433	A114	20c rose red	18	15
434	A115	2fr dk gray grn	1.50	10
435	A114	4fr blue	4.50	2.00

Issued to publicize the Charles V Exhibition, Ghent, 1955.

Emile Verhaeren, by Montald Constant
A116

1955, May 11 **Engraved**

436	A116	20c dk gray	22	7

Issued to commemorate the centenary of the birth of Emile Verhaeren, poet.

Allegory of Textile Manufacture
A117

1955, May 11

437	A117	2fr vio brn	1.40	18

Issued to publicize the second International Textile Exhibition, Brussels, June 1955.

"The Foolish Virgin" by Rik Wouters
A118

"Departure of Volunteers from Liege, 1830" by Charles Soubre
A119

1955, June 10

438	A118	1.20fr ol grn	1.25	1.25
439	A118	2fr violet	1.75	15

Issued to publicize the third biennial exhibition of sculpture, Antwerp, June 11–Sept. 10, 1955.

1955, Sept. 10 **Photogravure**

440	A119	20c grnsh sl	25	25
441	A119	2fr chocolate	1.25	22

Issued to publicize the exhibition "The Romantic Movement in Liege Province," Sept. 10 - Oct. 31, 1955; and to mark the 125th anniversary of Belgium's independence from the Netherlands.

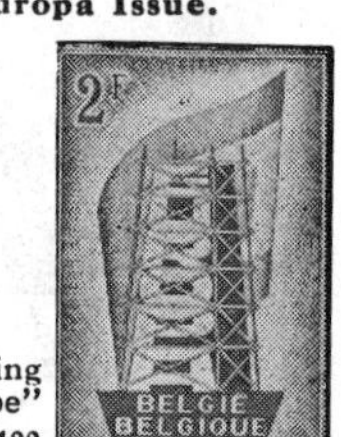

Pelican Giving Blood to Young
A120

Buildings of Tournai, Ghent and Antwerp
A121

1956, Jan. 14 **Engraved**

442	A120	2fr brt car	70	18

Issued in honor of the blood donor service of the Belgian Red Cross.

1956, July 14 **Photogravure**

443	A121	2fr brt ultra	50	18

Issued to publicize the Scheldt exhibition (Scaldis) at Tournai, Ghent and Antwerp, July–Sept. 1956.

Europa Issue.

"Rebuilding Europe"
A122

1956, Sept. 15 **Engraved**

444	A122	2fr lt grn	4.00	15
445	A122	4fr purple	10.00	1.00

Issued to symbolize the cooperation among the six countries comprising the Coal and Steel Community.

Train on Map of Belgium and Luxembourg—A123

1956, Sept. 29

446	A123	2fr dk bl	70	18

Issued to mark the electrification of the Brussels-Luxembourg railroad.

Edouard Anseele
A124

"The Atom" and Exposition Emblem
A125

1956, Oct. 27

447	A124	20c vio brn	15	6

Issued to commemorate the centenary of the birth of Edouard Anseele, statesman, and in connection with an exhibition held in his honor at Ghent.

1957-58 **Unwmkd.**

448	A125	2fr car rose	85	12
449	A125	2.50fr grn ('58)	85	18
450	A125	4fr brt vio bl	1.75	30
451	A125	5fr cl ('58)	1.40	1.20

Issued to publicize the 1958 World's Fair at Brussels.

Emperor Maximilian I Receiving Letter
A126

1957, May 19

452	A126	2fr claret	70	15

Issued for the Day of the Stamp, May 19, 1957.

Sikorsky S-58 Helicopter
A127

1957, June 15

453	A127	4fr gray grn & brt bl	1.00	1.00

Issued to publicize the 100,000th passenger carried by Sabena helicopter service, June 15, 1957.

Zeebrugge Harbor
A128

1957, July 6

454	A128	2fr dk bl	55	15

Issued to commemorate the 50th anniversary of the completion of the port of Zeebrugge-Bruges.

Leopold I Entering Brussels, 1831
A129

Leopold I Arriving at Belgian Border
A130

1957, July 17 **Photogravure**

455	A129	20c dk gray grn	18	12
456	A130	2fr lilac	90	35

Issued to commemorate the 126th anniversary of the arrival in Belgium of King Leopold I.

Boy Scout and Girl Scout Emblems
A131

Design: 4fr, Robert Lord Baden-Powell, painted by David Jaggers (vert.).

Engraved.

1957, July 29 *Perf. 11½* Unwmkd.

457	A131	80c gray	50	25
458	A131	4fr lt grn	1.50	1.00

Issued to commemorate the centenary of the birth of Lord Baden-Powell, founder of the Boy Scout movement.

"Kneeling Woman" by Lehmbruck A132

"United Europe" A133

1957, Aug. 20 Photogravure

459	A132	2.50fr dk bl grn	1.75	2.00

Issued to commemorate the fourth Biennial Exposition of Sculpture, Antwerp, May 25–Sept. 15.

Europa Issue, 1957.

1957, Sept. 16 Engr. *Perf. 11½*

460	A133	2fr dk vio brn	1.75	18
461	A133	4fr dk bl	2.50	75

Issued to publicize a united Europe for peace and prosperity.

Types of 1951 (Lion) and 1953 (Baudouin).

Typographed.

1957–70 *Perf. 13½x14* Unwmkd.

462	A108	30c gray grn	10	3

Photogravure.

Perf. 11½

463	A111	2.50fr red brn	60	3
a.		2.50fr org brn ('70)	1.75	3
464	A111	5fr violet	2.00	3

No. 463a was also issued in coils with black control number on back of every 5th stamp. The coil is on luminescent paper.

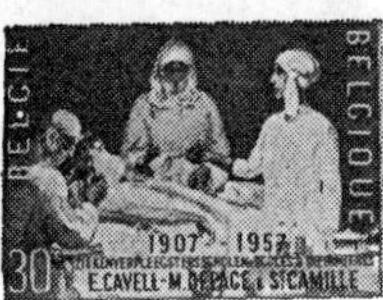

Queen Elisabeth Assisting at Operation, by Allard L'Olivier

A134

Engraved.

1957, Nov. 23 *Perf. 11½* Unwmkd.

465	A134	30c rose lil	15	10

Issued to commemorate the 50th anniversary of the founding of the Edith Cavell-Marie Depage and St. Camille schools of nursing.

Post Horn and Historic Postal Insignia

A135

1958, Mar. 16 Photo. *Perf. 11½*

466	A135	2.50fr gray	45	10

Postal Museum Day.

United Nations Issue

International Labor Organization

A136

Allegory of U. N.

A137

Designs: 1fr, Food and Agriculture Organization. 2fr, World Bank. 2.50fr, UNESCO. 3fr, U. N. Pavilion. 5fr, International Telecommunication Union. 8fr, International Monetary Fund. 11fr, World Health Organization. 20fr, U. P. U.

Engraved.

1958, Apr. 17 *Perf. 11½* Unwmkd.

467	A136	50c gray	1.40	1.40
468	A136	1fr claret	40	40
469	A137	1.50fr dp ultra	40	40
470	A137	2fr gray brn	1.25	1.25
471	A136	2.50fr ol grn	40	40
472	A136	3fr grnsh bl	1.25	1.25
473	A137	5fr rose lil	80	80
474	A136	8fr red brn	1.50	1.50
475	A136	11fr dl lil	2.00	2.00
476	A136	20fr car rose	2.50	2.50
		Nos. 467-476 (10)	11.90	11.90

World's Fair, Brussels, Apr. 17–Oct. 19. See Nos. C15–C20.

Nos. 467–476 were postally valid only at the United Nations Pavilion at the Brussels Fair. Proceeds from the sale of these stamps went toward financing the U. N. exhibits.

Eugène Ysaye

A138

1958, Sept. 1

477	A138	30c dk bl & plum	15	7

Issued to commemorate the centenary of the birth of Eugène Ysaye (1858–1931), violinist and composer.

Europa Issue, 1958

Common Design Type

1958, Sept. 13 Photogravure

Size: 24½x35mm.

478	CD1	2.50fr brt red & bl	38	6
479	CD1	5fr brt bl & red	55	55

Issued to show the European Postal Union at the service of European integration.

Baudouin Types of 1952–53

1958–62 Photogravure *Perf. 11½*

Size: 21x24mm.

480	A111	2fr green	25	3
481	A111	3fr rose lil	50	3
482	A111	3.50fr brt yel grn	75	5
482A	A111	4.50fr dk red brn ('62)	80	5
483	A111	6fr dp pink	75	5
483A	A111	6.50fr gray ('60)	70.00	14.00
483B	A111	7fr bl ('60)	75	5
484	A111	7.50fr grysh brn	62.50	18.50
485	A111	8fr bluish gray	1.00	8
486	A111	8.50fr claret	25.00	35
487	A111	9fr gray	67.50	90
488	A111	30fr red org	5.00	15

Engraved.

Size: 24½x35mm.

489	A110	100fr rose red	7.50	35
		Nos. 480-489 (13)	242.30	34.59

Nos. 480–482A were also issued in coils with black control number on back of every fifth stamp. These coils are on luminescent paper.

No. 482A is inscribed 1962.

Infant and U. N. Emblem

A140

Charles V and Jean-Baptiste of Thurn and Taxis

A141

1958, Dec. 10 Engraved

490	A140	2.50fr bl gray	70	10

Issued to commemorate the tenth anniversary of the signing of the Universal Declaration of Human Rights.

1959, Mar. 15 Unwmkd.

491	A141	2.50fr green	70	15

Issued for the Day of the Stamp. Design from painting by J.-E. van den Bussche.

NATO Emblem

A142

City Hall, Audenarde

A143

1959, Apr. 3 Photo. *Perf. 11½*

492	A142	2.50fr dp red & dk bl	1.00	15
493	A142	5fr emer & dk bl	2.00	1.65

Issued to commemorate the 10th anniversary of the North Atlantic Treaty Organization.

1959, Aug. 17 Engraved

494	A143	2.50fr dp cl	45	6

Pope Adrian VI, by Jan van Scorel

A144

1959, Aug. 31 *Perf. 11½*

495	A144	2.50fr dk red	38	10
496	A144	5fr Prus bl	90	80

Issued to commemorate the 500th anniversary of the birth of Pope Adrian VI.

Common Design Types pictured in section at front of book.

Europa Issue, 1959

Common Design Type

1959, Sept. 19 Photogravure

Size: 24 x 35½mm.

497	CD2	2.50fr dk red	25	12
498	CD2	5fr brt grnsh bl	60	60

No. 497 inscribed Belgie-Belgique.

Boeing 707

A146

Engraved and Photogravure

1959, Dec. 1 *Perf. 11½*

499	A146	6fr dk bl gray & car	2.25	1.50

Issued to commemorate the inauguration of jet flights by Sabena Airlines.

Lion Type of 1951

1959–60 Typographed. *Perf. 13½x14*

Size: 17½x21mm.

500	A108	2c org brn ('60)	8	3
501	A108	3c brt lil ('60)	8	3
502	A108	15c brt pink	5	3

Photogravure

Perf. 11½

Size: 20½x24½mm.

502A	A108	50c lt bl ('61)	1.50	15
503	A108	1fr car rose	15	3
		Nos. 500-503 (5)	1.86	27

No. 502A–503 were also issued in coils with black control number on back of every fifth stamp.

Countess of Taxis

A147

Indian Azalea

A148

Engraved

1960, Mar. 21 *Perf. 11½*

504	A147	3fr dk bl	2.00	18

Issued to honor Alexandrine de Rye, Countess of Taxis, Grand Mistress of the Netherlands Posts, 1628–1645, and to publicize the day of the stamp, March 21, 1960. The painting of the Countess is by Nicholas van der Eggermans.

1960, Mar. 28 Unwmkd.

Flowers: 3fr, Begonia. 6fr, Anthurium and bromelia.

505	A148	40c dl vio & dp car	35	15
506	A148	3fr emer, red & org yel	1.65	15
507	A148	6fr dk bl, grn & brt red	2.75	1.60

Issued to publicize the 24th Ghent International Flower Exhibition, Apr. 23–May 2, 1960.

Steel Workers, by Constantin Meunier

A149

Design: 3fr, The sower, field and dock workers, from "Monument to Labor," Brussels, by Constantin Meunier (horiz.).

Engraved and Photogravure

1960, Apr. 30 ***Perf. 11½***

508 A149 40c cl & brt red 35 25
509 A149 3fr brn & brt red 2.00 50

Issued to commemorate the 75th anniversary of the Socialist Party of Belgium.

Congo River Boat Pilot
A150

Designs: 40c, Medical team. 1fr, Planting tree. 2fr, Sculptors. 2.50fr, Shot put. 3fr, Congolese officials. 6fr, Congolese and Belgian girls playing with doll. 8fr, Boy pointing on globe to independent Congo.

1960, June 30 **Photo.** ***Perf. 11½***

Size: 35x24mm.

510 A150 10c brt red 40 15
511 A150 40c rose cl 60 20
512 A150 1fr brt lil 2.10 75
513 A150 2fr gray grn 2.00 90
514 A150 2.50fr blue 2.00 70
515 A150 3fr dk bl gray 2.25 40

Size: 51x35mm.

516 A150 6fr vio bl 6.00 2.25
517 A150 8fr dk brn 13.00 10.00
Nos. 510-517 (8) 28.35 15.35

Independence of Congo.

Europa Issue, 1960

Common Design Type

1960, Sept. 17

Size: 35x24½mm.

518 CD3 3fr claret 1.40 25
519 CD3 6fr gray 2.75 65

Children Examining Stamp and Globe
A152

H. J. W. Frère-Orban
A153

1960, Oct. 1 **Photo.** ***Perf. 11½***

520 A152 40c bis & blk +label 30 30

Issued to promote stamp collecting among children. Issued in sheets of 30 with alternating label. Label shows post horn and inscription in Flemish and French.

Photogravure and Engraved

1960, Oct. 17 **Unwmkd.**

Portrait in Brown

521 A153 10c org yel 30 20
522 A153 40c bl grn 50 25
523 A153 1.50fr brt vio 1.75 1.50
524 A153 3fr red 2.25 30

Centenary of Communal Credit Society.

King Baudouin and Queen Fabiola—A154

1960, Dec. 13 **Photo.** ***Perf. 11½***

Portraits in Dark Brown

525 A154 40c green 25 15
526 A154 3fr red lil 1.40 18
527 A154 6fr dl bl 2.25 90

Issued to commemorate the wedding of King Baudouin and Dona Fabiola de Mora y Aragon, Dec. 15, 1960.

No. 462 Surcharged

15c

1961 **Typographed** ***Perf. 13½x14***

528 A108 15c on 30c gray grn 60 7
529 A108 20c on 30c gray grn 70 25

See also No. 657.

No. 462 Surcharged and Precanceled

1961

530 A108 15c on 30c gray grn 2.00 12
531 A108 20c on 30c gray grn 3.00 2.25

The surcharges on Nos. 530-531 are combined with the precancellations. See note after No. 197.

Nicolaus Rockox, by Anthony Van Dyck
A155

Seal of Jan Bode, Alderman of Antwerp, 1264
A156

Engraved and Photogravure

1961, Mar. 18 ***Perf. 11½***

532 A155 3fr bis, blk & brn 75 15

Issued to commemorate the 400th anniversary of the birth of Nicolaus Rockox, mayor of Antwerp.

1961, Apr. 16 **Photogravure**

533 A156 3fr buff & brn 75 15

Issued for Stamp Day, April 16.

Senate Building, Brussels, Laurel and Sword
A157

Engraved and Photogravure

1961, Sept. 14 ***Perf. 11½*** **Unwmkd.**

534 A157 3fr brn & Prus grn 65 12
535 A157 6fr dk brn & dk car 1.40 90

Issued to commemorate the 50th Conference of the Interparliamentary Union, Brussels, Sept. 14-22.

Europa Issue, 1961

Common Design Type

1961, Sept. 16 **Photogravure**

Size: 35x25½mm.

536 CD4 3fr yel grn & dk grn 30 10
537 CD4 6fr org brn & blk 75 35

Atomic Reactor Plant, BR2, Mol
A159

Designs: 3fr, Atomic Reactor BR3 (vert.). 6fr, Atomic Reactor plant BR3.

1961, Nov. 8 ***Perf. 11½*** **Unwmkd.**

538 A159 40c dk bl grn 18 10
539 A159 3fr red lil 55 6
540 A159 6fr brt bl 1.10 1.00

Issued to publicize the atomic nuclear research center at Mol.

Horta Museum
A160

1962, Feb. 15 **Engraved**

541 A160 3fr red brn 65 10

Issued to honor Baron Victor Horta (1861-1947), architect.

Postrider, 16th Century
A161

Engraved and Photogravure

1962, March 25 ***Perf. 11½***

Chalky Paper

542 A161 3fr brn & sl grn 75 15

Stamp Day. See No. 631.

Gerard Mercator
A162

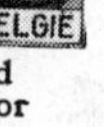

Bro. Alexis-Marie Gochet
A163

Engraved and Photogravure

1962, Apr. 14 **Unwmkd.**

543 A162 3fr sep & gray 75 15

Issued to commemorate the 450th anniversary of the birth of Mercator (Gerhard Kremer, 1512-1594), geographer and map maker.

1962, May 19 **Engr.** ***Perf. 11½***

Portrait: 3fr, Canon Pierre-Joseph Triest.

544 A163 2fr dk bl 45 15
545 A163 3fr gldn brn 75 10

Issued to honor Brother Alexis-Marie Gochet (1835-1910), geographer and educator, and Canon Pierre-Joseph Triest (1760-1836), educator and founder of hospitals and orphanages.

Europa Issue, 1962

Common Design Type

1962, Sept. 15 **Photogravure**

Size: 35x24mm.

546 CD5 3fr dp car, cit & blk 38 10
547 CD5 6fr ol, cit & blk 1.15 50

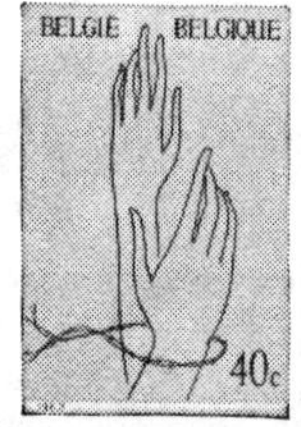

Hand with Barbed Wire and Freed Hand
A165

Engraved and Photogravure

1962, Sept. 16

548 A165 40c lt bl & blk 18 6

Issued in memory of concentration camp victims.

Adam, by Michelangelo, Broken Chain and U.N. Emblem
A166

1962, Nov. 24 ***Perf. 11½***

549 A166 3fr gray & blk 50 15
550 A166 6fr lt redsh brn & dk brn 75 40

Issued to publicize the U.N. Declaration of Human Rights.

Henri Pirenne
A167

1963, Jan. 15 **Engraved**

551 A167 3fr ultra 65 15

Issued to commemorate the centenary of the birth of Henri Pirenne (1862-1935), historian.

Swordsmen and Ghent Belfry
A168

Designs: 3fr, Modern fencers. 6fr, Arms of the Royal and Knightly Guild of St. Michael (vert.).

Engraved and Photogravure

1963, Mar. 23 *Perf. 11½* Unwmkd.

552	A168	1fr brn red & pale bl	25	18
553	A168	3fr dk vio & yel grn	35	10
554	A168	6fr gray, blk, red, bl & gold	85	50

Issued to commemorate the 350th anniversary of the granting of a charter to the Ghent guild of fencers.

Stagecoach
A169

1963, Apr. 7

555	A169	3fr gray & ocher	60	10

Stamp Day. See No. 632.

Hotel des Postes, Paris, Stagecoach and Stamp, 1863
A170

Engraved

1963, May 7 *Perf. 11½* Unwmkd.

556	A170	6fr dk brn, gray & yel grn	1.00	65

Issued to commemorate the centenary of the first International Postal Conference, Paris, 1863.

"Peace," Child in Rye Field
A171

Engraved and Photogravure

1963, May 8

557	A171	3fr grn, blk, yel & brn	50	12
558	A171	6fr buff, blk, brn & org	85	45

Issued to publicize the May 8th Movement for Peace. (On May 8, 1945, World War II ended in Europe).

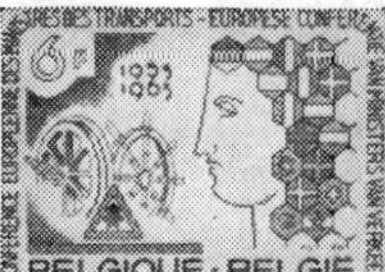

Allegory and Shields of 17 Member Nations
A172

1963, June 13 *Perf. 11½* Unwmkd.

559	A172	6fr bl & blk	1.00	45

10th anniversary of the Conference of European Transport Ministers.

Seal of Union of Belgian Towns
A173

1963, June 17

560	A173	6fr grn, red, blk & gold	90	45

50th anniversary of the International Union of Municipalities.

Caravelle over Brussels National Airport
A174

Photogravure and Engraved

1963, Sept. 1 *Perf. 11½* Unwmkd.

561	A174	3fr grn & gray	65	15

40th anniversary of SABENA airline.

Europa Issue, 1963

Common Design Type

1963, Sept. 14 Photogravure

Size: 35x24mm.

562	CD6	3fr blk, dl red & lt brn	1.90	12
563	CD6	6fr blk, lt bl & lt brn	3.00	50

Jules Destrée
A176

Design: No. 565, Henry Van de Velde.

Engraved

1963, Nov. 16 *Perf. 11½* Unwmkd.

564	A176	1fr rose lil	20	15
565	A176	1fr green	20	15

Issued to commemorate the centenary of the birth of Jules Destrée (1863–1936), statesman and founder of the Royal Academy of French Language and Literature (No. 564), and of Henry Van de Velde (1863–1957), architect (No. 565).

No. 564 incorrectly inscribed "1864."

Development of the Mail, Bas-relief
A177

Engraved and Photogravure

1963, Nov. 23

566	A177	50c dl red, sl & blk	25	7

50th anniversary of the establishment of postal checking service.

Dr. Armauer G. Hansen
A178

Designs: 2fr, Leprosarium. 5fr, Father Joseph Damien.

1964, Jan. 25 *Perf. 11½* Unwmkd.

567	A178	1fr brn org & blk	35	25
568	A178	2fr brn org & blk	45	30
569	A178	5fr brn org & blk	60	40
a.		Souvenir sheet of 3	2.75	2.75

Issued to publicize the fight against leprosy. No. 569a contains one each of Nos. 567–569; brown inscription and orange and brown emblem in margin. Size: 137x97 mm. Sold for 12fr.

Andreas Vesalius
A179

Jules Boulvin
A180

Design: 2fr, Henri Jaspar.

Engraved and Photogravure

1964, March 2 *Perf. 11½* Unwmkd.

570	A179	50c pale grn & blk	20	7
571	A180	1fr pale grn & blk	25	10
572	A180	2fr pale grn & blk	40	18

Issued to commemorate 400th anniversary of the death of Andreas Vesalius (1514–64), anatomist (50c); honor Jules Boulvin (1855–1920), mechanical engineer (1fr) and to commemorate the 25th anniversary of the death of Henri Jaspar (1870–1939), satesman and lawyer (2fr).

Postilion of Liège, 1830–40
A181

1964, Apr. 5 Engraved *Perf. 11½*

573	A181	3fr black	50	6

Issued for Stamp Day 1964.

Arms of Ostend
A182

1964, May 16 Photogravure

574	A182	3fr ultra, ver, gold & blk	40	6

Millennium of Ostend.

Flame, Hammer and Globe
A183

Designs: 1fr, "SI" and globe. 2fr, Flame over wavy lines.

1964, July 18 *Perf. 11½* Unwmkd.

575	A183	50c dk bl & red	20	10
576	A183	1fr dk bl & red	25	12
577	A183	2fr dk bl & red	38	25

Issued to commemorate the centenary of the First Socialist International, founded in London, Sept. 28, 1864.

Europa Issue, 1964

Common Design Type

1964, Sept. 12 Photo. *Perf. 11½*

Size: 24x35½mm.

578	CD7	3fr yel grn, dk car & gray	45	15
579	CD7	6fr car rose, yel grn & bl	60	50

Benelux Issue

King Baudouin, Queen Juliana and Grand Duchess Charlotte
A185

1964, Oct. 12

580	A185	3fr ol, lt grn & mar	50	10

Issued to commemorate the 20th anniversary of the customs union of Belgium, Netherlands and Luxembourg.

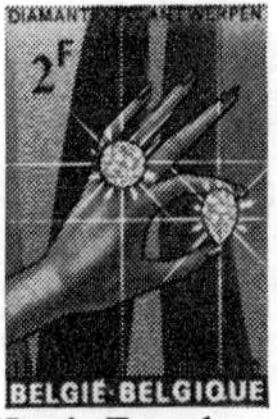

Hand, Round and Pear-shaped Diamonds
A186

Symbols of Textile Industry
A187

1965, Jan. 23 *Perf. 11½* Unwmkd.

581	A186	2fr ultra, dp car & blk	45	30

Issued to publicize the Diamond Exhibition "Diamantexpo," Antwerp, July 10–28, 1965.

1965, Jan. 25 Photogravure

582	A187	1fr bl, red & blk	30	10

Issued to publicize the eighth textile industry exhibition "Textirama," Ghent, Jan. 29–Feb. 2, 1965.

Vriesia A188 — Paul Hymans A189

Designs: 2fr, Echinocactus. 3fr, Stapelia.

Engraved and Photogravure

1965, Feb. 13

583	A188	1fr multi	28	20
584	A188	2fr multi	40	20
585	A188	3fr multi	45	15
a.		Souv. sheet of 3	3.25	3.25

Issued to publicize the 25th Ghent International Flower Exhibition, Apr. 24–May 3, 1965.

No. 585a contains one each of Nos. 583–585, and was issued Apr. 26. It carries the UNRWA and Belgian Postal emblems in the margin. Sold for 20fr.

1965, Feb. 24 Engraved *Perf. 11½*

586	A189	1fr dl pur	20	7

Issued to commemorate the centenary of the birth of Paul Hymans (1865–1941), Belgian Foreign Minister and first president of the League of Nations.

Peter Paul Rubens A190 — Sir Rowland Hill as Philatelist A191

Portraits: 2fr, Frans Snyders. 3fr, Adam van Noort. 6fr, Anthony Van Dyck. 8fr, Jacob Jordaens.

Photogravure and Engraved

1965, Mar. 15

Portraits in Sepia

587	A190	1fr car rose	30	20
588	A190	2fr bl grn	25	30
589	A190	3fr plum	35	15
590	A190	6fr dp car	45	25
591	A190	8fr dk bl	70	60
		Nos. 587-591 (5)	2.05	1.50

Issued to commemorate the founding of the General Savings and Pensions Bank.

1965, Mar. 27 Engraved *Perf. 11½*

592	A191	50c bl grn	15	7

Issued to publicize youth philately. The design is from a mural by J. E. Van den Bussche in the General Post Office, Brussels.

Postmaster, c. 1833 A192 — Staircase, Affligem Abbey A194

Telephone, Globe and Teletype Paper A193

1965, Apr. 26 *Perf. 11½* Unwmkd.

593	A192	3fr emerald	40	7

Issued for Stamp Day.

1965, May 8 Photogravure

594	A193	2fr dl pur & blk	32	18

Issued to commemorate the centenary of the International Telecommunication Union.

1965, May 27 Engraved

595	A194	1fr gray bl	25	10

St. Jean Berchmans and his Birthplace A195

Engraved and Photogravure

1965, May 27

596	A195	2fr dk brn & red brn	32	12

Issued to honor St. Jean Berchmans (1599–1621), Jesuit "Saint of the Daily Life."

TOC H Lamp and Arms of Poperinge A196 — Farmer with Tractor A197

1965, June 19 Photo. *Perf. 11½*

597	A196	3fr ol bis, blk & car	32	7

Issued to commemorate the 50th anniversary of the founding of Talbot House in Poperinge, which served British soldiers in World War I, and where the TOC H Movement began (Christian Social Service; TOC H is army code for Poperinge Center).

Engraved and Photogravure

1965, July 17 *Perf. 11½* Unwmkd.

Design: 3fr, Farmer with horse-drawn roller.

598	A197	50c bl, ol, bis brn & blk	15	10
599	A197	3fr bl, ol grn, ol & blk	30	10

Issued to commemorate the 75th anniversary of the Belgian Farmers' Association (Boerenbond).

Europa Issue, 1965

Common Design Type

1965, Sept. 25 *Perf. 11½*

Size: 35½x24mm.

600	CD8	1fr dl rose & blk	25	18
601	CD8	3fr grnsh gray & blk	35	12

King Leopold I A199 — Joseph Lebeau A200

1965, Nov. 13 Engraved

602	A199	3fr sepia	32	10
603	A199	6fr brt vio	60	40

Issued to commemorate the centenary of the death of King Leopold I (1790–1865). The designs of the vignettes are similar to the 30c and 1fr of 1865.

1965, Nov. 13 Photogravure

604	A200	1fr multi	90	12

Issued to commemorate the centenary of the death of Joseph Lebeau (1794–1865), Foreign Minister.

Tourist Issue

Grapes and Houses, Hoeilaart A201 — Bridge and Castle, Huy A202

1965, Nov. 13 Engraved *Perf. 11½*

605	A201	50c vio bl, lt bl & yel grn	25	7
606	A202	50c sl grn, lt bl & red brn	25	7

See also Nos. 666, 669.

Queen Elisabeth Type of Semi-Postal Issue, 1956

1965, Dec. 23 Photo. *Perf. 11½*

607	SP305	3fr dk gray	40	15

Issued in memory of Queen Elisabeth (1876–1965).

A dark frame has been added in design of No. 607; "1956" date has been changed to "1965;" inscription in bottom panel "Koningin Elisabeth Reine Elisabeth 3F."

"Peace on Earth" A203

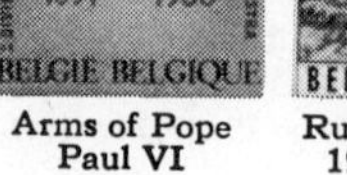

Arms of Pope Paul VI A204 — Rural Mailman, 19th Century A205

Design: 1fr, "Looking toward a Better Future" (family, new buildings, sun and landscape).

1966, Feb. 12 Photo. *Perf. 11½*

608	A203	50c multi	20	10
609	A203	1fr ocher, blk & bl	25	12
610	A204	3fr gray, gold, car & blk	35	15

Issued to commemorate the 75th anniversary of the encyclical by Pope Leo XIII "Rerum Novarum," which proclaimed the general principles for the organization of modern industrial society.

1966, Apr. 17 Photo. Unwmkd.

611	A205	3fr blk, dl yel & pale lil	35	7

Issued for Stamp Day 1966.

Lion Type of 1951 and Baudouin Type of 1953

Perf. 13½x14 (25c, 75c, 1.50fr); 11½ (60c, 12fr); 13½x13 (2fr)

Typo. (25c, 75c, 1.50fr, 2fr); Photo. (60c, 12fr)

1966–69

Size: 17½x21mm. (25c, 75c); 20½x24½mm. (60c); 17x20½mm. (1.50fr, 2fr)

612	A108	25c lt bl grn	8	3
613	A108	60c lil rose	9.00	2.50
614	A108	75c bluish lil	80	5
614A	A108	1.50fr dk sl grn ('69)	8	3
614B	A108	2fr emer ('68)	60	5
615	A111	12fr lt bl grn	1.25	25
		Nos. 612-615 (6)	11.81	2.91

Iguanodon, Natural Science Institute A206

Arend-Roland Comet, Observatory A207

Designs: No. 617, Ancestral head and spiral pattern, Kasai; Central Africa Museum. No. 618, Snowflakes, Meteorological Institute. No. 619, Seal of Charles V, Royal Archives. No. 620, Medieval scholar, Royal Library. 8fr, Satellite and rocket, Space Aeronautics Institute.

1966, May 28 Engr. and Photo.

616	A206	1fr grn & blk	20	10
617	A206	2fr gray, blk & brn org	15	12
618	A206	2fr bl, blk & yel	15	12
619	A207	3fr dp rose, blk & gold	30	7
620	A207	3fr multi	30	7
621	A207	6fr ultra, yel & blk	40	18
622	A207	8fr multi	50	50
		Nos. 616-622 (7)	2.00	1.16

Issued to publicize the national scientific heritage.

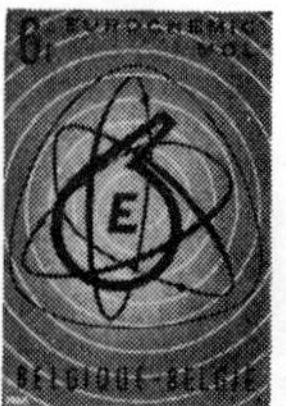

Atom Symbol and Retort A208 — August Kekulé, Benzene Ring A209

Engraved and Photogravure

1966, July 9 *Perf. 11½* Unwmkd.

623 A208 6fr gray, blk & red 75 35

Issued to publicize the European chemical plant, EUROCHEMIC, at Mol.

1966, July 9

624 A209 3fr brt bl & blk 35 12

Issued to honor August Friedrich Kekulé (1829–96), chemistry professor at University of Ghent (1858–67).

No. 611 Overprinted with Red and Blue Emblem

1966, July 11 Photogravure

625 A205 3fr multi 35 12

Issued to commemorate the 19th International P.T.T. Congress (Postal, Telegraph and Telephone Administrations), Brussels, July 11–15.

Rik Wouters, Self-portrait
A210

1966, Sept. 6 Photo. *Perf. 11½*

626 A210 60c multi 25 12

Issued to commemorate the 50th anniversary of the death of Rik Wouters (1882–1916), painter.

Europa Issue, 1966

Common Design Type

1966, Sept. 24 Engraved *Perf. 11½*

Size: 24x34mm.

627 CD9 3fr brt grn 35 15
628 CD9 6fr brt rose lil 85 50

Tourist Issue

Town Hall, Lier
A212

Castle Bouillon
A213

1966, Nov. 11 Engraved *Perf. 11½*

629 A212 2fr brn, lt bl & ind 55 8
630 A213 2fr dk brn, grn & ocher 55 8

See also Nos. 646–647, 667–668, 691.

Types of 1962–1963 Overprinted in Black and Red

1966, Nov. 11 Engraved and Photo.

631 A161 60c sep & grnsh gray 12 10
632 A169 3fr sep & pale bis 35 10

75th anniversary, Royal Federation of Philatelic Circles of Belgium. Overprint shows emblem of International Philatelic Federation (F.I.P.).

Lions Emblem
A214

Engraved and Photogravure

1967, Jan. 14 *Perf. 11½*

633 A214 3fr gray, blk & bl 30 12
634 A214 6fr lt grn, blk & vio 60 25

Issued to commemorate the 50th anniversary of the founding of the International Association of Lions Clubs.

Pistol by Leonhard Cleuter
A215

1967, Feb. 11 Photogravure

635 A215 2fr dp car, blk & cr 35 10

Fire Arms Museum in Liège.

International Tourist Year Emblem
A216

1967, Feb. 11

636 A216 6fr ver, ultra & blk 60 22

International Tourist Year, 1967.

Birches and Trientalis
A217

Design: No. 638, Dunes, beach grass, privet and blue thistles.

1967, Mar. 11 Photo. *Perf. 11½*

637 A217 1fr multi 18 8
638 A217 1fr multi 18 8

Issued to publicize the nature preserves at Hautes Fagnes and Westhoek.

Paul E. Janson
A218

1967, Apr. 15 Engraved *Perf. 11½*

639 A218 10fr blue 85 45

Issued in memory of Paul Emile Janson (1872–1944), lawyer and statesman.

Postilion
A219

1967, Apr. 16 Photo. and Engr.

640 A219 3fr rose red & cl 40 10

Issued for Stamp Day, 1967.

See also No. 645.

Europa Issue, 1967

Common Design Type

1967, May 2 Photogravure

Size: 24x35mm.

641 CD10 3fr blk, lt bl & red 45 12
642 CD10 6fr blk, grnsh gray & yel 70 45

Flax, Shuttle and Mills
A221

1967, June 3 Photo. *Perf. 11½*

643 A221 6fr tan & multi 60 25

Belgian linen industry.

Old Kursaal, Ostend
A222

1967, June 3 Engraved and Photo.

644 A222 2fr dk brn, lt bl & yel 30 12

700th anniversary of Ostend as a city.

Type of 1967 Inscribed: "FITCE"

Engraved and Photogravure

1967, June 24 *Perf. 11½*

645 A219 10fr ultra, sep & emer 90 45

Issued to commemorate the meeting of the Federation of Common Market Telecommunications Engineers, Brussels, July 3–8.

Tourist Issue

Type of 1966

Designs: No. 646, British War Memorial, Ypres. No. 647, Castle, Spontin.

1967, July 15 Engraved

646 A213 1fr grn, lt bl, sal & brn 30 5
647 A213 1fr ind, lt bl & ol 30 5

Caesar Crossing Rubicon, 15th Century Tapestry
A223

Design: No. 649, Emperor Maximilian Killing a Boar, 16th century tapestry.

1967, Sept. 2 Photo. *Perf. 11½*

648 A223 1fr multi 20 12
649 A223 1fr multi 20 12

Issued for the Charles Plisnier and Lodewijk de Raet Foundations.

Arms of University of Ghent
A224

Princess Margaret of York
A225

Design: No. 651, Arms of University of Liège.

Engraved and Photogravure

1967, Sept. 30 *Perf. 11½*

650 A224 3fr gray & multi 30 10
651 A224 3fr gray & multi 30 10

Issued to commemorate the 150th anniversaries of the Universities of Ghent and Liège.

1967, Sept. 30 Photogravure

652 A225 6fr multi 65 30

British Week, Sept. 28–Oct. 2.

"Virga Jesse," Hasselt
A226

1967, Nov. 11 Engraved *Perf. 11½*

653 A226 1fr sl bl 20 12

Christmas, 1967.

Hand Guarding Worker
A227

Military Mailman, 1916, by James Thiriar
A228

1968, Feb. 3 Photo. *Perf. 11½*

655 A227 3fr multi 32 7

Issued to publicize industrial safety.

Engraved and Photogravure

1968, Mar. 17 *Perf. 11½*

656 A228 3fr sep, lt bl & brn 35 7

Issued for Stamp Day, 1968.

No. 394 Surcharged Like Nos. 528–529.

1968 Typographed *Perf. 13½x14*

657 A108 15c on 50c bl 12 5

View of Grammont and Seal of Baudouin VI
A229

Stamp of 1866, No. 23
A230

Historic Sites: 3fr, Theux-Franchimont fortress, sword and seal. 6fr, Neolithic cave and artifacts, Spiennes. 10fr, Roman oil lamp and St. Medard's Church, Wervik.

1968, Apr. 13 Photo. *Perf. 11½*

659 A229 2fr bl, blk, lil & rose 30 10
660 A229 3fr org, blk & car 32 12
661 A229 6fr ultra, ind & bis 50 25
662 A229 10fr tan, blk, yel & gray 65 55

1968, Apr. 13 Engr. *Perf. 13*

663 A230 1fr black 15 10

Centenary of the Malines Stamp Printery.

Europa Issue, 1968
Common Design Type

1968, Apr. 27 Photo. *Perf. 11½*

Size: 35x24mm.

664 CD11 3fr dl grn, gold & blk 35 12
665 CD11 6fr car, sil & blk 65 42

Tourist Issue
Types of 1965–66

Designs: No. 666, City Hall, Louvain. No. 667, Ourthe Valley. No. 668, Fountain and Kursaal, Spa. No. 669, Windmill at Bokrijk.

1968 Engraved *Perf. 11½*

666 A201 1fr brt rose lil, lt bl & blk 25 7
667 A213 1fr blk, grnsh bl & ol 25 10
668 A213 2fr bl, brt grn & blk 25 10
669 A202 2fr blk, lt bl & yel 25 10

Issue dates: 2fr values, June 24. 1fr values, Dec. 16.

St. Laurent Abbey, Liège
A232

Designs: 3fr, Gothic Church, Lisseweghe. 6fr, Barges in Zandvliet locks. 10fr, Ronquieres canal ship lift.

Engraved and Photogravure

1968, Sept. 7 *Perf. 11½*

670 A232 2fr ultra, gray ol & sep 35 18
671 A232 3fr ol bis, gray & sep 45 10
672 A232 6fr ind, brt bl & sep 55 25
673 A232 10fr bis, brt bl & sep 80 50

See also No. 675.

Christmas Candle
A233

Engraved and Photogravure

1968, Dec. 7 *Perf. 11½*

674 A233 1fr multi 12 7

Christmas, 1968.

Type of 1968

Design: 6fr, Ship in Neuzen Lock, Ghent Canal.

1968, Dec. 14

675 A232 6fr blk, grnsh bl & ol 55 25

Opening of lock at Neuzen, Netherlands.

St. Albertus Magnus—A234

1969, Feb. 15 Engraved *Perf. 11½*

676 A234 2fr sepia 30 12

The Church of St. Paul in Antwerp (16th century) was destroyed by fire in Apr. 1968.

Ruins of Aulne Abbey, Gozee
A235

1969, Feb. 15 Engr. and Photo.

677 A235 3fr brt pink & blk 32 10

Aulne Abbey was destroyed in 1794 during the French Revolution.

The Travelers, Roman Sculpture
A236

Broodjes Chapel, Antwerp
A237

1969, Mar. 15 Engraved *Perf. 11½*

678 A236 2fr vio brn 25 10

2,000th anniversary of city of Arlon.

1969, Mar. 15 Engraved & Photo.

679 A237 3fr gray & blk 35 10

Issued to commemorate the 150th anniversary of public education in Antwerp.

Lion Type of 1951 and Baudouin Type of 1953

1969–72 Photo. *Perf. 13½x12½*

Size: 17½x22mm.

680 A108 1fr rose 10.00 4.00
680A A111 1.50fr gray ('70) 65 45
b. Bklt pane of 10 8.50
c. Bklt. pane of 6 (3#680A + 3#681C) 20.00
680D A108 2fr emer ('72) 60 7
e. Booklet pane of 6 (4 #680D + 2 #681C) 5.50
f. Booklet pane of 5 (#680D,#681D + label) 8.00
680G A111 2.50fr org brn ('70) 12.50 10.00
h. Bklt. pane of 6 (#680G + 5#681C) 22.50
681 A111 3fr lil rose 1.25 50
a. Bklt pane of 5 + label 35.00
b. Bklt pane of 8 (2#680 + 6#681) 25.00
681C A111 3.50fr brt yel grn ('70) 1.00 10
681D A111 4.50fr dl red brn ('72) 2.00 7
Nos. 680-681D (7) 28.00 15.19

Nos. 680–681D were issued in booklet panes only and have 1 or 2 straight edges. All panes have a large selvage, the size of 2, 4 or 6 stamps, with inscription or map of Belgium showing postal zones.

Post Office Train
A238

1969, Apr. 13 Photo. *Perf. 11½*

682 A238 3fr multi 30 7

Issued for Stamp Day.

Europa Issue, 1969
Common Design Type

1969, Apr. 26

Size: 35x24mm.

683 CD12 3fr lt grn, brn & blk 40 15
684 CD12 6fr sal, rose car & blk 70 45

NATO Type of 1959 Redrawn and Dated "1949–1969"

1969, May 31 Photo. *Perf. 11½*

685 A142 6fr org brn & ultra 75 45

Issued to commemorate the 20th anniversary of the North Atlantic Treaty Organization.

No. 685 inscribed Belgique-Belgie and OTAN-NAVO.

Construction Workers, by F. Leger
A240

Bicyclist
A241

1969, May 31

686 A240 3fr multi 32 7

Issued to commemorate the 50th anniversary of the International Labor Organization.

1969, July 5 Photo. *Perf. 11½*

687 A241 6fr rose & multi 65 30

Issued to publicize the World Bicycling Road Championships, Terlaemen to Zolder, Aug. 10.

Ribbon in Benelux Colors
A242

1969, Sept. 6 Photo. *Perf. 11½*

688 A242 3fr blk, red, ultra & yel 38 10

Issued to commemorate the 25th anniversary of the signing of the customs union of Belgium, Netherlands and Luxembourg.

Annevoie Garden and Pascali Rose
A243

Design: No. 690, Lochristi Garden and begonia.

1969, Sept. 6

689 A243 2fr multi 32 15
690 A243 2fr multi 32 15

Tourist Issue
Type of 1966 and

View of Furnes
A244

Design: No. 691, Mountain Road, Vielsalm.

1969, Sept. 6 Engraved

691 A213 2fr blk, lt bl & yel grn 30 12
692 A244 2fr car, lt bl & dk brn 30 12

See Nos. 711–712.

Armstrong, Collins, Aldrin and Map Showing Tranquillity Base
A245

1969, Sept. 20 Photogravure

693 A245 6fr black 65 32

See note after Algeria No. 427. See also No. B846.

Wounded Veteran
A246

Mailman
A247

1969, Oct. 11 Engr. *Perf. 11½*

694	A246	1fr bl gray	20	7

Issued to publicize the national war veterans' aid organization (O.N.I.G.). The design is similar to type SP10.

1969, Oct. 18 Photogravure

695	A247	1fr dp rose & multi	15	7

Issued to publicize youth philately. Design by Danielle Saintenoy, 14.

Kennedy Tunnel Under the Schelde, Antwerp
A248

Design: 6fr, Three highways crossing near Loncin.

1969, Nov. 8 Engraved *Perf. 11½*

696	A248	3fr multi	60	12
697	A248	6fr multi	70	45

Issued to publicize the John F. Kennedy Tunnel under the Schelde and the Walloon auto route and interchange near Loncin.

Henry Carton de Wiart, by Gaston Geleyn
A249

1969, Nov. 8

698	A249	6fr sepia	60	25

Issued to commemorate the centenary of the birth of Count Henry Carton de Wiart (1869–1951), statesman.

The Census at Bethlehem (detail), by Peter Brueghel
A250

1969, Dec. 13 Photogravure

699	A250	1.50fr multi	25	7

Christmas, 1969.

Symbols of Bank's Activity, 100fr Coin
A251

1969, Dec. 13

Engraved and Photogravure

700	A251	3.50fr lt ultra, blk & sil	30	7

Issued to commemorate the 50th anniversary of the Industrial Credit Bank (Société nationale de crédit à l'industrie).

Camellia
A252

Beeches in Botanical Garden
A253

Flowers: 2.50fr, Water lily. 3.50fr, Azalea.

1970, Jan. 31 Photo. *Perf. 11½*

701	A252	1.50fr multi	15	10
702	A252	2.50fr multi	45	28
703	A252	3.50fr multi	40	15
a.		Souvenir sheet of 3	3.25	3.25

Ghent International Flower Exhibition.

No. 703a contains one each of Nos. 701–703, and was issued Apr. 25. It carries gray United Nations and U.N. Refugee emblems in margin. Size: 121x90mm. Sold for 25fr.

Engraved and Photogravure

1970, Mar. 7 *Perf. 11½*

Design: 7fr, Birches.

704	A253	3.50fr yel & multi	60	10
705	A253	7fr grn & multi	75	40

European Nature Conservation Year.

Mailman
A254

1970, Apr. 4 Photogravure

706	A254	1.50fr multi	25	7

Issued for Youth Stamp Day.

New UPU Headquarters and Monument, Bern
A255

1970, Apr. 12 Engr. and Photo.

707	A255	3.50fr grn & lt grn	60	8

Issued to commemorate the opening of the new Universal Postal Union Headquarters, Bern.

Europa Issue, 1970

Common Design Type

1970, May 1 Photo. *Perf. 11½*

Size: 35x24mm.

708	CD13	3.50fr rose cl, yel & blk	50	15
709	CD13	7fr ultra, pink & blk	70	45

Cooperative Alliance Emblem
A257

1970, June 27 Photo. *Perf. 11½*

710	A257	7fr blk & org	65	22

Issued to commemorate the 75th anniversary of the International Cooperative Alliance.

Tourist Type of 1969 and

Ship in Ghent Terneuzen Lock, Zelzate
A258

Designs: No. 711, Romanesque Cathedral and Gothic fountain, Nivelles (vert.). No. 712, Water mill, Kasterlee. No. 714, Clock Tower, Virton (vert.).

1970 Engr. & Photo.

711	A244	1.50fr sl, sky bl & bis	30	10
712	A244	1.50fr blk, bl & ol	30	10
713	A258	2.50fr ind & lt bl	45	15
714	A258	2.50fr dk pur & ocher	35	15

Issue dates: Nos. 711–712, July 6. Nos. 713–714, June 27.

Lion Type of 1951

1970–73 Typo. *Perf. 13½x14*

Size: 17½x21mm.

714A	A108	2fr emer ('73)	12	5
715	A108	2.50fr brown	22	8
716	A108	3fr brt pink	25	5

No. 714A differs from No. 614B in size and in some design details. On No. 714A, the "2" has a thicker base and the dash below "F" is thinner.

King Baudouin
A259

1970–73 Engraved *Perf. 11½*

Size: 24x21mm.

717	A259	1.75fr grn ('71)	1.50	15
717A	A259	2.25fr gray grn ('72)	1.50	15
717B	A259	3fr emer ('73)	25	3
718	A259	3.50fr org brn	1.00	5
719	A259	3.50fr brn ('71)	75	5
720	A259	4fr bl ('72)	1.25	5
720A	A259	4.50fr brn ('72)	60	5
720B	A259	5fr lil ('72)	30	5
720C	A259	6fr rose car ('72)	35	12
721	A259	7fr ver ('71)	40	8
722	A259	8fr blk ('72)	50	12
723	A259	9fr ol bis ('71)	1.75	8
724	A259	10fr rose car ('71)	1.00	8
724A	A259	12fr Prus bl ('72)	1.00	10
725	A259	15fr lt vio ('71)	90	10
726	A259	18fr stl bl ('71)	4.50	20
727	A259	20fr vio bl ('71)	1.20	10
727A	A259	30fr ocher ('72)	1.75	15
		Nos. 717-727A (18)	20.50	1.71

No. 718 was issued Sept. 7, 1970, King Baudouin's 40th birthday, and is inscribed "1930–1970." Dates are omitted on other stamps of type A259.

Nos. 720 and 720B were also issued in coils in 1973 and Nos. 720C and 722 in 1978, with black control number on back of every fifth stamp.

See Nos. 802–804, 890–902, 924–925, 980–981.

U.N. Headquarters, N.Y.
A260

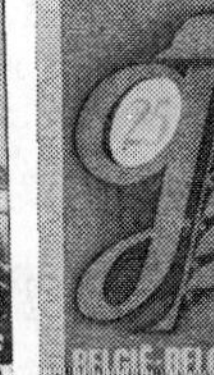

Fair Emblem
A261

1970, Sept. 12 Engr. and Photo.

728	A260	7fr dk brn & Prus bl	65	25

25th anniversary of the United Nations.

1970, Sept. 19

729	A261	1.50fr bis, org & brn	25	7

Issued to publicize the 25th International Fair at Ghent, Sept. 12–27.

Queen Fabiola
A262

The Mason, by Georges Minne
A263

1970, Sept. 19

730	A262	3.50fr lt bl & blk	35	7

Issued to publicize the Queen Fabiola Foundation for Mental Health.

Engraved and Photogravure

1970, Oct. 17 *Perf. 11½*

731	A263	3.50fr dl yel & sep	38	7

Issued to commemorate the 50th anniversary of the National Housing Society.

Man, Woman and City—A264

1970, Oct. 17 Photogravure

732	A264	2.50fr blk & multi	38	18

Issued to commemorate the 25th anniversary of the Social Security System.

Madonna with the Grapes, by Jean Gossaert
A265

1970, Nov. 14 Engraved *Perf. 11½*

733	A265	1.50fr dk brn	22	7

Christmas 1970.

Arms of Eupen, Malmédy and Saint-Vith
A266

Engraved and Photogravure

1970, Dec. 12 *Perf. 11½*

734	A266	7fr sep & dk brn	60	25

The 50th anniversary of the return of the districts of Eupen, Malmédy and Saint-Vith.

Automatic Telephone
A267

Touring Club Emblem
A269

"Auto"
A268

1971, Jan. 16 Photo. *Perf. 11½*

735 A267 1.50fr multi 25 7

Automatization of Belgian telephone system.

1971, Jan. 16

736 A268 2.50fr car & blk 38 18

Fiftieth Automobile Show, Brussels, Jan. 19–31.

1971, Feb. 13

737 A269 3.50fr ultra & multi 38 7

Belgian Touring Club, 75th anniversary.

Tournai Cathedral
A270

1971, Feb. 13 Engraved

738 A270 7fr brt bl 75 32

Cathedral of Tournai, 8th centenary.

Redrawn
Baudouin Type of 1953

1971–72 Photo. *Perf. 11½*

Size: 21x24mm.

738A A111 2.50fr org brn 75 7
738B A111 4.50fr brn ('72) 2.50 1.35
738C A111 7fr blue 90 12

On Nos. 738A–738C the 2, 4 and 7 are 3mm high. The background around the head is white. On Nos. 463, 482A and 483B the 2, 4 and 7 are 2½mm high, tinted background.

"The Letter Box," by T. Lobrichon
A271

1971, March 13 Engr. *Perf. 11½*

739 A271 1.50fr dk brn 25 8

Youth philately.

Albert I, Jules Destrée and Academy—A272

Engraved and Photogravure

1971, Apr. 17 *Perf. 11½*

740 A272 7fr gray & blk 65 30

50th anniversary of the founding of the Royal Academy of Language and French Literature.

Mailman
A273

1971, Apr. 25

741 A273 3.50fr multi 38 7

Stamp Day.

Europa Issue, 1971
Common Design Type

1971, May 1 Photogravure

Size: 35x24mm.

742 CD14 3.50fr ol & blk 45 10
743 CD14 7fr dk ol grn & blk 90 45

Radar Ground Station
A275

1971, May 15 Photo. *Perf. 11½*

744 A275 7fr multi 65 25

3rd World Telecommunications Day.

Antarctic Explorer, Ship and Penguins—A276

1971, June 19 Photo. *Perf. 11½*

745 A276 10fr multi 1.10 60

Tenth anniversary of the Antarctic Treaty pledging peaceful uses of and scientific cooperation in Antarctica.

Orval Abbey
A277

1971, June 26 Engraved *Perf. 11½*

746 A277 2.50fr chocolate 32 15

9th centenary of the Abbey of Notre Dame, Orval.

Georges Hubin
A278

1971, June 26 Engr. and Photo.

747 A278 1.50fr vio bl & blk 32 8

Georges Hubin (1863–1947), socialist leader and Minister of State.

Mr. and Mrs. Goliath, the Giants of Ath
A279

View of Ghent—A280

1971, Aug. 7 Photogravure

748 A279 2.50fr multi 30 12

Engraved

749 A280 2.50fr gray brn 30 15

Test Tubes and Insulin Molecular Diagram—A281

1971, Aug. 7 Photogravure

750 A281 10fr lt gray & multi 85 45

50th anniversary of the discovery of insulin.

City Hall and Belfry, Mons—A282

Family and "50"—A283

1971 Engraved *Perf. 11½*

Designs: 1.50fr, City Hall, Cloth Guild and statue of Margarethe of Austria, Malines (horiz.). No. 753, St. Martin's Church, Aalst. No. 754, Abbey and fountain, St. Hubert.

751 A282 1.50fr dk bl & buff 40 8
752 A282 2.50fr vio, buff & blk 25 8
753 A282 2.50fr vio, lt bl, blk & ol 40 8
754 A282 2.50fr vio bl & yel 40 8

Tourist issue.

1971, Sept. 11 Photogravure

755 A283 1.50fr grn & multi 25 12

50th anniversary of the Belgian Large Families League.

Achaemenidaen Tomb, Buzpar, and Persian Coat of Arms—A284

Engraved and Photogravure

1971, Oct. 2 *Perf. 11½*

756 A284 7fr multi 65 25

2500th anniversary of the founding of the Persian empire by Cyrus the Great.

Dr. Jules Bordet
A285

Flight into Egypt, Anonymous
A286

Portrait: No. 758, Stijn Streuvels.

1971, Oct. 2 Engraved

757 A285 3.50fr sl grn 35 8
758 A285 3.50fr dk brn 35 8

No. 757 honors Dr. Jules Bordet (1870–1945), serologist and immunologist; No. 758, Stijn Streuvels (1871–1945), novelist whose pen name was Frank Lateur.

1971, Nov. 13 Photogravure

759 A286 1.50fr multi 20 12

Christmas 1971.

Federation Emblem
A287

Book Year Emblem
A288

1971, Nov. 13

760 A287 3.50fr blk, ultra & gold 38 10

25th anniversary of the Federation of Belgian Industries (FIB).

1972, Feb. 19

761 A288 7fr bis, blk & bl 65 30

International Book Year 1972.

Coins of Belgium and Luxembourg
A289

1972, Feb. 19 **Engr. & Photo.**

762 A289 1.50fr org blk & sil 38 15

Economic Union of Belgium and Luxembourg, 50th anniversary.

Traffic Signal and Road Signs
A290

1972, Feb. 19 **Photogravure**

763 A290 3.50fr bl & multi 38 10

Via Secura (road safety), 25th anniversary.

Belgica '72 Emblem
A291

1972, Mar. 27

764 A291 3.50fr choc, bl & lil 38 7

International Philatelic Exhibition, Brussels, June 24–July 9.

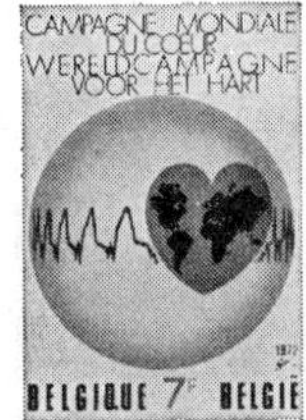

"Your Heart is your Health"
A292

Auguste Vermeylen
A293

1972, Mar. 27

765 A292 7fr blk, gray, red & bl 65 30

World Health Day.

1972, Mar. 27

766 A293 2.50fr multi 30 15

Centenary of the birth of Auguste Vermeylen (1872–1945), Flemish writer and educator. Portrait by Isidore Opsomer.

Astronaut on Moon
A294

1972, Apr. 23

767 A294 3.50fr multi 38 12

Stamp Day 1972.

Europa Issue 1972
Common Design Type

1972, Apr. 29

Size: 24x35mm.

768 CD16 3.50fr lt bl & multi 45 10
769 CD16 7fr rose & multi 70 45

"Freedom of the Press"
A296

1972, May 13 **Photo.** ***Perf. 11½***

770 A296 2.50fr org brn, buff & blk 38 12

50th anniversary of the BELGA news information agency and 25th Congress of the International Federation of Newspaper Editors (F.I.E.J.), Brussels, May 15–19.

Freight Cars with Automatic Coupling
A297

1972, June 3

771 A297 7fr bl & multi 65 30

International Railroad Union, 50th anniversary.

View of Couvin
A298

Design: No. 773, Aldeneik Church, Maaseik (vert.).

1972, June 24 **Engr.** ***Perf. 13½x14***

772 A298 2.50fr bl, vio brn & sl grn 60 30
773 A298 2.50fr dk brn & bl 60 30

Beatrice, by Gustave de Smet
A299

Radar Station, Intelsat 4
A300

1972, Sept. 9 **Photo.** ***Perf. 11½***

774 A299 3fr multi 32 12

Youth philately.

1972, Sept. 16

775 A300 3.50fr lt bl, sil & blk 40 10

Opening of the Lessive satellite earth station.

Frans Masereel, Self-portrait
A301

Adoration of the Kings, by Felix Timmermans
A302

1972, Oct. 21

776 A301 4.50fr lt ol & blk 55 6

Frans Masereel (1889–1972), wood engraver.

1972, Nov. 11 **Photo.** ***Perf. 11½***

777 A302 3.50fr blk & multi 32 12

Christmas 1972.

Maria Theresa, Anonymous
A303

1972, Dec. 16 **Photo.** ***Perf. 11½***

778 A303 2fr multi 32 18

200th anniversary of the Belgian Academy of Science, Literature and Art, founded by Empress Maria Theresa.

WMO Emblem, Meterological Institute, Ukkel
A304

1973, Mar. 24 **Photo.** ***Perf. 11½***

779 A304 9fr bl & multi 75 30

Centenary of international meteorological cooperation.

"Fire"
A305

Man and WHO Emblem
A306

1973, Mar. 24

780 A305 2fr multi 60 18

National industrial fire prevention campaign.

1973, Apr. 7

781 A306 8fr dk red, ocher & blk 75 35

25th anniversary of World Health Organization.

Europa Issue 1973
Common Design Type

1973, Apr. 28

Size: 35x24mm.

782 CD16 4.50fr org brn, vio bl & yel 45 10
783 CD16 8fr ol, dk bl & yel 90 45

Thurn and Taxis Courier
A308

Arrows Circling Globe
A309

1973, Apr. 28 ***Perf. 11½***

Engraved and Photogravure

784 A308 4.50fr blk & red brn 40 7

Stamp Day.

1973, May 12 **Photogravure**

785 A309 3.50fr dp ocher & multi 35 7

5th International Telecommunications Day.

Workers' Sports Exhibition Poster, Ghent, 1913
A310

1973, May 12

786 A310 4.50fr multi 45 15

60th anniversary of the International Workers' Sports Movement.

Fair Emblem
A311

1973, May 12 **Photo.** ***Perf. 11½***

787 A311 4.50fr multi 40 10

25th International Fair, Liège, May 12–27.

DC-10 and 1923 Biplane over Brussels Airport—A312

Design: 10fr, Tips biplane, 1908.

1973, May 19 **Engr. & Photo.**

788 A312 8fr gray bl, blk & ultra 70 35
789 A312 10fr grn, lt bl & blk 1.50 45

50th anniversary of SABENA, Belgian airline (No. 788) and 25th anniversary of the "Vieilles Tiges" Belgian flying pioneers' society (No. 789).

Adolphe Sax and Tenor Saxophone
A313

Fresco from Bathhouse, Ostend
A314

1973, Sept. 15 **Photogravure**

790 A313 9fr grn, blk & bl 65 25

Adolphe Sax (1814-1894), inventor of saxophone.

1973, Sept. 15

791 A314 4.50fr multi 40 10

Year of the Spa.

St. Nicholas Church, Eupen
A315

Charley, by Henri Evenepoel
A316

1973, Oct. 1 **Engraved** ***Perf. 13***

792 A315 2fr plum, sep & lt vio 25 12

1973, Oct. 13 **Photo.** ***Perf. 11½***

793 A316 3fr multi 32 12

Youth philately.

Luminescent Paper

Starting with No. 794, all stamps are on luminescent paper unless otherwise noted.

Jean-Baptiste Moens
A317

1973, Oct. 13 **Photo. & Engr.**

794 A317 10fr gray & multi 90 40

50th anniversary of the Belgian Stamp Dealers' Association. Printed in sheets of 12 stamps and 12 labels showing association emblem.

Adoration of the Shepherds, by Hugo van der Goes
A318

Louis Pierard, by M. I. Ianchelevici
A319

1973, Nov. 17 **Engr.** ***Perf. 11½***

795 A318 4fr blue 40 12

Christmas 1973.

1973, Nov. 17 **Photo. & Engr.**

796 A319 4fr ver & buff 45 12

Louis Pierard (1886-1952), journalist, member of Parliament.

Highway, Automobile Club Emblem
A320

1973, Nov. 17 **Photogravure**

797 A320 5fr yel & multi 45 12

50th anniversary of the Vlaamse Automobile Club.

Early Microphone, Emblem of Radio Belgium
A321

1973, Nov. 24 **Photo. & Engr.**

798 A321 4fr bl & blk 38 12

50th anniversary of Radio Belgium.

Town Hall, Léau
A322

Design: 4fr, Chimay Castle.

1973, Nov. 26 **Engraved** ***Perf. 13***

799 A322 3fr blk, lt bl & mar 45 12
800 A322 4fr grnsh blk & grnsh bl 22 12

Felicien Rops, Self-portrait
A323

Photogravure and Engraved

1973, Dec. 8 ***Perf. 11½***

801 A323 7fr tan & blk 60 25

Felicien Rops (1833-1898), painter and engraver.

King Type of 1970-73

1973 Photogravure *Perf. 12½x13½*

Size: 22x17mm.

802 A259 3fr emerald 3.75 15
a. Booklet pane of 4 (#802 and 3 #803) + labels 10.00
803 A259 4fr blue 1.00 5
804 A259 5fr lilac 60 5
a. Booklet pane of 4 + labels 2.75

Nos. 802-804 were issued in booklet panes only and have 1 or 2 straight edges, except No. 802 which has only one. Stamps within the panes are tête bêche and each pane has 2 labels showing Belgian postal emblem, also a large selvage, the size of 6 stamps, with zip code instruction.

See No. 923a.

King Albert
A324

Sun, Bird, Flowers and Girl
A325

1974, Feb. 16 **Photo.** ***Perf. 11½***

805 A324 4fr Prus grn & blk 42 18

King Albert, 1875-1934.

1974, Mar. 25 **Photo.** ***Perf. 11½***

806 A325 3fr vio & multi 45 15

Protection of the environment.

NATO Emblem
A326

1974, Apr. 20 **Photo.** ***Perf. 11½***

807 A326 10fr dp to lt bl 85 35

25th anniversary of the signing of the North Atlantic Treaty.

Hubert Krains
A327

"Destroyed City," by Ossip Zadkine
A328

Engraved and Photogravure

1974, Apr. 27 ***Perf. 11½***

808 A327 5fr blk & gray 40 8

Stamp Day.

Europa Issue 1974

1974, May 4

Design: 10fr, Solidarity, by Georges Minne.

809 A328 5fr blk & red 60 10
810 A328 10fr blk & ultra 1.10 45

Children
A329

1974, May 18 **Photo.** ***Perf. 11½***

811 A329 4fr lt bl & multi 40 15

10th Lay Youth Festival.

Planetarium, Brussels
A330

Soleilmont Abbey Ruins—A331

Engraved and Photogravure

1974, June 22 ***Perf. 11½***

Designs: 4fr, Pillory, Braine-le-Chateau. 7fr, Fountain, Ghent (procession symbolic of Chamber of Rhetoric). 10fr, Belfry, Bruges (vert.).

812 A330 3fr sky bl & blk 40 10
813 A330 4fr lil rose & blk 50 10
814 A331 5fr lt grn & blk 55 12
815 A331 7fr dl yel & blk 75 35
816 A330 10fr blk, bl & brn 90 40
Nos. 812-816 (5) 3.10 1.07

Historic buildings and monuments.

"BENE-LUX"
A332

1974, Sept. 7 **Photo.** ***Perf. 11½***

865 A332 5fr bl grn, dk grn & lt bl 40 8

30th anniversary of the signing of the customs union of Belgium, Netherlands and Luxembourg.

Jan Vekemans, by Cornelis de Vos
A333

1974, Sept. 14

866 A333 3fr multi 38 12

Youth philately.

Leon Tresignies, Willebroek Canal Bridge
A334

1974, Sept. 28 **Engr. & Photo.**

867 A334 4fr brn & ol grn 32 12

60th death anniversary of Corporal Leon Tresignies (1886-1914), hero of World War I.

Montgomery Blair, UPU Emblem
A335

Design: 10fr, Heinrich von Stephan and UPU emblem.

Engraved and Photogravure

1974, Oct. 5 ***Perf. 11½***

868 A335 5fr grn & blk 60 12
869 A335 10fr brick red & blk 90 35

Centenary of Universal Postal Union.

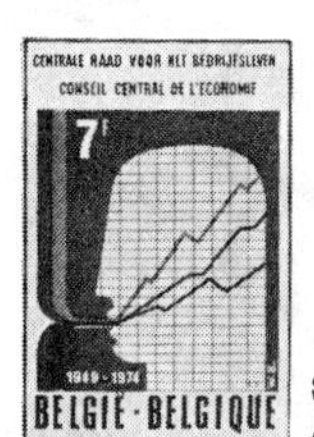

Symbolic Chart
A336

1974, Oct. 12 Photo. *Perf. 11½*

870 A336 7fr multi 75 30

Central Economic Council, 25th anniversary.

Rotary Emblem
A337

1974, Oct. 19

871 A337 10fr multi 75 38

Rotary International of Belgium.

Wild Boar (Regiment's Emblem)
A338

1974, Oct. 26

872 A338 3fr multi 40 15

Granting of the colors to the Ardennes Chasseurs Regiment, 40th anniversary.

Aarshot Church
A339

Gemmenich Border: Belgium, Germany, Netherlands
A340

Design: No. 875, St. Monan and Church, Nassogne.

1974, Nov. 4 Engraved *Perf. 13*

873 A339 3fr brn blk & yel 35 15
874 A340 4fr grnsh blk & bl 45 15
875 A340 4fr grnsh blk & bl 40 15

Tourist issue. 3fr is not luminescent.

Angel, by Van Eyck Brothers
A341

1974, Nov. 16 *Perf. 11½*

876 A341 4fr rose lil 40 15

Christmas 1974. The Angel shown is from the triptyque "The Mystical Lamb" in the Saint-Bavon Cathedral, Ghent.

Adolphe Quetelet, by J. Odevaere
A342

1974, Dec. 14 Engr. & Photo.

877 A342 10fr blk & buff 75 30

Death centenary of Adolphe Quetelet (1796–1874), statistician, astronomer and Secretary of Royal Academy of Brussels.

Lion Type of 1951

1974–75 Typo. *Perf. 13½x14*

Size: 17½x21mm.

878 A108 5c brt pink 5 5
881 A108 2.50fr lt brn ('81) 16 4
882 A108 4fr brt rose lil 30 5
883 A108 4.50fr blue 1.40 3
884 A108 5fr brt lil ('75) 32 5

Baudouin Type of 1970–73

1974–77 Engraved *Perf. 11½*

Size: 24x21mm.

890 A259 2.50fr gray grn 25 3
891 A259 3.25fr vio brn ('75) 38 3
893 A259 4.50fr grnsh bl 30 3
894 A259 6.50fr vio blk 45 3
895 A259 7.50fr brt pink ('75) 45 3
896 A259 9fr red brn ('80) 55 6
897 A259 11fr gray ('76) 70 30
898 A259 13fr sl ('75) 85 6
899 A259 14fr gray grn ('76) 85 15
900 A259 16fr grn ('77) 90 8
901 A259 17fr dl mag ('75) 1.00 15
902 A259 18fr grnsh bl ('80) 1.10 12
903 A259 22fr black 9.50 5.50
904 A259 22fr lt grn ('79) 1.35 30
905 A259 25fr lil ('75) 1.50 15
906 A259 35fr emer ('80) 1.85 20
910 A259 40fr dk bl ('77) 2.10 22
911 A259 45fr brn ('80) 2.75 35
Nos. 890-911 (18) 26.83 7.79

Themabelga Emblem
A343

Neoregelia Carolinae
A344

1975, Feb. 15 Photo. *Perf. 11½*

912 A343 6.50fr grn, blk & org 60 10

Themabelga, International Thematic Stamp Exhibition, Brussels, Dec. 13–21, 1975.

1975, Feb. 22

Flowers: 5fr, Coltsfoot. 6.50fr, Azalea.

913 A344 4.50fr multi 28 15

Photogravure and Engraved

914 A344 5fr multi 45 15
915 A344 6.50fr multi 65 15

Ghent International Flower Exhibition, Apr. 26–May 5.

School Emblem, Man Leading Boy
A345

Engraved and Photogravure

1975, Mar. 15 *Perf. 11½*

916 A345 4.50fr blk & multi 40 8

Centenary of the founding of the Charles Buls Normal School for Boys, Brussels.

Davids Foundation Emblem
A346

1975, Mar. 22 Photogravure

917 A346 5fr yel & multi 40 6

Centenary of the Davids Foundation, a Catholic organization for the promotion of Flemish through education and books.

King Albert
A347

Mailman, 1840, by James Thiriar
A348

1975, Apr. 5 Engr. & Photo.

918 A347 10fr blk & mar 75 35

King Albert (1875–1934), birth centenary.

1975, Apr. 19 Engr. *Perf. 11½*

919 A348 6.50fr dl mag 60 8

Stamp Day 1975.

St. John, from Last Supper, by Bouts
A349

Concentration Camp Symbols
A350

Europa Issue 1975

Design: 10fr, Woman's Head, detail from "Trial by Fire," by Dirk Bouts.

1975, Apr. 26 Engr. & Photo.

920 A349 6.50fr blk, grn & bl 70 25
921 A349 10fr blk, ocher & red 60 20

1975, May 3 Photogravure

Design: "B" denoted political prisoners, "KG" prisoners of war.

922 A350 4.50fr multi 40 12

Liberation of concentration camps, 30th anniversary.

Lion Type of 1951 and King Type of 1970–73

Perf. 13½x12½, 12½x13½

1975 Photogravure

Size: 17x22mm., 22x17mm.

923 A108 50c lt bl 30 3
a. Booklet pane of 4 (#923, 924 and 2#804) + labels 1.00
b. Booklet pane of 4 (#923 and 3#925) + labels 1.35
924 A259 4.50fr grnsh bl 50 5
925 A259 6.50fr dl pur 55 6

Nos. 923–925 were issued in booklet panes only. Nos. 923–924 have 1 straight edge, No. 925 has 1 or 2. Stamps within the panes are tete-beche and each pane has 2 labels showing Belgian postal emblem, also a large selvage, the size of 6 stamps, with zip code instructions.

Hospice of St. John, Bruges
A351

Church of St. Loup, Namur
A352

Design: 10fr, Martyrs' Square, Brussels.

1975, May 12 Engr. *Perf. 11½*

926 A351 4.50fr dp rose lil 38 18
927 A352 5fr sl grn 45 18
928 A351 10fr brt bl 75 30

European Architectural Heritage Year.

Church Tower, Dottignies
A353

Grand-Place, Sint-Truiden—A354

1975, May 24

929 A353 4.50fr multi 90 22
930 A354 5fr multi 45 12

Tourism. No. 929 is not luminescent.

Library, Louvain University, Ryckmans and Cerfaux
A355

1975, June 7 Photo. *Perf. 11½*

931 A355 10fr dl bl & sep 75 30

25th anniversary of Louvain Bible Colloquium, founded by Professors Gonzague Ryckmans (1887–1969) and Lucien Cerfaux (1883–1968).

"Metamorphose" by Pol Mara
A356

Marie Popelin, Palace of Justice, Brussels
A357

1975, June 14

932 A356 7fr multi 60 30

Queen Fabiola Mental Health Foundation.

1975, June 21 Engr. & Photo.

933 A357 6.50fr grn & cl 60 10

International Women's Year 1975. Marie Popelin (1846–1913), first Belgian woman doctor of law.

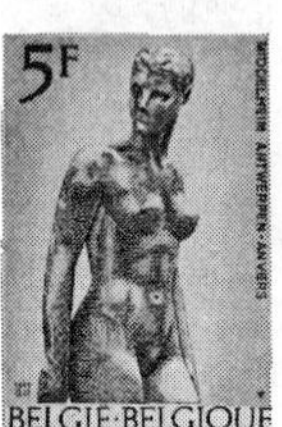

Assia, by Charles Despiau
A358

Cornelia Vekemans, by Cornelis de Vos
A359

Engraved & Photogravure

1975, Sept. 6 *Perf. 11½*

934 A358 5fr yel grn & blk 38 15

Middelheim Outdoor Museum, 25th anniversary.

1975, Sept. 20 Photogravure

935 A359 4.50fr multi 35 15

Youth philately.

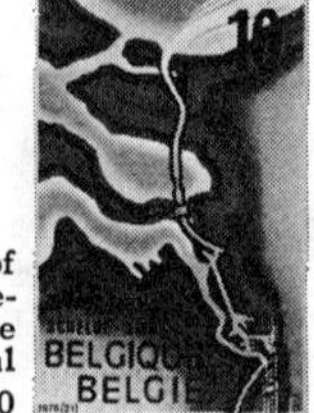

Map of Schelde-Rhine Canal
A360

1975, Sept. 20

936 A360 10fr multi 75 25

Opening of connection between the Schelde and Rhine, Sept. 23, 1975.

National Bank, W. F. Orban, Founder
A361

Photogravure and Engraved

1975, Oct. 11 *Perf. 12½x13*

937 A361 25fr multi 1.75 45

National Bank of Belgium, 125th anniversary.

Edmond Thieffry and Plane, 1925
A362

1975, Oct. 18 *Perf. 11½*

938 A362 7fr blk & lil 55 25

First flight Brussels to Kinshasa, Congo, 50th anniversary.

"Seat of Wisdom" St. Peter's, Louvain
A363

Photogravure and Engraved

1975, Nov. 8 *Perf. 11½*

939 A363 6.50fr bl, blk & grn 45 8

University of Louvain, 550th anniversary.

Angels, by Rogier van der Weyden
A364

1975, Nov. 15

940 A364 5fr multi 40 15

Christmas 1975.

Willemsfonds Emblem
A365

American Bicentennial Emblem
A366

1976, Feb. 21 Photo. *Perf. 11½*

941 A365 5fr multi 38 10

125th anniversary of the Willems Foundation, which supports Flemish language and literature.

1976, Mar. 13 Photo. *Perf. 11½*

942 A366 14fr gold, red, bl & blk 1.00 45

American Bicentennial.

No. 942 printed checkerwise in sheets of 30 stamps and 30 gold and black labels which show medal with 1626 seal of New York. Black engraved inscription on labels commemorates arrival of first Walloon settlers in Nieu Nederland.

Cardinal Mercier
A367

Symbolic of V.E.V.
A368

1976, Mar. 20 Engraved

943 A367 4.50fr brt rose lil 45 15

Désiré Joseph Cardinal Mercier (1851–1926), professor at Louvain University, spiritual and patriotic leader during World War I, 50th death anniversary.

1976, Apr. 3 Photo. *Perf. 11½*

944 A368 6.50fr multi 50 6

Flemish Economic Organization (Vlaams Ekonomisch Verbond), 50th anniversary.

General Post Office, Brussels
A369

1976, Apr. 24 Engr. *Perf. 11½*

945 A369 6.50fr sepia 50 6

Stamp Day.

Europa Issue 1976

Potter's Hands
A370

Design: 6.50fr, Basket maker (vert.).

1976, May 8 Photogravure

946 A370 6.50fr multi 70 12

947 A370 14fr multi 90 42

Truck on Road
A371

1976, May 8

948 A371 14fr blk, yel & red 1.00 42

15th International Road Union Congress, Brussels, May 9–13.

Queen Elisabeth
A372

1976, May 24 *Perf. 11½*

949 A372 14fr green 1.00 42

Queen Elisabeth (1876–1965), birth centenary.

Ardennes Draft Horses
A373

1976, June 19

950 A373 5fr multi 45 12

Ardennes Draft Horses Association, 50th anniversary.

Souvenir Sheets

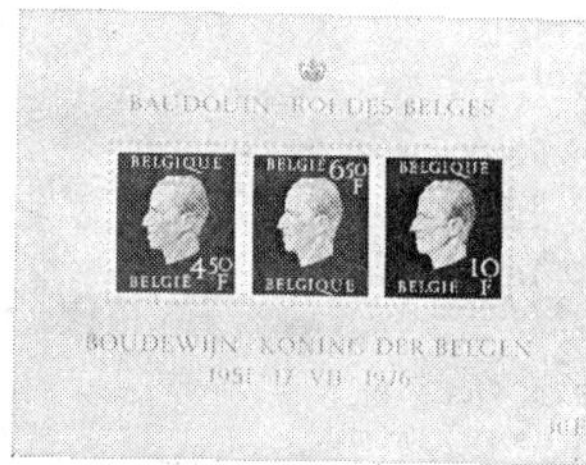

King Baudouin—A374

1976, June 26

951	A374	Sheet of 3	4.25	4.25
a.		4.50fr gray	1.25	1.25
b.		6.50fr ocher	1.25	1.25
c.		10fr brick red	1.25	1.25
952	A374	Sheet of 2	8.50	8.50
a.		20fr yel grn	3.25	3.25
b.		30fr Prus bl	3.25	3.25

25th anniversary of the reign of King Baudouin. Nos. 951–952 have silver marginal inscriptions. Size: 110x82mm. No. 951 sold for 30fr, No. 952 for 70fr. The surtax went to a new foundation for the improvement of living conditions in honor of the King.

Electric Train and Society Emblem
A375

1976, Sept. 11 Photo. *Perf. 11½*

953 A375 6.50fr multi 55 8

National Belgian Railroad Society, 50th anniversary.

William of Nassau, Prince of Orange
A376

1976, Sept. 11 Engraved

954 A376 10fr sl grn 70 18

400th anniversary of the pacification of Ghent.

New Subway Train
A377

1976, Sept. 18 Photogravure

955 A377 6.50fr multi 55 8

Opening of first line of Brussels subway.

Young Musician, by W. C. Duyster A378

1976, Oct. 2 Photo. ***Perf. 11½***

956	A378	4.50fr multi	60	18

Young musicians and youth philately.

Charles Bernard A379

St. Jerome in the Mountains, by Le Patinier A380

Blind Leading the Blind, by Breughel the Elder A381

Design: No. 958, Fernand Victor Toussaint van Boelaere.

1976, Oct. 16 Engraved

957	A379	5fr violet	40	10
958	A379	5fr red brn & sep	40	10
959	A380	6.50fr dk brn	60	8
960	A381	6.50fr sl grn	60	8

Charles Bernard (1875–1961), French-speaking journalist; Toussaint van Boelaere (1875–1947), Flemish journalist; No. 950, Charles Plisnier Belgian-French Cultural Society. No. 960, Association for Language Promotion.

Remouchamps Caves A382

Hunnegem Priory, Gramont, and Madonna A383

Designs: No. 963, River Lys and St. Martin's Church. No. 964, Ham-sur-Heure Castle.

1976, Oct. 23 Engr. ***Perf. 13***

961	A382	4.50fr multi	40	12
962	A383	4.50fr multi	40	12
963	A383	5fr multi	45	15
964	A383	5fr multi	45	15

Tourism. Nos. 961–962 are not luminescent.

Nativity, by Master of Flemalle A384

1976, Nov. 20 ***Perf. 11½***

965	A384	5fr violet	35	15

Christmas 1976.

Rubens' Monogram—A385

Photogravure and Engraved

1977, Feb. 12 ***Perf. 11½***

966	A385	6.50fr lil & blk	55	6

Peter Paul Rubens (1577–1640), painter, 400th birth anniversary.

King Type of 1970–73 and

Heraldic Lion A386

1977–78 Typo. ***Perf. 13½x14***

Size: 17x20mm.

967	A386	50c brn ('80)	4	3
968	A386	1fr brt lil	6	3
969	A386	1.50fr gray ('78)	10	3
970	A386	2fr yel ('78)	14	3
971	A386	2.75fr Prus bl ('80)	20	5
972	A386	3fr vio ('78)	18	3
973	A386	4fr red brn ('80)	28	6
974	A386	4.50fr lt ultra	30	5
975	A386	5fr grn ('80)	35	8
976	A386	6fr dl red brn	42	3

Perf. 13½x12½, 12½x13½

1978, Aug. Photogravure

Size: 17x22mm, 22x17mm.

977	A386	1fr brt lil	35	3
a.		Booklet pane of 4 (#977-978 and 2 #980)	1.50	
b.		Booklet pane of 4 (#977, 979 and 2 #981)	2.00	
978	A386	2fr yellow	40	3
979	A386	3fr violet	55	3
980	A259	6fr carmine	42	5
981	A259	8fr gray	65	8

Nos. 977–981 were issued in booklets only. Nos. 977–979 have one straight edge, Nos. 980–981 have 2. Nos. 980 and 981 are tete-beche within the panes. Each pane has 2 labels showing Belgian postal emblem, also a large selvage, the size of 6 stamps, with zip code instructions. Nos. 977–981 are not luminescent.

Anniversary Emblem A387

1977, Mar. 14 Photo. ***Perf. 11½***

982	A387	6.50fr sil & multi	50	6

Royal Belgian Association of Civil and Agricultural Engineers, 50th anniversary.

Birds and Lions Emblem A388

1977, Mar. 28

983	A388	14fr multi	90	35

Belgian District No. 112 of Lions International, 25th anniversary.

Pillar Box, 1852 A389

1977, Apr. 23 Engraved

984	A389	6.50fr sl grn	50	6

Stamp Day 1977.

Europa Issue 1977

Gileppe Dam, Jalhay A390

Design: 14fr, War Memorial, Yser at Nieuport.

1977, May 7 Photo. ***Perf. 11½***

985	A390	6.50fr multi	85	10
986	A390	14fr multi	85	45

Mars and Mercury Association Emblem A391

1977, May 14

987	A391	5fr multi	32	12

Mars and Mercury Association of Reserve and Retired Officers, 50th anniversary.

Prince de Hornes Coat of Arms A392

Conversion of St. Hubertus A394

Battle of the Golden Spur, from Oxford Chest—A393

Design: 6.50fr, Froissart writing book.

1977, June 11 Engr. ***Perf. 11½***

988	A392	4.50fr violet	40	12
989	A393	5fr red	42	12
990	A394	6.50fr dk brn	50	6
991	A394	14fr sl grn	70	45

300th anniversary of the Principality of Overijse (4.50fr); 675th anniversary of the Battle of the Golden Spur (5fr); 600th anniversary of publication of first volume of the Chronicles of Jehan Froissart (6.50fr); 1250th anniversary of the death of St. Hubertus (14fr).

Rubens, Self-portrait A395

1977, June 25 Photogravure

992	A395	5fr multi	45	18
a.		Souvenir sheet of 3	2.10	2.10

Peter Paul Rubens (1577–1640), painter, 400th birth anniversary. No. 992a contains 3 No. 992; decorative margin. Size: 100x152mm. Sold for 20fr.

Open Book, from The Lamb of God, by Van Eyck Brothers—A396

1977, Sept. 3 Photo. ***Perf. 11½***

993	A396	10fr multi	65	35

International Federation of Library Associations (IFLA), 50th Anniversary Congress, Brussels, Sept. 5–10.

Gymnast and Soccer Player A397

Designs: 6.50fr, Fencers in wheelchairs (horiz.). 10fr, Basketball players. 14fr, Hockey players.

1977, Sept. 10

994	A397	4.50fr multi	22	12
995	A397	6.50fr multi	35	6
996	A397	10fr multi	60	18
997	A397	14fr multi	90	45

Workers' Gymnastics and Sports Center, 50th anniversary (4.50fr); sport for the Handicapped (6.50fr); 20th European Basketball Championships (10fr); First World Hockey Cup (14fr).

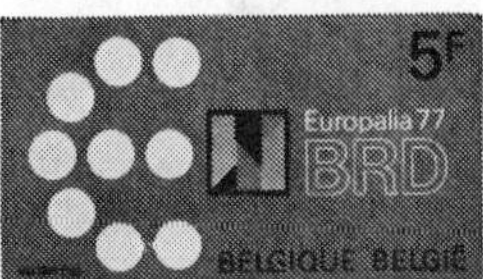

Europalia 77 Emblem—A398

1977, Sept. 17

998	A398	5fr gray & multi	40	12

5th Europalia Arts Festival, featuring German Federal Republic, Belgium, Oct.–Nov. 1977.

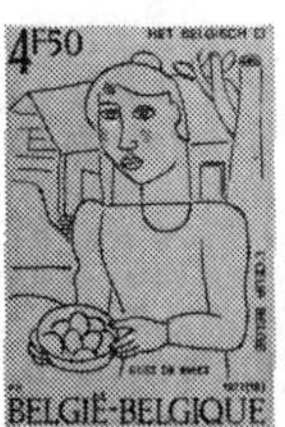

The Egg Farmer, by Gustave De Smet
A399

1977, Oct. 8 Engr. & Photo.

999 A399 4.50fr bis & blk 32 12

Publicity for Belgian eggs.

Mother and Daughter with Album, by Constant Cap
A400

1977, Oct. 15 Engraved

1000 A400 4.50fr dk brn 32 12

Youth Philately.

Bailiff's House, Gembloux
A401

Market Square, St. Nicholas
A402

Designs: No. 1002, St. Aldegonde Church and Cultural Center. No. 1004, Statue and bridge, Liège.

1977, Oct. 22

1001 A401 4.50fr multi 22 15
1002 A401 4.50fr multi 22 15
1003 A402 5fr multi 40 15
1004 A402 5fr multi 40 12

Tourism. Nos. 1001-1004 are not luminescent.
See Nos. 1017-1018, 1039-1040.

Nativity, by Rogier van der Weyden
A403

1977, Nov. 11 Engraved

1005 A403 5fr rose red 35 15

Christmas 1977.

Symbols of Transportation and Map
A404

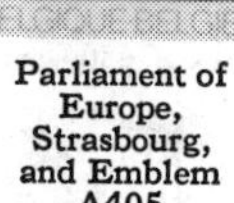

Parliament of Europe, Strasbourg, and Emblem
A405

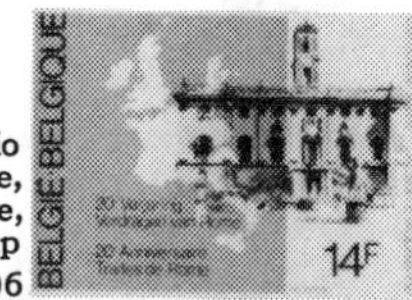

Campidoglio Palace, Rome, and Map
A406

Design: No. 1009, Paul-Henri Spaak and map of 19 European member countries.

1978, Mar. 18 Photo. *Perf. 11½*

1006 A404 10fr bl & multi 3.25 45
1007 A405 10fr bl & multi 3.25 45
1008 A406 14fr bl & multi 3.25 1.10
1009 A406 14fr bl & multi 3.25 1.10

European Action: 25th anniversary of the European Transport Ministers' Conference; 1st general elections for European Parliament; 20th anniversary of the signing of the Treaty of Rome; Paul-Henri Spaak (1899–1972), Belgian statesman who worked for the establishment of European Community.

Grimbergen Abbey—A407

1978, Apr. 1 Engraved

1010 A407 4.50fr red brn 32 12

850th anniversary of the Premonstratensian Abbey at Grimbergen.

Emblem
A408

No. 39 with First Day Cancel
A409

1978, Apr. 8 Photogravure

1011 A408 8fr multi 55 6

Ostend Chamber of Commerce and Industry, 175th anniversary.

1978, Apr. 15

1012 A409 8fr multi 55 6

Stamp Day.

Europa Issue

Pont des Trous, Tournai
A410

Design: 8fr, Antwerp Cathedral, by Vaclav Hollar (vert.).

Photogravure and Engraved

1978, May 6 *Perf. 11½*

1013 A410 8fr multi 60 8
1014 A410 14fr multi 85 35

Virgin of Ghent, Porcelain Plaque
A411

Paul Pastur Workers' University, Charleroi
A412

1978, Sept. 16 Photo. *Perf. 11½*

1015 A411 6fr multi 35 15
1016 A412 8fr multi 55 6

Municipal education in Ghent, 150th anniversary; Paul Pastur Workers' University, Charleroi, 75th anniversary. Nos. 1015–1016 are not luminescent.

Types of 1977 and

Tourist Guide, Brussels
A413

Designs: No. 1017, Jonathas House, Enghien. No. 1018, View of Wetteren and couple in local costume. No. 1020, Prince Carnival, Eupen-St. Vith.

1978, Sept. 25 Photo. & Engr.

1017 A401 4.50fr multi 28 15
1018 A402 4.50fr multi 28 15
1019 A413 6fr multi 42 15
1020 A413 6fr multi 42 15

Tourism. Nos. 1017–1020 are not luminescent.

Emblem
A414

1978, Oct. 7 Photogravure

1021 A414 8fr red & blk 55 8

Royal Flemish Engineer's Organization, 50th anniversary.

Young Philatelist
A415

1978, Oct. 14 Engr. *Perf. 11½*

1022 A415 4.50fr dk vio 32 8

Youth philately.

Nativity, Notre Dame, Huy
A416

1978, Nov. 18 Engr. *Perf. 11½*

1023 A416 6fr black 42 15

Christmas 1978.

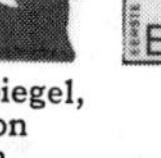

Tyll Eulenspiegel, Lay Action Emblem
A417

European Parliament Emblem
A418

1979, Mar. 3 Photo. *Perf. 11½*

1024 A417 4.50fr multi 32 6

10th anniversary of Lay Action Centers.

1979, Mar. 3

1025 A418 8fr multi 1.75 12

European Parliament, first direct elections, June 7–10.

St. Michael Banishing Lucifer
A419

1979, Mar. 17 Photo. & Engr.

1026 A419 4.50fr rose red & blk 28 12
1027 A419 8fr brt grn & blk 56 25

Millennium of Brussels.

NATO Emblem and Monument
A420

1979, Mar. 31 Photogravure

1028 A420 30fr multi 2.10 1.00

North Atlantic Treaty Organization, 30th anniversary.

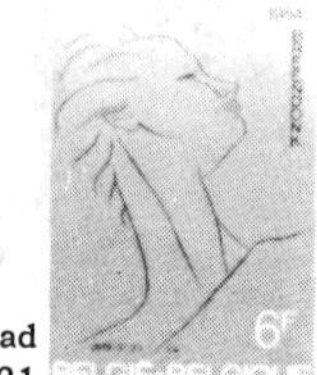

Prisoner's Head
A421

1979, Apr. 7 Photo. & Engr.

1029 A421 6fr org & blk 40 12

25th anniversary of the National Political Prisoners' Monument at Breendonk.

Belgium No. Q2
A422

1979, Apr. 21 Photo. *Perf. 11½*

1030 A422 8fr multi 56 12

Stamp Day 1979.

Europa Issue 1979

Mail Coach and Truck—A423

Design: 14fr, Chappe's heliograph, Intelsat satellite and dish antenna.

Photo. & Engr.

1979, Apr. 28 *Perf. 11½*
1031 A423 8fr multi 75 25
1032 A423 14fr multi 90 35

Chamber of Commerce Emblem
A424

1979, May 19 Photo. *Perf. 11½*
1033 A424 8fr multi 56 12

Verviers Chamber of Commerce and Industry, 175th anniversary.

"50" Emblem
A425

1979, June 9 Photo. *Perf. 11½*
1034 A425 4.50fr gold & ultra 32 6

National Fund for Professional Credit, 50th anniversary.

Merchants, Roman Bas-relief—A426

1979, June 9
1035 A426 10fr multi 60 12

Belgian Chamber of Trade and Commerce, 50th anniversary.

"Tintin" as Philatelist
A427

1979, Sept. 29 Photo. *Perf. 11½*
1036 A427 8fr multi 50 20

Youth philately.

Tourism Types of 1977

Designs: No. 1037, Belfry, Thuin. No. 1038, Royal Museum of Central Africa, Tervuren. No. 1039, St. Nicholas Church and cattle, Ciney. No. 1040, St. John's Church and statue of Our Lady, Poperinge.

Perf. 11½ (#1037, 1039), 13 (#1038, 1040)

1979, Oct. 22 **Photo & Engr.**
1037 A401 5fr multi 28 8
1038 A402 5fr multi 28 8
1039 A401 6fr multi 35 10
1040 A402 6fr multi 35 10

Francois Auguste Gevaert
A429

Piano, String Instruments
A430

Design: 6fr, Emmanuel Durlet.

Photo. & Engr.

1979, Nov. 3 *Perf. 11½*
1041 A429 5 fr brown 28 8
1042 A429 6fr brown 35 10
1043 A430 14fr brown 90 20

Francois Auguste Gevaert (1828-1908), musicologist and composer; Emmanuel Durlet (1893-1977), pianist; Queen Elisabeth Musical Chapel Foundation, 40th anniversary.

Virgin and Child, Notre Dame, Foy
A431

1979, Nov. 24 **Photo. & Engr.**
1044 A431 6fr lt grnsh bl 35 10

Christmas 1979.

Independence, 150th Anniversary
A432

1980, Jan. 26 **Photo** *Perf. 11½*
1045 A432 9fr 60 25

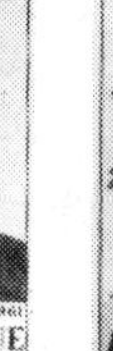

Frans van Cauwelaert
A433

Spring Flowers
A434

1980, Feb. 25 **Engraved**
1046 A433 5fr gray 35 8

Frans van Cauwelaert (1880-1961), Minister of State.

1980, Mar. 10 **Photo.**
Multicolored
1047 A434 5fr *shown* 28 8
1048 A434 6.50fr *Summer flowers* 35 10
1049 A434 9fr *Autumn flowers* 65 15

Ghent Flower Show, Apr. 19-27.

Telephone and Telegraph Administration, 50th Anniversary—A435

1980, Apr. 14 **Photo.** *Perf. 11½*
1050 A435 10fr multi 70 20

Belgium No. C4—A436

1980, Apr. 21
1051 A436 9fr multi 55 15

Stamp Day.

Europa Issue 1980

St. Benedict, by Hans Memling—A437

Design: 14fr, Margaret of Austria (1480-1530).

1980, Apr. 28
1052 A437 9fr multi 80 15
1053 A437 14fr multi 1.25 20

Palais des Nations, Brussels—A438

1980, May 10 **Photo.** *Perf. 11½*
1054 A438 5fr multi 35 10

4th Interparliamentary Conference for European Cooperation and Security, Brussels, May 12-18.

Golden Carriage, 1780, Mons—A439

Design: No. 1056, Canal landscape, Damme.

1980, May 17
1055 A439 6.50fr multi 40 10
1056 A439 6.50fr multi 40 10

Tourism.

Souvenir Sheet

Royal Mint Theater, Brussels—A440

1980, May 31 **Photo. & Engr.** *Perf. 11½*
1057 A440 50fr black 5.25 5.75

150th anniversary of independence. Multicolored decorative margin; sold for 75fr. Size: 100½x151mm.

King Baudouin, 50th Birthday—A441

1980, Sept. 6 **Photo.** *Perf. 11½*
1058 A441 9fr rose cl 60 15

View of Chiny—A442

Portal and Court, Diest—A443

1980 **Engr.** *Perf. 13*
1059 A442 5fr multi 35 10
1060 A443 5fr multi 35 10

Tourism. Nos. 1059-1060 are not luminescent. Issue dates: No. 1059, Sept. 27; No. 1060, Dec. 13. See Nos. 1072-1075.

Emblem of Belgian Heart League—A444

1980, Oct. 4 **Photo.** *Perf. 11½*
1061 A444 14fr bl & mag 85 20

Heart Week, Oct. 20-25.

Rodenbach Statue, Roulers—A445

1980, Oct. 11
1062 A445 9fr multi 55 15

Albrecht Rodenbach (1856-1880), poet.

Youth Philately—A446

1980, Oct. 27 **Photo.** ***Perf. 11½***
1063 A446 5fr multi 35 .10

National Broadcasting Service, 50th Anniversary—A447

1980, Nov. 10
1064 A447 10fr gray & blk 60 40

Garland and Nativity, by Daniel Seghers, 17th Century—A448

1980, Nov. 17
1065 A448 6.50fr multi 40 12

Christmas 1980.

Baron de Gerlache, by F.J. Navez A449

Leopold I, By Geefs A450

Design: 9fr, Baron de Stassart, by F.J. Navez.

1981, Mar. 16 **Photo.** ***Perf. 11½***
1066 A449 6fr multi 40 8
1067 A449 9fr multi 60 12

Photogravure & Engraved

1068 A450 50fr multi 3.00 1.50

Sesquicentennial of Chamber of Deputies, Senate and Dynasty.

Europa Issue 1981

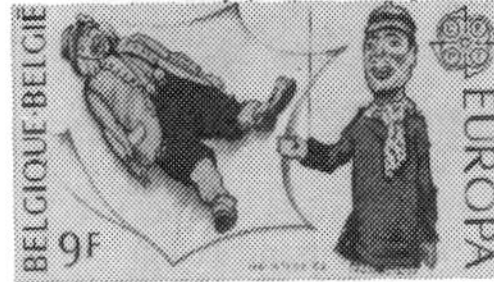

Tchantchès and Op-Signoorke, Puppets—A451

1981, May 4 **Photo. & Engr.** ***Perf. 11½***
1069 A451 9fr shown 55 12
1070 A451 14fr d'Artagnan and Woltje 85 20

Impression of M.A. de Cock (Founder of Post Museum)—A452

1981, May 18 **Photo.**
1071 A452 9fr multi 60 12

Stamp Day.

Tourism Types of 1980

Designs: No. 1072, Virgin and Child statue, Our Lady's Church, Tongre-Notre Dame. No. 1073, Egmont Castle, Zottegem. No. 1074, Eau d'Heure River. No. 1075, Tongerlo Abbey, Antwerp.

1981, June 15 **Engr.** ***Perf. 11½***
1072 A442 6fr multi 35 8
1073 A442 6fr multi 35 8
1074 A443 6.50fr multi 45 12
1075 A443 6.50fr multi 45 12

Soccer Player A453

E. Remouchamps, Founder—A454

1981, Sept. 5 **Photo.** ***Perf. 11½***
1076 A453 6fr multi 42 8

Soccer in Belgium centenary; Royal Antwerp Soccer Club.

1981, Sept. 5 **Photo. & Engr.**
1077 A454 6.50fr multi 45 12

Walloon Language and Literature Club 125th anniv.

Audit Office Sesquicentennial—A455

1981, Sept. 12 **Engr.**
1078 A455 10fr tan & dk brn 60 20

French Horn—A456

1981, Sept. 12 **Photo.**
1079 A456 6.50fr multi 45 12

Vredekring (Peace Circle) Band of Antwerp centenary.

Souvenir Sheet

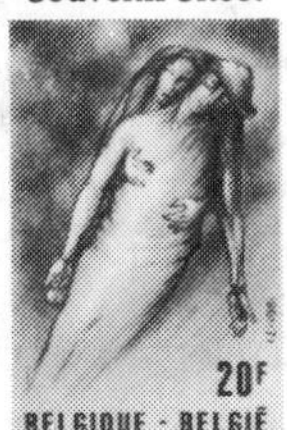

Pieta, by Ben Genaux—A457

1981, Sept. 19 **Photo.** ***Perf. 11½***
1080 A457 20fr multi 1.75 1.75

Mining disaster at Marcinelle, 25th anniv. Red brown and black margin shows mine fire. Size: 150x100mm. Sold for 30fr.

Mausoleum of Marie of Burgundy and Charles the Bold, Bruges—A458

1981, Oct. 10 **Photo. & Engr.**
1081 A458 50fr multi 3.00 1.25

Youth Philately—A459

1981, Oct. 24 **Photo.**
1082 A459 6fr multi 38 8

King Baudouin—A459a

King Baudouin—A460

1981, Nov. 5 **Photo. & Engr.** ***Perf. 11½***
1090 A459a 10fr blue 50 20
1099 A460 50fr lt grnsh bl & bl 2.75 1.00
1100 A460 65fr pale lil & blk 3.75 1.25
1102 A460 100fr lt bis brn & dk bl 5.75 2.00

Max Waller, Movement Founder A461

The Spirit Drinkers, by Gustave van de Woestyne A462

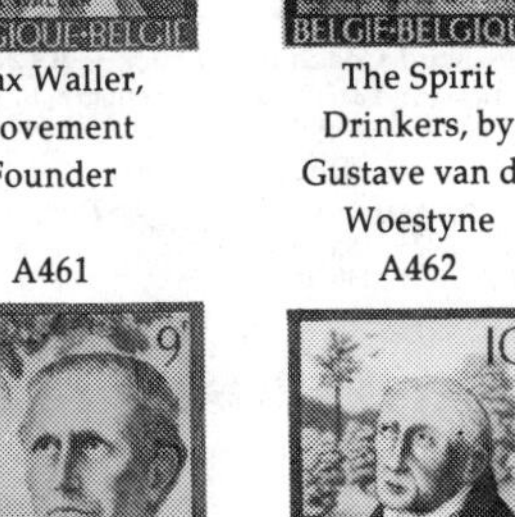

Fernand Severin, Poet, 50th Death Anniv. A463

Jan van Ruusbroec, Flemish Mystic, 500th Birth Anniv. A464

Thought and Man TV Series, 25th Anniv. A465

Nativity, 16th Cent. Engraving A466

1981, Nov. 7
1104 A461 6fr multi 35 8
1105 A462 6.50fr multi 38 8
1106 A463 9fr multi 55 12
1107 A464 10fr multi 60 20
1108 A465 14fr multi 80 25
Nos. 1104-1108 (5) 2.68 73

La Jeune Belgique cultural movement centenary (6fr).

1981, Nov. 21
1109 A466 6.50fr multi 38 8

Christmas 1981.

Royal Conservatory of Music Sesquicentennial—A467

Design: 9fr, Judiciary sesquicentennial.

1982, Jan. 25 **Photo.** ***Perf. 11½***
1110 A467 6.50fr multi 38 8
1111 A467 9fr multi 55 12

Galaxy and Microscope
A468

1982, Mar. 1

1112	A468	6fr multi		32	8
1113	A468	14fr multi		75	25
1114	A468	50fr multi		2.75	1.00

Radio-isotope production, Natl. Radio-elements Institute, Fleurus (6fr); Royal Belgian Observatory (14fr); centenary of TB bacillus discovery (50fr).

Joseph Lemaire (1882-1966), Minister of State—A469

1982, Apr. 17 **Photo.** ***Perf. 11½***

1115	A469	6.50fr multi	33	8

Europa 1982—A470

1982, May 1

1116	A470	10fr Universal suffrage	50	20
1117	A470	17fr Edict of Tolerance, 1781	85	30

Stamp Day—A471

1982, May 22 **Photo. & Engr.** ***Perf. 11½***

1118	A471	10fr multi	50	20

67th World Esperanto Congress, Anvers—A472

1982, June 7 **Photo.** ***Perf. 11½***

1119	A472	12fr Tower of Babel	60	25

Tourism Type of 1980

Designs: No. 1120, Tower of Gosselies. No. 1121, Zwijveke Abbey, Dendermonde. No. 1122, Stavelot Abbey. No. 1123, Villers-la-Ville Abbey ruins. No. 1124, Geraardsbergen Abbey entrance. No. 1125, Beveren Pillory.

1982, June 21 **Photo. & Engr.**

1120	A443	7fr lt bl & blk	35	15
1121	A443	7fr lt grn & blk	35	15
1122	A442	7.50fr tan & dk brn	38	18
1123	A442	7.50fr	38	18
1124	A443	7.50fr	38	18
1125	A443	7.50fr	38	18

Self Portrait, by L.P. Boon (b. 1912)
A473

Designs: 10fr, Adoration of the Shepherds, by Hugo van der Goes (1440-1482). 12fr, The King on His Throne, carving by M. de Ghelderode (1898-1962). 17fr, Madonna and Child, by Pieter Paulus (1881-1959).

1982, Sept. 13 **Photo.** ***Perf. 11½***

1126	A473	7fr multi	35	15
1127	A473	10fr multi	50	20
1128	A473	12fr multi	60	25
1129	A473	17fr multi	85	35

1982, Sept. 27

1130	A474	17fr multi	85	35

Youth Philately and Scouting Year—A475

1982, Oct. 2 **Photo.** ***Perf. 11½***

1131	A475	7fr multi	35	15

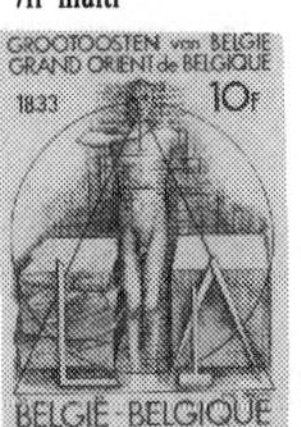

Grand Orient Lodge of Belgium Sesquicentennial—A476

1982, Oct. 16 **Photo. & Engr.**

1132	A476	10fr Man taking oath	50	20

Cardinal Joseph Cardijn (1882-1967)—A477

1982, Nov. 13 **Photo.** ***Perf.***

1133	A477	10fr multi	50	20

St. Francis of Assisi (1182-1226)—A478

1982, Nov. 27

1134	A478	20fr multi	1.00	40

Horse-drawn Trolley—A479

1983, Feb. 12 **Photo.** ***Perf. 11½***

1135	A479	7.50fr shown	38	18
1136	A479	10fr Electric trolley	50	20
1137	A479	50fr Trolley, diff.	2.50	1.00

Intl. Fed. for Periodical Press, 24th World Congress, Brussels, May 11-13—A480

1983, Mar. 19 **Photo.** ***Perf. 11½***

1138	A480	20fr multi	1.40	40

Homage to Women—A481

1983, Apr. 16

1139	A481	8fr Operator	55	16
1140	A481	11fr Homemaker	80	22
1141	A481	20fr Executive	1.40	40

Stamp Day—A482

1983, Apr. 23

1142	A482	11fr multi	80	22

SEMI-POSTAL STAMPS.

St. Martin of Tours Dividing His Cloak with a Beggar
SP1 SP2

Perf. 14

1910, June 1 Typo. Unwmkd.

B1	SP1	1c gray	2.50	2.00
B2	SP1	2c pur brn	20.00	17.50
B3	SP1	5c pck bl	5.50	4.00
B4	SP1	10c brn red	5.00	4.00
B5	SP2	1c gray grn	5.25	3.50
B6	SP2	2c vio brn	15.00	11.00
B7	SP2	5c pck bl	5.25	4.25
B8	SP2	10c carmine	5.00	4.00
		Nos. B1-B8 (8)	63.50	50.25

Overprinted "1911" in Black.

1911, Apr. 1

B9	SP1	1c gray	27.50	20.00
B10	SP1	2c pur brn	75.00	65.00
B11	SP1	5c pck bl	7.50	6.00
B12	SP1	10c brn red	7.50	6.00
a.		Double overprint		
B13	SP2	1c gray grn	55.00	45.00
a.		Inverted overprint		
B14	SP2	2c vio brn	50.00	42.50
B15	SP2	5c pck bl	7.50	6.00
a.		Double overprint		
B16	SP2	10c carmine	7.50	6.00
		Nos. B9-B16 (8)	237.50	196.50

Overprinted "CHARLEROI—1911".

1911, June

B17	SP1	1c gray	7.00	4.50
B18	SP1	2c pur brn	22.50	20.00
B19	SP1	5c pck bl	13.50	12.00
B20	SP1	10c brn red	10.00	9.00
B21	SP2	1c gray grn	8.00	6.00
B22	SP2	2c vio brn	25.00	22.50
B23	SP2	5c pck bl	10.00	9.00
B24	SP2	10c carmine	8.00	8.00
		Nos. B17-B24 (8)	104.00	91.00

Nos. B1–B24 were sold at double face value, except the 10c denominations which were sold for 15c. The surtax benefited the national anti-tuberculosis organization.

SP3

Mérode Monument SP4 — King Albert I SP5

1914, Oct. 3 Lithographed

B25	SP3	5c grn & red	1.75	1.00
B26	SP3	10c red	50	50
B27	SP3	20c vio & red	26.50	23.50

1914, Oct. 3

B28	SP4	5c grn & red	7.00	4.25
B29	SP4	10c red	7.00	4.25
B30	SP4	20c vio & red	85.00	65.00

Counterfeits of Nos. B25–B30 abound.

1915, Jan. 1 *Perf. 12, 14*

B31	SP5	5c grn & red	13.50	4.25
a.		Perf. 12x14	25.00	17.50
B32	SP5	10c rose & red	20.00	7.50
B33	SP5	20c vio & red	75.00	17.50
a.		Perf. 14x12	450.00	325.00
b.		Perf. 12	85.00	47.50

Nos. B25–B33 were sold at double face value. The surtax benefited the Red Cross.

Types of Regular Issue of 1915 Surcharged in Red:

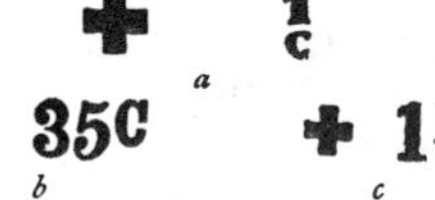

1918, Jan. 15 Typographed *Perf. 14*

B34	A46 (a)	1c +1c dp org	55	55
B35	A46 (a)	2c +2c brn	65	65
B36	A46 (a)	5c +5c bl grn	2.50	2.25
B37	A46 (a)	10c +10c red	4.50	3.75
B38	A46 (a)	15c +15c brt vio	6.50	5.25
B39	A46 (a)	20c +20c plum	15.00	11.00
B40	A46 (a)	25c +25c ultra	16.00	12.50

Engraved.

B41	A47 (b)	35c +35c lt vio & blk	21.00	18.50
B42	A48 (b)	40c +40c dl red & blk	21.00	18.50
B43	A49 (b)	50c +50c turq bl & blk	25.00	24.00
B44	A50 (c)	1f +1f bluish sl	72.50	57.50
B45	A51 (c)	2f +2f dp gray grn	190.00	165.00
B46	A52 (c)	5f +5f brn	475.00	425.00
B47	A53 (c)	10f +10f dp bl	1,000.	750.00
		Nos. B34-B47 (14)	1,850.20	1,494.45

Discus Thrower SP6 — Runner SP8

Racing Chariot SP7

1920, May 20 Engraved *Perf. 12*

B48	SP6	5c +5c dp grn	5.50	5.00
B49	SP7	10c +5c car	5.50	4.25
B50	SP8	15c +15c dk brn	11.50	3.75

Issued to commemorate the 7th International Olympic Games of 1920. The surtax was to benefit wounded soldiers. Imperforates exist.

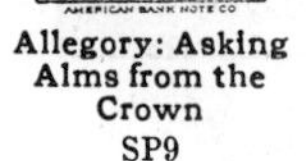

Allegory: Asking Alms from the Crown SP9 — Wounded Veteran SP10

1922, May 20

B51	SP9	20c +20c brn	2.50	3.25

1923, July 5

B52	SP10	20c +20c sl gray	4.00	4.50

The surtax on Nos. B51–B52 was to aid wounded veterans.

SP11 SP12

St. Martin, by Van Dyck
SP13 SP14

1925, Dec. 15 Typo. *Perf. 14*

B53	SP11	15c +15c dl vio & red	50	50
B54	SP11	30c +5c gray & red	35	40
B55	SP11	1fr +10c chlky bl & red	2.00	1.75

The surtax on Nos. B53–B55 benefited the National Anti-Tuberculosis League.

1926, Feb. 10

B56	SP12	30c +30c bluish grn (red surch.)	90	1.10
B57	SP13	1fr +1fr lt bl	14.00	15.00
B58	SP14	1fr +1fr lt bl	2.25	3.00

The surtax on Nos. B56–B58 aided victims of the Meuse flood.

Lion and Cross of Lorraine SP15 — Queen Elisabeth and King Albert SP16

1926, Dec. 6 Typographed *Perf. 14*

B59	SP15	5c +5c dk brn	30	30
B60	SP15	20c +5c red brn	1.25	1.10
B61	SP15	50c +5c dl vio	60	22

Engraved

Perf. 11½.

B62	SP16	1.50fr +25c dk bl	2.00	2.00
B63	SP16	5fr +1fr rose red	15.00	15.00
		Nos. B59-B63 (5)	19.15	18.62

The surtax on Nos. B59–B63 was used to benefit tubercular war veterans.

Boat Adrift
SP17

1927, Dec. 15 Engr. *Perf. 11½, 14*

B64	SP17	25c +10c dk brn	1.50	1.50
B65	SP17	35c +10c yel grn	1.50	1.50
B66	SP17	60c +10c dp vio	1.25	65
B67	SP17	1.75fr +25c dk bl	3.75	3.75
B68	SP17	5fr +1fr plum	9.50	10.00
		Nos. B64-B68 (5)	17.50	17.40

The surtax on these stamps was divided among several charitable associations.

Ogives of Orval Abbey SP18 — Monk Carving Capital of Column SP19

Ruins of Orval Abbey SP20

Design: 60c+15c, 1.75fr+25c, 3fr+1fr, Countess Matilda recovering her ring.

1928, Sept. 15 Photo. *Perf. 11½*

B69	SP18	5c +5c red & gold	65	55
B70	SP18	25c +5c dk vio & gold	1.10	1.10

Engraved.

B71	SP19	35c +10c dp grn	2.50	2.50
B72	SP19	60c +15c red brn	3.50	75
B73	SP19	1.75fr +25c dk bl	11.00	7.25
B74	SP19	2fr +40c dp vio	20.00	22.50
B75	SP19	3fr +1fr red	22.50	25.00

Perf. 14.

B76	SP20	5fr +5fr rose lake	32.50	35.00
B77	SP20	10fr +10fr ol brn	32.50	37.50
		Nos. B69-B77 (9)	126.25	132.15

The surtax on these stamps was to be used toward the restoration of the ruined Abbey of Orval.

St. Waudru, Mons SP22 — St. Rombaut, Malines SP23

Designs: 25c + 15c, Cathedral of Tournai. 60c + 15c, St. Bavon, Ghent. 1.75fr + 25c, St. Gudule, Brussels. 5fr + 5fr, Louvain Library.

1928, Dec. 1 Photo. *Perf. 14, 11½*

B78	SP22	5c +5c car	50	40
a.		Booklet pane of 9		
B79	SP22	25c +15c ol brn	75	60
a.		Booklet pane of 9		

Engraved.

B80	SP23	35c +10c dp grn	1.75	2.00
a.		Booklet pane of 4		
B81	SP23	60c +15c red brn	75	40
a.		Booklet pane of 4		
B82	SP23	1.75fr +25c vio bl	21.00	14.00
B83	SP23	5fr +5fr red vio	25.00	27.50
		Nos. B78-B83 (6)	49.75	44.90

The surtax was for anti-tuberculosis work.

Orval Abbey Stamps of 1928 Overprinted in Blue or Red

1929, Aug. 19

B84	SP18	5c +5c red & gold	150.00	165.00

B85	SP18	25c	+5c dk vio & gold (R)	150.00	165.00
B86	SP19	35c	+10c dp grn (R)	150.00	165.00
B87	SP19	60c	+15c red brn	150.00	165.00
B88	SP19	1.75fr	+25c dk bl (R)	150.00	165.00
B89	SP19	2fr	+40c dp vio (R)	150.00	165.00
B90	SP19	3fr	+1fr red	150.00	165.00
B91	SP20	5fr	+5fr rose lake	150.00	165.00
B92	SP20	10fr	+10fr dk brn (R)	150.00	165.00
			Nos. B84-B92 (9)	1,350.	1,485.

Issued in commemoration of the laying of the first stone toward the restoration of the ruined Abbey of Orval. Forgeries of the overprint exist.

Waterfall at Coo
SP28

Bayard Rock, Dinant
SP29

Designs: 35c+10c, Menin Gate, Ypres. 60c+15c, Promenade d'Orleans, Spa. 1.75fr+25c, Antwerp Harbor. 5fr+5fr, Quai Vert, Bruges.

1929, Dec. 2 Engr. *Perf. 11½, 14*

B93	SP28	5c	+5c red brn	25	35
B94	SP29	25c	+15c gray blk	1.00	1.20
B95	SP28	35c	+10c grn	1.50	1.75
B96	SP28	60c	+15c rose lake	75	40
B97	SP28	1.75fr	+25c dp bl	10.00	6.75
B98	SP29	5fr	+5fr dl vio	42.50	45.00
			Nos. B93-B98 (6)	56.00	55.45

Bornhem
SP34

Beloeil
SP35

Gaesbeek
SP36

Designs: 25c + 15c, Wynendaele. 70c + 15c, Oydonck. 1fr+25c, Ghent. 1.75fr+25c, Bouillon.

1930, Dec. 1 Photo. *Perf. 14*

B99	SP34	10c	+5c vio	38	30
B100	SP34	25c	+15c ol brn	1.00	70

Engraved.

B101	SP35	40c	+10c brn vio	1.25	1.25
B102	SP35	70c	+15c gray blk	75	50
B103	SP35	1fr	+25c rose lake	5.50	5.25
B104	SP35	1.75fr	+25c dp bl	6.25	4.25
B105	SP36	5fr	+5fr gray grn	42.50	52.50
			Nos. B99-B105 (7)	57.63	64.75

Prince Leopold
SP41

Queen Elisabeth
SP42

Philatelic Exhibition Issue.

Souvenir Sheet.

1931, July 18 Photo. *Perf. 14*

B106	SP41	2.45fr	+55c car brn	160.00	185.00

Issued in sheets measuring 122x159mm. Sold exclusively at the Brussels Philatelic Exhibition, July 18th to 21st, 1931. The surtax was for the Veterans' Relief Fund.

1931, Dec. 1 Engraved

B107	SP42	10c	+5c red brn	80	55
B108	SP42	25c	+15c dk vio	1.75	2.00
B109	SP42	50c	+10c dk grn	1.75	1.40
B110	SP42	75c	+15c blk brn	1.75	65
B111	SP42	1fr	+25c rose lake	16.50	9.00
B112	SP42	1.75fr	+25c ultra	13.00	6.75
B113	SP42	5fr	+5fr brn vio	90.00	100.00
			Nos. B107-B113 (7)	125.55	120.35

The surtax was for the National Anti-Tuberculosis League.

Désiré Cardinal Mercier
SP43

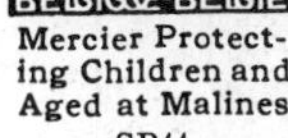

Mercier Protecting Children and Aged at Malines
SP44

Mercier as Professor at Louvain University
SP45

Mercier in Full Canonicals, Giving His Blessing
SP46

1932, June 10 Photo. *Perf. 14½x14*

B114	SP43	10c	+10c dk vio	1.00	1.00
B115	SP43	50c	+30c brt vio	4.00	4.00
B116	SP43	75c	+25c ol brn	3.50	2.50
B117	SP43	1fr	+2fr brn red	11.00	14.00

Engraved.

Perf. 11½.

B118	SP44	1.75fr	+75c dp bl	125.00	135.00
B119	SP45	2.50fr	+2.50fr dk brn	110.00	125.00
B120	SP44	3fr	+4.50fr dl grn	110.00	125.00
B121	SP45	5fr	+20fr vio brn	150.00	135.00
B122	SP46	10fr	+40fr brn lake	275.00	350.00
			Nos. B114-B122 (9)	789.50	891.50

Issued in commemoration of Cardinal Mercier and to obtain funds to erect a monument to his memory.

Belgian Infantryman
SP47

Sanatorium at Waterloo
SP48

1932, Aug. 4 *Perf. 14½x14*

B123	SP47	75c	+3.25fr red brn	80.00	85.00
B124	SP47	1.75fr	+4.25fr dk bl	80.00	85.00

Issued in commemoration of the Belgian soldiers who fought in World War I and to obtain funds to erect a national monument to their glory.

1932, Dec. 1 Photo. *Perf. 13½x14*

B125	SP48	10c	+5c dk vio	1.00	90
B126	SP48	25c	+15c red vio	2.50	1.75
B127	SP48	50c	+10c red brn	2.00	1.75
B128	SP48	75c	+15c ol brn	2.00	1.10
B129	SP48	1fr	+25c dp red	17.50	15.00
B130	SP48	1.75fr	+25c dp bl	14.00	13.00
B131	SP48	5fr	+5fr gray grn	150.00	150.00
			Nos. B125-B131 (7)	189.00	183.50

The surtax was for the assistance of the National Anti-Tuberculosis Society at Waterloo.

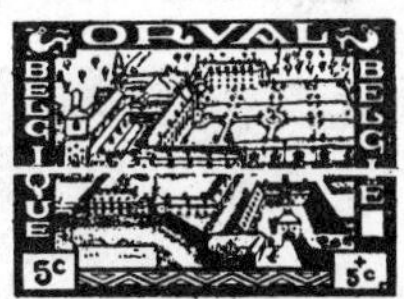

View of Old Abbey—SP49

Ruins of Old Abbey
SP50

Count de Chiny Presenting First Abbey to Countess Matilda
SP56

Restoration of Abbey in XVI and XVII Centuries
SP57

Abbey in XVIII Century, Maria Theresa and Charles V
SP58

Madonna and Arms of Seven Abbeys
SP60

Designs: 25c + 15c, Guests, courtyard. 50c + 25c, Transept. 75c + 50c, Bell Tower. 1fr + 1.25fr, Fountain. 1.25fr + 1.75fr, Cloisters. 5fr + 20fr, Duke of Brabant placing first stone of new abbey.

1933, Oct. 15 *Perf. 14*

B132	SP49	5c	+5c dl grn	80.00	90.00
B133	SP50	10c	+15c ol grn	60.00	80.00
B134	SP49	25c	+15c dk brn	60.00	80.00
B135	SP50	50c	+25c red brn	60.00	80.00
B136	SP50	75c	+50c dp grn	60.00	80.00
B137	SP50	1fr	+1.25fr cop red	60.00	80.00
B138	SP49	1.25fr	+1.75fr gray blk	60.00	80.00
B139	SP56	1.75fr	+2.75fr bl	70.00	90.00
B140	SP57	2fr	+3fr mag	70.00	85.00
B141	SP58	2.50fr	+5fr dl brn	80.00	85.00
B142	SP56	5fr	+20fr vio	80.00	90.00

Perf. 11½.

B143	SP60	10fr	+40fr bl	500.00	450.00
			Nos. B132-B143 (12)	1,240.	1,370.

The surtax was for a fund to aid in the restoration of Orval Abbey. Counterfeits exist.

"Tuberculosis Society"
SP61

Peter Benoit
SP62

1933, Dec. 1 Engr. *Perf. 14x13½*

B144	SP61	10c	+5c blk	1.75	1.50
B145	SP61	25c	+15c vio	4.50	4.75

B146	SP61	50c	+10c red brn	4.00	4.00
B147	SP61	75c	+15c blk brn	16.50	1.00
B148	SP61	1fr	+25c cl	18.50	17.50
B149	SP61	1.75fr	+25c vio bl	21.00	16.50
B150	SP61	5fr	+5fr lil	210.00	225.00
			Nos. B144-B150 (7)	276.25	270.25

The surtax was for anti-tuberculosis work.

1934, June 1 **Photogravure**

B151	SP62	75c	+25c ol brn	15.00	12.00

The surtax was to raise funds for the Peter Benoit Memorial.

King Leopold III
SP63 SP64

1934, Sept. 15

B152	SP63	75c	+25c ol blk	37.50	42.50
a.			Sheet of 20	1,400.	1,400.
B153	SP64	1fr	+25c red vio	35.00	35.00
a.			Sheet of 20	1,400.	1,400.

The surtax aided the National War Veterans' Fund. Sold for 4.50fr a set at the Exhibition of War Postmarks 1914–18, held at Brussels by the Royal Philatelic Club of Veterans. The price included an exhibition ticket. Sold at Brussels post office Sept. 18–22. No. B152 printed in sheets of 20 (4x5) and 100 (10x10). No. B153 printed in sheets of 20 (4x5) and 150 (10x15).

1934, Sept. 24

B154	SP63	75c	+25c vio	5.00	4.25
B155	SP64	1fr	+25c red brn	15.00	18.50

The surtax aided the National War Veterans' Fund. No. B154 printed in sheets of 100 (10x10); No. B155 in sheets of 150 (10x15). These stamps remained in use one year.

Crusader
SP65

1934, Nov. 17 **Engr.** ***Perf. 13½x14***

B156	SP65	10c	+5c blk & red	1.50	1.00
B157	SP65	25c	+15c brn & red	3.25	2.50
B158	SP65	50c	+10c dl grn & red	4.00	2.50
B159	SP65	75c	+15c vio brn & red	3.00	1.25
B160	SP65	1fr	+25c rose & red	16.50	15.00
B161	SP65	1.75fr	+25c ultra & red	14.00	13.00
B162	SP65	5fr	+5fr brn vio & red	165.00	200.00
			Nos. B156-B162 (7)	207.25	235.25

The surtax was for anti-tuberculosis work.

Prince Baudouin, Princess Josephine and Prince Albert
SP66

1935, Apr. 10 **Photogravure**

B163	SP66	35c	+15c dk grn	1.75	1.50
B164	SP66	70c	+30c red brn	1.75	1.25
B165	SP66	1.75fr	+50c dk bl	7.00	7.25

Surtax was for Child Welfare Society.

Brussels Exhibition Issue.

Stagecoach—SP67

1935, Apr. 27

B166	SP67	10c	+10c ol blk	1.75	1.65
B167	SP67	25c	+25c bis brn	6.00	5.00
B168	SP67	35c	+25c dk grn	6.00	5.75

Nos. B166–B168 were printed in sheets of 10. Price, set of 3, $175.

Franz von Taxis SP68 Queen Astrid SP69

Souvenir Sheet.

1935, May 25 **Engr.** ***Perf. 14***

B169	SP68	5fr	+5fr grnsh blk	210.00	225.00

Issued in sheets measuring 91½x117 mm., containing one stamp.

Nos. B166–B169 were issued for the Brussels Philatelic Exhibition (SITEB).

Queen Astrid Memorial Issue.

1935, Dec. 1 **Photo.** ***Perf. 11½***

Borders in Black.

B170	SP69	10c	+5c ol blk	25	25
B171	SP69	25c	+15c brn	50	45
B172	SP69	35c	+5c dk grn	75	50
B173	SP69	50c	+10c rose lil	1.00	85
B174	SP69	70c	+5c gray blk	25	25
B175	SP69	1fr	+25c red	3.25	2.50
B176	SP69	1.75fr	+25c bl	5.00	4.50
B177	SP69	2.45fr	+55c dk vio	5.50	5.75
			Nos. B170-B177 (8)	16.50	15.05

The surtax was divided among several charitable organizations.

Borgerhout Philatelic Exhibition Issue.

Souvenir Sheet.

Town Hall, Borgerhout
SP70

1936, Oct. 3

B178	SP70	70c	+30c pur brn	67.50	65.00

Issued in sheets, measuring 115x126 mm., containing one stamp.

Town Hall and Belfry of Charleroi SP71 Prince Baudouin SP72

Charleroi Youth Exhibition.

Souvenir Sheet.

1936, Oct. 18 **Engraved**

B179	SP71	2.45fr	+55c gray bl	67.50	60.00

Issued in sheets, measuring 95x120 mm., containing one stamp.

1936, Dec. 1 **Photo.** ***Perf. 14x13½***

B180	SP72	10c	+5c dk brn	20	20
B181	SP72	25c	+5c vio	50	50
B182	SP72	35c	+5c dk grn	50	50
B183	SP72	50c	+5c vio brn	75	60
B184	SP72	70c	+5c ol grn	50	30
B185	SP72	1fr	+25c cer	2.00	1.40
B186	SP72	1.75fr	+25c ultra	2.50	1.90
B187	SP72	2.45fr	+2.55fr vio rose	6.25	6.25
			Nos. B180-B187 (8)	13.20	11.65

The surtax was for the assistance of the National Anti-Tuberculosis Society.

1937, Jan. 10

B188	SP72	2.45fr	+2.55fr sl	3.25	3.25

Issued in commemoration of International Stamp Day. The surtax was for the benefit of the Brussels Postal Museum, the Royal Belgian Philatelic Federation and the Anti-Tuberculosis Society.

Queen Astrid and Prince Baudouin SP73 Queen Mother Elisabeth SP74

1937, Apr. 15 ***Perf. 11½***

B189	SP73	10c	+5c mag	20	20
B190	SP73	25c	+5c ol blk	45	35
B191	SP73	35c	+5c dk grn	45	40
B192	SP73	50c	+5c vio	65	90
B193	SP73	70c	+5c sl	45	25
B194	SP73	1fr	+25c dk car	1.75	1.65
B195	SP73	1.75fr	+25c dp ultra	3.00	2.50
B196	SP73	2.45fr	+1.55fr dk brn	6.25	5.75
			Nos. B189-B196 (8)	13.20	12.00

The surtax was to raise funds for Public Utility Works.

SP74a

1937, Sept. 15 ***Perf. 14x13½***

B197	SP74	70c	+5c int blk	65	60
B198	SP74	1.75fr	+25c brt ultra	1.40	1.40

Souvenir Sheet.

Perf. 11½.

B199	SP74a		Sheet of four	45.00	35.00
a.			1.50fr+2.50fr red brn	10.00	8.00
b.			2.45fr+3.55fr red vio	8.00	7.25

Nos. B197–B199 were issued for the benefit of the Queen Elisabeth Music Foundation in connection with the Eugene Ysaye international competition.

No. B199 contains two se-tenant pairs of Nos. B199a and B199b. Size: 111x145mm. On sale one day, Sept. 15, at Brussels.

Princess Josephine-Charlotte
SP75

1937, Dec. 1 ***Perf. 14x13½***

B200	SP75	10c	+5c sl grn	20	20
B201	SP75	25c	+5c lt brn	40	38
B202	SP75	35c	+5c yel grn	45	38
B203	SP75	50c	+5c ol gray	55	55
B204	SP75	70c	+5c brn red	45	25
B205	SP75	1fr	+25c red	1.50	1.25
B206	SP75	1.75fr	+25c vio bl	1.50	1.65
B207	SP75	2.45fr	+2.55fr mag	9.00	5.75
			Nos. B200-B207 (8)	14.05	10.41

King Albert Memorial Issue

Souvenir Sheet

King Albert Memorial—SP76

1938, Feb. 17 ***Perf. 11½***

B208	SP76	2.45fr	+7.55fr brn vio	20.00	21.00

Issued in connection with the dedication of the monument to King Albert. Sheet size: 143x115mm.

King Leopold III in Military Plane
SP77

1938, Mar. 15

B209	SP77	10c	+5c car brn	20	20
B210	SP77	35c	+5c dp grn	90	1.00
B211	SP77	70c	+5c gray blk	1.40	70
B212	SP77	1.75fr	+25c ultra	3.50	3.25
B213	SP77	2.45fr	+2.55fr pur	6.75	6.75
			Nos. B209-B213 (5)	12.75	11.90

The surtax was for the benefit of the National Fund for Aeronautical Propaganda.

Basilica of Koekelberg
SP78

Interior View of the Basilica of Koekelberg
SP79

1938, June 1 **Photogravure**

B214 SP78	10c +5c lt brn		30	30
B215 SP78	35c +5c grn		75	65
B216 SP78	70c +5c gray grn		85	70
B217 SP78	1fr +25c car		1.75	1.50
B218 SP78	1.75fr +25c ultra		2.00	1.90
B219 SP78	2.45fr +2.55fr brn vio		9.50	8.00

Engraved.

B220 SP79	5fr +5fr dl grn	20.00	20.00
Nos. B214-B220 (7)		35.15	33.05

The surtax was for a fund to aid in completing the National Basilica of the Sacred Heart at Koekelberg.

Nos. B214, B216 and B218 are different views of the exterior of the Basilica.

Souvenir Sheet

Interior of Koekelberg Basilica
SP80

1938, July 21 **Engr.** ***Perf. 14***

B221 SP80	5fr +5fr lt vio	20.00	22.50

Sheet size 94x120mm.

Stamps of 1938 Surcharged in Black:

40c (a) 2Fr50 2Fr50 (b)

1938, Nov. 10 ***Perf. 11½***

B222 SP78 (a)	40c on 35c+5c grn	50	50
B223 SP78 (a)	75c on 70c+5c gray grn	75	75
B224 SP78 (b)	2.50fr +2.50fr on 2.45fr+2.55fr	9.50	11.00

Prince Albert of Liège
SP81

1938, Dec. 10 **Photo.** ***Perf. 14x13½***

B225 SP81	10c +5c brn	30	30
B226 SP81	30c +5c mag	1.10	75
B227 SP81	40c +5c ol gray	85	85
B228 SP81	75c +5c sl grn	1.10	40
B229 SP81	1fr +25c dk car	1.75	1.90
B230 SP81	1.75fr +25c ultra	2.00	1.90
B231 SP81	2.50fr +2.50fr dp grn	10.00	12.00
B232 SP81	5fr +5fr brn lake	25.00	20.00
Nos. B225-B232 (8)		42.10	38.10

Henri Dunant
SP82

Florence Nightingale
SP83

King Leopold and Royal Children
SP85

Queen Mother Elisabeth and Royal Children
SP84

Queen Astrid
SP86

Queen Mother Elisabeth and Wounded Soldier
SP87

1939, Apr. 1 **Photo.** ***Perf. 11½***

The Cross is Printed in Carmine.

B233 SP82	10c +5c brn	30	30
B234 SP83	30c +5c brn car	90	85
B235 SP84	40c +5c ol gray	75	50
B236 SP85	75c +5c sl blk	2.00	40
B237 SP84	1fr +25c brt rose	8.00	4.00
B238 SP85	1.75fr +25c brt ultra	2.25	2.50
B239 SP86	2.50fr +2.50fr dl vio	3.25	4.25
B240 SP87	5fr +5fr gray grn	11.00	12.50
Nos. B233-B240 (8)		28.45	25.30

75th anniversary of the founding of the International Red Cross Society.

Rubens' House, Antwerp
SP88

"Albert and Nicolas Rubens"
SP89

Arcade, Rubens' House
SP90

"Helena Fourment and Her Children"
SP91

Rubens and Isabelle Brandt
SP92

Peter Paul Rubens
SP93

"The Velvet Hat"
SP94

"Descent from the Cross"
SP95

1939, July 1

B241 SP88	10c +5c brn	35	35
B242 SP89	40c +5c brn car	1.10	1.10
B243 SP90	75c +5c ol blk	1.85	1.40
B244 SP91	1fr +25c rose	3.50	4.00
B245 SP92	1.50fr +25c sep	3.75	4.00
B246 SP93	1.75fr +25c dp ultra	4.50	4.75
B247 SP94	2.50fr +2.50fr brt red vio	21.00	22.50
B248 SP95	5fr +5fr sl gray	27.50	27.50
Nos. B241-B248 (8)		63.55	65.60

Issued to honor Peter Paul Rubens. The surtax was used to restore Rubens' home in Antwerp.

"Martin van Nieuwenhove" by Hans Memling
SP96

1939, July 1

B249 SP96	75c +75c ol blk	6.00	6.00

Issued in honor of Hans Memling, (1430?–1495), Flemish painter.

Twelfth Century Monks at Work
SP97

Reconstructed Tower Seen through Cloister
SP98

Monks Laboring in the Fields
SP99

Orval Abbey, Aerial View
SP100

Bishop Heylen of Namur, Madonna and Abbot General Smets of the Trappists
SP101

King Albert I and King Leopold III and Shrine—SP102

1939, July 20

B250	SP97	75c	+75c ol blk	6.50	7.00
B251	SP98	1fr	+1fr rose red	5.50	4.75
B252	SP99	1.50fr	+1.50fr dl brn	5.50	4.75
B253	SP100	1.75fr	+1.75fr saph	6.00	5.00
B254	SP101	2.50fr	+2.50fr brt red vio	15.00	13.00
B255	SP102	5fr	+5fr brn car	13.00	13.00
			Nos. B250-B255 (6)	51.50	47.50

The surtax was used for the restoration of the Abbey of Orval.

Belfry at Bruges SP103 — Belfry at Furnes SP104

Designs (Belfries): 30c + 5c, Thuin. 40c + 5c, Lierre. 75c + 5c, Mons. 1.75fr+25c, Namur. 2.50fr + 2.50fr, Alost. 5fr + 5fr, Tournai.

1939, Dec. 1 Photo. *Perf. 14x13½*

B256	SP103	10c	+5c ol gray	35	25
B257	SP103	30c	+5c brn org	50	50
B258	SP103	40c	+5c brt red vio	60	50
B259	SP103	75c	+5c ol blk	60	50

Engraved

B260	SP104	1fr	+25c rose car	2.00	2.00
B261	SP104	1.75fr	+25c dk bl	2.50	2.50
B262	SP104	2.50fr	+2.50fr dp red brn	13.00	12.50
B263	SP104	5fr	+5fr pur	17.50	18.50
			Nos. B256-B263 (8)	37.05	37.25

Arms of Mons SP111 — Arms of Ghent SP112

Designs (Coats of Arms): 40c + 10c, Arel. 50c + 10c, Bruges. 75c + 15c, Namur. 1fr + 25c, Hasselt. 1.75fr. + 50c, Brussels. 2.50fr + 2.50fr, Antwerp. 5fr + 5fr, Liege.

1940–41 Typographed *Perf. 14x13½*

B264	SP111	10c	+5c multi ('41)	25	25
B265	SP112	30c	+5c multi	42	35
B266	SP111	40c	+10c multi	55	40
B267	SP112	50c	+10c multi	60	50
B268	SP111	75c	+15c multi	65	35
B269	SP112	1fr	+25c multi ('41)	90	90
B270	SP111	1.75fr	+50c multi ('41)	1.10	1.00
B271	SP112	2.50fr	+2.50fr multi ('41)	3.00	3.25
B272	SP111	5fr	+5fr multi ('41)	3.75	3.50
			Nos. B264-B272 (9)	11.22	10.50

The surtax was used for winter relief.

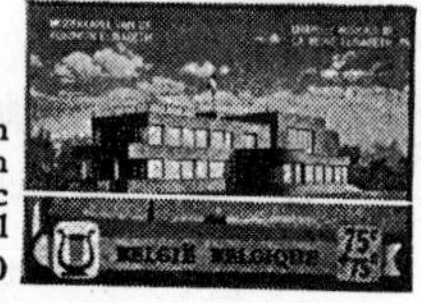

Queen Elisabeth Music Chapel SP120

Bust of Prince Albert of Liège SP121

1940, Nov. Photo. *Perf. 11½*

B273	SP120	75c	+75c sl	3.50	3.25
B274	SP120	1fr	+1fr rose red	2.00	1.75
B275	SP121	1.50fr	+1.50fr Prus grn	2.25	2.25
B276	SP121	1.75fr	+1.75fr ultra	2.50	2.25
B277	SP120	2.50fr	+2.50fr brn org	5.00	3.25
B278	SP121	5fr	+5fr red vio	6.25	5.25
			Nos. B273-B278 (6)	21.50	18.00

The surtax was for the Queen Elisabeth Music Foundation. Nos. B273–B278 were not authorized for postal use, but were sold to advance subscribers either mint or cancelled to order. See also Nos. B317–B318.

Souvenir Sheets.

Arms of Various Cities SP122

Typographed.

1941, May *Perf. 14x13½, Imperf.*

Cross and City Name in Carmine.

B279	SP122	Sheet of nine	17.50	22.50
a.		10c+5c sl	1.40	1.50
b.		30c+5c emer	1.40	1.50
c.		40c+10c choc	1.40	1.50
d.		50c+10c lt vio	1.40	1.50
e.		75c+15c dl pur	1.40	1.50
f.		1fr+25c car	1.40	1.50
g.		1.75fr+50c dl bl	1.40	1.50
h.		2.50fr+2.50fr ol gray	1.40	1.50
i.		5fr+5fr dl vio	4.25	5.00

The sheets measure 106x148 mm. The surtax was used for relief work.

Painting SP123 — Sculpture SP124

Monks Studying Plans of Orval Abbey SP128

Designs: 40c+60c, 2fr+3.50fr, Monk carrying candle. 50c+65c, 1.75fr+2.50fr, Monk praying. 75c+1fr, 3fr+5fr, Two monks singing.

1941, June Photo. *Perf. 11½*

B281	SP123	10c	+15c brn org	60	60
B282	SP124	30c	+30c ol gray	50	60
B283	SP124	40c	+60c dp brn	50	60
B284	SP124	50c	+65c vio	50	60
B285	SP124	75c	+1fr brt red vio	60	75
B286	SP124	1fr	+1.50fr rose red	75	75
B287	SP123	1.25fr	+1.75fr dp yel grn	75	75
B288	SP123	1.75fr	+2.50fr dp ultra	85	1.00
B289	SP123	2fr	+3.50fr red vio	85	1.00
B290	SP124	2.50fr	+4.50fr dl red brn	90	1.40
B291	SP124	3fr	+5fr dk ol grn	95	1.40
B292	SP128	5fr	+10fr grnsh blk	2.50	3.50
			Nos. B281-B292 (12)	10.25	12.95

The surtax was used for the restoration of the Abbey of Orval.

Maria Theresa SP129 — Charles the Bold SP130

Portraits (in various frames): 35c+5c, Charles of Lorraine. 50c+10c, Margaret of Parma. 60c+10c, Charles V. 1fr+15c, Johanna of Castile. 1.50fr+1fr, Philip the Good. 1.75fr+1.75fr, Margaret of Austria. 3.25fr+3.25fr, Archduke Albert. 5fr+5fr, Archduchess Isabella.

1941-42 Photogravure.

B293	SP129	10c	+5c ol blk	10	10
B294	SP129	35c	+5c dl grn	15	15
B295	SP129	50c	+10c brn	15	15
B296	SP129	60c	+10c pur	15	15
B297	SP129	1fr	+15c brt car rose	15	15
B298	SP129	1.50fr	+1fr red vio	60	60
B299	SP129	1.75fr	+1.75fr ryl bl	65	65
B300	SP130	2.25fr	+2.25fr dl red brn	75	80
B301	SP129	3.25fr	+3.25fr lt brn	1.25	1.35
B302	SP129	5fr	+5fr sl grn	1.25	1.35
			Nos. B293-B302 (10)	5.20	5.45

Souvenir Sheet.

Archduke Albert and Archduchess Isabella SP139

B302A	SP139	Sheet of two ('42)	6.50	7.25
b.		3.25fr+6.75fr turq bl	3.00	3.25
c.		5fr+10fr dk car	3.00	3.25

The sheets measure 77x59mm.
The surtax was for the benefit of National Social Service Work among soldiers' families.

Souvenir Sheets.

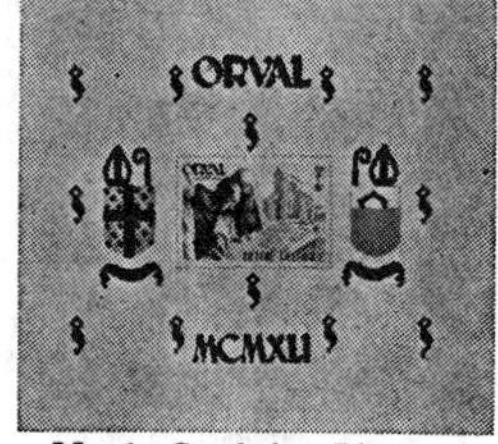

Monks Studying Plans of Orval Abbey SP140

1941, Oct. Photo. *Perf. 11½*

Inscribed "Belgie-Belgique".

B303	SP140	5fr	+15fr ultra	11.00	15.00

Imperf.

Inscribed "Belgique-Belgie".

B304	SP140	5fr	+15fr ultra	11.00	15.00

The sheets measure 185x165 mm. and are inscribed in black, gold and ultramarine.
The surtax was for the restoration of Orval Abbey.
No. B304 exists perforated.
In 1942 these sheets were privately trimmed and overprinted "1142 1942" and ornament.

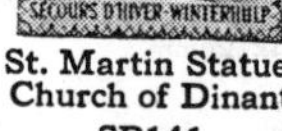

St. Martin Statue, Church of Dinant SP141 — Lennik, Saint-Quentin SP142

St. Martin's Church, Saint-Trond SP146

Designs (Statues of St. Martin): 50c+10c, 3.25fr +3.25fr, Beck, Limburg. 60c+10c, 2.25fr+2.25fr, Dave on the Meuse. 1.75fr+50c, Hal, Brabant.

1941–42 Photogravure *Perf. 11½*

B305	SP141	10c	+5c chnt	22	20
B306	SP142	35c	+5c dk bl grn	30	30
B307	SP142	50c	+10c vio	38	32
B308	SP142	60c	+10c dp brn	45	40
B309	SP142	1fr	+15c car	50	45
B310	SP141	1.50fr	+25c sl grn	60	60
B311	SP142	1.75fr	+50c dk ultra	70	65
B312	SP142	2.25fr	+2.25fr red vio	75	75
B313	SP142	3.25fr	+3.25fr brn vio	85	85
B314	SP146	5fr	+5fr dk ol grn	1.40	1.00
			Nos. B305-B314 (10)	6.15	5.52

Souvenir Sheets.

Inscribed "Belgie-Belgique".

No.	Design	Denom.	Description	Unused	Used
B315	SP146	5fr	+20fr vio brn ('42)	15.00	20.00

Imperf.

Inscribed "Belgique-Belgie"

No.	Design	Denom.	Description	Unused	Used
B316	SP146	5fr	+20fr vio brn ('42)	15.00	20.00

Nos. B315-B316 contain one stamp each. Size: 105x139mm.

In 1956, the Bureau Européen de la Jeunesse et de l'Enfance privately overprinted Nos. B315-B316: "Congrès Européen de l'education 7-12 Mai 1956," in dark red and dark green respectively. A black bar obliterates "Winterhulp-Secours d'Hiver."

Souvenir Sheets.

Queen Elisabeth Music Chapel
SP147

1941, Dec. 1 Photo. *Perf. 11½*

Inscribed "Belgique-Belgie".

No.	Design	Denom.	Description	Unused	Used
B317	SP147	10fr	+15fr ol blk	3.00	4.50

Imperf.

Inscribed "Belgie-Belgique".

No.	Design	Denom.	Description	Unused	Used
B318	SP147	10fr	+15fr ol blk	3.00	4.50

Issued in sheets measuring 105x139mm. The surtax was for the Queen Elisabeth Music Foundation. These sheets were perforated with the monogram of Queen Elisabeth in 1942.

In 1954 Nos. B317-B318 were overprinted to commemorate the birth centenary of Edgar Tinel, composer. Inscriptions in French, border in brown on No. B317; inscriptions in Flemish, border in green on No. B318. These overprinted sheets were not postally valid.

Jean Bollandus
SP148

Christophe Plantin
SP156

Designs: 35c+5c, Andreas Vesalius. 50c+10c, Simon Stevinus. 60c+10c, Jean Van Helmont. 1fr+15c, Rembert Dodoens. 1.75fr+50c, Gerardus Mercator. 3.25fr+3.25fr, Abraham Ortelius. 5fr+5fr, Justus Lipsius.

Photogravure.

1942, May 15 *Perf. 14x13½*

No.	Design	Denom.	Description	Unused	Used
B319	SP148	10c	+5c dl brn	7	7
B320	SP148	35c	+5c gray grn	12	12
B321	SP148	50c	+10c fawn	12	12
B322	SP148	60c	+10c grnsh blk	12	12

Engraved.

No.	Design	Denom.	Description	Unused	Used
B323	SP148	1fr	+15c brt rose	18	12
B324	SP148	1.75fr	+50c dl bl	70	70
B325	SP148	3.25fr	+3.25fr lil rose	45	45
B326	SP148	5fr	+5fr vio	65	65

Perf. 13½x14.

No.	Design	Denom.	Description	Unused	Used
B327	SP156	10fr	+30fr red org	3.00	3.00
			Nos. B319-B327 (9)	5.41	5.35

The surtax was used to help fight tuberculosis.

No. B327 was sold by subscription at the Brussels Post Office, July 1-10, 1942.

Belgian Prisoner
SP158

1942, Oct. 1 *Perf. 11½*

No.	Design	Denom.	Description	Unused	Used
B331	SP158	5fr	+45fr ol gray, with Label	12.00	12.00

The surtax was for prisoners of war. A brown label, inscribed "1942 POUR NOS PRISONNIERS/ VOOR ONZE GEVANGENEN," alternates with the stamps in the sheet.

SP159

SP164

SP162

SP168

Various Statues of St. Martin

1942-43

No.	Design	Denom.	Description	Unused	Used
B332	SP159	10c	+5c org	12	12
B333	SP159	35c	+5c dk bl grn	18	18
B334	SP159	50c	+10c dp brn	18	18
B335	SP162	60c	+10c blk	22	22
B336	SP159	1fr	+15c brt rose	22	22
B337	SP164	1.50fr	+25c grnsh blk	90	80
B338	SP164	1.75fr	+50c dk bl	95	85
B339	SP162	2.25fr	+2.25fr brn	95	85
B340	SP162	3.25fr	+3.25fr brt red vio	95	85
B341	SP168	5fr	+10fr hn brn	1.35	1.20
B342	SP168	10fr	+20fr rose brn & vio brn ('43)	2.25	2.25

Inscribed "Belgique-Belgie".

No.	Design	Denom.	Description	Unused	Used
B343	SP168	10fr	+20fr gldn brn & vio brn ('43)	2.25	2.25
			Nos. B332-B343 (12)	10.52	9.97

The surtax was for winter relief.

Issue dates: Nos. B332-B341, Nov. 12, 1942. Nos. B342-B343, Apr. 3, 1943.

Prisoners of War—SP170

Design: No. B345, Two prisoners with package from home.

1943, May Photo. *Perf. 11½*

No.	Design	Denom.	Description	Unused	Used
B344	SP170	1fr	+30fr ver	4.50	5.50
B345	SP170	1fr	+30fr brn rose	4.50	5.50

The surtax was used for prisoners of war.

Roof Tiler
SP172

Coppersmith
SP173

Designs: (Statues in Petit Sablon Park, Brussels). 35c+5c, Blacksmith. 60c+10c, Gunsmith. 1fr+15c, Armsmith. 1.75fr+75c, Goldsmith. 3.25fr+3.25fr, Fishdealer. 5fr+25fr, Watchmaker.

1943, June 1

No.	Design	Denom.	Description	Unused	Used
B346	SP172	10c	+5c chnt brn	10	10
B347	SP172	35c	+5c grn	15	12
B348	SP173	50c	+10c dk brn	15	12
B349	SP173	60c	+10c sl	15	15
B350	SP173	1fr	+15c dl rose brn	60	38
B351	SP173	1.75fr	+75c ultra	1.20	95
B352	SP173	3.25fr	+3.25fr brt red vio	1.25	1.30
B353	SP173	5fr	+25fr dk pur	1.25	1.50
			Nos. B346-B353 (8)	4.85	4.62

The surtax was for the control of tuberculosis.

"O"
SP180

"ORVAL"
SP185

Designs: 60c+1.90fr, "R." 1fr+3fr, "V." 1.75fr+5.25fr, "A." 3.25fr+16.75fr, "L."

1943, Oct. 9

No.	Design	Denom.	Description	Unused	Used
B354	SP180	50c	+1fr ol blk	1.50	1.40
B355	SP180	60c	+1.90fr dl vio	60	55
B356	SP180	1fr	+3fr rose brn	60	55
B357	SP180	1.75fr	+5.25fr dk bl	60	55
B358	SP180	3.25fr	+16.75fr dk bl grn	1.10	1.00
B359	SP185	5fr	+30fr dp brn	2.25	2.00
			Nos. B354-B359 (6)	6.65	6.05

The surtax aided restoration of Orval Abbey.

St. Léonard Church, Léau
SP186

St. Martin Church, Courtrai
SP190

Basilica of St. Martin, Angre
SP191

Notre Dame, Hal
SP193

St. Martin—SP194

Designs: 35c+5c, St. Martin Church, Dion-le-Val. 50c+15c, St. Martin Church, Alost. 60c+20c, St. Martin Church, Liege. 3.25fr+11.75fr, St. Martin Church, Loppem. No. B369, St. Martin, beggar and Meuse landscape.

1943-44

No.	Design	Denom.	Description	Unused	Used
B360	SP186	10c	+5c dp brn	12	12
B361	SP186	35c	+5c dk bl grn	22	18
B362	SP186	50c	+15c ol blk	22	18
B363	SP186	60c	+20c brt red vio	25	22
B364	SP190	1fr	+1fr rose brn	45	22
B365	SP191	1.75fr	+4.25fr dp ultra	2.75	2.50
B366	SP186	3.25fr	+11.75fr red lil	2.75	2.50
B367	SP193	5fr	+25fr dk bl	3.75	4.00
B368	SP194	10fr	+30fr gray grn ('44)	3.25	3.50
B369	SP194	10fr	+30fr blk brn ('44)	3.25	3.50
			Nos. B360-B369 (10)	17.01	16.92

Surtax for winter relief.

The surtax was for winter relief.

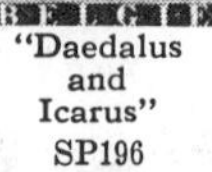
"Daedalus and Icarus"
SP196

Sir Anthony Van Dyck, Self-portrait
SP200

Paintings by Van Dyck: 50c+2.50fr. "The Good Samaritan." 60c+3.40fr, Detail of "Christ Healing the Paralytic." 1fr+5fr, "Madonna and Child." 5fr+30fr, "St. Sebastian."

1944, Apr. 16 Photo. *Perf. 11½*

Crosses in Carmine.

B370	SP196	35c	+1.65fr dk sl grn	70	75
B371	SP196	50c	+2.50fr grnsh blk	70	75
B372	SP196	60c	+3.40fr blk brn	80	85
B373	SP196	1fr	+5fr dk car	1.00	1.00
B374	SP200	1.75fr	+8.25fr int bl	1.50	1.40
B375	SP196	5fr	+30fr cop brn	1.60	1.75
			Nos. B370-B375 (6)	6.30	6.50

The surtax was for the Belgian Red Cross.

Jan van Eyck
SP202

Godfrey of Bouillon
SP203

Designs: 50c+25c, Jacob van Maerlant. 60c+40c, Jean Joses de Dinant. 1fr+50c, Jacob van Artevelde. 1.75fr+4.25fr, Charles Joseph de Ligne. 2.25fr+8.25fr, Andre Gretry. 3.25fr+11.25fr, Jan Moretus-Plantin. 5fr+35fr, Jan van Ruysbroeck.

1944, May 31

B376	SP202	10c	+15c dk pur	65	60
B377	SP203	35c	+15c grn	55	60
B378	SP203	50c	+25c chnt brn	55	60
B379	SP203	60c	+40c ol blk	55	60
B380	SP203	1fr	+50c rose brn	55	60
B381	SP203	1.75fr	+4.25fr ultra	55	60
B382	SP203	2.25fr	+8.25fr grnsh blk	1.50	1.35
B383	SP203	3.25fr	+11.25fr dk brn	90	80
B384	SP203	5fr	+35fr sl bl	1.75	1.10
			Nos. B376-B384 (9)	7.55	6.85

The surtax was for prisoners of war.

Sons of Aymon Astride Bayard
SP211

Brabo Slaying the Giant Antigoon
SP212

Till Eulenspiegel Singing to Nele
SP214

Designs: 50c+10c, St. Hubert converted by stag with crucifix. 1fr+15fr, St. George slaying the dragon. 1.75fr+5.25fr, Genevieve of Brabant with son and roe-deer. 3.25fr+11.75fr, Tchantches wrestling with the Saracen. 5fr+25fr, St. Gertrude rescuing the knight with the cards.

1944, June 25

B385	SP211	10c	+5c choc	10	10
B386	SP212	35c	+5c dk bl grn	15	15
B387	SP211	50c	+10c dl vio	15	15
B388	SP214	60c	+10c blk brn	15	15
B389	SP214	1fr	+15c rose brn	15	15
B390	SP214	1.75fr	+5.25fr ultra	85	75
B391	SP211	3.25fr	+11.75fr grnsh blk	95	90
B392	SP211	5fr	+25fr dk bl	1.20	1.10
			Nos. B385-B392 (8)	3.70	3.45

The surtax was for the control of tuberculosis.

Nos. B385–B389 were overprinted "Breendonk+10fr." in 1946 by the Union Royale Philatelique for an exhibition at Brussels. They had no postal validity.

Union of the Flemish and Walloon Peoples in their Sorrow
SP219

Union in Reconstruction
SP220

Photogravure

1945, May 1 *Perf. 11½* Unwmkd.

B395	SP219	1fr	+30fr car	2.00	2.25
B396	SP220	1¾fr	+30fr brt ultra	2.00	2.25

1945, July 21

Size: 34½x23½mm.

B397	SP219	1fr	+9fr scar	40	50
B398	SP220	1fr	+9fr car rose	40	50

The surtax was for the postal employees' relief fund.

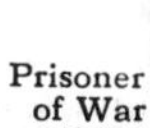
Prisoner of War
SP221

Reunion
SP222

Awaiting Execution
SP223

Symbolical Figures "Recovery of Freedom"
SP225

Design: 70c+30c, 3.50fr+3.50fr, Member of Resistance Movement.

1945, Sept. 10

B399	SP221	10c	+15c org	10	10
B400	SP222	20c	+20c dp pur	12	12
B401	SP223	60c	+25c sep	18	18
B402	SP221	70c	+30c dp yel grn	22	18
B403	SP221	75c	+50c org brn	25	25
B404	SP222	1fr	+75c brt bl grn	30	28
B405	SP223	1.50fr	+1fr brt red	30	28
B406	SP221	3.50fr	+3.50fr brt bl	2.25	2.25
B407	SP225	5fr	+40fr brn	2.00	2.00
			Nos. B399-B407 (9)	5.72	5.64

The inscriptions are transposed on Nos. B403–B406.

The surtax was for the benefit of prisoners of war, displaced persons, families of executed victims and members of the Resistance Movement.

Arms of West Flanders
SP226

Arms of Provinces: 20c+20c, Luxembourg. 60c+25c, East Flanders. 70c+30c, Namur. 75c+50c, Limburg. 1fr+75c, Hainaut. 1.50fr+1fr, Antwerp. 3.50fr+1.50fr, Liege. 5fr+45fr, Brabant.

1945, Dec. 1

B408	SP226	10c	+15c sl blk & sl gray	10	10
B409	SP226	20c	+20c rose car & rose	25	22
B410	SP226	60c	+25c dk brn & pale brn	25	22
B411	SP226	70c	+30c dk grn & lt grn	25	25
B412	SP226	75c	+50c org brn & pale org brn	30	25
B413	SP226	1fr	+75c pur & lt pur	25	25
B414	SP226	1.50fr	+1fr car & rose	25	25
B415	SP226	3.50fr	+1.50fr dp bl & gray bl	45	30
B416	SP226	5fr	+45fr dp mag & cer	4.00	4.00
			Nos. B408-B416 (9)	6.10	5.84

The surtax was for tuberculosis prevention.

Father Joseph Damien
SP227

Father Damien Comforting Leper
SP229

Leper Colony, Molokai Island, Hawaii
SP228

Photogravure.

1946, July 15 *Perf. 11½* Unwmkd.

B417	SP227	65c	+75c dk bl	1.65	1.50
B418	SP228	1.35fr	+2fr brn	1.65	1.50
B419	SP229	1.75fr	+18fr rose brn	1.90	1.75

The surtax was for the erection of a museum in Louvain.

Symbols of Wisdom and Patriotism
SP230

"In Memoriam"
SP232

François Bovesse
SP231

1946, July 15

B420	SP320	65c	+75c vio	1.65	1.50
B421	SP231	1.35fr	+2fr dk org brn	1.65	1.50
B422	SP232	1.75fr	+18fr car rose	2.10	1.75

The surtax was for the erection of a "House of the Fine Arts" at Namur.

Emile Vandervelde
SP233

Sower
SP235

Vandervelde, Laborer and Family
SP234

1946, July 15

B423	SP233	65c +75c dk sl grn	2.00	1.65
B424	SP234	1.35fr +2fr dk vio bl	2.00	1.65
B425	SP235	1.75fr +18fr dp car	2.25	2.00
		Nos. B417-B425 (9)	16.85	14.80

The surtax was for the Emile Vandervelde Institute, to promote social, economic and cultural activities.

Pepin of Herstal
SP236

Arms of Malines
SP241

Designs: 1fr+50c, Charlemagne. 1.50fr +1fr, Godfrey of Bouillon. 3.50fr+1.50fr, Robert of Jerusalem. Nos. B430–B431, Baldwin of Constantinople.

1946, Sept. 15 Engr. *Perf. 11½x11*

B426	SP236	75c +25c grn	75	80
B427	SP236	1fr +50c vio	1.00	1.00
B428	SP236	1.50fr +1fr plum	1.25	1.25
B429	SP236	3.50fr +1.50fr brt bl	1.50	1.75
B430	SP236	5fr +45fr red vio	12.50	16.50
B431	SP236	5fr +45fr red org	17.50	22.50
		Nos. B426-B431 (6)	34.50	43.80

The surtax on Nos. B426–B429 was for the benefit of former prisoners of war, displaced persons, the families of executed patriots, and former members of the Resistance Movement.

The surtax on Nos. B430–B431 was divided among several welfare, national celebration and educational organizations.

Issue dates: Nos. B426–B429, Apr. 15; No. B430, Sept. 15; No. B431, Nov. 15.

See also Nos. B437–B441, B465–B466, B472–B476.

1946, Dec. 2 *Perf. 11½*

Designs (Coats of Arms): 90c+60c, Dinant. 1.35fr+1.15fr, Ostend. 3.15fr+1.85fr, Verviers. 4.50fr+45.50fr, Louvain.

B432	SP241	65c +35c rose car	50	50
B433	SP241	90c +60c lem	65	70
B434	SP241	1.35fr +1.15fr dp grn	90	1.25
B435	SP241	3.15fr +1.85fr bl	2.25	2.75

B436	SP241	4.50fr +45.50fr dk vio brn	17.50	20.00
		Nos. B432-B436 (5)	21.80	25.20

The surtax was for anti-tuberculosis work
See also Nos. B442-B446.

Type of 1946.

Designs: 65c+35c, John II, Duke of Brabant. 90c+60c, Count Philip of Alsace. 1.35fr+1.15fr, William the Good. 3.15fr+1.85fr, Bishop Notger of Liege. 20fr+20fr, Philip the Noble.

1947, Sept. 25 Engr. *Perf. 11½x11*

B437	SP236	65c +35c Prus grn	90	1.00
B438	SP236	90c +60c yel grn	1.15	1.50
B439	SP236	1.35fr +1.15fr car	1.75	2.25
B440	SP236	3.15fr +1.85fr ultra	4.00	5.25
B441	SP236	20fr +20fr red vio	57.50	55.00
		Nos. B437-B441 (5)	65.30	65.00

The surtax was for victims of World War II.

Arms Type of 1946 Dated "1947"

Coats of Arms: 65c+35c, Nivelles. 90c+60c, St. Trond. 1.35fr+1.15fr, Charleroi. 3.15fr+1.85fr, St. Nicolas. 20fr+20fr, Bouillon.

1947, Dec. 15 *Perf. 11½*

B442	SP241	65c +35c org	90	80
B443	SP241	90c +60c dp cl	75	90
B444	SP241	1.35fr +1.15fr dk brn	1.15	1.00
B445	SP241	3.15fr +1.85fr dp bl	2.75	2.50
B446	SP241	20fr +20fr dk grn	25.00	22.50
		Nos. B442-B446 (5)	30.55	27.70

The surtax was for anti-tuberculosis work.

St. Benedict and King Totila
SP247

Achel Abbey
SP248

Designs: 3.15fr+2.85fr, St. Benedict, legislator and builder. 10fr+10fr, Death of St. Benedict.

1948, Apr. 5 Photogravure

B447	SP247	65c +65c red brn	1.50	1.75
B448	SP248	1.35fr +1.35fr gray	2.25	2.50
B449	SP247	3.15fr +2.85fr dp ultra	4.75	6.00
B450	SP247	10fr +10fr brt red vio	16.50	16.50

The surtax was to aid the Abbey of the Trappist Fathers at Achel.

St. Begga and Chèvremont Castle
SP249

Chèvremont Basilica and Convent
SP250

Designs: 3.15fr+2.85fr, Madonna of Chevremont and Chapel. 10fr+10fr, Madonna of Mt. Carmel.

1948, Apr. 5 Unwmkd.

B451	SP249	65c +65c bl grn	1.50	1.75
B452	SP250	1.35fr +1.35fr dk car rose	2.25	2.40
B453	SP249	3.15fr +2.85fr dp bl	4.75	6.00
B454	SP249	10fr +10fr dp brn	16.50	16.50

The surtax was to aid the Basilica of the Carmelite Fathers of Chèvremont.

Anseele Monument Showing French Inscription
SP251

Designs: 90c + 60c, View of Ghent. 1.35fr+1.15fr, Van Artevelde monument, Ghent. 3.15fr+1.85fr. Anseele Monument, Flemish inscription.

1948, June 21 *Perf. 14x13½*

B455	SP251	65c +35c rose red	2.40	2.25
B456	SP251	90c +60c gray	4.50	3.75
B457	SP251	1.35fr +1.15fr hn brn	3.00	2.75
B458	SP251	3.15fr +1.85fr brt bl	9.00	9.00
a.		Souvenir sheet of 4	67.50	75.00

Issued to honor Edouard Anseele, statesman, founder of the Belgian Socialist Party.

No. B458a contains one each of Nos. B455–B458. Size: 144x81mm. Sold for 50fr.

Statue "The Unloader"
SP252

Underground Fighter
SP253

1948, Sept. 4 *Perf. 11½x11*

B460	SP252	10fr +10fr gray grn	35.00	35.00
B461	SP253	10fr +10fr red brn	22.50	22.50

The surtax was used toward erection of monuments at Antwerp and Liège.

Portrait Type of 1946 and SP254

Double Barred Cross
SP254

Designs: 4fr+3.25fr, Isabella of Austria. 20fr+20fr, Archduke Albert of Austria.

1948, Dec. 15 Photo. *Perf. 13½x14*

B462	SP254	20c +5c dk sl grn	45	40
B463	SP254	1.20fr +30c mag	1.25	1.40
B464	SP254	1.75fr +25c red	1.85	2.00

Engraved

Perf. 11½x11

B465	SP236	4fr +3.25fr ultra	11.00	10.00
B466	SP236	20fr +20fr Prus grn	52.50	45.00
		Nos. B462-B466 (5)	67.05	58.80

The surtax was divided among several charities.

Souvenir Sheets

Rogier van der Weyden Paintings—SP255

Paintings by van der Weyden (No. B466A): 90c, Virgin and Child. 1.75fr, Christ on the Cross. 4fr, Mary Magdalene.

Paintings by Jordaens (No. B466B): 90c, Woman Reading. 1.75fr, The Flutist. 4fr, Old Woman Reading Letter.

1949, Apr. 1 Photo. *Perf. 11½*

B466A	SP255	Sheet of 3	125.00	150.00
c.		90c dp brn	37.50	42.50
d.		1.75fr dp rose lil	37.50	42.50
e.		4fr dk vio bl	37.50	42.50
B466B	SP255	Sheet of 3	125.00	150.00
f.		90c dk vio	37.50	42.50
g.		1.75fr red	37.50	42.50
h.		4fr bl	37.50	42.50

The surtax went to various cultural and philanthropic organizations. Nos. B466A and B466B have dark brown and orange decorative border. Size: 140x90½mm. Sheets sold for 50fr each.

Guido Gezelle
SP256

1949, Nov. 15 Photo. *Perf. 14x13½*

B467	SP256	1.75fr +75c dk Prus grn	3.50	4.00

Issued to commemorate the 50th anniversary of the death of Guido Gezelle, poet. The surtax was for the Guido Gezelle Museum, Bruges.

Portrait Type of 1946 and

Arnica
SP257

Designs: 65c+10c, Sand grass. 90c+10c, Wood myrtle. 1.20fr+30c, Field poppy. 1.75fr+25c, Philip the Good. 3fr+1.50fr, Charles V. 4fr+2fr, Maria-Christina. 6fr+3fr, Charles of Lorraine. 8fr+4fr, Maria-Theresa.

1949, Dec. 20 Typo. *Perf. 13½x14*

B468	SP257	20c	+5c multi	75	60
B469	SP257	65c	+10c multi	1.50	1.75
B470	SP257	90c	+10c multi	2.40	2.25
B471	SP257	1.20fr	+30c multi	2.85	2.75

Engraved

Perf. 11½x11

B472	SP236	1.75fr	+25c red org	1.50	1.25
B473	SP236	3fr	+1.50fr dp cl	11.00	12.00
B474	SP236	4fr	+2fr ultra	12.00	14.00
B475	SP236	6fr	+3fr choc	22.50	22.50
B476	SP236	8fr	+4fr dl grn	20.00	18.50
	Nos. B468-476 (9)			74.50	75.60

The surtax was apportioned among several welfare organizations.

Arms of Belgium and Great Britain
SP258

British Memorial
SP260

Design: 2.50fr+50c, British tanks at Hertain.

Engraved.

1950, Mar. 15 *Perf. 13½x14, 11½*

B477	SP258	80c	+20c grn	2.00	1.90
B478	SP258	2.50fr	+50c red	7.50	6.50
B479	SP260	4fr	+2fr dp bl	11.00	10.00

Issued to commemorate the 6th anniversary of the liberation of Belgian territory by the British army.

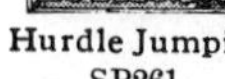

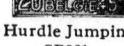

Hurdle Jumping
SP261

Relay Race
SP262

Designs: 90c+10c, Javelin throwing. 4fr+2fr, Pole vault. 8fr+4fr, Foot race.

Inscribed: "Heysel 1950."

Perf. 14x13½, 13½x14.

1950, July 1 Engr. Unwmkd.

B480	SP261	20c	+5c brt grn	1.25	1.10
B481	SP261	90c	+10c vio brn	3.50	3.25
B482	SP262	1.75fr	+25c car	4.25	3.75
a.	Souvenir sheet			55.00	50.00
B483	SP261	4fr	+2fr lt bl	42.50	37.50
B484	SP261	8fr	+4fr dp grn	52.50	45.00
	Nos. B480-B484 (5)			104.00	90.60

Issued to publicize the European Athletic Games, Brussels, August 1950.

No. B482a measures 89 x 68½ mm., and contains a single copy of No. B482 with inscriptions typographed in black in upper and lower margins.

The margins of No. B482a were trimmed in April, 1951, and an overprint ("25 Francs pour le Fonds Sportif—25e Fofre Internationale Bruxelles") was added in red in French and in black in Flemish by a private committee. These pairs of altered sheets were sold at the Brussels Fair.

Gentian
SP263

Tombeek Sanatorium
SP265

Sijsele Sanatorium
SP264

Designs: 65c+10c, Cotton Grass. 90c+10c, Foxglove. 1.20fr+30c, Limonia. 4fr+2fr, Jauche Sanatorium.

Typographed.

1950, Dec. 20 *Perf. 14x13½*

Cross in Red.

B485	SP263	20c	+5c mar, bl & emer	60	60
B486	SP263	65c	+10c brn, buff & emer	1.75	1.40
B487	SP263	90c	+10c bluish grn, dp mag & yel grn	2.25	2.25
B488	SP263	1.20fr	+30c vio bl, bl & grn	2.75	2.75

Engraved.

Perf. 11½.

B489	SP264	1.75fr	+25c car	2.00	1.75
B490	SP264	4fr	+2fr bl	15.00	13.00
B491	SP265	8fr	+4fr bl grn	25.00	27.50
	Nos. B485-B491 (7)			49.35	49.25

The surtax was for tuberculosis prevention and other charitable purposes.

Chemist
SP266

Allegory of Peace
SP268

Colonial Instructor and Class
SP267

1951, Mar. 27 Unwmkd.

B492	SP266	80c	+20c grn	2.25	2.50
B493	SP267	2.50fr	+50c vio brn	13.00	12.50
B494	SP268	4fr	+2fr dp bl	15.00	15.00

The surtax was for the reconstruction fund of the United Nations Educational, Scientific and Cultural Organization.

Monument to Political Prisoners
SP269

Fort of Breendonk
SP270

Design: 8fr+4fr, Monument: profile of figure on pedestal.

1951, Aug. 20 Photo. *Perf. 11½*

B495	SP269	1.75fr	+25c blk brn	3.00	3.00
B496	SP270	4fr	+2fr bl & sl gray	23.50	22.50
B497	SP269	8fr	+4fr dk bl grn	27.50	27.50

The surtax was for the erection of a national monument.

Queen Elisabeth
SP271

1951, Sept. 22

B498	SP271	90c	+10c grnsh gray	2.10	2.00
B499	SP271	1.75fr	+25c plum	3.00	2.75
B500	SP271	3fr	+1fr grn	20.00	18.50
B501	SP271	4fr	+2fr gray bl	27.50	22.50
B502	SP271	8fr	+4fr sep	32.50	25.00
	Nos. B498-B502 (5)			85.10	70.75

The surtax was for the Queen Elisabeth Medical Foundation.

Cross, Sun Rays and Dragon
SP272

Beersel Castle
SP273

Horst Castle
SP274

Castles: 4fr+2fr, Lavaux St. Anne. 8fr+4fr, Veves.

1951, Dec. 17 Engr. Unwmkd.

B503	SP272	20c	+5c red	30	40
B504	SP272	65c	+10c dp ultra	90	1.00
B505	SP272	90c	+10c sep	1.25	1.40
B506	SP272	1.20fr	+30c rose vio	1.50	1.60
B507	SP273	1.75fr	+75c red brn	1.75	2.00
B508	SP274	3fr	+1fr yel grn	15.00	11.00
B509	SP273	4fr	+2fr bl	18.50	15.00
B510	SP274	8fr	+4fr gray	24.00	19.00
	Nos. B503-B510 (8)			63.20	51.40

The surtax was for anti-tuberculosis work. See also Nos. B523–B526, B547–B550.

Main Altar
SP275

Basilica of the Sacred Heart Koekelberg
SP276

Procession Bearing Relics of St. Albert of Louvain
SP277

1952, Mar. 1 Photo. *Perf. 11½*

B511	SP275	1.75fr	+25c blk brn	2.00	1.90
B512	SP276	4fr	+2fr ind	15.00	14.00

Engraved.

B513	SP277	8fr	+4fr vio brn	21.00	18.50
a.	Souv. sheet			160.00	150.00

No. B513a measures 122x72mm., and contains one each of Nos. B511-B513, with inscriptions in indigo and black brown. Sold for 30 fr.

Issued to commemorate the 25th anniversary of the Cardinalate of J. E. Van Roey, Primate of Belgium. The surtax was for the Basilica.

Beaulieu Castle, Malines
SP278

August Vermeylen
SP279

1952, May 14 Engraved

Laid Paper.

B514	SP278	40fr	+10fr lt grnsh bl	285.00	250.00

Issued on the occasion of the 13th Universal Postal Union Congress, Brussels, 1952.

1952, Oct. 24 *Perf. 11½* Unwmkd.

Portraits: 80c+40c, Karel Van de Woestijne. 90c+45c, Charles de Coster. 1.75fr+75c, M. Maeterlinck. 4fr+2fr, Emile Verhaeren. 8fr+4fr, Hendrik Conscience.

Photogravure.

B515	SP279	65c	+30c pur	2.50	2.00

B516	SP279	80c	+40c dk grn	3.75	2.50
B517	SP279	90c	+45c sep	3.25	3.25
B518	SP279	1.75fr	+75c cer	3.75	3.50
B519	SP279	4fr	+2fr bl vio	35.00	32.50
B520	SP279	8fr	+4fr dk brn	35.00	40.00
		Nos. B515-B520 (6)		83.25	83.75

1952, Nov. 15

Portraits: 4fr, Emile Verhaeren. 8fr, Hendrik Conscience.

B521	SP279	4fr	(+9fr) bl	90.00	85.00
B522	SP279	8fr	(+9fr) dk car rose	90.00	85.00

On Nos. B521–B522, the denomination is repeated at either side of the stamp. The surtax is expressed on se-tenant labels bearing quotations of Verhaeren (in French) and Conscience (in Flemish).

A 9-line black overprint was privately applied to these labels: "Conference Internationale de la Musique Bruxelles UNESCO International Music Conference Brussels 1953*"

Type of 1951 Dated "1952," and

Arms of Malmédy
SP281

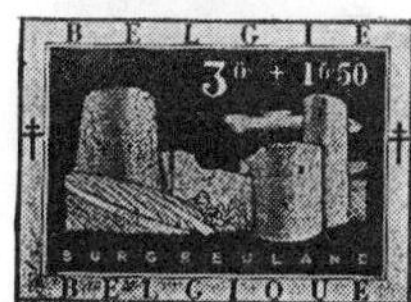

Castle Ruins, Burgreuland
SP282

Designs: 4fr+2fr, Vesdre Dam, Eupen. 8fr+4fr, St. Vitus, patron saint of Saint-Vith.

1952, Dec. 15 **Engraved**

B523	SP272	20c	+5c red brn	30	40
B524	SP272	80c	+20c grn	90	1.00
B525	SP272	1.20fr	+30c lil rose	1.75	1.50
B526	SP272	1.50fr	+50c ol brn	1.75	1.50
B527	SP281	2fr	+75c car	3.00	3.50
B528	SP282	3fr	+1.50fr choc	16.50	16.50
B529	SP281	4fr	+2fr bl	15.00	15.00
B530	SP281	8fr	+4fr vio brn	24.00	22.50
		Nos. B523-B530 (8)		63.20	61.90

The surtax on Nos. B523–B530 was for anti-tuberculosis and other charitable works.

Walthère Dewé
SP283

Princess Josephine-Charlotte
SP284

1953, Feb. 16 **Photogravure**

B531	SP283	2fr	+1fr brn car	4.00	3.75

The surtax was for the construction of a memorial to Walthère Dewé, Underground leader in World War II.

1953, Mar. 14 **Cross in Red**

B532	SP284	80c	+20c ol grn	1.50	1.65
B533	SP284	1.20fr	+30c brn	1.75	2.00
B534	SP284	2fr	+50c rose lake	2.25	2.25
a.		Bklt pane of 8		90.00	90.00
B535	SP284	2.50fr	+50c crim	15.00	15.00
B536	SP284	4fr	+1fr brt bl	11.00	11.00
B537	SP284	5fr	+2fr sl grn	15.00	15.00
		Nos. B532-B537 (6)		46.50	46.90

The surtax was for the Belgian Red Cross.

The selvage of No. B534a is inscribed in French or Dutch. The price is for the French.

Boats at Dock
SP285

Bridge and Citadel, Namur
SP286

Allegory
SP287

Designs: 1.20fr+30c, Bridge at Bouillon. 2fr+50c, Antwerp waterfront. 4fr+2fr, Wharf at Ghent. 8fr+4fr, Meuse River at Freyr.

1953, June 22 ***Perf. 11½*** **Unwmkd.**

B538	SP285	80c	+20c grn	1.50	1.25
B539	SP285	1.20fr	+30c redsh brn	2.00	1.90
B540	SP285	2fr	+50c sep	2.75	2.75
B541	SP286	2.50fr	+50c dp mag	15.00	12.50
B542	SP286	4fr	+2fr vio bl	21.00	13.00
B543	SP286	8fr	+4fr gray blk	24.00	15.00
		Nos. B538-B543 (6)		66.25	46.40

The surtax was used to promote tourism in the Ardenne-Meuse region and for various cultural works.

1953, Oct. 26 **Engraved**

B544	SP287	80c	+20c grn	6.25	4.00
B545	SP287	2.50fr	+1fr rose car	57.50	50.00
B546	SP287	4fr	+1.50fr bl	70.00	65.00

The surtax was for the European Bureau of Childhood and Youth.

Type of 1951 Dated "1953," and

Ernest Malvoz
SP288

Robert Koch
SP289

Portraits: 3fr+1.50fr, Carlo Forlanini. 4fr+2fr, Leon Charles Albert Calmette.

1953, Dec. 15

B547	SP272	20c	+5c bl	25	35
B548	SP272	80c	+20c rose vio	1.00	1.25
B549	SP272	1.20fr	+30c choc	1.25	1.60
B550	SP272	1.50fr	+50c dk gray	1.50	2.00
B551	SP288	2fr	+75c dk grn	2.50	3.25
B552	SP288	3fr	+1.50fr dk red	14.00	15.00
B553	SP288	4fr	+2fr ultra	12.50	12.50
B554	SP289	8fr	+4fr choc	15.00	16.50
		Nos. B547-B554 (8)		48.00	52.45

The surtax was for anti-tuberculosis and other charitable works.

King Albert I Statue
SP290

Albert I Monument, Namur
SP291

Design: 9fr+4.50fr, Cliffs of Marche-les-Dames.

1954, Feb. 17 **Photogravure**

B555	SP209	2fr	+50c chnt brn	3.00	2.50
B556	SP291	4fr	+2fr bl	17.50	16.50
B557	SP290	9fr	+4.50fr ol blk	20.00	22.50

Issued to commemorate the 20th anniversary of the death of King Albert I. The surtax aided in the erection of the monument pictured on B556.

Political Prisoners' Monument
SP292

Camp and Fort, Breendonk
SP293

Design: 9fr+4.50fr, Political prisoners' monument (profile).

1954, Apr. 1 ***Perf. 11½*** **Unwmkd.**

B558	SP292	2fr	+1fr red	15.00	12.50
B559	SP293	4fr	+2fr dk brn	32.50	27.50
B560	SP292	9fr	+4.50fr ol grn	35.00	30.00

The surtax was used toward the creation of a monument to political prisoners.

Gatehouse and Gateway
SP294

Nuns in Courtyard
SP295

Our Lady of the Vine
SP296

Designs: 2fr+1fr, Swans in stream. 7fr+3.50fr Nuns at well. 8fr+4fr, Statue above door.

1954, May 15

B561	SP294	80c	+20c dk bl grn	3.00	2.00
B562	SP294	2fr	+1fr crim	13.00	10.00
B563	SP295	4fr	+2fr vio	20.00	18.50
B564	SP295	7fr	+3.50fr lil rose	35.00	40.00
B565	SP295	8fr	+4fr brn	32.50	35.00
B566	SP296	9fr	+4.50fr gray bl	90.00	57.50
		Nos. B561-B566 (6)		193.50	163.00

The surtax was for the Friends of the Beguinage of Bruges.

Child's Head
SP297

"The Blind Man and the Paralytic," by Antoine Carte
SP298

1954, Dec. 1 **Engraved**

B567	SP297	20c	+5c dk grn	45	50
B568	SP297	80c	+20c dk gray	1.20	1.25
B569	SP297	1.20fr	+30c org brn	1.85	1.75
B570	SP297	1.50fr	+50c pur	2.50	2.50
B571	SP298	2fr	+75c rose car	11.00	6.50
B572	SP298	4fr	+1fr brt bl	22.50	18.50
		Nos. B567-B572 (6)		39.50	31.00

The surtax was for anti-tuberculosis work.

Ernest Solvay
SP299

Jean-Jacques Dony
SP300

Portraits: 1.20fr+30c, Egide Walschaerts. 25fr+50c, Leo H. Baekeland. 3fr+1fr, Jean-Etienne Lenoir. 4fr+2fr, Emile Fourcault and Emile Gobbe.

Photogravure.

1955, Oct. 22 *Perf. 11½* Unwmkd.

B573	SP299	20c	+ 5c brn & dk brn	30	40
B574	SP300	80c	+ 20c vio	1.25	80
B575	SP299	1.20fr	+ 30c ind	1.50	1.25
B576	SP300	2fr	+ 50c dp car	5.50	4.25
B577	SP300	3fr	+ 1fr dk grn	15.00	15.00
B578	SP299	4fr	+ 2fr brn	15.00	15.00
	Nos. B573-B578 (6)			38.55	36.70

Issued in honor of Belgian scientists.
The surtax was for the benefit of various cultural organizations.

"The Joys of Spring" by E. Canneel
SP301

Einar Holböll
SP302

Portraits: 4fr+2fr, John D. Rockefeller. 8fr+4fr, Sir Robert W. Philip.

1955, Dec. 5 *Perf. 11½* Unwmkd.

B579	SP301	20c	+ 5c red lil	50	40
B580	SP301	80c	+ 20c grn	1.00	1.25
B581	SP301	1.20fr	+ 30c redsh brn	1.25	1.75
B582	SP301	1.50fr	+ 50c vio bl	1.75	2.00
B583	SP302	2fr	+ 50c car	8.50	7.25
B584	SP302	4fr	+ 2fr ultra	17.50	18.50
B585	SP302	8fr	+ 4fr ol gray	22.50	22.50
	Nos. B579-B585 (7)			53.00	53.65

The surtax was for anti-tuberculosis work.

Palace of Charles of Lorraine
SP303

Queen Elisabeth and Sonata by Mozart
SP304

Design: 2fr+1 fr, Mozart at age 7.

1956, Mar. 5 Engraved

B586	SP303	80c	+ 20c stl bl	90	1.25
B587	SP303	2fr	+ 1fr rose lake	5.50	6.00
B588	SP304	4fr	+ 2fr dl pur	9.00	9.50

Issued to commemorate the 200th anniversary of the birth of Wolfgang Amadeus Mozart, composer.
The surtax was for the benefit of the Pro-Mozart Committee in Belgium.

Queen Elisabeth
SP305

1956, Aug. 16 Photogravure

B589	SP305	80c	+ 20c sl grn	1.20	1.25
B590	SP305	2fr	+ 1fr dp plum	4.00	3.50
B591	SP305	4fr	+ 2fr brn	6.50	6.25

Issued in honor of the 80th birthday of Queen Elisabeth. The surtax went to the Queen Elisabeth Foundation.
See also No. 607.

Ship with Cross
SP306

Rehabilitation
SP308

Infant on Scales
SP307

Design: 4fr+2fr, X-Ray examination.

1956, Dec. 17 Engraved

B592	SP306	20c	+ 5c redsh brn	65	40
B593	SP306	80c	+ 20c grn	1.00	1.20
B594	SP306	1.20fr	+ 30c dl lil	1.00	1.00
B595	SP306	1.5fr	+ 50c lt sl bl	1.10	1.60
B596	SP307	2fr	+ 50c ol grn	3.00	3.00
B597	SP307	4fr	+ 2fr dl pur	13.00	11.50
B598	SP308	8fr	+ 4fr dp car	13.00	13.00
	Nos. B592-B598 (7)			32.75	31.70

The surtax was for anti-tuberculosis work.

Charles Plisnier and Albrecht Rodenbach
SP309

Portraits: 80c+20c, Emiel Vliebergh and Maurice Wilmotte. 1.20fr+30c, Paul Pastur and Julius Hoste. 2fr+50c, Lodewijk de Raet and Jules Destree. 3fr+1fr, Constantin Meunier and Constant Permeke. 4fr+2fr, Lieven Gevaert and Edouard Empain.

Photogravure.

1957, June 8 *Perf. 11½* Unwmkd.

B599	SP309	20c	+ 5c brt vio	30	40
B600	SP309	80c	+ 20c lt red brn	60	60
B601	SP309	1.20f	+ 30c blk brn	75	85
B602	SP309	2fr	+ 50c cl	2.25	2.10
B603	SP309	3fr	+ 1fr dk ol grn	4.25	4.25
B604	SP309	4fr	+ 2fr vio bl	6.00	5.50
	Nos. B599-B604 (6)			14.15	13.70

The surtax was for the benefit of various cultural organizations.

Dogs and Antarctic Camp
SP310

1957, Oct. 18 Engr. *Perf. 11½*

B605	SP310	5fr + 2.50fr gray, org & vio brn	3.75	4.50
a.		Sheet of four	150.00	175.00
b.		bl, sl and red brn	35.00	45.00

Surtax for Belgian Antarctic Expedition, 1957–58.
No. B605a contains 4 No. B605b. Inscribed "Expedition Antarctique Belge 1957–1958" in French and Flemish. Size: 115x83mm.

Gen. Patton's Grave and Flag
SP311

Gen. George S. Patton, Jr.
SP312

Designs: 2.50fr+50c, Memorial, Bastogne. 3fr+1fr, Gen. Patton decorating Brig. Gen. Anthony C. McAuliffe. 6fr+3fr, Tanks of 1918 and 1944.

1957, Oct. 28 Photogravure

Size: 36x25mm., 25x36mm.

B606	SP311	1fr	+ 50c dk gray	2.00	2.25
B607	SP311	2.50fr	+ 50c ol grn	2.25	2.75
B608	SP311	3fr	+ 1fr red brn	3.75	4.50
B609	SP312	5fr	+ 2.50fr grysh bl	9.00	11.00

Size: 53x35mm.

B610	SP311	6fr	+ 3fr pale brn car	12.50	12.50
	Nos. B606-B610 (5)			29.50	33.00

The surtax was for the General Patton Memorial Committee and Patriotic Societies.

Adolphe Max
SP313

1957, Nov. 10 Engraved

B611	SP313	2.50fr	+ 1fr ultra	2.50	3.00

18th anniversary of the death of Adolphe Max, mayor of Brussels. The surtax was for the national "Adolphe Max" fund.

"Chinels," Fosses
SP314

"Op Signoorken," Malines
SP315

Infanta Isabella Shooting Crossbow
SP316

Legends: 1.50fr+50c, St. Remacle and the wolf. 2fr+1fr, Longman and the pea soup. 5fr+2fr, The Virgin with Inkwell (vert.). 6fr+2.50fr, "Gilles" (clowns), Binche.

Engraved and Photogravure.

1957, Dec. 14

B612	SP314	30c	+ 20c pur & org yel	25	35
B613	SP315	1fr	+ 50c brn & lt bl	75	60
B614	SP314	1.50fr	+ 50c gray & red	1.50	1.00
B615	SP315	2fr	+ 1fr gray & brt grn	1.25	1.75
B616	SP316	2.50fr	+ 1fr bl grn & lil	1.50	1.75
B617	SP316	5fr	+ 2fr bl & dk gray	6.25	5.50
B618	SP316	6fr	+ 2.50fr vio brn & red org	7.50	7.50
	Nos. B612-B618 (7)			19.00	18.45

The surtax was for anti-tuberculosis work.
See also Nos. B631–B637.

Benelux Gate—SP317

Designs: 1fr+50c, Civil Engineering Pavilion. 1.50fr+50c, Ruanda-Urundi Pavilion. 2.50fr+1fr, Belgium 1900. 3fr+1.50fr, Atomium. 5fr+3fr, Telexpo Pavilion.

Engraved.

1958, Apr. 15 ***Perf. 11½*** **Unwmkd.**

Size: 35½x24½mm.

B619	SP317	30c	+20c brn red, vio bl & sep	30	35
B620	SP317	1fr	+50c gray bl, dk brn & emer	45	60
B621	SP317	1.50fr	+50c grnsh bl, pur & cit	60	75
B622	SP317	2.50fr	+1fr ultra, red & brn red	75	75
B623	SP317	3fr	+1.50fr gray, car & lt ultra	1.75	1.75

Size: 49x33mm.

B624	SP317	5fr	+3fr gray, ultra & red lil	1.75	1.85
	Nos. B619-B624 (6)			5.60	6.05

World's Fair, Brussels, Apr. 17–Oct. 19.

Marguerite van Eyck by Jan van Eyck
SP318

Christ Carrying Cross, by Hieronymus Bosch
SP319

Paintings: 1.50fr+50c, St. Donatien, Jan Gossart. 2.50fr+1fr, Self-portrait, Lambert Lombard. 3fr+150fr, The Rower, James Ensor. 5fr+3fr, Henriette, Henri Evenepoel.

1958, Oct. 30 Photo. ***Perf. 11½***

Various Frames
in Ochre and Brown.

B625	SP318	30c	+20c dk ol grn	55	65
B626	SP319	1fr	+50c mar	1.50	1.60
B627	SP318	1.50fr	+50c vio bl	2.00	2.00
B628	SP318	2.50fr	+1fr dk brn	3.00	3.25
B629	SP319	3fr	+1.50fr dl red	4.50	5.25
B630	SP318	5fr	+3fr brt bl	12.50	12.50
	Nos. B625-B630 (6)			24.05	25.25

The surtax was for the benefit of various cultural organizations.

Type of 1957.

Legends: 40c+10c, Elizabeth, Countess of Hoogstraten. 1fr+50c, Jean de Nivelles. 1.50fr+50c, St. Evermare play, Russon. 2fr+1fr, The Penitents of Furnes. 2.50fr+1fr, Manger and "Pax." 5fr+2fr, Sambre-Meuse procession. 6fr+2.50fr, Our Lady of Peace and "Pax" (vert.).

Engraved and Photogravure

1958, Dec. 6 ***Perf. 11½*** **Unwmkd.**

B631	SP314	40c	+10 ultra & brt grn	45	35
B632	SP315	1fr	+50 gray brn & org	75	55
B633	SP315	1.50fr	+50c cl & brt grn	1.10	75
B634	SP314	2fr	+1fr brn & red	1.40	1.00
B635	SP316	2.50fr	+1fr vio brn & bl grn	4.25	3.75

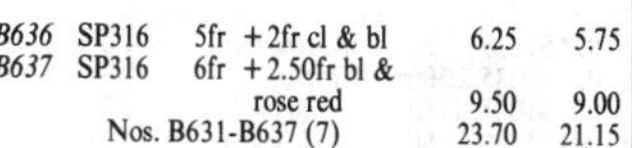

B636	SP316	5fr	+2fr cl & bl	6.25	5.75
B637	SP316	6fr	+2.50fr bl & rose red	9.50	9.00
	Nos. B631-B637 (7)			23.70	21.15

The surtax was for anti-tuberculosis work.

"Europe of the Heart"
SP320

1959, Feb. 25 Photo. **Unwmkd.**

B638	SP320	1fr	+50c red lil	1.25	90
B639	SP320	2.50fr	+1fr dk grn	2.50	3.25
B640	SP320	5fr	+2.50fr dp brn	4.25	4.75

The surtax was for aid for displaced persons.

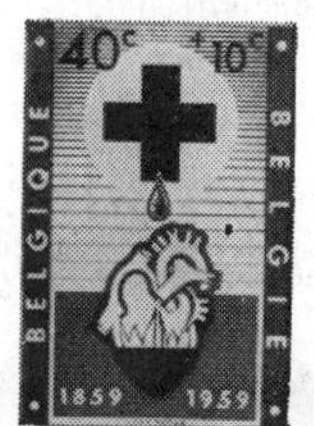

Allegory of Blood Transfusion
SP321

Henri Dunant and Battlefield at Solferino—SP322

Design: 2.50fr+1fr, 3fr+1.50fr, Red Cross, broken sword and drop of blood (horiz.).

1959, June 10 Photo. ***Perf. 11½***

B641	SP321	40c	+10c bl gray & car	60	60
B642	SP321	1fr	+50c brn & car	1.15	1.00
B643	SP321	1.50fr	+50c dl vio & car	1.50	1.40
B644	SP321	2.50fr	+1fr sl grn & car	2.25	2.50
B645	SP321	3fr	+1.50fr vio bl & car	5.25	5.50
B646	SP322	5fr	+3fr dk brn & car	8.00	7.25
	Nos. B641-B646 (6)			18.75	18.25

Issued to commemorate the centenary of the International Red Cross idea. The surtax was for the Red Cross and patriotic organizations.

Philip the Good
SP323

Arms of Philip the Good
SP324

Designs: 1fr+50c, Charles the Bold. 1.50fr+50c, Emperor Maximilian of Austria. 2.50fr+1fr, Philip the Fair. 3fr+1.50fr, Charles V. Portraits from miniatures by Simon Bening (c. 1483–1561).

1959, July 4 **Engraved**

B647	SP323	40c	+10c multi	60	65
B648	SP323	1fr	+50c multi	1.20	1.40
B649	SP323	1.50fr	+50c multi	1.75	1.25
B650	SP323	2.50fr	+1fr multi	2.75	2.75
B651	SP323	3fr	+1.50fr multi	5.25	5.00
B652	SP324	5fr	+3fr multi	9.00	8.50
	Nos. B647-B652 (6)			20.55	19.55

The surtax was for the Royal Library, Brussels.

Portraits show Grand Masters of the Order of the Golden Fleece.

Whale, Antwerp
SP325

Carnival, Stavelot
SP326

Designs: 1fr+50c, Dragon, Mons. 2fr+50c, Prince Carnival, Eupen. 3fr+1fr, Jester and cats, Ypres. 6fr+2fr, Holy Family (horiz.). 7fr+3fr, Madonna, Liége (horiz.).

Engraved and Photogravure

1959, Dec. 5 ***Perf. 11½***

B653	SP325	40c	+10c cit, Prus bl & red	50	45
B654	SP325	1fr	+50c ol & grn	80	65
B655	SP325	2fr	+50c lt brn, org & cl	1.00	85
B656	SP326	2.50fr	+1fr gray, pur & ultra	1.75	1.25
B657	SP326	3fr	+1fr gray, mar & yel	3.50	2.25
B658	SP326	6fr	+2fr ol, brt bl & hn brn	6.00	5.50
B659	SP326	7fr	+3fr chlky bl & org yel	9.00	8.00
	Nos. B653-B659 (7)			22.55	18.95

The surtax was for anti-tuberculosis work.

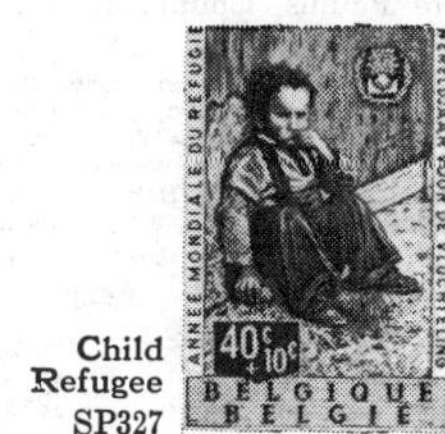

Child Refugee
SP327

Designs: 3fr+1.50fr, Man. 6fr+3fr, Woman.

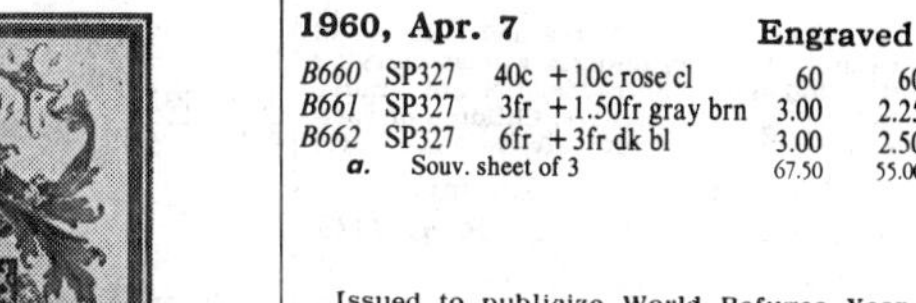

1960, Apr. 7 **Engraved**

B660	SP327	40c	+10c rose cl	60	60
B661	SP327	3fr	+1.50fr gray brn	3.00	2.25
B662	SP327	6fr	+3fr dk bl	3.00	2.50
a.	Souv. sheet of 3			67.50	55.00

Issued to publicize World Refugee Year, July 1, 1959–June 30, 1960.

No. B662a contains one each of Nos. B660–B662 with colors changed: 40c+10c, dull purple; 3fr+1.50fr, red brown; 6fr+3fr, henna brown. Black marginal inscription and uprooted oak emblem. Size: 121x92mm.

Parachutists and Plane
SP328

Designs: 2fr+50c, 2.50fr+1fr, Parachutists coming in for landing (vert.) 3fr+1fr, 6fr+2fr, Parachutist walking with parachute.

Photogravure and Engraved

1960, June 13 ***Perf. 11½***

B663	SP328	40c	+10c lt ultra & blk	32	32
B664	SP328	1fr	+50c bl & blk	1.50	1.50
B665	SP328	2fr	+50c bl, blk & ol	2.75	2.25
B666	SP328	2.50fr	+1fr grnsh bl, blk & gray ol	4.00	4.00
B667	SP328	3fr	+1fr bl, blk & sl grn	6.00	5.00
B668	SP328	6fr	lt vio bl, blk & ol	7.00	7.00
	Nos. B663-B668 (6)			21.57	20.07

The surtax was for various patriotic and cultural organizations.

Mother and Child, Planes and Rainbow
SP329

Designs: 40c+10c, Brussels Airport, planes and rainbow. 6fr+3fr, Rainbow connecting Congo and Belgium, and planes (vert.)

Photogravure

1960, Aug. 3 ***Perf. 11½*** **Unwmkd.**

Size: 35x24mm.

B669	SP329	40c	+10c grnsh bl	60	60
B670	SP329	3fr	+1.50fr brt red	5.50	4.75

Size: 35x52mm.

B671	SP329	6fr	+3fr vio	8.50	5.75

The surtax was for refugees from Congo.

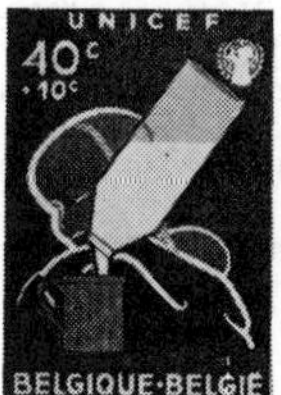

Infant, Milk Bottle and Mug
SP330

Designs: 1fr+50c, Nurse and children of 3 races. 2fr+50c, Refugee woman carrying gift clothes. 2.50fr+1fr, Negro nurse weighing infant. 3fr+1fr, Children of various races dancing. 6fr+2fr, Refugee boys.

Photogravure and Engraved

1960, Oct. 8 ***Perf. 11½***

B672	SP330	40c	+10c gldn brn, yel & bl grn	65	40
B673	SP330	1fr	+50c ol gray, mar & sl	2.25	1.40
B674	SP330	2fr	+50c vio, pale brn & brt grn	2.50	1.75
B675	SP330	2.50fr	+1fr dk red, sep & lt bl	3.50	2.25
B676	SP330	3fr	+1fr bl grn, red org & dl vio	3.75	2.75
B677	SP330	6fr	+2fr ultra, emer & brn	5.50	5.25
			Nos. B672-B677 (6)	18.15	13.80

Issued for the United Nations Children's Fund, UNICEF.

Tapestry
SP331

Belgian handicrafts: 1fr+50c, Cut crystal vases (vert.). 2fr+50c, Lace (vert.). 2.50fr+1fr, Metal plate & jug. 3fr+1fr, Diamonds. 6fr+2fr, Ceramics.

Photogravure and Engraved

1960, Dec. 5 ***Perf. 11½***

B678	SP331	40c	+10c bl, bis & brn	65	65
B679	SP331	1fr	+50c ind & org brn	1.75	1.40
B680	SP331	2fr	+50c dk red brn, blk & cit	3.00	2.25
B681	SP331	2.50fr	+1fr choc & yel	4.50	4.00
B682	SP331	3fr	+1fr org brn, blk & ultra	6.25	5.00
B683	SP331	6fr	+2fr dp blk & yel	8.25	6.75
			Nos. B678-B683 (6)	24.40	20.05

The surtax was for anti-tuberculosis work.

Jacob Kats and Abbe Nicolas Pietkin
SP332

Portraits: 1fr+50c, Albert Mockel and J. F. Willems. 2fr+50c, Jan van Rijswijck and Xavier M. Neujean. 2.50fr+1fr, Joseph Demarteau and A. Van de Perre. 3fr+1fr, Canon Jan-Baptist David and Albert du Bois. 6fr+2fr, Henri Vieuxtemps and Willem de Mol.

Photogravure and Engraved

1961, Apr. 22 ***Perf. 11½*** **Unwmkd.**

Portraits in Gray Brown

B684	SP332	40c	+10c ver & mar	90	65
B685	SP332	1fr	+50c bis brn & mar	1.75	1.50
B686	SP332	2fr	+50c yel & crim	3.25	2.85
B687	SP332	2.50fr	+1fr pale cit & dk grn	4.25	3.25
B688	SP332	3fr	+1fr lt & dk bl	5.50	4.50
B689	SP332	6fr	+2fr lil & ultra	9.50	6.50
			Nos. B684-B689 (6)	25.15	19.25

The surtax was for the benefit of various cultural organizations.

White Rhinoceros — **SP333**

Antonius Cardinal Perrenot de Granvelle — **SP334**

Animals: 1fr+50c, Przewalski horses. 2fr+50c, Okapi. 2.50fr+1fr, Giraffe (horiz.). 3fr+1fr, Lesser panda (horiz.). 6fr+2fr, European elk (horiz.).

Photogravure

1961, June 5 ***Perf. 11½*** **Unwmkd.**

B690	SP333	40c	+10c bis brn & dk brn	85	55
B691	SP333	1fr	+50c gray & brn	2.50	1.75
B692	SP333	2fr	+50c dp rose & blk	3.50	2.75
B693	SP333	2.50fr	+1fr red org & brn	2.75	2.25
B694	SP333	3fr	+1fr org & brn	3.25	2.50
B695	SP333	6fr	+2fr bl & bis brn	4.50	3.25
			Nos. B690-B695 (6)	17.35	13.05

The surtax was for various philanthropic organizations.

1961, July 29 **Engraved**

Designs: 3fr+1.50fr, Arms of Cardinal de Granvelle. 6fr+3fr, Tower and crosier, symbolic of collaboration between Malines and the Archbishopric.

B696	SP334	40c	+10c mag, car & brn	45	40
B697	SP334	3fr	+1.50fr multi	1.75	1.25
B698	SP334	6fr	+3fr mag pur & bis	4.00	3.00

Issued to commemorate the 400th anniversary of Malines as an Archbishopric.

Mother and Child by Pierre Paulus — **SP335**

Castle of the Counts of Male — **SP336**

Paintings: 1fr+50c, Mother Love, Francois-Joseph Navez. 2fr+50c, Motherhood, Constant Permeke. 2.50fr+1fr, Madonna and Child, Rogier van der Weyden. 3fr+1fr, Madonna with Apple, Hans Memling. 6fr+2fr, Madonna of the Forget-me-not, Peter Paul Rubens.

1961, Dec. 2 **Photo.** ***Perf. 11½***

Gold Frame

B699	SP335	40c	+10c dp brn	45	45
B700	SP335	1fr	+50c brt bl	85	65
B701	SP335	2fr	+50c rose red	1.40	1.10
B702	SP335	2.50fr	+1fr mag	2.25	1.50
B703	SP335	3fr	+1fr vio bl	2.75	2.00
B704	SP335	6fr	+2fr dk sl grn	4.25	3.25
			Nos. B699-B704 (6)	11.95	8.95

The surtax was for anti-tuberculosis work.

1962, Mar. 12 **Engr.** ***Perf. 11½***

Designs: 90c+10c, Royal library (horiz.). 1fr+50c, Church of Our Lady, Tongres. 2fr+50c, Collegiate Church, Soignies (horiz.). 2.50fr+1fr, Church of Our Lady, Malines. 3fr+1fr, St. Denis Abbey, Broqueroi. 6fr+2fr, Cloth Hall, Ypres (horiz.).

B705	SP336	40c	+10c brt grn	35	35
B706	SP336	90c	+10c lil rose	60	50
B707	SP336	1fr	+50c dl vio	90	75
B708	SP336	2fr	+50c vio	1.10	1.10
B709	SP336	2.50fr	+1fr red brn	2.25	1.75
B710	SP336	3fr	+1fr bl grn	2.75	2.00
B711	SP336	6fr	+2fr car rose	3.65	2.75
			Nos. B705-B711 (7)	11.60	9.20

The surtax was for various cultural and philanthropic organizations.

Andean Cock of the Rock — **SP337**

Handicapped Child — **SP338**

Birds: 1fr+50c, Red lory. 2fr+50c, Guinea touraco. 2.50fr+1fr, Keel-billed toucan. 3fr+1fr, Great bird of paradise. 6fr+2fr, Congolese peacock.

Engraved and Photogravure

1962, June 23 ***Perf. 11½*** **Unwmkd.**

Birds in Natural Colors

B712	SP337	40c	+10c bl	50	50
B713	SP337	1fr	+50c ultra & car	90	75
B714	SP337	2fr	+50c blk & car rose	90	90
B715	SP337	2.50fr	+1fr grnsh bl & ver	1.75	1.75
B716	SP337	3fr	+1fr red brn & grn	2.75	2.25
B717	SP337	6fr	+2fr red & ultra	4.75	3.25
			Nos. B712-B717 (6)	11.55	9.40

The surtax was for various philanthropic organizations.

Photogravure

1962, Sept. 22 ***Perf. 11½*** **Unwmkd.**

Handicapped Children: 40c+10c, Reading Braille. 2fr+50c, Deaf-mute girl with earphones and electronic equipment (horiz.). 2.50fr+1fr, Child with ball (cerebral palsy). 3fr+1fr, Girl with crutches (polio). 6fr+2fr, Sitting boys playing ball (horiz.).

B718	SP338	40c	+10c choc	35	35
B719	SP338	1fr	+50c rose red	65	65
B720	SP338	2fr	+50c brt lil	1.40	1.10
B721	SP338	2.50fr	+1fr dl grn	1.50	1.40
B722	SP338	3fr	+1fr dk bl	2.75	2.00
B723	SP338	6fr	+2fr dk brn	3.50	3.00
			Nos. B718-B723 (6)	10.15	8.50

The surtax was for various institutions for handicapped children.

Queen Louise-Marie
SP339

Belgian Queens: No. B725, like No. B724 with "ML" initials. 1fr+50c, Marie-Henriette. 2fr+1fr, Elisabeth. 3fr+1.50fr, Astrid. 8fr+2.50fr, Fabiola.

Photogravure and Engraved

1962, Dec. 8 ***Perf. 11½***

B724	SP339	40c	+10c gray, blk & gold ("L")	35	35
B725	SP339	40c	+10c gray, blk & gold ("ML")	35	35
B726	SP339	1fr	+50c gray, blk & gold	1.25	1.00
B727	SP339	2fr	+1fr gray, blk & gold	2.25	1.50
B728	SP339	3fr	+1.50fr gray, blk & gold	2.25	1.75
B729	SP339	8fr	+2.50fr gray, blk & gold	3.50	2.75
			Nos. B724-B729 (6)	9.95	7.70

The surtax was for anti-tuberculosis work.

British War Memorial (Porte de Menin), Ypres
SP340

1962, Dec. 26 **Engr.** ***Perf. 11½***

B730	SP340	1fr	+50c blk, grn, bl & red brn	1.20	1.20

Millennium of the city of Ypres. Issued in sheets of eight.

Peace Bell Ringing over Globe — **SP341**

The Sower by Brueghel — **SP342**

Engraved and Photogravure

1963, Feb. 18 ***Perf. 11½*** **Unwmkd.**

B731	SP341	3fr	+1.50fr blk, bl, org & grn	3.50	3.50
a.			Sheet of 4	16.50	16.50
B732	SP341	6fr	+3fr blk, brn & org	2.50	2.50

The surtax was for the installation of the Peace Bell (Bourdon de la Paix) at Koekelberg Basilica and for the benefit of various cultural organizations.

No. B731 was issued in sheets of 4. The sheet is inscribed "Bourdon de la Paix," repeated in Flemish, and measures 85x115 mm. No. B732 was issued in sheets of 30.

1963, Mar. 21 ***Perf. 11½***

Designs: 3fr+1fr, The Harvest, by Brueghel (horiz.). 6fr+2fr, "Bread," by Anton Carte (horiz.).

B733	SP342	2fr	+1fr grn, ocher & blk	45	45

B734 SP342 3fr +1fr red lil, ocher & blk 1.10 1.00

B735 SP342 6fr +2fr red brn, cit & blk 1.75 1.50

Issued for the "Freedom from Hunger" campaign of the U.N. Food and Agriculture Organization.

Speed Racing
SP343

Designs: 2fr+1fr, Bicyclists at check point (horiz.). 3fr+1.50fr, Team racing (horiz.). 6fr+3fr, Pace setters.

Engraved

1963, July 13 *Perf. 11½* Unwmkd.

B736 SP343 1fr +50c multi 40 45

B737 SP343 2fr +1fr bl, car, blk & ol gray 65 65

B738 SP343 3fr +1.50fr multi 90 90

B739 SP343 6fr +3fr multi 1.40 1.40

Issued to commemorate the 80th anniversary of the founding of the Belgian Bicycle League. The surtax was for athletes at the 1964 Olympic Games.

Princess Paola with Princess Astrid
SP344

Prince Albert and Family
SP345

Designs: 40c+10c, Prince Philippe. 2fr+50c, Princess Astrid. 2.50fr+1fr, Princess Paola. 6fr+2fr, Prince Albert.

1963, Sept. 28 Photogravure

Cross in Red

B740 SP344 40c +10c dk car rose & buff 35 35

B741 SP344 1fr +50c sl & buff 65 65

B742 SP344 2fr +50c dk car rose & buff 90 90

B743 SP344 2.50fr +1fr brt bl & buff 1.40 1.10

B744 SP345 3fr +1fr gray brn & buff 1.50 1.40

B745 SP345 3fr +1fr sl grn & buff 3.50 3.00

a. Bklt pane of 8 75.00 75.00

B746 SP344 6fr +2fr sl & buff 2.75 2.25

Nos. B740-B746 (7) 11.05 9.65

Issued to commemorate the centenary of the International Red Cross. No. B745 issued only in booklet panes of 8, which are in two forms: French and Flemish inscriptions in top and bottom margins transposed.

Daughter of Balthazar Gerbier, Painted by Rubens
SP346

Jesus, St. John and Cherubs by Rubens
SP347

Portraits (Rubens' sons): 1fr+40c, Nicolas, 2 yrs. old. 2fr+50c, Franz. 2.50fr+1fr, Nicolas, 6 yrs. old. 3fr+1fr, Albert.

Photogravure and Engraved

1963, Dec. 7 *Perf. 11½* Unwmkd.

B747 SP346 50c +10c buff, gray & dk brn 25 25

B748 SP346 1fr +40c buff, red brn & dk brn 55 55

B749 SP346 2fr +50c buff, vio brn & dk brn 90 80

B750 SP346 2.50fr +1fr buff, grn & dk brn 1.50 1.40

B751 SP346 3fr +1fr buff, red brn & dk brn 1.75 1.60

B752 SP347 6fr +2fr buff & gray 1.50 1.50

Nos. B747-B752 (6) 6.45 6.10

The surtax was for anti-tuberculosis work.

See also No. B771.

John Quincy Adams and Lord Gambier Signing Treaty of Ghent, by Amédée Forestier—SP348

1964, May 16 Photo. *Perf. 11½*

B753 SP348 6fr +3fr dk bl 2.75 2.75

Issued to commemorate the 150th anniversary of the signing of the Treaty of Ghent between the United States and Great Britain, Dec. 24, 1814.

Philip van Marnix
SP349

Portraits: 3fr+1.50fr, Ida de Bure Calvin. 6fr+3fr, Jacob Jordaens.

1964, May 30 Engraved

B754 SP349 1fr +50c bl gray 40 40

B755 SP349 3fr +1.50fr rose pink 85 65

B756 SP349 6fr +3fr redsh brn 1.10 1.10

Issued to honor Protestantism in Belgium. The surtax was for the erection of a Protestant church.

Foot Soldier, 1918
SP350

Battle of Bastogne
SP351

Designs: 2fr+1fr, Flag bearer, Guides Regiment, 1914. 3fr+1.50fr, Trumpeter of the Grenadiers and drummers, 1914.

1964, Aug. 1 Photo. *Perf. 11½*

B757 SP350 1fr +50c multi 30 28

B758 SP350 2fr +1fr multi 50 50

B759 SP350 3fr +1.50fr multi 70 70

Issued to commemorate the 50th anniversary of the German aggression against Belgium in 1914. The surtax aided patriotic undertakings.

1964, Aug. 1 Unwmkd.

Design: 6fr+3fr, Liberation of the estuary of the Escaut.

B760 SP351 3fr +1fr multi 45 45

B761 SP351 6fr +3fr multi 1.10 1.10

Issued to commemorate Belgium's Resistance and liberation of World War II. The surtax was to help found an International Student Center at Antwerp and to aid cultural undertakings.

Souvenir Sheets

Rogier van der Weyden Paintings
SP352

Descent From the Cross
SP353

Designs: 1fr, Philip the Good. 2fr, Portrait of a Lady. 3fr, Man with Arrow.

1964, Sept. 19 Photo. *Perf. 11½*

B762 SP352 Sheet of 3 6.00 6.00

a. 1fr multi 1.75 1.75

b. 2fr multi 1.75 1.75

c. 3fr multi 1.75 1.75

Engraved

B763 SP353 8fr red brn, sheet of 1 6.00 6.00

Issued to commemorate the 5th centenary of the death of the painter Rogier van der Weyden (Roger de La Pasture, 1400–1464). The surtax went to various cultural organizations. Sheets have gray brown frames and marginal inscriptions. Size of sheets: 153x114mm. Size of stamps: 24x36mm. (Nos. B762a,b,c); 54x35mm. (No. B763). No. B762 sold for 14fr, No. B763 for 16fr.

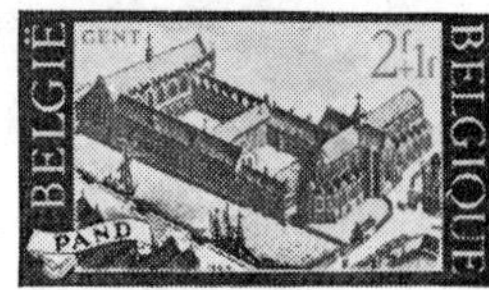

Ancient View of the Pand
SP354

Design: 3fr+1fr, Present view of the Pand from Lys River.

1964, Oct. 10 Photogravure

B764 SP354 2fr +1fr blk, grnsh bl & ultra 55 45

B765 SP354 3fr +1fr lil rose, bl & dk brn 80 80

The surtax was for the restoration of the Pand Dominican Abbey in Ghent.

Type of 1963 and

Child of Charles I, Painted by Van Dyck
SP355

Designs: 1fr+40c, William of Orange with his bride, by Van Dyck. 2fr+1fr, Portrait of a small boy with dogs by Erasmus Quellin and Jan Fyt. 3fr+1fr, Alexander Farnese by Antonio Moro. 4fr+2fr, William II, Prince of Orange by Van Dyck. 6fr+3fr, Artist's children by Cornelis De Vos.

1964, Dec. 5 Engraved *Perf. 11½*

B766 SP355 50c +10c rose cl 20 20

B767 SP355 1fr +40c car rose 30 28

B768 SP355 2fr +1fr vio brn 60 60

B769 SP355 3fr +1fr gray 50 50

B770 SP355 4fr +2fr vio bl 60 60

B771 SP347 6fr +3fr brt pur 90 90

Nos. B766-B771 (6) 3.10 3.08

The surtax was for anti-tuberculosis work.

Liberator, Shaking Prisoner's Hand, Concentration Camp
SP356

Designs: 1fr+50c, Prisoner's hand reaching for the sun. 3fr+1.50fr, Searchlights and tank breaking down barbed wire (horiz.). 8fr+5fr, Rose growing amid the ruins (horiz.).

Engraved and Photogravure

1965, May 8 *Perf. 11½* Unwmkd.

B772 SP356 50c +50c tan, blk & buff 20 20

B773 SP356 1fr +50c multi 25 25

B774	SP356	3fr +1.50fr dl lil & blk	50	50
B775	SP356	8fr +5fr multi	90	90

Issued to commemorate the 20th anniversary of the liberation of the concentration camps for political prisoners and prisoners of war.

Stoclet House, Brussels
SP357

Stoclet House: 6fr+3fr, Hall with marble foundation (vert.). 8fr+4fr, View of house from garden.

1965, June 21

B776	SP357	3fr +1fr sl & tan	40	40
B777	SP357	6fr +3fr sep	70	70
B778	SP357	8fr +4fr vio brn & tan	90	90

Issued to commemorate the 95th anniversary of the birth of the Austrian architect Josef Hoffmann (1870–1956), builder of the art nouveau residence of Adolphe Stoclet, engineer and financier.

Jackson's Chameleon
SP358

Animals from Antwerp Zoo: 2fr+1fr, Common iguanas. 3fr+1.50fr, African monitor. 6fr+3fr, Komodo monitor. 8fr+4fr, Nile softshell turtle.

1965, Oct. 16 Photo. *Perf. 11½*

B779	SP358	1fr +50c multi	20	20
B780	SP358	2fr +1fr multi	25	25
B781	SP358	3fr +1.50fr multi	38	38
B782	SP358	6fr +3fr multi	75	75

Miniature Sheet

B783	SP358	8fr +4fr multi	3.00	3.00

The surtax was for various cultural and philanthropic organizations. No. B783 contains one stamp (52x35mm.) and has gray animal border. Size: 117x95mm.

Boatmen's and Archers' Guild Halls
SP359

Buildings on Grand-Place, Brussels: 1fr+40c, Brewers' Hall. 2fr+1fr, "King of Spain." 3fr+1.50fr, "Dukes of Brabant." 10fr+4.50fr, Tower of City Hall and St. Michael.

1965, Dec. 4 Engraved *Perf. 11½*

Size: 35x24mm.

B784	SP359	50c +10c ultra	20	20
B785	SP359	1fr +40c bl grn	30	30
B786	SP359	2fr +1fr rose cl	40	40
B787	SP359	3fr +1.50fr vio	50	50

Size: 24x44mm.

B788	SP359	10fr +4.50fr sep & gray	70	70
		Nos. B784-B788 (5)	2.10	2.10

The surtax was for anti-tuberculosis work.

Souvenir Sheets

Queen Elisabeth
SP360

Design: No. B790, Types of 1931 and 1956.

1966, Apr. 16 Photo. *Perf. 11½*

B789	SP360	Sheet of 2	3.25	3.25
a.		SP74 3fr dk brn & gray grn	1.40	1.40
b.		SP87 3fr dk brn, yel grn & gold	1.40	1.40
B790	SP360	Sheet of 2	3.25	3.25
a.		SP42 3fr dk brn & dl bl	1.40	1.40
b.		SP304 3fr dk brn & gray	1.40	1.40

The surtax went to various cultural organizations.

Each sheet contains two stamps plus label with the Queen's initial; sold for 20fr. Dark brown marginal inscription. Size: 81½x115mm.

Luminescent Paper

was used in printing Nos. B789–B790, B801–B806, B808–B809, B811–B823, B825–B831, B833–B835, B837–B840, B842–B846, B848–B850, B852–B854, B856–B863, and from B865 onward unless otherwise noted.

Diver
SP361

Design: 10fr+4fr, Swimmer at start.

1966, May 9 Engraved

B791	SP361	60c +40c Prus grn, ol & org brn	20	20
B792	SP361	10fr +4fr ol grn, org brn & mag	90	90

Issued to publicize the importance of swimming instruction.

Minorites' Convent, Liège
SP362

Designs: 1fr+50c, Val-Dieu Abbey, Aubel. 2fr+1fr, View and seal of Huy. 10fr+4.50fr, Statue of Ambiorix by Jules Bertin, and tower, Tongeren.

1966, Aug. 27 Engr. *Perf. 11½*

B793	SP362	60c +40c bl, vio brn & org brn	13	13
B794	SP362	1fr +50c vio brn, bl & grnsh bl	20	18
B795	SP362	2fr +1fr car rose, vio brn & org brn	32	25
B796	SP362	10fr +4.50fr brt grn, vio brn & sl bl	1.00	90

The surtax was for various patriotic and cultural organizations.

Surveyor and Dog Team
SP363

Designs: 3fr+1.50fr, Adrien de Gerlache and "Belgica." 6fr+3fr, Surveyor, weather balloon and ship. 10fr+5fr, Penguins and "Magga Dan" (ship used for 1964, 1965 and 1966 expeditions).

1966, Oct. 8 Engraved *Perf. 11½*

B797	SP363	1fr +50c bl grn	20	20
B798	SP363	3fr +1.50fr pale vio	35	35
B799	SP363	6fr +3fr dk car	55	55

Souvenir Sheet

Engraved and Photogravure

B800	SP363	10fr +5fr dk gray, sky bl & dk red	1.40	1.40

Issued to publicize Belgian Antarctic expeditions. No. B800 contains one stamp (52x35mm.); inscriptions, map of Antarctica and observation post in margin. Size: 130x95mm.

Boy with Ball and Dog
SP364

Designs: 2fr+1fr, Girl skipping rope. 3fr+1.50fr, Girl and boy blowing soap bubbles. 6fr+3fr, Girl and boy rolling hoops (horiz.). 8fr+3.50fr, Four children at play and cat (horiz.).

Engraved and Photogravure

1966, Dec. 3 *Perf. 11½*

B801	SP364	1fr +1fr pink & blk	15	15
B802	SP364	2fr +1fr lt bluish grn & blk	25	25
B803	SP364	3fr +1.50fr lt vio & blk	32	32
B804	SP364	6fr +3fr pale sal & dk brn	50	50
B805	SP364	8fr +3.50fr lt yel grn & dk brn	70	60
		Nos. B801-B805 (5)	1.92	1.82

The surtax was for anti-tuberculosis work.

Souvenir Sheet

Refugees
SP365

Designs: 1fr, Boy receiving clothes. 2fr, Tibetan children. 3fr, African mother and children.

1967, Mar. 11 Photo. *Perf. 11½*

B806	SP365	Sheet of 3	2.50	2.50
a.		1fr blk & yel	60	60
b.		2fr blk & bl	60	60
c.		3fr blk & org	60	60

Issued to help refugees around the world. Sheet has black border with Belgian P.T.T. and U.N. Refugee emblems. Size: 110x76 mm. Sold for 20fr.

Robert Schuman
SP366

Kongolo Memorial, Gentinnes
SP367

Colonial Brotherhood Emblem
SP368

1967, June 24 Engraved *Perf. 11½*

B807	SP366	2fr +1fr gray bl	55	55

Engraved and Photogravure

B808	SP367	5fr +2fr brn & ol	65	65
B809	SP368	10fr +5fr multi	1.10	90

Issued to commemorate respectively: Robert Schuman (1886–1963), French statesman, one of the founders of European Steel and Coal Community, first president of European Parliament (2fr+1fr); Kongolo Memorial, erected in memory of missionary and civilian victims in the Congo (5fr+2fr); a memorial for African Troops, Brussels (10fr+5fr).

Preaching Fool from "Praise of Folly" by Erasmus
SP369

Erasmus, by Quentin Massys
SP370

Designs: 2fr+1fr, Exhorting Fool from Praise of Folly. 5fr+2fr, Thomas More's Family, by Hans Holbein (horiz.). 6fr+3fr, Pierre Gilles (Aegidius), by Quentin Massys.

Photogravure and Engraved (SP369); Photogravure (SP370)

1967, Sept. 2 *Perf. 11* Unwmkd.

B810	SP369	1fr +50c tan, blk, bl & car	18	18
B811	SP369	2fr +1fr tan, blk & car	25	25
B812	SP370	3fr +1.50fr multi	38	38
B813	SP369	5fr +2fr tan, blk & car	45	45
B814	SP370	6fr +3fr multi	60	60
		Nos. B810-B814 (5)	1.86	1.86

Issued to commemorate Erasmus (1466(?)–1536), Dutch scholar and his era.

Souvenir Sheet

Pro-Post Association Emblem
SP371

Engraved and Photogravure

1967, Oct. 21 *Perf. 11½*

B815 SP371 10fr +5fr multi 1.50 1.50

Issued to publicize the POSTPHILA Philatelic Exhibition, Brussels, Oct. 21–29. No. B815 has black marginal inscription and ornaments. Size: 112x77mm.

Detail from Brueghel's "Children's Games"
SP372

Designs: Various Children's Games. Singles of Nos. B816–B821 arranged in 2 rows of 3 show complete painting by Pieter Brueghel.

1967, Dec. 9 Photo. *Perf. 11½*

B816 SP372 1fr +50c multi 22 22
B817 SP372 2fr +50c multi 32 32
B818 SP372 3fr +1fr multi 35 35
B819 SP372 6fr +3fr multi 55 55
B820 SP372 10fr +4fr multi 80 80
B821 SP372 13fr +6fr multi 1.40 1.40
Nos. B816-B821 (6) 3.64 3.64

Queen Fabiola Holding Refugee Child from Congo
SP373

Design: 6fr+3fr, Queen Elisabeth and Dr. Depage.

1968, Apr. 27 Photo. *Perf. 11½*

Cross in Red

B822 SP373 6fr +3fr sep & gray 65 65
B823 SP373 10fr +5fr sep & gray 1.10 1.10

The surtax was for the Red Cross.

Woman Gymnast and Calendar Stone
SP374

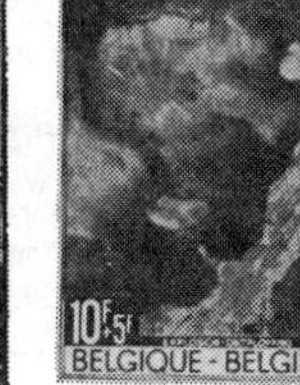

Yachting and "The Swimmer" by Andrien
SP375

"Explosion"
SP376

Designs: 2fr+1fr, Weight lifter and Mayan motif. 3fr+1.50fr, Hurdler, colossus of Tula and animal head from Kukulkan. 6fr+2fr, Bicyclists and Chichen Itza Temple.

Engraved and Photogravure

1968, May 27 *Perf. 11½*

B824 SP374 1fr +50c multi 18 18
B825 SP374 2fr +1fr multi 28 28
B826 SP374 3fr +1.50fr multi 35 35
B827 SP374 6fr +2fr multi 65 65

Photogravure

B828 SP375 13fr +5fr multi 1.50 1.50
Nos. B824-B828 (5) 2.96 2.96

Issued to publicize the 19th Olympic Games, Mexico City, Oct. 12–27.

1968, June 22 Photogravure

Designs (Paintings by Pol Mara): 12fr+5fr, "Fire." 13fr+5fr, "Tornado."

B829 SP376 10fr +5fr multi 90 90
B830 SP376 12fr +5fr multi 1.25 1.25
B831 SP376 13fr +5fr multi 1.50 1.50

The surtax was for disaster victims.

Undulate Triggerfish
SP377

Tropical Fish: 3fr+1.50fr, Angelfish. 6fr+3fr, Turkeyfish (Pterois volitans). 10fr+5fr, Orange butterflyfish.

Engraved and Photogravure

1968, Oct. 19 *Perf. 11½*

B832 SP377 1fr +50c multi 32 32
B833 SP377 3fr +1.50fr multi 50 45
B834 SP377 6fr +3fr multi 90 80
B835 SP377 10fr +5fr multi 1.00 1.00

King Albert and Queen Elisabeth Entering Brussels—SP378

Tomb of the Unknown Soldier and Eternal Flame, Brussels
SP379

Designs: 1fr+50c, King Albert, Queen Elisabeth and Crown Prince Leopold on balcony, Bruges (vert.). 6fr+3fr, King and Queen entering Liège.

1968, Nov. 9 Photo. *Perf. 11½*

B836 SP378 1fr +50c multi 32 35
B837 SP378 3fr +1.50fr multi 50 45
B838 SP378 6fr +3fr multi 90 80

Engraved and Photogravure

B839 SP379 10fr +5fr multi 1.00 1.00

Issued to commemorate the 50th anniversary of the victory in World War I.

Souvenir Sheet

The Painter and the Amateur, by Peter Brueghel
SP380

1969, May 10 Engraved *Perf. 11½*

B840 SP380 10fr +5fr sep 3.00 3.00

Issued to publicize the POSTPHILA 1969 Philatelic Exhibition, Brussels, May 10–18. Size of stamp: 40x47mm.; size of sheet: 90x123mm.

Huts, by Ivanka D. Pancheva, Bulgaria
SP381

Msgr. Victor Scheppers
SP382

Children's Drawings and UNICEF Emblem: 3fr+1.50fr, "My Art" (Santa Claus), by Claes Patric, Belgium. 6fr+3fr, "In the Sun" (young boy), by Helena Rejchlova, Czechoslovakia. 10fr+5fr, "Out for a Walk" by Phillis Sporn, USA (horiz.).

1969, May 31 Photo. *Perf. 11½*

B841 SP381 1fr +50c multi 22 22
B842 SP381 3fr +1.50fr multi 35 35
B843 SP381 6fr +3fr multi 75 75
B844 SP381 10fr +5fr multi 1.10 1.10

The surtax was for philanthropic purposes.

1969, July 5 Engraved

B845 SP382 6fr +3fr rose cl 1.40 1.40

Issued to commemorate Msgr. Victor Scheppers (1802–77), prison reformer and founder of the Brothers of Mechlin (Scheppers).

Souvenir Sheet

Moon Landing Type of 1969

Design: 20fr+10fr, Armstrong, Collins and Aldrin and moon with Tranquillity Base (vert.).

1969, Sept. 20 Photo. *Perf. 11½*

B846 A245 20fr +10fr ind 7.25 7.25

See note after No. 693. No. B846 contains one stamp. Margin has commemorative inscription and picture of Armstrong stepping on moon. Size: 94x129mm.

Heads from Alexander the Great Tapestry, 15th Century
SP383

Designs from Tapestries: 3fr+1.50fr, Fiddler from "The Feast," c. 1700. 10fr+4fr, Head of beggar from "The Healing of the Paralytic," 16th century.

1969, Sept. 20

B847 SP383 1fr +50c multi 25 25
B848 SP383 3fr +1.50fr multi 52 52
B849 SP383 10fr +4fr multi 1.25 1.25

The surtax was for philanthropic purposes.

Bearded Antwerp Bantam
SP384

Engraved and Photogravure

1969, Nov. 8 *Perf. 11½*

B850 SP384 10fr +5fr multi 2.00 2.00

Angel Playing Lute
SP385

Designs from Stained Glass Windows: 1.50fr+50c, Angel with trumpet, St. Waudru's, Mons. 7fr+3fr, Angel with viol, St. Jacques', Liege. 9fr+4fr, King with bagpipes, Royal Art Museum, Brussels.

1969, Dec. 13 Photogravure

Size: 24x35mm.

B851 SP385 1.50fr +50c multi 28 28
B852 SP385 3.50fr +1.50fr multi 55 55
B853 SP385 7fr +3fr multi 80 80

Size: 35x52mm.

B854 SP386 9fr +4fr multi 1.10 1.10

The surtax was for philanthropic purposes.

Farm and Windmill, Open-air Museum, Bokrijk
SP386

Belgian Museums: 3.50fr+1.50fr, Stage Coach Inn, Courcelles. 7fr+3fr, "The Thresher of Trevires," Gallo-Roman sculpture, Gaumais Museum, Virton. 9fr+4fr, "The Sovereigns," by Henry Moore, Middelheim Museum, Antwerp.

Engraved and Photogravure

1970, May 30 ***Perf. 11½***

B855 SP386 1.50fr +50c multi 45 45
B856 SP386 3.50fr +1.50fr multi 65 65
B857 SP386 7fr +3fr multi 90 90
B858 SP386 9fr +4fr multi 1.10 1.10

The surtax went to various culture organizations.

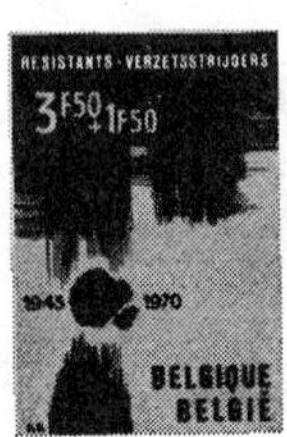

"Resistance"
SP387

Design: 7fr+3fr, "Liberation of Camps." The designs were originally used as book covers.

1970, July 4 Photo. ***Perf. 11½***

B859 SP387 3.50fr +1.50fr blk, gray grn & dp car 65 65
B860 SP387 7fr +3fr blk, lil & dp car 90 90

Issued to honor the Resistance Movement and to commemorate the 25th anniversary of the liberation of concentration camps.

Fishing Rod and Reel
SP388

Design: 9fr+4fr, Hockey stick and puck (vert.).

Engraved and Photogravure

1970, Sept. 19 ***Perf. 11½***

B861 SP388 3.50fr +1.50fr multi 65 65
B862 SP388 9fr +4fr brt grn & multi 1.50 1.50

Souvenir Sheet

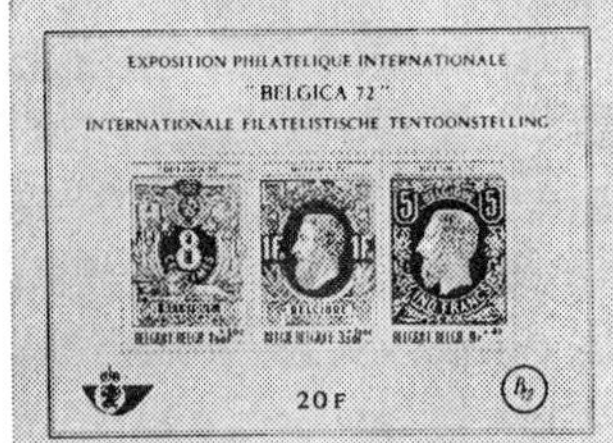

Belgium Nos. 31, 36 and 39
SP389

Engraved and Photogravure

1970, Oct. 10 ***Perf. 11½***

B863 SP389 20fr sheet of 3 7.25 7.25
a. 1.50fr+50c blk & dl lil 2.00 2.00
b. 3.50fr+1.50fr blk & lil 2.00 2.00
c. 9fr+4fr blk & red brn 2.00 2.00

Issued to publicize BELGICA 72 International Philatelic Exhibition, Brussels, June 24–July 9. No. B863 has black marginal inscription and lilac frame. Size: 130x97mm.

Camille Huysmans (1871–1968)
SP390

"Anxious City" (Detail) by Paul Delvaux
SP391

Portraits: 3.50fr+1.50fr, Joseph Cardinal Cardijn (1882–1967). 7fr+3fr, Maria Baers (1883–1959). 9fr+4fr, Paul Pastur (1866–1938).

Engraved and Photogravure

1970, Nov. 14 ***Perf. 11½***

Portraits in Sepia

B864 SP390 1.50fr +50c car rose 28 28
B865 SP390 3.50fr +1.50fr lil 65 65
B866 SP390 7fr +3fr grn 1.00 1.00
B867 SP390 9fr +4fr bl 1.40 1.40

1970, Dec. 12 **Photogravure**

Design: 7fr+3fr, "The Memory," by René Magritte.

B868 SP391 3.50fr +1.50fr multi 68 68
B869 SP391 7fr +3fr multi 1.15 1.15

Notre Dame du Vivier, Marche-les-Dames
SP392

Design: 7fr+3fr, Turnhout Beguinage and Beguine.

1971, March 13 ***Perf. 11½***

B870 SP392 3.50fr +1.50 multi 65 65
B871 SP392 7fr +3fr multi 1.20 1.20

The surtax was for philanthropic purposes.

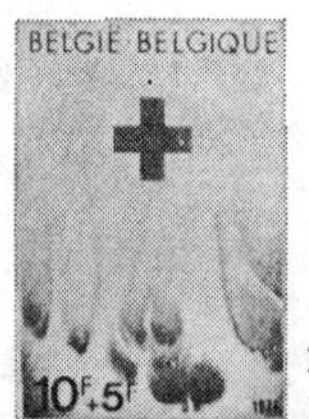

Red Cross
SP393

1971, May 22 Photo. ***Perf. 11½***

B872 SP393 10fr +5fr crim & blk 1.75 1.50

Belgian Red Cross.

Discobolus and Munich Cathedral
SP394

Festival of Flanders
SP395

Engraved and Photogravure

1971, June 19 ***Perf. 11½***

B873 SP394 7fr +3fr bl & blk 2.25 2.25

Publicity for the 20th Summer Olympic Games, Munich 1972.

1971, Sept. 11 Photo. ***Perf. 11½***

Design: 7fr+3fr, Wallonia Festival.

B874 SP395 3.50fr +1.50fr multi 55 55
B875 SP395 7fr +3fr multi 1.00 1.00

Attre Palace—SP396

Steen Palace, Elewijt
SP397

Design: 10fr+5fr, Royal Palace, Brussels.

1971, Oct. 23 **Engraved**

B876 SP396 3.50fr +1.50fr sl grn 1.10 1.10
B877 SP397 7fr +3fr red brn 1.50 1.50
B878 SP396 10fr +5fr vio bl 2.75 2.75

Surtax was for BELGICA 72, International Philatelic Exposition.

Ox Fly
SP398

Insects: 1.50fr+50c, Luna moth (vert.). 7fr+3fr, Wasp, polistes gallicus. 9fr+4fr, Tiger beetle (vert.).

1971, Dec. 11 Photo. ***Perf. 11½***

B879 SP398 1.50fr +50c multi 45 45
B880 SP398 3.50fr +1.50fr multi 60 60
B881 SP398 7fr +3fr multi 1.10 1.10
B882 SP398 9fr +4fr multi 1.40 1.40

Surtax was for philanthropic purposes.

Leopold I on No. 1
SP399

Epilepsy Emblem
SP400

Designs: 2fr+1fr, Leopold I on No. 5. 2.50fr+1fr, Leopold II on No. 45. 3.50fr+1.50fr, Leopold II on No. 48. 6fr+3fr, Albert I on No. 135. 7fr+3fr, Albert I on No. 214. 10fr+5fr, Albert I on No. 231. 15fr+7.50fr, Leopold III on No. 290. 20fr+10fr, King Baudouin on No. 718.

Engraved and Photogravure

1972, June 24 ***Perf. 11½***

"B" in Gold

B883 SP399 1.50fr +50c brn & blk 70 70
B884 SP399 2fr +1fr brick red & brn 80 80
B885 SP399 2.50 +1fr car & blk 1.25 1.25
B886 SP399 3.50fr +1.50fr vio & blk 1.50 1.50
B887 SP399 6fr +3fr rose lil & blk 2.00 2.00
B888 SP399 7fr +3fr rose car & blk 2.75 2.75
B889 SP399 10fr +5fr sl bl & blk 3.25 3.25
B890 SP399 15fr +7fr gray grn & bl grn 4.50 4.50
B891 SP399 20fr +10fr red brn & brn 7.00 7.00
Nos. B883-B891 (9) 23.75 23.75

Belgica 72, International Philatelic Exhibition, Brussels, June 24–July 9. Nos. B883–B891 issued in sheets of 10 and of 20 (2 tête bêche sheets with gutter between). Belgica 72 emblem in stamp color and gray blue border and inscription in margin. Sold in complete sets.

1972, Sept. 9 Photo. ***Perf. 11½***

B892 SP400 10fr +5fr multi 1.50 1.50

The surtax was for the William Lennox Center for epilepsy research and treatment.

Gray Lag Goose
SP401

Designs: 4.50fr+2fr, Lapwing. 8fr+4fr, Stork. 9fr+4.50fr, Kestrel (horiz.).

1972, Dec. 16 Photo. ***Perf. 11½***

B893 SP401 2fr +1fr multi 55 55
B894 SP401 4.50fr +2fr multi 80 80
B895 SP401 8fr +4fr multi 1.30 1.30
B896 SP401 9fr +4.50fr multi 1.85 1.85

Bijloke Abbey, Ghent—SP402

Designs: 4.50fr+2fr, St. Ursmer Collegiate Church, Lobbes. 8fr+4fr, Park Abbey, Heverle. 9fr+4.50fr, Abbey, Floreffe.

1973, Mar. 24 Engr. ***Perf. 11½***

B897 SP402 2fr +1fr sl grn 90 90
B898 SP402 4.50fr +2fr brn 1.40 1.40
B899 SP402 8fr +4fr rose lil 1.75 1.75
B900 SP402 9fr +4.50fr brt bl 2.25 2.25

Basketball
SP403

1973, Apr. 7 **Photo. & Engr.**

B901 SP403 10fr +5fr multi 1.75 1.75

First World Basketball Championships of the Handicapped, Bruges, Apr. 16–21.

Dirk Martens' Printing Press
SP404

Lady Talbot, by Petrus Christus
SP405

Hadrian and Marcus Aurelius Coins
SP406

Council of Malines, by Coussaert—SP407

Designs: 3.50fr+1.50fr, Head of Amon and Tutankhamen's cartouche. 10fr+5fr, Three-master of Ostend Merchant Company.

Photo. & Engr.; Photo. (B906)

1973, June 23 **Perf. 11½**

B902	SP404	2fr	+1fr multi	90	90
B903	SP404	3.50fr	+1.50fr multi	1.10	1.10
B904	SP405	4.50fr	+2fr multi	1.75	1.75
B905	SP406	8fr	+4fr multi	3.00	3.00
B906	SP407	9fr	+4.50fr multi	4.00	4.00
B907	SP407	10fr	+5fr multi	5.50	5.50
	Nos. B902-B907 (6)			16.25	16.25

Historical Anniversaries: 500th anniversary of first book printed in Belgium (B902); 50th anniversary of Queen Elisabeth Egyptological Foundation (B903); 500th anniversary of death of painter Petrus Christus (B904); Discovery of Roman treasure at Luttre-Liberchies (B905); 500th anniversary of Great Council of Malines (B906); 250th anniversary of the Ostend Merchant Company (B907).

No. B902 is not luminescent.

Queen of Hearts
SP408

Symbol of Blood Donations
SP409

Old Playing Cards: No. B909, King of Clubs. No. B910, Jack of Diamonds. No. B911, King of Spades.

1973, Dec. 8 **Photo.** **Perf. 11½**

B908	SP408	5	+2.50fr multi	1.50	1.50
B909	SP408	5	+2.50fr multi	1.50	1.50
B910	SP408	5	+2.50fr multi	1.50	1.50
B911	SP408	5	+2.50fr multi	1.50	1.50

Surtax was for philanthropic purposes. Nos. B908–B911 printed se-tenant in sheets of 24 (4x6).

1974, Feb. 23 **Photo.** **Perf. 11½**

Design: 10fr+5fr, Traffic lights, Red Cross (symbolic of road accidents).

B912	SP409	4fr	+2fr multi	90	90
B913	SP409	10fr	+5fr multi	1.50	1.50

The Red Cross as blood collector and aid to accident victims.

Armand Jamar, Self-portrait
SP410

Van Gogh, Self-portrait and House at Cuesmes
SP411

Designs: 5fr+2.50fr, Anton Bergmann and view of Lierre. 7fr+3.50fr, Henri Vieuxtemps and view of Verviers. 10fr+5fr, James Ensor, self-portrait, and masks.

1974, Apr. 6 **Photo.** **Perf. 11½**

Size: 24x35mm.

B914	SP410	4fr	+2fr multi	90	90
B915	SP410	5fr	+2.50fr multi	1.15	1.15
B916	SP410	7fr	+3.50fr multi	1.50	1.50

Size: 35x52mm.

B917	SP410	10fr	+5fr multi	2.25	2.25

1974, Sept. 21 **Photo.** **Perf. 11½**

B918	SP411	10fr	+5fr multi	2.00	2.00

Opening of Vincent van Gogh House at Cuesmes, where he worked as teacher.

Gentian
SP412

Spotted Cat's Ear
SP414

Badger
SP413

Design: 7fr+3.50fr, Beetle.

1974, Dec. 8 **Photo.** **Perf. 11½**

B919	SP412	4fr	+2fr multi	60	60
B920	SP413	5fr	+2.50fr multi	1.10	1.10
B921	SP413	7fr	+3.50fr multi	1.40	1.40
B922	SP414	10fr	+5fr multi	1.65	1.65

Pesaro Palace, Venice
SP415

St. Bavon Abbey, Ghent
SP416

Virgin and Child, by Michelangelo
SP417

1975, Apr. 12 **Engr.** **Perf. 11½**

B923	SP415	6.50fr	+2.50fr brn	1.10	1.10
B924	SP416	10fr	+4.50 vio brn	1.75	1.75
B925	SP417	15fr	+6.50fr brt bl	2.25	2.25

Surtax was for various cultural organizations.

Frans Hemerijckx and Leprosarium, Kasai
SP418

1975, Sept. 13 **Photo.** **Perf. 11½**

B926	SP418	20fr	+10fr multi	2.75	2.75

Dr. Frans Hemerijckx (1902–1969), tropical medicine and leprosy expert.

Emile Moyson
SP419

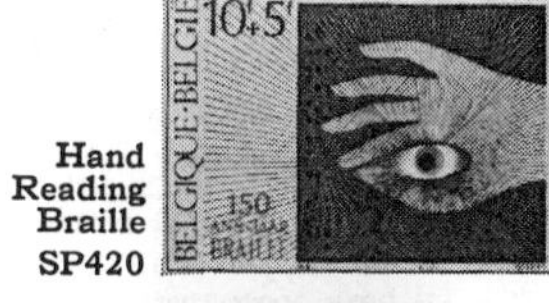

Hand Reading Braille
SP420

Beheading of St. Dympna
SP421

Design: 6.50fr+3fr, Dr. Ferdinand Augustin Snellaert.

1975, Nov. 22 **Engr.** **Perf. 11½**

B927	SP419	4.50fr	+2fr lil	90	90
B928	SP419	6.50fr	+3fr grn	1.00	1.00

Engraved and Photogravure

B929	SP420	10fr	+5fr multi	1.50	1.50

Photogravure

B930	SP421	13fr	+6fr multi	2.25	2.25

Emile Moyson (1838–1868), freedom fighter for the rights of Flemings and Walloons; Dr. Snellaert (1809–1872), physician and Flemish patriot; Louis Braille (1809–1852), sesquicentennial of invention of Braille system of writing for the blind; St. Dympna, patron saint of Geel, famous for treatment of mentally ill.

The Cheese Vendor
SP421

Designs (THEMABELGA Emblem and): No. B932, Potato vendor. No. B933, Basket carrier. No. B934, Shrimp fisherman with horse (horiz.). No. B935, Knife grinder (horiz.). No. B936, Milk vendor with dog cart (horiz.).

Engraved and Photogravure

1975, Dec. 13 **Perf. 11½**

B931	SP421	4.50fr	+1.50fr multi	65	65
B932	SP421	6.50fr	+3fr multi	90	90
B933	SP421	6.50fr	+3fr multi	1.00	1.00
B934	SP421	10fr	+5fr multi	1.50	1.50
B935	SP421	10fr	+5fr multi	1.50	1.50
B936	SP421	30fr	+15fr multi	4.25	4.25
	Nos. B931-B936 (6)			9.80	9.80

THEMABELGA International Topical Philatelic Exhibition, Brussels, Dec. 13–21. Issued in sheets of 10 (5x2).

Blackface Fund Collector
SP422

1976, Feb. 14 **Photo.** **Perf. 11½**

B937	SP422	10fr	+5fr multi	1.50	1.50

Centenary of the "Conservatoire Africain" philanthropic society, and to publicize the Princess Paola crèches.

Swimming and Olympic Emblem
SP423

Designs (Montreal Olympic Games Emblem and): 5fr+2fr, Running (vert.). 6.50fr+2.50fr, Equestrian.

1976, Apr. 10 **Photo.** **Perf. 11½**

B938	SP423	4.50fr	+1.50fr multi	45	45
B939	SP423	5fr	+2fr multi	65	65
B940	SP423	6.50fr	+2.50fr multi	90	90

21st Olympic Games, Montreal, Canada, July 17–Aug. 1.

Queen Elisabeth Playing Violin
SP424

Engraved and Photogravure

1976, May 1 **Perf. 11½**

B941	SP424	14fr	+6fr blk & cl	1.85	1.85

Queen Elisabeth International Music Competition, 25th anniversary.

Souvenir Sheet

Jan Olieslagers, Bleriot Monoplane, Aero Club Emblem—SP425

Engraved and Photogravure

1976, June 12 ***Perf. 11½***

B942	SP425	25fr +10fr multi	5.00	5.00

Royal Belgian Aero Club, 75th anniversary, and Jan Olieslagers (1883–1942), aviation pioneer. No. B942 has blue marginal decorations and black inscription. Size: 83x116mm.

Adoration of the Shepherds (detail), by Rubens
SP426

Dwarf, by Velazquez
SP427

Rubens Paintings (Details): 4.50fr, Descent from the Cross. No. B945, The Virgin with the Parrot. No. B946, Adoration of the Kings. No. B947, Last Communion of St. Francis. 30fr+15fr, Virgin and Child.

1976, Sept. 4 **Photo.** ***Perf. 11½***

Size: 30x52mm.

B943	SP426	4.50fr +1.50fr multi	90	90

Size: 24x35mm.

B944	SP426	6.50fr +3fr multi	1.25	1.25
B945	SP426	6.50fr +3fr multi	1.25	1.25
B946	SP426	10fr +5fr multi	1.75	1.75
B947	SP426	10fr +5fr multi	2.00	2.00

Size: 30x52mm.

B948	SP426	30fr +15fr multi	3.50	3.50
		Nos. B943-B948 (6)	10.65	10.65

Peter Paul Rubens (1577–1640), Flemish painter, 400th birth anniversary.

1976, Nov. 6 **Photo.** ***Perf. 11½***

B949	SP427	14fr +6fr multi	1.50	1.50

Surtax was for the National Association for the Mentally Handicapped.

Dr. Albert Hustin
SP428

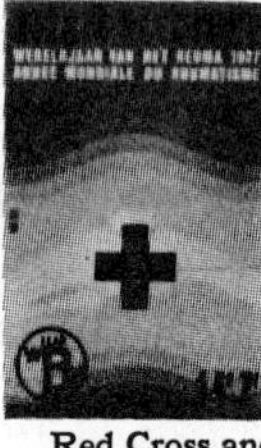

Red Cross and Rheumatism Year Emblem
SP429

1977, Feb. 19 **Photo.** ***Perf. 11½***

B950	SP428	6.50fr +2.50 multi	1.10	1.10
B951	SP429	14fr +7fr multi	1.50	1.50

Belgian Red Cross.

Bordet Atheneum, Empress Maria Theresa
SP430

Conductor and Orchestra, by E. Tytgat
SP431

Lucien Van Obbergh, Stage
SP432

Humanistic Society Emblem
SP433

Camille Lemonnier
SP434

Design: No. B953, Marie-Therese College, Herve, and coat of arms.

1977, Mar. 21 **Photo.** ***Perf. 11½***

B952	SP430	4.50fr +1fr multi	55	55
B953	SP430	4.50fr +1fr multi	55	55
B954	SP431	5fr +2fr multi	65	65
B955	SP432	6.50fr +2fr multi	90	90
B956	SP433	6.50fr +2fr blk & red	90	90

Engraved

B957	SP434	10fr +5fr sl bl	1.40	1.40
		Nos. B952-B957 (6)	4.95	4.95

Bicentenaries of the Jules Bordet Atheneum, Brussels, and the Marie-Therese College, Herve (Nos. B952–B953); 50th anniversaries of the Brussels Philharmonic Society, and Artists' Union (Nos. B954–B955); 25th anniversary of the Flemish Humanistic Organization (No. B956); 75th anniversary of the French-speaking Belgian writers' organization (No. B957).

Young Soccer Players
SP435

1977, Apr. 18 **Photogravure**

B958	SP435	10fr +5fr multi	1.50	1.50

30th International Junior Soccer Tournament.

Albert-Edouard Janssen, Financier
SP436

Famous Men: No. B960, Joseph Wauters (1875–1929), editor of Le Peuple, and newspaper. No. B961, Jean Capart (1877–1947), Egyptologist, and hieroglyph. No. B962, August de Boeck (1865–1937), composer, and score.

1977, Dec. 3 **Engr.** ***Perf. 11½***

B959	SP436	5fr +2.50fr brn	60	60
B960	SP436	5fr +2.50 red	60	60
B961	SP436	10fr +5fr mag	1.10	1.10
B962	SP436	10fr +5fr bl gray	1.10	1.10

Abandoned Child
SP437

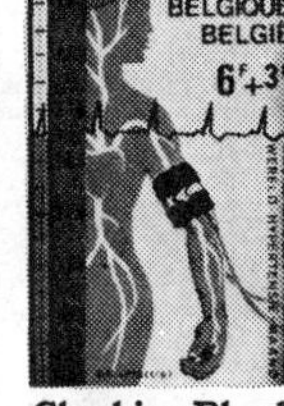

Checking Blood Pressure
SP438

De Mick Sanatorium, Brasschaat—SP439

1978, Feb. 18 **Photo.** ***Perf. 11½***

B963	SP437	4.50fr +1.50fr multi	65	65
B964	SP438	6fr +3fr multi	90	90
B965	SP439	10fr +5fr multi	1.10	1.10

Help for abandoned children (No. B963); fight against hypertension (No. B964); fight against tuberculosis (No. B965).

Actors and Theater
SP440

Karel van de Woestijne
SP441

Designs: No. B967, Harquebusier, Harquebusier Palace and coat of arms. 10fr+5fr, John of Austria and his signature.

Engraved and Photogravure

1978, June 17 ***Perf. 11½***

B966	SP440	6fr +3fr multi	75	75
B967	SP440	6fr +3fr multi	75	75

Engraved

B968	SP441	8fr +4fr blk	90	90
B969	SP441	10fr +5fr blk	1.25	1.25

Centenary of Royal Flemish Theater, Brussels (No. B966); 400th anniversary of Harquebusiers' Guild of Visé, Liège (No. B967); Karel van de Woestijne (1878–1929), poet (No. B968); 400th anniversary of signing of Perpetual Edict by John of Austria (No. B969).

Lake Placid '80 and Belgian Olympic Emblems
SP442

Designs (Moscow '80 Emblem and): 8fr+3.50fr, Kremlin Towers and Belgian Olympic Committee emblem. 7fr+3fr, Runners from Greek vase, Lake Placid '80 emblem and Olympic rings. 14fr+6fr, Olympic flame, Lake Placid '80 and Belgian emblems, Olympic rings.

1978, Nov. 4 **Photo.** ***Perf. 11½***

B970	SP442	6fr +2.50fr multi	90	90
B971	SP442	8fr +3.50fr multi	1.10	1.10

Souvenir Sheet

B972		Sheet of 2	3.50	3.50
a.	SP442	7fr+3fr multi	1.10	1.10
b.	SP442	14fr+6fr multi	1.75	1.75

Surtax was for 1980 Olympic Games. No. B972 has marginal inscription, Olympic Flame and Rings in blue and brown. Size: 150x100mm.

Great Synagogue, Brussels
SP443

Dancers
SP444

Father Pire, African Village
SP445

1978, Dec. 2 **Engr.** ***Perf. 11½***

B973	SP443	6fr +2fr sep	55	55

Photogravure

B974	SP444	8fr +3fr multi	80	80
B975	SP445	14fr +7fr multi	1.40	1.40

Centenary of Great Synagogue of Brussels; Flemish Catholic Youth Action Organization, 50th anniversary; Nobel Peace Prize awarded to Father Dominique Pire for his "Heart Open to the World" movement, 20th anniversary.

Young People Giving First Aid SP446

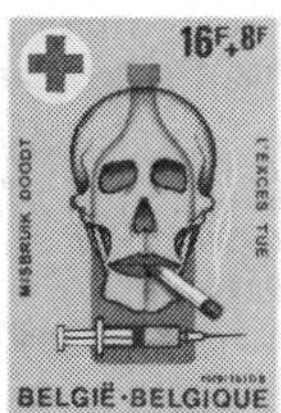

Skull with Bottle, Cigarette, Syringe SP447

1979, Feb. 10 Photo. *Perf. 11½*

B976	SP446	8fr +3fr multi	1.10	1.10
B977	SP447	16fr +8fr multi	1.50	1.50

Belgian Red Cross.

Beatrice Soetkens with Statue of Virgin Mary SP448

Details from Tapestries, 1516–1518, Showing Legend of Our Lady of Sand: 8fr+3fr, Francois de Tassis accepting letter from Emperor Frederick III (beginning of postal service). 14fr+7fr, Arrival of statue, Francois de Tassis and Philip the Fair. No. B981, Statue carried in procession by future Emperor Charles V and his brother Ferdinand. No. B982, Ship carrying Beatrice Soetkens with statue to Brussels (horiz.).

1979, May 5 Photo. *Perf. 11½*

B978	SP448	6fr +2fr multi	50	50
B979	SP448	8fr +3fr multi	70	70
B980	SP448	14fr +7fr multi	1.40	1.40
B981	SP448	20fr +10fr multi	1.90	1.90

Souvenir Sheet

B982	SP448	20fr +10fr multi	1.75	1.75

The surtax was for festivities in connection with the millennium of Brussels. No. B982 has multicolored margin showing entire tapestry with burghers receiving letter from kneeling messenger. Size: 100x 150mm.

Notre Dame Abbey, Brussels—SP449

Designs: 8fr+3fr, Beauvoorde Castle. 14fr+7fr, First issue of "Courrier de L'Escaut" and Barthelemy Dumortier, founder. 20fr+10fr, Shrine of St. Hermes, Renaix.

Engraved and Photogravure

1979, Sept. 15 *Perf. 11½*

B983	SP449	6fr +2fr multi	65	65
B984	SP449	8fr +3fr multi	80	80
B985	SP449	14fr +7fr multi	1.10	1.10
B986	SP449	20fr +10fr multi	2.00	2.00

50th anniversary of restoration of Notre Dame de la Cambre Abbey; historic Beauvoorde Castle, 15th century; sesquicentennial of the regional newspaper "Le Courrier de L'Escaut;" 850th anniversary of the consecration of the Collegiate Church of St. Hermes, Renaix.

Grand-Hornu Coal Mine—SP450

1979, Oct. 22 Engraved *Perf. 11½*

B987	SP450	10fr +5fr blk	90	90

Henry Heyman SP451

Veterans Organization Medal SP452

Boy and IYC Emblem—SP453

1979, Dec. 8 Photo. *Perf. 11½*

B988	SP451	8fr +3fr multi	65	65
B989	SP452	10fr +5fr multi	90	90
B990	SP453	16fr +8fr multi	1.40	1.40

Henri Heyman (1879-1958), Minister of State; Disabled Veterans' Organization, 50th anniversary; International Year of the Child.

Ivo Van Damme, Olympic Rings—SP454

1980, May 3 Photo. *Perf. 11½*

B991	SP454	20fr +10fr multi	1.75	1.75

Ivo Van Damme (1954-1976), silver medalist, 800-meter race, Montreal Olympics, 1976. Surtax was for Van Damme Memorial Foundation.

Queen Louis, King Leopold I—SP455

150th Anniversary of Independence (Queens and Kings): 9fr+3fr, Marie Henriette. Leopold II. 14fr+6fr, Elisabeth, Albert I. 17fr+8fr, Astrid, Leopold III. 25fr+10fr, Fabiola, Baudouin.

1980, May 31 Photo. & Engr. *Perf. 11½*

B992	SP455	6.50 +1.50fr multi	45	45
B993	SP455	9 +3fr multi	65	65
B994	SP455	14 +6fr multi	1.10	1.10
B995	SP455	17 +8fr multi	1.50	1.50
B996	SP455	25 +10fr multi	2.00	2.00
		Nos. B992-B996 (5)	5.70	5.70

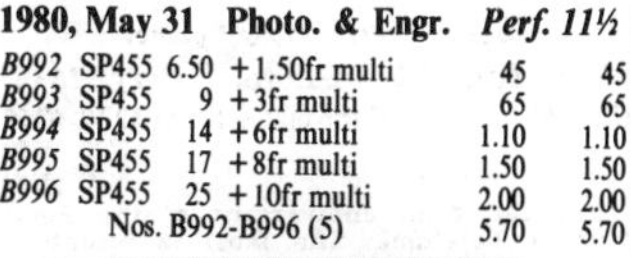

Miner, by Constantine Meunier—SP456

Seal of Bishop Notger, First Prince-Bishop—SP457

Designs: 9fr+3fr, Brewer, 16th century, from St. Lambert's reliquary (vert.). 25fr+10fr, Virgin and Child, 13th century, St. John's Collegiate Church, Liège.

1980, Sept. 13 Photo. *Perf. 11½*

B997	SP456	9 +3fr multi	65	65
B998	SP456	17 +6fr multi	1.25	1.25
B999	SP456	25 +10fr multi	2.00	2.00

Souvenir Sheet

B1000	SP457	20 +10fr multi	3.00	3.00

Millennium of the Principality of Liège. No. B1000 has gray and brown margin showing baptism of Centurion Cornelius from baptismal font in St. Bartholomew's Church, Liège. Size: 150x100mm.

Visual and Oral Handicaps—SP458

International Year of the Disabled: 10fr+5fr, Cerebral handicap (vert.).

1981, Feb. 9 Photo. *Perf. 11½*

B1001	SP458	10 +5fr multi	1.00	1.00
B1002	SP458	25 +10fr multi	2.50	2.50

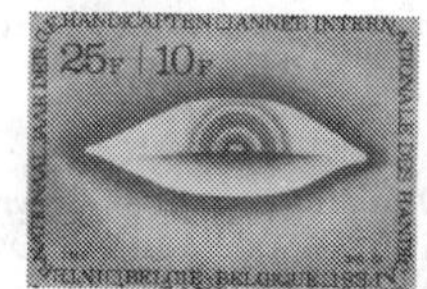

Dove with Red Cross Carrying Globe—SP459

Design: 10fr+5fr, Atomic model (vert.).

1981, Apr. 6 Photo. *Perf. 11½*

B1003	SP459	10 +5fr multi	90	90
B1004	SP459	25 +10fr multi	1.75	1.75

Red Cross and: 15th International Radiology Congress, Brussels, June 24-July 1 (No. B1003); international disaster relief (No. B1004).

Ovide Decroly—SP460

1981, June 1 Photo. *Perf. 11½*

B1005	SP460	35 +15fr multi	2.75	2.75

Ovide Decroly (1871-1932), developer of educational psychology.

Mounted Police Officer—SP461

Anniversaries: 9fr+4fr, Gendarmerie (State Police Force), 150th. 20fr+7fr, Carabineers Regiment, 150th. 40fr+20fr, Guides Regiment.

1981, Dec. 7 Photo *Perf. 11½*

B1006	SP461	9 +4fr multi	65	65
B1007	SP461	20 +7fr multi	1.40	1.40
B1008	SP461	40 +20fr multi	3.25	3.25

Billiards—SP462

1982, Mar. 29 Photo. *Perf. 11½*

B1009	SP462	6 +2fr shown	42	42
B1010	SP462	9 +4fr Cycling	70	70
B1011	SP462	10 +5fr Soccer	75	75
B1012	SP462	50 +14fr Yachting	3.25	3.25

Souvenir Sheet

B1013		Sheet of 4	5.00	5.00
a.	SP462	25fr like #B1009	1.20	1.20
b.	SP462	25fr like #B1010	1.20	1.20
c.	SP462	25fr like #B1011	1.20	1.20
d.	SP462	25fr like #B1012	1.20	1.20

No. B1013 shows designs in changed colors. Size: 105x100mm.

Christmas 1982—SP463

1982, Nov. 6 Photo. *Perf.*

B1014	SP463	10 +1fr multi	55	55

Surtax was for tuberculosis research.

Belgica '82 Intl. Stamp Exhibition, Brussels, Dec. 11-19—SP464

Messengers (Prints). Nos. B1016-B1018 vert.

1982, Dec. 11 Photo. & Engr. *Perf. 11½*

B1015	SP464	7 +2fr multi	45	45
B1016	SP464	7.50 +2.50fr multi	50	50
B1017	SP464	10 +3fr multi	65	65
B1018	SP464	17 +7fr multi	1.20	1.20
B1019	SP464	20 +9fr multi	1.50	1.50
B1020	SP464	25 +10fr multi	1.75	1.75

Souvenir Sheet

B1021	SP464	50 +25fr multi	3.75	3.75

No. B1021 contains one stamp (48x37mm.); multicolored margin continues design. Size: 125x90mm.

AIR POST STAMPS.

Fokker FVII/3m over Ostend
AP1

Designs: 1.50fr, Plane over St. Hubert. 2fr, over Namur. 5fr, over Brussels.

Photogravure.

1930, Apr. 30 *Perf. 11½* Unwmkd.

C1	AP1	50c blue	1.00	60
C2	AP1	1.50fr blk brn	4.50	5.75
C3	AP1	2fr dp grn	4.00	1.40
C4	AP1	5fr brn lake	4.50	2.50

1930, Dec. 5

C5	AP1	5fr dk vio	65.00	60.00

Issued for use on a mail carrying flight from Brussels to Leopoldville, Belgian Congo, starting Dec. 7.
Nos. C1–C5 exist imperforate.

Nos. C2 and C4 Surcharged in Carmine or Blue

1Fr 1Fr

1935, May 23

C6	AP1	1fr on 1.50fr blk brn (C)	1.00	1.25
C7	AP1	4fr on 5fr brn lake (Bl)	16.00	9.50

DC-4 Skymaster, Sabena Airline
AP5

1946-54 Engraved *Perf. 11½*

C8	AP5	6fr blue	75	25
C9	AP5	8.50fr vio brn	1.00	70
C10	AP5	50fr yel grn	7.50	75
a.		Perf. 12x11½ ('54)	125.00	90
C11	AP5	100fr gray	11.00	1.10
a.		Perf. 12x11½ ('54)	80.00	1.25

The French and Flemish inscriptions are transposed on Nos. C9 and C11.

Evolution of Postal Transportation
AP6

1949, July 1

C12	AP6	50fr dk brn	25.00	21.00

Centenary of Belgian postage stamps.

Glider—AP7

Design: 7fr, "Tipsy" plane.

1951, June 18 Photo. *Perf. 13½*

C12A	AP7	Strip of 2 + label	62.50	67.50
b.		6fr dk bl	27.50	30.00
c.		7fr car rose	27.50	30.00

For the 50th anniversary of the Aero Club of Belgium. The label is inscribed "1901 — 1951 + 37FR. BELGIE BELGIQUE" and carries the club emblem. The strip sold for 50fr.

1951, July 25 *Perf. 13½*

C13	AP7	6fr sepia	5.25	15
C14	AP7	7fr Prus grn	5.25	1.10

United Nations Issue

Types of Regular Issue, 1958

Designs: 5fr, International Civil Aviation Organization. 6fr, World Meteorological Organization. 7.50fr, Protection of Refugees. 8fr, General Agreement on Tariffs and Trade. 9fr, UNICEF. 10fr, Atomic Energy Agency.

Engraved.

1958, Apr. 17 *Perf. 11½* Unwmkd.

C15	A137	5fr dl bl	38	38
C16	A136	6fr yel grn	75	75
C17	A137	7.50fr lilac	45	45
C18	A136	8fr sepia	45	45
C19	A137	9fr carmine	1.00	1.00
C20	A136	10fr redsh brn	1.25	1.25
		Nos. C15-C20 (6)	4.28	4.28

World's Fair, Brussels, Apr. 17–Oct. 19. See note after No. 476.

AIR POST SEMI-POSTAL STAMPS.

American Soldier in Combat
SPAP1

Engraved.
Perf. 11x11½

1946, June 15 Unwmkd.

CB1	SPAP1	17.50fr +62.50fr dl brn	2.25	2.75
CB2	SPAP1	17.50fr +62.50fr dl gray grn	2.25	2.75

The French and Flemish inscriptions are transposed on No. CB2. The surtax was to erect an American memorial at Bastogne.

An overprint, "Hommage a Roosevelt", was privately applied to Nos. CB1 and CB2 in 1947 by the Association Belgo-Americaine.

In 1950 another private overprint was applied, in red, to Nos. CB1-2. It consists of "16-12-1944, 25-1-1945, Dedication July 16, 1950" and outlines of the American eagle emblem and the Bastogne Memorial. Similar overprints were applied to Nos. 265 and 345.

Flight Allegory
SPAP2

1946, Sept. 7 *Perf. 11½*

CB3	SPAP1	2fr +8fr brt vio	1.00	1.25

The surtax was for the benefit of aviation.

A particular stamp may be scarce, but if few want it, its market potential may remain relatively low.

Nos. B417–B425 Surcharged in Various Arrangements in Red or Dark Blue

POSTE AERIENNE
LUCHTPOST
1F

LUCHTPOST
+ POSTE AERIENNE
2F 1F +2F

Type I. Top line "POSTE AERIENNE."
Type II. Top line "LUCHTPOST."

1947, May 18 Photo. *Perf. 11½*

CB4	SP227	1fr	+2fr on 65c+75c dk bl (R)	1.40	1.40
a.		Type II		1.40	1.40
CB5	SP228	1.50fr	+2.50fr on 1.35fr+2fr brn (Bl)	1.40	1.40
a.		Type II		1.40	1.40
CB6	SP229	2fr	+45fr on 1.75fr+18fr rose brn (Bl)	1.40	1.40
a.		Type II		1.40	1.40
CB7	SP230	1fr	+2fr on 65c+75c vio (R)	1.40	1.40
a.		Type II		1.40	1.40
CB8	SP231	1.50fr	+2.50fr on 1.35fr+2fr dk org brn (Bl)	1.40	1.40
a.		Type II		1.40	1.40
CB9	SP232	2fr	+45fr on 1.75fr+18fr car rose (Bl)	1.40	1.40
a.		Type II		1.40	1.40
CB10	SP233	1fr	+2fr on 65c+75c dk sl grn (R)	1.40	1.40
a.		Type II		1.40	1.40
CB11	SP234	1.50fr	+2.50fr on 1.35fr+2fr dk vio bl (R)	1.40	1.40
a.		Type II		1.40	1.40
CB12	SP235	2fr	+45fr on 1.75fr+18fr dp car (Bl)	1.40	1.40
a.		Type II		1.40	1.40
			Nos. CB4-CB12, CB4a-CB12a (18)	25.20	25.20

In 1948 Nos. CB4–CB12 and CB4a–CB12a were punched with the letters "IMABA," and the inscription "Imaba du 21 au 29 aout 1948" was applied to the backs. Price $20.

Helicopter Leaving Airport
SPAP3

1950, Aug. 7

CB13	SPAP3	7fr +3fr bl	6.00	9.00

The surtax was for the National Aeronautical Committee.

SPECIAL DELIVERY STAMPS

From 1874 to 1903 certain hexagonal telegraph stamps were used as special delivery stamps.

Town Hall, Brussels — SD1 **Eupen** — SD2

Designs: 2.35fr, Street in Ghent. 3.50fr, Bishop's Palace, Liege. 5.25fr, Notre Dame Cathedral, Antwerp.

Photogravure.

1929 *Perf. 11½.* Unwmkd.

E1	SD1	1.75fr dk bl	1.40	40
E2	SD1	2.35fr carmine	4.00	60
E3	SD1	3.50fr dk vio	9.00	8.50
E4	SD1	5.25fr ol grn	8.50	7.25

1931

E5	SD2	2.45fr dk grn	20.00	3.25
		Nos. E1-E5 (5)	42.90	20.00

No. E5 Surcharged in Red

2Fr 50

X

1932

E6	SD2	2.50fr on 2.45fr dk grn	20.00	2.00

POSTAGE DUE STAMPS.

D1 D2

Typographed.

1870 *Perf. 15.* Unwmkd.

J1	D1	10c green	11.00	3.00
a.		Half used as 5c on piece		12.00
J2	D1	20c ultra	40.00	4.00

1895-09 *Perf. 14.*

J3	D2	5c yel grn	45	35
J4	D2	10c org brn	12.50	2.00
J5	D2	10c car ('00)	45	35
J6	D2	20c ol grn	45	35
J7	D2	30c pale bl ('09)	65	42
J8	D2	50c yel brn	18.50	7.50
J9	D2	50c gray ('00)	1.50	85
J10	D2	1fr carmine	42.50	25.00
J11	D2	1fr ocher ('00)	14.00	8.50
		Nos. J3-J11 (9)	91.00	45.32

1916 Redrawn

J12	D2	5c bl grn	11.00	6.00
J13	D2	10c carmine	11.50	4.75
J14	D2	20c dp gray grn	18.50	12.50
J15	D2	30c brt bl	5.75	4.50
J16	D2	50c gray	57.50	52.50
		Nos. J12-J16 (5)	104.25	80.25

In the redrawn stamps the lions have a heavy, colored outline. There is a thick vertical line at the outer edge of the design on each side.

D3 D4

1919 *Perf. 14*

J17	D3	5c green	90	40
J18	D3	10c carmine	1.75	40
J19	D3	20c gray grn	10.00	60
J20	D3	30c brt bl	3.00	40
J21	D3	50c gray	4.25	60
		Nos. J17-J21 (5)	19.90	2.40

1922-32

J22	D4	5c dk gray	15	15
J23	D4	10c green	18	15
J24	D4	20c dp brn	20	15
J25	D4	30c ver ('24)	35	15
a.		30c rose red	1.25	60
J26	D4	40c red brn ('25)	38	15
J27	D4	50c ultra	3.00	15
J28	D4	70c red brn ('29)	45	15
J29	D4	1fr vio ('25)	75	15
J30	D4	1fr rose lil ('32)	60	15
J31	D4	1.20fr ol grn ('29)	1.10	60
J32	D4	1.50fr ol grn ('32)	1.10	60
J33	D4	2fr vio ('29)	1.25	25
J34	D4	3.50fr dp bl ('29)	1.50	30
		Nos. J22-J34 (13)	11.01	3.10

1934-46 *Perf. 14x13½.*

J35	D4	35c grn ('35)	60	60
J36	D4	50c slate	38	15
J37	D4	60c car ('38)	60	35
J38	D4	80c sl ('38)	45	25
J39	D4	1.40fr gray ('35)	1.10	50
J39A	D4	3fr org brn ('46)	1.75	80
J39B	D4	7fr brt red vio ('46)	3.75	4.00
		Nos. J35-J39B (7)	8.63	6.65

See also Nos. J54–J61.

D5

D6

1945 Typographed *Perf. 12½*

Inscribed "TE BETALEN" at Top.

J40	D5	10c gray ol	15	15
J41	D5	20c ultra	15	15
J42	D5	30c carmine	12	10
J43	D5	40c blk vio	12	10
J44	D5	50c dl bl grn	15	10
J45	D5	1fr sepia	22	10
J46	D5	2fr red org	28	15

Inscribed "A PAYER" at Top.

J47	D5	10c gray ol	15	15
J48	D5	20c ultra	15	15
J49	D5	30c carmine	12	10
J50	D5	40c blk vio	12	10
J51	D5	50c dl bl grn	15	10
J52	D5	1fr sepia	22	10
J53	D5	2fr red org	28	15
		Nos. J40-J53 (14)	2.38	1.70

Type of 1922–32.

1949 Typographed. *Perf. 14x13½.*

J54	D4	65c emerald	7.50	7.25
J55	D4	1.80fr red	14.00	10.00
J56	D4	5fr red brn	3.75	60
J57	D4	8fr lil rose	9.00	8.50
J58	D4	10fr dk vio	7.50	7.25
		Nos. J54-J58 (5)	41.75	33.60

1953

J59	D4	1.60fr lil rose	9.00	10.00
J60	D4	2.40fr gray lil	8.00	2.75
J61	D4	4fr dp bl	9.00	1.25

1966-70 Photogravure

J62	D6	1fr brt pink	8	5
J63	D6	2fr bl grn	13	10
J64	D6	3fr blue	18	13
J65	D6	5fr purple	30	20
J66	D6	6fr bis brn	38	25
J67	D6	7fr red org ('70)	42	28
J68	D6	20fr sl grn	1.75	1.10
		Nos. J62-J68 (7)	3.24	2.11

MILITARY STAMPS

King Baudouin
M1 M2

Photogravure

1967, July 17 *Perf. 11* Unwmkd.

M1	M1	1.50fr grnsh gray	2.00	75

1971-75 Engraved *Perf. 11½*

M2	M2	1.75fr green	7.50	2.00
M3	M2	2.25fr gray grn ('73)	6.00	1.75
M4	M2	2.50fr gray grn ('74)	3.50	1.50
M5	M2	3.25fr vio brn ('75)	1.10	42

Nos. M1–M3 are luminescent, Nos. M4–M5 are not.

MILITARY PARCEL POST STAMP.

Type of Parcel Post Stamp of 1938 Surcharged with New Value and "M" in Blue.

1939 *Perf. 13½* Unwmkd.

MQ1	PP19	3fr on 5.50fr cop red	50	25

OFFICIAL STAMPS.

For franking the official correspondence of the Administration of the Belgian National Railways.

Regular Issue of 1921-27 Overprinted in Black

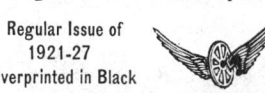

1929-30 *Perf. 14.* Unwmkd.

O1	A58	5c gray	28	30
O2	A58	10c bl grn	42	50
O3	A58	35c bl grn	55	40
O4	A58	60c ol grn	60	35
O5	A58	1.50fr brt bl	9.50	5.50
O6	A58	1.75fr ultra ('30)	2.50	2.75
		Nos. O1-O6 (6)	13.85	9.80

Same Overprint, in Red or Black, on Regular Issues of 1929-30.

1929-31

O7	A63	5c sl (R)	25	40
O8	A63	10c ol grn (R)	50	50
O9	A63	25c rose red (Bk)	1.40	1.00
O10	A63	35c dp grn (R)	1.50	60
O11	A63	40c red vio (Bk)	1.50	50
O12	A63	50c dp bl (R) ('31)	1.10	40
O13	A63	60c rose (Bk)	5.25	4.75
O14	A63	70c org brn (Bk)	5.75	1.25
O15	A63	75c blk vio (R) ('31)	4.00	1.00
		Nos. O7-O15 (9)	21.25	10.40

Overprinted on Regular Issue of 1932.

1932

O16	A73	10c ol grn (R)	75	75
O17	A74	35c dp grn	17.50	1.00
O18	A71a	75c bis brn (R)	2.00	42

Overprinted on No. 262 in Red.

1935 *Perf. 13½x14*

O19	A80	70c ol blk	3.50	40

Regular Stamps of 1935–36 Overprinted in Red.

1936-38 *Perf. 13½, 13½x14, 14.*

O20	A82	10c ol bis	20	30
O21	A82	35c green	30	32
O22	A82	50c dk bl	60	32
O23	A83	70c brown	3.00	75

Overprinted in Black or Red on Regular Issue of 1938.

Perf. 13½x14.

O24	A82	40c red vio (Bk)	40	32
O25	A85	75c ol gray (R)	90	22
		Nos. O20-O25 (6)	5.40	2.23

Regular Issues of 1935-41 Overprinted in Red or Dark Blue

1941-44 *Perf. 14, 14x13½, 13½x14.*

O26	A82	10c ol bis	22	15
a.		Inverted overprint		30.00
O27	A82	40c red vio	75	75
O28	A82	50c dk bl	22	15
a.		Inverted overprint		
O29	A83a	1fr rose car (Bl)	60	35
O30	A85	1fr rose pink (Bl)	15	12
O31	A83a	2.25fr grnsh blk ('44)	60	65
O32	A84	2.25fr gray vio	45	50
		Nos. O26-O32 (7)	2.99	2.67

Nos. O21, O23 and O25 Surcharged with New Values in Black or Red.

1942

O33	A82	10c on 35c grn	25	28
O34	A83	50c on 70c brn	20	22
O35	A85	50c on 75c ol gray (R)	20	22

O1

O2

1946-48 *Perf. 14.* Unwmkd.

O36	O1	10c ol bis	30	25
O37	O1	20c brt vio	2.00	75
O38	O1	50c dk bl	38	25
O39	O1	65c red lil ('48)	3.75	1.10
O40	O1	75c lil rose	30	30
O41	O1	90c brn vio	3.85	50
		Nos. O36-O41 (6)	10.58	3.15

Types A99, A101 and A102 with "B" Emblem Added to Design.

1948 *Perf. 11½.*

O42	A99	1.35fr red brn	3.25	1.00
O43	A99	1.75fr dk gray grn	4.25	35
O44	A101	3fr brt red vio	17.50	4.75
O45	A102	3.15fr dp bl	9.00	10.00
O46	A102	4fr brt ultra	15.00	18.50
		Nos. O42-O46 (5)	49.00	34.60

1953-66 Typo. *Perf. 13½x14*

O47	O2	10c orange	75	75
O48	O2	20c red lil	90	60
O49	O2	30c gray grn ('58)	90	1.00
O50	O2	40c ol gray	60	40
O51	O2	50c lt bl	80	45
O51A	O2	60c lil rose ('66)	1.75	1.00
O52	O2	65c red lil	37.50	42.50
O53	O2	80c emerald	1.75	80
O54	O2	90c dp bl	3.75	1.25
O55	O2	1fr rose	45	40
		Nos. O47-O55 (10)	49.15	49.15

King Baudouin
O3 O4

1954-70 Photogravure *Perf. 11½*

O56	O3	1.50fr gray	1.25	30
O57	O3	2fr rose red	45.00	60
O58	O3	2fr bl grn ('59)	1.25	30
O59	O3	2.50fr red brn ('58)	28.50	60
O60	O3	3fr red lil ('58)	2.50	45
O61	O3	3.50fr yel grn ('70)	90	45
O62	O3	4fr brt bl	2.75	75
O63	O3	6fr car rose ('58)	6.00	1.25
		Nos. O56-O63 (8)	88.15	4.70

Type of 1953–66 Redrawn

1970-75 Typo. *Perf. 13½x14*

O66	O2	1.50fr grnsh gray ('75)	25	10
O68	O2	2.50fr brown	15	10

1971-73 Engraved *Perf. 11½*

O71	O4	3.50fr org brn ('73)	2.00	85
O72	O4	4.50fr brn ('73)	1.25	70
O73	O4	7fr red	42	40
O74	O4	15fr violet	90	80

Nos. O71–O74 are on luminescent paper.

1974-78

O75	O4	3fr yel grn	7.50	1.85
O76	O4	4fr blue	2.50	90
O77	O4	4.50fr grnsh bl ('75)	75	30
O78	O4	5fr lilac	35	25
O79	O4	6fr car ('78)	38	30
O80	O4	6.50fr blk ('76)	75	65
O81	O4	8fr bluish blk ('78)	55	40
O82	O4	9fr lt red brn ('80)	55	50
O83	O4	10fr rose car	65	45
O84	O4	25fr lil ('76)	1.50	1.25
O85	O4	30fr org brn ('78)	2.10	1.50
		Nos. O75-O85 (11)	17.58	8.35

Heraldic Lion
O5

1977 Typographed *Perf. 13½x14*

O95	O5	4fr red brn	35	25
O96	O5	5fr grn ('80)	30	20

NEWSPAPER STAMPS.

Parcel Post Stamps of 1923-27 Overprinted **JOURNAUX DAGBLADEN 1928**

Perf. 14½x14, 14x14½.

1928 Unwmkd.

P1	PP12	10c vermilion	20	30
P2	PP12	20c turq bl	28	30
P3	PP12	40c ol grn	28	30
P4	PP12	60c orange	55	60
P5	PP12	70c dk brn	35	30
P6	PP12	80c violet	40	50
P7	PP12	90c slate	1.75	1.25
a.		Inverted overprint		
P8	PP13	1fr brt bl	75	40
a.		1fr ultra	8.25	3.50
P10	PP13	2fr ol grn	1.25	42
P11	PP13	3fr org red	1.50	60
P12	PP13	4fr rose	1.75	80
a.		Inverted overprint		
P13	PP13	5fr violet	1.75	75
P14	PP13	6fr bis brn	2.75	1.25
P15	PP13	7fr orange	3.50	1.75
P16	PP13	8fr dk brn	4.00	2.00
P17	PP13	9fr red vio	8.00	2.25
P18	PP13	10fr bl grn	5.50	2.00
P19	PP13	20fr magenta	11.00	4.75
		Nos. P1-P8, P10-P19 (18)	45.56	20.52

Parcel Post Stamps of 1923-28 Overprinted **JOURNAUX DAGBLADEN**

1929-31

P20	PP12	10c vermilion	30	25
P21	PP12	20c turq bl	30	25
P22	PP12	40c ol grn	40	28
a.		Inverted overprint		
P23	PP12	60c orange	50	50
P24	PP12	70c dk brn	60	30
P25	PP12	80c violet	75	35
P26	PP12	90c gray	2.00	1.25
a.		Inverted overprint		
P27	PP13	1fr ultra	65	35
a.		1fr brt bl	3.25	70
P28	PP13	1.10fr org brn ('31)	10.00	2.00
P29	PP13	1.50fr gray vio ('31)	10.00	2.50
P30	PP13	2fr ol grn	1.50	38
P31	PP13	2.10fr sl gray ('31)	37.50	12.50
P32	PP13	3fr org red	1.75	60
P33	PP13	4fr rose	1.75	1.00
P34	PP13	5fr violet	2.75	80
P35	PP13	6fr bis brn	3.25	1.25
P36	PP13	7fr orange	3.75	1.25
P37	PP13	8fr dk brn	4.00	1.40
P38	PP13	9fr red vio	4.75	2.00
P39	PP13	10fr bl grn	4.00	1.40
P40	PP13	20fr magenta	12.50	6.00
		Nos. P20-P40 (21)	103.00	36.61

PARCEL POST AND RAILWAY STAMPS.

Prices for used stamps are for copies with railway cancellations. Stamps with postal cancellations sell for twice as much.

Coat of Arms
PP1

Typographed.

1879–82 ***Perf. 14*** **Unwmkd.**

Q1	PP1	10c vio brn	40.00	2.40
Q2	PP1	20c blue	135.00	11.00
Q3	PP1	25c grn ('81)	165.00	6.50
Q4	PP1	50c carmine	1,150.	5.00
Q5	PP1	80c yellow	1,200.	35.00
Q6	PP1	1fr gray ('82)	120.00	14.00

Used copies of Nos. Q1–Q6 with pinholes, a normal state, sell for half price.

PP2

Most of the stamps of 1882-1902 (Nos. Q7 to Q28) are without watermark. Twice in each sheet of 100 stamps they have one of three watermarks: (1) A winged wheel and "Chemins de Fer de l'Etat Belge", (2) Coat of Arms of Belgium and "Royaume de Belgique", (3) Larger Coat of Arms, without inscription.

1882-94 ***Perf. 15x14½.***

Q7	PP2	10c brn ('86)	15.00	75
Q8	PP2	15c gray ('94)	9.00	7.50
Q9	PP2	20c bl ('86)	57.50	2.75
a.		20c ultra ('90)	55.00	2.75
Q10	PP2	25c yel grn ('91)	47.50	3.25
a.		25c bl grn ('87)	60.00	3.25
Q11	PP2	50c carmine	50.00	35
Q12	PP2	80c brnsh buff	50.00	60
Q13	PP2	80c lemon	62.50	2.25
Q14	PP2	1fr lavender	250.00	2.10
Q15	PP2	2fr yel buff ('94)	200.00	45.00

Counterfeits exist.

PP3

Name of engraver below frame.

1895–97

Numerals in Black, except 1fr, 2fr.

Q16	PP3	10c red brn ('96)	8.00	35
Q17	PP3	15c gray	8.00	5.25
Q18	PP3	20c blue	16.50	75
Q19	PP3	25c green	16.50	1.25
Q20	PP3	50c carmine	18.50	35
Q21	PP3	60c vio ('96)	32.50	45
Q22	PP3	80c ol yel ('96)	25.00	45
Q23	PP3	1fr lil brn	120.00	90
Q24	PP3	2fr yel buff ('97)	125.00	2.75

Counterfeits exist.

1902 **Numerals in Black.**

Q25	PP3	30c orange	20.00	1.25
Q26	PP3	40c green	22.50	1.25
Q27	PP3	70c blue	32.50	50
a.		Numerals omitted	275.00	
Q28	PP3	90c red	45.00	75

Winged Wheel
PP4

Without engraver's name.

1902–14 ***Perf. 15***

Q29	PP3	10c yel brn & sl	18	12
Q30	PP3	15c sl & vio	28	22
Q31	PP3	20c ultra & yel brn	18	15
Q32	PP3	25c yel grn & red	28	22
Q33	PP3	30c org & bl grn	28	15
Q34	PP3	35c bis & bl grn ('12)	50	30
Q35	PP3	40c bl grn & vio	28	18
Q36	PP3	50c pale rose & vio	18	15
Q37	PP3	55c lil brn & ultra ('14)	50	30
Q38	PP3	60c vio & red	25	15
Q39	PP3	70c bl & red	22	12
Q40	PP3	80c lem & vio brn	18	12
Q41	PP3	90c red & yel grn	25	15
Q42	PP4	1fr vio brn & org	25	12
Q43	PP4	1.10fr rose & blk ('06)	30	20
Q44	PP4	2fr ocher & bl grn	30	18
Q45	PP4	3fr blk & ultra	50	30
Q46	PP4	4fr yel grn & red ('13)	1.75	1.00
Q47	PP4	5fr org & bl grn ('13)	85	90
Q48	PP4	10fr ol yel & brn vio ('13)	1.40	85
		Nos. Q29-Q48 (20)	8.91	5.88

Exist imperforate.

Regular Issues of 1912–13 Handstamped in Violet

CHEMINS DE FER
SPOORWEGEN

1915 ***Perf. 14***

Q49	A42	5c green	120.00	120.00
Q50	A43	10c red	600.00	600.00
Q51	A45	10c red	120.00	120.00
a.		With engraver's name	385.00	385.00
Q52	A43	20c ol grn	*1,000.*	*1,000.*
Q53	A45	20c ol grn	140.00	140.00
a.		With engraver's name	385.00	385.00
Q54	A45	25c ultra	140.00	140.00
a.		With engraver's name	385.00	385.00
Q55	A43	35c bis brn	200.00	200.00
Q55A	A43	40c green	*1,350.*	*1,350.*
Q56	A45	40c green	140.00	140.00
Q57	A43	50c gray	165.00	165.00
Q58	A43	1fr orange	210.00	210.00
Q59	A43	2fr violet	*1,200.*	*1,200.*
Q60	A44	5fr plum	*2,350.*	*2,350.*

Excellent forgeries of this overprint exist.

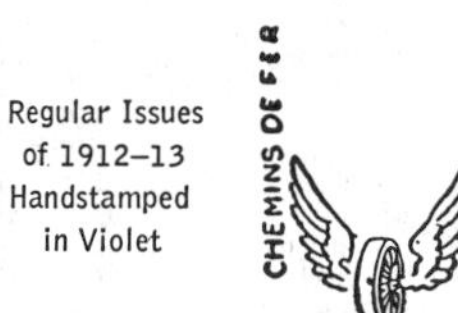

Locomotive
PP5 PP6

1916 **Lithographed** ***Perf. 13½***

Q61	PP5	10c pale bl	1.00	35
Q62	PP5	15c ol grn	1.25	70
Q63	PP5	20c red	1.85	75
Q64	PP5	25c lt brn	1.85	1.00
Q65	PP5	30c lilac	1.50	45
Q66	PP5	35c gray	1.25	45
Q67	PP5	40c org yel	2.75	1.75
Q68	PP5	50c bister	2.00	35
Q69	PP5	55c brown	2.75	1.80
Q70	PP5	60c gray vio	2.25	35
Q71	PP5	70c green	1.85	35
Q72	PP5	80c red brn	2.00	45
Q73	PP5	90c blue	2.50	45
Q74	PP6	1fr gray	2.00	35
Q75	PP6	1.10fr ultra (*Franken*)	20.00	13.00
Q76	PP6	2fr red	22.50	35
Q77	PP6	3fr violet	22.50	70
Q78	PP6	4fr emerald	25.00	1.40
Q79	PP6	5fr brown	28.50	2.00
Q80	PP6	10fr orange	28.50	1.75
		Nos. Q61-Q80 (20)	173.80	28.75

Type of 1916 Inscribed "FRANK" instead of "FRANKEN."

1920

Q81	PP6	1.10fr ultra	3.00	70

PP7 PP8

1920 ***Perf. 14.***

Q82	PP7	10c bl grn	1.25	28
Q83	PP7	15c ol grn	1.50	1.00
Q84	PP7	20c red	1.50	30
Q85	PP7	25c gray brn	2.00	80
Q86	PP7	30c red vio	9.50	11.50
Q87	PP7	40c pale org	9.50	70
Q88	PP7	50c bister	6.25	60
Q89	PP7	55c pale brn	5.00	2.25
Q90	PP7	60c dk vio	7.50	80
Q91	PP7	70c green	11.50	1.40
Q92	PP7	80c red brn	35.00	1.25
Q93	PP7	90c dl bl	6.25	55
Q94	PP8	1fr gray	52.50	1.10
Q95	PP8	1.10fr ultra	17.00	2.50
Q96	PP8	1.20fr dk grn	12.50	45
Q97	PP8	1.40fr blk brn	7.50	45
Q98	PP8	2fr vermilion	57.50	75
Q99	PP8	3fr red vio	70.00	1.00
Q100	PP8	4fr yel grn	62.50	75
Q101	PP8	5fr bis brn	62.50	75
Q102	PP8	10fr brn org	70.00	50
		Nos. Q82-Q102 (21)	508.75	29.68

PP9

PP10

Types PP7 and PP9 differ in the position of the wheel and the tablet above it.

Types PP8 and PP10 differ in the bars below "FR".

There are many other variations in the designs.

1920-21 **Typographed.**

Q103	PP9	10c carmine	55	25
Q104	PP9	15c yel grn	50	25
Q105	PP9	20c bl grn	1.25	20
Q106	PP9	25c ultra	1.40	35
Q107	PP9	30c chocolate	1.50	35
Q108	PP9	35c org brn	1.75	45
Q109	PP9	40c orange	2.00	25
Q110	PP9	50c rose	2.00	25
Q111	PP9	55c yel ('21)	4.00	1.75
Q112	PP9	60c dl rose	2.00	25
Q113	PP9	70c emerald	4.00	30
Q114	PP9	80c violet	3.50	20
Q115	PP9	90c lemon	16.50	15.00
Q116	PP9	90c claret	7.50	50
Q117	PP10	1fr buff	8.25	50
Q118	PP10	1fr red brn	7.50	35
Q119	PP10	1.10fr ultra	2.75	75
Q120	PP10	1.20fr orange	3.25	20
Q121	PP10	1.40fr yellow	15.00	90
Q122	PP10	1.60fr turq bl	25.00	50
Q123	PP10	1.60fr emerald	55.00	50
Q124	PP10	2fr pale rose	27.50	30
Q125	PP10	3fr dp rose	25.00	30
Q126	PP10	4fr emerald	25.00	40
Q127	PP10	5fr lt vio	21.00	30
Q128	PP10	10fr lemon	120.00	2.50
Q129	PP10	10fr dk brn	22.50	28
Q130	PP10	15fr dp rose ('21)	22.50	32
Q131	PP10	20fr dk bl ('21)	300.00	2.00
		Nos. Q103-Q131 (29)	728.70	30.45

PP11

1922 **Engraved.** ***Perf. 11½.***

Q132	PP11	2fr black	4.75	15
Q133	PP11	3fr brown	47.50	28
Q134	PP11	4fr green	12.50	18
Q135	PP11	5r claret	12.50	18
Q136	PP11	10fr yel brn	13.00	25
Q137	PP11	15fr rose red	13.50	42
Q138	PP11	20fr blue	85.00	38
		Nos. Q132-Q138 (7)	188.75	1.84

PP12

PP13

Perf. 14x13½, 13½x14.

1923–40 **Typographed**

Q139	PP12	5c red brn	35	35
Q140	PP12	10c vermilion	25	12
Q141	PP12	15c ultra	40	42
Q142	PP12	20c turq bl	25	10
Q143	PP12	30c brn vio ('27)	40	15
Q144	PP12	40c ol grn	32	10
Q145	PP12	50c mag ('27)	32	5
Q146	PP12	60c orange	40	15
Q147	PP12	70c dk brn ('24)	25	5
Q148	PP12	80c violet	32	10
Q149	PP12	90c sl ('27)	1.85	25
Q150	PP13	1fr ultra	45	5
Q151	PP13	1fr brt bl ('28)	1.10	10
Q152	PP13	1.10fr orange	4.50	22
Q153	PP13	1.50fr turq bl	5.00	32
Q154	PP13	1.70fr dp brn ('31)	1.40	25
Q155	PP13	1.80fr claret	8.00	35
Q156	PP13	2fr ol grn ('24)	45	25
Q157	PP13	2.10fr gray grn	10.00	42
Q158	PP13	2.40fr dp vio	9.00	65
Q159	PP13	2.70fr gray ('24)	20.00	25
Q160	PP13	3fr org red	70	12
Q161	PP13	3.30fr brn ('24)	21.00	45
Q162	PP13	4fr rose ('24)	95	15
Q163	PP13	5fr vio ('24)	1.40	15
Q163A	PP13	5fr brn vio ('40)	75	45

Q164	PP13	6fr bis brn ('27)	95	10
Q165	PP13	7fr org ('27)	1.60	10
Q166	PP13	8fr dp brn ('27)	1.40	12
Q167	PP13	9fr red vio ('27)	3.50	15
Q168	PP13	10fr bl grn ('27)	1.60	12
Q168A	PP13	10fr blk ('40)	4.00	3.50
Q169	PP13	20fr mag ('27)	3.25	12
Q170	PP13	30fr turq grn ('31)	9.50	25
Q171	PP13	40fr gray ('31)	50.00	55
Q172	PP13	50fr bis ('27)	15.00	30
		Nos. Q139-Q172 (36)	180.61	11.33

See also Nos. Q239–Q262.

Stamps of this and later issues overprinted "Bagages Reisgod" are revenues used on baggage.

PP14

1924 **Green Surcharge.**

Q173	PP14	2.30fr on 2.40fr vio	5.00	40
a.		Inverted surcharge	75.00	

Type of Regular Issue of 1926-27 Overprinted

COLIS POSTAL POSTCOLLO

1928 ***Perf. 14.***

Q174	A61	4fr buff	5.50	80
Q175	A61	5fr bister	5.50	1.00

Central P.O., Brussels
PP15

1929–30 **Engraved** ***Perf. 11½***

Q176	PP15	3fr blk brn	3.00	60
Q177	PP15	4fr gray	2.00	15
Q178	PP15	5fr carmine	2.40	15
Q179	PP15	6fr vio brn ('30)	35.00	32.50

No. Q179 Surcharged in Blue

X4 4X

1933

Q180	PP15	4(fr) on 6fr vio brn	30.00	35

Modern Locomotive
PP16

1934 **Photogravure** ***Perf. 13½x14***

Q181	PP16	3fr dk grn	6.75	2.50
Q182	PP16	4fr red vio	2.00	12
Q183	PP16	5fr dp rose	5.50	15

Modern Railroad Train
PP17

Old Railroad Train
PP18

Perf. 14x13½, 13½x14.

1935 **Engraved.**

Q184	PP17	10c rose car	45	18
Q185	PP17	20c violet	60	15
Q186	PP17	30c blk brn	75	15
Q187	PP17	40c dk bl	90	20
Q188	PP17	50c org red	1.00	15
Q189	PP17	60c green	1.10	25
Q190	PP17	70c ultra	1.40	20
Q191	PP17	80c ol blk	1.10	25
Q192	PP17	90c rose lake	1.50	70
Q193	PP18	1fr brn vio	1.50	15
Q194	PP18	2fr gray blk	3.00	20
Q195	PP18	3fr red org	3.25	25
Q196	PP18	4fr vio brn	4.25	25
Q197	PP18	5fr plum	4.50	25
Q198	PP18	6fr dp grn	5.25	25
Q199	PP18	7fr dp vio	6.00	20
Q200	PP18	8fr ol blk	8.25	30
Q201	PP18	9fr dk bl	9.00	25
Q202	PP18	10fr car lake	9.00	20
Q203	PP18	20fr green	42.50	30
Q204	PP18	30fr violet	115.00	1.20
Q205	PP18	40fr blk brn	120.00	2.25
Q206	PP18	50fr rose car	120.00	1.60
Q207	PP18	100fr ultra	300.00	30.00
		Nos. Q184-Q207 (24)	760.30	39.88

Centenary of Belgian State Railway.

Winged Wheel
PP19

Surcharge in Red or Blue.

1938 **Photogravure** ***Perf. 13½***

Q208	PP19	5fr on 3.50fr dk grn (R)	11.50	85
Q209	PP19	5fr on 4.50fr rose vio (Bl)	50	10
Q210	PP19	6fr on 5.50fr cop red (Bl)	60	15
a.		Half used as 3fr on piece		3.50

See also Nos. MQ1, Q297–Q299.

Symbolizing Unity Achieved Through Railroads
PP20

1939 **Engraved** ***Perf. 13½x14***

Q211	PP20	20c redsh brn	5.00	5.50
Q212	PP20	50c vio bl	5.00	5.50
Q213	PP20	2fr rose red	5.00	5.50
Q214	PP20	9fr sl grn	5.00	5.50
Q215	PP20	10fr dk vio	5.00	5.50
		Nos. Q211-Q215 (5)	25.00	27.50

Issued in commemoration of the Railroad Exposition and Congress held at Brussels.

Parcel Post Stamps of 1925-27 Overprinted in Blue or Carmine

Perf. 14½x14, 14x14½.

1940 **Unwmkd.**

Q216	PP12	10c vermilion	12	10
Q217	PP12	20c turq bl (C)	12	10
Q218	PP12	30c brn vio	15	10
Q219	PP12	40c ol grn (C)	12	12
Q220	PP12	50c magenta	15	10
Q221	PP12	60c orange	22	30
Q222	PP12	70c dk brn	18	20
Q223	PP12	80c vio (C)	18	12
Q224	PP12	90c sl (C)	27	30
Q225	PP13	1fr ultra (C)	25	25
Q226	PP13	2fr ol grn (C)	33	25
Q227	PP13	3fr org red	33	25
Q228	PP13	4fr rose	33	25
Q229	PP13	5fr vio (C)	33	25
Q230	PP13	6fr bis brn	50	32
Q231	PP13	7fr orange	50	25
Q232	PP13	8fr dp brn	50	25
Q233	PP13	9fr red vio	50	25
Q234	PP13	10fr bl grn (C)	50	30
Q235	PP13	20fr magenta	1.50	30
Q236	PP13	30fr turq grn (C)	2.50	1.50
Q237	PP13	40fr gray (C)	3.75	3.50
Q238	PP13	50fr bister	4.50	1.65
		Nos. Q216-Q238 (23)	17.83	11.01

1941 **Types of 1923-40.**

Q239	PP12	10c dl ol	15	10
Q240	PP12	20c lt vio	15	10
Q241	PP12	30c fawn	15	10
Q242	PP12	40c dl bl	15	15
Q243	PP12	50c lt grn	15	5
Q244	PP12	60c gray	25	15
Q245	PP12	70c chlky grn	25	15
Q246	PP12	80c orange	28	25
Q247	PP12	90c rose lil	28	25
Q248	PP13	1fr lt yel grn	28	20
Q249	PP13	2fr vio brn	42	20
Q250	PP13	3fr slate	50	20
Q251	PP13	4fr dl ol	60	20
Q252	PP13	5fr rose lil	80	20
Q253	PP13	5fr black	1.15	40
Q254	PP13	6fr org ver	1.00	30
Q255	PP13	7fr lilac	1.00	15
Q256	PP13	8fr chlky grn	1.00	20
Q257	PP13	9fr blue	1.25	15
Q258	PP13	10fr rose lil	1.25	15
Q259	PP13	20fr mlky bl	2.75	15
Q260	PP13	30fr orange	6.50	40
Q261	PP13	40fr rose	8.00	40
Q262	PP13	50fr brt red vio	10.00	25
		Nos. Q239-Q262 (24)	38.31	4.85

Adjusting Tie Plates
PP21

Engineer at Throttle
PP22

Freight Station Interior
PP23

Signal and Electric Train
PP24

1942 **Engraved** ***Perf. 14x13½***

Q263	PP21	9.20fr red org	85	85
Q264	PP22	12.30fr dp grn	85	85
Q265	PP23	14.30fr dk car	1.10	1.25

Perf. 11½.

Q266	PP24	100fr ultra	27.50	27.50

Engineer at Throttle
PP25

Adjusting Tie Plates
PP26

Freight Station Interior
PP27

1945–46 **Photogravure** **Unwmkd.**

Nos. Q268, Q270, Q272, Q274, Q287 and Q289 are inscribed "Belgique-Belgie", Nos. Q277, Q279, Q281 and Q283 are inscribed "Belgie-Belgique".

Q267	PP25	10c ol blk ('46)	20	4
Q268	PP25	20c dp vio	20	4
Q269	PP25	30c chnt brn ('46)	20	12
Q270	PP25	40c dp bl ('46)	20	10
Q271	PP25	50c pck grn	20	6
Q272	PP25	60c blk ('46)	25	15
Q273	PP25	70c emer ('46)	35	30
Q274	PP25	80c orange	60	20
Q275	PP25	90c brn vio ('46)	35	30
Q276	PP26	1fr bl grn ('46)	20	12
Q277	PP26	2fr blk brn	25	10
Q278	PP26	3fr grnsh blk ('46)	1.50	22
Q279	PP26	4fr dk bl	35	20
Q280	PP26	5fr sepia	35	5
Q281	PP26	6fr dk ol grn ('46)	1.75	18
Q282	PP26	7fr dk vio ('46)	60	18
Q283	PP26	8fr red org	60	10
Q284	PP26	9fr dp bl ('46)	75	7
Q285	PP27	10fr dk red ('46)	2.75	15
Q286	PP27	10fr sep ('46)	1.40	30
Q287	PP27	20fr dk yel grn ('46)	60	4
Q288	PP27	30fr dp vio	90	4
Q289	PP27	40fr rose pink	75	5
Q290	PP27	50fr brt bl ('46)	10.00	12
		Nos. Q267-Q290 (24)	25.30	3.23

Mercury
PP28

1945–46 ***Perf. 13½x13***

Q291	PP28	3fr emer ('46)	75	25
Q292	PP28	5fr ultra	25	18
Q293	PP28	6fr red	28	15

Inscribed "Belgique-Belgie".

Q294	PP28	3fr emer ('46)	75	25
Q295	PP28	5fr ultra	25	18
Q296	PP28	6fr red	28	15
		Nos. Q291-Q296 (6)	2.56	1.16

Winged Wheel Type of 1938.
Carmine Surcharge.

1946 ***Perf. 13½x14***

Q297	PP19	8fr on 5.50fr brn	90	20
Q298	PP19	10fr on 5.50fr dk bl	1.10	30
Q299	PP19	12fr on 5.50fr vio	1.75	25

Railway Crossing
PP29

1947 **Engraved** ***Perf. 12½***

Q300	PP29	100fr dk grn	10.00	25

Crossbowman with Train
PP30

1947 **Photogravure** ***Perf. 11½***

Q301	PP30	8fr dk ol brn	1.10	25
Q302	PP30	10fr gray & bl	1.25	30
Q303	PP30	12fr dk vio	1.85	40

Surcharged with
New Value and Bars in Carmine.

1948

Q304	PP30	9fr on 8fr dk ol brn	1.10	25
Q305	PP30	11fr on 10fr gray & bl	1.25	40
Q306	PP30	13.50fr on 12fr dk vio	1.75	35

Delivery of Parcel
PP31

1948

Q307	PP31	9fr chocolate	5.00	12
Q308	PP31	11fr brn car	5.50	12
Q309	PP31	13.50fr gray	7.50	35

Locomotive of 1835
PP32

Various Locomotives.
Lathe Work in Frame Differs.

1949 **Engraved** ***Perf. 12½***

Q310	PP32	½fr dk brn	38	12
Q311	PP32	1fr car rose	55	12
Q312	PP32	2fr dp ultra	60	15
Q313	PP32	3fr dp mag	1.20	12
Q314	PP32	4fr bl grn	1.50	15
Q315	PP32	5fr org red	1.50	15
Q316	PP32	6fr brn vio	1.75	18
Q317	PP32	7fr yel grn	2.50	12
Q318	PP32	8fr grnsh bl	2.75	15
Q319	PP32	9fr yel brn	3.75	18
Q320	PP32	10fr citron	4.50	12
Q321	PP32	20fr orange	7.50	12
Q322	PP32	30fr blue	11.00	12
Q323	PP32	40fr lil rose	13.00	18
Q324	PP32	50fr violet	15.00	25
Q325	PP32	100fr red	40.00	18
		Nos. Q310-Q325 (16)	107.48	2.41

See also No. Q337.

Engraved; Center Typographed.

Q326	PP32	10fr car rose & blk	5.25	70

1949 **Engraved**

Design: Electric locomotive.

Q327	PP32	60fr blk brn	16.50	30

Opening of Charleroi-Brussels electric railway line, Oct. 15, 1949.

Mailing Parcel Post
PP33

Sorting
PP34

Loading
PP35

1950–52 ***Perf. 12, 12½***

Q328	PP33	11fr red org	4.75	25
Q329	PP33	12fr red vio ('51)	12.00	1.20
Q330	PP34	13fr dk bl grn	4.25	20
Q331	PP34	15fr ultra ('51)	11.00	40
Q332	PP35	16fr gray	4.50	20
Q333	PP33	17fr brn ('52)	6.00	40
Q334	PP35	18fr brt car ('51)	10.00	50
Q335	PP35	20fr brn org ('52)	6.00	45
		Nos. Q328-Q335 (8)	58.50	3.60

Mercury and Winged Wheel
PP36

1951

Q336	PP36	25fr dk bl	11.00	9.00

Issued to commemorate the 25th anniversary of the founding of the National Society of Belgian Railroads.

Type of 1949.

1952 ***Perf. 11½*** **Unwmkd.**

Design: Electric locomotive.

Q337	PP32	300fr red vio	80.00	65

Nos. Q331, Q328 and Q334 Surcharged with New Value and "X" in Red, Blue or Green.

1953 ***Perf. 12.***

Q338	PP34	13fr on 15fr ultra (R)	37.50	1.10
Q339	PP33	17fr on 11fr red org (Bl)	22.50	85
Q340	PP35	20fr on 18fr brt car (G)	17.50	1.40

Electric Train, 1952
PP37

1953 **Engraved**

Q341	PP37	200fr dk yel grn & vio brn	150.00	4.75
Q342	PP37	200fr dk grn	125.00	1.25

No. Q341 was issued to commemorate the opening of the railway link connecting Brussels North and South Stations, Oct. 4, 1952.

New North Station, Brussels
PP38

Chapelle Station, Brussels—PP39

Designs: No. Q348, 15fr, Congress Station. 10fr, 20fr, 30fr, 40fr, 50fr, South Station. 100fr, 200fr, 300fr, Central Station.

1953-57 ***Perf. 11½*** **Unwmkd.**

Q343	PP38	1fr bister	30	3
Q344	PP38	2fr slate	45	8
Q345	PP38	3fr bl grn	60	3
Q346	PP38	4fr orange	1.10	3
Q347	PP38	5fr red brn	1.10	3
Q348	PP38	5fr dk red brn	6.50	25
Q349	PP38	6fr rose vio	1.20	4
Q350	PP38	7fr brt grn	1.20	4
Q351	PP38	8fr rose red	1.50	4
Q352	PP38	9fr brt grnsh bl	2.00	4
Q353	PP38	10fr lt grn	2.00	4
Q354	PP38	15fr dl red	8.50	18
Q355	PP38	20fr blue	3.00	3
Q356	PP38	30fr purple	5.25	3
Q357	PP38	40fr brt pur	6.75	3
Q358	PP38	50fr lil rose	8.00	3
Q359	PP39	60fr brt pur	12.00	12
Q360	PP39	80fr brn vio	16.50	15
Q361	PP39	100fr emerald	15.00	10
Q361A	PP39	200fr brt vio bl	37.50	1.40
Q361B	PP39	300fr lil rose	57.50	2.00
		Nos. Q343-Q361B (21)	187.95	4.72

Issue dates: No. Q347, 20fr and 30fr, 1953; 80fr, 1955; 200fr, 1956; 300fr, 1957. Rest of set, 1954.

See Nos. Q407, Q431–Q432.

Electric Train
PP40

Mercury and Winged Wheel
PP41

1954

Q362	PP40	13fr chocolate	9.00	25
Q363	PP40	18fr dk bl	9.50	12
Q364	PP40	21fr lil rose	10.00	60

Nos. Q362-Q364 Surcharged with New Value and "X" in Blue, Red or Green.

1956

Q365	PP40	14fr on 13fr choc (B)	9.00	25
Q366	PP40	19fr on 18fr dk bl (R)	9.50	30
Q367	PP40	22fr on 21fr lil rose (G)	10.00	50

1957 **Engraved.** ***Perf. 11½***

Q368	PP41	14fr brt grn	8.50	25
Q369	PP41	19fr ol gray	10.00	35
Q370	PP41	22fr car rose	10.00	60

Nos. Q369-Q370 Surcharged with New Value and "X" in Pink or Green.

1959

Q371	PP41	20fr on 19fr ol gray (P)	27.50	38
Q372	PP41	20fr on 22fr car rose (G)	27.50	85

Old North Station, Brussels
PP42

1959 **Engraved** ***Perf. 11½***

Q373	PP42	20fr ol grn	16.50	45

See also No. Q381.

Diesel and Electric Locomotives and Association Emblem
PP43

1960 ***Perf. 11½*** **Unwmkd.**

Q374	PP43	20fr red	75.00	50.00
Q375	PP43	50fr dk bl	75.00	42.50
Q376	PP43	60fr red lil	75.00	42.50
Q377	PP43	70fr emerald	75.00	42.50

Issued to commemorate the 75th anniversary of the International Association of Railway Congresses.

No. Q373 Surcharged with New Value and "X" in Red.

1961

Q378	PP42	24fr on 20fr ol grn	80.00	45

South Station, Brussels
PP44

1962 ***Perf. 11½*** **Unwmkd.**

Q379	PP44	24fr dl red	9.00	45

No. Q379 Surcharged with New Value and "X" in Light Green

1963

Q380	PP44	26fr on 24fr dl red	9.00	45

Type of 1959

Design: 26fr, Central Station, Antwerp.

1963 Engraved *Perf. 11½*

Q381	PP42	26fr blue	9.50	75

No. Q381 Surcharged in Red

1964, Apr. 20

Q382	PP42	28fr on 26fr bl	9.50	65

Type of 1959.

Design: 28fr, St. Peter's Station, Ghent.

1965 Engraved *Perf. 11½*

Q383	PP42	28fr red lil	9.00	1.25

Nos. Q383 Surcharged with New Value and "X" in Green

1966

Q384	PP42	35fr on 28fr red lil	9.00	1.25

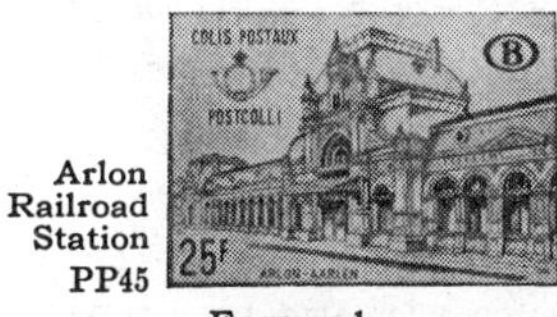

Arlon Railroad Station PP45

Engraved

1967, Aug. *Perf. 11½* Unwmkd.

Q385	PP45	25fr bister	22.50	30
Q386	PP45	30fr bl grn	12.00	45
Q387	PP45	35fr dp bl	13.00	75

Electric Train PP46

Designs: 2fr, 3fr, 4fr, 5fr, 6fr, 7fr, 8fr, 9fr, like 1fr. 10fr, 20fr, 30fr, 40fr, Train going right. 50fr, 60fr, 70fr, 80fr, 90fr, Train going left. 100fr, 200fr, 300fr, Diesel train.

1968-73 Engraved *Perf. 11½*

Q388	PP46	1fr ol bis	8	4
Q389	PP46	2fr slate	15	10
Q390	PP46	3fr bl grn	20	4
Q391	PP46	4fr orange	28	8
Q392	PP46	5fr brown	35	8
Q393	PP46	6fr plum	45	4
Q394	PP46	7fr brt grn	50	8
Q395	PP46	8fr carmine	55	8
Q396	PP46	9fr blue	60	8
Q397	PP46	10fr green	70	4
Q398	PP46	20fr dk bl	1.40	4
Q399	PP46	30fr dk pur	2.00	4
Q400	PP46	40fr brt lil	2.75	4
Q401	PP46	50fr brt pink	3.50	5
Q402	PP46	60fr brt vio	4.75	8
Q402A	PP46	70fr dp bis ('73)	5.50	1.75
Q403	PP46	80fr dk brn	6.00	25
Q403A	PP46	90fr yel grn ('73)	6.00	2.25
Q404	PP46	100fr emerald	8.00	50
Q405	PP46	200fr vio bl	16.00	1.25
Q406	PP46	300fr lil rose	32.50	2.10
		Nos. Q388-Q406 (21)	92.26	9.01

Types of 1953-68

Designs: 10fr, Congress Station, Brussels. 40fr, Arlon Station. 500fr, Electric train going left.

1968, June Engraved *Perf. 11½*

Q407	PP38	10fr gray	90	10
Q408	PP45	40fr vermilion	27.50	15
Q409	PP46	500fr yellow	37.50	2.50

Nos. Q385, Q387 and Q408 Surcharged with New Value and "X"

1970, Dec.

Q410	PP45	37fr on 25fr bis	67.50	4.50
Q411	PP45	48fr on 35fr dp bl	20.00	6.75
Q412	PP45	53fr on 40fr ver	25.00	9.00

Ostend Station PP47

1971, March Engraved *Perf. 11½*

Q413	PP47	32fr bis & blk	2.25	90
Q414	PP47	37fr gray & blk	2.75	1.25
Q415	PP47	42fr bl & blk	3.25	1.40
Q416	PP47	44fr brt rose & blk	3.50	1.50
Q417	PP47	46fr vio & blk	3.50	1.50
Q418	PP47	50fr brick red & blk	4.00	1.65
Q419	PP47	52fr sep & blk	4.00	1.65
Q420	PP47	54fr yel grn & blk	4.50	1.75
Q421	PP47	61fr grnsh bl & blk	4.50	2.00
		Nos. Q413-Q421 (9)	32.25	13.60

Nos. Q413-Q416, Q419-Q421 Surcharged wth New Value and "X"

1971, Dec. 15

Denomination in Black

Q422	PP47	34fr on 32fr bis	2.50	85
Q423	PP47	40fr on 37fr gray	3.00	85
Q424	PP47	47fr on 44fr brt rose	3.50	1.00
Q425	PP47	53fr on 42fr bl	4.00	1.00
Q426	PP47	56fr on 52fr sep	4.50	1.25
Q427	PP47	59fr on 54fr yel grn	5.00	1.25
Q428	PP47	66fr on 61fr grnsh bl	6.00	1.40
		Nos. Q422-Q428 (7)	28.50	7.60

Track, Underpinning of Railroad Car and Emblems—PP48

1972, Mar. Photogravure

Q429	PP48	100fr emer, red & blk	22.50	3.00

Centenary of International Railroad Union.

Congress Emblem PP49

1974, Apr. Photo. *Perf. 11½*

Q430	PP49	100fr yel, blk & red	18.50	2.50

4th International Symposium on Railroad Cybernetics, Washington, D.C., Apr. 1974.

Type of 1953-1957

1975, June 1 Engr. *Perf. 11½*

Q431	PP38	20fr emerald	1.40	80
Q432	PP38	50fr blue	3.50	2.00

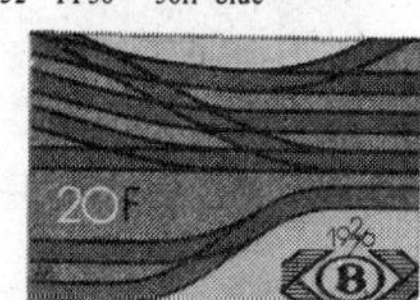

Railroad Tracks PP50

1976, June 10 Photo. *Perf. 11½*

Q433	PP50	20fr ultra & multi	6.50	1.25
Q434	PP50	50fr brt grn & multi	4.25	2.75
Q435	PP50	100fr dp org & multi	8.50	6.00
Q436	PP50	150fr brt lil & multi	12.00	10.00

Railroad Station PP51

1977 Photo. *Perf. 11½*

Q437	PP51	1000fr multi	57.50	*45.00*

Freight Car—PP52

Designs: 2fr, 3fr, 4fr, 5fr, 6fr, 7fr, 8fr, 9fr, Freight car. 10fr, 20fr, 30fr, 40fr, Hopper car. 50fr, 60fr, 70fr, 80fr, 90fr, Maintenance car. 100fr, 200fr, 300fr, 500fr, Liquid fuel car.

1980, Dec. 16 Engraved *Perf. 11½*

Q438	PP52	1fr bis brn & blk	8	3
Q439	PP52	2fr cl & blk	12	4
Q440	PP52	3fr brt bl & blk	18	5
Q441	PP52	4fr grnsh blk & blk	25	6
Q442	PP52	5fr sep & blk	30	10
Q443	PP52	6fr dp org & blk	35	12
Q444	PP52	7fr pur & blk	42	14
Q445	PP52	8fr black	48	14
Q446	PP52	9fr grn & blk	52	15
Q447	PP52	10fr yel bis & blk	58	20
Q448	PP52	20fr grnsh bl & blk	1.10	40
Q449	PP52	30fr bis & blk	1.75	60
Q450	PP52	40fr lt lil & blk	2.50	80
Q451	PP52	50fr dk brn & blk	2.90	1.00
Q452	PP52	60fr ol & blk	3.50	1.20
Q453	PP52	70fr vio bl & blk	4.00	1.40
Q454	PP52	80fr vio brn & blk	4.50	1.60
Q455	PP52	90fr lil rose & blk	5.25	1.80
Q456	PP52	100fr crim rose & blk	5.75	2.00
Q457	PP52	200fr brn & blk	11.50	4.00
Q458	PP52	300fr ol gray & blk	17.50	6.00
Q459	PP52	500fr dl pur & blk	30.00	10.00
		Nos. Q438-Q459 (22)	93.53	31.83

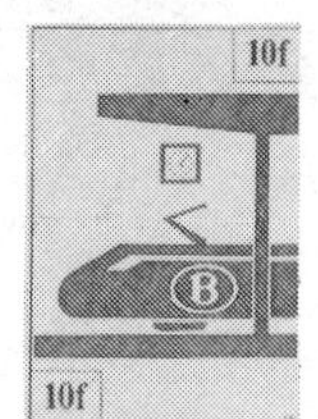

Train in Station—PP53

1982 Engr. *Perf. 11½*

Q460	PP53	10fr red & blk	70	20
Q461	PP53	20fr grn & blk	1.40	40
Q462	PP53	50fr sep & blk	3.50	1.00
Q463	PP53	100fr bl & blk	7.00	2.00

OCCUPATION STAMPS.

Issued under German Occupation.

German Stamps of 1906-11 Surcharged

Belgien
3 Centimes
a

* 1Fr.25C. *

Belgien
b

Wmkd. Lozenges. (125)

1914-15 *Perf. 14, 14½.*

N1	A16 (a)	3c on 3pf brn	45	30
N2	A16 (a)	5c on 5pf grn	38	25
N3	A16 (a)	10c on 10pf car	55	25
N4	A16 (a)	25c on 20pf ultra	60	45
N5	A16 (a)	50c on 40pf lake & blk	2.50	2.00
N6	A16 (a)	75c on 60pf mag	1.25	1.50
N7	A16 (a)	1fr on 80pf lake & blk, *rose*	2.50	2.50
N8	A17 (b)	1fr 25c on 1m car	22.50	15.00
N9	A21 (b)	2fr 50c on 2m gray bl	17.50	17.50
		Nos. N1-N9 (9)	48.23	39.75

German Stamps of 1906-18 Surcharged

Belgien 3 Cent. *c*

Belgien 1F. *d*

* 1F.25Cent. *

Belgien
e

1916-18

N10	A22 (c)	2c on 2pf db	25	25
N11	A16 (c)	3c on 3pf brn	30	20
N12	A16 (c)	5c on 5pf grn	30	25
N13	A22 (c)	8c on 7½pf org	25	25
N14	A16 (c)	10c on 10pf car	25	20
N15	A22 (c)	15c on 15pf yel brn	55	27
N16	A22 (c)	15c on 15pf dk vio	15	20
N17	A16 (c)	20c on 25pf org & blk, *yel*	30	30
N18	A16 (c)	25c on 20pf ultra	30	20
a.		25c on 20pf bl	35	25
N19	A16 (c)	40c on 30pf org & blk, *buff*	35	33
N20	A16 (c)	50c on 40pf lake & blk	30	30
N21	A16 (c)	75c on 60pf mag	55	*11.00*
N22	A16 (d)	1f on 80pf lake & blk, *rose*	1.10	*3.75*
N23	A17 (e)	1f 25c on 1m car	2.25	1.65
N24	A21 (e)	2f 50c on 2m gray bl	20.00	19.00
a.		2f50c on 1m car (error)		*5,500.*
N25	A20 (e)	6f 25c on 5m sl & car	27.50	32.50
		Nos. N10-N25 (16)	54.70	*70.65*

A similar series of stamps without "Belgien" was used in parts of Belgium and France while occupied by German forces. See France Nos. N15-N26.

BENADIR

(See Vol. IV, Somalia.)

BENIN

(bĕ·nēn')

French Colony

LOCATION—On the western coast of Africa, bordering on the Gulf of Guinea.

GOVT.—French Possession.

AREA—8,627 sq. mi.

POP.—493,000 (approx.).

CAPITAL—Benin.

In 1895 the French possessions known as Benin were incorporated into the colony of Dahomey and postage stamps of Dahomey superseded those of Benin. Dahomey took the name Benin when it became a republic in 1975.

100 Centimes = 1 Franc

Handstamped on Stamps of French Colonies **BÉNIN**

Black Overprint.

1892 ***Perf. 14x13½.*** **Unwmkd.**

1	A9	1c *bluish*	90.00	75.00
2	A9	2c brn, *buff*	72.50	62.50
3	A9	4c cl, *lav*	27.50	22.50
4	A9	5c grn, *grnsh*	8.00	7.25
5	A9	10c *lavender*	42.50	32.50
6	A9	15c blue	16.50	6.25
7	A9	20c red, *grn*	140.00	110.00
8	A9	25c *rose*	50.00	30.00
9	A9	30c brn, *yelsh*	100.00	80.00
10	A9	35c *orange*	100.00	80.00
11	A9	40c red, *straw*	80.00	72.50
12	A9	75c car, *rose*	200.00	165.00
13	A9	1fr brnz grn, *straw*	210.00	175.00

Red Overprint.

14	A9	15c blue	55.00	37.50

Blue Overprint.

15	A9	5c grn, *grnsh*	1,300.	325.00
15A	A9	15c blue	1,300.	325.00

Nos. 1–13 all exist with overprint inverted, and several with it double. These sell for slightly more than normal stamps. The overprints of Nos. 1–15A are of four types, three without accent mark on "E." They exist diagonal.

Counterfeits exist of Nos. 1–19.

Additional Surcharge Red or Black **40**

1892

16	A9	01c on 5c grn, *grnsh*	150.00	115.00
17	A9	40c on 15c bl	115.00	37.50
18	A9	75c on 15c bl	450.00	350.00
19	A9	75c on 15c bl (Bk)	1,850.	1,500.

Navigation and Commerce
A3 A4

1893 **Typographed.**

Name of Colony in Blue or Carmine.

20	A3	1c *bluish*	1.60	1.40
21	A3	2c brn, *buff*	2.00	1.80
22	A3	4c cl, *lav*	2.50	1.75
23	A3	5c grn, *grnsh*	2.75	2.25
24	A3	10c *lavender*	2.75	2.75
25	A3	15c bl, quadrille paper	15.00	9.50
26	A3	20c red, *grn*	8.50	4.50
27	A3	25c *rose*	18.50	11.00
28	A3	30c brn, *bis*	9.50	8.00
29	A3	40c red, *straw*	2.75	1.90
30	A3	50c car, *rose*	2.25	1.90
31	A3	75c vio, *org*	4.00	3.50
32	A3	1fr brnz grn, *straw*	28.50	25.00
		Nos. 20-32 (13)	100.60	75.25

1894

33	A4	1c *bluish*	1.40	1.10
34	A4	2c brn, *buff*	1.40	1.10
35	A4	4c cl, *lav*	1.40	1.10
36	A4	5c grn, *grnsh*	1.75	1.10
37	A4	10c *lavender*	2.75	2.00
38	A4	15c bl, quadrille paper	4.00	1.85
39	A4	20c red, *grn*	4.00	3.25
40	A4	25c *rose*	5.00	2.75
41	A4	30c brn, *bis*	2.75	2.25
42	A4	40c red, *straw*	8.50	5.50
43	A4	50c car, *rose*	9.50	6.00
44	A4	75c vio, *org*	6.00	4.50
45	A4	1fr brnz grn, *straw*	1.35	1.35
		Nos. 33-45 (13)	49.80	33.85

People's Republic

LOCATION—West Coast of Africa.

GOVT.—Republic.

AREA—43,483 sq. mi.

POP.—3,290,000 (est. 1977).

CAPITAL—Porto-Novo.

The Republic of Dahomey proclaimed itself the People's Republic of Benin on Nov. 30, 1975. See Dahomey for stamps issued before then.

Allamanda Cathartica A83 Flag Bearers, Arms of Benin A84

Photogravure

1975, Dec. 8 ***Perf. 13*** **Unwmkd.**

Flowers: 35fr, Ixora coccinea. 45fr, Hibiscus. 60fr, Phaemeria magnifica.

342	A83	10fr lil & multi	15	10
343	A83	35fr gray & multi	35	20
344	A83	45fr multi	50	35
345	A83	60fr bl & multi	60	45

1976, Apr. 30 **Litho.** ***Perf. 12***

Designs: 60fr, Speaker, wall with "PRPB," flag and arms of Benin. 100fr, Flag and arms of Benin.

346	A84	50fr ocher & multi	40	30
347	A84	60fr ocher & multi	45	30
348	A84	100fr multi	80	60

Proclamation of the People's Republic of Benin, Nov. 30, 1975.

A. G. Bell, Satellite and 1876 Telephone—A85

1976, July 9 **Litho.** ***Perf. 13***

349	A85	200fr lil, red & brn	1.65	70

Centenary of first telephone call by Alexander Graham Bell, Mar. 10, 1876.

Dahomey Nos. 277–278 Surcharged

1976, July 19 **Photo.** ***Perf. 12½x13***

350	A57	50fr on 1fr multi	40	18
351	A57	60fr on 2fr multi	50	20

Scouts Cooking—A86

Design: 70fr, Three Scouts.

1976, Aug. 16 **Litho.** ***Perf. 12½x13***

352	A86	50fr blk, lil & brn	40	30
353	A86	70fr blk, ol & red brn	55	40

African Jamboree, Nigeria 1976.

Blood Bank, Cotonou—A87

Designs: 50fr, Accident and first aid station. 60fr, Blood donation.

1976, Sept. 24 **Litho.** ***Perf. 13***

354	A87	5fr multi	5	3
355	A87	50fr multi	40	30
356	A87	60fr multi	50	35

National Blood Donors Day.

Manioc A88

Designs: 50fr, Corn. 60fr, Cacao. 150fr, Cotton.

1976, Oct. 4 **Litho.** ***Perf. 13x12½***

357	A88	20fr multi	15	10
358	A88	50fr multi	40	30
359	A88	60fr multi	45	30
360	A88	150fr multi	1.25	90

National Agricultural production campaign.

Classroom A89

1976, Oct. 25

361	A89	50fr multi	40	30

Third anniversary of KPARO newspaper, used in local language studies.

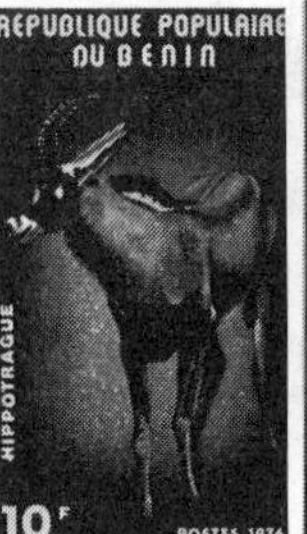

Roan Antelope A90 Flags, Wall, Broken Chains A91

Designs: 30fr, Buffalo. 50fr, Hippopotamus (horiz.). 70fr, Lion.

1976, Nov. 8 **Photogravure**

362	A90	10fr multi	10	6
363	A90	30fr multi	25	18
364	A90	50fr multi	40	30
365	A90	70fr multi	55	35

Penjari National Park.

1976, Nov. 30 **Litho.** ***Perf. 12½***

Design: 150fr, Corn, raised hands with weapons.

366	A91	40fr multi	30	20
367	A91	150fr multi	1.20	90

First anniversary of proclamation of the People's Republic of Benin.

Table Tennis, Map of Africa (Games' Emblem)—A92

Design: 50fr, Stadium, Cotonou.

1976, Dec. 26 **Litho.** ***Perf. 13***

368	A92	10fr multi	10	6
369	A92	50fr multi	40	30

West African University Games, Cotonou, Dec. 26–31.

Europafrica Issue

Planes over Africa and Europe A93

1977, May 13 **Litho.** ***Perf. 13***

370	A93	200fr multi	1.60	1.20

Snake A94

Designs: 3fr, Tortoise. 5fr, Zebus. 10fr, Cats.

1977, June 13 **Litho.** ***Perf. 13x13½***

371	A94	2fr multi	3	3
372	A94	3fr multi	3	3
373	A94	5fr multi	5	3
374	A94	10fr multi	10	6

Patients at Clinic
A95

1977, Aug. 2 Litho. *Perf. 12½*

375	A95	100fr multi	85	60

World Rheumatism Year.

Karate, Map of Africa
A96

Designs: 100fr, Javelin, map of Africa, Benin flag (horiz.). 150fr, Hurdles.

1977, Aug. 30 Litho. *Perf. 12½*

376	A96	90fr multi	70	55
377	A96	100fr multi	85	60
378	A96	150fr multi	1.25	90
a.		Souvenir sheet of 3	2.75	2.75

2nd West African Games, Lagos, Nigeria. No. 378a contains one each of Nos. 376-378; black marginal inscription. Size: 143x92mm.

Chairman Mao
A97

Lister and Vaporizer
A98

1977, Sept. 9 Litho. *Perf. 13x12½*

379	A97	100fr multi	85	60

Chairman Mao Tse-tung (1893-1976), Chinese communist leader, first death anniversary.

1977, Sept. 20 Engr. *Perf. 13*

Design: 150fr, Scalpels and flames, symbols of antisepsis, and Red Cross.

380	A98	150fr multi	1.20	90
381	A98	210fr multi	1.75	1.25

Joseph Lister (1827-1912), surgeon, founder of antiseptic surgery, birth sesquicentennial.

Guelede Mask, Ethnographic Museum, Porto Novo—A99

Designs: 50fr, Jar, symbol of unity, emblem of King Ghezo, Historical Museum, Abomey (vert.). 210fr, Abomey Museum.

1977, Oct. 17 *Perf. 13*

382	A99	50fr red & multi	40	30
383	A99	60fr blk, bl & bis	50	35
384	A99	210fr multi	1.75	1.25

Atacora Falls
A100

Mother and Child, Owl of Wisdom
A101

Designs: 60fr, Pile houses, Ganvie (horiz.). 150fr, Round huts, Savalou.

1977, Oct. 24 Litho. *Perf. 12½*

385	A100	50fr multi	40	30
386	A100	60fr multi	50	35
387	A100	150fr multi	1.25	90
a.		Souvenir sheet of 3	2.80	2.80

Tourist publicity. No. 387a contains one each of Nos. 385-387; black marginal inscription. Size: 143x91mm.

Perf. 12½x13, 13x12½

1977, Dec. 3 Photogravure

Design: 150fr, Chopping down magical tree (horiz.).

388	A101	60fr multi	50	35
389	A101	150fr multi	1.25	90

Campaign against witchcraft.

Battle Scene—A102

1978, Jan. 16 Litho *Perf. 12½*

390	A102	50fr multi	50	28

Victory of people of Benin over imperialist forces.

Map, People and Houses of Benin
A103

1978, Feb. 1

391	A103	50fr multi	50	28

General population and dwellings census.

Alexander Fleming, Microscope and Penicillin—A104

1978, Mar. 12 Litho. *Perf. 13*

392	A104	300fr multi	3.00	1.65

Alexander Fleming (1881-1955), 50th anniversary of discovery of penicillin.

Abdoulaye Issa, Weapons and Fighters
A105

1978, Apr. 1 *Perf. 12½x13*

393	A105	100fr red, blk & gold	1.00	55

First anniversary of death of Abdoulaye Issa and National Day of Benin's Youth.

El Hadj Omar and Horseback Rider
A106

Design: 90fr, L'Almamy Samory Toure (1830-1900) and horseback riders.

1978, Apr. 10 *Perf. 13x12½*

394	A106	90fr red & multi	90	50
395	A106	100fr multi	1.00	55

African heroes of resistance against colonialism.

ITU Emblem, Satellite, Landscape
A107

1978, May 17 Litho. *Perf. 13*

396	A107	100fr multi	1.00	55

10th World Telecommunications Day.

Soccer Player, Stadium, Argentina '78 Emblem—A108

Designs (Argentina '78 Emblem and): 300fr, Soccer players and ball (vert.). 500fr, Soccer player, globe with ball on map.

1978, June 1 Litho. *Perf. 12½*

397	A108	200fr multi	2.00	1.10
398	A108	300fr multi	3.00	1.65
399	A108	500fr multi	5.00	2.75
a.		Souvenir sheet of 3	11.00	11.00

11th World Cup Soccer Championship, Argentina, June 1-25. No. 399a contains 3 stamps similar to Nos. 397-399 in changed colors; red marginal inscription and blue border. Size: 190x120mm.

Nos. 397-399a Overprinted in Red Brown:
a. FINALE / ARGENTINE: 3 / HOLLANDE: 1
b. CHAMPION / 1978 / ARGENTINE
c. 3e BRESIL / 4e ITALIE

1978, June 25 Litho. *Perf. 12½*

400	A108 (a)	200fr multi	2.00	1.10
401	A108 (b)	300fr multi	3.00	1.65
402	A108 (c)	500fr multi	5.00	2.75
a.		Souvenir sheet of 3	11.00	11.00

Argentina's victory in 1978 Soccer Championship.

Games' Flag over Africa, Basketball Players—A109

Designs (Games' Emblem and): 60fr, Map of Africa and volleyball players. 80fr, Map of Benin and bicyclists.

1978, July 13 *Perf. 13x12½*

403	A109	50fr lt bl & multi	50	28
404	A109	60fr ultra & multi	60	35
405	A109	80fr multi	80	50
a.		Souvenir sheet of 3	2.00	2.00

3rd African Games, Algiers, July 13-28. No. 405a contains 3 stamps in changed colors similar to Nos. 403-405; rose lilac and black margin. Size: 208-80mm.

Martin Luther King, Jr.
A110

1978, July 30 *Perf. 12½*

406	A110	300fr multi	3.00	1.65

Martin Luther King, Jr. (1929-1968), American civil rights leader.

Kanna Taxi, Oueme
A111

Designs: 60fr, Leatherworker and goods. 70fr, Drummer and tom-toms. 100fr, Metalworker and calabashes.

1978, Aug. 26

407	A111	50fr multi	50	28
408	A111	60fr multi	60	35
409	A111	70fr multi	70	42
410	A111	100fr multi	1.00	55

Getting to know Benin through its provinces.

Map of Italy and Exhibition Poster—A112

1978, Aug. 26 Litho. *Perf. 13*

411 A112 200fr multi 2.00 1.10

Riccione 1978 Philatelic Exhibition.

Turkeys A113

Poultry: 20fr, Ducks. 50fr, Chicken. 60fr, Guinea fowl.

1978, Oct. 5 Photo. *Perf. 12½x13*

412 A113 10fr multi 10 10
413 A113 20fr multi 20 20
414 A113 50fr multi 50 50
415 A113 60fr multi 60 60

Poultry breeding.

Royal Messenger, UPU Emblem A114

Designs (UPU Emblem and): 60fr, Boatsman, ship and car (vert.). 90fr, Special messenger and plane (vert.).

Perf. 13x12½, 12½x13

1978, Oct. 16

416 A114 50fr multi 50 50
417 A114 60fr multi 60 60
418 A114 90fr multi 90 90

Centenary of change of "General Postal Union" to "Universal Postal Union."

Raoul Follereau A115

1978, Dec. 17 Litho. *Perf. 12½*

419 A115 200fr multi 2.00 2.00

Raoul Follereau (1903–1977), apostle to the lepers and educator of the blind.

See "Special Notices" at the front of this volume for data on the listing methods of this Catalogue, abbreviations, condition, prices and examination.

IYC Emblem A116

Designs: 20fr, Globe as balloon carrying children. 50fr, Children of various races surrounding globe.

1979, Feb. 20 Litho. *Perf. 12x13*

420 A116 10fr multi 10 10
421 A116 20fr multi 20 20
422 A116 50fr multi 50 50

International Year of the Child.

Hydrangea A117

Flowers: 25fr, Assangokan. 30fr, Geranium. 40fr, Water lilies (horiz.).

Perf. 13x12½, 12½x13

1979, Feb. 28 Lithographed

423 A117 20fr multi 20 20
424 A117 25fr multi 25 25
425 A117 30fr multi 30 30
426 A117 40fr multi 40 40

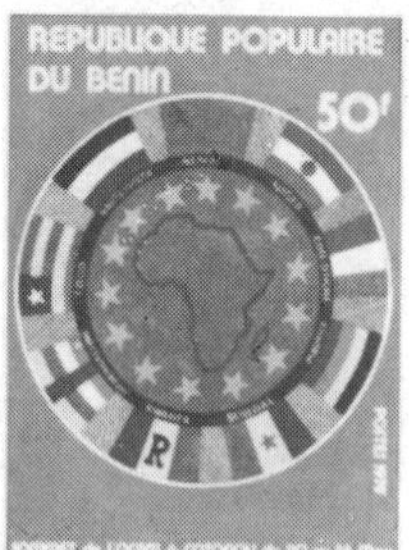

Emblem: Map of Africa and Members' Flags A118

Designs: 60fr, Map of Benin and flags. 80fr, OCAM flag and map of Africa showing member states.

1979, Mar. 20 Litho. *Perf. 12x13*

427 A118 50fr multi 50 50
428 A118 60fr multi 60 60
429 A118 80fr multi 80 80

OCAM Summit Conference, Cotonou, Mar. 20–28.

Tower, Waves, Satellite, ITU Emblem A119

1979, May 17 Litho. *Perf. 12½*

430 A119 50fr multi 50 50

World Telecommunications Day.

Bank Building and Sculpture A120

1979, May 26 Litho. *Perf.*

431 A120 50fr multi 50 50

Opening of Headquarters of West African Savings Bank in Dakar.

Guelede Mask, Abomey Tapestry, Malaconotus Bird—A121

Design: 50fr, Jet, canoe, satellite, UPU and exhibition emblems.

1979, June 8 Litho. *Perf. 13*

432 A121 15fr multi 15 15

Engraved

433 A121 50fr multi 50 50

Philexafrique II, Libreville, Gabon, June 8–17. Nos. 432, 433 each printed in sheets of 10 with 5 labels showing exhibition emblem.

Nos. 427-429 Overprinted: "26 au 28 juin 1979" and Dots

1979, June 26

434 A118 50fr multi 50 50
435 A118 60fr multi 60 60
436 A118 80fr multi 80 80

2nd OCAM Summit Conference, June 26-28.

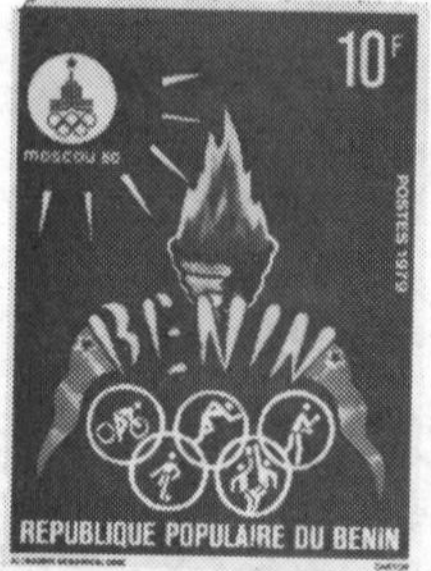

Olympic Flame and Emblems—A122

Pre-Olympic Year: 50fr, High jump.

1979, July 1 Litho.

437 A122 10fr multi 10 10
438 A122 50fr multi 50 50

Antelope—A123

Animals: 10fr, Giraffes, map of Benin (vert.) 20fr, Chimpanzee 50fr, Elephants, map of Benin (vert).

1979, Oct.1 Litho. *Perf. 13*

439 A123 5fr multi 5 5
440 A123 10fr multi 10 10
441 A123 20fr multi 20 20
442 A123 50fr multi 50 50

Map of Africa, Emblem and Jet—A124

1979, Dec. 12 Litho. *Perf. 12½*

443 A124 50fr multi 50 50
444 A124 60fr multi 60 60

ASECNA (Air Safety Board), 20th anniversary.

Mail Services—A125

Design: 50fr, Post Office and headquarters (vert.).

1979, Dec. 19 Litho. *Perf. 13*

445 A125 50fr multi 50 50
446 A125 60fr multi 60 60

Office of Posts and Telecommunications, 20th anniversary.

Lenin and Globe—A126

1980, Apr. 22 Litho. *Perf. 12½*

447 A126 50fr *shown* 50 50
448 A126 150fr *Lenin in library* 1.50 1.50

Lenin, 110th birth anniversary.

Cotonou Club Emblem A127

Galileo, Astrolabe A128

1980, Feb. 23 Litho. *Perf. 12½*

449	A127	90fr	*shown*	90	90
450	A127	200fr	*Rotary emblem on globe*, horiz.	2.00	2.00

Rotary International, 75th anniversary.

1980, Apr. 2

451	A128	70fr	*shown*	70	70
452	A128	100fr	*Copernicus, solar system*	1.00	1.00

Discovery of Pluto, 50th anniversary.

Abu Simbel, UNESCO Emblem—A129

1980, Apr. 15 *Perf. 13*

453	A129	50fr	*Column*, vert.	50	50
454	A129	60fr	*Ramses II*, vert.	60	60
455	A129	150fr	*shown*	1.50	1.50

UNESCO campaign to save Nubian monuments, 20th anniversary.

Monument, Martyrs' Square, Cotonou—A130

Designs: Various monuments in Martyrs' Square. Cotonou. 60fr, 70fr, 100fr, horiz.

1980, May 2 *Perf. 12½x13, 13x12½*

456	A130	50fr	multi	50	50
457	A130	60fr	multi	60	60
458	A130	70fr	multi	70	70
459	A130	100fr	multi	1.00	1.00

Tinbo—A131

Musical Instruments: 5fr, Assan (vert.). 15fr, Tam-tam sato (vert.). 20fr, Kora. 30fr, Gangan. 50fr, Sinhoun.

1980, May 20 *Perf. 12½*

460	A131	5fr	multi	5	5
461	A131	10fr	multi	10	10
462	A131	15fr	multi	15	15
463	A131	20fr	multi	20	20
464	A131	30fr	multi	30	30
465	A131	50fr	multi	50	50
			Nos. 460-465 (6)	1.30	1.30

First Non-stop Flight, Paris-New York—A132

1980, June 2 Litho. *Perf. 12½*

466	A132	90fr	*shown*	90	90
467	A132	100fr	*Dieudonne Coste, Maurice Bellonte*	1.00	1.00

Lunokhod I on the Moon—A133

1980, June 15 Engraved *Perf. 13*

468	A133	90fr	multi	90	90

Lunokhod I Soviet unmanned moon mision, 10th anniversary. See No. C290.

Olympic Flame and Mischa, Moscow '80 Emblem—A134

1980, July 16 Litho. *Perf. 12½*

469	A134	50fr	*shown*	50	50
470	A134	60fr	*Equestrian*, vert.	60	60
471	A134	70fr	*Judo*	70	70
472	A134	200fr	*Flag, sports, globe*, vert.	2.00	2.00
473	A134	300fr	*Weight lifting*, vert.	3.00	3.00
			Nos. 469-473 (5)	6.80	6.80

22nd Summer Olympic Games, Moscow, July 19-Aug. 3.

Telephone and Rising Sun—A135

World Telecommunications Day: 50fr, Farmer on telephone (vert.).

1980, May 17 Litho. *Perf. 12½*

474	A135	50fr	multi	50	50
475	A135	60fr	multi	60	60

Cotonou West African Community Village—A136

Designs: Views of Cotonou.

1980, July 26 *Perf. 13x13½*

476	A136	50fr	multi	50	50
477	A136	60fr	multi	60	60
478	A136	70fr	multi	70	70

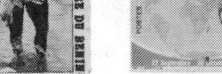

Agbadja Dancers—A137

Designs: Dancers and musicians.

1980, Aug. 1 *Perf. 12½*

479	A137	30fr	multi	30	30
480	A137	50fr	multi	50	50
481	A137	60fr	multi	60	60

Fisherman

A138

Philippines under Magnifier

A139

Designs: 5fr, Throwing net. 15fr, Canoe and shore fishing. 20fr, Basket traps. 50fr, Hauling net. 60fr, River fishing. All horiz.

1980, Sept. 1

482	A138	5fr	multi	5	5
483	A138	10fr	multi	10	10
484	A138	15fr	multi	15	15
485	A138	20fr	multi	20	20
486	A138	50fr	multi	50	50
487	A138	60fr	multi	60	60
			Nos. 482-487 (6)	1.60	1.60

1980, Sept. 27 *Perf. 13x13½, 13½x13*

World Tourism Conference, Manila, Sept. 27: 60fr, Emblem on flag, hand pointing to Manila on globe (horiz.).

488	A139	50fr	multi	50	50
489	A139	60fr	multi	60	60

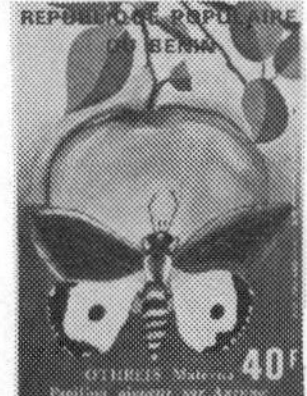

Othreis Materna—A140

1980, Oct. 1 *Perf. 12½*

490	A140	40fr	shown	40	40
491	A140	50fr	Othreis fullonia	50	50
492	A140	200fr	Oryctes sp.	2.00	2.00

African Postal Union, 5th Anniversary

A141

Clasped Hands Breaking Chain, UN Emblem

A142

1980, Oct. 24 Photo. *Perf. 13½*

493	A141	75fr	multi	75	75

1980, Nov. 4 *Perf. 12½x13*

494	A142	30fr	shown	30	30
495	A142	50fr	Freed prisoner	50	50
496	A142	60fr	Man holding torch	60	60

Declaration of human rights, 30th anniversary.

Self-portrait, by Vincent van Gogh, 1888—A143

1980, Dec. 1 Litho. *Perf. 13*

497	A143	100fr	shown	1.00	1.00
498	A143	300fr	Facteur Roulin	3.00	3.00

Vincent Van Gogh (1853-1890), artist.

Offenbach and Scene from Orpheus in the Underworld—A144

1980, Dec. 15 Engr.

499	A144	50fr	shown	50	50
500	A144	60fr	Paris Life	60	60

Jacques Offenbach (1819-1880), composer.

Kepler and Satellites—A145

1980, Dec. 20

501	A145	50fr	Kepler, diagram, vert.	50	50
502	A145	60fr	shown	60	60

Johannes Kepler (1571-1630), astronomer, 350th death anniversary.

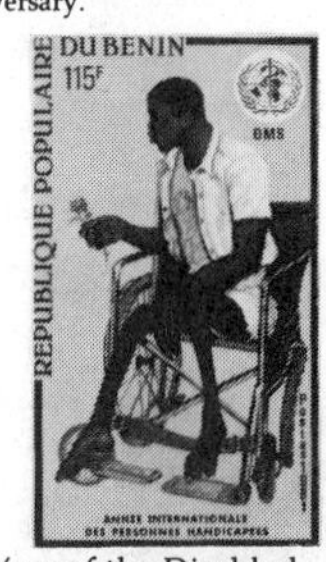

Intl. Year of the Disabled—A146

1981, Apr. 10 Litho. *Perf. 12½*

503	A146	115fr	multi	1.15	1.15

20th Anniv. of Manned Space Flight—A147

1981, May 30 *Perf. 13*

504	A147	500fr	multi	5.00	5.00

13th World Telecommunications Day—A148

1981, May 30 **Litho.** ***Perf. 12½***

505 A148 115fr multi 1.15 1.15

Amaryllis A149

1981, June 20 ***Perf. 12½***

506 A149 10fr shown 10 10
507 A149 20fr Eischornia crassipes, vert. 20 20
508 A149 80fr Parkia biglobosa, vert. 80 80

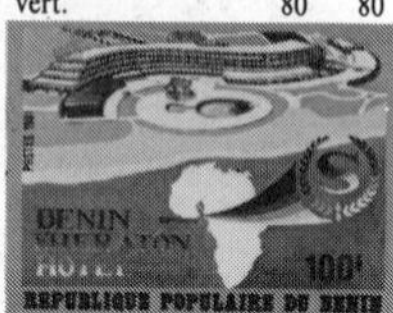

Benin Sheraton Hotel—A150

1981, July 1

509 A150 100fr multi 1.00 1.00

Guinea Pig A151

1981, July 31 ***Perf. 13x13½***

510 A151 5fr shown 5 5
511 A151 60fr Cat 60 60
512 A151 80fr Dogs 80 80

World UPU Day—A152

1981, Oct. 9 **Engr.** ***Perf. 13***

513 A152 100fr red brn & blk 1.00 1.00

25th Intl. Letter Writing Week, Oct. 6-12—A153

1981, Oct. 15

514 A153 100fr dk bl & pur 1.00 1.00

West African Economic Community A154

1981, Nov. 20 **Litho.** ***Perf. 12½***

515 A154 60fr multi 60 60

West African Rice Development Assoc. 10th Anniv.—A155

1981, Dec. 10 ***Perf. 13x13½***

516 A155 60fr multi 60 60

TB Bacillus Centenary—A156

1982, Mar. 1 **Litho.** ***Perf. 13***

517 A156 115fr multi 1.15 1.15

West African Economic Community, 5th Summit Conference—A157

1982, May 27 ***Perf. 12½***

518 A157 60fr multi 60 60

1982 World Cup—A158

1982, June 1 ***Perf. 13***

519 A158 90fr Players 90 90
520 A158 300fr Flags on leg 3.00 3.00

France No. B349 Magnified, Map of France—A159

1982, June 11

521 A159 90fr multi 90 90

PHILEXFRANCE '82 Stamp Exhibition, Paris, June 11-21.

George Washington—A160

1982, Mar. 10 **Litho.** ***Perf. 14***

522 A160 200fr Washington, flag, map 2.00 2.00

Nos. 519-520 Overprinted with Finalists Names.

1982, Aug. 16 ***Perf. 12½***

523 A158 90fr multi 90 90
524 A158 300fr multi 3.00 3.00

Italy's victory in 1982 World Cup.

Bluethroat—A161

1982, Sept. 1 ***Perf. 14x14½, 14½x14***

525 A161 5fr Daoelo gigas, vert. 5 5
526 A161 10fr shown 10 10
527 A161 15fr Swallow, vert. 15 15
528 A161 20fr Kingfisher, weaver bird, vert. 20 20
529 A161 30fr Great sedge warbler 30 30
530 A161 60fr Common warbler 60 60
531 A161 80fr Owl, vert. 80 80
532 A161 100fr Cockatoo, vert. 1.00 1.00
Nos. 525-532 (8) 3.20 3.20

ITU Plenipotentiaries Conference, Nairobi, Sept.—A162

1982, Sept. 26 ***Perf. 13***

533 A162 200fr Map 2.00 2.00

13th World UPU Day—A163

1982, Oct. 9 **Engr.** ***Perf. 13***

534 A163 100fr Monument 1.00 1.00

Nos. 411, 482, 510 Overprinted in Red or Blue:
#537 "RICCIONE 1982"
#536 "UAPT 1982"
#535 "Croix Rouge / 8 Mai 1982"

1982, Nov. **Litho.** ***Perf. 13, 12½, 13x13½***

535 A138 60fr on 5fr multi 60 60
536 A151 60fr on 5fr multi 60 60
537 A112 200fr multi (Bl) 2.00 2.00

Visit of French Pres. Francois Mitterand—A164

1983, Jan. 15 **Litho.** ***Perf. 12½x13***

538 A164 90fr multi 90 90

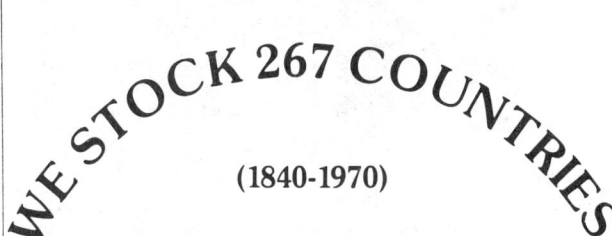

AIR POST STAMPS

People's Republic

Nativity, by Aert van Leyden
AP84

Paintings: 85fr, Adoration of the Kings, by Rubens (vert.). 140fr, Adoration of the Shepherds, by Charles Lebrun. 300fr, The Virgin with the Blue Diadem, by Raphael (vert.).

1975, Dec. 19 Litho. ***Perf. 13***

C240	AP84	40fr gold & multi	40	15
C241	AP84	85fr gold & multi	85	30
C242	AP84	140fr gold & multi	1.20	50
C243	AP84	300fr gold & multi	2.75	1.25

Christmas 1975.

Slalom, Innsbruck Olympic Emblem—AP85

Designs (Innsbruck Olympic Games Emblem and): 150fr, Bobsledding (vert.). 300fr, Figure skating, pairs.

1976, June 28 Litho. ***Perf. 12½***

C244	AP85	60fr multi	50	20
C245	AP85	150fr multi	1.25	50
C246	AP85	300fr multi	2.50	1.10

12th Winter Olympic Games, Innsbruck, Austria, Feb. 4–15.

Dahomey Nos. C235–C237 Overprinted: "POPULAIRE / DU BENIN" and Bars, with Surcharge Added on Nos. C236—C237

1976, July 4 Engr. ***Perf. 13***

C247	AP82	135fr multi	1.10	50
C248	AP82	210fr on 300fr multi	1.75	70
C249	AP82	380fr on 500fr multi	3.00	1.30

The overprint includes a bar covering "DU DAHOMEY" in shades of brown; "POPULAIRE DU BENIN" is blue on Nos. C247–C248, red on No. C249. The surcharge and bars over old value are blue on No. C248, red, brown on No. C249.

Long Jump—AP86

Designs (Olympic Rings and): 150fr, Basketball (vert.). 200fr, Hurdles.

1976, July 16 Photo. ***Perf. 13***

C250	AP86	60fr multi	50	20
C251	AP86	150fr multi	1.25	50
C252	AP86	200fr multi	1.65	70
a.		Souvenir sheet of 3	3.50	3.50

21st Olympic Games, Montreal, Canada, July 17–Aug 1. No. C252a contains one each of Nos. C250–C252; brown marginal inscription. Size:150x120mm.

Konrad Adenauer and Cologne Cathedral—AP87

Design: 90fr, Konrad Adenauer (vert.).

1976, Aug. 27 Engr. ***Perf. 13***

C253	AP87	90fr multi	70	30
C254	AP87	250fr multi	2.00	80

Konrad Adenauer (1876–1967), German Chancellor, birth centenary.

Children's Heads and Flying Fish (Dahomey Type A32)—AP88

Design: 210fr, Lion cub's head and Benin type A3 (vert.).

1976, Sept. 13

C255	AP88	60fr Prus bl & vio bl	50	20
C256	AP88	210fr multi	1.65	70

JUVAROUEN 76, International Youth Philatelic Exhibition, Rouen, France, Apr. 25–May 2.

Apollo 14 Emblem and Blast-off
AP89

Design: 270fr, Landing craft and man on moon.

1976, Oct. 18 Engr. ***Perf. 13***

C257	AP89	130fr multi	1.00	45
C258	AP89	270fr multi	2.25	95

Apollo 14 Moon Mission, 5th anniversary.

Annunciation, by Master of Jativa
AP90

Paintings: 60fr, Nativity, by Gerard David. 270fr, Adoration of the Kings, Dutch School. 300fr, Flight into Egypt, by Gentile Fabriano (horiz.).

1976, Dec. 20 Litho. ***Perf. 12½***

C259	AP90	50fr gold & multi	40	25

C260	AP90	60fr gold & multi	50	35
C261	AP90	270fr gold & multi	2.25	95
C262	AP90	300fr gold & multi	2.50	1.50

Christmas 1976.

Gamblers and Lottery Emblem
AP91

1977, Mar. 13 Litho. *Perf. 13*

C263	AP91	50fr multi	40	30

National lottery, 10th anniversary.

Sassenage Castle, Grenoble—AP92

1977, May 16 *Perf. 12½*

C264	AP92	200fr multi	1.65	1.20

10th anniversary of International French Language Council.

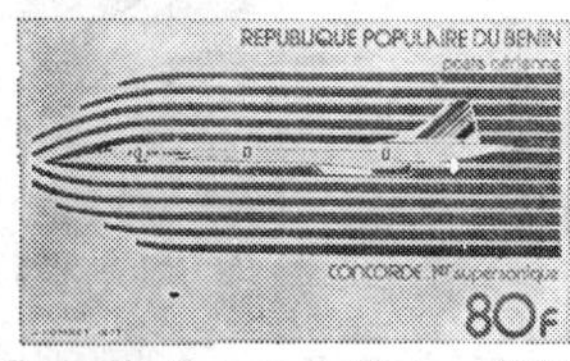

Concorde, Supersonic Plane—AP93

Designs: 150fr, Zeppelin. 300fr, Charles A. Lindbergh and Spirit of St. Louis. 500fr, Charles Nungesser and François Coli, French aviators lost over Atlantic, 1927.

1977, July 25 Engr. *Perf. 13*

C265	AP93	80fr ultra & red	65	50
C266	AP93	150fr multi	1.25	90
C267	AP93	300fr multi	2.50	1.80
C268	AP93	500fr multi	4.00	3.00

Aviation history.

Soccer Player
AP94

Design: 200fr, Soccer players and Games' emblem.

1977, July 28 Litho. *Perf. 12½x12*

C269	AP94	60fr multi	50	30
C270	AP94	200fr multi	1.65	1.20

World Soccer Cup elimination games.

Miss Haverfield, by Gainsborough
AP95

Designs: 150fr, Self-portrait, by Rubens. 200fr, Anguish, man's head by Da Vinci.

1977, Oct. 3 Engr. *Perf. 13*

C271	AP95	100fr sl grn & mar	80	60
C272	AP95	150fr red brn & dk brn	1.25	90
C273	AP95	200fr brn & red	1.65	1.20

Birth anniversaries: Thomas Gainsborough (1727–1788); Peter Paul Rubens (1577–1640); Leonardo da Vinci (1452–1519).

No. C265 Overprinted:
"1er VOL COMMERCIAL / 22.11.77 PARIS NEW-YORK"

1977, Nov. 22 Engr. *Perf. 13*

C274	AP93	80fr ultra & red	65	50

Concorde, first commercial flight, Paris to New York.

Viking on Mars—AP96

Designs: 150fr, Isaac Newton, apple globe, stars. 200fr, Vladimir M. Komarov, spacecraft and earth. 500fr, Dog Laika, rocket and space.

1977, Nov. 28 Engr. *Perf. 13*

C275	AP96	100fr multi	80	60
C276	AP96	150fr multi	1.25	90
C277	AP96	200fr multi	1.65	1.20
C278	AP96	500fr multi	4.00	3.00

Operation Viking on Mars; 250th death anniversary of Isaac Newton (1642–1727); 10th death anniversary of Russian cosmonaut Vladimir M. Komarov; 20th anniversary of first living creature in space.

Monument, Red Star Place, Cotonou—AP97

Litho.; Gold Embossed

1977 Nov. 30 *Perf. 12½*

C279	AP97	500fr multi	4.00	2.50

Common Design Types
pictured in section at front of book.

Suzanne Fourment, by Rubens
AP98

Design: 380fr, Nicholas Rubens, By Rubens.

1977, Dec. 12 Engr. *Perf. 13*

C280	AP98	200fr multi	1.65	1.20
C281	AP98	380fr cl & ocher	3.00	2.10

Peter Paul Rubens (1577–1640), 400th birth anniversary.

Parthenon and UNESCO Emblem
AP99

Designs: 70fr, Acropolis and frieze showing Pan-Athenaic procession (vert.). 250fr, Parthenon and frieze showing horsemen (vert.).

1978, Sept. 22 Litho. *Perf. 12½x12*

C282	AP99	70fr multi	70	40
C283	AP99	250fr multi	2.50	1.50
C284	AP99	500fr multi	5.00	3.00

Save the Parthenon in Athens campaign.

Philexafrique II—Essen Issue
Common Design Types

Designs: No. C285, Buffalo and Dahomey No. C33. No. C286, Wild ducks and Baden No. 1.

1978, Nov. 1 Litho. *Perf. 12½*

C285	CD138	100fr multi	1.00	60
C286	CD139	100fr multi	1.00	60

Nos. C285–C286 printed se-tenant.

Wilbur and Orville Wright and Flyer—AP100

1978, Dec. 28 Engr. *Perf. 13*

C287	AP100	500fr multi	5.00	3.00

75th anniversary of 1st powered flight.

Cook's Ships, Hawaii, World Map
AP101

Design: 50fr, Battle at Kowrowa.

1979, June 1 Engr. *Perf. 13*

C288	AP101	20fr multi	20	20
C289	AP101	50fr multi	50	50

Capt. James Cook (1728-1779), explorer, death bicentenary.

Lunokhod Type of 1980

1980, June 15 Engraved *Perf. 13*
Size: 27x48mm.

C290	A133	210fr multi	2.10	2.10

Soccer Players
AP102

1981, Mar. 31 Litho. *Perf. 13*

C291	AP102	200fr Ball, globe	2.00	2.00
C292	AP102	500fr shown	5.00	5.00

ESPANA '82 World Soccer Cup eliminations.

Prince Charles and Lady Diana, London Bridge—AP103

1981, July 29 Litho. *Perf. 12½*

C293	AP103	500fr multi	5.00	5.00

Royal wedding.

Three Musicians, by Pablo Picasso (1881-1973)—AP104

1981, Nov. 2 Litho. *Perf. 12½x13, 13x12½*

C294	AP104	300fr Dance, vert.	3.00	3.00
C295	AP104	500fr shown	5.00	5.00

1300th Anniv. of Bulgaria—AP105

1981, Dec. 2 Litho. *Perf. 13*

C296	AP105	100fr multi	1.00	1.00

Visit of Pope John Paul II—AP106

1982, Feb. 17 Litho. *Perf. 13*

C297	AP106	80fr multi	80	80

20th Anniv. of John Glenn's Flight—AP107

1982, Feb. 21 Litho. *Perf. 13*

C298	AP107	500fr multi	5.00	5.00

Scouting Year—AP108

1982, June 1 *Perf. 12½*

C299	AP108	105fr multi	1.05	1.05

Nos. C256, C275 Surcharged.

1982, Nov. Engr. *Perf. 13*

C300	AP88	50fr on 210fr multi	50	50
C301	AP96	50fr on 100fr multi	50	50

Monet in Boat, by Claude Monet (1832-1883)—AP109

1982, Dec. 6 Litho. *Perf. 13x12½*

C302	AP109	300fr multi	3.00	3.00

Christmas 1982—AP110

Virgin and Child Paintings.

1982, Dec. 20 *Perf. 12½x13*

C303	AP110	200fr Matthias Grunewald	2.00	2.00
C304	AP110	300fr Correggio	3.00	3.00

POSTAGE DUE STAMPS.

French Colony

Handstamped in Black on Postage Due Stamps of French Colonies **BÉNIN**

1894 *Imperf.* Unwmkd.

J1	D1	5c black	85.00	37.50
J2	D1	10c black	85.00	37.50
J3	D1	20c black	85.00	37.50
J4	D1	30c black	85.00	37.50

Nos. J1–J4 exist with overprint in various positions.

People's Republic

Pineapples D6

Mail Delivery D7

Designs: 20fr, Cashew (vert.). 40fr, Oranges. 50fr, Akee. 80fr, Mail delivery by boat.

1978, Sept. 5 Photo. *Perf. 13*

J44	D6	10fr multi	8	8
J45	D6	20fr multi	18	18
J46	D6	40fr multi	32	32
J47	D6	50fr multi	40	40
		Engraved		
J48	D7	60fr multi	50	50
J49	D7	80fr multi	60	60
		Nos. J44-J49 (6)	2.08	2.08

PARCEL POST STAMPS

Nos. 448, 459, 473 Overprinted "Colis Postaux"

1982, Nov. Litho. *Perf. 12½, 13x12½*

Q1	A126	100fr on 150fr multi	1.00	1.00
Q2	A130	100fr multi	1.00	1.00
Q3	A134	300fr multi	3.00	3.00

BERGEDORF

See Early German States group preceding Germany.

BHUTAN

(bo͞ot·än'; bo͞o·tăn')

LOCATION—Eastern Himalayas.
GOVT.—Kingdom.
AREA—18,147 sq. mi.
POP.—1,035,000 (est. 1974).
CAPITAL—Thimphu.

100 Chetrum = 1 Ngultrum or Rupee.

Postal Runner
A1

Designs: 3ch, 70ch, Archer. 5ch, 1.30nu, Yak. 15ch, Map of Bhutan, portrait of Druk Gyalpo (Dragon King) Ugyen Wangchuk (1867–1902) and Paro Dzong (fortress-monastery). 33ch, Postal runner. All horiz. except 2ch and 33ch.

Perf. 14x14½, 14½x14

1962, Oct. 10 Litho. Unwmkd.

1	A1	2ch red & gray	5	5
2	A1	3ch red & ultra	5	5
3	A1	5ch grn & brn	30	30
4	A1	15ch red, blk & org yel	8	8
5	A1	33ch bl grn & lil	15	15
6	A1	70ch dp ultra & lt bl	35	35
7	A1	1.30nu bl & blk	75	75
		Nos. 1-7 (7)	1.73	1.73

Nos. 1–7 were issued for inland use in April, 1962, and became valid for international mail on Oct. 10, 1962.

Refugee Year Emblem and Arms of Bhutan
A2

1962, Oct. 10 *Perf. 14½x14*

8	A2	1nu dk bl & dk car rose	80	80
9	A2	2nu yel grn & red lil	1.40	1.40

World Refugee Year.

Equipment of Ancient Warrior
A3

Boy Filling Grain Box and Wheat Emblem
A4

1963 *Perf. 14x14½* Unwmkd.

10	A3	33ch multi	35	35
11	A3	70ch multi	35	35
12	A3	1.30nu multi	80	80

Bhutan's membership in Colombo Plan.

1963, Sept. 17 *Perf. 13½x14*

13	A4	20ch lt bl, yel & red brn	30	30
14	A4	1.50nu rose lil, bl & red brn	1.25	1.25

Issued for the "Freedom from Hunger" Campaign of the U.N. Food and Agriculture Organization.

Masked Dancer—A5

Various Bhutanese Dancers (Five Designs; 2ch, 5ch, 20ch, 1nu, 1.30nu vertical)

1964, Mar. *Perf. 14½x14, 14x14½*

Dancers Multicolored

15	A5	2ch bl grn & brn	5	5
16	A5	3ch lt vio & blk	7	7
17	A5	5ch lt ultra & dk bl	7	7
18	A5	20ch yel & red	8	8
19	A5	33ch gray & blk	15	15
20	A5	70ch emer & blk	35	35
21	A5	1nu cit & red	60	60
22	A5	1.30nu bis & dk bl	70	70
23	A5	2nu org & blk	1.10	1.10
		Nos. 15-23 (9)	3.17	3.17

Stone Throwing
A6

Sport: 5ch, 33ch, Boxing. 1nu, 3nu, Archery. 2nu, Soccer.

1964, Oct. 10 Litho. *Perf. 14½*

24	A6	2ch emer & multi	5	5
25	A6	5ch org & multi	7	7
26	A6	15ch brt cit & multi	8	8
27	A6	33ch rose lil & multi	20	20
28	A6	1nu multi	70	70
29	A6	2nu rose lil & multi	1.10	1.10
30	A6	3nu lt bl & multi	1.50	1.50
		Nos. 24-30 (7)	3.62	3.62

Issued to commemorate the 18th Olympic Games, Tokyo, Oct. 10–25. See No. B4.
Nos. 24–30 exist imperf. Price $4.

Flags of the World at Half-mast
A7

1964, Nov. 22 *Perf. 14½* Unwmkd.

Flags in Original Colors

31	A7	33ch stl gray	20	20
32	A7	1nu silver	75	75
33	A7	3nu gold	1.75	1.75
a.		Souv. sheet of 2, perf. 13½	3.50	3.50

Issued in memory of those who died in the service of their country. Nos. 31–33 exist imperf.

No. 33a contains 2 stamps similar to Nos. 32–33 with flag of Bhutan and gold inscription in margin. Size: 83x118mm. Sheet exists imperf.; price $2.

Primrose
A8

Flowers: 5ch, 33ch, Gentian. 50ch, 1nu, Rhododendron. 75ch, 2nu, Peony.

1964, Dec. Lithographed *Perf. 13*

34	A8	2ch lt bl, vio bl & grn	3	3
35	A8	5ch vio, grn & yel	4	4
36	A8	15ch yel, vio & grn	10	10
37	A8	33ch gray, vio bl & grn	15	15
38	A8	50ch lt gray, grn & car	25	25
39	A8	75ch lt grn, yel & brn	40	40
40	A8	1nu pink, grn & dk gray	45	45
41	A8	2nu sep, yel & grn	95	95
		Nos. 34-41 (8)	1.92	1.92

Nos. 5, 40, 32, 41 and 33 Overprinted: "WINSTON CHURCHILL 1874–1965"

1965, Feb. 27

42	A1	33ch bl grn & lil	25	25
43	A8	1nu pink, grn & dk gray	65	65
44	A7	1nu sil & multi	65	65
45	A8	2nu sep, yel & grn	1.10	1.10
46	A7	3nu gold & multi	1.50	1.50
		Nos. 42-46 (5)	4.15	4.15

Issued in memory of Sir Winston Churchill (1874–1965), British statesman. The overprint is in three lines on Nos. 42–43 and 45; in two lines on Nos. 43 and 46.

Nos. 44 and 46 exist imperf. Price, both, $4.50.

Skyscraper, Pagoda and World's Fair Emblem—A9

Designs: 10ch, 2nu, Pieta by Michelangelo and statue of Khmer Buddha. 20ch, Skyline of New York and Bhutanese village. 33ch, George Washington Bridge, N. Y., and foot bridge, Bhutan.

1965, Apr. 21 Litho. *Perf. 14½*

47	A9	1ch bl & multi	5	5
48	A9	10ch grn & multi	8	8
49	A9	20ch rose lil & multi	12	12
50	A9	33ch bis & multi	18	18
51	A9	1.50nu bis & multi	75	75
52	A9	2nu multi	1.00	1.00
a.		Souv. sheet of 2, perf. 13½	2.75	2.75
		Nos.47-52 (6)	2.18	2.18

Issued to commemorate the New York World's Fair, 1964–65.

Nos. 47–52 exist imperf.; price $3.50.

No. 52a contains two stamps similar to Nos. 51–52. World's Fair emblems in margin in bister and inscription in black. Size: 118½x86½mm. Exists imperf.; price $2.

Telstar, Short-wave Radio and ITU Emblem—A10

Designs (ITU Emblem and): 2nu, Telstar and Morse key. 3nu, Syncom and ear phones.

1966, March 2 Litho. *Perf. 14½*

53	A10	35ch multi	15	15
54	A10	2nu multi	80	80
55	A10	3nu multi	1.25	1.25

Issued to commemorate the centenary (in 1965) of the International Telecommunication Union. Souvenir sheets exist containing two stamps similar to Nos. 54–55, perf. 13½ and imperf. Dark blue margin with white inscription and pictures of satellites in space. Size: 119x78mm. Price, 2 sheets, $5.

Leopard
A11

Animals: 1ch, 4nu, Asiatic black bear. 4ch, 2nu, Pigmy hog. 8ch, 75ch, Tiger. 10ch, 1.50nu, Dhole (Asiatic hunting dog). 1nu, 5nu, Takin (goat).

1966 Lithographed *Perf. 13*

Animals in Natural Colors

56	A11	1ch yel & blk	10	10
57	A11	2ch pale grn & blk	10	10
58	A11	4ch lt cit & blk	10	10
59	A11	8ch lt bl & blk	10	10
60	A11	10ch lt lil & blk	10	10
61	A11	75ch lt yel grn & blk	30	30
62	A11	1nu lt grn & blk	75	75
63	A11	1.50nu lt bl grn & blk	60	60
64	A11	2nu dl org & blk	75	75
65	A11	3nu bluish lil & blk	1.10	1.10
66	A11	4nu lt grn & blk	1.50	1.50
67	A11	5nu pink & blk	2.00	2.00
		Nos. 56-67 (12)	7.50	7.50

Issue dates: Nos. 56–60, 62, March 28; Nos. 61, 63–67, Apr. 26.

Nos. 6–9, 20–23 Surcharged

10 CH

1965(?) *Perf. 14½x14, 14x14½*

68	A2	5ch on 1nu dk bl & dk car rose		
69	A2	5ch on 2nu yel grn & red lil		
70	A5	10ch on 70ch multi		
71	A5	10ch on 2nu multi		
72	A1	15ch on 70ch dp ultra & lt bl		
73	A1	15ch on 1.30nu bl & blk		
74	A5	20ch on 1nu multi		
75	A5	20ch on 1.30nu multi		
		Nos. 68-75 (8)	*110.00*	

The surcharges on Nos. 68–69 contain two bars at left and right obliterating the denomination on both sides of the design. Four bars on Nos. 72–73.

Simtokha Dzong
A12

Tashichho Dzong—A13

Daga Dzong
A14

Designs: 5ch, Rinpung Dzong. 50ch, Tongsa Dzong. 1nu, Lhuntsi Dzong.

Perf. 14½x14 (A12), 13½ (A13, A14)

1966–70 Photogravure

76	A12	5ch org brn ('67)	4	4
77	A13	10ch dk grn & rose vio ('68)	6	6
78	A12	15ch brown	10	8
79	A12	20ch green	20	20
80	A13	50ch bl grn ('68)	30	20
81	A14	75ch dk bl & ol gray ('70)	30	30
82	A14	1nu dk vio & vio bl ('70)	40	40
		Nos. 76-82 (7)	1.40	1.28

Sizes: 5ch, 15ch, 20ch, 37x20½mm. 10ch, 53½x28½mm. 50ch, 35½x25½ mm.

Certain unlisted issues of Bhutan, starting in 1966, are mentioned and briefly described in "For the Record" at the back of this volume.

Mahatma Gandhi—A14a

1969, Oct. 2 Litho. ***Perf. 13x13½***

83	A14a	20ch lt bl & brn	60	60
84	A14a	2nu lem & brn ol	1.50	1.50

Mohandas K. Gandhi (1869–1948), leader in India's struggle for independence, birth centenary.

Various Forms of Mail Transport, UPU Headquarters, Bern—A14b

1970, Feb. 25 Photo. ***Perf. 13½***

85	A14b	3ch ol grn & gold	15	15
86	A14b	10ch red brn & gold	15	15
87	A14b	20ch Prus bl & gold	20	20
88	A14b	2.50nu dp mag & gold	1.00	1.00
		Nos. 85-88 (4)	1.25	1.25

New Headquarters of Universal Postal Union, Bern, Switzerland.
Exist imperf. Price $4.

Wangdiphodrang Dzong and Bridge
A15

1971–73 Photogravure ***Perf. 13½***

89	A15	2ch gray ('73)	5	5
90	A15	3ch dp red lil ('73)	5	5
91	A15	4ch vio ('73)	5	5
92	A15	5ch dk grn	15	15
93	A15	10ch org brn	15	15
94	A15	15ch dp bl	15	15
95	A15	20ch dp plum	15	15
		Nos. 89-95 (7)	75	75

U.N. Emblem and Bhutan Flag
A16

Designs (Bhutan Flag and): 10ch, U.N. Headquarters, New York. 20ch, Security Council Chamber and mural by Per Krohg. 3nu, General Assembly Hall.

1971, Sept. 21 Photo. ***Perf. 13½***

96	A16	5ch gold, bl & multi	3	3
97	A16	10ch gold & multi	3	3
98	A16	20ch gold & multi	6	6
99	A16	3nu gold & multi	85	85
		Nos. 96-99, C1-C3 (7)	5.22	5.22

Bhutan's admission to the United Nations. Exist imperf.

Boy Scout Crossing Stream in Rope Sling—A17

Designs (Emblem and Boy Scouts): 20ch, 2nu, mountaineering. 50ch, 6nu, reading map. 75ch, as 10ch.

1971, Nov. 30 Litho. ***Perf. 13½***

143	A17	10ch gold & multi	5	5
144	A17	20ch gold & multi	7	7
145	A17	50ch gold & multi	17	17
146	A17	75ch sil & multi	25	25
147	A17	2nu sil & multi	65	65
148	A17	6nu sil & multi	2.00	2.00
a.		Souvenir sheet of 2	2.75	2.75
		Nos. 143-148 (6)	3.19	3.19

60th anniversary of the Boy Scouts. No. 148a contains one each of Nos. 147–148 and 2 labels. Silver fleur-de-lis pattern on labels and margin. Size: 92½x92½mm. Exist imperf.

Nos. 87–90 Overprinted in Gold

UNHCR
UNRWA
1971

1971, Dec. 23

149	A16	5ch gold & multi	5	5
150	A16	10ch gold & multi	5	5
151	A16	20ch gold & multi	7	7
152	A16	3nu gold & multi	1.00	1.00
		Nos. 149-152, C4-C6 (7)	5.57	5.57

World Refugee Year. Exist imperf.

Book Year Emblem
A17a

1972, May 15 Photo. ***Perf. 13½x13***

153	A17a	2ch multi	8	8
154	A17a	3ch multi	8	8
155	A17a	5ch multi	12	8
156	A17a	20ch multi	75	60

International Book Year.

King Jigme Singye Wangchuk and Royal Crest—A18

Designs (King and): 25ch, 90ch, Flag of Bhutan. 1.25nu, Wheel with 8 good luck signs. 2nu, 4nu, Punakha Dzong, former winter capital. 3nu, 5nu, Crown. 5ch, same as 10ch.

1974, June 2 Litho. ***Perf. 13½***

157	A18	10ch mar & multi	5	5
158	A18	25ch gold & multi	10	10
159	A18	1.25nu multi	45	45
160	A18	2nu gold & multi	70	70
161	A18	3nu multi	1.00	1.00
		Nos. 157-161 (5)	2.30	2.30

Souvenir Sheets

Perf. 13½, Imperf.

162	A18	Sheet of 2	2.00	2.00
a.		5ch mar & multi	5	
b.		5nu red org & multi	1.70	
163	A18	Sheet of 2	2.15	2.15
a.		90ch gold & multi	45	
b.		4nu gold & multi	1.40	

Coronation of King Jigme Singye Wangchuk, June 2, 1974. Nos. 162–163 have maroon and multicolored borders with picture of the king wearing peacock crown. Size: 177x127mm.

Mailman on Horseback
A19

Old and New Locomotives
A20

Designs (UPU Emblem, Carrier Pigeon and): 3ch, Sailing and steam ships. 4ch, Old biplane and jet. 25ch, Mail runner and jeep.

1974, Oct. 9 Litho. ***Perf. 14½***

164	A19	1ch grn & multi	3	3
165	A20	2ch lil & multi	3	3
166	A20	3ch ocher & multi	3	3
167	A20	4ch yel grn & multi	3	3
168	A20	25ch sal & multi	10	10
		Nos. 164-168, C7-C9 (8)	1.82	1.82

Centenary of Universal Postal Union. Issued in sheets of 50 and sheets of 5 plus label with multicolored margin. Exist imperf.

Family and WPY Emblem—A21

1974, Dec. 17 ***Perf. 13½***

169	A21	25ch bl & multi	6	6
170	A21	50ch org & multi	12	12
171	A21	90ch ver & multi	22	22
172	A21	2.50nu brn & multi	60	60
a.		Souv. sheet, 10nu	3.50	3.50

Sephisa Chandra
A22

Designs: Indigenous butterflies.

1975, Sept. Lithographed ***Perf. 14½***

Multicolored

173	A22	1ch *shown*	3	3
174	A22	2ch *Lethe kansa*	3	3
175	A22	3ch *Neope bhadra*	3	3
176	A22	4ch *Euthalia duda*	3	3
177	A22	5ch *Vindula erota*	3	3
178	A22	10ch *Bhutanitis Lidderdale*	5	5
179	A22	3nu *Limenitis zayla*	1.25	1.25
180	A22	5nu *Delis thysbe*	2.00	2.00
		Nos. 173-180 (8)	3.45	3.45

Souvenir Sheet

Perf. 13

181	A22	10nu *Dabasa gyas*	3.50	3.50

No. 181 contains one stamp; Bhutanese landscape in multicolored margin. Size: 115x90mm.

Apollo and Apollo-Soyuz Emblem—A23

Design: No. 183, Soyuz and emblem.

1975, Oct. Litho. ***Perf. 14x13½***

182	A23	10nu multi	3.00	3.00
183	A23	10nu multi	3.00	3.00
a.		Souvenir sheet of 2, 15nu	10.00	10.00

Apollo Soyuz link-up in space, July 17. Nos. 182–183 printed se-tenant in sheets of 10. No. 183a contains two 15nu stamps similar to Nos. 182–183; light green margin with U.S. and U.S.S.R. flags and Apollo-Soyuz emblem. Size: 130x90 mm. Exist imperf.

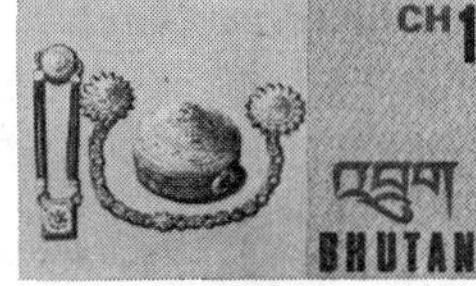

Jewelry
A24

Designs: 2ch, Coffee pot, bell and sugar cup. 3ch, Container and drinking horn. 4ch, Pendants and box cover. 5ch, Painter. 15ch, Silversmith. 20ch, Wood carver with tools. 1.50nu, Mat maker. 5nu, 10nu, Printer.

1975, Nov. ***Perf. 14½***

184	A24	1ch multi	3	3
185	A24	2ch multi	3	3
186	A24	3ch multi	3	3
187	A24	4ch multi	3	3
188	A24	5ch multi	3	3
189	A24	15ch multi	5	5
190	A24	20ch multi	6	6
191	A24	1.50nu multi	45	45
192	A24	10nu multi	3.00	3.00
		Nos. 184-192 (9)	3.71	3.71

Souvenir Sheet

Perf. 13

193	A24	5nu multi	1.50	1.50

Handicrafts and craftsmen. No. 193 contains one stamp; multicolored margin with black inscription. Size: 105x80mm.

King Jigme Singye Wangchuk
A25

Designs: 25ch, 90ch, 1nu, 2nu, 4nu, like 15ch. 1.30nu, 3nu, 5nu, Coat of arms. Sizes (Diameter): 15ch, 1nu, 1.30nu, 38mm. 25ch, 2nu, 3nu, 49mm. 90ch, 4nu, 5nu, 63mm.

Lithographed, Embossed on Gold Foil

1975, Nov. 11 ***Imperf.***

194	A25	15ch emerald	5	5
195	A25	25ch emerald	8	8
196	A25	90ch emerald	28	28
197	A25	1nu brt car	30	30
198	A25	1.30nu brt car	40	40
199	A25	2nu brt car	60	60
200	A25	3nu brt car	90	90
201	A25	4nu brt car	1.20	1.20
202	A25	5nu brt car	1.50	1.50
		Nos. 194-202 (9)	5.31	5.31

King Jigme Singye Wangchuk's 20th birthday.

Rhododendron Cinnabarinum
A28

Designs (Rhododendron): 2ch, Campanulatum. 3ch, Fortunei. 4ch, Red arboreum. 5ch, Pink arboreum. 1nu, Falconeri. 3nu, Hodgsonii. 5nu, Keysii. 10nu, Cinnabarinum.

1976, Feb. 15 Litho. ***Perf. 15***

203	A28	1ch rose & multi	3	3
204	A28	2ch lt grn & multi	3	3
205	A28	3ch gray & multi	3	3
206	A28	4ch lil & multi	3	3
207	A28	5ch ol gray & multi	3	3
208	A28	1nu brn org & multi	30	24
209	A28	3nu ultra & multi	90	72
210	A28	5nu gray & multi	1.50	1.20
		Nos. 203-210 (8)	2.85	2.31

Souvenir Sheet

Perf. 13½

211	A28	10nu multi	3.50	3.50

No. 211 contains one stamp; multicolored margin showing rhododendrons around pool. Size: 105x80mm.

Slalom and Olympic Games Emblem
A29

Designs (Olympic Games Emblem and): 2ch, 4-men bobsled. 3ch, Ice hockey. 4ch, Cross-country skiing. 5ch, Figure skating, women's. 2nu, Downhill skiing. 4nu, Speed skating. 6nu, Ski jump. 10nu, Figure skating, pairs.

1976, Mar. 29 Litho. ***Perf. 13½***

212	A29	1ch multi	3	3
213	A29	2ch multi	3	3
214	A29	3ch multi	3	3
215	A29	4ch multi	3	3
216	A29	5ch multi	3	3
217	A29	2nu multi	60	45
218	A29	4nu multi	1.20	90
219	A29	10nu multi	3.00	2.25
		Nos. 212-219 (8)	4.95	3.75

Souvenir Sheet

220	A29	6nu multi	2.00	2.00

12th Winter Olympic Games, Innsbruck, Austria, Feb. 4–15. No. 220 has orange and brown margin showing ski jump. Size: 78x104mm.

Orchid
A30

Designs: Various orchids.

1976, June Litho. ***Perf. 14½***

221	A30	1ch multi	3	3
222	A30	2ch multi	3	3
223	A30	3ch multi	3	3
224	A30	4ch multi	3	3
225	A30	5ch multi	3	3
226	A30	2nu multi	60	45
227	A30	4nu multi	1.20	90
228	A30	6nu multi	1.80	1.35
		Nos. 221-228 (8)	3.75	2.85

Souvenir Sheet

Perf. 13½

229	A30	10nu multi	3.25	1.65

No. 229 contains one stamp; multicolored margin with orchid design. Size: 106x80mm.

Double Carp Design—A31

Designs: Various symbolic designs and Colombo Plan emblem.

1976, July 1 Litho. ***Perf. 14½***

230	A31	3ch red & multi	3	3
231	A31	4ch ver & multi	3	3
232	A31	5ch multi	3	3
233	A31	25ch bl & multi	15	15
234	A31	1.25nu multi	38	30
235	A31	2nu yel & multi	60	48
236	A31	2.50nu vio & multi	75	60
237	A31	3nu multi	90	72
		Nos. 230-237 (8)	2.87	2.34

Colombo Plan, 25th anniversary.

Bandaranaike Conference Hall—A32

1976, Aug. 16 Litho. ***Perf. 13½***

238	A32	1.25nu multi	45	30
239	A32	2.50nu multi	85	60

5th Summit Conference of Non-aligned Countries, Colombo, Sri Lanka, Aug. 9–19.

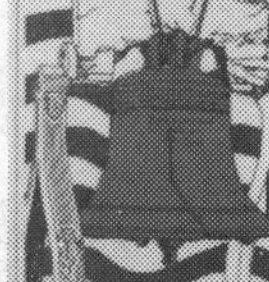

Queen Elizabeth II
A33

Liberty Bell
A34

Spirit of St. Louis
A35

Bhutanese Archer, Olympic Rings
A36

Designs: No. 242, Alexander Graham Bell. No. 245, LZ 3 Zeppelin docking, 1907. No. 246, Alfred B. Nobel.

1978, Nov. 15 Litho. ***Perf. 14½***

240	A33	20nu multi	5.00	5.00
241	A34	20nu multi	5.00	5.00
242	A33	20nu multi	5.00	5.00
243	A35	20nu multi	5.00	5.00
244	A36	20nu multi	5.00	5.00
245	A35	20nu multi	5.00	5.00
246	A33	20nu multi	5.00	5.00
		Nos. 240-246 (7)	35.00	

Commemoration: 25th anniversary of coronation of Queen Elizabeth II; American Bicentennial; centenary of first telephone call by Alexander Graham Bell; Charles A. Lindbergh crossing the Atlantic, 50th anniversary; Olympic Games; 75th anniversary of the Zeppelin; 75th anniversary of Nobel Prize. Seven souvenir sheets exist, each 25nu, commemorating same events with different designs. Size: 103x80mm.

Issues of 1967–1976 Surcharged with New Value and Bars

Perforations and Printing as Before

1978 **Multicolored**

252	A16	25ch on 3nu (#99)		
253	A17	25ch on 6nu (#148)		
254	A21	25ch on 2.50nu (#172)		
255	A22	25ch on 3nu (#179)		
256	A22	25ch on 5nu (#180)		
257	A23	25ch on 10nu (#182)		
258	A23	25ch on 10nu (#183)		
259	A24	25ch on 10nu (#192)		
260	A28	25ch on 5nu (#210)		
261	A29	25ch on 4nu (#218)		
262	A29	25ch on 10nu (#219)		
263	A30	25ch on 4nu (#227)		
264	A30	25ch on 6nu (#228)		
265	A31	25ch on 2.50nu (#236)		
266		25ch on 5nu *Girl Scout*		
267		25ch on 3nu *INDIPEX*		
268		25ch on 4nu *Dog*		
269		25ch on 8nu *Dogs*		
		Nos. 252-269, C11-C18 (26)	*60.00*	*60.00*

Nos. 266–269 on unlisted issues (see For the Record).

Mother and Child, IYC Emblem
A37

IYC Emblem and: 5nu, Mother and two children. 10nu, Boys with blackboards and stylus.

1979, June Litho. ***Perf. 14x13½***

289	A37	2nu multi	65	50
290	A37	5nu multi	1.60	1.25
291	A37	10nu multi	3.20	2.50
	a.	Souvenir sheet of 3	5.50	4.50

International Year of the Child. No. 291a contains Nos. 289–291, perf. 15x13½, and label; olive green decorative margin. Size: 130x103mm.

Conference Emblem and Dove—A38

Design: 10nu, Emblem and Bhutanese symbols.

1979, Sept. 3 Litho. ***Perf. 14x13½***

292	A38	25ch multi	8	6
293	A38	10nu multi	3.25	2.50

6th Non-Aligned Summit Conference, Havana, August 1979.

Silver Rattle, Dorji—A39

Antiques: 10ch, Silver handbell, Dilbu (vert.). 15ch, Cylindrical jar, Jadum (vert.). 25ch, Ornamental teapot, Jamjee. 1nu, Leather container, Kem (vert.). 1.25nu, Brass teapot, Jamjee. 1.70nu, Vessel with elephant-head legs, Sangphor (vert.). 2nu, Teapot with ornamental spout, Jamjee (vert.). 3nu, Metal pot on claw-shaped feet, Yangtho (vert.). 4nu, Dish inlaid with precious stones, Battha. 5nu, Metal circular flask, Chhap (vert.).

1979, Dec. 17 Photo. ***Perf. 14***

294	A39	5ch multi	3	3
295	A39	10ch multi	3	3
296	A39	15ch multi	5	3
297	A39	25ch multi	8	6
298	A39	1nu multi	32	25
299	A39	1.25nu multi	40	32
300	A39	1.70nu multi	55	45
301	A39	2nu multi	65	50
302	A39	3nu multi	97	75
303	A39	4nu multi	1.30	1.00
304	A39	5nu multi	1.60	1.25
		Nos. 294-304 (11)	5.98	4.67

Hill, Rinpiang Dzong
A40

Hill Statue, Stamps of Bhutan and : 2nu, Dzong. 5nu, Ounsti Dzong. 10nu, Lingzi Dzong, Gt. Britain Type 81. 20nu, Rope bridge, Penny Black.

1980, May 6 **Litho.** ***Perf. 14x13½***

305	A40	1nu multi	32	25
306	A40	2nu multi	65	50
307	A40	5nu multi	1.60	1.25
308	A40	10nu multi	3.25	2.50

Souvenir Sheet

309	A40	20nu multi	6.50	5.00

Sir Rowland Hill (1795-1879), originator of penny postage. No. 309 has multicolored margin showing postal runner and Hill. Size: 102x103mm.

Kichu Lhakhang Monastery, Phari—A41

Guru Padma Sambhava's Birthday: Monasteries.

1981, July 11 **Litho.** ***Perf. 14***

310	A41	1nu Dungtse, Phari (vert.)	32	25
311	A41	2nu shown	65	50
312	A41	2.25nu Kurjey	75	55
313	A41	3nu Tangu, Thimphu	1.00	75
314	A41	4nu Cheri, Thimphu	1.30	1.00
315	A41	5nu Chorten, Kora	1.65	1.25
316	A41	7nu Tak-Tsang, Phari (vert.)	2.30	1.75
		Nos. 310-316 (7)	7.97	6.05

Prince Charles and Lady Diana
A42

1981, Sept. 10 **Litho.** ***Perf. 14½***

317	A42	1nu St. Paul's Cathedral	32	25
318	A42	5nu like #317	1.65	1.25
319	A42	20nu shown	6.50	4.00
320	A42	25nu like #319	8.25	5.25

Souvenir Sheet

321	A42	20nu Wedding procession	6.50	4.00

Royal wedding. Nos. 318-319 issued in sheets of 5 plus label. No. 321 has multicolored decorative margin. Size: 69x91mm.

Orange-bellied Chloropsis—A43

1982, Apr. 19 **Litho.** ***Perf. 14***

322	A43	2nu shown	65	50
323	A43	3nu Monal pheasant	1.00	75
324	A43	5nu Ward's trogon	1.65	1.25
325	A43	10nu Mrs. Gould's sunbird	3.25	2.50

Souvenir Sheet

326	A43	25nu Maroon oriole	8.25	6.25

No. 326 has multicolored margin showing birds, map. Size: 95x101mm.

1982 World Cup—A44

Designs: Various soccer players.

1982, June 25 **Litho.** ***Perf. 14½x14***

327	A44	1nu multi	32	25
328	A44	2nu multi	65	50
329	A44	3nu multi	1.00	75
330	A44	20nu multi	6.50	5.00

Souvenir Sheets

331	A44	25nu multi	8.50	6.25

Nos. 331 have multicolored margins continuing design and listing finalists (Algeria, etc. or Hungary, etc.). Sizes: 80x118mm.

21st Birthday of Princess Diana—A45

1982, Aug.

332	A45	1nu St. James' Palace	32	25
332A	A45	10nu Diana, Charles	3.25	2.50
332B	A45	15nu Windsor Castle	5.00	4.00
333	A45	25m Wedding	8.50	6.25

Souvenir Sheet

334	A45	20nu Diana	6.50	5.00

No. 334 has multicolored margin showing family tree, Franklin Roosevelt. Size: 104x75mm.

10nu, 15 nu issued only in sheets of 5 plus label.

Scouting Year—A46

1982, Aug. 23 **Litho.** ***Perf. 14***

335	A46	3nu Baden-Powell, vert.	1.00	75
336	A46	5nu Eating around fire	1.65	1.25
337	A46	15nu Reading map	5.00	3.75
338	A46	20nu Pitching tents	6.75	5.00

Souvenir Sheet

339	A46	25nu Mountain climbing	8.25	6.25

No. 339 has multicolored margin continuing design. Size: 91x70mm.

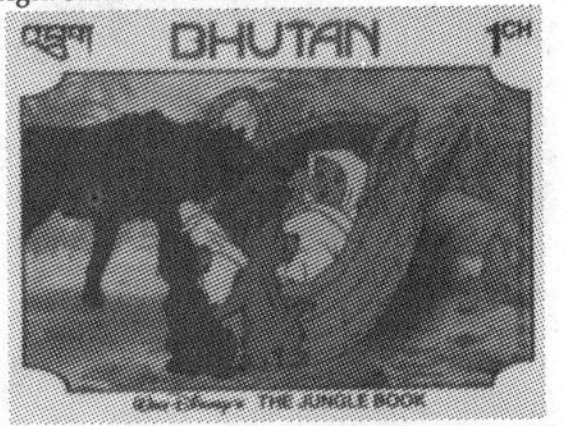

Rama and Cubs with Mowgli—A47

Designs: Scenes from Walt Disney's The Jungle Book.

1982, Sept. 1 ***Perf. 11***

340	A47	1ch multi	3	3
341	A47	2ch multi	3	3
342	A47	3ch multi	3	3
343	A47	4ch multi	3	3
344	A47	5ch multi	3	3
345	A47	10ch multi	3	3
346	A47	30ch multi	10	8
347	A47	2nu multi	65	50
348	A47	20nu multi	6.50	5.00
		Nos. 340-348 (9)	7.43	5.76

Souvenir Sheets
Perf. 13½

349	A47	20nu Baloo and Mowgli in forest	6.50	5.00
350	A47	20nu Baloo and Mowgli floating	6.50	5.00

Nos. 349-350 have multicolored margins. Size: 127x102mm.

George Washington Surveying—A48

1982, Nov. 15 **Litho.** ***Perf. 15***

351	A48	50ch shown	16	12
352	A48	1nu FDR, Harvard	32	25
353	A48	2nu Washington at Valley Forge	65	50
354	A48	3nu FDR, family	1.00	75
355	A48	4nu Washington, Battle of Monmouth	1.30	1.00
356	A48	5nu FDR, White House	1.65	1.25
357	A48	15nu Washington, Mt. Vernon	5.00	3.75
358	A48	20nu FDR, CHurchill, Stalin	6.50	5.00
		Nos. 351-358 (8)	16.58	12.62

Souvenir Sheets

359	A48	25nu Washington, vert.	8.25	6.25
360	A48	25nu FDR, vert.	8.25	6.25

George Washington (1732-1799) and Franklin D. Roosevelt (1882-1945). Size of Nos. 359-360: 103x73mm.

Nos. 332, 333-334 Overprinted:
"ROYAL BABY / 21.6.82"

1982, Nov. 19

360A	A45	1nu multi	32	32
360B	A45	25nu multi	8.50	6.25

Souvenir Sheet

360C	A45	20nu multi	6.50	5.00

Birth of Prince William of Wales, June 21.

500th Birth Anniv. of Raphael—A51

Portraits.

1983, Mar.

375	A51	1nu Angelo Doni	32	25
376	A51	4nu Maddalena Doni	1.30	1.00
377	A51	5nu Baldassare Castiglione	1.65	1.25
378	A51	20nu La Donna Velata	6.50	5.00

Souvenir Sheets

379	A51	25nu Expulsion of Heliodorus	8.25	6.25
380	A51	25nu Mass of Bolsena	8.25	6.25

SEMI-POSTAL STAMPS

Nos. 10–12 Surcharged

INNSBRUCK 1964

+50ch

Perf. 14x14½

1964, March Litho. Unwmkd.

B1	A3	33ch +50ch multi	3.75	3.75
B2	A3	70ch +50ch multi	3.75	3.75
B3	A3	1.30nu +50ch multi	3.75	3.75

Issued to commemorate the 9th Winter Olympic Games, Innsbruck, Jan. 29–Feb. 9, 1964.

Olympic Games Type of Regular Issue, 1964

Souvenir Sheet

Designs: 1nu+50ch, Archery. 2nu+50ch, Soccer.

1964, Oct. 10 ***Perf. 13½, Imperf.***

B4	A6	Sheet of 2	6.00	6.00
a.		1nu + 50ch multi	75	75
b.		2nu + 50ch multi	1.75	1.75

18th Olympic Games, Tokyo, Oct. 10–25. No. B4 has multicolored border. Size: 86x117½mm.

AIR POST STAMPS

U.N. Type of Regular Issue

Designs (Bhutan Flag and): 2.50nu, U.N. Headquarters, New York. 5nu, Security Council Chamber and mural by Per Krohg. 6nu, General Assembly Hall.

1971, Sept. 21 Photo. ***Perf. 13½***

C1	A16	2.50nu sil & multi	75	75
C2	A16	5nu sil & multi	1.50	1.50
C3	A16	6nu sil & multi	2.00	2.00

Bhutan's admission to the United Nations. Exist imperf.

Nos. C1–C3 Overprinted in Gold: "UNHCR / UNRWA / 1971" Like Nos. 153–156

1971, Dec. 23 Litho. ***Perf. 13½***

C4	A16	2.50nu silver & multi.	80	80
C5	"	5nu " "	1.60	1.60
C6	"	6nu " "	2.00	2.00

World Refugee Year. Exist imperf.

UPU Types of 1974

Designs (UPU Emblem, Carrier Pigeon and): 1nu, Mail runner and jeep. 1.40nu, 10nu, Old and new locomotives. 2nu, Old biplane and jet.

1974, Oct. 9 Litho. ***Perf. 14½***

C7	A19	1nu sal. & multi.	35	35
C8	A20	1.40nu lilac & multi.	55	55
C9	"	2nu multicolored	70	70

Souvenir Sheet

Perf. 13

C10	A20	10nu lil & multi	3.75	3.75

Centenary of Universal Postal Union. No. C10 contains one stamp; yellow and multicolored margin with UPU emblem and black inscription. Size: 91x78mm. Nos. C7–C9 were issued in sheets of 50 and sheets of 5 plus label with multicolored margin. Exist imperf.

Issues of 1968–1974 Surcharged 25ch and Bars

Perforations and Printing as Before

1968 Multicolored

C11	A16	25ch on 5nu (#C2)
C12	"	25ch on 6nu (#C3)
C13	A20	25ch on 1.40nu (#C8)
C14	"	25ch on 2nu (#C9)
C15		25ch on 4nu *Mythological creature*
C16		25ch on 10nu *Mythological creature*
C17		25ch on 5nu *INDIPEX*
C18		25ch on 6nu *INDIPEX*

Nos. C15–C18 on unlisted issues (see For the Record).

BOHEMIA AND MORAVIA

Listed under Czechoslovakia.

BOLIVIA

(bô·lĭv′ĭ·ȧ)

LOCATION—In the central part of South America, separated from the Pacific Coast by Chile and Peru.

GOVT.—Republic.

AREA—424,160 sq. mi.

POP.—5,950,000 (est. 1977).

CAPITAL—Sucre. (La Paz is the actual seat of government.)

100 Centavos = 1 Boliviano

100 Centavos = 1 Peso Boliviano (1963)

On February 21st, 1863, the Bolivian Government decreed contracts for carrying the mails should be let to the highest bidder, the service to commence on the day the bid was accepted, and stamps used for the payment of postage. On March 18th, 1863, the contract was awarded to Sr. Justiniano Garcia and was in effect until April 29th, 1863, when it was rescinded by the government. Stamps in the form illustrated above were prepared in denominations of ½, 1, 2 and 4 reales. All values exist in black and in blue. It is said that used copies exist on covers, but the authenticity of these covers remains to be established.

Condor
A1

A2

A3

72 varieties of each of the 5c, 78 varieties of the 10c, 30 varieties of each of the 50c and 100c.

The plate of the 5c stamps was entirely re-engraved four times and retouched at least six times. Various states of the plate have distinguishing characteristics, each of which is typical of most, though not all the stamps in a sheet. These characteristics (usually termed types) are found in the shading lines at the right side of the globe. (a.): vertical and diagonal lines; (b.): diagonal lines only; (c.): diagonal and horizontal with traces of vertical lines; (d): diagonal and horizontal lines; (e.): horizontal lines only; (f.): no lines except the curved ones forming the outlines of the globe.

Engraved.

1867-68 *Imperf.* Unwmkd.

1	A1	5c bl grn (b)	7.00	*20.00*
a.		5c bl grn (a)	7.00	*20.00*
b.		5c dp grn (a)	7.00	*20.00*
c.		5c ol grn, thick paper (a)	50.00	40.00
d.		5c yel grn, thick paper (a)	125.00	125.00
e.		5c yel grn, thick paper (b)	125.00	125.00
f.		5c yel grn, thin paper (a,b)	5.00	7.00
2	A1	5c grn (d)	6.00	11.00
a.		5c grn (c)	7.00	11.00
b.		5c grn (e)	6.00	11.00
c.		5c grn (f)	6.00	11.00
3	A1	5c vio ('68)	350.00	250.00
a.		5c rose lil ('68)	350.00	250.00
4	A3	10c brown	400.00	250.00
5	A2	50c orange	27.50	42.50
6	A2	50c bl ('68)	*425.00*	*300.00*
a.		50c dk bl ('68)	*425.00*	*300.00*
7	A3	100c blue	85.00	*110.00*
8	A3	100c grn ('68)	175.00	175.00
a.		100c pale bl grn ('68)	175.00	175.00

Used prices are for postally canceled copies. Pen cancellations usually indicate that the stamps have been used fiscally and such stamps sell for about one-fifth as much as those with postal cancellations.

Nos. 2-8 have been reprinted.

(9 stars)

(11 stars)

Coat of Arms
A4 A5

1868-69 *Perf. 12*

Nine Stars

10	A4	5c green	25.00	12.50
11	A4	10c vermilion	35.00	12.50
12	A4	50c blue	55.00	32.50
13	A4	100c orange	55.00	37.50
14	A4	500c black	650.00	625.00

Eleven Stars

15	A5	5c green	12.50	7.50
16	A5	10c vermilion	17.50	12.50
a.		Half used as 5c as cover		500.00
17	A5	50c blue	42.50	20.00
18	A5	100c dp org	37.50	20.00
19	A5	500c black	*1,600.*	*1,800.*

Arms and "The Law"
A6

1878 Various Frames. *Perf. 12*

20	A6	5c ultra	12.50	5.00
21	A6	10c orange	10.00	4.00
a.		Half used as 5c on cover		50.00
22	A6	20c green	30.00	5.00
a.		Half used as 10c on cover		200.00
23	A6	50c dl car	125.00	15.00

(11 stars)

(9 stars)

Numerals Upright
A7 A8

1887 *Rouletted*

24	A7	1c rose	3.00	1.25
25	A7	2c violet	3.00	1.25
26	A5	5c blue	10.00	2.00
27	A5	10c orange	10.00	2.00

1890 *Perf. 12*

28	A8	1c rose	2.75	1.50
29	A8	2c violet	6.00	2.00
30	A4	5c blue	3.50	1.50
31	A4	10c orange	7.50	1.75
32	A4	20c dk grn	17.50	2.50
33	A4	50c red	7.50	2.50
34	A4	100c yellow	17.50	6.00
		Nos. 28-34 (7)	62.25	17.75

1893 Lithographed. *Perf. 11.*

35	A8	1c rose	5.00	2.00
a.		Imperf. pair	50.00	
b.		Imperf. vert., pair	30.00	
c.		Horizontal pair, imprf. between	50.00	
36	A8	2c violet	5.00	2.00
a.		Block of 4 imperf. vert. and horiz. through center	75.00	
b.		Horizontal pair, imperf. between	40.00	
37	A7	5c blue	7.00	2.00
a.		Imperf. horiz., pair	40.00	
b.		Horizontal pair imperf. between	50.00	
38	A8	10c orange	20.00	3.00
a.		Horizontal pair, imperf. between	75.00	
39	A8	20c dk grn	65.00	20.00
a.		Imperf. pair, vert. or horiz.	200.00	
b.		Pair, imperf. btwn., vert. or horiz.	200.00	
		Nos. 35-39 (5)	102.00	29.00

Coat of Arms
A9

Engraved.

Thin Paper.

1894 *Perf. 14, 14½.* Unwmkd.

40	A9	1c bister	2.00	1.00
41	A9	2c red org	2.00	1.00
42	A9	5c green	2.00	1.00
43	A9	10c yel brn	2.00	1.00
44	A9	20c dk bl	6.00	2.50
45	A9	50c claret	15.00	3.50
46	A9	100c brn rose	35.00	12.50
		Nos. 40-46 (7)	64.00	22.50

Stamps of type A9 on thick paper were surreptitiously printed in Paris on the order of an official and without government authorization. Some of these stamps were substituted for part of a shipment of stamps on thin paper, which had been printed in London on government order. When the thick paper stamps reached Bolivia they were at first repudiated but afterwards were allowed to do postal duty. A large quantity of the thick paper stamps were fraudulently cancelled in Paris with a cancellation of heavy bars forming an oval.

To be legitimate, copies of the thick paper stamps must have been bought at post offices in Bolivia, or must have genuine cancellations of Bolivia.

The 10c blue on thick paper is not known to have been issued.

President Tomás Frías
A10

President José M. Linares
A11

Pedro Domingo Murillo
A12

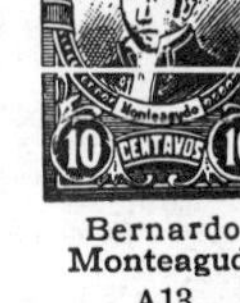

Bernardo Monteagudo
A13

Gen. José Ballivián
A14

Gen. Antonio José de Sucre
A15

Simón Bolívar
A16

Coat of Arms
A17

1897 Lithographed. *Perf. 12.*

47	A10	1c pale yel grn	2.00	1.25
a.		Imperf. horiz. pair	75.00	
b.		Vertical pair, imperf. between	75.00	
48	A11	2c red	3.50	2.50
49	A12	5c dk grn	3.50	1.25
a.		Horizontal pair, imperf. between	75.00	
50	A13	10c brn vio	3.50	1.25
a.		Vertical pair, imperf. between	75.00	
51	A14	20c lake & blk	7.50	1.50
a.		Imperf., pair		200.00
52	A15	50c orange	7.50	3.00
53	A16	1b Prus bl	7.50	7.50
54	A17	2b red, yel, grn & blk	45.00	60.00
		Nos. 47-54 (8)	80.00	78.25

Excellent forgeries of No. 54 exist.

Nos. 40-44 Handstamped in Violet or Blue

E.F.
1899

1899 *Perf. 14½.*

55	A9	1c yel bis	25.00	25.00
56	A9	2c red org	30.00	30.00
57	A9	5c green	20.00	20.00
58	A9	10c yel brn	25.00	20.00
59	A9	20c dk bl	40.00	40.00
		Nos. 55-59 (5)	140.00	135.00

The handstamp is found inverted, double, etc. Forgeries of this handstamp are plentiful. "E.F." stands for Estado Federal.

The 50c and 100c (Nos. 45-46) with similar handstamp are considered bogus.

Antonio José de Sucre
A18

Thin Paper.

1899 Engraved *Perf. 11½, 12*

62	A18	1c gray bl	2.25	1.00
63	A18	2c brnsh red	1.50	1.00
64	A18	5c dk grn	5.00	2.00
65	A18	10c yel org	2.25	1.50
66	A18	20c rose pink	3.00	1.00
67	A18	50c bis brn	5.00	2.50
68	A18	1b gray vio	2.50	2.00
		Nos. 62-68 (7)	21.50	11.00

1901

69	A18	5c dk red	2.50	1.00

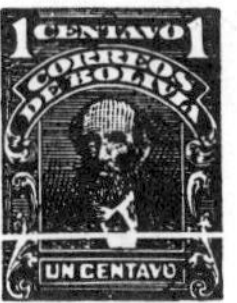

Col. Adolfo Ballivián
A19

Eliodoro Camacho
A20

President Narciso Campero
A21

José Ballivián
A22

Gen. Andrés Santa Cruz
A23

Coat of Arms
A24

1901-02 Engraved.

70	A19	1c claret	50	25
71	A20	2c green	60	35
73	A21	5c scarlet	60	40
74	A22	10c blue	1.50	25
75	A23	20c vio & blk	80	25
76	A24	2b brown	4.50	4.00
		Nos. 70-71, 73-76 (6)	8.50	5.50

1904 Lithographed

77	A19	1c claret	3.00	1.00

In No. 70 the panel above "CENTAVO" is shaded with continuous lines. In No. 77 the shading is of dots.

See also Nos. 103-105, 107, 110.

Coat of Arms of Dept. of La Paz
A25

Murillo
A26

José Miguel Lanza
A27

Ismael Montes
A28

1909 Lithographed *Perf. 11*

78	A25	5c bl & blk	13.00	6.00
79	A26	10c grn & blk	13.00	6.00
80	A27	20c org & blk	13.00	6.00
81	A28	2b red & blk	13.00	6.00

Centenary of Revolution of July, 1809.
Nos. 78-81 exist imperf. and tête bêche. Nos. 79-81 exist with center inverted.

Miguel Betanzos
A29

Col. Ignacio Warnes
A30

Murillo
A31

Monteagudo
A32

Esteban Arce
A33

Antonio José de Sucre
A34

Simón Bolívar
A35

Manuel Belgrano
A36

Dated 1809-1825.

1909 *Perf. 11½.*

82	A29	1c lt brn & blk	75	60
83	A30	2c grn & blk	90	75
84	A31	5c red & blk	90	50
85	A32	10c dl bl & blk	90	50
86	A33	20c vio & blk	1.00	75
87	A34	50c ol bis & blk	1.50	1.00
88	A35	1b gray brn & blk	1.50	1.50
89	A36	2b choc & blk	2.00	1.50
		Nos. 82-89 (8)	9.45	7.10

Issued in commemoration of the War of Independence, 1809-1825.

Warnes
A37

Betanzos—A38

Arce—A39

Dated 1910-1825.

1910 *Perf. 13x13½.*

92	A37	5c grn & blk	40	20
a.		Imperf., pair	5.00	
93	A38	10c cl & ind	40	20
a.		Imperf., pair	7.50	
94	A39	20c dl bl & ind	85	50
a.		Imperf., pair	5.00	

Issued in commemoration of the War of Independence.

Nos. 92-94 may be found with parts of a papermaker's watermark: "A I & Co/ EXTRA STRONG/9303."

Nos. 71 and 75 Surcharged in Black

5 Centavos 1911

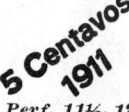

1911 *Perf. 11½, 12.*

95	A20	5c on 2c grn	60	30
a.		Inverted surcharge	7.00	7.00
b.		Double surcharge		
c.		Period after "1911"	5.00	1.25
d.		Blue surcharge	100.00	75.00

96	A23	5c on 20c vio & blk	20.00	20.00
a.		Inverted surch.	45.00	45.00

No. 83 Handstamp Surcharged in Green

97	A30	20c on 2c grn & blk		1,100.

This provisional was issued by local authorities at Villa Bella, a town on the Brazilian border. The 20c surcharge was applied after the stamp had been affixed to the cover. Excellent forgeries of No. 96-97 exist.

"Justice"
A40 A41

1912

Black or Dark Blue Overprint.

98	A40	2c grn (Bk)	60	40
a.		Inverted overprint	7.50	
99	A41	10c ver (Bl)	1.25	70
a.		Inverted overprint	7.50	

A42

A43

Red or Black Overprint.

Engraved.

100	A42	5c org (R)	50	50
a.		Inverted overprint	6.00	
b.		Pair, one without overprint	15.00	
c.		Black overprint	75.00	

Red or Black Surcharge.

101	A43	10c on 1c bl (R)	50	25
a.		Inverted surch.	7.50	
b.		Double surch.	7.50	
c.		Double surcharge, one inverted	8.50	
d.		Black surcharge	200.00	200.00

Revenue Stamp Surcharged "CORREOS / 10 Cts. / — 1917 —" in Red

1917 Lithographed

102		10c on 1c bl	1,650.	1,500.

Design similar to type A43.

Frías
A45

Sucre
A46

Bolívar
A47

1913 Engraved. *Perf. 12.*

103	A19	1c car rose	50	40
104	A20	2c vermilion	50	30
105	A21	5c green	60	20
106	A45	8c yellow	1.00	90
107	A22	10c gray	1.00	40
108	A46	50c dl vio	2.00	1.00
109	A47	1b sl bl	3.00	2.00
110	A24	2b black	6.00	4.00
		Nos. 103-110 (8)	14.60	9.20

Monolith of Tiahuanacu
A48

Mt. Potosí
A49

Lake Titicaca
A50

Mt. Illimani
A51

Legislature Building
A53

FIVE CENTAVOS.

Type I. Numerals have background of vertical lines. Clouds formed of dots.

Type II. Numerals on white background. Clouds near the mountain formed of wavy lines.

1916-17 Lithographed. *Perf. 11½.*

111	A48	½c brown	30	30
a.		Imperf. vert., pair	7.50	
112	A49	1c gray grn	35	20
a.		Imperf., pair	2.50	
113	A50	2c car & blk	35	20
a.		Imperf., pair	2.50	
b.		Imperf. horiz.		
c.		Center inverted	20.00	20.00
d.		Imperf., center inverted	22.50	
114	A51	5c dk bl (I)	75	35
a.		Imperf., pair	2.50	
b.		Imperf. horiz., pair	5.00	
c.		Imperf. vert., pair	5.00	
115	A51	5c dk bl (II)	75	15
a.		Imperf., pair	3.50	
116	A53	10c org & bl	1.25	15
a.		Imperf., pair	5.00	
b.		No period after "Legislativo"	1.25	25
c.		Center inverted	60.00	60.00
d.		Vertical pair, imperf. between	7.50	
		Nos. 111-116 (6)	3.75	1.35

Coat of Arms
A54 A55

Printed by the American Bank Note Co.

1919-20 Engraved. *Perf. 12.*

118	A54	1c carmine	35	35
119	A54	2c dk vio	6.00	4.00
120	A54	5c dk grn	50	15
121	A54	10c vermilion	50	15
122	A54	20c dk bl	2.00	50
123	A54	22c lt bl	1.25	1.25
124	A54	24c purple	1.25	75
125	A54	50c orange	6.00	1.00
126	A55	1b red brn	7.50	2.00
127	A55	2b blk brn	12.50	7.50
		Nos. 118-127 (10)	37.85	17.65

Printed by Perkins, Bacon & Co., Ltd.

Types of 1919-20 Issue.

Re-engraved.

1923-27 *Perf. 13½.*

128	A54	1c car ('27)	25	15
129	A54	2c dk vio	35	20

130	A54	5c dp grn	1.00	15
131	A54	10c vermilion	20.00	17.50
132	A54	20c sl bl	2.00	35
135	A54	50c orange	4.00	1.00
136	A55	1b red brn	1.00	50
137	A55	2b blk brn	75	50
		Nos. 128-137 (8)	29.35	20.35

The stamps of 1919–20 are perf. 12, those of 1923 are perf. 13½. The two issues may thus be readily distinguished. There are many differences in the designs of the two issues but they are too minute to be illustrated or described.

See also Nos. 144–146.

Stamps of 1919–20 Surcharged in Blue, Black or Red — **Habilitada 15 cts.**

1924 *Perf. 12.*

138	A54	5c on 1c car (Bl)	50	35
a.		Inverted surcharge	7.50	7.50
b.		Double surcharge	7.50	7.50
139	A54	15c on 10c ver (Bk)	1.00	60
a.		Inverted surcharge	10.00	10.00
140	A54	15c on 22c lt bl (Bk)	1.00	50
a.		Inverted surcharge	9.00	9.00
b.		Double surcharge, one inverted		
c.		Red surcharge	35.00	

Same Surcharge on No. 131.

Perf. 13½

142	A54	15c on 10c ver (Bk)	50	40
a.		Inverted surch.	10.00	10.00

No. 121 Surcharged — **Habilitada 15 cts.**

Perf. 12.

143	A54	15c on 10c ver (Bk)	60	50
a.		Inverted surch.	10.00	10.00
b.		Double surcharge	8.50	8.50
		Nos. 138-143 (5)	3.60	2.35

Printed by Waterlow & Sons.

Type of 1919-20 Issue.

Second Re-engraving.

1925 *Perf. 12½* **Unwmkd.**

144	A54	5c dp grn	75	35
145	A54	15c ultra	75	20
146	A54	20c dk bl	50	20

These stamps may be identified by the perforation.

Miner
A56

Condor Looking Toward the Sea
A57

Designs: 2c, Sower. 5c, Torch of Eternal Freedom. 10c, National flower (kantuta). 15c, Pres. Bautista Saavedra. 50c, Liberty head. 1b, Archer on horse. 2b, Mercury. 5b, Gen. A. J. de Sucre.

1925 Engraved. *Perf. 14.*

150	A56	1c dk grn	1.50	1.00
151	A56	2c rose	1.50	1.00
152	A56	5c red, *grn*	1.50	50
153	A56	10c car, *yel*	1.75	1.00
154	A56	15c red brn	1.00	50
155	A57	25c ultra	1.25	75
156	A56	50c dp vio	1.25	75
157	A56	1b red	2.25	2.00
158	A57	2b orange	3.50	3.00
159	A56	5b blk brn	4.00	3.00
		Nos. 150-159 (10)	19.50	13.50

Issued to commemorate the centenary of the Republic.

Stamps of 1919-27 Surcharged in Blue, Black or Red — **1927 5 CENTAVOS**

1927

160	A54	5c on 1c car (Bl)	1.50	1.25
a.		Inverted surcharge	6.00	6.00
b.		Black surcharge	30.00	30.00

Perf. 12.

162	A54	10c on 24c pur (Bk)	1.50	1.25
a.		Inverted surcharge	40.00	40.00
b.		Red surcharge	30.00	30.00

Coat of Arms
A66

Printed by Waterlow & Sons.

1927 Lithographed. *Perf. 13½.*

165	A66	2c yellow	50	35
166	A66	3c pink	60	50
167	A66	4c red brn	60	50
168	A66	20c lt ol grn	90	35
169	A66	25c dp bl	90	50
170	A66	30c violet	90	75
171	A66	40c orange	2.00	75
172	A66	50c dp brn	2.00	75
173	A55	1b red	2.25	75
174	A55	2b plum	3.50	1.00
175	A55	3b ol grn	3.50	2.50
176	A55	4b claret	5.00	3.00
177	A55	5b bis brn	6.00	2.00
		Nos. 165-177 (13)	28.65	13.70

Type of 1927 Issue Overprinted — *Octubre*  *1927*

1927

178	A66	5c dk grn	35	25
179	A66	10c slate	50	25
180	A66	15c carmine	75	50

Stamps of 1919-27 Surcharged — **15 cts. 1928**

Perf. 12, 12½, 13½

1928 Red Surcharge.

181	A54	15c on 20c dk bl (No. 122)	10.00	10.00
182	A54	15c on 20c sl bl (No. 132)	10.00	10.00
a.		Black surcharge	35.00	
183	A54	15c on 20c dk bl (No. 146)	225.00	225.00

Black Surcharge.

184	A54	15c on 24c pur (No. 124)	2.00	1.50
a.		Inverted surcharge	5.00	5.00
b.		Blue surcharge	55.00	
185	A54	15c on 50c org (No. 125)	60.00	60.00
186	A54	15c on 50c org (No. 135)	1.50	1.00
		Nos. 181-186 (6)	308.50	307.50

Condor
A67

Hernando Siles
A68

Map of Bolivia
A69

Printed by Perkins, Bacon & Co., Ltd.

1928 Engraved. *Perf. 13½.*

189	A67	5c green	50	10
190	A68	10c slate	50	10
191	A69	15c car lake	1.00	15

Stamps of 1913-17 Surcharged in Various Colors — **0.03 Centavos R. S. 21-4 1930**

1930 *Perf. 12, 11½.*

193	A20	1c on 2c ver (Bl)	1.00	1.00
a.		"0.10" for "0.01"	15.00	15.00
194	A50	3c on 2c car & blk (Br)	1.25	1.00
195	A48	25c on ½c brn (Bk)	1.00	75
196	A50	25c on 2c car & blk (V)	1.00	75

The lines of the surcharges were spaced to fit the various shapes of the stamps. The surcharges exist inverted, double, etc.

Trial printings were made of the surcharges on Nos. 193 and 194 in black and on No. 196 in brown.

Mt. Potosí
A70

Mt. Illimani
A71

Eduardo Abaroa
A72

Map of Bolivia
A73

Sucre
A74

Bolívar
A75

1931 Engraved. *Perf. 14.*

197	A70	2c green	60	50
198	A71	5c lt bl	50	25
199	A72	10c red org	60	25
200	A73	15c violet	1.00	25
201	A73	35c carmine	2.00	1.00
202	A73	45c orange	2.00	1.00
203	A74	50c gray	1.00	75
204	A75	1b brown	2.00	2.00
		Nos. 197-204 (8)	9.70	6.00

See also Nos. 207, 241.

Symbols of 1930 Revolution—A76

1931 Lithographed. *Perf. 11.*

205	A76	15c scarlet	3.00	50
a.		Pair, imperf. between		
206	A76	50c brt vio	1.00	75
a.		Pair, imperf. between	10.00	

Revolution of June 25, 1930.

Map Type of 1931. Without Imprint.

1932 Lithographed.

207	A73	15c violet	1.50	40

Stamps of 1927-31 Surcharged — **Habilitada A 15 Cts. D. S. 13-7.1933**

1933 *Perf. 13½, 14.*

208	A66	5c on 1b red	60	30
a.		Without period after "Cts"	1.25	1.25
209	A73	15c on 35c car	30	30
210	A73	15c on 45c org	30	30
a.		Inverted surcharge	3.00	3.00
211	A66	15c on 50c dp brn	60	25
212	A66	25c on 40c org	60	20
		Nos. 208-212 (5)	2.40	1.35

The hyphens in "13-7-33" occur in three positions.

Coat of Arms
A77

1933 Engraved *Perf. 12*

213	A77	2c bl grn	35	20
214	A77	5c blue	25	15
215	A77	10c red	60	40
216	A77	15c dp vio	35	20
217	A77	25c dk bl	90	60
		Nos. 213-217 (5)	2.45	1.55

Mariano Baptista
A78

Map of Bolivia
A79

1935

218	A78	15c dl vio	75	30

1935

219	A79	2c dk bl	35	25
220	A79	3c yellow	35	25
221	A79	5c vermilion	35	20
222	A79	5c bl grn	35	20
223	A79	10c blk brn	35	20
224	A79	15c dp rose	40	20
225	A79	15c ultra	40	20
226	A79	20c yel grn	50	25

No.	Type	Description	Unused	Used
227	A79	25c lt bl	50	20
228	A79	30c dp rose	90	35
229	A79	40c orange	90	30
230	A79	50c gray vio	90	20
231	A79	1b yellow	90	60
232	A79	2b ol brn	2.00	1.25
		Nos. 219-232 (14)	9.15	4.65

Regular Stamps of 1925-33 Surcharged in Black

Comunicaciones D. S. 25-2-37 0.05

1937 ***Perf. 11, 12, 13½.***

No.	Type	Description	Unused	Used
233	A77	5c on 2c bl grn	30	30
234	A77	15c on 25c dk bl	40	40
235	A77	30c on 25c dk bl	60	60
236	A55	45c on 1b red brn	75	75
237	A55	1b on 2b plum	90	90
a.		"1" missing	5.00	5.00
238	A77	2b on 25c dk bl	90	90

"Comunicaciones" on one line.

No.	Type	Description	Unused	Used
239	A76	3b on 50c brt vio	1.25	1.25
a.		"3" of value missing	6.00	6.00
240	A76	5b on 50c brt vio	2.00	2.00
		Nos. 233-240 (8)	7.10	7.10

President Siles—A80

1937 ***Perf. 14*** **Unwmkd.**

No.	Type	Description	Unused	Used
241	A80	1c yel brn	40	35

Native School
A81

Oil Wells
A82

Modern Factories
A83

Torch of Knowledge
A84

Map of the Sucre-Camiri R. R.
A85

Allegory of Free Education
A86

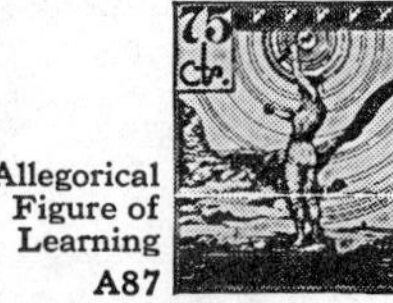

Allegorical Figure of Learning
A87

Symbols of Industry
A88

Modern Agriculture
A89

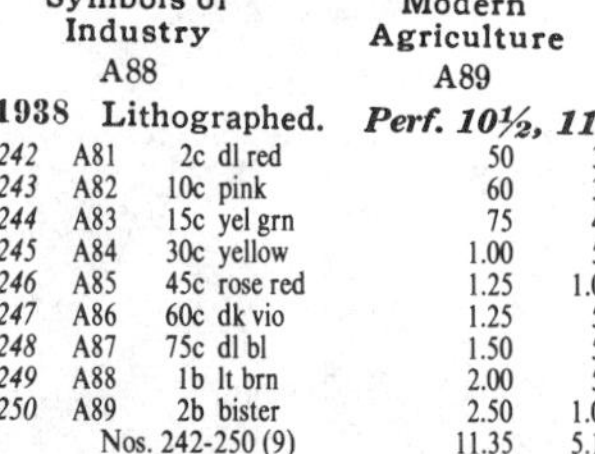

1938 Lithographed. ***Perf. 10½, 11.***

No.	Type	Description	Unused	Used
242	A81	2c dl red	50	35
243	A82	10c pink	60	35
244	A83	15c yel grn	75	40
245	A84	30c yellow	1.00	50
246	A85	45c rose red	1.25	1.00
247	A86	60c dk vio	1.25	50
248	A87	75c dl bl	1.50	50
249	A88	1b lt brn	2.00	50
250	A89	2b bister	2.50	1.00
		Nos. 242-250 (9)	11.35	5.10

Llamas
A90

Vicuna
A91

Coat of Arms
A92

Cocoi Herons
A93

Chinchilla
A94

Toco Toucan
A95

Condor
A96

Jaguar
A97

Perf. 10½, 11½x10½

1939, Jan. 21

No.	Type	Description	Unused	Used
251	A90	2c green	1.00	75
252	A90	4c fawn	1.00	75
253	A90	5c red vio	1.00	50
254	A91	10c black	1.00	75
255	A91	15c emerald	1.00	85
256	A91	20c dk sl grn	1.00	50
257	A92	25c lemon	90	40
258	A92	30c dk bl	90	50
259	A93	40c vermilion	2.00	60
260	A93	45c gray	2.00	60
261	A94	60c rose red	2.00	1.00
262	A94	75c sl bl	2.00	1.00
263	A95	90c orange	2.50	1.00
264	A95	1b blue	3.00	1.00
265	A96	2b rose lake	4.00	1.00
266	A96	3b dk vio	5.00	1.50
267	A97	4b brn org	6.00	2.00
268	A97	5b gray brn	7.50	2.50
		Nos. 251-268 (18)	43.80	17.20

Imperforate counterfeits of some values exist.

Flags of 21 American Republics
A98

1940, Apr. **Litho.** ***Perf. 10½***

No.	Type	Description	Unused	Used
269	A98	9b multi	3.50	3.00

Pan American Union, 150th anniversary.

Statue of Murillo
A99

Pedro Domingo Murillo
A102

Urns of Murillo and Sagarnaga
A100

Dream of Murillo
A101

1941, Apr. 15

No.	Type	Description	Unused	Used
270	A99	10c dl vio brn	15	10
271	A100	15c lt grn	25	15
a.		Imperf. (pair)	5.00	
272	A101	45c car rose	25	20
a.		Double impression		
273	A102	1.05b dk ultra	50	25

Issued to commemorate the 130th anniversary of the death (by execution) of Pedro Domingo Murillo (1759–1810), patriot.

First Stamp of Bolivia and 1941 Airmail Stamp—A103

1942. Oct. **Litho.** ***Perf. 13½***

No.	Type	Description	Unused	Used
274	A103	5c pink	1.25	1.00
275	A103	10c orange	1.25	1.00
276	A103	20c yel grn	2.00	1.00
277	A103	40c car rose	2.50	1.25
278	A103	90c ultra	5.00	1.50
279	A103	1b violet	7.00	3.50
280	A103	10b ol bis	22.50	15.00
		Nos. 274-280 (7)	41.50	24.25

Issued in commemoration of the first School Philatelic Exposition held in La Paz, October, 1941.

Gen. Ballivian Leading Cavalry Charge, Battle of Ingavi
A104

1943 **Photogravure** ***Perf. 12½***

No.	Type	Description	Unused	Used
281	A104	2c lt bl grn	15	10
282	A104	3c orange	15	10
283	A104	25c dp plum	25	15
284	A104	45c ultra	35	20
285	A104	3b scarlet	1.00	60
286	A104	4b brt rose lil	1.25	75
287	A104	5b blk brn	2.00	1.00
		Nos. 281-287 (7)	5.15	2.90

Souvenir Sheets.

Perf. 13, Imperf.

No.	Type	Description	Unused	Used
288	A104	Sheet of 4	3.50	3.00
289	A104	Sheet of 3	10.00	9.00

Centenary of the Battle of Ingavi, 1841. No. 288 contains 4 stamps similar to Nos. 281–284, No. 289 three stamps similar to Nos. 285–287; black marginal inscriptions. Size: 139x100mm.

Potosí
A107

Quechisla
A108

Miner
A109

Dam
A110

Mine Interior
A111

Chaquiri Dam
A112

Entrance to Pulacayo Mine
A113

1943 Engraved. *Perf. 12½.*

No.	Type	Denomination		
290	A107	15c red brn	35	25
291	A108	45c vio bl	35	25
292	A109	1.25b brt rose vio	50	40
293	A110	1.50b emerald	50	40
294	A111	2b brn blk	60	50
295	A112	2.10b lt bl	75	60
296	A113	3b red org	1.00	90
		Nos. 290-296 (7)	4.05	3.30

General José Ballivián and Cathedral at Trinidad
A114

1943, Nov. 18

No.	Type	Denomination		
297	A114	5c dk grn & brn	15	15
298	A114	10c dl pur & brn	20	20
299	A114	30c rose red & brn	25	25
300	A114	45c brt ultra & brn	35	35
301	A114	2.10b dp org & brn	50	50
		Nos. 297-301, C91-C95 (10)	3.40	2.80

Department of Beni centenary.

"Honor—Work—Law"
A115

"United for the Country"
A116

1944 Lithographed *Perf. 13½*

No.	Type	Denomination		
302	A115	20c orange	10	10
303	A115	90c ultra	15	10
304	A116	1b brt red vio	20	15
305	A116	2.40b dl brn	30	20

1945

No.	Type	Denomination		
306	A115	20c green	5	5
307	A115	90c dp rose	15	10
		Nos. 302-307, C96-C99 (10)	2.05	1.25

Nos. 302–307 were issued to commemorate the Revolution of Dec. 20, 1943.

Leopold Benedetto Vincenti, Joseph Ignacio de Sanjines and Bars of Anthem
A117

1946, Aug. 21 Litho. *Perf. 10½*

No.	Type	Denomination		
308	A117	5c rose vio & blk	20	15
309	A117	10c ultra & blk	20	15
310	A117	15c bl grn & blk	20	15
311	A117	30c ver & brn	25	20
a.		Souvenir sheet	1.25	1.25
312	A117	90c dk bl & brn	25	20
313	A117	2b blk & brn	60	25
a.		Souvenir sheet	2.50	2.50
		Nos. 308-313 (6)	1.70	1.10

Issued to commemorate the centenary of the adoption of Bolivia's national anthem.

Nos. 311a and 313a measure 86x136½ mm., contain respectively one each of Nos. 311 and 313, and are imperforate. The price of each sheet included a surtax of 4 bolivianos.

Nos. 248 and 262 Surcharged in Carmine, Black or Orange

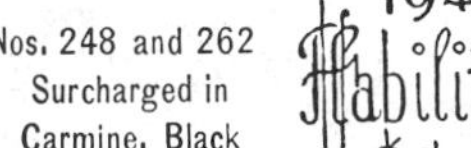

1947, Mar. 12 *Perf. 10½, 11*

No.	Type	Denomination		
314	A87	1.40b on 75c dl bl (C)	20	8
315	A94	1.40b on 75c sl bl (Bk)	20	8
316	A94	1.40b on 75c sl bl (C)	20	8
317	A94	1.40b on 75c sl bl (O)	20	8
		Nos. 314-317, C112 (5)	1.10	62

People Attacking Presidential Palace
A118

Arms of Bolivia and Argentina
A119

1947, Sept. Litho. *Perf. 13½*

No.	Type	Denomination		
318	A118	20c bl grn	5	4
a.		Imperf. (pair)		
319	A118	50c lil rose	10	6
320	A118	1.40b grnsh bl	15	8
a.		Imperf. (pair)		
321	A118	3.70b dl org	25	12
322	A118	4b violet	35	20
323	A118	10b olive	75	45
		Nos. 318-323, C113-C117 (11)	2.90	1.90

Issued to commemorate the first anniversary of the Revolution of July 21, 1946.

1947, Oct. 23

No.	Type	Denomination		
324	A119	1.40b dp org	12	8

Issued to commemorate the meeting of Presidents Enrique Hertzog of Bolivia and Juan D. Peron of Argentina at Yacuiba on October 23, 1947. See also No. C118.

Statue of Christ above La Paz
A120

Designs: 2b, Child kneeling before cross of Golgotha. 3b, St. John Bosco. No. 328, Virgin of Copacabana. No. 329, Pope Pius XII blessing University of La Paz.

1948, Sept. 26 *Perf. 11½* Unwmkd.

No.	Type	Denomination		
325	A120	1.40b bl & yel	50	18
326	A120	2b yel grn & sal	75	22
327	A120	3b grn & gray	1.50	30
328	A120	5b vio & sal	2.00	35
329	A120	5b red brn & lt grn	2.50	35
		Nos. 325-329, C119-C123 (10)	13.50	3.45

Issued to publicize the 3rd Inter-American Congress of Catholic Education.

Map and Emblem of Bolivia Auto Club
A125

Pres. Gregorio Pacheco, Map and Post Horn
A126

1948, Oct. 20

No.	Type	Denomination		
330	A125	5b ind & sal	4.00	25

Issued to publicize the International Automobile Races of South America, September–October 1948. See also No. C124.

1950, Jan. 2 Litho. *Perf. 11½*

No.	Type	Denomination		
331	A126	1.40b vio bl	15	10
332	A126	4.20b red	15	10
		Nos. 331-332, C125-C127 (5)	70	60

Issued to commemorate the 75th anniversary of the formation of the Universal Postal Union.

No. 273 Surcharged in Black

Bs.2.- Habilitada

D.S.6-VII-50

1950 *Perf. 10½*

No.	Type	Denomination		
333	A102	2b on 1.05b dk ultra	25	10

Crucifix and View of Potosí
A127

Symbols of United Nations
A128

Perf. 11½

1950, Sept. 14 Litho. Unwmkd.

No.	Type	Denomination		
334	A127	20c violet	10	6
335	A127	30c dp org	10	6
336	A127	50c lil rose	10	6
337	A127	1b carmine	15	6
338	A127	2b blue	20	6
339	A127	6b chocolate	35	15
		Nos. 334-339 (6)	1.00	45

Issued to commemorate the 400th anniversary of the appearance of a crucifix at Potosi.

1950, Oct. 24

No.	Type	Denomination		
340	A128	60c ultra	2.00	20
341	A128	2b green	2.50	35

Issued to commemorate the 5th anniversary of the formation of the United Nations, October 24, 1945. See also Nos. C138–C139.

Gate of the Sun and Llama
A129

Church of San Francisco
A130

Designs: 40c, Avenue Camacho. 50c, Consistorial Palace. 1b, Legislative Palace. 1.40b, Communications Bldg. 2b, Arms. 3b, La Gasca ordering Mendoza to found La Paz. 5b, Capt. Alonso de Mendoza founding La Paz. 10b, Arms; portrait of Mendoza.

1951, Mar. Engraved *Perf. 12½*

Center in Black.

No.	Type	Denomination		
342	A129	20c green	10	10
343	A130	30c dp org	10	10
344	A129	40c bis brn	10	10
345	A129	50c dk red	10	10
346	A129	1b dp pur	15	15
347	A129	1.40b dk vio bl	20	20
348	A129	2b dp pur	20	20
349	A129	3b red lil	30	20
a.		Sheet, Nos. 345, 346, 348, 349	1.75	1.75
b.		Sheet, imperf.	1.75	1.75
350	A129	5b dk red	35	25
a.		Sheet, Nos. 344, 347, 350	1.75	1.75
b.		Sheet, imperf.	1.75	1.75
351	A129	10b sepia	75	35
a.		Sheet, Nos. 342, 343, 351	1.75	1.75
b.		Sheet, imperf.	1.75	1.75
		Nos. 342-351, C140-C149 (20)	6.70	6.10

Issued to commemorate the 400th anniversary of the founding of La Paz.

The souvenir sheets measure 150x100 mm., and contain marginal inscriptions in black.

Boxing
A131

Designs: 50c, Tennis. 1b, Diving. 1.40b, Soccer. 2b, Skiing. 3b, Handball. 4b, Cycling.

Engraved

1951, July 1 *Perf. 12½* Unwmkd.

Center in Black.

No.	Type	Denomination		
352	A131	20c dp bl	25	10
353	A131	50c red	25	15
354	A131	1b claret	30	15
355	A131	1.40b yellow	30	20
356	A131	2b brt car	75	35
357	A131	3b yel brn	1.25	75
a.		Sheet, Nos. 352, 353, 356, 357	3.50	3.50
b.		Sheet, imperf.	3.50	3.50
358	A131	4b vio bl	1.50	75
a.		Sheet, Nos. 354, 355, 358	3.00	3.00
b.		Sheet, imperf.	3.00	3.00
		Nos. 352-358, C150-C156 (14)	12.45	5.85

The stamps were intended to commemorate the 5th athletic championship matches held at La Paz, October 1948.

The sheets measure 150x100 mm., and contain marginal inscriptions in black.

Eagle and Flag of Bolivia
A132

1951, Nov. 5 Litho. *Perf. 11½*

Flag in Red, Yellow and Green.

No.	Type	Denomination		
359	A132	2b aqua	15	15
360	A132	3.50b ultra	15	15
361	A132	5b purple	25	20
362	A132	7.50b gray	50	20
363	A132	15b dp car	60	40
364	A132	30b sepia	1.25	75
		Nos. 359-364 (6)	2.90	1.85

Issued to commemorate the centenary of the adoption of Bolivia's national flag.

Eduardo Abaroa
A133

Queen Isabella I
A134

1952, Mar. *Perf. 11*

No.	Type	Denomination		
365	A133	80c dk car	15	5
366	A133	1b red org	15	15
367	A133	2b emerald	25	15
368	A133	5b ultra	30	20
369	A133	10b lil rose	50	25
370	A133	20b dk brn	1.00	60
		Nos. 365-370, C157-C162 (12)	6.90	4.05

Issued to commemorate the 73rd anniversary of the death of Eduardo Abaroa.

1952, July 16 *Perf. 13½* Unwmkd.

371 A134 2b vio bl 15 10
372 A134 6.30b carmine 35 25

Issued to commemorate the 500th anniversary of the birth of Queen Isabella I of Spain. See also Nos. C163–C164.

Columbus Lighthouse
A135

1952, July 16 Lithographed

373 A135 2b vio bl, *bl* 25 20
374 A135 5b car, *sal* 50 30
375 A135 9b emer, *grn* 75 50
Nos. 373-375, C165-C168 (7) 2.55 1.58

Miner
A136

1953, Apr. 9

376 A136 2.50b vermilion 10 8
377 A136 8b violet 15 12

Issued to publicize the nationalization of the mines.

Gualberto Villarroel, Victor Paz Estenssoro and Hernan Siles Zuazo
A137

1953, Apr. 9 *Perf. 11½*

378 A137 50c rose lil 5 5
379 A137 1b brt rose 10 10
380 A137 2b vio bl 10 10
381 A137 3b lt grn 15 15
382 A137 4b yel org 15 15
383 A137 5b dl vio 25 15
Nos. 378-383, C169-C175 (13) 2.80 2.20

Issued to commemorate the first anniversary of the Revolution of Apr. 9, 1952.

Map of Bolivia and Cow's Head
A138

Designs: 17b, Same as 5b. 25b, 85b, Map and ear of wheat.

1954, Aug. 2 *Perf. 12x11½*

384 A138 5b car rose 5 4
385 A138 17b aqua 15 7
386 A138 25b chlky bl 25 8
387 A138 85b blk brn 50 25
Nos. 384-387, C176-C181 (10) 4.65 1.44

Nos. 384–385 were issued to commemorate the agrarian reform laws of 1953–54. Nos. 386–387 commemorate the 1st National Congress of Agronomy.

Oil Refinery
A139

Perf. 12x11½

1955, Oct. 9 Unwmkd.

388 A139 10b ultra & lt ultra 10 10
389 A139 35b rose car & rose 15 10
390 A139 40b dk & lt yel grn 15 10
391 A139 50b red vio & lil rose 20 10
392 A139 80b brn & bis brn 35 15
Nos. 388-392, C182-C186 (10) 5.65 3.00

Nos. 342-351, Surcharged with New Values and Bars in Ultramarine.

1957, Feb. 14 Engr. *Perf. 12½*

Center in Black.

393 A129 50b on 3b red lil 15 5
394 A129 100b on 2b dp pur 15 5
395 A129 200b on 1b dp pur 20 10
396 A129 300b on 1.40b dk vio bl 25 10
397 A129 350b on 20c grn 35 10
398 A129 400b on 40c bis brn 35 10
399 A130 600b on 30c dp org 50 15
400 A129 800b on 50c dk red 60 15
401 A129 1000b on 10b sep 60 25
402 A129 2000b on 5b dk red 1.00 40
Nos. 393-402 (10) 4.15 1.45

See also Nos. C187–C196.

CEPAL Building, Santiago de Chile, and Meeting Hall in La Paz
A140

1957, May 15 Litho. *Perf. 13*

403 A140 150b gray & ultra 15 5
404 A140 350b bis brn & gray 30 10
405 A140 550b chlky bl & brn 35 15
406 A140 750b dp rose & grn 50 20
407 A140 900b grn & brn blk 75 25
Nos. 403-407, C197-C201 (10) 8.90 4.75

Issued to commemorate the seventh session of the C. E. P. A. L. (Comision Economica para la America Latina de las Naciones Unidas), La Paz.

Presidents Siles Zuazo and Aramburu
A141

1957, Dec. 15 *Perf. 11½* Unwmkd.

408 A141 50b red org 15 5
409 A141 350b blue 40 10
410 A141 1000b redsh brn 75 15
Nos. 408-410, C202-C204 (6) 2.90 70

Issued to commemorate the opening of the Santa Cruz-Yacuiba Railroad and the meeting of the Presidents of Bolivia and Argentina.

Flags of Bolivia and Mexico and Presidents Hernan Siles Zuazo and Adolfo Lopez Mateos
A142

1960, Jan. 30 Litho. *Perf. 11½*

411 A142 350b olive 25 8
412 A142 600b red brn 35 15
413 A142 1500b blk brn 75 25
Nos. 411-413, C205-C207 (6) 4.60 1.53

Issued for an expected visit of Mexico's President Adolfo Lopez Mateos. On sale Jan. 30–Feb. 1, 1960.

Indians and Mt. Illimani
A143

Refugee Children
A144

1960, Mar. 26 Unwmkd.

414 A143 500b ol bis 35 10
415 A143 1000b blue 60 20
416 A143 2000b brown 1.25 50
417 A143 4000b green 2.50 75
Nos. 414-417, C208-C211 (8) 24.70 10.30

1960, Apr. 7 *Perf. 11½*

418 A144 50b brown 15 5
419 A144 350b claret 20 6
420 A144 400b stl bl 25 8
421 A144 1000b gray brn 75 25
422 A144 3000b sl grn 1.50 70
Nos. 418-422, C212-C216 (10) 6.70 4.64

Issued to publicize World Refugee Year, July 1, 1959–June 30, 1960.

Jaime Laredo
A145

Rotary Emblem and Nurse with Children
A146

1960, Aug. 15 Litho. *Perf. 11½*

423 A145 100b olive 40 10
424 A145 350b dp rose 60 10
425 A145 500b Prus grn 75 15
426 A145 1,000b brown 1.00 25
427 A145 1,500b vio bl 1.75 35
428 A145 5,000b gray 6.00 1.25
Nos. 423-428, C217-C222 (12) 25.25 8.10

Issued to honor violinist Jaime Laredo.

1960, Nov. 19 *Perf. 11½*

429 A146 350b grn, yel & dp bl 25 10
430 A146 500b brn, yel & dp bl 35 10
431 A146 600b vio, yel & dp bl 50 15
432 A146 1,000b gray, yel & dp bl 60 25
Nos. 429-432, C223-C226 (8) 8.45 3.65

Issued for the Children's Hospital, sponsored by the Rotary Club of La Paz.

Designs from Gate of the Sun
A147 A148

Designs: Various prehistoric gods and ornaments from Tiahuanacu excavations.

Lithographed

1960, Dec. 16 *Perf. 13x12, 12x13*

Gold Background.

Surcharge in Black or Dark Red (#436)

Size: 21x23, 23x21mm.

433 A147 50b on ½c red 75 50
434 A147 100b on 1c red 50 25
435 A147 200b on 2c blk 1.50 15
436 A147 300b on 5c grn 35 20
437 A147 350b on 10c grn 35 1.25
438 A148 400b on 15c ind 50 25
439 A148 500b on 20c red 50 25
440 A148 500b on 50c red 60 25
441 A148 600b on 22½c grn 75 40
442 A148 600b on 60c vio 90 50
443 A148 700b on 25c vio 1.25 30
444 A148 700b on 1b grn 1.75 1.00
445 A148 800b on 30c red 85 30
446 A148 900b on 40c grn 75 40
447 A148 1000b on 2b bl 90 50
448 A148 1800b on 3b gray 9.00 6.00

Perf. 11

Size: 49½x23mm.

449 A148 4000b on 4b gray 65.00 55.00

Perf. 11x13½

Size: 49x53mm.

450 A147 5000b on 5b gray 17.50 12.50
Nos. 433-450 (18) 103.70 80.00

Nos. 433–450 were not regularly issued without surcharge. Price (set), $20.

The decree for Nos. 433–450 stipulated that seven were for air mail (500b on 50c, 600b on 60c, 700b on 1b, 1,000b, 1,800b, 4,000b and 5,000b), but the overprinting failed to include "Aereo."

The 800b surcharge also exists on the 1c red and gold. This was not listed in the decree.

Miguel de Cervantes
A149

Nuflo de Chaves
A150

1961, Nov. Photo. *Perf. 13x12½*

451 A149 600b ocher & dl vio 50 12

Issued to commemorate Cervantes' appointment as Chief Magistrate of La Paz. See also No. C230.

1961, Nov. Unwmkd.

452 A150 1500b dk bl, *buff* 75 30

Issued to commemorate the 400th anniversary of the founding of Santa Cruz de la Sierra. See also Nos. 468, C246.

People below Eucharist Symbol
A151

Hibiscus
A152

1962, Mar. 19 Litho. *Perf. 10½*

453 A151 1000b gray grn, red & yel 1.00 50

Issued to commemorate the Fourth National Eucharistic Congress, Santa Cruz, 1961. See also No. C231.

Nos. 418–422 Surcharged Horizontally with New Value and Bars or Greek Key Border Segment

1962, June *Perf. 11½*

454 A144 600b on 50b brn 30 20
455 A144 900b on 350b cl 40 20
456 A144 1,000b on 400b stl bl 60 25
457 A144 2,000b on 1,000b gray brn 75 40

458 A144 3,500b on 3,000b sl grn 1.25 75
Nos.454-458, C232-C236 (10) 9.20 4.80

Old value obliterated with two short bars on No. 454; four short bars on Nos. 455–456 and Greek key border on Nos. 457–458. The Greek key obliteration comes in two positions: two full "keys" on top, and one full and two half keys on top.

1962, June 28 Litho. ***Perf. 10½***

Flowers in Natural Colors

Flowers: 400b, Bicolored vanda. 600b, Lily. 1000b, Orchid.

459 A152 200b sl bl 30 10
460 A152 400b brown 30 15
461 A152 600b dk bl 60 20
462 A152 1000b violet 1.00 35
Nos. 459-462, C237-C240 (8) 9.80 4.65

Infantry A153 — Anti-Malaria Emblem A154

Designs: 500b, Cavalry. 600b, Artillery. 2000b, Engineers.

1962, Sept. 5 ***Perf. 11½***

Insigne in Red, Yellow & Green

463 A153 400b blk, mar & buff 15 10
464 A153 500b blk, lt & dk grn 20 15
465 A153 600b blk & pale bis 25 20
466 A153 2000b blk & brn 75 50
Nos. 463-466, C241-C244 (8) 4.30 2.95

Issued in honor of Bolivia's Armed Forces.

1962, Oct. 4

467 A154 600b dk & lt vio & yel 40 20

Issued for the World Health Organization drive to eradicate malaria. See No. C245.

Portrait Type of 1961.

Design: 600b, Alonso de Mendoza.

1962 Photogravure ***Perf. 13x12½***

468 A150 600b rose vio, *bluish* 40 20

Soccer and Flags A155

Design: 1p, Goalkeeper catching ball (vert.).

1963, Mar. 21 Litho. ***Perf. 11½***

Flags in National Colors

469 A155 60c gray 60 15
470 A155 1p gray 90 25

Issued to publicize the 21st South American Soccer Championships. See also Nos. C247–C248.

Globe and Wheat Emblem A156

1963, Aug. 1 ***Perf. 11½*** **Unwmkd.**

471 A156 60c dk bl, bl & yel 35 15

Issued for the "Freedom from Hunger" campaign of the U.N. Food and Agriculture Organization. See also No. C249.

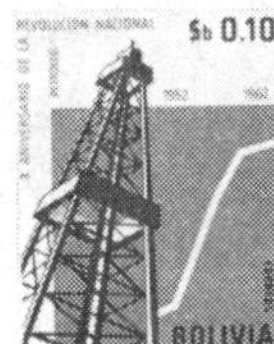

Oil Derrick and Chart A157

Designs: 60c, Map of Bolivia. 1p, Students.

1963, Dec. 21 Litho. ***Perf. 11½***

472 A157 10c grn & dk brn 15 10
473 A157 60c ocher & dk brn 40 15
474 A157 1p dk bl, grn & yel 50 25
Nos. 472-474, C251-C253 (6) 3.90 1.95

Issued to commemorate the 10th anniversary of the Revolution of Apr. 9, 1952.

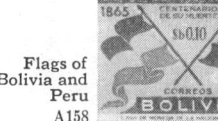

Flags of Bolivia and Peru A158

1966, Aug. 10 ***Perf. 13½*** **Wmk. 90**

Flags in National Colors

475 A158 10c blk & tan 15 10
476 A158 60c blk & lt grn 30 15
477 A158 1p blk & gray 50 20
478 A158 2p blk & rose 75 30
Nos. 475-478, C254-C257 (8) 4.15 1.85

Issued to commemorate the centenary (in 1965) of the death of Marshal Andrés Santa Cruz (1792–1865), president of Bolivia and of Peru-Bolivian Confederation.

Children A159

Lithographed

1966, Dec. 16 ***Perf. 13½*** **Unwmkd.**

479 A159 30c ocher & sep 25 10

Issued to help poor children. See No. C258.

Map and Flag of Bolivia and Generals Ovando and Barrientos A160

1966, Dec. 16 Litho. ***Perf. 13½***

Flag in Red, Yellow and Green

480 A160 60c vio brn & tan 30 10
481 A160 1p dl grn & tan 45 15

Issued to honor Generals Rene Barrientos Ortuno and Alfredo Ovando C., co-Presidents, 1965–66. See also Nos. C259–C260.

A161

Various Issues 1957–60 and Type A161 Surcharged with New Values and Bars

1966, Dec. 21

On No. 403:
"Centenario de la / Cruz Roja / Internacional"

482 A140 20c on 150b gray & ultra 15 5

On Nos. 405–406:
"Homenaje a la / Generala / J. Azurduy de / Padilla"

483 A140 30c on 550b chlky bl & brn 15 5
484 A140 2.80p on 750b dp rose & grn 90 50

On No. 424:
"CL Aniversario / Heroinas Coronilla"

485 A145 60c on 350b dp rose 25 10

Nos. 429–430 Surcharged

486 A146 1.60p on 350b multi 60 25
487 A146 2.40p on 500b multi 90 40

Revenue Stamps of 1946 surcharged with New Value, "X" and:
"XXV Aniversario / Gobierno Busch"

488 A161 20c on 5b red 15 5

Overprinted:
"XX Aniversario / Gob. Villaroel"

489 A161 60c on 2b grn 25 10

Overprinted:
"Centenario do / Rurrenabaque"

490 A161 1p on 10b brn 40 15

Overprinted:
"XXV Aniversario / Dpto. Pando"

491 A161 1.60p on 50c vio 60 25
Nos. 482-491, C261-C272 (22) 14.20 10.20

Sower A162 — "Macheteros" A163

1967, Sept. 20 Litho. ***Perf. 13½x13***

492 A162 70c multi 50 15

Issued to commemorate the 50th anniversary of Lions International. See Nos. C273–C273a.

1968, June 24 ***Perf. 13½x13***

Designs (Folklore characters): 60c, Chunchos. 1p, Wiphala. 2p, Diablada.

493 A163 30c gray & multi 15 8
494 A163 60c sky bl & multi 25 15
495 A163 1b gray & multi 40 20
496 A163 2b gray ol & multi 75 30
Nos. 493-496, C274-C277 (8) 4.45 2.43

Issued to publicize the 9th Congress of the Postal Union of the Americas and Spain.

A souvenir sheet exists containing 4 imperf. stamps similar to Nos. 493–496. Bister and gray marginal inscription. Size: 131x81½mm.

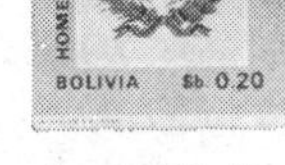

Arms of Tarija A164 — Pres. Gualberto Villaroël A165

1968, Oct. 29 Litho. ***Perf. 13½x13***

497 A164 20c pale sal & multi 15 6
498 A164 30c gray & multi 15 8
499 A164 40c dl yel & multi 20 10
500 A164 60c lt yel grn & multi 30 12
Nos. 497-500, C278-C281 (8) 4.40 2.11

Battle of Tablada sesquicentennial.

1968, Nov. 6 **Unwmkd.**

501 A165 20c sep & org 20 6
502 A165 30c sep & dl bl grn 20 6
503 A165 40c sep & dl rose 20 8
504 A165 50c sep & yel grn 25 10
505 A165 1b sep & ol bis 50 15
Nos. 501-505 (5) 1.35 45

Issued to commemorate the 4th centenary of the founding of Cochabamba. See Nos. C282–C286.

ITU Emblem A166

1968, Dec. 3 Litho. ***Perf. 13x13½***

506 A166 10c gray, blk & yel 25 6
507 A166 60c org, blk & ol 50 10

Issued to commemorate the centenary (in 1965) of the International Telecommunication Union. See Nos. C287–C288.

Polychrome Painted Clay Cup, Inca Period A167

1968, Nov. 14 ***Perf. 13½x13***

508 A167 20c dk bl grn & multi 25 6
509 A167 60c vio bl & multi 50 10

Issued to commemorate the 20th anniversary (in 1966) of UNESCO (United Nations Educational, Scientific and Cultural Organization). See Nos. C289–C290.

John F. Kennedy A168 — Tennis Player A169

1968, Nov. 22 ***Perf. 13x13½***

510 A168 10c yel grn & blk 20 10
511 A168 4b vio & blk 2.50 75

Issued in memory of Pres. John F. Kennedy (1917–1963).

A souvenir sheet contains one imperf. stamp similar to No. 511. Green marginal inscription. Size: 131x81½mm.

See Nos. C291–C292.

1968, Dec. 10 ***Perf. 13x13½***

512 A169 10c gray, blk & lt brn 20 10
513 A169 20c yel, blk & lt brn 20 10
514 A169 30c ultra, blk & lt brn 20 10

Issued to commemorate the 32nd South American Tennis Championships, La Paz, 1965. See Nos. C293–C294.

A souvenir sheet exists containing 3 imperf. stamps similar to Nos. 512–514. Light brown marginal inscription. Size: 131x81½mm.

Issue of 1863
A170

1968, Dec. 23 Litho. *Perf. 13x13½*

515	A170	10c yel grn, brn & blk	20	10
516	A170	30c lt bl, brn & blk	20	10
517	A170	2b gray, brn & blk	35	20
		Nos. 515-517, C295-C297 (6)	4.50	2.25

Issued to commemorate the centenary of Bolivian postage stamps. See Nos. C295–C297.

A souvenir sheet exists containing 3 imperf. stamps similar to Nos. 515–517. Yellow green marginal inscription. Size: 131x81½mm.

Rifle Shooting
A171

Sports: 50c, Equestrian. 60c, Canoeing.

1969, Oct. 29 Litho. *Perf. 13x13½*

518	A171	40c red brn, org & blk	20	10
519	A171	50c emer, red & blk	20	10
520	A171	60c bl, emer & blk	35	15
		Nos. 518-520, C299-C301 (6)	4.60	2.10

Issued to commemorate the 19th Olympic Games, Mexico City, Oct. 12–27, 1968.

A souvenir sheet exists containing 3 imperf. stamps similar to Nos. 518–520. Marginal inscription in red brown, emerald and blue. Size: 130½x81mm.

Temenis Laothoe Violetta
A172

Butterflies: 10c, Papilio crassus. 20c, Catagramma cynosura. 30c, Eunica eurota flora. 80c, Ituna phenarete.

1970, Apr. 24 Litho. *Perf. 13x13½*

521	A172	5c pale lil & multi	15	5
522	A172	10c pink & multi	15	5
523	A172	20c gray & multi	15	5
524	A172	30c yel & multi	15	5
525	A172	80c multi	35	20
		Nos. 521-525, C302-C306 (10)	8.20	3.35

A souvenir sheet exists containing 3 imperf. stamps similar to Nos. 521–523. Black marginal inscription. Size: 129½x80mm.

Boy Scout
A173

Design: 10c, Girl Scout planting rose bush.

1970, June 17 *Perf. 13½x13*

526	A173	5c multi	20	5
527	A173	10c multi	20	5

Issued to honor the Bolivian Scout movement. See Nos. C307–C308.

No. 437 Surcharged "EXFILCA 70 / $b. 0.30" and Two Bars in Red

1970, Dec. 6 Litho. *Perf. 13x12*

528	A147	30c on 350b on 10c gold & grn	20	10

EXFILCA 70, 2nd Interamerican Philatelic Exhibition, Caracas, Venezuela, Nov. 27–Dec. 6.

Nos. 455 and 452 Surcharged in Black or Red

1970, Dec. Photo. *Perf. 11½*

529	A144	60c on 900b on 350b cl	35	12
533	A150	1.20b on 1500b dk bl, *buff* (R)	65	20

Amaryllis Yungacensis
A174

Sica Sica Church, EXFILIMA Emblem
A175

Bolivian Flowers: 30c, Amaryllis escobar uriae (horiz.). 40c, Amaryllis evansae (horiz.). 2b, Gymnocalycium chiquitanum.

Perf. 13x13½, 13½x13

1971, Aug. 9 Litho. Unwmkd.

534	A174	30c gray & multi	15	10
535	A174	40c multi	15	10
536	A174	50c multi	25	20
537	A174	2b multi	75	50
		Nos. 534-537, C310-C313 (8)	5.90	2.50

1971, Nov. 6 *Perf. 14x13½*

538	A175	20c red & multi	25	10

EXFILIMA '71, 3rd Inter-American Philatelic Exhibition, Lima, Peru, Nov. 6–14.

Pres. Hugo Banzer Suarez
A176

1972, Jan. 24 Litho. *Perf. 13½*

539	A176	1.20b blk & multi	75	20

Bolivia's development, Aug. 19, 1971, to Jan. 24, 1972.

Chiriwano de Achocalla Dance
A177

Folk Dances: 40c, Rueda Chapaca. 60c, Kena-kena. 1b, Waca Thokori.

1972, Mar. 23 Litho. *Perf. 13½x13*

540	A177	20c red & multi	10	10
541	A177	40c rose lil & multi	25	20
542	A177	60c cr & multi	35	25
543	A177	1b cit & multi	50	35
		Nos. 540-543, C314-C315 (6)	2.95	1.40

Madonna and Child by B. Bitti
A178

Tarija Cathedral, EXFILBRA Emblem
A179

Paintings: 10c, Nativity, by Melchor Perez de Holguín. 50c, Coronation of the Virgin, by G. M. Berrio. 70c, Harquebusier, anonymous. 80c, St. Peter of Alcantara, by Holguín.

1972 Lithographed *Perf. 14x13½*

544	A178	10c gray & multi	15	10
545	A178	50c sal & multi	30	10
546	A178	70c lt grn & multi	35	15
547	A178	80c buff & multi	40	20
548	A178	1b multi	50	25
		Nos. 544-548, C316-C319 (9)	4.50	1.95

Bolivian paintings. Issue dates: 1b, Aug. 17; others, Dec. 4.

1972, Aug. 26

549	A179	30c multi	25	10

4th Inter-American Philatelic Exhibition, EXFILBRA, Rio de Janeiro, Brazil, Aug. 26–Sept. 2.

Echinocactus Notocactus
A180

Designs: Various cacti.

1973, Aug. 6 Litho. *Perf. 13½*

550	A180	20c crim & multi	15	5
551	A180	40c multi	20	8
552	A180	50c multi	25	10
553	A180	70c multi	35	12
		Nos. 550-553, C321-C323 (7)	3.20	1.25

Power Station, Santa Isabel
A181

Designs: 20c, Tin industry. 90c, Bismuth industry. 1b, Natural gas plant.

1973, Nov. 26 Litho. *Perf. 13½*

554	A181	10c gray & multi	10	5
555	A181	20c tan & multi	10	5
556	A181	90c lt grn & multi	40	12
557	A181	1b yel & multi	40	15
		Nos. 554-557, C324-C325 (6)	2.25	87

Bolivia's development.

Cattleya Nobilior
A182

Orchids: 50c, Zygopetalum bolivianum. 1b, Huntleya melagris.

1974, May 15 *Perf. 13½*

558	A182	20c gray & multi	15	5
559	A182	50c lt bl & multi	25	10
560	A182	1b cit & multi	40	15
		Nos. 558-560, C327-C330 (7)	7.80	2.45

UPU and Philatelic Exposition Emblems—A183

1974, Oct. 9

561	A183	3.50b grn, blk & bl	1.50	60

Centenary of Universal Postal Union; PRENFIL-UPU Philatelic Exhibition, Buenos Aires, Oct. 1–12; EXPO-UPU Philatelic Exhibition, Montevideo, Oct. 20–27.

Gen. Sucre, by I. Wallpher
A184

1974, Dec. 9 Litho. *Perf. 13½*

562	A184	5b multi	1.75	75

Sesquicentennial of the Battle of Ayacucho.

Lions Emblem and Steles
A185

1975, Mar. Litho. *Perf. 13½*

563	A185	30c red & multi	50	10

Lions International in Bolivia, 25th anniversary.

España 75 Emblem
A186

1975, Mar.

564	A186	4.50b yel, red & blk	1.25	50

España 75 International Philatelic Exhibition, Madrid, Apr. 4–13.

Emblem
A187

1975 Lithographed *Perf. 13½*

565	A187	2.50b lil, blk & sil	1.00	40

First meeting of Postal Ministers, Quito, Ecuador, March 1974, and for the Cartagena Agreement.

Pando Coat of Arms
A188

Designs: Departmental coats of arms.

1975, July 16 Litho. *Perf. 13½*
Gold & Multicolored

566 A188 20c *shown* 10 10
567 A188 2b *Chuquisaca* 75 50
568 A188 3b *Cochabamba* 1.00 75
Nos. 566-568, C336-C341 (9) 4.35 3.50

Sesquicentennial of Republic of Bolivia.

Simón Bolívar
A189

Presidents and Statesmen of Bolivia: 30c, Victor Paz Estenssoro. 60c, Tomas Frias. 1b, Ismael Montes. 2.50b, Aniceto Arce. 7b, Bautista Saavedra. 10b, José Manuel Pando. 15b, José Maria Linares. 50b, Simón Bolívar.

1975 Litho. *Perf. 13½*
Size: 24x32mm.

569 A189 30c multi 15 5
569A A189 60c multi 20 10
570 A189 1b multi 30 15
571 A189 2.50b multi 75 35
572 A189 7b multi 2.00 1.00
573 A189 10b multi 3.00 1.50
574 A189 15b multi 4.00 2.00

Size: 28x39mm.

575 A189 50b multi 15.00
Nos. 569-575, C346-C353 (16) 53.90

Sesquicentennial of Republic of Bolivia.

"EXFIVIA 75"
A190

1975, Dec. 1 Litho. *Perf. 13½*

576 A190 3b multi 1.00 50
a. Souvenir sheet 2.25 1.75

EXFIVIA 75, first Bolivian Philatelic Exposition. No. 576a contains one stamp similar to No. 576 with simulated perforations. Multicolored margin shows emblems of various international philatelic exhibitions. Size: 130x80mm. Sold for 5b.

Chiang Kai-shek, Flags of Bolivia and China
A191

1976, Apr. 4 Litho. *Perf. 13½*

577 A191 2.50b multi, red circle 90 40
578 A191 2.50b multi, bl circle 90 40

Pres. Chiang Kai-shek of China (1887–1975), first death anniversary.
Erroneous red of sun's circle on Chinese flag of No. 577 was corrected on No. 578 with a dark blue overlay.

Naval Insignia
A192

1976, Apr. Litho. *Perf. 13½*

579 A192 50c bl & multi 35 10

Navy anniversary.

Geological Map, Pickax and Lamp
A193

1976, May

580 A193 4b multi 1.25 75

Bolivian Geological Institute.

Lufthansa Jet, Bolivian and German Colors—A194

1976, May

581 A194 3b multi 1.25 50

Lufthansa, 50th anniversary.

Boy Scout and Scout Emblem
A195

1976, May Litho. *Perf. 13½*

582 A195 1b multi 50 30

Bolivian Boy Scouts, 60th anniversary.

Battle Scene, U.S. Bicentennial Emblem
A196

1976, May 25

583 A196 4.50b bis & multi 2.00 1.00

American Bicentennial.
A souvenir sheet contains one stamp similar to No. 583 with simulated perforations. Multicolored, inscribed margin shows U.S. flags of 1776 and 1976. Size: 130x80mm.

Family, Map of Bolivia
A197

Brother Vicente Bernedo
A198

1976 *Perf. 13½*

584 A197 2.50b multi 75 50

National Census 1976.

1976, Oct.

585 A198 1.50b multi 50 25

Brother Vicente Bernedo de Potosi (1544–1619), missionary to the Indians.

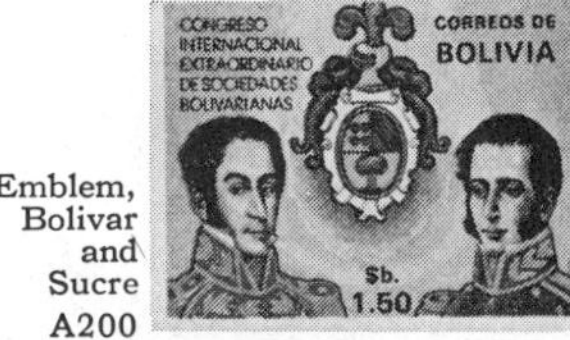

Policeman with Dog, Rainbow over La Paz
A199

1976, Oct.

586 A199 2.50b multi 75 40

Bolivian Police, 150 years of service.

Emblem, Bolivar and Sucre
A200

1976, Nov. 18 Litho. *Perf. 13½*

587 A200 1.50b multi 75 40

International Congress of Bolivarian Societies.

Pedro Poveda, View of La Paz
A201

1976, Dec.

588 A201 1.50b multi 50 25

Pedro Poveda (1874–1936), educator.

A202

1976, Dec. 17 *Perf. 10½*

594 A202 20c brown 10 5
595 A202 1b ultra 30 10
596 A202 1.50b green 50 10

Boy and Girl
A203

1977, Feb. 4 Litho. *Perf. 13½*

599 A203 50c multi 20 5

Christmas 1976, and for 50th anniversary of the Inter-American Children's Institute.

Staff of Aesculapius
A204

Supreme Court, La Paz
A205

1977, Mar. 18 Litho. *Perf. 13½x13*

600 A204 3b multi 90 15

National Seminar on Chagas' disease, Cochabamba, Feb. 21–26.

1977, May 3

Designs: 4b, Manuel Maria Urcullu, first President of Supreme Court. 4.50b, Pantaleon Dalence, President 1883–1889.

601 A205 2.50b multi 45 12
602 A205 4b multi 65 18
603 A205 4.50b multi 75 20

Sesquicentennial of Bolivian Supreme Court.

Newspaper Mastheads
A206

Map of Bolivia, Tower and Flag
A207

Designs: 2.50b, Alfredo Alexander and Hoy (horiz.). 3b, José Carrasco and El Diario (horiz.). 4b, Demetrio Canelas and Los Tiempos. 5.50b, Frontpage of Presencia.

1977, June Lithographed *Perf. 13½*

604 A206 1.50b multi 35 10
605 A206 2.50b multi 50 15
606 A206 3b multi 65 20
607 A206 4b multi 75 25
608 A206 5.50b multi 1.00 30
Nos. 604-608 (5) 3.25 1.00

Bolivian newspapers and their founders.

1977, June

609 A207 3b multi 75 25

90th anniversary of Oruro Club.

Games' Poster
A208

Tin Miner and Emblem
A209

1977, Oct. 20 Litho. *Perf. 13½*

610 A208 5b bl & multi 1.00 30

8th Bolivian Games, La Paz, Oct. 1977.

1977, Oct. 31 Litho. *Perf. 13*

611 A209 3b multi 75 25

Bolivian Mining Corporation, 25th anniversary.

Miners, Globe, Tin Symbol
A210

Map of Bolivia, Radio Masts
A211

1977, Nov. 3

612 A210 6b sil & multi 1.25 40

International Tin Symposium, La Paz, Nov. 14–21.

1977, Nov. 11

613 A211 2.50b bl & multi 50 12

Radio Bolivia, ASBORA, 50th anniversary.

No. 450 Surcharged with New Value, 3 Bars and "EXFIVIA–77"

1977, Nov. 25 Litho. *Perf. 11x13½*

614 A147 5b on 5000b on 5b gold & gray 1.10 25

EXFIVIA '77 Philatelic Exhibition, Cochabamba.

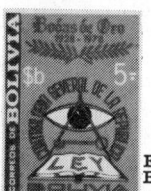

Eye, Compass, Book of Law
A212

1978, May 3 Litho. *Perf. 13½x13*

615 A212 5b multi 1.00 25

Audit Department, 50th anniversary.

Mt. Illimani
A213

Pre-Columbian Monolith
A214

Design: 1.50b, Mt. Cerro de Potosi.

Perf. 11x10½, 10½x11

1978, June 1 Litho.

616	A213	50c bl & Prus bl	15	3
617	A214	1b brn & lem	25	4
618	A213	1.50b red & bl gray	40	6

COLORS

Please refer to page v for a complete list of color abbreviations used in this book.

Unused Prices

Catalogue prices for unused stamps through 1960 are for hinged copies in fine condition.

Never-hinged unused stamps issued before 1961 often sell above Catalogue prices. Current never-hinged prices for various countries will be found in the Scott StampMarket Update.

Andean Countries, Staff of Aesculapius
A215

Map of Americas with Bolivia
A216

1978, June 1 *Perf. 10½x11*

626 A215 2b org & blk 50 15

Health Ministers of Andean Countries, 5th meeting.

1978, June 1

627 A216 2.50b dp ultra & red 50 20

World Rheumatism Year.

Central Bank Building
A217

1978, July 26 Litho. *Perf. 13½*

628 A217 7b multi 1.50 40

50th anniversary of Bank of Bolivia.

Jesus and Children
A218

1979, Feb. 20 Litho. *Perf. 13½*

629 A218 8b multi 1.40 25

International Year of the Child.

Antofagasta Cancel
A219

Eduardo Abaroa, and Chain
A220

Designs: 1b, La Chimba cancel. 1.50b, Mejillones cancel. 5.50b, View of Antofagasta (horiz.). 6.50b, Woman in chains, symbolizing captive province. 8b, Map of Antofagasta Province, 1876. 10b, Arms of province.

1979, Mar. 23 Litho. *Perf. 10½*

630	A219	50c buff & blk	10	3
631	A219	1b pink & blk	18	3
632	A219	1.50b pale grn & blk	28	6

Perf. 13½

633	A220	5.50b multi	95	25
634	A220	6.50b multi	1.20	28
635	A220	7b multi	1.25	28
636	A220	8b multi	1.40	35
637	A220	10b multi	1.75	48
		Nos. 630-637 (8)	7.11	1.76

Centenary of loss of Antofagasta coastal area to Chile.

Emblem and Map of Bolivia
A221

Gymnast
A222

1979, Mar. 26 *Perf. 13½x13*

638 A221 3b multi 55 12

Radio Club of Bolivia.

Perf. 13x13½, 13½x13

1979, Mar. 27

Design: 6.50b, Runner and Games emblem (horiz.).

639	A222	6.50b multi	1.20	28
640	A222	10b multi	1.75	48

Southern Cross Sports Games, Bolivia, Nov. 3–12, 1978.

A souvenir sheet contains 1 stamp similar to No. 640 with simulated perforations. Multicolored margin shows various exhibition and sports emblems. Sold for 20b. Size: 80x130mm.

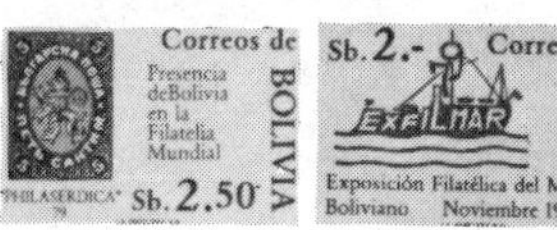

Bulgaria No. 1
A223

EXFILMAR Emblem
A224

1979, Mar. 30 *Perf. 10½*

641 A223 2.50b multi 45 12

PHILASERDICA '79 International Philatelic Exhibition, Sofia, Bulgaria, May 18–27.

1979, Apr. 2

642 A226 6b multi 1.10 30

Bolivian Maritime Philatelic Exhibition, La Paz, Nov. 18–28.

OAS Emblem, Map of Bolivia—A226

1979, Oct. 22 Litho. *Perf. 14×13½*

644 A226 6b multi 1.10 30

Organization of American States, 9th Congress, La Paz, Oct.-Nov.

Franz Tamayo
A227

Bolivian and Japanese Flags, Hospital
A228

U.N. Emblem and Meeting
A229

Radio Tower and Waves
A230

1979, Dec.

645	A227	2.80b blk & gray	50	15
646	A228	5b multi	90	25
648	A229	5b multi	90	25
649	A230	6b multi	1.10	30

Franz Tamayo, lawyer, birth centenary; Japanese-Bolivian health care cooperation; CEPAL, 18th Congress, La Paz, Sept. 18-26; Bolivian National Radio, 50th anniversary.

Puerto Suarez Iron Ore Deposits—A231

1979 Litho. *Perf. 13½x14*

650 A231 9.50b multi 1.70 45

Bolivia No. 19, EXFILMAR Emblem, Bolivian Flag—A232

1980 Litho. *Perf. 13½*

651 A232 4b multi 72 16

EXFILMAR, Bolivian Maritime Philatelic Exhibition, La Paz, Nov. 18-28, 1979.

Juana Azurduy on Horseback—A233

1980 Litho. *Perf. 14x13½*

652 A233 4b multi 72 16

Juana Azurduy de Padilla, independence fighter, birth bicentenary.

La Salle and World Map—A234

1980 *Perf. 13½x14*
653 A234 9b multi 1.60 40

St. Jean Baptiste de la Salle (1651-1719), educator.

"Victory" in Chariot, Madrid, Exhibition Emblem, Flags of Bolivia and Spain—A235

1980, Oct. **Litho.** *Perf. 13½x14*
654 A235 14b multi 2.50 65

ESPAMER '80 Stamp Exhibition, Madrid.

Map of South America, Flags of Argentina, Bolivia and Peru—A236

1980, Oct. *Perf. 14x13½*
655 A236 2b multi 36 8

Ministers of Public Works and Transport of Argentina, Bolivia and Peru meeting.

Santa Cruz-Trinidad Railroad, Inauguration of Third Section—A237

1980, Oct.
656 A237 3b multi 52 12

Flag on Provincial Map
A238

Ara Macao
A239

1981, May 11 Litho. *Perf. 14x13½, 13½x14*

657	A238	1b Soldier, flag, map	18	4
658	A238	3b Flag, map	52	12
659	A238	40b shown	7.25	1.60
660	A238	50b Soldier, civilians, horiz.	9.00	2.00

July 17 Revolution memorial.

1981, May 11 *Perf. 14x13½*

Designs: Parrots.

661	A239	4b shown	72	16
662	A239	7b Ara chloroptera	1.25	32
663	A239	8b Ara ararauna	1.50	35
664	A239	9b Ara rubrogenys	1.60	40
665	A239	10b Ara auricollis	1.75	42
666	A239	12b Anodorynchus hyacinthinus	2.25	60
667	A239	15b Ara militaris	2.75	75
668	A239	20b Ara severa	3.50	85
		Nos. 661-668 (8)	15.32	3.85

Christmas 1981
A240

1981, Dec. 7 **Litho.** *Perf. 10½*
669 A240 1b Virgin and Child, vert. 18 4
670 A240 2b Child, star 36 8

American Airforces Commanders' 22nd Conference, Buenos Aires—A241

1982, Apr. 12 **Litho.** *Perf. 13½*
671 A241 14b multi 2.50 70

75th Anniv. of Cobija
A242

Simon Bolivar Birth Bicentenary (1983)
A243

1982, July 8 **Litho.** *Perf. 13½*
672 A242 28b multi 62 24

1982, July 12
673 A243 18b multi 40 16

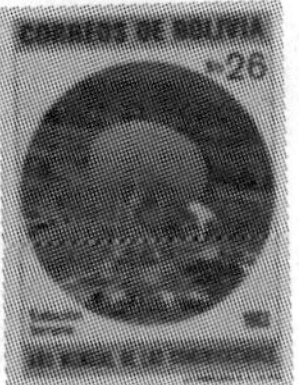

1983 World Telecommunications Day
A244

1982 World Cup
A245

1982, July 15
674 A244 26b Receiving station 58 20

1982, July 21 *Perf. 11*
675 A245 4b shown 10 4
676 A245 100b Final Act, by Picasso 2.25 90

Girl Playing Piano—A246

1982, July 25 *Perf. 13½*
677 A246 16b Boy playing soccer 35 14
678 A246 20b shown 45 18

Bolivian-Chinese Agricultural Cooperation, 1972-1982—A247

1982, Aug. 12
679 A247 30b multi 65 26

First Bolivian-Japanese Gastroenterology Conference, La Paz, Jan—A248

1982, Aug. 26
680 A248 22b multi 50 20

10th Anniv. of Bolivian Philatelic Federation—A249

1982, Aug. 31 **Litho.** *Perf. 14x13½*
681 A249 19b Stamps 40 15

Pres. Hernando Siles Birth Centenary—A250

1982, Sept. 1
682 A250 20b tan & dk brn 45 18

Scouting Year
A251

Cochabamba Philatelic Center, 25th Anniv.
A252

1982, Sept. 3 *Perf. 11*
683 A251 5b Baden-Powell 12 5

1982, Sept. 14
684 A252 3b multi 6 3

Cochabamba Superior Court of Justice Sesquicentennial—A253

1982 **Litho.** *Perf. 13½*
685 A253 10b multi 25 10

Enthronement of Virgin of Copacabana, 400th Anniv.
A254

Navy Day
A255

1982, Nov. 15 **Litho.** *Perf. 13½*
686 A254 13b multi 34 15

1982, Nov. 17
687 A255 14b Port Busch Naval Base 35 15

Christmas 1982—A256

1982, Nov. 19 *Perf. 11*
688 A256 10b grn & gray 25 10

10th Youth Soccer Championship, Jan. 22-Feb. 13—A257

1983, Feb. 13 **Litho.** *Perf. 13½*
689 A257 50b multi 1.25 50

AIR POST STAMPS.

Aviation School
AP1 AP2

Engraved.

1924, Dec. *Perf. 14* **Unwmkd.**

C1	AP1	10c ver & blk	35	35
a.		Inverted center	1,100.	
C2	AP1	15c car & blk	1.50	1.00
C3	AP1	25c dk bl & blk	75	50
C4	AP1	50c org & blk	1.50	1.00
C5	AP2	1b red brn & blk	1.50	1.50
C6	AP2	2b blk brn & blk	3.00	3.00
C7	AP2	5b dk vio & blk	5.00	5.00
		Nos. C1-C7 (7)	13.60	12.35

Issued to commemorate the establishing of the National Aviation School.

These stamps were available for ordinary postage. Nos. C1, C3, C5 and C6 exist imperforate. Proofs of the 2b with inverted center exist imperforate and privately perforated.

Emblem of Lloyd Aéreo Boliviano
AP3

1928 **Lithographed.** *Perf. 11.*

C8	AP3	15c green	1.50	85
a.		Imperf. (pair)	35.00	
C9	AP3	20c dk bl	30	15
C10	AP3	35c red brn	1.00	50

Graf Zeppelin Issues.

Nos. C1-C5 Surcharged or Overprinted in Various Colors:

CORREO AEREO
R. S. 6-V-1930
5 Cts.
a

CORREO AEREO
R. S.
6-V- 1930
b

1930, May 6 *Perf. 14.*

C11	AP1 (a)	5c on 10c ver & blk (G)	15.00	15.00
C12	AP1 (b)	10c ver & blk (Bl)	15.00	15.00
C13	AP1 (b)	10c ver & blk (Br)	750.00	1,000.
C14	AP1 (b)	15c car & blk (V)	15.00	15.00
C15	AP1 (b)	25c dk bl & blk (R)	15.00	15.00
C16	AP1 (b)	50c org & blk (Br)	15.00	15.00
C17	AP1 (b)	50c org & blk (R)	750.00	1,000.
C18	AP2 (b)	1b red brn & blk (gold)	175.00	150.00

Experts consider the 50c with silver overprint to be a trial color proof.

Surcharged or Overprinted in Bronze Inks of Various Colors.

C19	AP1 (a)	5c on 10c ver & blk (G)	85.00	85.00
C20	AP1 (b)	10c ver & blk (Bl)	70.00	70.00
C21	AP1 (b)	15c car & blk (V)	85.00	85.00
C22	AP1 (b)	25c dk bl & blk (cop)	85.00	85.00
C23	AP2 (b)	1b red brn & blk (gold)	175.00	175.00

Issued in commemoration of the flight of the airship Graf Zeppelin from Europe to Brazil and return via Lakehurst, N.J.

Nos. C11 to C18 exist with the surcharges inverted, double, or double with one inverted, but the regularity of these varieties is questioned.

Nos. C19 to C23 were intended for use on postal matter forwarded by the Graf Zeppelin.

No. C18 was overprinted with light gold or gilt bronze ink. No. C23 was overprinted with deep gold bronze ink. Nos. C13 and C17 were overprinted with trial colors but were sold with the regular printings. The 5c on 10c is known surcharged in black and in blue.

Air Post Stamps of 1928 Issue, Surcharged

Z 1930
Bs. 3.—

1930, May 6 *Perf. 11.*

C24	AP3	1.50b on 15c grn	40.00	40.00
a.		Inverted surcharge	80.00	80.00
b.		Comma instead of period after "1"	50.00	50.00
C25	AP3	3b on 20c dk bl	40.00	40.00
a.		Inverted surcharge	80.00	80.00
b.		Comma instead of period after "3"	55.00	55.00
C26	AP3	6b on 35c red brn	60.00	65.00
a.		Inverted surcharge	135.00	135.00
b.		Comma instead of period after "6"	75.00	75.00

Airplane and Bullock Cart AP6 — Airplane and River Boat AP7

1930, July 24 **Litho.** *Perf. 14*

C27	AP6	5c dp vio	75	50
C28	AP7	15c red	75	50
C29	AP7	20c yellow	75	50
C30	AP6	35c yel grn	75	25
C31	AP7	50c dp bl	75	25
C32	AP6	1b lt brn	75	25
C33	AP7	2b dp rose	75	35
C34	AP6	3b slate	4.00	2.25
		Nos. C27-C34 (8)	9.25	4.85

Nos. C27 to C34 exist imperforate.

Air Service Emblem
AP8

1932, Sept. 16 *Perf. 11.*

C35	AP8	5c ultra	1.25	75
C36	AP8	10c gray	75	35
C37	AP8	15c dk rose	1.25	1.00
C38	AP8	25c orange	1.25	1.00
C39	AP8	30c green	1.00	50
C40	AP8	50c violet	1.00	50
C41	AP8	1b dk brn	1.00	50
		Nos. C35-C41 (7)	7.50	4.60

Map of Bolivia
AP9

1935, Feb. 1 **Engraved.** *Perf. 12.*

C42	AP9	5c brn red	25	20
C43	AP9	10c dk grn	25	20
C44	AP9	20c dk vio	25	20
C45	AP9	30c ultra	25	20
C46	AP9	50c orange	40	20
C47	AP9	1b bis brn	40	35
C48	AP9	1½b yellow	1.00	20
C49	AP9	2b carmine	1.00	40
C50	AP9	5b green	2.00	50
C51	AP9	10b dk brn	3.00	1.00
		Nos. C42-C51 (10)	8.80	3.45

Air Post Stamps of 1924-30 Surcharged in Red or Green

Correo Aéreo
D. S. 25-2-37
0.05
c

1937, Oct. 6 *Perf. 11, 14.*

C52	AP6	5c on 35c yel grn (R)	50	40
a.		"Carreo"	15.00	
C53	AP3	50c on 35c red brn (R)	60	40
C54	AP3	50c on 35c red brn (R)	75	60
a.		Inverted surcharge	25.00	
C55	AP3	1b on 35c red brn (R)	1.50	75
C56	AP1	2b on 50c org & blk (R)	2.00	1.00
C57	AP1	12b on 10c ver & blk (G)	7.50	5.00
a.		Inverted surcharge	30.00	
C58	AP1	15b on 10c ver & blk (G)	7.50	3.00

Regular Postage Stamps of 1925 Surcharged in Green or Red

Correo
Aéreo
D. S.
25-2-37
Bs. 4.—
d

Perf. 14.

C59	A56 (d)	3b on 50c dp vio (G)	2.00	1.50
C60	A56 (d)	4b on 1b red (G)	2.50	2.00
C61	A57 (c)	5b on 2b org (G)	3.00	2.50
C62	A56 (d)	10b on 5b blk brn (R)	7.50	5.00
a.		Double surcharge	50.00	
		Nos. C52-C62 (11)	35.35	22.15

Courtyard of Potosí Mint
AP10

Miner
AP11

Emancipated Woman
AP12

Pincers, Torch and Good Will Principles
AP15

Airplane over Field
AP13

Airplanes and Liberty Monument
AP14

Airplane over River
AP16

Emblem of New Government
AP17

Transport Planes over Map of Bolivia
AP18

1938, May **Lithographed.** *Perf. 10½.*

C63	AP10	20c dp rose	35	30
C64	AP11	30c gray	35	30
C65	AP12	40c yellow	35	30
C66	AP13	50c yel grn	50	30
C67	AP14	60c dl bl	50	30
C68	AP15	1b dl red	75	30
C69	AP16	2b bister	1.75	30
C70	AP17	3b lt brn	1.75	30
C71	AP18	5b dk vio	2.50	30
		Nos. C63-C71 (9)	8.80	2.70

Chalice
AP19

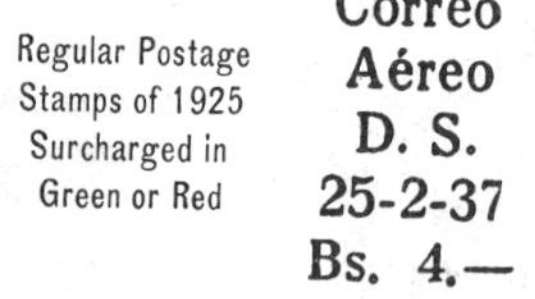

Virgin of Copacabana
AP20

Jesus Christ
AP21

Church of San Francisco, La Paz
AP22

St. Anthony of Padua
AP23

Lithographed.

1939, July 19 ***Perf. 13½, 10½.***

C72	AP19	5c dl vio	90	50
a.		Pair, imperf. between	60.00	
C73	AP20	30c lt bl grn	75	30
C74	AP21	45c vio bl	90	30
a.		Vertical pair, imperf. between	85.00	
C75	AP22	60c carmine	90	60
C76	AP23	75c vermilion	1.25	1.00
C77	AP23	90c dp bl	1.00	40
C78	AP22	2b dl brn	1.75	40
C79	AP21	4b dp plum	2.50	60
C80	AP20	5b lt bl	5.00	40
C81	AP19	10b yellow	12.50	40
		Nos. C72-C81 (10)	27.45	4.90

Issued to commemorate the second National Eucharistic Congress.

Plane over Lake Titicaca
AP24

Mt. Illimani and Condor
AP25

1941, Aug. 21 ***Perf. 13½.***

C82	AP24	10b dl grn	7.00	75
C83	AP24	20b lt ultra	8.00	1.25
C84	AP25	50b rose lil	15.00	1.75
C85	AP25	100b ol bis	35.00	6.00

Counterfeits exist.

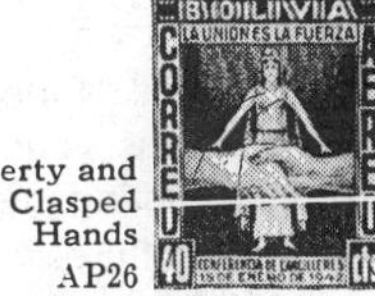

Liberty and Clasped Hands
AP26

1942, Nov. 12

C86	AP26	40c rose lake	50	35
C87	AP26	50c ultra	50	35
C88	AP26	1b org brn	60	50
C89	AP26	5b magenta	2.00	35
a.		Double impression		
C90	AP26	10b dl brn vio	6.00	2.50
		Nos. C86-C90 (5)	9.60	4.05

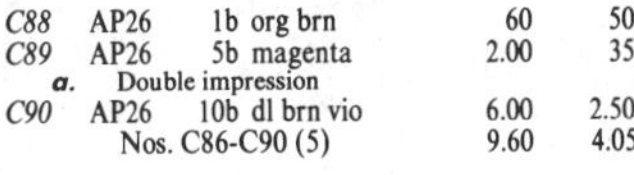

Issued to commemorate the Conference of Chancellors held January 15, 1942.

General José Ballivián; Old and Modern Transportation
AP27

1943, Nov. 18 **Engr.** ***Perf. 12½***

C91	AP27	10c rose vio & brn	15	15
C92	AP27	20c emer & brn	20	15
C93	AP27	30c rose car & brn	30	25
C94	AP27	3b bl & brn	40	30
C95	AP27	5b blk & brn	90	50
		Nos. C91-C95 (5)	1.95	1.35

Department of Beni centenary.

Condor and Sun Rising
AP28

Plane
AP29

Lithographed.

1944, Sept. 19 ***Perf. 13½.***

C96	AP28	40c red vio	15	10
C97	AP28	1b lt vio	20	10
C98	AP29	1.50b yel grn	25	10
C99	AP29	2.50b dk gray bl	50	25

Revolution of Dec. 20, 1943.

Map of National Airways
AP30

Map of Bolivian Air Lines
AP31

1945, May 31 ***Perf. 11***

C100	AP30	10c red	15	10
a.		Imperf. (pair)	12.50	
C101	AP30	50c yellow	20	10
a.		Imperf. (pair)	20.00	
C102	AP30	90c lt grn	30	10
C103	AP30	5b lt ultra	50	20
C104	AP30	20b dp brn	1.50	60
		Nos. C100-C104 (5)	2.65	1.10

10th anniversary of first flight, La Paz to Tacna, Peru, by Panagra Airways.

Centers in Red and Blue.

1945, Sept. 15 ***Perf. 13½.***

C105	AP31	20c violet	12	10
C106	AP31	30c org brn	12	10
C107	AP31	50c brt bl grn	12	10
C108	AP31	90c brt vio	12	10
C109	AP31	2b blue	20	15
C110	AP31	3b magenta	30	20
C111	AP31	4b ol bis	50	25
		Nos. C105-C111 (7)	1.48	1.00

Issued to commemorate the 20th anniversary of the founding of Lloyd Aéreo Boliviano.

No. C76 Surcharged in Blue

1947, Mar. 23

C112	AP23	1.40b on 75c ver	30	30

Mt. Illimani
AP32

Arms of Bolivia and Argentina
AP33

1947, Sept. 15 **Litho.** ***Perf. 11½***

C113	AP32	1b rose car	10	10
C114	AP32	1.40b emerald	15	10
C115	AP32	2.50b blue	25	20
C116	AP32	3b dp org	35	30
C117	AP32	4b rose lil	40	25
		Nos. C113-C117 (5)	1.25	95

Issued to commemorate the first anniversary of the Revolution of July 21, 1946.

1947, Oct. 23 ***Perf. 13½***

C118	AP33	2.90b ultra	40	40
a.		Imperf. (pair)	30.00	
b.		Perf. 10½	7.50	6.00

Issued to commemorate the meeting of Presidents Enrique Hertzog of Bolivia and Juan D. Perón of Argentina at Yacuiba, Oct. 23, 1947.

Types of Regular Issue of 1948.

Designs: 2.50b, Statue of Christ above La Paz. 3.70b, Child kneeling before cross. No. C121, St. John Bosco. No. C122, Virgin of Copacabana. 13.60b, Pope Pius XII blessing University of La Paz.

1948, Sept. 26 ***Perf. 11½.***

C119	A120	2.50b ver & yel	1.00	50
C120	A120	3.70b rose & cr	1.25	50
C121	A120	4b rose lil & gray	1.25	40
C122	A120	4b lt ultra & sal	1.25	25
C123	A120	13.60b ultra & lt grn	1.50	40
		Nos. C119-C123 (5)	6.25	2.05

Issued to publicize the 3rd Inter-American Congress of Catholic Education.

Type of Regular Issue of 1948

1948, Oct.

C124	A125	10b emer & sal	3.00	30

Issued to publicize the International Automobile Races of South America, September–October 1948.

Pres. Gregorio Pacheco, Map and Post Horn
AP34

L. A. B. Plane
AP35

1950, Jan. 2 **Unwmkd.**

C125	AP34	1.40b org brn	15	15
C126	AP34	2.50b orange	10	10
C127	AP34	3.30b rose vio	15	15

Issued to commemorate the 75th anniversary of the formation of the Universal Postal Union.

Nos. C100 and C104 Surcharged in Black

XV ANIVERSARIO PANAGRA Bs 4.- 1935-1950

1950, May 31 ***Perf. 11.***

C128	AP30	4b on 10c red	15	15
C129	AP30	10b on 20b dp brn	40	30
a.		Inverted surcharge	25.00	25.00

Issued to commemorate the 15th anniversary of Panagra air services in Bolivia.

1950, Sept. 15 **Litho.** ***Perf. 13½***

C130	AP35	20c red org	15	15
C131	AP35	30c purple	15	15
C132	AP35	50c green	15	15
C133	AP35	1b orange	15	15
C134	AP35	3b ultra	15	15
C135	AP35	15b carmine	50	20
C136	AP35	50b chocolate	1.50	50
		Nos. C130-C136 (7)	2.75	1.45

Issued to commemorate the 25th anniversary of the founding of Lloyd Aéreo Boliviano. No. C132 exists imperforate.

No. C116 Surcharged in Black

Triunfo de la Democracia 24 de Sept.49 Bs. 1.40

1950, Sept. 24 ***Perf. 11½***

C137	AP32	1.40b on 3b dp org	25	25

Issued to commemorate the 1st anniversary of the ending of the Civil War of Aug. 24–Sept. 24, 1949.

Symbols of United Nations
AP36

1950, Oct. 24 **Unwmkd.**

C138	AP36	3.60b crim rose	1.00	25
C139	AP36	4.70b blk brn	1.25	25

Issued to commemorate the 5th anniversary of the formation of the United Nations, October 24, 1945.

Gate of the Sun and Llama
AP37

Church of San Francisco
AP38

Designs: 40c, Avenue Camacho. 50c, Consistorial Palace. 1b, Legislative Palace. 2b, Communications Bldg. 3b, Arms. 4b, La Gasca ordering Mendoza to found La Paz. 5b, Capt. Alonso de Mendoza founding La Paz. 10b, Arms; portrait of Mendoza.

1951, Mar. 1 **Engr.** ***Perf. 12½.***

Center in Black.

C140	AP37	20c carmine	20	20
C141	AP38	30c dk vio bl	20	20
C142	AP37	40c dk bl	20	20
C143	AP37	50c bl grn	25	25
C144	AP37	1b red	30	30
C145	AP37	2b red org	50	50

C146	AP37	3b dp bl	50	50
C147	AP37	4b vermilion	60	60
a.		Souv. sheet of 4	1.50	1.50
C148	AP37	5b dk grn	60	60
a.		Souv. sheet of 3	1.50	1.50
C149	AP37	10b red brn	1.00	1.00
a.		Souv. sheet of 3	1.50	1.50
		Nos. C140-C149 (10)	4.35	4.35

400th anniversary of the founding of La Paz.

No. C147a contains C143–C145, C147; No. C148a contains C142, C146, C148; No. C149a contains 140, C141, C149. Black marginal inscriptions. Perf. and imperf., size: 150x100mm.

Horsemanship

AP39

Designs: 30c, Basketball. 50c, Fencing. 1b, Hurdling. 2.50b, Javelin throwing. 3b, Relay race. 5b, La Paz stadium.

1951, Aug. 23 **Unwmkd.**

Center in Black.

C150	AP39	20c purple	35	10
C151	AP39	30c rose vio	50	15
C152	AP39	50c dp red org	75	15
C153	AP39	1b chocolate	75	15
C154	AP39	2.50b orange	1.00	60
C155	AP39	3b blk brn	1.50	75
a.		Souv. sheet of 3	6.00	5.00
C156	AP39	5b red	3.00	1.50
a.		Souv. sheet of 4	7.00	6.50
		Nos. C150-C156 (7)	7.85	3.40

The stamps were intended to commemorate the 5th South American Games and the 2nd National Sports Congress held at La Paz, October 1948.

No. C155a contains C153–C155; No. C156a contains C150–C152, C156. Black marginal inscriptions. Perf. and imperf., size: 150x100mm.

Eduardo Abaroa AP40

Queen Isabella I AP41

1952, Mar. 24 Litho. ***Perf. 11***

C157	AP40	70c rose red	15	15
C158	AP40	2b org yel	20	25
C159	AP40	3b yel grn	20	25
C160	AP40	5b blue	25	25
C161	AP40	50b rose lil	1.75	75
C162	AP40	100b gray blk	2.00	1.00
		Nos. C157-C162 (6)	4.55	2.65

Issued to commemorate the 73rd anniversary of the death of Eduardo Abaroa.

1952, July 16 ***Perf. 13½***

C163	AP41	50b emerald	60	40
C164	AP41	100b brown	1.25	50

Issued to commemorate the 500th anniversary of the birth of Queen Isabella I of Spain. Exist imperforate.

Columbus Lighthouse

AP42

1952, July 16

C165	AP42	2b rose lil, *sal*	15	15
C166	AP42	3.70b bl grn, *bl*	15	15
C167	AP42	4.40b org, *sal*	25	10
C168	AP42	20b dk brn, *cr*	50	18

No. C168 exists imperforate.

Soldiers AP43

Gualberto Villarroel, Victor Paz Estenssoro and Hernan Siles Zuazo

AP44

Perf. 13½ (AP43), 11½ (AP44)

1953, Apr. 9 Lithographed

C169	AP44	3.70b chocolate	20	20
C170	AP43	6b red vio	20	20
C171	AP44	9b brn rose	20	20
C172	AP44	10b aqua	20	20
C173	AP44	16b vermilion	20	20
C174	AP43	22.50b dk brn	40	30
C175	AP44	40b gray	60	20
		Nos. C169-C175 (7)	2.00	1.50

Issued to commemorate the first anniversary of the Revolution of Apr. 9, 1952. Nos. C170 and C174 exist imperf.

Pres. Victor Paz Estenssoro Embracing Indian

AP45

Map and Peasant

AP46

1954, Aug. 2 ***Perf. 12x11½.***

C176	AP45	20b org brn	15	10
C177	AP46	27b brt pink	15	20
C178	AP46	30b red org	25	15
C179	AP46	45b vio brn	40	10
C180	AP45	100b bl grn	75	10
C181	AP46	300b yel grn	2.00	35
		Nos. C176-C181 (6)	3.70	1.00

Nos. C176 and C180 were issued to commemorate the 3rd Inter-American Indian Congress. Nos. C177–C179 and C181 commemorate the agrarian reform laws of 1953–1954.

Oil Derricks

AP47

Map of South America and La Paz Arms

AP48

1955, Oct. 9 ***Perf. 10½***

C182	AP47	55b dk & lt grnsh bl	15	10
C183	AP47	70b dk gray & gray	25	10
C184	AP47	90b dk & lt grn	30	15

Perf. 13.

C185	AP47	500b red lil	1.50	60
C186	AP47	1000b blk brn & fawn	2.50	1.50
		Nos. C182-C186 (5)	4.70	2.45

Nos. C140–C149 Surcharged with New Values and Bars in Black or Carmine.

1957 **Engraved.** ***Perf. 12½***

Center in Black

C187	AP37	100b on 3b dp bl (C)	15	10
C188	AP37	200b on 2b red org	15	10
C189	AP37	500b on 4b ver	25	15
C190	AP37	600b on 1b red	25	15
C191	AP37	700b on 20c car	40	20
C192	AP37	800b on 40c dk bl (C)	50	30
C193	AP38	900b on 30c dk vio bl (C)	60	15
C194	AP37	1800b on 50c bl grn (C)	1.00	50
C195	AP37	3000b on 5b dk grn (C)	1.50	90
C196	AP37	5000b on 10b red brn (C)	2.50	1.75
		Nos. C187-C196 (10)	7.30	4.30

Lithographed.

1957, May 25 ***Perf. 12*** **Unwmkd.**

C197	AP48	700b lil & vio	60	40
C198	AP48	1200b pale brn	75	60
C199	AP48	1350b rose car	1.00	75
C200	AP48	2700b bl grn	2.00	1.00
C201	AP48	4000b vio bl	2.50	1.25
		Nos. C197-C201 (5)	6.85	4.00

Issued to commemorate the seventh session of the C. E. P. A. L. (Comision Economica para la America Latina de las Naciones Unidas), La Paz.

Type of Regular Issue, 1957

1957, Dec. 19 ***Perf. 11½***

C202	A141	600b magenta	35	10
C203	A141	700b vio bl	50	18
C204	A141	900b pale grn	75	12

Issued to commemorate the opening of the Santa Cruz-Yacuiba Railroad and the meeting of the Presidents of Bolivia and Argentina.

Type of Regular Issue, 1960.

1960, Jan. 30

C205	A142	400b rose cl	75	15
C206	A142	800b sl bl	1.00	30
C207	A142	2000b slate	1.50	60

Issued for an expected visit of Mexico's Pres. Adolfo Lopez Mateos. On sale Jan. 30-Feb. 1, 1960.

Gate of the Sun, Tiahuanacu

AP49

Uprooted Oak Emblem

AP50

1960, Mar. 26 Litho. ***Perf. 11½***

C208	AP49	3,000b gray	2.00	75
C209	AP49	5,000b orange	3.00	1.50
C210	AP49	10,000b rose cl	6.00	2.50
C211	AP49	15,000b bl vio	9.00	4.00

1960, Apr. 7 ***Perf. 11½***

C212	AP50	600b ultra	50	50
C213	AP50	700b lt red brn	50	50
C214	AP50	900b dk bl grn	60	50
C215	AP50	1,800b violet	1.00	1.00
C216	AP50	2,000b gray	1.25	1.00
		Nos. C212-C216 (5)	3.85	3.50

Issued to publicize World Refugee Year, July 1, 1959–June 30, 1960.

No. C215 exists with "1961" overprint in dark carmine, but was not regularly issued in this form.

Jaime Laredo AP51

Lithographed

1960, Aug. 15 ***Perf. 11½*** **Unwmkd.**

C217	AP51	600b rose vio	1.25	40
C218	AP51	700b ol gray	1.50	50
C219	AP51	800b vio brn	1.50	50
C220	AP51	900b dk bl	2.00	50
C221	AP51	1,800b green	2.50	1.50
C222	AP51	4,000b dk gray	6.00	2.50
		Nos. C217-C222 (6)	14.75	5.90

Issued to honor the violinist Jaime Laredo.

Type of Regular Issue, 1960.
(Children's Hospital)

1960, Nov. 21 ***Perf. 11½***

C223	A146	600b red brn, yel & dp bl	60	35
C224	A146	1,000b ol grn, yel & dp bl	90	35
C225	A146	1,800b plum, yel & dp bl	1.25	60
C226	A146	5,000b blk, yel & dp bl	4.00	1.75

Issued for the Children's Hospital, sponsored by the Rotary Club of La Paz.

Pres. Paz Estenssoro and Pres. Getulio Vargas of Brazil

AP52

1960, Dec. 14 Litho. ***Perf. 11½***

C227	AP52	1,200b on 10b org & blk	1.25	1.00

Exists with surcharge inverted.

No. C227 without surcharge was not regularly issued, although a decree authorizing its circulation was published. Counterfeits of surcharge exist.

Pres. Paz Estenssoro and Pres. Frondizi of Argentina

AP53

Design: 4,000b, Flags of Bolivia and Argentina.

1961, May 23 ***Perf. 10½***

C228	AP53	4,000b brn, red, yel, grn & bl	1.00	90
C229	AP53	6,000b dk grn & blk	1.50	1.25

Issued to commemorate the visit of the President of Argentina, Dr. Arturo Frondizi, to Bolivia.

See "Special Notices" at the front of this volume for data on the listing methods of this Catalogue, abbreviations, condition, prices and examination.

Miguel de Cervantes
AP54

1961, Oct. Photogravure *Perf. 13*

C230	AP54	1400b pale grn & dk ol grn	75	35

Issued to commemorate Cervantes' appointment as Chief Magistrate of La Paz.

Virgin of Cotoca and Symbol of Eucharist
AP55

Planes and Parachutes
AP56

1962, Mar. 19 Litho. *Perf. 10½*

C231	AP55	1400b brn, pink & yel	1.00	50

Issued to commemorate the 4th National Eucharistic Congress, Santa Cruz, 1961.

Nos. C212–C216 Surcharged Vertically with New Value and Greek Key Border.

1962, June *Perf. 11½* Unwmkd.

C232	AP50	1,200b on 600b ultra	1.00	50
C233	AP50	1,300b on 700b lt red brn	90	50
C234	AP50	1,400b on 900b dk bl grn	1.00	50
C235	AP50	2,800b on 1,800b vio	1.50	75
C236	AP50	3,000b on 2,000b gray	1.50	75
		Nos. C232-C236 (5)	5.90	3.00

The overprinted segment of Greek key border on Nos. C232–C236 comes in two positions: two full "keys" on top, and one full and two half keys on top.

Flower Type of 1962

Flowers: 100b, 1,800b, Cantua buxifolia. 800b, 10,000b, Cantua bicolor.

1962, June 28 Litho. *Perf. 10½*

Flowers in Natural Colors

C237	A152	100b dk bl	10	10
C238	A152	800b green	50	25
C239	A152	1,800b violet	1.00	50
a.		Souv. sheet of 3	5.00	5.00
C240	A152	10,000b dk bl	6.00	3.00

No. C239a contains 3 imperf. stamps similar to Nos. C237–C239, but with the 1,800b background color changed to dark violet blue. Green marginal inscriptions. Size: 130x80mm.

1962, Sept. 5 Litho. *Perf. 11½*

Designs: 1,200b, 5,000b, Plane and oxcart. 2,000b, Aerial photography (plane over South America).

Emblem in Red, Yellow & Green

C241	AP56	600b blk & bl	35	20
C242	AP56	1200b multi	50	30
C243	AP56	2000b multi	60	50
C244	AP56	5000b multi	1.50	1.00

Armed Forces of Bolivia.

Malaria Type of 1962

Design: Inscription around mosquito, laurel around globe.

1962, Oct. 4

C245	A154	2000b ind, grn & yel	1.25	75

Issued for the World Health Organization drive to eradicate malaria.

Type of Regular Issue, 1961

Design: 1,200b Pedro de la Gasca (1485–1567).

Photogravure

1962 *Perf. 13x12½* Unwmkd.

C246	A150	1,200b brn, *yel*	50	30

Condor, Soccer Ball and Flags
AP57

Alliance for Progress Emblem
AP58

Design: 1.80p, Map of Bolivia, soccer ball, goal and flags.

1963, Mar. 21 Litho. *Perf. 11½*

Flags in National Colors

C247	AP57	1.40p blk, ocher & red	1.50	1.00
C248	AP57	1.80p blk, red & ocher	1.50	1.00

Issued to publicize the 21st South American Soccer Championships.

Freedom from Hunger Issue

Type of Regular Issue

Design: 1.20p, Wheat, globe and wheat emblem.

1963, Aug. 1 *Perf. 11½* Unwmkd.

C249	A156	1.20p dk grn, bl & yel	1.00	75

Issued for the "Freedom from Hunger" campaign of the U.N. Food and Agriculture Organization.

1963, Nov. 15 *Perf. 11½*

C250	AP58	1.20p dl yel, ultra & grn	1.25	50

Issued to commemorate the second anniversary of the Alliance for Progress, which aims to stimulate economic growth and raise living standards in Latin America.

Type of Regular Issue, 1963

Designs: 1.20p, Ballot box and voters. 1.40p, Map and farmer breaking chain. 2.80p, Miners.

1963, Dec. 21 *Perf. 11½*

C251	A157	1.20p gray, dk brn & rose	60	30
C252	A157	1.40p bis & grn	75	40
C253	A157	2.80p sl & buff	1.50	75

Issued to commemorate the 10th anniversary of the Revolution of Apr. 9, 1952.

Andrés Santa Cruz
AP59

Lithographed

1966, Aug. 10 *Perf. 13½* Wmk. 90

C254	AP59	20c dp bl	15	10
C255	AP59	60c dp grn	30	15
C256	AP59	1.20p red brn	75	25
C257	AP59	2.80p black	1.25	60

Issued to commemorate the centenary (in 1965) of the death of Marshal Andrés Santa Cruz (1792–1865), president of Bolivia and of Peru-Bolivia Confederation.

Children Type of 1966

Design: 1.40p, Mother and children.

1966, Dec. 16 *Perf. 13½* Unwmkd.

C258	A159	1.40p gray bl & blk	1.50	65

Issued to help poor children.

Co-Presidents Type of Regular Issue

1966, Dec. 16 Litho. *Perf. 12½*

Flag in Red, Yellow and Green

C259	A160	2.80p gray & tan	2.50	1.50
C260	A160	10p sep & tan	3.00	1.75
a.		Souv. sheet of 4	10.00	10.00

Issued to honor Generals Rene Barrientos Ortuno and Alfredo Ovando C., Co-Presidents, 1965–66.

No. C260a contains 4 imperf. stamps similar to Nos. 480–481 and C259–C260. Dark green marginal inscription. Size: 135x82mm.

Various Issues 1954–62 Surcharged with New Values and Bars

1966, Dec. 21

On No. C177:
"XII Aniversario / Reforma / Agraria"

C261	AP46	10c on 27b brt pink	20	20

On No. C182:
"XXV / Aniversario Paz / del Chaco"

C262	AP47	10c on 55b dk & lt grnsh bl	20	20

On No. C199:
"Centenario de / Tupiza"

C263	AP48	60c on 1350b rose car	30	30

On No. C200:
"XXV / Aniversario / Automovil Club / Boliviano"

C264	AP48	2.80p on 2700b bl grn	3.00	2.50

On No. C201:
"Centenario de la / Cruz Roja / Internacional"

C265	AP48	4p on 4000b vio bl	2.00	1.50

On No. C219:
"CL Aniversario / Heroinas Coronilla"

C266	AP51	1.20p on 800b vio brn	60	50

On No. C222:
"Centenario Himno / Paceño"

C267	AP51	1.40p on 4,000b dk gray	60	50

Nos. C224–C225 Surcharged

C268	A146	1.40p on 1,000b multi	60	60
C269	A146	1.40p on 1,800b multi	60	60

On Nos. C238–C239:
"Aniversario / Centro Filatelico / Cochabamba"

C270	A152	1.20p on 800b multi	50	40
C271	A152	1.20p on 1,800b multi	50	40

Revenue Stamp of 1946 Surcharged with New Value "X" and:
"XXV Aniversario / Dpto. Pando / Aéreo"

C272	A161	1.20p on 1b dk bl	75	60
		Nos. C261-C272 (12)	9.85	8.30

Lions Emblem and Pre-historic Sculptures
AP60

1967, Sept. 20 Litho. *Perf. 13x13½*

C273	AP60	2p red & multi	1.25	1.00
a.		Souv. sheet of 2	5.00	5.00

Issued to commemorate the 50th anniversary of Lions International. No. C273a contains 2 imperf. stamps similar to Nos. 492 and C273. Black marginal inscription. Size: 129x80mm.

Folklore Type of Regular Issue

Designs (Folklore characters): 1.20p, Pujllay. 1.40p, Ujusiris. 2p, Morenada. 3p, Auki-aukis.

1968, June 24 *Perf. 13½x13*

C274	A163	1.20b lt yel grn & multi	40	25
C275	A163	1.40b gray & multi	50	30
C276	A163	2b dk ol bis & multi	75	40
C277	A163	3b sky bl & multi	1.25	75

Issued to publicize the 9th Congress of the Postal Union of the Americas and Spain.

A souvenir sheet exists containing 4 imperf. stamps similar to Nos. C274–C277. Bister and gray marginal inscription. Size: 131x81½mm.

Moto Mendez
AP61

1968, Oct. 29 Litho. *Perf. 13½x13*

C278	AP61	1b dp org & multi	50	25
C279	AP61	1.20b lt ultra & multi	60	25
C280	AP61	2b bis brn & multi	1.00	50
C281	AP61	4b bluish lil & multi	1.50	75

Battle of Tablada sesquicentennial.

Pres. Guálberto Villaroël
AP62

1968, Nov. 6 *Perf. 13x13½*

C282	AP62	1.40b org & blk	50	40
C283	AP62	3b lt bl & blk	1.00	60
C284	AP62	4b rose & blk	1.25	75
C285	AP62	5b gray grn & blk	1.50	1.00
C286	AP62	10b pale pur & blk	3.00	2.00
		Nos. C282-C286 (5)	7.25	4.75

4th centenary of Cochabamba.

ITU Type of Regular Issue

1968, Dec. 3 Litho. *Perf. 13x13½*

C287	A166	1.20b gray, blk & yel	40	20
C288	A166	1.40b bl, blk & gray ol	50	30

Issued to commemorate the centenary (in 1965) of the International Telecommunication Union.

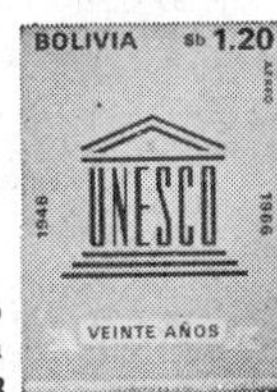

UNESCO Emblem
AP63

1968, Nov. 14 ***Perf. 13½x13***

C289	AP63	1.20b pale vio & blk	50	25
C290	AP63	2.80b yel grn & blk	1.00	50

Issued to commemorate the 20th anniversary (in 1966) of UNESCO (United Nations Educational, Scientific and Cultural Organization).

Kennedy Type of Regular Issue

1968, Nov. 22 **Unwmkd.**

C291	A168	1b grn & blk	50	30
C292	A168	10b scar & blk	3.50	2.00

Issued in memory of Pres. John F. Kennedy, 1917–1963.

A souvenir sheet contains one imperf. stamp similar to No. C291. Dark violet marginal inscription. Size: 131x81½mm.

Tennis Type of Regular Issue

1968, Dec. 10 ***Perf. 13x13½***

C293	A169	1.40b org, blk & lt brn	50	35
C294	A169	2.80b sky bl, blk & lt brn	1.00	75

Issued to commemorate the 32nd South American Tennis Championships, La Paz, 1965.

A souvenir sheet exists containing one imperf. stamp similar to No. C293. Light brown marginal inscription. Size: 131x 81½mm.

Stamp Centenary Type of Regular Issue

Design: 1.40b, 2.80b, 3b, Bolivia No. 1.

1968, Dec. 23 Litho. ***Perf. 13x13½***

C295	A170	1.40b org, grn & blk	75	35
C296	A170	2.80b pale rose, grn & blk	1.50	75
C297	A170	3b lt vio, grn & blk	1.50	75

Issued to commemorate the centenary of Bolivian postage stamps.

A souvenir sheet exists containing 3 imperf. stamps similar to Nos. C295–C297. Dark brown marginal inscription. Size: 131x81½mm.

Franklin D. Roosevelt
AP64

1969, Oct. 29 Litho. ***Perf. 13½x13***

C298	AP64	5b brn, blk & buff	2.00	1.50

Issued to honor Franklin D. Roosevelt (1882–1945), 32nd President of the United States.

Olympic Type of Regular Issue

Sports: 1.20b, Woman runner (vert.). 2.80b, Discus thrower (vert.). 5b, Hurdler.

Perf. 13½x13, 13x13½

1969, Oct. 29 **Lithographed**

C299	A171	1.20b yel grn, bis & blk	60	25
C300	A171	2.80b red, org & blk	1.25	50
C301	A171	5b bl, lt bl, red & blk	2.00	1.00

Issued to commemorate the 19th Olympic Games, Mexico City, Oct. 12–27, 1968.

A souvenir sheet exists containing 3 imperf. stamps similar to Nos. C299–C301. Marginal inscription in blue, yellow green and red brown. Size: 130½x81mm.

Butterfly Type of Regular Issue

Butterflies: 1b, Metamorpha dido wernichei. 1.80b, Heliconius felix. 2.80b, Morpho casica. 3b, Papilio yuracares. 4b, Heliconius melitus.

1970, Apr. 24 Litho. ***Perf. 13x13½***

C302	A172	1b sal & multi	50	20
C303	A172	1.80b lt bl & multi	75	40
C304	A172	2.80b multi	1.50	75
C305	A172	3b multi	2.00	75
C306	A172	4b multi	2.50	85
		Nos. C302-C306 (5)	7.25	2.95

A souvenir sheet exists containing 3 imperf. stamps similar to Nos. C302–C304. Black marginal inscription. Size: 129½x 80mm.

Scout Type of Regular Issue

Designs: 50c, Boy Scout building brick wall. 1.20b, Bolivian Boy Scout emblem.

1970, June 17 Litho. ***Perf. 13½x13***

C307	A173	50c yel & multi	20	10
C308	A173	1.20b multi	40	20

Issued to honor the Bolivian Boy Scout movement.

No. C228 Surcharged

1970, Dec. **Litho.** ***Perf. 10½***

C309	AP53	1.20b on 4,000b multi	40	20

Flower Type of Regular Issue

Bolivian Flowers: 1.20b, Amaryllis pseudopardina (horiz.). 1.40b, Rebutia kruegeri. 2.80b, Lobivia pentlandii (horiz.). 4b, Rebutia tunariensis.

Perf. 13x13½, 13½x13

1971, Aug. 9 **Litho.** **Unwmkd.**

C310	A174	1.20b multi	60	20
C311	A174	1.40b multi	75	25
C312	A174	2.80b multi	1.25	40
C313	A174	4b multi	2.00	75

Two souvenir sheets of 4 exist. One contains imperf. stamps similar to Nos. 534–535 and C310, C312. The other contains imperf. stamps similar to Nos. 536–537, C311, C313. Black marginal inscriptions. Size: 130x80mm.

Dance Type of Regular Issue

Folk Dances: 1.20b, Kusillo. 1.40b, Taquirari.

1972, Mar. 23 Litho. ***Perf. 13½x13***

C314	A177	1.20b yel & multi	75	25
C315	A177	1.40b org & multi	1.00	25

Two souvenir sheets of 3 exist. One contains imperf. stamps similar to Nos. 542–543, C314. The other contains imperf. stamps similar to Nos. 540–541, C315. Sheets have Sapporo '72 Olympic Games emblem in multicolor and marginal inscriptions in yellow, green and orange. Size: 80x129mm.

Painting Type of Regular Issue

Bolivian Paintings: 1.40b, Portrait of Chola Paceña, by Cecilio Guzmán de Rojas. 1.50b, Adoration of the Kings, by G. Gamarra. 1.60b, Adoration of Pachamama (mountain), by A. Borda. 2b, The Kiss of the Idol, by Guzman de Rojas.

1972 **Lithographed** ***Perf. 13½***

C316	A178	1.40b multi	60	25
C317	A178	1.50b multi	60	25
C318	A178	1.60b multi	60	25
C319	A178	2b multi	1.00	40

Two souvenir sheets of 2 exist. One contains imperf. stamps similar to Nos. 548 and C318. The other contains imperf. stamps similar to Nos. C317 and C319. Sheets have "Munich 1972," Olympic and Munich emblems in margins. Size: 129x80mm.

Issue dates: 1.40b, Dec. 4. Others, Aug. 17.

Bolivian Coat of Arms
AP65

1972, Dec. 4 ***Perf. 13½x14***

C320	AP65	4b lt bl & multi	2.00	1.50

Cactus Type of Regular Issue

Designs: Various cacti.

1973, Aug. 6 **Litho.** ***Perf. 13½***

C321	A180	1.20b tan & multi	50	20
C322	A180	1.90b org & multi	75	30
C323	A180	2b multi	1.00	40

Development Type of Regular Issue

Designs: 1.40b, Highway 1Y4. 2b, Bus crossing bridge.

1973, Nov. 26 **Litho.** ***Perf. 13½***

C324	A181	1.40b sal & multi	50	20
C325	A181	2b multi	75	30

Bolivia's development.

Santos-Dumont and 14-Bis Plane
AP66

1973, July 20

C326	AP66	1.40b yel & blk	1.00	50

Centenary of the birth of Alberto Santos-Dumont (1873–1932), Brazilian aviation pioneer.

Orchid Type of 1974

Orchids: 2.50b, Cattleya luteola (horiz.). 3.80b, Stanhopaea. 4b, Catasetum (horiz.). 5b, Maxillaria.

1974 **Lithographed** ***Perf. 13½***

C327	A182	2.50b multi	1.00	35
C328	A182	3.80b rose & multi	1.50	50
C329	A182	4b multi	2.00	60
C330	A182	5b sal & multi	2.50	70

Air Force Emblem, Plane over Map of Bolivia
AP67

Designs: 3.80b, Plane over Andes. 4.50b, Triple decker and jet. 8b, Rafael Pabon and double decker. 15b, Jet and "50."

1974 **Lithographed** ***Perf. 13x13½***

C331	AP67	3b multi	1.00	75
C332	AP67	3.80b multi	1.50	1.00
C333	AP67	4.50b multi	1.50	1.00
C334	AP67	8b multi	2.50	2.00
C335	AP67	15b multi	5.00	3.00
		Nos. C331-C335 (5)	11.50	7.75

Bolivian Air Force, 50th anniversary.

Coat of Arms Type of 1975

Designs: Departmental coats of arms.

1975, July 16 **Litho.** ***Perf. 13½***

Gold & Multicolored

C336	A188	20c *Beni*	10	10
C337	A188	30c *Tarija*	15	10
C338	A188	50c *Potosi*	15	15
C339	A188	1b *Oruro*	35	30
C340	A188	2.50b *Santa Cruz*	75	75
C341	A188	3b *La Paz*	1.00	75
		Nos. C336-C341 (6)	2.50	2.15

Sesquicentennial of Republic of Bolivia.

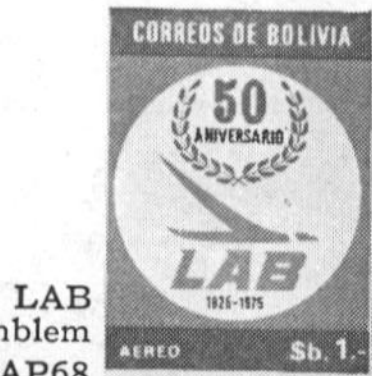

LAB Emblem
AP68

Bolivia on Map of Americas
AP69

Map of Bolivia, Plane and Kyllmann
AP70

1975 **Lithographed** ***Perf. 13½***

C342	AP68	1b gold, bl & blk	25	15
C343	AP69	1.50b multi	35	25
C344	AP70	2b multi	50	35

Lloyd Aereo Boliviano, 50th anniversary, founded by Guillermo Kyllmann.

Bolivar, Presidents Perez and Banzer, and Flags
AP71

1975, Aug. 4 **Litho.** ***Perf. 13½***

C345	AP71	3b gold & multi	1.00	75

Visit of Pres. Carlos A. Perez of Venezuela.

Bolivar Type of 1975.

Presidents and Statesmen of Bolivia: 50c, Rene Barrientes O. 2b, Francisco B. O'Connor. 3.80b, Gualberto Villarroel. 4.20b, German Busch. 4.50b, Hugo Banzer Suarez. 20b, José Ballivian. 30b, Andres de Santa Cruz. 40b, Antonio Jose de Sucre.

1975 **Litho.** ***Perf. 13½***

Size: 24x33mm.

C346	A189	50c multi	25	15
C347	A189	2b multi	75	40
C348	A189	3.80b multi	1.00	75
C349	A189	4.20b multi	1.50	1.00

Size: 28x39mm.

C350	A189	4.50b multi	1.50	1.00

Size: 24x33mm.

C351	A189	20b multi	6.00	4.00
C352	A189	30b multi	7.50	5.00
C353	A189	40b multi	10.00	7.00
		Nos. C346-C353 (8)	28.50	19.30

UPU Emblem
AP72

1975, Dec. 7 **Litho.** ***Perf. 13½***

C358	AP72	25b bl & multi	6.00	3.50

Centenary of Universal Postal Union (in 1974).

POSTAGE DUE STAMPS.

D1

Engraved.

1931 *Perf. 14, 14½.* **Unwmkd.**

J1	D1	5c ultra	2.00	1.25
J2	D1	10c red	2.00	1.25
J3	D1	15c yellow	2.00	1.25
J4	D1	30c dp grn	2.00	1.25
J5	D1	40c dp vio	2.00	1.25
J6	D1	50c blk brn	2.00	1.25
		Nos. J1-J6 (6)	12.00	7.50

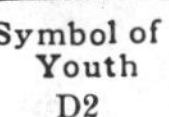

Symbol of Youth
D2

Torch of Knowledge
D3

Symbol of the Revolution of May 17, 1936
D4

1938 **Lithographed.** *Perf. 11.*

J7	D2	5c dp rose	90	75
a.		Pair, imperf. between		
J8	D3	10c green	90	75
J9	D4	30c gray bl	90	75

POSTAL TAX STAMPS.

Worker
PT1

Symbols of Communications
PT2

Imprint: "LITO. UNIDAS LA PAZ."

Perf. 13½x10½, 10½, 13½.

1939 **Lithographed.** **Unwmkd.**

RA1	PT1	5c dl vio	50	15
a.		Double impression		

Redrawn

Imprint: "TALL. OFFSET LA PAZ."

1940 *Perf. 12x11, 11.*

RA2	PT1	5c violet	40	15
a.		Horizontal pair, imperf. between	2.50	
b.		Imperf. horiz., pair		

Tax of Nos. RA1–RA2 was for the Workers' Home Building Fund.

1944–45 **Lithographed** *Perf. 10½*

RA3	PT2	10c salmon	40	15
RA4	PT2	10c bl ('45)	40	15

A 30c orange inscribed "Centenario de la Creacion del Departmento del Beni" was issued in 1946 and required to be affixed to all air and surface mail to and from the Department of Beni in addition to regular postage. Five higher denominations in the same scenic design were used for local revenue purposes.

Type of 1944 Redrawn.

1947-48 *Perf. 10½.* **Unwmkd.**

RA5	PT2	10c carmine	30	5
RA6	PT2	10c org yel ('48)	25	5
RA7	PT2	10c yel brn ('48)	25	5
RA8	PT2	10c emer ('48)	25	5

Post horn and envelope reduced in size.

Condor, Envelope and Post Horn
PT3

Communication Symbols
PT4

1951-52

RA9	PT3	20c dp org	40	20
a.		Imperf., pair		
RA10	PT3	20c grn ('52)	40	20
RA11	PT3	20c bl ('52)	40	20

1952–54 *Perf. 13½, 10½, 10½x12*

RA12	PT4	50c green	50	20
RA13	PT4	50c carmine	50	20
RA14	PT4	3b green	50	20
RA15	PT4	3b ol bis	75	60
RA16	PT4	5b vio ('54)	75	20
		Nos. RA12-RA16 (5)	3.00	1.40

No. RA10 and Type of 1951-52.
Surcharged with New Value in Black.

1953 *Perf. 10½.*

RA17	PT3	50c on 20c grn	40	20
RA18	PT3	50c on 20c red vio	40	20

Postman Blowing Horn
PT5

1954-55 *Perf. 10½.* **Unwmkd.**

RA19	PT5	1b brown	30	15
RA20	PT5	1b car rose ('55)	30	15

Nos. RA15 and RA14 Surcharged in Black "Bs. 5.—/D. S./21-IV-55"

1955 *Perf. 10½, 10½x12*

RA21	PT4	5b on 3b ol bis	30	10
RA22	PT4	5b on 3b grn	30	10

Tax of Nos. RA3–RA22 was for the Communications Employees Fund.

No. RA21 is known with surcharge in thin type of different font and with comma added after "55".

Plane over Airport
PT6

Planes
PT7

Lithographed.

1955 *Perf. 10½, 12, 13½,* **Unwmkd.**

RA23	PT6	5b dp ultra	40	10
a.		Vertical pair imperf. between		

Perf. 11½

RA24	PT7	10b lt grn	30	10

PT8

PT9

1955 **Lithographed** *Perf. 10½*

RA25	PT8	5b red	40	10

Perf. 12

RA26	PT9	20b dk brn	40	20

Tax of Nos. RA23–RA26 was for the building of new airports.

General Alfredo Ovando and Three Men
PT10

1970, Sept. 26 Litho. *Perf. 13x13½*

RA27	PT10	20c blk & red	25	15

See No. RAC1.

Pres. German Busch
PT11

1971, May 13 Litho. *Perf. 13x13½*

RA28	PT11	20c lil & blk	30	10

AIR POST POSTAL TAX STAMPS

Type of Postal Tax Issue

1970, Sept. 26 Litho. *Perf. 13x13½*

Design: 30c, General Ovando and oil well.

RAC1	PT10	30c blk & grn	25	15

Pres. Gualberto Villarroel, Refinery
PTAP1

1971, May 25 Litho. *Perf. 13x13½*

RAC2	PTAP1	30c lt bl & blk	25	15

Type of 1971 Inscribed:
"XXV ANIVERSARIO DE SU GOBIERNO"

1975 **Litho.** *Perf. 13x13½*

RAC3	PTAP1	30c lt bl & blk	25	15

BOSNIA AND HERZEGOVINA

(bŏz'ni·*ȧ* & hĕr'tsĕ·gô·vē'nä)

LOCATION—In what is now Jugoslavia, between Dalmatia and Serbia.

GOVT.—Provinces of Turkey under Austro-Hungarian occupation, 1879-1908; provinces of Austria-Hungary 1908-1918.

AREA—19,768 sq. mi.

POP.—2,000,000 (approx. 1918).

CAPITAL—Sarajevo.

Following World War I Bosnia and Herzegovina united with the kingdoms of Montenegro and Serbia, and Croatia, Dalmatia and Slovenia, to form the Kingdom of Jugoslavia (See Jugoslavia.)

100 Novcica(Neukreuzer) = 1 Florin (Gulden)

100 Heller = 1 Krone (1900)

Coat of Arms
A1

Type I. The heraldic eaglets on the right side of the escutcheon are entirely blank. The eye of the lion is indicated by a very small dot, which sometimes fails to print. All values except the ½n exist in this type.

Type II. There is a colored line across the lowest eaglet. A similar line sometimes appears on the middle eaglet. The eye of the lion is formed by a large dot which touches the outline of the head above it. All values are found in this type.

Type III. The eaglets and eye of the lion are similar to type I. Each tail feather of the large eagle has two lines of shading and the lowest feather does not touch the curved line below it. In types I and II there are several shading lines in these feathers, and the lowest feather touches the curved line. Only the 5n is found in type III.

Varieties of the Numerals.

2 NOVCICA:

A. The "2" has curved tail. All are type I.
B. The "2" has straight tail. All are type II.

15 NOVCICA:

C. The serif of the "1" is short and forms a wide angle with the vertical stroke.

D. The serif of the "1" forms an acute angle with the vertical stroke.

The numerals of the 5n were retouched several times and show minor differences, especially in the flag.

Other Varieties.

½ NOVCICA:

All printings of the ½n are type II.

There is a black dot between the curved ends of the ornaments near the lower spandrels.

G. This dot touches the curve at its right. Stamps of this (first) printing are lithographed.

H. This dot stands clear of the curved lines. Stamps of this (second) printing are typographed.

10 NOVCICA:

Ten stamps in each sheet of type II show a small cross in the upper section of the right side of the escutcheon.

Wmk. 91

Lithographed.

Wmkd. BRIEF-MARKEN or (from 1890) ZEITUNGS-MARKEN in Double-lined Capitals, Across the Sheet (91)

Perf. 9 to 13½ and Compound

1879–94 Type 1.

1	A1	½n blk (type II) ('94)	10.00	17.50
2	A1	1n gray	10.00	1.00
c.		1n gray lil		5.00
4	A1	2n yellow	11.00	1.50
5	A1	3n green	12.50	1.75
6	A1	5n rose red	22.50	50
7	A1	10n blue	55.00	1.00
8	A1	15n brown	75.00	5.00
9	A1	20n gray grn ('93)	275.00	6.25
10	A1	25n violet	65.00	6.00

No. 2c was never issued. It is usually cancelled by blue pencil marks and "mint" copies generally have been cleaned.

Typographed.

Perf. 10½ to 13 and Compound.

1894-98 Type II.

1a	A1	½n black	12.50	15.00
2a	A1	1n gray	3.50	50
4a	A1	2n yellow	2.25	50
5a	A1	3n green	3.50	65
6a	A1	5n rose red	60.00	50
7a	A1	10n blue	4.25	50
8a	A1	15n brown	3.50	2.00
9a	A1	20n gray grn	5.50	3.50
10a	A1	25n violet	8.50	5.00

Type III.

6b	A1	5n rose red ('98)	2.25	50

All the preceding stamps exist in various shades.

Nos. 1a to 10a were reprinted in 1911 in lighter colors, on very white paper and perf. 12½. Price, set $25.

A2

A3

Perf. 10½, 12½ and Compound

1900 Typographed.

No.	Type	Value	Unused	Used
11	A2	1h gray blk	38	7
12	A2	2h gray	38	7
13	A2	3h yellow	40	12
14	A2	5h green	38	3
15	A2	6h brown	75	15
16	A2	10h red	38	3
17	A2	20h rose	100.00	5.00
18	A2	25h blue	1.10	25
19	A2	30h bis brn	110.00	6.00
20	A2	40h orange	175.00	10.00
21	A2	50h red lil	1.25	45
22	A3	1k dk rose	1.50	65
23	A3	2k ultra	2.00	1.75
24	A3	5k dl bl grn	4.50	4.50
		Nos. 11-24 (14)	398.02	29.07

All values of this issue except the 3h exist on ribbed paper.

Nos. 17, 19 and 20 were reprinted in 1911. The reprints are in lighter colors and on whiter paper than the originals. Reprints of Nos. 17 and 19 are perf. 10½ and those of No. 20 are perf. 12½. Price $2 each.
perf. 12½. Price each $2.50.

Numerals in Black.

1901-04 ***Perf. 12½.***

No.	Type	Value	Unused	Used
25	A2	20h pink ('02)	1.10	35
26	A2	30h bis brn ('03)	1.10	45
27	A2	35h blue	1.35	50
a.		35h ultra	8.00	1.00
28	A2	40h org ('03)	1.50	80
29	A2	45h grnsh bl ('04)	1.20	55
		Nos. 25-29 (5)	6.25	2.65

Nos. 11-16, 18, 21-29 exist imperf. Most of Nos. 11-29 exist perf. 6½; compound with 12½; part perf.; in pairs imperf. between. These were supplied only to some high-ranking officials and never sold at any P.O.

View of Deboj
A4

The Carsija at Sarajevo
A17

Designs: 2h, View of Mostar. 3h, Pliva Gate, Jajce. 5h, Narenta Pass and Prenj River. 6h, Rama Valley. 10h, Vrbas Valley. 20h, Old Bridge, Mostar. 25h, Bey's Mosque, Sarajevo. 30h, Donkey post. 35h, Jezero and tourists' pavilion. 40h, Mail wagon. 45h, Bazaar at Sarajevo. 50h, Postal car. 2k, St. Luke's Campanile, Jajce. 5k, Emperor Franz Josef.

Perf. 6½, 9½, 10½ and 12½, also Compounds.

1906 Engraved. **Unwmkd.**

No.	Type	Value	Unused	Used
30	A4	1h black	15	15
31	A4	2h violet	20	15
32	A4	3h olive	20	15
33	A4	5h dk grn	20	15
34	A4	6h brown	35	25
a.		Perf. 13½	20.00	20.00
35	A4	10h carmine	20	15
36	A4	20h dk brn	1.00	30
a.		Perf. 13½	60.00	35.00
37	A4	25h dp bl	3.00	1.25
38	A4	30h green	3.25	50
39	A4	35h myr grn	3.50	50
40	A4	40h org red	3.50	50
41	A4	45h brn red	3.50	1.50
42	A4	50h dl vio	3.75	1.00
43	A17	1k maroon	9.00	2.00
44	A17	2k gray grn	12.50	11.00
45	A17	5k dl bl	10.00	9.00
		Nos. 30-45 (16)	54.30	28.55

Nos. 30-45 exist imperf. Price, set $65 unused, $42.50 canceled.

Birthday Jubilee Issue.

Designs of 1906 Issue, with "1830-1910" in label at bottom.

1910 ***Perf. 12½.***

No.	Type	Value	Unused	Used
46	A4	1h black	50	22
47	A4	2h violet	60	22
48	A4	3h olive	60	30
49	A4	5h dk grn	70	15
50	A4	6h org brn	75	30
51	A4	10h carmine	70	15
52	A4	20h dk brn	2.00	1.85
53	A4	25h dp bl	4.50	3.75
54	A4	30h green	3.50	3.25
55	A4	35h myr grn	4.50	3.25
56	A4	40h org red	4.50	4.00
57	A4	45h brn red	7.50	7.25
58	A4	50h dl vio	7.50	7.50
59	A17	1k maroon	7.50	7.50
60	A17	2k gray grn	30.00	22.50
61	A17	5k dl bl	5.00	5.00
		Nos. 46-61 (16)	80.35	67.19

80th birthday of Emperor Franz Josef.

Scenic Type of 1906.

Designs (Views): 12h, Jaice. 60h, Konjica. 72h, Vishegrad.

1912

No.	Type	Value	Unused	Used
62	A4	12h ultra	6.50	3.75
63	A4	60h dl bl	3.50	4.50
64	A4	72h carmine	15.00	17.50

Price, imperf. set, $75.

Emperor Franz Josef
A23 A24

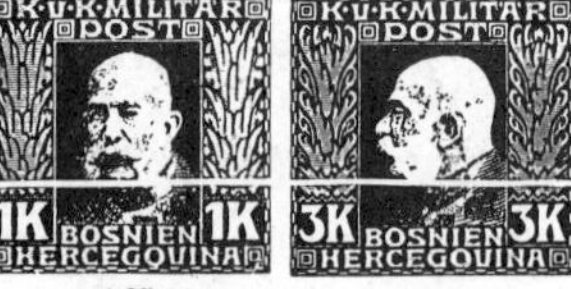

A25 A26

1912-14 Various Frames.

No.	Type	Value	Unused	Used
65	A23	1h ol grn	70	4
66	A23	2h brt bl	70	4
67	A23	3h claret	70	3
68	A23	5h green	70	3
69	A23	6h dk gray	70	7
70	A23	10h rose car	70	3
71	A23	12h dp ol grn	2.00	30
72	A23	20h org brn	7.50	6
73	A23	25h ultra	3.75	10
74	A23	30h org red	3.75	7
75	A24	35h myr grn	3.75	7
76	A24	40h dk vio	11.00	7
77	A24	45h ol brn	5.00	25
78	A24	50h sl bl	5.00	10
79	A24	60h brn vio	4.25	10
80	A24	72h dk bl	5.00	4.25
81	A25	1k brn vio, *straw*	20.00	50
82	A25	2k dk gray, *bl*	10.00	35
83	A26	3k car, *grn*	17.50	10.00
84	A26	5k dk vio, *gray*	35.00	30.00
85	A25	10k dk ultra, *gray* ('14)	135.00	110.00
		Nos. 65-85 (21)	272.70	156.46

Price, imperf. set, $450.

A27

A28

1916-17 ***Perf. 12½***

No.	Type	Value	Unused	Used
86	A27	3h dk gray	25	28
87	A27	5h ol grn	38	50
88	A27	6h violet	42	50
89	A27	10h bister	2.00	2.25
90	A27	12h bl gray	50	70
91	A27	15h car rose	10	7
92	A27	20h brown	45	60
93	A27	25h blue	35	50
94	A27	30h dk grn	35	50
95	A27	40h vermilion	35	50
96	A27	50h green	35	50
97	A27	60h lake	38	55
98	A27	80h org brn	85	15
a.		Perf. 11½	5.00	4.50
99	A27	90h dk vio	90	70
a.		Perf. 11½	500.00	500.00
101	A28	2k cl, *straw*	60	70
102	A28	3k grn, *bl*	1.85	2.65
103	A28	4k car, *grn*	8.00	9.50
104	A28	10k dp vio, *gray*	20.00	27.50
		Nos. 86-104 (18)	38.08	48.65

Price, imperf. set, $50.

Emperor Karl I
A29 A30

1917 ***Perf. 12½***

No.	Type	Value	Unused	Used
105	A29	3h ol gray	20	28
a.		Perf. 11½	100.00	75.00
b.		Perf. 12½x11½	20.00	19.00
106	A29	5h ol grn	15	20
107	A29	6h violet	50	75
108	A29	10h org brn	25	7
a.		Perf. 11½x12½	70.00	60.00
b.		Perf. 11½		
109	A29	12h blue	75	1.00
110	A29	15h brt rose	15	7
111	A29	20h red brn	15	15
112	A29	25h ultra	1.25	65
113	A29	30h gray grn	35	25
114	A29	40h ol bis	38	20
115	A29	50h dp grn	1.25	65
116	A29	60h car rose	1.25	55
a.		Perf. 11½	20.00	17.50
117	A29	80h stl bl	35	28
118	A29	90h dl vio	1.50	1.50
119	A30	2k car, *straw*	80	50
120	A30	3k grn, *bl*	20.00	22.50
121	A30	4k car, *grn*	8.00	8.50
122	A30	10k dp vio, *gray*	5.00	6.75
		Nos. 105-122 (18)	42.28	44.85

Price, imperf. set, $100.

Nos. 47 and 66 Overprinted in Red **1918**

1918

No.	Type	Value	Unused	Used
126	A4	2h violet	75	75
a.		Overprinted "1913"	9.00	9.00
b.		Inverted overprint	25.00	25.00
c.		Same as "a" inverted	80.00	80.00
d.		Double overprint	20.00	20.00
e.		Same as "a" double	80.00	80.00
f.		Double overprint, one inverted	22.50	
g.		Same as "a", double, one inverted	45.00	
127	A23	2h brt bl	75	75
a.		Pair, one without overprint		
b.		Inverted overprint	25.00	25.00
c.		Double overprint	20.00	20.00
d.		Double overprint, one inverted	15.00	

Emperor Karl I
A31

1918 Typo. ***Perf. 12½, Imperf.***

No.	Type	Value	Unused	Used
128	A31	2h orange	9.00	
129	A31	3h dk grn	9.00	
130	A31	5h lt grn	9.00	
131	A31	6h bl grn	9.00	
132	A31	10h brown	9.00	
133	A31	20h brick red	9.00	
134	A31	25h ultra	9.00	
135	A31	45h dk sl	9.00	
136	A31	50h lt bluish grn	9.00	
137	A31	60h bl vio	9.00	
138	A31	70h ocher	9.00	
139	A31	80h rose	9.00	
140	A31	90h vio brn	9.00	

Engraved

No.	Type	Value	Unused	Used
141	A30	1k ol grn, *grnsh*	*2,000.*	
		Nos. 128-140 (13)	117.00	

Nos. 128–141 were prepared for use in Bosnia and Herzegovina, but were not issued there. They were sold after the Armistice at the Vienna post office for a few days.

SEMI-POSTAL STAMPS.

Nos. 33 and 35 Surcharged in Red **1914. 7 Heller**

1914 ***Perf. 12½.*** **Unwmkd.**

No.	Type	Value	Unused	Used
B1	A4	7h on 5h dk grn	75	75
a.		Pair, one without surcharge		
B2	A4	12h on 10h car	80	80

Various minor varieties of the surcharge include "4" with open top, narrow "4" and wide "4".

Nos. B1–B2 exist with double and inverted surcharges. Price about $20 each.

Nos. 33 and 35 Surcharged in Red or Blue **1915. 7 Heller**

1915 ***Perf. 12½***

No.	Type	Value	Unused	Used
B3	A4	7h on 5h dk grn (R)	17.50	17.50
a.		Perf. 9½	125.00	125.00
B4	A4	12h on 10h car (Bl)	50	50

Nos. B3–B4 exist with double and inverted surcharges. Price about $18.50 each.

Nos. 68 and 70 Surcharged in Red or Blue **1915 7 Heller.**

1915

No.	Type	Value	Unused	Used
B5	A23	7h on 5h grn (R)	1.00	90
a.		"1915" at top and bottom	40.00	40.00
B6	A23	12h on 10h rose car (Bl)	3.00	2.50
a.		Surcharged "7 Heller."	40.00	40.00

Nos. B5–B6 are found in three types differing in length of surcharge lines: I, date 18mm., denomination 14mm. II, date 16mm., denomination 14mm. III, date 18mm., denomination 16mm.

Nos. B5–B6 exist with double and inverted surcharges. Price $15 each.

Nos. B5a and B6a exist double and inverted.

❖ 1916. ❖

Nos. 68 and 70 Surcharged in Red or Blue

7 Heller.

1916

B7	A23	7h on 5h grn (R)	75	1.00
B8	A23	12h on 10h rose car (Bl)	75	1.00

Nos. B7–B8 exist with double and inverted surcharges. Price $12.50 each.

Wounded Soldier SP1 — Blind Soldier SP2

1916 Engraved.

B9	SP1	5h (+2h) grn	1.00	1.00
B10	SP2	10h (+2h) mag	1.50	1.50

Nos. B9–B10 exist imperf. Price, set $27.50.

Nos. 89, 91 Overprinted

WITWEN- UND WAISENWOCHE 1917

1917

B11	A27	10h bister	25	38
B12	A27	15h car rose	25	38

Nos. B11–B12 exist imperf. Price, set $12.50.
Nos. B11–B12 exist with double and inverted overprint. Price $9 each.

Design for Memorial Church at Sarajevo—SP3

Archduke Francis Ferdinand SP4

Duchess Sophia and Archduke Francis Ferdinand SP5

1917 Typo. *Perf. 11½, 12½*

B13	SP3	10h vio blk	30	50
B14	SP4	15h claret	30	50
B15	SP5	40h dp bl	30	50

Assassination of Archduke Ferdinand and Archduchess Sophia. Sold at a premium of 2h each which helped build a memorial church at Sarajevo.
Nos. B13–B15 exist imperf. Price, set $2.50.

Blind Soldier SP6 — Emperor Karl I SP8

Design: 15h, Wounded soldier.

1918 Engraved *Perf. 12½*

B16	SP6	10h (+10h) grnsh bl	75	75
B17	SP6	15h (+10h) red brn	75	75

Nos. B16–B17 exist imperf. Price, set $18.50.

1918 Typographed. *Perf. 12½x13.*

Design: 15h, Empress Zita.

B18	SP8	10h gray grn	50	60
B19	SP8	15h brn red	50	60
B20	SP8	40h violet	50	60

Sold at a premium of 10h each which went to the "Karl's Fund."
Nos. B18–B20 exist imperf. Price, set $22.50.

POSTAGE DUE STAMPS.

D1

D2

Perf. 9½, 10½, 12½ and Compound.

1904 Unwmkd.

J1	D1	1h blk, red & yel	60	7
J2	D1	2h blk, red & yel	65	25
J3	D1	3h blk, red & yel	65	7
J4	D1	4h blk, red & yel	65	7
J5	D1	5h blk, red & yel	65	7
J6	D1	6h blk, red & yel	45	7
J7	D1	7h blk, red & yel	3.50	3.25
J8	D1	8h blk, red & yel	3.50	70
J9	D1	10h blk, red & yel	90	15
J10	D1	15h blk, red & yel	80	22
J11	D1	20h blk, red & yel	4.25	25
J12	D1	50h blk, red & yel	3.00	20
J13	D1	200h blk, red & grn	14.00	1.50
		Nos. J1-J13 (13)	33.60	6.87

Price, imperf. set, $75.

1916–18 *Perf. 12½*

J14	D2	2h red ('18)	50	50
J15	D2	4h red ('18)	38	38
J16	D2	5h red	50	50
J17	D2	6h red ('18)	38	38
J18	D2	10h red	45	45
J19	D2	15h red	3.75	3.75
J20	D2	20h red	45	45
J21	D2	25h red	1.40	1.40
J22	D2	30h red	1.25	1.25
J23	D2	40h red	10.00	10.00
J24	D2	50h red	32.50	32.50
J25	D2	1k dk bl	4.00	4.00
J26	D2	3k dk bl	19.00	19.00
		Nos. J14-J26 (13)	74.56	74.56

Nos. J25 and J26 have colored numerals on a white tablet.

Price, imperf. set, $150.

NEWSPAPER STAMPS.

Bosnian Girl N1

1913 *Imperf.* Unwmkd.

P1	N1	2h ultra	90	90
P2	N1	6h violet	2.75	2.75
P3	N1	10h rose	2.50	2.50
P4	N1	20h green	3.50	3.50

After Bosnia and Herzegovina became part of Jugoslavia stamps of type N1 perforated, also imperforate copies surcharged with new values, were used as regular postage stamps.

SPECIAL HANDLING STAMPS.

"Lightning" SH1

Engraved.

1916 *Perf. 12½.* Unwmkd.

QE1	SH1	2h vermilion	30	30
a.		Perf. 11½x12½	125.00	125.00
QE2	SH1	5h dp grn	50	50
a.		Perf. 11½	17.50	17.50

BRAZIL

(brȧ·zĭl')

Brasil (after 1918)

LOCATION—On the north and east coasts of South America, bordering on the Atlantic Ocean.

GOVT.—Republic.

AREA—3,287,000 sq. mi.

POP.—112,240,000 (est. 1977).

CAPITAL—Brasilia.

Brazil was an independent empire from 1822 to 1889 when a constitution was adopted and the country became officially known as The United States of Brazil.

1000 Reis = 1 Milreis

100 Centavos = 1 Cruzeiro (1942)

Prices of Brazil Nos. 1–13 vary according to condition. Quotations are for fine copies. Very fine to superb specimens sell at much higher prices, and inferior or poor copies sell at reduced prices, depending on the condition of the individual specimen.

Issues of the Empire.

A1

Engraved

Grayish or Yellowish Paper.

1843, Aug. 1 *Imperf.* Unwmkd.

1	A1	30r black	1,250.	450.00
a.		In pair with No. 2		*35,000.*
2	A1	60r black	650.00	250.00
3	A1	90r black	2,500.	1,000.

Early impressions of Nos. 1 to 3 bring higher prices than quoted which are for copies from worn plates.

A2

A3

Grayish or Yellowish Paper.

1844-46

7	A2	10r black	65.00	30.00
8	A2	30r black	75.00	37.50
9	A2	60r black	65.00	30.00
10	A2	90r black	400.00	150.00
11	A2	180r black	2,500.	1,500.
12	A2	300r black	4,500.	2,000.
13	A2	600r black	4,000.	2,250.

Nos. 8, 9 and 10 exist on thick paper and are considerably scarcer.

Grayish or Yellowish Paper.

1850, Jan. 1

21	A3	10r black	30.00	17.50
22	A3	20r black	70.00	90.00
23	A3	30r black	8.50	1.50
24	A3	60r black	8.50	1.50
25	A3	90r black	80.00	10.00
26	A3	180r black	80.00	50.00
27	A3	300r black	240.00	75.00
28	A3	600r black	275.00	75.00

All values except the 90r were reprinted in 1910 on very thick paper.

1854

37	A3	10r blue	12.50	11.00
38	A3	30r blue	35.00	40.00

A4

1861

39	A4	280r red	150.00	125.00
40	A4	430r yellow	225.00	150.00

Nos. 39 and 40 have been reprinted on thick white paper with white gum. They are printed in aniline inks and the colors are brighter than those of the originals.

1866 *Perf. 13½.*

41	A3	10r black	25.00	20.00
42	A3	10r blue	25.00	20.00
43	A3	20r black	225.00	100.00
44	A3	30r black	150.00	100.00
45	A3	30r blue	*500.00*	*500.00*
46	A3	60r black	60.00	12.50
47	A3	90r black	300.00	175.00
48	A3	180r black	300.00	175.00
49	A4	280r red	300.00	300.00
50	A3	300r black	600.00	350.00
51	A4	430r yellow	275.00	250.00
52	A3	600r black	300.00	175.00

Fraudulent perforations abound.

Emperor Dom Pedro A5

A6

A7

A8

A8a

A9

A9a

Thick or Thin White Wove Paper.

1866, July 1 ***Perf. 12***

53	A5	10r vermilion	8.00	3.00
a.		Bluish paper	200.00	200.00
54	A6	20r red lil	10.00	2.25
a.		20r dl vio	22.50	6.00
b.		Bluish paper	100.00	30.00
56	A7	50r blue	20.00	1.50
a.		Bluish paper	75.00	15.00
57	A8	80r sl vio	40.00	4.00
a.		Bluish paper	85.00	25.00
58	A8a	100r bl grn	17.50	50
a.		100r yel grn	12.50	50
b.		Bluish paper	225.00	60.00
59	A9	200r black	50.00	4.00
60	A9a	500r orange	175.00	30.00
		Nos. 53-60 (7)	320.50	45.25

The 10r and 20r exist imperf. on both white and bluish paper. Some authorities consider them proofs.

Nos. 58 and 65 are found in two types.

1876–77 ***Rouletted.***

61	A5	10r ver ('77)	30.00	25.00
62	A6	20r red lil ('77)	35.00	20.00
63	A7	50r bl ('77)	35.00	4.50
64	A8	80r vio ('77)	90.00	12.50
65	A8a	100r green	17.50	90
66	A9	200r blk ('77)	35.00	4.50
a.		Diagonal half used as 100r on cover		
67	A9a	500r orange	150.00	35.00
		Nos. 61-67 (7)	392.50	102.40

A10

A11

A12

A13

A14

A15

A16

A17

A18

A19

A20

1878-79 ***Rouletted.***

68	A10	10r vermilion	5.50	2.50
69	A11	20r violet	5.75	1.75
70	A12	50r blue	10.00	1.25
71	A13	80r lake	12.50	6.00
72	A14	100r green	12.00	70
73	A15	200r black	80.00	10.00
a.		Diagonal half used as 100r on cover		
74	A16	260r dk brn	45.00	20.00
75	A18	300r bister	45.00	5.00
76	A19	700r red brn	125.00	90.00
77	A20	1000r gray lil	150.00	35.00
		Nos. 68-77 (10)	490.75	172.20

1878, Aug. 21 ***Perf. 12***

78	A17	300r org & grn	50.00	15.00

Nos. 68-78 exist imperforate.

A21

A22

A23

Small Heads

1881, July 15 Laid Paper

Perf. 13, 13½ and Compound

79	A21	50r blue	70.00	15.00
80	A22	100r ol grn	225.00	17.50
81	A23	200r pale red brn	400.00	90.00

On Nos. 79 and 80 the hair above the ear curves forward. On Nos. 83 and 88 it is drawn backward. On the stamps of the 1881 issue the beard is smaller than in the 1882–85 issues and fills less of the space between the neck and the frame at the left.

See also No. 88.

A24

A25

A26

A27

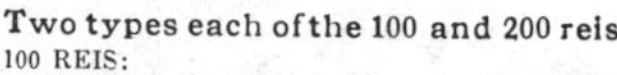
Two types each of the 100 and 200 reis.

100 REIS:

Type I. Groundwork formed of diagonal crossed lines and horizontal lines.

Type II. Groundwork formed of diagonal crossed lines and vertical lines.

200 REIS:

Type I. Groundwork formed of diagonal and horizontal lines.

Type II. Groundwork formed of diagonal crossed lines.

Larger Heads.

Perf. 12½ to 14 and Compound.

1882–84 Laid Paper

82	A24	10r black	4.50	4.50
83	A25	100r ol grn, type I	25.00	2.00
a.		100r dk grn, type I	25.00	2.00
b.		100r dk grn, type II	100.00	8.00
84	A26	200r pale red brn, type I	55.00	20.00
85	A27	200r pale rose, type II	30.00	3.50
a.		Diagonal half used as 100r on cover		20.00

See also No. 86.

A28 A29

A30

Three types of A29.

Type I. Groundwork formed of horizontal lines.

Type II. Groundwork formed of diagonal crossed lines.

Type III. Groundwork solid.

Perf. 13, 13½, 14 and Compound

1884-85

86	A24	10r orange	1.50	1.50
87	A28	20r sl grn	6.00	1.50
a.		20r ol grn	4.00	2.00
88	A21	50r bl, head larger	15.00	2.50
89	A29	100r lil, type III	200.00	16.00
a.		100r lil, type II	100.00	10.00
90	A29	100r lil, type I	50.00	1.75
91	A30	100r lilac	50.00	1.50

A31

Perf. 13, 13½, 14 and Compound.

1885

92	A31	100r lilac	25.00	85
a.		Imperf., pair	75.00	75.00

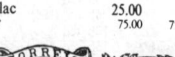

Southern Cross Crown

A32 A33 A34

1887

93	A32	50r chlky bl	15.00	3.00
94	A33	300r gray bl	75.00	8.00
95	A34	500r olive	50.00	7.50

A35

A36

Entrance to Bay of Rio de Janeiro

A37

1888

96	A35	100r lilac	25.00	75
a.		Imperf., pair	60.00	60.00
97	A36	700r violet	15.00	*50.00*
98	A37	1000r dl bl	100.00	50.00

Issues of the Republic.

Southern Cross

A38

Wove Paper, Thin to Thick.

Perf. 12½ to 14, 11 to 11½, and 12½ to 14 x 11 to 11½, Rough or Clean-Cut.

1890–91 Engr.; Typo. (#102)

99	A38	20r gray grn	1.50	1.25
a.		20r bl grn	1.50	1.25
b.		20r emer	10.00	5.00
100	A38	50r gray grn	2.50	1.00
a.		50r ol grn	10.00	1.00
b.		50r yel grn	10.00	5.00
c.		50r dk sl grn	10.00	5.00
d.		Horizontal pair, imperf. between		
101	A38	100r lil rose	250.00	5.00
102	A38	100r red lil, redrawn	50.00	2.00
a.		Tête bêche pair	*10,000.*	
103	A38	200r purple	12.50	1.25
a.		200r vio	15.00	2.25
b.		200r vio bl	20.00	2.50
104	A38	300r sl vio	50.00	2.50
a.		300r gray	50.00	7.50
b.		300r gray bl	100.00	10.00
c.		300r dk vio	25.00	6.00
105	A38	500r ol bis	16.00	10.00
a.		500r ol gray	16.00	10.00
106	A38	500r slate	16.00	8.00
107	A38	700r chocolate	20.00	20.00
a.		700r fawn	22.50	22.50
108	A38	1000r bister	20.00	4.00
a.		1000r yel buff	25.00	7.50
		Nos. 99-108 (10)	438.50	55.00

The redrawn 100r may be distinguished by the absence of the curved lines of shading in the left side of the central oval. The pearls in the oval are not well aligned and there is less shading at right and left of "CORREIO" and "100 REIS."

A 100 reis stamp of type A38 but inscribed "BRAZIL" instead of "E. U. DO BRAZIL" was not placed in issue but postmarked copies are known. A reprint on thick paper was made in 1910.

No. 101 exists imperf., not regularly issued.

Liberty Head

A39

Liberty Head

A40

Perf. 12½ to 14, 11 to 11½ and 12½ to 14 x 11 to 11½

1891, May 1 Typographed

109	A39	100r bl & red	20.00	50
a.		Head inverted	100.00	75.00
b.		Tête bêche pair	500.00	500.00
c.		100r ultra & red	22.50	60

Perf. 11, 11½, 13, 13½, 14 and Compound.

1893, Jan. 18 **Lithographed**

No.	Type	Description	Unused	Used
111	A40	100r rose	35.00	50

Sugarloaf Mountain

A41 A41a

A42

Liberty Head Hermes

A42a A43

Perf. 11 to 11½, 12½ to 14 and 12½ to 14x11 to 11½.

1894–97 **Unwmkd.**

No.	Type	Description	Unused	Used
112	A41	10r rose & bl	2.00	50
113	A41a	10r rose & bl	1.50	35
114	A41a	20r org & bl	1.75	40
115	A41a	50r dk bl & bl	7.50	1.50
116	A42	100r car & blk	12.50	25
a.		Vertical pair, imperf. between	90.00	
118	A42a	200r org & blk	3.00	25
a.		Imperf. horiz., pair	60.00	
b.		Vertical pair, imperf. between	60.00	
119	A42a	300r grn & blk	25.00	50
120	A42a	500r bl & blk	25.00	1.00
121	A42a	700r lil & blk	17.50	1.50
122	A43	1000r grn & vio	85.00	1.50
124	A43	2000r blk & gray lil	175.00	25.00
		Nos. 112-124 (11)	355.75	32.75

The head of No. 116 exists in five types. See also Nos. 140-150A, 159-161, 166-171d.

Newspaper Stamps Surcharged:

100 200

1898 1898

100 200

a *b*

100

1898

100

c

Surcharged on 1889 Issue of type N1.

1898 ***Rouletted***

Green Surcharge.

No.	Type	Description	Unused	Used
125	(b)	700r on 500r yel	10.00	10.00
126	(c)	1000r on 700r yel	30.00	30.00
a.		Surcharged "700r"	400.00	400.00
127	(c)	2000r on 1000r yel	20.00	12.50
128	(c)	2000r on 1000r brn	17.50	6.00

Violet Surcharge.

No.	Type	Description	Unused	Used
129	(a)	100r on 50r brn yel	3.50	6.00
130	(c)	100r on 50r brn yel	45.00	40.00
131	(c)	300r on 200r blk	3.50	1.25
a.		Double surcharge	75.00	60.00

The surcharge on No. 130 is handstamped. The impression is blurred and lighter in color than on No. 129. The two surcharges differ most in the shapes and serifs of the figures "1."

Counterfeits exist of No. 126a.

Black Surcharge.

No.	Type	Description	Unused	Used
132	(b)	200r on 100r vio	3.00	1.25
a.		Double surcharge	75.00	60.00
b.		Inverted surcharge	75.00	65.00
132C	(b)	500r on 300r car	4.50	2.50
133	(b)	700r on 500r grn	7.00	2.25

Blue Surcharge.

No.	Type	Description	Unused	Used
134	(b)	500r on 300r car	6.00	2.25

Red Surcharge.

No.	Type	Description	Unused	Used
135	(c)	1000r on 700r ultra	20.00	12.50
a.		Inverted surcharge	150.00	150.00

Surcharged on 1890-94 Issues:

200 1898

1898 50 RÉIS 50

d *e*

Perf. 11 to 14 and Compound.

Black Surcharge.

No.	Type	Description	Unused	Used
136	N3 (e)	20r on 10r bl	1.25	2.50
137	N2 (d)	200r on 100r red lil	11.00	6.50
a.		Double surcharge	75.00	75.00

Blue Surcharge.

No.	Type	Description	Unused	Used
138	N3 (e)	50r on 20r grn	2.50	4.00
a.		Double surcharge		
138B	N2 (d)	200r on 100r red lil	9.00	8.00

Red Surcharge.

No.	Type	Description	Unused	Used
139	N3 (e)	100r on 50r grn	8.00	10.00
a.		Blue surch.	15.00	15.00

The surcharge on Nos. 139 and 139a exists double, inverted, one missing, etc.

Types of 1894–97

Perf. 5½ to 7 and 11 to 11½x5½ to 7

No.	Type	Description	Unused	Used
140	A41a	10r rose & bl	6.00	3.00
141	A41a	20r org & bl	8.00	1.50
142	A41a	50r dk bl & lt bl	9.00	5.00
143	A42	100r car & blk	12.50	1.50
144	A42a	200r org & blk	12.50	2.00
145	A42a	300r grn & blk	55.00	5.00

Perf. 8½ to 9½ and 8½ to 9½x11 to 11½

No.	Type	Description	Unused	Used
146	A41a	10r rose & bl	5.00	2.50
147	A41a	20r org & bl	15.00	1.75
147A	A41a	50r dk bl & bl	125.00	25.00
148	A42	100r car & blk	25.00	1.25
149	A42a	200r org & blk	10.00	1.25
150	A42a	300r grn & blk	50.00	3.25
150A	A43	1000r grn & vio	120.00	5.00

Issue of 1890-93 Surcharged in Violet or Magenta

1899

50 RÉIS

Perf. 11 to 11½, 12½ to 14 and Compound

1899, June 25

No.	Type	Description	Unused	Used
151	A38	50r on 20r gray grn	1.50	1.50
a.		Double surcharge		
152	A38	100r on 50r gray grn	1.50	1.50
a.		Pair, one without surcharge		
b.		Double surch.	30.00	
153	A38	300r on 200r pur	8.00	8.00
a.		Double surcharge		
154	A38	500r on 300r sl vio	20.00	10.00
a.		500r on 300r gray lil	16.00	8.00
b.		Pair, one without surcharge	250.00	
155	A38	700r on 500r ol bis	20.00	5.00
a.		Pair, one without surcharge	250.00	
b.		Double surcharge		
156	A38	1000r on 700r choc	11.00	5.00
157	A38	1000r on 700r fawn	12.50	5.00
a.		Pair, one without surcharge	250.00	
b.		Double surcharge		
158	A38	2000r on 1000r yel buff	37.50	5.00
a.		2000r on 1000r bis	37.50	5.00
b.		Pair, one without surcharge	250.00	
		Nos. 151-158 (8)	112.00	41.00

Types of 1894–97

Perf. 11, 11½, 13 and Compound.

1900

No.	Type	Description	Unused	Used
159	A41a	50r green	8.50	50
160	A42	100r rose	17.50	40
a.		Frame around inner oval	90.00	3.50
161	A42a	200r blue	20.00	40

Three types exist of No. 161, all of which have the frame around inner oval.

Cabral Arrives at Brazil

A44

Independence Proclaimed

A45

"Emancipation of Slaves" Allegory, Republic of Brazil

A46 A47

1900, Jan. 1 **Litho.** ***Perf. 12½***

No.	Type	Description	Unused	Used
162	A44	100r red	6.00	5.50
a.		Imperf. (pair)	300.00	300.00
163	A45	200r grn & yel	6.00	5.50
164	A46	500r blue	6.00	5.50
165	A47	700r emerald	6.00	5.50

Discovery of Brazil, 400th anniversary.

Wmk. 97 Wmk. 98

Types of 1894–97.

Wmkd. (97? or 98?)

1905 ***Perf. 11, 11½***

No.	Type	Description	Unused	Used
166	A41a	10r rose & bl	4.00	1.25
167	A41a	20r org & bl	6.00	60
168	A41a	50r green	12.50	50
169	A42	100r rose	17.50	25
170	A42a	200r dk bl	15.00	25
171	A42a	300r grn & blk	17.50	1.50
		Nos. 166-171 (6)	72.50	4.35

Positive identification of Wmk. 97 or 98 places stamp in specific watermark groups below.

Wmkd.

"CORREIO FEDERAL REPUBLICA DOS ESTADOS UNIDOS DO BRAZIL"

in Sheet. (97)

No.	Type	Description	Unused	Used
166b	A41a	10r rose & bl	37.50	13.00
167b	A41a	20r org & bl	22.50	5.00
168b	A41a	50r green	45.00	6.00
169b	A42	100r rose	225.00	6.00
170b	A42a	200r dk bl	45.00	2.50
171b	A42a	300r grn & blk	275.00	35.00
171A	A43	1000r grn & vio	275.00	30.00
		Nos. 166b-171A (7)	925.00	97.50

Wmkd.

"IMPOSTO DE CONSUMO REPUBLICA DOS ESTADOS UNIDOS DO BRAZIL"

in Sheet. (98)

No.	Type	Description	Unused	Used
166c	A41a	10r rose & bl	55.00	22.50
167c	A41a	20r org & bl	50.00	12.50
168c	A41a	50r green	110.00	22.50
169c	A42	100r rose	45.00	2.50
170c	A42a	200r dk bl	45.00	1.00
171d	A42a	300r grn & blk	225.00	35.00
		Nos. 166c-171d (6)	530.00	96.00

Allegory, Pan-American Congress

A48

1906, July 23 **Litho.** **Unwmkd.**

No.	Type	Description	Unused	Used
172	A48	100r car rose	35.00	15.00
173	A48	200r blue	60.00	7.50

Third Pan-American Congress.

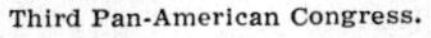

Aristides Lobo Benjamin Constant

A48a A49

Pedro Alvares Cabral Eduardo Wandenkolk

A50 A51

Manuel Deodoro da Fonseca
A52

Floriano Peixoto
A53

Prudente de Moraes
A54

Manuel Ferraz de Campos Salles
A55

Francisco de Paula Rodrigues Alves
A56

Liberty Head
A57

A58

A59

1906–16 Engraved *Perf. 12*

174	A48a	10r bluish sl	40	6
175	A49	20r anil vio	25	6
176	A50	50r green	50	8
a.		Booklet pane of 6 ('08)	20.00	25.00
177	A51	100r anil rose	1.10	5
a.		Imperf. vert., coil ('16)	4.00	50
b.		Booklet pane of 6 ('08)	30.00	35.00
178	A52	200r blue	1.10	8
a.		Booklet pane of 6 ('08)	17.50	22.50
179	A52	200r ultra ('15)	1.50	8
a.		Imperf. vert., coil ('16)	2.00	50
180	A53	300r gray blk	3.50	15
181	A54	400r ol grn	20.00	1.50
182	A55	500r dk vio	4.50	20
183	A54	600r ol grn ('10)	1.50	50
184	A56	700r red brn	4.50	2.00
185	A57	1000r vermilion	37.50	60
186	A58	2000r yel grn	4.50	40
187	A58	2000r Prus bl ('15)	15.00	50
188	A59	5000r car rose	6.00	1.25
		Nos. 174-188 (15)	101.85	7.51

Allegorical Emblems: Liberty, Peace, Industry, etc.
A60

1908, July 14

189	A60	100r carmine	20.00	1.00

National Exhibition, Rio de Janeiro.

Emblems of Peace Between Brazil and Portugal
A61

1908, July 14

190	A61	100r red	7.50	75

Issued to commemorate the centenary of the opening of Brazilian ports to foreign commerce. Medallions picture King Carlos I of Portugal and Pres. Affonso Penna of Brazil.

Bonifacio, Bolívar, Hidalgo, O'Higgins, San Martin, Washington
A62

1909

191	A62	200r dp bl	3.50	50

Nilo Peçanha
A63

Baron of Rio Branco
A64

1910, Nov. 15

192	A63	10,000r brown	6.00	1.00

1913–16

193	A64	1000r dp grn	1.50	30
194	A64	1000r sl ('16)	11.00	30

Cabo Frio
A65

Wmk. 99

Wmkd. "CORREIO." (99)

1915, Nov. 13 Litho. *Perf. 11½*

195	A65	100r dk grn, *yelsh*	3.00	1.75

Founding of the town of Cabo Frio, 300th anniversary.

Bay of Guajara
A66

1916, Jan. 5

196	A66	100r carmine	6.50	2.25

City of Belem, 300th anniversary.

Revolutionary Flag
A67

1917, Mar. 6

197	A67	100r dp bl	20.00	6.00

Centenary of Revolution of Pernambuco, Mar. 6, 1817.

Rodrígues Alves
A68

Engraved.

1917, Aug. 31 *Perf. 12* Unwmkd.

198	A68	5000r red brn	50.00	12.50

Liberty Head
A69 A70

Perf. 12½, 13, 13x13½.

1918-20 Typographed. Unwmkd.

200	A69	10r org brn	25	15
201	A69	20r slate	25	15
202	A69	25r ol gray ('20)	25	15
203	A69	50r green	16.00	1.75
204	A70	100r rose	85	15
a.		Imperf. (pair)		
205	A70	300r red org	15.00	1.75
206	A70	500r dl vio	15.00	75
		Nos. 200-206 (7)	47.60	4.85

Wmk. 100

Because of the spacing of this watermark, a few stamps in each sheet may show no watermark.

Wmkd.

CASA DA MOEDA in Sheet. (100)

207	A69	10r red brn	4.00	1.25
a.		Imperf. (pair)		
207B	A69	20r slate	1.00	80
c.		Imperf. (pair)		
208	A69	25r ol gray ('20)	50	30
209	A69	50r green	50	10
210	A70	100r rose	27.50	10
a.		Imperf. (pair)		
211	A70	200r dl bl	5.50	30
212	A70	300r orange	27.50	3.50
213	A70	500r dl vio	27.50	4.50
214	A70	600r orange	1.50	1.00
		Nos. 207-214 (9)	95.50	11.85

"Education"
A72

1918 Engraved. *Perf. 11½.*

215	A72	1000r blue	3.00	20
216	A72	2000r red brn	25.00	5.00
217	A72	5000r dk vio	6.00	5.00

Watermark note below No. 257 also applies to Nos. 215–217.

See also Nos. 233–234, 283–285, 404, 406, 458, 460.

Railroad
A73

"Industry"
A74

"Aviation"
A75

Mercury
A76

"Navigation"
A77

Perf. 13½x13, 13x13½

1920-22 Typographed. Unwmkd.

218	A73	10r red vio	40	10
219	A73	20r ol grn	40	10
220	A74	25r brn vio	30	10
221	A74	50r bl grn	50	10
222	A74	50r org brn ('22)	80	20
223	A75	100r rose red	1.00	10
224	A75	100r org ('22)	2.50	20
225	A75	150r vio ('21)	80	20
226	A75	200r blue	1.50	15
227	A75	200r rose red ('22)	1.75	15
228	A76	300r ol gray	8.00	25
229	A76	400r dl bl ('22)	11.00	1.75
230	A76	500r red brn	11.00	40
		Nos. 218-230 (13)	39.95	3.80

See also Nos. 236–257, 265–266, 268–271, 273–274, 276–281, 302–311, 316–322, 326–340, 357–358, 431–434, 436–441, 461–463B, 467–470, 472–474, 488–490, 492–494.

***Perf. 11, 11½* Engr. Wmk. 100**

231	A77	600r red org	1.25	20
232	A77	1000r claret	3.00	15
a.		Perf. 8½	20.00	3.00
233	A72	2000r dl vio	15.00	40
234	A72	5000r brown	17.50	5.00

Nos. 233 and 234 are inscribed "BRASIL CORREIO". Watermark note below No. 257 also applies to Nos. 231–234.

See also No. 282.

King Albert of Belgium and President Epitacio Pessoa
A78

1920, Sept. 19 Engr. *Perf. 11½x11*

235	A78	100r dl red	1.00	75

This stamp was issued to commemorate the visit of the King and Queen of Belgium to Brazil.

Types of 1920–22 Issue.

Perf. 13x13½, 13x12½.

1922-29 Typographed Wmk. 100

236	A73	10r red vio	20	10
237	A73	20r ol grn	20	10
238	A75	20r gray vio ('29)	15	10

239 A74 25r brn vio 25 10
240 A74 50r bl grn 8.50 4.00
241 A74 50r org brn ('23) 35 25
a. Booklet pane of 6
242 A75 100r rose red 15.00 30
243 A75 100r org ('26) 40 10
a. Booklet pane of 6
244 A75 100r turq grn ('28) 25 15
245 A75 150r violet 2.00 15
246 A75 200r blue 275.00 7.50
247 A75 200r rose red 30 15
a. Booklet pane of 6
248 A75 200r ol grn ('28) 2.50 2.00
249 A76 300r ol gray 75 20
a. Booklet pane of 6
250 A76 300r rose red ('29) 25 20
251 A76 400r blue 35 15
252 A76 400r org ('29) 75 50
253 A76 500r red brn 6.00 40
a. Booklet pane of 6
254 A76 500r ultra ('29) 7.00 15
255 A76 600r brn org ('29) 5.00 2.50
256 A76 700r dl vio ('29) 5.50 1.75
257 A76 1000r turq bl ('29) 8.00 60
Nos. 236-257 (22) 338.70 21.45

Because of the spacing of the watermark, a few stamps in each sheet show no watermark.

"Agriculture"
A79

1922 *Perf. 13x13½.* Unwmkd.

258 A79 40r org brn 50 10
259 A79 80r grnsh bl 40 20

See also Nos. 263, 267, 275.

Declaration of Ypiranga
A80

Dom Pedro I and José Bonifacio
A81

National Exposition and President Pessoa
A82

Engraved.

1922, Sept. 7 *Perf. 14* Unwmkd.

260 A80 100r ultra 1.50 40
261 A81 200r red 2.50 30
262 A82 300r green 4.50 30

Issued in commemoration of the centenary of independence and the National Exposition of 1922.

Agriculture Type of 1922
Typographed

1923 *Perf. 13½x12* Wmk. 100

263 A79 40r org brn 35 15

Brazilian Army Entering Bahia
A83

Perf. 13

1923, July 12 Litho. Unwmkd.

264 A83 200r rose 9.00 4.50

Centenary of the taking of Bahia from the Portuguese.

Wmk. 193

Types of 1920–22 Issues
Typographed
Wmkd.
ESTADOS UNIDOS DO BRASIL. (193)

1924 *Perf. 13x13½*

265 A73 10r red vio 4.50 3.00
266 A73 20r ol grn 5.00 3.00
267 A79 40r org brn 3.50 50
268 A74 50r org brn 3.00 5.00
269 A75 100r orange 3.50 25
270 A75 200r rose 5.00 20
271 A76 400r blue 3.00 3.00
Nos. 265-271 (7) 27.50 14.95

Arms of Equatorial Confederation, 1824
A84

Perf. 11

1924, July 2 Litho. Unwmkd.

272 A84 200r bl, blk, yel, & red 3.50 2.25
a. Red omitted 450.00 450.00

Centenary of the Equatorial Confederation.

Wmk. 101

Types of 1920–22 Issues.
Wmkd. Stars and CASA DA MOEDA. (101)
Perf. 9½ to 13½ and Compound.

1924–28 Typographed

273 A73 10r red vio 15 8
274 A73 20r ol gray 15 8
275 A79 40r org brn 30 12
276 A74 50r org brn 30 10
277 A75 100r red org 60 10
278 A75 200r rose 40 10
279 A76 300r ol gray ('25) 7.00 65
280 A76 400r blue 2.00 20
281 A76 500r red brn 9.00 30

Engraved.

282 A77 600r red org ('26) 75 15
283 A72 2000r dl vio ('26) 2.00 15
284 A72 5000r brn ('26) 8.50 50
285 A72 10,000r rose ('28) 10.00 60
Nos. 273-285 (13) 41.15 3.13

Nos. 283 to 285 are inscribed "BRASIL CORREIO".

Ruy Barbosa
A85

1925 *Perf. 11½* Wmk. 100

286 A85 1000r claret 4.00 2.00
a. Unwmkd. 15.00 8.00

1926 Wmk. 101

287 A85 1000r claret 1.75 25

"Justice"
A86

Scales of Justice and Map of Brazil
A87

Wmk. 206

Wmkd.
Star-framed CM, Multiple (206)

1927, Aug. 11 Typo. *Perf. 13½x13*

288 A86 100r dp bl 1.00 50
289 A87 200r rose 1.00 50

Issued in commemoration of the centenary of the founding of the law courses.

Liberty Holding Coffee Leaves
A88

1928, Mar. 5

290 A88 100r bl grn 1.50 60
291 A88 200r carmine 1.00 50
292 A88 300r ol blk 8.50 40

Issued to commemorate the bicentenary of the introduction of the coffee tree in Brazil.

Official Stamps of 1919 Surcharged in Red or Black **700 Réis**

Engraved.

1928 *Perf. 11, 11½* Wmk. 100

293 O3 700r on 500r org (R) 3.25 2.25
a. Inverted surcharge 500.00 500.00
294 O3 1000r on 100r rose red (Bk) 2.25 40
295 O3 2000r on 200r dl bl (R) 3.00 60
296 O3 5000r on 50r grn (R) 3.00 75
a. Inverted surcharge
297 O3 10,000r on 10r ol grn (R) 16.00 1.25
Nos. 293-297 (5) 27.50 5.25

Nos. 293 to 297 were used for ordinary postage.

Stamps in the outer rows of the sheets are often without watermark.

Ruy Barbosa
A89

Perf. 9, 9½x11, 11, and Compound.

1929 Wmk. 101

300 A89 5000r bl vio 6.50 75

For other stamps of type A89, see Nos. 323, 405 and 459.

Wmk. 218

Types of 1920-21 Issue.
Typographed.
Wmkd. E U BRASIL Multiple. (218) (Letters 8 mm. high.)

Wmk. 218 exists both in vertical alignment and in echelon.

1929 *Perf. 13½x12½.*

302 A75 20r gray vio 15 8
a. Wmk. in echelon 20 15
303 A75 50r red brn 15 8
a. Wmk. in echelon 75.00 35.00
304 A75 100r turq grn 25 8
305 A75 200r ol grn 12.00 2.50
306 A76 300r rose red 60 8
a. Wmk. in echelon 75 30
307 A76 400r orange 75 25
308 A76 500r ultra 9.00 50
a. Wmk. in echelon 125.00 17.50
309 A76 600r brn org 6.50 60
310 A76 700r dp vio 2.50 10
311 A76 1000r turq bl 4.00 10
a. Wmk. in echelon 15.00 9.00
Nos. 302-311 (10) 35.90 4.37

Architectural Fantasies
A90 A91

Architectural Fantasy
A92

Perf. 13x13½

1930, June 20 **Wmk. 206**

312	A90	100r turq bl	1.75	1.00
313	A91	200r ol gray	3.00	75
314	A92	300r rose red	5.00	1.25

Issued in connection with the Fourth Pan-American Congress of Architects and Exposition of Architecture.

Wmk. 221

Types of 1920-21 Issues.

Wmkd. ESTADOS UNIDOS DO BRASIL, Multiple. (221)

(Letters 6 mm. high.)

1930 ***Perf. 13x12½.***

316	A75	20r gray vio	10	10
317	A75	50r red brn	15	10
318	A75	100r turq bl	20	10
319	A75	200r ol grn	2.00	50
320	A76	300r rose red	45	15
321	A76	500r ultra	1.00	15
322	A76	1000r turq bl	20.00	1.00
		Nos.316-322 (7)	23.90	2.10

Barbosa Type of 1929.

1930 Engraved ***Perf. 11***

323	A89	5000r bl vio	850.00

Imperforates

Since 1930, imperforate or partly perforated sheets of nearly all commemorative and some definitive issues have become obtainable.

Wmk. 222

Types of 1920-29 Issue.

Wmkd. CORREIO BRASIL and 5 Stars in Squared Circle. (222)

Perf. 11, 13½x13, 13x12½.

1931-34 Typographed

326	A75	10r dp brn	10	5
327	A75	20r gray vio	10	5
328	A74	25r brn vio ('34)	10	50
330	A75	50r bl grn	15	10
331	A75	50r red brn	10	8
332	A75	100r orange	25	8
334	A75	200r dp car	35	8
335	A76	300r ol grn	50	8
336	A76	400r ultra	70	8
337	A76	500r red brn	2.50	10
338	A76	600r brn org	2.50	10
339	A76	700r dp vio	6.50	10
340	A76	1000r turq bl	15.00	10
		Nos. 326-340 (13)	28.85	1.50

Getulio Vargas and João Pessoa
A93

Vargas and Pessoa—A94

Oswaldo Aranha
A95 A96

Antonio Carlos
A97

Pessoa Vargas
A98 A99

Lithographed.

1931, Apr. 29 ***Perf. 14*** **Unwmkd.**

342	A93	10r +10r lt bl	20	1.00
343	A93	20r +20r yel brn	20	1.00
344	A95	50r +50r dl grn, red & yel	20	20
a.		Red missing at left	1.25	1.25
345	A93	100r +50r org	40	40
346	A93	200r +100r grn	40	40
347	A94	300r +150r multi	40	40
348	A93	400r +200r dp rose	1.50	90
349	A93	500r +250r dk bl	1.00	80
350	A93	600r +300r brn vio	70	2.00
351	A94	700r +350r multi	1.25	75
352	A96	1000r +500r brt grn, red & yel	3.00	30
353	A97	2000r +1000r gray blk & red	6.00	75
354	A98	5000r +2500r blk & red	25.00	7.00
355	A99	10000r +5000r brt grn & yel	60.00	15.00
		Nos.342-355 (14)	100.25	30.90

Issued to commemorate the Revolution of Oct. 3, 1930. Prepared as semipostal stamps, Nos. 342-355 were sold as ordinary postage stamps with stated surtax ignored.

Nos. 306, 320 and 250 Surcharged **1931 200 Réis**

Wmkd. E U BRASIL Multiple. (218)

1931, July 20 ***Perf. 13½x12½***

356	A76	200r on 300r rose red	1.00	75
a.		Wmk. in echelon	25.00	25.00
b.		Inverted surcharge	25.00	

Perf. 13x12½ **Wmk. 221**

357	A76	200r on 300r rose red	30	15
a.		Inverted surcharge	40.00	40.00

Perf. 13½x12½ **Wmk. 100**

358	A76	200r on 300r rose red	40.00	40.00

Map of South America Showing Meridian of Tordesillas
A100

João Ramalho and Tibiriçá
A101

Martim Affonso de Souza
A102

King John III of Portugal
A103

Disembarkation of M. A. de Souza at São Vicente
A104

Typographed.

1932, June 3 ***Perf. 13*** **Wmk. 222**

359	A100	20r dk vio	20	20
360	A101	100r black	50	40
361	A102	200r purple	1.25	20
362	A103	600r red brn	2.50	1.00

Perf. 9½, 11, 9½x11.

Engraved **Wmk. 101**

363	A104	700r ultra	3.00	1.50
		Nos.359-363 (5)	7.45	3.30

Nos. 359 to 363 commemorate the fourth centenary of the first colonization of Brazil at Sao Vicente, in 1532, under the hereditary captaincy of Martim Affonso de Souza.

Revolutionary Issue.

Map of Brazil
A105

Soldier and Flag
A106

Allegory: Freedom, Justice, Equality
A107

Soldier's Head
A108

"LEX" and Sword
A109

Symbolical of Law and Order
A110

Symbolical of Justice
A111

Perf. 11½

1932, Sept. 13 Litho. **Unwmkd.**

364	A105	100r brn org	60	3.00
365	A106	200r dk car	50	1.00
366	A107	300r gray grn	3.00	5.00
367	A108	400r dk bl	10.00	10.00
368	A105	500r blk brn	10.00	10.00
369	A107	600r red	10.00	10.00
370	A106	700r violet	4.50	10.00
371	A108	1000r orange	2.50	10.00
372	A109	2000r dk brn	20.00	20.00
373	A110	5000r yel grn	25.00	30.00
374	A111	10000r plum	27.50	40.00
		Nos. 364-374 (11)	113.60	149.00

Issued by the revolutionary forces in the state of Sao Paulo during the revolt of September, 1932. Subsequently the stamps were recognized by the Federal Government and placed in general use.

Excellent counterfeits of Nos. 373 and 374 exist.

Counterfeit cancellations abound.

City of Vassouras and Illuminated Memorial
A112

Typographed.

1933, Jan. 15 ***Perf. 12*** **Wmk. 222**

375	A112	200r rose red	1.50	75

Commemorative of the centenary of the founding of the city of Vassouras.

No. 306 Surcharged **200 RÉIS**

Perf. 13½x12½

1933, July 28 **Wmk. 218**

376	A76	200r on 300r rose red	85	75
a.		Wmk.218 in echelon (No. 306a)	25.00	25.00
b.		Wmk. 100 (No. 250)	55.00	55.00

Same Surcharge on No. 320.

Perf. 13x12½. **Wmk. 221**

377	A76	200r on 300r rose red	50	40
a.		Inverted surcharge	35.00	
b.		Double surcharge	35.00	

Religious Symbols and Inscriptions
A113

Typographed

1933, Sept. 3 *Perf. 13* Wmk. 222

378	A113	200r dk red	1.00	60

Issued in commemoration of the First National Eucharistic Congress in Brazil.

"Flag of the Race"
A114

1933, Aug. 18

379	A114	200r dp red	1.00	60

Commemorating the raising of the "Flag of the Race" and the 441st anniversary of the sailing of Columbus from Palos, Spain, August 3, 1492.

Republic Figure, Flags of Brazil and Argentina
A115

Wmk. 236

Engraved.

1933, Oct. 7 *Perf. 11½* Wmk. 101

380	A115	200r blue	60	35

Wmkd.

Coat of Arms in Sheet (236)

Watermark (reduced illustration) covers 22 stamps in sheet.

Thick Laid Paper.

Perf. 11, 11½.

381	A115	400r green	90	70
382	A115	600r brt rose	3.50	3.50
383	A115	1000r lt vio	5.00	3.00

Issued in commemoration of the visit of President Justo of the Argentine Republic to Brazil, October 2nd to 7th, 1933.

Allegory: "Faith and Energy"
A116

Allegory of Flight
A117

1933 Typographed. Wmk. 222

384	A116	200r dk red	30	15
385	A116	200r dk vio	35	10

See also Nos. 435, 471 and 491.

Wmk. 236

1934, Apr. 15 Engraved *Perf. 12*

386	A117	200r blue	75	1.00

Issued in commemoration of the first National Aviation Congress at Sao Paulo.

A118

Perf. 11

1934, May 12 Typo. Wmk. 222

387	A118	200r dk ol	50	50
388	A118	400r carmine	2.50	2.50
389	A118	700r ultra	2.50	1.50
390	A118	1000r orange	6.00	1.50

Issued in commemoration of the Seventh International Fair at Rio de Janeiro.

Christ of Corcovado
A119

1934, Oct. 20

392	A119	300r dk red	3.00	3.00
a.		Tête bêche pair	9.00	9.00
393	A119	700r ultra	12.00	7.50
a.		Tête bêche pair	35.00	35.00

Visit of Eugenio Cardinal Pacelli, later Pope Pius XII, to Brazil.

The three printings of Nos. 392–393, distinguishable by shades, sell for different prices.

José de Anchieta
A120

Thick Laid Paper.

1934, Nov. 8 *Perf. 11, 12* Wmk. 236

394	A120	200r yel brn	90	25
395	A120	300r violet	75	40
396	A120	700r blue	3.00	2.50
397	A120	1000r lt grn	6.00	1.50

Issued in commemoration of the 400th anniversary of the birth of Jose de Anchieta, S.J. (1534–1597), Portuguese missionary and "father of Brazilian literature."

"Brazil" and "Uruguay"
A121 A122

Perf. 11

1935, Jan. 8 Typo. Wmk. 222

398	A121	200r orange	90	50
399	A122	300r yellow	1.25	75
400	A122	700r ultra	4.00	3.50
401	A121	1000r dk vio	11.00	5.00

Visit of President Terra of Uruguay.

View of Town of Igarassu
A123

1935, July 1

402	A123	200r mar & brn	1.50	75
403	A123	300r vio & ol brn	1.50	60

Issued in commemoration of the 400th anniversary of the founding of the captaincy of Pernambuco.

Types of 1918-29.

Thick Laid Paper.

Perf. 9½, 11, 12, 12x11.

1934–36 Engraved Wmk. 236

404	A72	2000r violet	1.25	25
405	A89	5000r bl vio ('36)	12.50	50
406	A72	10000r cl ('36)	10.00	1.00

No. 404 is inscribed "BRASIL CORREIO".

Revolutionist
A124

Bento Gonçalves da Silva
A125

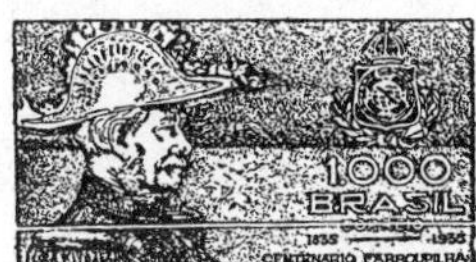

Duke of Caxias
A126

1935, Sept. 20 *Perf. 11, 12*

407	A124	200r black	1.00	75
408	A124	300r rose lake	1.00	60
409	A125	700r dl bl	4.50	3.00
410	A126	1000r lt vio	4.50	2.50

Centenary of the "Ragged" Revolution.

Federal District Coat of Arms
A127

Perf. 11

1935, Oct. 19 Typo. Wmk. 222

411	A127	200r blue	4.00	3.00

Issued in commemoration of the Eighth International Sample Fair held at Rio de Janeiro.

Coutinho's Ship
A128

Arms of Fernandes Coutinho
A129

1935, Oct. 25

412	A128	300r maroon	3.50	1.00
413	A129	700r turq bl	4.50	2.50

Issued in commemoration of the 400th anniversary of the establishment of the first Portuguese colony at Espirito Santo by Vasco Fernandes Coutinho.

Gavea, Rock near Rio de Janeiro
A130

Wmk. 245

Wmkd. Multiple

"CASA DA MOEDA DO BRASIL"

and Small Formée Cross. (245)

1935, Oct. 12 *Perf. 11*

414	A130	300r brn & vio	2.00	1.50
415	A130	300r blk & turq bl	2.00	1.50
416	A130	300r Prus bl & ultra	2.00	1.50
417	A130	300r crim & blk	2.00	1.50

"Child's Day," Oct. 12.

Viscount of Cairú
A131

Perf. 11, 12x11

1936, Jan. 20 Engraved Wmk. 236

418	A131	1200r violet	10.00	5.00

Issued in commemoration of the centenary of the death of José da Silva Lisboa, Viscount of Cairu (1756-1835).

View of Cametá
A132

1936, Feb. 26 *Perf. 11, 12*

419	A132	200r brn org	1.75	1.25
420	A132	300r green	1.75	75

Issued in commemoration of the 300th anniversary of the founding of the city of Cameta, Dec. 24, 1635.

Coining Press
A133

Thick Laid Paper.

1936, Mar. 24 *Perf. 11*

421	A133	300r pur brn, *cr*	1.25	75

Issued in commemoration of the first Numismatic Congress at Sao Paulo, March, 1936.

Carlos Gomes—A134

"Il Guarany"
A135

1936, July 11 *Perf. 11, 11x12*

Thick Laid Paper.

422	A134	300r dl rose	90	60
423	A134	300r blk brn	90	60
424	A135	700r ocher	3.50	1.75
425	A135	700r blue	5.00	2.50

Issued in commemoration of the 100th anniversary of the birth of Antonio Carlos Gomes, who composed the opera "Il Guarany."

Scales of Justice
A136

Perf. 11

1936, July 4 Typo. **Wmk. 222**

426	A136	300r rose	1.00	45

First National Judicial Congress.

Federal District Coat of Arms
A137

Wmk. 249

Wmkd. "CORREIO BRASIL" Multiple. (249)

1936, Nov. 13 Typographed

427	A137	200r rose red	1.25	1.00

Issued in commemoration of the Ninth International Sample Fair held at Rio de Janeiro.

Eucharistic Congress Seal
A138

1936, Dec. 17 *Perf. 11½* **Wmk. 245**

428	A138	300r grn, yel, bl & blk	1.25	75

Issued in commemoration of the Second National Eucharistic Congress in Brazil.

Botafogo Bay
A139

Thick Laid Paper.
Engraved.

1937, Jan. 2 *Perf. 11* **Wmk. 236**

429	A139	700r blue	1.50	75
430	A139	700r black	1.50	75

Issued to commemorate the birth centenary of Francisco Pereira Passos, engineer who planned the modern city of Rio de Janeiro.

Types of 1920-21, 1933.

Perf. 11, 11½ and Compound.

1936-37 Typographed. **Wmk. 249**

431	A75	10r dp brn	15	10
432	A75	20r dl vio	15	10
433	A75	50r bl grn	15	10
434	A75	100r orange	25	10
435	A116	200r dk vio	25	10
436	A76	300r ol grn	25	10
437	A76	400r ultra	35	10
438	A76	500r lt brn	75	10
439	A76	600r brn org ('37)	1.75	10
440	A76	700r dp vio	1.75	10
441	A76	1000r turq bl	3.50	10
		Nos. 431-441 (11)	9.30	1.10

Massed Flags and Star of Esperanto
A140

1937, Jan. 19

442	A140	300r green	1.75	75

Ninth Brazilian Esperanto Congress.

Bay of Rio de Janeiro
A141

Perf. 12½

1937, June 9 **Unwmkd.**

443	A141	300r org red & blk	75	75
444	A141	700r bl & dk brn	2.00	75

Issued in commemoration of the Second South American Radio Communication Conference held in Rio de Janeiro, June 7 to 19, 1937.

Globe
A142

1937, Sept. 4 *Perf. 11, 12* **Wmk. 249**

445	A142	300r green	1.50	75

50th anniversary of Esperanto.

Monroe Palace, Rio de Janeiro
A143

Botanical Garden, Rio de Janeiro
A144

1937, Sept. 30 *Perf. 12½* **Unwmkd.**

446	A143	200r lt brn & bl	75	50
447	A144	300r org & ol grn	75	50
448	A143	2000r grn & cer	6.00	6.00
449	A144	10000r lake & ind	50.00	30.00

Brig. Gen. José da Silva Paes
A145

Eagle and Shield
A146

1937, Oct. 11 *Perf. 11½* **Wmk. 249**

450	A145	300r blue	1.00	40

Bicentenary of Rio Grande do Sul.

1937, Dec. 2 Typo. *Perf. 11*

451	A146	400r dk bl	1.25	50

Issued in commemoration of the 150th anniversary of the Constitution of the United States of America.

Bags of Brazilian Coffee
A147

Frame Engr., Center Typo.
Center Typographed.

1938, Jan. 17 *Perf. 12½* **Unwmkd.**

452	A147	1200r multi	6.00	1.00

Arms of Olinda
A148

Perf. 11, 11x11½.

1938, Jan. 24 Engraved Wmk. 249

453	A148	400r violet	75	40

Issued in commemoration of the fourth centenary of the founding of the city of Olinda.

Independence Memorial, Ypiranga
A149

1938, Jan. 24 Typo. *Perf. 11*

454	A149	400r brn ol	1.00	40

Issued to commemorate the proclamation of Brazil's independence by Dom Pedro, Sept. 7, 1822.

Iguaçu Falls
A150

Engraved.

1938, Jan. 10 *Perf. 12½* **Unwmkd.**

455	A150	1000r sep & yel brn	2.00	1.25
456	A150	5000r ol blk & grn	22.50	8.50

Couto de Magalhães
A151

Perf. 11, 11x11½

1938, Mar. 17 **Wmk. 249**

457	A151	400r dl grn	75	35

Issued to commemorate the centenary of the birth of General Couto de Magalhaes (1837–1898), statesman, soldier, explorer, writer, developer.

Types of 1918–38

Perf. 11, 12x11, 12x11½, 12.

1938 Engraved **Wmk. 249**

458	A72	2000r bl vio	8.00	15
459	A89	5000r vio bl	14.00	15
a.		5000r dp bl	30.00	90
460	A72	10000r rose lake	35.00	1.20

No. 458 is inscribed "BRASIL CORREIO".

Types of 1920-22.
Typographed.

1938 *Perf. 11.* **Wmk. 245**

461	A75	50r bl grn	40	80
462	A75	100r orange	40	80
463	A76	300r ol grn	40	50

463A	A76	400r ultra	100.00	60.00
463B	A76	500r red brn	60	2.00
		Nos. 461-463B (5)	101.80	64.10

National Archives Building
A152

1938, May 20 **Wmk. 249**

464	A152	400r brown	75	35

Centenary of National Archives.

Souvenir Sheets.

Sir Rowland Hill
A153

1938, Oct. 22 ***Imperf.***

465	A153	400r dl grn, sheet of 10	20.00	15.00
a.		Single stamp	1.25	1.25

Issued in commemoration of the Brazilian International Philatelic Exposition (Brapex).

Issued in sheets measuring 106x118 mm. A few perforated sheets exist.

President Vargas
A154

1938, Nov. 10 ***Perf. 11***

Without Gum

466	A154	400r sl bl, sheet of 10	7.00	7.00
a.		Single stamp	65	65

Issued in commemoration of the Constitution of Brazil, set up by President Vargas, Nov. 10, 1937. Size: 113x135½mm.

Wmk. 256

Types of 1920-33.

Wmkd.

"CASA+DA+MOEDA+DO+BRAZIL" in 8mm. Letters (256)

1939 Typographed. ***Perf. 11.***

467	A75	10r red brn	30	30
468	A75	20r dl vio	15	15
469	A75	50r bl grn	15	10
470	A75	100r yel org	20	10
471	A116	200r dk vio	35	10
472	A76	400r ultra	1.25	10
473	A76	600r dl org	1.00	10
474	A76	1000r turq bl	7.50	10
		Nos. 467-474 (8)	10.90	1.05

View of Rio de Janeiro
A155

View of Santos
A156

1939, June 14 Engraved **Wmk. 249**

475	A155	1200r dl vio	2.50	25

1939, Aug. 23

476	A156	400r dl bl	60	30

Centenary of founding of Santos.

Chalice Vine and Blossoms
A157

Eucharistic Congress Seal
A158

1939, Aug. 23

477	A157	400r green	2.00	50

Issued in commemoration of the first South American Botanical Congress held in January, 1938.

1939, Sept. 3

478	A158	400r rose red	60	30

Third National Eucharistic Congress.

Duke of Caxias, Army Patron
A159

1939, Sept. 12 Photo. ***Rouletted***

479	A159	400r dp ultra	60	40

Issued for Soldiers' Day.

George Washington
A159a

Grover Cleveland
A159c

Emperor Pedro II
A159b

Statue of Friendship, Given by U. S. A.
A159d

Engraved.

1939, Oct. 7 ***Perf. 12*** **Unwmkd.**

480	A159a	400r yel org	75	40
481	A159b	800r dk grn	45	25
482	A159c	1200r rose car	1.00	25
483	A159d	1600r dk bl	1.00	40

New York World's Fair.

Benjamin Constant
A160

Fonseca on Horseback
A161

Manuel Deodoro da Fonseca and President Vargas
A162

Rouletted

1939, Nov. 15 Photo. **Wmk. 249**

484	A160	400r dp grn	60	30
485	A162	1200r chocolate	1.50	40

Engraved ***Perf. 11***

486	A161	800r gray blk	90	45

Issued in commemoration of the 50th anniversary of the Proclamation of the Republic.

President Roosevelt, President Vargas and Map of the Americas
A163

1940, Apr. 14

487	A163	400r sl bl	1.25	60

Pan American Union, 50th anniversary.

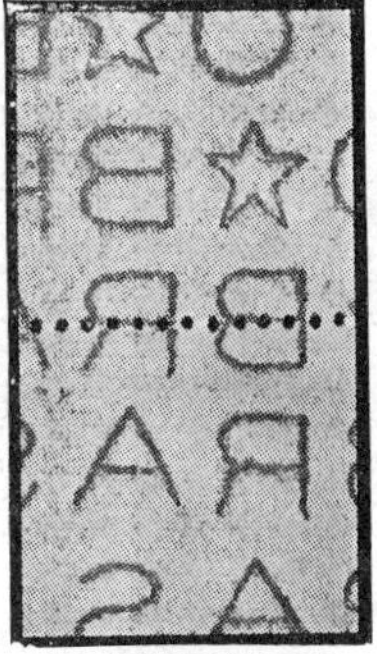

Wmk. 264

Types of 1920-33.

Wmkd.

"☆ CORREIO ☆ BRASIL ☆"

Multiple. Letters 7mm. high. (264)

1940-41 Typographed. ***Perf. 11.***

488	A75	10r red brn	10	25
489	A75	20r dl vio	15	25
489A	A75	50r bl grn ('41)	75	75
490	A75	100r yel org	1.00	8
491	A116	200r violet	75	8
492	A76	400r ultra	2.50	8
493	A76	600r dl org	2.50	8
494	A76	1000r turq bl	12.50	8
		Nos. 488-494 (8)	20.25	1.65

Map of Brazil
A164

1940, Sept. 7 **Engraved**

495	A164	400r carmine	65	35
a.		Unwmkd.	75.00	50.00

Issued in commemoration of the 9th Brazilian Congress of Geography held at Florianopolis.

Victoria Regia Water Lily
A165

President Vargas
A166

Relief Map of Brazil
A167

1940, Oct. 30 ***Perf. 11*** **Wmk. 249**

Without Gum

496	A165	1000r dl vio	3.50	2.50
a.		Sheet of ten	35.00	40.00
497	A166	5000r red	14.00	6.50
a.		Sheet of ten	140.00	175.00
498	A167	10,000r sl bl	15.00	3.50
a.		Sheet of ten	150.00	175.00

New York World's Fair.

All three sheets exist unwatermarked and also with papermaker's watermark of large globe and "AMERICA BANK" in sheet. A few imperforate sheets also exist.

Joaquim Machado de Assis
A168

Pioneers and Buildings of Porto Alegre
A169

1940, Nov. 1

499	A168	400r black	75	40

Birth centenary of Joaquim Maria Machado de Assis, poet and novelist.

1940, Nov. 2 **Wmk. 264**

500	A169	400r green	60	35

Issued to commemorate the bicentenary of the colonization of Porto Alegre.

Proclamation of King John IV of Portugal
A173

1940, Dec. 1 **Wmk. 249**

501	A173	1200r bl blk	2.00	50

Issued in commemoration of the 800th anniversary of Portuguese independence and the 300th anniversary of the restoration of the monarchy.

No. 501 was also printed on paper with papermaker's watermark of large globe and "AMERICA BANK." Unwatermarked copies are from these sheets.

Brazilian Flags and Head of Liberty
A175

Calendar Sheet and Inscription "Day of the Fifth General Census of Brazil"
A176

Engraved.

1940, Dec. 18 ***Perf. 11*** **Wmk. 256**

502	A175	400r dl vio	75	40
b.		Unwmkd.	60.00	60.00

Wmk. 245

502A	A175	400r dl vio	50.00	50.00

Issued in commemoration of the 10th anniversary of the inauguration of President Vargas.

Typographed.

1941, Jan. 14 ***Perf. 11*** **Wmk. 256**

503	A176	400r bl & red	45	20

Wmk. 245

504	A176	400r bl & red	3.50	1.00

Fifth general census of Brazil.

The only foreign revenue stamps listed in this Catalogue are those authorized for prepayment of postage.

King Alfonso Henriques
A177

Father Antonio Vieira
A178

Salvador Corrêia de Sa e Benevides
A179

President Carmona of Portugal and President Vargas
A180

Photogravure.

1940-41 ***Rouletted*** **Wmk. 264**

504A	A177	200r pink	20	15
505	A178	400r ultra	30	20
506	A179	800r brt vio	35	20
506A	A180	5400r sl grn	2.25	80

Wmk. 249

507	A177	200r pink	6.00	4.00
507A	A178	400r ultra	30.00	10.00
508	A180	5400r sl grn	3.50	1.75
		Nos. 504A-508 (7)	42.60	17.10

Issued in commemoration of the 800th anniversary of Portuguese Independence.

José de Anchieta
A181

Amador Bueno
A182

Engraved

1941, Aug. 1 ***Perf. 11*** **Wmk. 264**

509	A181	1000r gray vio	1.75	1.00

Society of Jesus, 400th anniversary.

1941, Oct. 20 ***Perf. 11½***

510	A182	400r black	80	50

Issued in commemoration of the 300th anniversary of the acclamation of Amador Bueno (1572-1648) as king of Sao Paulo.

Air Force Emblem
A183

1941, Oct. 20 ***Perf. 11***

511	A183	5400r sl grn	6.00	3.50

Issued in connection with Aviation Week, as propaganda for the Brazilian Air Force.

Petroleum
A184

Agriculture
A185

Steel Industry
A186

Commerce
A187

Marshal Peixoto
A188

Count of Porto Alegre
A189

Admiral J. A. C. Maurity
A190

"Armed Forces"
A191

Vargas
A192

Typographed

1941-42 ***Perf. 11*** **Wmk. 264**

512	A184	10r yel brn	10	5
513	A184	20r ol grn	10	5
514	A184	50r ol bis	10	5
515	A184	100r bl grn	20	5
516	A185	200r brn org	50	5
517	A185	300r lil rose	25	15
518	A185	400r grnsh bl	75	10
519	A185	500r salmon	35	10
520	A186	600r violet	75	10
521	A186	700r brt rose	35	15
522	A186	1000r gray	2.00	10
523	A186	1200r dl bl	4.00	10
524	A187	2000r gray vio	3.00	10

Engraved

525	A188	5000r blue	6.00	15
526	A189	10,000r rose red	7.50	1.00
527	A190	20,000r dp brn	7.50	1.25
528	A191	50,000r red ('42)	20.00	5.00
529	A192	100,000r bl ('42)	40	6.00
		Nos. 512-529 (18)	53.85	14.55

Nos. 512 to 527 and later issues come on thick or thin paper. The stamps on both papers also exist with three vertical green lines printed on the back, a control mark.

See also Nos. 541-587, 592-593, 656-670.

Bernardino de Campos
A193

Prudente de Morais
A194

1942, Jan. 25

533	A193	1000r red	2.50	75
534	A194	1200r blue	6.00	50

Issued in commemoration of the 100th anniversary of the birth of Bernardino de Campos and Prudente de Morais, lawyers and statesmen of Brazil.

Head of Indo-Brazilian Bull
A195

1942, May 1 ***Perf. 11½*** **Wmk. 264**

535	A195	200r blue	75	40
536	A195	400r org brn	75	40
a.		Wmk. 267	60.00	60.00

Issued in commemoration of the second Agriculture and Livestock Show of Central Brazil held at Uberaba. Wmk. 267 is illustrated with Nos. 573-587.

Outline of Brazil and Torch of Knowledge
A196

Map of Brazil Showing Goiania
A197

Perf. 11

1942, July 5 **Typo.** **Wmk. 264**

537	A196	400r org brn	70	35

8th Brazilian Congress of Education.

1942, July 5

538	A197	400r lt vio	70	40

Founding of Goiania city.

Seal of Congress
A198

1942, Sept. 20 **Wmk. 264**

539	A198	400r ol bis	50	25
a.		Wmk. 267	20.00	15.00

Issued to commemorate the 4th National Eucharistic Congress at Sao Paulo. Wmk. 267 is illustrated with Nos. 573-587.

Types of 1941-42.

1942-47 ***Perf. 11.*** **Wmk. 245**

541	A184	20r ol grn	10	40
542	A184	50r ol bis	10	10
543	A184	100r bl grn	40	40
544	A185	200r brn org	65	50
545	A185	400r grnsh bl	40	10
546	A186	600r lt vio	3.00	10
547	A186	700r brt rose	35	80
548	A186	1200r dl bl	1.25	15
549	A187	2000r gray vio ('47)	12.50	7.50

Engraved

550	A188	5000r blue	7.50	40
551	A189	10,000r rose red	6.00	1.50
552	A190	20,000r dp brn ('47)	4.50	45
553	A192	100,000r blue	3.50	6.00
		Nos. 541-553 (13)	40.25	18.40

Wmk. 268

Types of 1941-42.
Wmkd.
"CASA+DA+MOEDA+DO+BRASIL"
in 6mm. Letters. (268)

1941-47 Typographed. *Perf. 11.*

554	A184	20r ol grn	20	15
555	A184	50r ol bis ('47)	60	60
556	A184	100r bl grn ('43)	20	15
557	A185	200r brn org ('43)	20	10
558	A185	300r lil rose ('43)	15	10
559	A185	400r grnsh bl ('42)	35	15
560	A185	500r sal ('43)	20	10
561	A186	600r violet	70	8
562	A186	700r brt rose ('45)	40	8
563	A186	1000r gray	75	8
564	A186	1200r dp bl ('44)	75	15
565	A187	2000r gray vio ('43)	3.50	10

Engraved

566	A188	5000r bl ('43)	4.00	15
567	A189	10,000r rose red ('43)	8.50	45
568	A190	20,000r dp brn ('42)	20.00	50
569	A191	50,000r red ('42)	20.00	3.50
a.		50,000r dk brn red ('47)	15.00	3.50
570	A192	100,000r blue	65	65
		Nos. 554-570 (17)	61.15	7.09

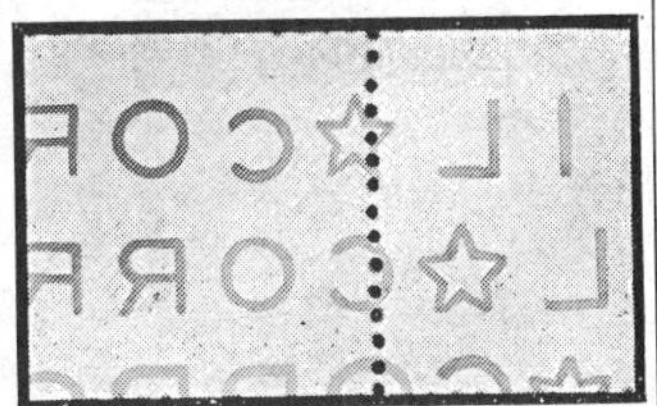

Wmk. 267

Wmkd.
"☆ CORREIO ☆ BRASIL ☆"
Multiple in Small Letters
(5 mm. high). (267)

Types of 1941-42.

1942-47 Typographed Wmk. 267

573	A184	20r ol grn ('43)	20	10
574	A184	50r ol bis ('43)	10	10
575	A184	100r bl grn ('43)	25	10
576	A185	200r brn org ('43)	30	35
577	A185	400r grnsh bl	30	10
578	A185	500r sal ('43)	75.00	10.00
579	A186	600r vio ('43)	60	40
580	A186	700r brt rose ('47)	50	1.50
581	A186	1000r gray ('44)	1.00	15
582	A186	1200r dl bl	2.00	10
583	A187	2000r gray vio	3.50	10

Engraved

584	A188	5000r blue	6.00	20
585	A189	10,000r rose red ('44)	6.00	1.50
586	A190	20,000r dp brn ('45)	12.00	60
587	A191	50,000r red ('43)	35.00	7.50
		Nos. 573-587 (15)	142.75	22.80

1942 Typographed Wmk. 249

592	A184	100r bl grn	5.00	3.50
593	A186	600r violet	5.00	1.00

Map Showing Amazon River
A199

1943, Mar. 19 *Perf. 11* Wmk. 267

607	A199	40c org brn	50	50

Issued in commemoration of the 400th anniversary of the discovery of the Amazon River.

Reproduction of Brazil Stamp of 1866
A200

Adaptation of 1843 "Bull's-eye"
A201

1943, Mar. 28 Wmk. 267

608	A200	40c violet	75	40
a.		Wmk. 268	*1,000.*	

Centenary of city of Petropolis.

1943, Aug. 1 Engraved *Imperf.*

609	A201	30c black	1.00	50
610	A201	60c black	1.25	50
611	A201	90c black	1.00	50

Centenary of the first postage stamp of Brazil. The 30c and 90c exist unwatermarked; prices $25 and $65.

Souvenir Sheet.

A202

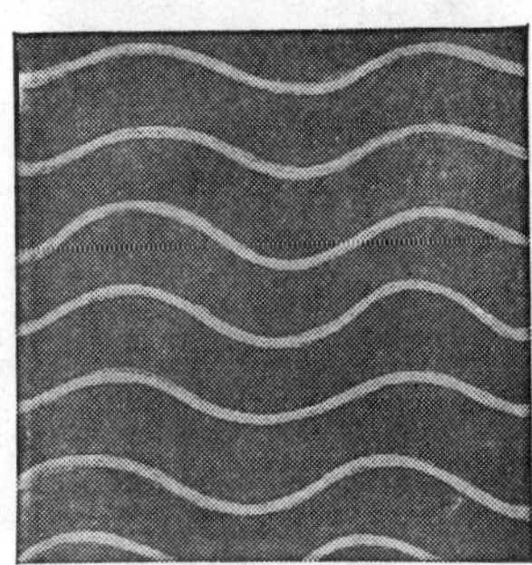

Wmk. 281

Wmkd. Wavy Lines. (281)
Horizontally or Vertically.
Without Gum.

1943 Engraved *Imperf.*

612	A202	Sheet of three	10.00	9.00
a.		30c blk	2.50	2.50
b.		60c blk	2.50	2.50
c.		90c blk	2.50	2.50

Sheet measures $125\frac{1}{2}$x$94\frac{1}{2}$mm.

Ubaldino do Amaral
A203

"Justice"
A204

Perf. 11, 12

1943, Aug. 27 Typo. Wmk. 264

613	A203	40c dl sl grn	50	25
a.		Wmk. 267	17.50	17.50

Birth centenary of Ubaldino do Amaral, banker and statesman.

1943, Aug. 30 Wmk. 267

614	A204	2cr brt rose	1.00	75

Centenary of Institute of Brazilian Lawyers.

Indo-Brazilian Bull
A205

1943, Aug. 30 Engraved

615	A205	40c dk red brn	1.25	75

9th Livestock Show at Bahia.

José Barbosa Rodrigues
A206

1943, Nov. 13 Typographed

616	A206	40c bluish grn	60	25

Birth centenary of José Barbosa Rodrigues, botanist.

Charity Hospital, Santos
A207

1943, Nov. 7 Engraved

617	A207	1cr blue	75	40

400th anniversary of Charity Hospital, Santos.

Pedro Americo
A208

Perf. 11

1943, Dec. 16 Typo. Wmk. 267

618	A208	40c brn org	50	30

Issued to commemorate the birth centenary of Pedro Americo de Figueirido e Melo (1843–1905), artist-hero and statesman.

Gen. A. E. Gomes Carneiro
A209

1944, Feb. 9 Engraved

619	A209	1.20cr rose	1.00	50

50th anniversary of the Lapa siege.

Statue of Baron of Rio Branco
A210

1944, May 13 Typographed

620	A210	1cr blue	75	40

Issued to commemorate the unveiling of a statue of the Baron of Rio Branco.

Duke of Caxias
A211

Granite Paper.

1944, May 13 *Perf. 12* Unwmkd.

621	A211	1.20cr bl grn & pale org	90	50

Centenary of pacification of Sao Paulo and Minas Gerais in an independence movement in 1842.

YMCA Seal
A212

1944, June 7 Litho. *Perf. 11*
Granite Paper.

622	A212	40c dp bl, car & yel	40	30

Centenary of Young Men's Christian Assn.

Chamber of Commerce
Rio Grande
A213

Engraved.

1944, Sept. 25 *Perf. 12* **Wmk. 268**

623	A213	40c lt yel brn	40	35

Issued to commemorate the centenary of the Chamber of Commerce of Rio Grande.

Martim F. R. de Andrada
A214

1945, Jan. 30 *Perf. 11*

624	A214	40c blue	40	35

Issued to commemorate the centenary of the death of Martim F. R. de Andrada, statesman.

Meeting of Duke of Caxias and David Canabarro
A215

1945, Mar. 19 Photogravure

625	A215	40c ultra	40	25

Centenary of the pacification of Rio Grande do Sul.

Globe and "Esperanto"
A216

1945, Apr. 16

626	A216	40c lt bl grn	60	30

10th Esperanto Congress, Rio de Janeiro, Apr. 14–22.

Baron of Rio Branco's Bookplate
A217

1945, Apr. 20 *Perf. 11* **Wmk. 268**

627	A217	40c violet	30	25

Issued to commemorate the centenary of the birth of José Maria da Silva Paranhos, Baron of Rio Branco.

Tranquility
A218

Glory
A219

Victory
A220

Peace
A221

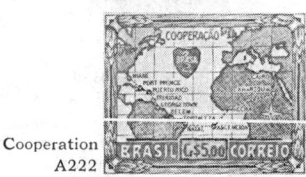

Cooperation
A222

Rouletted 7

1945, May 8 Engraved **Wmk. 268**

628	A218	20c dk rose vio	25	25
629	A219	40c dk car	28	25
630	A220	1cr dl org	60	50
631	A221	2cr stl bl	1.50	75
632	A222	5cr green	3.00	1.00
		Nos. 628-632 (5)	5.63	2.75

Victory of the Allied Nations in Europe.
Nos. 628–632 exist on thin card, imperf. and unwatermarked.

Francisco Manoel da Silva
A223

Perf. 12

1945, May 30 Typo. **Wmk. 245**

633	A223	40c brt rose	75	40
a.		Wmk. 268	11.00	11.00

Issued to commemorate the 150th anniversary of the birth of Francisco Manoel da Silva (1795–1865), composer (in 1831) of the national anthem.

Bahia Institute of Geography and History
A224

1945, May 30 *Perf. 11* **Wmk. 268**

634	A224	40c lt ultra	35	25

Issued to commemorate the 50th anniversary of the founding of the Institute of Geography and History at Bahia.

Emblems of 5th Army and B. E. F.
A225 A226

U.S. Flag and Shoulder Patches
A227

Brazilian Flag and Shoulder Patches—A228

Victory Symbol and Shoulder Patches
A229

1945, July 18 Lithographed

635	A225	20c multi	25	25
636	A226	40c multi	25	25
637	A227	1cr multi	1.25	75
638	A228	2cr multi	1.75	1.00
639	A229	5cr multi	5.00	1.25
		Nos. 635-639 (5)	8.50	3.50

Issued in honor of the Brazilian Expeditionary Force and the United States Fifth Army Battle against the Axis in Italy.

Radio Tower and Map
A230

1945, Sept. 3 Engraved

640	A230	1.20cr gray	60	25

Third Inter-American Conference on Radio Communications.
No. 640 was reproduced on a souvenir card with blue background and inscriptions. Size: 145x161mm.

A 40c lilac stamp, picturing the International Bridge between Argentina and Brazil and portraits of Presidents Justo and Vargas, was prepared late in 1945. It was not issued, but later was sold, without postal value, to collectors. Price, 15 cents.

Adm. Saldanha da Gama
A231

1946, Apr. 7

641	A231	40c gray blk	30	30

Issued to commemorate the centenary of the birth of Admiral Luiz Felipe Saldanha da Gama (1846–1895).

Princess Isabel d'Orleans-Braganca
A232

1946, July 29 **Unwmkd.**

642	A232	40c black	35	35

Issued to commemorate the centenary of the birth of Princess Isabel d'Orleans-Braganca.

Post Horn, V and Envelope
A233

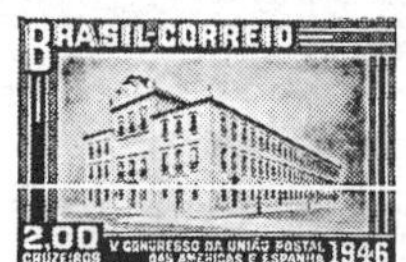

Post Office, Rio de Janeiro
A234

Bay of Rio de Janeiro and Plane
A235

Perf. 11

1946, Sept. 2 Litho. **Wmk. 268**

643	A233	40c blk & pale org	30	25

Perf. 12½ Engraved Unwmkd.

Center in Ultramarine.

644	A234	2cr slate	75	25
645	A234	5cr org brn	4.50	1.50
646	A234	10cr dk vio	5.00	1.50

Center in Brown Orange.

647	A235	1.30cr dk grn	50	50
648	A235	1.70cr car rose	75	50
649	A235	2.20cr dp ultra	75	75
		Nos. 643-649 (7)	12.30	5.25

Nos. 643 to 649 were issued to commemorate the 5th Postal Union Congress of the Americas and Spain.
No. 643 was reproduced on a souvenir card with inscriptions and marginal illustrations of the Palacio da Fazenda, Rio de Janeiro. Size: 188x239mm. Sold for 10 cruzeiros.

Liberty
A236

Perf. 11x11½

1946, Sept. 18 Wmk. 268

650 A236 40c blk & gray 20 15
a. Unwmkd. 15.00

Adoption of the Constitution of 1946.

Columbus Lighthouse, Dominican Republic
A237

1946, Sept. 14 Litho. *Perf. 11*

651 A237 5cr Prus grn 6.50 2.50

Orchid
A238

Gen. A. E. Gomes Carneiro
A239

1946, Nov. 8 Wmk. 268

652 A238 40c ultra, red & yel 55 30
a. Unwmkd. 27.50

Issued to publicize the 4th National Exhibition of Orchids, Rio de Janeiro, November, 1946.

Perf. 10½x12

1946, Dec. 6 Engraved Unwmkd.

653 A239 40c dp grn 20 20

Issued to commemorate the centenary of the birth of General Antonio Ernesto Gomes Carneiro.

Brazilian Academy of Letters
A240

1946, Dec. 14 *Perf. 11*

654 A240 40c blue 25 20

Issued to commemorate the 50th anniversary of the foundation of the Brazilian Academy of Letters, Rio de Janeiro.

Antonio de Castro Alves—A241

1947, Mar. 14 Litho. Wmk. 267

655 A241 40c bluish grn 25 25

Issued to commemorate the birth centenary of Antonio de Castro Alves (1847–1871), poet.

Types of 1941–42,
Values in Centavos or Cruzeiros.
Typographed

1947–54 *Perf. 11* Wmk. 267

656	A184	2c olive	10	8
657	A184	5c yel brn	10	8
658	A184	10c green	10	8
659	A185	20c brn org	10	8
660	A185	30c dk lil rose	20	8
661	A185	40c blue	20	8
b.		Wmk. 268	750.00	50.00
661A	A185	50c salmon	25	8
662	A186	60c lt vio	35	8
663	A186	70c brt rose ('54)	25	10
664	A186	1cr gray	60	10
665	A186	1.20cr dl bl	80	10
a.		Wmk. 268	6.00	9.00
666	A187	2cr gray vio	1.80	8

Engraved

667	A188	5cr blue	6.50	10
668	A189	10cr rose red	6.50	10

Perf. 11, 13.

669	A190	20cr dp brn	12.50	60
670	A191	50cr red	25.00	40
		Nos. 656-670 (16)	55.35	2.22

The 5cr, 20cr and 50cr also exist with perf. 12 to 13.

Pres. Gonzalez Videla of Chile
A242

1947, June 26 *Perf. 12x11* Unwmkd.

671 A242 40c dk brn org 25 20

Issued to commemorate the visit of President Gabriel Gonzalez Videla of Chile, June 1947.

A souvenir folder contains four impressions of No. 671, measures 6½x8¼ inches and has marginal inscriptions, including a coat of arms, in blue.

"Peace" and Western Hemisphere
A243

1947, Aug. 15 *Perf. 11x12*

672 A243 1.20cr blue 35 25

Issued to commemorate the Inter-American Defense Conference at Rio de Janeiro, August–September, 1947.

Pres. Harry S Truman, Map and Statue of Liberty
A244

1947, Sept. 1 Typo. *Perf. 12x11*

673 A244 40c ultra 30 25

Visit of U.S. President Harry S Truman to Brazil, Sept. 1947.

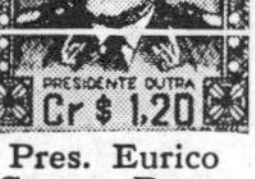

Pres. Eurico Gaspar Dutra
A245

Mother and Child
A246

Engraved.

1947, Sept. 7 *Perf. 11* Wmk. 268

674 A245 20c green 20 20
675 A245 40c rose car 25 15
676 A245 1.20cr dp bl 50 22

The souvenir sheet containing Nos. 674–676 is listed as No. C73A. See also No. 679.

1947, Oct. 10 Typo. Unwmkd.

677 A246 40c brt ultra 25 20

Issued to mark Child Care Week, 1947.

Arms of Belo Horizonte
A247

Globe
A248

1947, Dec. 12 Engraved Wmk. 267

678 A247 1.20cr rose car 60 25

Issued to commemorate the 50th anniversary of the founding of the city of Belo Horizonte.

Dutra Type of 1947.

1948 Engraved. Wmk. 267

679 A245 20c green 3.00 3.00

1948, July 10 Lithographed

680 A248 40c dl grn & pale lil 50 20

Issued to commemorate the International Exposition of Industry and Commerce, Petropolis, 1948.

Arms of Paranagua
A249

Child Reading Book
A250

1948, July 29

681 A249 5cr bis brn 3.00 1.00

Issued to commemorate the 300th anniversary of the founding of the city of Paranagua, July 29, 1648.

1948, Aug. 1

682 A250 40c green 30 20

National Education Campaign.

No. 682 was reproduced on a souvenir card with brown orange background and inscriptions. Size: 124x157mm.

Tiradentes
A251

Symbolical of Cancer Eradication
A252

1948, Nov. 12

683 A251 40c brn org 25 20

Issued to commemorate the 200th anniversary of the birth of Joaquim José da Silva Xavier (Tiradentes).

1948, Dec. 14

684 A252 40c claret 25 20

Anti-cancer publicity.

Adult Student
A253

1949, Jan. 3 *Perf. 12x11* Wmk. 267

685 A253 60c red vio & pink 25 15

Campaign for adult education.

"Battle of Guararapes," by Vitor Meireles—A254

1949, Feb. 15 *Perf. 11½x12*

686 A254 60c lt bl 1.25 60

Issued to commemorate the 300th anniversary of the Second Battle of Guararapes.

Church of São Francisco de Paula
A255

Manuel de Nobrega
A256

Engraved.

1949, Mar. 8 *Perf. 11x12* Unwmkd.

687 A255 60c dk brn 30 25
a. Souvenir sheet 40.00 40.00

Bicentenary of city of Ouro Fino, state of Minas Gerais.

No. 687a contains one imperf. stamp similar to No. 687, with dates in lower margin. Size: 70x89mm.

1949, Mar. 29 *Imperf.*

688 A256 60c violet 25 25

Issued to commemorate the 400th anniversary of the founding of the City of Salvador.

Emblem of Brazilian Air Force and Plane—A257

1949, June 18

689 A257 60c bl vio 25 25

Issued to honor the Brazilian Air Force.

Star and Angel
A258

Lithographed.

1949 *Perf. 11x12.* Wmk. 267

690 A258 60c pink 25 25

Issued to publicize the first Ecclesiastical Congress, Salvador, Bahia.

"U. P. U." Encircling Globe
A259

1949, Oct. 22 Typo. *Perf. 12x11*

691 A259 1.50cr blue 40 20

Issued to commemorate the 75th anniversary of the formation of the Universal Postal Union.

Ruy Barbosa
A260

Engraved.

1949, Dec. 14 *Perf. 12* Unwmkd.

692 A260 1.20cr rose car 75 40

Centenary of birth of Ruy Barbosa.

Joaquim Cardinal Arcoverde
A261

Perf. 11x12

1950, Feb. 27 Litho. Wmk. 267

693 A261 60c rose 30 25

Issued to commemorate the birth centenary of Joaquim Cardinal Arcoverde A. Cavalcanti.

Grapes and Factory
A262

1950, Mar. 15 *Perf. 12x11*

694 A262 60c rose lake 20 20

Issued to commemorate the 75th anniversary of Italian immigration to the state of Rio Grande do Sul.

Virgin of the Globe
A263

Globe and Soccer Players
A264

1950, May 31 *Perf. 11x12*

695 A263 60c blk & lt bl 30 20

Issued to commemorate the centenary of the establishment in Brazil of the Daughters of Charity of St. Vincent de Paul.

1950, June 24

696 A264 60c ultra, bl & gray 1.00 50

4th World Soccer Championship.

Symbolical of Brazilian Population Growth
A265

1950, July 10 Typo. *Perf. 12x11*

697 A265 60c rose lake 30 20

Issued to publicize the 6th Brazilian census.

Dr. Oswaldo Cruz
A266

1950, Aug. 23 Litho. *Perf. 11x12*

698 A266 60c org brn 30 25

Issued to publicize the 5th International Congress of Microbiology.

View of Blumenau and Itajai River
A267

1950, Sept. 9 *Perf. 12x11* Wmk. 267

699 A267 60c brt pink 25 20

Centenary of the founding of Blumenau.

Amazonas Theater, Manaus
A268

1950, Sept. 27

700 A268 60c lt brn red 20 20

Centenary of Amazonas Province.

Arms of Juiz de Fora
A269

1950, Oct. 24 *Perf. 11x12*

701 A269 60c carmine 25 25

Centenary of the founding of Juiz de Fora.

Post Office at Recife
A270

1951, Jan. 10 Typo. *Perf. 12x11*

702 A270 60c carmine 20 20
703 A270 1.20cr carmine 30 20

Issued to commemorate the opening of the new building of the Pernambuco Post Office.

Arms of Joinville
A271

Jean-Baptiste de La Salle
A272

1951, Mar. 9 *Perf. 11x12*

704 A271 60c org brn 20 20

Centenary of the founding of Joinville.

1951, Apr. 30 Lithographed

705 A272 60c blue 30 25

Issued to commemorate the 300th anniversary of the birth of Jean-Baptiste de La Salle.

Heart and Flowers
A273

Sylvio Romero
A274

1951, May 13 Engraved

706 A273 60c dp plum 30 25

Issued to honor Mother's Day, May 14, 1951.

1951, Apr. 21 Lithographed

707 A274 60c dl vio brn 20 20

Issued to commemorate the centenary of the birth of Sylvio Romero (1851–1914), poet and author.

João Caetano, Stage and Masks
A275

1951, July 9 *Perf. 12x11*

708 A275 60c lt gray bl 25 20

Issued to publicize the first Brazilian Theater Congress, Rio de Janeiro, July 9–13, 1951.

Orville A. Derby
A276

First Mass Celebrated in Brazil
A277

1951, July 23 *Perf. 11x12*

709 A276 2cr slate 40 40

Issued to commemorate the centenary of the birth (in New York State) of Orville A. Derby, geologist.

1951, July 25

710 A277 60c dl brn & buff 30 25

Issued to publicize the 4th Inter-American Congress on Catholic Education, Rio de Janeiro, 1951.

Euclides Pinto Martins
A278

1951, Aug. 16 *Perf. 12x11*

711 A278 3.80cr brn & cit 2.25 35

Issued to commemorate the 29th anniversary of the first flight from New York City to Rio de Janeiro.

Monastery of the Rock
A279

1951, Sept. 8

712 A279 60c dl brn & cr 25 25

Founding of Vitoria, 4th centenary.

Santos-Dumont and Model Plane Contest
A280

Dirigible and Eiffel Tower
A281

Lithographed.

1951, Oct. 19 ***Perf. 11x12*** **Wmk. 267**

713	A280	60c sal & dk brn	75	50

Engraved

Unwmkd.

714	A281	3.80cr dk pur	2.25	50

Issued to publicize the Week of the Wing and to commemorate the 50th anniversary of Santos-Dumont's flight around the Eiffel Tower.

In December 1951, Nos. 713 and 714 were privately overprinted: "Exposicao Filatelica Regional Distrito Federal 15-XII-1951 23-XII-1951." These were attached to souvenir sheets bearing engraved facsimiles of Nos. 38, 49 and 51, which were sold by Clube Filatelico do Brasil to mark its 20th anniversary. The overprinted stamps on the sheets were cancelled, but 530 "unused" sets were sold by the club.

Farmers and Ear of Wheat
A282

1951, Nov. 10 **Litho.** **Wmk. 267**

715	A282	60c dp grn & gray	40	30

Issued to publicize Festival of Grain at Bagé, 1951.

Map and Open Bible
A283

1951, Dec. 9 ***Perf. 12x11***

716	A283	1.20cr brn org	75	40

Issued to publicize the Day of the Bible.

Queen Isabella A284 — Henrique Oswald A285

1952, Mar. 10 ***Perf. 11x12***

717	A284	3.80cr lt bl	1.00	30

Issued to commemorate the 500th anniversary of the birth of Queen Isabella I of Spain.

1952, Apr. 22

718	A285	60c brown	30	25

Issued to commemorate the centenary of the birth of Henrique Oswald (1852–1931), composer.

Vicente Licinio Cardoso A286 — Map and Symbol of Labor A287

1952, May 2

719	A286	60c gray bl	30	25

4th Brazilian Homeopathic Congress.

1952, Apr. 30

720	A287	1.50cr brnsh pink	40	25

Issued to publicize the 5th International Labor Organization Conference for American Countries.

Gen. Polidoro da Fonseca A288 — Luiz de Albuquerque M. P. Caceres A289

Portraits: 5cr, Baron de Capanema. 10cr, Minister Eusebio de Queiros.

Engraved

1952, May 11 ***Perf. 11*** **Unwmkd.**

721	A288	2.40cr lt car	50	35
722	A288	5cr blue	3.50	45
723	A288	10cr dk bl grn	3.50	45

Centenary of telegraph in Brazil.

Perf. 11x12

1952, June 8 **Litho.** **Wmk. 267**

724	A289	1.20cr vio bl	30	20

Issued to commemorate the 200th anniversary of the founding of the city of Mato Grosso.

Symbolizing the Glory of Sports
A290

1952, July 21 ***Perf. 12x11***

725	A290	1.20cr dp bl & bl	85	40

Fluminense Soccer Club, 50th anniversary.

José Antonio Saraiva A291 — Emperor Dom Pedro A292

1952, Aug. 16 ***Perf. 11x12***

726	A291	60c lil rose	20	20

Issued to commemorate the centenary of the founding of Terezina, capital of Piaui State.

1952, Sept. 3 **Wmk. 267**

727	A292	60c lt bl & blk	25	20

Issued for Stamp Day and the 2nd Philatelic Exhibition of Sao Paulo.

Flag-encircled Globe
A293

1952, Oct. 24 ***Perf. 13½***

728	A293	3.80cr blue	1.50	50

Issued to publicize United Nations Day.

View of Sao Paulo, Sun and Compasses
A294

1952, Nov. 8 **Litho.** ***Perf. 12x11***

729	A294	60c dl bl, yel & gray grn	30	25

City Planning Day.

Father Diogo Antonio Feijo
A295

1952, Nov. 9 ***Perf. 11x12***

730	A295	60c fawn	20	20

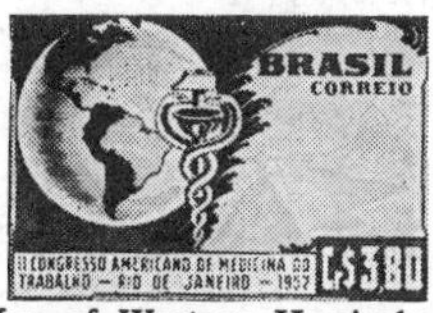

Rodolpho Bernardelli and His "Christ and the Adultress"
A297

1952, Dec. 18 ***Perf. 12x11***

732	A297	60c gray bl	25	20

Issued to commemorate the centenary of the birth of Rodolpho Bernardelli, sculptor and painter.

Map of Western Hemisphere and View of Rio de Janeiro
A298

1952, Sept. 20

733	A298	3.80cr vio brn & lt grn	90	30

Issued to commemorate the 2nd Congress of American Industrial Medicine, Rio de Janeiro, 1952.

Arms and Head of Pioneer
A299

Coffee, Cotton and Sugar Cane
A300

Designs: 2.80cr, Jesuit monk planting tree. 3.80cr and 5.80cr, Spiral, symbolizing progress.

1953, Jan. 25 **Litho.** ***Perf. 11***

734	A299	1.20cr ol brn & blk brn	75	50
735	A300	2cr ol grn & yel	2.50	50
736	A300	2.80cr red brn & dp org	1.75	30
737	A300	3.80cr dk brn & yel grn	1.50	30
738	A300	5.80cr int bl & yel grn	1.00	30
		Nos. 734-738 (5)	7.50	1.90

400th anniversary of Sao Paulo.

Ledger and Winged Cap
A301

1953, Feb. 22 ***Perf. 12x11***

739	A301	1.20cr dl brn & fawn	40	20

6th Brazilian Accounting Congress.

Joao Ramalho
A302

Engraved

1953, Apr. 8 ***Perf. 11½*** **Wmk. 264**

740	A302	60c blue	25	20

Issued to commemorate the fourth centenary of the founding of the city of Santo Andre.

Aarao Reis and Plan of Belo Horizonte
A303

1953, May 6 **Photogravure**

741	A303	1.20cr red brn	35	25

Issued to commemorate the centenary of the birth of Aarao Leal de Carvalho Reis (1853–1936), civil engineer.

Training Ship Almirante Saldanha
A304

1953, May 16

742 A304 1.50cr vio bl 50 30

Issued to commemorate the fourth globe-circling voyage of the training ship Almirante Saldanha.

Joaquim Jose Rodrigues Torres, Viscount of Itaborai
A305

1953, July 5 Photogravure

743 A305 1.20cr violet 30 20

Centenary of the Bank of Brazil.

Lamp and Rio-Petropolis Highway
A306

1953, July 14

744 A306 1.20cr gray 30 20

Issued to publicize the tenth International Congress of Nursing, Petropolis, 1953.

Bay of Rio de Janeiro
A307

1953, July 15

745 A307 3.80cr dk bl grn 60 20

Issued to publicize the fourth World Congress of Baptist Youth, July 1953.

Arms of Jau and Map
A308

1953, Aug. 15 Engraved

746 A308 1.20cr purple 30 20

Centenary of the city of Jau.

Ministry of Health and Education Building, Rio
A309

Maria Quiteria de Jesus Medeiros
A310

1953, Aug. 1

747 A309 1.20cr dp grn 30 20

Issued to publicize the Day of the Stamp and the first Philatelic Exhibition of National Education.

1953, Aug. 21 Photogravure

748 A310 60c vio bl 25 20

Issued to commemorate the centenary of the death of Maria Quiteria de Jesus Medeiros (1792–1848), independence heroine.

Pres. Odria of Peru
A311

Duke of Caxias Leading his Troops
A312

1953, Aug. 25

749 A311 1.40cr rose brn 30 20

Issued to publicize the visit of Gen. Manuel A. Odria, President of Peru, Aug. 25, 1953.

Engraved (60c, 5.80cr); Photo.
Identical Frames.

1953, Aug. 25

Designs: 1.20cr, Caxias' tomb. 1.70cr, 5.80cr, Portrait of Caxias. 3.80cr, Arms of Caxias.

750 A312 60c dp grn 50 25
751 A312 1.20cr dp cl 75 25
752 A312 1.70cr sl grn 75 25
753 A312 3.80cr rose brn 1.25 25
754 A312 5.80cr gray vio 1.25 25
Nos. 750-754 (5) 4.50 1.25

Issued to commemorate the 150th anniversary of the birth of Luis Alves de Lima e Silva, Duke of Caxias.

Quill Pen, Map and Tree
A313

Horacio Hora
A314

1953, Sept. 12 Photogravure

755 A313 60c ultra 25 20

5th National Congress of Journalism.

1953, Sept. 17 Litho. Wmk. 267

756 A314 60c org & dp plum 25 20

Issued to commemorate the centenary of the birth of Horacio Pinto de Hora (1853–1890), painter.

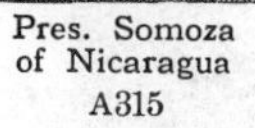

Pres. Somoza of Nicaragua
A315

Auguste de Saint-Hilaire
A316

1953, Sept. 24 Photo. Wmk. 264

757 A315 1.40cr dk vio brn 30 20

Issued to publicize the visit of Gen. Anastasio Somoza, president of Nicaragua.

1953, Sept. 30

758 A316 1.20cr dk brn car 40 25

Issued to commemorate the centenary of the death of Auguste de Saint-Hilaire, explorer and botanist.

José Carlos do Patrocinio
A317

Clock Tower, Crato
A318

1953, Oct. 9 Photogravure

759 A317 60c dk sl gray 25 20

Issued to commemorate the centenary of the birth of José Carlos do Patrocinio, (1853–1905), journalist and abolitionist.

1953, Oct. 17

760 A318 60c bl grn 25 20

Centenary of the city of Crato.

Joao Capistrano de Abreu
A319

Allegory: "Justice"
A320

1953, Oct. 23

761 A319 60c dl bl 30 30
762 A319 5cr purple 2.00 30

Issued to commemorate the centenary of the birth of Joao Capistrano de Abreu (1853–1927), historian.

1953, Nov. 17

763 A320 60c indigo 25 20
764 A320 1.20cr dp mag 25 20

Issued to commemorate the 50th anniversary of the Treaty of Petropolis.

Farm Worker in Wheat Field
A321

Teacher and Pupils
A322

1953, Nov. 29 Photo. *Perf. 11½*

766 A321 60c dk grn 30 20

Issued to publicize the Third National Wheat Festival, Erechim, 1953.

1953, Dec. 14

767 A322 60c red 25 25

Issued to publicize the First National Conference of Primary School Teachers, Salvador, 1953.

Zacarias de Gois e Vasconsellos
A323

Alexandre de Gusmão
A324

Design: 5cr, Porters with Trays of Coffee Beans.

1953-54 Photogravure.

Inscribed: "Centenario do Parana."

768 A323 2cr org brn & blk ('54) 1.00 40
a. Buff paper 90 40
769 A323 5cr dp org & blk 2.00 40

Centenary of the state of Paraná.

1954, Jan. 13

770 A324 1.20cr brn vio 30 20

Issued to commemorate the 200th anniversary of the death of Alexandre de Gusmao (1695–1753), statesman, diplomat and writer.

Symbolical of Sao Paulo's Growth
A325

Arms and View of Sao Paulo
A326

Designs: 2cr, Priest, settler and Indian. 2.80cr, José de Anchieta.

1954, Jan. 25 ***Perf. 11½x11***

771 A325 1.20cr dk vio brn 1.25 50
a. Buff paper 1.75 1.00
772 A325 2cr lil rose 1.75 60
773 A325 2.80cr pur gray 1.75 1.00

Engraved.
Perf. 11x11½.

774 A326 3.80cr dl grn 1.75 50
a. Buff paper 3.00 2.50
775 A326 5.80cr dl red 2.00 60
a. Buff paper 4.00 75
Nos. 771-775 (5) 8.50 3.20

400th anniversary of Sao Paulo.

J. Fernandes Vieira, A. Vidal de Negreiros, A. F. Camarao and H. Dias
A327

Perf. 11x11½

1954, Feb. 18 Photo. Unwmkd.

776 A327 1.20cr ultra 40 30

Issued to commemorate the 300th anniversary of the recovery of Pernambuco from the Dutch.

Sao Paulo and Minerva
A328

1954, Feb. 24

777 A328 1.50cr dp plum 30 25

Issued to publicize the 10th International Congress of Scientific Organizations, Sao Paulo, 1954.

Stylized Grapes, Jug and Map — A329
Monument of the Immigrants — A330

1954, Feb. 27 Photo. ***Perf. 11½x11***

778 A329 40c dp cl 30 25

Grape Festival, Rio Grande do Sul.

1954, Feb. 28

779 A330 60c dp vio bl 30 25

Issued to commemorate the unveiling of the Monument to the Immigrants of Caxias do Sul.

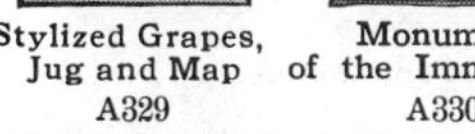

First Brazilian Locomotive
A331

Perf. 11x11½

1954, Apr. 30 **Unwmkd.**

781 A331 40c carmine 50 25

Issued to commemorate the centenary of the first railroad engine built in Brazil.

Pres. Chamoun of Lebanon
A332

1954, May 12 Photo. ***Perf. 11½x11***

782 A332 1.50cr maroon 35 30

Issued to commemorate the visit of Pres. Camille Chamonn of Lebanon, 1954.

Sao Jose College, Rio de Janeiro
A333

J. B. Champagnat Marcelin — A334
Apolonia Pinto — A335

1954, June 6 ***Perf. 11x11½, 11½x11***

783 A333 60c purple 30 20
784 A334 1.20cr vio bl 35 25

Issued to commemorate the 50th anniversary of the founding of the Marist Brothers in Brazil.

1954, June 21 **Photogravure**

785 A335 1.20cr brt grn 15 12

Issued to commemorate the centenary of the birth of Apolonia Pinto (1854–1937), actress.

Adm. Margues Tamandare
A336

Portraits: 2c, 5c, 10c, Admiral Margues Tamandare. 20c, 30c, 40c, Oswaldo Cruz. 50c, 60c, 90c, Joaquim Murtinho. 1cr, 1.50cr, 2cr, Duke of Caxias. 5cr, 10cr, Ruy Barbosa. 20cr, 50cr, José Bonifacio.

1954-60 ***Perf. 11x11½*** **Wmk. 267**

No.	Type	Value	Color	Unused	Used
786	A336	2c	vio bl	15	12
787	A336	5c	org red	10	5
788	A336	10c	brt grn	15	5
789	A336	20c	magenta	15	5
790	A336	30c	dk gray grn	25	5
791	A336	40c	rose red	50	5
792	A336	50c	violet	30	5
793	A336	60c	gray grn	15	5
794	A336	90c	org ('55)	75	15
795	A336	1cr	brown	15	5
796	A336	1.50cr	blue	10	5
a.			Wmk. 264	20.00	10.00
797	A336	2cr	dk bl grn ('56)	50	5
798	A336	5cr	rose lil ('56)	35	10
799	A336	10cr	lt grn ('60)	75	10
800	A336	20cr	crim rose ('59)	75	10
801	A336	50cr	ultra ('59)	4.00	20
			Nos. 786-801 (16)	9.10	1.27

See also Nos. 890, 930–933.

Boy Scout Waving Flag (Statue) — A337
Baltasar Fernandes, Explorer — A338

Perf. 11½x11

1954, Aug. 2 **Unwmkd.**

802 A337 1.20cr vio bl 60 30

Issued to publicize the International Boy Scout Encampment, Sao Paulo, 1954.

1954, Aug. 15

803 A338 60c dk red 30 25

300th anniversary of city of Sorocaba.

Adeodato Giovanni Cardinal Piazza — A339
Our Lady of Aparecida, Map of Brazil — A340

1954, Sept. 2

804 A339 4.20cr red org 75 35

Issued to commemorate the visit of Adeodato Cardinal Piazza, papal legate to Brazil.

1954

Design: 1.20cr, Virgin standing on globe.

805 A340 60c claret 75 35
806 A340 1.20cr vio bl 1.00 30

No. 805 was issued to commemorate the 1st Congress of Brazil's Patron Saint (Our Lady of Aparecida); No. 806, the centenary of the proclamation of the dogma of the Immaculate Conception. Both stamps also commemorate the Marian Year.

Issue dates: 60c, Sept. 6; 1.20cr, Sept. 8.

Benjamin Constant and Hand Reading Braille
A341

1954, Sept. 27 **Photo.** **Unwmkd.**

807 A341 60c dk grn 30 20

Issued to commemorate the centenary of the founding of the Benjamin Constant Institute.

River Battle of Riachuelo
A342

Admiral F. M. Barroso — A343
Dr. Christian F. S. Hahnemann — A344

1954, Oct. 6 ***Perf. 11x11½, 11½x11***

808 A342 40c redsh brn 50 25
809 A343 60c purple 40 25

Issued to commemorate the 150th anniversary of the birth of Admiral Francisco Manoel Barroso da Silva (1804–82).

1954, Oct. 8 ***Perf. 11½x11***

810 A344 2.70cr dk grn 40 25

Issued to publicize the first World Congress of Homeopathic Medicine.

Nizia Floresta — A345
Ears of Wheat — A346

1954, Oct. 12

811 A345 60c lil rose 30 25

Issued to commemorate the reburial of the remains of Nizia Floresta (Dio Nizia Pinto Lisboa), writer and educator.

1954, Oct. 22

812 A346 60c ol grn 40 25

4th National Wheat Festival, Carazinho.

Basketball Player and Ball-Globe — A347
Allegory of the Spring Games — A348

1954, Oct. 23 **Photogravure**

813 A347 1.40cr org red 50 30

Issued to publicize the second World Basketball Championship Matches, 1954.

Perf. 11½x11

1954, Nov. 6 **Wmk. 267**

814 A348 60c red brn 40 25

Issued to publicize the 6th Spring Games.

San Francisco Hydroelectric Plant
A349

1955, Jan. 15 ***Perf. 11x11½***

815 A349 60c brn org 20 15

Issued to publicize the inauguration of the San Francisco Hydroelectric Plant.

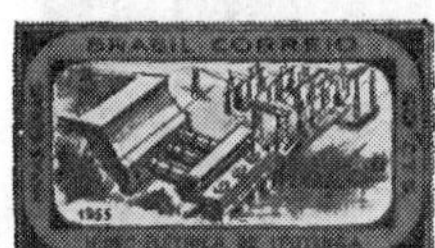

Itutinga Hydroelectric Plant
A350

1955, Feb. 3

816 A350 40c blue 20 15

Issued to publicize the inauguration of the Itutinga Hydroelectric Plant at Lavras.

Rotary Emblem
and Bay of Rio de Janeiro
A351

1955, Feb. 23 ***Perf. 12x11½***

817 A351 2.70cr sl gray & blk 75 25

Rotary International, 50th anniversary.

Fausto Cardoso Palace
A352

1955, Mar. 17 ***Perf. 11x11½***

818 A352 40c hn brn 25 25

Centenary of Aracaju.

Aviation Symbols
A353

1955, Mar. 13 **Photo.** ***Perf. 11½***

819 A353 60c dk gray grn 20 15

Issued to publicize the third National Aviation Congress at Sao Paulo, Mar. 6–13.

Arms of Botucatu
A354

1955, Apr. 14

820 A354 60c org brn 25 20
821 A354 1.20cr brt grn 35 20

Centenary of Botucatu.

Young Racers at Starting Line
A355

Perf. 11½

1955, Apr. 30 **Photo.** **Unwmkd.**

823 A355 60c org brn 35 20

5th Children's Games.

Marshal Hermes da Fonseca
A356

Congress Altar, Sail and Sugar-loaf Mountain
A357

1955, May 12 **Wmk. 267**

824 A356 60c purple 25 20

Issued to commemorate the centenary of the birth of Marshal Hermes da Fonseca.

Engr.; Photo. (2.70cr)

1955, July 17 ***Perf. 11½*** **Unwmkd.**

Designs: 2.70cr, St. Pascoal. 4.20cr, Aloisi Benedetto Cardinal Masella.

825 A357 1.40cr green 25 25
826 A357 2.70cr dp cl 50 40
827 A357 4.20cr blue 60 25

Issued to commemorate the 36th World Eucharistic Congress in Rio de Janeiro.

Girl Gymnasts
A358

Granite Paper

1955, Nov. 12 **Engraved**

828 A358 60c rose lil 35 20

Issued to publicize the 7th Spring Games.

José B. Monteiro Lobato
A359

1955, Dec. 8 **Granite Paper**

829 A359 40c dk grn 20 15

Issued in honor of José B. Monteiro Lobato, author.

Adolfo Lutz
A360

Lt. Col. Vilagran Cabrita
A361

1955, Dec. 18 **Granite Paper**

830 A360 60c dk grn 20 15

Issued to commemorate the centenary of the birth of Adolfo Lutz, public health pioneer.

1955, Dec. 22 **Photo.** **Wmk. 267**

831 A361 60c vio bl 20 15

Issued to commemorate the centenary of the First Battalion of Engineers.

Salto Grande Hydroelectric Dam
A362

Granite Paper.

1956, Jan. 15 ***Perf. 11½*** **Unwmkd.**

832 A362 60c brick red 20 15

Arms of Mococa
A363

"G" and Globe
A364

Photogravure

1956, Apr. 17 ***Perf. 11½*** **Wmk. 256**

833 A363 60c brick red 20 15

Centenary of Mococa, Sao Paulo.

Granite Paper

1956, Apr. 14 **Unwmkd.**

834 A364 1.20cr vio bl 30 20

18th International Geographic Congress, Rio de Janeiro, August 1956.

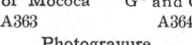

Girls' Foot Race
A365

1956, Apr. 28 **Photogravure**

Granite Paper.

835 A365 2.50cr brt bl 50 20

6th Children's Games.

Plane over Map of Brazil
A366

1956, June 12 ***Perf. 11½*** **Wmk. 267**

836 A366 3.30cr brt vio bl 1.00 25

Issued to commemorate the 25th anniversary of the National Airmail Service.

Fireman Rescuing Child
A367

1956, July 2 **Wmk. 264**

837 A367 2.50cr crimson 60 25
a. Buff paper 2.25 1.00

Centenary of the Fire Brigade.

Map of Brazil and Open Book
A368

1956, Sept. 8 **Wmk. 267**

838 A368 2.50cr brt vio bl 40 20

Issued to commemorate the 50th anniversary of the arrival of the Marist Brothers in Northern Brazil.

Church and Monument, Franca
A369

1956, Sept. 7 **Engraved**

839 A369 2.50cr dk bl 40 20

Centenary of city of Franca, Sao Paulo.

Woman Hurdler
A370

1956, Sept. 22 **Photo.** **Unwmkd.**

Granite Paper.

840 A370 2.50cr dk car 1.00 25

Issued to publicize the 8th Spring Games.

Forest and Map of Brazil
A371

1956, Sept. 30 ***Perf. 11½*** **Wmk. 267**

841 A371 2.50cr dk grn 35 20

Issued to publicize education in forestry.

Baron da Bocaina
A372

1956, Oct. 8 **Engraved** **Wmk. 268**

842 A372 2.50cr redsh brn 35 20

Issued to commemorate the centenary of the birth of Baron da Bocaina, who introduced the special delivery mail system to Brazil.

Marbleized Paper

Paper with a distinct wavy-line or marbleized watermark (which Brazilians call *marmorizado* paper) has been found on many stamps of Brazil, 1956–68, including Nos. 843–845, 847, 851–854, 858–858A, 864, 878, 880, 882, 884, 886–887, 896, 909, 918, 920–921, 925–928, 936–939, 949, 955–958, 960, 962–964, 978–979, 983, 985–987, 997–998, 1002–1003, 1005, 1009–1012, 1017, 1024, 1026, 1055, 1075, 1078, 1082, C82, C82a, C83–C87, C96, C99, C109.

Quantities are much less than those of stamps on regular paper.

Panama Stamp Showing Pres. Juscelino Kubitschek
A373

1956, Oct. 12 Photo. Wmk. 267

843 A373 3.30cr grn & blk 1.00 25

Issued on America Day, Oct. 12, to commemorate the meeting of the Presidents and the Pan-American Conference at Panama City, July 21-22.

Symbolical of Steel Production
A374

Photogravure.

1957, Jan. 31 *Perf. 11½* Wmk. 267

844 A374 2.50cr chocolate 40 15

Issued to commemorate the second expansion of the National Steel Company at Volta Redonda.

Joaquim E. Gomes da Silva
A375

Granite Paper.

1957, Mar. 1 Photo. Unwmkd.

845 A375 2.50cr dk bl grn 35 15

Issued to commemorate the centenary of the birth (in 1856) of Joaquim E. Gomes da Silva.

Allan Kardec
A376

Engraved.

1957, Apr. 18 *Perf. 11½* Wmk. 268

846 A376 2.50cr dk brn 35 15

Issued in honor of Allan Kardec, pen name of Leon Hippolyto Denizard Rivail, and for the centenary of the publication of his "Codification of Spiritism."

Boy Gymnast
A377

Granite Paper.

1957, Apr. 27 Photo. Unwmkd.

847 A377 2.50cr lake 75 25

7th Children's Games.

Pres. Craveiro Lopes — A378 | Stamp of 1932 — A379

1957, June 7 Engraved Wmk. 267

848 A378 6.50cr blue 75 25

Issued to commemorate the visit of Gen. Francisco Higino Craveiro Lopes, President of Portugal.

1957, July 9 Photogravure

849 A379 2.50cr rose 30 15

Issued to commemorate the 25th anniversary of the movement for a constitution.

St. Antonio Monastery, Pernambuco
A380

1957, Aug. 24 Engraved Wmk. 267

850 A380 2.50cr dp mag 30 15

Issued to commemorate the 300th anniversary of the emancipation of the Franciscan province of St. Antonio in Pernambuco State.

Volleyball — A381 | Basketball — A382

1957, Sept. 28 Photo. *Perf. 11½*

851 A381 2.50cr dl org red 75 25

Issued for the 9th Spring Games.

1957, Oct. 12

852 A382 3.30cr org & brt grn 75 25

Issued to commemorate the second Women's International Basketball Championship, Rio de Janeiro.

Count of Pinhal and Sao Carlos
A383

1957, Nov. 4 *Perf. 11½* Wmk. 267

853 A383 2.50cr rose 60 25

Issued to commemorate the centenary of the city of Sao Carlos and to honor the Count of Pinhal, its founder.

Auguste Comte
A384

1957, Nov. 15

854 A384 2.50cr dk red brn 50 25

Issued to commemorate the centenary of the death of Auguste Comte, French mathematician and philosopher.

Radio Station
A385

1957, Dec. 10 Wmk. 268

855 A385 2.50cr dk grn 35 15

Opening of Sarapui Central Radio Station.

Admiral Tamandare and Warship
A386

Design: 3.30cr, Aircraft carrier.

1957–58 Photogravure

856 A386 2.50cr lt bl 45 20

Engraved

857 A386 3.30cr grn ('58) 50 20

Issued to commemorate the 150th anniversary of the birth of Admiral Joaquim Marques de Tamandare, founder of the Brazilian navy.

Coffee Plant and Symbolic "R"
A387

Photogravure.

1957–58 *Perf. 11½* Wmk. 267

858 A387 2.50cr magenta 85 35

Unwmkd.

Granite Paper.

858A A387 2.50cr mag ('58) 75 35

Issued to commemorate the centenary (in 1956) of the city of Ribeirao Preto in Sao Paulo state.

Dom John VI—A388

1958, Jan. 28 Engraved Wmk. 268

859 A388 2.50cr magenta 50 25

Issued to commemorate the 150th anniversary of the opening of the ports of Brazil to foreign trade.

Bugler
A389

1958, Mar. 18 Wmk. 267

860 A389 2.50cr red 60 25

Issued to commemorate the 150th anniversary of the Brazilian Marine Corps.

Station at Rio and Locomotive of 1858 — A390 | Court House — A391

Photogravure.

1958, Mar. 29 *Perf. 11½* Wmk. 267

861 A390 2.50cr red brn 50 25

Issued to commemorate the centenary of the Central Railroad of Brazil.

1958, Apr. 1 Engraved Wmk. 256

862 A391 2.50cr green 35 15

Issued to commemorate the 150th anniversary of the Military Superior Court.

Emblem and Brazilian Pavilion
A392

1958, Apr. 17 Wmk. 267

863 A392 2.50cr dk bl 30 25

World's Fair, Brussels, Apr. 17–Oct. 19.

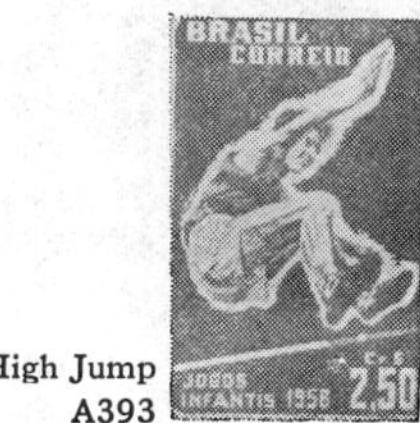

High Jump
A393

1958, Apr. 20 Photo. Unwmkd.
Granite Paper

864 A393 2.50cr crim rose 45 15

8th Children's Games.

Marshal Mariano da Silva Rondon
A394

1958, Apr. 19 Engraved Wmk. 267

865 A394 2.50cr magenta 35 15

Issued to honor Marshal Mariano da Silva Rondon and the "Day of the Indian."

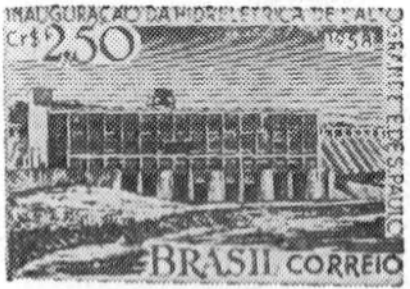
Hydroelectric Station
A395

1958, Apr. 28 *Perf. 11½* Wmk. 267

866 A395 2.50cr magenta 25 15

Opening of Sao Paulo State power plant.

National Printing Plant
A396

1958, May 22 Photogravure

867 A396 2.50cr redsh brn 25 15

Issued to commemorate the 150th anniversary of the founding of the National Printing Plant.

Marshal Osorio
A397

1958, May 24

868 A397 2.50cr brt vio 25 15

Issued to commemorate the 150th anniversary of the birth of Marshal Manoel Luiz Osorio.

Pres. Ramon Villeda Morales
A398

Fountain
A399

Engraved.

1958, June 7 *Perf. 11½* Wmk. 267

869 A398 6.50cr dk grn 2.00 75
a. Wmk. 268 4.00 3.00

Issued to commemorate the visit of Pres. Ramon Villeda Morales of Honduras.

1958, June 13

870 A399 2.50cr dk grn 35 15

Issued to commemorate the 150th anniversary of the Botanical Garden, Rio de Janeiro.

Symbols of Agriculture A400 — Prophet Joel A401

1958, June 18 Photogravure

871 A400 2.50cr rose car 25 15

Issued to commemorate the 50th anniversary of Japanese immigration to Brazil.

1958, June 21 Engraved

872 A401 2.50cr dk bl 30 15

Issued to commemorate the bicentenary of the Cathedral of Bom Jesus at Matosinhos.

Stylized Globe
A402

1958, July 10 Photogravure

873 A402 2.50cr dk brn 25 15

Issued to publicize the International Investment Conference, Belo Horizonte.

Julio Bueno Brandao
A403

1958, Aug. 1 *Perf. 11½* Wmk. 268

874 A403 2.50cr red brn 25 15

Issued to commemorate the centenary of the birth of Julio Bueno Brandao, President of Minas Gerais.

Palacio Tiradentes
(House of Congress)
A404

1958, July 24 Engraved

875 A404 2.50cr sepia 25 15

Issued to honor the 47th Interparliamentary Conference, Rio de Janeiro, July 24–Aug. 1.

Presidential Palace, Brasilia
A405

1958, Aug. 8 Photo. Wmk. 267

876 A405 2.50cr ultra 35 15

Issued to publicize the construction of Brazil's new capital, Brasilia.

Freighters
A406

1958, Aug. 22

877 A406 2.50cr blue 45 15

Issued in honor of the Brazilian merchant marine.

Joaquim Caetano da Silva
A407

1958, Sept. 2 Unwmkd.
Granite Paper

878 A407 2.50cr redsh brn 35 15

Issued in honor of Joaquim Caetano da Silva, scientist and historian.

Giovanni Gronchi
A408

Archers
A409

1958, Sept. 4 Engraved Wmk. 268

879 A408 7cr dk bl 75 15

Issued to commemorate the visit of Italy's President Giovanni Gronchi to Brazil.

Perf. 11½

1958, Sept. 21 Photo. Unwmkd.
Granite Paper

880 A409 2.50cr red org 60 20

Issued to publicize the 10th Spring Games.

Elderly Couple A410 — Machado de Assis A411

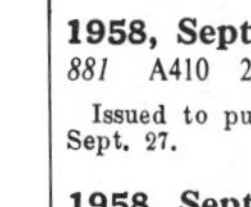

1958, Sept. 27 Wmk. 267

881 A410 2.50cr magenta 40 15

Issued to publicize the Day of the Old People, Sept. 27.

1958, Sept. 28 Unwmkd.

882 A411 2.50cr red brn 35 15

Issued to commemorate the 50th anniversary of the death of Joaquim Maria Machado de Assis, writer.

Pres. Vargas and Oil Derrick
A412

1958, Oct. 6 Wmk. 268

883 A412 2.50cr blue 25 15

Issued to commemorate the 5th anniversary of Pres. Getulio D. Vargas' oil law.

Globe
A413

Gen. Lauro Sodré
A414

Perf. 11½

1958, Nov. 14 Photo. Wmk. 267

884 A413 2.50cr blue 50 15

Issued to commemorate the seventh Inter-American Congress of Municipalities.

1958, Nov. 15 Engraved

885 A414 3.30cr green 15 15

Issued to commemorate the centenary of the birth of Gen. Lauro Sodré.

U. N. Emblem
A415

Soccer Player
A416

1958, Dec. 26 Photo. *Perf. 11½*

886 A415 2.50cr brt bl 35 15

Issued to commemorate the tenth anniversary of the signing of the Universal Declaration of Human Rights.

1959, Jan. 20

887 A416 3.30cr emer & red brn 50 20

World Soccer Championships of 1958.

Railroad Track and Map
A417

Pres. Sukarno of Indonesia
A418

1959, Apr. ***Perf. 11½*** **Wmk. 267**

888 A417 2.50cr dp org 30 20

Issued to commemorate the centenary of the linking of Patos and Campina Grande by railroad.

1959, May 20

889 A418 2.50cr blue 25 15

Visit of President Sukarno of Indonesia.

Dom John VI
A419

Boy Polo Players
A420

Perf. 10½x11½

1959, June 12 **Wmk. 267**

890 A419 2.50cr crimson 30 10

1959, June 13 ***Perf. 11½***

891 A420 2.50cr org brn 35 15

9th Children's Games.

Loading Freighter
A421

Organ and Emblem
A422

1959, July 10

892 A421 2.50cr dk grn 35 15

Issued to honor the merchant marine.

1959, July 16 Photogravure

893 A422 3.30cr magenta 20 15

Issued to commemorate the bicentenary of the Carmelite Order in Brazil.

Joachim Silverio de Souza
A423

Symbolic Road
A424

1959, July 20 ***Perf. 11½***

894 A423 2.50cr red brn 20 15

Issued to commemorate the birth centenary of Joachim Silverio de Souza, first bishop of Diamantina, Minas Gerais.

1959, Sept. 27 **Wmk. 267**

895 A424 3.30cr bl grn & ultra 25 15

11th International Roadbuilding Congress.

Girl Athlete
A425

1959, Oct. 4

896 A425 2.50cr lil rose 40 20

11th Spring Games.

Map of Parana—A426

1959, Sept. 27

897 A426 2.50cr dk grn 25 15

Issued to commemorate the 25th anniversary of the founding of Londrina, Parana.

Globe and Snipes
A427

Lusignan Cross
A428

1959, Oct. 22 ***Perf. 11½***

898 A427 6.50cr dl grn 15 15

Issued to commemorate the World Championship of Snipe Class Sailboats, Porto Alegre, won by Brazilian yachtsmen.

1959, Oct. 24 **Engraved**

899 A428 6.50cr dl bl 15 15

Issued to commemorate the 4th International Conference on Brazilian-Portuguese Studies, Univeristy of Bahia, Aug. 10–20.

Factory Entrance and Order of Southern Cross
A429

Corcovado Christ, Globe and Southern Cross
A430

1959, Nov. 19 Photogravure

900 A429 3.30cr org red 15 15

Issued to commemorate the 50th anniversary of the Pres. Vargas Gunpowder Factory.

1959, Nov. 26 ***Perf. 11½***

901 A430 2.50cr blue 40 15

Universal Thanksgiving Day.

Burning Bush—A431

1959, Dec. 24 **Wmk. 267**

902 A431 3.30cr lt grn 15 15

Centenary of Presbyterian work in Brazil.

Piraja da Silva and Schistosoma Mansoni
A432

1959, Dec. 28

903 A432 2.50cr rose vio 35 15

Issued to commemorate the 25th anniversary of the discovery and identification of schistosoma mansoni, a parasite of the fluke family, by Dr. Piraja da Silva.

Luiz de Matos—A433

1960, Jan. 3 Photogravure

904 A433 3.30cr red brn 15 15

Birth centenary of Luiz de Matos.

L. L. Zamenhof
A434

Adél Pinto
A435

Perf. 11½

1960, Mar. 10 **Wmk. 267**

905 A434 6.50cr emerald 15 15

Issued to commemorate the birth centenary of Lazarus Ludwig Zamenhof (1859–1917), Polish oculist who invented Esperanto in 1887.

1960, Mar. 19 **Engr.** **Wmk. 268**

906 A435 11.50cr rose red 15 15

Issued to commemorate the centenary of the birth of Adél Pinto, civil engineer and railroad expert.

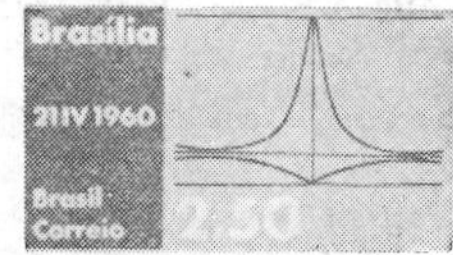

Presidential Palace, Colonnade
A436

Design: 27cr, Plan of Brasilia (like No. C98).

Perf. 11x11½

1960 **Photogravure** **Wmk. 267**

907 A436 2.50cr brt grn 40 15

908 A436 27cr salmon 1.00 1.00

Nos. 907-908, C95-C98 (6) 3.20 1.75

No. 907 issued Apr. 21 to commemorate the inauguration of Brazil's new capital, Brasilia, Apr. 21, 1960.

No. 908 issued Sept. 12 to commemorate the birthday of Pres. Juscelino Kubitschek. It measures 105x46½mm., carrying at center a 27cr in design of No. C98, flanked by the chief design features of Nos. 907, C95–C97, with Kubitschek signature below. Issued in sheets of 4 with wide horizontal gutter.

Grain, Coffee, Cotton and Cacao
A437

Paulo de Frontin
A438

Perf. 11½x11

1960, July 28 **Wmk. 267**

909 A437 2.50cr brown 30 15

Centenary of Ministry of Agriculture.

1960, Oct. 12 **Wmk. 268**

910 A438 2.50cr org red 20 15

Issued to commemorate the centenary of the birth of Paulo de Frontin, engineer.

Girl Athlete Holding Torch
A439

1960, Oct. 18 ***Perf. 11½x11***

911 A439 2.50cr bl grn 30 15

12th Spring Games.

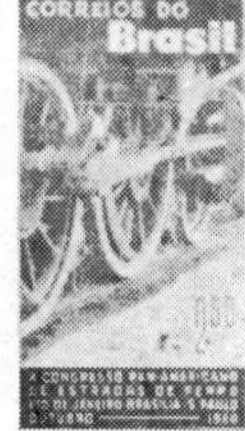

Volleyball and Net
A440

Locomotive Wheels
A441

Perf. 11½x11

1960, Nov. 12 **Wmk. 268**

912 A440 11cr blue 50 20

International Volleyball Championships.

1960, Oct. 15 ***Perf. 11½x11***

913 A441 2.50cr ultra 20 10

10th Pan-American Railroad Congress.

Symbols of Flight
A442

1960, Dec. 16 Photo. *Perf. 11½*

914 A442 2.50cr brn & yel 20 15

Issued to commemorate the International Fair of Industry and Commerce, Rio de Janeiro.

Emperor Haile Selassie I
A443

1961, Jan. 31 *Perf. 11½x11*

915 A443 2.50cr dk brn 20 15

Issued to commemorate the visit of Emperor Haile Selassie I of Ethiopia to Brazil, Dec. 1960.

Map of Brazil, Open Book and Sacred Heart Emblem
A444

Perf. 11x11½

1961, Mar. 13 Wmk. 268

916 A444 2.50cr blue 30 15

The 50th anniversary of the operation in Brazil of the Order of the Blessed Heart of Mary.

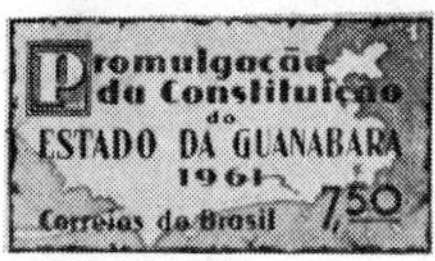

Map of Guanabara
A445

1961, March 27 Wmk. 267

917 A445 7.50cr org brn 25 15

Issued to commemorate the promulgation of the constitution of the state of Guanabara.

Arms of Agulhas Negras
A446

Brazil and Senegal Linked on Map
A447

Design: 3.30cr, Dress helmet and sword.

Perf. 11½x11

1961, Apr. 23 Wmk. 267

918 A446 2.50cr green 35 15
919 A446 3.30cr rose car 15 15

Issued to commemorate the sesquicentennial of the Agulhas Negras Military Academy.

1961, Apr. 28 Photogravure

920 A447 27cr ultra 50 20

Issued to commemorate the visit of Afonso Arinos, Brazilian foreign minister, to Senegal to attend its independence ceremonies.

View of Ouro Preto, 1711
A448

1961, June 6 *Perf. 11x11½*

921 A448 1cr orange 20 20

250th anniversary of Ouro Preto.

War Arsenal
A449

1961, June 20 Wmk. 256

924 A449 5cr dk red brn 40 15

Issued to commemorate the 150th anniversary of the War Arsenal, Rio de Janeiro.

Coffee Bean and Branch
A450

Rabindranath Tagore
A451

Perf. 11½x11

1961, June 26 Wmk. 267

925 A450 20cr redsh brn 1.50 25

Issued to commemorate the 8th Directorial Committee meeting of the International Coffee Convention, Rio de Janeiro, June 26, 1961.

1961, July 28 Photo. Wmk. 267

926 A451 10cr rose car 30 15

Issued to commemorate the centenary of the birth of Rabindranath Tagore, Indian poet.

Stamp of 1861 and Map of English Channel
A452

Design: 20cr, 430r stamp of 1861 and map of Netherlands.

1961, Aug. 1 *Perf. 11x11½*

927 A452 10cr rose 75 20
928 A452 20cr sal pink 1.75 30

Centenary of 1861 stamp issue.

Portrait Type of 1954–60

Designs as Before.

1961 *Perf. 11x11½* Wmk. 268

930 A336 1cr brown 1.25 65
931 A336 2cr dk bl grn 1.75 65
932 A336 5cr red lil 4.00 40
933 A336 10cr emerald 7.50 40

The 1cr, 5cr and 10cr have patterned background.

Sun, Clouds, Rain and Weather Symbols
A453

Dedo de Deus Peak
A454

1962, March 23 *Perf. 11½x11*

936 A453 10cr red brn 1.25 30

World Meteorological Day, Mar. 23.

1962, Apr. 14 Photo. Wmk. 267

937 A454 8cr emerald 25 25

Issued to commemorate the 50th anniversary of the climbing of Dedo de Deus (Finger of God) peak.

Dr. Gaspar Vianna and Leishmania Protozoa
A455

1962, Apr. 24 *Perf. 11x11½*

938 A455 8cr blue 25 15

Issued to commemorate the 50th anniversary of the discovery by Gaspar Oliveiro Vianna (1885–1914) of a cure for leishmaniasis.

Henrique Dias—A456

1962, June 18 Wmk. 267

939 A456 10cr dk vio brn 50 15

Issued to commemorate the 300th anniversary of the death of Henrique Dias, Negro military leader who fought against the Dutch and Spaniards.

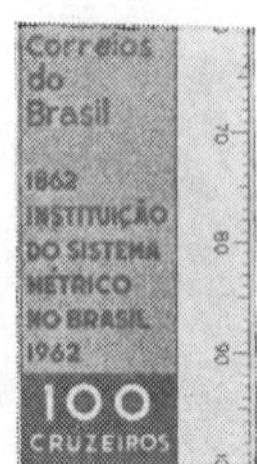

Millimeter Gauge
A457

Sailboats, Snipe Class
A458

1962, June 26 *Perf. 11½x11*

940 A457 100cr car rose 60 20

Issued to commemorate the centenary of the introduction of the metric system in Brazil.

1962, July 21 Photo. Wmk. 267

941 A458 8cr Prus grn 30 15

Issued to commemorate the 13th Brazilian championships for Snipe Class sailing.

Julio Mesquita—A459

1962, Aug. 18 *Perf. 11x11½*

942 A459 8cr dl brn 30 15

Issued to commemorate the centenary of the birth of Julio Mesquita, journalist and founder of Sao Paulo.

Empress Leopoldina
A460

1962, Sept. 7 *Perf. 11½x11*

943 A460 8cr rose cl 25 15

140th anniversary of independence.

Buildings, Brasilia—A461

Perf. 11x11½

1962, Oct. 24 Wmk. 267

944 A461 10cr orange 60 15

Issued to commemorate the 51st Interparliamentary Conference, Brasilia.

Pouring Ladle
A462

1962, Oct. 26 *Perf. 11½x11*

945 A462 8cr orange 25 15

Issued to mark the inauguration of the Usiminas State Iron and Steel Foundry at Belo Horizonte, Minas Gerais.

UPAE Emblem
A463

1962, Nov. 19 *Perf. 11x11½*

946 A463 8cr brt mag 20 15

Issued to commemorate the 50th anniversary of the founding of the Postal Union of the Americas and Spain, UPAE.

Chimney and Cogwheel Forming "10"
A464

1962, Nov. 26 ***Perf. 11½x11***

947 A464 10cr lt bl grn 40 15

Issued to commemorate the 10th anniversary of the National Economic and Development Bank.

Quintino Bocaiuva
A465

Soccer Player and Globe
A466

Perf. 11½x11

1962, Dec. 27 Photo. **Wmk. 267**

948 A465 8cr brn org 20 15

Issued to commemorate the 50th anniversary of the death of Quintino Bocaiuva, journalist.

1963, Jan. 14

949 A466 10cr bl grn 12 7

World Soccer Championship of 1962.

Carrier Pigeon
A467

Lithographed

1963, Jan. ***Perf. 14*** **Unwmkd.**

950 A467 8cr yel, dk bl, red & grn 25 15

Souvenir Sheet

Imperf.

951 A467 100cr yel, dk bl, red & grn 1.40 1.20

Issued to commemorate 300 years of Brazilian postal service. No. 951 contains one stamp. Black inscription and ultramarine border. Size: 145x57mm.

Issue dates: 8cr, Jan. 25; 100cr, Jan. 31.

Severino Neiva
A468

Perf. 10½x11½

1963, Jan. 31 Photo. **Wmk. 267**

952 A468 8cr brt vio 25 10

Radar Tracking Station and Rockets
A469

"Cross of Unity"
A470

Perf. 11½x11

1963, Mar. 15 **Wmk. 268**

953 A469 21cr lt ultra 30 15

Issued to publicize the International Aeronautics and Space Exhibition, Sao Paulo.

1963 ***Perf. 11½x11*** **Wmk. 267**

954 A470 8cr red lil 20 15

Issued to commemorate Vatican II, the 21st Ecumenical Council of the Roman Catholic Church.

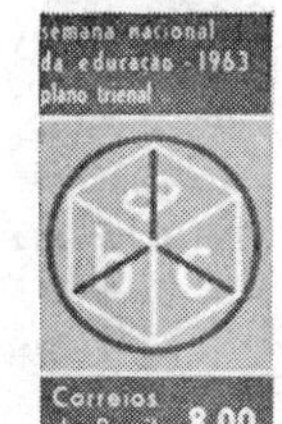

"ABC" in Geometric Form
A471

Basketball Player
A472

1963, Apr. 22 Photo. **Wmk. 267**

955 A471 8cr brt bl & lt bl 20 15

Issued for Education Week, Apr. 22–27, in connection with the 3-year alphabetization program.

1963, May 15

956 A472 8cr dp lil rose 35 15

Issued to commemorate the 4th International Basketball Championships, Rio de Janeiro, May 10–25, 1963.

Games Emblem
A473

"OEA" and Map of the Americas
A474

1963, May 22 ***Perf. 11½x11***

957 A473 10cr car rose 60 15

4th Pan American Games, Sao Paulo.

1963, June 6

958 A474 10cr org & dp org 60 15

Issued to commemorate the 15th anniversary of the charter of the Organization of American States.

José Bonifacio de Andrada
A475

1963, June 13

959 A475 8cr dk brn 20 15

Issued to commemorate the bicentenary of the birth of José Bonifacio de Andrada de Silva, statesman.

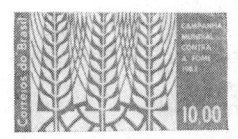

Wheat
A476

Perf. 11x11½

1963, June 19 Photo. **Wmk. 267**

960 A476 10cr blue 50 15

Issued for the "Freedom from Hunger" campaign of the U.N. Food and Agriculture Organization.

Centenary Emblem
A477

João Caetano
A478

1963, Aug. 19 ***Perf. 11½x11***

961 A477 8cr yel org & red 30 15

Centenary of International Red Cross.

1963, Aug. 24 ***Perf. 11½x11***

962 A478 8cr slate 30 15

Death centenary of João Caetano, actor.

Symbols of Agriculture, Industry and Atomic Energy
A479

Hammer Thrower
A480

1963, Aug. 28

963 A479 10cr car rose 40 15

Issued to commemorate the first anniversary of the Atomic Development Law.

1963, Sept. 13

964 A480 10cr gray 75 10

International College Students' Games, Porto Alegre.

Marshal Tito
A481

Compass Rose, Map of Brazil and View of Rio de Janeiro
A482

1963, Sept. 19

965 A481 80cr sepia 60 30

Visit of Marshal Tito of Jugoslavia.

1963, Sept. 20

966 A482 8cr lt bl grn 20 15

8th International Leprology Congress.

Oil Derrick and Storage Tank
A483

1963, Oct. 3 ***Perf. 11x11½***

967 A483 8cr dk sl grn 20 15

Issued to commemorate the 10th anniversary of Petrobras, the national oil company.

"Spring Games"—A484

1963, Nov. 5 Photo. **Wmk. 267**

968 A484 8cr yel & org 25 20

1963 Spring Games.

Borges de Medeiros
A485

1963, Nov. 29 ***Perf. 11½x11***

969 A485 8cr red brn 20 15

Issued to commemorate the centenary of the birth of Dr. Borges de Medeiros (1863–1962), Governor of Rio Grande do Sul.

São João del Rei
A486

1963, Dec. 8 ***Perf. 11x11½***

970 A486 8cr vio bl 20 15

250th anniversary of São João del Rei.

Dr. Alvaro Alvim
A487

1963, Dec. 19

971 A487 8cr dk gray 20 15

Issued to commemorate the centenary of the birth of Dr. Alvaro Alvim (1863–1928), X-ray specialist and martyr of science.

Viscount de Mauá
A488

Mandacaru Cactus and Emblem
A489

1963, Dec. 28 ***Perf. 11½x11***

972 A488 8cr rose car 20 15

Issued to commemorate the sesquicentennial of the birth of Viscount de Mauá, founder of first Brazilian railroad.

1964, Jan. 23 Photo. Wmk. 267

973 A489 8cr dl grn 25 15

Issued to commemorate the 10th anniversary of the Bank of Northeast Brazil.

Coelho Netto
A490

Lauro Müller
A491

1964, Feb. 21 ***Perf. 11½x11***

974 A490 8cr brt vio 20 15

Birth centenary of Coelho Netto, writer.

1964, March 8 Wmk. 267

975 A491 8cr dp org 20 15

Issued to commemorate the centenary of the birth of Lauro Siverino Müller, politician and member of the Brazilian Academy of Letters.

Child Holding Spoon
A492

1964, March 25 ***Perf. 11x11½***

976 A492 8cr yel brn & yel 25 15

Issued for "School Meals Week."

Chalice Rock
A493

Allan Kardec
A494

1964, Apr. 9 Engraved *Perf. 11½x11*

977 A493 80cr red org 40 20

Issued for tourist publicity.

1964, Apr. 18 Photogravure

978 A494 30cr sl grn 75 15

Issued to commemorate the centenary of "O Evangelho" (Gospel) of the codification of Spiritism.

Heinrich Lübke
A495

Pope John XXIII
A496

Perf. 11½x11

1964, May 8 Photo. Wmk. 267

979 A495 100cr red brn 60 18

Issued to commemorate the visit of President Heinrich Lübke of Germany.

1964, June 29 Wmk. 267

980 A496 20cr dk car rose 30 20
a. Unwmkd. 30 20

Issued in memory of Pope John XXIII.

Pres. Senghor of Senegal
A497

1964, Sept. 19 Wmk. 267

981 A497 20cr dk brn 40 15

Issued to commemorate the visit of Léopold Sédar Senghor, President of Senegal.

Botafago Bay and Sugarloaf Mountain—A498

Designs: 100cr, Church of Our Lady of the Rock (vert.). 200cr, Copacabana beach.

Perf. 11x11½, 11½x11

1964–65 Photogravure

983 A498 15cr org & bl 40 25
984 A498 100cr brt grn & red brn, *yel* 50 18
985 A498 200cr blk & red 2.50 35
a. Souv. sheet of 3 ('65) 1.75 1.75

Issued to commemorate the 4th centenary of Rio de Janeiro. See Nos. 993–995a.

No. 985a contains three imperf. stamps similar to Nos. 983–985, but printed in brown with marginal inscriptions and border in deep orange. Size: 129x79mm. Sold for 320cr. Issued Dec. 30, 1965.

A souvenir card containing one lithographed facsimile of No. 984, imperf., exists, but has no franking value. Marginal inscriptions in green. Size: 100x125mm. Sold by P.O. for 250cr.

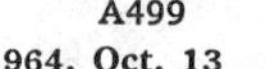

Pres. Charles de Gaulle
A499

Pres. John F. Kennedy
A500

1964, Oct. 13 ***Perf. 11½x11***

986 A499 100cr org brn 30 15

Issued to commemorate the visit of Charles de Gaulle, President of France, Oct. 13–15.

1964, Oct. 24 Photo. Wmk. 267

987 A500 100cr slate 30 15

Issued in memory of President John F. Kennedy (1917–63).

"Prophet" by A. F. Lisbao
A501

1964, Nov. 18 ***Perf. 11½x11***

988 A501 10cr slate 10 6

Issued to commemorate the 150th anniversary of the death of the sculptor Antonio Francisco Lisbao, "O Aleijadinho" (The Cripple).

Antonio Goncalves Dias
A502

Designs: 30cr, Euclides da Cunha. 50cr, Prof. Angelo Moreira da Costa Lima. 200cr, Tiradentes. 500cr, Dom Pedro I. 1000cr, Dom Pedro II.

1965–66 *Perf. 11x11½* Wmk. 267

989 A502 30cr brt bluish grn ('66) 1.50 25
989A A502 50cr dl brn ('66) 1.50 10
990 A502 100cr blue 60 10
991 A502 200cr brn org 1.25 10
992 A502 500cr red brn 5.00 50
992A A502 1000cr sl bl ('66) 6.00 1.50
Nos. 989-992A (6) 15.85 2.55

Statue of St. Sebastian, Guanatаro Bay
A503

The Arches
A504

Design: 35cr, Estacio de Sá (1520–67), founder of Rio de Janeiro.

1965 Photogravure *Perf. 11½*

Size: 24x37mm.

993 A503 30cr bl & rose red 60 15

Lithographed and Engraved

Perf. 11x11½

994 A504 30cr lt bl & blk 60 15

Photogravure

Perf. 11½

Size: 21x39mm.

995 A503 35cr blk & org 25 25
a. Souv. sheet of 3 2.25 2.25

Issued to commemorate the 4th centenary of Rio de Janeiro. Issue dates: No. 993, Mar. 5. No. 994, Nov. 30. No. 995, July 28. No. 995a, Dec. 30.

No. 995a contains three imperf. stamps similar to Nos. 993–995, but printed in deep orange with marginal inscriptions and border in brown. Size: 130x79mm. Sold for 100cr.

Sword and Cross
A505

1965, Apr. 15 *Perf. 11½* Wmk. 267

996 A505 120cr gray 40 15

Issued to commemorate the first anniversary of the democratic revolution.

Vital Brazil
A506

Shah of Iran
A507

1965, Apr. 28 *Perf. 11½* Wmk. 267

997 A506 120cr dp org 50 15

Centenary of birth of Vital Brazil, M.D.

A souvenir card containing one impression similar to No. 997, imperf., exists, printed in dull plum. Sold by P.O. for 250cr. Size: 114x180mm.

1965, May 5 Photogravure

998 A507 120cr rose cl 40 15

Issued to commemorate the visit of Shah Mohammed Riza Pahlavi of Iran.

Marshal Mariano da Silva Rondon
A508

Lions' Emblem
A509

1965, May 7 **Engraved**

999 A508 30cr claret 50 15

Issued to commemorate the centenary of the birth of Marshal Mariano da Silva Rondon (1865–1958), explorer and expert on Indians.

1965, May 14 Photogravure

1000 A509 35cr pale vio & blk 30 15

Issued to commemorate the 12th convention of the Lions Clubs of Brazil, Rio de Janeiro, May 11–16.

ITU Emblem, Old and New Communication Equipment
A510

1965, May 21 ***Perf. 11½*** **Wmk. 267**

1001 A510 120cr yel & grn 50 20

Issued to commemorate the centenary of the International Telecommunication Union.

Epitácio Pessoa
A511

Statue of Admiral Barroso
A512

1965, May 23 Photogravure

1002 A511 35cr bl gray 20 15

Issued to commemorate the centenary of the birth of Epitácio da Silva Pessoa (1865–1942), jurist, president of Brazil, 1919–22.

1965, June 11

1003 A512 30cr blue 40 15

Centenary of the naval battle of Riachuelo.

A souvenir card containing one lithographed facsimile of No. 1003, imperf., exists. Size: 100x139½mm.

José de Alencar and Indian Princess
A513

1965, June 24 ***Perf. 11½x11***

1004 A513 30cr dp plum 50 15

Issued to commemorate the centenary of the publication of "Iracema" by José de Alencar.

A souvenir card containing one lithographed facsimile of No. 1004, printed in rose red and imperf., exists. Size: 100x141½mm.

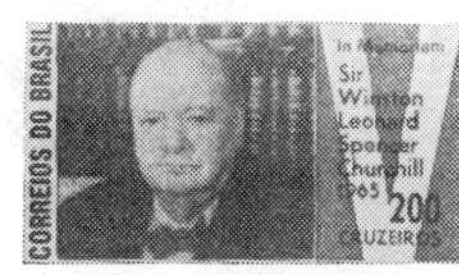

Winston Churchill
A514

1965, June 25 ***Perf. 11x11½***

1005 A514 200cr slate 1.00 25

Issued in memory of Sir Winston Spencer Churchill (1874–1965), statesman and World War II leader.

Scout Jamboree Emblem
A515

1965, July 17 Photogravure

1006 A515 30cr dl bl grn 50 15

Issued to commemorate the First Pan-American Boy Scout Jamboree, Fundao Island, Rio de Janeiro, July 15–25.

ICY Emblem
A516

1965, Aug. 25 ***Perf. 11½*** **Wmk. 267**

1007 A516 120cr dl bl & blk 40 15

International Cooperation Year, 1965.

Leoncio Correias
A517

Emblem
A518

1965, Sept. 1 ***Perf. 11½x11***

1008 A517 35cr sl grn 20 15

Issued to commemorate the centenary of the birth of Leoncio Correias, poet.

1965, Sept. 4

1009 A518 30cr brt rose 30 15

Issued to publicize the Eighth Biennial Fine Arts Exhibition, Sao Paulo, Nov.–Dec., 1965.

Pres. Saragat of Italy
A519

1965, Sept. 11 **Photo.** **Wmk. 267**

1010 A519 100cr sl grn, *pink* 25 12

Visit of Pres. Giuseppe Saragat of Italy.

Grand Duke and Duchess of Luxembourg
A520

1965, Sept. 17 ***Perf. 11x11½***

1011 A520 100cr brn ol 25 12

Issued to commemorate the visit of Grand Duke Jean and Grand Duchess Josephine Charlotte of Luxembourg.

Biplane
A521

1965, Oct. 8 **Photo.** ***Perf. 11½x11***

1012 A521 35cr ultra 25 15

Issued to publicize the 3rd Aviation Week Philatelic Exhibition, Rio de Janeiro.

A souvenir card carries one impression of this 35cr, imperf. Size: 102x140mm. Sold for 100cr.

Flags of OAS Members
A522

1965, Nov. 17 ***Perf. 11x11½***

1013 A522 100cr brt bl & blk 40 20

Issued to commemorate the second meeting of Foreign Ministers of the Organization of American States, Rio de Janeiro.

King Baudouin and Queen Fabiola of Belgium—A523

1965, Nov. 18

1014 A523 100cr gray 40 20

Visit of King and Queen of Belgium.

"Coffee Beans"
A524

Perf. 11½x11

1965, Dec. 21 **Photo.** **Wmk. 267**

1015 A524 30cr brown 60 15

Brazilian coffee publicity.

Conveyor and Loading Crane
A525

1966, Apr. 1 ***Perf. 11x11½***

1016 A525 110cr tan & dk sl grn 40 25

Issued to commemorate the opening of the new terminal of the Rio Doce Iron Ore Company at Tubarao.

Pouring Ladle and Steel Beam
A526

Prof. de Rocha Dissecting Cadaver
A527

Perf. 11½x11

1966, Apr. 16 **Photo.** **Wmk. 267**

1017 A526 30cr *dp org* 35 15

Issued to commemorate the 25th anniversary of the National Steel Company (nationalization of the steel industry).

1966, Apr. 26

1018 A527 30cr brt bluish grn 60 15

Issued to commemorate the 50th anniversary of the discovery and description of Rickettsia prowazeki, the cause of typhus fever, by Prof. Henrique de Rocha Lima.

Battle of Tuiuti
A528

Perf. 11x11½

1966, May 24 **Photo.** **Wmk. 267**

1019 A528 30cr gray grn 60 15

Centenary of the Battle of Tuiuti.

Symbolic Water Cycle
A529

CORREIO - 1966
BRASIL
100 CRUZEIROS
VISITA DO PRESIDENTE DE ISRAEL SR. ZALMAN SHAZAR

Pres. Shazar of Israel
A530

1966, July 1 ***Perf. 11½x11***

1020	A529	100cr lt brn & bl	45	20

Hydrological Decade (UNESCO), 1965–74.

1966, July 18 Photo. **Wmk. 267**

1021	A530	100cr ultra	50	20

Visit of Pres. Zalman Shazar of Israel.

Imperial Academy of Fine Arts
A531

Perf. 11x11½

1966, Aug. 12 Engr. **Wmk. 267**

1022	A531	100cr red brn	40	20

150th anniversary of French art mission.

Military Service Emblem
A532

1966, Sept. 6 Photo. ***Perf. 11x11½***

1023	A532	30cr yel, ultra & grn	40	15
a.		With commemorative border	2.25	2.25

Issued to publicize the new Military Service Law. No. 1023a, issued in sheets of four, measures 103½x47mm. It carries at left a single 30cr, type A532, in deeper tones of yellow and ultramarine, Wmk. 264. Top and bottom "frames" in ultramarine are inscribed "Departamento dos Correios e Telégrafos" and "100 Cruzeiros." Inscription at right: "Bloco Comemorativo da Nova Lei do Serviço Militar." Without gum. Sold for 100cr.

Rubén Dario
A533

Perf. 11½x11

1966, Sept. 20 Photo. **Wmk. 267**

1024	A533	100cr brt rose lil	40	15

Issued to commemorate the 50th anniversary of the death of Rubén Dario (pen name of Felix Rubén Garcia Sarmiento (1867–1916), Nicaraguan poet, newspaper correspondent and diplomat.

Ceramic Candlestick from Santarém
A534

1966, Oct. 6 ***Perf. 11x11½***

1025	A534	30cr dk brn, *sal*	40	15

Centenary of Goeldi Museum at Belém.

Arms of Santa Cruz
A535

Perf. 11½x11

1966, Oct. 15 Photo. **Wmk. 267**

1026	A535	30cr sl grn	45	15

Issued to publicize the First National Tobacco Exposition, Santa Cruz.

UNESCO Emblem
A536

1966, Oct. 24 Engraved ***Perf. 11½***

1027	A536	120cr black	60	25
a.		With commemorative border	1.75	1.75

Issued to commemorate the 20th anniversary of UNESCO (United Nations Educational, Scientific and Cultural Organization). No. 1027a issued in sheets of 4 with red control number measures 102x48mm. It carries at right a design similar to No. 1027. Inscribed at left: "Bloco comemorativo do 20° aniversario da UNESCO," "Cr$150" and "Departamento dos Correios e Telegrafos". Unwatermarked granite paper, without gum. Sold for 150cr.

Captain Antonio Correia Pinto and Map of Lages
A537

Formée Cross and Southern Cross
A538

Perf. 11½x11

1966, Nov. 22 Photo. **Wmk. 267**

1028	A537	30cr sal pink	35	15

Issued to commemorate the bicentenary of the arrival of Capt. Antonio Correia Pinto.

1966, Dec. 4 ***Perf. 11½***

1029	A538	100cr bl grn	45	15

Issued to commemorate LUBRAPEX 1966 philatelic exhibition at the National Museum of Fine Arts, Rio de Janeiro.

Madonna and Child
A539

Madonna and Child
A540

Perf. 11½x11

1966, Dec. Photo. **Wmk. 267**

1030	A539	30cr bl grn	30	15

Perf. 11½

1031	A540	35cr sal & ultra	25	20
a.		150cr sal & ultra	1.75	1.75

Christmas 1966.

No. 1031a measures 46x103mm. and is printed in sheets of 4. It is inscribed "Pax Hominibus" (but not "Brasil Correio") and carries the Madonna shown on No. 1031. Issued without gum.

Issue dates: 30cr, Dec. 8; 35cr, Dec. 22; 150cr, Dec. 28.

Arms of Laguna
A541

1967, Jan. 4 Engr. ***Perf. 11x11½***

1032	A541	60cr sepia	25	15

Issued to commemorate the centenary of the Post and Telegraph Agency of Laguna, Santa Catarina.

Railroad Bridge
A542

1967, Feb. 16 Photo. **Wmk. 267**

1033	A542	50cr dp org	60	20

Centenary of the Santos-Jundiai railroad.

Black Madonna of Czestochowa, Polish Eagle and Cross
A543

1967, Mar. 12 ***Perf. 11x11½***

1034	A543	50cr yel, bl & rose red	60	20

Issued to commemorate the thousandth anniversary of the adoption of Christianity in Poland.

Research Rocket
A544

Anita Garibaldi
A545

1967, March 23 ***Perf. 11½x11***

1035	A544	50cr blk & brt bl	75	30

World Meteorological Day, March 23.

Perf. 11x11½

1967–69 Photo. **Wmk. 267**

Portraits: 1c, Mother Joana Angelica. 2c, Marilia de Dirceu. 3c, Dr. Rita Lobato. 6c, Ana Neri. 10c, Darcy Vargas.

1036	A545	1c dp ultra	15	5
1037	A545	2c red brn	15	5
1038	A545	3c brt grn	25	8
1039	A545	5c black	50	8
1040	A545	6c brown	50	8
1041	A545	10c dk sl grn ('69)	2.75	75
		Nos. 1036-1041 (6)	4.30	1.09

Issue dates: 1c, May 3; 2c, Aug. 14; 3c, June 7; 5c, Apr. 14; 6c, May 14, 1967; 10c, June 18, 1969.

VARIG Airlines
A546

Madonna and Child, by Robert Feruzzi
A548

Lions Emblem and Globes
A547

1967, May 8 ***Perf. 11½x11***

1046	A546	6c brt bl & blk	30	25

40th anniversary of VARIG Airlines.

1967, May 9 Engr. ***Perf. 11x11½***

1047	A547	6c green	50	25
a.		Souv. sheet	1.25	1.25

Issued to commemorate the 50th anniversary of Lions International. No. 1047a contains one imperf. stamp similar to No. 1047. Green inscription and Lions emblem in margin. Size: 131x80mm. Sold for 15c.

1967, May 14 Photo. ***Perf. 11½x11***

1048	A548	5c violet	30	25
a.		15c, souv. sheet	1.25	1.25

Issued for Mother's Day. No. 1048a contains one 15c imperf. stamp in design of No. 1048. Violet marginal inscription. Size: 129x77mm.

Prince Akihito and Princess Michiko
A549

1967, May 25 ***Perf. 11x11½***

1049	A549	10c blk & pink	40	20

Issued to commemorate the visit to Brazil of Crown Prince Akihito and Princess Michiko of Japan.

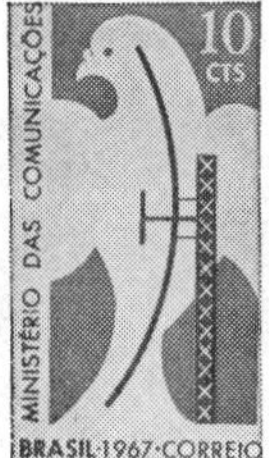

Carrier Pigeon and Radar Screen
A550

Brother Vicente do Salvador
A551

Perf. 11½x11

1967, June 20 Photo. Wmk. 267

1050	A550	10c sl & brt pink	40	20

Issued to commemorate the opening of the Communications Ministry in Brasilia.

1967, June 28 Engraved

1051	A551	5c brown	35	25

Issued to commemorate the 400th anniversary of the birth of Brother Vicente do Salvador (1564–1636), founder of Franciscan convent in Rio de Janeiro, and historian.

Boy, Girl and 4-S Emblem
A552

1967, July 12 Photo. ***Perf. 11½***

1052	A552	5c grn & blk	30	20

National 4-S (4-H) Day.

Möbius Strip
A553

1967, July 21 ***Perf. 11x11½***

1053	A553	5c brt bl & blk	30	25

Issued to commemorate the 6th Brazilian Mathematical Congress.

Fish
A554

1967, Aug. 1 ***Perf. 11½***

1054	A554	5c slate	50	25

Bicentenary of city of Piracicaba.

Golden Rose and Papal Arms
A555

1967, Aug. 15

1055	A555	20c mag & yel	1.25	50

Issued to commemorate the offering of a golden rose by Pope Paul VI to the Virgin Mary of Fatima (Our Lady of Peace), Patroness of Brazil.

General Sampaio
A556

King Olaf of Norway
A557

1967, Aug. 25 Engr. ***Perf. 11½x11***

1056	A556	5c blue	30	25

Issued to honor General Antonio de Sampaio, hero of the Battle of Tutui.

1967, Sept. 8 Photogravure

1057	A557	10c brn org	30	25

Visit of King Olaf of Norway.

Sun over Sugar Loaf, Botafogo Bay
A558

Nilo Peçanha
A559

Photogravure and Embossed

1967, Sept. 25 ***Perf. 11½*** **Wmk. 267**

1058	A558	10c blk & dp org	30	20

Issued to commemorate the 22nd meeting of the International Monetary Fund, International Bank for Reconstruction and Development, International Financial Corporation and International Development Association.

Perf. 11½x11

1967, Oct. 1 Photo. Wmk. 267

1059	A559	5c brn vio	30	25

Issued to commemorate the centenary of the birth of Nilo Peçanha (1867–1924), President of Brazil 1909–1910.

Virgin of the Apparition and Basilica of Aparecida
A560

Cockerel, Festival Emblem
A561

1967, Oct. 11 ***Perf. 11½***

1060	A560	5c ultra & dl yel	50	25
a.		Souv. sheet of 2	1.75	1.75

Issued to commemorate the 250th anniversary of the discovery of the statue of Our Lady of the Apparition, now in the National Basilica of the Apparition at Aparecida do Norte.

No. 1060a contains imperf. 5c and 10c stamps similar to No. 1060. Blue marginal inscriptions with pink and blue design. Issued Dec. 27, 1967, for Christmas. Size: 77½x129mm.

Engraved and Photogravure

1967, Oct. 16 ***Perf. 11½x11***

1061	A561	20c blk & multi	75	40

Second International Folksong Festival.

Balloon, Plane and Rocket
A562

Perf. 11x11½

1967, Oct. 18 Photo. Unwmkd.

1062	A562	10c blue	60	35
a.		15c, souv. sheet	1.50	1.50

Issued for the Week of the Wing, Oct. 18–23. No. 1062a contains one imperf. 15c stamp similar to No. 1062, blue marginal design and inscription; it was issued Oct. 23. Size: 130x75mm.

Pres. Arthur Bernardes
A563

Portraits of Brazilian Presidents: 20c, Campos Salles. 50c, Wenceslau Pereira Gomes Braz. 1cr, Washington Pereira de Souza Luiz. 2cr, Castello Branco.

Perf. 11x11½

1967–68 Photogravure Wmk. 267

1063	A563	10c blue	30	20
1064	A563	20c dk red brn	1.00	20
		Engraved		
1065	A563	50c blk ('68)	4.00	30
1066	A563	1cr lil rose ('68)	6.00	30
1067	A563	2cr emer ('68)	1.50	30
		Nos. 1063-1067 (5)	12.80	1.30

Carnival of Rio
A564

Ships, Anchor and Sailor
A565

1967, Nov. 22 ***Perf. 11½x11***

1070	A564	10c lem, ultra & pink	40	25
a.		15c, souv. sheet	1.50	1.50

Issued for International Tourist Year, 1967. No. 1070a contains a 15c imperf. stamp in design of No. 1070. Pink marginal design and inscription. Size: 76x 130mm. Issued Nov. 24.

1967, Dec. 6

1071	A565	10c ultra	40	30

Issued for Navy Week.

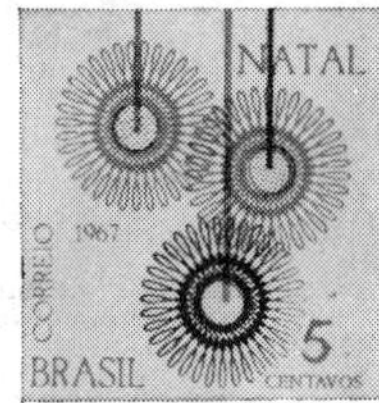

Christmas Decorations
A566

1967, Dec. 8 ***Perf. 11½***

1072	A566	5c car, yel & bl	40	25

Christmas 1967.

Olavo Bilac, Planes, Tank and Aircraft Carrier—A567

Perf. 11x11½

1967, Dec. 16 Photo. Wmk. 267

1073	A567	5c brt bl & yel	40	25

Issued for Reservists' Day and to honor Olavo Bilac, sponsor of compulsory military service.

Rodrigues de Carvalho
A568

1967, Dec. 18 Engr. ***Perf. 11½x11***

1074	A568	10c green	30	25

Issued to commemorate the centenary of the birth of Rodrigues de Carvalho, poet and lawyer.

Orlando Rangel
A569

Photogravure

1968, Feb. 29 ***Perf. 11x11½***

1075	A569	5c lt grnsh bl & blk	60	35

Issued to commemorate the centenary of the birth of Orlando de Fonseca Rangel, pioneer of pharmaceutical industry in Brazil.

Virgin of Paranagua and Diver
A570

Map of Brazil Showing Manaus
A571

1968, Mar. 9 *Perf. 11½x11*

1076 A570 10c dk sl grn & brt yel grn 50 30

Issued to commemorate the 250th anniversary of the first underwater explorations at Paranagua.

1968, Mar. 13 Photo. **Wmk. 267**

1077 A571 10c yel, grn & red 40 30

Issued to publicize the free port of Manaus on the Amazon River.

Human Rights Flame
A572

Paul Harris and Rotary Emblem
A573

1968, Mar. 21 *Perf. 11½x11*

1078 A572 10c bl & sal 40 30
International Human Rights Year.

1968, Apr. 19 Litho. **Unwmkd.**
Without Gum

1079 A573 20c grn & org brn 1.50 70

Issued to commemorate the centenary of the birth of Paul Percy Harris (1868–1947), founder of Rotary International.

Pedro Alvares Cabral and his Fleet—A574

Design: 20c, First Mass celebrated in Brazil.

1968 Without Gum *Perf. 11½*

1080 A574 10c multi 85 50
1081 A574 20c multi 1.15 60

Issued to commemorate the 500th anniversary of the birth of Pedro Alvares Cabral, navigator, who took possession of Brazil for Portugal.
Issue dates: 10c, Apr. 22; 20c, July 11.

College Arms
A575

1968, Apr. 22 Photo. **Wmk. 267**

1082 A575 10c vio bl, red & gold 80 35

Centenary of St. Luiz College, São Paulo.

Motherhood, by Henrique Bernardeli
A576

1968, May 12 Litho. **Unwmkd.**
Without Gum

1083 A576 5c multi 50 30
Issued for Mother's Day.

Harpy Eagle
A577

Photogravure and Engraved

1968, May 28 **Wmk. 267**

1084 A577 20c brt bl & blk 1.75 60
Sesquicentennial of National Museum.

Brazilian and Japanese Women
A578

1968, June 28 Litho. **Unwmkd.**
Without Gum

1085 A578 10c yel & multi 80 50

Issued to commemorate the inauguration of Varig's direct Brazil-Japan airline.

Horse Race
A579

Perf. 11x11½

1968, July 16 Litho. **Unwmkd.**
Without Gum

1086 A579 10c multi 50 30
Centenary of the Jockey Club of Brazil.

Musician Wren—A580

Designs: 10c, Red-crested cardinal (vert.). 50c, Royal flycatcher (vert.).

Perf. 11½x11, 11x11½

1968–69 Engraved **Sheet Wmk.**
Without Gum

1087 A580 10c multi ('69) 75 30
1088 A580 20c multi 1.25 30
1089 A580 50c multi 1.75 60

Some stamps in each sheet of Nos. 1087–1089 show parts of a two-line papermaker's watermark: "WESTERPOST / INDUSTRIA BRASILEIRA" with diamond-shaped emblem between last two words. Entire watermark appears in one sheet margin.
Issue dates: 10c, Aug. 20, 1969. 20c, July 19, 1968. 50c, Aug. 2, 1968.

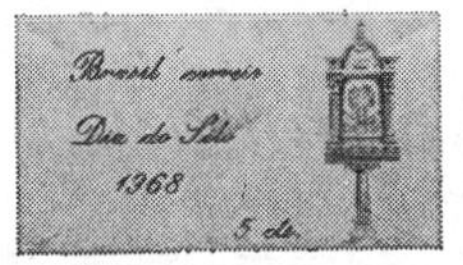

Mailbox and Envelope
A581

Photogravure and Engraved

1968, Aug. 1 *Perf. 11* **Wmk. 267**

1091 A581 5c cit, blk & grn 25 20

Issued for Stamp Day, 1968 and to commemorate the 125th anniversary of the first Brazilian postage stamps.

Emilio Luiz Mallet
A582

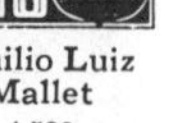

Map of South America
A583

Perf. 11½x11

1968, Aug. 25 Engraved **Wmk. 267**

1092 A582 10c pale pur 25 20
Issued to honor Marshal Emilio Luiz Mallet, Baron of Itapevi, patron of the marines.

1968, Sept. 5 **Photogravure**

1093 A583 10c dp org 20 20
Visit of President Eduardo Frei of Chile.

Seal of Portuguese Literary School
A584

Photogravure and Engraved

1968, Sept. 10 *Perf. 11½*

1094 A584 5c pink & grn 25 20
Centenary of Portuguese Literary School.

Map of Brazil and Telex Tape
A585

1968, Sept. Photo. *Perf. 11x11½*

1095 A585 20c cit & brt grn 60 25

Linking of 25 Brazilian cities by teletype.

Soldiers' Heads on Medal
A586

Perf. 11½x11

1968, Sept. 24 Litho. **Unwmkd.**
Without Gum

1096 A586 5c bl & gray 30 25
8th American Armed Forces Conference.

Clef, Notes and Sugarloaf Mountain
A587

1968, Sept. 30 *Perf. 11½*
Without Gum

1097 A587 6c blk, yel & red 60 30
Third International Folksong Festival.

Catalytic Cracking Plant
A588

1968, Oct. 4 **Without Gum**

1098 A588 6c bl & multi 60 40

Issued to commemorate the 15th anniversary of Petrobras, the national oil company.

Child Protection
A589

Whimsical Girl
A590

Design: 5c, School boy walking toward the sun.

Perf. 11½x11, 11x11½

1968, Oct. 16 Litho. Unwmkd.
Without Gum

1099	A590	5c gray & lt bl	50	40
1100	A589	10c brt bl, dk red & blk	60	30
1101	A590	20c multi	75	30

Issued to commemorate the 22nd anniversary of the United Nations Children's Fund.

Children with Books
A591

1968, Oct. 23 *Perf. 11x11½*
Without Gum

1102 A591 5c multi 35 25

Issued to publicize Book Week.

U.N. Emblem and Flags
A592

Perf. 11½x11

1968, Oct. 24 Without Gum

1103 A592 20c blk & multi 75 35

Issued to commemorate the 20th anniversary of the World Health Organization.

Jean Baptiste Debret, Self-portrait
A593

Perf. 11x11½

1968, Oct. 30 Litho. Unwmkd.
Without Gum

1104 A593 10c dk gray & pale yel 50 25

Issued to commemorate the bi-centenary of the birth of Jean Baptiste Debret, (1768–1848), French painter who worked in Brazil (1816–31). Design includes his "Burden Bearer."

Queen Elizabeth II
A594

1968, Nov. 4 *Perf. 11½*
Without Gum

1105 A594 70c lt bl & multi 1.75 1.00

Issued to commemorate the visit of Queen Elizabeth II of Great Britain.

Francisco Braga
A595

Perf. 11½x11

1968, Nov. 19 Wmk. 267

1106 A595 5c dl red brn 40 25

Issued to commemorate the centenary of the birth of Antonio Francisco Braga, composer of the Hymn of the Flag.

Brazilian Flag
A596

1968, Nov. 19 *Perf. 11½* Unwmkd.
Without Gum

1107 A596 10c multi 50 30

Issued for Flag Day.

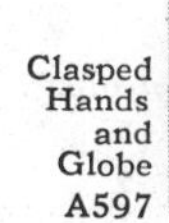

Clasped Hands and Globe
A597

Perf. 11x11½

1968, Nov. 25 Typo. Unwmkd.
Without Gum

1108 A597 5c multi 30 25

Issued for Voluntary Blood Donor's Day.

Old Locomotive—A598

1968, Nov. 28 Litho. *Perf. 11½*
Without Gum

1109 A598 5c multi 1.00 50

Centenary of the São Paulo Railroad.

Bell
A599

Francisco Caldas, Jr.
A600

Design: 6c, Santa Claus and boy.

1968 Without Gum *Perf. 11½x11*

1110	A599	5c multi	50	25
1111	A599	6c multi	50	25

Christmas 1968.
Issue dates: 5c, Dec. 12; 6c, Dec. 20.

1968, Dec. 13 Without Gum

1112 A600 10c crim & blk 35 20

Issued to commemorate the centenary of the birth of Francisco Caldas, Jr., journalist and founder of Correio de Povo, newspaper.

Map of Brazil, War Memorial and Reservists' Emblem
A601

Perf. 11x11½

1968, Dec. 16 Photo. Wmk. 267

1113 A601 5c bl grn & org brn 50 25

Issued for Reservists' Day.

Radar Antenna
A602

Viscount of Rio Branco
A603

Perf. 11½x11

1969, Feb. 28 Litho. Unwmkd.
Without Gum

1114 A602 30c ultra, lt bl & blk 1.25 60

Issued to publicize the inauguration of EMBRATEL, satellite communications ground station bringing U.S. television to Brazil via Telstar.

1969, Mar. 16 Without Gum

1115 A603 5c blk & buff 35 25

Issued to commemorate the 150th anniversary of the birth of José Maria da Silva Paranhos, Viscount of Rio Branco (1819–1880), statesman.

St. Gabriel
A604

1969, Mar. 24 Without Gum

1116 A604 5c multi 50 25

Issued to honor St. Gabriel as patron saint of telecommunications.

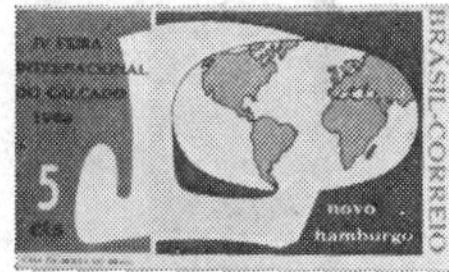

Shoemaker's Last and Globe
A605

Perf. 11x11½

1969, Mar. 29 Litho. Unwmkd.
Without Gum

1117 A605 5c multi 35 25

Issued to publicize the 4th International Shoe Fair, Novo Hamburgo.

Allan Kardec
A606

1969, Mar. 31 Photo. Wmk. 267

1118 A606 5c brt grn & org brn 40 25

Issued to commemorate the centenary of the death of Allan Kardec (pen name of Leon Hippolyto Denizard Rivail, 1803–1869), French physician and spiritist.

Men of 3 Races and Arms of Cuiabá
A607

1969, Apr. 8 Litho. Unwmkd.
Without Gum

1119 A607 5c blk & multi 30 25

Issued to commemorate the 250th anniversary of the founding of Cuiabá, capital of Matto Grosso.

State Mint—A608

1969, Apr. 11 *Perf. 11½*
Without Gum

1120 A608 5c ol bis & org 60 40

Issued to commemorate the opening of the state money printing plant.

Brazilian Stamps and Emblem
A609

Perf. 11x11½

1969, Apr. 30 Litho. Unwmkd.

Without Gum

1121	A609	5c multi	40	25

Issued to commemorate the 50th anniversary of the São Paulo Philatelic Society.

St. Anne, Baroque Statue
A610

1969, May 8 ***Perf. 11½***

Without Gum

1122	A610	5c lem & multi	60	40

Issued for Mother's Day.

ILO Emblem
A611

Perf. 11x11½

1969, May 13 Photo. Wmk. 267

1123	A611	5c dp rose red & gold	40	20

Issued to commemorate the 50th anniversary of the International Labor Organization.

Diving Platform and Swimming Pool
A612

Mother and Child at Window
A613

Lithographed and Photogravure

Perf. 11½x11

1969, June 13 Unwmkd.

Without Gum

1124	A612	20c bis brn, blk & bl grn	1.00	60

40th anniversary of the Cearense Water Sports Club, Fortaleza.

1969 Lithographed ***Perf. 11½***

Designs: 20c, Modern sculpture by Felicia Leirner. 50c, "The Sun Sets in Brasilia," by Danilo di Prete. 1cr, Angelfish, painting by Aldemir Martins.

Size: 24x36mm.

1125	A613	10c org & multi	85	30

Size: 33x34mm.

1126	A613	20c red & multi	80	60

Size: 33x53mm.

1127	A613	50c yel & multi	3.00	1.50

Without Gum

1128	A613	1cr gray & multi	3.50	1.50

Issued to publicize the 10th Biennial Art Exhibition, São Paulo, Sept.–Dec. 1969.

Angelfish
A614

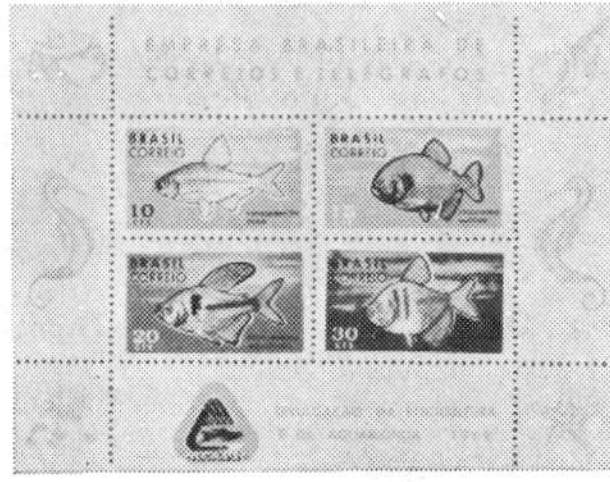

Fish
A615

Fish: 10c, Tetra. 15c, Piranha. No. 1130c, Megalamphodus megalopterus. 30c, Black tetra.

Perf. 11½

1969, July 21 Litho. Wmk. 267

1129	A614	20c multi	1.00	50

Souvenir Sheet

Perf. 10½x11½

1969, July 24 Unwmkd.

1130	A615	Sheet of four	3.50	3.50
a.		10c yel & multi	75	75
b.		15c brt bl & multi	75	75
c.		20c grn & multi	75	75
d.		30c org & multi	75	75

Issued to publicize the work of ACAPI, an organization devoted to the preservation and development of fish in Brazil.

No. 1130 contains 4 stamps (size: 38½x21mm.). Greenish margin with commemorative inscription, marine life design and ACAPI emblem. Size: 132½x98½mm.

L. O. Teles de Menezes
A616

Mailman
A617

Perf. 11½x11

1969, July 26 Photo. Wmk. 267

1131	A616	50c dp org & bl grn	2.00	1.00

Centenary of Spiritism press in Brazil.

1969, Aug. 1

1132	A617	30c blue	2.00	1.00

Issued for Stamp Day.

Map of Brazil
A618

Gen. Tasso Fragoso
A620

Railroad Bridge
A619

Lithographed

1969, Aug. 25 ***Perf. 11½*** **Unwmkd.**

Without Gum

1133	A618	10c lt ultra, grn & yel	50	25

Perf. 11x11½

1134	A619	20c multi	1.00	40

Engraved ***Perf. 11½x11*** **Wmk. 267**

With Gum

1135	A620	20c green	1.00	50

No. 1133 honors the Army as guardian of security; No. 1134, as promoter of development. No. 1135 commemorates the birth centenary of Gen. Tasso Fragoso.

Jupia Dam, Parana River
A621

Perf. 11½

1969, Sept. 10 Litho. Unwmkd.

Without Gum

1136	A621	20c lt bl & multi	50	50

Issued to commemorate the inauguration of the Jupia Dam, part of the Urubupunga hydroelectric system serving Sao Paulo.

Gandhi and Spinning Wheel
A622

1969, Oct. 2 ***Perf. 11x11½***

1137	A622	20c yel & blk	50	30

Issued to commemorate the centenary of the birth of Mohandas K. Gandhi (1869–1948), leader in India's fight for independence.

Santos Dumont, Eiffel Tower and Module Landing on Moon
A623

1969, Oct. 17 ***Perf. 11½***

Without Gum

1138	A623	50c dk bl & multi	2.50	1.50

Man's first landing on the moon, July 20, 1969. See note after U.S. No. C76.

Smelting Plant
A624

1969, Oct. 26 ***Perf. 11½*** **Unwmkd.**

Without Gum

1139	A624	20c multi	50	40

Expansion of Brazil's steel industry.

Steel Furnace
A625

1969, Oct. 31 Litho. Without Gum

1140	A625	10c yel & multi	50	40

25th anniversary of Acesita Steel Works.

Water Vendor, by J. B. Debret
A626

Design: 30c, Street Scene, by Debret.

1969–70 Without Gum

1141	A626	20c multi	1.25	50
1141A	A626	30c multi	1.25	1.00

Issued to commemorate the 200th anniversary of the birth of Jean Baptiste Debret (1768–1848), painter.

Issue dates: 20c, Nov. 5, 1969; 30c, May 19, 1970.

Exhibition Emblem
A627

1969, Nov. 15 ***Perf. 11½x11***

Without Gum

1142 A627 10c multi 50 25

Issued to publicize the ABUEXPO 69 Philatelic Exposition, Sao Paulo, Nov. 15–23.

Plane—A628

1969, Nov. 23 Without Gum

1143 A628 50c multi 3.00 1.50

Issued to publicize the year of the expansion of the national aviation industry.

Pelé Scoring
A629

1969–70 Without Gum

1144 A629 10c multi 75 75

Souvenir Sheet

Imperf.

1145 A629 75c multi ('70) 7.50 6.00

Issued to commemorate the 1,000th goal scored by Pelé, Brazilian soccer player.

No. 1145 contains one imperf. stamp with simulated perforations, commemorative marginal inscription. Size: 80x119 mm.

Issued dates: 10c, Nov. 28, 1969. 75c, Jan. 23, 1970.

Madonna and Child from Villa Velha Monastery
A630

Lithographed

1969, Dec. ***Perf. 11½*** **Unwmkd.**

Without Gum

1146 A630 10c gold & multi 50 25

Souvenir Sheet

Imperf.

1147 A630 75c gold & multi 6.00 5.00

Christmas 1969.

No. 1147 has simulated perforations; commemorative inscription and Christmas decorations in margin. Size: 136x102mm.

Issue dates: 10c, Dec. 8; 75c, Dec. 18.

Destroyer and Submarine
A631

Perf. 11x11½

1969, Dec. 9 Engraved Wmk. 267

1148 A631 5c bluish gray 50 25

Issued for Navy Day.

Dr. Herman Blumenau
A632

1969, Dec. 26 ***Perf. 11½*** **Wmk. 267**

1149 A632 20c gray grn 1.25 40

Issued to commemorate the 150th anniversary of the birth of Dr. Herman Blumenau (1819–1899), founder of Blumenau, Santa Catarina State.

Carnival Scene—A633

Sugarloaf Mountain, Mask, Confetti and Streamers
A634

Designs: 5c, Jumping boy and 2 women (vert.). 20c, Clowns. 50c, Drummer.

1969–70 **Litho.** **Unwmkd.**

Without Gum

1150 A633 5c multi 60 30
1151 A633 10c multi 60 30
1152 A633 20c multi 75 40
1153 A634 30c multi ('70) 3.50 1.75
1154 A634 50c multi ('70) 3.00 1.75
Nos. 1150-1154 (5) 8.45 4.50

Carico Carnival, Rio de Janeiro.

Issue dates: Nos. 1150–1152, Dec. 29, 1969. Nos. 1153–1154, Feb. 5, 1970.

Opening Bars of "Il Guarani" with Antonio Carlos Gomes Conducting
A635

1970, Mar. 19 **Litho.** ***Perf. 11½***

Without Gum

1155 A635 20c blk, yel, gray & brn 75 40

Issued to commemorate the centenary of the opera Il Guarani, by Antonio Carlos Gomes.

Church of Penha
A636

1970, Apr. 6 ***Perf. 11½*** **Unwmkd.**

Without Gum

1156 A636 20c blk & multi 40 20

Issued to commemorate the 400th anniversary of the Church of Penha, State of Esperito Santo.

Assembly Building
A637

Designs: 50c, Reflecting Pool. 1cr, Presidential Palace.

1970, Apr. 21 Without Gum

1157 A637 20c multi 1.25 60
1158 A637 50c multi 3.25 1.50
1159 A637 1cr multi 3.25 1.50

10th anniversary of Brasilia.

Symbolic Water Design
A638

1970, May 5 ***Perf. 11½*** **Unwmkd.**

Without Gum

1161 A638 50c multi 2.50 1.00

Issued to publicize the Rondon Project for the development of the Amazon River basin.

Marshal Manoel Luiz Osorio and Osorio Arms—A639

1970, May 8 Without Gum

1162 A639 20c multi 2.00 75

Issued to commemorate the inauguration of the Marshal Osorio Historical Park.

Madonna, from San Antonio Monastery, Rio de Janeiro
A640

Detail from Brasilia Cathedral
A641

1970, May 10 Without Gum

1163 A640 20c multi 60 50

Issued for Mother's Day.

1970, May 27 Engraved Wmk. 267

1164 A641 20c lt yel grn 40 30

8th National Eucharistic Congress, Brasilia.

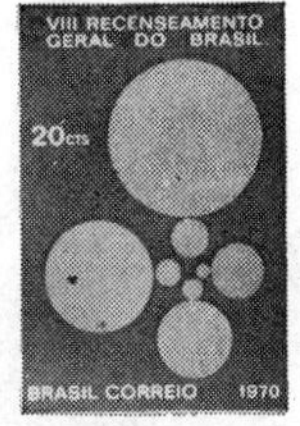

Census Symbol
A642

Lithographed

1970, June 22 ***Perf. 11½*** **Unwmkd.**

Without Gum

1165 A642 20c grn & yel 75 40

Issued to publicize the 8th general census.

Soccer Cup, Maps of Brazil and Mexico
A643

Swedish Flag and Player Holding Rimet Cup—A644

Designs: 2cr, Chilean flag and soccer. 3cr, Mexican flag and soccer.

1970 Without Gum

1166 A643 50c blk, lt bl & gold 1.00 1.00
1167 A644 1cr pink & multi 4.00 1.50
1168 A644 2cr gray & multi 6.00 1.50
1169 A644 3cr multi 5.00 1.00

Issued to commemorate the 9th World Soccer Championships for the Jules Rimet Cup, Mexico City, May 30–June 21. No. 1166 commemorates Brazil's victory.

Issue dates: No. 1166, June 24; Nos. 1167–1169, Aug. 4.

Corcovado Christ and Map of South America A645

1970, July 18 **Without Gum**

1170	A645	50c brn, dk red & bl	2.50	1.25

Issued to publicize the 6th World Congress of Marist Brothers' Alumni.

Pandiá Calógeras A646

Perf. 11½x11

1970, Aug. 25 Photo. **Unwmkd.**

1171	A646	20c bl grn	75	50

Issued to honor Pandiá Calógeras, Minister of War.

Brazilian Military Emblems and Map A647

Perf. 11x11½

1970, Sept. 8 Litho. **Unwmkd.**

Without Gum

1172	A647	20c gray & multi	60	50

25th anniversary of victory in World War II.

Annunciation (Brazilian Primitive Painting) A648

1970, Sept. 29 ***Perf. 11½***

Without Gum

1173	A648	20c multi	2.00	1.00

Issued for St. Gabriel's (patron saint of communications) Day.

Boy in Library A649

U.N. Emblem A650

1970, Oct. 23 **Without Gum**

1174	A649	20c multi	1.75	1.00

Issued to publicize Book Week.

1970, Oct. 24 **Without Gum**

1175	A650	50c dk bl, lt bl & sil	2.00	1.50

25th anniversary of the United Nations.

Rio de Janeiro, 1820—A651

Designs: 50c, LUBRAPEX 70 emblem. 1 cr, Rio de Janeiro with Sugar Loaf Mountain, 1970. No. 1179, like 20c.

1970, Oct. **Without Gum**

1176	A651	20c multi	2.00	1.00
1177	A651	50c yel brn & blk	3.50	1.50
1178	A651	1cr multi	3.00	2.00

Souvenir Sheet

Imperf.

1179	A651	1cr multi	6.00	2.00

Issued to commemorate LUBRAPEX 70, third Portuguese-Brazilian Philatelic Exhibition, Rio de Janeiro, Oct. 24–31. No. 1179 contains one stamp, black marginal inscription. Size: 60x80mm.

Issue dates: Nos. 1176–1178, Oct. 27. No. 1179, Oct. 31.

Holy Family by Candido Portinari A652

1970, Dec. Litho. ***Perf. 11½***

Without Gum

1180	A652	50c multi	1.50	1.00

Souvenir Sheet

Imperf.

1181	A652	1cr multi	6.00	2.00

Christmas 1970. No. 1181 contains one stamp with simulated perforations. Light yellow green margin with red and black inscription. Size: 106x52mm. Issue dates: 50c, Dec. 1; 1cr, Dec. 8.

Battleship A653

CIH Emblem A654

1970, Dec. 11 Litho. ***Perf. 11½***

Without Gum

1182	A653	20c multi	1.50	75

Navy Day.

1971, Mar. 28 Litho. ***Perf. 11½***

Without Gum

1183	A654	50c blk & red	2.00	1.00

Third Inter-American Housing Congress, Mar. 27–Apr. 3.

Links Around Globe A655

1971, Mar. 31 Litho. ***Perf. 12½x11***

Without Gum

1184	A655	20c grn, yel, blk & red	85	50

International year against racial discrimination.

Morpho Melacheilus A656

Design: 1cr, Papilio thoas brasiliensis.

Perf. 11x11½

1971, Apr. 28 Litho. **Unwmkd.**

Without Gum

1185	A656	20c multi	1.50	1.00
1186	A656	1cr multi	6.00	5.00

Madonna and Child A657

1971, May 9 Litho. ***Perf. 11½***

Without Gum

1187	A657	20c multi	1.75	40

Mother's Day, 1971.

Basketball A658

1971, May 19 **Without Gum**

1188	A658	70c multi	2.25	1.00

6th World Women's Basketball Championship.

Map of Trans-Amazon Highway

A660 A659

Lithographed

1971, July 1 ***Perf. 11½*** **Unwmkd.**

Without Gum

1189	A659	40c multi	3.00	1.00
1190	A660	1cr multi	3.00	1.25

Trans-Amazon Highway. Nos. 1189–1190 printed se-tenant in sheets of 28 (4x7). Horizontal rows contain 2 pairs of 1189–1190 with a label between. Each label carries different inscription.

Man's Head, by Victor Mairelles de Lima A661

Design: 1cr, Arab Violinist, by Pedro Américo.

1971, Aug. 1 **Without Gum**

1191	A661	40c pink & multi	2.75	1.00
1192	A661	1cr gray & multi	3.25	1.50

Stamp Day.

Duke of Caxias and Map of Brazil A662

1971, Aug. 23 **Photogravure**

1193	A662	20c yel grn & red brn	75	60

Army Day.

Anita Garibaldi A663

1971, Aug. 30 Litho. **Without Gum**

1194	A663	20c multi	75	50

Anita Garibaldi (1821–1849), heroine in liberation of Brazil.

Xavante Jet and Santos Dumont's Plane, 1910—A664

1971, Sept. 6 **Without Gum**

1195	A664	40c yel & multi	1.75	75

First flight of Xavante jet plane.

Flags and Map of Central American Nations
A665

"71" in French Flag Colors
A666

1971, Sept. 15 Without Gum

1196 A665 40c ocher & multi 1.60 60

Sesquicentennial of the independence of Central American nations.

1971, Sept. 16 Without Gum

1197 A666 1.30cr ultra & multi 2.00 1.00

French Exhibition.

Black Mother, by Lucilio de Albuquerque
A667

Archangel Gabriel
A668

1971, Sept. 28 Without Gum

1198 A667 40c multi 1.00 60

Centenary of law guaranteeing personal freedom starting at birth.

Perf. 11½x11

1971, Sept. 29 Without Gum

1199 A668 40c multi 1.00 75

St. Gabriel's Day.

Bridge over River
A669

Children's Drawings: 35c, People crossing bridge. 60c, Woman with hat.

1971, Oct. 25 ***Perf. 11½***

Without Gum

1200 A669 35c pink, bl & blk 1.00 60
1201 A669 45c blk & multi 1.25 60
1202 A669 60c ol & multi 1.25 60

Children's Day.

Werkhäuserii Superba
A670

1971, Nov. 16 Without Gum

1203 A670 40c bl & multi 2.00 75

In memory of Carlos Werkhauser, botanist.

Greek Key Pattern "25"
A671

Design: 40c, like 20c but inscribed "sesc / servicio social / do comercio."

1971, Dec. 3

Without Gum

1204 A671 20c blk & bl 1.50 50
1205 A671 40c blk & org 1.50 50

25th anniversary of SENAC (national apprenticeship system) and SESC (commercial social service). Nos. 1204–1205 printed se-tenant.

Gunboat
A672

1971, Dec. 8 ***Perf. 11***

Without Gum

1206 A672 20c bl & multi 1.00 50

Navy Day.

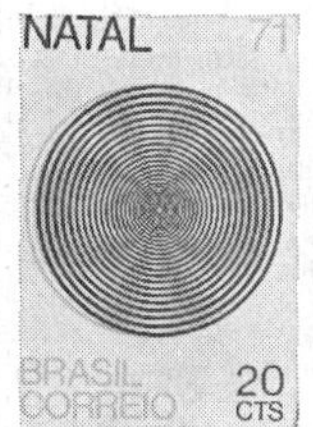

Cross and Circles
A673

Washing of Bonfim Church, Salvador, Bahia
A674

1971, Dec. 11

1207 A673 20c car & bl 90 75
1208 A673 75c sil & gray 90 75
1209 A673 1.30cr blk, yel, grn & bl 5.00 1.50

Christmas 1971.

1972, Feb. 18 Litho. ***Perf. 11½x11***

Designs: 40c, Grape Festival, Rio Grande do Sul. 75c, Festival of the Virgin of Nazareth, Belém. 1.30cr, Winter Arts Festival, Ouro Preto.

Without Gum

1210 A674 20c sil & multi 2.25 75
1211 A674 40c sil & multi 2.25 75
1212 A674 75c sil & multi 2.75 1.75
1213 A674 1.30cr sil & multi 4.50 1.50

Pres. Lanusse and Flag of Argentina
A675

1972, Mar. 13 ***Perf. 11x11½***

Without Gum

1214 A675 40c bl & multi 3.00 2.25

Visit of Lt. Gen. Alejandro Agustin Lanusse, president of Argentina.

Presidents Castello Branco, Costa e Silva and Garrastazu Medici—A676

1972, Mar. 29 Without Gum

1215 A676 20c emer & multi 1.50 60

Anniversary of 1964 revolution.

Post Office Emblem
A677

Perf. 11½x11

1972, Apr. 10 Photo. **Unwmkd.**

1216 A677 20c red brn 2.00 50

No. 1216 is luminescent.

Pres. Thomas and Portuguese Flag
A678

1972, Apr. 22 Litho. ***Perf. 11***

Without Gum

1217 A678 75c ol brn & multi 2.50 1.50

Visit of Pres. Américo Thomas of Portugal to Brazil, Apr. 22–27.

Soil Research (CPRM)
A679

1972, May 3 ***Perf. 11½***

Without Gum; Multicolored

1218 A679 20c *shown* 2.25 50
1219 A679 40c *Offshore oil rig* 2.25 1.00
1220 A679 75c *Hydroelectric dam* 2.50 2.00
1221 A679 1.30cr *Iron ore production* 3.00 1.50

Industrial development. Stamps are inscribed with names of industrial firms.

Souvenir Sheet

Poster for Modern Art Week 1922
A680

1972, May 5

1222 A680 1cr blk & car 7.00 2.50

50th anniversary of Modern Art Week. No. 1222 contains one stamp. Silver margin with black inscription. Size: 78x110 mm.

Mailman, Map of Brazil and Letters
A681

Designs: 45c, "Telecommunications" (vert.). 60c, Tropospheric scatter system. 70c, Road map of Brazil and worker.

1972, May 26 Without Gum

1223 A681 35c bl & multi 2.50 50
1224 A681 45c sil & multi 1.75 75
1225 A681 60c blk & multi 1.50 75
1226 A681 70c multi 1.75 75

Unification of communications in Brazil.

Development Type and

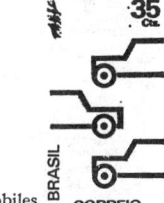

Automobiles
A682

Designs: 45c, Ships. 70c, Ingots.

Perf. 11x11½, 11½x11

1972, June 21 Photogravure

1227 A682 35c blk, mag & org 2.00 50

Lithographed

1228 A679 45c lil & multi 2.00 60
1229 A679 70c vio & multi 2.50 1.00

Industrial development. The 35c is luminescent.

Soccer
A683

Designs: 75c, Folk music. 1.30cr, Plastic arts.

Perf. 11½x11

1972, July 7 Photo. **Unwmkd.**

1230 A683 20c blk & yel 1.25 50
1231 A683 75c blk & ver 2.50 1.00
1232 A683 1.30cr blk & ultra 2.50 75

150th anniversary of independence. No. 1230 publicizes the 1972 sports tournament, a part of independence celebrations. Nos. 1230–1232 are luminescent.

Souvenir Sheet

Shout of Independence, by Pedro Américo de Figueiredo e Melo
A684

1972, July 19 Litho. *Perf. 11½*
Without Gum

1233	A684	1cr multi	3.50	1.25

4th Interamerican Philatelic Exhibition, EXFILBRA, Rio de Janeiro, Aug 26–Sept. 2. No. 1233 contains one stamp (55x 37mm.). Black and multicolored margin with white inscription. Size: 125x87mm.

Figurehead—A685

Designs: 60c, Gauchos dancing fandango. 75c, Acrobats (capoeira). 1.15cr, Karajá (ceramic) doll. 1.30cr, Mock bullfight (bumba meu boi).

1972, Aug. 6 Without Gum

1234	A685	45c multi	1.50	1.00
1235	A685	60c org & multi	1.50	1.00
1236	A685	75c gray & multi	1.50	1.25
1237	A685	1.15cr multi	1.00	1.25
1238	A685	1.30cr yel & multi	4.50	2.50
		Nos. 1234-1238 (5)	10.00	7.00

Brazilian folklore.

Map of Brazil, by Diego Homem, 1568
A686

Designs: 1cr, Map of Americas, by Nicholas Visscher, 1652. 2cr, Map of Americas, by Lopo Homem, 1519.

1972, Aug. 26 Litho. *Perf. 11½*
Without Gum

1239	A686	70c multi	2.50	1.75
1240	A686	1cr multi	5.00	3.00
1241	A686	2cr multi	3.00	2.50

4th Inter-American Philatelic Exhibition, EXFILBRA, Rio de Janeiro, Aug. 26–Sept. 2.

Dom Pedro Proclaimed Emperor, by Jean Baptiste Debret—A687

Designs: 30c, Founding of Brazil (people with imperial flag; vert.). 1cr, Coronation of Emperor Dom Pedro (vert.). 2cr, Dom Pedro commemorative medal. 3.50cr, Independence Monument, Ipiranga.

1972, Sept. 4 Litho. *Perf. 11½x11*

1242	A687	30c yel & grn	2.50	2.50
1243	A687	70c pink & rose lil	1.50	1.00
1244	A687	1cr buff & red brn	10.00	2.50
1245	A687	2cr pale yel & blk	5.00	2.50
1246	A687	3.50cr gray & blk	3.50	3.50
		Nos. 1242-1246 (5)	22.50	12.00

Sesquicentennial of independence.

Souvenir Sheet

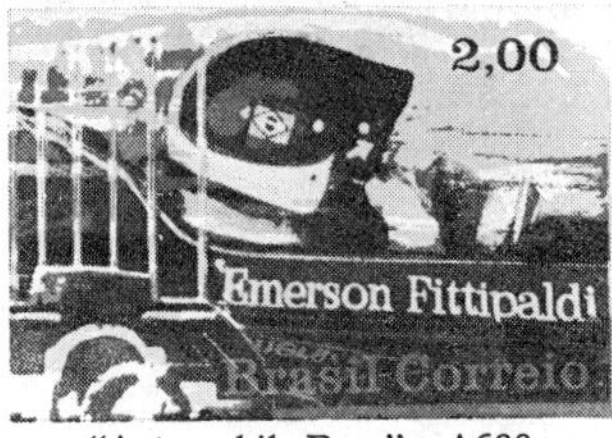

"Automobile Race"—A688

1972, Nov. 14 *Perf. 11½*

1247	A688	2cr multi	5.00	4.00

Emerson Fittipaldi, Brazilian world racing champion. No. 1247 contains one stamp. Multicolored margin with race car design and black inscription. Size: 120x 86½mm.

Numeral and Post Office Emblem
A689

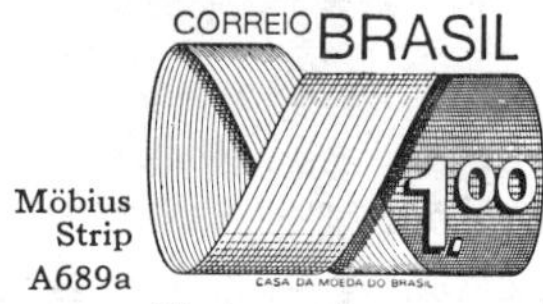

Möbius Strip
A689a

Photogravure

1972–75 *Perf. 11½x11* Unwmkd.

1248	A689	5c orange	10	5
a.		Wmk. 267	50	8
1249	A689	10c brn ('73)	20	5
a.		Wmk. 267	4.00	8
1250	A689	15c brt bl ('75)	10	5
1251	A689	20c ultra	10	5
1252	A689	25c sep ('75)	10	5
1253	A689	30c dp car	20	10
1254	A689	40c dk grn ('73)	25	10
1255	A689	50c olive	25	10
1256	A689	70c red lil ('75)	25	10

Engraved *Perf. 11½*

1257	A689a	1cr lil ('74)	40	10
1258	A689a	2cr grnsh bl ('74)	75	40
1259	A689a	4cr org & vio ('75)	1.00	50
1260	A689a	5cr brn, car & buff ('74)	1.00	50
1261	A689a	10cr grn, blk & buff ('74)	1.75	75
		Nos. 1248-1261 (14)	6.45	2.90

The 5cr and 10cr have beige lithographed multiple Post Office emblem underprint.

Nos. 1248–1261 are luminescent. Nos. 1248a and 1249a are not.

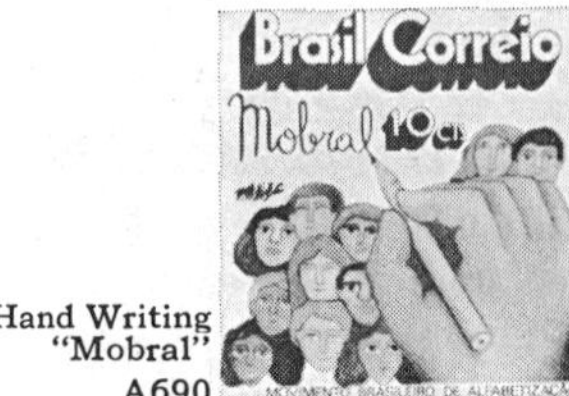

Hand Writing "Mobral"
A690

Designs: 20c, Multiracial group and population growth curve. 1cr, People and hands holding house. 2cr, People, industrial scene and upward arrow.

1972, Nov. 28 Litho. *Perf. 11½*
Without Gum

1262	A690	10c blk & multi	50	50
1263	A690	20c blk & multi	1.75	75
1264	A690	1cr blk & multi	6.50	30
1265	A690	2cr blk & multi	1.75	1.00

Publicity for: "Mobral" literacy campaign (10c); Centenary of census (20c); Housing and retirement fund (1cr); Growth of gross national product (2cr).

Congress Building, Brasilia, by Oscar Niemeyer, and "Os Guerreiros," by Bruno Giorgi—A691

1972, Dec. 4 Without Gum

1266	A691	1cr bl, blk & org	8.00	6.00

Meeting of National Congress, Brasilia, Dec. 4–8.

Holy Family (Clay Figurines)
A692

Retirement Plan
A693

1972, Dec. 13 Photo. *Perf. 11½x11*

1267	A692	20c ocher & blk	75	50

Christmas 1972. Luminescent.

Perf. 11½x11, 11x11½

1972, Dec. 20 Lithographed

Designs: No. 1269, School children and traffic lights (horiz.). 70c, Dr. Oswaldo Cruz with Red Cross, caricature. 2cr, Produce, fish and cattle (horiz.).

Without Gum

1268	A693	10c blk, bl & dl org	75	50
1269	A693	10c org & multi	1.25	1.00
1270	A693	70c blk, red & brn	7.50	1.50
1271	A693	2cr grn & multi	12.50	5.00

Publicity for: Agricultural workers' assistance program (No. 1268); highway and transportation development (No. 1269); centenary of the birth of Dr. Oswaldo Cruz (1872–1917), Director of Public Health Institute (70c); agricultural and cattle export (2cr). Nos. 1268–1271 are luminescent.

Sailing Ship, Navy
A694

Designs: 10c, Monument, Brazilian Expeditionary Force. No. 1274, Plumed helmet, Army. No. 1275, Rocket, Air Force.

Lithographed and Engraved

1972, Dec. 28 *Perf. 11x11½*
Without Gum

1272	A694	10c brn, dk brn & blk	75	40
1273	A694	30c lt ultra, grn & blk	75	40
1274	A694	30c yel grn, bl grn & blk	75	40
1275	A694	30c lil, mar & blk	75	40

Armed Forces Day. Nos. 1272–1275 are se-tenant in blocks of 4 with greenish blue label showing Navy, Army and Air Force insignia in black.

The first price column gives the catalogue value of an unused stamp, the second that of a used stamp.

Rotary Emblem and Cog-wheels
A695

1973, Mar. 21 Litho. Unwmkd.
Perf. 11½

1276	A695	1cr ultra, grnsh bl & yel	2.50	2.50

Rotary International serving Brazil 50 years.

Swimming
A696

Designs: No. 1278, Gymnastics. No. 1279, Volleyball (vert.).

1973 Photo. *Perf. 11x11½, 11½x11*

1277	A696	40c brt bl & red brn	75	50
1278	A696	40c grn & org brn	3.75	1.00
1279	A696	40c vio & org brn	1.75	50

Issue dates: No. 1277, Apr. 19; No. 1278, May 22; No. 1279, Oct. 15.

Flag of Paraguay
A697

Perf. 11½

1973, Apr. 27 Litho. Unwmkd.

1280	A697	70c multi	1.75	50

Visit of Pres. Alfredo Stroessner of Paraguay, Apr. 25–27.

"Communications"
A698

Design: 1cr, Neptune, map of South America and Africa.

1973, May 5 *Perf. 11x11½*

1281	A698	70c multi	1.00	1.00
1282	A698	1cr multi	6.00	3.00

Inauguration of the Ministry of Communications Building, Brasilia (70c); and of the first underwater telephone cable between South America and Europe, Bracan 1 (1cr).

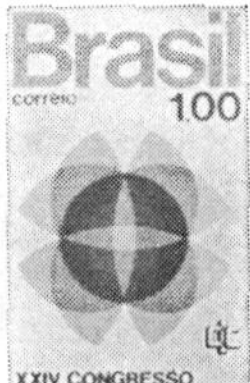

Congress Emblem
A699

1973, May 19 *Perf. 11½x11*

1283 A699 1cr org & pur 6.00 3.00

24th Congress of the International Chamber of Commerce, Rio de Janeiro, May 19–26.

Swallow-tailed Manakin
A700

Birds: No. 1285, Orange-backed oriole. No. 1286, Brazilian ruby (hummingbird).

1973 Lithographed *Perf. 11x11½*

1284 A700 20c multi 50 20
1285 A700 20c multi 50 20
1286 A700 20c multi 50 20

Issue dates: No. 1284, May 26; No. 1285, June 6; No. 1286, June 19.

Tourists
A701

1973, June 28 Litho. *Perf. 11x11½*

1287 A701 70c multi 1.50 1.00

National Tourism Year.

Conference at Itu
A702

Satellite and Multi-spectral Image
A703

1973 *Perf. 11½x11*

1288 A702 20c *shown* 75 20
1289 A702 20c *Decorated wagon* 75 20
1290 A702 20c *Indian* 75 25
1291 A702 20c *Graciosa Road* 75 25

Centenary of the Itu Convention (1288); sesquicentennial of the July 2 episode (1289); 400th anniversary of the founding of Niteroi (1290); centenary of Graciosa Road (1291).

Issue dates: No. 1291, July 29; others July 2.

1973, July 11 *Perf. 11½*

Designs: 70c, Official opening of Engineering School, 1913. 1cr, Möbius strips and "IMPA."

1292 A703 20c blk & multi 30 50
1293 A703 70c dk bl & multi 2.50 75
1294 A703 1cr lil & multi 3.50 75

Institute for Space Research (20c); School of Engineering, Itajubá, 60th anniversary (70c); Institute for Pure and Applied Mathematics (1cr).

Santos-Dumont and 14-Bis Plane
A704

Designs (Santos-Dumont and): 70c, No. 6 Balloon and Eiffel Tower. 2cr Demoiselle plane.

Lithographed and Engraved

1973, July 20 *Perf. 11x11½*

1295 A704 20c lt grn, brt grn & brn 1.00 60
1296 A704 70c yel, rose red & brn 2.50 60
1297 A704 2cr bl, vio bl & brn 2.75 1.00

Centenary of the birth of Alberto Santos-Dumont (1873–1932), aviation pioneer.

Mercator Map
A705

Design: No. 1299, Same, red border on top and at left.

Photogravure & Engraved

1973, Aug. 1 **Wmk. 267**

1298 A705 40c red & blk 90 75
1299 A705 40c red & blk 90 75
Block of 4 6.00 6.00

Stamp Day. Nos. 1298–1299 are printed se-tenant horizontally and tête bêche vertically in sheets of 55. Blocks of 4 have red border all around.

Gonçalves Dias
A706

Perf. 11½x11

1973, Aug. 10 **Wmk. 267**

1300 A706 40c vio & blk 1.00 50

Sesquicentenary of the birth of Antonio Gonçalves Dias (1823–1864), poet.

Souvenir Sheet

Copernicus and Sun—A707

Perf. 11x11½

1973, Aug. 15 Litho. Unwmkd.

1301 A707 1cr multi 3.00 1.50

500th anniversary of the birth of Nicolaus Copernicus (1473–1543), Polish astronomer. No. 1301 contains one stamp; multicolored margin. Size: 124x86mm.

Folklore Festival Banner
A708

1973, Aug. 22 *Perf. 11½*

1302 A708 40c ultra & multi 1.25 60

Folklore Day, Aug. 22.

Masonic Emblem
A709

1973, Aug. 24 Photo. *Perf. 11x11½*

1303 A709 1cr Prus bl 3.00 2.00

Free Masons of Brazil, 1822–1973.

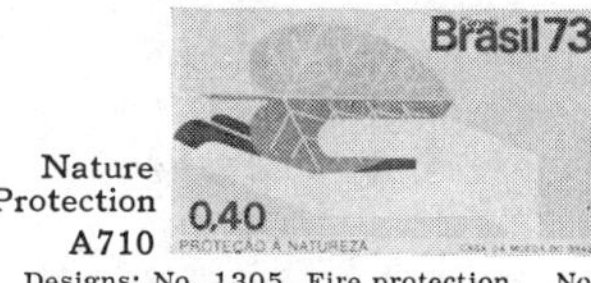

Nature Protection
A710

Designs: No. 1305, Fire protection. No. 1306, Aviation safety. No. 1307, Safeguarding cultural heritage.

1973, Sept. 20 Litho. *Perf. 11x11½*

1304 A710 40c brt grn & multi 75 40
1305 A710 40c dk bl & multi 75 40
1306 A710 40c lt bl & multi 75 40
1307 A710 40c pink & multi 75 40

Souvenir Sheet

St. Gabriel and Proclamation of Pope Paul VI—A711

Lithographed and Engraved

1973, Sept. 29 *Perf. 11½* **Unwmkd.**

1308 A711 1cr bis & blk 3.50 2.00

1st National Exhibition of Religious Philately, Rio de Janeiro, Sept. 29–Oct. 6. No. 1308 contains one stamp; bister margin and black inscription. Size: 123x87½mm.

St. Teresa
A712

Photogravure and Engraved

Perf. 11½x11

1973, Sept. 30 **Wmk. 267**

1309 A712 2cr dk org & brn 6.00 2.50

Centenary of the birth of St. Teresa of Lisieux, the Little Flower (1873–1897), Carmelite nun.

Monteiro Lobato and Emily
A713

Perf. 11½

1973, Oct. 12 Litho. Unwmkd.

Multicolored

1310 A713 40c *shown* 75 50
1311 A713 40c *Aunt Nastacia* 75 50
1312 A713 40c *Snubnose, Peter and Rhino* 75 50
1313 A713 40c *Viscount de Sabugosa* 75 50
1314 A713 40c *Dona Benta* 1.00 50
Block of 5 + label 3.50 3.50

Monteiro Lobato, author of children's books. Nos. 1310–1314 printed in sheets of 30 stamps and 6 labels.

Soapstone Sculpture of Isaiah (detail)
A714

Baroque Art in Brazil: No. 1316, Arabesque, gilded wood carving (horiz.). 70c, Father José Mauricio Nuñes Garcia and music score. 1cr, Church door, Salvador, Bahia. 2cr, Angels, church ceiling painting by Manoel da Costa Athayde (horiz.).

1973, Nov. 5

1315 A714 40c multi 1.00 30
1316 A714 40c multi 1.00 30
1317 A714 70c multi 2.00 75
1318 A714 1cr multi 9.00 2.00
1319 A714 2cr multi 7.50 2.00
Nos. 1315-1319 (5) 20.50 5.35

Old and New Telephones
A715

1973, Nov. 28 *Perf. 11x11½*

1320 A715 40c multi 50 40

50th anniversary of Brazilian Telephone Company.

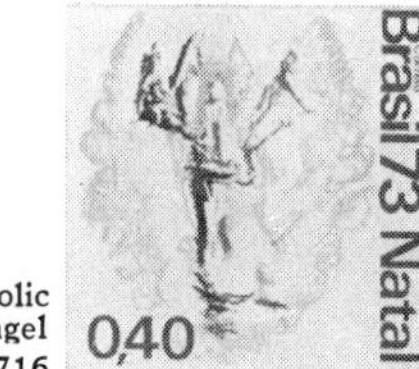

Symbolic Angel
A716

1973, Nov. 30 *Perf. 11½*

1321 A716 40c ver & multi 50 40

Christmas 1973.

"Gaiola"
A717

Designs: River boats.

1973, Nov. 30 Litho. *Perf. 11x11½*

Multicolored

1322 A717 40c *shown* 75 35
1323 A717 70c *"Regatao"* 1.25 40
1324 A717 1cr *"Jangada"* 7.00 3.00
1325 A717 2cr *"Saveiro"* 6.00 3.00

Nos. 1322–1325 are luminescent.

Scales of Justice
A718

1973, Dec. 5 *Perf. 11½*

1326 A718 40c mag & vio 75 35

To honor the High Federal Court, created in 1891. Luminescent.

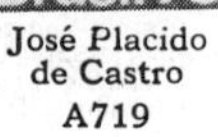

José Placido de Castro
A719

Scarlet Ibis and Victoria Regia
A720

Lithographed and Engraved
Perf. 11½x11

1973, Dec. 12 **Wmk. 267**

1327	A719	40c lil rose & blk	1.00	35

Centenary of the birth of José Placido de Castro, liberator of the State of Acre.

Perf. 11½x11

1973, Dec. 28 Litho. **Unwmkd.**

Designs: 70c, Jaguar and spathodea campanulata. 1cr, Scarlet macaw and carnauba palm. 2cr, Rhea and coral tree.

1328	A720	40c brn & multi	1.50	50
1329	A720	70c brn & multi	3.50	1.25
1330	A720	1cr bis & multi	2.00	1.25
1331	A720	2cr bis & multi	8.00	3.00

Nos. 1328–1331 are luminescent.

Saci Pereré, Mocking Goblin
A721

Characters from Brazilian Legends: 80c, Zumbi, last chief of rebellious slaves. 1cr, Chico Rei, African king. 1.30cr, Little Black Boy of the Pasture. 2.50cr, Iara, Queen of the Waters.

Perf. 11½x11

1974, Feb. 28 Litho. **Unwmkd.**

Size: 21x39mm.

1332	A721	40c multi	1.00	25
1333	A721	80c multi	1.25	75
1334	A721	1cr multi	2.00	50

Size: 32½x33mm.

Perf. 11½

1335	A721	1.30cr multi	5.00	1.75
1336	A721	2.50cr multi	5.00	2.50
		Nos. 1332-1336 (5)	14.25	5.75

Nos. 1332–1336 are luminescent.

Pres. Costa e Silva Bridge
A722

1974, Mar. 11

1337	A722	40c multi	75	35

Inauguration of the Pres. Costa e Silva Bridge, Rio Niteroi, connecting Rio de Janeiro and Guanabara State.

"The Press"
A723

1974, Mar. 25 ***Perf. 11½***

Multicolored

1338	A723	40c *shown*	60	40
1339	A723	40c *"Radio"*	60	40
1340	A723	40c *"Television"*	90	40

Communications Commemorations: No. 1338, bicentenary of first Brazilian newspaper, published in London by Hipolito da Costa; No. 1339, founding of the Radio Sociedade do Rio de Janeiro by Roquette Pinto; No. 1340, installation of first Brazilian television station by Assis Chateaubriand. Luminescent.

"Reconstruction"
A724

1974, Mar. 31

1341	A724	40c multi	1.00	50

10 years of progress. Luminescent.

Corcovado Christ, Marconi, Colors of Brazil and Italy
A725

1974, Apr. 25 Litho. ***Perf. 11½***

1342	A725	2.50cr multi	6.00	2.50

Centenary of the birth of Guglielmo Marconi (1874–1937), Italian physicist and inventor. Luminescent.

Stamp Printing Press, Stamp Designing
A726

1974, May 6

1343	A726	80c multi	1.00	50

Brazilian mint.

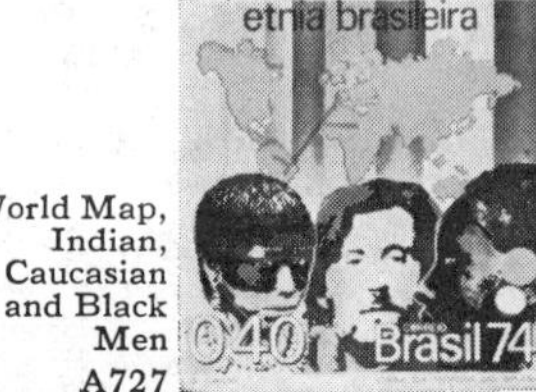

World Map, Indian, Caucasian and Black Men
A727

Designs (World Map and): No. 1345, Brazilians. No. 1346, Cabin and German horseback rider. No. 1347, Italian farm wagon. No. 1348, Japanese woman and torii.

1974, May 11 **Unwmkd.**

1344	A727	40c multi	50	35
1345	A727	40c multi	50	35
1346	A727	2.50cr multi	3.50	1.50
1347	A727	2.50cr multi	4.50	1.50
1348	A727	2.50cr multi	2.50	1.50
		Nos. 1344-1348 (5)	11.50	5.20

Ethnic and migration influences in Brazil.

Sandstone Cliffs, Sete Cidades National Park—A728

Design: 80c, Ruins of Cathedral of São Miguel das Missões.

Lithographed and Engraved

1974, June 8 ***Perf. 11x11½***

1349	A728	40c multi	1.00	50
1350	A728	80c multi	1.00	50

Tourist publicity.

Souvenir Sheet

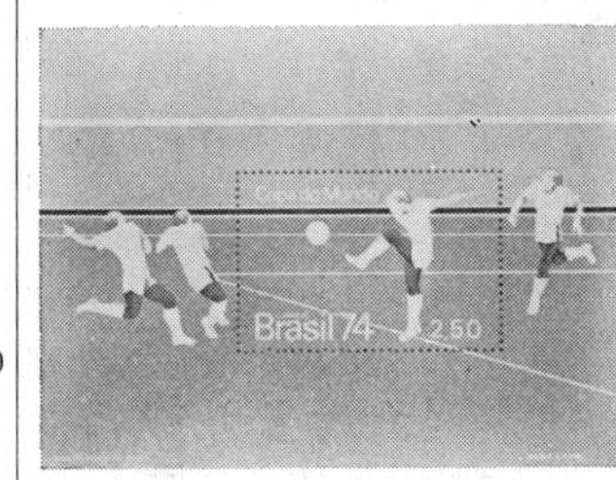

Soccer—A729

1974, June 20 Litho. ***Perf. 11½***

1351	A729	2.50cr multi	3.00	3.00

World Cup Soccer Championship, Munich, June 13–July 7. No. 1351 has multicolored margin. Size: 130x95mm.

Church and College, Caraça
A730

1974, July 6 Litho. ***Perf. 11x11½***

1352	A730	40c multi	75	35

Bicentenary of the College (Seminary) of Caraça.

Wave on Television Screen
A731

1974, July 15 ***Perf. 11½***

1353	A731	40c blk & bl	50	40

TELEBRAS, Third Brazilian Congress of Telecommunications, Brasilia, July 15–20.

Fernão Dias Paes
A732

1974, July 21 ***Perf. 11½***

1354	A732	20c grn & multi	50	30

3rd centenary of the expedition led by Fernão Dias Paes exploring Minas Gerais and the passage from South to North in Brazil.

Mexican Flag
A733

1974, July 24 Litho. ***Perf. 11½***

1355	A733	80c multi	3.00	1.25

Visit of Pres. Luis Echeverria Alvares of Mexico, July 24–29.

Flags of Brazil and Germany
A734

1974, Aug. 5 ***Perf. 11x11½***

1356	A734	40c multi	1.00	50

World Cup Soccer Championship, 1974, victory of German Federal Republic.

Souvenir Sheet

Congress Emblem—A735

1974, Aug. 7 ***Perf. 11½***

1357	A735	1.30cr multi	1.00	75

5th World Assembly of the World Council for the Welfare of the Blind, São Paulo, Aug. 7–16. No. 1357 has ocher margin with black inscription. Stamp and margin inscribed in Braille with name of Assembly. Size: 126x88½mm.

Raul Pederneiras, Caricature by J. Carlos
A736

Lithographed and Engraved

1974, Aug. 15 ***Perf. 11½x11***

1358	A736	40c buff, blk & ocher	50	40

Centenary of the birth of Raul Pederneiras (1874–1953), journalist, professor of law and fine arts.

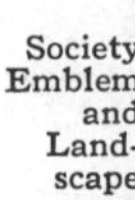

Society Emblem and Landscape
A737

Perf. 11x11½

1974, Aug. 19 **Lithographed**

1359	A737	1.30cr multi	1.75	1.00

13th Congress of the International Union of Building and Savings Societies.

Souvenir Sheet

Five Women, by Di Cavalcanti—A738

1974, Aug. 26 **Litho.** ***Perf. 11½***

1360	A738	2cr multi	3.00	1.50

LUBRAPEX 74, 5th Portuguese-Brazilian Philatelic Exhibition, São Paulo, Nov. 26–Dec. 4. No. 1360 has gray marginal inscription. Size of stamp: 37x55mm., size of sheet: 87x125mm.

"UPU" and World Map
A739

1974, Oct. 9 **Litho.** ***Perf. 11½***

1361	A739	2.50cr blk & brt bl	6.00	1.50

Centenary of Universal Postal Union.

Hammock (Antillean Arawak Culture)
A740

Bilro Lace
A741

Singer of "Cord" Verses
A742

Ceramic Figure by Master Vitalino
A743

1974, Oct. 16 **Litho.** ***Perf. 11½***

1362	A740	50c dp rose lil	1.50	50
1363	A741	50c lt & dk bl	1.50	50
1364	A742	50c yel & red brn	1.50	50
1365	A743	50c brt yel & dk brn	1.50	50

Popular Brazilian crafts.

Branch of Coffee
A744

1974, Oct. 27 ***Perf. 11*** **Unwmkd.**

1366	A744	50c multi	1.75	75

Centenary of city of Campinas.

Hornless Tabapuã
A745

Animals of Brazil: 1.30cr, Creole horse. 2.50cr, Brazilian mastiff.

1974, Nov. 10 ***Perf. 11½***

1367	A745	80c multi	50	50
1368	A745	1.30cr multi	1.00	1.00
1369	A745	2.50cr multi	5.00	2.50

Angel
A746

1974, Nov. 18 ***Perf. 11½x11***

1370	A746	50c ultra & multi	85	40

Christmas 1974.

Solteira Island Hydroelectric Dam
A747

1974, Nov. 18 ***Perf. 11½***

1371	A747	50c blk & yel	2.50	1.00

Inauguration of the Solteira Island Hydroelectric Dam over Parana River.

The Girls, by Carlos Reis
A748

1974, Nov. 26

1372	A748	1.30cr multi	1.00	50

LUBRAPEX 74, 5th Portuguese-Brazilian Philatelic Exhibition, São Paulo, Nov. 26–Dec. 4.

Youths, Judge, Scales
A749

1974, Dec. 20 **Litho.** ***Perf. 11½***

1373	A749	90c yel, red & bl	50	35

Juvenile Court of Brazil, 50th anniversary.

Long Distance Runner
A750

1974, Dec. 23

1374	A750	3.30cr multi	1.25	75

São Silvestre long distance running, 50th anniversary.

News Vendor, 1875, Masthead, 1975
A751

1975, Jan. 4

1375	A751	50c multi	1.75	75

Centenary of the newspaper "O Estado de S. Paulo."

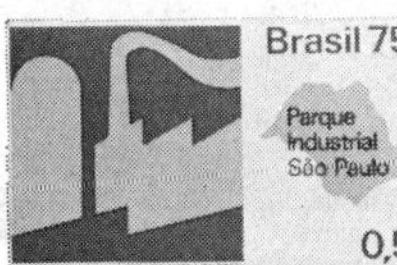

São Paulo Industrial Park
A752

Designs: 1.40cr, Natural rubber industry, Acre. 4.50cr, Manganese mining, Amapá.

1975, Jan. 24 **Litho.** ***Perf. 11x11½***

1376	A752	50c vio bl & yel	2.00	50
1377	A752	1.40cr yel & brn	75	75
1378	A752	4.50cr yel & blk	2.25	50

Economic development.

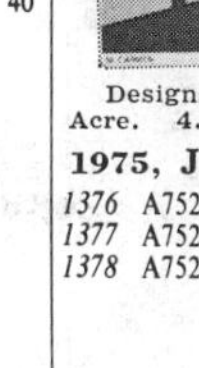

Fort of the Holy Cross
A753

Designs: No. 1380, Fort of the Three Kings. No. 1381, Fort of Montserrat. 90c, Fort of Our Lady of Help.

Lithographed, Engraved

1975, Mar. 14 ***Perf. 11½***

1379	A753	50c yel & red brn	75	40
1380	A753	50c yel & red brn	75	40
1381	A753	50c yel & red brn	75	40
1382	A753	90c yel & red brn	75	60

Colonial forts.

House on Stilts, Amazon Region
A754

Designs: 50c, Modern houses and plan of Brasilia. 1.40cr, Indian hut, Rondonia. 3.30cr, German-style cottage (Enxaimel), Santa Catarina.

1975, Apr. 18 **Litho.** ***Perf. 11½***

1383	A754	50c yel & multi	1.50	75
1384	A754	50c yel & multi	3.00	1.50
1385	A754	1cr yel & multi	75	50
1386	A754	1.40cr yel & multi	2.00	1.00
1387	A754	1.40cr yel & multi	1.00	50
1388	A754	3.30cr yel & multi	1.00	50
1389	A754	3.30cr yel & multi	2.00	1.00
		Nos. 1383-1389 (7)	11.25	5.75

Brazilian architecture. Nos. 1383–1384, 1386–1387, 1388–1389 printed se-tenant in sheets of 50. Nos. 1383, 1386, 1388 have yellow strip at right side, others at left; No. 1385 has yellow strip on both sides.

Astronotus Ocellatus
A755

Designs: Brazilian fresh-water fish.

1975, May 2 **Litho.** ***Perf. 11½***

Pale Green and Multicolored

1390	A755	50c *shown*	75	40
1391	A755	50c *Colomesus psitacus*	75	40
1392	A755	50c *Phallocerus caudimaculatus*	75	40
1393	A755	50c *Symphysodon discus*	75	40

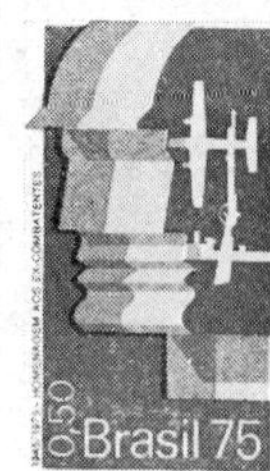

Soldier's Head in Brazil's Colors, Plane, Rifle and Ship
A756

Brazilian Otter
A757

1975, May 8 ***Perf. 11½x11***

1394	A756	50c vio bl & multi	75	35

In honor of the veterans of World War II, on the 30th anniversary of victory.

1975, June 17 Litho. *Perf. 11½*

Designs: 70c, Brazilian pines (horiz.). 3.30cr, Marsh cayman (horiz.).

1395	A757	70c bl, grn & blk	1.50	35
1396	A757	1cr multi	1.00	35
1397	A757	3.30cr multi	1.00	60

Nature protection.

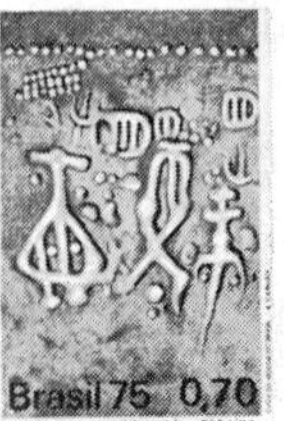

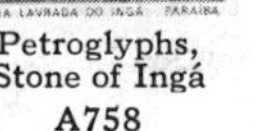

Petroglyphs, Stone of Ingá
A758

Marjoara Vase, Pará
A759

Vinctifer Comptoni, Petrified Fish
A760

1975, July 8 Litho. *Perf. 11½*

1398	A758	70c multi	1.00	40
1399	A759	1cr multi	75	40
1400	A760	1cr multi	75	40

Archaeological discoveries.

Immaculate Conception, Franciscan Monastery, Vitoria
A761

Post and Telegraph Ministry
A762

1975, July 15

1401	A761	3.30cr bl & multi	1.50	60

Holy Year 1975 and 300th anniversary of establishment of the Franciscan Province in Southern Brazil.

1975, Aug. 8 Engr. *Perf. 11½*

1402	A762	70c dk car	1.25	30

Stamp Day 1975.

Sword Dance, Minas Gerais
A763

Folk Dances: No. 1404, Umbrella Dance, Pernambuco. No. 1405, Warrior's Dance, Alagoas.

1975, Aug. 22 Litho. *Perf. 11½*

1403	A763	70c gray & multi	75	35
1404	A763	70c pink & multi	75	35
1405	A763	70c yel & multi	75	35

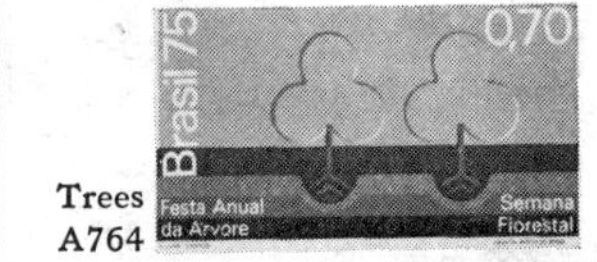

Trees
A764

1975, Sept. 15 *Perf. 11x11½*

1406	A764	70c multi	60	25

Annual Tree Festival.

Globe, Radar and Satellite
A765

1975, Sept. 16 *Perf. 11½*

1407	A765	3.30cr multi	1.25	75

Inauguration of 2nd antenna of Tangua Earth Station, Rio de Janeiro State.

Woman Holding Flowers and Globe
A766

1975, Sept. 23

1408	A766	3.30cr multi	1.50	60

International Women's Year 1975.

Tile, Railing and Column, Alcantara
A767

Cross and Monastery, São Cristovão
A768

Design: No. 1411, Jug and Clock Tower, Goiás (vert.).

1975, Sept. 27 Litho. *Perf. 11½*

1409	A767	70c multi	75	30
1410	A768	70c multi	75	30
1411	A768	70c multi	75	30

Historic cities.

"Books teach how to live"
A769

1975, Oct. 23 Litho. *Perf. 11½*

1412	A769	70c multi	40	25

Day of the Book.

ASTA Congress Emblem
A770

1975, Oct. 27 *Perf. 11x11½*

1413	A770	70c multi	50	25

American Society of Travel Agents, 45th World Congress, Rio de Janeiro, Oct. 27–Nov. 1.

Angels
A771

1975, Nov. 11

1414	A771	70c red & brn	50	20

Christmas 1975.

Map of Americas, Waves
A772

Dom Pedro II
A773

1975, Nov. 19 *Perf. 11½x12*

1415	A772	5.20cr gray & multi	2.25	1.25

2nd Interamerican Conference of Telecommunications (CITEL), Rio de Janeiro, Nov. 19–27.

1975, Dec. 2 Engr. *Perf. 12*

1416	A773	70c vio brn	1.25	50

Dom Pedro II (1825–1891), emperor of Brazil, birth sesquicentennial.

People and Cross
A774

1975, Dec. 4 Litho. *Perf. 11x11½*

1417	A774	70c lt bl & dp bl	1.00	50

National Day of Thanksgiving.

Guarapari Beach, Espirito Santo
A775

Designs: No. 1419, Salt Stone beach, Piaui. No. 1420, Cliffs, Rio Grande Do Sul.

1975, Dec. 19 Litho. *Perf. 11½*

1418	A775	70c multi	50	25
1419	A775	70c multi	50	25
1420	A775	70c multi	50	25

Tourist publicity.

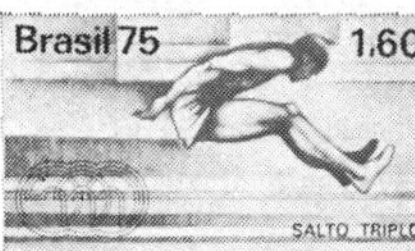

Triple Jump, Games Emblem
A776

1975, Dec. 22 *Perf. 11x11½*

1421	A776	1.60cr bl grn & blk	35	25

Triple jump world record by Joao Carlos de Oliveira in 7th Pan-American Games, Mexico City, Oct. 12–26.

UN Emblem and Headquarters
A777

1975, Dec. 29 *Perf. 11½*

1422	A777	1.30cr dp bl & vio bl	35	20

United Nations, 30th anniversary.

Light Bulbs, House and Sun
A778

Design: No. 1424, Gasoline drops, car and sun.

1976, Jan. 16

1423	A778	70c multi	50	20
1424	A778	70c multi	50	15

Energy conservation.

Concorde—A779

1976, Jan. 21 Litho. *Perf. 11x11½*

1425	A779	5.20cr bluish blk	1.25	65

First commercial flight of supersonic jet Concorde from Paris to Rio de Janeiro, Jan. 21.

Souvenir Sheet

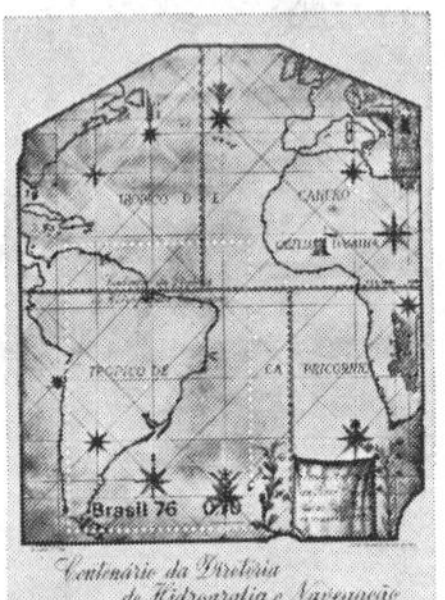

Nautical Map of South Atlantic, 1776—A780

1976, Feb. 2 *Perf. 11½*

1426	A780	70c sal & multi	75	50

Centenary of the Naval Hydrographic and Navigation Institute. Size: 88x123mm.

Telephone Lines, 1876 Telephone
A781

1976, Mar. 10 Litho. *Perf. 11x11½*

1427	A781	5.20cr org & bl	1.00	50

Centenary of first telephone call by Alexander Graham Bell, March 10, 1876.

Eye and Exclamation Point
A782

Kaiapo Body Painting
A783

1976, Apr. 7 Litho. *Perf. 11½x11*

1428	A782	1cr vio red brn & brn	75	40

World Health Day: "Foresight prevents blindness."

1976, Apr. 19 Litho. *Perf. 11½*

Designs: No. 1430, Bakairi ceremonial mask. No. 1431, Karajá feather headdress.

1429	A783	1cr lt vio & multi	40	30
1430	A783	1cr lt vio & multi	40	30
1431	A783	1cr lt vio & multi	40	30

Preservation of indigenous culture.

Itamaraty Palace, Brasilia
A784

1976, Apr. 20

1432	A784	1cr multi	1.00	75

Diplomats' Day. Itamaraty Palace, designed by Oscar Niemeyer, houses the Ministry of Foreign Affairs.

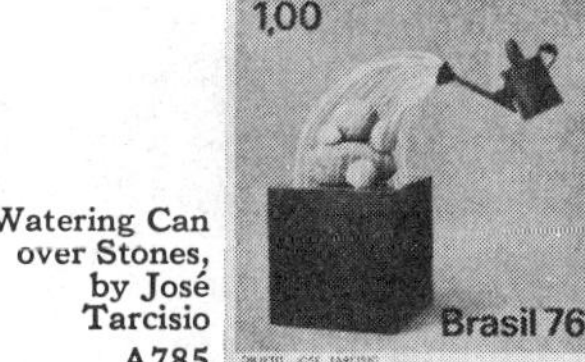

Watering Can over Stones, by José Tarcisio
A785

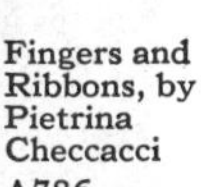

Fingers and Ribbons, by Pietrina Checcacci
A786

1976, May 14 Litho. *Perf. 11½*

1433	A785	1cr multi	60	35
1434	A786	1.60cr multi	60	35

Modern Brazilian art.

Basketball
A787

Orchid
A788

Designs (Olympic Rings and): 1.40cr, Yachting. 5.20cr, Judo.

1976, May 21 Litho. *Perf. 11½*

1435	A787	1cr emer & blk	20	15
1436	A787	1.40cr dk bl & blk	25	15
1437	A787	5.20cr org & blk	60	50

21st Olympic Games, Montreal, Canada, July 17–Aug. 1.

1976, June 4 *Perf. 11½x11*

Design: No. 1439, Golden-faced lion monkey.

1438	A788	1cr multi	50	30
1439	A788	1cr multi	50	30

Nature protection.

Film Camera, Brazilian Colors
A789

1976, June 19

1440	A789	1cr vio bl, brt grn & yel	35	25

Brazilian film industry.

Bahia Woman
A790

Designs: 10c, Oxcart driver (horiz.). 20c, Raft fishermen (horiz.). 30c, Rubber plantation worker. 40c, Cowboy (horiz.). 50c, Gaucho. 80c, Gold panner. 1cr, Banana plantation worker. 1.10cr, Grape harvester. 1.30cr, Coffee picker. 1.80cr, Farmer gathering wax palms. 2cr, Potter. 5cr, Sugar cane cutter. 7cr, Salt mine worker. 10cr, Fisherman. 15cr, Coconut seller. 20cr, Lacemaker.

Perf. 11½x11, 11x11½

1976–78 Photogravure

1441	A790	10c red brn ('77)	10	5
1442	A790	15c brown	50	5
1443	A790	20c vio bl	10	5
1444	A790	30c lil rose	10	5
1445	A790	40c org ('77)	15	5
1446	A790	50c citron	10	5
1447	A790	80c sl grn	15	6
1448	A790	1cr black	20	8
1449	A790	1.10cr mag ('77)	20	8
1450	A790	1.30cr red ('77)	20	10
1451	A790	1.80cr dk vio bl ('78)	30	10

Engraved

1452	A790	2cr brn ('77)	40	10
1453	A790	5cr dk pur ('77)	90	10
1454	A790	7cr violet	30	10
1455	A790	10cr yel grn ('77)	1.00	10
1456	A790	15cr gray grn ('78)	2.50	15
1457	A790	20cr blue	2.50	10
		Nos. 1441-1457 (17)	9.70	1.37

See Nos. 1653-1679.

Hyphessobrycon Innesi
A791

Designs: Brazilian fresh-water fish.

1976, July 12 Litho. *Perf. 11x11½*

Multicolored

1460	A791	1cr *shown*	35	15
1461	A791	1cr *Copeina arnoldi*	35	15
1462	A791	1cr *Prochilodus insignis*	35	15
1463	A791	1cr *Crenicichla lepidota*	35	15
1464	A791	1cr *Ageneiosus*	35	15
1465	A791	1cr *Corydoras reticulatus*	35	15
		Nos. 1460-1465 (6)	2.10	90

Nos. 1460–1465 printed se-tenant in sheets of 36.

Santa Marta Lighthouse
A792

1976, July 29 Engr. *Perf. 12x11½*

1466	A792	1cr blue	50	30

300th anniversary of the city of Laguna.

Children on Magic Carpet
A793

1976, Aug. 1 Litho. *Perf. 11½x12*

1467	A792	1cr multi	25	20

Stamp Day.

Nurse's Lamp and Head
A794

1976, Aug. 12 Litho. *Perf. 11½*

1468	A794	1cr multi	40	20

Brazilian Nurses' Association, 50th anniversary.

Puppet, Soldier
A795

Winner's Medal
A796

Designs: 1.30cr, Girl's head. 1.60cr, Hand with puppet head on each finger (horiz.).

1976, Aug. 20

1469	A795	1cr multi	40	20
1470	A795	1.30cr multi	40	20
1471	A795	1.60cr multi	40	20

Mamulengo puppet show.

1976, Aug. 21

1472	A796	5.20cr multi	1.25	50

27th International Military Athletic Championships, Rio de Janeiro, Aug. 21–28.

Family Protection
A797

1976, Sept. 12

1473	A797	1cr lt & dk bl	35	20

National organizations SENAC and SESC helping commercial employees to improve their living standard, both commercially and socially.

Dying Tree
A798

1976, Sept. 20 Litho. *Perf. 11½*

1474	A798	1cr gray & multi	25	20

Protection of the environment.

Atom Symbol, Electron Orbits
A799

1976, Sept. 21

1475	A799	5.20cr multi	1.25	50

20th General Conference of the International Atomic Energy Agency, Rio de Janeiro, Sept. 21–29.

Train in Tunnel
A800

1976, Sept. 26

1476	A800	1.60cr multi	40	25

Inauguration of Sao Paulo subway, first in Brazil.

St. Francis and Birds
A801

1976, Oct. 4

1477	A801	5.20cr multi	1.25	50

St. Francis of Assisi, 750th death anniversary.

Ouro Preto School of Mining
A802

1976, Oct. 12 Engr. *Perf. 12x11½*

1478	A802	1cr dk vio	1.00	50

Ouro Preto School of Mining, centenary.

Three Kings
A803

Designs: Children's drawings.

1976, Nov. 4 Litho. *Perf. 11½*

Multicolored

1479	A803	80c *shown*	25	10
1480	A803	80c *Santa Claus on donkey*	25	10
1481	A803	80c *Virgin and Child and Angels*	25	10
1482	A803	80c *Angels with candle*	25	10
1483	A803	80c *Nativity*	25	10
		Nos. 1479-1483 (5)	1.25	50

Christmas 1976. Nos. 1479–1483 printed se-tenant in sheets of 35.

Souvenir Sheet

30,000 Reis Banknote—A804

1976, Nov. 5 Litho. *Perf. 11½*

1484	A804	80c multi	60	40

Opening of 1000th branch of Bank of Brazil, Barra do Bugres, Mato Grosso. No. 1484 contains one stamp. Size of stamp: 38x56½mm.; size of sheet: 125x87mm.

Virgin of Monte Serrat, by Friar Agostinho
A805

St. Joseph, 18th Century Wood Sculpture
A806

Designs: 5.60cr, The Dance, by Rodolfo Bernadelli, 19th century. 6.50cr, The Caravel, by Bruno Giorgi, 20th century abstract sculpture.

1976, Nov. 5

1485	A805	80c multi	30	6
1486	A806	5cr multi	75	25
1487	A805	5.60cr multi	90	25
1488	A806	6.50cr multi	1.25	25

Development of Brazilian sculpture.

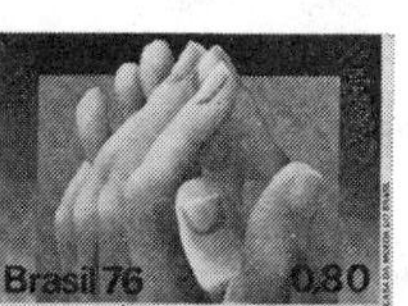

Praying Hands
A807

1976, Nov. 25

1489	A807	80c multi	85	50

National Day of Thanksgiving.

Sailor, 1840
A808

Design: 2cr, Marine's uniform, 1808.

1976, Dec. 13 Litho. *Perf. 11½x11*

1490	A808	80c multi	50	25
1491	A808	2cr multi	50	25

Brazilian Navy.

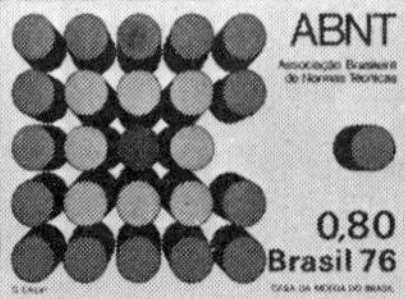

"Natural Resources and Development"
A809

1976, Dec. 17 *Perf. 11½*

1492	A809	80c multi	35	20

Brazilian Bureau of Standards, founded 1940.

Wheel of Life
A810

Designs: 5.60cr, Beggar, sculpture by Agnaldo dos Santos. 6.50cr, Benin mask.

1977, Jan. 14

1493	A810	5cr multi	50	25
1494	A810	5.60cr multi	60	25
1495	A810	6.50cr multi	90	45

FESTAC '77, 2nd World Black and African Festival, Lagos, Nigeria, Jan. 15–Feb. 12.

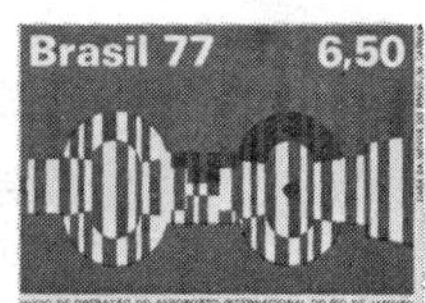

A811

1977, Jan. 20 Litho. *Perf. 11½*

1496	A811	6.50cr bl & yel grn	90	45

Rio de Janeiro International Airport.

Seminar Emblem with Map of Americas
A812

Salicylate, Microphoto
A813

1977, Feb. 6

1497	A812	1.10cr gray, vio bl & bl	50	10

6th Inter-American Budget Seminar.

1977, Apr. 10 Litho. *Perf. 11½*

1498	A813	1.10cr multi	30	10

International Rheumatism Year.

Lions International Emblem
A814

1977, Apr. 16

1499	A814	1.10cr multi	30	20

25th anniversary of Brazilian Lions International.

Heitor Villa Lobos
A815

1977, Apr. 26 *Perf. 11x11½*

Multicolored

1500	A815	1.10cr *shown*	30	12
1501	A815	1.10cr *Chiquinha Gonzaga*	30	12
1502	A815	1.10cr *Noel Rosa*	30	12

Brazilian composers.

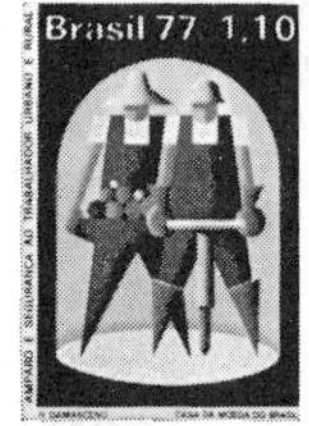

Farmer and Worker
A816

Medicine Bottles and Flask
A817

1977, May 8 Litho. *Perf. 11½*

1503	A816	1.10cr grn & multi	25	12
1504	A817	1.10cr lt & dk grn	25	12

Support and security for rural and urban workers (No. 1503) and establishment in 1971 of Medicine Distribution Center (CEME) for low-cost medicines (No. 1504).

Churchyard Cross, Porto Seguro
A818

Views, Porto Seguro: 5cr, Beach and boats. 5.60cr, Our Lady of Pena Chapel. 6.50cr, Town Hall.

1977, May 25 Litho. *Perf. 11½*

1505	A818	1.10cr multi	25	15
1506	A818	5cr multi	75	40
1507	A818	5.60cr multi	1.00	50
1508	A818	6.50cr multi	25	20

Centenary of Brazil's membership in Universal Postal Union.

Diario de Porto Alegre
A819

1977, June 1

1509	A819	1.10cr multi	25	20

150th anniversary of Diario de Porto Alegre, newspaper.

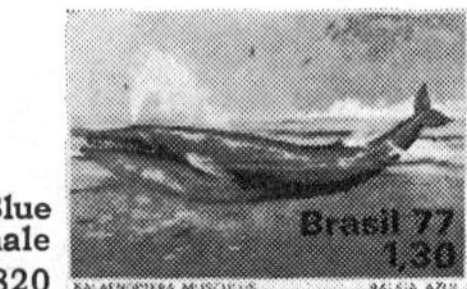

Blue Whale
A820

1977, June 3

1510	A820	1.30cr multi	30	20

Protection of marine life.

"Life and Development"
A821

1977, June 20

1511	A821	1.30cr multi	30	20

National Development Bank, 25th anniversary.

Train Leaving Tunnel
A822

1977, July 8 Engr. *Perf. 11½*

1512	A822	1.30cr black	30	20

Centenary of São Paulo-Rio de Janeiro railroad.

Vasum Cassiforme — A823

Caduceus, Formulas for Water and Fluoride — A824

Sea Shells: No. 1514, Strombus goliath. No. 1515, Murex tenuivaricosus.

1977, July 14 Lithographed

1513	A823	1.30cr bl & multi	35	20
1514	A823	1.30cr brn & multi	35	20
1515	A823	1.30cr grn & multi	35	20

1977, July 15 *Perf. 11½x11*

1516	A824	1.30cr multi	30	20

3rd International Odontology Congress, Rio de Janeiro, July 15–21.

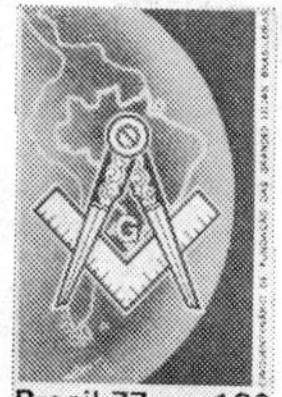

Masonic Emblem, Map of Brazil — A825

"Stamps Don't Sink or Lose their Way" — A826

1977, July 18 *Perf. 11½*

1517	A825	1.30cr bl, lt bl & blk	30	20

50th anniversary of the founding of the Brazilian Grand Masonic Lodge.

1977, Aug. 1

1518	A826	1.30cr multi	30	20

Stamp Day 1977.

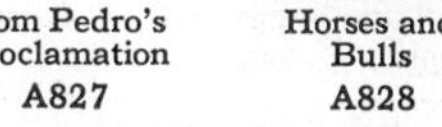

Dom Pedro's Proclamation — A827

Horses and Bulls — A828

1977, Aug. 11 Litho. *Perf. 11½*

1519	A827	1.30cr multi	35	20

150th anniversary of Brazilian Law School.

Perf. 11½x11, 11x11½

1977, Aug. 20 Lithographed

Designs: No. 1521, King on horseback. No. 1522, Joust (horiz.).

1520	A828	1.30cr ocher & multi	40	20
1521	A828	1.30cr bl & multi	40	20
1522	A828	1.30cr yel & multi	40	20

Brazilian folklore.

2000-reis Doubloon
A829

Brazilian Colonial Coins: No. 1524, 640r pataca. No. 1525, 20r copper "vintem."

1977, Aug. 31 *Perf. 11½*

1523	A829	1.30cr vio bl & multi	30	15
1524	A829	1.30cr dk red & multi	30	15
1525	A829	1.30cr yel & multi	30	15

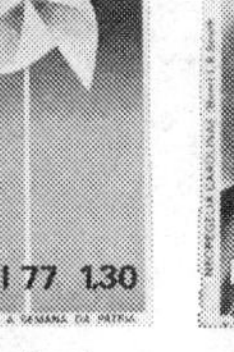

Pinwheel — A830

Neoregelia Carolinae — A831

1977, Sept. 1

1526	A830	1.30cr multi	30	15

National Week.

1977, Sept. 21 Litho. *Perf. 11½*

1527	A831	1.30cr multi	30	15

Nature preservation.

Pen, Pencil, Letters
A832

1977, Oct. 15 Litho. *Perf. 11½*

1528	A832	1.30cr multi	30	15

Primary education, sesquicentennial.

Dome and Telescope
A833

1977, Oct. 15

1529	A833	1.30cr multi	30	15

National Astrophysics Observatory, Brasópolis, sesquicentennial.

"Jahu" Hydroplane (Savoia Marchetti S-55)
A834

Design: No. 1531, PAX, dirigible.

1977, Oct. 17

1530	A834	1.30cr multi	40	15
1531	A834	1.30cr multi	40	15

50th anniversary of crossing of South Atlantic by Joao Ribeiro de Barros from Genoa to Sao Paulo (No. 1530) and 75th anniversary of the PAX airship (No. 1531).

O'Guarani
A835

1977, Oct. 24

1532	A835	1.30cr multi	30	15

Book Day and to honor José Martiniano de Alencar, writer, jurist.

Waves
A836

1977, Nov. 5 Litho. *Perf. 11½*

1533	A836	1.30cr multi	30	15

Amateur Radio Operators' Day.

Nativity
A837

Designs (Folk Art): 2cr, Annunciation. 5cr, Nativity.

1977, Nov. 10

1534	A837	1.30cr bis & multi	35	15
1535	A837	2cr bis & multi	50	15
1536	A837	5cr bis & multi	1.00	25

Christmas 1977.

Emerald
A838

Designs: No. 1538, Topaz. No. 1539, Aquamarine.

1977, Nov. 19

1537	A838	1.30cr multi	35	20
1538	A838	1.30cr multi	35	20
1539	A838	1.30cr multi	35	20

PORTUCALE 77, 2nd International Topical Exhibition, Porto, Nov. 19–20.

Angel with Cornucopia
A839

1977, Nov. 24 Litho. *Perf. 11½*

1540	A839	1.30cr multi	30	20

National Thanksgiving Day.

Army's Railroad Construction Battalion—A840

Designs: No. 1542, Navy's Amazon flotilla. No. 1543, Air Force's postal service (plane).

1977, Dec. 5

1541	A840	1.30cr multi	30	20
1542	A840	1.30cr multi	30	20
1543	A840	1.30cr multi	30	20

Civilian services of armed forces.

Varig Emblem, Jet
A841

1977, Dec. *Perf. 11x11½*

1544	A841	1.30cr bl & blk	30	20

50th anniversary of Varig Airline.

Sts. Cosme and Damiao Church, Igaracu — A842

Woman Holding Sheaf — A843

Brazilian Architecture: 7.50cr, St. Bento Monastery Church, Rio de Janeiro. 8.50cr, Church of St. Francis of Assisi, Ouro Preto. 9.50cr, St. Anthony Convent Church, Joao Pessoa.

1977, Dec. 8

1545	A842	2.70cr multi	50	15
1546	A842	7.50cr multi	1.00	35
1547	A842	8.50cr multi	1.25	40
1548	A842	9.50cr multi	1.50	45

1977, Dec. 19 *Perf. 11½*

1549	A843	1.30cr multi	30	20

Brazilian diplomacy.

Soccer Ball and Foot
A844

Designs: No. 1551, Soccer ball in net. No. 1552, Symbolic soccer player.

1978, Mar. 1 Litho. *Perf. 11½*

1550 A844 1.80cr multi 35 20
1551 A844 1.80cr multi 35 20
1552 A844 1.80cr multi 35 20

11th World Cup Soccer Championship, Argentina, June 1–25.

"La Fosca" on La Scala Stage and Carlos Gomes
A845

1978, Feb. 9

1553 A845 1.80cr multi 35 20

Bicentenary of La Scala in Milan, and to honor Carlos Gomes (1836–1893), Brazilian composer.

Symbols of Postal Mechanization
A846

1978, Mar. 15 Litho. *Perf. 11½*

1554 A846 1.80cr multi 35 20

Opening of Postal Staff College.

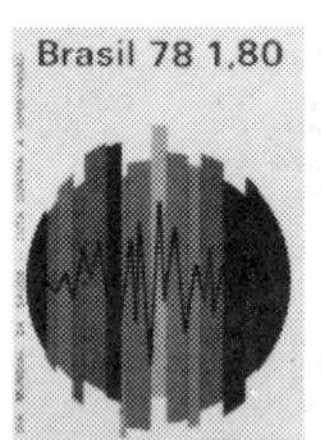

Hypertension Chart
A847

Waves from Antenna Uniting World
A848

1978, Apr. 4

1555 A847 1.80cr multi 35 20

World Health Day, fight against hypertension.

1978, May 17 Litho. *Perf. 12x11½*

1556 A848 1.80cr multi 35 20

10th World Telecommunications Day.

Brazilian Canary
A849

Birds: 8.50cr, Cotinga. 9.50cr, Tanager fastuosa.

1978, June 5 *Perf. 11½x12*

1557 A849 7.50cr multi 1.00 30
1558 A849 8.50cr multi 1.25 40
1559 A849 9.50cr multi 1.50 50

Inocencio Serzedelo Correa and Manuel Francisco Correa, 1893
A850

1978, June 20 Litho. *Perf. 11x11½*

1560 A850 1.80cr multi 35 20

85th anniversary of Union Court of Audit.

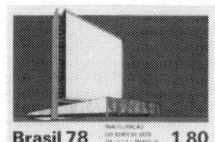

Post and Telegraph Building
A851

1978, June 22 *Perf. 11½*

1561 A851 1.80cr multi 35 25

Souvenir Sheet

Imperf.

1562 A851 7.50cr multi 2.00 50

Inauguration of Post and Telegraph Building (ECT), Brasilia, and for BRAPEX, 3rd Brazilian Philatelic Exhibition, Brasilia, June 23–28 (No. 1562). No. 1562 has buff margin with black inscription. Size: 70x 90mm.

Ernesto Geisel
A852

1978, June 22 Engr. *Perf. 11½*

1563 A852 1.80cr dl grn 35 20

Ernesto Geisel, President of Brazil.

Savoia-Marchetti S-64, Map of South Atlantic
A853

1978, July 3 Lithographed

1564 A853 1.80cr multi 35 20

50th anniversary of first crossing of South Atlantic by Carlos del Prete and Arturo Ferrarin.

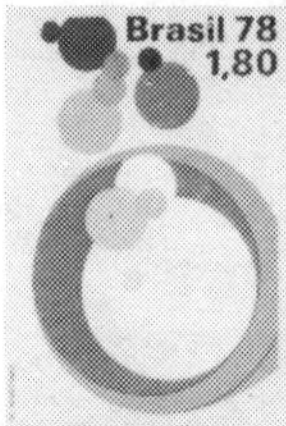

Symbolic of Smallpox Eradication
A854

Brazil No. 68
A855

1978, July 25

1565 A854 1.80cr multi 35 20

Eradication of smallpox.

1978, Aug. 1

1566 A855 1.80cr multi 35 25

Stamp Day, centenary of the "Barba Branca" (white beard) issue.

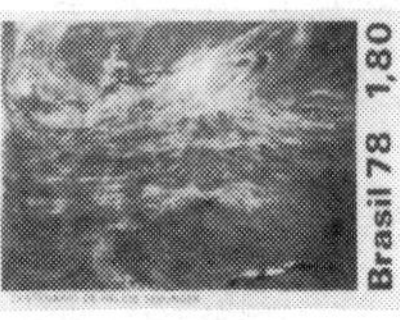

Stormy Sea, by Seelinger
A856

1978, Aug. 4

1567 A856 1.80cr multi 35 25

Helios Seelinger, painter, birth centenary.

Guitar Players
A857

Musicians and Instruments: No. 1569, Flutes. No. 1570, Percussion instruments.

1978, Aug. 22 Litho. *Perf. 11½*

1568 A857 1.80cr multi 35 15
1569 A857 1.80cr multi 35 15
1570 A857 1.80cr multi 30 20

Children at Play
A858

1978, Sept. 1 Litho. *Perf. 11½*

1571 A858 1.80cr multi 30 20

National Week.

Collegiate Church
A859

1978, Sept. 6 Engraved

1572 A859 1.80cr red brn 35 20

Restoration of patio of Collegiate Church, Sao Paulo.

Justice by A. Geschiatti
A860

1978, Sept. 18 Lithographed

1573 A860 1.80cr blk & ol 35 20

Federal Supreme Court, sesquicentennial.

Iguacu Falls
A861

Design: No. 1575, Yellow ipecac.

1978, Sept. 21

1574 A861 1.80cr multi 35 20
1575 A861 1.80cr multi 35 20

Iguacu National Park.

Stages of Intelsat Satellite
A862

1978, Oct. 9 Litho. *Perf. 11½*

1576 A862 1.80cr multi 35 20

Flag of Order of Christ
A863

Brazilian Flags: No. 1578, Principality of Brazil. No. 1579, United Kingdom. No. 1580, Imperial Brazil. No. 1581, National flag (current).

1978, Oct. 13

1577 A863 1.80cr multi 25 20
1578 A863 1.80cr multi 25 20
1579 A863 1.80cr multi 25 20
1580 A863 8.50cr multi 1.25 50
1581 A863 8.50cr multi 1.25 50
a. Block of 5 + label 3.50

7th LUBRAPEX Philatelic Exhibition, Porto Alegre. Nos. 1577–1581 printed se-tenant in blocks of 5 plus label showing Acorianos monument.

Mail Street Car
A864

Mail Transportation: No. 1583, Overland mail truck. No. 1584, Mail delivery truck. 7.50cr. Railroad mail car. 8.50cr, Mail coach. 9.50cr, Post riders.

1978, Oct. 21 *Perf. 11x11½*

1582 A864 1.80cr multi 25 10
1583 A864 1.80cr multi 25 10
1584 A864 1.80cr multi 25 10
1585 A864 7.50cr multi 1.25 45
1586 A864 8.50cr multi 1.50 50
1587 A864 9.50cr multi 1.50 55
Nos. 1582-1587 (6) 5.00 1.80

18th Universal Postal Union Congress, Rio de Janeiro, 1979. Nos. 1582–1587 printed se-tenant.

Brasil 78 1,80

Gaucho Herding Cattle, and Cactus
A865

1978, Oct. 23 *Perf. 11½x11*

1588 A865 1.80cr multi 35 20

Joao Guimaraes Rosa, poet and diplomat, 70th birthday.

A little time given to study of the arrangement of the Scott Catalogue can make it easier to use effectively.

St. Anthony's Hill, by Nicholas A. Taunay
A866

Landscape Paintings: No. 1590, Castle Hill, by Victor Meirelles. No. 1591, View of Sabara, by Alberto da Veiga Guignard. No. 1592, View of Pernambuco, by Frans Post.

1978, Nov. 6 Litho. *Perf. 11½*

1589 A866 1.80cr multi 35 20
1590 A866 1.80cr multi 35 20
1591 A866 1.80cr multi 35 20
1592 A866 1.80cr multi 35 20

Angel with Harp
A867

Designs: No. 1594, Angel with lute. No. 1595, Angel with oboe.

1978, Nov. 10

1593 A867 1.80cr multi 35 20
1594 A867 1.80cr multi 35 20
1595 A867 1.80cr multi 35 20

Christmas 1978.

Symbolic Candles
A868

1978, Nov. 23

1596 A868 1.80cr blk, gold & car 35 20

National Thanksgiving Day.

Red Crosses and Activities—A869

1978, Dec. 5 Litho. *Perf. 11x11½*

1597 A869 1.80cr blk & red 30 20

70th anniversary of Brazilian Red Cross.

Paz Theater, Belem
A870

Designs: 12cr, José de Alencar Theater, Portaleza. 12.50cr, Municipal Theater, Rio de Janeiro.

1978, Dec. 6 *Perf. 11½*

1598 A870 10.50cr multi 2.00 60
1599 A870 12cr multi 2.25 75
1600 A870 12.50cr multi 2.50 78

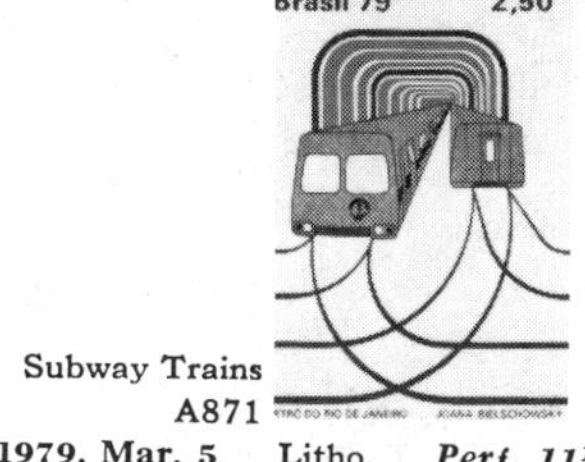

Subway Trains
A871

1979, Mar. 5 Litho. *Perf. 11½*

1601 A871 2.50cr multi 50 20

Inauguration of Rio de Janeiro's subway system.

Old and New Post Offices—A872

Designs: No. 1603, Old and new mail boxes. No. 1604, Manual and automatic mail sorting. No. 1605, Old and new planes. No. 1606, Telegraph and telex machine. No. 1607, Mailmen's uniforms.

1979, Mar. 20 Litho. *Perf. 11x11½*

1602 A872 2.50cr multi 50 15
1603 A872 2.50cr multi 50 15
1604 A872 2.50cr multi 50 15
1605 A872 2.50cr multi 50 15
1606 A872 2.50cr multi 50 15
1607 A872 2.50cr multi 50 15
Nos. 1602-1607 (6) 3.00 90

10th anniversary of the new Post and Telegraph Department, and 18th Universal Postal Union Congress, Rio de Janeiro, Sept.–Oct., 1979.

O'Day 23 Class Yacht
A873

Yachts and Stamp Outlines: 10.50cr, Penguin Class. 12cr, Hobie Cat Class. 12.50cr, Snipe Class.

1979, Apr. 18 Litho. *Perf. 11x11½*

1608 A873 2.50cr multi 70 40
1609 A873 10.50cr multi 1.25 70
1610 A873 12cr multi 1.25 75
1611 A873 12.50cr multi 1.50 75

Brasiliana '79, 3rd World Thematic Stamp Exhibition, São Conrado, Sept. 15–23.

Children, IYC Emblem
A874

1979, May 30 Litho. *Perf. 11½*

1612 A874 2.50cr multi 30 20

International Year of the Child and Children's Book Day.

Giant Water Lily
A875

Designs: 12cr, Amazon manatee. 12.50cr, Arrau (turtle).

1979, June 5 Litho. *Perf. 11½*

1613 A875 10.50cr multi 1.25 60
1614 A875 12cr multi 1.25 60
1615 A875 12.50cr multi 1.25 60

Amazon National Park, nature conservation.

Bank Emblem
A876

1979, June 7

1616 A876 2.50cr multi 30 15

Northwest Bank of Brazil, 25th anniversary.

Physician Tending Patient 15th Cent. Woodcut—A877

1979, June 30

1617 A877 2.50cr multi 30 15

National Academy of Medicine, 50th anniversary.

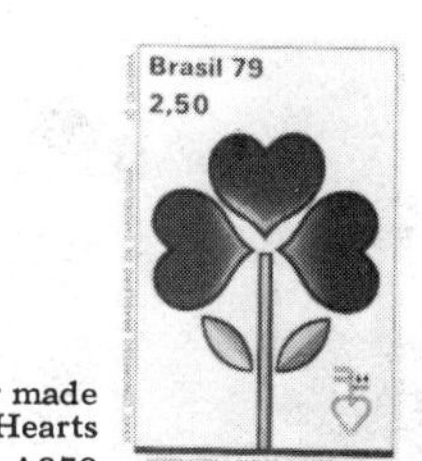

Flower made of Hearts
A878

1979, July 8 Litho. *Perf. 11½*

1618 A878 2.50cr multi 30 15

35th Brazilian Cardiology Congress.

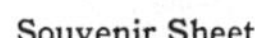
Souvenir Sheet

Hotel Nacional, Rio de Janeiro
A879

1979, July 16

1619 A879 12.50cr multi 2.00 1.25

Brasiliana '79 comprising 1st Inter-American Exhibition of Classical Philately and 3rd World Topical Exhibition, Rio de Janeiro, Sept. 15–23. No. 1619 has multicolored margin showing hang glider. Size: 87x125mm.

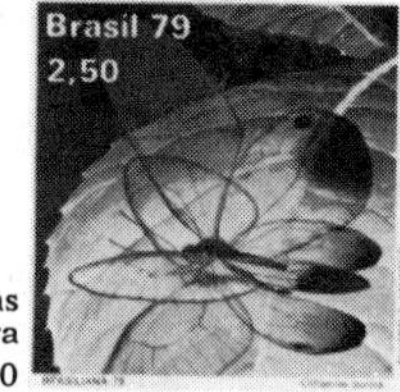

Cithaerias Aurora
A880

Moths: 10.50cr, Evenus regalis. 12cr, Diaethria clymena janeira. 12.50cr, Caligo eurilochus.

1979, Aug. 1

1620 A880 2.50cr multi 30 15
1621 A880 10.50cr multi 1.25 60
1622 A880 12cr multi 1.25 60
1623 A880 12.50cr multi 1.25 60

Stamp Day 1979.

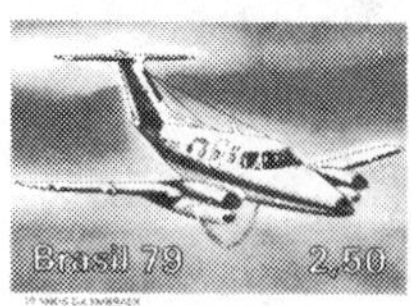

EMB-121 Xingo
A881

1979, Aug. 19 Litho. *Perf. 11½*

1624 A881 2.50cr vio bl 35 20

Embraer, Brazilian aircraft company, 10th anniversary.

Symbolic Southern Sky over Landscape
A882

1979, Sept. 12

1625 A882 3.20cr multi 35 20

National Week.

Our Lady of the Apparition
A883

1979, Sept. 8 Litho. *Perf. 11½*

1626 A883 2.50cr multi 35 20

Statue of Our Lady of the Apparition, 75th anniversary of coronation.

"UPU," Envelope and Mail Transport
A884

"UPU" and: No. 1628, Post Office emblems. 10.50cr, Globe. 12cr, Flags of Brazil and U.N. 12.50cr, UPU emblem.

1979, Sept. 12 *Perf. 11x11½*

1627	A884	2.50cr multi	35	20
1628	A884	2.50cr multi	35	20
1629	A884	10.50cr multi	1.25	60
1630	A884	12cr multi	1.40	75
1631	A884	12.50cr multi	1.40	75
		Nos. 1627-1631 (5)	4.75	2.50

18th Universal Postal Union Congress, Rio de Janeiro, Sept.–Oct. 1979.

Pyramid Fountain, Rio de Janeiro
A885

Fountains: 10.50cr, Facade, Marilia, Ouro Preto (horiz.). 12cr, Boa Vista, Recife.

Perf. 12x11½, 11½x12

1979, Sept. 15

1632	A885	2.50cr multi	30	20
1633	A885	10.50cr multi	1.25	60
1634	A885	12cr multi	1.40	75

Brasiliana '79, 1st Interamerican Exhibition of Classical Philately.

Church of the Glory
A886

Landscapes by Leandro Joaquim: 12cr, Fishing on Guanabara Bay. 12.50cr, Boqueirao Lake and Carioca Arches.

1979, Sept. 15 *Perf. 11½*

1635	A886	2.50cr multi	35	20
1636	A886	12cr multi	1.40	75
1637	A886	12.50cr multi	1.40	75

Brasiliana '79, 3rd World Topical Exhibition, São Conrado, Sept. 15–23.

World Map
A887

1979, Sept. 20

1638	A887	2.50cr multi	30	20

3rd World Telecommunications Exhibition, Geneva, Sept. 20–26.

"UPU" and UPU Emblem
A888

1979, Oct. 9 **Litho.** *Perf. 11½×11*

1639	A888	2.50cr multi	30	20
1640	A888	10.50cr multi	1.25	60
1641	A888	12cr multi	1.40	75
1642	A888	12.50cr multi	1.40	75

Universal Postal Union Day.

IYC Emblem, Feather Toy—A889

IYC Emblem and Toys: No. 1644, Bumble bee, ragdoll. No. 1645, Flower, top. No. 1646, Wooden acrobat.

1979, Oct. 12 *Perf. 11½*

1643	A889	2.50cr multi	35	20
1644	A889	3.20cr multi	35	25
1645	A889	3.20cr multi	35	25
1646	A889	3.20cr multi	35	25

International Year of the Child.

Adoration of the Kings—A890

Christmas 1979: No. 1648, Nativity. No. 1649, Jesus and the Elders in the Temple.

1979, Nov. 12 **Litho.** *Perf. 11½*

1647	A890	3.20cr multi	35	25
1648	A890	3.20cr multi	35	25
1649	A890	3.20cr multi	35	25

Souvenir Sheet

Hands Reading Braille—A891

Lithographed and Embossed

1979, Nov. 20. *Perf. 11½*

1650	A891	3.20cr multi	35	25

Publication of Braille script, 150th anniversary. Multicolored margin shows extension of stamp design with Braille printed and embossed. Size: 127×87½mm.

Wheat Harvester
A892

Steel Mill
A893

1979, Nov. 22

1651	A892	3.20cr multi	35	25

Thanksgiving 1979.

1979, Nov. 23

1652	A893	3.20cr multi	35	25

COSIPA Steelworks, São Paulo, 25th anniversary.

Type of 1976

Designs: 70c, Women grinding coconuts. 2cr, Coconuts. 2.50cr, Basket weaver. 3cr, Mangoes. 3.20cr, River boatman. 4cr, Corn. 5cr, Onions. 7cr, Oranges. 10cr, Maracuja. 12cr, Pineapple. 17cr, Guarana. 20cr, Sugar cane. 21cr, Harvesting ramie (China grass). 24cr, Beekeeping. 27cr, Man leading pack mule. 30cr, Silkworm. 34cr, Cacao. 42cr, Soybeans. 50cr, Wheat. 66cr, Grapes. 100cr, Cashews. 140cr, Tomatoes. 500cr, Cotton.

1979-80 **Photo.** *Perf. 11×11½, 11½×11*

1655	A790	70c	gray grn	20	20
1658	A790	2cr	yel brn ('82)	3	3
1659	A790	2.50cr	sepia	15	10
1660	A790	3cr	red ('82)	5	3
1661	A790	3.20cr	blue	15	10
1663	A790	4cr	org ('80)	15	10
1663A	A790	5cr	dk pur ('82)	8	5
1664	A790	7cr	org ('81)	85	40
1665	A790	10cr	bl grn ('82)	15	8
1666	A790	12cr	dk grn ('81)	18	10
1667	A790	17cr	brn org ('82)	26	14
1667A	A790	20cr	ol ('82)	30	16
1668	A790	21cr	purple	50	10
1670	A790	24cr	('82)	36	20
1671	A790	27cr	sep ('79)	60	10
1672	A790	30cr	('82)	45	25
1674	A790	34cr	brn ('80)	75	10
1677	A790	42cr	grn ('80)	1.00	10
1678	A790	50cr	yel org ('82)	75	40
1679	A790	66cr	pur ('81)	3.50	*1.00*
1679A	A790	100cr	dk red brn ('81)	1.50	80
1679B	A790	140cr	red ('82)	2.10	1.00
1679C	A790	500cr	brn ('82)	7.50	4.00

Brasil 80 3,20

Plant Inside Raindrop—A896

Light Bulb Containing: 17cr+7cr, Sun. 20cr+8cr, Windmill. 21cr+9cr, Dam.

1980, Jan. 2 **Litho.** *Perf. 12*

1680	A896	3.20cr multi	25	15
1681	A896	24cr (17+7)	2.50	1.25
1682	A896	28cr (20+8)	3.00	1.50
1683	A896	30cr (21+9)	3.50	1.75

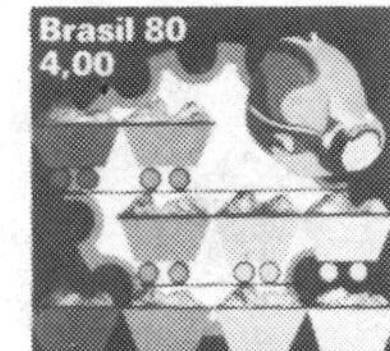

Anthracite Industry—A897

1980, Mar. 19 **Litho.** *Perf. 11½*

1684	A897	4cr multi	40	25

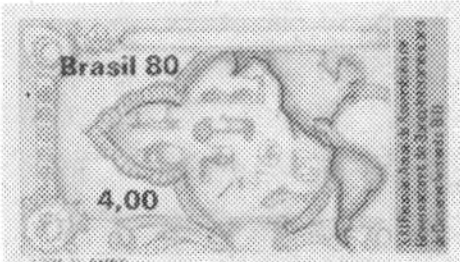

Map of Americas, Symbols of Development—A898

1980, Apr. 14 **Litho.** *Perf. 11x11½*

1685	A898	4cr multi	40	25

21st Assembly of Inter-American Development Bank Governors, Rio de Janeiro, Apr. 14-16.

Tapirape Mask, Mato Grosso—A899

1980, Apr. 18 *Perf. 11½*

1686	A899	4cr *shown*	40	25
1687	A899	4cr *Tukuna mask, Amazonas,* vert.	40	25
1688	A899	4cr *Kanela mask, Maranhao,* vert.	40	25

Brazilian Television, 30th Anniversary—A900

1980, May 5 **Litho.** *Perf. 11½*

1689	A900	4cr multi	35	25

Duke of Caixas, by Miranda
A901

The Worker, by Candido Partinari
A902

1980, May 7

1690	A901	4cr multi	35	25

Duke of Caixas, death centenary.

1980, May 18

Paintings: 28cr, Mademoiselle Pogany, by Constantin Brancusi. 30cr, The Glass of Water, by Francisco Aurelio de Figueiredo.

1691	A902	24cr multi	2.75	1.50
1692	A902	28cr multi	2.75	1.75
1693	A902	30cr multi	3.25	1.85

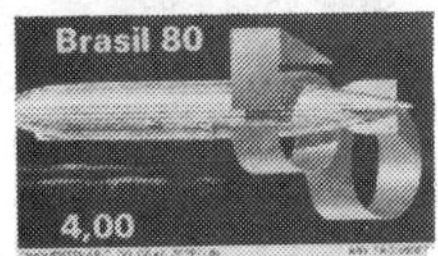

Graf Zeppelin, 50th Anniversary of Atlantic Crossing—A903

1980, June **Litho.** ***Perf. 11x11½***

1694	A903	4cr multi	50	25

Pope John Paul II, St. Peter's, Rome, Congress Emblem—A904

Pope, Emblem and Brazilian Churches: No. 1693, Fortaleza (vert.). 24cr, Apericida. 28cr, Rio de Janeiro. 30cr, Brasilia.

1980, June 24 ***Perf. 12***

1695	A904	4cr multi	50	25
1696	A904	4cr multi	50	25
1697	A904	24cr multi	2.75	1.50
1698	A904	28cr multi	2.75	1.75
1699	A904	30cr multi	3.50	1.90
		Nos. 1695-1699 (5)	10.00	5.65

Visit of Pope John Paul II to Brazil, June 30-July 12; 10th National Eucharistic Congress, Fortaleza, July 9-16.

First Transatlantic Flight, 50th Anniversary—A905

1980, June **Litho.** ***Perf. 11x11½***

1700	A905	4cr multi	40	25

Souvenir Sheet

Yacht Sail, Exhibition Emblem—A906

1980, June ***Perf. 11½***

1701	A906	30cr multi	5.00	2.00

Brapex IV Stamp Exhibition, Fortaleza, June 13-21. Multicolored margin shows sails on water. Size: 125x88mm.

Rowing, Moscow '80 Emblem—A907

1980, June 30

1702	A907	4cr *shown*	50	25
1703	A907	4cr *Target shooting*	50	25
1704	A907	4cr *Bicycling*	50	25

22nd Summer Olympic Games, Moscow, July 19-Aug. 3.

Rondon Community Works Project—A908

1980, July 11

1705	A908	4cr multi	50	25

Helen Keller and Anne Sullivan—A909

1980, July 28

1706	A909	4cr multi	50	25

Helen Keller (1880-1968), blind deaf writer and lecturer taught by Anne Sullivan (1867-1936).

Souvenir Sheet

São Francisco River Canoe—A910

1980, Aug. 1 **Litho.** ***Perf. 11½***

1707	A910	24cr multi	4.00	1.50

Stamp Day. Light blue and black margin shows river canoe, Postal and Telegraph Museum emblem. Size: 125½x86½mm.

Microscope, Red Cross, Insects, Brick and Tile Houses—A911

1980, Aug. 5 ***Perf. 11½x11***

1708	A911	4cr multi	50	25

National Health Day.

Brazilian Postal Administration, 15th Anniversary—**A912**

1980, Sept. 16 **Litho.** ***Perf. 12***

1709	A912	5cr multi	60	30

Souvenir Sheet

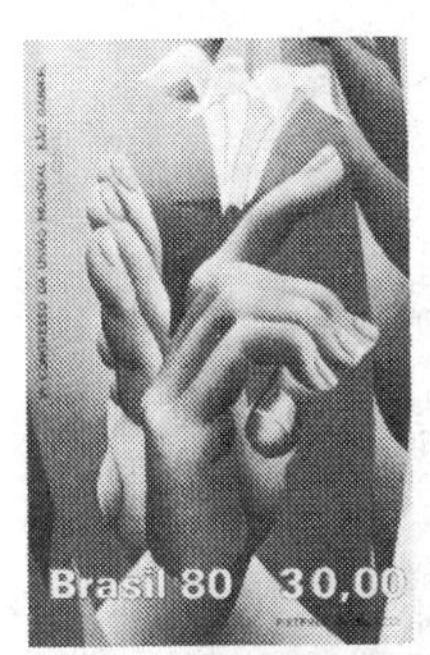

St. Gabriel World Union, 6th Congress—**A913**

1980, Sept. 29 ***Perf. 11½x12***

1710	A913	30cr multi	4.00	2.00

No. 1710 has red and orange margin. Size: 125x86mm.

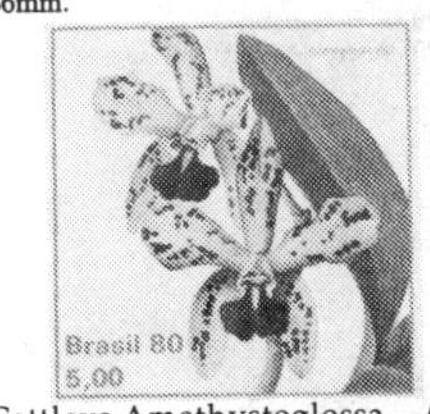

Cattleya Amethystoglossa—**A914**

1980, Oct. 3 ***Perf. 11½***

1711	A914	5cr *shown*	50	30
1712	A914	5cr *Laelia cinnabarina*	50	30
1713	A914	24cr *Zygopetalum crinitum*	3.00	1.50
1714	A914	28cr *Laelia tenebrosa*	3.50	1.75

Espamer 80, American-European Philatelic Exhibition, Madrid, Oct. 3-12.

Red-tailed Amazon Parrot
A915

Capitao Rodrigo, Hero of Erico Verissimo's "O Continento"
A916

Parrots: No. 1716, Vinaceous Amazon. No. 1717, Brown-backed. No. 1718, Red-spectacled.

1980, Oct. 18 **Litho.** ***Perf. 12***

1715	A915	5cr multi	50	25
1716	A915	5cr multi	50	25
1717	A915	28cr multi	3.25	1.75
1718	A915	28cr multi	3.25	1.75

Lubrapex '80 Stamp Exhibition, Lisbon, Oct. 18-26.

1980, Oct. 23

1719	A916	5cr multi	50	25

Book Day.

Flight into Egypt—A917

1980, Nov. 5

1720	A917	5cr multi	50	25

Christmas 1980.

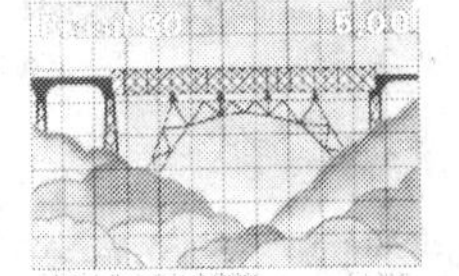

Sound Waves and Oscillator Screen—A918

1980, Nov. 7

1721	A918	5cr multi	50	25

Telebras Research Center inauguration.

Carvalho Viaduct, Paranagua-Curitiba Railroad—A919

1980, Nov. 10

1722	A919	5cr multi	50	25

Engineering Club centenary.

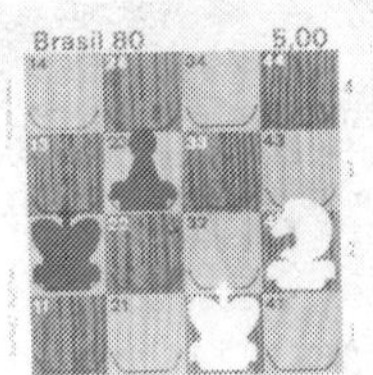

Portable Chess Board—A920

1980, Nov. 18 **Litho.** ***Perf. 11½***

1723	A920	5cr multi	50	25

Postal chess contest.

Sun and Wheat—A921

1980, Nov. 27 *Perf. 11½x11*
1724 A921 5cr multi 50 25

Thanksgiving 1980.

Father Anchieta Writing "Virgin Mary, Mother of God" on Sand of Iperoig Beach—A922

1980, Dec. 8 *Perf. 12*
1725 A922 5cr multi 50 25

Christ Carrying Cross, By O Aleijadinho—A923

Antonio Francisco Lisboa (O Aleijadinho), 250th Birth Anniversary: Paintings of the life of Christ: a. Mount of Olives. B. Arrest in the Garden. c. Flagellation. d. Crown of Thorns. f. Crucifixion.

1980, Dec. 29
1726 Block of 6 4.00 4.00
a.-f. A923 5cr any single 60 30

Agricultural Productivity—A924

1981, Jan. 2 **Litho.** *Perf. 11x11½*
1727 A924 30cr *shown* 3.50 1.75
1728 A924 35cr *Domestic markets* 4.25 2.00
1729 A924 40cr *Exports* 4.75 2.00

Boy Scout and Campfire—A925

1981, Jan. 22 **Litho.** *Perf. 11x11½*
1730 A925 5cr shown 60 30
1731 A925 5cr Scouts cooking 60 30
1732 A925 5cr Scout, tents 60 30

4th Pan-American Scout Jamboree.

Souvenir Sheet

Mailman, 1930—A926

1981, Mar. 11 **Litho.** *Perf. 11*
1733 Sheet of 3 7.25 3.75
a. A926 30cr shown 1.80 90
b. A926 35cr Mailman, 1981 2.40 1.20
c. A926 40cr Telegram messenger, 1930 3.00 1.50

Department of Posts and Telegraphs, 50th anniversary. No. 1733 has black marginal inscription. Size: 100x70mm.

The Hunter and the Jaguar, by Felix Taunay (1795-1881)—A927

1981, Apr. 10 **Litho.** *Perf. 11*
1734 A927 30cr multi 3.60 1.80

Size: 70x90mm.

Lima Barreto and Rio de Janeiro, 1900—A928

1981, May 13 **Litho.** *Perf. 11½*
1735 A928 7cr multi 85 42

Lima Barreto, writer, birth centenary.

Maraca Indian Funerary Urn A929

1981, May 18
1736 A929 7cr shown 85 42
1737 A929 7cr Marajoara triangular jug 85 42
1738 A929 7cr Tupi-Guarani bowl 85 42

Lophornis Magnifica—A930

Designs: Hummingbirds.

1981, May 22 *Perf. 11½*
1739 A930 7cr shown 85 42
1740 A930 7cr Phaethornis pretrei 85 42
1741 A930 7cr Chrysolampis mosquitus 85 42
1742 A930 7cr Heliactin cornuta 85 42

Rotary Emblem and Faces—A931

1981, May 31
1743 A931 7cr Emblem, hands 85 42
1744 A931 35cr shown 4.25 2.00

72nd Convention of Rotary Intl., Sao Paulo.

Environmental Protection—A932

1981, June 5 *Perf. 12*
1745 A932 7cr shown 85 42
1746 A932 7cr Forest 85 42
1747 A932 7cr Clouds (air) 85 42
1748 A932 7cr Village (soil) 85 42

Nos. 1745-1748 se-tenant.

Biplane, 1931 (Airmail Service, 50th Anniv.)—A933

1981, June 10 *Perf. 11½*
1749 A933 7cr multi 85 42

Madeira-Mamore Railroad, 50th Anniv. of Nationalization—A934

1981, July 10 **Litho.** *Perf. 11x11½*
1750 A934 7cr multi 85 42

66th Intl. Esperanto Congress, Brasilia A935

1981, July 26 *Perf. 12*
1751 A935 7cr grn & blk 85 42

No. 79—A936

1981, Aug. 1
1752 A936 50cr shown 6.00 3.00
1753 A936 55cr No. 80 6.50 3.25
1754 A936 60cr No. 81 7.00 3.50

Stamp Day; centenary of "small head" stamps.

Institute of Military Engineering, 50th Anniv.—A937

1981, Aug. 11 **Litho.** *Perf. 11½*
1755 A937 12cr multi 16 8

Reisado Dancers—A938

1981, Aug. 22
1756 A938 50cr Dancers, diff. 70 35
1757 A938 55cr Sailors 78 38
1758 A938 60cr shown 85 42

Intl. Year of the Disabled—A939

1981, Sept. 17 **Litho.** *Perf. 11½*
1759 A939 12cr multi 18 10

Virgin of Nazareth Statue A941

Christ the Redeemer Statue, Rio de Janeiro, 50th Anniv. A942

1981, Oct. 10 **Litho.** *Perf. 12*
1764 A941 12cr multi 18 10

Candle Festival of Nazareth, Belem.

1981, Oct. 12
1765 A942 12cr multi 18 10

World Food Day—A943

1981, Oct. 16
1766 A943 12cr multi 18 10

75th Anniv. of Santos-Dumont's First Flight—A944

1981, Oct. 23 **Litho.** *Perf. 12*

1767 A944 60cr multi 90 50

Father José de Santa Rita Durao, Titlepage of his Epic Poem Caramuru, Diego Alvares Correia (Character)—A945

1981, Oct. 29

1768 A945 12cr multi 18 10

Caramuru publication centenary; World Book Day.

Christmas 1981—A946

Designs: Creches and figurines. 55cr, 60cr vert.

1981, Nov. 10 **Litho.** *Perf. 12*

1769 A946 12cr multi 18 10
1770 A946 50cr multi 70 35
1771 A946 55cr multi 78 38
1772 A946 60cr multi 90 50

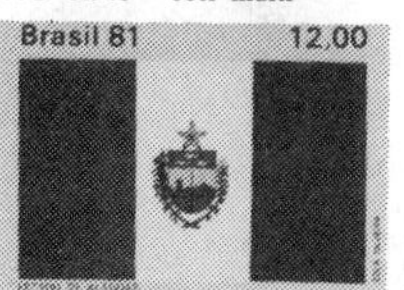

State Flags A947

Designs: a. Alagoas. b. Bahia. c. Federal District. d. Pernambuco. e. Sergipe.

1981, Nov. 19

1773 Block of 5 plus label 1.00 50
a.-e. A497 12cr, any single 18 10

Label shows arms of Brazil.

Thanksgiving 1981—A948

1981, Nov. 26 **Litho.** *Perf. 11½*

1776 A948 12cr multi 18 10

Ministry of Labor, 50th Anniv.—A949

1981, Nov. 26

1777 A949 12cr multi 18 10

School of Engineering, Itajuba A950

1981, Nov. 30 *Perf. 11x11½*

1778 A950 15cr lt grn & pur 25 12

Theodomiro C. Santiago, founder, birth centenary.

Sao Paulo State Police Sesquicentennial A951

1981, Dec. 15 **Litho.** *Perf. 12*

1779 A951 12cr Policeman with saxophone 18 10
1780 A951 12cr Mounted policemen 18 10

Army Library Centenary A952

1981, Dec. 17

1781 A952 12cr multi 18 10

Souvenir Sheet

Philatelic Club of Brazil, 50th Anniv. A953

1981, Dec. 18 *Perf. 11*

1782 A953 180cr multi 2.75 1.50

No. 1782 has multicolored margin showing "Bull's Eye" stamps designs, emblem. Size: 89x69mm.

Brigadier Eduardo Gomes—A954

1982, Jan. 20 **Litho.** *Perf. 11x11½*

1783 A954 12cr bl & blk 18 10

Birth Centenary of Henrique Lage, Industrialist—A956

1982, Mar. 14 **Litho.** *Perf. 11½*

1785 A956 17cr multi 26 16

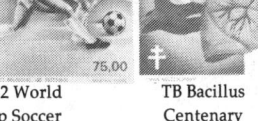

1982 World Cup Soccer A957

TB Bacillus Centenary A958

Designs: Various soccer players.

1982, Mar. 19

1786 A957 75cr multi 1.15 70
1787 A957 80cr multi 1.20 75
1788 A957 85cr multi 1.25 76

Souvenir Sheet
Imperf.

1789 Sheet of 3 4.50 4.50
a. A957 100cr like #1786 1.50
b. A957 100cr like #1787 1.50
c. A957 100cr like #1788 1.50

No. 1789 has black marginal inscription. Size: 125x87mm.

1982, Mar. 24 *Perf. 12*

1790 A958 90cr Microscope, lung 1.35 80
1791 A958 100cr Lung, pills 1.50 90

Nos. 1790-1791 se-tenant.

A959

1982, Apr. 17 **Litho.** *Perf. 11*

1792 Sheet of 3 3.75 2.25
a. A959 75cr Laelia Purpurata 1.15 70
b. A959 80cr Oncidium flexuosum 1.20 75
c. A959 85cr Cleistes revoluta 1.30 80

BRAPEX V Stamp Exhibition, Blumenau. No. 1792 has black marginal inscription. Size: 100x70mm.

Oil Drilling Centenary—A960

1982, Apr. 18 *Perf. 11½*

1793 A960 17cr multi 26 14

400th Birth Anniv. of St. Vincent de Paul—A961

1982, Apr. 24 **Litho.** *Perf. 11½*

1794 A961 17cr multi 26 14

Seven Steps of Guaira (Waterfalls)—A962

1982, Apr. 29

1795 A962 17cr Fifth Fall 26 14
1796 A962 21cr Seventh Fall 32 22

Ministry of Communications, 15th Anniv.—A963

1982, May 15

1797 A963 21cr multi 32 22

Museology Course, Natl. Historical Museum, 50th Anniv.—A964

1982, May 18

1798 A964 17cr blk & sal pink 26 14

Vale de Rio Duce Mining Company—A965

1982, June 1

1799 A965 17cr Gears 26 14

Martin Afonso de Souza Reading Charter to Settlers—A966

1982, June 3 Litho. *Perf. 11½*

1800	A966	17cr multi	26	14

Town of Sao Vincente, 450th anniv.

Armadillo—A967

1982, June 4

1801	A967	17cr shown	26	14
1802	A967	21cr Wolves	32	22
1803	A967	30cr Deer	45	25

Film Strip and Award—A968

1982, June 19

1804	A968	17cr multi	26	14

20th anniv. of Golden Palm award for The Promise Keeper, Cannes Film Festival.

Souvenir Sheet

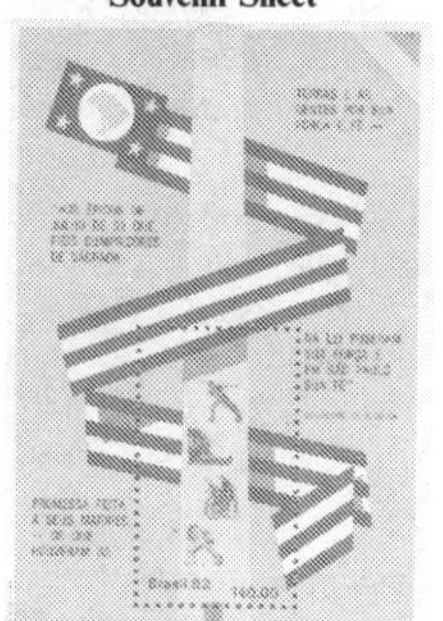

50th Anniv. of Constitutionalist Revolution—A969

1982, July 9 Litho. *Perf. 11*

1805	A969	140cr multi	2.25	1.25

Multicolored margin continues design. Size: 70x100mm.

Church of Our Lady of O'Sabara A970

St. Francis of Assisi, 800th Birth Anniv. A971

Baroque Architecture, Minas Gerais State: No. 1807, Church of Our Lady of the Rosary, Diamantina (horiz.). No. 1808, Town Square, Mariana (horiz.).

1982, July 16 *Perf. 11½*

1806	A970	17cr multi	26	14
1807	A970	17cr multi	26	14
1808	A970	17cr multi	26	14

1982, July 24

1809	A971	21cr multi	32	22

Stamp Day and Centenary of Pedro II "Large Head" Stamps—A972

1982, Aug. 1

1810	A972	21cr No. 82	32	22

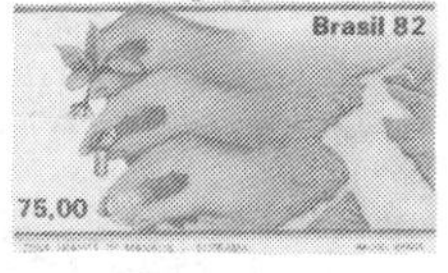

Port of Manaus Free Trade Zone—A973

1982, Aug. 15 *Perf. 11x11½*

1811	A973	75cr multi	1.15	70

Scouting Year—A974

1982, Aug. 21 Litho. *Perf. 11*

1812		Sheet of 2	4.25	2.50
a.	A974	85cr Baden-Powell	1.30	75
b.	A974	185cr Scout	2.80	1.75

Black marginal inscription, emblem. Size: 100x70mm.

Orixas Folk Costumes of African Origin—A975

1982, Aug. 21 *Perf. 11½*

1813	A975	20cr Iemanja	30	16
1814	A975	20cr Xango	30	16
1815	A975	20cr Oxumare	30	16

10th Anniv. of Central Bank of Brazil Currency Museum—A976

1982, Aug. 31

1816	A976	25cr 12-florin coin, 1645, obverse and reverse	38	20
1817	A976	25cr Emperor Pedro's 6.40-reis coronation coin, 1822	38	20

National Week—A977

1982, Sept. 1

1818	A977	25cr Don Pedro proclaiming independence	38	20

St. Theresa of Avila (1515-1582)—A978

1982, Oct. 4

1819	A978	85cr Portrait	1.30	75

Type of 1979

Designs: 24cr, Beekeeping. 30cr, Silkworm.

1982, Sept. Photo. *Perf. 11½x11*

1670	A790	24cr ('82)	36	20
1672	A790	30cr ('82)	45	25

Instruments —A979

1982, Oct. 15 Litho. *Perf. 11½x11*

1820	A979	75cr shown	1.15	70
1821	A979	80cr Dancers	1.20	72
1822	A979	85cr Musicians	1.30	75
a.		Souvenir sheet of 3	3.75	2.25

Lubrapex '82, 4th Portuguese-Brazilian Stamp Exhibition. No. 1822a contains Nos. 1820-1822 (perf. 11). Size: 100x70mm.

Aviation Industry Day—A980

1982, Oct. 17 *Perf. 12*

1823	A980	24cr Embraer EMB-312 trainer plane	36	20

Bastos Tigre, Poet, Birth Centenary, and "Saudade" Text—A981

1982, Oct. 29

1824	A981	24cr multi	36	20

Book Day.

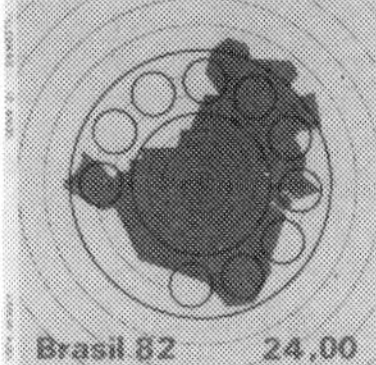

10th Anniv. of Brazilian Telecommunications Co.—A982

1982, Nov. 9 Litho. *Perf. 11½*

1825	A982	24cr multi	36	20

Christmas 1982—A983

Children's Drawings.

1982, Nov. 10

1826	A983	24cr Nativity	36	20
1827	A983	24cr Angels	36	20
1828	A983	30cr Nativity, diff.	45	45
1829	A983	30cr Flight into Egypt	45	45

State Flags—A984

1982, Nov. 19

1830	A984	24cr Ceara	36	20
1831	A984	24cr Espirito Santo	36	20
1832	A984	24cr Paraiba	36	20
1833	A984	24cr Rio Grande do Norte	36	20
1834	A984	24cr Rondonia	36	20
		Nos. 1830-1834 (5)	1.80	1.00

Thanksgiving 1982—A985

1982, Nov. 25

1835	A985	24cr multi	36	20

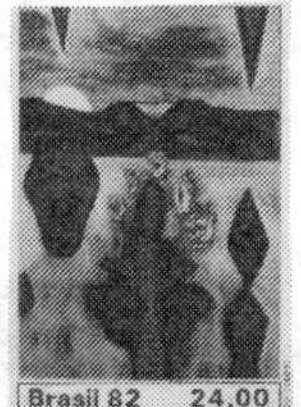

Homage to the Deaf—A986

1982, Dec. 1

1836	A986	24cr multi	36	20

Naval Academy Bicentenary—A987

Training Ships.

1982, Dec. 14

1837	A987	24cr Brazil	36	20
1838	A987	24cr Benjamin Constant	36	20
1839	A987	24cr Almirante Saldanha	36	20

Souvenir Sheet

No. 12—A988

1982, Dec. 18 **Litho.** ***Perf. 11***

1840	A988	200cr multi	3.00	1.50

BRASILIANA '83 Intl. Stamp Exhibition, Rio de Janeiro, July 29-Aug. 7. Multicolored margin shows Regional Administration building. Size: 100x70mm.

Brasiliana '83 Carnival—A989

1983, Feb. 9 **Litho.** ***Perf. 11½***

1841	A989	24cr Samba drummers	18	10
1842	A989	130cr Street parade	1.00	50
1843	A989	140cr Dancer	1.05	52
1844	A989	150cr Male dancer	1.10	55

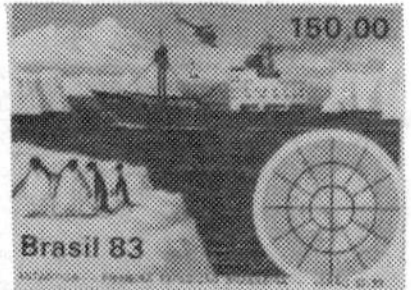

Antarctic Expedition—A990

1983, Feb. 20 **Litho.** ***Perf. 11½***

1845	A990	150cr Support ship Barano de Teffe	1.10	55

50th Anniv. of Women's Rights—A991

1983, Mar. 8

1846	A991	130cr multi	1.00	50

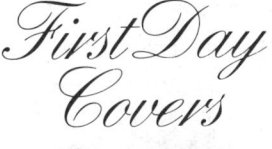

SEMI-POSTAL STAMPS

National Philatelic Exhibition Issue.

SP1

Wmkd. Coat of Arms in Sheet. (236)

1934, Sept. 16 Engraved *Imperf.*

Thick Paper

B1	SP1	200r +100r dp cl	75	1.25
B2	SP1	300r +100r ver	75	1.25
B3	SP1	700r +100r brt bl	8.00	10.00
B4	SP1	1000r +100r blk	8.00	10.00

The surtax was to help defray the expenses of the exhibition. Issued in sheets of 60, inscribed "EXPOSICAO FILATELICA NACIONAL".

Red Cross Nurse and Soldier
SP2

Perf. 11

1935, Sept. 19 Typo. Wmk. 222

B5	SP2	200r +100r pur & red	1.00	1.00
B6	SP2	300r +100r ol brn & red	1.00	75
B7	SP2	700r +100r turq bl & red	12.00	7.00

3rd Pan-American Red Cross Conference. Exist imperf.

Three Wise Men and Star of Bethlehem
SP3

Angel and Child
SP4

Southern Cross and Child
SP5

Mother and Child
SP6

Perf. 10½

1939, Dec. 20 Litho. Wmk. 249

B8	SP3	100r +100r chlky bl & bl blk	50	50
a.		Horiz. or vert. pair, imperf. between	45.00	
B9	SP4	200r +100r brt grnsh bl	1.00	1.00
a.		Horizontal pair, imperf. between	45.00	
B10	SP5	400r +200r ol grn & ol	1.00	25
B11	SP6	1200r +400r crim & brn red	5.00	1.50
a.		Vertical pair, imperf. between	45.00	

The surtax was distributed to charitable institutions.

AIR POST STAMPS.

Official Stamps of 1913 Surcharged

SERVIÇO AEREO 200 Rs.

1927, Dec. 28 *Perf. 12* Unwmkd.

Center in Black.

C1	O2	50r on 10r gray	15	15
a.		Inverted surcharge	225.00	
b.		Top ornaments missing	45.00	
C2	O2	200r on 1000r blk brn	2.00	2.00
a.		Double surch.	225.00	
C3	O2	200r on 2000r red brn	2.00	3.00
a.		Double surch.	225.00	
C4	O2	200r on 5000r brn	1.50	1.50
a.		Double surch.	225.00	
b.		Double surcharge, one inverted	250.00	
c.		Triple surch.	350.00	
C5	O2	300r on 500r org	1.50	1.50
C6	O2	300r on 600r vio	60	50
b.		Pair, one without surch.		
C6A	O2	500r on 10r gray	275.00	300.00
C7	O2	500r on 50r gray	1.50	50
a.		Double surch.	225.00	225.00
C8	O2	1000r on 20r ol grn	90	25
a.		Double surch.	225.00	
C9	O2	2000r on 100r ver	2.50	1.75
a.		Pair, one without surcharge	900.00	
C10	O2	2000r on 200r bl	2.50	1.75
C11	O2	2000r on 10,000r blk	2.00	60
C12	O2	5000r on 20,000r bl	4.00	2.50
C13	O2	5000r on 50,000r grn	4.00	3.00
C14	O2	5000r on 100,000r org	20.00	20.00
C15	O2	10,000r on 500,000r brn	20.00	17.50
C16	O2	10,000r on 1,000,000r dk brn	20.00	15.00
		Nos. C1-C6, C7-C16 (16)	85.15	71.50

Nos. C1, C1b, C7, C8 and C9 have small diamonds printed over the numerals in the upper corners.

Monument to de Gusmão
AP1

Santos-Dumont's Airship
AP2

Augusto Severo's Airship "Pax"
AP3

Santos-Dumont's Biplane "14 Bis"
AP4

Ribeiro de Barros's Seaplane "Jahu"
AP5

Perf. 11, 12½x13, 13x13½.

1929 Typographed. Wmk. 206

C17	AP1	50r bl grn	25	20
C18	AP2	200r red	1.25	20
C19	AP3	300r brt bl	1.50	20
C20	AP4	500r red vio	2.00	20
C21	AP5	1000r org brn	5.00	40
		Nos. C17-C21 (5)	10.00	1.20

See also Nos. C32-C36.

Bartholomeu de Gusmão
AP6

Augusto Severo
AP7

Alberto Santos-Dumont
AP8

Perf. 9, 11 and Compound.

1929-30 Engraved. Wmk. 101

C22	AP6	2000r lt grn ('30)	10.00	25
C23	AP7	5000r carmine	10.00	1.00
C24	AP8	10,000r ol grn	10.00	1.25

See also Nos. C37, C40.

Allegory: Airmail Service between Brazil and the United States
AP9

1929 Typographed Wmk. 206

C25	AP9	3000r violet	10.00	65

See also Nos. C38, C41. Nos. C23-C25 exist imperforate.

Air Post Stamps of 1929 Surcharged in Blue or Red

ZEPPELIN 2$500

1931, Aug. 16 *Perf. 12½x13½.*

C26	AP2	2500r on 200r red (Bl)	20.00	22.50
C27	AP3	5000r on 300r brt bl (R)	22.50	27.50

No. C25 Surcharged

2.500 REIS

1931, Sept. 2 *Perf. 11*

C28	AP9	2500r on 3000r vio	17.50	17.50
a.		Inverted surcharge	200.00	
b.		Surcharged on front and back	175.00	

Regular Issues of 1928-29 Surcharged

ZEPPELIN 3$500

Perf. 11, 11½.

1932, May Wmk. 101

C29	A89	3500r on 5000r gray lil	20.00	22.50
C30	A72	7000r on 10,000r rose	20.00	22.50
a.		Vert. pair, imperf. between	200.00	
b.		Horiz. pair, imperf. between	250.00	

Imperforates

Since 1933, imperforate or partly perforated sheets of nearly all of the airmail issues have become available.

Flag and Airplane
AP10

Typographed

1933, June 7 *Perf. 11.* Wmk. 222

C31	AP10	3500r grn, yel & dk bl	4.00	85

See also Nos. C39, C42.

1934 Wmk. 222

C32	AP1	50r bl grn	60	60
C33	AP2	200r red	1.25	60
C34	AP3	300r brt bl	2.50	1.25
C35	AP4	500r red vio	1.25	50
C36	AP5	1000r org brn	3.00	40
		Nos. C32-C36 (5)	8.60	3.35

Engraved.

1934 *Perf. 12x11.* Wmk. 236

Thick Laid Paper.

C37	AP6	2000r lt grn	4.00	1.00

Types of 1929, 1933.

Perf. 11, 11½, 12.

1937-40 Typographed Wmk. 249

C38	AP9	3000r violet	20.00	1.50
C39	AP10	3500r grn, yel & dk bl	2.00	1.25

Engraved.

C40	AP7	5000r ver ('40)	4.50	60

Watermark note after No. 501 also applies to No. C40.

Types of 1929-33.

Perf. 11, 11½x12

1939-40 Typographed Wmk. 256

C41	AP9	3000r violet	90	50
C42	AP10	3500r bl, dl grn & yel ('40)	60	40

Map of the Western Hemisphere Showing Brazil
AP11

1941, Jan. 14 Engr. *Perf. 11*

C43	AP11	1200r dk brn	2.50	50

5th general census of Brazil.

Nos. 506A and 508 Overprinted in Carmine

AÉREO "10 Nov." 937-941

Rouletted.

1941, Nov. 10 Wmk. 264

C45	A180	5400r sl grn	2.00	1.00
a.		Overprint inverted	175.00	

Issued in commemoration of the fourth anniversary of President Vargas' new constitution.

Nos. 506A and 508 Surcharged in Black

AÉREO
"10 Nov."
937-942
Cr.$ 5,40

1942, Nov. 10 Wmk. 264

C47 A180 5.40cr on 5400r sl grn 2.00 1.00
a. Wmk. 249 60.00 60.00
b. Surcharge inverted 75.00 75.00

Issued in commemoration of the fifth anniversary of President Vargas' new constitution.

The status of No. C47a is questioned.

Southern Cross and Arms of Paraguay
AP12

Wmk. 270

Wmkd. Wavy Lines and Seal. (270)

1943, May 11 Engr. *Perf. 12½*

C48 AP12 1.20cr lt gray bl 1.00 50

Issued in commemoration of the visit of President Higinio Morinigo of Paraguay.

Map of South America
AP13

Wmk. 271

Wmkd. Wavy Lines. (271)

1943, June 30 *Perf. 12½.*

C49 AP13 1.20cr multi 1.00 50

Visit of President Penaranda of Bolivia.

Numeral of Value
AP14

1943, Aug. 7

C50 AP14 1cr blk & dl yel 3.00 2.00
a. Double impression 50.00
C51 AP14 2cr blk & pale grn 4.00 2.00
a. Double impression 60.00
C52 AP14 5cr blk & pink 5.00 2.75

Centenary of Brazil's first postage stamps.

Souvenir Sheet.

AP15

Imperf.

Without Gum

C53 AP15 Sheet of three 37.50 35.00
a. 1cr blk & dl yel 10.00 10.00
b. 2cr blk & pale grn 10.00 10.00
c. 5cr blk & pink 10.00 10.00

Issued to commemorate the 100th anniversary of the first postage stamps of Brazil and the second Philatelic Exposition (Brapex). Printed in panes of 6 sheets, perforated 12½ between. Each sheet is perforated on two or three sides. Size approximately 155x155mm. Inscriptions are printed in light brown.

Law Book
AP16

1943, Aug. 13 *Perf. 12½*

C54 AP16 1.20cr rose & lil rose 60 25

Issued to commemorate the second Inter-American Conference of Lawyers.

Semi-Postal Stamps of 1939 Surcharged in Red, Carmine or Black

AÉREO
20
Cts.

1944, Jan. 3 *Perf. 10½* Wmk. 249

C55 SP5 20c on 400r+200r ol grn & ol (R) 50 50
C56 SP5 40c on 400r+200r ol grn & ol (Bk) 1.00 35
C57 SP5 60c on 400r+200r ol grn & ol (C) 1.00 25
C58 SP5 1cr on 400r+200r ol grn & ol (Bk) 1.25 30
C59 SP5 1.20cr on 400r+200r ol grn & ol (C) 1.50 30
Nos. C55-C59 (5) 5.25 1.70

No. C59 is known with surcharge in black but its status is questioned.

Bartholomeu de Gusmão and the "Aerostat"
AP17

Engraved

1944, Oct. 23 *Perf. 12* Wmk. 268

C60 AP17 1.20cr rose car 50 20

Week of the Wing.

L. L. Zamenhof
AP18

1945, Apr. 16 Litho. *Perf. 11*

C61 AP18 1.20cr dl brn 60 30

Issued to commemorate the Esperanto Congress held in Rio de Janeiro, April 14–22, 1945.

Map of South America
AP19

Baron of Rio Branco
AP20

1945, Apr. 20

C62 AP19 1.20cr gray brn 50 25
C63 AP20 5cr rose lil 1.50 40

Issued to commemorate the centenary of the birth of José Maria de Silva Paranhos, Baron of Rio Branco.

Dove and Flags of American Republics
AP21

Perf. 12x11

1947, Aug. 15 Engr. Unwmkd.

C64 AP21 2.20cr dk bl grn 50 25

Issued to commemorate the Inter-American Defense Conference at Rio de Janeiro August–September, 1947.

Santos-Dumont Monument, St. Cloud, France
AP22

Bay of Rio de Janeiro and Rotary Emblem
AP23

1947, Nov. 15 Typo. *Perf. 11x12*

C65 AP22 1.20cr org brn & ol 50 25

Issued to commemorate the Week of the Wing and to honor the Santos-Dumont monument which was destroyed in World War II.

1948, May 16 Engraved. *Perf. 11.*

C66 AP23 1.20cr dp cl 60 40
C67 AP23 3.80r dl vio 1.25 40

Issued in honor of the 39th convention of Rotary International, Rio de Janeiro, May 1948.

Hotel Quitandinha, Petropolis
AP24

1948, July 10 Litho. Wmk. 267

C68 AP24 1.20cr org brn 35 25
C69 AP24 3.80cr violet 65 30

Issued to commemorate the International Exposition of Industry and Commerce, Petropolis, 1948.

Musician and Singers
AP25

1948, Aug. 13 Engraved. Unwmkd.

C70 AP25 1.20cr blue 50 20

Issued to commemorate the centenary of the establishment of the National School of Music.

Luis Batlle Berres
AP26

1948, Sept. 2 Typographed.

C71 AP26 1.70cr blue 35 25

Issued to commemorate the visit of President Luis Batlle Berres of Uruguay, September, 1948.

Merino Ram
AP27

Perf. 12x11.

1948, Oct. 10 **Wmk. 267**

C72 AP27 1.20cr dp org 70 30

Issued to publicize the International Livestock Exposition at Bagé.

Eucharistic Congress Seal
AP28

Engraved.

1948, Oct. 23 ***Perf. 11*** **Unwmkd.**

C73 AP28 1.20cr dk car rose 40 30

Issued to commemorate the 5th National Eucharistic Congress, Porto Alegre, October 24 to 31.

Souvenir Sheet

AP28a

Without Gum

1948, Dec. 14 **Engraved** ***Imperf.***

C73A AP28a Sheet of three 50.00 60.00

No. C73A contains one each of Nos. 674-676. Issued in honor of President Eurico Gaspar Dutra and the armed forces. Exists both with and without number on back. Measures 130x75mm. Marginal inscriptions typographed in black.

Church of Prazeres, Guararapes
AP29

Perf. 11½x12.

1949, Feb. 15 **Litho.** **Wmk. 267**

C74 AP29 1.20cr pink 1.50 75

Issued to commemorate the 300th anniversary of the Second Battle of Guararapes.

Thomé de Souza Meeting Indians
AP30

Perf. 11x12.

1949, Mar. 29 **Engr.** **Unwmkd.**

C75 AP30 1.20cr blue 35 25

Issued to commemorate the 400th anniversary of the founding of the City of Salvador.

A souvenir folder, issued with No. C75, has an engraved 20cr red brown postage stamp portraying John III printed on it, and a copy of No. C75 affixed to it and postmarked. Paper is laid, inscriptions are in red brown and size of folder front is 100x150mm. Price, $5.

Franklin D. Roosevelt
AP31

1949, May 20 ***Imperf.*** **Unwmkd.**

C76 AP31 3.80cr dp bl 1.00 80
a. Souvenir sheet 9.00 10.00

No. C76a measures 85x110mm., with deep blue inscriptions in upper and lower margins. It also exists with papermaker's watermark.

Joaquim Nabuco
AP32

1949, Aug. 30 ***Perf. 12***

C77 AP32 3.80cr rose lil 70 40
a. Wmk. 256, imperf. 25.00

Issued to commemorate the centenary of the birth of Joaquim Nabuco (1849–1910), lawyer and writer.

Maracanã Stadium
AP33

Soccer Player and Flag
AP34

Perf. 11x12, 12x11

1950, June 24 **Litho.** **Wmk. 267**

C78 AP33 1.20cr ultra & sal 1.25 40
C79 AP34 5.80cr bl, yel grn & yel 3.50 50

Issued to publicize the 4th World Soccer Championship at Rio de Janeiro.

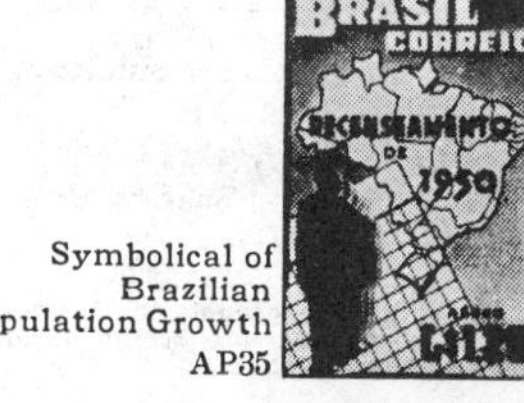

Symbolical of Brazilian Population Growth
AP35

1950, July 10 ***Perf. 12x11***

C80 AP35 1.20cr red brn 40 15

Issued to publicize the 6th Brazilian census.

J. B. Marcelino Champagnat
AP36

Engraved.

1956, Sept. 8 ***Perf. 11½*** **Wmk. 267**

C81 AP36 3.30cr rose lil 35 15

Issued to commemorate the 50th anniversary of the arrival of the Marist Brothers in Northern Brazil.

Santos-Dumont's 1906 Plane
AP37

1956, Oct. 16 **Photogravure**

C82 AP37 3cr dk bl grn 1.25 30
a. Souvenir sheet of four 1.75 1.75
b. 3cr dk car 35 25
C83 AP37 3.30cr brt ultra 30 10
C84 AP37 4cr dp cl 60 10
C85 AP37 6.50cr red brn 20 10
C86 AP37 11.50cr org red 1.25 35
Nos. C82-C86 (5) 3.60 95

Issued to commemorate the 50th anniversary of the first flight by Santos-Dumont.

No. C82a measures 123½x156mm. and contains four copies of No. C82b. Inscribed in dark carmine in four languages: "50TH ANNIVERSARY OF THE FIRST FLIGHT OF THE HEAVIER THAN THE AIR." Issued Oct. 14, 1956.

Lord Baden-Powell
AP38

1957, Aug. 1 **Unwmkd.**

Granite Paper

C87 AP38 3.30cr dp red lil 40 15

Issued to commemorate the centenary of the birth of Lord Baden-Powell, founder of the Boy Scouts.

U.N. Emblem, Soldier and Map of Suez Canal Area
AP39

Engraved.

1957, Oct. 24 ***Perf. 11½*** **Wmk. 267**

C88 AP39 3.30cr dk bl 30 20

Issued to honor the Brazilian contingent of the United Nations Emergency Force.

Basketball Player
AP40

1959, May 30 **Photo.** ***Perf. 11½***

C89 AP40 3.30cr brt red brn & bl 40 15

Brazil's victory in the World Basketball Championships of 1959.

Symbol of Flight
AP41

1959, Oct. 21 **Wmk. 267**

C90 AP41 3.30cr dp ultra 20 10

Issued to publicize Week of the Wing.

Caravelle
AP42

1959, Dec. 18 ***Perf. 11½***

C91 AP42 6.50cr ultra 15 10

Inauguration of Brazilian jet flights.

Pres. Adolfo Lopez Mateos
AP43

Pres. Dwight D. Eisenhower
AP44

1960, Jan. 19 **Photo.** **Wmk. 267**

C92 AP43 6.50cr brown 15 10

Issued to commemorate the visit of President Adolfo Lopez Mateos of Mexico.

1960, Feb. 23 ***Perf. 11½***

C93 AP44 6.50cr dp org 20 12

Visit of Pres. Dwight D. Eisenhower.

World Refugee Year Emblem
AP45

Tower at Brasilia
AP46

1960, Apr. 7 **Wmk. 268**
C94 AP45 6.50cr blue 15 10

Issued to publicize World Refugee Year, July 1, 1959–June 30, 1960.

Type of Regular Issue and AP46.

Designs: 3.30cr, Square of the Three Entities. 4cr, Cathedral. 11.50cr, Plan of Brasilia.

Perf. 11x11½, 11½x11

1960, Apr. 21 Photo. **Wmk. 267**

C95	A436	3.30cr	violet	20	15
C96	A436	4cr	blue	1.25	15
C97	AP46	6.50cr	rose car	15	15
C98	A436	11.50cr	brown	20	15

Issued to commemorate the inauguration of Brazil's new capital, Brasilia, Apr. 21, 1960.

Chrismon and Oil Lamp
AP47

1960, May 16 ***Perf. 11x11½***
C99 AP47 3.30cr lil rose 15 15

Issued to publicize the Seventh National Eucharistic Congress at Curitiba.

Cross, Sugarloaf Mountain and Emblem—AP48

1960, July 1 **Wmk. 267**
C100 AP48 6.50cr brt bl 15 10

Issued to commemorate the 10th Congress of the World Baptist Alliance, Rio de Janeiro.

Boy Scout
AP49

Caravel
AP50

1960, July 23 ***Perf. 11½x11***
C101 AP49 3.30cr org ver 15 10

Boy Scouts of Brazil, 50th anniversary.

1960, Aug. 5 Engraved Wmk. 268
C102 AP50 6.50cr black 15 10

Issued to commemorate the 500th anniversary of the birth of Prince Henry the Navigator.

Maria E. Bueno
AP51

Photogravure

1960, Dec. 15 ***Perf. 11x11½***
C103 AP51 6cr pale brn 15 10

Issued to commemorate the victory at Wimbledon of Maria E. Bueno, women's singles tennis champion.

War Memorial, Sugarloaf Mountain and Allied Flags
AP52

1960, Dec. 22 **Wmk. 268**
C104 AP52 3.30cr lil rose 15 10

Issued to commemorate the reburial of Brazilian servicemen of World War II.

Power Line and Map
AP53

Malaria Eradication Emblem
AP54

1961, Jan. 20 ***Perf. 11½x11***
C105 AP53 3.30cr lil rose 10 10

Issued to commemorate the inauguration of Three Marias Dam and hydroelectric station in Minas Gerais.

Engraved

1962, May 24 **Wmk. 267**
C106 AP54 21cr blue 10 10

Issued for the World Health Organization drive to eradicate malaria.

F. A. de Varnhagen
AP55

1966, Feb. 17 Photo. **Wmk. 267**
C107 AP55 45cr red brn 30 15

Issued to commemorate the 150th anniversary of the birth of Francisco Adolfo de Varnhagen, Viscount of Porto Seguro (1816–1878), historian and diplomat.

Map of the Americas and Alliance for Progress Emblem
AP56

1966, March 14 ***Perf. 11x11½***
C108 AP56 120cr grnsh bl & vio bl 40 15

Issued to commemorate the fifth anniversary of the Alliance for Progress.

A souvenir card contains one impression of No. C108, imperf. Black inscriptions. Size: 113x160mm.

Nun and Globe
AP57

Face of Jesus from Shroud of Turin
AP58

1966, Mar. 25 Photo. ***Perf. 11½x11***
C109 AP57 35cr violet 20 10

Issued to commemorate the centenary of the arrival of the teaching Sisters of St. Dorothea.

1966, June 3 Photo. **Wmk. 267**
C110 AP58 45cr brn org 25 15

Issued to commemorate Vatican II, the 21st Ecumenical Council of the Roman Catholic Church, Oct. 11, 1962–Dec. 8, 1965.

A souvenir card contains one impression of No. C110, imperf. Brown orange inscription and head of Jesus in margin. Size: 100x39mm.

Admiral Mariz e Barros
AP59

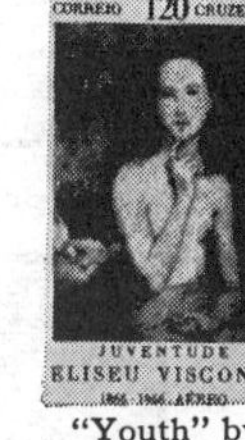

"Youth" by Eliseu Visconti
AP60

1966, June 13 Photo. **Wmk. 267**
C111 AP59 35cr red brn 20 10

Death centenary of Admiral Antonio Carlos Mariz e Barros, who died in the Battle of Itaperu.

1966, July 31 ***Perf. 11½x11***
C112 AP60 120cr red brn 50 20

Birth centenary of Eliseu Visconti, painter.

SPECIAL DELIVERY STAMP.

No. 191 Surcharged **1000 REIS EXPRESSO**

1930 ***Perf. 12*** **Unwmkd.**
E1 A62 1000r on 200r dp bl 3.00 1.50
a. Inverted surcharge 450.00

POSTAGE DUE STAMPS.

D1

D2

Typographed.

1889 ***Rouletted.*** **Unwmkd.**

J1	D1	10r	carmine	1.50	75
J2	D1	20r	carmine	1.75	1.30
J3	D1	50r	carmine	3.50	2.00
J4	D1	100r	carmine	2.00	1.00
J5	D1	200r	carmine	30.00	10.00
J6	D1	300r	carmine	4.00	5.00
J7	D1	500r	carmine	4.00	5.00
J8	D1	700r	carmine	7.00	7.00
J9	D1	1000r	carmine	7.00	7.00
		Nos. J1-J9 (9)		60.75	39.05

1890

J10	D1	10r	orange	50	20
J11	D1	20r	ultra	75	20
J12	D1	50r	olive	1.00	20
J13	D1	200r	magenta	3.00	30
J14	D1	300r	bl grn	2.00	65
J15	D1	500r	slate	2.50	2.25
J16	D1	700r	purple	3.50	4.00
J17	D1	1000r	dk vio	5.00	5.00
		Nos. J10-J17 (8)		18.25	12.80

Perf. 11 to 11½, 12½ to 14 and Compound.

1895-1901

J18	D2	10r	dk bl ('01)	1.00	50
J19	D2	20r	yel grn	10.00	3.00
J20	D2	50r	yel grn ('01)	6.25	6.25
J21	D2	100r	brick red	7.00	40
J22	D2	200r	violet	4.50	25
a.		200r	gray lil ('98)	6.50	1.25
J23	D2	300r	dl bl	3.00	1.25
J24	D2	2000r	brown	10.00	10.00
		Nos. J18-J24 (7)		41.75	21.65

1906 **Wmk. 97**
J25 D2 100r brick red 6.50 2.00

Wmkd. (97? or 98?)
J26 D2 200r violet 6.00 1.00
a. Wmk. 97 150.00 65.00
b. Wmk. 98 10.00 15.00

D3

D4

Engraved

1906–10 ***Perf. 12*** **Unwmkd.**

J28	D3	10r	slate	15	10
J29	D3	20r	brt vio	15	10
J30	D3	50r	dk grn	20	10
J31	D3	100r	carmine	1.50	50
J32	D3	200r	dp bl	65	25
J33	D3	300r	gray blk	25	50
J34	D3	400r	ol grn	80	75
J35	D3	500r	dk vio	30.00	30.00
J36	D3	600r	vio ('10)	1.00	1.00
J37	D3	700r	red brn	25.00	25.00
J38	D3	1000r	red	1.25	1.75
J39	D3	2000r	green	3.75	4.50
J40	D3	5000r	choc ('10)	75	5.00
		Nos. J28-J40 (13)		65.45	69.55

Typographed.

1919-23 ***Perf. 12½, 11, 11x10½.***

J41	D4	5r	red brn	15	30
J42	D4	10r	violet	30	30
J43	D4	20r	ol gray	25	20
J44	D4	50r	grn ('23)	25	25
J45	D4	100r	red	1.50	1.25
J46	D4	200r	blue	7.00	2.00
J47	D4	400r	brn ('23)	1.75	1.35
		Nos. J41-J47 (7)		11.20	5.65

Perf. 12½, 12½x13½.

1924-35 **Wmk. 100**

J48	D4	5r	red brn	25	20
J49	D4	100r	red	75	30
J50	D4	200r	sl bl ('29)	75	50
J51	D4	400r	dp brn ('29)	1.50	1.00
J52	D4	600r	dk vio ('29)	1.75	1.10
J53	D4	600r	org ('35)	75	50
		Nos. J48-J53 (6)		5.75	3.60

1924 ***Perf. 11x10½.*** **Wmk. 193**
J54 D4 100r red 30.00 30.00
J55 D4 200r sl bl 3.00 3.00

Perf. 11x10½, 13x13½.

1925-27 **Wmk. 101**

J56	D4	20r	ol gray	25	20
J57	D4	100r	red	1.00	40
J58	D4	200r	sl bl	3.00	50

J59	D4	400r brown	2.50	1.75
J60	D4	600r dk vio	5.00	3.50
		Nos. J56-J60 (5)	11.75	6.35

Wmkd. E U BRASIL Multiple. (218)

1929-30 ***Perf. 12½x13½.***

J61	D4	100r lt red	25	20
J62	D4	200r bl blk	40	25
J63	D4	400r brown	40	25
J64	D4	1000r myr grn	75	50

Perf. 11, 12½x13, 13.

1931-36 **Wmk. 222**

J65	D4	10r lt vio ('35)	15	10
J66	D4	20r blk ('33)	20	15
J67	D4	50r bl grn ('35)	30	25
J68	D4	100r rose red ('35)	30	25
J69	D4	200r sl bl ('35)	40	35
J70	D4	400r blk brn ('35)	1.75	1.75
J71	D4	600r dk vio	30	25
J72	D4	1000r myr grn	50	40
J73	D4	2000r brn ('36)	1.00	1.00
J74	D4	5000r ind ('36)	1.25	1.25
		Nos. J65-J74 (10)	6.15	5.75

1938 ***Perf. 11.*** **Wmk. 249**

J75	D4	200r sl bl	1.00	75

1940 **Typographed.** **Wmk. 256**

J76	D4	10r lt vio	50	50
J77	D4	20r black	50	50
J79	D4	100r rose red	50	50
J80	D4	200r myr grn	50	50

1942 **Wmk. 264**

J81	D4	10r lt vio	15	10
J82	D4	20r ol blk	15	10
J83	D4	50r lt bl grn	15	10
J84	D4	100r vermilion	30	30
J85	D4	200r gray bl	30	30
J86	D4	400r claret	30	30
J87	D4	600r rose vio	20	20
J88	D4	1000r dk bl grn	20	20
J89	D4	2000r dp yel brn	50	50
J90	D4	5000r indigo	30	30
		Nos. J81-J90 (10)	2.55	2.40

1949 **Wmk. 268**

J91	D4	10c pale rose lil	4.00	3.50
J92	D4	20r black	20.00	15.00

No. J92 exists in shades of gray ranging to gray olive.

OFFICIAL STAMPS

Pres. Affonso Penna
O1

Pres. Hermes da Fonseca
O2

Engraved

1906, Nov. 15 ***Perf. 12*** **Unwmkd.**

O1	O1	10r org & grn	20	15
O2	O1	20r org & grn	35	15
O3	O1	50r org & grn	1.20	15
O4	O1	100r org & grn	35	15
O5	O1	200r org & grn	65	15
O6	O1	300r org & grn	1.75	30
O7	O1	400r org & grn	3.50	65
O8	O1	500r org & grn	2.00	50
O9	O1	700r org & grn	3.00	2.00
O10	O1	1000r org & grn	2.00	75
O11	O1	2000r org & grn	2.50	90
O12	O1	5000r org & grn	7.00	90
O13	O1	10,000r org & grn	9.00	50
		Nos. O1-O13 (13)	33.50	7.25

The portrait is the same but the frame differs for each denomination of this issue.

1913, Nov. 15 **Center in Black**

O14	O2	10r gray	30	20
O15	O2	20r ol grn	30	20
O16	O2	50r gray	35	15
O17	O2	100r vermilion	65	15
O18	O2	200r blue	75	25
O19	O2	500r orange	2.50	60
O20	O2	600r violet	3.50	90
O21	O2	1000r blk brn	3.75	75
O22	O2	2000r red brn	4.50	75
O23	O2	5000r brown	5.00	1.00
O24	O2	10,000r black	7.00	3.75
O25	O2	20,000r blue	25.00	25.00
O26	O2	50,000r green	30.00	30.00
O27	O2	100,000r org red	100.00	100.00
O28	O2	500,000r brown	160.00	165.00
O29	O2	1,000,000r dk brn	175.00	185.00
		Nos. O14-O29 (16)	518.60	513.70

The portrait is the same on all denominations of this series but there are eight types of the frame. Though all the stamps are inscribed "Correio" (postage) the higher values were used only for fiscal purposes.

Pres. Wenceslau Braz
O3

Perf. 11, 11½

1919, Apr. 11 **Wmk. 100**

O30	O3	10r ol grn	40	1.00
O31	O3	50r green	50	50
O32	O3	100r rose red	75	40
O33	O3	200r dl bl	1.00	40
O34	O3	500r orange	6.50	7.50
		Nos. O30-O34 (5)	9.15	9.80

The official decree called for eleven stamps in this series but only five were issued.

See Nos. 293–297.

NEWSPAPER STAMPS.

N1

Lithographed.

1889, Feb. 1 ***Rouletted*** **Unwmkd.**

P1	N1	10r yellow	2.50	3.00
a.		Pair, imperf. between	125.00	175.00
P2	N1	20r yellow	6.00	7.00
P3	N1	50r yellow	10.00	6.00
P4	N1	100r yellow	4.00	3.00
P5	N1	200r yellow	2.50	1.50
P6	N1	300r yellow	3.00	1.50
P7	N1	500r yellow	17.50	8.00
P8	N1	700r yellow	3.00	10.00
P9	N1	1000r yellow	3.00	10.00
		Nos. P1-P9 (9)	51.50	50.00

1889, May 1

P10	N1	10r olive	50	20
P11	N1	20r green	50	25
P12	N1	50r brn yel	65	25
P13	N1	100r violet	1.35	1.00
P14	N1	200r black	1.25	1.00
P15	N1	300r carmine	8.00	8.00
P16	N1	500r green	40.00	35.00
P17	N1	700r ultra	20.00	25.00
P18	N1	1000r brown	5.00	15.00
		Nos. P10-P18 (9)	77.25	85.70

N2

N3

White Wove Paper Thin to Thick
Perf. 11 to 11½, 12½ to 14 and 12½ to 14x11 to 11½

1890 **Typographed**

P19	N2	10r blue	4.50	3.75
a.		10r ultra	4.50	3.75
P20	N2	20r emerald	17.50	7.50
P21	N2	100r violet	6.00	4.50

1890-93

P22	N3	10r blue	50	25
a.		10r ultra	1.25	50
P23	N3	10r ultra, *buff*	1.00	50
P24	N3	20r green	1.00	60
a.		20r emer	1.25	75
P25	N3	50r yel grn ('93)	5.00	4.00

POSTAL TAX STAMPS.

Icarus from the Santos-Dumont Monument at St. Cloud, France
PT1

Perf. 13½x12½, 11.

1933, Oct. 1 **Typo.** **Wmk. 222**

RA1	PT1	100r dp brn	50	10

No. RA1 was issued in commemoration of the Brazilian aviator, Santos-Dumont. It did not pay postage but its use was obligatory as a tax on all correspondence sent to countries in South America, the United States and Spain. Its use on correspondence to other countries was optional. The money obtained from its sale was added to funds for the construction of airports throughout Brazil.

Father Joseph Damien and Children
PT2

Father Bento Dias Pacheco
PT3

Perf. 12x11

1952, Nov. 24 **Litho.** **Wmk. 267**

RA2	PT2	10c yel brn	25	15

1953, Nov. 30

RA3	PT2	10c yel grn	25	15

1954, Nov. 22 **Photo.** ***Perf. 11½***

RA4	PT3	10c vio bl	20	15

1955, Nov. 24

RA5	PT3	10c dk car rose	20	15

1957, Nov. 24

RA6	PT3	10c org red	20	10

1958, Nov. 24

RA7	PT3	10c dp emer	15	10

1961, Nov. 24

RA8	PT3	10c red lil	15	10

1962, Nov. 24

RA9	PT3	10c chocolate	15	10

1963, Nov. 24

RA10	PT3	10c slate	15	10

1964, Nov. 24

RA11	PT3	2cr dp mag	15	10

1965, Nov. 24

RA12	PT3	2cr violet	15	10

1966, Nov. 24

RA13	PT3	2cr orange	15	10

1968, Nov. 25

RA14	PT3	5c brt yel grn	1.25	60

1969, Nov. 28

RA15	PT3	5c dp plum	15	10

Eunice Weaver
PT4

Father Nicodemos
PT5

1971, Nov. 24

RA16	PT4	10c sl grn	40	25

1973, Nov. 24

RA17	PT4	10c brt rose lil	20	10

1975, Nov. 24 **Litho.** **Unwmkd.**

RA18	PT5	10c sepia	20	10

Use of Nos. RA2–RA18 was required for one week. The tax was for the care and treatment of lepers.

POSTAL TAX SEMI-POSTAL STAMP.

Icarus
PTSP1

Typographed.

1947, Nov. 15 ***Perf. 11*** **Wmk. 267**

RAB1	PTSP1	40c + 10c brt red	35	20
a.		Pair, imperf. between	40.00	

Issued to commemorate Aviation Week, November 15-22, 1947, and compulsory on all domestic correspondence during that week.

BREMEN BRUNSWICK

See Early German States group preceding Germany.

BULGARIA

(bŭl·gâr'ĭ·ȧ; bo͝ol·gâr'ĭ·ȧ)

LOCATION—In southeastern Europe bordering on the Black Sea in the east and the Danube River on the north.

GOVT.—Republic.

AREA—42,796 sq. mi.

POP.—8,760,000 (est. 1976).

CAPITAL—Sofia.

In 1885 Bulgaria, then a principality under the suzerainty of the Sultan of Turkey, was joined by Eastern Rumelia. Her independence of Turkey was established in 1908.

100 Centimes = 1 Franc

100 Stotinki = 1 Lev (1881)

Lion of Bulgaria
A1 A2 A3

Wmk. 168

Typographed.

Laid Paper.

Wmkd. ЭЗГВ & Wavy Lines (168)

1879, June 1 *Perf. 14½x15*

1	A1	5c blk & yel	60.00	20.00
2	A1	10c blk & grn	150.00	40.00
3	A1	25c blk & vio	150.00	15.00
a.		Imperf.		
4	A1	50c blk & bl	175.00	35.00
5	A2	1fr blk & red	60.00	20.00

1881, June 10

6	A3	3s red & sil	15.00	2.25
7	A3	5s blk & org	20.00	2.25
a.		Background inverted		2,500.
8	A3	10s blk & grn	72.50	6.00
9	A3	15s red & grn	90.00	6.00
10	A3	25s blk & vio	225.00	22.50
11	A3	30s bl & fawn	25.00	6.50

1882, Dec. 4

12	A3	3s org & yel	90	60
a.		Background inverted		2,500.
13	A3	5s grn & pale grn	6.50	60
a.		5s rose & pale rose (error)	2,250.	1,750.
14	A3	10s rose & pale rose	9.00	60
15	A3	15s red vio & pale lil	6.50	35
16	A3	25s bl & pale bl	6.50	60
17	A3	30s vio & grn	7.50	75
18	A3	50s bl & pink	7.50	90

See also Nos. 207–210, 286.

A4

A5

Surcharged in Black, Carmine or Vermilion

1884, May 1

Typographed Surcharge

19	A4	3s on 10s rose (Bk)	175.00	50.00
20	A4	5s on 30s bl & fawn (C)	75.00	32.50
20A	A4	5s on 30s bl & fawn (Bk)	2,500.	2,500.
21	A5	15s on 25s bl (C)	200.00	32.50

On some values the surcharge may be found inverted or double.

1885, June

Lithographed Surcharge

21B	A4	3s on 10s rose (Bk)	40.00	32.50
21C	A4	5s on 30s bl & fawn (V)	40.00	32.50
21D	A5	15s on 25s bl (V)	40.00	32.50
22	A5	50s on 1fr blk & red (Bk)	150.00	125.00

Forgeries of Nos. 19–22 are plentiful.

Word below left star in oval has 5 letters

A6

Third letter below left star is "A"

A7

1885, May 25

23	A6	1s gray vio & pale gray	12.50	4.50
24	A7	2s sl grn & pale gray	12.50	3.50

Word below left star has 4 letters

A8

Third letter below left star is "b" with cross-bar in upper half

A9

A10

1886–87

25	A8	1s gray vio & pale gray	85	20
26	A9	2s sl grn & pale gray	85	20
27	A10	1 l blk & red ('87)	25.00	5.00

A11

Perf. 10½, 11, 11½, 13, 13½.

1889 Wove Paper. Unwmkd.

28	A11	1s lilac	20	5
29	A11	2s gray	75	10
30	A11	3s bis brn	50	10
31	A11	5s yel grn	25	4
a.		Vertical pair, imperf. between		
32	A11	10s rose	1.50	12
33	A11	15s orange	80	10
34	A11	25s blue	1.25	12
35	A11	30s dk brn	10.50	8
36	A11	50s green	75	30
37	A11	1 l org red	65	35
		Nos. 28-37 (10)	17.15	1.36

The 10s orange is a proof.

Nos. 28–34 are known imperforate. Price, set $225. See Nos. 39, 41–42.

No. 35 Surcharged in Black **15**

1892, Jan. 26

38	A11	15s on 30s brn	9.00	1.00
a.		Inverted surcharge	100.00	75.00

1894 *Perf. 10½, 11, 11½.*

Pelure Paper.

39	A11	10s red	10.00	50
a.		Imperf.	80.00	

No. 26 Surcharged in Red **01**

Wmkd. Wavy Lines. (168)

1895, Oct. 25 *Perf. 14½x15*

Laid Paper.

40	A9	1s on 2s sl grn & pale gray	60	20
a.		Inverted surcharge	9.00	6.00
b.		Double surcharge	90.00	90.00
c.		Pair, one without surcharge	175.00	175.00

This surcharge on No. 24 is a proof.

Wmkd. Coat of Arms in the Sheet.

1896, Apr. 30 *Perf. 11½, 13*

Wove Paper.

41	A11	2 l rose & pale rose	4.00	3.00
42	A11	3 l blk & buff	4.00	3.00

Coat of Arms

A14

Cherry Wood Cannon

A15

1896, Feb. 2 *Perf. 13*

43	A14	1s bl grn	50	15
44	A14	5s dk bl	50	15
45	A14	15s purple	75	30
46	A14	25s red	7.00	1.50

Baptism of Prince Boris.

Examples of Nos. 41–46 from sheet edges show no watermark.

Nos. 43, 45–46 were also printed on rough unwatermarked paper.

1901, Apr. 20 Litho. **Unwmkd.**

53	A15	5s carmine	1.25	1.50
54	A15	15s yel grn	1.25	1.50

Insurrection of Independence in April, 1876, 25th anniversary.

Exist imperf. Forgeries exist.

Nos. 30 and 36 Surcharged in Black

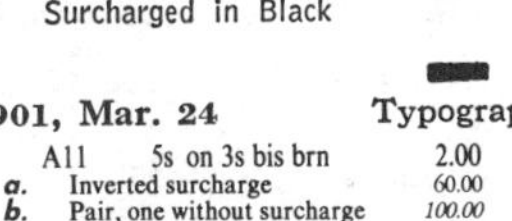

1901, Mar. 24 Typographed

55	A11	5s on 3s bis brn	2.00	1.25
a.		Inverted surcharge	60.00	60.00
b.		Pair, one without surcharge	100.00	100.00
56	A11	10s on 50s grn	2.50	1.25
a.		Inverted surcharge	70.00	70.00
b.		Pair, one without surcharge	100.00	100.00

Tsar Ferdinand

A17

Fighting at Shipka Pass

A18

ONE LEVA:

Type I. The numerals in the upper corners have, at the top, a sloping serif on the left side and a short straight serif on the right.

Type II. The numerals in the upper corners are of ordinary shape without the serif at the right.

1901–05 Typo. *Perf. 12½*

57	A17	1s vio & gray blk	15	4
58	A17	2s brnz grn & ind	15	3
a.		Imperf.		
59	A17	3s org & ind	20	6
60	A17	5s emer & brn	3.50	4
61	A17	10s rose & blk	2.25	4
62	A17	15s cl & gray blk	1.00	5
63	A17	25s bl & blk	1.00	5
64	A17	30s bis & gray blk	22.50	12
65	A17	50s dk bl & brn	1.25	9
66	A17	1 l red org & brnz grn, type I	3.00	25
67	A17	1 l brn red & brnz grn, II('05)	60.00	2.00
68	A17	2 l car & blk	6.00	1.50
69	A17	3 l sl & red brn	7.50	3.50
		Nos. 57-69 (13)	108.50	7.77

1902, Aug. 29 Litho. *Perf. 11½*

70	A18	5s lake	1.25	60
71	A18	10s bl grn	1.25	60
72	A18	15s blue	6.00	3.00

Battle of Shipka Pass, 1877.

Imperf. copies are proofs.

Excellent forgeries of Nos. 70 to 72 exist.

No. 62 Surcharged in Black **10**

1903, Oct. 1 *Perf. 12½*

73	A17	10s on 15s cl & gray blk	8.50	40
a.		Invtd. surch.	80.00	70.00
b.		Double surcharge	80.00	70.00
c.		Pair, one without surcharge	150.00	150.00
d.		10s on 10s rose & blk	350.00	350.00

Ferdinand in 1887 and 1907

A19

1907, Aug. 12 Litho. *Perf. 11½*

74	A19	5s dp grn	7.50	1.25
75	A19	10s red brn	13.00	1.25
76	A19	25s dp bl	20.00	2.50

Accession to the throne of Ferdinand I, 20th anniversary.

Nos. 74–76 imperf. are proofs. Nos. 74–76 exist in pairs imperforate between.

Stamps of 1889 Overprinted **1909**

1909

77	A11	1s lilac	1.50	50
a.		Inverted overprint	30.00	25.00
b.		Double overprint, one inverted	35.00	35.00
78	A11	5s yel grn	1.50	50
a.		Inverted ovpt.	30.00	30.00
b.		Double overprint	30.00	30.00

With Additional Surcharge **5** or **10**

79	A11	5s on 30s brn (Bk)	2.25	35
a.		"5" double	30.00	30.00
b.		"1990" for "1909"	1,000.	800.00
80	A11	10s on 15s org (Bk)	2.25	75
a.		Inverted surcharge	20.00	20.00
b.		"1909" omitted	40.00	40.00
81	A11	10s on 50s dk grn (R)	2.25	75
a.		"1990" for "1909"	150.00	150.00
b.		Black surcharge	75.00	75.00

Stamps of 1901 Surcharged with Value Only.

83	A17	5s on 15s cl & gray blk (Bl)	2.25	75
a.		Inverted surcharge	25.00	25.00
84	A17	10s on 15s cl & gray blk (Bl)	5.00	50
a.		Inverted surcharge	25.00	25.00
85	A17	25s on 30s brn bis & gray blk (R)	7.50	1.00
a.		Double surcharge	100.00	100.00
b.		"2" of "25" omitted	125.00	125.00
c.		Blue surcharge	400.00	250.00

1910

Surcharged in Blue

5

1910, Oct.

87	A17	1s on 3s org & ind	5.00	1.00
a.		"1910" omitted	25.00	
88	A17	5s on 15s cl & gray blk	1.75	75

Tsar Assen's Tower (Crown over lion)
A20

Tsar Ferdinand
A21

City of Trnovo
A22

Tsar Ferdinand
A23

Tsar Ferdinand
A24

Isker River
A25

Ferdinand
A26

Rila Monastery (Crown at upper right)
A27

Tsar and Princes
A28

Ferdinand in Robes of Ancient Tsars
A29

Monastery of Holy Trinity
A30

View of Varna
A31

1911, Feb. 14 Engraved *Perf. 12*

89	A20	1s myr grn	15	4
90	A21	2s car & blk	15	5
91	A22	3s lake & blk	40	8
92	A23	5s grn & blk	1.00	4
93	A24	10s dp red & blk	1.25	4
94	A25	15s brn bis	3.00	10
95	A26	25s ultra & blk	50	6
96	A27	30s bl & blk	7.50	15
97	A28	50s ocher & blk	17.50	20
a.		Center inverted		*3,000.*
98	A29	1 l chocolate	6.50	25
99	A30	2 l dl pur & blk	1.50	90
100	A31	3 l bl vio & blk	7.00	3.00
		Nos. 89-100 (12)	46.45	4.91

See also Nos. 114–120, 161–162.

Tsar Ferdinand
A32

1912, Aug. 2 Typo. *Perf. 12½*

101	A32	5s ol grn	3.00	1.00
a.		5s pale grn	*350.00*	*150.00*
102	A32	10s claret	4.50	2.25
103	A32	25s slate	6.00	2.50

25th year of reign of Tsar Ferdinand.

ОСВОБ. ВОЙНА

Nos. 89–95 Overprinted in Various Colors

1912-1913

1913, Aug. 6 Engr.

104	A20	1s myr grn (C)	20	10
105	A21	2s car & blk (Bl)	20	10
107	A22	3s lake & blk (Bl Bk)	30	15
108	A23	5s grn & blk (R)	20	8
109	A24	10s dp red & blk (BK)	45	7
110	A25	15s brn bis (G)	90	35
111	A26	25s ultra & blk	4.00	50
		Nos. 104-111 (7)	6.25	1.35

Victory over the Turks in Balkan War of 1912–1913.

10 ст.

No. 95 Surcharged in Red

1915, July 6

112	A26	10s on 25s ultra & blk	50	10

No. 28 Surcharged in Green

3 СТОТИНКИ

113	A11	3s on 1s lil	4.50	4.50

Types of 1911 Re-engraved.

1915, Nov. 7 *Perf. 11½, 14*

114	A20	1s dk bl grn	5	3
115	A23	5s grn & brn vio	1.25	5
116	A24	10s red brn & brnsh blk	20	4
117	A25	15s ol grn	30	4
118	A26	25s ind & blk	20	4
119	A27	30s ol grn & red brn	20	4
120	A29	1 l dk brn	60	40
		Nos. 114-120 (7)	2.80	64

No. 114 is 19½mm. wide; No. 89, 18½mm. No. 118 is 19¾mm. wide; No. 95, 18¼mm. No. 120 is 20mm. wide; No. 98, 19mm. The re-engraved stamps also differ from the 1911 issue in many details of design. Nos. 114-120 exist imperforate.

The 5s and 10s exist perf. 14x11½.

For Nos. 114–116 and 118 overprinted with Cyrillic characters and "1916–1917," see Romania Nos. 2N1–2N4.

Coat of Arms
A33

Peasant and Bullock
A34

Soldier and Mt. Sonichka
A35

View of Nish
A36

Town and Lake Okhrida
A37

Demir-Kapiya (Iron Gate)
A37a

View of Gevgeli
A38

Perf. 11½, 12½x13, 13x12½.

1917–19 Typographed

122	A33	5s green	40	15
123	A34	15s slate	15	6
124	A35	25s blue	15	6
125	A36	30s orange	15	10
126	A37	50s violet	75	30
126A	A37a	2 l brn org ('19)	75	35
127	A38	3 l claret	1.00	75
		Nos. 122-127 (7)	3.35	1.77

Commemorative of the liberation of Macedonia. A 1 l dark green was prepared but not issued. Price $1.50.

View of Veles
A39

Monastery of St. Clement at Okhrida
A40

1918 *Perf. 13x14*

128	A39	1s gray	5	4
129	A40	5s green	5	5

Tsar Ferdinand
A41

Plowing with Oxen
A42

1918, July 1 *Perf. 12½x13*

130	A41	1s dk grn	4	4
131	A41	2s dk brn	4	4
132	A41	3s indigo	35	15
133	A41	10s brn red	35	15

30th anniversary of Tsar Ferdinand's accession to the throne.

1919 *Perf. 13½x13.*

134	A42	1s gray	4	4

Sobranye Palace
A43

Tsar Boris III
A44

1919 *Perf. 11½x12, 12x11½*

135	A43	1s black	3	3
137	A43	2s ol grn	3	3

1919, Oct. 3

138	A44	3s org brn	3	3
139	A44	5s green	4	3
140	A44	10s rose red	3	3
141	A44	15s violet	3	3
142	A44	25s dp bl	3	3
143	A44	30s chocolate	15	4
144	A44	50s yel brn	10	3
		Nos. 138-144 (7)	41	22

First anniversary of enthronement of Tsar Boris III.

Nos. 135–144 exist imperforate.

Birthplace of Vazov at Sopot and Cherrywood Cannon
A47

"The Bear Fighter"—a Character from "Under the Yoke"
A48

Ivan Vazov in 1870 and 1920
A49

Vazov
A50

The Monk Paisii
A52

Homes of Vazov
at Plovdiv and Sofia
A51

1920, Oct. 20 Photo. *Perf. 11½*

147	A47	30s brn red	10	5
148	A48	50s dk grn	15	7
149	A49	1 l db	30	15
150	A50	2 l lt brn	85	35
151	A51	3 l blk vio	1.25	40
152	A52	5 l dp bl	1.50	50
		Nos. 147-152 (6)	4.15	1.52

Issued to commemorate the 70th birthday of Ivan Vazov (1850–1921), Bulgarian poet and novelist.

Several values of this series exist imperforate and in pairs imperforate between.

Tsar Ferdinand
A53 A54

Mt. Shar
A55

Bridge over Vardar River
A56

View of Ohrid
A57

Typographed.

1921, June 11 ***Perf. 13x14, 14x13***

153	A53	10s claret	5	5
154	A54	10s claret	5	5
155	A55	10s claret	5	5
156	A56	10s rose lil	5	5
157	A57	20s blue	30	25
		Nos. 153-157 (5)	50	45

Nos. 153–157 were intended to be issued in 1915 to commemorate the liberation of Macedonia. They were not put in use until 1921. A 50s violet was prepared but never placed in use. Price $1.

View of Sofia
A58

"The Liberator,"
Monument to Alexander II
A59

Monastery at Shipka Pass
A62

Tsar Boris III
A63

Harvesting Grain
A64

Tsar Assen's Tower
(No crown over lion)
A65

Rila Monastery
(Rosette at upper right)
A66

1921–23 Engraved ***Perf. 12***

158	A58	10s bl gray	8	3
159	A59	20s dp grn	8	3
160	A63	25s bl grn ('22)	8	3
161	A22	50s orange	8	3
162	A22	50s dk bl ('23)	3.00	3.00
163	A62	75s dl vio	20	4
164	A62	75s dp bl ('23)	35	12
165	A63	1 l carmine	35	15
166	A63	1 l dp bl ('22)	35	5
167	A64	2 l brown	40	6
168	A65	3 l brn vio	45	9
169	A66	5 l lt bl	3.00	30
170	A63	10 l vio brn	8.00	1.25
		Nos. 158-170 (13)	16.42	5.18

Bourchier in
Bulgarian Costume
A67

James David
Bourchier
A68

View of Rila Monastery
A69

1921, Dec. 31

171	A67	10s red org	5	5
172	A67	20s orange	5	5
173	A68	30s dp gray	7	5
174	A68	50s bluish gray	7	5
175	A68	1 l dl vio	25	7
176	A69	1½ l ol grn	25	15
177	A69	2 l dp grn	25	15
178	A69	3 l Prus bl	65	30
179	A69	5 l red brn	1.25	50
		Nos. 171-179 (9)	2.89	1.37

Issued to commemorate the death of James D. Bourchier, Balkan correspondent of the London Times.

Postage Due Stamps of 1919-22 Surcharged

10
СТОТИНКИ
a

1924

182	D6	10s on 20s yel	4	4
183	D6	20s on 5s gray grn	4	4
a.		20s on 5s emer	10.00	10.00
184	D6	20s on 10s vio	4	4
185	D6	20s on 30s org	4	4

Nos. 182 to 185 were used for ordinary postage.

Regular Issues of 1919-23 Surcharged in Blue or Red:

1 ЛЕВЪ
b

3 ЛЕВА
c

186	A43 (a)	10s on 1s blk (R)	4	4
187	A44 (b)	1 l on 5s emer (Bl)	15	4
188	A22 (c)	3 l on 50s dk bl (R)	30	15
189	A63 (b)	6 l on 1 l car (Bl)	90	30
		Nos. 182-189 (8)	1.55	69

The surcharge of No. 188 comes in three types: normal, thick and thin.

Nos. 182, 184–189 exist with inverted surcharge.

Lion of Bulgaria
A70 A71

Tsar Boris III
A72

New Sofia Cathedral
A73

Harvesting
A74

1925 Typo. ***Perf. 13, 11½***

191	A70	10s red & bl, *pink*	7	3
192	A70	15s car & org, *bl*	7	3
193	A70	30s blk & buff	7	4
a.		Cliche of 15s in plate of 30s		
194	A71	50s choc, *grn*	10	5
195	A72	1 l dl grn	60	4
196	A73	2 l dk grn & buff	1.25	5
197	A74	4 l lake & yel	1.25	5
		Nos. 191-197 (7)	3.41	29

Several values of this series exist imperforate and in pairs imperforate between. See also Nos. 199, 201.

Cathedral of Sveta Nedelya, Sofia,
Ruined by Bomb—A75

1926 ***Perf. 11½***

198	A75	50s gray blk	20	10

A76

A77

Type A72 Re-engraved.
(Shoulder at left does not touch frame.)

1926

199	A76	1 l gray	75	4
a.		1 l grn	75	4
201	A76	2 l ol brn	85	4

Center Embossed.

202	A77	6 l dp bl & pale lem	2.00	15
203	A77	10 l brn blk & brn org	6.50	1.25

Christo Botev
A78

Tsar Boris III
A79

1926, June 2

204	A78	1 l ol grn	50	18
205	A78	2 l sl vio	1.00	18
206	A78	4 l red brn	1.25	60

Issued to commemorate the 50th anniversary of the death of Christo Botev (1847-1876), Bulgarian revolutionary and poet.

Lion Type of 1881.

1927-29 ***Perf. 13.***

207	A3	10s dk red & db	10	3
208	A3	15s blk & org ('29)	10	4
209	A3	30s dk bl & bis brn ('28)	10	4
a.		30s ind & buff	10	4
210	A3	50s blk & rose red ('28)	15	3

1928, Oct. 3 ***Perf. 11½***

211	A79	1 l ol grn	1.25	4
212	A79	2 l dp brn	1.50	5

St. Clement
A80

Konstantin Miladinov
A81

George S. Rakovski
A82

Drenovo Monastery
A83

Paisii
A84

Tsar Simeon
A85

Lyuben Karavelov
A86

Vassil Levski
A87

Georgi Benkovski
A88

Tsar Alexander II
A89

1929, May 12

213	A80	10s dk vio	15	10
214	A81	15s vio brn	15	4
215	A82	30s red	15	4
216	A83	50s ol grn	30	4
217	A84	1 l org brn	75	10
218	A85	2 l dk bl	1.00	15
219	A86	3 l dl grn	2.25	50
220	A87	4 l ol brn	3.00	25
221	A88	5 l brown	2.25	40
222	A89	6 l Prus grn	2.75	1.00
		Nos. 213-222 (10)	12.75	2.62

Issued to commemorate the millenary of Tsar Simeon and the 50th anniversary of the liberation of Bulgaria from the Turks.

Royal Wedding Issue.

Tsar Boris and Fiancée, Princess Giovanna
A90

Queen Ioanna and Tsar Boris
A91

1930, Nov. 12 ***Perf. 11½***

223	A90	1 l green	30	30
224	A91	2 l dl vio	40	40
225	A90	4 l rose red	40	40
226	A91	6 l dk bl	45	45

Fifty-five copies of a miniature sheet incorporating one each of Nos. 223-226 were printed and given to royal, governmental and diplomatic personages.

Tsar Boris III
A92 A93

Perf. 11½, 12x11½, 13.

1931-37 **Unwmkd.**

227	A92	1 l bl grn	30	3
228	A92	2 l carmine	50	3
229	A92	4 l red org ('34)	1.00	5
230	A92	4 l yel org ('37)	40	4
231	A92	6 l dp bl	85	5
232	A92	7 l dp bl ('37)	35	6
233	A92	10 l sl blk	10.00	60
234	A92	12 l lt brn	50	15
235	A92	14 l lt brn ('37)	45	25
236	A93	20 l cl & org brn	1.25	45
		Nos. 227-236 (10)	15.60	1.71

Nos. 230–233 and 235 have outer bars at top and bottom as shown on cut A92; Nos. 227–229 and 234 are without outer bars.

See also Nos. 251, 252, 279–280, 287.

Balkan Games Issues.

Gymnast
A95

Soccer
A96

Riding
A97

Swimmer
A100

"Victory"
A101

Designs: 6 l, Fencing. 10 l, Bicycle race.

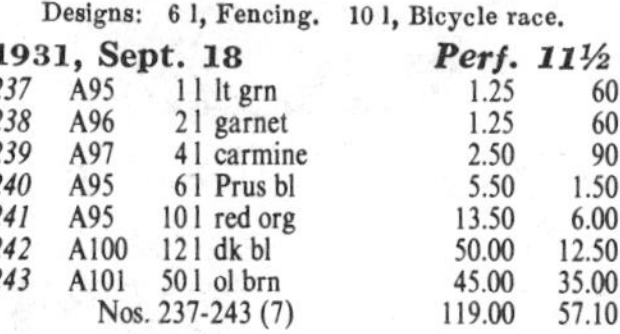

1931, Sept. 18 ***Perf. 11½***

237	A95	1 l lt grn	1.25	60
238	A96	2 l garnet	1.25	60
239	A97	4 l carmine	2.50	90
240	A95	6 l Prus bl	5.50	1.50
241	A95	10 l red org	13.50	6.00
242	A100	12 l dk bl	50.00	12.50
243	A101	50 l ol brn	45.00	35.00
		Nos. 237-243 (7)	119.00	57.10

1933, Jan. 5

244	A95	1 l bl grn	1.75	1.25
245	A96	2 l blue	3.00	1.25
246	A97	4 l brn vio	4.25	1.50
247	A95	6 l brt rose	9.00	2.50
248	A95	10 l ol brn	42.50	15.00
249	A100	12 l orange	90.00	32.50
250	A101	50 l red brn	175.00	160.00
		Nos. 244-250 (7)	325.50	214.00

Nos. 244–250 were sold only at the philatelic agency.

Boris Type of 1931.
Outer Bars at Top and Bottom Removed.

1933 ***Perf. 13.***

251	A92	6 l dp bl	90	4

Type of 1931 Surcharged in Blue **2**

1934

252	A92	2(l) on 3 l ol brn	7.00	50

Soldier Defending Shipka Pass
A102

Shipka Battle Memorial
A103

Color-Bearer
A104

Widow and Orphans
A106

Veteran of the War of Liberation, 1878
A105

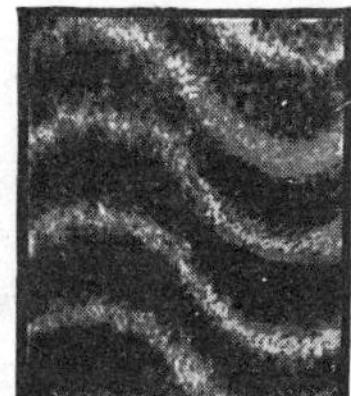
Wmk. 145

Wmkd. Wavy Lines. (145)

1934, Aug. 26 ***Perf. 10½, 11½***

253	A102	1 l green	60	40
254	A103	2 l pale red	60	25
255	A104	3 l bis brn	1.75	1.25
256	A105	4 l dk car	1.50	60
257	A104	7 l dk bl	2.75	2.00
258	A106	14 l plum	8.00	8.00
		Nos. 253-258 (6)	15.20	12.50

Issued to commemorate the unveiling of the Shipka Pass Battle memorial.

An unwatermarked miniature sheet incorporating one each of Nos. 253-258 was put on sale in 1938 in five cities at a price of 8,000 leva. Printing: 100 sheets.

1934, Sept. 21

259	A102	1 l brt grn	60	40
260	A103	2 l dl org	60	25
261	A104	3 l yellow	1.75	1.25
262	A105	4 l rose	1.50	60
263	A104	7 l blue	2.75	2.00
264	A106	14 l ol bis	8.00	8.00
		Nos. 259-264 (6)	15.20	12.50

An unwatermarked miniature sheet incorporating one each of Nos. 259–263 was issued.

Velcho A. Djamjiyata
A108

Capt. G. S. Mamarchev
A109

1935, May 5 ***Perf. 11½***

265	A108	1 l dp bl	1.25	35
266	A109	2 l maroon	1.25	40

Issued in commemoration of the centenary of a Bulgarian uprising against the Turks.

Soccer Game
A110

Cathedral of Alexander Nevski
A111

Symbolical of Victory
A113

Soccer Team
A112

Player and Trophy
A114

The Trophy
A115

1935, June 14

267	A110	1 l green	1.75	1.50
268	A111	2 l bl gray	4.75	2.25
269	A112	4 l crimson	7.75	3.75
270	A113	7 l brt bl	15.00	4.25
271	A114	14 l orange	15.00	6.00
272	A115	50 l lil brn	135.00	125.00
		Nos. 267-272 (6)	179.25	142.75

5th Balkan Soccer Tournament.

Gymnast on Parallel Bars
A116

Youth in "Yunak" Costume
A117

Girl in "Yunak" Costume
A118

Pole Vaulting
A119

Stadium, Sofia
A120

Yunak Emblem
A121

1935, July 10

273	A116	1 l green	2.50	1.50
274	A117	2 l lt bl	3.00	1.50
275	A118	4 l carmine	7.25	3.00
276	A119	7 l dk bl	7.25	4.50
277	A120	14 l dk brn	7.25	4.50
278	A121	50 l red	85.00	80.00
		Nos. 273-278 (6)	112.25	95.00

Issued to commemorate the 8th tournament of the Yunak Gymnastic Organization at Sofia, July 12-14.

Boris Type of 1931.
Wmkd. Wavy Lines. (145)

1935 *Perf. 12½, 13*

279	A92	1 l green	50	3
280	A92	2 l carmine	25.00	5

Janos Hunyadi
A122

King Ladislas Varnenchik
A123

Varna Memorial
A124

King Ladislas III
A125

Battle of Varna, 1444
A126

1935, Aug. 4 *Perf. 10½, 11½*

281	A122	1 l brn org	1.25	1.00
282	A123	2 l maroon	1.25	1.00
283	A124	4 l vermilion	5.50	3.75
284	A125	7 l dl bl	2.50	1.50
285	A126	14 l green	2.50	1.50
		Nos. 281-285 (5)	13.00	8.75

Issued to commemorate the Battle of Varna, and the death of the Polish King, Ladislas Varnenchik (1424-1444).

Lion Type of 1881.

1935 *Perf. 13.* **Wmk. 145**

286	A3	10s dk red & db	1.00	15

Boris Type of 1933.
Outer Bars at Top and Bottom Removed.

287	A92	6 l gray bl	75	10

Dimitr Monument
A127

Haji Dimitr
A128

Haji Dimitr and Stefan Karaja
A129

Taking the Oath
A130

Birthplace of Dimitr
A131

1935, Oct. 1 *Perf. 11½* **Unwmkd.**

288	A127	1 l green	1.75	60
289	A128	2 l brown	2.25	1.25
290	A129	4 l car rose	5.00	4.00
291	A130	7 l blue	7.00	6.50
292	A131	14 l orange	7.00	6.50
		Nos. 288-292 (5)	23.00	18.85

Issued to commemorate the 67th anniversary of the death of the Bulgarian patriots, Haji Dimitr and Stefan Karaja.

Numeral
A132

Lion
A133

1936-39 *Perf. 13x12½, 13*

293	A132	10s red org ('37)	4	3
294	A132	15s emerald	4	3
295	A133	30s maroon	8	3
296	A133	30s yel brn ('37)	8	3
297	A133	30s Prus bl ('37)	10	3
298	A133	50s ultra	12	3
299	A133	50s dk car ('37)	15	3
300	A133	50s sl grn ('39)	6	3
		Nos. 293-300 (8)	67	24

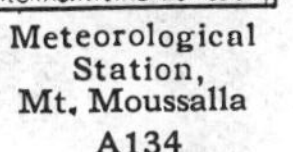

Meteorological Station, Mt. Moussalla
A134

Peasant Girl
A135

Town of Nessebr
A136

1936, Aug. 16 Photo. *Perf. 11½*

301	A134	1 l purple	1.40	1.00
302	A135	2 l ultra	1.40	90
303	A136	7 l dk bl	3.75	2.25

Issued to commemorate the fourth Geographical and Ethnographical Congress, Sofia, August, 1936.

Sts. Cyril and Methodius
A137

Displaying the Bible to the People
A138

1937, June 2

304	A137	1 l dk grn	25	20
305	A137	2 l dk plum	25	20
306	A138	4 l vermilion	45	30
307	A137	7 l dk bl	2.00	1.50
308	A138	14 l rose red	2.00	1.50
		Nos. 304-308 (5)	4.95	3.70

Millennium of Cyrillic alphabet.

Princess Marie Louise
A139

Tsar Boris III
A140

1937, Oct. 3

310	A139	1 l yel grn	35	8
311	A139	2 l brn red	35	12
312	A139	4 l scarlet	40	20

Issued in honor of Princess Marie Louise.

1937, Oct. 3

313	A140	2 l brn red	35	25

Issued to commemorate the 19th anniversary of the accession of Tsar Boris III to the throne. See No. B11.

National Products Issue.

Peasants Bundling Wheat
A141

Sunflower
A142

Wheat
A143

Chickens and Eggs
A144

Cluster of Grapes
A145

Rose and Perfume Flask
A146

Strawberries
A147

Girl Carrying Grape Clusters
A148

Rose
A149

Tobacco Leaves
A150

1938 *Perf. 13.*

316	A141	10s orange	4	4
317	A141	10s red org	4	4
318	A142	15s brt rose	30	6
319	A142	15s dp plum	30	6
320	A143	30s gldn brn	10	6
321	A143	30s cop brn	10	6
322	A144	50s black	10	6
323	A144	50s indigo	10	9
324	A145	1 l yel grn	75	7
325	A145	1 l green	75	7
326	A146	2 l rose pink	50	8
327	A146	2 l rose brn	50	6
328	A147	3 l dp red lil	1.00	20
329	A147	3 l brn lake	1.00	20
330	A148	4 l plum	80	20
331	A148	4 l gldn brn	80	20
332	A149	7 l vio bl	1.50	75
333	A149	7 l dp bl	1.50	75
334	A150	14 l dk brn	2.25	1.25
335	A150	14 l red brn	2.25	1.25
		Nos. 316-335 (20)	14.68	5.55

Several values of this series exist imperforate.

Crown Prince Simeon
A151 A153

Designs: 2 l, Same portrait as 1 l, value at lower left. 14 l, Similar to 4 l, but no wreath.

1938, June 16

336	A151	1 l brt grn	10	6
337	A151	2 l rose pink	12	6
338	A153	4 l dp org	13	8
339	A151	7 l ultra	75	50
340	A151	14 l dp brn	75	50
		Nos. 336-340 (5)	1.85	1.20

First birthday of Prince Simeon.

Tsar Boris III
A155 A156

Various Portraits of Tsar.

1938, Oct. 3

341	A155	1 l lt grn	10	6
342	A156	2 l rose brn	60	8
343	A156	4 l gldn brn	15	6
344	A156	7 l brt ultra	30	30
345	A156	14 l dp red lil	35	35
		Nos. 341-345 (5)	1.50	85

20th anniversary, reign of Tsar Boris III.

Early Locomotive
A160

Designs: 2 l, Modern locomotive. 4 l, Train crossing bridge. 7 l, Tsar Boris in cab.

1939, Apr. 26

346	A160	1 l yel grn	15	8
347	A160	2 l cop brn	15	8
348	A160	4 l red org	1.00	30
349	A160	7 l dk bl	2.25	1.50

Issued in commemoration of the 50th anniversary of Bulgarian State Railways.

Post Horns and Arrows
A164

Central Post Office, Sofia
A165

1939, May 14 Typographed

350	A164	1 l yel grn	12	6
351	A165	2 l brt car	18	6

Issued in commemoration of the 60th anniversary of the establishment of the postal system.

Gymnast on Bar
A166

Yunak Emblem
A167

Discus Thrower
A168

Athletic Dancer
A169

Weight Lifter
A170

1939, July 7 Photogravure

352	A166	1 l yel grn & pale grn	20	15
353	A167	2 l brt rose	20	15
354	A168	4 l brn & gldn brn	35	35
355	A169	7 l dk bl & bl	1.00	1.00
356	A170	14 l plum & rose vio	4.25	4.25
		Nos. 352-356 (5)	6.00	5.90

Issued to commemorate the 9th tournament of the Yunak Gymnastic Organization at Sofia, July 4–8.

Tsar Boris III
A171

Bulgaria's First Stamp
A172

1940-41 Typographed.

356A	A171	1 l dl grn ('41)	75	3
357	A171	2 l brt crim	20	4

1940, May 19 Photo. *Perf. 13*

Design: 20 l, Similar design, scroll dated "1840–1940."

358	A172	10 l ol blk	1.50	1.50
359	A172	20 l indigo	1.50	1.50

Centenary of first postage stamp. Exist imperf.

Peasant Couple and Tsar Boris
A174

Flags over Wheat Field and Tsar Boris
A175

Tsar Boris and Map of Dobrudja
A176

1940, Sept. 20

360	A174	1 l sl grn	5	4
361	A175	2 l rose red	10	7
362	A176	4 l dk brn	15	8
363	A176	7 l dk bl	60	40

Issued in commemoration of the return of Dobrudja from Romania.

Fruit
A177

Bees and Flowers
A178

Plowing
A179

Shepherd and Sheep
A180

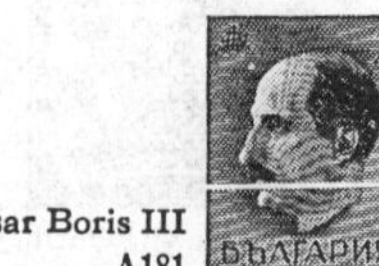

Tsar Boris III
A181

Perf. 10, 10½x11½, 11½, 13.

1940-44 Typographed. Unwmkd.

364	A177	10s red org	3	3
365	A178	15s blue	4	3
366	A179	30s ol brn ('41)	4	3
367	A180	50s violet	15	4
368	A181	1 l brt grn	5	3
369	A181	2 l rose car	7	3
370	A181	4 l red org	15	3
371	A181	6 l red vio ('44)	35	4
372	A181	7 l blue	35	4
373	A181	10 l bl grn ('41)	40	15
		Nos. 364-373 (10)	1.63	45

See No. 440.

1940-41 *Perf. 13.* Wmk. 145

373A	A180	50s vio ('41)	10	3
374	A181	1 l brt grn	10	3
375	A181	2 l rose car	15	3
376	A181	7 l dl bl	40	8
377	A181	10 l bl grn	60	20
		Nos. 373A-377 (5)	1.35	37

Watermarked vertically or horizontally.

P. R. Slaveikov
A182

Sofronii, Bishop of Vratza
A183

Saint Ivan Rilski
A184

Martin S. Drinov
A185

Monk Khrabr
A186

Kolio Ficheto
A187

1940, Sept. 23 Photo. Unwmkd.

378	A182	1 l brt bl grn	7	4
379	A183	2 l brt car	8	5
380	A184	3 l dp red brn	15	8
381	A185	4 l red org	12	8
382	A186	7 l dp bl	1.20	75
383	A187	10 l dp red brn	1.60	1.10
		Nos. 378-383 (6)	3.22	2.10

Issued in commemoration of the liberation of Bulgaria from the Turks in 1878.

Johannes Gutenberg
A188

N. Karastoyanov, First Bulgarian Printer
A189

1940, Dec. 16

384	A188	1 l sl grn	10	8
385	A189	2 l org brn	10	8

Issued in commemoration of the 500th anniversary of the invention of the printing press and the 100th anniversary of the first Bulgarian printing press.

Christo Botev
A190

Monument to Botev
A192

Botev with his Insurgent Band
A191

1941, May 3

386	A190	1 l dk bl grn	10	5
387	A191	2 l crim rose	15	5
388	A192	3 l dk brn	75	60

Issued in honor of Christo Botev, patriot and poet.

Palace of Justice, Sofia
A193

Designs: 20 l, Workers' hospital. 50 l, National Bank.

1941-43 Engraved *Perf. 11½*

389	A193	14 l lt gray brn ('43)	30	15
390	A193	20 l gray grn ('43)	45	25
391	A193	50 l lt bl gray	2.50	2.00

Macedonian Woman
A196

City of Okhrida
A200

Outline of Macedonia and Tsar Boris III
A197

View of Aegean Sea
A198

Poganovski Monastery
A199

1941, Oct. 3 Photo. *Perf. 13*

392	A196	1 l sl grn	5	4
393	A197	2 l crimson	6	4
394	A198	2 l red org	9	4
395	A199	4 l org brn	10	8
396	A200	7 l dp gray bl	60	50
		Nos. 392-396 (5)	90	70

Issued to commemorate the acquisition of Macedonian territory from neighboring countries.

Peasant Working in a Field
A201

Designs: 15s, Plowing. 30s, Apiary. 50s, Women harvesting fruit. 3 l, Shepherd and sheep. 5 l, Inspecting cattle.

1941-44

397	A201	10s dk vio	4	4
398	A201	10s dk bl	4	4
399	A201	15s Prus bl	4	4
400	A201	15s dk ol brn	4	4
401	A201	30s red org	5	4
402	A201	30s dk sl grn	5	3
403	A201	50s bl vio	6	3
404	A201	50s red lil	8	3
405	A201	3 l hn brn	75	40
406	A201	3 l dk brn ('44)	1.75	1.75
407	A201	5 l sepia	90	75
408	A201	5 l vio bl ('44)	1.75	1.75
		Nos. 397-408 (12)	5.55	4.94

Girls Singing
A207

Boys in Camp
A208

Raising Flag
A209

Folk Dancers
A211

Camp Scene
A210

1942, June 1 Photogravure

409	A207	1 l dk bl grn	8	5
410	A208	2 l scarlet	15	6
411	A209	4 l ol gray	15	6
412	A210	7 l dp bl	20	15
413	A211	14 l fawn	40	30
		Nos. 409-413 (5)	98	62

National "Work and Joy" movement.

Wounded Soldier
A212

Soldier's Farewell
A213

Designs: 4 l, Aiding wounded soldier. 7 l, Widow and orphans at grave. 14 l, Tomb of Unknown Soldier. 20 l, Queen Ioanna visiting wounded.

1942, Sept. 7

414	A212	1 l sl grn	8	6
415	A213	2 l brt rose	8	6
416	A213	4 l yel org	8	5
417	A213	7 l dk bl	9	5
418	A213	14 l brown	12	8
419	A213	20 l ol blk	20	10
		Nos. 414-419 (6)	65	40

Issued to aid war victims. No. 419 was printed in sheets of 50, alternating with 50 labels.

Legend of Kubrat
A218

Cavalry Charge
A219

Designs: 30s, Rider of Madara. 50s, Christening of Boris I. 1 l, School, St. Naum. 2 l, Crowning of Tsar Simeon by Boris I. 3 l, Golden era of Bulgarian literature. 4 l, Sentencing of the Bogomil Basil. 5 l, Proclamation of 2nd Bulgarian Empire. 7 l, Ivan Assen II at Trebizond. 10 l, Deporting the Patriarch Jeftimi. 14 l, Wandering minstrel. 20 l, Monk Paisii. 30 l, Monument, Shipka Pass.

1942, Oct. 12

420	A218	10s bluish blk	4	4
421	A219	15s Prus grn	4	4
422	A219	30s dk rose vio	4	4
423	A219	50s indigo	4	4
424	A219	1 l sl grn	5	5
425	A219	2 l crimson	5	5
426	A219	3 l brown	5	5
427	A219	4 l orange	6	6
428	A219	5 l grnsh blk	6	6
429	A219	7 l dk bl	7	7
430	A219	10 l brn blk	15	15
431	A219	14 l ol blk	15	15
432	A219	20 l hn brn	50	50
433	A219	30 l black	75	75
		Nos. 420-433 (14)	2.05	2.05

Tsar Boris III
A234

Wmk. 275

Designs: Various portraits of Tsar.

Wmkd. Entwined Curved Lines. (275)

Perf. 13, Imperf.

1944, Feb. 28 Photogravure

Frames in Black.

434	A234	1 l ol grn	5	5
435	A234	2 l red brn	12	12
436	A234	4 l brown	14	14
437	A234	5 l gray vio	25	25
438	A234	7 l sl bl	25	25
		Nos. 434-438 (5)	81	81

Issued in memory of Tsar Boris III (1894–1943).

Tsar Simeon II
A239

Perf. 11½, 13

1944, June 12 Typo. Unwmkd.

439	A239	3 l red org	30	4

Shepherd Type of 1940

1944

440	A180	50s yel grn	25	10

Parcel Post Stamps of 1944 Overprinted in Black or Orange

ВСИЧКО ЗА ФРОНТА

1945, Jan. 25 *Perf. 11½*

448	PP5	1 l dk car	3	3
449	PP5	7 l rose lil	5	3
450	PP5	20 l org brn	7	3
451	PP5	30 l dk brn car	15	3
452	PP5	50 l red org	30	15
453	PP5	100 l bl (O)	70	35

The overprint reads: "Everything for the Front".

No. 448 with Additional Surcharge of New Value in Black.

454	PP5	4 l on 1 l dk car	5	3
		Nos. 448-454 (7)	1.35	65

Nos. 368 to 370 Overprinted in Black

СЪБИРАЙТЕ СТАРО ЖЕЛЪЗО

1945, Mar. 15 *Perf. 11½, 13*

455	A181	1 l brt grn	5	3
456	A181	2 l rose car	8	3
457	A181	4 l red org	12	4

The overprint reads: "Collect old iron."

Overprinted in Black

СЪБИРАЙТЕ ХАРТИЕНИ ОТПАДЪЦИ

458	A181	1 l brt grn	5	3
459	A181	2 l rose car	8	3
460	A181	4 l red org	12	4

The overprint reads: "Collect discarded paper."

Overprinted in Black

СЪБИРАЙТЕ ВСЪКАКВИ ПАРЦАЛИ

461	A181	1 l brt grn	5	3
462	A181	2 l rose car	8	3

463	A181	4 l red org	12	4
		Nos. 455-463 (9)	75	30

The overprint reads: "Collect all kinds of rags."

Oak Tree
A245

Imperf., Perf. 11½.

1945 Lithographed Unwmkd.

464	A245	4 l vermilion	8	6
465	A245	10 l blue	8	6

Imperf.

466	A245	50 l brn lake	25	20

Slav Congress, Sofia, March, 1945.

A246

A247

Lion Rampant
A248

Arms of Bulgaria
A249

A251

A252

Arms of Bulgaria
A253 A254

Two types of 2 l and 4 l: Type I: Large crown close to coat of arms. Type II: Smaller crown standing high.

1945-46 Photogravure *Perf. 13*

469	A246	30s yel grn	3	3
470	A247	50s pck grn	3	3
471	A248	1 l dk grn	3	3
472	A249	2 l choc (I)	4	3
a.		Type II	3	3
473	A249	4 l dk bl (I)	8	3
a.		Type II	5	3
475	A251	5 l red vio	5	3
476	A251	9 l sl gray	6	3
477	A252	10 l Prus bl	8	3
478	A253	15 l brown	10	4
479	A254	20 l carmine	20	6
480	A254	20 l gray blk	20	6
		Nos. 469-480 (11)	90	40

Breaking Chain A255 — 1 Lev Coin A256

Water Wheel A257 — Coin and Symbols of Agriculture and Industry A258

Lithographed.

1945, June 4 *Imperf.* Unwmkd.

Laid Paper.

481	A255	50 l brn red, *pink*	10	8
482	A255	50 l org, *pink*	10	8
483	A256	100 l gray bl, *pink*	15	12
484	A256	100 l brn, *pink*	15	12
485	A257	150 l dk ol gray, *pink*	35	25
486	A257	150 l dl car, *pink*	35	25
487	A258	200 l dp bl, *pink*	60	50
488	A258	200 l ol grn, *pink*	60	50
		Nos. 481-488 (8)	2.40	1.90

Souvenir Sheets.

489	Sheet of four	2.50	2.50
a.	50 l vio bl	25	25
b.	100 l vio bl	25	25
c.	150 l vio bl	25	25
d.	200 l vio bl	25	25
490	Sheet of four	2.50	2.50
a.	50 l brn org	25	25
b.	100 l brn org	25	25
c.	150 l brn org	25	25
d.	200 l brn org	25	25

Nos. 481 to 490 were issued to publicize Bulgaria's Liberty Loan.

Nos. 489 and 490 measure 90x122mm. and contain one each of types A255-A258. Margin inscription: "March 9, 1935, Sofia" in Bulgarian characters.

Olive Branch
A260

1945, Sept. 1 Typo. *Perf. 13*

491	A260	10 l org brn & yel grn	7	5
492	A260	50 l dl red & dp grn	30	15

Victory of Allied Nations, World War II.

September 9, 1944
A261

Numeral and Broken Chain
A262

1945, Sept. 7

493	A261	1 l gray grn	3	3
494	A261	4 l dp bl	3	3
495	A261	5 l rose lil	3	3
496	A262	10 l lt bl	5	3
497	A262	20 l brt car	25	12
498	A261	50 l brt bl grn	60	30
499	A261	100 l org brn	65	50
		Nos. 493-499 (7)	1.64	1.04

Issued to commemorate the 1st anniversary of Bulgaria's liberation.

Old Postal Savings Emblem— A263

First Bulgarian Postal Savings Stamp
A264

Child Putting Coin in Bank
A265

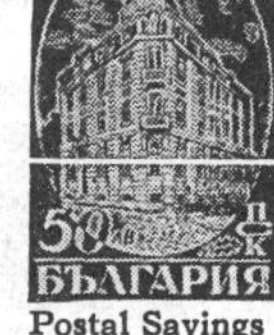

Postal Savings Building, Sofia
A266

1946, Apr. 12

500	A263	4 l brn org	6	4
501	A264	10 l dk ol	15	5
502	A265	20 l ultra	15	6
503	A266	50 l sl gray	75	75

Issued to commemorate the 50th anniversary of Bulgarian Postal Savings.

Refugee Children
A267

Nurse Assisting Wounded Soldier
A269

Wounded Soldier
A268

Design: 35 l, 100 l, Red Cross hospital train.

1946, Apr. 4

Cross in Carmine

504	A267	2 l dk ol	5	5
505	A268	4 l violet	10	5
506	A267	10 l plum	10	6
507	A268	20 l ultra	12	6
508	A269	30 l brn org	15	10
509	A268	35 l gray blk	20	20
510	A269	50 l vio brn	30	30
511	A268	100 l gray brn	1.00	1.00
		Nos. 504-511 (8)	2.02	1.82

See also Nos. 553 to 560.

Advancing Troops
A271

Grenade Thrower
A272

Attacking Planes
A274

Designs: 5 l, Horse-drawn cannon. 9 l, Engineers building pontoon bridge. 10 l, 30 l, Cavalry charge. 40 l, Horse-drawn supply column. 50 l, Motor transport column. 60 l, Infantry, tanks and planes.

1946, Aug. 9 Typo. Unwmkd.

512	A271	2 l dk red vio	4	4
513	A272	4 l dk gray	4	4
514	A271	5 l dk org red	4	4
515	A274	6 l blk brn	5	4
516	A271	9 l rose lil	5	4
517	A271	10 l dp vio	5	4
518	A271	20 l dp bl	30	15
519	A271	30 l red org	30	15
520	A271	40 l dk ol bis	35	20
521	A271	50 l dk grn	35	20
522	A271	60 l red brn	50	35
		Nos. 512-522 (11)	2.07	1.29

Bulgaria's participation in World War II.

Arms of Russia and Bulgaria
A279

Lion Rampant
A280

1946, May 23

523	A279	4 l red org	8	8
525	A279	20 l turq grn	20	15

Issued to commemorate the Congress of the Bulgarian-Soviet Association, May 1946.

The 4 l exists in dk car rose and 20 l in blue, price, set $10.

1946, May 25 *Imperf.*

526	A280	20 l blue	35	25

Issued to commemorate the Day of the Postage Stamp, May 26, 1946.

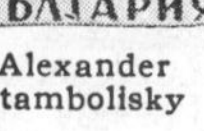

Alexander Stambolisky
A281

Flags of Albania, Romania, Bulgaria and Jugoslavia
A282

1946, June 13 *Perf. 12*

527	A281	100 l red org	3.50	3.50

Issued to commemorate the 23rd anniversary of the death of Alexander Stambolisky, agrarian leader.

1946, July 6 *Perf. 11½*

528	A282	100 l blk brn	90	90

Issued to publicize the 1946 Balkan Games.
Sheet of 100 arranged so that all stamps are tête bêche vertically and horizontally, except two center rows in left pane which provide 10 vertical pairs that are not tête bêche vertically.

St. Ivan Rilski
A283

Rila Monastery
A286

A284

A285

Views of Rila Monastery
A287

1946, Aug. 26

529	A283	1 l red brn	7	6
530	A284	4 l blk brn	8	6
531	A285	10 l dk grn	15	8
532	A286	20 l dp bl	20	10
533	A287	50 l dk red	90	75
		Nos. 529-533 (5)	1.40	1.05

Millenary of Rila Monastery.

People's Republic

A288

1946, Sept. 15 Typographed

534	A288	4 l brn lake	4	4
535	A288	20 l dl bl	5	5
536	A288	50 l ol bis	20	20

No. 535 is inscribed "BULGARIA" in Latin characters.
Issued to commemorate the referendum of September 8, 1946, resulting in the establishment of the Bulgarian People's Republic.

Partisan Army
A289

Snipers
A290

Soldiers: Past and Present
A291

Design: 30 l, Partisans advancing.

1946, Dec. 2

537	A289	1 l vio brn	3	3
538	A290	4 l dl grn	4	3
539	A291	5 l chocolate	5	3
540	A290	10 l crimson	5	4
541	A289	20 l ultra	30	15
542	A290	30 l ol bis	30	15
543	A291	50 l black	35	30
		Nos. 537-543 (7)	1.12	73

Relief Worker and Children
A294

Child with Gift Parcels
A295

Waiting for Food Distribution
A296

Mother and Child
A297

1946, Dec. 30

545	A294	1 l dk vio brn	3	3
546	A295	4 l brt red	4	4
547	A295	9 l ol bis	5	4
548	A294	10 l sl gray	10	4
549	A296	20 l ultra	15	6
550	A297	30 l dp brn org	15	10
551	A296	40 l maroon	30	20
552	A294	50 l pck grn	50	40
		Nos. 545-552 (8)	1.32	91

"Bulgaria" is in Latin characters on No. 548.

Red Cross Types of 1946

1947, Jan. 31

Cross in Carmine

553	A267	2 l ol bis	5	5
554	A268	4 l ol blk	5	5
555	A267	10 l bl grn	10	10
556	A268	20 l brt bl	25	25
557	A269	30 l yel grn	35	35
558	A268	35 l grnsh gray	40	40
559	A269	50 l hn brn	60	60
560	A268	100 l dk bl	1.00	1.00
		Nos. 553-560 (8)	2.80	2.80

Laurel Branch, Allied and Bulgarian Emblems
A298

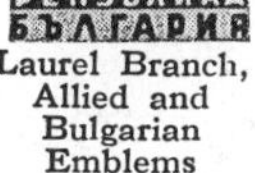
Dove of Peace
A299

1947, Feb. 28

561	A298	4 l olive	5	5
562	A299	10 l brn red	6	6
563	A299	20 l dp bl	20	20

Issued to commemorate the return to peace at the close of World War II. "Bulgaria" in Latin characters on No. 563.

A302

Guerrilla Fighters
A303 A304

1947, Jan. 21 *Perf. 11½*

567	A302	10 l choc & brn org	30	30
568	A303	20 l dk bl & bl	30	30
569	A304	70 l dp cl & rose	15.00	15.00

Issued to honor the anti-fascists.

Hydroelectric Station
A305

Miner
A306

Symbols of Industry
A307

Tractor
A308

1947, Aug. 6

570	A305	4 l ol grn	8	5
571	A306	9 l red brn	15	12
572	A307	20 l dp bl	25	25
573	A308	40 l ol brn	60	60

Exhibition Building
A309

Former Home of Alphonse de Lamartine
A310

Symbols of Agriculture and Horticulture
A311

Perf. 11x11½, 11½x11.

1947, Aug. 31 Litho. Unwmkd.

574	A309	4 l scarlet	7	3
575	A310	9 l brn lake	9	5
576	A311	20 l brt ultra	35	12

Issued to publicize the Plovdiv International Fair, 1947. See No. C54.

Basil Evstatiev Aprilov
A312

1947, Oct. 19 Photo. *Perf. 11*

577	A312	40 l brt ultra	40	25

Issued to commemorate the centenary of the death of Basil Evstatiev Aprilov, educator and historian. See also No. 603.

Balkan Games Issue.

Bicycle Race
A313

Basketball
A314

Chess
A315

Designs: 20 l, Soccer players. 60 l, Four flags of participating nations.

1947, Sept. 29 Typo. *Perf. 11½*

578	A313	2 l plum	30	20
579	A314	4 l dk ol grn	30	20
580	A315	9 l org brn	60	20
581	A315	20 l brt ultra	1.25	30
582	A315	60 l vio brn	2.50	1.50
		Nos. 578-582 (5)	4.95	2.40

People's Theater, Sofia
A316

National Assembly
A317

Central Post Office, Sofia
A318

Presidential Mansion
A319

1947-48 Typographed *Perf. 12½*

583	A316	50s yel grn	4	3
584	A317	50s yel grn	4	3
585	A318	1 l green	4	3
586	A319	1 l green	4	3
587	A316	2 l brn lake	4	3
588	A317	2 l lt brn	4	3
589	A316	4 l dp bl	6	4
590	A317	4 l dp bl	8	4
591	A316	9 l carmine	40	4
592	A317	20 l dp bl	85	30
		Nos. 583-592 (10)	1.63	60

On Nos. 583–592 inscription reads "Bulgarian Republic." No. 592 is inscribed in Latin characters.

Redrawn.

НАРОДНА

added to inscription.

593	A318	1 l green	6	3
594	A318	2 l brn lake	8	3
595	A318	4 l dp bl	10	4

Cyrillic inscription beneath design on Nos. 593–595 reads "Bulgarian People's Republic".

Geno Kirov
A320

Actors' Portraits: 1 l, Zlatina Nedeva. 2 l, Ivan Popov. 3 l, Athanas Kirchev. 4 l, Elena Snejina. 5 l, Stoyan Bachvarov.

Lithographed

1947, Dec. 8 *Perf. 10½* Unwmkd.

596	A320	50s bis brn	5	4
597	A320	1 l lt bl grn	5	4
598	A320	2 l sl grn	6	5
599	A320	3 l dp bl	10	6
600	A320	4 l scarlet	12	8
601	A320	5 l red brn	12	8
		Nos. 596-601, B22-B26 (11)	1.95	1.80

National Theater, 50th anniversary.

Merchant Ship "Fatherland"
A321

1947, Dec. 19

602	A321	50 l Prus bl, *cr*	60	35

B. E. Aprilov
A322

Bulgarian Worker
A323

1948, Feb. 19 *Perf. 11*

603	A322	4 l brn car, *cr*	10	10

Issued to commemorate the centenary of the death of Basil Evstatiev Aprilov, educator and historian.

1948, Feb. 29 Photo. *Perf. 11½x12*

604	A323	4 l dp bl, *cr*	20	10

2nd Bulgarian Workers' Congress.

Self-education
A324

Accordion Player
A325

Factory Recess
A326

Girl Throwing Basketball
A327

1948, Mar. 31 Photogravure

605	A324	4 l red	6	6
606	A325	20 l dp bl	20	15
607	A326	40 l dl grn	30	15
608	A327	60 l brown	80	50

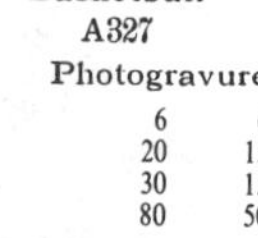

Nicholas Vaptzarov
A328

Portraits: 9 l, P. K. Iavorov. 15 l, Christo Smirnenski. 20 l, Ivan Vazov. 45 l, P. R. Slaveikov.

1948, May 18 Litho. *Perf. 11*

Cream Paper.

611	A328	4 l brt ver	7	4
612	A328	9 l lt brn	8	5
613	A328	15 l claret	10	6
614	A328	20 l dp bl	15	15
615	A328	45 l green	50	50
		Nos. 611-615 (5)	90	80

Soviet Soldier
A329

Civilians Offering Gifts to Soldiers
A330

Designs: 20 l, Soldiers, 1878 and 1944. 60 l, Stalin and Spasski Tower.

1948, July 5 Photogravure

Cream Paper.

616	A329	4 l brn org	6	5
617	A330	10 l ol grn	6	5
618	A330	20 l dp bl	15	12
619	A329	60 l ol brn	65	60

Issued to honor the Soviet Army.

Demeter Blagoev
A331

Monument to Bishop Andrey
A332

Designs: 9 l, Gabriel Genov. 60 l, Marching youths.

1948, Sept. 6 Lithographed

Cream Paper.

620	A331	4 l dk brn	4	4
621	A331	9 l brn org	5	5
622	A332	20 l dp bl	12	9
623	A332	60 l brown	90	75

No. 623 is inscribed in Cyrillic characters.
Issued to commemorate the 25th anniversary of the National Insurrection of 1923.

Christo Smirnenski
A333

Battle of Grivitza, 1877
A334

1948, Oct. 2 Photo. *Perf. 11½*

Cream Paper

624	A333	4 l blue	7	4
625	A333	16 l red brn	15	6

Issued to commemorate the 25th anniversary of the death of Christo Smirnenski, poet, 1898–1923.

1948, Nov. 1

626	A334	20 l blue	20	12

Issued to publicize Romanian-Bulgarian friendship. See Nos. C56–C57.

Bath, Gorna Banya
A335

Bath, Bankya
A336

Mineral Bath, Sofia
A337

Maliovitza
A338

1948-49 Typographed. *Perf. 12½.*

627	A335	2 l red brn	15	3
628	A336	3 l red org	15	3
629	A337	4 l dp bl	20	3
630	A338	5 l vio brn	18	3
631	A336	10 l red vio	25	3
632	A338	15 l ol grn ('49)	35	5
633	A335	20 l dp bl	1.25	20
		Nos. 627-633 (7)	2.53	40

Latin characters on No. 633. See also No. 653.

Emblem of the Republic
A339

1948–50

634	A339	50s red org	4	3
634A	A339	50s org brn ('50)	6	3
635	A339	1 l green	6	3
636	A339	9 l black	20	8

Botev's Birthplace, Kalofer
A340

Christo Botev
A341

Cyrillic Inscription:
"Chr. Botev 1848-1948."

Designs: 9 l, Steamer "Radetzky." 15 l, Kalofer village. 20 l, Botev in uniform. 40 l, Botev's mother. 50 l, Pen, pistol and wreath.

Photogravure.

1948, Dec. 21 *Perf. 11x11½, 11½*

Cream Paper.

638	A340	1 l dk grn	3	3
639	A341	4 l vio brn	4	3
640	A340	9 l violet	5	3
641	A340	15 l brown	8	6
642	A341	20 l blue	20	10
643	A340	40 l red brn	45	30
644	A341	50 l ol blk	60	45
		Nos. 638-644 (7)	1.45	1.00

Issued to commemorate the centenary of the birth of Christo Botev, Bulgarian national poet.

Lenin
A342

Lenin Speaking
A343

1949, Jan. 24 *Perf. 11½* Unwmkd.

Cream Paper.

645	A342	4 l brown	15	7
646	A343	20 l brn red	50	35

25th anniversary of the death of Lenin.

Road Construction
A344

Designs: 5 l, Tunnel construction. 9 l, Locomotive. 10 l, Textile worker. 20 l, Female tractor driver. 40 l, Workers in truck.

1949, Apr. 6 *Perf. 10½*

Inscribed: "CHM".

Cream Paper.

647	A344	4 l dk red	15	5
648	A344	5 l dk brn	20	8
649	A344	9 l dk sl grn	35	15
650	A344	10 l violet	40	20
651	A344	20 l dl bl	75	60
652	A344	40 l brown	1.50	1.00
		Nos. 647-652 (6)	3.35	2.08

Issued to honor the Workers' Cultural Brigade.

Type of 1948.

Redrawn.

Country Name and "POSTA" in Latin Characters.

1949 Typographed *Perf. 12½*

653	A337	20 l dp bl	80	15

Miner
A345

1949 *Perf. 11x11½.*

654	A345	4 l dk bl	25	8

George Dimitrov
A347

A348

1949, July 10 Photogravure

656	A347	4 l red brn	20	3
657	A348	20 l dk bl	60	35

Issued in tribute to Prime Minister George Dimitrov, 1882–1949.

Power Station
A349

Grain Towers
A350

Farm Machinery
A351

Tractor Parade
A352

Agriculture and Industry
A353

Perf. 11½x11, 11x11½.

1949, Aug. 5

658	A349	4 l ol grn	12	3
659	A350	9 l dk red	25	10
660	A351	15 l purple	30	15
661	A352	20 l blue	1.00	70
662	A353	50 l org brn	3.00	1.50
		Nos. 658-662 (5)	4.67	2.48

Issued to publicize Bulgaria's Five Year Plan.

Grenade and Javelin Throwers
A354

Boy and Girl Athletes
A357

Hurdlers
A355

Motorcycle and Tractor
A356

1949, Sept. 5

663	A354	4 l brn org	35	20
664	A355	9 l ol grn	75	35
665	A356	20 l vio bl	1.50	1.00
666	A357	50 l red brn	4.00	2.25

Frontier Guards
A358 A359

1949, Oct. 31

667	A358	4 l chnt brn	15	5
668	A359	20 l gray bl	75	45

See also No. C60.

George Dimitrov
A360

Allegory of Labor
A361

Laborers of Both Sexes
A362

Workers and Flags of Bulgaria and Russia
A363

Perf. 11½

1949, Dec. 13 Photo. **Unwmkd.**

669	A360	4 l org brn	15	5
670	A361	9 l purple	30	8
671	A362	20 l dl bl	45	35
672	A363	50 l red	1.00	95

Joseph V. Stalin
A364

Stalin and Dove
A365

1949, Dec. 21

673	A364	4 l dp org	20	8
674	A365	40 l rose brn	90	70

Issued to commemorate the 70th anniversary of the birth of Joseph V. Stalin.

Kharalamby Stoyanov
A366

Communications Strikers
A368

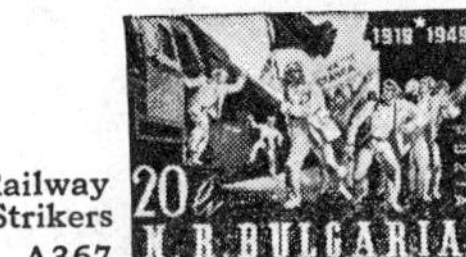

Railway Strikers
A367

1950, Feb. 15

675	A366	4 l yel brn	15	5
676	A367	20 l vio bl	30	15
677	A368	60 l brn ol	90	75

Issued to commemorate the 30th anniversary (in 1949) of the General Railway and Postal Employees' Strike of 1919.

Miner
A369

Shipbuilding
A371

Locomotive
A370

Tractor
A372

Farm Machinery
A373

Stalin Central Heating Plant
A374

Textile Worker
A375

1950-51 *Perf. 11½, 13.*

678	A369	1 l ol	12	4
679	A370	2 l gray blk	20	4
680	A371	3 l gray bl	30	4
681	A372	4 l dk bl grn	2.50	75
682	A373	5 l hn brn	60	10
682A	A373	9 l gray blk ('51)	30	6
683	A374	10 l dp plum ('51)	40	10
684	A375	15 l dk car ('51)	60	6
685	A375	20 l dk bl ('51)	1.00	60
		Nos. 678-685 (9)	6.02	1.79

No. 685 is inscribed in Latin characters.

See Nos. 750–751A.

Vassil Kolarov
A377

1950, Mar. 6 *Perf. 11½*

Size: 21½x31½ mm.

686	A377	4 l red brn	7	5

Size: 27x39½ mm.

687	A377	20 l vio bl	60	30

Issued in memory of Vassil Kolarov (1877–1950).

No. 687 has altered frame and is inscribed in Latin characters.

Stanislav Dospevski, Self-portrait
A378

King Kaloyan and Desislava
A379

Plowman Resting, by Christo Stanchev
A380

Statue of Dimtcho Debelianov, by Ivan Lazarov
A381

"Harvest," by V. Dimitrov
A382

Design: 9 l, Nikolai Pavlovich, self-portrait.

1950, Apr. 15 *Perf. 11½*

688	A378	1 l dk ol grn	35	15
689	A379	4 l dk red	1.00	30
690	A378	9 l chocolate	1.00	30
691	A380	15 l brown	1.75	35
692	A380	20 l dp bl	2.25	1.10
693	A381	40 l red brn	3.25	1.75
694	A382	60 l dp org	4.50	2.25
		Nos. 688-694 (7)	14.10	6.20

Latin characters on No. 692.

Ivan Vazov and Birthplace
A383

1950, June 26

695	A383	4 l ol grn	12	10

Issued to commemorate the centenary of the birth of Ivan Vazov (1850-1921), poet.

Road Building
A384

Men of Three Races and "Stalin" Flag
A385

Perf. 11½x11, 11x11½

1950, Sept. 19

696	A384	4 l brn red	5	4
697	A385	20 l vio bl	45	30

2nd National Peace Conference.

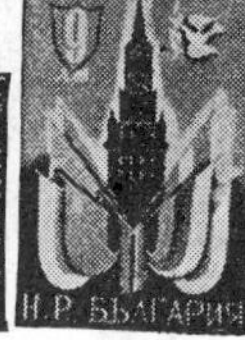

Molotov, Kolarov, Stalin and Dimitrov
A386

Spasski Tower and Flags
A387

Russian and Bulgarian Women
A388

Loading Russian Ship
A389

Photogravure.

1950, Oct. 10 *Perf. 11½* **Unwmkd.**

698	A386	4 l brown	10	4
699	A387	9 l rose car	15	6
700	A388	20 l gray bl	35	30
701	A389	50 l dk grnsh bl	1.50	90

Issued to commemorate the 2nd anniversary of the Soviet-Bulgarian treaty of mutual assistance.

St. Constantine Sanatorium
A390

Children at Seashore
A391

Design: 5 l, Rest home.

1950 Typographed

702	A390	1 l dk grn	6	3
703	A391	2 l carmine	20	3
704	A390	5 l dp org	30	15
705	A391	10 l dp bl	75	35

Originally prepared in 1945 as "Sunday Delivery Stamps," this issue was released for ordinary postage in 1950.

Runners
A393

Designs: 9 l, Cycling. 20 l, Putting the Shot. 40 l, Volleyball.

1950, Aug. 21 Photo. *Perf. 11*

706	A393	4 l dk grn	35	20
707	A393	9 l red brn	60	50
708	A393	20 l gray bl	90	75
709	A393	40 l plum	2.50	1.75

Marshal Fedor I. Tolbukhin
A394

Natives Greeting Tolbukhin
A395

Perf. 11½x11, 11x11½.

1950, Dec. 10 Photo. **Unwmkd.**

710	A394	4 l claret	15	10
711	A395	20 l dk bl	80	35

Issued to publicize the return of Dobrich and part of the province of Dobruja from Romania to Bulgaria.

Dimitrov's Birthplace
A396

George Dimitrov
A397 A398

Various Portraits, Inscribed:

Г.ДИМИТРОВ

1950, July 2 *Perf. 10½*

712	A396	50s ol grn	20	3
713	A397	50s brown	20	3
714	A397	1 l redsh brn	30	3
715	A396	2 l gray (*Dimitrov Museum, Sofia*)	30	4
716	A397	4 l claret	55	15
717	A397	9 l red brn	75	35
718	A398	10 l brn red	80	75
719	A396	15 l ol gray	80	75
720	A396	20 l dk bl	2.25	1.10
		Nos. 712-720, C61 (10)	9.65	4.73

Issued to commemorate the first anniversary of the death of George Dimitrov, statesman. No. 720 is inscribed in Latin characters.

A. S. Popov
A400

1951, Feb. 10

722	A400	4 l red brn	35	18
723	A400	20 l dk bl	75	35

No. 723 is inscribed in Latin characters.

Arms of Bulgaria
A401 A402

Typographed

1950 *Perf. 13* **Unwmkd.**

724	A401	2 l dk brn	6	3
725	A401	3 l rose	7	3
726	A402	5 l carmine	10	4
727	A402	9 l aqua	25	5

Nos. 724-727 were prepared in 1947 for official use but were issued as regular postage stamps Oct. 1, 1950.

Heroes Chankova, Antonov-Malchik, Dimitrov and Dimitrova
A403

Stanke Dimitrov-Marek
A404

George Kirkov
A405

George Dimitrov at Leipzig
A406

Natcho Ivanov and Avr. Stoyanov
A407

Portraits: 9 l, Anton Ivanov. 15 l, Christo Michailov.

1951, Mar. 25 Photo. *Perf. 11½*

728	A403	1 l red vio	20	6
729	A404	2 l dk red brn	20	8
730	A405	4 l car rose	20	10
731	A405	9 l org brn	75	15
732	A405	15 l ol brn	1.25	45
733	A406	20 l dk bl	1.75	1.00
734	A407	50 l ol gray	3.25	1.75
		Nos. 728-734 (7)	7.60	3.59

First Bulgarian Tractor
A408

First Steam Roller
A409

First Truck
A410

Bulgarian Embroidery
A411

Designs: 15 l, Carpet. 20 l, Tobacco and roses. 40 l, Fruits.

Perf. 11x10½

1951, Mar. 30 Photo. Unwmkd.

735	A408	1 l ol brn	15	4
736	A409	2 l violet	20	4
737	A410	4 l red brn	30	10
738	A411	9 l purple	45	15
739	A409	15 l dp plum	80	40
740	A411	20 l vio bl	90	50
741	A410	40 l dp grn	1.75	1.50

Perf. 13.

Size: 23x18½ mm.

742	A408	1 l purple	6	3
743	A409	2 l Prus grn	15	3
744	A410	4 l red brn	20	5
		Nos. 735-744 (10)	4.96	2.84

See also Nos. 894, 973.

Turkish Attack on Mt. Zlee Dol
A412

Designs: 4 l, Georgi Benkovski speaking to rebels. 9 l, Cherrywood cannon of 1876 and Russian cavalry, 1945. 20 l, Rebel, 1876 and partisan, 1944. 40 l, Benkovski and Dimitrov.

1951, May 3 *Perf. 10½*

Cream Paper.

745	A412	1 l redsh brn	20	15
746	A412	4 l dk grn	20	15
747	A412	9 l vio brn	75	50
748	A412	20 l dp bl	90	80
749	A412	40 l dk red	1.25	1.00
		Nos. 745-749 (5)	3.30	2.60

Issued to commemorate the 75th anniversary of the "April" revolution.

Industrial Types of 1950.

1951 *Perf. 13*

750	A369	1 l violet	15	3
751	A370	2 l dk brn	15	3
751A	A372	4 l dk yel grn	1.00	10

Demeter Blagoev Addressing 1891 Congress at Busludja
A413

1951 Photogravure *Perf. 11*

752	A413	1 l purple	35	15
753	A413	4 l dk grn	50	15
754	A413	9 l dp cl	90	60

Issued to commemorate the 60th anniversary of the first Congress of the Bulgarian Social-Democratic Party.

See also Nos. 1174–1176.

Day Nursery
A414

Designs: 4 l, Model building construction. 9 l, Playground. 20 l, Children's town.

1951, Oct. 10 Unwmkd.

755	A414	1 l brown	15	6
756	A414	4 l dp plum	35	15
757	A414	9 l bl grn	1.00	45
758	A414	20 l dp bl	1.75	1.00

Issued to publicize Children's Day, Sept. 25, 1951.

Order of Labor
A415 A416

1952, Feb. 1 *Perf. 13*

Reverse of Medal

759	A415	1 l red brn	5	3
760	A415	4 l bl grn	10	3
761	A415	9 l dk bl	40	15

Obverse of Medal

762	A416	1 l carmine	5	3
763	A416	4 l green	10	3
764	A416	9 l purple	40	15
		Nos. 759-764 (6)	1.10	42

No. 764 has numeral at lower left and different background.

Workers and Symbols of Industry
A417

Design: 4 l, Flags and heads of George Dimitrov and V. Tchervenkov.

1951, Dec. 29 *Perf. 11*

Inscribed: "16 XII 1951."

765	A417	1 l ol blk	7	3
766	A417	4 l chocolate	15	5

Issued to publicize the Third Congress of Bulgarian General Workers' Professional Union.

Dimitrov and Chemical Works
A418

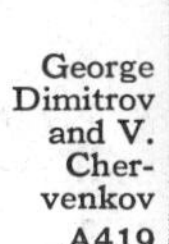

George Dimitrov and V. Chervenkov
A419

Portrait: 80s, Dimitrov.

Photogravure.

1952, June 18 *Perf. 11* **Unwmkd.**

767	A418	16s brown	45	30
768	A419	44s brn car	75	45
769	A418	80s brt bl	1.50	90

Issued to commemorate the 70th anniversary of the birth of George Dimitrov.

Vassil Kolarov Dam
A420

Republika Power Station
A421

1952, May 16 *Perf. 13*

770	A420	4s dk grn	6	4
771	A420	12s purple	9	4
772	A420	16s red brn	13	5
773	A420	44s rose brn	80	15
774	A420	80s brt bl	2.50	35
		Nos. 770-774 (5)	3.58	63

No. 774 is inscribed in Latin characters.

1952, June 30 *Perf. 13, Pin Perf.*

775	A421	16s dk brn	35	4
776	A421	44s magenta	1.00	20

Nikolai I. Vapzarov
A422

Designs: Various portraits.

1952, July 23 *Perf. 10½*

777	A422	16s rose brn	25	15
778	A422	44s dk red brn	65	20
779	A422	80s dk ol brn	1.75	1.00

Issued to commemorate the 10th anniversary of the death of Nikolai I. Vapzarov, poet and revolutionary.

Dimitrov and Youth Conference
A423

Designs: 16s, Resistance movement incident. 44s, Frontier guards and industrial scene. 80s, George Dimitrov and young workers.

1952, Sept. 1 *Perf. 11x11½*

780	A423	2s brn car	15	4
781	A423	16s purple	20	15
782	A423	44s dk grn	75	50
783	A423	80s dk brn	1.50	1.00

Issued to commemorate the 40th anniversary of the founding conference of the Union of Social Democratic Youth.

Assault on the Winter Palace
A424

Designs: 8s, Volga-Don Canal. 16s, Symbols of world peace. 44s, Lenin and Stalin. 80s, Himlay hydroelectric station.

Photogravure.

1952, Nov. 6 *Perf. 11½* **Unwmkd.**

Dated: "1917-1952."

784	A424	4s red brn	6	4
785	A424	8s dk grn	9	4
786	A424	16s dk bl	13	5
787	A424	44s brown	35	30
788	A424	80s ol brn	1.00	60
		Nos. 784-788 (5)	1.63	1.03

Issued to commemorate the 35th anniversary of the Russian revolution.

Vassil Levski
A425

Design: 44s, Levski and comrades.

1953, Feb. 19 Cream Paper *Perf. 11*

789	A425	16s brown	15	6
790	A425	44s brn blk	35	15

Issued to commemorate the 80th anniversary of the death of Vassil Levski, patriot.

Ferrying Artillery and Troops into Battle
A426

Soldier
A427

Mother and Children
A428

Designs: 44s, Victorious soldiers. 80s, Soldier welcomed. 1 l, Monuments.

1953, Mar. 3 *Perf. 10½*

791	A426	8s Prus grn	20	4
792	A427	16s dp brn	25	6
793	A426	44s dk sl grn	60	20
794	A426	80s dl red brn	1.25	65
795	A426	1 l black	1.50	1.25
		Nos. 791-795 (5)	3.80	2.20

Issued to commemorate the 75th anniversary of Bulgaria's independence from Turkey.

1953, Mar. 9

796	A428	16s sl grn	10	5
797	A428	16s brt bl	10	5

Issued to commemorate Women's Day.

Certain countries cancel stamps in full sheets and sell them (usually with gum) for less than face value. Dealers generally sell "CTO" (canceled to order) stamps for much less than postally used copies.

Woodcarvings at Rila Monastery
A429 A430

Designs: 12s, 16s, 28s, Woodcarvings, Rila Monastery. 44s, Carved Ceilings, Trnovo. 80s, 1 l, 4 l, Carvings, Pasardjik.

Photogravure.

1953 Perf. 13. Unwmkd.

798	A429	2s gray brn	5	3
799	A430	8s dk sl grn	7	3
800	A430	12s brown	20	3
801	A430	16s rose lake	50	3
802	A429	28s dk ol grn	65	5
803	A430	44s dk brn	1.00	8
804	A430	80s ultra	1.35	12
805	A430	1 l vio bl	2.25	35
806	A430	4 l rose lake	4.50	1.50
		Nos. 798-806 (9)	10.57	2.22

Karl Marx A431 "Capital" A432

1953, Apr. 30 Perf. 10½

807	A431	16s brt bl	15	10
808	A432	44s dp brn	45	30

70th anniversary of the death of Karl Marx.

Labor Day Parade A433 Joseph V. Stalin A434

1953, Apr. 30 Perf. 13

809	A433	16s brn red	20	5

Issued to publicize Labor Day, May 1, 1953.

1953, May 23 Perf. 13x13½

810	A434	16s dk gray	20	5
811	A434	16s dk brn	20	5

Death of Joseph V. Stalin, Mar. 5, 1953.

Georgi Delchev A435 Battle Scene A436

Peasants Attacking Turkish Troops—A437

1953, Aug. 8 Perf. 13

812	A435	16s dk brn	8	4
813	A436	44s purple	45	20
814	A437	1 l dp cl	75	30

Issued to commemorate the 50th anniversary of the Ilinden Revolt (Nos. 812 and 814) and the Preobrazhene Revolt (No. 813).

Soldier and Rebels A438

Design: 44s, Soldier guarding industrial construction.

1953, Sept. 18

815	A438	16s dp cl	10	5
816	A438	44s grnsh bl	35	15

Issued to publicize Army Day.

George Dimitrov and Vassil Kolarov A439 Demeter Blagoev A440

Designs: 16s, Citizens in revolt. 44s, Attack.

1953, Sept. 22

817	A439	8s ol gray	10	4
818	A439	16s dk red brn	15	5
819	A439	44s cerise	65	35

September Revolution, 30th anniversary.

1953, Sept. 21

Portraits: 44s, G. Dimitrov and D. Blagoev.

820	A440	16s brown	30	5
821	A440	44s red brn	45	20

Issued to commemorate the 50th anniversary of the formation of the Social Democratic Party.

Railway Viaduct A441 Pouring Molten Metal A442

Designs: 16s, Welder and storage tanks. 80s, Harvesting machine.

1953, Oct. 17

826	A441	8s brt bl	7	4
827	A441	16s grnsh blk	12	4
828	A442	44s brn red	35	18
829	A441	80s orange	60	45

Month of Bulgarian-Russian friendship.

Belladonna A443 Kolarov Library, Sofia A444

Medicinal Flowers: 4s, Jimson weed. 8s, Sage. 12s, Dog rose. 16s, Gentian. 20s, Poppy. 28s, Peppermint. 40s, Bear grass. 44s, Coltsfoot. 80s, Cowslip. 1 l, Dandelion. 2 l, Foxglove.

Photogravure.

1953 Perf. 13. Unwmkd.

White or Cream Paper

830	A443	2s dl bl	6	3
831	A443	4s brn org	6	3
832	A443	8s bl grn	10	6
833	A443	12s brn org	12	6
834	A443	12s bl grn	12	6
835	A443	16s vio bl	25	8
836	A443	16s dp red brn	25	8
837	A443	20s car rose	35	8
838	A443	28s dk gray grn	50	8
839	A443	40s dk bl	60	25
840	A443	44s brown	60	30
841	A443	80s yel brn	1.00	65
842	A443	1 l hn brn	3.00	80
843	A443	2 l purple	5.50	2.25
a.		Souvenir sheet	35.00	35.00
		Nos. 830-843 (14)	12.51	4.81

No. 843a contains 12 stamps, one of each denomination above, printed in dark green, with floral border and frame of inscriptions. Size: 161x172mm. Sold for 6 leva.

1953, Dec. 16

854	A444	44s brown	30	15

Issued to commemorate the 75th anniversary of the founding of the Kolarov Library, Sofia.

Singer and Accordionist A445 Lenin and Stalin A446

Design: 44s, Dancers.

1953, Dec. 26

855	A445	16s red brn	10	4
856	A445	44s dk grn	30	15

1954, Mar. 13

Designs: 44s, Lenin statue. 80s, Lenin mausoleum, Moscow. 1 l, Lenin.

Cream Paper.

857	A446	16s brown	15	3
858	A446	44s rose brn	35	5
859	A446	80s blue	50	20
860	A446	1 l dp ol grn	75	50

30th anniversary of the death of Lenin.

Demeter Blagoev and Followers A447

Design: 44s, Blagoev at desk.

1954, Apr. 28 Cream Paper

861	A447	16s dp red brn	15	4
862	A447	44s blk brn	45	15

Issued to commemorate the 30th anniversary of the death of Demeter Blagoev.

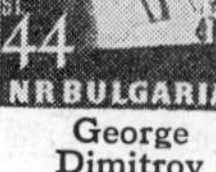

George Dimitrov A448 Dimitrov and Refinery A449

1954, June 11 Cream Paper

863	A448	44s lake	20	8
864	A449	80s brown	45	12

Issued to commemorate the 5th anniversary of the death of George Dimitrov.

Train Leaving Tunnel A450

1954, July 30 Cream Paper

865	A450	44s dk grn	60	15
866	A450	44s blk brn	60	15

Day of the Railroads, Aug. 1, 1954.

Miner at Work A451

1954, Aug. 19 Cream Paper

867	A451	44s grnsh blk	30	10

Issued to publicize Miners' Day.

Academy of Science A452

1954, Oct. 27 Cream Paper

868	A452	80s black	75	35

Issued to commemorate the 85th anniversary of the foundation of the Bulgarian Academy of Science.

Gymnastics A453 Horsemanship A454

Designs: 44s, Wrestling. 2 l, Skiing.

1954, Dec. 21

869	A453	16s dk gray grn	90	30
870	A453	44s brn red	90	30
871	A454	80s cop brn	2.25	1.00
872	A453	2 l vio bl	5.25	3.00

Welcoming Liberators A455 Soldier's Return A456

Designs: 28s, Refinery. 44s, Dimitrov and workers. 80s, Girl and boy. 1 l, George Dimitrov.

1954, Oct. 4 Cream Paper

873	A455	12s brn car	5	3
874	A456	16s dp car	5	3
875	A455	28s indigo	15	4
876	A455	44s redsh brn	20	5
877	A456	80s dp bl	90	35
878	A456	1 l dk grn	90	35
		Nos. 873-878 (6)	2.25	85

10th anniversary of Bulgaria's liberation.

Recreation at Workers' Rest Home
A457

Metal Worker and Furnace
A458

Portraits: 80s, Dimitrov, Blagoev, and Kirkov.

Photogravure.

1954, Dec. 28 ***Perf. 13*** **Unwmkd.**

Cream Paper

879	A457	16s dk grn	15	4
880	A458	44s brn org	20	6
881	A457	80s dp vio bl	75	35

Issued to commemorate the 50th anniversary of Bulgaria's trade union movement.

Geese
A459

Designs: 4s, Chickens. 12s, Hogs. 16s, Sheep. 28s, Telephone building. 44s, Communist party headquarters. 80s, Apartment buildings. 1 l, St. Kiradgieff Mills.

1955–56

882	A459	2s dk bl grn	10	3
883	A459	4s ol grn	15	3
884	A459	12s dk red brn	30	5
885	A459	16s brn org	60	8
886	A459	28s vio bl	25	6
887	A459	44s lil red, *cr*	45	7
a.		44s brn red	3.75	20
888	A459	80s dk red brn	65	15
889	A459	1 l dk bl grn	1.35	35
		Nos. 882-889 (8)	3.85	82

Issue dates: No. 887, Apr. 20, 1956; others, Feb. 19, 1955.

Textile Worker
A460

Mother and Child
A461

Design: 16s, Woman feeding calf.

1955, Mar. 5

890	A460	12s dk brn	6	3
891	A460	16s dk grn	12	3
892	A461	44s dk car rose	35	10
893	A461	44s blue	45	10

Women's Day, Mar. 8, 1955.

No. 744 Surcharged In Blue.

1955, Mar. 8 ***Perf. 13***

894	A410	16s on 4 l red brn	75	3

May Day Demonstration of Workers
A462

Sts. Cyril and Methodius
A463

Design: 44s, Three workers and globe.

1955, Apr. 23 Photogravure

895	A462	16s car rose	9	5
896	A462	44s blue	28	10

Labor Day, May 1, 1955.

1955, May 21 Cream Paper

Designs: 8s, Paisii Hilendarski. 16s, Nicolas Karastoyanov's printing press. 28s, Christo Botev. 44s, Ivan Vazov. 80s, Demeter Blagoev and socialist papers. 2 l, Blagoev printing plant, Sofia.

897	A463	4s dp bl	3	3
898	A463	8s olive	4	3
899	A463	16s black	8	5
900	A463	28s hn brn	15	6
901	A463	44s brown	30	8
902	A463	80s rose red	65	30
903	A463	2 l black	1.50	90
		Nos. 897-903 (7)	2.75	1.45

Issued to commemorate the 1100th anniversary of the creation of the Cyrillic alphabet. Latin lettering at bottom on Nos. 901-903.

Sergei Rumyantzev
A464

Mother and Children
A465

Portraits: 16s, Christo Jassenov. 44s, Geo Milev.

Cream Paper

1955, June 30 ***Perf. 13*** **Unwmkd.**

904	A464	12s org brn	15	4
905	A464	16s lt brn	20	4
906	A464	44s grnsh blk	45	20

Issued to commemorate the 25th anniversary of the deaths of Sergei Rumyanchev, Christo Jassenov and Geo Milev. Latin lettering at bottom of No. 906.

1955, July 30 Cream Paper

907	A465	44s brn car	35	15

Issued to commemorate the World Congress of Mothers in Lausanne, 1955.

Young People of Three Races
A466

Friedrich Engels and Book
A467

1955, July 30 Cream Paper

908	A466	44s blue	35	8

Issued to commemorate the fifth World Festival of Youth in Warsaw, July 31–Aug. 14, 1955.

1955, July 30

909	A467	44s brown	35	15

Issued to commemorate the 60th anniversary of the death of Friedrich Engels.

Entrance to Fair, 1892
A468

Statuary Group at Fair, 1955
A469

Designs: 44s, "Fruit of our Land." 80s, Woman holding Fair emblem.

1955, Aug. 31 Cream Paper

910	A468	4s dp brn	3	3
911	A469	16s dk car rose	5	3
912	A468	44s ol blk	25	12
913	A469	80s dp bl	65	20

Issued to commemorate the 16th International Plovdiv Fair. Latin lettering on Nos. 912–913.

Friedrich von Schiller
A470

Portraits: 44s, Adam Mickiewicz. 60s, Hans Christian Andersen. 80s, Baron de Montesquieu. 1 l, Miguel de Cervantes. 2 l, Walt Whitman.

1955, Oct. 31 Cream Paper

914	A470	16s brown	20	5
915	A470	44s brn red	60	15
916	A470	60s Prus bl	90	15
917	A470	80s black	95	15
918	A470	1 l rose vio	2.25	60
919	A470	2 l ol grn	2.50	1.00
		Nos. 914-919 (6)	7.40	2.10

Issued in honor of various anniversaries of famous writers. Nos. 918 and 919 are issued in sheets alternating with labels without franking value. The labels show title pages for Leaves of Grass and Don Quixote in English and Spanish, respectively. Latin lettering on Nos. 915–919.

Karl Marx Industrial Plant
A471

Friendship Monument
A472

I. V. Michurin
A473

Designs: 4s, Alexander Stambolisky Dam. 16s, Bridge over Danube. 1 l, Vladimir V. Mayakovsky.

1955, Dec. 1 **Unwmkd.**

920	A471	2s sl blk	3	3
921	A471	4s dp bl	3	3
922	A471	16s dk bl grn	6	4
923	A472	44s red brn	30	8
924	A473	80s dk grn	40	12
925	A473	1 l gray blk	75	18
		Nos. 920-925 (6)	1.57	48

Issued to publicize Russian-Bulgarian friendship.

Library Seal
A474

Krusto Pishurka
A475

Portrait: 44s, Bacho Kiro.

1956, Feb. 10 ***Perf. 11x10½***

Cream Paper

926	A474	12s car lake	5	3
927	A475	16s dp brn	10	3
928	A475	44s sl blk	30	12

Issued to commemorate the 100th anniversary of the National Library. Latin lettering at bottom of No. 928.

Canceled to Order

Beginning about 1956, some issues were sold in sheets canceled to order. Prices in second column when much less than unused are for "CTO" copies. Postally used stamps are valued at slightly less than, or the same as, unused.

Quinces
A476

Cherrywood Cannon
A477

Designs: 8s, Pears. 16s, Apples. 44s, Grapes.

1956 Photogravure ***Perf. 13***

929	A476	4s carmine	1.25	8
930	A476	8s bl grn	50	10
931	A476	16s lil rose	1.25	5
932	A476	44s dp vio	1.25	20

Latin lettering on No. 932. See also Nos. 964–967.

1956, Apr. 28 ***Perf. 11x10½***

Design: 44s, Cavalry attack.

933	A477	16s dk cl	10	4
934	A477	44s dk sl grn	25	15

Issued to commemorate the 80th anniversary of the April (1876) Uprising against Turkish rule.

Demeter Blagoev and Birthplace
A478

Cherries
A479

1956, May 30 ***Perf. 11***

935	A478	44s Prus bl	30	10

Issued to commemorate the centenary of the birth of Demeter Blagoev (1856–1924), writer.

1956 ***Perf. 13*** **Unwmkd.**

Designs: 12s, Plums. 28s, Peaches. 80s, Strawberries.

936	A479	2s rose car	7	3
937	A479	12s blue	15	3
938	A479	28s org brn	30	5
939	A479	80s dp car	90	35

Latin lettering on No. 939.

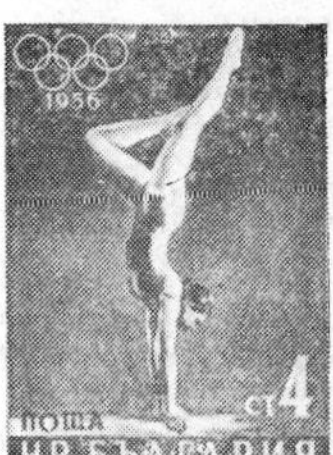

Gymnastics
A480

Pole Vaulting
A481

Designs: 12s, Discus throw. 44s, Soccer. 80s, Basketball. 1 l, Boxing.

Perf. 11x10½, 10½x11

1956, Aug. 29

940	A480	4s brt ultra	15	5
941	A480	12s brick red	20	6
942	A481	16s yel brn	35	20
943	A481	44s dk grn	60	35
944	A480	80s dk red brn	1.50	95
945	A481	1 l dp mag	2.25	1.25
		Nos. 940-945 (6)	5.05	2.86

Latin lettering on Nos. 943–945.

Issued to publicize the forthcoming 16th Olympic Games at Melbourne, Nov. 22–Dec. 8, 1956.

Tobacco, Rose and Distillery
A482

People's Theater
A483

1956, Sept. 1 **Perf. 13**

946	A482	44s dp car	60	20
947	A482	44s ol grn	60	20

17th International Plovdiv Fair.

1956, Nov. 16 **Unwmkd.**

Design: 44s, Dobri Woinikoff and Sawa Dobroplodni, dramatists.

948	A483	16s dl red brn	15	6
949	A483	44s dk bl grn	35	15

Bulgarian Theater centenary.

Benjamin Franklin
A484

Cyclists, Palms and Pyramids
A485

Portraits: 20s, Rembrandt. 40s, Mozart. 44s, Heinrich Heine. 60s, G. B. Shaw. 80s, Dostoevski. 1 l, Henrik Ibsen. 2 l, Pierre Curie.

1956, Dec. 29

950	A484	16s dk ol grn	15	4
951	A484	20s brown	20	4
952	A484	40s dk car rose	30	6
953	A484	44s dk vio brn	35	8
954	A484	60s dk sl	45	15
955	A484	80s dk brn	50	10
956	A484	1 l bluish grn	1.00	50
957	A484	2 l Prus grn	2.25	65
		Nos. 950-957 (8)	5.20	1.62

Issued in honor of great personalities of the world.

1957, Mar. 6 **Photo.** **Perf. 10½**

958	A485	80s hn brn	75	30
959	A485	80s Prus grn	75	30

Fourth Egyptian bicycle race.

Woman Technician
A486

"New Times" Review
A487

Designs: 16s, Woman and children. 44s, Woman feeding chickens.

960	A486	12s dp bl	6	3
961	A486	16s hn brn	8	3
962	A486	44s sl grn	35	12

Women's Day, Mar. 8, 1957. Latin lettering on 44s.

1957, Mar. 8 **Unwmkd.**

963	A487	16s dp car	20	7

Issued to commemorate the 60th anniversary of the founding of the "New Times" review.

Fruit Type of 1956.

Designs: 4s, Quinces. 8s, Pears. 16s, Apples. 44s, Grapes.

1957 Photogravure. **Perf. 13**

964	A476	4s yel grn	4	3
965	A476	8s brn org	8	3
966	A476	16s rose red	15	3
967	A476	44s org yel	80	10

Latin lettering on No. 967.

Sts. Cyril and Methodius
A488

Basketball
A489

1957, May 22 **Perf. 11**

968	A488	44s ol grn & buff	50	15

Issued for the centenary of the first public veneration of Sts. Cyril and Methodius, inventors of the Cyrillic alphabet.

1957, June 20 Photo. Perf. 10½x11

969	A489	44s dk grn	1.25	30

Issued to commemorate the 10th European Basketball Championship at Sofia.

Dancer and Spasski Tower, Moscow
A490

1957, July 18 **Perf. 13**

970	A490	44s blue	35	15

Issued to publicize the Sixth World Youth Festival in Moscow.

George Dimitrov—A491

1957, July 18

971	A491	44s dp car	50	15

75th anniversary of the birth of George Dimitrov (1882–1949).

Vassil Levski
A492

1957, July 18 **Perf. 11**

972	A492	44s grnsh blk	50	15

Issued to commemorate the 120th anniversary of the birth of Vassil Levski, patriot and national hero.

No. 742 Surcharged in Carmine.

1957 **Perf. 13** **Unwmkd.**

973	A408	16s on 1 l pur	12	3

Trnovo and Lazarus L. Zamenhof
A493

1957, July 27

974	A493	44s sl grn	75	20

Issued to commemorate the 50th anniversary of the Bulgarian Esperanto Society and the 70th anniversary of Esperanto.

Bulgarian Veteran of 1877 War and Russian Soldier
A494

Design: 44s, Battle of Shipka Pass.

1957, Aug. 13

975	A494	16s dk bl grn	15	3
976	A494	44s brown	45	7

Issued to commemorate the 80th anniversary of Bulgaria's liberation from the Turks. Latin lettering on No. 976.

Woman Planting Tree
A495

Red Deer in Forest
A496

Designs: 16s, Dam, lake and forest. 44s, Plane over forest. 80s, Fields on edge of forest.

1957, Sept. 16 **Photo.** **Perf. 13**

977	A495	2s dp grn	4	3
978	A496	12s dk brn	7	3
979	A496	16s Prus bl	8	3
980	A496	44s Prus grn	20	8
981	A496	80s yel grn	45	18
		Nos. 977-981 (5)	84	35

Latin lettering on Nos. 980 and 981.

Lenin
A497

Designs: 16s, Cruiser "Aurora." 44s, Dove over map of communist area. 60s, Revolutionaries and banners. 80s, Oil refinery.

1957, Oct. 29 **Perf. 11**

982	A497	12s chocolate	15	3
983	A497	16s Prus grn	30	4
984	A497	44s dp bl	60	12
985	A497	60s dk car rose	70	30
986	A497	80s dk grn	1.25	40
		Nos. 982-986 (5)	3.00	89

Issued to commemorate the 40th anniversary of the Communist Revolution. Latin lettering on Nos. 984–985.

Globes
A498

1957, Oct. 4 **Perf. 13**

987	A498	44s Prus bl	30	18

Issued to commemorate the fourth International Trade Union Congress, Leipzig, Oct. 4-15.

Vassil Kolarov Hotel
A499

Health Resorts: 4s, Skis and Pirin Mountains. 8s, Old house at Koprivspitsa. 12s, Rest home at Velingrad. 44s, Momin-Prochod Hotel. 60s, Nesebr Hotel, shoreline and peninsula. 80s, Varna beach scene. 1 l, Hotel at Varna.

1958 Photogravure **Perf. 13**

988	A499	4s blue	3	3
989	A499	8s org brn	6	3
990	A499	12s dk grn	6	5
991	A499	16s green	10	3
992	A499	44s dk bl grn	18	8
993	A499	60s dp bl	30	12
994	A499	80s fawn	45	20
995	A499	1 l dk red brn	75	30
		Nos. 988-995 (8)	1.93	84

Issued to publicize various Bulgarian health resorts. Latin lettering on 44s, 60s, 80s, and 1 l.

Issue dates: Nos. 991–994, Jan. 20. Others, July 5.

Mikhail I. Glinka
A500

Portraits: 16s, Jan A. Komensky (Comenius). 40s, Carl von Linné. 44s, William Blake. 60s, Carlo Goldoni. 80s, Auguste Comte.

1957, Dec. 30

996	A500	12s dk brn	25	3
997	A500	16s dk grn	25	3
998	A500	40s Prus bl	60	7
999	A500	44s maroon	60	10
1000	A500	60s org brn	75	12
1001	A500	80s dp plum	2.25	1.00
		Nos. 996-1001 (6)	4.70	1.35

Issued to honor famous men of other countries. Latin lettering on Nos. 999–1001.

Young Couple, Flag, Dimitrov
A501

People's Front Salute
A502

1958, Dec. 28 *Perf. 11*

1002 A501 16s car rose 18 7

Issued to commemorate the 10th anniversary of Dimitrov's Union of the People's Youth.

1958, Dec. 28

1003 A502 16s dk vio brn 18 7

15th anniversary of the People's Front.

Hare
A503

Animals: 12s, Red deer (doe) (vert.). 16s, Red deer (stag). 44s, Chamois. 80s, Brown bear. 1 l, Wild boar.

Photogravure.

1958, Apr. 5 *Perf. 10½* **Unwmkd.**

1004 A503 2s lt & dk ol grn 6 3
1005 A503 12s sl grn & red brn 15 3
1006 A503 16s bluish grn & dk red brn 18 3
1007 A503 44s bl & brn 25 10
1008 A503 80s bis & dk brn 80 22
1009 A503 1 l stl bl & dk brn 1.10 35
Nos. 1004-1009 (6) 2.54 76

Price, imperf. set $5.

Marx and Lenin—A504

Designs: 16s, Marchers and flags. 44s, Lenin blast furnaces.

1958, July 2 *Perf. 11*

1010 A504 12s dk brn 12 3
1011 A504 16s dk car 15 4
1012 A504 44s dk bl 60 15

Issued to commemorate the 7th Congress of the Bulgarian Communist Party.

Wrestlers
A505

1958, June 20 *Perf. 10½*

1013 A505 60s dk car rose 1.00 65
1014 A505 80s dp brn 1.50 90

World Wrestling Championship, Sofia.

Chessmen and Globe
A506

Photogravure

1958, July 18 *Perf. 10½* **Unwmkd.**

1015 A506 80s grn & yel grn 1.75 1.25

5th World Students' Chess Games, Varna.

Conference Emblem
A507

1958, Sept. 24

1016 A507 44s blue 35 15

Issued to commemorate the World Trade Union Conference of Working Youth, Prague, July 14–20.

Swimmer
A508

Designs: 28s, Dancer (vertical). 44s, Volleyball (vertical).

1958, Sept. 19 *Perf. 11x10½*

1017 A508 16s brt bl 15 7
1018 A508 28s brn org 30 15
1019 A508 44s brt grn 45 15

1958 Students' Games.

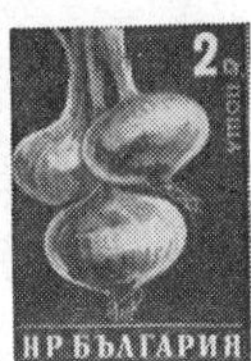

Onions
A509

Vegetables: 12s, Garlic. 16s, Peppers. 44s, Tomatoes. 80s, Cucumbers. 1 l, Eggplant.

1958, Sept. 20 *Perf. 13*

1020 A509 2s org brn 3 3
1021 A509 12s Prus bl 3 3
1022 A509 16s dk grn 6 5
1023 A509 44s dp car 15 5
1024 A509 80s dp grn 45 12
1025 A509 1 l brt pur 75 15
Nos. 1020-1025 (6) 1.47 43

See No. 1072.

Price, imperf. set $4.50.

Plovdiv Fair Building
A510

1958, Sept. 14 *Perf. 11* **Unwmkd.**

1026 A510 44s dp car 45 12

18th International Plovdiv Fair.

Attack
A511

Design: 44s, Fighter dragging wounded man.

1958, Sept. 23 Photo. *Perf. 11*

1027 A511 16s org ver 12 6
1028 A511 44s lake 35 10

Issued to commemorate the 35th anniversary of the September Revolution.

Emblem, Brussels Fair
A512

1958, Oct. 13 *Perf. 11*

1029 A512 1 l blk & brt bl 2.50 2.50

Brussels World's Fair, Apr. 17-Oct. 19.

Price imperf. $10.

Runner at Finish Line
A513

Woman Throwing Javelin
A514

Sports: 60s, High jumper. 80s, Hurdler. 4 l, Shot putter.

1958, Nov. 30

1030 A513 16s red brn, *pnksh* 35 20
1031 A514 44s ol, *yelsh* 35 20
1032 A514 60s dk bl, *bluish* 65 30
1033 A514 80s dp grn, *grnsh* 80 30
1034 A513 4 l dp rose cl, *pnksh* 5.50 2.25
Nos. 1030-1034 (5) 7.65 3.25

1958 Balkan Games.
Latin lettering on Nos. 1032–1033.

Christo Smirnenski
A515

1958, Dec. 22

1035 A515 16s dk car 15 6

Issued to commemorate the 60th anniversary of the birth of Christo Smirnenski, poet, 1898–1923.

Girls Harvesting
A516

Girl Tending Calves
A517

Designs: 16s, Boy and girl laborers. 40s, Boy pushing wheelbarrow. 44s, Headquarters building.

1959, Nov. 29 **Photogravure**

1036 A516 8s dk ol grn 5 3
1037 A517 12s redsh brn 7 3
1038 A516 16s vio brn 8 3
1039 A517 40s Prus bl 15 5
1040 A516 44s dp car 75 20
Nos. 1036-1040 (5) 1.10 34

Issued to commemorate the 4th Congress of Dimitrov's Union of People's Youth.

UNESCO Building, Paris
A518

1959, Mar. 28 *Perf. 11* **Unwmkd.**

1041 A518 2 l dp red lil, *cr* 1.75 1.25

Opening of UNESCO Headquarters, Paris, Nov. 3, 1958.

Price imperf. $5.

Skier
A519

Soccer Players
A520

1959, Mar. 28 *Perf. 11*

1042 A519 1 l bl, *cr* 1.50 75

Forty years of skiing in Bulgaria.

1959, Mar. 25

1043 A520 2 l chnt, *cr* 1.75 1.00

Issued to commemorate the 1959 European Youth Soccer Championship.

Russian Soldiers Installing Telegraph Wires
A251

First Bulgarian Postal Coach
A522

Designs: 60s, Stamp of 1879. 80s, First Bulgarian automobile. 1 l, Television tower. 2 l, Strike of railroad and postal workers, 1919.

1959, May 4

No.	Type	Description	Unused	Used
1044	A521	12s dk grn & cit	8	3
1045	A522	16s dp plum	12	3
1046	A521	60s dk brn & yel	30	10
1047	A522	80s hn brn & sal	40	20
1048	A521	1 l blue	60	25
1049	A522	2 l dk red brn	1.50	1.25
		Nos. 1044-1049 (6)	3.00	1.86

Issued to commemorate the 80th anniversary of the Bulgarian post. Latin lettering on Nos. 1046-1049.

Two imperf. souvenir sheets exist with olive borders and inscriptions. One contains one copy of No. 1046 in black & ochre, and measures 92x121mm. The other sheet contains one copy each of Nos. 1044-1045 and 1047-1048 in changed colors: 12s, olive green & ochre; 16s, deep claret & ochre; 80s, dark red & ochre; 1 l, olive & ochre. Each sheet sold for 5 leva.

Price, each $30.

Great Tits—A523

Birds: 8s, Hoopoe. 16s, Great spotted woodpecker (vert.). 45s, Gray partridge (vert.). 60s, Rock partridge. 80s, European cuckoo. 1 l, Wood thrush (vert.). 1.25 l, Eurasian jay. $15 each.

1959, June 30 Photogravure

No.	Type	Description	Unused	Used
1050	A523	2s ol & sl grn	5	3
1051	A523	8s dp org & blk	7	3
1052	A523	16s chnt & dk brn	15	10
1053	A523	45s brn & blk	20	15
1054	A523	60s dp bl & gray	45	20
1055	A523	80s dp bl grn & gray	80	30
		Nos. 1050-1055 (6)	1.72	81

Bagpiper
A524

Designs: 12s, Acrobats. 16s, Girls exercising with hoops. 20s, Male dancers. 80s, Ballet dancers. 1 l, Ceramic pitcher. 16s, 20s, 80s are horizontal.

1959, Aug. 29 *Perf. 11* Unwmkd.

Surface-colored Paper.

No.	Type	Description	Unused	Used
1056	A524	4s dk ol	4	3
1057	A524	12s scarlet	5	3
1058	A524	16s maroon	7	4
1059	A524	20s dk bl	30	10
1060	A524	80s brt grn	60	30
1061	A524	1 l brn org	95	50
		Nos. 1056-1061 (6)	2.01	1.00

Issued to publicize the 7th International Youth Festival, Vienna. Latin inscriptions on Nos. 1060-1061.

Partisans in Truck
A525

Designs: 16s, Partisans and soldiers shaking hands. 45s, Refinery. 60s, Tanks. 80s, Harvester. 1.25 l, Children with flag (vert.).

1959, Sept. 8

No.	Type	Description	Unused	Used
1062	A525	12s red & Prus grn	3	3
1063	A525	16s red & dk pur	6	3
1064	A525	45s red & int bl	12	5
1065	A525	60s red & ol grn	15	8
1066	A525	80s red & brn	50	15
1067	A525	1.25 l red & dp brn	1.10	45
		Nos. 1062-1067 (6)	1.96	79

15th anniversary of Bulgarian liberation.

Soccer—A526

1959, Oct. 10 *Perf. 11.* Unwmkd.

No.	Type	Description	Unused	Used
1068	A526	1.25 l dp grn, *yel*	5.00	3.50

50 years of Bulgarian soccer.

Price, set imperf. in changed colors, $10 unused, $6 canceled.

Batak Defenders
A527

1959, Aug. 8

No.	Type	Description	Unused	Used
1069	A527	16s dp cl	30	15

Issued to commemorate the 300th anniversary of the settlement of Batak.

Post Horn and Letter
A528

Bird-shaped Lyre
A529

Design: 1.25 l, Dove and letter.

1959, Nov. 23

No.	Type	Description	Unused	Used
1070	A528	45s emer & blk	35	10
1071	A528	1.25 l lt bl, red & blk	65	30

Issued for International Letter Writing Week Oct. 5-11.

Type of 1958 Surcharged "45 CT." in Dark Blue.

Design: Tomatoes.

1959 Photogravure *Perf. 13*

No.	Type	Description	Unused	Used
1072	A509	45s on 44s scar	75	15

1960, Feb. 23 *Perf. 10½* Unwmkd.

Design: 1.25 l, Lyre.

No.	Type	Description	Unused	Used
1073	A529	80s emer & blk	45	15
1074	A529	1.25 l brt red & blk	75	30

Issued to commemorate the 50th anniversary of Bulgaria's State Opera.

N. I. Vapzarov
A530

Parachute and Radio Tower
A531

1959, Dec. 14 *Perf. 11*

No.	Type	Description	Unused	Used
1075	A530	80s yel grn & red brn	45	12

Issued to commemorate the 50th anniversary of the birth of N. I. Vapzarov, poet and patriot.

1959, Dec. 3 Photogravure

No.	Type	Description	Unused	Used
1076	A531	1.25 l dp grnsh bl & yel	1.75	75

Issued to publicize the third Congress of Voluntary Participants in Defense.

Cotton Picker
A532

Harvester Combine
A533

Designs: 2s, Kindergarten. 4s, Woman doctor and child. 10s, Woman milking cow. 12s, Woman holding tobacco leaves. 15s, Woman working loom. 16s, Stalin textile mill, Dimitrovgrad. 25s, Rural electrification. 28s, Woman picking sunflowers. 40s, "Cold-well" hydroelectric dam. 45s, Miner. 60s, Foundry worker. 80s. Woman harvesting grapes. 1 l, Worker and peasant with cogwheel. 1.25 l, Industrial worker. 2 l, Party leader.

1959-61 Photogravure *Perf. 13*

No.	Type	Description	Unused	Used
1077	A533	2s brn org ('60)	4	3
1077A	A532	4s gldn brn ('61)	4	3
1078	A532	5s dk grn	4	3
1079	A533	10s red brn ('61)	4	3
1080	A532	12s red brn	5	3
1081	A532	15s red lil ('60)	6	3
1082	A533	16s dp vio ('60)	6	3
1083	A533	20s orange	8	3
1084	A532	25s brt bl ('60)	8	3
1085	A532	28s brt grn	15	3
1086	A533	40s brt grnsh bl	25	3
1087	A532	45s choc ('60)	20	3
1088	A533	60s scarlet	35	10
1089	A533	80s ol ('60)	45	12
1090	A532	1 l maroon	50	12
1090A	A533	1.25 l dl bl ('61)	1.75	50
1091	A532	2 l dp car ('60)	1.25	35
		Nos. 1077-1091 (17)	5.39	1.55

Issued to commemorate the early completion of the 5-year plan (in 1959).

L. L. Zamenhof
A534

Path of Lunik 3
A535

1959, Dec. 5 *Perf. 11* Unwmkd.

No.	Type	Description	Unused	Used
1092	A534	1.25 l dk grn & yel grn	90	60

Issued to commemorate the centenary of the birth (in 1859) of Lazarus Ludwig Zamenhof, inventor of Esperanto.

1960, Mar. 28 *Perf. 11*

No.	Type	Description	Unused	Used
1093	A535	1.25 l Prus bl & brt yel	4.50	3.50

Flight of Lunik 3 around moon.
Price, imperf. $9.

Skier
A536

1960, Apr. 15 Lithographed

No.	Type	Description	Unused	Used
1094	A536	2 l ultra, blk & brn	1.50	50

8th Winter Olympics, Squaw Valley, CA, Feb. 18-29.

Price, imperf. $4 unused, $2 canceled.

Vela Blagoeva
A537

Portraits: 28s, Anna Maimunkova. 45s, Vela Piskova. 60s, Rosa Luxemburg. 80s, Klara Zetkin. 1.25 l, N. K. Krupskaya.

1960, Apr. 27 Photo. *Perf. 11*

No.	Type	Description	Unused	Used
1095	A537	16s rose & red brn	5	3
1096	A537	28s cit & ol	8	3
1097	A537	45s ol grn & sl grn	20	3
1098	A537	60s lt bl & Prus bl	20	10
1099	A537	80s red org & dp brn	45	15
1100	A537	1.25 l dl yel & ol	75	30
		Nos. 1095-1100 (6)	1.73	64

International Women's Day, Mar. 8, 1960.

Lenin
A538

Design: 45s, Lenin sitting.

1960, May 12

No.	Type	Description	Unused	Used
1101	A538	16s red brn	35	20
1102	A538	45s sal pink & blk	75	30

90th anniversary of the birth of Lenin.

Women Playing Basketball
A539

1960, June 3 ***Perf. 11***

1103	A539	1.25 l yel & sl grn	1.25	50

Issued to commemorate the seventh European Women's Basketball championships.

Parachutist
A541

Design: 1.25 l, Parachutes.

1960, June 29 **Lithographed**

1105	A541	16s lil & dk bl	60	30
1106	A541	1.25 l bl & cl	1.50	45

Issued to commemorate the 5th International Parachute Championships.

Yellow Gentian
A542

Flowers: 5s, Tulips. 25s, Turk's-cap lily. 45s, Rhododendron. 60s, Lady's-slipper. 80s, Violets.

1960, July 27 Photo. ***Perf. 11***

1107	A542	2s beige, grn & yel	15	3
1108	A542	5s yel grn, grn & car rose	15	3
1109	A542	25s pink, grn & org	20	3
1110	A542	45s pale lil, grn & rose lil	35	15
1111	A542	60s yel, grn & org	75	15
1112	A542	80s gray, grn & vio bl	90	35
		Nos. 1107-1112 (6)	2.50	74

Soccer
A543

Sports: 12s, Wrestling. 16s, Weight lifting. 45s, Woman gymnast. 80s, Canoeing. 2 l, Runner.

1960, Aug. 29 ***Perf. 11*** **Unwmkd.**

Athletes' Figures in Pink

1113	A543	8s brown	3	3
1114	A543	12s violet	4	4
1115	A543	16s Prus bl	8	8
1116	A543	45s dp plum	20	10
1117	A543	80s blue	30	20
1118	A543	2 l dp grn	1.25	50
		Nos. 1113-1118 (6)	1.90	95

17th Olympic Games, Rome, Aug. 25-Sept. 11. Price, set imperf. in changed colors, $7.

Globes
A544

Photogravure

1960, Oct. 12 ***Perf. 11*** **Unwmkd.**

1125	A544	1.25 l bl & ultra	60	30

Issued to commemorate the 15th anniversary of the World Federation of Trade Unions.

Alexander Popov
A545

1960, Oct. 12

1126	A545	90s bl & blk	75	20

Issued to commemorate the centenary of the birth of Alexander Popov, radio pioneer.

Bicyclists
A546

1960, Sept. 22

1127	A546	1 l yel, red org & blk	1.25	90

The 10th Tour of Bulgaria Bicycle Race.

Jaroslav Vésin
A547

1960, Nov. 22 ***Perf. 11*** **Unwmkd.**

1128	A547	1 l brt cit & ol grn	2.25	1.25

Birth centenary of Jaroslav Vésin, painter.

U.N. Headquarters
A548

Costume of Kyustendil
A549

1961, Jan. 14 Photo. ***Perf. 11***

1129	A548	1 l brn & yel	1.50	1.00
a.		Souvenir sheet	5.50	5.50

15th anniv. of the UN. No. 1129 sold for 2 l. Price, imperf. $4.50.

No. 1129a sold for 2.50 l and contains one copy of No. 1129, imperf. in dark olive and pink with orange marginal inscription. Size: 74x58mm.

1961, Jan. 28

Designs (Regional Costumes): 16s, Pleven. 28s, Sliven. 45s, Sofia. 60s, Rhodope. 80s, Karnobat.

1130	A549	12s sal, sl grn & yel	10	3
1131	A549	16s pale lil, brn vio & buff	10	3
1132	A549	28s pale grn, sl grn & rose	15	7
1133	A549	45s bl & red	30	8
1134	A549	60s grnsh bl, Prus bl & yel	50	15
1135	A549	80s yel, sl grn & pink	65	30
		Nos. 1130-1135 (6)	1.80	66

Theodor Tiro (Fresco)
A550

Designs: 60s, Boyana Church. 1.25 l, Duchess of Dessislava (fresco).

1961, Jan. 28 **Photogravure**

1136	A550	60s yel grn, blk & grn	50	15
1137	A550	80s yel, sl grn & org	50	15
1138	A550	1.25 l yel grn, hn brn & buff	1.00	35

700th anniversary of murals in Boyana Church.

Clock Tower, Vratsa
A551

Wooden Jug
A552

Designs: 12s, Clock tower, Bansko. 20s, Anguchev House, Mogilitsa. 28s, Oslekov House, Koprivspitsa (horiz.). 40s, Pasha's house, Melnik (horiz.). 45s, Lion sculpture. 60s, Man on horseback, Madara. 80s, Fresco, Bratchkovo monastery. 1 l, Tsar Assen coin.

1961, Feb. 25 ***Perf. 11*** **Unwmkd.**

Denomination and Stars in Vermilion.

1139	A551	8s ol grn	3	3
1140	A551	12s lt vio	3	3
1141	A552	16s dk red brn	5	3
1142	A551	20s brt bl	5	3
1143	A551	28s grnsh bl	8	5
1144	A551	40s red brn	12	7
1145	A552	45s ol gray	15	8
1146	A552	60s slate	30	10
1147	A552	80s dk ol gray	50	12
1148	A552	1 l green	75	30
		Nos. 1139-1148 (10)	2.06	84

Capercaillie
A553

Birds: 4s, Dalmatian pelican. 16s, Ring-necked pheasant. 80s, Great bustard. 1 l, Lammergeier. 2 l, Hazel hen.

1961, March 31

1149	A553	2s blk, sal & Prus grn	4	3
1150	A553	4s blk, yel grn & org	4	3
1151	A553	16s brn, lt grn & org	7	3
1152	A553	80s brn, bluish grn & yel	35	5
1153	A553	1 l blk, lt bl & yel	50	18
1154	A553	2 l brn, bl & yel	1.25	60
		Nos. 1149-1154 (6)	2.25	92

Radio Tower and Winged Anchor
A554

1961, Apr. 1 ***Perf. 11*** **Unwmkd.**

1155	A554	80s brt grn & blk	45	15

Issued to commemorate the 50th anniversary of the Transport Workers' Union.

T. G. Shevchenko
A555

Water Polo
A556

1961, Apr. 27

1156	A555	1 l ol & blk	2.00	1.25

Issued to commemorate the centenary of the death of Taras G. Shevchenko, Ukrainian poet.

1961, May 15

Designs: 5s, Tennis. 16s, Fencing. 45s, Throwing the discus. 1.25 l, Sports Palace. 2 l, Basketball. 5 l, Sports Palace, different view. 5s, 16s, 45s and 1.25 l, are horizontal.

Black Inscriptions

1157	A556	4s lt ultra	4	3
1158	A556	5s org ver	5	3
1159	A556	16s ol grn	15	3
1160	A556	45s dl bl	20	6
1161	A556	1.25 l yel brn	75	20
1162	A556	2 l lilac	95	45
		Nos. 1157-1162 (6)	2.14	80

Souvenir Sheet

Imperf.

1163	A556	5 l yel grn, dl bl & yel	10.00	10.00

Nos. 1157-1163 were issued to publicize the 1961 World University Games, Sofia, Aug. 26-Sept. 3.
No. 1163 measures 66x66mm.

Price, #1157-1162 in changed colors, imperf. $6.

Monk Seal—A557

Black Sea Fauna: 12s, Jellyfish. 16s, Dolphin. 45s, Black Sea sea horse (vert.). 1 l, Starred sturgeon. 1.25 l, Thornback ray.

1961, June 19 ***Perf. 11***

1164	A557	2s grn & blk	3	3
1165	A557	12s Prus grn & pink	4	3
1166	A557	16s ultra & vio bl	6	3
1167	A557	45s lt bl & brn	18	5
1168	A557	1 l yel grn & Prus grn	50	20
1169	A557	1.25 l lt vio bl & red brn	90	35
		Nos. 1164-1169 (6)	1.71	69

Hikers
A558

Designs: 4s, "Sredetz" hostel (horiz.). 16s, Tents. 1.25 l, Mountain climber.

1961, Aug. 25 Litho. ***Perf. 11***

1170	A558	4s yel grn, yel & blk	4	3
1171	A558	12s lt bl, cr & blk	5	3
1172	A558	16s grn, cr & blk	6	3
1173	A558	1.25 l bis, cr & blk	65	15

"Know Your Country" campaign.

Demeter Blagoev Addressing 1891 Congress at Busludja
A559

1961, Aug. 5 Photogravure

1174	A559	45s dk red & buff	20	15
1175	A559	80s bl & pink	35	20
1176	A559	2 l dk brn & pale cit	90	50

Issued to commemorate the 70th anniversary of the first Congress of the Bulgarian Social-Democratic Party.

The Golden Girl
A560

Fairy Tales: 8s, The Living Water. 12s, The Golden Apple. 16s, Krali-Marko, hero. 45s, Samovila-Vila, Witch. 80s, Tom Thumb.

1961, Oct. 10 ***Perf. 11*** **Unwmkd.**

1177	A560	2s bl, blk & org	15	3
1178	A560	8s rose lil, blk & gray	20	3
1179	A560	12s bl grn, blk & pink	30	3
1180	A560	16s red, blk, bl & gray	45	20
1181	A560	45s ol grn, blk & pink	80	30
1182	A560	80s ocher, blk & dk car	1.25	45
		Nos. 1177-1182 (6)	3.15	1.04

Caesar's Mushroom
A561

Miladinov Brothers and Title Page
A562

Designs: Various mushrooms.

1961, Dec. 20 Photo. ***Perf. 11***

Denominations in Black

1183	A561	2s lem & red	5	3
1184	A561	4s ol grn & red brn	5	3
1185	A561	12s bis & red brn	5	3
1186	A561	16s lil & red brn	5	4
1187	A561	45s car rose & yel	20	7
1188	A561	80s brn org & sep	35	15
1189	A561	1.25 l vio & dk brn	60	20
1190	A561	2 l org brn & brn	1.00	60
		Nos. 1183-1190 (8)	2.35	1.15

Price, denomination in dark grn, imperf. set $5 unused, $3 canceled.

1961, Dec. 21 ***Perf. 10½*** **Unwmkd.**

1191	A562	1.25 l ol & blk	50	15

Issued to commemorate the centenary of the publication of "Collected Folksongs" by the Brothers Miladinov, Dimitri and Konstantin.

Nos. 1079-85, 1087, 988, 1023, 1084, 1090-91 and 806 Surcharged with New Value in Black, Red or Violet.

1962, Jan. 1

1192	A533	1s on 10s red brn	3	3
1193	A532	1s on 12s red brn	3	3
1194	A532	2s on 15s red lil	7	3
1195	A533	2s on 16s dp vio (R)	7	3
1196	A533	2s on 20s org	7	3
a.		"2 CT." on 2 lines	7	4
1197	A532	3s on 25s brt bl (R)	12	4
a.		Black surch.	7.50	5.00
1198	A532	3s on 28s brt grn (R)	12	3
1199	A532	5s on 45s choc	18	5
1200	A499	5s on 44s dk bl grn (R)	18	15
1201	A509	5s on 44s dp car (V)	18	30
1202	A532	10s on 1 l mar	35	65
1203	A532	20s on 2 l dp car	75	15
1204	A430	40s on 4 l rose lake (V)	1.50	30
		Nos. 1192-1204 (13)	3.65	1.82

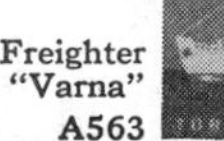

Freighter "Varna"
A563

Designs: 5s, Tanker "Komsomoletz." 20s, Liner "G. Dimitrov."

1962, Mar. 1 Photo. ***Perf. 10½***

1205	A563	1s lt grn & brt bl	4	3
1206	A563	5s lt bl & grn	20	6
1207	A563	20s gray bl & grnsh bl	75	20

Dimitrov working as Printer
A564

Roses
A565

Design: 13s, Griffin, emblem of state printing works.

1962, March 19 **Unwmkd.**

1208	A564	2s ver, blk & yel	5	3
1209	A564	13s red org, blk & yel	45	15

Issued to commemorate the 80th anniversary (in 1961) of the George Dimitrov state printing works.

1962, March 28

Various Roses in Natural Colors

1210	A565	1s dp vio	3	3
1211	A565	2s sal & dk car	4	3
1212	A565	3s gray & car	8	4
1213	A565	4s dk grn	15	4
1214	A565	5s ultra	20	10
1215	A565	6s bluish grn & dk car	60	30
1216	A565	8s cit & car	1.25	45
1217	A565	13s blue	2.50	1.00
		Nos. 1210-1217 (8)	4.85	1.99

Malaria Eradication Emblem and Mosquito—A566

Design: 20s, Malaria eradication emblem.

1962, Apr. 19

1218	A566	5s org brn, yel & blk	60	20
1219	A566	20s emer, yel & blk	1.25	60

WHO drive to eradicate malaria.

Price, imperf. $6 unused, $3.50 canceled.

Lenin and First Issue of Pravda
A567

1962, May 4 ***Perf. 10*** **Unwmkd.**

1220	A567	5s dp rose & sl	60	20

Issued to commemorate the 50th anniversary of Pravda, Russian newspaper founded by Lenin.

Blackboard and Book
A568

1962, May 21 Photogravure

1221	A568	5s Prus bl, blk & yel	20	6

The 1962 Teachers' Congress.

Soccer Player and Globe
A569

1962, May 26 ***Perf. 10½***

1222	A569	13s brt grn, blk & lt brn	1.10	35

World Soccer Championship, Chile, May 30-June 17.

Price, imperf. in changed colors, $5.50 unused, $3.50 canceled.

George Dimitrov
A570

1962, June 18 Photogravure

1223	A570	2s dk grn	15	3
1224	A570	5s turq bl	50	20

Issued to commemorate the 80th anniversary of the birth of George Dimitrov (1882-1949), communist leader and premier of the Bulgarian Peoples' Republic.

Bishop
A571

Chessmen: 2s, Rook. 3s, Queen. 13s, Knight. 20s, Pawn.

1962, July 7 ***Perf. 10½*** **Unwmkd.**

1225	A571	1s gray, emer & blk	3	3
1226	A571	2s gray, lem & blk	5	3
1227	A571	3s gray, lil & blk	15	3
1228	A571	13s gray, dk org & blk	60	20
1229	A571	20s gray, bl & blk	95	50
		Nos. 1225-1229 (5)	1.78	79

Issued to commemorate the 15th Chess Olympics, Varna. Nos. 1225-1229 were also issued imperf. in changed colors. Price $4 unused, $1.50 canceled.

An imperf. souvenir sheet contains one 20s horizontal stamp showing five chessmen. Lilac and gray border of sea horses and waves. Size: 75x66mm. Price $7.50.

Rila Mountain
A572

Designs: 2s, Pirin mountain. 6s, Nesebr, Black Sea. 8s, Danube. 13s, Vidin Castle. 1 l, Rhodope mountain.

1962–63 ***Perf. 13***

1230	A572	1s dk bl grn	5	3
1231	A572	2s blue	6	4
1232	A572	6s grnsh bl	15	4
1233	A572	8s lilac	20	4
1234	A572	13s yel grn	60	15
1234A	A572	1 l dp grn ('63)	4.50	65
		Nos. 1230-1234A (6)	5.56	95

XXXV КОНГРЕС
1962

No. 974 Surcharged in Red

13 =

1962, July 14 ***Perf. 13***

1235	A493	13s on 44s sl grn	3.00	1.75

Issued to commemorate the 25th Bulgarian Esperanto Congress, Burgas, July 14–16.

Girl and Festival Emblem
A573

Design: 5s, Festival emblem.

1962, Aug. 18 **Photo.** ***Perf. 10½***

1236	A573	5s grn, lt bl & pink	20	6
1237	A573	13s lil, lt bl & gray	60	15

Issued to commemorate the 8th Youth Festival for Peace and Friendship, Helsinki, July 28–Aug. 6, 1962.

Parnassius Apollo—A574

1962, Sept. 13

Various Butterflies in Natural Colors

1238	A574	1s pale cit & dk grn	4	3
1239	A574	2s rose & brn	7	3
1240	A574	3s buff & red brn	10	3
1241	A574	4s gray & brn	12	3
1242	A574	5s lt gray & brn	15	3
1243	A574	6s gray & blk	20	4
1244	A574	10s pale grn & blk	1.25	30
1245	A574	13s buff & red brn	1.75	65
		Nos. 1238-1245 (8)	3.68	1.14

Planting Machine—A575

Designs: 2s, Electric locomotive. 3s, Blast furnace. 13s, Blagoev and Dimitrov and Communist flag.

1962, Nov. 1 ***Perf. 11½***

1246	A575	1s bl grn & dk ol grn	3	3
1247	A575	2s bl & Prus bl	7	3
1248	A575	3s car & brn	15	4
1249	A575	13s plum, red & blk	60	20

Bulgarian Communist Party, 8th Congress.

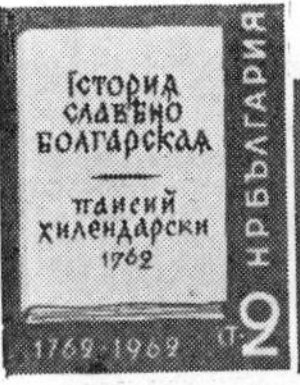

Title Page of "Slav-Bulgarian History"
A576

Paisii Hilendarski Writing History
A577

1962, Dec. 8 ***Perf. 10½*** **Unwmkd.**

1250	A576	2s ol grn & blk	7	3
1251	A577	5s brn org & blk	30	5

Issued to commemorate the 200th anniversary of "Slav-Bulgarian History" by Paisii.

Aleco Konstantinov
A578

1963, Mar. 5 **Photo.** ***Perf. 11½***

1252	A578	5s red, grn & blk	22	12

Issued to commemorate the centenary of the birth of Aleco Konstantinov (1863–1897), writer. Printed with alternating red brown and black label showing Bai Ganu, hero from Konstantinov's books.

Arms of Bulgaria
A579

Sofia University
A580

Designs: No. 1255, Levski Stadium, Sofia. No. 1256, Arch, Nissaria. No. 1257, Parachutist.

1963, Feb. 20 ***Perf. 10*** **Unwmkd.**

1253	A579	1s brn red	3	3
1254	A580	1s red brn	3	3
1255	A580	1s bl grn	3	3
1256	A580	1s dk grn	3	3
1257	A580	1s brt bl	3	3
		Nos. 1253-1257 (5)	15	15

Vassil Levski
A581

Boy, Girl and Dimitrov
A582

1963, Apr. 11 **Photogravure**

1258	A581	13s grnsh bl & buff	75	30

Issued to commemorate the 90th anniversary of the death of Vassil Levski, revolutionary leader in the fight for liberation from the Turks.

1963, Apr. 25 ***Perf. 11½*** **Unwmkd.**

Design: 13s, Girl with book and boy with hammer.

1259	A582	2s org, ver, red brn & blk	8	5
1260	A582	13s bluish grn, brn & blk	50	12

Issued to commemorate the 10th Congress of Dimitrov's Union of the People's Youth.

Red Squirrel
A583

Sun Coast Promenade
A584

Animals: 2s, Hedgehog. 3s, European polecat. 5s, Pine marten. 13s, Badger. 20s, Otter. (2s, 3s, 13s, horiz.)

1963, Apr. 30

Red Numerals

1261	A583	1s grn & brn, *grnsh*	3	3
1262	A583	2s grn & blk *yel*	4	3
1263	A583	3s grn & brn, *bis*	7	3
1264	A583	5s vio & red brn, *lil*	15	6
1265	A583	13s red brn & blk, *pink*	75	20
1266	A583	20s blk & brn, *bl*	1.25	35
		Nos. 1261-1266 (6)	2.29	70

1963, Mar. 12 ***Perf. 13*** **Unwmkd.**

Black Sea Resorts: 2s, 3s, 13s, Views of Gold Sand. 5s, 20s, Sun Coast.

1267	A584	1s blue	5	3
1268	A584	2s vermilion	35	3
1269	A584	2s car rose	50	3
1270	A584	3s ocher	30	3
1271	A584	5s lilac	30	3
1272	A584	13s bl grn	1.00	12
1273	A584	20s green	1.75	35
		Nos. 1267-1273 (7)	4.25	62

Freestyle Wrestling
A585

Design: 20s, Freestyle wrestling (horiz.).

1963, May 31 ***Perf. 11½***

1274	A585	5s yel bis & blk	15	10
1275	A585	20s org brn & blk	75	30

Issued to commemorate the 15th International Freestyle Wrestling Competitions, Sofia.

"Women for Peace"
A586

1963, June 24 ***Perf. 11½*** **Unwmkd.**

1276	A586	20s bl & blk	75	30

Issued to commemorate the World Congress of Women, Moscow, June 24–29.

Esperanto Emblem and Arms of Sofia
A587

Moon, Earth and Lunik 4
A588

1963, June 29 **Photogravure**

1277	A587	13s multi	75	30

Issued to commemorate the 48th World Esperanto Congress, Sofia, Aug. 3–10.

1963, July 22

Designs: 2s, Radar equipment. 3s, Satellites and moon.

1278	A588	1s ultra	5	5
1279	A588	2s red lil	6	5
1280	A588	3s grnsh bl	15	5

Issued to commemorate Russia's rocket to the moon, Apr. 2, 1963.

= MOSTRA
13
EUROPEISTICA·1963
RICCIONE

Nos. 1211–1212 and 1215 Overprinted or Surcharged in Green, Ultramarine or Black

1963, Aug. 31 ***Perf. 10½***

Roses in Natural Colors

1281	A565	2s sal & dk car (G)	30	15
1282	A565	5s on 3s gray & dk car (U)	45	20
1283	A565	13s on 6s bluish grn & dk car	1.00	50

Issued to commemorate the International Stamp Fair, Riccione, Aug. 31.

Women's Relay Race
A589

Designs: 2s, Hammer thrower. 3s, Women's long jump. 5s, Men's high jump. 13s, Discus thrower.

Perf. 11½

1963, Sept. 13 **Photo.** **Unwmkd.**

Flags in National Colors

1284	A589	1s sl grn	10	3
1285	A589	2s purple	15	3
1286	A589	3s Prus bl	20	5
1287	A589	5s maroon	60	35
1288	A589	13s chnt brn	2.50	1.50
		Nos. 1284-1288 (5)	3.55	1.96

Issued to publicize the Balkan Games. A multicolored, 50s, imperf. souvenir sheet shows design of women's relay race. Size: 74x70mm. Price $4 unused, $3 canceled.

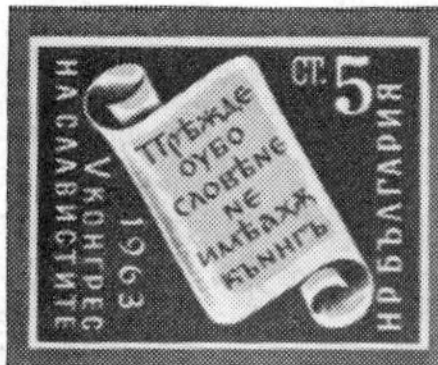

"Slav-Bulgarian History"
A590

1963, Sept. 19 ***Perf. 10½***

1289	A590	5s sal pink, sl & yel	20	4

5th International Slavic Congress.

Revolutionists A591 Christo Smirnenski A592

1963, Sept. 22 ***Perf. 11½***

1290	A591	2s brt red & blk	15	3

Issued to commemorate the 40th anniversary of the September Revolution.

1963, Oct. 28 ***Perf. 10½***

1291	A592	13s pale lil & ind	45	15

Issued to commemorate the 65th anniversary of the birth of Christo Smirnenski, poet.

Columbine A593 Horses A594

1963, Oct. 9 **Photo.** ***Perf. 11½***

Multicolored

1292	A593	1s *shown*	4	3
1293	A593	2s *Edelweiss*	5	5
1294	A593	3s *Primrose*	10	5
1295	A593	5s *Water lily*	15	6
1296	A593	6s *Tulips*	20	8
1297	A593	8s *Larkspur*	25	12
1298	A593	10s *Alpine clematis*	75	30
1299	A593	13s *Anemone*	1.35	45
		Nos. 1292-1299 (8)	2.89	1.14

1963, Dec. 28 ***Perf. 10½*** **Unwmkd.**

Designs: 2s, Charioteer and chariot. 3s, Trumpeters. 5s, Woman carrying tray with food. 13s, Man holding bowl. 20s, Woman in armchair. Designs are from a Thracian tomb at Kazanlik.

1300	A594	1s gray, org & dk red	5	3
1301	A594	2s gray, ocher & pur	5	3
1302	A594	3s gray, dl yel & sl grn	8	5
1303	A594	5s pale grn, ocher & brn	20	6
1304	A594	13s pale grn, bis & blk	65	15
1305	A594	20s pale grn, org & dk car	1.00	35
		Nos. 1300-1305 (6)	2.03	67

World Map and Emblem
A595

Designs: 2s, Blood transfusion. 3s, Nurse bandaging injured wrist. 5s, Red Cross nurse. 13s, Henri Dunant.

1964, Jan. 27 ***Perf. 10½***

1306	A595	1s lem, blk & red	4	3
1307	A595	2s ultra, blk & red	5	3
1308	A595	3s gray, sl, blk & red	6	3
1309	A595	5s brt bl, blk & red	15	6
1310	A595	13s org yel, blk & red	45	18
		Nos. 1306-1310 (5)	75	33

Centenary of International Red Cross.

Speed Skating—A596

Sports: 2s, 50s, Women's figure skating. 3s, Cross-country skiing. 5s, Ski jump. 10s, Ice hockey goalkeeper. 13s, Ice hockey players.

1964, Feb. 21 ***Perf. 10½*** **Unwmkd.**

1311	A596	1s grnsh bl, ind & ocher	5	3
1312	A596	2s brt pink, ol grn & dk sl grn	5	3
1313	A596	3s dl grn, dk grn & brn	8	3
1314	A596	5s bl, blk & yel brn	20	3
1315	A596	10s gray, org & blk	50	15
1316	A596	13s lil, blk & lil rose	90	30
		Nos. 1311-1316 (6)	1.78	57

Miniature Sheet

Imperf.

1317	A596	50s gray, Prus grn & pink	6.00	4.50

Issued to commemorate 9th Winter Olympic Games, Innsbruck, Jan. 29–Feb. 9, 1964.

No. 1317 measures 64x67½mm.

Mask of Nobleman, 2nd Century
A597

Designs: 2s, Thracian horseman. 3s, Ceramic jug. 5s, Clasp and belt. 6s, Copper kettle. 8s, Angel. 10s, Lioness. 13s, Scrub woman, contemporary sculpture.

1964, Mar. 14 **Photo.** ***Perf. 10½***

Gray Frame

1318	A597	1s dp grn & red	4	3
1319	A597	2s ol gray & red	5	3
1320	A597	3s bis & red	10	6
1321	A597	5s ind & red	30	6
1322	A597	6s org brn & red	35	8
1323	A597	8s brn red & red	50	10
1324	A597	10s ol & red	60	15
1325	A597	13s gray ol & red	90	35
		Nos. 1318-1325 (8)	2.84	86

2,500 years of Bulgarian art.

"The Unborn Maid"
A598

Fairy Tales: 2s, Grandfather's Glove. 3s, The Big Turnip. 5s, The Wolf and the Seven Kids. 8s, Cunning Peter. 13s, The Wheat Cake.

1964, Apr. 17 ***Perf. 10½*** **Unwmkd.**

1326	A598	1s bl grn, red & org brn	4	3
1327	A598	2s ultra, ocher & blk	5	3
1328	A598	3s cit, red & blk	6	4
1329	A598	5s dp rose, brn & blk	15	4
1330	A598	8s yel grn, red & blk	30	15
1331	A598	13s lt vio bl, grn & blk	95	35
		Nos. 1326-1331 (6)	1.55	64

Ascalaphus Otomanus
A599

Insects: 2s, Nemoptera coa. (vert.). 3s, Saga natalia (grasshopper). 5s, Rosalia alpina (vert.). 13s, Anisoplia austriaca (vert.). 20s, Scolia flavitrons.

1964, May 16 **Photo.** ***Perf. 11½***

1332	A599	1s brn org, yel & blk	5	3
1333	A599	2s dl bl grn, bis & blk	6	5
1334	A599	3s gray, grn & blk	10	8
1335	A599	5s lt ol grn, blk & vio	15	10
1336	A599	13s vio, bis & blk	65	18
1337	A599	20s gray bl, yel & blk	1.00	30
		Nos. 1332-1337 (6)	2.01	74

Soccer
A600

Designs: 13s, Women's volleyball. 60s, Map of Europe and European Women's Volleyball Championship Cup (rectangular, size: 60x69mm.).

1964, June 8 ***Perf. 11½*** **Unwmkd.**

1338	A600	2s bl, dk bl, ocher & red	20	10
1339	A600	13s bl, dk bl, ocher & red	75	30

Miniature Sheet

Imperf.

1340	A600	60s ultra, ocher, red & gray	3.00	2.50

Issued to commemorate the 50th anniversary of the Levski Physical Culture Association.

Peter Beron and Title Page of Primer—A601

1964, June 22 ***Perf. 11½***

1341	A601	20s red brn & dk brn, *grysh*	1.50	1.25

Issued to commemorate the 140th anniversary of the publication of the first Bulgarian primer.

Robert Stephenson's "Rocket" Locomotive, 1825
A602

Designs: 2s, Modern steam locomotive. 3s, Diesel locomotive. 5s, Electric locomotive. 8s, Freight train on bridge. 13s, Diesel locomotive and tunnel.

1964, July 1 **Photo.** ***Perf. 11½***

1342	A602	1s org brn, blk, bis & gray	4	3
1343	A602	2s org brn, blk, Prus bl & ol	5	3
1344	A602	3s org brn, blk, grn & gray	6	3
1345	A602	5s org brn, blk & bl	20	4
1346	A602	8s org brn, blk, bl & gray	35	5
1347	A602	13s org brn, blk, yel & gray	75	15
		Nos. 1342-1347 (6)	1.45	33

German Shepherd
A603

1964, Aug. 22 **Photogravure**

Multicolored

1348	A603	1s *shown*	3	3
1349	A603	2s *Setter*	4	3
1350	A603	3s *Poodle*	6	3
1351	A603	4s *Pomeranian*	15	4
1352	A603	5s *St. Bernard*	18	4
1353	A603	6s *Terrier*	35	15
1354	A603	10s *Pointer*	1.50	60
1355	A603	13s *Dachshund*	3.00	1.00
		Nos. 1348-1355 (8)	5.31	1.92

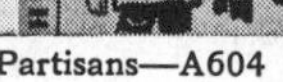

Partisans—A604

Designs: 2s, People welcoming Soviet army. 3s, Russian aid to Bulgaria. 4s, Blast furnace, Kremikovski. 5s, Combine. 6s, Peace demonstration. 8s, Sentry. 13s, Demeter Blagoev and George Dimitrov.

1964, Sept. 9 ***Perf. 11½*** **Unwmkd.**

Flag in Red

1356	A604	1s lt & dp ultra	4	3
1357	A604	2s ol bis & dp ol	5	3

1358	A604	3s rose lil & mar	6	3
1359	A604	4s lt vio & vio	6	3
1360	A604	5s org & red brn	20	4
1361	A604	6s bl & dp bl	25	5
1362	A604	8s lt grn & grn	30	6
1363	A604	13s fawn & red brn	55	12
		Nos. 1356-1363 (8)	1.51	39

Issued to commemorate the 20th anniversary of People's Government of Bulgaria.

No. 967 Surcharged

мм панаир
ПЛОВДИВ - 1964
ST 20

1964, Sept. 13 *Perf. 13*

1364	A476	20s on 44s org yel	1.00	45

International Plovdiv Fair.

Gymnast on Parallel Bars — A606

Vratcata Mountain Road — A607

Sports: 2s, Long jump. 3s, Woman diver. 5s, Soccer. 13s, Women's volleyball. 20s, Wrestling.

1964, Oct. 10 *Perf. 11½*

1366	A606	1s pale grn, grn & red	4	3
1367	A606	2s pale vio, vio bl & red	5	3
1368	A606	3s bl grn, brn & red	6	5
1369	A606	5s pink, pur & red	15	8
1370	A606	13s bl, Prus grn & red	50	15
1371	A606	20s yel, grn & red	1.00	35
		Nos. 1366-1371 (6)	1.80	69

Issued for the 18th Olympic Games, Tokyo. Oct. 10–25. See No. B27.

1964, Oct. 26 Photo. *Perf. 12½x13*

Bulgarian Views: 2s, Ritlite mountain road. 3s, Pines, Malovica peak. 4s, Pobitite rocks. 5s, Erkupria. 6s, Rhodope mountain road.

1372	A607	1s dk sl grn	3	3
1373	A607	2s brown	3	3
1374	A607	3s grnsh bl	8	3
1375	A607	4s dk red brn	20	3
1376	A607	5s dp grn	30	3
1377	A607	6s bl vio	35	5
		Nos. 1372-1377 (6)	99	20

Mail Coach, Plane and Rocket
A608

1964, Oct. 3 *Perf. 11½* **Unwmkd.**

1378	A608	20s grnsh bl	1.75	90

Issued to commemorate the first national stamp exhibition, Sofia, Oct. 3–18. Issued in sheets of 12 stamps and 12 labels (woman's head and inscription, 5x5) arranged around one central label showing stylized bird design.

Students Holding Book
A609

1964, Dec. 30 Photogravure

1379	A609	13s lt bl & blk	60	15

Issued to commemorate the 8th International Students' Congress, Sofia.

500-Year-Old Walnut Tree at Golemo Drenovo—A610

Designs: Various Old Trees.

1964, Dec. 28

1380	A610	1s blk, buff & cl brn	3	3
1381	A610	2s blk, pink & dp cl	5	3
1382	A610	3s blk, yel & dk brn	6	3
1383	A610	4s blk, lt bl & Prus bl	8	3
1384	A610	10s blk, pale grn & grn	45	10
1385	A610	13s blk, pale bis & dk ol grn	80	30
		Nos. 1380-1385 (6)	1.47	52

Soldiers' Monument
A611

1965, Jan. 1 **Unwmkd.**

1386	A611	2s red & blk	30	10

Issued to honor Bulgarian-Soviet friendship.

Olympic Medal Inscribed "Olympic Glory"
A612

1965, Jan. 27 Photo. *Perf. 11½*

1387	A612	20s org brn, gold & blk	90	35

Issued to commemorate Bulgarian victories in the 1964 Olympic Games.

"Victory Over Fascism"
A613

Design: 13s, "Fight for Peace" (dove and globe).

1965, Apr. 16 *Perf. 11½*

1388	A613	5s gray, blk & ol bis	15	5
1389	A613	13s gray, blk & bl	45	20

Issued to commemorate the 20th anniversary of victory over Fascism, May 9, 1945.

Vladimir M. Komarov and Section of Globe
A614

Designs: 2s, Konstantin Feoktistov. 5s, Boris B. Yegorov. 13s, Komarov, Feoktistov and Yegorov. 20s, Spaceship Voskhod.

1965, Feb. 15 Photogravure

1390	A614	1s pale lil & dk bl	3	3
1391	A614	2s lt bl, ind & dl vio	3	3
1392	A614	5s pale grn, grn & ol grn	15	5
1393	A614	13s pale pink, dp rose & mar	35	15
1394	A614	20s lt bl, vio bl, grnsh bl & yel	75	30
		Nos. 1390-1394 (5)	1.31	56

Russian 3-man space flight, Oct. 12-13, 1964.

Imperfs. in changed colors. Four low values se-tenant.

Price, set $3 unused, $1.50 canceled.

Bullfinch
A615

Birds: 2s, European golden oriole. 3s, Common rock thrush. 5s, Barn swallow. 8s, European roller. 10s, European goldfinch. 13s, Rosy pastor starling. 20s, Nightingale.

1965, Apr. 20 *Perf. 11½* **Unwmkd.**

Birds in Natural Colors

1395	A615	1s bl grn	4	3
1396	A615	2s rose lil	10	3
1397	A615	3s rose	15	3
1398	A615	5s brt bl	20	5
1399	A615	8s citron	45	6
1400	A615	10s gray	1.75	45
1401	A615	13s lt vio bl	1.75	45
1402	A615	20s emerald	3.00	90
		Nos. 1395-1402 (8)	7.44	2.00

Sting Ray
A616

Black Sea Fish: 2s, Belted bonito. 3s, Hogfish. 5s, Gurnard. 10s, Scad. 13s, Turbot.

1965, June 10 Photo. *Perf. 11½*

Gray Frames

1403	A616	1s org, blk & gold	3	3
1404	A616	2s ultra, ind & sil	4	3
1405	A616	3s emer, blk & gold	10	3
1406	A616	5s dp car, blk & gold	20	10
1407	A616	10s grnsh bl, blk & sil	1.00	30
1408	A616	13s red brn, blk & gold	1.40	60
		Nos. 1403-1408 (6)	2.77	1.09

Plane, Bus, Train, Ship and Whale
A617

ITU Emblem and Communications Symbols
A618

1965, Apr. 30

1409	A617	13s multi	45	15

Issued to publicize the fourth International Conference of Transport, Dock and Fishery Workers, Sofia, May 10–14.

1965, May 17

1410	A618	20s multi	90	35

Issued to commemorate the centenary of the International Telecommunication Union.

Col. Pavel Belyayev and Lt. Col. Alexei Leonov
A619

Design: 20s, Leonov floating in space.

1965, May 20 **Unwmkd.**

1411	A619	2s gray, dl bl & dk brn	15	8
1412	A619	20s multi	2.25	90

Space flight of Voskhod 2 and the first man floating in space, Lt. Col. Alexei Leonov.

ICY Emblem
A620

1965, May 15 Photogravure

1413	A620	20s org, ol & blk	90	30

International Cooperation Year, 1965.

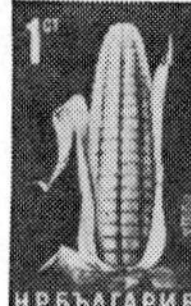

Corn A621 — Marx and Lenin A622

Designs: 2s, Wheat. 3s, Sunflowers. 4s, Sugar beet. 5s, Clover. 10s, Cotton. 13s, Tobacco.

1965, Apr. 1 ***Perf. 12½x13***

1414	A621	1s org yel	3	3
1415	A621	2s brt grn	5	3
1416	A621	3s dp org	8	3
1417	A621	4s olive	15	3
1418	A621	5s brt rose	30	3
1419	A621	10s grnsh bl	90	10
1420	A621	13s bister	1.25	30
		Nos. 1414-1420 (7)	2.76	55

1965, June ***Perf. 10½***

1421	A622	13s red & dk brn	60	20

Issued to commemorate the 6th Conference of Postal Ministers of Communist Countries, Peking, June 21–July 15.

Film and UNESCO Emblem A623

1965, June 30

1422	A623	13s dp bl, blk & lt gray	60	20

Balkan Film Festival, Varna.

Ballerina A624

1965, July 10 **Photogravure**

1423	A624	5s dp lil rose & blk	65	30

Issued to publicize the Second International Ballet Competition, Varna.

Map of Balkan Peninsula and Dove with Letter—A625

Col. Pavel Belyayev and Lt. Col. Alexei Leonov—A626

Designs: 2s, Sailboat and modern buildings. 3s, Fish and plants. 13s, Symbolic sun and rocket. 40s, Map of Balkan Peninsula and dove with letter (like 1s).

1965, July 23–Aug. 7 ***Perf. 10½***

1424	A625	1s sil, dp ultra & yel	5	3
1425	A625	2s sil, pur & yel	6	3
1426	A625	3s gold, grn & yel	15	8
1427	A625	13s gold, hn brn & yel	75	60
1428	A626	20s sil, bl & brn	1.10	75
		Nos. 1424-1428 (5)	2.11	1.49

Miniature Sheet

Imperf.

1429	A625	40s gold & brt bl	2.25	1.75

Balkaphila 1905 Philatelic Exhibition, Varna, Aug. 7-15, and visit of Russian astronauts Belyayev and Leonov The 20s and 40s were issued Aug. 7.

No. 1429 has gold denomination and inscription in margin. Size: 69×61½mm.

Price, #1428 imperf. in changed colors, $1.10.

Woman Gymnast A627

Designs: 2s, Woman gymnast on parallel bars. 3s, Weight lifter. 5s, Automobile and chart. 10s, Women basketball players. 13s, Automobile and map of rally.

1965, Aug. 14 ***Perf. 10½***

1430	A627	1s crim, brn & blk	4	3
1431	A627	2s rose vio, dp cl & blk	5	3
1432	A627	3s dp car, brn & blk	6	3
1433	A627	5s fawn, red brn & blk	20	3
1434	A627	10s dp lil rose, dp cl & blk	80	15
1435	A627	13s lil, cl & blk	95	20
		Nos. 1430-1435 (6)	2.10	47

Issued to commemorate various sports events in Bulgaria during May–June, 1965.

No. 989 Surcharged

2 Ст

ПЪРВИ НАЦИОНАЛЕН
СЪБОР НА НАРОДНОТО
ТВОРЧЕСТВО
12-15.VIII
1965

1965, Aug. 12 ***Perf. 13***

1436	A499	2s on 8s org brn	90	60

Issued to publicize the First National Folklore Competition, Aug. 12–15.

Escaping Prisoners A628

Apples A629

1965, July 23 ***Perf. 10½***

1437	A628	2s slate	20	15

Issued to commemorate the 40th anniversary of the escape of political prisoners from Bolshevik Island.

1965, July 1 ***Perf. 13***

Fruit: 2s, Grapes. 3s, Pears. 4s, Peaches. 5s, Strawberries. 6s, Walnuts.

1438	A629	1s dp org	3	3
1439	A629	2s lt ol grn	3	3
1440	A629	3s bister	5	3
1441	A629	4s orange	6	3
1442	A629	5s car rose	18	3
1443	A629	6s yel brn	60	15
		Nos. 1438-1443 (6)	95	30

Dressage—A630

Horsemanship: 2s, Three-day test. 3s, Jumping. 5s, Race. 10s, Steeplechase. 13s, Hurdle race.

1965, Sept. 30 ***Perf. 10½*** **Unwmkd.**

1444	A630	1s bluish gray, blk & dk vio	4	3
1445	A630	2s buff, blk & hn brn	4	3
1446	A630	3s gray, blk & dk car rose	5	3
1447	A630	5s gray ol, dk grn & red brn	8	5
1448	A630	10s lt gray, blk & dk red brn	75	30
1449	A630	13s sal, dk grn & dk red brn	1.25	45
		Nos. 1444-1449 (6)	2.21	89

See also No. B28.

Smiling Children A631

Designs: 2s, Two girl Pioneers. 3s, Bugler. 5s, Pioneer with model plane. 8s, Two singing girls in national costume. 13s, Running boy.

1965, Oct. 24 **Photogravure**

1450	A631	1s dk bl grn & yel grn	3	3
1451	A631	2s vio & dp rose	3	3
1452	A631	3s ol & lem	15	3
1453	A631	5s dp bl & bis	15	6
1454	A631	8s ol bis & org	45	20
1455	A631	13s rose car & vio	1.00	35
		Nos. 1450-1455 (6)	1.81	70

Issued to honor the Dimitrov Pioneer Organization.

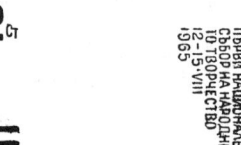

U-52 Plane over Trnovo A632

Designs: 2c, IL-14 over Plovdiv. 3s, Mi-4 Helicopter over Dimitrovgrad. 5s, Tu-104 over Ruse. 13s, IL-18 over Varna. 20s, Tu-114 over Sofia.

1965, Nov. 25 ***Perf. 10½***

1456	A632	1s gray, bl & red	3	3
1457	A632	2s gray, lil & red	3	3
1458	A632	3s gray, grnsh bl & red	7	5
1459	A632	5s gray, org & red	12	8
1460	A632	13s gray, bis & red	80	24
1461	A632	20s gray, lt grn & red	1.10	60
		Nos. 1456-1461 (6)	2.15	1.03

Issued to publicize the development of Bulgarian Civil Air Transport.

IQSY Emblem, and Earth Radiation Zones A633

Designs (IQSY Emblem and): 2s, Sun with corona. 13s, Solar eclipse.

1965, Dec. 15 **Photo.** ***Perf. 10½***

1462	A633	1s grn, yel & ultra	3	3
1463	A633	2s yel, red lil & red	5	3
1464	A633	13s bl, yel & blk	60	20

International Quiet Sun Year, 1964–65.

"North and South Bulgaria" A634

"Martenitsa" Emblem A635

1965, Dec. 6

1465	A634	13s brt yel grn & blk	75	35

Issued to commemorate the centenary of the Union of North and South Bulgaria.

1966, Jan. 10 **Photo.** ***Perf. 10½***

"Spring" in Folklore: 2s, Drummer. 3s, Bird ornaments. 5s, Dancer "Lazarka." 8s, Vase with flowers. 13s, Bagpiper.

1466	A635	1s rose lil, vio bl & gray	3	3
1467	A635	2s gray, blk & crim	3	3
1468	A635	3s red, vio & gray	5	3
1469	A635	5s lil, blk & crim	9	3
1470	A635	8s rose lil, brn & pur	30	7
1471	A635	13s bl, blk & rose lil	75	20
		Nos. 1466-1471 (6)	1.25	39

Church of St. John the Baptist, Nessebr—A636

Designs: 1s, Christ, fresco from Bojana Church. 2s, Ikon "Destruction of Idols" (horiz.). 3s, Bratchkovo Monastery. 4s, Zemen Monastery (horiz.). 13s, Nativity, ikon from Arbanassi. 20s, Ikon "Virgin and Child," 1342.

1966, Feb. 25 **Litho.** ***Perf. 11½***

1472	A636	1s gray & multi	40	40
1473	A636	2s gray & multi	30	25
1474	A636	3s multi	30	25
1475	A636	4s multi	30	25
1476	A636	5s multi	40	30
1477	A636	13s gray & multi	50	30
1478	A636	20s multi	90	75
		Nos. 1472-1478 (7)	3.10	2.50

2,500 years of art in Bulgaria.

Georgi Benkovski and T. Kableshkov—A637

Designs: 1s, Proclamation of April Uprising, Koprivstitsa. 3s, Dedication of flag, Panaguriste. 5s, V. Petleshkov and Z. Dyustabanov. 10s, Botev landing at Kozlodui. 13s, P. Volov and Ilarion Dragostinov.

1966, March 3 Photo. *Perf. 10½*

Center in Black

1479	A637	1s red brn & gold	3	3
1480	A637	2s brt red & gold	4	3
1481	A637	3s ol grn & gold	6	3
1482	A637	5s stl bl & gold	12	3
1483	A637	10s brt rose lil & gold	35	4
1484	A637	13s lt vio & gold	65	15
		Nos. 1479-1484 (6)	1.25	31

Issued to commemorate the 90th anniversary of the April Uprising against the Turks.

Elephant A638

Animals from Sofia Zoo: 2s, Tiger. 3s, Chimpanzee. 4s, Siberian ibex. 5s, Polar bear. 8s, Lion. 13s, Bison. 20s, Kangaroo.

1966, May 23 Lithographed

1485	A638	1s yel, blk & gray	4	3
1486	A638	2s dl yel, org yel & blk	4	3
1487	A638	3s pale grn, bis & blk	6	3
1488	A638	4s tan, brn & blk	15	3
1489	A638	5s lt bl & blk	20	4
1490	A638	8s pale rose, bis & blk	20	15
1491	A638	13s cit, brn & blk	65	30
1492	A638	20s pale lil, bis & blk	1.50	60
		Nos. 1485-1492 (8)	2.84	1.21

WHO Headquarters, Geneva A639

1966, May 3 Photogravure

1493	A639	13s dp bl & sil	90	20

Issued to commemorate the inauguration of the World Health Organization Headquarters, Geneva.

Worker A640

1966, May 9 Photo. *Perf. 10½*

1494	A640	20s gray & rose	90	20

Sixth Trade Union Congress.

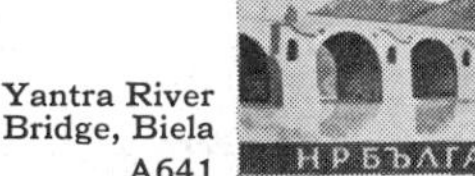

Yantra River Bridge, Biela A641

Designs: No. 1496, Maritsa River Bridge, Svilengrad. No. 1497, Fountain, Samokov. No. 1498, Ruins of Fort, Kaskovo. 8s, Old Fort, Ruse. 13s, House, Gabrovo.

1966, Feb. 10 Photo. *Perf. 13*

1495	A641	1s Prus bl	3	3
1496	A641	1s brt grn	3	3
1497	A641	2s ol grn	5	3
1498	A641	2s dk red brn	5	3
1499	A641	8s red brn	35	10
1500	A641	13s dk bl	60	20
		Nos. 1495-1500 (6)	1.11	42

Souvenir Sheet

Moon Allegory—A642

1966, Apr. 29 *Imperf.*

1501	A642	60s blk, plum & sil	3.25	2.50

Issued to commemorate the first Russian soft landing on the moon by Luna 9, Feb. 3, 1966. Size: 70x50mm.

Steamer Radetzky and Bugler—A643

1966, May 28 *Perf. 10½*

1502	A643	2s multi	15	5

Issued to commemorate the 90th anniversary of the participation of the Danube steamer Radetzky in the uprising against the Turks.

Standard Bearer Nicola Simov-Kuruto A644

1966, May 30

1503	A644	5s bis, grn & ol	30	12

Issued to honor Nicola Simov-Kuruto, hero of the Turkish War.

UNESCO Emblem A645

1966, June 8

1504	A645	20s gold, blk & ver	90	35

Issued to commemorate the 20th anniversary of UNESCO (United Nations Educational, Scientific and Cultural Organization).

Youth Federation Badge—A646

1966, June 6 Photo. *Perf. 10½*

1505	A646	13s sil, bl & blk	45	20

Issued to publicize the 7th Assembly of the International Youth Federation.

Soccer—A647

Designs: Various soccer scenes. 50s, Jules Rimet Cup.

1966, June 27

1506	A647	1s gray, yel brn & blk	3	3
1507	A647	2s gray, crim & blk	4	3
1508	A647	5s gray, ol bis & blk	15	5
1509	A647	13s gray, ultra & blk	45	20
1510	A647	20s gray, Prus bl & blk	75	35
		Nos. 1506-1510 (5)	1.42	66

Miniature Sheet

Imperf.

1511	A647	50s gray, dp lil rose & gold	3.00	2.25

Issued to commemorate the World Soccer Cup Championship, Wembley, England, July 11–30. Size of No. 1511: 60x64mm.

Woman Javelin Thrower—A648

Designs: No. 1513, Runner. No. 1514, Young man and woman carrying banners (vert.).

1966 Photo. *Perf. 10½*

1512	A648	2s grn, yel & ver	5	3
1513	A648	13s dp grn, yel & sal pink	45	15
1514	A648	13s bl, lt bl & sal	50	20

Nos. 1512–1513 commemorate the 3rd Spartacist Games; issued Aug. 10. No. 1514 commemorates the 3rd congress of the Bulgarian Youth Federation; issued May 25.

Wrestlers Nicolas Petrov and Dan Kolov—A649

1966, July 29

1515	A649	13s bis brn, dk brn & lt ol grn	60	20

3rd International Wrestling Championships.

Map of Balkan Countries, Globe and UNESCO Emblem A650

1966, Aug. 26 *Perf. 10½x11½*

1516	A650	13s ultra, lt grn & pink	35	15

First Congress of Balkanologists.

Children with Building Blocks A651

Designs: 2s, Bunny and teddy bear with book. 3s, Children as astronauts. 13s, Children with pails and shovel.

1966, Sept. 1 *Perf. 10½*

1517	A651	1s dk car, org & blk	3	3
1518	A651	2s emer, blk & red brn	5	3
1519	A651	3s ultra, org & blk	10	3
1520	A651	13s bl, rose & blk	75	20

Issued for Children's Day.

Yuri A. Gagarin and Vostok 1 A652

Designs: 2s, Gherman S. Titov and Vostok 2. 3s, Andrian G. Nikolayev, Pavel R. Popovich, and Vostoks 3 & 4. 5s, Valentina Tereshkova, Valeri Bykovski and Vostoks 5 and 6. 8s, Vladimir M. Komarov, Boris B. Yegorov, Konstantin Feoktistov and Voskhod 1. 13s, Pavel Belyayev, Alexei Leonov and Voskhod 2.

1966, Sept. 29 Photo. *Perf. 11½x11*

1521	A652	1s sl & gray	3	3
1522	A652	2s plum & gray	3	3
1523	A652	3s yel brn & gray	6	4
1524	A652	5s brn red & gray	8	6
1525	A652	8s ultra & gray	20	10
1526	A652	13s Prus bl & gray	45	20
		Nos. 1521-1526, B29 (7)	2.10	1.21

Russian space explorations.

St. Clement, 14th Century Wood Sculpture A653

1966, Oct. 27 Photo. *Perf. 11½x11*

1527	A653	5s red, buff & brn	35	5

Issued to commemorate the 1050th anniversary of the birth of St. Clement of Ochrida.

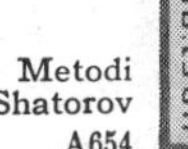

Metodi Shatorov A654

Portraits: 3s, Vladimir Trichkov. 5s, Valcho Ivanov. 10s, Raiko Daskalov. 13s, General Vladimir Zaimov.

1966, Nov. 8 ***Perf. 11x11½***

Gold Frame, Black Denomination

1528	A654	2s crim & bl vio	3	3
1529	A654	3s mag & blk	5	3
1530	A654	5s car rose & dk bl	15	5
1531	A654	10s org & ol	35	10
1532	A654	13s red & brn	45	15
		Nos. 1528-1532 (5)	1.03	36

Issued to honor fighters against fascism.

George Dimitrov
A655

Steel Worker
A656

1966, Nov. 14 Photo. ***Perf. 11½x11***

1533	A655	2s mag & blk	5	3
1534	A656	20s fawn, gray & blk	65	20

Bulgarian Communist Party, 9th Congress.

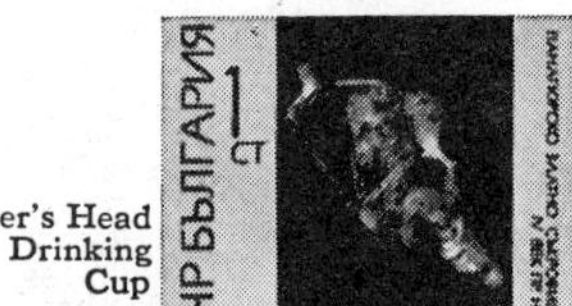

Deer's Head Drinking Cup
A667

Gold Treasure: 2s, 6s, 10s, Various Amazon's head jugs. 3s, Ram's head cup. 5s, Circular plate. 8s, Deer's head cup. 13s, Amphora. 20s, Ram drinking horn.

1966, Nov. 28 ***Perf. 12x11½***

Vessels in Gold and Brown; Black Inscriptions

1535	A667	1s gray & vio	3	3
1536	A667	2s gray & grn	7	3
1537	A667	3s gray & dk bl	10	3
1538	A667	5s gray & red brn	15	3
1539	A667	6s gray & Prus bl	18	4
1540	A667	8s gray & brn ol	1.25	15
1541	A667	10s gray & sep	1.25	20
1542	A667	13s gray & dk vio bl	1.25	30
1543	A667	20s gray & vio brn	1.50	50
		Nos. 1535-1543 (9)	5.78	1.31

The gold treasure from the 4th century B.C. was found near Panagyurishte in 1949.

Tourist House, Bansko
A668

Tourist Houses: No. 1545, Belogradchik. No. 1546, Triavna. 20s, Rila.

1966, Nov. 29 Photo. ***Perf. 11x11½***

1544	A668	1s dk bl	4	3
1545	A668	2s dk grn	4	3
1546	A668	2s brn red	4	3
1547	A668	20s lilac	75	15

Decorated Tree
A669

Design: 13s, Jug with bird design.

1966, Dec. 12 ***Perf. 11***

1548	A669	2s grn, pink & gold	3	3
1549	A669	13s brn lake, rose, emer & gold	50	20

Issued for New Year, 1967.

Pencho Slavikov, Author
A670

Dahlia
A671

Portraits: 2s, Dimcho Debeljanov, author. 3s, P. H. Todorov, author. 5s, Dimitri Dobrovich, painter. 8s, Ivan Markvichka, painter. 13s, Ilya Bezhkov, painter.

1966, Dec. 15 ***Perf. 10½x11***

1550	A670	1s bl, ol & org	3	3
1551	A670	2s org, brn & gray	3	3
1552	A670	3s ol, bl & org	5	3
1553	A670	5s gray, red brn & org	8	3
1554	A670	8s lil, dk gray & bl	20	8
1555	A670	13s bl, vio & lil	50	20
		Nos. 1550-1555 (6)	89	40

1966, Dec. 29

Flowers: No. 1557, Clematis. No. 1558, Foxglove. No. 1559, Narcissus. 3s, Snowdrop. 5s, Petunia. 13s, Tiger lily. 20s, Bellflower.

Flowers in Natural Colors

1556	A671	1s gray & lt brn	5	5
1557	A671	1s gray & dl bl	5	5
1558	A671	2s gray & dl lil	10	5
1559	A671	2s gray & brn	10	5
1560	A671	3s gray & dk grn	15	6
1561	A671	5s gray & dp ultra	20	12
1562	A671	13s gray & brn	65	25
1563	A671	20s gray & ultra	95	40
		Nos. 1556-1563 (8)	2.25	1.03

Ring-necked Pheasant
A672

Game: 2s, Rock partridge. 3s, Gray partridge. 5s, Hare. 8s, Roe deer. 13s, Red deer.

1967, Jan. 28 ***Perf. 11x10½***

1564	A672	1s lt ultra, dk brn & ocher	3	3
1565	A672	2s pale yel grn & dk grn	3	3
1566	A672	3s lt bl, blk & cr	10	3
1567	A672	5s lt grn & blk	15	4
1568	A672	8s pale bl, dk brn & ocher	60	15
1569	A672	13s bl & dk brn	95	35
		Nos. 1564-1569 (6)	1.86	63

Bulgaria No. 1, 1879
A673

Thracian Coin, 6th Century, B.C.
A674

1967, Feb. 4 Photo. ***Perf. 10½***

1570	A673	10s emer, blk & yel	1.10	50

Issued to publicize the 10th Congress of the Bulgarian Philatelic Union.

1967, March 30 ***Perf. 11½x11***

Coins: 2s, Macedonian tetradrachma, 2nd century, B.C. 3s, Tetradrachma of Odessus, 2nd century, B.C. 5s, Philip II of Macedonia, 4th century, B.C. 13s, Thracian King Seuthus VII, 4th century, B.C., obverse and reverse. 20s, Apollonian coin, 5th century, B.C., obverse and reverse.

Size: 25x25mm.

1571	A674	1s brn, blk & sil	3	3
1572	A674	2s red lil, blk & sil	3	3
1573	A674	3s grn, blk & sil	5	3
1574	A674	5s brn org, blk & sil	20	4

Size: 37½x25mm.

1575	A674	13s brt bl, blk & brnz	1.25	50
1576	A674	20s vio, blk & sil	1.75	1.10
		Nos. 1571-1576 (6)	3.31	1.73

Partisans Listening to Radio
A675

Design: 20s, George Dimitrov addressing crowd and Bulgarian flag.

1967, Apr. 20 ***Perf. 11x11½***

1577	A675	1s red, gold, buff & sl grn	5	3
1578	A675	20s red, gold, dl red, grn & blk	75	30

Issued to commemorate the 25th anniversary of the Union of Patriotic Front Organizations.

Nikolas Kofardjiev
A676

Portraits: 2s, Petko Napetov. 5s, Petko D. Petkov. 10s, Emil Markov. 13s, Traitcho Kostov.

1967, Apr. 24 ***Perf. 11½x11***

1579	A676	1s brn red, gray & blk	3	3
1580	A676	2s ol grn, gray & blk	5	3
1581	A676	5s brn, gray & blk	8	5
1582	A676	10s dp bl, gray & blk	17	10
1583	A676	13s mag, gray & blk	50	12
		Nos. 1579-1583 (5)	83	33

Issued to honor fighters against fascism.

Symbolic Flower and Flame
A677

1967, May 18 Photo. ***Perf. 11x11½***

1584	A677	13s gold, yel & lt grn	60	12

First Cultural Congress, May 18–19.

Gold Sand Beach and ITY Emblem
A678

Designs: 20s, Hotel, Pamporovo. 40s, Nessebr Church.

1967, June 12 Photo. ***Perf. 11x11½***

1585	A678	13s ultra, yel & blk	35	15
1586	A678	20s Prus bl, blk & buff	50	20
1587	A678	40s brt grn, blk & ocher	1.35	65

Issued for International Tourist Year, 1967.

Angora Cat
A679

Cats: 2s, Siamese (horiz.). 3s, Abyssinian. 5s, Black European. 13s, Persian (horiz.). 20s, Striped domestic.

Perf. 11½x11, 11x11½

1967, June 19

1588	A679	1s dl vio, dk brn & buff	3	3
1589	A679	2s ol, sl & brt bl	10	3
1590	A679	3s dl bl & brn	15	3
1591	A679	5s grn, blk & yel	20	4
1592	A679	13s dl red brn, sl & org	75	20
1593	A679	20s gray grn, brn & buff	1.10	50
		Nos. 1588-1593 (6)	2.33	83

Scene from Opera "The Master of Boyana" by K. Iliev
A680

Songbird on Keyboard
A681

1967, June 19

1594	A680	5s gray, vio bl & dp car	15	3
1595	A681	13s gray, dp car & dk bl	45	15

Issued to commemorate the 3rd International Competition for Young Opera Singers.

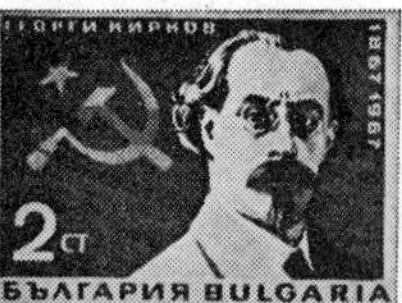

George Kirkov
A682

1967, June 24 ***Perf. 11x11½***

1596	A682	2s rose red & dk brn	15	3

Issued to commemorate the centenary of the birth of George Kirkov (1867–1919), revolutionist.

Symbolic Tree and Stars
A683

1967, July 28 Photo. ***Perf. 11½x11***

1597	A683	13s dp bl, car & blk	50	20

Issued to commemorate the 11th Congress of Dimitrov's Union of the People's Youth.

Roses and Distillery
A684

Designs: No. 1599, Chick and incubator. No. 1600, Cucumbers and hothouse. No. 1601, Lamb and sheep farm. 3s, Sunflower and oil mill. 4s, Pigs and pig farm. 5s, Hops and hop farm. 6s, Corn and irrigation system. 8s, Grapes and Bolgar tractor. 10s, Apples and cultivated tree. 13s, Bees and honey. 20s, Bee, blossoms and beehives.

1967 ***Perf. 11x11½***

1598	A684	1s multi	3	3
1599	A684	1s dk car, yel & blk	3	3
1600	A684	2s vio, lt grn & blk	3	3
1601	A684	2s brt grn, gray & blk	3	3
1602	A684	3s yel grn, yel & blk	5	3
1603	A684	4s brt pur, yel & blk	7	4
1604	A684	5s ol bis, yel grn & blk	10	8
1605	A684	6s ol, brt grn & blk	15	10
1606	A684	8s grn, bis & blk	20	12
1607	A684	10s multi	30	15
1608	A684	13s grn, bis brn & blk	60	24
1609	A684	20s grnsh bl, brt pink & blk	75	30
		Nos. 1598-1609 (12)	2.34	1.18

Issue dates: Nos. 1598–1601, 1607 and 1609, July 15; Nos. 1602–1606 and 1608, July 24.

Map of Communist Countries, Spasski Tower
A685

Designs: 2s, Lenin speaking to soldiers. 3s, Fighting at Wlodaja, 1918. 5s, Marx, Engels and Lenin. 13s, Oil refinery. 20s, Molniya communication satellite.

1967, Aug. 25 ***Perf. 11***

1610	A685	1s multi	3	3
1611	A685	2s mag & ol	3	3
1612	A685	3s mag & dl vio	5	3
1613	A685	5s mag & red	8	5
1614	A685	13s mag & ultra	30	12
1615	A685	20s mag & bl	75	20
		Nos. 1610-1615 (6)	1.24	46

Issued to commemorate the 50th anniversary of the Russian October Revolution.

Rod, "Fish" and Varna
A686

1967, Aug. 29 Photo. ***Perf. 11***

1616	A686	10s multi	45	15

7th World Angling Championships, Varna.

Skiers and Winter Olympics' Emblem—A687

Sports and Emblem: 2s, Ski jump. 3s, Biathlon. 5s, Ice hockey. 13s, Figure skating couple.

1967, Sept. 20 Photo. ***Perf. 11***

1617	A687	1s dk bl grn, red & blk	3	3
1618	A687	2s ultra, blk & ol	3	3
1619	A687	3s vio brn, bl & blk	5	3
1620	A687	5s grn, yel & blk	8	5
1621	A687	13s vio bl, blk & buff	45	10
		Nos. 1617-1621, B31 (6)	2.14	90

Issued to publicize the 10th Winter Olympic Games, Grenoble, France, Feb. 6–18, 1968.

Bogdan Mountain
A688

Mountain Peaks: 2s, Czerny. 3s, Ruen (vert.). 5s, Persenk. 10s, Botev. 13s, Rila (vert.). 20s, Vihren.

1967, Sept. 25 Engr. ***Perf. 11½***

1622	A688	1s sl grn & yel	3	3
1623	A688	2s sep & pale bl	3	3
1624	A688	3s ind & lt bl	5	3
1625	A688	5s sl grn & lt bl	10	5
1626	A688	10s dp cl & lt bl	18	6
1627	A688	13s dk gray & lt bl	30	15
1628	A688	20s ind & rose	75	30
		Nos. 1622-1628 (7)	1.44	65

George Rakovski
A689

1967, Oct. 20 Photo. ***Perf. 11***

1629	A689	13s yel grn & blk	60	20

Issued to commemorate the centenary of the death of George Rakovski, revolutionary against Turkish rule.

Yuri A. Gagarin, Valentina Tereshkova and Alexei Leonov
A690

Designs: 2s, Lt. Col. John H. Glenn, Jr., and Maj. Edward H. White. 5s, Earth and Molniya 1. 10s, Gemini 6 and 7. 13s, Luna 13 moon probe. 20s, Gemini 10 and Agena rocket.

1967, Nov. 25

1630	A690	1s Prus bl, blk & yel	3	3
1631	A690	2s dl bl, blk & dl yel	3	3
1632	A690	5s vio bl, grnsh bl & blk	8	5
1633	A690	10s dk bl, blk & red	30	10
1634	A690	13s grnsh bl, brt yel & blk	50	12
1635	A690	20s dl bl, blk & red	80	45
		Nos. 1630-1635 (6)	1.74	78

Achievements in space exploration.

View of Trnovo
A691

Various Views of Trnovo

1967, Dec. 5 Photogravure ***Perf. 11***

1636	A691	1s multi	3	3
1637	A691	2s multi	3	3
1638	A691	3s multi	5	3
1639	A691	5s multi	15	5
1640	A691	13s multi	35	15
1641	A691	20s multi	60	30
		Nos. 1636-1641 (6)	1.21	59

Issued to publicize the restoration of the ancient capital Veliko Trnovo.

Ratchenitza Folk Dance, by Ivan Markvichka
A692

1967, Dec. 9

1642	A692	20s gold & gray grn	1.75	1.25

Issued to commemorate the Belgo-Bulgarian Philatelic Exposition, Brussels, Dec. 9–10. Printed in sheets of 8 stamps and 8 labels.

Canceled-to-order stamps are often from remainders. Most collectors of canceled stamps prefer postally used specimens.

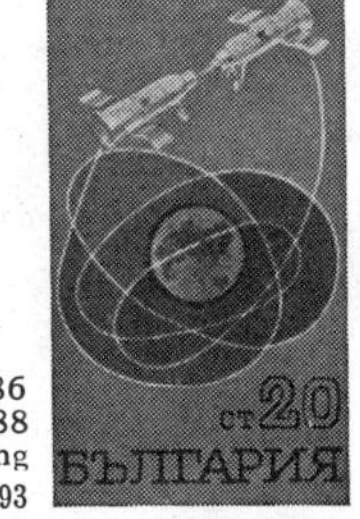

Cosmos 186 and 188 Docking
A693

Design: 40s, Venus 4 and orbits around Venus (horiz.).

1968, Jan.

1643	A693	20s vio, gray & pink	75	30
1644	A693	40s rose car, gray, sil & blk	1.50	60

Issued to commemorate the docking maneuvers of the Russian spaceships Cosmos 186 and Cosmos 188, Nov. 1, 1967, and the flight to Venus of Venus 4, June 12–Nov. 18, 1967.

Crossing the Danube, by Orenburgski
A694

Paintings: 2s, Flag of Samara, by J. Veschin (vert.). 3s, Battle of Pleven by Orenburgski. 13s, Battle of Orlovo Gnezdo, by N. Popov (vert.). 20s, Welcome for Russian Soldiers, by D. Gudienov.

1968, Jan. 25 Photo. ***Perf. 11***

1645	A694	1s gold & dk grn	5	3
1646	A694	2s gold & dk bl	5	3
1647	A694	3s gold & cl brn	5	3
1648	A694	13s gold & dk vio	60	20
1649	A694	20s gold & Prus grn	75	35
		Nos. 1645-1649 (5)	1.50	64

Issued to commemorate the 90th anniversary of the liberation from Turkey.

Shepherds, by Zlatyn Boyadjiev
A695

Paintings: 2s, Wedding dance, by V. Dimitrov. (vert.). 3s, Partisans' Song, by Ilya Petrov. 5s, Portrait of Anna Penchovich, by Nikolai Pavlovich (vert.). 13s, Self-portrait, by Zachary Zograf (vert.). 20s, View of Old Plovdiv, by T. Lavrenov. 60s, St. Clement of Ochrida, by A. Mitov.

1967, Dec. Litho. ***Perf. 11½***

Size: 45x38mm., 38x45mm.

1650	A695	1s gray & multi	8	3
1651	A695	2s gray & multi	15	3

Size: 55x35mm.

1652	A695	3s gray & multi	20	15

Size: 38x45mm., 45x38mm.

1653	A695	5s gray & multi	45	15
1654	A695	13s gray & multi	1.25	35
1655	A695	20s gray & multi	1.50	75
		Nos. 1650-1655 (6)	3.63	1.46

Miniature Sheet

Imperf.

Size: 65x84mm.

1656	A695	60s multi	4.50	4.50

Marx Statue, Sofia

A696

Maxim Gorky

A697

1968, Feb. 20 Photo. ***Perf. 11***

1657	A696	13s blk & red	50	15

150th anniversary of birth of Karl Marx.

1968, Feb. 20

1658	A697	13s ver & grnsh blk	50	15

Issued to commemorate the centenary of the birth of Maxim Gorky (1868–1936), Russian writer.

Folk Dancers—A698

Designs: 5s, Runners. 13s, Doves. 20s, Festival poster, (head, flowers and birds). 40s, Globe and Bulgaria No. 1 under magnifying glass.

1968, Mar. 20

1659	A698	2s multi	5	3
1660	A698	5s multi	10	5
1661	A698	13s multi	25	8
1662	A698	20s multi	60	30
1663	A698	40s multi	1.25	65
		Nos. 1659-1663 (5)	2.25	1.11

Issued to publicize the 9th Youth Festival for Peace and Friendship, Sofia, July 28–Aug. 6.

Bellflower

A699

Flowers: 2s, Gentian. 3s, Crocus. 5s, Iris. 10s, Dog-tooth violet. 13s, Sempervivum. 20s, Dictamnus.

1968, Apr. 25 ***Perf. 11***

Flowers in Natural Colors

1664	A699	1s dl bl & blk	3	3
1665	A699	2s yel grn & blk	3	3
1666	A699	3s gray grn & blk	5	3
1667	A699	5s brn org & blk	15	5
1668	A699	10s ultra & blk	20	10
1669	A699	13s rose lil & blk	75	12
1670	A699	20s ol & blk	90	35
		Nos. 1664-1670 (7)	2.11	71

"The Unknown Hero," Tale by Ran Bosilek

A700

Design: 20s, The Witch and the Young Man (Hans Christian Andersen fairy tale.)

1968, Apr. 25 Photo. ***Perf. 10½***

1671	A700	13s blk & multi	60	20
1672	A700	20s blk & multi	75	45

Bulgarian-Danish Philatelic Exhibition.

Memorial Church, Shipka

A701

Steeplechase

A702

1968, May 3

1673	A701	13s multi	90	35

Bulgarian Stamp Exhibition in West Berlin.

1968, June 24 Photo. ***Perf. 10½***

Designs (Olympic Rings and): 1s, Gymnast on bar. 3s, Fencer. 10s, Boxer. 13s, Woman discus thrower.

1674	A702	1s red & blk	3	3
1675	A702	2s gray, blk & rose brn	3	3
1676	A702	3s mag, gray & blk	5	3
1677	A702	10s grnsh bl, blk & lem	20	5
1678	A702	13s vio bl, gray & pink	75	20
		Nos. 1674-1678, B33 (6)	2.16	84

Issued to publicize the 19th Olympic Games, Mexico City, Oct. 12–27.

Battle of Buzluja

A703

Design: 13s, Haji Dimitr and Stefan Karaja.

1968, July 1

1679	A703	2s sil & red brn	5	3
1680	A703	13s gold & sl grn	45	15

Issued to commemorate the centenary of the death of the patriots Haji Dimitr and Stefan Karaja.

Lakes of Smolian

A704

Cinereous Vulture

A705

Bulgarian Scenes: 2s, Ropotamo Lake. 3s, Erma-Idreloto mountain pass. 8s, Isker River dam. 10s, Slanchev Breg (sailing ship). 13s, Cape Caliacra. 40s, Old houses, Sozopol. 2 1, Chudnite Skali ("Strange Mountains").

1968 Photogravure ***Perf. 13***

1681	A704	1s Prus grn	3	3
1682	A704	2s dk grn	3	3
1683	A704	3s dk brn	5	3
1684	A704	8s ol grn	15	8
1685	A704	10s redsh brn	18	10
1686	A704	13s dk ol grn	35	12
1687	A704	40s Prus bl	1.10	45
1688	A704	2 l sepia	7.00	1.50
		Nos. 1681-1688 (8)	8.89	2.34

1968, July 29 ***Perf. 10½***

Designs: 2s, Crowned crane. 3s, Zebra. 5s, Leopard. 13s, Indian python. 20s, African crocodile.

1689	A705	1s ultra, blk & tan	3	3
1690	A705	2s org brn, blk & yel	3	3
1691	A705	3s yel grn & blk	10	5
1692	A705	5s brn red, blk & yel	30	6
1693	A705	13s dp grn, blk & tan	60	18
1694	A705	20s dl bl, blk & gray grn	65	25
		Nos. 1689-1694 (6)	1.71	60

Centenary of the Sofia Zoo.

Human Rights Flame

A706

1968, July 8

1695	A706	20s dp bl & gold	75	30

International Human Rights Year, 1968.

Congress Hall, Varna, and Emblem

A707

1968, Sept. 17 Photo. ***Perf. 10½***

1696	A707	20s bis, grn & red	60	15

Issued to publicize the 56th International Dental Congress, Varna.

Flying Swans

A708

Rose

A709

Stag Beetle

A710

Designs: 2s, Jug. 20s, Five Viking ships.

1968 Photogravure ***Perf. 10½***

1697	A709	2s grn & ocher	1.00	1.00
1698	A708	5s dp bl & gray	1.00	1.00
1699	A709	13s dp plum & lil rose	1.00	1.00
1700	A708	20s dp vio & gray	1.00	1.00

Issued to publicize cooperation with the Scandinavian countries. Nos. 1697 and 1700 are printed with connecting label showing bridge made of flags of Scandinavian countries.

Issue dates: 5s, 13s, Sept. 12. Others, Nov. 22.

Perf. 12½x13, 13x12½

1968, Aug. 26

Insects: No. 1702, Ground beetle (Procerus scabrosus). No. 1703, Ground beetle (Calosoma sycophania). No. 1704, Scarab beetle (horiz.). No. 1705, Saturnid moth (horiz.).

1701	A710	1s brn ol	3	3
1702	A710	1s dk bl	3	3
1703	A710	1s dk grn	3	3
1704	A710	1s org brn	3	3
1705	A710	1s magenta	3	3
		Nos. 1701-1705 (5)	15	15

Turks Fighting Insurgents, 1688

A711

1968, Aug. 22 ***Perf. 10½***

1706	A711	13s multi	60	15

Issued to commemorate the 280th anniversary of the Tchiprovtzi insurrection.

Christo Smirnenski—A712

1968, Sept. 28 Litho. ***Perf. 10½***

1707	A712	13s gold, red org & blk	60	15

Issued to commemorate the 70th birthday of Christo Smirnenski (1898–1923), poet.

Dalmatian Pelican

A713

Birds: 2s, Little egret. 3s, Crested grebe. 5s, Common tern. 13s, European spoonbill. 20s, Glossy ibis.

1968, Oct. 28 Photogravure

1708	A713	1s sil & multi	5	3
1709	A713	2s sil & multi	5	3
1710	A713	3s sil & multi	8	5
1711	A713	5s sil & multi	15	8
1712	A713	13s sil & multi	60	20
1713	A713	20s sil & multi	90	50
		Nos. 1708-1713 (6)	1.83	89

Issued to publicize the Srebirna wild life reservation.

Carrier Pigeon

A714

1968, Oct. 19

1714	A714	20s emerald	75	30
a.		Sheet of 4 + labels	3.75	3.00

Issued to publicize the 2nd National Stamp Exhibition in Sofia, Oct. 25–Nov. 15. No. 1714a contains 4 No. 1714 and 5 decorative labels of two types with commemorative inscriptions. Gold frame. Size: 133x161½mm. No. 1714 was issued only as sheet No. 1714a.

Man and Woman from Lovetch
A715

Regional Costumes: 1s, Silistra. 3s, Jambol. 13s, Chirpan. 20s, Razgrad. 40s, Ihtiman.

1968, Nov. 20 Litho. *Perf. 13½*

1715	A715	1s dp org & multi	3	3
1716	A715	2s Prus bl & multi	6	3
1717	A715	3s multi	7	3
1718	A715	13s multi	35	8
1719	A715	20s multi	75	25
1720	A715	40s grn & multi	1.50	65
		Nos. 1715-1720 (6)	2.76	1.07

St. Arsenius
A716

Designs (10th century Murals and Icons): 2s, Procession with relics of St. Ivan Rilsky (horiz.). 3s, St. Michael Torturing the Soul of the Rich Man. 13s, St. Ivan Rilsky. 20s, St. John. 40s, St. George. 1 l, Procession meeting relics of St. Ivan Rilsky (horiz.).

Perf. 11½x12½, 12½x11½

1968, Nov. 25 Photogravure

1721	A716	1s gold & multi	3	3
1722	A716	2s gold & multi	3	3
1723	A716	3s gold & multi	15	3
1724	A716	13s gold & multi	65	20
1725	A716	20s gold & multi	1.25	45
1726	A716	40s gold & multi	2.00	95
		Nos. 1721-1726 (6)	4.11	1.69

Souvenir Sheet

Imperf.

1727	A716	1 l gold & multi	6.00	5.00

Issued to commemorate the millenium of Rila Monastery. No. 1727 also publicizes "Sofia 1969," International Philatelic Exhibition, May 31–June 8, 1969. No. 1727 contains one stamp (size: 57x51mm.), gray margin with emblems of Philatelic Exhibition. Size: 100x75mm.

Medlar
A717

Herbs: No. 1729, Camomile. 2s, Lily-of-the-valley. 3s, Belladonna. 5s, Mallow. 10s, Buttercup. 13s, Poppies. 20s, Thyme.

1969, Jan. 2 Litho. *Perf. 10½*

1728	A717	1s blk, grn & org red	3	3
1729	A717	1s blk, grn & yel	3	3
1730	A717	2s blk, emer & grn	3	3
1731	A717	3s blk & multi	5	3
1732	A717	5s blk & multi	7	4
1733	A717	10s blk, grn & yel	16	8
1734	A717	13s blk & multi	30	15
1735	A717	20s blk, lil & grn	65	30
		Nos. 1728-1735 (8)	1.32	69

Silkworms and Spindles
A718

Designs: 2s, Silkworm, cocoons and pattern. 3s, Cocoons and spinning wheel. 5s, Cocoons, woof-and-warp diagram. 13s, Silk moth, cocoon and spinning frame. 20s, Silk moth, eggs and shuttle.

1969, Jan. 30 Photo. *Perf. 10½*

1736	A718	1s bl, grn, sl & blk	3	3
1737	A718	2s dp car, sil & blk	3	3
1738	A718	3s Prus bl, sil & blk	5	3
1739	A718	5s pur, ver, sil & blk	8	6
1740	A718	13s red lil, ocher, sil & blk	35	15
1741	A718	20s grn, org, sil & blk	60	30
		Nos. 1736-1741 (6)	1.14	60

Bulgarian silk industry.

Attack and Capture of Emperor Nicephorus
A719

Sts. Cyril and Methodius, Mural, Troian Monastery
A720

Designs (Manasses Chronicle): No. 1742, Death of Ivan Asen. 3s, Khan Kroum feasting after victory. No. 1748, Invasion of Bulgaria by Prince Sviatoslav of Kiev. No. 1750, Russian invasion and campaigns of Emperor John I Zimisces, c. 972 A.D. 40s, Tsar Ivan Alexander, Jesus and Constantine Manasses.

Horizontal designs: No. 1743, Kings Nebuchadnezzar, Balthazar, Darius and Cyrus. No. 1745, Kings Cambyses, Gyges and Darius. 5s, King David and Tsar Ivan Alexander. No. 1749, Persecution of Byzantine army after battle of July 26, 811. No. 1751, Christening of Bulgarian Tsar Boris, 865. 60s, Arrival of Tsar Simeon in Constantinople and his succeeding surprise attack on that city.

1969 Photo. *Perf. 14x13½, 13½x14*

Gold Frame

1742	A719	1s multi	3	3
1743	A719	1s multi	3	3
1744	A719	2s multi	3	3
1745	A719	2s multi	3	3
1746	A719	3s multi	5	3
1747	A719	5s multi	15	5
1748	A719	13s multi	35	8
1749	A719	13s multi	35	12
1750	A719	20s multi	75	20
1751	A719	20s multi	75	20
1752	A719	40s multi	1.50	75
1753	A719	60s multi	1.75	90
		Nos. 1742-1753 (12)	5.77	2.45

1969, Mar. 23

1754	A720	28s gold & multi	1.25	60

Post Horn
A721

Designs: 13s, Bulgaria Nos. 1 and 534. 20s, Street fighting at Stačkata, 1919.

1969, Apr. 15 Photo. *Perf. 10½*

1755	A721	2s grn & yel	3	3
1756	A721	13s multi	45	10
1757	A721	20s dk bl & lt bl	75	30

Issued to commemorate the 90th anniversary of the Bulgarian postal administration.

The Fox and the Rabbit
A722

Children's Drawings: 2s, Boy reading to wolf and fox. 13s, Two birds and cat, singing together.

1969, Apr. 21

1758	A722	1s emer, org & blk	3	3
1759	A722	2s org, lt bl & blk	3	3
1760	A722	13s lt bl, ol & blk	60	20

Issued for Children's Week.

ILO Emblem
A723

1969, Apr. 28

1761	A723	13s dl grn & blk	45	15

Issued to commemorate the 50th anniversary of the International Labor Organization.

St. George and SOPHIA 69 Emblem
A724

Designs: 2s, Virgin Mary and St. John Bogoslov. 3s, Archangel Michael. 5s, Three Saints. 8s, Jesus Christ. 13s, Sts. George and Dimitrie. 20s, Christ, the Almighty. 40s, St. Dimitrie. 60s, The 40 Martyrs. 80s, The Transfiguration.

1969, Apr. 30 *Perf. 11x12*

1762	A724	1s gold & multi	3	3
1763	A724	2s gold & multi	3	3
1764	A724	3s gold & multi	5	3
1765	A724	5s gold & multi	10	4
1766	A724	8s gold & multi	15	5
1767	A724	13s gold & multi	35	8
1768	A724	20s gold & multi	65	20
1769	A724	40s gold & multi	1.00	50
a.		Sheet of four	5.25	5.25
1770	A724	60s gold & multi	2.25	1.00
1771	A724	80s gold & multi	3.00	1.25
		Nos. 1762-1771 (10)	7.61	3.21

Issued to show old Bulgarian art from the National Art Gallery. No. 1769a contains 4 of No. 1769 with center label showing Alexander Nevski Shrine. See note on SOPHIA 69 after Nos. C112–C120.

St. Cyril Preaching
A725

St. Sophia Church
A726

Design: 28s, St. Cyril and followers.

1969, June 20 Litho. *Perf. 10½*

1772	A275	2s sil, grn & red	15	5
1773	A275	28s sil, dk bl & red	95	45

Issued to commemorate the 1100th anniversary of the death of St. Cyril (827–869), apostle to the Slavs, inventor of Cyrillic alphabet. Issued in sheets of 25 with se-tenant labels; Cyrillic inscription on label of 2s, Glagolitic inscription on label of 28s.

1969, May 25 *Perf. 13x12½*

Sofia Through the Ages: 1s, Roman coin with inscription "Ulpia Serdica." 2s, Roman coin with Aesculapius Temple. 4s, Bojana Church. 5s, Sobranie Parliament. 13s, Vasov National Theater. 20s, Alexander Nevski Shrine. 40s, Clement Ochrida University. 1 l, Coat of arms.

1774	A726	1s gold & bl	3	3
1775	A726	2s gold & ol grn	3	3
1776	A726	3s gold & red brn	5	3
1777	A726	4s gold & pur	7	3
1778	A726	5s gold & plum	10	3
1779	A726	13s gold & brt grn	30	8
1780	A726	20s gold & vio bl	60	20
1781	A726	40s gold & dp car	1.50	35
		Nos. 1774-1781 (8)	2.68	78

Souvenir Sheet

Imperf.

1782	A726	1 l grn, gold & red	3.00	3.00

Issued to show historic Sofia in connection with the International Philatelic Exhibition, Sofia, May 31–June 8.

No. 1782 contains one stamp (size: 43½x43½mm.). Emblems of 8 preceding philatelic exhibitions in metallic ink in margin; gold inscription. Size: 80x72mm.

No. 1782 was overprinted in green "IBRA '73" and various symbols, and released May 4, 1973, for the Munich Philatelic Exhibition. The overprint also exists in gray.

St. George
A727

1969, June 9 Litho. *Perf. 11½*

1783	A727	40s sil, blk & pale rose	1.50	75

Issued to commemorate the 38th FIP (Féderation Internationale de Philatelie) Congress, June 9–11.

Hand Planting Sapling
A728

1969, Apr. 28 Photo. ***Perf. 11***

1784	A728	2s ol grn, blk & lil	5	3

Issued to publicize 25 years of the reforestation campaign.

Partisans
A729

Designs: 2s, Combine harvester. 3s, Dam. 5s, Flutist and singers. 13s, Factory. 20s, Lenin, Dimitrov, Russian and Bulgarian flags.

1969, Sept. 9

1785	A729	1s blk, pur & org	3	3
1786	A729	2s blk, ol bis & org	3	3
1787	A729	3s blk, bl grn & org	5	3
1788	A729	5s blk, brn red & org	15	3
1789	A729	13s blk, bl & org	45	15
1790	A729	20s blk, brn & org	75	30
		Nos. 1785-1790 (6)	1.46	57

25th anniversary of People's Republic.

Women Gymnasts
A730

Design: 20s, Wrestlers.

1969, Sept. Photo. ***Perf. 11***

1791	A730	2s bl, blk & pale brn	3	3
1792	A730	20s red org & multi	60	30

Third National Spartakiad.

Tchanko Bakalov Tcherkovski
A731

1969, Sept.

1793	A731	13s multi	45	15

Birth centenary of Tchanko Bakalov Techerkovski, poet.

Woman Gymnast
A732

Designs: 2s, Two women with hoops. 3s, Woman with hoop. 5s, Two women with spheres.

1969, Oct.

Gymnasts in Light Gray

1794	A732	1s grn & dk bl	3	3
1795	A732	2s bl & dk bl	3	3
1796	A732	3s emer & sl grn	8	5
1797	A732	5s org & pur	12	8
		Nos. 1794-1797, B35-B36(6)	1.51	1.06

Issued to publicize the World Championships for Artistic Gymnastics, Varna.

The Priest Rilski, by Zachary Zograf
A733

Paintings from the National Art Gallery. 2s, Woman at Window, by Vasil Stoilov. 3s, Workers at Rest, by Nenko Balkanski (horiz.). 4s, Woman Dressing (Nude), by Ivan Nenov. 5s, Portrait of a Woman, by N. Pavlovich. 13s, Falstaff, by Duzunov Kr. Sarafov. No. 1804, Portrait of a Woman, by N. Mihajlov (horiz.). No. 1805, Workers at Mealtime, by Stojan Sotirov (horiz.). 40s, Self-portrait, by Tcheno Togorov.

Perf. 11½x12, 12x11½

1969, Nov. 10

1798	A733	1s gold & multi	3	3
1799	A733	2s gold & multi	3	3
1800	A733	3s gold & multi	5	3
1801	A733	4s gold & multi	7	3
1802	A733	5s gold & multi	10	3
1803	A733	13s gold & multi	45	15
1804	A733	20s gold & multi	90	30
1805	A733	20s gold & multi	90	30
1806	A733	40s gold & multi	1.75	95
		Nos. 1798-1806 (9)	4.28	1.85

Roman Bronze Wolf—A734

Design: 2s, Roman statue of woman, found at Silistra (vert.).

1969, Oct. Photogravure ***Perf. 11***

1807	A734	2s sil, ultra & gray	5	5
1808	A734	13s sil, dk grn & gray	60	15

City of Silistra's 1,800th anniversary.

Worker and Factory
A735

1969 ***Perf. 13***

1809	A735	6s ultra & blk	15	8

25th anniversary of the factory militia.

European Hake—A736

Designs: No. 1811, Deep-sea fishing trawler. Fish: 2s, Atlantic horse mackerel. 3s, Pilchard. 5s, Dentex macrophthalmus. 10s, Chub mackerel. 13s, Otolithes macrognathus. 20s, Lichia vadigo.

1969 ***Perf. 11***

1810	A736	1s ol grn & blk	3	3
1811	A736	1s ultra, ind & gray	3	3
1812	A736	2s lil & blk	3	3
1813	A736	3s vio bl & blk	5	3
1814	A736	5s rose cl, pink & blk	15	6
1815	A736	10s gray & blk	30	10
1816	A736	13s ver, sal & blk	45	12
1817	A736	20s ocher & blk	90	30
		Nos. 1810-1817 (8)	1.94	70

Marin Drinov
A737

1969, Nov. 10 Litho. ***Perf. 11***

1818	A737	20s blk & red org	60	20

Issued to commemorate the centenary of the Bulgarian Academy of Science, founded by Marin Drinov.

Trapeze Artists
A738

Pavel Bania Sanatorium
A739

Circus Performers: 2s, Jugglers. 3s, Jugglers with loops. 5s, Juggler and bear on bicycle. 13s, Woman and performing horse. 20s, Musical clowns.

1969 Photogravure ***Perf. 11***

1819	A738	1s dk bl & multi	5	3
1820	A738	2s dk grn & multi	5	3
1821	A738	3s dk vio & multi	8	3
1822	A738	5s multi	12	8
1823	A738	13s multi	50	24
1824	A738	20s multi	75	36
		Nos. 1819-1824 (6)	1.55	77

1969, Dec. Photogravure ***Perf. 10½***

Health Resorts: 5s, Chisar Sanatorium. 6s, Kotel Children's Sanatorium. 20s, Narechen Polyclinic.

1825	A739	2s blue	5	3
1826	A739	5s ultra	9	6
1827	A739	6s green	12	10
1828	A739	20s emerald	60	18

G. S. Shonin, V. N. Kubasov and Spacecraft
A740

Designs: 2s, A. V. Filipchenko, V. N. Volkov, V. V. Gorbatko and spacecraft. 3s, Vladimir A. Shatalov, Alexei S. Yeliseyev and spacecraft. 28s, Three spacecraft in orbit.

1970, Jan. Photo. ***Perf. 11***

1829	A740	1s rose car, ol grn & blk	3	3
1830	A740	2s bl, dl cl & blk	3	3
1831	A740	3s grnsh bl, vio & blk	5	5
1832	A740	28s vio bl, lil rose & lt bl	90	35

Issued to commemorate the Russian space flights of Soyuz 6, 7 and 8, Oct. 11–13, 1969.

Khan Krum and Defeat of Emperor Nicephorus, 811
A741

Bulgarian History: 1s, Khan Asparuch and Bulgars crossing the Danube (679). 3s, Conversion of Prince Boris to Christianity, 865. 5s, Tsar Simeon and battle of Akhelo, 917. 8s, Tsar Samuel defeating the Byzantines, 976. 10s, Tsar Kaloyan defeating Emperor Baldwin, 1205. 13s, Tsar Ivan Assen II defeating Greek King Theodore Komnine, 1230. 20s, Coronation of Tsar Ivailo, 1277.

1970, Feb. ***Perf. 10½***

1833	A741	1s gold & multi	3	3
1834	A741	2s gold & multi	5	3
1835	A741	3s gold & multi	5	3
1836	A741	5s gold & multi	10	6
1837	A741	8s gold & multi	14	6
1838	A741	10s gold & multi	30	10
1839	A741	13s gold & multi	45	15
1840	A741	20s gold & multi	75	30
		Nos. 1833-1840 (8)	1.87	76

See also Nos. 2126–2133.

Bulgarian Pavilion, EXPO '70
A742

1970 ***Perf. 12½***

1841	A742	20s brn, sil & org	90	60

Issued to publicize EXPO '70 International Exposition, Osaka, Japan, Mar. 15–Sept. 13, 1970.

Soccer
A743

Designs: Various views of soccer game.

1970, Mar. 4 Photo. ***Perf. 12½***

1842	A743	1s bl & multi	5	4
1843	A743	2s rose car & multi	5	4
1844	A743	3s ultra & multi	7	5
1845	A743	5s grn & multi	12	10
1846	A743	20s emer & multi	60	20
1847	A743	40s red & multi	1.35	45
		Nos. 1842-1847 (6)	2.24	88

Issued to publicize the 9th World Soccer Championships for the Jules Rimet Cup, Mexico City, May 30–June 21, 1970. See No. B37.

Lenin
A744

Designs: 13s, Lenin portrait. 20s, Lenin writing.

1970, Apr. 22

1848	A744	2s vio bl & multi	3	3
1849	A744	13s brn & multi	50	15
1850	A744	20s multi	90	20

Centenary of birth of Lenin (1870–1924).

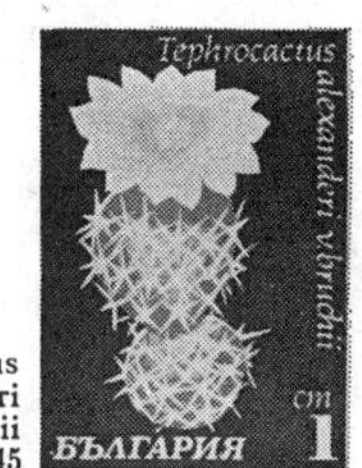

Tephrocactus Alexanderi V. Bruchii
A745

Cacti: 2s, Opuntia drummondii. 3s, Hatiora cilindrica. 5s, Gymnocalycium vatteri. 8s, Heliantho cereus grandiflorus. 10s, Neochilenia andreaeana. 13s, Peireskia vargasii v. longispina. 20s, Neobesseya rosiflora.

1970 Photogravure *Perf. 12½*

1851	A745	1s multi	3	3
1852	A745	2s dk grn & multi	3	3
1853	A745	3s multi	5	3
1854	A745	5s bl & multi	10	5
1855	A745	8s brn & multi	30	5
1856	A745	10s vio bl & multi	1.25	20
1857	A745	13s brn red & multi	1.25	30
1858	A745	20s pur & multi	1.50	50
		Nos. 1851-1858 (8)	4.51	1.19

Rose
A746

Designs: Various Roses.

1970, June 8 Litho. *Perf. 13½*

1859	A746	1s gray & multi	3	3
1860	A746	2s gray & multi	3	3
1861	A746	3s gray & multi	5	3
1862	A746	4s gray & multi	7	3
1863	A746	5s gray & multi	15	3
1864	A746	13s gray & multi	35	15
1865	A746	20s gray & multi	70	30
1866	A746	28s gray & multi	1.50	75
		Nos. 1859-1866 (8)	2.88	1.35

Gold Bowl
A747

Designs: Various bowls and art objects from Gold Treasure of Thrace.

1970, June 15 Photo. *Perf. 12½*

1867	A747	1s blk, bl & gold	3	3
1868	A747	2s blk, lt vio & gold	3	3
1869	A747	3s blk, ver & gold	7	5
1870	A747	5s blk, yel grn & gold	10	6
1871	A747	13s blk, org & gold	45	15
1872	A747	20s blk, lil & gold	80	35
		Nos. 1867-1872 (6)	1.48	67

EXPO Emblem, Rose and Bulgarian Woman
A748

Designs (EXPO Emblem and): 2s, Three women. 3s, Woman and fruit. 28s, Dancers. 40s, Mt. Fuji and pavilions.

1970, June 20

1873	A748	1s gold & multi	10	5
1874	A748	2s gold & multi	10	5
1875	A748	3s gold & multi	12	5
1876	A748	28s gold & multi	1.10	40

Miniature Sheet

Imperf.

1877	A748	40s gold & multi	1.50	1.00

Issued to publicize EXPO '70 International Exposition, Osaka, Japan, Mar. 15–Sept. 13. No. 1877 contains one stamp with simulated perforations; gray margin with blue border and roses. Size: 75½x 90mm.

Ivan Vasov
A749

1970, Aug. 1 Photo. *Perf. 12½*

1878	A749	13s vio bl	60	15

Issued to commemorate the 120th anniversary of the birth of Ivan Vasov, author.

U.N. Emblem—A750

1970, Aug. 1

1879	A750	20s Prus bl & gold	60	30

25th anniversary of the United Nations.

George Dimitrov
A751

Retriever
A752

1970, Aug.

1880	A751	20s blk, gold & org	75	30

Issued to commemorate the 70th anniversary of BZNC (Bulgarian Communist Party).

1970 Photo. *Perf. 12½*

Dogs: 1s, Golden retriever (horiz.). 3s, Great Dane. 4s, Boxer. 5s, Cocker spaniel. 13s, Doberman pinscher. 20s, Scottish terrier. 28s, Russian greyhound (horiz).

1881	A752	1s multi	5	4
1882	A752	2s multi	5	4
1883	A752	3s multi	7	5
1884	A752	4s multi	10	6
1885	A752	5s multi	12	8
1886	A752	13s multi	60	15
1887	A752	20s multi	80	45
1888	A752	28s multi	1.35	50
		Nos. 1881-1888 (8)	3.14	1.37

Volleyball
A753

Designs: No. 1890, Two women players. No. 1891, Woman player. No. 1892, Man player.

1970, Sept. Photo. *Perf. 12½*

1889	A753	2s dk red brn, bl & blk	5	5
1890	A753	2s ultra, org & blk	5	5
1891	A753	20s Prus bl, yel & blk	90	20
1892	A753	20s grn, yel & blk	90	20

World Volleyball Championships.

Enrico Caruso and "I Pagliacci" by Ruggiero Leoncavallo
A754

Opera Singers and Operas: 2s, Christina Morfova and "The Bartered Bride" by Bedrich Smetana. 3s, Peter Reitchev and "Tosca" by Giacomo Puccini. 10s, Svetana Tabakova and "The Flying Dutchman" by Richard Wagner. 13s, Katia Popova and "The Masters" by Paroshkev Hadjev. 20s, Feodor Chaliapin and "Boris Godunov" by Modest Musorgski.

1970, Oct. 15 Photo. *Perf. 14*

1893	A754	1s blk & multi	8	8
1894	A754	2s blk & multi	8	8
1895	A754	3s blk & multi	8	8
1896	A754	10s blk & multi	18	12
1897	A754	13s blk & multi	35	15
1898	A754	20s blk & multi	1.25	35
		Nos. 1893-1898 (6)	2.02	86

Issued to honor opera singers in their best roles.

Ivan Assen II Coin—A755

Coins from 14th Century with Ruler's Portrait: 2s, Theodor Svetoslav. 3s, Mikhail Chichman. 13s, Ivan Alexander and Mikhail Assen. 20s, Ivan Sratsimir. 28s, Ivan Chichman (initials).

1970, Nov. *Perf. 12½*

1899	A755	1s buff & multi	5	5
1900	A755	2s gray & multi	5	5
1901	A755	3s multi	8	5
1902	A755	13s multi	32	12
1903	A755	20s lt bl & multi	75	24
1904	A755	28s multi	1.00	36
		Nos. 1899-1904 (6)	2.25	87

Fireman
A756

Design: 3s, Fire engine.

1970 Lithographed *Perf. 12½*

1905	A756	1s blk, gray & yel	3	3
1906	A756	3s blk, gray & red	15	3

Fire protection publicity.

Bicyclists
A757

Congress Emblem
A758

1970 Photogravure

1907	A757	20s grn, yel & pink	75	25

For the 20th Bulgarian bicycle race.

1970

1908	A758	13s gold & multi	45	15

For the 7th World Congress of Sociology, Varna, Sept. 14–19.

Beethoven
A759

Friedrich Engels
A760

1970

1909	A759	28s lil rose & dk bl	90	30

Bicentenary of the birth of Ludwig van Beethoven (1770–1827), composer.

1970 Photogravure *Perf. 12½*

1910	A760	13s ver, tan & brn	60	15

Sesquicentennial of the birth of Friedrich Engels (1820–1895), German socialist, collaborator of Karl Marx.

Miniature Sheets

Luna 16
A761

Design (Russian moon mission): 80s, Lunokhod 1, unmanned vehicle on moon (horiz.).

1970 Photogravure *Imperf.*

1911	A761	80s plum, sil, blk & bl	3.25	3.00
1912	A761	1 l vio bl, sil & red	5.00	3.75

No. 1911 commemorates Lunokhod 1, Nov. 10–17. Size: 60x72mm. No. 1912, Luna 16 mission, Sept. 12–24. Size: 50x68mm.

Issue dates: 80s, Dec. 18; 1 lev, Nov. 10.

Snowflake
A762

1970, Dec. 15 Photo. *Perf. 12½x13*

1913	A762	2s ultra & multi	5	3

New Year 1971.

Birds and Flowers
A763

Folk Art: 2s, Bird and flowers. 3s, Flying birds. 5s, Birds and flowers. 13s, Sun. 20s, Tulips and pansies.

1971, Jan. 25 *Perf. 12½x13½*

1914	A763	1s multi	3	3
1915	A763	2s multi	3	3
1916	A763	3s multi	3	3
1917	A763	5s multi	10	6
1918	A763	13s multi	30	10
1919	A763	20s multi	90	20
		Nos. 1914-1919 (6)	1.39	45

Spring 1971.

Girl, by Zeko Spiridonov
A764

Modern Bulgarian Sculpture: 2s, Third Class (people looking through train window), by Ivan Funev. 3s, Bust of Elin Pelin, by Marko Markov. 13s, Bust of Nina, by Andrej Nikolov. 20s, Monument to P. K. Yavorov (kneeling woman), by Ivan Lazarov. 28s, Engineer, by Ivan Funev. 1 l, Refugees, by Sekul Krimov (horiz.).

1971, Feb. *Perf. 12½*

1920	A764	1s gold & vio	6	6
1921	A764	2s gold & dk ol grn	6	6
1922	A764	3s gold & rose brn	10	8
1923	A764	13s gold & dk grn	35	20
1924	A764	20s gold & red brn	60	30
1925	A764	28s gold & dk brn	90	48
		Nos. 1920-1925 (6)	2.07	1.18

Souvenir Sheet
Imperf.

1926	A764	1 l gold, dk brn & buff	3.25	3.00

No. 1926 has green marginal inscription. Size: 60x72mm.

Runner
A765

Design: 20s, Woman putting the shot.

1971, Mar. 13 Photo. *Perf. 12½x13*

1927	A765	2s brn & multi	5	5
1928	A765	20s dp grn, org & blk	1.40	35

2nd European Indoor Track and Field Championships.

Bulgarian Secondary School, Bolgrad
A766

Educators: 20s, Dimiter Mitev, Prince Bogoridi and Sava Radoulov.

1971, March 16 *Perf. 12½*

1929	A766	2s sil, brn & grn	3	3
1930	A766	20s sil, brn & vio	75	20

First Bulgarian secondary school, 1858, in Bolgrad, USSR.

Communards
A767

1971, Mar. 18 Photo. *Perf. 12½x13*

1931	A767	20s rose mag & blk	75	30

Centenary of the Paris Commune.

Dimitrov Facing Goering, Quotation, FIR Emblem
A768

1971, Apr. 11 *Perf. 12½*

1932	A768	2s grn, gold, blk & red	3	3
1933	A768	13s plum, gold, blk & red	90	15

International Federation of Resistance Fighters (FIR), 20th anniversary.

George S. Rakovski
A769

1971, Apr. 14

1934	A769	13s ol & blk brn	45	15

150th anniversary of birth of George S. Rakovski (1821–1867), revolutionary against Turkish rule.

Edelweiss Hotel, Borovets
A770

Designs: 2s, Panorama Hotel, Pamporovo. 4s, Boats at Albena, Black Sea. 8s, Boats at Rousalka. 10s, Shtastlivetsa Hotel, Mt. Vitosha.

1971 *Perf. 13*

1935	A770	1s brt grn	3	3
1936	A770	2s ol gray	5	3
1937	A770	4s brt bl	7	3
1938	A770	8s blue	20	5
1939	A770	10s bluish grn	30	7
		Nos. 1935-1939 (5)	65	21

Technological Progress—A771

Designs: 1s, Mason with banner (vert.). 13s, Two men and doves (vert.).

1971, Apr. 20 Photo. *Perf. 12½*

1940	A771	1s gold & multi	3	3
1941	A771	2s gray bl & multi	3	3
1942	A771	13s lt grn & multi	50	20

Tenth Congress of Bulgarian Communist Party.

Panayot Pipkov and Anthem
A772

1971, May 20

1943	A772	13s sil, blk & brt grn	50	18

Birth centenary of Panayot Pipkov, composer.

Mammoth
A773

Prehistoric Animals: 2s, Bear (vert.). 3s, Hipparion (horse). 13s, Platybelodon. 20s, Dinotherium (vert.). 28s, Saber-tooth tiger.

1971, May 29 *Perf. 12½*

1944	A773	1s dl bl & multi	6	5
1945	A773	2s lil & multi	6	5
1946	A773	3s multi	10	8
1947	A773	13s multi	50	14
1948	A773	20s dp grn & multi	75	20
1949	A773	28s multi	1.50	35
		Nos. 1944-1949 (6)	2.97	87

Khan Asparuch Crossing Danube, 679 A.D., by Boris Angelushev—A774

Historical Paintings: 3s, Reception at Trnovo, by Ilya Petrov. 5s, Chevartov's Troops at Benkovsky, by P. Morozov. 8s, Russian Gen. Gurko and People in Sofia, 1878, by D. Gudjenko. 28s, People Greeting Red Army, by S. Venov.

1971, Mar. 6 *Perf. 13½x14*

1950	A774	2s gold & multi	5	3
1951	A774	3s gold & multi	5	3
1952	A774	5s gold & multi	20	6
1953	A774	8s gold & multi	35	8
a.		Souv. sheet of 4	1.10	1.10
1954	A774	28s gold & multi	2.50	1.25
		Nos. 1950-1954 (5)	3.15	1.45

No. 1953a contains one each of Nos. 1950–1953. Gold decoration in gutter between stamps. Size: 137½x130mm.

In 1973, No. 1953a was surcharged 1 lev and overprinted "Visitez la Bulgarie", airline initials and emblems, and, on the 5s stamp, "Par Avion".

Freed Black, White and Yellow Men
A775

1971, May 20 Photo. *Perf. 12½*

1955	A775	13s bl, blk & yel	60	20

International Year against Racial Discrimination.

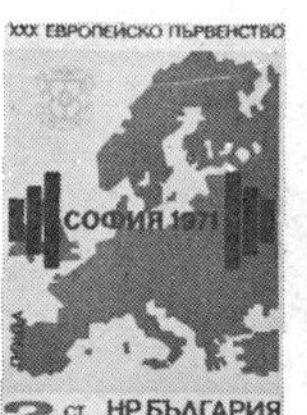

Map of Europe, Championship Emblem
A776

"XXX" Supporting Barbell
A777

1971, June 19

1956	A776	2s lt bl & multi	3	3
1957	A777	13s yel & multi	75	20

30th European Weight Lifting Championships, Sofia, June 19–27.

Facade, Old House, Koprivnica
A778

Designs: Decorated facades of various old houses in Koprivnica.

1971, July 10 Photo. *Perf. 12½*

1958	A778	1s grn & multi	5	4
1959	A778	2s brn & multi	5	4
1960	A778	6s vio & multi	15	9
1961	A778	13s dk red & multi	75	18

Frontier Guard and German Shepherd
A779

1971, July 31 *Perf. 13*

1962	A779	2s grn & ol grn	5	3

25th anniversary of the Frontier Guards.

Congress of Busludja, Bas-relief A780

1971, July 31 ***Perf. 12½***

1963	A780	2s dk red & ol grn	15	3

80th anniversary of the first Congress of the Bulgarian Social Democratic party.

Young Woman, by Ivan Nenov A781

Paintings: 2s, Lazarova in Evening Gown, by Stefan Ivanov. 3s, Performer in Dress Suit, by Kyril Zonev. 13s, Portrait of a Woman, by Detchko Uzunov. 20s, Woman from Kalotina, by Vladimir Dimitrov. 40s, Gorjanin (Mountain Man), by Stoyan Venev.

1971, Aug. 2 ***Perf. 14x13½***

1964	A781	1s grn & multi	5	5
1965	A781	2s grn & multi	5	5
1966	A781	3s grn & multi	5	5
1967	A781	13s grn & multi	35	8
1968	A781	20s grn & multi	75	45
1969	A781	40s grn & multi	1.75	80
		Nos. 1964-1969 (6)	3.00	1.48

National Art Gallery.

Wrestlers A782

Designs: 13s, Wrestlers.

1971, Aug. 27 ***Perf. 12½***

1970	A782	2s grn, blk & bl	5	3
1971	A782	13s red org, blk & bl	60	15

European Wrestling Championships.

Young Workers A783 — Post Horn Emblem A784

1971 Photogravure ***Perf. 13***

1972	A783	2s dk bl	5	3

25th anniversary of the Young People's Brigade.

1971, Sept. 15 ***Perf. 12½***

1973	A784	20s dp grn & gold	65	30

8th meeting of postal administrations of socialist countries, Varna.

FEBS Waves Emblem—A785

1971, Sept. 20

1974	A785	13s blk, red & mar	75	30

7th Congress of European Biochemical Association (FEBS), Varna.

Statue of Republic A786

Design: 13s, Bulgarian flag.

1971, Sept. 20 ***Perf. 13x12½***

1975	A786	2s gold, yel & dk red	5	3
1976	A786	13s gold, grn & red	60	20

25th anniversary of the Bulgarian People's Republic.

Cross Country Skiing and Winter Olympics Emblem A787

Sport and Winter Olympics Emblem: 2s, Downhill skiing. 3s, Ski jump and skiing. 4s, Women's figure skating. 13s, Ice hockey. 28s, Slalom skiing. 1 l, Torch and stadium.

1971, Sept. 25 ***Perf. 12½***

1977	A787	1s dk grn & multi	6	5
1978	A787	2s vio bl & multi	6	5
1979	A787	3s ultra & multi	6	5
1980	A787	4s dp plum & multi	9	5
1981	A787	13s dk bl & multi	50	10
1982	A787	28s multi	1.50	50
		Nos. 1977-1982 (6)	2.27	80

Miniature Sheet

Imperf.

1983	A787	1 l multi	4.50	3.25

11th Winter Olympic Games, Sapporo, Japan, Feb. 3–13, 1972.
Size of No. 1983: 70x80mm.

Factory, Botevgrad A788

Industrial Buildings: 2s, Petro-chemical works, Pleven (vert.). 10s, Chemical works, Vratsa. 13s, Maritsa-Istok Power Station, Dimitrovgrad. 40s, Electronics works, Sofia.

1971 Photogravure ***Perf. 13***

1984	A788	1s violet	5	3
1985	A788	2s orange	6	3
1986	A788	10s dp pur	20	9
1987	A788	13s lil rose	30	12
1988	A788	40s dp brn	90	25
		Nos. 1984-1988 (5)	1.51	52

UNESCO Emblem A789

1971, Nov. 4 ***Perf. 12½***

1989	A789	20s lt bl, blk, gold & red	75	30

25th anniversary of the United Nations Educational, Scientific and Cultural Organization (UNESCO).

Soccer Player, by Kyril Zonev (1896–1971) A790

Paintings by Kyril Zonev: 2s, Landscape (horiz.). 3s, Self-portrait. 13s, Lilies. 20s, Landscape (horiz.). 40s, Portrait of a Young Woman.

1971, Nov. 10 ***Perf. 11x12***

1990	A790	1s gold & multi	8	8
1991	A790	2s gold & multi	8	8
1992	A790	3s gold & multi	8	8
1993	A790	13s gold & multi	32	18
1994	A790	20s gold & multi	65	35
1995	A790	40s gold & multi	1.50	48
		Nos. 1990-1995 (6)	2.71	1.25

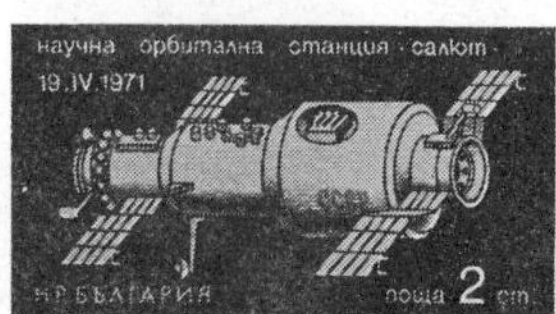

Salyut Space Station—A791

Astronauts Dobrovolsky, Volkov and Patsayev—A792

Designs: 13s, Soyuz 11 space transport. 40s, Salyut and Soyuz 11 joined.

1971, Dec. 20 ***Perf. 12½***

1996	A791	2s dk grn, yel & red	5	5
1997	A791	13s multi	30	20
1998	A791	40s dk bl & multi	1.35	60

Souvenir Sheet

Imperf.

1999	A792	80s multi	3.00	2.50

Salyut-Soyuz 11 space mission, and in memory of the Russian astronauts Lt. Col. Georgi T. Dobrovolsky, Vladislav N. Volkov and Victor I. Patsayev, who died during the Soyuz 11 space mission, June 6–30, 1971. Size of No. 1999: 70x73½mm.

Oil Tanker Vihren—A793

1972, Jan. 8 Photo. ***Perf. 12½***

2000	A793	18s lil rose, vio & blk	60	20

Bulgarian shipbuilding industry.

Goce Delchev A794

Portraits: 5s, Jan Sandanski. 13s, Damjan Gruev.

1972, Jan. 21 Photo. ***Perf. 12½***

2001	A794	2s brick red & blk	5	5
2002	A794	5s grn & blk	11	6
2003	A794	13s lem & blk	45	15

Centenary of the births of Bulgarian patriots Delchev (1872–1903) and Sandanski, and of Macedonian Gruev (1871–1906).

Gymnast with Ball, Medals—A795

Designs: 18s, Gymnast with hoop, and medals. 70s, Gymnasts with hoops, and medals.

1972, Feb. 10

2004	A795	13s grn, brn, red & gold	60	15
2005	A795	18s brn, grn, red & gold	75	30

Miniature Sheet

Imperf.

2006	A795	70s gold, brn, grn & red	3.00	2.50

5th World Women's Gymnastic Championships, Havana, Cuba.
Size of No. 2006: 61½x73mm.

View of Melnik, by Petar Mladenov A796

Paintings from National Art Gallery: 2s, Plower, by Pencho Georgiev. 3s, Funeral, by Alexander Djendov. 13s, Husband and Wife, by Vladimir Dimitrov. 20s, Nursing Mother, by Nenko Balkanski. 40s, Paisii Hilendarski Writing History, by Koio Denchev.

1972, Feb. 20 ***Perf. 13½x14***

2007	A796	1s grn & multi	6	5
2008	A796	2s grn & multi	6	5
2009	A796	3s grn & multi	10	8
2010	A796	13s grn & multi	35	12
2011	A796	20s grn & multi	60	20
2012	A796	40s grn & multi	1.35	45
		Nos. 2007-2012 (6)	2.52	95

Paintings from National Art Gallery.

Worker A797 — Singing Harvesters A798

1972, Mar. 7 *Perf. 12½*

2013	A797	13s sil & multi	35	15

7th Bulgarian Trade Union Congress.

Perf. 11½x12, 12x11½

1972, Mar. 31

Designs: Paintings by Vladimir Dimitrov.

Olive Brown & Multicolored

2014	A798	1s *shown*	8	5
2015	A798	2s *Harvester*	8	5
2016	A798	3s *Women Diggers*	12	10
2017	A798	13s *Fabric Dyers*	35	20
2018	A798	20s *"My Mother"*	60	30
2019	A798	40s *Self-portrait*	1.35	50
		Nos. 2014-2019 (6)	2.58	1.20

90th anniversary of birth of Vladimir Dimitrov, painter.

"Your Heart is your Health" A799 — St. Mark's Basilica and Wave A800

1972, Apr. 30 *Perf. 12½*

2020	A799	13s red, blk & grn	60	20

World Health Day.

1972, May 6 *Perf. 13x12½*

Design: 13s, Ca' D'Oro and wave.

2021	A800	2s ol grn, bl grn & lt bl	5	5
2022	A800	13s red brn, vio & lt grn	60	20

UNESCO campaign to save Venice.

Dimitrov in Print Shop, 1901—A801

Designs: Life of George Dimitrov.

1972, May 8 Photo. *Perf. 12½*

Gold and Multicolored

2023	A801	1s *shown*	6	5
2024	A801	2s *Dimitrov as leader of 1923 uprising*	6	5
2025	A801	3s *Leipzig trial, 1933*	6	5
2026	A801	5s *as Communist functionary, 1955*	9	6
2027	A801	13s *as leader and teacher, 1948*	21	9
2028	A801	18s *addressing youth rally, 1948*	30	13
2029	A801	28s *with Pioneers, 1948*	75	20
2030	A801	40s *Mausoleum*	1.50	45
2031	A801	80s *Portrait*	3.00	75
a.		Souvenir sheet	3.75	3.00
		Nos. 2023-2031 (9)	6.03	1.83

90th anniversary of the birth of George Dimitrov (1882–1949), communist leader.

No. 2031a contains one imperf. stamp similar to No. 2031, but in different colors. Gold marginal inscription. Size: 86x82mm.

Price, #2031 imperf. in slightly changed colors, $6.

Paisii A802

Design: 2s, Flame and quotation.

1972, May 12

2032	A802	2s gold, grn & brn	3	3
2033	A802	13s gold, grn & brn	45	15

250th anniversary of the birth of the monk Paisii Hilendarski (1722–1798), writer of Bulgarian-Slavic history.

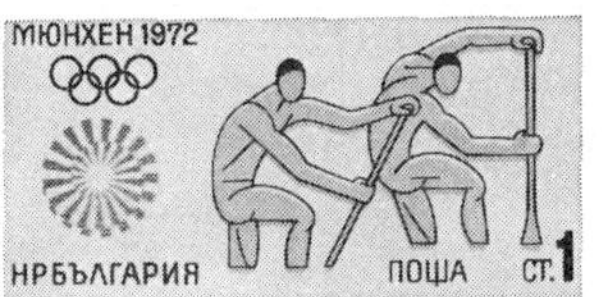

Canoeing, Motion and Olympic Emblems—A803

Designs (Motion and Olympic emblems and): 2s, Gymnastics. 3s, Swimming, women's. 13s, Volleyball. 18s, Jumping. 40s, Wrestling. 80s, Stadium and sports.

1972, June 25

Figures of Athletes in Silver & Black

2034	A803	1s lt bl & multi	5	5
2035	A803	2s org & multi	8	8
2036	A803	3s multi	10	10
2037	A803	13s yel & multi	35	25
2038	A803	18s multi	45	25
2039	A803	40s pink & multi	1.35	50
		Nos. 2034-2039 (6)	2.38	1.23

Miniature Sheet

Imperf.

Size: 62x60mm.

2040	A803	80s gold, ver & yel	2.75	2.25

20th Olympic Games, Munich, Aug. 26–Sept. 11.

Angel Kunchev A804

1972, June 30 Photo. *Perf. 12½*

2041	A804	2s mag, dk pur & gold	5	3

Centenary of the death of Angel Kunchev, patriot and revolutionist.

Zlatni Pyassatsi A805

1972, Sept. 16 **Multicolored**

2042	A805	1s *shown*	5	3
2043	A805	2s *Drouzhba*	5	3
2044	A805	3s *Slunchev Bryag*	8	5
2045	A805	13s *Primorsko*	30	18
2046	A805	28s *Roussalka*	75	40
2047	A805	40s *Albena*	1.25	50
		Nos. 2042-2047 (6)	2.48	1.19

Bulgarian Black Sea resorts.

Bronze Medal, Olympic Emblems, Canoeing A806

Designs (Olympic Emblems and): 2s, Silver medal, broad jump. 3s, Gold medal, boxing. 18s, Gold medal, wrestling. 40s, Gold medal, weight lifting.

1972, Sept. 29

2048	A806	1s Prus bl & multi	5	5
2049	A806	2s dk grn & multi	5	5
2050	A806	3s org brn & multi	5	5
2051	A806	18s ol & multi	45	20
2052	A806	40s multi	1.10	45
		Nos. 2048-2052 (5)	1.70	80

Bulgarian victories in 20th Olympic Games.

Stoj Dimitrov A807

Resistance Fighters: 2s, Cvetko Radoinov. 3s, Bogdan Stivrodski. 5s, Mirko Laiev. 13s, Nedelyo Nikolov.

1972, Oct. 30 Photo. *Perf. 12½x13*

2053	A807	1s ol & multi	5	5
2054	A807	2s multi	5	5
2055	A807	3s multi	6	6
2056	A807	5s multi	10	4
2057	A807	13s multi	30	9
		Nos. 2053-2057 (5)	56	29

"50 Years USSR" A808

1972, Nov. 3 Photo. *Perf. 12½x13*

2058	A808	13s gold, red & yel	30	15

50th anniversary of Soviet Union.

Turk's-cap Lily A809

Protected Plants: 2s, Gentian. 3s, Sea daffodil. 4s, Globe flower. 18s, Primrose. 23s, Pulsatilla vernalis. 40s, Snake's-head.

1972, Nov. 25 *Perf. 12½*

Flowers in Natural Colors

2059	A809	1s ol bis	5	5
2060	A809	2s ol bis	5	5
2061	A809	3s ol bis	8	5
2062	A809	4s ol bis	10	8
2063	A809	18s ol bis	40	25
2064	A809	23s ol bis	60	40
2065	A809	40s ol bis	1.10	70
		Nos. 2059-2065 (7)	2.38	1.58

No. 2052 Overprinted in Red — СВЕТОВЕН ПЪРВЕНЕЦ

1972, Nov. 27

2066	A806	40s multi	1.00	35

Bulgarian weight lifting Olympic gold medalists.

Dobri Chintulov—A810

1972, Nov. 28 Photo. *Perf. 12½*

2067	A810	2s gray, dk & lt grn	15	3

Dobri Chintulov, writer, 150th birth anniversary.

Forehead Band—A811

Designs (14th–19th Century Jewelry): 2s, Belt buckles. 3s, Amulet. 8s, Pendant. 23s, Earrings. 40s, Necklace.

1972, Dec. 27 Engr. *Perf. 14x13½*

2068	A811	1s red brn & blk	5	3
2069	A811	2s emer & blk	5	3
2070	A811	3s Prus bl & blk	7	5
2071	A811	8s dk red & blk	16	12
2072	A811	23s red org & multi	65	30
2073	A811	40s vio & blk	1.25	60
		Nos. 2068-2073 (6)	2.23	1.13

Skin Divers—A812

Designs: 2s, Shelf-1 underwater house and divers. 18s, Diving bell and diver (vert.). 40s, Elevation balloon and divers (vert.).

1973, Jan. 24 Photo. *Perf. 12½*

2074	A812	1s lt bl, blk & yel	3	3
2075	A812	2s blk, bl & org yel	3	3
2076	A812	18s blk, Prus bl & dl org	45	20
2077	A812	40s blk, ultra & bis	1.35	60

Bulgarian deep-sea research in the Black Sea.

A souvenir sheet of four contains imperf. 20s stamps in designs of Nos. 2074–2077 with colors changed. Gray marginal inscriptions. Size: 118x99mm. Sold for 1 lev. Price $4 unused, $2.50 canceled.

Execution of Levski, by Boris Angelushev
A813

Design: 20s, Vassil Levski, by Georgi Danchev.

1973, Feb. 19 *Perf. 13x12½*

2078	A813	2s dl rose & Prus grn	3	3
2079	A813	20s dl grn & brn	1.10	30

Centenary of the death of Vassil Levski (1837–1873), patriot, executed by the Turks.

Kukersky Mask, Elhovo Region
A814

Nicolaus Copernicus
A815

Kukersky Masks at pre-Spring Festival: 2s, Breznik. 3s, Hissar. 13s, Radomir. 20s, Karnobat. 40s, Pernik.

1973, Feb. 26 *Perf. 12½*

2080	A814	1s dp rose & multi	10	8
2081	A814	2s emer & multi	10	8
2082	A814	3s vio & multi	10	8
2083	A814	13s multi	45	18
2084	A814	20s multi	60	30
2085	A814	40s multi	3.00	1.75
		Nos. 2080-2085 (6)	4.35	2.47

1973, Mar. 21 Photo. *Perf. 12½*

2086	A815	28s ocher, blk & cl	1.25	60

500th anniversary of the birth of Nicolaus Copernicus (1473–1543), Polish astronomer.

Vietnamese Worker and Rainbow
A816

1973, Apr. 16

2087	A816	18s lt bl & multi	45	20

Peace in Viet Nam.

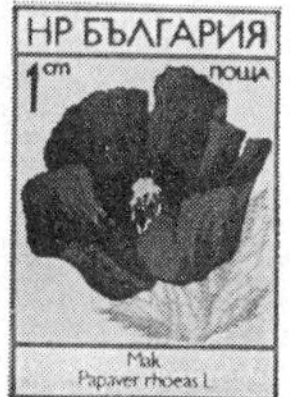

Poppy
A817

Designs: Wild flowers.

1973, May Photo. *Perf. 13*

Multicolored

2088	A817	1s *shown*	5	5
2089	A817	2s *Daisy*	6	5
2090	A817	3s *Peony*	7	5
2091	A817	13s *Centaury*	35	15
2092	A817	18s *Corn cockle*	2.25	1.50
2093	A817	28s *Ranunculus*	90	45
		Nos. 2088-2093 (6)	3.68	2.25

Christo Botev
A818

1973, June 2

2094	A818	2s pale grn, buff & brn	6	5
2095	A818	18s pale brn, gray & grn	75	50

125th anniversary of the birth of Christo Botev (1848–1876), poet.

"Suffering Worker"—A819

Design: 1s, Asen Halachev and revolutionists.

1973, June 6 Photo. *Perf. 13*

2096	A819	1s gold, red & blk	3	3
2097	A819	2s gold, org & dk brn	5	5

50th anniversary of Pleven uprising.

Muskrat
A820

Perf. 12½x13, 13x12½

1973, June 29 Lithographed

Multicolored

2098	A820	1s *shown*	5	5
2099	A820	2s *Racoon*	5	5
2100	A820	3s *Mouflon (vert.)*	7	5
2101	A820	12s *Fallow deer (vert.)*	25	15
2102	A820	18s *European bison*	35	20
2103	A820	40s *Elk*	2.50	2.00
		Nos. 2098-2103 (6)	3.27	2.50

Aleksandr Stamboliski—A821

1973, June 14 Photo. *Perf. 12½*

2104	A821	18s dp brn & org	45	35
a.		18s org	2.50	1.50

50th anniversary of the death of Aleksandr Stamboliski (1879–1923), leader of Peasants' Party and premier.

Trade Union Emblem
A822

Stylized Sun, Olympic Rings
A823

1973, Aug. 27 Photo. *Perf. 12½*

2105	A822	2s yel & multi	5	3

8th Congress of World Federation of Trade Unions, Varna, Oct. 15–22.

1973, Aug. 29 *Perf. 13*

Designs: 28s, Emblem of Bulgarian Olympic Committee and Olympic rings. 80s, Soccer, emblems of Innsbruck and Montreal 1976 Games (horiz.).

2106	A823	13s multi	75	60
2107	A823	28s multi	95	75

Souvenir Sheet

2108	A823	80s multi	3.75	3.50

contains one stamp. Blue and gray green margin shows emblems of various Olympic committees and games. Size: 60x77½ mm. It also exists imperf.; also with violet margin, imperf.

Revolutionists with Communist Flag
A824

Designs: 5s, Revolutionists on flatcar blocking train. 13s, Raising Communist flag (vert.). 18s, George Dimitrov and Vassil Kolarov.

1973, Sept. 22 Photo. *Perf. 12½*

2109	A824	2s mag & multi	5	3
2110	A824	5s mag & multi	9	6
2111	A824	13s mag & multi	30	15
2112	A824	18s mag & multi	1.00	70

50th anniversary of the September Revolution.

Warrior Saint
A825

Murals from Boyana Church: 1s, Tsar Kaloyan and 2s, his wife Dessislava. 5s, "St. Wystratti." 10s, Tsar Constantine Assen. 13s, Deacon Laurentius. 18s, Virgin Mary. 20s, St. Ephraim. 28s, Jesus. 80s, Jesus in the Temple (horiz.).

1973, Sept. 24

2113	A825	1s gold & multi	10	8
2114	A825	2s gold & multi	10	8
2115	A825	3s gold & multi	12	8
2116	A825	5s gold & multi	15	12
2117	A825	10s gold & multi	30	12
2118	A825	13s gold & multi	35	20
2119	A825	18s gold & multi	60	30
2120	A825	20s gold & multi	75	35
2121	A825	28s gold & multi	2.25	75
		Nos. 2113-2121 (9)	4.72	2.08

Miniature Sheet

Imperf.

2122	A825	80s gold & multi	4.50	3.75

No. 2122 contains one stamp with simulated perforations. Gold margin with view of Boyana Church. Size: 56x76½mm.

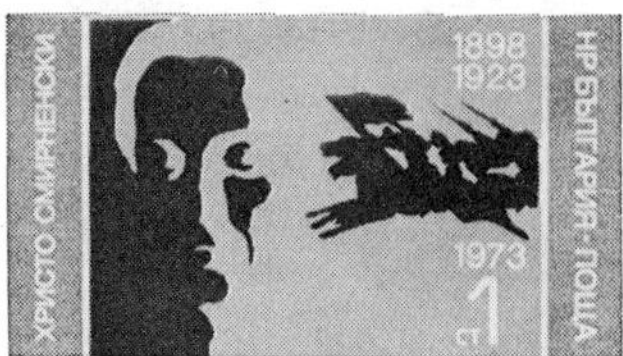

Christo Smirnenski—A826

1973, Sept. 29 Photo. *Perf. 12½*

2123	A826	1s multi	3	3
2124	A826	2s vio bl & multi	15	5

75th anniversary of the birth of Christo Smirnenski (1898–1923), poet.

Human Rights Flame
A827

1973, Oct. 10

2125	A827	13s dk bl, red & gold	45	30

25th anniversary of the Universal Declaration of Human Rights.

Type of 1970

History of Bulgaria: 1s, Tsar Theodor Svetoslav receiving Byzantine envoys. 2s, Tsar Mihail Shishman's army in battle with Byzantines. 3s, Tsar Ivan Alexander's victory at Russocastro. 4s, Patriarch Euthimius at the defense of Turnovo. 5s, Tsar Ivan Shishman leading horsemen against the Turks. 13s, Momchil attacking Turks at Umour. 18s, Tsar Ivan Stratsimir meeting King Sigismund's crusaders. 28s, The Boyars Balik, Theodor and Dobrotitsa, meeting ship bringing envoys from Anne of Savoy.

1973, Oct. 23 *Perf. 13*

Silver and Black Vignettes

2126	A741	1s ol bis	8	8
2127	A741	2s Prus bl	8	8
2128	A741	3s lilac	10	8
2129	A741	4s green	12	8
2130	A741	5s violet	15	10
2131	A741	13s org & brn	24	18
2132	A741	18s ol grn	45	24
2133	A741	28s yel brn & brn	1.25	60
		Nos. 2126-2133 (8)	2.47	1.44

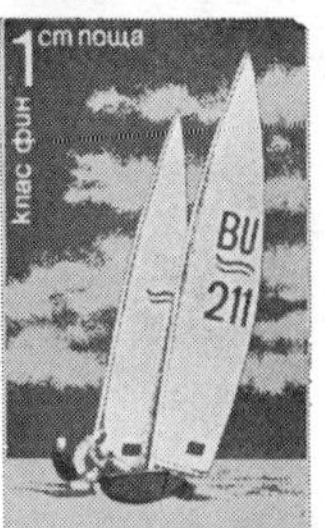

Fin Class
A828

1973, Oct. 29 Lithographed *Perf. 13*

Sailboats: 2s, Flying Dutchman. 3s, Soling class. 13s, Tempest class. 20s, Class 470. 40s, Tornado class.

2134	A828	1s ultra & multi	8	8
2135	A828	2s grn & multi	8	8
2136	A828	3s dk bl & multi	10	8
2137	A828	13s dl vio & multi	35	20

2138	A828	20s gray bl & multi	60	35
2139	A828	40s multi	3.00	2.00
		Nos. 2134-2139 (6)	4.21	2.79

Price, set imperf. in changed colors, $12.50.

Village, by Bencho Obreshkov
A829

Paintings: 2s, Mother and Child, by Stoyan Venev. 3s, Rest (woman), by Tsenko Boyadjiev. 13s, Flowers in Vase, by Sirak Skitnik. 18s, Meri Kuneva (portrait), by Ilya Petrov. 40s, Winter in Plovdiv, by Zlatyu Boyadjiev. 13s, 18s, 40s, vertical.

Perf. 12½x12, 12x12½

1973, Nov. 10

2140	A829	1s gold & multi	8	8
2141	A829	2s gold & multi	8	8
2142	A829	3s gold & multi	8	8
2143	A829	13s gold & multi	30	15
2144	A829	18s gold & multi	60	20
2145	A829	40s gold & multi	1.50	80
		Nos. 2140-2145 (6)	2.64	1.39

Souvenir Sheet

Paintings by Stanislav Dospevski: No. 2146a, Domnica Lambreva. No. 2146b, Self-portrait. Both vertical.

2146	A829	Sheet of 2	3.25	3.00
a.		50s gold & multi	1.00	75
b.		50s gold & multi	1.00	75

Bulgarian paintings. No. 2146 commemorates the 150th birth anniv. of Stanislav Dospevski; gold margin and brown inscription. Size: 100x96mm.

Souvenir Sheet

Soccer—A830

1973, Dec. 10 Photo. ***Perf. 13***

2147	A830	28s multi	3.75	3.00

No. 2147 sold for 1 l. Size: 65x100mm. Exists overprinted for Argentina 78.

Angel and Ornaments
A831

Designs: 1s, Attendant facing right. 2s, Passover table and lamb. 3s, Attendant facing left. 8s, Abraham and ornaments. 13s, Adam and Eve. 28s, Expulsion from Garden of Eden.

1974, Jan. 21 Photo. ***Perf. 13***

2148	A831	1s fawn, yel & brn	10	8
2149	A831	2s fawn, yel & brn	10	8
2150	A831	3s fawn, yel & brn	12	10
2151	A831	5s sl grn & yel	15	10
2152	A831	8s sl grn & yel	25	12
2153	A831	13s lt brn, yel & ol	40	24
2154	A831	28s lt brn, yel & ol	90	50
		Nos. 2148-2154 (7)	2.02	1.22

Woodcarvings from Rozhen Monastery, 19th century. Nos. 2148–2150, 2151 2152, 2153–2154 printed se-tenant.

Lenin, by N. Mirtchev—A832

Design: 18s, Lenin visiting Workers, by W. A. Serov.

1974, Jan. 28 Litho. ***Perf. 12½x12***

2155	A832	2s ocher & multi	5	5
2156	A832	18s ocher & multi	45	18

50th anniversary of the death of Lenin.

1974, Jan. 28

Design: Demeter Blagoev at Rally, by G. Kowachev.

2157	A832	2s multi	5	5

50th anniversary of the death of Demeter Blagoev, founder of Bulgarian Communist Party.

Sheep
A833

Designs: Domestic animals.

1974, Feb. 1 Photo. ***Perf. 13***

Multicolored

2158	A833	1s *shown*	8	8
2159	A833	2s *Goat*	8	8
2160	A833	3s *Pig*	8	8
2161	A833	5s *Cow*	12	8
2162	A833	13s *Buffalo cow*	30	18
2163	A833	20s *Horse*	45	30
		Nos. 2158-2163 (6)	1.11	80

Comecon Emblem
A834

1974, Feb. 11 Photo. ***Perf. 13***

2164	A834	13s sil & multi	40	14

25th anniversary of the Council of Mutual Economic Assistance.

Soccer—A835

Designs: Various soccer action scenes.

1974, Mar. Photo. ***Perf. 13***

2165	A835	1s dl grn & multi	8	8
2166	A835	2s brt grn & multi	8	8
2167	A835	3s sl grn & multi	10	8
2168	A835	13s ol & multi	30	18
2169	A835	28s bl grn & multi	60	32
2170	A835	40s emer & multi	1.00	50
		Nos. 2165-2170 (6)	2.16	1.24

Souvenir Sheet

2171	A835	1 l grn & multi	3.25	2.25

World Soccer Championship, Munich, June 13–July 7. No. 2171 contains one stamp. Red margin with emblem and inscription in white; soccer cup in yellow and gold. Size: 67x78½mm. No. 2171 exists imperf.

Salt Production
A836

Children's Paintings: 1s, Cosmic Research for Peaceful Purposes. 3s, Fire Dancers. 28s, Russian-Bulgarian Friendship (train and children). 60s, Spring (birds).

1974, Apr. 15 Photo. ***Perf. 13***

2172	A836	1s lil & multi	8	8
2173	A836	2s lt grn & multi	8	8
2174	A836	3s bl & multi	8	8
2175	A836	28s sl & multi	2.00	1.10

Souvenir Sheet

Imperf.

2176	A836	60s bl & multi	3.00	2.50

Third World Youth Philatelic Exhibition, Sofia, May 23–30. No. 2176 contains one stamp with simulated perforations, rose and lilac border. Size: 70x70mm.

Folk Singers
A837

Designs: 2s, Folk dancers (men). 3s, Bagpiper and drummer. 5s, Wrestlers. 13s, Runners (women). 18s, Gymnast.

1974, Apr. 25 ***Perf. 13***

2178	A837	1s ver & multi	5	5
2179	A837	2s org brn & multi	5	5
2180	A837	3s brn red & multi	5	5
2181	A837	5s bl & multi	15	5
2182	A837	13s ultra & multi	70	20
2183	A837	18s vio bl & multi	45	15
		Nos. 2178-2183 (6)	1.45	55

4th Amateur Arts and Sports Festival

Aster
A838

Flowers: 2s, Petunia. 3s, Fuchsia. 18s, Tulip. 20s, Carnation. 28s, Pansy. 80s, Sunflower.

1974, May Photogravure ***Perf. 13***

2184	A838	1s grn & multi	5	5
2185	A838	2s vio bl & multi	5	5
2186	A838	3s ol & multi	5	5
2187	A838	18s brn & multi	28	16
2188	A838	20s multi	45	30
2189	A838	28s dl bl & multi	95	35
		Nos. 2184-2189 (6)	1.83	96

Souvenir Sheet

2190	A838	80s multi	2.00	1.75

No. 2190 contains one stamp. Deep ultramarine margin with white inscription and flower design. Size: 78x60mm.

Automobiles and Emblems
A839

1974, May 15 Photo. ***Perf. 13***

2191	A839	13s multi	21	15

International Automobile Federation (FIA) Spring Congress, Sofia, May 20–24.

Old and New Buildings, UNESCO Emblem
A840

1974, June 15

2192	A840	18s multi	28	15

UNESCO Executive Council, 94th Session, Varna.

Postrider
A841

Designs: 18s, First Bulgarian mail coach. 28s, UPU Monument, Bern.

1974, Aug. 5

2193	A841	2s ocher, blk & vio	3	3
2194	A841	18s ocher, blk & grn	45	20

Souvenir Sheet

2195	A841	28s ocher, blk & bl	2.25	1.75

Centenary of Universal Postal Union. No. 2195 contains one stamp, multicolored marginal inscription. Size: 79x58mm. Exists imperf.

Pioneer and Komsomol Girl
A842

"Bulgarian Communist Party"
A843

Designs: 2s, Pioneer and birds. 60s, Emblem with portrait of George Dimitrov.

1974, Aug. 12

2196	A842	1s grn & multi	3	3
2197	A842	2s bl & multi	3	3

Souvenir Sheet

2198	A842	60s red & multi	3.00	2.50

30th anniversary of Dimitrov Pioneer Organization, Sepremvriiche. No. 2198 contains one stamp, gold margin with black inscription. Size: 60x83mm.

1974, Aug. 20

Symbolic Designs: 2s, Russian liberators. 5s, Industrialization. 13s, Advanced agriculture and husbandry. 18s, Scientific and technical progress.

2199	A843	1s bl gray & multi	3	3
2200	A843	2s bl gray & multi	3	3

2201	A843	5s gray & multi	9	3
2202	A843	13s gray & multi	21	9
2203	A843	18s gray & multi	40	15
		Nos. 2199-2203 (5)	76	33

30th anniversary of the People's Republic.

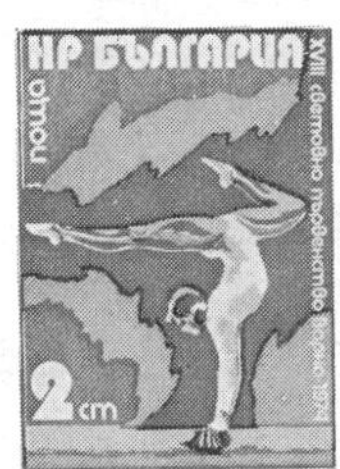

Gymnast on Parallel Bars
A844

Design: 13s, Gymnast on vaulting horse.

1974, Oct. 18 Photo. *Perf. 13*

2204	A844	2s multi	5	5
2205	A844	13s multi	35	16

18th Gymnastic Championships, Varna.

Souvenir Sheet

Symbols of Peace—A845

1974, Oct. 29 Photo. *Perf. 13*

2206	A845	Sheet of 4, multi	2.50	2.25
a.		13s *Doves*	25	15
b.		13s *Map of Europe*	25	15
c.		13s *Olive Branch*	25	15
d.		13s *Inscription*	25	15

1974 European Peace Conference. "Peace" in various languages written on Nos. 2206a–2206c. No. 2206 has yellow, brown and lilac margin. Size: 97½x117 mm. Sold for 60s. Exists imperf.

Nib and Envelope
A846

1974, Nov. 20

2207	A846	2s yel, blk & grn	3	3

Introduction of postal zone numbers.

Flowers
A847

1974, Dec. 5

2208	A847	2s emer & multi	3	3

St. Todor, Ceramic Icon
A848

Apricot Blossoms
A849

Designs: 2s, Medallion, Veliko Turnovo. 3s, Carved capital. 5s, Silver bowl. 8s, Goblet. 13s, Lion's head finial. 18s, Gold plate with Cross. 28s, Breastplate with eagle.

1974, Dec. 18 Photogravure *Perf. 13*

2209	A848	1s org & multi	5	5
2210	A848	2s pink & multi	5	5
2211	A848	3s bl & multi	5	5
2212	A848	5s lt vio & multi	9	5
2213	A848	8s brn & multi	20	8
2214	A848	13s multi	30	16
2215	A848	18s red & multi	45	22
2216	A848	28s ultra & multi	1.00	50
		Nos. 2209-2216 (8)	2.19	1.16

Art works from 9th–12th centuries.

1975, Jan. Photogravure *Perf. 13*

Fruit Tree Blossoms: 2s, Apple. 3s, Cherry. 19s, Pear. 28s, Peach.

2217	A849	1s org & multi	5	5
2218	A849	2s multi	5	5
2219	A849	3s car & multi	5	5
2220	A849	19s lem & multi	30	15
2221	A849	28s ver & multi	65	25
		Nos.2217-2221 (5)	1.10	55

Tree and Book
A850

1975, Mar. 25 Photo. *Perf. 13*

2222	A850	2s gold & multi	3	3

Forestry High School, 50th anniversary.

Souvenir Sheet

Farmers' Activities (Woodcuts)—A851

1975, Mar. 25

2223	A851	Sheet of 4 multi	1.00	75
a.		2s *Farmer with ax and flag*		
b.		5s *Farmers on guard*		
c.		13s *Dancing couple*		
d.		18s *Woman picking fruit*		

Bulgarian Agrarian Peoples' Union, 75th anniversary. No. 2223 has orange and green margin. Size: 102x95mm.

Michelangelo, Self-portrait
A852

Designs: 13s, Night (horiz.). 18s, Day (horiz.). Both designs after sculptures from Medici Tomb, Florence.

1975

2224	A852	2s plum & dk bl	5	5
2225	A852	13s vio bl & plum	21	9
2226	A852	18s brn & grn	45	15

Souvenir Sheet

2227	A852	2s ol & red	1.65	1.50

500th birth anniversary of Michelangelo Buonarotti (1475–1564), Italian sculptor, painter and architect. No. 2227 issued to publicize ARPHILA 75 International Philatelic Exhibition, Paris, June 6–16. Marginal inscriptions and border in gold, red and green. Sheet sold for 60s. Size: 69x83mm.

Issue dates: Nos. 2224–2226, Mar. 28. No. 2227, Mar. 31.

Souvenir Sheet

Spain No. 1 and España 75 Emblem—A853

1975, Apr. 4

2228	A853	40s multi	4.75	3.00

España 75 International Philatelic Exhibition, Madrid, Apr. 4–13. No. 2228 contains one stamp; bright ultramarine margin with white design and inscription, bister post horn. Size: 70x102mm.

Gabrov Costume
A854

Regional Costumes: 3s, Trnsk. 5s, Vidin. 13s, Gocedelchev. 18s, Risen.

1975, Apr. Photogravure *Perf. 13*

2229	A854	2s bl & multi	5	5
2230	A854	3s emer & multi	5	5
2231	A854	5s org & multi	12	8
2232	A854	13s ol & multi	25	12
2233	A854	18s multi	50	20
		Nos. 2229-2233 (5)	97	50

Red Star and Arrow
A855

Standard Kilogram and Meter
A856

Design: 13s, Dove and broken sword.

1975, May 9

2234	A855	2s red, blk & gold	3	3
2235	A855	13s bl, blk & gold	30	15

Victory over Fascism, 30th anniversary.

1975, May 9 *Perf. 13x13½*

2236	A856	13s sil, lil & blk	21	9

Centenary of International Meter Convention, Paris, 1875.

IWY Emblem, Woman's Head
A857

Ivan Vasov
A858

1975, May 20 Photo. *Perf. 13*

2237	A857	13s multi	30	9

International Women's Year 1975.

1975, May

Design: 13s, Ivan Vasov, seated.

2238	A858	2s buff & multi	3	3
2239	A858	13s gray & multi	21	9

125th birth anniversary of Ivan Vasov.

Nikolov and Sava Kokarechkov
A859

Designs: 2s, Mitko Palaouzov and Ivan Vassilev. 5s, Nicolas Nakev and Stevtcho Kraychev. 13s, Ivanka Pachkoulova and Detelina Mintcheva.

1975, May 30

2240	A859	1s multi	5	5
2241	A859	2s multi	5	5
2242	A859	5s multi	9	5
2243	A859	13s multi	30	15

Teen-age resistance fighters, killed during World War II.

Aleksei A. Leonov and Soyuz
A860

Designs: 18s, Thomas P. Stafford and Apollo. 28s, Apollo and Soyuz over earth. 1 l, Apollo Soyuz link-up.

1975, July 15

2244	A860	13s bl & multi	21	9
2245	A860	18s pur & multi	35	15
2246	A860	28s multi	90	35

Souvenir Sheet

2247	A860	1 l vio & multi	3.00	2.25

Apollo Soyuz space test project (Russo-American cooperation), launching July 15; link-up July 17. No. 2247 contains one stamp. Apollo-Soyuz emblem, Russian and American flags in margin. Size: 75x83mm.

Mother Feeding Child, by John E. Millais
A861

Etchings: 2s, The Dead Daughter, by Goya. 3s, Reunion, by Bemkov. 13s, Seated Nude, by Renoir. 20s, Man in a Fur Hat, by Rembrandt. 40s, The Dream, by Daumier (horiz.). 1 l, Temptation, by Dürer.

Photogravure and Engraved

1975, Aug. *Perf. 12x11½, 11½x12*

2248	A861	1s yel grn & multi	5	5
2249	A861	2s org & multi	5	5
2250	A861	3s lil & multi	5	5
2251	A861	13s lt bl & multi	21	9
2252	A861	20s ocher & multi	36	20
2253	A861	40s rose & multi	1.10	35
		Nos. 2248-2253 (6)	1.82	79

Souvenir Sheet

2254	A861	1 l emer & multi	2.50	2.25

World Graphics Exhibition. No. 2254 contains one stamp; gray green marginal inscription and border. Size: 80x95mm.

Letter "Z" from 12th Century Manuscript
A862

Whimsical Globe
A863

Initials from Illuminated Manuscripts: 2s, "B" from 17th century prayerbook. 3s, "V" from 16th century Bouhovo Gospel. 8s, "B" from 14th century Turnovo collection. 13s, "V" from Dobreisho's Gospel, 13th century. 18s, "E" from 11th century Enina book of the Apostles.

1975, Aug. Litho. *Perf. 11½*

2255	A862	1s multi	3	3
2256	A862	2s multi	3	3
2257	A862	3s multi	3	3
2258	A862	8s multi	13	5
2259	A862	13s multi	21	9
2260	A862	18s multi	35	15
		Nos. 2255-2260(6)	78	38

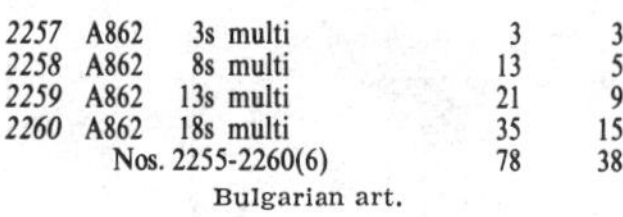

Bulgarian art.

1975, Aug. Photo. *Perf. 13*

2261	A863	2s multi	3	3

Festival of Humor and Satire.

Lifeboat Dju IV and Gibraltar-Cuba Route
A864

1975, Aug. 5 Photo. *Perf. 13*

2262	A864	13s multi	30	15

Oceanexpo 75, First International Ocean Exhibition, Okinawa, July 20, 1975–Jan. 18, 1976.

Sts. Cyril and Methodius
A865

Sts. Constantine and Helena
A866

St. Sophia Church, Sofia, Woodcut by V. Zahriev—A867

1975, Aug. 21

2263	A865	2s ver, yel & brn	5	5
2264	A866	13s grn, yel & brn	30	15

Souvenir Sheet

2265	A867	50s org & multi	1.35	1.25

Balkanphila V, philatelic exhibition, Sofia, Sept. 27–Oct. 5. No. 2265 has bluish gray and orange margin. Size: 89x85mm.

Peace Dove and Map of Europe
A868

1975, Nov. Photogravure *Perf. 13*

2266	A868	18s ultra, rose & yel	35	30

European Security and Cooperation Conference, Helsinki, Finland, July 30–Aug. 1. No. 2266 printed in sheets of 5 stamps and 4 labels, arranged checkerwise.

Acherontia Atropos
A869

Designs: Moths.

1975 Photo. *Perf. 13*

2267	A869	1s *shown*	3	3
2268	A869	2s *Daphnis nerii*	3	3
2269	A869	3s *Smerinthus ocellata*	5	3
2270	A869	10s *Deilephila nicea*	18	8
2271	A869	13s *Choerocampa elpenor*	21	9
2272	A869	18s *Macroglossum fuciformis*	60	30
		Nos. 2267-2272 (6)	1.10	56

Soccer Player
A870

1975, Sept. 21

2273	A870	2s multi	3	3

8th Inter-Toto (soccer pool) Soccer Championships, Varna.

Constantine's Rebellion Against the Turks, 1403—A871

Designs (Woodcuts): 2s, Campaign of Vladislav III, 1443–1444. 3s, Battles of Turnovo, 1598 and 1686. 10s, Battle of Liprovsko, 1688. 13s, Guerrillas, 17th century. 18s, Return of exiled peasants.

1975, Nov. 27 Photo. *Perf. 13*

2274	A871	1s bis, grn & blk	5	5
2275	A871	2s bl, car & blk	5	5
2276	A871	3s yel, lil & blk	8	6
2277	A871	10s org, grn & blk	24	8
2278	A871	13s grn, lil & blk	30	12
2279	A871	18s pink, grn & blk	45	20
		Nos. 2274-2279 (6)	1.17	56

Bulgarian history.

Red Cross and First Aid—A872

Design: 13s, Red Cross and dove.

1975, Dec. 1

2280	A872	2s red brn, red & blk	3	3
2281	A872	13s bl grn, red & blk	21	9

90th anniversary of Bulgarian Red Cross.

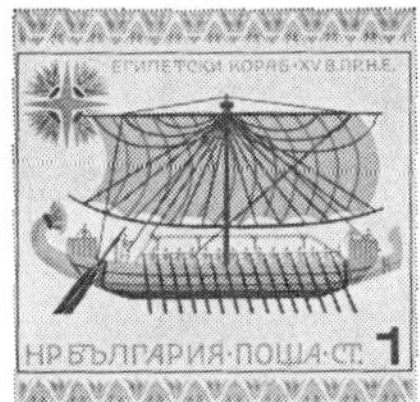

Egyptian Galley
A873

Historic Ships: 2s, Phoenician galley. 3s, Greek trireme. 5s, Roman galley. 13s, Viking longship. 18s, Venetian galley.

1975, Dec. 15 Photo. *Perf. 13*

2282	A873	1s multi	5	5
2283	A873	2s multi	5	5
2284	A873	3s multi	5	6
2285	A873	5s multi	12	6
2286	A873	13s multi	30	15
2287	A873	18s multi	45	20
		Nos. 2282-2287 (6)	1.02	57

See Nos. 2431-2436, 2700-2705.

Souvenir Sheet

Ethnographical Museum, Plovdiv
A874

1975, Dec. 17

2288	A874	Sheet of 3	5.25	5.00
a.		80s grn, yel & dk brn	1.50	1.25

European Architectural Heritage Year. No. 2288 contains 3 stamps and 3 labels showing stylized bird. Olive margin and inscription. Size: 160x96½mm.

Dobri Hristov
A875

1975, Dec. *Perf. 13*

2289	A875	5s brt grn, yel & brn	10	3

Dobri Hristov, musician, birth centenary.

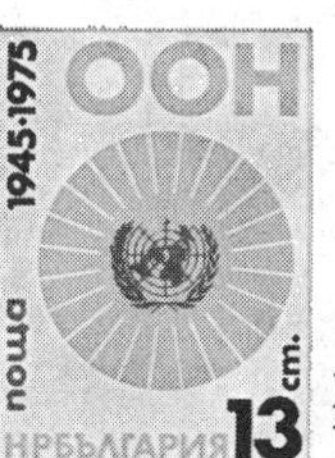

United Nations Emblem
A876

1975, Dec.

2290	A876	13s gold, blk & mag	22	10

United Nations, 30th anniversary.

Glass Ornaments
A877

Design: 13s, Peace dove, decorated ornament.

1975, Dec. 22 Photo. *Perf. 13*

2291	A877	2s brt vio & multi	3	3
2292	A877	13s gray & multi	22	10

New Year 1976.

Downhill Skiing—A878

Designs (Winter Olympic Games Emblem and): 2s, Cross country skier (vert.). 3s, Ski jump. 13s, Biathlon (vert.). 18s, Ice hockey (vert.). 23s, Speed skating (vert.). 80s, Figure skating, pair (vert.).

1976, Jan. 30 *Perf. 13½*

2293	A878	1s sil & multi	3	3
2294	A878	2s sil & multi	3	3
2295	A878	3s sil & multi	3	3
2296	A878	13s sil & multi	21	9
2297	A878	18s sil & multi	28	20
2298	A878	23s sil & multi	60	35
		Nos. 2293-2298 (6)	1.18	73

Souvenir Sheet

2299	A878	80s sil & multi	2.25	1.75

12th Winter Olympic Games, Innsbruck, Austria, Feb. 4–15. No. 2299 has light blue margin with white inscription. Size: 71x80mm.

Electric Streetcar, Sofia, 1976
A879

Design: 13s, Streetcar and trailer, 1901.

1976, Jan. 12 Photo. *Perf. 13½x13*

2300	A879	2s gray & multi	3	3
2301	A879	13s gray & multi	35	15

75th anniversary of Sofia streetcars.

Stylized Bird
A880

Designs: 5s, Dates "1976" and "1956" and star. 13s, Hammer and sickle. 50s, George Dimitrov.

1976, Mar. 1 *Perf. 13*

2302	A880	2s gold & multi	3	3
2303	A880	5s gold & multi	15	3
2304	A880	13s gold & multi	25	9

Souvenir Sheet

2305	A880	50s gold & multi	1.10	90

11th Bulgarian Communist Party Congress. No. 2305 contains one stamp; crimson margin. Size: 56x64mm.

A. G. Bell and Telephone, 1876
A881

1976, Mar. 10

2306	A881	18s dk brn, yel & ocher	40	20

Centenary of first telephone call by Alexander Graham Bell, Mar. 10, 1876.

Mute Swan—A882

Waterfowl: 2s, Ruddy shelduck. 3s, Common shelduck. 5s, Garganey teal. 13s, Mallard. 18s, Red-crested pochard.

1976, Mar. 27 Litho. *Perf. 11½*

2307	A882	1s vio bl & multi	3	3
2308	A882	2s yel grn & multi	3	3
2309	A882	3s bl & multi	3	3
2310	A882	5s multi	10	3
2311	A882	13s pur & multi	21	9
2312	A882	18s grn & multi	35	15
		Nos. 2307-2312 (6)	75	36

Guerrillas—A883

Designs (Woodcuts by Stoev): 2s, Peasants with rifle and proclamation. 5s, Raina Knaginia with horse and guerrilla. 13s, Insurgents with cherrywood cannon.

1976, Apr. 5 Photo. *Perf. 13*

2313	A883	1s multi	3	3
2314	A883	2s multi	3	3
2315	A883	5s multi	9	3
2316	A883	13s multi	21	9

Centenary of uprising against Turkey.

Guard and Dog
A884

Design: 13s, Men on horseback, observation tower.

1976, May 15

2317	A884	2s multi	3	3
2318	A884	13s multi	30	9

30th anniversary of Border Guards.

Construction Worker
A885

1976, May 20

2319	A885	2s multi	3	3

Young Workers Brigade, 30th anniversary.

Busludja, Bas-relief
A886

AES Complex
A887

Design: 5s, Memorial building.

1976, May 28 Photo. *Perf. 13*

2320	A886	2s grn & multi	3	3
2321	A886	5s vio bl & multi	10	3

First Congress of Bulgarian Social Democratic Party, 85th anniversary.

1976, Apr. 7

Designs: 8s, Factory. 10s, Apartment houses. 13s, Refinery. 20s, Hydroelectric station.

2322	A887	5s green	9	3
2323	A887	8s maroon	13	5
2324	A887	10s green	18	8
2325	A887	13s violet	30	12
2326	A887	20s brt grn	36	16
		Nos. 2322-2326 (5)	1.06	44

Five-year plan accomplishments.

Children Playing Around Table
A888

Designs (Kindergarten Children): 2s, with doll carriage and hobby horse. 5s, playing ball. 23s, in costume.

1976, June 15

2327	A888	1s grn & multi	3	3
2328	A888	2s yel & multi	3	3
2329	A888	5s lil & multi	10	3
2330	A888	23s rose & multi	45	18

Demeter Blagoev
A889

Christo Botev
A890

1976, May 28

2331	A889	13s bluish blk, red & gold	30	15

Demeter Blagoev (1856–1924), writer, political leader, 120th birth anniversary.

1976, May 25

2332	A890	13s ocher & sl grn	30	15

Christo Botev (1848–1876), poet, death centenary. Printed se-tenant with yellow green and ocher label, inscribed with poem.

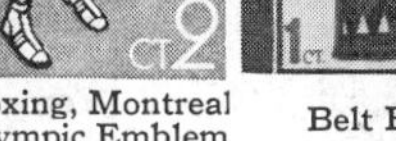

Boxing, Montreal Olympic Emblem
A891

Belt Buckle
A892

Designs (Montreal Olympic Emblem): 1s, Wrestling (horiz.). 3s, 1 l, Weight lifting. 13s, One-man kayak. 18s, Woman gymnast. 28s, Woman diver. 40s, Woman runner.

1976, June 25

2333	A891	1s org & multi	3	3
2334	A891	2s multi	3	3
2335	A891	3s lil & multi	3	3
2336	A891	13s multi	20	8
2337	A891	18s multi	35	15
2338	A891	28s bl & multi	46	25
2339	A891	40s lem & multi	80	45
		Nos. 2333-2339 (7)	1.90	1.02

Souvenir Sheet

2340	A891	1 l org & multi	2.00	1.65

21st Olympic Games, Montreal, Canada, July 17–Aug. 1. No. 2340 contains one stamp; multicolored margin. Size: 69x79mm.

1976, July 30 Photo. *Perf. 13*

Thracian Art (8th–4th Centuries): 2s, Brooch. 3s, Mirror handle. 5s, Helmet cheek cover. 13s, Gold ornament. 18s, Lion's head (harness decoration). 20s, Knee guard. 28s, Jeweled pendant.

2341	A892	1s brn & multi	3	3
2342	A892	2s bl & multi	3	3
2343	A892	3s multi	3	3
2344	A892	5s cl & multi	9	3
2345	A892	13s pur & multi	21	9
2346	A892	18s multi	35	15
2347	A892	20s multi	40	16
2348	A892	28s multi	65	25
		Nos. 2341-2348 (8)	1.79	77

Composite of Bulgarian Stamp Designs—A893

1976, June 5

2349	A893	50s red & multi	1.35	1.20

International Federation of Philately (F.I.P.), 50th anniversary and 12th Congress. No. 2349 has multicolored margin. Size: 73x102mm.

Partisans at Night, by Tsanko Lavrenov—A894

Paintings: 5s, Old Town, by Stanko Davrelov. 13s, Seated Woman, by Petrov (vert.). 18s, Seated Boy, by Petrov (vert.). 28s, The Visit, by Davrelov (vert.). 80s, Ilya Petrov, self-portrait (vert.).

1976, Aug. 11 Photo. *Perf. 14*

2350 A894 2s multi 3 3
2351 A894 5s multi 9 3
2352 A894 13s ultra & multi 21 9
2353 A894 18s multi 28 15
2354 A894 28s multi 50 25
Nos. 2350-2354 (5) 1.11 55

Souvenir Sheet

2354A A894 80s multi 1.75 1.50

No. 2354A has green border. Size: 60x83mm.

Souvenir Sheet

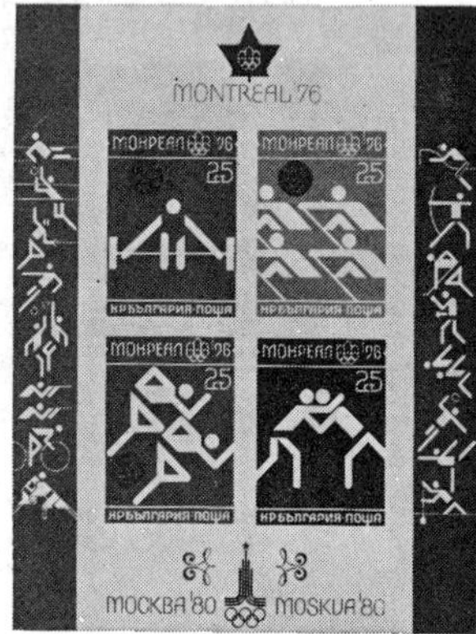

Olympic Sports and Emblems A895

1976, Sept. 6 Photo. *Perf. 13*

Multicolored

2355 A895 Sheet of 4 2.00 1.65
a. 25s *Weight Lifting* 40 25
b. 25s *Rowing* 40 25
c. 25s *Running* 40 25
d. 25s *Wrestling* 40 25

Medalists, 21st Olympic Games, Montreal. No. 2355 has gold margin, green and red inscription. Size: 98x117mm.

Souvenir Sheet

Fresco and UNESCO Emblem—A896

1976, Dec. 3

2356 A896 50s red & multi 1.10 95

U.N. Educational, Scientific and Cultural Organization, 30th anniversary. No. 2356 has brown and orange margin. Size: 71x 80mm.

"The Pianist" by Jendov A897

Fish and Hook A898

Designs (Caricatures by Jendov): 5s, Imperialist "Trick or Treat." 13s, The Leader, 1931.

1976, Sept. 30 Photo. *Perf. 13*

2357 A897 2s grn & multi 3 3
2358 A897 5s pur & multi 9 3
2359 A897 13s mag & multi 21 9

Alex Jendov (1901–1953), caricaturist.

1976, Sept. 21 Photo. *Perf. 13*

2360 A898 5s multi 9 3

World Sport Fishing Congress, Varna.

St. Theodore A899

Frescoes: 3s, St. Paul. 5s, St. Joachim. 13s, Melchizedek. 19s, St. Porphyrius. 28s, Queen. 1 l, The Last Supper.

1976, Oct. 4 Litho. *Perf. 12x12½*

2361 A899 2s gold & multi 3 3
2362 A899 3s gold & multi 3 3
2363 A899 5s gold & multi 9 3
2364 A899 13s gold & multi 25 9
2365 A899 19s gold & multi 35 20
2366 A899 28s gold & multi 50 25
Nos. 2361-2366 (6) 1.25 63

Miniature Sheet

Perf. 12

2367 A899 1 l gold & multi 2.00 1.50

Frescoes from Zemen Monastery, 14th century. No. 2367 has gold and vermilion border. Size: 60x75mm.

Document A900

1976, Oct. 5

2368 A900 5s multi 9 3

State Archives, 25th anniversary.

Cinquefoil A901

Designs: 1s, Chestnut. 5s, Holly. 8s, Yew. 13s, Daphne. 23s, Judas tree.

1976, Oct. 14 Photo. *Perf. 13*

2369 A901 1s car & grn 3 3
2370 A901 2s grn & multi 3 3
2371 A901 5s multi 9 3
2372 A901 8s multi 13 5
2373 A901 13s brn & multi 21 9
2374 A901 23s multi 45 20
Nos. 2369-2374 (6) 94 43

Dimitri Polianov A902

1976, Nov. 19

2375 A902 2s dk pur & ocher 3 3

Dimitri Polianov (1876–1953), poet, birth centenary.

Christo Boteff, by Zlatyu Boyadjiev A903

Paintings: 2s, Partisan Carrying Cherrywood Cannon, by Ilya Petrov. 3s, "Necklace of Immortality" (man's portrait), by Detchko Uzunov. 13s, "April 1876," by Georgi Popoff. 18s, Partisans, by Stoyan Venev. 60s, The Oath, by Svetlin Ruseff.

1976, Dec. 8

2376 A903 1s bis & multi 3 3
2377 A903 2s bis & multi 3 3
2378 A903 3s bis & multi 3 3
2379 A903 13s bis & multi 21 9
2380 A903 18s bis & multi 28 10
Nos. 2376-2380 (5) 58 28

Souvenir Sheet

Imperf.

2381 A903 60s gold & multi 1.25 90

Uprising against Turkish rule, centenary. No. 2381 contains one stamp; gold border. Size: 44x82mm.

"Pollution" and Tree—A904

Design: 18s, "Pollution" obscuring sun.

1976, Nov. 10 *Perf. 13*

2382 A904 2s ultra & multi 3 3
2383 A904 18s bl & multi 35 15

Protection of the environment.

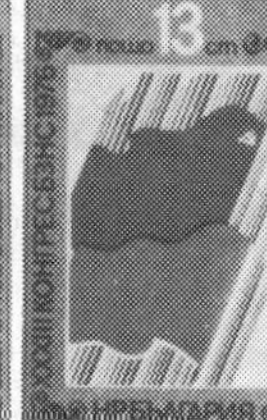

Congress Emblem A904a

Flags A904b

1976, Nov. 28 Photo. *Perf. 13*

2384 A904a 2s multi 3 3
2384A A904b 13s multi 22 15

33rd BSIS Congress (Bulgarian Socialist Party).

Tobacco Workers, by Stajkov A905

Paintings by Stajkov: 2s, View of Melnik. 13s, Shipbuilder.

1976, Dec. 16 Photo. *Perf. 13*

2385 A905 1s multi 3 3
2386 A905 2s multi 3 3
2387 A905 13s multi 21 15

Veselin Stajkov (1906–1970), painter, 70th birth anniversary.

Snowflake A906

1976, Dec. 20

2388 A906 2s sil & multi 5 3

New Year 1977.

Zachary Stoyanov A907

1976, Dec. 30

2389 A907 2s multi 3 3

Zachary Stoyanov (1851–1889), historian, 125th birth anniversary.

Bronze Coin of Septimus Severus A908

Roman Coins: 2s, 13s, 18s, Bronze coins of Caracalla (diff.). 23s, Copper coin of Diocletian.

1977, Jan. 28 Photo. *Perf. 13½x13*

2390 A908 1s gold & multi 3 3
2391 A908 2s gold & multi 3 3

2392	A908	13s gold & multi	21	9
2393	A908	18s gold & multi	35	20
2394	A908	23s gold & multi	50	30
		Nos. 2390-2394 (5)	1.12	65

Coins struck in Serdica (modern Sofia).

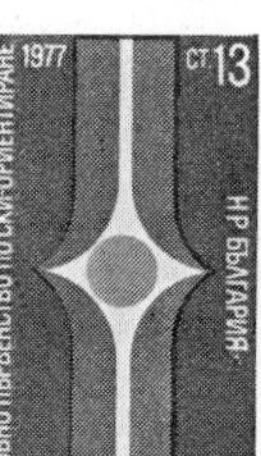

Skis and Compass A909

Tourist Congress Emblem A910

1977, Feb. 14 ***Perf. 13***

2395	A909	13s ultra, red & lt bl	21	15

2nd World Ski Orienteering Championships.

1977, Feb. 24 **Photo.** ***Perf. 13***

2396	A910	2s multi	3	3

5th Congress of Bulgarian Tourist Organization.

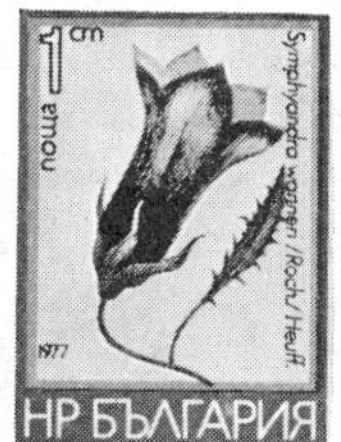

Bellflower A911

Designs: Various bellflowers.

1977, Mar. 2

2397	A911	1s yel & multi	3	3
2398	A911	2s rose & multi	3	3
2399	A911	3s lt bl & multi	3	3
2400	A911	13s multi	21	9
2401	A911	43s yel & multi	75	40
		Nos. 2397-2401 (5)	1.05	58

Vasil Kolarov A912

Union Congress Emblem A913

1977, Mar. 21 **Photo.** ***Perf. 13***

2402	A912	2s bl & blk	3	3

Vasil Kolarov (1877–1950), politician.

1977, Mar. 25

2403	A913	2s multi	3	3

8th Bulgarian Trade Union Congress, Apr. 4–7.

Wolf—A914

Wild Animals: 2s, Red fox. 10s, Weasel. 13s, European wildcat. 23s, Jackal.

1977, May 16 Litho. ***Perf. 12½x12***

2404	A914	1s multi	3	3
2405	A914	2s multi	3	3
2406	A914	10s multi	18	6
2407	A914	13s multi	21	9
2408	A914	23s multi	45	20
		Nos. 2404-2408 (5)	90	41

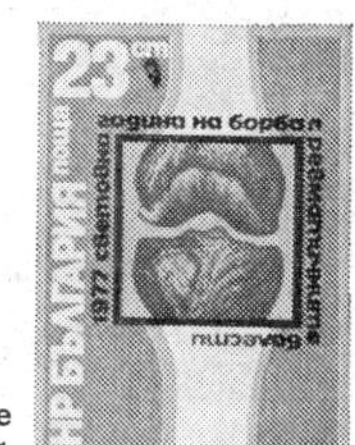

Diseased Knee A915

1977, Mar. 31 **Photo.** ***Perf. 13***

2409	A915	23s multi	40	25

World Rheumatism Year.

Writers' Congress Emblem A916

1977, June 7

2410	A916	23s lt bl & yel grn	40	18

International Writers Congress: "Peace, the Hope of the Planet." No. 2410 printed in sheets of 8 stamps and 4 labels with signatures of participating writers.

Old Testament Trinity, Sofia, 16th Century A917

Icons: 1s, St. Nicholas, Nessebur, 13th century. 3s, Annunciation, Royal Gates, Veliko Turnovo, 16th century. 5s, Christ Enthroned, Nessebur, 17th century. 13s, St. Nicholas, Elena, 18th century. 23s, Presentation of the Virgin, Rila Monastery, 18th century. 35s, Virgin and Child, Tryavna, 19th century. 40s, St. Demetrius on Horseback, Provadia, 19th century. 1 l, The 12 Holidays, Rila Monastery, 18th century.

1977, May 10 **Photo.** ***Perf. 13***

2411	A917	1s blk & multi	3	3
2412	A917	2s grn & multi	3	3
2413	A917	3s brn & multi	3	3
2414	A917	5s bl & multi	10	3
2415	A917	13s ol & multi	21	9
2416	A917	23s mar & multi	40	18
2417	A917	35s grn & multi	60	30
2418	A917	40s dp ultra & multi	80	50
		Nos. 2411-2418 (8)	2.20	1.19

Miniature Sheet

Imperf.

2419	A917	1 l gold & multi	2.00	1.75

Bulgarian icons. No. 2419 has decorative orange border. Size: 101x100mm.

Souvenir Sheet

St. Cyril A918

1977, June 7 **Photo.** ***Perf. 13***

2420	A918	1 l gold & multi	2.00	1.60

1150th anniversary of the birth of St. Cyril (827–869), reputed inventor of Cyrillic alphabet. No. 2420 has violet blue and gold margin showing ancient Cyrillic writing. Size: 103x87mm.

Congress Emblem A919

1977, May 9

2421	A919	2s red, gold & grn	3	3

13th Komsomol Congress.

Newspaper Masthead—A920

1977, June 3 **Photo.** ***Perf. 13***

2422	A920	2s multi	3	3

Centenary of Bulgarian daily press and 50th anniversary of Rabotnichesko Delo newspaper.

Patriotic Front Emblem A921

Weight Lifting A922

1977, May 26

2423	A921	2s gold & multi	3	3

8th Congress of Patriotic Front.

1977, June 15

2424	A922	13s dp brn & multi	22	10

European Youth Weight Lifting Championships, Sofia, June.

Women Basketball Players A923

1977, June 15 ***Perf. 13***

2425	A923	23s multi	40	18

7th European Women's Basketball Championships.

Wrestling—A924

Designs (Games' Emblem and): 13s, Running. 23s, Basketball. 43s, Women's gymnastics.

1977, Apr. 15

2426	A924	2s multi	3	3
2427	A924	13s multi	21	9
2428	A924	23s multi	40	18
2429	A924	43s multi	75	20

UNIVERSIADE '77, University Games, Sofia, Aug. 18–27.

TV Tower, Berlin A925

1977, Aug. 12 **Litho.** ***Perf. 13***

2430	A925	25s bl & dk bl	45	36

SOZPHILEX 77 Philatelic Exhibition, Berlin, Aug. 19–28.

Ship Type of 1975

Historic Ships: 1s, Hansa cog. 2s, Santa Maria, caravelle. 3s, Golden Hind, frigate. 12s, Santa Catherina, carrack. 13s, La Corone, galleon. 43s, Mediterranean galleass.

1977, Aug. 29 **Photo.** ***Perf. 13***

2431	A873	1s multi	3	3
2432	A873	2s multi	3	3
2433	A873	3s multi	3	3
2434	A873	12s multi	20	6
2435	A873	13s multi	22	10
2436	A873	43s multi	85	35
		Nos. 2431-2436 (6)	1.36	60

Ivan Vasov National Theater A926

Buildings, Sofia: 13s, Party Headquarters. 23s, House of the People's Army. 30s, Clement Ochrida University. 80s, National Gallery. 1 l, National Assembly.

1977, Apr. 30 Photogravure *Perf. 13*

2437	A926	12s red, *gray*	20	8
2438	A926	13s red brn, *gray*	21	9
2439	A926	23s bl, *gray*	40	18
2440	A926	30s ol, *gray*	55	30
2441	A926	80s vio, *gray*	1.40	80
2442	A926	1 l cl, *gray*	1.75	1.00
		Nos. 2437-2442 (6)	4.51	2.45

Map of Europe A927

1977 June10

2443	A927	23s brn, bl & grn	40	18

21st Congress of the European Organization for Quality Control, Varna.

Union of Earth and Water, by Rubens A928

Rubens Paintings: 23s, Venus and Adonis. 40s, Pastoral Scene (man and woman). 1 l, Portrait of a Lady in Waiting.

1977, Sept. 23 Litho. *Perf. 12*

2444	A928	13s gold & multi	21	9
2445	A928	23s gold & multi	40	18
2446	A928	40s gold & multi	70	20

Souvenir Sheet

2447	A928	1 l gold & multi	2.00	1.60

Peter Paul Rubens (1577–1640), 400th birth anniversary. No. 2447 has gold border. Size: 72x88mm.

George Dimitrov A929

1977, June 17 Photo. *Perf. 13*

2448	A929	13s red & dp cl	21	9

George Dimitrov (1882–1947), first Prime Minister of Bulgaria.

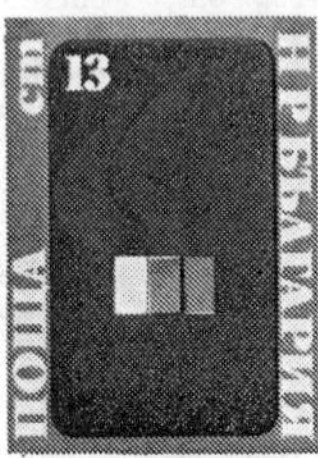

Flame with Star A930

Smart Pete on Donkey, by Ilija Beskor A931

1977, May 17

2449	A930	13s gold & multi	21	9

3rd Bulgarian Culture Congress.

1977, May 19

2450	A931	2s multi	3	3

11th National Festival of Humor and Satire, Gabrovo.

Elin Pelin A932 Dr. Pirogov A934

13th Canoe World Championships A933

Albena, Black Sea—A933a

Writers: 2s, Pelin (Dimitur Ivanov Stojanov, (1877-1949). 5s Peju K. Jaworov (1878-1914). Artists: 13s, Boris Angelushev (1902-1966). 23s, Ceno Todorov (Ceno Todorov Dikov, 1877-1953). Each printed with label showing scenes from authors' works or illustrations by the artists.

1977, Aug. 26 Photo. *Perf. 13*

2451	A932	2s gold & brn	3	3
2452	A932	5s gold & gray grn	10	3
2453	A932	13s gold & cl	21	9
2454	A932	23s gold & bl	40	18

1977, Sept. 1 Photo. *Perf. 13*

2455	A933	2s shown	3	3
2456	A933	23s 2-man canoe	40	18

1977, Oct. 5 Photo. *Perf. 13*

2456A	A933a	35s shown	60	28
2456B	A933a	43s Rila Monastery	75	35

Nos. 2456A-2456B se-tenant.

1977, Oct. 14 Photo. *Perf. 13*

2457	A934	13s ol, ocher & brn	21	9

Centenary of visit by Russian physician N. J. Pirogov during war of liberation from Turkey.

Peace Decree, 1917 A935

Old Soldier with Grandchild A936

Designs: 13s, Lenin, 1917. 23s, "1917" as a flame.

1977, Oct. 21

2458	A935	2s blk, buff & red	3	3
2459	A935	13s multi	21	9
2460	A935	23s multi	40	18

60th anniversary of Russian October Revolution.

1977, Sept. 30

Designs (Festival Posters): 13s, "The Bugler." 23s, Liberation Monument, Sofia (detail). 25s, Samara flag.

2461	A936	2s multi	3	3
2462	A936	13s multi	21	9
2463	A936	23s multi	40	18
2464	A936	25s multi	45	30

Liberation from Turkish rule, centenary.

Souvenir Sheet

Games' and Sports Emblems—A937

1977, Aug. 10 Photo. *Perf. 13½x13*

2465	A937	1 l multi	2.00	1.60

University Games '77, Sofia. No. 2465 has multicolored margin. Size: 83x75mm.

Conference Building—A938

1977, Sept. 12 *Perf. 13½*

2466	A938	23s multi	40	18

64th Interparliamentary Union Conference, Sofia.

Ornament A940

Design: 13s, Different ornament.

1977, Dec. 1

2468	A940	2s gold & multi	3	3
2469	A940	13s sil & multi	21	9

New Year 1978.

Railroad Bridge—A941

1977, Nov. 9

2470	A941	13s grn, yel & gray	21	9

Transport Organization, 50th anniversary.

Petko Ratchev Slaveikov A942

1977, Nov. 15

2471	A942	8s gold & vio brn	14	5

Petko Ratchev Slaveikov (1827–95), poet, birth sesquicentennial. No. 2471 printed in sheets of 8 stamps and 8 labels in 4 alternating vertical rows. Pink and black label shows woman rocking cradle.

Soccer Player A943

Design: 23s, Soccer player and Games' emblem. 50s, Soccer players.

1978, Jan. 30 Photo. *Perf. 13*

2472	A943	13s multi	21	9
2473	A943	23s multi	40	18

Souvenir Sheet

2474	A943	50s ultra & multi	1.00	80

11th World Cup Soccer Championship, Argentina, June 1–25.

No. 2474 contains one stamp; cup and Argentina '78 emblem in margin. Size: 75x62mm.

Todor Zhivkov and Leonid I. Brezhnev A944

Ostankino Tower, Moscow, Bulgarian Post Emblem A945

1977, Sept. 7 **Photo.** ***Perf. 13***

2475	A944	18s gold, car & brn	30	15

Bulgarian-Soviet Friendship. No. 2475 issued in sheets of 3 stamps and 3 labels.

1978, Mar. 1

2476	A945	13s multi	21	9

20th anniversary of the Comecon Postal Organization (Council of Mutual Economic Assistance).

Leo Tolstoy A946

Shipka Pass Monument A947

Portraits: 5s, Fedor Dostoevski. 13s, Ivan Sergeevich Turgenev. 23s, Vasili Vasilievich Vershchagin. 25s, Giuseppe Garibaldi. 35s, Victor Hugo.

1978, Mar. 28 **Photo.** ***Perf. 13***

2477	A946	2s yel & dk grn	3	3
2478	A946	5s lem & brn	8	4
2479	A946	13s tan & sl grn	21	9
2480	A946	23s gray & vio brn	40	18
2481	A946	25s yel grn & blk	45	20
2482	A946	35s lt bl & vio bl	60	28
		Nos. 2477-2482 (6)	1.77	82

Souvenir Sheet

2483	A947	50s multi	95	60

Centenary of Bulgaria's liberation from Ottoman rule. No. 2483 has yellow ornaments in margin. Size: 55x73mm.

Bulgarian and Russian Colors A948

1978, Mar. 18

2484	A948	2s multi	3	3

30th anniversary of Russo-Bulgarian cooperation.

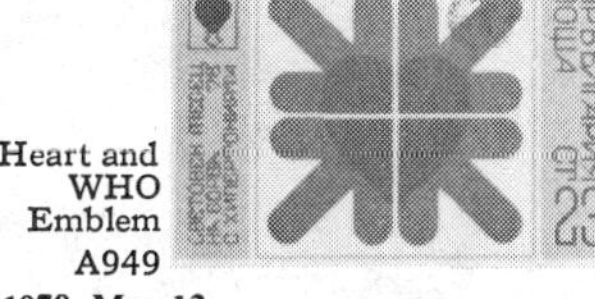

Heart and WHO Emblem A949

1978, May 12

2485	A949	23s gray, red & org	40	18

World Health Day, fight against hypertension.

Goddess A950

Ceramics (2nd–4th Centuries) and Exhibition Emblem: 5s, Mask of bearded man. 13s, Vase. 23s, Vase. 35s, Head of Silenus. 53s, Cock.

1978, Apr. 26

2486	A950	2s grn & multi	3	3
2487	A950	5s multi	8	4
2488	A950	13s multi	21	9
2489	A950	23s multi	40	18
2490	A950	35s multi	60	28
2491	A950	53s car & multi	95	45
		Nos. 2486-2491 (6)	2.27	1.07

Philaserdica Philatelic Exhibition.

Nikolai Roerich, by Svyatoslav Roerich A951

"Mind and Matter," by Andrei Nikolov A952

1978, Apr. 5

2492	A951	8s multi	15	6
2493	A952	13s multi	22	10

Nikolai K. Roerich (1874–1947) and Andrei Nikolov (1878–1959), artists.

Bulgarian Flag and Red Star—A953

1978, Apr. 18

2494	A953	2s vio bl & multi	3	3

Bulgarian Communist Party Congress.

Young Man, by Albrecht Dürer A954

Paintings: 23s, Bathsheba at Fountain, by Rubens. 25s, Portrait of a Man, by Hans Holbein the Younger. 35s, Rembrandt and Saskia, by Rembrandt. 43s, Lady in Mourning, by Tintoretto. 60s, Old Man with Beard, by Rembrandt. 80s, Knight in Armor, by Van Dyck.

1978, June 19 **Photo.** ***Perf. 13***

2495	A954	13s multi	21	9
2496	A954	23s multi	40	18
2497	A954	25s multi	45	20
2498	A954	35s multi	60	28
2499	A954	43s multi	75	35
2500	A954	60s multi	1.10	40
2501	A954	80s multi	1.40	45
		Nos. 2495-2501 (7)	4.91	1.95

Dresden Art Gallery paintings.

Doves and Festival Emblem—A955

1978, May 31

2502	A955	13s multi	21	9

11th World Youth Festival, Havana, July 28–Aug. 5.

Fritillaria Stribrnyi A956

Rare Flowers: 2s, Fritillaria drenovskyi. 3s, Lilium rhodopaeum. 13s, Tulipa urumoffii. 23s, Lilium jankae. 43s, Tulipa rhodopaea.

1978, June 27

2503	A956	1s multi	3	3
2504	A956	2s multi	3	3
2505	A956	3s multi	3	3
2506	A956	13s multi	21	9
2507	A956	23s multi	40	18
2508	A956	43s multi	75	35
		Nos. 2503-2508 (6)	1.45	71

Yacht Cor Caroli and Map of Voyage A957

1978, May 19 **Photo.** ***Perf. 13***

2509	A957	23s multi	40	18

First Bulgarian around-the-world voyage, Capt. Georgi Georgiev, Dec. 20, 1976–Dec. 20, 1977.

Market, by Naiden Petkov—A958

Views of Sofia: 5s, Street, by Emil Stoichev. 13s, Street, by Boris Ivanov. 23s, Tolbukhin Boulevard, by Nikola Tanev. 35s, National Theater, by Nikola Petrov. 53s, Market, by Anton Mitov.

1978, Aug. 28 **Litho.** ***Perf. 12½x12***

2510	A958	2s multi	3	3
2511	A958	5s multi	10	3
2512	A958	13s multi	22	10
2513	A958	23s multi	40	18
2514	A958	35s multi	60	28
2515	A958	53s multi	95	45
		Nos. 2510-2515 (6)	2.30	1.07

Miniature Sheet

Sleeping Venus, by Giorgione—A959

1978, Aug. 7 **Photo.** ***Imperf.***

2516	A959	1 l multi	2.00	1.50

No. 2516 has light green decorative margin. Size: 71x71mm.

View of Varna—A960

1978, July 13 **Photo.** ***Perf. 13***

2517	A960	13s multi	22	10

63rd Esperanto Congress, Varna, July 29–Aug. 5.

Black Woodpecker A961

Woodpeckers: 2s, Syrian. 3s, Three-toed. 13s, Middle spotted. 23s, Lesser spotted. 43s, Green

1978, Sept. 1

2518	A961	1s multi	3	3
2519	A961	2s multi	3	3
2520	A961	3s multi	5	3
2521	A961	13s multi	22	10
2522	A961	23s multi	40	18
2523	A961	43s multi	75	35
		Nos. 2518-2523 (6)	1.48	72

Battle A962

1978, Sept. 5

2524	A962	2s red & brn	3	3

55th anniversary of September uprising.

Souvenir Sheet

National Theater, Sofia A963

Photogravure and Engraved

1978, Sept. 1 ***Perf. 12x11½***

Multicolored

2525	Sheet of 4	3.00	2.00
a.	A963 40s *shown*	70	40
b.	A963 40s *Festival Hall, Sofia*	70	40
c.	A963 40s *Charles Bridge, Prague*	70	40
d.	A963 40s *Belvedere Palace, Prague*	70	40

PRAGA '78 and PHILASERDICA '79 Philatelic Exhibitions. No. 2525 has pink marginal inscriptions and PRAGA and PHILASERDICA emblems. Size: 153x112mm.

Black and White Hands, Human Rights Emblem
A964

1978, Oct. 3 Photo. ***Perf. 13x13½***

2526 A964 13s multi 22 10

Anti-Apartheid Year.

Gotse Deltchev
A965

Bulgarian Calculator
A966

1978, Aug. 1 Photo. ***Perf. 13***

2527 A965 13s multi 22 10

Gotse Deltchev (1872–1903), patriot.

1978, Sept. 3

2528 A966 2s multi 3 3

International Sample Fair, Plovdiv.

Guerrillas—A967

1978, Aug. 1

2529 A967 5s blk & rose red 10 3

75th anniversary of the Ilinden and Preobrazhene revolts.

"Pipe Line" and Flags
A968

1978, Oct. 3

2530 A968 13s multi 22 10

Construction of gas pipe line from Orenburg to Russian border.

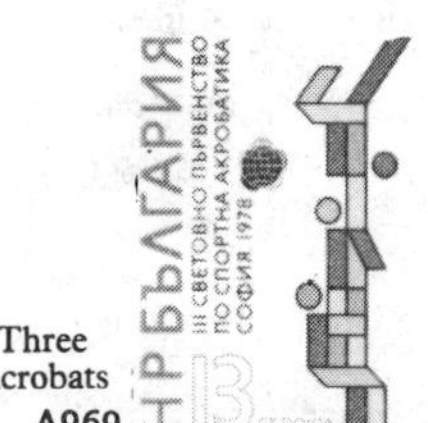

Three Acrobats
A969

1978, Oct. 4 ***Perf. 13x13½***

2531 A969 13s multi 22 10

3rd World Acrobatic Championships, Sofia, Oct. 6-8.

Christo G. Danov
A970

1978, Sept. 18 Photo. ***Perf. 13***

2532 A970 2s dp cl & ocher 3 3

Christo G. Danov (1828–1911), 1st Bulgarian publisher. No. 2532 printed with se-tenant label showing early printing press.

Insurgents, by Todor Panajotov
A971

1978, Sept. 20

2533 A971 2s multi 3 3

Vladaja mutiny, 60th anniversary.

Salvador Allende
A972

Human Rights Flame
A973

1978, Oct. 11 Photo. ***Perf. 13***

2534 A972 13s dk brn & org red 22 10

Salvador Allende (1908–1973), president of Chile.

1978, Oct. 18

2535 A973 23s multi 40 18

Universal Declaration of Human Rights, 30th anniversary.

"Strength for my Arm" by Zlatyu Boyadjiev
A974

Bulgarian Paintings: 1s, Levski and Matei Mitkaloto, by Kalina Tasseva. 3s, Rumena, woman military leader, by Nikola Mirchev (horiz.). 13s, Kolju Ficeto, by Elza Goeva. 23s, Family, National Revival Period, by Naiden Petkov.

Perf. 12x12½, 12½x12

1978, Oct. 25 Lithographed

2536 A974 1s multi 3 3
2537 A974 2s multi 3 3
2538 A974 3s multi 5 2
2539 A974 13s multi 22 10
2540 A974 23s multi 40 18
Nos. 2536-2540 (5) 73 36

1300th anniversary of Bulgaria (in 1981).

Souvenir Sheet

Tourism Building, Plovdiv
A975

Design: No. 2541b, Chrelo Tower, Rila Cloister.

1978, Nov. 1 Photo. ***Perf. 13***

2541 Sheet of 5 4.00 2.75
a. A975 43s multi 75 40
b. A975 43s multi 75 40

Conservation of European architectural heritage. No. 2541 contains 3 No. 2541a, 2 No. 2541b and ornamental label. Lilac marginal inscription. Size: 116x116mm.

Ferry, Map of Black Sea with Route
A976

1978, Nov. 1 Photo. ***Perf. 13***

2542 A976 13s multi 22 10

Opening of Ilychovsk-Varna Ferry.

Bird, from Marble Floor, St. Sofia Church
A977

1978, Nov. 20

2543 A977 5s multi 10 3

3rd Bulgaria '78, National Philatelic Exhibition, Sofia. Printed se-tenant with label showing emblems of Bulgaria '78 and Philaserdica '79.

Initial, 13th Century Gospel
A978

Designs: 13s, St. Cyril, miniature, 1567. 23s, Book cover, 16th century. 80s, St. Methodius, miniature, 13th century.

1978, Dec. 15 Photo. ***Perf. 13***

2544 A978 2s multi 3 3
2545 A978 13s multi 22 10
2546 A978 23s multi 40 18

Souvenir Sheet

2547 A978 80s multi 1.50 1.25

Centenary of the Cyril and Methodius National Library. No. 2547 shows Gospel page. Size: 63x95mm.

Bulgaria No. 53
A979

Bulgarian Stamps: 13s, No. 534. 23s, No. 968. 35s, No. 1176 (vert.). 53s, No. 1223 (vert.). 1 l, No. 1.

1978, Dec. 30

2548 A979 2s ol grn & red 3 3
2549 A979 13s ultra & rose car 22 10
2550 A979 23s rose lil & ol grn 40 18
2551 A979 35s brt bl & blk 60 28
2552 A979 53s ver & sl grn 95 45
Nos. 2548-2552 (5) 2.20 1.04

Souvenir Sheet

2553 A979 1 l multi 2.00 1.50

Philaserdica '79, International Philatelic Exhibition, Sofia, May 18–27, 1979, and centenary of Bulgarian stamps. No. 2553 has green and black marginal inscription and UPU emblem. Size: 62x88mm. See Nos. 2560–2564.

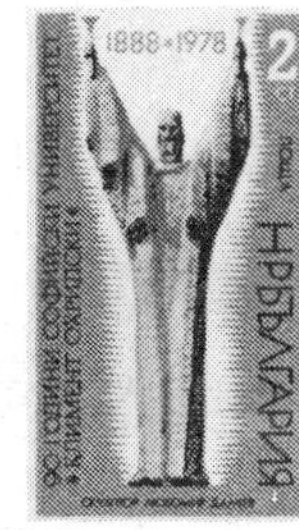

St. Clement of Ochrida
A980

1978, Dec. 8

2554 A980 2s multi 3 3

Clement of Ochrida University, 90th anniversary.

Ballet Dancers
A981

1978, Dec. 22

2555 A981 13s multi 22 10

Bulgarian ballet, 50th anniversary.

Nikola Karastojanov
A982

1978, Dec. 12

2556 A982 2s multi 3 3

Nikola Karastojanov (1778–1874), printer. No. 2556 printed se-tenant with label showing printing press.

COLORS

Please refer to page v for a complete list of color abbreviations used in this book.

Christmas Tree Made of Birds
A983

Design: 13s, Post horn.

1978, Dec. 22

2557	A983	2s multi	3	3
2558	A983	13s multi	22	10

New Year 1979.

COMECON Building, Moscow, Members' Flags—A984

1979, Jan. 25 Photo. ***Perf. 13***

2559	A984	13s multi	22	10

Council for Mutual Economic Aid (COMECON), 30th anniversary.

Philaserdica Type of 1978

Designs as Before

1979, Jan. 30

2560	A979	2s brt bl & red	3	3
2561	A979	13s grn & dk car	22	10
2562	A979	23s org brn & multi	40	18
2563	A979	35s dl red & blk	65	28
2564	A979	53s vio & dk ol	65	45
		Nos. 2560-2564 (5)	1.90	1.04

Philaserdica '79.

Bank Building, Commemorative Coin
A985

1979, Feb. 13

2565	A985	2s yel, gray & sil	3	3

Centenary of Bulgarian People's Bank.

Aleksander Stamboliski
A986

1979, Feb. 28

2566	A986	2s org & dk brn	3	3

Aleksander Stamboliski (1879–1923), leader of peasant's party and premier.

Flower with Child's Face, IYC Emblem
A987

Stylized Heads, World Association Emblem
A988

1979, Mar. 8

2568	A987	23s multi	40	18

International Year of the Child.

1979, Mar. 20

2569	A988	13s multi	22	10

8th World Congress for the Deaf, Varna, June 20–27.

"75" and Trade Union Emblem
A989

1979, Mar. 20

2570	A989	2s sl grn & org	3	3

75th anniversary of Bulgarian Trade Unions.

Souvenir Sheet

Sculptures in Sofia—A990

Designs: 2s, Soviet Army Monument (detail). 5s, Mother and Child, Central Railroad Station. 13s, 23s, 25s, Bas-relief from Monument of the Liberators.

1979, Apr. 2 Photo. ***Perf. 13***

2571	A990	Sheet of 5 + label	1.50	1.00
a.		2s multi	3	
b.		5s multi	10	
c.		13s multi	22	
d.		23s multi	40	
e.		25s multi	45	

Centenary of Sofia as capital. No. 2571 has ultramarine and red border. Size: 106x103mm.

Rocket Launch, Space Flight Emblems
A991

Designs (Intercosmos and Bulgarian-USSR Flight Emblems and): 25s, Link-up (horiz.). 35s, Parachute descent. 1 l, Globe, emblems and orbit (horiz.).

1979, Apr. 11

2572	A991	12s multi	20	10
2573	A991	25s multi	45	20
2574	A991	35s multi	50	30

Souvenir Sheet

2575	A991	1 l multi	2.00	

First Bulgarian cosmonaut on Russian space flight. No. 2575 has space emblems in margin. Size: 68x85mm.

Nicolai Rukavishnikov
A992

Design: 13s, Rukavishnikov and Soviet cosmonaut Georgi Ivanov.

1979, May 14 Photo. ***Perf. 13***

2576	A992	2s multi	3	3
2577	A992	13s multi	22	10

Col. Nicolai Rukavishnikov, first Bulgarian astronaut.

Souvenir Sheet

Thracian Gold-leaf Collar—A993

1979, May 16

2578	A993	1 l multi	2.00	1.50

48th International Philatelic Federation Congress, Sofia, May 16–17. No. 2578 has ultramarine and carmine decorative margin. Size: 77x86mm.

Post Horn, Carrier Pigeon, Jet, Globes and UPU Emblem—A994

Designs (Post Horn, Globes and ITU Emblem): 5s, 1st Bulgarian and modern telephones. 13s, Morse key and teleprinter. 23s, Old radio transmitter and radio towers. 35s, Bulgarian TV tower and satellite.

1979, May 8 ***Perf. 13½x13***

2579	A994	2s multi	3	3
2580	A994	5s multi	10	3
2581	A994	13s multi	22	10
2582	A994	23s multi	40	18
2583	A994	35s multi	60	28
		Nos. 2579-2583 (5)	1.35	62

Souvenir Sheet

Design: 50s, Ground receiving station.

Perf. 13

2584	A994	50s vio, blk & gray	95	40

International Telecommunications Day and centenary of Bulgarian Postal and Telegraph Services. No. 2584 has ocher marginal inscription and emblems. Size of stamp: 39x28mm. Size of sheet: 65x70mm.

Hotel Vitosha—New Otani
A996

1979, May 20

2586	A996	2s ultra & pink	3	3

Philaserdica '79 Day.

Horseman Receiving Gifts, by Karellia and Boris Kuklievi—A997

1979, May 23

2587	A997	2s multi	3	3

Bulgarian-Russian Friendship Day.

Man on Donkey, by Boris Angeloushev
A998

Four Women, by Albrecht Dürer
A999

1979, May 23 Photo. ***Perf. 13½***

2588	A998	2s multi	3	3

12th National Festival of Humor and Satire, Gabrovo.

Lithographed and Engraved

1979, May 31 ***Perf. 14×13½***

Dürer Engravings: 23s, Three Peasants. 25s, The Cook and his Wife. 35s, Portrait of Helius Eobanus Hessus. 80s, Rhinoceros (horiz.).

2589	A999	13s multi	22	10
2590	A999	23s multi	40	18
2591	A999	25s multi	45	20
2592	A999	35s multi	60	28

Souvenir Sheet

Imperf.

2593	A999	80s multi	1.50	1.00

Albrecht Dürer (1471–1528), German engraver and painter. No. 2593 has lilac and brown decorative margin. Size: 81x81mm.

Unused Prices

Catalogue prices for unused stamps through 1960 are for hinged copies in fine condition.

R. Todorov (1879–1916)
A1000

Bulgarian Writers: No. 2595, Dimitri Dymov (1909–1966). No. 2596, S. A. Kostov (1879–1939).

1979, June 26 Photo. *Perf. 13*

2594	A1000	2s multi	3	3
2595	A1000	2s sl grn & yel grn	3	3
2596	A1000	2s dp cl & yel	3	3

Nos. 2594–2596 each printed se-tenant with label showing title page or character from writer's work.

Moscow '80 Emblem, Runners—A1001

Moscow '80 Emblem and: 13s, Pole vault (horiz.). 25s, Discus. 35s, Hurdles (horiz.). 43s, High jump (horiz.). 1 l, Long jump.

1979, May 15 Litho. *Perf. 13*

2597	A1001	2s multi	3	3
2598	A1001	13s multi	22	10
2599	A1001	25s multi	45	20
2600	A1001	35s multi	60	28
2601	A1001	43s multi	75	35
2602	A1001	1 l multi	2.00	1.60
		Nos. 2597-2602 (6)	4.05	2.56

22nd Summer Olympic Games, Moscow, July 19-Aug. 3, 1980.

Rocket—A1002

Designs: 5s, Flags of U.S.S.R. and Bulgaria. 13s, "35."

1979, Sept. 4 Photogravure

2603	A1002	2s multi	3	3
2604	A1002	5s multi	10	3
2605	A1002	13s multi	22	10

35th anniversary of liberation.

COLORS

Please refer to page v for a complete list of color abbreviations used in this book.

Moscow '80 Emblem, Gymnast—A1003

Designs: Moscow '80 Emblem and gymnasts. 13s horiz.

1979, July 31 Photo. *Perf. 13*

2606	A1003	2s multi	3	3
2607	A1003	13s multi	22	10
2608	A1003	25s multi	45	20
2609	A1003	35s multi	60	28
2610	A1003	43s multi	75	35
2611	A1003	1 l multi	1.75	75
		Nos. 2606-2611 (6)	3.80	1.71

Souvenir Sheet

2612	A1003	2 l multi	4.00	3.00

22nd Summer Olympic Games, Moscow, July 19-Aug. 3, 1980. No. 2612 has light and dark blue margin showing Moscow '80 emblem; black control number. Size: 67x89mm.

Theater Institute, 18th Congress
A1004

1979, July 8 Photo. *Perf. 13*

2613	A1004	13s ultra & blk	22	10

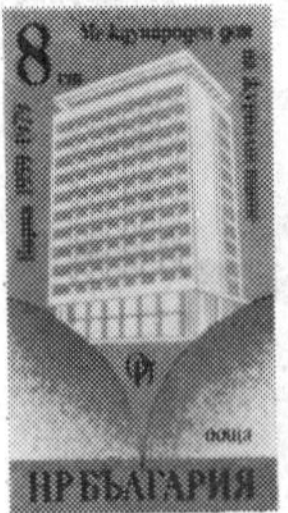

Journalists' Vacation House, Varna, 20th Anniversary—A1005

1979, July 17

2614	A1005	8s multi	14	5

Icon Type of 1977

Virgin and Child by: 13s, 23s, Nesebar, 16th century (diff.). 35s, 43s, Sozopol, 16th century (diff.). 53s, Samokov, 19th century. Inscribed 1979.

1979, Aug. 7 Litho. *Perf. 12½*

2615	A917	13s multi	22	10
2616	A917	23s multi	38	20
2617	A917	35s multi	60	30
2618	A917	43s multi	72	36
2619	A917	53s multi	90	45
		Nos. 2615-2619 (5)	2.82	1.41

Anton Besenschek—A1006

1979, Aug. 9 Photo. *Perf. 13x13½*

2620	A1006	2s dk ol grn & pale yel	3	3

Bulgarian stenography centenary.

Bulgarian Alpine Club, 50th Anniversary—A1007

1979, Aug. 28 *Perf. 13*

2621	A1007	2s multi	3	3

Public Health Ordinance—A1008

1979, Aug. 31 *Perf. 13½*

2622	A1008	2s multi	3	3

Public Health Service centenary. No. 2622 printed with label showing Dimitar Mollov, founder.

Isotope Measuring Device—A1009

1979, Sept. 8 *Perf. 13½x13*

2623	A1009	2s multi	3	3

International Sample Fair, Plovdiv.

Games' Emblem—A1010

1979, Sept. 20 *Perf. 13*

2624	A1010	5s multi	10	3

Universiada '79, World University Games, Mexico City, Sept.

Sofia Locomotive Sports Club, 50th Anniversary—A1011

1979, Oct. 2

2625	A1011	2s bl & org red	3	3

Ljuben Karavelov—A1012

1979, Oct. 4 Photo. *Perf. 13*

2626	A1012	2s bl & sl grn	3	3

Ljuben Karavelov (1837-1879), poet and freedom fighter.

Biathlon, Lake Placid '80 Emblem—A1013

1979, Oct. 20

2627	A1013	2s *shown*	3	3
2628	A1013	13s *Speed skating*	22	10
2629	A1013	23s *Downhill skiing*	40	18
2630	A1013	43s *Luge*	75	35

Souvenir Sheet

Imperf.

2631	A1013	1 l *Slalom*	2.25	1.75

13th Winter Olympic Games, Lake Placid, N.Y., Feb. 12-24. No. 2631 has gold and bluish green margin showing Lake Placid '80 emblem. Size: 70x78mm.

Woman from Thrace, by Decko Uzunov—A1014

Decko Uzunov, 80th Birthday: 12s, Apparition in Red. 23s, Composition.

1979, Oct. 31 *Perf. 14*

2632	A1014	12s multi	20	8
2633	A1014	13s multi	22	10
2634	A1014	23s multi	40	18

Swimming, Moscow '80 Emblem—A1016

1979, Nov. 30 **Photo.** *Perf. 13*

2636	A1016	2s *Two-man kayak*, vert.	3	3
2637	A1016	13s *Swimming*, vert.	22	10
2638	A1016	25s *shown*	45	20
2639	A1016	35s *One-man kayak*	60	28
2640	A1016	43s *Diving*, vert	75	35
2641	A1016	1 l *Diving*, vert. (diff.)	1.75	75
		Nos. 2636-2641 (6)	3.80	1.71

Souvenir Sheet

2642	A1016	2 l *Water polo*, vert.	3.50	3.50

22nd Summer Olympic Games, Moscow, July 19-Aug. 3, 1980. No. 2642 has multicolored margin showing Moscow '80 emblem; black control number. Size: 66x88mm.

Nikola Wapzarov—A1017

1979, Dec. 7 **Photo.** *Perf. 13*

2643	A1017	2s cl & rose	3	3

Nikola Wapzarov (1909-1942), painter and freedom fighter. No. 2643 printed with label showing smoke stacks.

The First Socialists, by Bojan Petrov A1018

Paintings: 13s, Dimitar Blagoev Reading Newspaper, by Dimitar Gjudshenov, 1892. 25s, Workers' Party March, by Sotir Sotirov, 1917. 35s, Dawn in Plovdiv, by Johann Leviev (vert.).

1979, Dec. 10 Litho. *Perf. 12½x12, 12x12½*

2644	A1018	2s multi	3	3
2645	A1018	13s multi	22	10
2646	A1018	25s multi	50	22
2647	A1018	35s multi	70	30

Unused Prices

Catalogue prices for unused stamps through 1960 are for hinged copies in fine condition.

Never-hinged unused stamps issued before 1961 often sell above Catalogue prices. Current never-hinged prices for various countries will be found in the Scott StampMarket Update.

Procession with Relics, 9th Century Fresco—A1020

Frescoes of Sts. Cyril and Methodius, St. Clement's Basilica, Rome: 13s, Reception by Pope Hadrian II. 23s, Burial of Cyril the Philosopher, 18th century. 25s, St. Cyril. 35s, St. Methodius.

1979, Dec. 25

2655	A1020	2s multi	3	3
2656	A1020	13s multi	22	10
2657	A1020	23s multi	40	18
2658	A1020	25s multi	45	20
2659	A1020	35s multi	60	28
		Nos. 2655-2659 (5)	1.70	79

Bulgarian Television Emblem—A1021

1979, Dec. 29 *Perf. 13½*

2660	A1021	5s vio bl & lt bl	10	3

Bulgarian television, 25th anniversary. No. 2660 printed with label showing Sofia television tower.

Doves in Girl's Hair—A1022

Design: 2s, Children's heads, mosaic (vert.).

1979 *Perf. 13*

2661	A1022	2s multi	3	3
2662	A1022	13s multi	22	10

International Year of the Child. Issue dates: 2s, July 17; 13s, Dec. 14.

Puppet on Horseback, IYC Emblem

A1023

Thracian Rider, Votive Tablet, 3rd Century

A1024

1980, Jan. 22 **Photo.** *Perf. 13*

2663	A1023	2s multi	3	3

UNIMA, International Puppet Theater Organization, 50th anniversary (1979); International Year of the Child (1979).

National Archaeological Museum Centenary; 13s, Deines stele, 5th century B.C.

1980, Jan. 29 **Photo.** *Perf. 13x13½*

2664	A1024	2s brn & gold	3	3
2665	A1024	13s multi	22	10

Dimitrov Meeting Lenin in Moscow, by Alexander Poplilov A1026

1980, Mar. 28 *Perf. 12x12½*

2667	A1026	13s multi	22	10

Lenin, 110th birth anniversary.

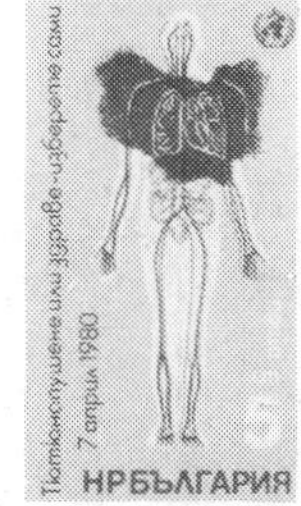

Circulatory System, Lungs Enveloped in Smoke—A1027

1980, Apr. 7 *Perf. 13*

2668	A1027	5s multi	10	3

World Health Day, fight against cigarette smoking.

Souvenir Sheet

Intercosmos Emblem, Cosmonauts—A1028

1980, Apr. 22 *Perf. 12*

2675	A1028	50s multi	90	40

Intercosmos cooperative space program. Multicolored margin shows planets, stars and emblems. Size: 111x102mm.

Penio Penev (1930-1959), Poet—A1029

1980, Apr. 22 **Photo.** *Perf. 13*

2676	A1029	5s multi	10	3

Se-tenant with label showing quote from author's work.

Penny Black—A1030

1980, Apr. 24 *Perf. 13*

2678	A1030	25s dk red & sep	45	20

London 1980 International Stamp Exhibition, May 6-14; printed se-tenant with label showing Rowland Hill between every two stamps.

Dimiter H. Tchorbadjiiski, Self-portrait—A1031

1980, Apr. 29

2679	A1031	5s *shown*	10	3
2680	A1031	13s *"Our People"*	22	10

Nikolai Giaurov

A1032

Raising Red Flag Reichstag Building, Berlin

A1033

1980, Apr. 30

2681	A1032	5s multi	10	3

Nikolai Giaurov (b. 1930), opera singer; printed se-tenant with label showing. Boris Godunov.

1980, May 6 *Perf. 13x13½*

Armistice, 35th Anniversary: 13s, Soviet Army memorial, Berlin-Treptow.

2682	A1033	5s multi	10	3
2683	A1033	13s multi	22	10

Numeral—A1034

1979 *Perf. 14*

2684	A1034	2s ultra	3	3
2685	A1034	5s rose car	10	3

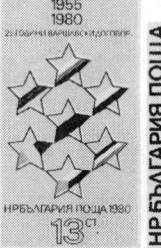

Warsaw Pact, 25th Anniversary A1035

Sharpshooting, Moscow '80 Emblem A1036

1980, May 14 **Photo.** *Perf. 13*

2686	A1035	13s multi	22	10

1980, June 10

2687	A1036	2s *shown*	3	3
2688	A1036	13s *Judo*, horiz.	22	10
2689	A1036	25s *Wrestling*, horiz.	45	20
2690	A1036	35s *Archery*	60	28
2691	A1036	43s *Fencing*, horiz.	75	35
2692	A1036	1 l *Fencing*	1.75	75
		Nos. 2687-2692 (6)	3.80	1.71

Souvenir Sheet

2693	A1036	2 l *Boxing*	3.50	3.50

22nd Summer Olympic Games, Moscow, July 19-Aug. 3. No. 2693 has magenta and dark blue margin, black control number. Size: 63x89mm.

10th Intl. Ballet Competition, Varna—A1037

1980, Sept. **Photo.** *Perf. 13*

2694	A1037	13s multi	22	10

Hotel Europa, Sofia—A1038

Hotels: No. 2696, Bulgaria, Burgas, vert. No. 2697, Plovdiv, Plovdiv. No. 2698, Riga, Russe, vert. No. 2699, Varna, Djuba.

1980, July 11

2695	A1038	23s lt ultra & multi	40	18
2696	A1038	23s org & multi	40	18
2697	A1038	23s gray & multi	40	18
2698	A1038	23s bl & multi	40	18
2699	A1038	23s yel & multi	40	18
		Nos. 2695-2699 (5)	2.00	90

See No. 2766.

Ship Type of 1975

Ships of 16th, 17th Centuries: 5s, Christ of Lubeck, galleon. 8s, Roman galley. 13s, Eagle, Russian galleon. 23s, Mayflower. 35c, Maltese galley. 53, Royal Louis, galleon.

1980, July 14

2700	A873	5s multi	10	3
2701	A873	8s multi	15	5
2702	A873	13s multi	22	10
2703	A873	23s multi	40	18
2704	A873	35s multi	60	28
2705	A873	53s multi	95	45
		Nos. 2700-2705 (6)	2.42	1.09

15th World Parachute Championships, Kazanluk—A1039

1980

2706	A1039	13s *shown*	22	10
2707	A1039	25s *Parachutist*	45	20

Int'l Year of the Child, 1979—A1040

Designs: Children's drawings and IYC emblem. 43s, Tower. 5s, 25s, 43s, vert.

Perf. 12½x12, 12x12½

1980 **Lithographed**

2708	A1040	3s multi	5	3
2709	A1040	5s multi	10	3
2710	A1040	8s multi	15	5
2711	A1040	13s multi	22	10
2712	A1040	25s multi	45	20
2713	A1040	35s multi	60	28
2714	A1040	43s multi	75	35
		Nos. 2708-2714 (7)	2.32	1.04

Helicopter, Missile Transport, Tank—A1041

1980, Sept. 23 **Photo.** *Perf. 13*

2715	A1041	3s *shown*	5	3
2716	A1041	5s *Jet, radar, rocket*	10	3
2717	A1041	8s *Helicopter, ships*	15	5

Bulgarian People's Army, 35th anniversary.

St. Anne, by Leonardo da Vinci—A1042

Da Vinci Paintings: 8s, 13s, Annunciation (diff.). 25s, Adoration of the Kings. 35s, Lady with the Ermine. 50s, Mona Lisa.

1980, Nov.

2718	A1042	5s multi	10	3
2719	A1042	8s multi	15	5
2720	A1042	13s multi	22	10
2721	A1042	25s multi	45	20
2722	A1042	35s multi	60	28
		Nos. 2718-2722 (5)	1.52	66

Souvenir Sheet

Imperf.

2723	A1042	50s multi	1.00	50

No. 2723 has multicolored margin showing human figure. Size: 57½x81mm.

International Peace Conference, Sofia—A1043

1980, Sept. 4 **Photo.** *Perf. 13*

2724	A1043	25s multi	45	20

Jordan Jowkov (1880-1937), Writer—A1044

1980, Sept. 19

2725	A1044	5s multi	10	3

Se-tenant with label showing scene from Jowkov's work.

International Samples Fair, Plovdiv—A1045

1980, Sept. 24 *Perf. 13½x13*

2726	A1045	5s multi	10	3

World Ski Racing Championship, Velingrad—A1046

1981, Jan. 17 **Photo.** *Perf. 13*

2727	A1046	43s multi	75	35

Hawthorn—A1047

Designs: Medicinal herbs.

1981, Jan.

2728	A1047	3s shown	5	3
2729	A1047	5s St. John's wort	10	3
2730	A1047	13s Common elder	22	10
2731	A1047	25s Blackberries	45	20
2732	A1047	35s Lime	60	28
2733	A1047	43s Wild briar	75	35
		Nos. 2728-2733 (6)	2.17	99

Slalom—A1048

1981, Feb. 27 **Photo.** *Perf. 13*

2734	A1048	43s multi	75	35

Evian Alpine World Ski Cup Championship, Borovets.

Nuclear Traces, Research Institute—A1049

1981, Mar. 10 *Perf. 13½x13*

2735	A1049	13s gray & blk	22	10

Nuclear Research Institute, Dubna, USSR, 25th anniversary.

Congress Emblem—A1050

1981, Mar. 12 *Perf. 13½*

2736	A1050	5s shown	10	3
2737	A1050	13s Stars	22	10
2738	A1050	23s Teletape	40	18

Souvenir Sheet

2739	A1050	50s Dimiter Blagoev, Gerogi Dimitrov	1.00	75

12th Bulgarian Communist Party Congress. Nos. 2736-2738 each printed se-tenant with label. No. 2739 has red marginal inscription. Size: 65x87mm.

Arabian Horse A1051

1980, Nov. 27 **Litho.** *Perf. 12½x12*

2740	A1051	3s multi	5	3
2741	A1051	5s multi	10	3
2742	A1051	13s multi	22	10
2743	A1051	23s multi	40	18
2744	A1051	35s multi	60	28
		Nos. 2740-2744 (5)	1.37	62

Vassil Stoin, Ethnologist, Birth Centenary—A1052

1980, Dec. 5 Photo. *Perf. 13½x13*

2745 A1052 5s multi 10 3

New Year—A1053

1980, Dec. 8 *Perf. 13*

2746 A1053 5s shown 10 3
2747 A1053 13s Cup, date 22 10

Vienna Hofburg Palace—A1054

1981, May 15 Photo. *Perf. 13*

2748 A1054 35s multi 60 28

WIPA 1981 Intl. Philatelic Exhibition, Vienna, May 22-31.

34th Farmers' Union Congress—A1055

1981, May 18 *Perf. 13½*

2749 A1055 5s shown 10 3
2750 A1055 8s Flags 15 6
2751 A1055 13s Flags, diff. 22 10

Wild Cat A1056

1981, May 27

2752 A1056 5s shown 10 3
2753 A1056 13s Boar 22 10
2754 A1056 23s Mouflon 40 18
2755 A1056 25s Mountain goat 45 20
2756 A1056 35s Stag 60 28
2757 A1056 53s Roe deer 95 45
Nos. 2752-2757 (6) 2.72 1.24

Souvenir Sheet
Perf. 13½x13

2758 A1056 1 l Stag (diff.) 2.00 1.50

EXPO '81 Intl. Hunting Exhibition, Plovdiv. Nos. 2752-2757 each se-tenant with labels showing various hunting rifles. No. 2758 contains one stamp (48½x39mm.); multicolored margin shows hunter with bird. Size: 79x104mm.

25th Anniv. of UNESCO Membership A1057

1981, June 11 *Perf. 13*

2759 A1057 13s multi 22 10

DWVY-1 Aircraft—A1058

1981, June 24 Litho. *Perf. 12½*

2760 A1058 5s shown 10 3
2761 A1058 12s LAS-7 22 10
2762 A1058 25s LAS-8 45 20
2763 A1058 35s DAR-1 60 28
2764 A1058 45s DAR-3 80 38
2765 A1058 55s DAR-9 1.00 50
Nos. 2760-2765 3.17 1.49

Hotel Type of 1980

1981, July 13 Photo. *Perf. 13*

2766 A1038 23s Veliko Tirnovo Hotel 40 18

Flying Figure, Sculpture by Velichko Minekov—A1059

Bulgarian Social Democratic Party Buzludja Congress, 90th Anniv. (Minkov Sculpture): 13s, Advancing Female Figure.

1981, July 16 *Perf. 13½*

2767 A1059 5s multi 10 5
2768 A1059 13s multi 22 10

Kukeri, by Georg Tschapkanov A1060

Statistics Office Centenary A1061

1981, May 28 Photo. *Perf. 13*

2769 A1060 5s multi 10 5

13th Natl. Festival of Humor and Satire.

1981, June 9

2770 A1061 5s multi 10 5

Gold Jug—A1063

Designs: Goldsmiths' works, 7th-9th cent.

1981, July 21

2772 A1063 5s multi 10 5
2773 A1063 13s multi 22 10
2774 A1063 23s multi 40 18
2775 A1063 25s multi 45 20
2776 A1063 35s multi 60 28
2777 A1063 53s multi 95 45
Nos. 2772-2777 (6) 2.72 1.26

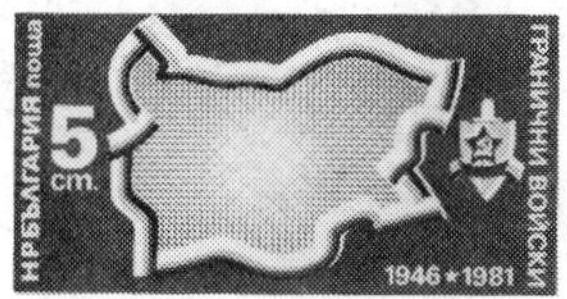

35th Anniv. of Frontier Force—A1064

1981, July 28 *Perf. 13½x13*

2778 A1064 5s multi 10 5

1300th Anniv. of First Bulgarian State—A1065

Designs: No. 2779, Sts. Cyril and Methodius. No. 2780, 9th cent. bas-relief. 8s, Floor plan, Round Church, Preslav, 10th cent. 12s, Four Evangelists of King Ivan Alexander, miniature, 1356. No. 2783, King Ivan Asen II memorial column. No. 2784, Warriors on horseback. 16s, April uprising, 1876. 23s, Russian liberators, Tirnovo. 25s, Social Democratic Party founding, 1891. 35s, September uprising, 1923. 41s, Fatherland Front. 43s, Prime Minister George Dimitrov, 5th Communist Party Congress, 1948. 50s, Lion, 10th cent. bas-relief. 53s, 10th Communist Party Congress. 55s, Kremikovski Metalurgical Plant, 1 l, Breshnev, Gen. Todor Jovkov.

1981, Aug. 10

2779 A1065 5s multi 10 5
2780 A1065 5s multi 10 5
2781 A1065 8s multi 15 6
2782 A1065 12s multi 22 10
2783 A1065 13s multi 24 10
2784 A1065 13s multi 24 10
2785 A1065 16s multi 30 12
2786 A1065 23s multi 40 18
2787 A1065 25s multi 45 20
2788 A1065 35s multi 60 28
2789 A1065 41s multi 70 32
2790 A1065 43s multi 75 35
2791 A1065 53s multi 95 45
2792 A1065 55s multi 1.00 50
Nos. 2779-2792 (14) 6.20 2.86

Souvenir Sheets

2793 A1065 50s multi 1.00 50
2794 A1065 1 l multi 2.00 1.00

Nos. 2791-2794 have multicolored margins showing flags and arms. Size: 83x75mm.

European Volleyball Championship A1066

1981, Sept. 16 *Perf. 13*

2795 A1066 13s multi 24 10

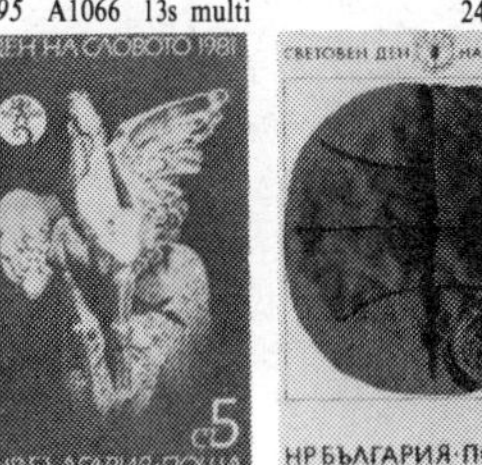

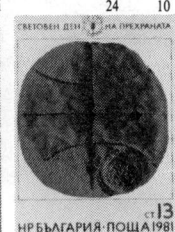

Pegasus, Bronze Sculpture (Word Day) A1067

World Food Day A1068

1981, Oct. 2

2796 A1067 5s ol & cr 10 5

1981, Oct. 16

2797 A1068 13s multi 24 10

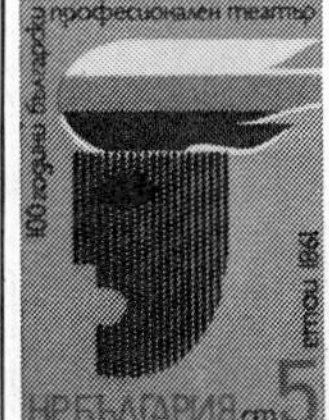

Professional Theater Centenary—A1069

1981, Oct. 30

2798 A1069 5s multi 10 5

Anti-Apartheid Year—A1070

1981, Dec. 2

2799 A1070 5s multi 10 5

Espana '82 World Cup Soccer—A1071

Designs: Various soccer players.

1981, Dec.

2800 A1071 5s multi 10 5
2801 A1071 13s multi 24 10
2802 A1071 43s multi 75 35
2803 A1071 53s multi 95 45

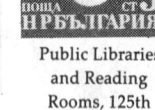

Heritage Day—A1072

1981, Nov. 21 **Photo.** ***Perf. 13***
2804 A1072 13s multi 24 10

Bagpipe A1073

Public Libraries and Reading Rooms, 125th Anniv. A1074

1982, Jan. 14
2805 A1073 13s shown 24 10
2806 A1073 25s Flutes 45 20
2807 A1073 30s Rebec 55 25
2808 A1073 35s Flute, recorder 60 28
2809 A1073 44s Mandolin 80 38
Nos. 2805-2809 (5) 2.64 1.21

1982, Jan. 20
2810 A1074 5s dk grn 10 5

Souvenir Sheet

Intl. Decade for Women (1975-1985)—A1075

1982, Mar. 8
2811 A1075 1 l multi 2.00 1.00

Size: 65x78mm.

New Year 1982—A1076

1981, Dec. 22 **Photo.** ***Perf. 13***
2812 A1076 5s Ornament 10 5
2813 A1076 13s Ornament, diff. 24 10

The Sofia Plains, by Nicolas Petrov (1881-1916)—A1077

1982, Feb. 10 ***Perf. 12½***
2814 A1077 5s shown 10 5
2815 A1077 13s Girl Embroidering 24 10
2816 A1077 30s Fields of Peshtera 55 25

25th Anniv. of UNICEF (1981)—A1078

Mother and Child Paintings.

1982, Feb. 25 ***Perf. 14***
2817 A1078 53s Vladamir Dimitrov 95 45
2817 A1078 53s Basil Stoilov 95 45
2819 A1078 53s Ivan Milev 95 45
2820 A1078 53s Liliana Russeva 95 45

Figures, by Vladamir Dimitrov (1882-1961)—A1079

1982, Mar. 8 **Litho.**
2821 A1079 5s shown 10 5
2822 A1079 8s Landscape 15 6
2823 A1079 13s View of Istanbul 24 10
2824 A1079 25s Harvesters, vert. 45 20
2825 A1079 30s Woman in a Landscape, vert. 55 25
2826 A1079 35s Peasant Woman, vert. 60 28
Nos. 2821-2826 (6) 2.09 94

Souvenir Sheet

2827 A1079 50s Self-portrait 1.00 50

No. 2827 contains one stamp (54x32mm.); olive green and brown margin. Size: 65x58mm.

Trade Union Congress—A1080

1982, Apr. 8 **Photo.** ***Perf. 13½***
2828 A1080 5s Dimitrov reading union paper 10 5
2829 A1080 5s Culture Palace 10 5

Nos. 2828-2829 se-tenant with label showing text.

Marsh Snowdrop A1081

Designs: Medicinal plants.

1982, Apr. 10 **Photo.** ***Perf. 13***
2830 A1081 3s shown 6 3
2831 A1081 5s Chicory 10 5
2832 A1081 8s Chamaenerium angustifolium 15 6
2833 A1081 13s Solomon's seal 24 10
2834 A1081 25s Violets 45 20
2835 A1081 35s Centaury 60 28
Nos. 2830-2835 (6) 1.60 72

Cosmonauts' Day A1082

1982, Apr. 12 ***Perf. 13½***
2836 A1082 13s Salyut-Soyuz link-up 24 10

Se-tenant with label showing K.E. Tsiolkovsky (space pioneer).

Souvenir Sheet

SOZFILEX Stamp Exhibition—A1083

1982, May 7 ***Perf. 13***
2837 A1083 50s Dimitrov, emblems 1.00 50

Size: 62x82mm.

14th Komsomol Congress (Youth Communists)—A1084

1982, May 25
2838 A1084 5s multi 10 5

PHILEXFRANCE '82 Intl. Stamp Exhibition, Paris, June 11-21—A1085

1982, May 28
2839 A1085 42s France #1, Bulgaria #1 72 32

19th Cent. Fresco—A1086

Designs: Various floral pattern frescoes.

1982, June 8 ***Perf. 11½***
2840 A1086 5s red & multi 10 5
2841 A1086 13s grn & multi 24 10
2842 A1086 25s vio & multi 45 20
2843 A1086 30s ol grn & multi 55 25
2844 A1086 42s bl & multi 72 32
2845 A1086 60s brn & multi 1.10 50
Nos. 2840-2845 (6) 3.16 1.42

Souvenir Sheet

George Dimitrov (1882-1949), First Prime Minister—A1087

1982, June 15 ***Perf. 13***
2846 A1087 50s multi 1.00 50

Multicolored margin shows natl. colors, olive branch. Size: 77x52mm.

9th Congress of the National Front—A1088

1982, June 21 **Photo.** *Perf. 13*

2847 A1088 5s Dimitrov 10 5

35th Anniv. of Balkan Bulgarian Airline—A1089

1982, June 28 *Perf. 13½x13*

2848 A1089 42s multi 72 32

Nuclear Disarmament—A1090

1982, July 15 *Perf. 13*

2849 A1090 13s multi 24 10

Ludmila Jirkova (b. 1942), Artist—A1091

1982, July **Photo.** *Perf. 13*

2850	A1091	5s multi	10	5
2851	A1091	13s multi	24	10

Souvenir Sheet

2852 A1091 1 l multi 2.00 1.00

No. 2852 has multicolored margin showing Jirkova's paintings. Size: 62x67mm.

5th Congress of Bulgarian Painters—A1092

1982, July 27 *Perf. 13½*

2853 A1092 5s multi 10 5

Se-tenant with label showing text.

10th Anniv. of UN Conference on Human Environment, Stockholm—A1093

1982, Nov. 10 *Perf. 13*

2854 A1093 13s dk bl & grn 24 10

SEMI-POSTAL STAMPS

Regular Issues of 1911-20 Surcharged:

ЗА НАШИТЬ ПЛЬННИЦИ
1
a

ЗА НАШИТЬ ПЛЬННИЦИ 5
b

ЗА НАШИТЬ ПЛЬННИЦИ 50
c

Perf. 11½x12, 12x11½.

1920, June 20 **Unwmkd.**

B1	A43 (a)	2s +1s ol grn	3	3
B2	A44 (b)	5s +2½s grn	4	4
B3	A44 (b)	10s +5s rose	4	4
B4	A44 (b)	15s +7½s vio	4	4
B5	A44 (b)	25s +12½s dp bl	5	5
B6	A44 (b)	30s +15s choc	5	5
B7	A44 (b)	50s +25s yel brn	5	5
B8	A29 (c)	1 l +50s dk brn	15	15
B9	A37a (a)	2 l +1 l brn org	30	30
B10	A38 (a)	3 l +1½ l cl	60	60
		Nos. B1-B10 (10)	1.35	1.35

Surtax aided ex-prisoners of war.
Price, #B1-B7 imperf., $12.50.

Souvenir Sheet

SP1

1937, Nov. 22 **Photo.** ***Imperf.***

B11 SP1 2 l +18 l ultra 6.00 6.00

Issued to commemorate the 19th anniversary of the accession of Tsar Boris III to the throne. Size: 80x115mm.

Stamps of 1917-21 Surcharged in Black

Наводнението
1939
1+1
лева

1939, Oct. 22 ***Perf. 12½, 12***

B12	A34	1 l +1 l on 15s sl	8	8
B13	A69	2 l +1 l on 1½ l ol grn	15	15
B14	A69	4 l +2 l on 2 l dp grn	20	20
B15	A69	7 l +4 l on 3 l Prus bl	60	60
B16	A69	14 l +7 l on 5 l red brn	1.10	1.10
		Nos. B12-B16 (5)	2.13	2.13

The surtax aided victims of the Sevlievo flood.
The surcharge on Nos. B13–B16 omits "leva."

Map of Bulgaria
SP2

1947, June 6 Typo. ***Perf. 11½***

B17	SP2	20 l +10 l dk brn red & grn	60	60

Issued to commemorate the 30th Jubilee Esperanto Congress, Sofia, 1947.

Postman SP3 — Radio Towers SP6

Designs: 10 l+5 l, Lineman. 20 l+10 l, Telephone operators.

1947, Nov. 5

B18	SP3	4 l +2 l ol brn	7	7
B19	SP3	10 l +5 l brt red	15	15
B20	SP3	20 l +10 l dp ultra	15	15
B21	SP6	40 l +20 l choc	75	75

Christo Ganchev
SP7

Actors' Portraits: 10 l+6 l, Adriana Budevska. 15 l+7 l, Vasil Kirkov. 20 l+15 l, Sava Ognianov. 30 l+20 l, Krostyu Sarafov.

1947, Dec. 8 Litho. ***Perf. 10½***

B22	SP7	9 l +5 l Prus grn	10	10
B23	SP7	10 l +6 l car lake	20	20
B24	SP7	15 l +7 l rose vio	20	20
B25	SP7	20 l +15 l ultra	30	30
B26	SP7	30 l +20 l vio brn	65	65
		Nos. B22-B26 (5)	1.45	1.45

National Theater, 50th anniversary.

Souvenir Sheet

Olympic Emblem—SP8

1964, Oct. 10 Litho. ***Imperf.***

B27	SP8	40s +20s bis, red & bl	3.25	2.50

Issued to commemorate the 18th Olympic Games, Tokyo, Oct. 10–25. No. B27 measures 60x68mm.

Horsemanship Type of 1965
Miniature Sheet

Design: 40s+20s, Hurdle race.

1965, Sept. 30 Photo. ***Imperf.***

B28	A630	40s +20s bluish gray, gold & vio blk	3.00	2.25

No. B28 measures 80x79mm.

Space Exploration Type of 1966

Designs: 20s+10s, Yuri A. Gagarin, Alexei Leonov and Valentina Tereshkova. 30s+10s, Rocket and globe.

1966, Sept. 29 Photo. ***Perf. 11½x11***

B29	A652	20s +20s pur & gray	1.25	75

Miniature Sheet
Imperf.

B30	A652	30s +10s gray, fawn & blk	2.25	1.75

Issued to publicize Russian space explorations. No. B30 measures 59x51mm.

Winter Olympic Games Type of 1967

Sports and Emblem: 20s+10s, Slalom. 40s+10s, Figure skating couple.

1967, Sept. Photo. ***Perf. 11***

B31	A687	20s +10s multi	1.50	60

Souvenir Sheet
Imperf.

B32	A687	40s +10s multi	2.25	1.75

Issued to publicize the 10th Winter Olympic Games, Grenoble, France, Feb. 6–8, 1968. No. B32 has silver and bister marginal design. Size: 68x68mm.

Type of Olympic Games Issue, 1968

Designs: 20s+10s, Rowing. 50s+10s, Stadium, Mexico City, and communications satellite.

1968, June 24 Photo. ***Perf. 10½***

B33	A702	20s +10s vio bl, gray & pink	1.10	50

Miniature Sheet
Imperf.

B34	A702	50s +10s gray, blk & Prus bl	2.25	1.75

Issued to publicize the 19th Olympic Games, Mexico City, Oct. 12–27. No. B34 measures 75x75mm.

Sports Type of Regular Issue, 1969

Designs: 13s+5s, Woman with ball. 20s+10s, Acrobatic jump.

1969, Oct. Photo. ***Perf. 11***

Gymnasts in Light Gray

B35	A732	13s +5s brt rose & vio	35	20
B36	A732	20s +10s cit & bl grn	90	50

Issued to publicize the Championships for Artistic Gymnastics in Varna.

Miniature Sheet

Soccer Ball
SP9

1970, Mar. 4 Photo. ***Imperf.***

B37	SP9	80s +20s org, blk, sil & bl	3.00	3.00

Issued to publicize the 9th World Soccer Championships for the Jules Rimet Cup, Mexico City, May 30–June 21, 1970. No. B37 measures 55x73½mm.

Souvenir Sheet

Yuri A. Gagarin—SP10

1971, Apr. 12 Photo. ***Imperf.***

B38	SP10	40s +20s multi	2.25	1.75

10th anniversary of the first man in space. No. B38 measures 80x53mm.

Bulgarian Lion, Magnifying Glass, Stamp Tongs
SP11

1971, July 10 Photo. ***Perf. 12½***

B39	SP11	20s +10s brn org, blk & gold	1.25	60

11th Congress of Bulgarian Philatelists, Sofia, July, 1971.

AIR POST STAMPS.

Regular Issues of 1925-26 Overprinted in Various Colors

1927-28 ***Perf. 11½.*** **Unwmkd.**

C1	A76	2 l ol (R) ('28)	1.25	75
C2	A74	4 l lake & yel (Bl)	1.25	75
C3	A77	10 l brn blk & brn org (G) ('28)	20.00	17.50

Overprinted Vertically and Surcharged with New Value.

C4	A77	1(l) on 6 l dp bl & pale lem (C)	1.25	75
a.		Inverted surcharge	*450.00*	*400.00*
b.		Pair, one without surcharge	*600.00*	

Nos. C2-C4 overprinted in changed colors were not issued, price set $15.

Dove Delivering Message AP1 — Junkers Plane, Rila Monastery AP2

1931, Oct. 28 Typographed.

C5	AP1	1(l) dk grn	25	10
C6	AP1	2(l) maroon	25	10
C7	AP1	6(l) dp bl	40	20
C8	AP1	12(l) carmine	40	30
C9	AP1	20(l) dk vio	1.00	60
C10	AP1	30(l) dp org	1.50	1.25
C11	AP1	50(l) org brn	3.00	1.50
		Nos. C5-C11 (7)	6.80	4.05

Counterfeits exist.

1932, May 9

C12	AP2	18 l bl grn	17.50	17.50
C13	AP2	24 l dp red	17.50	17.50
C14	AP2	28 l ultra	17.50	17.50

1938, Dec. 27

C15	AP1	1(l) vio brn	20	10
C16	AP1	2(l) green	20	15
C17	AP1	6(l) dp rose	75	30
C18	AP1	12(l) pck bl	90	35

Counterfeits exist.

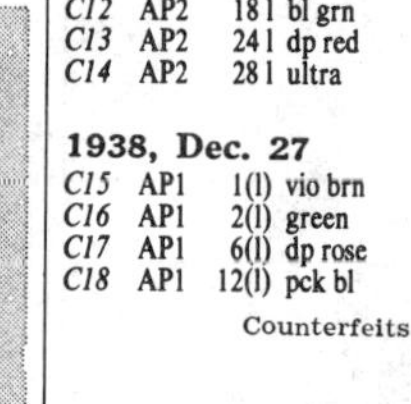

Mail Plane AP3 — Plane over Tsar Assen's Tower AP4

Designs: 4 l, Plane over Bachkovski Monastery. 6 l, Bojurishte Airport, Sofia. 10 l, Plane, train and motorcycle. 12 l, Planes over Sofia Palace. 16 l, Plane over Pirin Valley. 19 l, Plane over Rila Monastery. 30 l, Plane and Swallow. 45 l, Plane over Sofia Cathedral. 70 l, Plane over Shipka Monument. 100 l, Plane and Royal Cipher.

Photogravure.

1940, Jan. 15 ***Perf. 13.***

C19	AP3	1 l dk grn	8	6
C20	AP4	2 l crimson	1.00	6
C21	AP4	4 l red org	15	8
C22	AP3	6 l dp bl	25	10
C23	AP4	10 l dk brn	40	20
C24	AP3	12 l dl brn	65	35
C25	AP3	16 l brt bl vio	75	50
C26	AP3	19 l sapphire	90	75
C27	AP4	30 l rose lake	1.25	1.00
C28	AP4	45 l gray vio	3.00	1.75
C29	AP4	70 l rose pink	3.00	2.00
C30	AP4	100 l dp sl bl	8.50	7.50
		Nos. C19-C30 (12)	19.93	14.35

Nos. 368 and 370 Overprinted in Black

1945, Jan. 26

C31	A181	1 l brt grn	5	5
C32	A181	4 l red org	5	5

A similar overprint on Nos. O4, O5, O7 and O8 was privately applied.

Type of Parcel Post Stamps of 1944 Surcharged or Overprinted in Various Colors

Imperf.

C37	PP5	10 l on 100 l dl yel (Bl)	12	10
C38	PP5	45 l on 100 l dl yel (C)	18	15
C39	PP5	75 l on 100 l dl yel (G)	30	25
C40	PP5	100 l dl yel (V)	50	35

Plane and Sun AP16 — Pigeon with Letter AP17

Plane and Letter
AP18

Wings and Posthorn
AP19

Winged Letter
AP20

Plane and Sun
AP21

Pigeon and Posthorn
AP22

Mail Plane
AP23

Conventionalized Figure Holding Pigeon
AP24

1946, July 15 Litho. ***Perf. 13***

C41	AP16	1 l dl lil	5	4
C42	AP16	2 l sl gray	5	4
C43	AP17	4 l vio blk	6	5
C44	AP18	6 l blue	6	5
C45	AP19	10 l turq grn	6	5
C46	AP19	12 l yel brn	8	6
C47	AP20	16 l rose vio	8	6
C48	AP19	19 l carmine	12	6
C49	AP21	30 l orange	18	6
C50	AP22	45 l lt ol grn	25	18
C51	AP22	75 l red brn	35	10
C52	AP23	100 l sl blk	80	35
C53	AP24	100 l red	80	35
		Nos. C41-C53 (13)	2.94	1.45

No. C47 exists imperf. Price $90.

People's Republic

Plane over Plovdiv
AP25

1947, Aug. 31 Photo. ***Imperf.***

C54	AP25	40 l dl ol grn	60	60

Plovdiv International Fair, 1947.

Baldwin's Tower
AP26

1948, May 23 Litho. ***Perf. 11½***

C55	AP26	50 l ol brn, *cr*	1.10	90

Issued to commemorate Stamp Day and the 10th Congress of Bulgarian Philatelic Societies, June 1948.

Romanian and Bulgarian Parliament Buildings
AP27

Romanian and Bulgarian Flags, Bridge over Danube
AP28

1948, Nov. 3 Photogravure

Cream Paper

C56	AP27	40 l ol gray	30	15
C57	AP28	100 l red vio	75	65

Issued to publicize Romanian-Bulgarian friendship.

Mausoleum of Pleven
AP29

1949, June 26

C58	AP29	50 l brown	2.25	2.25

Issued to commemorate the 7th Congress of Bulgarian Philatelic Associations, June 26–27, 1949.

Symbols of the U.P.U.
AP30

Frontier Guard and Dog
AP31

1949, Oct. 10 ***Perf. 11½***

C59	AP30	50 l vio bl	1.50	85

Issued to commemorate the 75th anniversary of the formation of the Universal Postal Union.

1949, Oct. 31

C60	AP31	60 l ol blk	1.50	1.25

Dimitrov Mausoleum
AP32

1950, July 3 ***Perf. 10½.***

C61	AP32	40 l ol brn	3.50	1.50

Issued to commemorate the first anniversary of the death of George Dimitrov, statesman.

Belogradchic Rocks
AP33

Air View of Plovdiv Fair
AP34

Designs: 16s, Beach, Varna. 20s, Harvesting grain. 28s, Rila monastery. 44s, Studena dam. 60s, View of Dimitrovgrad. 80s, View of Trnovo. 1 l, University building, Sofia. 4 l, Partisans' Monument.

1954, Apr. 1 ***Perf. 13*** **Unwmkd.**

C62	AP33	8s ol blk	6	3
C63	AP34	12s rose brn	6	3
C64	AP33	16s brown	6	3
C65	AP33	20s brn red, *cr*	15	3
C66	AP33	28s dp bl, *cr*	20	3
C67	AP33	44s vio brn, *cr*	20	5
C68	AP33	60s red brn, *cr*	35	8
C69	AP34	80s dk grn, *cr*	35	20
C70	AP33	1 l dk bl grn, *cr*	1.75	60
C71	AP34	4 l dp bl	3.75	1.50
		Nos. C62-C71 (10)	6.93	2.58

Glider on Mountainside
AP35

Designs: 60s, Glider over airport. 80s, Three gliders.

1956, Oct. 15 Photogravure

C72	AP35	44s brt bl	20	10
C73	AP35	60s purple	45	15
C74	AP35	80s dk bl grn	60	20

Issued to commemorate the 30th anniversary of glider flights in Bulgaria.

Passenger Plane
AP36

1957, May 21 ***Perf. 13*** **Unwmkd.**

C75	AP36	80s dp bl	80	65

Issued to commemorate the tenth anniversary of civil aviation in Bulgaria.

Sputnik 3 over Earth
AP37

1958, Nov. 28 ***Perf. 11***

C76	AP37	80s brt grnsh bl	3.50	3.00

International Geophysical Year, 1957-58.
Price, imperf. $7.50.

Lunik 1 Leaving Earth for Moon
AP38

1959, Feb. 28 ***Perf. 10½***

C77	AP38	2 l brt bl & ocher	5.50	4.50

Launching of 1st man-made satellite to orbit moon.

Price, imperf. in slightly different colors, $8.50 unused, $7.50 canceled.

Statue of Liberty and Tu-110 Airliner
AP39

Perf. 10½

1959, Nov. 11 **Photo.** **Unwmkd.**

C78	AP39	1 l vio bl & pink	2.00	1.00

Visit of Khrushchev to U.S.
Price, imperf. $6 unused, $5 canceled.

Lunik 2 and Moon
AP40

1960, June 23 **Litho.** ***Perf. 11***

C79	AP40	1.25 l bl, blk & yel	4.00	3.00

Russian rocket to the Moon, Sept. 12, 1959.

Sputnik 5 and Dogs Belka and Strelka
AP41

1961, Jan. 14 **Photo.** ***Perf. 11***

C80	AP41	1.25 l brt grnsh bl & org	4.50	3.75

Russian rocket flight of Aug. 19, 1970.

Maj. Yuri A. Gagarin and Vostok 1—AP42

1961, Apr. 26 **Unwmkd.**

C81	AP42	4 l grnsh bl, blk & red	5.00	3.00

First manned space flight, Apr. 12, 1961.

Soviet Space Dogs
AP43

1961, June 28 ***Perf. 11***

C82	AP43	2 l sl & dk car	3.00	1.75

Venus-bound Rocket
AP44

1961, June 28

C83	AP44	2 l brt bl, yel & org	5.00	3.00

Issued to commemorate the Soviet launching of the Venus space probe, Feb. 12, 1961.

Maj. Gherman Titov
AP45

Design: 1.25 l, Spaceship Vostok 2.

1961, Nov. 20 **Photo.** ***Perf. 11x10½***

C84	AP45	75s dk ol grn & gray grn	3.00	1.75
C85	AP45	1.25 l vio bl, lt bl & pink	3.25	2.25

Issued to commemorate the first manned space flight around the world, Maj. Gherman Titov of Russia, Aug. 6–7, 1961.

Iskar River Narrows
AP46

Designs: 2s, Varna and sailboat. 3s, Melnik. 10s, Trnovo. 40s, Pirin mountains.

1962, Feb. 3 ***Perf. 13*** **Unwmkd.**

C86	AP46	1s bl grn & gray bl	3	3
C87	AP46	2s bl & pink	5	3
C88	AP46	3s brn & ocher	25	3
C89	AP46	10s blk & lem	60	6
C90	AP46	40s dk grn & grn	1.50	50
		Nos. C86-C90 (5)	2.43	65

Ilyushin Turboprop Airliner
AP47

1962, Aug. 18 ***Perf. 11***

C91	AP47	13s bl & blk	60	30

15th anniversary of TABSO airline.

Konstantin E. Tsiolkovsky and Rocket Launching—AP48

Design: 13s, Earth, moon and rocket on future flight to the moon.

1962, Sept. 24 ***Perf. 11***

C92	AP48	5s dp grn & gray	2.25	1.25
C93	AP48	13s ultra & yel	1.25	50

Issued to commemorate the 13th meeting of the International Astronautical Federation.

Maj. Andrian G. Nikolayev
AP49

Designs: 2s, Lt. Col. Pavel R. Popovich. 40s, Vostoks 3 and 4 in orbit.

1962, Dec. 9 **Photo.** **Unwmkd.**

C94	AP49	1s bl, sl grn & blk	15	3
C95	AP49	2s bl grn, grn & blk	30	3
C96	AP49	40s dk bl grn, pink & blk	2.00	1.25

First Russian group space flight of Vostoks 3 and 4, Aug. 12–15, 1962.

Spacecraft "Mars 1" Approaching Mars—AP50

Design: 13s, Rocket launching spacecraft, Earth, Moon and Mars.

1963, Feb. 25 ***Perf. 11*** **Unwmkd.**

C97	AP50	5s multi	75	30
C98	AP50	13s multi	1.50	45

Issued to commemorate the launching of the Russian spacecraft "Mars 1," Nov. 1, 1962.

Lt. Col. Valeri F. Bykovski
AP51

Designs: 2s, Lt. Valentina Tereshkova. 5s, Globe and trajectories.

1963, Aug. 26 ***Perf. 11½*** **Unwmkd.**

C99	AP51	1s pale vio & Prus bl	5	4
C100	AP51	2s cit & red brn	8	5
C101	AP51	5s rose & dk red	25	6

Issued to commemorate the space flights of Valeri Bykovski, June 14–19, and Valentina Tereshkova, first woman cosmonaut, June 16–19, 1963. An imperf. souvenir sheet contains one 50s stamp showing Spasski tower and globe in lilac and red brown. Light blue border with red brown inscription. Size: 77x67mm. ~ice

See also No. CB3.

Nos. C99-C100 Surcharged in Magenta or Green

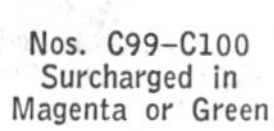

1964, Aug. 22

C102	AP51	10s on 1s pale vio & Prus bl (M)	50	30
C103	AP51	20s on 2s cit & red brn (G)	95	35

Issued to commemorate the International Space Exhibition in Riccione, Italy. Overprint in Italian on No. C103.

St. John's Monastery, Rila
AP52

Design: 13s, Notre Dame, Paris; French inscription.

1964, Dec. 22 **Photo.** ***Perf. 11½***

C104	AP52	5s pale brn & blk	20	5
C105	AP52	13s lt ultra & sl bl	90	30

Issued to commemorate the philatelic exhibition at St. Ouen (Seine) organized by the Franco-Russian Philatelic Circle and philatelic organizations in various People's Democracies.

Paper Mill, Bukijovtz
AP53

Designs: 10s, Metal works, Plovdiv. 13s, Metal works, Kremikovtsi. 20s, Oil refinery, Stara-Zagora. 40s, Fertilizer plant, Stara-Zagora. 1 l, Rest home, Meded.

1964–68 ***Perf. 13*** **Unwmkd.**

C106	AP53	8s grnsh bl	20	4
C107	AP53	10s red lil	30	6
C108	AP53	13s brt vio	45	8
C109	AP53	20s sl bl	90	15
C110	AP53	40s dk ol grn	1.50	35
C111	AP53	1 l red ('68)	3.25	65
		Nos. C106-C111 (6)	6.60	1.33

Three-master AP54 Veliko Turnovo AP55

Means of Communication: 2s, Postal coach. 3s, Old steam locomotive. 5s, Early cars. 10s, Montgolfier balloon. 13s, Early plane. 20s, Jet planes. 40s, Rocket and satellites. 1 l, Postrider.

1969, Mar. 31 **Photo.** ***Perf. 13x12½***

C112	AP54	1s gray & multi	3	3
C113	AP54	2s gray & multi	3	3
C114	AP54	3s gray & multi	5	3
C115	AP54	5s gray & multi	8	3
C116	AP54	10s gray & multi	20	10
C117	AP54	13s gray & multi	30	15
C118	AP54	20s gray & multi	50	30
C119	AP54	40s gray & multi	1.10	60
		Nos. C112-C119 (8)	2.29	1.27

Miniature Sheet

Imperf.

C120	AP54	1 l gold & org	3.00	3.00

Issued to publicize SOFIA 1969 Philatelic Exhibition, Sofia, May 31–June 8. No. C120 contains one stamp, silver marginal inscription. Size: 57x54mm.

1973, July 30 **Photo.** ***Perf. 13***

Designs: Historic buildings in various cities.

Multicolored

C121	AP55	2s *shown*	3	3
C122	AP55	13s *Roussalka*	35	15
C123	AP55	20s *Plovdiv*	1.75	1.50
C124	AP55	28s *Sofia*	75	40

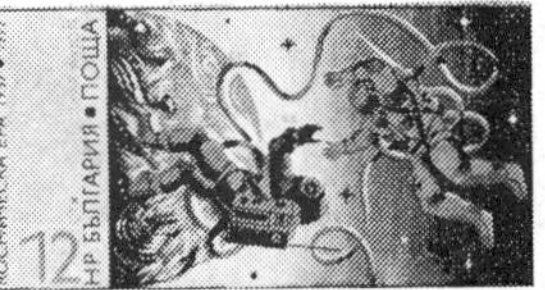

Alexei Leonov Floating in Space—AP56

Designs: 25s, Mariner 6, US spacecraft. 35s, Venera 4, USSR Venus probe.

1977, Oct. 14 **Photo.** ***Perf. 13½***

C125	AP56	12s multi	20	8
C126	AP56	25s multi	40	20
C127	AP56	35s multi	62	28

Space era, 20 years.

TU-154, Balkanair Emblem
AP57

1977 ***Perf. 13***

C128	AP57	35s ultra & multi	62	28

30th anniversary of Bulgarian airline, Balkanair. No. C128 issued in sheets of 6 stamps and 3 labels (in lilac) with commemorative inscription and Balkanair emblem.

Baba Vida Fortress
AP58

Design: 35s, Peace Bridge, connecting Rousse, Bulgaria, with Giurgiu, Romania.

1978 **Photo.** ***Perf. 13***

C130	AP59	25s multi	45	20
C131	AP59	35s multi	62	28

The Danube, European Intercontinental Waterway. Issued in sheets containing 5 each of Nos. C129–C130 and 2 labels, one showing course of Danube, the other hydrofoil and fish.

Red Cross
AP59

1978, Mar. Photo. *Perf. 13*

C132	AP60	25s multi	45	20

Centenary of Bulgarian Red Cross.

AIR POST SEMI-POSTAL STAMPS.

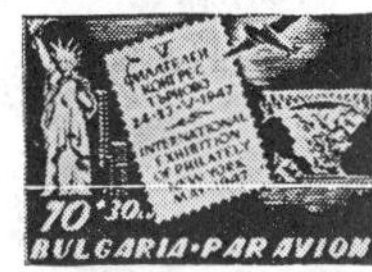

Statue of Liberty, Plane and Bridge
SPAP1

Lithographed.

1947, May 24 *Perf. 11½.* Unwmkd.

CB1	SPAP1	70 l +30 l red brn	1.50	1.25

Issued to honor the 5th Philatelic Congress, Trnovo, and the Centenary International Philatelic Exhibition, New York, May, 1947.

Bulgarian Worker
SPAP2

Photogravure.

1948, Feb. 28 *Perf. 12x11½.*

CB2	SPAP2	60 l (+16 l) hn brn, *cr*	60	45

Issued to commemorate the 2nd Bulgarian Workers' Congress, and sold by subscription only, at a premium of 16 levas over face value.

Type of Air Post Stamps, 1963

Design: Valeri Bykovski and Valentina Tereshkova.

1963, Aug. 26 *Perf. 11½* Unwmkd.

CB3	AP51	20s +10s pale bluish grn & dk grn	1.25	60

See note after No. C101.

SPECIAL DELIVERY STAMPS.

Postman on Bicycle
SD1

Postman on Motorcycle
SD3

Mail Car
SD2

Photogravure.

1939 *Perf. 13* Unwmkd.

E1	SD1	5 l dp bl	60	20
E2	SD2	6 l cop brn	25	20
E3	SD3	7 l gldn brn	40	20
E4	SD2	8 l red org	60	20
E5	SD1	20 l brt rose	1.25	60
		Nos. E1-E5 (5)	3.10	1.40

POSTAGE DUE STAMPS.

D1

D2

Large Lozenge Perf. 5½ to 6½.

1884 Typographed. Unwmkd.

J1	D1	5s orange	210.00	25.00
J2	D1	25s lake	100.00	17.50
J3	D1	50s blue	7.50	7.50

1886 *Imperf.*

J4	D1	5s orange	100.00	4.75
J5	D1	25s lake	175.00	4.75
J6	D1	50s blue	5.50	4.75

1887 *Perf. 11½.*

J7	D1	5s orange	12.50	1.75
J8	D1	25s lake	12.50	1.75
J9	D1	50s blue	5.00	1.75

Same, Redrawn.
24 horizontal lines of shading in upper part instead of 30 lines.

1892 *Perf. 10½, 11½*

J10	D1	5s orange	12.50	2.00
J11	D1	25s lake	12.50	2.00

1893 Pelure Paper.

J12	D2	5s orange	13.50	5.50

D3

D4

Imperf.

1895 Ordinary Paper

J13	D3	30s on 50s bl	7.50	3.00

Perf. 10½, 11½

J14	D3	30s on 50s bl	7.50	3.50

Wmkd. Coat of Arms in the Sheet.

1896 *Perf. 13*

J15	D4	5s orange	4.75	1.00
J16	D4	10s purple	3.00	1.00
J17	D4	30s green	3.00	75

Nos. J15–J17 are also known on unwatermarked paper from the edges of sheets.

In 1901 a cancellation, "T" in circle, was applied to Nos. 60–65 and used provisionally as postage dues.

D5

D6

1901–04 *Perf. 11½* Unwmkd.

J19	D5	5s dl rose	30	15
J20	D5	10s yel grn	65	15
J21	D5	20s dl bl ('04)	5.50	25
J22	D5	30s vio brn	60	25
J23	D5	50s org ('02)	8.50	6.00
		Nos. J19-J23 (5)	15.55	6.80

Nos. J19–J23 exist imperf. and in pairs imperf. between. Price, imperf., $250.

Thin Semi-Transparent Paper.

1915 *Perf. 11½* Unwmkd.

J24	D6	5s green	20	5
J25	D6	10s purple	30	5
J26	D6	20s dl rose	30	8
J27	D6	30s dp org	1.25	30
J28	D6	50s dp bl	45	20
		Nos. J24-J28 (5)	2.50	68

1919–21 *Perf. 11½, 12x11½*

J29	D6	5s emerald	15	6
a.		5s gray grn ('21)	45	20
J30	D6	10s violet	15	6
J31	D6	20s salmon	10	6
a.		20s yel	15	7
J32		30s orange	10	8
a.		30s red org ('21)	1.00	1.00
J33	D6	50s blue	15	6
J34	D6	1 l emer ('21)	15	4
J35	D6	2 l rose ('21)	20	4
J36	D6	3 l brn org ('21)	30	4
		Nos. J29-J36 (8)	1.30	44

Stotinki values of the above series surcharged 10s or 20s were used as ordinary postage stamps. See Nos. 182–185.

The 1919 printings are on thicker white paper with clean-cut perforations, the 1921 printings on thicker grayish paper with rough perforations.

Most of this series exist imperforate and in pairs imperforate between.

Heraldic Lion
D7

Lion of Trnovo
D8

National Arms
D9

1932, Aug. 15 Thin Paper

J37	D7	1 l ol bis	60	45
J38	D7	2 l rose brn	60	45
J39	D7	6 l brn vio	1.75	75

1933, Apr. 10

J40	D8	20s dk brn	3	3
J41	D8	40s dp bl	4	3
J42	D8	80s car rose	4	3
J43	D9	1 l org brn	30	20
J44	D9	2 l olive	45	35
J45	D9	6 l dl vio	20	12
J46	D9	14 l ultra	30	20
		Nos. J40-J46 (7)	1.36	96

National Arms
D10

Arms of the People's Republic
D11

1947, June Typo. *Perf. 10½*

J47	D10	1 l chocolate	4	4
J48	D10	2 l dp cl	4	4
J49	D10	8 l dp org	6	6
J50	D10	20 l blue	20	15

1951 *Perf. 11½x10½*

J51	D11	1 l chocolate	3	3
J52	D11	2 l claret	3	3
J53	D11	8 l red org	30	20
J54	D11	20 l dp bl	90	75

OFFICIAL STAMPS.

Bulgarian Coat of Arms
O1 O2

Typographed

1942 *Perf. 13* Unwmkd.

O1	O1	10s yel grn	3	3
O2	O1	30s red	3	3
O3	O1	50s bister	3	3
O4	O2	1 l vio bl	3	3
O5	O2	2 l dk grn	4	3
O6	O2	3 l lilac	6	4
O7	O2	4 l rose	8	3
O8	O2	5 l carmine	10	4
		Nos. O1-O8 (8)	40	26

1944 *Perf. 10½x11½*

O9	O2	1 l blue	30	20
O10	O2	2 l brt red	35	25

Lion Rampant
O3 O4

O5

1945 *Imperf.*

O11	O5	1 l pink	3	3

Perf. 10½x11½, Imperf.

O12	O3	2 l bl grn	3	3
O13	O4	3 l bis brn	3	3
O14	O4	4 l lt ultra	3	3
O15	O5	5 l brn lake	4	3
		Nos. O11-O15 (5)	16	15

In 1950, four stamps prepared for official use were issued as regular postage stamps. See Nos. 724–727.

PARCEL POST STAMPS.

Weighing Packages
PP1

Parcel Post
PP2

Designs: 3 l, 8 l, 20 l, Parcel post truck. 4 l, 6 l, 10 l, Motorcycle.

Perf. 12½x13½, 13½x12½.

1941-42 Photogravure. Unwmkd.

Q1	PP1	1 l sl grn	3	3
Q2	PP2	2 l crimson	4	3
Q3	PP2	3 l dl brn	4	3
Q4	PP2	4 l red org	4	3
Q5	PP1	5 l dp bl	4	3
Q6	PP1	5 l sl grn ('42)	4	3
Q7	PP2	6 l red vio	4	3
Q8	PP2	6 l hn brn ('42)	4	3
Q9	PP1	7 l dk bl	4	3
Q10	PP1	7 l dk brn ('42)	6	4
Q11	PP2	8 l brt bl grn	6	3
Q12	PP2	8 l grn ('42)	6	3
Q13	PP2	9 l ol gray	6	4
Q14	PP2	9 l dp ol ('42)	8	4
Q15	PP2	10 l orange	6	3
Q16	PP2	20 l gray vio	35	6
Q17	PP2	30 l dl blk	45	7
Q18	PP2	30 l sep ('42)	30	6
		Nos. Q1-Q18 (18)	1.83	67

Arms of Bulgaria
PP5

1944 Lithographed. *Imperf.*

Q21	PP5	1 l dk car	3	3
Q22	PP5	3 l bl grn	3	3
Q23	PP5	5 l dl bl grn	4	3
Q24	PP5	7 l rose lil	6	3
Q25	PP5	10 l dp bl	6	3
Q26	PP5	20 l org brn	8	3
Q27	PP5	30 l dk brn car	15	4
Q28	PP5	50 l red org	45	10
Q29	PP5	100 l blue	75	15
		Nos. Q21-Q29 (9)	1.65	47

POSTAL TAX STAMPS.

The use of stamps Nos. RA1 to RA18 was compulsory on letters, etc., to be delivered on Sundays and holidays. The money received from their sale was used toward maintaining a sanatorium for employees of the post, telegraph and telephone services.

View of Sanatorium
PT1

Sanatorium, Peshtera
PT2

Typographed.

1925–29 *Perf. 11½* Unwmkd.

RA1	PT1	1 l *grnsh bl*	3.00	15
RA2	PT1	1 l choc ('26)	3.00	10
RA3	PT1	1 l org ('27)	3.50	15
RA4	PT1	1 l pink ('28)	6.00	20
RA5	PT1	1 l vio, *pnksh* ('29)	5.00	20
RA6	PT2	2 l bl grn	40	15
RA7	PT2	2 l vio ('27)	40	20
RA8	PT2	5 l dp bl	3.25	1.00
RA9	PT2	5 l rose ('27)	4.00	50
		Nos. RA1-RA9 (9)	28.55	2.65

St. Constantine Sanatorium
PT3

1930–33

RA10	PT3	1 l red brn & ol grn	7.50	15
RA11	PT3	1 l ol grn & yel ('31)	75	15
RA12	PT3	1 l red vio & ol brn ('33)	75	15

Trojan Rest Home
PT4

Sanatorium
PT5

Wmkd. Wavy Lines. (145)

1935 *Perf. 11, 11½.*

RA13	PT4	1 l choc & red org	45	10
RA14	PT4	1 l emer & ind	45	10
RA15	PT5	5 l red brn & ind	2.25	45

St. Constantine Sanatorium
PT6

Children at Seashore
PT7

Rest Home
PT8

Photogravure.

1941 *Perf. 13* Unwmkd.

RA16	PT6	1 l dk ol grn	4	3
RA17	PT7	2 l red org	15	4
RA18	PT8	5 l dp bl	30	15

BURMA

See British Commonwealth Section of Vol. I.

BURUNDI

(bo͞o·ro͞on'dē)

LOCATION—Central Africa, adjoining the ex-Belgian Congo Republic, Rwanda and Tanganyika.

GOVT.—Republic.

AREA—10,739 sq. mi.

POP.—3,970,000 (est. 1977).

CAPITAL—Bujumbura.

Burundi was established as an independent country on July 1, 1962. With Rwanda, it had been a United Nations trusteeship territory (Ruanda-Urundi) administered by Belgium. A military coup overthrew the monarchy Nov. 28, 1966.

100 Centimes = 1 Franc

Royaume
du

Flower Issue of Ruanda-Urundi, 1953 Overprinted:

Burundi

Photogravure

1962, July 1 *Perf. 11½* Unwmkd.

Flowers in Natural Colors

1	A86	25c dk grn & dl org	15	15
2	A86	40c grn & sal	15	15
3	A86	60c bl grn & pink	30	30
4	A86	1.25fr dk grn & bl	22.00	22.00
5	A86	1.50fr vio & ap grn	75	75
6	A86	5fr dp plum & lt bl grn	90	90
7	A86	7fr dk grn & fawn	1.75	1.75
8	A86	10fr dp plum & pale ol	2.50	2.50
		Nos. 1-8 (8)	28.50	28.50

Animal Issue of Ruanda-Urundi, 1959–61 with Similar Overprint or Surcharge in Black or Violet Blue.

Size: 23x33mm., 33x23mm.

9	A28	10c brn, crim & blk brn	5	3
10	A29	20c gray, ap grn & blk	5	3
11	A28	40c mag, blk & gray grn	5	3
12	A29	50c grn, org yel & brn	6	3
a.		Larger ovpt. and bar	10	10
13	A28	1fr brn, ultra & blk	15	15
14	A29	1.50fr blk, gray & org (VB)	15	15
15	A28	2fr grnsh bl, ind & brn	15	15
16	A29	3fr brn, dp car & blk	15	15
17	A29	3.50fr on 3fr brn, dp car & blk	20	20
18	A29	4fr on 10fr multi ("XX" 6 mm wide)	30	30
a.		"XX" 4 mm wide	90	90
19	A29	5fr multi	30	30
20	A29	6.50fr red, org yel & brn	50	35
21	A29	8fr bl, mag & blk	60	45
a.		vio bl ovpt.	1.25	1.25
22	A29	10fr multi	60	60

Size: 45x26½mm.

23	A29	20fr multi	1.25	1.25
24	A29	50fr red, org, dp bl & brn (ovpt. bars 2mm wide)	2.50	2.25
a.		Ovpt. bars 4mm wide	3.75	2.25
		Nos. 9-24 (16)	7.06	6.42

On No. 12a, "Burundi" is 13mm. long; bar is continuous line across sheet. On No. 12, "Burundi" is 10mm.; bar is 29mm. No. 12a was issued in 1963.

Two types of overprint exist on 10c, 40c, 1fr and 2fr: I, "du" is below "me"; bar 22½mm. II, "du" below "oy"; bar 20 mm.

The 50c and 3fr exist in two types, besides the larger 50c overprint listed as No. 12: I, "du" is closer to "Royaume" than to "Burundi"; bar is less than 29mm; wording is centered above bar. II, "du" is closer to "Burundi"; bar is more than 30mm.; wording is off-center leftward.

King Mwami Mwambutsa IV and Royal Drummers—A1

Flag and Arms of Burundi
A2

Design: 2fr, 8fr, 50fr, Map of Burundi and King.

Photogravure

1962, Sept. 27 *Perf. 14* Unwmkd.

25	A1	50c dl rose car & dk brn	5	3
26	A2	1fr dk grn, red & emer	10	3
27	A1	2fr brn ol & dk brn	18	3
28	A1	3fr ver & dk brn	42	20
29	A2	4fr Prus bl, red & emer	30	5
30	A1	8fr vio & dk brn	60	12
31	A1	10fr brt grn & dk brn	75	18
32	A2	20fr brn, red & emer	1.75	38
33	A1	50fr brt pink & dk brn	3.25	75
		Nos. 25-33 (9)	7.40	1.77

Issued to commemorate Burundi's independence, July 1, 1962.

Ruanda-Urundi Nos. 151–152 Surcharged:

HOMMAGE A
DAG HAMMARSKJÖLD
3<u>50</u>F
ROYAUME du BURUNDI

Photogravure, Surcharge Engraved

1962, Oct. 31 *Perf. 11½*

Inscription in French

34	A92	3.50fr on 3fr ultra & red	33	25
35	A92	6.50fr on 3fr ultra & red	60	50
36	A92	10fr on 3fr ultra & red	90	75

Inscription in Flemish

37	A92	3.50fr on 3fr ultra & red	33	25
38	A92	6.50fr on 3fr ultra & red	60	50
39	A92	10fr on 3fr ultra & red	90	75
		Nos. 34-39 (6)	3.66	3.00

Issued in memory of Dag Hammarskjold, Secretary General of the United Nations, 1953–61.

King Mwami Mwambutsa IV, Map of Burundi and Emblem—A3

1962, Dec. 10 Photo. *Perf. 14*

40	A3	8fr yel, bl grn & blk brn	1.00	30
41	A3	50fr gray grn, bl grn & blk brn	2.75	70

Issued for the World Health Organization drive to eradicate malaria.

Stamps of type A3 without anti-malaria emblem are listed as Nos. 27, 30 and 33.

Sowing Seed over Africa
A4

1963, Mar. 21 *Perf. 14x13*

42	A4	4fr ol & dl pur	15	10
43	A4	8fr dp org & dl pur	35	25

44	A4	15fr emer & dl pur	50	40

Issued for the "Freedom from Hunger" campaign of the U.N. Food and Agriculture Organization.

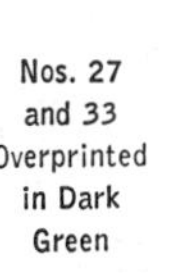
Nos. 27 and 33 Overprinted in Dark Green

1963, June 19 ***Perf. 14*** **Unwmkd.**

45	A1	2fr brn ol & dk brn	3.75	3.00
46	A1	50fr brt pink & dk brn	4.25	3.00

Conquest and peaceful use of outer space.

Types of 1962 Inscribed: "Premier Anniversaire" in Red or Magenta

1963, July 1 **Photogravure**

47	A2	4fr ol, red & emer (R)	25	8
48	A1	8fr org & dk brn (M)	40	15
49	A1	10fr lil & dk brn (M)	65	25
50	A2	20fr gray, red & emer (R)	1.65	50

First anniversary of independence.

Nos. 26 and 32 Surcharged in Brown

1963, Sept. 24 ***Perf. 14*** **Unwmkd.**

51	A2	6.50fr on 1fr dk grn, red & emer	75	20
52	A2	15fr on 20fr brn, red & emer	1.50	50

Red Cross Flag over Globe with Map of Africa
A5

1963, Sept. 26 ***Perf. 14x13***

53	A5	4fr emer, car & gray	30	12
54	A5	8fr brn ol, car & gray	60	25
55	A5	10fr bl, car & gray	90	35
56	A5	20fr lil, car & gray	1.85	60

Centenary of International Red Cross.

"1962", Arms of Burundi, U.N. and UNESCO Emblems
A6

U.N. Agency Emblems: 8fr, International Telecommunications Union. 10fr, World Meteorological Organization. 20fr, Universal Postal Union. 50fr, Food and Agriculture Organization.

1963, Nov. 4 ***Perf. 14*** **Unwmkd.**

57	A6	4fr yel, ol grn & blk	25	10
58	A6	8fr pale lil, Prus bl & blk	45	12
59	A6	10fr bl, lil & blk	60	18
60	A6	20fr yel grn, grn & blk	1.10	30
61	A6	50fr yel, red brn & blk	2.75	60
a.		Souv. sheet of 2	6.75	6.75
		Nos. 57-61 (5)	5.15	1.30

Issued to commemorate the first anniversary of Burundi's admission to the United Nations. No. 61a contains two imperf. stamps with simulated perforations similar to Nos. 60–61. The 20fr stamp shows the FAO and the 50fr the WMO emblems. Gray margin with black inscription. Size: 111x73½mm.

UNESCO Emblem, Scales and Map—A7

Designs: 3.50fr, 6.50fr, Scroll, scales and "UNESCO". 10fr, 20fr, Abraham Lincoln, broken chain and scales.

Lithographed

1963, Dec. 10 ***Perf. 14x13½***

62	A7	50c pink, lt bl & blk	3	3
63	A7	1.50fr org, lt bl & blk	7	5
64	A7	3.50fr fawn, lt grn & blk	18	15
65	A7	6.50fr lt vio, lt grn & blk	35	18
66	A7	10fr bl, bis & blk	60	20
67	A7	20fr pale brn, ocher, bl & blk	1.20	35
		Nos. 62-67 (6)	2.43	96

Issued to commemorate the 15th anniversary of the Universal Declaration of Human Rights and the centenary of the American Emancipation Proclamation (Nos. 66–67).

Ice Hockey A8 — Impala A9

Designs: 3.50 fr, Women's figure skating. 6.50fr, Torch. 10fr, Men's speed skating. 20fr, Slalom.

Photogravure

1964, Jan 25 ***Perf. 14*** **Unwmkd.**

68	A8	50c ol, blk & gold	10	3
69	A8	3.50fr lt brn, blk & gold	30	10
70	A8	6.50fr pale gray, blk & gold	60	20
71	A8	10fr gray, blk & gold	90	27
72	A8	20fr tan, blk & gold	1.75	65
		Nos. 68-72 (5)	3.65	1.25

Issued to publicize the 9th Winter Olympic Games, Innsbruck, Jan. 29–Feb. 9, 1964.

A souvenir sheet contains two stamps (10fr+5fr and 20fr+5fr) in tan, black and gold. Size: 121x65mm.

Canceled to Order

Starting about 1964, prices in the used column are for "canceled to order" stamps. Postally used copies sell for much more.

1964 **Lithographed**

Animals: 1fr, 5fr, Hippopotamus (horiz.). 1.50fr, 10fr, Giraffe. 2fr, 8fr, Cape buffalo (horiz.). 3fr, 6.50fr, Zebra (horiz.). 3.50fr, 15fr, Defassa waterbuck. 20fr, Cheetah. 50fr, Elephant. 100fr, Lion.

Perf. 14x13, 13x14

Size: 21½x35mm., 35x21½mm.

73	A9	50c multi	8	3
74	A9	1fr multi	10	3
75	A9	1.50fr multi	12	4
76	A9	2fr multi	15	4
77	A9	3fr multi	25	6
78	A9	3.50fr multi	28	7

Size: 26x42mm., 42x26mm.

79	A9	4fr multi	30	8
80	A9	5fr multi	38	10
81	A9	6.50fr multi	45	10
82	A9	8fr multi	50	20
83	A9	10fr multi	65	20
84	A9	15fr multi	1.00	33

Perf. 14

Size: 53x33mm.

85	A9	20fr multi	1.35	40
86	A9	50fr multi	3.50	65
87	A9	100fr multi	6.50	1.35
		Nos. 73-87 (15)	15.61	3.68

See also Nos. C1–C7.

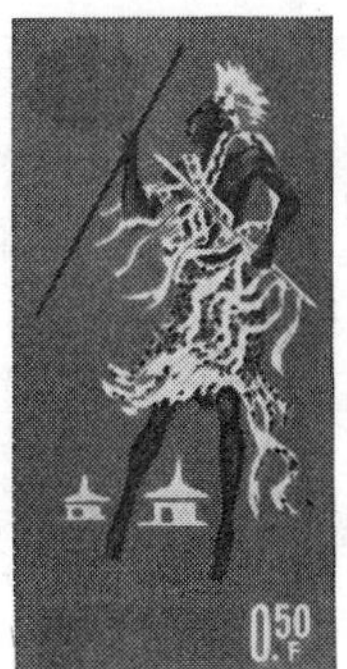

Burundi Dancer
A10

Designs: Various Dancers and Drummers.

Lithographed

1964, Aug. 21 ***Perf. 14*** **Unwmkd.**

Dancers Multicolored

88	A10	50c gold & emer	8	3
89	A10	1fr gold & vio bl	10	5
90	A10	4fr gold & brt bl	25	10
91	A10	6.50fr gold & red	40	18
92	A10	10fr gold & brt bl	60	25
93	A10	15fr gold & emer	90	30
94	A10	20fr gold & red	1.25	45
a.		Souv. sheet of 3	5.00	5.00

1965, Sept. 10

Dancers Multicolored

88a	A10	50c sil & emer	8	5
89a	A10	1fr sil & vio bl	8	5
90a	A10	4fr sil & brt bl	20	10
91a	A10	6.50fr sil & red	30	15
92a	A10	10fr sil & brt bl	50	20
93a	A10	15fr sil & emer	60	35
94b	A10	20fr sil & red	90	60
c.		Souv. sheet of 3	4.00	4.00

Issued to commemorate the New York World's Fair, 1964–65. No. 94a contains one each of Nos. 92–94, gold background and bright blue border. No. 94c, dated "1965" in yellow, contains one each of Nos. 92a–94b, silver background and bright blue border. Size of souvenir sheets: 120x100mm.

Pope Paul VI and King Mwami Mwambutsa IV—A11

22 Sainted Martyrs
A12

Designs: 4fr, 14fr, Pope John XXIII and King Mwami.

1964, Nov. 12 **Photo.** ***Perf. 12***

95	A11	50c brt bl, gold & red brn	5	3
96	A12	1fr mag, gold & sl	5	5
97	A11	4fr pale rose lil, gold & brn	20	8
98	A12	8fr red, gold & brn	45	15
99	A11	14fr lt grn, gold & brn	90	30
100	A11	20fr red brn, gold & grn	1.60	60
		Nos. 95-100 (6)	3.25	1.21

Issued to commemorate the canonization of 22 African martyrs, Oct. 18, 1964.

Shot Put A13 — African Purple Gallinule A14

Sports: 1fr, Discus. 3fr, Swimming (horiz.). 4fr, Running. 6.50fr, Javelin, woman. 8fr, Hurdling (horiz.). 10fr, Broad jump (horiz.). 14fr, Diving, woman. 18fr, High jump (horiz.). 20fr, Vaulting (horiz.).

1964, Nov. 18 **Litho.** ***Perf. 14***

101	A13	50c ol & multi	4	3
102	A13	1fr brt pink & multi	6	5
103	A13	3fr multi	15	10
104	A13	4fr multi	18	12
105	A13	6.50fr multi	30	18
106	A13	8fr lt bl & multi	40	20
107	A13	10fr multi	50	25
108	A13	14fr multi	75	30
109	A13	18fr bis & multi	90	40
110	A13	20fr gray & multi	1.00	50
		Nos. 101-110 (10)	4.28	2.13

Issued to commemorate the 18th Olympic Games, Tokyo, Oct. 10–25, 1964. See also No. B8.

1965 ***Perf. 14*** **Unwmkd.**

Birds: 1fr, 5fr, Little bee eater. 1.50fr, 6.50fr, Secretary bird. 2fr, 8fr, Yellow-billed stork. 3fr, 10fr, Congo peacock. 3.50fr, 15fr, African anhinga. 20fr, Saddle-billed stork. 50fr, Abyssinian ground hornbill. 100fr, Crowned crane.

Birds in Natural Colors

Size: 21x35mm.

111	A14	50c tan, grn & blk	4	3

112	A14	1fr pink, mag & blk	5	3
113	A14	1.50fr bl & blk	6	3
114	A14	2fr yel grn, dk grn & blk	8	3
115	A14	3fr yel, brn & blk	10	5
116	A14	3.50fr yel grn, dk grn & blk	10	6

Size: 26x43mm.

117	A14	4fr tan, grn & blk	12	8
118	A14	5fr pink, mag & blk	15	8
119	A14	6.50fr bl & blk	20	10
120	A14	8fr yel grn, dk grn & blk	25	10
121	A14	10fr yel, brn & blk	35	12
122	A14	15fr yel grn, dk grn & blk	50	15

Size: 33x53mm.

123	A14	20fr rose lil & blk	65	60
124	A14	50fr yel, brn & blk	1.90	40
125	A14	100fr grn, yel & blk	3.75	80
		Nos. 111-125 (15)	8.30	2.66

Issue dates: Nos. 111–116, Mar. 31. Nos. 117–122, Apr. 16. Nos. 123–125, Apr. 30.

See also Nos. C8–C16.

Relay Satellite and Morse Key
A15

Designs: 3fr, Telstar and old telephone handpiece. 4fr, Relay satellite and old wall telephone. 6.50fr, Orbiting Geophysical Observatory and radar screen. 8fr, Telstar II and headphones. 10fr, Sputnik II and radar aerial. 14fr, Syncom and transmission aerial. 20fr, Interplanetary Explorer and tracking aerial.

1965, July 3 Litho. *Perf. 13*

126	A15	1fr multi	5	5
127	A15	3fr multi	10	5
128	A15	4fr multi	10	10
129	A15	6.50fr multi	20	15
130	A15	8fr multi	30	18
131	A15	10fr multi	35	20
132	A15	14fr multi	50	28
133	A15	20fr multi	60	35
		Nos. 126-133 (8)	2.20	1.36

Issued to commemorate the centenary of the International Telecommunication Union. Perf. and imperf. souvenir sheets of two contain one each of Nos. 131 and 133. Bluish black margin and gold inscription. Size: 120x86mm. Price, both sheets, $7.50.

Globe and ICY Emblem—A16

Designs: 4fr, Map of Africa and U.N. development emblem. 8fr, Map of Asia and Colombo Plan emblem. 10fr, Globe and U.N. emblem. 18fr, Map of the Americas and Alliance for Progress emblem. 25fr, Map of Europe and EUROPA emblems. 40fr, Map of Outer Space and satellite with U.N. wreath.

1965, Oct. 1 Litho. *Perf. 13*

134	A16	1fr ol grn & multi	5	3
135	A16	4fr dl bl & multi	15	3
136	A16	8fr pale yel & multi	30	12
137	A16	10fr lil & multi	40	12
138	A16	18fr sal & multi	65	20
139	A16	25fr gray & multi	1.00	20
140	A16	40fr bl & multi	1.60	25
a.		Souv. sheet of 3	4.50	4.50
		Nos. 134-140 (7)	4.15	95

Issued for the International Cooperation Year. No. 140a contains one each of Nos. 138–140. Gray margin with multicolored inscription. Size: 101½x100mm.

Protea
A17

Flowers: 1fr, 5fr, Crossandra. 1.50fr, 6.50fr, Ansellia. 2fr, 8fr, Thunbergia. 3fr, 10fr, Schizoglossum. 3.50fr, 15fr, Dissotis. 4fr, 20fr, Protea. 50fr, Gazania. 100fr, Hibiscus. 150fr, Markhamia.

1966 *Perf. 13½* Unwmkd.

Size: 26x26mm.

141	A17	50c multi	3	3
142	A17	1fr multi	3	3
143	A17	1.50fr multi	5	3
144	A17	2fr multi	7	3
145	A17	3fr multi	10	3
146	A17	3.50fr multi	10	3

Size: 31x31mm.

147	A17	4fr multi	12	5
148	A17	5fr multi	15	8
149	A17	6.50fr multi	20	10
150	A17	8fr multi	25	12
151	A17	10fr multi	30	15
152	A17	15fr multi	60	20

Size: 39x39mm.

153	A17	20fr multi	70	20
154	A17	50fr multi	1.65	50
155	A17	100fr multi	3.25	75
156	A17	150fr multi	5.00	1.10
		Nos. 141-156 (16)	12.60	3.43

Issue dates: Nos. 141–147, Feb. 28; Nos. 148–153, May 18; Nos. 154–156, June 15.

See also Nos. C17–C25.

Souvenir Sheets

Allegory of Prosperity and Equality Tapestry by Peter Colfs—A18

1966, Nov. 4 Litho. *Perf. 13½*

157	A18	Sheet of 7 (1.50fr)	1.25	75
158	A18	Sheet of 7 (4fr)	3.00	2.00

Issued to commemorate the 20th anniversary of UNESCO (United Nations Educational, Scientific and Cultural Organization). Each sheet contains 6 stamps showing a reproduction of the Colfs tapestry from the lobby of the General Assembly Building, New York, and one stamp with the UNESCO emblem plus a label. The labels on Nos. 157–158 and C26 are inscribed in French or English. The 3 sheets with French inscription have light blue marginal border. The 3 sheets with English inscription have pink border. Size: 203x124mm. See also No. C26.

Republic

Nos. 141–152, 154–156 Overprinted

REPUBLIQUE DU BURUNDI

1967 Lithographed *Perf. 13½*

Size: 26x26mm.

159	A17	50c multi	5	3
160	A17	1fr multi	5	3
161	A17	1.50fr multi	6	3
162	A17	2fr multi	8	3
163	A17	3fr multi	12	3
164	A17	3.50fr multi	15	3

Size: 31x31mm.

165	A17	4fr multi	1.00	60
166	A17	5fr multi	18	5
167	A17	6.50fr multi	20	5
168	A17	8fr multi	30	5
169	A17	10fr multi	35	7
170	A17	15fr multi	50	10

Size: 39x39mm.

171	A17	50fr multi	5.00	2.00
172	A17	100fr multi	9.50	4.00
173	A17	150fr multi	7.75	3.50
		Nos. 159-173 (15)	25.29	10.60

Nos. 111, 113, 116, 118–125 Overprinted "REPUBLIQUE DU BURUNDI" and Horizontal Bar.

1967 Lithographed *Perf. 14*

Birds in Natural Colors

Size: 21x35mm.

174	A14	50c multi	1.65	1.00
175	A14	1.50fr bl & blk	5	3
176	A14	3.50fr multi	12	3

Size: 26x43mm.

177	A14	5fr multi	15	5
178	A14	6.50fr bl & blk	18	5
179	A14	8fr multi	25	5
180	A14	10fr yel, brn & blk	50	7
181	A14	15fr multi	90	10

Size: 33x53mm.

182	A14	20fr multi	2.00	75
183	A14	50fr multi	5.00	2.25
184	A14	100fr multi	8.00	4.50
		Nos. 174-184 (11)	18.80	8.88

Haplochromis Multicolor
A19
Various Tropical Fish.

1967 Photogravure *Perf. 13½*

Size: 42x19mm.

186	A19	50c multi	6	3
187	A19	1fr multi	6	3
188	A19	1.50fr multi	8	3
189	A19	2fr multi	10	3
190	A19	3fr multi	15	3
191	A19	3.50fr multi	18	3

Size: 50x25mm.

192	A19	4fr multi	18	5
193	A19	5fr multi	20	5
194	A19	6.50fr multi	25	5
195	A19	8fr multi	30	5
196	A19	10fr multi	35	7
197	A19	15fr multi	55	10

Size: 59x30mm.

198	A19	20fr multi	75	20
199	A19	50fr multi	2.00	35
200	A19	100fr multi	4.25	60
201	A19	150fr multi	6.50	85
		Nos. 186-201 (16)	15.96	2.55

Issue Dates: Nos. 186–191, Apr. 4; Nos. 192–197, Apr. 28; Nos. 198–201, May 18.

See also Nos. C46–C54.

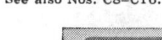

Ancestor Figures, Ivory Coast
A20

African Art: 1fr, Seat of Honor, Southeast Congo. 1.50fr, Antelope head, Aribinda Region. 2fr, Buffalo mask, Upper Volta. 4fr, Funeral figures, Southwest Ethiopia.

1967, June 5 Photo. *Perf. 13½*

202	A20	50c sil & multi	5	5
203	A20	1fr sil & multi	5	5
204	A20	1.50fr sil & multi	10	5
205	A20	2fr sil & multi	12	5
206	A20	4fr sil & multi	18	5
		Nos. 202-206, C36-C40 (10)	3.50	2.00

Scouts on Hiking Trip
A21

Designs: 1fr, Cooking at campfire. 1.50fr, Lord Baden-Powell. 2fr, Boy Scout and Cub Scout giving Scout sign. 4fr, First aid.

1967, Aug. 9 Photo. *Perf. 13½*

207	A21	50c sil & multi	5	6
208	A21	1fr sil & multi	8	6
209	A21	1.50fr sil & multi	10	6
210	A21	2fr sil & multi	12	8
211	A21	4fr sil & multi	18	8
		Nos. 207-211, C41-C45 (10)	4.08	1.64

Issued to commemorate the 60th anniversary of the Boy Scouts and the 12th Boy Scout World Jamboree, Farragut State Park, Idaho, Aug. 1–9.

The Gleaners, by Francois Millet
A22

Paintings Exhibited at EXPO '67: 8fr, The Water Carrier of Seville, by Velazquez. 14fr, The Triumph of Neptune and Amphitrite, by Nicolas Poussin. 18fr, Acrobat Standing on a Ball, by Picasso. 25fr, Marguerite van Eyck, by Jan van Eyck. 40fr, St. Peter Denying Christ, by Rembrandt.

1967, Oct. 12 Photo. *Perf. 13½*

212	A22	4fr multi	25	8
213	A22	8fr multi	35	10
214	A22	14fr multi	50	12
215	A22	18fr multi	65	20
216	A22	25fr multi	1.00	35
217	A22	40fr multi	1.50	50
a.		Souv. sheet of 2	2.50	2.00
		Nos. 212-217 (6)	4.25	1.35

Issued to commemorate EXPO '67 International Exhibition, Montreal, Apr. 28–Oct. 27. Printed in sheets of 10 stamps and 2 labels inscribed in French or English. No. 217a contains one each of Nos. 216–217. Blue margin with black and red inscription. Size: 105x105mm. Exists imperf.

Place de la Revolution and Pres. Michel Micombero
A23

Designs: 5fr, President Michel Micombero and flag. 14fr, Formal garden and coat of arms. 20fr, Modern building and coat of arms.

1967, Nov. 23 *Perf. 13½*

218	A23	5fr multi	25	10
219	A23	14fr multi	60	20
220	A23	20fr multi	90	20
221	A23	30fr multi	1.20	45

First anniversary of the Republic.

Madonna by Carlo Crivelli
A24

Designs: 1fr, Adoration of the Shepherds by Juan Bautista Mayno. 4fr, Holy Family by Anthony Van Dyck. 14fr, Nativity by Maitre de Moulins.

1967, Dec. 7 Photo. *Perf. 13½*

222	A24	1fr multi	6	5
223	A24	4fr multi	15	10
224	A24	14fr multi	50	30
225	A24	26fr multi	1.20	50

Christmas 1967.

Printed in sheets of 25 and one corner label inscribed "Noel 1967" and giving name of painting and painter.

Slalom
A25

Designs: 10fr, Ice hockey. 14fr, Women's skating. 17fr, Bobsled. 26fr, Ski jump. 40fr, Speed skating. 60fr, Hand holding torch, and Winter Olympics emblem.

1968, Feb. 16 Photo. *Perf. 13½*

226	A25	5fr sil & multi	20	4
227	A25	10fr sil & multi	35	5
228	A25	14fr sil & multi	50	10
229	A25	17fr sil & multi	55	10
230	A25	26fr sil & multi	90	15
231	A25	40fr sil & multi	1.40	25
232	A25	60fr sil & multi	2.10	40
		Nos. 226-232 (7)	6.00	1.09

Issued to publicize the 10th Winter Olympic Games, Grenoble, France, Feb. 6–18. Issued in sheets of 10 stamps and label.

The Lacemaker, by Vermeer
A26

Paintings: 1.50fr, Portrait of a Young Man, by Botticelli. 2fr, Maja Vestida, by Goya (horiz.).

1968, Mar. 29 Photo. *Perf. 13½*

233	A26	1.50fr gold & multi	8	5
234	A26	2fr gold & multi	12	8
235	A26	4fr gold & multi	25	12
		Nos. 233-235, C59-C61 (6)	3.15	1.30

Issued in sheets of 6.

Moon Probe
A27

Designs: 6fr, Russian astronaut walking in space. 8fr, Weather satellite. 10fr, American astronaut walking in space.

1968, May 15 Photo. *Perf. 13½*

Size: 35x35mm.

236	A27	4fr sil & multi	20	10
237	A27	6fr sil & multi	30	10
238	A27	8fr sil & multi	40	10
239	A27	10fr sil & multi	45	15
		Nos. 236-239, C62-C65 (8)	4.75	1.28

Issued to publicize peaceful space explorations.

A souvenir sheet contains one 25fr stamp in Moon Probe design and one 40fr in Weather Satellite design. Margin in silver and deep red lilac; black inscription. Stamp size: 41x41mm. Sheet size: 109x83mm. Price $2.

Sheet exists imperf. Price $3.

Salamis Aethiops
A28

Butterflies: 1fr, 5fr, Graphium ridleyanus. 1.50fr, 6.50fr, Cymothoe. 2fr, 8fr, Charaxes eupale. 3fr, 10fr, Papilio bromius. 3.50fr, 15fr, Teracolus annae. 20fr, Salamis aethiops. 50fr, Papilio zonobia. 100fr, Danais chrysippus. 150fr, Salamis temora.

1968

Size: 30x33½mm.

240	A28	50c gold & multi	5	3
241	A28	1fr gold & multi	5	3
242	A28	1.50fr gold & multi	6	3
243	A28	2fr gold & multi	8	5
244	A28	3fr gold & multi	10	6
245		3.50fr gold & multi	12	6

Size: 33½x37½mm.

246	A28	4fr gold & multi	12	8
247	A28	5fr gold & multi	15	8
248	A28	6.50fr gold & multi	20	8
249	A28	8fr gold & multi	25	8
250	A28	10fr gold & multi	30	10
251	A28	15fr gold & multi	60	15

Size: 41x46mm.

252	A28	20fr gold & multi	90	20
253	A28	50fr gold & multi	1.80	25
254	A28	100fr gold & multi	3.50	55
255	A28	150fr gold & multi	5.50	80
		Nos. 240-255 (16)	13.78	2.63

Issue dates: Nos. 240–245, June 7; Nos. 246–251, June 28. Nos. 252–255, July 19.

See also Nos. C66–C74.

Women, Along the Manzanares, by Goya
A29

Paintings: 7fr, The Letter, by Pieter de Hooch. 11fr, Woman Reading a Letter, by Gerard Terborch. 14fr, Man Writing a Letter, by Gabriel Metsu.

1968, Sept. 30 Photo. *Perf. 13½*

256	A29	4fr multi	15	8
257	A29	7fr multi	25	12
258	A29	11fr multi	40	18
259	A29	14fr multi	60	25
		Nos. 256-259, C84-C87 (8)	5.25	1.58

International Letter Writing Week.

Soccer
A30

Designs: 7fr, Basketball. 13fr, High jump. 24fr, Relay race. 40fr, Javelin.

1968, Oct. 24

260	A30	4fr gold & multi	10	3
261	A30	7fr gold & multi	18	6
262	A30	13fr gold & multi	35	10
263	A30	24fr gold & multi	70	20
264	A30	40fr gold & multi	1.15	30
		260-264, C88-C92 (10)	7.43	2.09

Issued to commemorate the 19th Olympic Games, Mexico City, Oct. 12–27. Printed in sheets of 8.

Virgin and Child, by Fra Filippo Lippi
A31

Paintings: 5fr, The Magnificat, by Sandro Botticelli. 6fr, Virgin and Child, by Albrecht Durer. 11fr, Madonna del Gran Duca, by Raphael.

1968, Nov. 26 Photo. *Perf. 13½*

265	A31	3fr multi	15	8
266	A31	5fr multi	20	10
267	A31	6fr multi	24	15
268	A31	11fr multi	45	25
a.		Souv. sheet of 4	1.50	1.50
		Nos. 265-268, C93-C96 (8)	3.14	1.48

Christmas 1968.

No. 268a contains one each of Nos. 265–268, decorative border and inscription. Size: 120x120mm. See Nos. C93–C96.

WHO Emblem and Map of Africa
A32

1969, Jan. 22

269	A32	5fr gold, dk grn & yel	18	8
270	A32	6fr gold, vio & ver	28	12
271	A32	11fr gold, pur & red lil	45	20

Issued to commemorate the 20th anniversary of the World Health Organization in Africa.

Nos. 265–268 Overprinted in Silver

1969, Feb. 17 Photo. *Perf. 13½*

272	A31	3fr multi	15	8
273	A31	5fr multi	20	10
274	A31	6fr multi	25	15
275	A31	11fr multi	45	25
		Nos. 272-275, C100-C103 (8)	3.70	1.71

Issued to commemorate man's first flight around the moon by the U.S.A. spacecraft Apollo 8, Dec. 21–27, 1968.

Map of Africa, and CEPT Emblem
A33

Designs: 14fr, Plowing with tractor. 17fr, Teacher and pupil. 26fr, Maps of Europe and Africa and CEPT (Conference of European Postal and Telecommunications Administrations) emblem (horiz.).

1969, Mar. 12 Photo. *Perf. 13*

276	A33	5fr multi	20	8
277	A33	14fr multi	60	20

278	A33	17fr multi	75	25
279	A33	26fr multi	1.00	30

Issued to commemorate the 5th anniversary of the Yaoundé (Cameroun) Agreement, creating the European and African-Malgache Economic Community.

Resurrection, by Gaspard Isenmann
A34

Paintings: 14fr, Resurrection by Antoine Caron. 17fr, Noli me Tangere, by Martin Schongauer. 26fr, Resurrection, by El Greco.

1969, Mar. 24

280	A34	11fr gold & multi	45	15
281	A34	14fr gold & multi	55	20
282	A34	17fr gold & multi	75	25
283	A34	26fr gold & multi	1.10	30
a.		Souv. sheet of 4	3.00	3.00

Easter 1969.
No. 283a contains one each of Nos. 280–283; gold and blue border and inscription. Size: 100½x125mm.

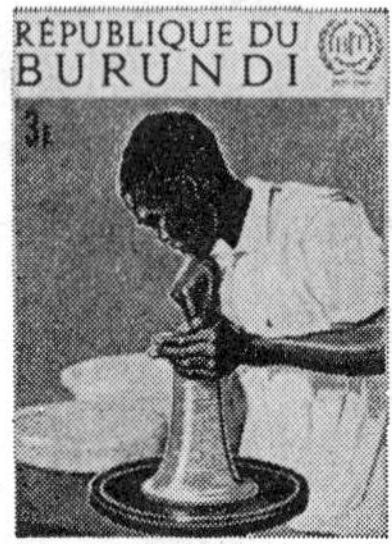

Potter
A35

Designs (BIT Emblem and): 5fr, Farm workers. 7fr, Foundry worker. 10fr, Woman testing corn crop.

1969, May 17 Photo. ***Perf. 13½***

284	A35	3fr multi	12	6
285	A35	5fr multi	20	6
286	A35	7fr multi	30	12
287	A35	10fr multi	40	18

Issued to commemorate the 50th anniversary of the International Labor Organization.

Industry and Bank's Emblem
A36

Designs (African Development Bank Emblem and): 17fr, Communications. 30fr, Education. 50fr, Agriculture.

1969, July 29 Photo. ***Perf. 13½***

288	A36	10fr gold & multi	35	10
289	A36	17fr gold & multi	60	20
290	A36	30fr gold & multi	1.00	30
291	A36	50fr gold & multi	1.60	50
a.		Souv. sheet of 4	3.75	3.75

Issued to publicize the 5th anniversary of the African Development Bank. No. 291a contains one each of Nos. 288–291, gold decorative border. Size: 103x124mm.

Girl Reading Letter, by Vermeer
A37

Paintings: 7fr, Graziella (young woman), by Auguste Renoir. 14fr, Woman writing a letter, by Gerard Terborch. 26fr, Galileo Galilei, painter unknown. 40fr, Ludwig van Beethoven, painter unknown.

1969, Oct. 24 Photo. ***Perf. 13½***

292	A37	4fr multi	18	5
293	A37	7fr multi	30	10
294	A37	14fr multi	65	18
295	A37	26fr multi	1.10	28
296	A37	40fr multi	1.50	40
a.		Souv. sheet of 2	3.50	3.50
		Nos. 292-296 (5)	3.73	1.01

Issued for International Letter Writing Week, Oct. 7–13.
No. 296a contains one each of Nos. 295–296. Buff decorative margin with commemorative inscription. Size: 133x75mm.

Moon Landing Issue

Rocket Launching
A38

Designs: 6.50fr, Rocket in space. 7fr, Separation of landing module from capsule. 14fr, 26fr, Landing module landing on moon. 17fr, Capsule in space. 40fr, Neil A. Armstrong leaving landing module. 50fr, Astronaut on moon.

1969, Nov. 6 Photo. ***Perf. 13½***

297	38	4fr bl & multi	30	10
298	38	6.50fr vio bl & multi	42	25
299	38	7fr vio bl & multi	42	25
300	38	14fr blk & multi	70	38
301	38	17fr vio bl & multi	1.10	50
		Nos. 297-301, C104-C106 (8)	7.24	3.58

Souvenir Sheet

302	A38	Souvenir sheet of 3	6.00	6.00
a.		26fr multi	1.00	1.00
b.		40fr multi	1.50	1.50
c.		50fr multi	2.00	2.00

See note after Algeria No. 427.
On. No. 302 stamp designs extend into inscribed margin. Size: 140x88mm.

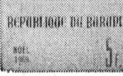

Madonna and Child, by Rubens
A39

Paintings: 6fr, Madonna and Child with St. John, by Giulio Romano. 10fr, Magnificat Madonna, by Botticelli.

1969, Dec. 2 Photogravure

303	A39	5fr gold & multi	15	8
304	A39	6fr gold & multi	25	10
305	A39	10fr gold & multi	50	15
a.		Souvenir sheet of 3	1.50	1.50
		Nos. 303-305, C107-C109 (6)	4.45	1.28

Christmas 1969.
No. 305a contains one each of Nos. 303–305. Gold frame with inscription. Size: 110x87mm.

Sternotomis Bohemani
A40

Designs: Various Beetles and Weevils.

1970 ***Perf. 13½***

Size: 39x28mm.

306	A40	50c sil & multi	3	3
307	A40	1fr sil & multi	3	3
308	A40	1.50fr sil & multi	4	3
309	A40	2fr sil & multi	5	3
310	A40	3fr sil & multi	8	3
311	A40	3.50fr sil & multi	9	3

Size: 46x32mm.

312	A40	4fr sl & multi	10	3
313	A40	5fr sl & multi	13	3
314	A40	6.50fr sl & multi	17	3
315	A40	8fr sl & multi	20	3
316	A40	10fr sl & multi	25	3
317	A40	15fr sl & multi	50	4

Size: 52x36mm.

318	A40	20fr sl & multi	65	6
319	A40	50fr sl & multi	1.60	35
320	A40	100fr sl & multi	3.25	70
321	A40	150fr sl & multi	4.75	1.00
		Nos. 306-321, C110-C118 (25)	22.12	4.53

Issue dates: Nos. 306–313, Jan. 20; Nos. 314–318, Feb. 17; Nos. 319–321, Apr. 3.

Jesus Condemned to Death
A41

Stations of the Cross, by Juan de Aranoa y Carredano: 1.50fr, Jesus carries His Cross. 2fr, Jesus falls the first time. 3fr, Jesus meets His mother. 3.50fr, Simon of Cyrene helps carry the cross. 4fr, Veronica wipes the face of Jesus. 5fr, Jesus falls the second time.

1970, Mar. 16 Photo. ***Perf. 13½***

322	A41	1fr gold & multi	5	5
323	A41	1.50fr gold & multi	6	6
324	A41	2fr gold & multi	8	6
325	A41	3fr gold & multi	15	6
326	A41	3.50fr gold & multi	18	8
327	A41	4fr gold & multi	22	10
328	A41	5fr gold & multi	30	10
a.		Souv. sheet of 7 + label	1.10	1.10
		Nos. 322-328, C119-C125 (14)	5.09	2.18

Easter 1970.
No. 328a contains one each of Nos. 322–328 and label showing three crosses. Gold decorative border. Size: 154x123mm.

Parade and EXPO '70 Emblem
A42

Designs (EXPO '70 Emblem and): 6.50fr, Aerial view. 7fr, African pavilions. 14fr, Pagoda (vert.). 26fr, Recording pavilion and pool. 40fr, Tower of the Sun (vert.). 50fr, Flags of participating nations.

1970, May 5 Photo. ***Perf. 13½***

329	A42	4fr gold & multi	15	3
330	A42	6.50fr gold & multi	25	5
331	A42	7fr gold & multi	30	6
332	A42	14fr gold & multi	50	12
333	A42	26fr gold & multi	80	18
334	A42	40fr gold & multi	1.25	30
335	A42	50fr gold & multi	1.75	40
		Nos. 329-335 (7)	5.00	1.14

Issued to publicize EXPO '70 International Exhibition, Osaka, Japan, March 15–Sept. 13, 1970. See No. C126.

White Rhinoceros—A43

Designs, FAUNA: Camel, dromedary, okapi, addax, Burundi cow (2 stamps of each animal in 2 different poses). MAP OF THE NILE: Delta and pyramids, dhow, cataract, Blue Nile and crowned crane, Victoria Nile and secretary bird, Lake Victoria and source of Nile on Mt. Gikizi.

1970, July 8 Photo. ***Perf. 13½***

336	A43	7fr multi	30	10
a.		Sheet of 18	5.50	2.75

Issued in sheets of 18 (3x6) stamps of different designs, to publicize the southernmost source of the Nile on Mt. Gikizi in Burundi. See No. C127.

Winter Wren, Firecrest, Skylark and Crested Lark—A44

Birds: 2fr, 3.50fr and 5fr, vertical; others horizontal.

1970, Sept. 30 Photo. ***Perf. 13½***

Stamp Size: 44x33mm.

Gold Frame & Multicolored; Birds in Natural Colors

337	A44	2fr Block of four	38	12
a.		*Northern shrike*	9	
b.		*European starling*	9	
c.		*Yellow wagtail*	9	
d.		*Bank swallow*	9	
338	A44	3fr Block of four	62	15
a.		*Winter wren*	15	
b.		*Firecrest*	15	
c.		*Skylark*	15	
d.		*Crested lark*	15	
339	A44	3.50fr Block of four	70	20
a.		*Woodchat shrike*	16	
b.		*Common rock thrush*	16	
c.		*Black redstart*	16	
d.		*Ring ouzel*	16	
340	A44	4fr Block of four	80	20
a.		*European Redstart*	18	
b.		*Hedge sparrow*	18	
c.		*Gray wagtail*	18	
d.		*Meadow pipit*	18	
b.		A91 20fr like #571	60	

341 A44 5fr Block of four 1.00 20
 a. *Eurasian hoopoe* 24
 b. *Pied flycatcher* 24
 c. *Great reed warbler* 24
 d. *Eurasian kingfisher* 24
342 A44 6.50fr Block of four 1.30 25
 a. *House martin* 30
 b. *Sedge warbler* 30
 c. *Fieldfare* 30
 d. *European Golden oriole* 30
 Nos. 337-342, C132-C137 (12 blocks of 4) 26.75 5.67

Nos. 337–342 are printed in sheets of 16 containing 4 blocks of 4.

Library, U.N. Emblem—A45

Designs: 5fr, Students taking test, and emblem of University of Bujumbura. 7fr, Students in laboratory and emblem of Ecole Normale Supérieure of Burundi. 10fr, Students with electron-microscope and Education Year emblem.

1970, Oct. 23

343 A45 3fr gold & multi 12 4
344 A45 5fr gold & multi 20 5
345 A45 7fr gold & multi 30 8
346 A45 10fr gold & multi 40 10

Issued for International Education Year.

Pres. and Mrs. Michel Micombero
A46

Designs: 7fr, Pres. Michel Micombero and Burundi flag. 11fr, Pres. Micombero and Revolution Memorial.

1970, Nov. 28 Photo. *Perf. 13½*

347 A46 4fr gold & multi 15 6
348 A46 7fr gold & multi 25 12
349 A46 11fr gold & multi 40 17
 a. Souvenir sheet of 3 1.00 1.00

Issued to commemorate the 4th anniversary of independence. No. 349a contains 3 stamps similar to Nos. 347–349, but inscribed "Poste Aerienne." Dark gray and gold margin with commemorative inscription. Size: 125x143mm. Exists imperf.

See Nos. C140–C142.

Lenin with Delegates
A47

Designs (Lenin, Paintings): 5fr, addressing crowd. 6.50fr, with soldier and sailor. 15fr, speaking from balcony. 50fr, Portrait.

1970, Dec. 31 Photo. *Perf. 13½*

Gold Frame

350 A47 3.50fr dk red brn 14 6
351 A47 5fr dk red brn 20 8
352 A47 6.50fr dk red brn 28 12
353 A47 15fr dk red brn 60 25
354 A47 50fr dk red brn 2.00 35
 Nos. 350-354 (5) 3.22 86

Lenin's birth centenary (1870–1924).

Lion
A48

1971, March 19 Photo. *Perf. 13½*

Multicolored

Size: 38x38mm.

355 A48 1fr Strip of four 22 12
 a. *Lion* 5
 b. *Cape buffalo* 5
 c. *Hippopotamus* 5
 d. *Giraffe* 5
356 A48 2fr Strip of four 35 15
 a. *Hartebeest* 8
 b. *Black rhinoceros* 8
 c. *Zebra* 8
 d. *Leopard* 8
357 48 3fr Strip of four 50 25
 a. *Grant's gazelles* 12
 b. *Cheetah* 12
 c. *African white-backed vultures* 12
 d. *Johnston's okapi* 12
358 A48 5fr Strip of four 85 40
 a. *Chimpanzee* 20
 b. *Elephant* 20
 c. *Spotted hyenas* 20
 d. *Beisa* 20
359 A48 6fr Strip of four 1.00 45
 a. *Gorilla* 24
 b. *Gnu* 24
 c. *Wart hog* 24
 d. *Cape hunting dog* 24
360 A48 11fr Strip of four 2.00 90
 a. *Sable antelope* 45
 b. *Caracal lynx* 45
 c. *Ostriches* 45
 d. *Bongo* 45
 Nos. 355-360, C146-C151 (12 strips of 4) 22.67 5.82

The Resurrection, by Il Sodoma
A49

Paintings: 6fr, Resurrection, by Andrea del Castagno. 11fr, Noli me Tangere, by Correggio.

1971, Apr. 2

361 A49 3fr gold & multi 15 5
362 A49 6fr gold & multi 30 10
363 A49 11fr gold & multi 55 15
 a. Souvenir sheet of 3 1.10 1.10
 Nos. 361-363, C143-C145 (6) 2.80 88

Easter 1971. No. 363a contains one each of Nos. 361–363. Red and gold margin. Size: 120x85mm. Sheet exists imperf.

Young Venetian Woman, by Dürer
A50

Dürer Paintings: 11fr, Hieronymus Holzschuher. 14fr, Emperor Maximilian I. 17fr, Holy Family, from Paumgartner Altar. 26fr, Haller Madonna. 31fr, Self-portrait, 1498.

1971, Sept. 20

364 A50 6fr multi 25 12
365 A50 11fr multi 45 22
366 A50 14fr multi 55 28
367 A50 17fr multi 70 35
368 A50 26fr multi 1.00 50
369 A50 31fr multi 1.25 60
 a. Souvenir sheet of 2 2.50 2.50
 Nos. 364-369 (6) 4.20 2.07

International Letter Writing Week. Paintings by Dürer. 500th anniversary of the birth of Albrecht Dürer (1471–1528), German painter and engraver. No. 369a contains one each of Nos. 368–369. Tan margin with portrait of Erasmus. Size: 137x80mm. Exists imperf.

Nos. 364–369, 369a Overprinted in Black and Gold:

"VIème CONGRES / DE L'INSTITUT INTERNATIONAL / DE DROIT D'EXPRESSION FRANCAISE"

1971, Oct. 8

370 A50 6fr multi 25 6
371 A50 11fr multi 45 12
372 A50 14fr multi 55 15
373 A50 17fr multi 70 20
374 A50 26fr multi 1.00 30
375 A50 31fr multi 1.25 35
 a. Souvenir sheet of 2 2.50 2.50
 Nos. 370-375 (6) 4.20 1.18

6th Congress of the International Legal Institute of the French-speaking Area, Usumbura, Aug. 10–19.

Madonna and Child, by Il Perugino
A51

Paintings of the Madonna and Child by: 5fr, Andrea del Sarto. 6fr, Luis de Morales.

1971, Nov. 2 Photo. *Perf. 13½*

376 A51 3fr dk grn & multi 12 4
377 A51 5fr dk grn & multi 20 6
378 A51 6fr dk grn & multi 27 8
 a. Souvenir sheet of 3 75 75
 Nos. 376-378,C153-C155 (6) 2.79 1.13

Christmas 1971. No. 378a contains one each of Nos. 376–378. Multicolored border. Size: 125x81mm. Sheet exists imperf.

Lunar Orbiter
A52

Designs: 11fr, Vostok. 14fr, Luna 1. 17fr, Apollo 11 astronaut on moon. 26fr, Soyuz 11. 40fr, Lunar Rover (Apollo 15).

1972, Jan. 15

379 A52 6fr gold & multi 35 18
380 A52 11fr gold & multi 45 22
381 A52 14fr gold & multi 55 28
382 A52 17fr gold & multi 80 40
383 A52 26fr gold & multi 80 65
384 A52 40fr gold & multi 1.25 65
 a. Souvenir sheet of 6 4.25 4.25
 Nos. 379-384 (6) 4.20 2.38

Conquest of space. See No. C156.

No. 384a contains one each of Nos. 379–384 inscribed "APOLLO 16." Multicolored margin inscribed "La Conquête de l'Espace." Size: 134x135mm.

Slalom and Sapporo '72 Emblem
A53

Designs (Sapporo '72 Emblem and): 6fr, Figure skating, pairs. 11fr, Figure skating, women's. 14fr, Ski jump. 17fr, Ice hockey. 24fr, Speed skating, men's. 26fr, Snow scooter. 31fr, Downhill skiing. 50fr, Bobsledding.

1972, Feb. 3

385 A53 5fr sil & multi 15 5
386 A53 6fr sil & multi 20 7
387 A53 11fr sil & multi 35 10
388 A53 14fr sil & multi 45 15
389 A53 17fr sil & multi 55 15
390 A53 24fr sil & multi 75 18
391 A53 26fr sil & multi 80 20
392 A53 31fr sil & multi 1.00 25
393 A53 50fr sil & multi 1.60 40
 Nos. 385-393 (9) 5.85 1.55

11th Winter Olympic Games, Sapporo, Japan, Feb. 3–13. Printed in sheets of 12. See No. C157.

Issue dates: Nos. 385–390, Feb. 1; Nos. 391–393, Feb. 21.

Ecce Homo, by Quentin Massys
A54

Paintings: 6.50fr, Crucifixion, by Rubens. 10fr, Descent from the Cross, by Jacopo da Pontormo. 18fr, Pietà, by Ferdinand Gallegos. 27fr, Trinity, by El Greco.

1972, Mar. 20 Photo. *Perf. 13½*

394 A54 3.50fr gold & multi 8 4
395 A54 6.50fr gold & multi 25 8
396 A54 10fr gold & multi 35 12
397 A54 18fr gold & multi 65 20

398	A54	27fr gold & multi	95	30
a.		Souvenir sheet of 5+label	2.50	2.50
		Nos. 394-398 (5)	2.28	74

Easter 1972. Printed in sheets of 8 with label. No. 398a contains one each of Nos. 394–398 and decorative label. Dark brown and gold margin. Size: 120x 157mm. Exists imperf.

Gymnastics, Olympic Rings and "Motion"
A55

1972, May 19

Gold and Multicolored

399	A55	5fr *shown*	18	6
400	A55	6fr *Javelin*	20	7
401	A55	11fr *Fencing*	42	13
402	A55	14fr *Bicycling*	52	17
403	A55	17fr *Pole vault*	65	20
		Nos. 399-403, C158-C161 (9)	5.62	1.81

Souvenir Sheet

404	A55	Souv. sheeet of 2	2.50	2.50
a.		31fr *Discus*	90	90
b.		40fr *Soccer*	1.20	1.20

20th Olympic Games, Munich, Aug. 26–Sept. 11. No. 404 has multicolored margin with Olympic flag, "Motion" and commemorative inscription. Size: 126x80mm.

Prince Rwagasore, Pres. Micombero, Burundi Flag, Drummers
A56

Designs: 7fr, Rwagasore, Micombero, flag, map of Africa, globe. 13fr, Micombero, flag, globe.

1972, Aug. 24 Photo. *Perf. 13½*

405	A56	5fr sil & multi	15	5
406	A56	7fr sil & multi	25	8
407	A56	13fr sil & multi	45	15
a.		Souvenir sheet of 3	1.00	
		Nos. 405-407, C162-C164 (6)	2.85	95

10th anniversary of independence.

No. 407a contains one each of Nos. 405–407. Silver and light blue margin with black inscription. Size: 146x80mm.

Madonna and Child, by Andrea Solario
A57

Paintings of the Madonna and Child by: 10fr, Raphael. 15fr, Botticelli.

1972, Nov. 2

408	A57	5fr lt bl & multi	15	5
409	A57	10fr lt bl & multi	30	10
410	A57	15fr lt bl & multi	45	15
a.		Souvenir sheet of 3	1.00	
		Nos. 408-410, C165-167 (6)	3.45	1.07

Christmas 1972. Sheets of 20 stamps and one label. No. 410a contains one each of Nos. 408–410. Deep carmine and gold border. Size: 128x81mm.

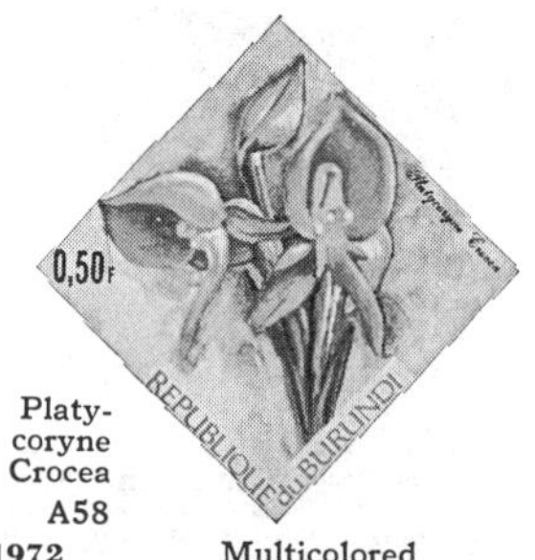

Platycoryne Crocea
A58

1972 **Multicolored**

Size: 33x33mm.

411	A58	50c *shown*	3	3
412	A58	1fr *Cattleya trianaei*	3	3
413	A58	2fr *Eulophia cucullata*	7	3
414	A58	3fr *Cymbidium hamsey*	10	5
415	A58	4fr *Thelymitra pauciflora*	13	6
416	A58	5fr *Miltassia*	17	8
417	A58	6fr *Miltonia*	20	10

Size: 38x38mm.

418	A58	7fr Like 50c	23	12
419	A58	8fr Like 1fr	27	13
420	A58	9fr Like 2fr	30	15
421	A58	10fr Like 3fr	35	17
		Nos. 411-421, C168-C174 (18)	6.35	2.09

Orchids. Issue dates: Nos. 411–417, Nov. 6; Nos. 418–421, Nov. 29.

Henry Morton Stanley—A59

Designs: 7fr, Porters, Stanley's expedition. 13fr, Stanley entering Ujiji.

1973, Mar. 19 Photo. *Perf. 13½*

422	A59	5fr gold & multi	15	5
423	A59	7fr gold & multi	20	7
424	A59	13fr gold & multi	40	13
		Nos. 422-424, C175-C177 (6)	2.55	85

Exploration of Africa by David Livingstone (1813–1873) and Henry Morton Stanley (John Rowlands; 1841–1904).

Crucifixion, by Roger van der Weyden
A60

Paintings: 5fr, Flagellation of Christ, by Caravaggio. 13fr, The Burial of Christ, by Raphael.

1973, Apr. 10

425	A60	5fr gold & multi	15	5
426	A60	7fr gold & multi	20	7
427	A60	13fr gold & multi	40	13
a.		Souvenir sheet of 3	1.00	1.00
		Nos. 425-427, C178-C180 (6)	3.00	85

Easter 1973. No. 427a contains one each of Nos. 425–427. Multicolored margin. Size: 121x73mm.

INTERPOL Emblem, Flag—A61

Design: 10fr, INTERPOL flag and emblem. 18fr, INTERPOL Headquarters and emblem.

1973, May 19 Photo. *Perf. 13½*

428	A61	5fr sil & multi	15	5
429	A61	10fr sil & multi	30	12
430	A61	18fr sil & multi	55	22
		Nos. 428-430, C181-C182 (5)	2.75	1.09

50th anniversary of International Criminal Police Organization (INTERPOL).

Signs of the Zodiac, Babylon—A62

Designs: 5fr, Greek and Roman gods representing planets. 7fr, Ptolemy (No. 433a) and Ptolemaic solar system. 13fr, Copernicus (No. 434a) and heliocentric system.

1973, July 27 Photo. *Perf. 13½*

Gold and Multicolored

431	A62	3fr Block of four	32	12
a.		3fr in UL	8	3
b.		3fr in UR	8	3
c.		3fr in LL	8	3
d.		3fr in LR	8	3
432	A62	5fr Block of four	60	12
a.		5fr in UL	15	3
b.		5fr in UR	15	3
c.		5fr in LL	15	3
d.		5fr in LR	15	3
433	A62	7fr Block of four	80	20
a.		7fr in UL	20	5
b.		7fr in UR	20	5
c.		7fr in LL	20	5
d.		7fr in LR	20	5
434	A62	13fr Block of four	1.60	40
a.		13fr in UL	40	10
b.		13fr in UR	40	10
c.		13fr in LL	40	10
d.		13fr in LR	40	10
e.		Souvenir sheet of 4	3.50	3.50
		Nos. 431-434, C183-C186 (8 blocks of 4)	18.32	4.54

500th anniversary of the birth of Nicolaus Copernicus (1473–1543), Polish astronomer.

Nos. 431–434 are printed in sheets of 32 containing 8 blocks of 4. No. 434e contains one each of Nos. 431–434. Gold and multicolored margin. Size: 136x136mm.

Flowers and Butterflies—A63

Designs: Each block of 4 contains 2 flower and 2 butterfly designs. The 1fr, 2fr, 5fr and 11fr have flower designs listed as "a" and "d" numbers, butterflies as "b" and "c" numbers; the arrangement is reversed for the 3fr and 6fr.

1973, Sept. 3 Photo. *Perf. 13*

Stamp Size: 34x41½mm.

Gold and Multicolored

435	A63	1fr Block of 4	16	12
a.		*Protea cynaroides*	4	3
b.		*Precis octavia*	4	3
c.		*Epiphora bauhiniae*	4	3
d.		*Gazania longiscapa*	4	3
436	A63	2fr Block of 4	32	12
a.		*Kniphofia*	8	3
b.		*Cymothoe coccinata*	8	3
c.		*Nudaurelia zambesina*	8	3
d.		*Freesia refracta*	8	3
437	A63	3fr Block of 4	48	12
a.		*Calotis eupompe*	12	3
b.		*Narcissus*	12	3
c.		*Cineraria hybrida*	12	3
d.		*Cyrestis camillus*	12	3
438	A63	5fr Block of 4	80	20
a.		*Iris tingitana*	20	5
b.		*Pappilio demodocus*	20	5
c.		*Catopsilia avelaneda*	20	5
d.		*Nerine sarniensis*	20	5
439	A63	6fr Block of 4	98	25
a.		*Hypolimnas dexithea*	24	6
b.		*Zantedeschia tropicalis*	24	6
c.		*Sandersonia aurantiaca*	24	6
d.		*Drurya antimachus*	24	6
440	A63	11fr Block of 4	1.80	45
a.		*Nymphaea capensis*	45	10
b.		*Pandoriana pandora*	45	10
c.		*Precis orythia*	45	10
d.		*Pelargonium domestica*	45	10
		Nos. 435-440, C187-C192 (12 blocks of 4)	24.39	6.21

Virgin and Child, by Giovanni Bellini
A64

Virgin and Child by: 10fr, Jan van Eyck. 15fr, Giovanni Boltraffio.

1973, Nov. 13 Photo. *Perf. 13*

441	A64	5fr gold & multi	15	3
442	A64	10fr gold & multi	30	8
443	A64	15fr gold & multi	45	12
a.		Souvenir sheet of 3	1.00	1.00
		Nos. 441-443, C193-C195 (6)	3.45	93

Christmas 1973. No. 443a contains one each of Nos. 441–443 with multicolored margin. Size: 143x79mm.

Pietá, by Paolo Veronese
A65

Paintings: 10fr, Virgin and St. John, by van der Weyden. 18fr, Crucifixion, by van der Weyden. 27fr, Burial of Christ, by Titian. 40fr, Pietá, by El Greco.

1974, Apr. 19 Photo. *Perf. 14x13½*

444	A65	5fr gold & multi	15	5
445	A65	10fr gold & multi	30	10
446	A65	18fr gold & multi	55	18
447	A65	27fr gold & multi	85	25
448	A65	40fr gold & multi	1.35	30
a.		Souvenir sheet of 5	3.25	3.25
		Nos. 444-448 (5)	3.20	88

Easter 1974. No. 448a contains one each of Nos. 444–448, rose brown and gold margin. Size: 145x120mm.

Fish—A66

Designs: Fish.

1974, May 30 Photo. *Perf. 13*

Stamp Size: 35x35mm.

Multicolored

No.	Type	Description	Unused	Used
449	A66	1fr Block of 4	12	12
a.		*Haplochromis multicolor*	3	3
b.		*Pantodon buchholzi*	3	3
c.		*Tropheus duboisi*	3	3
d.		*Distichodus sexfasciatus*	3	3
450	A66	2fr Block of 4	24	12
a.		*Pelmatochromis kribensis*	6	3
b.		*Nannaethiops tritaeniatus*	6	3
c.		*Polycentropsis abbreviata*	6	3
d.		*Hemichromis bimaculatus*	6	3
451	A66	3fr Block of 4	36	12
a.		*Ctenopoma acutirostre*	9	3
b.		*Synodontis angelicus*	9	3
c.		*Tilapia melanopleura*	9	3
d.		*Aphyosemion bivittatum*	9	3
452	A66	5fr Block of 4	60	12
a.		*Monodactylus argenteus*	15	3
b.		*Zanclus canescens*	15	3
c.		*Pygoplites diacanthus*	15	3
d.		*Cephalopholis argus*	15	3
453	A66	6fr Block of 4	72	18
a.		*Priacanthus arenatus*	18	4
b.		*Pomacanthus arcuatus*	18	4
c.		*Scarus guacamaia*	18	4
d.		*Zeus faber*	18	4
454	A66	11fr Block of 4	1.32	32
a.		*Lactophrys quadricornis*	33	8
b.		*Balistes vetula*	33	8
c.		*Acanthurus bahianus*	33	8
d.		*Holocanthus ciliaris*	33	8
		Nos. 449-454, C207-C212 (12 blocks of 4)	18.04	4.08

Soccer and Cup A67

Designs: Various soccer scenes and cup.

1974, July 4 Photogravure *Perf. 13*

No.	Type	Description	Unused	Used
455	A67	5fr gold & multi	15	
456	A67	6fr gold & multi	18	
457	A67	11fr gold & multi	33	
458	A67	14fr gold & multi	42	
459	A67	17fr gold & multi	50	
a.		Souvenir sheet of 3	2.75	2.75
		Nos. 455-459, C196-C198 (8)	4.16	

World Soccer Championship, Munich, June 13–July 7. No. 459a contains 3 stamps similar to Nos. C196–C198 without "Poste Aerienne." Gold and multicolored margin with picture of Munich City Hall. Size: 88x142mm.

Nos. 455–459 and 459a exist imperf.

Flags over UPU Headquarters, Bern A68

Designs: No. 461, G.P.O., Usumbura. No. 462, Mailmen ("11F" in UR). No. 463, Mailmen ("11F" in UL). No. 464, UPU emblem. No. 465, Means of transportation. No. 466, Pigeon over globe showing Burundi. No. 467, Swiss flag, pigeon over map showing Bern.

1974, July 23

No.	Type	Description	Unused	Used
460	A68	6fr gold & multi	24	
461	A68	6fr gold & multi	24	
462	A68	11fr gold & multi	45	
463	A68	11fr gold & multi	45	
464	A68	14fr gold & multi	55	
465	A68	14fr gold & multi	55	
466	A68	17fr gold & multi	70	
467	A68	17fr gold & multi	70	
a.		Souvenir sheet of 8	4.25	4.25
		Nos. 460-467, C199-C206 (16)	13.48	2.00

Centenary of Universal Postal Union. Stamps of same denomination printed se-tenant (continuous design) in sheets of 40.

No. 467a contains one each of Nos. 460–467. Violet, gold and light blue margin. Size: 96x162mm.

St. Ildefonso Writing Letter, by El Greco A69

Paintings: 11fr, Lady Sealing Letter, by Chardin. 14fr, Titus at Desk, by Rembrandt. 17fr, The Love Letter, by Vermeer. 26fr, The Merchant G. Gisze, by Holbein. 31fr, Portrait of Alexandre Lenoir, by David.

1974, Oct. 1 Photo. *Perf. 13*

No.	Type	Description	Unused	Used
468	A69	6fr gold & multi	18	
469	A69	11fr gold & multi	33	
470	A69	14fr gold & multi	42	
471	A69	17fr gold & multi	50	
472	A69	26fr gold & multi	78	
473	A69	31fr gold & multi	93	
a.		Souvenir sheet of 2	2.00	2.00
		Nos. 468-473 (6)	3.14	

International Letter Writing Week, Oct. 6–12. No. 473a contains one each of Nos. 472–473. Multicolored margin. Size: 95 x105mm. Sheet exists imperf.

Virgin and Child, by Bernaert van Orley A70

Paintings of the Virgin and Child: 10fr, by Hans Memling. 15fr, by Botticelli.

1974, Nov. 7 Photo. *Perf. 13*

No.	Type	Description	Unused	Used
474	A70	5fr gold & multi	15	
475	A70	10fr gold & multi	30	
476	A70	15fr gold & multi	45	
a.		Souvenir sheet of 3	1.00	1.00
		Nos. 474-476, C213-C215 (6)	3.45	2.50

Christmas 1974. Sheets of 20 stamps and one label. No. 476a contains one each of Nos. 474–476, gold and multicolored margin. Size: 137x90mm. Sheet exists imperf.

Apollo-Soyuz Space Mission and Emblem—A71

1975, July 10 Photo. *Perf. 13*

Multicolored

No.	Type	Description	Unused	Used
477	A71	26fr Block of 4	1.60	
a.		*A.A. Leonov, V.N. Kubasov, Soviet flag*	40	
b.		*Soyuz and Soviet flag*	40	
c.		*Apollo and American flag*	40	
d.		*D.K. Slayton, V.D. Brand, T.P. Stafford, American flag*	40	
478	A71	31fr Block of 4	2.20	
a.		*Apollo-Soyuz link-up*	55	
b.		*Apollo, blast-off*	55	
c.		*Soyuz, blast-off*	55	
d.		*Kubasov, Leonov, Slayton, Brand, Stafford*	55	
		Nos.477-478, C216-C217 (4 blocks of 4)	8.20	2.00

Apollo Soyuz space test project (Russo-American cooperation), launching July 15; link-up, July 17. Nos. 477–478 are printed in sheets of 32 containing 8 blocks of 4.

Addax A72

1975, July 31 Photo. *Perf. 13½*

Multicolored

No.	Type	Description	Unused	Used
479	A72	1fr Strip of four	12	
a.		*shown*	3	
b.		*Roan antelope*	3	
c.		*Nyala*	3	
d.		*White rhinoceros*	3	
480	A72	2fr Strip of four	24	
a.		*Mandrill*	6	
b.		*Eland*	6	
c.		*Salt's dik-dik*	6	
d.		*Thomson's gazelles*	6	
481	A72	3fr Strip of four	36	
a.		*African small-clawed otter*	9	
b.		*Reed buck*	9	
c.		*Indian civet*	9	
d.		*Cape buffalo*	9	
482	A72	5fr Strip of four	60	
a.		*White-tailed gnu*	15	
b.		*African wild asses*	15	
c.		*Black-and-white colobus monkey*	15	
d.		*Gerenuk*	15	
483	A72	6fr Strip of four	72	
a.		*Dama gazelle*	18	
b.		*Black-backed jackal*	18	
c.		*Sitatungas*	18	
d.		*Zebra antelope*	18	
484	A72	11fr Strip of four	1.32	
a.		*Fennec*	33	
b.		*Lesser kudus*	33	
c.		*Blesbok*	33	
d.		*Serval*	33	
		Nos. 479-484, C218-C223 (12 strips of 4)	18.02	2.25

Jonah, by Michelangelo A73

Designs: Paintings from Sistine Chapel.

1975, Dec. 3 Photo. *Perf. 13*

Multicolored

No.	Type	Description	Unused	Used
485	A73	5fr *shown*	15	
486	A73	5fr *Libyan Sybil*	15	
487	A73	13fr *Prophet Isaiah*	40	
488	A73	13fr *Delphic Sybil*	40	
489	A73	27fr *Daniel*	80	
490	A73	27fr *Cumaean Sybil*	80	
a.		Souvenir sheet of 6	3.00	3.00
		Nos. 485-490, C228-C233 (12)	8.04	1.25

Michelangelo Buonarotti (1475–1564), Italian sculptor, painter and architect. Stamps of same denominations printed se-tenant in sheets of 18 stamps and 2 labels. No. 490a contains one each of Nos. 485–490; brown & gold margin, black inscription. Size: 137x111mm.

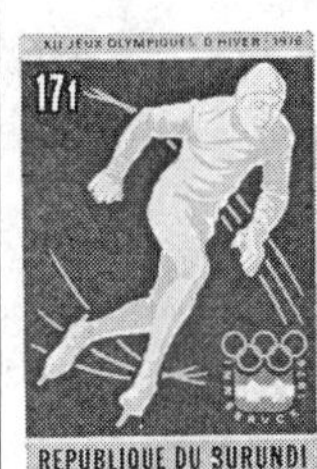

Speed Skating A74 — Basketball A75

Designs (Innsbruck Games Emblem and): 24fr, Figure skating, women's. 26fr, Two-man bobsled. 31fr, Cross-country skiing.

1976, Jan. 23 Photo. *Perf. 14x13½*

No.	Type	Description	Unused	Used
491	A74	17fr dp bl & multi	50	
492	A74	24fr multi	72	
493	A74	26fr multi	76	
494	A74	31fr plum & multi	93	
a.		Souvenir sheet of 3	3.25	3.25
		Nos. 491-494, C234-C236 (7)	6.03	75

12th Winter Olympic Games, Innsbruck, Austria, Feb. 4–15.

No. 494a contains 3 stamps similar to Nos. C234–C236, perf. 13½, without "POSTE AERIENNE." Multicolored margin with snowflakes and Games' emblem. Size: 130x62½mm.

1976, May 3 Litho. *Perf. 13½*

Designs (Montreal Games Emblem and): Nos. 496, 499, 503b, Pole vault. Nos. 497, 500, 503d, Running. Nos. 498, 501, 503a, Soccer. No. 502, 503c, Basketball.

No.	Type	Description	Unused	Used
495	A75	14fr bl & multi	42	
496	A75	14fr ol & multi	42	
497	A75	17fr mag & multi	50	
498	A75	17fr ver & multi	50	
499	A75	28fr ol & multi	80	
500	A75	28fr mag & multi	80	
501	A75	40fr ver & multi	1.20	
502	A75	40fr bl & multi	1.20	
		Nos. 495-502, C237-C242 (14)	12.26	1.75

Souvenir Sheet

No.	Type	Description	Unused	Used
503	A75	Sheet of 4	3.20	60
a.		14fr red & multi	42	
b.		17fr ol & multi	50	
c.		28fr bl & multi	80	
d.		40fr mag & multi	1.20	

21st Olympic Games, Montreal, Canada, July 17–Aug. 1. Stamps of same denomination printed se-tenant in sheets of 20.

No. 503 has gold inscription, black Montreal Olympic emblem and multicolored band in margin. Size: 115x120mm.

Virgin and Child, by Dirk Bouts

A76

Virgin and Child by: 13fr, Giovanni Bellini. 27fr, Carlo Crivelli.

1976, Oct. 18 Photo. *Perf. 13½*

504	A76	5fr gold & multi	15	
505	A76	13fr gold & multi	40	
506	A76	27fr gold & multi	80	
a.		Souvenir sheet of 3	1.50	
		Nos. 504-506, C250-C252 (6)	4.03	80

Christmas 1976. Sheets of 20 stamps and descriptive label. No. 506a contains one each of Nos. 504-506; multicolored margin. Size: 123x80mm.

St. Veronica, by Rubens

A77

Paintings by Rubens: 21fr, Christ on the Cross. 27fr, Descent from the Cross. 35fr, The Deposition.

1977, Apr. 5 Photo. *Perf. 13*

507	A77	10fr gold & multi	30
508	A77	21fr gold & multi	62
509	A77	27fr gold & multi	80
510	A77	35fr gold & multi	1.05
a.		Souvenir sheet of 4	3.00

Easter 1977. Sheets of 30 stamps and descriptive label. No. 510a contains 4 stamps similar to Nos. 507-510 inscribed "POSTE AERIENNE." Multicolored margin. Size: 111x85mm.

Alexander Graham Bell — A78

Intelsat Satellite, Modern and Old Telephones — A79

Designs: No. 513, Switchboard operator, c. 1910, and wall telephone. No. 514, Intelsat and radar. No. 515, A.G. Bell and first telephone. No. 516, Satellites around globe and videophone.

1977, May 17 Photo. *Perf. 13*

511	A78	10fr multi	16
512	A79	10fr multi	16
513	A78	17fr multi	28
514	A79	17fr multi	28
515	A78	26fr multi	45
516	A79	26fr multi	45
		Nos. 511-516, C253-C256 (10)	3.44

Centenary of first telephone call by Alexander Graham Bell, Mar. 10, 1876. Stamps of same denomination printed se-tenant in sheets of 32.

Buffon's Kob

A80

1977, Aug. 22 Photo. *Perf. 14x14½*

Multicolored

517	A80	2fr Strip of four	24
a.		*shown*	6
b.		*Marabous*	6
c.		*Brindled gnu*	6
d.		*River hog*	6
518	A80	5fr Strip of four	60
a.		*Zebras*	15
b.		*Shoebill*	15
c.		*Striped hyenas*	15
d.		*Chimpanzee*	15
519	A80	8fr Strip of four	96
a.		*Flamingos*	24
b.		*Nile crocodiles*	24
c.		*Green mamba*	24
d.		*Greater kudus*	24
520	A80	11fr Strip of four	1.36
a.		*Hyrax*	34
b.		*Cobra*	34
c.		*Jackals*	34
d.		*Verreaux's eagles*	34
521	A80	21fr Strip of four	2.56
a.		*Honey badger*	64
b.		*Harnessed antelopes*	64
c.		*Secretary bird*	64
d.		*Klipspringer*	64
522	A80	27fr Strip of four	2.80
a.		*African big-eared fox*	70
b.		*Elephants*	70
c.		*Vulturine guineafowl*	70
d.		*Impalas*	70
		Nos. 517-522, C258-C263 (12 strips of 4)	33.92

The Goose Girl, by Grimm

A81

Fairy Tales: 5fr, by Grimm Brothers. 11fr, by Aesop. 14fr, by Hans Christian Andersen. 17fr, by Jean de La Fontaine. 26fr, English fairy tales.

1977, Sept. 14 *Perf. 14*

Multicolored

523	A81	5fr Block of four	60
a.		*shown*	15
b.		*The Two Wanderers*	15
c.		*The Man of Iron*	15
d.		*Snow White and Rose Red*	15
524	A81	11fr Block of four	1.36
a.		*The Quarreling Cats*	34
b.		*The Blind and the Lame*	34
c.		*The Hermit and the Bear*	34
d.		*The Fox and the Stork*	34
525	A81	14fr Block of four	1.68
a.		*The Princess and the Pea*	42
b.		*The Old Tree Mother*	42
c.		*The Ice Maiden*	42
d.		*The Old House*	42
526	A81	17fr Block of four	2.00
a.		*The Oyster and the Suitors*	50
b.		*The Wolf and the Lamb*	50
c.		*Hen with the Golden Egg*	50
d.		*The Wolf as Shepherd*	50
527	A81	26fr Block of four	3.20
a.		*Three Heads in the Well*	80
b.		*Mother Goose*	80
c.		*Jack and the Beanstalk*	80
d.		*Alice in Wonderland*	80
		Nos. 523-527 (5 blocks of four)	8.84

Security Council Chamber, UN Nos. 28, 46, 37, C7—A82

Designs (UN Stamps and): 8fr, UN General Assembly, interior. 21fr, UN Meeting Hall.

1977, Oct. 10 Photo. *Perf. 13½*

528	A82	8fr Block of four	96
a.		No. 25	24
b.		No. C5	24
c.		No. 23	24
d.		No. 2	24
529	A82	10fr Block of four	1.20
a.		No. 28	30
b.		No. 46	30
c.		No. 37	30
d.		No. C7	30
530	A82	21fr Block of four	2.48
a.		No. 45	62
b.		No. 42	62
c.		No. 17	62
d.		No. 13	62
e.		Souvenir sheet of 3	1.30
		Nos. 528-530, C264-C266 (6 blocks of 4)	14.92

25th anniversary (in 1976) of the United Nations Postal Administration. No. 530e contains 8fr in design of No. 529d, 10fr in design of No. 530b, 21fr in design of No. 528c; silver margin. Size: 128x76mm.

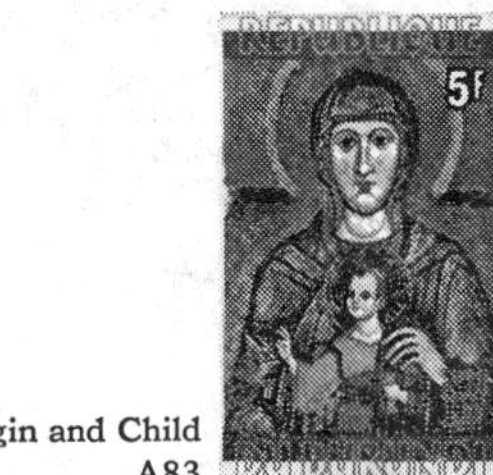

Virgin and Child

A83

Designs: Paintings of the Virgin and Child.

1977, Oct. 31 Photo. *Perf. 14x13*

531	A83	5fr By Meliore Toscano	15
532	A83	13fr By J. Lombardos	40
533	A83	27fr By Emmanuel Tzanes, 1610-1680	80
a.		Souvenir sheet of 3	1.50
		Nos. 531-533, C267-C269 (6)	4.05

Christmas 1977. Sheets of 24 stamps with descriptive label. No. 533a contains one each of Nos. 531-533; gold and multicolored margin. Size: 130x72mm.

Cruiser Aurora, Russia Nos. 211, 303, 1252, 187—A84

Designs (Russian Stamps and): 8fr, Kremlin, Moscow. 11fr, Pokrovski Cathedral, Moscow. 13fr, Labor Day parade, 1977 and 1980 Olympic Games emblem.

1977, Nov. 14 Photo. *Perf. 13*

534	A84	5fr Block of four	60
a.		No. 211	15
b.		No. 303	15
c.		No. 1252	15
d.		No. 187	15
535	A84	8fr Block of four	96
a.		No. 856	24
b.		No. 1986	24
c.		No. 908	24
d.		No. 2551	24
536	A84	11fr Block of four	1.36
a.		No. 3844b	34
b.		No. 3452	34
c.		No. 3382	34
d.		No. 3837	34
537	A84	13fr Block of four	1.60
a.		No. 4446	40
b.		No. 3497	40
c.		No. 2926	40
d.		No. 2365	40
		Nos. 534-537 (4 blocks of 4)	4.52

60th anniversary of Russian October Revolution.

Ship at Dock, Arms and Flag—A85

Burundi Arms and Flag and: 5fr, Men at lathes. 11fr, Male leopard dance. 14fr, Coffee harvest. 17fr, Government Palace.

1977, Nov. 25 Photo. *Perf. 13½*

538	A85	1fr sil & multi	3
539	A85	5fr sil & multi	15
540	A85	11fr sil & multi	35
541	A85	14fr sil & multi	42
542	A85	17fr sil & multi	50
		Nos. 538-542 (5)	1.45

15th anniversary of independence.

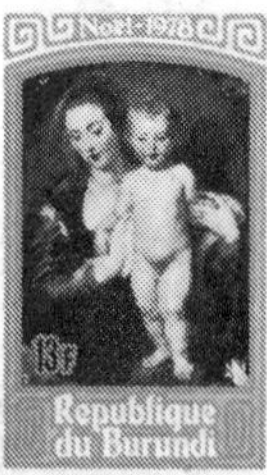

Virgin and Child, by Rubens

A86

Paintings of the Virgin and Child by: 13fr, Rubens. 17fr, Solario. 27fr, Tiepolo. 31fr, Gerard David. 40fr, Bellini.

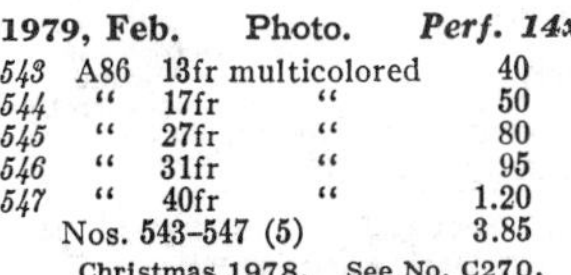

1979, Feb. Photo. *Perf. 14x13*

543	A86	13fr multicolored	40
544	"	17fr "	50
545	"	27fr "	80
546	"	31fr "	95
547	"	40fr "	1.20
		Nos. 543-547 (5)	3.85

Christmas 1978. See No. C270.

Abyssinian Hornbill—A87

1979 Photo. *Perf. 13½×13*

Multicolored

548	A87	1fr *shown*	3
549	A87	2fr *Snakebird*	6
550	A87	3fr *Melittophagus pusillus*	10
551	A87	5fr *Flamingo*	15
552	A87	8fr *Afropavo congensis*	25
553	A87	10fr *Gallinule*	30
554	A87	20fr *Martial eagle*	60
555	A87	27fr *Ibis*	80
556	A87	50fr *Saddle-billed stork*	1.50
		Nos. 548-556 (9)	3.79

See Nos. C273-C281.

Mother and Infant, IYC Emblem—A88

IYC Emblem and: 20fr, Infant. 27fr, Girl with doll. 50fr, Children in Children's Village.

1979, July 19 Photo. *Perf. 14*

557	A88	10fr multi	30
558	A88	20fr multi	60
559	A88	27fr multi	80
560	A88	50fr multi	1.50

International Year of the Child. See No. B82.

Virgin and Child, by del Garbo—A89

Virgin and Child by: 27fr, Giovanni Penni. 31fr, G. Romano. 50fr, Jacopo Bassano.

1979, Oct. 12

561	A89	20fr multi	60
562	A89	27fr multi	80
563	A89	31fr multi	95
564	A89	50fr multi	1.50
		Nos. 561-564, B83-B86 (8)	7.85

Christmas 1979. See Nos. C271, CB48.

Rowland Hill, Penny Black—A90

Stamps of Burundi: 27fr, German East Africa Nos. 17, N17. 31fr, Nos. 4, 24. 40fr, Nos. 29, 294. 60fr, Heinrich von Stephan, Nos. 464-465.

1979, Nov. 6

565	A90	20fr multi	60
566	A90	27fr multi	80
567	A90	31fr multi	95
568	A90	40fr multi	1.20
569	A90	60fr multi	1.80
		Nos. 565-569 (5)	5.35

Sir Rowland Hill (1795-1879), originator of penny postage. See No. C272.

A91

1980, Oct. 24 Photo. *Perf. 13x13½*

570	A91	20fr 110-meter hurdles	60
571	A91	20fr Hurdles, Thomas Munkelt	60
572	A91	20fr Hurdles, R.D.A.	60
573	A91	30fr Discus	90
574	A91	30fr Discus, V. Rasshchupkin	90
575	A91	30fr Discus, U.R.S.S.	90
576	A91	40fr Soccer, Tchecoslovaquie	1.20
577	A91	40fr "Football"	1.20
578	A91	40fr shown	1.20
		Nos. 570-578 (9)	8.10

22nd Summer Olympic Games, Moscow, July 19-Aug. 3. Stamps of same denomination se-tenant.

Virgin and Child, by Mainardi—A92

Christmas 1980 (Paintings): 30fr, Holy Family, by Michelangelo. 40fr, Virgin and Child, by di Cosimo. 45fr, Holy Family, by Fra Bartolomeo.

1980, Dec. 12 Photo. *Perf. 13½x13*

579	A92	10fr multi	30
580	A92	30fr multi	90
581	A92	40fr multi	1.20
582	A92	45fr multi	1.35
		Nos. 579-582, B87-B90 (8)	7.85

UPRONA Party National Congress, 1979—A93

1980, Dec. 29 *Perf. 14x13½*

583	A93	10fr multi	30
584	A93	40fr multi	1.20
585	A93	45fr multi	1.35

Johannes Kepler, Dish Antenna—A94

1981, Feb. 12 *Perf. 14*

586	A94	10fr shown	30
587	A94	40fr Satellite	1.20
588	A94	45fr Satellite, diff.	1.35
	a.	Souvenir sheet of 3	3.00

350th death anniversary of Johannes Kepler and first earth satellite station in Burundi. No. 588a contains Nos. 586-588; gold and red margin shows trajectory. Size: 78x109mm.

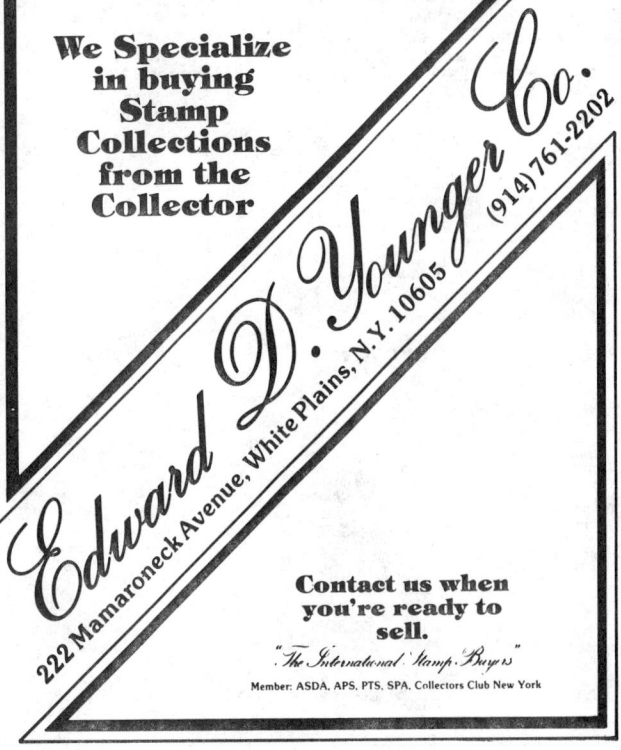

SEMI-POSTAL STAMPS

Prince Louis Rwagasore
SP1

Prince and Stadium—SP2

Design: 1.50fr+75c, 6.50fr+3fr, Prince and memorial monument.

Perf. 14x13, 13x14

1963, Feb. 15 Photo. Unwmkd.

B1	SP1	50c +25c brt vio	4	4
B2	SP2	1fr +50c red org & dk bl	6	6
B3	SP2	1.50fr +75c lem & dk vio	10	8
B4	SP1	3.50fr +1.50fr lil rose	15	12
B5	SP2	5fr +2fr rose pink & dk bl	25	15
B6	SP2	6.50fr +3fr gray ol & dk vio	30	20
		Nos. B1-B6 (6)	90	65

Issued in memory of Prince Louis Rwagasore (1932–61), son of King Mwami Mwambutsa IV and Prime Minister. The surtax was for the stadium and monument in his honor.

Red Cross Type of Regular Issue
Souvenir Sheet

1963, Sept. 26 Litho. *Imperf.*

B7	A5	Sheet of four	4.00	4.00
a.		4fr+2fr fawn, red & blk	65	65
b.		8fr+2fr grn, red & blk	75	75
c.		10fr+2fr gray, red & blk	85	85
d.		20fr+2fr ultra, red & blk	1.25	1.25

Issued to commemorate the centenary of the International Red Cross. The surtax was for Red Cross work in Burundi. Pale yellow margin with black and red inscription. Size: 90x140mm.

Olympic Type of Regular Issue
Souvenir Sheet

Designs: 18fr+2fr, Hurdling (horiz.). 20fr+5fr, Vaulting (horiz.).

1964, Nov. 18 *Perf. 13½*

B8	A13	Sheet of two	5.00	4.50
a.		18fr+2fr yel grn & multi	2.00	1.75
b.		20fr+5fr brt pink & multi	2.00	1.75

Issued to commemorate the 18th Olympic Games, Tokyo, Oct. 10–25, 1964. No. B8 has ornamental red brown border and black and blue marginal inscriptions. Size: 115x71mm.

Scientist with Microscope and Map of Burundi—SP3

Lithographed and Photogravure

1965, Jan. 28 *Perf. 14½* Unwmkd.

B9	SP3	2fr +50c tan, red & dk brn	12	8
B10	SP3	4fr +1.50fr pink, red & grn	28	12
B11	SP3	5fr +2.50fr ocher, red & vio	40	16
B12	SP3	8fr +3fr gray, red & dk bl	50	25
B13	SP3	10fr +5fr grnsh gray, red & red brn	75	32
		Nos. B9-B13 (5)	2.05	93

Souvenir Sheet
Perf. 13x13½

B14	SP3	10fr +10fr pale ol, red & dk brn	1.75	1.75

Issued for the fight against tuberculosis. No. B14 contains one stamp. Tan, red & dark brown margin. Size: 100x71mm.

Coat of Arms, 10fr Coin, Reverse
SP4

Designs (Coins of Various Denominations): 4fr+50c, 8fr+50c, 15fr+50c, 40fr+50c, King Mwambutsa IV, obverse.

Litho.; Embossed on Gilt Foil

1965, Aug. 9 *Imperf.*

Diameter: 39mm.

B15	SP4	2fr +50c crim & org	15	10
B16	SP4	4fr +50c ultra & ver	25	15

Diameter: 45mm.

B17	SP4	6fr +50c org & gray	35	25
B18	SP4	8fr +50c bl & mag	45	30

Diameter: 56mm.

B19	SP4	12fr +50c lt grn & red lil	70	50
B20	SP4	15fr +50c yel grn & lt lil	85	65

Diameter: 67mm.

B21	SP4	25fr +50c vio bl & buff	1.40	1.00
B22	SP4	40fr +50c brt pink & red brn	2.25	1.50
		Nos. B15-B22 (8)	6.40	4.45

Stamps are backed with patterned paper in blue, orange and pink engine-turned design.

Prince Louis Rwagasore and Pres. John F. Kennedy
SP5

Designs: 4fr+1fr, 20fr+5fr, Prince Louis and memorial. 20fr+2fr, 40fr+5fr, Pres. John F. Kennedy and library shelves. 40fr+2fr, King Mwambutsa IV at Kennedy grave, Arlington (vert.).

1966, Jan. 21 Photo. *Perf 13½*

B23	SP5	4fr +1fr gray bl & dk brn	20	5
B24	SP5	10fr +1fr pale grn, ind & brn	35	10
B25	SP5	20fr +2fr lil & dp grn	75	15
B26	SP5	40fr +2fr gray grn & dk brn	1.25	20

Souvenir Sheet

B27	SP5	Sheet of two	4.00	3.00
a.		20fr+5fr gray bl & dk brn	1.50	1.20
b.		40fr+5fr lil & dp grn	2.00	1.50

Issued in memory of Prince Louis Rwagasore and President John F. Kennedy. No. B27 has brown margin with picture of King Mwambutsa IV and inscription. Size: 75x90mm.

Republic

Winston Churchill and St. Paul's, London
SP6

Designs: 15fr+2fr, Tower of London and Churchill. 20fr+3fr, Big Ben and Churchill.

1967, March 23 Photo. *Perf.13½*

B28	SP6	4fr +1fr multi	20	6
B29	SP6	15fr +2fr multi	70	20
B30	SP6	20fr +3fr multi	90	35

Issued in memory of Sir Winston Churchill (1874–1965), statesman and World War II leader.

A souvenir sheet contains one airmail stamp, 50fr+5fr, with Churchill portrait centered, marginal decorations and inscriptions. Size: 80x80mm. Exists perf. and imperf. Price, each sheet, $3.50.

Nos. B28–B30 Overprinted

1967, July 14 Photo. *Perf. 13½*

B31	SP6	4fr +1fr multi	30	12
B32	SP6	15fr +2fr multi	85	40
B33	SP6	20fr +3fr multi	1.25	60

50th anniversary of Lions International. Exist with dates transposed.

The souvenir sheets described below No. B30 also received this Lions overprint. Price, each $3.50.

Blood Transfusion and Red Cross
SP7

Designs: 7fr+1fr, Stretcher bearers and wounded man. 11fr+1fr, Surgical team. 17fr+1fr, Nurses tending blood bank.

1969, June 26 Photo. *Perf. 13½*

B34	SP7	4fr +1fr multi	20	3
B35	SP7	7fr +1fr multi	30	8
B36	SP7	11fr +1fr multi	60	8
B37	SP7	17fr +1fr multi	65	15
		Nos. B34-B37, CB9-CB11 (7)	4.95	1.24

Issued to commemorate the 50th anniversary of the League of Red Cross Societies.

Pope Paul VI and Map of Africa—SP8

Designs: 3fr+2fr, 17fr+2fr, Pope Paul VI (vert.). 10fr+2fr, Flag made of flags of African Nations. 14fr+2fr, View of St. Peter's, Rome. 40fr+2fr, 40fr+5fr, Martyrs of Uganda. 50fr+2fr, 50fr+5fr, Pope on Throne. All designs include portrait of Pope Paul VI.

1969, Sept. 12 Photo. *Perf. 13½*

B38	SP8	3fr +2fr multi	15	3
B39	SP8	5fr +2fr multi	30	5
B40	SP8	10fr +2fr multi	45	10
B41	SP8	14fr +2fr multi	65	12
B42	SP8	17fr +2fr multi	75	15
B43	SP8	40fr +2fr multi	1.50	35
B44	SP8	50fr +2fr multi	1.75	40
		Nos. B38-B44 (7)	5.55	1.20

Souvenir Sheet

B45	SP8	Sheet of 2	4.00	3.50
a.		40fr+5fr multi	1.75	1.50
b.		50fr+5fr multi	2.00	1.75

Issued to commemorate the visit of Pope Paul VI to Uganda, July 31–Aug. 2. No. B45 contains 2 stamps, yellow margin with black inscription and church window design. Size: 80x102mm.

Virgin and Child, by Albrecht Dürer
SP9

Paintings: 11fr+1fr, Madonna of the Eucharist, by Sandro Botticelli. 20fr+1fr, Holy Family, by El Greco.

1970, Dec. 14 Photo. *Perf. 13½*

Gold Frame

B46	SP9	6.50fr +1fr multi	30	10
B47	SP9	11fr +1fr multi	45	15
B48	SP9	20fr +1fr multi	85	28
a.		Souvenir sheet of 3	1.75	1.75
		Nos. B46-B48, CB12-CB14 (6)	4.30	1.42

Christmas 1970. No. B48a contains one each of Nos. B46–B48 with ornamental border and inscription. Size: 135x75mm.

Nos. 376–378 Surcharged in Gold and Black

1971, Nov. 27

B49	A51	3fr +1fr multi	22	10
B50	A51	5fr +1fr multi	30	15
B51	A51	6fr +1fr multi	38	18
a.		Souvenir sheet of 3	1.10	1.10
		Nos. B49-B51, CB19-CB21 (6)	3.00	1.11

25th anniversary of the United Nations International Children's Fund (UNICEF). No. B51a contains 3 stamps similar to Nos. B49–B51 with 2fr surtax each. Size: 125x81mm.

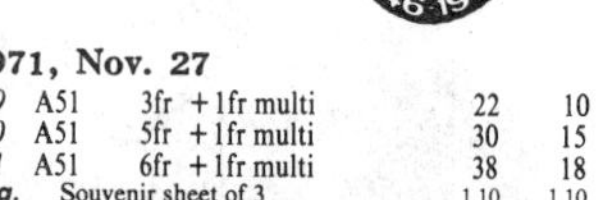

"La Polenta," by Pietro Longhi
SP10

Designs: 3fr+1fr, Archangel Michael, Byzantine icon from St. Mark's 6fr+1fr, "Gossip," by Pietro Longhi. 11fr+1fr, "Diana's Bath," by Giovanni Batista Pittoni. All stamps inscribed UNESCO.

1971, Dec. 27

B52	SP10	3fr +1fr gold & multi	15	6
B53	SP10	5fr +1fr gold & multi	24	10
B54	SP10	6fr +1fr gold & multi	28	12
B55	SP10	11fr +1fr gold & multi	48	20
a.		Souvenir sheet of 4	1.20	1.00
		Nos. B52-B55, CB22-CB25 (8)	3.68	1.48

The surtax was for the UNESCO campaign to save the treasures of Venice. No. B55a contains 4 stamps similar to Nos. B52–B55, but with 2fr surtax instead 1f. Gold and black ornamental margin. Size: 113x131½mm. Sheet exists imperf.

Nos. 408–410 Surcharged "+1F" in Silver

1972, Dec. 12 Photo. *Perf. 13½*

B56	A57	5fr +1fr multi	20	7
B57	A57	10fr +1fr multi	40	13
B58	A57	15fr +1fr multi	60	20
a.		Souvenir sheet of 3	1.40	1.40
		Nos. B56-B58, CB26-CB28 (6)	3.65	1.17

Christmas 1972. No. B58a contains 3 stamps similar to Nos. B56–B58, but with 2fr surtax. Deep carmine and gold border. Size: 128x81mm.

Nos. 441–443 Surcharged "+1F" in Silver

1973, Dec. 14 Photo. *Perf. 13*

B59	A64	5fr +1fr multi	20	6
B60	A64	10fr +1fr multi	40	12
B61	A64	15fr +1fr multi	60	18
a.		Souvenir sheet of 3	1.25	1.25
		Nos. B59-B61, CB29-CB31 (6)	3.80	1.18

Christmas 1973. No. B61a contains 3 stamps similar to Nos. B59–B61 with 2fr surtax each. Size: 143x79mm.

Christmas Type of 1974

1974, Dec. 2 Photogravure *Perf. 13*

B62	A70	5fr +1fr multi	25	15
B63	A70	10fr +1fr multi	40	25
B64	A70	15fr +1fr multi	60	38
a.		Souvenir sheet of 3	1.50	1.50
		Nos. B62-B64, CB32-CB34 (6)	4.30	1.35

No. B64a contains 3 stamps similar to Nos. B62–B64 with 2fr surtax each. Size: 137x90mm.

Nos. 485–490 Surcharged "+1 F" in Silver and Black

1975, Dec. 22 Photo. *Perf. 13*

Multicolored

B65	A73	5fr +1fr #485	20	
B66	A73	5fr +1fr #486	20	
B67	A73	13fr +1fr #487	45	
B68	A73	13fr +1fr #488	45	
B69	A73	27fr +1fr #489	85	
B70	A73	27fr +1fr #490	85	
a.		Souvenir sheet of 6	3.50	3.50
		Nos. B65-B70, CB35-CB40 (12)	8.60	1.75

Michelangelo Buonarroti (1475–1564), 500th birth anniversary. No. B70a contains 6 stamps similar to Nos. B65–B70 with 2fr surcharge each. Size: 132x106 mm.

Nos. 504–506 Surcharged "+1f" in Silver and Black

1976, Nov. 25 Photo. *Perf. 13½*

B71	A76	5fr +1fr multi	18	
B72	A76	13fr +1fr multi	45	
B73	A76	27fr +1fr multi	85	
a.		Souvenir sheet of 3	1.75	1.75
		Nos. B71-B73, CB41-CB43 (6)	4.33	1.50

Christmas 1976. No. B73a contains 3 stamps similar to Nos. B71–B73 with 2fr surtax each. Size: 123x80mm.

Nos. 531–533 Surcharged "+1fr" in Silver and Black

1977 Photo. *Perf. 14x13*

B74	A83	5fr +1fr multi	18	
B75	A83	13fr +1fr multi	45	
B76	A83	27fr +1fr multi	85	
a.		Souvenir sheet of 3	1.75	1.75
		Nos. B74-B76, CB44-CB46 (6)	4.31	

Christmas 1977. No. B76a contains 3 stamps similar to Nos. B74–B76 with 2fr surtax each. Size: 130x71mm.

Christmas Type of 1979

1979, Feb. Photo. *Perf. 14x13*

B77	A86	13fr +1fr multi	45	
B78	A86	17fr +1fr multi	55	
B79	A86	27fr +1fr multi	85	
B80	A86	31fr +1fr multi	1.00	
B81	A86	40fr +1fr multi	1.25	
		Nos. B77-B81 (5)	4.10	

Christmas 1978.

IYC Type of 1979

1979, July 19 Photo. *Perf. 14*

B82	Sheet of 4, multi	3.75	3.00
a.	+2fr *like* #557	35	25
b.	+2fr *like* #558	65	45
c.	+2fr *like* #559	88	60
d.	+2fr *like* #560	1.50	1.00

International Year of the Child. No. B82 has multicolored margin showing detail from Virgin and Child by Rubens, IYC emblem. Size: 131x85mm.

Christmas Type of 1979

1979, Dec. 10 Photo *Perf. 13½*

B83	A89	20fr +1fr *like* #561	65	
B84	A89	27fr +1fr *like* #562	85	
B85	A89	31fr +1fr *like* #563	95	
B86	A89	50fr +2fr *like* #564	1.55	

Christmas Type of 1980

1981, Jan. 16 Photo. *Perf. 13½x13*

B87	A92	10fr +1fr *like* #579	35	
B88	A92	30fr +1fr *like* #580	95	
B89	A92	40fr +1fr *like* #581	1.25	
B90	A92	50fr +1fr *like* #582	1.55	

Christmas 1980.

AIR POST STAMPS

Animal Type of Regular Issue.

Animals: 6fr, Zebra. 8fr, Cape buffalo (bubalis). 10fr, Impala (vert.). 14fr, Hippopotamus. 15fr, Defassa waterbuck (vert.). 20fr, Cheetah. 50fr, Elephant.

Lithographed

1964, July 2 *Perf. 14* Unwmkd.

Border in Gold

Size: 42x21mm., 21x42mm.

C1	A9	6fr multi	40	5
C2	A9	8fr multi	50	8
C3	A9	10fr multi	65	10
C4	A9	14fr multi	90	15
C5	A9	15fr multi	1.00	18

Size: 53x32½mm.

C6	A9	20fr multi	1.35	30
C7	A9	50fr multi	3.50	75
		Nos. C1-C7 (7)	8.30	1.61

Bird Type of Regular Issue

Birds: 6fr, Secretary bird. 8fr, African anhinga. 10fr, African peacock. 14fr, Bee eater. 15fr, Yellow-billed stork. 20fr, Saddle-billed stork. 50fr, Abyssinian ground hornbill. 75fr, Martial eagle. 130fr, Lesser flamingo.

1965, June 10 Litho. *Perf. 14*

Birds in Natural Colors, Border in Gold.

Size: 26x43mm.

C8	A14	6fr multi	20	5
C9	A14	8fr multi	25	8
C10	A14	10fr multi	30	10
C11	A14	14fr multi	45	12
C12	A14	15fr multi	45	15

Size: 33x53mm.

C13	A14	20fr multi	60	13
C14	A14	50fr multi	1.50	40
C15	A14	75fr multi	2.20	50
C16	A14	130fr multi	4.00	75
		Nos. C8-C16 (9)	9.95	2.28

Flower Type of Regular Issue

Flowers: 6fr, Dissotis. 8fr, Crossandra. 10fr, Ansellia. 14fr, Thunbergia. 15fr, Schizoglossum. 20fr, Gazania. 50fr, Protea. 75fr, Hibiscus. 130fr, Markhamia.

1966, Oct. 10 *Perf. 13½* Unwmkd.

Gold Background.

Size: 31x31mm.

C17	A17	6fr multi	15	5
C18	A17	8fr multi	20	8
C19	A17	10fr multi	25	10
C20	A17	14fr multi	35	12
C21	A17	15fr multi	35	15

Size: 39x39mm.

C22	A17	20fr multi	50	18
C23	A17	50fr multi	1.25	40
C24	A17	75fr multi	1.85	50
C25	A17	130fr multi	3.35	75
		Nos. C17-C25 (9)	8.25	2.33

Souvenir Sheet

Tapestry Type of Regular Issue

1966, Nov. 4 *Perf. 13½* Unwmkd.

C26	A18	Sheet of 7 (14fr)	3.50	2.00

See note after No. 158.

Republic

Nos. C17–C25, Overprinted

REPUBLIQUE

DU

BURUNDI

1967 Lithographed *Perf. 13½*

Size: 31x31mm.

Gold Background

C27	A17	6fr multi	38	13
C28	A17	8fr multi	45	15
C29	A17	10fr multi	50	17
C30	A17	14fr multi	75	25
C31	A17	15fr multi	75	25

Size: 39x39mm.

C32	A17	20fr multi	1.10	35
C33	A17	50fr multi	3.00	1.00
C34	A17	75fr multi	4.75	1.00
C35	A17	130fr multi	6.50	2.10
		Nos. C27-C35 (9)	18.18	5.40

Nos. C8–C16 Overprinted "REPUBLIQUE / DU / BURUNDI" and Horizontal Bar

1967 Lithographed *Perf. 14*

Birds in Natural Colors, Border in Gold

Size: 26x43mm.

C35A	A14	6fr multi	*30*
C35B	A14	8fr multi	*35*
C35C	A14	10fr multi	*40*
C35D	A14	14fr multi	*60*
C35E	A14	15fr multi	*75*

Size: 33x53mm

C35F	A14	20fr multi	*1.20*
C35G	A14	50fr multi	*3.00*
C35H	A14	75fr multi	*4.75*
C35I	A14	130fr multi	*5.50*
		Nos. C35A-C35I (9)	*16.85*

African Art Type of Regular Issue

African Art: 10fr, Spirit of Bakutu figurine, Equatorial Africa. 14fr, Pearl throne of Sultan of the Bamum, Cameroun. 17fr, Bronze head of Mother Queen of Benin, Nigeria. 24fr, Statue of 109th Bakouba king, Kata-Mbula, Central Congo. 26fr, Baskets and lances, Burundi.

1967, June 5 Photo. *Perf. 13½*

C36	A20	10fr gold & multi	30	20
C37	A20	14fr gold & multi	40	20
C38	A20	17fr gold & multi	45	20
C39	A20	24fr gold & multi	65	40
C40	A20	26fr gold & multi	1.20	75
		Nos. C36-C40 (5)	3.00	1.75

Boy Scout Type of Regular Issue

Designs: 10fr, Scouts on hiking trip. 14fr, Cooking at campfire. 17fr, Lord Baden-Powell. 24fr, Boy Scout and Cub Scout giving Scout sign. 26fr, First aid.

1967, Aug. 9 *Perf. 13½*

C41	A21	10fr gold & multi	30	20
C42	A21	14fr gold & multi	45	20
C43	A21	17fr gold & multi	55	20
C44	A21	24fr gold & multi	85	35
C45	A21	26fr gold & multi	1.40	35
		Nos. C41-C45 (5)	3.55	1.30

Issued to commemorate the 60th anniversary of the Boy Scouts and the 12th Boy Scout World Jamboree, Farragut State Park, Idaho, Aug. 1–9.

A souvenir sheet of 2 contains one each of Nos. C44–C45 and 2 labels in the designs of Nos. 208–209 with commemorative inscriptions was issued Jan. 8, 1968. Size: 100x100mm.

Fish Type of Regular Issue

Designs: Various Tropical Fish

1967, Sept. 8 Photo. *Perf. 13½*

Size: 50x23mm.

C46	A19	6fr multi	20	5
C47	A19	8fr multi	25	6
C48	A19	10fr multi	30	8
C49	A19	14fr multi	45	10
C50	A19	15fr multi	45	12

Size: 58x27mm.

C51	A19	20fr multi	65	14
C52	A19	50fr multi	1.50	25
C53	A19	75fr multi	2.25	35
C54	A19	130fr multi	4.00	60
		Nos. C46-C54 (9)	10.05	1.75

Boeing 707 of Air Congo and ITY Emblem

AP1

Designs: 14fr, Boeing 727 of Sabena over lake. 17fr, Vickers VC10 of East African Airways over lake. 26fr, Boeing 727 of Sabena over airport.

1967, Nov. 3 Photo. *Perf. 13*

C55	AP1	10fr blk, yel brn & sil	25	10
C56	AP1	14fr blk, org & sil	40	15
C57	AP1	17fr blk, brt bl & sil	50	20
C58	AP1	26fr blk, brt rose lil & sil	85	30

Issued to commemorate the opening of the jet airport at Bujumbura and for International Tourist Year, 1967.

Paintings Type of Regular Issue

Paintings: 17fr, Woman with Cat, by Renoir. 24fr, The Jewish Bride, by Rembrandt (horiz.). 26fr, Pope Innocent X, by Velazquez.

1968, Mar. 29 Photo. *Perf. 13½*

Light Green and Gold Frame

C59	A26	17fr multi	70	30
C60	A26	24fr multi	90	35
C61	A26	26fr multi	1.10	40

Issued in sheets of 6.

Space Type of Regular Issue

Designs: 14fr, Moon Probe. 18fr, Russian astronaut walking in space. 25fr, Weather satellite. 40fr, American astronaut walking in space.

1968, May 15 Photo. *Perf. 13½*

Size: 41x41mm.

C62	A27	14fr sil & multi	50	10
C63	A27	18fr sil & multi	60	18
C64	A27	25fr sil & multi	90	20
C65	A27	40fr sil & multi	1.40	35

Issued to publicize peaceful space explorations.

Butterfly Type of Regular Issue

Butterflies: 6fr, Teracolus annae. 8fr, Graphium ridleyanus. 10fr, Cymothoe. 14fr, Charaxes eupale. 15fr, Papilio bromius. 20fr, Papilio zenobia. 50fr, Salamis aethiops. 75fr, Danais chrysippus. 130fr, Salamis temora.

1968, Sept. 9 Photo. *Perf. 13½*

Size: 38x42mm.

C66	A28	6fr gold & multi	20	3
C67	A28	8fr gold & multi	25	4
C68	A28	10fr gold & multi	30	5
C69	A28	14fr gold & multi	45	5
C70	A28	15fr gold & multi	50	8

Size: 44x49mm.

C71	A28	20fr gold & multi	75	12
C72	A28	50fr gold & multi	1.75	18
C73	A28	75fr gold & multi	2.50	25
C74	A28	130fr gold & multi	4.50	40
		Nos. C66-C74 (9)	11.20	1.20

Painting Type of Regular Issue

Paintings: 17fr, The Letter, by Jean H. Fragonard. 26fr, Young Woman Reading Letter, by Jan Vermeer. 40fr, Lady Folding Letter, by Elisabeth Vigée-Lebrun. 50fr, Mademoiselle Lavergne, by Jean Etienne Liotard.

1968, Sept. 30 Photo. *Perf. 13½*

C84	A29	17fr multi	45	12
C85	A29	26fr multi	85	20
C86	A29	40fr multi	1.15	28
C87	A29	50fr multi	1.40	35

Issued for International Letter Writing Week, Oct. 7-13.

Olympic Games Type of 1968

Designs: 10fr, Shot put. 17fr, Running. 26fr, Hammer throw. 50fr, Hurdling. 75fr, Broad jump.

1968, Oct. 24

C88	A30	10fr gold & multi	25	8
C89	A30	17fr gold & multi	45	12
C90	A30	26fr gold & multi	75	20
C91	A30	50fr gold & multi	1.40	40
C92	A30	75fr gold & multi	2.10	60
		Nos. C88-C92 (5)	4.95	1.40

Issued to commemorate the 19th Olympic Games, Mexico City, Oct. 12-27.

Christmas Type of 1968

Paintings: 10fr, Virgin and Child, by Correggio. 14fr, Nativity, by Federigo Baroccio. 17fr, Holy Family, by El Greco. 26fr, Adoration of the Magi, by Maino.

1968, Nov. 26 Photo. *Perf. 13½*

C93	A31	10fr multi	30	15
C94	A31	14fr multi	45	20
C95	A31	17fr multi	55	25
C96	A31	26fr multi	80	30
a.		Souv. sheet of 4	2.25	

No. C96a contains one each of Nos. C93-C96, decorative border and inscriptions. Size: 120x120mm.

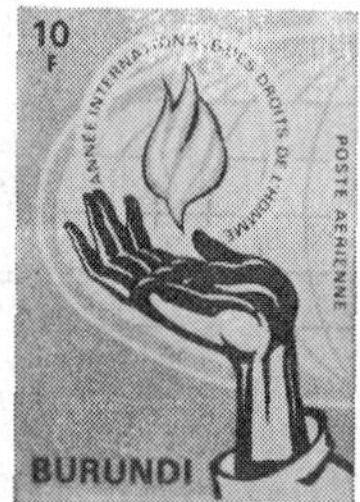

Human Rights Flame, Hand and Globe
AP2

1969, Jan. 22

C97	AP2	10fr multi	30	10
C98	AP2	14fr multi	42	10
C99	AP2	26fr lil & multi	80	25

International Human Rights Year, 1968.

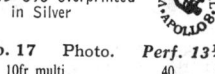

Nos. C93-C96 Overprinted in Silver

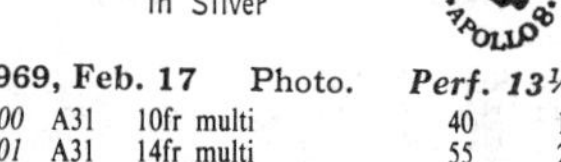

1969, Feb. 17 Photo. *Perf. 13½*

C100	A31	10fr multi	40	15
C101	A31	14fr multi	55	25
C102	A31	17fr multi	70	28
C103	A31	26fr multi	1.00	45

Issued to commemorate man's first flight around the moon by the U.S. spacecraft Apollo 8, Dec. 21-27, 1968.

Moon Landing Type of 1969

Designs: 26fr, Neil A. Armstrong leaving landing module. 40fr, Astronaut on moon. 50fr, Splashdown in the Pacific.

1969, Nov. 6 Photo. *Perf. 13½*

C104	A38	26fr gold & multi	1.00	50
C105	A38	40fr gold & multi	1.50	75
C106	A38	50fr gold & multi	1.80	85

See note after Algeria No. 427.

Christmas Type of 1969

Paintings: 17fr, Madonna and Child, by Benvenuto da Garofalo. 26fr, Madonna and Child, by Jacopo Negretti. 50fr, Madonna and Child, by Il Giorgione. All horizontal.

1969, Dec. 2 Photogravure

C107	A39	17fr gold & multi	75	15
C108	A39	26fr gold & multi	1.00	25
C109	A39	50fr gold & multi	1.80	55
a.		Souvenir sheet of 3	3.00	3.00

No. C109a contains one each of Nos. C107-C109. Gold frame with black and red inscription. Size: 87x110mm.

Insect Type of Regular Issue

Designs: Various Beetles and Weevils.

1970 *Perf. 13½*

Size: 46x32mm.

C110	A40	6fr gold & multi	15	3
C111	A40	8fr gold & multi	20	3
C112	A40	10fr gold & multi	25	3
C113	A40	14fr gold & multi	45	3
C114	A40	15fr gold & multi	50	4

Size: 52x36mm.

C115	A40	20fr gold & multi	65	6
C116	A40	50fr gold & multi	1.60	50
C117	A40	75fr gold & multi	2.40	50
C118	A40	130fr gold & multi	4.00	80
		Nos. C110-C118 (9)	10.20	2.02

Issue dates: Nos. C110-C115, Jan. 20. Nos. C116-C118, Feb. 27.

Easter Type of 1970

Stations of the Cross, by Juan de Aranoa y Carredano: 8fr, Jesus meets the women of Jerusalem. 10fr, Jesus falls a third time. 14fr, Jesus stripped. 15fr, Jesus nailed to the cross. 18fr, Jesus dies on the cross. 20fr, Descent from the cross. 50fr, Jesus laid in the tomb.

1970, Mar. 16 Photo. *Perf. 13½*

C119	A41	8fr gold & multi	25	10
C120	A41	10fr gold & multi	30	12
C121	A41	14fr gold & multi	45	18
C122	A41	15fr gold & multi	50	20
C123	A41	18fr gold & multi	55	22
C124	A41	20fr gold & multi	60	25
C125	A41	50fr gold & multi	1.40	60
a.		Souv. sheet of 7 + label	3.50	3.50
		Nos. C119-C125 (7)	4.05	1.67

No. C125a contains one each of Nos. C119-C125 and label showing Ascension. Gold decorative border. Size: 154x123mm.

EXPO '70 Type of Regular Issue

Souvenir Sheet

Designs: 40fr, Tower of the Sun (vert.). 50fr, Flags of participating nations (vert.).

1970, May 5 Photo. *Perf. 13½*

C126	A42	Souv. sheet of 2	2.75	2.75
a.		40fr multi	95	95
b.		50f multi	1.20	1.20

Issued to publicize EXPO '70 International Exhibition, Osaka, Japan, March 15-Sept. 13, 1970. No. C126 has gold and black decorative border. Size: 104½x80mm.

Rhinoceros Type of Regular Issue

Designs, FAUNA: Camel, dromedary, okapi, rhinoceros, addax, Burundi cow (2 stamps of each animal in 2 different poses). MAP OF THE NILE: Delta and pyramids, dhow, cataract, Blue Nile and crowned crane, Victoria Nile and secretary bird, Lake Victoria and source of Nile on Mt. Gikizi.

1970, July 8 Photo. *Perf. 13½*

C127	A43	14fr multi	56	20
a.		Sheet of 18	10.50	

Issued in sheets of 18 (3x6) stamps of different designs, to publicize the southernmost source of the Nile on Mt. Gikizi in Burundi.

U.N. Emblem and Headquarters, N.Y.
AP3

Designs (U.N. Emblem and): 11fr, Security Council and mural by Per Krohg. 26fr, Pope Paul VI and U Thant. 40fr, Flags in front of U.N. Headquarters, N.Y.

1970, Oct. 23 Photo. *Perf. 13½*

C128	AP3	7fr gold & multi	20	5
C129	AP3	11fr gold & multi	35	8
C130	AP3	26fr gold & multi	75	15
C131	AP3	40fr gold & multi	1.20	25
a.		Souvenir sheet of 2	2.00	1.75

Issued to commemorate the 25th anniversary of the United Nations. No. C131a contains 2 stamps similar to Nos. C130-C131 but without "Poste Aerienne"; blue margin with gold ornament, black inscription and U.N. emblem. Size: 123x80mm. Exists imperf.

Bird Type of Regular Issue

Birds: 8fr, 14fr, 30fr, vertical; 10fr, 20fr, 50fr, horizontal.

1970 Photogravure *Perf. 13½*

Gold Frame & Multicolored; Birds in Natural Colors

Stamp size: 52x44mm.

C132	A44	8fr Block of four	1.10	25
a.		*Northern shrike*	25	6
b.		*European starling*	25	6
c.		*Yellow wagtail*	25	6
d.		*Bank swallow*	25	6
C133	A44	10fr Block of four	1.60	35
a.		*Winter wren*	38	8
b.		*Firecrest*	38	8
c.		*Skylark*	38	8
d.		*Crested lark*	38	8
C134	A44	14fr Block of four	2.10	50
a.		*Woodchat shrike*	50	12
b.		*Common rock thrush*	50	12
c.		*Black redstart*	50	12
d.		*Ring ouzel*	50	12
C135	A44	20fr Block of four	3.40	65
a.		*European redstart*	80	15
b.		*Hedge sparrow*	80	15
c.		*Gray wagtail*	80	15
d.		*Meadow pipit*	80	15
C136	A44	30fr Block of four	5.25	1.05
a.		*Eurasian hoopoe*	1.20	25
b.		*Pied flycatcher*	1.20	25
c.		*Great reed warbler*	1.20	25
d.		*Eurasian kingfisher*	1.20	25
C137	A44	50fr Block of four	8.50	1.75
a.		*House martin*	2.00	40
b.		*Sedge warbler*	2.00	40
c.		*Fieldfare*	2.00	40
d.		*European Golden oriole*	2.00	40
		Nos. C132-C137 (6 blocks of 4)	21.95	4.55

Nos. C132-C137 are printed in sheets of 16 containing 4 blocks of 4.

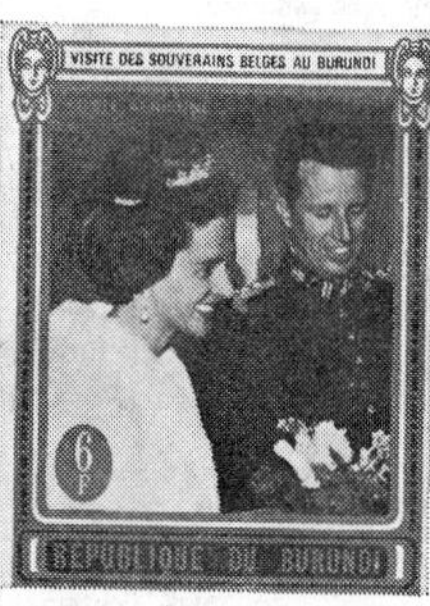

Queen Fabiola and King Baudouin of Belgium
AP4

Designs: 20fr, Pres. Michel Micombero and King Baudouin. 40fr, Pres. Micombero and coats of arms of Burundi and Belgium.

1970, Nov. 28 Photo. *Perf. 13½*

C140	AP4	6fr gold, dp brn & dp plum	30	10
C141	AP4	20fr gold, dp brn & dp plum	90	30
C142	AP4	40fr gold, dp brn & dp plum	1.85	60
a.		Souvenir sheet of 3	3.00	3.00

Issued to commemorate the visit of the King and Queen of Belgium. No. C142a contains 3 stamps similar to Nos. C140-C142, but without "Poste Aerienne." Deep plum and gold margin with commemorative inscription. Size: 143½x108mm.

Easter Type of Regular Issue

Paintings of the Resurrection: 14fr, by Louis Borrassá. 17fr, Piero della Francesca. 26fr, Michel Wohlgemuth.

1971, Apr. 2 Photo. *Perf. 13½*

C143	A49	14fr gold & multi	50	15
C144	A49	17fr gold & multi	55	18
C145	A49	26fr gold & multi	75	25
a.		Souvenir sheet of 3	1.90	1.50

Easter 1971. No. C145a contains one each of Nos. C143-C145. Red and gold margin. Size: 120x85mm. Sheet exists imperf.

Animal Type of Regular Issue

1971 Photogravure *Perf. 13½*

Multicolored

Size: 44x44mm.

C146	A48	10fr Strip of four	1.25	25
a.		*Lion*	30	6
b.		*Cape buffalo*	30	6
c.		*Hippopotamus*	30	6
d.		*Giraffe*	30	6
C147	A48	14fr Strip of four	2.25	45
a.		*Hartebeest*	50	10
b.		*Black rhinoceros*	50	10
c.		*Zebra*	50	10
d.		*Leopard*	50	10
C148	A48	17fr Strip of four	2.50	50
a.		*Grant's gazelles*	60	12
b.		*Cheetah*	60	12
c.		*African white-backed vultures*	60	12
d.		*Johnston's okapi*	60	12
C149	A48	24fr Strip of four	3.25	65
a.		*Chimpanzee*	75	15
b.		*Elephant*	75	15
c.		*Spotted Hyenas*	75	15
d.		*Beisa*	75	15

C150 A48 26fr Strip of four 4.00 80
a. *Gorilla* 90 20
b. *Gnu* 90 20
c. *Warthog* 90 20
d. *Cape hunting dog* 90 20
C151 A48 31fr Strip of four 4.50 90
a. *Sable antelope* 1.00 22
b. *Caracal lynx* 1.00 22
c. *Ostriches* 1.00 22
d. *Bongo* 1.00 22
Nos. C146-C151 (6 strips of 4) 17.75 3.55

No. C146 Overprinted in Gold and Black

LUTTE CONTRE LE RACISME ET
LA DISCRIMINATION RACIALE

1971, July 20 Photo. *Perf. 13½*

C152 A48 10fr Strip of four 1.20 24
a. *Lion* 30 5
b. *Cape buffalo* 30 5
c. *Hippopotamus* 30 5
d. *Giraffe* 30 5

International Year Against Racial Discrimination.

Christmas Type of Regular Issue

Paintings of the Madonna and Child by: 14fr, Cima de Conegliano. 17fr, Fra Filippo Lippi. 31fr, Leonardo da Vinci.

1971, Nov. 2 Photo. *Perf. 13½*

C153 A51 14fr red & multi 55 25
C154 A51 17fr red & multi 65 30
C155 A51 31fr red & multi 1.00 40
a. Souvenir sheet of 3 2.25 2.25

Christmas 1971. No. C155a contains one each of Nos. C153-C155. Multicolored margin. Size: 125x81mm. Sheet exists imperf.

Spacecraft Type of Regular Issue
Souvenir Sheet

1972, Jan. 15 Photo. *Perf. 13½*

C156 A52 Sheet of 6, multi 3.00 2.00
a. 6fr *Lunar Orbiter* 15 8
b. 11fr *Vostok* 30 15
c. 14fr *Luna I* 35 18
d. 17fr *Apollo 11 astronaut on moon* 42 20
e. 26fr *Soyuz 11* 70 35
f. 40fr *Lunar rover (Apollo 15)* 95 50

Conquest of space. No. C156 has dark blue and multicolored margin. Size: 134x135mm.

Sapporo '72 Type of Regular Issue
Souvenir Sheet

Designs (Sapporo '72 Emblem and): 26fr, Snow scooter. 31fr, Downhill skiing. 50fr, Bobsledding.

1972, Feb. 3

C157 A53 Sheet of 3 3.00 2.50
a. 26fr sil & multi 70 50
b. 31fr sil & multi 80 60
c. 50fr sil & multi 1.25 80

11th Winter Olympic Games, Sapporo, Japan, Feb. 3-13. No. C157 contains 3 stamps, arranged vertically. Silver decorative margin with blue and black inscription. Size: 106x125mm.

Olympic Games Type of 1972

1972, July 24 Photo. *Perf. 13½*

Gold and Multicolored

C158 A55 24fr *Weight lifting* 72 23
C159 A55 26fr *Hurdles* 78 25
C160 A55 31fr *Discus* 95 30
C161 A55 40fr *Soccer* 1.20 40

20th Olympic Games, Munich, Aug. 26-Sept. 11.

Independence Type of 1972

Designs: 15fr, Prince Rwagasore, Pres. Micombero, Burundi flag, drummers. 18fr, Rwagasore, Micombero, flag, map of Africa, globe. 27fr, Micombero, flag, globe.

1972, Aug. 24 Photo. *Perf. 13½*

C162 A56 15fr gold & multi 50 17
C163 A56 18fr gold & multi 60 20
C164 A56 27fr gold & multi 90 30
a. Souvenir sheet of 3 2.25 2.25

10th anniversary of independence.

No. C164a contains one each of Nos. C162-C164. Gold and light blue margin with black inscription. Size: 146x80mm.

Christmas Type of 1972

Paintings of the Madonna and Child by: 18fr, Sebastiano Mainardi. 27fr, Hans Memling. 40fr, Lorenzo Lotto.

1972, Nov. 2 Photo. *Perf. 13½*

C165 A57 18fr dk car & multi 55 17
C166 A57 27fr dk car & multi 80 25
C167 A57 40fr dk car & multi 1.20 35
a. Souvenir sheet of 3 2.75 2.75

Christmas 1972. No. C167a contains one each of Nos. C165-C167, slate green and gold border. Size: 128x81mm.

Orchid Type of Regular Issue

1973, Jan. 18 Photo. *Perf. 13½*

Multicolored

Size: 38x38mm.

C168 A58 13fr *Thelymitra pauciflora* 42 10
C169 A58 14fr *Miltassia* 45 12
C170 A58 15fr *Miltonia* 50 13
C171 A58 18fr *Platycoryne crocea* 55 15
C172 A58 20fr *Cattleya trinaei* 60 17
C173 A58 27fr *Eulophia cucullata* 85 20
C174 A58 36fr *Cymbidium hamsey* 1.10 27
Nos. C168-C174 (7) 4.47 1.14

African Exploration Type of 1973

Designs: 15fr, Livingstone writing his diary. 18fr, "Dr. Livingstone, I presume." 27fr, Livingstone and Stanley discussing expedition.

1973, Mar. 19 Photo. *Perf. 13½*

C175 A59 15fr gold & multi 45 15
C176 A59 18fr gold & multi 55 18
C177 A59 27fr gold & multi 80 27
a. Souvenir sheet of 3 2.10 2.10

Exploration of Africa by David Livingstone and Henry Morton Stanley. No. C177a contains 3 stamps similar to Nos. C175-C177, but without "Poste Aerienne." Gold and violet decorative margin. Size: 100x140mm.

Easter Type of 1973

Paintings: 15fr, Christ at the Pillar, by Guido Reni. 18fr, Crucifixion, by Mathias Grunewald. 27fr, Descent from the Cross, by Caravaggio.

1973, Apr. 10

C178 A60 15fr gold & multi 55 15
C179 A60 18fr gold & multi 70 18
C180 A60 27fr gold & multi 1.00 27
a. Souvenir sheet of 3 2.10 2.10

Easter 1973. No. C180a contains one each of Nos. C178-C180. Multicolored margin. Size: 121x73mm.

INTERPOL Type of Regular Issue

Designs: 27fr, INTERPOL emblem and flag. 40fr, INTERPOL flag and emblem.

1973, May 19 Photo. *Perf. 13½*

C181 A61 27fr gold & multi 80 32
C182 A61 40fr gold & multi 95 38

50th anniversary of International Criminal Police Organization (INTERPOL).

Copernicus Type of Regular Issue

Designs: 15fr, Copernicus (C183a), Earth, Pluto, and Jupiter. 18fr, Copernicus (No. C184a), Venus, Saturn, Mars. 27fr, Copernicus (No. C185a), Uranus, Neptune, Mercury. 36fr, Earth and various spacecrafts.

1973, July 27 Photo. *Perf. 13½*

Gold and Multicolored

C183 A62 15fr Block of four 2.40 60
a. 15fr in UL 60 15
b. 15fr in UR 60 15
c. 15fr in LL 60 15
d. 15fr in LR 60 15
C184 A62 18fr Block of four 2.80 70
a. 18fr in UL 70 17
b. 18fr in UR 70 17
c. 18fr in LL 70 17
d. 18fr in LR 70 17
C185 A62 27fr Block of four 4.20 1.00
a. 27fr in UL 1.05 25
b. 27fr in UR 1.05 25
c. 27fr in LL 1.05 25
d. 27fr in LR 1.05 25
C186 A62 36fr Block of four 5.60 1.40
a. 36fr in UL 1.40 35
b. 36fr in UR 1.40 35
c. 36fr in LL 1.40 35
d. 36fr in LR 1.40 35
e. Souvenir sheet of 4 15.00 15.00

500th anniversary of the birth of Nicolaus Copernicus (1473-1543), Polish astronomer. Nos. C183-C186 are printed in sheets of 32 containing 8 blocks of 4. No. C186e contains one each of Nos. C183-C186. Gold and multicolored margin. Size: 136x136mm.

Flower-Butterfly Type of 1973

Designs: Each block of 4 contains 2 flower and 2 butterfly designs. The 10fr, 14fr, 24fr and 31fr have flower designs listed as "a" and "d" numbers, butterflies as "b" and "c" numbers; the arrangement is reversed for the 17fr and 26fr.

1973, Sept. 28 Photo. *Perf. 13*

Stamp Size: 35x45mm.

Gold and Multicolored

C187 A63 10fr Block of 4 1.60 40
a. *Protea cynaroides* 40 10
b. *Precis octavia* 40 10
c. *Epiphora bauhiniae* 40 10
d. *Gazania longiscapa* 40 10
C188 A63 14fr Block of 4 2.25 55
a. *Kniphofia* 55 13
b. *Cymothoe coccinata* 55 13
c. *Nudaurelia zambesina* 55 13
d. Freesia refracta 55 13
C189 A63 17fr Block of 4 2.60 65
a. *Calotis eupompe* 65 15
b. *Narcissus* 65 15
c. *Cineraria hybrida* 65 15
d. *Cyrestis camillus* 65 15
C190 A63 24fr Block of 4 3.80 95
a. *Iris tingitana* 95 23
b. *Papilio demodocus* 95 23
c. *Catopsilia avelaneda* 95 23
d. *Nerine sarniensis* 95 23
C191 A63 26fr Block of 4 4.40 1.10
a. *Hypolimnas dexithea* 1.10 25
b. *Zantedeschia tropicalis* 1.10 25
c. *Sandersonia aurantiaca* 1.10 25
d. *Drurya antimachus* 1.10 25
C192 A63 31fr Block of 4 5.20 1.30
a. *Nymphaea capensis* 1.30 30
b. *Pandoriana pandora* 1.30 30
c. *Precis orythia* 1.30 30
d. *Pelargonium domestica* 1.30 30
Nos. C187-C192 (6 blocks of 4) 19.85 4.95

Christmas Type of 1973

Virgin and Child by: 18fr, Raphael. 27fr, Pietro Perugino. 40fr, Titian.

1973, Nov. 19

C193 A64 18fr gold & multi 55 15
C194 A64 27fr gold & multi 80 22
C195 A64 40fr gold & multi 1.20 33
a. Souvenir sheet of 3 2.75 2.75

Christmas 1973. No. C195a contains one each of Nos. C193-C195 with multicolored margin. Size: 143x79mm.

Soccer Type of Regular Issue

Designs: Various soccer scenes and cup.

1974, July 4 Photogravure *Perf. 13*

C196 A67 20fr gold & multi 60
C197 A67 26fr gold & multi 78
C198 A67 40fr gold & multi 1.20

World Cup Soccer Championships, Munich, June 13-July 7. For souvenir sheet see No. 459a.

UPU Type of 1974

Designs: No. C199, Flags over UPU Headquarters, Bern. No. C200, G.P.O., Usumbura. No. C201, Mailmen ("26F" in UR). No. C202, Mailmen ("26F" in UL). No. C203, UPU emblem. No. C204, Means of transportation. No. C205, Pigeon over globe showing Burundi. No. C206, Swiss flag, pigeon over map showing Bern.

1974, July 23

C199 A68 24fr gold & multi 95
C200 A68 24fr gold & multi 95
C201 A68 26fr gold & multi 1.00
C202 A68 26fr gold & multi 1.00
C203 A68 31fr gold & multi 1.25
C204 A68 31fr gold & multi 1.25
C205 A68 40fr gold & multi 1.60
C206 A68 40fr gold & multi 1.60
a. Souvenir sheet of 8 10.00 10.00
Nos. C199-C206 (8) 9.60

Centenary of Universal Postal Union. Stamps of same denomination printed se-tenant (continuous design) in sheets of 40. No. C206a contains one each of Nos. C199-C206. Violet, gold and light blue margin. Size: 96x162mm.

Fish Type of 1974

1974, Sept. 9 Photo. *Perf. 13*

Size: 35x35mm.

Multicolored

C207 A66 10fr Block of 4 1.20 25
a. *Haplochromis multicolor* 30 6
b. *Pantodon buchholzi* 30 6
c. *Tropheus duboisi* 30 6
d. *Distichodus sexfasciatus* 30 6
C208 A66 14fr Block of 4 1.68 35
a. *Pelmatochromis kribensis* 42 8
b. *Nannaethiops tritaeniatus* 42 8
c. *Polycentropsis abbreviata* 42 8
d. *Hemichromis bimaculatus* 42 8
C209 A66 17fr Block of 4 2.00 40
a. *Ctenopoma acutirostre* 50 10
b. *Synodontis angelicus* 50 10
c. *Tilapia melanopleura* 50 10
d. *Aphyosemion bivittatum* 50 10
C210 A66 24fr Block of four 2.90 60
a. *Monodactylus argenteus* 72 15
b. *Zanclus canescens* 72 15
c. *Pygoplites diacanthus* 72 15
d. *Cephalopholis argus* 72 15
C211 A66 26fr Block of 4 3.15 70
a. *Priacanthus arenatus* 78 17
b. *Pomacanthus arcutus* 78 17
c. *Scarus guacamaia* 78 17
d. *Zeus faber* 78 17
C212 A66 31fr Block of 4 3.75 80
a. *Lactophrys quadricornis* 93 20
b. *Balistes vetula* 93 20
c. *Acanthurus bahianus* 93 20
d. *Holocanthus ciliaris* 93 20
Nos. C207-C212 (6 blocks of 4) 14.68 3.10

Christmas Type of 1974

Paintings of the Virgin and Child: 18fr, by Hans Memling. 27fr, by Filippino Lippi. 40fr, by Lorenzo di Gredi.

1974, Nov. 7 Photo. *Perf. 13*

C213 A70 18fr gold & multi 55 45
C214 A70 27fr gold & multi 80 65
C215 A70 40fr gold & multi 1.20 95
a. Souvenir sheet of 3 3.00 3.00

Christmas 1974. Sheets of 20 stamps and one label. No. C215a contains one each of Nos. C213-C215, gold and multicolored border. Size: 137x90mm. Sheet exists imperf.

Apollo-Soyuz Type of 1975.

1975, July 10 Photo. *Perf. 13*

Multicolored

C216 A71 27fr Block of 4 1.80
a. *A.A. Leonov, V.N. Kubasov, Soviet flag* 45
b. *Soyuz and Soviet flag* 45
c. *Apollo and American flag* 45
d. *Slayton, Brand, Stafford, American flag* 45
C217 A71 40fr Block of 4 2.60
a. *Apollo-Soyuz link-up* 65
b. *Apollo, blast-off* 65
c. *Soyuz, blast-off* 65
d. *Kubasov, Leonov, Slayton, Brand, Stafford* 65

Apollo Soyuz space test project (Russo-American cooperation), launching July 15; link-up, July 17. Nos. C216-C217 are printed in sheets of 32 containing 8 blocks of 4.

Animal Type of 1975

1975, Sept. 17 Photo. *Perf. 13½*

Multicolored

C218 A72 10fr Strip of four 1.20
a. *Addax* 30
b. *Roan antelope* 30
c. *Nyala* 30
d. *White rhinoceros* 30
C219 A72 14fr Strip of four 1.68
a. *Mandrill* 42
b. *Eland* 42
c. *Salt's dik-dik* 42
d. *Thomson's gazelles* 42
C220 A72 17fr Strip of four 2.00
a. *African small-clawed otter* 50
b. *Reed buck* 50
c. *Indian civet* 50
d. *Cape buffalo* 50

C221 A72 24fr Strip of four 2.88
a. *White-tailed gnu* 72
b. *African wild asses* 72
c. *Black-and-white colobus monkey* 72
d. *Gerenuk* 72
C222 A72 26fr Strip of four 3.15
a. *Dama gazelle* 76
b. *Black-backed jackal* 76
c. *Sitatungas* 76
d. *Zebra antelope* 76
C223 A72 31fr Strip of four 3.75
a. *Fennec* 93
b. *Lesser kudus* 93
c. *Blesbok* 93
d. *Serval* 93
Nos. C218-C223 (6 strips of 4) 14.66

Nos. C218–C219 Overprinted in Black and Silver with IWY Emblem and: "ANNEE INTERNATIONALE / DE LA FEMME"

1975, Nov. 19 Photo. *Perf. 13½*

C224 A72 10fr Strip of four 1.20 24
a. *Addax* 30 5
b. *Roan antelope* 30 5
c. *Nyala* 30 5
d. *White rhinoceros* 30 5
C225 A72 14fr Strip of four 1.68 35
a. *Mandrill* 42 8
b. *Oryx* 42 8
c. *Dik-dik* 42 8
d. *Thomson's gazelles* 42 8

International Women's Year 1975.

Nos. C222–C223 Overprinted in Black and Silver with U.N. Emblem and: "30ème ANNIVERSAIRE DES/ NATIONS UNIES"

1975, Nov. 19

C226 A72 26fr Strip of four 3.15 60
a. *Dama gazelle* 76 15
b. *Wild dog* 76 15
c. *Sitatungas* 76 15
d. *Striped duiker* 76 15
C227 A72 31fr Strip of four 3.75 65
a. *Fennec* 93 15
b. *Lesser kudus* 93 15
c. *Blesbok* 93 15
d. *Serval* 93 15

United Nations, 30th anniversary.

Michelangelo Type of 1975

Designs: Paintings from Sistine Chapel.

1975, Dec. 3 Photo. *Perf. 13*

C228 A73 18fr *Zachariah* 54
C229 A73 18fr *Joel* 54
C230 A73 31fr *Erythrean Sybil* 93
C231 A73 31fr *Prophet Ezekiel* 93
C232 A73 40fr *Persian Sybil* 1.20
C233 A73 40fr *Prophet Jeremiah* 1.20
a. Souvenir sheet of 6 5.50
Nos. C228-C233 (6) 5.34

Michelangelo Buonarotti (1475–1564), Italian sculptor, painter and architect. Stamps of same denominations printed se-tenant in sheets of 18 stamps and 2 labels. No. C233a contains one each of Nos. C228–C233, green & gold margin, black inscription. Size: 137x111mm.

Olympic Games Type, 1976

Designs (Olympic Games Emblem and): 18fr, Ski jump. 36fr, Slalom. 50fr, Ice hockey.

1976, Jan. 23 Photo. *Perf. 14x13½*

C234 A74 18fr ol brn & multi 54
C235 A74 36fr grn & multi 1.08
C236 A74 50fr pur & multi 1.50
a. Souvenir sheet of 4 3.10 2.00

12th Winter Olympic Games, Innsbruck, Austria, Feb. 4–15.

No. C236a contains 4 stamps similar to Nos. 491–494, perf. 13½, inscribed "POSTE AERIENNE." Multicolored margin with snowflakes and Games' emblem. Size: 100x103mm.

Hurdles—AP5

Designs (Montreal Games Emblem and): Nos. C238, C241, C243b, High jump. Nos. C239, C242, C243a, Athlete on rings. No. C240, C243c, Hurdles.

1976, May 3 Litho. *Perf. 13½*

C237 AP5 27fr grn & multi 78
C238 AP5 27fr dk bl & multi 78
C239 AP5 31fr ocher & multi 93
C240 AP5 31fr grn & multi 93
C241 AP5 50fr dk bl & multi 1.50
C242 AP5 50fr ocher & multi 1.50
Nos. C237-C242 (6) 6.42

Souvenir Sheet

C243 AP5 Sheet of 3 3.40 60
a. 27fr ocher & multi 78
b. 31fr dk bl & multi 95
c. 50fr grn & multi 1.50

21st Olympic Games, Montreal, Canada, July 17–Aug. 1. Stamps of same denomination printed se-tenant in sheets of 20.

No. C243 has gold inscription, Montreal Olympic emblem and multicolored band in margin. Size: 100x120mm.

Battle of Bunker Hill, by John Trumbull

AP6 AP7

Paintings: 26fr, Franklin, Jefferson and John Adams. 36fr, Declaration of Independence, by John Trumbull.

1976, July 16 Photo. *Perf. 13*

C244 AP6 18fr gold & multi 54
C245 AP7 18fr gold & multi 54
C246 AP6 26fr gold & multi 76
C247 AP7 26fr gold & multi 76
C248 AP6 36fr gold & multi 1.05
C249 AP7 36fr gold & multi 1.05
a. Souvenir sheet of 6 5.00 3.00
Nos. C244-C249 (6) 4.70

American Bicentennial. Stamps of same denomination printed se-tenant in sheets of 50. No. C249a contains one each of Nos. C244–C249 with Bicentennial emblem in margin. Size: 102x148mm.

Christmas Type of 1976

Paintings: 18fr, Virgin and Child with St. Anne, by Leonardo da Vinci. 31fr, Holy Family with Lamb, by Raphael. 40fr, Madonna of the Basket, by Correggio.

1976, Oct. 18 Photo. *Perf. 13½*

C250 A76 18fr gold & multi 54
C251 A76 31fr gold & multi 94
C252 A76 40fr gold & multi 1.20
a. Souvenir sheet of 3 2.80 1.75

Christmas 1976. Sheets of 20 stamps and descriptive label. No. C252a contains one each of Nos. C250–C252; multicolored margin. Size: 123x80mm.

A.G. Bell Type 1977

Designs: 10fr, A.G. Bell and first telephone. Nos. C253, 17fr, A.G. Bell speaking into microphone. Nos. C254, C257e, Satellites around globe and videophone. No. C255, Switchboard operator, c.1910, and wall telephone. Nos. C256, 26fr, Intelsat satellite, modern and old telephones. No. C257c, Intelsat and radar.

1977, May 17 Photo. *Perf. 13*

C253 A78 18fr multi 28
C254 A79 18fr multi 28
C255 A78 36fr multi 55
C256 A79 36fr multi 55

Souvenir Sheet

C257 Sheet of 5 3.50 2.00
a. A78 10fr multi 30 14
b. A78 17fr multi 50 22
c. A79 18fr multi 54 25
d. A79 26fr multi 80 45
e. A79 36fr multi 1.05 50

Centenary of first telephone call by Alexander Graham Bell, Mar. 10, 1876. No. C257 contains 3 postage (10fr, 17fr, 26fr) and 2 air post stamps (18fr, 36fr). Multicolored margin with ITU emblem and old telephone. Size: 120x135mm.

Animal Type of 1977

1977, Aug. 22 Photo. *Perf. 14x14½*

Multicolored

C258 A80 9fr Strip of four 1.10
a. *Buffon's kob* 26
b. *Marabous* 26
c. *Brindled gnu* 26
d. *River hog* 26
C259 A80 13fr Strip of four 1.60
a. *Zebras* 40
b. *Shoebill* 40
c. *Striped hyenas* 40
d. *Chimpanzee* 40
C260 A80 30fr Strip of four 3.60
a. *Flamingos* 90
b. *Nile Crocodiles* 90
c. *Green mamba* 90
d. *Greater kudus* 90
C261 A80 35fr Strip of four 4.20
a. *Hyrax* 1.05
b. *Cobra* 1.05
c. *Jackals* 1.05
d. *Verreaux's eagles* 1.05
C262 A80 54fr Strip of four 6.50
a. *Honey badger* 1.62
b. *Harnessed antelopes* 1.62
c. *Secretary bird* 1.62
d. *Klipspringer* 1.62
C263 A80 70fr Strip of four 8.40
a. *African big-eared fox* 2.10
b. *Elephants* 2.10
c. *Vulturine guineafowl* 2.10
d. *Impalas* 2.10
Nos. C258-C263 (6 strips of 4) 25.40

UN Type of 1977

Designs (UN Stamps and): 24fr, UN buildings by night. 27fr, UN buildings and view of Manhattan. 35fr, UN buildings by day.

1977, Oct. 10 Photo. *Perf. 13½*

C264 A82 24fr Block of four 2.88
a. No. 77 72
b. No. 78 72
c. No. 40 72
d. No. 32 72
C265 A82 27fr Block of four 3.20
a. No. 50 80
b. No. 21 80
c. No. 30 80
d. No. 44 80
C266 A82 35fr Block of four 4.20
a. No. C6 1.05
b. No. 105 1.05
c. No. 4 1.05
d. No. 1 1.05
e. Souvenir sheet of 3 2.75

25th anniversary (in 1976) of the United Nations Postal Administration. No. C266e contains 24fr in design of No. C265b, 27fr in design of No. C266a, 35fr in design of No. C264c; silver margin. Size: 128x76 mm.

Christmas Type of 1977

Designs: Paintings of the Virgin and Child.

1977, Oct. 31 Photo. *Perf. 14x13*

C267 A83 18fr Master of Moulins 55
C268 A83 31fr Workshop of Lorenzo de Credi 95
C269 A83 40fr Palma Vecchio 1.20
a. Souvenir sheet of 3 3.00 2.00

Christmas 1977. Sheets of 24 stamps and descriptive label. No. C269a contains one each of Nos. C267–C269; gold and multicolored margin. Size: 130x72mm.

Souvenir Sheet

Type of 1979

1979, Feb. Photo. *Perf. 14x13½*

C270 Sheet of 5, multi 4.00
a. *like #543* 40
b. *like #544* 50
c. *like #545* 80
d. *like #546* 95
e. *like #547* 1.20

Christmas 1978. No. C270 has green, gold and black margin. Size: 114x120mm.

Christmas Type of 1979

Souvenir Sheet

1979, Oct. 12 *Perf. 13½*

C271 Sheet of 4, multi 4.00 2.50
a. *like #561* 60 32
b. *like #562* 80 45
c. *like #563* 95 55
d. *like #564* 1.50 85

Christmas 1979.

Hill Type of 1979

Souvenir Sheet

1979, Nov.6

C272 Sheet of 5, multi 5.50 3.50
a. *like #565* 60 32
b. *like #566* 80 45
c. *like #567* 95 55
d. *like #568* 1.20 70
e. *like #569* 1.80 1.00

Sir Rowland Hill (1795-1879), originator of penny postage.

Bird Type of 1979

1979 Photo. *Perf. 13½x13*

Multicolored

C273 A87 6fr *like #548* 18
C274 A87 13fr *like #549* 40
C275 A87 18fr *like #550* 55
C276 A87 26fr *like #551* 78
C277 A87 31fr *like #552* 95
C278 A87 36fr *like #553* 1.10
C279 A87 40fr *like #554* 1.20
C280 A87 54fr *like #555* 1.65
C281 A87 70fr *like #556* 2.10
Nos. C273-C281 (9) 8.91

Olympic Type of 1980

Souvenir Sheet

1980, Oct. 24 Photo. *Perf. 13½*

C282 Sheet of 9 8.50
a. A91 20fr like #570 60
b. A91 20fr like #571 60
c. A91 20fr like #572 60
d. A91 30fr like #573 90
e. A91 30fr like #574 90
f. A91 30fr like #575 90
g. A91 40fr like #576 1.20
h. A91 40fr like #577 1.20
i. A91 40fr like #578 1.20

22nd Summer Olympic Games, Moscow, July 19-Aug. 3. No. C282 has multicolored margin showing Moscow '80 emblem. Size: 144½x 112mm.

Christmas Type of 1980

Souvenir Sheet

1980, Dec. 12 Photo. *Perf. 13½x13*

C283 Sheet of 4 3.75 2.75
a. *like #579* 30 20
b. *like #580* 90 60
c. *like #581* 1.20 80
d. *like #582* 1.35 90

Multicolored decorative margin. Size: 133½x104mm.

UPRONA Type of 1980

Souvenir Sheet

1980, Dec. 29 *Perf. 14½x13½*

C284 Sheet of 3 3.00
a. A93 10fr like #583 30
b. A93 40fr like #584 1.20
c. A93 45fr like #585 1.35

No. C284 has light blue and gold decorative margin. Size: 109x68mm.

AIR POST SEMI-POSTAL STAMPS

Coin Type of Semi-Postal Issue

Designs (Coins of Various Denominations): 3fr+1fr, 11fr+1fr, 20fr+1fr, 50fr+1fr, Coat of Arms, reverse. 5fr+1fr, 14fr+1fr, 30fr+1fr, 100fr+1fr, King Mwambutsa IV, obverse.

1965, Nov. 15 *Imperf.*

Lithographed; Embossed on Gilt Foil

Diameter: 39mm.

CB1	SP4	3fr +1fr lt & dk vio	10	10
CB2	SP4	5fr +1fr pale grn & red	15	15

Diameter: 45mm.

CB3	SP4	11fr +1fr org & lil	30	30
CB4	SP4	14fr +1fr red & emer	40	40

Diameter: 56mm.

CB5	SP4	20fr +1fr ultra & blk	55	55
CB6	SP4	30fr +1fr dp org & mar	80	80

Diameter: 67mm.

CB7	SP4	50fr +1fr bl & vio bl	1.35	1.35
CB8	SP4	100fr +1fr rose & dp cl	2.75	2.75
		Nos. CB1-CB8 (8)	6.40	6.40

Stamps are backed with patterned paper in blue, orange, and pink engine-turned design.

Red Cross Type of Semi-Postal Issue

Designs: 26fr+3fr, Laboratory. 40fr+3fr, Ambulance and thatched huts. 50fr+3fr, Red Cross nurse with patient.

1969, June 26 **Photo.** *Perf. 13½*

CB9	SP7	26fr +3fr multi	75	20
CB10	SP7	40fr +3fr multi	1.10	30
CB11	SP7	50fr +3fr multi	1.35	40

Issued to commemorate the 50th anniversary of the League of Red Cross Societies. Perf. and imperf. souvenir sheets exist containing 3 stamps similar to Nos. CB9–CB11, but without "Poste Aerienne." Gold frame with green commemorative inscription. Size: 90½x97mm.

Christmas Type of Semi-Postal Issue

Paintings: 14fr+3fr, Virgin and Child, by Velázquez. 26fr+3fr, Holy Family, by Joos van Cleve. 40fr+3fr, Virgin and Child, by Rogier van der Weyden.

1970, Dec. 14 **Photo.** *Perf. 13½*

CB12	SP9	14fr +3fr multi	50	17
CB13	SP9	26fr +3fr multi	90	30
CB14	SP9	40fr +3fr multi	1.30	42
a.		Souvenir sheet of 3	3.00	3.00

No. CB14a contains one each of Nos. CB12–CB14 with ornamental border and inscription. Size: 135x75mm.

No. C147 Surcharged in Gold and Black

+2F

LUTTE CONTRE

L'ANALPHABETISME

1971, Aug. 9 **Photo.** *Perf. 13½*

CB15	A48	14fr +2fr Strip of four	1.60	32
a.		*Hartebeest*	40	8
b.		*Black rhinoceros*	40	8
c.		*Zebra*	40	8
d.		*Leopard*	40	8

UNESCO campaign against illiteracy.

No. C148 Surcharged in Gold and Black

+1F

AIDE INTERNATIONALE
AUX REFUGIES

1971, Aug. 9 **Multicolored**

CB16	A48	17fr +1fr Strip of four	1.85	35
a.		*Grant's gazelles*	45	8
b.		*Cheetah*	45	8
c.		*African white-backed vultures*	45	8
d.		*Johnston's okapi*	45	8

International help for refugees.

Nos. C150–C151 Surcharged in Black and Gold

75eme ANNIVERSAIRE DES
JEUX OLYMPIQUES MODERNES
(1896 - 1971)

a

JEUX PRE-OLYMPIQUES
MUNICH 1972

b

1971, Aug. 16

CB17	A48(a)	26fr +1fr Strip of four	4.50	90
a.		*Gorilla*	1.10	22
b.		*Gnu*	1.10	22
c.		*Warthog*	1.10	22
d.		*Cape hunting dog*	1.10	22
CB18	A48(b)	31fr +1fr Strip of four	6.00	1.20
a.		*Sable antelope*	1.50	30
b.		*Caracal lynx*	1.50	30
c.		*Ostriches*	1.50	30
d.		*Bongo*	1.50	30

75th anniversary of modern Olympic Games (No. CB17); Olympic Games, Munich, 1972 (No. CB18).

Nos. C153–C155 Surcharged

1971, Nov. 27 **Photo.** *Perf. 13½*

CB19	A51	14fr +1fr multi	50	15
CB20	A51	17fr +1fr multi	60	20
CB21	A51	31fr +1fr multi	1.00	33

25th anniversary of the United Nations International Children's Fund (UNICEF).

Casa D'Oro, Venice
SPAP1

Views in Venice: 17fr+1fr, Doge's Palace. 24fr+1fr, Church of Sts. John and Paul. 31fr+1fr, Doge's Palace and Piazzetta at Feast of Ascension, by Canaletto.

1971, Dec. 27

CB22	SPAP1	10fr +1fr gold & multi	33	15
CB23	SPAP1	17fr +1fr gold & multi	55	22
CB24	SPAP1	24fr +1fr gold & multi	75	30
CB25	SPAP1	31fr +1fr gold & multi	90	35
a.		Souvenir sheet of 4	3.00	3.00

The surtax was for the UNESCO campaign to save the treasures of Venice. No. CB25a contains 4 stamps similar to Nos. CB22–CB25, but with 2fr surtax instead 1fr. Gold and black ornamental margin. Size: 113x131½mm. Sheet exists imperf.

Nos. C165–C167 Surcharged "+1F" in Silver

1972, Dec. 12 **Photo.** *Perf. 13½*

CB26	A57	18fr +1fr multi	50	17
CB27	A57	27fr +1fr multi	85	25
CB28	A57	40fr +1fr multi	1.10	35
a.		Souvenir sheet of 3	2.50	2.50

Christmas 1972. No. CB28a contains 3 stamps similar to Nos. CB26–CB28 but with 2fr surtax. Slate green and gold border. Size: 128x81mm.

Nos. C193–C195 Surcharged "+1F" in Silver

1973, Dec. 14 **Photo.** *Perf. 13*

CB29	A64	18fr +1fr multi	55	17
CB30	A64	27fr +1fr multi	80	25
CB31	A64	40fr +1fr multi	1.25	40
a.		Souvenir sheet of 3	3.00	3.00

Christmas 1973. No. CB31 contains 3 stamps similar to Nos. CB29–CB31 with 2fr surtax each. Size: 143x79mm.

Christmas Type of 1974

1974, Dec. 2 **Photogravure** *Perf. 13*

CB32	A70	18fr +1fr multi	65	40
CB33	A70	27fr +1fr multi	1.00	60
CB34	A70	40fr +1fr multi	1.40	85
a.		Souvenir sheet of 3	3.50	3.50

Christmas 1974. No. CB34a contains 3 stamps similar to Nos. CB32–CB34 with 2fr surtax. Size: 137x90mm.

Nos. C228–C233 Surcharged "+ 1 F" in Silver and Black

1975, Dec. 22 **Photo.** *Perf. 13*

Multicolored

CB35	A73	18fr +1fr #C228	60	
CB36	A73	18fr +1fr #C229	60	
CB37	A73	31fr +1fr #C230	95	
CB38	A73	31fr +1fr #C231	95	
CB39	A73	40fr +1fr #C232	1.25	
CB40	A73	40fr +1fr #C233	1.25	
a.		Souvenir sheet of 6	6.00	6.00
		Nos. CB35-CB40 (6)	5.60	

Michelangelo Buonarroti (1475–1564), 500th birth anniversary. No. CB40a contains 6 stamps similar to Nos. CB35–CB40 with 2fr surtax each. Size: 132x106mm.

Nos. C250–C252 Surcharged "+1f" in Silver and Black

1976, Nov. 25 **Photo.** *Perf. 13½*

CB41	A76	18fr +1fr multi	60	
CB42	A76	31fr +1fr multi	1.00	
CB43	A76	40fr +1fr multi	1.25	
a.		Souvenir sheet of 3	3.00	3.00

Christmas 1976. No. CB43a contains 3 stamps similar to Nos. CB41–CB43 with 2fr surtax each. Size: 123x80mm.

Nos. C267–C269 Surcharged "+1fr" in Silver and Black

1977 **Photo.** *Perf. 14x13*

CB44	A83	18fr +1fr multi	58	
CB45	A83	31fr +1fr multi	1.00	
CB46	A83	40fr +1fr multi	1.25	
a.		Souvenir sheet of 3	3.00	3.00

Christmas 1977. No. CB46a contains 3 stamps similar to Nos. CB44–CB46 with 2fr surtax each. Size: 130x71mm.

Type of 1979

Souvenir Sheet

1979, Feb. **Photo.** *Perf. 14x13*

CB47		Sheet of 5	4.50
a.	A86	13fr +2fr multi	50
b.	A86	17fr +2fr multi	60
c.	A86	27fr +2fr multi	90
d.	A86	31fr +2fr multi	1.05
e.	A86	40fr +2fr multi	1.30

Christmas 1978. No. CB47 has gold, black and blue border. Size: 115x121mm.

Christmas Type of 1979

Souvenir Sheet

1979, Dec. 10 **Photo.** *Perf. 13½*

CB48		Sheet of 4	4.50
a.	A89	20fr +2fr *like* #561	68
b.	A89	27fr +2fr *like* #562	90
c.	A89	31fr +2fr *like* #563	1.00
d.	A89	50fr +2fr *like* #564	1.60

No. CB48 has multicolored decorative margin. Size: 86x110mm.

Christmas Type of 1980

Souvenir Sheet

1981, Jan. 16 **Photo.** *Perf. 13½x13*

CB49		Sheet of 4	4.50
a.	A92	10+2fr *like* #579	40
b.	A92	30+2fr *like* #580	1.00
c.	A92	40+2fr *like* #581	1.30
d.	A92	50+2fr *like* #582	1.60

Christmas 1980. Multicolored decorative margin. Size: 133x104mm.

CAMBODIA

(kăm·bō'dĭ·ȧ)

Khmer Republic

LOCATION—Southern Indo-China.

GOVT.—Republic

AREA—69,866 sq. mi.

POP.—7,640,000 (est. 1974).

CAPITAL—Phnom Penh.

Before 1951, Cambodia used stamps of Indo-China. In October, 1970, the Kingdom of Cambodia became the Khmer Republic.

100 Cents = 1 Piaster

100 Cents = 1 Riel (1955)

Imperforates

Most Cambodia stamps exist imperforate in issued and trial colors, and also in small presentation sheets in issued colors.

Apsaras

A1

King Norodom Sihanouk

A3

Enthronement Hall

A2

Engraved.

1951-52 *Perf. 13* Unwmkd.

No.	Type	Description	Unused	Used
1	A1	10c dk bl grn	55	55
2	A1	20c cl & org brn	35	20
3	A1	30c pur & ind	35	20
4	A1	40c ultra & brt bl grn	35	20
5	A2	50c dk grn & dk ol grn	35	20
6	A3	80c bl blk & dk bl grn	70	70
7	A2	1pi ind & pur	90	90
8	A3	1.10pi dp car & brt red	90	90
9	A3	1.50pi blk brn & red brn	1.25	90
10	A1	1.50pi dp car & cer	1.25	90
11	A2	1.50pi ind & dp ultra	1.25	1.10
12	A3	1.90pi ind & dp ultra	1.75	1.60
13	A2	2pi dp car & org brn	1.60	1.00
14	A3	3pi dp car & org brn	2.25	1.60
15	A1	5pi ind & pur	9.00	4.00
a.		Souvenir sheet of 1 ('52)	25.00	
16	A2	10pi pur & ind	16.50	8.00
a.		Souvenir sheet of 1 ('52)	25.00	
17	A3	15pi dk pur & pur	22.50	11.00
a.		Souvenir sheet of 1 ('52)	30.00	
		Nos. 1-17 (17)	61.80	33.95

No. 9 issued in 1951, others in 1952.

Nos. 15a, 16a and 17a contain single copies respectively of the 5pi, 10pi and 15pi. They were sold in a booklet for 30pi. Size: 128x89mm.

Phnom Daun Penh

A4

East Gate, Angkor Thom

A5

Arms of Cambodia

A6

Methods of Mail Transport

A7

1954-55 *Perf. 13* Unwmkd.

No.	Type	Description	Unused	Used
18	A4	10c rose car	6	6
a.		Souvenir sheet of 5 ('55)	25.00	
19	A4	20c dk grn	6	6
20	A4	30c indigo	6	6
21	A4	40c dk pur	6	6
22	A4	50c dk vio brn	6	6
23	A5	70c chocolate	20	20
a.		Souvenir sheet of 5 ('55)	25.00	
24	A5	1pi red vio	20	20
25	A5	1.50pi red	20	20
26	A6	2pi rose red	40	40
a.		Souvenir sheet of 5 ('55)	25.00	
27	A6	2.50pi green	60	60
28	A7	2.50pi bl grn	80	60
a.		Souvenir sheet of 5 ('55)	25.00	
29	A6	3pi ultra	90	75
30	A7	4pi blk brn	1.00	1.00
31	A6	4.50pi purple	1.20	1.00
32	A7	5pi rose red	1.25	1.00
33	A6	6pi chocolate	1.50	1.00
34	A7	10pi purple	1.50	1.50
35	A7	15pi dp bl	2.00	1.85
36	A5	20pi ultra	4.00	2.50
37	A5	30pi bl grn	6.00	5.00
		Nos. 18-37 (20)	22.05	18.10

The four souvenir sheets each contain five different stamps: No. 18a (10c, 20c, 30c, 40c, 50c); No. 23a (70c, 1pi, 1.50pi, 20pi, 30pi); No. 26a (2pi, 2.50pi green, 3pi, 4.50pi, 6pi); No. 28a (2.50pi blue green, 4pi, 5pi, 10pi, 15pi). Size of Nos. 18a, 26a and 28a: 120x120mm. Size of No. 23a: 160x92mm.

King Norodom Suramarit

A8

King Norodom Suramarit and Queen Kossamak Nearirat Serey Vathana

A9

Portraits: 50c (No. 39), 2.50r, 4r, 6r, 15r, Queen Kossamak Nearirat Serey Vathana.

Perf. 14x13(A8), 13(A9)

1955, Nov. 24 Engr. Unwmkd.

No.	Type	Description	Unused	Used
38	A8	50c violet	10	10
39	A8	50c indigo	10	10
40	A8	1r car lake	15	15
41	A9	1.50r dk brn	40	40
42	A9	2r blk & ind	40	30
43	A8	2r dp ultra	25	40
44	A8	2.50r dk vio brn	40	40
45	A9	3r brn org & car	40	40
46	A8	4r dk grn	60	60
47	A9	5r blk & dk grn	60	60
48	A8	6r dp plum	1.00	75
49	A8	7r dk brn	1.25	75
50	A9	10r brn car & vio	1.00	1.00
51	A8	15r purple	1.75	1.25
52	A8	20r dp grn	2.25	2.00
		Nos. 38-52 (15)	10.65	9.20

Issued to commemorate the coronation of King Norodom Suramarit and Queen Kossamak Nearirat Serey Vathana.

See also Nos. 74-75.

King Norodom Suramarit

A10

Prince Sihanouk, Globe and Flags

A11

Portrait: 3r, 5r, 50r, Queen Kossamak Nearirat Serey Vathana.

1956, Mar. 8 *Perf. 13*

No.	Type	Description	Unused	Used
53	A10	2r dk red	1.00	1.00
54	A10	3r dk bl	1.50	1.50
55	A10	5r yel grn	2.25	2.25
56	A10	10r dk grn	5.50	5.50
57	A10	30r dk vio	12.00	12.00
58	A10	50r rose lil	22.50	22.50
		Nos. 53-58 (6)	44.75	44.75

Issued to commemorate the coronation of King Norodom Suramarit and Queen Kossamak Nearirat Serey Vathana.

1957, Mar. 1

No.	Type	Description	Unused	Used
59	A11	2r grn, ultra & car	60	45
60	A11	4.50r ultra	60	45
61	A11	8.50r carmine	60	45

Issued to commemorate the first anniversary of Cambodia's admission to the United Nations (in 1956).

Type of Semi-Postal Stamps, 1957.

1957, May 12 *Perf. 13* Unwmkd.

No.	Type	Description	Unused	Used
62	SP1	1.50r vermilion	55	55
63	SP1	6.50r bluish vio	70	70
64	SP1	8r dk grn	70	70

Issued to commemorate the 2500th anniversary of the birth of Buddha.

King Ang Duong

A12

1958, Mar. 4

No.	Type	Description	Unused	Used
65	A12	1.50r pur & brn	20	20
66	A12	5r ol gray & ol	50	40
67	A12	10r cl & dl brn	1.00	60
a.		Souvenir sheet of 3	3.50	3.50

Issued to honor King Ang Duong (1795-1860).

No. 67a contains one each of Nos. 65-67. Sold for 25r. Size: 155x93mm.

King Norodom I

A13

1958-59 Engraved *Perf. 12½x13*

No.	Type	Description	Unused	Used
68	A13	2r ultra & ol	40	40
69	A13	6r org & sl grn	80	80
70	A13	15r grn & ol gray	1.20	1.20
a.		Souvenir sheet of 3 ('59)	3.50	3.50

Issued in honor of King Norodom I (1835-1904).

No. 70a contains one each of Nos. 68-70. Sold for 32r. Size: 155x93mm.

Issue dates: Nos. 68-70, Nov. 3, 1958. No. 70a, Jan. 31, 1959.

Children of the World

A14

1959, Dec. 9 *Perf. 13* Unwmkd.

No.	Type	Description	Unused	Used
71	A14	20c rose vio	6	6
72	A14	50c blue	12	12
73	A14	80c rose car	20	20

Issued to promote friendship among the children of the world.

Nos. 49 and 52 with Black Border.

1960 *Perf. 14x13*

No.	Type	Description	Unused	Used
74	A8	7r dk brn & blk	1.25	1.25
75	A8	20r dp grn & blk	1.25	1.25

Issued to commemorate the death of King Norodom Suramarit.

Port of Sihanoukville, Prince Sihanouk and Serpent Naga

A15

(double size) 20r

1960, Apr. *Perf. 13x12½*

No.	Type	Description	Unused	Used
76	A15	2r car & sep	40	40
a.		Cambodian 20r	1.20	1.20
77	A15	5r ultra & dp brn	40	40
a.		Cambodian 20r	1.60	1.60
78	A15	20r lil & dk bl	1.40	1.00

Issued to commemorate the opening of the port of Sihanoukville. By error the denomination in Cambodian on the 2r and 5r was engraved as 20r; it was corrected later.

Ceremonial Plow
A16

1960 *Perf. 12*

79	A16	1r magenta	40	40
80	A16	2r brown	40	40
81	A16	3r bluish grn	40	40

Feast of the Sacred Furrow.

Works of Sangkum Issue

Fight Against Illiteracy
A17

Water Conservation, Dam at Chhouksar
A18

Dove, Factory and Books
A19

Buddhist Ceremony
A20

Designs: 6r, Workman and house. 10r, Woman in rice field.

1960, Sept. 1 Engraved *Perf. 13*

82	A17	2r dk grn, brn & dk bl	22	18
a.		Souvenir sheet of 3	3.50	3.50
83	A18	3r brn & grn	32	27
a.		Souvenir sheet of 3	3.50	3.50
84	A19	4r rose car, vio & grn	35	32
85	A17	6r brn, org & grn	45	40
86	A17	10r ultra, grn & bis	90	80
87	A20	25r dk car, red & mag	2.25	1.65
		Nos. 82-87 (6)	4.49	3.62

No. 82a contains one each of Nos. 82, 85 and 87, and sold for 42r. No. 83a contains one each of Nos. 83, 84 and 86, and sold for 23r. Marginal inscriptions in bister. Size: 149x100mm. Nos. 82a–83a were issued Dec. 5, 1960.

Cambodian Flag and Dove
A21

Frangipani
A22

1960, Dec. 24 Engraved *Perf. 13*

Flag in Ultramarine and Red.

88	A21	1.50r brn & grn	25	25
89	A21	5r org red	35	35
90	A21	7r grn & ultra	85	85
a.		Souvenir sheet of 3	1.75	1.75
b.		Souvenir sheet of 3 (colors changed)	4.50	4.50

Issued as peace propaganda.

No. 90a contains one each of Nos. 88–90 and sold for 16r. No. 90b contains one of each denomination with colors changed to: 1.50r orange red, 5r green & ultramarine, 7r brown & green. No. 90b sold for 20r. Marginal inscriptions in bistre. Size: 146½x93mm.

1961, July 1 *Perf. 13* Unwmkd.

Flowers: 5r, Oleander. 10r, Amaryllis.

91	A22	2r lil rose, yel & grn	30	30
92	A22	5r ultra, lil rose & grn	50	50
93	A22	10r vio, car & grn	1.25	1.25
a.		Souv. sheet of 3	2.75	2.75

No. 93a contains one each of Nos. 91–93. Gold marginal inscription. Size: 130x100mm. Sold for 20r.

Krishna in Chariot, Khmer Frieze
A23

Independence Monument
A24

1961–63 Typo. *Perf. 14x13½*

94	A23	1r lilac	10	10
94A	A23	2r bl ('63)	1.25	75
95	A23	3r emerald	25	25
96	A23	6r orange	45	25
a.		Souv. sheet of 3	4.75	4.75

Issued to honor Cambodian armed forces.

No. 94A issued in coils. No. 96a contains one each of Nos. 94, 95, 96. Orange marginal inscriptions. Size: 149x85mm. Sold for 12r.

1961, Nov. 9 Engr. *Perf. 13x12½*

97	A24	2r green	30	30
98	A24	4r gray brn	30	30
a.		Souvenir sheet of 2	1.20	1.20
		Nos. 97-98, C15-C17 (5)	6.70	5.10

Issued to commemorate the tenth anniversary of Independence. No. 98a contains one each of Nos. 97–98 with gold marginal inscription. Size: 150x85mm.

Nos. 27 and 31 Overprinted in Red: "VIe CONFERENCE MONDIALE BOUDDIQUE 12-11-1961"

1961, Nov. 11 *Perf. 13*

99	A6	2.50pi (r) grn	35	35
100	A6	4.50pi (r) pur	50	50

Sixth World Conference of Buddhism.

Highway (American Aid)
A25

Foreign Aid: 2r, Power station (Czech aid). 4r, Textile factory (Chinese aid). 5r, Hospital (Russian aid). 6r, Airport (French aid).

1961, Dec. Engraved *Perf. 13*

101	A25	2r org & rose car	20	12
102	A25	3r bl, grn & org brn	30	20
103	A25	4r dl bl, org brn & mag	35	22
104	A25	5r dl grn & lil rose	40	35
105	A25	6r dk bl & org brn	55	40
a.		Souvenir sheet of 5	2.50	2.50
		Nos. 101-105 (5)	1.80	1.29

Issued to publicize foreign aid to Cambodia. No. 105a contains one each of Nos. 101–105 with bistre marginal inscription. Size: 148x84mm.

Malaria Eradication Emblem
A26

1962, Apr. 7 *Perf. 13* Unwmkd.

106	A26	2r mag & brn	25	18
107	A26	4r grn & dk brn	38	32
108	A26	6r vio & ol bis	45	38

Issued for the World Health Organization drive to eradicate malaria.

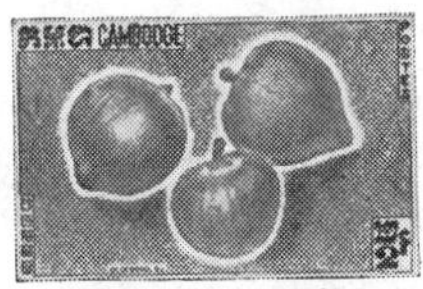

Turmeric—A27

Fruits: 4r, Cinnamon. 6r, Mangosteens.

1962, June 4 Engraved

109	A27	2r gray & bis	45	40
110	A27	4r dk bl grn & ol gray	45	40
111	A27	6r dk bl, grn & mag	70	60
a.		Souv. sheet of 3	2.00	2.00

Nos. 111a contains one each of Nos. 109–111 with marginal inscription in gray. Size: 149x84mm. Sold for 15r.

Pineapples
A28

Designs: 5r, Sugar cane. 9r, Sugar palms.

1962 *Perf. 13* Unwmkd.

112	A28	2r bluish grn & brn	40	35
113	A28	5r brn & grn	50	40
114	A28	9r Prus grn & brn	75	50

No. 73 Surcharged

1962, Nov. 9 *Perf. 13*

115	A14	50c on 80c rose car	30	30

No. 97 Surcharged with New Value in Red and Overprinted in Black with Two Bars and: "INAUGURATION / DU / MONUMENT"

1962

116	A24	3r on 2r grn	25	18

Dedication of Independence Monument.

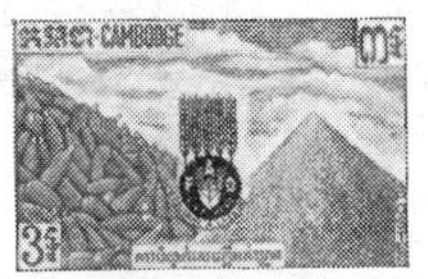

Corn, Rice and FAO Emblem
A29

1963, Mar. 21 Engraved *Perf. 13*

117	A29	3r multi	55	45
118	A29	6r org red, vio bl & ocher	55	45

Issued for the "Freedom from Hunger" campaign of the U.N. Food and Agriculture Organization.

Preah Vihear, Ancient Temple
A30

Tonsay Lake
A31

1963, June 15 *Perf. 12½x13*

119	A30	3r cl, brn & sl grn	25	25
120	A30	6r org, sl grn & grnsh blk	50	38
121	A30	15r bl, choc & grn	1.00	85

Return by Thailand of Preah Vihear on the Mekong River.

No. 44 Surcharged with New Value and Bars

1963 Engraved *Perf. 14x13*

122	A8	3r on 2½r dk vio brn	35	35

Perf. 12x12½, 12½x12

1963, Aug. 1 Photogravure

Designs: 7r, Popokvil Falls. 20r, Beach (horiz.).

123	A31	3r multi	20	20
124	A31	7r multi	45	30
125	A31	20r multi	1.20	70

UNESCO Emblem, Scales and Globe
A32

1963, Dec. 10 Engraved *Perf. 13*

126	A32	1r vio bl, rose cl & grn	20	20

127	A32	3r yel grn, vio bl & rose cl	35	35
128	A32	12r rose cl, yel grn & vio bl	75	75

Issued to commemorate the 15th anniversary of the Universal Declaration of Human Rights.

Kouprey
A33

1964, March 3 Perf. 13 Unwmkd.

129	A33	50c grn, dk brn & org brn	15	15
130	A33	3r org, brn, dk brn & grn	25	25
131	A33	6r bl, dk brn & grn	40	30

Black-billed Magpie
A34

Birds: 6r, Kingfisher. 12r, Gray heron.

1964, May 2 Engraved Perf. 13

132	A34	3r dk bl, ind & grn	20	20
133	A34	6r ind, org & brn	40	40
134	A34	12r Prus grn, ind & red brn	85	85

Emblem of Royal Cambodian Airline
A35

1964 Perf. 13x12½ Unwmkd.

135	A35	1.50r rose car & pur	20	20
136	A35	3r ver & dk bl	25	20
137	A35	7.50r ultra & car	60	50

Issued to commemorate the 8th anniversary of the Royal Cambodian Airline.

Prince Norodom Sihanouk
A36

1964 Engraved Perf. 12½x13

138	A36	2r purple	18	18
139	A36	3r red brn	25	25
140	A36	10r dk bl	70	60

Issued to commemorate the 10th anniversary of the Sangkum (political party).

Woman Weaver
A37

Khmer Handicrafts: 3r, Metal worker. 5r, Basket maker.

1965, Feb. 1 Perf. 13x12½

141	A37	1r multi	15	15
142	A37	3r red lil, red brn & gray ol	35	25
143	A37	5r grn, dk brn & car	40	30

Nos. 139-140 Overprinted in Black or Red: "CONFERENCE / DES PEUPLES / INDOCHINOIS"

1965, Mar. 1 Perf. 12½x13

144	A36	3r red brn	40	40
145	A36	10r dk bl (R)	60	40

Conference of the people of Indo-China.

ITU Emblem, Old and New Communication Equipment
A38

1965, May 17 Engraved Perf. 13

146	A38	3r grn & ol bis	30	30
147	A38	4r red & bl	40	30
148	A38	10r vio & rose lil	70	60

Issued to commemorate the centenary of the International Telecommunication Union.

Cotton Plant
A39

Designs: 3r, Peanut plant. 7.50r, Coconut palm.

1965, Aug. 2 Perf. 12½x13

149	A39	1.50r org, sl grn & pur	25	25
150	A39	3r bl, yel, grn & brn	38	38
151	A39	7.50r org brn & sl grn	70	70

Preah Ko Temple, Rolouoh
A40

Temples at Angkor: 5r, Baksei Chamkrong, Rolouoh. 7r, Banteay Srei (Citadel of Women). 9r, Angkor Wat. 12r, Bayon, Angkor Thom.

1966, Feb. 1 Engraved Perf. 13

152	A40	3r gray ol, sal & dl grn	32	28
153	A40	5r lil, dk grn & redsh brn	45	40
154	A40	7r dk grn, redsh brn & bis	50	45
155	A40	9r vio bl, pur & dk grn	85	55
156	A40	12r dk grn, rose car & ver	1.10	75
		Nos. 152-156 (5)	3.22	2.43

WHO Headquarters, Geneva
A41

1966, July 1 Photo. Perf. 12½x13

WHO Emblem in Blue and Yellow

157	A41	2r blk & pale rose	20	15
158	A41	3r blk & yel grn	25	20
159	A41	5r blk & lt bl	35	25

Issued to commemorate the inauguration of World Health Headquarters, Geneva.

Tree Planting
A42

UNESCO Emblem
A43

1966, July 22 Engr. Perf. 12½x13

160	A42	1r brn, dl brn & brt grn	15	10
161	A42	3r org, dl brn & brt grn	25	20
162	A42	7r gray, dl brn & brt grn	50	30

Issued for Arbor Day.

1966 Photogravure Perf. 13

163	A43	3r multi	30	30
164	A43	7r multi	50	30

Issued to commemorate the 20th anniversary of UNESCO (United Nations Educational, Scientific and Cultural Organization).

Wrestlers and Games' Emblem
A44

Designs (Games Emblem and): 3r, Stadium, Phnom Penh. 7r, Swordsmen. 10r, Indian club swingers. Bas-reliefs from Angkor Wat.

1966, Nov. 25 Engraved Perf. 13

165	A44	3r vio bl	25	20
166	A44	4r green	30	20
167	A44	7r dk car rose	45	25
168	A44	10r dk brn	60	40

Issued to commemorate the GANEFO Games.

Indian Wild Boar
A45

Designs: 5r, Muntjac (vert.). 7r, Elephant.

Perf. 13x12½, 12½x13

1967, Feb. 20 Engraved

169	A45	3r brt bl, grn & blk	25	20
170	A45	5r multi	35	20
171	A45	7r multi	50	30

Nos. 152-153, 155-156 and 121 Overprinted in Red: "ANNEE INTERNATIONALE DU TOURISME 1967"

1967, Apr. 27 Engr. Perf. 13

172	A40	3r multi	30	30
173	A40	5r multi	40	30
174	A40	9r multi	60	55
175	A40	12r multi	70	70
176	A30	15r multi	85	85
		Nos. 172-176 (5)	2.85	2.70

International Tourist Year, 1967.

No. 154 Overprinted in Red: "MILLENAIRE / DE BANTEAY SREI / 967-1967"

1967, Apr. 27

177	A40	7r multi	65	35

Issued to commemorate the millennium of the Banteay Srei Temple at Angkor.

Royal Ballet Dancer
A46

Various Dancers

1967, June Engraved Perf. 13

178	A46	1r orange	15	15
179	A46	3r Prus bl	30	25
180	A46	5r ultra	45	35
181	A46	7r car rose	60	55
182	A46	10r multi	90	70
		Nos. 178-182 (5)	2.40	2.00

Issued to publicize the Cambodian Royal Ballet.

Nos. 128 and 70 Surcharged in Red

Journée Internationale
de l'Alphabétisation
8-9-67
6ʳ

1967, Sept. 8 Engraved

183	A32	6r on 12r multi	50	40
184	A13	7r on 15r grn & ol gray	60	45

Issued for International Literacy Day, Sept. 8. The surcharge on No. 184 is adapted to fit the shape of the stamp.

Symbolic Water Cycle
A47

1967, Nov. 1 Typo. Perf. 13x14

185	A47	1r blk, bl & org	15	15
186	A47	6r lil, lt bl & org	40	25
187	A47	10r dk bl, emer & org	65	40

Hydrological Decade (UNESCO), 1965-74.

Royal University, Kompong Cham
A48

Designs: 6r, Engineering School, Pnompenh. 9r, University Center, Sangkum Reastr Niyum.

1968, Mar. 1 Engraved *Perf. 13*

188	A48	4r vio bl & multi	30	30
189	A48	6r sl & multi	45	45
190	A48	9r Prus bl & multi	65	45

Vaccination and WHO Emblem
A49

Design: 7r, Malaria control and WHO emblem (man spraying DDT).

1968, July 8 Engraved *Perf. 13*

191	A49	3r ultra	20	18
192	A49	7r dp bl	45	30

Issued for the 20th anniversary of the World Health Organization.

Stadium, Mexico City
A50

Designs: 2r, Wrestling. 3r, Bicycling. 5r, Boxing (vert.). 7.50r, Torch bearer (vert.).

1968, Oct. 12 Engraved *Perf. 13*

193	A50	1r brn ol, grn & brn red	17	15
194	A50	2r brn, dk bl & rose cl	20	17
195	A50	3r plum, Prus bl & sep	30	25
196	A50	5r dk pur	38	30
197	A50	7.50r multi	42	38
		Nos. 193-197 (5)	1.47	1.25

Issued to commemorate the 19th Olympic Games, Mexico City, Oct. 12–27.

Red Cross Team
A51

1968, Nov. 1 Engraved *Perf. 13*

198	A51	3r Prus bl, grn & red	30	15

Issued to honor the Cambodian Red Cross.

Prince Norodom Sihanouk
A52

Design: 8r, Soldiers wading through swamp.

1968, Nov. 9

199	A52	7r emer, ultra & pur	50	30
200	A52	8r bl, grn & dp brn	60	30

15th anniversary of independence.

Human Rights Flame and Prince Sihanouk
A53

1968, Dec. 10 Engraved *Perf. 13*

201	A53	3r blue	25	18
202	A53	5r brt plum	40	25
203	A53	7r multi	50	30

International Human Rights Year.

ILO Emblem
A54

1969, May 1 Engraved *Perf. 13*

204	A54	3r ultra	22	18
205	A54	6r dp car	35	25
206	A54	9r bl grn	50	30

Issued to commemorate the 50th anniversary of the International Labor Organization.

Globe, Red Cross, Crescent, Lion and Sun Emblems
A55

1969, May 8

207	A55	1r bl, red & yel	15	15
208	A55	3r sl grn, red & vio brn	22	20
209	A55	10r brt lil, red & brn	60	30

Issued to commemorate the 50th anniversary of the League of Red Cross Societies.

Papilio Oeacus—A56

Butterflies: 4r, Papilio agamenon. 8r, Danaus plexippus.

1969, Oct. 10 Engraved *Perf. 13*

210	A56	3r lil, blk & yel	25	25
211	A56	4r ver, blk & grn	35	35
212	A56	8r yel grn, dk brn & org	60	45

Map of Cambodia and Diesel Engine
A57

Designs: Various railroad stations and trains.

1969, Nov. 27 Engraved *Perf. 13*

213	A57	3r multi	25	20
214	A57	6r sl grn & lt brn	35	28
215	A57	8r black	45	38
216	A57	9r dk grn & bl	50	38

Issued to publicize the new rail link between Phnom Penh and Sihanoukville.

Tripletail
A58

Fish: 7r, Sleeper goby. 9r, Snakehead.

1970, Jan. 29 Photo. *Perf. 13*

217	A58	3r multi	18	12
218	A58	7r multi	35	27
219	A58	9r multi	45	35

Wat Maniratanaram
A59

Monasteries: 2r, Wat Tepthidaram (vert.). 6r, Wat Patumavati. 8r, Wat Unnalom.

1970, Apr. 29 Photo. *Perf. 13*

220	A59	2r multi	12	10
221	A59	3r multi	25	15
222	A59	6r multi	38	25
223	A59	8r multi	50	38

U.P.U. Headquarters and Monument, Bern—A60

1970, May 20

224	A60	1r grn & multi	5	5
225	A60	3r scar & multi	6	6
226	A60	4r dp bl & multi	10	8
227	A60	10r brn & multi	18	15

Issued to commemorate the inauguration of the new Universal Postal Union Headquarters in Bern.

Open Book and Satellite Earth Receiving Station
A61

1970, May 17 Photo. *Perf. 13*

228	A61	3r dk vio bl & multi	10	5
229	A61	4r sl grn & multi	12	8
230	A61	9r brn ol & multi	18	15

World Telecommunications Day.

Nelumbium Speciosum
A62

Flowers: 4r, Eichhornia crassipes. 13r, Nymphea lotus.

1970, Aug. 17 Photo. *Perf. 13*

231	A62	3r multi	8	8
	a.	Cambodian and Arabic 3's transposed	1.25	
232	A62	4r multi	12	12
233	A62	13r multi	20	20

Elephant God, Bas-relief at Banteay Srei
A63

1970, Sept. 21 Engraved *Perf. 13*

234	A63	3r lil rose & dp grn	10	6
235	A63	4r bl grn, grn & lil rose	12	7
236	A63	7r bl grn, dk brn & grn	18	10

Issued for World Meteorological Day.

Khmer Republic

Globe, Rocket, Dove and U.N. Emblem—A64

1970, Nov. 9 Photo. *Perf. 12½x12*

237	A64	3r blk & multi	10	7
238	A64	5r brn red & multi	12	10
239	A64	10r dp vio & multi	18	10

25th anniversary of the United Nations.

Education Year Emblem
A65

1970, Nov. 9 Engr. *Perf. 13x12½*

240	A65	1r blue	4	4
241	A65	3r brt rose lil	10	6
242	A65	8r bl grn	20	10

Issued for International Education Year.

Chuon-Nath—A66

1971, Jan. 27 Photo. *Perf. 13*

243	A66	3r ol grn & multi	7	5
244	A66	8r pur & multi	12	8
245	A66	9r vio & multi	18	10

In memory of Chuon-Nath (1883–1969), Cambodian language expert.

Soldiers in Battle
A67

1971, March 18 Photo. *Perf. 13*

246	A67	1r gray & multi	4	4
247	A67	3r bis & multi	15	10
248	A67	10r bl & multi	50	25

National territorial defense.

U.N. Emblem, Men of Four Races
A68

1971, March 21

249	A68	3r bl & multi	6	5
250	A68	7r grn & multi	12	10
251	A68	8r brt rose & multi	18	12

International year against racial discrimination.

General Post Office, Phnom Penh
A69

1971, Apr. 19

252	A69	3r bl & multi	15	10
253	A69	9r lil rose & multi	45	20
254	A69	10r blk & multi	50	25

Symbolic Globe and Waves—A70

Design: 7r, 8r, ITU emblem and waves.

1971, May 17 Photo. ***Perf. 13***

255	A70	3r grn, blk & bl	5	5
256	A70	4r yel & multi	13	5
257	A70	7r lil, blk & red	8	8
258	A70	8r sal pink, blk & red	15	10

3rd World Telecommunications Day.

Erythrina Indica
A71

Wild Flowers: 3r, Bauhinia variegata. 6r, Butea frondosa. 10r, Lagerstroemia floribunda (vert.).

1971, July 5 ***Perf. 13x12½, 12½x13***

259	A71	2r lt ultra & multi	8	5
260	A71	3r yel grn & multi	10	8
261	A71	6r bl & multi	18	12
262	A71	10r brn & multi	30	25

Khmer Coat of Arms
A72

Flag and Square of the Republic
A73

1971, Oct. 9 Engraved ***Perf. 13***

263	A72	3r brt grn & bis	8	5
264	A73	3r pur & multi	8	5
265	A73	4r dp cl & multi	8	5
266	A72	8r org & bis	10	7
267	A72	10r lt brn & bis	15	8
a.		Souvenir sheet of 3	1.00	1.00
268	A73	10r sl grn & multi	15	8
a.		Souvenir sheet of 3	85	85
		Nos. 263-268 (6)	64	38

First anniversary of the Republic. No. 267a contains one each of Nos. 263, 266–267 with olive marginal inscriptions. Sold for 25fr. No. 268a contains one each of Nos. 264–265 and 268 with purple marginal inscription. Sold for 20r. Size of sheets: 129x100mm.

UNICEF Emblem
A74

1971, Dec. 11

269	A74	3r blk brn	6	5
270	A74	5r ultra	10	6
271	A74	9r dk pur & brn red	18	10

25th anniversary of the United Nations International Children's Fund (UNICEF).

Book Year Emblem
A75

1972, Feb. 7

272	A75	3r bl, grn & vio	8	5
273	A75	8r vio, grn & bl	15	8
274	A75	9r emer & multi	18	10
a.		Souvenir sheet of 3	90	90

International Book Year 1972. No. 274a contains one each of Nos. 272–274 with emerald marginal inscription. Size: 159x99mm. Sold for 23r.

Lion of St. Mark
A76

Designs: 5r, Waves engulfing St. Mark's Basilica. 10r, Bridge of Sighs (vert.).

1972, Feb. 7 Engraved ***Perf. 13***

275	A76	3r lil rose & org brn	8	5
276	A76	5r yel grn & org brn	15	7
277	A76	10r org brn, bl & yel grn	25	18
a.		Souvenir sheet of 3	85	85

UNESCO campaign to save Venice. No. 277a contains one each of Nos. 275–277. Yellow green marginal inscription. Size: 140x99mm. Sold for 23r.

U.N. Emblem
A77

1972, Mar. 28

278	A77	3r dp car	8	5
279	A77	6r dp bl	18	12
280	A77	9r dp org	20	17
a.		Souvenir sheet of 3	90	90

25th anniversary. United Nations Economic Commission for Asia and the Far East (ECAFE), No. 280a contains one each of Nos. 278–280. Deep blue marginal inscription. Size: 138x100mm. Sold for 23r.

Dancing Apsarases
A78

"UIT"
A79

1972, May 5 Engraved ***Perf. 13***

281	A78	1r gldn brn	5	5
282	A78	3r violet	8	6
283	A78	7r rose cl	18	15
284	A78	8r ol brn	20	15
285	A78	9r bl grn	22	18
286	A78	10r ultra	25	20
287	A78	12r purple	28	25
288	A78	14r Prus bl	35	28
		Nos. 281-288 (8)	1.61	1.32

1972, May 17 Lithographed

Size: 35½x22mm.

289	A79	3r blk, yel & grnsh bl	10	5
290	A79	9r blk, dp lil rose & bl grn	25	13
291	A79	14r blk, brn & bl grn	35	25

4th World Telecommunications Day.

"Human Environment"
A80

1972, June 5 Engraved

292	A80	3r org, plum & grn	10	7
293	A80	12r brt grn & plum	40	25
294	A80	15r plum & brt grn	48	32
a.		Souv. sheet of 3	1.10	1.10

U.N. Conference on Human Environment, Stockholm, June 5–16. No. 294a contains one each of Nos. 292–294. Green marginal inscription. Size: 129x100mm. Sold for 35r.

Javan Rhinoceros
A81

1972, Aug. 1 Engraved ***Perf. 13***

Multicolored

295	A81	3r *shown*	6	5
296	A81	4r *Serow*	6	5
297	A81	6r *Malayan sambar*	10	7
298	A81	7r *Banteng*	12	8
299	A81	8r *Water buffalo*	12	8
300	A81	10r *Gaur*	15	10
		Nos. 295-300 (6)	61	43

Nos. 263, 267, 134, 293, 294 Overprinted in Red

XXe JEUX OLYMPIQUES
MUNICH 1972

1972, Sept. 9 Engr. ***Perf. 13***

301	A72	3r brt grn & bis	15	10
302	A72	10r org & bis	45	30
303	A34	12r multi	60	35
304	A80	12r brt grn & plum	60	35
305	A80	15r plum & brt grn	80	50
		Nos. 301-305 (5)	2.60	1.60

20th Olympic Games, Munich, Aug. 26–Sept. 11.

Raising Khmer Flag
A82

1972, Oct. 9 Photo. ***Perf. 12½x13***

306	A82	3r multi	8	5
307	A82	5r brt rose & multi	10	6
308	A82	9r yel grn & multi	16	10

2nd anniversary of the establishment of the Khmer Republic.

Stupa and Crest
A83

Apsaras
A84

1973, May 12 Engraved ***Perf. 13***

309	A83	3r ocher & multi	7	5
310	A83	12r yel grn & multi	15	18
311	A83	14r bl & multi	20	23
a.		Souvenir sheet of 3	90	90

New Constitution. No. 311a contains one each of Nos. 309–311 with brown marginal inscription. Size: 128½x99mm. Sold for 34r.

1973, July 23 Engraved ***Perf. 13***

Sculptures from Angkor Wat: 8r, 10r, Devata (different).

312	A84	3r brn blk	7	5
313	A84	8r Prus grn	13	13
314	A84	10r ol bis	17	17
a.		Souvenir sheet of 3	75	75

No. 314a contains one each of Nos. 312–314 with black marginal inscription. Size: 130x100mm. Sold for 25r.

INTERPOL Emblem
A85

Marshal Lon Nol
A86

1973, Oct. 2 Engraved ***Perf. 13***

315	A85	3r grn & multi	8	5
316	A85	7r red brn & multi	15	13
317	A85	10r ol & multi	20	20
a.		Souvenir sheet of 3	80	80

50th anniversary of the International Criminal Police Organization. No. 317a contains one each of Nos. 315–317; black marginal inscription. Size: 123x100mm. Sold for 30r.

1973, Oct. 9

318	A86	3r lt grn, blk & brn	12	7
319	A86	8r brn, ol & blk	25	15
320	A86	14r blk & brn	42	25
a.		Souvenir sheet of 3	1.10	1.10

Marshal Lon Nol, first president of the Republic. No. 320a contains stamps similar to Nos. 318–320 in changed colors; greenish black marginal inscription. Size: 129x99mm. Sold for 50r.

Nos. 248, 243 and 307 Surcharged with New Value, 2 Bars and Overprinted in Red or Silver: "4th ANNIVERSAIRE/DE LA REPUBLIQUE"

1974 Photo. *Perf. 13, 12½x13*

No.	Type	Description	Unused	Used
321	A67	10r multi (R)	4	3
322	A66	50r on 3r multi (S)	20	15
323	A82	100r on 5r multi (S)	45	30

4th anniversary of independence.

Copernicus and "Nerva"—A87

Designs: Copernicus, various spacecraft and events.

1974, Sept. 10 Litho. *Perf. 13*

Multicolored

No.	Type	Description	Unused	Used
324	A87	1r *shown*		
325	A87	5r *Mariner II*		
326	A87	10r *Apollo*		
327	A87	25r *Telstar*		
328	A87	50r *Space walk*		
329	A87	100r *Moon landing*		
330	A87	150r *Separation of spaceship and module*		
		Nos. 324-330, C32-C33 (9)	*17.50*	*17.50*

500th anniversary of the birth of Nicolaus Copernicus (1473-1543), Polish astronomer.

Carrier Pigeon and UPU Emblem

A88

Design: 60r, Sailing ship and UPU emblem.

1974, Nov. 2

No.	Type	Description	Unused	Used
331	A88	10r multi	4	3
332	A88	60r multi	25	15

Centenary of Universal Postal Union. A souvenir sheet containing one No. 332 exists. See No. C34.

Importation Prohibited

The U.S. Treasury Department prohibited the importation of stamps of Cambodia (Khmer Republic) as of Apr. 17, 1975.

SEMI-POSTAL STAMPS.

Nos. 8, 12, 14 and 15 Surcharged in Black

+60c
AIDE A L'ÉTUDIANT

1952, Oct. 20 *Perf. 13* Unwmkd.

No.	Type	Description	Unused	Used
B1	A3	1.10pi +40c dp car & brt red	4.25	4.25
B2	A3	1.90pi +60c ind & dp ultra	4.25	4.25
B3	A3	3pi +1pi dp car & org brn	4.25	4.25
B4	A1	5pi +2pi ind & pur	4.25	4.25

Preah Stupa

SP1

1957, Mar. 15 Engraved *Perf. 13*

No.	Type	Description	Unused	Used
B5	SP1	1.50r +50c ind, ol & red	60	60
B6	SP1	6.50r +1.50r red lil, ol & red	1.00	1.00
B7	SP1	8r +2r bl, ol & red	1.50	1.50

Issued to commemorate the 2500th anniversary of the birth of Buddha. See Nos. 62-64.

Type of Regular Issue, 1959, with Red Typographed Surcharge

+ 0,30

1959, Dec. 9

No.	Type	Description	Unused	Used
B8	A14	20c +20c rose vio	6	6
B9	A14	50c +30c bl	12	12
B10	A14	80c +50c rose car	18	18

The surtax was for the Red Cross.

Nos. 107-108 Surcharged and Overprinted in Red: "1863-1963 CENTENAIRE DE LA CROIX ROUGE"

1963, Oct. 1 *Perf. 13* Unwmkd.

No.	Type	Description	Unused	Used
B11	A26	4r +40c grn & dk brn	60	60
B12	A26	6r +60c vio & ol bis	75	75

Centenary of International Red Cross.

Nos. 263, 267, 293-294, 134 Surcharged in Red

SECOURS AUX VICTIMES DE GUERRE

1972, Nov. 15 Engr. *Perf. 13*

No.	Type	Description	Unused	Used
B13	A72	3r +2r multi	15	20
B14	A72	10r +6r multi	40	30
B15	A80	12r +7r multi	50	35
B16	A34	12r +7r multi	50	35
B17	A80	15r +8r multi	85	65
		Nos. B13-B17 (5)	2.40	1.85

Surtax was for war victims. Surcharge arranged differently on Nos. B15-B17.

AIR POST STAMPS.

Kinnari

AP1

Engraved

1953, Apr. 16 *Perf. 13* Unwmkd.

No.	Type	Description	Unused	Used
C1	AP1	50c dp grn	55	55
a.		Souvenir sheet of 4	50.00	50.00
C2	AP1	3pi red brn	65	55
a.		Souvenir sheet of 3	50.00	50.00
C3	AP1	3.30pi rose vio	90	65
C4	AP1	4pi dk brn & dp bl	1.10	65
C5	AP1	5.10pi brn, red & org	1.35	90
C6	AP1	6.50pi dk brn & lil rose	1.35	1.50
a.		Souvenir sheet of 2	50.00	50.00
C7	AP1	9pi lil rose & dp grn	2.00	2.00
C8	AP1	11.50pi multi	3.75	3.00
C9	AP1	30pi dk brn, bl grn & org	5.75	3.50
		Nos. C1-C9 (9)	17.40	13.30

No. C1a contains one each of the 50c, 3.30pi, 5.10pi and 30pi, and sold for 50pi. No. C2a contains one each of the 3pi, 4pi and 11.50pi, and sold for 25pi. No C6a contains one each of the 6.50pi and 9pi, and sold for 20pi. Marginal inscriptions in brown. Size: 129x100mm.

AP2

1957, Dec. 11

No.	Type	Description	Unused	Used
C10	AP2	50c maroon	12	8
C11	AP2	1r emerald	20	15
C12	AP2	4r ultra	90	55
C13	AP2	50r car rose	5.00	4.50
C14	AP2	100r grn, bl & car	8.00	6.00
a.		Souvenir sheet of 5	17.50	17.50
		Nos. C10-C14 (5)	14.22	11.28

No. C14a contains one each of Nos. C10-C14, and sold for 160r. Size: 159x93mm.

Independence Type of 1961

1961, Nov. 9 *Perf. 13x12½*

No.	Type	Description	Unused	Used
C15	A24	7r multi	75	40
C16	A24	30r grn, car & ultra	2.00	1.60
C17	A24	50r ind, grn & ol	3.50	2.50
a.		Souvenir sheet of 3	8.00	8.00

Issued to commemorate the tenth anniversary of Independence. No. C17a contains one each of Nos. C15-C17 with gold marginal inscription. Size: 150x85mm.

No. C15 Surcharged with New Value in Red and Overprinted in Black with Two Bars and: "INAUGURATION DU MONUMENT"

1962, Nov. 9

No.	Type	Description	Unused	Used
C18	A24	12r on 7r multi	1.10	90

Dedication of Independence Monument.

Hanuman, Monkey God

AP3

1964, Sept. 1 Engraved *Perf. 13*

No.	Type	Description	Unused	Used
C19	AP3	5r multi	50	27
C20	AP3	10r ol bis, lil rose & grn	70	35
C21	AP3	20r vio, bl & ol bis	1.10	55
C22	AP3	40r bl, ol bis & dk bl	2.50	1.10
C23	AP3	80r multi	4.00	3.25
		Nos. C19-C23 (5)	8.80	5.52

Nos. C19-C22 Surcharged in Red

12ᶠ
JEUX
OLYMPIQUES
TOKYO-1964

1964, Oct.

No.	Type	Description	Unused	Used
C24	AP3	3r on 5r multi	40	32
C25	AP3	6r on 10r multi	55	50
C26	AP3	9r on 20r multi	80	70
C27	AP3	12r on 40r multi	1.20	1.00

18th Olympic Games, Tokyo, Oct. 10-25.

Certain unlisted issues of Cambodia, starting in 1972, are mentioned and briefly described in "For the Record" at the back of this volume.

Garuda, 12th Century, Angkor Thom

AP4

1973, Jan. 18 Engraved *Perf. 13*

No.	Type	Description	Unused	Used
C28	AP4	3r carmine	8	6
C29	AP4	30r vio bl	65	50
C30	AP4	50r dl pur	1.10	80
C31	AP4	100r dl grn	2.25	1.50

Copernicus Type of 1974

Designs: 200r, Copernicus and Skylab III. 250r, Copernicus, Concorde and solar eclipse.

1974, Sept. 10 Litho. *Perf. 13*

No.	Type	Description	Unused	Used
C32	A87	200r multi		
C33	A87	250r multi		

500th anniversary of the birth of Nicolaus Copernicus (1473-1543), Polish astronomer. A souvenir sheet containing No. C32 is perf., size 110x82mm. A souvenir sheet containing No. C33 is imperf., size 83x111 mm.

UPU Type of 1974

Design: 700r, Rocket, globe and UPU emblem.

1974, Nov. 2

No.	Type	Description	Unused	Used
C34	A88	700r gold & multi	2.80	2.00

Centenary of Universal Postal Union. A souvenir sheet containing one No. C34 exists.

POSTAGE DUE STAMPS

D1

Frieze, Angkor Wat

D2

Typographed.

1957 ***Perf. 13½*** **Unwmkd.**

Denomination in Black.

J1	D1	10c ver & pale bl	12	12
J2	D1	50c ver & pale bl	18	18
J3	D1	1r ver & pale bl	22	22
J4	D1	3r ver & pale bl	33	33
J5	D1	5r ver & pale bl	60	60
		Nos. J1-J5 (5)	1.45	1.45

1974, Feb. 18 Engr. ***Perf. 12½x13***

J6	D2	2r ocher	8	6
J7	D2	6r green	13	10
J8	D2	8r dp car	20	15
J9	D2	10r vio bl	27	20

CAMEROUN

(kăm′ĕr·ōōn)

(Kamerun)

LOCATION—On the west coast of Africa, north of the equator.

GOVT.—Republic.

AREA—182,964 sq. mi.

POP.—6,670,000 (est. 1977).

CAPITAL—Yaoundé.

Before World War I, Cameroun (Kamerun) was a German Protectorate. It was occupied during the War by Great Britain and France and in 1922 was mandated to these countries by the League of Nations. The French mandated part became the independent State of Cameroun Jan. 1, 1960. The Southern Cameroons, a United Kingdom Trust Territory, joined this state to form the Federal Republic of Cameroun Oct. 1, 1961. The name was changed to United Republic of Cameroon on May 20, 1972.

Stamps of Southern Cameroons are listed under Cameroons in Vol. I.

100 Pfennig = 1 Mark
12 Pence = 1 Shilling
100 Centimes = 1 Franc

Issued under German Dominion.

A1

A2

Stamps of Germany, 1889-1900, Overprinted in Black.

1897 ***Perf. 13½x14½*** **Unwmkd.**

1	A1	3pf yel brn	15.00	16.50
a.		3pf red brn	22.50	30.00
b.		3pf dk brn	8.75	37.50
2	A1	5pf green	7.50	4.00
3	A2	10pf carmine	5.50	5.50
4	A2	20pf ultra	6.50	7.50
5	A2	25pf orange	30.00	40.00
6	A2	50pf red brn	25.00	35.00
		Nos. 1-6 (6)	89.50	108.50

Kaiser's Yacht "Hohenzollern"
A3 A4

Typographed.

1900 ***Perf. 14*** **Unwmkd.**

7	A3	3pf brown	1.75	1.75
8	A3	5pf green	30.00	1.00
9	A3	10pf carmine	80.00	1.50
10	A3	20pf ultra	40.00	2.50
11	A3	25pf org & blk, *yel*	1.75	7.50
12	A3	30pf org & blk, *sal*	2.25	6.00
13	A3	40pf lake & blk	2.25	6.00
14	A3	50pf pur & blk, *sal*	2.75	7.50
15	A3	80pf lake & blk, *rose*	3.50	10.00

Engraved.

Perf. 14½x14

16	A4	1m carmine	100.00	75.00
17	A4	2m blue	7.50	75.00
18	A4	3m blk vio	8.00	125.00
19	A4	5m sl & car	150.00	650.00
		Nos. 7-19 (13)	429.75	968.75

Wmk. 125

Typographed.

1905-18 Wmkd. Lozenges. (125)

20	A3	3pf brn ('18)	1.00	
21	A3	5pf grn ('06)	1.00	2.00
a.		Booklet pane of 6	12.50	
b.		Booklet pane of 6,(2 No. 21 + 4 No. 22)	75.00	
22	A3	10pf carmine	1.00	1.00
a.		Booklet pane of 6	12.50	
23	A3	20pf ultra ('14)	2.50	190.00
24	A4	1m car ('15)	3.00	
25	A4	5m sl & car ('13)	25.00	4,500.

The 3pf and 1m were not placed in use.

Issued under British Occupation.

Stamps of German Cameroun Surcharged

C. E. F.
1 d.
2

Wmkd. Lozenges (125)
(*54-56, 65)
Unwmkd. (Other Values.)

1915 ***Perf. 14, 14½***

Blue Surcharge.

53	A3	½p on 3pf brn	3.75	5.50
54	A3	½p on 5pf grn	1.50	2.00
a.		Double surcharge	300.00	180.00
b.		blk surcharge	2.75	3.25
55	A3	1p on 10pf car	1.50	2.00
a.		"1" with thin serifs	16.00	20.00
b.		Double surcharge	72.50	85.00
c.		Black surcharge	12.00	17.50
d.		"C.E.F." omitted	1,600.	
e.		"1d" double	1,500.	

Black Surcharge.

56	A3	2p on 20pf ultra	1.25	2.00
57	A3	2½p on 25pf org & blk, *yel*	3.00	5.00
a.		Double surcharge	2,000.	
58	A3	3p on 30pf org & blk, *sal*	3.00	5.00
59	A3	4p on 40pf lake & blk	3.00	5.00
60	A3	6p on 50pf pur & blk, *sal*	3.00	5.00
61	A3	8p on 80pf lake & blk, *rose*	3.00	5.00

Surcharged

C. E. F.
1s.

62	A4	1sh on 1m car	125.00	150.00
a.		"S" inverted	525.00	550.00
63	A4	2sh on 2m bl	125.00	150.00
a.		"S" inverted	525.00	550.00
64	A4	3sh on 3m blk vio	125.00	150.00
a.		"S" inverted	525.00	550.00
b.		Double surcharge	3,000.	
65	A4	5sh on 5m sl & car	125.00	150.00
a.		"S" inverted	525.00	550.00
		Nos. 53-65 (13)	523.00	636.50

The letters "C. E. F." are the initials of "Cameroons Expeditionary Force."

Issued under French Occupation.

Stamps of Gabon, 1910, Overprinted

Corps Expéditionnaire
Franco-Anglais
CAMEROUN

1915 ***Perf. 13½x14.*** **Unwmkd.**

101	A10	10c red & car	15.00	7.50
102	A13	1c choc & org	50.00	16.50
103	A13	2c blk & choc	90.00	75.00
104	A13	4c vio & dp bl	90.00	75.00
105	A13	5c ol gray & grn	15.00	7.50
105A	A13	10c red & car	*10,000.*	*11,000.*
106	A13	20c ol brn & dk vio	90.00	85.00
107	A14	25c dp bl & choc	30.00	13.00
108	A14	30c gray blk & red	90.00	72.50
109	A14	35c dk vio & grn	27.50	11.50
a.		Double ovpt.	800.00	800.00
110	A14	40c choc & ultra	90.00	75.00
111	A14	45c car & vio	100.00	80.00
112	A14	50c bl grn & gray	100.00	90.00
113	A14	75c org & choc	135.00	90.00
114	A15	1fr dk brn & bis	115.00	100.00
115	A15	2fr car & brn	140.00	100.00
		Nos. 101-105, 106-115 (15)	1,177.50	898.50

The overprint is vertical, reading up, on Nos. 101–106, 114–115, and horizontal on Nos. 107–113.

Stamps of Middle Congo, Issue of 1907, Overprinted

Occupation
Francaise
du Cameroun

1916 **Unwmkd.**

116	A1	1c ol gray & brn	42.50	42.50
117	A1	2c vio & brn	55.00	50.00
118	A1	4c bl & brn	55.00	50.00
119	A1	5c dk grn & bl	15.00	13.50
120	A2	35c vio brn & bl	62.50	50.00
121	A2	45c vio & red	37.50	35.00

The overprint is horizontal on Nos. 116–119, and vertical, reading down, on Nos. 120–121.

Same Overprint
On Stamps of French Congo, 1900.

Wmkd. Branch of Thistle. (122)

122	A4	15c dl vio & ol grn	30.00	30.00
a.		Inverted overprint	67.50	67.50

Wmkd. Branch of Rose Tree. (123)

123	A5	20c yel grn & org	90.00	50.00
124	A5	30c car rose & org	50.00	35.00
125	A5	40c org brn & brt grn	37.50	35.00
126	A5	50c gray vio & lil	42.50	35.00
127	A5	75c red vio & org	47.50	32.50

Wmkd. Branch of Olive. (124)

128	A6	1fr gray lil & ol	62.50	50.00
129	A6	2fr car & brn	62.50	50.00
		Nos. 116-129 (14)	690.00	558.50

The overprint is horizontal on No. 122; vertical, reading down or up, on Nos. 123–129.

Counterfeits exist of Nos. 101–129.

Stamps of Middle Congo, Issue of 1907 Overprinted

CAMEROUN
Occupation
Française

1916-17 **Unwmkd.**

130	A1	1c ol gray & brn	6	6
131	A1	2c vio & brn	7	6
132	A1	4c bl & brn	12	12
133	A1	5c dk grn & bl	15	13
a.		Booklet pane of 4		
134	A1	10c car & bl	45	35
135	A1	15c brn vio & rose ('17)	50	28
a.		Booklet pane of 4		
136	A1	20c brn & bl	28	18
137	A2	25c bl & grn	32	25
a.		Triple ovpt.	165.00	
138	A2	30c scar & grn	22	22
a.		Double ovpt.	165.00	
139	A2	35c vio brn & bl	35	30
140	A2	40c dl grn & brn	50	35
141	A2	45c vio & red	55	38
142	A2	50c bl grn & red	55	45
143	A2	75c brn & bl	70	45
144	A3	1fr dp grn & vio	55	45
145	A3	2fr vio & gray grn	3.75	2.75
146	A3	5fr bl & rose	4.25	3.25
		Nos. 130-146 (17)	13.37	10.03

Nos. 130 to 146 exist on ordinary paper and, with the exception of No. 132, on chalk surfaced paper. Nos. 137 to 146 are known with inverted "S" in "Francaise."

On Nos. 137 to 146 there is a space of 7mm. between "Cameroun" and "Occupation."

Provisional French Mandate.

Types of Middle Congo, 1907, Overprinted

CAMEROUN

1921

147	A1	1c ol grn & org	4	4
148	A1	2c brn & rose	4	4
149	A1	4c gray & lt grn	12	12
150	A1	5c dl red & org	12	12
a.		Double overprint	375.00	
151	A1	10c bl grn & lt grn	15	15
152	A1	15c bl & org	15	15
153	A1	20c red brn & ol	18	18
154	A2	25c sl & org	22	15
155	A2	30c rose & ver	22	15
156	A2	35c gray & ultra	30	30
157	A2	40c ol grn & org	22	22
158	A2	45c brn & rose	25	18
159	A2	50c bl & ultra	22	20
160	A2	75c red brn & lt grn	25	22
161	A3	1fr sl & org	75	70
162	A3	2fr ol grn & rose	2.50	2.10
163	A3	5fr dl red & gray	3.25	3.25
		Nos. 147-163 (17)	8.98	8.27

The 2c, 4c, 15c, 25c and 50c exist with overprint omitted.

Nos. 152, 162, 163, 158, 160 Surcharged with New Value and Bars.

1924-25

164	A1	25c on 15c bl & org ('25)	30	30
165	A3	25c on 2fr ol grn & rose	30	30
166	A3	25c on 5fr red & gray	32	32
a.		Pair, one without new value and bars		
167	A2	65c on 45c brn & rose ('25)	80	80
168	A2	85c on 75c red brn & lt grn ('25)	80	80
		Nos. 164-168 (5)	2.52	2.52

French Mandate

Herder and Cattle Crossing Sanaga River—A5

Tapping Rubber Tree A6 — Rope Suspension Bridge A7

1925–38 Typo. *Perf. 14x13½*

No.	Type	Description	Unused	Used
170	A5	1c ol grn & brn vio, *lav*	5	5
171	A5	2c rose & grn, *grnsh*	5	5
172	A5	4c bl & blk	8	8
173	A5	5c org & red vio, *lav*	6	5
174	A5	10c red brn & org, *yel*	12	12
175	A5	15c sl grn & grn	12	12
176	A5	15c lil & red ('27)	40	35

Perf. 13½x14.

No.	Type	Description	Unused	Used
177	A6	20c ol brn & red brn	12	12
178	A6	20c grn ('26)	12	12
179	A6	20c brn red & ol brn ('27)	12	12
180	A6	25c lt grn & blk	28	12
181	A6	30c bluish grn & ver	12	12
182	A6	30c dk grn & grn ('27)	22	12
183	A6	35c brn & blk	12	12
184	A6	35c dl grn & grn ('38)	45	35
185	A6	40c org & vio	45	38
186	A6	45c dp rose & cer	12	12
187	A6	45c vio & org brn ('27)	1.10	80
188	A6	50c lt grn & cer	12	7
189	A6	55c ultra & car ('38)	60	50
190	A6	60c red vio & blk	12	12
191	A6	60c brn red ('26)	8	8
192	A6	65c ind & brn	8	8
193	A6	75c ind & dp bl	30	22
194	A6	75c org brn & red vio ('27)	28	12
195	A6	80c car & brn ('38)	55	45
196	A6	85c dp rose & bl	28	18
197	A6	90c brn red & cer ('27)	1.10	45

Perf. 14x13½.

No.	Type	Description	Unused	Used
198	A7	1fr ind & brn	35	28
199	A7	1fr dl bl ('26)	25	20
200	A7	1fr ol brn & red vio ('27)	38	22
201	A7	1fr grn & dk brn ('29)	65	45
202	A7	1.10fr rose red & dk brn ('28)	2.00	1.75
203	A7	1.25fr gray & dp bl ('33)	2.25	1.40
204	A7	1.50fr dl bl ('27)	45	25
205	A7	1.75fr brn & org ('33)	50	40
206	A7	1.75fr dk bl & lt bl ('38)	50	35
207	A7	2fr dl grn & brn org	80	28
208	A7	3fr ol brn & red vio ('27)	2.75	60
209	A7	5fr brn & blk, *bluish*	1.25	70
a.		Cliché of 2fr in plate of 5fr	850.00	
210	A7	10fr org & vio ('27)	5.00	2.50
211	A7	20fr rose & ol grn ('27)	9.50	4.50
		Nos. 170-211 (42)	34.24	19.46

Common Design Types pictured in section at front of book.

No. 199 Surcharged with New Value and Bars in Red.

1926

No.	Type	Description	Unused	Used
212	A7	1.25fr on 1fr dl bl	22	22

Colonial Exposition Issue.
Common Design Types
Name of Country in Black.

1931 Engraved. *Perf. 12½.*

No.	Type	Description	Unused	Used
213	CD70	40c dp grn	1.50	1.50
214	CD71	50c violet	2.25	2.00
215	CD72	90c red org	2.25	2.00
216	CD73	1.50fr dl bl	2.25	2.00

Paris International Exposition Issue.
Common Design Types

1937 *Perf. 13.*

No.	Type	Description	Unused	Used
217	CD74	20c dp vio	60	60
218	CD75	30c dk grn	50	50
219	CD76	40c car rose	50	50
220	CD77	50c dk brn	40	40
221	CD78	90c red	60	60
222	CD79	1.50fr ultra	60	60
		Nos. 217-222 (6)	3.20	3.20

French Colonial Art Exhibition.
Common Design Type
Souvenir Sheet.

1937 *Imperf.*

No.	Type	Description	Unused	Used
222A	CD77	3fr org red & blk	2.25	2.25

Size: 118x99mm.

New York World's Fair Issue.
Common Design Type

1939 *Perf. 12½x12.*

No.	Type	Description	Unused	Used
223	CD82	1.25fr car lake	45	45
224	CD82	2.25fr ultra	45	45

Mandara Woman A19 — Falls on M'bam River near Banyo A20

Elephants
A21

Man in Yaré
A22

1939–40 Engraved *Perf. 13*

No.	Type	Description	Unused	Used
225	A19	2c blk brn	4	4
226	A19	3c magenta	4	4
227	A19	4c dp ultra	6	6
228	A19	5c red brn	8	8
229	A19	10c dp bl grn	5	5
230	A19	15c rose red	12	6
231	A19	20c plum	12	6
232	A20	25c blk brn	25	25
233	A20	30c dk red	22	18
234	A20	40c ultra	28	28
235	A20	45c sl grn	80	60
236	A20	50c brn car	28	22
237	A20	60c pck bl	30	28
238	A20	70c plum	1.00	1.00
239	A21	80c Prus bl	75	70
240	A21	90c Prus bl	30	28
241	A21	1fr car rose	45	40
242	A21	1fr choc ('40)	55	32
243	A21	1.25fr car rose	1.40	1.10
244	A21	1.40fr org red	55	45
245	A21	1.50fr chocolate	38	35
246	A21	1.60fr blk brn	90	85
247	A21	1.75fr dk bl	30	30
248	A21	2fr dk grn	45	45
249	A21	2.25fr dk bl	30	30
250	A21	2.50fr brt red vio	55	45
251	A21	3fr dk vio	30	28
252	A22	5fr blk brn	45	35
253	A22	10fr brt red vio	80	60
254	A22	20fr dk grn	1.25	85
		Nos. 225-254 (30)	13.32	11.23

Stamps of 1925–40 Overprinted in Black or Orange "CAMEROUN FRANCAIS 27.8.40."

1940 *Perf. 14x13½, 13½x14, 13.*

No.	Type	Description	Unused	Used
255	A19	2c blk brn (O)	28	28
256	A19	3c mag (Bk)	28	28
257	A19	4c dp ultra (O)	35	35
258	A19	5c red brn (Bk)	1.10	1.10
259	A19	10c dp bl grn (O)	22	22
260	A19	15c rose red (Bk)	38	38
260A	A19	20c plum (O)	3.75	2.75
261	A20	25c blk brn (Bk)	30	28
b.		Inverted ovpt.	120.00	120.00
261A	A20	30c dk red (Bk)	3.25	2.25
262	A20	40c ultra (Bk)	1.25	75
263	A20	45c sl grn (Bk)	90	60
264	A6	50c lt grn & cer (Bk)	45	32
a.		Inverted ovpt.	100.00	
265	A20	60c pck bl (Bk)	1.35	1.00
266	A20	70c plum (Bk)	50	50
267	A21	80c Prus bl (O)	1.40	1.20
268	A21	90c Prus bl (O)	35	35
269	A21	1.25fr car rose (Bk)	50	35
270	A21	1.40fr org red (Bk)	80	60
271	A21	1.50fr choc (Bk)	35	35
272	A21	1.60fr blk brn (O)	55	55
273	A21	1.75fr dk bl (O)	75	75
274	A21	2.25fr dk bl (O)	40	40
275	A21	2.50fr brt red vio (Bk)	40	38
276	A7	5fr brn & blk, *bluish* (Bk)	6.25	5.50
277	A22	5fr blk brn (Bk)	7.25	6.25
278	A7	10fr org & vio (Bk)	9.00	8.00
278A	A22	10fr brt red vio (Bk)	20.00	12.50
279	A7	20fr rose & ol grn (Bk)	22.50	18.50
279A	A22	20fr dk grn	95.00	95.00

Same Overprint on Stamps of 1939.
Perf. 12½x12.

No.	Type	Description	Unused	Used
280	CD82	1.25fr car lake (Bk)	1.40	1.40
281	CD82	2.25fr ultra (Bk)	1.40	1.40
		Nos. 255-281 (31)	182.66	164.54

Issued to note Cameroun's affiliation with General de Gaulle's "Free France" movement.

Cattle Fording Sanaga River and Marshal Petain
A22a

1941 Engraved *Perf. 12½x12*

No.	Type	Description	Unused	Used
281A	A22a	1fr green	38	
281B	A22a	2.50fr dk bl	38	

Nos. 281A–281B were issued by the Vichy government, and were not placed on sale in Cameroun.

Lorraine Cross and Joan of Arc Shield
A23

1941 Photo. *Perf. 14x14½*

No.	Type	Description	Unused	Used
282	A23	5c brown	4	4
283	A23	10c dk bl	4	4
284	A23	25c emerald	6	6
285	A23	30c dp org	6	6
286	A23	40c dk sl grn	4	4
287	A23	80c red brn	12	5
288	A23	1fr dp red lil	5	5
289	A23	1.50fr brt red	13	5
290	A23	2fr gray blk	15	12
291	A23	2.50fr brt ultra	20	15
292	A23	4fr dl vio	35	30
293	A23	5fr bister	45	35
294	A23	10fr dp brn	50	30
295	A23	20fr dp grn	85	55
		Nos. 282-295 (14)	3.04	2.16

Eboue Issue
Common Design Type
Engraved.

1945 *Perf. 13.* Unwmkd.

No.	Type	Description	Unused	Used
296	CD91	2fr black	18	18
297	CD91	25fr Prus grn	45	45

Surcharged with New Values and Bars in Red, Carmine or Black.

1946 *Perf. 14x14½.*

No.	Type	Description	Unused	Used
297A	A23	50c on 5c brn (R)	18	18
298	A23	60c on 5c brn (R)	22	22
a.		Inverted surcharge	52.50	
299	A23	70c on 5c brn (R)	22	22
300	A23	1.20fr on 5c brn (C)	22	22
301	A23	2.40fr on 25c emer	12	12
302	A23	3fr on 25c emer	30	30
302A	A23	4.50fr on 25c emer	55	55
303	A23	15fr on 2.50fr brt ultra (C)	55	55
		Nos. 297A-303 (8)	2.36	2.36

Zebu and Herder
A25

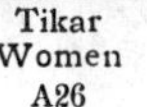

Tikar Women
A26

Porters Carrying Bananas
A27

Bowman
A28

Lamido Horsemen
A29

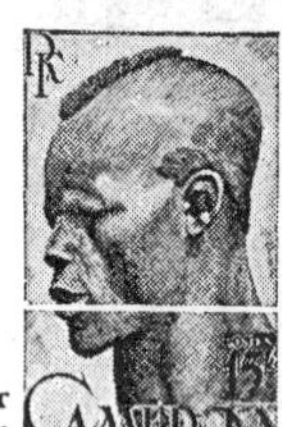
Farmer
A30

Perf. 12½x12, 12x12½.

1946 Engraved.

304	A25	10c bl grn	3	3
305	A25	30c brn org	3	3
306	A25	40c brt ultra	4	4
307	A26	50c ol brn	4	4
308	A26	60c dp plum	8	8
309	A26	80c chnt brn	12	12
310	A27	1fr org red	6	6
311	A27	1.20fr dp grn	22	15
312	A27	1.50fr dk car	65	55
313	A28	2fr black	6	6
314	A28	3fr dk car	12	5
314A	A28	3.60fr red brn	40	30
315	A28	4fr dp bl	22	12
316	A29	5fr brn car	30	12
317	A29	6fr ultra	35	12
318	A29	10fr sl grn	35	4
319	A30	15fr grnsh bl	75	18
320	A30	20fr dk grn	90	12
321	A30	25fr black	1.25	30
		Nos. 304-321 (19)	5.97	2.51

Imperforates

Most Cameroun stamps from 1952 onward exist imperforate in issued and trial colors, and also in small presentation sheets in issued colors.

Military Medal Issue.

Common Design Type

Engraved and Typographed.

1952 *Perf. 13.* **Unwmkd.**

322	CD101	15fr multi	2.25	1.40

Issued to commemorate the centenary of the creation of the French Military Medal.

Porters Carrying Bananas
A32

Picking Coffee Beans
A33

1954 Engraved

323	A32	8fr red vio, org brn & vio bl	20	8
324	A32	15fr brn red, yel & blk brn	50	12
325	A33	40fr blk brn, org brn & lil rose	45	10

FIDES Issue

Common Design Type

Designs: 5fr, Plowmen. 15fr, Wouri bridge. 20fr, Technical instruction. 25fr, Mobile medical station.

1956 *Perf. 13* **Unwmkd.**

326	CD103	5fr org brn & dk brn	25	15
327	CD103	15fr aqua, sl & blk	30	10
328	CD103	20fr grnsh bl & dp ultra	45	25
329	CD103	25fr dp ultra	65	40

Coffee Issue

Coffee—A35

1956 Engraved *Perf. 13*

330	A35	15fr car & brt red	25	12

Autonomous Government

Flag and Woman Holding Child
A36

1958

331	A36	20fr multi	45	10

Issued to commemorate the anniversary of the installation of the first autonomous government of Cameroun.

Men Looking to the Sun
A37

1958

332	A37	20fr sep & brn red	50	40

Issued to commemorate the tenth anniversary of the signing of the Universal Declaration of Human Rights.

Flower Issue

Common Design Type

Design: 20fr, Randia malleifera.

1959 Photogravure *Perf. 12½x12*

333	CD104	20fr dp grn, yel & rose	40	20

Loading Bananas
A38

Harvesting Bananas
A39

1959 Engraved. *Perf. 13*

334	A38	20fr dk grn & org	30	8
335	A39	25fr mar & sl grn	40	10

Independent State

Map and Flag of Cameroun
A40

Prime Minister Ahmadou Ahidjo
A41

Engraved.

1960 *Perf. 13* **Unwmkd.**

336	A40	20fr multi	40	10
337	A41	25fr blk, grn & pale lem	45	15

Declaration of independence, Jan. 1, 1960.

Uprooted Oak Emblem
A42

1960

338	A42	30fr red brn, ultra & yel grn	60	55

Issued to publicize World Refugee Year, July 1, 1959–June 30, 1960.

C.C.T.A. Issue

Common Design Type

1960

339	CD106	50fr dl cl & sl	1.00	60

U.N. Headquarters, New York, and Flag—A43

1961, May 20 *Perf. 13*

Flag in Green, Red and Yellow

340	A43	15fr grn, dk bl & brn	40	35
341	A43	25fr dk bl & grn	45	35
342	A43	85fr red, dk bl & vio brn	1.35	1.20

Issued to commemorate Cameroun's admission to the United Nations, Sept. 20, 1960.

Federal Republic

Stamps of 1946-60 Surcharged in Red or Black:

REPUBLIQUE FEDERALE 2d

Two types of 2sh6p:
I. Large figures. "2/6" measures 8x3¾mm.
II. Small figures. "2/6" measures 6x2½mm.

Engraved

1961, Oct. 1 *Perf. 12x12½, 13*

343	A27	½p on 1fr org red (#310)	25	25
344	A28	1p on 2fr blk (#313)	35	25
345	A34	1½p on 5fr org brn & dk brn (#326)	35	25
346	A29	2p on 10fr sl grn (#318)	40	30
347	CD103	3p on 15fr aqua, sl & blk (#327)	45	35
348	A35	4p on 15fr car & brt red (Bk) (#330)	60	45
349	A38	6p on 20fr dk grn & org (#334)	75	50
350	A41	1sh on 25fr blk, grn & pale lem (#337)	1.50	1.25
351	A42	2sh6p on 30fr red brn, ultra & yel grn (#338) (I)	2.50	2.50
a.		Type II	6.50	6.50
		Nos. 343-351 (9)	7.15	6.10

Issued for use in the former United Kingdom Trust Territory of Southern Cameroons.

The "Republique Federale" overprint is in one line on Nos. 345, 347–349, in two vertical lines on No. 350. See Nos. C38–C40.

President Ahidjo and Prime Minister Foncha
A45

Engraved

1962, Jan. 1 *Perf. 13* **Unwmkd.**

352	A45	20fr vio & choc	4.50	4.00
353	A45	25fr dk grn & brn	6.50	6.00
354	A45	60fr car & dl grn	22.50	20.00

Same Surcharged for Use in Southern Cameroons

= 3 d

355	A45	3p on 20fr vio & choc	70.00	70.00
356	A45	6p on 25fr dk grn & brn	70.00	70.00
357	A45	2sh6p on 60fr car & dl grn	70.00	70.00

Issued to commemorate the reunification of the former French and British Sections of Cameroun. It is reported that Nos. 352–357 were withdrawn after a few days and destroyed.

Mustache Monkey
A46

Designs: 1fr, 4fr, Elephant, Ntem Falls. 1.50fr, 3fr, Buffon's kob, Dschang. 2fr, 5fr, Hippopotamus. 6fr, 15fr, Mustache monkey. 8fr, 30fr, Manatee, Lake Ossa. 10fr, 25fr, Buffalo, Batouri. 20fr, 40fr, Giraffes, Waza Reservation (vert.).

Engraved

1962 *Perf. 12* **Unwmkd.**

358	A46	50c brn, brt grn & bl	10	3
359	A46	1fr gray brn, bl grn & org	10	3
360	A46	1.50fr brn, lt grn & sl grn	10	4
361	A46	2fr dk gray, grnsh bl & grn	10	4

No.	Type	Description	Unused	Used
362	A46	3fr brn, org & lil rose	10	6
363	A46	4fr brn, yel grn & bl grn	12	6
364	A46	5fr gray brn, grn & sal	15	8
365	A46	6fr brn, yel & bl	18	10
366	A46	8fr dk bl, red & grn	25	15
367	A46	10fr ol blk, org & brt bl	25	8
368	A46	15fr brn, Prus bl & bl	30	8
369	A46	20fr brn & gray	40	12
370	A46	25fr red brn, grn & yel	60	30
371	A46	30fr blk, org & bl	85	40
372	A46	40fr dp cl, yel grn & blk	1.20	60
		Nos. 358-372 (15)	4.80	2.17

See also Nos. 396–397.

African and Malgasy Union Issue

Common Design Type

1962, Sept. 8 Photo. *Perf. 12½x12*

373	CD110	30fr multi	1.00	70

Issued to commemorate the first anniversary of the African and Malgasy Union.

Village and Map of Cameroun
A48

Designs: 20fr, 25fr, Sun rising over city. 50fr, Hands holding scroll.

1962, Oct. 1 Engr. *Perf. 13*

374	A48	9fr pur, ol & dk brn	20	20
375	A48	18fr grn, org brn & dk bl	35	25
376	A48	20fr lil rose, ol bis & ind	35	25
377	A48	25fr bl, red org & sep	50	30
378	A48	50fr dk red, sep & bl	1.00	75
		Nos. 374-378 (5)	2.40	1.75

Issued to commemorate the first anniversary of the reunification of Cameroun.

"School under the Trees"
A49

1962, Nov. 5 Photo. *Perf. 12x12½*

379	A49	20fr ver, emer & yel	40	20

Literacy and popular education campaign.

Telstar and Globe
A50

1963, Feb. 9 Engraved *Perf. 13*

Size: 36x22mm.

380	A50	1fr dk bl, ol & pur	5	5
381	A50	2fr dk bl, cl & grn	8	8
382	A50	3fr dk grn, ol & dp cl	12	12
383	A50	25fr grn, dp cl & brt bl	70	60

Issued to commemorate the first television connection of the United States and Europe through the Telstar satellite, July 11–12, 1962. See No. C45.

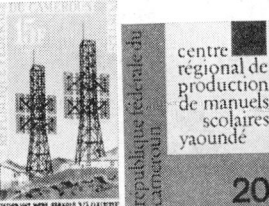

High Frequency Transmission Station, Mt. Bankolo
A51

"Yaoundé—Regional Center of Textbook Production"
A52

Design: 20fr, Station and wiring plan.

1963, May 18 Photo. *Perf. 12x12½*

384	A51	15fr multi	25	20
385	A51	20fr multi	35	25

Issued to publicize the high frequency telegraph connection Douala-Yaoundé. See No. C46.

1963, Aug. 10 *Perf. 12½* Unwmkd.

386	A52	20fr emer, blk & red	35	20
387	A52	25fr org, blk & red	45	25
388	A52	100fr gold, blk & red	1.75	1.00

Issued to publicize the UNESCO regional center for the production of school books at Yaounde.

Pres. Ahmadou Ahidjo and Flag
A53

Design: 18fr, Flag and map of Cameroun.

1963, Oct. 1 *Perf. 12x12½*

Flag in Green, Red and Yellow

389	A53	9fr grn, bl & dk brn	15	15
390	A53	18fr grn, bl & lil	30	25
391	A53	20fr grn, blk & yel grn	35	30

Second anniversary of reunification.

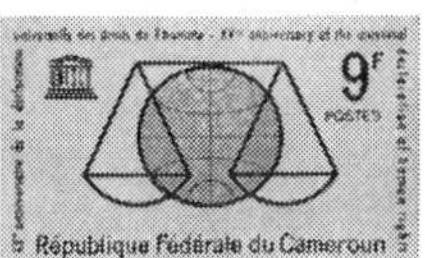

Scales, Globe, UNESCO Emblem
A54

1963, Dec. 10 Photo. *Perf. 12½x12*

392	A54	9fr ultra, blk & sal	15	12
393	A54	18fr brt yel grn, blk & rose red	30	20
394	A54	25fr rose red, blk & brt yel grn	40	30
395	A54	75fr yel, blk & ultra	1.35	75

Issued to commemorate the 15th anniversary of the Universal Declaration of Human Rights.

Animal Type of 1962

Design: 10fr, 25fr, Lion, Waza National Park, North Cameroun.

1964, June 20 Engr. *Perf. 13*

396	A46	10fr red brn, bis & grn	25	10
397	A46	25fr grn & bis	50	25

Soccer Game in Stadium
A55

Designs: 18fr, Pile of sports equipment. 30fr, Stadium (outside), flags and map of Africa.

1964, July 11 Engraved *Perf. 13*

398	A55	10fr grn, bl & red brn	20	10
399	A55	18fr car, grn & vio	30	20
400	A55	30fr blk, dk bl & org brn	50	30

Tropics Cup Games, Yaounde, July 11–19.

Europafrica Issue, 1964

Common Design Type and

Palace of Justice, Yaounde
A56

Design: 40fr, Emblems of Science, Agriculture, Industry and Education and two sunbursts.

1964, July 20 Photo. *Perf. 12x13*

401	A56	15fr multi	50	40
402	CD116	40fr multi	1.00	85

Issued to commemorate the first anniversary of the economic agreement between the European Economic Community and the African and Malgache Union.

Hurdling and Olympic Flame
A57

Design: 10fr, Runners (vert.).

1964, Oct. 10 Engraved *Perf. 13*

403	A57	9fr red, yel grn & blk	85	60
404	A57	10fr red, vio & ol gray	85	60

18th Olympic Games, Tokyo, Oct. 10–25. See Nos. C49, C49a.

Bamileke Dance Dress
A58

Ntem Falls, Ebolowa Region
A59

Designs: 18fr, Dance mask, Bamenda region. 25fr, Fulani horseman, North Cameroun (horiz.).

1964 *Perf. 13* Unwmkd.

405	A58	9fr red, yel grn & bl	15	10
406	A58	18fr bl, red & brn	30	20
407	A59	20fr dk car, grn & ol	35	20
408	A58	25fr dk brn, org & car	45	30

See also No. C50.

Cooperation Issue

Common Design Type

1964, Nov. 7 Engraved

409	CD119	18fr dk bl, yel grn & dk brn	35	20
410	CD119	30fr red brn, bl grn & dk brn	60	25

Memorial Stone
A60

Diesel Train
A61

1965, Jan. 1 Engraved *Perf. 13*

411	A60	12fr bl, ind & grn	25	15

Typographed

Perf. 14x13

412	A61	20fr rose car, yel & grn	40	20

Issued to commemorate the laying of the first rail of the Mbanga-Kumba Railroad, March 28, 1964.

Red Cross Station and Ambulance
A62

Design: 50fr, Red Cross nurse and infant (vert.).

1965, May 8 Engraved *Perf. 13*

413	A62	25fr car, sl grn & ocher	45	25
414	A62	50fr gray, red & red brn	90	45

Issued for the Cameroun Red Cross.

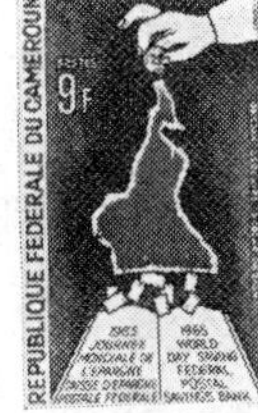

Coins Inserted in Map of Cameroun, and Bankbook
A63

Savings Bank Building
A64

Design: 20fr, Bankbook and coins inserted in cacao pod-shaped bank (horiz.).

1965, June 10

Size: 22x37mm.

415	A63	9fr grn, red & org	20	20

Size: 48x27mm., 27x48mm

416	A64	15fr choc, ultra & grn	30	25
417	A63	20fr ocher, brt grn & brn	35	30

Federal Postal Savings Banks.

Soccer Players and Africa Cup
A65

Engraved

1965, June 26 ***Perf. 13*** **Unwmkd.**

418	A65	9fr car, brn & yel	20	15
419	A65	20fr car, sl bl & yel	35	25

Issued to honor the Cameroun Oryx Club, winner of the club champions' Africa Cup, February 1965.

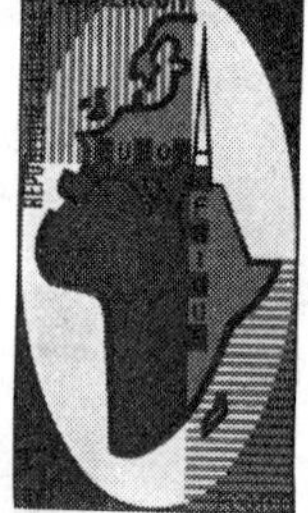

Symbolic Map of Europe and Africa
A66

Designs: 40fr, Delegates around conference table.

1965, July 20 Photo. ***Perf. 12x12½***

420	A66	5fr car, blk & lil	10	10
421	A66	40fr brn, buff, grn & ultra	70	50

Issued to commemorate the second anniversary of the economic agreement between the European Economic Community and the African and Malgache Union.

UPU Monument, Bern
A67

1965, July 26 Engraved ***Perf. 13***

422	A67	30fr blk & red	55	40

Issued to commemorate the fifth anniversary of Cameroun's admission to the UPU.

ICY Emblem—A68

1965, Sept. 11 ***Perf. 13*** **Unwmkd.**

423	A68	10fr dk bl & car rose	25	25

Issued for the International Cooperation Year, 1964–65. See also No. C57.

Pres. Ahidjo and Government House
A69

Design: 9fr, 20fr, Pres. Ahidjo and Government House (vert.).

Perf. 12x12½, 12½x12

1965, Oct. 1 Photo. **Unwmkd.**

Portrait in Dark Brown; Building in Gray

424	A69	9fr dp red, brt pink, & brt bl	15	12
425	A69	18fr brt yel & blk	30	18
426	A69	20fr vio bl, brt bl & org	35	20
427	A69	25fr yel grn & blk	45	25

Reelection of Pres. Ahmadou Ahidjo.

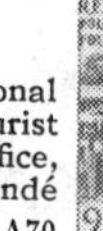

National Tourist Office, Yaoundé
A70

Designs: 9fr, Pouss Musgum houses. 18fr, Great Calao's dance (North Cameroun). 20fr, Gate of Sultan's Palace, Foumban (vert.).

1965 Engraved ***Perf. 13***

428	A70	9fr brn, rose red & grn	15	10
429	A70	18fr brt bl, brn & grn	30	25
430	A70	20fr bl, brn & choc	35	20
431	A70	25fr mar, emer & gray	35	20

See also No. C58.

Mountain Hotel, Buea—A71

Designs: 20fr, Hotel of the Deputies, Yaoundé. 35fr, Dschang Health Center.

1966

432	A71	9fr sl grn, rose cl & brn	20	15
433	A71	20fr brt bl, sl grn & blk	35	20
434	A71	35fr brn, sl grn & car	60	45
		Nos. 432-434, C63-C69 (10)	8.55	4.75

Issue dates: Nos. 432–433, Apr. 6; No. 434, June 4.

Bas-relief, Foumban
A72

Designs: 18fr, Ekoi mask (vert.). 20fr, Mother and child, carving, Bamiléké (vert.). 25fr, Ceremonial stool, Bamoun.

1966, Apr. 15 **Unwmkd.**

435	A72	9fr red & blk	25	15
436	A72	18fr brt grn, org brn & choc	35	25
437	A72	20fr brt bl, red brn & pur	45	25
438	A72	25fr pur & dk brn	50	30

Issued to commemorate the International Negro Arts Festival, Dakar, Senegal, Apr. 1–24.

WHO Headquarters, Geneva
A73

1966, May 3 Photo. ***Perf. 12½x13***

439	A73	50fr ultra, red brn & yel	85	50

Issued to commemorate the inauguration of the World Health Organization Headquarters, Geneva.

ITU Headquarters, Geneva
A74

1966, May 3 Photo. ***Perf. 12½x13***

440	A74	50fr ultra & yel	85	50

Issued to publicize the International Telecommunication Union Headquarters, Geneva.

Phaeomeria Magnifica
A75

"6" and Men Dancing around U.N. Emblem
A76

Flowers: 18fr, Hibiscus (rose of China). 20fr, Mountain rose.

1966, May 20 ***Perf. 12x12½***

Flowers in Natural Colors

Size: 22x36mm.

441	A75	9fr red brn	15	10
442	A75	18fr green	30	15
443	A75	20fr dk grn	35	15
		Nos. 441-443, C70-C72 (6)	3.60	1.15

See also No. 469.

1966, Sept. 20 Engraved ***Perf. 13***

Design: 50fr, U.N. General Assembly (horiz.).

444	A76	50fr ultra, grn & vio brn	85	20
445	A76	100fr red brn, grn & ultra	1.75	75

Issued to commemorate the 6th anniversary of Cameroun's admission to the United Nations.

Prime Minister's Residence, Buea
A77

Designs (Prime Minister's Residences): 18fr, at Yaoundé, front view. 20fr, at Yaoundé, side view. 25fr, at Buea, front view.

1966, Oct. 1 Photogravure

446	A77	9fr multi	15	12
447	A77	18fr multi	30	18
448	A77	20fr multi	35	15
449	A77	25fr multi	40	25

5th anniversary of re-unification.

Learning to Write and UNESCO Emblem
A78

Design: No. 451, Children's heads and UNICEF emblem.

1966, Nov. 24 Engraved ***Perf. 13***

450	A78	50fr red lil, bl & brn	85	45
451	A78	50fr red lil, blk & brt bl	85	45

No. 450 commemorates the 20th anniversary of UNESCO (United Nations Educational, Scientific and Cultural Organization), No. 451 commemorates the 20th anniversary of UNICEF (United Nations International Children's Emergency Fund).

Independence Proclamation
A79

1967, Jan. 1 Engraved ***Perf. 13***

452	A79	20fr grn, red & yel	45	35

7th anniversary of independence.

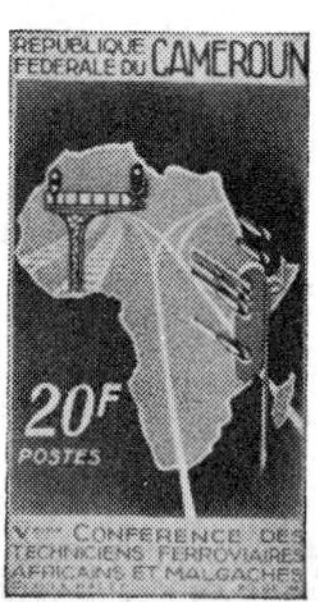

Map of Africa and Madagascar, Railroad Tracks and Symbols
A80

Design: 25fr, Map of Africa and Madagascar and train.

1967, Feb. 21 Photo. ***Perf. 13***

453	A80	20fr multi	35	25
454	A80	25fr multi	45	25

Issued to commemorate the 5th Conference of African and Madagascan Railroad Technicians.

Lions Emblem and Forest—A81

Design: 100fr, Lions emblem and palms.

1967, Mar. 3

455	A81	50fr multi	85	50
456	A81	100fr multi	1.75	1.00

Lions International, 50th anniversary.

Jet and I.C.A.O. Emblem
A82

Dove and I.A.E.A. Emblem
A83

Perf. 13x12½, 12½x13

1967, March 15 Photogravure

457	A82	50fr ultra, lt bl, brn & gold	85	50
458	A83	50fr ultra & emer	85	50

Issued to honor United Nations agencies: No. 457, the International Civil Aviation Organization; No. 458, the International Atomic Energy Agency.

Rotary International Emblem
A84

1967, Apr. 17 Photo. ***Perf. 12½***

459	A84	25fr crim, vio bl & gold	45	25

Issued to commemorate the 10th anniversary of the Douala, Cameroun, branch of Rotary International.

Pomelo
A85

Bird-of-Paradise Flower
A86

Fruit: 2fr, Papaya. 3fr, Custard apple. 4fr, Breadfruit. 5fr, Coconut. 6fr, Mango. 8fr, Avocado. 10fr, Pineapple. 30fr, Bananas.

1967, May 10 Photo. ***Perf. 12x12½***

460	A85	1fr multi	7	5
461	A85	2fr multi	7	5
462	A85	3fr multi	12	5
463	A85	4fr multi	12	5
464	A85	5fr multi	15	6
465	A85	6fr multi	20	6
466	A85	8fr multi	25	10
467	A85	10fr multi	30	12
468	A85	30fr multi	70	30
		Nos. 460-468 (9)	1.98	84

1967, June 22 Photo. ***Perf. 12x12½***
Size: 22x36mm.

469	A86	15fr lt bl & multi	25	10

Sanaga Falls and ITY Emblem
A87

1967, Aug. 14 Photo. ***Perf. 13x12½***

470	A87	30fr multi	50	30

Issued for International Tourist Year 1967.

Art of Cameroun: Coconut Harvest
A88

Designs (Carved Bas-reliefs): 20fr, Lion hunt. 30fr, Women carrying baskets. 100fr, Carved chest.

1967, Sept. 22 ***Perf. 12½x13***

471	A88	10fr brn, bl & car	15	10
472	A88	20fr brn, yel & grn	35	20
473	A88	30fr emer, brn & car	50	20
474	A88	100fr red org, brn & emer	1.75	70

Coat of Arms
A89

1968, Jan. 1 Litho. ***Perf. 12½x13***

475	A89	30fr gold & multi	60	30

Spiny Lobster
A90

Designs (Fish and Crustaceans): 10fr, River crayfish. 15fr, Nile mouth-breeder. 20fr, Sole. 25fr, Common pike. 30fr, Crab. 40fr, Spadefish (vert.). 50fr, Shrimp (vert.). 55fr, African snakehead. 60fr, Threadfin.

1968, July 25 Engraved ***Perf. 13***

476	A90	5fr brn, vio bl & dl grn	10	5
477	A90	10fr ultra, brn ol & sl	15	6
478	A90	15fr sal, red lil & sep	20	10
479	A90	20fr red brn, dp bl & sep	25	12
480	A90	25fr lt brn, emer & sl	40	15
481	A90	30fr mag, dk bl & dk brn	50	15
482	A90	40fr sl bl & org	60	20
483	A90	50fr emer, gray & rose car	75	30
484	A90	55fr lt brn, Prus bl & dk brn	85	40
485	A90	60fr brn, bl grn & ind	1.00	50
		Nos. 476-485 (10)	4.80	2.03

Tanker, Refinery and Map of Area Served—A91

1968, July 30 Photo. ***Perf. 12½***

486	A91	30fr multi	45	20

Issued to commemorate the opening of the Port Gentil (Gabon) Refinery, June 12, 1968.

Human Rights Flame
A92

1968, Sept. 14 Photo. ***Perf. 12½x13***

487	A92	15fr bl & sal	25	12

Issued for International Human Rights Year. See also No. C110.

Pres. Ahmadou Ahidjo
A93

1969, Apr. 10 Photo. ***Perf. 12½x12***

488	A93	30fr car & multi	45	20

Chocolate Vat
A94

Designs: 30fr, Chocolate factory. 50fr, Candy making (vert.).

1969, Apr. 24 Engraved ***Perf. 13***

489	A94	15fr red brn, ind & choc	25	10
490	A94	30fr grn, blk & red brn	45	20
491	A94	50fr brn & multi	75	30

Cameroun chocolate industry.

Fertility Symbol, Abbia
A95

Diesel Train on Bridge
A96

Art and Folklore from Abbia: 10fr, Two toucans (horiz.). 15fr, Forest symbol. 30fr, Vulture attacking monkey (horiz.). 70fr, Oliphant player.

1969, May 30 Engraved ***Perf. 13***

492	A95	5fr ultra, Prus bl & brt rose lil	10	6
493	A95	10fr bl, ol gray & org	18	8
494	A95	15fr ultra, dk red & blk	20	15
495	A95	30fr brt bl, lem & grn	45	18
496	A95	70fr brt bl, dk grn & ver	1.10	50
		Nos. 492-496 (5)	2.03	97

Perf. 12½x13, 13x12½

1969, July 11 Photogravure

Design: 30fr, Kumba Railroad station (horiz.).

497	A96	30fr bl & multi	45	20
498	A96	50fr blk & multi	85	40

Opening of Mbanga-Kumba Railroad.

Development Bank Issue
Common Design Type

1969, Sept. 10 Engraved ***Perf. 13***

499	CD130	30fr vio bl, grn & ocher	50	20

Issued to commemorate the 5th anniversary of the African Development Bank.

ASECNA Issue
Common Design Type

1969, Dec. 12 Engraved ***Perf. 13***

500	CD132	100fr sl grn	1.50	90

Red Sage
A99

Design: 30fr, Passionflower.

1970, Mar. 24 Photo. ***Perf. 12x12½***
Size: 22x36½mm.

501	A99	15fr yel grn & multi	25	15
502	A99	30fr multi	40	15

See Nos. C140–C141.

U.P.U. Headquarters Issue
Common Design Type

1970, May 20 Engraved ***Perf. 13***

503	CD133	30fr bl, pur & grn	45	18
504	CD133	50fr gray, red & bl	75	25

Brewery
A100

Design: 30fr, Cellar with barrels.

1970, July 9 Engraved ***Perf. 13***

505	A100	15fr brn, gray & dk grn	20	15
506	A100	30fr bl grn, dk brn & brn red	40	15

Cameroun brewing industry.

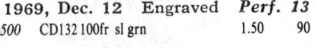

Ozila Dancers A101 — Cameroun Doll A102

Design: 50fr, Ozila dancer and drummer.

1970, Oct. 19 Engraved *Perf. 13*

507	A101	30fr multi	40	15
508	A101	50fr red & multi	75	30

1970, Nov. 2

Designs: 15fr, Doll in short skirt. 30fr, Doll with basket on back.

509	A102	10fr car & multi	20	12
510	A102	15fr dk grn & multi	28	15
511	A102	30fr brn red & multi	50	20

Cogwheels and Grain A103

1970, Feb. 9 Photo. *Perf. 13*

512	A103	30fr multi	40	20

Europafrica Economic Conference.

Federal University, Yaoundé A104

1971, Jan. 19 Engraved

513	A104	50fr multi	60	20

Inauguration of Federal University at Yaoundé.

Presidents Ahidjo and Pompidou, Flags of Cameroun and France A105

1971, Feb. 9 Photogravure *Perf. 13*

514	A105	30fr multi	60	50

Visit of Georges Pompidou, President of France.

Young People, Globe, Map of Cameroun A106

1971, Feb. 11

515	A106	30fr bl & multi	35	13

Fifth National Youth Festival, Feb. 11.

Gerbera Hybrida A107 — Men of Four Races—A108

Designs: 40fr, Opuntia polyantha (cactus). 50fr, Hemerocallis hybrida (lily).

1971, Mar. 14 Photogravure

516	A107	20fr multi	27	10
517	A107	40fr grn & multi	45	22
518	A107	50fr bl & multi	60	20

1971, March 21 *Perf. 13x12½*

Design: 30fr, Hands and globe.

519	A108	20fr grn & multi	25	7
520	A108	30fr ultra & multi	40	13

International year against racial discrimination.

Crowned Cranes at Waza Camp A109

Designs: 20fr, Canoe on Sanaga River. 30fr, Sanaga River.

1971, Apr. 9. Engraved *Perf. 13*

521	A109	10fr red, grn & blk	12	8
522	A109	20fr dk grn, brn & red	27	8
523	A109	30fr red, dk grn & brt bl	35	12

International Court, The Hague A110

1971, June 14 Engr. *Perf. 13*

524	A110	50fr ultra, org brn & sl grn	60	25

25th anniversary of the International Court in The Hague, Netherlands.

Liana Bridge A111 — Bamoun Horseman A113

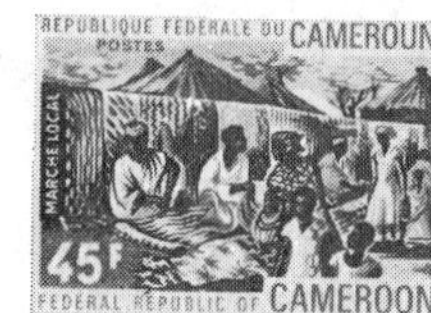

Local Market A112

1971, Aug. 16 Photo. *Perf. 13*

525	A111	40fr multi	50	20
526	A112	45fr multi	55	20

1971, Sept. 18

African Art: 15fr, Animal fetish statuette.

527	A113	10fr brn & yel	12	5
528	A113	15fr dp brn & org yel	18	8

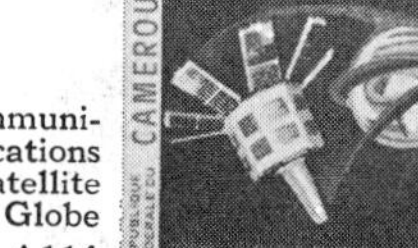

Communications Satellite and Globe A114

1971, Oct. 14 *Perf. 13x12½*

529	A114	40fr Prus bl, sl grn & org	45	18

Pan-African telecommunications system.

UNICEF Emblem A115

Design: 50fr, UNICEF emblem and grain (vert.).

1971, Dec. 11 Engraved *Perf. 13*

530	A115	40fr sl grn, bl grn & plum	60	30
531	A115	50fr dp bl, dk red & lt grn	85	40

25th anniversary of the United Nations International Children's Fund (UNICEF).

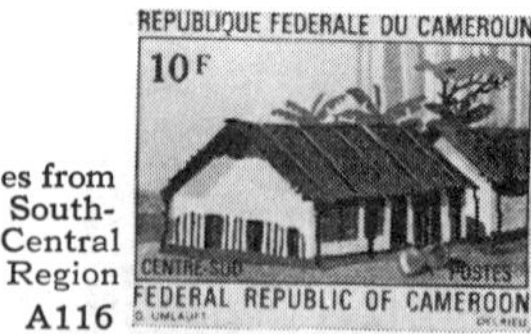

Houses from South-Central Region A116

Design: 15fr, Adamaua round houses.

1972, Jan. 15 Photo. *Perf. 13*

532	A116	10fr dk bl & multi	10	8
533	A116	15fr blk & multi	20	12

Giraffe A117

Designs: 5fr, Home industries. 10fr, Smith (horiz.). 15fr, Women carrying burdens.

Perf. 13x13½, 13½x13

1972, Feb. 18 Lithographed

534	A117	2fr multi	8	3
535	A117	5fr blk, org & red	12	4
536	A117	10fr multi	20	5
537	A117	15fr multi	25	10

Youth Day 1972.

Soccer Players and Field—A118

1972, Feb. 22 *Perf. 13½*

Designs: 20fr, African Soccer Cup (vert.). 45fr, Team captains shaking hands (vert.).

538	A118	20fr gray & multi	25	15
539	A118	40fr gray & multi	50	30
540	A118	45fr yel & multi	60	35

African Soccer Cup, Yaoundé, Feb. 23–Mar. 5.

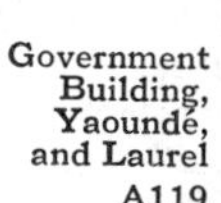

Government Building, Yaoundé, and Laurel A119

1972, Apr. 6 Photo. *Perf. 12½x12*

541	A119	40fr multi	35	20

110th session of Inter-Parliamentary Council, Yaoundé, Apr. 1972.

"Fantasia," North Cameroun A120

Bororo Woman A121

Design: 40fr, Boat on Wouri River and Mt. Cameroun.

Perf. 13x12½, 12½x13

1972, Apr. 24

542	A120	15fr dk vio & multi	25	10
543	A121	20fr multi	25	10
544	A120	40fr multi	40	20

Chemical Apparatus A122

1972, May 15 Engraved *Perf. 13*

545	A122	40fr lil, red & grn	35	18

President Ahmadou Ahidjo Prize.

United Republic

Solanum Macranthum A123

Design: 45fr, Wax plant.

1972, July 20 Photo. ***Perf. 13***

546 A123 40fr multi 40 18
547 A123 45fr yel & multi 42 20

Charaxes Ameliae
A124

Design: 45fr, Papilio tynderaeus.

1972, Aug. 20 Photo. ***Perf. 13***

548 A124 40fr bl, dk bl & gold 50 25
549 A124 45fr lt grn, blk & gold 55 30

No. 468 Surcharged

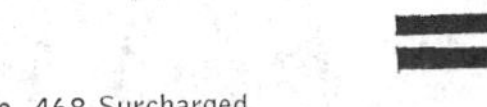

40 F

1972, Aug. 30 Photo. ***Perf. 12x12½***

550 A85 40fr on 30fr multi 40 20

Resurrection Lily A125

Great Blue Touraco A126

Flowers: 45fr, Candlestick cassia. 50fr, Amaryllis.

1972, Sept. 16 ***Perf. 13***

551 A125 40fr lt grn & multi 40 20
552 A125 45fr multi 45 25
553 A125 50fr lt bl & multi 55 30

Perf. 12½x13, 13x12½

1972, Nov. 20 Lithographed

Design: 45fr, Red-faced lovebirds (horiz.).

554 A126 10fr yel & multi 10 7
555 A126 45fr yel & multi 45 20

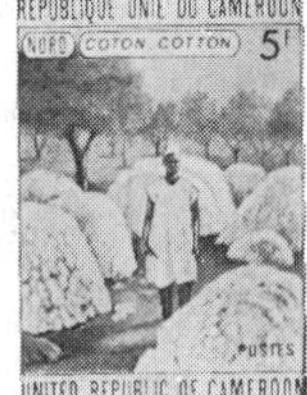

Cotton (North)
A127

Designs: 10fr, Cacao (south central). 15fr, Logging (southeast and southern coast). 20fr, Coffee (west). 45fr, Tea (northwest and southwest).

1973, Mar. 26 Photo. ***Perf. 12½x13***

556 A127 5fr blk & multi 6 6
557 A127 10fr blk & multi 8 8
558 A127 15fr blk & multi 13 10
559 A127 20fr blk & multi 18 15
560 A127 45fr blk & multi 45 20
Nos. 556-560 (5) 90 59

Third 5-Year Plan.

Flag and Map of Cameroun, Pres. Ahidjo and No. 331—A128

Design: 20fr, Proclamation of independence, Pres. Ahidjo and No. 336.

1973, May 20 Engr. ***Perf. 13***

561 A128 10fr ultra & multi 10 10
562 A128 20fr multi 20 12

First anniversary of the United Republic of Cameroun. See Nos. C200–C201.

Bamoun Mask A129

Dr. Hansen A130

Designs: Various Bamoun masks.

1973, July 10 Engraved ***Perf. 13***

563 A129 5fr grn, brn & blk 5 5
564 A129 10fr lil, brn & blk 10 6
565 A129 45fr red, brn & blk 35 20
566 A129 100fr ultra, brn & blk 80 50

1973, July 25 Engraved ***Perf. 13***

567 A130 45fr multi 40 20

Centenary of the discovery by Dr. Armauer G. Hansen of the Hansen bacillus, the cause of leprosy.

No. 556 Surcharged with New Value, 2 Bars, and Overprinted in Ultramarine: "SECHERESSE/SOLIDARITE AFRICAINE"

1973, Aug. 16 Photo. ***Perf. 12½x13***

568 A127 100fr on 5fr multi 80 60

African solidarity in drought emergency.

Dancers, South West Africa A131

WMO Emblem A132

Designs: Southwest African dances.

1973, Aug. 17 ***Perf. 13***

569 A131 10fr multi 8 6
570 A131 25fr multi 20 15
571 A131 45fr multi 45 20

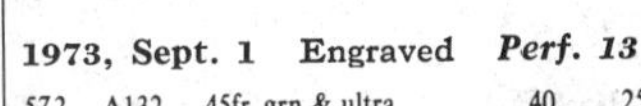

1973, Sept. 1 Engraved ***Perf. 13***

572 A132 45fr grn & ultra 40 25

Centenary of international meteorological cooperation.

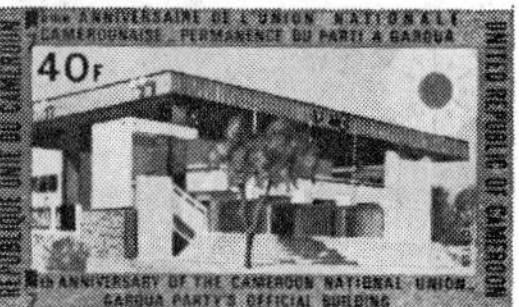

Garoua Party Headquarters—A133

1973, Sept. 1 Photogravure

573 A133 40fr multi 40 25

7th anniversary of Cameroun National Union.

African Postal Union Issue, 1973

Common Design Type

1973, Sept. 12 Engraved

574 CD137 100fr brt bl, bl & sl grn 90 60

11th anniversary of African and Malagasy Posts and Telecommunications Union (UAMPT).

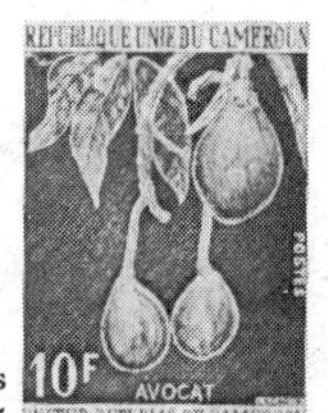

Avocados
A135

1973, Sept. 20

Multicolored

575 A135 10fr *shown* 15 6
576 A135 20fr *Mangos* 25 13
577 A135 45fr *Plums* 45 20
578 A135 50fr *Custard apple* 65 25

Kirdi Village
A136

Views: 45fr, Mabas village. 50fr, Fishing village.

1973, Oct. 25 Engraved ***Perf. 13***

579 A136 15fr blk, bis & grn 20 10
580 A136 45fr mag, brn & org 45 25
581 A136 50fr grn, blk & org 50 30

Handshake on Map of Africa
A137

1974, May 15 Engr. ***Perf. 12½x13***

582 A137 40fr car & multi 35 18
583 A137 45fr ind & multi 40 20

10th anniversary of the Organization for African Unity.

Spinning Mill
A138

1974, May 25 Engr. ***Perf. 13x12½***

584 A138 45fr multi 40 25

CICAM Industrial Complex.

Carved Panel from Bilinga
A139

Cameroun Art (Carvings): 40fr, Detail from Bubinga chair. 45fr, Detail Acajou Ngollon panel.

1974, May 30

585 A139 10fr brt grn & ocher 10 6
586 A139 40fr red & brn 35 20
587 A139 45fr bl & rose brn 40 25

Zebu
A140

1974, June 1 ***Perf. 13½***

588 A140 40fr multi 35 23

North Cameroun cattle raising. See No. C210.

Laying Rail Section
A141

Designs: 5fr, Map showing line Yaoundé to Ngaoundéré (vert.). 40fr, Welding rail joint (vert.). 100fr, Train on Djerem River Bridge.

Perf. 12½x13, 13x12½

1974, June 10 Engraved

589 A141 5fr multi 8 4
590 A141 20fr multi 18 10
591 A141 40fr multi 35 20
592 A141 100fr multi 85 65

Opening of Yaoundé-Ngaoundéré railroad line.

No. 466 Surcharged

1974, June 1 Photo. ***Perf. 12x12½***

593 A85 40fr on 8fr multi 40 20

UPU Emblem, Hands Holding Letters
A142

1974, Oct. 8 Engraved ***Perf. 13***

594 A142 40fr multi 35 20

Centenary of Universal Postal Union. See Nos. C218–C219.

Presidents and Flags of Cameroun, CAR, Congo, Gabon and Meeting Center—A143

1974, Dec. 8 Photogravure ***Perf. 13***

595 A143 40fr gold & multi 35 20

10th anniversary of Central African Customs and Economic Union (Union Douanière et Economique de l'Afrique Centrale, UDEAC). See also No. C223.

No. 589 Surcharged in Violet Blue

= 100F

10 DECEMBRE 1974

1974, Dec. 10 Engr. *Perf. 12½x13*

596 A141 100fr on 5fr multi 80 70

Virgin of Autun, 15th Century Sculpture A144

Design: 45fr, Virgin and Child, by Luis de Morales (c. 1509–1586).

1974, Dec. 20 Photogravure *Perf. 13*

597 A144 40fr gold & multi 35 25
598 A144 45fr gold & multi 40 30

Christmas 1974.

Cockscomb A145

1975, Mar. 10 Photo. *Perf. 13*

Multicolored

599 A145 5fr *shown* 8 5
600 A145 40fr *Costus spectabilis* 35 20
601 A145 45fr *Mussaenda erythrophylla* 38 25

Tropical plants.

Fishing by Night—A146

Design: 45fr, Fishing by day.

1975, Apr. 1 Engr. *Perf. 13*

602 A146 40fr bl & multi 35 20
603 A146 45fr bl & multi 40 25

Afo Akom Statue and Chief's Stool A147

1975, Apr. 1 Photogravure

604 A147 40fr multi 30 20
605 A147 45fr multi 35 20
606 A147 200fr multi 1.60 1.10

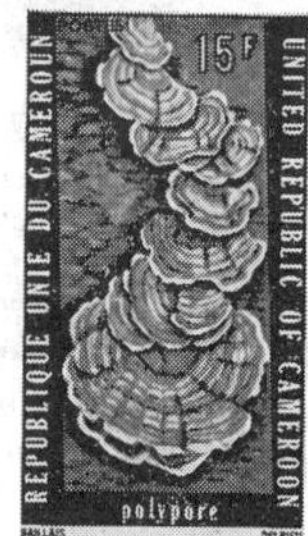

Tree Fungus A148

Design: 40fr, Chrysalis.

1975, Apr. 14

607 A148 15fr brn & multi 15 10
608 A148 40fr blk & multi 40 23

Ministry of Posts and Telecommunications A149

1975, July 21 Engraved *Perf. 13*

609 A149 40fr brn, grn & Prus bl 35 25
610 A149 45fr Prus bl, brn & grn 40 30

Presbyterian Church, Elat A150

Designs: No. 612, Foumban Mosque. 45fr, Catholic Church, Ngaoundere.

1975, Aug. 20 Engr. *Perf. 13*

611 A150 40fr multi 32 20
612 A150 40fr multi 32 20
613 A150 45fr multi 38 25

Plowing A151

Design: No. 615, Corn harvest (vert.).

Perf. 13x12½, 12½x13

1975, Dec. 15 Photogravure

614 A151 40fr dp grn & multi 32 20
615 A151 40fr dp grn & multi 32 20

Green revolution.

Zamengoe Satellite Monitoring Station—A152

Design: 100fr, Radar (vert.).

1976, May 20 Litho. *Perf. 13*

616 A152 40fr multi 30 25
617 A152 100fr multi 85 60

Porcelain Rose A153

Design: 50fr, Flower of North Cameroun.

1976, July 20 Litho. *Perf. 12½*

618 A153 40fr multi 30 20
619 A153 50fr multi 40 25

Leopard Dance A154

Telephone Exchange A155

1976, Sept. 15 Litho. *Perf. 12*

620 A154 40fr gray & multi 32 25

See Nos. C233–C234.

1976, Oct. 5 *Perf. 13*

621 A155 50fr multi 45 30

Centenary of first telephone call by Alexander Graham Bell, Mar. 10, 1876.

Young Men Building House—A156

Design: 45fr, Young women working in field.

1976, Oct. 10 Litho. *Perf. 12*

622 A156 40fr multi 32 25
623 A156 45fr multi 40 25

10th National Youth Day.

Konrad Adenauer, Cologne Cathedral A157

1976, Oct. 20

624 A157 100fr multi 85 60

Konrad Adenauer (1876–1967), German chancellor, birth centenary.

Party Headquarters, Douala—A158

Design: No. 626, Party Headquarters, Yaoundé.

1976, Dec. 28 Litho. *Perf*

625 A158 50fr org & multi 40 30
626 A158 50fr bl & multi 40 30

10th anniversary of the Cameroun National Union.

Bamoun Copper Pipe A159

Ostrich A160

1977, Feb. 4 Litho. *Perf. 12½*

627 A159 50fr multi 40 30

2nd World Black and African Festival, Lagos, Nigeria, Jan. 15–Feb. 12. See No. C239.

1977, Mar. 20 Litho. *Perf. 12*

Design: 50fr, Crowned cranes.

628 A160 30fr multi 25 15
629 A160 50fr multi 40 25

Cameroun No. 609 and Switzerland No. 3L1—A161

1977, June 5 Litho. *Perf. 12*

630 A161 50fr multi 40 30

Jufilex Philatelic Exhibition, Bern, Switzerland. See Nos. C252–C253.

No. 617 Overprinted in French and English in Red: "To the Welfare of the / families of martyrs and / freedom fighters of Palestine."

1977, Aug. 22 Litho. *Perf. 13*

635 A152 100fr multi 85 60

Palestinian fighters and their families.

Chairman Mao and Great Wall A164

1977, Sept. 9 Engr. *Perf. 13*

636 A164 100fr ol & brn 85 60

Mao Tse-tung (1893–1976), Chinese communist leader, first death anniversary.

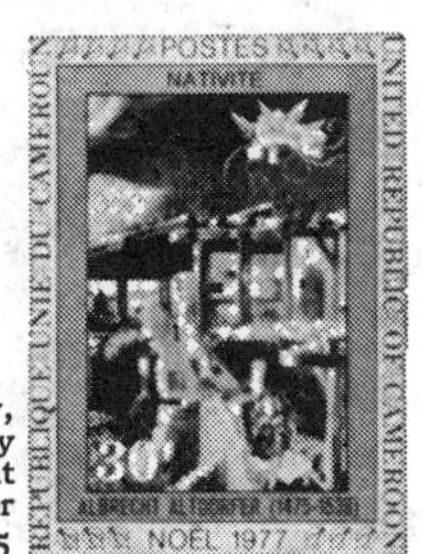

Nativity, by Albrecht Altdorfer
A165

Design: 50fr, Madonna of the Grand Duke, by Raphael.

1977, Dec. 15 Litho. *Perf. 12½x12*

637	A165	30fr multi	25	20
638	A165	50fr multi	40	30

Christmas 1977. See Nos. C264–C265.

Gazelle and Rotary Emblem
A166

Pres. Ahidjo, Flag and Map of Cameroun
A167

1978, Feb. 11 Litho. *Perf. 12*

639	A166	50fr org & multi	40	30

Rotary Club of Yaoundé, 20th anniversary.

1978, Apr. 3 Litho. *Perf. 12½*

640	A167	50fr multi	40	20

New flag of Cameroun. See No. C266.

Cardioglossa Escalerae
A168

Design: 60fr, Cardioglossa elegans.

1978, Apr. 5

641	A168	50fr multi	40	25
642	A168	60fr multi	50	35

See No. C267.

Jules Verne and "From Earth to Moon"
A169

1978, Oct. 10 Litho. *Perf. 12*

643	A169	250fr multi	2.50	2.00

Jules Verne (1828–1905), science fiction writer, birth sesquicentennial. See No. C276.

Hypolimnas Salmacis Drury—A170

Butterflies: 25fr, Euxanthe trajanus ward. 30fr, Euphaedra cyparissa cramer.

1978, Oct. 15

644	A170	20fr multi	20	15
645	A170	25fr multi	25	20
646	A170	30fr multi	30	20

Men Planting Seedlings
A171

1978, Oct. 30 *Perf. 12½*

647	A171	10fr multi	10	8
648	A171	15fr multi	15	10

Green barrier against the desert.

Carved Bamun Drum
A172

Designs: 60fr, String instrument (Gueguerou; horiz.).

1978, Nov. 20 Litho. *Perf. 12½*

649	A172	50fr multi	50	30
650	A172	60fr multi	60	40

See No. C277.

Pres. Ahidjo, Giscard D'Estaing, Flags of Cameroun and France—A173

1979, Feb. 8 Photo. *Perf. 13*

651	A173	60fr multi	60	40

Visit of Pres. Valery Giscard D'Estaing of France to Cameroun.

Human Rights Emblem, Globe, Scroll and African—A174

1979, Feb. 11 Litho. *Perf. 12x12½*

652	A174	5fr multi	5	3

Universal Declaration of Human Rights, 30th anniversary (in 1978). See No. C278.

Boy and Girl Greeting Sun
A175

1979, Aug. 15 Litho. *Perf. 12*

653	A175	50fr multi	50	30

International Year of the Child.

Rhinoceros
A176

Protected Animals: No. 655, Giraffe (vert.). No. 656, Gorilla. No. 657, Leopard. No. 658, Elephant (vert.).

1979, Sept. 20 *Perf. 12½*

654	A176	50fr multi	50	30
655	A176	60fr multi	60	40
656	A176	60fr multi	60	40
657	A176	100fr multi	1.00	60
658	A176	100fr multi	1.00	60
		Nos. 654-658 (5)	3.70	2.30

Eugene Jamot, Map of Cameroun, Tsetse Fly—A177

1979, Nov. 5 Engr. *Perf. 13*

659	A177	50fr multi	50	30

Eugene Jamot (1879-1937), discoverer of sleeping sickness cure.

Annunciation, by Fra Filippo Lippi
A178

Paintings: 50fr, Rest During the Flight to Egypt, C. 1620. No. 622, Flight into Egypt, by Jan Joest. No. 663, Nativity, by Joest. 100fr, Nativity, by Botticelli.

1979, Dec. 6 Litho. *Perf. 12½×12*

660	A178	10fr multi	10	6
661	A178	50fr multi	50	30
662	A178	60fr multi	60	40
663	A178	60fr multi	60	40
664	A178	100fr multi	1.00	60
		Nos. 660-664 (5)	2.80	1.76

Christmas 1979. Nos. 662-663 printed se-tenant.

Pepper Capense—A179

Medicinal Plants: 60fr, Bracken fern.

1979, Dec. 15 Litho. *Perf. 12½*

665	A179	50fr multi	50	30
666	A179	60fr multi	60	40

Pres. Ahidjo, Cameroun Map, Arms and No. 331—A180

1980, Feb. 12 Litho. *Perf. 12½*

667	A180	50fr multi	50	30

Independence, 20th anniversary.

Congress Building, Bafoussam—A181

1980, Feb. 12

668	A181	50fr multi	50	30

Cameroun National Union, 3rd Ordinary Congress, Bafoussam, Feb. 12-17.

Rotary Emblem, Map of Cameroun—A182

Rotary International, 75th Anniversary: No. 670, Anniversary emblem.

1980, Mar. 15 **Litho.** ***Perf. 12½***

669 A182 200fr multi 2.00 1.20
670 A182 200fr multi 2.00 1.20
a. Souvenir sheet of 2 4.00 2.50

No. 670a contains Nos. 669-670; multicolored margin shows emblems of various Rotary clubs. Size: 175x140mm.

Voacanga Medicinal Beans—A183

1980, Dec. 3 **Litho.** ***Perf. 12½***

671 A183 50fr *shown* 50 30
672 A183 60fr *Voacanga tree,* vert. 60 40
673 A183 100fr *Voacanga flower,* vert. 1.00 60

Violet Mellowstone—A184

1980, Dec. 5

674 A184 50fr *shown* 50 30
675 A184 60fr *Patula* 60 40
676 A184 100fr *Cashmere bouquet* 1.00 60

Occupation of Mecca by Mohammed, 1350th Anniversary—A185

1980, Dec. 9

677 A185 50fr multi 50 30

Bororo Girls and Roumsiki Peaks—A187

1980, Dec. 29

680 A187 50fr *shown* 50 30
681 A187 60fr *Dschang tourist center* 60 40

Banana Tree—A188

1981, Feb. 5

682 A188 50fr *shown* 50 30
683 A188 60fr *Cattle,* vert 60 40

Girl on Crutches—A189

1981, Feb. 20 **Litho.** ***Perf. 12½***

684 A189 60fr shown 60 40
685 A189 150fr Boy in motorized wheelchair 1.50 1.00

International Year of the Disabled.

Air Terminal, Douala Airport—A190

1981, Apr. 4 **Litho.** ***Perf. 12½***

686 A190 100fr shown 1.00 65
687 A190 200fr Boeing 747 2.00 1.40
688 A190 300fr Douala Intl. Airport 3.00 2.00

Cameroun Airlines, 10th anniv.

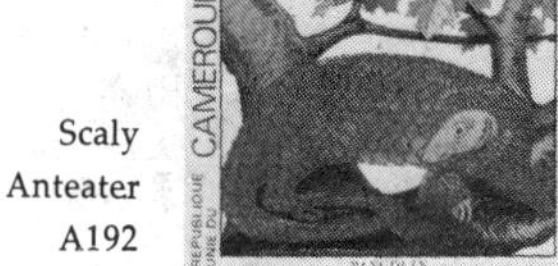

Pres. Ahidjo Presenting Trophy to Canon Soccer Team—A191

1981, Apr. 20

689 A191 60fr shown 60 40
690 A191 60fr Union team captain 60 40

1979 African Soccer Cup champions.

Scaly Anteater A192

Designs: Endangered species.

1981, July 20 **Litho.** ***Perf. 12½***

691 A192 50fr Moutourou 50 32
692 A192 50fr Tortoise 50 32
693 A192 100fr shown 1.00 65

Prince Charles and Lady Diana, St. Paul's Cathedral—A193

1981, July 29 **Litho.** ***Perf. 12½***

694 A193 500fr shown 5.00 3.25
695 A193 500fr Couple, royal coach 5.00 3.25
a. Souvenir sheet of 2 10.00 6.50

Royal wedding. No. 695a contains Nos. 694-695; multicolored margin shows flowers. Size: 145x94mm.

Bafoussam-Bamenda Highway A194

1981, Sept. 10 **Litho.** ***Perf. 12½***

696 A194 50fr multi 50 32

Freighter Cam Iroko (Cameroun Shipping Line)—A195

1981, Sept. 25

697 A195 60fr multi 60 40

20th Anniv. of Reunification—A196

1981, Oct. 10 ***Perf. 12½x13***

698 A196 50fr multi 50 32

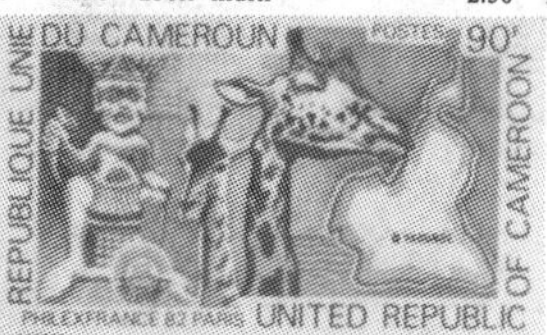

Medicinal Plants—A197

1981, Dec. 31 **Litho.** ***Perf. 12½***

699 A197 60fr Voacanga thouarsii 60 40
700 A197 70fr Cassia alata 70 45

Easter 1982—A198

Paintings: 100fr, Christ in the Garden of Olives, by Delacroix. 200fr, Descent from the Cross, by Giotto. 250fr, Pieta in the Countryside, by Bellini.

1982, Apr. 10 **Litho.** ***Perf. 13***

701 A198 100fr multi 1.00 65
702 A198 200fr multi 2.00 1.20
703 A198 250fr multi 2.50 1.55

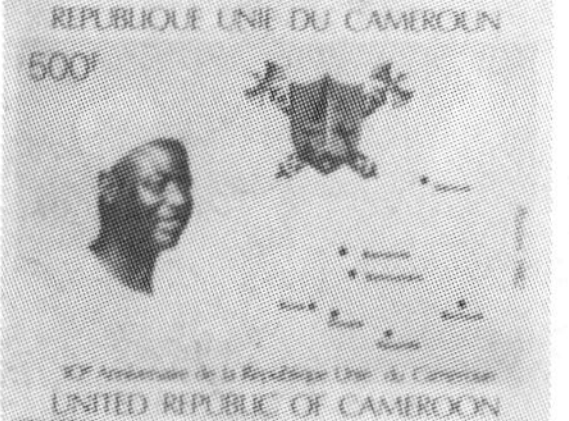

PHILEXFRANCE '82 Stamp Exhibition, Paris, June 11-21—A199

1982, Apr. 25 ***Perf. 12***

704 A199 90fr multi 90 60

Snakeskin Handbag—A200

1982, Apr. 30 ***Perf. 12½***

705 A200 60fr shown 60 40
706 A200 70fr Clay water jug 70 50

10th Anniv. of Republic—A201

1982, May 20 ***Perf. 13***

707 A201 500fr multi 5.00 3.00

African Slender-snouted Crocodile (Endangered Species)—A186

1980, Dec. 24

678 A186 200fr *shown* 2.00 1.20
679 A186 300fr *Buffon's antelope,* vert. 3.00 1.80

Town Hall, Douala—A202

1982, June 15 **Litho.** ***Perf. 12½***

708	A202	40fr shown	40	30
709	A202	60fr Yaounde	60	40

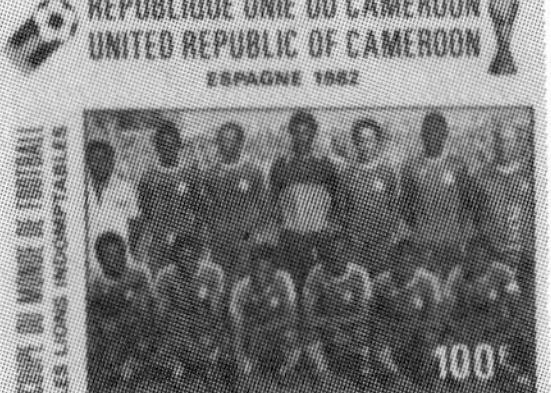

1982 World Cup—A203

1982, July 10 ***Perf. 13***

710	A203	100fr Natl. team	1.00	65
711	A203	200fr Semi-finalists	2.00	1.20
712	A203	300fr Players, vert.	3.00	1.90
713	A203	400fr Natl. team 2nd lineup	4.00	2.50
a.		Souvenir sheet of 2	8.00	5.00

No. 713a contains 2 Nos. 713; multicolored margin. Size: 217x95mm.

Partridge—A204

1982 ***Perf. 12½x13***

714	A204	10fr shown	10	6
715	A204	15fr Turtle dove	15	10
716	A204	20fr Swallow	20	12
717	A204	200fr Bongo antelope	2.00	1.20
718	A204	300fr Black colobus	3.00	1.90
		Nos. 714-718 (5)	5.45	3.38

Issue dates: 200fr, 300fr, July 20; others Aug. 10.

Scouting Year—A205

1982, Sept. 30 **Litho.** ***Perf. 13x12½***

719	A205	200fr Campfire	2.00	1.20
720	A205	400fr Baden-Powell	4.00	2.50

25th Anniv. of the Presbyterian Church in Cameroun—A206

1982, Oct. 30 ***Perf. 13x12½, 12½x13***

721	A206	45fr Buea Chapel	45	45
722	A206	60fr Nyasoso Chapel, vert.	60	40

ITU Plenipotentiaries Conference, Nairobi, Sept.—A207

1982, Oct. 5 **Litho.** ***Perf. 12½x13***

723	A207	70fr multi	70	45

Italy's Victory in 1982 World Cup—A208

1982, Nov. ***Perf. 13***

724	A208	500fr Cup, globe	5.00	3.00
725	A208	1000fr	10.00	6.00

30th Anniv. of Customs Cooperation Council—A209

1983, Jan. 10 ***Perf.***

726	A209	250fr Emblem	2.50	1.50
727	A209	250fr Headquarters, Brussels	2.50	1.50

2nd Yaounde Medical Conference—A210

1983, Jan. 23 **Litho.** ***Perf. 13***

728	A210	60fr grn & multi	60	30
729	A210	70fr brn & multi	70	35

SEMI-POSTAL STAMPS.

Curie Issue

Common Design Type

1938 ***Perf. 13*** **Unwmkd.**

B1	CD80 1.75fr +50c brt ultra		3.50	3.25

French Revolution Issue

Common Design Type

1939 **Photogravure.**

Name and Value Typo. in Black.

B2	CD83	45(c) +25(c) grn	4.00	4.00
B3	CD83	70(c) +30(c) brn	4.00	4.00
B4	CD83	90(c) +35(c) red org	4.00	4.00
B5	CD83	1.25fr +1fr rose pink	4.50	4.50
B6	CD83	2.25fr +2fr bl	5.50	5.50
		Nos. B2-B6 (5)	22.00	22.00

Stamps of 1925–33 Surcharged in Black

OEUVRES DE GUERRE

+ 2 frs.

1940 ***Perf. 14x13½.***

B7	A7	1.25fr +2fr gray & dp bl	6.25	6.25
B8	A7	1.75fr +3fr brn & org	6.25	6.25
B9	A7	2fr +5fr dl grn & brn org	6.25	6.25

The surtax was used for war relief work.

Regular Stamps of 1939 Surcharged in Black **+ 5 Frs. SPITFIRE**

1940 ***Perf. 13.***

B10	A20	25c +5fr blk brn	62.50	57.50
B11	A20	45c +5fr sl grn	62.50	57.50
B12	A20	60c +5fr pck bl	75.00	67.50
B13	A20	70c +5fr plum	75.00	67.50

The surtax was used to purchase Spitfire planes for the Free French army.

Common Design Type and

Military Doctor
SP2

Cameroun Militiaman
SP4

1941 **Photogravure** ***Perf. 13½***

B13A	SP2	1fr +1fr red	65
B13B	CD86	1.50fr +3fr mar	65
B13C	SP4	2.50fr +1fr dk bl	65

Nos. B13A-B13C were issued by the Vichy government, and were not placed on sale in Cameroun.

Nos. 281A-281B were surcharged "OEUVRES COLONIALES" and surtax (including change of denomination of the 2.50fr to 50c). These were issued in 1944 by the Vichy government, and not placed on sale in Cameroun.

New York World's Fair Stamps, 1939 Surcharged in Black

+ SPITFIRE 10fr. Général de GAULLE

1941 ***Perf. 12½x12.***

B14	CD82	1.25fr +10fr car lake	55.00	42.50
B15	CD82	2.25fr +10fr ultra	55.00	42.00

New York World's Fair Stamps, 1939, Surcharged in Black or Blue **+ 10 Frs. AMBULANCE LAQUINTINIE**

1941

B16	CD82	1.25fr +10fr car lake (Bl)	11.00	7.50
B17	CD82	2.25fr +10fr ultra (Bk)	11.00	7.50

The surtax was used to purchase ambulances for the Free French army.

Regular Stamps of 1933–39 Surcharged in Black **Valmy + 100 frs.**

1943

Perf. 14x13½, 13, 12½x12.

B21	A7	1.25fr +100 gray & dp bl	5.00	5.00
B22	A21	1.25fr +100fr car rose	5.00	5.00
B23	CD82	1.25fr +100fr car lake	5.00	5.00
B24	A21	1.50fr +100fr choc	5.00	5.00
B25	CD82	2.25fr +100fr ultra	5.00	5.00
		Nos. B21-B25 (5)	25.00	25.00

Red Cross Issue

Common Design Type

1944 Photogravure. ***Perf. 14½x14.***

B28	CD90	5fr +20fr rose	1.00	1.00

The surtax was for the French Red Cross and national relief.

Tropical Medicine Issue

Common Design Type

1950 **Engraved** ***Perf. 13***

B29	CD100	10fr +2fr dk bl grn & dk grn	2.25	2.25

The surtax was for charitable work.

Independent State

Map and Flag
SP7

Engraved

1961, Mar. 25 ***Perf. 13*** **Unwmkd.**

B30	SP7	20fr +5fr grn, car & yel	70	70
B31	SP7	25fr +10fr multi	80	80
B32	SP7	30fr +15fr car, yel & grn	1.25	1.25

The surtax was for the Red Cross.

Federal Republic

Map of Cameroun, Lions Emblem and Physician Helping Leper
SP8

1962, Jan. 28

B33	SP8	20fr +5fr blk, mar & red brn	50	50
B34	SP8	25fr +10fr ultra, mar & red brn	75	75
B35	SP8	50fr +15fr grn, mar & red brn	1.25	1.25

Issued for leprosy relief work.

Anti-Malaria Issue

Common Design Type

1962, Apr. 7 ***Perf. 12½x12***

B36	CD108	25fr +5fr rose lil	60	60

Issued for the World Health Organization drive to eradicate malaria.

Freedom from Hunger Issue

Common Design Type

1963, Mar. 21 **Engraved** ***Perf. 13***

B37	CD112	18fr +5fr grn, dk ultra & brn	45	35
B38	CD112	25fr +5fr red brn & grn	65	45

AIR POST STAMPS.

Common Design Type

Photogravure.

1942 ***Perf. 14½x14.*** **Unwmkd.**

C1	CD87	1fr dk org	15	15
C2	CD87	1.50fr brt red	15	15
C3	CD87	5fr brn red	15	15
C4	CD87	10fr black	35	35
C5	CD87	25fr ultra	40	40
C6	CD87	50fr dk grn	55	55
C7	CD87	100fr plum	70	70
		Nos. C1-C7 (7)	2.45	2.45

Victory Issue

Common Design Type

1946, May 8 **Engraved** ***Perf. 12½***

C8	CD92	8fr dk vio brn	30	30

Issued to commemorate the European victory of the Allied Nations in World War II.

Chad to Rhine Issue

Common Design Types

1946, June 6

C9	CD93	5fr dk bl grn	38	38
C10	CD94	10fr dk rose vio	42	42
C11	CD95	15fr red	45	45
C12	CD96	20fr brt bl	50	50
C13	CD97	25fr org red	65	65
C14	CD98	50fr gray	75	75
		Nos. C9-C14 (6)	3.15	3.15

Plane and Map
AP9

Seaplane Alighting
AP10

Plane and Freighters
AP11

1946 **Photogravure** ***Perf. 13, 13½***

C15	AP9	25c brn red	5	5
C16	AP9	50c green	5	5
C17	AP9	1fr brt vio	7	7
C18	AP10	2fr ol grn	12	12
C19	AP10	3fr chocolate	12	12
C20	AP10	4fr dp ultra	12	12
C21	AP10	6fr bl grn	18	18
C22	AP10	7fr brt vio	20	20
C23	AP10	12fr orange	2.75	2.75
C24	AP10	20fr crimson	55	55
C25	AP11	50fr dk ultra	65	65
		Nos. C15-C25 (11)	4.86	4.86

Nos. C15 to C25 were "issued" in 1941 in France by the Vichy Government, but were not sold in Cameroun until 1946.

V8

This 100fr stamp and eight denominations of types AP9, AP10 and AP11 without "RF" monogram were issued by the Vichy Government in 1943-44, but were not on sale in Cameroun.

Birds over Mountains
AP12

Cavalry and Plane
AP13

Warrior, Dance Mask and Nose of Plane
AP14

Engraved

1947, Feb. 10 ***Perf. 12½.*** **Unwmkd.**

C26	AP12	50fr dk grn	90	45
C27	AP13	100fr brn red	2.00	30
C28	AP14	200fr black	3.75	70

U.P.U. Issue

Common Design Type

1949, July ***Perf. 13.***

C29	CD99	25fr multi	2.50	2.00

Issued to commemorate the 75th anniversary of the Universal Postal Union.

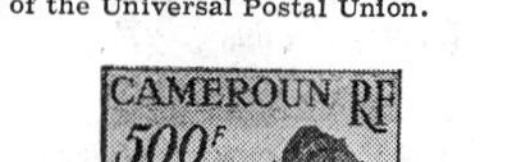

Humsiki Peak
AP16

1953, Feb. 16

C30	AP16	500fr grnsh blk, dk vio & vio bl	8.50	1.75

Edéa Dam and Sacred Ibis
AP17

1953, Nov. 18

C31	AP17	15fr choc, brn lake & ultra	1.20	50

Issued to publicize the official dedication of Edea Dam on the Sanaga River.

Liberation Issue
Common Design Type

1954, June 6

C32	CD102	15fr dk grnsh bl & bl grn	1.75	1.50

10th anniversary of the liberation of France.

Dr. Eugene Jamot, Research Laboratory and Tsetse Flies
AP19

1954, Nov. 29

C33	AP19	15fr dk grn, ind & dk brn	1.40	1.25

Issued to commemorate the 75th anniversary of the birth of Dr. Eugene Jamot.

Logging—AP20

Designs: 100fr, Giraffes. 200fr, Port of Douala.

1955, Jan. 24

C34	AP20	50fr ol grn, brn & vio brn	70	15
C35	AP20	100fr grnsh bl, brn & dk brn	2.00	30
C36	AP20	200fr dk grn, choc & dp ultra	2.75	50

Federal Republic

Air Afrique Issue
Common Design Type
Engraved

1962, Feb. 17 *Perf. 13* Unwmkd.

C37	CD107	25fr mar, pur & lt grn	60	55

Founding of Air Afrique (African Airlines).

The lack of a price for a listed item does not necessarily indicate rarity.

Nos. C35-C36 and C30 Surcharged in Red with New Value, Bars and: "REPUBLIQUE FEDERALE"

Two types of 5sh:
I. "5/-" measures 6½x4mm.
II. "5/" measures 3¾x3mm. No dash after diagonal line.
Three types of 10sh:
I. "10/-" measures 9x3¾mm.
II. "10/-" measures 7x2½–3mm.
III. "1" of "10/" vertically in line with last "E" of "FEDERALE".
Two types of £1:
I. "REPUBLIQUE / FEDERALE" 17¼ mm. wide.
II. "REPUBLIQUE / FEDERALE" 22mm. wide.

1961, Oct. 1 Engraved *Perf. 13*

C38	AP20	5sh on 100fr (I)	4.00	4.00
a.		Type II	10.00	10.00
C39	AP20	10sh on 200fr (I)	8.00	8.00
a.		Type II	35.00	35.00
b.		Type III	8.00	8.00
C40	AP16	£1 on 500fr (I)	15.00	15.00
a.		Type II	22.50	22.50

Issued for use in the former United Kingdom Trust Territory of Southern Cameroons.

Kapsikis Mokolo—AP21

Designs: 50fr, Cocotieres Hotel, Douala. 100fr, Cymothoe sangaris butterflies. 200fr, Ostriches, Waza Reservation.

1962, June 15

C41	AP21	50fr sl grn, bl & dl red	75	45
C42	AP21	100fr multi	1.65	60
C43	AP21	200fr dk grn, blk & bis	3.50	1.00
C44	AP21	500fr vio brn, bl & ocher	7.50	2.50

Telstar Type of Regular Issue

1963, Feb. 9
Size: 48x27mm.

C45	A50	100fr dk grn & red brn	1.75	1.00

See note after No. 383.

Edéa Relay Station
AP22

1963, May 18 Photo. *Perf. 12x12½*

C46	AP22	100fr multi	1.75	1.00

Issued to publicize the high frequency telegraph connection Douala-Yaounde.

African Postal Union Issue
Common Design Type

1963, Sept. 8 *Perf. 12½* Unwmkd.

C47	CD114	85fr ultra, ocher & red	1.75	1.50

Air Afrique Issue, 1963
Common Design Type

1963, Nov. 19 *Perf. 13x12*

C48	CD115	50fr pink, gray, blk & grn	85	60

Olympic Games Type of 1964

Design: 300fr, Greco-Roman wrestlers (ancient).

1964, Oct. 10 Engraved *Perf. 13*

C49	A57	300fr red, dk brn & dl grn	5.00	3.00
a.		Sheet of 3	6.50	6.50

Issued to commemorate the 18th Olympic Games, Tokyo, Oct. 10-25. No. C49a contains one each of Nos. 403-404 and C49. Size: 168x99mm.

Kribi Port—AP25

1964, Oct. 26 *Perf. 13* Unwmkd.

C50	AP25	50fr red brn, ultra & grn	85	50

Black Rhinoceros—AP26

1965, Dec. 15 Engraved *Perf. 13*

C51	AP26	250fr brn red, grn & dk brn	4.50	1.75

Pres. John F. Kennedy—AP27

1964, Dec. 8 Photogravure *Perf. 12½*

C52	AP27	100fr grn, yel grn & brn	1.75	1.75
a.		Souv. sheeet of 4	7.00	7.00

Issued in memory of Pres. John F. Kennedy (1917-63). No. C52a contains 4 No. C52; green marginal inscription. Size: 128x90mm.

Abraham Lincoln—AP28

1965, Apr. 20 *Perf. 13* Unwmkd.

C53	AP28	100fr multi	1.65	1.25

Abraham Lincoln, death centenary.

Syncom Satellite and ITU Emblem
AP29

1965, May 17 Engraved

C54	AP29	70fr red, dk bl, & blk	1.25	90

Centenary of International Telecommunication Union.

Winston Churchill
AP30

Design: 18fr, Churchill, battleship and oak leaves with acorns.

Perf. 13x12½

1965, May 28 Photo. Unwmkd.

C55	AP30	12fr org, dk brn & ultra	1.00	75
C56	AP30	18fr org, dk brn, & ultra	1.00	75
a.		Strip of 2 + label	2.50	2.00

Issued in memory of Sir Winston Spencer Churchill, statesman and World War II leader. No. C56a contains Nos. C55-C56 and label between inscribed "Sir Winston Churchill 1874 1965."

ICY Type of Regular Issue

1965, Sept. 11 Engraved *Perf. 13*

C57	A68	100fr dk red & dk bl	1.65	1.10

International Cooperation Year, 1964-65.

Racing Boat, Sanaga River, Edéa
AP31

1965, Oct. 27 *Perf. 13* Unwmkd.

C58	AP31	50fr brn, dk grn & sl	90	50

Edward H. White Floating in Space and Gemini IV—AP32

Designs: 50fr, Vostok 6. 200fr, Gemini V and REP (rendezvous evaluation pod). 500fr, Gemini VI & VII rendezvous.

1966, March 30 Engraved *Perf. 13*

C59	AP32	50fr car rose & dk sl grn	85	50
C60	AP32	100fr red lil & vio bl	1.65	1.00
C61	AP32	200fr ultra & dk pur	3.00	2.00
C62	AP32	500fr brt bl & ind	8.00	4.50

Man's conquest of space.

Hotel Type of Regular Issue

Designs: 18fr, Mountain Hotel, Buea. 25fr, Hotel Akwa Palace, Douala. 50fr, Terminus Hotel, Yaoundé. 60fr, Imperial Hotel, Yaoundé. 85fr, Independence Hotel, Yaoundé. 100fr, Hunting Lodge, Mora (vert.). 150fr, Boukarous (round huts), Waza Camp.

1966

C63	A71	18fr sl grn, brt bl & blk	25	20
C64	A71	25fr car, ultra & sl	40	25
C65	A71	50fr choc, grn & ocher	85	50

C66	A71	60fr choc, grn & brt bl	90	50
C67	A71	85fr dk car rose, dl bl & grn	1.25	75
C68	A71	100fr brn, grn & sl	1.65	75
C69	A71	150fr brn, dl bl & ocher	2.10	1.00
		Nos. C63-C69 (7)	7.40	3.95

Issue dates: Nos. C63–C64, Apr. 6; Nos. C65–C69, June 4.

Flower Type of Regular Issue

Flowers: 25fr, Hibiscus mutabilis. 50fr, Delonix regia. 100fr, Bougainvillea.

1966, May 20 Photo. *Perf. 12½*

Flowers in Natural Colors

Size: 26x45mm.

C70	A75	25fr sl grn	40	15
C71	A75	50fr brt grnsh bl	75	20
C72	A75	100fr gold	1.65	40

Military Police—AP33

Design: 25fr, "Army," soldier, tanks and parachutes. 60fr, "Navy," and "Vigilante." 100fr, "Air Force," plane.

1966, June 21 Engraved *Perf. 13*

C73	AP33	20fr vio bl, org brn & dl pur	30	20
C74	AP33	25fr dk grn, dl pur & brn	40	25
C75	AP33	60fr bl grn, bl & ind	1.00	45
C76	AP33	100fr brn, Prus bl & car rose	1.65	1.00

Issued to honor Cameroun's armed forces.

Wembley Stadium, London

AP34

Design: 200fr, Soccer.

1966, July 20

C77	AP34	50fr grn, cop red & sl	85	40
C78	AP34	200fr red, bl & grn	3.00	1.75

Issued to commemorate the 8th World Cup Soccer Championship, Wembley, England, July 11–30.

Air Afrique Issue, 1966

Common Design Type

1966, Aug. 31 Photo. *Perf. 13*

C79	CD123	25fr red lil, blk & gray	40	20

Issued to commemorate the introduction of DC-8F planes by Air Afrique.

Yaoundé Cathedral—AP35

Designs: 18fr, Buea Cathedral. 30fr, Orthodox Church, Yaoundé. 60fr, Mosque, Garoua.

1966, Dec. 19 Engraved *Perf. 13*

C80	AP35	18fr choc, bl & grn	30	25
C81	AP35	25fr brn, grn & brt vio	40	25
C82	AP35	30fr lil, grn & dl red	45	30
C83	AP35	60fr mar, brt grn & grn	1.00	50

Pioneer A and Moon—AP36

Designs: 50fr, Ranger 6. 100fr, Luna 9. 250fr, Luna 10.

1967, Apr. 30 Engraved *Perf. 13*

C84	AP36	25fr grn, bl & bis	40	25
C85	AP36	50fr grn, dk pur & brn	85	50
C86	AP36	100fr red brn, brt bl & lil	1.75	1.00
C87	AP36	250fr red brn, sl & brn	4.00	3.00

"Conquest of the Moon."

Flower Type of Regular Issue

Flowers: 200fr, Thevetia Peruviana. 250fr, Amaryllis.

1967, June 22 Photo. *Perf. 12½*

Size: 26x46mm.

C88	A86	200fr multi	3.00	1.35
C89	A86	250fr multi	4.00	1.75

African Postal Union Issue, 1967

Common Design Type

1967, Sept. 9 Engraved *Perf. 13*

C90	CD124	100fr red brn, Prus bl & brt lil	1.60	1.00

Skis, Ice Skates, Olympic Flame and Emblem

AP38

1967, Oct. 11 Engr. *Perf. 13*

C91	AP38	30fr ultra & sep	55	30

Issued to publicize the 10th Winter Olympic Games, Grenoble, Feb. 6–8, 1968.

Cameroun Exhibit, EXPO '67

AP39

Designs: 100fr, Bangwa house poles carved with ancestor figures. 200fr, Canadian Pavilions.

1967, Oct. 18

C92	AP39	50fr mag, ol & mar	75	35
C93	AP39	100fr dk grn, mar & dk brn	1.75	80
C94	AP39	200fr brn, lil rose & sl grn	3.50	1.75

Issued to commemorate EXPO '70, International Exhibition, Montreal, Apr. 28–Oct. 27, 1967.

See note after No. C116 regarding 1969 moon overprint.

Konrad Adenauer and Cologne Cathedral

AP40

Design: 70fr, Adenauer and Chancellery, Bonn.

1967, Dec. 1 Photo. *Perf. 12½*

C95	AP40	30fr multi	50	30
C96	AP40	70fr multi	1.25	60
a.		Strip of 2 + label	1.80	1.00

Issued in memory of Konrad Adenauer (1876–1967), chancellor of West Germany (1949–63). No. C96a contains Nos. C95–C96 and label between showing the CEPT design of the 1967 Europa issues.

Pres. Ahidjo, King Faisal and View of Mecca—AP41

Design: 60fr, Pres. Ahidjo, Pope Paul VI and view of Rome.

1968, Feb. 18 Photo. *Perf. 12½*

C97	AP41	30fr multi	45	25
C98	AP41	60fr multi	90	45

Issued to commemorate President Ahidjo's pilgrimage to Mecca and visit to Rome.

Earth on Television Transmitted by Explorer VI—AP42

Designs: 30fr, Molniya spacecraft. 40fr, Earth on television screen transmitted by Molniya.

1968, Apr. 20 Engraved *Perf. 13*

C99	AP42	20fr multi	30	15
C100	AP42	30fr multi	45	25
C101	AP42	40fr multi	60	30

Telecommunication by satellite.

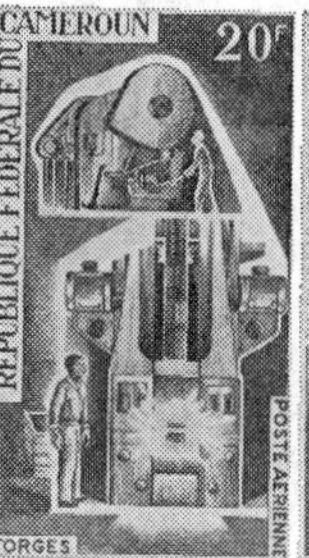

Forge—AP43 Boxing—AP44

Designs: No. C103, Tea harvest. No. C104, Trans-Cameroun railroad (diesel train emerging from tunnel). 40fr, Rubber harvest. 60fr, Douala Harbor (horiz.).

1968, June 5 Engraved *Perf. 13*

C102	AP43	20fr red brn, dk grn & ind	30	15
C103	AP43	30fr dk brn, grn & ultra	45	25
C104	AP43	30fr ind, sl grn & bis brn	45	25
C105	AP43	40fr ol bis, dk grn & bl grn	50	30
C106	AP43	60fr ultra, dk brn & sl	90	60
		Nos. C102-C106 (5)	2.60	1.55

Issued to publicize the Second Economic Development Five-Year Plan.

1968, Aug. 19 Engraved *Perf. 13*

Design: 50fr, Broad jump. 60fr, Athlete on rings.

C107	AP44	30fr brt grn, dk grn & choc	45	25
C108	AP44	50fr brt grn, brn red & choc	75	45
C109	AP44	60fr brt grn, ultra & choc	90	50
a.		Min. sheet of 3	2.25	2.25

Issued to commemorate the 19th Olympic Games, Mexico City, Oct. 12–27. No. C109a contains one each of Nos. C107–C109. Size: 128x99mm.

Human Rights Type of Regular Issue

1968, Sept. 14 Photo. *Perf. 12½x13*

C110	A92	30fr grn & brt pink	40	22

International Human Rights Year, 1968.

Martin Luther King, Jr.

AP45

Portraits: No. C112, Mahatma Gandhi and map of India. 40fr, John F. Kennedy. 60fr, Robert F. Kennedy. No. C115, Rev. Martin Luther King, Jr. No. C116, Mahatma Gandhi.

1968, Dec. 5 Photo. *Perf. 12½*

C111	AP45	30fr bl & blk	50	30
C112	AP45	30fr multi	50	30
C113	AP45	40fr pink & blk	60	40
C114	AP45	60fr bluish lil & blk	90	60
C115	AP45	70fr yel grn & blk	1.00	70
a.		Souv. sheet of 4	3.00	3.00

C116 AP45 70fr multi 1.00 70
Nos. C111-C116 (6) 4.50 3.00

Issued to honor exponents of non-violence. The 2 King stamps (Nos. C111 and C115), the 2 Gandhi stamps (Nos. C112 and C116) and the 2 Kennedy stamps (Nos. C113–C114) are each printed as triptychs with a descriptive label between. No. C115a contains one each of Nos. C112–C115; black marginal inscription. Size: 122x160mm.

In 1969 Nos. C111–C116 and C94 were overprinted in carmine capitals: "Premier Homme / sur la Lune / 20 Juillet 1969" and "First Man / Landing on Moon / 20 July 1969".

PHILEXAFRIQUE Issue

The Letter, by Armand Cambon
AP46

1968, Dec. 10
C117 AP45 100fr multi 1.65 1.25

Issued to publicize PHILEXAFRIQUE, Philatelic Exhibition in Abidjan, Feb. 14–23, 1969. Printed with alternating light green label.

2nd PHILEXAFRIQUE Issue

Common Design Type

Design: 50fr, Cameroun No. 199 and Wouri Bridge.

1969, Feb. 14 Engraved *Perf. 13*
C118 CD128 50fr sl grn, ol & dl bl 85 85

Issued to commemorate the opening of PHILEXAFRIQUE, Abidjan, Feb. 14.

Caladium Bicolor
AP47

Flowers: 50fr, Aristolochia elegans. 100fr, Gloriosa simplex.

1969, May 14 Photo. *Perf. 12½*
C119 AP47 30fr lil & multi 45 30
C120 AP47 50fr grn & multi 85 50
C121 AP47 100fr brn & multi 1.50 80

Issued to publicize the 3rd International Flower Show, Paris, Apr. 23–Oct. 5.

Douala Post Office—AP48

Designs: 50fr, Buèa Post Office. 100fr, Bafoussam Post Office.

1969, June 19 Engraved *Perf. 13*
C122 AP48 30fr grn, vio bl & brn 35 20
C123 AP48 50fr sl, emer & red brn 70 40
C124 AP48 100fr dk brn, brt grn & brn 1.40 75

Coronation of Napoleon I, by Jacques Louis David
AP49

Napoleon Crossing Saint Bernard, after J. L. David
AP50

1969, July 4 Photo. *Perf. 12x12½*
C125 AP49 30fr vio bl & multi 75 30

Embossed on Gold Foil
Die-cut Perf. 10
C126 AP50 1000fr gold 25.00 25.00

Bicentenary of birth of Napoleon I.

William E. B. Dubois (1868–1963), American Writer—AP51

Portraits: 15fr, Dr. Price Mars, Haiti (1876–1969). No. C128, Aimé Cesaire, Martinique (1913–). No. C130, Langston Hughes, U.S. (1902–1967). No. C131, Marcus Garvey, Jamaica (1887–1940). 100fr, René Maran, Martinique (1887–1960).

1969, Sept. 25 Photo. *Perf. 12½*
C127 AP51 15fr lt bl & blk 20 10
C128 AP51 30fr lem & blk 40 20
C129 AP51 30fr rose brn & blk 40 20
C130 AP51 50fr gray & blk 65 35
C131 AP51 50fr emer & blk 65 35
C132 AP51 100fr yel & blk 1.35 85
a. Min. sheet of 6 4.00 4.00
Nos. C127-C132 (6) 3.65 2.05

Issued to honor Negro writers.

No. C132a contains one each of Nos. C127–C132. Size: 114x125mm.

ILO Emblem
AP52

1969, Oct. 29 Photo. *Perf. 13*
C133 AP52 30fr blk, bl grn & gray 50 20
C134 AP52 50fr blk, dp lil rose & gray 85 40

Issued to commemorate the 50th anniversary of the International Labor Organization.

Armstrong, Collins and Aldrin Splashdown in the Pacific
AP53

Design: 500fr, Landing module and Neil A. Armstrong's first step on moon.

1969, Nov. 29 Photo. *Perf. 12½*
C135 AP53 200fr multi 3.00 1.50
C136 AP53 500fr multi 6.50 3.75

See note after Algeria No. 427.

Pres. Ahidjo, Arms and Map of Cameroun—AP54

Embossed on Gold Foil

1970, Jan. 1 *Die-cut Perf. 10*
C137 AP54 1000fr gold & multi 12.50 12.50

10th anniversary of independence.

Hotel Mont Fébé, Yaoundé
AP55

1970, Jan. 15 Engraved *Perf. 13*
C138 AP55 30fr lt brn, sl grn & gray 50 20

Demand as well as supply determine a stamp's market value. The first is as important as the other.

Lenin
AP56

1970, Jan. 25 Photo. *Perf. 12½*
C139 AP56 50fr org & blk 70 40

Issued to commemorate the centenary of the birth of Nikolai Lenin (1870–1924), Russian Communist leader.

Plant Type of Regular Issue

Designs: 50fr, Cleome speciosa (caper). 100fr, Mussaenda erythrophylla (madder).

1970, Mar. 24 Photo. *Perf. 12½*
Size: 26x46mm.
C140 A99 50fr blk & multi 60 40
C141 A99 100fr multi 1.20 60

Map of Africa and Lions Emblem Pinpointing Yaoundé—AP57

1970, May 2 Photo. *Perf. 12½*
C142 AP57 100fr multi 1.35 75

Issued to commemorate the 13th Lions International Congress of District 13, Yaoundé, May 2, 1970.

U.N. Emblem and Doves—AP58

Design: 50fr, U.N. emblem and dove (vert.).

1970, June 26 Engraved *Perf. 13*
C143 AP58 30fr brn & org 40 25
C144 AP58 50fr Prus bl & sl bl 65 35

25th anniversary of the United Nations.

Japanese Pavilion and EXPO Emblem—AP59

Designs (EXPO Emblem and): 100fr, Map of Japan (vert.). 150fr, Australian pavilion.

1970, Aug. 1 Engraved *Perf. 13*
C145 AP59 50fr ind, lt grn & ver 65 35
C146 AP59 100fr bl, lt grn & red 1.35 65
C147 AP59 150fr choc, bl & gray 2.00 1.00

Issued to commemorate EXPO '70 International Exhibition, Osaka, Japan, Mar. 15–Sept. 13.

Charles de Gaulle AP60 — **Pelé and Team AP61**

Design: 200fr, de Gaulle in uniform.

1970, Aug. 27

C148	AP60	100fr grn, vio bl & ol brn	1.50	75
C149	AP60	200fr ol brn, vio bl & grn	3.00	1.40
a.		Strip of 2 + label	5.00	2.50

Issued to commemorate the 30th anniversary of the rallying of the Free French.

Nos. C148-C149 were printed in same sheet flanking a label showing maps of Cameroun and France, and Cross of Lorraine.

1970, Oct. 14 Photo. *Perf. 12½*

Designs: 50fr, Aztec Stadium, Mexico City (horiz.). 100fr, Mexican soccer team (horiz.).

C150	AP61	50fr multi	75	35
C151	AP61	100fr multi	1.50	75
C152	AP61	200fr multi	3.00	1.50

Issued to publicize the 9th World Soccer Championships for the Jules Rimet Cup, Mexico City, May 30-June 21, and the final victory of Brazil over Italy.

Ludwig van Beethoven AP62

1970, Nov. 23 Engraved *Perf. 13*

C153	AP62	250fr multi	2.75	1.50

Issued to commemorate the bicentenary of the birth of Ludwig van Beethoven (1770-1827), composer.

Christ at Emmaus, by Rembrandt AP63

Design: 150fr, The Anatomy Lesson, by Rembrandt.

1970, Dec. 5 Photo. *Perf. 12x12½*

C154	AP63	70fr grn & multi	80	40
C155	AP63	150fr multi	1.80	90

Charles Dickens AP64

Designs: 50fr, Scenes from David Copperfield. 100fr, Dickens holding quill.

1970, Dec. 22 *Perf. 13*

C156	AP64	40fr blk & rose	50	25
C157	AP64	50fr bis & multi	60	30
C158	AP64	100fr rose & multi	1.20	60

Death centenary of Charles Dickens (1812-1870), English novelist. Nos. C156-C158 printed se-tenant.

De Gaulle Type of 1970 Overprinted with Black Border and: "IN MEMORIAM / 1890-1970"

1971, Jan. 15 Engraved *Perf. 13*

C159	AP60	100fr vio bl, emer & brn red	1.20	60
C160	AP60	200fr brn red, emer & vio bl	2.40	1.20
a.		Strip of 2 + label	4.25	2.00

In memory of Gen. Charles de Gaulle (1890-1970), President of France.

Timber Storage, Douala—AP65

Designs (Industrialization): 70fr, ALUCAM aluminum plant, Edea (vert.). 100fr, Mbakaou Dam.

1971, Feb. 14 Engraved *Perf. 13*

C161	AP65	40fr dk red, bl grn & ol brn	50	20
C162	AP65	70fr ol brn, sl grn & brt bl	80	40
C163	AP65	100fr Prus bl, yel grn & red brn	1.20	60

Relay Race—AP66

Designs: 50fr, Torch bearer (vert.). 100fr, Discus.

1971, Apr. 24 Engraved *Perf. 13*

C164	AP66	30fr dk brn, ver & ind	40	20
C165	AP66	50fr blk, bl & choc	70	35
C166	AP66	100fr multi	1.25	50

75th anniversary of revival of Olympic Games.

Fishing Trawler—AP67

Designs: 40fr, Local fishermen, Northern Cameroun. 70fr, Fishing harbor, Douala. 150fr, Shrimp boats, Douala.

1971, May 14 Engraved *Perf. 13*

C167	AP67	30fr lt brn, bl & grn	35	20
C168	AP67	40fr sl grn, bl & dk brn	45	25
C169	AP67	70fr dk brn, bl & red org	85	40
C170	AP67	150fr multi	1.80	90

Cameroun fishing industry.

Cameroun No. 123 and War Memorial, Yaoundé—AP68

Designs (Cameroun Stamps): 25fr, No. C33 and Jamot memorial. 40fr, No. 431 and government buildings, Yaoundé. 50fr, No. 19 and Imperial German postal emblem. 100fr, No. 101 and World War II memorial.

1971, Aug. 1 Engraved *Perf. 13*

C171	AP68	20fr grn, ocher & dk brn	25	10
C172	AP68	25fr dk brn, vio bl & sl grn	30	15
C173	AP68	40fr grn, mar & sl	45	25
C174	AP68	50fr dk brn, blk & ver	60	30
C175	AP68	100fr mar, sl grn & org	1.20	60
		Nos. C171-C175 (5)	2.80	1.40

PHILATECAM 1971 Philatelic Exhibition.

Cameroun Flag, Pres. Ahidjo and Reunification Highway—AP69

Typo., Silk Screen, Embossed

1971, Oct. 1 *Perf. 12½*

C176	AP69	250fr gold & multi	3.75	3.00

PHILATECAM Philatelic Exhibition, Yaoundé-Douala.

African Postal Union Issue, 1971

Common Design Type

1971, Nov. 13 Photo. *Perf. 13x13½*

C177	CD135	100fr bl & multi	1.35	65

Annunciation, by Fra Angelico AP71

Paintings: 45fr, Virgin and Child, by Andrea del Sarto. 150fr, Christ Child with Lamb, detail from Holy Family, by Raphael (vert.).

Perf. 13x13½, 13½x13

1971, Dec. 19

Brown Inscriptions

C178	AP71	40fr multi	40	20
C179	AP71	45fr multi	60	30
C180	AP71	150fr multi	2.00	90

Christmas 1971.

Cameroun Airlines Emblem AP72

1972, Feb. 2 Photo. *Perf. 12½x12*

C181	AP72	50fr lt bl & multi	60	30

Inauguration of Cameroun Airlines.

Doge's Palace, by Ippolito Caffi AP73

Paintings: 100fr, 200fr, Details from "Regatta on the Grand Canal," by School of Canaletto.

1972 Photogravure *Perf. 13*

C182	AP73	40fr gold & multi	50	25
C183	AP73	100fr gold & multi	1.20	60
C184	AP73	200fr gold & multi	2.50	1.20

UNESCO campaign to save Venice.

Astronauts Patsayev, Dobrovolsky and Volkov—AP74

1972, May 1 Photo. *Perf. 13x13½*

C185	AP74	50fr multi	60	25

Salute-Soyuz 11 space mission, and in memory of the Russian astronauts Victor I. Patsayev, Georgi T. Dobrovolsky and Vladislav N. Volkov, who died during Soyuz 11 space mission, June 6-30, 1971.

U.N. Headquarters, Chinese Flag and Gate of Heavenly Peace AP75

1972, May 19 *Perf. 13*

C186	AP75	50fr blk, scar & gold	50	25

Admission of People's Republic of China to United Nations.

United Republic

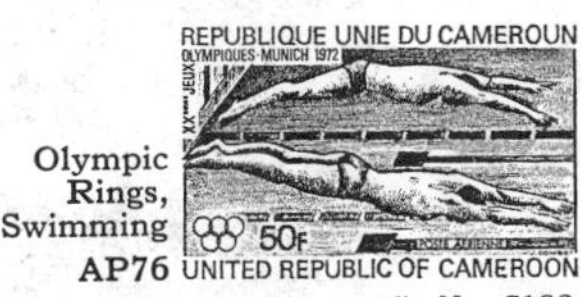

Olympic Rings, Swimming
AP76

Designs (Olympic Rings and): No. C188, Boxing (vert.). 200fr, Equestrian.

1972, Aug. 1 Engraved *Perf. 13*

C187 AP76 50fr lake & sl grn 60 30
C188 AP76 50fr choc & sl 60 30
C189 AP76 200fr cl, gray & dk brn 2.25 1.10
a. Min. sheet of 3 3.25 3.25

20th Olympic Games, Munich, Aug. 26–Sept. 11. No. C189a contains stamps similar to Nos. C187–C189, but in changed colors. The 50fr (swimming) is Prussian blue, violet & brown; the 50c (boxing) lilac, Prussian blue & brown; the 200fr, Prussian blue & brown. Size: 139x99mm.

Nos. C187–C189 Overprinted in Red or Black

NATATION MARK SPITZ
MEDAILLES D'OR
a

SUPER WELTER
KOTTYSCH
MEDAILLE D'OR
b

CONCOURS COMPLET
MEADE
MEDAILLE D'OR
c

1972, Oct. 23 Engraved *Perf. 13*

C190 AP76 (a) 50fr lake & sl grn (R) 60 30
C191 AP76 (b) 50fr choc & sl 60 30
C192 AP76 (c) 200fr cl, gray & dk brn 2.50 1.20

Gold Medal Winners in 20th Olympic Games: Mark Spitz, USA, swimming (C190); Dieter Kottysch, West Germany, light middleweight boxing (C191); Richard Meade, Great Britain, 3-day equestrian (C192).

Madonna with Angels, by Cimabue
AP77

Design: 140fr, Madonna of the Rose Arbor, by Stefan Lochner.

1972, Dec. 21 Photo. *Perf. 13*

C193 AP77 45fr gold & multi 60 30
C194 AP77 140fr gold & multi 1.40 70

Christmas 1972.

St. Teresa, the Little Flower
AP78

Design: 100fr, Lisieux Cathedral and St. Teresa.

1973, Jan. 2 Engraved

C195 AP78 45fr vio bl, pur & mar 50 25
C196 AP78 100fr mag, ultra & brn 1.00 55

Centenary of the birth of St. Teresa of Lisieux (1873–1897), Carmelite nun.

African Unity Hall, Addis Ababa and Emperor Haile Selassie—AP79

1973, Mar. 14 Photo. *Perf. 13*

C197 AP79 45fr yel & multi 40 25

80th birthday of Emperor Haile Selassie of Ethiopia.

Corn, Grain, Healthy and Starving People—AP80

1973, Apr. 10 Typo. *Perf. 13*

C198 AP80 45fr multi 40 20

World Food Program, 10th anniversary.

Hearts and Blood Vessels
AP81

1973, May 5 Engraved

C199 AP81 50fr dk car rose & dk vio bl 40 25

"Your Heart is Your Health" and for the 25th anniversary of the World Health Organization.

Type of Regular Issue

Designs: 45fr, Map of Cameroun, Pres. Ahidjo and No. C176. 70fr, National colors and commemorative inscriptions.

1973, May 20 Engr. *Perf. 13*

C200 A128 45fr grn & multi 40 25
C201 A128 70fr red & multi 60 40

First anniversary of the United Republic of Cameroun.

Scout Emblem and Flags
AP82

1973, July 31 Typo. *Perf. 13*

C202 AP82 40fr multi 40 25
C203 AP82 45fr multi 45 30
C204 AP82 100fr multi 85 65

Cameroun's admission to the World Scout Conference, Mar. 26, 1971.

African Weeks Issue

Head and City Hall, Brussels
AP83

1973, Sept. 17 Engraved *Perf. 13*

C205 AP83 40fr dp brn & rose cl 40 25

African Weeks, Brussels, Sept. 15–30.

Map of Africa with Cameroun
AP84

1973, Sept. 29 Engraved *Perf. 13*

C206 AP84 40fr blk, red & grn 50 25

Help for handicapped children.

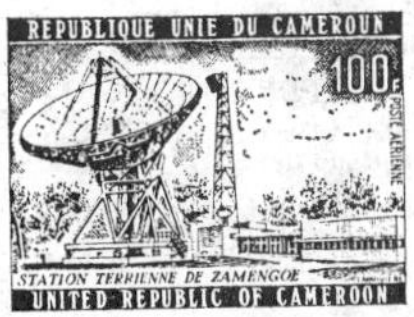

Zamengoe Radar Station
AP85

1973, Dec. 8 Engraved *Perf. 13*

C207 AP85 100fr bl, lt brn & grn 85 60

Chancellor Rolin Madonna, by Van Eyck
AP86

Design: 140fr, Nativity, by Federigo Barocci.

1973, Dec. 11 Photo. *Perf. 13*

C208 AP86 45fr gold & multi 45 30
C209 AP86 140fr gold & multi 1.50 1.10

Christmas 1973.

Zebu Type of 1974

Design: Zebu herd.

1974, June 1 Lithographed *Perf. 13*

C210 A140 45fr multi 40 20

North Cameroun cattle raising.

Churchill and Union Jack
AP87

1974, July 10 Engraved *Perf. 13*

C211 AP87 100fr blk, bl & red 90 60

Birth centenary of Winston Churchill (1874–1965).

Soccer, Arms of Frankfurt, Dortmund, Gelsenkirchen and Stuttgart—AP88

Designs: 100fr, Soccer and arms of Berlin, Hamburg, Hanover and Düsseldorf. 200fr, Soccer cup and game.

1974, Aug. 5 Photo. *Perf. 13*

C212 AP88 45fr gray, sl & org 40 20
C213 AP88 100fr gray, sl & org 85 60
C214 AP88 200fr org, sl & bl 1.65 1.00
Strip of 3, Nos. C212-C214 3.25 2.00

World Cup Soccer Championship, Munich, June 13–July 7. Nos. C212–C214 printed se-tenant in sheets containing 5 triptychs.

Nos. C212–C214 Overprinted in Dark Blue: "7th JULY 1974 / R.F.A. 2 HOLLANDE 1 / 7 JUILLET 1974"

1974, Sept. 16 Photo. *Perf. 13*

C215 AP88 45fr multi 40 25
C216 AP88 100fr multi 85 65
C217 AP88 200fr multi 1.65 1.20
Strip of 3, Nos. C215-C217 3.25 2.25

World Cup Soccer Championship, 1974, victory of German Federal Republic.

UPU Type of 1974

Designs: 100fr, Cameroun No. 503. 200fr, Cameroun No. C29.

1974, Oct. 8 Engraved *Perf. 13*

C218 A142 100fr bl & multi 80 60
C219 A142 200fr red & multi 1.65 1.10

Centenary of Universal Postal Union.

Copernicus and Planets Circling Sun
AP89

1974, Oct. 15 Engraved *Perf. 13*

C220 AP89 250fr multi 2.00 1.50

500th anniversary of the birth of Nicolaus Copernicus (1473–1543), Polish astronomer.

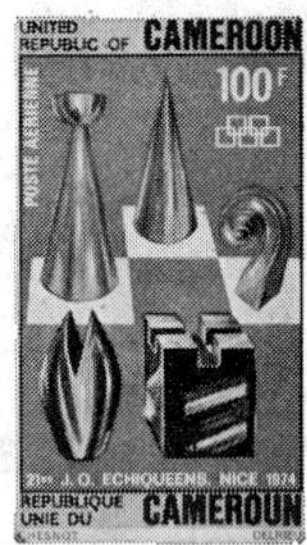

Chess Pieces AP90

1974, Nov. 3 Photo. ***Perf. 13x12½***

C221	AP90	100fr multi	75	65

21st Chess Olympiad, Nice, France, June 6–30.

Mask and ARPHILA Emblem—AP91

1974, Nov. 30 Engraved ***Perf. 13***

C222	AP91	50fr choc & mag	40	25

ARPHILA 75, Paris, June 6–16, 1975.

Presidents and Flags of Cameroun, CAR, Gabon and Congo—AP92

1974, Dec. 8 Photogravure

C223	AP92	100fr gold & multi	80	60

See note after No. 595.

Man Landing on Moon—AP93

1974, Dec. 15 Engraved

C224	AP93	200fr brn, bl & car	1.60	1.20

5th anniversary of man's first landing on the moon.

Charles de Gaulle and Félix Eboué—AP94

1975, Feb. 24 Typo. ***Perf. 13***

C225	AP94	45fr multi	50	25
C226	AP94	200fr multi	2.10	1.20

Félix A. Eboué (1884–1944), Governor of Chad, first colonial governor to join Free French in WWII, 30th death anniversary.

Marquis de Lafayette AP95

Designs: 140fr, George Washington and soldiers. 500fr, Benjamin Franklin and Independence Hall.

1975, Oct. 20 Engr. ***Perf. 13***

C227	AP95	100fr vio bl & multi	80	60
C228	AP95	140fr brn & multi	1.10	90
C229	AP95	500fr grn & multi	4.00	2.50

American Bicentennial.

The Burning Bush, by Nicolas Froment AP96

Painting: 500fr, Adoration of the Kings, by Gentile da Fabriano (horiz.).

1975, Dec. 25 Photo. ***Perf. 13***

C230	AP96	50fr gold & multi	50	25
C231	AP96	500fr gold & multi	4.75	2.50

Christmas 1975.

Concorde and Route: Paris–Dakar–Rio de Janeiro—AP97

1976, July 20 Litho. ***Perf. 13***

C232	AP97	500fr lt bl & multi	4.50	2.50
a.		Souvenir sheeet	5.50	5.50

First commercial flight of supersonic jet Concorde from Paris to Rio de Janeiro, Jan. 21. No. C232a contains one stamp; black marginal inscription giving specifications of Concorde. Size: 130x93mm. Sold for 600fr.

Dance Type of 1976

Designs: 50fr, Dancers and drummer. 100fr, Woman dancer.

1976, Sept. 15 Litho. ***Perf. 12***

C233	A154	50fr gray & multi	40	30
C234	A154	100fr gray & multi	80	50

Virgin and Child, by Giovanni Bellini—AP98

Paintings: 30fr, Adoration of the Shepherds, by Le Brun. 60fr, Adoration of the Kings, by Rubens. 500fr, The Newborn, by Georges de la Tour.

1976, Dec. 15 Litho. ***Perf. 12½***

C235	AP98	30fr gold & multi	25	15
C236	AP98	60fr gold & multi	50	35
C237	AP98	70fr gold & multi	55	40
C238	AP98	500fr gold & multi	4.00	2.50
a.		Souvenir sheet of 4	5.50	5.50

Christmas 1976. No. C238a contains one each of Nos. C235–C238; black and gold marginal inscription. Size: 150x120 mm.

Festival Type of 1977

Design: 60fr, Traditional Chief on his throne, sculpture.

1977, Feb. 4 Litho. ***Perf. 12½***

C239	A159	60fr multi	50	35

2nd World Black and African Festival, Lagos, Nigeria, Jan. 15–Feb. 12.

Crucifixion, by Matthias Grunewald—AP99

Paintings: 125fr, Christ on the Cross, by Velazquez (vert.). 150fr, The Deposition, by Titian.

1977, Apr. 2 Litho. ***Perf. 12½***

C240	AP99	50fr gold & multi	40	30
C241	AP99	125fr gold & multi	1.00	60
C242	AP99	150fr gold & multi	1.25	80
a.		Souvenir sheet of 3	2.75	2.75

Easter 1977. No. C242a contains one each of Nos. C240–C242, perf. 12; black and gold marginal inscription and black control number. Size: 210x115mm. Sold for 350fr.

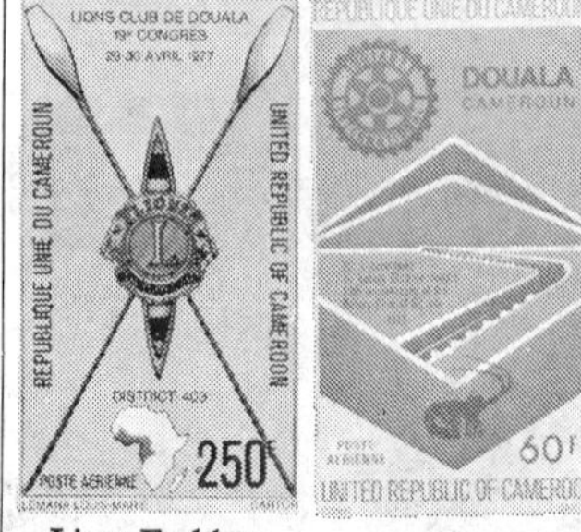

Lions Emblem, Map of Africa AP100

Rotary Emblem AP101

1977, Apr. 29 Litho. ***Perf. 12½***

C243	AP100	250fr multi	2.00	1.50

Lions Club of Douala, 19th Congress, Apr. 29–30.

1977, May 18

C244	AP101	60fr multi	50	35

Rotary Club of Douala, 20th anniversary.

Antoine de Saint-Exupéry AP102

Charles Lindbergh and Spirit of St. Louis—AP103

Designs: 50fr, Jean Mermoz and his plane. 80fr, Maryse Bastié and her plane. 100fr, Sikorsky S-43. 300fr, Concorde.

1977, May 20 Engr. ***Perf. 13***

C245	AP103	50fr org & bl	40	30
C246	AP102	60fr mag & org	50	35
C247	AP103	80fr mag & bl	60	45
a.		Souvenir sheet of 3	1.75	1.75
C248	AP103	100fr grn & yel	80	60
C249	AP103	300fr multi	2.50	1.85
C250	AP103	500fr multi	4.00	2.75
a.		Souvenir sheet of 3	8.50	8.50
		Nos. C245-C250 (6)	8.80	6.30

Aviation pioneers and events. No. C247a contains one each of Nos. C245–C247; blue marginal inscription. Size: 170x100mm. Sold for 200fr. No. C250a contains one each of Nos. C248–C250; blue marginal inscription. Size: 190x100mm. Sold for 1000fr.

Sassenage Castle, Grenoble—AP104

1977, May 21 Litho. ***Perf. 12½***

C251	AP104	70fr multi	55	40

10th anniversary of International French Language Council.

Jufilex Type of 1977

Designs: 70fr, Switzerland (Zurich) No. 1L1 and Cameroun No. 16. 100fr, Switzerland (Geneva) No. 2L1 and Cameroun No. 254.

1977, June 5 Litho. ***Perf. 12***

C252	A161	70fr multi	55	40
C253	A161	100fr multi	80	60

Jufilex Philatelic Exhibition, Bern, Switzerland.

Diseased Knee, WHO Emblem AP105

1977, Oct. 15 Engr. ***Perf. 13***

C260	AP105	70fr multi	55	40

World Rheumatism Year.

Nos. C249 and C232 Overprinted in Red:
"PREMIER VOL PARIS – NEW YORK / FIRST FLIGHT PARIS – NEW YORK / 22 Nov. 1977–22nd Nov. 1977"

Perf. 13

1977, Nov. 22 **Engr., Litho.**

C262	AP103	300fr multi	2.50	1.85
C263	AP97	500fr multi	4.00	3.00

Concorde, first commercial flight Paris to New York.

Christmas Type of 1977

Paintings: 60fr, Virgin and Child with 4 Saints, by Bellini (horiz.). 400fr, Adoration of the Shepherds, by George de la Tour (horiz.).

1977, Dec. 15 **Litho.** ***Perf. 12x12½***

C264	A165	60fr multi	50	35
C265	A165	400fr multi	3.50	2.50

Christmas 1977.

Flag Type of 1978

Design: 60fr, New flag, Pres. Ahidjo and spear.

1978, Apr. 3 **Litho.** ***Perf. 12½***

C266	A167	60fr multi	50	25

New flag of Cameroun.

Frog Type of 1978

Design: 100fr, Cardioglossa trifasciata.

1978, Apr. 5

C267	A168	100fr multi	85	60

L'Arlesienne, by Van Gogh AP106

Painting: No. C269, Burial of Christ, by Albrecht Dürer.

1978, May 15 **Litho.** ***Perf. 12½***

C268	AP106	200fr multi	2.00	1.60
C269	AP106	200fr multi	2.00	1.60

Vincent Van Gogh (1853–1890), 125th birth anniversary and Albrecht Dürer (1471–1528), 450th death anniversary.

Leprosy Distribution on World Map, Raoul Follereau—AP107

1978, June 6 **Litho.** ***Perf. 12***

C270	AP107	100fr multi	1.00	80

25th World Leprosy Day.

Capt. Cook and Siege of Quebec AP108

Design: 250fr, Capt. Cook, Adventure and Resolution, map of voyages.

1978, July 26 **Engr.** ***Perf. 13***

C271	AP108	100fr multi	1.00	80
C272	AP108	250fr multi	2.50	2.00

Capt. James Cook (1728–1779), explorer.

Argentine Soccer Team, Coat of Arms and Rimet Cup—AP109

Designs: 200fr, Two soccer players (vert.). 1000fr, Soccer ball illuminating world map (vert.).

1978, Sept. 1 **Litho.** ***Perf. 13***

C273	AP109	100fr multi	1.00	80
C274	AP109	200fr multi	2.00	1.60
C275	AP109	1000fr multi	10.00	8.00

11th World Cup Soccer Championship, Argentina, June 1–25.

Jules Verne Type of 1978

Design: 400fr, Jules Verne and "20,000 Leagues Under the Sea" (horiz.).

1978, Oct. 10 **Litho.** ***Perf. 12***

C276	A169	400fr multi	4.00	3.20

Jules Verne (1828–1905), science fiction writer, birth sesquicentennial.

Musical Instrument Type of 1978

Design: 100fr, Man playing Mvet zither.

1978, Nov. 20 **Litho.** ***Perf. 12½***

C277	A172	100fr multi	1.00	60

Human Rights Type of 1979

1979, Feb. 11 **Litho.** ***Perf. 12x12½***

C278	A174	500fr multi	5.00	4.00

Universal Declaration of Human Rights, 30th anniversary (in 1978).

Lions Emblem, Map of District 403 AP110

1979, Apr. 26 **Litho.** ***Perf. 12½***

C279	AP110	60fr multi	60	40

21st Congress of Lions Club of Yaounde.

Penny Black, Hill, Cameroun No. 9 AP111

1979, Aug. 30 **Engraved** ***Perf. 13***

C280	AP111	100fr multi	1.00	60

Sir Rowland Hill (1795–1879), originator of penny postage.

See "Special Notices" at the front of this volume for data on the listing methods of this Catalogue, abbreviations, condition, prices and examination.

"TELECOM 79" AP112

1979, Sept. 26 **Litho.** ***Perf. 13x12½***

C281	AP112	100fr multi	1.00	60

3rd World Telecommunications Exhibition, Geneva, Sept. 20–26.

Pope Paul VI—AP113

1979, Oct. 23 **Engraved** ***Perf. 12½×13***

Multicolored

C282	AP113	100fr *shown*	1.00	65
C283	AP113	100fr *John Paul I*	1.00	65
C284	AP113	100fr *John Paul II*	1.00	65

"Double Eagle" over French Coastline AP114

Design: No. C286, Balloonists and balloon.

1979, Dec. 15 **Litho.** ***Perf. 12½***

C285	AP114	500fr multi	5.00	3.00
C286	AP114	500fr multi	5.00	3.00

First Transatlantic balloon crossing.

100-Meter Race—AP115

Designs: 150fr, Figure skating pairs. 200fr, Javelin. 300fr, Wrestling.

1980, Dec. 18 **Litho.** ***Perf. 12½***

C287	AP115	100fr yel brn & brn	1.00	60
C288	AP115	150fr bl & brn	1.50	90
C289	AP115	200fr grn & brn	2.00	1.20
C290	AP115	300fr red & brn	3.00	1.80

22nd Summer Olympic Games, Moscow, July 19-Aug. 3; 13th Winter Olympic Games, Lake Placid, Feb. 12-24 (150fr).

Alan Shepard and Freedom 7—AP116

1981, Sept. 15 **Litho.** ***Perf. 12½***

C291	AP116	500fr shown	5.00	3.00
C292	AP116	500fr Yuri Gagarin, Vostok I	5.00	3.00

Manned space flight, 20th anniv.

4th African Scouting Conference, Abidjan, June AP117

1981, Oct. 5

C293	AP117	100fr Emblem, salute, badge	1.00	65
C294	AP117	500fr Scout saluting	5.00	3.00
C295	AP118	500fr multi	5.00	3.00

Guernica (detail), by Pablo Picasso (1881-1973)—AP118

Design: No. C296, Landscape, by Paul Cezanne (1839-1906).

1981, Nov. 10 **Litho.** ***Perf. 12½***

C296	AP118	500fr multi	5.00	3.00

Christmas 1981—AP119

Designs: 50fr, Virgin and Child, by Froment (vert.). 60fr, San Zeno Altarpiece, by Mantegna (vert.). 400fr, Flight into Egypt, by Giotto.

1981, Dec. 1 **Litho.** ***Perf. 12½***

C297	AP119	50fr multi	50	30
C298	AP119	60fr multi	60	40
C299	AP119	400fr multi	4.00	2.40
		Souvenir sheet of 3	5.25	3.25

No. C299a contains Nos. C297-C299 (perf. 13x13½); green and gold marginal inscription. Size: 190x112mm.

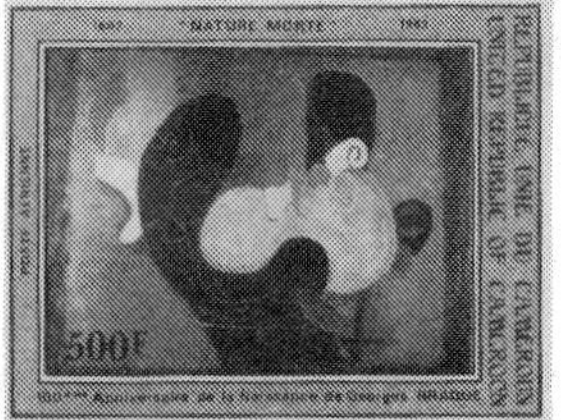

Still Life, by Georges Braque (1882-1963)—AP120

Paintings: No. C301, Olympia, by Edouard Manet (1832-1883).

1982, Dec. 5 **Litho.** ***Perf. 13***

C300	AP120	500fr multi	5.00	3.00
C301	AP120	500fr multi	5.00	3.00

AIR POST SEMI-POSTAL STAMPS.

V9 V10

Stamps of the designs shown above were issued in 1942 by the Vichy Government, but were not placed on sale in Cameroun.

POSTAGE DUE STAMPS.

Man Felling Tree
D1

Typographed.

1925-27 ***Perf. 14x13½*** **Unwmkd.**

J1	D1	2c lt bl & blk	12	12
J2	D1	4c ol bis & red vio	12	12
J3	D1	5c vio & blk	22	22
J4	D1	10c red & blk	22	22
J5	D1	15c gray & blk	28	28
J6	D1	20c ol grn & blk	35	35
J7	D1	25c yel & blk	42	42
J8	D1	30c bl & org	50	50
J9	D1	50c brn & blk	55	55
J10	D1	60c bl grn & rose red	70	70
J11	D1	1fr dl red & grn, *grnsh*	90	90
J12	D1	2fr red & vio ('27)	1.65	1.65
J13	D1	3fr org brn & ultra ('27)	2.25	2.25
		Nos. J1-J13 (13)	8.28	8.28

Carved Figures
D2 D3

1939 **Engraved** ***Perf. 14x13***

J14	D2	5c brt red vio	6	6
J15	D2	10c Prus bl	35	35
J16	D2	15c car rose	6	6
J17	D2	20c blk brn	6	6
J18	D2	30c ultra	8	8
J19	D2	50c dk grn	15	15
J20	D2	60c brn vio	18	18
J21	D2	1fr dk vio	38	38
J22	D2	2fr org red	60	60
J23	D2	3fr dk bl	90	90
		Nos. J14-J23 (10)	2.82	2.82

A 10c stamp, type D2, without "RF" was issued in 1944 by the Vichy Government, but was not placed on sale in Cameroun.

1947 ***Perf. 13.*** **Unwmkd.**

J24	D3	10c dk red	5	5
J25	D3	30c dp org	5	5
J26	D3	50c grnsh blk	6	6
J27	D3	1fr dk car	12	12
J28	D3	2fr dp yel grn	22	22
J29	D3	3fr dp red lil	28	28
J30	D3	4fr dp ultra	28	28
J31	D3	5fr red brn	35	35
J32	D3	10fr pck bl	50	50
J33	D3	20fr sepia	90	90
		Nos. J24-J33 (10)	2.81	2.81

Federal Republic

Hibiscus
D4

Flowers: No. J35, Erythrine. No. J36, Plumeria lutea. No. J37, Ipomoea. No. J38, Hoodia gordonii. No. J39, Grinum. No. J40, Ochna. No. J41, Gloriosa. No. J42, Costus spectabilis. No. J43, Bougainvillea spectabilis. No. J44, Delonix regia. No. J45, Haemanthus. No. J46, Ophthalmophyllum. No. J47, Titanopsis. No. J48, Amorphophallus. No. J49, Zingiberacee.

Engraved

1963, Apr. 10 ***Perf. 11*** **Unwmkd.**

J34	D4	50c car, bl, grn & yel	5	5
J35	D4	50c car, bl, grn & yel	5	5
J36	D4	1fr mag, grn & yel	6	6
J37	D4	1fr mag, grn & yel	6	6
J38	D4	1.50fr dk grn, lil & yel	7	7
J39	D4	1.50fr dk grn, lil & yel	7	7
J40	D4	2fr org ver, yel & grn	12	12
J41	D4	2fr org ver, yel & grn	12	12
J42	D4	5fr mag, grn & yel	15	15
J43	D4	5fr mag, grn & yel	15	15
J44	D4	10fr crim, grn & yel	32	32
J45	D4	10fr crim, grn & yel	32	32
J46	D4	20fr grn, yel & lil	60	60
J47	D4	20fr grn, yel & lil	60	60
J48	D4	40fr lil & yel	1.10	1.10
J49	D4	40fr lil & yel	1.10	1.10
		Nos. J34-J49 (16)	4.94	4.94

The two types of each value in Nos. J34–J49 were printed tête bêche, se-tenant at the base.

MILITARY STAMP

M1

Typographed

1963, July 1 ***Perf. 13*** **Unwmkd.**

M1	M1	rose cl	2.00	2.00

CAMPIONE D'ITALIA

The 1944 issues of this Italian enclave within the borders of Switzerland are not listed because of their local nature. These stamps were valid only on mail going from Campione d'Italia to Switzerland. Letters going to other countries required Swiss stamps in addition.

CAPE JUBY

(kăp jōō'bĭ)

LOCATION — Northwest coast of Africa in Spanish Sahara.

GOVT.—Spanish administration.

AREA—12,700 sq. mi.

POP.—9,836.

CAPITAL—Villa Bens (Cape Juby).

By agreement with France, Spain's Sahara possessions were extended to include Cape Juby and in 1916 Spanish troops occupied the territory. It is attached for administrative purposes to Spanish Sahara.

100 Centimos = 1 Peseta

Stamps of Rio de Oro, 1914 Surcharged in Violet, Red or Green

CABO JUBI 5 CÉNTIMOS

1916 *Perf. 13.* **Unwmkd.**

No.	Type	Description	Unused	Used
1	A6	5c on 4p rose (V)	100.00	22.50
2	A6	10c on 10p dl vio (R)	37.50	22.50
3	A6	15c on 50c dk brn (G)	50.00	35.00
4	A6	15c on 50c dk brn (R)	37.50	22.50
5	A6	40c on 1p red vio (G)	75.00	40.00
6	A6	40c on 1p red vio (R)	67.50	25.00
		Nos. 1-6 (6)	367.50	167.50

Nos. 1–6 exist with inverted surcharge. Prices about twice those quoted.

Stamps of Spain, 1876–1917, Overprinted in Red or Black

CABO JUBY

1919 *Imperf.*

No.	Type	Description	Unused	Used
7	A21	¼c bl grn (R)	30	6
		Perf. 13x12½, 14.		
8	A46	2c dk brn (Bk)	30	6
a.		Double overprint	20.00	9.00
b.		Double overprint (Bk+R)	55.00	37.50
9	A46	5c grn (R)	70	6
a.		Double overprint	20.00	9.00
b.		Inverted overprint	28.50	18.50
10	A46	10c car (Bk)	80	12
a.		Double overprint (Bk+R)	55.00	37.50
11	A46	15c ocher (Bk)	3.75	25
b.		Double overprint	20.00	9.00
c.		Red control #	4.50	4.50
d.		As "c," inverted ovpt.	15.00	
12	A46	20c ol grn (R)	20.00	3.50
13	A46	25c dp bl (R)	3.50	38
a.		Double overprint	20.00	9.00
14	A46	30c bl grn (R)	3.50	50
15	A46	40c rose (Bk)	3.50	50
16	A46	50c sl bl (R)	4.00	50
17	A46	1p lake (Bk)	11.50	3.50
18	A46	4p dp vio (R)	42.50	15.00
19	A46	10p org (Bk)	57.50	16.50
		Nos. 7-19 (13)	151.85	40.93

Nos. 8–19 have blue control number on back.

Nos. 8–13, 15, 17–19 exist imperf.

Same Overprint on Stamps of Spain, 1920–21.

1922 *Imperf.*

No.	Type	Description	Unused	Used
20	A47	1c bl grn (R)	25.00	14.00

Perf. 13x12½.

Engraved.

Blue Control Number on Back.

No.	Type	Description	Unused	Used
23	A46	20c violet	150.00	75.00

A 2c litho. exists, price $300.

Same Overprint on Stamps of Spain, 1922–23.

1925 *Perf. 13½x13.*

No.	Type	Description	Unused	Used
25	A49	5c red vio	7.00	3.00
26	A49	10c bl grn	20.00	3.00
28	A49	20c violet	40.00	10.00

Spain #331, 2c ol grn, exists.

Price $240 unused, $80 canceled

Seville-Barcelona Exposition Issue.

Stamps of Spain, 1929, Overprinted CABO JUBY in Red or Blue.

1929 *Perf. 11.*

No.	Type	Description	Unused	Used
29	A52	5c rose lake (Bl)	30	25
30	A53	10c grn (R)	30	25
31	A50	15c Prus bl (R)	30	25
32	A51	20c pur (R)	30	25
33	A50	25c brt rose (Bl)	30	25
34	A52	30c blk brn (Bl)	38	42
35	A53	40c dk bl (R)	38	42
36	A51	50c dp org (Bl)	65	75
37	A52	1p bl blk (R)	15.00	8.00
38	A53	4p dp rose (Bl)	17.50	16.50
39	A53	10p brn (Bl)	17.50	11.50
		Nos. 29-39 (11)	52.91	38.84

Stamps of Spanish Morocco, 1928-33, Overprinted in Black or Red

Cabo Juby

1934 *Perf. 14.*

No.	Type	Description	Unused	Used
40	A7	1c brt rose (Bk)	38	42
41	A2	2c dk vio (R)	3.75	50
42	A2	5c dp bl (R)	3.75	75
43	A2	10c dk grn (Bk)	7.50	1.25
43A	A10	10c dk grn (R)	2.50	2.10
44	A2	15c org brn (Bk)	16.50	5.50
45	A7	20c sl grn (R)	7.00	3.75
46	A3	25c cop red (Bk)	3.75	3.50
47	A10	30c red brn (Bk)	7.00	3.75
48	A13	40c dp bl (R)	22.50	13.00
49	A13	50c red org (Bk)	40.00	20.00
50	A4	1p yel grn (Bk)	27.50	12.00
51	A5	2.50p red vio (Bk)	60.00	27.50
52	A6	4p ultra (R)	75.00	35.00

No. 43A and 1c, 20c, 30c, 40c, 50c, with control numbers.

Same Overprint in Black on Stamp of Spanish Morocco, 1932.

No.	Type	Description	Unused	Used
53	A2	1c car rose ("Ct")	1.75	75
		Nos. 40-53 (15)	278.88	129.77

Stamps of Spanish Morocco, 1933–35, Overprinted in Black, Blue or Red

CABO JUBY

1935–36

No.	Type	Description	Unused	Used
54	A8	2c grn (R)	65	18
55	A9	5c mag (Bk)	2.50	25
55A	A10	10c dk grn (R) ('36)	13.00	2.75
56	A11	15c yel (Bl)	5.25	1.75
57	A12	25c crim (Bk)	45.00	27.50
58	A8	1p sl blk (R)	1.50	4.50
59	A9	2.50p brn (Bl)	35.00	17.50
60	A11	4p yel grn (R)	42.50	20.00
61	A12	5p blk (R)	42.50	27.50
		Nos. 54-61 (9)	187.90	101.93

Same Overprint in Black or Red on Stamps of Spanish Morocco, 1935.

1935 *Perf. 13½.*

No.	Type	Description	Unused	Used
62	A14	25c vio (R)	3.75	1.75
63	A15	30c crim (Bk)	3.75	1.50
64	A14	40c org (Bk)	5.00	1.75
65	A15	50c brt bl (R)	10.00	1.75
66	A14	60c dk bl grn (R)	12.00	4.25
67	A15	2p brn lake (Bk)	57.50	27.50

Same Overprint on Stamps of Spanish Morocco, 1933.

Perf. 13½, 14.

No.	Type	Description	Unused	Used
68	A7	1c brt rose (Bk)	28	12
		Perf. 14		
69	A7	20c sl grn (R)	5.00	2.75
		Nos. 62-69 (8)	97.28	41.37

Same Overprint on Stamps of Spanish Morocco, 1937.

1937 *Perf. 13½.*

No.	Type	Description	Unused	Used
70	A21	1c dk bl (Bk)	12	12
71	A21	2c org brn (Bk)	12	12
72	A21	5c cer (Bk)	12	12
73	A21	10c emer (Bk)	12	12
74	A21	15c brt bl (Bk)	18	18
75	A21	20c red brn (Bk)	18	18
76	A21	25c mag (Bk)	18	18
77	A21	30c red org (Bk)	18	18
78	A21	40c org (Bk)	90	75
79	A21	50c ultra (R)	90	75
80	A21	60c yel grn (Bk)	90	75
81	A21	1p bl vio (Bk)	90	75
82	A21	2p Prus bl (Bk)	52.50	50.00
83	A21	2.50p gray blk (R)	52.50	50.00
84	A21	4p dk brn (Bk)	52.50	50.00
85	A22	10p vio blk (R)	52.50	50.00
		Nos. 70-85 (16)	214.80	204.20

Issued in commemoration of the First Year of the Revolution.

Same Overprint in Black on Types of Spanish Morocco, 1939.

Designs: 5c, Spanish quarter. 10c, Moroccan quarter. 15c, Street scene, Larache. 20c, Tetuan.

1939 **Photogravure.** *Perf. 13½.*

No.	Type	Description	Unused	Used
86	A25	5c vermilion	65	50
87	A25	10c dp grn	65	50
88	A25	15c brn lake	65	65
89	A25	20c brt bl	65	65

Same Overprint in Black or Red on Stamps of Spanish Morocco, 1940.

1940 *Perf. 11½x11.*

No.	Type	Description	Unused	Used
90	A26	1c dk brn (Bk)	18	6
91	A27	2c ol grn (R)	18	6
92	A28	5c dk bl (R)	18	6
93	A29	10c dk red lil (Bk)	25	6
94	A30	15c dk grn (R)	25	6
95	A31	20c pur (R)	25	6
96	A32	25c blk brn (R)	25	18
97	A33	30c brt grn (Bk)	25	18
98	A34	40c sl grn (R)	75	25
99	A35	45c org ver (Bk)	75	25
100	A36	50c brn org (Bk)	75	25
101	A37	70c saph (R)	2.00	70
102	A38	1p ind & brn (Bk)	4.25	70
103	A39	2.50p choc & dk grn (Bk)	9.00	4.00
104	A40	5p dk cer & sep (Bk)	9.00	4.00
105	A41	10p dk ol grn & brn org (Bk)	27.50	16.50
		Nos. 90-105 (16)	55.79	27.37

Stamps of Spanish Morocco, 1944, Overprinted in Black or Red

CABO JUBY

1944 *Perf. 12½.* **Unwmkd.**

No.	Type	Description	Unused	Used
106	A47	1c choc & lt bl	10	10
107	A48	2c sl grn & lt grn	10	10
108	A49	5c choc & grnsh blk (R)	10	10
109	A50	10c brt ultra & red org	10	10
110	A51	15c sl grn & lt grn	10	10
111	A52	20c dp cl & blk (R)	10	10
112	A53	25c lt bl & choc	10	10
113	A47	30c yel grn & brt ultra (R)	10	10
114	A48	40c choc & red vio	10	10
115	A49	50c brt ultra, & red brn	10	10
116	A50	75c yel grn & brt ultra (R)	75	42
117	A51	1p brt ultra & choc	75	42
118	A52	2.50p blk & brt ultra (R)	2.25	1.75
119	A53	10p sal & gray blk (R)	14.00	12.50
		Nos. 106-119 (14)	18.75	16.09

Same Overprint on Stamps of Spanish Morocco, 1946.

1946 *Perf. 10½x10.*

No.	Type	Description	Unused	Used
120	A54	1c pur & brn	10	10
121	A55	2c dk Prus grn & vio blk (R)	10	10
122	A54	10c dp org & vio bl	10	10
123	A55	15c dk bl & bl grn	10	10
124	A54	25c yel grn & ultra	10	10
125	A56	40c dk bl & brn (R)	10	10
126	A55	45c blk & rose	25	25
127	A57	1p dk Prus grn & dp bl	90	42
128	A58	2.50p dp org & grnsh gray (R)	2.50	2.00
129	A59	10p dk bl & gray (R)	9.00	6.25
		Nos. 120-129 (10)	13.25	9.52

Same Overprint in Carmine, Black or Brown on Stamps of Spanish Morocco, 1948.

1948 *Perf. 10, 10x10½*

No.	Type	Description	Unused	Used
130	A64	2c pur & brn	7	7
131	A65	5c dp cl & vio	7	7
132	A66	15c brt ultra & bl grn (Bk)	7	7
133	A67	25c blk & Prus grn	7	7
134	A65	35c brt ultra & gray blk	10	10
135	A68	50c red & vio (Br)	10	10
136	A66	70c dk gray grn & ultra (Bk)	10	10
137	A67	90c cer & dk gray grn (Bk)	10	10
138	A68	1p brt ultra & vio (Br)	30	30
139	A64	2.50p vio brn & sl grn	90	65
140	A69	10p blk & dp ultra	2.75	2.00
		Nos. 130-140 (11)	4.63	3.63

SEMI-POSTAL STAMPS.

Types of Semi-Postal Stamps of Spain, 1926, Overprinted

CABO-JUBY

1926 *Perf. 12½, 13* **Unwmkd.**

No.	Type	Description	Unused	Used
B1	SP1	1c orange	7.50	4.25
B2	SP2	2c rose	7.50	4.25
B3	SP3	5c blk brn	2.00	1.75
B4	SP4	10c dk grn	1.25	1.00
B5	SP1	15c dk vio	75	75
B6	SP4	20c vio brn	75	75
B7	SP5	25c dp car	75	75
B8	SP1	30c ol grn	75	75
B9	SP3	40c ultra	7	7
B10	SP2	50c red brn	7	7
B11	SP4	1p vermilion	7	7
B12	SP3	4p bister	90	60
B13	SP5	10p lt vio	1.40	1.00
		Nos. B1-B13 (13)	23.76	16.06

AIR POST STAMPS.

Spanish Morocco, Nos. C1 to C10

Overprinted in Black CABO JUBY

1938, June 1 *Perf. 13½.* **Unwmkd.**

C1	AP1	5c brown	25	7
C2	AP1	10c brt grn	25	7
C3	AP1	25c crimson	18	7
C4	AP1	40c lt bl	2.75	1.75
C5	AP2	50c brt mag	25	7
C6	AP2	75c dk bl	25	38
C7	AP1	1p sepia	25	38
C8	AP1	1.50p dp vio	1.50	80
C9	AP1	2p dp red brn	3.75	2.00
C10	AP1	3p brn blk	10.00	6.50
		Nos. C1-C10 (10)	19.43	12.09

Strait of Gibraltar
AP3

Designs: 5c, Ketama landscape. 10c, Mosque, Tangier. 15c, Velez. 90c, Sanjurjo.

1942, Apr. 1 Photo. *Perf. 12½*

C11	AP3	5c dp bl	10	10
C12	AP3	10c org brn	10	10
C13	AP3	15c grnsh blk	10	10
C14	AP3	90c dk rose	75	50
C15	AP3	5p black	2.75	1.75
		Nos. C11-C15 (5)	3.80	2.55

SPECIAL DELIVERY STAMPS.

Special Delivery Stamp of Spain Overprinted "CABO JUBY" as on Nos. 7-28.

1919 *Perf. 14* **Unwmkd.**

E1	SD1	20c red (Bk)	2.00	1.25
a.		Inverted overprint		
b.		Double overprint	28.50	16.50

Spanish Morocco No. E4 Overprinted in Red

Cabo Juby

1934

E2	SD2	20c black	7.50	7.00

Spanish Morocco No. E5 Overprinted in Black

CABO JUBY

1935

E3	SD3	20c vermilion	3.75	1.25

Same Overprint on Spanish Morocco, No. E6.

1937 *Perf. 13½.*

E4	SD4	20c brt car	90	75

Issued in commemoration of the First Year of the Revolution.

Same Overprint on Spanish Morocco, No. E8.

1940 *Perf. 11½x11.*

E5	SD5	25c scarlet	60	38

SEMI-POSTAL SPECIAL DELIVERY STAMP.

Type of Semi-Postal Special Delivery Stamp of Spain, 1926, Overprinted CABO-JUBY

1926 *Perf. 12½, 13.* **Unwmkd.**

EB1	SPSD1	20c ultra & blk	2.25	1.50

CAPE VERDE

(kāp vûrd)

LOCATION—A group of ten islands and five islets in the Atlantic Ocean, lying about 500 miles due west of Senegal.

GOVT.—Republic.

AREA—1,557 sq. mi.

POP.—300,000 (1976).

CAPITAL—Praia.

The Portuguese territory of Cape Verde became independent July 5, 1975.

1000 Reis = 1 Milreis
100 Centavos = 1 Escudo (1913)

Crown of Portugal
A1

King Luiz
A2

Typographed.

1877 *Perf. 12½, 13½.* **Unwmkd.**

1	A1	5r black	2.50	2.00
2	A1	10r yellow	17.50	12.50
3	A1	20r bister	2.00	1.75
4	A1	25r rose	2.00	1.50
a.		Perf. 13½	10.00	6.00
5	A1	40r blue	70.00	45.00
a.		Cliche of Mozambique in Cape Verde plate, in pair with #5	1,100.	900.00
b.		As "a," perf. 13½	1,750.	1,750.
6	A1	50r green	70.00	45.00
7	A1	100r lilac	7.50	3.00
8	A1	200r orange	5.00	3.75
a.		Perf. 13½	13.50	9.00
9	A1	300r brown	7.50	5.00

1881-85

10	A1	10r green	2.50	2.00
11	A1	20r car ('85)	4.50	3.00
a.		Perf. 13½	37.50	30.00
12	A1	25r vio ('85)	3.00	2.50
13	A1	40r yel buff	3.00	2.00
a.		Imperf.	1.00	
b.		Cliche of Mozambique in Cape Verde plate, in pair with #13	85.00	85.00
c.		As "b," imperf.	27.50	
14	A1	50r blue	5.50	4.50

Reprints of the 1877-85 issues are on smooth white chalky paper, ungummed, and on thin white paper with shiny white gum. They are perf. 13½. Price $1 each.

Embossed.
Chalk-Surfaced Paper.

1886 *Perf. 12½, 13½*

15	A2	5r black	3.00	2.00
16	A2	10r green	3.25	2.25
17	A2	20r carmine	4.50	3.00
a.		Perf.13½	5.50	4.50
18	A2	25r violet	4.50	2.25
19	A2	40r chocolate	5.00	2.50
a.		Perf. 13½	7.50	5.00
20	A2	50r blue	5.00	2.50
21	A2	100r yel brn	5.25	3.00
22	A2	200r gray lil	11.00	8.00
23	A2	300r orange	12.50	10.00

The 25, 50 and 100r have been reprinted in aniline colors with clean-cut perf. 13½. Price $2 each.

King Carlos
A3 A4

Typographed.

1894-95 *Perf. 11½, 12½, 13½.*

24	A3	5r orange	1.20	90
25	A3	10r redsh vio	1.25	1.10
26	A3	15r chocolate	2.75	2.00
a.		Perf. 12½	110.00	75.00
27	A3	20r lavender	2.75	1.75
28	A3	25r dp grn	3.00	2.00
a.		Perf. 12½	3.50	3.50
29	A3	50r lt bl	3.00	2.00
a.		Perf. 13½	7.50	3.00
30	A3	75r car ('95)	10.00	6.00
a.		Perf. 13½	25.00	15.00
31	A3	80r yel grn ('95)	15.00	10.00
a.		Perf. 13½	20.00	12.50
32	A3	100r brn, *buff* ('95)	7.50	3.00
a.		Perf. 12½	37.50	15.00
33	A3	150r car, *rose* ('95)	20.00	16.50
a.		Perf. 12½	125.00	100.00
b.		Perf. 11½	37.50	25.00
34	A3	200r dk bl, *lt bl* ('95)	17.50	12.50
a.		Perf. 12½	110.00	80.00
35	A3	300r dk bl, *sal* ('95)	22.50	13.50

1898-1903 *Perf. 11½.*

Name and Value in Black except 500r

36	A4	2½r gray	30	20
37	A4	5r orange	30	20
38	A4	10r lt grn	30	20
39	A4	15r brown	3.75	1.50
40	A4	15r gray grn ('03)	1.25	1.00
41	A4	20r gray vio	1.25	50
42	A4	25r sea grn	2.50	1.00
a.		Perf. 12½	62.50	20.00
43	A4	25r car ('03)	1.25	30
44	A4	50r dk bl	2.50	1.00
45	A4	50r brn ('03)	2.50	2.00
46	A4	65r sl bl ('03)	12.50	*12.50*
47	A4	75r rose	6.00	3.00
48	A4	75r lil ('03)	2.25	1.75
49	A4	80r violet	6.00	3.50
50	A4	100r dk bl, *bl*	2.00	1.25
51	A4	115r org brn, *pink* ('03)	12.50	*12.50*
52	A4	130r brn, *straw* ('03)	12.50	*12.50*
53	A4	150r brn, *straw*	6.00	4.00
54	A4	200r red vio, *pnksh*	2.50	2.00
55	A4	300r dk bl, *rose*	7.50	3.75
56	A4	400r dl bl, *straw* ('03)	7.50	6.00
57	A4	500r blk & red, *bl* ('01)	7.50	3.75
58	A4	700r vio, *yelsh* ('01)	20.00	12.50
		Nos. 36-58 (23)	120.65	*86.90*

Regular Issues Surcharged in Red or Black

65 RÉIS

Two spacing types of surcharge. See note above Angola No. 61.

On Issue of 1886.

1902, Dec. 1 *Perf. 12½, 13½*

59	A2	65r on 5r blk (R)	4.00	3.00
60	A2	65r on 200r gray lil	4.00	3.00
61	A2	65r on 300r org	4.00	3.00
62	A2	115r on 10r grn	4.00	3.00
63	A2	115r on 20r rose	4.00	3.00
a.		Perf. 13½	30.00	20.00
64	A2	130r on 50r bl	4.00	3.00
65	A2	130r on 100r brn	4.00	3.00
66	A2	400r on 25r vio	2.25	1.75
67	A2	400r on 40r choc	3.00	2.75
a.		Perf. 13½	30.00	22.50

On Issue of 1894.

Perf. 11½, 12½, 13½.

68	A3	65r on 10r red vio	6.50	4.00
69	A3	65r on 20r lav	6.00	3.00
70	A3	65r on 100r brn, *buff*	6.00	4.00
a.		Perf 12½	15.00	10.00
71	A3	115r on 5r org	3.25	2.50
a.		Inverted surcharge	15.00	15.00
72	A3	115r on 25r bl grn	3.00	2.40
a.		Perf. 11½	17.50	8.00
73	A3	115r on 150r car, *rose*	6.00	5.00
a.		Perf. 13½	25.00	15.00
74	A3	130r on 75r car	3.25	2.75
a.		Perf. 13½	37.50	25.00
75	A3	130r on 80r yel grn	3.00	2.75
76	A3	130r on 200r dk bl, *bl*	4.00	3.00
77	A3	400r on 50r lt bl	4.50	3.00
a.		Inverted surcharge	40.00	40.00
b.		Perf. 13½	62.50	45.00
78	A3	400r on 300r dk bl, *sal*	2.00	1.50

On Newspaper Stamp of 1893.

79	N1	400r on 2½r brn	1.75	1.50
a.		Inverted surcharge	12.50	
b.		Perf. 12½	37.50	25.00
		Nos. 59-79 (21)	82.50	60.90

Reprints of Nos. 59, 66, 67, and 77 have shiny white gum and clean-cut perforation 13½. Price $1 each.

Overprinted in Black PROVISORIO

On Nos. 39, 42, 44, 47

1902-03 *Perf. 11½*

80	A4	15r brown	1.50	1.25
81	A4	25r sea grn	1.50	1.25
82	A4	50r bl ('03)	1.75	1.40
83	A4	75r rose ('03)	2.75	2.00
a.		Invtd. ovpt.	20.00	20.00

No. 46 Surcharged in Black

50 RÉIS

1905, July 1

84	A4	50r on 65r sl bl	2.50	2.25

Stamps of 1898-1903 Overprinted in Carmine or Green

REPUBLICA

1911, Aug. 20

85	A4	2½r gray	35	25
86	A4	5r orange	35	25
87	A4	10r lt grn	1.00	80
88	A4	15r gray grn	70	35
89	A4	20r gray vio	1.00	1.00
90	A4	25r car (G)	1.00	50
91	A4	50r brown	6.50	4.50
92	A4	75r red lil	1.25	75
93	A4	100r dk bl, *bl*	1.25	1.00
94	A4	115r org brn, *pink*	90	*2.00*
95	A4	130r brn, *straw*	90	*2.00*
96	A4	200r red vio, *pnksh*	5.00	5.00
97	A4	400r dl bl, *straw*	2.00	2.00
98	A4	500r blk & red, *bl*	2.25	1.75
99	A4	700r vio, *straw*	2.25	1.75
		Nos. 85-99 (15)	26.70	*23.90*

King Manuel II
A5

Overprinted in Carmine or Green.

1912 *Perf. 11½x12*

100	A5	2½r violet	20	*2.00*
101	A5	5r black	20	18
102	A5	10r gray grn	35	25
103	A5	20r car (G)	2.00	1.25
104	A5	25r vio brn	50	30
105	A5	50r dk bl	4.50	2.75
106	A5	75r bis brn	90	60
107	A5	100r brn, *lt grn*	90	60
108	A5	200r dk grn, *sal*	1.25	90
109	A5	300r *azure*	1.25	90

Perf. 14½x15.

110	A5	400r blk & bl	3.00	2.75
111	A5	500r ol grn & vio brn	3.00	2.75
		Nos. 100-111(12)	18.05	*15.23*

Vasco da Gama Issue of Various Portuguese Colonies. Common Design Types CD20-CD27 Surcharged

REPUBLICA
CABO VERDE
¼ C.

On Stamps of Macao.

1913, Feb. 13 *Perf. 12½ to 16*

112	¼c on ½a bl grn	1.25	1.25
113	½c on 1a red	1.25	1.25
114	1c on 2a red vio	1.25	1.25
115	2½c on 4a yel grn	1.25	1.25
116	5c on 8a dk bl	6.00	6.00
117	7½c on 12a vio brn	5.50	5.50
118	10c on 16a bis brn	2.50	2.50
119	15c on 24a bis	5.00	5.00
	Nos. 112-119 (8)	24.00	24.00

On Stamps of Portuguese Africa.

Perf. 14 to 15.

120	¼c on 2½r bl grn	1.00	1.00
121	½c on 5r red	1.00	1.00
122	1c on 10r red vio	1.00	1.00
123	2½c on 25r yel grn	1.00	1.00
124	5c on 50r dk bl	2.00	2.00
125	7½c on 75r vio brn	3.00	3.00
126	10c on 100r bis brn	2.50	2.50
127	15c on 150r bis	3.00	3.00
	Nos. 120-127 (8)	14.50	14.50

On Stamps of Timor.

128	¼c on ½a bl grn	1.25	1.25
129	½c on 1a red	1.25	1.25
130	1c on 2a red vio	1.25	1.25
131	2½c on 4a yel grn	1.25	1.25
132	5c on 8a dk bl	5.50	5.50
133	7½c On 12a vio brn	5.50	5.50
134	10c on 16a bis brn	2.75	2.75
135	15c on 24a bis	3.00	3.00
	Nos. 128-135 (8)	21.75	21.75

No. 75 Overprinted in Red

REPUBLICA

1913 *Perf. 11½, 12½, 13½.*

137	A3	130r on 80r yel grn	3.50	2.75

Nos. 73 and 76 overprinted but not issued. Prices, $10, $12.

Same Overprint on No. 83 in Green

1914 *Perf. 12*

139	A4	75r rose	3.50	2.75
a.		"PROVISORIO" double (G and R)	30.00	27.50

Ceres
A6

Perf. 11½, 12x11½, 15x14.

1914-26 Typographed.

Name and Value in Black.

144	A6	¼c ol brn	10	10
a.		Imperf.		
145	A6	½c black	10	10
146	A6	1c bl grn	1.25	1.00
147	A6	1c yel grn ('22)	10	10
148	A6	1½c lil brn	10	10
149	A6	2c carmine	18	15
150	A6	2c gray ('26)	25	*3.00*
151	A6	2½c lt vio	10	5
152	A6	3c org ('22)	35	25
153	A6	4c rose ('22)	12	*2.00*
154	A6	4½c gray ('22)	18	*3.00*
155	A6	5c dp bl	1.25	60
156	A6	5c brt bl ('22)	18	18
157	A6	6c lil ('22)	20	*3.00*
158	A6	7c ultra ('22)	20	*3.00*
159	A6	7½c yel brn	20	*3.00*
160	A6	8c slate	65	50
161	A6	10c org brn	20	15
162	A6	12c bl grn ('22)	30	25
163	A6	15c plum	7.50	5.50
164	A6	15c brn rose ('22)	25	15
165	A6	20c yel grn	20	15
166	A6	24c ultra ('26)	1.50	1.50
167	A6	25c choc ('26)	1.50	1.50
168	A6	30c brn, *grn*	5.00	5.00
169	A6	30c gray grn ('22)	35	25
170	A6	40c brn, *pink*	5.00	5.00
171	A6	40c turq bl ('22)	75	22
172	A6	50c org, *sal*	5.00	5.00
173	A6	50c vio ('26)	1.00	40
174	A6	60c dk bl ('22)	90	60
175	A6	60c rose ('26)	1.00	75
176	A6	80c brt rose ('22)	3.50	1.50
177	A6	1e grn *bl*	5.00	5.00
178	A6	1e rose ('22)	5.00	3.00
179	A6	1e dp bl ('26)	4.00	2.00
180	A6	2e dk vio ('22)	5.00	3.00
181	A6	5e buff ('26)	8.00	6.00
182	A6	10e pink ('26)	15.00	10.00
183	A6	20e pale turq ('26)	40.00	22.50
		Nos. 144-183 (40)	121.46	*99.55*

Provisional Issue of 1902 Overprinted in Carmine

REPUBLICA

1915 *Perf. 11½, 12½, 13½*

184	A2	115r on 10r grn	1.75	1.75
a.		Perf. 13½	20.00	20.00
185	A2	115r on 20r rose	2.00	2.00
a.		Perf. 13½	20.00	20.00
186	A2	130r on 50r bl	1.75	1.75
187	A2	130r on 100r brn	1.25	1.25
188	A3	115r on 5r org	75	50
a.		Invtd. ovpt.	22.50	
189	A3	115r on 25r bl grn	1.25	1.10
a.		Perf. 11½	20.00	20.00
190	A3	115r on 150r car, *rose*	1.00	1.00
191	A3	130r on 75r car	1.25	1.25
192	A3	130r on 80r yel grn	1.25	1.25
a.		Inverted overprint	22.50	
193	A3	130r on 200r bl, *bl*	1.25	1.25
a.		Perf. 12½	55.00	45.00
		Nos. 184-193 (10)	13.50	13.10

War Tax Stamps of Portuguese Africa Surcharged

CABO VERDE
CORREIOS
½ C.

1921, Feb. 3 *Perf. 15x14, 11½*

194	WT1	¼c on 1c grn	30	30
195	WT1	½c on 1c grn	45	30
a.		"1/2" instead of "½"	8.50	8.50
196	WT1	1c green	45	35

Nos. 127 and 126 Surcharged

2 C.

Perf. 14 to 15.

197	CD27	2c on 15c on 150r bis	1.50	1.50
198	CD26	4c on 10c on 100r bis brn	1.75	1.50
a.		On No. 118(error)	100.00	100.00

No. 50 Surcharged

6 C.
REPUBLICA

Perf. 12.

200	A4	6c on 100r dk bl, *bl*	1.75	1.00
a.		Accent on "U" of surch.	7.50	7.50

Stamps of 1913-15 Surcharged

$04

1922, Apr. *Perf. 11½, 12½, 13½*

On No. 137

201	A3	4c on 130r on 80r yel grn	2.00	2.00

On Nos. 191-193

202	A3	4c on 130r on 75r car	2.50	2.50
203	A3	4c on 130r on 80r yel grn	2.00	2.00
204	A3	4c on 130r on 200r bl, *bl*	1.25	90
a.		Perf. 12½	20.00	20.00

Surcharge of Nos. 201-204 with smaller $ occurs once in sheet of 28. Price eight times normal.

Nos. 78-79 Surcharged

República
40 C.

1925 *Perf. 13½, 11½*

205	A3	40c on 400r on 300r bl, *sal*	90	60
206	N1	40c on 400r on 2½r brn	65	60

No. 176 Surcharged

70 C.

1931, Nov. *Perf. 12x11½*

214	A6	70c on 80c brt rose	3.00	2.25

Ceres
A7

Wmkd. Maltese Cross. (232)

1934, May 1 *Perf. 12x11½*

215	A7	1c bister	10	*1.00*
216	A7	5c ol brn	10	10
217	A7	10c violet	10	10
218	A7	5c black	10	10
219	A7	20c gray	10	10
220	A7	30c dk grn	13	10
221	A7	40c red org	40	25
222	A7	45c brt bl	75	50
223	A7	50c brown	75	50
224	A7	60c ol grn	75	50
225	A7	70c brn org	1.00	1.00
226	A7	80c emerald	1.00	40
227	A7	85c dp rose	2.50	2.00
228	A7	1e maroon	2.00	1.00
229	A7	1.40e dk bl	3.00	2.50
230	A7	2e dk vio	3.50	1.00
231	A7	5e ap grn	14.00	6.00
232	A7	10e ol bis	22.00	12.50
233	A7	20e orange	50.00	22.50
		Nos. 215-233 (19)	102.28	*52.15*

Vasco da Gama Issue

Common Design Types

1938 *Perf. 13½x13.* **Unwmkd.**

Name and Value in Black.

234	CD34	1c gray grn	5	*1.00*
235	CD34	5c org brn	10	*1.00*
236	CD34	10c dk car	10	10
237	CD34	15c dk vio brn	75	45
238	CD34	20c slate	35	25
239	CD35	30c rose vio	30	25
240	CD35	35c brt grn	50	30
241	CD35	40c brown	30	25
242	CD35	50c brt red vio	30	25
243	CD36	60c gray blk	45	40
244	CD36	70c brn vio	45	30
245	CD36	80c orange	45	35
246	CD36	1e red	60	30
247	CD37	1.75e blue	1.75	80
248	CD37	2e dk bl grn	2.25	1.00
249	CD37	5e ol grn	7.00	2.00
250	CD38	10e bl vio	9.50	5.00
251	CD38	20e red brn	30.00	6.00
		Nos. 234-251 (18)	55.20	*20.00*

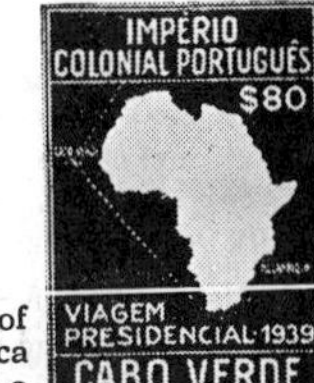

Outline Map of Africa
A8

1939, June 23 Litho. *Perf. 11½x12*

252	A8	80c vio, *pale rose*	5.00	3.50
253	A8	1.75e bl, *pale bl*	25.00	8.50
254	A8	20e brn, *buff*	80.00	27.50

Issued to commemorate the visit of the President of Portugal to this colony in 1939.

Nos. 239 and 221 Surcharged with New Value and Bars in Black.

1948 *Perf. 13½x13* **Unwmkd.**

255	CD35	10c on 30c rose vio	1.50	2.00

Perf. 12x11½ **Wmk. 232**

256	A7	25c on 40c red org	1.50	2.00

Machado Pt., Sao Vicente
A9

Brava Creek, Sao Nicoláo
A10

Designs: 10c, Ribeira Grande. 1e, Harbor, Sao Vicente. 1.75e, Mindelo, distant view. 2e, Joao de Evora Beach. 5e, Mindelo. 10e, Volcano, Fire Island. 20e, Mt. Paul.

Perf. 14½

1948, Oct. 1 Litho. **Unwmkd.**

257	A9	5c vio brn & bis	40	40
258	A9	10c ol grn & pale grn	40	25
259	A10	50c mag & lil rose	1.00	50
260	A10	1e brn vio & rose lil	2.50	1.50
261	A10	1.75e ultra & grnsh bl	3.00	2.50
262	A10	2e dk brn & buff	12.00	3.75
263	A10	5e ol grn & yel	16.00	8.00
264	A10	10e red & cr	25.00	14.00
265	A10	20e dk vio & bis	60.00	27.50
		Nos. 257-265 (9)	120.30	58.40

Common Design Types pictured in section at front of book

Lady of Fatima Issue.
Common Design Type

1948, Dec.

266	CD40	50c dk bl	10.00	7.50

U.P.U Symbols
A10a

1949, Oct. *Perf. 14*

267	A10a	1e red vio & pink	6.25	4.25

U.P.U., 75th anniversary

Holy Year Issue
Common Design Types

1950, May *Perf. 13x13½*

268	CD41	1e org brn	75	50
269	CD42	2e slate	3.50	2.25

Holy Year Conclusion Issue
Common Design Type

1951, Oct. *Perf. 14* **Unwmkd.**

270	CD43	2e pur & lil	1.50	1.50

Stamps of 1938 Surcharged with New Value and Bars in Black.
Perf. 13½x13

1951, May 21 **Unwmkd.**

271	CD35	10c on 35c brt grn	50	*1.50*
272	CD36	20c on 70c brn vio	75	*1.50*
273	CD36	40c on 70c brn vio	1.50	*2.00*
274	CD36	50c on 80c org	2.50	*3.00*
275	CD37	1e on 1.75e bl	3.00	*4.00*
276	CD38	2e on 10e bl vio	5.00	*7.50*
a.		1e on 10e bl vio	100.00	100.00
		Nos. 271-276 (6)	13.25	*19.50*

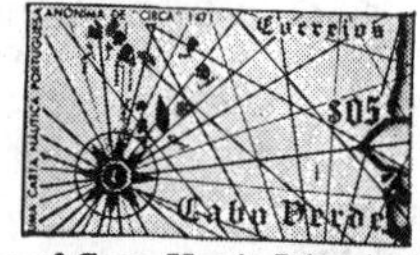

Map of Cape Verde Islands, 1502
A11

Vicente Dias and Gonçalo de Cintra
A12

Portraits: 30c, Diogo Alfonso and Alvaro Fernandes. 50c, Lançarote and Soeiro da Costa. 1e, Diogo Gomes and Antonio da Nola. 2e, Prince Henry and Prince Henry the Navigator. 3e, Antao Gonçalves and Dinis Dias. 5e, Alfonso Goncalves Baldaia and Joao Fernandes. 10e, Dinis Eanes da Gra and Alvaro de Freitas. 20e, Map of Cape Verde Islands, 1502.

1952, Feb. 24 *Perf. 14*

277	A11	5c multi	10	10
278	A12	10c multi	10	10
279	A12	30c multi	10	10
280	A12	50c multi	13	10
281	A12	1e multi	20	13
282	A12	2e multi	1.25	20
283	A12	3e multi	3.75	40
284	A12	5e multi	3.00	50
285	A12	10e multi	6.00	1.50
286	A11	20e multi	12.00	2.50
		Nos. 277-286 (10)	26.63	5.63

Medical Congress Issue.
Common Design Type
Design: Hypodermic Injection.

1952, June *Perf. 13½*

287	CD44	20c ol grn & dk brn	50	40

No. 247 Surcharged with New Values and "X" in Black.

1952, Jan. 25 *Perf. 13½x13*

288	CD37	10c on 1.75e bl	1.75	1.75
289	CD37	20c on 1.75e bl	1.75	1.75
290	CD37	50c on 1.75e bl	6.00	6.00
291	CD37	1e on 1.75e bl	75	75
292	CD37	1.50e on 1.75e bl	75	75
		Nos. 288-292 (5)	11.00	11.00

Facade of Jeronymos Convent
A13

Lithographed.

1953, Jan. *Perf. 13½* **Unwmkd.**

293	A13	10c brn & pale ol	25	25
294	A13	50c pur & fawn	30	25
295	A13	1e dk grn & fawn	70	25

Issued to commemorate the Exhibition of Sacred Missionary Art held at Lisbon in 1951.

Stamp of Portugal and Arms of Colonies
A13a

1953 Photogravure
Stamp and Arms Multicolored.

296	A13a	50c lil rose & gray	1.25	60

Centenary of Portuguese stamps.

Sao Paulo Issue
Common Design Type

1954 Lithographed. *Perf. 13½*

297	CD46	1e grn, cr & gray	30	20

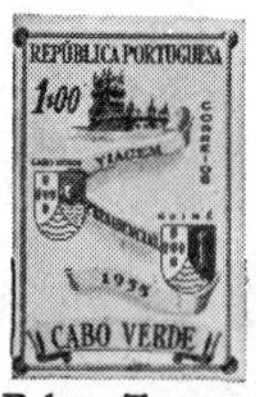

Belem Tower, Lisbon, and Colonial Arms
A14

Arms of Praia
A15

1955, May 15 Litho. *Perf. 13½*

298	A14	1e multi	30	20
299	A14	1.60e buff & multi	50	30

Issued to publicize the visit of Pres. Francisco H. C. Lopes.

1958, June 14 *Perf. 12x11½*

300	A15	1e multi	30	20
301	A15	2.50e pink & multi	60	30

Centenary of city of Praia.

Fair Emblem, Globe and Arms
A15a

1958 *Perf. 12x11½*

302	A45	2e multi	50	40

World's Fair, Brussels, Apr. 17–Oct. 19.

Tropical Medicine Congress Issue
Common Design Type
Design: Aloe vera.

1958, Sept. 5 *Perf. 13½*

303	CD47	3e multi	3.50	2.00

Prince Henry
A16

Antonio da Nola
A17

1960, June 25 Litho. *Perf. 13½*

304	A16	2e multi	50	40

Issued to commemorate the 500th anniversary of the death of Prince Henry the Navigator.

1960, Oct. *Perf. 14½* **Unwmkd.**
Design: 2.50e, Diogo Gomes.

305	A17	1e multi	30	20
306	A17	2.50e multi	80	40

Discovery of Cape Verde, 500th anniversary.

School Children
A18

1960

307	A18	2.50e multi	60	50

Issued to commemorate the 10th anniversary of the Commission for Technical Cooperation in Africa South of the Sahara (C.C.T.A.).

Arms of Praia
A19

Designs: Arms of various cities and towns of Cape Verde.

1961, July Litho. *Perf. 13½*
Multicolored

308	A19	5c *shown*	5	5
309	A19	15c *Nova Sintra*	5	5
310	A19	20c *Ribeira Brava*	5	5
311	A19	30c *Assomada*	10	10
312	A19	1e *Maio*	65	13
313	A19	2e *Mindelo*	50	13
314	A19	2.50e *Santa Maria*	90	18
315	A19	3e *Pombas*	1.50	28
316	A19	5e *Sal-Rei*	1.50	25
317	A19	7.50e *Tarrafal*	1.00	28
318	A19	15e *Maria Pia*	1.50	60
319	A19	30e *San Felipe*	3.25	1.25
		Nos. 308-319 (12)	11.05	3.35

Sports Issue
Common Design Type

Sports: 50c, Throwing javelin. 1e, Discus throwing. 1.50e, Cricket. 2.50e, Boxing. 4.50e, Hurding. 12.50e, Golf.

1962, Jan. 18 *Perf. 13½*
Multicolored Design

320	CD48	50c lt brn	10	10
321	CD48	1e lt grn	70	25
322	CD48	1.50e lt bl grn	40	20
323	CD48	2.50e pale vio bl	60	30
324	CD48	4.50e orange	1.00	60
325	CD48	12.50e beige	2.25	1.50
		Nos. 320-325 (6)	5.05	2.95

Anti-Malaria Issue
Common Design Type
Design: Anopheles pretoriensis.

1962 Lithographed *Perf. 13½*

326	CD49	2.50e multi	1.00	70

Issued for the World Health Organization drive to eradicate malaria.

Airline Anniversary Issue
Common Design Type

1963, Oct. *Perf. 14½* **Unwmkd.**

327	CD50	2.50e gray & multi	60	40

Issued to commemorate the 10th anniversary of Transportes Aéreos Portugueses.

National Overseas Bank Issue
Common Design Type
Design: 1.50e, José da Silva Mendes Leal.

1964, May 16 *Perf. 13½*

328	CD51	1.50e multi	60	50

Issued to commemorate the centenary of the National Overseas Bank of Portugal.

ITU Issue
Common Design Type

1965, May 17 Litho. *Perf. 14½*

329	CD52	2.50e buff & multi	1.50	1.00

Issued to commemorate the centenary of the International Telecommunication Union.

Militia Drummer, 1806
A20

Designs: 1e, Soldier, Militia, 1806. 1.50e, Grenadier officer, 1833. 2.50e, Grenadier, 1833. 3e, Cavalry officer, 1834. 4e, Grenadier, 1835. 5e, Artillery officer, 1848. 10e, Drum major, infantry, 1856.

1965, Dec. 1 Litho. *Perf. 14½*

330	A20	50c multi	12	12
331	A20	1e multi	27	18
332	A20	1.50e multi	45	18
333	A20	2.50e multi	1.00	35
334	A20	3e multi	1.50	50
335	A20	4e multi	1.00	50
336	A20	5e multi	1.00	65
337	A20	10e multi	2.50	1.60
		Nos. 330-337 (8)	7.84	4.08

National Revolution Issue
Common Design Type
Design: 1e, Dr. Adriano Moreira School and Health Center.

1966, May 28 Litho. *Perf. 12*

338	CD53	1e multi	30	30

National Revolution, 40th anniversary.

Navy Club Issue
Common Design Type
Designs: 1e, Capt. Fontoura da Costa and gunboat Mandovy. 1.50e, Capt. Carvalho Araujo and minesweeper Augusto Castilho.

1967, Jan. 31 Litho. *Perf. 13*

339	CD54	1e multi	60	30
340	CD54	1.50e multi	1.00	40

Centenary of Portugal's Navy Club.

Virgin Mary Statue
A21

Pres. Rodrigues Thomaz
A22

1967, May 13 Litho. *Perf. 12½x13*

341 A21 1e multi 20 15

Issued to commemorate the 50th anniversary of the apparition of the Virgin Mary to 3 shepherd children at Fatima.

1968, Feb. 9 Litho. *Perf. 13½*

342 A22 1e multi 25 20

Issued to commemorate the 1968 visit of Pres. Americo de Deus Rodrigues Thomaz.

Cabral Issue

Pedro Alvares Cabral
A23

Design: 1e, Cantino's world map, 1502 (horiz.).

1968, Apr. 22 Litho. *Perf. 14*

343 A23 1e multi 70 40
344 A23 1.50e multi 80 40

See note after Angola No. 545.

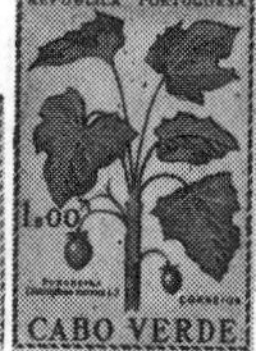

São Vicente Harbor
A24

Physic Nut
A25

Designs: 1.50e, Peanut plant. 2.50e, Castor-oil plant. 3.50e, Yams. 4e, Date palm. 4.50e, Guavas. 5e, Tamarind. 10e, Bitter cassava. 30e, Woman carrying fruit baskets.

1968, Oct. 15 Litho. *Perf. 14*

345 A24 50c multi 6 3
346 A25 1e multi 10 5
347 A25 1.50e multi 15 15
348 A25 2.50e multi 25 12
349 A25 3.50e multi 33 15
350 A25 4e multi 35 18
351 A25 4.50e multi 50 18
352 A25 5e multi 60 18
353 A25 10e multi 1.00 35
354 A25 30e multi 3.00 1.25
Nos. 345-354 (10) 6.34 2.64

Admiral Coutinho Issue

Common Design Type

Design: 30c, Adm. Coutinho and map showing route of first flight from Lisbon to Rio de Janeiro (vert.).

1969, Feb. 17 Litho. *Perf. 14*

355 CD55 30c multi 20 10

Issued to commemorate the centenary of the birth of Admiral Carlos Viegas Gago Coutinho (1869–1959), explorer and aviation pioneer.

Vasco da Gama
A26

King Manuel I
A27

Vasco da Gama Issue

1969, Aug. 29 Litho. *Perf. 14*

356 A26 1.50e multi 25 10

Issued to commemorate the 500th anniversary of the birth of Vasco da Gama (1469–1524), navigator.

Administration Reform Issue

Common Design Type

1969, Sept. 25 Litho. *Perf. 14*

357 CD56 2e multi 40 20

King Manuel I Issue

1969, Dec. 1 Litho. *Perf. 14*

358 A27 3e multi 60 30

Issued to commemorate the 500th anniversary of the birth of King Manuel I.

Marshal Carmona Issue

Common Design Type

Design: 2.50e, Antonio Oscar Carmona in marshal's uniform.

1970, Nov. 15 Litho. *Perf. 14*

359 CD57 2.50e multi 50 25

Galleons on Sanaga River
A28

1972, May 25 Litho. *Perf. 13*

360 A28 5e lil rose & multi 75 40

4th centenary of the publication of The Lusiads by Luiz Camoëns.

Olympic Games Issue

Common Design Type

Design: 4e, Basketball and boxing, Olympic emblem.

1972, June 20 *Perf. 14x13½*

361 CD59 4e multi 75 40

20th Olympic Games, Munich, Aug. 26–Sept. 11.

Lisbon-Rio de Janeiro Flight Issue

Common Design Type

Design: 3.50e, "Lusitania" landing at San Vicente.

1972, Sept. 20 Litho. *Perf. 13½*

362 CD60 3.50e multi 75 40

WMO Centenary Issue

Common Design Type

1973, Dec. 15 Litho. *Perf. 13*

363 CD61 2.50e ultra & multi 50 30

Centenary of international meteorological cooperation.

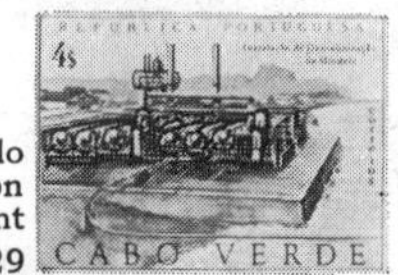

Mindelo Desalination Plant
A29

1974 Lithographed *Perf. 13½*

364 A29 4e multi 75 40

Opening of the Mindelo desalination plant.

Republic

No. 343 Overprinted: "INDEPENDENCIA / 5–Julho–75"

1975, Dec. 19 Litho. *Perf. 14*

365 A23 1e multi 25 15

Proclamation of Independence.

Amilcar Cabral, Flag and Crowd
A30

1976, Jan. 20

366 A30 5e multi 1.00 75

3rd anniversary of the assassination of Amilcar Cabral (1924–1973), revolutionary leader.

Rising Sun, Coat of Arms, Liberated People—A31

1976, July 5 Litho. *Perf. 14*

367 A31 50c multi 8 6
368 A31 3e multi 32 25
369 A31 15e multi 1.60 1.20
370 A31 50e multi 6.50 4.00
a. Miniature sheet of 4 *15.00 15.00*

First anniversary of independence. No. 370a contains one each of Nos. 367–370. Size: 154x110mm.

No. 351 Overprinted with Row of Stars and: "REPUBLICA / DE"

1976 Litho. *Perf. 14*

372 A25 4.50e multi 3.00 1.00

Amilcar Cabral, Map and Flag of Cape Verde—A32

1976, Sept. 19 *Perf. 14*

373 A32 1e multi 50 20

Party of International Action (PAICC), 20th anniversary.

Electronic Tree and ITU Emblem
A33

Ashtray
A34

1977, May 17 Litho. *Perf. 13½x13*

374 A33 5.50e multi 45 25

World Telecommunications Day.

1977, July 5 Litho. *Perf. 14*

Carved Coconut Shells: 30c, Bell on stand. 50c, Lamp with Adam and Eve. 1e, Hollow shell with Nativity. 1.50e, Desk lamp. 5e, Jar. 10e, Jar with hinged cover. 20e, Tobacco jar with palms. 30e, Stringed instrument.

375 A34 20c lil & multi 12 4
376 A34 30c rose & multi 20 4
377 A34 50c sal & multi 12 8
378 A34 1e lt grn & multi 20 12
379 A34 1.50e org yel & multi 25 20
380 A34 5e gray & multi 40 12
381 A34 10e lt bl & multi 80 20
382 A34 20e yel & multi 1.50 80
383 A34 30e rose lil & multi 2.50 1.25
Nos. 375-383 (9) 6.09 2.85

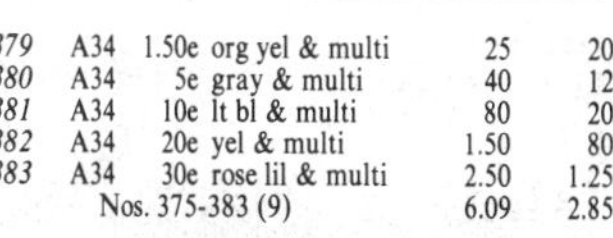

Cape Verde No. 1 and Coat of Arms
A35

Congress Emblem
A36

1977, Sept. 12 Litho. *Perf. 13½*

384 A35 4e bl & multi 42 12
385 A35 8e lil & multi 85 28

Centenary of Cape Verde stamps.

1977, Nov. 15 *Perf. 14*

386 A36 3.50e multi 38 10

African Party of Independence of Guinea-Bissau and Cape Verde (PAIGC), 3rd congress, Nov. 15–20.

No. 363 Overprinted with Row of Stars and: "REPUBLICA / DE"

1978, May 1 *Perf. 12*

387 CD61 2.50e ultra & multi 30 10

No. 355 Surcharged with New Value and Bars

1978, May 1 *Perf. 14*

388 CD55 3e on 30c multi 35 12

Antenna and ITU Emblem—A37

1978, May 17 Litho. *Perf. 14*

389 A37 3.50e sil & multi 45 15

10th World Telecommunications Day.

Freighter Cabo Verde—A38

1978, June 25 Litho. *Perf. 14*

391 A38 1e multi 20 10

First ship of Cape Verde merchant marine.

Map of Africa and Equality Emblem
A39

1978, June 21

392	A39	4.50e multi	90	20

Anti-Apartheid Year.

Human Rights Emblem
A40

1978, Dec. 10 Litho. *Perf. 14*

393	A40	1.50e multi	30	5
394	A40	2e multi	40	15

Universal Declaration of Human Rights, 30th anniversary.

1.50

Children and Balloons, IYC Emblem
A41

IYC Emblem and Child's Drawing: 3.50e, Children and flowers.

1979, June 1 Litho. *Perf. 14*

395	A41	1.50e multi	30	5
396	A41	3.50e multi	70	15

International Year of the Child.

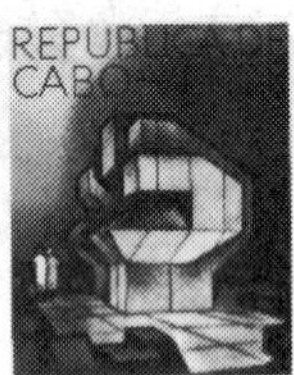

Pindjiguiti Massacre Monument—A42

1979, Aug. 3 *Perf. 13*

397	A42	4.50e multi	90	15

Massacre of Pindjiguiti, 20th anniversary.

Centenary of Mindelo—A43

1980, Apr. 23 Litho. *Perf. 12½*

398	A43	4e multi	80	15

Flag of Cape Verde
A44

Stylized Bird, "V"
A45

1980 Litho. *Perf. 12½*

399	A44	4e multi	80	15
400	A45	4e multi	80	15
401	A45	7e multi	1.40	20
402	A45	11e multi	2.25	30

5th anniversary of independence No. 399 issued June 1.

Running—A46

1980, June 6

403	A46	1e *shown*	20	15
404	A46	2.50e *Boxing*	50	15
405	A46	3e *Basketball*	60	15
406	A46	4e *Volleyball*	80	15
407	A46	20e *Swimming*	4.00	60
408	A46	50e *Tennis*	10.00	1.50
		Nos. 403-408 (6)	16.10	2.70

Souvenir Sheet
Perf. 13

409	A46	30e *Soccer*, horiz.	*8.00*

22nd Summer Olympic Games, Moscow, July 19-Aug. 3. No. 409 has multicolored margin showing Misha, the bear, and Olympic flame. Size: 99x67mm.

Thunnus Alalunga—A47

1980, Nov. 11 Litho. *Perf. 13*

410	A47	50c shown	10	10
411	A47	4.50e Trachurus trachurus	90	15
412	A47	8e Muraena helena	1.60	30
413	A47	10e Corvina nigra	2.00	30
414	A47	12e Katsuwonus pelamis	2.40	45
415	A47	50e Prionace glauca	10.00	1.50
		Nos. 410-415 (6)	17.00	2.80

Lochnera Rosea
A48

1980

416	A48	50c shown	10	10
417	A48	4.50e Poinciana regia-bojer	90	15
418	A48	8e Mirabilis jalapa	1.60	30
419	A48	10e Nerium oleander	2.00	30
420	A48	12e Bougainvillia litoralis	2.40	30
421	A48	30e Hibiscus	6.00	90
		Nos. 416-421 (6)	13.00	2.05

Arca Verde—A49

1980, Nov. 30 Litho. *Perf. 12½x12*

422	A49	3e shown	60	15
423	A49	5.50e Ilha do Maio	1.10	15
424	A49	7.50e Ilha de Komo	1.50	30
425	A49	9e Boa Vista	1.80	30
426	A49	12e Santo Antao	2.40	30
427	A49	30e Santiago	6.00	90
		Nos. 422-427 (6)	13.40	2.10

Desert Erosion Prevention Campaign—A50

1981, Mar. 30 Litho. *Perf. 13*

428	A50	4.50e multi	90	20
429	A50	10.50e multi	2.10	35

6th Anniv. of Constitution
A51

1981, Apr. 15

430	A51	4.50e multi	90	20

Souvenir Sheet

Austria No. B336
A52

1981, May 18

431	A52	50e multi	10.00

WIPA '81 Philatelic Exhibition, Vienna, Austria, May 22-31. No. 431 has multicolored margin showing Prince Eugene statue, exhibition emblem. Size: 108x63mm.

Antenna—A53

1981, Aug. 25 Litho. *Perf. 12½*

432	A53	4.50e shown	90	15
433	A53	8e Dish antenna	1.60	30
434	A53	20e Dish antenna, diff.	4.00	75

Intl. Year of the Disabled—A54

1981, Dec. 25 Litho. *Perf. 12½*

435	A54	4.50e multi	18

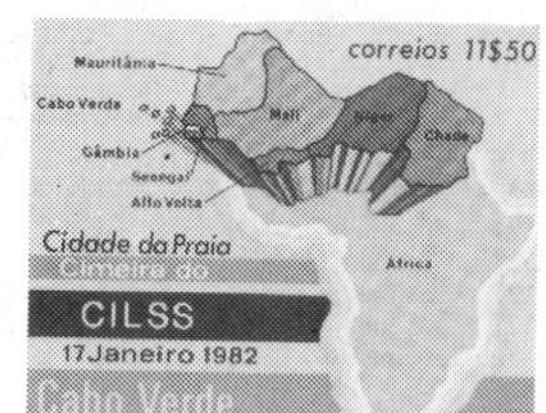

Purple Gallinule—A55

1981, Dec. 30

436	A55	1e Egret, vert.	4
437	A55	4.50e Barn owl, vert.	18
438	A55	8e Passerine, vert.	30
439	A55	10e shown	40
440	A55	12e Guinea fowl	50
		Nos. 436-440 (5)	1.42

Souvenir Sheet
Perf. 13

441	A55	50e Razo. Isld. lark	3.00

No. 441 contains one stamp (31x39mm.); multicolored margin continues design. Size: 80x56mm.

CILSS Congress, Praia, Jan. 17—A56

1982, Jan. 17 *Perf. 13x12½*

442	A56	11.50e multi	48

Cabo Verde TAÇA AMILCAR CABRAL 4$50

Amilcar Cabral Soccer Championship—A57

Designs: Soccer players and flags.

1982, Feb. 10 Litho. *Perf. 12½*

443	A57	4.50e multi	18
444	A57	7.50e multi	28
445	A57	11.50e multi	48

1982 World Cup—A58

Designs: Soccer players and ball.

1982, Apr. 25

446	A58	1.50e multi	4
447	A58	4.50e multi	18
448	A58	8e multi	30
449	A58	10.50e multi	42
450	A58	12e multi	50
451	A58	20e multi	80
		Nos. 446-451 (6)	2.24

Souvenir Sheet

452	A58	50e multi	2.00

No. 452 has multicolored margin continuing design. Size: 83x91mm.

First Anniv of Women's Organization—A59

1982, Apr. 15 Litho. *Perf. 12½x12*

453	A59	4.50e Marching	18
454	A59	8e Farming	30
455	A59	12e Child care	50

Return of Barque Morrissey-Ernestina—A60

1982, July 5 Litho.

456	A60	12e multi	50

Butterflies—A61

1982, July 5 Litho. *Perf. 13*

457	A61	2e Hypolimnas misippus	8
458	A61	4.50e Melanitis lede	18
459	A61	8e Catopsilia florella	30
460	A61	10.50e Colias electo	42
461	A61	11.50e Danaus chrysippus	48
462	A61	12e Papilio demodecus	50
		Nos. 457-462 (6)	1.96

AIR POST STAMPS.

Common Design Type
Name and Value in Black
Perf. 13½x13.

1938, July 26 **Unwmkd.**

C1	CD39	10c scarlet	50	45
C2	CD39	20c purple	50	45
C3	CD39	50c orange	50	45
C4	CD39	1e ultra	50	45
C5	CD39	2e lil brn	1.50	1.00
C6	CD39	3e dk grn	2.25	1.50
C7	CD39	5e red brn	6.00	1.50
C8	CD39	9e rose car	10.00	3.00
C9	CD39	10e magenta	14.00	4.50
		Nos. C1-C9 (9)	35.75	13.30

No. C7 exists with overprint "Exposicao Internacional de Nova York, 1939–1940" and Trylon and Perisphere.

POSTAGE DUE STAMPS.

D1

D2

Typographed.

1904 *Perf. 12.* **Unwmkd.**

J1	D1	5r yel grn	28	50
J2	D1	10r slate	28	50
J3	D1	20r yel brn	50	60
J4	D1	30r red org	90	1.00
J5	D1	50r gray brn	50	1.00
J6	D1	60r red brn	6.50	6.50
J7	D1	100r lilac	1.50	1.75
J8	D1	130r dl bl	1.50	1.75
J9	D1	200r carmine	1.75	2.00
J10	D1	500r dl vio	4.50	5.00
		Nos. J1-J10 (10)	18.21	20.60

Overprinted in Carmine or Green

1911

J11	D1	5r yel grn	20	20
J12	D1	10r slate	20	20
J13	D1	20r yel brn	30	25
J14	D1	30r orange	30	25
J15	D1	50r gray brn	30	25
J16	D1	60r red brn	60	40
J17	D1	100r lilac	60	40
J18	D1	130r dl bl	70	50
J19	D1	200r car (G)	1.25	75
J20	D1	500r dl vio	1.75	1.75
		Nos. J11-J20 (10)	6.20	4.95

1921 *Perf. 11½.*

J21	D2	½c yel grn	12	25
J22	D2	1c slate	12	25
J23	D2	2c red brn	12	25
J24	D2	3c orange	12	25
J25	D2	5c gray brn	12	25
J26	D2	6c lt brn	12	12
J27	D2	10c red vio	12	12
J28	D2	13c dl bl	50	75
J29	D2	20c carmine	50	75
J30	D2	50c gray	1.25	1.50
		Nos. J21-J30 (10)	3.09	4.49

Common Design Type
Photogravure and Typographed.

1952 *Perf. 14.* **Unwmkd.**

Numeral in Red, Frame Multicolored.

J31	CD45	10c chocolate	8	8
J32	CD45	30c blk brn	12	12
J33	CD45	50c dk bl	8	8
J34	CD45	1e dk bl	25	25
J35	CD45	2e red brn	50	50
J36	CD45	5e ol grn	1.00	1.00
		Nos. J31-J36 (6)	2.03	2.03

NEWSPAPER STAMP.

N1

1893 Typo. *Perf. 11½* **Unwmkd.**

P1	N1	2½r brown	1.00	60
a.		Perf. 12½	2.00	1.50
b.		Perf. 13½	5.75	3.00

POSTAL TAX STAMPS.

Pombal Issue
Common Design Types
Engraved.

1925 *Perf. 12½.* **Unwmkd.**

RA1	CD28	15c dl vio & blk	50	50
RA2	CD29	15c dl vio & blk	50	50
RA3	CD30	15c dl vio & blk	50	50

St. Isabel
PT1

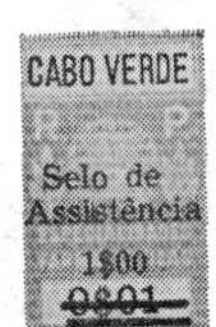

PT2

1948 **Lithographed** *Perf. 11*

RA4	PT1	50c dk grn	2.75	2.25
RA5	PT1	1e hn brn	5.50	5.50

No. RA5 Surcharged with New Value and Bars

1959

RA6	PT1	50c on 1e hn brn	3.00	3.00

Perf. 14

RA7	PT1	50c car rose	1.75	1.00
RA8	PT1	1e blue	1.75	1.00

St. Isabel Type Redrawn

1967–72 **Lithographed** *Perf. 14*
Multicolored

RA9	PT1	30c (bl panel)	30	30
RA10	PT1	50c (lil rose panel)	75	75
RA11	PT1	50c (red panel) ('72)	*2.00*	*2.00*
RA12	PT1	1e (brn panel)	1.00	1.00
RA13	PT1	1e (red lil panel) ('72)	*2.00*	*2.00*
		Nos. RA9-RA13 (5)	*6.05*	*6.05*

Nos. RA9–RA13 are inscribed "ASSISTENCIA" in large letters in bottom panel and "PORTUGAL" and "CABO VERDE" in small letters in upper left corner.

Revenue Stamps Surcharged in Green, Blue or Black

1967–72 **Typographed** *Perf. 12*
Black "CABO VERDE" & Value
Pale Green Burelage

RA14	PT2	50c on 1c org (Bl) ('71)	2.00	75
a.		Black surcharge ('68?)	*10.00*	*8.75*
RA15	PT2	50c on 2c org (G) ('69)	1.75	1.00
a.		Blue surcharge	2.00	1.00
b.		Black surcharge ('68?)	*10.00*	*8.00*
c.		Inverted surcharge (Bk)		
RA16	PT2	50c on 3c org (G) ('72)	1.00	75
RA17	PT2	50c on 5c org (G) ('72)	1.00	75
RA18	PT2	50c on 10c org (G) ('71)	1.75	1.00
RA19	PT2	1e on 1c org (Bk)	7.50	4.00
RA20	PT2	1e on 2c org (G) ('71)	1.50	1.50
a.		Blue surcharge ('71)	1.50	1.00
b.		Black surcharge	7.50	4.00
		Nos. RA14-RA20 (7)	16.50	9.75

POSTAL TAX DUE STAMPS.

Pombal Issue.
Common Design Types

1925 *Perf. 12½.* **Unwmkd.**

RAJ1	CD31	30c dl vio & blk	45	50
RAJ2	CD32	30c dl vio & blk	45	50
RAJ3	CD33	30c dl vio & blk	45	50

CARINTHIA

See Austria and Jugoslavia.

CAROLINE ISLANDS

(kăr'ô-līn)

LOCATION—A group of about 549 small islands in the West Pacific Ocean, north of the Equator.
GOVT.—Former German colony.
AREA—550 sq. mi.
POP.—40,000 (approx. 1915.)

100 Pfennig = 1 Mark

Stamps of Germany 1889–90 Overprinted in Black

Overprinted at 56° Angle.

1900 *Perf. 13½x14½.* **Unwmkd.**

1	A9	3pf dk brn	17.50	20.00
2	A9	5pf green	22.50	20.00
3	A10	10pf carmine	25.00	25.00
4	A10	20pf ultra	30.00	35.00
5	A10	25pf orange	75.00	80.00
6	A10	50pf red brn	75.00	80.00
		Nos. 1-6 (6)	245.00	260.00

1899 Overprinted at 48° Angle.

1a	A9	3pf lt brn	700.00	950.00
2a	A9	5pf green	850.00	750.00
3a	A10	10pf carmine	110.00	200.00
4a	A10	20pf ultra	110.00	200.00
5a	A10	25pf orange	*2,000.*	*4,000.*
6a	A10	50pf red brn	1,250.	2,350.

Kaiser's Yacht "Hohenzollern"
A3 A4

1900–10 **Typographed** *Perf. 14*

7	A3	3pf brown	1.25	1.50
8	A3	5pf green	1.25	*2.25*
9	A3	10pf carmine	1.25	*6.00*
a.		Half used as 5pf on cover, back-stamped ('05)		*500.00*
10	A3	20pf ultra	1.75	*10.00*
a.		Half used as 10pf on cover ('10)		*5,500.*
11	A3	25pf org & blk, *yel*	2.25	*17.50*
12	A3	30pf org & blk, *sal*	2.25	17.50
13	A3	40pf lake & blk	2.25	*20.00*
14	A3	50pf pur & blk, *sal*	2.75	*25.00*
15	A3	80pf lake & blk, *rose*	4.00	*30.00*

Engraved.
Perf. 14½x14

16	A4	1m carmine	5.50	*75.00*
17	A4	2m blue	9.50	*85.00*
18	A4	3m blk vio	14.00	*175.00*
19	A4	5m sl & car	225.00	*700.00*
		Nos. 7-19 (13)	273.00	

No. 9a is known as the "typhoon provisional" the stock of 5pf stamps having been destroyed during a typhoon. Covers (cards) without backstamp, price about $90.

Forged cancellations are found on Nos. 7–19.

No. 7 Handstamp Surcharged **5 Pf**

1910, July 12

20	A3	5pf on 3pf brn		*5,500.*

Price is for stamp tied to cover. Stamps on piece sell for about one-third less.

Surcharge exists inverted, price $4,250; double, price $4,500.

Wmk. 125

Typographed

1915–19 **Wmkd. Lozenges. (125)**

21	A3	3pf brn ('19)	1.25	
22	A3	5pf green	20.00	

Engraved.

23	A4	5m sl & car	27.50	

Nos. 21–23 were never placed in use.

CARPATHO-UKRAINE

(Listed under Czechoslovakia).

CASTELLORIZO

(käs·tĕl'lō·rē'tsō)
(Castelrosso)

LOCATION—A Mediterranean island in the Dodecanese group lying close to the coast of Asia Minor and about 60 miles east of Rhodes.
GOVT.—Former Italian Colony.
AREA—4 sq. mi.
POP.—2,238 (1936).

Formerly a Turkish possession, Castellorizo was occupied by the French in 1915 and ceded to Italy after World War I.

Issued under French Occupation.

25 Centimes = 1 Piastre
100 Centimes = 1 Franc

Stamps of French Offices in Turkey Overprinted **B. N. F.** **CASTELLORIZO**

1920 *Perf. 14x13½* **Unwmkd.**

1	A2	1c gray	22.50	22.50
a.		Inverted ovpt.	50.00	50.00
b.		Double ovpt.	55.00	55.00
2	A2	2c vio brn	22.50	22.50
3	A2	3c red org	22.50	22.50
a.		Inverted overprint	50.00	50.00
4	A2	5c green	22.50	22.50
a.		Inverted overprint	50.00	50.00
5	A3	10c rose	27.50	27.50
6	A3	15c pale red	35.00	35.00
a.		Inverted overprint	90.00	90.00
7	A3	20c brn vio	40.00	40.00
8	A5	1pi on 25c bl	40.00	40.00

No.	Type	Description	Unused	Used
9	A3	30c lilac	40.00	40.00
10	A4	40c red & pale bl	85.00	85.00
a.		Inverted ovpt.	350.00	350.00
11	A6	2pi on 50c bis brn & lav	95.00	95.00
a.		Inverted ovpt.	350.00	350.00
12	A6	4pi on 1fr cl & ol grn	110.00	110.00
a.		Double ovpt.	400.00	400.00
b.		Inverted ovpt.	400.00	400.00
13	A6	20pi on 5fr dk bl & buff	275.00	275.00
a.		Double overprint	700.00	700.00
		Nos. 1-13 (13)	837.50	837.50

On Nos. 10–13 the overprint is placed vertically.

No. 1–9 were overprinted in blocks of 25. Position 4 had "CASTELLORIZO" inverted and Positions 8 and 18 had "CASTELLORISO". The later variety also occurred in the setting of the form for Nos. 10–13.

"B. N. F." are the initials of "Base Navale Francaise".

Overprinted in Black or Red

O. N. F.
Castellorizo

1920

On Stamps of French Offices in Turkey

No.	Type	Description	Unused	Used
14	A2	1c gray	10.00	10.00
15	A2	2c vio brn	10.00	10.00
16	A2	3c red org	12.50	12.50
17	A2	5c grn (R)	12.50	12.50
19	A3	10c rose	12.50	12.50
20	A3	15c pale red	15.00	15.00
21	A3	20c brn vio	32.50	32.50
22	A5	1pi on 25c bl (R)	25.00	25.00
a.		Inverted ovpt.		
23	A3	30c lil (R)	25.00	25.00
24	A4	40c red & pale bl	25.00	25.00
25	A6	2pi on 50c bis brn & lav	25.00	25.00
26	A6	4pi on 1fr cl & ol grn	32.50	32.50
28	A6	20pi on 5fr dk bl & buff	160.00	160.00
		Nos. 14-28 (13)	397.50	397.50

On Nos. 25, 26 and 28 the two lines of the overprint are set wider apart than on the lower values.

"O.N.F." are the initials of "Occupation Navale Francaise."

Overprint on 8pi on 2fr (#37), price $450.

On Stamps of France.

No.	Type	Description	Unused	Used
30	A22	10c red	13.00	9.00
a.		Inverted ovpt.		70.00
31	A22	25c bl (R)	13.00	9.00
a.		Inverted ovpt.		70.00

This overprint exists on 8 other 1900–1907 denominations of France (5c, 15c, 20c, 30c, 40c, 50c, 1fr, 5fr). These are believed not to have been issued or postally used.

Stamps of France, 1900-1907, Handstamped in Black or Violet

1920

No.	Type	Description	Unused	Used
33	A22	5c green	75.00	75.00
34	A22	10c red	75.00	75.00
35	A22	20c vio brn	75.00	75.00
36	A22	25c blue	75.00	75.00
37	A18	50c bis brn & lav	500.00	500.00
38	A18	1fr cl & ol grn (V)	500.00	500.00
		Nos. 33-38 (6)	1,300.	1,300.

Nos. 1–38 are considered speculative.

Forgeries of overprints on Nos. 1–38 exist. They abound of Nos. 33–38.

Stamps of French Offices in Turkey handstamped "Occupation Francaise Castellorizo" were made privately.

Issued under Italian Dominion.

100 Centesimi = 1 Lira

Italian Stamps of 1906-20 Overprinted **CASTELROSSO**

Wmkd. Crown. (140)

1922 *Perf. 14*

No.	Type	Description	Unused	Used
51	A48	5c green	90	1.00
52	A48	10c claret	35	1.00
53	A48	15c slate	35	1.00
54	A50	20c brn org	35	1.00
a.		Double ovpt.	65.00	
55	A49	25c blue	35	1.00
56	A49	40c brown	4.75	4.00
57	A49	50c violet	4.75	4.00
58	A49	60c carmine	4.75	4.00
59	A49	85c chocolate	85	1.75
		Nos. 51-59 (9)	17.40	18.75

Map of Castellorizo; Flag of Italy
A1

1923

No.	Type	Description	Unused	Used
60	A1	5c gray grn	45	75
61	A1	10c dl rose	45	75
62	A1	25c dl bl	45	75
63	A1	50c gray lil	45	75
64	A1	1 l brown	45	75
		Nos. 60-64 (5)	2.25	3.75

Italian Stamps of 1901-20 Overprinted

1924

No.	Type	Description	Unused	Used
65	A48	5c green	55	1.20
66	A48	10c claret	55	1.20
67	A48	15c slate	55	1.20
68	A50	20c brn org	55	1.20
69	A49	25c blue	55	1.20
70	A49	40c brown	55	1.20
71	A49	50c violet	55	1.20
72	A49	60c carmine	55	1.75
a.		Double ovpt.	65.00	
73	A49	85c red brn	55	2.10
74	A46	1 l brn & grn	55	2.75
		Nos. 65-74 (10)	5.50	15.00

Ferrucci Issue.

Types of Italian Stamps of 1930, Overprinted in Red or Blue **CASTELROSSO**

1930 **Wmkd. Crowns. (140)**

No.	Type	Description	Unused	Used
75	A102	20c violet	75	85
76	A103	25c dk grn	75	85
77	A103	50c black	75	85
78	A103	1.25 l dp bl	75	85
79	A104	5 l + 2 l dp car (Bl)	2.00	2.25
		Nos. 75-79 (5)	5.00	5.65

Garibaldi Issue.

Types of Italian Stamps of 1932, Overprinted in Red or Blue **CASTELROSSO**

1932

No.	Type	Description	Unused	Used
80	A138	10c brown	3.50	4.00
81	A138	20c red brn (Bl)	3.50	4.00
82	A138	25c dp grn	3.50	4.00
83	A138	30c bluish sl	3.50	4.00
84	A138	50c red vio (Bl)	3.50	4.00
85	A141	75c cop red (Bl)	3.50	4.00
86	A141	1.25 l dl bl	3.50	4.00
87	A141	1.75 l + 25c brn	3.50	4.00
88	A144	2.55 l + 50c org (Bl)	3.50	4.00
89	A145	5 l + 1 l dl vio	3.50	4.00
		Nos. 80-89 (10)	35.00	40.00

CENTRAL AFRICA

LOCATION—Western Africa, north of equator.
GOVT.—Empire.
AREA—241,313 sq. mi.
POP.—2,610,000 (est. 1974).
CAPITAL—Bangui.

The former French colony of Ubangi-Shari, a unit in French Equatorial Africa, proclaimed itself the Central African Republic Dec. 1, 1958. It became the Central African Empire Dec. 4, 1976.

100 Centimes = 1 Franc

Central African Republic

Premier Barthélemy Boganda and Flag
A1

Design: 25fr, Barthélemy Boganda and flag (horiz.).

Engraved.

1959 *Perf. 13* **Unwmkd.**

No.	Type	Description	Unused	Used
1	A1	15fr multi	25	20
2	A1	25fr multi	40	20

Issued to commemorate the first anniversary of the establishment of the Republic and to honor Premier Barthélemy Boganda (1910–1959).

Imperforates

Most stamps of Central African Republic exist imperforate in issued and trial colors, and also in small presentation sheets in issued colors.

C.C.T.A. Issue

Common Design Type

1960 *Perf. 13* **Unwmkd.**

No.	Type	Description	Unused	Used
3	CD106	50fr lt grn & dk bl	1.15	85

Dactyloceras Widenmanni—A2

Designs: Various butterflies.

1960-61

No.	Type	Description	Unused	Used
4	A2	50c bl grn & dk red ('61)	4	3
5	A2	1fr multi	4	3
6	A2	2fr dk grn & brn ('61)	6	5
7	A2	3fr yel grn & dk red ('61)	6	6
8	A2	5fr dk sl grn, pale grn & ol brn	8	8
9	A2	10fr multi	20	10
10	A2	20fr multi	35	18
11	A2	85fr multi	1.35	80
		Nos. 4-11 (8)	2.18	1.33

No. 2 Overprinted:
"FETE NATIONALE 1-12-1960"

1960

No.	Type	Description	Unused	Used
12	A1	25fr multi	1.10	1.10

National Holiday, Dec. 1, 1960.

Common Design Types pictured in section at front of book.

Louis Pasteur and Pasteur Institute, Bangui
A3

1961, Feb. 25 *Perf. 13* **Unwmkd.**

No.	Type	Description	Unused	Used
13	A3	20fr multi	65	65

Opening of Pasteur Institute at Bangui.

Flag, Map, and U.N. Emblem
A4

1961, Mar. 4 **Engraved**

No.	Type	Description	Unused	Used
14	A4	15fr multi	30	20
15	A4	25fr multi	40	30
16	A4	85fr multi	1.35	1.10

Issued to commemorate the admission of Central African Republic to the United Nations.

No. 15 Overprinted in Green:
"FETE NATIONALE 1-12-61" and Star

1961, Dec. 1

No.	Type	Description	Unused	Used
17	A4	25fr multi	1.40	1.40

National Holiday, Dec. 1.

No. 16 Surcharged in Red Brown:
"U.A.M. CONFERENCE DE BANGUI
25-27 Mars 1962"

1962, March 25

No.	Type	Description	Unused	Used
18	A4	50fr on 85fr multi	1.20	1.20

Issued to commemorate the conference of the African and Malgache Union at Bangui, March 25–27.

Abidjan Games Issue

Common Design Type

Designs: 20fr, Hurdling. 50fr, Bicycling.

1962, July 21 Photo. *Perf. 12½x12*

No.	Type	Description	Unused	Used
19	CD109	20fr multi	30	25
20	CD109	50fr multi	80	55

See No. C6.

African-Malgache Union Issue

Common Design Type

1962, Sept. 8 **Unwmkd.**

No.	Type	Description	Unused	Used
21	CD110	30fr multi	55	45

Issued to commemorate the first anniversary of the African and Malgache Union.

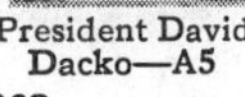

President David Dacko—A5

Soldiers with Flag—A6

1962 *Perf. 12*

No.	Type	Description	Unused	Used
22	A5	20fr multi	30	12
23	A5	25fr multi	35	15

1963, Aug. 13 **Photogravure**

No.	Type	Description	Unused	Used
24	A6	20fr blk & multi	30	20

National Army, third anniversary.

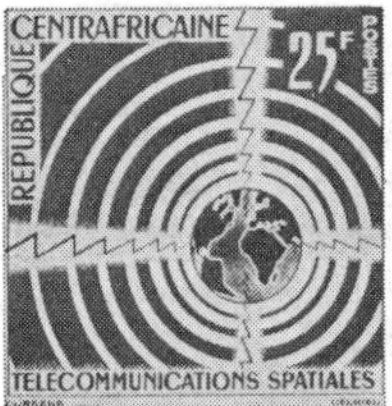

Waves Around Globe
A6a

Design: 100fr, Orbit patterns around globe.

1963, Sept. 19 ***Perf. 12½*** **Unwmkd.**

25	A6a	25fr plum & grn	45	40
26	A6a	100fr org, bl & grn	1.75	1.65

Issued to publicize space communications.

Young Pioneers
A7

1963, Oct. 14 **Engr.** ***Perf. 12½***

27	A7	50fr grnsh bl, vio bl & brn	70	50

Issued to honor Young Pioneers.

Boali Falls
A8

1963, Oct. 28 ***Perf. 13***

28	A8	30fr bl, grn & red brn	45	30

Colotis Evippe
A9

Designs: Various butterflies.

1963, Nov. 18 **Photo.** ***Perf. 12½x13***

29	A9	1fr multi	15	15
30	A9	3fr multi	20	20
31	A9	4fr multi	25	25
32	A9	60fr multi	1.00	1.00

UNESCO Emblem, Scales and Tree—A9a

1963, Dec. 10 ***Perf. 13***

33	A9a	25fr grn, ol & red brn	45	35

Issued to commemorate the 15th anniversary of the Universal Declaration of Human Rights.

Leaves and IQSY Emblem
A10

1964, Apr. 20 **Engr.** ***Perf. 13***

34	A10	25fr org, Prus grn & bis	1.10	1.00

International Quiet Sun Year, 1964–65.

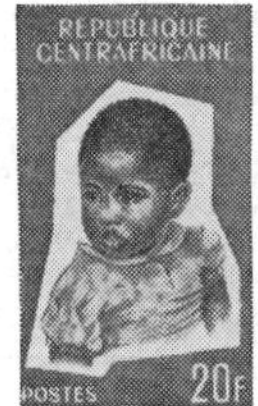

Child
A11

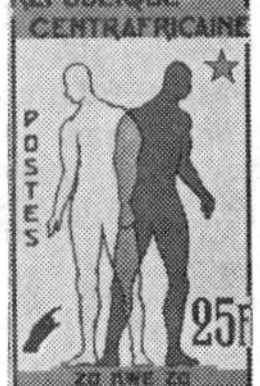

"All Men Are Men"
A12

Designs: Heads of Children.

1964, Aug. 13 ***Perf. 13*** **Unwmkd.**

35	A11	20fr rose lil, red brn & lt ol grn	35	25
36	A11	25fr brick red, red brn & bl	40	30
37	A11	40fr lt ol grn, red brn & rose lil	60	45
38	A11	50fr dl cl, red brn & lt grn	80	50
a.		Min. sheet of 4	2.25	2.25

No. 38a contains one each of Nos. 35–38. Size: 144x99mm.

Cooperation Issue
Common Design Type

1964, Nov. 7 **Engraved**

39	CD119	25fr grn, mag & dk brn	45	30

1964, Dec. 1 **Litho.** ***Perf. 13x12½***

40	A12	25fr multi	42	20

Issued to publicize National Unity.

Putting Yoke on Oxen
A13

Designs: 50fr, Ox pulling harrow. 85fr, Team of oxen in field. 100fr, Hay wagon.

1965, Apr. 28 **Engr.** ***Perf. 13***

41	A13	25fr sl grn, sep & rose	40	30
42	A13	50fr sl grn, lt bl & brn	75	45
43	A13	85fr bl, grn & red brn	1.25	75
44	A13	100fr multi	1.50	1.00

Telegraph Receiver by Pouget-Maisonneuve—A14

Designs: 30fr, Chappe telegraph (vert.). 50fr, Doignon regulator (vert.). 85fr, Pouillet telegraph transcriber.

1965, May 17 **Unwmkd.**

45	A14	25fr red, grn & ultra	40	30
46	A14	30fr lake & grn	50	35
47	A14	50fr car & vio	85	50
48	A14	85fr red lil & sl	1.25	80

Issued to commemorate the centenary of the International Telecommunication Union.

"Health"
A15

Designs: 25fr, "Clothes;" shuttle, cloth and women. 60fr, "Teaching;" student and school. 85fr, "Food;" mother feeding child, tractor in wheat field.

1965, June 10 **Engr.** ***Perf. 13***

49	A15	25fr ultra, brt grn & brn	40	30
50	A15	50fr ultra, brn & grn	75	50
51	A15	60fr grn, ultra & brn	90	65
52	A15	85fr multi	1.35	75

Issued to publicize the slogans and aims of "M.E.S.A.N." (Mouvement d'Evolution Sociale de l'Afrique Noire). See No. C30.

Caterpillars and Moth on Coffee Branch
A16

Designs: 3fr, Hawk moth and caterpillar on coffee leaves (horiz.). 30fr, Platyedra moth and larvae on cotton plant.

1965, Aug. 25 **Engr.** ***Perf. 13***

53	A16	2fr dk pur, dp org & sl grn	5	5
54	A16	3fr blk, sl grn & red	8	8
55	A16	30fr red lil, red & sl grn	1.00	40

Issued to publicize plant protection.

Boy Scout, Tents and Animals
A17

Design: 25fr, Campfire and Scout emblem.

1965, Sept. 27 ***Perf. 13*** **Unwmkd.**

56	A17	25fr red org, bl & red lil	40	22
57	A17	50fr brn & Prus bl	80	55

Issued to honor the Boy Scouts.

Nos. 30, 1 and 22 Surcharged in Black or Brown

5 F

Engraved; Photogravure
Perf. 13, 12, 12½x13

1965, Aug. 26 **Unwmkd.**

58	A9	2fr on 3fr multi	1.75	1.75
59	A1	5fr on 15fr multi	1.75	1.75
60	A5	10fr on 20fr multi (Br)	2.00	2.00

The surcharges are adjusted to shape of stamps.

U.N. Emblem and Wheat
A18

1965, Oct. 16 **Engraved** ***Perf. 13***

61	A18	50fr ocher, sl grn & brt bl	90	60

Issued for the "Freedom from Hunger Campaign" of the United Nations Food and Agriculture Organization.

Diamond Cutter
A19

1966, March 14 **Engraved** ***Perf. 13***

62	A19	25fr car rose, dk pur & brn	40	25

Nos. 43–44 Surcharged

5 F

1966, Feb.

63	A13	5fr on 85fr multi	25	25
64	A13	10fr on 100fr multi	45	45

Issue dates: No. 63, Feb. 17. No. 64, Feb. 15.

Statue of Mbaka Woman Porter
A20

WHO Headquarters, Geneva
A21

1966, Apr. 9 **Photo.** ***Perf. 13x12½***

65	A20	25fr multi	40	25

Issued to commemorate the International Negro Arts Festival. Dakar, Senegal, Apr. 1–24.

1966, May 3 **Photo.** **Unwmkd.**

66	A21	25fr pur, bl & yel	40	25

Issued to commemorate the inauguration of the World Health Organization Headquarters, Geneva.

Eulophia Cucullata
A22

Orchids: 5fr, Lissochilus horsfalii. 10fr, Tridactyle bicaudata. 15fr, Polystachya. 20fr, Eulophia alta. 25fr, Microcelia macrorrhynchium.

1966, May 16 **Photo.** ***Perf. 12x12½***
Orchids in Natural Colors

67	A22	2fr dk red	8	5
68	A22	5fr brn org & vio	10	8
69	A22	10fr bl grn & blk	15	10
70	A22	15fr lt grn & dk brn	25	15
71	A22	20fr dk grn	35	20
72	A22	25fr lt ultra & brn	45	20
		Nos. 67-72 (6)	1.38	78

Congo Forest Mouse
A23

Rodents: 10fr, One-stripe mouse. 20fr, Dollman's tree mouse (vert.).

1966, Sept. 15 **Photo.** ***Perf. 12½x12***

73	A23	5fr yel & multi	12	10
74	A23	10fr tan & multi	18	10
75	A23	20fr lt grn & multi	35	25

UNESCO Emblem A24 — Pres. Jean Bedel Bokassa A25

1966, Dec. 5 Photo. *Perf. 13*

76	A24	30fr multi	45	25

Issued to commemorate the 20th anniversary of UNESCO (United Nations Educational, Scientific and Cultural Organization).

1967, Jan. 1 *Perf. 12x12½*

77	A25	30fr yel grn, blk & bis brn	50	25

No. 72 Surcharged with New Value and "XX"

1967, May 8 Photo. *Perf. 12x12½*

78	A22	10fr on 25fr multi	20	10

See also No. C43.

Central Market, Bangui A26

1967, Aug. 8 Photo. *Perf. 12½x13*

79	A26	30fr multi	50	30

Safari Hotel, Bangui A27

1967, Sept. 26 Photo. *Perf. 12½x13*

80	A27	30fr multi	50	30

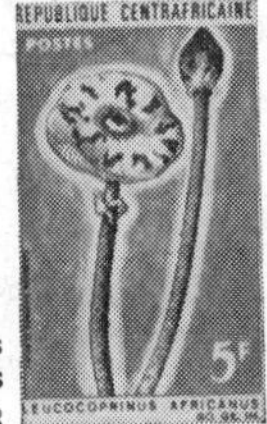

Leucocoprinus Africanus A28

Various Mushrooms

1967, Oct. 3 Engraved *Perf. 13*

81	A28	5fr dk brn, ol & ocher	12	10
82	A28	10fr dk brn, ultra & yel	18	13
83	A28	15fr dk brn, sl grn & yel	25	17
84	A28	30fr multi	60	25
85	A28	50fr multi	85	50
		Nos. 81-85 (5)	2.00	1.15

Map, Radio Tower, Projector and People—A29

1967, Oct. 31

86	A29	30fr emer, ocher & ind	50	30

Radiovision service.

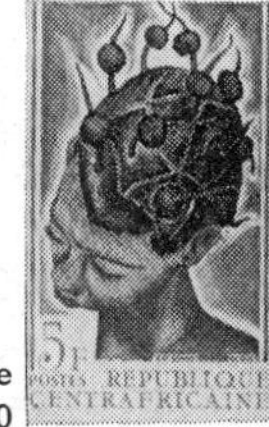

African Hair Style A30

Various African Hair Styles.

1967, Nov. 7 Engraved *Perf. 13*

87	A30	5fr ultra, dk brn & bis brn	10	8
88	A30	10fr car, dk brn & bis brn	20	12
89	A30	15fr dp grn, dk brn & bis brn	25	15
90	A30	20fr org, dk brn & bis brn	35	15
91	A30	30fr red lil, dk brn & bis brn	50	25
		Nos. 87-91 (5)	1.40	75

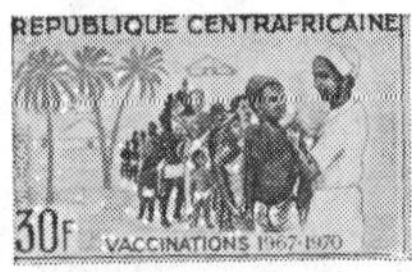

Nurse Vaccinating Children A31

1967, Nov. 14

92	A31	30fr dk red brn & brt grn	50	25

Vaccination campaign, 1967–70.

Douglas DC-3 A32

Designs: 2fr, Beechcraft Baron. 5fr, Douglas DC-4.

1967, Nov. 24

93	A32	1fr brn red, ind & grn	6	6
94	A32	2fr brt bl, blk & brt pink	6	6
95	A32	5fr grnsh bl, blk & emer	13	12
		Nos. 93-95, C47-C49 (6)	11.85	6.14

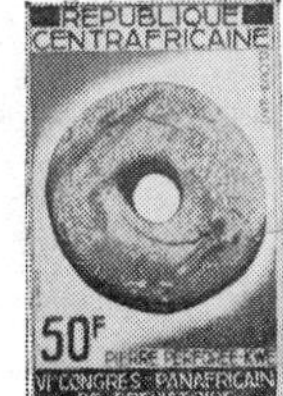

Pierced Stone, Kwe Tribe A33

Designs: 30fr, Primitive dwelling at Toulou (horiz.). 100fr, Megaliths, Bouar. 130fr, Rock painting (people), Toulou (horiz.).

1967, Dec. 26 Engraved *Perf. 13*

96	A33	30fr crim, ind & mar	50	30
97	A33	50fr ol brn, ocher & dk grn	80	40
98	A33	100fr dk brn, brt bl & brn	1.60	70
99	A33	130fr dk red, brn & dk grn	2.00	90

Issued to publicize the 6th Pan-African Prehistoric Congress, Dakar.

Tanker, Refinery and Map of Area Served—A33a

1968, July 30 Photo. *Perf. 12½*

100	A33a	30fr multi	40	20

Issued to commemorate the opening of the Port Gentil (Gabon) Refinery, June 12, 1968.

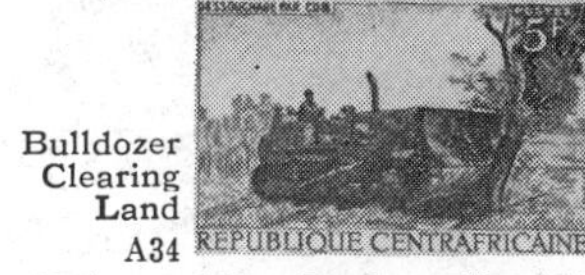

Bulldozer Clearing Land A34

Designs: 10fr, Baoule cattle. 20fr, 15,000-spindle spinning machine. No. 104, Automatic Diederichs looms. No. 105, Bulldozer.

1968, Oct. 1 Engraved *Perf. 13*

101	A34	5fr blk, grn & dk brn	7	5
102	A34	10fr blk, pale grn & bis brn	18	15
103	A34	20fr grn, red brn & yel	30	18
104	A34	30fr brn, ol & ultra	50	20
105	A34	30fr ind, red brn & sl grn	50	20
		Nos. 101-105 (5)	1.55	78

Issued to publicize "Operation Bokassa."

Bangui Mosque A35

1968, Oct. 14

106	A35	30fr grn, bl & ocher	45	20

Hunting Knife of Baya and Boufi Tribes—A36

Designs: 20fr, Hunting knife of Nzakara tribe. 30fr, Crossbow of Babinga and Babenzele (pygmy) tribes.

1968, Nov. 19 Engraved *Perf. 13*

107	A36	10fr lem, Prus bl & ultra	15	12
108	A36	20fr ultra, dk ol & sl grn	30	17
109	A36	30fr sl grn, ultra & brn org	45	17

"Ville de Bangui," 1958 A37

River Boats: 30fr, "J. B. Gouandjia," 1968. 50fr, "Lamblin," 1944.

1968, Dec. 10 Engraved *Perf. 13*

Size: 36x22mm.

110	A37	10fr mag, brt grn & vio bl	15	10
111	A37	30fr bl, grn & brn	50	20
112	A37	50fr brn, sl & ol grn	85	40
		Nos. 110-112, C62-C63 (5)	5.00	2.40

Woman Javelin Thrower A38

Sport Designs: 10fr, Women runners. 15fr, Soccer.

1969, Mar. 18 Photo. *Perf. 13x12½*

113	A38	5fr multi	10	6
114	A38	10fr multi	17	10
115	A38	15fr multi	25	12
		Nos. 113-115, C71-C72 (5)	2.77	1.23

BIT and ILO Emblems and Worker A39

1969, May 20 Photo. *Perf. 12½x13*

116	A39	30fr dp bl, grn & ol brn	40	15
117	A39	50fr dp car, grn & ol brn	75	35

Issued to commemorate the 50th anniversary of the International Labor Organization.

Pres. Jean Bedel Bokassa A40

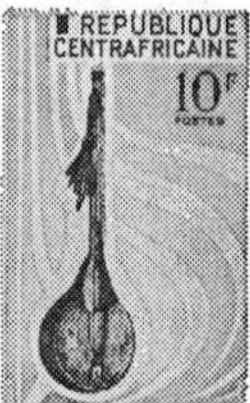

Garayah A41

1969, Dec. 1 Litho. *Perf. 13x13½*

118	A40	30fr ver & multi	40	20

ASECNA Issue

Common Design Type

1969, Dec. 12 Engraved *Perf. 13*

119	CD132	100fr dp bl	1.50	70

1970, Jan. 6 Engraved *Perf. 13*

Musical Instuments: 15fr, Ngombi (harp; horiz.). 30fr, Xylophone (horiz.). 50fr, Ndala (lute; horiz.). 130fr, Gatta and babyon (drums).

120	A41	10fr yel grn, dk grn & ocher	15	12
121	A41	15fr bl grn, ocher & dk brn	25	15
122	A41	30fr mar, ocher & dk brn	45	20
123	A41	50fr rose car & ind	75	45
124	A41	130fr brt bl, brn & ol	2.00	70
		Nos. 120-124 (5)	3.60	1.62

U.P.U. Headquarters Issue

Common Design Type

1970, May 20 Engraved *Perf. 13*

125	CD133	100fr ultra, ver & red brn	1.00	50

Loading Platform and Flour Storage Bins
A42

Designs: 50fr, Flour milling machinery. 100fr, View of mill.

1970, Feb. 24 Litho. ***Perf. 14***

126	A42	25fr sl & multi	35	18
127	A42	50fr lil & multi	70	32
128	A42	100fr red & multi	1.40	75

Inauguration of SICPAD (Société Industrielle Centrafricaine des Produits Alimentaires et Dérivés, a part of Operation Bokassa, Feb. 22, 1968.

Pres. Bokassa
A43

1970, Aug. 13 Litho. ***Perf. 14***

129	A43	30fr multi	3.25	2.75
130	A43	40fr multi	4.75	3.50

Cheese Factory, Sarki—A44

Silk Worm
A45

Designs: 10fr, M'Bali Ranch. 20fr, Zebu (vert.).

Perf. 13x13½, 13½x13

1970, Sept. 15

131	A44	5fr red & multi	20	10
132	A44	10fr red & multi	4.00	3.50
133	A44	20fr red & multi	65	45
134	A45	40fr red & multi	1.10	75
		Nos. 131-134, C83 (5)	7.95	5.90

Issued to publicize Operation Bokassa, a national development plan.

Gnathonemus Monteiri—A46

River Fish: 20fr, Mormyrus proboscirostris. 30fr, Marcusenius wilverthi. 40fr, Gnathonemus elephas. 50fr, Gnathonemus curvirostris.

1971, Apr. 6 Photo. ***Perf. 12½***

135	A46	10fr multi	15	10
136	A46	20fr multi	30	20
137	A46	30fr multi	50	25
138	A46	40fr multi	65	25
139	A46	50fr multi	80	40
		Nos. 135-139 (5)	2.40	1.20

Berberati Cathedral
A47

1971, July 20 Litho. ***Perf. 13½***

140	A47	5fr grn & multi	10	8

New Roman Catholic Cathedral at Berberati.

Charles de Gaulle
A48

Gray Galago
A49

1971, Aug. 20 ***Perf. 13½x13***

141	A48	100fr brt bl & multi	1.50	1.10

In memory of Gen. Charles de Gaulle (1890–1970), president of France.

1971, Oct. 25 Photo. ***Perf. 13***

Designs: 40fr, Elegant galago. 100fr, Calabar potto (horiz.). 150fr, Bosman's potto (horiz.). 200fr, Oustalet's colobo (horiz.).

142	A49	30fr pink & multi	50	40
143	A49	40fr lt bl & multi	70	50
144	A49	100fr multi	1.40	1.00
145	A49	150fr multi	2.25	1.25
146	A49	200fr multi	3.25	1.50
		Nos. 142-146 (5)	8.10	4.65

Alan B. Shepard
A50

Designs: No. 148, Yuri Gagarin. No. 149, Edwin E. Aldrin, Jr. No. 150, Alexei Leonov. No. 151, Neil A. Armstrong on moon. No. 152, Lunokhod I on moon.

1971, Nov. 19 Litho. ***Perf. 14***

147	A50	40fr vio & multi	50	25
148	A50	40fr vio & multi	50	25
149	A50	100fr multi	1.35	60
150	A50	100fr multi	1.35	60
151	A50	200fr red & multi	2.50	1.00
152	A50	200fr red & multi	2.50	1.00
		Nos. 147-152 (6)	8.70	3.70

Space achievements of United States and Russia.

"Operation Bokassa" and Pres. Bokassa
A51

1971, Dec. 1 Photo. ***Perf. 13***

153	A51	40fr red & multi	60	22

12th anniversary of independence.

Racial Equality Emblem
A52

1971, Dec. 6 Lithographed

154	A52	50fr multi	60	25

International Year Against Racial Discrimination.

Bokassa School Emblem and Cadets—A53

Book Year Emblem
A54

1972, Jan. 1 Photogravure

155	A53	30fr gold & multi	45	20

J. B. Bokassa Military School.

1972, Mar. 11 Photo. ***Perf. 12½x13***

156	A54	100fr red brn, gold & org	1.10	65

International Book Year 1972.

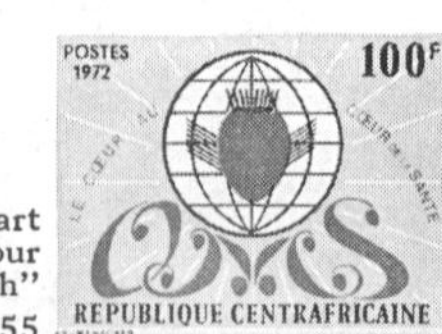

"Your Heart is your Health"
A55

1972, Apr. 7 Photo. ***Perf. 13x12½***

157	A55	100fr yel, blk & car	1.10	65

World Health Day.

Red Cross Workers in Village
A56

1972, May 8 ***Perf. 13***

158	A56	150fr multi	2.00	90

25th World Red Cross Day.

Globe
A57

1972, May 17 Lithographed

159	A57	50fr yel, blk & dp org	60	30

4th World Telecommunications Day.

Pres. and Mrs. Bokassa and Family—A58

1972, May 28 ***Perf. 14***

160	A58	30fr yel & multi	40	15

Mother's Day. Mothers' gold medal awarded to Catherine Bokassa.

Pres. Bokassa Planting Cotton, Map of Africa
A59

1972, June 5 Photo. ***Perf. 13***

161	A59	40fr yel & multi	50	25

Operation Bokassa, a national development plan.

Postal Checking and Savings Center
A60

1972, June 21

162	A60	30fr yel org & multi	40	18

REPUBLIQUE CENTRAFRICAINE

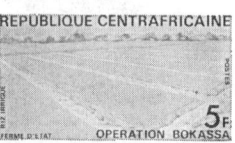

POSTES

5F

OPERATION BOKASSA

Irrigated Rice Fields—A61

"Le Pacifique" Apartment House
A62

Designs: 25fr, Plowing rice field. No. 166, Swimming pool, Hotel St. Sylvestre. No. 167, Entrance, Hotel St. Sylvestre. No. 168, J. B. Bokassa University.

1972 Lithographed ***Perf. 13x13½***

163	A61	5fr multi	7	6
164	A61	25fr multi	32	15

Engraved *Perf. 13*

165	A62	30fr multi	35	15
166	A62	30fr multi	35	15
167	A62	40fr multi	45	25
168	A62	40fr multi	45	20
		Nos. 163-168 (6)	1.99	96

Operation Bokassa. Issue dates: 5fr, 25fr, Nov. 10; No. 165, June 27; Nos. 166-167, Dec. 9; No. 168, Aug. 26.

Bull Chasing Woman on Clock Face A63

Designs (Scenes Painted on Clock Faces): 10fr, Men and open cooking fire. 20fr, Fishermen. 30fr, Palms, monkeys and giraffe. 40fr, Warriors.

1972, July 31 Photo. *Perf. 12½*

169	A63	5fr dk red & multi	8	4
170	A63	10fr brt bl & multi	10	6
171	A63	20fr grn & multi	25	10
172	A63	30fr yel & multi	45	20
173	A63	40fr vio & multi	50	30
		Nos. 169-173 (5)	1.38	70

HORCEN Central African clock and watch factory.

Protestant Youth Center—A64

Design: 10fr, Postal runner carrying mail in cleft stick (vert.).

1972, Aug. 12 *Perf. 13*

174	A64	10fr multi	15	8
175	A64	20fr multi	25	10
		Nos. 174-175, C95-C98 (6)	5.50	2.48

Centraphilex 1972, Central African Philatelic Exhibition, Bangui.

Mail Truck A65

1972, Oct. 23 Photo. *Perf. 13*

176	A65	100fr ocher & multi	1.35	50

Universal Postal Union Day.

Mother Teaching Child to Write A66

Central African Mothers: 10fr, Caring for infant. 15fr, Combing child's hair. 20fr, Teaching to read. 180fr, Nursing. 190fr, Teaching to walk.

1972, Dec. 27 *Perf. 13½x13*

177	A66	5fr multi	8	4
178	A66	10fr lil & multi	12	7
179	A66	15fr dl org & multi	20	8
180	A66	20fr yel grn & multi	25	12
181	A66	180fr multi	2.25	75
182	A66	190fr pink & multi	2.25	1.10
		Nos. 177-182 (6)	5.15	2.16

Farmer Carrying Sheaf—A67

1973, May 30 Photo. *Perf. 13*

183	A67	50fr vio bl & multi	55	35

10th anniversary of the World Food Program.

Garcinia Punctata A68

African Flora: 20fr, Bertiera racemosa. 30fr, Corynanthe pachyceras. 40fr, Combretodendron africanum. 50fr, Xylopia Villosa (vert.).

1973, June 8

184	A68	10fr pale bl & multi	10	7
185	A68	20fr multi	20	10
186	A68	30fr lt gray & multi	40	15
187	A68	40fr multi	40	30
188	A68	50fr multi	50	35
		Nos. 184-188 (5)	1.60	97

Pygmy Chameleon A69

1973, June 26 Photo. *Perf. 13*

189	A69	15fr multi	20	10

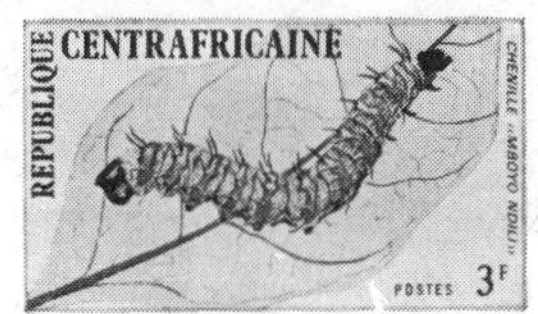

Caterpillar—A70

Designs: Various caterpillars.

1973, Aug. 6 Photo. *Perf. 13*

190	A70	3fr multi	5	5
191	A70	5fr multi	8	5
192	A70	25fr multi	30	15

No. 184 Surcharged with New Value, 2 Bars, and Overprinted in Red: "SECHERESSE SOLIDARITE AFRICAINE"

1973, Aug. 16

193	A68	100fr on 10fr multi	90	75

African solidarity in drought emergency.

African Postal Union Issue

Common Design Type

1973, Sept. 12 Engraved *Perf. 13*

194	CD137	100fr dk brn, red org & ol	90	65

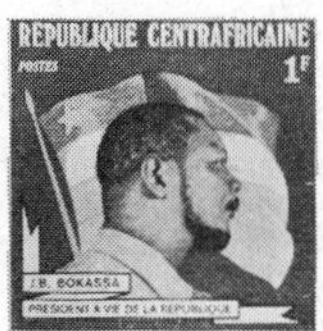

Pres. Bokassa and CAR Flag A71

1973, Nov. 30 Photo. *Perf. 12½*

195	A71	1fr brn & multi	3	3
196	A71	2fr pur & multi	5	5
197	A71	3fr vio bl & multi	5	5
198	A71	5fr ocher & multi	5	5
199	A71	10fr multi	10	7
200	A71	15fr org & multi	15	10
201	A71	20fr multi	20	15
202	A71	30fr dk grn & multi	30	20
203	A71	40fr dk brn & multi	40	30
		Nos. 195-203, C117-C118 (11)	2.83	2.05

INTERPOL Emblem A72

1973, Dec. 20 *Perf. 13x12½*

204	A72	50fr yel & multi	50	40

50th anniversary of the International Criminal Police Organization.

Catherine Bokassa Center A73

Design: 40fr, Ambulance in front of Catherine Bokassa Center.

1974, Jan. 24 Engraved *Perf. 13*

205	A73	30fr multi	25	18
206	A73	40fr multi	32	25

Catherine Bokassa Center for Mothers and Children.

Cigarette-making Machine A74

Designs: 10fr, Cigarette in ashtray, and factory. 30fr, Hand lighting cigarette, and Administration Building.

1974, Jan. 29

207	A74	5fr sl grn & multi	7	5
208	A74	10fr sl grn & multi	10	10
209	A74	30fr sl grn & multi	25	15

Publicity for Centra cigarettes.

"Communications" A75

1974, June 8 Photo. *Perf. 12½x13*

210	A75	100fr multi	1.00	70

World Telecommunications Day.

People and WPY Emblem A76

1974, June 20 Engraved *Perf. 13*

211	A76	100fr red, sl grn & brn	1.00	70

World Population Year.

Mother, Child, WHO Emblem A77

1974, July 10

212	A77	100fr multi	1.00	45

26th anniversary of World Health Organization.

Hoeing—A78

Designs: 10fr, Battle scene ("yesterday"). 15fr, Pastoral scene ("today"). 20fr, Rice planting. 25fr, Storehouse. 40fr, Veterans Headquarters. Borders show tanks and tractors.

1974, Nov. 15 Litho. *Perf. 13*

213	A78	10fr multi	10	7
214	A78	15fr multi	12	8
215	A78	20fr multi	18	10
216	A78	25fr multi	22	15
217	A78	30fr multi	25	15
218	A78	40fr multi	35	15
		Nos. 213-218 (6)	1.22	70

Veterans' activities.

Presidents and Flags of Cameroun, CAR, Congo, Gabon and Meeting Center—A79

1974, Dec. 8 Photogravure *Perf. 13*

219	A79	40fr gold & multi	40	22

See No. C126 and note after Cameroun No. 595.

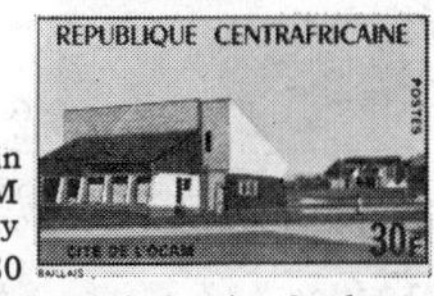

House in OCAM City A80

Designs: Scenes in housing development, OCAM City.

1975, Feb. 1 Photo. *Perf. 13*

220	A80	30fr multi	30	17
221	A80	40fr multi	40	22
222	A80	50fr multi	45	30
223	A80	100fr multi	90	65

1975, Feb. 22

Designs: Cottage scenes in J. B. Bokassa "pilot village."

224	A80	25fr multi	20	12
225	A80	30fr multi	25	15
226	A80	40fr multi	40	20

Foreign Ministry A81

Television Station
A82

1975, Feb. 28 *Perf. 13x12½*

227	A81	40fr multi	40	18

Perf. 13

228	A82	40fr multi	40	18

Public buildings, Bangui.

Bokassa's Saber—A83

Design: 40fr, Bokassa's baton.

1975, Feb. 22 Photo. *Perf. 13*

229	A83	30fr dp bl & multi	25	17
230	A83	40fr vio bl & multi	35	20

Jean Bedel Bokassa, President for Life and Marshal of the Republic. See Nos. C127-C128.

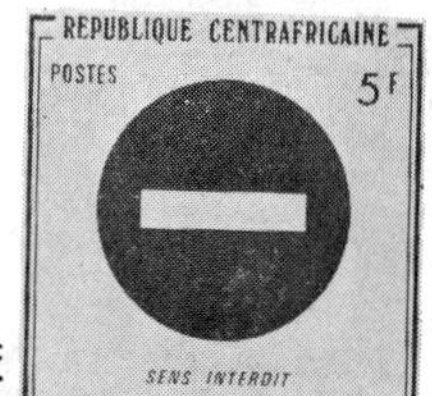

Do Not Enter
A84

Traffic Signs: 10fr, Stop. 20fr, No parking. 30fr, School. 40fr, Intersection.

1975, Mar. 20

231	A84	5fr ultra & red	5	5
232	A84	10fr ultra & red	10	8
233	A84	20fr ultra & red	15	10
234	A84	30fr ultra & multi	20	17
235	A84	40fr ultra & multi	40	20
		Nos. 231-235 (5)	90	60

Buffon's Kob
A85

Designs: 15fr, Wart hog. 20fr, Waterbuck. 30fr, Lion.

1975, June 24 Photo. *Perf. 13*

236	A85	10fr dl grn & multi	10	7
237	A85	15fr lem & multi	15	8
238	A85	20fr yel grn & multi	20	13
239	A85	30fr lt bl & multi	30	17

Crane Lifting Log onto Truck
A86

Designs: 10fr, Forest (vert.). 15fr, Tree felling (vert.). 100fr, Log pile. 150fr, Logs transported by raft. 200fr, Lumberyard.

1975, Nov. 28 Engr. *Perf. 13*

240	A86	10fr multi	8	5
241	A86	15fr multi	12	8
242	A86	50fr multi	40	25
243	A86	100fr multi	75	55
244	A86	150fr multi	1.10	90
245	A86	200fr multi	1.50	1.10
		Nos. 240-245 (6)	3.95	2.93

Promotion of Central African wood.

Women's Heads and Various Occupations—A87

1975, Dec. 10 Photogravure

246	A87	40fr multi	35	20
247	A87	100fr multi	75	55

International Women's Year 1975.

Alexander Graham Bell
A88

1976, Mar. 25 Litho. *Perf. 12½x13*

248	A88	100fr yel & blk	75	50

Centenary of first telephone call by Alexander Graham Bell, Mar. 10, 1876.

Satellite and ITU Emblem—A89

Design: No. 250, UPU emblem, various forms of mail transport.

1976 Engr. *Perf. 13*

249	A89	100fr vio bl, cl & grn	75	50
250	A89	100fr car, grn & ocher	90	70

World Telecommunications Day (No. 249); Universal Postal Union Day (No. 250).

Soyuz on Launching Pad—A90

Design: 50fr, Apollo rocket.

1976, June 14 Litho. *Perf. 14x13½*

251	A90	40fr multi	42	18
252	A90	50fr multi	55	25
		Nos. 251-252, C135-C137 (5)	6.97	2.91

Apollo Soyuz space test project, Russo-American cooperation, launched July 15, link-up July 17, 1975.

Drurya Antimachus—A91

Butterfly: 40fr, Argema mittrei (vert.).

1976, Sept. 20 Litho. *Perf. 12½*

253	A91	30fr ocher & multi	25	15
254	A91	40fr ultra & multi	35	20

See Nos. C145-C146.

Slalom, Piero Gros—A92

Design: 60fr, Karl Schnabel and Toni Innauer.

1976, Sept. 23 *Perf. 13½*

255	A92	40fr multi	42	20
256	A92	60fr multi	65	32
		Nos. 255-256, C147-C149 (5)	6.92	3.17

12th Winter Olympic Games winners, Innsbruck.

Viking Components
A93

Design: 60fr, Viking take-off.

1976, Dec.

257	A93	40fr multi	42	18
258	A93	60fr multi	65	30
		Nos. 257-258, C151-C153 (5)	6.92	2.88

Viking Mars project.

Empire

Stamps of 1973-76 Overprinted with Bars and "EMPIRE CENTRAFRICAIN" in Black, Green, Violet Blue, Silver, Carmine, Brown or Red

Printing and Perforations as Before

1977, March

Multicolored

259	A70	3fr (#190; B)	5	5
260	A78	10fr (#213;B)	12	10
261	A84	10fr (#232;VB)	12	10
262	A85	10fr (#236;C)	15	12
263	A85	15fr (#237;C)	20	15
264	A86	15fr (#241;B)	17	12
265	A78	20fr (#215;B)	20	18
266	A85	20fr (#238;C)	20	18
267	A78	25fr (#216;B)	25	20
268	A80	25fr (#224;B)	25	20
269	A80	30fr (#220;VB)	30	25
270	A80	30fr (#225;B)	30	25
271	A85	30fr (#239;C)	30	25
272	A79	40fr (#219;B)	35	30
273	A80	40fr (#221;VB)	40	30
274	A80	40fr (#226;B)	35	30
275	A81	40fr (#227;B & S)	35	30
276	A82	40fr (#228;B)	35	30
277	A84	40fr (#235;VB)	30	25
278	A91	40fr (#254;B)	30	25
279	A86	50fr (#242;Br)	45	35
280	A75	100fr (#210;B)	90	70
281	A76	100fr (#211;B)	90	70
282	A77	100fr (#212;G)	1.00	80
283	A88	100fr (#248;R)	1.00	80
284	A89	100fr (#249;B)	1.00	80
285	A89	100fr (#250;B)	1.00	80
		Nos. 259-285 (27)	11.26	9.10

Stamps of 1975-76 Overprinted "EMPIRE CENTRAFRICAIN" in Black on Silver Panel

1977, Apr. 1

286	A83	40fr multi (#230)	30	25
287	A90	40fr multi (#251)	40	30
288	A92	40fr multi (#255)	30	25
289	A93	40fr multi (#257)	30	25
290	A90	50fr multi (#252)	50	35
291	A92	60fr multi (#256)	50	35
292	A93	60fr multi (#258)	50	35
		Nos. 286-292 (7)	2.80	2.10

Pierre and Marie Curie—A94

Design: 60fr, Wilhelm C. Roentgen.

1977, Apr. 1 Litho. *Perf. 13½*

293	A94	40fr multi	35	18
294	A94	60fr multi	60	30
		Nos. 293-294, C180-C182 (5)	6.80	2.88

Nobel Prize winners.

Italy No. C42 and Faustine Temple, Rome—A95

Design: 60fr, Russia No. C12 and St. Basil's Cathedral, Moscow.

1977, Apr. 11 Litho. *Perf. 11*

295	A95	40fr multi	35	18
296	A95	60fr multi	60	30
		Nos. 295-296, C184-C186 (5)	6.80	2.88

75th anniversary of the Zeppelin.

Lindbergh over Paris—A96

Designs: 60fr, Santos Dumont and "14 bis." 100fr, Bleriot and monoplane. 200fr, Roald Amundsen and "N24." 300fr, Concorde. 500fr, Lindbergh and Spirit of St. Louis.

1977, Sept. 30 Litho. *Perf. 13½*

297	A96	50fr multi	50	25
298	A96	60fr multi	60	30
299	A96	100fr multi	95	38
300	A96	200fr multi	1.90	80
301	A96	300fr multi	3.00	1.20
		Nos. 297-301 (5)	6.95	2.93

Souvenir Sheet

302	A96	500fr multi	4.75	2.25

History of aviation, famous fliers. No. 302 has multicolored margin showing Spirit of St. Louis and Concorde. Size: 117x91½mm.

Shot on Goal—A97

Designs: 60fr, Heading ball in net. 100fr, Backfield defense. 200fr, Argentina '78 poster. 300fr, Mario Zagalo and stadium. 500fr, Ferenc Puskas.

1977, Nov. 18 Litho. *Perf. 13½*

303	A97	50fr multi	50	25
304	A97	60fr multi	60	30
305	A97	100fr multi	95	35
306	A97	200fr multi	1.90	80
307	A97	300fr multi	3.00	1.20
		Nos. 303-307 (5)	6.95	2.90

Souvenir Sheet

308	A97	500fr multi	4.75	2.25

World Soccer Championships, Argentina, June 1–25, 1978. No. 308 has multicolored margin showing Argentina '78 emblem, World Cup and Stadium. Size: 120x81mm.

Emperor Bokassa I, Central African Flag A98

1977, Dec. 4 Litho. *Perf. 13½*

309	A98	40fr multi	30	25
310	A98	60fr multi	50	35
311	A98	100fr multi	80	60
312	A98	150fr multi	1.20	90
		Nos. 309-312, C188-C189 (6)	6.90	4.60

Coronation of Emperor Bokassa I, Dec. 4.

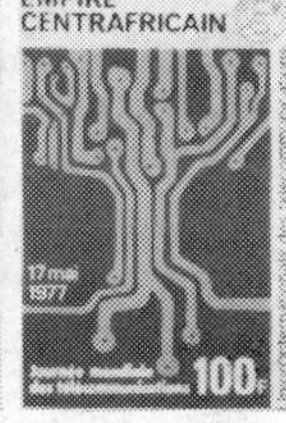

Lilium A99 — Electronic Tree, ITU Emblem A100

Design: 10fr, Hibiscus.

1977 Litho. *Perf. 13½x14*

313	A99	5fr multi	5	3
314	A99	10fr multi	10	5

1977

315	A100	100fr blk, org & brn	1.20	90

World Telecommunications Day.

Bible and People A101

1977 Litho. *Perf. 14x13½*

316	A101	40fr multi	40	20

Bible Week.

People and Rotary Emblem A102

1977

317	A102	60fr multi	60	30

Rotary Club of Bangui, 20th anniversary.

Holy Family, by Rubens A103

Rubens Paintings: 150fr, Marie de Medicis. 200fr, Son of artist. 300fr, Neptune. 500fr, Marie de Medicis (different).

1978, Jan. 26

318	A103	60fr multi	60	30
319	A103	150fr multi	1.40	60
320	A103	200fr multi	1.90	80
321	A103	300fr multi	3.00	1.20

Souvenir Sheet

322	A103	500fr gold & multi	4.75	2.25

Peter Paul Rubens (1577–1640), 400th birth anniversary. No. 322 contains one stamp; multicolored margin shows entire painting. Size: 89x116mm.

Rhinoceros—A104

Endangered Animals and Wildlife Fund Emblem: 50fr, Slender-nosed crocodile. 60fr, Leopard (vert.). 100fr, Giraffe (vert.). 200fr, Elephant. 300fr, Gorilla (vert.).

1978, Feb. 21 Litho. *Perf. 13½*

323	A104	40fr multi	35	18
324	A104	50fr multi	50	25
325	A104	60fr multi	60	30
326	A104	100fr multi	95	42
327	A104	200fr multi	1.90	80
328	A104	300fr multi	3.00	1.25
		Nos. 323-328 (6)	7.30	3.20

Bokassa Sports Palace A105

Design: 60fr, Sports Palace, side view.

1978 *Perf. 14*

329	A105	40fr multi	32	25
330	A105	60fr multi	50	35

Automatic Telephone Exchange, Bangui—A106

1978

331	A106	40fr multi	40	20
332	A106	60fr multi	60	30

Diligence and Satellite—A107

Designs (UPU Emblem and): 50fr, Steam locomotive and communications via satellite. 60fr, Paddle-wheel steamer and ship-to-shore communication via satellite. 80fr, Old mail truck and satellite.

1978, May 17 *Perf. 13½*

333	A107	40fr multi	40	20
334	A107	50fr multi	50	25
335	A107	60fr multi	60	30
336	A107	80fr multi	80	40
		Nos. 333-336, C191-C192 (6)	5.30	2.65

Century of progress of posts and telecommunications.

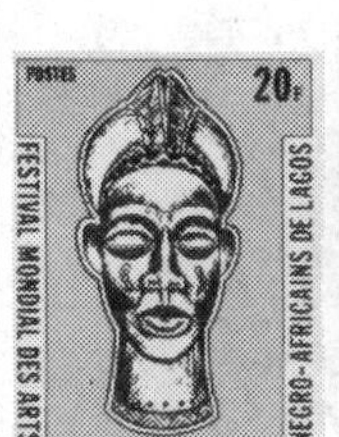

Mask A108 — Capt. Cook on "Endeavour" A109

Designs: 30fr, Mask. 60fr, Women dancers (horiz.). 100fr, Men dancers (horiz.).

Perf. 13½x14, 14x13½

1978, July 11 Lithographed

337	A108	20fr blk & yel	20	10
338	A108	30fr blk & brt bl	30	15
339	A108	60fr blk & multi	60	30
340	A108	100fr blk & multi	1.00	50

Black-African World Arts Festival, Lagos.

1978, Aug. 30 *Perf. 14½*

Designs: 60fr, Resolution off Hawaii (horiz.). 200fr, Hawaiians welcoming Capt. Cook (horiz.). 350fr, Masked rowers in Hawaiian boat (horiz.).

341	A109	60fr multi	60	30
342	A109	80fr multi	80	40
343	A109	200fr multi	2.00	1.00
344	A109	350fr multi	3.50	1.75

Capt. James Cook (1728–1779), explorer.

Dürer, Self-portrait A110

Dürer Paintings: 80fr, The Four Apostles. 200fr, Virgin and Child. 350fr, Emperor Maximilian I.

1978, Oct. 24 Litho. *Perf. 13½*

345	A110	60fr multi	60	30
346	A110	80fr multi	80	40
347	A110	200fr multi	2.00	1.00
348	A110	350fr multi	3.50	1.75

Albrecht Dürer (1471–1528), German painter.

Tutankhamen's Gold Mask A111

Treasures of Tutankhamen: 60fr, King and Queen, gold back panel of throne. 80fr, Gilt folding chair. 100fr, King wearing crowns of Upper and Lower Egypt, painted wood sculpture. 120fr, Lion's head. 150fr, Tutankhamen, wood stature. 180fr, Gold throne. 250fr, Gold miniature coffin.

1978, Nov. 22

349	A111	40fr multi	40	20
350	A111	60fr multi	60	30
351	A111	80fr multi	80	40
352	A111	100fr multi	1.00	50
353	A111	120fr multi	1.20	60
354	A111	150fr multi	1.50	75
355	A111	180fr multi	1.80	90
356	A111	250fr multi	2.50	1.25
		Nos. 349-356 (8)	9.80	4.90

Tutankhamen, c. 1358 B.C., King of Egypt.

Lenin at Smolny Institute A112

Designs: 60fr, 200fr, 300fr, Various Lenin portraits. 100fr, Ulyanov family (horiz.). 150fr, Lenin, Cruiser "Aurora" and flag (horiz.). 500fr, "Aurora" and star.

1978, Nov. *Perf. 14*

357	A112	40fr multi	40	20
358	A112	60fr multi	60	30
359	A112	100fr blk & gold	1.00	50
360	A112	150fr blk, gold & red	1.50	75
361	A112	200fr multi	2.00	1.00
362	A112	300fr multi	3.00	1.50
		Nos. 357-362 (6)	8.50	4.25

Souvenir Sheet

363	A112	500fr multi	5.25	

60th anniversary of the Soviet Union. No. 363 has red marginal inscription and hammer and sickle emblem. Size: 78x110mm.

Catherine Bokassa A113

Design: 60fr, Emperor Bokassa.

1978, Dec. 4 Litho. *Perf. 13*

364	A113	40fr multi	40	20
365	A113	60fr multi	60	30

First anniversary of coronation. See No. C202.

Rowland Hill, Letter Scale and G.B. No. 1—A114

Designs (Rowland Hill and): 50fr, U.S. No. 1, mailman on bicycle. 60fr, Austria No. P4 and 19th century mailman. 80fr, Switzerland No. 2L1, postilion and mail-coach.

1978, Dec. 9 Litho. *Perf. 13½*

366	A114	40fr multi	40	20
367	A114	50fr multi	50	25
368	A114	60fr multi	60	30
369	A114	80fr multi	80	40
		Nos. 366-369, C203-C204 (6)	5.30	2.65

Sir Rowland Hill (1795–1879), originator of penny postage.

Nos. 303–307 Overprinted in Silver: "VAINQUEUR : ARGENTINE"

1978, Dec. 27

370	A97	50fr multi	50	25
371	A97	60fr multi	60	30
372	A97	100fr multi	1.00	50
373	A97	200fr multi	2.00	1.00
374	A97	300fr multi	3.00	1.50
		Nos. 370-374 (5)	7.10	3.55

Souvenir Sheet

No. 308 Overprinted in Silver: "ARGENTINE – PAYS BAS 3–1 / 25 juin 1978"

375	A97	500fr multi	5.00	2.50

Argentina's victory in World Cup Soccer Championship 1978.

Children Painting and Dutch Portrait—A115

Designs (UNICEF, Eagle Emblems and): 50fr, Eskimo children skiing, and ski jump. 60fr, Children with toy racing car, and Carl Benz with early car model. 80fr, Children launching rocket, and Intelsat.

1979, Mar. 6 Litho. *Perf. 13½*

376	A115	40fr multi	40	20
377	A115	50fr multi	50	25
378	A115	60fr multi	60	30
379	A115	80fr multi	80	40
		Nos. 376-379, C206-C207 (6)	5.30	2.65

International Year of the Child.

High Jump, Moscow '80 Emblem and "M" A116

Designs (Moscow '80 Emblem, Various Sports and): 50fr, Bicycling and "O". 60fr, Weight lifting and "C". 80fr, Judo and "K".

1979, Mar. 16 Litho. *Perf. 13*

380	A116	40fr multi	32	15
381	A116	50fr multi	40	20
382	A116	60fr multi	48	25
383	A116	80fr multi	65	30
		Nos. 380-383, C209-C210 (6)	4.25	2.10

22nd Olympic Games, Moscow, July 19–Aug. 3, 1980. Background letters on Nos. 380–383, C209–C210 spell "Mockba." A 1500fr gold embossed stamp showing emblems and Discobolus exists.

Memorial, Bangui, Butterfly, Hibiscus—A117

Design: 150fr, Canoe, truck and letters.

1979, June 8 Litho. *Perf. 12x12½*

384	A117	60fr multi	48	25
385	A117	150fr multi	1.20	60

Philexafrique II, Libreville, Gabon, June 8–17. No. 384, 385 each printed in sheets of 10 with 5 labels showing exhibition emblem.

Schoolgirl A118

1979, July 25 Litho. *Perf. 12½x12*

386	A118	70fr multi	55	22

International Bureau of Education, Geneva, 50th anniversary.

Chicken A119

Designs: 20fr, Bull. 40fr, Sheep.

1979, Aug. *Perf. 13*

387	A119	10fr multi	8	4
388	A119	20fr multi	16	8
389	A119	40fr multi	32	15

National Husbandry Association. See No. C211.

Souvenir Sheet

Virgin and Child, by Dürer A120

1979, Aug. *Perf. 13½*

390	A120	500fr lt grn & dl red	4.00	1.85

Albrecht Dürer (1471–1528), German engraver and printer. No. 390 has dull red and light green margin showing entire etching. Size: 90x115mm.

Nos. 257-258 Overprinted "ALUNISSAGE/APOLLO XI/ JUILLET 1969" and Emblem

1979, Nov. 11 Litho. *Perf. 13½*

391	A93	40fr multi	32	15
392	A93	60fr multi	48	25
		Nos. 391-392, C212-C214 (5)	5.60	2.80

Apollo 11 moon landing, 10th anniversary.

Girl and Rose—A121

1979, Dec. 15 Multicolored

393	A121	30fr *Butterfly and girl*, vert.	24	12
394	A121	40fr *shown*	32	16
395	A121	60fr *Hansel and Gretel*, vert.	48	24
396	A121	200fr *Cinderella*	1.60	80
397	A121	250fr *Mermaid*, vert.	2.00	1.00
		Nos. 393-397 (5)	4.64	2.32

International Year of the Child.

Locomotive, U.S. Type A27, Hill—A122

Locomotives, Hill and Stamps: 100fr, France No. 1. 150fr, Germany type All. 250fr, Great Britain No. 32. 500fr, CAR No. 2.

1979, Dec. 20

398	A122	60fr multi	48	24
399	A122	100fr multi	80	40
400	A122	150fr multi	1.20	60
401	A122	250fr multi	2.00	1.00

Souvenir Sheet

402	A122	500fr multi	4.25	2.25

Sir Rowland Hill (1795-1879), originator of penny postage. No. 402 has multicolored margin showing Hill and Penny Black. Size: 116×78½mm.

Basketball, Moscow '80 Emblem—A123

Pre-Olympic Year: Men's or women's basketball.

1979, Dec. 28 Litho. *Perf. 14½*

403	A123	50fr multi	40	20
404	A123	125fr multi	1.00	50
405	A123	200fr multi	1.60	80
406	A123	300fr multi	2.40	1.20
407	A123	500fr multi	4.00	2.00
		Nos. 403-407 (5)	9.40	4.70

Nos. 313-314, 337-338 Overprinted "REPUBLIQUE CENTRAFRICAINE" in Black on Silver Panel and

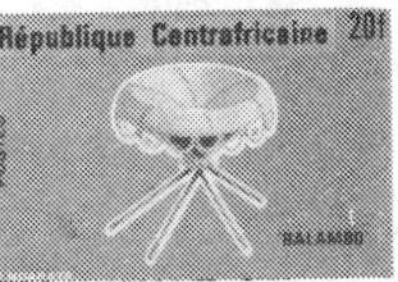

Balambo Chair—A124

1980, Mar. 20 Litho. *Perf. 13½x14, 14x13½*

408	A99	5fr multi	4	3
409	A99	10fr multi	8	4
410	A124	20fr multi	16	8
411	A108	20fr multi	16	8
412	A108	30fr multi	24	12
		Nos. 408-412 (5)	68	35

Viking Satellite—A125

1980, Apr. 8 *Perf. 13½*

413	A125	40fr *shown*	32	16
414	A125	50fr *Apollo-Soyuz*	40	20
415	A125	60fr *Voyager*	48	24
416	A125	100fr *European Space Agency emblem, flags*	80	40
		Nos. 413-416, C221-C222 (6)	4.80	2.40

Walking, Olympic Medal, Moscow '80 Emblem—A126

1980, July 25 Litho. *Perf. 13½*

417	A126	30fr *shown*	24	12
418	A126	40fr *Relay race*	32	16
419	A126	70fr *Running*	55	25
420	A126	80fr *High jump*	65	32
		Nos. 417-420, C231-C232 (6)	3.76	1.85

Agricultural Development—A127

1980, Nov. 4 **Litho.** ***Perf. 13½***

No.	Type	Value	Description	Unused	Used
421	A127	30fr	*shown*	24	12
422	A127	40fr	*Telecommunications*	32	16
423	A127	70fr	*Engineering*	55	25
424	A127	100fr	*Civil engineering*	80	40
			Nos. 421-424, C234-C235 (6)	4.71	2.33

Europe-Africa cooperation.

Nos. 403-407 Overprinted with Medal and Country

1980, Nov. 12 ***Perf. 14½***

No.	Type	Value	Description	Unused	Used
425	A123	50fr	multi	40	20
426	A123	125fr	multi	1.00	50
427	A123	200fr	multi	1.60	80
428	A123	300fr	multi	2.40	1.20
429	A123	500fr	multi	4.00	2.00
			Nos. 425-429 (5)	9.40	4.70

Virgin and Child, by Raphael A128

African Postal Union, 5th Anniversary A129

Christmas 1980: Virgin and Child paintings by Raphael.

1980, Dec. 20 ***Perf. 12½***

No.	Type	Value	Description	Unused	Used
430	A128	60fr	multi	50	25
431	A128	150fr	multi	1.20	60
432	A128	250fr	multi	2.00	1.00

1980, Dec. 24 **Photo.** ***Perf. 13½***

No.	Type	Value	Description	Unused	Used
433	A129	70fr	multi	55	25

Peruvian Soccer Team, Soccer Cup—A130

1981, Jan. 13 **Litho.** ***Perf. 13½***

No.	Type	Value	Description	Unused	Used
434	A130	10fr	shown	8	4
435	A130	15fr	Scotland	12	6
436	A130	20fr	Mexico	16	8
437	A130	25fr	Sweden	20	10
438	A130	30fr	Austria	25	12
439	A130	40fr	Poland	32	16
440	A130	50fr	France	40	20
441	A130	60fr	Italy	50	25
442	A130	70fr	Germany	60	30
443	A130	80fr	Brazil	65	32
			Nos. 434-443, C237-C238 (12)	5.68	2.83

ESPANA '82 World Cup Soccer Championship.

13th World Telecommunications Day—A131

1981, May 17 **Litho.** ***Perf. 12½***

No.	Type	Value	Description	Unused	Used
444	A131	150fr	multi	1.20	60

Apollo 15 Crew on Moon—A132

Space Exploration: Columbia space shuttle.

1981, June 10 **Litho.** ***Perf. 14***

No.	Type	Value	Description	Unused	Used
445	A132	100fr	multi	80	40
446	A132	150fr	multi	1.20	60
447	A132	200fr	multi	1.60	80
448	A132	300fr	multi	2.40	1.20

Souvenir Sheet

No.	Type	Value	Description	Unused	Used
449	A132	500fr	multi	4.00	2.00

No. 449 has multicolored margin continuing design of stamp. Size: 103x78mm.

Family of Acrobats with Monkey, by Picasso—A133

Picasso Birth Centenary: 50fr, The Balcony. 80fr, The Artist's Son as Pierrot. 100fr, The Three Dancers.

1981, June 30 ***Perf. 13½***

No.	Type	Value	Description	Unused	Used
450	A133	40fr	multi	32	16
451	A133	50fr	multi	40	20
452	A133	80fr	multi	65	32
453	A133	100fr	multi	80	40
			Nos. 450-453, C245-C246 (6)	4.97	2.48

First Anniv. of Zimbabwe's Independence—A134

1981, July 9 **Litho.** ***Perf. 12½***

No.	Type	Value	Description	Unused	Used
454	A134	100fr	multi	80	80
455	A134	150fr	multi	1.20	60
456	A134	200fr	multi	1.60	80

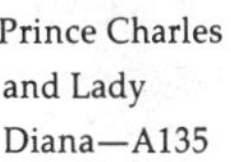

Prince Charles and Lady Diana—A135

1981, July, 24 ***Perf. 14***

No.	Type	Value	Description	Unused	Used
457	A135	75fr	Charles	60	30
458	A135	100fr	Diana	80	40
459	A135	150fr	St. Paul's Cathedral	1.20	60
460	A135	175fr	shown	1.40	70

Souvenir Sheet

No.	Type	Value	Description	Unused	Used
461	A135	500fr	Couple	4.00	2.00

Royal Wedding. No. 461 has multicolored margin showing flowers. Size: 70x91mm.

Nos. 417-420 Overprinted with Event, Winner and Country in Gold.

1981 **Litho.** ***Perf. 13½***

No.	Type	Value	Description	Unused	Used
462	A126	30fr	multi	24	12
463	A126	40fr	multi	32	16
464	A126	70fr	multi	55	25
465	A126	80fr	multi	65	32
			Nos. 462-465, C248-C249 (6)	3.76	1.85

Prince Charles and Lady Diana—A136

1981, Aug. 20 **Litho.** ***Perf. 13½***

No.	Type	Value	Description	Unused	Used
466	A136	40fr	shown	32	16
467	A136	50fr	Crowned Prince of Wales	40	20
468	A136	80fr	Diana	65	32
469	A136	100fr	Naval training	80	40
			Nos. 466-469, C251-C252 (6)	4.97	2.48

Royal wedding.

1906 Renault—A137

1981, Sept. 22 **Litho.** ***Perf. 12½***

No.	Type	Value	Description	Unused	Used
470	A137	20fr	shown	16	8
471	A137	40fr	Mercedes-Benz, 1937	32	16
472	A137	50fr	Matra-Ford, 1969	40	20
473	A137	110fr	Tazio Nuvolari, 1927	90	45
474	A137	150fr	Jackie Stewart, 1965	1.20	60
			Nos. 470-474 (5)	2.98	1.49

Souvenir Sheet
Perf. 10

No.	Type	Value	Description	Unused	Used
475	A137	450fr	Finish line, 1914	3.75	2.00

Grand Prix of France, 75th anniv. No. 475 has multicolored margin continuing design. Size: 104x80mm.

World Food Day—A138

1981, Oct. 16

No.	Type	Value	Description	Unused	Used
476	A138	90fr	multi	72	36
477	A138	110fr	multi	90	45

Navigators and their Ships—A139

1981, Sept. 4 **Litho.** ***Perf. 13½***

No.	Type	Value	Description	Unused	Used
478	A139	40fr	C.V. Rietschoten	32	16
479	A139	50fr	M. Pajot	40	20
480	A139	60fr	K. Jaworski	50	25
481	A139	80fr	M. Birch	65	32
			Nos. 478-481, C254-C255 (6)	4.27	2.13

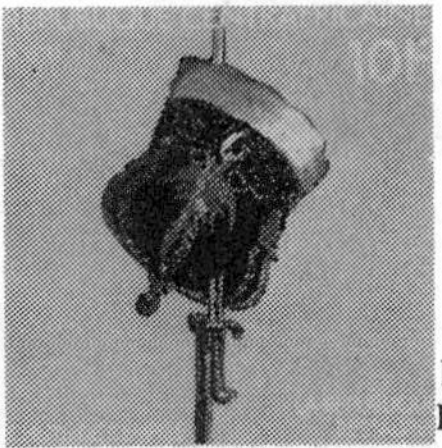

Downfall of Empire—A140

1981, Oct. 6

No.	Type	Value	Description	Unused	Used
482	A140	5fr	Sword through crown	4	3
483	A140	10fr	like #482	8	4
484	A140	25fr	Victory holding map	20	10
485	A140	60fr	like #484	50	25
486	A140	90fr	Toppled Bokassa statue	72	36
487	A140	500fr	like #486	4.00	2.00
			Nos. 482-487 (6)	5.54	2.78

Komba A141

1981, Nov. 17

No.	Type	Value	Description	Unused	Used
488	A141	50fr	shown	40	20
489	A141	90fr	Dodoro, horiz.	72	36
490	A141	140fr	Kaya, horiz.	1.15	60

Central African States Bank—A142

1981, Dec. 12 **Litho.** ***Perf. 12½x13***

No.	Type	Value	Description	Unused	Used
491	A142	90fr	multi	72	36
492	A142	110fr	multi	90	45

Christmas 1981
A143

Virgin and Child Paintings.

1981, Dec. 24

493 A143 50fr Fra Angelico, 1430 40 20
494 A143 60fr Cosimo Tura, 1484 50 25
495 A143 90fr Bramantino 72 36
496 A143 110fr Memling 90 45
Nos. 493-496, C260-C261 (6) 5.27 2.66

Scouting Year—A144

1982, Jan. 13 ***Perf. 12½***

497 A144 100fr Hiking 80 40
498 A144 150fr Scouts, horiz. 1.20 60
499 A144 200fr Hiking 1.60 80
500 A144 300fr Salute, flag, vert. 2.40 1.20

Souvenir Sheet

501 A144 500fr Scout, Baden-Powell, vert. 4.00 2.00

No. 501 contains one stamp (perf. 13); multicolored margin shows hike, emblem. Size: 84x113mm.

Elephant—A145

1982, Jan. 22 ***Perf. 13½***

502 A145 60fr shown 50 25
503 A145 90fr Giraffes 72 36
504 A145 100fr Addaxes 80 40
505 A145 110fr Okapi 90 45
Nos. 502-505, C263-C264 (6) 9.32 4.66

Norman Rockwell Illustrations—A146

1982, Feb. 17 ***Perf. 13½x14***

506 A146 30fr Grandfather snowman 25 12
507 A146 60fr Croquet players 50 25
508 A146 110fr Women talking 90 45
509 A146 150fr Searching 1.20 60

AT 16 Dirigible—A147

1982, Feb. 27 **Litho.** ***Perf. 13½***

510 A147 5fr shown 4 3
511 A147 10fr Beyer-Garrat locomotive 8 4
512 A147 20fr Bugatti 24 "Royale," 1924 16 8
513 A147 110fr Vickers "Valentia," 1928 90 45
Nos. 510-513, C266-C267 (6) 7.58 3.85

Bellvue Garden, by Edouard Manet (1832-1883)—A148

Anniversaries: 400fr, Goethe (1749-1832) (vert.). Nos. 519-520, Princess Diana, 21st birthday, July 1 (vert.). 300fr, George Washington (1732-1799) (vert.).

1982, Apr. 6 **Litho.** ***Perf. 13***

517 A148 200fr multi 1.60 80
517A A148 300fr multi 2.40 1.25
518 A148 400fr multi 3.25 1.60
519 A148 500fr multi 4.00 2.00

Souvenir Sheet

520 A148 500fr multi 4.00 2.00

No. 520 has multicolored margin showing flowers. Size: 80x104mm.

23rd Olympic Games, Los Angeles, 1984—A149

1982, July 24 **Litho.** ***Perf. 13½***

521 A149 5fr Soccer 4 3
522 A149 10fr Boxing 8 4
523 A149 20fr Running 16 8
524 A149 110fr Long jump 90 45
Nos. 521-524, C269-C270 (6) 7.68 3.85

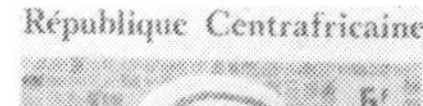

21st Birthday of Princess Diana—A150

Portraits.

1982, July 20 **Litho.** ***Perf. 13½***

525 A150 5fr multi 4 3
526 A150 10fr multi 8 4
527 A150 20fr multi 16 8
528 A150 110fr multi 90 45
Nos. 525-528, C272-C273 (6) 7.68 3.85

Nos. 457-461 Overprinted in Blue: "NAISSANCE ROYALE 1982"

1982, Aug. 20 ***Perf. 14***

529 A135 75fr multi 60 30
530 A135 110fr multi 90 45
531 A135 150fr multi 1.25 60
532 A135 175fr multi 1.40 70

Souvenir Sheet

533 A135 500fr multi 4.00 2.00

Birth of Prince William of Wales, June 21.

Sakpa Basket—A152

Baskets and bowls.

1982, Sept. 2 ***Perf. 13***

538 A152 5fr shown 4 3
539 A152 10fr like 5fr 8 4
540 A152 25fr Ngbenda gourd, vert. 20 10
541 A152 60fr like 25fr 48 24
542 A152 120fr Ta ti ngou jugs 1.00 50
543 A152 175fr Kangu bowls 1.60 80
544 A152 300fr Kolongo bowls, vert. 2.50 1.25
Nos. 538-544 (7) 5.90 2.96

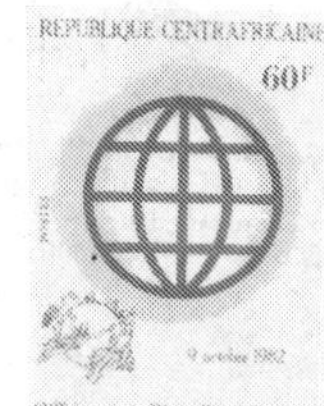

13th World UPU Day—A153

1982, Oct. 9

549 A153 60fr multi 48 24
550 A153 120fr multi 1.00 50

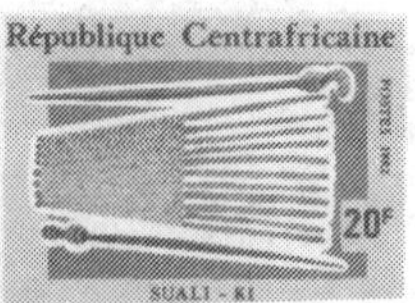

Comb and Hairpins—A154

1982, Oct. 20 ***Perf. 13x12½***

551 A154 20fr multi 16 8
552 A154 30fr multi 24 12
553 A154 60fr multi 48 24
554 A154 80fr multi 65 32
555 A154 120fr multi 1.00 50
Nos. 551-555 (5) 2.53 1.26

Artist Pierre Ndarata and No. 69—A155

1982, Oct. ***Perf. 13***

556 A155 40fr Jean Tubind at easel, vert. 32 16
557 A155 70fr shown 56 28
558 A155 90fr like 70fr 72 36
559 A155 140fr like 40fr 1.35 68

TB Bacillus Centenary—A156

1982, Nov. 30 ***Perf. 13½x13***

560 A156 100fr vio & blk 80 40
561 A156 120fr red org & blk 1.00 50
562 A156 175fr bl & blk 1.60 80

10th Anniv. of UN Conference on Human Environment—A157

1982, Dec. 8

563 A157 120fr multi 1.00 50
564 A157 150fr multi 1.20 60
565 A157 300fr multi 2.50 1.25

Granary—A158

1982, Dec. 15 ***Perf. 13***

566 A158 60fr multi 48 24
567 A158 80fr multi 65 32
568 A158 120fr multi 1.00 50
569 A158 200fr multi 1.60 80

ITU Plenipotentiaries Conference, Nairobi, Sept.—A159

1982, Dec.

570 A159 100fr multi 80 40
571 A159 120fr multi 1.00 50

SEMI-POSTAL STAMPS
Central African Republic
Anti-Malaria Issue
Common Design Type
Perf. 12½x12

1962, Apr. 7 Engraved Unwmkd.

B1 CD108 25fr +5fr sl 70 70

Issued for the World Health Organization drive to eradicate malaria.

Freedom from Hunger Issue
Common Design Type

1963, Mar. 21 *Perf. 13*

B2 CD112 25fr +5fr bis, Prus grn & brn 65 65

Guinea Fowl and Partridge
SP1

Designs: 10fr+5fr, Yellow-backed duiker and snail. 20fr+5fr, Elephant, tortoise and hippopotamus playing tug-of-war. 30fr+10fr, Cuckoo and tortoise. 50fr+20fr, Patas monkey and leopard.

1971, Feb. 9 Photo. *Perf. 12½x12*

B3	SP1	5fr +5fr multi	1.20	60
B4	SP1	10fr +5fr multi	1.75	1.25
B5	SP1	20fr +5fr multi	2.50	1.75
B6	SP1	30fr +10fr multi	3.50	2.50
B7	SP1	50fr +20fr multi	7.00	5.00
		Nos. B3-B7 (5)	15.95	11.10

Lengué Dancer
SP2

Dancers: 40fr+10fr, Le Lengué. 100fr+40fr, Teke. 140fr+40fr, Englabolo.

1971 Lithographed *Perf. 13*

B8	SP2	20fr +5fr multi	35	20
B9	SP2	40fr +10fr multi	65	40
B10	SP2	100fr +40fr multi	1.75	90
B11	SP2	140fr +40fr multi	2.25	1.20

AIR POST STAMPS
Central African Republic

Abyssinian Roller—AP1

Birds: 200fr, Gold Coast touraco. 500fr, African fish eagle.

Engraved

1960, Sept. 3 *Perf. 13* Unwmkd.

C1	AP1	100fr vio bl, org brn & emer	1.50	65
C2	AP1	200fr multi	3.00	1.25
C3	AP1	500fr Prus bl, emer & red brn	7.50	3.00

Olympic Games Issue
French Equatorial Africa No. C37 Surcharged in Red Like Chad No. C1.

1960, Dec. 15 *Perf. 13*

C4 AP8 250fr on 500fr grnsh blk, blk & sl 6.50 6.50

Issued to commemorate the 17th Olympic Games, Rome, Aug. 25–Sept. 11.

Air Afrique Issue
Common Design Type

1962, Feb. 17 *Perf. 13* Unwmkd.

C5 CD107 50fr vio, lt grn & red brn 75 70

Founding of Air Afrique airline.

Pole Vault
AP1a

1962, July 21 Photo. *Perf. 12x12½*

C6 AP1a 100fr grn, yel, brn & blk 1.50 1.00

Abidjan games.

Red-faced Lovebirds—AP2

Bird: 50fr, Great blue touraco.

1962-63 Engraved *Perf. 13*

C7	AP2	50fr sl grn, bl grn & org	75	35
C8	AP2	250fr multi ('63)	3.75	2.10

Issue dates: 50fr, Nov. 15, 1962; 250fr, Mar. 11, 1963.

Runner with Torch and Palm Branch
AP3

1962, Dec. 24

C9 AP3 100fr gray grn, brn & car 1.50 1.00

Tropics Cup Games, Bangui, Dec. 24–31.

African Postal Union Issue
Common Design Type

1963, Sept. 8 Photo. *Perf. 12½*

C10 CD114 85fr emer, ocher & red 1.25 85

Sun Shining on Africa—AP4

1963, Nov. 9 *Perf. 13x12*

C11 AP4 25fr bl, yel & vio bl 40 30

Issued for African unity.

Europafrica Issue
Common Design Type

1963, Nov. 30 *Perf. 12x13*

C12 CD116 50fr ultra, yel & dk brn 1.35 1.10

Diesel Engine—AP5

Designs: Various Locomotives; 25fr, 50fr, vertical.

1963, Dec. 1 Engraved *Perf. 13*

C13	AP5	20fr brn, cl & dk grn	30	30
C14	AP5	25fr brn, bl & choc	40	30
C15	AP5	50r brn, red lil & vio	80	60
C16	AP5	100fr brn, grn & dl red brn	1.65	1.20
a.		Min. sheet of 4	3.25	3.25

Bangui-Douala railroad project.
No. C16a contains one each of Nos. C13–C16. Size: 189x99mm.

Bangui Cathedral—AP6

1964, Jan. 21 *Perf. 13* Unwmkd.

C17 AP6 100fr yel grn, org brn & bl 1.50 90

Radar Tracking Station and WMO Emblem—AP7

1964, Mar. 23 Engr. *Perf. 13*

C18 AP7 50fr org brn, bl & pur 75 65

World Meteorological Day.

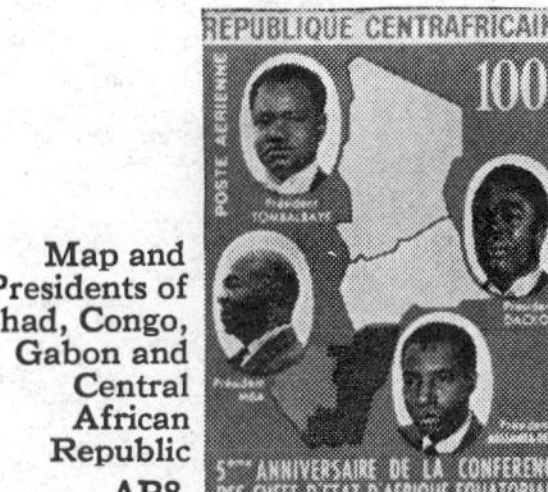

Map and Presidents of Chad, Congo, Gabon and Central African Republic
AP8

1964, June 23 Photo. *Perf. 12½*

C19 AP8 100fr multi 1.50 1.00

Issued to commemorate the 5th anniversary of the Conference of Chiefs of State of Equatorial Africa.

Javelin Throwers—AP9

Designs: 50fr, Basketball game. 100fr, Four runners. 250fr, Swimmers, one in water.

1964, June 23 Engraved *Perf. 13*

C20	AP9	25fr grn, dk brn & lt vio bl	40	20
C21	AP9	50fr blk, car & grn	75	40
C22	AP9	100fr grn, vio bl & dk brn	1.50	80
C23	AP9	250fr grn, blk & car	3.75	2.25
a.		Min. sheet	6.50	6.50

Issued for the 18th Olympic Games, Tokyo, Oct. 10–25, 1964.
No. C23a contains one each of Nos. C20–C23. Size: 128½x99mm.

John F. Kennedy
AP10

1964, July 4 Photo. *Perf. 12½*

C24	AP10	100fr lil, brn & blk	1.65	1.35
a.		Min. sheet of 4	7.50	7.50

Issued in memory of President John F. Kennedy.

Industrial Symbols, Maps of Africa and Europe
AP11

1964, Dec. 19 *Perf. 13x12* Unwmkd.

C25 AP11 50fr yel, org & grn 75 70

See note after Cameroun No. 402.

International Cooperation Year Emblem—AP12

1965, Jan. 2 *Perf. 13*

C26 AP12 100fr red brn, yel & bl 1.50 90

International Cooperation Year.

Nimbus Weather Satellite
AP13

1965, Mar. 23 Engraved *Perf. 13*

C27 AP13 100fr org brn, ultra & blk 1.60 1.00

Fifth World Meteorological Day.

Lincoln and Statue of Liberty
AP14

1965, Apr. 15 Photo. *Perf. 13*

C28 AP14 100fr bluish grn, ind & bis 1.60 90

Centenary of death of Abraham Lincoln.

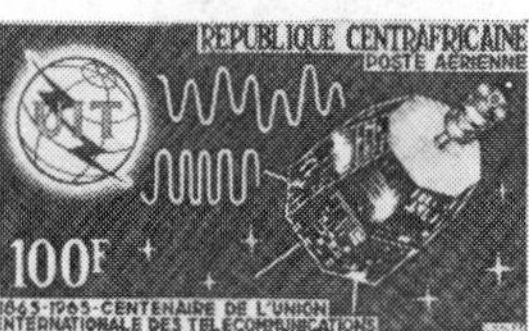

ITU Emblem and Relay Satellite
AP15

1965, May 17 Engr. *Perf. 13*

C29 AP15 100fr dk grn vio bl & brn 1.60 90

Issued to commemorate the centenary of the International Telecommunication Union.

"Housing," New Home in Village
AP16

1965, June 10 Unwmkd.

C30 AP16 100fr ultra, brn & sl grn 1.50 90

See note after No. 52.

Europafrica Issue

Tractor, Cotton Picker, Cotton, Sun and Emblem
AP17

1965, Nov. 7 Photo. *Perf. 12x13*

C31 AP17 50fr multi 70 50

See note after Chad No. C11.

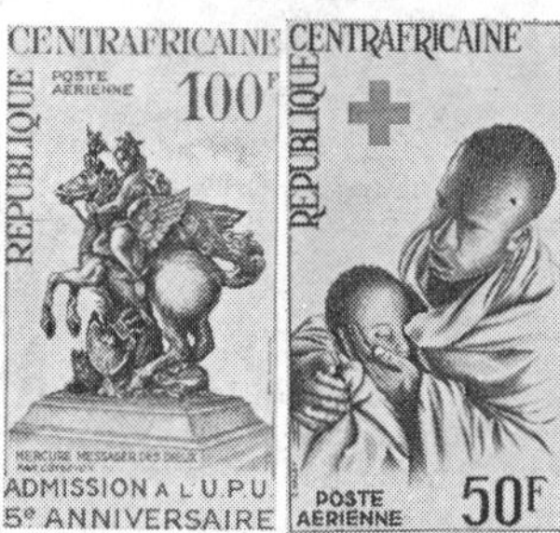

Mercury by Antoine Coysevox
AP18

Father Holding Sick Child
AP19

1965, Dec. 5 Engraved *Perf. 13*

C32 AP18 100fr red brn, bl & blk 1.60 1.00

Issued to commemorate the fifth anniversary of Central African Republic's admission to the Universal Postal Union.

1965, Dec. 12

Design: 100fr, Mother and child.

C33 AP19 50fr dk bl, car & blk 75 50
C34 AP19 100fr red brn, red & brt grn 1.50 1.00

Issued to honor the Red Cross.

Air Afrique Issue
Common Design Type

1966, Aug. 31 Photo. *Perf. 13*

C35 CD123 25fr bl, blk & lem 40 15

Issued to commemorate the introduction of DC-8F planes by Air Afrique.

Surveyor Spacecraft on Moon
AP20

Designs: No. C37, Luna 9 on Moon and Earth. 200fr, Rocket take-off, Jules Verne's "From the Earth to the Moon."

1966, Oct. 24 Photo. *Perf. 12x12½*

C36 AP20 130fr multi 2.00 1.20
C37 AP20 130fr multi 2.00 1.20
C38 AP20 200fr multi 3.00 1.80
a. Souv. sheet of 3 8.00 8.00

Issued to commemorate the conquest of the Moon. No. C38a contains one each of Nos. C36–C38, black marginal inscription and control number. Size: 132x158mm.

Eugene A. Cernan, Gemini 9 and Agena Rocket
AP21

Design: No. C40, Pavel R. Popovich and rocket.

1966, Nov. 14 Photo. *Perf. 13*

C39 AP21 50fr multi 75 35
C40 AP21 50fr multi 75 35

Issued to honor American and Russian astronauts.

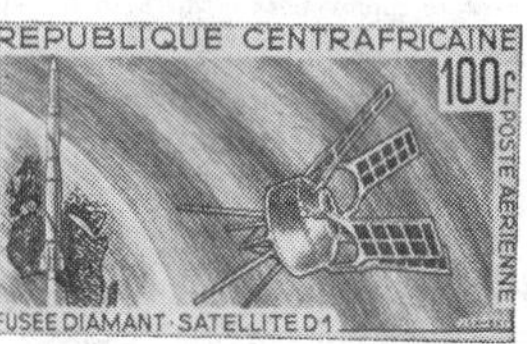

Diamant Rocket, D-1 Satellite and Globe with Map of Africa
AP22

1966, Nov. 14 Engraved

C41 AP22 100fr brt rose lil & brn 1.60 70

Issued to commemorate the launching of France's first satellite, Nov. 26, 1965, and the launching of the D-1 satellite, Feb. 17, 1966.

Exchange of Agricultural and Industrial Products between Africa and Europe
AP23

1966, Dec. 5 Photo. *Perf. 12x13*

C42 AP23 50fr multi 75 45

See note after Gabon No. C46.

No. C35 Surcharged XIX

1967, May 8 *Perf. 13*

C43 CD123 5fr on 25fr multi 15 10

The surcharge obliterates the "2" of the original 25fr denomination.

DC-8F Over M'Poko Airport, Bangui—AP24

1967, July 3 Engraved *Perf. 13*

C44 AP24 100fr sl, dk grn & brn 1.60 75

View of EXPO '67, Montreal
AP25

1967, July 17

C45 AP25 100fr vio bl, dk red brn & dk grn 1.50 70

Issued to commemorate the International Exposition, EXPO '67, Montreal, Apr. 28–Oct. 27.

African Postal Union Issue, 1967
Common Design Type

1967, Sept. 9 Engraved *Perf. 13*

C46 CD124 100fr brt grn, dk car rose & plum 1.50 70

Potez 25 TOE—AP26

Designs: 200fr, Junkers 52. 500fr, Caravelle 11R.

1967, Nov. 24 Engraved *Perf. 13*

C47 AP26 100fr brt bl, brn & gray grn 1.60 65
C48 AP26 200fr dk brn, grn & ind 2.75 1.25
C49 AP26 500fr bl, ind & org brn 7.25 4.00

Presidents Boganda and Bokassa
AP27

1967, Dec. 1 Photo. *Perf. 12½*

C50 AP27 130fr org, red, lt bl & blk 2.00 1.35

9th anniversary of the republic.

Pres. Jean Bedel Bokassa
AP28

1968, Jan. 1 *Perf. 12½x12*

C51 AP28 30fr multi 50 30

Human Rights Flame, Men and Globe—AP29

1968, Mar. 26 Photo. *Perf. 13*

C52 AP29 200fr brt grn, vio & ver 3.00 1.50

International Human Rights Year.

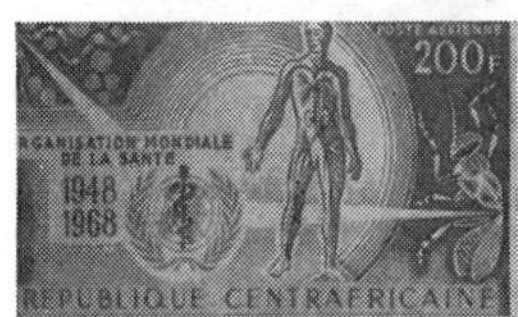

Man, WHO Emblem and Tsetse Fly—AP30

1968, Apr. 8 **Engraved**

C53 AP30 200fr multi 3.00 1.50

Issued to commemorate the 20th anniversary of the World Health Organization.

Javelin Thrower — AP31

Space Probe Landing on Venus — AP32

Design: No. C55, Downhill skier.

1968, Apr. 16 **Engraved** ***Perf. 13***

C54 AP31 200fr choc, dk red & Prus bl 3.00 1.60
C55 AP31 200fr dk red, choc & Prus bl 3.00 1.60

The 1968 Olympic Games.

1968, Apr. 23

C56 AP32 100fr ultra, dk & brt grn 1.50 70

Issued to commemorate the Venus exploration by Venus IV, Oct. 18, 1967.

Marie Curie and "Cancer Destroyed"—AP33

1968, Apr. 30

C57 AP33 100fr vio, brt bl & brn 1.50 70

Issued to commemorate the centenary of the birth of Marie Curie (1867–1934), scientist.

Nos. C36-C37 and C47-C48 Surcharged with New Value

Photogravure; Engraved

1968, Sept. 16 ***Perf. 12x12½, 13***

C58 AP20 5fr on 130fr multi 10 8
C59 AP26 10fr on 100fr multi 15 10
C60 AP26 20fr on 200fr multi 30 12
C61 AP20 50fr on 130fr multi 80 55

On No. C58 the old denomination has been obliterated with "XIX", on No. C61 the obliteration is a rectangular bar. On Nos. C59-C60 the last zero of the old denomination has been obliterated with a black square.

River Boat Type of Regular Issue

Craft: 100fr, "Pie X," Bangui, 1894. 130fr, "Ballay," Bangui, 1891.

1968, Dec. 10 **Engraved** ***Perf. 13***

Size: 48x27mm.

C62 A37 100fr bl, dk brn & ol 1.50 70
C63 A37 130fr brt pink, sl grn & sl 2.00 1.00

PHILEXAFRIQUE Issue

Mme. de Sévigné, French School, 17th Century
AP34

1968, Dec. 17 **Photo.** ***Perf. 12½***

C64 AP34 100fr brn & multi 1.60 1.40

Issued to publicize PHILEXAFRIQUE, Philatelic Exhibition in Abidjan, Feb. 14–23. Printed with alternating brown label.

2nd PHILEXAFRIQUE Issue

Common Design Type

Design: 50fr, Ubangi No. J16, cotton field and Pres. Bokassa.

1969, Feb. 14 **Engraved** ***Perf. 13***

C65 CD128 50fr bis brn, blk & dk grn 90 90

Issued to commemorate the opening of PHILEXAFRIQUE, Abidjan, Feb. 14.

Holocerina Angulata Aur.—AP35

Butterflies and Moths: 20fr, Nudaurelia dione fabr. 30fr, Eustera troglophylla hamp. (vert.). 50fr, Aurivillius aratus west. 100fr, Epiphora albida druce.

1969, Feb. 25 **Photogravure**

C66 AP35 10fr yel & multi 15 6
C67 AP35 20fr vio & multi 30 15
C68 AP35 30fr multi 45 20
C69 AP35 50fr multi 85 40
C70 AP35 100fr multi 1.65 80
Nos. C66-C70 (5) 3.40 1.61

Boxing—AP36

Sport Design: 100fr, Basketball.

1969, Mar. 18 **Photo.** ***Perf. 13***

C71 AP36 50fr multi 75 35
C72 AP36 100fr yel & multi 1.50 60

Apollo 8 over Moonscape—AP37

1969, May 27 **Photo.** ***Perf. 13***

C73 AP37 200fr dp bl, gray & yel 3.00 1.35

Issued to commemorate the U.S. Apollo 8 mission, the first men in orbit around the moon, Dec. 21–27, 1968.

Market Cross, Nuremberg, and Toys—AP38

1969, June 3

C74 AP38 100fr blk, brt rose lil & emer 1.50 1.00

Issued to publicize the International Toy Fair in Nuremberg, Germany.

Napoleon as First Consul, by Anne-Louis Girodet-Trioson
AP39

Designs: 130fr, Napoleon meeting Emperor Francis II, by Antoine Jean Gros (horiz.). 200fr, The Wedding of Napoleon and Marie-Louise, by Georges Rouget (horiz.).

1969, Nov. 4 **Photo.** ***Perf. 12½***

C75 AP39 100fr multi 1.75 1.25
C76 AP39 130fr brn & multi 2.50 1.50
C77 AP39 200fr multi 4.00 3.00

Issued to commemorate the bicentenary of the birth of Napoleon Bonaparte (1769–1821).

Pres. Bokassa, Map of Africa and Flag — AP40

Franklin Delano Roosevelt — AP41

1970, Jan. 1 ***Die-cut*** ***Perf. 10½***

Embossed on Gold Foil

C78 AP40 2000fr gold 25.00 25.00

1970 **Lithographed** ***Perf. 13½x14***

Design: No. C80, Lenin.

C79 AP41 100fr gold, yel, blk & bl 1.35 80
C80 AP41 100fr gold, yel, blk & red 1.25 70

No. C79 issued to commemorate the 25th anniversary of the death of Pres. Franklin Delano Roosevelt (1882–1945); Nos. C80 commemorates the centenary of the birth of Lenin (1870–1924).

Issue dates: No. C79, Apr. 29; No. C80, Apr. 22.

No. C73 Overprinted in Red:

ATTERRISSAGE
d'APOLLO 12
19 novembre 1969

1970, June 1 Photogravure ***Perf. 13***

C81 AP37 200fr multi 8.50 6.50

Issued to commemorate the moon landing mission of Apollo 12, Nov. 14–24, 1969.

AP42

1970, Sept. 15 **Litho.** ***Perf. 10***

C82 AP42 Triptych 2.50 1.25
a. 100fr *Dancer* 1.25 50
b. 100fr *Still life* 1.25 50

Issued to publicize Knokphila 70, 6th International Philatelic Exhibition at Knokke, Belgium, July 4–10. The two stamps and violet blue label are printed se-tenant and imperf. between stamps and label.

Sericulture Type of Regular Issue

1970, Sept. 15 ***Perf. 10***

C83 A45 140fr multi 2.00 1.10

Issued to publicize Operation Bokassa, a plan for the development of the country.

C.A.R. Flag, EXPO Emblem and Pavilion
AP43

1970, Dec. 18 **Litho.** ***Perf. 13½x13***

C84 AP43 200fr red & multi 2.75 1.35

International Exposition EXPO '70, Osaka, Japan.

Soccer
AP44

1970, Dec. 8 ***Perf. 13x13½***

C85 AP44 200fr multi 2.75 1.35

World Soccer Championships, Mexico, May 30–June 21, 1970.

Dove
AP45

1970, Dec. 31

C86 AP45 200fr bl, yel & blk 2.75 1.35

25th anniversary of the United Nations.

Presidents Mobutu, Bokassa, and Tombalbaye—AP46

1971, Jan. 10

C87	AP46	140fr multi	2.00	90

Return of Central African Republic to the United States of Central Africa which also includes Congo Democratic Republic and Chad.

Satellite over Globe—AP47

1971, May 17 Photo. *Perf. 12½*

C88	AP47	100fr multi	1.35	65

3rd World Telecommunications Day.

African Postal Union Issue, 1971

Common Design Type

Design: 100fr, Carved head and UAMPT building, Brazzaville, Congo.

1971, Nov. 13 Photo. *Perf. 13x13½*

C89	CD135	100fr bl & multi	1.35	65

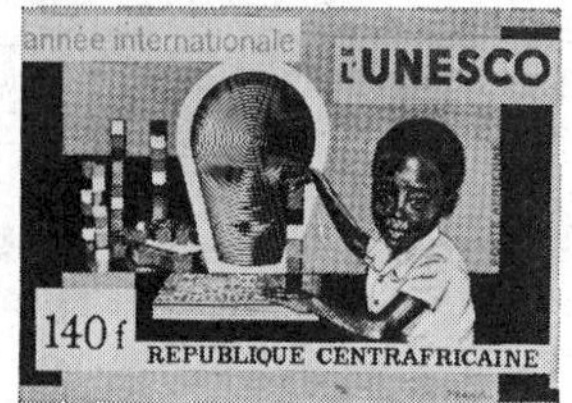

Child and Education Year Emblem—AP48

1971, Nov. 11 Litho. *Perf. 13x13½*

C90	AP48	140fr multi	1.75	75

25th anniversary of the United Nations Educational, Scientific and Cultural Organization (UNESCO).

Fight Against Cancer AP49

Gamal Abdel Nasser AP50

1971, Nov. 20 Photo. *Perf. 12½*

C91	AP49	100fr grn & multi	1.35	60

1972, Jan. 15

C92	AP50	100fr dk red, blk & bis	1.25	60

In memory of Gamal Abdel Nasser (1918–1970), president of Egypt.

Olympic Rings and Boxing—AP51

Design: No. C94, Track and Olympic rings (vert.).

1972, May 26 Engraved *Perf. 13*

C93	AP51	100fr brn org & sep	1.50	60
C94	AP51	100fr grn & vio	1.50	60
a.		Miniature sheet of 2	3.00	3.00

20th Olympic Games, Munich, Aug. 26–Sept. 10. No. C94a contains 2 stamps similar to Nos. C93–C94, but in changed colors. The boxing stamp is red lilac and green, the track stamp ocher and red lilac. Size: 129x98mm.

Tiling's Mail Rocket, 1931, and Mailman—AP52

Designs: 50fr, DC-3 and mailman riding camel (vert.). 150fr, Sirio satellite and rocket (vert.). 200fr, Intelsat 4 and rocket.

1972, Aug. 12

C95	AP52	40fr bl, org & ind	50	25
C96	AP52	50fr bl, brn & org	60	25
C97	AP52	150fr brn, org & gray	1.75	80
C98	AP52	200fr brn, bl & org	2.25	1.00
a.		Souv. sheet of 4	5.25	5.25

Centraphilex 1972, Central African Philatelic Exhibition, Bangui. No. C98a contains one each of Nos. C95–C98. Brown marginal inscription. Size: 200x99½mm.

Europafrica Issue

Arrows with Symbols of Agriculture and Industry AP53

1972, Nov. 17 Litho. *Perf. 13*

C99	AP53	100fr multi	1.10	60

Nos. C93–C94, C94a Overprinted

a. POIDS-MOYEN / LEMECHEV MEDAILLE D'OR

b. LONGUER / WILLIAMS MEDAILLE D'OR

1972, Nov. 24 Engraved

C100	AP51 (a)	100fr brn org & sep	1.35	60
C101	AP51 (b)	100fr grn & vio	1.35	60
a.		Miniature sheet of 2	3.00	3.00

Gold Medal Winners in 20th Olympic Games: Viatscheslav Lemechev, USSR, middleweight boxing (C100); Randy Williams, USA, broad jump (C101).

Lunar Rover and Module—AP54

1972, Dec. 18 Engr. *Perf. 13*

C102	AP54	100fr sl grn, bl & gray	1.20	65

Apollo 16 U.S. moon mission, Apr. 15–27, 1972.

Virgin and Child, by Francesco Pesellino AP55

Design: 150fr, Adoration of the Child with St. John the Baptist and St. Romuald, by Fra Filippo Lippi.

1972, Dec. 25 Photogravure

C103	AP55	100fr gold & multi	1.25	65
C104	AP55	150fr gold & multi	1.85	1.00

Christmas 1972.

Parthenon, Athens, Spyridon Louis, Marathon, 1896—AP56

Designs (Olympic Rings and): 40fr, Arc de Triomphe, Paris, H. Barrelet, single scull, 1900. 50fr, Old Courthouse and Western Arch, St. Louis, Myer Prinstein, triple jump, 1904. 100fr, Tower, London, Henry Taylor, swimming, 1908. 150fr, City Hall, Stockholm, Greco-Roman wrestling, 1912.

1972, Dec. 28 Engraved

C105	AP56	30fr brt grn, mag & brn	40	12
C106	AP56	40fr vio bl, emer & brn	50	18
C107	AP56	50fr car rose, vio bl & Prus bl	60	25
C108	AP56	100fr sl, red lil & brn	1.25	55
C109	AP56	150fr red lil, blk & Prus bl	1.85	90
		Nos. C105-C109 (5)	4.60	2.00

Olympic Games 1896–1912.

WHO Emblem, Surgeon and Nurse—AP57

1973, Apr. 7 Photo. *Perf. 13*

C110	AP57	100fr multi	1.25	70

World Health Organization, 25th anniversary.

World Map, Arrows, Waves AP58

1973, May 17 Litho. *Perf. 12½*

C111	AP58	200fr lt bl, dp org & blk	2.00	1.20

5th International Telecommunications Day.

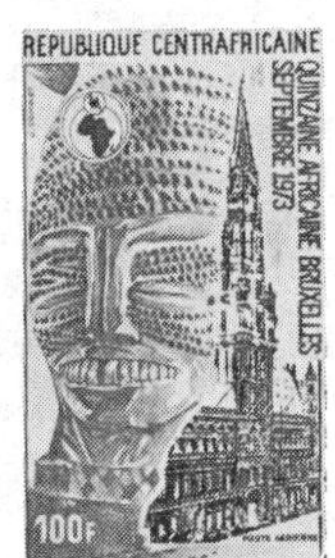

Head and City Hall, Brussels AP58a

1973, Sept. 17 Engr. *Perf. 13*

C112	AP58a	100fr pur, ocher & brn	1.25	70

African Weeks, Brussels, Sept. 15–30, 1973.

Europafrica Issue

Map of Central African Republic with Industry and Agriculture, Young Man—AP59

1973, Sept. 28 Engraved *Perf. 13*

C113	AP59	100fr sep, grn & org	1.10	70

Carrier Pigeon with Letter and UPU Emblem—AP60

1973, Oct. 9 Photogravure

C114	AP60	200fr multi	2.25	1.40

Universal Postal Union Day.

WMO Emblem, Weather Map—AP61

1973, Oct. 20 Engraved *Perf. 13*

C115	AP61	150fr brt ultra & sl grn	1.50	75

Centenary of international meteorological cooperation.

Copernicus, Heliocentric System
AP62

1973, Nov. 2 **Photogravure**

C116	AP62	100fr gold & multi	1.15	70

500th anniversary of the birth of Nicolaus Copernicus (1473–1543), Polish astronomer.

Pres. Bokassa
AP63

Pres. Bokassa
AP64

Rocket Launch and Apollo 17 Badge
AP65

1973, Nov. 30 **Photo.** ***Perf. 12½***

C117	AP63	50fr multi	50	35
C118	AP64	100fr multi	1.00	70

1973, Dec. 15 **Engraved** ***Perf. 13***

Designs: 65fr, Capsule over moonscape (horiz.). 100fr, Moon landing (horiz.). 150fr, Astronauts on moon. 200fr, Splash-down with parachutes and badge.

C119	AP65	50fr ver, gray grn & brn	50	40
C120	AP65	65fr dk brn, brn red & sl grn	60	50
C121	AP65	100fr ver, sl & choc	1.00	70
C122	AP65	150fr brn, ol & sl grn	1.40	1.00
C123	AP65	200fr red, bl & sl grn	2.00	1.40
		Nos. C119-C123 (5)	5.50	4.00

Apollo 17 U.S. moon mission, Dec. 7–19, 1972.

St. Teresa
AP66

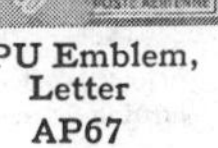

UPU Emblem, Letter
AP67

1973, Dec. 25

C124	AP66	500fr vio bl & grnsh bl	5.00	3.00

Centenary of the birth of St. Teresa of the Infant Jesus, the Little Flower (1873–1897), Carmelite nun.

1974, Oct. 9 **Engraved** ***Perf. 13***

C125	AP67	500fr multi	5.00	3.50

Centenary of Universal Postal Union.

Presidents and Flags of Cameroun, CAR, Gabon and Congo
AP68

1974, Dec. 8 **Photogravure** ***Perf. 13***

C126	AP68	100fr gold & multi	90	65

See note after Cameroun No. 595.

Marshal Bokassa
AP69

Design: 100fr, Bokassa in Marshal's uniform with cape.

1975, Feb. 22 **Photo.** ***Perf. 13***

C127	AP69	50fr tan & multi	40	30
C128	AP69	100fr tan & multi	80	60

Jean Bedel Bokassa, President for Life and Marshal of the Republic.

Mask, Map of Africa, Arphila Emblem
AP70

Albert Schweitzer and Dugout, Lambarene
AP71

1975, Aug. 25 **Engr.** ***Perf. 13***

C129	AP70	100fr brt bl, red brn & red	1.00	50

ARPHILA 75 International Philatelic Exhibition, Paris, June 6–16.

1975, Sept. 30 **Engr.** ***Perf. 13***

C130	AP71	200fr blk, ultra & ol	2.00	1.00

Dr. Albert Schweitzer (1875–1965), medical missionary and musician.

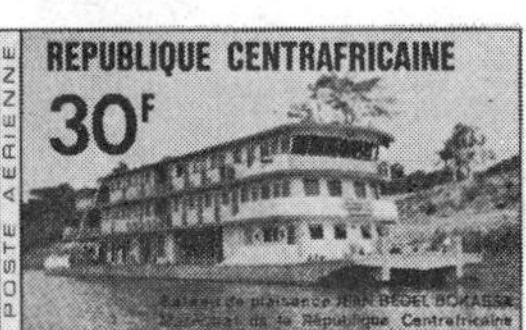

Pres. Bokassa's Houseboat, Bow—AP72

Design: 40fr, Pres. Bokassa's houseboat, stern.

1976, Feb. 22 **Litho.** ***Perf. 13***

C131	AP72	30fr multi	25	15
C132	AP72	40fr multi	35	20

Monument to Franco-CAR Cooperation
AP73

Presidents and Flags of France and CAR
AP74

1976, Mar. 5

C133	AP73	100fr multi	80	50
C134	AP74	200fr multi	1.60	1.00

Official visit of Pres. Valery Giscard d'Estaing to Central African Republic, Mar. 5–8.

Apollo Soyuz Type, 1976

Designs: 100fr, Soyuz space ship. 200fr, Apollo space ship. 300fr, Astronauts and cosmonauts in cabin. 500fr, Apollo and Soyuz after link-up.

1976, June 14 **Litho.** ***Perf. 14x13½***

C135	A90	100fr multi	1.00	38
C136	A90	200fr multi	2.00	85
C137	A90	300fr multi	3.00	1.25

Souvenir Sheet

C138	A90	500fr multi	4.75	2.25

Apollo Soyuz space test project, Russo-American cooperation, launched July 15, link-up July 17. No. C138 has multicolored margin showing Apollo Soyuz insignia. Size: 103½x78mm.

French Hussar
AP75

Uniforms: 125fr, Scottish "Black Watch." 150fr, German dragoon. 200fr, British grenadier. 250fr, American ranger. 450fr, American dragoon.

1976, July 4 ***Perf. 13½***

C139	AP75	100fr multi	95	30
C140	AP75	125fr multi	1.20	50
C141	AP75	150fr multi	1.50	60
C142	AP75	200fr multi	1.90	70
C143	AP75	250fr multi	2.25	90
		Nos. C139-C143 (5)	7.80	3.00

Souvenir Sheet

C144	AP75	450fr multi	4.25	1.90

American Bicentennial. No. C144 has U.S. Bicentennial emblem in tri-color in margin, black inscription. Size: 118x80 mm.

Acherontia Atropos—AP76

Design: 100fr, Papilio nireus and heniocha marnois.

1976, Sept. 20 **Litho.** ***Perf. 12½***

C145	AP76	50fr multi	40	25
C146	AP76	100fr multi	80	50

Olympic Winners Type, 1976

Designs: 100fr, Women's figure skating, Dorothy Hamill (vert.). 200fr, Ice skating, Alexander Gorshkov and Ludmilla Pakhomova. 300fr, Men's figure skating, John Curry (vert.). 500fr, Down-hill skiing, Rosi Mittermaier (vert.).

1976, Sept. 23 **Litho.** ***Perf. 13½***

C147	A92	100fr multi	95	40
C148	A92	200fr multi	1.90	90
C149	A92	300fr multi	3.00	1.35

Souvenir Sheet

C150	A92	500fr multi	4.75	2.25

12th Winter Olympic Games winners, Innsbruck. No. C150 has multicolored margin showing Olympic flags and eternal flame, black inscriptions. Size: 103x78 mm.

Viking Mars Type, 1976

Designs: 100fr, Phases of Mars landing. 200fr, Viking descending on Mars (horiz.). 300fr, Viking probe. 500fr, Viking flight to Mars (horiz.).

1976, Dec.

C151	A93	100fr multi	95	35
C152	A93	200fr multi	1.90	85
C153	A93	300fr multi	3.00	1.20

Souvenir Sheet

C154	A93	500fr multi	4.75	2.25

Viking Mars project. No. C154 has multicolored margin showing flight control room. Size: 102x77mm.

Empire

Stamps of 1973–76 Overprinted with Bars and "EMPIRE CENTRAFRICAIN" in Black, Violet Blue or Gold

Printing and Perforations as Before

1977, March

Multicolored

C155	AP68	100fr (#C126;B)	90	70
C156	AP70	100fr (#C129;VB)	90	70
C157	AP73	100fr (#C133;G)	90	70
C158	AP71	200fr (#C130;B)	2.00	1.50
C159	AP67	500fr (#C125;B)	5.50	4.00
		Nos. C155-C159 (5)	10.20	7.60

No bar on No. C159.

Stamps of 1976 Overprinted "EMPIRE CENTRAFRICAIN" in Black on Silver Panel

1977, Apr. 1

C160	AP76	50fr multi (#C145)	50	30
C161	A90	100fr multi (#C135)	90	70
C162	AP75	100fr multi (#C139)	80	60
C163	AP76	100fr multi (#C146)	80	60

C164	A92	100fr multi (#C147)	80	60
C165	A93	100fr multi (#C151)	80	60
C166	AP75	125fr multi (#C140)	1.00	80
C167	AP75	150fr multi (#C141)	1.20	90
C168	A90	200fr multi (#C136)	2.00	1.50
C169	AP75	200fr multi (#C142)	1.60	1.20
C170	A92	200fr multi (#C148)	1.60	1.20
C171	A93	200fr multi (#C152)	1.60	1.20
C172	AP75	250fr multi (#C143)	2.00	1.50
C173	A90	300fr multi (#C137)	3.00	2.25
C174	A92	300fr multi (#C149)	2.50	1.85
C175	A93	300fr multi (#C153)	2.50	1.85
		Nos. C160-C175 (16)	23.60	17.65

Souvenir Sheets

C176	AP75	450fr multi (#C144)	3.75	3.75
C177	A90	500fr multi (#C138)	4.00	4.00
C178	A92	500fr multi (#C150)	4.00	4.00
C179	A93	500fr multi (#C154)	4.00	4.00

Overprint on type AP75 is in upper and lower case letters.

Nobel Prize Type, 1977

Designs: 100fr, Rudyard Kipling. 200fr, Ernest Hemingway. 300fr, Luigi Pirandello. 500fr, Rabindranath Tagore.

1977, Apr. 1 Litho. *Perf. 13½*

C180	A94	100fr multi	95	35
C181	A94	200fr multi	1.90	85
C182	A94	300fr multi	3.00	1.20

Souvenir Sheet

C183	A94	500fr multi	4.75	2.25

Nobel Prize winners. No. C183 has multicolored margin with black inscription. Size: 118x80mm.

Zeppelin Type of 1977

Designs: 100fr, Germany No. C42 and North Pole. 200fr, Germany No. C44 and Science and Industry Building, Chicago. 300fr, Germany No. C35 and Brandenburg Gate, Berlin. 500fr, U.S. No. C14 and U.S. Capitol, Washington, D.C.

1977, Apr. 11 Litho. *Perf. 11*

C184	A95	100fr multi	95	35
C185	A95	200fr multi	1.90	85
C186	A95	300fr multi	3.00	1.20

Souvenir Sheet

C187	A95	500fr multi	4.75	2.25

75th anniversary of Zeppelin. No. C187 has multicolored margin showing early Zeppelin and 15 Zeppelin stamps from various countries. Size: 129x90mm.

Bokassa Type of 1977

1977, Dec. 4 Litho. *Perf. 13½*

C188	A98	200fr multi	1.60	1.00
C189	A98	300fr multi	2.50	1.50
a.		Souvenir sheet, 500fr	4.00	3.00

Coronation of Emperor Bokassa I, Dec. 4. No. C189a contains a horizontal stamp in similar design; multicolored margin with eagle and government buildings. Size: 112x80mm. A 2500fr gold embossed horizontal stamp in similar design exists.

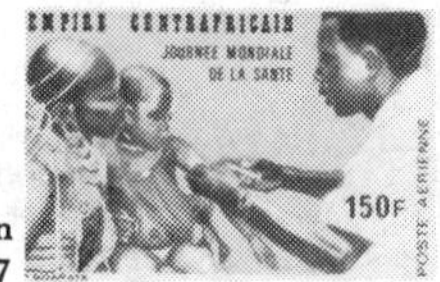

Vaccination AP77

1977 Litho. *Perf. 14x13½*

C190	AP77	150fr multi	1.50	75

World Health Day.

Communications Type of 1978

Designs: 100fr, Balloon and spaceships docking in space. 200fr, Hydrofoil and Concorde. 500fr, Tom-tom and Zeppelin.

1978, May 17 Litho. *Perf. 13½*

C191	A107	100fr multi	1.00	50
C192	A107	200fr multi	2.00	1.00

Souvenir Sheet

C193	A107	500fr multi	5.50	3.50

Century of progress of posts and telecommunications. No. C193 contains one stamp (53x35mm.); multicolored margin shows allegory of posts. Size: 104x70mm.

Clement Ader and his Plane—AP78

Designs: 50fr, Wilbur and Orville Wright and plane. 60fr, John W. Alcock, Arthur W. Brown and plane. 100fr, Alan Cobham and plane 150fr, Claude Dornier and hydroplane. 500fr, Wilbur and Orville Wright and plane.

1978, Sept. 19 *Perf. 14*

C194	AP78	40fr multi	45	20
C195	AP78	50fr multi	55	25
C196	AP78	60fr multi	65	30
C197	AP78	100fr multi	1.10	50
C198	AP78	150fr multi	1.60	75
		Nos. C194-C198 (5)	4.35	2.00

Souvenir Sheet

C199	AP78	500fr multi	5.50	

History of aviation. No. C199 has multicolored margin showing Concorde. Size: 116x80mm.

Philexafrique II—Essen Issue
Common Design Types

Designs: No. C200, Crocodile and Central African Rep. No. C3. No. C201, Birds and Mecklenburg-Schwerin No. 1.

1978, Nov. 1 Litho. *Perf. 12½*

C200	CD138	100fr multi	1.00	50
C201	CD139	100fr multi	1.00	50

Nos. C200–C201 printed se-tenant.

Bokassa Type 1978

Design: 150fr, Catherine and Jean Bedel Bokassa (horiz.).

1978, Dec. 4 Litho. *Perf. 13*

C202	A113	150fr multi	1.50	75

First anniversary of coronation. A 1000fr gold embossed souvenir sheet showing Emperor Bokassa exists.

Rowland Hill Type of 1978

Designs (Rowland Hill and): 100fr, Mailman and Tuscany No. 23. 200fr, Balloon and France No. 1. 500fr, Central Africa Nos. 1–2.

1978, Dec. 27

C203	A114	100fr multi	1.00	50
C204	A114	200fr multi	2.00	1.00

Souvenir Sheet

C205	A114	500fr multi	5.00	2.50

Sir Rowland Hill (1795–1879), originator of penny postage. No. C205 contains one stamp (37½x39mm.); multicolored margin shows Penny Black. Size: 83x85mm. 1500fr gold embossed stamp and souvenir sheet exist.

IYC Type of 1979

Designs (UNICEF, Eagle Emblems and): 100fr, Chinese girl flying kites and German Do-X flying boat, 1929. 200fr, Boys playing leapfrog, hurdler and Olympic emblem. 500fr, Child with abacus and Albert Einstein with his equation.

1979, Mar. 6 *Perf. 13½*

C206	A115	100fr multi	1.00	50
C207	A115	200fr multi	2.00	1.00

Souvenir Sheet

C208	A115	500fr multi	5.00	2.50

International Year of the Child. No. C208 contains one stamp (56x33mm.); multicolored margin shows various spacecraft. Size: 110x79mm. 1500fr gold embossed stamp and souvenir sheet exist.

Olympic Type of 1979

Designs (Moscow '80 Emblem, various Sports and): 100fr, Hurdles and "B". 200fr, Broad jump and "A".

1979, Mar. 16 Litho. *Perf. 13*

C209	A116	100fr multi	1.00	50
C210	A116	200fr multi	2.00	1.00

22nd Olympic Games, Moscow, July 19–Aug. 3, 1980. A 1500fr gold embossed souvenir sheet exists showing diver, runner and javelin.

Type of 1979

Design: 60fr, Horse.

1979, Aug. Litho. *Perf. 13*

C211	A119	60fr multi	48	25

National Husbandry Association.

Nos. C151-C154 Overprinted "ALUNISSAGE/APOLLO XI/ JUILLET 1969" and Emblem in Black or Silver

1979, Oct. Litho. *Perf. 14×13½*

C212	A93	100fr multi	80	40
C213	A93	200fr multi	1.60	80
C214	A93	300fr multi	2.40	1.20

Souvenir Sheet

C215	A93	500fr multi (S)	4.25	2.25

Apollo 11 moon landing, 10th anniversary.

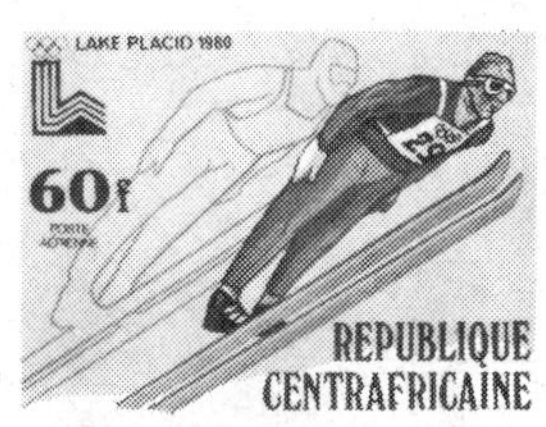

Ski Jump, Lake Placid '80 Emblem AP79

Lake Placid Emblem and: 100fr, Downhill skiing. 200fr, Hockey. 300fr, Slalom. 500fr, Bobsledding.

1979, Nov. 11 Litho. *Perf. 13½*

C216	AP79	60fr multi	48	25
C217	AP79	100fr multi	80	40
C218	AP79	200fr multi	1.60	80
C219	AP79	300fr multi	2.40	1.20

Souvenir Sheet

C220	AP79	500fr multi	4.25	2.25

13th Winter Olympics Games, Lake Placid, N.Y., Feb. 12-24, 1980. No.C 220 has multicolored margin showing skiers. Size 113×78mm.

Space Type of 1980

1980, Apr. 8 Litho. *Perf. 13½*

C221	A125	150fr *Early satellites*	1.20	60
C222	A125	200fr *Space shuttle*	1.60	80

Souvenir Sheet

C223	A125	500fr *Apollo 11, Armstrong*	4.00	2.00

Space explorations No. C223 has multicolored margin showing Neil Armstrong on moon. Size: 85x58½mm.

Nos. C216-C220 Overprinted:

a. VAINQUEUR / INNAVER / AUTRICHE

b. VAINQUEUR / MOSER-PROELL / AUTRICHE

c. VAINQUEUR / ETATS-UNIS

d. VAINQUEUR / STENMARK / SUEDE

e. VAINQUEURS / SCHAERER-BENZ / SUISSE

1980, May 12 Litho. *Perf. 13½*

C224	AP79 (a)	60fr multi	48	25
C225	AP79 (b)	100fr multi	80	40
C226	AP79 (c)	200fr multi	1.60	80
C227	AP79 (d)	300fr multi	2.40	1.20

Souvenir Sheet

C228	AP79 (e)	500fr multi	4.00	2.00

World Telecommunications Day—AP80

1980, June 26 Litho. *Perf. 12½*

C229	AP80	100fr multi	80	40
C230	AP80	150fr multi, vert.	1.20	60

Olympic Type of 1980

1980, July 25 Litho. *Perf. 13½*

C231	A126	100fr *Boxing*	80	40
C232	A126	150fr *Hurdles*	1.20	60

Souvenir Sheet

C233	A126	250fr *Long jump*	2.00	1.00

22nd Summer Olympic Games, Moscow, July 19-Aug. 3. No. C233 contains one stamp (39x36mm); multicolored margin shows satellite, Olympic rings, Moscow '80 emblem, Kremlin. Size: 87x84mm.

Europe-Africa Type of 1980

1980, Nov. 4 Litho. *Perf. 13½*

C234	A127	150fr *Meteorology*	1.20	60
C235	A127	200fr *Aviation*	1.60	80

Souvenir Sheet

C236	A127	500fr *Concorde jet*	4.00	2.00

No. C236 contains one stamp (41½x29mm.); multicolored margin showing jet, flags and maps. Size: 89x64½mm.

Soccer Type of 1981

1981, Jan. 13 Litho. *Perf. 13½*

C237	A130	100fr Netherlands	80	40
C238	A130	200fr Spain	1.60	80

Souvenir Sheet

C239	A130	500fr Argentina	4.00	2.00

ESPANA '82 World Cup Soccer Championship. No. C239 has multicolored margin showing soccer scenes and teams. Size: 119x87mm.

Jacob Wrestling with the Angel, by Rembrandt—AP81

Rembrandt Paintings: 90fr, Christ during the Storm. 150fr, Jeremiah Mourning the Destruction of Jerusalem. 250fr, Tobit Accusing Anne of Theft of a Goat. 500fr, Belshazzar's Feast (horiz.).

1981, Feb. 20 *Perf. 12½*

C240	AP81	60fr multi	50	25
C241	AP81	90fr multi	70	35
C242	AP81	150fr multi	1.20	60
C243	AP81	250fr multi	2.00	1.00

Souvenir Sheet

C244	AP81	500fr multi	4.00	2.00

No. C244 has gray and light brown margin showing figures by Rembrandt. Size: 105x80mm.

Picasso Type of 1981

Paintings: 150fr, Woman in Mirror with Self-portrait. 200fr, Woman Sleeping, The Dream. 500fr, Portrait of Maia (the Artist's Daughter).

1981, June 30 **Litho.** ***Perf. 13½***

C245	A133	150fr multi	1.20	60
C246	A133	200fr multi	1.60	80

Souvenir Sheet

C247	A133	500fr multi	4.00	2.00

No. C247 contains one stamp (42x46mm.); multicolored margin shows entire painting. Size: 78½x113½mm.

Nos. C231-C233 Overprinted with Event, Winner and Country in Gold.

1981 **Litho.** ***Perf. 13½***

C248	A126	100fr multi	80	40
C249	A126	150fr multi	1.20	60

Souvenir Sheet

C250	A126	250fr multi	2.00	1.00

Royal Wedding Type of 1981

1981, Aug. 20 **Litho.** ***Perf. 13½***

C251	A136	150fr Prince of Wales arms	1.20	60
C252	A136	200fr Palace	1.60	80

Souvenir Sheet

C253	A136	500fr St. Paul's Cathedral	4.00	2.00

No. C253 contains one stamp (60x32mm.); multicolored margin shows arms. Size: 120x70mm.

Navigator Type of 1981

1981, Sept. 4 **Litho.** ***Perf. 13½***

C254	A139	100fr O. Kersauson	80	40
C255	A139	200fr Chichester	1.60	80

Souvenir Sheet

C256	A139	500fr A. Colas	4.00	2.00

No. C256 has multicolored margin showing ships. Size: 100x80mm.

Lizard—AP82

1981, Oct. 30 ***Perf. 12½x13***

C257	AP82	30fr shown	25	12
C258	AP82	60fr Snake	50	25
C259	AP82	110fr Crocodile	90	45

Christmas Type of 1981

1981, Dec. 24 ***Perf. 13½***

C260	A143	140fr Correggio	1.15	60
C261	A143	200fr Gentileschi, 1610	1.60	80

Souvenir Sheet

C262	A143	500fr Holy Family, by Cranach	4.00	2.00

No. C262 contains one stamp (41x50mm.); multicolored margin shows entire painting. Size: 81x98mm.

Animal Type of 1982

1982, Jan. 22 **Litho.** ***Perf. 13½***

C263	A145	300fr Mandrill	2.40	1.20
C264	A145	500fr Lion	4.00	2.00

Souvenir Sheet

C265	A145	600fr Nile crocodiles	5.00	2.50

No. C265 contains one stamp (47x38mm.); multicolored margin shows crocodiles. Size: 100x80mm.

Transportation Type of 1982

1982, Feb. 27 **Litho.** ***Perf. 13½***

C266	A147	300fr Savannah cargo ship	2.40	1.25
C267	A147	500fr Columbia space shuttle	4.00	2.00

Souvenir Sheet

C268	A147	600fr Spirit of Locomotion emblem	5.00	2.50

No. C268 contains one stamp (39x43mm.); multicolored margin shows modes of transportation. Size: 101x81mm.

Olympic Type of 1982

1982, July 24 **Litho.** ***Perf. 13½***

C269	A149	300fr Diving	2.50	1.25
C270	A149	500fr Equestrian	4.00	2.00

Souvenir Sheet

C271	A149	600fr Basketball	5.00	2.50

No. C271 contains one stamp (38x56mm.); multicolored margin shows city views. Size: 80x108mm.

Diana Type of 1982

1982, July 20 **Litho.** ***Perf. 13½***

C272	A150	300fr multi	2.50	1.25
C273	A150	500fr multi	4.00	2.00

Souvenir Sheet

C274	A150	600fr multi	5.00	2.50

No. C274 contains one stamp (56x32mm.). Size: 120x75mm.

Christmas 1982—AP83

Raphael Paintings.

1982, Dec. ***Perf. 13***

C275	AP83	150fr Beautiful Gardener	1.20	60
C276	AP83	500fr Holy Family	4.00	2.00

AIR POST SEMI-POSTAL STAMPS

Central African Republic

Isis of Kalabsha
SPAP1

Engraved

1964, March 7 *Perf. 13* Unwmkd.

CB1	SPAP1	25fr +10fr ol, ultra & brt pink	1.00	1.00
CB2	SPAP1	50fr +10fr dk bl grn, ol & red brn	1.50	1.50
CB3	SPAP1	100fr +10fr ol gray, lil & mar	2.50	2.50

Issued to publicize the UNESCO world campaign to save historic monuments in Nubia.

African Infants and Globe—SPAP2

1971, Dec. 11 Litho. *Perf. 13x13½*

CB4	SPAP2	140fr +50fr multi	2.50	1.50

25th anniversary of the United Nations International Children's Fund (UNICEF), and Children's Day.

POSTAGE DUE STAMPS

Central African Republic

Sternotomis Virescens—D1

Beetles: No. J2, Sternotomis gama. No. J3, Augosoma centaurus. No. J4, Phosphorus virescens and ceroplesis carabarica. No. J5, Cetoine scaraboidae. No. J6, Ceroplesis S.P. No. J7, Macrorhina S.P. No. J8, Cetoine scaraboidae. No. J9, Phryneta leprosa. No. J10, Taurina longiceps. J11, Monohamus griseoplagiatus. J12, Jambonus trifasciatus.

Engraved

1962, Oct. 15 *Perf. 11* Unwmkd.

J1	D1	50c grn & dp org	5	5
J2	D1	50c grn & dp org	5	5
J3	D1	1fr blk, brn & lt grn	10	10
J4	D1	1fr blk, brn & lt grn	10	10
J5	D1	2fr blk, org & yel grn	10	10
J6	D1	2fr blk & red org	10	10
J7	D1	5fr brn, org & grn	18	18
J8	D1	5fr brn, org, grn & red	18	18
J9	D1	10fr blk, grn & brn	45	45
J10	D1	10fr blk, brn & grn	45	45
J11	D1	25fr blk, bl grn & brn	70	70
J12	D1	25fr blk, brn & bl grn	70	70
		Nos. J1-J12 (12)	3.16	3.16

Each two stamps of the same denomination are printed together in the sheet, se-tenant at the base.

MILITARY STAMPS

Central African Republic

No. 1 Overprinted **FM**

Engraved

1962, Jan. 1 *Perf. 13* Unwmkd.

M1	A1	bl, car, grn & yel	12.50	12.50

No. 1 Overprinted **=** **FM**

1963

M2	A1	bl, car, grn & yel	13.50	13.50

OFFICIAL STAMPS

Central African Republic

Coat of Arms
O1

Imprint: "d'après G. RICHER SO.GE.IM."

Perf. 13x12½

1965-69 Litho. Unwmkd.

Arms in Original Colors

O1	O1	1fr blk & brn org	6	6
O2	O1	2fr blk & vio	7	6
O3	O1	5fr blk & gray	10	6
O4	O1	10fr blk & grn	28	12
O5	O1	20fr blk & red brn	45	32
O6	O1	30fr blk & emer ('69)	80	60
O7	O1	50fr blk & dk bl	1.00	80
O8	O1	100fr blk & bis	2.10	1.25
O9	O1	130fr blk & ver ('69)	3.25	2.50
O10	O1	200fr blk & cl	4.50	3.00
		Nos. O1-O10 (10)	12.61	8.77

Redrawn

Imprint: "d'après G. RICHER DELRIEU"

1971 Photo. *Perf. 12x12½*

Arms in Original Colors

O11	O1	5fr blk & gray	18	18
O12	O1	30fr blk & emer	45	28
O13	O1	40fr blk & dp cl	60	35
O14	O1	100fr blk & bis	1.40	70
O15	O1	140fr blk & lt bl	2.50	1.00
O16	O1	200fr blk & cl	3.25	1.60
		Nos. O11-O16 (6)	8.38	4.11

Empire

Nos. O11, O13-O16 Overprinted with Bar and "EMPIRE CENTRAFRICAIN"

1977 Lithographed *Perf. 12x12½*

O17	O1	5fr multi	18	15
O18	O1	40fr multi	35	28
O19	O1	100fr multi	80	55
O20	O1	140fr multi	1.20	85
O21	O1	200fr multi	1.85	1.35
		Nos. O17-O21 (5)	4.38	3.18

Type of 1965 Inscribed: "EMPIRE CENTRAFRICAIN"

1978, July Litho. *Perf. 12½*

O22	O1	1fr multi	3	3
O23	O1	2fr multi	3	3
O24	O1	5fr multi	5	5
O25	O1	10fr multi	12	12
O26	O1	15fr multi	15	15
O27	O1	20fr multi	20	20
O28	O1	30fr multi	30	30
O29	O1	40fr multi	40	40
O30	O1	50fr multi	50	50
O31	O1	60fr multi	60	60
O32	O1	100fr multi	1.00	1.00
O33	O1	130fr multi	1.30	1.30
O34	O1	140fr multi	1.40	1.40
O35	O1	200fr multi	2.00	2.00
		Nos. O22-O35 (14)	8.08	8.08

CENTRAL LITHUANIA

(lĭth'ů-ā'nĭ-ȧ)

LOCATION—North of Poland and east of Lithuania.

CAPITAL—Vilnius.

At one time Central Lithuania was a grand duchy of Lithuania but at the end of the 18th Century it fell under Russian rule. After World War I, Lithuania regained her sovereignty but certain areas were occupied by Poland. During the Russo-Polish war this territory was seized by Lithuania whose claim was promptly recognized by the Soviet Government. Under the leadership of the Polish General Zeligowski the territory was recaptured and it was during this occupation the stamps of Central Lithuania came into being. Subsequently the territory became a part of Poland.

100 Fennigi = 1 Markka

Coat of Arms
A1

Perf. 11½, Imperf.

1920–21 Typo. Unwmkd.

1	A1	25f red	30	50
2	A1	25f dk grn ('21)	30	50
3	A1	1m blue	30	50
4	A1	1m dk brn ('21)	30	50
5	A1	2m violet	30	50
6	A1	2m org ('21)	30	50
		Nos. 1-6 (6)	1.80	3.00

Lithuanian Stamps of 1919 Surcharged in Blue or Black

Wmkd. Wavy Lines. (145)

Perf. 11½x12, 12½x11½, 14

1920, Nov. 23

13	A5	2m on 15sk lil	10.00	10.00
a.		Invtd surch.	*250.00*	
14	A5	4m on 10sk red	10.00	10.00
a.		Invtd surch.	*250.00*	
15	A5	4m on 20sk dl bl (Bk)	10.00	10.00
a.		Invtd surch.	*250.00*	
16	A5	4m on 30sk buff	10.00	10.00
a.		Invtd surch.	*250.00*	
17	A6	6m on 50sk lt grn	10.00	10.00
a.		4m on 50sk lt grn (error)	*250.00*	
b.		10m on 50sk lt grn (error)	*250.00*	
18	A6	6m on 60sk vio & red	10.00	10.00
a.		4m on 60sk vio & red (error)	*250.00*	
b.		10m on 60sk vio & red (error)	*250.00*	
19	A6	6m on 75sk bis & red	10.00	10.00
a.		4m on 75sk bis & red (error)	*250.00*	
b.		10m on 75sk bis & red (error)	*250.00*	
20	A8	10m on 1auk gray & red	15.00	15.00
a.		Invtd. surch.	*375.00*	
21	A8	10m on 3auk lt brn & red	*400.00*	*500.00*
22	A8	10m on 5auk bl grn & red	*400.00*	*500.00*
		Nos. 13-22 (10)	*885.00*	*1,085.*

Reprints of Nos. 17a, 17b, 18a, 18b, 19a, 19b. Price, each $75.

Counterfeits of Nos. 21–22 exist.

Lithuanian Girl
A2

Warrior
A3

Holy Gate of Vilnius
A4

Tower and Cathedral, Vilnius
A5

Rector's Insignia
A6

Gen. Lucien Zeligowski
A7

Perf. 11½, Imperf.

1920 Litho. Unwmkd.

23	A2	25f gray	25	40
24	A3	1m orange	25	40
25	A4	2m claret	50	60
26	A5	4m gray grn & buff	50	60
27	A6	6m rose & gray	1.00	1.25
28	A7	10m brn & yel	2.50	3.00
		Nos. 23-28 (6)	5.00	6.25

St. Anne's Church, Vilnius
A8

White Eagle and White Knight Vytis
A10

St. Stanislas Cathedral, Vilnius
A9

Queen Hedwig and King Ladislas II Jagello
A11

Coat of Arms of Vilnius
A12

Poczobut Astronomical Observatory
A13

Union of Lithuania and Poland
A14

Tadeusz Kosciuszko and Adam Mickiewicz
A15

1921 *Perf. 11½, 13½, 14, Imperf.*

35	A8	1(m) dk gray & yel	50	75
36	A9	2(m) rose & grn	50	75
37	A10	3(m) dk grn	50	75
38	A11	4(m) brn & buff	50	75
39	A12	5(m) red brn	50	75
40	A13	6(m) sl & buff	50	1.00
41	A14	10(m) red vio & buff	1.25	1.75
42	A15	20(m) blk brn & buff	1.50	1.75
		Nos. 35-42 (8)	5.75	8.25

Peasant Girl Sowing
A16

Allegory: Peace and Industry
A19

White Eagle and Vytis
A17

Great Theater at Vilnius
A18

Gen. Zeligowski Entering Vilnius
A20

Gen. Zeligowski
A21

1921–22 *Perf. 11½, Imperf.*

53	A16	10m brn ('22)	2.50	2.75
54	A17	25m red & yel ('22)	3.00	3.00
55	A18	50m dk bl ('22)	3.50	3.50
56	A19	75m vio ('22)	5.50	5.50
57	A20	100m bl & bis	2.75	3.50
58	A21	150m ol grn & brn	3.00	3.75
		Nos. 53-58 (6)	20.25	22.00

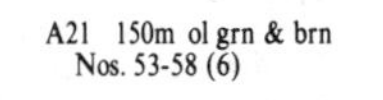

Nos. 53–56 commemorate the opening of the National Parliament; Nos. 57–58, the anniversary of the entry of General Zeligowski into Vilnius.

SEMI-POSTAL STAMPS.

Nos. 1–6 Surcharged in Black or Red

NA
ŚLĄSK
2 M.

1921 *Perf. 11½, Imperf.* Unwmkd.

B1	A1	25f +2m red (Bk)	90	1.25
B2	A1	25f +2m dk grn	90	1.25
B3	A1	1m +2m bl	1.25	1.50
B4	A1	1m +2m dk brn	1.25	1.50
B5	A1	2m +2m vio	1.50	1.75
B6	A1	2m +2m org	1.25	1.50
		Nos. B1-B6 (6)	7.05	8.75

The surcharge means "For Silesia 2 marks." The stamps were intended to provide a fund to assist the plebiscite in Upper Silesia.

Nos. 25, 26 Surcharged:

+1 (*a*) +1 M (*b*)

Perf. 11½, Imperf.

B13	A4 (a)	2m +1(m) cl	1.40	1.75
B14	A5 (b)	4m +1m gray grn & buff	1.40	2.00

Nos. 25–26, 28 with inset

10M

Perf. 11½, Imperf.

B17	A4	2m +1m cl	75	75
B18	A5	4m +1m gray grn & buff	75	75
B19	A7	10m +2m brn & yel	75	75
		Nos. B13-B19 (5)	5.05	6.00

POSTAGE DUE STAMPS.

University, Vilnius
D1

Castle Ruins, Troki
D3

Castle Hill, Vilnius
D2

Holy Gate, Vilnius
D4

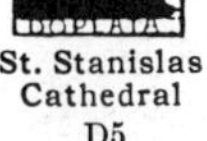

St. Stanislas Cathedral
D5

St. Anne's Church, Vilnius
D6

Perf. 11½, Imperf.

1920–21 Unwmkd.

J1	D1	50f red vio	40	50
J2	D2	1m green	40	50
J3	D3	2m red vio	40	50
J4	D4	3m red vio	60	75
J5	D5	5m red vio	60	75
J6	D6	20m scarlet	1.50	2.00
		Nos. J1-J6 (6)	3.90	5.00

CHAD

(chäd)

(Tchad)

LOCATION—In Central Africa south of Libya.

GOVT.—Republic.

AREA—495,752 sq. mi.

POP.—4,200,000 (est. 1977).

CAPITAL—N'djamena (formerly Fort Lamy).

A former dependency of Ubangi-Shari, Chad became a separate French colony in 1920. In 1934 the colonies of Chad, Gabon, Middle Congo and Ubangi-Shari were grouped in a single administrative unit known as French Equatorial Africa, with the capital at Brazzaville. The Republic of Chad was proclaimed Nov. 28, 1958.

100 Centimes = 1 Franc

Types of Middle Congo, 1907-17, Overprinted **TCHAD**

Perf. 14x13½, 13½x14.

1922 **Unwmkd.**

No.	Type	Description	Unused	Used
1	A1	1c red & vio	8	8
a.		Overprint omitted	67.50	
2	A1	2c ol brn & sal	18	18
a.		Ovpt. omitted	110.00	
3	A1	4c ind & vio	22	22
4	A1	5c choc & grn	35	35
5	A1	10c dp grn & gray grn	50	50
6	A1	15c vio & red	60	60
7	A1	20c grn & vio	2.00	2.00
8	A2	25c ol brn & brn	3.75	3.75
9	A2	30c rose & pale rose	45	45
10	A2	35c dl bl & dl rose	1.00	1.00
11	A2	40c choc & grn	1.00	1.00
12	A2	45c vio & grn	95	95
13	A2	50c dk bl & pale bl	75	75
14	A2	60c on 75c vio, *pnksh*	1.50	1.50
a.		"TCHAD" omitted	90.00	
b.		"60" omitted	90.00	
15	A1	75c red & vio	75	75
16	A3	1fr ind & sal	4.50	4.50
17	A3	2fr ind & vio	6.75	6.75
18	A3	5fr ind & ol brn	6.25	6.25
		Nos. 1-18 (18)	31.50	31.50

Stamps of 1922 Overprinted in Various Colors:

AFRIQUE EQUATORIALE FRANÇAISE — *a*

AFRIQUE EQUATORIALE FRANÇAISE — *b*

1924-33

No.	Type	Description	Unused	Used
19	A1 (a)	1c red & vio	5	5
a.		"TCHAD" omitted	55.00	
b.		Dbl. ovpt.	45.00	
20	A1 (a)	2c ol brn & sal	5	5
a.		"TCHAD" omitted	55.00	
b.		Dbl. ovpt.	45.00	
21	A1 (a)	4c ind & vio	5	5
a.		"TCHAD" omitted	275.00	
22	A1 (a)	5c choc & grn (Bl)	45	30
a.		"TCHAD" omitted	57.50	
23	A1 (a)	5c choc & grn	25	25
a.		"TCHAD" omitted	72.50	
24	A1 (a)	10c dp grn & gray grn (Bl)	22	22
25	A1 (a)	10c dp grn & gray grn	22	18
26	A1 (a)	10c red org & blk ('25)	20	20
27	A1 (a)	15c vio & red	25	25
28	A1 (a)	20c grn & vio	25	25
29	A2 (b)	25c ol brn & brn	25	20
30	A2 (b)	30c rose & pale rose	12	10
31	A2 (b)	30c gray & bl (R) ('25)	12	12
32	A2 (b)	30c dk grn & grn ('27)	45	45
a.		"Afrique Equatoriale Francaise" omitted	85.00	
33	A2 (b)	35c ind & dl rose	18	12
34	A2 (b)	40c choc & grn	45	45
a.		Dbl. overprint (R + Bk)	90.00	
35	A2 (b)	45c vio & grn	30	30
a.		Dbl. overprint (R + Bk)	90.00	
36	A2 (b)	50c dk bl & pale bl	30	30
a.		Inverted overprint	55.00	
37	A2 (b)	50c grn & vio ('25)	45	45
38	A2 (b)	65c org brn & bl ('28)	75	75
39	A2 (b)	75c red & vio	30	30
40	A2 (b)	75c dp bl & lt bl (R) ('25)	22	22
a.		"TCHAD" omitted	55.00	
41	A2 (b)	75c rose & dk brn ('28)	90	90
42	A2 (b)	90c brn red & pink ('30)	3.00	3.00
43	A3 (b)	1fr ind & sal	65	60
44	A3 (b)	1.10fr dl grn & bl ('28)	95	95
45	A3 (b)	1.25fr org brn & lt bl ('33)	3.00	3.00
46	A3 (b)	1.50fr ultra & bl ('30)	3.00	3.00
47	A3 (b)	1.75fr ol brn & vio ('33)	21.00	21.00
48	A3 (b)	2fr ind & vio	1.00	85
49	A3 (b)	3fr red vio ('30)	4.00	4.00
50	A3 (b)	5fr ind & ol brn	1.00	90
		Nos. 19-50 (32)	44.38	43.76

Types of 1922 Overprinted Type "b" and Surcharged with New Values.

1924-27

No.	Type	Description	Unused	Used
51	A2	60c on 75c dk vio, *pnksh*	20	20
a.		"60" omitted	67.50	
52	A3	65c on 1fr brn & ol grn ('25)	60	60
53	A3	85c on 1fr brn & ol grn ('25)	60	60
54	A2	90c on 75c brn red & rose red ('27)	55	55
55	A3	1.25fr on 1fr dk bl & ultra (R) ('26)	18	18
a.		"Afrique Equatoriale Francaise" omitted	55.00	
56	A3	1.50fr on 1fr ultra & bl ('27)	60	60
57	A3	3fr on 5fr org brn & dl red ('27)	1.75	1.75
58	A3	10fr on 5fr ol grn & cer ('27)	5.00	5.00
59	A3	20fr on 5fr vio & ver ('27)	6.25	6.25
		Nos. 51-59 (9)	15.73	15.73

Colonial Exposition Issue.

Common Design Types

Name of Country in Black.

1931 **Engraved** *Perf. 12½*

No.	Type	Description	Unused	Used
60	CD70	40c dp grn	2.00	2.00
61	CD71	50c violet	2.00	2.00
62	CD72	90c red org	2.00	2.00
63	CD73	1.50fr dl bl	2.00	2.00

Common Design Types pictured in section at front of book.

Republic

"Birth of the Republic"
A1

"Solidarity of the Community"
A2

Engraved.

1959 *Perf. 13* **Unwmkd.**

No.	Type	Description	Unused	Used
64	A1	15fr ultra, grn & mar	27	15
65	A2	25fr dk grn & dp cl	40	15

Issued to commemorate the first anniversary of the proclamation of the Republic.

Imperforates

Most Chad stamps from 1959 onward exist imperforate in issued and trial colors, and also in small presentation sheets in issued colors.

C.C.T.A. Issue

Common Design Type

1960

No.	Type	Description	Unused	Used
66	CD106	50fr rose lil & dk pur	90	80

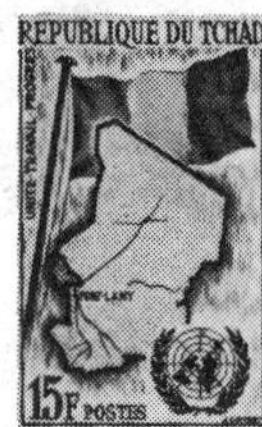

Flag and Map of Chad and U.N. Emblem
A3

Engraved

1961, Jan. 11 *Perf. 13* **Unwmkd.**

Flag in blue, yellow and carmine.

No.	Type	Description	Unused	Used
67	A3	15fr brn & dk bl	35	25
68	A3	25fr org brn & dk bl	45	25
69	A3	85fr sl grn & dk bl	1.50	85

Admission of Chad to United Nations.

Chari Bridge and Hippopotamus
A4

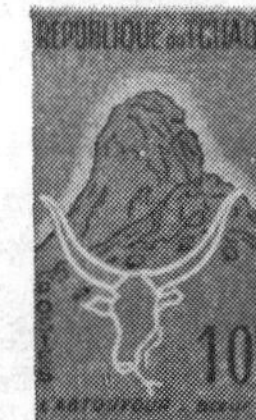

Abtouyoua Mountain and Ox
A5

Designs: 50c, Biltine and dorcas gazelle. 1fr, Logone and elephant. 2fr, Batha and lion. 3fr, Salamat and buffalo. 4fr, Ouaddai and Kudu. 15fr, Bessada and giant eland. 20fr, Tibesti mountains and mouflon. 25fr, Rocherg and antelope. 30fr, Kanem and cheetah. 60fr, Borkou and oryx. 85fr, Gorge of Archet and addax.

Typographed

1961-62 *Perf. 13½x14, 14x13½*

No.	Type	Description	Unused	Used
70	A5	50c yel grn & dk grn ('62)	3	3
71	A5	1fr bl grn & dk bl grn ('62)	4	3
72	A5	2fr dk red brn & blk ('62)	4	3
73	A5	3fr ocher & dl grn ('62)	6	6
74	A5	4fr dk crim & blk ('62)	8	8
75	A4	5fr yel & blk	10	10
76	A5	10fr pink & blk	15	10
77	A5	15fr lil & blk ('62)	25	8
78	A5	20fr red & blk	30	15
79	A5	25fr bl & blk ('62)	40	15
80	A5	30fr ultra & blk ('62)	50	20
81	A5	60fr yel & ol grn ('62)	90	30
82	A5	85fr org & blk	1.20	50
		Nos. 70-82 (13)	4.05	1.81

First anniversary of Independence.

Abidjan Games Issue

Common Design Type

Designs: 20fr, Relay race. 50fr, High jump.

1962, July 21 Photo. *Perf. 12½x12*

No.	Type	Description	Unused	Used
83	CD109	20fr brn, lt grn & blk	35	20
84	CD109	50fr brn, lt grn & blk	75	50

See No. C8.

African-Malgache Union Issue

Common Design Type

1962, Sept. 8 **Unwmkd.**

No.	Type	Description	Unused	Used
85	CD110	30fr dk bl, bluish grn, red & gold	50	45

Issued to commemorate the first anniversary of the African and Malgache Union.

Pres. Ngarta Tombalbaye
A7

1963, Apr. 22 *Perf. 12x12½*

No.	Type	Description	Unused	Used
86	A7	20fr multi	30	15
87	A7	85fr multi	1.20	45

Space Communciations Issue

Waves Around Globe
A8

Design: 100fr, Orbit patterns around globe.

Photogravure

1963, Sept. 19 *Perf. 12½* **Unwmkd.**

No.	Type	Description	Unused	Used
88	A8	25fr grn & pur	40	35
89	A8	100fr pink & ultra	1.50	1.10

Ancestral Mask
A9

Excavated Sao Art: 5fr, Clay weight. 25fr, Ancestral clay statuette. 60fr, Gazelle, bronze. 80fr, Bronze pectoral.

1963, Dec. 2 Engraved *Perf. 13*

90	A9	5fr brt grn & red brn	10	5
91	A9	15fr gray, dl cl & red	25	15
92	A9	25fr dk bl & org brn	40	25
93	A9	60fr org brn & sl grn	90	40
94	A9	80fr org red & ol	1.20	40
		Nos. 90-94 (5)	2.85	1.25

UNESCO Emblem, Scales and Tree—A10

1963, Dec. 10

95	A10	25fr grn & mar	40	30

Issued to commemorate the 15th anniversary of the Universal Declaration of Human Rights.

Potter
A11

Designs: 30fr, Boatmaker. 50fr, Weaver. 85fr, Smiths.

Engraved

1964, Feb. 5 *Perf. 12½* Unwmkd.

96	A11	10fr bl, blk & org	15	10
97	A11	30fr yel, blk & car	45	20
98	A11	50fr grn, blk & car	75	30
99	A11	85fr pur, blk & yel	85	50

Barograph and WMO Emblem
A12

1964, March 23 *Perf. 13*

100	A12	50fr red lil, pur & ultra	85	45

Fourth World Meteorological Day.

Cotton
A13

Design: 25fr, Royal poinciana.

1964, Apr. 6 Photo. *Perf. 12½x13*

101	A13	20fr multi	40	20
102	A13	25fr multi	40	20

Co-operation Issue
Common Design Type

1964, Nov. 7 Engraved *Perf. 13*

103	CD119	25fr ver, dk bl & dk brn	40	30

National Guard and Map of Chad
A14

Design: 25fr, Infantry, flag and map (vert.).

Perf. 12½x13, 13x12½

1964, Dec. 11 Photogravure

104	A14	20fr multi	35	20
105	A14	25fr lt bl & multi	40	20

Issued to honor the army of Chad.

Aoudad or Barbary Sheep
A15

Animals: 10fr, Addax. 20fr, Oryx. 25fr, Derby's eland (vert.). 30fr, Giraffe, buffalo and lion, Zakouma Park (vert.). 85fr, Great kudu at water hole.

Perf. 12½x12, 12x12½

1965, Jan. 11 Unwmkd.

106	A15	5fr dk brn, ultra & yel	7	4
107	A15	10fr ultra, org & blk	18	12
108	A15	20fr multi	30	15
109	A15	25fr multi	40	20
110	A15	30fr multi	45	25
111	A15	85fr multi	1.25	65
		Nos. 106-111 (6)	2.65	1.41

Olsen Perforator
A16

Designs: 60fr, Mildé telephone (vert.). 100fr, Distributor of Baudot telegraph.

1965, May 17 Engraved *Perf. 13*

112	A16	30fr choc, red, grn & ver	45	30
113	A16	60fr red brn, sl grn & ver	90	60
114	A16	100fr sl grn, red brn & ver	1.40	1.00

Issued to commemorate the centenary of the International Telecommunication Union.

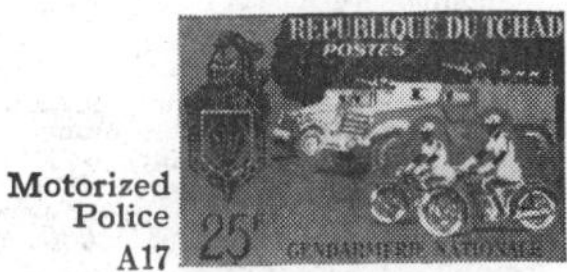

Motorized Police
A17

Perf. 12½x12

1965, June 22 Photo. Unwmkd.

115	A17	25fr ol, dk grn, gold & brn	40	25

Issued to honor the national police.

Guitar
A18

Musical Instruments from National Museum: 1fr, Drum and stool (vert.). 3fr, Shoulder drums (vert.). 15fr, Viol. 60fr, Harp (vert.).

1965, Oct. 26 Engraved *Perf. 13*

Size: 22x36, 36x22mm.

116	A18	1fr car, emer & brn	6	3
117	A18	2fr red, brt lil & brn	6	3
118	A18	3fr red & sep	6	6
119	A18	15fr red, ocher & sl grn	25	15
120	A18	60fr mar & sl grn	90	40
		Nos. 116-120, C23 (6)	2.68	1.12

Head and Bowl
A19

WHO Headquarters, Geneva
A20

Sao Art: 20fr, Head. 60fr, Head with crown. 80fr, Circlet with human head. From excavations at Bouta Kebira and Gawi.

1966, Apr. 1 Engr. *Perf. 13*

121	A19	15fr ol, choc & ultra	20	15
122	A19	20fr dk red, brn & bl grn	30	20
123	A19	60fr brt bl, choc & ver	90	50
124	A19	80fr brn org, grn & pur	1.20	60

Issued to publicize the International Negro Arts Festival, Dakar, Senegal, Apr. 1–24.

No. 86 Surcharged with New Value and Two Bars in Orange

1966, Apr. 15 Photo. *Perf. 12x12½*

125	A7	25fr on 20fr multi	40	20

1966, May 3

126	A20	25fr car, lt ultra & yel	40	30
127	A20	32fr emer, ultra & yel	45	35

Issued to commemorate the inauguration of the World Health Organization Headquarters, Geneva.

Staff of Mercury and Map of Africa
A21

1966, May 24 *Perf. 12½x12*

128	A21	30fr multi	45	20

Central African Customs and Economic Union (Union Douaniere et Economique de l'Afrique Centrale, UDEAC).

Soccer Player
A22

Design: 60fr, Soccer player facing left.

1966, July 12 Engraved *Perf. 13*

129	A22	30fr grn, bl grn & mar	45	25
130	A22	60fr dk bl, gray & car	90	50

Issued to commemorate the 8th World Cup Soccer Championship, Wembley, England, July 11–30.

Young Men, Flag and Emblem
A23

Photogravure

1966, Aug. 11 *Perf. 12½x13*

131	A23	25fr dk bl & multi	40	25

Chad Youth Movement.

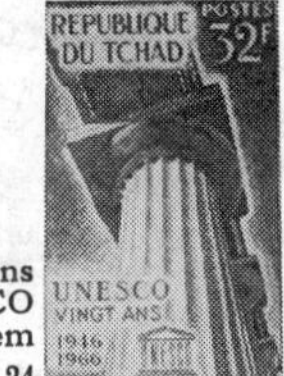

Greek Columns and UNESCO Emblem
A24

1966, Aug. 23 Engr. *Perf. 13*

132	A24	32fr sl bl, vio & car rose	50	30

Issued to commemorate the 20th anniversary of UNESCO (United Nations Educational, Scientific and Cultural Organization).

Reconstructed Skull of Chadanthropus
A25

1966, Sept. 20 Engraved *Perf. 13*

133	A25	30fr gray, red & ocher	45	20

Issued to commemorate Yves Coppens' discovery of Lake Chad man.

Stone Axe
A26

Prehistoric Tools: 30fr, Flint arrow head. 85fr, Bone harpoon. 100fr, Sandstone millstone with grinder.

1966, Dec. 11 Engraved *Perf. 13*

134	A26	25fr dp bl, red & dk brn	32	18
135	A26	30fr brn, dp bl & blk	45	22
136	A26	85fr dk red, brt bl & brn	1.20	55
137	A26	100fr Prus grn, dk brn & bis brn	1.40	70
a.		Min. sheet of 4	3.75	3.75

No. 137a contains one each of Nos. 134–137. Size: 128x99mm.

Map of Chad and Various Sports
A27

1967, Apr. 10 Photo. *Perf. 12x12½*

138 A27 25fr multi 40 25

Issued for Sports Day, Apr. 10, 1967.

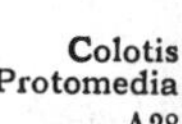

Colotis Protomedia
A28

Various Butterflies.

1967, May 23 Photo. *Perf. 12½x12*

139 A28 5fr bl & multi 10 8
140 A28 10fr emer & multi 20 12
141 A28 20fr org & multi 30 20
142 A28 130fr red & multi 1.75 90

WHO Headquarters, Brazzaville
A29

1967, Sept. 23 Photo. *Perf. 12½x13*

143 A29 30fr vio bl & multi 45 25

Issued to commemorate the opening of the Regional Office of the United Nations World Health Organization, Brazzaville.

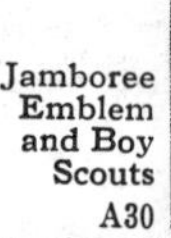

Jamboree Emblem and Boy Scouts
A30

Design: 32fr, Jamboree emblem and Boy Scout.

1967, Oct. 17 Photo. *Perf. 12½x13*

144 A30 25fr multi 35 15
145 A30 32fr multi 50 25

Issued to publicize the 12th Boy Scout World Jamboree, Farragut State Park, Idaho, Aug. 1-9.

Great Mills of Chad
A31

Design: 30fr, Lake reclamation project, grain fields.

1967, Nov. 14 Engraved *Perf. 13*

146 A31 25fr brt bl, ind & sep 35 15
147 A31 30fr ultra, emer & ol brn 40 25

Economic development of Chad.

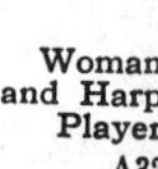

Woman and Harp Player
A32

Rock Paintings: 30fr, Giraffes. 50fr, Camel rider hunting ostrich.

1967, Dec. 19 Engraved *Perf. 13*

Size: 36x22mm.

148 A32 15fr bl, sal & mar 20 12
149 A32 30fr grnsh bl, sal & mar 45 25
150 A32 50fr emer, sal & mar 75 32
Nos. 148-150, C38-C39 (5) 4.75 2.24

Issued to commemorate the Balloud expedition in the Ennedi Mountains. See also Nos. 163-166.

Rotary Emblem
A33

Map of Chad, WHO Emblem, Well, Physicians, Mother and Child
A34

1968, Jan. 9 Photo. *Perf. 13x12½*

151 A33 50fr multi 75 35

Rotary Club of Chad, 10th anniversary.

1968, Apr. 6 *Perf. 13x12½*

152 A34 25fr multi 35 20
153 A34 32fr multi 50 30

Issued to commemorate the 20th anniversary of the World Health Organization.

"Water" Aiding Agriculture and Industry—A35

1968, Apr. 23 Engraved *Perf. 13*

154 A35 50fr grnsh bl, brn & brt grn 70 30

Hydrological Decade (UNESCO), 1965-74.

National Administration School
A36

1968, Aug. 20 Engraved *Perf. 13*

155 A36 25fr sl, brn red & rose vio 35 20

Boy Learning to Write
A37

1968, Sept. 10

156 A37 60fr dk bl, dk brn & blk 75 35

Issued for National Literacy Day.

Cotton Harvest
A38

Loom, Fort Archambault Factory
A39

Tiger Moth
A40

1968, Sept. 24 Engraved *Perf. 13*

157 A38 25fr Prus bl, choc & dk grn 35 13
158 A39 30fr brt grn, ol & ultra 45 20

Issued to publicize the cotton industry.

1968, Oct. 1 Photogravure

Designs (Moths): 30fr, Owlet. 50fr, Saturnid (Gynanisa maja). 100fr, Saturnid (Epiphora bauhiniae).

159 A40 25fr multi 30 15
160 A40 30fr multi 40 20
161 A40 50fr multi 70 35
162 A40 100fr multi 1.25 50

Rock Paintings Type of 1967

Rock Paintings: 2fr, Archers. 10fr, Costumes (4 women, 1 man). 20fr, Funeral vigil. 25fr, Dispute.

1968, Nov. 19 Engraved *Perf. 13*

Size: 36x22mm.

163 A32 2fr scar, sal & brn 6 5
164 A32 10fr pur, sal & dk red 15 6
165 A32 20fr grn, sal & mar 30 15
166 A32 25fr bl, sal & mar 40 20

Man and Human Rights Flame
A41

St. Paul
A42

1968, Dec. 10 Engraved *Perf. 13*

167 A41 32fr grn, brt bl & red 50 30

International Human Rights Year.

1969, May 6 Litho. *Perf. 12½x13*

Apostles: 1fr, St. Peter. 2fr, St. Thomas. 5fr, St. John the Evangelist. 10fr, St. Bartholomew. 20fr, St. Matthew. 25fr, St. James the Less. 30fr, St. Andrew. 40fr, St. Jude. 50fr, St. James the Greater. 85fr, St. Philip. 100fr, St. Simon.

168 A42 50c multi 4 3
169 A42 1fr multi 5 3
170 A42 2fr multi 5 3
171 A42 5fr multi 8 3
172 A42 10fr multi 15 8
173 A42 20fr multi 28 15
174 A42 25fr multi 35 17
175 A42 30fr multi 42 20
176 A42 40fr multi 55 25
177 A42 50fr multi 65 30
178 A42 85fr multi 1.00 55
179 A42 100fr multi 1.20 60
Nos. 168-179 (12) 4.82 2.42

Issued to commemorate the Jubilee Year of the Catholic Church in Chad. Nos. 168-179 printed se-tenant in sheets of 12 (4x3).

Tractors and Trucks
A43

1969, June 19 Engraved *Perf. 13*

180 A43 32fr grn, red brn & ind 40 25

Issued to commemorate the 50th anniversary of the International Labor Organization.

Deborah Meyer, U.S., 200 Meter Freestyle
A44

Woman with Flowers, by Veneto
A45

Winners of 1968 Olympic Games: No. 182, Roland Matthes, East Germany, 100 meter backstroke. No. 183, Klaus DiBiasi, Italy, springboard diving. No. 184, Bruno Cipolla, Primo Baran and Renzo Sambo, Italy, pair with coxswain. No. 185, Annemarie Zimmermann and Rosewitha Esser, West Germany, women's kayak tandem. No. 186, Sailing, Great Britain. No. 187, Pierre Trentin, France, 1000 meter bicycling. No. 188, Pier Franco Vianelli, Italy, 196 kilometer bicycle road race. No. 189, Daniel Morelon and Pierre Trentin, France, tandem. No. 190, Daniel R. Rebillard, France, 4000 meter pursuit (bicycle). No. 191, Ingrid Becker, West Germany, pentathlon. No. 192, Jean J. Guyon, France, equestrian. No. 193, Olympic dressage team, West Germany. No. 194, Bernd Klinger, West Germany, small bore rifle. No. 195, Manfred Wolke, East Germany, welterweight. No. 196, Randy Matson, U.S., shot put. No. 197, Colette Besson, France, 400 meter run. No. 198, Mohammed Gammoudi, Tunisia, 5,000 meter run. No. 199, Tommie Smith, U.S., 200 meter run. No. 200, David Hemery, Great Britain, 200 meter hurdles. No. 201, Willie Davenport, U.S., 110 meter hurdles. No. 202, Bob Beamon, U.S., broad jump. No. 203, Sawao Kato, Japan, all around gymnastics. No. 204, Dick Fosbury, U.S., high jump.

Paintings: No. 206, Holy Family, by Murillo (horiz.). No. 207, Adoration of the Kings, by Rubens. No. 208, Portrait of an African Woman, by Bezombes. No. 209, Three Negroes, by Rubens. No. 210, Mother and Child, by Gauguin.

Lithographed

1969, June 30 *Perf. 12½x13*

Multicolored

No.	Type	Description	Unused	Used
181	A44	1fr *Meyer*	35	35
182	A44	1fr *Matthes*	35	35
183	A44	1fr *DiBiasi*	35	35
184	A44	1fr *Cipolla, Baran & Sambo*	35	35
185	A44	1fr *Zimmermann & Esser*	35	35
186	A44	1fr *Sailing, Great Britain*	35	35
187	A44	1fr *Trentin*	35	35
188	A44	1fr *Vianelli*	35	35
189	A44	1fr *Morelon & Trentin*	35	35
190	A44	1fr *Rebillard*	35	35
191	A44	1fr *Becker*	35	35
192	A44	1fr *Guyon*	35	35
193	A44	1fr *Dressage, Germ.*	35	35
194	A44	1fr *Klinger*	35	35
195	A44	1fr *Wolke*	35	35
196	A44	1fr *Matson*	35	35
197	A44	1fr *Besson*	35	35
198	A44	1fr *Gammoudi*	35	35
199	A44	1fr *Smith*	35	35
200	A44	1fr *Hemery*	35	35
201	A44	1fr *Davenport*	35	35
202	A44	1fr *Beamon*	35	35
203	A44	1fr *Kato*	35	35
204	A44	1fr *Fosbury*	35	35

Perf. 12½x13, 13x12½

No.	Type	Description	Unused	Used
205	A45	1fr *Veneto*	35	35
206	A45	1fr *Murillo*	35	35
207	A45	1fr *Rubens*	35	35
208	A45	1fr *Bezombes*	35	35
209	A45	1fr *Rubens*	35	35
210	A45	1fr *Gauguin*	35	35
		Nos. 181-210 (30)	10.50	10.50

Issued to stress the brotherhood of mankind.

Cochlospermum Tinctorium A46

Flowers: 4fr, Parkia biglobosa. 10fr, Pancratium trianthum. 15fr, Morning glory.

1969, July 8 Photo. *Perf. 12½x13*

No.	Type	Description	Unused	Used
211	A46	1fr pink, yel & blk	5	5
212	A46	4fr dk grn, yel & red	5	5
213	A46	10fr dk grn, yel & gray	15	8
214	A46	15fr vio bl & multi	20	10

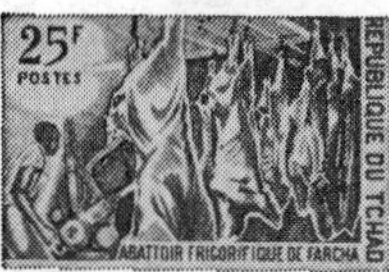

Meat Freezer, Farcha A47

Design: 30fr, Cattle at Farcha slaughterhouse.

1969, Aug. 19 Engraved *Perf. 13*

No.	Type	Description	Unused	Used
215	A47	25fr sl grn, ocher & red brn	32	18
216	A47	30fr red brn, sl grn & gray	38	25

Economic development in Chad.

Development Bank Issue

Common Design Type

1969, Sept. 10

No.	Type	Description	Unused	Used
217	CD130	30fr dl red, grn & ocher	40	20

Issued to commemorate the 5th anniversary of the African Development Bank.

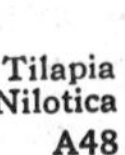

Tilapia Nilotica A48

Fish: 3fr, Citharinus latus. 5fr, Tetraodon fahaka strigosus. 20fr, Hydrocyon forskali.

1969, Nov. 25 Engraved *Perf. 13*

No.	Type	Description	Unused	Used
218	A48	2fr choc, grn & gray	5	3
219	A48	3fr gray, red & bl	8	5
220	A48	5fr ocher, blk & yel	10	8
221	A48	20fr blk, red & grn	32	18

ASECNA Issue

Common Design Type

1969, Dec. 12 Engraved *Perf. 13*

No.	Type	Description	Unused	Used
222	CD132	30fr orange	30	15

Pres. François Tombalbaye A49 — Lenin A50

1970, Jan. 11 Litho. *Perf. 14*

No.	Type	Description	Unused	Used
223	A49	25fr multi	38	20

1970, Apr. 22 Photo. *Perf. 11½*

No.	Type	Description	Unused	Used
224	A50	150fr gold, blk & buff	1.85	1.00

Issued to commemorate the centenary of the birth of Lenin (1870-1924), Russian communist leader.

U.P.U. Headquarters Issue

Common Design Type

1970, May 20 Engraved *Perf. 13*

No.	Type	Description	Unused	Used
225	CD133	30fr dk red, pur & brn	40	12

Adult Education Class and U.N. Emblem A52

1970, June 16 Litho. *Perf. 14*

No.	Type	Description	Unused	Used
226	A52	100fr bl & multi	1.20	30

Issued for International Education Year.

Bull's Head, Symbols of Weather and Agriculture—A53 — Ahmed Mangue A54

1970, July 22 Engr. *Perf. 13*

No.	Type	Description	Unused	Used
227	A53	50fr org, gray & grn	55	15

Issued for World Meteorological Day.

Lithographed and Engraved

1970, Sept. 15 *Perf. 13*

No.	Type	Description	Unused	Used
228	A54	100fr gold, car & blk	1.10	25

Issued in memory of Ahmed Mangue, Minister of Education.

Tanner A55

Designs: 2fr, Cloth dyer (vert.). 3fr, Camel turning oil press (horiz.). 4fr, Water carrier. 5fr, Copper worker (horiz.).

1970, Oct. 10 Engraved *Perf. 13*

No.	Type	Description	Unused	Used
229	A55	1fr ol brn, bl & brn	5	5
230	A55	2fr dk brn, ol & ind	5	5
231	A55	3fr pur, ol brn & rose car	4	4
232	A55	4fr choc, lem & bl grn	6	6
233	A55	5fr red, choc & sl grn	5	5
		Nos. 229-233 (5)	25	25

OCAM Headquarters, Map of Africa, Stars A57

1970, Oct. 24 Photo. *Perf. 12x12½*

No.	Type	Description	Unused	Used
234	A56	32fr dk bl & multi	40	25

25th anniversary of United Nations.

1971, Jan. 23 Photo. *Perf. 12½x12*

No.	Type	Description	Unused	Used
235	A57	30fr dk grn & multi	40	25

OCAM (Organisation Commune Africaine, Malgache et Mauricienne) Summit Conference, N'djamena, Jan. 22-30.

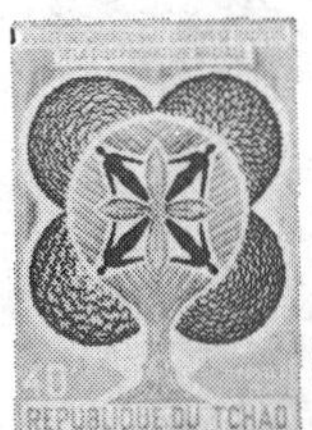

Symbolic Tree A58

1971, March 21 Engraved *Perf. 13*

No.	Type	Description	Unused	Used
236	A58	40fr bl grn, dk red & grn	50	25

International year against racial discrimination.

Map of Africa, Radar Antenna A59

Designs (Map of Africa and): 40fr, Communications tower. 50fr, Communications satellite.

1971, May 17 Engraved *Perf. 13*

No.	Type	Description	Unused	Used
237	A59	5fr ultra, org & dk red	10	8
238	A59	40fr pur, emer & brn	40	20
239	A59	50fr dk red, blk & brn	60	30

3rd World Telecommunications Day.

UNICEF Emblem and Children A60

1971, Dec. 11

No.	Type	Description	Unused	Used
240	A60	50fr Prus bl, emer & brt pink	60	30

25th anniversary of the United Nations International Children's Fund (UNICEF).

Gorane Nangara Dancers A61

Dancers: 15fr, Girls' initiation dance, Yondo. 30fr, Women of M'Boum (vert.). 40fr, Men of Sara Kaba (vert.).

1971, Dec. 18 Litho. *Perf. 13*

No.	Type	Description	Unused	Used
241	A61	10fr blk & multi	15	5
242	A61	15fr brn org & multi	25	8
243	A61	30fr bl & multi	50	15
244	A61	40fr yel grn & multi	65	18

Presidents Pompidou and Tombalbaye, Map with Paris and Fort Lamy—A62

1972, Jan. 25 Photo. *Perf. 13*

No.	Type	Description	Unused	Used
245	A62	40fr bl & multi	50	30

Visit of Pres. Georges Pompidou of France, Jan. 1972.

Examination

The Catalogue editors cannot undertake to appraise, identify or pass upon genuineness or condition of stamps.

Canceled-to-order stamps are often from remainders. Most collectors of canceled stamps prefer postally used specimens.

President Tombalbaye
A63

1972, Apr. 13 Litho. *Perf. 13*

246	A63	30fr multi	30	15
247	A63	40fr multi	40	20

See Nos. C112-C113.

Downhill Skiing—A64

Designs: 75fr, Women's figure skating. 150fr, Luge.

1972, Apr. 13 *Perf. 13½*

248	A64	25fr multi	25	13
249	A64	75fr multi	75	38
250	A64	150fr multi	1.50	75
		Nos. 248-250, C114-C115 (5)	5.80	2.91

11th Winter Olympic Games, Sapporo, Japan.

Heart
A65

Gorrizia Dubiosa
A66

1972, Apr. 25 Engraved *Perf. 13*

251	A65	100fr pur, bl & car	1.20	25

"Your heart is your health," World Health Month.

1972, May 6 Photogravure

Insects: 2fr, Spider (argiope sector). 3fr, Silk spider (nephila senegalense). 4fr, Beetle (oryctes boas). 5fr, Dragonfly (hemistigma albipunctata).

252	A66	1fr grn & multi	8	6
253	A66	2fr bl & multi	8	6
254	A66	3fr car rose & multi	8	6
255	A66	4fr yel grn & multi	8	6
256	A66	5fr dp grn & multi	8	6
		Nos. 252-256 (5)	40	30

Scout Greeting—A67

Designs: 70fr, Mountain climbing. 80fr, Canoeing.

1972, May 15

257	A67	30fr multi	30	15
258	A67	70fr multi	70	35
259	A67	80fr multi	80	40
		Nos. 257-259, C118-C119 (5)	4.00	2.25

Scout Jamboree.

Hurdles, Motion and Olympic Emblems
A68

Designs (Motion and Olympic Emblems and): 130fr, Gymnast on rings. 150fr, Swimming. 300fr, Bicycling.

1972, June 9 Litho. *Perf. 13½*

260	A68	50fr blk & multi	60	18
261	A68	130fr blk & multi	1.40	38
262	A68	150fr blk & multi	1.80	45

Souvenir Sheet

263	A68	300fr blk & multi	3.50	3.00

20th Olympic Games, Munich, Aug. 26-Sept. 10. No. 263 contains one stamp. Black marginal inscription and multicolored torch. Size: 101x86mm.

Ski Jump, Kasaya, Japan—A69

Designs: 75fr, Cross-country skiing, P. Tyldum, Sweden. 100fr, Figure-skating, pairs, L. Rodnina and A. Ulanov, USSR. 130fr, Men's speed skating, A. Schenk, Netherlands.

1972, June 15 *Perf. 14½*

264	A69	25fr gold & multi	25	13
265	A69	75fr gold & multi	75	38
266	A69	100fr gold & multi	1.00	50
267	A69	130fr gold & multi	1.30	65
		Nos. 264-267, C130-C131, (6)	6.80	3.41

11th Winter Olympic Games, gold-medal winners. Nos. 264-267 exist se-tenant with label showing earth satellite.

TV Tower and Weight-lifting—A70

Designs (TV Tower, Munich and): 40fr, Woman sprinter. 60fr, Soccer goalkeeper.

1972, Aug. 15 Litho. *Perf. 14½*

268	A70	20fr gold & multi	20	10
269	A70	40fr gold & multi	40	20
270	A70	60fr gold & multi	60	30
		Nos. 268-270, C135-C137 (6)	4.90	2.45

20th Summer Olympic Games, Munich. Nos. 268-270 exist se-tenant with label showing arms of Munich.

Dromedary
A71

Domestic Animals: 30fr, Horse. 40fr, Dog. 45fr, Goat.

1972, Aug. 29 Engraved *Perf. 13*

271	A71	25fr pur & bis	35	12
272	A71	30fr red lil & ind	40	15
273	A71	40fr emer & lt brn	50	15
274	A71	45fr dk bl & brn	55	20

Tobacco Cultivation
A72

Design: 50fr, Plowing.

1972, Oct. 24 Engraved *Perf. 13*

275	A72	40fr dk brn, dk car & sl grn	40	20
276	A72	50fr ultra, brn & sl grn	50	25

Massa Warrior
A73

Design: 20fr, Moundang warrior.

1972, Nov. 15 Photo. *Perf. 14x13*

277	A73	15fr org & multi	25	20
278	A73	20fr yel & multi	30	25

King Faisal and Pres. Tombalbaye
A74

1972, Nov. 17 Litho. *Perf. 13*

279	A74	100fr gold & multi	1.00	60

Visit of King Faisal of Saudi Arabia. See No. C143.

Gen. Gowon and Pres. Tombalbaye
A75

1972, Dec. 7

280	A75	70fr multi	75	40

Visit of Gen. Yakubu Gowon of Nigeria.

Olympic Emblem and 100-meter Sprint, Valeri Borzov, USSR—A76

Designs (Olympic Emblem and): 20fr, Shotput, Komar, Poland. 40fr, Hammer throw, Bondartchuk, USSR. 60fr, Discus, Danek, Czechoslovakia.

1972, Dec. 22 *Perf. 11*

281	A76	10fr multi	10	5
282	A76	20fr multi	20	10
283	A76	40fr multi	40	20
284	A76	60fr multi	60	30
		Nos. 281-284, C148-C149 (6)	5.30	2.65

20th Summer Olympic Games, winners.

Olympic Emblem and Fencing, Woyda, Poland—A77

Designs (Olympic Emblem and): 30fr, 3-day equestrian event, Richard Meade, Gt. Britain. 50fr, Two-man sculls, Brietzke-Mager, East Germany.

1972, Dec. 22

285	A77	20fr gold & multi	20	10
286	A77	30fr gold & multi	30	15
287	A77	50fr gold & multi	50	25
		Nos. 285-287, C151-C152 (5)	5.00	2.50

20th Summer Olympic Games, winners.

Soviet Flag and Shield
A78

1972, Dec. 30 Lithographed *Perf. 12*

288	A78	150fr red & multi	1.35	65

50th anniversary of the Soviet Union.

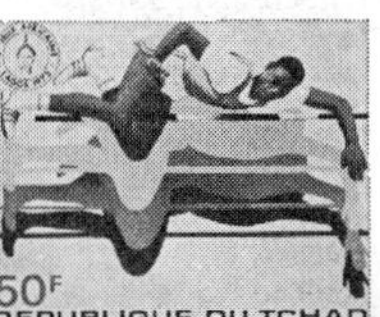

High Jump
A79

Designs (Games Emblem and): 125fr, Running. 200fr, Shot put. 250fr, Discus.

1973, Jan. 17 Litho. *Perf. 13½x13*

289	A79	50fr vio bl & multi	50	22
290	A79	125fr ol & multi	1.20	60
291	A79	200fr lil & multi	2.00	1.00

Souvenir Sheet

292 A79 250fr brn & multi 3.00 3.00

2nd African Games, Lagos, Nigeria, Jan. 7–18. No. 292 contains one stamp. Ultramarine margin with inscription and black Games emblems. Size: 101½x 85mm.

No. 271 Surcharged with New Value, 2 Bars, and Overprinted in Red: "SECHERESSE SOLIDARITE AFRICAINE"

1973, Aug. 16 Engr. *Perf. 13*

293 A71 100fr on 25fr multi 1.00 65

African solidarity in drought emergency.

African Postal Union Issue

Common Design Type

1973, Sept. 17 Engraved *Perf. 13*

294 CD137 100fr cl, sl grn & brn ol 1.00 60

Dinothrombium Tinctorium

A80

Rotary Emblem

A81

1974, Sept. 3 Photogravure *Perf. 13*

Multicolored

295 A80 25fr *shown* 22 12

296 A80 30fr *Bupreste sternocera* 25 15

297 A80 40fr *Diptere hyperechia* 35 20

298 A80 50fr *Chrysis* 45 27

299 A80 100fr *Longicorn beetle* 85 40

300 A80 130fr *Spider* 1.10 50

Nos. 295-300 (6) 3.22 1.64

1975, Apr. 11 Typo. *Perf. 13*

301 A81 50fr multi 45 25

Rotary International, 70th anniversary.

Craterostigma Plantagineum

A82

Flowers: 10fr, Tapinanthus globiferus. 15fr, Commelina forskalaei (vert.). 20fr, Adenium obesum. 25fr, Yellow hibiscus. 30fr, Red hibiscus. 40fr, Kigelia africana.

1975, Sept. 25 Photo. *Perf. 13*

302 A82 5fr org & multi 5 5

303 A82 10fr gray bl & multi 8 5

304 A82 15fr yel grn & multi 13 8

305 A82 20fr lt brn & multi 17 10

306 A82 25fr lil & multi 20 12

307 A82 30fr bis & multi 25 13

308 A82 40fr ultra & multi 32 18

Nos. 302-308 (7) 1.20 71

A. G. Bell, Satellite and Waves

A83

1976, June 10 Litho. *Perf. 12½*

309 A83 100fr bl, brn & ocher 80 50

310 A83 125fr lt grn, brn & ocher 1.00 60

Centenary of first telephone call by Alexander Graham Bell, Mar. 10, 1876.

Ice Hockey, USSR—A84

Design: 90fr, Ski jump, Karl Schnabl, Austria.

1976, June 21 *Perf. 14*

311 A84 60fr multi 60 30

312 A84 90fr multi 85 35

12th Winter Olympic Games, winners. See Nos. C178—C180.

High Hurdles—A85

1976, July 12 Litho. *Perf. 13½*

313 A85 45fr multi 45 25

21st Summer Olympic Games, Montreal, Canada.

See Nos. C187—C190.

Mars Landing and Viking Rocket

A86

Design (Mars Landing and): 90fr, Viking trajectory, Earth to Mars.

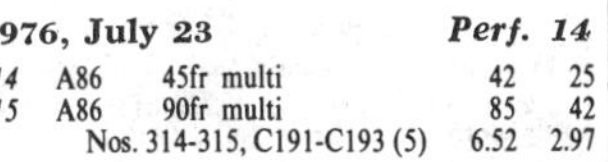

1976, July 23 *Perf. 14*

314 A86 45fr multi 42 25

315 A86 90fr multi 85 42

Nos. 314-315, C191-C193 (5) 6.52 2.97

Viking Mars project.

Robert Koch, Medicine—A87

Design: 90fr, Anatole France, literature.

1976, Dec. 15

316 A87 45fr multi 50 25

317 A87 90fr multi 85 42

Nos. 316-317, C196-C198 (5) 7.05 3.12

Nobel Prize winners.

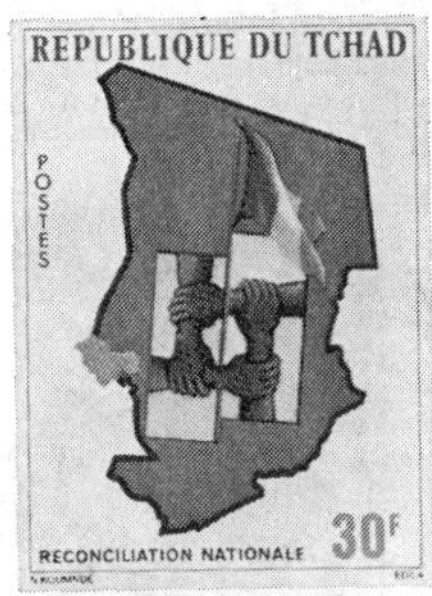

Map and Flag of Chad, Clasped Hands

A88

Designs: 60fr, like 30fr. 120fr, Map of Chad, people and various occupations.

1976, Sept. 15 Litho. *Perf. 12½x13*

318 A88 30fr multi 25 18

319 A88 60fr org & multi 50 30

320 A88 120fr brn & multi 1.00 65

National reconciliation.

Freed Political Prisoners—A89

Designs: 60fr, Parade of cadets. 120fr, like 30fr.

1976, Sept. 25 Litho. *Perf. 12½*

321 A89 30fr bl & multi 25 18

322 A89 60fr blk & multi 50 30

323 A89 120fr red & multi 1.00 65

Revolution of Apr. 13, 1975, first anniversary.

Decorated Calabashes—A90

Designs: Various pyrographed calabashes.

1976, Nov. Litho. *Perf. 12½x13*

324 A90 30fr multi 25 18

325 A90 60fr multi 50 30

326 A90 120fr multi 1.00 65

Germany No. C57 and Friedrichshafen, Germany—A91

1977, Mar. 30 *Perf. 14*

327 A91 100fr multi 95 42

Nos. 327, C206-C209 (5) 7.20 3.07

75th anniversary of the Zeppelin.

Elizabeth II in Coronation Regalia and Clergy—A92

Design: 450fr, Elizabeth II and Prince Philip.

1977, June 15 Litho. *Perf. 14x13½*

328 A92 250fr multi 2.35 70

Souvenir Sheet

329 A92 450fr multi 4.25 2.00

25th anniversary of the reign of Elizabeth II. No. 329 has multicolored margin showing Buckingham Palace and heraldic supporters. Size: 110x91mm.

Simon Bolivar—A93

Famous Personalities: 175fr, Joseph J. Roberts. No. 332, Queen Wilhelmina of Netherlands. No. 333, Charles de Gaulle. 325fr, King Baudouin and Queen Fabiola of Belgium.

1977, June 15 *Perf. 13½x14*

330 A93 150fr multi 1.40 50

331 A93 175fr multi 1.60 60

332 A93 200fr multi 1.85 65

333 A93 200fr multi 1.85 65

334 A93 325fr multi 3.25 1.00

Nos. 330-334 (5) 9.95 3.40

Post and Telecommunications Emblem—A94

Map of Chad and Waves — A95

Society Emblem — A96

Perf. 13 (A94); 12½ (A95); 13½x13 (A96)

1977, Aug. 15 Lithographed

335	A94	30fr yel & blk	25	18
336	A95	60fr multi	50	30
337	A96	120fr multi	1.00	65

Telecommunications (30fr); National Telecommunications School, 10th anniversary (60fr); International Telecommunication Society of Chad (120fr).

WHO Emblem and Man (Back Pain) A97

Designs (WHO Emblem and): 60fr, Woman's head (neck pain; horiz.). 120fr, Leg (knee pain).

Perf. 12½x13, 13x12½

1977, Nov. 10 Engraved

338	A97	30fr multi	25	18
339	A97	60fr multi	50	30
340	A97	120fr multi	1.00	65

World Rheumatism Year.

World Cup Emblems and Saving a Goal—A98

Designs (Argentina '78, World Cup Emblems and): 60fr, Heading the ball. 100fr, Referee whistling a goal. 200fr, World Cup poster. 300fr, Pelé. 500fr, Helmut Schoen and Munich stadium.

1977, Nov. 25 Litho. ***Perf. 13½***

341	A98	40fr multi	35	15
342	A98	60fr multi	60	27
343	A98	100fr multi	95	42
344	A98	200fr multi	1.90	75
345	A98	300fr multi	3.00	1.15
		Nos. 341-345 (5)	6.80	2.74

Souvenir Sheet

346	A98	500fr multi	4.75	1.85

World Cup Soccer Championship, Argentina '78. No. 346 has multicolored margin showing Argentina '78 emblem and stadium. Size: 119x80½mm.

Nos. 328-329 Overprinted in Silver: "ANNIVERSAIRE DU COURONNEMENT 1953-1978"

1978, Sept. 13 ***Perf. 14x13½***

347	A92	250fr multi	2.00	1.00

Souvenir Sheet

348	A92	450fr multi	4.00

25th anniversary of coronation of Queen Elizabeth II. Size of No. 348: 111x92mm.

Abraham and Melchisedek, by Rubens—A99

Rubens Paintings: 120fr, Helene Fourment (vert.). 200fr, David and the Elders of Israel. 300fr, Anne of Austria (vert.). 500fr, Marie de Medicis (vert.).

1978, Nov. 23 Litho. ***Perf. 13½***

349	A99	60fr multi	60	30
350	A99	120fr multi	1.20	60
351	A99	200fr multi	2.00	1.00
352	A99	300fr multi	3.00	1.50

Souvenir Sheet

353	A99	500fr multi	5.50

Peter Paul Rubens (1577-1640). No. 353 has multicolored margin showing entire painting. Size: 78x103mm.

Dürer Portrait A100

Dürer Paintings: 150fr, Jacob Muffel. 250fr, Young Woman. 350fr, Oswolt Krel.

1978, Nov. 23

354	A100	60fr multi	60	30
355	A100	150fr multi	1.50	75
356	A100	250fr multi	2.50	1.25
357	A100	350fr multi	3.50	1.75

Albrecht Dürer (1471-1528), German painter.

Head, Village and Fly A101

1978, Nov. 28 ***Perf. 13***

358	A101	60f multi	60	30

National Health Day.

Nos. 341-346 Overprinted in Silver:
a. 1962 BRESIL-TCHECOSLOVAQUIE / 3-1
b. 1966 / GRANDE BRETAGNE / - ALLEMAGNE (RFA) / 4-2
c. 1970 BRESIL-ITALIE 4-1
d. 1974 ALLEMAGNE (RFA)- / PAY BAS 2-1
e. 1978 / ARGENTINE -/ PAY BAS / 3-1
f. ARGENTINE -PAYS BAS / 3-1

1978, Dec. 30 Litho. ***Perf. 13½***

359	A98(a)	40fr multi	40	20
360	A98(b)	60fr multi	60	30
361	A98(c)	100fr multi	1.00	50
362	A98(d)	200fr multi	2.00	1.00
363	A98(e)	300fr multi	3.00	1.50
		Nos. 359-363 (5)	7.00	3.50

Souvenir Sheet

364	A98(f)	500fr multi	5.00	2.50

World Soccer Championship winners. Size of No. 364: 119x80½mm.

UPU Emblems, Camel Caravan, Satellites—A102

Design: 150fr, Obus woman and houses, Massa Territory, hibiscus.

1979, June 8 Litho. ***Perf. 12x12½***

365	A102	60fr multi	60	30
366	A102	150fr multi	1.50	75

Philexafrique II, Libreville, Gabon, June 8-17. Nos. 365, 366 each printed in sheets of 10 with 5 labels showing exhibition emblem.

Wildlife Fund Emblem and Gazelle A103

Protected Animals: 50fr, Addax. 60fr, Oryx antelope. 100fr, Cheetah. 150fr, Zebra. 300fr, Rhinoceros.

1979, Sept. 15 Litho. ***Perf. 14½***

367	A103	40fr multi	40	20
368	A103	50fr multi	50	25
369	A103	60fr multi	60	30
370	A103	100fr multi	1.00	50
371	A103	150fr multi	1.50	75
372	A103	300fr multi	3.00	1.50
		Nos. 367-372 (6)	7.00	3.50

Souvenir Sheet

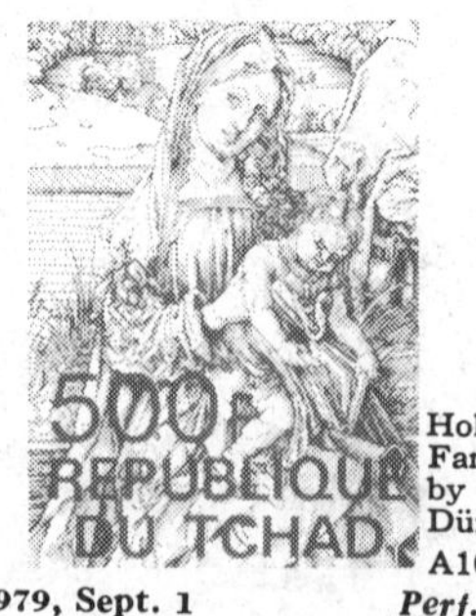

Holy Family, by Dürer A104

1979, Sept. 1 ***Perf. 13½***

373	A104	500fr brn & dl red	5.50	2.75

Albrecht Dürer (1471-1528), German engraver and painter. No. 373 has brown and dull red margin showing entire etching. Size: 90x115mm.

See "Special Notices" at the front of this volume for data on the listing methods of this Catalogue, abbreviations, condition, prices and examination.

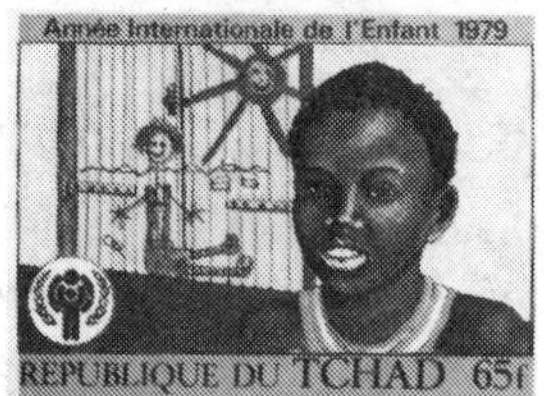

Boy and Handpainted Doors—A105

IYC Emblem and: 75fr, Oriental girl. 100fr, Caucasian girl, doves. 150fr, African boys. 250fr, Pencil and outlines of child's hands.

1979, Sept. 19 Litho. ***Perf. 13½***

374	A105	65fr multi	65	32
375	A105	75fr multi	75	38
376	A105	100fr multi	1.00	50
377	A105	150fr multi	1.50	75

Souvenir Sheet

378	A105	250fr multi	2.75	1.40

International Year of the Child. No. 378 has multicolored margin showing IYC emblem, children and trains. Size: 103x78mm.

Nos. 314-315 Overprinted "ALUNISSAGE/APOLLO XI/ JUILLET 1969" and Emblem

1979, Nov. 26 Litho. ***Perf. 13½x14***

379	A86	45fr multi	45	22
380	A86	90fr multi	90	45
		Nos. 379-380, C240-C242 (5)	6.85	3.42

Apollo 11 moon landing, 10th anniversary.

Ski Jump, Lake Placid '80 Emblem A106

Lake Placid '80 Emblem and: 20fr, Slalom (vert.). 40fr, Biathlon (vert.). 150fr, Women's slalom (vert.). 350fr, Cross-country skiing. 500fr, Downhill skiing.

1979, Dec. 18 ***Perf. 14½***

381	A106	20fr multi	20	10
382	A106	40fr multi	40	20
383	A106	60fr multi	60	30
384	A106	150fr multi	1.50	75
385	A106	350fr multi	3.50	1.75
386	A106	500fr multi	5.00	2.50
		Nos. 381-386 (6)	11.20	5.60

13th Winter Olympic Games, Lake Placid, N.Y., Feb. 12-24, 1980.

Jet over Map of Africa—A107

1980, Feb. 20 Litho. ***Perf. 12½***

387	A107	15fr yel & multi	15	8
388	A107	30fr bl & multi	30	15
389	A107	60fr red & multi	60	30

ASECNA (Air Safety Board), 20th anniversary.

21st Birthday of Princess Diana—A109

1982, July 2 **Litho.** ***Perf. 13½***

395	A109	30fr 1961	30	15
396	A109	40fr 1965	40	20
397	A109	50fr 1967	50	25
398	A109	60fr 1975	60	30
		Nos. 395-398, C260-C261 (6)	5.60	2.80

1984 Olympic Games, Los Angeles—A110

1982, Aug. 2 **Litho.** ***Perf. 13½***

399	A110	30fr Gymnast	30	15
400	A110	40fr Equestrian	40	20
401	A110	50fr Judeo	50	25
402	A110	60fr High jump	60	30
403	A110	80fr Hurdles	80	40
404	A110	300fr Woman gymnast	3.00	1.50
		Nos. 399-404(6)	5.60	2.80

Souvenir Sheet

405	A110	500fr Relay race	5.00	2.50

No. 405 contains one stamp (56x39mm.); multicolored margin continues design. Size: 110x82mm. Nos. 403-405 airmail.

Scouting Year—A111

Scouts from various countries.

1982

406	A111	30fr West Germany	30	15
407	A111	40fr Upper Volta	40	20
408	A111	50fr Mali	50	25
409	A111	60fr Scotland	60	30
410	A111	80fr Kuwait	80	40
411	A111	300fr Chad	3.00	1.50
		Nos. 401-411 (6)	5.60	2.80

Souvenir Sheet

412	A111	500fr Chad, diff.	5.00	2.50

No. 412 contains one stamp (53x35mm.); multicolored margin shows banner around globe. Size: 110x75mm. Nos. 410-412 airmail.

SEMI-POSTAL STAMPS

Anti-Malaria Issue

Common Design Type

Perf. 12½x12

1962, Apr. 7 Engraved Unwmkd.

B1 CD108 25fr +5fr org 85 85

Issued for the World Health Organization drive to eradicate malaria.

Freedom from Hunger Issue

Common Design Type

1963, Mar. 21 ***Perf. 13***

B2 CD112 25fr +5fr dk grn, dk bl & brn 75 75

Red Cross, Mother and Children
SP1

1974, Oct. 2 Photo. ***Perf. 12½x13***

B3 SP1 30fr +10fr multi 35 30

Red Cross of Chad, first anniversary.

AIR POST STAMPS

Olympic Games Issue

French Equatorial Africa No. C37 Surcharged in Red

XVII• OLYMPIADE 1960 250F REPUBLIQUE DU TCHAD

Engraved

1960, Dec. 15 ***Perf. 13*** **Unwmkd.**

C1 AP8 250fr on 500fr grnsh blk, blk & sl 8.50 8.50

Issued to commemorate the 17th Olympic Games, Rome, Aug. 25–Sept. 11. Surcharge 46mm. wide; illustration reduced.

Red Bishops AP1 Discus Thrower AP2

Designs (birds in pairs): 100fr, Scarlet-chested sunbird. 200fr, African paradise flycatcher. 250fr, Malachite kingfisher. 500fr, Nubian carmine bee-eater.

Engraved

1961-63 ***Perf. 13*** **Unwmkd.**

C2 AP1 50fr dk grn, mag & blk 80 15
C3 AP1 100fr multi 1.50 70
C4 AP1 200fr multi 3.00 1.25
C5 AP1 250fr dk bl, grn & dp org ('63) 3.75 1.85
C6 AP1 500fr multi 7.50 4.00
Nos. C2-C6 (5) 16.55 7.95

Air Afrique Issue

Common Design Type

1962, Feb. 17 ***Perf. 13*** **Unwmkd.**

C7 CD107 25fr lt bl, org brn & blk 45 25

Issued to commemorate the founding of Air Afrique (African Airlines).

Abidjan Games Issue

Photogravure

1962, July 21 ***Perf. 12x12½***

C8 AP2 100fr brn, lt grn & blk 1.50 85

African Postal Union Issue

Common Design Type

1963, Sept. 8 ***Perf. 12½*** **Unwmkd.**

C9 CD114 85fr dk bl, ocher & red 1.20 65

Air Afrique Issue, 1963

Common Design Type

1963, Nov. 19 ***Perf. 13x12***

C10 CD115 50fr multi 1.10 75

Europafrica Issue

Common Design Type

1963, Nov. 30 Photo. ***Perf. 12x13***

C11 CD116 50fr dp grn, yel & dk brn 75 55

Mail Truck and Broussard Plane
AP4

Engraved

1963, Dec. 16 ***Perf. 13*** **Unwmkd.**

C12 AP4 100fr sl grn, ultra & red brn 1.50 50

Chiefs of State Issue

Map and Presidents of Chad, Congo, Gabon and Central African Republic
AP4a

1964, June 23 Photo. ***Perf. 12½***

C13 AP4a 100fr multi 1.35 65

See note after Central African Republic No. C19.

Europafrica Issue, 1964

Globe and Emblems of Industry and Agriculture—AP5

1964, July 20 ***Perf. 13x12***

C14 AP5 50fr brn, pur & dp org 65 45

See note after Cameroun No. 402.

Soccer—AP6

Designs: 50fr, Javelin throw (vert.). 100fr, High jump (vert.). 200fr, Runners.

1964, Aug. 12 Engr. ***Perf. 13***

C15 AP6 25fr yel grn, sl grn & org brn 35 25
C16 AP6 50fr org brn, ind & brt bl 75 50
C17 AP6 100fr blk, red & brt grn 1.50 1.00
C18 AP6 200fr bis, blk & car 3.00 1.65
a. Min. sheet of 4 6.00 6.00

Issued for the 18th Olympic Games, Tokyo, Oct. 10–25, 1964. No. C18a contains one each of Nos. C15–C18. Size: 191x99mm.

Communications Symbols
AP7

1964, Nov. 2 Litho. ***Perf. 12½x13***

C19 AP7 25fr lil, dk brn & lt red brn 40 20

Issued to commemorate the Pan-African and Malagasy Posts and Telecommunications Congress, Cairo, Oct. 24–Nov. 6.

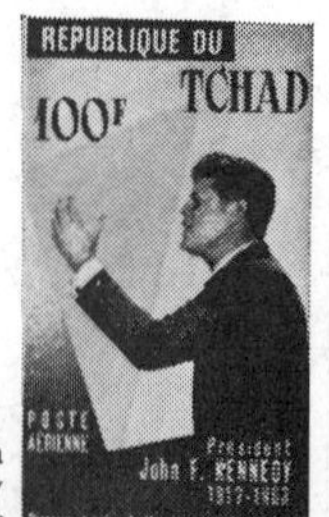

President John F. Kennedy
AP8

1964, Nov. 3 Photo. ***Perf. 12½***

C20 AP8 100fr multi 1.75 1.25
a. Souv. sheet of 4 7.00 7.00

Issued in memory of Pres. John F. Kennedy (1917–1963). No. C20a contains 4 No. C20; black marginal inscription. Size: 90x129mm.

ICY Emblem
AP9

1965, July 5 Photo. ***Perf. 13***

C21 AP9 100fr multi 1.50 85

International Cooperation Year, 1965.

Abraham Lincoln—AP10

1965, Sept. 7 ***Perf. 13*** **Unwmkd.**

C22 AP10 100fr multi 1.50 85

Centenary of death of Abraham Lincoln.

Musical Instrument Type of Regular Issue

Design: 100fr, Xylophone (marimba).

1965, Oct. 26 Engraved ***Perf. 13***

Size: 48x27mm.

C23 A18 100fr ocher, brt bl & vio bl 1.35 45

Winston Churchill
AP11

1965, Nov. 23 Engraved ***Perf. 13***

C24 AP11 50fr dk grn & blk 75 35

Issued in memory of Sir Winston Spencer Churchill (1874–1965), statesman and World War II leader.

Dr. Albert Schweitzer and Outstretched Hands
AP12

1966, Feb. 15 Photo. ***Perf. 12½***

C25 AP12 100fr multi 1.50 75

Issued in memory of Dr. Albert Schweitzer (1875–1965), medical missionary, theologian and musician.

Air Afrique Issue, 1966

Common Design Type

1966, Aug. 31 Photo. ***Perf. 13***

C26 CD123 30fr yel grn, blk & gray 45 25

Issued to commemorate the introduction of DC-8F planes by Air Afrique.

White-throated Bee-eater—AP13

Birds: 50fr, Blue-eared glossy starling. 200fr, African pygmy kingfisher. 250fr, Red-throated bee-eater. 500fr, Little green bee-eater.

1966-67 Photo. *Perf. 13x12½*

C27 AP13 50fr gold & multi 50 25
C28 AP13 100fr bluish gray & multi 1.00 45
C29 AP13 200fr grnsh gray & multi 2.00 1.00
C30 AP13 250fr pale bl & multi 2.50 1.20
C31 AP13 500fr pale sal & multi 5.00 2.50
Nos. C27-C31 (5) 11.00 5.40

Issue dates: 100fr, 200fr, 500fr, Oct. 18, 1966. Others, Mar. 21, 1967.

Congress Hall—AP14

1967, Jan. 5 Photo. *Perf. 12½*

C32 AP14 25fr multi 40 20

Opening of the new Congress Hall.

Breguet 19 Biplane—AP15

Planes: 30fr, Latécoère 631 hydroplane. 50fr, Douglas DC-3. 100fr, Piper Cherokee 6.

1967, Aug. 1 Engr. *Perf. 13*

C33 AP15 25fr sky bl, sl grn & lt brn 40 20
C34 AP15 30fr sky bl, ind & grn 45 25
C35 AP15 50fr sky bl, ol bis & sl grn 75 40
C36 AP15 100fr dk bl, sl grn & dk red 1.50 75

First anniversary of Air Chad.

African Postal Union Issue, 1967

Common Design Type

1967, Sept. 9 Engraved *Perf. 13*

C37 CD124 100fr ol, brt pink & red brn 1.35 70

Rock Painting Type of Regular Issue

Rock Paintings: 100fr, Masked dancers. 125fr, Rabbit hunt.

1967, Dec. 19 Engraved *Perf. 13*

Size: 48x27mm.

C38 A32 100fr brt grn, sal & mar 1.50 65
C39 A32 125fr ultra, sal & mar 1.85 90

Issued to commemorate the Balloud expedition in the Ennedi Mountains.

Downhill Skiing—AP16

Design: 100fr, Ski jump (vert.).

1968, Feb. 5 Engraved *Perf. 13*

C40 AP16 30fr red lil, brt grn & dk ol 45 25
C41 AP16 100fr vio bl, brt bl & sl grn 1.50 85

Issued to commemorate the 10th Winter Olympic Games, Grenoble, France, Feb. 6–18.

Konrad Adenauer AP17

1968, Mar. 19 Photo. *Perf. 12½*

C42 AP17 52fr grn, dk brn & lt lil 80 45
a. Souv. sheet of 4 3.25 3.25

Issued in memory of Konrad Adenauer (1876–1967), chancellor of West Germany (1949–63). No. C42a contains four No. C42. Margin with black inscription and 1967 CEPT (Europa) emblem. Size: 120½x169mm.

The Snake Charmer, by Henri Rousseau—AP18

Design: 130fr, "War" by Henri Rousseau.

1968, May 14 Photo. *Perf. 13½*

Size: 41x41mm.

C43 AP18 100fr ultra & multi 1.50 60

Size: 48x35mm. *Perf. 12½*

C44 AP18 130fr brn & multi 1.80 80

Hurdlers—AP19

Design: 80fr, Relay race.

1968, Oct. 16 Engraved *Perf. 13*

C45 AP19 32fr cop red, grn & choc 50 20
C46 AP19 80fr ultra, choc & car 1.00 30

Issued to commemorate the 19th Olympic Games, Mexico City, Oct. 12–27.

PHILEXAFRIQUE Issue

The Actor Wolf (Bernard), by Jacques L. David AP20

1969, Jan. 15 Photo. *Perf. 12½*

C47 AP20 100fr multi 1.50 90

Issued to publicize PHILEXAFRIQUE, Philatelic Exhibition in Abidjan, Feb. 14–23. Printed with alternating lilac rose label.

2nd PHILEXAFRIQUE Issue

Common Design Type

Design: 50fr, Chad No. J12 and Moundang Dancers.

1969, Feb. 14 Engraved *Perf. 13*

C48 CD128 50fr red, brt bl, brn & grn 75 50

Issued to commemorate the opening of PHILEXAFRIQUE, Abidjan, Feb. 14.

Gustav Nachtigal and Tibesti Gorge, 1869
AP21

Design: No. C50, Heinrich Barth and Lake Chad, 1851.

1969, Feb. 17

C49 AP21 100fr vio bl, dk brn & brn 1.25 35
C50 AP21 100fr grn, pur & bl 1.25 35

Issued to honor the German explorers Gustav Nachtigal (1834–1885) and Heinrich Barth (1821–1865), and to commemorate the state visit of the President of West Germany Heinrich Lubke.

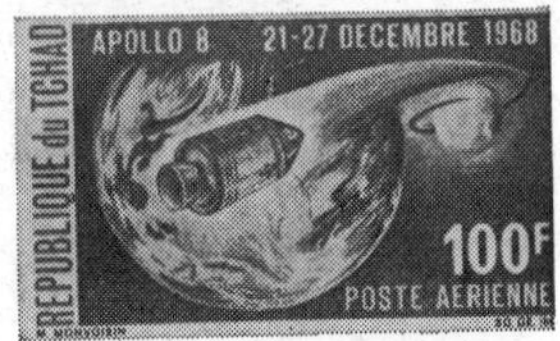

Apollo 8, Earth and Moon
AP22

1969, Apr. 10 Photo. *Perf. 13*

C51 AP22 100fr multi 1.25 65

Issued to commemorate the U.S. Apollo 8 mission, the first men in orbit around the moon, Dec. 21–27, 1968.

Mahatma Gandhi AP23

Portraits: No. C53, John F. Kennedy. No. C54, Rev. Dr. Martin Luther King, Jr. No. C55, Robert F. Kennedy.

1969, May 20 Photo. *Perf. 12½*

C52 AP23 50fr blk & lt grn 65 35
C53 AP23 50fr blk & tan 65 35
C54 AP23 50fr blk & pink 65 35
C55 AP23 50fr blk & lt vio bl 65 35
a. Souv. sheet of 4 3.00 3.00

Issued to honor exponents of non-violence. No. C55a contains one each of Nos. C52–C55. Black marginal inscription. Size: 120x159mm.

Presidents Tombalbaye and Mobutu, Map and Flags of Chad and Congo—AP24

Embossed on Gold Foil

1969 *Die-cut Perf. 13½*

C56 AP24 1000fr gold, dk bl & red 16.00 16.00

Issued to commemorate the first anniversary of the establishment of the Union of Central African States, comprising Chad, Congo Democratic Republic and Central African Republic.

Napoleon Visiting Hospital, by Alexandre Veron-Bellecourt
AP25

Paintings: 85fr, Battle of Wagram, by Horace Vernet. 130fr, Battle of Austerlitz, by Francois Pascal Gerard.

1969, July 23 Photo. *Perf. 12x12½*

C57 AP25 30fr multi 60 45
C58 AP25 85fr multi 1.50 1.10
C59 AP25 130fr multi 2.50 1.75

Bicentenary of birth of Napoleon I.

Apollo 11 Issue

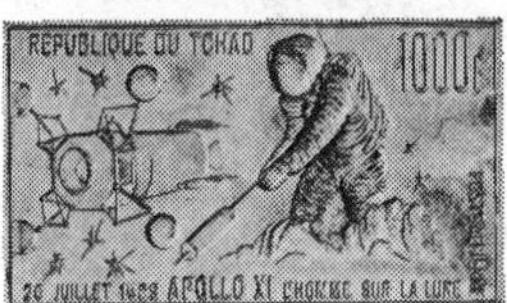

Astronaut on Moon—AP26

Embossed on Gold Foil

1969, Oct. 17 *Die-cut Perf. 13½*

C60 AP26 1000fr gold 16.00 16.00

See note after Algeria No. 427.

Village Life, by Goto Narcisse
AP27

Designs: No. C62, Women at the Market, by Iba N'Diaye. No. C63, Woman with Flowers, by Iba N'Diaye (vert.).

Perf. 12x12½, 12½x12

1970 Photogravure

C61 AP27 100fr multi 1.10 30
C62 AP27 250fr grn & multi 3.00 70
C63 AP27 250fr brn & multi 3.00 70

Issue dates: Mar. 17, 100fr. Aug. 28, Nos. C62–C63.

EXPO Emblem and Osaka Print
AP28

Designs (EXPO Emblem and): 100fr, Tower of the Sun. 125fr, Osaka print (diff. design).

1970, June 30 Engraved *Perf. 13*

C64	AP28	50fr bl, red brn & sl grn	70	18
C65	AP28	100fr red, yel grn & Prus bl	1.35	28
C66	AP28	125fr blk, dk red & bis	1.60	40

Issued to publicize EXPO '70 International Exhibition, Osaka, Japan, Mar. 15–Sept. 13.

Nos. C28–C30 Surcharged in Carmine with New Value and Bars and Overprinted:
a. "APOLLO XI / 1er débarquement sur la lune / 20 juillet 1969"
b. "APOLLO XII / Exploration de la lune / 19 novembre 1969"
c. "APOLLO XIII / Exploit spatial / 11–17 avril 1970"

1970, July 9 Photo. *Perf. 13x12½*

C67	AP13 (a)	50fr on 100fr multi	65	40
C68	AP13 (b)	100fr on 200fr multi	1.30	60
C69	AP13 (c)	125fr on 250fr multi	1.60	80

Space missions of Apollo 11, 12 and 13.

DC-8 "Fort Lamy" over Airport
AP29

1970, Aug. 5 *Perf. 12½*

C70	AP29	30fr dk sl grn & multi	40	15

The Visitation, Venetian School, 15th Century
AP30

Paintings, Venetian School: 25fr, Nativity, 15th century. 30fr, Virgin and Child, c. 1350.

1970, Dec. 15 Photo. *Perf. 12½x12*

C71	AP30	20fr gold & multi	30	15
C72	AP30	25fr gold & multi	32	20
C73	AP30	30fr gold & multi	40	25

Christmas 1970. See Nos. C105–C108.

Post Office Mauritius and Emblem
AP31

Designs (PHILEXOCAM Emblem and): 20fr, Tuscany No. 23. 30fr, France No. 8. 60fr, United States No. 2. 80fr, Japan No. 8. 100fr, Saxony No. 1.

1971, Jan. 23 Engraved *Perf. 13*

C74	AP31	10fr lt bl grn, bis & dk bl	15	5
C75	AP31	20fr brt grn, blk & bis	25	8
C76	AP31	30fr mar, blk & org brn	40	15
C77	AP31	60fr car lake, org brn & blk	70	25
C78	AP31	80fr bl, bis brn & dl bl	90	38
C79	AP31	100fr bl, dl bl & bis brn	1.35	45
a.		Souvenir sheet of 6	4.00	4.00
		Nos. C74-C79 (6)	3.75	1.36

Publicity for PHILEXOCAM, philatelic exhibition, Fort Lamy, Jan. 23–30. No. C79a contains one each of Nos. C74–C79 with orange brown marginal inscription. Size: 158x130mm.

Gamal Abdel Nasser
AP32

1971, Feb. 16 Photo. *Perf. 12½*

C80	AP32	75fr multi	75	20

In memory of Gamal Abdel Nasser (1918–1970), President of Egypt.

Presidents Mobutu, Bokassa and Tombalbaye—AP33

1971, Apr. 28 Photo. *Perf. 13*

C81	AP33	100fr multi	1.00	50

Return of Central African Republic to the United States of Central Africa which also includes Congo Democratic Republic and Chad.

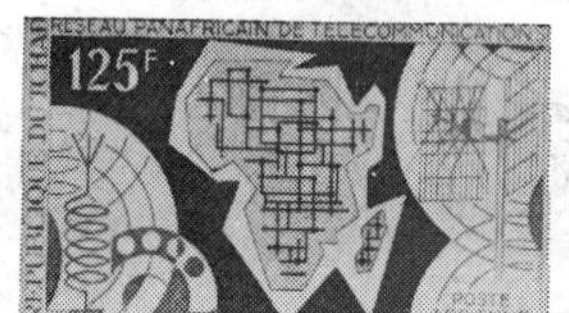

Map of Africa, Communications Network and Symbols—AP34

1971, May 17 Engraved *Perf. 13*

C82	AP34	125fr ultra, sl grn & brn red	1.40	30

Pan-African telecommunications system.

Boys Around Campfire, Torii
AP35

1971, Aug. 24 Photo. *Perf. 12½*

C83	AP35	250fr multi	2.75	85

13th Boy Scout World Jamboree, Asagiri Plain, Japan, Aug. 2–10.

White Egret—AP36

1971, Sept. 28 Photo. *Perf. 13x12½*

C84	AP36	1000fr blk, dk bl & ocher	10.00	7.00

Greek Marathon Runners—AP37

Designs: 45fr, Ancient Olympic Stadium. 75fr, Greek wrestlers. 130fr, Olympic Stadium, Athens, 1896.

1971, Oct. 5 *Perf. 12½*

C85	AP37	40fr multi	50	25
C86	AP37	45fr multi	55	35
C87	AP37	75fr multi	85	40
C88	AP37	130fr multi	1.40	75

75th anniversary of modern Olympic Games.

Duke Ellington
AP38

Portraits: 50fr, Sidney Bechet. 100fr, Louis Armstrong.

1971, Oct. 20 Lithographed *Perf. 13*

C89	AP38	50fr multi	65	18
C90	AP38	75fr lt bl & multi	90	23
C91	AP38	100fr multi	1.25	35

Famous American jazz musicians.

Charles de Gaulle
AP39

Design: No. C93, Félix Eboué.

Lithographed and Embossed

1971, Nov. 9 *Perf. 12½*

C92	AP39	200fr grn, yel grn & gold	3.50	3.50
C93	AP39	200fr bl, lt bl & gold	3.50	3.50
a.		Souvenir sheet of 2	7.50	7.50

First anniversary of the death of Charles de Gaulle (1890–1970), president of France. No. C93a contains one each of Nos. C92–C93 with brown and ocher label carrying commemorative inscription and de Gaulle's signature. Size: 110x70mm.

African Postal Union Issue, 1971
Common Design Type

Design: 100fr, Sao antelope head and UAMPT building, Brazzaville, Congo.

1971, Nov. 13 Photo. *Perf. 13x13½*

C94	CD135	100fr bl & multi	1.10	35

Apollo 15 Rocket
AP40

Designs: 80fr, Apollo 15 capsule (horiz.). 150fr, Lunar module on Moon (horiz.). 250fr, Astronaut making tests. 300fr, Moon-buggy. No. C100, Successful splashdown (horiz.). No. C101, Apollo 15 insignia.

1972, Jan. 5 Litho. *Perf. 13½*

C95	AP40	40fr multi	32	15
C96	AP40	80fr multi	65	33
C97	AP40	150fr multi	1.20	60
C98	AP40	250fr multi	2.00	1.00
C99	AP40	300fr multi	2.40	1.20
C100	AP40	500fr multi	4.00	2.00
		Nos. C95-C100 (6)	10.57	5.28

Souvenir Sheet

C101	AP40	500fr multi	4.00	1.85

Apollo 15 moon landing. No. C101 has multicolored margin with American flag, and portraits of the families of astronauts Scott, Worden and Irwin. Size: 103x84 mm.

Soyuz 2 Link-up—AP41

Designs: 30fr, Soyuz 2 on launching pad (vert.). 50fr, No. C108, Cosmonauts in uniform. 200fr, V. I. Patzaev. No. C106, V. N. Volkov. 400fr, G. L. Dobrovolsky. No. C109, Three cosmonauts.

1972, Jan. 5 *Perf. 13½x13*

C102	AP41	30fr multi	25	13
C103	AP41	50fr multi	40	20
C104	AP41	100fr multi	80	40
C105	AP41	200fr multi	1.60	80
C106	AP41	300fr multi	2.40	1.20
C107	AP41	400fr multi	3.25	1.60
		Nos. C102-C107 (6)	8.70	4.33

Souvenir Sheets

C108	AP41	300fr multi	3.00	1.50
C109	AP41	400fr multi	4.00	2.00

Soyuz 2 link-up project. No. C108 has multicolored margin depicting launching pad, No. C109, Moscow sky-line. Size: 100x79mm.

Bobsledding—AP42

Design: 100fr, Slalom.

1972, Feb. 24 Engraved *Perf. 13*

C110 AP42 50fr Prus bl & rose red 60 20
C111 AP42 100fr red lil & sl grn 1.20 35

11th Winter Olympic Games, Sapporo, Japan, Feb. 3–13.

Pres. Tombalbaye Type, 1972

1972, Apr. 13 Litho. *Perf. 13*

C112 A63 70fr multi 70 35
C113 A63 80fr multi 80 40

11th Winter Olympic Type, 1972

Designs: 130fr, Speed skating. No. C115, Ice hockey. No. C116, Ski jumping. 250fr, 4-man bobsled.

1972, Apr. 13 *Perf. 13½*

C114 A64 130fr multi 1.30 65
C115 A64 200fr multi 2.00 1.00

Souvenir Sheets

C116 A64 200fr multi 2.00 1.00
C117 A64 250fr multi 2.50 1.25

11th Winter Olympic Games, Sapporo, Japan. Nos. C116 and C117 have multicolored margins showing Japanese religious figures. Size: 99x79mm.

Scout Jamboree Type, 1972

Designs: 100fr, Cooking preparation. 120fr, Lord Baden Powell. 250fr, Hiking.

1972, May 15

C118 A67 100fr multi 1.00 60
C119 A67 120fr multi 1.20 75

Souvenir Sheet

C120 A67 250fr multi 2.50 1.50

Scout Jamboree. No. C120 has multicolored margin showing African veldt and ostrich. Size: 102x81mm.

Zebras—AP43

Designs: 30fr, Mandrills. 100fr, African elephants. 130fr, Gazelles. 150fr, Hippopotamuses. 200fr, Lion cub.

1972, May 15 Litho. *Perf. 13*

C121 AP43 20fr multi 20 10
C122 AP43 30fr multi 30 15
C123 AP43 100fr multi 1.00 50
C124 AP43 130fr multi 1.30 65
C125 AP43 150fr multi 1.50 75
Nos. C121-C125 (5) 4.30 2.15

Souvenir Sheet

C126 AP43 200fr multi 2.00 1.00

African wild animals. No. C126 has multicolored margin showing map of Africa, sun and various animals. Size: 102½x79 mm.

See "Special Notices" at the front of this volume for data on the listing methods of this Catalogue, abbreviations, condition, prices and examination.

View of Venice, by Caffi—AP44

Paintings by Ippolito Caffi: 40fr, Sailing ship and Doge's Palace (vert.). 140fr, Grand Canal (vert.).

1972, May 23 Photo.

C127 AP44 40fr gold & multi 50 15
C128 AP44 45fr gold & multi 60 20
C129 AP44 140fr gold & multi 1.50 1.00

UNESCO campaign to save Venice.

11th Winter Olympic Winners Type, 1972

Designs: 150fr, Slalom, B. Cochran, U.S. 200fr, Women's figure skating, B. Schuba, Austria. 250fr, Ice hockey, USSR. 300fr, 2-man bobsled. W. Zimmerer and P. Utzschneider, West Germany.

1972, June 15 *Perf. 14½*

C130 A69 150fr gold & multi 1.50 75
C131 A69 200fr gold & multi 2.00 1.00

Souvenir Sheets

C132 A69 250fr gold & multi 2.00 1.25
C133 A69 300fr gold & multi 3.00 1.75

11th Winter Olympic gold medal winners. Nos. C130–C131 exist se-tenant with label showing earth satellite. Nos. C132–C133 have multicolored margins showing satellite orbiting earth. Size: 127x89mm.

Daudet, "Tartarin de Tarascon," Book Year Emblem—AP45

1972, July 22 Engraved *Perf. 13*

C134 AP45 100fr dk red, lil & dk brn 1.20 30

International Book Year, 1972, and to honor Alphonse Daudet (1840–1897), French writer.

20th Summer Olympics Type, 1972

Designs (TV Tower, Munich and): 100fr, Gymnast. 120fr, Pole vault. 150fr, Fencing. 250fr, Hammer throw. 300fr, Boxing.

1972, Aug. 15

C135 A70 100fr gold & multi 1.00 50
C136 A70 120fr gold & multi 1.20 60
C137 A70 150fr gold & multi 1.50 75

Souvenir Sheets

C138 A70 250fr gold & multi 2.50 1.25
C139 A70 300fr gold & multi 3.00 1.50

20th Summer Olympic Games, Munich, Nos. C135–C137 exist se-tenant with label showing arms of Munich. Nos. C138–C139 have multicolored margin with Munich views. Size: 127x89mm.

Lunokhod on Moon—AP46

Design: 100fr, Luna 16 on moon and rocket in flight (vert.).

1972, Sept. 19

C140 AP46 100fr dk bl, pur & bis 1.20 50
C141 AP46 150fr sl, brn & lil 1.80 75

Russian moon missions.

Farcha Laboratory, Cattle, Scientist—AP47

1972, Nov. 11 Photo. *Perf. 13*

C142 AP47 75fr yel & multi 70 35

20th anniversary of the Farcha Laboratory for veterinary research.

King Faisal and Holy Kaaba, Mecca—AP48

1972, Nov. 17

C143 AP48 75fr multi 75 40

Visit of King Faisal of Saudi Arabia.

Christmas Type of 1970

Designs: 40fr, Virgin and Child, by Giovanni Bellini. 75fr, Virgin and Child, by Dall'Occhio. 80fr, Nativity, by Fra Angelico (horiz.). 95fr, Adoration of the Kings, by Il Perugino.

1972, Dec. 15 Photo. *Perf. 13*

C144 AP30 40fr gold & multi 50 15
C145 AP30 75fr gold & multi 85 25
C146 AP30 80fr gold & multi 1.00 28
C147 AP30 95fr gold & multi 1.10 38

Christmas 1972.

20th Summer Olympic Winners Type, 1972

Designs (Olympic Emblems and): 150fr, Pole vault, Nordwig, East Germany. 250fr, Hurdles, Milburn, U.S. 300fr, Javelin, Wolfermann, West Germany.

1972, Dec. 22

C148 A76 150fr multi 1.50 75
C149 A76 250fr multi 2.50 1.25

Souvenir Sheet

C150 A76 300fr multi 3.00 1.50

20th Summer Olympic Games winners. No. C150 has multicolored margin showing Olympic emblems. Size: 111½x82 mm.

Summer Olympic Winners Type, 1972

Designs (Olympic Emblem and): 150fr, Dressage, Mancinelli, Italy. No. C152; Finn class sailing, Serge Maury, France. No. C153, Swimming, Mark Spitz.

1972, Dec. 22 Litho. *Perf. 11*

C151 A77 150fr gold & multi 1.50 75
C152 A77 250fr gold & multi 2.50 1.25

Souvenir Sheet

C153 A77 250fr multi 2.50 1.25

20th Summer Olympic Games, winners. No. C153 has gold and multicolored margin showing Olympic emblem and flame. Size: 111x82½mm.

Copernicus and Solar System AP49

1973, Mar. 31 Engraved *Perf. 13*

C154 AP49 250fr gray, mag & brn 2.75 1.50

500th anniversary of the birth of Nicolaus Copernicus (1473–1543), Polish astronomer.

Skylab over Africa—AP50

Design: 150fr, Skylab.

1974, Aug. 6 Engraved *Perf. 13*

C155 AP50 100fr mar, bl & ol 1.00 55
C156 AP50 150fr brn, bl & sl grn 1.40 75

Exploits of Skylab, U.S. manned space station.

Soccer—AP51

Designs: 125fr, 150fr, Soccer players; 125fr, vertical.

1974, Oct. 22 Engraved *Perf. 13*

C157 AP51 50fr dl red & choc 45 25
C158 AP51 125fr red & dp grn 1.10 65
C159 AP51 150fr grn & rose red 1.35 75

World Cup Soccer Championship, Munich, June 13–July 7.

Family and WPY Emblem AP52

1974, Nov. 11

C160 AP52 250fr multi 2.25 1.40

World Population Year.

Mail Delivery by Canoe—AP53

Designs (UPU Emblem and): 40fr, Diesel train. 100fr, Jet. 150fr, Spacecraft.

1974, Dec. 20 Engraved *Perf. 13*

C161 AP53 30fr car & multi 28 18
C162 AP53 40fr ultra & blk 35 20
C163 AP53 100fr brn, ultra & blk 90 55
C164 AP53 150fr grn, lil & ol 1.40 85

Centenary of Universal Postal Union.

Women of Different Races, IWY Emblem—AP54

1975, June 25 Photo. *Perf. 13*

C165 AP54 250fr bl & multi 2.10 1.25

International Women's Year 1975.

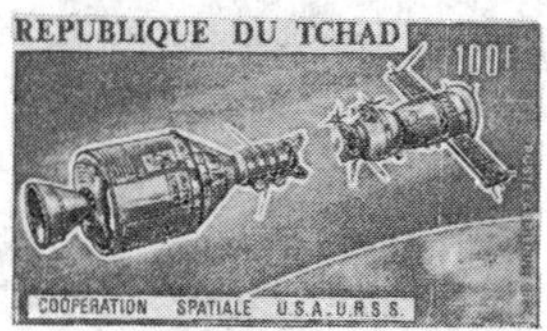

Apollo and Soyuz Before Link-up—AP55

Design: 130fr, Apollo and Soyuz after link-up.

1975, July 15 Engr. *Perf. 13*

C166 AP55 100fr ultra, choc & grn 1.00 50
C167 AP55 130fr vio bl, brn & grn 1.20 75

Apollo Soyuz space test project (Russo-American space cooperation), launching July 15; link-up July 17.

Soccer Player, View of Montreal AP56

Designs (Olympic Rings, Montreal Skyline): 100fr, Discus thrower. 125fr, Runner.

1975, Oct. 14 Engr. *Perf. 13*

C168 AP56 75fr car & sl grn 70 38
C169 AP56 100fr car, choc & bl grn 1.00 50
C170 AP56 125fr brn, bl & car 1.25 75

Pre-Olympic Year 1975.

Nos. C166-C167 Overprinted: "JONCTION / 17 JUILLET 1975"

1975, Nov. 4 Engr. *Perf. 13*

C171 AP55 100fr multi 1.00 50
C172 AP55 130fr multi 1.20 70

Apollo-Soyuz link-up in space, July 17.

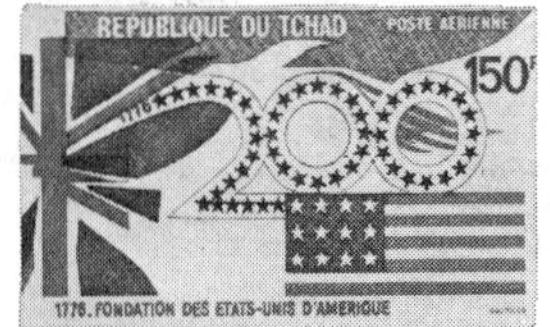

Stylized British and American Flags, "200"—AP57

1975, Dec. 5 Engr. *Perf. 13*

C173 AP57 150fr vio bl, car & ol bis 1.35 75

American Bicentennial.

Adoration of the Shepherds, by Murillo—AP58

Paintings: 75fr, Adoration of the Shepherds, by Georges de La Tour. 80fr, Virgin and Child with Bible, by Rogier van der Weyden (vert.). 100fr, Holy Family, by Raphael (vert.).

1975, Dec. 15 Litho. *Perf. 13x12½*

C174 AP58 40fr yel & multi 40 20
C175 AP58 75fr yel & multi 70 38
C176 AP58 80fr yel & multi 80 40
C177 AP58 100fr yel & multi 1.00 45

Christmas 1975.

12th Winter Olympic Winners Type, 1976

Designs: 250fr, 4-man bobsled, West Germany. 300fr, Speed skating, J. E. Storholt, Norway. 500fr, Downhill skiing, F. Klammer, Austria.

1976, June 21 *Perf. 14*

C178 A84 250fr multi 2.40 1.10
C179 A84 300fr multi 2.85 1.35

Souvenir Sheet

C180 A84 500fr multi 4.75 2.00

12th Winter Olympic Games winners, Innsbruck. No. C180 has multicolored margin showing snowflakes. Size: 114x78mm.

Paul Revere's Ride and Portrait by Copley—AP59

Designs: 125fr, George Washington crossing Delaware. 150fr, Lafayette offering his services to America. 200fr, Rochambeau at Yorktown with Washington. 250fr, Benjamin Franklin presenting Declaration of Independence. 400fr, Count de Grasse's victory at Cape Charles.

1976, July 4 Litho. *Perf. 14*

C181 AP59 100fr multi 95 45
C182 AP59 125fr multi 1.20 60
C183 AP59 150fr multi 1.40 70
C184 AP59 200fr multi 1.90 85
C185 AP59 250fr multi 2.50 95
Nos. C181-C185 (5) 7.95 3.55

Souvenir Sheet

C186 AP59 400fr multi 4.00 1.85

American Bicentennial. No. C186 has multicolored margin showing George Washington and his staff. Size: 113x78mm.

Summer Olympics Type, 1976

Designs: 100fr, Boxing. 200fr, Pole vault. 300fr, Shot put. 500fr, Sprint.

1976, July 12

C187 A85 100fr multi 90 50
C188 A85 200fr multi 1.85 85
C189 A85 300fr multi 2.75 1.10

Souvenir Sheet

C190 A85 500fr multi 4.00 2.00

21st Summer Olympic Games, Montreal. No. C190 has multicolored margin showing Olympic stadium. Size: 103x77mm.

Viking Mars Project Type, 1976

Designs (Mars Lander and): 100fr, Viking landing on Mars. 200fr, Capsule over Mars. 250fr, Lander over Mars. 450fr, Lander and probe.

1976, July 23 Litho. *Perf. 14*

C191 A86 100fr multi 95 50
C192 A86 200fr multi 1.90 85
C193 A86 250fr multi 2.40 95

Souvenir Sheet

C194 A86 450fr multi 4.25 2.00

Viking Mars project, No. C194 has multicolored margin showing Viking probe. Size: 114x89mm.

Concorde—AP60

1976, Oct. 15 Litho. *Perf. 12½*

C195 AP60 250fr bl, blk & ver 2.00 75

First commercial flight of supersonic jet Concorde, Jan. 21.

Nobel Prize Type, 1976

Designs: 100fr, Albert Einstein, physics. 200fr, Dag Hammarskjold, peace. 300fr, Shinichiro Tomanaga, physics. 500fr, Alexander Fleming, medicine.

1976, Dec. 15

C196 A87 100fr multi 95 50
C197 A87 200fr multi 1.90 85
C198 A87 300fr multi 2.85 1.10

Souvenir Sheet

C199 A87 500fr multi 4.75 2.00

Nobel Prize winners. No. C199 has multicolored margin showing reverse and obverse of Nobel medal. Size: 116x79mm.

Adoration of the Shepherds, by Gerard van Honthorst—AP61

Paintings: 30fr, Nativity, by Albrecht Altdorfer (vert.). 60fr, Nativity, by Hans Holbein (vert.). 150fr, Adoration of the Kings, by Gerard David.

1976, Dec. 22 Litho. *Perf. 12½*

C200 AP61 30fr gold & multi 25 15
C201 AP61 60fr gold & multi 50 30
C202 AP61 120fr gold & blk 1.00 60
C203 AP61 150fr gold & blk 1.20 70

Christmas 1976.

Lesdiguières Bridge, by Jongkind—AP62

Design: 120fr, Sailing Ship and Boats, by Johan Barthold Jongkind (1819–1891).

1976, Dec. 27 Photo. *Perf. 13*

C204 AP62 100fr multi 80 45
C205 AP62 120fr multi 1.00 60

Centenary of impressionism.

Zeppelin Type of 1977

Designs: 125fr, Germany No. C40 and North Pole. 150fr, Germany No. C45 and Chicago department store. 175fr, Germany No. C38 and scenes of New York and London. 200fr, 500fr, U.S. No. C15 and New York.

1977, Mar. 30 *Perf. 11*

C206 A91 125fr multi 1.20 50
C207 A91 150fr multi 1.40 60
C208 A91 175fr multi 1.65 70
C209 A91 200fr multi 2.00 85

Souvenir Sheet

C210 A91 500fr multi 4.75 2.00

75th anniversary of the Zeppelin. No. C210 has multicolored margin showing world map with cancellations of Zeppelin flights. Size: 130x91mm.

Sassenage Castle, Grenoble—AP63

1977, May 21 Litho. *Perf. 12½*

C211 AP63 100fr multi 80 45

10th anniversary of the International French Language Council.

Lafayette and Ships—AP64

Designs: 120fr, Abraham Lincoln, eagle and flags (vert.). 150fr, James Madison and family.

1977, July 30 Engr. *Perf. 13*

C212 AP64 100fr multi 80 60
C213 AP64 120fr multi 1.00 70
C214 AP64 150fr multi 1.20 90

American Bicentennial.

Lindbergh and Spirit of St. Louis—AP65

Designs: 100fr, Concorde. 150fr, 200fr, 300fr, Various Lindbergh portraits and Spirit of St. Louis.

1977, Sept. 27

C215	AP65	100fr multi.	80	60
C216	"	120fr "	1.00	70
C217	"	150fr "	1.20	90
C218	"	200fr "	1.60	1.10
C219	"	300fr "	2.40	1.65
		Nos. C215-C219 (5)	7.00	4.95

Charles A. Lindbergh's solo transatlantic flight from New York to Paris, 50th anniversary, and first supersonic transatlantic flight of Concorde.

Mariner 10—AP66

Spacecraft: 200fr, Lunokhod on moon, Luna 21. 300fr, Viking on Mars.

1977, Oct. 10 Engr. *Perf. 13*

C220	AP66	100fr multi.	80	60
C221	"	200fr "	1.60	1.20
C222	"	300fr "	2.40	1.60

Running AP67

Designs: 60fr, Volleyball. 120fr, Soccer. 125fr, Basketball.

1977, Oct. 24 Engr. *Perf. 13*

C223	AP67	30fr multicolored	25	20
C224	"	60fr "	50	35
C225	"	120fr "	1.00	70
C226	"	125fr "	1.00	75

No. C215 Overprinted:
"PARIS NEW – YORK / 22.11.77"

1977, Nov. 22

C227	AP65	100fr multi.	80	60

Concorde, first commercial flight Paris to New York.

Virgin and Child, by Rubens AP68

Rubens Paintings: 60fr, Virgin and Child and Two Donors. 100fr, Adoration of the Shepherds. 125fr, Adoration of the Kings.

1977, Dec. 20 Litho. *Perf. 12½x12*

C228	AP68	30fr multicolored	25	20
C229	"	60fr "	50	35
C230	"	100fr "	80	60
C231	"	125fr "	1.00	75

Christmas 1977.

Antoine de Saint-Exupéry—AP69

Designs: 50fr, Wilbur and Orville Wright and Flyer. 80fr, Hugo Junkers and his plane. 100fr, Gen. Italo Balbo and his plane. 120fr, Concorde. 500fr, Wilbur and Orville Wright and Flyer.

1978, Oct. 25 Litho. *Perf. 13½*

C232	AP69	40fr multicolored	40	20
C233	"	50fr "	50	25
C234	"	80fr "	80	40
C235	"	100fr "	1.00	50
C236	"	120fr "	1.20	60
		Nos. C232-C236 (5)	3.90	1.95

Souvenir Sheet

C237	AP69	500fr multi.	5.50	

History of aviation and 75th anniversary of 1st powered flight. No. C237 has multicolored margin showing Concorde in flight. Size: 104x99mm.

Philexafrique II—Essen Issue
Common Design Types

Designs: No. C238, Rhinoceros and Chad No. C6. No. C239, Kingfisher and Mecklenburg-Strelitz No. 1.

1978, Nov. 1 *Perf. 12½*

C238	CD138	100fr multi.	1.00	50
C239	CD139	100fr "	1.00	50

Nos. C238-C239 printed se-tenant.

Nos. C191-C194 Overprinted
"ALUNISSAGE/APOLLO XI/ JUILLET 1969"

1979, Nov. 26 Litho. *Perf. 13½×14*

C240	A86	100fr multi	1.00	50
C241	A86	200fr multi	2.00	1.00
C242	A86	250fr multi	2.50	1.25

Souvenir Sheet

C243	A86	450fr multi	4.75	2.50

Apollo 11 moon landing, 10th anniversary.

Hurdles, Moscow '80 Emblem—AP70

Moscow '80 Emblem and: 30fr, Field hockey. 250fr, Swimming. 350fr, Running. 500fr, Yachting.

1979, Nov. 30 *Perf. 13½*

C244	AP70	15fr multi	15	8
C245	AP70	30fr multi	30	15
C246	AP70	250fr multi	2.50	1.25
C247	AP70	350fr multi	3.50	1.75

Souvenir Sheet

C248	AP70	500fr multi	5.25	2.75

Pre-Olympic Year. No. C248 has multicolored margin showing Moscow '80 emblem. Size: 118×80mm.

Austria Jubilee Issue of 1910, Canoe, Hill AP71

Hill, Stamps and Vessels: 100fr, U.S. type A97, dhow. 200fr, France No. 21, Sidewheeler. 300fr, Holstein No. 16, ocean liner. 500fr, Chad No. J13, ocean liner.

1979, Dec. 3 *Perf. 14×13½*

C249	AP71	65fr multi	65	35
C250	AP71	100fr multi	1.00	50
C251	AP71	200fr multi	2.00	1.00
C252	AP71	300fr multi	3.00	1.50

Souvenir Sheet

C253	AP71	500fr multi	5.25	2.75

Sir Rowland Hill (1795-1879), originator of penny postage. No. C253 has multicolored margin showing early stamps. Size: 114×91mm.

Nos. C244-C245, C249-C250 Overprinted: "POSTES 1981" in Red or Overprinted and Surcharged Silver on Red.

1981, Nov. 15 Litho. *Perf. 13½, 14x13½*

C254	AP70	30fr on 15fr multi	30	15
C255	AP70	30fr multi	30	15
C256	AP71	60fr on 65fr multi	60	30
C257	AP71	60fr on 100fr multi	60	30

Diana Type of 1982

1982, July 2 Litho. *Perf. 13½*

C260	A109	80fr 1977	80	40
C261	A109	300fr 1980	3.00	1.50

Souvenir Sheet

C262	A109	500fr 1981	5.00	2.50

No. C262 has multicolored margin showing family tree. Size: 78x75mm.

AIR POST SEMI-POSTAL STAMPS

Ramses II Battling the Hittites (from Abu Simbel)
SPAP1

Engraved

1964, March 9 *Perf. 13* Unwmkd.

CB1	SPAP1 10fr	+ 5fr red, grn & vio	35	30
CB2	SPAP1 25fr	+ 5fr red, grn & vio brn	60	50
CB3	SPAP1 50fr	+ 5fr red, grn & sl grn	1.00	90

Issued to publicize the UNESCO world campaign to save historic monuments in Nubia.

Lions Emblem
SPAP2

1967, July 5 Photo. *Perf. 13*

CB4	SPAP2 50fr	+ 10fr multi	90	35

Issued to commemorate the 50th anniversary of Lions International and to publicize the Lions work for the blind.

POSTAGE DUE STAMPS

Postage Due Stamps of France Overprinted

TCHAD

A. E. F.

1928 *Perf. 14x13½* Unwmkd.

J1	D2	5c	lt bl	12	12
J2	D2	10c	gray brn	12	12
J3	D2	20c	ol grn	23	23
J4	D2	25c	brt rose	32	32
J5	D2	30c	lt red	35	35
J6	D2	45c	bl grn	50	50
J7	D2	50c	brn vio	60	60
J8	D2	60c	yel brn	65	65
J9	D2	1fr	red brn	65	65
J10	D2	2fr	org red	2.00	2.00
J11	D2	3fr	brt vio	1.10	1.10
			Nos. J1-J11 (11)	6.64	6.64

Huts
D3

Canoe
D4

Typographed.

1930 *Perf. 14x13½, 13½x14.*

J12	D3	5c	dp bl & ol	28	28
J13	D3	10c	dk red & brn	32	32
J14	D3	20c	grn & brn	50	50
J15	D3	25c	lt bl & brn	55	55
J16	D3	30c	bis brn & Prus bl	55	55
J17	D3	45c	Prus bl & ol	65	65
J18	D3	50c	red vio & brn	75	75
J19	D3	60c	gray lil & bl blk	1.00	1.00
J20	D4	1fr	bis brn & bl blk	1.00	1.00
J21	D4	2fr	vio & brn	1.85	1.85
J22	D4	3fr	dp red & brn	18.50	18.50
			Nos. J12-J22 (11)	25.95	25.95

In 1934 stamps of Chad were superseded by those of French Equatorial Africa.

Republic

Rhinoceros—D5

Tibesti Pictographs: No. J24, Kudu. No. J25, Two antelopes. No. J26, Three antelopes. No. J27, Ostrich. No. J28, Horned bull. No. J29, Bull. No. J30, Wild swine. No. J31, Elephant. No. J32, Rhinoceros. No. J33, Warrior with spear and shield. No. J34, Masked archer.

Engraved

1962, Apr. 20 *Perf. 13* Unwmkd.

J23	D5	50c	ol bis	8	8
J24	D5	50c	brn red	8	8
J25	D5	1fr	blue	10	10
J26	D5	1fr	green	10	10
J27	D5	2fr	vermilion	18	18
J28	D5	2fr	maroon	18	18
J29	D5	5fr	sl grn	20	20
J30	D5	5fr	vio bl	20	20
J31	D5	10fr	brown	55	55
J32	D5	10fr	org brn	55	55
J33	D5	25fr	car rose	1.10	1.10
J34	D5	25fr	violet	1.10	1.10
			Nos. J23-J34 (12)	4.42	4.42

The two designs of the same denomination are printed se-tenant.

Kanem Doll
D6

Dolls: 2fr, Kotoko. 5fr, Leather doll. 10fr, Kotoko. 25fr, Guera.

1969, Sept. 19 Engr. *Perf. 14x13*

J35	D6	1fr	grn, ver & brn	5	5
J36	D6	2fr	ver, yel grn & brn	7	5
J37	D6	5fr	grn, brn & sl grn	15	10
J38	D6	10fr	grn, lil & brn	20	15
J39	D6	25fr	rose, bl & brn	35	25
			Nos. J35-J39 (5)	82	60

MILITARY STAMPS

Flag Bearer and Map of Chad
M1

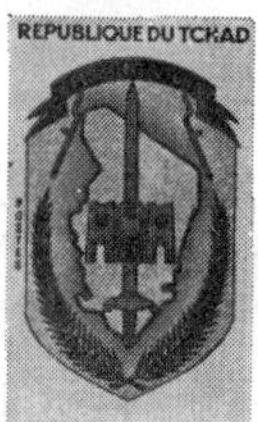

1st Regiment Emblem
M2

No. 78 Overprinted "F.M."

1965 Typo. *Perf. 14x13½*

M1	A5	20fr red & blk	110.00	110.00

Lithographed

1968 *Perf. 13x12½* Unwmkd.

M2	M1	tan & multi	75	50

1972, Jan. 21 Photo. *Perf. 13*

M3	M2	bl & multi	80	50

OFFICIAL STAMPS

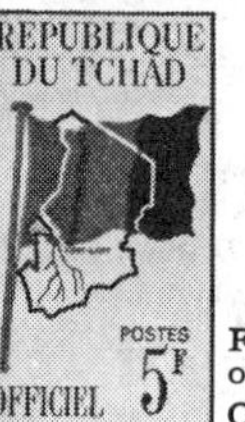

Flag and Map of Chad
O1

Perf. 13½x14

1966–71 Typographed Unwmkd.

Flag in blue, yellow and carmine.

O1	O1	1fr	lt bl	6	3
O2	O1	2fr	gray	6	3
O3	O1	5fr	black	7	4
O4	O1	10fr	vio bl	15	12
O5	O1	25fr	orange	35	18
O6	O1	30fr	brt grn	45	25
O7	O1	40fr	car ('71)	55	25
O8	O1	50fr	red lil	70	30
O9	O1	85fr	green	1.10	55
O10	O1	100fr	brown	1.60	60
O11	O1	200fr	red	2.75	1.00

CHILE

(chē'lā ; chĭl'ē)

LOCATION — Southwest coast of South America.
GOVT.—Republic.
AREA—286,397 sq. mi.
POP.—10,660,000 (est. 1977).
CAPITAL—Santiago.

100 Centavos = 1 Peso
1000 Milésimos = 100 Centésimos = 1 Escudo (1960)
100 Centavos = 1 Peso (1975)

> Prices of early Chile stamps vary according to condition. Quotations for Nos. 1–14 are for fine copies. Very fine to superb specimens sell at much higher prices, and inferior or poor copies sell at reduced prices, depending on the condition of the individual specimen.
>
> Pen cancellations are common on the 1862–67 issues. Such stamps sell for much less than the quoted prices which are for those with handstamped postal cancellations.

Christopher Columbus
A1

Wmkd.

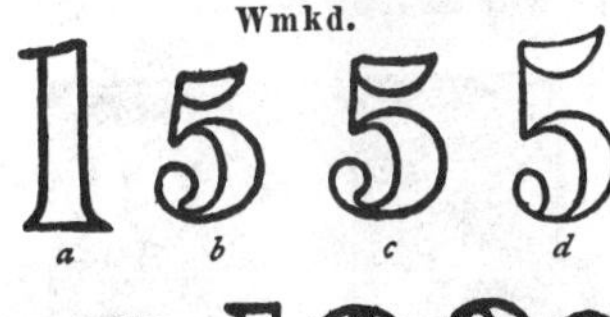

a b c d

10 10 20

e f g

London Prints.

Engraved.

1853 *Imperf.* **Wmk. b.**

Blued Paper.

No.	Type	Description	Unused	Used
1	A1	5c brn red	*500.00*	55.00
a.		White paper		90.00

Wmk. e.

White Paper.

No.	Type	Description	Unused	Used
2	A1	10c dp brt bl	*800.00*	100.00
a.		Blued paper		*650.00*
b.		Diagonal half used as 5c on cover		*600.00*

Santiago Prints.

Impressions Fine and Clear.
White Paper.

1854 **Wmks. b and e.**

No.	Type	Description	Unused	Used
3	A1	5c pale red brn	450.00	45.00
a.		5c dp red brn	*500.00*	50.00
b.		5c chnt	*800.00*	150.00
4	A1	5c brnt sien	*1,500.*	200.00
a.		5c dl choc	*2,750.*	1,000.
5	A1	10c dp bl	*1,250.*	125.00
a.		10c sl bl		125.00
b.		10c grnsh bl		1,000.
c.		Half used as 5c on cover		500.00
6	A1	10c lt dl bl	*1,250.*	125.00
a.		10c pale bl		125.00
b.		Diagonal half used as 5c on cover		375.00

Lithographed.

No.	Type	Description	Unused	Used
7	A1	5c red brn	*2,250.*	275.00
a.		5c pale brn	*1,600.*	225.00

London Print.

Engraved.

1855 Blued Paper **Wmk. c.**

No.	Type	Description	Unused	Used
8	A1	5c brn red	175.00	12.50

Santiago Prints.

Impressions Worn and Blurred.
White Paper.

1856-62 **Wmks. b and e.**

No.	Type	Description	Unused	Used
9	A1	5c rose red ('58)	40.00	6.00
a.		5c car red ('62)	100.00	20.00
b.		5c org red ('61)	250.00	150.00
c.		5c dl redsh brn ('57)	250.00	25.00
d.		Printed on both sides		*550.00*
e.		Double impression		
10	A1	10c dp bl	200.00	25.00
a.		10c sky bl ('57)	200.00	25.00
b.		10c lt bl	200.00	25.00
c.		10c ind bl	250.00	75.00
d.		Half used as 5c on cover		150.00

London Prints.

1862 **Wmks. a, f and g.**

No.	Type	Description	Unused	Used
11	A1	1c lem yel	30.00	37.50
a.		Double impression		*850.00*
12	A1	10c brt bl	50.00	10.00
a.		10c dp bl	50.00	10.00
b.		Blued paper	125.00	25.00
c.		Wmkd. "20" (error)	*4,000.*	*2,000.*
d.		Half used as 5c on cover		150.00
13	A1	20c green	75.00	45.00
a.		20c emer		

Santiago Print.

1865 **Wmk. d.**

No.	Type	Description	Unused	Used
14	A1	5c rose red	30.00	12.50
a.		5c car red	35.00	12.50
b.		Printed on both sides		*225.00*
c.		Laid paper		*200.00*
d.		Double impression		*200.00*

The 5c rose red (shades) on unwatermarked paper, either wove or ribbed, and on paper watermarked Chilean arms in the sheet are reprints made about 1870.

No. 13 has been reprinted in the color of issue and in fancy colors, both from the original engraved plate and from lithographic transfers. The reprints are on paper without watermark or with watermark CHILE and Star.

A2

A3

1867 *Perf. 12* **Unwmkd.**

No.	Type	Description	Unused	Used
15	A2	1c orange	17.50	2.50
		Pen cancellation		25
16	A2	2c black	25.00	3.75
		Pen cancellation		40
17	A2	5c red	17.50	1.25
		Pen cancellation		10
18	A2	10c blue	17.50	2.50
		Pen cancellation		25
19	A2	20c green	25.00	3.75
		Pen cancellation		35

Unused prices for Nos. 15-19 are for stamps with original gum.

1877 ***Rouletted***

No.	Type	Description	Unused	Used
20	A3	1c gray	2.50	1.25
21	A3	2c orange	15.00	3.75
22	A3	5c dl lake	17.50	1.00
23	A3	10c blue	15.00	2.50
a.		Diagonal half used as 5c on cover		
24	A3	20c green	16.00	3.75

The panel inscribed "CENTAVO" is straight on No. 22.

A4

A5

Columbus
A6

1878–99 ***Rouletted***

No.	Type	Description	Unused	Used
25	A4	1c grn ('81)	1.00	20
26	A4	2c rose ('81)	1.25	20
27	A5	5c dl lake ('78)	5.00	50
28	A5	5c ultra ('83)	1.25	10
29	A5	10c org ('85)	2.00	40
a.		10c yel	8.00	1.00
30	A5	15c dk grn ('92)	1.50	50
31	A5	20c gray ('86)	1.25	50
32	A5	25c org brn ('92)	2.00	50
33	A5	30c rose car ('99)	5.00	2.00
34	A5	50c lil ('78)	50.00	10.00
35	A5	50c vio ('85)	2.50	1.00
36	A6	1p dk brn & blk ('92)	25.00	2.00
a.		Imperf. horiz. or vert. pair	125.00	
		Nos. 25-36 (12)	97.75	17.90

Columbus
A7 A8

1894 **Re-engraved.**

No.	Type	Description	Unused	Used
37	A7	1c bl grn	1.00	20
38	A7	2c car lake	1.00	20

In type A4 there is a small colorless ornament at each side of the base of the numeral, above the "E" and "V" of "CENTAVO". In type A7 these ornaments are missing, the figure "1" is broader than in type A4 and the head of the figure "2" is formed by a curved line instead of a ball.

1900–01

Type I. There is a heavy shading of short horizontal lines below "Chile" and the adjacent ornaments.

Type II. There is practically no shading below "Chile" and the ornaments.

Type I.

No.	Type	Description	Unused	Used
39	A8	1c yel grn	1.00	20
40	A8	2c brn rose	2.00	20
41	A8	5c dp bl	12.50	20
42	A8	10c violet	7.50	40
a.		Horizontal pair, imperf. between		
43	A8	20c gray	5.00	1.00
44	A8	30c dp org ('01)	6.00	1.00
45	A8	50c red brn	7.50	1.75
a.		horizontal pair, imperf. between	75.00	
		Nos. 39-45 (7)	41.50	4.75

Type II.

No.	Type	Description	Unused	Used
46	A8	1c yel grn ('01)	1.00	20
47	A8	2c rose ('01)	1.00	20
48	A8	5c dl bl ('01)	5.00	20
a.		Printed on both sides		
49	A8	10c vio ('01)	6.00	50

Columbus
A9 A10

1900 Black Surcharge

No.	Type	Description	Unused	Used
50	A9	5c on 30c rose car	1.00	20
a.		Inverted surcharge	37.50	20.00
b.		Double surcharge	125.00	80.00
c.		Double surcharge, both inverted	125.00	80.00
d.		Double surcharge, one inverted	125.00	80.00
e.		Surcharged on front and back	125.00	80.00

1901–02 ***Perf. 12***

No.	Type	Description	Unused	Used
51	A10	1c green	35	20
52	A10	2c carmine	50	20
53	A10	5c ultra	1.00	10
54	A10	10c red & blk	2.50	40
55	A10	30c vio & blk	7.50	40
56	A10	50c red org & blk	9.00	3.00
		Nos. 51-56 (6)	20.85	4.30

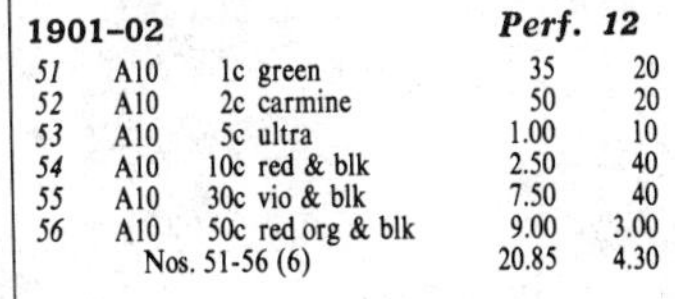

No. 44 Surcharged in Dark Blue

1903 ***Rouletted.***

No.	Type	Description	Unused	Used
57	A8	10c on 30c org	2.50	50
a.		Inverted surcharge	25.00	15.00
b.		Double surcharge	30.00	15.00
c.		Double surch., one inverted	30.00	15.00
d.		Double surch., both inverted	30.00	15.00
e.		Stamp design printed on both sides		

Pedro de Valdivia
A11

Coat of Arms
A12

A13

Telegraph Stamps Surcharged or Overprinted in Black

Type I. Animal at left has neither mane nor tail.
Type II. Animal at left has mane and tail.

1904 ***Perf. 12.***

No.	Type	Description	Unused	Used
58	A11	1c on 20c ultra	35	20
a.		Imperf. horiz. pair	50.00	50.00
b.		Inverted surcharge	60.00	60.00
59	A13	2c yel brn, I	35	20
a.		Inverted overprint	25.00	25.00
b.		Pair, one without overprint	60.00	60.00
60	A13	5c red, I	60	20
a.		Inverted overprint	25.00	25.00
c.		Pair, one without overprint	60.00	60.00
61	A13	10c ol grn, I	2.00	60
a.		Inverted overprint	60.00	60.00

Perf. 12½ to 16.

No.	Type	Description	Unused	Used
62	A13	2c yel, brn, II	6.00	4.00
63	A11	3c on 5c brn red	50.00	50.00
a.		Inverted surcharge		
64	A12	3c on 1p brn, II	50	30
a.		Double surcharge	60.00	60.00
65	A13	5c red, II	10.00	7.50
a.		Inverted overprint		
66	A13	10c ol grn, II	20.00	12.00
67	A11	12c on 5c brn red	1.25	50
a.		No star at left of "Centavos"	2.50	1.50
b.		Inverted surcharge	50.00	50.00
c.		Double surcharge	60.00	60.00
		Nos. 62-67 (6)	87.75	74.30

Counterfeits exist of the overprint and surcharge varieties of Nos. 57–67.

Columbus
A14 A15

Columbus
A16

1905-09 ***Perf. 12.***

No.	Type	Description	Unused	Used
68	A14	1c green	30	20
69	A14	2c carmine	30	20
70	A14	3c yel brn	75	30
71	A14	5c ultra	75	10
72	A15	10c gray & blk	1.50	20
73	A15	12c lake & blk	6.50	2.50
74	A15	15c vio & blk	1.50	20
75	A15	20c org brn & blk	3.00	20
76	A15	30c bl grn & blk	4.00	30
77	A15	50c ultra & blk	4.00	30
78	A16	1p gold, grn & gray	16.00	9.00
		Nos. 68-78 (11)	38.60	13.50

A 20c dull red and black, type A15, was prepared but not issued. Price $125. "Specimen" copies of Nos. 74, 76-78 exist, punched to prevent postal use.

Nos. 73, 78 Surcharged in Blue or Red

ISLAS DE
JUAN FERNANDEZ
5
a

ISLAS DE
JUAN FERNANDEZ
10 Cts.
b

1910

No.	Type	Description	Unused	Used
79	A15 (a)	5c on 12c lake & blk (Bl)	60	20
80	A16 (b)	10c on 1p gold, grn & gray (R)	1.50	40
81	A16 (b)	20c on 1p gold, grn & gray (R)	2.00	80
82	A16 (b)	1p gold, grn & gray (R)	4.00	1.50

The 1p is overprinted "ISLAS DE JUAN FERNANDEZ" only. The use of these stamps throughout Chile was authorized.

Independence Centenary Issue.

Oath of Independence
A17

Monument to
O'Higgins
A26

Gen. Manuel
Blanco Encalada
A29

Designs: 2c, Battle of Chacabuco. 3c, Battle of Roble. 5c, Battle of Maipú. 10c, Naval Engagement of "Lautaro" and "Esmeralda." 12c, Capturing the "Maria Isabel." 15c, First Sortie of Liberating Forces. 20c, Abdication of O'Higgins. 25c, Chile's First Congress. 50c, Monument to José M. Carrera. 1p, Monument to San Martin. 5p, Gen. José Ignacio Zenteno. 10p, Adm. Lord Thomas Cochrane.

1910 Center in Black.

No.	Type	Description	Unused	Used
83	A17	1c dk grn	35	20
a.		Center inverted	6,500.	
84	A17	2c lake	35	20
85	A17	3c red brn	1.00	60
86	A17	5c dp bl	50	10
87	A17	10c gray brn	1.00	40
88	A17	12c vermilion	2.75	1.20
89	A17	15c slate	2.25	60
90	A17	20c red org	3.50	1.00
91	A17	25c ultra	4.50	2.00
92	A26	30c violet	3.50	1.00
93	A26	50c ol grn	8.00	3.00
94	A26	1p yel org	17.50	7.50
95	A29	2p red	17.50	7.50
96	A29	5p yel grn	50.00	25.00
97	A29	10p dk vio	45.00	22.50
		Nos. 83-97 (15)	157.70	72.80

Columbus
A32

De Valdivia
A33

Mateo de
Toro Zambrano
A34

Bernardo
O'Higgins
A35

Ramón Freire
A36

F. A. Pinto
A37

Joaquín Prieto
A38

Manuel Bulnes
A39

Manuel
Montt
A40

José
Joaquín Pérez
A41

Federico
Errázuriz Zanartu
A42

Aníbal
Pinto
A43

Designs: 2p, Domingo Santa María. 5p, José de Balmaceda. 10p, Federico Errázuriz Echaurren.

Outer backgrounds consist of horizontal and diagonal lines.

1911 Engraved. ***Perf. 12.***

No.	Type	Description	Unused	Used
98	A32	1c dp grn	25	10
99	A33	2c scarlet	25	10
100	A34	3c sepia	75	40
101	A35	5c dk bl	25	5
102	A36	10c gray & blk	75	20
a.		Center inverted	900.00	700.00
103	A37	12c car & blk	1.25	20
104	A38	15c vio & blk	1.00	20
a.		Center inverted	900.00	
105	A39	20c org red & blk	2.00	20
a.		Center inverted	62.50	62.50
106	A40	25c lt bl & blk	2.50	75
107	A41	30c bis brn & blk	3.50	30
108	A42	50c myr grn & blk	4.50	30
109	A43	1p grn & blk	8.00	40
110	A43	2p ver & blk	15.00	1.50
111	A43	5p ol grn & blk	55.00	10.00
112	A43	10p org yel & blk	47.50	8.00
		Nos. 98-112 (15)	142.50	22.70

See also Nos. 117, 121, 123, 127-128, 133-141, 143, 155A, 157-161, 165-169, 171-172.

Columbus
A47

Toro Z.
A48

Freire
A49

O'Higgins
A50

1912-13 Engraved. ***Perf. 12.***

No.	Type	Description	Unused	Used
113	A47	2c scarlet	20	10
114	A48	4c blk brn	30	10
115	A49	8c gray	1.00	20
116	A50	10c bl & blk	1.00	10
a.		Center inverted	600.00	500.00
b.		Imperf. horizontally or vertically, pair	60.00	
117	A37	14c car & blk	1.00	20
121	A38	40c vio & blk	5.00	60
123	A40	60c lt bl & blk	11.00	1.75
		Nos. 112-123 (7)	19.50	3.05

See also Nos. 125-126, 131, 164, 170, 173.

Cochrane
A52

Columbus
A53

1915 Engraved. ***Perf. 13½x14.***

No.	Type	Description	Unused	Used
124	A52	5c sl bl	50	10
a.		Imperf., pair	12.50	

See also Nos. 155, 162-163.

1918

No.	Type	Description	Unused	Used
125	A49	8c slate	10.00	60

No. 125 is from a plate made in Chile to resemble No. 115. The top of the head is further from the oval, the spots of color enclosed in the figures "8" are oval instead of round, and there are many small differences in the design.

1921 Worn Plate.

No.	Type	Description	Unused	Used
126	A49	8c gray	30.00	9.00

No. 126 differs from No. 125 in not having diagonal lines in the frame and only a few diagonal lines above the shoulders (due to wear), while No. 125 has diagonal lines in the oval up to the level of the forehead.

1915-25 Typo. ***Perf. 13½x14½***

No.	Type	Description	Unused	Used
127	A32	1c gray grn	25	10
128	A33	2c red	25	10
129	A53	4c brn ('18)	35	10

Frame Litho.; Head Engraved

No.	Type	Description	Unused	Used
131	A50	10c bl & blk	1.75	5
a.		10c dk bl & blk	1.75	
b.		Imperf., pair	125.00	
c.		Center inverted	375.00	
133	A38	15c vio & blk	1.25	10
134	A39	20c org red & blk	2.25	10
a.		20c brn org & blk	2.25	10
135	A40	25c dl bl & blk	75	20
136	A41	30c bis brn & blk	2.25	20
137	A42	50c dp grn & blk	2.25	20

Perf. 14

No.	Type	Description	Unused	Used
138	A43	1p grn & blk	12.00	30
139	A43	2p red & blk	14.00	20
a.		2p ver & blk	45.00	1.00
140	A43	5p ol grn & blk ('20)	37.50	1.00
141	A43	10p org & blk ('25)	40.00	2.50
		Nos. 127-141 (13)	114.85	5.15

The frames have crosshatching on the 15c, 20c, 30c, 2p, 5p and 10p. They have no crosshatching on the 10c, 25c, 50c and 1p.

Nos. 131a and 134a are printed from new head plates which give blacker and heavier impressions. No. 131a exists with; (a) frame lithographed and head engraved; (b) frame typographed and head engraved; (c) frame typographed and head lithographed. No. 134a is with frame typographed and head engraved.

A 4c stamp with portrait of Balmaceda and a 14c with portrait of Manuel de Salas were prepared but not placed in use. Both stamps were sent to the paper mill at Puente Alto for destruction. They were not all destroyed as some were privately preserved and sold. Price $7.50 each.

Columbus
A54

Manuel Rengifo
A55

Types of 1915-20 Re-drawn.

1918-20 ***Perf. 13½x14½***

No.	Type	Description	Unused	Used
143	A32	1c gray grn ('20)	35	20
144	A54	4c brown	60	20

No. 143 has all the lines much finer and clearer than No. 127. The white shirt front is also much less shaded.

1921

No.	Type	Description	Unused	Used
145	A55	40c dk vio & blk	2.25	20

Pan-American Congress Building
A56

Admiral Juan José Latorre
A57

1923, Apr. 25 Typo. ***Perf. 14½x14***

No.	Type	Description	Unused	Used
146	A56	2c red	25	15
147	A56	4c brown	25	15

Typographed; Center Engraved.

No.	Type	Description	Unused	Used
148	A56	10c bl & blk	25	15
149	A56	20c org & blk	60	20
150	A56	40c dl vio & blk	1.00	30
151	A56	1p grn & blk	1.25	50
152	A56	2p red & blk	4.50	60
153	A56	5p dk grn & blk	16.50	4.00
		Nos. 146-153 (8)	24.60	6.05

Fifth Pan-American Congress.

Typographed; Head Engraved.

1927 ***Perf. 13½x14½***

No.	Type	Description	Unused	Used
154	A57	80c dk brn & blk	2.75	80

Wmk. 215

Wmkd.

Small Star in Shield, Multiple. (215)

Types of 1915-25 Issues. Inscribed: "Chile Correos".

1928–31 Engr. *Perf. 13½x14½*

155	A52	5c sl bl	1.00	30

Frame Typo.; Center Engraved

155A	A38	15c vio & blk	*400.00*	
156	A55	40c dk vio & blk	65	10
157	A42	50c dp grn & blk	2.50	10

Perf. 14

158	A43	1p grn & blk	1.00	10
159	A43	2p red & blk	4.00	20
160	A43	5p ol grn & blk	8.00	40
161	A43	10p org & blk	8.00	1.50
		Nos. 155, 156-161 (7)	25.15	2.70

Paper of Nos. 155-161 varies from thin to thick.

Types of 1915-25 Issues. Inscribed: "Correos de Chile"

Perf. 13½x14½

1928 Engraved.

162	A52	5c dp bl	50	10

1929 Lithographed.

163	A52	5c lt grn	50	10

Frame Litho.; Center Engraved

164	A50	10c bl & blk	2.00	10
165	A38	15c vio & blk	2.25	10
166	A39	20c org red & blk	5.00	12
167	A40	25c bl & blk	85	10
168	A41	30c brn & blk	65	30
169	A42	50c dp grn & blk	50	10
		Nos. 163-169 (7)	11.75	92

Redrawn.

Frame Typo.; Center Litho.

1929

170	A50	10c bl & blk	2.50	6
171	A38	15c vio & blk	2.00	20
172	A39	20c org red & blk	3.00	25

1931 Unwmkd.

173	A50	10c bl & blk	75	30

In the redrawn stamps the lines behind the portraits are heavier and completely fill the ovals. There are strong diagonal lines above the shoulders. On No. 170 the head is larger than on Nos. 164 and 173.

A58

Prosperity of Saltpeter Trade

A59 A60

Perf. 13½x14

1930, July 21 Litho. Wmk. 215

Size: 20x25 mm.

175	A58	5c yel grn	50	20
176	A58	10c red brn	50	20
177	A58	15c violet	50	20
178	A59	25c dp gray	2.00	60
179	A60	70c dk bl	5.00	1.50

Perf. 14

Size: 24½x30 mm.

180	A60	1p dk gray grn	3.75	75
		Nos. 175-180 (6)	12.25	3.45

Issued to commemorate the centenary of the first shipment of saltpeter from Chile, July 21, 1830.

Manuel Bulnes

A61

Bernardo O'Higgins

A62

1931 *Perf. 13½, 14*

181	A61	20c dk brn	1.25	10

1932

182	A62	10c dp bl	1.50	10

Mariano Egana

A63

Joaquín Tocornal

A64

1934 *Perf. 13½x14*

183	A63	30c magenta	75	20

Perf. 14

184	A64	1.20p brt bl	1.25	30

Centenary of the constitution.

José Joaquín Pérez

A65

1934 *Perf. 13½x14*

185	A65	30c brt pink	2.00	10

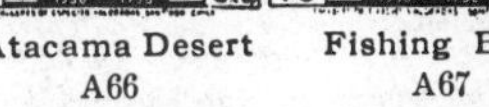

Atacama Desert

A66

Fishing Boats

A67

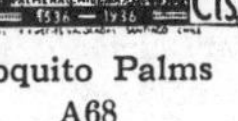

Coquito Palms

A68

Sheep

A69

Mining

A70

Lonquimay Forest

A71

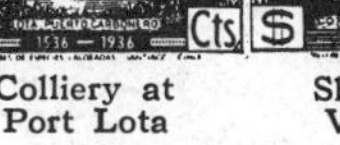

Colliery at Port Lota

A72

Shipping at Valparaiso

A73

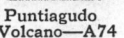

Puntiagudo Volcano—A74

Diego de Almagro—A75

Cattle

A76

Mining Saltpeter

A77

Perf. 14

1936, Mar. 1 Litho. Wmk. 215

186	A66	5c vermilion	35	20
187	A67	10c violet	25	15
188	A68	20c magenta	25	15
189	A69	25c grnsh bl	2.50	80
190	A70	30c lt grn	25	15
191	A71	40c blk, *cr*	2.50	75
192	A72	50c bl, *bluish*	1.25	30

Engraved.

193	A73	1p dk grn	1.25	50
194	A74	1.20p dp bl	1.50	70
195	A75	2p dk brn	1.50	85
196	A76	5p cop red	4.00	2.00
197	A77	10p dk vio	10.00	7.00
		Nos. 186-197 (12)	25.60	13.55

Issued in commemoration of the 400th anniversary of the discovery of Chile by Diego de Almagro.

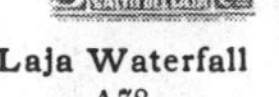

Laja Waterfall

A78

Agriculture

A79

Boldo Tree

A79a

Nitrate Industry

A80

Mineral Spas

A81

Copper Mine

A82

Mining

A83

Fishing in Chiloé

A84

Osorno Volcano

A85

Mercantile Marine

A86

Lake Villarrica

A87

State Railways

A88

Perf. 13½x14

1938–40 Lithographed Wmk. 215

198	A78	5c brn car ('39)	25	10
199	A79	10c sal pink ('39)	25	10
200	A79a	15c brn org ('40)	25	10
201	A80	20c lt bl	25	10
202	A81	30c brt pink	25	10
203	A82	40c lt grn ('39)	25	6
204	A83	50c violet	25	10

Perf. 14

Engraved.

205	A84	1p org brn	25	10
206	A85	1.80p dp bl	65	30
207	A86	2p car lake	25	10
208	A87	5p dk sl grn	50	10
209	A88	10p rose vio ('40)	1.25	10
		Nos. 198-209 (12)	4.65	1.36

See also Nos. 217–227.

Map of the Americas

A89

Perf. 14

1940, Sept. 11 Litho. Unwmkd.

210	A89	40c dl grn & yel grn	25	10

Pan American Union, 50th anniversary.

Camilo Henríquez
A90

Founding of Santiago
A93

Designs: 40c, Pedro de Valdivia. 1.10p, Benjamin Vicuna Mackenna. 3.60p, Diego Barros Arana.

Perf. 14½x14, 14½.

1941, Jan. 23 Engraved Wmk. 215

211	A90	10c car lake	25	15
212	A90	40c green	40	12
213	A90	1.10p red	1.25	75
214	A93	1.80p blue	1.25	75
215	A90	3.60p indigo	3.75	2.50
		Nos. 211-215 (5)	6.90	4.27

400th anniversary of Santiago.

Types of 1938.
Lithographed.

1942-46 *Perf. 13½x14.* Unwmkd.

217	A79	10c sal pink ('43)	25	10
218	A79a	15c brn org ('43)	25	10
219	A80	20c lt bl ('43)	25	10
220	A81	30c brt pink ('43)	30	10
221	A82	40c yel grn	1.00	10
222	A83	50c vio ('43)	25	10

Engraved.
Perf. 14.

223	A84	1p brn org	2.00	10
225	A86	2p car lake ('43)	25	10
226	A87	5p dk sl grn ('43)	65	10
227	A88	10p rose vio ('46)	1.00	10
		Nos. 217-227 (10)	6.20	1.00

Valentin Letelier
A95

University of Chile
A98

Designs: 40c, Andrés Bello. 90c, Manuel Bulnes. 1.80p, Manuel Montt.

1942, Nov. 1 *Perf. 14x14½, 14 (1p)*

228	A95	30c rose red	25	10
229	A95	40c dp grn	25	10
230	A95	90c rose vio	1.50	1.00
231	A98	1p dp brn	1.00	60
232	A95	1.80p dk bl	3.00	2.00
		Nos. 228-232 (5)	6.00	3.80

University of Chile centenary. See also No. C89.

Manuel Bulnes
A100

Map Showing Strait of Magellan
A104

Designs: 30c, Juan Williams Wilson. 40c, Diego Duble Almeida. 1p, José Mardones.

1944, Mar. 2 Litho. *Perf. 14*

233	A100	15c black	25	15
234	A100	30c dp rose	25	15
235	A100	40c yel grn	25	15
236	A100	1p brn car	1.25	40
237	A104	1.80p ultra	1.75	1.00
		Nos. 233-237 (5)	3.75	1.85

Issued to commemorate the 100th anniversary of the occupation of the Strait of Magellan.

Red Cross and Lamp of Life
A105

Serpent and Cup
A106

1944, Oct. 18 Unwmkd.

238	A105	40c grn, red & blk	35	15
239	A106	1.80p ultra & red	90	50

Issued to commemorate the 80th anniversary of the International Red Cross Society.

Bernardo O'Higgins
A107

"Embrace of Maipú"
(O'Higgins Joining San Martin)
A108

Designs: 40c, Abdication of O'Higgins. 1.80p, Battle of Rancagua.

1945 Engr. *Perf. 14 (15c), 14½*

Center in Black.

240	A107	15c carmine	25	15
241	A108	30c brown	35	15
242	A108	40c dp grn	35	15
243	A108	1.80p dk bl	1.75	1.20

Issued to commemorate the centenary of the death of Bernardo O'Higgins in 1842.

Proposed Columbus Lighthouse
A111

Perf. 14

1945, Sept. 10 Litho. Wmk. 215

244	A111	40c lt grn	35	20

Issued in honor of the discovery of America by Columbus and the Memorial Lighthouse to be erected in his memory.

Andrés Bello
A112

1946 Engraved.

245	A112	40c dk grn	25	10
246	A112	1.80p dk bl	25	15

Issued to commemorate the 80th anniversary of the death of Andrés Bello, poet and educator.

Map Showing Chile's Claims of Antarctic Territory
A113

1947, May 12 Litho. *Perf. 14½*

247	A113	40c carmine	50	15
248	A113	2.50p dp bl	1.00	40

Eusebio Lillo and Ramon Carnicer
A114

1947, Sept. 18 Engraved

249	A114	40c dk grn	25	12

Centenary of national anthem.

Miguel de Cervantes Saavedra
A115

1947, Oct. 11 Wmk. 215

250	A115	40c dk car	35	20

Issued to commemorate the 400th anniversary of the birth of Miguel de Cervantes Saavedra, novelist, playwright and poet.

Arturo Prat Chacón and Iquique Naval Battle
A116

1948, Dec. 24 *Perf. 14½*

251	A116	40c dp bl	25	8

Issued to commemorate the centenary of the birth of Arturo Prat Chacon, Chilean naval hero.

Bernardo O'Higgins
A117

Lithographed.

1948 *Perf. 13½x14.* Wmk. 215

252	A117	60c black	12	10

See also No. 262.

No. 203 Surcharged in Black

VEINTE
CTS.

1948

253	A82	20c on 40c lt grn	12	10

Chilean Pigeons
A118

American Skunk
A119

Designs not illustrated, FAUNA: Chilean Otter. Southern sea lions. Sugar-cane borer moth. Emperor penguins. Bat. Chinchilla. Grant's stag beetle. Trevally (fish). Chilean slender lizard. Crested caracara. Red-gartered coot. Chilean guemal (deer). Spiny rock lobster. Tile-fish. Praying mantis. Torrent duck. Red conger. FLORA: Araucarian pine (monkey puzzle tree). Evening primrose. Chilean red bell flower. Loxodon (flower). Boldo tree. Coquito palm trees.

Lithographed.

1948, Dec. 6 *Perf. 14* Wmk. 215

254	A118	60c ultra	40	20
	a.	Block of 25	12.50	
255	A119	2.60p green	65	35
	a.	Block of 25	20.00	

Issued in panes of 100 stamps, divisible into four blocks of 25 different designs.

The stamps commemorate the centenary (in 1944) of the publication of the first volume of Claudio Gay's Natural History of Chile. See also No. C124.

Benjamin Vicuna Mackenna
A121

1949, Mar. 22 Engr. *Perf. 13½x14*

257	A121	60c dp bl	15	10

See also No. C126.

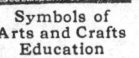

Symbols of Arts and Crafts Education
A122

Heinrich von Stephan
A123

Design: 2.60p, Badge and book.

Lithographed.

1949, Nov. 11 ***Perf. 14*** **Unwmkd.**

258 A122 60c lil rose 25 10
259 A122 2.60p vio bl 60 30

Issued to commemorate the centenary of the foundation of Chile's School of Arts and Crafts. See also Nos. C127–C128.

1950, Jan. 6 **Engraved**

260 A123 60c dp car 25 10
261 A123 2.50p dp bl 65 30

Issued to commemorate the 75th anniversary of the formation of the Universal Postal Union. See also Nos. C129–C130.

O'Higgins Type of 1948.

1950 **Lithographed** ***Perf. 13x14***

262 A117 60c black 12 8

Gen. José de San Martín
A124

Queen Isabella I
A125

Perf. 14

1951, Mar. 16 **Engr.** **Wmk. 215**

263 A124 60c dp bl 15 8

Issued to commemorate the centenary of the death of Gen. José de San Martin. See also No. C165.

1952, Mar. 20

264 A125 60c brt bl 15 8

Issued to commemorate the 500th anniversary of the birth of Queen Isabella I of Spain. See also No. C166.

Bernardo O'Higgins
A126

Mateo de Toro Zambrano
A127

Lithographed.

1952 ***Perf. 13½x14*** **Unwmkd.**

265 A126 1p dk bl grn 10 8

See also No. 275.

Nos.252 and 262 Surcharged "40 Ctvs." in Red.

1952, Sept.

266 A117 40c on 60c blk 12 8

Wmk. 215

267 A117 40c on 60c blk 10 8

1953, Mar. 13 **Wmk. 215**

268 A127 80c green 10 8

See also No. 285.

Valdivia Arms
A128

Old Fort
A129

Designs: 3p, Modern Valdivia. 5p, Street in ancient Valdivia.

1953, May ***Perf. 14***

269 A128 1p brt ultra 25 10
270 A129 2p dl rose vio 25 10
271 A129 3p bl grn 35 20
272 A129 5p dp brn 35 20
Nos. 269-272, C167 (5) 2.45 90

Issued to commemorate the 4th centenary of the founding of Valdivia, capital of Valdivia province.

José Toribio Medina
A130

1953, June **Engraved** ***Perf. 14½***

273 A130 1p brown 20 15
274 A130 2.50p dp bl 35 20

Issued to commemorate the centenary of the birth of Jose Toribio Medina (1852–1930), historian and bibliographer.

O'Higgins Type of 1952.

Lithographed.

1953, Oct. ***Perf. 13½x14*** **Wmk. 215**

275 A126 1p dk bl grn 10 8

Stamp of 1853
A131

1953, Oct. 15 **Engr.** ***Perf. 14½***

276 A131 1p chocolate 25 15

Centenary of Chile's first postage stamps. Souvenir sheet including No. 276 is noted below No. C168.

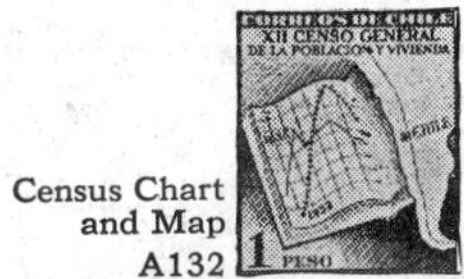

Census Chart and Map
A132

1953, Nov. 5 **Litho.** ***Perf. 13½x14***

277 A132 1p bl grn 15 10
278 A132 2.50p vio bl 25 10
279 A132 3p chocolate 35 20
280 A132 4p carmine 50 20

Issued to publicize the 12th general census of population and housing.

Arms of Angol
A133

Ignacio Domeyko
A134

1954, May 28 ***Perf. 14*** **Unwmkd.**

281 A133 2p dp car 15 8

Issued to commemorate the 400th anniversary of the founding of Angol, capital of Malleco province.

1954, Aug. 16 **Engr.** ***Perf. 13½x14***

282 A134 1p grnsh bl 10 5

Issued to commemorate the 150th anniversary of the birth of Ignacio Domeyko (1802–1889), mineralogist and educator. See also No. C171.

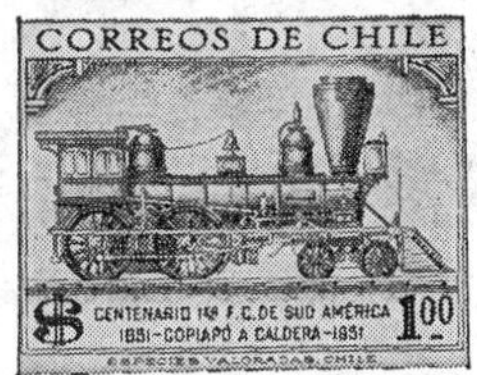

Early Steam Locomotive—A135

Perf. 14½

1954, Sept. 10 **Wmk. 215**

283 A135 1p red 18 10

Issued to commemorate the centenary (in 1951) of the first South American railroad. See also No. C172.

Adm. Arturo Prat Chacón
A136

Arms of Viña del Mar
A137

Lithographed.

1954 ***Perf. 14*** **Unwmkd.**

284 A136 2p dk vio bl 12 8

Issued to commemorate the 75th anniversary of the naval Battle of Iquique.

Toro Zambrano Type of 1953

1954, Nov. 6 ***Perf. 13½x14***

285 A127 80c green 12 6

1955, Mar. 5 ***Perf. 14*** **Wmk. 215**

Design: 2p, Arms of Valparaiso.

286 A137 1p vio bl 10 8
287 A137 2p carmine 15 8

Issued to publicize the first International Philatelic Exhibition, Valparaiso, March 1955.

Dr. Alejandro del Rio
A138

1955, May 24 ***Perf. 13½x14***

288 A138 2p vio bl 12 8

14th Pan-American Sanitary Conference.

Christ of the Andes, Emblems of Chile, Argentina
A139

1955, Aug. 31 ***Perf. 14½*** **Unwmkd.**

289 A139 1p vio bl 20 10

Issued to publicize the reciprocal visits of Presidents Juan D. Peron and Carlos Ibanez del Campo. See also No. C173.

Manuel Rengifo
A140

Portraits: 5p, Mariano Egana. 50p, Diego Portales.

1955–56 ***Perf. 14x14½*** **Unwmkd.**

290 A140 3p vio bl 12 8
291 A140 5p dk car rose 20 8
292 A140 50p rose lil ('56) 2.00 40

Issued to commemorate the centenary of the death of Joaquin Prieto (1786–1854), soldier and political leader; president, 1831–41. See No. QRA1.

Jose M. Carrera
A141

Ramón Freire
A142

Portraits: 5p, Manuel Bulnes. 10p, Pres. Francisco A. Pinto. 50p, Manuel Montt.

Lithographed

1956–58 ***Perf. 14x14½*** **Unwmkd.**

293 A141 2p purple 12 6
293A A142 3p lt vio bl 12 6
294 A141 5p redsh brn (19½x23mm) 12 6
a. Size 19x22mm 12 8
295 A142 10p vio (19x22¼mm) 15 6
a. Perf. 13½x14 (19¼x22½mm) ('58) 60 8
296 A141 50p rose red 40 10
Nos. 293-296 (5) 91 34

No. 294 has yellow gum; No. 294a, white gum.

Wmk. 215

297 A141 2p dl pur 12 8
298 A142 3p vio bl 12 8

Federico Santa Maria
A143

Gabriela Mistral
A144

Engraved.

1957, Jan. 31 ***Perf. 14*** **Unwmkd.**

299 A143 5p dk red brn 20 8

Issued to commemorate the 25th anniversary of the Federico Santa Maria Technical University. See Nos. C190–C191.

Souvenir sheet including No. 299 is noted below No. C191.

1958, Jan. 10

300 A144 10p red brn 20 5

Issued in honor of Gabriela Mistral, poet and educator. See also No. C192.

Arms of Osorno A145 — Arms of Santiago A146

Design: 50p, Garcia Hdo. de Mendoza.

1958, Mar. 23 Lithographed *Perf. 14*

301 A145 10p carmine 20 10

Engraved

302 A145 50p green 50 15

Issued to commemorate the 400th anniversary of the founding of the city of Osorno, capital of Osorno province.

Souvenir sheet including No. 302 in red brown is noted below No. C193.

1958, Oct. 18 *Perf. 14* Unwmkd.

303 A146 10p dk vio 20 6

Issued to publicize the National Philatelic Exposition, Santiago, Oct. 18–26.

Souvenir sheet including No. 303 in deep red is noted below No. C194.

Symbolical Savings Bank A147 — Modern Map of Antarctica A148

1958, Dec. 18

304 A147 10p dk bl 20 6

Issued to commemorate the centenary of the Savings Bank for Public Employees.

Souvenir sheet including No. 304 in violet is noted below No. C195.

1958, Aug. 28 *Perf. 14* Unwmkd.

305 A148 40p rose car 25 10

Issued to commemorate the International Geophysical Year, 1957–1958. See No. C214.

Antarctic Map and 'La Araucana' A149 — Map of Strait of Magellan, 1588 A150

1958 Lithographed. *Perf. 14*

310 A149 10p vio bl 20 10

Engraved.

311 A150 200p dl pur 2.50 75

See also Nos. C199–C200.

Valdivia River Bridge A153

1959, Feb. 9 Engraved *Perf. 14*

319 A153 40p green 25 10

Issued to commemorate the centenary of the German School in Valdivia and to publicize the Valdivia Philatelic Exhibition, Feb. 9–18.

Souvenir sheet including No. 319 is noted below No. C213.

Strait of Magellan, Map by Pedro Sarmiento de Gamboa, c. 1582 A154

1959, Aug. 27 Lithographed

320 A154 10p dl pur 25 10

Issued to commemorate the 400th anniversary of the Juan Ladrillero expedition to explore the Strait of Magellan, 1557–1558. See also No. C215.

Diego Barros Arana A155 — Henri Dunant A156

1959, Aug. 27

321 A155 40p ultra 25 10

Issued to commemorate the 50th anniversary of the death of Diego Barros Arana (1830–1907), historian. See No. C216.

1959, Oct. 6 *Perf. 14* Unwmkd.

322 A156 20p red & red brn 20 6

Issued to commemorate the centenary of the Red Cross idea. See No. C217.

Manuel Bulnes A157 — Francisco A. Pinto A158

Choshuenco Volcano A159

Designs: No. 326, Choshuenco volcano, redrawn. 5c, Manuel Montt. 10c, Maule River Valley. 20c, 1e, Inca Lake.

1960–67 Lithographed *Perf. 13x14*

323 A157 5m bluish grn 8 5
324 A158 1c carmine 8 5

Perf. 14

Size: 29x25mm.

325 A159 2c ultra ('61) 10 5

Perf. 14x13

Size: 23½x18mm.

326 A159 2c ultra ('62) 8 5

Perf. 13x14

327 A157 5c blue 12 5

Perf. 14

Size: 29x25mm.

328 A159 10c grn ('62) 30 10
329 A159 20c Prus bl ('62) 50 15
329A A159 1e bluish grn ('67) 60 25
Nos. 323-329A (8) 1.86 75

On No. 325 "Volcan Choshuenco" is at upper left, below "Correos." On No. 326, it is at bottom, above "Centesimos."

Refugee Family A160

1960, Apr. 7 *Perf. 14½*

330 A160 1c green 20 10

Issued to publicize World Refugee Year, July 1, 1959–June 30, 1960. A souvenir sheet is noted below No. C218.

Type of Air Post Issue, 1962, and

Arms of Chile A161

José M. Carrera A162

Designs: No. 332, Palace of Justice. 5c, National Memorial. 10c, Manuel de Toro y Zambrano and Martinez de Rozas. 20c, Manuel de Salas and Juan Egana. 50c, Manuel Rodriguez and Juan Mackenna.

Wmk. 215 (#331, 1e); Unwmkd.

1960–65 Engraved *Perf. 14½*

331 A161 1c mar & sep 25 10
332 A161 1c brn & cl ('62) 20 5
333 A162 5c grn & Prus grn ('61) 20 5
334 AP54 10c brn & vio brn ('64) 25 5
334A AP54 20c ind & bl grn ('65) 25 6
335 AP54 50c red brn & mar ('65) 40 15
336 A162 1e gray ol & brn 1.50 60
Nos.331-336, C218A-C220D (14) 6.50 2.62

Issued to commemorate the 150th anniversary of the formation of the first National Government. A souvenir sheet is noted below No. C220B. See also No. C285.

Family A163

Design: 10c, Various buildings.

Lithographed

1960, Jan. 18 *Perf. 14* Unwmkd.

337 A163 5c green 25 8
338 A163 10c brt vio 25 8

Issued to publicize the 13th population census (No. 337) and the second housing census (No. 338).

Chamber of Deputies A164

1961, Aug. 14 *Perf. 14½* Unwmkd.

339 A164 2c red brn 75 10

Issued to commemorate the 150th anniversary of the first National Congress. See also No. C245.

Soccer Players and Globe A165

Design: 5c, Goalkeeper and stadium (vert.).

1962, May 30 Engr. *Perf. 14½*

340 A165 2c blue 25 10
341 A165 5c green 35 10

Issued to commemorate the World Soccer Championship, Chile, May 30–June 17.

Note on souvenir sheet follows No. C247.

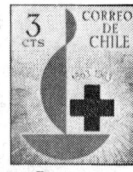

Mother and Child A166 — Centenary Emblem A167

1963, Mar. 21 Litho. *Perf. 14*

342 A166 3c maroon 15 5

Issued for the "Freedom from Hunger" campaign of the U.N. Food and Agriculture Organization. See also No. C248.

1963, Aug. 23 *Perf. 14* Unwmkd.

343 A167 3c red & gray 18 8

Issued to commemorate the centenary of the International Red Cross. See No. C249.

Fireman Carrying Woman A168 — Enrique Molina A169

1963, Dec. 20 *Perf. 14* Unwmkd.

344 A168 3c violet 15 8

Issued to commemorate the centenary of the Santiago Fire Brigade. See No. C250.

1964, Nov. 14 Litho. *Perf. 14*

Design: No. 346, Msgr. Carlos Casanueva.

345 A169 4c bis brn 15 4
346 A169 4c rose cl 10 4

Issued to honor Enrique Molina, founder of the University of Concepcion, and Msgr. Carlos Casanueva, rector of the Catholic University, 1920–53. See Nos. C257–C258.

Easter Island Statue
A170

Copihue, National Flower
A171

Design: 30c, Robinson Crusoe.

1965–69 Litho. *Perf. 14x14½*

347 A170 6c rose lil 10 6
347A A170 10c rose pink ('68) 10 6

Perf. 14

348 A171 15c yel grn & rose red 15 8
348A A171 20c yel grn & rose red ('69) 10 6

Perf. 14x14½

349 A170 30c rose cl 25 15

Skier
A172

Lorenzo Sazie
A173

1965, Aug. 30 *Perf. 14*

350 A172 4c bl grn 10 6

World Skiing Championships, Chile, 1966.

1966, Feb. 9 Litho. *Perf. 14x14½*

351 A173 1e green 75 10

Issued to commemorate the centenary of the death of Dr. Lorenzo Sazie, dean of the Faculty of Medicine, University of Santiago.

German Riesco, President in 1901–1906
A174

Portrait: 30c, Jorge Montt (1847–1922), president in 1891–1896.

1966 *Perf. 13x14* Unwmkd.

354 A174 30c violet 12 5
355 A174 50c dl brn 12 5

William Wheelwright and S.S. Chile
A175

1966, Aug. 2 *Perf. 14½*

358 A175 10c ultra & lt bl 10 8

Issued to commemorate the 125th anniversary (in 1965) of the arrival of the paddle steamers "Chile" and "Peru." See also No. C268.

Learning to Read
A176

1966, Aug. 13 Litho. *Perf. 14*

359 A176 10c red brn 10 8

Literacy campaign.

U.N. and ICY Emblems
A177

1966, Oct. 28 *Perf. 14½* Unwmkd.

360 A177 1e grn & brn 1.25 20

International Cooperation Year, 1965. See No. C269.

Capt. Luis Pardo and Ship in Antarctica—A178

1967, Jan. Litho. *Perf. 14½*

361 A178 20c turq bl 15 10

Issued to commemorate the 50th anniversary of the rescue of the Shackleton South Pole expedition by Capt. Luis Pardo of Chile. See also No. C271.

Family
A179

Trees and Mountains
A180

1967, Apr. 13 *Perf. 14* Unwmkd.

362 A179 10c mag & blk 6 4

Issued to publicize the 8th International Conference for Family Planning, Santiago, April 1967. See also No. C272.

1967, June 9 Litho. *Perf. 14½*

363 A180 10c bl grn & lt bl 6 4

Reforestation Campaign. See No. C274.

Lions Emblem
A181

1967, July 12 Litho. *Perf. 14*

364 A181 20c Prus bl & yel 20 10

Issued to commemorate the 50th anniversary of Lions International. See also Nos. C275–C276.

Chilean Flag
A182

1967, Oct. 20 *Perf. 14½* Unwmkd.

365 A182 80c crim & ultra 20 10

Issued to commemorate the sesquicentennial of the national flag. See No. C277.

José Maria Cardinal Caro
A183

1967, Dec. 4 Engraved *Perf. 14½*

366 A183 20c dp car 75 20

Issued to commemorate the centenary of the birth of José Maria Cardinal Caro, the first Chilean cardinal. See No. C279.

San Martin and O'Higgins
A184

1968, Apr. 23 Litho. Unwmkd.

367 A184 3e blue 12 6

Issued to commemorate the sesquicentennial of the Battles of Chacabuco and Maipu. See No. C280.

Farm Couple
A185

1968, June 18 *Perf. 14½*

368 A185 20c blk, org & grn 25 10

Agrarian reforms. See No. C281.

Juan I. Molina
A186

1968, Aug. 27 Litho. *Perf. 14½*

369 A186 2e red lil 12 6

Issued to honor Juan I. Molina, educator and scientist. See also No. C282.

Hand Holding Cogwheel
A187

1968, Sept. *Perf. 14x14½*

370 A187 30c dp car 12 6

Fourth census of manufacturers.

Map of Chiloé Province, Sailing Ship and Coastal Vessel
A188

1968, Oct. 7 *Perf. 14½*

371 A188 30c ultra 12 6

Issued to commemorate the anniversaries of the founding of five towns in Chiloé Province. See also No. C283.

Automobile Club Emblem
A189

1968, Nov. 10 Engr. *Perf. 14½x14*

372 A189 1e car rose 12 6

Issued to commemorate the 40th anniversary of the Automobile Club of Chile. See No. C284.

Francisco Garcia Huidobro
A190

Design: 5e, King Philip V of Spain.

1968, Dec. 31 Litho. *Perf. 14½*

373 A190 2e pale rose & ultra 12 6
374 A190 5e brn & yel grn 15 8

Issued to commemorate the 225th anniversary of the founding of the State Mint (Casa de Moneda de Chile). See Nos. C288–C289.

Satellite and Radar Station
A191

1969, May 20 Litho. *Perf. 14½*

375 A191 30c blue 10 5

Issued to publicize the inauguration of ENTEL-Chile, the first commercial satellite communications ground station, Longovilo. See No. C290.

Red Cross, Crescent and Lion and Sun Emblems—A192

1969, Sept. Lithographed *Perf. 14½*

376 A192 2e vio bl & red 10 6

Issued to commemorate the 50th anniversary of the League of Red Cross Societies. See No. C291.

Rapel Hydro-electric Plant
A193

1969, Nov. 18 Litho. *Perf. 14½*

377 A193 40c green 12 8

See No. C292.

Col. Rodriguez Monument
A194

1969, Nov. 24

378 A194 2e rose cl 12 6

Issued to commemorate the 150th anniversary of the death of Col. Manuel Rodriguez. See No. C293.

EXPO '70 Emblem
A195

1969, Dec. 2 Litho. *Perf. 14*

379 A195 3e blue 8 5

Issued to publicize EXPO '70 International Exhibition, Osaka, Japan, March 15–Sept. 13, 1970. See No. C294.

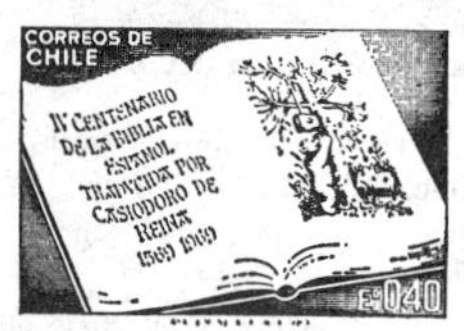

Open Book
A196

1969, Dec. 3 *Perf. 14½*

380 A196 40c red brn 8 5

Issued to commemorate the 400th anniversary of the translation of the Bible into Spanish by Casiodoro de Reina. See No. C295.

Globes and ILO Emblem
A197

1969, Dec. 17 *Perf. 14½*

381 A197 1e grn & blk 8 5

Issued to commemorate the 50th anniversary of the International Labor Organization. See No. C296.

Human Rights Flame
A198

1969, Dec. 18

382 A198 4e bl & red 8 5

Human Rights Year, 1968. See No. C297.

Policarpo Toro and Easter Island
A199

1970, Jan. 26 *Perf. 14½*

383 A199 5e lilac 8 5

Issued to commemorate the 80th anniversary of the acquisition of Easter Island. See No. C298.

Sailing Ship and Arms of Valdivia
A200

1970, Feb. 4 Litho. *Perf. 14½*

384 A200 40c dk car 10 6

Issued to commemorate the 150th anniversary of the capture of Valdivia during Chile's war of independence by Thomas Cochrane (1775–1860), naval commander. See No. C299.

Paul Harris and Rotary Emblem
A201

1970, Mar. 18 Lithographed *Perf. 14*

385 A201 10e vio bl 10 5

Issued to commemorate the centenary of the birth of Paul Harris (1868–1947), founder of Rotary International. See No. C300.

Mahatma Gandhi
A202

Santo Domingo Church, Santiago, Chile
A203

1970, Apr. 1 Litho. *Perf. 14½*

386 A202 40c bl grn 10 4

Issued to commemorate the centenary of the birth of Mohandas K. Gandhi (1869–1948), leader in India's fight for independence. See No. C301.

1970, Apr. 30 Engraved

Designs: 2e, Casa de Moneda de Chile (horiz.). 3e, Pedro de Valdivia. 5e, Bridge (horiz.). 10e, Ambrosio O'Higgins.

387 A203 2e vio brn 10 6
388 A203 3e dk red 8 5
389 A203 4e dk bl 8 5
390 A203 5e brown 12 6
391 A203 10e green 12 8
Nos. 387-391 (5) 50 30

Issued to commemorate the exploration and development of Chile by Spanish explorers.

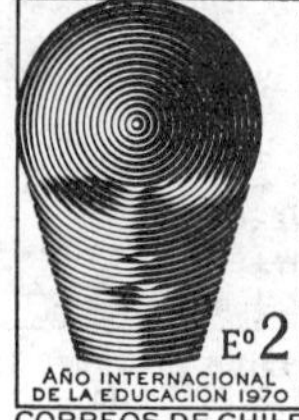

Education Year Emblem
A204

Virgin and Child
A205

1970, July 17 Litho. *Perf. 14½*

392 A204 2e claret 8 5

Issued for International Education Year. See No. C302.

1970, July 28

393 A205 40c green 8 6

Issued to publicize the O'Higgins National Shrine at Maipu. See No. C303.

Torch and Snake—A206

Copper Symbol, Chile Arms
A207

1970, Aug. 11

394 A206 40c cl & lt bl 6 4

Issued to commemorate the International Cancer Congress, Houston, Texas, May 22–29. See No. C304.

1970, Oct. 21 Litho. *Perf. 14½*

395 A207 40c car & lt red brn 6 4

Issued to commemorate the nationalization of the copper industry. See No. C305.

Dove and World Map
A208

1970, Oct. 22

396 A208 3e rose mag & pur 8 5

Issued to commemorate the 25th anniversary of the United Nations. See No. C306.

No. 375 Surcharged in Red

1970, Dec. 24 Litho. *Perf. 14½*

397 A191 52c on 30c bl 10 8

Freighter and Ship's Wheel
A209

1971, Jan. 18 Litho. *Perf. 14*

398 A209 52c dp car 8 5

National Maritime Commission. See No. C307.

Bernardo O'Higgins and Ship
A210

1971, Feb. 3 *Perf. 14½*

399 A210 5e grnsh bl & grn 8 5

The 150th anniversary of the expedition to liberate Peru from Spanish rule. See No. C309.

Youth, Girl and U.N. Emblem
A211

1971, Feb. 11 Litho. *Perf. 14½*

400 A211 52c dk bl & brn 8 5

First meeting in Latin America of the Executive Council of UNICEF (U.N. Children's Fund), Santiago, May 20–31, 1969. See No. C310.

Chilean Boy Scout Emblem
A212

1971, Feb. 10 *Perf. 14*

401 A212 1e grn & brn 8 5

Founding of Chilean Boy Scouts, 60th anniversary. See No. C311.

Satellite and Radar Station
A213

1971, May 25 Litho. *Perf. 14½*

402 A213 40c dl grn 10 6

First commercial Chilean satellite communications ground station, Longovilo. See No. C312.

Diver with Harpoon Gun
A214

1971, Sept. 1

403 A214 1.15e lt & dk grn 12 5
404 A214 2.35e vio bl & dp vio bl 8 5

10th World Championship of Underwater Fishing.

Ferdinand Magellan and Sailing Ship
A215

1971, Nov. 3

405 A215 35c lt vio & brn vio 8 5

450th anniversary of first trip through and discovery of the Strait of Magellan, Oct. 21–Nov. 28, 1520.

Dagoberto Godoy and Plane over Andes
A216

1971, Nov. 4

406 A216 1.15e bl & grn 8 5

First trans-Andean flight, Dec. 12, 1918.

Virgin of San Cristobal
A217

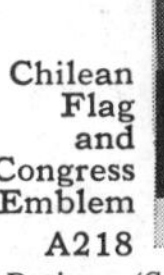

Chilean Flag and Congress Emblem
A218

Designs (Congress Emblem and): 4.35e, Church of San Francisco. 9.35e, Central post office (horiz.). 18.35e, La Posada (Inn) del Corregidor (horiz.).

1971

407 A217 1.15e dk bl 15 8
408 A218 2.35e ultra & car 10 5
409 A217 4.35e brn red 10 5
410 A217 9.35e violet 12 5
411 A217 18.35e lil rose 15 8
Nos. 407-411 (5) 62 31

10th Congress of the Postal Union of the Americas and Spain, Santiago. Issue dates: 2.35e, 4.35e, Nov. 5; 1.15e, Nov. 11; 9.35e, Nov. 18; 18.35e, Nov. 19.

Observation Dome, Cerro el Tololo Observatory
A219

1971, Dec. 18

412 A219 1.95e lt & dk bl 8 5

Boeing 707 over Easter Island
A220

1971, Dec. 18

413 A220 2.35e dk brn & yel 8 5

Inauguration of flights to Easter Island.

Alonso de Ercilla y Zuniga
A221

1972, Mar. 20 Engraved *Perf. 14*

414 A221 1e dk red 8 5

4th centenary (in 1969) of "La Araucana," by Alonso de Ercilla y Zuniga (1533–1596), Spanish author. See No. C313.

Map of Antarctica and Dog Sled
A222

1972, Mar. 20 Litho. *Perf. 14½x15*

415 A222 1.15e vio bl & blk 10 5
416 A222 3.50e bl grn & grn 8 5

10th anniversary (in 1971) of the Antarctic Treaty pledging peaceful uses of and scientific cooperation in Antarctica.

"Your Heart is your Health"
A223

1972, Apr. 2 Litho. *Perf. 14½*

417 A223 1.15e blk & car 8 5

World Health Day.

People and Statement by Pres. Allende
A224

Conference Hall and U.N. Emblem
A225

1972, Apr. 13 Litho. *Perf. 14½*

418 A224 35c dl grn & buff 10 8
419 A225 1.15e ultra & pur 8 5
420 A224 4e dk pur & pale rose 12 8
421 A225 6e org & vio bl 10 5

3rd United Nations Conference on Trade and Development (UNCTAD III), Santiago, Apr.–May 1972. Design A224 is perforated horizontally in the middle.

Soldier, 1822, Andes, Military College Emblem
A226

1972, June 9

422 A226 1.15e bl & yel 8 5

Sesquicentennial of Bernardo O'Higgins Military College.

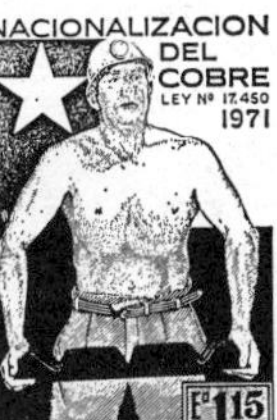

Miner Holding Copper Ingot, Chilean Flag
A227

Sailing Ship
A228

1972, July 11 Litho. *Perf. 15x14½*

423 A227 1.15e bl & rose red 8 5
424 A227 5e bl, blk & rose red 10 5

Nationalization of copper industry.

1972, Aug. 4

425 A228 1.15e vio brn 8 5

Sesquicentennial of the Arturo Pratt Naval Training School.

Mt. Calan Observatory
A229

1972, Aug. 31 Litho. *Perf. 14½*

426 A229 50c ultra 10 6

University of Chile Mt. Calan Observatory.

Carrier Pigeon
A230

1972, Oct. 9 Litho. *Perf. 14½*

427 A230 1.15e red lil & vio 8 5

International Letter Writing Week, Oct. 9–15.

René Schneider and Army Flag—A231

1972, Oct. 25 *Perf. 14*

428 A231 2.30e multi 8 5

2nd anniversary of the death of Gen. René Schneider. No. 428 is perforated vertically in the middle.

Book and Young People
A232

1972, Oct. 31 *Perf. 14½*

429 A232 50c blk & dp org 8 5

International Book Year 1972.

Guitar and Earthen Jar
A233

Designs: 2.65e, Fish and produce. 3.50e, Stove, pots and rug (vert.).

1972, Nov. 20 Litho. *Perf. 14½*

430 A233 1.15e red & blk 8 5
431 A233 2.65e ultra & rose lake 8 5
432 A233 3.50e red & red brn 8 5

Tourism Year of the Americas.

José M. Carrera Before Execution
A234

Map of Antarctica, Flag at O'Higgins Base
A235

1973, Feb. 1 Litho. *Perf. 14½*

433 A234 2.30e lt ultra 8 5

Sesquicentennial of the death of José Miguel Carrera (1785–1821), Chilean revolutionist and dictator.

1973, Feb. 8

434 A235 10e ultra & red 8 5

25th anniversary of the Bernardo O'Higgins Antarctic Base.

Naval Air Service Emblem, Destroyer
A236

La Silla Observatory
A237

1973, Mar. 16 Litho. *Perf. 14½*

435 A236 20e brt bl & ocher 8 5

Chilean Naval Aviation, 50th anniversary.

1973, Apr. 25 Litho. *Perf. 14½*

436 A237 2.30e ultra & blk 8 5

INTERPOL Emblem
A238

Designs: 50e, Fingerprint over globe.

1973, Sept. 23 Litho. *Perf. 14½*

437 A238 30e bis & ultra 12 8
438 A238 50e blk & red 25 8

50th anniversary of International Criminal Police Organization.

Grapes A239

Design: 100e, Globe inscribed "Chile Exporta Vino."

1973, Dec. 10 Litho. *Perf. 14½*

439	A239	20e buff & lil	12	8
440	A239	100e bl & cl	12	8

Chilean wine export.

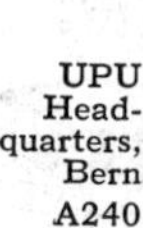

UPU Headquarters, Bern A240

1974, Apr. 4

441	A240	500e on 45c grn	8	5

Centenary of Universal Postal Union. No. 441 was not issued without dark green surcharge and overprint.

Bernardo O'Higgins, Armed Forces Emblems—A241

1974, Apr. 11 Litho. *Perf. 14½*

Multicolored

442	A241	30e *shown*	8	5
443	A241	30e *Soldiers with mortar*	8	5
444	A241	30e *Navy anti-aircraft gunners*	8	5
445	A241	30e *Pilot in cockpit*	8	5
446	A241	30e *Mounted policeman*	8	5
		Nos. 442-446 (5)	40	25

Honoring the Armed Forces.

Soccer Ball and Globe A242

Traffic Police A243

Design: 1000e, Soccer ball and stadium (horiz.).

1974 Lithographed *Perf. 14*

447	A242	500e dk red & org	10	6
448	A242	1000e bl & ind	20	10

World Cup Soccer Championship, Munich, June 13–July 7.

A souvenir sheet contains 2 imperf. stamps similar to Nos. 447–448, with blue marginal inscription. Printed on thin card. Size: 90x119mm.

Nos. 386, 355 Surcharged

1974, June Litho. *Perf. 14½*

449	A202	100e on 40c bl grn	10	5

Perf. 13x14

450	A174	300e on 50c dl brn	10	5

1974, June 20 *Perf. 14½*

451	A243	30e red brn & grn	12	5

Traffic safety.

Santiago-Fiji Air Service—A244

1974, Sept. 5 Litho. *Perf. 14½x14*

Brown & Green

452	A244	Block of 4	1.25	50
a.		200e *Easter Island turtle*	25	10
b.		200e *Polynesian dancer*	25	10
c.		200e *Map of Fiji Islands*	25	10
d.		200e *Kangaroo*	25	10

Inauguration of air service by LAN (Chile's national airline) from Santiago to Easter Island, Tahiti, Fiji, Australia.

Globe Cut to Show Mantle and Core A245

1974, Sept. 9 *Perf. 14x14½*

453	A245	500e red brn & org	12	6

International Volcanology Congress, Santiago, Sept. 9–14.

No. 393 Surcharged in Brown

E°100

24 OCTUBRE 1974

INAUGURACION TEMPLO VOTIVO

1974, Oct. 24 Litho. *Perf. 14½*

454	A205	100e on 40c grn	12	8

Inauguration of the O'Higgins National Shrine at Maipu, Oct. 24, 1974.

Juan Fernandez Archipelago—A246

1974, Nov. 22 Litho. *Perf. 14½x14*

Blue & Brick Red

455	A246	Block of 4	75	50
a.		200e *Robinson Crusoe Island*	15	10
b.		200e *Chonta palms*	15	10
c.		200e *Mountain goat*	15	10
d.		200e *Crayfish*	15	10

400th anniversary of discovery of Juan Fernandez Archipelago.

O'Higgins and Bolivar A247

1974, Dec. 9 *Perf. 14½*

456	A247	100e red brn & buff	8	5

Sesquicentennial of the Battles of Junin and Ayacucho.

F. Vidal Gormaz and Institute Seal A248

Albert Schweitzer A249

1975, Jan. 22 Litho. *Perf. 14½*

457	A248	100e rose cl & bl	10	6

Centenary of the Naval Hydrographic Institute; F. Vidal Gormaz was first commandant.

1975, Apr. 7 Litho. *Perf. 14x14½*

458	A249	500e yel & red brn	12	6

Dr. Albert Schweitzer (1875–1965), medical missionary, birth centenary.

E° 70.-

No. 395 Surcharged in Red

Revalorizada 1975

1975, Apr. 7 *Perf. 14½*

459	A207	70e on 40c car & lt red brn	10	6

Volunteer Lifeboat Service—A250

1975, Apr. 15 Litho. *Perf. 14½x14*

Dark Blue & Gray Olive

460	A250	Block of 4	75	50
a.		150e *Lighthouse*	15	10
b.		150e *Shipwreck*	15	10
c.		150e *Lifeboat*	15	10
d.		150e *Sailor reaching for life preserver*	15	10

Valparaiso Volunteer Lifeboat service, 50th anniversary.

Frigate Lautaro A251

1975, May 21 Photo. & Engr.

Emerald & Black

461	A251	500e *shown*	20	10
462	A251	500e *Corvette Baquedano*	20	10
463	A251	500e *Cruiser Chacabuco*	20	10
464	A251	500e *Brigantine Goleta Esmeralda*	20	10

Orange & Black

465	A251	800e *Frigate Lautaro*	25	10
466	A251	800e *Corvette Baquedano*	25	10
467	A251	800e *Cruiser Chacabuco*	25	10
468	A251	800e *Brigantine Goleta Esmeralda*	25	10

Ultramarine & Black

469	A251	1000e *Frigate Lautaro*	35	12
470	A251	1000e *Corvette Baquedano*	35	12
471	A251	1000e *Cruiser Chacabuco*	35	12
472	A251	1000e *Brigantine Goleta Esmeralda*	35	12
		Nos.461-472 (12)	3.20	1.28

Shipwreck of training frigate Lautaro, 30th anniversary. Stamps of same denomination printed se-tenant in sheets of 25 (5x5) with 7 Lautaro stamps and 6 each of the others.

A souvenir card contains impressions of Nos. 469–472 with ultramarine and orange marginal inscription and decoration. Size: 118x150mm.

Happy Mother, by Alfredo Valenzuela P. A252

Diego Portales, Finance Minister A253

Paintings: No. 474, Young Girl, by Francisco Javier Mandiola. No. 475, Lucia Guzman, by Pedro Lira Rencoret. No. 476, Woman, by Magdalena Mira Mena.

1975, Oct. 13 Litho. *Perf. 14½*

473	A252	50c multi	12	8
474	A252	50c multi	12	8
475	A252	50c multi	12	8
476	A252	50c multi	12	8

International Women's Year 1975. Gray inscription on back, printed beneath gum, gives details about painting shown.

A souvenir card contains impressions of Nos. 473–476 with black and blue marginal inscription and decoration. Size: 149x120 mm.

1975–78 Litho. *Perf. 13x14*

477	A253	10c gray grn	8	5
478	A253	20c vio ('76)	8	5
479	A253	30c org ('76)	8	5
480	A253	50c lt brn	8	5
481	A253	1p blue	8	5
482	A253	1.50p ocher ('76)	10	5
483	A253	2p gray ('77)	10	5
483A	A253	2.50p cit ('78)	10	5
484	A253	5p rose cl	20	5
		Nos. 477-484 (9)	90	45

Cochrane and Liberating Squadron, 1820—A254

Designs: No. 486, Capture of Valdivia, 1820. No. 487, Capture of Three-master Esmeralda, 1820. No. 488, Cruiser Cochrane, 1874. No. 489, Destroyer Cochrane, 1962.

1976, Jan. 6 ***Perf. 14½***

485	A254	1p multi	12	8
486	A254	1p multi	12	8
487	A254	1p multi	12	8
488	A254	1p multi	12	8
489	A254	1p multi	12	8
		Nos. 485-489 (5)	60	40

Lord Thomas Cochrane, first commander of Chilean Navy, birth bicentenary. Nos. 485–489 printed se-tenant.

Flags of Chile and Bolivia A255

1976, May 25 **Litho.** ***Perf. 14½***

490	A255	1.50p multi	15	8

Sesquicentennial of Bolivia's independence.

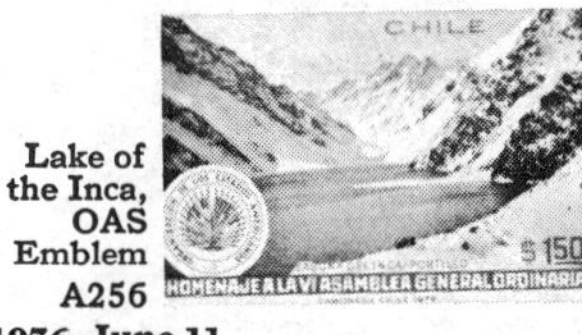

Lake of the Inca, OAS Emblem A256

1976, June 11

491	A256	1.50p multi	12	8

6th General Assembly of the Organization of American States.

George Washington A257

1976, July

492	A257	5p multi	35	15

American Bicentennial.

Minerva and Academy Emblem A258

1976, July

493	A258	2.50p multi	12	8

Polytechnic Military Academy, 50th anniversary.

Araucan Indian A259

Designs: 2p, Condor with broken chain. 3p, Winged woman, symbolizing rebirth.

1976, Sept. 20 **Litho.** ***Perf. 14½***

494	A259	1p bl & multi	12	8
495	A259	2p bl & multi	15	8
496	A259	3p yel & multi	25	12

3rd anniversary of the Military Junta. Nos. 494–496 printed se-tenant.

View, Antarctica A260

1977, Feb. 10 **Litho.** ***Perf. 14½***

497	A260	2p multi	12	6

Visit of President Augusto Pinochet to Antarctica.

School Emblem, Planted Field A261

Justice A262

1977, Mar. 10 ***Perf. 14½***

498	A261	2p multi	12	6

Centenary of advanced agricultural education.

1977, Mar. 30 **Litho.** ***Perf. 14½***

499	A262	2p brn & sl	12	6

Supreme Court of Justice, sesquicentennial.

Eye with Globe, Caduceus A263

1977, Mar. 30 **Litho.** ***Perf. 14½***

500	A263	2p multi	12	6

11th Pan-American Ophthalmological Congress.

Mounted Policeman A264

Designs: No. 502, Policewoman with children. No. 503, Paine Peaks and Osorno Volcano, crossed rifle emblem. No. 504, Crossed rifle emblem, mounted and motorcycle policemen, helicopter and automobile. (horiz.).

1977, Apr. 27

501	A264	2p multi	12	6
502	A264	2p multi	12	6
503	A264	2p multi	12	6
504	A264	2p multi	12	6

Chilean police organization, 50th anniversary.

Intelsat Satellite over Globe A265

1977, May 17 **Litho.** ***Perf. 14½***

505	A265	2p multi	12	6

World Telecommunications Day.

El Mercurio's First Front Page, Press and Ship—A266

1977, July 5 **Litho.** ***Perf. 14½***

506	A266	2p multi	12	6

El Mercurio de Valparaiso, first Chilean newspaper, 150th anniversary.

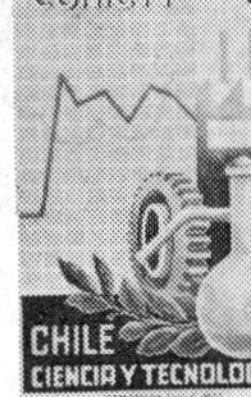

St. Francis, Birds and Cross A267

Science and Technology A268

1977, July 26 **Litho.** ***Perf. 14½***

507	A267	5p multi	25	12

St. Francis of Assisi, 750th death anniversary.

1977, Aug. 26 **Litho.** ***Perf. 14½***

508	A268	4p multi	20	10

Young Mother Weaving A269

Designs: No. 510, Handicapped boy in wheelchair and nurse. No. 511, Children dancing in circle (horiz.). No. 512, Old man and home (horiz.).

1977, Sept. 13 **Litho.** ***Perf. 14½***

509	A269	5p multi	25	8
510	A269	5p multi	25	8
511	A269	10p multi	50	12
512	A269	10p multi	50	12

4th anniversary of Government Junta and social services of armed forces.

Diego de Almagro A270

1977, Oct. 31 **Engr.** ***Perf. 14½***

513	A270	5p rose & car	25	6

Diego de Almagro (1475–1538), leader of Spanish expedition to Chile.

Bell, Letters, Dove and Child A271

1977, Dec. 12 **Litho.** ***Perf. 14½***

514	A271	2.50p multi	12	6

Christmas 1977.

Loading Timber A272

1978 **Litho.** ***Perf. 15***

515	A272	10p multi	50	12
516	A272	20p multi	1.00	12

No. 516 inscribed "CORREOS," ship is flying Chilean flag.

Papal Arms and Globe A273

University A274

1978 **Litho.** ***Perf. 14½***

521	A273	10p multi	50	12
522	A274	25p multi	1.25	20

World Peace Day (10p); Catholic University of Valparaiso, 50th anniversary (25p). Issue dates: 10p, July 28; 25p, July 31.

O'Higgins, by Gil de Castro A275

1978, Aug. 20 Litho. *Perf. 15*

523 A275 10p multi 50 12

Bernardo O'Higgins (1778–1842), soldier and statesman.

Chacabuco Victory Monument A276

1978, Sept. 11

524 A276 10p multi 50 12

160th anniversary of O'Higgins victory at Chacabuco, and 5th anniversary of military government.

Teacher Writing on Blackboard A277

1978, Sept. 21

525 A277 15p multi 75 12

10th anniversary and 9th Reunion of Interamerican Council for Education, Science and Culture (C.I.E.C.C.), Sept. 21–29.

First National Fleet, by Thomas Somerscales—A278

Design: 30p, Last Moments of Rancagua Battle, by Pedro Subercaseaux.

1978 Litho. *Perf. 15*

526 A278 20p multi 1.00 12
527 A278 30p multi 1.50 20

Bernardo O'Higgins (1778–1842), soldier and statesman.

Issue dates: 20p, Oct. 9; 30p, Oct. 2.

San Martin-O'Higgins Medal, by Rene Thenot, 1942—A279

1978, Oct. 20

528 A279 7p multi 35 8

José de San Martin and Bernardo O'Higgins, 200th birth anniversaries.

Council Emblem A280

1978, Nov. 27 Litho. *Perf. 14½*

529 A280 50p multi 3.00 50

International Council of Military Sports, 30th anniversary.

Three Kings A281 **Virgin and Child A282**

1978, Dec. 14 Litho. *Perf. 14½*

530 A281 3p multi 15 8
531 A282 11p multi 60 25

Christmas 1978.

Philippi Brothers A283

1978, Dec. 29 Litho. *Perf. 14½x15*

532 A283 3.50p multi 20 8

Bernardo E. Philippi (1811–1852) and Rodulfo A. Philippi (1808–1904), scientists and travelers.

No. 477 Surcharged in Bright Green

1979 Litho. *Perf. 13x14*

533 A253 3.50p on 10c gray grn 25 15

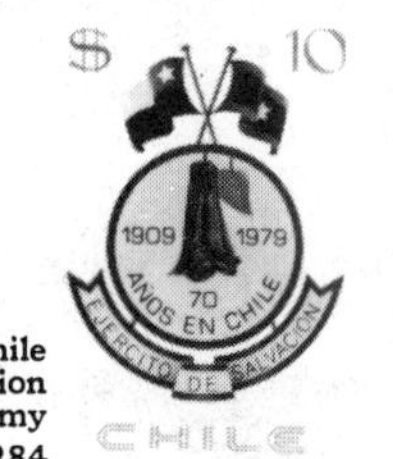

Flags of Chile and Salvation Army A284

1979, Mar. 17 Litho. *Perf. 14½*

534 A284 10p multi 75 50

Salvation Army in Chile, 70th anniversary.

Pope Paul VI A285

1979, Mar. 30

535 A285 11p multi 80 50

In memory of Pope Paul VI (1897–1978).

Battle of Maipu Monument A286

1979, Apr. 17 Litho. *Perf. 14½*

536 A286 8.50p multi 65 40

Bernardo O'Higgins (1778–1842), Liberator of Chile.

Battle of Angamos A287

Naval Battles: No. 538, Iquique. No. 539, Punta Gruesa.

1979, May 21 Litho. *Perf. 14½*

537 A287 3.50p multi 25 15
538 A287 3.50p multi 25 15
539 A287 3.50p multi 25 15

Centenary of victorious naval battles against Peru.

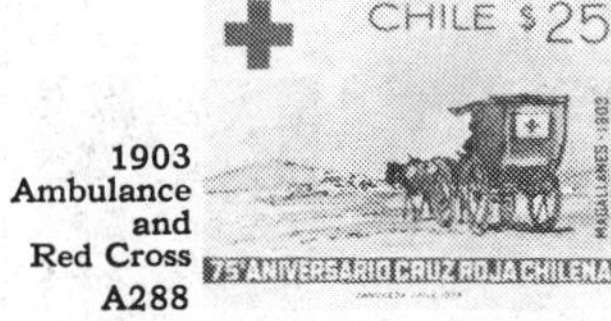

1903 Ambulance and Red Cross A288

1979, June 29 Litho. *Perf. 14½*

540 A288 25p multi 1.50 90

75th anniversary of Chilean Red Cross.

Diego Portales A289

1979-81 Litho. *Perf. 13½x13*

542 A289 1.50p ocher 10 5
543 A289 2p gray ('81) 12 10
545 A289 3.50p red 20 10
546 A289 4.50p bl grn ('81) 25 15
547 A289 5p rose cl 30 15
548 A289 6p emerald 35 20
Nos. 542-548(6) 1.32 75

People and Flag A290

1979, Aug. 28 Litho. *Perf. 14½*

551 A290 10p multi 60 35

Jugoslavian immigration, centenary.

Coat of Arms and Mt. Castillo—A290a

1979, Oct. 12 Litho. *Perf. 14½*

552 A290a 20p multi 1.20 75

Coyhaique sesquicentennial.

IYC Emblem, Playground—A291

IYC Emblem, Children's Drawings: 11p, Girl and shadow (vert.). 12p, Dancing.

1979, Oct. 9 *Perf. 14½*

553 A291 9.50p multi 60 35
554 A291 11p multi 65 40
555 A291 12p multi 70 40

International Year of the Child.

Telecom 79—A292

1979, Oct. 26 Litho. *Perf. 14½*

556 A292 15p multi 90 50

3rd World Telecommunications Exhibition, Geneva, Sept. 20-26.

Puerto Williams, 25th Anniversary A293

1979, Nov. 21

557 A293 3.50p multi 20 10

Adoration of the Kings—A294

1979, Dec. 4 Litho. *Perf. 15*

558 A294 3.50p multi 20 10

Christmas 1979.

Rafael Sotomayor, Minister of War
A295

Military Heroes: No. 560, Erasmo Escala. No. 561, Emilio Sotomayor. No. 562, Eleuterio Ramirez

1979, Dec. 29 *Perf. 13½*

559 A295 3.50p ocher & brn 20 10
560 A295 3.50p ocher & brn 20 10
561 A295 3.50p ocher & brn 20 10
562 A295 3.50p ocher & brn 20 10

Nos. 559-562 printed se-tenant in blocks of four.

Bell UH-1 Rescue Helicopter at Tinguiririca Volcano, by S.O. Mococain—A296

Air Force, 50th Anniversary: No. 564, Flying boat Catalina Skua over Antarctic, by E.F. Alvarez. No. 565, F5-E Tiger II over Andes, by M.M. Barria.

1980, Mar. 21 **Litho.** *Perf. 13½*

563 A296 3.50p *shown* 20 10
564 A296 3.50p *Jet* 20 10
565 A296 3.50p *Sea plane* 20 10

The Death of Bueras, by Pedro Leon Carmona—A297

1980, Apr. 14 **Litho.** *Perf. 13½*

566 A297 12p multi 70 40

Charge of Bueras, Battle of Maipo, 1818.

Rotary International, 75th Anniversary—A298

1980, Apr. 15

567 A298 10p multi 60 30

Gen. Manuel Baquedano, by Pedro Subercaseaux—A299

Gen. Pedro Lagos, Battle Scene, by Subercaseaux—A300

Battle of Morro de Arica Centenary (Subercaseaux Paintings): No. 570, Commander Juan J. San Martin, battle scene.

1980, June 7 **Litho.** *Perf. 13½*

568 A299 3.50p multi 20 10
569 A300 3.50p multi 20 10
570 A300 3.50p multi 20 10

Score and Perez's Silhouette—A301

1980, June 27 **Litho.** *Perf. 13½*

571 A301 6p multi 35 20

Osman Perez Freire (1880-1930), composer, and fragment from his song "Ay, Ay, Ay."

Mt. Gasherbrum II, Chilean Flag, Ice Pick—A302

1980, July 9

572 A302 15p multi 90 50

Chilean Himalayan expedition, June 1979.

"Charity," Stained-glass Window—A303

1980, July 18

573 A303 10p multi 60 30

Daughters of Charity, 125th anniversary in Chile.

Condor, Colors of Chile—A304

1980, Sept. 11 **Litho.** *Perf. 13½*

574 A304 3.50p multi 20 10

17th anniversary of constitution.

Inca Child Mummy

A305

Pablo Burchard, by Pedro Lira

A306

1980, Sept. 14

575 A305 5p *shown* 30 15
576 A305 5p *Claudio Gay* 30 15

National Museum of Natural History (founded by Claudio Gay, 1800-1873) sesquicentennial. Nos. 575-576 se-tenant with gutter between giving history of museums and mummy.

1980, Sept. 27 **Litho.** *Perf. 13½*

577 A306 3.50p multi 20 10

Museum of Fine Art centenary (directed by Burchard, 1932).

Santiago International Fair
A307

1980, Oct. 30

578 A307 3.50p multi 20 10

Nativity—A308

Christmas 1980: 3.50p, Family (vert.).

1980, Nov. 25 **Litho.** *Perf. 13½*

579 A308 3.50p multi 20 10
580 A308 10.50p multi 65

Infantryman 1879
A309

Congress Emblem
A310

Designs: Pacific War period uniforms, 1879. Nos. 581-584 se-tenant.

1980, Nov. 27

581 A309 3.50p *shown* 20 10
582 A309 3.50p *Cavalry officer* 20 10
583 A309 3.50p *Artillery officer* 20 10
584 A309 3.50p *Engineer colonel* 20 10

1980, Dec. 1

585 A310 11.50p multi 70 40

23rd International Congress of Military Medicine and Pharmacy.

Successful Eradication of Hoof and Mouth Disease—A311

1981, Jan. 16 **Litho.** *Perf. 13½*

586 A311 9.50p multi 45 15

Maoi Statues, Easter Island—A312

1981, Jan. 28 **Litho.** *Perf. 13½*

587 A312 3.50p shown 16 10
588 A312 3.50p Robinson Crusoe Island 16 10
589 A312 10.50p Penguins, Antarctic Territory 65 50

National Heroine Javiera Carrera, by O.M. Pizarro, Birth Bicentenary—A313

1981, Mar. 20

590 A313 3.50p multi 16 10

UPU Membership Centenary—A314

1981, Apr. 1

591 A314 3.50p multi 16 10

C130 Hercules Air Force Transport Plane Unloading Cargo—A315

1981, Apr. 21

592 A315 3.50p multi 16 10

Lieutenant Marsh Air Force Base, first anniversary.

13th World Telecom—munications Day—A316

1981, May 17 **Litho.** ***Perf. 13½***

593 A316 3.50p multi 16 10

Arturo Prat Naval Base A317

1981, June 23 **Litho.** ***Perf. 13½***

594 A317 3.50p multi 16 10

Capt. Jose Luis Araneda—A318

1981, June 26

595 A318 3.50p multi 16 10

Battle of Sangrar centenary.

Philatelic Society of Chile, 90th Anniv.—A319

1981, July 29 **Litho.** ***Perf. 13½***

596 A319 4.50p multi 20 10

Minister Recabarren and Chief Conuepan Giving Speeches, by Hector Robles Acuna—A320

1981, Aug. 7

597 A320 4.50p multi 20 10

Temuco city centenary.

Exports—A321

1981, Aug. 31 **Litho.** ***Perf. 13½***

598 A321 14p multi 65 35

Palacio de Moneda (Govt. Mint)—A322

1981, Sept. 11

599 A322 4.50p multi 20 15

Natl. liberation, 8th anniv.

St. Vincent de Paul, 400th Birth Anniv.—A323

1981, Sept. 27 **Litho.** ***Perf. 13½***

600 A323 4.50p multi 25 10

Andres Bello, Statesman, Birth Bicentenary

A324

1981, Sept. 29

601 A324 4.50p Coin 25 10
602 A324 9.50p Bust, books 50 15
603 A324 11.50p Statue, arms 60 25

2nd Congress of South American Uniformed Police—A325

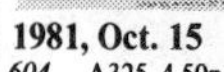

1981, Oct. 15

604 A325 4.50p multi 25 10

World Food Day—A326

1981, Oct. 16

605 A326 5.50p multi 30 10

Uniform Type of 1980

1879 Parade Uniforms. Nos. 544-547 se-tenant.

1981, Nov. 6 ***Perf. 13½***

606 A309 5.50p Infantry private 30 10
607 A309 5.50p Cadet 30 10
608 A309 5.50p Cavalryman 30 10
609 A309 5.50p Artilleryman 30 10

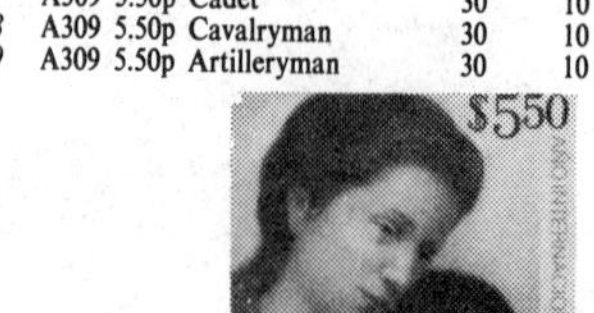

Intl. Year of the Disabled—A327

1981, Nov. 11

610 A327 5.50p multi 30 10

Christmas 1981—A328

1981, Nov. 25

611 A328 5.50p Nativity 30 10
612 A328 11.50p Three Kings 60 25

50th Anniv. of Federico Santa Maria Technical University—A329

1981, Dec. 1 **Litho.** ***Perf. 13½***

613 A329 5.50p multi 30 10

Dario Salas (1881-1941), Educator—A330

1981, Dec. 4

614 A330 5.50p multi 30 10

FIDA '82, 2nd Natl. Air Force Fair—A331

1982, Mar. 6 **Litho.** ***Perf. 13½***

615 A331 4.50p multi 25

1982 Constitution—A332

1982, Mar. 11

616 A332 4.50p Cardinal Caro, family 25
617 A332 11p Diego Portales 65
618 A332 30p Bernardo O'Higgins 1.80

Panamerican Institute of Geography and History, 12th General Assembly—A333

1982, Mar. 22 **Litho.** ***Perf.* 13½**
619 A333 4.50p multi 25

American Air Forces Cooperation System—A334

1982, Apr. 12
620 A334 4.50p multi 25

Pedro Montt—A335 Fish Exports—A336

1982
621 A335 4.50p lt vio 25

1982, May 3 **Litho.** ***Perf.* 13½**
622 A336 20p multi 1.20

Scouting Year—A337

1982, May 21 **Litho.** ***Perf.* 13**
623 Pair 50
a.-b. A337 4.50p multi 25

Battle of Concepcion Centenary—A338

Designs: Chacabuco Regiment officers killed in battle.

1982, June 18 **Litho.** ***Perf.* 13½**
624 Block of 4 1.00
a. A338 4.50p I. Carrera Pinto 25
b. A338 4.50p A. Perez Canto 25
c. A338 4.50p J. Montt Salamanca 25
d. A338 4.50p L. Cruz Martinez 25

UN World Assembly on Aging, July 26—Aug 6—A339

1982, Aug. 5
625 A339 4.50p multi 25

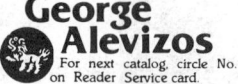

SEMI-POSTAL STAMPS.

S. S. Abtao and Captain Policarpo Toro—SP1

S. S. Abtao and Brother Eugenio Eyraud SP2

Perf. 14½x15

1940, Mar. 1 Engr. Unwmkd.

B1	SP1	80c +2.20p dk grn & lake	2.00	1.75
B2	SP2	3.60p +6.40p lake & dk grn	2.00	1.75

Issued in commemoration of the 50th anniversary of Chilean ownership of Easter Island. The surtax was used for charitable institutions.

These stamps were printed together in a sheet containing fifteen of each value, of which nine pairs are se-tenant.

Pedro de Valdivia SP3

Portraits: 10c+10c, Jose Toribio Medina.

1961, Apr. 29 Photo. *Perf. 13x12½*

B3	SP3	5c +5c pale brn & sl grn	1.00	25
B4	SP3	10c +10c buff & vio blk	75	25

Printed without charge by the Spanish Mint as a gift to Chile. The surtax was to aid the 1960 earthquake victims and to increase teachers' salaries. See also Nos. CB1–CB2.

No. 402 Surcharged in Dark Green

E° 27 + 3

"Centenario de la Organización Meteorológica Mundial IMO-W-MO 1973"

1974, Mar. 25 Litho. *Perf. 14½*

B5	A213	27e +3e on 40c dl grn	8	5

Centenary of international meteorological cooperation.

The 3e surtax of Nos. B5–B10 was for modernization of the postal system.

E° 27 + 3

No. 412 Surcharged in Dark Blue

"V Centenario del Nacimiento de Copérnico 1473 - 1973"

1974, Apr. 25 Litho. *Perf. 14½*

B6	A219	27e +3e on 1.95e lt & dk bl	8	5

500th anniversary of the birth of Nicolaus Copernicus (1473–1534), Polish astronomer.

E° 27 + 3

No. 329A Surcharged

" Centenario de la ciudad de Viña del Mar 1874 - 1974 "

1974, May 2 Litho. *Perf. 14*

B7	A159	27e +3e on 1e bluish grn	8	5

Centenary of the city of Viña del Mar.

No. 377 Surcharged

1974, June 7 Litho. *Perf. 14½*

B8	A193	47e +3e on 40c grn	8	5

Nos. 395 and 380 Surcharged in Red

1974

B9	A207	67e +3e on 40c multi	8	5
B10	A196	97e +3e on 40c red brn	8	5

Issue dates: No. B9, July 9; No. B10, June 20.

AIR POST STAMPS.

Bernardo O'Higgins AP1

Lithographed; Center Engraved

Black Surcharge.

1927 *Perf. 13½x14.* Unwmkd.

C1	AP1	40c on 10c blk brn & bl	300.00	35.00
C2	AP1	80c on 10c blk brn & bl	300.00	60.00
C3	AP1	1.20p on 10c blk brn & bl	300.00	60.00
C4	AP1	1.60p on 10c blk brn & bl	300.00	60.00
C5	AP1	2p on 10c blk brn & bl	300.00	60.00
		Nos. C1-C5 (5)	1,500.	275.00

Nos. C1 to C5 were issued for air post service between Santiago and Valparaiso, and are not known without surcharge.

Regular Issues of 1915–28 Overprinted or Surcharged in Black, Red or Blue

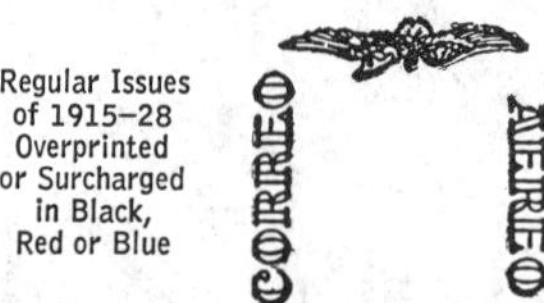

Inscribed: "Chile Correos".

1928–29 *Perf. 13½x14, 14*

C6	A39	20c brn org & blk (Bk)	50	20
C6A	A55	40c dk vio & blk (R)	50	20
C6B	A43	1p grn & blk (Bl)	1.50	60
C6C	A43	2p red & blk (Bl)	2.50	40
f.		2p ver & blk (Bl)	110.00	27.50
C6D	A43	5p ol grn & blk (Bl)	3.75	1.00
C6E	A50	6p on 10c dp bl & blk (R)	60.00	32.50
C7	A43	10p org & blk (Bk) ('29)	12.50	4.00
C8	A43	10p org & blk (Bl)	55.00	32.50
		Nos.C6-C8 (8)	136.25	71.40

On Nos. C6B to C6D, C7 and C8 the overprint is larger than on the other stamps of the issue.

Same Overprint or Surcharge on Nos. 155, 156, 158-161.

Inscribed: "Chile Correos".

1928-32 Wmk. 215

C9	A55	40c vio & blk (R)	60	30
C10	A43	1p grn & blk (Bl)	1.75	50
C11	A43	2p red & blk (Bl)	10.00	2.00
C12	A52	3p on 5c sl bl (R)	40.00	27.50
C13	A43	5p ol grn & blk (Bl)	7.50	2.00
C14	A43	10p org & blk (Bk)	40.00	10.00
		Nos. C9-C14 (6)	99.85	42.30

Same Overprint on Nos. 166-169, 172 and 158 in Black, Red or Blue.

Inscribed: "Correos de Chile"

1928-30

C15	A39	20c org red & blk (#166) (Bk) ('29)	1.25	60
C16	A39	20c org red & blk (#172) (Bk) ('30)	40	20
C17	A40	25c bl & blk (R)	60	20
C18	A41	30c brn & blk (Bk)	35	20
a.		Double ovpt., one inverted	*350.00*	*350.00*
C19	A42	50c dp grn & blk (R)	50	20
		Nos. C15-C19 (5)	3.10	1.40

Inscribed: "Chile Correos".

1932 *Perf. 13½x14, 14.*

C21	A43	1p yel grn & blk (Bk)	3.75	2.00

Condor on Andes AP1a

Airplane Crossing Andes AP3

Los Cerrillos Airport AP2

Lithographed.

1931 *Perf. 13½x14, 14½x14*

C22	AP1a	5c yel grn	35	20
C23	AP1a	10c yel brn	35	20
C24	AP1a	20c rose	35	20
C25	AP2	50c dk bl	1.75	50
C26	AP3	50c blk brn	85	40
C27	AP3	1p purple	75	30
C28	AP3	2p bl blk	1.50	40
a.		2p bluish sl	1.50	40
C29	AP2	5p lt red	3.75	35
		Nos. C22-C29 (8)	9.65	2.55

Airplane over City AP4

Wings over Chile AP5

Condor AP6

Airplane and Star of Chile AP7

Condor and Statue of Canpolican AP8

Two Airplanes over Globe AP9

Seaplane AP10

Airplane AP11

Airplane and Southern Cross AP12

Airplane and Symbols of Space AP13

Perf. 13½x14

1934–39 Engraved Wmk. 215

Size: 21x25 mm.

C30	AP4	10c yel grn ('35)	25	10
C31	AP4	15c dk grn ('35)	35	20
C32	AP4	20c dp bl ('36)	20	12
C33	AP5	30c blk brn ('35)	20	12
C34	AP5	40c ind ('38)	20	12
C35	AP5	50c dk brn ('36)	20	12
C36	AP6	60c vio blk ('35)	20	12
C37	AP7	70c bl ('35)	35	20
C38	AP8	80c ol blk ('35)	20	12

Perf. 14

Size: 24½x29 mm.

C39	AP9	1p sl blk	20	12
C40	AP9	2p grnsh bl	20	12
C41	AP10	3p org brn ('35)	25	15
C42	AP10	4p brn ('35)	25	15
C43	AP10	5p org red	25	15
C44	AP11	6p yel brn ('35)	35	20
a.		6p brn ('39)	3.75	2.00
C45	AP11	8p grn ('35)	30	15
C46	AP11	10p brn lake	35	20
C47	AP12	20p olive	35	20
C48	AP12	30p gray blk	35	20
C49	AP13	40p gray vio	1.00	60
C50	AP13	50p brn vio	1.00	60
		Nos. C30-C50 (21)	7.00	4.06

Nos. C30–C50 have been re-issued in slightly different colors, with white gum. The first printings are considerably scarcer. See also Nos. C90–C107B, C148–C154.

Types of 1931 Surcharged in Black or Red

Cts.80

Perf. 13½ x14, 14½ x14.

1940 Wmk. 215

C51	AP1a	80c on 20c lt rose	60	20
C52	AP2	1.60p on 5p lt red	3.75	1.25
C53	AP3	5.10p on 2p sl bl (R)	3.00	1.50

The surcharge on No. C52 measures 21½mm.

Plane and Weather Vane
AP14

Plane and Caravel
AP23

Designs (Plane and): 20c, Globe. 30c, Chilean flag. 40c, Star of Chile and Southern Cross. 50c, Mountains. 60c, Tree. 70c, Lakes. 80c, Shore. 90c, Sunrise. 2p, Compass. 3p, Telegraph lines. 4p, Rainbow. 5p, Factory. 10p, Snow-capped mountain.

Lithographed

1941-42 ***Perf. 14.*** **Wmk. 215**

C54	AP14	10c ol gray	25	15
C55	AP14	20c dp rose	25	15
C56	AP14	30c bl vio	25	15
C57	AP14	40c dl red brn	25	15
C58	AP14	50c red org ('42)	50	20
C59	AP14	60c dp grn	25	15
C60	AP14	70c rose	50	30
C61	AP14	80c ultra ('42)	2.50	50
C62	AP14	90c dk brn	75	30
C63	AP23	1p brt bl	50	30
C64	AP23	2p rose lake	75	40
C65	AP23	3p dk bl grn & yel grn	1.00	65
C66	AP23	4p bl vio & buff	1.50	85
C67	AP23	5p dk org red ('42)	12.50	6.00
C68	AP23	10p gray grn & bl grn	7.50	5.00
		Nos. C54-C68 (15)	29.25	15.25

The 1p, dated "1541-1941", commemorates the 400th anniversary of Santiago.

1942-46 **Unwmkd.**

C69	AP14	10c ultra ('43)	25	15
C70	AP14	10c rose lil ('45)	25	15
C71	AP14	20c dl grn ('43)	25	15
C72	AP14	20c cop brn ('45)	25	15
C73	AP14	30c dl vio ('44)	25	15
C74	AP14	30c ol blk ('45)	25	15
C75	AP14	40c red brn ('44)	50	20
C76	AP14	40c ultra ('45)	25	15
C77	AP14	50c rose ('43)	25	15
C78	AP14	50c org red ('45)	25	15
C79	AP14	60c orange	25	15
C79B	AP14	60c dp grn ('46)	25	15
C80	AP14	70c rose ('45)	75	40
C81	AP14	80c sl grn	25	15
C82	AP14	90c brn ('45)	75	40
C83	AP23	1p gray grn & lt bl ('43)	35	20
C84	AP23	2p org red ('43)	75	20
C85	AP23	3p dk pur & pale org ('43)	75	20
C86	AP23	4p bl grn & yel grn	75	40
C87	AP23	5p dk rose car ('43)	65	30
a.		5p dk car rose ('44)	30	20
C88	AP23	10p saph ('43)	75	40
		Nos. C69-C88 (21)	8.25	4.10

No. C83 is without dates "1541-1941." See Nos. C109-C123, C145-C147.

Coat of Arms and Plane
AP29

1942, Nov. 5 **Engr.** ***Perf. 14½***

C89	AP29	100p car lake	37.50	27.50

University of Chile centenary.

Types of 1934-39.
Engraved.

1944-55 ***Perf. 13½x14.*** **Unwmkd.**

C90	AP4	10c yel grn ('55)	35	25
C92	AP4	20c dp bl	20	12
C93	AP5	30c blk brn	20	12
C94	AP5	40c indigo	20	12
C95	AP5	50c dk brn ('47)	20	12
C96	AP6	60c sl vio	20	12
C97	AP7	70c bl ('48)	20	12
C98	AP8	80c ol blk	20	12

Perf. 14

C99	AP9	1p sl blk	20	12
C100	AP9	2p grnsh bl	35	15
C101	AP10	3p org brn ('45)	20	12
C102	AP10	4p brown	20	12
C103	AP10	5p org red	50	20
C104	AP11	6p yel brn ('46)	50	20
C105	AP11	8p green	50	20
C106	AP11	10p brn lake	1.25	20
C107	AP12	20p ol gray ('45)	1.00	20
a.		Imperf., pair	100.00	
C107B	AP13	50p rose vio ('50)	25.00	4.00
		Nos. C90-C107B (18)	31.45	6.60

Plane and Radio Tower
AP30

Lithographed.

1945 ***Perf. 14*** **Unwmkd.**

C108	AP30	1.60p brt vio	75	30

Types of 1941-42.

1946-48 **Wmk. 215**

C109	AP14	10c rose lil ('47)	20	12
C110	AP14	20c dk red brn ('48)	20	12
C111	AP14	20c dl grn ('48)	2.50	40
C112	AP14	30c blk ('48)	20	12
C113	AP14	40c ultra ('48)	20	12
C114	AP14	60c ol grn ('48)	20	12
C115	AP14	80c ol blk ('48)	20	12
C116	AP14	90c choc ('48)	25	15
C117	AP23	1p gray grn & lt bl ('48)	25	12
C118	AP30	1.60p brt vio	25	12
C119	AP30	1.80p brt vio ('48)	25	12
C119A	AP23	2p org red	50	15
C120	AP23	3p dk pur & pale org ('47)	2.00	40
C121	AP23	4p bl grn & yel grn ('48)	1.50	60
C122	AP23	5p rose car ('47)	1.00	30
C123	AP23	10p saph ('47)	1.25	30
		Nos. C109-C123 (16)	10.95	3.38

No. C117 is without dates "1541-1941."

Araucarian Pine
AP31

1948

C124	AP31	3p carmine	75	75
a.		Block of 25	25.00	

Issued in panes of 100 stamps, divisible into four blocks of 25 different designs, the same animals, insects, birds, fish, flowers and trees of Chile as illustrated and described for Nos. 254-255.

The stamps commemorate the centenary (in 1944) of the publication of the first volume of Claudio Gay's Natural History of Chile.

Air Line Emblem and Planes
AP32

Lithographed.

1949 ***Perf. 14.*** **Wmk. 215**

C125	AP32	2p ultra	50	30

Issued to commemorate the 20th anniversary of the establishment of Chile's National Air Line.

Benjamin Vicuna Mackenna
AP33

Factory, Badge and Book
AP34

1949, Mar. 22 **Engr.** ***Perf. 13½x14***

C126	AP33	3p dk car rose	25	15

Lithographed.

1949, Nov. 11 ***Perf. 14*** **Unwmkd.**

Design: 10p, Column and cogwheel.

C127	AP34	5p green	75	50
C128	AP34	10p red brn	1.25	80

Issued to commemorate the centenary of the founding of Chile's School of Arts and Crafts.

Plane and Globe—AP35

1950, Jan. **Engraved**

C129	AP35	5p green	35	30
C130	AP35	10p red brn	75	50

Issued to commemorate the 75th anniversary of the formation of the Universal Postal Union.

Plane over Snow-capped Mountain
AP36

Plane over Fishing Boat—AP37

Araucarian Pine and Plane
AP38

Plane Above River
AP39

Plane and: 40c, Coast and Sunrise. 2p, Chilean flag. 3p, Dock crane. 5p, Blast furnace. 10p, Mountain lake. 20p, Cable cars.

Imprint: "Especies Valoradas-Chile"

Lithographed.

1950-54 ***Perf. 14*** **Wmk. 215**

C135	AP36	20c yel brn ('54)	20	12
C136	AP36	40c pur ('52)	20	12
C137	AP37	60c lt bl ('53)	1.50	80
C138	AP38	1p dl grn	20	12
C139	AP38	2p brn red	20	12
C140	AP38	3p vio bl	20	12
C141	AP39	4p red org ('54)	20	12
C142	AP38	5p violet	20	12
C143	AP39	10p yel grn ('53)	25	12
C144	AP39	20p red brn ('54)	40	12
		Nos. C135-C144 (10)	3.55	1.88

See also Nos. C155-C164, C207-C212.

Nos. C115, C81 and C116 Surcharged with New Value in Carmine or Black.

1951-52 **Wmk. 215**

C145	AP14	40c on 80c ol blk (C) ('52)	25	12

Unwmkd.

C146	AP14	40c on 80c sl grn (C) ('52)	6.50	3.50

Wmk. 215

C147	AP14	1p on 90c choc	20	12

Types of 1934-39.

Engraved.

1951-53 ***Perf. 14*** **Unwmkd.**

C148	AP9	1p dp bl	20	12
C149	AP9	2p blue	35	15
C150	AP11	6p bis brn ('52)	50	20
C151	AP12	30p dk gray ('53)	5.00	75
C152	AP13	40p dk pur brn	15.00	2.00
C153	AP13	50p dk pur	25.00	8.00
		Nos. C148-C153 (6)	46.05	11.22

Wmk. 215

C154	AP13	50p dk pur ('52)	1.25	60

Types of 1950-54.

Designs as Before.

Imprint: "Especies Valoradas-Chile"

Lithographed.

1951-55 ***Perf. 14*** **Unwmkd.**

C155	AP36	20c yel brn ('54)	20	12
C156	AP36	40c purple	20	12
C157	AP37	60c lt bl ('53)	25	15
C158	AP38	1p dk bl grn ('55)	20	12
C159	AP38	2p brn red	20	12
C160	AP38	3p vio bl	20	12
C161	AP39	4p red org ('52)	35	20
C162	AP38	5p violet	35	20
C163	AP39	10p emerald	35	12
C164	AP39	20p brown	50	18
		Nos. C155-C164 (10)	2.80	1.45

San Martin Crossing Andes—AP40

Engraved.

1951, Mar. 16 *Perf. 14½.* Wmk. 215

C165	AP40	5p red vio	50	30

Issued to commemorate the centenary of the death of Gen. José de San Martín.

Isabella Type of Regular Issue, 1952.

1952, Mar. 21 *Perf. 14*

C166	A125	10p carmine	60	40

Issued for the 500th anniversary of the birth of Queen Isabella I of Spain.

A souvenir card without franking value was issued for the Hispano-Chilean Philatelic Exhibition at Santiago, Oct. 12, 1969. It contains 2 imperf. stamps similar to Nos. 264 and C166—60c green and 10p rose red. Size: 115x137½mm. Price $12.50.

Ancient Fortress AP42

1953, Apr. 28

C167	AP42	10p brn car	1.25	30

4th centenary of the founding of Valdivia.

Stamp Centenary Type of 1953.

1953, Oct. 15 Engraved *Perf. 14½*

C168	A131	100p dp grnsh bl	2.00	1.25

Issued to commemorate the centenary of Chile's first postage stamps.

An imperf. souvenir sheet contains one each of Nos. 276 and C168, with inscriptions in black at top and bottom center. Sheet measures 178x229mm. It is stated that this sheet was not valid for postage. Price $425.

Early Plane and Stylized Modern Version AP44

Engraved.

1954, May 26 *Perf. 14* Unwmkd.

C170	AP44	3p dp bl	20	12

Issued to commemorate the 25th anniversary of the founding of Chile's National Air Line.

Domeyko Type of Regular Issue, 1954.

1954, Aug. 16 *Perf. 13½x14*

C171	A134	5p org brn	25	15

Issued to commemorate the 150th anniversary (in 1952) of the birth of Ignacio Domeyko.

Railroad Type of Regular Issue, 1954.

1954, Sept. 10 *Perf. 14½* Wmk. 215

C172	A135	10p dk pur	50	25

Issued to commemorate the centenary (in 1951) of the first South American railroad.

An imperforate souvenir sheet contains one each of Nos. 283 and C172. Size: 174x232mm. Price, $300.

Presidential Visits Type of 1955

1955, May 24

C173	A139	100p red	1.50	1.25

Issued to publicize the reciprocal visits of Presidents Juan D. Peron and Carlos Ibanez del Campo.

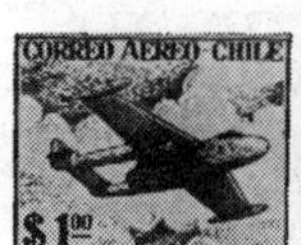

Jet Plane in Clouds AP48 — Comet Air Liner AP49

Designs: 2p, Helicopter over bridge. 10p, Oil derricks and plane. 50p, Control tower and plane. 200p, Beechcraft monoplane. 500p, Douglas DC-6.

***Perf. 14½x14, 14x13½* (AP49)**

1955-56 Engraved. Wmk. 215

C174	AP48	1p dp red lil ('56)	25	10
C175	AP48	2p pale brn ('56)	15	8
C176	AP48	10p bluish grn ('56)	15	8
C177	AP48	50p rose ('56)	75	30
C178	AP49	100p green	1.00	20
C179	AP49	200p dp ultra	6.25	1.00
C180	AP49	500p dk car	7.50	1.00
		Nos. C174-C180 (7)	16.05	2.76

Stamps similar to type AP49, but inscribed in escudo currency, are listed as type AP58.

1956-58 Unwmkd.

Designs: 5p, Train and plane. 20p, Jet plane and Easter Island statue.

C183	AP48	5p violet	15	8
C184	AP48	10p grn ('57)	15	8
C185	AP48	20p ultra	15	8
C186	AP48	50p rose ('57)	15	8
C187	AP49	100p bl grn ('57)	35	20
C188	AP49	200p dp ultra ('57)	50	20
C189	AP49	500p car ('58)	75	30
		Nos. C183-C189 (7)	2.20	1.02

Symbols of University Departments AP50

Design: 100p, View of the University.

1956, Dec. 15 *Perf. 14½* Unwmkd.

C190	AP50	20p green	35	20
C191	AP50	100p dk vio bl	1.25	75

Issued to commemorate the 25th anniversary of the Federico Santa Maria Technical University, Valparaiso.

A souvenir sheet contains one each of Nos. 299, C190—C191, imperf. It was not issued for postal use, though some served postally. Size: 127x160mm. Price, $30.

Mistral Type of Regular Issue, 1958

1958, Jan. 10 Engraved *Perf. 14*

C192	A144	100p green	25	15

Issued in honor of Gabriela Mistral, poet and educator.

Ambrosio O'Higgins AP51

1958, March 23

C193	AP51	100p lt bl	35	20

Issued to commemorate the 400th anniversary of the founding of the city of Osorno.

A souvenir sheet contains one each of Nos. 302 and C193, imperf. and printed in red brown. It was not issued for postal use, though some served postally. Size: 155x138mm. Price, $20.

Exhibition Type of Regular Issue

1958, Oct. 18 Unwmkd.

C194	A146	50p dl grn	20	12

Issued to publicize the National Philatelic Exhibition, Santiago, Oct. 18–26.

A souvenir sheet contains one each of Nos. 303 and C194, imperf. and printed in deep red. It was not issued for postal use, though some served postally. Size: 188x 220mm. Price, $20.

Bank Type of Regular Issue, 1958.

1958, Dec. 18 Engraved. *Perf. 14*

C195	A147	50p redsh brn	20	12

Issued to commemorate the centenary of the Savings Bank for Public Employees.

A souvenir sheet contains one each of Nos. 304 and C195, printed in dull violet, imperf. It was not issued for postal use, though some served postally. Price, $17.50.

Antarctic Types of Regular Issue

1958 Lithographed. *Perf. 14*

C199	A149	20p violet	25	12

Engraved.

C200	A150	500p dk bl	3.00	1.50

Symbols of Various Religions AP52

Engraved.

1959, Jan. 23 *Perf. 14½* Unwmkd.

C206	AP52	50p dk car rose	20	12

Issued to commemorate the 10th anniversary of the Universal Declaration of Human Rights.

Types of 1950–54.

Imprint: "Casa de Moneda de Chile."

Designs: 1p, Araucarian pine and plane. 10p, Plane over mountain lake. 20p, Plane and cable cars. 50p, Plane silhouette over shore. 100p, Plane over map of Antarctica. 200p, Plane over natural arch rock.

1959 Lithographed. *Perf. 14*

C207	AP38	1p dk bl grn	75	40
a.		Wmk. 215	37.50	
C208	AP39	10p emerald	50	12
C209	AP39	20p red brn	35	12
C210	AP39	50p yel grn	35	15
C211	AP39	100p car rose	35	15
C212	AP39	200p brt bl	50	12
		Nos. C207-C212 (6)	2.80	1.06

Carlos Anwandter AP53

1959, June 18 Engraved. *Perf. 14*

C213	AP53	20p rose car	25	12

Issued to commemorate the centenary of the German School in Valdivia, founded by Carlos Anwandter.

A souvenir sheet contains one each of Nos. 319 and C213, imperf. It was not issued for postal use, though some served postally. Price, $25.

IGY Type of Regular Issue, 1958.

1959, Aug. 28 *Perf. 14* Unwmkd.

C214	A148	50p green	20	12

Issued to commemorate the International Geophysical Year, 1957-58.

Ladrillero Type of Regular Issue.

1959, Aug. 28 Lithographed.

C215	A154	50p green	25	12

Issued to commemorate the 400th anniversary (in 1957) of the Juan Ladrillero expedition.

Barros Arana Type of Regular Issue.

1959, Aug. 28

C216	A155	100p purple	50	30

Issued to commemorate the 50th anniversary of the death of Diego Barros Arana (1830–1907), historian.

Red Cross Type of Regular Issue.

1959, Oct. 6

C217	A156	50p red & blk	35	20

Centenary of Red Cross idea.

WRY Type of Regular Issue, 1960.

1960, Apr. 7 *Perf. 14½* Unwmkd.

C218	A160	10c violet	35	20

Issued to publicize World Refugee Year, July 1, 1959—June 30, 1960.

A souvenir sheet contains two stamps similar to Nos. 330 and C218, the 1c printed in blue, the 10c airmail in maroon. The sheet is imperf., printed on thin cardboard and has border, inscriptions and WRY emblems in dark green with drab background. Size: 160x204mm. Price, $110.

Type of Regular Issue, 1960–62, and

José Agustin Eyzaguirre and José Miguel Infante—AP54

Designs: 2c, Palace of Justice. 5c, National memorial. No. C220, Arms of Chile. No. C220A, José Gaspar Marin and J. Gregorio Argomedo. 50c, Archbishop J. I. Cienfuegos and Brother Camilo Henriquez. 1e, Bernardo O'Higgins.

Engraved

1960-65 *Perf. 14½* Unwmkd.

C218A	AP54	2c mar & gray vio ('62)	20	12
C219	A162	5c vio bl & dl pur ('61)	25	15

Wmk. 215

C220	A161	10c dk brn & red brn	25	12

Unwmkd.

C220A	AP54	10c vio brn & brn ('64)	25	12
C220B	AP54	20c dk bl & dl pur ('64)	35	15
C220C	AP54	50c bl grn & ind ('65)	65	30
C220D	A162	1e dk red & red brn ('63)	1.50	60
		Nos. C218A-C220D (7)	3.45	1.56

Issued to commemorate the 150th anniversary of the formation of the first National Government.

A souvenir sheet contains two airmail stamps: a 5c brown similar to No. C219 (National Memorial) and a 10c green, type A161. The sheet is imperf., printed on heavy paper with papermaker's watermark, and has green inscriptions. Size: 120x 168mm. Price, $40.

Map and Rotary Emblem AP55

Lithographed

1960, Dec. 1 *Perf. 14* Unwmkd.

C221	AP55	10c blue	35	20

Issued to commemorate the South American Rotary Regional Conference, Santiago, 1960.

A souvenir sheet contains one 10c maroon, type AP55, with brown marginal inscription. Size: 118x158mm. Price, $17.50.

The souvenir sheet was overprinted in green "El Mundo Unida Contra la Malaria" and the outline of a mosquito, and released in October, 1962. Price, $35.

Plane over Mountain Lake
AP56

Designs: 1m, Araucarian pine and plane. 2m, Chilean flag and plane. 3m, Plane and dock crane. 4m, Plane above river (vignette like AP39). 5m, Blast furnace. 2c, Plane over cable cars. 5c, Plane silhouette over shore. 10c, Plane over map of Antarctica. 20c, Plane over natural arch rock.

Imprint: "Casa de Moneda de Chile."

1960–62 Lithographed *Perf. 14*

C222	AP56	1m orange	15	12
C223	AP56	2m yel grn	15	8
C224	AP56	3m violet	15	8
C225	AP56	4m gray ol	15	8
C226	AP56	5m brt bl grn	15	8
C227	AP56	1c ultra	15	8
C228	AP56	2c red brn ('61)	25	8
C229	AP56	5c yel grn ('61)	1.50	10
C230	AP56	10c car rose ('62)	40	10
C231	AP56	20c brt bl ('62)	40	10
		Nos. C222-C231 (10)	3.45	90

Oil Derricks and Douglas DC-6
AP57

Beechcraft Monoplane
AP58

Designs: 5m, Train and plane. 2c, Jet plane and Easter Island statue. 5c, Control tower and plane. 10c, Comet airliner. 50c, Douglas DC-6.

Lithographed

1960–67 *Perf. 14x13½* Unwmkd.

C234	AP57	5m red brn	8	5
C235	AP57	1c dl bl	8	5
C236	AP57	2c ultra ('62)	8	5
C237	AP57	5c rose red ('64)	8	5
C238	AP58	10c ultra ('67)	8	6
C239	AP58	20c car ('62)	8	5
C240	AP58	50c grn ('63)	8	5
		Nos. C234-C240 (7)	56	36

Stamps similar to type AP58, but inscribed in peso ($) currency, are listed as type AP49.

Congress Type of Regular Issue.

1961, Oct. 5 *Perf. 14½*

C245	A164	10c gray grn	1.00	40

Issued to commemorate the 150th anniversary of the first National Congress.

Soccer Type of Regular Issue, 1962.

Designs: 5c, Goalkeeper and stadium (vert.). 10c, Soccer players and globe.

Engraved

1962, May 30 *Perf. 14½* Unwmkd.

C246	A165	5c rose lil	20	10
C247	A165	10c dk car	35	20

Issued to commemorate the World Soccer Championship, Chile, May 30–June 17.

A souvenir sheet of four contains one each of Nos. 340–341, C246–C247, imperf., with light brown marginal inscriptions. Size: 123x194mm. Sold for 7.50 escudos (face value, 22 centavos). Price, $7.50.

Hunger Type of Regular Issue.

Design: 20c, Mother with empty bowl (horiz.).

1963, Mar. 21 Litho. *Perf. 14*

C248	A166	20c green	15	8

Issued for the "Freedom from Hunger" campaign of the U.N. Food and Agriculture Organization.

Red Cross Type of Regular Issue.

Design: 20c, Centenary emblem and plane silhouette (horiz.).

1963, Sept. 6 *Perf. 14* Unwmkd.

C249	A167	20c gray & red	18	10

Centenary of International Red Cross.

Fire Engine of 1860's
AP59

1963, Dec. 20 Litho. *Perf. 14½*

C250	AP59	30c red	18	10

Centenary of the Santiago Fire Brigade.

Western Hemisphere
AP60

1964, Apr. 9 *Perf. 14½* Unwmkd.

C254	AP60	4c ultra	10	5

Issued in memory of President John F. Kennedy and to honor the Alliance for Progress.

Battle of Rancagua
AP61

1965, May 7 Engraved *Perf. 14½*

C255	AP61	5c dl grn & sep	10	5

Issued to commemorate the sesquicentennial of the Battle of Rancagua, Oct. 7, 1814.

ITU Emblem, Old and New Communication Equipment
AP62

1965, May 7 Litho. *Perf. 14½x14*

C256	AP62	40c red & mar	15	6

Issued to commemorate the centenary of the International Telecommunication Union.

Portrait Type of 1964

Portraits: No. C257, Enrique Molina. No. C258, Msgr. Carlos Casanueva.

1965, June Litho. *Perf. 14*

C257	A169	60c brt vio	15	8
C258	A169	60c green	10	6

See note after No. 346.

Skier Type of Regular Issue 1965

Design: 20c, Skier (horiz.).

1965, Aug. 30 *Perf. 14* Unwmkd.

C259	A172	20c ultra	15	8

World Skiing Championships, Chile, 1966.

Fishing Boats, Angelmo Harbor
AP63

Aviators' Monument
AP64

1965

C260	AP63	40c brown	10	6

Perf. 14x14½

C262	AP64	1e car rose	20	8

Andrés Bello
AP65

1965, Nov. 29 Engraved Unwmkd.

C263	AP65	10c dk car rose	18	10

Issued to commemorate the centenary of the death of Andrés Bello (1780?–1865), Venezuela-born writer and educator.

Skiers
AP66

Basketball
AP67

1966, Apr. 6 Litho. *Perf. 14*

C264	AP66	4e dk bl & red brn	75	20

World Skiing Championships, Partillo, Aug. 1966.

1966, Apr. 28

C265	AP67	13c rose car	10	5

International Basketball Championships.

Slalom
AP68

Perf. 14½x15

1966, July 20 Litho. Unwmkd.

C266	AP68	75c rose car & lil	15	8
C267	AP68	3e ultra & lt bl	25	10

International Skiing Championships, Partillo, August 1966. A souvenir sheet of 2 contains imperf. stamps similar to Nos. C266–C267. Marginal inscription in ultramarine and rose carmine. No gum. Size: 109x140mm. Price $3.50.

Ship Type of Regular Issue

1966 Lithographed *Perf. 14½*

C268	A175	70c Prus grn & yel grn	15	10

See note below No. 358.

ICY Type of Regular Issue

1966, Oct. 28 *Perf. 14½* Unwmkd.

C269	A177	3e bl & car	65	20

International Cooperation Year, 1965.

A souvenir sheet of 2 contains imperf. stamps similar to Nos. 360 and C269. Brown marginal inscription. No gum. Size: 111x140mm. Price $3.

Chilean Flag and Ships
AP69

1966, Nov. 21 Litho. *Perf. 14*

C270	AP69	13c dl red brn	12	6

Centenary of the city of Antofagasta.

Pardo Type of Regular Issue

Design: 40c, Pardo and map of Chile's claim to Antarctica.

1967, Jan. 6 *Perf. 14½* Unwmkd.

C271	A178	40c ultra	10	6

See note below No. 361.

Family Type of Regular Issue

1967, Apr. 13 Litho. *Perf. 14*

C272	A179	80c brt bl & blk	15	8

Issued to publicize the 8th International Conference for Family Planning, Santiago, April 1967.

Ruben Dario and Title Page of "Azul"
AP70

1967, May 15 Engr. *Perf. 14½*

C273	AP70	10c dk bl	10	8

Issued to commemorate the centenary of the birth of Ruben Dario (pen name of Felix Ruben Garcia Sarmiento, 1867–1916), Nicaraguan poet, newspaper correspondent and diplomat.

Tree Type of Regular Issue

1967, June 9 Lithographed

C274	A180	75c grn & pale rose	12	6

Reforestation Campaign.

Lions Type of Regular Issue

1967 Lithographed *Perf. 14*

C275	A181	1e pur & yel	15	8
C276	A181	5e bl & yel	1.25	20

Issued to commemorate the 50th anniversary of Lions International. A souvenir sheet without franking value contains 3 imperf. stamps, 20c, 1e and 5e, in violet blue and yellow. Marginal inscription and design in violet blue and yellow. Size: 110x140mm. Price, $10.

Issue dates: 1e, July 12; 5e, Aug. 11.

Flag Type of Regular Issue

1967, Oct. 20 *Perf. 14½* Unwmkd.

C277	A182	50c ultra & crim	15	10

Sesquicentennial of the national flag.

ITY Emblem
AP71

1967, Nov. 22 Litho. *Perf. 14½*

C278 AP71 30c lt vio bl & blk 10 6

Issued for International Tourist Year, 1967.

Caro Type of Regular Issue, 1967.

1967, Dec. 4 Engraved *Perf. 14½*

C279 A183 40c violet 75 30

Issued to commemorate the centenary of the birth of José Maria Cardinal Caro.

Type of Regular Issue, 1968

1968, Apr. 23 Litho. *Perf. 14½*

C280 A184 2e brt vio 12 8

Issued to commemorate the sesquicentennial of the Battles of Chacabuco and Maipu. A souvenir sheet of 2 contains imperf. stamps similar to Nos. 367 and C280. Gold marginal inscription commemorates the battles and the First Trans-Andes Philatelic Week, Apr. 4–10. Price, $5. A second sheet exists with the 2e in green and the 3e in brown. Size: 139½x100mm. Price, $5.

Farm Type of Regular Issue

1968, June 18 Unwmkd.

C281 A185 50c blk, org & grn 15 8

Issued to publicize the agrarian reforms.

Juan I. Molina
AP72

1968, Aug. 27 Litho. *Perf. 14½*

C282 AP72 1e brt grn 12 6

Issued to honor Juan I. Molina, educator and scientist.

Map of Chiloé Province AP73 **British Crown and Map of Chile AP74**

Lithographed

1968, Oct. 7 *Perf. 14½* Unwmkd.

C283 AP73 1e rose cl 12 8

Issued to commemorate the anniversaries of the founding of five towns in Chiloé Province.

Auto Club Type of Regular Issue

1968, Nov. 10 Engr. *Perf. 14½x14*

C284 A189 5e ultra 20 10

Issued to commemorate the 40th anniversary of the Automobile Club of Chile.

1968, Nov. 12 Litho. *Perf. 14½*

Designs: 50c, Chilean coat of arms (horiz.; similar to type A161). 3e, British coat of arms (horiz.).

C285 AP74 50c grn & brn 25 10
C286 AP74 3e bl & org brn 15 8

Engraved

C287 AP74 5e pur & mag 25 15

Visit of Queen Elizabeth II of Great Britain, Nov. 11–18. A souvenir sheet of 3 contains imperf., lithographed stamps similar to Nos. C285–C287. Dark blue marginal inscription. Size: 124½x190mm. The souvenir sheet also publicizes the British-Chilean Philatelic Exhibition. Price, $10.

First Coin Minted in Chile and Coin Press
AP75

Design: 1e, Chile No. 128.

1968, Dec. 31 Litho. *Perf. 14½*

C288 AP75 50c ocher & vio brn 10 6
C289 AP75 1e lt bl & dp org 10 6

Issued to commemorate the 225th anniversary of the founding of the State Mint (Casa de Moneda de Chile). A souvenir sheet of 4 contains imperf. stamps similar to Nos. 373–374, C288–C289. Brown marginal inscription. Size: 150x119mm. Price, $2.50.

Satellite Type of Regular Issue

1969, May 20 Litho. *Perf. 14½*

C290 A191 2e rose lil 12 8

Issued to publicize the inauguration of ENTEL-Chile, the first commercial satellite communications ground station, Longovilo.

Red Cross Type of Regular Issue

1969, Sept. Litho. *Perf. 14½*

C291 A192 5e blk & red 10 6

Issued for the 50th anniversary of the League of Red Cross Societies. A souvenir card contains 2 imperf. stamps similar to Nos. 376 and C291, with red marginal inscription. Size: 109x140 mm. Price $4.

Dam Type of Regular Issue

1969, Nov. 18 Litho. *Perf. 14½*

C292 A193 3e blue 15 8

Rodriguez Type of Regular Issue

1969, Nov. 24

C293 A194 30c brown 15 8

Issued to commemorate the 150th anniversary of the death of Col. Manuel Rodriguez.

EXPO '70 Type of Regular Issue

1969, Dec. 1 Litho. *Perf. 14*

C294 A195 5e red 18 10

Issued to publicize EXPO '70 International Exposition, Osaka, Japan, March 15–Sept. 13, 1970.

Bible Type of 1969

1969, Dec. 2 *Perf. 14½*

C295 A196 1e green 10 5

Issued to commemorate the 400th anniversary of the translation of the Bible into Spanish by Casiodoro de Reina.

ILO Type of Regular Issue

1969, Dec. 17 *Perf. 14½*

C296 A197 2e rose lil & blk 15 8

Issued to commemorate the 50th anniversary of the International Labor Organization.

Human Rights Year Type of 1969

1969, Dec. 18

C297 A198 4e brn & red 15 8

Human Rights Year, 1968.
A souvenir sheet of 2 contains imperf. stamps similar to Nos. 382 and C297. Blue commemorative marginal inscription. Size: 110x140mm. Price, $4.50.

Easter Island Type of 1970

1970, Jan. 26

C298 A199 50c dl grnsh bl 15 8

Issued to commemorate the 80th anniversary of the acquisition of Easter Island.

Ship Type of Regular Issue

1970, Feb. 4 Litho. *Perf. 14½*

C299 A200 2e dp ultra 25 6

Issued to commemorate the 150th anniversary of the capture of Valdivia during Chile's war of independence by Thomas Cochrane (1775–1860), naval commander.

Rotary Type of Regular Issue

1970, Mar. 18 Lithographed *Perf. 14*

C300 A201 1e rose cl 12 6

Issued to commemorate the centenary of the birth of Paul Harris (1868–1947), founder of Rotary International.

Gandhi Type of Regular Issue

1970, Apr. 1 Litho. *Perf. 14½*

C301 A202 1e red brn 15 8

Issued to commemorate the centenary of the birth of Mohandas K. Gandhi (1869–1948), leader in India's fight for independence.

Education Year Type of 1970

1970, July 17 Litho. *Perf. 14½*

C302 A204 4e red brn 15 8

Issued for International Education Year.

National Shrine Type of 1970

1970, July 28 Litho. *Perf. 14½*

C303 A205 1e ultra 10 5

Issued to publicize the O'Higgins National Shrine at Maipu.

Cancer Type of Regular Issue

1970, Aug. 11

C304 A206 2e brn & lt ol 15 10

Issued to commemorate the International Cancer Congress, Houston, Texas, May 22–29.

Copper Type of Regular Issue

1970, Oct. 21 Litho. *Perf. 14½*

C305 A207 3e grn & lt red brn 15 8

Nationalization of the copper industry.

United Nations Type of 1970

1970, Oct. 22

C306 A208 5e dk car & grn 50 8

United Nations, 25th anniversary.

Freighter Type of Regular Issue

1971, Jan. 18 Litho. *Perf. 14*

C307 A209 5e lt red brn 10 6

National Maritime Commission.

No. C290 Surcharged in Red

1971, Jan. 21 Litho. *Perf. 14½*

C308 A191 52c on 2e rose lil 25 6

Liberation Type of Regular Issue

1971, Feb. 3 *Perf. 14½*

C309 A210 1e gray bl & brn 8 5

The 150th anniversary of the expedition to liberate Peru.

UNICEF Type of Regular Issue

1971, Feb. 11 Litho. *Perf. 14½*

C310 A211 2e bl & grn 8 5

First meeting in Latin America of the Executive Council of UNICEF, Santiago, May 20–31, 1969.

Boy Scout Type of Regular Issue

1971, Feb. 10 *Perf. 14*

C311 A212 5c dk car & ol 15 8

Founding of Chilean Boy Scouts, 60th anniversary.

Satellite Type of Regular Issue

1971, May 25 Litho. *Perf. 14½*

C312 A213 2e brown 15 10

First commercial Chilean satellite communications ground station, Longovilo.

De Ercilla Type of Regular Issue

1972, Mar. 20 Engraved *Perf. 14*

C313 A221 2e Prus bl 15 10

4th centenary (in 1969) of "La Araucana," by Alonso de Ercilla y Zuniga (1533–1596).
A souvenir card contains impressions of Nos. 414 and C313 with black marginal inscription commemorating España 75 Philatelic Exhibition. Size: 165x220mm.

AIR POST SEMI-POSTAL STAMPS

Type of Semi-Postal Stamps, 1961.

Portraits: 10c+10c, Alonso de Ercilla. 20c+20c, Gabriela Mistral.

Perf. 13x12½

1961, Apr. 29 Photo. Unwmkd.

CB1 SP3 10c +10c sal & choc 1.00 30
CB2 SP3 20c +20c gray & dp cl 1.00 30

Printed without charge by the Spanish Mint as a gift to Chile. The surtax was to aid the 1960 earthquake victims and to increase teachers' salaries.

ACKNOWLEDGMENT OF RECEIPT STAMPS.

AR1

1894 *Perf. 11½.* Unwmkd.

H1 AR1 5c brown 50 50
a. Imperf., pair 3.00

The black stamp of design similar to AR1 inscribed "Avis de Paiement" was prepared for use on notices of payment of funds but was not regularly issued.

POSTAGE DUE STAMPS.

D1 D2

Handstamped

1894 *Perf. 13* Unwmkd.

No.	Type	Denomination	Unused	Used
J1	D1	2c blk, *straw*	15.00	7.00
J2	D1	4c blk, *straw*	15.00	7.00
J3	D1	6c blk, *straw*	15.00	7.00
J4	D1	8c blk, *straw*	15.00	7.00
J5	D2	10c blk, *straw*	15.00	7.00
J6	D1	16c blk, *straw*	15.00	7.00
J7	D1	20c blk, *straw*	15.00	7.00
J8	D1	30c blk, *straw*	15.00	7.00
J9	D1	40c blk, *straw*	15.00	7.00
J1a	D1	2c blk, *yel*	62.50	60.00
J2a	D1	4c blk, *yel*	50.00	40.00
J3a	D1	6c blk, *yel*	37.50	35.00
J4a	D1	8c blk, *yel*	15.00	12.50
J5a	D2	10c blk, *yel*	15.00	12.50
J6a	D1	16c blk, *yel*	15.00	12.50
J7a	D1	20c blk, *yel*	15.00	12.50
J8a	D1	30c blk, *yel*	15.00	12.50
J9a	D1	40c blk, *yel*	15.00	12.50

Counterfeits exist.

D3

1895 Lithographed. *Perf. 11.*

J19	D3	1c red, *yel*	5.00	2.00
J20	D3	2c red, *yel*	5.00	2.00
J21	D3	4c red, *yel*	4.00	2.00
J22	D3	6c red, *yel*	5.00	2.00
J23	D3	8c red, *yel*	3.00	2.00
J24	D3	10c red, *yel*	3.00	2.00
J25	D3	20c red, *yel*	2.00	1.25
J26	D3	40c red, *yel*	3.00	2.00
J27	D3	50c red, *yel*	3.00	2.00
J28	D3	60c red, *yel*	6.00	3.00
J29	D3	80c red, *yel*	6.00	3.50
J30	D3	1p red, *yel*	6.00	3.50
		Nos. J19-J30 (12)	51.00	27.25

Nos. J19–J30 were printed in sheets of 100 (10x10) containing all 12 denominations.

Counterfeits of Nos. J19–J42 exist.

1896 *Perf. 13½.*

J31	D3	1c red, *straw*	85	50
J32	D3	2c red, *straw*	85	50
J33	D3	4c red, *straw*	85	50
J34	D3	6c red, *straw*	2.00	75
J35	D3	8c red, *straw*	85	50
J36	D3	10c red, *straw*	85	50
J37	D3	20c red, *straw*	85	50
J38	D3	40c red, *straw*	12.50	10.00
J39	D3	50c red, *straw*	12.50	10.00
J40	D3	60c red, *straw*	12.50	10.00
J41	D3	80c red, *straw*	12.50	10.00
J42	D3	100c red, *straw*	25.00	20.00
		Nos. J31-J42 (12)	82.10	63.75

D4

D5

1898 *Perf. 13.*

J43	D4	1c scarlet	50	30
J44	D4	2c scarlet	1.25	60
J45	D4	4c scarlet	50	30
J46	D4	10c scarlet	50	30
J47	D4	20c scarlet	50	30
		Nos. J43-J47 (5)	3.25	1.80

1924 *Perf. 11½, 12½.*

J48	D5	2c bl & red	75	50
J49	D5	4c bl & red	75	50
J50	D5	8c bl & red	75	50
J51	D5	10c bl & red	75	50
J52	D5	20c bl & red	75	30
J53	D5	40c bl & red	75	50
J54	D5	60c bl & red	75	50
J55	D5	80c bl & red	75	50
J56	D5	1p bl & red	1.00	60
J57	D5	2p bl & red	2.00	1.25
J58	D5	5p bl & red	2.00	1.25
		Nos. J48-J58 (11)	11.00	6.90

Nos. J48–J58 were printed in sheets of 150 containing all 11 denominations, and in sheets of 50 containing the five lower denominations, providing various se-tenants.

All values of this issue exist imperforate, also with center inverted, but are not believed to have been regularly issued. Those with inverted centers sell for about 10 times normal stamps.

OFFICIAL STAMPS.

For Domestic Postage.

O1

Single-lined frame.
Control number in violet.

1907 *Imperf.* **Unwmkd.**

O1	O1	dl bl, "CARTA" in org	27.50	22.50
O2	O1	red, "OFICIO" in bl	27.50	22.50
O3	O1	vio, "PAQUETE" in red	27.50	22.50
O4	O1	org, *bl*, "EP" in vio	27.50	22.50

The diagonal inscription in differing color indicates type of usage: CARTA for letters of ordinary weight; OFICIO, heavy letters to 100 grams; PAQUETE, parcels to 100 grams; E P (Encomienda Postal), heavier parcels; C (Certificado), as on No. O8, registration including postage.

Varieties include CARTA, PAQUETE and E P inverted, OFICIO omitted, etc.

Double-lined frame.
Large control number in black.

Perf. 11.

O5	O1	bl, "CARTA" in yel	7.00	6.25
O6	O1	red, "OFICIO" IN bl	7.00	5.00
O7	O1	brn, "PAQUETE" in grn	7.00	5.00
O8	O1	grn, "C" in red	135.00	110.00

Nos. O5–O8 exist in tête bêche pairs; with CARTA, OFICIO or PAQUETE double or inverted, and other varieties.

Counterfeits of Nos. O1–O8 exist.

For Foreign Postage.

Regular Issues of 1892-1909 Overprinted in Red

a

On Stamps of 1904-09.

1907 *Perf. 12.*

O9	A14	1c green	7.50	7.50
a.		Inverted ovpt.	25.00	
O10	A12	3c on 1p brn	20.00	20.00
a.		Inverted ovpt.	75.00	
O11	A14	5c ultra	15.00	15.00
a.		Inverted ovpt.	50.00	
O12	A15	10c gray & blk	15.00	15.00
O13	A15	15c vio & blk	20.00	20.00
O14	A15	20c org brn & blk	20.00	20.00
O15	A15	50c ultra & blk	62.50	62.50

On Stamp of 1892.
Rouletted.

O16	A6	1p dk brn & blk	150.00	125.00

Counterfeits of Nos. O9–O16 exist.

Regular Issues of 1915-25 Overprinted in Red or Blue

OFICIAL
b

1926 *Perf. 13½x14, 14.*

O17	A52	5c sl bl (R)	1.50	40
O18	A50	10c bl & blk (R)	2.50	60
O19	A39	20c org red & blk (Bl)	1.00	30
O20	A42	50c dp grn & blk (Bl)	1.00	30
O21	A43	1p grn & blk (R)	3.75	50
O22	A43	2p ver & blk (Bl)	2.50	80
		Nos. O17-O22 (6)	12.25	2.90

Nos. O21 and O22 are overprinted vertically at each side.

Nos. O17 to O22 were for the use of the Biblioteca Nacional.

Regular Issue of 1915-25 Overprinted in Red

Servicio del
ESTADO
c

1928 *Perf. 13½x14, 14.*

O23	A50	10c bl & blk	5.00	1.50
O24	A39	20c brn org & blk	2.50	75
O25	A40	25c dl bl & blk	6.00	75
O26	A42	50c dp grn & blk	3.75	75
O27	A43	1p grn & blk	3.75	1.00
		Nos. O23-O27 (5)	21.00	4.75

The overprint on Nos. O23 to O26 is 16½mm. high; on No. O27 it is 20mm.

Regular Issues of 1928-30 Overprinted in Red

Servicio del
ESTADO
d

On Stamp Inscribed: "Correos de Chile".

1930-31

O28	A50	10c bl & blk	2.50	1.00

Wmkd.

Small Star in Shield, Multiple. (215)

On Stamps Inscribed: "Correos de Chile".

O29	A50	10c bl & blk	5.00	2.00
O30	A39	20c org red & blk	75	35
O31	A40	25c bl & blk	75	35
O32	A42	50c dp grn & blk	1.25	50

On Stamps Inscribed: "Chile Correos".

O33	A42	50c dp grn & blk	1.25	50
O34	A43	1p grn & blk	1.25	75
		Nos. O28-O34 (7)	12.75	5.45

Same Overprint on No. 181.

1933 *Perf. 13½x14.*

O35	A61	20c dk brn	75	35

Same Overprint in Red on No. 182.

1935 **Wmk. 215**

O36	A62	10c dp bl	75	50

No. 163 Overprinted Type "b" in Red.
Inscribed: "Correos de Chile".

1934

O37	A52	5c lt grn	65	50

Overprint "b" on No. 182.

1935

O38	A62	10c dp bl	65	50

Same Overprint in Black on No. 181.

1936 *Perf. 13½x14.* **Wmk. 215**

O39	A61	20c dk brn	7.50	50

Overprint "b" in Red on No. 158.

1938 *Perf. 14.*

O40	A43	1p grn & blk	2.00	1.00

Nos. 204 and 205 Overprinted Type "d" in Black.

1939 *Perf. 13½x14, 14.*

O41	A83	50c violet	3.75	1.25
O42	A84	1p org brn	5.00	3.50

Stamps of 1938–40 Overprinted Type "b" in Black, Red or Blue.

1940-46 *Perf. 13½x14, 14.*

O43	A79	10c sal pink ('45)	2.00	1.50
O44	A79a	15c brn org	1.00	35
O45	A80	20c lt bl (R) ('42)	1.25	50
O46	A81	30c brn pink (Bl)	65	35
O47	A82	40c lt grn	65	35
O48	A83	50c vio ('45)	3.75	75
O49	A84	1p org brn ('42)	2.50	75
O50	A85	1.80p dp bl (R) ('45)	10.00	6.25
O51	A86	2p car lake ('42)	2.00	1.25
		Nos. O43-O51 (9)	23.80	12.05

Overprint "b" in Black on Nos. 223, 225.

Unwmkd.

O58	A84	1p brn org	2.50	1.25
O59	A86	2p car lake ('46)	4.50	1.50

Regular Issues of 1938–43 Overprinted Diagonally in Carmine, Black or Blue

OFICIAL
e

1948-54 **Unwmkd., Wmk. 215**

Perf. 13½x14, 14.

O60	A80	20c lt bl, #219 (C)	65	35
O61	A81	30c brt pink, #202 (Bl) ('54)	1.25	50
O62	A82	40c brt grn, #203 ('54)	2.50	1.25
O63	A83	50c vio #222 ('49)	75	35
O64	A84	1p org brn, #205	2.50	1.00
O65	A86	2p car lake, #207 ('54)	1.00	50
O66	A87	5p dk sl grn, #208 (C) ('51)	2.50	1.00
		Nos. O60-O66 (7)	11.15	4.95

Overprint "e" Diagonally on Nos. 265 and 275 in Red or Black.

1953-55 **Unwmkd., Wmk. 215**

Perf. 13½x14, 13x14

O67	A126	1p dk bl grn, #265 (R)	1.00	50
O68	A126	1p dk bl grn, #265 (Bk) ('55)	75	50
O69	A126	1p dk bl grn, #275 (R) ('55)	75	50

Overprint "e" Horizontally on Nos. 207, 209 in Black or Blue

1955-56 *Perf. 14.* **Wmk. 215**

O70	A86	2p car lake ('56)	2.50	75
O71	A88	10p rose vio (Bl)	3.00	1.75

Overprint "e" Horizontally on Nos. 293–295 and Types of 1956 Regular Issue in Black or Red.

1956 *Perf. 14x14½.* **Unwmkd.**

O72	A141	2p purple	1.00	60
O73	A142	3p lt vio bl (R)	3.00	2.00
O74	A141	5p redsh brn	75	30
O75	A142	10p vio (19x22¼mm) (R)	3.00	1.75
a.		Perf. 13½x14 (19½x22½mm) ('58)	50	30
O76	A141	50p rose red	2.50	1.00

No. 310 Overprinted in Red Vertically, Reading Down, Similar to Type "e."

Size of Overprint: 21x2½mm.

1958 Lithographed *Perf. 14*

O77	A149	10p vio bl	*250.00*	*25.00*

Overprint "e" Horizontally on No. 327 in Red.

1960 *Perf. 13x14* **Unwmkd.**

O79	A157	5c blue	2.50	1.00

Methods and style of listing are detailed in "Special Notices" at the front of this volume.

POSTAL TAX STAMPS

Talca Issue.

A 10c blue postal tax stamp, inscribed "Bicentenario de Talca" and picturing a coat of arms, was issued in 1942. It was sold only in Talca and was required for a time on all domestic letters sent from that city. The tax helped pay for Talca's bicentenary celebration. Price 10 cents.

Nos. 326 and 347 Surcharged

E° 0,10
Art. 77
LEY
17272

Lithographed

1970 ***Perf. 14x13*** **Unwmkd.**

RA1	A159	10c on 2c ultra	10	8

Perf. 14x14½

RA2	A170	10c on 6c rose lil	10	8

Chilean Arms
PT1

Perf. 14½x14

1970, Apr. 23 Litho. Unwmkd.

RA3	PT1	10c blue	15	8

No. RA3 Surcharged in Red

E°0,15 E°0,15

a b

1971-72

RA4	PT1 (a)	15c on 10c bl	5	5
RA5	PT1 (b)	15c on 10c bl ('72)	10	8

Type of 1970

1972, July Litho. *Perf. 14½x14*

RA6	PT1	15c rose red	15	8

No. RA6 Surcharged in Ultramarine

E°0,20

1972-73

RA7	PT1	20c on 15c rose red	12	6
RA8	PT1	50c on 15c rose red ('73)	15	8

No. RA8 has 9 bars instead of 8.

The surtax on Nos. RA1-RA8 was for modernization of postal system. Compulsory on all inland mail.

PARCEL POST POSTAL TAX STAMP

Pres. J. J. Prieto V.
PPT1

Lithographed

1957, Apr. 8 *Perf. 14* Unwmkd.

QRA1	PPT1	15p green	25	15

The surtax aided the Prieto Foundation. No. QRA1 was required on parcel post entering or leaving Chile.

CHINA

(chī'nȧ)

LOCATION—Eastern Asia.
GOVT.—Republic.
AREA—2,903,475 sq. mi.
POP.—462,798,093 (1948).

10 Candareen = 1 Mace
10 Mace = 1 Tael
100 Cents = 1 Dollar (Yuan) (1897)

Issues of the Imperial Maritime Customs Post.

Imperial Dragon
A1

Typographed

1878 *Perf. 12½* Unwmkd.

Thin Paper.

Stamps printed 2½ mm. apart.

1	A1	1c green	60.00	20.00
a.		Imperf. (pair)	500.00	
2	A1	3c brn red	40.00	10.00
a.		Imperf. (pair)	400.00	
3	A1	5c orange	65.00	10.00
a.		Imperf. (pair)	500.00	

Imperforate proofs of Nos. 1-3 have an extra circle near the dragon's lower left foot.

1882

Thin or Pelure Paper.

Stamps printed 4½ mm apart.

4	A1	1c green	100.00	45.00
5	A1	3c brn red	140.00	12.50
6	A1	5c org yel	1,650.	300.00

1883

Rough to smooth Perf. 12½.

Medium to Thick Opaque Paper.

Stamps printed 2 to 3¼ mm. apart.

7	A1	1c green	60.00	15.00
a.		Vertical pair, imperf. between	1,500.	
8	A1	3c brn red	85.00	10.00
a.		Vertical pair, imperf. between		*1,500.*
9	A1	5c yellow	125.00	10.00

Nos. 1 to 9 were printed from plates of 25, 20 or 15 individual copper dies, but only No. 5 exists in the 15-die setting. Many different printings and plate settings exist. All values occur in a wide variety of shades and papers. The effect of climate on certain papers has produced the varieties on so-called toned papers in Nos. 1 to 15.

Counterfeits, frequently with forged cancellations, occur in all early Chinese issues.

Imperial Dragon
A2

Wmk. 103

Wmkd. Yin-Yang Symbol. (103)

1885 *Perf. 12½*

10	A2	1c green	10.00	2.50
a.		Vertical pair, imperf. between	500.00	
b.		Horiz. pair, imperf. between		
11	A2	3c lilac	12.00	3.50
a.		Horizontal pair, imperf. between		250.00
b.		Vertical pair, imperf. between		300.00
12	A2	5c grnsh yel	20.00	5.00
a.		5c bis brn	35.00	8.00
b.		Vertical pair, imperf. between	600.00	
c.		Horizontal pair, imperf. between		525.00

1888 *Perf. 11½-12*

13	A2	1c green	3.00	1.00
14	A2	3c lilac	5.00	1.25
b.		Double impression		
15	A2	5c grnsh yel	7.00	1.25
b.		Horiz. pair, imperf. vert.		400.00
c.		Double impression	250.00	150.00

Nos. 10 to 15 were printed from plates made of 40 individual copper dies, arranged in two panes of 20 each. Several different settings exist of all values.

Imperforates of Nos. 13-15 are considered proofs by most authorities.

Stamps overprinted "Formosa" in English or Chinese are proofs.

"Shou" and "Wu Fu"
A3

Dragon and Hydrangea Leaves
A4

"Pa Kua" Signs in Corners
A5

Dragon and Peony
A6

Carp, the Messenger Fish
A7

Dragon, "Pa Kua" and Immortelle
A8

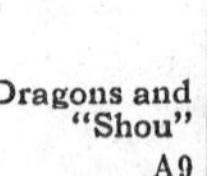

Dragons and "Shou"
A9

Dragons and Giant Peony
A10

Junk on the Yangtse
A11

Lithographed in Shanghai.

1894

16	A3	1c org red	4.00	2.00
a.		Vertical pair, imperf. between	250.00	200.00
b.		Horizontal pair, imperf. between	250.00	250.00
c.		Imperf. horizontally (pair)	150.00	150.00
17	A4	2c green	4.00	2.00
a.		Horizontal pair, imperf. between	225.00	
18	A5	3c org yel	3.50	1.25
a.		Vertical pair, imperf. between	200.00	200.00
b.		Horizontal pair, imperf. between	200.00	200.00
19	A6	4c rose pink	17.50	6.50
a.		Horizontal pair, imperf. between	300.00	
20	A7	5c dl org	27.50	12.50
a.		Horizontal pair, imperf. between	250.00	
21	A8	6c brown	7.00	2.50
a.		Vertical pair, imperf. between	200.00	
b.		Horizontal pair, imperf. between	200.00	
22	A9	9c dl grn	20.00	5.00
a.		Imperf., pair	200.00	
b.		Imperf. vert., pair	250.00	
c.		Imperf. horiz., pair	200.00	
d.		Vertical pair, imperf. between	250.00	
e.		Tête bêche pair	150.00	150.00
f.		Tête bêche pair, imperf. horizontally	750.00	
g.		Tête bêche pair, imperf. vertically	600.00	
h.		Vert. strip of 3, imperf. between	300.00	
23	A10	12c orange	40.00	10.00
24	A11	24c carmine	65.00	22.50
a.		Vertical pair, imperf. between	650.00	

Nos. 16 to 24 were issued to commemorate the 60th birthday of Tsz'e Hsi, the Empress Dowager. All values exist in several distinct shades.

On March 20, 1896, the Customs Post was changed, by Imperial Edict, to a National Post and the dollar was adopted as the unit of currency. The effective date of the Imperial Edict was January 1, 1897 and until that date the Customs Post continued operating.

Time was required to work out details of the Imperial Post and design new stamps. As a provisional measure, stocks of Nos. 16 to 24 were ordered surcharged with new values in dollars and cents. It is believed that only the Shanghai office stock of Nos. 16 to 24 (plus any reserve stock at the printer's) was surcharged with small figures of value. Other post offices throughout China were instructed to return all unoverprinted stocks on receipt of the new surcharges.

Early in the year it was apparent that all stamps would be exhausted before the new issues were ready (Nos. 86 to 97), and since the stones from which Nos. 16 to 24 had been printed no longer existed, new stones were made from the original transfers. A printing from the new stones was made early in 1897 and surcharged with large figures of value spaced 2½mm. below the Chinese characters. During the surcharging, sheets from the 1894 (original) printing were received from outlying post offices and surcharged as they arrived. A small quantity of the 1897 printing reached the public without surcharge (Nos. 16n to 24n).

Additional stamps were still required and another printing was made from the new stones and surcharged with large figures, but in a new setting with 1½mm. between the Chinese characters and the value. Additional sheets of the 1894 printing were received from the most distant post offices and were also surcharged with the 1½mm. setting. Thus there are four different sets of the large-figure surcharges. All these stamps were regularly issued but no attempt was made by the post office to separate printings. Some values are difficult to distinguish as to printing, particularly in used condition.

1897 Lithographed in Shanghai.

16n	A3	1c red org	150.00
17n	A4	2c yel grn	100.00
18n	A5	3c chr yel	95.00
p.		3c yel buff	300.00
19n	A6	4c pale rose	150.00
20n	A7	5c yellow	90.00
21n	A8	6c red brn	200.00
22n	A9	9c yelsh grn	250.00
23n	A10	12c pale org yel	300.00
24n	A11	24c rose red	275.00

Nos. 16n to 24n were new printings from new stones. These stamps were prepared solely for surcharging and were not regularly issued without surcharge. The colors of the 1897 printings are pale or dull; the gum is thin and white. The 1894 printing has a thicker, yellowish gum.

The set of nine values on thick unwatermarked paper is a special printing ordered by P. G. von Mollendorf, a Customs official, for presentation purposes. Price, set, $100.

Issues of the Chinese Government Post.

Preceding Issues Surcharged in Black

貳洋暫
分銀作
2
cents.

Small Numerals.

Surcharged on Nos. 13–15.

1897, Jan. 2 *Perf. 11½–12.*

25	A2	1c on 1c grn	7.50	2.00
26	A2	2c on 3c lil	20.00	5.00
27	A2	5c on 5c grnsh yel	17.50	4.00

Surcharged on Nos. 16–24.

28	A5	½c on 3c org yel	5.00	1.75
a.		'1' instead of '½'	100.00	100.00
b.		Horizontal pair, imperf.between	250.00	
c.		Imperf. horizontally (pair)	125.00	125.00
d.		Double surcharge	300.00	
e.		Vert. pair, imperf. between	300.00	
29	A3	1c on 1c org red	2.25	1.25
a.		Inverted surcharge	600.00	500.00
30	A4	2c on 2c grn	2.50	1.25
a.		Imperf. vertically (pair)	200.00	
b.		Vertical pair, imperf. between	250.00	
c.		Double surcharge	300.00	
d.		Inverted surcharge	600.00	
e.		Horizontal pair, imperf. between	225.00	
31	A6	4c on 4c rose pink	2.50	1.50
a.		Double surch.	300.00	300.00
b.		Vertical pair, imperf. between	225.00	225.00
c.		Horizontal pair, imperf. between	225.00	225.00
32	A7	5c on 5c dl org	3.50	1.50
a.		Vertical pair, imperf. between	300.00	
33	A8	8c on 6c brn	4.00	2.00
a.		Vertical pair, imperf. between	175.00	175.00
b.		Vertical strip of three, imperf. between	250.00	250.00
c.		Horizontal pair, imperf. between	225.00	225.00
34	A8	10c on 6c brn	12.00	6.00
a.		10c on 6c choc	12.00	6.00
b.		Vertical pair, imperf. between	175.00	175.00
c.		Imperf. vertically (pair)	250.00	
35	A9	10c on 9c dl grn	17.50	8.00
a.		Double surcharge	400.00	400.00
b.		Invtd. surch.	750.00	750.00
36	A10	10c on 12c org	30.00	15.00
a.		Imperf. horizontally (pair)	150.00	
37	A11	30c on 24c car	45.00	25.00
a.		Vert. pair, imperf. between	1,250.	

Preceding Issues Surcharged in Black

貳洋暫
分銀作
2
cents.

Large Numerals
Numerals 2½mm. below Chinese characters.

1897, March

Surcharged on Nos. 16 to 24.

38	A5	½c on 3c org yel	375.00	100.00
b.		Inverted surch.		400.00
39	A3	1c on 1c org red	55.00	40.00
40	A4	2c on 2c grn	100.00	60.00
41	A6	4c on 4c rose pink	110.00	45.00
b.		Horiz. pair, imperf. between	1,750.	
42	A7	5c on 5c dl org	32.50	22.50
43	A8	8c on 6c brn	375.00	375.00
44	A9	10c on 9c dl grn	125.00	60.00
45	A10	10c on 12c org	1,200.	250.00
46	A11	30c on 24c car	275.00	250.00
b.		2mm spacing between '30' and 'cents.'		1,250.

Same Surcharge on Nos. 16n to 24n.

47	A5	½c on 3c chr yel	1.40	75
a.		'cen' for 'cent'	150.00	135.00
b.		Vertical pair, imperf. between	135.00	135.00
c.		Imperf. horizontally (pair)	75.00	75.00
d.		As 'a,' imperf. horiz. (pair)	750.00	750.00
48	A3	1c on 1c red org	2.75	1.75
a.		Horiz. pair, imperf. between		250.00
49	A4	2c on 2c yel grn	2.25	1.00
50	A6	4c on 4c pale rose	3.25	2.00
a.		Horizontal pair, imperf. between	150.00	150.00
51	A7	5c on 5c yel	4.50	2.75
52	A8	8c on 6c red brn	20.00	12.00
53	A9	10c on 9c yelsh grn	25.00	11.00
a.		10c on 9c emer	25.00	12.50
54	A10	10c on 12c pale org yel	20.00	12.50
55	A11	30c on 24c rose red	60.00	30.00
a.		2mm spacing between '30' and 'cents'	300.00	150.00
b.		Vertical pair, imperf. between	2,000.	

Numerals 1½mm. below Chinese characters.

1897, May

Surcharged on Nos. 16 to 24.

56	A5	½c on 3c org yel	50.00	35.00
57	A3	1c on 1c org red	60.00	50.00
58	A4	2c on 2c grn	3,500.	100.00
59	A6	4c on 4c rose pink	40.00	35.00
60	A7	5c on 5c dl org	30.00	27.50
61	A8	8c on 6c brn	225.00	200.00
62	A9	10c on 9c dl grn	40.00	25.00
63	A10	10c on 12c org	200.00	175.00
64	A11	30c on 24c car	2,000.	

Same Surcharge on Nos. 16n to 24n.

65	A5	½c on 3c yel	75	60
a.		Invtd. surch.	250.00	200.00
b.		½mm spacing	800.00	700.00
66	A3	1c on 1c red org	1.50	1.00
67	A4	2c on 2c yel grn	2.50	1.50
a.		Inverted surcharge	700.00	
68	A6	4c on 4c pale rose	45.00	30.00
a.		Inverted surcharge	200.00	200.00
69	A7	5c on 5c yel	50.00	30.00
70	A9	10c on 9c gray grn	35.00	15.00
a.		Inverted surcharge	150.00	125.00
71	A10	10c on 12c brn org	75.00	25.00
72	A11	30c on 24c pale rose	1,500.	600.00

Same Surcharge (1½mm. Spacing) on Type A12, and

A12

A12a

Redrawn Designs.
Printed from New Stones.

1897

73	A12	½c on 3c yel	75.00	32.50
a.		½mm spacing	300.00	250.00
74	A12a	2c on 2c yel grn	16.00	2.00
a.		Horizontal pair, imperf. between	300.00	

Nos. 73 and 74 were surcharged on stamps printed from new stones, which differ slightly from the originals. On No. 73 the numeral "3" and symbols in the four corner panels have been enlarged and strengthened. On No. 74, the numeral "2" has a thick, flat base.

Surcharged on 1888 Issue.

75	A2	1c on 1c grn	75.00
76	A2	2c on 3c lil	150.00
77	A2	5c on 5c grnsh yel	40.00

Nos. 75–77 were not regularly issued.

Type A13 Surcharged in Black:

A13

政郵清大
分壹當
one cent
a

政郵清大
貳洋暫
分銀作
2 cents
b

政郵清大
貳洋暫
分銀作
2
cents
c

政郵清大
肆洋暫
分銀作
4
cents.
d

政郵清大
肆洋暫
分銀作
4
cents.
e

政郵清大
當壹圓
1 dollar.
f

政郵清大
當壹圓
1 dollar
g

1897 *Perf. 12 to 15.* **Unwmkd.**

78	A13 (a)	1c on 3c red	7.00	2.00
a.		No period after 'cent'	22.50	22.50
b.		Central character with large 'box'	10.00	8.00
79	A13 (b)	2c on 3c red	25.00	10.00
a.		Invtd. surch.	225.00	225.00
b.		Inverted 'S' in 'CENTS'	30.00	27.50
c.		No period after 'CENTS'	30.00	27.50
d.		Comma after 'CENTS'	30.00	27.50
e.		Double surch.	750.00	
f.		Double surcharge, both inverted	1,500.	
g.		Double surch. (blk. & grn.)	1,750.	
80	A13 (c)	2c on 3c red	7.50	2.50
81	A13 (d)	4c on 3c red	1,250.	1,000.
a.		Double surch. (blk. & vio.)	2,000.	1,500.
82	A13 (e)	4c on 3c red	45.00	15.00
83	A13 (f)	$1 on 3c red	20,000.	20,000.
a.		No period after 'r'		
84	A13 (g)	$1 on 3c red	150.00	65.00
85	A13 (g)	$5 on 3c red	1,650.	1,250.
a.		Inverted surcharge	2,000.	2,000.

A few copies of the 3c red exist without surcharge; one cancelled. No. 79 with green surcharge is a trial printing.

Dragon
A14

Carp
A15

Wild Goose
A16

"Imperial Chinese Post".
Lithographed in Japan.
Perf. 11, 11½, 12.

1897, Aug. 16 **Wmk. 103**

86	A14	½c pur brn	1.25	75
a.		Horizontal pair, imperf. between	150.00	
87	A14	1c yellow	1.50	60
88	A14	2c orange	1.00	40
a.		Imperf. horizontally (pair)	175.00	
89	A14	4c brown	1.75	75
a.		Horizontal pair, imperf. between	275.00	
90	A14	5c rose red	2.75	85
91	A14	10c dk grn	6.00	70
92	A15	20c maroon	12.00	3.50
93	A15	30c red	15.00	5.00
94	A15	50c yel grn	17.50	9.00
a.		50c blk grn	150.00	
b.		50c bl grn	250.00	
95	A16	$1 car & rose	75.00	25.00
a.		Imperf. vertically (pair)	900.00	
96	A16	$2 org & yel	250.00	250.00
a.		Imperf. vertically (pair)	1,000.	
97	A16	$5 yel grn & pink	150.00	150.00

The inner circular frames and outer frames of Nos. 86 to 91 differ for each denomination.

No. 97 imperforate was not regularly issued. Copies have been privately perforated and offered as No. 97. Shades occur in most values of this issue.

Dragon
A17

Carp
A18

Wild Goose
A19

Engraved in London.
"Chinese Imperial Post".

1898 *Perf. 12 to 16.* **Wmk. 103**

98	A17	½c chocolate	40	10
a.		Vertical pair, imperf. between		135.00
99	A17	1c ocher	40	8
a.		Vertical pair, imperf. between	50.00	50.00
b.		Horizontal pair, imperf. between	100.00	100.00
100	A17	2c scarlet	60	8
a.		Vertical pair, imperf. between	30.00	30.00
b.		Imperf. vertically (pair)		
101	A17	4c org brn	1.40	10
a.		Vertical pair, imperf. between	75.00	
b.		Imperf. vertically (pair)	40.00	40.00
c.		Horiz. pair, imperf. between	125.00	125.00
d.		Horiz. strip of 3, imperf. between	150.00	150.00
102	A17	5c salmon	1.75	50
a.		Vertical pair, imperf. between	60.00	60.00
b.		Horizontal pair, imperf. between	65.00	65.00
103	A17	10c dk bl grn	1.75	20
a.		Vert. or horiz. pair, imperf. between	65.00	65.00
104	A18	20c claret	6.00	85
a.		Horizontal pair, imperf. between	150.00	
b.		Imperf. horiz. (pair)	100.00	100.00
105	A18	30c dl rose	7.00	60
a.		Horizontal pair, imperf. between	150.00	
b.		Imperf. horizontally (pair)	150.00	
106	A18	50c lt grn	12.00	2.00
a.		Vertical pair, imperf. between	200.00	
107	A19	$1 red & pale rose	45.00	4.00

108	A19	$2 brn, red & yel	60.00	15.00
109	A19	$5 dp grn & sal	125.00	30.00
a.		Horizontal pair, imperf. between	1,100.	
b.		Vert. pair, imperf. between	1,200.	

No. 98 surcharged "B. R. A.—5—Five Cents" in three lines in black or green, was surcharged by British military authorities shortly after the Boxer riots for use from military posts in an occupied area along the Peking-Mukden railway. Usually canceled in violet.

1902–03 ***Perf. 12 to 16*** **Unwmkd.**

110	A17	½c brown	30	8
a.		Horiz. or vert. pair, imperf. between	65.00	65.00
111	A17	1c ocher	30	8
a.		Horizontal pair, imperf. between	30.00	30.00
b.		Vertical pair, imperf. between	35.00	35.00
c.		Vert. pair, imperf. horiz.	25.00	25.00
112	A17	2c scarlet	60	8
a.		Horiz. or vert. pair, imperf. between	30.00	30.00
c.		Vert. pair, imperf. horiz.	25.00	25.00
d.		Horiz. pair, imperf. vert.	25.00	25.00
e.		Vert. strip of 3 imperf. between	40.00	40.00
113	A17	4c org brn	90	20
a.		Horiz. or vert. pair, imperf. between	45.00	45.00
114	A17	5c rose red	6.50	1.00
a.		Vertical pair, imperf. between	100.00	
b.		Vert. pair, imperf. horiz.	50.00	
115	A17	5c orange	6.50	1.00
a.		5c yel	60.00	10.00
b.		Vertical pair, imperf. between	75.00	
c.		Horizontal pair, imperf. between	90.00	
116	A17	10c green	5.00	15
a.		Vertical pair, imperf. between	35.00	
b.		Horizontal pair, imperf. between	40.00	
c.		Vert. pair, imperf. horiz.	35.00	
d.		Vert. strip of 3, imperf. between	85.00	
117	A18	20c red brn	4.00	25
a.		Horizontal pair, imperf. between	90.00	
b.		Vertical pair, imperf. between	75.00	
118	A18	30c dl red	6.50	35
a.		Vertical pair, imperf. between	135.00	
119	A18	50c yel grn	7.50	40
120	A19	$1 red & pale rose	30.00	1.00
121	A19	$2 brn red & yel	60.00	5.00
122	A19	$5 dp grn & sal	90.00	25.00
		Nos. 110-122 (13)	218.10	34.59

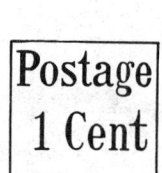

Diagonal Half of No. 112 Surcharged on Stamp and Envelope

Postage
1 Cent
Paid

1903

123	A17	1c on half of 2c scar, on cover		250.00

Excellent forgeries of No. 123 are plentiful, particularly on pieces of cover.

1905-10

124	A17	2c grn ('08)	50	5
a.		Horizontal pair, imperf. between	50.00	50.00
b.		Vertical pair, imperf. between	60.00	60.00
c.		Imperf. vertically (pair)	50.00	
d.		Horiz. strip of 4, imperf. between	125.00	
125	A17	3c sl grn ('10)	75	6
a.		Horiz. or vert. pair, imperf. between	65.00	
126	A17	4c ver ('09)	1.00	12
127	A17	5c violet	1.50	12
a.		5c lil	2.00	12
b.		Horiz. or vert. pair, imperf. between	65.00	
d.		Vert. pair, imperf. horiz.	35.00	
128	A17	7c mar ('10)	4.00	70
129	A17	10c ultra ('08)	2.75	10
a.		Horiz. or vert. pair, imperf. between	100.00	
c.		Vert. pair, imperf. horiz.	75.00	50.00
130	A18	16c ol grn ('07)	15.00	1.50
		Nos. 124-130 (7)	25.50	2.65

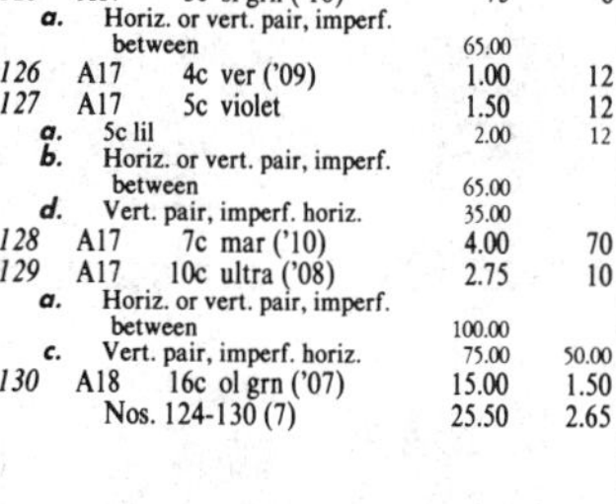

Temple of Heaven, Peking
A20

1909 ***Perf. 14***

131	A20	2c org & grn	1.00	35
132	A20	3c org & bl	1.25	50
133	A20	7c org & brn vio	1.50	50

Issued to commemorate the first year of the reign of Hsuan T'ung, who later became Henry Pu-yi and then Emperor Kang Teh of Manchukuo.

Stamps of 1902-10
Overprinted with Chinese Characters.

1912 ***Perf. 12 to 16***

Foochow Issue.

Overprinted in Red or Black 立中時臨

134	A17	3c sl grn (R)	50.00	30.00
135	A19	$1 red & pale rose (Bk)	450.00	400.00
136	A19	$2 brn red & yel (Bk)	600.00	500.00
137	A19	$5 dp grn & sal (Bk)	650.00	500.00

The overprint "Ling Shih Chung Li" or "Provisional Neutrality," signified that the Post Office was conducted neutrally by agreement between the Manchu and opposing forces.

Nanking Issue

Overprinted in Red or Black

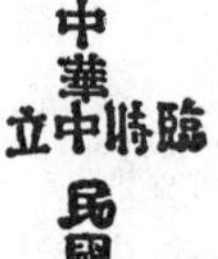

138	A17	1c ocher (R)	30.00	25.00
139	A17	3c sl grn (R)	25.00	20.00
140	A17	7c mar (Bk)	110.00	100.00
141	A18	16c ol grn (R)	350.00	300.00
142	A18	50c yel grn (R)	650.00	600.00
143	A19	$1 red & pale rose (Bk)	600.00	550.00
144	A19	$2 brn red & yel (Bk)	1,000.	1,000.
145	A19	$5 dp grn & sal (Bk)	2,000.	2,000.

Vertical overprint reads: "Chung Hwa Min Kuo" (Republic of China).

Stamps of this issue were also used in Shanghai and Hankow.

Additional values were overprinted but not issued. Excellent forgeries of the overprints of Nos. 134–145 exist.

Issues of the Republic

Overprinted in Black or Red 中華民國 *a*

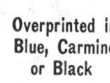

Overprinted by the Maritime Customs Statistical Department, Shanghai.

146	A17	½c brn (Bk)	35	6
a.		Inverted overprint	3.50	3.00
b.		Double overprint	35.00	
147	A17	1c ocher (R)	40	6
a.		Vert. pair, imperf. horiz.	40.00	40.00
b.		Invtd. ovpt.	35.00	25.00
c.		Double overprint	40.00	40.00
d.		Horizontal pair, imperf. between	40.00	40.00
e.		Horiz. pair, imperf. vert.	25.00	
f.		Pair, one without overprint	25.00	
148	A17	2c grn (R)	50	5
a.		Vertical pair, imperf. between	50.00	50.00
149	A17	3c sl grn (R)	80	5
a.		Inverted overprint	45.00	20.00
b.		Horiz. or vert. pair, imperf. between	60.00	60.00
d.		Horiz. pair, imperf. vert.	45.00	
150	A17	4c ver (Bk)	85	10
a.		Vertical pair, imperf. between	350.00	
151	A17	5c vio (R)	1.40	12
a.		Horizontal pair, imperf. between		
152	A17	7c mar (Bk)	2.00	40
153	A17	10c ultra (R)	1.75	10
a.		Double overprint	75.00	
b.		Pair, one without overprint	300.00	
c.		Brnsh red overprint	6.00	4.00
d.		Inverted overprint	100.00	100.00
154	A18	16c ol grn (R)	3.50	1.00
155	A18	20c red brn (Bk)	4.00	30
156	A18	30c rose red (Bk)	5.00	50
157	A18	50c yel grn (R)	7.00	40
158	A19	$1 red & pale rose (Bk)	30.00	1.00
a.		Inverted overprint		*1,750.*
159	A19	$2 brn red & yel (Bk)	42.50	5.00
a.		Inverted overprint	110.00	125.00
160	A19	$5 dp grn & sal (Bk)	110.00	100.00
		Nos. 146-160 (15)	210.05	109.14

Stamps with blue overprint similar to the preceding were not an official issue but were privately made by a printer in Tientsin.

Overprinted in Red

b

Overprinted by the Commercial Press, Shanghai

Type "b" differs from "a" in that the top character is shifted slightly to right and the bottom character is larger and has small "legs".

161	A17	1c ocher (R)	1.50	12
a.		Inverted overprint	40.00	40.00
b.		Vertical pair, imperf. between	60.00	
c.		Double ovpt.	55.00	
162	A17	2c grn (R)	15.00	12
a.		Inverted overprint	650.00	400.00
b.		Vertical pair, imperf. between	85.00	
c.		Horizontal pair, imperf. between	100.00	
d.		Horiz. strip of 3, imperf. btwn.	250.00	

Overprinted in Blue, Carmine or Black

Overprinted by Waterlow & Sons, London.

163	A17	½c brn (Bl)	20	5
a.		Vertical pair, imperf. between	350.00	350.00
164	A17	1c ocher (C)	20	5
a.		Horizontal pair, imperf. between	55.00	
165	A17	2c grn (C)	30	5
166	A17	3c sl grn (C)	60	5
a.		Inverted overprint		450.00
167	A17	4c ver (Bk)	90	15
168	A17	5c vio (C)	1.00	20
169	A17	7c mar (Bk)	4.50	1.50
170	A17	10c ultra (C)	1.25	12
a.		Vertical pair, imperf. between	175.00	150.00
171	A18	16c ol grn (R)	4.50	1.00
172	A18	20c red brn (Bk)	4.00	50
173	A18	30c dl red (Bk)	5.00	50
174	A18	50c yel grn (R)	7.50	1.25
175	A19	$1 red & pale rose (Bk)	22.50	2.00
176	A19	$2 brn red & yel (Bk)	55.00	40.00
177	A19	$5 dp grn & sal (C)	110.00	100.00
		Nos. 163-177 (15)	217.45	147.42

Due to instructions issued to postmasters throughout China at the time of the Revolution, a number of them prepared unauthorized overprints using the same characters as the overprints prepared by the government. While many were made in good faith, some, like the blue overprints from Tientsin, were bogus, and the status of certain others is extremely dubious.

Dr. Sun Yat-sen
A21

1912, Dec. 14 ***Perf. 14½***

178	A21	1c orange	90	60
179	A21	2c yel grn	90	60
180	A21	3c sl grn	90	60
181	A21	5c rose lil	1.50	75
182	A21	8c dp brn	1.75	1.25
183	A21	10c dl bl	1.75	1.25
184	A21	16c ol grn	4.50	2.25
185	A21	20c maroon	5.00	1.75
186	A21	50c dk grn	15.00	9.00
187	A21	$1 brn red	40.00	17.50
188	A21	$2 yel brn	200.00	140.00
189	A21	$5 gray	90.00	50.00
		Nos. 178-189 (12)	362.20	225.55

Issued in honor of the leader of the Revolution.

President Yuan Shih-kai
A22

1912, Dec. 14

190	A22	1c orange	60	50
191	A22	2c yel grn	60	50
192	A22	3c sl grn	60	50
193	A22	5c rose lil	75	60
194	A22	8c dp brn	2.25	1.50
195	A22	10c dl bl	1.50	1.25
196	A22	16c ol grn	3.00	2.50
197	A22	20c maroon	3.75	2.50
198	A22	50c dk grn	16.50	10.00
199	A22	$1 brn red	25.00	15.00
200	A22	$2 yel brn	37.50	20.00

201 A22 $5 gray 80.00 60.00
Nos. 190-201 (12) 172.05 114.85

Issued in honor of the first president of the Republic.

Junk
A24

Reaping Rice
A25

Gateway, Hall of Classics, Peking
A26

DESIGN A24.

London Printing: Vertical shading lines under top panel fine, junk with clear diagonal shading lines on sails, right pennant of junk usually long, lines in water weak except directly under junk.

Peking Printing: Vertical shading lines under top panel and inner vertical frame line much heavier, water and sails of junk more evenly and strongly colored, white wave over "H" of "CHINA" pointed upward, touching the junk.

DESIGN A25.

London: Front hat brim thick and nearly straight, left foot touches shadow.

Peking: Front hat brim thin and strongly upturned, left foot and sickle clearly outlined in white, shadow of middle tree lighter than those of the right and left trees.

DESIGN A26.

London: Light colored walk clearly defined almost to the doorway, figure in right doorway "T" shaped with strong horizontal cross-bar, white panel in base of central tower rectangular, vertical stroke in top left character uniformly thick at its base, tree to right of doorway ends in minute dots.

Peking: Walk more heavily shaded near doorway, especially at right; figure in right doorway more like a "Y", white panel at base of central tower is a long oval, right vertical stroke in top left character incurved near its base, tree at right has five prominent dots at top.

London Printing: By Waterlow & Sons, London, perforated 14 to 15.

Peking Printing: By the Chinese Bureau of Engraving and Printing, Peking, perforated 14.

London Printing.

1913, May 5 *Perf. 14-15.*

202 A24 ½c blk brn 25 5
a. Horiz. or vert. pair, imperf. btwn. 90.00
203 A24 1c orange 25 5
a. Horizontal pair, imperf. between 90.00
b. Vertical pair, imperf. between 80.00
c. Horiz. strip of 5, imperf. between 225.00
204 A24 2c yel grn 60 5
a. Horizontal pair, imperf. between 125.00
205 A24 3c bl grn 90 5
a. Horizontal pair, imperf. between 90.00
b. Vertical pair, imperf. between 225.00
206 A24 4c scarlet 1.50 5
207 A24 5c rose lil 2.50 6
208 A24 6c gray 1.50 10
209 A24 7c violet 2.50 75
210 A24 8c brn org 2.75 20
211 A24 10c dk bl 2.75 6
a. Horizontal pair, imperf. between 200.00 200.00
b. Vertical pair, imperf. between 225.00 175.00
212 A25 15c brown 10.00 50
213 A25 16c ol grn 2.75 50
214 A25 20c brn red 4.50 15
215 A25 30c brn vio 6.00 20
a. Horiz. pair, imperf. between 225.00 175.00
216 A25 50c green 10.00 20
217 A26 $1 ocher & blk 30.00 35
218 A26 $2 bl & blk 40.00 2.50
219 A26 $5 scar & blk 70.00 20.00
220 A26 $10 yel grn & blk 400.00 350.00
Nos. 202-220 (19) 588.75 375.82

First Peking Printing.

1915 *Perf. 14.*

221 A24 ½c blk brn 25 5
222 A24 1c orange 25 5
a. Bklt. pane of 6 75.00
b. Bklt. pane of 4
223 A24 2c yel grn 35 5
224 A24 3c bl grn 50 5
a. Bklt. pane of 6 75.00
225 A24 4c scarlet 1.20 5
226 A24 5c rose lil 1.20 5
a. Bklt. pane of 4 75.00
227 A24 6c gray 1.50 12
228 A24 7c violet 1.75 50
229 A24 8c brn org 1.50 6
230 A24 10c dk bl 1.50 5
a. Bklt. pane of 4 75.00
231 A25 15c brown 10.00 75
232 A25 16c ol grn 3.00 20
233 A25 20c brn red 2.50 5
234 A25 30c brn vio 2.50 8
235 A25 50c green 4.00 6
236 A26 $1 ocher & blk 12.50 20
237 A26 $2 bl & blk 17.50 50
a. Center invtd. 4,000. 4,500.
238 A26 $5 scar & blk 40.00 3.50
239 A26 $10 yel grn & blk 175.00 60.00
Nos. 221-239 (19) 277.00 66.37

1919

240 A24 1½c violet 35 8
241 A25 13c brown 60 6
242 A26 $20 yel & blk 1,100. 900.00

Nos. 226 and 230 overprinted in red with five characters in vertical column were for postal savings use.

The higher values of the 1913-19 issues are often overprinted with Chinese characters, which are the names of various postal districts. Stamps were frequently stolen while in transit to post offices. The overprints served to protect them, since the stamps could only be used in the districts for which they were overprinted.

Yeh Kung-cho, Hsu Shi-chang and Chin Yun-peng
A27

1921, Oct. 10

243 A27 1c orange 4.00 75
244 A27 3c bl grn 4.00 75
245 A27 6c gray 4.00 75
246 A27 10c blue 4.00 75

National Post Office, 25th anniversary.

A28

1923 Red Surcharge.

247 A28 2c on 3c bl grn 1.00 5
a. Inverted surcharge 1,000. 900.00

Second Peking Printing.

A29

A30

A31

Types of 1913-19 Issues.

Re-engraved.

Type A29: Most of the whitecaps in front of the junk have been removed and the water made darker. The shading lines have been removed from the arabesques and pearls above the top inscription. The inner shadings at the top and sides of the picture have been cut away.

Type A30: The heads of rice in the side panels have a background of crossed lines instead of horizontal lines. The Temple of Heaven is strongly shaded and has a door. There are rows of pearls below the Chinese characters in the upper corners. The arabesques above the top inscription have been altered and are without shading lines.

Type A31: The curved line under the inscription at top is single instead of double. There are four vertical lines, instead of eight, at each side of the picture. The trees at the sides of the temple had foliage in the 1913-19 issues, but now the branches are bare. There are numerous other alterations in the design.

1923 *Perf. 14.*

248 A29 ½c blk brn 25 5
a. Horizontal pair, imperf. between 75.00 75.00
b. Horiz. pair, imperf. vert. 60.00 60.00
249 A29 1c orange 25 5
a. Imperf., pair 35.00
b. Horiz. pair, imperf. vert. 50.00
c. Booklet pane of 6 50.00
d. Booklet pane of 4 25.00
250 A29 1½c violet 30 5
251 A29 2c yel grn 40 5
252 A29 3c bl grn 35 5
a. Bklt. pane of 6 40.00
253 A29 4c gray 5.00 5
254 A29 5c claret 80 5
a. Bklt. pane of 4 85.00
255 A29 6c scarlet 1.00 5
256 A29 7c violet 1.50 6
257 A29 8c orange 1.25 5
258 A29 10c blue 1.25 5
a. Bklt. pane of 6 60.00
b. Bklt. pane of 2 75.00
259 A30 13c brown 5.00 8
260 A30 15c dp bl 2.00 5
261 A30 16c ol grn 2.50 10
262 A30 20c brn red 2.50 5
263 A30 30c purple 3.50 6
264 A30 50c dp grn 12.50 6
265 A31 $1 org brn & sep 11.50 10
266 A31 $2 bl & red brn 17.50 15
267 A31 $5 red & sl 35.00 35
268 A31 $10 grn & cl 85.00 11.50
269 A31 $20 plum & bl 175.00 22.50
Nos. 248-269 (22) 364.35 35.56

Nos. 249 and 275 exist with webbing watermark from experimental printing.

To prevent speculation and theft, the dollar denominations were overprinted with single characters in red for use in Kwangsi ($1-$20) and Kweichow ($1-$5).

See also Nos. 275, 324.

Temple of Heaven, Peking
A32

1923, Oct. 17 *Perf. 14*

270 A32 1c orange 1.75 30
271 A32 3c bl grn 2.00 50
272 A32 4c red 3.00 50
273 A32 10c blue 7.00 1.25

Adoption of Constitution, October, 1923.

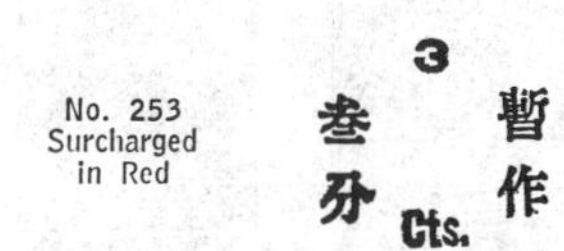

No. 253 Surcharged in Red

1925

274 A29 3c on 4c gray 2.00 10
a. Invtd. surch. 1,000. 1,000.
b. Vertical pair, imperf. between

Junk Type of 1923

1926

275 A29 4c ol grn 70 5
a. Imperf. vertically (pair) 75.00
b. Horiz. pair, imperf. between 90.00
c. Horiz. strip of 3, imperf. between 100.00

Marshal Chang Tso-lin
A34

President Chiang Kai-shek
A35

1928, Mar. 1 *Perf. 14*

276 A34 1c brn org 75 25
277 A34 4c ol grn 1.50 35
278 A34 10c dl bl 7.00 1.25
279 A34 $1 red 32.50 17.50

Issued to commemorate the assumption of office by Marshal Chang Tso-lin. The stamps of this issue were only available for postage in the Provinces of Chihli and Shantung and at the Offices in Manchuria and Sinkiang.

1929, May

280 A35 1c brn org 1.25 35
281 A35 4c ol grn 1.50 50
282 A35 10c dk bl 17.50 1.25
283 A35 $1 dk red 75.00 30.00

Issued to commemorate the unification of China.

Sun Yat-sen Mausoleum, Nanking
A36

1929, May 30 *Perf. 14*

284 A36 1c brn org 50 35
285 A36 4c ol grn 75 35
286 A36 10c dk bl 6.00 1.25
287 A36 $1 dk red 42.50 25.00

Issued in commemoration of Dr. Sun Yat-sen on the occasion of the transfer of his remains from Peiping to the mausoleum at Nanking.

Nos. 224 and 252 Surcharged in Red

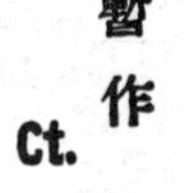

1930

288 A24 1c on 3c bl grn 1.50 35
289 A29 1c on 3c bl grn 40 5
a. No period after "Ct" 12.50 8.00

See Nos. 311, 325, 330.

Dr. Sun Yat-sen—A37

Type I. Double-lined circle in the sun.
Type II. Heavy, single-lined circle in the sun.

Engraved

Perf.

11½x12½, 12½x13, 12½, 13½.

Printed by De la Rue & Co., Ltd., London.

1931 Type I.

290 A37 1c orange 12 4
291 A37 2c ol grn 12 5

292	A37	4c green	35	4
293	A37	20c ultra	35	4
294	A37	$1 org brn & dk brn	3.00	8
295	A37	$2 bl & org brn	6.00	20
296	A37	$5 dl red & blk	9.00	60
		Nos. 290-296 (7)	18.94	1.05

Stamps issued prior to 1933 were printed by a wet-paper process, and owing to shrinkage such stamps are 1—1½ mm. narrower than the later dry-printed stamps. Early printings are perf. 12½x13. Nos. 304, 305 and 306 were later perf. 11½x12½.

1931-37 Type II.

297	A37	2c ol grn	5	4
a.		Bklt. pane of 6	22.50	
b.		Bklt. pane of 4	17.50	
298	A37	4c green	5	4
299	A37	5c grn ('33)	5	4
a.		Bklt. pane of 6	30.00	
b.		Bklt. pane of 4	22.50	
300	A37	15c dk grn	2.50	8
301	A37	15c scar ('34)	20	4
302	A37	20c ultra ('37)	20	4
303	A37	25c ultra	20	4
a.		Bklt. pane of 6	37.50	
304	A37	$1 org brn & dk brn	3.50	4
305	A37	$2 bl & org brn	7.00	10
306	A37	$5 dl red & blk	12.00	20
		Nos. 297-306 (10)	25.75	66

See Nos. 631 to 635 for other stamps of type A37.

"Nomads in the Desert"
A38

1932 *Perf. 14* Unwmkd.

307	A38	1c dp org	17.50	12.50
308	A38	4c ol grn	17.50	12.50
309	A38	5c claret	17.50	12.50
310	A38	10c dp bl	17.50	12.50

Issued to commemorate the Northwest Scientific Expedition of Sven Hedin. A small quantity of this issue was sold at face at Peking and several other cities. The bulk of the issue was given to Hedin and sold at $5 (Chinese) a set for funds to finance the expedition. Letters franked with these stamps were carried without additional charge.

No. 252 Surcharged in Black Like No. 288.

1932

311	A29	1c on 3c bl grn	1.00	10

Martyrs Issue.

Teng Keng
A39

Ch'en Ying-shih
A40

Chu Chih-hsin
A45

Sung Chiao-jen
A46

Huang Hsing
A47

Liao Chung-kai
A48

1932–34 *Perf. 14*

312	A39	½c blk brn	5	5
313	A40	1c org ('34)	5	5
a.		Booklet pane of 6	25.00	
b.		Booklet pane of 4	25.00	
314	A39	2½c rose lil ('33)	5	5
315	A48	3c dp brn ('33)	5	5
316	A45	8c brn org	15	5
317	A46	10c dl vio	20	5
318	A45	13c bl grn	15	5
319	A46	17c brn ol	15	5
320	A47	20c brn red	15	5
321	A48	30c brn vio	15	5
322	A47	40c orange	15	5
323	A40	50c grn ('34)	20	5
		Nos. 312-323 (12)	1.50	60

Perfs. 12 to 13 and compound and with secret marks are listed as Nos. 402-439. No. 316 re-drawn is No. 485.

Junk Type of 1923 Issue.

1933 *Perf. 14.*

324	A29	6c brown	14.00	25

No. 275 Surcharged in Red Like No. 288.

325	A29	1c on 4c ol grn	1.00	5
a.		No period after Ct		

Tan Yuan-chang
A49

1933, Jan. 9

326	A49	2c ol grn	1.00	30
327	A49	5c green	1.25	35
328	A49	25c ultra	6.00	1.00
329	A49	$1 red	37.50	18.00

Issued in commemoration of Tan Yuan-chang more commonly known as Tan Yen-kai, a prominent statesman in China since the revolution of 1912 and President of the Executive Department of the National Government. The stamps were placed on sale January 9, 1933, the date of the ceremony in celebration of the completion of the Tan Yuan-chang Memorial Hall and Tomb at Mukden.

No. 251 Surcharged in Red Like No. 288.

1935 *Perf. 14*

330	A29	1c on 2c yel grn	85	6

Emblem of New Life Movement
A50

Four Virtues of New Life
A51

Lighthouse
A52

1936, Jan. 1

331	A50	2c ol grn	75	25
332	A50	5c green	1.25	25
333	A51	20c dk bl	6.00	1.00
334	A52	$1 rose red	20.00	4.00

"New Life" movement.

Methods of Mail Transportation
A53

Maritime Scene
A54

Shanghai General Post Office
A55

Ministry of Communications, Nanking
A56

1936, Oct. 10

335	A53	2c orange	60	25
336	A54	5c green	75	20
337	A55	25c blue	5.00	60
338	A56	$1 dk car	20.00	2.50

Issued in commemoration of the 40th anniversary of the founding of the Chinese Post Office.

Nos. 260 and 261 Surcharged in Red

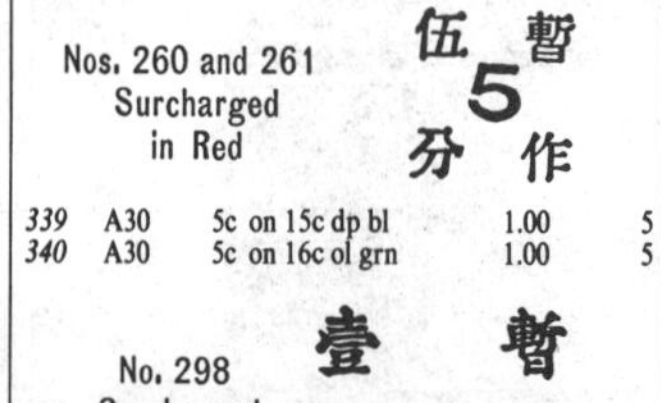

339	A30	5c on 15c dp bl	1.00	5
340	A30	5c on 16c ol grn	1.00	5

No. 298 Surcharged in Red

壹 暫
分 1 作

1937 Type II.

341	A37	1c on 4c grn	40	5
a.		Upper left character missing		

Nos. 322 and 303 Surcharged in Black or Red

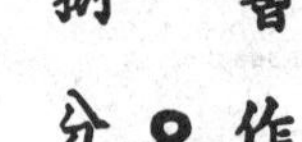

1938 *Perf. 12½, 14.*

342	A47	8c on 40c org (Bk)	60	4
343	A37	10c on 25c ultra (R)	60	4

Dr. Sun Yat-sen
A57

Type I. Coat button half circle. Six lines of shading above head. Top frame partially shaded with vertical lines.

Type II. Coat button complete circle. Nine lines of shading above head. Top frame partially shaded with vertical lines.

Type III. Coat button complete circle. Nine lines of shading above head. Top frame line fully shaded with vertical lines.

Engraved.

1938 *Perf. 12½* Unwmkd.

Printed by the Chung Hwa Book Co.

Type I.

344	A57	$1 hn & dk brn	20.00	2.00
345	A57	$2 dp bl & org brn	4.00	35
346	A57	$5 red & grnsh blk	35.00	8.00

1939 Type II.

347	A57	$1 hn & dk brn	3.00	20
348	A57	$2 dp bl & org brn	4.00	25

1939-41 Type III.

349	A57	2c ol grn	6	4
350	A57	3c dl cl	6	4
351	A57	5c green	6	4
352	A57	5c ol grn	6	4
353	A57	8c ol grn	6	4
354	A57	10c green	6	4
355	A57	15c scarlet	10	4
356	A57	15c dk vio brn ('41)	1.50	75
357	A57	16c ol gray	25	4
358	A57	25c dk bl	15	4
359	A57	$1 hn & dk brn	1.25	10
360	A57	$2 dp bl & org brn	1.40	10
a.		Imperf., pair	250.00	
361	A57	$5 red & grnsh blk	60	10
362	A57	$10 dk grn & dl pur	4.50	60
363	A57	$20 rose lake & dk bl	10.00	2.50
		Nos. 349-363 (15)	20.11	4.51

Several values exist imperforate, but these were not regularly issued. No. 361 imperforate was sold as waste paper.

See also Nos. 368–401, 506–524.

Chinese and American Flags and Map of China
A58

Frame Engr., Center Litho.

1939, July 4 *Perf. 12* Unwmkd.

Printed by American Bank Note Co.

Flag in Deep Rose and Ultramarine.

364	A58	5c dk grn	75	30
365	A58	25c dp bl	1.50	60
366	A58	50c brown	1.75	1.25
367	A58	$1 rose car	3.50	2.25

Issued in commemoration of the 150th anniversary of the Constitution of the United States of America.

Type of 1939-41 Issue. Re-engraved.

2c, 1939-41

Re-engraved.

8c, 1939-41

Re-engraved.

1940 *Perf. 12½.*

368	A57	2c ol grn	10	5
369	A57	8c ol grn	10	5

Type of 1938–41 Issue.

1940 *Perf. 14* Unwmkd.

Type III.

370	A57	2c ol grn	40	20
371	A57	5c green	1.00	35
372	A57	$1 hn & dk brn	25.00	5.00
373	A57	$2 dp bl & org brn	6.00	1.50
374	A57	$5 red & grnsh blk	5.00	85
375	A57	$10 dk grn & dl pur	5.00	60
		Nos. 370-375 (6)	42.40	8.50

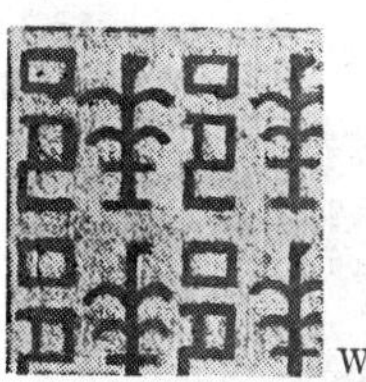

Wmk. 261

Type of 1939-41. Wmkd. Character Yu (Post) Multiple. (261)

1940 *Perf. 12½.*

Type III.

376	A57	$1 hn & dk brn	1.00	15
377	A57	$2 dp bl & org brn	2.00	25
378	A57	$5 red & grnsh blk	2.50	75
379	A57	$10 dk grn & dl pur	3.50	1.50
380	A57	$20 rose lake & dp bl	6.00	2.50
		Nos. 376-380 (5)	15.00	5.15

Printed by the Dah Tung Book Co.

Type III with secret marks.

Five Cent.

Type III
Characters joined.

Secret Mark.
Characters not joined.

Eight Cent.

Type III
Characters not joined.

Secret Mark.
Characters joined.

Ten Cent.

Type III
Characters sharp and well-proportioned.

Secret Mark.
Characters coarse and varying in thickness.

Dollar Values.

Type III

Secret Mark.

1940 *Perf. 14.* Unwmkd.

381	A57	5c green	5	4
382	A57	5c ol grn	5	4
383	A57	8c ol grn	35	5
a.		Without 'star' in uniform button	50	15
384	A57	10c green	5	4
385	A57	30c scarlet	5	4
386	A57	50c dk bl	8	4
387	A57	$1 org brn & sep	12	4
388	A57	$2 dp bl & yel brn	20	4
389	A57	$5 red & sl grn	25	12
390	A57	$10 dk grn & dl pur	1.00	25
391	A57	$20 rose lake & dk bl	2.00	50
		Nos. 381-391 (11)	4.20	1.20

Type III with secret marks.

1940 *Perf. 14.* Wmk. 261

392	A57	5c green	5	4
393	A57	5c ol grn	5	4
394	A57	10c green	5	4
395	A57	30c scarlet	5	4
396	A57	50c dk bl	5	4
397	A57	$1 org brn & sep	15	4
398	A57	$2 dp bl & yel brn	75	5
399	A57	$5 red & sl grn	2.00	25
400	A57	$10 dk grn & dl pur	6.00	1.25
401	A57	$20 rose lake & dk bl	7.50	2.00
		Nos. 392-401 (10)	16.65	3.79

Nos. 383, 384, 385, 397, 400 and 401 exist perf. 12½, but were not issued with this perforation.

Types of 1932-34. Martyrs Issue with secret mark.

1932-34 Issue.
In the left Chinese character in bottom row, the two parts are not joined.

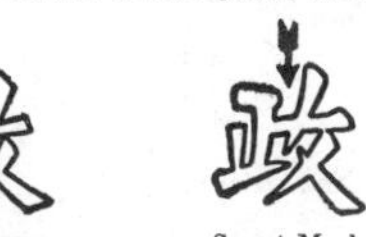

Secret Mark, 1940-41 Issue.
The two parts are joined.

Perf. 12½, 13 and Compound.

1940-41 Wmk. 261

402	A39	½c ol blk	6	3
403	A40	1c orange	6	3
404	A46	2c dp bl ('41)	6	3
405	A39	2½c rose lil	6	3
406	A48	3c dp yel brn	6	3
407	A39	4c pale vio ('41)	6	3
408	A48	5c dl red org ('41)	6	3
409	A45	8c dp org	6	3
410	A46	10c dl vio	6	3
411	A45	13c dp yel grn	6	3
412	A48	15c brn car	6	3
413	A46	17c brn ol	6	3
414	A47	20c lt bl	6	3
415	A45	21c ol brn ('41)	6	3
416	A40	25c red vio ('41)	6	3
417	A46	28c ol ('41)	6	3
418	A48	30c brn car	6	3
a.		Vert. pair, imperf. btwn.	125.00	
419	A47	40c orange	6	3
420	A40	50c green	6	3

Unwmkd.

421	A39	½c ol blk	6	3
422	A40	1c orange	6	3
a.		Without secret mark	75	50
b.		Horiz. pair, imperf. vert.	25.00	
423	A46	2c dp bl	6	3
a.		Vert. pair, imperf. horiz.	6.00	
b.		Horiz. pair, imperf. between	125.00	
424	A39	2½c rose lil	6	3
425	A48	3c dp yel brn	6	3
426	A39	4c pale vio	6	3
427	A48	5c dl red org	6	3
428	A45	8c dp org	6	3
429	A46	10c dl vio	6	3
430	A45	13c dp yel grn	6	3
431	A48	15c brn car	6	3
432	A46	17c brn ol	6	3
433	A47	20c lt bl	6	3
a.		Vert. pair, imperf. horiz.	100.00	
b.		Horiz. pair, imperf. vert.	100.00	
434	A45	21c ol brn	6	3
435	A40	25c rose vio	6	3
436	A46	28c olive	6	3
437	A48	30c brn car	1.00	25
438	A47	40c orange	6	3
439	A40	50c green	6	3
		Nos. 402-439 (38)	3.22	1.36

Several values exist imperforate, but they were not regularly issued.

Regional Surcharges.

The regional surcharges, Nos. 440 to 448, 482 to 484, 486 to 491 and 525 to 549, have been given a general listing according to the basic stamps, with black or red surcharges. The surcharges of the individual provinces, plus Hong Kong and Shanghai, are noted in small type beneath each major listing. These surcharges are identified by the following italic letters:

a—Hong Kong
b—Shanghai
bx—Anhwei
c—Hunan
d—Kansu
e—Kiangsi
f—Eastern Szechwan
g—Chekiang
h—Fukien
i—Kwangsi
j—Kwantung
k—Western Szechwan
l—Yunnan
m—Honan
n—Shensi
o—Kweichow
p—Hupeh

The numeral following each italic letter is the surcharge denomination.

In listings that include more than one region, the lowest price is used for the major.

Regional Surcharges on Stamps of 1939-40:

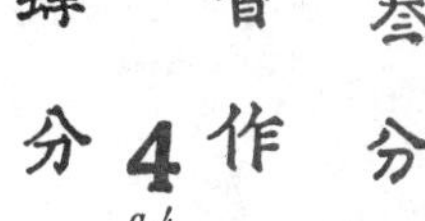

a 4
Hong Kong

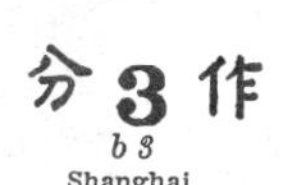

b 3
Shanghai

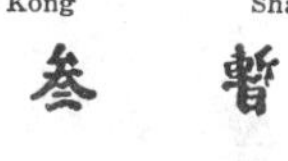

c 3
Hunan

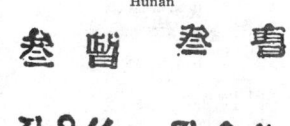

d 3-I *d 3*-II
Kansu

e 3
Kiangsi

f 3
Eastern Szechwan

g 3
Chekiang

1940-41 *Perf. 12½, 14.* Unwmkd.

Parenthetical number indicates basic stamp.

Carmine Surcharge.

440		A57 (a4) 4c on 5c ol grn (#382)	8	10
a.		Lower right character duplicated at left	12.50	14.00

Black Surcharge.

441		A57 (b3) 3c on 5c grn (#351)	12	15
442		A57 3c on 5c ol grn (#352)	40	30
		(c3) Hunan	35	25
		(d3-I) Kansu	40	40
		(d3-II) Kansu	40	40
443		A57 (b3) 3c on 5c grn (#381)	12	15
444		A57 3c on 5c ol grn (#382)	12	15
		(b3) Shanghai	12	15
		(e3) Kiangsi	12	15
		(f3) Eastern Szechwan	15	15
r.		Lower left character duplicated at right (Kiangsi)	30.00	35.00

1940-41 *Perf. 14.* Wmk. 261

445		A57 3c on 5c grn (#392)	12	15
		(b3) Shanghai	12	15
		(c3) Hunan	25	30
		(e3) Kiangsi	12	15
r.		Lower left character duplicated at right (Kiangsi)	20.00	20.00
446		A57 3c on 5c ol grn (#393)	25	25
		(b3) Shanghai	25	25
		(f3) Eastern Szechwan	40	50
r.		Lower left character duplicated at right (Eastern Szechwan)	30.00	35.00

Red Surcharge.

447		A57 (g3) 3c on 5c grn (#392)	90	30
448		A57 (g3) 3c on 5c ol grn (#393)	2.00	1.75

Dr. Sun Yat-sen
A59

Engraved

1941 *Perf. 12* Unwmkd.

Printed by American Bank Note Co.

449	A59	½c sepia	4	4
450	A59	1c orange	4	4
451	A59	2c brt ultra	4	4
452	A59	5c green	4	4
453	A59	8c red org	4	4
454	A59	8c turq grn	4	4
455	A59	10c brt grn	4	4
456	A59	17c olive	1.00	35
457	A59	25c rose vio	4	4
458	A59	30c scarlet	4	4

No.	Type	Description	Unused	Used
459	A59	50c dk bl	6	5
460	A59	$1 brn & blk	10	4
461	A59	$2 bl & blk	10	7
a.		Center invert.	5,000.	
462	A59	$5 scar & blk	20	10
463	A59	$10 grn & blk	2.00	20
464	A59	$20 rose vio & blk	60	40
		Nos. 449-464 (16)	4.42	1.57

Industry and Agriculture
A60

1941, June 21 ***Perf. 12½***

Printed by Chung Hwa Book Co.

No.	Type	Description	Unused	Used
465	A60	8c green	5	5
466	A60	21c red brn	10	10
467	A60	28c dk ol grn	12	12
468	A60	33c vermilion	18	15
469	A60	50c dp ultra	20	18
470	A60	$1 dk vio	50	40
		Nos. 465-470 (6)	1.15	1.00

Issued to promote the Thrift Movement and its aim to "Save for Reconstruction."

Souvenir Sheet.

A61

Typographed
Imperf.

No.	Type	Description	Unused	Used
471	A61	Sheet of six	10.00	10.00
a.		8c dl grn	1.00	1.00
b.		21c dk org brn	1.00	1.00
c.		28c dl yel grn	1.00	1.00
d.		33c red	1.00	1.00
e.		50c dl bl	1.00	1.00
f.		$1 dk vio	1.00	1.00

Issued in sheets measuring 155x171mm. without gum.

This sheet exists with additional blue marginal overprints in Russia, French and Chinese reading "Souvenir of the Exhibition of the Russian Philatelic Society in China, Shanghai, China, Feb. 28, 1943."

The overprinting was applied by the society, and when so overprinted this sheet had no franking power.

Stamps of 1939-41 Overprinted in Carmine or Blue

中華民國創立
三十週年紀念
三十年十月十日

1941, Oct. 10 ***Perf. 12½, 14, 13***

No.	Type	Description	Unused	Used
472	A40	1c dl org (Bl)	4	4
473	A57	2c ol grn (C)	4	4
474	A39	4c pale vio (C)	4	4
475	A57	8c ol grn (#369) (C)	5	5
476	A57	10c grn (#354) (C)	5	5
477	A57	16c ol gray (#257) (C)	5	5
478	A45	21c ol brn (C)	7	7
479	A46	28c ol (C)	20	15
480	A57	30c scar (Bl)	30	25
481	A57	$1 hn & dk brn (#359) (Bl)	50	40
		Nos. 472-481 (10)	1.34	1.14

Chinese Republic, 30th anniversary.

e7 Kiangsi — f7 Eastern Szechwan

g7 Chekiang — h7 Fukien

1941 ***Perf. 12½, 14*** **Unwmkd.**

No.	Type	Description	Unused	Used
482	A57	7c on 8c ol grn (#353)	15	15
		(g7) Chekiang	15	15
		(h7) Fukien	15	15
483	A57 (f7)	7c on 8c ol grn (#369)	12	12
484	A57	7c on 8c ol grn (#383)	15	15
		(e7) Kiangsi	15	15
		(g7) Chekiang	25	25
		(h7) Fukien	15	15
a.		Without "star" in uniform button	35.00	

Type of 1932-34 Re-engraved.

1941 ***Perf. 14*** **Unwmkd.**

No.	Type	Description	Unused	Used
485	A45	8c dp org	1.75	2.00

The original stamps are 19½mm. wide, the re-engraved 21mm.

Eleven other values of the Martyrs Issue and types A37 and A57 exist re-engraved, but were not issued.

c1 Hunan — e1 Kiangsi

h1 Fukien — i1 Kwangsi

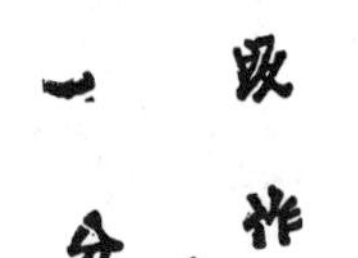

j1 Kwangtung

1942 **Red Surcharge.**

No.	Type	Description	Unused	Used
486	A39	1c on ½c blk brn (#312)	20	15
		(c1) Hunan	20	25
		(i1) Kwangsi	20	25
487	A39	1c on ½c ol blk (#421)	20	25
		(c1) Hunan	20	25
		(e1) Kiangsi	20	25
		(h1) Fukien	20	25
		(i1) Kwangsi	20	25
488	A59	1c on ½c sep (#449)	12	20
		(c1) Hunan	12	20
		(j1) Kwangtung	12	20

c40 Hunan — f40 Eastern Szechwan

k40 Western Szechwan — l40 Yunnan

Red Surcharge.

No.	Type	Description	Unused	Used
489	A57	40c on 50c dk bl (#386)	25	25
		(f40) Eastern Szechwan	25	25
		(k40) Western Szechwan	1.00	1.00
		(l40) Yunnan	85	85
a.		Inverted surcharge (Yunnan)	60.00	

Wmk. 261.

No.	Type	Description	Unused	Used
490	A40 (c40)	40c on 50c grn (#420)	20	15

Unwmkd.

No.	Type	Description	Unused	Used
491	A59 (c40)	40c on 50c dk bl (#459)	12	8

Dr. Sun Yat-sen
A62

Central Trust Printing.
Perf. 10½-11, 11½-12½, 13 and Compounds

1942-43 **Typo.** **Without Gum**

No.	Type	Description	Unused	Used
492	A62	10c dp grn ('43)	6	6
493	A62	16c dl ol brn	3.00	3.00
a.		Perf. 10½	100.00	75.00
494	A62	20c dk ol grn ('43)	6	6
a.		Perf. 11	5.00	5.00
495	A62	25c brn vio	6	6
496	A62	30c dl ver	6	6
a.		Perf. 11	1.75	1.75
497	A62	40c dk red brn ('43)	40	6
a.		Perf. 11x13	35.00	
b.		Perf. 11	10.00	10.00
498	A62	50c sage grn	6	5
a.		Perf. 11	1.00	1.00
499	A62	$1 rose lake	6	6
a.		Perf. 11	20.00	20.00
500	A62	$1 dl grn ('43)	6	6
501	A62	$1.50 dp bl ('43)	6	6
a.		Perf. 11	200.00	
502	A62	$2 dk bl grn	6	6
503	A62	$3 dk yel ('43)	6	6
504	A62	$4 red brn	6	6
505	A62	$5 cer ('43)	6	6
		Nos. 492-505 (14)	4.12	3.77

Many shades and part-perforate varieties exist. See Nos. 550 to 563 for other stamps of type A62 with secret mark and new values and colors.

Type of 1938.
Thin Paper Without Gum.
Engraved.

1942-44 ***Imperf.*** **Unwmkd.**

No.	Type	Description	Unused	Used
506	A57	$10 red brn	10	8
507	A57	$20 bl grn	15	10
508	A57	$20 rose red ('44)	3.00	50
509	A57	$30 dl vio ('43)	30	25
510	A57	$40 rose red ('43)	10	5
511	A57	$50 blue	75	75
512	A57	$100 org brn ('43)	1.00	75

Rouletted.

No.	Type	Description	Unused	Used
513	A57	$5 lil gray ('44)	1.50	35
a.		Rouletted x perf. 12½	15.00	
514	A57	$10 red brn	1.25	25
515	A57	$50 blue	1.50	60
a.		Rouletted x imperf.		
		Nos. 506-515 (10)	9.65	3.68

1942-45 ***Perf. 12½ to 15.***

No.	Type	Description	Unused	Used
516	A57	$4 dp bl ('43)	10	6
517	A57	$5 lil gray ('43)	10	7
518	A57	$10 red brn	10	7
519	A57	$20 bl grn ('43)	10	10
520	A57	$20 rose red ('45)	22.50	22.50
521	A57	$30 dl vio ('43)	10	10
522	A57	$40 rose ('43)	50	25
523	A57	$50 blue	25	20
524	A57	$100 org brn ('45)	22.50	22.50
		Nos. 516-524 (9)	46.25	45.85

No. 493 Overprinted in Black or Red

國內平信
附加已付

1942

No.	Type	Description	Unused	Used
525	A62	16c dl ol brn (Bk)	15.00	15.00
		(c) Hunan	175.00	
		(i) Kwangsi	15.00	15.00
		(k) Western Szechwan	35.00	35.00
		(m) Honan	300.00	300.00
r.		Perf. 10½ (Kwangsi)	250.00	
		(n) Shensi	50.00	50.00
s.		Inverted ovpt. (Shensi)	85.00	
526	A62	16c dl ol brn (R)	3.00	4.00
		(bx) Anhwei	125.00	125.00
		(d) Kansu	3.00	4.00
		(e) Kiangsi	8.50	8.50
		(f) Eastern Szechwan	10.00	10.00
r.		Perf. 10½ (E. Szechwan)	300.00	
		(h) Fukien	35.00	35.00
		(j) Kwangtung	225.00	250.00
		(l) Yunnan	9.00	9.00
		(o) Kweichow	30.00	30.00
		(p) Hupeh, perf. 10½	275.00	275.00
s.		Horiz. pair, imperf. between (Yunnan)	150.00	
t.		Perf. 13 (Hupeh)	600.00	400.00

This overprint means "Domestic Ordinary Letter Surcharge Paid." It was applied in various sizes and types by 14 districts, 9 using red ink, 5 using black. (The Anhwei overprint comes in two types.) These overprinted stamps were briefly sold for $1.16 before the government ordered their sale suspended. The vertical bars and 50c surcharge of Nos. 527-528 were then applied.

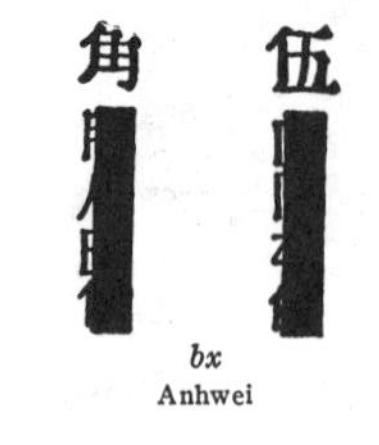

bx
Anhwei

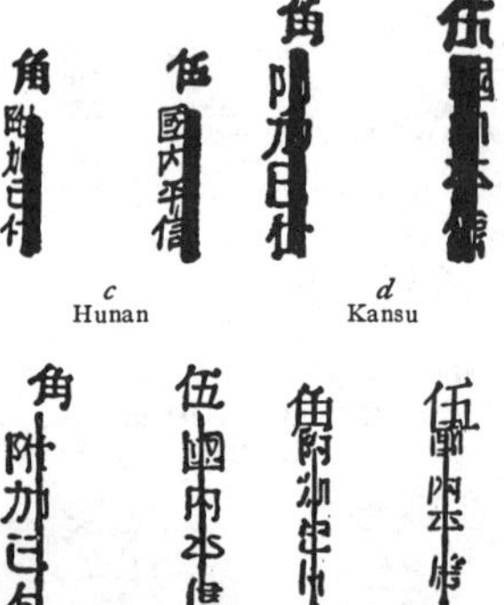

c Hunan — d Kansu

e Kiangsi — f Eastern Szechwan

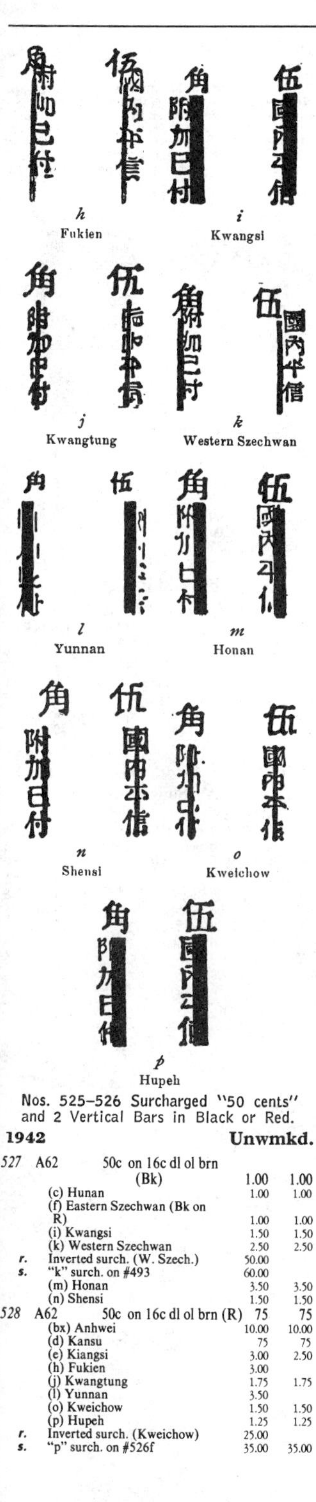

h Fukien

i Kwangsi

j Kwangtung

k Western Szechwan

l Yunnan

m Honan

n Shensi

o Kweichow

p Hupeh

Nos. 525–526 Surcharged "50 cents" and 2 Vertical Bars in Black or Red.

1942 **Unwmkd.**

No.	Type	Description	Unused	Used
527	A62	50c on 16c dl ol brn (Bk)	1.00	1.00
		(c) Hunan	1.00	1.00
		(f) Eastern Szechwan (Bk on R)	1.00	1.00
		(i) Kwangsi	1.50	1.50
		(k) Western Szechwan	2.50	2.50
	r.	Inverted surch. (W. Szech.)	50.00	
	s.	"k" surch. on #493	60.00	
		(m) Honan	3.50	3.50
		(n) Shensi	1.50	1.50
528	A62	50c on 16c dl ol brn (R)	75	75
		(bx) Anhwei	10.00	10.00
		(d) Kansu	75	75
		(e) Kiangsi	3.00	2.50
		(h) Fukien	3.00	
		(j) Kwangtung	1.75	1.75
		(l) Yunnan	3.50	
		(o) Kweichow	1.50	1.50
		(p) Hupeh	1.25	1.25
	r.	Inverted surch. (Kweichow)	25.00	
	s.	"p" surch. on #526f	35.00	35.00

Many varieties of Nos. 527–528 exist, including narrow or wide spacing between the two top characters, or between the vertical bars, or both.

Surcharges on stamps perf. 10½ (basic No. 493a) usually sell at much higher prices."

General Issue

c 50 Hunan

f 50 Eastern Szechwan

g 50 Chekiang

i 50 Kwangsi

j 50 Kwangtung

k 50 Western Szechwan

m 50 Honan

n 50 Shensi

o 50 Kweichow

No. 493 Surcharged in Black, Red or Carmine.

1943 **Unwmkd.**

No.	Type	Description	Unused	Used
529	A62	50c on 16c dl ol brn (Bk)	1.00	1.00
		(m50) Honan	1.50	1.50
		(n50) Shensi	1.00	1.00
	r.	Perf. 11x13 (Shensi)	50.00	
530	A62	50c on 16c dl ol brn (R, C)	25	25
	a.	General Issue (C)	25	25
		General Issue (C) (c50) Hunan	1.00	1.00
	r.	Inverted surch. (Hunan)	35.00	
		(f50) Eastern Szechwan	75	75
		(g50) Chekiang	10.00	
		(i50) Kwangsi	1.50	1.50
		(j50) Kwangtung	1.25	1.25
		(k50) Western Szechwan	2.00	2.00
		(m50) Honan	2.50	2.50
		(o50) Kweichow	1.25	1.25
	s.	"05" instead of "50" (Kweichow)	250.00	

Many varieties of Nos. 529–530 exist, such as narrow or wide spacing horizontally or vertically between the overprinted Chinese characters.

Surcharges on No. 493a (perf. 10½) usually sell at much higher prices.

The General Issue type, No. 530a, was distributed to all head offices, which in turn supplied the post offices under their direction. It is surcharged in carmine; the other stamps listed under No. 530 are surcharged in red or carmine.

The lack of a price for a listed item does not necessarily indicate rarity.

c 20 Hunan

d 20 Kansu

e 20 Kiangsi

f 20 Eastern Szechwan

h 20 Fukien

i 20 Kwangsi

j 20 Kwangtung

k 20 Western Szechwan

l 20 Yunnan

m 20 Honan

n 20 Shensi

o 20 Kweichow

p 20 Hupeh

1943 **Unwmkd.**

No.	Type	Description	Unused	Used
531	A45	20c on 13c bl grn (#318) (Bk)	8	10
		(d20) Kansu	25	30
		(k20) Western Szechwan	10	12
		(n20) Shensi	8	10
532	A45	20c on 13c bl grn (#318) (R)	12	12
		(c20) Hunan	350.00	
		(e20) Kiangsi	35.00	
		(i20) Kwangsi	12	12
		(j20) Kwangtung	12.00	12.00
		(p20) Hupeh	20	30

Wmk. 261

No.	Type	Description	Unused	Used
533	A45	20c on 13c dp yel grn (#411) (Bk)	10	12
		(d20) Kansu	30	30
		(k20) Western Szechwan	15	15
		(l20) Yunnan	90	90
		(m20) Honan	35.00	
		(n20) Shensi	10	12
534	A45	20c on 13c dp yel grn (#411) (R)	10	10
		(c20) Hunan	15	15
		(e20) Kiangsi	12	12
		(f20) Eastern Szechwan	10	10
		(h20) Fukien	25	25
		(i20) Kwangsi	20	20
		(j20) Kwangtung	5.00	5.00
		(o20) Kweichow	35	25
		(p20) Hupeh	10	10

Unwmkd.

No.	Type	Description	Unused	Used
535	A45	20c on 13c dp yel grn (#430) (Bk)	10	12
		(d20) Kansu	15	20
		(k20) Western Szechwan	8.00	8.00
		(l20) Yunnan	18	20
		(m20) Honan	35	35
		(n20) Shensi	10	12
536	A45	20c on 13c dp yel grn (#430) (R)	10	12
		(c20) Hunan	1.25	1.25
		(e20) Kiangsi	15	20
		(f20) Eastern Szechwan	10	12
		(i20) Kwangsi	10	12
		(j20) Kwangtung	10	12
		(o20) Kweichow	20	20
		(p20) Hupeh	10	12
537	A57	20c on 16c ol gray (#357) (Bk)	8	10
		(c20) Hunan	8	10
		(d20) Kansu	10	12
		(k20) Western Szechwan	10	12
		(m20) Honan	75	75
		(n20) Shensi	8	10
538	A57	20c on 16c ol gray (#357) (R)	15	20
		(c20) Hunan	65	70
		(e20) Kiangsi	15	20
		(i20) Kwangsi	15	20
		(j20) Kwangtung	15.00	16.50
		(o20) Kweichow	15	20

Wmk. 261.

No.	Type	Description	Unused	Used
539	A46	20c on 17c brn ol (#413) (R)	10	12
		(c20) Hunan	25	30
		(i20) Kwangsi	10	12
		(j20) Kwangtung	10.00	10.00

Unwmkd.

No.	Type	Description	Unused	Used
540	A46	20c on 17c brn ol (#432) (Bk)	12	15
		(d20) Kansu	90	1.00
		(k20) Western Szechwan	12	15
		(m20) Honan	8.50	9.00
541	A46	20c on 17c brn ol (#432) (R)	15	20
		(e20) Kiangsi	15	20
		(j20) Kwangtung	15	20
		(o20) Kweichow	15	20
542	A59 (m20)	20c on 17c ol (#456) (Bk)	60.00	65.00
543	A59 (c20)	20c on 17c ol (#456) (R)	1.25	1.25

Wmk. 261.

No.	Type	Description	Unused	Used
544	A45 (e20)	20c on 21c ol brn (#415) (R)	25	30

Unwmkd.

No.	Type	Description	Unused	Used
545	A45	20c on 21c ol brn (#434) (Bk)	8	8
		(c20) Hunan	8	8
		(d20) Kansu	15	20
		(k20) Western Szechwan	10	12
		(l20) Yunnan	10	12
		(m20) Honan	25	30
546	A45	20c on 21c ol brn (#434) (R)	8	8
		(e20) Kiangsi	12	15
		(f20) Eastern Szechwan	8	8
		(h20) Fukien	12	15
		(i20) Kwangsi	8	10
		(j20) Kwangtung	8	10
		(o20) Kweichow	15	15
		(p20) Hupeh	12	15

Wmk. 261.

547 A46(e20)20c on 28c ol (#417) (R) 250.00 275.00

Unwmkd.

548 A46 20c on 28c ol (#436) (Bk) 10 12
(d20) Kansu 6.00 6.00
(k20) Western Szechwan 10.00 10.00
(l20) Yunnan 10 12
(m20) Honan 10.00 10.00
549 A46 20c on 28c ol (#436) (R) 8 8
(c20) Hunan 8 8
(e20) Kiangsi 10 12
(h20) Fukien 8 8
(i20) Kwangsi 10 12
(j20) Kwangtung 10 12
(o20) Kweichow 25 25

Many varieties of Nos. 531-549 exist, such as narrow or wide spacing between the overprinted Chinese characters, and "20" higher or lower than illustrated.

Type of 1942-43.
Pacheng Printing.

1944-46 ***Perf. 12*** **Unwmkd.**
Without Gum

550 A62 30c chocolate 25 15
551 A62 $1 green 2.00 1.50
552 A62 $2 dk vio brn 6 8
a. Imperf., pair 3.00
553 A62 $2 dk bl grn 8 8
a. Perf. 10½ 75.00 80.00
554 A62 $2 dp bl 10 10
555 A62 $3 lt yel 7 5
556 A62 $4 vio brn 6 8
a. Imperf., pair 50.00
557 A62 $5 car ('46) 5 5
a. Perf. 10½ 75.00 80.00
558 A62 $6 gray vio ('45) 4 3
559 A62 $10 red brn ('45) 4 4
a. Imperf., pair 50.00
560 A62 $20 dp ultra ('46) 4 3
561 A62 $50 dk grn ('46) 6 3
562 A62 $70 lil ('46) 6 4
563 A62 $100 lt brn ('46) 6 4
Nos. 550-563 (14) 2.97 2.30

In the Pacheng printing of the Central Trust type stamps, the secret mark "C" has been added below the lower left foliate ornament beneath the sun emblem. On the $3, it is below the right ornament. New values also include a "P" at right of sun emblem on the $6 and $10, and at right of necktie on the $20. Some values of Pacheng printing exist on paper with elephant watermark in sheet.

Dr. Sun Yat-sen
A63

Allegory of Savings
A64

Typographed

1944-46 ***Perf. 12½*** **Unwmkd.**
Without Gum.

565 A63 40c brn red 8 3
566 A63 $2 gray brn 8 3
567 A63 $3 red 8 3
a. $3 org red 1.00 75
568 A63 $3 lt red brn ('45) 25 15
569 A63 $6 pale lil gray ('45) 8 5
570 A63 $10 dl lake ('45) 8 5
571 A63 $20 rose ('45) 8 5
a. Perf. 15½ 30.00
572 A63 $50 lt brn ('46) 8 3
573 A63 $70 rose vio ('46) 10 3
Nos. 565-573 (9) 91 45

1944-45 **Engraved** ***Perf. 13***
Without Gum.

574 A64 $40 ind ('45) 8 4
575 A64 $50 yel grn ('45) 8 4
576 A64 $100 yel brn 8 4
577 A64 $200 dk grn ('45) 10 7

All four values were printed on thick paper; the first three were also printed on thin paper.

Dr. Sun Yat-sen
A65 A66

Lithographed

1944, Dec. 25 **Without Gum**

578 A65 $2 dp grn 12 12
579 A65 $5 fawn 18 18
580 A65 $6 dl rose vio 30 30
581 A65 $10 vio bl 60 60
582 A65 $20 carmine 85 85
Nos. 578-582 (5) 2.05 2.05

50th anniversary of the Kuomintang.

1945, Mar. 12 **Without Gum**

583 A66 $2 gray grn 8 8
584 A66 $5 red brn 15 15
585 A66 $6 dk vio bl 18 18
586 A66 $10 lt bl 30 30
587 A66 $20 rose 40 40
588 A66 $30 buff 60 60
Nos. 583-588 (6) 1.71 1.71

Issued to commemorate the 20th anniversary of the death of Dr. Sun Yat-sen.

Dr. Sun Yat-sen
A67

1945-46 **Without Gum** ***Perf. 12½***

589 A67 $2 green 8 3
590 A67 $5 dl grn 8 3
591 A67 $10 dk bl 8 3
a. Imperf., pair 25.00
592 A67 $20 car ('46) 8 3
a. Imperf., pair 50.00

Statue of Liberty, Map of China, Flags of Great Britain, China and United States, and Chiang Kai-shek
A68

Engraved

1945, July 7 ***Perf. 12*** **Unwmkd.**
Flags in Dark Blue and Red.

593 A68 $1 dp bl 15 15
594 A68 $2 dl grn 30 30
595 A68 $5 ol gray 30 30
596 A68 $6 brown 75 75
597 A68 $10 rose lil 1.10 1.10
598 A68 $20 car rose 2.00 2.00
Nos. 593-598 (6) 4.60 4.60

Issued to commemorate the signing of a Treaty in 1943 between Great Britain, the United States and China.

President Lin Sen
A69

President Chiang Kai-shek
A70

1945, Aug. ***Perf. 12*** **Unwmkd.**

599 A69 $1 dp ultra & blk 8 8
600 A69 $2 myr grn & blk 8 8
601 A69 $5 red & blk 12 12
602 A69 $6 pur & blk 30 30
603 A69 $10 choc & blk 40 40
604 A69 $20 ol grn & blk 70 70
Nos. 599-604 (6) 1.68 1.68

Issued in memory of President Lin Sen (1864-1943).

1945, Oct. 10
Flag in Rose Red and Violet Blue.

605 A70 $2 green 25 25
606 A70 $4 dk bl 25 25
607 A70 $5 ol gray 25 25
608 A70 $6 bis brn 60 60
609 A70 $10 gray 85 85
610 A70 $20 red vio 1.40 1.40
Nos. 605-610 (6) 3.60 3.60

Issued to commemorate the inauguration of Chiang Kai-shek as president, October 10, 1943.

President Chiang Kai-shek
A71

1945, Oct. 10 **Typo.** ***Perf. 13***
Without Gum.
Flag in Carmine and Blue.

611 A71 $20 grn & bl 10 8
612 A71 $50 bis brn & bl 20 12
613 A71 $100 blue 18 15
614 A71 $300 rose red & bl 18 15

Issued to commemorate the Victory of the Allied Nations over Japan.

C. N. C. Surcharges.

The green surcharges on Nos. 615 to 621, and the surcharges on Nos. 647 to 721, and 768 to 774 represent Chinese National Currency and were applied at Shanghai.

Stamps of 1938-41 Surcharged in Black with Chinese Characters and New Value in Checkered Rectangle at Bottom, Re-surcharged in Green

壹 國
角 幣

1945 ***Perf. 12, 12½***

615 A57 10c on $20 on 3c dl cl (#350) 5 4
616 A46 15c on $30 on 2c dp bl (#423) 5 10
a. Horiz. pair, imperf. between 75.00
b. Vert. pair, imperf. between 65.00
617 A59 25c on $50 on 1c org (#450) 5 10
618 A57 50c on $100 on 3c dl cl (#350) 5 10
619 A40 $1 on $200 on 1c org (#422) 5 10
a. Horiz. pair, imperf. between 90.00
620 A57 $2 on $400 on 3c dl cl (#350) 5 10
621 A59 $5 on $1000 on 1c org (#450) 5 10

The black (first) surcharges on Nos. 615 to 621 represent Nanking puppet government currency.

In the green surcharge, the characters at the left express the new value and are either two or four in number.

Types of 1932-34, Re-engraved, Overprinted in Black 北 華 and Surcharged in Green with Horizontal Bar and Four or Five Chinese Characters.

Perf. 14.

622 A47 $10 on 20c brn red 2.00 2.00
623 A47 $20 on 40c org 8.00 8.00
a. Green surcharge inverted 20.00
624 A48 $50 on 30c vio brn 5.00 5.00

These provisional surcharges were applied in Honan in National currency to stamps of the Hwa Pei (North China) government. The black overprint reads: "Hwa Pei."

The two-character "Hwa Pei" overprint was applied to various stamps in 1941-43 by the North China puppet government. See Nos. 8N1-8N53, 8N60-8N84.

Dr. Sun Yat-sen
A72 A73

1945, Dec. **Typo.** ***Perf. 12***
Without Gum.

625 A72 $20 dp car 6 6
626 A72 $30 dp bl 6 6
627 A72 $40 orange 6 6
628 A72 $50 green 6 6
629 A72 $100 dk brn 8 8
630 A72 $200 brn vio 9 9
Nos. 625-630 (6) 41 41

Type of 1931-37.
Perf. 12½, 13x12½, 13½.

1946 **Unwmkd.**

631 A37 $1 dk vio 8 6
632 A37 $2 ol grn 8 6
633 A37 $20 brt yel grn 8 6
634 A37 $30 chocolate 8 6
635 A37 $50 red org 8 6
Nos.631-635 (5) 40 30

1946-47 **Engraved** ***Perf. 14***
Without Gum.

636 A73 $20 carmine 6 5
637 A73 $30 dk bl ('47) 6 5
638 A73 $50 purple 6 5
639 A73 $70 red org ('47) 6.00 1.00
640 A73 $100 dk car 6 5
641 A73 $200 ol grn ('47) 8 5
642 A73 $500 brt bl grn ('47) 12 5
643 A73 $700 red brn ('47) 15 5
644 A73 $1000 rose lake 25 5
645 A73 $3000 blue 60 5
646 A73 $5000 dp grn & ver 75 8
Nos. 636-646 (11) 8.19 1.53

Stamps of 1932-41 Surcharged in Black

Perf. 12½, 13, 13x12, 14.
Wmk. 261

647 A45 $20 on 8c dp org (#409) 8 10
648 A39 $30 on ½c ol blk (#402) 500.00 500.00
649 A45 $50 on 21c ol brn (#415) 8 10
650 A45 $70 on 13c dp yel grn (#411) 8 10
651 A46 $100 on 28c ol (#417) 8 10

Unwmkd.

652 A39 $3 on 2½c rose lil (#424) 50 75
653 A48 $10 on 15c brn car (#431) 8 10
654 A45 $20 on 8c dp org (#428) 8 10
655 A47 $20 on 20c lt bl (#433) 8 10
656 A39 $30 on ½c ol blk (#421) 8 10
657 A45 $50 on 21c ol brn (#434) 8 10

657A A45 $70 on 13c bl grn (#318) 50.00 60.00
658 A45 $70 on 13c dp yel grn (#430) 8 10
659 A46 $100 on 28c ol (#436) 8 10

Stamps of 1931-1946 Surcharged in Black or Carmine

伍 拾 圓 國 幣 50.00

Perf. 12½, 13, 14

1946-47 **Wmk. 261**

660 A57 $50 on 5c grn (#392) 8 10
661 A57 $50 on 5c ol grn (#393) 15.00 16.50
662 A48 $50 on 5c dl red org (#408) 5 10
663 A40 $100 on 1c org (#403) 5 10

Perf. 12, 12½, 12½x13, 13, 14.

1946-47 **Unwmkd.**

664 A57 $20 on 3c dl cl (#350) 8 10
665 A45 $20 on 8c dp org (#428) 8 10
666 A57 $50 on 3c dl cl (#350) 8 10
667 A57 $50 on 5c ol grn (#352) 8 10
668 A57 $50 on 5c ol grn (#382) 8 10
669 A48 $50 on 5c dl red org (#427) 8 10
670 A59 $50 on 5c grn (#452) 8 10
671 A62 $50 on $1 dl grn (#500) 8 10
672 A40 $100 on 1c org (#422) 8 10
a. Without secret mark (No. 422a) 50.00
673 A57 $100 on 3c dl cl (#350) 8 10
674 A57 $100 on 8c ol grn (#353) 10.00 10.00
675 A57 $100 on 8c ol grn (#369) 8 10
676 A57 $100 on 8c ol grn (#383) 8 10
a. Without "star" in uniform button (No. 383a) 15.00 15.00
677 A59 $100 on 8c turq grn (#454) 8 10
678 A37 $100 on $1 dk vio (#631) 20 10
679 A73 $100 on $20 car (#636) 85 15
680 A57 $200 on 10c grn (#354) 8 10
681 A57 $200 on 10c grn (#384) 8 10
682 A37 $200 on $4 dl bl 10 10
a. Double surch. 15.00
683 A62 $250 on $1.50 dp bl (#501) 8 10
a. Perf. 11 175.00
684 A37 $250 on $2 ol grn (#632) 8 10
685 A37 $250 on $5 car 10 10
686 A57 $300 on 10c grn (#354) 8 10
687 A59 $300 on 10c brt grn (#455) 8 10
688 A57 $500 on 3c dl cl (#350) 8 10
689 A37 $500 on $20 brt yel grn (#633) 8 10
690 A37 $800 on $30 choc (#634) 8 10
691 A37 $1000 on 2c ol grn (#297) 35 20
692 A62 $1000 on $2 dk vio brn (#552) 12 12
a. Imperf., pair 15.00 15.00
693 A62 $1000 on $2 dk bl grn (#553) 8 8
694 A62 $1000 on $2 dp bl (#554) 8 8
695 A67 $1000 on $2 grn (#589) 10 12
696 A62 $2000 on $5 car (#557) 8 8
697 A67 $2000 on $5 dl grn (C) (#590) 15 20
Nos. 664-697 (34) 13.97 13.53

Nos. 682 and 685 wer not issued without surcharge. No. 682 is perf. 13x13½; No. 685, perf. 12x12½.

The characters at the left express the new value and vary in number.

Stamps of 1938-41 Surcharged in Black

伍 拾 圓 國 幣 50.00

Perf. 12, 12½, 13, 14.

1946 **Wmk. 261**

698 A45 $20 on 8c dp org (#409) 80.00 90.00
699 A57 $50 on 5c grn (#392) 8 15
700 A57 $50 on 5c ol grn (#393) 8 15

1946-48 **Unwmkd.**

700A A57 $20 on 5c grn (#381) 375.00
701 A57 $20 on 8c ol grn (#353) 6 10
702 A57 $20 on 8c ol grn (#369) 25 30
703 A57 $20 on 8c ol grn (#383) 6 10
a. Without "star" in uniform button (No. 383a) 2.50 2.50
b. Inverted surch. 12.50
c. Double surcharge, one on back 15.00 16.00
d. Double surch. 20.00
704 A45 $20 on 8c dp org (#428) 6 10
a. Double surch. 12.50
705 A59 $20 on 8c red org (#453) 6 10
706 A59 $20 on 8c turq grn (#454) 6 10
a. Inverted surch. 12.50
b. Double surcharge 12.50
707 A57 $50 on 5c grn (#351) 20 25
708 A57 $50 on 5c ol grn (#352) 6 10
a. Inverted surch. 20.00
709 A57 $50 on 5c grn (#381) 6 10
710 A57 $50 on 5c ol grn (#382) 6 10
711 A48 $50 on 5c dl red org (#427) 6 10
a. Inverted surch. 25.00
712 A59 $50 on 5c grn (#452) 6 10
a. Double surch. 20.00

Stamps of 1939-41 Surcharged in Blue or Red

拾 圓 國 幣 10.00

1946 *Perf. 12½.* **Wmk. 261**

713 A40 $10 on 1c org (Bl) (#403) 5 10
a. Inverted surch. 30.00
714 A48 $20 on 3c dp yel grn (#406) (Bl) 250.00 150.00

1946 *Perf. 12, 12½, 13* **Unwmkd.**

715 A40 $10 on 1c org (Bl) (#422) 5 10
a. Without secret mark (No. 422a) 5.00 6.00
b. Inverted surcharge 7.50 9.00
716 A59 $10 on 1c org (Bl) (#450) 5 10
a. Double surch. 20.00
717 A57 $20 on 2c ol grn (R) (#368) 5 10
718 A59 $20 on 2c brt ultra (R) (#451) 4 10
a. Inverted surch. 12.50
b. Double surch. 12.50
719 A57 $20 on 3c dl cl (Bl) (#350) 4 10
a. Double surch. 20.00
720 A48 $20 on 3c dp yel brn (Bl) (#425) 4 15
721 A39 $30 on 4c pale vio (R) (#426) 4 15
a. Inverted surch. 8.00

President Chiang Kai-shek
A74

Perf. 14, 10½-11½

1946, Oct. 31 Engraved Unwmkd.

722 A74 $20 carmine 12 15
723 A74 $30 green 12 15
724 A74 $50 vermilion 12 15
725 A74 $100 yel grn 12 15
726 A74 $200 yel org 12 15
727 A74 $300 magenta 12 15
Nos. 722-727 (6) 72 90

60th birthday of Chiang Kai-shek.

Perf. 14 stamps were printed by Dah Tung Book Co. and have no gum. Perf. 10½-11½ stamps were printed by Dah Yeh Printing Co.; the earlier ones are gumless, the later ones gummed.

Assembly House, Nanking—A75

1946, Nov. 15 **Litho.** *Perf. 14*

Without Gum

728 A75 $20 green 6 10
729 A75 $30 blue 6 10
730 A75 $50 dk brn 6 10
a. Horiz. pair, imperf. between 50.00 60.00
731 A75 $100 carmine 6 10

Convening of National Assembly.

Entrance to Dr. Sun Yat-sen Mausoleum
A76

Dr. Sun Yat-sen
A77

1947, May 1 **Engraved**

732 A76 $100 dp grn 10 12
733 A76 $200 dp bl 10 12
734 A76 $250 carmine 10 12
735 A76 $350 lt brn 10 12
736 A76 $400 dp cl 10 12
Nos. 732-736 (5) 50 60

First anniversary of return of Chinese National Government to Nanking.

1947 *Perf. 12½, 11½x12½*

737 A77 $500 ol grn 10 4
738 A77 $1000 grn & car 10 4
739 A77 $2000 dp bl & red brn 15 6
740 A77 $5000 org red & blk 15 6

Confucius
A78

Confucius' Lecturing School
A79

Tomb of Confucius
A80

Temple of Confucius
A81

1947, Aug. 27 **Litho.** *Perf. 14*

Without Gum

741 A78 $500 car rose 8 5

Engraved.

742 A79 $800 yel brn 8 5
743 A80 $1250 bl grn 8 5
744 A81 $1800 blue 8 6

Sun Yat-sen and Plum Blossoms
A82

Chinese Flag and Map of Taiwan
A83

1947-48 **Engraved** *Perf. 14*

Without Gum

745 A82 $150 dk bl 8 3
746 A82 $250 dp lil 35 3
747 A82 $500 bl grn 6 6
748 A82 $1000 red 6 3
749 A82 $2000 vermilion 15 3
750 A82 $3000 blue 5 3
751 A82 $4000 gray ('48) 15 3
752 A82 $5000 dk brn 6 3
753 A82 $6000 rose lil ('48) 15 3
754 A82 $7000 lt red brn ('48) 15 3
755 A82 $10,000 dp bl & car 50 3
756 A82 $20,000 car & yel grn 35 3
757 A82 $50,000 grn & dk bl 35 3
758 A82 $100,000 dl yel & ol grn ('48) 35 3
759 A82 $200,000 vio brn & dp bl ('48) 85 15
760 A82 $300,000 sep & org brn ('48) 85 15
761 A82 $500,000 dk Prus grn & sep ('48) 1.25 15
Nos. 745-761 (17) 5.76 90

See also Nos. 788-799.

1947, Oct. 25 **With Gum**

762 A83 $500 carmine 10 15
763 A83 $1250 dp grn 10 15

Second anniversary, restoration of Taiwan to China.

Mobile Post Office
A84

Street-Corner Branch Post Office
A85

1947, Nov. 5

764	A84	$500 carmine	8	10
765	A85	$1000 lilac	8	10
766	A85	$1250 green	8	10
767	A84	$1800 dp bl	8	10

Stamps and Type of 1943-47 Surcharged in Black or Green

伍 國
佰
圓 500.00 幣

Perf. 12½, 13, 14.

1947-48 **Unwmkd.**

768	A37	$500 on $20 brt yel grn (#633)	8	6
769	A73	$1250 on $70 red org(#639)	8	10
770	A82	$1800 on $350 yel org	8	10
771	A62	$2000 on $3 dk yel ('48) (#503)	8	10
772	A63	$2000 on $3 red (#567)	8	10
a.		On #567a	2.50	1.00
773	A62	$3000 on $3 lt yel ('48) (#555)	8	10
774	A63	$3000 on $3 lt red brn (G) ('48) (#568)	8	10
		Nos. 768-774 (7)	56	66

The characters at the left express the new value and vary in number.

No. 640 Surcharged

伍 國
千
圓 5000 幣

1948, Aug. ***Perf. 14***

775	A73	$5000 on $100 dk car	1.75	2.00

No. 775 received its surcharge in Kwangsi for use in that province.

Map of China and Mail-carrying Vehicles—A86

Rural Mail Delivery—A87

Early and Modern Mail Transportation
A88

1947, Dec. 16 **Engraved** ***Perf. 12***

776	A86	$100 violet	5	10
777	A87	$200 brt grn	5	10
778	A87	$300 red brn	5	10
779	A88	$400 scarlet	5	10
780	A88	$500 brt vio bl	5	10
		Nos. 776-780 (5)	25	50

Issued to commemorate the 50th anniversary of the Chinese Postal Administration.

National Assembly Building and New Constitution
A89

1947, Dec. 25 ***Perf. 14***

Without Gum.

781	A89	$2000 brt red	8	10
782	A89	$3000 blue	8	10
783	A89	$5000 dp grn	8	10

Issued to commemorate the first anniversary of the adoption of China's new constitution, Dec. 25, 1946.

Chinese Stamps of 1947 and 1912
A90

Lithographed

1948, Mar. 20 ***Perf. 14, Imperf.***

Without Gum

784	A90	$5000 dk car rose	18	18
a.		Vert. pair, imperf. between	30.00	
785	A90	$5000 dk grn	18	18
a.		Vert. pair, imperf. between	20.00	

Issued to commemorate stamp exhibitions at Nanking, Mar. 20 (No. 784), and at Shanghai, May 19 (No. 785).

Sun Yat-sen Memorial Hall, Taipei
A91

1948, Apr. 28 **Engraved** ***Perf. 14***

786	A91	$5000 violet	12	20
787	A91	$10000 red	12	20

Issued to commemorate the third anniversary of the restoration of Formosa to China.

Sun Yat-sen Type of 1947–48

1948 **Without Gum**

788	A82	$20000 rose pink	10	15
789	A82	$30000 chocolate	10	15
790	A82	$40000 green	5	4
791	A82	$50000 dp bl	5	4
792	A82	$100000 dl grn	10	4
793	A82	$200000 brn vio	15	4
794	A82	$300000 yel grn	15	4
795	A82	$500000 lil rose	30	8
796	A82	$1000000 claret	25	8
797	A82	$2000000 vermilion	60	15
798	A82	$3000000 ol bis	1.00	25
799	A82	$5000000 ultra	1.75	50
		Nos. 788-799 (12)	4.60	1.56

Zeros for "cents" omitted.

Early Ship and Modern Hai Tien
A92

Passenger Ship Kiang Ya
A93

1948, Aug. 16 **Without Gum**

800	A92	$20000 blue	6	8
801	A92	$30000 rose lil	6	8
802	A93	$40000 yel brn	6	8
803	A93	$60000 vermilion	6	8

Issued to commemorate the 75th anniversary of the China Merchants' Steam Navigation Company.

Type of 1947-48 Surcharged in Black

圓仟伍作改☆☆
5000.00
☆☆

1948 ***Perf. 14*** **Unwmkd.**

804	A82	$4000 on $100 car	6	8
805	A82	$5000 on $100 car	6	8
806	A82	$8000 on $700 red brn	6	8

Stamps of 1942-46 Surcharged in Black or Red

圓仟伍作改
5000.00

1948 ***Perf. 12½, 13***

807	A62	$5000 on $1 dl grn (#500)	8	8
808	A62	$5000 on $1 grn (#551)	2.00	2.00
809	A62	$5000 on $2 dk bl grn (#502)	8	10
810	A72	$10000 on $20 dp car (#625)	8	10
811	A62	$20000 on 10c dp grn (#492)	8	10
812	A62	$20000 on 50c sage grn (R) (#498)	8	10
813	A62	$30000 on 30c dl ver (#496)	8	10
a.		Perf. 10½	15.00	
		Nos. 807-813 (7)	2.48	2.58

Nos. 492, 556 and 558 Surcharged in Black or Carmine

圓仟伍萬壹作改
15000

1948

814	A62	$15,000 on 10c dp grn	12	15
815	A62	$15,000 on $4 vio brn	12	15
816	A62	$15,000 on $6 gray vio (C)	12	15

No. 498, 494 and 504 Surcharged in Black

圓萬肆作改
40000

1948 ***Perf. 11½, 13.*** **Unwmkd.**

817	A62	$15,000 on 50c sage grn	12	15
818	A62	$40,000 on 20c dk ol grn	12	15
a.		Perf. 11	5.00	5.00
819	A62	$60,000 on $4 red brn	12	15

Gold Yuan Surcharges
(Nos. 820–885E)

Stamps of 1942-47 Surcharged in Black, Carmine or Red

金
圓
1/2 分

1948 ***Perf. 14, 13, 11***

820	A62	½c on 30c dl ver (#496)	8	10
821	A82	½c on $500 bl grn (Bk) (#747)	8	10
822	A82	½c on $500 bl grn (C) (#747)	8	10
823	A73	1c on $20 car (#636)	8	10
824	A62	2c on $1.50 dp bl (R) (#501)	8	10
825	A62	3c on $5 cer (#505)	8	10
826	A62	4c on $1 rose lake (#499)	8	10
827	A62	5c on 50c sage grn (#498)	8	10
a.		Perf. 11	3.00	3.00
		Nos. 820-827 (8)	64	80

On No. 820–827, the position of the surcharged denomination and "Gold Yuan" characters varies, the aim being to obliterate the original denomination.

Stamps of 1940-48 Surcharged in Black, Violet, Carmine, Blue or Green

壹 金
角 10 圓

Perf. 12, 12½, 13, 14, 12½x13.

1948–49

828	A63	5c on $20 rose (#571)	8	10
829	A72	5c on $30 dp bl (C) (#626)	8	10
a.		Double surch.	10.00	
830	A57	10c on 2c ol grn (#368)	8	10
831	A39	10c on 2½c rose lil (#424)	8	12
832	A62	10c on 25c brn vio (V) (#495)	8	10
833	A63	10c on 40c brn red (#565)	6	10
834	A62	10c on $1 dl grn (#500)	6	10
834A	A62	10c on $1 grn (#551)	25.00	25.00
835	A63	10c on $2 gray brn (#566)	8	10
836	A62	10c on $20 ultra (C) (#560)	8	12
836A	A63	10c on $20 rose (#571)	25.00	25.00
837	A67	10c on $20 car (#592)	12	12
837A	A73	10c on $20 car (#636)	75	60
838	A72	10c on $30 dp bl (C) (#626)	8	10
839	A63	10c on $70 rose vio (#573)	8	10
a.		Double surch.	8.00	
840	A82	10c on $7000 lt red brn (#754)	8	20
841	A82	10c on $20,000 rose pink (#788)	8	40
842	A63	20c on $6 pale lil gray (#569)	8	10
843	A37	20c on $30 choc (#634)	8	12
844	A73	20c on $30 dk bl (C) (#637)	8	10
845	A73	20c on $100 dk car (#640)	8	10
a.		Inverted surch.	11.00	
b.		Double surch.	12.50	
846	A39	50c on ½c blk brn (#312)	15.00	15.00
847	A39	50c on ½c ol blk (#421)	8	10
a.		Inverted surch.	17.50	
848	A62	50c on 20c dk ol grn (#494)	8	10
849	A62	50c on 30c dl ver (Bl) (#496)	8	10
850	A62	50c on 40c dk red brn (V) (#497)	8	10
a.		Perf. 11	3.00	3.50
851	A63	50c on 40c brn red (V) (#565)	8	10
852	A62	50c on $4 vio brn (#556)	8	12
853	A62	50c on $4 vio brn (Bl) (#556)	8	12
854	A62	50c on $20 dp ultra (C) (#560)	8	10
855	A67	50c on $20 car (V) (#592)	8	10
856	A73	50c on $20 car (#636)	8	10
857	A62	50c on $70 lil (C) (#562)	8	10

858	A82	50c on $6000 rose lil (#753)	20	20
859	A82	50c on $6000 rose lil (Bl) (#753)	12	15
860	A62	$1 on 30c choc (#550)	10	12
a.		Perf. 11	30.00	
861	A62	$1 on 40c dk red brn (#497)	8	12
a.		Perf. 11	2.50	3.00
862	A62	$1 on $1 rose lake (#499)	8	10
863	A62	$1 on $5 car (#557)	8	10
864	A63	$2 on $2 gray brn (R) (#566)	8	10
865	A72	$2 on $20 dp car (#625)	8	10
866	A73	$2 on $100 dk car (#640)	8	10
867	A46	$5 on 17c brn ol (#432)	8	10
868	A63	$5 on $2 gray brn (#566)	10	12
869	A82	$5 on $3000 bl (C) (#750)	8	10
870	A47	$8 on 20c lt bl (#433)	8	10
871	A82	$8 on $30,000 choc (C) (#789)	10	12
872	A47	$10 on 40c org (#438)	8	10
873	A63	$10 on $2 gray brn (G) (#566)	8	10
874	A63	$10 on $2 gray brn (C) (#566)	10	12
875	A63	$20 on $2 gray brn (C) (#566)	10	12
875A	A73	$20 on $20 car (#636)	60	60
876	A62	$50 on 30c dl ver (#496)	8	10
877	A63	$50 on $2 gray brn (Bl) (#566)	12	15
878	A73	$80 on $20 car (#636)	15	20
879	A62	$100 on $1 grn (#551)	15	20
a.		Perf. 11	30.00	
880	A63	$100 on $2 gray brn (C) (#566)	15	20
880A	A82	$50,000 on $20,000 rose pink (#788)	35	30
880B	A82	$100,000 on $30,000 choc (V) (#789)	40	30

Wmk. 261.

881	A39	10c on 2½c rose lil (#405)	8	10
882	A39	50c on ½c ol blk (#402)	8	10
		Nos. 828-882 (61)	71.93	73.34

Characters at left express the new value. Style of characters and numerals varies.

Nos. Q7 to Q9 Surcharged in Black or Carmine

金圓伍佰圓 改作郵票 500.00

1948 ***Perf. 12½*** **Unwmkd.**

883	PP2	$200 on $3000 red org	8	10
884	PP2	$500 on $5000 dk bl (C)	10	12
885	PP2	$1000 on $10,000 vio	15	20

Nos. 788-791 Surcharged in Gold Yuan in Red or Black at Foochow

金圓 念萬圓 200000

1949, Apr. 30 ***Perf. 14*** **Unwmkd.**

885A	A82	$20,000 on $40,000 grn	3.00	3.00
885B	A82	$50,000 on $30,000 choc (B)	3.00	3.00
885C	A82	$100,000 on $20,000 rose pink (B)	3.00	3.00
885D	A82	$200,000 on $40,000 grn	3.00	3.00
885E	A82	$200,000 on $50,000 dp bl	3.00	3.00
		Nos. 883A-885E (5)	15.00	15.00

Nos. 885A–885E were issued in Fukien Postal District.

Dr. Sun Yat-sen
A94

Engraved.

1949 ***Perf. 14*** **Unwmkd.**

Without Gum.

886	A94	$1 orange	5	4
887	A94	$10 green	5	4
888	A94	$20 vio brn	5	4
889	A94	$50 dk Prus grn	8	8
890	A94	$100 org brn	5	4
891	A94	$200 red org	6	6
892	A94	$500 rose lil	5	4
893	A94	$800 car rose	20	10
894	A94	$1000 blue	5	4

Redrawn. Engraved.

Perf. 12½

894A	A94	$10 green	20	15
b.		Perf. 14	2.00	2.00
894C	A94	$20 vio brn	10	10
d.		Perf. 14	40	25
		Nos. 886-894C (11)	94	73

Small "T" at left of necktie on Nos. 894A–894d.

Redrawn.

1949 **Lithographed** ***Perf. 12½***

Without Gum

895	A94	$50 grnsh gray	7	7
896	A94	$100 dk org brn	5	5
897	A94	$200 org red	5	5
898	A94	$1000 dp bl	6	6
899	A94	$5000 lt bl	6	6
900	A94	$10,000 sepia	6	6
		Nos. 895-900 (6)	35	35

Diagonal lines have been added to the background of the redrawn design.
See also Nos. 945–958, 973–981.

中華民國郵政
50
金圓伍角

Plane, Train and Ship
A95

Two types, 50c on $20:
- I. Thick numerals in "20." Vertical stroke in lower right corner of vignette. (Dah Tung Book Co.)
- II. Thin "20." No vertical stroke in corner. (Central Trust.)

Two types, $2 on $50, $10 on $30, $100 on $50 and $300 on $50:
- III. "Y" in lower right corner of vignette. (Dah Yeh Printing Co.)
- IV. No "Y" in corner. (Dah Tung, Central Trust or Chung Ming.)

Two types, $50 on $300 and $1000 on $100:
- V. Projection on left frame column below foliate ornament. (Dah Yeh Printing Co.)
- VI. No projection. (Dah Tung Book Co.)

Gold Yuan Surcharge in Various Colors on Revenue Stamps.

Lithographed;

Nos. 923, 933, 935 - 936 Engraved.

1949 ***Perf. 12½, 13, 14***

Without Gum.

915	A95	50c on $20 red brn, I (Bk)	8	4
a.		50c on $20 brn, II (Bk)	8	5
916	A95	$1 on $15 red org (Bk)	8	4
917	A95	$2 on $50 dk bl, IV (C)	8	4
d.		Type III	25	15
917A	A95	$3 on $50 dk bl (Bl)	7	6
917C	A95	$3 on $50 dk bl (Bk)	8	4
918	A95	$5 on $500 brn (Dk Br)	8	4
919	A95	$10 on $30 dk vio, III (Bl)	8	4
a.		Type IV	40	40
b.		Dbl. surch., IV		
920	A95	$15 on $20 org brn (Bl)	8	4
921	A95	$25 on $20 org brn (G)	8	4
922	A95	$50 on $50 dk bl (R O)	8	4
923	A95	$50 on $300 grn, VI (C)	8	4
a.		$50 on $300 yel grn, V (C)	10	10
924	A95	$80 on $50 dk bl (Dk Br)	8	4
925	A95	$100 on $50 dk bl, IV (Bk)	8	4
a.		Type III	35	10
926	A95	$200 on $50 dk bl (Bk)	8	4
927	A95	$200 on $500 brn (Bl)	20	15
928	A95	$300 on $50 dk bl, III (C)	8	4
a.		Type IV	40	40
929	A95	$300 on $50 dk bl (Br)	30	25
930	A95	$500 on $15 red org (Bl)	15	15
931	A95	$500 on $30 dk vio (Bk)	15	15
932	A95	$1000 on $50 dk bl (C)	20	20
933	A95	$1000 on $100 ol grn, V (Bk)	20	20
a.		Type VI	2.50	2.50
934	A95	$1500 on $50 dk bl (Bl)	1.00	60
935	A95	$2000 on $300 grn (Bl)	20	10
936	A95	$5000 on $100 ol grn (C)	100.00	
		Nos. 915-935 (23)	3.59	2.42

No. 936 was officially authorized, but never issued.

Key pattern of overprinted border inverted and in 2 or 3 detached sections at top and bottom.

Hankow Prints.

Lithographed.

Without Gum.

937	A95	$50 on $10 sl grn (Bk)	1.00	75
938	A95	$100 on $10 sl grn (Bl)	3.00	1.75
939	A95	$500 on $10 sl grn (Bk)	3.00	1.75
940	A95	$1000 on $10 sl grn (Bl)	1.25	35
941	A95	$5000 on $20 red brn (Bl)	2.00	50
942	A95	$10,000 on $20 red brn (Bk)	1.75	75
943	A95	$50,000 on $20 red brn (Bl)	1.75	75
944	A95	$100,000 on $20 red brn (Bk)	1.75	75
944A	A95	$500,000 on $20 red brn (Bl)	125.00	37.50
944B	A95	$2,000,000 on $20 red brn (G)	225.00	100.00
944C	A95	$5,000,000 on $20 red brn (Bl)	450.00	200.00
		Nos. 937-944C (11)	815.50	344.85

The basic revenue stamps of Nos. 915-944C were the work of several printers. There are three main types, differing in the bottom label. Nos. 922 and 925 are in a second type: Nos. 923 and 930 in a third. Varieties of paper, color and overprint exist.
Counterfeits exist of Nos. 944A–944C.

Type of 1949 Redrawn.

1949 **Without Gum** ***Perf. 12½***

945	A94	$500 rose lil	7	7
946	A94	$2000 violet	8	8
947	A94	$20,000 ap grn	8	8
948	A94	$50,000 rose pink	15	15
949	A94	$80,000 brn red	50	50
950	A94	$100,000 bl grn	25	25
		Nos. 945-950 (6)	1.13	1.13

Zeros for "cents" omitted on No. 950.

Redrawn Coarse Impression

1949 **Litho.** **Without Gum**

Size: 18¼x20¾mm.

951	A94	$50 green	50	35
952	A94	$1000 dp bl	40	20
953	A94	$5000 carmine	50	30
954	A94	$10,000 brown	40	20
955	A94	$20,000 orange	50	40
956	A94	$50,000 blue	50	40
957	A94	$200,000 violet	50	40
958	A94	$500,000 vio brn	50	40
		Nos. 951-958 (8)	3.80	2.65

Zeros for "cents" omitted on Nos. 957-958.

Locomotive and Ship
A96

1949, May 1 **Litho.** ***Perf. 12½***

Without Gum

959	A96	orange	85	40
a.		Rouletted	1.50	1.20

Nos. 959, C62, E12 and F2 were printed without denomination and sold at the daily rate of the yuan. This was necessitated by the gold yuan inflation.

Revenue Stamps Overprinted in Black

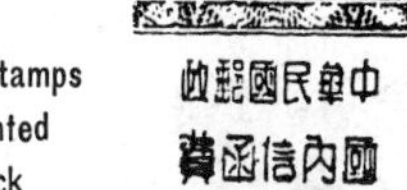

1949, May ***Perf. 12½, 13, 14***

Without Gum

960	A95	$30 dk vio	60.00	40.00

Engraved.

961	A95	$200 vio brn	7.00	5.00
962	A95	$500 dk grn	7.00	5.00

A similar overprint appears on Nos. C63, E13 and F3, differing in second and third characters of bottom row.

Silver Yuan Surcharge in Various Colors

中華郵政
郵資壹角
10

1949 **Lithographed**

963	A95	1c on $5000 brn (G)	60	40
964	A95	4c on $100 ol grn (Bl)	25	30
965	A95	4c on $3000 org (Bk)	25	30
966	A95	10c on $50 dk bl (RV)	25	30
967	A95	10c on $1000 car (Bk)	40	25
a.		Inverted surch.	50.00	
968	A95	20c on $1000 red (V)	40	80
b.		Inverted surch.	17.50	
968A	A95	50c on $30 dk vio (C)	30	50
969	A95	50c on $50 dk bl (C)	1.25	50
970	A95	$1 on $50 dk bl (Bk)	75	50
		Nos. 963-970 (9)	4.45	3.85

Nos. 963-965 and 967 are engraved.

Sun Type of 1949 Redrawn.

Coarse Impression.

Perf. 12½, 13 or Compound

1949

973	A94	1c ap grn	25	50
974	A94	2c orange	35	50
975	A94	4c bl grn	10	10
976	A94	10c dp lil	10	25
977	A94	16c org red	75	1.25
978	A94	20c blue	30	30
979	A94	50c dk brn	2.00	2.00

980	A94	100c dp bl	100.00	100.00
981	A94	500c scarlet	125.00	125.00
		Nos. 973-981 (9)	228.85	229.90

Flying Geese Over Globe — A97

Pigeons, Globe and Wreath — A98

1949, May Litho. *Perf. 12½*

Without Gum

984	A97	$1 brn org	3.00	2.00
985	A97	$2 blue	6.00	2.50
986	A97	$5 car rose	9.00	5.00
987	A97	$10 bl grn	17.50	6.50

Five other denominations—10c, 16c, 50c, $20 and $50—were also printed at Shanghai, but were not issued.

Engraved and Typographed.

1949, Aug. 1 Without Gum *Imperf.*

988	A98	$1 org red & blk	2.50	3.00

Issued to commemorate the 75th anniversary of the formation of the Universal Postal Union.

Exists with black denomination omitted.

Summer Palace, Peiping — A99

Bronze Bull and Kunming Lake — A100

Engraved and Typographed.

1949, Aug. *Rouletted*

Without Gum

989	A99	15c org brn & grn	18	30
990	A100	40c dl grn & car	22	30
a.		2nd and 3rd characters at top transposed	40.00	50.00

Silver Yuan Surcharge in Black on 1949 Sun Yat-sen Issues

1 壹 分

1949 *Perf. 12½, 14*

991	A94	1c on $100 org brn (890)	2.00	1.50
992	A94	1c on $100 dk org brn (896)	2.25	1.75
993	A94	2½c on $500 rose lil (892)	2.50	2.00
a.		Inverted surch.	15.00	
994	A94	2½c on $500 rose lil (945)	2.50	2.00
995	A94	15c on $10 grn (887)	5.00	4.00
a.		Inverted surch.	15.00	
996	A94	15c on $20 vio brn (894C)	7.50	6.00
		Nos. 991-996 (6)	21.75	17.25

Silver Yuan Surcharge in Black or Carmine

5 伍 分

997	A94	2½c on $50 grn (951)	60	50
998	A94	2½c on $50,000 bl (956)	60	50
999	A94	5c on $1000 dp bl (952) (C)	1.00	75
1000	A94	5c on $20,000 org (955)	1.00	75
1001	A94	5c on $200,000 vio (957) (C)	1.00	1.00
1002	A94	5c on $500,000 vio brn (958)	1.00	1.00
1003	A94	10c on $5000 car (953)	1.50	1.25
1004	A94	10c on $10,000 brn (954)	1.50	1.00
1005	A94	15c on $200 red org (891)	2.00	2.00
1006	A94	25c on $100 dk org brn (896)	4.00	4.00
		Nos. 997-1006 (10)	14.20	12.75

Republic of China (Taiwan)

LOCATION (since 1949)—Taiwan (Formosa).

GOVT.—Republic.

AREA—13,892 sq. mi.

POP.—16,700,000 (est. 1978).

CAPITAL—Taipei.

Stamps issued and used in Taiwan after Communist forces occupied the Chinese mainland include Taiwan Nos. 91–96, 101–103, J10–J17.

Type of 1949 with Value Omitted Surcharged in Various Colors

壹 臺 圓 幣 1 00

1950, Jan. 1 *Perf. 12½* Unwmkd.

1007	A97	$1 grn (Bk)	15.00	1.50
1008	A97	$2 grn (C)	20.00	5.00
1009	A97	$5 grn (V)	250.00	20.00
1010	A97	$10 grn (Br)	300.00	75.00
1011	A97	$20 grn (Dk Bl)	600.00	275.00
		Nos. 1007-1011 (5)	1,185.	376.50

Two printings of the $1 and $2 show minor differences.

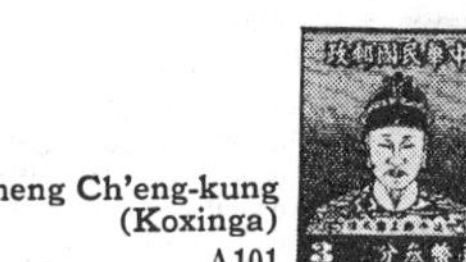

Cheng Ch'eng-kung (Koxinga) — A101

1950, June 26 Typo. *Rouletted*

Without Gum.

1012	A101	3c dk gray grn	35	10
1013	A101	10c org brn	35	10
1014	A101	15c org yel	4.00	1.00
1015	A101	20c emerald	75	15
1016	A101	30c claret	11.00	5.00
1017	A101	40c red org	1.25	15
1018	A101	50c chocolate	1.50	25
1019	A101	80c carmine	2.50	1.25
1020	A101	$1 ultra	3.00	15
1021	A101	$1.50 green	8.00	1.00
1022	A101	$1.60 blue	11.00	75
1023	A101	$2 red vio	15.00	75
1024	A101	$5 aqua	40.00	4.50
		Nos. 1012-1024 (13)	98.70	15.15

Part perforate pairs exist of the 10c, 20c, and 80c.

Stamps of 1947-48 Surcharged in Carmine or Black

臺幣叁分 3

1950, Mar. 25 *Perf. 14*

1025	A82	3c on $30,000 choc	1.50	1.25
1026	A82	3c on $40,000 grn (C)	1.50	1.25
1027	A82	3c on $50,000 dp bl (C)	2.00	1.25
1028	A82	5c on $200,000 brn vio	2.00	1.25
1029	A82	10c on $4000 gray	4.00	2.00
a.		Inverted surch.	50.00	
1030	A82	10c on $6000 rose lil	5.00	2.00
a.		Inverted surch.	125.00	
1031	A82	10c on $20,000 rose pink	6.00	3.00
1032	A82	10c on $2,000,000 ver	6.00	3.00
a.		Inverted surch.	75.00	
1033	A82	20c on $500,000 lil rose	6.50	3.50
a.		Inverted surch.	100.00	
1034	A82	20c on $1,000,000 cl	6.50	5.00
a.		Inverted surch.	100.00	
1035	A82	30c on $3,000,000 ol bis	12.50	7.50
1036	A82	50c on $5,000,000 ultra (C)	20.00	15.00
		Nos. 1025-1036 (12)	73.50	46.00

Allegory of Election — A102

Perf. 12x12½, Imperf.

1951, Mar. 20 Engraved Unwmkd.

Without Gum

1037	A102	40c carmine	3.00	35
a.		Horiz. pair, imperf. btwn.	60.00	
1038	A102	$1 dp bl	6.00	1.25
1039	A102	$1.60 purple	9.00	1.50
1040	A102	$2 brown	14.00	3.00

Adoption of local self-government in Taiwan.

Souvenir Sheet.

Imperf.

1041	A102	$2 dp bl grn	37.50	37.50

Marginal inscriptions publicize Postal Commemorative Day, Mar. 20, 1951. Size: 100x71 mm.

Type A97 Surcharged — A103

Farmer and Scroll Announcing Tax Reduction — A104

Surcharge in Various Colors.

1951, July 19 Without Gum *Perf. 12½*

1042	A103	$5 grn (R Br)	14.00	3.00
1043	A103	$10 grn (Bk)	37.50	4.00
1044	A103	$20 grn (R)	150.00	17.50
1045	A103	$50 grn (P)	300.00	35.00

1952, Jan. 1 *Imperf., Perf. 14*

Without Gum

1046	A104	20c red org	3.00	1.75
1047	A104	40c dk grn	6.00	2.25
1048	A104	$1 brown	8.00	5.00
1049	A104	$1.40 dp bl	14.00	9.00
1050	A104	$2 dk gray	20.00	10.00
1051	A104	$5 brn car	27.50	12.00
		Nos. 1046-1051 (6)	78.50	40.00

Land tax reduction of 37.5% in Taiwan.

Pres. Chiang Kai-shek, Flag and Followers — A105

Imperf., Perf. 14

1952, Mar. 1 Unwmkd.

Without Gum

Flag in Violet Blue and Carmine.

1052	A105	40c rose car	3.50	60
a.		Vert. pair, imperf. btwn.	35.00	
1053	A105	$1 dp grn	6.00	2.00
1054	A105	$1.60 brn org	14.00	1.25
a.		Horiz. pair, imperf. btwn.	90.00	
1055	A105	$2 brt bl	17.50	5.00
1056	A105	$5 vio brn	22.50	3.00
		Nos. 1052-1056 (5)	63.50	11.85

Issued to commemorate the 2nd anniversary of Chiang Kai-shek's return to the presidency.

See Nos. 1064 - 1069.

Nos. 975, 976, 978 and 979 Surcharged in Black

叁 臺 分 幣 3

1952 *Perf. 12½.*

1057	A94	3c on 4c bl grn	1.75	75
1058	A94	3c on 10c dp lil	1.75	75
a.		Inverted surch.		
1059	A94	3c on 20c bl	1.75	75
1060	A94	3c on 50c dk brn	1.75	75

Geese Type of 1949 with Value Omitted Surcharged

臺幣壹拾圓 10 00

1952, Dec. 8

1061	A97	$10 grn (P)	40.00	7.50
1062	A97	$20 grn (R)	150.00	15.00
1063	A97	$50 grn (Bk)	650.00	225.00

Chiang Type of 1952 Redrawn.

Perf. 12½

1953, Mar. 1 Engraved Unwmkd.

Without Gum

Flag in Dark Blue & Carmine.

1064	A105	10c red org	4.00	40
1065	A105	20c green	4.00	45
1066	A105	40c rose pink	7.50	60
1067	A105	$1.40 blue	15.00	75
1068	A105	$2 brown	20.00	1.50
1069	A105	$5 rose vio	40.00	2.50
		Nos. 1064-1069 (6)	90.50	6.20

Third anniversary of Chiang Kai-shek's return to presidency.

Many differences in redrawn design.

Price, imperf. set, $100

Nos. 1020, 1014, 1016 and 1022 Surcharged in Various Colors

3 cts. 叁 分

1953–54 *Rouletted.*

1070	A101	3c on $1 ultra (C)	1.50	25
1070A	A101	10c on 15c org yel (G) ('54)	12.50	50
1071	A101	10c on 30c cl (Bl)	1.50	30
1072	A101	20c on $1.60 bl (Bk)	1.50	30

Chinese characters and ornamental device at bottom differ on each value.

Nurse and Patients — A106

1953, July 1 Litho. *Perf. 12½*

Without Gum

Cross in Red, Burelage Color in Italics.

No.	Type	Description	Unused	Used
1073	A106	40c brn, *buff*	6.00	60
1074	A106	$1.60 bl, *bl*	9.00	70
1075	A106	$2 grn, *yel*	22.50	1.25
1076	A106	$5 red org, *org*	30.00	3.50

Issued to honor the Chinese Anti-Tuberculosis Association.

Pres. Chiang Kai-shek
A107

1953, Oct. 31 Engraved

Without Gum

No.	Type	Description	Unused	Used
1077	A107	10c dk brn	50	10
1078	A107	20c lilac	1.50	10
1079	A107	40c dp grn	1.50	12
1080	A107	50c dp pink	1.50	10
1081	A107	80c brn bis	10.00	40
1082	A107	$1 dp ol grn	4.00	15
1083	A107	$1.40 dp bl	7.50	60
1084	A107	$1.60 dp car	10.00	50
1085	A107	$1.70 ap grn	5.00	1.50
1086	A107	$2 brown	6.00	20
1087	A107	$3 dk bl	35.00	3.00
1088	A107	$4 aqua	15.00	1.00
1089	A107	$5 red org	8.00	1.25
1090	A107	$10 dk grn	12.50	2.00
1091	A107	$20 dk brn lake	35.00	4.50
a.		Souvenir folder	40.00	
		Nos. 1077-1091 (15)	153.00	15.52

67th birthday of Pres. Chiang Kai-shek.
No. 1091a contains Nos. 1077–1091 imperf., arranged in 3 sheets of 5 stamps each.

Silo Highway Bridge
A108

Forest of Evergreens
A109

Design: $1.60 and $5, Silo bridge, side view.

Without Gum

1954, Jan. 28 *Perf. 12½* Unwmkd.

Various Frames.

No.	Type	Description	Unused	Used
1092	A108	40c vermilion	2.00	50
1093	A108	$1.60 bl vio	27.50	75
1094	A108	$3.60 sepia	11.00	1.50
1095	A108	$5 magenta	35.00	2.50
a.		Souv. sheet	40.00	

Opening of Silo bridge, 1st anniversary.
No. 1095a contains one each of Nos. 1092–1095 imperforate.

1954, Mar. 12 *Perf. 12x12½*

Design: $10, Nursery.

Without Gum

No.	Type	Description	Unused	Used
1096	A109	40c bl grn	12.00	60
1097	A109	$10 red vio	30.00	3.50

Issued to publicize forest conservation.

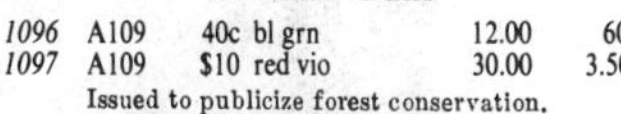

Runner
A110

Globe, Bridge and Ship
A111

1954, Mar. 29 Without Gum

No.	Type	Description	Unused	Used
1098	A110	40c dp ultra	15.00	1.25
1099	A110	$5 carmine	30.00	5.00

Issued to publicize 11th Youth Day, March 29, 1954.

1954, Oct. 21 *Perf. 12*

Without Gum

No.	Type	Description	Unused	Used
1100	A111	40c red org	11.00	30
1101	A111	$5 dp bl	7.00	1.50

Issued to publicize the second Overseas Chinese Day, October 21, 1954.

Ex-Prisoner with Broken Chains
A112

Designs: $1, Ex-prisoner with torch and flag, UN emblem. $1.60, Torch and date.

1955, Jan. 23

No.	Type	Description	Unused	Used
1102	A112	40c bl grn	1.75	40
a.		Vert. pair, imperf. btwn.	150.00	
1103	A112	$1 sepia	14.00	1.75
1104	A112	$1.60 lake	17.50	1.60

Issued to honor anti-Communist Chinese prisoners who fought with the North Korean army, released January 23, 1955.

Nos. 1019–1021, 1017 Surcharged in Brown, Blue or Green:

a

b

c

1955 *Rouletted*

No.	Type	Description	Unused	Used
1105	A101 (a)	3c on $1 ultra (Br)	2.00	60
1106	A101 (b)	10c on 80c car (Bl)	2.00	60
1107	A101 (b)	10c on $1.50 grn (Bl)	2.00	60
1108	A101 (c)	20c on 40c red org (G)	2.00	60

Hand Planting Evergreen Tree
A113

Chiang Kai-shek, Flags, Building
A114

Design: $50, Seedling and map of Taiwan.

1955, Apr. 1 *Perf. 12*

Without Gum

No.	Type	Description	Unused	Used
1109	A113	$20 dp car	14.00	1.50
1110	A113	$50 blue	25.00	5.50

Issued to publicize forest conservation.

1955, May 20 Engraved *Perf. 12*

Without Gum

No.	Type	Description	Unused	Used
1111	A114	20c olive	1.50	10
1112	A114	40c bl grn	2.00	10
1113	A114	$2 car rose	4.00	60
1114	A114	$7 dp ultra	8.50	1.25
a.		Souvenir sheet of 4	20.00	20.00

No. 1114a contains one each of Nos. 1111–1114, imperforate, with ornamental border typographed in red.
First anniversary of Pres. Chiang Kai-shek's re-election.

Armed Forces Emblem
A115

1955, Sept. 3 Without Gum

No.	Type	Description	Unused	Used
1115	A115	40c dk bl	1.75	20
1116	A115	$2 org ver	12.50	60
1117	A115	$7 bl grn	11.50	1.25
a.		Sheet of three	32.50	32.50

Armed Forces Day, Sept. 3.
No. 1117a measures 147x104mm. and contains one each of Nos. 1115–1117.

Nos. 1017, 1018 and C64 Surcharged in Magenta

1955 Typographed *Rouletted*

No.	Type	Description	Unused	Used
1118	A101	20c on 40c red org	2.25	60
1119	A101	20c on 50c choc	2.25	60
1120	AP6	20c on 60c dp bl	2.25	60

Flags of U.N. and China
A116

1955, Oct. 24 Engraved *Perf. 11½*

Without Gum.

No.	Type	Description	Unused	Used
1121	A116	40c dk bl	1.75	20
1122	A116	$2 dk car rose	6.00	60
1123	A116	$7 sl grn	5.25	1.25

Issued to commemorate the tenth anniversary of the United Nations, Oct. 24, 1955.

Pres. Chiang Kai-shek
A117

Birthplace of Sun Yat-sen
A118

1955, Oct. 31 Photo. *Perf. 13½*

No.	Type	Description	Unused	Used
1124	A117	40c dk bl, red & brn	1.75	20
1125	A117	$2 grn, red & dk bl	4.50	60
1126	A117	$7 brn, red & grn	6.00	1.25
a.		Souvenir sheet of 3	12.50	12.50

69th birthday of Pres. Chiang Kai-shek.
No. 1126a measures 147x105 mm. and contains one each of Nos. 1124–1126, imperf.

1955, Nov. 12 Engraved *Perf. 12*

Without Gum

No.	Type	Description	Unused	Used
1127	A118	40c blue	1.75	20
1128	A118	$2 red brn	4.00	75
1129	A118	$7 rose lake	6.00	1.25

90th anniversary, birth of Sun Yat-sen.

No. 959a Surcharged in Bright Green

角貳

0.20

1956 Litho. *Rouletted*

No.	Type	Description	Unused	Used
1130	A96	20c on org	35	15

See also No. 1213.

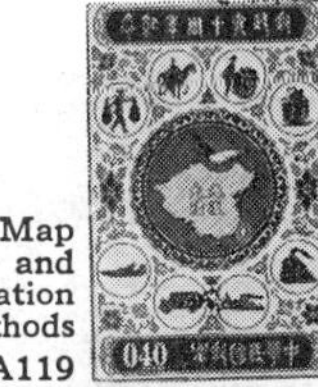

China Map and Transportation Methods
A119

Wmk. 281

Wmkd. Wavy Lines (281).

1956, Mar. 20 Engraved *Perf. 12*

Without Gum

No.	Type	Description	Unused	Used
1131	A119	40c dk car	40	15
1132	A119	$1 int blk	75	40
1133	A119	$1.60 chocolate	1.50	20
1134	A119	$2 dk grn	2.00	40

Issued to commemorate the 60th anniversary of the founding of the modern Chinese postal system.

Souvenir Sheets

Imperf.

No.	Type	Description	Unused	Used
1135	A119	$2 magenta	4.50	4.50
1136	A119	$2 red	4.50	4.50

Issued for the exhibition for the 60th anniversary of the modern Chinese postal system, March 20, 1956.
Nos. 1135-36 measure 148x103mm. Marginal floral design and inscription in red and silver (No. 1135), and red and gold (No. 1136).

Children at Play
A120

Early and Modern Locomotives
A121

1956, Apr. 4 *Perf. 12* Unwmkd.

Without Gum.

No.	Type	Description	Unused	Used
1137	A120	40c emerald	50	10
1138	A120	$1.60 dk bl	1.25	20
1139	A120	$2 dk car	1.75	70

Children's Day, Apr. 4, 1956.

1956, June 9 Wmk. 281 (vert.)

Without Gum

No.	Type	Description	Unused	Used
1140	A121	40c rose car	1.25	10
1141	A121	$2 blue	1.25	15
1142	A121	$8 green	3.75	75

75th anniversary of Chinese Railroads.

Pres. Chiang Kai-shek
A122 A123

A124
Various Portraits of Chiang

Perf. 14½x13½,
14½ (A123), 13½x14½

1956, Oct. 31 Photo. Unwmkd.

1143	A122	20c	red org	40	10
1144	A122	40c	car rose	1.20	10
1145	A123	$1	brt ultra	90	20
1146	A123	$1.60	red lil	1.50	20
1147	A124	$2	red brn	3.50	25
1148	A124	$8	brt grnsh bl	8.00	1.00
			Nos. 1143-1148 (6)	15.50	1.85

Issued in honor of the 70th birthday of Pres. Chiang Kai-shek.

Types of Special Delivery, Air Post and Registration Stamps of 1949 Surcharged in Black or Maroon

分叁

a

分叁 角壹

$0.10

b *c*

Lithographed.

1956 *Rouletted* Unwmkd.

Without Gum.

1150	SD2 (a)	3c	red vio	85	20
a.			Perf. 12½	1.25	60
1151	AP5 (b)	3c	bl grn (M)	85	20
1152	R2 (c)	10c	brt red	85	20

Telecommunications Emblem and Radio Tower
A125

Engraved.

1956, Dec. 28 *Perf. 12* Wmk. 281

Without Gum.

1153	A125	40c	dp ultra	18	10
1154	A125	$1.40	carmine	30	10
1155	A125	$1.60	dk grn	45	10
1156	A125	$2	chocolate	2.50	30

Issued to commemorate the 75th anniversary of the founding of the Chinese telegraph service.

Map of China Mother Instructing Mencius
A126 A127

Pin Perf., Perf. 12x12½

1957 Lithographed. Wmk. 281

Without Gum.

1157	A126	3c	brt bl	35	6
1158	A126	10c	violet	35	10
1159	A126	20c	red org	35	10
1160	A126	40c	rose red	35	10

Unwmkd.

1161	A126	$1	org brn	60	10
1162	A126	$1.60	green	90	20
			Nos. 1157-1162 (6)	2.90	66

Map inscription reads: "Recovery of Mainland."

See also Nos. 1177-82.

Engraved

1957, May 12 *Perf. 12* Unwmkd.

Design: $3, Mother tattooing Yueh Fei.

Without Gum

1163	A127	40c	green	50	20
1164	A127	$3	redsh brn	1.25	35

Issued to honor Mother's Day, 1957.

Badge of Chinese Boy Scouts
A128

1957, Aug. 11 Without Gum

1165	A128	40c	lilac	25	10
1166	A128	$1	green	45	15
1167	A128	$1.60	dk bl	65	20

Issued to commemorate the centenary of the birth of Lord Baden-Powell and to publicize the World Scout Jubilee Jamboree, England, Aug. 1-12.

Globe, Radio Tower and Microphone—A129

1957, Sept. 16 Without Gum

1168	A129	40c	vermilion	25	10
1169	A129	50c	brt rose lil	45	20
1170	A129	$3.50	dk bl	1.10	35

Issued to commemorate the 30th anniversary of Chinese broadcasting.

Map of Taiwan
A130

1957, Oct. 26 Without Gum

1171	A130	40c	bl grn	45	10
1172	A130	$1.40	lt ultra	1.15	35
1173	A130	$2	gray	1.50	40

Issued to commemorate the start of construction on the Cross Island Highway, Taiwan.

Freighter "Hai Min" and River Boat "Kiang Foo"
A131

1957, Dec. 16 Engraved *Perf. 12*

Without Gum.

1174	A131	40c	dp ultra	25	10
1175	A131	80c	rose lake	60	15
1176	A131	$2.80	vermilion	1.50	50

Issued to commemorate the 85th anniversary of the establishment of the China Merchants Steam Navigation Co.

Type of 1957.

1957, Dec. 25 Typo. Unwmkd.

Pin Perf., Perf. 12x12½

Without Gum.

Dark Blue Frames.

1177	A126	3c	brt bl	30	10
1178	A126	10c	violet	30	15
1179	A126	20c	brick red	30	15
a.			Booklet pane of 6		
b.			Booklet pane of 4		
1180	A126	40c	rose red	70	25
a.			Booklet pane of 6		
b.			Booklet pane of 4		
1181	A126	$1	dp org brn	70	15
a.			Booklet pane of 6		
1182	A126	$1.60	dp grn	1.00	15
			Nos. 1177-1182 (6)	3.30	95

Butterfly Mme. Chiang Kai-shek Orchid
A132 A133

Photogravure.

1958, Mar. 20 *Perf. 13½* Unwmkd.

Various Insects in Natural Colors

1183	A132	10c	pale grn, grn & blk	30	10
1184	A132	40c	lem, pink, grn & blk	30	15
1185	A132	$1	yel grn & mar	45	15
1186	A132	$1.40	yel, org & blk	60	20
1187	A132	$1.60	pale brn & dk pur	70	20
1188	A132	$2	brt yel, org & blk	90	30
			Nos. 1183-1188 (6)	3.25	1.10

1958, Mar. 20

Orchids: 20c, Formosan Wilson (horiz.). $1.40, Klotzsch. $3, Fitzgerald (horiz.).

Orchids in Natural Colors.

1189	A133	20c	chocolate	30	15
1190	A133	40c	purple	45	15
1191	A133	$1.40	dk vio brn	60	25
1192	A133	$3	dk bl	90	50

World Health Organization Emblem
A134

1958, May 28 Engraved *Perf. 12*

Without Gum.

1193	A134	40c	dk bl	15	10
1194	A134	$1.60	brick red	40	10
1195	A134	$2	dp red lil	75	30

Issued to commemorate the 10th anniversary of the World Health Organization.

President's Mansion, Taipei
A135

Wmk. 323
Wmk. 323 is found with "Yu" in various arrangements.

Wmkd.

Seal Character 'Yu' (323)

1958, Sept. 20 Engraved *Perf. 12*

Without Gum

1196	A135	$10	bl grn	3.50	10
a.			Granite paper ('63)	3.00	10
1197	A135	$20	car rose	5.00	30
a.			Granite paper ('63)	4.50	10
1198	A135	$50	red brn	20.00	1.75
1199	A135	$100	dk bl	35.00	3.50

See also Nos. 1349-1351.

Taiwan Farm Scene
A136

1958, Oct. 1 Unwmkd.

Without Gum

1200	A136	20c	emerald	15	8
1201	A136	40c	black	15	8
1202	A136	$1.40	brt mag	60	10
1203	A136	$3	ultra	1.40	40

Issued to commemorate the tenth anniversary of the Joint Commission on Rural Reconstruction.

Pres. Chiang Kai-shek
A137

1958, Oct. 31 Photo. *Perf. 13½*

Without Gum.

1204	A137	40c	multi	40	15

Issued to honor Pres. Chiang Kai-shek on his 72nd birthday.

UNESCO Building, Paris
A138

1958, Nov. 3 Engraved ***Perf. 12***
Without Gum.

1205	A138	20c dk bl	12	8
1206	A138	40c green	18	8
1207	A138	$1 40 org ver	70	10
1208	A138	$3 red lil	1.00	40

Issued to commemorate the opening of UNESCO (U. N. Educational, Scientific and Cultural Organization) Headquarters in Paris, Nov. 3.

Flame from Liberty Torch Encircling Globe
A139

1958, Dec. 10 Unwmkd.
Without Gum

1209	A139	40c green	12	8
1210	A139	60c gray brn	18	8
1211	A139	$1 carmine	50	15
1212	A139	$3 ultra	1.00	40

Issued to commemorate the tenth anniversary of the signing of the Universal Declaration of Human Rights.

No. 959a Surcharged In Bright Green

0.20

Rouletted

1958, Dec. 11 Litho. Unwmkd.
Without Gum

1213	A96	20c on org	30	10

Ballot Box, Scales and Constitution
A140

1958, Dec. 25 Engraved ***Perf. 12***
Without Gum.

1214	A140	40c green	18	8
1215	A140	50c dl pur	25	8
1216	A140	$1.40 car rose	75	15
1217	A140	$3.50 dk bl	1.25	50

Issued to commemorate the 10th anniversary of the adoption of the constitution.

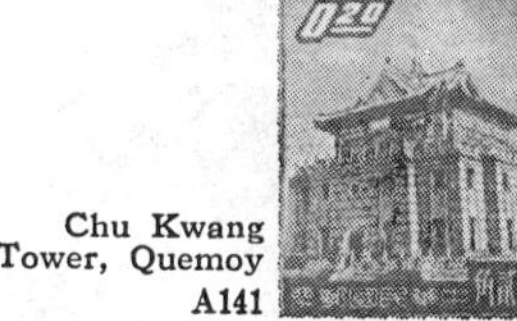

Chu Kwang Tower, Quemoy
A141

Lithographed.

1959–60 ***Perf. 12*** Wmk. 323
Without Gum.

1218	A141	3c orange	12	5
1218A	A141	5c lt yel grn ('60)	12	8
1219	A141	10c lilac	12	5
1220	A141	20c ultra	12	5
1221	A141	40c brown	18	5
1222	A141	50c bluish grn	30	5
1223	A141	$1 rose red	50	5
1224	A141	$1.40 yel grn	70	5
1225	A141	$2 gray grn	70	8
1226	A141	$2.80 rose pink	1.20	8
1227	A141	$3 sl bl	1.20	9
		Nos. 1218-1227 (11)	5.26	68

See also Nos. 1270–1283.

ILO Emblem and Headquarters, Geneva
A142

1959, June 15 Engraved ***Perf. 12***
Without Gum

1228	A142	40c blue	12	6
1229	A142	$1.60 dk brn	30	6
1230	A142	$3 brt bl grn	60	15
1231	A142	$5 org ver	1.50	40

Issued to commemorate the 40th anniversary of the International Labor Organization.

Bugler and Tents
A143

1959, July 8 Unwmkd.
Without Gum

1232	A143	40c carmine	20	10
1233	A143	50c dk bl	60	15
1234	A143	$5 green	1.50	50

Issued to publicize the 10th World Boy Scout Jamboree, at Makiling National Park, Philippines, July 17–26.

Inscribed Stone, Mt. Tai-wu, Quemoy
A144

Map of Taiwan Straits
A145

1959, Sept. 3 Engraved ***Perf. 12***
Without Gum.

1235	A144	40c brown	20	10
1236	A145	$1.40 ultra	50	15
1237	A145	$2 green	1.10	30
1238	A144	$3 dk bl	1.40	40

Defense of Quemoy and Matsu islands.

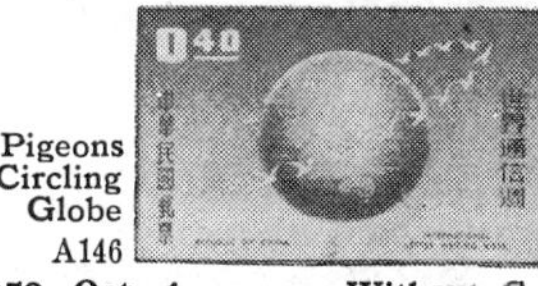

Pigeons Circling Globe
A146

1959, Oct. 4 Without Gum

1239	A146	40c blue	15	10
1240	A146	$1 rose car	30	15
1241	A146	$2 gray brn	50	10
1242	A146	$3.50 red org	1.10	40

Issued for International Letter Writing Week, Oct. 4–10.

National Taiwan Science Hall, Taipei—A147

Design: $3, Front view.

1959, Nov. 12 Photo. ***Perf. 13x13½***

1243	A147	40c multi	85	15
1244	A147	$3 multi	1.75	45

Emblem
A148

1959, Dec. 7 Engraved ***Perf. 12***
Without Gum

1245	A148	40c bl grn	25	10
1246	A148	$1.60 red lil	60	15
1247	A148	$3 orange	1.00	30

Issued to commemorate the 10th anniversary of the International Confederation of Free Trade Unions.

Sun Yat-sen, Lincoln and Flags
A149

Perf. 13½, 12

1959, Dec. 25 Photo. Unwmkd.

1248	A149	40c multi	30	10
1249	A149	$3 multi	1.40	20

Issued to honor Sun Yat-sen and Abraham Lincoln as "Leaders of Democracy."

Mailman on Motorcycle Delivering Night Mail
A150

Postal Launch
A151

1960, Mar. 20 Engraved ***Perf. 11½***
Without Gum

1250	A150	$1.40 dk vio brn	65	15
1251	A151	$1.60 ultra	85	20

Issued to publicize the Prompt Delivery Service.

WRY Uprooted Oak Emblem
A152

1960, Apr. 7 Photo. ***Perf. 13***

1252	A152	40c blk, red brn & emer	25	10
1253	A152	$3 blk, red org & grn	65	30

Issued to publicize World Refugee Year, July 1, 1959–June 30, 1960.

Cross Island Highway, Taiwan
A153

Design: $1, $2, Road through tunnel (vert.).

Perf. 11½

1960, May 9 Engr. Unwmkd.
Without Gum

1254	A153	40c green	30	10
1255	A153	$1 dk bl	95	40
1256	A153	$2 brn vio	40	20
1257	A153	$3 brown	1.25	25
a.		Souv. sheet of 2, wmk. 323	22.50	22.50

Issued to commemorate the opening of the Cross Island Highway, Taiwan.

No. 1257a contains imperf. copies of Nos. 1255 and 1257, with multicolored pictorial background and marginal inscriptions in red. Size: 144x103mm.

Red Overprint on Nos. 1237–1238
Chinese and English:
"Welcome U.S. President
Dwight D. Eisenhower 1960"

1960, June 18 ***Perf. 12*** Unwmkd.

1258	A145	$2 green	50	15
a.		Invtd. ovpt.	135.00	135.00
1259	A144	$3 dk bl	1.00	40

Issued to commemorate President Eisenhower's visit to China, June 18, 1960.

Phonopost
A154

1960, June 27 Without Gum

1260	A154	$2 red org	70	20

Issued to publicize the Phonopost Service of the Chinese armed forces.

Two Horses and Groom, by Han Kan
A155

Paintings from Palace Museum, Taichung: $1, Two Riders, by Wei Yen. $1.60, Flowers and Birds by Hsiao Yung (vert.). $2, Pair of Mandarin Ducks by Monk Hui Ch'ung.

1960, Aug. 4 Photo. *Perf. 13*

1261 A155 $1 ol gray, blk & brn 85 30
1262 A155 $1.40 bis brn, blk & fawn 1.00 30
1263 A155 $1.60 multi 1.40 40
1264 A155 $2 beige, blk & gray grn 2.50 75

Chinese paintings, 7th–11th centuries.

Youth Corps Flag and Summer Activities **Reforestation**
A156 **A157**

Design: $3, similar to 50c (horiz.).

1960, Aug. 20 Engraved *Perf. 12*
Without Gum

1265 A156 50c sl grn 40 10
1266 A156 $3 cop brn 1.40 40

Summer activities of China Youth Corps.

1960, Aug. 29 Photo. *Perf. 13½x13*

Designs: $2, Protection of forest. $3, Timber industry.

1267 A157 $1 multi 50 10
1268 A157 $2 multi 1.20 40
1269 A157 $3 multi 1.20 40
a. Souvenir sheet of 3 1.75 1.75

Issued to commemorate the Fifth World Forestry Congress, Seattle, Washington, Aug. 29–Sept. 10.

No. 1269a contains Nos. 1267–1269 assembled as a triptych, 65½x40mm. and imperf., but with simulated black perforations. Marginal inscriptions in carmine. Size of sheet: 99x144½mm.

Chu Kwang Tower, Quemoy **Diver**
A158 **A159**

Lithographed

1960–61 *Perf. 12* Wmk. 323
Without Gum

1270 A158 3c lt red brn 15 5
1271 A158 40c pale vio 15 5
1272 A158 50c org ('61) 15 5
1273 A158 60c rose lil 15 5
1274 A158 80c pale grn 20 5
1275 A158 $1 gray grn ('61) 1.25 5
1276 A158 $1.20 gray ol 60 5
1277 A158 $1.50 ultra 60 6
1278 A158 $2 car rose ('61) 1.35 8
1279 A158 $2.50 pale bl 1.35 8
1280 A158 $3 bluish grn 90 8
1281 A158 $3.20 lt red brn 2.25 8
1282 A158 $3.60 vio bl ('61) 2.00 18
1270B A158 10c emer ('63) 75 4

1962–64 Granite Paper
Without Gum

1270a A158 3c lt red brn 30 4
1271a A158 40c pale vio 30 4
1274a A158 80c pale grn 50 4
1275a A158 $1 gray grn ('63) 2.00 4
1278a A158 $2 car rose 2.25 7
1281a A158 $3.20 red brn ('64) 2.25 6
1282A A158 $4 brt bl grn 4.00 15
1283 A158 $4.50 vermilion 3.50 25
Nos. 1270-1283 (14) 26.95 1.64
1283a A158 $4.50 vermilion 2.25 20
Nos. 1270a-1283a (9) 2.25 20

Two types of No. 1271a: I. Seven lines in "0" of "40." II. Eight lines in "0."

Perf. 12½

1960, Oct. 25 Photo. Unwmkd.

Sports: 80c, Discus thrower. $2, Basketball. $2.50, Soccer. $3, Hurdling. $3.20, Runner.

1284 A159 50c ultra, yel & org 35 10
1285 A159 80c rose cl, pur & yel 35 15
1286 A159 $2 blk, red org & yel 60 25
1287 A159 $2.50 org & blk 90 30
1288 A159 $3 multi 1.00 50
1289 A159 $3.20 multi 1.65 60
Nos. 1284-1289 (6) 4.85 1.90

Bronze Wine Container, 1751–1111 B.C.
A160

Flat Bowl, 1111–771 B.C.
A161

Designs: $1, Cauldron, 1111–771 B.C. $1.20, Porcelain vase, 960–1126 A.D. $1.50, Perforated tube, 1111–771 B.C. $2, Jug in shape of monk's cap, 1368–1661 A.D. $2.50, Jade flower vase, 1368–1661, A.D.

Art Series I

1961–62 Photo. *Perf. 13*

1290 A160 80c lt ol, blk & dk vio 60 12
1291 A160 $1 sal, bl & blk 65 15
1292 A160 $1.20 yel, brn & ultra 85 30
1293 A160 $1.50 lil, bl & sep 85 40
1294 A160 $2 pale grn, dk grn & red brn 1.20 30
1295 A160 $2.50 grnsh bl & dk vio 1.50 35
Nos. 1290-1295 (6) 5.65 1.62

Art Series II

Designs: 80c, Palace perfumer, 1662–1911. $1, Corn vase, 770–221 B.C. $2, Jade tankard, 960–1126 A.D. $4, Glazed washer, 1127–1279 A.D. $4.50, Jade chimera, 8 B.C.–206 A.D.

1296 A160 80c pink, brn, bl & yel 40 10
1297 A160 $1 cit, blk & brn 1.20 20
1298 A161 $1.50 sal & ind 1.20 50
1299 A160 $2 bl, blk & rose 1.20 40
1300 A161 $4 red, blk & bluish gray 4.00 40
1301 A161 $4.50 grnsh bl, blk & brn 3.75 1.00
Nos. 1296-1301 (6) 11.75 2.60

Art Series III (1962)

Designs: 80c, Topaz twin wine vessels, 1662–1911 A.D. $1, Squat pouring vase, 1751–1111 B.C. $2.40, Vase, 1368–1661 A.D. $3, Wine vase, 1751–1111 B.C. $3.20, Covered porcelain jar, 1662–1911 A.D. $3.60, Perforated disc, 206 B.C.–8 A.D.

1302 A160 80c crim, blk & ocher 30 10
1303 A160 $1 bl & vio blk 40 10
1304 A160 $2.40 hn brn, blk & bl 1.35 40
1305 A160 $3 bl, blk & pink 3.00 1.25
1306 A160 $3.20 ultra, lt grn & red 4.00 25
1307 A160 $3.60 yel, blk & brn 3.00 75
Nos. 1302-1307 (6) 12.05 2.85

Issued to publicize ancient Chinese art treasures.

Farmer with Mechanized Plow **Madame Chiang Kai-shek and League Emblem**
A162 **A163**

1961, Feb. 4 Engraved *Perf. 12*
Without Gum

1308 A162 80c rose vio 25 10
1309 A162 $2 green 85 40
1310 A162 $3.20 vermilion 85 20

Issued to publicize the 1961 agricultural census.

Photogravure

1961, March 8 *Perf. 13* Unwmkd.
Portrait in Black

1311 A163 80c lt grn & car rose 60 10
1312 A163 $1 yel grn & car rose 1.50 25
1313 A163 $2 org brn & car rose 1.50 25
1314 A163 $3.20 lil & car rose 3.25 50

Issued to commemorate the 10th anniversary of the Chinese Women's Anti-Aggression League.

Spiny Lobster and Mail Order Service Emblem **Jeme Tien-yow and Pataling Tunnel**
A164 **A165**

1961, Mar. 20 Engraved *Perf. 11½*
Without Gum

1315 A164 $3 sl grn 1.20 25

Issued to publicize the mail order service for consumer goods.

1961, Apr. 26 *Perf. 11½*
Without Gum

Design: $2, Jeme Tien-yow and 1909 locomotive (horiz.).

1316 A165 80c lilac 25 10
1317 A165 $2 black 1.25 40

Issued to commemorate the centenary of the birth of Jeme Tien-yow, builder of the Peking-Kalgan railroad.

Map of China inscribed: "Recovery of the Mainland"
A166

Pres. Chiang Kai-shek
A167

1961, May 20 Photo. *Perf. 13½*

1318 A166 80c multi 75 15
1319 A167 $2 multi 2.50 75
a. Souvenir sheet of 2 1.75 1.75

Issued to commemorate the first anniversary of Pres. Chiang Kai-shek's 3rd term inauguration.

No. 1319a contains one each of Nos. 1318–1319, imperf, with simulated perforations and red marginal inscription. Without gum. Size: 135x100mm.

Convair 880-M, Biplane of 1921 and Flag
A168

1961, July 1 *Perf. 13x12½*

1320 A168 $10 multi 3.00 40

40th anniversary of civil air service.

Sun Yat-sen and Chiang Kai-shek
A169

Flag and Map of China
A170

Photogravure

1961, Oct. 10 *Perf. 13½* Unwmkd.

1321	A169	80c gray, lt brn & sl	75	10
1322	A170	$5 gray, ultra, red & beige	2.75	90
a.		Souvenir sheet of 2	2.50	2.50

Issued to commemorate the 50th anniversary of the Republic of China. No. 1322a contains one each of Nos. 1321–1322, imperf. with simulated perforations and red marginal inscription. No gum. Size of sheet: 135x99mm.

Lotus Pond
A172

Green Lake **A171** **Oil Refinery** **A173**

Taiwan Scenery: $2, Sun-Moon Lake. $3.20, Wulai waterfalls.

Perf. 13½x14, 14x13½

1961, Oct. 31 Unwmkd.

1323	A171	80c multi	50	15
1324	A172	$1 multi	1.50	50
1325	A172	$2 multi	1.50	50
1326	A171	$3.20 multi	3.00	75

1961, Nov. 14 *Perf. 11½*

Designs: $1.50, Steel works. $2.50, Aluminum plant. $3.20, Fertilizer plant (horiz.).

1327	A173	80c multi	50	10
1328	A173	$1.50 multi	1.50	80
1329	A173	$2.50 multi	1.50	80
1330	A173	$3.20 multi	3.00	70

Issued to publicize Chinese industrial development and in connection with the Golden Jubilee Convention of the Chinese Institute of Engineers, Nov. 13–16.

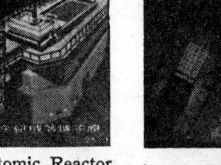

Atomic Reactor, Tsing-Hwa University **A174** **Atomic Reactor in Operation** **A175**

Design: $3.20, Atomic symbol and laboratory, Tsing-Hwa (horiz.).

1961–62 Photogravure *Perf. 12½*

1331	A174	80c multi	1.00	10
1332	A175	$2 multi ('62)	2.25	1.40
1333	A175	$3.20 multi ('62)	3.25	90

Issued to commemorate the inauguration on Apr. 13, 1961, of the first Chinese atomic reactor at the National Tsing-Hwa University Institute of Nuclear Science.

Microwave Reflector and Telegraph Wires
A176

Design: $3.20, Microwave parabolic antenna and mountains (horiz.).

1961, Dec. 28 *Perf. 12½*

1334	A176	80c multi	50	12
1335	A176	$3.20 multi	2.75	90

Issued to commemorate the 80th anniversary of Chinese telecommunications.

Mechanical Postal Equipment and Twine Tying Machine—A176a

Perf. 11½

1962, Mar. 20 Engraved Wmk. 323

Without Gum

1336	A176a	80c chocolate	1.00	10

Yu Shan Observatory **A177** **Observation Balloon, Earth and Cumulus Clouds** **A178**

Design: $1, Map showing route of typhoon Pamela, Sept. 1961 (horiz.).

1962 Without Gum

1337	A177	80c brown	30	10
1338	A178	$1 bluish blk	2.25	40
1339	A178	$2 green	2.25	80

Issue dates: 80c, $2, Mar. 23; $1, May 7. World Meteorological Day, Mar. 23.

Child Receiving Milk, U.N. Emblem—A179

1962, Apr. 4 Without Gum

1340	A179	80c rose red	25	10
1341	A179	$3.20 green	1.75	75
a.		Souvenir sheet of 2	1.50	1.50

Issued to commemorate the 15th anniversary of UNICEF (United Nations Children's Emergency Fund.) No. 1341a contains one each of Nos. 1340–1341 imperf. with simulated perforations and red marginal inscription. Size: 135x100mm.

Malaria Eradication Emblem
A180

Photogravure

1962, Apr. 7 *Perf. 12½* Unwmkd.

1342	A180	80c dk bl, red & lt grn	60	10
1343	A180	$3.60 brn, pink & grn	1.40	75

Issued for the World Health Organization drive to eradicate malaria.

Yu Yu-jen **A181** **Cheng Ch'eng-kung (Koxinga)** **A182**

1962, Apr. 24 *Perf. 13*

1344	A181	80c gray, blk & pink	65	10

Issued to honor Yu Yu-jen, newspaper reporter, revolutionary leader and co-worker of Sun Yat-sen, on his 84th birthday.

1962, Apr. 29

1345	A182	80c dp cl	50	10
1346	A182	$2 dk grn	1.10	25

Issued to commemorate the 300th anniversary (in 1961) of the recovery of Taiwan from the Dutch by Koxinga.

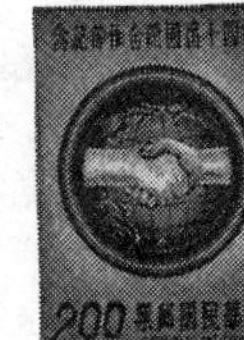

Emblem of International Cooperative Alliance **A183** **Clasped Hands Across Globe** **A184**

Engraved

1962, July 7 *Perf. 12* Wmk. 323

Without Gum

1347	A183	80c brown	60	10
1348	A184	$2 violet	1.75	50

Issued to publicize the International Cooperative Movement and to commemorate the 40th International Cooperative Day, July 7, 1962.

Mansion Type of 1958

1962, July 20 Without Gum

1349	A135	$5 gray grn	2.00	6
a.		Granite paper ('63)	2.25	10
1350	A135	$5.60 violet	2.50	8
a.		Granite paper ('63)	3.50	10
1351	A135	$6 orange	2.75	10
a.		Granite paper ('63)	3.75	10

"Art and Science"
A185

Designs: $2, "Education," book and UNESCO emblem (horiz.). $3.20, "Communications," globes (horiz.).

1962, Aug. 28 *Perf. 12* Wmk. 323

Without Gum

1352	A185	80c lil rose	25	15
1353	A185	$2 rose cl	1.00	60
1354	A185	$3.20 yel grn	1.25	40

Issued to publicize the activities of UNESCO in China.

Emperor T'ai Tsung, T'ang Dynasty, 627–649—A186

Emperors: $2, T'ai Tsu, Sung dynasty, 960–975. $3.20, T'ai Tsu, Yuan dynasty (Genghis Khan), 1206–27. $4, T'ai Tsu, Ming dynasty, 1368–98.

1962, Sept. 20 Photo. Unwmkd.

1355	A186	80c multi	1.00	20
1356	A186	$2 multi	4.50	1.35
1357	A186	$3.20 multi	5.00	1.10
1358	A186	$4 multi	4.50	1.65

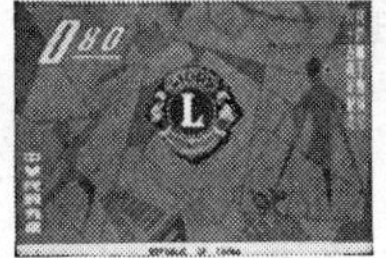

Lions International Emblem
A187

1962, Oct. 8 *Perf. 13*

1359	A187	80c multi	75	10
1360	A187	$3.60 multi	2.25	85
a.		Souvenir sheet of 2	2.00	2.00

Issued to commemorate the 45th anniversary of Lions International. No. 1360a contains one each of Nos. 1359–1360, imperf. with simulated perforations and gold marginal inscription. Size: 100x75mm.

Pole Vaulting
A188

Shooting
A189

1962, Oct. 25 *Perf. 13* Unwmkd.

1361	A188	80c multi	85	15
1362	A189	$3.20 multi	1.65	40

Sports meet.

Young Farmers and 4-H Emblem

A190

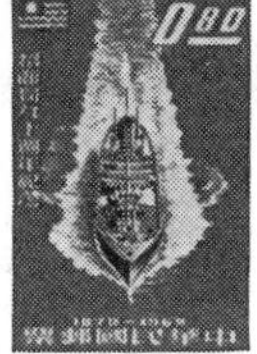

Flag and Liner of China Merchants' Steam Navigation Co.

A191

Design: $3.20, 4-H emblem and rice.

Engraved

1962, Dec. 7 *Perf. 12* Wmk. 323

Without Gum

1363	A190	80c carmine	40	10
1364	A190	$3.20 green	1.00	50
a.		Souvenir sheet of 2	1.25	1.25

Issued to commemorate the 10th anniversary of the 4-H Club in China. No. 1364a contains one each of Nos. 1363-1364, imperf. with simulated perforations and red lithographed marginal inscription. Size: 135x100mm.

Photogravure

1962, Dec. 16 *Perf. 13½* Unwmkd.

Design: $3.60, Company's Pacific navigation chart and freighter (horiz.).

1365	A191	80c multi	75	10
1366	A191	$3.60 multi	2.25	85

Issued to commemorate the 90th anniversary of the China Merchants' Steam Navigation Co., Ltd.

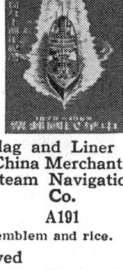

Farm Woman, Tractor and Plane Dropping Food over Mainland

A192

Photogravure

1963, Mar. 21 *Perf. 12½* Unwmkd.

1367	A192	$10 multi	3.50	90

Issued for the "Freedom from Hunger" campaign of the U.N. Food and Agriculture Organization.

Torch, Young Couple and Martyrs' Monument, Canton

A193

Engraved

1963, Mar. 29 *Perf. 11½* Wmk. 323

Without Gum

1368	A193	80c purple	35	8
1369	A193	$3.20 green	1.75	40

Issued for the 20th Youth Day.

Swallows, Pagoda and AOPU Emblem

A194

Designs: $2, Northern gannet (horiz.). $6, Japanese crane and pine.

Photogravure

1963, Apr. 1 *Perf. 13* Unwmkd.

1370	A194	80c multi	1.50	15
1371	A194	$2 multi	1.50	15
1372	A194	$6 multi	5.00	1.75

Issued to commemorate the first anniversary of the formation of the Asian-Oceanic Postal Union, AOPU.

Refugee Girl (Li Ying) and Map of China

A195

Refugees Fleeing Mainland

A196

Engraved

1963, June 27 *Perf. 11½* Wmk. 323

Without Gum

1373	A195	80c bluish blk	75	15
1374	A196	$3.20 dp cl	1.65	25

Issued to commemorate the first anniversary of the evacuation of Chinese mainland refugees from Hong Kong to Taiwan. Designs from photographs of refugees.

Nurse and Red Cross

A197

Basketball Player, Stadium and Asian Cup

A198

Design: $10, Globe and Red Cross.

Photogravure

1963, Sept. 1 *Perf. 12½* Unwmkd.

1375	A197	80c blk & car	1.50	20
1376	A197	$10 sl, gray & car	5.50	2.00

Centenary of International Red Cross.

Engraved

1963, Nov. 20 *Perf. 12* Wmk. 323

Without Gum

Design: $2, Hands reaching for ball and Asian cup.

1377	A198	80c lil rose	35	10
1378	A198	$2 violet	2.25	75

Issued to commemorate the 2nd Asian Basketball Championship, Taipei, Nov. 20.

U.N. Emblem, Torch and Men

A199

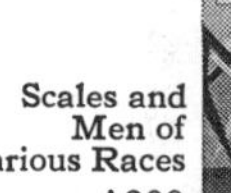

Scales and Men of Various Races

A200

1963, Dec. 10 *Perf. 11½* Wmk. 323

Without Gum

1379	A199	80c brt grn	25	8
1380	A200	$3.20 maroon	75	20

Universal Declaration of Human Rights, 15th anniversary.

Village and Orchids

A201

"Kindle the Fire of Conscience"

A202

Perf. 13½x13

1963, Dec. 17 Photo. Unwmkd.

1381	A201	40c multi	80	10
1382	A202	$4.50 multi	2.75	75

Issued to commemorate the contribution of the Good-People-Good-Deeds campaign to improve ethical standards.

Sun Yat-sen and Book, "Three Principles of the People"

A203

1963, Dec. 25 *Perf. 13*

1383	A203	$5 bl & multi	2.50	30

"Land-to-the-Tillers" program, 10th anniversary.

Torch

A204

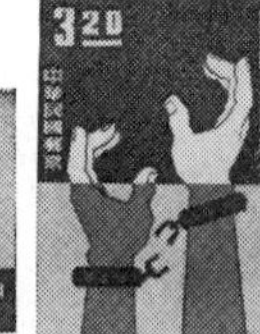

Hands Unchained

A205

Engraved

1964, Jan. 23 *Perf. 11½* Wmk. 323

Without Gum

1384	A204	80c red org	20	8
1385	A205	$3.20 indigo	1.00	15

Liberty Day, 10th anniversary.

Broadleaf Cactus

A206

Wu Chih-hwei

A207

Designs: $1, Crab cactus. $3.20, Nopalxochia. $5, Grizzly bear cactus.

Photogravure

1964, Feb. 27 *Perf. 12½* Unwmkd.

Plants in Original Colors

1386	A206	80c dp plum & fawn	40	10
1387	A206	$1 dk bl & car	1.00	40
1388	A206	$3.20 green	1.50	10
1389	A206	$5 lil & yel	2.00	40

Perf. 11½

1964, Mar. 25 Engraved Wmk. 323

Without Gum

1390	A207	80c blk brn	65	8

Issued to commemorate the centenary of the birth of Wu Chih-hwei (1865-1953), politician and leader of the Kuomintang.

Chu Kwang Tower, Quemoy

A208

Lithographed

1964-66 *Perf. 13x12½* Wmk. 323

Granite Paper; Without Gum

1391	A208	3c sepia	10	5
1392	A208	5c brt yel grn ('65)	10	5
1393	A208	10c yel grn	10	5
1394	A208	20c sl grn ('65)	10	5
1395	A208	40c rose red	10	5
1396	A208	50c brown	10	5
1397	A208	80c org ('65)	20	5
1398	A208	$1 vio ('65)	25	5
1399	A208	$1.50 brt lil ('66)	35	15
1400	A208	$2 lil rose	35	6
1401	A208	$2.50 ultra ('65)	35	6
1402	A208	$3 slate	60	10
1403	A208	$3.20 brt bl	75	6
1404	A208	$4 brt grn	90	8
		Nos. 1391-1404 (14)	4.35	91

Nurses Holding Candles

A209

Florence Nightingale and Student Nurse

A210

1964, May 12 Engr. *Perf. 11½*

Without Gum

1406	A209	80c vio bl	50	8
1407	A210	$4 red	1.50	25

Issued for Nurses Day.

Shihmen Reservoir

A211

Designs: $1, Irrigation system. $3.20, Main dam and power plant. $5, Spillway.

Photogravure

1964, June 14 *Perf. 12½* Unwmkd.

1408	A211	80c multi	60	10
1409	A211	$1 multi	60	10
1410	A211	$3.20 multi	1.20	15
1411	A211	$5 multi	3.00	75

Completion of Shihmen Reservoir.

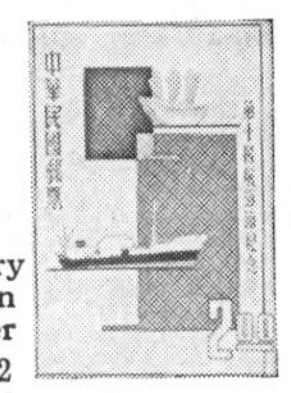

15th Century Ship, Modern Liner
A212

Perf. 11½

1964, July 11 Engr. Wmk. 323

Without Gum

1412 A212 $2 orange 45 8
1413 A212 $3.60 brt grn 85 20

China's 10th Navigation Day.

Bananas
A213

Photogravure

1964, July 25 *Perf. 14* Unwmkd.

Multicolored

1414 A213 80c *shown* 60 8
1415 A213 $1 *Oranges* 1.20 40
1416 A213 $3.20 *Pineapple* 1.50 25
1417 A213 $4 *Watermelon* 2.50 65

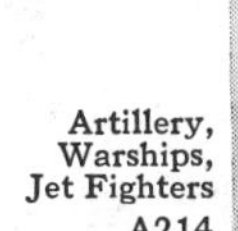

Artillery, Warships, Jet Fighters
A214

Engraved

1964, Sept. 3 *Perf. 11½* Wmk. 323

Without Gum

1418 A214 80c dk bl 30 8
1419 A214 $6 vio brn 1.65 40

Issued for the 10th Armed Forces Day.

Unisphere, Flags of China and U.S.
A215

Chinese Pavilion, N.Y. World's Fair
A216

1964, Sept. 10 Photo. Unwmkd.

1420 A215 80c vio & multi 60 8
1421 A216 $5 bl & multi 2.75 45

New York World's Fair, 1964-65.
See also Nos. 1450-1451.

Cowboy Carrying Calf, and Ranch
A217

Bicycling
A218

Engraved

1964, Sept. 24 *Perf. 11½* Wmk. 323

Without Gum

1422 A217 $2 brn lake 75 10
1423 A217 $4 dk vio bl 1.75 40

Animal Protection Week, Sept. 24-30.

1964, Oct. 10 Without Gum

Sports: $1, Runner. $3.20, Gymnast on rings. $10, High jump.

1424 A218 80c vio bl 35 6
1425 A218 $1 rose red 65 10
1426 A218 $3.20 dl bl grn 1.20 10
1427 A218 $10 lilac 3.50 1.50

18th Olympic Games, Tokyo, Oct. 10-25.

Hsü Kuang-chi
A219

Pharmaceutical Industry
A220

Textile Industry
A221

1964, Nov. 8 Engraved *Perf. 11½*

Without Gum

1428 A219 80c indigo 75 8

Issued to honor Hsü Kuang-chi (1562-1633), scholar and statesman.

1964, Nov. 11 Photo. Unwmkd.

Designs: $2, Chemical industry. $3.60, Cement industry.

1429 A220 40c multi 50 8
1430 A221 $1.50 multi 1.25 40
1431 A220 $2 multi 1.50 15
1432 A221 $3.60 multi 2.50 30

Dr. Sun Yat-sen
A222

Eleanor Roosevelt and Scales of Justice
A223

1964, Nov. 24 Engraved Wmk. 323

Without Gum

1433 A222 80c green 60 8
1434 A222 $3.60 purple 1.20 25

Founding of the Kuomintang by Sun Yat-sen, 70th anniversary.

Photogravure

1964, Dec. 10 *Perf. 13* Unwmkd.

1435 A223 $10 vio & brn 1.65 40

Issued to honor Eleanor Roosevelt (1884-1962) on the 16th anniversary of the Universal Declaration of Human Rights.

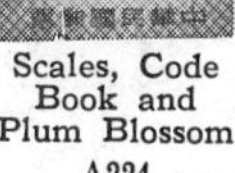

Scales, Code Book and Plum Blossom
A224

Rotary Emblem and Mainspring
A225

Engraved

1965, Jan. 11 *Perf. 11½* Wmk. 323

Without Gum

1436 A224 80c car rose 25 8
1437 A224 $3.20 dl sl grn 75 20

The 20th Judicial Day.

1965, Feb. 23 *Perf. 11½* Wmk. 323

Without Gum

1438 A225 $1.50 vermilion 30 8
1439 A225 $2 emerald 85 15
1440 A225 $2.50 blue 1.00 25

Rotary International, 60th anniversary.

Double Carp Design
A226

Madame Chiang Kai-shek
A227

Engraved

1965, Mar. 29 *Perf. 11½* Wmk. 323

Granite Paper; Without Gum

1441 A226 $5 purple 4.00 10
1442 A226 $5.60 dp bl 2.50 30
1443 A226 $6 brown 2.00 20
1444 A226 $10 lil rose 4.00 20
1445 A226 $20 rose car 5.00 40
1446 A226 $50 green 10.00 1.25
1447 A226 $100 crim rose 22.50 2.25
Nos. 1441-1447 (7) 50.00 4.70

1965, Apr. 17 Photo. Unwmkd.

1448 A227 $2 multi 1.75 10
1449 A227 $6 sal & multi 4.50 1.00

Chinese Women's Anti-Aggression League, 15th anniversary.

Unisphere and Chinese Pavilion
A228

"100 Birds Paying Homage to Queen Phoenix" and Unisphere
A229

1965, May 8

1450 A228 $2 bl & multi 1.25 10
1451 A229 $10 red, ocher & bis 5.00 75

New York World's Fair, 1964-65.

ITU Emblem, Old and New Communication Equipment—A230

Design: $5, similar to 80c (vert.).

Perf. 13½x13, 13x13½

1965, May 17 Photo. Unwmkd.

1452 A230 80c multi 30 8
1453 A230 $5 multi 1.90 50

Issued to commemorate the centenary of the International Telecommunication Union.

Red Sea Bream
A231

Fish: 80c, White pomfret. $2, Skipjack (vert.). $4, Moonfish.

1965, July 1 *Perf. 13*

1454 A231 40c multi 25 6
1455 A231 80c multi 50 6
1456 A231 $2 multi 75 8
1457 A231 $4 multi 1.50 30

Issued for Fishermen's Day.

Confucius
A232

ICY Emblem
A233

Portraits: $2.50, Yueh Fei. $3.50, Wen Tien-hsiang. $3.60, Mencius.

Engraved

1965-66 *Perf. 11½* Wmk. 323

Without Gum

1458 A232 $1 dp car 50 6
1459 A232 $2.50 blk brn 50 8
1460 A232 $3.50 dk red 1.00 15
1461 A232 $3.60 dk bl 1.50 20

Issue dates: Nos. 1458, 1461, Sept. 28, 1965. Nos. 1459-1460, Sept. 3, 1966.
The $2.50 and $3.50 have colored background.
See also Nos. 1507-1508.

Photogravure

1965, Oct. 24 *Perf. 13* Unwmkd.

Design: $6, ICY emblem (horiz.).

1462 A233 $2 brn, blk & gold 65 8
1463 A233 $6 brt grn, red & gold 2.50 1.00

International Cooperation Year, 1965.

Street Crossing and Traffic Light
A234

Sun Yat-sen
A235

Engraved

1965, Nov. 1 *Perf. 11½* Wmk. 323

Without Gum

1464 A234 $1 brn vio 80 8
1465 A234 $4 crim rose 1.40 20

Issued to publicize traffic safety.

Photogravure

1965, Nov. 12 *Perf. 13½* Unwmkd.

Designs: $4, Dr. Sun Yat-sen, portrait at right. $5, Sun Yat-sen and flags (horiz.).

1466 A235 $1 multi 50 8
1467 A235 $4 multi 1.00 25
1468 A235 $5 multi 2.50 1.00

A little time given to study of the arrangement of the Scott Catalogue can make it easier to use effectively.

Children with New Year's Firecrackers
A236

Dragon Dance, "Dragon Playing Ball"
A237

1965, Dec. 1 Photo. *Perf. 13*

1469	A236	$1 multi	1.30	10
1470	A237	$4.50 multi	1.50	75

Lien Po from "Marshal and Prime Minister Reconciled"
A238

Facial Paintings for Chinese Operas: $3, Kuan Yü from "Reunion at Ku City." $4, Gen. Chang Fei from "The Battle of Chang Pan Hill." $6, Buddha from "The Flower-Scattering Angel."

1966, Feb. 15 *Perf. 11½* Unwmkd.

1471	A238	$1 ol & multi	2.25	30
1472	A238	$3 multi	2.00	25
1473	A238	$4 multi	2.25	30
1474	A238	$6 ver & multi	3.50	2.00

Postal Service Emblem Held by Carrier Pigeon
A239

Stone, Mt. Tai-wu, Quemoy, and Mailman
A240

Designs (postal service emblem and): $3, Postal Museum. $4, Mailman climbing symbolic slope.

1966, Mar. 20 Photo. *Perf. 12½*

1475	A239	$1 grn & multi	50	8
1476	A240	$2 multi	50	8
1477	A240	$3 multi	75	15
1478	A239	$4 multi	1.50	50

China postal service, 70th anniversary.

Fishing on a Snowy Day, "Five Dynasties" (907–960)
A241

Paintings from Palace Museum: $3.50, Calves on the Plain, Sung artist (960–1126). $4.50, Winter landscape, Sung artist (960–1126). $5, Magpies, by Lin Ch'un, Southern Sung dynasty (1127–1279).

1966, May 20 Photo. *Perf. 13*

1479	A241	$2.50 blk, brn & red	1.00	8
1480	A241	$3.50 bis brn, blk & gray	75	10
1481	A241	$4.50 blk, buff & sl	75	40
1482	A241	$5 multi	2.25	50

Issued to commemorate the inauguration of Pres. Chiang Kai-shek for a fourth term.

Dragon Boat Race
A242

Lion Dance
A243

Design: $4, Lady Chang O flying to the Moon.

1966 Unwmkd.

1483	A242	$2.50 multi	1.75	8
1484	A242	$4 multi	1.25	8
1485	A243	$6 multi	1.00	25

Issued for the Dragon Boat, Mid-Autumn and Lunar New Year Festivals. Issue dates: $2.50, June 23; $4, Sept. 29; $6, Nov. 26.

Flags of China and Argentina
A244

1966, July 9 Photogravure *Perf. 13*

1486	A244	$10 multi	1.75	25

Issued to commemorate the 150th anniversary of Argentina's Independence.

Lin Sen
A245

Flying Geese
A246

Engraved

1966, Aug. 1 *Perf. 11½* Wmk. 323

Without Gum

1487	A245	$1 dk brn	60	8

Issued to commemorate the centenary of the birth of Lin Sen (1867–1943), Chairman of the Nationalist Government of China (1931–43).

1966–67 *Perf. 11½ rough*

Granite Paper; Without Gum

1496	A246	$3.50 brown	30	5
1497	A246	$4 vermilion	40	5
1498	A246	$4.50 brt grn	50	15
1499	A246	$5 rose lil	50	5
1500	A246	$5.50 yel grn ('67)	50	15
1501	A246	$6 brt bl	1.50	40
1502	A246	$6.50 violet	1.00	25
1503	A246	$7 black	85	5
1504	A246	$8 car rose ('67)	1.00	15
		Nos. 1496-1504 (9)	6.55	1.30

The $4.50, $5, $6, $7 and $8 were reissued with gum in 1970–71.

Pres. Chiang Kai-shek in Chung San Robe
A247

Design: $5, Chiang Kai-shek in marshal's uniform.

Photogravure

1966, Oct. 31 *Perf. 13* Unwmkd.

1505	A247	$1 multi	60	10
1506	A247	$5 multi	2.40	50

Issued to commemorate Chiang Kai-shek's inauguration for a fourth term as president, May 20, 1966.

Famous Men Type of 1965–66 with Frame Line

Portraits: No. 1507, Tsai Yuan-pei (1868–1940), educator. No. 1508, Chiu Ching (1875–1907), woman educator and revolutionist.

Engraved

1967 *Perf. 11½* Wmk. 323

Without Gum

1507	A232	$1 vio bl	60	8
1508	A232	$1 black	60	6

Issue dates: No. 1507, Jan. 11. No. 1508, July 15.

No. 1507 is on granite paper.

Motorized Mailman and Microwave Station
A248

"Transportation" and Radar Weather Station
A249

Photogravure

1967, Mar. 15 *Perf. 13* Unwmkd.

1511	A248	$1 multi	60	5
1512	A249	$5 multi	1.20	20

Issued to publicize the progress in communication and transportation services.

Pres. Chiang Kai-shek and Chinese Flag
A250

Chu Yuan, 332–295 B.C.
A251

Design: $4, Different frame.

1967, May 20 Lithographed *Perf. 13*

1513	A250	$1 multi	90	8
1514	A250	$4 multi	1.85	20

First anniversary of President Chiang Kai-shek's 4th-term inauguration.

Engraved

1967, June 12 *Perf. 11½* Wmk. 323

Portraits: $2, Li Po (705–760). $2.50, Tu Fu (712–770). $3, Po Chu-i (772–846).

Granite Paper; Without Gum

1515	A251	$1 black	50	5
1516	A251	$2 brown	75	8
1517	A251	$2.50 brn blk	90	20
1518	A251	$3 grnsh blk	90	15

Issued for Poets' Day.

Hotei, Wood Carving
A252

World Map
A253

Handicrafts: $2.50, Vase and plate. $3, Dolls. $5, Palace lanterns.

Photogravure

1967, Aug. 12 *Perf. 11½* Unwmkd.

1519	A252	$1 gray & multi	30	8
1520	A252	$2.50 multi	60	8
1521	A252	$3 multi	85	15
1522	A252	$5 multi	1.40	40

Taiwan handicraft industry.

Engraved

1967, Sept. 25 *Perf. 11½* Wmk. 323

Granite Paper; Without Gum

1523	A253	$1 vermilion	10	6
1524	A253	$5 blue	50	25

Issued to commemorate the first Conference of the World Anti-Communist League, WACL, Taipei, Sept. 25–29.

Players on Stilts: "The Fisherman and the Woodcutter"
A254

Photogravure

1967, Oct. 10 *Perf. 13* Unwmkd.

1525	A254	$4.50 multi	50	25

Issued for the 56th National Day.

Maroon Oriole—A255

Formosan Birds: $1, Formosan barbet (vert.). $2.50, Formosan green pigeon. $3, Formosan blue magpie. $5, Crested serpent eagle (vert.). $8, Mikado pheasants.

1967, Nov. 25 Photo. *Perf. 11*

Granite Paper

1526	A255	$1 multi	20	15
1527	A255	$2 multi	40	15
1528	A255	$2.50 multi	40	20
1529	A255	$3 multi	50	20
1530	A255	$5 multi	1.00	30
1531	A255	$8 multi	1.50	75
		Nos. 1526-1531 (6)	4.00	1.75

Chung Hsing Pagoda
A256

Buddha, Changhua
A257

Designs: $2.50, Seashore, Yeh Liu Park. $5, National Palace Museum, Taipei.

Photogravure

1967, Dec. 10 *Perf. 13* Unwmkd.

1532	A256	$1 multi	25	8
1533	A257	$2.50 multi	75	30
1534	A257	$4 multi	1.00	20
1535	A257	$5 multi	1.75	50

Issued for International Tourist Year 1967.

China Park, Manila, and Flags
A258

1967, Dec. 30 *Perf. 13½*

1536	A258	$1 multi	35	6
1537	A258	$5 multi	1.10	25

Sino-Philippine Friendship Year 1966–67.

Sun Yat-sen Building, Yangmingshan
A259 A259a

Perf. 13x12½

1968–75 Lithographed Wmk. 323

Granite Paper

1538	A259	5c lt brn	10	4
1539	A259	10c grnsh blk	10	4
1540	A259	50c brt rose lil	10	3
a.		Booklet pane of 4	65	
1541	A259	$1 vermilion	20	3
a.		Booklet pane of 4	1.25	
1542	A259	$1.50 emerald	30	5
1543	A259	$2 plum	30	4
1544	A259	$2.50 blue	30	4
a.		Booklet pane of 4	1.75	
1545	A259	$3 grnsh bl	60	5
		Nos. 1538-1545 (8)	2.00	32

Coil Stamps

Perf. 13 Horiz.

Photo. Unwmkd.

1546	A259a	$1 car rose ('70)	25	15
1547	A259a	$1 ver ('75)	20	6

Issue dates: 50c, $1, $2.50, Jan. 23, 1968; No. 1546, Mar. 20, 1970; No. 1547, Jan. 28, 1975; others July 11, 1968.

Inscription on No. 1546 is in color with white background. On No. 1547 it is white with colored background.

Harvesting Sugar Cane
A260

Jade Cabbage, 1662–1911
A261

Photogravure

1968, Mar. 1 *Perf. 13* Unwmkd.

1548	A260	$1 ol & multi	40	10
1549	A260	$4 multi	60	30

1968, Mar. 29 *Perf. 13* Unwmkd.

Ancient Art Treasures: $1.50, Jade battle axe. $2, Porcelain flower bowl, 960–1126 A.D. (horiz.). $2.50, Cloisonné enamel vase, 1723–1736 A.D. $4, Agate flower holder in shape of finger citrus, 1662–1911 A.D. (horiz.). $5, Sacrificial kettle, 1111–771 B.C.

1550	A261	$1 rose & multi	25	8
1551	A261	$1.50 bl & multi	50	25
1552	A261	$2 bl & multi	60	10
1553	A261	$2.50 dl rose & multi	60	25
1554	A261	$4 pink & multi	65	30
1555	A261	$5 bl & multi	1.00	40
		Nos. 1550-1555 (6)	3.60	1.38

View of City in Cathay (1)—A262

Views: No. 1557, City and wall of Forbidden City (2). No. 1558, Wall at right, bridge at left (3). No. 1559, Queen's ship landing at left (4). No. 1560, Palace (5). $5, City wall and gate. $8, Suburb around Great Bridge. Design from scroll "A City in Cathay," painted 1736.

1968, June 18 Photo. ***Perf. 13½***

Size: 50x29mm.

1556	A262	$1 multi	25	9
1557	A262	$1 multi	25	9
1558	A262	$1 multi	25	9
1559	A262	$1 multi	25	9
1560	A262	$1 multi	25	9

Size: 60x31mm. *Perf. 13x13½*

1561	A262	$5 multi	1.50	80
1562	A262	$8 multi	2.25	90
		Nos. 1556-1562 (7)	5.00	2.15

Nos. 1556–1560 printed se-tenant in sheet of 50 with horizontal strips of five containing one of each.

See also Nos. 1610–1614.

Entrance Gate, Taroko Gorge
A263

Design: $8, Sun Yat-sen Building, Yangmingshan.

1968, Feb. 12 Photo. ***Perf. 13***

1563	A263	$5 multi	1.00	25
1564	A263	$8 multi	1.00	25

The 17th Annual Conference of the Pacific Area Travel Association.

Vice President Chen Cheng
A264

Flying Geese
A265

1968, Mar. 5

1565	A264	$1 brn & multi	50	5

Issued in memory of Vice President Chen Cheng (1898–1965).

Lithographed

1968, Mar. 20 *Perf. 12* Wmk. 323

Granite Paper

1566	A265	$1 vermilion	30	12

Souvenir Sheet

Imperf.

1567	A265	$3 green	75	75

Issued to commemorate the 90th anniversary of Chinese postage stamps. No. 1567 contains one stamp with simulated perforations, yellow decorative margin with red inscription. Size: 75x100mm.

WHO Emblem and "20"
A266

Symbolic Water Cycle
A267

1968, Apr. 7 Engraved *Perf. 12*

Granite Paper

1568	A266	$1 green	30	5
1569	A266	$5 scarlet	75	30

Issued to commemorate the 20th anniversary of the World Health Organization.

Lithographed

1968, June 6 *Perf. 11½* Wmk. 323

Granite Paper

1570	A267	$1 grn & org	35	8
1571	A267	$4 brt bl & org	75	8

Hydrological Decade (UNESCO) 1965–74.

Broadcasting to Mainland China
A268

Dual Carriers for F.M. Broadcasting
A269

Lithographed

1968, Aug. 1 *Perf. 12* Wmk. 323

Granite Paper

1572	A268	$1 bl, vio bl & gray	35	8
1573	A269	$4 lt ultra & ver	75	15

Issued to commemorate the 40th anniversary of the Broadcasting Corporation of China, and the inauguration of frequency modulation broadcasting.

Human Rights Flame
A270

Crop Improvement and Extension Work
A271

1968, Sept. 3 Granite Paper

1574	A270	$1 multi	30	15
1575	A270	$5 multi	60	15

International Human Rights Year 1968.

Lithographed

1968, Sept. 30 *Perf. 12* Wmk. 323

Granite Paper

1576	A271	$1 yel, bis & dk brn	25	5
1577	A271	$5 yel, emer & dk grn	75	50

Joint Commission on Rural Reconstruction, 20th anniversary.

Javelin
A272

Designs: $2.50, Weight lifting. $5, Pole vault (horiz.). $8, Woman hurdling (horiz.).

Photogravure

1968, Oct. 12 *Perf. 13* Unwmkd.

1578	A272	$1 multi	25	5
1579	A272	$2.50 multi	35	15
1580	A272	$5 multi	60	10
1581	A272	$8 pink & multi	85	30

Issued to commemorate the 19th Olympic Games, Mexico City, Oct. 12–27.

Pres. Chiang Kai-shek and Whampoa Military Academy
A273

Designs: $2, Pres. Chiang Kai-shek reviewing forces of the Northern Expedition. $2.50, Suppression of bandits, reconstruction work and New Life Movement emblem. $3.50, Marco Polo Bridge near Peking and victory parade, Nanking. $4, Original copy of Constitution of Republic of China. $5, Nationalist Chinese flag flying over mainland China.

1968, Oct. 31 *Perf. 11½x12*

1582	A273	$1 multi	35	8
1583	A273	$2 multi	50	20
1584	A273	$2.50 multi	50	20
1585	A273	$3.50 multi	60	20
1586	A273	$4 multi	75	40
1587	A273	$5 multi	1.00	40
		Nos. 1582-1587 (6)	3.70	1.48

Chiang Kai-shek's achievements for China.

Cock
A274

1968, Nov. 12 Litho. *Perf. 12*

Granite Paper

No.	Type	Description	Unused	Used
1588	A274	$1 pink & multi	4.50	15
1589	A274	$4.50 lil & multi	4.50	2.25

Issued for use on New Year's greetings.

Flag
A275

1968, Dec. 25 *Perf. 12½* Wmk. 323

Granite Paper

No.	Type	Description	Unused	Used
1590	A275	$1 multi	35	6
1591	A275	$5 lt bl & multi	75	20

Constitution of the Republic of China, 20th anniversary.

Jade Belt Buckle, 1662–1911
A276

Ancient Art Treasures: $1.50, Yellow jade vase, 960–1126 A.D. (vert.). $2, Cloisonné enamel square teapot, 1662–1911 A.D. $2.50, Kuei, sacrificial bronze vessel, 722–481 B.C. $4, Heavenly ball vase, 1368–1661 A.D. (vert.). $5, Gourd-shaped vase, 1662–1911 A.D. (vert.).

Photogravure

1969, Jan. 15 *Perf. 13* Unwmkd.

No.	Type	Description	Unused	Used
1592	A276	$1 dl rose & multi	25	5
1593	A276	$1.50 rose & multi	30	15
1594	A276	$2 brt rose & multi	30	10
1595	A276	$2.50 lt bl & multi	50	20
1596	A276	$4 tan & multi	65	20
1597	A276	$5 pale bl & multi	90	40
		Nos. 1592-1597 (6)	2.90	1.10

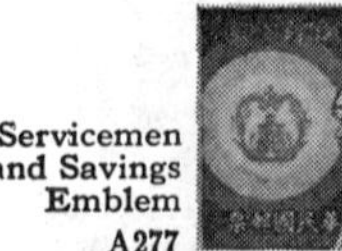

Servicemen and Savings Emblem
A277

Engraved

1969, Feb. 1 *Perf. 12* Wmk. 323

Granite Paper

No.	Type	Description	Unused	Used
1598	A277	$1 dl red brn	30	8
1599	A277	$4 dp bl	85	15

Issued to commemorate the 10th anniversary of the Military Savings Program.

Ti (Flute)
A278

Musical Instruments: $2.50, Sheng (13 bamboo pipes connected at the base). $4, P'i p'a (lute). $5, Cheng (zither).

Photogravure

1969, Mar. 16 *Perf. 13* Unwmkd.

No.	Type	Description	Unused	Used
1600	A278	$1 buff & multi	20	5
1601	A278	$2.50 lt ap grn & multi	35	10
1602	A278	$4 pink & multi	75	40
1603	A278	$5 lt grnsh bl & multi	75	25

Sun Yat-sen Building and Kuomintang Emblem—A279

Double Carp Design
A280

1969, Mar. 29 Litho. *Perf. 13½*

No.	Type	Description	Unused	Used
1604	A279	$1 multi	25	5

Issued to commemorate the 10th National Congress of the Chinese Nationalist Party (Kuomintang), Mar. 29. A $2.50 stamp portraying Sun Yat-sen and Chiang Kai-shek was prepared but not issued.

Perf. 13½x12½

1969–74 Engr. Wmk. 323

Granite Paper

No.	Type	Description	Unused	Used
1606	A280	$10 dk bl ('74)	85	20
a.		Perf. 11½	1.75	15
1607	A280	$20 dk brn ('74)	1.75	20
a.		Perf. 11½	2.50	20
1608	A280	$50 grn ('74)	3.50	75
a.		Perf. 11½	6.50	75
1609	A280	$100 brt red ('74)	6.50	2.00
a.		Perf. 11½	10.00	2.50

The 1969 issue is 27mm. high; 1974, 28mm. See No. 1980.

Bridal Procession—A281

Designs: No. 1610, Musicians and standard bearer from bridal procession. $2.50, Emigrant farm family in oxcart. $5, Art gallery. $8, Roadside food stands. Designs from scroll "A City in Cathay," painted in 1736. Nos. 1610–1611 printed se-tenant in sheets of 30 (6x5).

Photogravure

1969, May 20 *Perf. 13½* Unwmkd.

No.	Type	Description	Unused	Used
1610	A281	$1 multi	25	10
1611	A281	$1 multi	25	10
1612	A281	$2.50 multi	65	40
1613	A281	$5 multi	75	50
1614	A281	$8 multi	1.25	80
		Nos. 1610-1614 (5)	3.15	1.90

ILO Emblem
A282

Perf. 11½

1969, June 15 Engr. Wmk. 323

Granite Paper

No.	Type	Description	Unused	Used
1615	A282	$1 dk bl	25	5
1616	A282	$8 dk car	85	30

International Labor Organization, 50th anniversary.

Family at Dinner Table and Dressing
A283

Pupils in Laboratory and Playing
A284

Designs: $2.50, Housecleaning and obeying traffic rules. $4, Recreation (music, fishing, basketball) and education.

Perf. 11½

1969, July 15 Engr. Wmk. 323

No.	Type	Description	Unused	Used
1617	A283	$1 brick red	20	5
1618	A283	$2.50 blue	75	25
1619	A283	$4 green	75	20

Model Citizen's Life Movement.

1969, Sept. 1 *Perf. 11½* Wmk. 323

Design: $1, $5, Pupils with book and various school activities (horiz.).

Granite Paper

No.	Type	Description	Unused	Used
1620	A284	$1 brt red	20	8
1621	A284	$2.50 brt grn	35	10
1622	A284	$4 dk bl	50	15
1623	A284	$5 brown	65	25

Issued to commemorate the first anniversary of the free 9-year education system.

Wild Flowers and Pheasants, by Lu Chih (Ming)
A285

Paintings: $2.50, Bamboo and birds, Sung dynasty. $5, Flowers and Birds, Sung dynasty. $8, Cranes and Flowers, by G. Castiglione, S.J. (1688–1766).

1969, Oct. 9 Photo. *Perf. 13½*

No.	Type	Description	Unused	Used
1624	A285	$1 multi	20	8
1625	A285	$2.50 multi	40	15
1626	A285	$5 multi	80	25
1627	A285	$8 multi	1.25	40

Golden Scepter Rose
A286

Rocket and Radar Station
A287

Roses: $1, "Charles Mollerin," called black rose. $5, Peace. $8, Josephine Bruce.

1969, Oct. 31 Litho. *Perf. 14*

No.	Type	Description	Unused	Used
1628	A286	$1 lt vio & multi	30	10
1629	A286	$2.50 lt bl & multi	50	20
1630	A286	$5 dl org & multi	85	50
1631	A286	$8 ap grn & multi	1.00	40

Engraved

1969, Nov. 21 *Perf. 11½* Wmk. 323

No.	Type	Description	Unused	Used
1632	A287	$1 rose cl	25	8

The 30th Air Defense Day.

Symbol of International Cooperation
A288

Pekingese
A289

1969, Nov. 25

No.	Type	Description	Unused	Used
1633	A288	$1 rose cl	35	8
1634	A288	$5 green	70	20

Issued to commemorate the 5th General Assembly of the Asian Parliamentary Union, Taipei, Nov. 24–28.

1969, Dec. 1 Lithographed *Perf. 12*

Granite Paper

No.	Type	Description	Unused	Used
1635	A289	50c red & multi	40	8
1636	A289	$4.50 grn & multi	2.50	60

Issued for use on New Year's greetings.

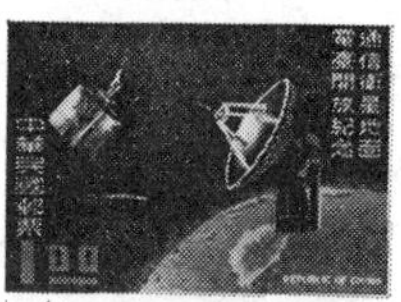

Satellite, Earth Station and Map of Taiwan
A290

Photogravure

1969, Dec. 28 *Perf. 13* Unwmkd.

No.	Type	Description	Unused	Used
1637	A290	$1 brn & multi	25	10
1638	A290	$5 vio bl & multi	70	30
1639	A290	$8 pur & multi	1.15	50

Issued to commemorate the inauguration of the Communication Satellite Earth Station at Chin-Shan-Li, Dec. 28.

Agate Grinding Stone, 1662–1911
A291

Ancient Art Treasures: $1, Carved lacquer ware vase, 1662–1911 (vert.). $2, White jade Chin-li-chih melons, 1662–1911. $2.50, Black jade shepherd and ram, 206 B.C.–220 A.D. $4, Chien-lung twin porcelain vase, 1736–1796 (vert.). $5, Ju porcelain vase with 3 bulls, 960–1126 (vert.).

1970, Jan. 23

No.	Type	Description	Unused	Used
1640	A291	$1 lt grnsh bl & multi	18	8
1641	A291	$1.50 pale bl & multi	30	15
1642	A291	$2 grn & multi	30	15
1643	A291	$2.50 pink & multi	40	15
1644	A291	$4 ol bis & multi	70	15
1645	A291	$5 ultra & multi	90	30
		Nos. 1640-1645 (6)	2.78	98

Hsuan Chuang
A292

Chu Hsi
A293

Design: $2.50, Hua To.

Engraved

1970, Feb. 20 *Perf. 11½* Wmk. 323

Granite Paper

No.	Type	Description	Unused	Used
1646	A292	$1 car rose	30	10
1647	A293	$2.50 bl grn	50	15
1648	A293	$4 blue	60	20

Issued in memory of Hsuan Chuang (602–664), who propagated Buddhism in China; Chu Hsi (1130–1200), who developed Neo-Confucianism, and Hua To (3rd century A.D.) physician and surgeon.

EXPO '70 Pavilion, Emblem and Flags of Participants
A294

Design: $5, Chinese pavilion, EXPO '70 emblem, exhibition and Chinese flags.

Photogravure

1970, Mar. 13 *Perf. 13* Unwmkd.

1649	A294	$5 org red & multi	60	25
1650	A294	$8 lt bl & multi	85	40

EXPO '70 International Exhibition, Osaka, Japan, Mar. 15–Sept. 13.

Nimbus III and WMO Emblem
A295

Design: $1, Agricultural meteorological station and tropical landscape (vert.).

Perf. 14x13½, 13½x14

1970, Mar. 23 Litho. Wmk. 323

Granite Paper

1651	A295	$1 grn & multi	30	8
1652	A295	$8 bl & multi	90	40

10th Annual World Meteorological Day.

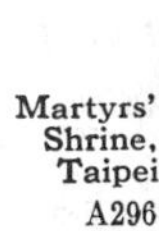

Martyrs' Shrine, Taipei
A296

Shrine's Gate
A297

Photogravure

1970, Mar. 29 *Perf. 13* Unwmkd.

1653	A296	$1 multi	30	8
1654	A297	$8 multi	90	40

Issued to commemorate the completion of the Martyrs' Shrine in Northern Taipei, dedicated to the memory of 72 young revolutionaries who died March 29, 1911.

Yueh Fei Fighting for Lost Territories
A298

Characters from Chinese Operas: $2.50, Emperor Shun and stepmother. $5, The Lady Warrior Chin Liang-yu. $8, Kuan Yu and groom.

1970, May 4 *Perf. 13½* Unwmkd.

1655	A298	$1 multi	30	10
1656	A298	$2.50 multi	50	25
1657	A298	$5 multi	75	30
1658	A298	$8 multi	1.25	50

"One Hundred Horses" (Detail) by Lang Shih-ning—A299

Three Horses Playing—A300

Designs (Horses): No. 1660, Trees in left background. No. 1661, Tree trunk in lower left corner. No. 1662, Group of trees at right. No. 1663, Barren tree at right. $8, Groom roping horses. Designs from scroll "One Hundred Horses" by Lang Shih-ning (Giuseppe Castiglione, 1688–1766). Nos. 1659–1663 printed se-tenant in sheets of 50 (5x10).

Photogravure

1970, June 18 *Perf. 13½* Unwmkd.

1659	A299	$1 multi	20	8
1660	A299	$1 multi	20	8
1661	A299	$1 multi	20	8
1662	A299	$1 multi	20	8
1663	A299	$1 multi	20	8
1664	A300	$5 bis & multi	85	60
1665	A300	$8 dl yel & multi	1.25	75
		Nos. 1659-1665 (7)	3.10	1.75

Lai-tsu Amusing his Old Parents
A301

Chinese Fairy Tales: No. 1667, Man disguised as deer, and hunters. No. 1668, Boy cooling his father's bed. No. 1669, Boy fishing through ice. No. 1670, Son reunited with old mother. No. 1671, Emperor tasting mother's medicine. No. 1672, Boy saving oranges for mother. No. 1673, Boy saving father from tiger.

Lithographed

1970, July 10 *Perf. 13½* Wmk. 323

Granite Paper

1666	A301	10c red & multi	5	3
1667	A301	10c car rose & multi	5	3
1668	A301	10c lt vio & multi	5	3
1669	A301	10c gray & multi	5	3
1670	A301	10c emer & multi	5	3
1671	A301	50c bis & multi	10	3
1672	A301	$1 sky bl & multi	20	3
1673	A301	$1 dp bl & multi	20	3
		Nos. 1666-1673 (8)	75	24

See also Nos. 1726–1733.

Man's First Step onto Moon
A302

Designs: $1, Pres. Chiang Kai-shek's message brought to the moon. $5, Neil A. Armstrong, Michael Collins, Edwin E. Aldrin, Jr., and moon (horiz.).

Perf. 13½x13, 13x13½

1970, July 21 Photo. Unwmkd.

1674	A302	$1 yel & multi	35	10
1675	A302	$5 lt yel grn & multi	65	25
1676	A302	$8 bl & multi	1.00	50

Issued to commemorate the first anniversary of man's first landing on the moon.

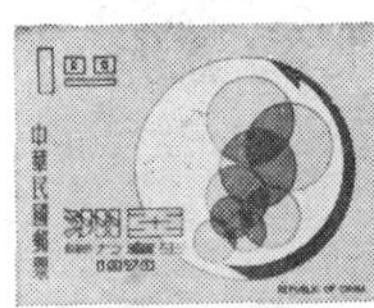

Asian Productivity Year Symbol
A303

Lithographed

1970, Aug. 18 *Perf. 13½* Wmk. 323

Granite Paper

1677	A303	$1 emer & multi	30	5
1678	A303	$5 bl & multi	65	20

Issued to publicize Asian Productivity Year.

Flags of China and U.N.
A304

1970, Sept. 19 *Perf. 12* Wmk. 323

Granite Paper

1679	A304	$5 bl, car & blk	75	20

Issued to commemorate the 25th anniversary of the United Nations.

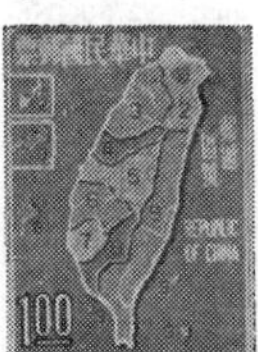

Postal Zone Map of Taiwan—A305

Postal Code Emblem—A306

1970, Oct. 8 Lithographed

1680	A305	$1 lt bl & multi	25	8
1681	A306	$2.50 grn & multi	60	25

Issued to publicize the postal code system.

Eleventh Month Scroll
A307

Designs: A scroll series, "Activities of the 12 Months," painted on silk by a group of painters of the Ch'ien Lung court (1736–1796). Chinese number in parenthesis at right of denomination tells month.

Perf. 13½x13

1970–71 Photo. Unwmkd.

Jan., Feb., Mar. Scrolls

(一) (二) (三)

1682	A307	$1 multi	90	20
1683	A307	$2.50 multi	1.25	30
1684	A307	$5 multi	2.00	50

Apr., May, June Scrolls

(四) (五) (六)

1685	A307	$1 multi	20	8
1686	A307	$2.50 multi	50	20
1687	A307	$5 multi	70	40

July, Aug., Sept. Scrolls

(七) (八) (九)

1688	A307	$1 multi	20	8
1689	A307	$2.50 multi	50	20
1690	A307	$5 multi	70	30

Oct., Nov., Dec. Scrolls

(十) (一十) (二十)

1691	A307	$1 multi	20	8
1692	A307	$2.50 multi	50	20
1693	A307	$5 multi	70	30
		Nos. 1682-1693 (12)	8.35	2.84

Issue dates: Nos. 1691–1693, Oct. 21, 1970. Nos. 1682–1684, Jan. 14, 1971. Nos. 1685–1687, Apr. 26, 1971. Nos. 1688–1690, Aug. 27, 1971.

Family at Home
A308

Piggy Bank
A309

Design: $4, Family of 5 going on an excursion (vert.).

Perf. 13½x14, 14x13½

1970, Nov. 11 Litho. Wmk. 323

Granite Paper

1694	A308	$1 multi	20	8
1695	A308	$4 yel grn & multi	60	20

Issued to publicize family planning.

1970, Dec. 1 *Perf. 12½x12*

Granite Paper

1696	A309	50c multi	35	8
1697	A309	$4.50 bl & multi	1.50	40

Issued for use on New Year's greetings.

Tibia Fusus Shells
A310

Rare Taiwan Shells: $2.50, Harpeola kurodai. $5, Conus stupa kuroda. $8, Entemnotrochus rumphii.

1971, Feb. 25 ***Perf. 13x13½***

1698	A310	$1	vio & multi	20	8
1699	A310	$2.50	multi	25	20
1700	A310	$5	org & multi	60	40
1701	A310	$8	grn & multi	1.00	25

Sun Yat-sen Building, Yangmingshan
A311

Passbook and Postal Savings Certificate
A312

Perf. 13½x12½

1971 Lithographed Wmk. 323

Granite Paper

1702	A311	5c	brown	8	4
1703	A311	10c	dk gray	8	4
1704	A311	50c	brt rose lil	10	4
1705	A311	$1	vermilion	10	4
1706	A311	$1.50	ultra	25	5
1707	A311	$2	plum	25	5
1708	A311	$2.50	emerald	50	5
1709	A311	$3	aqua	50	5
			Nos. 1702-1709 (8)	1.86	36

Perf. 13½x14

1971, Mar. 20 Litho. Wmk. 323

Design: $4, People and hand dropping coin into bank.

1712	A312	$1	yel grn & multi	15	8
1713	A312	$4	ver & multi	60	20

Publicizing Chinese Postal Savings Service.

Cooperation Emblem, Farmers
A313

Rock Monkey
A314

Design: $8, Chinese teaching rice farming to Africans (horiz.).

Photogravure

1971, May 20 ***Perf. 13*** **Unwmkd.**

1714	A313	$1	multi	20	8
1715	A313	$8	multi	90	40

Sino-African Technical Cooperation Committee, 10th anniversary.

1971, June 25 ***Perf. 11½***

Taiwan Animals: $2, White-face flying squirrel. $3, Chinese pangolin. $5, Formosan sika deer. ($2, $3, $5 are horiz.).

1716	A314	$1	gold & multi	25	15
1717	A314	$2	gold & multi	25	20
1718	A314	$3	gold & multi	50	20
1719	A314	$5	gold & multi	50	40

Pitcher
A315

Designs: $2.50, Players at base (horiz.). $4, Hitter and catcher.

1971, July 29 Photo. ***Perf. 13***

1720	A315	$1	multi	25	8
1721	A315	$2.50	multi	35	20
1722	A315	$4	multi	60	20

Pacific Regional competition for the 1971 Little League World Series.

Nos. 1541, 1544–1545 Overprinted in Magenta or Red

Perf. 13x12½

1971, Sept. 9 Litho. Wmk. 323

Granite Paper

1723	A259	$1	ver (M)	20	8
1724	A259	$2.50	bl (R)	50	25
1725	A259	$3	grnsh bl (R)	40	30

Chinese victory in 1971 Little League World Series, Williamsport, Pa., Aug. 24.

Fairy Tale Type of 1970

Chinese Fairy Tales (Filial Piety): No. 1726, Birds and elephant helping in rice field. No. 1727, Son gathering mulberries for mother. No. 1728, Son gathering firewood. No. 1729, Son, mother and bandits. No. 1730, Son carrying heavy burden. 50c, Son digging for bamboo shoots in winter. No. 1732, Man and wife working as slaves. No. 1733, Father, son and carriage.

1971, Sept. 22 ***Perf. 13½***

Granite Paper

1726	A301	10c	dp org & multi	8	4
1727	A301	10c	lil & multi	8	4
1728	A301	10c	ocher & multi	8	4
1729	A301	10c	dp car & multi	8	4
1730	A301	10c	lt ultra & multi	8	4
1731	A301	50c	multi	10	4
1732	A301	$1	emer & multi	20	5
1733	A301	$1	lt red brn & multi	20	5
			Nos. 1726-1733 (8)	90	34

Flag of China, "Double Ten" and Anniversary Emblems
A316

Designs (Flag of China and): $2.50, National anthem. $5, Gen. Chiang Kai-shek. $8, Sun Yat-sen.

1971, Oct. 10 Photo. ***Perf. 13***

1734	A316	$1	org & multi	20	8
1735	A316	$2.50	multi	30	15
1736	A316	$5	grn & multi	60	40
1737	A316	$8	ol & multi	75	40

60th National Day.

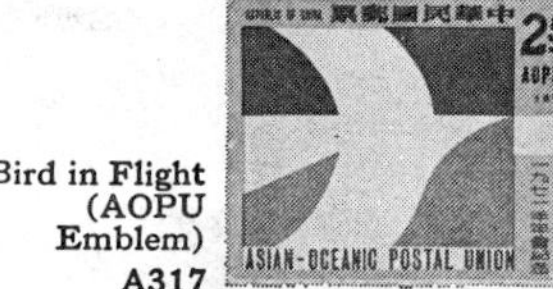

Bird in Flight (AOPU Emblem)
A317

Perf. 13½x14

1971, Nov. 8 Litho. Wmk. 323

1738	A317	$2.50	yel & multi	70	20
1739	A317	$5	org & multi	70	20

Asian-Oceanic Postal Union Executive Committee Session, Taipei, Nov. 8–15.

"White Frost Hawk," by Lang Shih-ning
A318

Dog Series I

Designs: $2, "Star-Glancing Wolf." $2.50, "Golden-Winged Face." $5, "Young Black Dragon." $8, "Young Gray Dragon."

Designs from painting series "Ten Prized Dogs," by Lang Shih-ning (Giuseppe Castiglione, 1688–1766).

Perf. 13½x13

1971, Nov. 16 Litho. Unwmkd.

Multicolored

1740	A318	$1	*Facing left*	25	8
1741	A318	$2	*Lying down*	30	10
1742	A318	$2.50	*Scratching*	35	20
1743	A318	$5	*Facing right*	70	30
1744	A318	$8	*Looking back*	1.20	60
			Nos. 1740-1744 (5)	2.80	1.28

Dog Series II

Designs: $1, "Black with Snow-white Paws." $2, "Yellow Leopard." $2.50, "Flying Magpie." $5, "Heavenly Lion." $8, "Mottled Tiger."

1972, Jan. 12

1745	A318	$1	*Facing right*	25	10
1746	A318	$2	*Walking*	30	10
1747	A318	$2.50	*Sleeping*	35	20
1748	A318	$5	*Facing left*	70	30
1749	A318	$8	*Sitting*	1.50	50
			Nos. 1745-1749 (5)	3.10	1.20

Squirrels—A319

Perf. 13½x12½

1971, Dec. 1 Wmk. 323

1750	A319	Block of 4, multi	60	40
a.		50c in UL corner	10	4
b.		50c in UR corner	10	4
c.		50c in LL corner	10	4
d.		50c in LR corner	10	4
1751	A319	Block of 4, multi	3.25	2.25
a.		$4.50 in UL corner	60	30
b.		$4.50 in UR corner	60	30
c.		$4.50 in LL corner	60	30
d.		$4.50 in LR corner	60	30

New Year 1972.

Flags of China and Jordan
A320

1971, Dec. 16 ***Perf. 13½***

Granite Paper

1752	A320	$5	multi	70	20

50th anniversary of the founding of the Hashemite Kingdom of Jordan.

Cargo Ship "Hai King"
A321

Design: $7, Ocean liner and map of Pacific Ocean (vert.).

1971, Dec. 16 ***Perf. 12½***

1753	A321	$4	grn, dk bl & red	45	20
1754	A321	$7	ocher & multi	70	20

Centenary of China Merchants Steam Navigation Co.

Downhill Skiing, Olympic Rings
A322

Designs: $5, Cross-country skiing. $8, Giant slalom.

1972, Feb. 3 ***Perf. 13½***

1755	A322	$1	org, blk & bl	20	8
1756	A322	$5	yel grn, dp org & blk	60	20
1757	A322	$8	red, gray & blk	70	20

11th Winter Olympic Games, Sapporo, Japan, Feb. 3–13.

Vase, 18th Century
A323

Porcelain Series I

Porcelain Masterworks of Ching Dynasty: $2, Covered jar. $2.50, Pitcher. $5, Vase with 5 openings and dragon design. $8, Covered jar with children design.

Perf. 11½

1972, Mar. 20 Photo. Unwmkd.

1758	A323	$1	vio & multi	30	8
1759	A323	$2	plum & bl	30	15
1760	A323	$2.50	org ver & bl	30	15
1761	A323	$5	bis brn & bl	60	25
1762	A323	$8	sl grn & multi	90	40
			Nos. 1758-1762 (5)	2.40	1.03

See also Nos. 1812–1821, 1864–1868.

Nine Flying Doves
A324

Perf. 13½x14

1972, Apr. 1 Litho. Wmk. 323

1763 A324 $1 lt bl & blk 20 8
1764 A324 $5 lt vio & blk 60 20

Asian-Oceanic Postal Union, 10th anniversary.

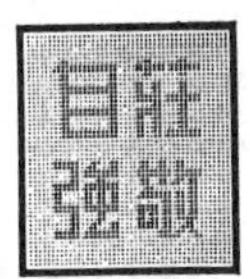

"Dignity with Self-reliance"
A325

Perf. 13½x12½

1972–75 Litho. Wmk. 323

1765 A325 5c brn & yel 5 3
1766 A325 10c bl & org 5 3
1767 A325 20c cl & yel grn ('75) 5 3
1768 A325 50c lil & lil rose 5 3
1769 A325 $1 red & brt bl 10 3
1770 A325 $1.50 yel & dk bl 20 4
1771 A325 $2 mar & org 20 6
1772 A325 $2.50 emer & ver 20 7
1773 A325 $3 red & lt grn 25 8
Nos. 1765-1773 (9) 1.15 40

Souvenir Sheet

Imperf.

1775 A325 Sheet of 2 1.00 1.00

No. 1775 commemorates ROCPEX '72 Philatelic Exhibition, Taipei, Oct. 24–Nov. 2. It contains 2 stamps similar to Nos. 1771 and 1773 with simulated perforations. Orange brown margin with white inscriptions. Size: 69x100mm.

Issue dates: $1, $1.50, $2, $3, May 20, 1972; 5c, 10c, 50c, $2.50, No. 1775, Oct. 24, 1972; 20c, 1975.

Emperor Shih-tsung's Procession
A326

Messengers on Horseback—A327

Designs from scrolls depicting Emperor Shih-tsung's (reigned 1522–1566) journey to and from tombs at Cheng-tien. No. 1776 shows land journey and is designed from right to left. No. 1779 shows return trip by boat and is designed from left to right. The five stamps of Nos. 1776 and 1780 are numbered 1 to 5 in Chinese (see illustrations with Nos. 1682–1686 for numerals).

1972 Photo. *Perf. 13½* Unwmkd.

Multicolored

1776 A326 Strip of 5, *Departure* 70 35
 a. $1 *shown* (1) 10 5
 b. $1 *Seven carriages* (2) 10 5
 c. $1 *Carriage drawn by 23 horses* (3) 10 5
 d. $1 *Procession* (4) 10 5
 e. $1 *Emperor under 2 canopies* (5) 10 5
1777 A327 $2.50 *shown* 40 8
1778 A327 $5 *Guards with flags, fans & spears* 60 20
1779 A327 $8 *Sedan chair carried by 28 men* 1.00 40
1780 A326 Strip of 5, *Return trip* 70 35
 a. $1 *Three barges* (1) 10 5
 b. $1 *Procession, sedan chairs* (2) 10 5
 c. $1 *Two barges with trunks* (3) 10 5
 d. $1 *Procession on land* (4) 10 5
 e. $1 *Procession, 2 sedan chairs* (5) 10 5
1781 A327 $2.50 *Courtiers at city welcoming Emperor* 40 8
1782 A327 $5 *Orchestra on horseback* 60 20
1783 A327 $8 *Barges* 90 40
Nos. 1776-1783 (8) 5.30 2.06

Issue dates: No. 1776–1779, June 14; Nos. 1780–1783, July 12.

First Day Covers
A328

Magnifying Glass, Tongs, Gauge
A329

Design: $2.50, Sun Yat-sen stamp of 1971 (type A311) under magnifying glass.

Wmk. 323

1972, Aug. 9 Engr. *Perf. 12*

1784 A328 $1 dk vio bl 20 5
1785 A328 $2.50 brt brn 25 8
1786 A329 $8 scarlet 75 20

Promotion of philately. Printed in sheets of 40. Each sheet contains 4 blocks of 10 stamps surrounded by margins with inscriptions.

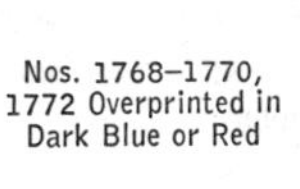

Nos. 1768–1770, 1772 Overprinted in Dark Blue or Red

Perf. 13½x12½

1972, Sept. 9 Litho. Wmk. 323

1787 A325 $1 red & brt bl (DB) 20 8
1788 A325 $1.50 yel & dk bl (R) 40 20
1789 A325 $2 mar & org (R) 40 8
1790 A325 $3 red & lt grn (DB) 40 15

China's championship victories in the Little League World Series, Gary, Ind., and in the Senior League World Series, Williamsport, Pa., Aug. 1972.

Emperor Yao (2357–2258 B.C.)
A330

Mountain Climbing
A331

Rulers: $4, Emperor Shun (ruled 2255–2208 B.C.). $4.50, Yü, the Great (ruled 2205–2198 B.C.). $5, King T'ang (ruled 1783–1754 B.C.). $5.50, King Wen (ruled 1171–1122 B.C.). $6, King Wu (ruled 1121–1114 B.C.). $7, Chou Kung (died 1105 B.C.). $8, Confucius (551–479 B.C.).

1972–73 Engraved *Perf. 12*

Granite Paper

1791 A330 $3.50 dk bl 25 20
1792 A330 $4 rose red 25 20
1793 A330 $4.50 bluish lil 30 20
1794 A330 $5 brt grn 35 20
1795 A330 $5.50 dp org ('73) 50 20
1796 A330 $6 dp cl ('73) 50 25
 a. Perf. 13½x12½ ('76) 50 25
1797 A330 $7 sep ('73) 50 25
 a. Perf. 13½x12½ ('76) 50 25
1798 A330 $8 ind ('73) 75 30
 a. gray, perf. 13½x12½ ('76) 75 30
Nos. 1791-1798 (8) 3.40 1.80

In the first printing, Nos. 1791-1794, 1796-1798 measure 32mm. high. In a 1974 reissue they are 33mm.

Photogravure

1972, Oct. 31 *Perf. 12* Unwmkd.

Designs (China Youth Corps emblem and): $2.50, Skiing (skiers forming circle). $4, Diving. $8, Parachute jumping.

1800 A331 $1 grn & multi 15 8
1801 A331 $2.50 bl & multi 30 8
1802 A331 $4 org & multi 40 20
1803 A331 $8 multi 90 40

China Youth Corps, 20th anniversary.

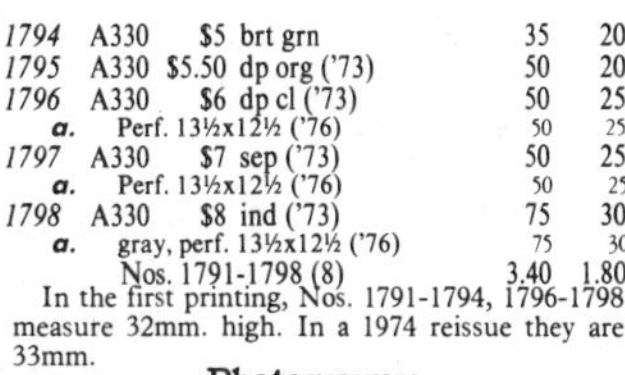

JCI Emblem
A332

1972, Nov. 12 Litho. Wmk. 323

1804 A332 $1 multi 20 8
1805 A332 $5 org & multi 50 15
1806 A332 $8 multi 75 40

27th Junior Chamber International (JCI) World Congress, Taipei, Nov. 12–19.

Electronic Mail Sorter
A333

Plane, Ship and Pier
A334

Design: $5, Highway overpass over railroad.

Engraved

1972, Nov. 12 *Perf. 11½* Wmk. 323

1807 A333 $1 red 20 8
1808 A334 $2.50 blue 35 15
1809 A334 $5 dk vio & brn 75 30

Progress of communications system on Taiwan.

Cow and Calf (Parental Love)
A335

1972, Dec. 1 Litho. *Perf. 12*

1810 A335 50c red & blk 30 8
1811 A335 $4.50 yel, red & brn 80 30

New Year 1973. Printed in sheets of 80, divided into 4 panes of 20, separated by vertical and horizontal gutters 2 rows wide. 20 red chops meaning "Happy New Year" are printed in the gutters.

Porcelain Type of 1972 and

Stem Bowl with Dragons
A336

Porcelain Series II

1973 Photogravure *Perf. 11½*

Porcelain Masterworks of Ming Dynasty: $1, Covered vase with fruits and flowers. $2, Vase with ornamental and floral design. $2.50, Vase imitating ancient bronze. $5, Flask with flowers of 4 seasons. $8, Garlic head vase.

1812 A323 $1 gray & multi 15 5
1813 A323 $2 lt brn & multi 20 8
1814 A323 $2.50 brt grn & multi 30 10
1815 A323 $5 ultra & multi 50 25
1816 A323 $8 ol & multi 75 40
Nos. 1812-1816 (5) 1.90 88

Porcelain Series III

Ming Porcelain: $2, Refuse container with dragons. $2.50, Covered jar with lotus. $5, Covered jar with horses. $8, Bowl with figures of immortals.

1817 A336 $1 gray & multi 15 5
1818 A336 $2 lt vio & multi 20 8
1819 A336 $2.50 dk red & multi 40 10
1820 A336 $5 bl & multi 40 20
1821 A336 $8 dp org & multi 75 30
Nos. 1817-1821 (5) 1.90 73

Issue dates: Nos. 1812–1816, Jan. 10; Nos. 1817–1821, Mar. 24.

See also Nos. 1865–1868.

Oyster Fairy and Fisherman's Dance—A337

1973, Feb. 7 Photo. *Perf. 11½*

Granite Paper

Multicolored

1822 A337 $1 *Kicking shuttlecock* (vert.) 35 5
1823 A337 $4 *shown* 60 20
1824 A337 $5 *Rowing boat over land* 60 20
1825 A337 $8 *Old man carrying young lady* (vert.) 90 30

Chinese folklore popular entertainment.

Bamboo Boat
A338

Taiwanese Handicrafts: $2.50, Painted marble vase (vert.). $5, Painted glass plate. $8, Doll, bridegroom carrying bride on back (vert.).

Perf. 13½x14½, 14½x13½

1973, Mar. 9 Photogravure

1826 A338 $1 multi 20 5
1827 A338 $2.50 multi 35 10
1828 A338 $5 multi 60 20
1829 A338 $8 multi 85 30

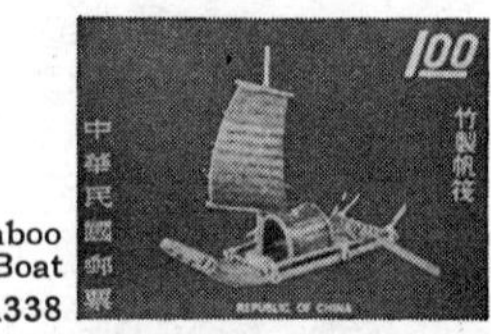

Federation Emblem, Cargo Hook, Crane
A339

Emblem, Tractor, New Buildings
A340

Perf. 12½

1973, Apr. 2 Litho. Wmk. 323

1830	A339	$1 sal & multi	10	5
1831	A340	$5 bl & blk	40	20

12th convention of International Federation of Asian and Western Pacific Contractors Association, Taipei, Apr. 2–10.

Pres. Chiang Kai-shek, Flag of China
A341

Lin Tse-hsü
A342

Design: $4, like $1 with different border.

Perf. 12

1973, May 20 Photo. Unwmkd.

1832	A341	$1 yel & multi	30	5
1833	A341	$4 dk grn & multi	65	20

First anniversary of Pres. Chiang Kai-shek's inauguration for a fifth term.

Engraved

1973, June 3 *Perf. 12* Wmk. 323

1834	A342	$1 sepia	15	6

Lin Tse-hsü (1785–1850), Governor of Hunan and Kwantung, who destroyed large quantity of opium at Humen, Kwantung, June 3, 1839.

Willows and Palace Gate in the Morning—A343

Lady Watering Peonies, Stone Ornament
A344

Design from scroll "Spring Morning in the Han Palace," by Chiu Ying. The five stamps of No. 1835 are numbered 1 to 5 and the five stamps of No. 1838 are numbered 6–10 in Chinese (see illustrations with Nos. 1682–1691 for numerals). The stamps are numbered and listed from right to left.

Perf. 11½

1973 Photogravure Unwmkd.

Multicolored; Granite Paper

1835	A343	Strip of 5	60	25
a.		$1 *shown* (1)	8	5
b.		$1 *Ladies feeding peacocks* (2)	8	5
c.		$1 *Lady watering peonies* (3)	8	5
d.		$1 *Pear tree in bloom* (4)	8	5
e.		$1 *Lady musicians* (5)	8	5
1836	A344	$5 *shown*	50	20
1837	A344	$8 *Lady musicians*	70	30
1838	A343	Strip of 5	60	25
a.		$1 *Ladies playing go* (6)	8	5
b.		$1 *Various games* (7)	8	5
c.		$1 *Talking and playing music* (8)	8	5

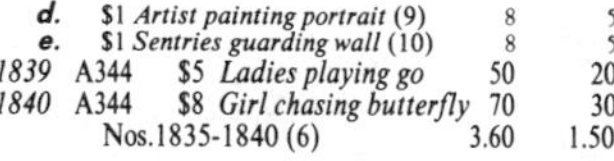

d.		$1 *Artist painting portrait* (9)	8	5
e.		$1 *Sentries guarding wall* (10)	8	5
1839	A344	$5 *Ladies playing go*	50	20
1840	A344	$8 *Girl chasing butterfly*	70	30
		Nos.1835-1840 (6)	3.60	1.50

Issue dates: Nos. 1835–1837, June 20; Nos. 1838–1840, July 18.

Fan, Bamboo Design, by Hsiang Te-hsin—A345

Wmk. 368

Wmkd. JEZ Multiple (368)

Designs: Painted fans, Ming dynasty.

1973, Aug. 15 Photo. *Perf. 12½x13*

1841	A345	$1 bis & multi	15	6
1842	A345	$2.50 bis & multi	30	8
1843	A345	$5 bis & multi	50	20
1844	A345	$8 bis & multi	80	30

See also Nos. 1934–1937.

Little League Emblem
A346

INTERPOL Emblem
A347

Wmk. 370

Wmkd. Geometrical Design (370)

1973, Sept. 9 Litho. *Perf. 13½*

1845	A346	$1 yel, car & dk bl	20	6
1846	A346	$4 yel, grn & dk bl	40	20

Chinese victory in Little League Twin Championships, Gary, Ind., and Williamsport, Pa.

1973, Sept. 11 Litho. Wmk. 370

Perf. 12

1847	A347	$1 bl & org	10	5
1848	A347	$5 grn & org	40	20
1849	A347	$8 mag & org	60	30

50th anniversary of International Criminal Police Organization.

Ch'iu Feng-chia
A348

Engraved

1973, Oct. 5 *Perf. 11½* Wmk. 323

1850	A348	$1 vio blk	20	8

2nd meeting of overseas Hakkas, Taipei, Oct. 5–7, and to honor Ch'iu Feng-chia (1864–1912), Hakka scholar, poet and revolutionist.

Tseng-wen Reservoir
A349

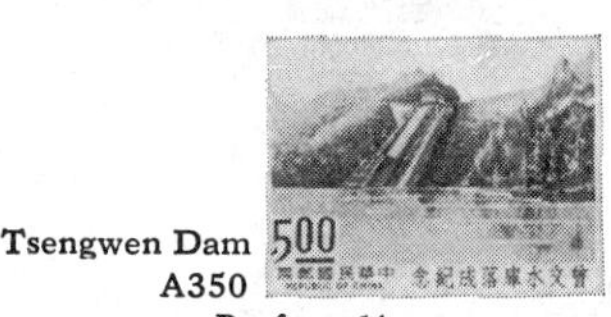

Tsengwen Dam
A350

Perf. 13½

1973, Oct. 31 Photo. Unwmkd.

Multicolored

1851	A349	Strip of 3	40	15
a.		$1 *Upper shore*	8	5
b.		$1 *shown*	8	5
c.		$1 *Lower shore*	8	5

Perf. 12x11½

1852	A350	$5 *shown*	50	20
1853	A350	$8 *Spillway*	70	30

Inauguration of Tsengwen Reservoir. No. 1851 printed se-tenant in sheets of 15.

Tiger
A351

Wmk. 370

1973, Dec. 1 Litho. *Perf. 12½*

1854	A351	50c multi	20	6
1855	A351	$4.50 multi	60	20

New Year 1974.

"Snow-dotted Eagle," by Lang Shih-ning—A352

Designs: No. 1857, "Comfortable Ride." No. 1858, "Red Flower Eagle." No. 1859, "Cloud-running Steed." No. 1860, "Sky-running steed." $2.50, "Red Jade Seat." $5, "Thunderclap Steed." $8, "Arabian Champion." Designs from painting series "Ten Prized Horses," by Lang Shih-ning (Giuseppe Castiglione, 1688–1766).

Perf. 13

1973 Lithographed Unwmkd.

Multicolored; Without Gum

1856	A352	50c *shown*	8	5
1857	A352	$1 *Pinto, blk tail*	18	3
1858	A352	$1 Facing left	18	5
1859	A352	$1 *Facing right*	18	5
1860	A352	$1 *Pinto, white tail*	18	5
1861	A352	$2.50 *Palomino*	40	8
1862	A352	$5 *Grazing*	60	20
a.		Souvenir sheet of 4	90	
1863	A352	$8 *Brown stallion*	1.00	25
		Nos. 1856-1863 (8)	2.80	76

Nos. 1857–1860 printed se-tenant in sheets of 50. No. 1862a contains 4 stamps with simulated perforations similar to Nos. 1856–1857, 1861–1862. Bluish green ornamental margin, black inscription. Size: 150x120mm.

Issue dates: 50c, $2.50, $5, Nov. 21; others Dec. 21.

Porcelain Types of 1972–73

Porcelain Series IV

Porcelain Masterworks of Sung Dynasty: $1, Vase. $2, Three-tiered vase. $2.50, Lotus-shaped bowl. $5, Incense burner. $8, Incense burner on stand.

1974, Jan. 16 Photo. *Perf. 11½*

1864	A323	$1 ultra & multi	12	5
1865	A336	$2 multi	25	8
1866	A336	$2.50 red & multi	30	8
1867	A336	$5 lil & multi	50	20
1868	A336	$8 grn & multi	70	30
		Nos.1864-1868 (5)	1.87	71

Juggler
A353

Taroko Gorge, Hualien
A354

Design: $8, Magician producing dishes from his robe (horiz.).

1974, Feb. 6 Photo. *Perf. 11½*

1869	A353	$1 yel & multi	15	5
1870	A353	$8 yel & multi	60	30

1974, Mar. 22 Photo. *Perf. 12*

Designs: $2.50, Luce Chapel, Tunghai University. $5, Tzu En Pagoda, Sun Moon Lake. $8, Goddess of Mercy, Keelung.

1871	A354	$1 multi	12	5
1872	A354	$2.50 multi	30	7
1873	A354	$5 multi	45	15
1874	A354	$8 multi	75	25

Taiwan landmarks.

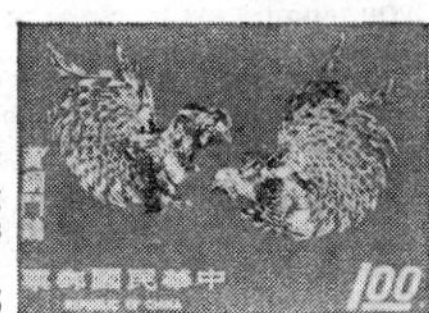

Fighting Cocks (Brass)
A355

Designs: $2.50, Grapes and bowl with fruit (imitation jade). $5, Fisherman (wood carving; vert.). $8, Basket with plastic roses (vert.).

Perf. 13½x14½, 14½x13½

1974, Apr. 10

1875	A355	$1 bl grn & multi	12	5
1876	A355	$2.50 brn & multi	30	8
1877	A355	$5 crim & multi	40	15
1878	A355	$8 multi	75	25

Taiwanese handicraft products.

Sun Yat-sen Memorial Hall
A356

Designs: $2.50, Reaching-moon Tower, Cheng Ching Lake. $5, Orchid Island (boats). $8, Penghu Interisland Bridge.

1974, May 15 Photo. *Perf. 11½*
Granite Paper

1879	A356	$1 bl & multi	12	5
1880	A356	$2.50 bl & multi	35	8
1881	A356	$5 bl & multi	40	15
1882	A356	$8 bl & multi	75	25

Taiwan landmarks.

Pres. Chiang and Gate of Whampoa Military Academy
A357

Marching Cadets and Entrance Gate
A358

Perf. 11½
1974, June 16 Engraved Wmk. 323

1883	A357	$1 car rose	30	3
1884	A358	$14 vio bl	1.20	50

50th anniversary of the founding of the Whampoa Military Academy.

Long-distance Runner and Olympic Rings
A359

The Boy Wang Ch'i Fighting Invaders
A360

Design: $8, Women's relay race and Olympic rings.

1974, June 23 Litho. *Perf. 12½*

1885	A359	$1 bl, blk & red	12	5
1886	A359	$8 pink, blk & red	65	25

80th anniversary of International Olympic Committee.

1974, July 15 *Perf. 13½* Wmk. 370

Folk Tales: No. 1888, T'i Ying pleading for her father before the Emperor. No. 1889, Wen Yen-po flushing out ball caught in tree. No. 1890, Boy Wang Hua returning gold piece he found. No. 1891, Pu Shih, a rich sheep raiser and benefactor. No. 1892, K'ung Yung as a child choosing smallest pear. No. 1893, Tung Yu studying. No. 1894, Szu Ma-kuang saving playmate from drowning in water jar.

1887	A360	50c ol & multi	5	4
1888	A360	50c ultra & multi	5	4
1889	A360	50c ocher & multi	5	4
1890	A360	50c red brn & multi	5	4
1891	A360	$1 grn & multi	10	4
1892	A360	$1 lil & multi	10	4
1893	A360	$1 bl & multi	10	4
1894	A360	$1 car & multi	10	4
		Nos. 1887-1894 (8)	60	32

Same denominations printed in blocks of four in sheets of 100.

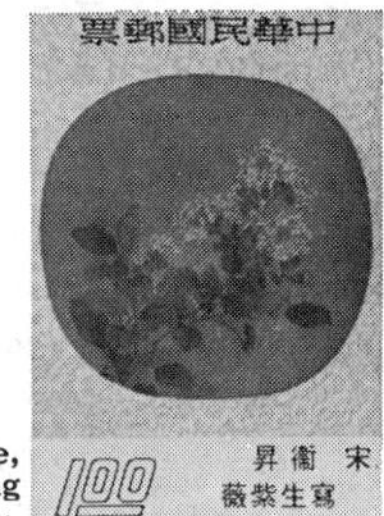

Myrtle, by Wei Sheng
A361

Silk Fan Paintings, Sung Dynasty (960–1279 A.D.): $2.50, Cabbage and Insects, by Hsu Ti. $5, Hibiscus, Cat and Dog, by Li Ti. $8, Pomegranate and Birds, by Wu Ping. Fans from National Palace Museum.

Perf. 13x12½
1974, Aug. 14 Photo. Wmk. 368

1895	A361	$1 multi	15	3
1896	A361	$2.50 multi	35	7
1897	A361	$5 multi	60	15
1898	A361	$8 multi	90	25

See Nos. 1950–1953.

Battle at Marco Polo Bridge, July 7, 1937
A362

Perf. 13½
1974, Sept. 3 Litho. Wmk. 370

1899	A362	$1 multi	10	5

Souvenir Sheet
Wmk. 323
Without Gum; Granite Paper

1900	A362	$1 multi, sheet of 8	80	
a.		Single stamp	10	

20th Armed Forces Day. No. 1900 commemorates Armed Forces Stamp Exhibition, Sun Yat-sen Memorial Hall, Sept. 3–9. Sheet has yellow ornamental margin with black inscription. Size: 106x146mm.

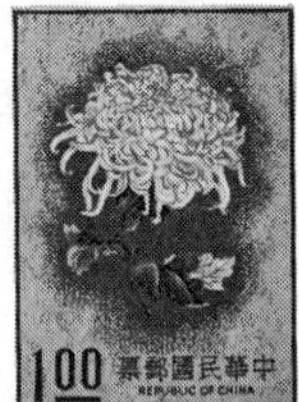

Chrysanthemum
A363

Designs: Various chrysanthemums.

Perf. 12
1974, Sept. 30 Photo. Unwmkd.
Granite Paper

1901	A363	$1 lil & multi	12	5
1902	A363	$2.50 multi	30	8
1903	A363	$5 org & multi	45	15
1904	A363	$8 multi	75	25

Rep. of China Pavilion, EXPO Emblem
A364

Map of Fair Grounds, Chinese Flag
A364a

Perf. 13
1974, Oct. 10 Litho. Wmk. 370

1905	A364	$1 multi	15	5
1906	A364a	$8 multi	60	25

EXPO '74, Spokane, Wash., May 4–Nov. 4. Theme, "Preserve the Environment."

Steel Mill, Kaohsiung
A365

Taichung Harbor
A366

Designs: $1, Taiwan North Link Railroad and map. $2, Oil refinery. $2.50, Electric train. $3.50, Taoyuan International Airport. $4, Taiwan North-South Highway and map. $4.50, Kaohsiung shipyard. $5, Su-ao Port.

Perf. 13x12½, 12½x13
1974, Oct. 31 Wmk. 323

1907	A365	50c lil, yel & brn	5	3
1908	A365	$1 grn & org	10	3
1909	A365	$2 bl & yel	15	5
1910	A365	$2.50 emer & org	15	8
1911	A366	$3 ocher & ultra	20	10
1912	A366	$3.50 sl grn & yel	25	12
1913	A366	$4 brn & yel	30	14
1914	A366	$4.50 ver & bl	30	15
1915	A366	$5 sep & dk bl	40	16
		Nos. 1907-1915 (9)	1.90	86

Major construction projects.
See Nos. 2009–2017, 2068–2076.

Agaricus Bisporus
A367

Edible Mushrooms: $2.50, Pleurotus ostreatus. $5, Dictyophora indusiata. $8, Flammulina velutipes.

Photogravure
1974, Nov. 15 *Perf. 11½* Unwmkd.

1916	A367	$1 multi	10	5
1917	A367	$2.50 multi	35	8
1918	A367	$5 multi	60	16
1919	A367	$8 multi	75	25

9th International Scientific Congress on the Cultivation of Edible Fungi, Taipei, Nov. 1974.

Batters and World Map
A368

Pitcher and Championship Banners
A369

Lithographed
1974, Nov. 24 *Perf. 13½* Wmk. 323

1920	A368	$1 multi	15	5
1921	A369	$8 multi	60	25

China's victory in 1974 Little League Baseball World Series Triple Championships.

Rabbit
A370

Acrobat with Iron Rod
A371

Perf. 12½
1974, Dec. 10 Photo. Wmk. 323

1922	A370	50c org & multi	10	5
1923	A370	$4.50 brn & multi	40	15

New Year 1975.

1975, Jan. 15 *Perf. 11½* Unwmkd.

Design: $5, Two acrobats spinning tops (horiz.).

Granite Paper

1924	A371	$4 yel & multi	30	15
1925	A371	$5 yel & multi	45	20

Children Watching Puppet Show—A372

Ceremonial New Year Greetings—A373

Designs from scroll "Festivals for the New Year," by Ting Kuan-p'eng. Nos. 1926a–1926e are numbered 1–5 in Chinese.

1975, Feb. 25 Photo. *Perf. 11½*
Multicolored; Granite Paper

1926	A372	Strip of 5	50	20
a.		$1 *Ceremonial New Year Greetings* (1)	8	5
b.		$1 *Man with trained monkey* (2)	8	5
c.		$1 *Crowd and musicians* (3)	8	5
d.		$1 *Picnic under a tree* (4)	8	5
e.		$1 *shown* (5)	8	5
1927	A373	$2.50 *shown*	35	8
1928	A373	$5 *Children buying firecrackers*	50	20
1929	A373	$8 *Children and man with trained monkey*	1.20	60

Sun Yat-sen Memorial Hall, Taipei
A374

Sun Yat-sen's Handwriting
A375

Sun Yat-sen, Bronze Statue in Memorial Hall
A376

Sun Yat-sen Memorial Hall, St. John's University, N.Y.
A377

Perf. 13½x14, 14x13½

1975, Mar. 12 **Lithographed**

1930	A374	$1 grn & multi	12	5
1931	A375	$4 yel grn & multi	35	15
1932	A376	$5 yel & multi	45	20
1933	A377	$8 gray & multi	75	30

Dr. Sun Yat-sen (1866–1925), statesman and revolutionary leader, 50th death anniversary.

Fan Type of 1973 Inscribed: "Landscape" (1st Characters, 水 山 2nd Row)

Designs: Painted fans, Ming Dynasty. Second row of inscription gives design description.

Perf. 12½x13

1975, Apr. 16 **Photo.** **Wmk. 368**

1934	A345	$1 bis & multi	12	4
1935	A345	$2.50 bis & multi	30	8
1936	A345	$5 bis & multi	45	20
1937	A345	$8 bis & multi	75	30

Yuan-chin coin, 1122–221 B.C.
A378

Ancient Chinese Coins: $4, Pan-liang, 221–207 B.C. $5, Five chu, 206 B.C.–220 A.D. $8, Five chu, 502–557 A.D.

Perf. 13

1975, May 20 **Litho.** **Wmk. 323**

1938	A378	$1 sal & multi	12	4
1939	A378	$4 yel & multi	30	15
1940	A378	$5 dl yel & multi	45	20
1941	A378	$8 lt vio & multi	75	30

The Cloth-bag Monk, by Chang Hung (1577–1668)
A379

Chinese Paintings: $4, Lao-tzu Riding Buffalo, by Chao Pu-chih (1053–1110). $5, Portrait of Shih-te, by Wang Wen (1497–1576). $8, Splashed-ink Immortal, by Liang K'ai (early 13th century).

Perf. 11½

1975, June 18 **Photo.** **Unwmkd.**

Granite Paper

1942	A379	$2 blk, buff & ver	15	8
1943	A379	$4 blk, gray & red	30	15
1944	A379	$5 blk, yel & ver	40	20
1945	A379	$8 tan, red & blk	75	30

Chu Yin Reading by the Light of Fireflies
A380

Folk Tales: No. 1947, Hua Mu-lan going to war for her father. No. 1948, King Kou Chien tasting gall. $5, Chou Ch'u killing tiger.

Perf. 14x13½

1975, July 16 **Litho.** **Wmk. 368**

1946	A380	$1 ol & multi	12	4
1947	A380	$2 bis brn & multi	18	8
1948	A380	$2 lt grn & multi	18	8
1949	A380	$5 bl & multi	50	16

See Nos. 2108–2111.

Cherry-Apple Blossoms, by Lin Ch'un
A381

Silk Fan Paintings, Sung Dynasty: $2, Spring Blossoms and Butterfly, by Ma K'uei. $5, Monkeys and Deer, by I Yüan-chih. $8, Tame Sparrow among Bamboo.

Perf. 13x12½

1975, Aug. 15 **Litho.** **Wmk. 323**

1950	A381	$1 multi	12	4
1951	A381	$2 multi	25	8
1952	A381	$5 multi	50	16
1953	A381	$8 multi	70	30

See Nos. 2001–2004.

Gen. Chang Tzu-chung (1891–1940)
A382

Portraits: No. 1955, Maj. Gen. Kao Chih-hong (1908–1937). No. 1956, Capt. Sha Shih-chiun (1896–1938). No. 1957, Maj. Gen. Hsieh Chin-yuan (1905–1941). No. 1958, Lt. Yen Hai-wen (1916–1937). No. 1959, Lt. Gen. Tai An-lan (1905–1942).

Perf. 12

1975, Sept. 3 **Engr.** **Wmk. 323**

1954	A382	$2 carmine	25	8
1955	A382	$2 sepia	25	8
1956	A382	$2 dl grn	25	8
1957	A382	$5 vio blk	60	20
1958	A382	$5 vio bl	60	20
1959	A382	$5 dk bl	60	20
		Nos. 1954-1959 (6)	2.55	84

Martyrs of the resistance fight against Japan.

Lotus Pond with Willows, by Madame Chiang—A383

Paintings by Madame Chiang Kai-shek: $5, Sun Breaks through Mountain Clouds. $8, A Pair of Pine Trees. $10, Fishing and Farming.

Perf. 13½

1975, Oct. 31 **Litho.** **Unwmkd.**

1960	A383	$2 multi	20	10
1961	A383	$5 multi	40	25
1962	A383	$8 multi	60	40
1963	A383	$10 multi	75	50

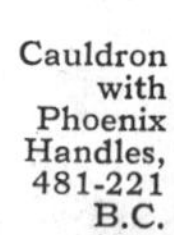

Cauldron with Phoenix Handles, 481-221 B.C.
A384

Ancient Bronzes: $2, Rectangular cauldron, 1122–722 B.C. (vert.). $8, Flat jar, 481–221 B.C. $10, 3-legged wine vessel, 1766–1122 B.C. (vert.).

1975, Nov. 12 **Photo.** ***Perf. 12***

1964	A384	$2 pink & multi	15	10
1965	A384	$5 lt bl & multi	40	25
1966	A384	$8 yel & multi	60	40
1967	A384	$10 lil & multi	75	50

Dragon, Nine-Dragon Wall, Peihai
A385

Techi Dam
A386

Perf. 12½

1975, Dec. 1 **Litho.** **Wmk. 323**

1968	A385	$1 org & multi	10	5
1969	A385	$5 grn & multi	40	20

New Year 1976.

1975, Dec. 17 ***Perf. 13½*** **Unwmkd.**

Design: $10, Panoramic view of Techi Dam.

1970	A386	$2 grn & multi	20	8
1971	A386	$10 bl & multi	85	40

Completion of Techi Dam, Tachia River.

Biathlon and Olympic Rings
A387

Designs (Olympic Rings and): $5, Luge. $8, Skiing.

1976, Jan. 15 **Litho.** ***Perf. 13½***

1972	A387	$2 bl & multi	20	8
1973	A387	$5 bl & multi	40	16
1974	A387	$8 bl & multi	60	25

12th Winter Olympic Games, Innsbruck, Austria, Feb. 4–15.

Chin, Oldest Chinese Instrument
A388

Musical Instruments: $5, Se, c. 2900 B.C. $8, Standing kong-ho (harp). $10, Sleeping kong-ho.

1976, Feb. 11 ***Perf. 14*** **Unwmkd.**

1975	A388	$2 yel & multi	20	8
1976	A388	$5 org & multi	40	16
1977	A388	$8 grnsh bl & multi	60	25
1978	A388	$10 multi	75	32

Double Carp Type of 1969.

Perf. 13½x12½

1976, Dec. 15 **Engraved** **Unwmkd.**

1980	A280	$14 car rose	1.00	25

Mail Collecting
A389

Mail Sorting
A390

Designs: $8, Mail transport. $10, Mail delivery.

Perf. 13½

1976, Mar. 20 **Litho.** **Wmk. 323**

1984	A389	$2 yel & multi	20	8
1985	A390	$5 grn & multi	40	16
1986	A390	$8 bl & multi	60	25
1987	A389	$10 org & multi	75	32
	a.	Souvenir sheet of 4	2.25	2.25

80th anniversary of postal service. No. 1987a contains one each of Nos. 1984–1987; buff margin with red inscription. Size: 130x100mm.

Pres. Chiang Kai-shek
A391

People Paying Homage—A392

Designs: No. 1990, Pres. Chiang lying in state. No. 1991, Hearse leaving funeral chapel. $5, People along funeral route. $8, Spirit tablet in Tzuhu Guest House. $10, Tzuhu Guest House, Pres. Chiang's burial place.

1976, Apr. 4

1988	A391	$2 gray & multi	20	8
1989	A392	$2 gray & multi	20	8
1990	A392	$2 gray & multi	20	8
1991	A392	$2 gray & multi	20	8
1992	A392	$5 gray & multi	35	20
1993	A392	$8 gray & multi	60	30
1994	A392	$10 gray & multi	65	40
		Nos. 1988-1994 (7)	2.40	1.22

Pres. Chiang Kai-shek (1887–1975), first death anniversary.

Flags of China and USA
A393

Perf. 13½

1976, May 29 Litho. Wmk. 323

1995	A393	$2 multi	20	8
1996	A393	$10 yel & multi	70	40

American Bicentennial.

Coin, 12th Century B.C.
A394

Cauldron, Shang Dynasty
A395

Bronze Shovel Coins (pu): $5, Pointed-feet coin, 481–221 B.C. $8, Round-feet coin, 722–481 B.C. $10, Square-feet coin, 3rd–2nd centuries B.C.

1976, June 16

1997	A394	$2 sal & multi	15	8
1998	A394	$5 lt bl & multi	40	16
1999	A394	$8 gray & multi	60	25
2000	A394	$10 multi	75	32

Fan Painting Type of 1975

Silk Fan Paintings, Sung Dynasty: $2, Hibiscus, by Li Tung. $5, Lilies, by Lin Ch'un. $8, Deer and Pine, by Mou Chung-fu. $10, Quail and Wild Flowers, by Li An-chung.

Perf. 13x12½

1976, July 14 Litho. Wmk. 323

2001	A381	$2 multi	20	8
2002	A381	$5 multi	40	20
2003	A381	$8 multi	60	30
2004	A381	$10 multi	75	35

1976, Aug. 25 Photo. *Perf. 11½*

Granite Paper

Ancient Bronzes: $5, 3-legged cauldron, Chou Dynasty (1122–722 B.C.). $8, Wine container, Chou Dynasty. $10, Wine vessel with spout, Shang Dynasty (1766–1122 B.C.).

2005	A395	$2 rose & multi	20	8
2006	A395	$5 lt bl & multi	40	16
2007	A395	$8 yel & multi	60	25
2008	A395	$10 lil & multi	75	32

Construction Types of 1974

Designs: $1, Taiwan North Link railroad and map. $2, Railroad electrification. $3, Taichung Harbor. $4, Taiwan North-South Highway and map. $5, Steel Mill, Kaohsiung. $6, Taoyuan International Airport. $7, Kao-hsiung shipyard. $8, Oil refinery. $9, Su-ao Port.

Perf. 13½x12½, 12½x13½

1976 Lithographed Wmk. 323

2009	A365	$1 car & grn	10	5
2010	A365	$2 org & multi	15	5
2011	A366	$3 vio & multi	20	10
2012	A366	$4 car & multi	25	15
2013	A365	$5 grn & brn	30	20
2014	A366	$6 brn & multi	35	20
2015	A366	$7 brn & multi	40	25
2016	A365	$8 car & grn	50	30
2017	A366	$9 ol & bl	50	30
		Nos. 2009-2017 (9)	2.75	1.60

Chiang Kai-shek and Mother
A396

Sun Yat-sen and Chiang Kai-shek at Canton Station—A397

Design: $5, Chiang Kai-shek, portrait.

1976, Oct. 31 Litho. *Perf. 13½*

2023	A396	$2 multi	20	8
2024	A396	$5 multi	40	20
2025	A397	$10 multi	75	40

Pres. Chiang Kai-shek, 90th anniversary of birth.

Flags of Kuomintang and China
A398

Sun Yat-sen and Chiang Kai-shek
A399

1976, Nov. 12 *Perf. 13½x14*

2026	A398	$2 multi	20	8
2027	A399	$10 multi	75	40
a.		Souvenir sheet of 2	1.00	1.00

11th National Kuomintang Congress, Taipei.

No. 2027a contains one each of Nos. 2026–2027; yellow margin with red inscription. Size: 110x87mm.

Brazen Serpent
A400

1976, Dec. 15 Wmk. 323 *Perf. 12½*

2028	A400	$1 red, lil & gold	10	5
2029	A400	$5 plum, yel & gold	40	16

New Year 1977.

Bird and Plum Blossoms, by Ch'en Hung-shou
A401

Chinese Paintings: $8, "Wintry Days" (pine), by Yang Wei-chen. $10, Rock and Bamboo, by Hsia Ch'ang.

Unwmkd.

1977, Jan. 12 Photo. *Perf. 11½*

Granite Paper

2030	A401	$2 multi	20	8
2031	A401	$8 multi	50	30
2032	A401	$10 multi	75	35

Black-naped Orioles—A402

Birds of Taiwan: $8, Common Kingfisher. $10, Chinese pheasant-tailed jacana.

1977, Feb. 16 Lithographed

2033	A402	$2 multi	20	8
2034	A402	$8 multi	50	30
2035	A402	$10 multi	75	35

See Nos. 2163-2165.

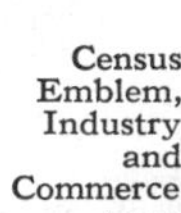

Census Emblem, Industry and Commerce
A403

Unwmkd.

1977, Mar. 16 Litho. *Perf. 13½*

2036	A403	$2 red & multi	20	8
2037	A403	$10 pur & multi	75	35

Industry and Commerce Census.

Green Mountains Rising into Clouds, by Madame Chiang—A404

Landscapes, by Madame Chiang Kai-shek: $5, Boat in the Beauty of Spring. $8, Scholar beside Waterfall. $10, Water Rises to Meet the Bridge.

Photogravure

1977, Mar. 31 *Perf. 11½* Unwmkd.

Granite Paper

2038	A404	$2 multi	20	5
2039	A404	$5 multi	40	12
2040	A404	$8 multi	60	20
2041	A404	$10 multi	75	25

League Emblem
A405

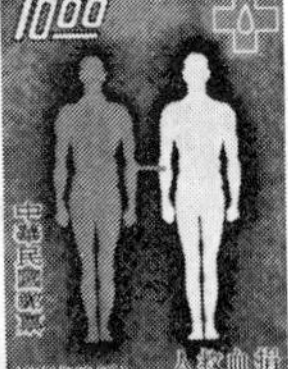

Blood Donation
A406

1977, Apr. 18 Litho. *Perf. 12½*

2042	A405	$2 car & multi	25	5
2043	A405	$10 grn & multi	80	25

10th World Anti-Communist League Conference.

1977, May 5 *Perf. 13½* Wmk. 323

Design: $2, Donating blood (horiz).

2044	A406	$2 red & blk	20	5
2045	A406	$10 red & blk	70	25

Blood donation movement.

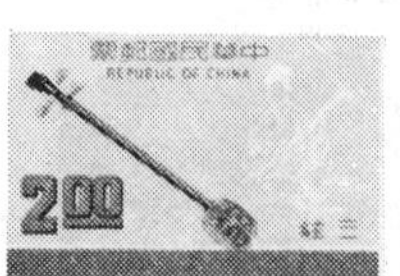

San-hsien
A407

Musical Instruments: $5, Tung-hsiao (bamboo flute). $8, Yang-chin (butterfly harpsichord). $10, Pai-hsiao (pipes). Background shows musician playing instrument.

Unwmkd.

1977, June 21 Photo. *Perf. 14*

2046	A407	$2 multi	20	5
2047	A407	$5 multi	40	12
2048	A407	$8 multi	60	20
2049	A407	$10 multi	75	25

Idea Leuconoe
A408

Protected Butterflies: $4, Hebomoia glaucippe formosana. $6, Stichophthalma howqua formosana. $10, Atrophaneura horishana.

1977, July 20 Litho. *Perf. 13½*

2050	A408	$2 ver & multi	20	5
2051	A408	$4 lt grn & multi	40	10
2052	A408	$6 lt bl & multi	60	15
2053	A408	$10 yel & multi	75	25

National Palace Museum A409

Temple A410

Children's Drawings: $2, Sea Goddess Festival. $4, Boats on Shore of Lan-yu.

Perf. 13½

1977, Aug. 27 Litho. Wmk. 323

2054	A409	$1 multi	10	3
2055	A409	$2 multi	20	5
2056	A409	$4 multi	30	10
2057	A410	$5 multi	40	12

8th Exhibition of World School Children's Art.

Carved Lacquer Plate, Wan-li Ware A411

Ancient Carved Lacquer Ware: $5, Bowl, Ching dynasty. $8, Round box, Ming dynasty. $10, Four-tiered box, Ching dynasty.

Perf. 13x14

1977, Sept. 28 Photo. Wmk. 368

2058	A411	$2 multi	20	5
2059	A411	$5 multi	40	12
2060	A411	$8 multi	60	20
2061	A411	$10 multi	75	25

Lions International, Emblem and Activities A412

Unwmkd.

1977, Oct. 8 Litho. *Perf. 13*

2062	A412	$2 multi	20	5
2063	A412	$10 multi	70	25

International Association of Lions Clubs, 60th anniversary.

Nos. 2069 and 2075 Overprinted in Claret

1977
中華民國青
年、青少年
及少年棒球
隊再獲世界
三冠軍紀念

Perf. 13½x12½

1977, Sept. 9 Litho. Unwmkd.

2064	A365	$2 org & multi	20	5
2065	A365	$8 car & grn	60	20

Little League baseball championship.

Chinese Quality Mark A413

Unwmkd.

1977, Oct. 14 Litho. *Perf. 13x12½*

2066	A413	$2 red & multi	20	5
2067	A413	$10 bl & multi	70	25

International Standardization Day.

Construction Types of 1974

Redrawn: Numerals Outlined

Designs as 1976 Issue.

Perf. 13½x12½, 12½x13½

1977 Lithographed Unwmkd.

Granite Paper

2068	A365	$1 car & dp grn	10	3
2069	A365	$2 ver & multi	15	5
2070	A366	$3 vio & multi	20	7
2071	A366	$4 car & multi	25	10
2072	A365	$5 grn & multi	30	12
2073	A366	$6 sep & multi	35	15
2074	A366	$7 sep & multi	40	18
2075	A365	$8 red lil & multi	50	20
2076	A366	$9 ol & multi	50	22
		Nos. 2068-2076 (9)	2.75	1.12

Numerals are in solid color on Nos. 1907–1915, 2009–2017; in outline on Nos. 2068–2076.

Man and Heart A414

Wmk. 323

1977, Nov. 12 Litho. *Perf. 13½x12½*

2077	A414	$2 multi	20	5
2078	A414	$10 multi	70	25

Physical health, cardiac care.

White Stallion A415

Design: $5, Two horses (horiz.). Designs from painting "100 Horses," by Lang Shih-ning.

Lithographed

1977, Dec. 1 *Perf. 12½* Unwmkd.

2079	A415	$1 red & multi	10	3
2080	A415	$5 emer & multi	40	15

New Year 1978.

First Page of Constitution A416

Pres. Chiang Accepting Constitution, 1946 A417

1977, Dec. 25 Litho. *Perf. 13½*

2081	A416	$2 multi	20	6
2082	A417	$10 multi	70	30

30th anniversary of the Constitution.

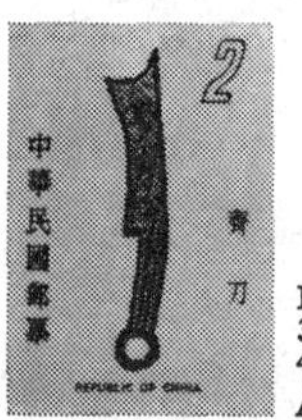

Knife Coin with 3 Characters, 403–221 B.C. A418

Designs: Ancient knife coins.

1978, Jan. 18 *Perf. 13½* Wmk. 323

2083	A418	$2 sal & multi	20	5
2084	A418	$5 lt bl & blk	40	16
2085	A418	$8 lt gray & multi	60	25
2086	A418	$10 tan & multi	75	32

China No. 1 and Flag of China A419

Designs: $5, No. 464 (Sun Yat-sen). $10, No. 1204 (Chiang Kai-shek).

1978, Feb. 21 Litho. *Perf. 13½*

2087	A419	$2 brn & multi	20	8
2088	A419	$5 bl & multi	40	16
2089	A419	$10 org & multi	75	32
	a.	Souvenir sheet of 3	1.50	

Centenary of Chinese postage stamps. No. 2089a contains one each of Nos. 2087–2089; orange and dark carmine margin. Size: 143x101mm.

Sun Yat-Sen Memorial Hall A420

China Nos. 2079 and 2 A421

Perf. 14x12½, 12½x14

1978, Mar. 20 Wmk. 323

2090	A420	$2 multi	25	8
2091	A421	$10 multi	75	32

ROCPEX '78 Philatelic Exhibition, Taipei, Mar. 20–29.

Chiang Kai-shek with Revolutionary Army—A422

Designs (Chiang Kai-shek); $2, as young man, 1912 (vert.). $8, Making speech at Mt. Lu, July 17, 1937. $10, Reviewing Armed Forces on National Day, 1956, and Chinese flags (vert.).

1978, Apr. 5 *Perf. 13½* Wmk. 323

2092	A422	$2 vio & multi	20	8
2093	A422	$5 grn & multi	40	16
2094	A422	$8 bl & multi	60	25
2095	A422	$10 vio bl & multi	75	32

Pres. Chiang Kai-shek (1887–1975).

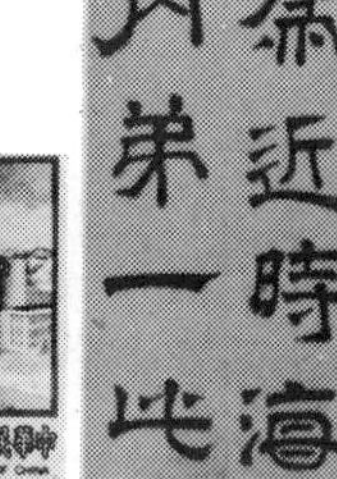

Nuclear Reactor and Plant A423

Poem by Wen Cheng-ming (1470–1559) A424

Perf. 13½x12½

1978, Apr. 28 Unwmkd.

2096	A423	$10 multi	65	32

First nuclear power plant on Taiwan.

Lithographed

1978, May 20 *Perf. 13½* Wmk. 323

Chinese Calligraphy: $2, Letter by Wang Hsi-chih (307–365). $4, Eulogy by Chu Sui-liang (596–658). $8, From Autobiography of Huai-su, Tang Dynasty. $10, Poem by Ch'ang Piao, Sung Dynasty.

2097	A424	$2 multi	15	8
2098	A424	$4 multi	25	16
2099	A424	$6 multi	35	24
2100	A424	$8 multi	50	32
2101	A424	$10 multi	60	40
		Nos. 2097-2101 (5)	1.85	1.20

Head and Dao Cancer Fund Emblem A425

Carved Lacquer Vase, Ming Dynasty A426

1978, June 15 Litho. *Perf. 13½*

2102	A425	$2 red, org & ol	15	8
2103	A425	$10 dk & lt bl & grn	60	40

Cancer prevention.

1978, July 12

Ancient Carved Lacquer Ware: $2, Box with dragon and cloud design, Ch'ing dynasty (horiz.). $5, Double box on legs, Ch'ing dynasty (horiz.). $8, Round box with peonies, Ming dynasty (horiz.).

2104	A426	$2 gray ol & multi	15	8
2105	A426	$5 gray ol & multi	30	16
2106	A426	$8 gray ol & multi	50	25
2107	A426	$10 gray ol & multi	60	32

Tsu Ti Practicing with his Sword
A427

Folk Tales: No. 2109, Pan Ch'ao, diplomat and governor. No. 2110, Tien Tan's "Fire Bull Battle." $5, Liang Hung-yu, a general's wife, who served as drummer in battle.

Perf. 13½

1978, Aug. 16 Litho. **Wmk. 323**

2108	A427	$1 multi	10	4
2109	A427	$2 bis & multi	15	8
2110	A427	$2 gray & multi	15	8
2111	A427	$5 multi	30	16

Nos. 2012 and 2014 Overprinted in Red

1978 中華民國青年青少年及少年棒球隊三獲世界三冠軍紀念

1978, Sept. 9 *Perf. 12½x13*

2112	A366	$4 multi	25	16
2113	A366	$6 multi	40	25

Triple championships won by Chinese teams in Little League World Series. "1978" overprint on $4 at left, on $6 at right.

Ixias Pyrene
A428

Protected Butterflies: $4, Euploea sylvestor swinhoei. $6, Cyrestis thyodamas formosana. $10, Byasa polyeuctes termessus.

1978, Sept. 20

2114	A428	$2 multi	15	8
2115	A428	$4 multi	25	16
2116	A428	$6 multi	35	25
2117	A428	$10 multi	60	40

Scout Symbols
A429

Tropical Tomatoes
A430

1978, Oct. 5 Litho. *Perf. 13½*

2118	A429	$2 multi	25	8
2119	A429	$10 multi	40	40

5th Chinese Boy Scout Jamboree, Cheng Ching Lake, Oct. 5–12.

1978, Oct. 23 **Wmk. 323**

Design: $10, Tropical tomatoes (horiz.).

2120	A430	$2 multi	10	8
2121	A430	$10 multi	50	40

International Symposium on Tropical Tomatoes, Taiwan, Oct. 23–28.

Sino-Saudi Bridge
A431

Design: $6, Buttresses of bridge, flags of Taiwan and Saudi Arabia (horiz.).

1978, Oct. 31

2122	A431	$2 multi	10	8
2123	A431	$6 multi	30	25

Completion of Sino-Saudi Bridge over Cho-Shui River.

National Flag
A432

1978-80 *Perf. 13½*

2124	A432	$1 red & dk bl	8	4
a.		Bklt. pane of 16 ($5, $6, $8, $10, 3 $1, 9 $2)	2.50	2.00
2125	A432	$2 red & dk bl	12	8
a.		Bklt. pane of 15 + label	1.50	
2126	A432	$3 multi ('80)	30	12
2127	A432	$4 multi ('80)	35	15
2128	A432	$5 multi	25	20
2129	A432	$6 multi	30	24
2130	A432	$7 multi ('80)	35	28
2131	A432	$8 multi	45	32
2132	A432	$10 multi ('79)	60	40
2133	A432	$12 multi ('80)	60	45
		Nos. 2124-2133 (10)	3.40	2.28

Two types exist: 1. Second line (red) below flag is same width as blue line. 2. Second line is a hairline, notably thinner. The $3, $4, $7 and $12 were issued only in type 2; Nos. 2134, 2124a, only in type 1; others in both types.

See Nos. 2288-2300.

Coil Stamp

1980, Jan. 15 *Perf. 12 Horiz.*

2134	A432	$2 multi	10	6

Three Rams, by Emperor Hsuan-tsung
A433

Taoyuan International Airport
A434

Wmk. 323

1978, Dec. 1 Litho. *Perf. 12½*

2135	A433	$1 multi	5	4
2136	A433	$5 multi	25	20

New Year 1979.

1978, Dec. 31 *Perf. 13½*

Design: $10, Passenger terminal and control tower (horiz.).

2137	A434	$2 multi	10	8
2138	A434	$10 multi	50	40

Completion of Taoyuan International Airport.

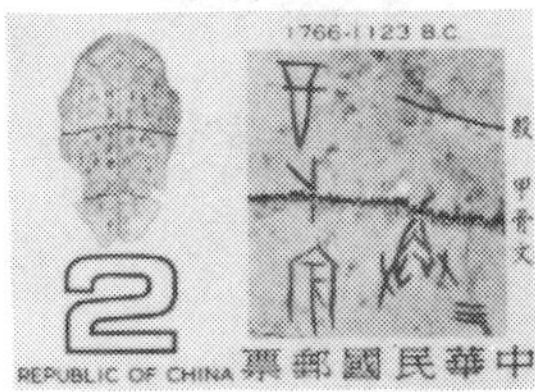

Oracle Bones and Inscription, 1766–1123 B.C.—A435

Antiquities and Inscriptions: $5, Leh-chi cauldron, 722–481 B.C. $8, Small seal (turtle), 206 B.C.–8 A.D. $10, Inscribed stone tablet, 175–183 A.D.

1979, Jan. 17

2139	A435	$2 multi	10	8
2140	A435	$5 multi	25	20
2141	A435	$8 multi	40	32
2142	A435	$10 multi	50	40

Origin and development of Chinese characters.

Chihkan Tower, 1653
A436

Taiwan Scenery: $5, Shrine of Confucius, 1665. $8, Shrine of Koxinga, 1661. $10, Eternal Castle and moat.

1979, Feb. 11 Litho. *Perf. 13½*

2143	A436	$2 multi	10	8
2144	A436	$5 multi	25	20
2145	A436	$8 multi	40	32
2146	A436	$10 multi	50	40

Children Playing on Winter Day, Sung Dynasty—A437

1979, Mar. 8

Multicolored

2147	A437	Block of four	1.00
a.		$5 in UL corner	25
b.		$5 in UR corner	25
c.		$5 in LL corner	25
d.		$5 in LR corner	25
e.		Souvenir sheet of 4	1.25

No. 2147e contains No. 2147; pink and black margin. Size: 101x145mm.

Lu Hao-tung
A438

Yellow Jade Brush Holder
A439

Wmk. 323

1979, Mar. 29 Engr. *Perf. 13x12½*

2148	A438	$2 blue	10	8

Lu Hao-tung (1868–1895), revolutionist.

Unwmkd.

1979, Apr. 12 Photo. *Perf. 12*

Ancient Brush Washers: $5, White jade, Ming Dynasty. $8, Dark green jade, Ch'ing Dynasty. $10, Bluish jade, Ch'ing Dynasty. All horiz.

Granite Paper

2149	A439	$2 multi	10	8
2150	A439	$5 multi	25	20
2151	A439	$8 multi	40	32
2152	A439	$10 multi	50	40

Plum Blossoms, National Flower
A440

City Houses and Garden
A441

Wmk. 323

1979, May 20 Engr. *Perf. 13x12½*

2153	A440	$10 dk bl	50	40
2154	A440	$20 brown	1.00	80
2155	A440	$50 dl grn	2.50	2.00
2156	A440	$100 vermilion	5.00	4.00
2156A	A440a	$500 ver & brn	25.00	15.00

Perf. 13x12½, 12½x13

1979, June 5 Lithographed

Design: $10, Rural landscape (horiz.).

2157	A441	$2 multi	10	8
2158	A441	$10 multi	50	40

Protection of the Environment.

Bankbook and Computer Department
A442

Designs: $2, Children at counter (vert.). $5, People standing in line (vert.). $10, Hand putting coin in savings bank, symbolic tree.

Lithographed

1979, July 1 *Perf. 13½* **Wmk. 323**

2159	A442	$2 multi	10	8
2160	A442	$5 multi	25	20
2161	A442	$8 multi	40	32
2162	A442	$10 multi	50	40

Postal savings, 60th anniversary.

Bird Type of 1977

Birds of Taiwan: $2, Swinoe's pheasant. $8, Steere's babbler. $10, Formosan yuhina.

1979, Aug. 8 *Perf. 11½*

2163	A402	$2 multi	10	8
2164	A402	$8 multi	40	32
2165	A402	$10 multi	50	40

Rowland Hill, Penny Black
A443

Perf. 13½x13

1979, Aug. 27 Litho. **Wmk. 323**

2166	A443	$10 multi	50	40

Sir Rowland Hill (1795–1879), originator of penny postage.

Jar with Rope Design, Shang Dynasty A444

Ancient Chinese Pottery: $5, Two-handled jar, Shang dynasty. $8, Red jar with "ears," Han dynasty. $10, Green glazed jar, Han dynasty.

1979, Sept. 12 *Perf. 13½*

2167	A444	$2 multi	12	8
2168	A444	$5 multi	30	20
2169	A444	$8 multi	45	32
2170	A444	$10 multi	60	40

Children and IYC Emblem A445

Wmk. 323

1979, Sept. 28 Litho. *Perf. 13½*

2171	A445	$2 multi	10	8
2172	A445	$10 multi	50	40

International Year of the Child.

Trade Symbols, Competition Emblem A446

Wmk. 323

1979, Nov. 11 Litho. *Perf. 13½*

2173	A446	$2 bl & multi	10	8
2174	A446	$10 grn & multi	50	40

10th National Vocational Training Competition, Taichung, Nov. 11.

Trees on a Winter Plain, by Li Ch'eng A447

Paintings: $5, Bamboo, Wen T'ung. $8, Old tree, bamboo and rock, by Chao Meng-fu. $10, Twin Pines, by Li K'an.

1979, Nov. 21

2175	A447	$2 multi	10	8
2176	A447	$5 multi	25	20
2177	A447	$8 multi	40	32
2178	A447	$10 multi	50	40

Monkey—A448

1979, Dec. 1 *Perf. 12½*

2179	A448	$1 yel & multi	5	3
2180	A448	$6 tan & multi	30	25

New Year 1980.

Rotary Emblem and "75"—A449

Rotary International, 75th Anniversary. $12, Anniversary emblem (vert.).

Wmk. 323

1980, Feb. 23 Litho. *Perf. 13½*

2181	A449	$2 multi	10	6
2182	A449	$12 multi	60	50

Mt. Hohuan—A450

Taiwan Landscapes (East-West Cross-Island Highway): $2, Tunnel of Nine Turns (vert.). $12, Bridge, Tien Hsiang (vert.).

1980, Mar. 1

2183	A450	$2 multi	10	6
2184	A450	$8 multi	40	24
2185	A450	$12 multi	60	50

Shih Chien-Ju—A451

1980, Mar. 29 Engr. *Perf. 13½×12½*

Granite Paper

2186	A451	$2 multi	10	6

Shih Chien-Ju (1879-1900), revolutionist.

Chung-cheng Memorial Hall—A452

1980, Apr. 4 Litho. *Perf. 13½*

2187	A452	$2 *shown*	10	6
2188	A452	$8 *Quotation*	40	24
2189	A452	$12 *Bronze statue*	60	50

Chiang Kai-shek (1887-1975), 5th anniversary of death.

Melon-shaped Jade Brush Washer, Ming Dynasty—A453

Jade Pottery: $2, Jar with dragons, Sung dynasty (vert.). $8, Monk's alms bowl, Ch'ing dynasty. $10, Yellow jade brush washer, Ch'ing dynasty.

1980, May 20 Photo. *Perf. 12*

Granite Paper

2190	A453	$2 multi	10	6
2191	A453	$5 multi	25	20
2192	A453	$8 multi	40	32
2193	A453	$10 multi	50	40

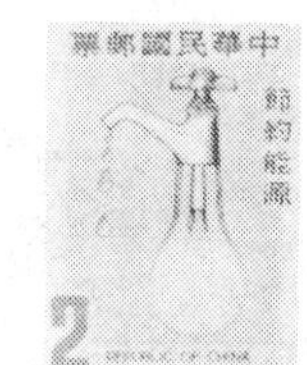

Energy Conservation—A454

1980, July 15 Litho. *Perf. 13½*

2194	A454	$2 multi	10	6
2195	A454	$12 multi	60	50

Soldier, T'ang Dynasty Pottery—A455

1980, Aug. 18 Litho. *Perf. 13½*

2196	A455	$2 *shown*	10	6
2197	A455	$5 *Roosters*	25	20
2198	A455	$8 *Horse*	40	32
2199	A455	$10 *Camel*	50	40

Confucius Returning Lost Article—A456

Folk Tales: $1, Grinding mortar into a needle. No. 2202, Wen Tien-hsiang in jail. $5, Sending coal in snow.

Wmk. 323

1980, Sept. 23 Litho. *Perf. 14x13½*

2200	A456	$1 multi	5	3
2201	A456	$2 multi	10	6
2202	A456	$2 multi	10	6
2203	A456	$5 multi	25	20

Railroad Electrification—A457

1980, Oct. 10 *Perf. 13½x14*

2204	A457	$2 *shown*	10	6
2205	A457	$2 *Taichung Harbor*	10	6
2206	A457	$2 *Chiang Kai-shek Airport*	10	6
2207	A457	$2 *Steel Mill*	10	6
2208	A457	$2 *Sun Yat-sen Freeway*	10	6
2209	A457	$2 *Nuclear power plant*	10	6
2210	A457	$2 *Petrochemical plants*	10	6
2211	A457	$2 *Su-ao Harbor*	10	6
2212	A457	$2 *Kaohsiung shipyard*	10	6
2213	A457	$2 *North link railroad*	10	6
a.		Souvenir sheet of 10	1.25	
		Nos. 2204-2213 (10)	1.00	60

Completion of major construction projects. Nos. 2204-2213 se-tenant. No. 2213a contains one each of Nos. 2204-2213. Size: 218x100mm.

10th National Savings Day—A458

Wmk. 323

1980, Oct. 25 Litho. *Perf. 13½*

2214	A458	$2 *Ancient coin and coin banks*	10	6
2215	A458	$12 *shown*	10	6

Landscape, by Ch'iu Ying, Ming Dynasty—A459

1980, Nov. 12 Litho. *Perf. 13½*

2216	A459	Block of 4	1.00	80
a.		$5 in UL corner	25	20
b.		$5 in UR corner	25	20
c.		$5 in LL corner	25	20
d.		$5 in LR corner	25	20
e.		Souvenir sheet	1.25	1.00

No. 2216e contains No. 2216a-2216d; yellow and brown decorative margin. Size: 102x145½mm.

Cock

A460

Faces, Flag, Census Form

A461

1980, Dec. 1 *Perf. 12½*

2217	A460	$1 multi	5	3
2218	A460	$6 multi	30	24
a.		Souvenir sheet of 4	75	

New Year 1980. No. 2218a contains 2 each Nos. 2217-2218; black marginal inscription. Size: 77x102mm.

1980, Dec. 13 *Perf. 13½*

2219	A461	$2 *shown*	10	6
2220	A461	$12 *Buildings*, horiz.	60	50

1980 population and housing census.

TIROS-N Satellite A462

Design: $10, Central weather bureau (horiz.).

1981, Jan. 28 Litho. *Perf. 13½*

2221	A462	$2 multi	10	6
2222	A462	$10 multi	50	50

Completion of meteorological satellite ground station, Taipei.

"Happiness"

A463

1981, Feb. 3 *Perf. 13½x12½*

New Year 1981 (Calligraphy): No. 2224, Wealth. No. 2225, Longevity. No. 2226, Joy. Nos. 2223-2226 se-tenant.

2223	A463	$5 multi	25	15
2224	A463	$5 multi	25	15
2225	A463	$5 multi	25	15
2226	A463	$5 multi	25	15

International Year of the Disabled—A464

1981, Feb. 19 Litho. *Perf. 13½*

2227	A464	$2 multi	10	6
2228	A464	$12 multi	60	55

Mt. Ali—A465

1981, Mar. 1

2229	A465	$2 shown	10	6
2230	A465	$7 Oluanpi Beach	35	28
2231	A465	$12 Sun Moon Lake	60	35

A $2 multicolored stamp for the 12th National Kuomintang Congress at Taipei was prepared for release Mar. 29, 1981, but not issued. It showed Sun Yat-sen, Chiang Kai-shek, flags of China and the Koumintang and a map of China.

Children in Forest—A467

Children's Day: Drawings.

1981, Apr. 4

2233	A467	$1 multi	5	3
2234	A467	$2 multi	10	6
2235	A467	$5 multi	25	20
2236	A467	$7 multi	35	28

Chiang Kai-shek Memorial Hall—A468

1981, Apr. 5 *Perf. 12½x13½*

2237	A468	20c bluish lil	3	3
2238	A468	40c crim rose	3	3
2239	A468	50c dl red brn	3	3

Chiang Kai-shek (1887-1975), 6th anniversary of death.

Cloisonne Enamel Brush Washer, 15th Cent.—A469

Cloisonne Enamel: $5, Ritual vessel, 15th cent. (vert.). $8, Plate, 17th cent. $10, Vase, Ming Dynasty (vert.).

1981, May 20 Photo. *Perf. 12*
Granite Paper

2240	A469	$2 multi	10	6
2241	A469	$5 multi	25	20
2242	A469	$8 multi	40	32
2243	A469	$10 multi	50	40

Early and Modern Locomotives A470

Linnaeus Crab

A471

Wmk. 323

1981, June 9 Litho. *Perf. 12½*

2244	A470	$2 shown	10	6
2245	A470	$14 Trains, horiz.	70	52

Railroad service centenary.

1981, June 14 *Perf. 13½*

2246	A471	$2 De Haan crab, horiz.	10	6
2247	A471	$5 shown	25	20
2248	A471	$8 Miers crab, horiz.	40	32
2249	A471	$14 Rathbun crab	70	52

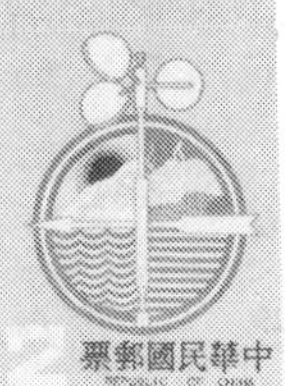

Central Weather Bureau, 40th Anniv.—A472

1981, July 1 Litho. *Perf. 13½*

2250	A472	$2 multi	10	6
2251	A472	$14 multi	70	50

Scene from The Cowherd and the Weaving Maid—A473

Designs: Scenes from the Cowherd and the Weaving Maid.

1981, Aug. 6 Litho. *Perf. 13½x14*

2252	A473	$2 multi	10	6
2253	A473	$4 multi	20	12
2254	A473	$8 multi	40	24
2255	A473	$14 multi	70	42

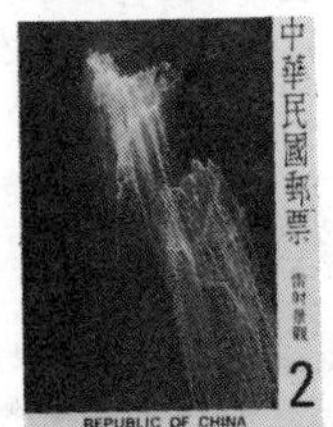

First Lasography Exhibition—A474

Lasography Designs.

1981, Aug. 15 *Perf. 13½*

2256	A474	$2 multi	10	6
2257	A474	$5 multi	25	15
2258	A474	$8 multi	40	24
2259	A474	$14 multi	70	42

Soccer Players

A475 A476

1981, Sept. 9 Litho. *Perf. 13½*

2260	A475	$5 multi	25	15
2261	A476	$5 multi	25	15

Sports Day. Se-tenant.

70th Anniv. of Republic: No. 2263, Eastward Expedition (soldiers on Hill). No. 2264, Northward Expedition (Chiang on horse). No. 2265, Resistance War with Japan (Chiang, fi st raised). No. 2266, Suppression of Communist Rebels (Battle scene). No. 2267, Counter-offensive and unification. $8, Chiang Kai-shek. $14, Sun Yat-sen.

Wmk. 323

1981 Litho. *Perf. 13½*

2262	A477	$2 multi	10	6
2263	A477	$2 multi	10	6
2264	A477	$2 multi	10	6
2265	A477	$2 multi	10	6
2266	A477	$3 multi	15	10
2267	A477	$3 multi	15	10
2268	A477	$8 multi	40	25
2269	A477	$14 multi	70	40
		Nos. 2262-2269 (8)	1.80	1.09
a.		Souvenir sheet of 8	2.00	1.25

No. 2269a contains Nos. 2262-2269; multicolored decorative margin. Size: 117x168mm. Nos. 2262-2269 issued Oct. 10; No. 2269a, Oct. 25.

ROCPEX TAIPEI '81 Intl. Philatelic Exhibition, Taipei, Oct. 25-Nov. 2 A478

1981, Oct. 25

2270	A478	$2 multi	10	6
2271	A478	$14 multi	70	40

Boys Playing Games (#2272a)—A479

Design: "One Hundred Boys," Sung Dynasty scroll. Two strips of 5 each in continuous design.

1981, Nov. 12

2272	Block of 10	1.00	60
a.-e.	single (top)	10	6
f.-j.	single (bottom)	10	6

New Year 1982 (Year of the Dog) A480

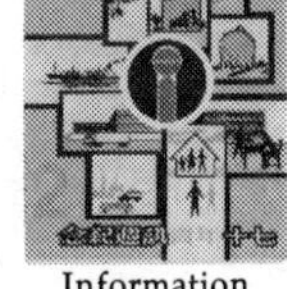

Information Week, Dec. 6-12

A481

Wmk. 323

1981, Dec. 1 Litho. *Perf. 12½*

2273	A480	$1 multi	5	3
2274	A480	$10 multi	50	30
a.		Souvenir sheet of 4	1.25	75

No. 2274a contains 2 each Nos. 2273-2274;black marginal inscription. Size: 78x103mm.

1981, Dec. 7 *Perf. 14x13½*

2275	A481	$2 multi	10	6

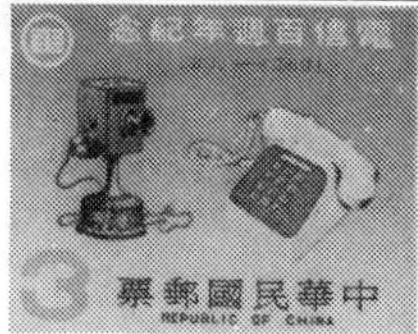

Telecommunications Centenary—A482

1981, Dec. 28 *Perf. 14x13½, 13½x14*

2276	A482	$2 Telephone, vert.	10	6
2277	A482	$3 Old, new phones	15	10
2278	A482	$8 Submarine cable	40	25
2279	A482	$18 Computers, vert.	90	65

Floral Arrangement—A483

Designs: Various floral arrangements in Ming vases.

Wmk. 323

1982, Jan. 23 **Litho.** *Perf. 13½*

2280	A483	$2 multi	10	6
2281	A483	$3 multi	15	10
2282	A483	$8 multi	40	25
2283	A483	$18 multi	90	65

The Ku Cheng Reunion—A484

Designs: Opera scenes.

Wmk. 323

1982, Feb. 15 **Litho.** *Perf. 13½*

2284	A484	$2 multi	10	6
2285	A484	$3 multi	15	10
2286	A484	$4 multi	20	12
2287	A484	$18 multi	90	65

Flag Type of 1978

1981 **Litho.** *Perf. 13½*

Panel Color

2288	A432	$1 red	5	3
2289	A432	$1.50 lt. ol	8	5
2290	A432	$2 dk. ol bis	10	6
2291	A432	$3 red	15	10
2292	A432	$4 bl	20	12
2293	A432	$5 sep	25	15
2294	A432	$6 org	30	20
2295	A432	$7 grn	35	22
2296	A432	$8 mag	40	25
2297	A432	$9 ol grn	45	28
2298	A432	$10 dk. pur	50	30
2299	A432	$12 lil	60	40
2300	A432	$14 dk. grn	70	45
		Nos. 2288-2300 (13)		

Second line (red) below flag is a hairline, notably thinner.

Tubercle Bacillus Centenary A485

Cheng Shih-liang, Revolutionary A486

Wmk.323

1982, Mar. 24 **Litho.** *Perf. 13½*

2309	A485	$2 multi	10	6

1982, Mar. 29 **Engr.** *Perf. 13½x12½*

Granite Paper

2310	A486	$2 car rose	10	6

Children's Day—A487

Designs: Various children's drawings. $2 vert.

1982, Apr. 4 **Litho.**

2311	A487	$2 multi	10	6
2312	A487	$3 multi	15	10
2313	A487	$5 multi	25	15
2314	A487	$8 multi	40	25

Dentists' Day—A488

1982, May 4 **Litho.** *Perf. 13½*

2315	A488	$2 Tooth, boy	10	6
2316	A488	$3 Flossing, brushing	15	10
2317	A488	$10 Examination	50	30

Champleve Enamel Cup and Saucer, 18th Cent.—A489

Painted Enamelware: $5, Cloisonne gold-plated duck Ch'ien-lung period (1736-1795) (vert.). $8, Incense burner, K'ang-hsi period (1662-1722). $12, Cloisonne pitcher, Ch'ien-lung period (vert.).

1982, May 20 **Photo.** *Perf. 12*

Granite Paper

2318	A489	$2 multi	10	6
2319	A489	$5 multi	25	16
2320	A489	$8 multi	40	26
2321	A489	$12 multi	60	40

Poets' Day—A490

Tang Dynasty Poetry Illustrations (618-906): $2, Spring Dawn, by Meng Hao-Jan. $3, On Looking for a Hermit and Not Finding Him, by Chia Tao. $5, Summer Dying, by Liu Yu-Hsi. $18, Looking at the Snow Drifts on South Mountain, by Tsu Yung.

Wmk. 323

1982, June 25 **Litho.** *Perf. 13½*

2322	A490	$2 multi	10	6
2323	A490	$3 multi	15	10
2324	A490	$5 multi	25	16
2325	A490	$18 multi	90	60

5th World Women's Softball Championship, Taipei, July 1-12—A491

1982, July 2

2326	A491	$2 lt grn & multi	10	6
2327	A491	$18 tan & multi	90	60

Scouting Year—A492

1982, July 18

2328	A492	$2 Crossing bridge, Baden-Powell	10	6
2329	A492	$18 Emblem, camp	90	60

Stamp in Tongs—A493

1982, Aug. 9

2330	A493	$2 shown	10	6
2331	A493	$18 Album stamps magnified	90	60

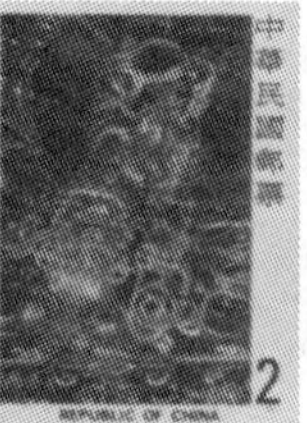

Carved Lion, Tsu Shih Temple A494

Hsun Kuan Saving Hsiang-cheng City A495

Tsu Shih Temple of Sanhsia Architecture: $3, Lion brackets (horiz.). $5, Sub-lintels. $18, Tiled roof (horiz.).

1982, Sept. 1 **Litho.** *Perf. 13½*

2332	A494	$2 multi	10	6
2333	A494	$3 multi	15	10
2334	A494	$5 multi	25	15
2335	A494	$18 multi	90	60

1982, Oct. 15 *Perf. 14x13½*

Designs: Scenes from The Thirty-Six Examples of Filial Piety, Folk Tale collection by Wu Yen-huan.

2336	A495	$1 multi	5	3
2337	A495	$2 multi	10	6
2338	A495	$3 multi	15	10
2339	A495	$5 multi	25	15

30th Anniv. of China Youth Corps—A496

1982, Oct. 31

2340	A496	$2 Riding	10	6
2341	A496	$3 Raising flag, vert.	15	10
2342	A496	$18 Mountain climbing	90	60

(Buddhist Saint) A497

New Year 1983 (Year of the Boar) A498

Paintings of Lohan, Hanging Scrolls by Liu Sung-nien, 13th cent.

Wmk. 323

1982, Nov. 12 **Litho.** *Perf. 13x12½*

2343	A497	$2 multi	10	6
2344	A497	$3 multi	15	10
2345	A497	$18 multi	90	60
a.		Souvenir sheet of 3	1.25	75

No. 2345a contains Nos. 2343-2345; marginal inscription. Size: 140x102mm.

1982, Dec. 1 *Perf. 12½*

2346	A498	$1 multi	5	3
2347	A498	$10 multi	50	30
a.		Souvenir sheet of 4	1.25	75

No. 2347a contains 2 each Nos. 2346-2347; marginal inscription. Size: 78x102mm.

Enamelware Type of 1982

Designs: $2, Square basin, Ch'ing Dynasty (1644-1911). $3, Vase, Ch'ien-lung period (1736-1795) (vert.). $4, Tea pot, Ch'ien-lung period. $18, Elephant vase, Ch'ing Dynasty (vert.).

1983, Jan. 5 **Photo.** *Perf. 12*

Granite Paper

2348	A489	$2 multi	10	6
2349	A489	$3 multi	15	10
2350	A489	$4 multi	20	12
2351	A489	$18 multi	90	60

Poetry Illustration Type of 1982

Sung Dynasty Poetry: $2, Seeing the Flowers Fade Away. $3, River. $5, Freckled with Clouds is the Azure Sky. $11, Yielding Fine Fragrance in the Snow. Nos. 2352-2355 vert.

Wmk. 323

1983, Feb. 10 **Litho.** *Perf. 13½*

2352	A490	$2 multi	10	6
2353	A490	$3 multi	15	8
2354	A490	$5 multi	25	16
2355	A490	$11 multi	55	30

Mt. Jade, Taiwan—A499

1983, Mar. 1

2356	A499	$2	Wawa Valley, vert.	10	6
2357	A499	$3	University Pond, vert.	15	8
2358	A499	$18	shown	90	60

400th Anniv. of Arrival of Matteo Ricci (1552-1610), Italian Missionary—A500

1983, Apr. 3 **Wmk. 323** **Litho.** *Perf. 14x13½*

2359	A500	$2	Globe	10	6
2360	A500	$18	Great Wall	90	60

SEMI-POSTAL STAMPS.

SP1

Red or Blue Surcharge.

1920, Dec. 1 *Perf. 14, 15* Unwmkd.

B1	SP1	1c on 2c grn	6.00	1.50
B2	SP1	3c on 4c scar (B)	8.50	2.50
B3	SP1	5c on 6c gray	12.50	3.50

The surcharge represents the actual franking value. The extra cent helped victims of the 1919 Yellow River flood.

War Refugees

SP2

Black Surcharge.

1944, Oct. 10 Engraved *Perf. 12*

B4	SP2	$2+$2 on 50c+50c brt ultra	25	25
B5	SP2	$4+$4 on 8c+8c brt grn	25	25
B6	SP2	$5+$5 on 21c+21c red brn	75	75
B7	SP2	$6+$6 on 28c+28c ol grn	1.25	1.25
B8	SP2	$10+$10 on 33c+33c red	1.75	1.75
B9	SP2	$20+$20 on $1+$1 vio	3.50	3.50
a.		Sheet of six	12.50	12.50
		Nos. B4-B9 (6)	7.75	7.75

The borders of each stamp differ slightly in design.

The surtax was for war refugees.

No. B9a measures 191x112mm. and contains one each of Nos. B4 to B9 with marginal inscriptions in olive green, red brown and bright green.

Nos. B4–B8 exist without surcharge, but were not regularly issued.

Great Wall of China

SP4

Chinese Refugee Family

SP5

Lithographed.

1948, July 5 *Perf. 14, Imperf.*

Without Gum.

Cross in Carmine.

B11	SP4	$5000 +$2000 vio	12	12
B12	SP4	$10,000 +$2000 brn	12	12
B13	SP4	$15,000 +$2000 gray	12	12
a.		Cross omitted	150.00	

The surtax was for anti-tuberculosis work.

Republic of China (Taiwan)

1954, Oct. 1 Engraved *Perf. 12*

Without Gum

B14	SP5	40c +10c dp bl	6.00	1.00
B15	SP5	$1.60 +40c lil rose	12.00	2.00
B16	SP5	$5 +$1 red	30.00	17.00

The surtax was used to aid in the evacuation of Chinese from North Viet Nam.

AIR POST STAMPS.

Curtiss "Jenny" over Great Wall

(Bars of Republic flag on tail.)

AP1

Engraved

1921, July 1 *Perf. 14* Unwmkd.

C1	AP1	15c bl grn & blk	17.50	8.50
C2	AP1	30c scar & blk	12.50	7.50
C3	AP1	45c dl vio & blk	12.50	7.50
C4	AP1	60c dk bl & blk	17.50	8.50
C5	AP1	90c ol grn & blk	17.50	10.00
		Nos. C1-C5 (5)	77.50	42.00

(Nationalist sun emblem on tail.)

AP2

1929, July 5

C6	AP2	15c bl grn & blk	2.50	50
C7	AP2	30c dk red & blk	4.00	1.00
C8	AP2	45c dk vio & blk	7.50	3.00
C9	AP2	60c dk bl & blk	7.50	3.00
C10	AP2	90c ol grn & blk	10.00	5.00
		Nos. C6-C10 (5)	31.50	12.50

Junkers F-13 over Great Wall

AP3

1932-37

C11	AP3	15c gray grn	10	6
C12	AP3	25c org ('33)	10	4
C13	AP3	30c red	25	10
C14	AP3	45c brn vio	10	8
C15	AP3	50c dk brn ('33)	10	8
C16	AP3	60c dk bl	10	8
C17	AP3	90c ol grn	25	10
C18	AP3	$1 yel grn ('33)	25	10
C19	AP3	$2 brn ('37)	25	10
C20	AP3	$5 brn car ('37)	1.00	75
		Nos. C11-C20 (10)	2.50	1.49

Type of 1932–37, with secret mark

1932–37 Issue. Lower part of left character joined.

Secret Mark, 1940–41 Issue. Separated.

Wmkd. Character Yu (Post) Multiple. (261)

Perf. 12, 12½, 12½x13, 13.

1940-41

C21	AP3	15c gray grn	10	6
C22	AP3	25c yel org	12	7
C23	AP3	30c red	10	6
a.		Vert. pair, imperf. between	150.00	
C24	AP3	45c dl rose vio ('41)	8	6
C25	AP3	50c brown	8	6
C26	AP3	60c dp bl ('41)	8	6
C27	AP3	90c ol ('41)	10	7
C28	AP3	$1 ap grn ('41)	12	10
C29	AP3	$2 lt brn ('41)	12	10
C30	AP3	$5 lake	12	10
		Nos. C21-C30 (10)	1.02	74

Unwmkd.

Perf. 12½, 13, 13½.

C31	AP3	15c gray grn ('41)	6	6
C32	AP3	25c lt org ('41)	6	6
C33	AP3	30c lt red ('41)	6	6
C34	AP3	45c dl rose vio ('41)	8	8
C35	AP3	50c brown	6	6
C36	AP3	60c bl ('41)	6	6
C37	AP3	90c lt ol ('41)	6	6
C38	AP3	$1 ap grn ('41)	10	10
C39	AP3	$2 lt brn ('41)	15	15
C40	AP3	$5 lake ('41)	12	12
		Nos. C31-C40 (10)	81	81

Nos. C11 and C12 Surcharged in Black

圓叁拾伍幣國

5300

1946, May 2 *Perf. 14* Unwmkd.

C41	AP3	$53 on 15c gray grn	20	20
C42	AP3	$73 on 25c org	550.00	600.00

Forgeries of No. C42 exist.

On Nos. C23, C21, C22, C29 and C30.

Perf. 13, 13x12, 12½.

Wmk. 261

C43	AP3	$23 on 30c red	8	10
C44	AP3	$53 on 15c gray grn	6.00	7.00
C45	AP3	$73 on 25c yel org	8	10
C46	AP3	$100 on $2 lt brn	8	10
C47	AP3	$200 on $5 lake	8	10

On Nos. C33, C31, C32, C39 and C40.

Perf. 13, 13x12, 13x12½, 12½.

Unwmkd.

C48	AP3	$23 on 30c lt red	5	5
a.		Inverted surcharge	100.00	
b.		"2300" omitted	50.00	
c.		Last character (kuo) of surch. omitted	50.00	
C49	AP3	$53 on 15c gray grn	5	5
a.		Horiz. pair, imperf. between		750.00
C50	AP3	$73 on 25c lt org	5	5
a.		Inverted surcharge	750.00	
C51	AP3	$100 on $2 lt brn	5	5
C52	AP3	$200 on $5 lake	5	5
a.		Inverted surcharge	75.00	

The surcharges on Nos. C41–C52 represent Chinese national currency and were applied at Shanghai.

Douglas DC-4 over Sun Yat-sen Mausoleum, Nanking

AP4

1946, Sept. 10 Litho. *Perf. 14*

Without Gum.

C53	AP4	$27 blue	15	10

No. C23 Surcharged in Black

圓萬壹作改

Perf. 13x12

1948, May 18 Wmk. 261

C54	AP3	$10,000 on 30c red	10	10

Same, in Black or Carmine, on Nos. C33, C32, C37, C36, C18 and C38.

Perf. 12½, 13x12½, 14

Unwmkd.

C55	AP3	$10,000 on 30c lt red	7	7
C56	AP3	$20,000 on 25c lt org	8	8
C57	AP3	$30,000 on 90c lt ol (C)	8	8
C58	AP3	$50,000 on 60c bl (C)	7	7
C59	AP3	$50,000 on $1 yel grn (C)	35.00	35.00
C60	AP3	$50,000 on $1 ap grn (C)	8	8

No. C53 Surcharged in Black

10000.00

Perf. 14.

C61	AP4	$10,000 on $27 bl	8	8
		Nos. C54-C61 (8)	35.56	35.56

Douglas DC-4 and Arrow

AP5

Lithographed

1949, May 2 *Perf. 12½* Unwmkd.

Without Gum.

C62	AP5	bl grn	1.25	1.50
a.		Rouletted	2.00	2.00

See note after No. 959.

Revenue Stamp Overprinted in Blue

政郵國民華中

費空航內國

1949, May Engraved *Perf. 14*

C63	A95	$100 ol grn	16.00	17.50

See note after No. 962.

Republic of China (Taiwan)

Cheng Ch'eng-kung (Koxinga)

AP6

Typographed.

Rouletted.

1950, Sept. 26 Unwmkd.

Without Gum.

C64	AP6	60c dp bl	11.00	2.00

Plane over City Gate, Taipei

AP7

Jet Planes above Chung Shan Bridge
AP8

Two Doves Near Koxinga Shrine
AP9

1954 Engraved *Perf. 11½*
Without Gum

C65	AP7	$1 dk brn	7.00	50
a.	Vert. pair, imperf. btwn.		300.00	
C66	AP8	$1.60 ol blk	4.50	40
a.	Vert. pair, imperf. btwn.		200.00	
b.	Horiz. pair, imperf. between		150.00	175.00
C67	AP9	$5 grnsh bl	5.50	50

No. C67 Surcharged in Red.

1958, Dec. 11

C68	AP9	$3.50 on $5 grnsh bl	1.25	25

Sea Gull
AP10

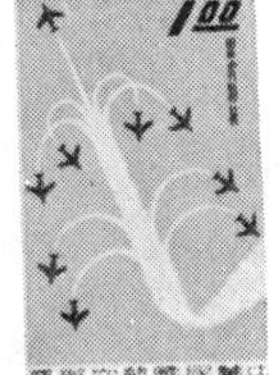

Sabre Jets in Bomb Burst Formation
AP11

1959, Mar. 20 Photo. *Perf. 13*

C69	AP10	$8 bl, gray & blk	1.20	20

1960, Feb. 29 *Perf. 13* Unwmkd.

Plane Formations: $2, Loop (horiz.). $5, Diamond formation passing over grounded plane (horiz.).

C70	AP11	$1 multi	1.50	35
C71	AP11	$2 multi	1.50	18
C72	AP11	$5 multi	3.00	40

Issued to honor the Chinese Air Force and the "Thunder Tiger" aerobatic team.

Jet Airliner over Pitan Bridge
AP12

Designs: $6, Jet over Tropic of Cancer monument, Kiai (vert.). $10, Jet over Lion Head mountain, Sinchu (vert.).

1963, Aug. 14 Photo. *Perf. 13*

C73	AP12	$2.50 multi	1.00	8
C74	AP12	$6 multi	1.75	12
C75	AP12	$10 multi	3.50	1.00

Boeing 727 over Chilin Pavilion, Grand Hotel
AP13

Design: $8, Boeing 727 over National Palace Museum, Taipei.

1967, Apr. 1 *Perf. 13* Unwmkd.

C76	AP13	$5 multi	90	10
C77	AP13	$8 multi	1.25	30

Wild Geese Flying over Mountains
AP14

Designs (Wild Geese flying over): $5, The sea. $8, The land (horiz.).

1969, Aug. 14 Photo. *Perf. 13*

C78	AP14	$2.50 multi	50	6
C79	AP14	$5 multi	75	12
C80	AP14	$8 multi	1.00	20

SPECIAL DELIVERY STAMPS.

Design: Dragon in irregular oval. Stamp 8x2½ inches, divided into four parts by perforation or serrate rouletting. Prices of Nos. E1–E8 are for used parts. Complete unused strips of four are exceptionally scarce.

"Chinese Imperial Post Office" in lines, repeated to form the background which is usually lighter in color than the rest of the design.

Dragon's head facing downward. Background with period after "POSTOFFICE".

No Date.

1905 *Perf. 11.* Unwmkd.

E1	10c grass grn	100.00

Serrate Roulette in Black.

E2	10c dp grn	80.00

1907-10

Dragon's head facing forward. Background with no period after "POSTOFFICE".

No Date.

E3	10c lt bluish grn	40.00

1909-11

Background with date at bottom.

E4	10c grn (Feb. 1909)	15.00
E5	10c bl grn (Jan. 1911)	10.00

1912

"Imperial Post Office" in serifed letters repeated to form the background.

No Date. No Border. Background of 30 or 28 lines.

E6	10c grn (30 lines)	20.00
a.	28 lines	25.00

Background of 35 lines of sans-serif letters. Colored Border

E8	10c green	20.00

On No. E8 the medallion in the third section has Chinese characters in the background instead of the usual English inscriptions. E6 and E8 occur with many types of four-character overprints reading "Republic of China," applied locally but unofficially at various post offices.

1913

Design: Wild Goose. Stamp 7½x2¾ inches, divided into five parts.

"Chinese Post Office" in sans-serif letters, repeated to form the background of 28 lines. With border.

Serrate Roulette in Black.

E9	10c green	125.00	10.00

Unused prices for Nos. E9–E10 are for complete strips of five parts. Used prices are for single parts.

1914

"Chinese Post Office" in antique letters, forming a background of 29 or 30 lines. No border.

Serrate Roulette in Green.

E10	10c green	35.00	1.00

On No. E9 the background is in sans-serif capitals, the Chinese and English inscriptions are on white tablets and the serial numbers are in black.

On No. E10 the background is in antique capitals and extends under the inscriptions. The serial numbers are in green.

NOTE:

In February, 1916, the Special Delivery Stamps were demonetized and became merely receipts without franking value. To mark this, four of the five sections of the stamp had the letters A, B, C, D either handstamped or printed on them.

SD1

Typographed.

1941 *Rouletted* Unwmkd.
Without Gum.

E11	SD1	($2) car & yel	11.00	2.25

Motorcycle Messenger
SD2

1949, July Litho. *Perf. 12½*
Without Gum.

E12	SD2	red vio	1.00	1.00
a.	Rouletted		1.50	1.50

See note after No. 959.

Revenue Stamp Overprinted in Purple Brown

中華民國郵政
國內快遞費

1949 Without Gum

E13	A95	$10 grnsh gray	7.50	7.50

See note after No. 962.

REGISTRATION STAMPS.

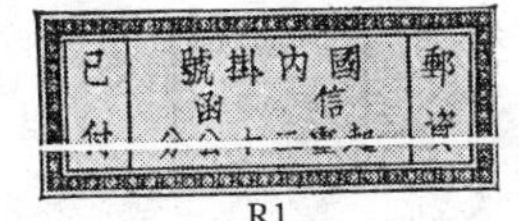

R1

Typographed.

1941 *Rouletted.* Unwmkd.
Without Gum.

F1	R1	($1.50) grn & buff	8.50	2.00

Mountain Scene
R2

1949, July Litho. *Perf. 12½*
Without Gum.

F2	R2	carmine	1.25	1.00
a.	Rouletted		1.25	1.00

See note after No. 959.

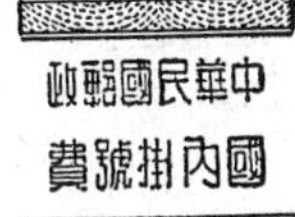

Revenue Stamp Overprinted in Carmine

1949

F3	A95	$50 dk bl	7.00	6.00

See note after No. 962.

POSTAGE DUE STAMPS.

Regular Issue of 1902-03 Overprinted in Black

POSTAGE DUE
資 欠

1904 *Perf. 14 to 15.* Unwmkd.

J1	A17	½c chocolate	5.50	1.25
J2	A17	1c ocher	5.50	1.00
J3	A17	2c scarlet	5.50	1.75
J4	A17	4c red brn	5.50	1.75
J5	A17	5c salmon	9.00	1.75
J6	A17	10c dk bl grn	11.00	2.00
a.	Vertical pair, imperf. between		250.00	
	Nos. J1-J6 (6)		42.00	9.50

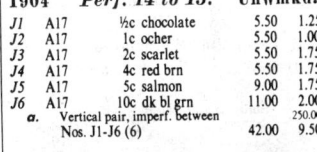

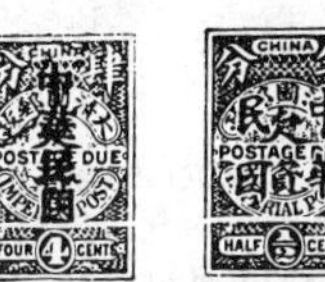

D1 D2 D3

1904 Engraved

J7	D1	½c blue	2.25	15
a.	Horizontal pair, imperf. between		150.00	150.00
J8	D1	1c blue	3.50	15
J9	D1	2c blue	2.00	15
a.	Horizontal pair, imperf. between		150.00	150.00
J10	D1	4c blue	4.50	35
J11	D1	5c blue	5.50	40
J12	D1	10c blue	5.50	75
J13	D1	20c blue	14.00	2.50
J14	D1	30c blue	17.50	3.00
	Nos. J7-J14 (8)		54.75	7.45

Arabic numeral of value at left on Nos. J12 to J14.

1911

J15	D1	1c brown	4.00	1.00
J16	D1	2c brown	6.00	1.50

The ½c, 4c, 5c and 20c in brown exist but were not issued as they arrived in China after the downfall of the Ching dynasty.

Issue of 1904 Overprinted in Red

立中時臨

1912

J19	D1	½c blue	250.00	225.00
J20	D1	4c blue	400.00	300.00
J21	D1	5c blue	425.00	400.00
J22	D1	10c blue	425.00	400.00
J23	D1	20c blue	1,100.	1,000.
J24	D1	30c blue	1,100.	1,000.

Nos. J15–J16 exist with this overprint, but were not regularly issued.

1912 Overprinted in Red.

J25	D2	½c blue	25	15
J26	D2	1c brown	30	20
a.	Horizontal pair, imperf. between		150.00	
b.	Inverted overprint		125.00	
J27	D2	2c brown	50	30
J28	D2	4c blue	1.50	40
J29	D2	5c blue	75.00	75.00
J30	D2	5c brown	1.50	50
a.	Inverted overprint		100.00	85.00
J31	D2	10c blue	3.00	65
J32	D2	20c blue	5.00	1.50
J33	D2	30c blue	10.00	4.00
	Nos. J25-J33 (9)		97.05	82.70

1912 Overprinted in Black.

J34	D3	½c blue	6.00	2.00
J35	D3	½c brown	1.00	35

J36	D3	1c brown	75	35
a.		Inverted overprint	125.00	
J37	D3	2c brown	2.00	65
J38	D3	4c blue	4.00	1.00
J39	D3	5c brown	4.00	1.25
a.		Horizontal pair, imperf. between	200.00	
J40	D3	10c blue	10.00	2.00
J41	D3	20c brown	20.00	7.00
J42	D3	30c blue	25.00	8.00
		Nos. J34-J42 (9)	72.75	22.60

D4

Printed by Waterlow & Sons.

1913, May ***Perf. 14, 15***

J43	D4	½c blue	50	15
a.		Horizontal pair, imperf. between	175.00	
J44	D4	1c blue	1.00	10
J45	D4	2c blue	1.00	15
J46	D4	4c blue	2.50	20
J47	D4	5c blue	3.00	20
J48	D4	10c blue	5.00	50
J49	D4	20c blue	7.50	80
J50	D4	30c blue	10.00	2.00
		Nos. J43-J50 (8)	30.50	4.10

Printed by the Chinese Bureau of Engraving & Printing.

1915 **Re-engraved** ***Perf. 14***

J51	D4	½c blue	60	10
J52	D4	1c blue	1.25	10
J53	D4	2c blue	1.25	10
J54	D4	4c blue	1.25	10
J55	D4	5c blue	1.75	25
J56	D4	10c blue	2.25	35
J57	D4	20c blue	6.00	40
J58	D4	30c blue	17.50	1.50
		Nos. J51-J58 (8)	31.85	2.90

In the upper part of the stamps of type D4 there is an ornament of five marks like the letter "V". Below this is a curved label with an inscription in Chinese characters. On the 1913 stamps there are two complete background lines between the ornament and the label. The 1915 stamps show only one unbroken line at this place. There are other minute differences in the engraving of the stamps of the two issues.

D5

1932 ***Perf. 14.***

J59	D5	½c orange	12	8
J60	D5	1c orange	12	8
J61	D5	2c orange	12	8
J62	D5	4c orange	25	25
J63	D5	5c orange	25	25
J64	D5	10c orange	50	35
J65	D5	20c orange	50	35
J66	D5	30c orange	50	35
		Nos. J59-J66 (8)	2.36	1.79

1940

Regular Stamps of 1939 Overprinted in Black or Red

欠 暫

資 作

J67	A57	$1 hn & dk brn (Bk)	1.00	1.00
J68	A57	$2 dl bl & org brn (R)	1.50	1.50

Type of 1932.
Printed by
The Commercial Press, Ltd.
Perf. 12½, 12½x13, 13.

1940-41 **Engraved.**

J69	D5	½c yel org	6	8
J70	D5	1c yel org	15	20
J71	D5	2c yel org ('41)	6	8
J72	D5	4c yel org	6	8
J73	D5	5c yel org ('41)	10	12
J74	D5	10c yel org ('41)	10	12
J75	D5	20c yel org ('41)	10	12
J76	D5	30c yel org	10	12
J77	D5	50c yel org	10	12
J78	D5	$1 yel org	10	12
J79	D5	$2 yel org	20	25
		Nos. J69-J79 (11)	1.13	1.41

D6

Thin Paper Without Gum.

1944 **Typographed** ***Perf. 13***

J80	D6	10c bluish grn	5	5
J81	D6	20c lt chlky bl	5	5
J82	D6	40c dl rose	5	5
J83	D6	50c bluish grn	5	5
J84	D6	60c dl bl	5	5
J85	D6	$1 dl rose	10	10
J86	D6	$2 lil brn	12	15
		Nos. J80-J86 (7)	47	50

D7

1945 **Without Gum** **Unwmkd.**

J87	D7	$2 rose car	5	6
J88	D7	$6 rose car	5	6
J89	D7	$8 rose car	5	6
J90	D7	$10 rose car	6	8
J91	D7	$20 rose car	6	8
J92	D7	$30 rose car	6	8
		Nos. J87-J92 (6)	33	42

D8

Thin Paper Without Gum.

1947 **Lithographed** ***Perf. 14***

J93	D8	$50 plum	6	8
J94	D8	$80 plum	6	8
J95	D8	$100 plum	6	8
J96	D8	$160 plum	6	8
J97	D8	$200 plum	6	8
J98	D8	$400 vio brn	6	8
J99	D8	$500 vio brn	6	8
a.		Vert. pair, imperf. between	10.00	
J100	D8	$800 vio brn	6	8
J101	D8	$2000 vio brn	6	8
		Nos. J93-J101 (9)	54	72

Type of 1945, Redrawn, Surcharged with New Value in Black.

1948 **Engraved.** ***Perf. 13½x14.***

Without Gum

J102	D7	$1000 on $20 dp cl	10	12
J103	D7	$2000 on $30 dp cl	10	12
J104	D7	$3000 on $50 dp cl	10	12
J105	D7	$4000 on $100 dp cl	10	12
J106	D7	$5000 on $200 dp cl	10	12
J107	D7	$10,000 on $300 dp cl	12	15
J108	D7	$20,000 on $500 dp cl	12	15
J109	D7	$30,000 on $1000 dp cl	15	20
		Nos. J102-J109 (8)	79	98

There are many differences in the redrawn design.

No. 627 Surcharged in Black

改作欠資

壹 金
分 圓
1

1949 ***Perf. 12***

J110	A72	1 (c) on $40 org	10	12
J111	A72	2 (c) on $40 org	10	12
J112	A72	5 (c) on $40 org	10	12
J113	A72	10 (c) on $40 org	10	12
J114	A72	20 (c) on $40 org	10	12
J115	A72	50 (c) on $40 org	12	15
J116	A72	$1 on $40 org	12	15
J117	A72	$2 on $40 org	12	15
J118	A72	$5 on $40 org	12	15
J119	A72	$10 on $40 org	20	25
		Nos. J110-J119 (10)	1.18	1.45

Republic of China (Taiwan)

No. 438 Surcharged in Green or Black

肆 臺
角 幣
資 欠
40 40

1951 ***Perf. 12½.*** **Unwmkd.**

J120	A47	40c on 40c org (G)	6.00	2.50
J121	A47	80c on 40c org (G)	6.00	2.50

Revenue Stamps Surcharged in Various Colors

政郵國民華中
角壹幣台資欠
10

Without Gum

1953 ***Perf. 12½, 14.*** **Unwmkd.**

J122	A95	10c on $50 dk bl (O)	6.00	2.50
J123	A95	20c on $100 ol grn (Dk Br)	6.00	2.50
J124	A95	40c on $20 org brn	7.50	75
J125	A95	80c on $500 sl grn (Dk Bl)	12.50	1.50
J126	A95	$1 on $30 dk vio (G)	12.50	5.00
		Nos. J122-J126 (5)	44.50	12.25

D9

Lithographed

1956 ***Perf. 12½*** **Unwmkd.**

Without Gum

J127	D9	20c rose car, & lt bl	25	10
J128	D9	40c grn & buff	25	10
J129	D9	80c brn & gray	50	10
J130	D9	$1 ultra & pink	50	15

No. 1197 Surcharged in Dark Violet

Engraved

1961, Dec. 28 ***Perf. 12*** **Wmk. 323**

Without Gum

J131	A135	$5 on $20 car rose	1.50	50

0 10
資 欠
壹
角

Nos. 1274, 1282-1283 Surcharged in Black, Carmine Rose or Blue

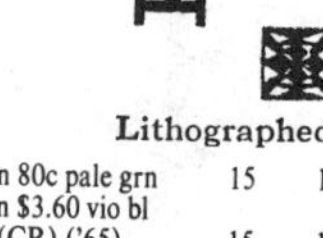

1964-65 **Lithographed**

J132	A158	10c on 80c pale grn	15	10
J133	A158	20c on $3.60 vio bl (CR) ('65)	15	10
J134	A158	40c on $4.50 ver (B) ('65)	25	10

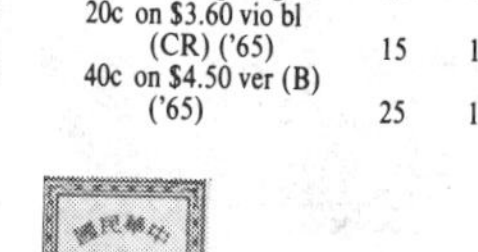

D10

1966-76 ***Perf. 12½*** **Wmk. 323**

Granite Paper; Without Gum

J135	D10	10c dk brn & lil	10	6
J136	D10	20c bl & yel	10	6
J137	D10	50c vio bl & lt bl ('70)	25	6
J138	D10	$1 pur & sal	20	6
J139	D10	$2 grn & lt bl	25	6
J140	D10	$5 red & sal	50	25
J141	D10	$10 lil rose & pink ('76)	1.00	50
		Nos. J135-J141 (7)	2.40	1.05

The 50c and $10 are gummed. The $1 and $2 were reissued with gum in 1968 and 1973 respectively.

The $10 is on ordinary paper.

PARCEL POST STAMPS

PP1

PP2

PP3

Engraved

1945-48 ***Perf. 13*** **Unwmkd.**

Without Gum.

Q1	PP1	$500 green	40	8
Q2	PP1	$1000 blue	40	8

No.	Type	Description	Unused	Used
Q3	PP1	$3000 rose red	1.00	13
Q4	PP1	$5000 brown	17.50	2.00
Q5	PP1	$10,000 lil gray	27.50	2.50
Q6	PP1	$20,000 red org	600.00	
		Nos. Q1-Q5 (5)	46.80	4.79

No. Q6 was prepared but not issued.

Perf. 12½.

No.	Type	Description	Unused	Used
Q7	PP2	$3000 red org	50	10
Q8	PP2	$5000 dk bl	60	12
Q9	PP2	$10,000 violet	60	20
Q10	PP2	$20,000 dk red	60	20

Perf. 13½

No.	Type	Description	Unused	Used
Q11	PP3	$1000 org yel	60	25
Q12	PP3	$3000 bl grn	75	25
Q13	PP3	$5000 org red	75	25
Q14	PP3	$7000 dl bl	75	25
Q15	PP3	$10,000 car rose	90	25
Q16	PP3	$30,000 olive	90	25
Q17	PP3	$50,000 indigo	90	25
Q18	PP3	$70,000 org brn	1.00	25
Q19	PP3	$100,000 dp plum	1.00	25

Denomination Tablet Without Inner Frame.

No.	Type	Description	Unused	Used
Q20	PP3	$200,000 dk grn	1.50	40
Q21	PP3	$300,000 pink	1.50	40
Q22	PP3	$500,000 vio brn	1.50	50
Q23	PP3	$3,000,000 sl bl	1.75	75
Q24	PP3	$5,000,000 lilac	1.75	75
Q25	PP3	$6,000,000 ol gray	2.00	85
Q26	PP3	$8,000,000 scarlet	2.00	1.00
Q27	PP3	$10,000,000 sage grn	3.00	1.25
		Nos. Q11-Q27 (17)	22.55	8.15

Zeros for "cents" omitted on Nos. Q23–Q27.

Parcel Post Stamps of 1945–48 Surcharged in Black or Carmine

圓拾圓金
10
圓拾圓金

1949 *Perf. 13½.* **Unwmkd.**

No.	Type	Description	Unused	Used
Q32	PP3	$10 on $3000 bl grn	40	10
Q33	PP3	$20 on $5000 org red	40	10
Q34	PP3	$50 on $10,000 car rose	40	10
Q35	PP3	$100 on $3,000,000 sl bl (C)	60	15
Q36	PP3	$200 on $5,000,000 lil	1.00	15
Q37	PP3	$500 on $1000 org yel	2.00	25
Q38	PP3	$1000 on $7500 dl bl	2.00	40
		Nos. Q32-Q38 (7)	6.80	1.25

Five characters in each line on Nos. Q33 to Q38.

MILITARY STAMPS.

No. 454 Overprinted in Dull Red 郵 軍

1943-44 *Perf. 12.* **Unwmkd.**

No.	Type	Description	Unused	Used
M1	A59	8c turq grn	1.25	1.00

Nos. 383, 453-454 Overprinted in Red 郵 軍

6mm. between characters.

Perf. 14, 12½.

No.	Type	Description	Unused	Used
M2	A57	8c ol grn	1.00	1.00
a.		8mm between characters	1.50	1.50
M3	A59	8c red org	135.00	
M4	A59	8c turq grn	2.50	1.75

No. 493 Overprinted in Red 郵 軍

Perf. 13.

No.	Type	Description	Unused	Used
M5	A62	16c dl ol brn	1.25	1.00
a.		Perf. 10½-11	75.00	

No. M5 overprinted in black is a proof.

Stamps of 1942–44 Overprinted in Carmine or Black 郵 軍

No.	Type	Description	Unused	Used
M6	A62	50c sage grn (C)	1.25	1.00
M7	A62	$1 rose lake (Bk)	1.25	1.00
M8	A62	$1 dl grn (Bk)	1.25	1.00
M9	A62	$2 dk bl grn (C)	2.50	2.00
M10	A62	$2 dk vio brn ('44) (Bk)	9.00	7.50

Nos. 383 and 357 Overprinted in Red 郵 軍

1944 *Perf. 12, 14.*

No.	Type	Description	Unused	Used
M11	A57	8c ol grn	1.50	1.50
a.		Right character inverted	75.00	
M12	A57	16c ol gray	7.00	6.00

Anti-Aircraft Guns
M1

Thin Paper Without Gum.

1945, Jan. 1 **Typo.** *Perf. 12½*

No.	Type	Description	Unused	Used
M13	M1	rose	60	75

Taiwan (Formosa)

100 Sen = 1 Yen
100 Cents = 1 Dollar

Stamps and Types of Japan (Taiwan) Overprinted in Black

中華民國
臺灣省

Lithographed.
Values in Sen and Yen.
Black Overprint.

1945 *Imperf.* **Unwmkd.**

Stamps Divided by Lines of Colored Dashes.

No.	Type	Description	Unused	Used
1	A1	3s carmine	50	40
2	A1	5s bl grn	60	30
3	A1	10s pale bl	75	30
a.		Inverted ovpt.	30.00	
b.		Double ovpt.	35.00	
4	A1	30s dk bl	1.00	1.00
5	A1	40s violet	1.25	75
6	A1	50s gray brn	75	75
7	A1	1y ol grn	85	1.00

Same Overprint on Types of Japan A99 and A100.

No.	Type	Description	Unused	Used
8	A99	5y gray grn	4.00	2.50
9	A100	10y brn vio	6.00	3.50
a.		Invtd. ovpt.	125.00	
		Nos. 1-9 (9)	15.70	10.50

The basic stamps of this issue were prepared by Japanese authorities for Taiwan use before the end of World War II when the island reverted to Chinese control. They are printed on crude buff or white wove paper. The overprint translates: "For Use in Taiwan, Chinese Republic."

A second overprinting of Nos. 2–3 was made with a different font.

China, Nos. 728-731, Surcharged in Black

限臺灣省貼用
70 錢拾柒

1946 *Perf. 14.*

No.	Type	Description	Unused	Used
10	A75	70s on $20 grn	10	7
a.		Inverted surcharge	125.00	
11	A75	1y on $30 bl	20	15
12	A75	2y on $50 dk brn	30	25
13	A75	3y on $100 car	30	25

Issued to commemorate the convening of the Chinese National Assembly.

China Issues and Types of 1940-1946 Surcharged in Black

用貼灣臺限
錢 拾
a

Perf.
12½, 12½x13, 13, 13x12½, 14.

1946–47

No.	Type	Description	Unused	Used
14	A46	2s on 2c dp bl ('47)	5	5
15	A48	5s on 5c dl red org	5	5
16	A39	10s on 4c pale vio	5	5
17	A48	30s on 15c brn car	5	5
18	A73	50s on $20 car ('47)	5	5
19	A37	65s on $20 brt yel grn ('47)	5	5
20	A47	1y on 20c lt bl	5	5
a.		Inverted surch.	60.00	
21	A37	1y on $30 choc ('47)	5	5
22	A37	2y on $50 red org ('47)	5	5
23	A73	3y on $100 dk car ('47)	10	10
24	A73	5y on $200 ol grn ('47)	10	10
25	A73	10y on $500 brt bl grn ('47)	10	10
26	A73	20y on $700 red brn ('47)	25	25
27	A73	50y on $1000 rose lake ('47)	50	50
28	A73	100y on $3000 bl ('47)	75	75
		Nos. 14-28 (15)	2.25	2.25

The bottom line of the surcharge expresses the new value and consists of 2, 3 or 4 characters.

Same Surcharge on China No. 412.

1947 *Perf. 13.* **Wmk. 261**

No.	Type	Description	Unused	Used
28A	A48	30s on 15c brn car	27.50	30.00

Type of China, 1946.
Inscribed:

貼 臺
用 灣

Engraved

1947 *Perf. 11, 11½.* **Unwmkd.**

No.	Type	Description	Unused	Used
29	A74	70c carmine	15	15
30	A74	$1 green	15	15
31	A74	$2 vermilion	15	15
32	A74	$3 yel grn	15	15
33	A74	$7 yel org	25	25
34	A74	$10 magenta	25	25
		Nos. 29-34 (6)	1.10	1.10

60th birthday of Chiang Kai-shek.

Type of China, 1947.
Inscribed: 用貼灣臺

1947 *Perf. 14*

No.	Type	Description	Unused	Used
35	A76	50c dp grn	15	15
36	A76	$3 dp bl	15	15
37	A76	$7.50 carmine	15	15
38	A76	$10 lt brn	15	15
39	A76	$20 dp cl	15	15
		Nos. 35-39 (5)	75	75

First anniversary of return of Chinese National Government to Nanking.

Dr. Sun Yat-sen
A1

1947, July 10 **Without Gum**

No.	Type	Description	Unused	Used
40	A1	$1 dk brn	5	5
41	A1	$2 org brn	5	5
42	A1	$3 bl grn	5	5
43	A1	$5 vermilion	5	5
44	A1	$9 dp bl	5	5
45	A1	$10 brt rose car	5	5
46	A1	$20 dp grn	5	5
47	A1	$50 rose lil	10	10
48	A1	$100 blue	18	18
49	A1	$200 dk red	15	15
		Nos. 40-49 (10)	78	78

The 30c gray and $7.50 orange were not regularly issued without surcharge.

Type of 1947 Surcharged in Black

改作伍佰圓
500.00
b

1948 *Perf. 14* **Unwmkd.**

No.	Type	Description	Unused	Used
51	A1	$25 on $100 bl	60	25
52	A1	$500 on $7.50 org	75	50
53	A1	$1000 on 30c gray	3.00	1.25

Stamps of China, 1943–48, Surcharged Type "a" in Black or Carmine.

1948–49 *Perf. 12½, 14*

No.	Type	Description	Unused	Used
54	A73	$5 on $70 red org	15	15
55	A62	$10 on $3 dk yel	20	20
56	A82	$10 on $150 dk bl (C)	15	15
57	A82	$20 on $250 dp lil (C)	15	15
58	A67	$100 on $20 car	100.00	100.00
59	A82	$1000 on $20,000 rose pink ('49)	1.00	50
		Nos. 54-59 (6)	101.65	101.15

The bottom line of the surcharge expresses the new value and consists of 2 or 3 characters.

Type of 1947.

1949 **Engraved.** *Perf. 14.*

No.	Type	Description	Unused	Used
63	A1	$25 ol grn	15	12
64	A1	$5000 ocher	25	15
65	A1	$10,000 ap grn	25	15
66	A1	$20,000 ol bis	25	15
67	A1	$30,000 indigo	25	15
68	A1	$40,000 vio brn	25	15
		Nos. 63-68 (6)	1.40	87

No. 42 and Type of 1947 Surcharged Type "b" in Black, Carmine Violet or Red Violet.

1949

No.	Type	Description	Unused	Used
69	A1	$300 on $3 bl grn	25	20
70	A1	$1000 on $3 bl grn (C)	75	20
71	A1	$2000 on $3 bl grn (V)	50	40
72	A1	$3000 on $3 bl grn (RV)	2.00	30
73	A1	$3000 on $7.50 org	16.50	1.50
		Nos. 69-73 (5)	20.00	2.60

Stamps of China, 1940-47, Surcharged Type "a" in Black or Carmine.

Perf. 12½, 13x13½, 14.

No.	Type	Description	Unused	Used
74	A39	$2 on 2½c rose lil (#424)	10	10
75	A72	$5 on $40 org (#627)	10	10
76	A73	$5 on $50 pur (C) (#638)	10	10
77	A73	$5 on $100 dk car (#640)	10	10
78	A57	$20 on 2c ol grn (#368)	15	15
81	A63	$100 on $20 rose (#571)	15	10
82	A67	$200 on $10 dk bl (C) (#591)	25	25
84	A57	$500 on $30 dl vio (#521)	20	20
86	A62	$800 on $4 red brn (#504)	50	50

87	A67	$5000 on $10 dk bl (#591)	85	85
88	A67	$10,000 on $20 car (#592)	2.00	1.50
89	A82	$200,000 on $3000 bl (C) (#750)	37.50	17.50
		Nos. 74-89 (12)	42.00	21.45

Northeastern Provinces No. 47, Surcharged in Green, Red Violet, Black or Blue

2 ★★★ 2

1949–50

91	A2	2c on $44 dk car rose (G)	2.25	1.00
92	A2	5c on $44 dk car rose (RV) ('50)	2.50	1.50
a.		vio surcharge	2.50	2.00
93	A2	10c on $44 dk car rose (RV) ('50)	4.50	90
94	A2	20c on $44 dk car rose (Bk) ('50)	7.00	2.35
a.		Double surcharge	27.50	
95	A2	30c on $44 dk car rose (Bl) ('50)	8.00	2.65
96	A2	50c on $44 dk car rose (Bl) ('50)	14.00	5.25
		Nos. 91-96 (6)	38.25	13.65

China 959a, Overprinted in Black 用貼灣臺限

Ovpt. 15mm. Wide.

1949 ***Rouletted 9½.*** **Unwmkd.**

97	A96	orange	20	15

China Nos. 567, 498 and 640 Surcharged Type "a" in Black.

1948–49 ***Perf. 12½, 13, 14*** **Unwmkd.**

98	A63	$20 on $3 red	75	20
99	A62	$50 on 50c sage grn	30	10
a.		Perf. 11	10.00	10.00
100	A73	$600 on $100 dk car	1.00	60

Bottom line of surcharge consists of 3 characters.

No. 99 has two settings of surcharge: I. Spacing 10mm. between rows of characters. II. Spacing 12mm.

Nos. 67, 47 and 68 Surcharged in Violet or Black 臺幣壹角 10

1949 ***Perf. 14.***

101	A1	2c on $30,000 ind (V)	1.75	1.50
102	A1	10c on $50 rose lil	3.00	1.25
103	A1	10c on $40,000 vio brn	2.00	1.50

Numerals slightly larger on Nos. 101 and 103.

For similar surcharges on China type A82 see China Nos. 1025–1036.

AIR POST STAMP.

China No. C62a, Overprinted in Black 用貼灣臺限

Ovpt. 15mm. Wide.

1949 ***Rouletted 9½*** **Unwmkd.**

C1	AP5	bl grn	40	40

SPECIAL DELIVERY STAMP.

China No. E12a, Overprinted in Black 用貼灣臺限

Ovpt. 12½mm. Wide.

1950 ***Rouletted 9½.*** **Unwmkd.**

E1	SD2	red vio	30	20

REGISTRATION STAMP.

China No. F2a Overprinted in Black 用貼灣臺限

Ovpt. 12mm. Wide.

1950 ***Rouletted 9½*** **Unwmkd.**

F1	R2	carmine	30	20

POSTAGE DUE STAMPS.

D1

Lithographed.

1948, Feb. 10 ***Perf. 14*** **Unwmkd.**

Without Gum

J1	D1	$1 blue	6	6
J2	D1	$3 blue	6	6
J3	D1	$5 blue	6	6
J4	D1	$10 blue	8	8
J5	D1	$20 blue	6	6
		Nos. J1-J5(5)	32	32

Nos. J1–J4 Surcharged in Carmine 改作伍拾圓 50.00

1948, Dec. 4

J6	D1	$50 on $1 bl	1.25	1.25
J7	D1	$100 on $3 bl	1.25	1.25
J8	D1	$300 on $5 bl	1.25	1.25
J9	D1	$500 on $10 bl	2.00	2.00

Nos. 70, 72 and 64 Handstamped in Violet 資 欠

1949, Aug. 5

J10	A1	$1000 on $3 bl grn	4.00	3.00
J11	A1	$3000 on $3 bl grn	3.50	3.00
J12	A1	$5000 ocher	3.00	3.00

No. 48 Surcharged in Various Colors 臺幣肆分 資 欠 4

1950

J13	A1	4c on $100 bl (Br)	1.00	75
J14	A1	10c on $100 bl (RV)	1.50	1.00
J15	A1	20c on $100 bl (Bk)	2.00	1.50
J16	A1	40c on $100 bl (C)	5.00	3.00
J17	A1	$1 on $100 bl (Bl)	8.00	5.50
		Nos. J13-J17 (5)	17.50	11.75

The indexes in each volume of the Scott Catalogue contain many listings which help to identify stamps.

PARCEL POST STAMPS.

Type of China, Parcel Post Stamps of 1945–48 With Added Inscription:

Engraved.

1949 ***Perf. 14.*** **Unwmkd.**

Q1	PP3	$100 bluish grn	50.00	10
Q2	PP3	$300 rose car	50.00	10
Q3	PP3	$500 ol grn	50.00	10
Q4	PP3	$1000 slate	50.00	15
Q5	PP3	$3000 dp plum	50.00	15
		Nos. Q1-Q5 (5)	250.00	60

Chinese characters in lower corners have colorless background; denomination tablet in color.

OCCUPATION STAMPS.

Issued Under Japanese Occupation.

Kwangtung.

(kwäng'dōōng')

China No. 297 Overprinted in Black 用貼區粵

1942 ***Perf. 12½*** **Unwmkd.**

1N1	A37	2c ol grn	80	75
a.		Inverted ovpt.	30.00	

Same Overprint in Red or Black on Stamps of China, 1939-41.

Perf. 12½, 14.

1N2	A57	3c dl cl (#350)	50	35
1N3	A57	8c ol grn (#383)	50	35
1N4	A57	10c grn (#354) (R)	50	35
1N5	A57	10c grn (#354) (R)	50	35
1N6	A57	16c ol gray (#357)	90	75
1N7	A57	30c scar (#385)	50	35
1N8	A57	50c dk bl (#386) (R)	50	35
1N9	A57	$1 org brn & sep (#387)	1.60	1.50
1N10	A57	$2 dp bl & yel brn (#388)	85	75
1N11	A57	$5 red & sl grn (#389)	1.60	1.50
1N12	A57	$10 dk grn & dl pur (#390)	3.50	3.00
1N13	A57	$20 rose lake & dk bl (#391)	1.65	1.50

Same Overprint on China Nos. 422 and 433.

Perf. 12½.

1N14	A40	1c orange	45	35
a.		Inverted ovpt.	32.50	30.00
1N15	A47	20c lt bl	85	75

Same Overprint on Stamps of China, 1941.

Perf. 12.

1N16	A59	1c orange	40	35
1N17	A59	5c green	40	35
1N18	A59	8c turq grn	40	35
1N19	A59	10c brt grn	40	35
1N20	A59	17c olive	85	75
1N21	A59	30c scarlet	85	75
1N22	A59	50c dk bl	85	75
		Nos.1N1-1N22 (22)	19.35	16.60

Stamps of China, 1939-41 Overprinted in Black 貼 粵 用 省

1942 ***Perf. 12½, 14***

1N23	A57	2c ol grn (#368)	40	35
1N24	A57	3c dl cl (#350)	40	35
1N25	A57	5c ol grn (#352)	40	35
1N26	A57	8c ol grn (#353)	125.00	
1N27	A57	8c ol grn (#369)	50	50
1N28	A57	10c grn (#354)	75	75
1N29	A57	16c ol gray (#357)	75	75
1N30	A57	25c dk bl (#358)	75	75
1N31	A57	30c scar (#385)	40	35
1N32	A57	50c dk bl (#386)	40	35
1N33	A57	$1 org brn & sep (#387)	1.25	1.25
1N34	A57	$2 dp bl & yel brn (#388)	1.25	1.25
1N35	A57	$5 red & sl grn (#389)	2.00	2.00
1N36	A57	$10 dk grn & dl pur (#390)	3.00	3.00
1N37	A57	$20 rose lake & dk bl (#391)	4.00	4.00
		Nos. 1N23-1N25, 1N27-1N37 (14)	16.25	16.00

Same Overprint on China Nos. 397–401.

1942 ***Perf. 14.*** **Wmk. 261**

1N38	A57	$1 org brn & sep	3.50	2.50
1N39	A57	$2 dp bl & yel brn	3.50	2.50
1N40	A57	$5 red & sl grn	4.50	3.00
1N41	A57	$10 dk grn & dl pur	4.50	3.00
1N42	A57	$20 rose lake & dk bl	7.00	5.00
		Nos. 1N38-1N42 (5)	23.00	16.00

Same Overprint on Stamps of China, 1941.

1942 ***Perf. 12.*** **Unwmkd.**

1N43	A59	2c brt ultra	20	10
1N44	A59	5c green	20	15
1N45	A59	8c red org	20	20
1N46	A59	8c turq grn	20	20
1N47	A59	10c brt grn	50	50
1N48	A59	17c olive	50	50
1N49	A59	25c rose vio	50	50
1N50	A59	30c scarlet	50	50
1N51	A59	50c dk bl	50	50
1N52	A59	$1 brn & blk	1.00	1.00
1N53	A59	$2 bl & blk	1.00	1.00
1N54	A59	$5 scar & blk	1.00	1.00
1N55	A59	$10 grn & blk	2.25	2.25
1N56	A59	$20 rose vio & blk	3.00	3.00
		Nos. 1N43-1N56 (14)	11.55	11.40

China Nos. 354 and 369 Surcharged in Black

1945 ***Perf. 12½*** **Unwmkd.**

1N57	A57	$200 on 10c grn	60.00	35.00
1N58	A57	$400 on 8c ol grn	60.00	35.00

China No. 422 Surcharged in Black 肆佰圓 暫售

1945

1N59	A40	$400 on 1c org	375.00	300.00

POSTAGE DUE STAMP.

China, No. J79 Surcharged Diagonally with New Value Between Parallel Lines in Black.

1945 ***Perf. 12½.*** **Unwmkd.**

1NJ1	D5	$100 on $2 yel org	375.00	375.00
a.		Inverted surch.	500.00	

MENG CHIANG (Inner Mongolia)

疆   

Characters 4mm. High — Characters 5mm. High

I — II

Nos. 297-298, 301-303 Overprinted

1941		Engraved	Wnwmkd.	
2N1	A37	2c #297, I	50	50
a.		Type II	60	60
2N2	A37	4c #298, II	9.00	9.00
a.		Type I	15.00	15.00
2N3	A37	15c #301, I	50	50
a.		Type II	1.00	1.00
2N4	A37	20c #302, II	1.50	1.00
a.		Type I	1.50	1.50
2N5	A37	25c #303, II	1.50	1.00
a.		Type I	14.00	14.00
		Type I, set of 5	31.50	31.50
		Type II, set of 5	13.60	12.60

On Nos. 312, 314, 318, 321

1941			Perf. 14	
2N6	A39	½c #312, I	90	90
a.		Type II	6.00	6.00
2N7	A39	2½c #314, II	35	30
a.		Type I	40	40
2N8	A45	13c #318, II	1.25	1.00
a.		Type II	32.50	32.50
2N9	A48	30c #321, II	27.50	27.50

On Stamps of 1939-41

1941			Perf. 12½	
2N10	A57	2c #368, II	35	35
2N11	A57	3c #350, I	25	25
a.		Type II	35	35
2N12	A57	5c #352, I	25	25
a.		Type II	35	35
2N13	A57	8c #353, I	25	25
a.		Type II	35	35
2N14	A57	8c #369, II	2.25	1.75
2N15	A57	10c #354, II	60	40
2N16	A57	16c #357, II	85	75
2N17	A57	$1 #359, II	3.50	3.50
a.		Type I	250.00	250.00
b.		#347, I	37.50	37.50
2N18	A57	$5 #361, II	20.00	20.00
		Type I, set of 5	288.25	288.25
		Type II, set of 9	28.60	27.80

On Stamps of 1940 with Secret Marks

1941		Perf. 14	Unwmkd.	
2N19	A57	5c #382, II	30	30
2N20	A57	8c #383, I	35	30
a.		Type II	16.50	16.50
2N21	A57	10c #384, I	35	30
a.		Type II	50	40
2N22	A57	30c #385, I	90	35
a.		Type II	1.25	90
2N23	A57	50c #386, I	1.25	75
a.		Type II	1.25	90
2N24	A57	$1 #387, I	3.50	3.50
a.		Type II	6.00	6.00
2N25	A57	$2 #388, I	4.00	4.00
a.		Type II	12.00	8.00
2N26	A57	$5 #389, I	14.00	14.00
a.		Type II	22.50	22.50
2N27	A57	$10 #390, II	22.50	22.50
a.		Type I	27.50	27.50
2N28	A57	$20 #391, II	32.50	32.50
a.		Type I	37.50	37.50
		Type I, set of 9	89.35	88.20
		Type II, set of 10	115.30	110.50

On Stamps of 1940 with Secret Marks

1941		Perf. 14	Wmk. 261	
2N29	A57	10c #394, II	1.25	90
2N30	A57	30c #395, II	1.75	1.75
a.		Type I	32.50	32.50
2N31	A57	50c #396, II	1.75	1.75

On Stamps of 1940-41 (Martyrs) with Secret Marks

1941		Perf. 12½, 13 & Comp.	Wmk. 261	
2N32	A39	½c #402, II	5.00	3.00
2N33	A40	1c #403, I	30	25
a.		Type II	30	30
2N34	A39	2½c #405, II	20.00	20.00
a.		Type I	22.50	22.50
2N35	A48	3c #406, II	30	30
2N36	A46	10c #410, II	2.00	1.75
a.		Type I	2.25	1.75
2N37	A46	17c #413, II	13.50	13.50
a.		Type I	22.50	22.50
2N38	A40	25c #416, II	1.75	60
2N39	A48	30c #418, II	16.50	14.00
a.		Type I	22.50	22.50
2N40	A47	40c #419, II	60	35
a.		Type I	1.75	1.75
2N41	A40	50c #420, I	3.50	1.75
a.		Type II	13.50	13.50
		Type I, set of 7	75.30	73.00
		Type II, set of 10	73.45	67.30

Unwmkd.

2N42	A39	½c #421, I	30	30
a.		Type II	30	30
2N43	A40	1c #422, I	30	30
a.		Type II	90	30
2N44	A46	2c #423, I	30	30
2N45	A48	3c #425, I	40	40
a.		Type II	50	30
2N46	A39	4c #426, II	60	30
2N47	A45	8c #428, II	4.00	4.00
a.		Type I	37.50	37.50
2N48	A46	10c #429, I	6.00	4.00
a.		Type II	16.50	16.50
2N49	A45	13c #430, I	1.75	90
a.		Type II	3.00	2.25
2N50	A48	15c #431, II	1.00	1.00
2N51	A46	17c #432, I	90	75
a.		Type II	1.00	75
2N52	A47	20c #433, II	1.00	50
a.		Type I	1.25	1.25
2N53	A45	21c #434, II	1.00	1.00
2N54	A40	25c #435, I	1.25	1.25
2N55	A46	28c #436, II	1.00	1.00
2N56	A40	50c #439, II	2.00	2.00
a.		Type I	3.50	1.75
		Type I, set of 11	53.45	48.70
		Type II, set of 13	32.80	30.20

China Nos. 297-298, 302 Surcharged in Black

疆 蒙 分 壹

1942		Perf. 12½, 13.	Unwmkd.	
2N57	A37	1c on 2c ol grn	90	90
2N58	A37	2c on 4c grn	90	75
2N59	A37	10c on 20c ultra	12.00	12.00

Same, on China No. 313.

Perf. 14.

2N60	A40	½c on 1c org	2.00	

Same, on Stamps of China, 1938-41

Perf. 12½.

2N61	A57	1c on 2c ol grn (#368)	50	30
2N62	A57	4c on 8c ol grn (#353)	2.50	2.00
a.		Inverted surch.	50.00	50.00
2N63	A57	4c on 8c ol grn (#369)	75	75
2N64	A57	5c on 10c grn (#354)	50	35
2N65	A57	8c on 16c ol gray (#357)	1.00	60
2N66	A57	50c on $1 hn & dk brn (#359)	2.50	2.50
a.		50c on $1 hn & dk brn (#347)	20.00	20.00
b.		50c on $1 hn & dk brn (#344)	200.00	200.00
2N67	A57	$1 on $2 dp bl & org brn (#360)	12.50	12.50

No. 2N66b was issued without gum.

Same, on Stamps of China, 1940.

Perf. 14.

2N68	A57	4c on 8c ol grn (#383)	25	25
2N69	A57	15c on 30c scar (#385)	60	60
a.		Inverted surch.	50.00	50.00
2N70	A57	25c on 50c dk bl (#386)	1.00	1.00
2N71	A57	50c on $1 org brn & sep (#387)	1.50	1.00
2N72	A57	$1 on $2 dp bl & yel brn (#388)	3.00	2.50
2N73	A57	$5 on $10 dk grn & dl pur (#390)	10.00	10.00
2N74	A57	$10 on $20 rose lake & dk bl (#391)	37.50	37.50

Same, on China No. 395.

1942		Perf. 14.	Wmk. 261	
2N75	A57	15c on 30c scar	25.00	25.00

Same, on China Nos. 418 and 419.

Perf. 12½, 13.

2N76	A48	15c on 30c brn car	12.00	12.00
2N77	A47	20c on 40c org	2.50	2.50

Same, on Stamps of China, 1940-41.

1942			Unwmkd.	
2N78	A40	½c on 1c org	20	20
2N79	A39	2c on 4c pale vio	40	35
2N80	A47	10c on 20c lt bl	75	60
2N81	A47	20c on 40c org	3.00	2.50
2N82	A40	25c on 50c grn	7.00	7.00

Same Surcharge on "New Peking" Prints.

Perf. 14.

2N83	A37	1c on 2c ol grn	15	15
2N84	A37	2c on 4c dl grn	15	15
2N85	A46	5c on 10c dl vio	30	30
2N86	A57	8c on 16c ol gray	30	30
2N87	A47	10c on 20c red brn	50	50
2N88	A48	15c on 30c brn car	75	75
2N89	A47	20c on 40c org	75	75
2N90	A40	25c on 50c grn	1.00	1.00
2N91	A57	50c on $1 org brn & sep	2.00	2.00
2N92	A57	$1 on $2 dp bl & org brn	14.00	14.00
2N93	A57	$5 on $10 dk grn & dl pur	17.50	17.50

The "New Peking" printings were made by the Chinese Bureau of Engraving and Printing for use in Japanese controlled areas of North China. They are on thin, poor quality paper, with dull gum or without gum and there are slight alterations in the designs.

Dragon-Carved Pillar and Doves
A1

Mining Coal
A2

Wmkd.

Characters in Circle in Sheet.

Perf. 12 x Pin-Perf. 12.

1943			Engraved	
2N94	A1	4f dp org	15	15
2N95	A1	8f dk bl	25	25

Issued to commemorate the 5th anniversary of the Inner Mongolia post and telegraph service.

The watermark, which is 40mm. in diameter and covers four stamps, occurs three times in the sheet.

Photogravure.

1943		Perf. 12.	Unwmkd.	
2N96	A2	8f Prus grn	12	12
2N97	A2	8f brn red	25	25

Issued to commemorate the 2nd anniversary of the "Greater East Asia War".

Flying Horse
A3

Yun Wang
A4

1944		Perf. 12½x12, 12x12½.		
2N98	A3	4f rose	15	15
2N99	A4	8f dl bl	25	25

Issued to commemorate the 5th anniversary of the founding of the Federal Autonomous Government of Mongolia, September 1, 1939.

Industrial Plant
A5

1944, Dec. 8		Photo. Perf. 12x12½		
2N100	A5	8f red brn	10	10

Issued to commemorate the 3rd anniversary of the "Greater East Asia War" and to encourage production increase.

New Peking Printings of 1942 Overprinted in Black 蒙疆

Engraved

1945 *Perf. 14.* **Unwmkd.**

Without Gum.

2N101 A37 2c ol grn 10 10
2N102 A37 4c dl grn 1.25 1.25
2N103 A37 5c green 10 10
2N104 A57 $1 org brn & sep 75 75
2N105 A57 $2 dp bl & org brn 3.00 3.00
2N106 A57 $5 red & grnsh blk 10.00 10.00

Same Overprint on New Peking Printings of Martyrs Issue

2N107 A40 1c orange 10 10
2N108 A45 8c dp org 10 10
2N109 A46 10c dl vio 15 15
2N110 A47 20c red brn 15 15
2N111 A48 30c brn car 10 10
2N112 A47 40c orange 10 10
2N113 A40 50c green 35 35
Nos. 2N101-2N113 (13) 16.25 16.25

Stamps of Meng Chiang, 1941 With Additional Surcharge in Red or Black 伍角

1945

2N114 A39 10c on ½c ol blk (#2N42) (R) 25 25
a. 10c on ½c ol blk (#2N42,II) 75
2N115 A40 10c on 1c org (#2N43,II) (R) 25 25
a. Without secret mark (China #313) 20.00 20.00
2N116 A37 50c on 2c ol grn (#2N1, II) (Bk) 40 40
2N117 A57 50c on 2c ol grn (#2N10) (Bk) 10 10
2N118 A39 50c on 4c pale vio (#2N46) (R) 25 25
2N119 A57 50c on 5c ol grn (#2N12, II) (R) 15 15
a. On #2N12, I
2N120 A57 50c on 5c ol grn (#2N19) (R) 25 25
Nos. 2N114-2N120 (7) 1.65 1.65

Same Surcharge on Nos. 2N32 and 2N33 II.

1945 **Wmk. 261**

2N121 A39 10c on ½c ol blk (R) 7.50 7.50
2N122 A40 10c on 1c org (R) 50 50

Same Surcharge on Nos. 2N107, 2N101-2N103 and 2N108

1945 **Unwmkd.**

2N123 A40 10c on 1c org (R) 20 20
2N124 A37 50c on 2c ol grn (Bk) 15 15
2N125 A37 50c on 4c dl grn (R) 2.50 2.50
2N126 A37 50c on 5c grn 20 20
2N127 A45 $1 on 8c dp org (R) 35 35
Nos. 2N123-2N127 (5) 3.40 3.40

Honan

河南 I　河南 II

Nos. 297-298, 301-303 Overprinted

1941 **Engraved** **Unwmkd.**

3N1 A37 2c #297, II 60 60
a. Type I 1.50 1.50
3N2 A37 4c #298, I 2.25 1.75
a. Type II 7.00 7.00
3N3 A37 15c #301, II 50 50
a. Type I 60 50
3N4 A37 20c #302, I 2.50 50
3N5 A37 25c #303, II 7.00 7.00

On Nos. 312, 314, 318, 321-322

1941 *Perf. 14*

3N6 A39 ½c #312, I 30 30
a. Type II 4.00 4.00
3N7 A39 2½c #314, II 25 25
a. Type I 30 30
3N8 A45 13c #318, II 50 30
a. Type I 37.50 37.50
3N9 A48 30c #321, II 4.00 2.00
3N10 A47 40c #322, II 37.50 37.50

On Stamps of 1939-41

1941 *Perf. 12½*

3N11 A57 2c #368, II 25 25
3N12 A57 3c #350, II 25 25
a. Type I 30 30
3N13 A57 5c #352, II 25 25
a. Type I 30 30
3N14 A57 8c #353, II 25 25
a. Type I 60 60
3N15 A57 10c #354, II 25 25
3N16 A57 16c #357, II 25 25
3N17 A57 $1 #359, II 4.00 3.25
a. Type I 165.00 165.00
b. On #347, I 30.00 30.00
3N18 A57 $5 #361, II 32.50 32.50

On Stamps of 1940 with Secret Marks

1941 *Perf. 14* *Unwmkd.*

3N20 A57 5c #382, II 90 25
3N21 A57 8c #383, II 25 25
3N22 A57 10c #384, II 25 25
3N23 A57 30c #385, II 1.25 40
a. Type I 1.50 1.00
3N24 A57 50c #386, I 1.50 1.25
a. Type II 3.50 2.25
3N25 A57 $1 #387, I 3.50 1.75
a. Type II 27.50 25.00
3N26 A57 $2 #388, I 5.00 4.00
a. Type II 6.00 3.50
3N27 A57 $5 #389, I 7.00 7.00
a. Type II 22.50 22.50
3N28 A57 $10 #390, II 20.00 20.00
a. Type I 65.00 65.00
3N29 A57 $20 #391, II 32.50 32.50
a. Type I 35.00 35.00
Type I, set of 7 73.50 70.00
Type II, set of 10 159.65 151.90

On Stamps of 1940 with Secret Marks

1941 *Perf. 14* *Wmk. 261*

3N30 A57 5c #392, II 7.00 1.25
3N31 A57 5c #393, II 3.50 50
3N32 A57 30c #395, II 4.00 1.75
a. Type I 7.00 3.50
3N33 A57 50c #396, II 7.00 7.00

On Stamps of 1940-41 (Martyrs) with Secret Marks

1941 *Perf. 12½, 13 & Comp.* *Wmk. 261*

3N34 A39 ½c #402, II 25 25
3N35 A40 1c #403, II 25 25
a. Type I 25 25
3N36 A39 2½c #405, II 6.00 3.50
3N37 A46 10c #410, I 90 30
a. Type II 2.25 1.75
3N38 A45 13c #411, II 25 25
3N39 A46 17c #413, II 50 25
a. Type I 4.00 1.75
3N40 A40 25c #416, II 50 25
3N41 A47 40c #419, II 75 25
a. Type I 6.00 1.50

Unwmkd.

3N42 A39 ½c #421, II 25 25
a. Type I 25 25
3N43 A40 1c #422, I 25 25
a. Type II 50 25
3N44 A46 2c #423, I 3.00 60
3N45 A48 3c #425, I 50 50
3N46 A39 4c #426, II 25 25
3N47 A46 10c #429, I 13.50 7.00
3N48 A45 13c #430, II 75 25
a. Type I 5.00 1.75
3N49 A48 15c #431, II 25 25
3N50 A46 17c #432, II 25 25
a. Type I 5.00 1.50
3N51 A47 20c #433, II 25 25
a. Type I 13.50 4.00
3N52 A45 21c #434, II 25 25
3N53 A40 25c #435, I 1.25 90
3N54 A46 28c #436, II 25 25
Type I, set of 9 42.25 16.75
Type II, set of 9 3.00 2.25

Overprinted in Red

新嘉坡
陷落紀念

1942

3N55 A39 4c #3N46 90 90
3N56 A57 8c #3N14 8.00 8.00
3N57 A57 8c #369, II 3.00 3.00

The fall of Singapore.

Overprinted in Red

滿洲國建國
十週年紀念

1942

3N58 A57 2c #3N19 2.50 2.50
3N59 A39 4c #407, II 3.50 3.50
3N60 A57 8c #369, II 15.00 15.00
3N61 A57 8c #3N14 15.00 15.00

Tenth Anniv. of the formation of Manchukuo.

Hopei

河北 I　河北 II

Nos. 297-298, 301-303 Overprinted

1941 **Engraved** **Unwmkd.**

4N1 A37 2c #297, II 40 40
a. Type I 60 60
4N2 A37 4c #298, I 75 60
a. Type II 27.50 27.50
4N3 A37 15c #301, II 40 40
a. Type I 1.50 90
4N4 A37 20c #302, II 60 60
4N5 A37 25c #303, II 2.25 1.75
a. Type I 37.50 37.50

On Nos. 312, 314, 318, 321

1941 *Perf. 14*

4N6 A39 ½c #312, II 25 25
a. Type I 50 50
4N7 A39 2½c #314, II 25 25
a. Type I 35 25
4N8 A45 13c #318, II 75 50
a. Type I 1.25 1.25
4N9 A48 30c #321, II 1.75 1.25

On Stamps of 1939-41

1941 *Perf. 12½*

4N10 A57 2c #368, II 25 25
4N11 A57 2c #349, II 25 25
4N12 A57 3c #350, II 25 25
a. Type I 90 60
4N13 A57 5c #352, II 25 25
a. Type I 50 50
4N14 A57 8c #353, II 25 25
a. Type I 60 60
4N15 A57 8c #369, II 75 30
4N16 A57 10c #354, II 25 25
4N17 A57 16c #357, II 25 25
4N18 A57 $1 #359, II 2.25 2.25
a. On #347, I 135.00 135.00
4N19 A57 $2 #360, II 2.25 2.25
a. Type I 25.00 25.00
4N20 A57 $5 #361, II 16.50 16.50
a. Type I 20.00 20.00
4N21 A57 $10 #362, II 55.00 55.00
4N22 A57 $20 #363, II 160.00 160.00
Type II, set of 13 238.50 238.05
Type I, set of 6 182.00 181.70

On Stamps of 1940 with Secret Marks

1941 *Perf. 14* *Unwmkd.*

4N24 A57 5c #382, II 25 25
a. Type I 25 25
4N25 A57 8c #383, II 25 25
a. Type I 27.50 27.50
4N26 A57 10c #384, II 25 25
a. Type I 60 50
4N27 A57 30c #385, II 25 25
4N28 A57 50c #386, II 75 25
a. Type I 90 75
4N29 A57 $1 #387, II 1.75 90
a. Type I 2.25 1.75
4N30 A57 $2 #388, II 6.00 1.75
a. Type I 11.00 7.00
4N31 A57 $5 #389, II 12.00 12.00
a. Type I 17.50 17.50
4N32 A57 $10 #390, II 16.50 16.50
a. Type I 22.50 22.50
4N33 A57 $20 #391, II 27.50 27.50
a. Type I 32.50 32.50
Type II, set of 10 65.50 59.90
Type I, set of 9 115.00 110.25

On Stamps of 1940 with Secret Marks

1941 *Perf. 14* *Wmk. 261*

4N34 A57 5c #392, II 25 25
4N35 A57 5c #393, II 25 25
4N36 A57 10c #394, II 25 25
4N37 A57 30c #395, II 50 50
a. Type I 1.50 1.25
4N38 A57 50c #396, II 75 60

On Stamps of 1940-41 (Martyrs) with Secret Marks

1941 *Perf. 12½, 13 & Comp.* *Wmk. 261*

4N39 A39 ½c #402, II 25 25
4N40 A40 1c #403, II 25 25
a. Type I 25 25
4N41 A46 2c #404, II 25 25
4N42 A39 2½c #405, II 25 25
4N43 A48 3c #406, II 25 25
4N44 A46 10c #410, II 50 50
a. Type I 50 30
4N45 A45 13c #411, II 50 50
4N46 A46 17c #413, II 50 50
a. Type I 90 75
4N47 A40 25c #416, II 60 50
4N48 A48 30c #418, II 60 50
a. Type I 9.00 9.00
4N49 A47 40c #419, II 60 50
a. Type I 1.75 1.50
Nos. 4N39-4N49 (11) 4.55 4.25

Unwmkd.

4N50 A39 ½c #421, II 25 25
a. Type I 25 25
4N51 A40 1c #422, II 25 25
a. Type I 25 25
4N52 A46 2c #423, I 50 50
4N53 A48 3c #425, II 25 25
a. Type I 50 50
4N54 A39 4c #426, II 50 50
4N55 A45 8c #428, II 50 50
a. Type I 75 60
4N56 A46 10c #429, II 50 50
4N57 A45 13c #430, II 75 75
a. Type I 75 60
4N58 A48 15c #431, II 50 50
4N59 A46 17c #432, II 60 50
a. Type I 1.50 1.00
4N60 A47 20c #433, II 50 50
a. Type I 1.50 1.00
4N61 A45 21c #434, II 50 50
4N62 A40 25c #435, II 75 50
a. Type I 1.50 1.00
4N63 A46 28c #436, II 50 50

Honan Singapore Overprint in Red

1942

4N64 A39 4c #4N54 50 50
4N65 A57 8c #4N25 1.50 1.50
4N66 A57 8c #4N14 1.75 1.75
4N67 A57 8c #4N23 2.00 2.00

Honan Anniv. of Manchukuo Overprint in Red

1942

4N68 A57 2c #4N22 3.00 3.00
4N69 A39 4c #4N54 1.25 1.25
4N70 A57 8c #4N14 25.00 25.00
4N71 A57 8c #4N25 3.00 3.00

Shansi

西 山 西 山

I II

Nos. 297-298, 301, 303 Overprinted

1941 Engraved Unwmkd.

No.	Design	Stamp	Unused	Used
5N1	A37	2c #297, II	90	50
a.		Type I	1.50	75
5N2	A37	4c #298, I	5.00	1.25
a.		Type II	55.00	32.50
5N3	A37	15c #301, I	75	50
a.		Type II	75	50
5N4	A37	25c #303, II	1.50	60
a.		Type I	22.50	22.50

On Nos. 312, 314, 318, 321

1941 Perf. 14

No.	Design	Stamp	Unused	Used
5N5	A39	½c #312, II	25	25
a.		Type I	60	30
5N6	A39	2½c #314, II	25	25
a.		Type I	50	50
5N7	A45	13c #318, II	60	60
a.		Type I	55.00	55.00
5N8	A48	30c #321, II	3.50	3.50

On Stamps of 1939-41

1941 Perf. 12½

No.	Design	Stamp	Unused	Used
5N9	A57	2c #368, II	50	50
5N10	A57	3c #350, II	50	50
a.		Type I	3.50	1.00
5N11	A57	5c #352, II	50	50
a.		Type I	90	40
5N12	A57	8c #353, II	50	50
a.		Type I	90	50
5N13	A57	8c #369, II	16.50	11.00
5N14	A57	10c #354, II	50	30
5N15	A57	16c #357, II	90	90
5N16	A57	$1 #359, II	4.00	2.25
5N17	A57	$2 #360, II	14.00	14.00
5N18	A57	$5 #361, II	25.00	25.00
		Nos. 5N9-5N18 (10)	62.90	55.45

On Stamps of 1940 with Secret Marks

1941 Perf. 14 Unwmkd.

No.	Design	Stamp	Unused	Used
5N19	A57	5c #382, II	25	25
5N20	A57	8c #383, II	50	50
5N21	A57	10c #384, II	50	50
a.		Type I	60	30
5N22	A57	30c #385, I	75	50
a.		Type II	75	75
5N23	A57	50c #386, I	90	75
a.		Type II	90	90
5N24	A57	$1 #387, I	5.00	2.50
a.		Type II	14.00	5.00
5N25	A57	$2 #388, I	7.00	2.50
a.		Type II	7.00	5.00
5N26	A57	$5 #389, II	9.00	9.00
a.		Type I	27.50	27.50
5N27	A57	$10 #390, II	14.00	14.00
a.		Type I	16.50	16.50
5N28	A57	$20 #391, II	25.00	25.00
a.		Type I	27.50	27.50
		Type II, set of 10	71.90	60.90
		Type I, set of 8	85.75	78.05

On Stamps of 1940 with Secret Marks

1941 Perf. 14 Wmk. 261

No.	Design	Stamp	Unused	Used
5N29	A57	5c #392, II	40	40
5N30	A57	5c #393, II	40	40
5N31	A57	10c #394, II	75	75
5N32	A57	30c #395, I	30.00	30.00
5N33	A57	50c #396, I	2.50	1.50
		Nos. 5N29-5N33 (5)	34.05	33.05

On Stamps of 1940-41 (Martyrs) with Secret Marks

1941 Perf. 12½, 13 & Comp. Wmk. 261

No.	Design	Stamp	Unused	Used
5N34	A39	½c #402, II	25	25
5N35	A40	1c #403, II	25	25
a.		Type I	25	25
5N36	A46	2c #404, II	50	50
5N37	A39	2½c #405, I	1.50	1.50
5N38	A46	10c #410, I	1.75	1.25
5N39	A45	13c #411, II	35	35
5N40	A46	17c #413, I	11.00	8.00
5N41	A40	25c #416, II	60	60
5N42	A48	30c #418, II	27.50	27.50
a.		Type I	27.50	27.50
5N43	A47	40c #419, II	60	60
a.		Type I	12.00	7.00
5N44	A40	50c #420, II	90	75
a.		Type I	15.00	9.00
		Type II, set of 8	30.95	30.80
		Type I, set of 7	69.00	54.50

Unwmkd.

No.	Design	Stamp	Unused	Used
5N45	A39	½c #421, II	25	25
a.		Type I	25	25
5N46	A40	1c #422, II	25	25
a.		Type I	25	25
5N47	A46	2c #423, II	25	25
5N48	A48	3c #425, I	2.00	1.25
5N49	A39	4c #426, II	25	25
5N50	A45	8c #428, I	5.00	1.75
a.		Type II	5.00	2.25
5N51	A46	10c #429, I	11.00	10.00
a.		Type II	20.00	20.00
5N52	A45	13c #430, I	6.50	1.25
a.		Type II	6.00	4.00
5N53	A48	15c #431, II	75	60
5N54	A46	17c #432, II	75	60
a.		Type I	90	90
5N55	A47	20c #433, II	75	60
a.		Type I	90	90
5N56	A45	21c #434, II	75	60
5N57	A40	25c #435, I	1.25	75
5N58	A46	28c #436, II	90	75
5N59	A40	50c #439, II	3.00	1.75
		Type I, set of 9	38.90	32.15
		Type II, set of 13	28.05	17.30

Honan Singapore Overprint in Red

1942

No.	Design	Stamp	Unused	Used
5N60	A39	4c #5N49	90	90
5N61	A57	8c #5N20	3.00	3.00
5N62	A57	8c #5N11	3.00	3.00
5N63	A57	8c #5N18	10.00	10.00

Honan Anniv. of Manchukuo Overprint in Red

1942

No.	Design	Stamp	Unused	Used
5N64	A57	2c #5N17	1.50	1.50
5N65	A39	4c #5N49	1.50	1.50
5N66	A57	8c #5N11	15.00	15.00
5N67	A57	8c #5N18	18.00	18.00
5N68	A57	8c #5N20	15.00	15.00
		Nos. 5N64-5N68 (5)	51.00	51.00

Shantung

東 山 東 山

I II

Nos. 297-298, 301-303 Overprinted

1941 Engraved Unwmkd.

No.	Design	Stamp	Unused	Used
6N1	A37	2c #297, II	25	25
a.		Type I	50	40
6N2	A37	4c #298, I	1.75	90
a.		Type II	1.75	1.25
6N3	A37	15c #301, II	25	25
a.		Type I	90	50
6N4	A37	20c #302, II	50	25
6N5	A37	25c #303, II	1.50	1.25
a.		Type I	80.00	80.00

On Nos. 312, 314, 318

1941 Perf. 14

No.	Design	Stamp	Unused	Used
6N6	A39	½c #312, II	25	25
a.		Type I	40	25
6N7	A39	2½c #314, II	25	25
a.		Type I	25	25
6N8	A45	13c #318, II	25	25
a.		Type I	9.00	7.00

On Stamps of 1939-41

1941 Perf. 12½

No.	Design	Stamp	Unused	Used
6N9	A57	2c #349, II	25	25
6N10	A57	2c #368, II	25	25
6N11	A57	3c #350, II	25	25
a.		Type I	50	25
6N12	A57	5c #352, II	25	25
a.		Type I	25	25
6N13	A57	8c #353, II	25	25
a.		Type I	25	25
6N14	A57	8c #369, II	25	25
6N15	A57	10c #354, II	25	25
6N16	A57	16c #357, II	60	60
6N17	A57	$1 #359, II	4.00	4.00
a.		Type I	135.00	135.00
b.		On No. 347, I	25.00	25.00
6N18	A57	$5 #361, II	20.00	20.00
		Nos. 6N9-6N18 (10)	26.35	26.35

On Stamps of 1940 with Secret Marks

1941 Perf. 14 Unwmkd.

No.	Design	Stamp	Unused	Used
6N20	A57	5c #382, II	25	25
6N21	A57	8c #383, I	20	20
a.		Type II	25	25
6N22	A57	10c #384, II	25	25
6N23	A57	30c #385, II	50	25
a.		Type I	1.25	1.25
6N24	A57	50c #386, II	90	75
a.		Type I	1.25	90
6N25	A57	$1 #387, II	90	75
a.		Type I	3.00	3.00
6N26	A57	$2 #388, II	2.50	2.00
a.		Type I	6.00	5.00
6N27	A57	$5 #389, II	7.00	6.00
a.		Type I	14.00	14.00
6N28	A57	$10 #390, II	16.50	16.50
a.		Type I	22.50	22.50
6N29	A57	$20 #391, II	25.00	25.00
a.		Type I	32.50	32.50

On Stamps of 1940 with Secret Marks

1941 Perf. 14 Wmk. 261

No.	Design	Stamp	Unused	Used
6N30	A57	5c #392, II	25	25
6N31	A57	5c #393, II	25	25
6N32	A57	10c #394, II	2.00	1.75
6N33	A57	30c #395, II	2.00	1.00
a.		Type I	7.00	6.00
6N34	A57	50c #396, II	1.50	75
a.		Type I	2.25	1.75
		Nos. 6N30-6N34 (5)	6.00	4.00

On Stamps of 1940-41 (Martyrs) with Secret Marks

1941 Perf. 12½, 13 & Comp. Wmk. 261

No.	Design	Stamp	Unused	Used
6N35	A39	½c #402, II	25	25
6N36	A40	1c #403, II	25	25
a.		Type I	25	25
6N37	A39	2½c #405, II	1.75	1.50
6N38	A46	10c #410, I	90	40
6N39	A45	13c #411, II	50	25
6N40	A46	17c #413, II	1.50	50
a.		Type I	3.00	1.25
6N41	A40	25c #416, II	50	50
6N42	A48	30c #418, I	9.00	9.00
6N43	A47	40c #419, II	50	50
a.		Type I	9.00	9.00
6N44	A40	50c #420, II	1.00	60
		Nos. 6N35-6N44 (10)	16.15	13.75

Unwmkd.

No.	Design	Stamp	Unused	Used
6N45	A39	½c #421, II	25	25
a.		Type I	25	25
6N46	A40	1c #422, II	25	25
a.		Type I	25	25
b.		On No. 422a, II	32.50	32.50
6N48	A46	2c #423, II	25	25
6N49	A48	3c #425, I	50	50
a.		Type II	75	50
6N50	A39	4c #426, II	25	25
6N51	A45	8c #428, II	25	25
a.		Type I	6.00	6.00
6N52	A46	10c #429, I	2.50	1.75
6N53	A45	13c #430, II	25	25
a.		Type I	60	60
6N54	A48	15c #431, II	25	25
6N55	A46	17c #432, II	25	25
a.		Type I	60	60
6N56	A47	20c #433, II	25	25
a.		Type I	60	60
6N57	A45	21c #434, II	25	25
6N58	A40	25c #435, I	90	75
6N59	A46	28c #436, II	50	30
6N60	A40	50c #439, II	3.00	3.00
		Type II, set of 13	6.75	6.30
		Type I, set of 9	12.20	11.30

Honan Singapore Overprint in Red

1942

No.	Design	Stamp	Unused	Used
6N61	A39	4c #6N50	50	50
6N62	A57	8c #6N13	3.00	3.00
6N63	A57	8c #6N21a	1.75	1.75
6N64	A57	8c #6N19	7.00	7.00

Honan Anniv. of Manchukuo Overprint in Red

1942

No.	Design	Stamp	Unused	Used
6N65	A57	2c #6N18	1.50	1.50
6N66	A39	4c #6N50	1.25	1.25
6N67	A57	8c #6N13	10.00	10.00
6N68	A57	8c #6N19	16.50	16.50
6N69	A57	8c #6N21a	1.50	1.50
		Nos. 6N65-6N69 (5)	30.75	30.75

Supeh

北 蘇 北 蘇

I II

Nos. 297-298, 301-302 Overprinted

1941 Engraved Unwmkd.

No.	Design	Stamp	Unused	Used
7N1	A37	2c #297, I	2.25	2.25
a.		Type II	5.00	5.00
7N2	A37	4c #298, I	15.00	15.00
7N3	A37	15c #301, I	60	50
a.		Type II	75	60
7N4	A37	20c #302, II	75	60

On Nos. 312, 314, 318

1941 Perf. 14

No.	Design	Stamp	Unused	Used
7N5	A39	½c #312, I	60	60
7N6	A39	2½c #314, II	50	50
a.		Type I	50	50
7N7	A45	13c #318, II	50	50
a.		Type I	55.00	55.00

On Stamps of 1939-41

1941 Perf. 12½

No.	Design	Stamp	Unused	Used
7N8	A57	2c #368, II	50	50
7N9	A57	3c #350, II	50	50
a.		Type I	7.00	6.00
7N10	A57	5c #352, II	50	50
a.		Type I	50	50
7N11	A57	8c #353, I	50	50
a.		Type II	1.75	1.75
7N12	A57	8c #369, II	16.50	16.50
7N13	A57	10c #354, II	50	50
7N14	A57	16c #357, II	50	50
7N15	A57	$1 #359, II	6.00	6.00
		Nos. 7N8-7N15 (8)	25.50	25.50

On Stamps of 1940 with Secret Marks

1941 Perf. 14 Unwmkd.

No.	Design	Stamp	Unused	Used
7N17	A57	5c #382, II	20	20
7N18	A57	8c #383, II	20	20
7N19	A57	10c #384, I	50	40
a.		Type II	60	40
7N20	A57	30c #385, II	75	40
a.		Type I	75	60
7N21	A57	50c #386, II	75	40
a.		Type I	1.25	75
7N22	A57	$1 #387, I	7.00	4.00
a.		Type II	14.00	14.00
7N23	A57	$2 #388, I	8.00	7.00
a.		Type II	8.00	8.00
7N24	A57	$5 #389, I	14.00	14.00
a.		Type II	37.50	37.50
7N25	A57	$10 #390, II	22.50	22.50
a.		Type I	27.50	27.50
7N26	A57	$20 #391, II	32.50	32.50
a.		Type I	32.50	32.50
		Type II, set of 10	117.00	116.10
		Type I, set of 8	91.50	86.75

On Stamps of 1940 with Secret Marks

1941 Perf. 14 Wmk. 261

No.	Design	Stamp	Unused	Used
7N27	A57	10c #394, II	50	30
7N28	A57	30c #395, I	3.00	2.25
7N29	A57	50c #396, I	3.00	2.25

On Stamps of 1940-41 (Martyrs) with Secret Marks

1941 *Perf. 12½, 13 & Comp.* *Wmk. 261*

7N30	A39	½c #402, II	25	25
7N31	A40	1c #403, II	25	25
a.		Type I	25	25
7N32	A46	2c #404, II	25	25
7N33	A39	½c #405, I	10.00	10.00
7N34	A46	10c #410, I	3.50	3.00
7N35	A45	13c #411, II	1.50	1.00
7N36	A46	17c #413, II	75	30
a.		Type I	27.50	27.50
7N37	A40	25c #416, II	75	50
7N38	A48	30c #418, I	3.50	3.00
7N39	A47	40c #419, II	60	40
a.		Type I	2.25	2.25
7N40	A40	50c #420, I	32.50	32.50
		Nos. 7N30-7N40 (11)	53.85	51.45

Unwmkd.

7N41	A39	½c #421, II	20	20
a.		Type I	25	25
7N42	A40	1c #422, II	20	20
7N43	A46	2c #423, I	2.25	1.75
7N44	A48	3c #425, I	50	50
7N45	A39	4c #426, II	25	25
7N46	A46	10c #429, I	16.50	16.50
7N47	A45	13c #430, I	60	60
7N48	A48	15c #431, II	60	30
7N49	A46	17c #432, II	75	50
a.		Type I	75	75
7N50	A47	20c #433, II	50	30
a.		Type I	1.50	1.25
7N51	A45	21c #434, II	50	30
7N52	A40	25c #435, I	1.50	1.25
a.		Type II	1.75	1.50
7N53	A46	28c #436, II	40	40
		Nos. 7N41-7N53 (13)	24.75	23.05

Honan Singapore Overprint in Red

1942

7N54	A37	4c #298, II	32.50	32.50
7N55	A39	4c #7N45	1.50	1.50
7N56	A57	8c #7N11a	3.00	3.00
7N57	A57	8c #7N16	7.00	7.00

Honan Anniv. of Manchukuo Overprint in Red

1942

7N58	A57	2c #7N15	1.75	1.75
7N59	A39	4c #7N45	1.25	1.25
7N60	A57	8c #7N11a	37.50	37.50
7N61	A57	8c #7N16	20.00	20.00

North China

For use in:

Honan, Hopei, Shansi, Shantung and Supeh (Northern Kiangsu).

Stamps of China, 1931–37 Surcharged North China (Hwa Pei) and Half of Original Value

北 華
分 壹

1942 *Perf. 14, 12½* **Unwmkd.**

8N1	A40	½c on 1c org (#313)	15	15
8N2	A37	1c on 2c ol grn (#297)	25	20
8N3	A37	2c on 4c grn (#298)	50	20
8N4	A45	4c on 8c brn org (#316)	90.00	

Same Surcharge on Stamps of 1938-41. *Perf. 12½*

8N5	A57	1c on 2c ol grn (#349)	1.25	1.25
8N6	A57	1c on 2c ol grn (#368)	30	15
8N7	A57	4c on 8c ol grn (#353)	75	40
8N8	A57	4c on 8c ol grn (#369)	15	15
8N9	A57	5c on 10c grn	15	15
8N10	A57	8c on 16c ol gray	50	20
8N11	A57	50c on $1 hn & dk brn (#359)	1.25	1.25
8N12	A57	50c on $1 hn & dk brn (#344)	200.00	200.00
8N13	A57	50c on $1 hn & dk brn (#347)	22.50	22.50
8N14	A57	$1 on $2 dp bl & org brn (#360)	3.00	3.00
8N15	A57	$1 on $2 dp bl & org brn (#345)	9.00	9.00
8N16	A57	$1 on $2 dp bl & org brn (#348)	50.00	50.00

No. 8N12 was issued without gum.

Same Surcharge on China Nos. 383-388, 390-391. *Perf. 14*

8N17	A57	4c on 8c ol grn	10	10
8N18	A57	5c on 10c grn	10	10
8N19	A57	15c on 30c scar	10	10
a.		Invtd. surch.	60.00	60.00
8N20	A57	25c on 50c dk bl	15	10
8N21	A57	50c on $1 org brn & sep	65	50
8N22	A57	$1 on $2 dp bl & yel brn	1.50	1.00
8N23	A57	$5 on $10 dk grn & dl pur	20.00	20.00
8N24	A57	$10 on $20 rose lake & dk bl	12.50	12.50

Same Surcharge on China Nos. 394-396. **Wmk. 261**

8N25	A57	5c on 10c grn	20	20
8N26	A57	15c on 30c scar	50	40
8N27	A57	25c on 50c dk bl	30	20

Same Surcharge on Stamps of 1940-41.

1942 *Perf. 12½, 13* **Wmk. 261**

8N28	A40	½c on 1c org	10	10
8N29	A46	1c on 2c dp bl	10	10
8N30	A45	4c on 8c dp org	7.00	7.00
8N31	A46	5c on 10c dl vio	10	10
8N32	A48	1c on 30c brn car	35	20
8N33	A47	20c on 40c org	20	10
8N34	A40	25c on 50c grn	50	30

Unwmkd.

8N35	A40	½c on 1c org (#422)	10	10
a.		½c on 1c org (#422a)	2.00	2.00
8N36	A46	1c on 2c dp bl	10	10
8N37	A39	2c on 4c pale vio	10	10
8N38	A45	4c on 8c dp org	10	10
8N39	Aa46	5c on 10c dl vio	10	10
8N40	A47	10c on 20c lt bl	10	10
8N41	A47	20c on 40c org	20	15
8N42	A40	25c on 50c grn	1.25	1.00

Same Surcharge on "New Peking" Prints. *Perf. 14*

8N43	A37	1c on 2c ol grn	10	10
8N44	A37	2c on 4c dl grn	10	10
a.		Inverted surch.	30.00	
8N45	A45	4c on 8c dp org	10	10
8N46	A57	8c on 16c ol gray	10	10
8N47	A47	10c on 20c red brn	15	10
8N48	A48	15c on 30c brn car	25	10
8N49	A47	20c on 40c org	20	10
a.		Inverted surch.	35.00	
8N50	A40	25c on 50c grn	30	15
8N51	A57	50c on $1 org brn & sep	20	10
8N52	A57	$1 on $2 dp bl & org brn	1.50	1.00
8N53	A57	$5 on $10 dk grn & dl pur	6.00	6.00

See note after No. 2N93.

Nos. 8N44, 8N17 and 8N46 with Additional Overprint in Red

邦友
界租 還交
念紀

1943 *Perf. 14* **Unwmkd.**

8N54	A37	2c on 4c dl grn	10	10
8N55	A57	4c on 8c ol grn	10	10
8N56	A57	8c on 16c ol gray	20	20

Issued to commemorate the return of the Foreign Concessions to China.

Nos. 8N44, 8N7 and 8N46 with Additional Overprint in Red

局總 政郵
立成
念紀年週五

1943, Aug. 15 *Perf. 14, 12½*

8N57	A37	2c on 4c dl grn	10	10
8N58	A57	4c on 8c ol grn	15	15
8N59	A57	8c on 16c ol gray	30	30

Issued to commemorate the fifth anniversary of the North China Postal Service.

Stamps of China, 1934-41, Overprinted in Black

北 華

1943, Nov. 1

8N60	A40	1c org (#313)	10	10
8N61	A40	1c org (#422)	10	10
8N62	A57	10c grn (#354)	10	10
8N63	A57	$2 dp bl & yel brn (#388)	12.00	10.00
8N64	A57	$5 red & grnsh blk (#361)	3.50	3.00
8N65	A57	$5 red & sl grn (#389)	3.00	2.50
8N66	A57	$10 dk grn & dl pur (#390)	10.00	9.00
8N67	A57	$20 rose lake & dk bl (#391)	70.00	60.00
		Nos. 8N60-8N67 (8)	98.80	84.80

Same Overprint on "New Peking" Prints.

8N68	A40	1c orange	10	10
8N69	A37	2c ol grn	10	10
8N70	A37	4c dl grn	10	10
8N71	A37	5c green	10	10
8N72	A57	9c ol grn	10	10
8N73	A46	10c dl vio	10	10
8N74	A57	16c ol gray	10	10
8N75	A57	18c ol gray	10	10
8N76	A47	20c henna	15	10
8N77	A48	30c brn car	15	10
8N78	A47	40c brt org	20	10
a.		Inverted ovpt.	30.00	30.00
8N79	A40	50c green	20	10
8N80	A57	$1 org brn & sep	50	25
8N81	A57	$2 bl & org brn	60	30
8N82	A57	$5 red & sl grn	1.25	1.00
8N83	A57	$10 dk grn & dl pur	2.50	2.50
8N84	A57	$20 rose lake & dk bl	5.00	5.00
		Nos. 8N68-8N84 (17)	11.35	10.25

See note after No. 2N93.

Nos. 8N70 and 8N62 with Additional Overprint in Red

戰 参
念紀年週一

1944, Jan. 9

8N85	A37	4c dl grn	15	15
8N86	A57	10c green	15	15

Issued to commemorate the first anniversary of the declaration of war against the Allies by North China.

Nos. 8N72, 8N75, 8N79 and 8N80 with Additional Overprint in Red

會員委務政
念紀年週四

1944, Mar. 30

8N87	A57	9c ol grn	15	15
8N88	A57	18c ol gray	20	20
8N89	A40	50c green	40	40
8N90	A57	$1 org brn & sep	75	75
a.		red ovpt. inverted	25.00	25.00

Issued to commemorate the fourth anniversary of the North China Political Council.

Shanghai-Nanking Nos. 9N101-9N104 Surcharged North China (Hwa Pei) and New Value in Red or Black

(a) 華北玖分 (b) 華北壹角捌分 (c) 華北叁角陸分 (d) 華北玖角

1944 *Perf. 12½x12, 12x12½*

8N91	OS1 (a)	9c on 50c org	10	10
8N92	OS1 (b)	18c on $1 grn (R)	15	15
a.		Dble. surch.	25.00	25.00
8N93	OS2 (c)	36c on $2 dp bl (R)	15	15
8N94	OS2 (d)	90c on $5 car rose	25	25

Nos. 8N72, 8N75, 8N79 and 8N80 Overprinted in Red or Blue

立成局總政郵
念紀年週六

1944, Aug. 15

8N95	A57	9c ol grn	10	10
8N96	A57	18c ol gray	10	10
8N97	A40	50c green	20	20
8N98	A57	$1 org brn & sep (Bl)	35	35

Issued to commemorate the sixth anniversary of the General Post Office Department of North China.

North China Nos. 8N76, 8N79-8N81 Overprinted in Blue or Black

席 主 汪
念 紀 典 葬

1944, Dec. 5

8N99	A47	20c hn (Bl)	12	12
8N100	A40	50c grn (Bl)	12	12
8N101	A57	$1 org brn & sep (Bl)	18	18
8N102	A57	$2 bl & org brn	18	18

Issued to commemorate the death of Wang Ching-wei, puppet ruler of China.

North China Nos. 8N76, 8N79-8N81 Overprinted in Red or Black

年週二戰參
念 紀

1945

8N103	A47	20c henna	12	12
8N104	A40	50c grn (R)	20	20
8N105	A57	$1 org brn & sep	20	20
8N106	A57	$2 bl & org brn	35	35

Issued to commemorate the second anniversary of the declaration of war.

Shanghai-Nanking
Nos. 9N105-9N106
Surcharged in Red

華北伍角

1945 *Perf. 12x12½*

8N107	OS3	50c on $3 lt org	10	10
8N108	OS3	$1 on $6 bl	15	15

Issued to commemorate the return of the foreign concessions in Shanghai.

Dragon Pillar OS1 — Dr. Sun Yat-sen OS2

Designs: $2, Long Bridge and White Pagoda. $5, Tower in Imperial City. $10, Marble Boat, Summer Palace.

Lithographed.

1945 *Perf. 14* **Unwmkd.**

Various Papers.

8N109	OS1	$1 dl yel	8	8
8N110	OS1	$2 dp bl	6	6
8N111	OS1	$5 carmine	15	15
8N112	OS1	$10 dl grn	15	15

Issued to commemorate the fifth anniversary of the North China Political Council.

1945

Without Gum; Various Papers.

8N113	OS2	$1 bister	15	10
8N114	OS2	$2 dk bl	18	10
8N115	OS2	$5 fawn	25	15
8N116	OS2	$10 sage grn	40	25
8N117	OS2	$20 dl vio	50	30
8N118	OS2	$50 brown	12.50	6.00
		Nos. 8N113-8N118 (6)	13.98	6.90

Nos. 8N113-8N118 without "Hwa Pei" overprint are proofs.

Wutai Mountain, Shansi OS3

Designs: $10, Kaifeng Iron Pagoda. $20, International Bridge, Tientsin. $30, Taishan Mountain, Shantung. $50, General Post Office, Peking.

1945, Aug. 15

Without Gum; Various Papers.

8N119	OS3	$5 gray grn	4	4
8N120	OS3	$10 dl brn	5	5
8N121	OS3	$20 dl pur	7	7
8N122	OS3	$30 sl bl	8	8
8N123	OS3	$50 carmine	15	15
		Nos. 8N119-8N123 (5)	39	39

Issued to commemorate the seventh anniversary of the North China Postal Directorate.

Shanghai and Nanking

China Nos. 299-303 Surcharged

貳角伍分 暫售 25 — a

陸圓 暫售 6.00 — b

1942-45 *Perf. 12½, 13½* **Unwmkd.**

9N1	A37 (b)	$6 on 5c grn	10	10
9N2	A37 (b)	$20 on 15c scar	10	10
9N3	A37 (b)	$500 on 15c dk grn	15	15
9N4	A37 (b)	$1000 on 20c ultra	15	15
9N5	A37 (b)	$1000 on 25c ultra	15	15

A $1000 on 20c ultramarine, No. 293, exists. Price $200.

Same Surcharge on Stamps of 1939-41.

Perf. 12½

9N6	A57 (a)	25c on 5c ol grn (#352)	10	10
9N7	A57 (a)	30c on 2c ol grn (#368)	10	10
9N8	A57 (a)	50c on 3c dl cl (#350)	10	10
9N9	A57 (a)	50c on 5c ol grn (#352)	10	10
9N10	A57 (a)	50c on 8c ol grn (#353)	10	10
9N11	A57 (b)	$1 on 8c ol grn (#353)	10	10
9N12	A57 (b)	$1 on 8c ol grn (#369)	5.00	5.00
9N13	A57 (b)	$1 on 15c dk vio brn (#356)	10	10
9N14	A57 (b)	$1.30 on 16c ol gray (#357)	10	10
9N15	A57 (b)	$1.50 on 3c dl cl (#350)	10	10
9N16	A57 (b)	$2 on 5c ol grn (#352)	10	10
9N17	A57 (b)	$2 on 10c grn (#354)	10	10
9N18	A57 (b)	$3 on 15c dk vio brn (#356)	10	10
9N19	A57 (b)	$4 on 16c ol gray (#357)	10	10
9N20	A57 (b)	$5 on 15c dk vio brn (#356)	10	10
9N21	A57 (b)	$6 on 5c grn (#351)	10	10
a.		Perf. 14 (#371)	15.00	15.00
9N22	A57 (b)	$6 on 5c ol grn (#352)	10	10
9N23	A57 (b)	$6 on 8c ol grn (#353)	10	10
9N24	A57 (b)	$6 on 8c ol grn (#369)	400.00	400.00
9N25	A57 (b)	$6 on 10c grn (#354)	10	10
9N26	A57 (b)	$10 on 10c grn (#354)	10	10
9N27	A57 (b)	$10 on 16c ol gray (#357)	10	10
9N28	A57 (b)	$20 on 3c dl cl (#350)	10	10
9N29	A57 (b)	$20 on 15c scar (#355)	10	10
9N30	A57 (b)	$20 on 15c dk vio brn (#356)	10	10
9N31	A57 (b)	$20 on $2 dp bl & org brn (#360)	50	50
9N32	A57 (b)	$100 on 3c dl cl (#350)	10	10
9N33	A57 (b)	$500 on 8c ol grn (#353)	40	40
9N34	A57 (b)	$500 on 8c ol grn (#369)	12.50	12.50
9N35	A57 (b)	$500 on 10c grn (#354)	10	10
9N36	A57 (b)	$500 on 15c scar (#355)	10	10
9N37	A57 (b)	$500 on 15c dk vio brn (#356)	10	10
9N38	A57 (b)	$500 on 16c ol gray (#357)	10	10
9N39	A57 (b)	$1000 on 25c dk bl (#358)	10	10
9N40	A57 (b)	$2000 on $5 red & grnsh blk (#361)	25	25
		Nos. 9N1-9N23, 9N25-9N40 (39)	22.20	22.20

Nos. 381-391 Surcharged with Type "b."

Perf. 14

9N41	A57	$1 on 8c ol grn	10	10
9N42	A57	$1.70 on 30c scar	10	10
a.		Perf. 12½	15	15
9N43	A57	$2 on 5c ol grn	10	10
9N44	A57	$2 on $1 org brn & sep	35	35
9N45	A57	$3 on 8c ol grn	10	10
a.		$3 on 8c ol grn (#383a)		
b.		"3" with flat top	10	10
9N46	A57	$6 on 5c grn	10	10
9N47	A57	$6 on 5c ol grn	10	10
9N48	A57	$6 on 8c ol grn	10	10
9N49	A57	$10 on 10c grn	10	10
a.		Perf. 12½	25	25
9N50	A57	$20 on $2 dp bl & yel brn	15	15
9N51	A57	$50 on 30c scar	10	10
9N52	A57	$50 on 50c dk bl	10	10
9N53	A57	$50 on $5 red & sl grn	15	15
9N54	A57	$50 on $20 rose lake & dk bl	60	60
9N55	A57	$100 on $10 dk grn & dl pur	30	30
9N56	A57	$200 on $20 rose lake & dk bl	10	10
9N57	A57	$500 on 8c ol grn	3.00	3.00
a.		$500 on 8c ol grn (#383a)	12.50	12.50
9N58	A57	$500 on 10c grn	15	15
9N59	A57	$1000 on 30c scar	15	15
9N60	A57	$1000 on 50c dk bl	15	15
9N61	A57	$1000 on $2 dp bl & yel brn	75	75
9N62	A57	$2000 on $5 red & sl grn	30	30

China Nos. 392-395 and 399-401 Surcharged with Type "b."

1942-45 *Perf. 14* **Wmk. 261**

9N63	A57	$2 on $1 org brn & sep, perf. 12½	30	30
9N64	A57	$6 on 5c grn	10	10
9N65	A57	$6 on 5c ol grn	10	10
9N66	A57	$50 on $5 red & sl grn	10	10
a.		Numeral tablet vio	10	10
9N67	A57	$100 on $10 dk grn & dl pur	15	15
9N68	A57	$200 on $20 rose lake & dk bl	15	15
9N69	A57	$500 on 10c grn	25	25
9N70	A57	$1000 on 30c scar	50	50
9N71	A57	$5000 on $10 dk grn & dl pur, perf. 12½	3.50	3.50
a.		Perf. 14	30.00	30.00
		Nos. 9N41-9N71 (31)	12.30	12.30

Nos. 9N63 and 9N71 were not issued without surcharge. A $50 on 30c scarlet exists.

Same Surcharge on Stamps of 1940-41.

Wmk. 261

Perf. 12½, 13

9N72	A46	$30 on 2c dp bl	35.00	35.00

A $7.50 on ½c and a $15 on 1c are known.

Unwmkd.

9N73	A39	$7.50 on ½c ol blk	10	10
9N74	A40	$15 on 1c org	10	10
a.		Without secret mark	30.00	30.00
9N75	A46	$30 on 2c dp bl	10	10
9N76	A40	$200 on 1c org	10	10
9N77	A45	$200 on 8c dp org	10	10
		Nos. 9N73-9N77 (5)	50	50

Same Surcharge on Stamps of 1941.

Perf. 12

9N78	A59 (a)	5c on ½c sep	10	10
9N79	A59 (a)	10c on 1c org	10	10
9N80	A59 (a)	20c on 1c org	10	10
9N81	A59 (a)	40c on 5c grn	10	10
9N82	A59 (b)	$5 on 5c grn	10	10
9N83	A59 (b)	$10 on 10c brt grn	10	10
9N84	A59 (b)	$50 on ½c sep	10	10
9N85	A59 (b)	$50 on 1c org	10	10
9N86	A59 (b)	$50 on 17c ol	10	10
9N87	A59 (b)	$200 on 5c grn	10	10
9N88	A59 (b)	$200 on 8c turq grn	10	10
9N89	A59 (b)	$200 on 8c red org	10	10
9N90	A59 (b)	$500 on $5 scar & blk	15	15
9N91	A59 (b)	$1000 on 1c org	15	15
9N92	A59 (b)	$1000 on 25c rose vio	25	25
9N93	A59 (b)	$1000 on 30c scar	25	25
9N94	A59 (b)	$1000 on $2 bl & blk	40	40
9N95	A59 (b)	$1000 on $10 grn & blk	25	25
9N96	A59 (b)	$2000 on $5 scar & blk	50	50
		Nos. 9N78-9N96 (19)	3.15	3.15

Stamps of China 1939-41 Surcharged in Red or Blue

收回租界紀念 三十二年 八月一日 貳角伍分

1943 *Perf. 12, 12½* **Unwmkd.**

9N97	A57	25c on 5c grn	5	5
9N98	A59	50c on 8c red org (Bl)	5	5
9N99	A57	$1 on 16c ol gray	10	10
9N100	A59	$2 on 50c dk bl	10	10

Issued to commemorate the return of the foreign concessions in Shanghai.

Wheat and Cotton
OS1

Purple Mountain, Nanking
OS2

Perf. 12½x12, 12x12½

1944 **Engraved.** **Unwmkd.**

9N101	OS1	50c orange	5	5
9N102	OS1	$1 green	5	5
9N103	OS2	$2 dp bl	5	5
9N104	OS2	$5 car rose	10	5

Issued to commemorate the fourth anniversary of the establishment of the puppet government at Nanking.

Map of Foreign Concessions in Shanghai
OS3

1944 *Perf. 12x12½*

9N105	OS3	$3 lt org	5	10
9N106	OS3	$6 blue	5	10

Issued to commemorate the first anniversary of the return of the foreign concessions in Shanghai.

Nos. 9N101-9N104 Surcharged in Black with Type "b."

1945, Mar. 30

9N107	OS1	$15 on 50c org	5	5
9N108	OS1	$30 on $1 grn	5	5
9N109	OS2	$60 on $2 dp bl	5	5
9N110	OS2	$200 on $5 car rose	10	10

China Nos. C31, C32, C36 and C38 Surcharged in Red, Green, Orange or Carmine

1945 ***Perf. 12½, 13.***

9N111	AP3	$150 on 15c gray grn (R)	5	5
9N112	AP3	$250 on 25c yel org (G)	5	5
9N113	AP3	$600 on 60c dp bl (O)	10	10
9N114	AP3	$1,000 on $1 ap grn (C)	15	15

Issued as air raid precaution propaganda.

AIR POST STAMPS

China Nos. C35 and C38 Surcharged in Black

10

付已費空航之片明內國

The surcharges on Nos. 9NC1–9NC7 were in Japanese currency because all air mail then was carried by Japanese planes.

1941 ***Perf. 12½*** **Unwmkd.**

The surcharges translate: (10c) "Airmail fee for postcard within the nation has been paid." (20c) "Airmail fee for letter within the nation has been paid."

9NC1	AP3	10(s) on 50c brn	10	10
9NC2	AP3	20(s) on $1 ap grn	10	10

Two types of surcharge exist on No. 9NC1.

Similar Surcharge on No. C28.

1941 ***Perf. 13*** **Wmk. 261**

9NC3	AP3	20(s) on $1 ap grn	7.50	7.50

Nos. C37 and C39 Surcharged

35

付已費空航函信本日寄

1941 ***Perf. 12½, 13*** **Unwmkd.**

The surcharges translate: (18c and 25c) "Airmail fee for postcard to Japan has been paid." (35c) "Airmail fee for letter to Japan has been paid."

9NC4	AP3	18(s) on 90c lt ol	10	10
9NC5	AP3	25(s) on 90c lt ol	10	10
9NC6	AP3	35(s) on $2 lt brn	10	10

No. 9NC6 with Additional Surcharge in Red

Perf. 12½.

9NC7	AP3	60(s) on 35 (s) on $2 lt brn	10	10

POSTAGE DUE STAMPS

Postage Due Stamps of China 1932 Surcharged in Black

改壹
作圓
1.00

1945 ***Perf. 14*** **Unwmkd.**

9NJ1	D5	$1 on 2c org	10	10
9NJ2	D5	$2 on 5c org	10	10
9NJ3	D5	$5 on 10c org	10	10
9NJ4	D5	$10 on 20c org	10	10

Northeastern Provinces.

中民
華國

With the end of World War II and the collapse of Manchukuo, the Northeastern Provinces reverted to China. In many Manchurian towns and cities, the Manchukuo stamps were locally handstamped in ideograms: "Republic of China," "China Postal Service" or "Temporary Use for China." A typical example is shown above.

Dr. Sun Yat-sen

A1 A2

Typographed.

Black Surcharge.

1946, Feb. ***Perf. 14*** **Unwmkd.**

1	A1	50c on $5 red	6	5
2	A1	50c on $10 grn	6	5
3	A1	$1 on $10 grn	6	5
4	A1	$2 on $20 brn vio	6	5
5	A1	$4 on $50 brn	12	10
		Nos. 1-5 (5)	36	30

The two characters at left express the new value.

Stamps of China, 1938–41 Overprinted 限東北貼用

1946, Apr. ***Perf. 12½, 13, 13½, 14***

6	A40	1c org (#422)	8	5
7	A48	3c dp yel brn (#425)	8	5
8	A48	5c dl red org (#427)	8	5
9	A57	10c grn (#354)	8	5
10	A57	10c grn (#384)	8	5
11	A47	20c lt bl (#433)	8	5
a.		Horiz. pair, imperf. between	40.00	
		Nos. 6-11 (6)	48	30

Without Gum.

1946, July **Engraved** ***Perf. 14***

12	A2	5c lake	12	8
13	A2	10c orange	12	8
14	A2	20c yel grn	12	8
15	A2	25c blk brn	12	8
16	A2	50c red org	12	8
17	A2	$1 blue	12	8
18	A2	$2 dk vio	12	8
19	A2	$2.50 indigo	12	8
20	A2	$3 brown	12	8
21	A2	$4 org brn	12	8
22	A2	$5 dk grn	12	8
23	A2	$10 crimson	12	8
24	A2	$20 olive	12	8
25	A2	$50 bl vio	12	8
		Nos. 12-25 (14)	1.68	1.12

Two types of $4, $10, $20 and $50: I. Character *kuo* directly left of sun emblem is open at upper and lower left corners of "box." Diagonal stroke from top center to lower right has no hook at bottom. II. Character is closed at left corners. Diagonal stroke has hook at bottom.

See also Nos. 47–52, 61–63.

China Nos. 728–731 Surcharged in Black

1946

26	A75	$2 on $20 grn	12	12
27	A75	$3 on $30 bl	12	12
28	A75	$5 on $50 dk brn	12	12
29	A75	$10 on $100 car	12	12

Convening of Chinese National Assembly.

Type of China, 1946. Inscribed:

東貼
北用

1947 **Engraved** ***Perf. 11, 11½***

30	A74	$2 carmine	10	10
31	A74	$3 green	10	10
32	A74	$5 vermilion	10	10
33	A74	$10 yel grn	12	12
34	A74	$20 yel org	12	12
35	A74	$30 magenta	12	12
		Nos. 30-35 (6)	66	66

60th birthday of Chiang Kai-shek.

Type of China, 1947.

Inscribed: 用貼北東

Engraved.

1947 ***Perf. 14*** **Unwmkd.**

36	A76	$2 dp grn	10	10
37	A76	$4 dp bl	10	10
38	A76	$6 carmine	10	10
39	A76	$10 lt brn	10	10
40	A76	$20 dp cl	10	10
		Nos. 36-40 (5)	50	50

First anniversary of return of Chinese National Government to Nanking.

China Nos. 644 to 646 and 634 Surcharged in Black

用貼北東限
改叁
作佰
圓
300.00

1947 ***Perf. 12½, 14.***

41	A73	$100 on $1000 rose lake	10	7
42	A73	$300 on $3000 bl	12	8
43	A73	$500 on $5000 dp grn & ver	15	8
44	A37	$500 on $30 choc	15	12

Type of 1946.

Without Gum.

1947 **Engraved** ***Perf. 14***

47	A2	$44 dk car rose	15.00	15.00
48	A2	$100 dp grn	5	5
49	A2	$200 rose brn	5	5
50	A2	$300 bluish grn	6	6
51	A2	$500 rose car	6	6
52	A2	$1000 dp org	8	8
		Nos. 47-52 (6)	15.30	15.30

Stamps and Types of 1946-47 Surcharged in Black or Red

1948 ***Perf. 14*** **Unwmkd.**

53	A2	$1500 on 20c yel grn	25	25
54	A2	$3000 on $1 bl	10	10
55	A2	$4000 on 25c blk brn (R)	10	10
56	A2	$8000 on 50c red org	10	10
57	A2	$10,000 on 10c org	15	15
58	A2	$50,000 on $109 dk grn (R)	30	33
59	A2	$100,000 on $65 dl grn	30	40
60	A2	$500,000 on $22 gray (R)	30	40
		Nos. 53-60 (8)	1.60	1.83

Type of 1946.

Without Gum

1949

61	A2	$22 gray	17.50
62	A2	$65 dl grn	20.00
63	A2	$109 dk grn	30.00

POSTAGE DUE STAMPS.

D1

Engraved.

Without Gum.

1947 ***Perf. 14*** **Unwmkd.**

J1	D1	10c dk bl	4	4
J2	D1	20c dk bl	4	4
J3	D1	50c dk bl	4	4
J4	D1	$1 dk bl	4	4
J5	D1	$2 dk bl	4	4
J6	D1	$5 dk bl	4	4
		Nos. J1-J6 (6)	24	24

Nos. J1 to J3 Surcharged in Red

拾改
圓作

1948

J7	D1	$10 on 10c dk bl	4	4
J8	D1	$20 on 20c dk bl	4	4
J9	D1	$50 on 50c dk bl	4	4

The surcharge reads "Changed to . . . . dollars." Characters at the left express the new value and vary on each denomination.

MILITARY STAMPS

No. 16 Surcharged in Black

郵軍
作暫
圓肆拾肆

1947 ***Perf. 14.*** **Unwmkd.**

M1	A2	$44 on 50c red org	1.75	1.75

The surcharge reads: "Army Post. Temporarily for 44 dollars."

China No. M11 Overprinted in Black 用貼北東限

Thin Paper Without Gum.

Perf. 12½.

M2	M1	rose	25	25

China No. M11 Overprinted in Black 用貼北東限

M3	M1	rose	3.50	3.00

PARCEL POST STAMP.

China No. Q25 Surcharged in Black

用貼北東限
伍改
拾
萬
圓作

Engraved.

1948 ***Perf. 13½*** **Unwmkd.**

Without Gum.

Q1	PP3	$500,000 on $5,000,000 lil	40.00

Anhwei Province

(ăn·(h)wā)

China Type A95 Handstamp Surcharged

1949, Mar. 16 **Lithographed**

1	A95	On $1000 car	15.00

SPECIAL DELIVERY STAMP

China Type A95 with Similar Surcharge

1949, Mar 16 — **Lithographed**

E1	A95	On $500 brn	15.00

REGISTRATION STAMP

China Type A95 with Similar Surcharge

1949, Mar. 16 — **Lithographed**

F1	A95	On $3000 org	15.00

ACKNOWLEDGMENT OF RECEIPT STAMP

China Type A95 with Similar Surcharge

1949, Mar. 16 — **Lithographed**

AR1	A95	On $20 red brn	15.00

Fukien Province

(fü·kyen)

Stamps of China, 1945–49, Surcharged

壹 郵

分 1 資

Without Gum

1949 — **Engraved** — ***Perf. 14***

1	A82	1c on $500 bl grn	4.00	4.00
2	A82	1c on $7000 lt red brn	7.50	7.50
3	A82	2c on $2,000,000 ver	1.75	1.75
4	A82	2½c on $50,000 dp bl	2.50	2.50
5	A73	4c on $100 dk car	1.75	1.75
6	A73	10c on $200 ol grn	1.75	1.75
7	A82	10c on $3000 bl	1.25	1.25
8	A82	10c on $4000 gray	1.50	1.50
9	A82	10c on $6000 rose lil	1.25	1.25
10	A82	10c on $100,000 dl grn	1.25	1.25
11	A82	10c on $1,000,000 cl	1.25	1.25
12	A82	40c on $200,000 brn vio	3.00	3.00

The surcharge on No. 2 is handstamped and in slightly larger characters.

Issue dates: No. 2, May 10; others, June.

China Nos. 973, 975–978 Overprinted

州 福

1949, June — **Litho.** — ***Perf. 12½, 13***

13	A94	1c ap grn	3.50	2.50
14	A94	4c bl grn	1.25	75
15	A94	10c dp lil	15.00	6.00
16	A94	16c org red	3.00	3.00
17	A94	20c blue	7.50	5.00

Same Overprint on China No. 959, 959a

Perf. 12½, Rouletted

1949, July — **Lithographed**

18	A96	orange	5.00	5.00

Same Overprint on Fukien Nos. 1, 3–4, 11 in Black or Red

1949, June — **Engraved** — ***Perf. 14***

19	A82	1c on $500 bl grn	30.00	22.50
20	A82	2c on $2,000,000 ver	5.00	4.00
21	A82	2½c on $50,000 dp bl	5.00	4.00
22	A82	10c on $4000 gray	10.00	8.00
23	A82	10c on $1,000,000 cl	30.00	22.50

AIR POST STAMP

China No. C62 Overprinted as Nos. 13–17

Perf. 12½, Rouletted

1949, July — **Lithographed**

C1	AP5	bl grn	5.00	5.00

SPECIAL DELIVERY STAMP

China No. E12 Overprinted as Nos. 13–17

Perf. 12½, Rouletted

1949, July — **Lithographed**

E1	SD2	red vio	5.00	5.00

REGISTRATION STAMP

China No. F2 Overprinted as Nos. 13–17

Perf. 12½, Rouletted

1949, July — **Lithographed**

F1	R2	carmine	5.00	5.00

Hunan Province

(hü·nän)

China No. 640 Surcharged

郵資已付 湘 國內平信

1949, May — **Engr.** — ***Perf. 14***

1	A73	On $100 dk car	1.75	1.75

The first printing of surcharge on No. 1 is in smaller characters.

China Nos. 797, 788, 750, 747 Surcharged

伍分

湘

1949, May — **Engr.** — ***Perf. 14***

2	A82	1c on $2,000,000 ver	3.00	3.00
3	A82	2c on $20,000 rose pink	3.00	3.00
4	A82	5c on $3000 bl	3.00	3.00
5	A82	10c on $500 bl grn	3.00	3.00

AIR POST STAMP

China No. 790 Surcharged

湘 國內航空

付已資郵

1949, May — **Engr.** — ***Perf. 14***

C1	A82	On $40,000 grn	1.75	1.75

SPECIAL DELIVERY STAMP

China No. 637 Surcharged as No. F1 in Red

1949, May — **Engr.** — ***Perf. 14***

E1	A73	On $30 dk bl	1.00	1.00

REGISTRATION STAMP

China No. 754 Surcharged

號掛內國

湘

付已資郵

1949, May — **Engr.** — ***Perf. 14***

F1	A73	On $7000 lt red brn	1.50	1.50

Hupeh Province

(hü·pā, -be)

China Type A95 Surcharged

改起華中

分壹資郵

1

1949, May — **Lithographed**

1	A95	1c on $20 red brn	6.50	6.50
2	A95	10c on $20 red brn	6.50	6.50

Kansu Province

(kan·sü, gän·sü)

China No. 959 Handstamped in Purple

區青寧甘限

用貼

1949, Aug. — **Litho.** — ***Perf. 12½***

1	A96	orange	125.00

AIR POST STAMP

Same Handstamp Overprinted on China No. C62 in Red

1949, Aug. — **Litho.** — ***Perf. 12½***

C1	AP5	bl grn	125.00

Counterfeits exist.

Kiangsi Province

(kyang·sē, jyäng·sē)

China Nos. 789–791 Surcharged

郵資已付 國內平信

贛

1949 — **Engraved** — ***Perf. 14***

1	A82	On $30,000 choc	3.00	3.00
2	A82	On $40,000 grn	5.00	5.00
3	A82	On $50,000 dp bl	5.00	5.00

AIR POST STAMP

Similar Surcharge on China No. 754

1949 — **Engraved** — ***Perf. 14***

C1	A82	On $7000 lt red brn	10.00	10.00

Third and fourth characters in right column of surcharge read "Air Mail" in Chinese on No. C1, "Registered" on Nos. F1–F2.

SPECIAL DELIVERY STAMP

Similar Surcharge on China No. 750

1949 — **Engraved** — ***Perf. 14***

E1	A82	On $3000 bl	4.00	4.00

See note below No. C1.

REGISTRATION STAMPS

Similar Surcharge on China Nos. 747 and 754

1949 — **Engraved** — ***Perf. 14***

F1	A82	On $500 bl grn	5.00	5.00
F2	A82	On $7000 lt red brn	6.00	6.00

See note below No. C1.

Kwangsi Province

(kwäng·sē, gwäng·sē)

China Nos. 811 and 818 Also Surcharged in Red

伍銀桂

分圓區

1949, May 21 — **Typographed**

6	A62	5c on $20,000 on 10c dp grn	4.00	4.00
7	A62	5c on $40,000 on 20c dk ol grn	7.50	7.50

China Stamps of 1946–48 Surcharged in Black or Red

桂區 分2圓銀 — a

銀圓壹角貨分 桂 區 — b

1949 — **Engraved** — ***Perf. 14***

Type "a" Surcharge

8	A82	½c on $500,000 lil rose	7.50	7.50
9	A82	1c on $200,000 brn vio	2.25	2.25
10	A82	2c on $300,000 yel grn	15.00	15.00
11	A73	5c on $3000 bl	2.25	2.25
12	A82	5c on $3000 bl	2.25	2.25
13	A82	5c on $40,000 grn	3.00	3.00

Type "b" Surcharge

14	A82	13c on $50,000 dp bl (R)	3.00	3.00
15	A82	13c on $50,000 dp bl	7.00	7.00
16	A82	17c on $7000 lt red brn	3.00	3.00
17	A82	21c on $100,000 dl grn	3.00	3.00

Shensi Province

(shen·sē)

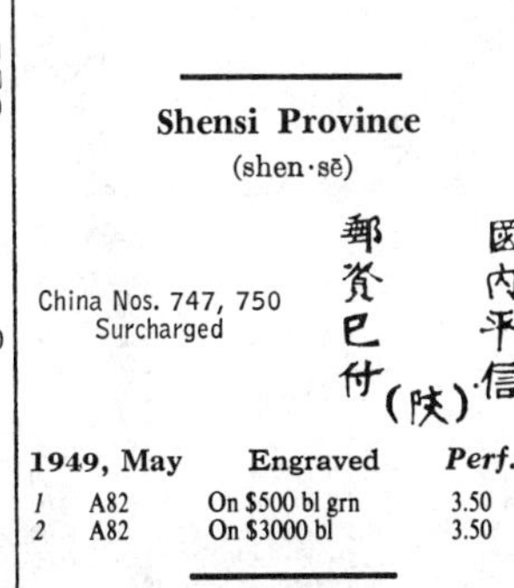

China Nos. 747, 750 Surcharged

郵資已付 (陝) 國內平信

1949, May — **Engraved** — ***Perf. 14***

1	A82	On $500 bl grn	3.50	3.50
2	A82	On $3000 bl	3.50	3.50

AIR POST STAMP

Similar Surcharge on China No. 754

1949, May — **Engraved** — ***Perf. 14***

C1	A82	On $7000 lt red brn	4.50	4.50

SPECIAL DELIVERY STAMP

Similar Surcharge on China No. 746 in Red

1949, May — **Engraved** — ***Perf. 14***

E1	A82	On $250 dp lil	3.50	3.50

REGISTRATION STAMPS

Similar Surcharge on China Nos. 626, 637 in Red

1949, May — **Typo.** — ***Perf. 12***

F1	A72	On $30 dp bl	7.00	7.00

Engr. — ***Perf. 14***

F2	A73	On $30 dk bl	3.50	3.50

Szechwan Province.

(se'chwän', sü'chwän')

Re-engraved Issue of China, 1923, Overprinted 用貼川四限

1933 *Perf. 14.* **Unwmkd.**

1	A29	1c orange	1.00	15
2	A29	5c claret	1.00	15
3	A30	50c dp grn	3.75	90

The overprint reads "For use in Szechwan Province exclusively".

Same Overprint on Sun Yat-sen Issue of 1931-37.

Type II.

1933-34 *Perf. 12½.*

4	A37	2c ol grn	15	20
5	A37	5c green	15	15
6	A37	15c dk grn	90	30
7	A37	15c scar ('34)	75	1.00
8	A37	25c ultra	75	20
9	A37	$1 org brn & dk brn	4.00	75
10	A37	$2 bl & org brn	8.00	1.75
11	A37	$5 dl red & blk	25.00	7.00
		Nos. 4-11 (8)	39.70	11.35

Same Overprint on Martyrs Issue of 1932-34.

1933 *Perf. 14*

12	A39	½c blk brn	30	15
13	A40	1c orange	15	15
14	A39	2½c rose lil	1.00	50
15	A48	3c dp brn	60	15
16	A45	8c brn org	75	15
17	A46	10c dl vio	1.50	15
18	A45	13c bl grn	1.50	15
19	A46	17c brn ol	2.00	75
20	A47	20c brn red	2.00	15
21	A48	30c brn vio	2.00	15
22	A47	40c orange	5.00	40
23	A40	50c green	10.00	50
		Nos. 12-23 (12)	26.80	3.35

Stamps of China, 1947–48, Surcharged

1949 Engraved *Perf. 14*

24	A82	On $150 dk bl	10.00	10.00
25	A82	On $250 dp lil	10.00	10.00
26	A82	On $500 bl grn	2.00	2.00
27	A82	On $1000 red	6.00	6.00
28	A82	On $2000 ver	2.00	2.00
29	A82	On $3000 bl	2.00	2.00
30	A82	On $4000 gray	2.00	2.00
31	A82	On $5000 dk brn	10.00	10.00
32	A82	On $6000 rose lil	2.00	2.00
33	A82	On $7000 lt red brn	10.00	10.00
34	A82	On $10,000 dk bl & car	2.00	2.00
35	A82	On $20,000 rose pink	4.00	4.00
36	A82	On $30,000 choc	2.00	2.00
37	A82	On $50,000 grn & dk bl	2.00	2.00
38	A82	On $50,000 dp bl	3.00	3.00
39	A82	On $100,000 dl yel & ol	3.50	3.50
40	A82	On $100,000 dl grn	4.00	4.00
41	A82	On $200,000 vio brn & dp bl	4.00	4.00
42	A82	On $200,000 brn vio	4.00	4.00
43	A82	On $300,000 sep & org brn		
44	A82	On $300,000 yel grn	7.50	7.50
45	A82	On $500,000 dk Prus grn & sep	2.00	2.00
46	A82	On $1,000,000 cl	6.50	6.50
47	A82	On $2,000,000 ver	4.00	4.00
48	A82	On $3,000,000 ol bis	4.00	4.00
49	A82	On $5,000,000 ultra	15.00	15.00

Several of Nos. 24–49 exist with inverted surcharge and a few with bottom character of left row repeated in right row, same position.

Counterfeits exist.

China No. 737 Surcharged in Purple

1949 *Perf. 12½*

50	A77	2c on $500 ol grn	7.00	7.00

China No. 975 Handstamp Surcharged in Purple

1949 **Lithographed**

51	A94	2½c on 4c bl grn	6.00	6.00

AIR POST STAMPS

China No. C55–C59, C61 Surcharged

Perf. 12½, 13x12½, 14

1949, July **Unwmkd.**

C1	AP3	On $10,000 on 30c lt red	2.00	2.00
a.		On #C54		500.00
C2	AP4	On $10,000 on $27 bl	3.50	3.50
a.		Second surch. invtd.		125.00
b.		On #C53		100.00
C3	AP3	On $20,000 on 25c lt org	3.50	3.50
C4	AP3	On $30,000 on 90c lt ol	4.50	4.50
C5	AP3	On $50,000 on 60c bl	30.00	30.00
C6	AP3	On $50,000 on $1 yel grn	5.00	5.00
		Nos. C1-C6 (6)	48.50	48.50

On No. C2 characters of overprint are arranged in two horizontal rows, and two of four lines are vertical.

REGISTRATION STAMPS

Stamps of China, 1944–47, Surcharged

Engr.; Typo. (A72)

1949 *Perf. 12, 13, 14*

F1	A64	On $100 yel brn	20.00
F2	A72	On $100 dk brn	30.00
F3	A64	On $200 dk grn	10.00
F4	A72	On $200 brn vio	10.00
F5	A73	On $200 ol grn	60.00
F6	A73	On $500 brt bl grn	60.00
F7	A73	On $700 red brn	85.00
F8	A73	On $5000 dp grn & ver	50.00
		Nos. F1-F8 (8)	325.00

PARCEL POST STAMP

China No. Q10 Surcharged

1949 Engr. *Perf. 12½*

Q1	PP2	1c on $20,000 dk red	75.00

No. Q1 is also found with surcharged value repeated in 5 characters at top of stamp.

Tsingtau

(tsing·tou, ching·dou)

China Nos. 890, 899, 945, 894 Handstamp Surcharged in Purple Blue or Red

Engr.; Litho.

1949, May *Perf. 14, 12½*

1	A94	1c on $100 org brn (P)	10.00	10.00
2	A94	4c on $5000 lt bl (P)	8.00	7.00
3	A94	6c on $500 rose lil (B)	7.00	6.00
4	A94	10c on $1000 bl (R)	7.00	6.00

Yunnan Province.

(yōōn'nän'; yün'-)

Stamps of China, 1923-26, Overprinted 用貼省滇限

The overprint reads "For exclusive use in the Province of Yunnan". It was applied to prevent stamps being purchased in the depreciated currency of Yunnan and used elsewhere.

1926 *Perf. 14.* **Unwmkd.**

1	A29	½c blk brn	15	10
2	A29	1c orange	20	10
3	A29	1½c violet	25	20
4	A29	2c yel grn	40	20
5	A29	3c bl grn	30	15
6	A29	4c ol grn	30	15
7	A29	5c claret	50	15
8	A29	6c red	40	25
9	A29	7c violet	40	30
10	A29	8c brn org	50	40
11	A29	10c dk bl	50	15
12	A30	13c brown	85	60
13	A30	15c dk bl	75	60
14	A30	16c ol grn	85	60
15	A30	20c brn red	1.25	25
16	A30	30c brn vio	2.00	60
17	A30	50c dp grn	1.75	75
18	A31	$1 org brn & sep	6.00	1.75
19	A31	$2 bl & red brn	12.50	5.00
20	A31	$5 red & sl	80.00	60.00
		Nos. 1-20 (20)	109.85	72.30

Unification Issue of China, 1929, Overprinted in Red

1929 *Perf. 14*

21	A35	1c brn org	75	30
22	A35	4c ol grn	1.00	50
23	A35	10c dk bl	2.25	1.25
24	A35	$1 dk red	40.00	32.50

Similar Overprint in Black on Sun Yat-sen Mausoleum Issue.

Characters 15½-16mm. apart.

25	A36	1c brn org	60	25
26	A36	4c ol grn	90	50
27	A36	10c dk bl	2.50	1.25
28	A36	$1 dk red	27.50	15.00

London Print Issue of China, 1931-37, Overprinted 用貼省滇限

1932-34 *Perf. 12½.* **Unwmkd.**

Type I (double circle).

29	A37	1c orange	50	50
30	A37	2c ol grn	75	75
31	A37	4c green	85	85
32	A37	20c ultra	1.25	1.25
33	A37	$1 org brn & dk brn	17.50	12.50
34	A37	$2 bl & org brn	35.00	22.50
35	A37	$5 dl red & blk	100.00	75.00
		Nos. 29-35 (7)	155.85	113.35

Type II (single circle).

36	A37	2c ol grn	40	20
37	A37	4c green	75	75
38	A37	5c green	50	50
39	A37	15c dk grn	2.50	1.75
40	A37	15c scar ('34)	1.50	1.50
41	A37	25c ultra	1.75	1.75
42	A37	$1 org brn & dk brn	20.00	12.50
43	A37	$2 bl & org brn	40.00	20.00
44	A37	$5 dl red & blk	90.00	75.00
		Nos. 36-44 (9)	157.40	113.95

Nos. 36–39, 41–44 were overprinted in London as well as in Peiping. The overprints differ in minor details. Price of London overprints (8), $350.

Tan Yuan-chang Issue of China, 1933, Overprinted

1933 *Perf. 14.*

45	A49	2c ol grn	75	40
46	A49	5c green	90	60
47	A49	25c ultra	2.00	1.25
48	A49	$1 red	25.00	18.00

Martyrs Issue of China, 1932-34 Overprinted 用貼省滇限

1933

49	A39	½c blk brn	25	20
50	A40	1c orange	30	20
51	A39	2½c rose lil	50	30
52	A48	3c dp brn	60	40
53	A45	8c brn org	1.25	75
54	A46	10c dl vio	85	40
55	A45	13c bl grn	1.00	40
56	A46	17c brn ol	2.00	75
57	A47	20c brn red	1.00	60
58	A48	30c brn vio	2.00	75
59	A47	40c orange	15.00	12.00
60	A40	50c green	15.00	12.00
		Nos. 49-60 (12)	39.75	28.75

China No. 324 was overprinted with characters arranged vertically, like Sinkiang No. 114, but was not issued.

China Stamps of 1945–49 Surcharged in Black or Blue

Engr.; Litho.; Typo.

1949 *Perf. 12, 12½, 14*

61	A82	1c on $200,000 brn vio	1.25	1.25
62	A82	1.2c on $40,000 grn	1.75	1.75
63	A94	6c on $200 red org	1.00	1.00
64	A94	10c on $20,000 org	1.00	1.00
65	A94	12c on $50 dk Prus grn (Bl)	1.25	1.25
66	A72	12c on $50 grnsh gray (Bl)	1.50	1.50
67	A72	12c on $200 brn vio (Bl)	75	75
68	A94	30c on $20 vio brn	1.00	1.00
69	A82	$1.20 on $100,000 dl grn	3.00	3.00

China No. 888 and 630 Surcharged

1949 Engr. *Perf. 14*

70	A94	4c on $20 vio brn	75.00

Typo. *Perf. 12*

71	A72	12c on $200 brn vio	100.00

Manchuria.

(măn·chŏŏr'ĭ·ȧ)

Kirin and Heilungkiang Issue.

Stamps of China, 1923-26, Overprinted 用貼黑吉限

The overprint reads: "For use in Ki-Hei District" the two names being abbreviated.

The intention of the overprint was to prevent the purchase of stamps in Manchuria, where the currency was depreciated, and their resale elsewhere.

1927 *Perf. 14.* **Unwmkd.**

1	A29	½c blk brn	10	10
2	A29	1c orange	10	10
3	A29	1½c violet	20	20
4	A29	2c yel grn	25	15
5	A29	3c bl grn	20	20
6	A29	4c ol grn	25	10
7	A29	5c claret	25	15
8	A29	6c red	35	20
9	A29	7c violet	35	25
10	A29	8c brn org	35	20
11	A29	10c dk bl	35	10
12	A30	13c brown	1.25	50
13	A30	15c dk bl	75	30
14	A30	16c ol grn	75	30
15	A30	20c brn red	1.25	50
16	A30	30c brn vio	1.25	50
17	A30	50c dp grn	4.00	50
18	A31	$1 org brn & sep	10.00	1.50
19	A31	$2 bl & red brn	15.00	7.50
20	A31	$5 red & sl	75.00	60.00
		Nos. 1-20 (20)	112.00	73.35

Several values of this issue exist with inverted overprint, double overprint and in pairs with one overprint omitted. These "errors" were not regularly issued. Forgeries also exist.

Chang Tso-lin Stamps of 1928 Overprinted in Red or Blue 貼 吉 用 黑

1928 *Perf. 14*

21	A34	1c brn org (R)	40	30
22	A34	4c ol grn (R)	75	50
23	A34	10c dl bl (R)	2.00	1.25
24	A34	$1 red (Bl)	22.50	15.00

Unification Issue of China, 1929, Overprinted in Red as in 1928.

1929

25	A35	1c brn org	75	40
26	A35	4c ol grn	1.00	60
27	A35	10c dk bl	3.00	1.75
28	A35	$1 dk red	40.00	25.00

Similar Overprint in Black on Sun Yat-sen Mausoleum Issue of China.

Characters 15-16mm. apart.

1929 *Perf. 14*

29	A36	1c brn org	75	75
30	A36	4c ol grn	75	75
31	A36	10c dk bl	2.00	1.50
32	A36	$1 dk red	25.00	15.00

Sinkiang.

(sĭn'kyăng'; shĭn'jyăng',-gyăng')

Stamps of China, 1913-19, Overprinted in Black or Red 限新省貼用 *a*

The first character of overprint "a" is ½ mm. out of alignment, to the left, and the overprint measures 16mm.

1915 *Perf. 14, 15.* **Unwmkd.**

1	A24	½c blk brn	35	25
2	A24	1c orange	35	15
3	A24	2c yel grn	40	25
4	A24	3c sl grn	40	25
5	A24	4c scarlet	50	30
6	A24	5c rose lil	60	50
7	A24	6c gray	75	50
8	A24	7c violet	1.00	90
9	A24	8c brn org	75	60
10	A24	10c dk bl	1.40	1.25
11	A25	15c brown	1.25	1.25
12	A25	16c ol grn	3.00	2.00
13	A25	20c brn red	3.00	2.00
14	A25	30c brn vio	4.00	2.00
15	A25	50c dp grn	10.00	7.50
16	A26	$1 ocher & blk (R)	50.00	20.00
a.		Second & third characters of ovpt. transposed	1,000.	
		Nos. 1-16 (16)	77.75	39.70

Stamps of China, 1913-19, Overprinted in Black or Red 限新省貼用 *b*

The five characters of overprint "b" are correctly aligned and measure 15½mm.

1916-19

17	A24	½c blk brn	40	15
18	A24	1c orange	40	15
19	A24	1½c violet	40	30
20	A24	2c yel grn	40	15
21	A24	3c sl grn	40	15
22	A24	4c scarlet	40	30
23	A24	5c rose lil	50	30
24	A24	6c gray	60	25
25	A24	7c violet	1.00	75
26	A24	8c brn org	35	15
27	A24	10c dk bl	25	15
28	A25	13c brown	1.00	40
29	A25	15c brown	1.00	50
30	A25	16c ol grn	60	30
31	A25	20c brn red	40	30
32	A25	30c brn vio	75	50
33	A25	50c dp grn	1.00	50
34	A26	$1 ocher & blk (R)	5.00	1.25
35	A26	$2 dk bl & blk (R)	10.00	2.50
36	A26	$5 scar & blk (R)	30.00	12.50
37	A26	$10 yel grn & blk (R)	100.00	60.00
38	A26	$20 yel & blk (R)	300.00	200.00
		Nos. 17-38 (22)	454.85	281.55

China Nos. 243–246 Overprinted 用貼省新限

1921 *Perf. 14*

39	A27	1c orange	75	60
40	A27	3c bl grn	1.00	1.00
41	A27	6c gray	3.00	2.00
42	A27	10c blue	25.00	20.00

Constitution Issue of China, 1923, Overprinted 貼 新 疆 用 省

1923

43	A32	1c orange	1.75	35
44	A32	3c bl grn	1.75	50
45	A32	4c red	5.00	75
46	A32	10c blue	12.50	5.00

Stamps of China, 1923-26, Overprinted Type "b" as in 1916-19, in Black or Red.

1924 **Re-engraved**

47	A29	½c blk brn	20	8
48	A29	1c orange	20	8
49	A29	1½c violet	20	8
50	A29	2c yel grn	20	8
51	A29	3c bl grn	25	8
52	A29	4c gray	2.00	1.25
53	A29	5c claret	35	8
54	A29	6c red	40	15
55	A29	7c violet	35	15
56	A29	8c org brn	5.00	2.00
57	A29	10c dk bl	35	15
58	A30	13c red brn	50	25
59	A30	15c dp bl	50	30
60	A30	16c ol grn	60	30
61	A30	20c brn red	60	20
62	A30	30c brn vio	1.00	25
63	A30	50c dp grn	1.25	40
64	A31	$1 org brn & sep (R)	5.00	75
65	A31	$2 bl & red brn (R)	10.00	2.00
66	A31	$5 red & sl (R)	35.00	5.00
67	A31	$10 grn & cl (R)	100.00	60.00
68	A31	$20 plum & bl (R)	150.00	100.00
		Nos. 47-68 (22)	313.95	173.63

See also Nos. 69, 114.

Same Overprint on China No. 275.

1926

69	A29	4c ol grn	40	12

Chang Tso-lin Stamps of China, 1928 Overprinted in Red or Blue 貼 新 用 疆

1928 *Perf. 14*

70	A34	1c brn org (R)	50	30
71	A34	4c ol grn (R)	1.00	60
72	A34	10c dl bl (R)	2.50	1.50
73	A34	$1 red (Bl)	22.50	15.00

Unification Issue of China, 1929, Overprinted in Red as in 1928.

1929

74	A35	1c brn org	75	50
75	A35	4c ol grn	1.25	1.00
76	A35	10c dk bl	3.00	2.00
77	A35	$1 dk red	42.50	25.00

Similar Overprint in Black on Sun Yat-sen Mausoleum Issue of China.

Characters 15mm. apart

1929 *Perf. 14*

78	A36	1c brn org	1.25	50
79	A36	4c ol grn	1.75	75
80	A36	10c dk bl	5.00	1.50
81	A36	$1 dk red	32.50	15.00

Stamps of Sun Yat-sen Issue of 1931-37 Overprinted 用貼省新限

1932 **Type I** *Perf. 12½*

82	A37	1c orange	50	60
83	A37	2c ol grn	1.00	1.25
84	A37	4c green	75	75
85	A37	20c ultra	1.00	1.25
86	A37	$1 org brn & dk brn	4.00	4.00
87	A37	$2 bl & org brn	6.00	5.00
88	A37	$5 dl red & blk	14.00	12.50
		Nos. 82-88 (7)	27.25	25.35

No. 83 was overprinted in Shanghai in 1938. The overprint differs in minor details.

1932–38 **Type II**

89	A37	2c ol grn	15	15
90	A37	4c green	15	15
91	A37	5c green	15	15
92	A37	15c dk grn	40	35
93	A37	15c scar ('34)	35	30
93A	A37	20c ultra ('38)	30	50
94	A37	25c ultra	35	30
95	A37	$1 org brn & dk brn	2.00	1.75
96	A37	$2 bl & org brn	3.00	3.00
97	A37	$5 dl red & blk	12.00	10.00
		Nos. 89-97 (10)	18.85	16.65

Nos. 89, 90 and 94 were overprinted in London, Peiping and Shanghai. Nos. 92, 95–97 exist with London and Peiping overprints. Nos. 91 and 93 exist with Peiping and Shanghai overprints. No. 93A is a Shanghai overprint. The overprints differ in minor details.

Tan Yuan-chang Issue of China, 1933, Overprinted as in 1928.

1933 *Perf. 14.*

98	A49	2c ol grn	40	30
99	A49	5c green	1.00	75
100	A49	25c ultra	2.00	1.50
101	A49	$1 red	25.00	20.00

Stamps of China Martyrs Issue of 1932-34 Overprinted 用貼省新限

1933-34

102	A39	½c blk brn	10	10
103	A40	1c orange	10	10
104	A39	2½c rose lil	10	10
105	A48	3c dp brn	10	10
106	A45	8c brn org	10	10
107	A46	10c dl vio	10	10
108	A45	13c bl grn	15	15
109	A46	17c brn ol	15	15
110	A47	20c brn red	25	25
111	A48	30c brn vio	25	25
112	A47	40c orange	35	35
113	A40	50c green	40	40
		Nos. 102-113 (12)	2.15	2.15

Nos. 102–113 were originally overprinted in Peiping. In 1938, Nos. 103–105, 108–112 were overprinted in Shanghai. The two overprints differ in minor details. No. 105, Shanghai overprint, is scarce. Price $35.

China No. 324 Overprinted Type "b" as in 1924.

1936 *Perf. 14.*

114	A29	6c brown	9.00	8.00

Stamps of China, 1939-40 Overprinted in Black.

1940–45 *Perf. 12½* **Unwmkd.**

Type III.

115	A57	2c ol grn	8	5
116	A57	3c dl cl ('41)	8	5
117	A57	5c green	8	5
118	A57	5c ol grn	8	5
119	A57	8c ol grn ('41)	8	5
120	A57	10c grn ('41)	8	5
121	A57	15c scarlet	8	5
122	A57	16c ol gray ('41)	15	5
123	A57	25c dk bl	8	5
124	A57	$1 hn & dk brn (type II)	2.50	2.50
125	A57	$2 dp bl & org brn (type I)	3.00	2.50
126	A57	$5 red & grnsh blk	10.00	10.00
		Nos. 115-126 (12)	16.29	15.45

Perf. 14.

With Secret Marks.

127	A57	8c ol grn (#383a)	8	5
a.		On #383	4.00	4.00
128	A57	10c grn ('41)	90	75
129	A57	30c scar ('45)	8	5
130	A57	50c dk bl ('45)	8	5
131	A57	$1 org brn & sep	15	10
132	A57	$2 dp bl & org brn	30	25
133	A57	$5 red & sl grn	45	40
134	A57	$10 dk grn & dl pur	1.00	1.00
135	A57	$20 rose lake & dk bl	1.75	1.50
		Nos. 127-135 (9)	4.79	4.15

Wmkd. Character Yu (Post). (261)

Perf. 14.

136	A57	5c ol grn	8	8
137	A57	10c green	15	10
138	A57	30c scarlet	15	15
139	A57	50c dk bl	18	18

Martyrs Issue, 1940-41, Overprinted in Black 用貼省新限

Perf. 12, 12½, 13, 13x12, 13½x13.

1941-45 **Wmk. 261**

140	A40	1c orange	15	10
141	A39	2½c rose lil	15	10
142	A45	8c dp org ('45)	90	75
143	A46	10c dl vio	15	10
144	A45	13c dp yel grn	40	30
145	A46	17c brn ol	50	40
146	A40	25c red vio ('45)	60	50
147	A47	40c org ('45)	90	75
		Nos. 140-147 (8)	3.75	3.00

Unwmkd.

148	A39	½c ol blk	8	5
149	A40	1c org ('45)	8	5
150	A46	2c dp bl ('45)	8	5

151	A48	3c dp yel brn	8	5
152	A39	4c pale vio ('45)	8	5
153	A45	8c dp org	8	5
154	A45	13c dp yel grn ('45)	12	10
155	A48	15c brn car ('45)	12	10
156	A46	17c brn ol ('45)	30	25
157	A47	20c lt bl ('45)	15	10
158	A45	21c ol brn ('45)	25	20
159	A46	28c ol ('45)	25	20
160	A47	40c org ('45)	1.50	1.25
161	A40	50c grn ('45)	25	20
		Nos. 148-161 (14)	3.42	2.70

Stamps of China, 1942–43 Overprinted in Carmine, Black or Red 用貼省新限

Without Gum.

1944 ***Perf. 12½, 13.***

162	A62	10c dp grn (C)	6	4
163	A62	20c dk ol grn (C)	6	4
164	A62	25c vio brn	6	4
165	A62	30c dk org	6	4
166	A62	40c red brn	6	4
167	A62	50c sage grn	6	4
a.		Perf. 11	1.00	1.00
168	A62	$1 rose lake	6	4
169	A62	$1 dl grn	6	4
170	A62	$1.50 dp bl (C)	6	4
171	A62	$2 dk bl grn (R)	6	4
172	A62	$3 yellow	6	4
173	A62	$5 cerise	6	4
		Nos. 162-173 (12)	72	48

Same Overprint on Stamps of China, 1942-43, in Black.

1944–46 ***Imperf.***

174	A57	$10 red brn	20.00	20.00
175	A57	$20 rose red	25	25
176	A57	$30 dl vio	40	35
177	A57	$40 rose red	45	40
178	A57	$50 bl ('46)	350.00	400.00
179	A57	$100 org brn	90	75

Perf. 13½.

180	A57	$4 dp bl	8	5
181	A57	$5 lil gray	8	5
182	A57	$10 red brn	8	5
183	A57	$20 bl grn	50	50
184	A57	$20 rose red	25.00	25.00
185	A57	$30 dl vio	65	60
186	A57	$40 rose	75	75
187	A57	$50 blue	1.00	1.00
188	A57	$100 org brn	25.00	25.00
		Nos. 174-177, 179-188 (14)	75.14	74.75

Nos. 162 and 164 Surcharged in Black 角貳分 改作壹

1944, Aug. 1

194	A62	12c on 10c dp grn	15	8
195	A62	24c on 25c brn vio	20	10

Stamps of China, 1940–41, Overprinted in Black at Chengtu, Szechwan 用貼省新限

1943

196	A57	10c grn (#354)	1.50	1.50
197	A47	20c lt bl (#433)	1.50	1.50

Perf. 14 **Wmk. 261**

198	A57	50c dk bl (#396)	1.50	1.50

China Nos. 565 and 567 Overprinted in Black 用貼省新限

1945 ***Perf. 12½*** **Unwmkd.**

200	A63	40c brn red	8	8
201	A63	$3 red	8	8

China Nos. 640–642, 788, 750, 753 Surcharged in Black or Red 伍分 改作 用貼省新限

1949 **Engraved** ***Perf. 14***

202	A73	1c on $100 dk car	2.00	2.00
203	A73	3c on $200 ol grn (R)	2.00	2.00
204	A73	5c on $500 brt bl grn (R)	2.00	2.00
205	A82	10c on $20,000 rose pink	3.50	3.50
206	A82	50c on $4000 gray (R)	4.00	4.00
207	A82	$1 on $6000 rose lil	10.00	10.00
		Nos. 202-207 (6)	23.50	23.50

AIR POST STAMPS.

Sinkiang Nos. 53, 57, 59, 32 Overprinted in Red 空航

1932-33 ***Perf. 14.*** **Unwmkd.**

C1	A29	5c cl ('33)	125.00	75.00
C2	A29	10c dk bl ('33)	125.00	60.00
C3	A30	15c dp bl	1,000.	250.00
C4	A25	30c brn vio	375.00	275.00

Counterfeits exist of Nos. C1–C19.

Air Post Stamps of China, 1932–37 Handstamped in Dull Red 用貼省新限

1942

C5	AP3	15c gray grn	1.00	75
C6	AP3	25c orange	200.00	200.00
C7	AP3	30c red	60	60
C8	AP3	45c brn vio	1.00	75
C9	AP3	50c dk brn	8.00	8.00
C10	AP3	60c dk bl	1.00	75
C11	AP3	90c ol grn	12.50	12.50
C12	AP3	$1 yel grn	1.00	75
		Nos. C5-C12 (8)	225.10	224.10

Same Handstamped Overprint on Air Post Stamps of China, 1940–41.

1942 ***Perf. 12½, 13, 13½*** **Wmk. 261**

C13	AP3	15c gray grn	65	50
C14	AP3	25c yel org	65	50

1942 **Unwmkd.**

C15	AP3	25c lt org	75	60
C16	AP3	30c lt red	75	75
C17	AP3	50c brown	1.00	75
C18	AP3	$2 lt brn	8.00	8.00
C19	AP3	$5 lake	8.00	8.00
		Nos. C15-C19 (5)	18.50	18.10

Twelve values exist with this overprint in black. Their status has not been determined. Inverted overprints exist in both red and black.

Official Perforated Characters

For use on official mail, various Sinkiang stamps were perforated with an arrangement of four Chinese characters ("For Official Business Only"). These include Nos. 1–38, 47—69, 114.

Offices in Tibet.

(tĭ·bĕt'; tĭb'ĕt)

12 Pies = 1 Anna
16 Annas = 1 Rupee

Stamps of China, Issues of 1902-10, Surcharged 分 年 Three Pies

1911 ***Perf. 12 to 16.*** **Unwmkd.**

1	A17	3p on 1c ocher	2.50	2.50
a.		Inverted surcharge	300.00	
2	A17	½a on 2c grn	2.50	2.50
3	A17	1a on 4c ver	2.50	2.50
4	A17	2a on 7c mar	3.50	3.50
5	A17	2½a on 10c ultra	5.00	5.00
6	A18	3a on 16c ol grn	8.50	8.50
a.		Large "S" in "Annas"	300.00	
7	A18	4a on 20c red brn	8.50	8.50
8	A18	6a on 30c rose red	15.00	15.00
9	A18	12a on 50c yel grn	35.00	35.00
10	A19	1r on $1 red & pale rose	125.00	125.00
11	A19	2r on $2 red & yel	350.00	350.00
		Nos. 1-11	558.00	558.00

CHINA, People's Republic of

LOCATION—Eastern Asia.
GOV'T.—Communist republic.
POP.—865,680,000 (est. 1977).
CAPITAL—Peking.

The communists completed their conquest of all mainland China in 1949. They established the Central Government and General Postal Administration in Peking. They ordered all but two regions to stop selling regional issues by June 30, 1950, extending validity one year from that date. The Northeast and Port Arthur-Dairen regions were exempted because their currency had a different value. These two regions stopped using separate issues at the end of 1950. Thereafter unified issues were used throughout mainland China.

After currency revaluation Mar. 1, 1955, reprints were prepared and put on sale by the Philatelic Agency in order to supply stocks of exhausted issues for collectors. Minor differences in design or paper distinguish the reprints. They are of commemorative and special issues up to the gymnastics set of 1952. Many exist canceled to order. Reprints are plentiful and inexpensive. Prices are for original issues. Reprint distinctions are footnoted.

Commemorative issues, beginning in 1949, and special issues, beginning in 1951, bear 4 numbers in lower margin: 1. Issue number. 2. Total of stamps in set. 3. Position of stamp in set. 4. Cumulative number of stamp (usually in parenthesis). A fifth number, the year of issue, was added in 1952.

The numbering system varies at times, with all numbers omitted on Nos. 938–1046.

In certain sets listings include parenthetically the position-in-set number. During some periods these parentheses in listings hold the stamp's cumulative number.

All stamps to the beginning of 1960 were issued without gum, except as noted. After that date, most stamps have gum, which is translucent and almost invisible. All issues are unwatermarked, unless otherwise noted.

100 fen = 1 yuan ($)

Prices fluctuate for most P.R.C. issues, and for Communist Regional issues. Information is inadequate or lacking about quantities printed and issued, existence of large stocks, and possible release of remainders.

Prices quoted represent averages and indicate relative values.

Lantern and Gate of Heavenly Peace
A1

Globe and Hand Holding Hammer
A2

1949, Oct. 8 Litho. *Perf. 12½*

1	A1	$30 blue	1.25	1.50
2	A1	$50 rose red	1.25	1.50
3	A1	$100 green	1.25	1.50
4	A1	$200 maroon	1.25	1.50

First session of Chinese People's Political Conference. See also Nos. 1L121–1L124.

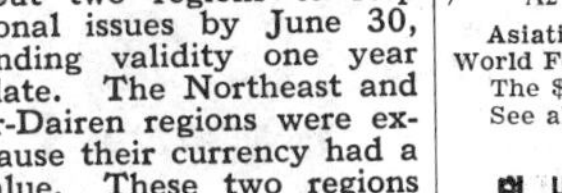

Original Reprint

Reprints have altered ornament on lantern base. On originals, it is a full oval; in reprints, only a partial circle. Price, set, 40 cents.

1949, Nov. 16

5	A2	$100 carmine	4.00	2.50
6	A2	$300 sl grn	4.00	1.50
7	A2	$500 dk bl	4.00	4.00

Asiatic and Australasian Congress of the World Federation of Trade Unions, Peking. The $100, imperf., is of dubious status. See also Nos. 1L133–1L135.

Original

Reprint

Reprints show heavier shading on index finger and thumb. Price, set, 40 cents.

Conference Hall, Peking
A3

Mao Tse-tung on Rostrum
A4

1950, Feb. 1 Engraved *Perf. 14*

8	A3	$50 red	3.00	3.00
9	A3	$100 blue	3.00	3.00
10	A4	$300 red brn	3.00	2.00
11	A4	$500 green	3.00	2.00

Chinese People's Political Conference. See also Nos. 1L136–1L139.

Original

Reprint

Nos. 8–9: First character in top inscription shows a square, reprints an oblong.

Nos. 10–11: Originals have heavy crosshatching and lines which touch back of head and top of rostrum. Reprints have lighter lines which do not touch head or top of rostrum.

Reprints, price set 80 cents.

Gate of Heavenly Peace (same size)
A5

First Issue: Top line of shading broken at right.

1950, Feb. 10 Litho. *Perf. 12½*

12	A5	$200 green	1.00	1.00
13	A5	$300 brn red	10	30
14	A5	$500 red	15	12
15	A5	$800 orange	10.00	12
16	A5	$1000 dl vio	15	10
17	A5	$2000 olive	1.00	50
18	A5	$5000 brt pink	15	1.00
19	A5	$8000 blue	15	3.00
20	A5	$10,000 brown	15	1.50
		Nos. 12-20 (9)	12.85	7.64

1950, June 9 Typographed

Second Issue: Top line of shading extends to frame line at right.

21	A5	$1000 dl vio	15	10
22	A5	$3000 red brn	15	10
23	A5	$10,000 brown	15	10

1949 Unit Issue of China Surcharged in Blue, Black, Green or Red

中國人民郵政 貳佰圓 200

1950, Mar. Litho. *Perf. 12½*

24	SD2	$100 on red vio (Bl)	3.00	3.00
a.		Rouletted	20	40
25	R2	$200 on red (Bk)	11.00	2.00
a.		Rouletted	1.50	50
26	AP5	$300 on bl grn (Bk)	20	85
a.		Rouletted	10	75
27	A96	$500 on org (G)	10	30
a.		Perf. 14	70.00	60.00
28	A96	$800 on org (R)	6.00	75
a.		Rouletted	1.50	20
b.		Perf. 14	90.00	50.00
29	A96	$1000 on org (Bk)	5	25
a.		Perf. 14	10	20
		Nos. 24-29 (6)	20.35	7.15

Harvesters with Ox
A6

1950, May

30	A6	$20,000 on $10,000 red	175.00	15.00

No. 30 is surcharged on an unissued stamp of East China.

Flag, Mao Tse-tung, Gate of Heavenly Peace
A7

1950, July 1 *Perf. 14*

Yellow Stars

31	A7	$800 grn & red	20.00	2.50
32	A7	$1000 brn & red	20.00	5.00
33	A7	$2000 dk brn & red	20.00	6.00
34	A7	$3000 dk bl & red	20.00	7.00

Inauguration of the People's Republic, Oct. 1, 1949. See also Nos. 1L150–1L153.

Original

Reprint

Originals have a single curved line in jacket button, reprints have an extra dot in button. Price, set 90 cents.

Sun Yat-sen Stamps of Northeastern Provinces Surcharged in Red, Black or Blue

中國人民郵政 伍拾圓 ☆ 50

1950, July 1 Engraved

35	A2	$50 on 20c yel grn (R)	50	4.00
36	A2	$50 on 25c blk brn (R)	1.50	1.75
37	A2	$50 on 50c red org (Bk)	15	50
38	A2	$100 on $2.50 ind (R)	35	50
39	A2	$100 on $3 brn (Bk)	8.00	50
40	A2	$100 on $4 org brn, Type II (Bl)	6.00	2.75
a.		Type I	30.00	40.00
41	A2	$100 on $5 dk grn (Bk)	8.00	50
42	A2	$100 on $10 crim (Bl)	8.00	4.00
43	A2	$400 on $20 ol, Type II (Bl)	8.00	4.00
a.		Type I	60.00	50.00
44	A2	$400 on $44 dk car rose (Bl)	20	2.50
45	A2	$400 on $65 dl grn (R)	20.00	8.00
46	A2	$400 on $100 dp grn (R)	8.00	2.50
47	A2	$400 on $200 rose brn (Bk)	30.00	3.50
48	A2	$400 on $300 bluish grn (R)	30.00	3.50
		Nos. 35-48 (14)	128.70	38.50

Flying Geese Type of China Surcharged in Red, Blue, Green, Brown or Black

中國人民郵政 貳佰圓 ★★ 200

1950, Aug. 1 *Perf. 12½, Imperf.*

49	A97	$50 on 10c dk bl (R)	5	25
50	A97	$100 on 16c ol, imperf. (Bl)	5	25
51	A97	$100 on 50c dl grn, imperf. (Bl)	5	12
52	A97	$200 on $1 org (G)	10	12
53	A97	$200 on $2 bl (Br)	1.25	20
54	A97	$400 on $5 car rose (Bk)	15	25
55	A97	$400 on $10 bl grn (Bk)	15	80
56	A97	$400 on $20 pur (Bk)	20	1.00
		Nos. 49-58 (8)	2.00	2.99

Dove of Peace, by Picasso
A8

Chinese Flag and "1"
A9

1950, Aug. 1 Engraved *Perf. 14*

57	A8	$400 brown	6.00	3.00
58	A8	$800 green	6.00	3.00
59	A8	$2000 blue	6.00	3.00

World Peace Campaign. See also Nos. 1L154–1L156.

Paper of originals appears bright under ultraviolet lamp. That of reprints looks dull. Price, set 40 cents.

1950 Engraved & Litho.

Flag in Red & Yellow

60	A9	$100 purple	10.00	4.00
61	A9	$400 red brn	10.00	7.00

62	A9	$800 green	10.00	4.00
63	A9	$1000 lt ol	10.00	5.00
64	A9	$2000 blue	10.00	7.00
		Nos. 60-64 (5)	50.00	27.00

First anniversary of the Chinese People's Republic. Size of $800: 38x46 mm.; others 26x32 mm.

Issue dates: No. 62, Oct. 1; others Oct. 31. See also Nos. 1L157-1L161.

Original ($800) Reprint

Reprints are a brighter red, leaves beside "1" are gray brown instead of reddish brown. On the $800 the arrangement of dots in background differs in relationship to large star. Price, set 80 cents.

(same size)

Gate of Heavenly Peace
A10

"Communication" and Map of China
A11

Third Issue: Cloud almost touches character at upper left. Cloud breaks inner frame line at top.

1950 **Lithographed**

65	A10	$100 lt grnsh bl	40.00	9.00
66	A10	$200 green	140.00	12.00
67	A10	$300 dk car	1.00	*5.00*
68	A10	$400 grnsh gray	40	*5.00*
69	A10	$500 carmine	25	*6.00*
70	A10	$800 orange	2.00	35
71	A10	$2000 gray ol	50	60
		Nos. 65-71 (7)	184.15	*37.95*

Issue dates: $800, Oct. 8; $500, $2000, Dec. 1; others, Oct. 6.

1950, Nov. 1 **Lithographed**

72	A11	$400 grn & brn	6.00	4.00
73	A11	$800 car & grn	6.00	3.00

First All-China Postal Conference, Peking.

Original Reprint

Originals have 3 lines below horizontal bar between 1st & 2nd character; reprints have 4. Price, set, 30 cents.

Stalin and Mao Tse-tung—A12

1950, Dec. 1 **Engraved** ***Perf. 14***

74	A12	$400 red	9.00	4.00
75	A12	$800 dp grn	9.00	3.00
76	A12	$2000 dk bl	9.00	4.00

Signing of Sino-Soviet Treaty of Friendship, Alliance and Mutual Assistance. See also Nos. 1L176-1L178.

Paper of originals appears bright under ultraviolet lamp. That of reprints looks dull. Price, set 85 cents.

East China Issue of 1949 Surcharged in Red, Black, Brown or Blue

Train and Postal Runner
A12a

1950, Dec. **Litho.** ***Perf. 12½***

77	A12a	$50 on $10 dp ultra (R)	5	10
78	A12a	$100 on $15 org ver (Bk)	6	10
a.		$100 on $15 red (Bk), perf. 14	10	10
79	A12a	$300 on $50 car (Bk)	3	20
80	A12a	$400 on $1600 vio bl (Br)	50	15
81	A12a	$400 on $2000 brn vio (Bl)	20	15
		Nos. 77-81 (5)	84	70

East China Issue of 1949 Surcharged in Red or Black

Chairman Mao
A12b

1950, Dec.

82	A12b	$50 on $10 ultra (R)	5	10
83	A12b	$400 on $15 ver (Bk)	3	10
84	A12b	$400 on $2000 grn (Bk)	20	10

(same size)

Gate of Heavenly Peace
A13 A14

Fourth Issue: Similar to 3rd issue, but large cloud does not break inner frame line at top.

1950-51 **Lithographed**

85	A13	$100 lt bl	1.00	1.00
86	A13	$200 dl grn	1.20	1.20
87	A13	$300 dl lil	25	*7.00*
88	A13	$400 gray grn	25	1.00
89	A13	$500 carmine	3	*1.50*
90	A13	$800 orange	50.00	1.25
a.		Imperf., pair	*600.00*	
91	A13	$1000 violet	35	1.00
92	A13	$2000 olive	110.00	4.00
93	A13	$3000 brown	5	*8.00*
94	A13	$5000 pink	3	*8.00*
		Nos. 85-94 (10)	163.16	*33.95*

Issue dates: $200, $300, $500, $800, $2000, $5000, Dec. 22, 1950; others June 8, 1951.

1951, Jan. 18 **Engraved** ***Perf. 14***

Fifth Issue: Colored network on surface in salmon.

95	A14	$10,000 brown	50	*10.00*
96	A14	$20,000 olive	50	*7.50*
97	A14	$30,000 green	12.00	*18.00*
98	A14	$50,000 violet	50.00	12.50
99	A14	$100,000 scarlet	1,000.	100.00
100	A14	$200,000 blue	1,000.	100.00
		Nos. 95-100 (6)	2,063.	*248.00*

Unit Issue of China Surcharged

中國人民郵政
伍
圓
5

1951, May 2 **Litho.** ***Perf. 12½***

101	SD2	$5 on rose lil	2.00	25
102	AP5	$10 on brt grn	15	8
103	R2	$15 on red	10	8
104	A96	$25 on org	40	8

Issued for use in Northeast China, but available for use throughout China. Nos. 101-104 rouletted were sold for philatelic purposes only.

Price, set $1.

Chairman Mao Tse-tung
A15

1951, July 1 **Engraved** ***Perf. 14***

105	A15	$400 chestnut	3.00	2.00
106	A15	$500 dp grn	3.00	2.00
107	A15	$800 crimson	3.00	2.00

30th anniversary of the Chinese Communist Party.

Reprints are on whiter, thinner and harder paper. Price, set, 40 cents.

Picasso Dove—A16

1951, Aug. 15 ***Perf. 12½***

108	A16	$400 org brn	5.00	2.50
109	A16	$800 bl grn	5.00	1.50
110	A16	$1000 dl vio	5.00	2.50

Reprints are perf. 14. Price, set 80 cents.

Remittance Stamp of China Surcharged in Carmine or Black

(same size)

A17

Engraved, Commercial Press

1951, Sept. ***Perf. 12½***

111	A17	$50 on $2 bl grn (C)	20	75

Typo., Kang Hwa Printing Co.

Roul. 9½

112	A17	$50 on $2 gray bl (C)	75	75
113	A17	$50 on $5 red org (Bk)	5	75
114	A17	$50 on $50 gray (C)	5.00	75

Litho., Central Trust Co.

Perf. 13

115	A17	$50 on $50 gray blk (C)	5	75

Litho., Chung Hwa Book Co.

Perf. 11½

116	A17	$50 on $50 gray (C)	25	75
a.		Perf. 11½x10	75	75
		Nos. 111-116 (6)	6.30	4.50

National Emblem
A18

1951, Oct. 1 ***Perf. 14***

Engraved; Background Network Lithographed in Yellow.

117	A18	$100 Prus bl	4.00	2.00
118	A18	$200 brown	4.00	1.50
119	A18	$400 orange	4.00	2.00
120	A18	$500 green	4.00	1.50
121	A18	$800 carmine	4.00	1.50
		Nos. 117-121 (5)	20.00	8.50

Reprints exist but difficult to distinguish; paper whiter, and colors slightly brighter. Price, set, 40 cents.

Price, set 60 cents.

Lu Hsun and Quotation
A19

1951, Oct. 19 **Litho.** ***Perf. 12½***

122	A19	$400 lilac	4.00	3.00
123	A19	$800 green	4.00	3.00

15th anniversary of the death of Lu Hsun (1881-1936), writer.

Original Reprint

Reprints have dot in triangle at lower right; no dot in original. Price, set, 30 cents.

Peasant Uprising, Chintien—A20

Design: Nos. 126-127, Coin of Taiping Regime and decrees of peasant government.

1951, Dec. 15 **Engraved** ***Perf. 14***

124	A20	$400 green	5.00	2.00
125	A20	$800 scarlet	5.00	2.00
126	A20	$800 orange	5.00	2.00
127	A20	$1000 dp bl	5.00	3.00

Centenary of Taiping Peasant Rebellion.

Original

Reprint

Reprints of Nos. 124-125 have additional short stroke at upper left.

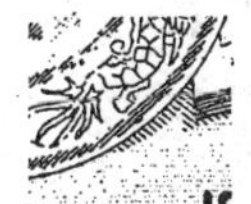
Original

Reprint

Reprints of Nos. 126-127 have two short strokes on scale near tail of right dragon on coin.
Price, Nos. 124-127, 35 cents.

Old and New Methods of Agriculture
A21

1952, Jan. 1

128	A21	$100 scarlet	4.00	3.00
129	A21	$200 brt bl	4.00	3.00
130	A21	$400 dp brn	4.00	2.00
131	A21	$800 green	4.00	2.00

Agrarian reform.

Original

Reprint

One short horizontal line between legs of plower; 2 lines in reprints. Price set, 30 cents.
Price, set 60 cents.

Potala Monastery, Lhasa
A22

Designs: Nos. 134-135, Farmer plowing with yaks.

1952, Mar. 15 ***Perf. 12½***

132	A22	$400 vermilion	5.00	3.00
133	A22	$800 claret	5.00	3.00
134	A22	$800 bl grn	5.00	2.00
135	A22	$1000 dl vio	5.00	2.00

Liberation of Tibet.

Reprints, perf. 14, have a small Chinese character at lower left of the vignette which is missing in the original. Price, set, 30 cents.

Children of Four Races
A23

Hammer and Sickle on Numeral 1
A24

1952, Apr. 12 **Lithographed**

136	A23	$400 dl grn	10	5
137	A23	$800 vio bl	10	5

International Child Protection Conference, Vienna.

1952, May 1

Designs: No. 139, Dove rising from worker's hand. No. 140, Dove, hammer, wheat and chimneys.

138	A24	$800 scarlet	5	5
139	A24	$800 bl grn	5	5
140	A24	$800 org brn	8	5

Labor Day.

Physical Exercises—A25

Stamps printed in blocks of four for each color, each block representing a specific setting-up exercise; exercises coincided with a national radio program. Where exercise positions are identical within the block, the serial number (in parenthesis) is the only means of differentiation.

1952, June 20

141	A25	$400 ver, blk. of 4	15.00	15.00
a.		*Right arm forward (1)*	2.00	1.00
b.		*Left arm forward (2)*	2.00	1.00
c.		*as "a" (3)*	2.00	1.00
d.		*as "b" (4)*	2.00	1.00
142	A25	$400 bl, blk. of 4	15.00	15.00
a.		*Arms outstretched (5)*	2.00	1.00
b.		*Knee-bend (6)*	2.00	1.00
c.		*as "a" (7)*	2.00	1.00
d.		*Rest (8)*	2.00	1.00
143	A25	$400 brn red, blk. of 4	15.00	15.00
a.		*Arms forward (9)*	2.00	1.00
b.		*Arms outstretched (10)*	2.00	1.00
c.		*as "b" (11)*	2.00	1.00
d.		*Rest (12)*	2.00	1.00
144	A25	$400 yel grn, blk. of 4	15.00	15.00
a.		*Arms outstretched (13)*	2.00	1.00
b.		*Sideways bend (14)*	2.00	1.00
c.		*as "a" (15)*	2.00	1.00
d.		*Hands on hips (16)*	2.00	1.00
145	A25	$400 red org, blk. of 4	15.00	15.00
a.		*as 144a (17)*	2.00	1.00
b.		*Alternate toe touch (18)*	2.00	1.00
c.		*as "a" (19)*	2.00	1.00
d.		*Rest (20)*	2.00	1.00
146	A25	$400 dl bl, blk. of 4	15.00	15.00
a.		*Stretch (21)*	2.00	1.00
b.		*Toe touch (22)*	2.00	1.00
c.		*Hands on floor (23)*	2.00	1.00
d.		*Rest (24)*	2.00	1.00
147	A25	$400 org, block of 4	15.00	15.00
a.		*Leg forward (25)*	2.00	1.00
b.		*Leg extended back (26)*	2.00	1.00
c.		*as "a" (27)*	2.00	1.00
d.		*Rest (28)*	2.00	1.00
148	A25	$400 dl pur, block of 4	15.00	15.00
a.		*Jumping jack (29)*	2.00	1.00
b.		*Rest (30)*	2.00	1.00
c.		*as "a" (31)*	2.00	1.00
d.		*as "b" (32)*	2.00	1.00
149	A25	$400 yel bis, blk. of 4	15.00	15.00
a.		*Left leg raised (33)*	2.00	1.00
b.		*Hands on hips (34)*	2.00	1.00
c.		*Right leg raised (35)*	2.00	1.00
d.		*as "b" (36)*	2.00	1.00
150	A25	$400 sky bl, blk. of 4	15.00	15.00
a.		*Arms raised forward (37)*	2.00	1.00
b.		*Arms above head (38)*	2.00	1.00
c.		*Arms outstretched (39)*	2.00	1.00
d.		*Rest (40)*	2.00	1.00
		Nos. 141-150 (10 blocks of 4)	150.00	150.00

Originals are on thin gray paper, colors darker. Reprints on thicker white paper, colors brighter.

Price, set $3.

Hunting, Wei Dynasty, A.D. 386-580—A26

Designs from Murals in Cave Temples at Tunhuang, Kansu Province: No. 152, Lady attendants, Sui Dynasty, 581-617 A.D. No. 153, Gandharvas (mythology), Tang Dynasty, 618-906. No. 154, Dragon, Tang Dynasty.

1952, July 1 **Engraved**

151	A26	$800 sl grn (1)	12	6
152	A26	$800 choc (2)	12	6
153	A26	$800 ind (3)	12	6
154	A26	$800 blk (4)	12	6

"Glorious Mother Country," 1st series.

Marco Polo Bridge, near Peking
A27

Designs: No. 156, Cavalry passing through Great Wall. No. 157, Departure of New Fourth Army. No. 158, Mao Tse-tung and Gen. Chu Teh planning counter-attack.

1952, July 7 **Litho.** ***Perf. 14***

155	A27	$800 brt bl	10	6
156	A27	$800 bl grn	10	6
157	A27	$800 plum	20	6
158	A27	$800 scarlet	5	6

15th anniversary of war against Japan.

Soldier and Tanks
A28

Designs: No. 159, Soldier, sailor and airman (vert.). No. 161, Sailor and warships. No. 162, Airman and planes.

1952, Aug. 1 **Engraved** ***Perf. 12½***

159	A28	$800 carmine	10	6
160	A28	$800 dp grn	20	6
161	A28	$800 purple	10	6
162	A28	$800 org brn	10	6

25th anniversary of People's Liberation Army.

Huai River Sluice Dam—A29

Designs: No. 164, Train on the Chengtu-Chungking Railway. No. 165, Oil refinery and derricks in the Northwest. No. 166, Mechanized state farm.

1952, Oct. 1 ***Perf. 14***

163	A29	$800 dk vio	10	6
164	A29	$800 red	10	6
165	A29	$800 dk vio brn	10	6
166	A29	$800 dp grn	10	6

"Glorious Mother Country," 2nd series.

Doves and Globe
A30

Designs: Nos. 167-168, Picasso dove over Pacific (vert.). $2500, as No. 169.

1952, Oct. 2 ***Perf. 14***

167	A30	$400 maroon	10	4
168	A30	$800 red	10	5
169	A30	$800 brn org	10	6
170	A30	$2500 dp grn	10	15

Peace Conference of the Asian and Pacific Regions.

Volunteers on the March—A31

Designs: No. 172, Chinese peasants loading supplies. No. 173, Volunteers attacking across river. No. 174, Meeting of Chinese and Korean troops.

1952, Oct. 25

171	A31	$800 bl grn (1)	10	6
172	A31	$800 ver (2)	10	6
173	A31	$800 vio (3)	15	6
174	A31	$800 lake brn (4)	20	6

2nd anniversary of Chinese Volunteers in Korea.

Woman Textile Worker
A32

Design: No. 176, Farm woman with sickle.

1953, Mar. 10

175	A32	$800 carmine	10	9
176	A32	$800 emerald	12	9

International Women's Day.

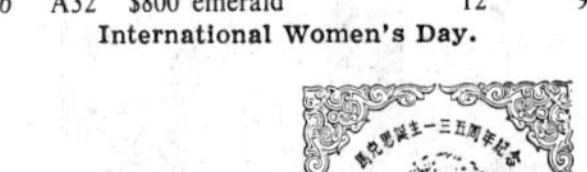

Textile Worker
A33

Karl Marx
A34

Designs: $200, Shepherdess. $250, Stone lion. $800, Lathe operator. $1600, Coal miners. $2000, Corner tower of Forbidden City, Peking.

1953 Litho. *Perf. 14; 12½* ($250)

177	A33	$50 magenta	10	8
178	A33	$200 emerald	8	10
179	A33	$250 ultra	10	10
180	A33	$800 bl grn	5	6
181	A33	$1600 gray	10	25
182	A33	$2000 red org	40	15
		Nos. 177-182 (6)	83	74

Issue dates: Nos. 177-181, Mar. 25; No. 182, May 23.

1953, May 20 **Engraved** ***Perf. 14***

183	A34	$400 dk brn	10	8
184	A34	$800 sl grn	10	8

135th anniversary of the birth of Karl Marx (1818-1883).

Workers and Banners
A35

1953, June 25

185	A35	$400 Prus bl	12	5
186	A35	$800 carmine	8	5

7th All-China Trade Union Congress.

Picasso Dove
A36

1953, July 25

187	A36	$250 bl grn	10	7
188	A36	$400 org brn	5	10
189	A36	$800 purple	8	12

World Peace.

Groom, Wei Dynasty, 386–580
A37

Scenes from Tunhuang Murals: No. 191, Court Players, Wei Dynasty. No. 192, Battle Scene, Sui Dynasty, 581–617. No. 193, Ox-drawn palanquin, Tang Dynasty, 618–906.

1953, Sept. 1

190	A37	$800 dp grn (1)	8	6
191	A37	$800 red org (2)	5	6
192	A37	$800 Prus bl (3)	12	6
193	A37	$800 car (4)	10	6

"Glorious Mother Country," 3rd series.

Stalin and Mao on Kremlin Terrace—A38

Statue of Stalin at Volga-Don Canal
A39

Designs: No. 195, Lenin proclaiming Soviet power. No. 197, Stalin as orator.

1953, Oct. 5

194	A38	$800 grn (1)	10	8
195	A38	$800 car (2)	15	8
196	A39	$800 brt bl (3)	12	8
197	A39	$800 org brn (4)	10	8

35th anniversary of the Russian October Revolution.

Stamps in same designs with two additional characters meaning "Soviet" in the single-line Chinese inscription, and in different colors, were unofficially released at several small post offices in Hunan, Fukien and Canton areas in February, 1953, but were withdrawn after only a small number had been sold.

Price, set $3500 unused, $2000 canceled.

Compass, 3rd Century B.C.
A40

Designs: No. 199, Seismoscope, later Han Dynasty. No. 200, Drum cart to measure distance, Chin Dynasty. No. 201, Armillary sphere, Ming Dynasty.

1953, Dec. 1

198	A40	$800 ind (1)	10	6
199	A40	$800 dk grn (2)	10	6
200	A40	$800 dk sl grn (3)	10	6
201	A40	$800 choc (4)	8	6

Major inventions by ancient and medieval Chinese scientists.
"Glorious Mother Country," 4th series.

Francois Rabelais
A41

(same size)
Gate of Heavenly Peace
A42

Designs: $400, José Marti, Cuban revolutionary. $800, Chu Yuan (350–275 B.C.), philosopher. $2200, Nicolaus Copernicus, astronomer.

1953, Dec. 30

202	A41	$250 sl grn (3)	8	5
203	A41	$400 brn blk (4)	8	5
204	A41	$800 ind (1)	8	5
205	A41	$2200 choc (2)	8	10

1954, April 16 Lithographed

Sixth Issue: Inscription at upper right.

206	A42	$50 carmine	5	5
207	A42	$100 lt bl	5	6
208	A42	$200 green	5	6
209	A42	$250 ultra	40	8
210	A42	$400 gray grn	5	8
211	A42	$800 orange	5	6
212	A42	$1600 gray	5	40
213	A42	$2000 olive	5	20
		Nos. 206-213 (8)	75	99

Textile Plant, Harbin
A43

Lenin
A44

1954, May 1 Engraved

Designs: $200, Tangku Harbor. $250, Tienshui-Lanchow railroad bridge, Kansu Province. $400, Heavy machine-building plant, Taiyuan, Shansi. No. 218, Automatic blast, furnace, Anshan, Manchuria. No. 219, Fushun open-cut coal mine. $2000, Automatic power plant, Northeast. $3200, Prospecting in Tayeh district, Hupeh.

214	A43	$100 brn ol	20	3
215	A43	$200 bl grn	15	3
216	A43	$250 violet	5	3
217	A43	$400 black	10	3
218	A43	$800 claret	5	3
219	A43	$800 indigo	5	3
220	A43	$2000 red	5	15
221	A43	$3200 dk brn	15	25
		Nos. 214-221 (8)	80	58

Economic progress.

1954, June 30 Engraved

Designs: $400, Lenin and Stalin Monument, Gorki (horiz.). $2000, Lenin proclaiming Soviet power.

222	A44	$400 dp grn	5	8
223	A44	$800 dk brn	20	12
224	A44	$2000 dp car	10	12

30th anniversary of the death of Lenin.

Pottery Vessels, Neolithic Period, 2000 B. C.—A45

Archeological Treasures: No. 226, Stone chime, Shang Dynasty, c. 1200 B.C. No. 227, Kuo Chi Tsu-pai bronze basin, Middle Chou Dynasty, 816 B.C. No. 228, Lacquered box and wine cup, Warring States Period, 403–221 B.C.

1954, Aug. 25

225	A45	$800 brown	9	6
226	A45	$800 indigo	9	6
227	A45	$800 Prus bl	9	6
228	A45	$800 dk car	9	6

"Glorious Mother Country," 5th series.

Pipe Production, Anshan Steel Mill
A46

Stalin Statue, by Tomsky
A47

Design: $800, Rolling mill, Anshan.

1954, Oct. 1

229	A46	$400 Prus grn	30	15
230	A46	$800 vio brn	30	15

1954, Oct. 15

Designs: $800, Stalin portrait. $2000, Stalin viewing hydroelectric plant.

Size: 21x45mm.

231	A47	$400 black	30	12

Size: 26x37mm.

232	A47	$800 blk brn	10	12

Size: 42x26mm.

233	A47	$2000 dp red	10	12

First anniversary of the death of Stalin.

Exhibition Building, Peking—A48

1954, Nov. 7

234	A48	$800 brn, *cr*	8.50	4.00

Russian Economic and Cultural Exhibition, Peking.

Apprentices and Lathe
A49

Design: $800, Heavy machinery and workers.

1954, Dec. 15

235	A49	$400 dk ol grn	15	10
236	A49	$800 brt red	10	10

Progress in technology.

Woman Worker Voting
A50

People Celebrating Opening of Congress—A51

1954, Dec. 30

237	A50	$400 dp cl	12	12
238	A51	$800 brt red	10	10

First National Congress.

Flags, Worker and Woman Holding Constitution—A52

1954, Dec. 30

239	A52	$400 brn, *buff*	15	7
240	A52	$800 brt red, *yel*	15	10

Adoption of Constitution.

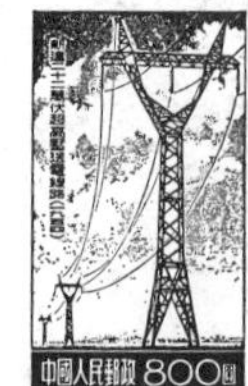

High-tension Pylon
A53

1955, Feb. 25

241	A53	$800 dk Prus bl	25	15

Development of electric power.

Factory Health Workers and Red Cross—A54

1955, June 25

Engraved; Cross Typographed

242	A54	8f dp grn & red	10.50	20

50th anniversary of Chinese Red Cross.

Stalin and Mao in Kremlin
A55

Soviet Specialist and Chinese Worker
A56

1955, July 25 **Engraved**

243	A55	8f brn red	8.00	15
244	A56	20f ol blk	10.00	25

5th anniversary of Sino-Soviet Friendship Treaty.

Chang Heng (78–139), Astronomer
A57

Portraits of Scientists: No. 246, Tsu Chung-chih (429–500), mathematician. No. 247, Chang Sui (683–727), astronomer. No. 248, Li Shih-chen (1518–1593), physician and pharmacologist.

1955, Aug. 25 ***Perf. 14***

245	A57	8f sep, *buff*	40	5
a.		Min. sheet, sep, *white*	2.00	1.00
246	A57	8f dp grn, *buff*	40	5
a.		Min. sheet, dp grn, *white*	2.00	1.00
247	A57	8f blk, *buff*	40	5
a.		Min. sheet, blk, *white*	2.00	1.00
248	A57	8f cl, *buff*	40	5
a.		Min. sheet, cl, *white*	2.00	1.00

Miniature sheets contain one imperf. stamp each. Size: 63x90mm.

Steel Pouring Ladle
A58

1955–56 **Lithographed**

Bluish Black Frames, Multicolored Centers.

Position-in-set number in ( ).

249	A58	8f *shown* (1)	25	5
250	A58	8f *High tension line* (2)	25	5
251	A58	8f *Mechanized coal mining* (3)	25	5
252	A58	8f *Tank cars and derricks* (4)	25	5
253	A58	8f *Heavy machine shop* (5)	25	5
254	A58	8f *Soldier on guard* (6)	25	5
255	A58	8f *Spinning machine* (7)	25	5
256	A58	8f *Workers discussing 5-year plan* (8)	25	5
257	A58	8f *Combine harvester* (9)	25	5
258	A58	8f *Milk production* (10)	25	5
259	A58	8f *Dam* (11)	25	5
260	A58	8f *Pottery industry* (12) ('56)	25	5
261	A58	8f *Truck* (13)	25	5
262	A58	8f *Ship at dock* (14)	25	5
263	A58	8f *Geological survey* (15)	25	5
264	A58	8f *Higher education* (16)	25	5
265	A58	8f *Family* (17)	25	5
266	A58	8f *Workers' rest home* (18) ('56)	25	5
		Nos.249-266 (18)	4.50	90

First Five Year Plan.
Issue dates: Nos. 249–257, Oct. 1, 1955; Nos. 258–259, 261–265, Dec. 15, 1955; Nos. 260, 266, Feb. 24, 1956.

Lenin A59 — Engels A60

1955, Dec. 15 **Engraved** ***Perf. 14***

267	A59	8f dk bl grn	7.00	10
268	A59	20f dk rose car	7.00	50

85th anniversary of the birth of Lenin.

1955, Dec. 15

269	A60	8f dp org	7.00	10
270	A60	20f brown	7.00	50

135th anniversary of the birth of Friedrich Engels (1820–1895), German socialist.

Storming Lu Ting Bridge
A61

Crossing Great Snow Mountains
A62

1955, Dec. 30

271	A61	8f dk red	5.00	20
272	A62	8f dk bl	5.00	20

Long March of Chinese Communist army, 20th anniversary.

Miner
A63

Gate of Heavenly Peace
A64

Designs: 1f, Machinist. 2f, Airman. 2½f, Nurse. 4f, Soldier. 8f, Steel worker. 10f, Scientist. 20f, Farm woman. 50f, Sailor.

1955–56 **Lithographed** ***Perf. 14***

273	A63	½f org brn	6.00	5
274	A63	1f purple	6.00	10
275	A63	2f green	6.00	5
276	A63	2½f bl ('56)	12.00	5
277	A63	4f gray ol	10.00	10
278	A63	8f red org (Peking printing)	10.00	20
a.		Perf. 12½ (Shanghai printing)	75.00	25.00
279	A63	10f cl ('56)	50.00	5
280	A63	20f dp bl	10.00	5
281	A63	50f gray	10.00	5
		Nos. 273-281 (9)	120.00	70

Engraved

282	A64	$1 cl ('56)	2.00	25
283	A64	$2 sep ('55)	4.00	25
284	A64	$5 ind ('56)	10.00	40
285	A64	$10 dp org ('56)	20.00	4.00
286	A64	$20 gray vio ('56)	40.00	10.00
		Nos. 282-286 (5)	76.00	14.90

Nos. 282–286 are the 7th Gate Issue.

Trucks, Mountains, Highway Map
A65

Suspension Bridge over Tatu River
A66

Design: No. 289, First truck arriving in Lhasa, and the Potala.

1956, Mar. 10 **Engraved**

287	A65	4f dp bl	25	10
288	A66	8f dk brn	25	10
289	A65	8f carmine	25	10

Completion of Sikang-Tibet and Chinghai-Tibet Highways.

Summer Palace and Marble Boat
A67

Famous Views of Imperial Peking: No. 291, Peihai Park with Jade Belt Marble Bridge. No. 292, Gate of Heavenly Peace. No. 293, Temple of Heaven. No. 294, Great Throne Hall, Forbidden City.

1956–57

290	A67	4f car rose (1)	50	10
291	A67	4f bl grn (2)	50	10
292	A67	8f red org (3) ('57)	50	10
293	A67	8f Prus bl (4)	50	10
294	A67	8f yel brn (5)	50	10
		Nos. 290-294 (5)	2.50	50

Issue dates: No. 292, Feb. 20, 1957; others, June 15, 1956.
No. 292 exists with sun rays in background.

Salt Making
A68

Designs: No. 296, Dwelling of the Eastern Han period. No. 297, Duck hunting and harvesting. No. 298, Carriage crossing bridge.

1956, Oct. 1

295	A68	4f gray ol	15	5
296	A68	4f sl bl	15	5
297	A68	8f gray brn	15	5
298	A68	8f sepia	15	5

Murals, Tung Han Dynasty, 250 B.C.–220 A.D., found near Chengtu.

Ancient Coins and "Save"
A69

1956, Oct. 1

299	A69	4f yel brn	4.00	12
300	A69	8f rose red	4.00	12

Promotion of saving.

Gate of Heavenly Peace
A70

Sun Yat-sen
A71

1956, Nov. 10

301	A70	4f dk grn	4.00	10
302	A70	8f brt red	4.00	10
303	A70	16f dk car	4.00	15

8th National Congress of the Communist Party of China.

1956, Nov. 12

304	A71	4f brn, *cr*	5.00	5
305	A71	8f dp bl, *cr*	5.00	70

90th anniversary of birth of Sun Yat-sen.

Weight Lifting
A72

Designs: No. 306, Shot put. No. 308, Track. No. 309, Soccer. No. 310, Bicycling.

1957, Mar. 20 **Litho.** ***Perf. 12½***

Hibiscus red and green; inscription in brown.

306	A72	4f dp car (2)	40	5
307	A72	4f red lil (5)	40	5
308	A72	8f dk bl grn (1)	40	5
309	A72	8f dp bl (3)	40	5
310	A72	8f dp yel brn (4)	40	5
		Nos. 306-310 (5)	2.00	25

First National Workers' Sports Meeting.

Truck Factory No. 1, Changchun
A73

Designs: 8f, Trucks rolling off assembly line.

1957, May 1 **Engraved** ***Perf. 14***

311	A73	4f lt brn	18	5
312	A73	8f sl grn	18	3

China's truck industry.

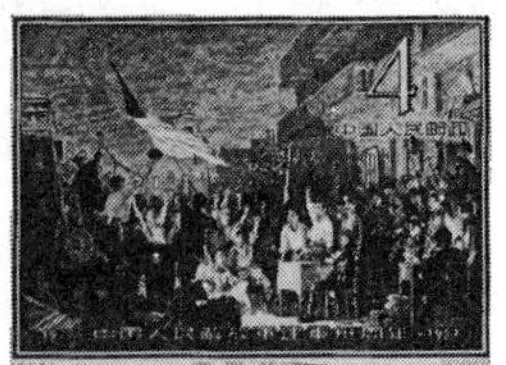

Nanchang Uprising—A74

Designs: No. 314, Mao and Chu Teh at Chingkanshan. No. 315, Crossing Yellow River. No. 316, Liberation of Nanking, Apr. 23, 1949.

1957

313	A74	4f blk vio (1)	6.00	15
314	A74	4f sl grn (2)	6.00	25
315	A74	8f red brn (3)	6.00	10
316	A74	8f dp bl (4)	6.00	10

30th anniversary of People's Liberation Army.

Issue dates: Nos. 313, 315, Aug. 10; No. 314, Aug. 30; No. 316, Dec. 30.

Congress Emblem A75

1957, Sept. 30

317	A75	8f chocolate	4.00	12
318	A75	22f indigo	4.00	12

4th International Trade Union Congress, Leipzig, Oct. 4–15.

Yangtze River Bridge A76

Design: 20f, Road leading to and over bridge.

1957, Oct. 1

319	A76	8f scarlet	40	10
320	A76	20f sl bl	40	5

Completion of Yangtze River Bridge at Wuhan.

Fireworks over Kremlin A77

Designs: 8f, Hammer and sickle over globe and broken chain. 20f, Stylized dove and olive branch. 22f, Hands of three races holding book with Marx and Lenin. 32f, Star and pylon.

1957, Nov. 7

321	A77	4f brt red	5.00	10
322	A77	8f chocolate	5.00	10
323	A77	20f dp grn	6.00	10
324	A77	22f red brn	6.00	10
325	A77	32f dp bl	6.50	35
		Nos. 321-325 (5)	28.50	75

40th anniversary of Russian October Revolution.

Map of Yellow River Basin—A78

Designs: No. 327, Sanmen Gorge dam and powerhouse. No. 328, Ocean liner on Yellow River. No. 329, Dam, irrigation canals and tree-bordered fields.

1957, Dec. 30

326	A78	4f dp org (1)	4.50	15
327	A78	4f dp bl (2)	4.50	50
328	A78	8f dp lake (3)	4.50	10
329	A78	8f bl grn (4)	4.50	10

Yellow River control plan.

Old Man and Young Drummer A79

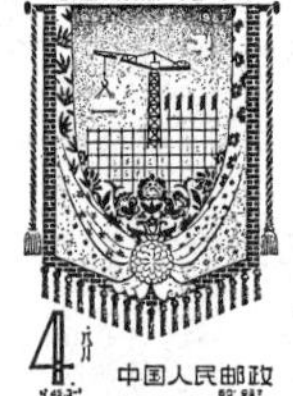

Crane, Dove and Flowers A80

1957, Dec. 30 **Lithographed**

Multicolored

330	A79	8f *shown* (1)	20	5
331	A79	8f *Plowman* (2)	20	5
332	A79	8f *Woman planting tree* (3)	20	5
333	A79	8f *Harvest* (4)	20	5

Agricultural cooperation.

1958, Jan. 30 **Engraved**

Designs (Congratulatory Banner and): 8f, Crane with hot ingots, cotton bolls and wheat. 16f, Train on bridge, ship and plane.

334	A80	4f emer, *cr*	25	5
335	A80	8f red, *cr*	25	5
336	A80	16f ultra, *cr*	25	5

Fulfillment of First Five-Year Plan.

Sungyu Pagoda, Honan A81

Trilobite, Kaoli A82

Ancient Pagodas: No. 338, Chienhsun Pagoda, Yunnan. No. 339, Sakyamuni Pagoda, Shansi. No. 340, Flying Rainbow Pagoda, Shansi.

1958, Mar. 15 **Engraved**

337	A81	8f sep (1)	35	5
338	A81	8f Prus bl (2)	35	5
339	A81	8f mar (3)	35	5
340	A81	8f dp grn (4)	35	5

1958, Apr. 15

Designs: 8f, Lufeng dinosaur. 16f, Choukoutien sino-megaceros.

341	A82	4f black	35	8
342	A82	8f sepia	35	8
343	A82	16f sl grn	35	8

Prehistoric animals of China.

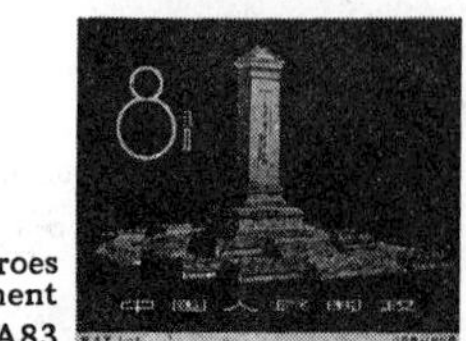

Heroes Monument A83

1958, May 1

344	A83	8f scarlet	12.00	40
a.		Souvenir sheet	12.00	9.00

Unveiling of People's Heroes Monument, Peking. No. 344a contains one imperf. stamp, scarlet marginal inscription. Size: 87x137mm. Issued May 30.

Karl Marx A84

Cogwheels and Factories—A85

Design: 22f, Marx Speaking to German Workers' Educational Association, London, painting by Zhukow.

1958, May 5

345	A84	8f chocolate	8.00	15
346	A84	22f dk grn	8.50	30

140th anniversary of the birth of Karl Marx (1818–1883).

1958, May 25

347	A85	4f brt grnsh bl	8.00	*3.00*
348	A85	8f red lil	8.00	1.00

8th All-China Trade Union Congress, Peking.

Dove over Globe A86

Mother and Child A87

1958, June 1

349	A86	8f vio bl	8.00	10
350	A86	20f bl grn	8.00	1.40

4th Congress of the International Democratic Women's Federation, Vienna, Austria, June 1958.

1958, June 1 **Lithographed**

Designs (Children): No. 352, Watering sunflowers. No. 353, Playing hide-and-seek. No. 354, Sailing toy boat.

351	A87	8f grn & multi (1)	5.00	15
352	A87	8f grn & multi (2)	5.00	15
353	A87	8f grn & multi (3)	5.00	15
354	A87	8f grn & multi (4)	5.00	15

Children's Day.

Kuan Han-ching A88

Designs (Operas): 4f, "Dream of Butterflies." 20f, "The Riverside Pavilion."

1958, June 20 **Engraved**

355	A88	4f ind, *cr*	7.50	*1.00*
356	A88	8f brn, *cr*	7.50	25
357	A88	20f blk, *cr*	10.00	35
a.		Souvenir sheet of 3, *white*	100.00	30.00

700th anniversary of publication of works of Kuan Han-ching (1210–1280), dramatist. No. 357a contains 3 imperf. stamps similar to Nos. 355–357. Dark brown marginal inscription. Size: 130x100mm. Issued June 28.

Planetarium A89

Design: 20f, Telescope and stars over Peking.

1958, June 25

358	A89	8f dk grn	9.00	35
359	A89	20f indigo	9.00	15

First Chinese planetarium, Peking.

Marx and Engels A90

Wild Goose and Broadcasting Tower A91

Design: 8f, Cover of first edition of the Communist Manifesto.

1958, July 1

360	A90	4f dk red vio	6.50	1.50
361	A90	8f Prus bl	6.50	15

110th anniversary of publication of the Communist Manifesto.

1958, July 10

362	A91	4f ultra	6.50	15
363	A91	8f dp grn	6.50	30

1st Conference of the Ministers of Posts and Telecommunications of Socialist Countries, Moscow, Dec. 3–17, 1957.

Peony and Doves A92

Bronze Weather Vane A93

Designs: 8f, Olive branch with ribbon and clouds. 22f, Atomic energy symbol over factories.

1958, July 20

364	A92	4f red	14.00	1.00
365	A92	8f green	14.00	12.00
366	A92	22f red brn	14.00	4.00

Congress for Disarmament and International Cooperation, Stockholm, July 17–22.

1958, Aug. 25

Designs: No. 368, Weather balloon. No. 369, Typhoon tower and weather map of Asia.

367	A93	8f yel bis & blk (1)	25	10
368	A93	8f bl & blk (2)	25	10
369	A93	8f brt grn & blk (3)	25	10

Meteorological services in ancient and modern China.

"5" Encircling IUS Emblem A94

1958, Sept. 4

370	A94	8f rose lil	6.50	15
371	A94	22f dp bl grn	6.50	25

5th Congress of the International Union of Students, Peking, Sept. 4–13.

Telegraph Building, Peking
A95

1958, Sept. 29

372 A95 4f grnsh blk 75 8
373 A95 8f rose red 75 8

Opening of Telegraph Building, Peking.

Exhibition Emblem and Exhortation
A96

Designs: No. 375, Dragon over clouds signifying "aiming high." No. 376, Flying horses, signifying "great leap forward" in production.

1958, Oct. 1

374 A96 8f sl grn (1) 6.75 10
375 A96 8f rose car (2) 6.75 10
376 A96 8f red brn (3) 6.75 10

National Exhibition of Industry and Communications, Peking.

Worker and Excavator
A97

Design: 8f, Completed dam and pylon.

1958, Oct. 25

377 A97 4f dk brn 15 10
378 A97 8f dp Prus bl 25 10

Completion of the 13 Ming Tombs Reservoir.

Sputnik over Armillary Sphere
A98

Designs: 8f, Sputnik 3 in orbit. 10f, Trajectories of 3 Sputniks over earth.

1958, Oct. 30

379 A98 4f scarlet 3.00 15
380 A98 8f dp vio bl 3.00 5
381 A98 10f dp grn 3.00 25

Anniversary of first earth satellite launched by the USSR.

Chinese and North Korean Soldiers
A99

Designs: No. 383, Chinese soldier embracing Korean woman. No. 384, Chinese girl presenting flowers to returning soldier.

1958, Nov. 20

382 A99 8f brt pur (1) 60 10
383 A99 8f chnt (2) 60 10
384 A99 8f rose car (3) 60 10

Return of the Chinese Volunteers from Korea.

Forest and Mountains
A100

Peony
A101

Designs: No. 386, Mounted forest patrol. No. 387, Mechanized lumbering (horiz.). No. 388, Tree-planting: "Turning the Country Green" (horiz.).

1958, Dec. 15

385 A100 8f dp bl grn (1) 75 30
386 A100 8f sl grn (2) 75 10
387 A100 8f dk pur (3) 75 10
388 A100 8f ind (4) 75 20

Afforestation.

1958, Sept. 25 **Lithographed**

Designs: 3f, Lotus. 5f, Chrysanthemums.

389 A101 1½f lil rose 7.00 15
390 A101 3f bl grn 7.00 30
391 A101 5f dp org 7.00 5

Atomic Reactor
A102

Design: 20f, Cyclotron.

1958, Dec. 30 **Engraved**

392 A102 8f dp bl 8.00 15
393 A102 20f dp brn 8.00 *1.00*

Inauguration of China's first atomic reactor and cyclotron, Peking.

Children Launching Model Planes
A103

Camel Carrying Load
A104

Designs: 8f, Gliders over trees. 10f, Parachutists descending. 20f, Small monoplanes in mid-air.

1958, Dec. 30

394 A103 4f carmine 45 10
395 A103 8f dp sl grn 45 5
396 A103 10f dk brn 45 5
397 A103 20f Prus bl 45 5

Sports-aviation publicity.

1959, Jan. 1

Designs: No. 399, Pomegranates. No. 400, Rooster. No. 401, Theatrical figure.

398 A104 8f vio & blk (1) 5.00 5
399 A104 8f dp bl grn & blk (2) 5.00 15
400 A104 8f red & blk (3) 5.00 20
401 A104 8f dp bl & blk (4) 5.00 15

Paper cut-outs (folk art).

Red Flag, Mao and Workers
A105

Women Workers and Atomic Model
A106

Designs: 8f, Traditional and modern blast furnaces. 10f, Steel works and workers.

1959

402 A105 4f brt red 8.00 15
403 A105 8f lake 8.00 15
404 A105 10f dp red 8.00 15

"Great Leap Forward" in steel production.

Issue dates: 4f, 8f, Feb. 19; 10f, May 25.

1959, Mar. 8

Design: 22f, Chinese and Soviet women holding banners dated "3.8".

405 A106 8f emer, *cr* 50 15
406 A106 22f mag, *cr* 50 5

International Women's Day.

Natural History Museum
A107

1959, Apr. 1

407 A107 4f grnsh bl 25 10
408 A107 8f ol brn 25 10

Opening of Museum of Natural History, Peking.

Wheat
A108

Designs on Chinese Flag: No. 410, Rice. No. 411, Cotton bolls. No. 412, Soybeans, rapeseed and peanuts.

1959, Apr. 25

409 A108 8f red (1) 40 10
410 A108 8f red (2) 40 10
411 A108 8f red (3) 40 10
412 A108 8f red (4) 40 10
Block of 4 (Nos. 409-412) 2.50 50

Successful harvest, 1958. Printed se-tenant in blocks of four.

Marx, Lenin and Workers
A109

Designs: 8f, Black, yellow and white fists holding banner. 22f, Steel workers parading with banners dated "5.1."

1959, May 1

413 A109 4f ultra 6.00 15
414 A109 8f red 6.00 5
415 A109 22f emerald 6.00 15

International Labor Day.

Peking Airport
A110

Design: 10f, Plane loading on runway.

1959, June 20

416 A110 8f lil & blk 6.00 10
417 A110 10f ol gray & blk 6.00 10

Opening of new Peking Airport.

Students with Marx-Lenin Banners
A111

Design: 8f, Workers with banners of Mao.

1959, July 1 **Photo.** ***Perf. 11x11½***

418 A111 4f gray, red & dk brn 10.00 2.00
419 A111 8f bis, red & dk brn 10.00 2.00

40th anniversary of the May 4th students' uprising.

Frederick Joliot-Curie
A112

Design: 22f, Three races, dove and olive branch.

1959, July 25 **Engraved** ***Perf. 11½***

420 A112 8f vio brn 7.00 *1.00*
421 A112 22f dk vio 7.00 5

10th anniversary of the World Peace Movement.

Stamp Printing Plant, Peking
A113

1959, Aug. 15 ***Perf. 11x11½***

422 A113 8f dp bl grn 12.50 90

Sino-Czechoslovak cooperation in stamp production.

Table Tennis
A114

1959, Aug. 30 **Litho.** ***Perf. 14***

423 A114 4f blk & bl 75 10
424 A114 8f blk & red 75 5

25th World Table Tennis Championships, Dortmund, German Democratic Republic.

Soviet Space Rocket
A115

1959, Sept. 10 **Photo.** ***Perf. 11½***

425 A115 8f Prus bl, red & blk 17.50 60

Launching of first Russian space rocket, Jan. 2, 1959.

Backyard Steel Production
A116

Mao and Gate of Heavenly Peace
A117

Designs: No. 426, Sun rising over "industry and agriculture." No. 428, Farming. No. 429, Trade. No. 430, Education. No. 431, Militia. No. 432, Communal dining. No. 433, Nursery. No. 434, Care for the aged. No. 435, Health services. No. 436, Flutist; culture and sports. No. 437, Flower symbolizing unity of industry, agriculture, trade, education and armed forces.

Position-in-set number in ( ).

1959, Sept. 25 **Engraved**

426	A116	8f rose (1)	30	8
427	A116	8f vio brn (2)	30	8
428	A116	8f dp org (3)	30	8
429	A116	8f sl grn (4)	30	8
430	A116	8f dp bl (5)	30	8
431	A116	8f ol (6)	30	8
432	A116	8f ind (7)	30	8
433	A116	8f lil rose (8)	30	8
434	A116	8f gray blk (9)	30	8
435	A116	8f emer (10)	30	8
436	A116	8f dk vio (11)	30	8
437	A116	8f red (12)	30	8
		Nos. 426-437 (12)	3.60	96

First anniversary of Peoples' Communes.

1959, Sept. 28 Photo. *Perf. 11½x11*

Designs: 8f, Marx, Lenin and Kremlin. 22f, Dove over globe.

With Gum

438	A117	8f lt brn & red	12.00	3.00
439	A117	8f dl bl & red	10.00	1.00
440	A117	22f bl grn & red	10.00	50

See note after No. 456.

National Emblem A118 — Blast Furnaces A119

1959, Oct. 1 Lithographed *Perf. 14*

441	A118	4f pale grn, red & gold	6.00	3.00
442	A118	8f gray, red & gold	7.00	50
443	A118	10f lt bl, red & gold	7.00	50
444	A118	20f pale brn, red & gold	7.00	2.00

Engraved and Photogravure

1959, Oct. 1 ***Perf. 11½x11***

Designs: No. 446, Large coal mine. No. 447, Planer, Wuhan heavy machinery plant. No. 448, Wuhan Yangtze River Bridge. No. 449, Combine harvester. No. 450, Hsinankiang hydroelectric station. No. 451, Spinning machine. No. 452, Kirin chemical fertilizer plant.

With Gum

445	A119	8f brn & rose red (1)	25	10
446	A119	8f brn & gray (2)	25	10
447	A119	8f brn & yel brn (3)	25	10
448	A119	8f brn & stl bl (4)	25	10
449	A119	8f brn & org (5)	25	10
450	A119	8f brn & ol (6)	25	10
451	A119	8f brn & bl grn (7)	25	15
452	A119	8f brn & vio (8)	25	15
		Nos. 445-452 (8)	2.00	90

Celebration at Gate of Heavenly Peace
A120

Mao Proclaiming Republic—A121

Designs: 10f, Workers and factory (vert.). No. 455, People rejoicing (vert.).

1959, Oct. 1 Lithographed *Perf. 14*

Inscribed: 1949–1959.

453	A120	8f cr & multi	2.00	25
454	A120	10f cr & multi	2.00	25
455	A120	20f cr & multi	2.00	25

Engraved

456	A121	20f dp car	22.50	8.50

Nos. 438–456 commemorate 10th anniversary of the Proclamation of the People's Republic of China.

Pioneer Bugler
A122

Exhibition Emblem, Communications Symbols
A123

Designs: No. 457, Pioneers' emblem. No. 459, Schoolgirl. No. 460, Girl using rain gauge. No. 461, Boy planting tree. No. 462, Girl figure skater.

1959, Nov. 10 Photo. *Perf. 11½*

457	A122	4f red yel & blk (1)	1.50	15
458	A122	4f Prus bl & red (2)	1.50	15
459	A122	8f brn & red (3)	1.50	15
460	A122	8f dk bl & red (4)	1.50	15
461	A122	8f red & grn (5)	1.50	15
462	A122	8f mag & red (6)	1.50	15
		Nos. 457-462 (6)	9.00	90

10th anniversary of the Young Pioneers. Black inscription on No. 457 engraved.

1959, Dec. 1 **Engraved**

Design: 8f, Exhibition emblem and chimneys.

463	A123	4f dk bl	25	8
464	A123	8f red	25	8

Exhibition of Industry and Communications, Peking.

Palace of Nationalities
A124

Engraved, Frame Litho.

1959, Dec. 10 ***Perf. 14***

465	A124	4f red & blk	1.25	10
466	A124	8f brt grn & blk	1.25	10

Inauguration of the Cultural Palace of Nationalities, Peking.

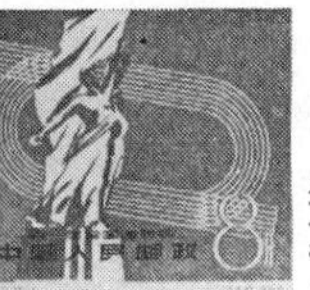

Athletes' Monument and Track
A125

Designs: No. 468, Parachuting. No. 469, Marksmanship. No. 470, Diving. No. 471, Table tennis. No. 472, Weight lifting. No. 473, High jump. No. 474, Rowing. No. 475, Track. No. 476, Basketball. No. 477, Traditional Chinese fencing. No. 478, Motorcycling. No. 479, Gymnastics. No. 480, Bicycling. No. 481, Horsemanship. No. 482, Soccer.

1959, Dec. 28 **Lithographed**

467	A125	8f bis, blk & gray (1)	60	10
468	A125	8f dl bl, blk & gray (2)	60	10
469	A125	8f red brn & blk (3)	60	10
470	A125	8f grn, blk & brn (4)	60	10
471	A125	8f brt grn, blk, brn & gray (5)	60	10
472	A125	8f gray, blk & brn (6)	60	10
473	A125	8f dl bl, blk & brn (7)	60	10
474	A125	8f Prus grn, blk & brn (8)	60	10
475	A125	8f org, blk & brn (9)	60	10
476	A125	8f dl vio, blk & brn (10)	60	10
477	A125	8f lt ol, blk & brn (11)	60	10
478	A125	8f bl, blk & gray (12)	60	10
479	A125	8f gray bl, blk, brn, & bl (13)	60	10
480	A125	8f gray, blk, brn, & vio (14)	60	10
481	A125	8f red org, blk, brn, & gray (15)	60	10
482	A125	8f lt gray, blk, brn, & red (16)	60	10
		Nos. 467-482 (16)	9.60	1.60

First National Sports Meeting, Peking.

Wheat and Main Pavilion
A126

Designs (Pavilion and): 8f, Meteorological symbols. 10f, Domestic animals. 20f, Fish.

1960, Jan. 20 **Engr. and Litho.**

Cream Background

483	A126	4f blk & org	25	10
484	A126	8f blk & dl bl	25	10
485	A126	10f blk & org brn	25	10
486	A126	20f blk & grnsh bl	25	20

Opening of the National Agricultural Exhibition Halls, Peking.

With Gum

From No. 487 onward all stamps were issued with gum except as noted.

Conference Hall, Tsunyi
A127

Designs: 8f, Mao addressing conference. 10f, Crossing Chinsha River.

Engr. (4f, 10f); Photo. (8f)

1960, Jan. 25 ***Perf. 11x11½***

487	A127	4f vio & bl	10.00	1.00
488	A127	8f red & multi	10.00	*5.00*
489	A127	10f sl grn	10.00	2.00

25th anniversary of the Communist Party Conference at Tsunyi.

Clara Zetkin (1857–1933)
A128

Chinese and Russian Workers
A129

Designs: 8f, Mother, child and dove. 10f, Woman tractor driver. 22f, Women of three races.

1960, Mar. 8 Photo. *Perf. 11½x11*

490	A128	4f blk & multi	75	75
491	A128	8f blk & multi	75	75
492	A128	10f blk & multi	75	75
493	A128	22f blk & multi	75	75

50th anniversary of International Women's Day.

1960, Mar. 10

Designs: 8f, Chinese and Russian flags. 10f, Chinese and Russian soldiers.

494	A129	4f dk brn	10.00	1.50
495	A129	8f red, yel & blk	10.00	1.50
496	A129	10f dp bl	12.00	5.00

10th anniversary of Sino-Soviet Treaty of Friendship. Black inscription engraved on No. 495.

Flags of Hungary and China
A130

Design: 8f, Parliament Building, Budapest.

1960, Apr. 4 ***Perf. 11x11½***

497	A130	8f yel, blk, red & grn	10.00	1.00
498	A130	8f bl, red & blk	10.00	4.00

15th anniversary of the liberation of Hungary.

Lenin Speaking
A131

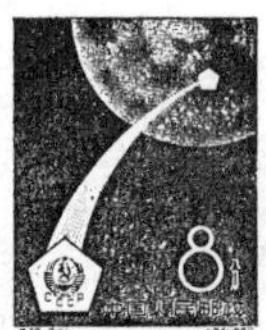

Lunik 2, Earth and Russian Arms
A132

Designs: 8f, Portrait of Lenin. 20f, Lenin talking with Smolny Palace guard.

Engr. (4f, 20f); Engr. & Photo. (8f).

1960, April 22 ***Perf. 11½x11***

499	A131	4f vio brn	10.00	2.00
500	A131	8f org red & blk	10.00	2.00
501	A131	20f dk brn	10.00	2.00

90th anniversary of the birth of Lenin.

1960, Apr. 30 Engraved *Perf. 11½*

Design: 10f, Lunik 3 over earth.

502	A132	8f red	3.00	15
503	A132	10f green	3.00	15

Russian space flights.

Pioneers and Flags of Czechoslovakia and China
A133

View of Prague with Charles Bridge
A134

Perf. 11½x11; 11x11½

1960, May 9 Photogravure

504	A133	8f yel & multi	9.00	2.50
505	A134	8f dp grn	9.00	1.50

15th anniversary of the liberation of Czechoslovakia.

Nostril Bouquet
A135

Designs: Various goldfish.
Position-in-set number in ( ).

1960, June 1 *Perf. 11x11½*

Multicolored

506	A135	4f *shown* (1)	7.50	50
507	A135	4f *Black-back dragon eye* (2)	7.50	50
508	A135	4f *Bubble eye* (3)	7.50	50
509	A135	4f *Red tiger head* (4)	7.50	50
510	A135	8f *Pearl scale* (5)	7.50	50
511	A135	8f *Blue dragon eye* (6)	7.50	50
512	A135	8f *Skyward eye* (7)	7.50	50
513	A135	8f *Red cap*(8)	7.50	50
514	A135	8f *Purple cap* (9)	7.50	4.00
515	A135	8f *Red head* (10)	7.50	4.00
516	A135	8f *Red and white dragon eye* (11)	7.50	4.00
517	A135	8f *Red dragon eye* (12)	7.50	4.00
		Nos. 506-517 (12)	90.00	20.00

Sow with Litter
A136

Designs: No. 519, Pig being inoculated. No. 520, Pigs. No. 521, Pig and mechanized feeding. No. 522, Pig and bales.

1960, June 15

518	A136	8f red & blk (1)	5.50	50
519	A136	8f dp grn & blk (2)	5.50	50
520	A136	8f lil rose & blk (3)	5.50	50
521	A136	8f lt yel grn & blk (4)	5.50	50
522	A136	8f org & blk (5)	5.50	1.25
		Nos. 518-522 (5)	27.50	3.25

Flag Inscribed "Serving the Workers"
A137

Flowers, Flags of North Korea and China
A138

Design: 8f, Inscribed stone seal.

Photogravure

1960, July 30 *Perf. 11½x11*

523	A137	4f lt grn, red, pink & brn	9.00	2.50

Engraved and Photogravure

524	A137	8f pale bl, red & bis	9.00	2.50

3rd National Congress for Literature and Arts, Peking.

1960, Aug. 15 Photogravure

Design: 8f, Flying horse of Korea.

525	A138	8f red & multi	9.00	2.50
526	A138	8f ultra, red & ind	9.00	2.50

15th anniversary of the liberation of Korea.

Railroad Station, Peking—A139

Design: 10f, Train arriving at station.

1960, Aug. 30 *Perf. 11½*

527	A139	8f bl, cr & brn	5.00	2.00
528	A139	10f bluish grn, cr & ind	5.00	2.00

Opening of new Peking Railroad Station.

Girls and Flags of North Viet Nam and China
A140

Lake of the Returning Sword, Hanoi
A141

Worker and Fresh-air Installation
A142

1960, Sept. 2 *Perf. 11x11½, 11½x11*

529	A140	8f red & multi	2.50	60
530	A141	8f red, gray grn & gray	2.50	40

15th anniversary of the Democratic Republic of North Viet Nam.

1960, Sept. 10 *Perf. 11½*

Designs: No. 532, Exterminator. No. 533, Window cleaning. No. 534, Medical examination of child. No. 535, Physical exercise.

531	A142	8f blk & org (1)	75	10
532	A142	8f ind & sl (2)	75	15
533	A142	8f brn & bl (3)	75	20
534	A142	8f mar & ocher (4)	75	30
535	A142	8f ind & brt grn (5)	75	25
		Nos. 531-535 (5)	3.75	1.00

National health campaign.

Great Hall of the People—A143

Design: 10fr, Inside view.

1960, Oct. 1

536	A143	8f yel & multi	5.50	2.50
537	A143	10f brn & multi	5.50	2.50

Completion of the Great Hall of the People, Peking.

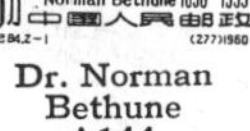

Dr. Norman Bethune
A144

Engels Addressing Congress at The Hague—A145

Design: No. 539, Dr. Bethune operating on a soldier.

Photo. (No. 538); Engr. (No. 539)

1960, Nov. 20 *Perf. 11½x11*

538	A144	8f red & multi	1.25	15
539	A144	8f sepia	1.25	15

Dr. Norman Bethune (1890-1939), Canadian surgeon with 8th Army.

Engr. (No. 540); Photo. (No. 541).

1960, Nov. 28

Designs: 10f, Portrait of Engels.

540	A145	8f brown	12.00	4.00
541	A145	10f bl & multi	12.00	4.00

140th anniversary of the birth of Friedrich Engels (1820-1895), German Socialist.

"Hwang Shi Ba"
A146

Freighter
A147

1960-61 Photogravure

Various Chrysanthemums in Natural Colors.

542	A146	4f bl gray (1)	5.00	60
543	A146	4f pink (2)	5.00	60
544	A146	8f dk gray (3)	5.00	60
545	A146	8f dp bl (4)	5.00	60
546	A146	8f grn (5)	5.00	60
547	A146	8f mag (6)	5.00	60
548	A146	8f ol (7)	5.00	60
549	A146	8f grnsh bl (8)	5.00	60
550	A146	10f gray (9)	5.00	60
551	A146	10f choc (10)	5.00	60
552	A146	20f dp bl (11)	5.00	60
553	A146	20f brt red (12)	5.00	60
554	A146	22f ol bis (13)	5.00	60
555	A146	22f car (14)	5.00	60
556	A146	30f grnsh gray (15)	5.00	60
557	A146	30f brt pink (16)	5.00	60
558	A146	35f dp grn (17)	5.00	60
559	A146	52f brt lil rose (18)	5.00	60
		Nos. 542-559 (18)	85.00	10.20

Issue dates: Nos. 548-550, 557-559, Dec. 10, 1960; Nos. 545-547, 554-556, Jan. 18, 1961; Nos. 542-544, Feb. 24, 1961.

1960, Dec. 15 *Perf. 11½*

Without Gum

560	A147	8f dp bl	8.00	1.25

Launching of first 10,000-ton Chinese-built freighter.

Pantheon, Paris
A148

Design: 8f, Proclamation of the Commune.

Engraved and Photogravure

1961, Mar. 18 *Perf. 11½x11*

561	A148	8f gray blk & red	4.00	1.00
562	A148	8f brn & red	4.00	1.00

90th anniversary of the Paris Commune.

Championship Symbol and Jasmine—A149

Designs: 10f, Table tennis racket and ball; Temple of Heaven. 20f, Table tennis match. 22f, Peking workers' gymnasium.

1961, Apr. 5 Photo. *Perf. 11*

563	A149	8f multi	60	15
564	A149	10f multi	60	10
565	A149	20f multi	60	10
566	A149	22f multi	60	25
a.		Souv. sheet of 4	90.00	75.00

26th World Table Tennis Championships, Peking. No. 566a contains one each of Nos. 563-566. Red and bister marginal inscription and decoration. Size: 150x100 mm.

Jeme Tien-yow
A150

Design: 10f, Train and tunnel, Peking-Changchow Railroad.

1961, June 20 *Perf. 11½x11*

567	A150	8f ol grn & blk	1.20	10
568	A150	10f org brn & brn	1.20	10

Centenary of the birth of Jeme Tien-yow, railroad construction engineer.

Congress Building, Shanghai—A151

Designs: 8f, August 1st Building, Nanchang. 10f, Provisional Central Government Office, Juikin. 20f, Pagoda Hill, Yenan. 30f, Gate of Heavenly Peace, Peking.

1961, July 1 ***Perf. 11½***

569	A151	4f gold, red & cl	7.50	25
570	A151	8f gold, red & bl grn	7.50	25
571	A151	10f gold, red & yel brn	7.50	50
572	A151	20f gold, red & ultra	7.50	25
573	A151	30f gold, red & org red	7.50	30
		Nos. 569-573 (5)	37.50	1.55

40th anniversary of the Chinese Communist Party.

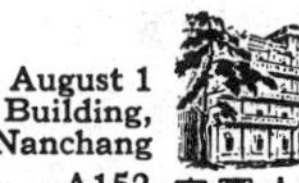

August 1 Building, Nanchang
A152

Designs: 1½f, 2f, as 1f. 3f, 4f, 5f, Trees and Sha Cho Pa Building, Juikin. 8f, 10f, 20f, Pagoda Hill, Yenan. 22f, 30f, 1059–1064.

1961–62 **Engraved** ***Perf. 11***
Without Gum
Size: 24x16mm

574	A152	1f vio bl	1.25	10
575	A152	1½f maroon	1.25	10
576	A152	2f indigo	1.25	10
577	A152	3f dl vio	1.25	10
578	A152	4f green	1.25	10
579	A152	5f gray	1.25	25
580	A152	8f sepia	1.25	5
581	A152	10f brt lil rose	1.25	5
582	A152	20f grnsh bl	1.25	5
583	A152	22f brown	1.25	5
584	A152	30f blue	1.25	5
585	A152	50f vermilion	1.25	5
		Nos. 574-585 (12)	15.00	1.05

Issue dates: 1f, 1½f, 5f, July 20, 1962; others July 20, 1961. See Nos. 647–654, 1059–1064.

Flowers, Flags of Mongolia and China
A153

Design: 10f, Parliament, Ulan Bator, and statue of Sukhe Bator.

1961, July 11 **Photo.** ***Perf. 11x11½***

586	A153	8f crim, ultra & yel	9.00	1.00
587	A153	10f org, blk & yel	9.00	*5.00*

40th anniversary of the Mongolian People's Republic.

Military Museum—A154

1961, Aug. 1 ***Perf. 11½***
Engraved and Photogravure

588	A154	8f gray bl, brn & grn	8.50	15
589	A154	10f gray, blk & grn	8.50	15

Opening of the People's Revolutionary Military Museum.

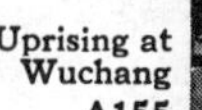

Uprising at Wuchang
A155

Sun Yat-sen
A156

Perf. 11x11½, 11½x11

1961, Oct. 10 **Photogravure**

590	A155	8f gray & blk	8.50	*1.75*
591	A156	10f tan & blk	8.50	25

50th anniversary of the 1911 Revolution.

Donkey **A157** **Rejoicing Tibetans** **A158**

Designs: 8f, 10f, 20f, 22f, Horses; 30f, 50f, Camels. Ceramic statuettes from Tang Dynasty (618–906) graves.

1961, Nov. 10 ***Perf. 11½x11***
Statuettes in Original Colors

592	A157	4f dl bl	1.00	25
593	A157	8f gray grn	1.00	25
594	A157	8f dp pur	1.00	25
595	A157	10f dp bl	1.00	20
596	A157	20f olive	1.00	25
597	A157	22f bl grn	1.00	10
598	A157	30f red brn	1.00	25
599	A157	50f slate	1.00	25
		Nos. 592-599 (8)	8.00	1.80

1961, Nov. 25

Designs: 8f, Woman sower. 10f, Celebration of bumper crop. 20f, People's representatives. 30f, Tibetan children.

600	A158	4f brn & ocher	10.00	5
601	A158	8f brn & lt bl grn	10.00	20
602	A158	10f brn & yel	10.00	5
603	A158	20f brn & rose	10.00	65
604	A158	30f brn & bluish gray	10.00	65
		Nos. 600-604 (5)	50.00	1.60

Rebirth of the Tibetan people.

Lu Hsun
A159

1962, Feb. 26

605	A159	8f red brn & blk	35	15

80th anniversary of the birth of Lu Hsun, writer.

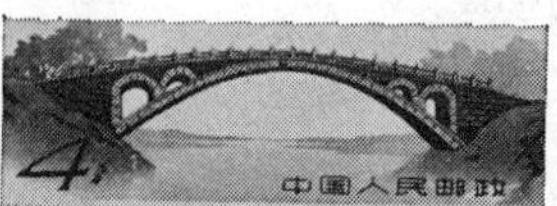

An Chi Bridge, Chao Hsien—A160

Bridges of Ancient China: 8f, Pao Tai, Soochow. 10f, Chu Pu, Kwan Hsien. 20f, Chen Yang, San Kiang.

1962, May 15 ***Perf. 11***

606	A160	4f dk gray bl	60	10
607	A160	8f dp grn	60	10
608	A160	10f brown	60	5
609	A160	20f grnsh bl	60	45

Tu Fu **A161** **Cranes and Bamboo** **A162**

Design: 4f, Tu Fu memorial pavilion, Chengtu.

1962, May 25 ***Perf. 11½x11***

610	A161	4f ol bis & blk	10.00	10
611	A161	8f grnsh bl & blk	10.00	10

Poet Tu Fu, 1,250th anniversary of birth.

1962, June 10

Designs: 10f, Two cranes in flight. 20f, Crane on rock.

612	A162	8f tan & multi	4.00	50
613	A162	10f bl & multi	4.00	40
614	A162	20f bis & multi	4.00	50

"The Sacred Crane," from paintings by Chen Chi-fo.

Cuban Soldier and Flag
A163

Designs: 10f, Sugar cane worker. 22f, Militiaman and woman.

1962, July 10 ***Perf. 11x11½***

615	A163	8f car, rose & blk	10.00	1.50
616	A163	10f grn & blk	10.00	50
617	A163	22f ultra & blk	10.00	6.00

Support of Cuba.

Torch and Map of Algeria **A164** **Mei Lan-fang** **A165**

Design: 22f, Algerian soldiers and flag.

1962, July 10 ***Perf. 11½x11***

618	A164	8f dp brn & red org	45	20
619	A164	22f ocher & dp brn	45	30

Support of Algeria.

1962 ***Perf. 11½x11, 11x11½***

Designs (Mei Lan-fang in Women's Roles): No. 621, Beating drum. No. 622, With fan. 10f, Lady Yu with swords. 20f, With bag. 22f, Heavenly Maiden (horiz.). 30f, With spinning wheel (horiz.). 50f, Kneeling (horiz.). $3, Scene from opera "Drunken Beauty."

620	A165	4f tan & multi	9.00	1.00
621	A165	8f tan & multi	9.00	1.00
622	A165	8f gray & multi	9.00	10
623	A165	10f gray & multi	9.00	1.00
624	A165	20f lt grn & multi	9.00	50
625	A165	22f cr & multi	9.00	4.00
626	A165	30f lt bl & multi	9.00	5.00
627	A165	50f buff & multi	9.00	6.00
		Nos. 620-627 (8)	72.00	18.60

Souvenir Sheet
Perf. 11

628	A165	$3 brn & multi	450.00	325.00

Stage art of Mei Lan-fang, actor.

Issue dates: 4f, 8f, 10f, Aug. 8; $3, Sept. 15; others Sept. 1. Imperfs. exist. *Price, set $200.*

No. 628 contains one stamp (48x58mm); Prussian blue margin with white ornamental design. Size: 108x147mm.

Flower Drum Dance, Han
A166

Folk Dances: 8f, Ordos, Mongolia. 10f, Catching shrimp, Chuang. 20f, Friend, Yi. 30f, Fiddle dance, Tibet. 50f, Tambourine dance, Uighur.

Cumulative numbers 246–251 at lower right.

1962, Oct. 15 **Litho.** ***Perf. 12½***
Without Gum

629	A166	4f cr & multi	40	5
630	A166	8f cr & multi	40	5
631	A166	10f cr & multi	40	10
632	A166	20f cr & multi	40	40
633	A166	30f cr & multi	40	30
634	A166	50f cr & multi	40	40
		Nos. 629-634 (6)	2.40	1.30

See Nos. 696–707.

Soldiers Storming Winter Palace—A167

Design: 8f, Lenin leading soldiers (vert.).

1962, Nov. 7 **Photo.** ***Perf. 11½***

635	A167	8f blk & red	13.00	20
636	A167	20f sl grn & red	13.00	60

45th anniversary of the Russian Revolution.

Monument and Map of Albania **A168** **Tsai Lun, Inventor of Papermaking** **A169**

Design: 10f, Albanian flag and Girl Pioneer.

1962, Nov. 28 ***Perf. 11½x11***

637	A168	8f Prus bl & sep	1.00	30
638	A168	10f red, yel, & blk	1.00	30

50th anniversary of Albanian independence.

1962, Dec. 1 ***Perf. 11½x11***

Designs: No. 640, Paper making. No. 641, Sun Szu-miao, physician. No. 642, Writing medical treatise. No. 643, Shen Ko, geologist. No. 644, Making field notes. No. 645, Kuo Shou-chin, astronomer. No. 646, Astronomical instrument.

Cumulative numbers 297–304 at lower right.

639	A169	4f multi	40	20
640	A169	4f multi	40	10
641	A169	8f multi	40	15
642	A169	8f multi	40	20
643	A169	10f multi	40	10
644	A169	10f multi	40	25
645	A169	20f multi	40	25
646	A169	20f multi	40	25
		Nos. 639-646 (8)	3.20	1.50

Scientists of ancient China.

Building Type of 1961

Designs: 1f, 2f, Building, Nanchang. 3f, 4f, Trees and Sha Cho Pa Building. 8f, 10f, 20f, Pagoda Hill, Yenan. 30f, Gate of Heavenly Peace, Peking.

Rough Perf. 12½

1962, Jan. **Lithographed**

Size: 21x16mm.

647	A152	1f ultra	35	10
648	A152	2f grnsh gray	35	10
649	A152	3f vio gray	35	10
650	A152	4f green	35	10
651	A152	8f dk ol, perf. 14	35	10
a.		Perf. 12½		50
652	A152	10f brt rose lil	35	10
653	A152	20f sl bl	35	10
654	A152	30f dl bl	35	10
		Nos. 647-654 (8)	2.80	80

Tank Monument, Havana
A170

Crowd in Havana—A171

Designs: No. 656, Cuban revolutionaries. No. 658, Crowd in Peking. No. 659, Cuban soldier. No. 660, Castro and Cuban flag.

Perf. 11½, 11x11½

1963, Jan. 1 **Photogravure**

655	A170	4f red & blk brn	8.50	15
656	A170	4f grn & blk	8.50	15
657	A171	8f dl red & brn	8.50	1.00
658	A171	8f dl red & brn	8.50	20
659	A170	10f ocher & blk	8.50	3.00
660	A170	10f red, bl & blk	8.50	*6.00*
		Nos. 655-660 (6)	51.00	*10.50*

4th anniversary of the Cuban revolution.

Green Dragontail
A172

Karl Marx
A173

Position-in-set number in ( ).

1963 **Without Gum** ***Perf. 11***

Butterflies in Natural Colors.

661	A172	4f *Tibetan clouded yel* (1)	1.25	15
662	A172	4f *Tritailed glory* (2)	1.25	15
663	A172	4f *Neumogeni jungle queen* (3)	1.25	15
664	A172	4f *Washan swordtail* (4)	1.25	40
665	A172	4f *Striped ringlet* (5)	1.25	15
666	A172	8f *shown* (6)	1.25	10
667	A172	8f *Dilunulated peacock* (7)	1.25	15
668	A172	8f *Yamfly* (8)	1.25	5
669	A172	8f *Golden kaiser-i-hind* (9)	1.25	5
670	A172	8f *Mushaell hairstreak* (10)	1.25	5
671	A172	10f *Yellow orange-tip* (11)	1.25	5
672	A172	10f *Great jay* (12)	1.25	10
673	A172	10f *Striped punch* (13)	1.25	5
674	A172	10f *Hainan violet-beak* (14)	1.25	5
675	A172	10f *Omeiskipper* (15)	1.25	5
676	A172	20f *Philippines birdwing* (16)	1.25	15
677	A172	20f *Richtofenis red apollo* (17)	1.25	15
678	A172	22f *Blue-banded king crow* (18)	1.25	20
679	A172	30f *Solskyi copper* (19)	1.25	35
680	A172	50f *Yunnan clipper* (20)	1.25	60
		Nos. 661-680 (20)	25.00	3.15

Issue dates: Nos. 666–675, July 15; others Apr. 5.

1963, May 5 ***Perf. 11½***

Designs: No. 682, "Workers of the World, Unite" on cover of first edition of Communist Manifesto. No. 683, Marx and Engels.

Without Gum

681	A173	8f blk, gold & sal (1)	8.75	3.00
682	A173	8f gold & red (2)	8.75	3.00
683	A173	8f gold & choc (3)	8.75	3.00

145th anniversary of birth of Karl Marx (1818–1883), German political philosopher.

Child with Top
A174

Designs (Child): No. 685, eating berries. No. 686, as traffic policeman. No. 687, with windmill. No. 688, listening to caged cricket. No. 689, with sword. No. 690, embroidering. No. 691, with umbrella. No. 692, playing with sand. No. 693, playing table tennis. No. 694, learning to add. No. 695, with kite.

1963, June 1 **Litho.** ***Perf. 12½***

Without Gum

Multicolored Designs

684	A174	4f grnsh gray (1)	45	5
685	A174	4f tan (2)	45	5
686	A174	8f gray (3)	45	5
687	A174	8f bl (4)	45	5
688	A174	8f tan (5)	45	5
689	A174	8f dp gray (6)	45	5
690	A174	8f cit (7)	45	5
691	A174	8f gray (8)	45	5
692	A174	10f grn (9)	45	15
693	A174	10f vio (10)	45	15
694	A174	20f bis (11)	45	40
695	A174	20f grn (12)	45	40
		Nos. 684-695 (12)	5.40	1.50

Children's Day.
Price, imperf set $9.

Dance Type of 1962

Folk Dances: 4f, Weavers' dance, Puyi. 8f, Kazakh. 10f, Olunchun. 20f, Labor dance, Kaochan. 30f, Reed pipe dance, Miao. 50f, Fan dance, Korea.

Cumulative numbers 261–266 at lower right.

1963, June 15 ***Perf. 12½***

Without Gum

696	A166	4f cr & multi	40	5
697	A166	8f cr & multi	40	5
698	A166	10f cr & multi	40	10
699	A166	20f cr & multi	40	25
700	A166	30f cr & multi	40	30
701	A166	50f cr & multi	40	50
		Nos. 696-701 (6)	2.40	1.25

1963, June 30 **Without Gum**

Folk Dances: 4f, "Wedding Ceremony," Yu. 8f, "Encircling Mountain Forest," Pai. 10f, Long drum dance, Yao. 20f, Third day of the third month dance, Li. 30f, Knife dance, Kawa. 50f, Peacock dance, Thai.

Cumulative numbers 279–284 at lower right.

702	A166	4f cr & multi	40	5
703	A166	8f cr & multi	40	5
704	A166	10f cr & multi	40	10
705	A166	20f cr & multi	40	30
706	A166	30f cr & multi	40	30
707	A166	50f cr & multi	40	40
		Nos. 702-707 (6)	2.40	1.20

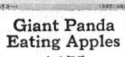

Giant Panda Eating Apples
A175

Table Tennis Player
A176

Designs: No. 709, Giant panda eating bamboo shoots. 10f, Two pandas (horiz.).

1963, Aug. 5 **Photo.** ***Perf. 11½x11***

Size: 28x38mm.

708	A175	8f pale bl & blk	3.00	15
709	A175	8f pale bl & blk	3.00	1.25

Size: 50x29mm. ***Perf. 11½***

710	A175	10f ol & blk	3.00	10

Price, imperf set $12.

1963, Sept. 10 **Engr.** ***Perf. 11½***

Design: No. 712, Trophies won by Chinese team.

711	A176	8f dk ol grn	8.00	30
712	A176	8f brown	8.00	5

27th World Table Tennis Championships.

Snub-nosed Langur
A177

Jade-green Screen Mountain
A178

Designs: 10f, Two monkeys playing. 22f, Two monkeys grooming.

Photogravure

1963, Sept. 23 ***Perf. 11½x11***

713	A177	8f gray & multi	1.00	10
714	A177	10f gray & multi	1.00	10
715	A177	22f gray & multi	1.00	30

Price, imperf set $8.

Engraved and Photogravure

1963, Oct. 15 ***Perf. 11½***

Hwang Shan Landscapes (Yellow Mountains), Anhwei Province. Nos. 724–731 horizontal.

Multicolored

716	A178	4f *shown* (1)	1.50	20
717	A178	4f *'Guests Welcoming Pines'* (2)	1.50	35
718	A178	4f *Pines and Rock Behind the Sea* (3)	1.25	25
719	A178	4f *Terrace of Keeping Cool* (4)	1.25	10
720	A178	8f *Mount of Heavenly Capital* (5)	1.50	20
721	A178	8f *Mount of Scissors* (6)	1.50	20
722	A178	8f *Forest of Ten Thousand Pines* (7)	1.50	20
723	A178	8f *'Brush Blooming in Dream'* (8)	1.50	20
724	A178	10f *Mount of Lotus Flower* (9)	1.50	20
725	A178	10f *Cumulus Cloud over West Sea* (10)	1.50	20
726	A178	10f *Old Pines of Hwang Shan* (11)	1.50	20
727	A178	10f *'Watching the Clouds over West Sea'*	1.25	10
728	A178	20f *Mount of Stalagmites* (13)	1.50	30
729	A178	22f *'Stone Monkey Watching the Sea'* (14)	1.50	25
730	A178	30f *Forest of Lions* (15)	1.50	*3.00*
731	A178	50f *Three Fairy Tales of Pen Lai* (16)	1.50	20
		Nos. 716-731 (16)	23.25	*6.15*

Soccer Player
A179

Athletes and Banners—A180

Designs: No. 733, Discus, women's. No. 734, Diving, men's. No. 735, Gymnastics, women's.

Engraved and Photogravure

1963, Nov. 17 ***Perf. 11***

732	A179	8f gray, red & blk (1)	6.75	20
733	A179	8f gray, ultra & blk (2)	6.75	10
734	A179	8f lt grn, brn & blk (3)	6.75	10
735	A179	8f gray, lil rose & blk (4)	6.75	10

Photogravure ***Perf. 11½***

736	A180	10f red & multi (5)	6.75	30
		Nos. 732-736 (5)	33.75	80

Games of the Newly Emerging Forces, Djakarta.

Clay Rooster and Goat
A181

Chinese Folk Toys: No. 738, Cloth camel. No. 739, Cloth tigers. No. 740, Clay ox and rider. No. 741, Cloth rabbit, wooden doll, clay roosters. No. 742, Straw rooster. No. 743, Cloth donkey and bird. No. 744, Clay lion. No. 745, Cloth tiger and tumbler doll.

1963, Dec. 10 Litho. *Perf. 11½*
Toys Multicolored; Without Gum

737	A181	4f bis (1)	25	8
738	A181	4f gray (4)	25	8
739	A181	4f lt bl (7)	25	8
740	A181	8f bis (2)	25	8
741	A181	8f gray (5)	25	8
742	A181	8f lt bl (8)	25	8
743	A181	10f bis (3)	25	8
744	A181	10f gray (6)	25	8
745	A181	10f lt bl (9)	25	8
		Nos. 737-745 (9)	2.25	72

Armed Vietnamese Family
A182

Flags of Cuba and China
A183

Design: No. 747, Militia with Vietnamese flag.

Photogravure

1963, Dec. 20 *Perf. 11½x11*

746	A182	8f tan, blk & red	1.50	15
747	A182	8f red & multi	1.50	25

Liberation of South Viet Nam.

1964, Jan. 1

Design: No. 749, Boy waving Cuban flag.

748	A183	8f red, yel, bl & ind	10.00	1.00
749	A183	8f multi	10.00	3.00

5th anniversary of the liberation of Cuba.

Woman Driving Tractor
A184

Women of the People's Commune: No. 751, harvesting. No. 752, picking cotton. No. 753, picking fruit. No. 754, reading book. No. 755, on guard duty.

1964, Mar. 8

750	A184	8f ol, pink & brn (1)	30	10
751	A184	8f brn yel & org (2)	30	10
752	A184	8f gray & multi (3)	30	10
753	A184	8f blk, org & bl (4)	30	10
754	A184	8f grn & multi (5)	30	10
755	A184	8f lil & multi (6)	30	10
		Nos. 750-755 (6)	1.80	60

Helpful notes abound in the "Information for Collectors" section at the front of this volume.

Chinese and African Men
A185

Design: No. 757, African drummer.

1964, Apr. 12 Photo. *Perf. 11*

756	A185	8f red & multi	25	10
757	A185	8f blk & dk brn	25	10

African Freedom Day.

Marx, Engels, Lenin and Stalin
A186

Design: No. 759, Banners and workers.

1964, May 1 *Perf. 11½*

758	A186	8f gold, red & blk	15.00	*5.00*
759	A186	8f gold, red & blk	15.00	*4.00*

Labor Day.

Orchard, Yenan
A187

Yenan, Shrine of the Chinese Revolution: No. 761, Central Auditorium, Yang Chia Ling. No. 762, Mao's office and residence. No. 763, Auditorium, Wang Chia Ping. No. 764, Border Region Assembly Hall. No. 765, Pagoda Hill and Bridge.

1964, July 1 Photo. *Perf. 11x11½*

760	A187	8f multi (1)	1.50	20
761	A187	8f multi (2)	1.50	20
762	A187	8f multi (3)	1.50	20
763	A187	8f multi (4)	1.50	20
764	A187	8f multi (5)	1.50	20
765	A187	52f multi (6)	1.50	85
		Nos. 760-765 (6)	9.00	1.85

Map and Flag of Viet Nam
A188

Alchemist's Glowing Crucible
A189

1964, July 20 *Perf. 11½*

766	A188	8f multi	18.00	1.00

Victory in South Viet Nam.

1964, Aug. 5 *Perf. 11½x11*

Position-in-set number in ( ).

Peonies in Natural Colors

767	A189	4f *shown* (1)	1.50	10
768	A189	4f *Night-shining jade* (2)	1.50	10
769	A189	8f *Pur. Kuo's cap* (3)	1.50	5
770	A189	8f *Chao pink* (4)	1.50	5
771	A189	8f *Yao yel* (5)	1.50	10
772	A189	8f *Twin beauty* (6)	1.50	5
773	A189	8f *Ice-veiled ruby* (7)	1.50	5
774	A189	10f *Gold-sprinkled Chinese ink* (8)	1.50	8
775	A189	10f *Cinnabar jar* (9)	1.50	8
776	A189	10f *Lan Tien jade* (10)	1.50	5
777	A189	10f *Imperial robe yel* (11)	1.50	8
778	A189	10f *Hu red* (12)	1.50	8
779	A189	20f *Pea green* (13)	1.50	1.50
780	A189	43f *Wei purple* (14)	1.50	1.50
781	A189	52f *Intoxicated celestial peach* (15)	1.50	1.50
		Nos. 767-781 (15)	22.50	5.37

Souvenir Sheet
Perf. 11½
Without Gum

782	A189	$2 *Glorious crimson & great gold pink*	80.00	50.00

No. 782 contains one stamp (48x59mm.). Bluish gray and silver border. Size: 77x136mm.

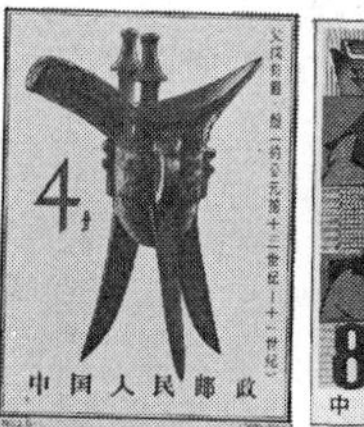

Wine Cup
A190

Grain Harvest
A191

Designs: Sacrificial bronze vessels of Yin dynasty, prior to 1050 B.C.

Engraved and Photogravure

1964, Aug. 25 *Perf. 11½x11*

Frames & Inscriptions Black, Vessels Multicolored

783	A190	4f *shown* (1)	1.00	60
784	A190	4f *Ku beaker* (2)	1.00	60
785	A190	8f *Kuang wine urn* (3)	1.00	8
786	A190	8f *Chia wine cup* (4)	1.00	8
787	A190	10f *Tsun wine vessel* (5)	1.00	10
788	A190	10f *Yu wine urn* (6)	1.00	10
789	A190	20f *Tsun wine vessel* (7)	1.00	20
790	A190	20f *Ceremonial cauldron* (8)	1.00	20
		Nos. 783-790 (8)	8.00	1.96

1964, Sept. 26 Photogravure

Designs: No. 792, Students planting trees. No. 793, Study period. No. 794, Scientific experimentation.

791	A191	8f multi (1)	40	10
792	A191	8f multi (2)	40	10
793	A191	8f multi (3)	40	10
794	A191	8f multi (4)	40	10

Youth helping in agriculture.

Marx, Engels, Trafalgar Square, London
A192

People with Banners
A193

1964, Sept. 28 *Perf. 11½*

795	A192	8f red, gold & red brn	37.50	18.50

Centenary of the First International.

1964, Oct. 1

Designs: No. 797, Gate of Heavenly Peace and Chinese flag. No. 798, People with banners, facing left.

796	A193	8f cr & multi (1)	7.00	25
797	A193	8f cr & multi (2)	7.00	25
798	A193	8f cr & multi (3)	7.00	25
a.		Souv. sheet of three	100.00	50.00
		Strip of three, Nos. 796-798	36.00	3.00

15th anniversary of the People's Republic. Nos. 796-798 printed se-tenant. No. 798a contains Nos. 796-798 as continuous design without separating perfs. Red and gold marginal inscription. Size: 153x114mm.

Oil Derricks
A194

Designs: 4f, Geological surveyors and truck (horiz.). 8f, "Christmas tree" and extraction accessories. 10f, Oil refinery. 20f, Tank cars (horiz.).

1964, Oct. 1

799	A194	4f lt bl & multi	12.00	10
800	A194	8f lt bl & multi	12.00	5
801	A194	8f lil & multi	12.00	15
802	A194	10f sl & multi	12.00	5
803	A194	20f brn & multi	14.00	*8.00*
		Nos. 799-803 (5)	62.00	*8.35*

Oil industry.

Albanian and Chinese Flags
A195

Design: 10f, Enver Hoxha and Albanian coat of arms.

1964, Nov. 29 *Perf. 11x11½*

804	A195	8f red & multi	13.00	*75*
805	A195	10f red, yel & blk	13.00	7.50

20th anniversary of the liberation of Albania.

Power Dam Construction
A196

Designs: No. 807, Installation of turbo-generator rotor. No. 808, Main dam. 20f, Pylon.

1964, Dec. 15 *Perf. 11½*

806	A196	4f multi	15.00	10
807	A196	8f multi	15.00	10
808	A196	8f multi	15.00	5
809	A196	20f multi	15.00	6.00

Hsin An Kiang Dam and hydroelectric power station.

Fertilizer Industry—A197

Designs (Chemical Industry): No. 811, Plastics. No. 812, Medicines. No. 813, Rubber. No. 814, Insecticides. No. 815, Industrial acids. No. 816, Industrial alkalies. No. 817, Synthetic fibers.

1964, Dec. 30 **Engr. & Photo.**

810	A197	8f red & blk (1)	50	15
811	A197	8f yel grn & blk (2)	50	10
812	A197	8f brn & blk (3)	50	10
813	A197	8f lil rose & blk (4)	50	10
814	A197	8f bl & blk (5)	50	10
815	A197	8f org & blk (6)	50	20
816	A197	8f vio & blk (7)	50	20
817	A197	8f brt grn & blk (8)	50	20
		Nos. 810-817 (8)	4.00	1.15

Mao Studying Map
A198

Mao Tse-tung
A199

Design: No. 819, Victory at Lushan Pass.

1965, Jan. 31 **Photo.** ***Perf. 11***

818	A198	8f red & multi	21.00	10.00
819	A198	8f red & multi	21.00	10.00
		Perf. 11½x11		
820	A199	8f gold & multi	21.00	10.00

Tsunyi Conference, 30th anniversary.

Conference Hall, Bandung—A200 **Lenin A201**

1965, Apr. 18 ***Perf. 11½x11***

Design: No. 822, Asians and Africans applauding.

821	A200	8f cr & multi	25	7
822	A200	8f cr & multi	25	8

10th anniversary of the Bandung, Indonesia, Conference, Apr. 1955.

1965, Apr. 25 ***Perf. 11½***

823	A201	8f red, choc & sal	18.50	6.00

95th anniversary of the birth of Lenin.

Chinese Player
A202

1965, Apr. 25 ***Perf. 11½***

Emerald, Gold, Red & Black

824	A202	8f *shown* (1)	10	8
825	A202	8f *European woman* (2)	10	8
826	A202	8f *Chinese woman* (3)	10	8
827	A202	8f *European man* (4)	10	8
		Block of 4	60	40

28th World Table Tennis Championships, Ljubljana, Jugoslavia, Apr. 15–25. Nos. 824–827 printed se-tenant.

Climbers on Mt. Minya Konka
A203

Marx and Lenin
A204

Mountain Climbers: No. 829, on Muztagh Ata. No. 830, on Mt. Jolmo Lungma (Mt. Everest). No. 831, Women camping on Kongur Tiubie Tagh. No. 832, on Shisha Pangma.

1965, May 25 **Engr. & Photo.**

828	A203	8f bl, blk & ol (1)	60	20
829	A203	8f bl, blk & ol (2)	60	20
830	A203	8f ultra, blk & gray (3)	60	20
831	A203	8f lt bl, blk & yel gray (4)	60	20
832	A203	8f ultra, blk & gray (5)	60	20
		Nos.828-832 (5)	3.00	1.00

Chinese mountaineering achievements, 1957–64.

1965, June 21 **Photo.** ***Perf. 11½x11***

833	A204	8f red, yel & blk	25.00	6.00

Postal Ministers' Congress, Peking.

Tseping Valley
A205

Chingkang Mountains, Cradle of the Chinese Revolution.

1965, July 1 ***Perf. 11x11½***

Multicolored

834	A205	4f *shown* (1)	2.50	10
835	A205	8f *San Wan Tsun* (2)	2.50	10
836	A205	8f *Octagon Bldg., Mao Ping* (3)	2.50	15
837	A205	8f *River and Bridge at Lung Shih* (4)	2.50	85
838	A205	8f *Ta Ching Tsun* (5)	2.50	8
839	A205	10f *Bridge across the Lung Yuan* (6)	2.50	8
840	A205	10f *Hwang Yang Mountain* (7)	2.50	1.50
841	A205	52f *Chingkang peaks* (8)	2.50	1.50
		Nos. 834-841 (8)	20.00	4.36

Soldiers with Books—A206

1965, Aug. 1 ***Perf. 11½***

Without Gum

Multicolored

842	A206	8f *shown* (1)	6.00	2.50
843	A206	8f *Soldiers reading Little Red Books* (2)	6.00	2.50
844	A206	8f *With shell and artillery* (3)	6.00	8
845	A206	8f *Rifle instruction* (4)	6.00	8
846	A206	8f *Sewing jacket* (5)	6.00	10
847	A206	8f *Bayonet charge*(6)	6.00	3.50
848	A206	8f *With banner* (7)	6.00	3.50
849	A206	8f *Military band* (8)	6.00	3.50
		Nos. 842-849 (8)	48.00	15.76

People's Liberation Army. Nos. 846–849 vertical.

"Welcome to Peking"
A207

Designs: No. 851, Chinese and Japanese young men. No. 852, Chinese and Japanese girls. No. 853, Musical entertainment. No. 854, Emblem of meeting.

1965, Aug. 25 ***Perf. 11½x11***

850	A207	4f yel & multi	45	10
851	A207	8f pink & multi	45	12
852	A207	8f multi	45	12
853	A207	10f multi	45	12
854	A207	22f lt bl & multi	35	25
		Nos. 850-854 (5)	2.15	71

Chinese-Japanese Youth Meeting, Peking.

North Vietnamese Soldier
A208

Peoples of the World—A209

Designs: No. 856, Soldier with guns. No. 857, Soldier giving victory salute.

1965, Sept. 2 ***Perf. 11½x11***

855	A208	8f red & red brn (1)	50	15
856	A208	8f red & blk (2)	50	15
857	A208	8f red & vio brn (3)	50	15
		Perf. 11½		
858	A209	8f blk & red (4)	50	15

Struggle of the people of Viet Nam.

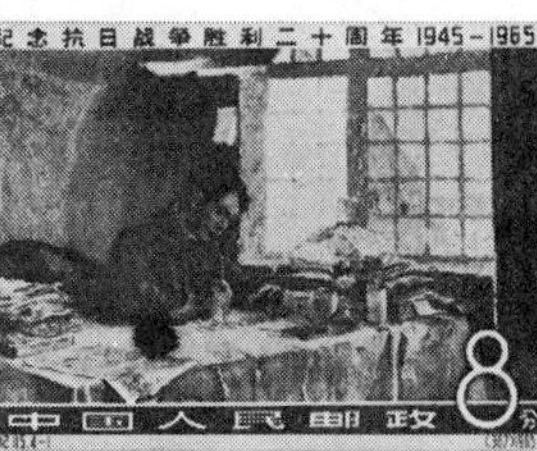

Mao Tse-tung at His Desk—A210

Crossing Yellow River
A211

Victory Monument
A212

Design: No. 862, Recruits in cart.

1965, Sept. 3 ***Perf. 11***

859	A210	8f red & multi (1)	8.25	2.00
		Perf. 11x11½, 11½x11		
860	A211	8f red & dk grn (2)	8.25	6.00
861	A212	8f red & dk brn (3)	8.25	50
862	A211	8f red & dk grn (4)	8.25	50

20th anniversary of victory over Japan.

Soccer
A213

National Games Opening Ceremonies—A214

Designs: No. 864, Archery. No. 865, Javelin. No. 866, Gymnastics. No. 867, Volleyball. No. 869, Bicycling. 20f, Diving. 22f, Hurdles. 30f, Weight lifting. 43f, Basketball.

Position-in-set number in ( ).

Perf. 11½x11, 11 (A214)

1965, Sept. 28

863	A213	4f red & multi (1)	5.00	10
864	A213	4f gray & multi (2)	5.00	10
865	A213	8f dk grn & multi (3)	5.00	10
866	A213	8f lil rose & multi (4)	5.00	10
867	A213	8f dp grn & multi (5)	5.00	10

868	A214	10f red, gold & multi (6)	5.00	10
869	A213	10f ol & multi (7)	5.00	10
870	A213	20f ultra & multi (8)	5.00	50
871	A213	22f org & multi (9)	5.00	60
872	A213	30f dp bl & multi (10)	5.00	1.00
873	A213	43f red lil & multi (11)	5.00	2.00
		Nos. 863-873 (11)	55.00	4.80

2nd National Games.

Government Building
A215

Textile Workers
A216

Designs: 4f, 20f, as 1f. 1½f, 5f, 22f, Gate of Heavenly Peace. 2f, 8f, 30f, People's Hall. 3f, 10f, 50f, Military Museum.

1965–66 ***Perf. 11½x11***

Without Gum

874	A215	1f brown	10	3
875	A215	1½f red lil	10	30
876	A215	2f green	10	3
877	A215	3f bl grn	10	3
878	A215	4f brt bl	10	5
879	A215	5f vio brn ('66)	15	5
880	A215	8f rose red	15	3
881	A215	10f gray ol	15	3
882	A215	20f violet	15	6
883	A215	22f orange	75	6
884	A215	30f yel grn	75	3
885	A215	50f dp bl ('66)	75	60
		Nos. 874-885 (12)	3.35	1.30

1965, Nov. 30

Multicolored

886	A216	8f *shown* (1)	10.00	5
887	A216	8f *Machine shop* (2)	10.00	10
888	A216	8f *Welder* (3)	10.00	5
889	A216	8f *Students* (4)	10.00	1.50
890	A216	8f *Militia* (5)	10.00	1.50
		Nos. 886-890 (5)	50.00	3.20

Women workers.

Soccer—A217

Children's Sports: No. 892, Racing. No. 893, Tobogganing and skating. No. 894, Gymnastics. No. 895, Swimming. No. 896, Rifle practice. No. 897, Jumping rope. No. 898, Table tennis.

1966, Feb. 25 ***Perf. 11***

891	A217	4f emer & multi (1)	7	5
892	A217	4f yel brn & multi (2)	7	5
893	A217	8f bl & multi (3)	15	10
894	A217	8f yel & multi (4)	15	10
895	A217	8f grnsh bl & multi (5)	15	10
896	A217	8f grn & multi (6)	15	10
897	A217	10f org & multi (7)	20	12
898	A217	52f grnsh gray & multi (8)	1.10	60
		Nos. 891-898 (8)	2.04	1.22

Mobile Transformer
A218

New Industrial Machinery: No. 900, Electron microscope (vert.). No. 901, Lathe. No. 902, Vertical boring and turning machine (vert.). No. 903, Gear-grinding machine. No. 904, Hydraulic press. No. 905, Milling machine. No. 906, Electron accelerator (vert.).

Perf. 11x11½, 11½x11

1966, Mar. 30 **Engr. and Photo.**

899	A218	4f yel & blk (1)	5.50	15
900	A218	8f blk & lt ultra (2)	5.50	15
901	A218	8f sal pink & blk (3)	5.50	15
902	A218	8f ol & blk (4)	5.50	15
903	A218	8f rose lil & blk (5)	5.50	15
904	A218	10f gray & blk (6)	5.50	1.00
905	A218	10f bl grn & blk (7)	5.50	1.00
906	A218	22f lil & blk (8)	5.50	1.00
		Nos. 899-906 (8)	44.00	3.75

Military and Civilian Workers
A219

Women in Various Occupations: No. 908, Train conductor. No. 909, Red Cross worker. No. 910, Kindergarten teacher. No. 911, Road sweeper. No. 912, Hairdresser. No. 913, Bus conductor. No. 914, Traveling saleswoman. No. 915, Canteen worker. No. 916, Rural mail carrier.

1966, May 10 ***Perf. 11x11½***

907	A219	8f red & multi (1)	25	12
908	A219	8f pale grn & multi (2)	25	12
909	A219	8f yel & multi (3)	25	12
910	A219	8f grn & multi (4)	25	12
911	A219	8f sal & multi (5)	25	12
912	A219	8f pale bl & bl (6)	25	12
913	A219	8f yel & multi (7)	25	12
914	A219	8f tan & multi (8)	25	12
915	A219	8f yel grn & multi (9)	25	12
916	A219	8f grn & multi (10)	25	12
		Nos. 907-916 (10)	2.50	1.20

Statue "Thunder-storm"
A220

Design: 22f, Open book and association emblem.

1966, June 27 **With Gum** ***Perf. 11***

917	A220	8f red & blk	1.00	10
918	A220	22f red, gold & yel	1.50	20

Afro-Asian Writers' Association Conference, Peking.

Sun Yat-sen
A221

1966, Nov. 12 ***Perf. 11½x11***

919	A221	8f sep & lt buff	12.50	5.00

Birth centenary of Sun Yat-sen.

Athletes Holding Portrait of Mao
A222

Two Women Athletes with Little Red Book
A223

Designs: No. 921, Athletes holding Little Red Books. No. 923, Athletes reading Mao texts.

1966, Dec. 31 ***Perf. 11***

920	A222	8f red & multi (1)	8.25	2.50
921	A222	8f red & multi (2)	8.25	2.50

Perf. 11x11½

922	A223	8f bl & multi (3)	8.25	2.50
923	A223	8f bl & multi (4)	8.25	2.50

1st Athletic Games of the New Emerging Nations.

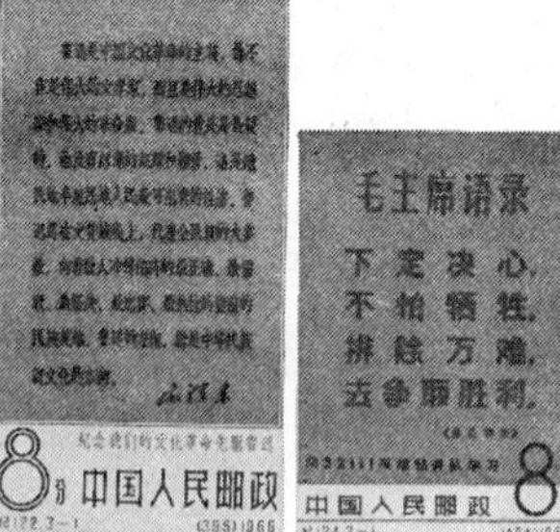

Appreciation of Lu Hsun by Mao
A224

"Be Resolute . . . ," by Mao Tse-tung
A225

Designs: No. 925, Portrait of Lu Hsun. No. 926, Lu Hsun's handwriting (3 vert. rows).

Engr. & Photo.; Photo. (No. 925)

1966, Dec. 31 ***Perf. 11½***

924	A224	8f red & blk (1)	9.00	3.00
925	A224	8f red & multi (2)	9.00	3.00
926	A224	8f red & blk (3)	9.00	3.00

Lu Hsun, Revolutionary writer (1881–1936).

Perf. 11½x11, 11½ (No. 928)

1967, Mar. 10 **Photogravure**

Designs: No. 928, Drilling crew fighting natural gas fire (horiz.). No. 929, Attempt to close fire-engulfed valve.

Sizes: Nos. 927, 929, 26x38mm.; No. 928, 49x29mm.

927	A225	8f red, gold & blk	7.50	3.00
928	A225	8f brick red & blk	7.50	3.00
929	A225	8f brick red & blk	7.50	3.00

Heroic oil well firefighters.

Liu Ying-chun
A226

1967, Mar. 25 ***Perf. 11½x11***

Multicolored

930	A226	8f *shown* (1)	6.00	2.00
931	A226	8f *With book by Mao* (2)	6.00	2.00
932	A226	8f *Holding bridle of horse* (3)	6.00	2.00
933	A226	8f *With film slide* (4)	6.00	2.00
934	A226	8f *Lecturing* (5)	6.00	2.00
935	A226	8f *Fatal attempt to stop runaway horse* (6)	6.00	2.00
		Nos. 930-935 (6)	36.00	12.00

In memory of soldier Liu Ying-chun, hero.

Industrial Growth—A227

Design: No. 937, Banners and people facing left: agricultural growth.

1967, Apr. 15 ***Perf. 11***

936	A227	8f red & multi	7.00	2.50
937	A227	8f red & multi	7.00	2.50

Third Five-Year Plan.

Mao Tse-tung
A228

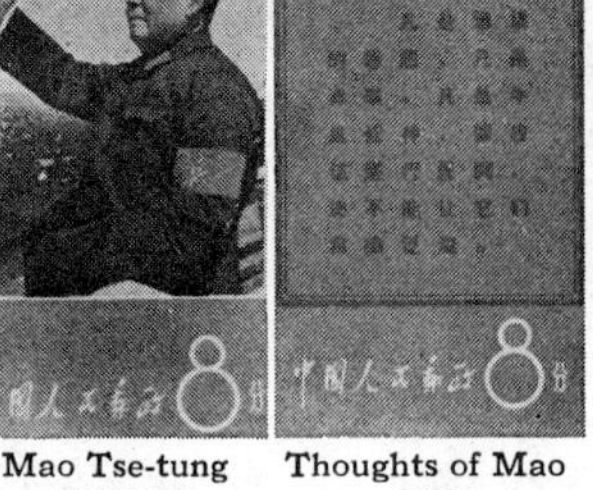

Thoughts of Mao
A229

1967, Apr. 20 ***Perf. 11½***

938	A228	8f red & multi	8.00	3.00

Red & Gold

939	A229	8f *39 characters*	8.00	3.00
940	A229	8f *50 characters*	8.00	3.00
941	A229	8f *39 characters in 6 lines*	8.00	3.00
942	A229	8f *53 characters*	8.00	3.00
943	A229	8f *46 characters*	8.00	3.00
		Strip of five	60.00	25.00

Gold & Red

944	A229	8f *41 characters*	8.00	3.00
945	A229	8f *49 characters*	8.00	3.00
946	A229	8f *35 characters*	8.00	3.00
947	A229	8f *22 characters*	8.00	3.00
948	A229	8f *29 characters*	8.00	3.00
		Strip of five	60.00	25.00
		Nos. 938-948 (11)	88.00	33.00

Thoughts of Mao Tse-tung. Nos. 939–943, Nos. 944–948 printed se-tenant in strips of 5 each.

No numbers appear below design on Nos. 938–1046.

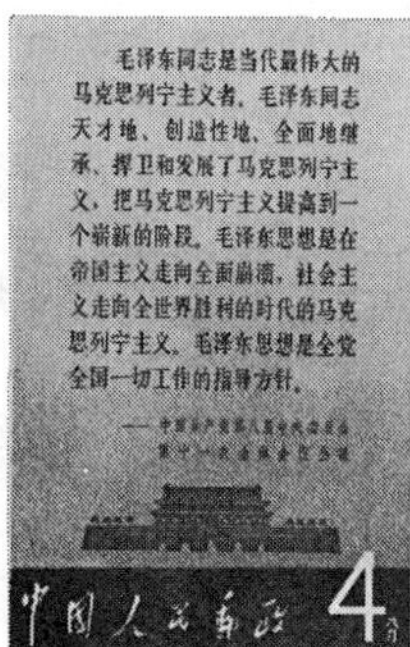

Text by Mao and Gate of Heavenly Peace
A230

Mao and Lin Piao
A231

Designs: No. 950, Mao and poem. No. 951, Mao among people of various races. No. 952, Mao facing left and Red Guards with books. No. 953, Mao with upraised right hand. No. 954, Mao leaning on rail (horiz.). 10f, Mao and Lin Piao in discussion (horiz.).

Engraved and Photogravure

1967 ***Perf. 11x11½***

Size: 36x56mm.

949	A230	4f yel, red & mar	8.00	2.00

Photogravure

950	A230	8f yel, brn, & red	8.00	2.00
951	A230	8f yel, red & multi	8.00	2.00
952	A230	8f yel, red & multi	8.00	2.00

Perf. 11

Size: 36x50, 50x36mm.

953	A231	8f blk & multi	8.00	2.00
954	A231	8f blk & multi	50.00	17.00
955	A231	8f lt bl & multi	20.00	17.00
956	A231	10f blk & multi	40.00	17.00
		Nos. 949-956 (8)	150.00	61.00

"Mao Tse-tung Our Great Teacher."
Issue dates: Nos. 949–953, May 1; Nos. 954–956, Sept. 20.

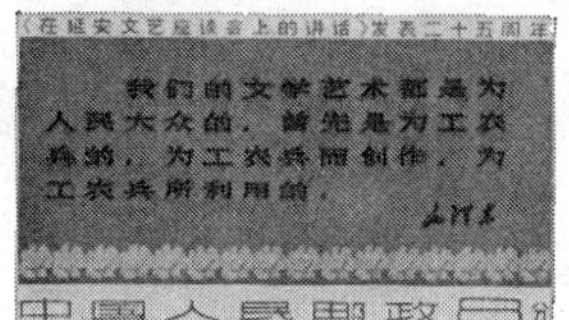

Mao Text (4 lines)—A232

Parade of Supporters—A233

Design: No. 958, Mao text (5 lines).

Engraved and Photogravure

1967, May 23 ***Perf. 11½***

957	A232	8f blk, red & yel	17.00	5.50
958	A232	8f blk, red & yel	17.00	5.50

Photogravure ***Perf. 11***

959	A233	8f multi	17.00	5.50

25th anniversary of Mao Tse-tung's "Talks on Literature and Art" in Yenan.

Mao Tse-tung
A234

1967 **Engraved** ***Perf. 11***

960	A234	4f brown	20.00	7.50
961	A234	8f carmine	20.00	7.50
962	A234	35f dk brn	20.00	7.50
963	A234	43f vermilion	20.00	7.50
964	A234	52f carmine	20.00	7.50
		Nos. 960-964 (5)	100.00	37.50

46th anniversary of Chinese Communist Party.
Issue dates: 8f, July 1, others September.

Mao, "Sun of the Revolution"—A235

Design: No. 966, Mao and people of various races.

1967, Oct. 1 ***Perf. 11½x11***

965	A235	8f multi	18.00	8.00
966	A235	8f multi	18.00	8.00

18th anniversary of the People's Republic of China.

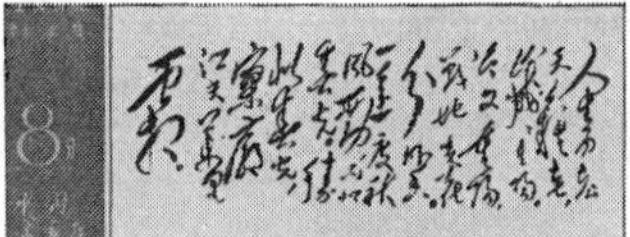

"September 9"—A236

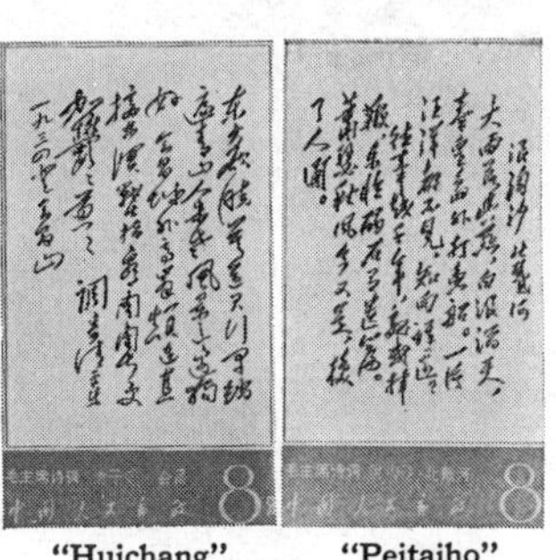

"Huichang" "Peitaiho"
A237 A238

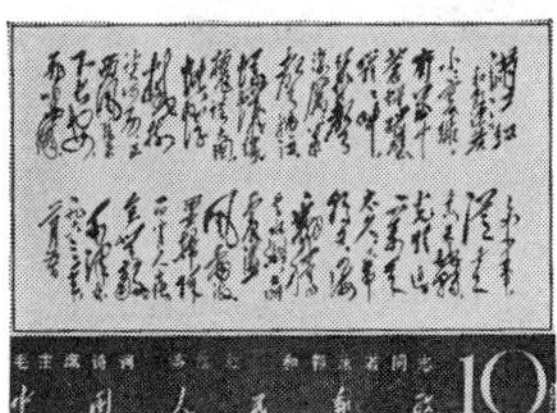

Reply to Comrade Kuo Mo-jo—A239

Mao Tse-tung Writing Poems—A240

Designs (Poems by Mao): No. 967, "The Long March." No. 968, "Liupanshan." No. 969, shown. No. 970, "The Cave of the Fairies." No. 971, "Snow." No. 972, "Lushan Pass." Nos. 973–974, shown. No. 975, "Conquest of Nanking." No. 976, "The Yellow Crane Pavilion." No. 977, "Swimming." No. 978, shown. No. 979, "Changsha."

1967–68 **Photogravure** ***Perf. 11***

Red and Yellow Frame; Poem Written in Black

Size: 79x18½mm.

967	A236	4f *9 characters, UL panel* ('68)	15.00	6.00
968	A236	4f *11 characters, UL panel* ('68)	15.00	6.00

Size: 60x24mm. ***Perf. 11½***

969	A236	8f *shown, 10 characters in UL panel*	7.00	2.00
970	A236	8f *21 characters in UL panel*	7.00	2.00
971	A236	8f *11 characters in UL panel*	15.00	6.00
972	A236	8f *9 characters in UL panel*	15.00	6.00

Size: 29x50mm.

973	A237	8f *shown*	7.00	2.00
974	A238	8f *shown*	15.00	6.00
975	A238	8f *3 rows in bottom panel*	7.00	2.00
976	A238	8f *2 rows in bottom panel*	15.00	6.00

Size: 52x38mm. ***Perf. 11***

977	A239	8f *3 short vert. rows, at left of poem*	15.00	6.00
978	A239	10f *shown*	15.00	6.00
979	A239	10f *undivided text*	7.00	2.00
980	A240	10f red, yel & multi	11.00	5.00
		Nos. 967-980 (14)	166.00	63.00

Poems by Mao Tse-tung.
Issue dates: Nos. 969–970, 980, Oct. 1, 1967; Nos. 973–974, 977, May 20, 1968; others July 20, 1968.

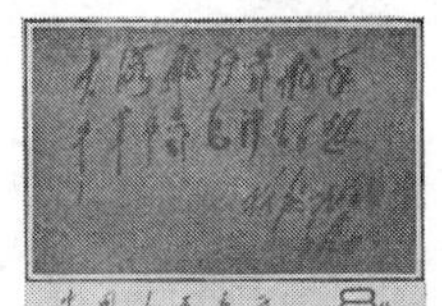

Lin Piao's Epigram on Mao Tse-tung
A241

1967, Dec. 26 Photo. ***Perf. 11x11½***

981	A241	8f red & gold	25.00	8.00

Mao and Parade of Artists—A242

"Raid on White Tiger Regiment"
A243

"Red Detachment of Women"—A244

1968 ***Perf. 11½x11; 11*** **(983, 990)**

Multicolored

982	A242	8f *shown* (56x36mm)	6.00	2.00
983	A242	8f *"The Red Lantern"* (vert.)	6.00	2.00
984	A243	8f *shown*	6.00	2.00
985	A243	8f *"Shachiapang" (women & soldier)*	6.00	2.00
986	A243	8f *"On the Dock"*	6.00	2.00
987	A243	8f *"Taking Bandits' Fort"if*	6.00	2.00
988	A244	8f *shown*	12.50	6.50
989	A244	8f *"The White-haired Girl"*	12.50	6.50
990	A242	8f *Mao with Orchestra & Chorus* (50x36mm)	10.00	4.50
		Nos. 982-990 (9)	71.00	29.50

Mao's direction for revolutionary literature and art.
Issue dates: Nos. 982–987, Jan. 30; Nos. 988–990, May 1.

"Unite still more closely. . ."—A245

1968, May 31 **Photo.** ***Perf. 11***

991	A245	8f red, gold & red brn	27.50	10.00

Mao Tse-tung's statement of support of Afro-Americans.

Statement about Cultural Revolution
A246

Directives of Chairman Mao: No. 993, Experiences of Revolutionary Committee. No. 994, Leadership role of Revolutionary Committee. No. 995, Basic principle of reform. No. 996, Purpose of Cultural Revolution.

1968, July 20 Photo. *Perf. 11½*
Red, Yellow & Brown

992	A246	8f *shown*	15.00	4.00
993	A246	8f *5 lines over signature*	15.00	4.00
994	A246	8f *4½ lines over signature*	15.00	4.00
995	A246	8f *4 lines over signature*	15.00	4.00
996	A246	8f *8 lines over signature*	15.00	4.00
		Strip of five	160.00	65.00

Printed se-tenant in horizontal strips of 5 within sheet.

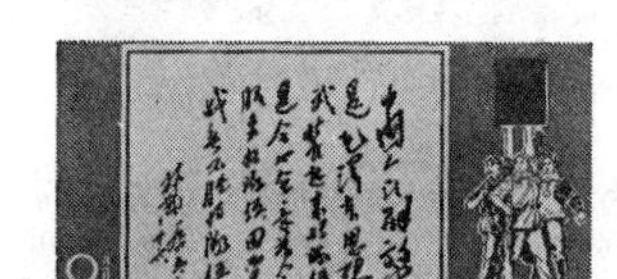

Lin Piao's Statement, July 26, 1965
A247

1968, Aug. 1 Engr. and Photo.

997	A247	8f red, gold & blk	12.50	5.00

41st anniversary of the Chinese People's Liberation Army.

Mao Tse-tung Going to An Yuan, 1921
A248

1968, Aug. 1 *Perf. 11x11½*

998	A248	8f multi	12.50	7.00

Shade varieties include varying amount of red in clouds.

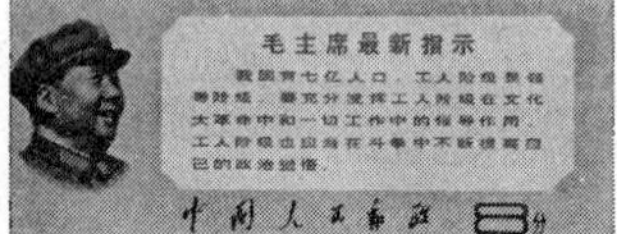

Directive of Chairman Mao—A249

1968, Nov. 30 *Perf. 11½*

999	A249	8f red & blk brn	25.00	8.00

China Map, Worker, Farmer and Soldier
A249a

1968, Nov. Photo. *Perf. 11½x11*

999A	A249a	8f red, bl & bis	*4,500.*	*2,500.*

Map inscribed: "The entire nation is red." Issued in Canton and quickly withdrawn because Taiwan appears white instead of red.

Woman, Miner and Soldier Holding Little Red Book
A250

1968, Dec. 26 *Perf. 11x11½*

1000	A250	8f multi	10.00	3.00

Yangtze Bridge, Nanking
A251

Road across Bridge—A252

Designs: No. 1003, Side view. 10f, Aerial view.

Litho., *Perf. 11½x11 (A251)*; Photo., *Perf. 11½ (A252)*
1969 Without Gum

1001	A251	4f multi	3.00	2.00
1002	A252	8f multi	8.00	4.00
1003	A252	8f multi	4.00	2.00
1004	A251	10f multi	4.00	2.00

Inauguration of Yangtze Bridge at Nanking on Dec. 29, 1968.

Singer and Pianist
A253

Designs (Piano Music from the Opera, "The Red Lantern"): No. 1006, Woman singer and pianist.

1969, Aug. Photo. *Perf. 11x11½*
Without Gum

1005	A253	8f multi	3.00	2.00
1006	A253	8f multi	3.00	2.00

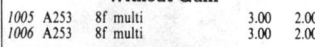

Harvest
A254

1969, Oct.
Multicolored

1007	A254	4f *shown*	2.00	2.00
a.		Brown omitted	150.00	75.00
1008	A254	8f *Two harvesters*	2.00	2.00
1009	A254	8f *Harvesters with Little Red Books*	7.00	3.00
1010	A254	10f *Red Cross worker examining baby*	2.00	1.00

Agriculture students.

Armed Forces and Slogan—A255

Guarding the Coast—A256

Designs: No. 1013, 43f, Snow patrol (vert.).

1969, Oct. *Perf. 11½*

1011	A255	8f red & multi	2.50	*2.00*
a.		Bayonets omitted	150.00	150.00
1012	A256	8f bl & multi	2.50	*2.00*
1013	A256	8f bl & multi	2.50	*2.00*
1014	A256	35f blk & multi	2.50	*3.00*
1015	A256	43f blk & multi	2.50	*3.00*
		Nos. 1011-1015 (5)	12.50	*12.00*

Defense of Chen Pao-tao (Damansky Islands) in Ussuri River.

Farm Woman
A257

Designs: 8f, Foundry worker. 10f, Soldier.

1969, Dec. *Perf. 10; 11½ (#1017)*
Without Gum

1016	A257	4f ver & dk pur	1.25	1.25
1017	A257	8f ver & dk brn	1.25	1.25
1018	A257	10f ver & blk	1.25	1.25

Perforation

Nos. 1016–1018 and some succeeding issues bear two kinds of perforation: clean (Peking) and rough (Shanghai).

Building
A258

Communist Party Building, Shanghai
A259

Agriculture Building, Canton
A260

Foundry Worker
A261

Two types of 8f Gate of Heavenly Peace:
I. Strong, definite halo around sun.
II. Halo missing, white shades gradually into red.

1969–72 Photo. *Perf. 10, 11½*
Multicolored; Without Gum

1019	A258	1f *shown*	5	*25*
1020	A259	1½f *shown*	1.00	1.00
a.		Perf. 11½	8.00	5.00
1021	A260	2f *shown*	5	*15*
1022	A260	3f *1929 Party Day House, PuTien*	8	5
1023	A260	4f *Mao's Home and Office, Yunnan*	10	*20*
1024	A261	5f *Woman Tractor Driver*	1.25	50
1025	A260	8f *Gate of Heavenly Peace, type II*	2.00	50
a.		Type I	1.50	60
1026	A259	8f *Heroes Monument*	1.50	1.00
a.		Perf. 11½	7.00	2.00
1027	A260	8f *Pagoda Hill, Yenan*	3.00	5.00
1028	A260	8f *Gate of Heavenly Peace (no sun)*	15	10
1029	A260	10f *Monument, Tsu Ping*	20	*30*
1030	A259	20f *Conference Hall, Tsunyi*	4.50	2.00
a.		Perf. 11½	4.00	4.00
1031	A260	20f *Highway ('72)*	30	30
1032	A260	22f *Shao Shan Village, Birthplace of Mao*	35	*50*
1033	A260	35f *Conference Hall*	50	50
1034	A260	43f *Chingkang Peaks*	60	50
1035	A259	50f *as 4f, different view*	4.50	2.00
1036	A260	52f *People's Hall, Peking*	80	50
1037	A261	$1 *shown ('70)*	4.50	4.00
a.		Perf. 11		
b.		Perf. 11½		
		Nos. 1019-1037 (19)	25.43	*19.35*

Kin Hsün-hua
A262

Mounted Patrol
A263

1970, Jan. Without Gum *Perf. 11½*

1045	A262	8f red & gray brn	4.00	4.00
a.		8f red & blk	8.00	8.00

Death of Kin Hsün-hua in Kirin border flood.

1970, Aug. 1 Without Gum

1046	A263	8f yel grn & multi	2.50	2.00

43rd anniversary of the People's Liberation Army.

Beginning with No. 1047 commemorative stamps carry a cumulative number in parenthesis at lower left and the year at lower right. Where such numbers help to identify, they are quoted in parenthesis.

Cpl. Yang Tse-jung
A264

Ensemble
A265

1970, Aug. 1

Perf. 11½x11, 11x11½

No.	Type	Description	Unused	Used
1047	A264	8f *shown* (1)	50	50
1048	A264	8f *Armed guards* (2)	50	50
1049	A264	8f *Yang leaping through forest* (3)	50	50
1050	A265	8f *shown* (4)	50	50
1051	A265	8f *Yang in folk costume* (5)	50	50
1052	A265	8f *Four actors* (6)	50	50
		Nos. 1047-1052 (6)	3.00	3.00

Scenes from opera "Taking Tiger Mountain by Strategy." Nos. 1048, 1052, horizontal.

Frontier Guard
A266

1971, Jan. Litho. *Perf. 11½*

Without Gum

No.	Type	Description	Unused	Used
1053	A266	4f multi	2.00	75
a.		Perf. 10	60	1.00
b.		Perf. 11½x10	4.00	
c.		Perf. 10x11½	9.00	

Banner of the Commune
A267

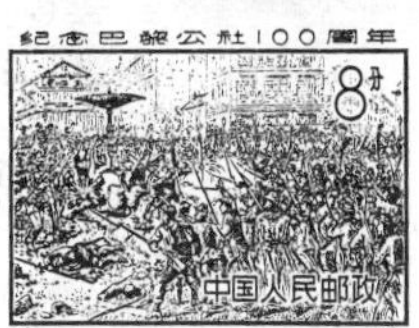

Street Battle, Paris, 1871
A268

Designs: 10f, Proclamation of the Commune. 22f, Rally.

1971, Mar. 18 Litho. and Engr.

Perf. 11½x11, 11x11½

No.	Type	Description	Unused	Used
1054	A267	4f sal & multi	45	70
1055	A268	8f ver, pink & brn	45	70
1056	A267	10f ver, pink & dk brn	45	70
1057	A268	22f ver, pink & dk brn	45	70

Centenary of the Paris Commune.

Redrawn Building Type of 1961

Designs: 2f, 3f, August 1 building, Nanchang. 4f, 52f, Gate of Heavenly Peace, Peking. 10f, 20f, Pagoda Hill, Yenan.

1971 Litho. *Perf. 11x11½*

Size: 21x16mm.

No.	Type	Description	Unused	Used
1059	A152	2f sl grn	3.00	3.00
1060	A152	3f sepia	3.00	3.00
1061	A152	4f brt pink	3.00	3.00
1062	A152	10f brt rose lil	3.00	3.00
1063	A152	20f dk bl grn	3.00	3.00
1064	A152	52f orange	3.00	3.00
		Nos. 1059-1064 (6)	18.00	18.00

Paper of Nos. 1059–1064 is white. That of Nos. 647–654 is toned.

Communist Party Building, Shanghai—A269

People and Factories
A270

Designs: No. 1068, Peasant Movement Training Institute. No 1069, Ching Kang Peaks. No. 1070, Conference Building, Tsunyi. No. 1071, Pagoda Hill, Yenan. No. 1073, People and People's Hall, Peking. No. 1074, People and Pagoda Hill, Yenan. 22f, Gate of Heavenly Peace, Peking.

Red and Gold Frame

1971, July 1 Photo. *Perf. 11½*

No.	Type	Description	Unused	Used
1067	A269	4f ver (12)	10	10
1068	A269	4f brt grn (13)	10	10
1069	A269	8f grnsh bl & red (14)	25	25
1070	A269	8f ol blk (15)	25	25
1071	A269	8f bis, grn & red (16)	25	25
1072	A270	8f yel, red & multi (18)	25	25
1073	A270	8f yel, red & multi (19)	25	25
1074	A270	8f yel, red & multi (20)	25	25
a.		Strip of 3 (#1072-1074)	1.00	1.00
1075	A269	22f red, gold & brn (17)	25	25
		Nos. 1067-1075 (9)	1.95	1.95

50th anniversary of the Chinese Communist Party. Nos. 1072–1074 printed se-tenant with continuous design.

Chinese Welcome
A271

Enver Hoxha
A272

Designs: No. 1077, Chinese and African players. No. 1078, Chinese and African girl players. 43f, Games' emblem.

1971, Nov. 3 Litho. *Perf. 11½*

No.	Type	Description	Unused	Used
1076	A271	8f lil rose & multi	20	20
1077	A271	8f lt yel & multi	20	20
1078	A271	8f dk grn & multi	20	20
1079	A271	43f grn, gold & org	1.00	1.00

Afro-Asian Table Tennis Games, Peking.

1971, Nov. 3 Photo. *Perf. 11*

Designs: No. 1081, Party's birthplace. No. 1082, Albanian flag. 52f, Albanian partisans (horiz.).

No.	Type	Description	Unused	Used
1080	A272	8f Prus bl & multi	3.00	3.00
1081	A272	8f buff & multi	1.00	1.00
1082	A272	8f red, yel & multi	1.00	1.00
1083	A272	52f lt bl & multi	1.00	1.00

30th anniversary of the founding of Albanian Communist Party.

Yenan Pagoda and 1942 Meeting House
A273

1972, May 23 Photogravure *Perf. 11*

Cumulative numbers in parenthesis.

Multicolored

No.	Type	Description	Unused	Used
1084	A273	8f *shown* (33)	75	75
1085	A273	8f *Uniformed choir* (34)	75	75
1086	A273	8f *"Brother & Sister"* (35)	75	75
1087	A273	8f *Outdoor performance* (36)	75	75
1088	A273	8f *"The Red Signal Lantern"* (37)	75	75
1089	A273	8f *Dancer from "The Red Company of Women"* (38)	75	75
		Nos. 1084-1089 (6)	4.50	4.50

30th anniversary of the publication of the Discussions on Literature and Art at the Yenan Forum.

Various Ball Games—A274

Workers' Gymnastics
A275

1972, June 10 Multicolored

No.	Type	Description	Unused	Used
1090	A274	8f *shown* (39)	16	16
1091	A275	8f *shown* (40)	16	16
1092	A275	8f *Tug of war* (41)	16	16
1093	A275	8f *Mountain climbers and tents* (42)	16	16
1094	A275	8f *Children diving & swimming* (43)	16	16
		Nos. 1090-1094 (5)	80	80

10th anniversary of Mao Tse-tung's edict on physical culture.

Ocean Freighter Fenglei—A276

1972, July 10 Photo. *Perf. 11½*

Multicolored

No.	Type	Description	Unused	Used
1095	A276	8f *shown* (29)	20	20
1096	A276	8f *Tanker Taching No. 30* (30)	20	20
1097	A276	8f *Cargo-passenger ship Changzeng* (31)	20	20
1098	A276	8f *Dredger Xienfeng* (32)	20	20

Table Tennis Players' Welcome
A277

Perf. 11½x11, 11x11½

1972, Sept. 2

Multicolored

No.	Type	Description	Unused	Used
1099	A277	8f *Championship emblem* (vert.) (45)	14	14
1100	A277	8f *shown* (46)	14	14
1101	A277	8f *Table tennis* (47)	14	14
1102	A277	22f *Women from different countries* (vert.) (48)	65	65

First Asian table tennis championships.

Wang Tsum-hu
A278

Workers on Cliffs along Canal
A279

Engraved and Photogravure

1972, Dec. 25 *Perf. 11½x11*

No.	Type	Description	Unused	Used
1103	A278	8f multi (44)	25	25

Wang Tsum-hu, the Iron Man, fighter for the working class.

1972, Dec. 30

Designs: No. 1105, Canal flowing through tunnel. No. 1106, Bridge. No. 1107, Canal along cliffs.

No.	Type	Description	Unused	Used
1104	A279	8f multi (49)	15	15
1105	A279	8f multi (50)	15	15
1106	A279	8f multi (51)	15	15
1107	A279	8f multi (52)	15	15

Construction of Red Flag Canal, Linhsien county, Honan.

Giant Panda
A280

Woman Coal Miner
A281

Designs: Pandas in various positions. The 8f stamps are horizontal.

Perf. 11½x11, 11x11½

1973, Jan. 15 Photogravure

Designs in Black and Red

1108	A280	4f lt yel grn (61)	1.00	1.00
1109	A280	8f buff (59)	1.00	1.00
1110	A280	8f lt tan (60)	1.00	1.00
1111	A280	10f pale grn (58)	1.00	1.00
1112	A280	20f pale bl gray (57)	1.00	1.00
1113	A280	43f pale lil (62)	1.00	1.00
		Nos. 1108-1113 (6)	6.00	6.00

1973, Mar. 8 Photo. *Perf. 11½x11*

Multicolored

1114	A281	8f *shown* (63)	20	20
1115	A281	8f *Committee member* (64)	20	20
1116	A281	8f *Telephone line worker* (65)	20	20

International Working Women's Day. Designs are after paintings from an exhibition for 30th anniversary of the Yenan Forum on Literature and Art.

Dancing Girl
A282

Tournament Emblem
A283

1973, June 1 Photo. *Perf. 11*

Yellow & Multicolored

1117	A282	8f *shown* (86)	15	15
1118	A282	8f *Musician, boy* (87)	15	15
1119	A282	8f *Girl with scarf* (88)	15	15
1120	A282	8f *Boy with tambourine* (89)	15	15
1121	A282	8f *Girl with drum* (90)	15	15
		Nos. 1117-1121 (5)	75	75

Nos. 1117–1121 printed se-tenant.

1973, Aug. 25 Photo. *Perf. 11½*

Designs: No. 1123, Visitors from Asia, Africa and Latin America arriving by plane. No. 1124, Woman player. 22f, African, Asian and Latin American women.

1122	A283	8f multi (91)	15	15
1123	A283	8f multi (92)	15	15
1124	A283	8f multi (93)	15	15
1125	A283	22f multi (94)	40	40

Asian, African and Latin American Table Tennis Friendship Invitational Tournament.

The White-haired Girl
A284

Designs: Scenes from the ballet "The White-haired Girl." Nos. 1126 and 1129 vertical.

1973, Sept. 25 Photo. *Perf. 11½*

1126	A284	8f multi (53)	20	20
1127	A284	8f multi (54)	20	20
1128	A284	8f multi (55)	20	20
1129	A284	8f multi (56)	20	20

Fair Building, Canton—A285

1973, Oct. 15 Photo. *Perf. 11*

1130	A285	8f multi (95)	15	15

Export Commodities Fall Fair, Canton.

Teapot with Blue Phoenix Design
A286

Designs: No. 1132, Silver pot with horse design. No. 1133, Black pottery horse. No. 1134, Woman, clay figurine. No. 1135, Carved stone pillar base. No. 1136, Galloping bronze horse. No. 1137, Bronze inkwell (toad). No. 1138, Bronze lamp, Chang Hsin Palace. No. 1139, Bronze tripod. No. 1140, Square bronze pot. 20f, Bronze wine vessel. 52f, Painted red clay tripod.

1973, Nov. 20 *Perf. 11½*

1131	A286	4f ol bis & multi (66)	10	10
1132	A286	4f ver & multi (67)	10	10
1133	A286	8f yel grn & multi (68)	14	14
1134	A286	8f brt rose & multi (69)	14	14
1135	A286	8f lt vio & multi (70)	14	14
1136	A286	8f yel bis & multi (71)	14	14
1137	A286	8f lt bl & multi (72)	14	14
1138	A286	8f gray & multi (73)	14	14
1139	A286	10f yel bis & multi (74)	18	18
1140	A286	10f dp org & multi (75)	18	18
1141	A286	20f lil & multi (76)	40	40
1142	A286	52f grn & multi (77)	1.00	1.00
		Nos. 1131-1142 (12)	2.80	2.80

Excavated works of art.

Marginal Markings

Marginal inscriptions on stamps of 1974 start at lower left with "J" for commemoratives and "T" for "special issues," followed by three numbers indicating (a) set sequence for the year, (b) total of stamps in set, and (c) number of stamp within set. At right appears the year date. Listings include the "c" number parenthetically.

Woman Gymnast
A287

Designs: No. 1144, Gymnast on rings. No. 1145, Aerial split over balance beam, woman. No. 1146, Gymnast on parallel bars. No. 1147, Uneven bars, woman. No. 1148, Gymnast on horse.

1974, Jan. 1 Photo. *Perf. 11½x11*

1143	A287	8f lt grn & multi (1)	15	15
1144	A287	8f lt vio & multi (2)	15	15
1145	A287	8f lt bl & multi (3)	15	15
1146	A287	8f sal & multi (4)	15	15
1147	A287	8f yel & multi (5)	15	15
1148	A287	8f lil rose & multi (6)	15	15
		Nos. 1143-1148 (6)	90	90

Girls Twirling Bamboo Diabolos—A288

Designs: No. 1149, Lion Dance (vert.). No. 1150, Handstand on chairs (vert.). No. 1152, Men balancing jar. No. 1153, Plate spinning (vert.). No. 1154, Twirling umbrella (vert.).

1974, Jan. 21 *Perf. 11*

1149	A288	8f brn & multi (1)	15	15
1150	A288	8f Prus bl & multi (2)	15	15
1151	A288	8f lil & multi (3)	15	15
1152	A288	8f dl bl & multi (4)	15	15
1153	A288	8f ol grn & multi (5)	15	15
1154	A288	8f gray & multi (6)	15	15
		Nos. 1149-1154 (6)	90	90

Traditional acrobatics.

Shao Shan
A289

Transportation by Railroad
A290

Designs: 1½f, Site of 1st National Communist Party Congress. 2f, Peasant Movement Institute, Kwangchow. 3f, Headquarters of Nanchang Uprising. 4f, Great Hall of the People, Peking. 5f, View of Wen Chia Shih. 8f, Tien An Men. 10f, Tzeping in Chingkang Mountains. 20f Site of Kutien Meeting. 22f, Tsunyi Conference site. 35f, Yenan (bridge). 43f, Hsi Pai Ho, Communist Party meeting site. 50f, Fairy Cave, Lushan. 52f, Monument to People's Heroes. $2, Trucks on mountain road.

1974 Litho. *Perf. 11*

Without Gum

1163	A289	1f sl grn & pale grn	5	5
1164	A289	1½f car & buff	5	5
1165	A289	2f dk bl & pale grn	5	5
1166	A289	3f dk ol & yel	5	5
1167	A289	4f red & yel	8	8
1168	A289	5f brn & lt yel	10	10
1169	A289	8f dl mag & buff	15	15
1170	A289	10f bl & pink	20	20
1171	A289	20f dk red & buff	40	40
1172	A289	22f vio & lt yel	45	45
1173	A289	35f mar & lt yel	60	60
1174	A289	43f red brn & buff	85	*1.50*
1175	A289	50f dk bl & pink	*6.00*	*1.00*
1176	A289	52f sep & buff	1.00	1.00

Photogravure & Engraved

1177	A290	$1 multi	2.00	75
1178	A290	$2 multi	4.00	1.25
		Nos. 1163-1178 (16)	*16.03*	*7.68*

Capital Stadium
A290a

Design: 8f, Hotel Peking.

1974, Dec. 1 Photo. *Perf. 11*

Without Gum

1179	A290a	4f blk & yel grn	10	*20*
1180	A290a	8f blk & ultra	15	15

"Veteran Secretary"
A291

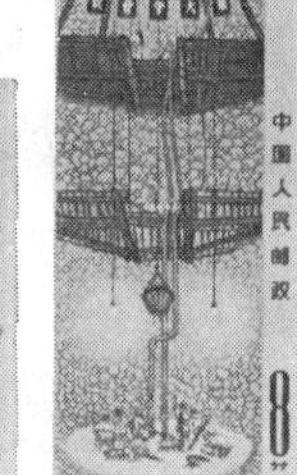

Well Diggers
A292

Designs: Nos. 1183–1186 horizontal.

1974, Apr. 20 Photo. *Perf. 11*

Multicolored

1181	A291	8f *shown* (1)	15	15
1182	A292	8f *shown* (2)	15	15
1183	A291	8f *Spring hoeing* (3)	15	15
1184	A291	8f *Farmers* (4)	15	15
1185	A292	8f *Farm* (5)	15	15
1186	A291	8f *Bumper crops* (6)	15	15
		Nos. 1181-1186 (6)	90	90

Paintings by farmers of Huhsien County, shown at exhibition in Peking.

Mailman on Motorcycle—A293

1974, May 15 Photo. *Perf. 11*

Multicolored

1187	A293	8f *shown* (1)	15	15
1188	A293	8f *People of the world* (2)	15	15
1189	A293	8f *Great Wall* (3)	15	15

Centenary of the Universal Postal Union.

Barefoot Doctor Inocculating Children—A294

Designs (Barefoot Doctors): No. 1191, Crossing stream at night to reach patient (vert.). No. 1192, Gathering herbs (vert.). No. 1193, Acupuncture treatment for farmer in the field.

Perf. 11x11½, 11½x11

1974, June 26 Photogravure

1190	A294	8f multi (82)	15	15
1191	A294	8f multi (83)	15	15
1192	A294	8f multi (84)	15	15
1193	A294	8f multi (85)	15	15

Steel Worker Wang Chin-hsi—A295

1974, Sept. 30 Photo. *Perf. 11*

Designs: No. 1195, Workers studying Mao's writings around campfire. No. 1196, Drilling for oil in winter. No. 1197, Scientific industrial management. No. 1198, Oil derricks and farms. Numbered T.4.

1194	A295	8f multi (5-1)	15	15
1195	A295	8f multi (5-2)	15	15
1196	A295	8f multi (5-3)	15	15
1197	A295	8f multi (5-4)	15	15
1198	A295	8f multi (5-5)	15	15
		Nos. 1194-1198 (5)	75	75

The workers of Taching as examples of achievement.

Members of Tachai Commune—A296

Designs: No. 1200, Farmers leveling mountains and fields in winter. No. 1201, Scientific farming. No. 1202, Trucks carrying surplus harvest. No. 1203, Young workers with banner. Numbered T.5.

1974, Sept. 30

1199	A296	8f multi (5-1)	15	15
1200	A296	8f multi (5-2)	15	15
1201	A296	8f multi (5-3)	15	15
1202	A296	8f multi (5-4)	15	15
1203	A296	8f multi (5-5)	15	15
		Nos. 1199-1203 (5)	75	75

The farmers of Tachai as examples of achievement.

Arms of Republic and Members of Ethnic Grops—A297

Taching Steel Worker
A298

Designs: No. 1206, Tachai farm woman. No. 1207, Soldier, planes and ships. Numbered J.3.

1974, Oct. 1

1204	A297	8f multi (1-1)	50	50
1205	A298	8f multi (3-1)	20	20
1206	A298	8f multi (3-2)	20	20
1207	A298	8f multi (3-3)	20	20

People's Republic of China, 25th anniversary. Nos. 1205–1207 printed se-tenant.

Export Commodities Fair Building, Canton—A299

1974, Oct. 15

1208	A299	8f multi	25	25

Chinese Export Commodities Fair, Canton.

Guerrillas' Monument, Permet, Albania
A300

Albanian Patriots and Coat of Arms
A301

1974, Nov. 29 Photo. *Perf. 11½x11*

1209	A300	8f multi	1.00	*1.00*
1210	A301	8f multi	1.00	*1.00*

Albania's liberation, 30th anniversary.

Water-cooled Generator—A302

Designs: No. 1212, Motorized rice sprouts transplanter. No. 1213, Universal cylindrical grinding machine. No. 1214, Open-air rock drill (vert.). All dated 1973.

Photogravure and Engraved

1974, Dec. 23 *Perf. 11*

1211	A302	8f vio & multi (78)	15	15
1212	A302	8f yel grn & multi (79)	15	15
1213	A302	8f ver & multi (80)	15	15
1214	A302	8f bl & multi (81)	15	15

Industrial products.

Congress Delegates—A303

Designs: No. 1216, Red flags, constitution and flowers. No. 1217, Worker, farmer and soldier, agriculture and industry. Numbered J.5.

1975, Jan. 25 Photo. *Perf. 11½*

1215	A303	8f gold & multi (3-1)	15	15
1216	A303	8f gold & multi (3-2)	15	15
1217	A303	8f gold & multi (3-3)	15	15

Fourth National People's Congress, Peking.

Teacher Studying Revolutionary Works
A304

Designs: No. 1219, Teacher, children and horse. No. 1220, Outdoors class. No. 1221, Class held in boat. Numbered T.9.

1975, Mar. 8 Photo. *Perf. 11*

1218	A304	8f multi (4-1)	15	15
1219	A304	8f multi (4-2)	15	15
1220	A304	8f multi (4-3)	15	15
1221	A304	8f multi (4-4)	15	15

Rural women teachers and for International Working Women's Day.

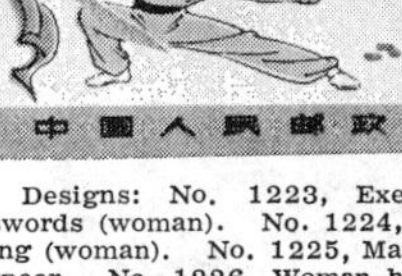

"Broad-sword," Encounter Position
A305

Designs: No. 1223, Exercise with 2 swords (woman). No. 1224, Graceful boxing (woman). No. 1225, Man leaping with spear. No. 1226, Woman holding cudgel. 43f, Two women with spears against man with cudgel.

1975, June 10 Photo. *Perf. 11x11½*

Size: 39x29mm.

1222	A305	8f red & multi (6-1)	30	30
1223	A305	8f red & multi (6-2)	30	30
1224	A305	8f red & multi (6-3)	30	30
1225	A305	8f red & multi (6-4)	30	30
1226	A305	8f red & multi (6-5)	30	30

Size: 59x29mm.

1227	A305	43f red & multi (6-6)	80	80
		Nos. 1222-1227 (6)	2.30	2.30

Wushu ("Kung Fu"), self-defense exercises. Tête bêche in sheets of 50 (5x10).

Mass Judgment and Criticisms
A306

Designs: No. 1229, Brigade leader writing wall newspaper. No. 1230, Study and criticism on battlefield (horiz.). No. 1231, Former "slave" led into battle by criticism of Lin Piao and Confucius (horiz.). Numbered T. 8.

Perf. 11½x11, 11x11½

1975, Aug. 20 Photogravure

1228	A306	8f red & multi (4-1)	15	15
1229	A306	8f red & multi (4-2)	15	15
1230	A306	8f red & multi (4-3)	15	15
1231	A306	8f red & multi (4-4)	15	15

Campaign to encourage criticism of Lin Piao and Confucius.

Athletes Studying Theory of Dictatorship of Proletariat—A307

Designs: No. 1232, Women athletes leading parade (vert.). No. 1234, Women volleyball players. No. 1235, Runner, soldier, farmer and worker (vert.). No. 1236, Young athlete and various sports. No. 1237, Athletes of various races and horse race. 35f, Children and diving tower (vert.). Numbered J. 6.

1975, Sept. 12 Photo. *Perf. 11½*

1232	A307	8f multi (7-1)	15	15
1233	A307	8f multi (7-2)	15	15
1234	A307	8f multi (7-3)	15	15
1235	A307	8f multi (7-4)	15	15
1236	A307	8f multi (7-5)	15	15
1237	A307	8f multi (7-6)	15	15
1238	A307	35f multi (7-7)	70	70
		Nos. 1232-1238 (7)	1.60	1.60

3rd National Sports Meet.

Mountaineers
A308

Mt. Everest
A309

Design: No. 1240, Mountaineers raising Chinese flag on summit (horiz.). Numbered T.15.

Perf. 11½x11, 11x11½

1975 Photogravure

1239	A308	8f multi (3-2)	15	15
1240	A308	8f multi (3-3)	15	15
1241	A309	43f multi (3-1)	80	80

Chinese Mt. Everest expedition.

Agricultural Workers with Book—A310

Designs: No. 1243, Workers carrying load. No. 1244, Woman driving harvester combine. Numbered J.7.

1975, Oct. 1 *Perf. 11½*

1242	A310	8f multi (3-1)	15	15
1243	A310	8f multi (3-2)	15	15
1244	A310	8f multi (3-3)	15	15

National Conference to promote learning from Tachai's achievements in agriculture.

Girl Giving Boy Red Scarf
A311

Designs (Children): No. 1246, Putting up wall posters criticizing Lin Piao and Confucius. No. 1247, Studying. No. 1248, Harvesting. 52f, Physical training. Numbered T.14.

1975, Dec. 1 Photo. *Perf. 11½*

1245	A311	8f multi (5-1)	15	15
1246	A311	8f multi (5-2)	15	15
1247	A311	8f multi (5-3)	15	15
1248	A311	8f multi (5-4)	15	15
1249	A311	52f multi (5-5)	1.00	1.00
		Nos. 1245-1249 (5)	1.60	1.60

Moral, intellectual and physical progress of Chinese children.

Woman Plowing Rice Field
A312

Designs: No. 1251, Mechanized rice planting. No. 1252, Drainage and irrigation. No. 1253, Woman spraying insecticide over cotton field. No. 1254, Combine. Numbered T.13.

1975, Dec. 15 ***Perf. 11***

1250	A312	8f multi (5-1)	15	15
1251	A312	8f multi (5-2)	15	15
1252	A312	8f multi (5-3)	15	15
1253	A312	8f multi (5-4)	15	15
1254	A312	8f multi (5-5)	15	15
		Nos. 1250-1254 (5)	75	75

Priority program of farm mechanization.

Farmland and Irrigation Canal
A313

Designs of Nos. 1255–1270 numbered J.8.

1976, Feb. 20 Photo. ***Perf. 11½***

Multicolored

1255	A313	8f *shown* (16-1)	20	20
1256	A313	8f *Irrigation canal* (16-2)	20	20
1257	A313	8f *Fertilizer plant* (16-3)	20	20
1258	A313	8f *Textile plant* (16-4)	20	20
1259	A313	8f *Anshan Iron and Steel Co.* (16-5)	20	20

Nos. 1255–1270 commemorate fulfillment of 4th Five-year Plan.

1976, Apr. 9

Multicolored

1260	A313	8f *Coal freight trains* (16-6)	20	20
1261	A313	8f *Hydroelectric station* (16-7)	20	20
1262	A313	8f *Ship building* (16-8)	20	20
1263	A313	8f *Oil industry* (16-9)	20	20
1264	A313	8f *Pipe line and port* (16-10)	20	20

1976, June 12

Multicolored

1265	A313	8f *Train on viaduct* (16-11)	20	20
1266	A313	8f *Scientific research* (16-12)	20	20
1267	A313	8f *Classroom* (16-13)	20	20
1268	A313	8f *Health Center* (16-14)	20	20
1269	A313	8f *Apartment houses* (16-15)	20	20
1270	A313	8f *Department store* (16-16)	20	20
		Nos. 1255-1270 (16)	3.20	3.20

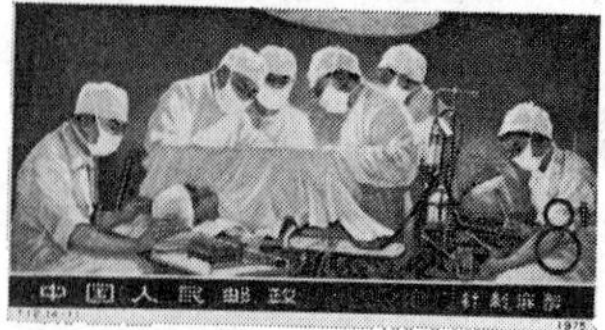

Heart Surgery with Acupuncture Anesthesia—A314

Designs (Operating Room and): No. 1272, Man driving tractor with severed arm restored. No. 1273, Man exercising broken arm in cast. No. 1274, Patient threading needle after cataract operation. Numbered T.12.

1976, Apr. 9 Photo. ***Perf. 11½***

1271	A314	8f brn & multi (4-1)	16	16
1272	A314	8f yel grn & multi (4-2)	16	16
1273	A314	8f bl grn & multi (4-3)	16	16
1274	A314	8f vio bl & multi (4-4)	16	16

Achievements in medical and health services.

Students in May 7 School—A315

Designs: No. 1276, Students as farm workers. No. 1277, Production brigade. Numbered J.9.

1976, May 7 Photo. ***Perf. 11½***

1275	A315	8f multi (3-1)	16	16
1276	A315	8f multi (3-2)	16	16
1277	A315	8f multi (3-3)	16	16

10th anniversary of Chairman Mao's May 7 Directive.

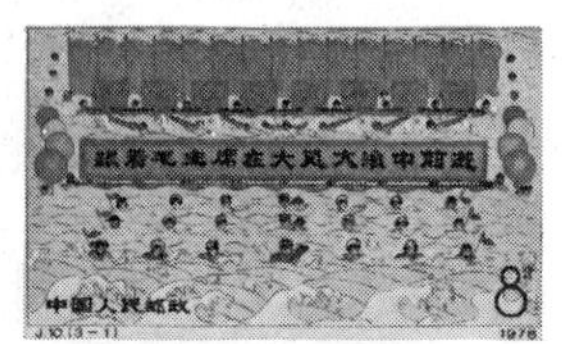

Mass Training in Swimming—A316

Designs: No. 1279, Swimmers crossing Yangtze River. No. 1280, Swimmers walking into the surf. Numbered J.10.

1976, July 16 Photo. ***Perf. 11½***

Size: 47x27mm.

1278	A316	8f multi (3-1)	16	16

Size: 35x27mm.

1279	A316	8f multi (3-2)	16	16
1280	A316	8f multi (3-3)	16	16

Chairman Mao's swim in Yangtze River, 10th anniversary.

Workers, Peasants and Soldiers Going to College—A317

Designs: No. 1282, Classroom. No. 1283, Instruction on construction site. No. 1284, Computer room. No. 1285, Graduates returning home. Numbered T.18.

1976, Sept. 6 Photo. ***Perf. 11½***

1281	A317	8f multi (5-1)	16	16
1282	A317	8f multi (5-2)	16	16
1283	A317	8f multi (5-3)	16	16
1284	A317	8f multi (5-4)	16	16
1285	A317	8f multi (5-5)	16	16
		Nos. 1281-1285 (5)	80	80

Success of proletarian education system.

Power Line Repair by Woman
A318

Designs: No. 1287, Insulator repair. No. 1288, Cherry picker. No. 1289, Transformer repair. Numbered T.16.

1976, Sept. 15

1286	A318	8f multi (4-1)	16	16
1287	A318	8f multi (4-2)	16	16
1288	A318	8f multi (4-3)	16	16
1289	A318	8f multi (4-4)	16	16

Maintenance of high power lines.

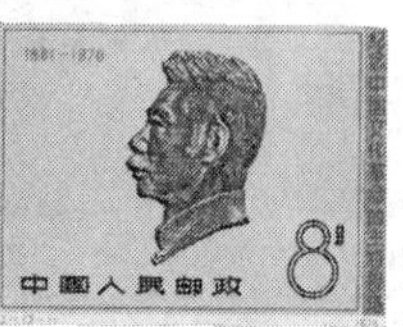

Lu Hsun
A319

Designs: No. 1291, Lu Hsun sick, writing in bed. No. 1292, Lu Hsun with worker, soldier and peasant. Numbered J.11.

Photogravure and Engraved

1976, Oct. 19 ***Perf. 11x11½***

1290	A319	8f multi (3-1)	16	16
1291	A319	8f multi (3-2)	16	16
1292	A319	8f multi (3-3)	16	16

Lu Hsun (1881–1936), writer and revolutionary leader.

Old Farmer Tying Towel on Student's Head
A320

Designs: No. 1294, Student teaching farm woman (horiz.). No. 1295, Students climbing mountain for new water resources. No. 1296, Student testing wheat (horiz.). 10f, Student feeding lamb. 20f, Frontier guards (horiz.). Numbered T.17.

1976, Dec. 22 Photo. ***Perf. 11½***

1293	A320	4f multi (6-1)	8	8
1294	A320	8f multi (6-2)	16	16
1295	A320	8f multi (6-3)	16	16
1296	A320	8f multi (6-4)	16	16
1297	A320	10f multi (6-5)	25	25
1298	A320	20f multi (6-6)	50	50
		Nos. 1293-1298 (6)	1.31	1.31

Students' efforts to help poor country people.

Mao's Home, Shaoshan—A321

Designs: No. 1300, School building. No. 1301, Farmers' Association building. 10f, Railroad station. All in Shaoshan. Numbered T.11.

1976, Dec. 26 ***Perf. 11***

1299	A321	4f multi (4-1)	8	8
1300	A321	8f multi (4-2)	16	16
1301	A321	8f multi (4-3)	16	16
1302	A321	10f multi (4-4)	25	25

Shaoshan, Mao's birthplace.

Chou En-lai
A322

Designs: No. 1304, Chou giving report at 10th Party Congress. No. 1305, Chou with Wang Chin-hsi, famous oil worker (horiz.). No. 1306, Chou with people of Tachai, 1973 (horiz.). Numbered J.13.

1977, Jan. 8 Photo. ***Perf. 11½***

1303	A322	8f multi (4-1)	16	16
1304	A322	8f multi (4-2)	16	16
1305	A322	8f multi (4-3)	16	16
1306	A322	8f multi (4-4)	16	16

Premier Chou En-lai (1898–1976), a founder of Chinese Communist Party, 1st death anniversary.

Liu Hu-lan, an Inspiration
A323

Designs: No. 1307, Liu Hu-lan monument. No. 1308, Mao Tse-tung quotation: "A great life—a glorious death." Numbered J.12.

1977, Jan. 31

1307	A323	8f multi (3-1)	20	20
1308	A323	8f multi (3-2)	20	20
1309	A323	8f multi (3-3)	20	20

Liu Hu-lan, Chinese heroine.

Uprising in Taiwan
A324

Design: 10f, Gate of Heavenly Peace, Peking; Sun Moon Lake, Taiwan, Taiwanese people holding PRC flag. Numbered J.14.

1977, Feb. 28 Photo. ***Perf. 11***

1310	A324	8f multi (2-1)	20	20
1311	A324	10f multi (2-2)	25	25

Uprising of the people of Taiwan, Feb. 28, 1947.

Sharpshooters—A325

Designs: No. 1313, Women horseback riders. No. 1314, Underground defense tunnel. Numbered T.10.

1977, Mar. 8 ***Perf. 11½***

1312	A325	8f multi (3-1)	16	16
1313	A325	8f multi (3-2)	16	16
1314	A325	8f multi (3-3)	16	16

Militia women.

Forestry
A326

Designs: 1f, Coal mining. 1½f, Sheep-herding. 2f, Export (loading railroad car onto ship). 4f, Hydroelectric station. 5f, Fishery. 8f, Combine in field. 10f, Radio tower and mail truck. 20f, Steel production. 30f, Trucks on mountain road. 40f, Textiles. 50f, Tractor assembly line. 60f, Offshore oil rigs and birds, setting sun. 70f, Railroad bridge, Yangtze Gorge. No numbers.

1977 Photogravure *Perf. 11½*

1315	A326	1f yel grn, red & blk	5	5
1316	A326	1½f bl grn, yel grn & brn	5	*50*
1317	A326	2f org, bl & blk	7	7
1318	A326	3f ol & dk grn	9	9
1319	A326	4f lil, org & blk	10	10
1320	A326	5f lt ol & ultra	12	10
1321	A326	8f red & yel	18	10
1322	A326	10f lt grn, org & bl	20	5
1323	A326	20f org, yel & brn	35	5
1324	A326	30f bl, lt grn & blk	45	10
1325	A326	40f multi	55	40
1326	A326	50f cit, red & blk	65	20
1327	A326	60f pur, yel & org	90	30
1328	A326	70f bl & multi	1.00	50
		Nos. 1315-1328 (14)	4.76	*2.61*

Address by Party Committee
A327

Designs: No. 1330, Planting new rice fields. No. 1331, Farmers reading wall newspaper. No. 1332, Land reclamation. Numbered T.22.

1977, Apr. 9 *Perf. 11x11½*

1329	A327	8f multi (4-1)	16	16
1330	A327	8f multi (4-2)	16	16
1331	A327	8f multi (4-3)	16	16
1332	A327	8f multi (4-4)	16	16

Building Tachai-type communities throughout China.

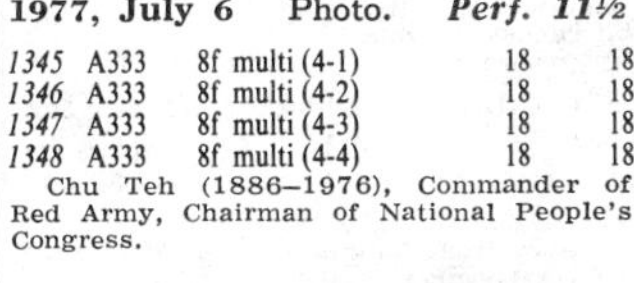

Worker at Microphone—A328

Designs: No. 1334, Drilling for oil during snowstorm. No. 1335, Crowd advancing under Red banner. No. 1336, Workers, industrial complex, rocket blast-off. Numbered J.15.

1977, Apr. 25 *Perf. 11*

1333	A328	8f multi (4-1)	16	16
1334	A328	8f multi (4-2)	16	16
1335	A328	8f multi (4-3)	16	16
1336	A328	8f multi (4-4)	16	16

Conference on learning from Taching workers in industry.

Mongolians Hailing Anniversary
A329

Designs: 10f, Iron and steel complex, iron ore train. 20f, Cattle grazing in improved pasture. Numbered J.16.

1977, May 1 *Perf. 11x11½*

1337	A329	8f multi (3-1)	16	16
1338	A329	10f multi (3-2)	20	20
1339	A329	20f multi (3-3)	40	40

30th anniversary of Inner Mongolian Autonomous Region.

1877 Flag of Romania and Oak Leaves
A330

Mihai Viteazu Memorial (16th Century Hero)
A331

Design: 10f, Battle of Smirdan, by N. Grigorescu. Numbered J.17.

1977, May 9 Photo. *Perf. 11*

1340	A330	8f multi (3-1)	16	16
1341	A331	10f multi (3-2)	20	20
1342	A331	20f multi (3-3)	40	40

Centenary of Romanian independence.

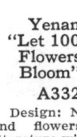

Yenan "Let 100 Flowers Bloom"
A332

Design: No. 1344, Hammer, sickle, gun and flowers; "Proletarian revolutionary literature will prosper." Numbered J.18.

1977, May, 23

1343	A332	8f grn, red & gold	16	16
1344	A332	8f lt brn, red & gold	16	16

Yenan Forum on Literature and Art, 35th anniversary.

Chu Teh
A333

Designs: No. 1346, Chu Teh, last address to Congress. No. 1347, Chu Teh at his desk (horiz.). No. 1348, Chu Teh on horseback as commander of Red Army. Numbered J.19.

1977, July 6 Photo. *Perf. 11½*

1345	A333	8f multi (4-1)	18	18
1346	A333	8f multi (4-2)	18	18
1347	A333	8f multi (4-3)	18	18
1348	A333	8f multi (4-4)	18	18

Chu Teh (1886–1976), Commander of Red Army, Chairman of National People's Congress.

Military under Mao's Banner
A334

Designs: No. 1350, Red Flag, Soldiers, Chingkang Mountains. No. 1351, Guerrilla fighters returning to base. No. 1352, Guerrillas crossing Yangtze. No. 1353, National defense. Numbered J.20.

1977, Aug. 1

1349	A334	8f multi (5-1)	18	18
1350	A334	8f multi (5-2)	18	18
1351	A334	8f multi (5-3)	18	18
1352	A334	8f multi (5-4)	18	18
1353	A334	8f multi (5-5)	18	18
		Nos. 1349-1353 (5)	90	90

Liberation Army Day, 50th anniversary of People's Army.

Gate of Heavenly Peace, People and Red Flags—A335

Designs: No. 1355, People marching under Red Flag with Mao's portrait. No. 1356, People marching under Red Flag with hammer and sickle. Numbered J.23.

1977, Aug. 22 Photo. *Perf. 11½x11*

1354	A335	8f multi (3-1)	25	25
1355	A335	8f multi (3-2)	25	25
1356	A335	8f multi (3-3)	25	25

11th National Congress of the Communist Party of China.

Chairman Mao
A336

Designs (Mao Portraits): No. 1358, as young man in Shansi. No. 1359, addressing Communist Party in Plenary Session. No. 1360, Proclaiming People's Republic at Gate of Heavenly Peace. No. 1361, at airport with Chou En-lai and Chu Teh (horiz.). No. 1362, Reviewing Army as old man. Numbered J.21.

1977, Sept. 9 Photo. *Perf. 11½*

1357	A336	8f multi (6-1)	18	18
1358	A336	8f multi (6-2)	18	18
1359	A336	8f multi (6-3)	18	18
1360	A336	8f multi (6-4)	18	18
1361	A336	8f multi (6-5)	18	18
1362	A336	8f multi (6-6)	18	18
		Nos. 1357-1362 (6)	1.08	1.08

Mao-Tse-tung (1893–1976), first death anniversary.

Mao Memorial Hall—A337

Design: No. 1364, Chairman Hua's inscription. Numbered J.22.

1977, Sept. 9

1363	A337	8f lt ultra & multi	50	50
1364	A337	8f lt grn, tan & gold	50	50

Completion of Mao Memorial Hall.

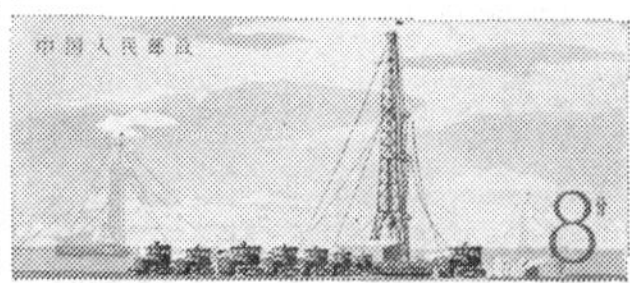

Tractors Moving Drilling Tower
A338

Designs: No. 1366, Shui Pow Tsi oil well and women workers. No. 1367, Construction of oil pipe line, Taching, and silos. No. 1368, Tung Fang Hung oil refinery, Peking. No. 1369, Taching oil loaded into tanker in harbor. 20f, Off-shore drilling platform "Pohai No. 1." Numbered T.19.

1978, Jan. 31 Photo. *Perf. 11*

1365	A338	8f multi (6-1)	16	16
1366	A338	8f multi (6-2)	16	16
1367	A338	8f multi (6-3)	16	16
1368	A338	8f multi (6-4)	16	16
1369	A338	8f multi (6-5)	16	16
1370	A338	20f multi (6-6)	40	40
		Nos. 1365-1370 (6)	1.20	1.20

Development of Chinese oil industry.

"Army Teaching Militia"—A339

Design: No. 1372, "Army helping with rice planting." Numbered T.23.

1978, Feb. 5 Photo. *Perf. 11*

1371	A339	8f multi (2-1)	16	16
1372	A339	8f multi (2-2)	16	16

Army and people working as a family.

Red Flags, Mao Tse-tung
A340

Constitution and Red Flags
A341

Design: No. 1375, Atom symbol over symbols of agriculture and industry. All designs include Great Hall of the People, Peking, and flowers. Numbered J.24.

1978, Feb. 26

1373	A340	8f multi (3-1)	16	16
1374	A341	8f multi (3-2)	16	16
1375	A340	8f multi (3-3)	16	16

5th National People's Congress.

Mao's Eulogy for Lei Feng
A342

Lei Feng, Studying Mao's Works
A343

Design: No. 1377, Chairman Hua's thoughts (5 lines). Numbered J.26.

1978, Mar. 5

1376	A342	8f gold & red (3-1)	25	25
1377	A342	8f gold & red (3-2)	25	25
1378	A343	8f multi (3-3)	25	25

Lei Feng (1940–1962), communist fighter; 15th anniversary of Chairman Mao's eulogy "Learn from Comrade Feng."

Hsiang Ching-yu A344 — Yang Kai-hui A345

Numbered J.27.

1978, Mar. 8

1379 A344 8f multi (2-1) 16 16
1380 A345 8f multi (2-2) 16 16

Hsiang Ching-yu, pioneer of Women's Movement, executed 1928; Yang Kai-hui, communist fighter, executed 1930.

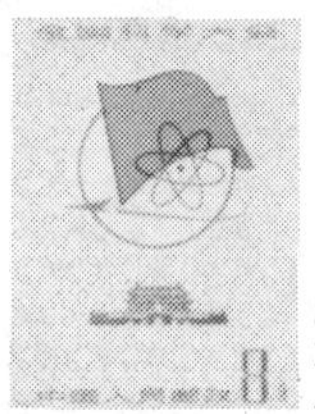

Conference Emblem
A346

Designs: No. 1382, Banners symbolizing industry, agriculture, defense and science. No. 1383, Red flag, atom symbol and globe. Numbered J.25.

1978, Mar. 18 Litho. *Perf. 11½x11*

1381 A346 8f gold & red (3-1) 16 16
1382 A346 8f multi (3-2) 16 16
1383 A346 8f multi (3-3) 16 16
a. Souvenir sheet of 3 4.25 4.25

National Science Conference. No. 1383a contains one each of Nos. 1381–1383 with simulated perforations; olive margin with atom symbols and inscription. Size: 140x 105mm. Sold for 50fen.

Release of Weather Balloon
A347

Weather Observations: No. 1385, Radar station, typhoon watch. No. 1386, Computer, weather maps. No. 1387, Local weather observers. No. 1388, Rockets intercepting hail clouds. Numbered T.24.

1978, Apr. 25 Photo. *Perf. 11x11½*

1384 A347 8f multi (5-1) 25 25
1385 A347 8f multi (5-2) 25 25
1386 A347 8f multi (5-3) 25 25
1387 A347 8f multi (5-4) 16 16
1388 A347 8f multi (5-5) 16 16
Nos. 1384-1388 (5) 1.07 1.07

Galloping Horse A348 — Children Playing Soccer A349

Designs: Galloping Horses, by Hsu Pei-hung (1895–1953). 40f, 50f, 60f, 70f, $5, horiz. Numbered T.28.

Perf. 11½x11, 11x11½

1978, May 5

1389 A348 4f multi (10-1) 6 6
1390 A348 8f multi (10-2) 16 16
1391 A348 8f multi (10-3) 16 16
1392 A348 10f multi (10-4) 20 20
1393 A348 20f multi (10-5) 40 40
1394 A348 30f multi (10-6) 50 50
1395 A348 40f multi (10-7) 65 65
1396 A348 50f multi (10-8) 80 80
1397 A348 60f multi (10-9) 1.00 1.00
1398 A348 70f multi (10-10) 1.20 1.20
Nos. 1389-1398 (10) 5.13 5.13

Souvenir Sheet

1399 A348 $5 multi 8.50 8.50

No. 1399 contains one stamp showing 4 horses (89x39mm.); black and silver margin shows floral damask pattern. Size: 147x98mm.

1978, June 1 *Perf. 11½*

Designs: No. 1401, Children on the beach. No. 1402, Little girls dancing. No. 1403, Children taking long walks. 20f, Children exercising for good health. Numbered T.21.

Size: 22x27mm.

1400 A349 8f multi (5-2) 16 16
1401 A349 8f multi (5-3) 16 16
1402 A349 8f multi (5-4) 16 16
1403 A349 8f multi (5-5) 16 16

Size: 48x28mm.

1404 A349 20f multi (5-1) 40 40
Nos. 1400-1404 (5) 1.04 1.04

Build up your health while young.

Synthetic Fiber Feeder
A350

Designs: No. 1406, Drawing out threads. No. 1407, Weaving. No. 1408, Dyeing and printing. No. 1409, Finished products. Numbered T.25.

1978, June 15 Photo. *Perf. 11½*

1405 A350 8f multi (5-1) 16 16
1406 A350 8f multi (5-2) 16 16
1407 A350 8f multi (5-3) 16 16
1408 A350 8f multi (5-4) 16 16
1409 A350 8f multi (5-5) 16 16
Nos. 1405-1409 (5) 80 80

Chemical fiber industry. Nos. 1405–1409 printed se-tenant in continuous design.

Conference Emblem A351 — "Develop Economy and Ensure Supplies" A352

Numbered J.28.

1978, June 20 *Perf. 13*

1410 A351 8f multi (2-1) 16 16
1411 A352 8f multi (2-2) 16 16

National Conference on Learning from Taching and Tachai in Finance and Trade.

The only foreign revenue stamps listed in this Catalogue are those authorized for prepayment of postage.

New Pastures, Mongolia
A353

Designs: No. 1413, Kazakh shepherds selecting sheep for breeding. No. 1414, Mechanized shearing of sheep, Tibet. Numbered T.27.

1978, June 30 Photo. *Perf. 11½*

1412 A353 8f multi (3-1) 16 16
1413 A353 8f multi (3-2) 16 16
1414 A353 8f multi (3-3) 16 16

Learning from Tachai in developing animal husbandry and new pastoral areas.

Coke Oven—A354

Designs: No. 1416, Iron furnace. No. 1417, Pouring steel. No. 1418, Steel rolling. No. 1419, Finished iron and steel products. Numbered T.26.

1978, July 22

1415 A354 8f multi (5-1) 16 16
1416 A354 8f multi (5-2) 16 16
1417 A354 8f multi (5-3) 16 16
1418 A354 8f multi (5-4) 16 16
1419 A354 8f multi (5-5) 16 16
Nos. 1415-1419 (5) 80 80

Iron and steel industry.

Iron Fist to Prevent Revisionism A355 — Jug in Shape of Sheep A356

Designs: No. 1421, "Carrying forward revolutionary tradition." No. 1422, "Strenuous training in military skills to wipe out enemy." Numbered T.32.

1978, Aug. 1 Photo. *Perf. 11½*

1420 A355 8f multi (3-1) 16 16
1421 A355 8f multi (3-2) 16 16
1422 A355 8f multi (3-3) 16 16

"Learn from Hard-boned 6th Company." (A military unit since 1939).

1978, Aug. 26

Arts and Crafts: 4f, Giant lion (toy; horiz.). No. 1425, Rhinoceros (lacquer ware; horiz). 10f, Cat (embroidery). 20f, Bag (weaving; horiz.). 30f, Teapot in shape of peacock (cloisonné). 40f, Plate with lotus, and swan-shaped box (lacquer ware; horiz.). 50f, Dragon flying in sky (ivory). 60f, Sun rising (jade; horiz.). 70f, Flight to human world (ivory). $3, Flying fairies (arts and crafts; horiz.). Numbered T.29.

1423 A356 4f multi (10-1) 7 7
1424 A356 8f multi (10-2) 16 16
1425 A356 8f multi (10-3) 16 16
1426 A356 10f multi (10-4) 20 20
1427 A356 20f multi (10-5) 40 40
1428 A356 30f multi (10-6) 50 50
1429 A356 40f multi (10-7) 65 65
1430 A356 50f multi (10-8) 80 80
1431 A356 60f multi (10-9) 1.00 1.00
1432 A356 70f multi (10-10) 1.20 1.20
Nos. 1423-1432 (10) 5.14 5.14

Souvenir Sheet

1433 A356 $3 multi 6.00 6.00

No. 1433 contains one stamp (85x36 mm.). Gold decorative margin. Size: 139x90mm.

Women, Atom Symbol, Rocket and Wheat
A357

1978, Sept. 8 Photo. *Perf. 11*

1434 A357 8f multi 50 30

4th National Women's Congress.

Ginseng A358 — Flag, Wheat, Cogwheel, Plane, Atom Symbols A359

Medicinal Plants: No. 1436, Horn of plenty. No. 1437, Blackberry lily. No. 1438, Balloonflower. 55f, Rhododendron dauricum. Numbered T.30.

1978, Sept. 15

1435 A358 8f multi (5-1) 16 16
1436 A358 8f multi (5-2) 16 16
1437 A358 8f multi (5-3) 16 16
1438 A358 8f multi (5-4) 16 16
1439 A358 55f multi (5-5) 1.10 1.10
Nos. 1435-1439 (5) 1.74 1.74

1978, Oct. 11 Photo. *Perf. 11*

1440 A359 8f multi 25 25

9th National Trade Union Congress.

Youth League Emblem
A360

1978, Oct. 16

1441 A360 8f multi 25 25

10th National Communist Youth League Congress.

Chinese and Japanese Girls Exchanging Gifts
A361

Great Wall and Mt. Fuji
A362

1978, Oct. 22

1442 A361 8f multi 25 25
1443 A362 55f multi 1.10 1.10

Signing of Sino-Japanese Peace and Friendship Treaty.

Moslem, Chinese and Mongolian People
A363

Chinsha River Bridge, West Szechuan
A364

Designs: No. 1445, Loading coal at Holan Mountain. 10f, Irrigated rice fields and boxthorn. Numbered J.29.

1978, Oct. 25

1444 A363 8f multi (3-1) 16 16
1445 A363 8f multi (3-2) 16 16
1446 A363 10f multi (3-3) 20 20

20th anniversary of founding of Ningsia Moslem Autonomous Region.

1978, Nov. 1 Photo. *Perf. 11½x11*

Highway Bridges: No. 1448, Hsinhong bridge, Wuhsi. No. 1449, Chiuhsikou bridge, Fengdu. No. 1450, Chinsha River bridge, West Szechuan. 60f, Shangyeh bridge, Sanmen. $2, Hsiang-kiang River bridge. Numbered T.31.

1447 A364 8f multi (5-1) 16 16
1448 A364 8f multi (5-2) 16 16
1449 A364 8f multi (5-3) 16 16
1450 A364 8f multi (5-4) 16 16
1451 A364 60f multi (5-5) 1.20 1.20
Nos. 1447-1451 (5) 1.84 1.84

Souvenir Sheet

1452 A364 $2 multi 6.00

No. 1452 contains one stamp (86x37 mm.). Ultramarine, white and gold margin shows tiny boats. Size: 145x69mm.

Mechanical Transplanting of Rice Seedlings
A365

Paintings: No. 1454, Spraying fields. No. 1455, Seed selection. No. 1456, Trade. No. 1457, Delivery of public grain in city. Numbered T.34.

1978, Nov. 30 *Perf. 11½*

1453 A365 8f multi (5-1) 40 40
1454 A365 8f multi (5-2) 40 40
1455 A365 8f multi (5-3) 40 40
1456 A365 8f multi (5-4) 40 40
1457 A365 8f multi (5-5) 40 40
Strip of 5 (#1453-1457) 2.50 2.50

Agricultural progress. Nos. 1453–1457 printed se-tenant in continuous design.

Dancers and Fireworks—A366

Designs: No. 1459, Industry (vert.). 10f, Agriculture (vert.). Numbered J.33.

1978, Dec. 11 Photo. *Perf. 11*

1458 A366 8f multi (3-1) 16 16
1459 A366 8f multi (3-2) 16 16
1460 A366 10f multi (3-3) 20 20

20th anniversary of Kwangsi Chuang Autonomous Region.

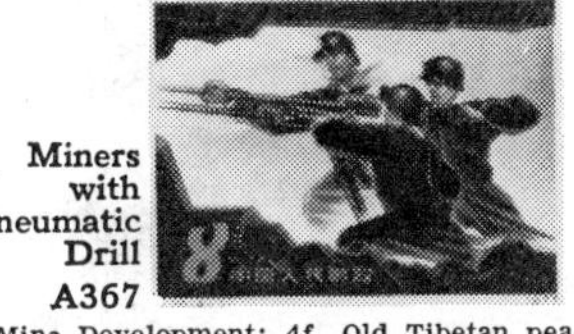

Miners with Pneumatic Drill
A367

Mine Development: 4f, Old Tibetan peasant reporting to surveyor. 10f, Open-cut mining with power shovel. 20f, Loaded electric train in pit. Numbered T.20.

1978, Dec. 29 Photo. & Engr.

1461 A367 4f multi (4-1) 8 8
1462 A367 8f multi (4-2) 16 16
1463 A367 10f multi (4-3) 20 20
1464 A367 20f multi (4-4) 40 40

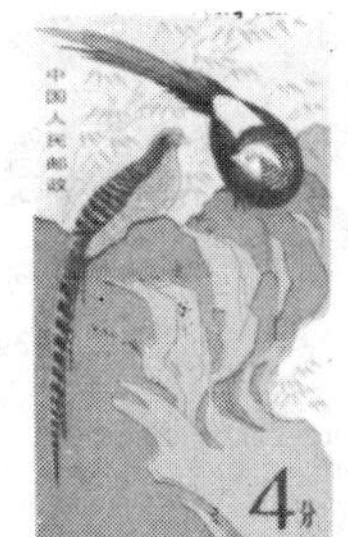

Golden Pheasants Roosting on Rock
A368

Golden Pheasants: 8f, In flight. 45f, Seeking food. Numbered T.35.

1979, Jan. 25 Photo. *Perf. 11½*

1465 A368 4f multi (3-1) 6
1466 A368 8f multi (3-2) 12
1467 A368 45f multi (3-3) 65

Albert Einstein and his Equation
A369

1979, Mar. 14 Photo. *Perf. 11½x11*

1468 A369 8f brn gold & blk 25 25

Albert Einstein (1879–1955), theoretical physicist.

Phoenix Battling Monster, Praying Woman
A370

Design: 60f, Man riding dragon to heaven. Designs from silk paintings found in Changsha tomb, Warring States Period (475–221 B.C.). Numbered T.33.

1979, Mar. 29 *Perf. 11*

1469 A370 8f multi (2-1) 12
1470 A370 60f multi (2-2) 90

Summer Palace
A371

Photo., Photo. & Engr. ($5)

1979-80 *Perf. 13*

1471 A371 $1 *Pagoda* ('80) 1.25
1472 A371 $2 *Shown* 2.25
1473 A371 $5 *Temple, Beihai Park* ('80) 7.50

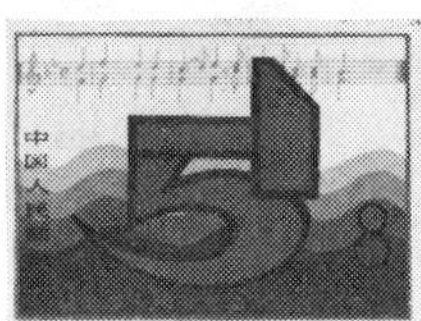

Hammer and Sickle "5 1" and Bars from "Internationale"
A372

1979, May 1 Photo. *Perf. 11*

1474 A372 8f multi 25 25

International Labor Day, 90th anniv.

"Tradition of May 4th Movement"
A373

Young Woman, Rocket, Antenna, Nuclear Reactor
A374

1979, May 4

1475 A373 8f multi 20
1476 A374 8f multi 20

60th anniversary of May 4th Movement.

IYC Emblem, Children Holding Balloons
A375

Children of Three Races, IYC Emblem
A376

1979, May 25 *Perf. 11½*

1477 A375 8f multi 12
1478 A376 60f multi 90

International Year of the Child.

Great Wall in Spring
A377

Designs (The Great Wall): No. 1480, in summer. No. 1481, in autumn. 60f, in winter. $2, Guard tower. Numbered T.38.

1979, June 25 Photo. *Perf. 11*

1479 A377 8f multi (4-1) 12
1480 A377 8f multi (4-2) 12
1481 A377 8f multi (4-3) 12
1482 A377 60f multi (4-4) 90

Souvenir Sheet

1483 A377 $2 multi 3.25

No. 1483 has blue gray and gold margin showing Great Wall and towers. Size: 140x78mm.

Roaring Tiger
A379

Manchurian Tiger: 8f, Two young tigers. 60f, Tiger at rest. Numbered T.40.

1979, July 20 *Perf. 11½x11*

1484 A379 4f multi (3-1) 6 6
1485 A379 8f multi (3-2) 12 12
1486 A379 60f multi (3-3) 90 90

Mechanical Harvesting—A380

Work of the Communes: No. 1488, Forestry. No. 1489, Raising ducks. No. 1490, Women weaving baskets. 10f, Fishing. Numbered T.39.

1979, Aug. 10 *Perf. 11½*

1487 A380 4f multi (5-1) 6
1488 A380 8f multi (5-2) 12
1489 A380 8f multi (5-3) 12
1490 A380 8f multi (5-4) 12
1491 A380 10f multi (5-5) 15

Souvenir Sheet

No. 1483 Overprinted with Gold Inscription and "1979"

1979, Aug. 25 Photo. *Perf. 11*

1492 A377 $2 multi 15.00

31st International Stamp Exhibition, Riccione, Italy. Size: 140x78mm. Numbered J41 (1-1).

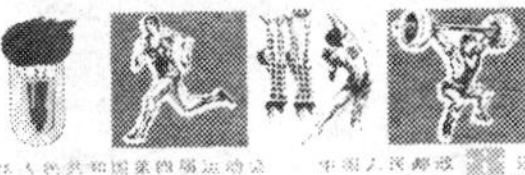

Games Emblem, Sports—A381

Emblem and: No. 1494, Soccer, badminton, high jump, speed skating. No. 1495, Fencing, skiing, gymnastics, diving. No. 1496, Motorcycling, table tennis, basketball, archery. No. 1497, Emblem only (vert.). Numbered J.43.

1979, Sept. 15 *Perf. 11½x11*

1493 A381 8f multi (4-1) 12
1494 A381 8f multi (4-2) 12
1495 A381 8f multi (4-3) 12
1496 A381 8f multi (4-4) 12

Souvenir Sheet
Perf. 11½

1497 A381 $2 multi 3.00

4th National Games. Nos. 1493–1496 printed se-tenant. No. 1497 has gray olive margin showing symbols of various sports. Size of stamp: 22x26mm., size of sheet: 57x62mm.

Flag and Rainbow—A382

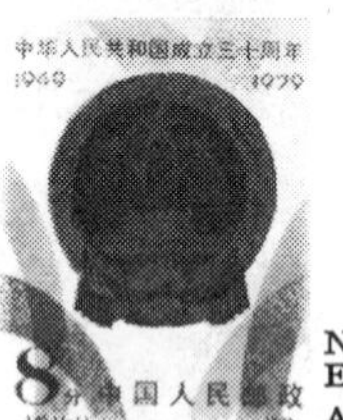

National Emblem A383

National Anthem A384

Dancers A385

Tractor, Aerial Crop Spraying, Irrigation A386

Designs: No. 1499, Flag and mountains. Nos. 1503–1505, various dances (numbered J.47). No. 1507, Atom symbol. No. 1509, Rocket, submarine, jets (Nos. 1506–1509 numbered J.48). No. 1510, National Emblem.

1979, Oct. 1 Photo. ***Perf. 11½***

1498 A382 8f multi 20
1499 A382 8f multi 20
1500 A383 8f multi 12

Engraved ***Perf. 11***

1501 A384 8f multi 25

Photogravure ***Perf. 11½***

1502 A385 8f multi (4-1) 20
1503 A385 8f multi (4-2) 20
1504 A385 8f multi (4-3) 20
1505 A385 8f multi (4-4) 20
Block of 4 (#1502-1505) 2.00
1506 A386 8f multi (4-1) 20
1507 A386 8f multi (4-2) 20
1508 A386 8f multi (4-3) 20
1509 A386 8f multi (4-4) 20

Souvenir Sheet

1510 A383 $1 multi 2.00

People's Republic of China, 30th anniversary. Nos. 1502–1505 printed in blocks of 4. No. 1510 has multicolored decorative margin. Size: 67x75mm.

Exhibition Emblem A387

Children Flying Model Planes A388

1979, Oct. 3

1511 A387 8f multi 25

Junior National Scientific and Technological Exhibition.

1979, Oct. 3

Designs: No. 1513, Girls and microscope. No. 1514, Children and telescope. No. 1515, Boy catching butterflies. No. 1516, Girl taking meteorological readings. No. 1517, Boys sailing model boat. No. 1518, Girl with book. Numbered T.41.

1512 A388 8f multi (6-1) 10
1513 A388 8f multi (6-2) 10
1514 A388 8f multi (6-3) 10
1515 A388 8f multi (6-4) 10
1516 A388 8f multi (6-5) 10
1517 A388 60f multi (6-6) 70
Nos. 1512-1517 (6) 1.20

Souvenir Sheet
Perf. 11

1518 A388 $2 multi 7.00

Study Science from Childhood. No. 1518 contains one stamp (90x40mm.). Light blue margin shows fish. Size: 148x 90mm.

Yu Shan Mountain—A389

Taiwan Landscapes: No. 1520, Sun and Moon Lake. No. 1521, Chihkan Tower. No. 1522, Suao-Hualien Highway. 55f, Tian Xiang Falls. 60f, Banping Mountain. Numbered T.42.

1979, Oct. 20 Photo. ***Perf. 11×11½***

1519 A389 8f multi (6-1) 12
1520 A389 8f multi (6-2) 12
1521 A389 8f multi (6-3) 12
1522 A389 8f multi (6-4) 12
1523 A389 55f multi (6-5) 80
1524 A389 60f multi (6-6) 90
Nos. 1519-1524 (6) 2.18

Arts Symbols—A390

Design: 8f, Seals and modernization symbols. Numbered J.39.

1979, Oct. 30

1525 A390 4f multi 10
1526 A390 8f multi 20

4th National Congress of Literary and Art Workers.

Train in Tunnel—A391

Railroads: No. 1520, Mountain bridge. No. 1521, Freight train. Numbered T.36.

Photogravure and Engraved
1979, Oct. 30

1527 A391 8f multi (3-1) 12
1528 A391 8f multi (3-2) 12
1529 A391 8f multi (3-3) 12

Chrysanthemum Petal—A392

Camellias: No. 1531, Lion head. No. 1532, Camellia chryantha. 10f, Small osmanthus leaf. 20f, Baby face. 30f, Cornelian. 40f, Peony camellia. 50f, Purple gown. 60f, Dwarf rose. 70f, Willow leaf spinel pink. $2, Red jewelry. Numbered T.37.

1979, Nov. 10 **Photo.** ***Perf. 11×11½***

1530 A392 4f multi (10-1) 6
1531 A392 8f multi (10-2) 12
1532 A392 8f multi (10-3) 12
1533 A392 10f multi (10-4) 15
1534 A392 20f multi (10-5) 30
1535 A392 30f multi (10-6) 45
1536 A392 40f multi (10-7) 60
1537 A392 50f multi (10-8) 75
1538 A392 60f multi (10-9) 90
1539 A392 70f multi (10-10) 1.10
Nos. 1530-1539 (10) 4.55

Souvenir Sheet
Perf. 11½×11

1540 A392 $2 multi 5.00 7.00

No. 1540 contains one stamp (86×36mm.), gold margin with white inscription. Size: 135×90mm.

Souvenir Sheet

No. 1540 Overprinted and Numbered in Gold in Margin.

1979, Nov. 10

1541 A392 $2 multi 14.00

People's Republic of China Philatelic Exhibition, Hong Kong, 1979. Numbered J.42 (1-1).

Norman Bethune Treating Soldier A393

Design: 70f, Bethune statue.

1979, Nov. 12

1542 A393 8f multi (2-2) 12
1543 A393 70f multi (2-1) 1.00

Dr. Norman Bethune, 40th death anniversary. Numbered J.50.

Central Archives Hall—A394

International Archives Weeks: No. 1545, Gold archive cabinet (vert.). 60f, Pavilion. Numbered J.51.

Perf. 11×11½, 11½×11
1979, Nov. 26 **Photo.**

1544 A394 8f multi (3-1) 12
1545 A394 8f multi (3-2) 12
1546 A394 60f multi (3-3) 90

Monkey King in Waterfall Cave—A395

Monkey King, Scenes from Pilgrimage to the West (Novel): No. 1548, Fighting Necha, son of Prince Li. No. 1549, In Mother Queen's peach orchard. No. 1550, In the alchemy furnace. 10f, Subduing the white bone demon. 20f, With palm leaf fan. 60f, In cobweb cave. 70f, Walking on scripture-seeking route. Numbered T.43.

1979, Dec. 1 ***Perf. 11½×11***

1547 A395 8f multi (8-1) 14
1548 A395 8f multi (8-2) 14
1549 A395 8f multi (8-3) 14
1550 A395 8f multi (8-4) 14
1551 A395 10f multi (8-5) 16
1552 A395 20f multi (8-6) 30
1553 A395 60f multi (8-7) 1.00
1554 A395 70f multi (8-8) 1.10
Nos. 1547-1554 (8) 3.12

Stalin Delivering Speech—A396

Design: No. 1555, Portrait of Stalin (vert.). Numbered J. 49.

Perf. 11×11½, 11½×11
1979, Dec. 21 **Engraved**

1555 A396 8f brn (2-1) 15
1556 A396 8f blk (2-2) 15

Joseph Stalin (1879-1953).

See "Special Notices" at the front of this volume for data on the listing methods of this Catalogue, abbreviations, condition, prices and examination.

Peony, by Qi Baishi—A397

1980 Photo. *Perf. 11½*

1557 A397 4f *shown* (16-1) 6
1558 A397 4f *Squirrels and grapes* (16-2) 6
1559 A397 8f *Crabs candle and wine* (16-3) 14
1560 A397 8f *Tadpoles in mountain spring* (16-4) 14
1561 A397 8f *Chicks* (16-5) 14
1562 A397 8f *Lotus* (16-6) 14
1563 A397 8f *Red plum* (16-7) 14
1564 A397 8f *Kingfisher* (16-8) 14
1565 A397 10f *Bottle gourd* (16-9) 15
1566 A397 20f *Voice of autumn* (16-10) 32
1567 A397 30f *Wisteria* (16-11) 45
1568 A397 40f *Chrysanthemums* (16-12) 60
1569 A397 50f *Shrimp* (16-13) 75
1570 A397 55f *Litchi* (16-14) 80
1571 A397 60f *Cabbages and mushrooms* (16-15) 90
1572 A397 70f *Peaches* (16-16) 1.10
Nos. 1557-1572 (16) 6.03

Souvenir Sheet

1980, May 20 Photo. *Perf. 11½*

1573 A397 $2 Evergreen 3.00

Qi Baishi paintings. Issue dates: Nos. 1557-1560, 1569-1572, Jan. 15; others, May 20. Numbered T. 44.

No. 1573 contains one stamp (37½x61mm); brown and tan margin shows portrait of Qi Baishi and inscription. Size: 120x86mm.

Meng Liang Mask from Hongyang Cave Opera—A398

Opera Masks. No. 1575, Li Kui, from Black Whirlwind. No. 1576, Huang Gai, from Meeting of Heroes. No. 1577, 10f, Lu Zhishen, from Wild Boar Forest. 20f, Lian Po, from Reconciliation between the General and Minister. 60f, Zhang Fei, from Reed Marsh. 70f, Dou Erdun, from Stealing the Emperor's Horse, Numbered T. 45.

1980, Jan. 25 *Perf. 11½x11*

1574 A398 4f multi (8-1) 6
1575 A398 4f multi (8-2) 6
1576 A398 8f multi (8-3) 14
1577 A398 8f multi (8-4) 14
1578 A398 10f multi (8-5) 13
1579 A398 20f multi (8-6) 30
1580 A398 60f multi (8-7) 90
1581 A398 70f multi (8-8) 1.00
Nos. 1574-1581 (8) 2.73

Speed Skating, Olympic Rings A399

Monkey, New Year A400

Olympic Rings and: No. 1582, Chinese flag. No. 1584, Figure skating. 60f, Downhill skiing. Numbered J. 54.

1980, Feb. 13

1582 A399 8f multi (4-1) 12
1583 A399 8f multi (4-2) 12
1584 A399 8f multi (4-3) 12
1585 A399 60f multi (4-4) 90

13th Winter Olympic Games, Lake Placid, N.Y., Feb. 12-24.

Engraved & Photogravure

1980, Feb. 15 *Perf. 11½*

1586 A400 8f multi 1.00

Clara Zetkin—A401

1980, Mar. 8 Photo. & Engr. *Perf. 11½x11*

1587 A401 8f blk & yel 25

International Working Women's Day, 70th anniversary, founded by Clara Zetkin (1857-1933).

Orchard—A402

Afforestation: 8f, Trees lining highway. 10f, Aerial seeding. 20f, Trees surrounding factory. Numbered T.48.

1980, Mar. 12 *Perf. 11x11½*

1588 A402 4f multi (4-1) 6
1589 A402 8f multi (4-2) 12
1590 A402 10f multi (4-3) 15
1591 A402 20f multi (4-4) 30

Apsaras, Symbols of Modernization—A403

1980, Mar. 15 Photo. *Perf. 11½*

1592 A403 8f multi 25

2nd National Conference of the Scientific and Technical Association of China.

Mail Transport by Ship—A404

1980, Mar. 20 *Perf. 11x11½*

1593 A404 2f *shown* (4-1) 3
1594 A404 4f *Bus* (4-2) 6
1595 A404 8f *Train* (4-3) 12
1596 A404 10f *Jet* (4-4) 15

Numbered T.49.

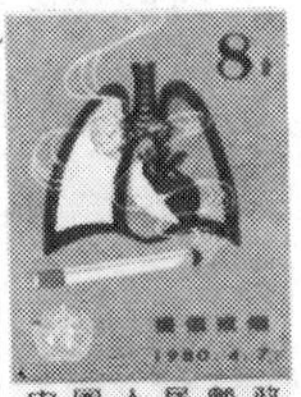

Lungs, Heart, Cigarette, WHO Emblem A405

Statue of Chien Chen (688-763) A406

1980, Apr. 7 *Perf. 11½x11*

1597 A405 8f *shown* (2-1) 12
1598 A405 60f *Faces* (2-2) 90

Fight against cigarette smoking. Numbered J.56.

1980, Apr. 13 *Perf. 11x11½, 11½x11*

Loan to China by Japan of statue of Chien Chen (Jian Zhen), Buddhist missionary to Japan (754-763): No. 1600, Chien Chen Memorial Hall, Yangchou (horiz.). 60f, Chien Chen's ship (horiz.). His name in Japan is Ganjin. Numbered J.55.

1599 A406 8f multi (3-1) 15
1600 A406 8f multi (3-2) 15
1601 A406 60f multi (3-3) 1.00

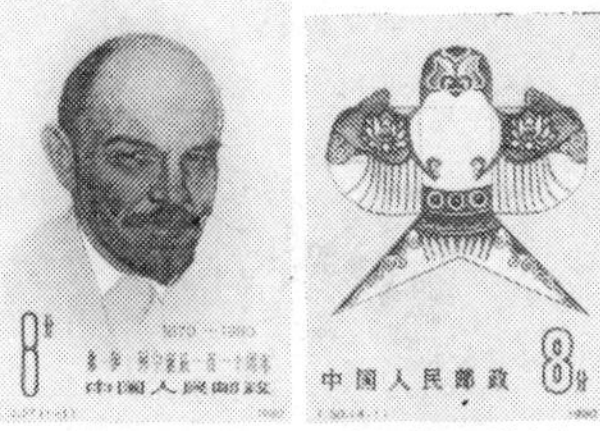

Lenin's 110th Birthday—A407

Swallow Chick Kite—A408

Photo. & Engr.

1980, Apr. 22 *Perf. 11½x11*

1602 A407 8f multi 25

1980, May 10 Photo. *Perf. 11½*

Designs: Kites. Numbered T.50.

1603 A408 8f *Shown* (4-1) 12
1604 A408 8f *Slender-swallow* (4-2) 12
1605 A408 8f *Semi-slender swallow* (4-3) 12
1606 A408 70f *Dual swallows* (4-4) 1.00

Hare Running from Fallen Papaya—A409

1980, June 1 Photo. *Perf. 11x11½*

1607 Strip of 4 60
a. A409 8f *Shown* (4-1) 12
b. A409 8f *Hare fox, monkey running away* (4-2) 12
c. A409 8f *Lion instructing animals* (4-3) 12
d. A409 8f *Discovery of fallen papaya* (4-4) 12

Gu Dong fairy tale. Nos. 1607a-1607d se-tenant with label telling story. Numbered T.51.

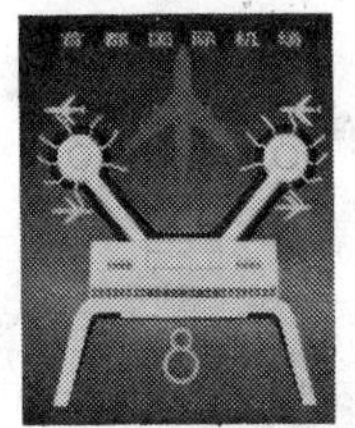

Terminal Building, Jets—A410

1980, June 20 *Perf. 11½*

1608 A410 8f *Shown* (2-1) 15
1609 A410 10f *Runways, jets* (2-2) 20

Peking International Airport opening. Numbered T.47.

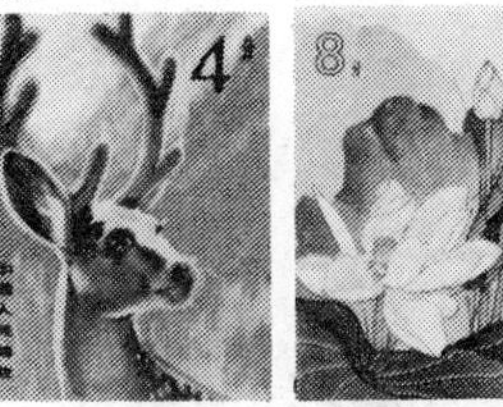

Sika Stag A411

White Lotus A412

1980, July 18 Photo. *Perf. 11½*

1610 A411 4f *Shown* (3-1) 10
1611 A411 8f *Doe and fawn* (3-2) 15
1612 A411 60f *Herd* (3-3) 90

Numbered T.52.

1980, Aug. 4

1613 A412 8f *Shown* (4-1) 25
1614 A412 8f *Rose-tipped snow* (4-2) 25
1615 A412 8f *Buddha's seat* (4-3) 25
1616 A413 70f *Variable charming face* (4-4) 1.75

Souvenir Sheet

1617 A412 $1 *Fresh lotus on rippling water* 2.50

Numbered T.54. No. 1617 contains one stamp (48x88mm); light gray decorative margin. Size: 70x145½mm.

Pearl Cave, Sword-cut Stone Sculptures—A413

Guilin Landscapes: No. 1619, Three mountains, distant views. No. 1620, Nine-horse fresco hill. No. 1621, Egrets around aged banyan. No. 1622, Western hills at sunset (vert.). No. 1623, Moonlight on Lijiang River (vert.). 60f, Spring-head, ancient ferry (vert.). 70f, Scenic path, Yangshue (vert.). Numbered T.53.

1980, Aug. 30 Photo. *Perf. 11½*

1618 A413 8f multi (8-1) 12
1619 A413 8f multi (8-2) 12
1620 A413 8f multi (8-3) 12
1621 A413 8f multi (8-4) 12
1622 A413 8f multi (8-5) 12
1623 A413 8f multi (8-6) 12
1624 A413 60f multi (8-7) 90
1625 A413 70f multi (8-8) 1.05
Nos. 1618-1625 (8) 2.67

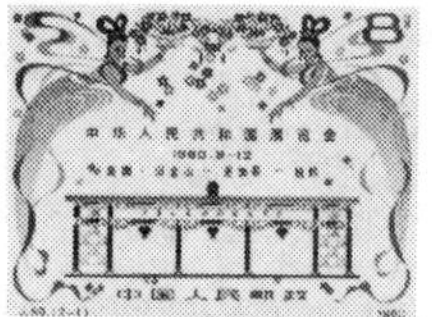

Entrance Gate and Good Fairies—A414

Great Wall, Symbols of Chicago, San Francisco and New York—A415

1980, Sept. 13 Photo. *Perf. 11x11½*

1626 A414 8f multi 12
1627 A415 70f multi 1.05

Exhibitions of the People's Republic of China in San Francisco, Chicago and New York, Sept.-Dec.

Sheets of 12 were sold only at U.S. exhibitions.

Romanian Flag, Warrior and Scroll—A416

1980, Sept. 20 Photo. *Perf. 11½x11*

1628 A416 8f multi 40

2050th anniversary of Dacia, first independent Romanian state.

UNESCO Exhibition of Drawings and Paintings—A417

Numbered J.60.

1980, Oct. 8 *Perf. 11½*

1629 A417 8f *Sea of Clouds, by Liu Haisu,* (3-1) 25 25
1630 A417 8f *Oriole and Magnolia, by Yu Feian,* vert., (3-2) 25 25
1631 A417 8f *Camels, by Wu Zuoren,* (3-3) 25 25

Quxi Tower, Tarrying Garden—A418

Designs: Scenes from Tarrying Garden. Numbered T.56.

1980, Oct. 25 Photo. *Perf. 11½*

1632 A418 8f *shown* (4-1) 12
1633 A418 8f *Yuancui Pavilion* (4-2) 12
1634 A418 10f *Hanbi Shanfang* (4-3) 15
1635 A418 60f *Guanyun Peak* (4-4) 90

Xu Guangpi (1562-1633), Agronomist A419 — Shooting, Olympic Rings A420

Scientists of Ancient China: No. 1637, Li Bing, hydraulic engineer, 3rd century B.C. No. 1638, Jia Sixie, agronomist, 5th century. 60f, Huang Daopo, textile expert, 13th century. Numbered J.58.

Photo. & Engr.

1980, Nov. 20 *Perf. 11½x11*

1636 A419 8f multi (4-1) 15
1637 A419 8f multi (4-2) 15
1638 A419 8f multi (4-3) 15
1639 A419 60f multi (4-4) 1.00

1980, Nov. 26 Photo.

1640 A420 4f *shown* (5-1) 6
1641 A420 8f *Gymnastics* (5-2) 12
1642 A420 8f *Diving* (5-3) 12
1643 A420 10f *Volleyball* (5-4) 15
1644 A420 60f *Archery* (5-5) 90
Nos. 1640-1644 (5) 1.35

Return to International Olympic Committee, 1st anniversary. Numbered J.62.

Chinese River Dolphin—A421

1980, Dec. 25 Photo. & Engr. *Perf. 11x11½*

1645 A421 8f *shown* (2-1) 12
a. Booklet pane of 6 90
1646 A421 60f *Dolphins* (2-2) 90
a. Booklet pane of 1 1.25

Cock—A422

1981, Jan. 5 Photo. & Engr. *Perf. 11½*

1647 A422 8f multi 25
a. Bklt. pane of 12 3.00

New Year 1981. Numbered T.58.

Early Morning in Xishuang Bana—A423

Photo.

1981, Jan. 20 *Perf. 11x11½, 11½x11*

1648 A423 4f *shown* (6-1) 6
1649 A423 4f *Dai mountain village* (6-2) 6
1650 A423 8f *Rainbow over Lanchang River* (6-3) 12
1651 A423 8f *Ancient temple,* vert. (6-4) 12
1652 A423 8f *Moonlit night,* vert. (6-5) 12
1653 A423 60f *Phoenix tree,* vert. (6-6) 90
Nos. 1648-1653 (6) 1.38

Flower Basket Palace Lantern—A424

Designs: Palace lanterns. Numbered T.60.

1981, Feb. 19 Photo. *Perf. 11½*

1654 A424 4f multi (6-1) 6
1655 A424 8f multi (6-2) 12
1656 A424 8f multi (6-3) 12
1657 A424 8f multi (6-4) 12
1658 A424 20f multi (6-5) 30
1659 A424 60f multi (6-6) 90
Nos. 1654-1659 (6) 1.62

Crossing River, Scene from Marking the Gunwale—A425

Designs: Scenes from Marking the Gunw ale fable.

1981, Mar. 10 Photo. *Perf. 11x11½*

1660 A425 8f Text (5-1) 12
1661 A425 8f shown (5-2) 12
1662 A425 8f Dropping sword in water (5-3) 12
1663 A425 8f Marking gunwale (5-4) 12
1664 A425 8f Searching for sword (5-5) 12
a. Bklt. pane of 10 (2 each #1660-1664) 1.75
Nos. 1660-1664 (5) 60

Nos. 1660-1664 se-tenant. Numbered T.59.

Chinese Juniper—A426

Designs: Miniature landscapes. Numbered T.61.

1981, Mar. 31 *Perf. 11½*

1665 A426 4f Chinese elm, vert. (6-1) 6
1666 A426 8f Juniper, vert. (6-2) 12
1667 A426 8f Maidenhair tree, vert. (6-3) 12
1668 A426 10f shown (6-4) 15
1669 A426 20f Wild kaki persimmon (6-5) 30
1670 A426 60f Single-seed juniper (6-6) 90

Vase with Tiger-shaped Handles—A427

Cizhou Kiln Ceramic Pottery: 4f, Vase with two tigers, Song Dynasty (vert.). No. 1672, Black glazed jar, Jin Dynasty. No. 1673, Amphora (vert.). No. 1674, Jar with two phoenixes (Yuan Dynasty). 10f, Flat flask, Yuan Dynasty. Numbered T.62.

1981, Apr. 15 Photo. *Perf. 11½x11*

1671 A427 4f multi (6-1) 6
1672 A427 8f multi (6-2) 12
1673 A427 8f multi (6-3) 12
1674 A427 8f multi (6-4) 12
1675 A427 10f multi (6-5) 15
1676 A427 60f multi (6-6) 90
Nos. 1671-1676 (6) 1.47

Panda Bear and Colored Stamps A428

1981, Apr. 29 Photo. *Perf. 11½x11*

1677 A428 8f shown (2-1) 12
1678 A428 60f Boat, bird (2-2) 90
a. Booklet (8 #1677, 1677-1678 se-tenant) 2.50

Qinchuan Steer—A429

Cattle Breeds: No. 1680, Binhu buffalo. No. 1681, Yak. No. 1682, Black and white dairy cows. 10f, Pasture red cow. 55f, Simmental cross-breed. Numbered T.63.

1981, May 5 *Perf. 11x11½*

1679 A429 4f multi (6-1) 6
1680 A429 8f multi (6-2) 12
1681 A429 8f multi (6-3) 12
1682 A429 8f multi (6-4) 12
1683 A429 10f multi (6-5) 15
1684 A429 55f multi (6-6) 85
Nos. 1679-1684 (6) 1.42

Mail Delivery Slogan A430 — 13th World Telecommunications Day A431

1981, May 9 *Perf. 11*

1685 A430 8f multi 12

Numbered J.70.

1981, May 17 *Perf. 11½x11*

1686 A431 8f multi 12

Numbered J.69.

Construction Worker A432

Telephone Building, Peking—A433

1981, May 20 *Perf. 11½*

1687 A432 8f shown (4-1) 12
1688 A432 8f Miner (4-2) 12
1689 A432 8f Children crossing street (4-3) 12
1690 A432 8f Farm worker (4-4) 12

National Safety Month. Numbered J.65.

1981, June 5 Engr. *Perf. 11½x11*

1691 A433 8f vio brn 12

Swaythling Cup, Men's Team Table Tennis—A434

36th World Table Tennis Championships Victory: No. 1692a, St. Bride Vase, men's singles (7-3). No. 1692b, Iran Cup, men's doubles (7-4). No. 1692c, G. Geist Prize, women's singles (7-5). No. 1692d, W.J. Pope Trophy, women's doubles (7-6). No. 1692e, Heydusek Prize, mixed doubles (7-7). No. 1694, Marcel Corbillon Cup, women's team. Nos. 1693-1694 printed in sheets of 16 (8 each) with 2 labels. Numbered J.71.

1981, June 30 Photo. *Perf. 11½x11*

1692 Strip of 5 60
a.-e. A434 8f multi 12
1693 A434 20f multi (7-1) 30
1694 A434 20f multi (7-2) 30

Chinese Communist Party, 60th Anniv.—A435

1981, July 1 Photo. *Perf. 11x11½*

1695 A435 8f multi 12

Hanpo Pass, Lushan Mountains—A436

1981, July 20 Photo. & Engr. *Perf. 12½x12*

1696 A436 8f Five-veteran Peak, vert. (7-1) 12
1697 A436 8f shown (7-2) 12
1698 A436 8f Yellow Dragon Pool, vert. (7-3) 12
1699 A436 8f Sunlit Peak (7-4) 12
1700 A436 8f Three-layer Spring, vert. (7-5) 12
1701 A436 8f Stone and pines (7-6) 12
1702 A436 60f Dragon-head Cliff, vert. (7-7) 90
Nos. 1696-1702 (7) 1.62

Numbered T.67.

Tremella Fuciformis A437

Designs: Edible mushrooms. Numbered T.66.

1981, Aug. 6 Photo. *Perf 11½*

1703 A437 4f shown (6-1) 6
1704 A437 8f Dictyophora indusiata (6-2) 12
1705 A437 8f Hericium erinaceus (6-3) 12
1706 A437 8f Russula rubra (6-4) 12
1707 A437 10f Lentinus edodes (6-5) 15
1708 A437 70f Agaricus bisporus (6-6) 1.05
Nos. 1703-1708 (6) 1.62

Quality Month A438

Lunan Stone Forest, Yunn A439

1981, Sept. 1 Photo. *Perf. 11½x11*

1709 A438 8f Silver medal (2-1) 12
1710 A438 8f Gold medal (2-2) 12

Numbered J.66.

1981, Sept. 18 *Perf. 11½*

Designs: Views of limestone formations, Lunan Stone Forest. Nos. 1711-1713 horiz. Numbered T.64.

1711 A439 8f multi (5-1) 12
1712 A439 8f multi (5-2) 12
1713 A439 8f multi (5-3) 12
1714 A439 10f multi (5-4) 15
1715 A439 70f multi (5-5) 1.05
Nos. 1711-1715 (5) 1.56

Lu Xun, Writer, Birth Centenary A440

1981, Sept. 25

1716 A440 8f shown (2-1) 12
1717 A440 20f Portrait (diff.) (2-2) 30

Numbered J.67.

Sun Yat-sen and Text—A441

70th Anniv. of 1911 Revolution: No. 1719, 72 Martyrs Grave, Huang Hua Gang. No. 1720, Hubei Provincial Government Headquarters, 1911. Numbered J.68.

1981, Oct. 10 Photo. *Perf. 11x11½*

1718 A441 8f multi (3-1) 12
1719 A441 8f multi (3-2) 12
1720 A441 8f multi (3-3) 12

Asian Conference of Parliamentarians on Population and Development, Peking, Oct. 27—A442

1981, Oct. 27 *Perf. 11½x11, 11x11½*

1721 A442 8f Tree, vert. (2-1) 12
1722 A442 70f shown (2-2) 1.05

Numbered J.73.

Huang Guo Shu Falls A443

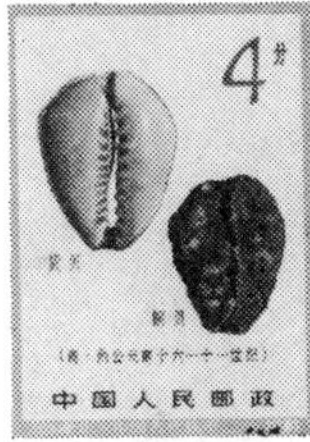

Cowrie Shell and Shell-shaped Coin A444

1981 Engr. *Perf. 13x13½, 11½(Photo.)*

1726 A443 3f shown 5
a. Photo. 5
1727 A443 4f Hainan Isld. ('82)
a. Photo. 6
1729 A443 8f Great Wall 12
a. Photo. 12
1730 A443 10f Immense Forest ('82)
a. Photo. 15
1731 A443 20f Mt. Tian
a. Photo. 30

1981, Oct. 29 Photo. & Engr. *Perf. 11½x11*

Ancient Coins. Numbered T.65.

1740 A444 4f shown (8-1) 6
1741 A444 4f Shovel (8-2) 6
1742 A444 8f Shovel, diff. (8-3) 12
1743 A444 8f Shovel, diff. (8-4) 12
1744 A444 8f Knife (8-5) 12
1745 A444 8f Knife (8-6) 12
1746 A444 60f Knife, diff. (8-7) 90
1747 A444 70f Gong (8-8) 1.05
Nos. 1740-1747 (8) 2.55

See Nos. 1765-1772.

Intl. Year of the Disabled—A445

1981, Nov. 10 Photo. *Perf. 11½x11*

1748 A445 8f multi 12

Numbered J.72.

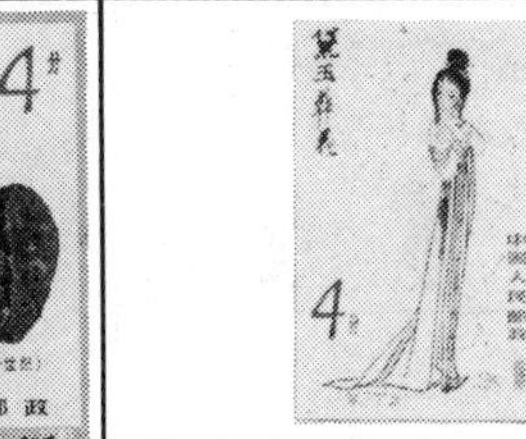

Twelve Beauties, from The Dream of Red Mansions, by Cao Xueqin—A446

1981-82 Photo. *Perf. 11*

1749 A446 4f Daiyu (12-1) 6
1750 A446 4f Baochai (12-2) 6
1751 A446 8f Yuanchun (12-3) 12
1752 A446 8f Yingchun (12-4) 12
1753 A446 8f Tanchun (12-5) 12
1754 A446 8f Xichun (12-6) 12
1755 A446 8f Xiangyun (12-7) 12
1756 A446 10f Liwan (12-8) 15
1757 A446 20f Xifeng (12-9) 30
1758 A446 30f Sister Qiao (12-10) 45
1759 A446 40f Keqing (12-11) 60
1760 A446 80f Miaoyu (12-12) 1.20
Nos. 1749-1760 (12) 3.42

Souvenir Sheet

1761 A446 $2 Baoyu, Daiyu 3.00

No. 1761 contains one stamp (59x39mm.); multicolored margin continues design. Size: 140x78mm. Issue dates: Nos. 1749, 1751, 1753, 1755, 1757, 1759, 1761, Nov. 20, 1981; others, Apr. 24, 1982. Numbered T.69.

Women's Team Victory in 3rd World Cup Volleyball Championship—A447

1981, Dec. 21 Photo.

1762 A447 8f Girl playing volleyball (2-1) 12
1763 A447 20f Girl holding trophy (2-2) 30

Numbered J.76.

New Year 1982 (Year of the Dog) -A448

1982, Jan. 5 Photo. & Engr. *Perf. 11½*

1764 A448 8f multi 12
a. Bklt. pane of 10 plus label 1.20

Numbered T.70.

Coin Type of 1981

1982, Feb. 12 Photo. & Engr.

1765 A444 4f Guilian mask (8-1) 6
1766 A444 4f Shu shovel (8-2) 6
1767 A444 8f Xia zhuan shovel (8-3) 12
1768 A444 8f Han Dan shovel (8-4) 12
1769 A444 8f Knife (8-5) 12
1770 A444 8f Ming knife (8-6) 12
1771 A444 70f Jin hua knife (8-7) 1.05
1772 A444 80f Yi Liu Hua coin (8-8) 1.20
Nos. 1765-1772 (8) 2.85

Numbered T.71.

Nie Er (1912-1935), Natl. Anthem Composer—A449

1982, Feb. 15 ***Perf. 11x11½***
1773 A449 8f multi 12

Numbered J.75.

Intl. Drinking Water and Sanitation Decade, 1981-1990—A450

1982, Mar. 1 ***Perf. 11½x11***
1774 A450 8f multi 12

Numbered J.77.

TB Bacillus Centenary—A451

1982, Mar. 24 ***Perf. 11x11½***
1775 A451 8f multi 12

Fire Control—A452

1982, May 8 **Photo.** ***Perf. 11½x11***
1776 A452 8f Water hoses (2-1) 12
1777 A452 8f Chemical extinguisher (2-2) 12

Numbered T.76.

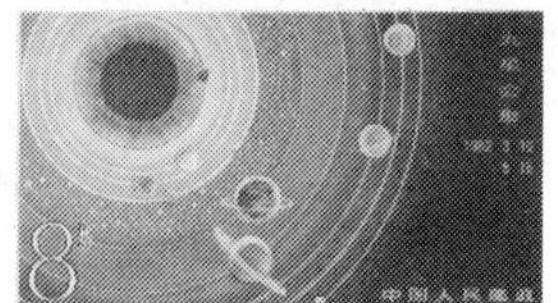

Syzygy of the Nine Planets, Mar. 10 and May 16—A453

1982, May 16 ***Perf. 11½***
1778 A453 8f multi 12

Numbered T.78.

Medicinal Herbs A454

Soong Ching Ling (1893-1981), Sun Yat-sens' Widow A455

1982, May 20 ***Perf. 11½x11***
1779 A454 4f Hemerocallis flava (6-1) 6
1780 A454 8f Fritillaria unibracteata (6-2) 12
1781 A454 8f Aconitum carmichaeli (6-3) 12
1782 A454 10f Lilium brownii (6-4) 15
1783 A454 20f Arisaema consanguineum (6-5) 30
1784 A454 70f Paeonia lactiflora (6-6) 1.05

Souvenir Sheet

1785 A454 $2 Iris tectorum maxim 3.00

No. 1785 contains one stamp (89x39mm.); gold and gray decorative margin. Size: 138x70mm. Nos. 1779-1784 numbered T.72.

1982, May 29 ***Perf. 11½***
1786 A455 8f Addressing Consultative Conference (2-1) 12
1787 A455 20f Portrait (2-2) 30

Numbered J.82.

Sable—A456

1982, June 20 **Photo.** ***Perf. 11½***
1788 A456 8f shown (2-1) 12
1789 A456 80f Sable, diff. (2-2) 1.20
a. Bklt. pane of 8: 6x8f plus sheetlet of 2 (8f, 80f) 2.25

Numbered T.68.

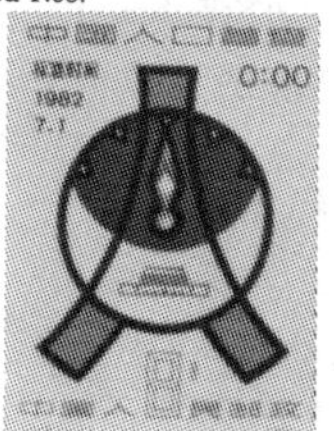

Natl. Census, July 1—A457

1982, June 30 ***Perf. 11½x11***
1790 A457 8f multi 12

Numbered J.78.

2nd UN Conference on Peaceful Uses of Outer Space, Vienna, Aug. 9-21—A458

1982, July 25 **Photo.** ***Perf. 11½x11***
1791 A458 8f 12

Numbered J.81.

Strolling in Autumn Woods, by Shen Zhou, Ming Dynasty—A459

Fan Paintings (Ming or Qing Dynasty): No. 1793, Jackdaw on Withered Tree, by Tang Yin. No. 1794, Bamboo and Sparrows, by Zhou Zhimian. 10f, Writing Poem under Pine, by Chen Hongshou and Bai Han. 20f, Chrysanthemums, by Yun Shouping, Qing. 70f, Birds, Crape Myrtle and Chinese Parasol, by Wang Wu, Qing.

1982, July 31 ***Perf. 11½***
1792 A459 4f multi (6-1) 6
1793 A459 8f multi (6-2) 12
1794 A459 8f multi (6-3) 12
1795 A459 10f multi (6-4) 15
1796 A459 20f multi (6-5) 30
1797 A459 70f multi (6-6) 1.05
Nos. 1792-1797 (6) 1.80

Numbered T.77.

60th Anniv. of Chinese Geological Society—A460

1982, Aug. 25 ***Perf. 11½x11***
1798 A460 8f multi 12

Numbered J.79.

Orpiment—A461

1982, Aug. 25 **Photo.** ***Perf. 11½x11***
1799 A461 4f shown (4-1) 6
1800 A461 8f Stibnite (4-2) 12
1801 A461 10f Cinnabar (4-3) 15
1802 A461 20f Wolframite (4-4) 30

Numbered T.73.

Souvenir Sheet

Messenger, Tomb Mural, Jiayu Pass, Wei-Jin Period—A462

1982, Aug. 25
1803 A462 $1 multi 1.50

All-China Philatelic Federation, First Congress. Pale green margin, black inscription. Size: 136x80mm. Numbered J.85.

12th Natl. Communist Party Congress A463

Hoopoe A464

1982, Sept. 1 ***Perf. 11½***
1804 A463 8f multi 12

Numbered J.86.

1982, Sept. 10 ***Perf. 11½x11***
1805 A464 8f shown (5-1) 12
1806 A464 8f Swallows (5-2) 12
1807 A464 8f Oriole (5-3) 12
1808 A464 20f Swifts (5-4) 30
1809 A464 70f Woodpecker (5-5) 1.05
Nos. 1805-1809 (5) 1.71

Souvenir Sheet

1810 A464 $2 Cuckoos 3.00

No. 1810 contains one stamp (56x36mm.); gray blue margin shows tree; black inscription. Size: 136x80mm. Numbered T.79.

Japan-China Relations Normalization, 10th Anniv. A465

World Food Day A466

Flower Paintings: 8f, Plum blossoms, by Guan Shanyue. 70f, Hibiscus, by Xiao Shufang.

1982, Sept. 29 *Perf. 11*

1811 A465 8f J.84 (2-1) 12
1812 A465 70f J.84 (2-2) 1.05

1982, Oct. 16

1813 A466 8f J.80 12

Guo Morou (1892-1978), Acad. of Sciences Pres. A467

Bodhisattva, 11th Cent. Sculpture A468

Designs: Portraits. Numbered J.87.

1982, Nov. 16 **Photo.** *Perf. 11½x11*

1814 A467 8f multi (2-1) 12
1815 A467 20f multi (2-2) 30

1982, Nov. 19 *Perf. 11*

Liao Dynasty Buddha Sculptures, Lower Huayan Monastery. Numbered T.74.

1816 A468 8f multi (4-1) 12
1817 A468 8f multi (4-2) 12
1818 A468 8f multi (4-3) 12
1819 A468 70f multi (4-4) 1.05

Souvenir Sheet
Perf. 11x11½

1820 A468 $2 multi 3.00

No. 1820 contains one stamp (36x55mm.); marginal inscription. Size: 130x80mm.

Dr. D.S. Kotnis, Indian Physician in 8th Army—A469

1982, Dec. 9 **Photo.** *Perf. 11½x11, 11x11½*

1821 A469 8f Portrait, vert. (2-1) 12
1822 A469 70f Riding horse (2-2) 1.05

Numbered J.83.

11th Communist Youth League Natl. Congress—A470

1982, Dec. 20 *Perf. 11x11½*

1823 A470 8f multi 12

Numbered J.88.

Bronze Wine Container—A471

Western Zhou Dynasty Bronze (1200-771 B.C.): No. 1825, Three-legged cooking pot. No. 1826, Food bowl. No. 1827, Three-legged cooking pot (diff.). No. 1828, Animal-shaped wine container. 10f, Wine container with lid. 20f, Round food bowl. 70f, Square wine container. Numbered T.75.

1982, Dec. 25 **Photo. & Engr.** *Perf. 11*

1824 A471 4f multi (8-1) 6
1825 A471 4f multi (8-2) 6
1826 A471 8f multi (8-3) 12
1827 A471 8f multi (8-4) 12
1828 A471 8f multi (8-5) 12
1829 A471 10f multi (8-6) 15
1830 A471 20f multi (8-7) 30
1831 A471 70f multi (8-8) 1.05
Nos. 1824-1831 (8) 1.98

New Year 1983 (Year of the Pig)—A472

1983, Jan. 5 *Perf. 11½*

1832 A472 8f multi 12
a. Bklt. pane of 12 1.50

Numbered T.80.

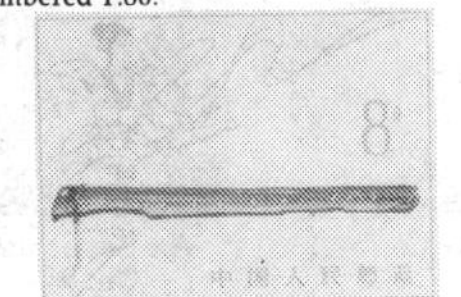

Stringed Instruments—A473

1983, Jan. 20 *Perf. 11½x11, 11x11½*

1833 A473 4f Konghou (5-1) 6
1834 A473 8f Ruan (5-2) 12
1835 A473 8f Qin, horiz. (5-3) 12
1836 A473 10f Piba (5-4) 15
1837 A473 70f Sanxian (5-5) 1.05
Nos. 1833-1837 (5) 1.50

Numbered T.81.

60th Anniv. of Peking-Hankow Railroad Workers' Strike—A474

1983, Feb. 7 **Photo.** *Perf. 11½x11*

1838 A474 8f Memorial Tower, Zhengzhou (2-1) 12
1839 A474 8f Monument, Jiangan (2-2) 12

Numbered J.89.

The Western Chamber, Traditional Opera, by Wang Shifu (1271-1368)—A475

Scenes from the opera.

1983, Feb. 21 **Photo.** *Perf. 11x11½*

1840 A475 8f multi (4-1) 12
1841 A475 8f multi (4-2) 12
1842 A475 10f multi (4-3) 15
1843 A475 80f multi (4-4) 1.25

Souvenir Sheet
Photo. & Engr. ***Perf. 12***

1844 A475 $2 multi 3.00

No. 1844 contains one stamp (27x48mm.). Size: 130x80mm. Numbered T.82.

Karl Marx (1818-1883)—A476

1983, Mar. 14 **Photo. & Engr.** *Perf. 11½x11*

1845 A476 8f Portrait (2-1) 12
1846 A476 20f Making speech (2-2) 30

Numbered J.90.

AIR POST STAMPS

Mail Plane and Temple of Heaven
AP1

1951, May 1 Engraved *Perf. 12½*

C1	AP1	$1000 carmine	5	10
C2	AP1	$3000 green	10	10
C3	AP1	$5000 orange	5	15
C4	AP1	$10,000 vio brn & grn	8	25
C5	AP1	$30,000 dk bl & brn	60	75
		Nos. C1-C5 (5)	88	1.35

Planes at Airport
AP2

Designs: 28f, Plane over winding mountain highway. 35f, Plane over railroad yard. 52f, Plane over ship.

1957-58 *Perf. 14*

C6	AP2	16f indigo	19.00	5
C7	AP2	28f ol blk	19.00	10
C8	AP2	35f slate	19.00	2.50
C9	AP2	52f Prus bl ('58)	19.00	50

POSTAGE DUE STAMPS

Grain and Cogwheel
D1

Numeral
D2

1950, Sept. 1 Typo. *Perf. 12½*

J1	D1	$100 stl bl	5	10
J2	D1	$200 stl bl	5	10
J3	D1	$500 stl bl	5	10
J4	D1	$800 stl bl	7.00	10
J5	D1	$1000 stl bl	15	40
J6	D1	$2000 stl bl	15	40
J7	D1	$5000 stl bl	10	60
J8	D1	$8000 stl bl	10	1.00
J9	D1	$10,000 stl bl	20	2.00
		Nos. J1-J9 (9)	7.85	4.80

1954, Aug. 18 Litho. *Perf. 14*

J10	D2	$100 red	15	8
J11	D2	$200 red	15	8
J12	D2	$500 red	15	8
J13	D2	$800 red	5	8
J14	D2	$1600 red	5	15
		Nos. J10-J14 (5)	55	47

MILITARY STAMPS

Red Star, 8-1 in Center
M1

1953, Aug. 1 Lithographed *Perf. 14*

M1	M1	$800 yel & red (Army)	9.00	15.00
M2	M1	$800 dp pur, org & red (Air Force)	150.00	
M3	M1	$800 org, bl & red (Navy)		

Nos. M2-M3 were not regularly issued.

NORTHEAST CHINA

The Northeast Liberation Area included the provinces of Liaoning, Kirin, Jehol and Heilungkiang—the area generally known as Manchuria under the Japanese. The first postwar issues were local overprints on stamps of Manchukuo. In early 1946, a Ministry of Posts and Telegraphs served the areas already liberated, and in August, 1946, a Communications Committee of the Political Council was established. In June, 1947, these postal services were subordinated to the Harbin General Post Office, and this was extended to Changchun on Oct. 22, 1948, and to Mukden on Nov. 4, 1948. It was rapidly extended to cover all Manchuria.

All Stamps Issued without Gum

Mao Tse-tung
A1 A2

Lithographed

1946, Feb. *Perf. 11* Unwmkd.

1L1	A1	$1 violet	5.00	5.00
1L2	A2	$2 vermilion	60	1.00
1L3	A2	$5 orange	60	1.00
a.		Booklet pane of 6	130.00	
1L4	A2	$10 blue	60	1.00
a.		Booklet pane of 6	130.00	

Price, imperf set $35.

Map of China, Lion, Hyena and Chiang Kai-shek
A3

1946, Dec. 12 *Perf. 10½*

1L5	A3	$1 violet	1.50	1.25
1L6	A3	$2 orange	1.50	1.25
1L7	A3	$5 org brn	5.00	4.00
1L8	A3	$10 lt grn	9.00	8.00
a.		Imperf. pair	30.00	

10th anniversary of the capture of Chiang Kai-shek at Sian.

Railroad Workers, Chengchow
A4

1947, Feb. 7 *Perf. 10½*

1L9	A4	$1 pink	25	90
1L10	A4	$2 dl grn	25	90
1L11	A4	$5 pink	1.00	1.00
1L12	A4	$10 dl grn	1.50	1.50

24th anniversary of the Chengchow railroad workers' strike and massacre.

Women (Worker, Soldier and Farmer)
A5

Wmkd. Chinese Characters in Sheet

1947, Mar. 8 *Perf. 10½x11*

1L13	A5	$5 brick red	50	60
1L14	A5	$10 brown	50	60

International Women's Day, March 8.

Same Overprinted in Green ("Northeast Postal Service")

東北郵政

1947, Mar. 18

1L15	A5	$5 brick red	2.50	3.25
1L16	A5	$10 brown	2.50	3.25

Children Carrying Banner
A6

1947, Apr. 4 *Perf. 11x10½*

Granite Paper

1L17	A6	$5 rose red	3.00	3.00
1L18	A6	$10 lt grn	3.00	3.00
1L19	A6	$30 orange	3.00	3.00

Children's Day.

Nos. 1L1-1L2 Surcharged in Red, Brown, Black, Blue or Green

改作伍拾圓 5000

1947, Apr. *Perf. 11* Unwmkd.

1L20	A1	$50 on $1 vio (R)	19.00	19.00
a.		Brown surcharge	19.00	19.00
1L21	A2	$50 on $2 ver	19.00	19.00
a.		Brown surcharge	19.00	19.00
1L22	A1	$100 on $1 vio	19.00	19.00
a.		Green surcharge	19.00	19.00
1L23	A2	$100 on $2 ver (Bl)	19.00	19.00
a.		Green surcharge	19.00	19.00

Farmer and Worker
A7

Ax Severing Chain
A8

Wmkd. Chinese Characters in Sheet

1947, May 1 *Perf. 10½x11*

Granite Paper

1L24	A7	$10 org red	75	75
1L25	A7	$30 ultra	1.00	1.00
1L26	A7	$50 gray grn	1.25	1.25

Labor Day. Price, imperf pairs, set $125.

1947, May 4 *Perf. 11*

1L27	A8	$10 brt grn	2.25	2.50
1L28	A8	$30 brown	2.25	2.50
1L29	A8	$50 violet	2.75	2.75

28th anniversary of the students' revolt at Peking University against the 1918 peace treaty.

Price, imperf pairs, set $175.

Workers with Banner: "Oppose Imperialist Aggression"
A9

1947, May 30 *Perf. 10½x11*

Banner in Red

1L30	A9	$2 brt lil	2.50	2.50
1L31	A9	$5 brt grn	2.50	2.50
1L32	A9	$10 yellow	2.50	2.50
1L33	A9	$20 violet	2.50	2.50
1L34	A9	$30 red brn	2.50	2.50
1L35	A9	$50 dk bl	2.50	2.50
1L36	A9	$100 brown	2.50	2.50
a.		Souvenir sheet of 7	60.00	
		Nos. 1L30-1L36 (7)	17.50	17.50

22nd anniversary of the Shanghai-Nanking Road incident. No. 1L36a is on granite paper and contains 7 imperf. stamps similar to Nos. 1L30-1L36. Multicolored marginal inscription. Size: 215x158mm.

Price, imperf pairs, ordinary paper, set $275.

Mao and Communist Flag
A10

1947, July 1 *Perf. 10½x11*

1L37	A10	$10 red	4.00	4.00
1L38	A10	$30 brt lil	4.00	4.00
1L39	A10	$50 rose brn	10.00	10.00
1L40	A10	$100 vermilion	12.00	12.00

26th anniversary of the founding of the Chinese Communist Party.

Hand Holding Rifle
A11

1947, July 7 *Perf. 10½*

1L41	A11	$10 orange	3.75	3.75
1L42	A11	$30 green	3.75	3.75
1L43	A11	$50 dl bl	3.75	3.75
1L44	A11	$100 brown	3.75	3.75
a.		Souvenir sheet of 4	45.00	50.00

10th anniversary of the start of Sino-Japanese War. No. 1L44a contains 4 imperf. stamps similar to Nos. 1L41-1L44. Brown marginal inscription. Size: 149x107mm.

White Mountain and Black Water, Northeast China
A12

Wmkd. Zigzag Lines (141)

1947, Aug. 15 *Perf. 10½*

1L45	A12	$10 brn org	10.00	10.00
1L46	A12	$30 lt ol grn	1.50	10.00
1L47	A12	$50 bl grn	1.50	10.00
1L48	A12	$100 sepia	10.00	10.00

2nd anniversary of the reoccupation of Northeast China and the surrender of Japan.

Nos. 1L1-1L2 Surcharged in Black, Red, Green or Blue

1947, Aug. 29 *Perf. 11* Unwmkd.

1L49	A1	$5 on $1 vio	20.00	20.00
a.		Red surcharge	20.00	20.00
b.		Green surcharge	20.00	20.00
1L50	A2	$10 on $2 ver	20.00	20.00
a.		Blue surcharge	20.00	20.00
b.		Green surcharge	20.00	20.00

Map of Manchuria
A13

1947, Sept. 18 **Unwmkd.**

White Paper

1L51	A13	$10 gray grn	6.00	6.00
1L52	A13	$20 rose lil	6.00	6.00
1L53	A13	$30 blk brn	6.00	6.00
1L54	A13	$50 carmine	6.00	6.00

16th anniversary of Japanese attack on Mukden, Sept. 18, 1931.

Northeast Political Council Offices
A14

Mao Tse-tung
(Value figures repeated)
A15

1947, Oct. 10 ***Perf. 10½***

1L55	A14	$10 yel org	25.00	25.00
1L56	A14	$20 rose red	25.00	25.00
1L57	A14	$100 brown	60.00	60.00

35th anniversary of the founding of the Chinese Republic.

1947, Oct. 10 White Paper *Perf. 11*

1L58	A15	$1 brown	20	1.50
1L59	A15	$5 gray grn	4.00	1.50
1L60	A15	$10 brt grn	12.00	8.00
1L61	A15	$15 bluish lil	12.00	8.00
1L62	A15	$20 brt rose	10	1.50
1L63	A15	$30 green	15	2.00
1L64	A15	$50 blk brn	12.00	8.00
1L65	A15	$90 blue	4.00	2.00
1L66	A15	$100 red	10	2.00
1L67	A15	$500 red org	25.00	15.00
		Nos. 1L58-1L67 (10)	69.55	49.50

Type A22 resembles A15, but has "YUAN" at upper right.

1947, Nov. **Redrawn**

White Paper

1L68	A15	$50 lt grn	75	1.50
1L69	A15	$150 red org	1.00	1.50
a.		Wmkd. Chinese characters	2.50	
1L70	A15	$250 bluish lil	25	1.50
a.		Wmkd. Chinese characters	1.00	1.50

1947, Dec. **Unwmkd.**

Newsprint

1L71	A15	$300 green	37.50	25.00
1L72	A15	$1,000 yellow	1.00	1.00
		Nos. 1L68-1L72 (5)	40.50	30.50

Panel below portrait 8½x3mm. on Nos. 1L68–1L70; 7x3mm. on No. 1L58–1L67. Nos. 1L68–1L70 have different ornamental border.

Nos. 1L71–1L72 without zeros for cents.

The $1, $90, $100 and $500 were also printed on newsprint; the $1,000 also on white paper.

Hand Holding Torch
A16

1947, Dec. 12 ***Perf. 11*** **Unwmkd.**

White Paper

1L73	A16	$30 rose red	5.00	5.00
1L74	A16	$90 dk bl	5.00	5.00
1L75	A16	$150 green	5.00	5.00

11th anniversary of the capture of Chiang Kai-shek at Sian.

Tomb of Gen. Li Chao-lin
A17

Globe and Banner
A18

Perf. 10½x11

1948, Mar. 9 **Unwmkd.**

1L76	A17	$30 green	5.00	5.00
a.		Granite paper, wmkd.	5.00	5.00
1L77	A17	$150 vio gray	10.00	10.00
a.		Granite paper, wmkd.	10.00	10.00

2nd anniversary of the assassination of Gen. Li Chao-lin, Commander of 3rd Army.

Wmkd. Chinese Characters in Sheet

1948, May 1 ***Perf. 11x10½***

1L78	A18	$50 red	6.00	10.00
1L79	A18	$150 green	1.00	15.00
1L80	A18	$250 lilac	1.00	30.00

Labor Day.

Student, Torch and Banner
A19

Perf. 10½x11

1948, May 4 **Unwmkd.**

Granite paper

1L81	A19	$50 green	8.50	8.00
1L82	A19	$150 brown	8.50	8.50
1L83	A19	$250 red	8.50	8.50

Youth Day, May 4.

Nos. 1L58, 1L61, 1L59, 1L63, 1L65, 1L2–1L4, 1L68–1L69, 1L71 Surcharged in Black, Blue, Red or Green

壹佰圓 10000 改作

1948–49 ***Perf. 11***

1L84	A15	$100 on $1 brn pur	60.00	45.00
a.		Blue surcharge	25.00	25.00
1L85	A15	$100 on $15 bluish lil	17.50	17.50
a.		Blue surcharge	25.00	25.00
1L86	A15	$300 on $5 gray grn (R)	50.00	25.00
1L87	A15	$300 on $30 grn (R)	8.50	10.00
1L88	A15	$300 on $90 bl (R)	8.50	10.00
1L89	A2	$500 on $2 ver	5.00	5.00
1L90	A15	$500 on $50 lt grn (R, '49)	25.00	20.00
1L91	A2	$1500 on $5 org (bl)	5.00	5.00
1L92	A15	$1500 on $150 red org (Gr, '49)	6.00	6.00
1L93	A2	$2500 on $10 bl (R)	5.00	5.00
1L94	A15	$2500 on $300 grn ('49)	5.00	5.00
		Nos. 1L84-1L94 (11)	195.50	153.50

Crane Operator
A20

Wmkd. Chinese Characters in Sheet

1948, May ***Perf. 11***

1L95	A20	$100 red & pink	50	50
1L96	A20	$300 vio brn & yel	1.50	1.50
1L97	A20	$500 bl & grn	1.50	1.50

6th All-China Labor Conference, Harbin.

Farmer, Worker and Soldier Saluting
A21

Mao Tse-tung
("YUAN" at upper right)
A22

Perf. 11x10½

1948, Dec. 3 **Unwmkd.**

White paper

1L98	A21	$500 vermilion	3.50	3.50
1L99	A21	$1500 brt grn	6.00	6.00
1L100	A21	$2500 brown	10.00	10.00

Liberation of Northeast China.

1949, Feb. ***Perf. 11***

1L101	A22	$300 olive	40	60
1L102	A22	$500 orange	1.00	1.00
1L103	A22	$1500 bl grn	40	60
1L104	A22	$4500 brown	40	60
1L105	A22	$6500 dk bl	40	70
		Nos. 1L101-1L105 (5)	2.60	3.50

See also type A15.

Workers, Globe and Flag
A23

Fields and Factories
A24

1949, May 1 ***Perf. 11½***

1L106	A23	$1000 red & dl bl	15	30
1L107	A23	$1500 red & pale bl	10	30
1L108	A23	$4500 rose & ol brn	15	40
1L109	A23	$6500 dl org & grn	60	50
1L110	A23	$10,000 mar & ultra	60	60
		Nos. 1L106-1L110 (5)	1.60	2.10

Labor Day.

1949 ***Perf. 10, 11***

1L111	A24	$5000 Prus bl	2.50	1.00
1L112	A24	$10,000 org brn	25	1.00
1L113	A24	$50,000 green	10	2.00
1L114	A24	$100,000 violet	15	8.00

Production in agriculture and industry.

Workers with Flags
A25

Heroes' Monument, Harbin
A26

1949, July 1 ***Perf. 11***

1L115	A25	$1500 vio, lt bl & red	5	25
1L116	A25	$4500 dk brn, lt bl & ver	1.00	30
1L117	A25	$6500 gray, lt bl & rose red	10	50

28th anniversary of the founding of the Chinese Communist Party.

1949, Aug. 15 ***Perf. 11½x11***

1L118	A26	$1500 brick red	10	50
1L119	A26	$4500 yel grn	25	50
1L120	A26	$6500 lt bl	1.00	50

4th anniversary of the Reoccupation, and the surrender of Japan.

東北貼用

(enlarged)

"Northeast Postal Service"

The following commemorative issues are similar to those of the People's Republic of China, with the 4 characters shown added in different sizes and various arrangements. Reprints were also issued similar to those of the PRC.

Chinese Lantern Type of PRC, 1949

1949, Sept. 12 **Litho.** ***Perf. 12½***

1L121	A1	$1000 dp bl	6.00	5.00
1L122	A1	$1500 scarlet	6.00	5.00
1L123	A1	$3000 green	6.00	5.00
1L124	A1	$4500 maroon	6.00	5.00

First session of Chinese People's Political Conference.

Reprints exist. Price, set 60 cents.

Factory
A27

1949, Oct. ***Perf. 11x10½***

1L125	A27	$1500 orange	15	40

Nos. 1L101, 1L103–1L105, 1L125 Surcharged in Black or Green

貳仟圓 2000 改作

1949, Nov. 20

1L126	A22	$2000 on $300 ol	12.00	2.50
1L127	A22	$2000 on $4500 pur brn (G)	70.00	15.00
1L128	A22	$2500 on $1500 bl grn	75	3.00
1L129	A22	$2500 on $6500 bl	35.00	10.00
1L130	A27	$5000 on $1500 org	50	50
1L131	A22	$20,000 on $4500 pur brn	30	3.00
1L132	A22	$35,000 on $300 ol	45	4.00
		Nos. 1L126-1L132(7)	119.00	38.00

Globe and Hammer Type of PRC

1949, Nov. 15 ***Perf. 12½***

1L133	A2	$5000 crimson	60.00	60.00
1L134	A2	$20,000 dp grn	60.00	60.00
1L135	A2	$35,000 vio bl	60.00	60.00

Asiatic and Australasian Congress of the World Federation of Trade Unions, Peking.

Reprints, price, set $25.

Mao and Conference Hall Types of PRC

1950, Feb. 1 ***Perf. 14***

1L136	A3	$1000 vermilion	11.00	11.00
1L137	A3	$1500 dp bl	11.00	11.00
1L138	A4	$5000 dk vio brn	11.00	11.00
1L139	A4	$20,000 green	11.00	11.00

First session of Chinese People's Political Conference.

Reprints exist. Price, set 75 cents.

Gate of Heavenly Peace (same size)
A28

1950 ***Perf. 10½***

Narrow horizontal shading

1L140 A28	$500 olive	25	50
1L141 A28	$1000 orange	25	50
1L142 A28	$1000 lil rose	25	50
1L143 A28	$2000 gray grn	10	15
1L144 A28	$2500 yellow	50	15
1L145 A28	$5000 dp org	7.00	20
1L146 A28	$10,000 brn org	50	50
1L147 A28	$20,000 vio brn	10	20
1L148 A28	$35,000 dp bl	10	35
1L149 A28	$50,000 brt grn	25	70
	Nos. 1L140-1L149 (10)	9.30	3.75

Flag and Mao Type of PRC

1950, July 1 ***Perf. 14***

Yellow Stars

1L150 A7	$5000 grn & red	12.50	9.00
1L151 A7	$10,000 brn & red	12.50	9.00
1L152 A7	$20,000 dk brn & red	12.50	9.00
1L153 A7	$30,000 dk vio bl & red	12.50	9.00

Inauguration of the People's Republic, Oct. 1, 1949.

Reprints exist. Price, set 75 cents.

Picasso Dove Type of PRC

1950, Aug. 1 Engraved ***Perf. 14***

1L154 A8	$2500 brown	5.00	4.00
1L155 A8	$5000 green	5.00	4.00
1L156 A8	$20,000 blue	5.00	4.00

World Peace Campaign.

Reprints exist. Price, set 50 cents.

Flag Type of PRC

1950, Oct. 1 Engraved & Litho.

Flag in Red & Yellow

1L157 A9	$1000 purple	10.00	10.00
1L158 A9	$2500 org brn	10.00	10.00
1L159 A9	$5000 dp grn	10.00	10.00
1L160 A9	$10,000 olive	10.00	10.00
1L161 A9	$20,000 blue	10.00	10.00
	Nos. 1L157-1L161 (5)	50.00	50.00

First anniversary of the Chinese People's Republic. Size of No. 1L159: 38x47mm., others 26x33mm. Reprints exist. Price, set, 35 cents.

Reprints exist. Price, set 60 cents.

Postal Conference Type of PRC

1950, Nov. 1 Lithographed

1L162 A11	$2500 grn & dp org	4.00	3.00
1L163 A11	$5000 car & grn	4.00	3.00

All-China Postal Conference, Peking.

Reprints exist. Price, set, 25 cents.

Gate of Heavenly Peace (same size)
A29

1950 ***Perf. 10½***

Wide horizontal shading

1L164 A29	$5000 orange	40	1.25
1L165 A29	$30,000 scarlet	25	*3.00*
1L166 A29	$100,000 violet	2.00	3.25

Wmkd. Zigzag Lines (141)

1L167 A29	$250 brown	20	30
1L168 A29	$500 olive	20	30
1L169 A29	$1000 lil rose	25	50
1L170 A29	$2000 dl grn ('51)	10	50
1L171 A29	$2500 yellow	15	50
1L172 A29	$5000 orange	20	50
1L173 A29	$10,000 brn org ('51)	30	50
1L174 A29	$12,500 maroon	10	50
1L175 A29	$20,000 dp brn ('51)	30	1.00
	Nos. 1L164-1L175 (12)	4.45	*12.10*

A $50,000 grn was prepared, but not issued, Price $3.50.

Stalin and Mao Tse-tung Type of PRC

Engraved

1950, Dec. 1 ***Perf. 14*** **Unwmkd.**

1L176 A12	$2500 red	2.00	2.00
1L177 A12	$5000 dp grn	2.00	2.00
1L178 A12	$20,000 dk bl	2.00	2.00

Signing of the Sino-Soviet Treaty of Friendship, Alliance and Mutual Assistance.

Reprints exist. Price, set 80 cents.

PARCEL POST STAMPS

Locomotive
PP1

Lithographed

1951 ***Imperf., perf. 10½***

1LQ1 PP1	$100,000 pur (P)	40.00
1LQ2 PP1	$300,000 brn (P, I)	150.00
1LQ3 PP1	$500,000 grnsh bl (P, I)	250.00
1LQ4 PP1	$1,000,000 ver (P, I)	400.00

PORT ARTHUR AND DAIREN

The Liaoning Postal Administration was established on April 1, 1946, in accordance with the Sino-Soviet Treaty, but was renamed one week later the Port Arthur and Dairen Postal Administration. On Apr. 3, 1947, it was combined with telecommunications and renamed the Kwantung Post and Telegraph General Administration. On May 1, 1949, the name was again changed to Port Arthur and Dairen Post and Telegraph Administration. Postal tariffs were based on local currency and both Manchukuo and Japanese stamps were overprinted for use.

With Gum

Manchukuo Nos. 162 and 94 Handstamp Surcharged in Violet ("Liaoning Post")

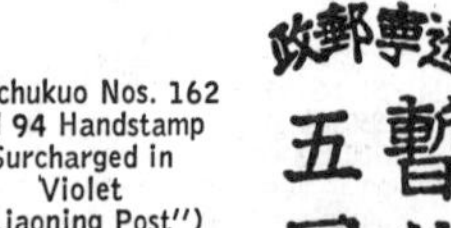

1946, Mar. 15

2L1	A19	20f on 30f buff	70.00	70.00
2L2	A18	1y on 12f org	40.00	40.00

Same Surcharge on Japan Nos. 260, 337, 195, 244, 263, 342 in Violet, Red or Black

1946, Apr. 1

2L3	A85	20f on 3s grn (V)	15.00	15.00
2L4	A151	1y on 17s gray vio (R)	12.00	12.00
2L5	A57	5y on 6s car	30.00	30.00
2L6	A57	5y on 6s crim	30.00	30.00
2L7	A88	5y on 6s org	20.00	20.00
2L8	A154	15y on 40s dk vio	90.00	90.00
		Nos. 2L1-2L8 (8)	307.00	307.00

Surcharge sideways on Nos. 2L5–2L6.

Japan Nos. 260 and 263 Surcharged

1946, Apr.

2L9	A85	1y on 3s grn	*350.00*	
2L10	A88	5y on 6s org	*230.00*	

Sha Ho Kow (suburb of Dairen) issue.

Manchukuo Nos. 84, 88 and 98 Handstamp Surcharged in Green, Red or Black

1946, May 1

2L11	A16	1y on 1f red brn (G)	18.00	18.00
2L12	A18	5y on 4f lt ol grn (R)	25.00	25.00
2L13	A19	15y on 30f chnt brn	50.00	50.00

Transfer of postal administration and Labor Day.

Manchukuo Nos. 159, 86 and 94 Surcharged in Green, Red or Black

1946, July 7

2L14	A17	1y on 6f crim rose (G)	15.00	15.00
2L15	A17	5y on 2f lt grn (R)	65.00	65.00
2L16	A18	15y on 12f dp org	90.00	90.00

9th anniversary of the outbreak of war with Japan.

Manchukuo Nos. 94, 84 and 158 Surcharged in Black, Green or Red

1946, Aug. 15

2L17	A18	1y on 12f dp org (B)	27.50	27.50
2L18	A16	5y on 1f red brn (G)	50.00	50.00
2L19	A10	15y on 5f gray blk (R)	100.00	100.00

Surrender of Japan, first anniversary.

Manchukuo Nos. 159, 94 and 86 Surcharged in Green, Black or Red

1946, Oct. 10

2L20	A17	1y on 6f crim rose (G)	27.50	27.50
2L21	A18	5y on 12f dp org (B)	50.00	50.00
2L22	A17	15y on 2f lt grn (R)	100.00	100.00

35th anniversary of Chinese revolution.

Manchukuo Nos. 84, 159 and 94 Surcharged in Black, Green or Blue

1946, Oct. 19

2L23	A16	1y on 1f red brn (B)	45.00	45.00
2L24	A17	5y on 6f crim rose (G)	70.00	70.00
2L25	A18	15y on 12f dp org (Bl)	110.00	110.00

10th anniversary of the death of Lu Hsun (1881–1936), writer.

Manchukuo Nos. 86, 159 and 95 Surcharged in Red, Green or Black

1947, Feb. 20

2L26	A16	1y on 2f lt grn (R)	45.00	45.00
2L27	A17	5y on 6f crim rose (G)	85.00	85.00
2L28	A10	15y on 13f dk red brn	140.00	140.00

29th anniversary of the Red (USSR) Army.

Manchukuo Nos. 86, 159 and 162 Surcharged in Red, Green or Black

1947, May 1

2L29	A17	1y on 2f lt grn (R)	22.50	22.50
2L30	A17	5y on 6f crim rose (G)	65.00	65.00
2L31	A19	15y on 30f buff	100.00	100.00

Labor Day.

Manchukuo Nos. 86, 88, 98 and 162 Surcharged ("Kwantung Postal Service, China")

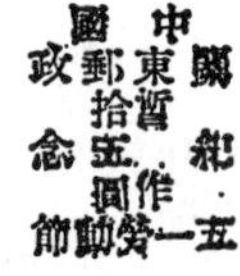

1947, Sept. 15

2L32	A17	5y on 2f lt grn	30.00	25.00
2L33	A18	15y on 4f lt ol grn	50.00	40.00
2L34	A19	20y on 30f red brn	75.00	60.00
2L35	A19	20y on 30f buff	80.00	75.00

Manchukuo Nos. 86 and 159 Surcharged in Red and Green

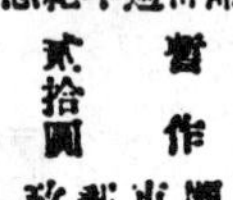

Sacred Golden Kite (same size)
A1

1948, Feb. 20

2L36	A17	10y on 2f lt grn (R)	100.00	100.00
2L37	A17	20y on 6f crim rose (G)	120.00	120.00
2L38	A1	100y on bl & red brn	500.00	500.00

30th anniversary of the Red (USSR) Army. No. 2L38 is on an ungummed label commemorating the 2600th anniversary of the Japanese Empire.

政郵華中
五 暫
圓 作
電郵東關

Japan No. 260 and Manchukuo Nos. 84, 86 and 88 Surcharged in Red, Blue or Black

1948, July

2L39	A85	5y on 3s grn (R)	80.00	80.00
2L40	A16	10y on 1f red brn (Bl)	125.00	125.00
2L41	A17	50y on 2f lt grn	250.00	250.00
2L42	A18	100y on 4f lt ol grn (R)	400.00	400.00

Smaller Characters on Bottom Line

2L43	A17	10y on 2f lt grn (R)	145.00	145.00
2L44	A16	50y on 1f red brn	180.00	180.00

政郵東關
年週一卅念紀
壹 暫
仟
圓 作
節命革月十

Stamps of Manchukuo Nos. 84, 86 and 88 Surcharged in Blue, Red or Black

1948, Nov. 1

2L45	A16	10y on 1f red brn (Bl)	500.00	
2L46	A17	50y on 2f lt grn (R)	500.00	
2L47	A18	100y on 4f lt ol grn	450.00	

31st anniversary of the Russian Revolution.

年八四祝慶
模勞業農東關
念紀會大覽展
拾 暫
圓 作
電郵東關

Manchukuo Nos. 86 and 161 Surcharged in Red or Green

1948, Nov. 15

2L48	A17	10y on 2f lt grn (R)	700.00	
2L49	A17	50y on 20f brn (G)	700.00	700.00

Kwantung Agricultural and Industrial Exhibition.

政郵東關

貳 暫
拾
圓 作

Manchukuo Nos. 86, 88 and 161 Surcharged in Red, Black or Green

1949, Jan.

2L50	A17	20y on 2f lt grn (R)	500.00	
2L51	A18	50y on 4f lt ol grn	700.00	
2L52	A17	100y on 20f brn (G)	700.00	

Without Gum

From No. 2L56 onward all stamps were issued without gum except as noted.

Farmer and Worker
A2

Train and Ship
A3

Ship at Dock
(*No. 2L55*)
A4

(*No. 2L56*)

1949 **Litho.** ***Perf. 11, 11½***

2L53	A2	5y pale grn	1.50	2.50
2L54	A3	10y orange	8.50	7.00
2L55	A4	50y vermilion	12.00	10.00
2L56	A4	50y red (redrawn)	20.00	7.00

Issue dates: Nos. 2L56, July 7; others Apr. 1.

Worker, Flag and Means of Transport
A5

1949, May 1 ***Perf. 11***

2L57	A5	10y rose pink	8.00	8.00
a.		10y ver	75.00	75.00

Labor Day. No. 2L57a is from a worn plate.

Mao Tse-tung and Red Flag
A6

Heroes' Monument, Dairen
A7

1949, July 1

2L59	A6	50y red	24.00	24.00

28th anniversary of the founding of the Chinese Communist Party.

1949, Sept.

2L60	A7	10y red, bl & ol	15.00	15.00
a.		10y red, bl & pale bl	100.00	100.00

4th anniversary of victory over Japan and opening of the Dairen Industrial Fair.

Nos. 2L53–2L54 Surcharged in Red or Black

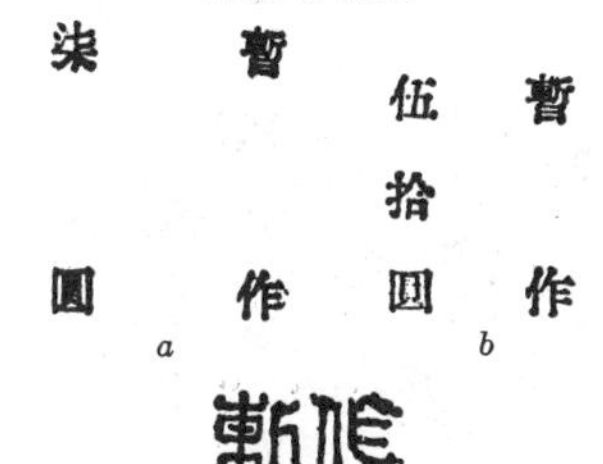

柒 暫
伍 暫
拾
圓 作 圓 作
a b

暫作
伍佰圓
c

With Gum

1949, Sept.

2L62	A2(a)	7y on 5y lt grn (R)	25.00	25.00
2L63	A2(a)	7y on 5y lt grn	25.00	25.00
2L64	A2(b)	50y on 5y lt grn (R)	70.00	70.00
2L65	A3(b)	100y on 10y org	350.00	350.00
2L66	A3(c)	500y on 10y org (R)	600.00	400.00
		Nos. 2L62-2L66 (5)	1,070.	870.00

Size of surcharge on No. 2L63: 16x19mm.
A 500y on 5y light green with red surcharge "c", and a 500y on 10y orange with surcharge "b" were prepared but not issued.

Stalin and Lenin
A8

1949, Nov. 7 ***Perf. 11x11½***

2L68	A8	10y dl bl grn (shades)	8.00	8.00

32nd anniversary of the Russian Revolution.

Workers Saluting Mao, Star and Flag
A9

1949, Nov. 16 ***Perf. 11***

2L69	A9	35y dk bl, red, & yel	9.00	9.00

Founding of the People's Republic of China.

Stalin
A10

(same size)

Gate of Heavenly Peace
A11

1949, Dec. 20 ***Perf. 11½***

2L70	A10	20y dl mag	21.00	21.00
2L71	A10	35y rose red	21.00	21.00

70th birthday of Stalin.

1950, Mar. 10 **Typo.** ***Perf. 10½***

2L72	A11	10y Prus bl	50	1.50
2L73	A11	20y dl grn	7.50	1.50
2L74	A11	35y red	50	1.00
2L75	A11	50y dp pur	30	1.00
2L76	A11	100y lil rose	50	1.00
		Nos. 2L72-2L76 (5)	9.30	6.00

NORTH CHINA

The North China Liberation Area included the provinces of Hopeh, Chahar, Shansi and Suiyuan. The original postal service, begun in the Shansi-Hopeh-Chahar Border Area in December, 1937, became the North China Postal and Telegraph Administration in May, 1949.

All Stamps Issued without Gum

Large Victory Issue

Cavalry Man Holding Nationalist Flag
A1

Perf. 10½

1946, Mar. **Wmk. Wavy Lines**

Granite Paper

Size: 34½x42mm.

3L1	A1	$1 red brn	1.00	1.00
a.		Newsprint	12.00	12.00
3L2	A1	$2 gray grn	1.00	1.00
3L3	A1	$4 vermilion	1.25	1.00
3L4	A1	$5 vio brn	1.25	1.00
3L5	A1	$8 vio bl	1.25	1.00
3L6	A1	$10 dp car	1.25	1.00
3L7	A1	$12 yellow	3.00	1.50
3L8	A1	$20 lt grn	7.00	7.00
		Nos. 3L1-3L8 (8)	17.00	14.50

Defeat of Japan.

Small Victory Issue

Perf. 10½x10, 9½ rough

1946, May **Unwmkd.**

Granite paper

Size: 20x21mm.

3L9	A1	$1 red org	1.00	1.00
3L10	A1	$2 green	1.50	1.00
3L11	A1	$3 lt lil	3.00	3.00
3L12	A1	$5 dl pur	4.00	10
3L13	A1	$8 dk bl	6.00	6.00
3L14	A1	$10 rose red	1.50	1.50
3L15	A1	$15 purple	*30.00*	*20.00*
3L16	A1	$20 green	3.00	3.00
3L17	A1	$30 brt grnsh bl	2.50	*3.50*
3L18	A1	$40 brt rose lil	3.00	*3.00*
3L19	A1	$50 brown	*20.00*	25
3L20	A1	$60 myr grn	*30.00*	75

Wmkd. Wavy Lines

3L21	A1	$100 orange	1.00	*2.00*
3L22	A1	$200 dl bl	1.00	*2.00*
3L23	A1	$500 rose	*10.00*	*25.00*
		Nos. 3L9-3L23 (15)	*117.50*	*72.10*

North China Postal and Telegraph Administration

Charging Infantrymen
A2

Agriculture and Industry
A3

1949, Jan. ***Imperf.*** **Unwmkd.**

White Paper

3L24	A2	50c brn lake	1.00	30
3L25	A2	$1 Prus bl	1.00	30

Newsprint

3L26	A2	$2 ap grn	1.00	30
3L27	A2	$3 dl vio	20	30

No.	Type	Description	Unused	Used
3L28	A2	$5 brown	1.00	30
3L29	A3	$6 dp rose	1.00	30
a.		White paper	1.25	30
3L30	A2	$10 bl grn	20	30
3L31	A2	$12 dp car	1.00	30
		Nos. 3L24-3L31 (8)	6.40	2.40

No. 3L29 issued in Peking, others in Tientsin.

Remittance Stamps of China Surcharged

壹 $1

叁 $3

A4

1949, Jan. Engraved *Perf. 13*

Small Central Characters

No.	Type	Description	Unused	Used
3L32	A4	50c on $50 brn blk	4.00	75
3L33	A4	$1 on $50 gray blk	3.00	75
3L34	A4	$3 on $50 gray	3.00	75

Large Central Characters

No.	Type	Description	Unused	Used
3L35	A4	50c on $50 blk	2.00	75
3L36	A4	$6 on $20 dk vio brn	2.00	60

Issued in Tientsin.

Sun Yat-sen Type A2 of Northeastern Provinces and China No. 640 Surcharged in Black, Red, Green or Blue

a b

c

Type "b," bottom character of left vertical row (yuan) differs. Type "c," top character of right vertical row differs.

1949, March 7 *Perf. 14*

No.	Type	Description	Unused	Used
3L37	A2 (a)	50c on 5c lake	25	3.00
3L38	A2 (a)	$1 on 10c org	25	1.00
3L39	A2 (a)	$2 on 20c yel grn	50.00	1.25
a.		Surch. inverted	100.00	
3L40	A2 (a)	$3 on 50c red org	25	3.00
3L41	A2 (a)	$4 on $5 dk grn	4.00	1.50
3L42	A2 (a)	$6 on $10 crim	1.00	1.00
3L43	A2 (a)	$10 on $300 bluish grn	1.25	2.00
3L44	A2 (a)	$12 on $1 bl	1.25	1.50
3L45	A2 (a)	$18 on $3 brn	1.25	75
3L46	A2 (b)	$20 on 50c red org (Bl)	1.25	25
3L47	A2 (a)	$20 on $20 ol, II	1.25	50
a.		Type I	10.00	10.00
3L48	A2 (a)	$30 on $2.50 ind (R)	1.25	2.00
3L49	A2 (a)	$40 on 25c blk brn (R)	1.10	1.00
3L50	A2 (a)	$50 on $109 dk grn (R)	9.00	2.00
3L51	A2 (b)	$80 on $1 bl (R)	15.00	1.00
3L52	A2 (a)	$100 on $65 dl grn (R)	18.00	1.50
3L53	A73 (b)	$100 on $100 dk car, surch. 16mm. wide (Bl)	18.00	1.30
a.		Surch. 14mm. wide	24.00	18.00

1949, Apr.

No.	Type	Description	Unused	Used
3L55	A2 (c)	$2 on 20c yel grn	1.25	1.50
3L56	A2 (c)	$3 on 50c red org	20	1.00
3L57	A2 (c)	$4 on $5 dk grn	1.25	2.00
3L58	A2 (c)	$6 on $10 crim, I	9.00	1.00
a.		Type II	9.00	1.00
3L59	A2 (c)	$12 on $1 bl	75	75

d e

1949, Apr.

No.	Type	Description	Unused	Used
3L60	A2 (d)	$1 on 25c blk brn (G)	15	2.50
3L61	A2 (d)	$10 on $300 bluish grn (R)	9.00	2.75
3L62	A2 (d)	$20 on 50c red org (G)	9.00	2.00
3L63	A2 (d)	$20 on $20 ol (R)	6.00	40
3L64	A2 (d)	$40 on 25c blk brn (R)	6.00	1.25
3L65	A2 (d)	$50 on $109 dk grn, surch. 15mm. wide (R)	9.00	1.25
a.		Surch. 13mm. wide	30.00	8.00
3L66	A2 (d)	$80 on $1 bl (R)	6.00	1.25

On Stamps of China

No.	Type	Description	Unused	Used
3L67	A73 (d)	$100 on $100 dk car (G)	14.00	4.00
3L68	A73 (d)	$300 on $700 red brn (Bl)	10.00	1.15
3L69	A82 (d)	$500 on $500 bl grn (R)	7.50	1.00
3L70	A82 (d)	$3000 on $3000 bl (R)	10.00	1.25

On Stamps of Northeastern Provinces

1949, Aug.

No.	Type	Description	Unused	Used
3L71	A2 (e)	$10 on $10 crim (Bl), II	6.00	1.15
a.		Type I	12.00	12.00
3L72	A2 (e)	$30 on 20c yel grn (R)	6.00	1.00
3L73	A2 (e)	$50 on $44 dk car rose (Bl)	6.00	50
3L74	A2 (e)	$100 on $3 brn (Bl)	10.00	1.25
3L75	A2 (e)	$200 on $4 org brn (Bl), II	14.00	4.00
a.		Type I	300.00	150.00

On China No. 754

No.	Type	Description	Unused	Used
3L76	A82	$10 on $7000 lt red brn (Bl)	10.00	4.00
		Nos. 3L37-3L76 (39)	275.45	61.50

Overprints on Nos. 3L71 and 3L76 have 2 characters in center row.

Farmer and Worker on Globe
A5

1949, May 1 Engraved *Perf. 14*

No.	Type	Description	Unused	Used
3L77	A5	$20 crimson	1.75	65
3L78	A5	$40 dk bl	1.75	80
3L79	A5	$60 brn org	1.75	65
3L80	A5	$80 dk grn	1.75	1.25
3L81	A5	$100 purple	1.75	1.00
		Nos. 3L77-3L81 (5)	8.75	4.35

Labor Day. Exist imperf. Price, set $9. Also issued in blocks of four, imperf. between, perf. around outer edges.

Mao Tse-tung (Chinese Numeral)
A6

Mao Tse-tung (Arabic Numeral)
A7

1949, July 1 *Perf. 14*

No.	Type	Description	Unused	Used
3L82	A6	$10 red	25	75
3L83	A7	$20 dk bl	25	15
3L84	A6	$50 orange	2.00	50
3L85	A7	$80 dk grn	30	25
3L86	A6	$100 purple	2.00	50
3L87	A7	$120 olive	20	25
3L88	A6	$140 vio brn	2.00	1.00
		Nos. 3L82-3L88 (7)	7.00	3.40

28th anniversary of the founding of the Chinese Communist Party.

Price, imperf set $25.

(same size)
Gate of Heavenly Peace
A8

Farmers and Factory
A9

1949, Nov. 26 Litho. *Perf. 12½*

No.	Type	Description	Unused	Used
3L89	A8	$50 orange	20	2.00
3L90	A8	$100 crimson	5	40
3L91	A8	$200 green	50	50
3L92	A8	$300 rose brn	7.00	1.00
3L93	A8	$400 blue	7.00	1.00
3L94	A8	$500 brown	7.00	60
3L95	A8	$700 violet	2.00	3.00
		Nos. 3L89-3L95 (7)	23.75	8.50

1949, Dec. Engraved *Perf. 14*

No.	Type	Description	Unused	Used
3L96	A9	$1000 orange	2.50	50
3L97	A9	$3000 dk bl	5	40
3L98	A9	$5000 crimson	10	75
3L99	A9	$10,000 red brn	10	1.50

PARCEL POST STAMPS

Parcel Post Stamps of China Nos. Q23–Q27 Surcharged in Red, Black or Blue

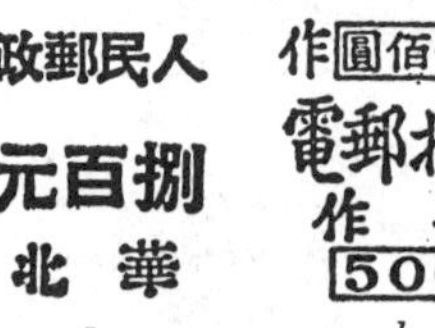

a b

1949, June

No.	Type	Description	Unused	Used
3LQ1	PP3 (a)	$300 on $6,000,000 ol gray (R)		15.00
3LQ2	PP3 (a)	$400 on $8,000,000 scar (Bl)		15.00
3LQ3	PP3 (a)	$500 on $10,000,000 sage grn (R)		18.00
3LQ4	PP3 (a)	$800 on $5,000,000 lil (R)		25.00
3LQ5	PP3 (a)	$1000 on $3,000,000 sl bl (R)		35.00

Surcharged Type "b"

No.	Type	Description	Unused	Used
3LQ6	PP3	$500 on $3,000,000 dk bl		25.00
3LQ7	PP3	$1000 on $5,000,000 vio gray		40.00
3LQ8	PP3	$3000 on $8,000,000 ver		75.00
3LQ9	PP3	$5000 on $10,000,000 dl grn		140.00
		Nos. 3LQ1-3LQ9 (9)		388.00

Nos. 3LQ8–3LQ9 have large numerals unboxed.

Remittance Stamps of China (like North China Type A4) Surcharged in Black or Red

a b

Peking Surcharge (a)

1949, June Litho. *Perf. 13*

No.	Description	Unused	Used
3LQ10	$6 on $5 ver	10.00	5.00
3LQ11	$20 on $50 gray	10.00	5.00
3LQ12	$50 on $20 dk vio brn	10.00	5.00
3LQ13	$100 on $10 ol grn	25.00	10.00

Tientsin Surcharge (b)

Engraved *Perf. 14*

No.	Description	Unused	Used
3LQ14	$20 on $1 brn org	10.00	6.00
a.	Perf. 12½	20.00	10.00
3LQ15	$30 on $2 dk grn	10.00	6.00
a.	Red surcharge	10.00	10.00
3LQ16	$30 on $10 ol grn	10.00	6.00
3LQ17	$100 on $10 gray grn (R)	10.00	6.00

Lithographed *Perf. 13*

No.	Description	Unused	Used
3LQ18	$50 on $5 red	10.00	6.00

Engraved *Perf. 12½*

No.	Description	Unused	Used
3LQ19	$20 on $1 org brn	25.00	18.00
3LQ20	$100 on $10 yel grn	60.00	50.00

Typographed *Roulette 9½*

No.	Description	Unused	Used
3LQ21	$30 on $2 bl grn (R)	50.00	30.00

The surcharge on No. 3LQ14a is without first and last lines.

Locomotive
PP1

1949, Nov. Engraved *Perf. 14*

No.	Type	Description	Unused	Used
3LQ22	PP1	$500 crimson	5.00	6.00
3LQ23	PP1	$1000 dp bl		10.00
3LQ24	PP1	$2000 green		15.00
3LQ25	PP1	$5000 dp ol		30.00
3LQ26	PP1	$10,000 orange		60.00
3LQ27	PP1	$20,000 red brn		150.00
3LQ28	PP1	$50,000 brn pur		300.00
		Nos. 3LQ22-3LQ28 (7)		571.00

NORTHWEST CHINA

The Northwest China Liberation Area consisted of the provinces of Sinkiang, Tsinghai, Ningsia and the western part of Shensi. The area was first established as the Shensi-Kansu-Ningsia Border Area in October, 1936, after the Long March to Yenan. Remote Sinkiang was not included until late 1949.

All Stamps Issued without Gum

Pagoda on Yenan Hill
A1

1945, Mar. Lithographed *Imperf.*

No.	Type	Description	Unused	Used
4L1	A1	$1 green	15.00	
a.		Rouletted 9	70.00	
4L2	A1	$5 dk bl	80.00	
a.		Rouletted 9	100.00	
4L3	A1	$10 rose red	14.00	
a.		Rouletted 9	70.00	
4L4	A1	$50 dl pur	10.00	
4L5	A1	$100 yel org	14.00	
		Nos. 4L1-4L5 (5)	133.00	

First issue; denomination in Chinese and Arabic. Heavy shading at top of vignette. Columns at sides.

Nos. 4L1–4L2 Surcharged in Red:

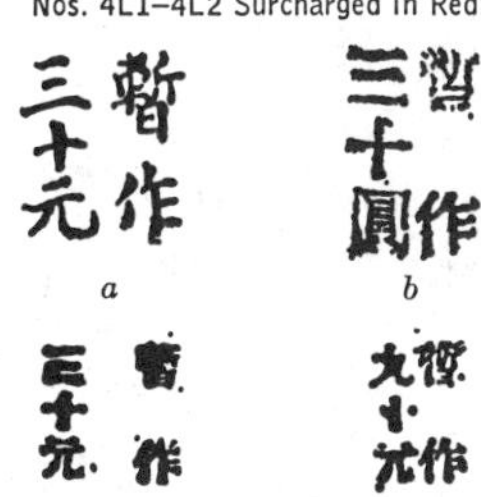

a b c d

1946, Nov.

4L6 A1 (a) $30 on $1 grn 20.00
4L7 A1 (b) $30 on $1 grn *125.00*
a. Rectangular lower left character *500.00*
4L8 A1 (c) $30 on $1 grn 15.00
4L9 A1 (b) $60 on $1 grn
4L10 A1 (d) $90 on $5 dk bl 20.00

Surcharges on Nos. 4L7a and 4L9 are type "b" as illustrated. Surcharge on No. 4L7 differs from "b," having lower left character as in type "a."

(same size)
Pagoda on Yenan Hill
A2 A3

1948, June

4L11 A2 $100 buff 125.00
4L12 A2 $300 rose pink 1.00
4L13 A2 $500 red 3.50
4L14 A2 $1000 blue 3.50
4L15 A2 $2000 yel grn 24.00
4L16 A2 $5000 dl pur 10.00
Nos. 4L11-4L16 (6) 167.00

Second issue; denominations in Chinese only. Many shades and proofs exist.

1948, Dec.

4L17 A3 10c yel org 1.50
4L18 A3 20c lemon 1.50
4L19 A3 $1 dk bl 1.50
4L20 A3 $2 vermilion 1.50
4L21 A3 $5 pale bl grn 9.00
4L22 A3 $10 violet 13.50
Nos. 4L17-4L22 (6) 28.50

Third issue; ornamental border at sides. Many shades exist.

Nos. 4L2 and 4L13 Surcharged in Red or Black

1949, Jan.

4L23 A1 $1 on $5 dk bl 45.00
4L24 A2 $2 on $500 red 20.00

Pagoda on Yenan Hill
A4

1949, May 1

4L25 A4 50c yel to ol 10 20
4L26 A4 $1 dl bl to ind 15 20
4L27 A4 $3 ol yel to org yel 10 20
4L28 A4 $5 bl grn 50 20
4L29 A4 $10 vio to dp vio 6.00 5.00
4L30 A4 $20 pink to rose red 1.50 2.00
Nos. 4L25-4L30 (6) 8.35 7.80

Fourth issue; light shading at top of vignette, columns without ornaments at sides. Many shades exist.

China Nos. 959, F2 and E12 Overprinted ("People's Post, Shensi")

人民郵政(陝)

1949, June 13 Engr. *Perf. 12½*

4L31 A96 orange 18.00 12.50
4L32 R2 carmine 25.00 18.50
4L33 SD2 red vio 25.00 18.50

Stamps of China, Sun Yat-sen Type of 1949, Overprinted in Black or Red ("People's Post, Shensi")

人民郵政 陝西

Lithographed; Engraved

1949, July 1 *Perf. 14, 12½*

4L34 A94 $10 grn (887) 1.00 50
4L35 A94 $20 vio brn (888) 2.00 1.00
4L36 A94 $20 vio brn (894C) 1.00 50
4L37 A94 $50 dk Prus grn (889; R) 5.00 2.00
4L38 A94 $50 grn (951) 5.00 1.50
4L39 A94 $100 org brn (890) 12.00 2.50
4L40 A94 $500 ros lil (892) 18.00 2.50
4L41 A94 $1000 dp bl (952; R) 25.00 1.25
4L42 A94 $2000 vio (946;R) 25.00 7.50
4L43 A94 $5000 car (953) 34.00 15.00
4L44 A94 $10,000 brn (954) 65.00 32.00
Nos. 4L34-4L44 (11) 193.00 66.25

Kansu-Ningsia-Tsinghai Area, Lanchow Overprints

China Nos. 959a, F2 and E12 Overprinted ("People's Post, Kansu")

人民郵政(甘)

1949, Oct. Engr. *Rouletted*

4L45 A96 orange 18.00 16.00

Perf. 12½

4L46 R2 carmine 25.00 16.00
4L47 SD2 red vio 25.00 16.00

Stamps of China, Sun Yat-sen Type of 1949, Overprinted ("People's Post, Kansu")

人民郵政(甘)

Engraved; Lithographed

1949, Oct. *Perf. 14, 12½*

4L48 A94 $10 grn (887) 3.25 1.50
4L49 A94 $20 vio brn (888) 3.25 3.00
4L50 A94 $50 dk Prus grn (889) 9.00 8.00
4L51 A94 $100 org brn (890) 3.25 3.00
4L52 A94 $100 dk org brn (896) 5.00 4.00
4L53 A94 $200 red org (891) 6.50 3.00
4L54 A94 $500 rose lil (892) 6.50 3.00
4L55 A94 $1000 bl (894) 3.25 3.00
4L56 A94 $1000 dp bl (898) 6.50 5.00
4L57 A94 $2000 vio (946) 11.00 9.00
4L58 A94 $5000 lt bl (899) 22.00 18.00
4L59 A94 $10,000 sep (900) 30.00 25.00
4L60 A94 $20,000 ap grn (947) 60.00 50.00
Nos. 4L48-4L60 (13) 169.50 135.50

China Nos. 959, F2 and 791–792 Surcharged in Black or Red ("People's Post, Sinkiang")

1949, Oct.

4L61 A96 $1 on org 16.00 16.00
4L62 R2 $3 on car 16.00 16.00
4L63 A82 10c on $50,000 dp bl (R) 16.00 16.00
4L64 A82 $1.50 on $100,000 dl grn (R) 16.00 16.00

Northwest People's Post

Mao Tse-tung
A5

Great Wall
A6

1949, Oct. 15 Litho. *Imperf.*

4L65 A5 $50 rose 2.50 1.50
a. Cliche of $200 in plate $50 120.00
4L66 A6 $100 dk bl 15 15
4L67 A5 $200 orange 15 75
4L68 A6 $400 sepia 2.50 50

EAST CHINA

The East China Liberation Area included the provinces of Shantung, Kiangsu, Chekiang, Anhwei and Fukien. The original postal service established in Shantung in 1941, became the East China Posts and Telegraph General Office in July, 1948.

All Stamps Issued without Gum

Mao Tse-tung
A1

Transportation and Tower
A2

1948, Mar. Litho. *Perf. 10½*

5L1 A1 $50 yel org 1.50 1.00
5L2 A1 $100 dp rose 5.00 3.50
5L3 A1 $200 dk vio bl 5.00 3.50
5L4 A1 $300 brt grn 5.00 3.50
5L5 A1 $500 dp bl 2.00 1.50
5L6 A1 $800 vermilion 5.00 4.00
5L7 A1 $1000 dk bl 10.00 8.00
5L8 A1 $5000 rose 20.00 15.00
5L9 A1 $10,000 dp car 35.00 25.00
Nos. 5L1-5L9 (9) 88.50 65.00

Many varieties, including unissued imperforates exist.

Perf. 9 to 11 and comp.

1949, Apr. Lithographed

5L10 A2 $1 yel grn 10 10
5L11 A2 $2 bl grn 10 10
5L12 A2 $3 dl red 10 10
5L13 A2 $5 pale brn (ovpt. 4x4 mm) 10 10
a. Without overprint 57.50 57.50
b. Overprint 3x3 mm 1.00 1.00
5L14 A2 $10 ultra 15 15
5L15 A2 $13 brt vio 15 15
5L16 A2 $18 brt bl 15 15
5L17 A2 $21 vermilion 20 20
5L18 A2 $30 gray 20 20
5L19 A2 $50 crimson 25 25
5L20 A2 $100 olive 6.00 6.00
Nos. 5L10-5L20 (11) 7.50 7.50

Seventh anniversary of Shantung Communist Postal Administration. The overprint on the $10, character "yu" meaning "Posts," obliterates Japanese flag on tower, erroneously included in design. Two sizes of overprint exist.

Price, imperfs of Nos. 5L10-5L12, 5L13a, 5L14-5L20 on different paper, set $75.

Train and Postal Runner (1949.2.7)
A3

Mao, Soldiers, Map
A4

Perf. 8 to 11

1949, Apr. Lithographed

5L21 A3 $1 brt emer 10 10
5L22 A3 $2 bl grn 10 10
5L23 A3 $3 dk red 5 10
5L24 A3 $5 brown 3 10
5L25 A3 $10 ultra 10 10
5L26 A3 $13 brt vio 5 10
5L27 A3 $18 brt bl 5 10
5L28 A3 $21 vermilion 5 10
5L29 A3 $30 slate 15 25
5L30 A3 $50 crimson 25 25
5L31 A3 $100 olive 50 50
Nos. 5L21-5L31 (11) 1.43 1.80

Seventh anniversary of Shantung Post Office, Feb. 7. Imperf. sets were sold by the Philatelic Dept., Tientsin P.O. Price $25. See Nos. 5L69-5L76.

Perf. 9½ to 11 comp.

1949, Apr.

5L32 A4 $1 brt emer 5 5
5L33 A4 $2 bl grn 5 5
5L34 A4 $3 dl red 5 5
5L35 A4 $5 brown 5 5
5L36 A4 $10 ultra 5 5
5L37 A4 $13 brt vio 5 5
5L38 A4 $18 brt bl 10 10
5L39 A4 $21 vermilion 10 10
5L40 A4 $30 gray 10 10
5L41 A4 $50 crimson 10 10
5L42 A4 $100 olive 75 65
Nos. 5L32-5L42 (11) 1.45 1.35

Victory of Hwai-Hai (Hwaiying and Haichow). Imperf. sets were sold by the Philatelic Dept., Tientsin P.O.

Price, set $45.

Stamps of China, Sun Yat-sen Type of 1949, Surcharged in Red or Black

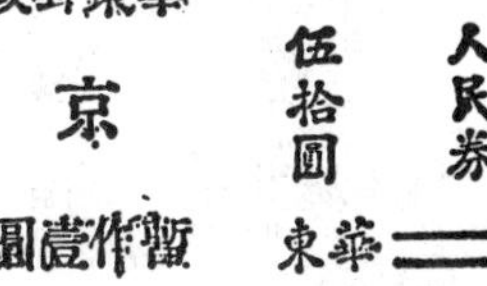

(Nanking) (Wuhu)
a b

1949, May 4 Engr. *Perf. 12½*

5L43 A94 (a) $1 on $10 grn (894A, R) 35 35
a. Perf. 13 3.00 3.00
5L44 A94 (a) $3 on $20 vio brn (894C) 35 35
a. Perf. 13 75 2.00
b. Perf. 14 6.00 6.00
c. Surch. inverted 75.00

Perf. 12½, 14

1949, May Lithographed, Engraved

5L45 A94 (b) $30 on $1000 dp bl (898) 4.00 2.00
5L46 A94 (b) $30 on $1000 bl (894) 4.00 2.00
5L47 A94 (b) $50 on $200 org red (897) 4.00 2.00
5L48 A94 (b) $100 on $5000 lt bl (899,R) 10.00 10.00
5L49 A94 (b) $300 on $10,000 sep (900,R) 30.00 30.00
5L50 A94 (b) $500 on $200 org red (897) 45.00 45.00
Nos. 5L45-5L50 (6) 97.00 91.00

Many varieties exist.

China Nos. 915a and 915 Surcharged in Green, Black or Red

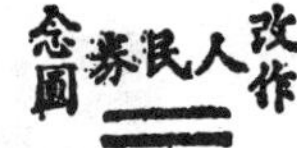

(East China)

1949, May Litho. Perf. 12½

No.	Type	Description	Unused	Used
5L51	A95	$5 on 50c on $20 brn, II (G)	16.00	16.00
5L52	A95	$10 on 50c on $20 brn, II	16.00	16.00
5L53	A95	$20 on 50c on $20 red brn, II (R)	16.00	16.00
a.		Type I (R)	18.00	18.00

Stamps of China, Sun Yat-sen Type of 1949, Surcharged in Black or Red

(Hangchow)

Engr., No. 5L57 Litho.

1949, June 25 Perf. 14, 12½

No.	Type	Description	Unused	Used
5L54	A94	$1 on $1 org (886)	1.50	1.50
5L55	A94	$3 on $20 vio brn (894C,R)	85	85
5L56	A94	$5 on $100 org brn (890)	4.00	2.00
5L57	A94	$5 on $100 dk org brn (896)	2.00	35
5L58	A94	$10 on $50 dk Prus grn (889,R)	20.00	17.50
5L59	A94	$13 on $10 grn (894A)	30	30
		Nos. 5L54-5L59 (6)	28.65	22.50

East China Liberation Area

Maps of Shanghai and Nanking
A5

1949, May 30 Litho. Perf. 8½ to 11

No.	Type	Description	Unused	Used
5L60	A5	$1 org ver	10	10
5L61	A5	$2 bl grn	10	10
5L62	A5	$3 brt vio	5	5
5L63	A5	$5 vio brn	6	5
5L64	A5	$10 ultra	10	5
5L65	A5	$30 slate	6	15
5L66	A5	$50 carmine	15	15
5L67	A5	$100 olive	15	12
5L68	A5	$500 orange	85	50
		Nos. 5L60-5L68 (9)	1.62	1.27

Liberation of Shanghai and Nanking. Many shades, paper and perforation varieties exist.

Train and Postal Runner Type Dated "1949"

1949, July–1950, Feb. Perf. 12½, 14

No.	Type	Description	Unused	Used
5L69	A3	$10 dp ultra	5	5
5L70	A3	$15 org ver	5	5
a.		$15 red, perf. 14	40	10
5L71	A3	$30 sl grn	3	5
a.		Perf. 12½	5	10
5L72	A3	$50 carmine	10	5
5L73	A3	$60 bl grn, perf. 14	5	10
5L74	A3	$100 ol, perf. 14	2.00	10
5L75	A3	$1600 vio bl ('50)	75	1.00
5L76	A3	$2000 brn vio ('50)	1.00	1.50
		Nos. 5L69-5L76 (8)	4.03	2.90

Chu Teh, Mao, Troops with Flags
A7

Mao Tse-tung
A8

1949, Aug. 17 Perf. 12½

No.	Type	Description	Unused	Used
5L77	A7	$70 orange	3	3
5L78	A7	$270 crimson	5	3
5L79	A7	$370 emerald	25	4
5L80	A7	$470 vio brn	65	4
5L81	A7	$570 blue	10	15
		Nos. 5L77-5L81 (5)	1.08	29

22nd anniversary of the People's Liberation Army.

1949, Oct.

No.	Type	Description	Unused	Used
5L82	A8	$10 dk bl	2.00	5.00
5L83	A8	$15 vermilion	2.50	2.50
5L84	A8	$70 brown	10	5
5L85	A8	$100 vio brn	3	5
5L86	A8	$150 orange	3	5
5L87	A8	$200 grnsh gray	3	5
5L88	A8	$500 gray bl	3	5
5L89	A8	$1000 rose	3	5
5L90	A8	$2000 emerald	3	10
		Nos. 5L82-5L90 (9)	4.78	7.90

Stamps of China, Sun Yat-sen Type of 1949 Surcharged in Black or Red

1949, Nov. Litho. Perf. 12½

No.	Type	Description	Unused	Used
5L91	A94	$400 on $200 org red (897)	22.00	80
5L92	A94	$1000 on $50 grnsh gray (895, R)	2.00	80
5L93	A94	$1200 on $100 dk org brn (896)	4	*1.50*
5L94	A94	$1600 on $20,000 ap grn (947)	4	*80*
5L95	A94	$2000 on $1000 dp bl (952,R)	4	*80*
a.		Perf. 14	50.00	25.00
		Nos. 5L91-5L95 (5)	24.12	*4.70*

PARCEL POST STAMPS

Parcel Post Stamps of China 1945–48 Surcharged

(Shantung)

1949, Aug. 1 Engraved Perf. 13

No.	Type	Description	Unused	Used
5LQ1	PP1	$200 on $500 grn	6.00	6.00
5LQ2	PP1	$500 on $1000 Bl	6.00	6.00

Perf. 13½

No.	Type	Description	Unused	Used
5LQ3	PP3	$200 on $200,000 dk grn	40.00	30.00
5LQ4	PP3	$200 on $10,000,000 sage grn	6.00	6.00
5LQ5	PP3	$500 on $7000 dl bl	55.00	50.00
5LQ6	PP3	$500 on $50,000 ind	6.00	6.00
5LQ7	PP3	$1000 on $10,000 car rose	6.00	6.00
5LQ8	PP3	$1000 on $100,000 dk rose brn	6.00	6.00
5LQ9	PP3	$1000 on $300,000 pink	6.00	6.00
5LQ10	PP3	$1000 on $500,000 vio brn	50.00	45.00
5LQ11	PP3	$1000 on $8,000,000 org ver	6.00	6.00
5LQ12	PP3	$2000 on $5,000,000 dl vio	9.00	9.00
5LQ13	PP3	$2000 on $6,000,000 brn blk	9.00	9.00
5LQ14	PP3	$3000 on $30,000 ol	20.00	17.50
5LQ15	PP3	$3000 on $70,000 org brn	20.00	17.50
5LQ16	PP3	$5000 on $3,000,000 dl bl	25.00	22.50
		Nos. 5LQ1-5LQ16 (16)	276.00	248.50

China No. 987 Surcharged

$200 $500 $1000 $2000 $5000 $10,000

1949, Sept. 7 Litho. Perf. 12½

No.	Type	Description	Unused	Used
5LQ17	A97	$200 on $10 bl grn	30.00	15.00
5LQ18	A97	$500 on $10 bl grn	30.00	15.00
5LQ19	A97	$1000 on $10 bl grn	30.00	15.00
5LQ20	A97	$2000 on $10 bl grn	30.00	15.00
5LQ21	A97	$5000 on $10 bl grn	30.00	15.00
5LQ22	A97	$10,000 on $10 bl grn	30.00	15.00
		Nos. 5LQ17-5LQ22 (6)	180.00	90.00

Flying Geese Type of China, 1949, and China Nos. 984–986 Surcharged in Red or Black

1950, Jan. 28

No.	Type	Description	Unused	Used
5LQ23	A97	$5000 on 10c bl vio (R)	90.00	50.00
5LQ24	A97	$10,000 on $1 brn org	90.00	50.00
5LQ25	A97	$20,000 on $2 bl	90.00	50.00
5LQ26	A97	$50,000 on $5 car rose	90.00	50.00

Parcel Post Stamps of China Nos. Q1–Q4 Surcharged in Red or Black

1950, Jan. 28 Engraved Perf. 13

No.	Type	Description	Unused	Used
5LQ27	PP1	$5000 on $500 grn (R)	20	*50.00*
5LQ28	PP1	$10,000 on $1000 bl (R)	120.00	50.00
5LQ29	PP1	$20,000 on $3000 bl grn	120.00	50.00
5LQ30	PP1	$50,000 on $5000 org red	20.00	50.00

CENTRAL CHINA

The Central Chinese Liberation Area included the provinces of Honan, Hupeh, Hunan and Kiangsi. The area was established between August and September, 1949, following the liberation of Hankow.

All Stamps Issued without Gum

Hupeh Postal and Telegraph Administration

Stamps of China, Sun Yat-sen Type of 1949, Surcharged ("Chinese P.O., Temporary Use")

Engraved; Lithographed

1949, June 4 Perf. 14, 12½

Thin parallel lines.

No.	Type	Description	Unused	Used
6L1	A94	$1 on $200 red org (891)	75	75
6L2	A94	$6 on 10,000 sep (900)	75	75
6L3	A94	$15 on $1 org (886)	75	75
6L4	A94	$30 on $100 org brn (890)	3.50	3.50
6L5	A94	$30 on $100 dk org brn (896)	75	75
6L6	A94	$50 on $20 vio brn (894C)	12.00	12.00
6L7	A94	$80 on $1000 dp bl (898)	2.25	2.25

Thick parallel lines.

No.	Type	Description	Unused	Used
6L8	A94	$1 on $200 red org (891)	3.50	3.50
6L9	A94	$3 on $5000 lt bl (899)	50	50
6L10	A94	$10 on $500 rose lil (892)	50	50
6L11	A94	$10 on $500 rose lil (945)	3.50	3.50
6L12	A94	$50 on $20 vio brn (888)	3.50	3.50
6L13	A94	$50 on $20 vio brn (894C)	1.00	1.00
6L14	A94	$80 on $1000 bl (894)	3.50	3.50
6L15	A94	$80 on $1000 dp bl (898)	16.00	16.00
6L16	A94	$100 on $50 dk Prus grn (899)	1.50	1.50
		Nos. 6L1-6L16 (16)	54.25	54.25

Kiangsi Postal and Telegraph Administration

Central Trust Revenue Stamps of China Surcharged ("People's Post, Kiangsi")

(same size)
A1

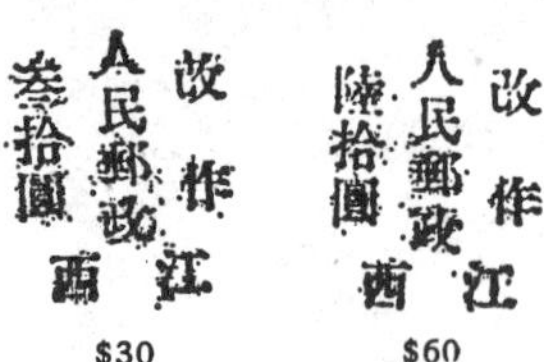

$30 $60

1949, June 20 Engr. Perf. 12½

No.	Type	Description	Unused	Used
6L17	A1	$3 on $30 pur	1.00	1.00
6L18	A1	$15 on $15 red org	1.00	1.00
6L19	A1	$30 on $50 dk bl	6.00	4.00
6L20	A1	$60 on $50 dk bl	1.00	1.00
6L21	A1	$130 on $15 red org	1.00	1.00

The $15 surcharge has 3 characters in left vertical row, the $130 surcharge has 5.

Same Surcharge on Sun Yat-sen Issues of China, 1945–49

Engraved, Litho. Perf. 14, 12½

No.	Type	Description	Unused	Used
6L22	A82	$1 on $250 dp lil (746)	5.00	1.00
6L23	A94	$5 on $1000 dp bl (898)	5.00	1.00
6L24	A94	$5 on $2000 vio (946)	5.00	1.00
6L25	A94	$5 on $5000 lt bl (899)	1.00	1.00
6L26	A94	$10 on $1000 bl (894)	5.00	4.00
6L27	A82	$20 on $4000 gray	1.00	1.00
6L28	A73	$30 on $100 dk car	5.00	4.00
6L29	A82	$30 on $20,000 rose pink	1.00	1.00
6L30	A94	$80 on $500 rose lil (945)	1.00	1.00
6L31	A94	$100 on $1000 dp bl (898)	1.00	1.00
6L32	A82	$200 on $250 dp lil	2.00	2.00
		Nos. 6L17-6L32 (16)	42.00	26.00

Central China Posts and Telegraph Administration

Farmer, Soldier and Worker
A2 A3

I. Top white line of square character (yuan) at upper left does not touch left vertical stroke. No gap in shading between soldier's feet.
II. Top line connects with left vertical stroke. Gap in shading between feet.

Perf. 10 to 11½ & Comp.

1949 Lithographed

6L33	A2	$1 orange	9.00	9.00
6L34	A2	$3 brn org	3.00	3.00
6L35	A2	$6 emerald	3.00	3.00
6L36	A3	$7 yel brn	50	50
6L37	A2	$10 bl grn	15	30
6L38	A3	$14 org brn	18.00	9.00
6L39	A2	$15 ultra	40	15
6L40	A2	$30 grn, I	10	15
a.		Type II	10	15
6L41	A3	$35 gray bl	15.00	9.00
6L42	A2	$50 rose vio	10.00	6.00
6L43	A3	$70 dp grn	15	15
6L44	A2	$80 pink	50	50
6L45	A3	$100 bl grn	30	30
6L46	A3	$220 rose red	4.00	4.00
		Nos. 6L33-6L46 (14)	64.10	45.05

Star Enclosing Map of Hankow Area
A4

Two types of $500:
I. Thick numerals of "500". No period after "500".
II. Thin numerals and period.
Two types of $1000:
I. No period after "1000".
II. Period after "1000".

1949, July

6L48	A4	$110 org brn	25	25
6L49	A4	$130 violet	5.00	25
6L50	A4	$200 dp org	10	25
6L51	A4	$290 brown	2.00	75
6L52	A4	$370 dk bl	2.00	50
6L53	A4	$500 lt bl, I	5.00	1.00
a.		$500 bl, II	25.00	6.00
6L54	A4	$1000 dk red, I	35.00	2.50
a.		$1000 dl red, II	25.00	4.50
6L55	A4	$5000 brown	1.00	2.00
6L56	A4	$10,000 brt pink	2.00	3.00
		Nos. 6L48-6L56 (9)	52.35	10.50

Hankow River Customs Building
A5

River Wall, Wuchang
A6

Design: $290, $370, River scene, Hanyang.

1949, Aug. 16 ***Perf. 11, Imperf.***

6L57	A5	$70 green	80	65
6L58	A5	$220 crimson	80	65
6L59	A5	$290 brown	80	65
6L60	A5	$370 brt bl	80	65
6L61	A6	$500 purple	80	65
6L62	A6	$1000 vermilion	80	65
		Nos. 6L57-6L62 (6)	4.80	3.90

Liberation of Hankow, Wuchang and Hanyang.

Nos. 6L35, 6L39 and 6L40 Surcharged in Red ("Honan People's Post")

柒 人
拾 民
圓 幣
省南河

1949, July

6L63	A2	$7 on $6 emer	8.50	8.50
6L64	A2	$14 on $15 ultra	10.00	10.00
6L65	A2	$70 on $30 grn	15.00	15.00

Surcharge shown is for $70. The $7 has 5 characters in left column and no bottom line.

Issues of 1949 Overprinted ("Honan People's Post")

人 河
民 南
幣 省

1949, Aug.

6L66	A2	$3 brn org	1.00	1.00
6L67	A3	$7 yel brn	1.00	1.00
6L68	A2	$10 bl grn	2.00	2.00
6L69	A3	$14 org brn	2.00	2.00
6L70	A2	$30 yel grn (6L40a)	2.00	2.00
6L71	A3	$35 gray bl	1.00	1.00
6L72	A2	$50 rose vio	7.50	7.50
6L73	A3	$70 dp grn	2.00	2.00
6L74	A4	$110 org brn	14.00	14.00
6L75	A3	$220 rose red	4.00	4.00
6L76	A4	$290 brown	14.00	14.00
6L77	A4	$370 blue	16.00	16.00
6L78	A4	$500 bl, II	24.00	24.00
6L79	A4	$1000 dk red, I	32.00	32.00
6L80	A4	$5000 brown	90.00	90.00
6L81	A4	$10,000 brt pink	200.00	200.00
		Nos. 6L66-6L81 (16)	412.50	412.50

Width of the overprint varies slightly.

Nos. 6L57–6L62 Overprinted ("Honan People's Post")

人 河
民 南
幣 省

1949, Aug. ***Perf. 11, Imperf.***

6L82	A5	$70 green	4.50	3.50
6L83	A5	$220 crimson	4.50	3.50
6L84	A5	$290 brown	4.50	3.50
6L85	A5	$370 brt bl	4.50	3.50
6L86	A6	$500 purple	4.50	3.50
6L87	A6	$1000 vermilion	4.50	3.50
		Nos. 6L82-6L87 (6)	27.00	21.00

Width of overprint on Nos. 6L82–6L85, 7mm.; on Nos. 6L86–6L87, 12mm.

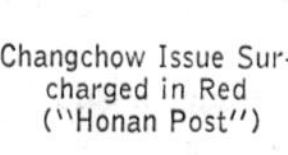

Changchow Issue Surcharged in Red ("Honan Post")

(same size)
Mao Tse-tung
A7

1949, Sept. ***Perf. 10***

6L88	A7	$290 on $30 yel grn	60.00	40.00
6L89	A7	$370 on $30 yel grn	100.00	60.00

Issues of 1949 Surcharged

作 改
圓 佰 貳
200⁰⁰

1950, Jan.

6L90	A2	$200 on $1 org	3.00	2.00
6L91	A2	$200 on $3 brn org	3.00	2.00
6L92	A2	$200 on $6 emer	3.00	2.00
6L93	A3	$200 on $7 yel brn	3.00	2.00
6L94	A3	$200 on $14 org brn	3.00	2.00
6L95	A3	$200 on $35 gray bl	3.00	2.00
6L96	A3	$200 on $70 dp grn	3.00	2.00
6L97	A2	$200 on $80 pink	3.00	2.00
6L98	A3	$200 on $220 rose red	3.00	2.00
6L99	A4	$200 on $370 bl	50	2.00
6L100	A3	$300 on $70 dp grn	1.00	2.00
6L101	A2	$300 on $80 pink	1.00	2.00
6L102	A3	$300 on $220 rose red	10	2.00
6L103	A2	$1200 on $3 brn org	30.00	15.00
6L104	A3	$1200 on $7 yel brn	6.00	3.00
6L105	A3	$1500 on $14 org brn	9.00	2.00
6L106	A2	$2100 on $1 org	35.00	15.00
6L107	A2	$2100 on $6 emer	35.00	15.00
6L108	A3	$2100 on $35 gray bl	13.00	2.50
6L109	A4	$5000 on $370 bl	5.00	3.00
		Nos. 6L90-6L109 (20)	162.60	81.50

Two types of surcharge exist, differing in spacing of characters in top row.

PARCEL POST STAMPS

Star and Map of Hankow
PP1

1949, Nov. **Litho.** ***Perf. 11, 11½***

6LQ1	PP1	$5000 brown	1.00	1.00
6LQ2	PP1	$10,000 scarlet	7.00	1.50
6LQ3	PP1	$20,000 dk sl grn	2.50	2.50
6LQ4	PP1	$50,000 vermilion	1.00	5.00

SOUTH CHINA

The South China Liberation Area included the provinces of Kwantung and Kwangsi and Hainan Island. The South China Postal and Telegraph Administration was organized on or about Nov. 4, 1949.

All Stamps Issued without Gum

Pearl River Bridge, Canton
A1

1949, Nov. 4 **Litho.** ***Imperf.***

7L1	A1	$10 green	5	5
7L2	A1	$20 sepia	5	5
7L3	A1	$30 violet	5	5
7L4	A1	$50 carmine	5	5
7L5	A1	$100 ultra	25	15
		Nos. 7L1-7L5 (5)	45	35

China Nos. 993–995 With Additional Overprint in Red ("Liberation of Swatow")

暫 解
用 放

1949, Nov. 9

7L6	A94	2½c on $500 rose lil (993)	12.50	12.50
a.		Handstamped	30.00	30.00
7L7	A94	2½c on $500 rose lil (994)	20.00	20.00
a.		Handstamped	30.00	30.00
7L8	A94	15c on $10 grn (995)	15.00	15.00
a.		Handstamped	40.00	40.00

On Unit Issues of China, 1949

7L9	A96	org (959)	15.00	12.00
7L10	AP5	bl grn (C62)	15.00	12.00
7L11	SD2	red vio (E12)	15.00	12.00
7L12	R2	car (F2)	15.00	12.00

On Sun Yat-sen and Flying Geese Issues of China

7L13	A94	2c org (974)	30.00	30.00
7L14	A94	4c bl grn (975)	350.00	250.00
7L15	A94	10c dp lil (976)	18.00	14.00
7L16	A94	20c bl (978)	18.00	14.00
7L17	A97	$1 brn org (984)	18.00	14.00
7L18	A97	$10 bl grn (987)	230.00	190.00
		Nos. 7L6-7L18 (13)	771.50	607.50

Nos. 7L1–7L3 Surcharged in Red or Green

300
圓佰叁作改

1950, Jan.

7L19	A1	$300 on $30 vio (R)	3.50	1.00
7L20	A1	$500 on $20 brn (R)	3.50	1.00
7L21	A1	$800 on $30 vio (G)	3.50	1.00
7L22	A1	$1000 on $10 gray grn (R)	3.50	1.00
7L23	A1	$1000 on $20 brn (R)	3.50	1.00
		Nos. 7L19-7L23 (5)	17.50	5.00

SOUTHWEST CHINA

The Southwest China Liberation Area included the provinces of Kweichow, Szechwan, Yunnan, Sikang and Tibet. The Southwest Postal and Telegraph Administration was organized on or about Nov. 15, 1949 after the liberation of Kweiyang, capital of Kweichow Province.

All Stamps Issued without Gum

Chu Teh, Mao and Troops
A1

1949, Dec. **Litho.** ***Perf. 12½***

8L1	A1	$10 dp bl	2.00	1.00
8L2	A1	$20 rose cl	15	50
8L3	A1	$30 dp org	10	50
8L4	A1	$50 gray grn	35	50
8L5	A1	$100 carmine	10	50
8L6	A1	$200 blue	50	60
8L7	A1	$300 bl vio	1.00	1.50
8L8	A1	$500 dk gray	2.50	2.50
8L9	A1	$1000 pale pur	5.00	5.00
8L10	A1	$2000 green	15.00	15.00
8L11	A1	$5000 orange	40.00	40.00
		Nos. 8L1-8L11 (11)	66.70	67.60

China Nos. 974–975, 984, 986–987 Surcharged ("Kweichow People's Post")

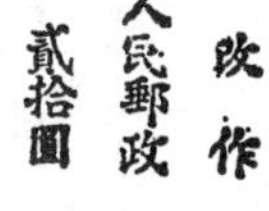

1949, Dec. 1 ***Perf. 12½***

8L12	A94	$20 on 2c org	5.00	5.00
8L13	A94	$50 on 4c bl grn	5.00	5.00
8L14	A97	$100 on $1 brn org	8.00	8.00
8L15	A97	$400 on $5 car rose	25.00	25.00
8L16	A97	$2000 on $10 bl grn	60.00	60.00
		Nos. 8L12-8L16 (5)	103.00	103.00

Map of China, Flag Planted in Southwest
A2

1950, Jan. **Litho.** ***Perf. 9 to 11½***

8L17	A2	$20 dk bl	10	5
8L18	A2	$30 green	50	20
8L19	A2	$50 red	20	10
8L20	A2	$100 brown	20	25

Liberation of the Southwest.

Nos. 8L5–8L6 Surcharged 圓仟貳作改

Perf. 12½

8L21 A1 $300 on $100 car 10.00 5.00
8L22 A1 $500 on $100 car 15 1.50
8L23 A1 $1200 on $100 car 1.00 3.00
8L24 A1 $1500 on $200 bl 1.00 3.00
8L25 A1 $2000 on $200 bl 20.00 15.00
Nos. 8L21-8L25 (5) 32.15 27.50

Nos. 8L5–8L6 Overprinted ("East Szechwan") (川東)

1950, Jan.

8L26 A1 $100 carmine 5.00 5.00
8L27 A1 $200 blue 5.00 5.00

Nos. 8L5–8L6 Hand-stamp Surcharged 壹仟伍百 改作

1950, Jan.

8L28 A1 $1200 on $100 car 25.00 20.00
8L29 A1 $1500 on $200 bl 25.00 20.00

Many varieties, including wide and narrow settings, exist.

Nos. 8L17–8L20 Surcharged in Black or Red

叁仟圓 改作 伍仟圓
$3000 $5000
壹萬圓 貳萬圓 伍萬圓
$10,000 $20,000 $50,000

1950 *Perf. 9 to 11½*

8L30 A2 $60 on $30 grn 17.50 6.00
8L31 A2 $150 on $30 grn 17.50 6.00
8L32 A2 $300 on $20 dk bl (R) 2.00 2.50
8L33 A2 $300 on $100 brn 16.00 6.00
8L34 A2 $1500 on $100 brn 24.00 15.00
8L35 A2 $3000 on $50 red 6.00 10.00
8L36 A2 $5000 on $50 red 5.00 12.00
8L37 A2 $10,000 on $50 red 45.00 25.00
8L38 A2 $20,000 on $50 red 3.00 20.00
8L39 A2 $50,000 on $50 red 5.00 30.00
Nos. 8L30-8L39 (10) 141.00 132.50

Nos. 8L5–8L7 Overprinted ("West Szechwan") 川 西

1950, Jan. *Perf. 12½*

8L40 A1 $100 carmine 20.00 20.00
8L41 A1 $200 pale bl 20.00 20.00
8L42 A1 $300 bl vio 20.00 20.00

Nos. 8L4–8L7 Surcharged 蓉 圓仟貳作改 $2000

1950, Jan.

8L43 A1 $500 on $100 car 8.00 6.00
a. Narrow spacing 60.00 50.00
8L44 A1 $800 on $100 car 8.00 6.00
8L45 A1 $1000 on $50 gray grn 10.00 8.00
8L46 A1 $2000 on $200 pale bl 17.50 14.00
8L47 A1 $3000 on $300 gray vio 32.50 27.50
Nos. 8L43-8L47 (5) 76.00 61.50

Two lines of surcharge 7mm. apart on No. 8L43, 4mm. on No. 8L43a.

China Nos. 975 and 977 Surcharged

政郵民人 政郵民人
蓉 圓百貳 $200 蓉 圓仟壹 $1000

Perf. 12½, 13 or Compound

1950, Jan.

8L48 A94 $100 on 4c bl grn 12.00 12.00
8L49 A94 $200 on 4c bl grn 24.00 24.00
8L50 A94 $800 on 16c org red 75.00 75.00
8L51 A94 $1000 on 16c org red 150.00 150.00

Unit Issue of China Overprinted ("Southwest People's Post") 人民郵政 西南

1950, Jan. **Engraved** *Perf. 12½*

8L52 A96 orange 125.00 80.00
a. Rouletted 125.00 80.00
8L53 SD2 red vio 125.00 80.00
8L54 R2 carmine 125.00 80.00

On No. 8L54, space between overprint columns is 3mm. and right column is raised to height of left.

Nos. 8L3, 8L17-8L20 Surcharged in Black or Red

改作 捌百元

1950, Mar. *Perf. 12½, 9 to 11½*

8L55 A1 $800 on $30 dp org 42.00 35.00
8L56 A2 $1000 on $50 red 9.00 7.50
8L57 A2 $2000 on $100 brn 12.00 9.00
8L58 A2 $4000 on $20 dk bl (R) 35.00 25.00
8L59 A2 $5000 on $30 gray grn 55.00 45.00
Nos. 8L55-8L59 (5) 153.00 121.50

SHANGHAI

(See Vol. IV.)

CILICIA

(sĭ·lĭsh'ĭ·ȧ; -lĭsh'ȧ)

LOCATION—A territory of Turkey, in southeastern Asia Minor.
GOVT.—Former French occupation.
AREA—6,238 sq. mi.
POP.—383,645.
PRINCIPAL TOWN—Seyhan.

British and French forces occupied Cilicia in 1918 and in 1919 its control was transferred to the French. Eventually part of Cilicia was assigned to the French Mandated Territory of Syria but by the Lausanne Treaty of 1923 which fixed the boundary between Syria and Turkey, Cilicia reverted to Turkey.

40 Paras = 1 Piaster

Issued under French Occupation.

The overprint on Nos. 2–93 is often found inverted, double, etc.
Numbers in parentheses are those of basic Turkish stamps.

Turkish Stamps of 1913–19 Handstamped CILICIE

Perf. 11½, 12, 12½, 13½.

1919 **Unwmkd.**

On Pictorial Issue of 1913.

2 A24 2pa red lil (254) 1.00 95
3 A25 4pa dk brn (255) 75 75
4 A27 6pa dk bl (257) 4.50 2.50
5 A32 1¾pi sl & red brn (262) 1.50 1.25

On Issue of 1915.

6 A17 1pi bl (300) 60 60
7 A21 20pa car rose (318) 60 60
9 A22 20pa car rose (330) 1.50 1.50

On Commemorative Issue of 1916.

10 A41 20pa ultra (347) 75 75
11 A41 1pi vio & blk (348) 90 90
12 A41 5pi yel brn & blk (349) 75 75

On Issue of 1916-18.

13 A44 10pa grn (424) 1.00 1.00
14 A47 50pa ultra (428) 3.25 1.85
15 A51 25pi car, *straw* (434) 1.10 1.10
16 A52 50pi car (437) 75 75
17 A52 50pi ind (438) 11.00 11.00

On Issue of 1917.

18 A53 5pi on 2pa Prus bl (547) 3.25 2.50

On Issue of 1919.

19 A47 50pa ultra (555) 3.00 1.75
20 A48 2pi org brn & ind (556) 1.10 1.00
21 A49 5pi pale bl & blk (557) 3.25 1.85

On Newspaper Stamp of 1916.

22 N3 5pa on 10pa gray grn (P137) 80 75

On Semi-Postal Stamps of 1916.

23 A17 1pi bl (B19) 55 55
24 A21 20pa car rose (B28) 70 60
25 A21 1pi ultra (B29) 3.50 2.75

Turkish Stamps of 1913–18 Handstamped CILICIE

1919

On Pictorial Issue of 1913.

31 A24 2pa red lil (254) 45 45
32 A25 4pa dk brn (255) 1.10 1.10

On Issue of 1915.

33 A17 1pi bl (300) 70 70
34 A22 20pa car rose (330) 60 60

On Commemorative Issue of 1916.

35 A41 20pa ultra (347) 90 90
36 A44 1pi vio & blk (348) 70 70

On Issue of 1917.

40 A53 5pi on 2pa Prus bl (547) 75 75

On Newspaper Stamp of 1916.

41 N3 5pa on 10pa gray grn (P137) 75 75

On Semi-Postal Stamps of 1916.

42 A17 1pi bl (B19) 1.25 1.10
43 A21 20pa car rose (B28) 45 45

Turkish Stamps of 1913-19 Handstamped *Cilicie*

1919

On Pictorial Issue of 1913.

51 A24 2pa red lil (254) 50 50
52 A25 4pa dk brn (255) 50 50

On Issue of 1915.

53 A17 1pi bl (300) 35 25
55 A22 5pa ocher (328) 1.60 1.40
56 A22 20pa car rose (330) 70 70

On Commemorative Issue of 1916.

57 A41 20pa ultra (347) 70 70
58 A41 1pi vio & blk (348) 80 80
59 A41 5pi yel brn & blk (349) 70 70

On Issue of 1916

59A A17 1pi bl (372) 30.00 18.50

On Issue of 1916-18.

60 A43 5pa org (421) 1.50 1.25
61 A46 1pi dl vio (426) 1.10 90
63 A52 50pi grn *straw* (439) 17.50 8.50

On Issue of 1917

64 A53 5pi on 2pa Prus bl (547) 3.25 2.75

On Newspaper Stamp of 1916.

65 N3 5pa on 10pa gray grn (P137) 70 70

On Newspaper Stamp of 1919.

65A N4 5pa on 2pa ol grn (P173)

On Semi-Postal Stamps of 1916.

66 A17 1pi bl (B19) 1.10 90
67 A19 20pa car (B26) 2.75 2.50
68 A21 20pa car rose (B28) 62.50 30.00
69 A21 20pa car rose (B31) 1.00 90

Turkey No. 424 Handstamped *T.E.O. Cilicie*

1919

71 A44 10pa green 50 50

Turkish Stamps of 1913-19 Overprinted in Black, Red or Blue T. E. O. Cilicie

1919

In this setting there are various broken and wrong font letters and the letter "i" is sometimes replaced by a "t."

On Pictorial Issue of 1913.

75 A30 1pi bl (R) (260) 40 25

On Issue of 1915.

76 A21 20pa car rose (318) 75 80

On Commemorative Issue of 1916.

77 A41 20pa ultra (347) 65 55
78 A41 1pi vio & blk (348) 45 30

On Issue of 1916-18.

79 A43 5pa org (Bl) (421) 20 20
80 A44 10pa grn (424) 25 25

81	A45	20pa dp rose (Bk) (425)	60	60
82	A45	20pa dp rose (Bl) (425)	20	20
83	A48	2pi org brn & ind (429)	30	25
83C	A49	5pi pale bl & blk (R) (430)	40	30
84	A51	25pi car, *straw* (434)	2.50	2.25
85	A52	50pi grn, *straw* (439)	42.50	30.00

On Issue of 1917.

85A	A53	5pi on 2pa Prus bl (547)		
86	A53	5pi on 2pa Prus bl (548)	2.75	2.50

On Newspaper Stamps of 1916–19

87	N3	5pa on 10pa gray grn (P137)	25	25
88	N4	5pa on 2pa ol grn (P173)	20	20

On Semi-Postal Stamps of 1915–17

89	A21	20pa car rose (B8)		
90	A21	20pa car rose (B28)	70	70
91	A41	10pa car (B42)	30	20
92	A11	10pa on 20pa vio brn (B38)	25	25
93	SP1	10pa red vio (B46)	70	40

It is understood that the Newspaper and Semi-Postal stamps overprinted "Cilicie" were used as ordinary postage stamps.

A1

Blue Surcharge.

1920 ***Perf. 11½.***

98	A1	70pa on 5pa red	35	35
99	A1	3½pi on 5pa red	35	35

Nos. 98-99 exist with surcharge double, inverted, double with one inverted, "OCCUPTTION," etc. Price, $1 to $2 each.

French Offices in Turkey No. 26 Surcharged — T. E. O 20 PARAS

1920 ***Perf. 14x13½***

100	A3	20pa on 10c rose red	32	32
a.		'PARAS' omitted	11.00	11.00
b.		Surcharged on back	2.50	2.50

Three types of "20" exist on No. 100.

Stamps of France, 1900-17, Surcharged — O. M. F. Cilicie 5 PARAS

1920

101	A16	5pa on 2c vio brn	30	30
102	A22	10pa on 5c grn	35	35
103	A22	20pa on 10c red	60	60
104	A22	1pi on 25c bl	1.00	1.00
105	A20	2pi on 15c gray grn	1.85	1.85
106	A18	5pi on 40c red & gray bl	2.25	2.25
107	A18	10pi on 50c bis brn & lav	2.75	2.75
108	A18	50pi on 1fr cl & ol grn	62.50	62.50
109	A18	100pi on 5fr dk bl & buff	525.00	525.00
		Nos. 101-109 (9)	596.60	596.60

Nos. 106 to 109 surcharged in four lines.

Stamps of France, 1917, Surcharged — O. M. F. Cilicie SAND. EST 20 PARAS

1920

110	A16	5pa on 2c vio brn	2.25	
111	A22	10pa on 5c grn	2.25	
112	A22	20pa on 10c red	1.50	
113	A22	1pi on 25c bl	1.50	
114	A20	2pi on 15c gray grn	4.50	
115	A18	5pi on 40c red & gray bl	32.50	
116	A18	20pi on 1fr cl & ol grn	52.50	
		Nos. 110-116 (7)	97.00	

On Nos. 115 and 116 "SAND. EST" is placed vertically. "Sand. Est" is an abbreviation of Sandjak de l'Est (Eastern County).

Nos. 110–116 were prepared for use, but never issued.

Stamps of France, 1900-17, Surcharged — O. M. F. Cilicie 10 PARAS

1920

117	A16	5pa on 2c vio brn	18	18
a.		Inverted surch.	6.00	5.25
b.		Double surcharge	8.00	
c.		"Cililie"	7.25	7.25
d.		Surch. 5 pi (error)	15.00	15.00
119	A22	10pa on 5c grn	22	22
a.		Inverted surcharge	6.00	5.25
b.		Surch. 5pa (error)	13.50	13.50
121	A22	20pa on 10c red	28	28
a.		Inverted surcharge	6.00	5.25
b.		Surch. 10pa (error)	15.00	15.00
122	A22	1pi on 25c bl	28	28
a.		Double surcharge	11.00	
b.		Inverted surcharge	6.00	5.25
123	A20	2pi on 15c gray grn	35	35
a.		Double surcharge	11.00	
b.		Inverted surcharge	6.00	5.25
124	A18	5pi on 40c red & gray bl	50	50
a.		Double surcharge	15.00	
b.		Inverted surcharge	9.00	8.00
c.		"PIASRTES"	12.50	12.50
125	A18	10pi on 50c bis brn & lav	60	60
a.		"PIASRTES"	12.50	12.50
126	A18	50pi on 1fr cl & ol grn	1.25	1.25
a.		"PIASRTES"	18.50	18.50
b.		Inverted surch.	18.50	16.50
127	A18	100pi on 5fr dk bl & buff	7.25	7.25
a.		"PIASRTES"	35.00	35.00
		Nos.117-127 (9)	10.91	10.91

This surcharge has "O.M.F." in thicker letters than the preceding issues.

There were two printings of this surcharge which may be distinguished by the space of 1 or 2mm. between "Cilicie" and the numeral.

The surcharge on Nos. 119b and 121b is always inverted.

AIR POST STAMPS.

Nos. 123 and 124 Handstamped

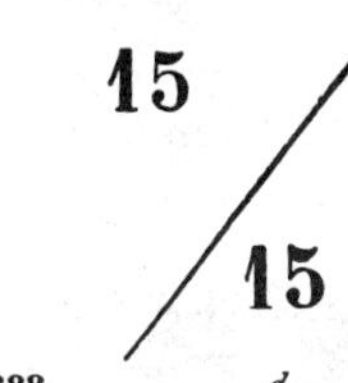

Perf. 14x13½

1920, July 15 **Unwmkd.**

C1	A20	2pi on 15c gray grn	*3,250.*	*3,250.*
C2	A18	5pi on 40c red & gray bl	*3,250.*	*3,250.*
a.		"PIASRTES"		

A very limited number of Nos. C1 and C2 were used on two air mail flights between Adana and Aleppo. At a later date impressions from a new handstamp were struck "to oblige" on stamps of the regular issue of 1920 (Nos. 123, 124, 125 and 126) that were in stock at the Adana Post Office.

Counterfeits exist.

POSTAGE DUE STAMPS.

Turkish Postage Due Stamps of 1914 Handstamped.

1919 ***Perf. 12.*** **Unwmkd.**

Handstamped CILICIE

J1	D1	5pa claret	1.25	1.25
J2	D2	20pa red	1.25	1.25
J3	D3	1pi dk bl	2.75	2.75
J4	D4	2pi slate	2.25	2.25

Handstamped CILICIE

J5	D1	5pa claret	1.25	1.25
J6	D2	20pa red	1.25	1.25
J7	D3	1pi dk bl	2.75	2.75
J8	D4	2pi slate	2.25	2.25

Handstamped *Cilicie*

J9	D1	5pa claret	1.25	1.25
J10	D2	20pa red	1.25	1.25
J11	D3	1pi dk bl	2.75	2.75
J12	D4	2pi slate	2.25	2.25

Postage Due Stamps of France Surcharged — O. M. F. Cilicie 2 PIASTRES

1921

J13	D2	1pi on 10c choc	3.25	3.25
J14	D2	2pi on 20c ol grn	3.25	3.25
J15	D2	3pi on 30c red	3.25	3.25
J16	D2	4pi on 50c vio brn	3.25	3.25

COCHIN CHINA

(kō'chin chī'nȧ; kŏch'in)

LOCATION — The southernmost state of French Indo-China in the Cambodian Peninsula.

GOVT.—French Colony.

AREA—26,476 sq. mi.

POP.—4,615,968.

CAPITAL—Saigon.

100 Centimes = 1 Franc

Surcharged in Black on Stamps of French Colonies:

5 (a) 5 C. CH. (b) 5 (c)

1886–87 ***Perf. 14x13½*** **Unwmkd.**

1	A9 (a)	5c on 25c yel, *straw*	85.00	62.50
2	A9 (b)	5c on 2c brn, *buff*	6.25	6.25
3	A9 (b)	5c on 25c yel, *straw*	7.25	7.25
4	A9 (c)	5c on 25c *rose* ('87)	20.00	18.50
a.		Double surcharge, one of type b	110.00	750.00
b.		Triple surcharge, two of type b	120.00	120.00
c.		Inverted surcharge		

15 / 15 (d)

1888

5	A9 (d)	15c on half of 30c brn, *bis*	17.50	

No. 5 was prepared but not issued.

The so-called Postage Due stamps were never issued.

Stamps of Cochin China were superseded by those of Indo-China in 1892.

COLOMBIA

(kō̇·lŏm'bē̇·ä)

LOCATION — On the northwest coast of South America, bordering on the Caribbean Sea and the Pacific Ocean.

GOVT.—Republic.

AREA—456,535 sq. mi. (estimated.)

POP.—25,167,500 (est. 1977).

CAPITAL—Bogotá.

In 1810 the Spanish Viceroyalty of New Granada gained its independence and with Venezuela and Ecuador formed the State of Greater Colombia. In 1832 this state split into three independent units as Venezuela, Ecuador and the Republic of New Granada. The name of the country has been successively Granadine Confederation (1858-61), United States of New Granada (1861), United States of Colombia (1861-85), Republic of Colombia (1885 to date).

100 Centavos = 1 Peso

Prices of early Colombia stamps vary according to condition. Quotations for Nos. 1–34 are for fine copies. Very fine to superb specimens sell at much higher prices, and inferior or poor copies sell at reduced prices, depending on the condition of the individual specimen.

In the earlier days many towns did not have handstamps for canceling and stamps were canceled with pen and ink. Pen cancellations, therefore, do not indicate fiscal use. (Postage stamps were not used for revenue purposes.) Prices of Nos. 1–128 are for pen-canceled specimens. Those with handstamped cancellations sell for considerably more.

Fractions of many Colombian stamps of both early and late issues are found canceled, their use to pay postage having been tolerated even though forbidden by the postal laws and regulations. Many are known to have been made for philatelic purposes.

Granadine Confederation

Coat of Arms

A1 A2

Type A1: Asterisks in frame. Wavy lines in background.

Type A2: Diamond-shaped ornaments in frame. Straight lines in background. Numerals larger.

Lithographed.

1859 ***Imperf.*** **Unwmkd.**

Wove Paper.

1	A1	2½c green	100.00	60.00
a.		2½c yel grn	100.00	60.00
2	A1	5c blue	70.00	60.00
a.		Tête bêche pair	*3,000.*	*6,500.*
3	A1	5c violet	75.00	75.00
b.		"50" instead of "5"		*8,500.*
4	A1	10c red brn	70.00	40.00
a.		10c buff	70.00	40.00
6	A1	20c blue	70.00	40.00
a.		20c gray bl	70.00	40.00
b.		Se-tenant with 5c	*30,000.*	
c.		Tête bêche pair	*20,000.*	*20,000.*
7	A1	1p carmine	50.00	50.00
a.		1p rose	50.00	50.00
8	A1	1p rose, *bluish*	350.00	

The 10c green is an essay.

Reprints of No. 7 are in brown rose or brown red. Wavy lines of background are much broken; no dividing lines between stamps.

1860 **Laid Paper.**

9	A2	5c lilac	350.00	250.00

Wove Paper.

10	A2	5c gray lil	75.00	60.00
a.		5c lil	75.00	60.00
11	A2	10c yel buff	50.00	40.00
a.		Tête bêche pair	5,000.	
12	A2	20c blue	175.00	125.00

United States of New Granada

Arms of New Granada
A3

1861

13	A3	2½c black	850.00	525.00
14	A3	5c yellow	200.00	125.00
a.		5c buff	200.00	125.00
16	A3	10c blue	600.00	200.00
17	A3	20c red	400.00	200.00
18	A3	1p pink	850.00	500.00

There are 54 varieties of the 5c, 20c, and 1 peso.
Forgeries exist of Nos. 13-18.

United States of Colombia

Coat of Arms
A4 A5 A6

1862

19	A4	10c blue	200.00	125.00
20	A4	20c red	*1,600.*	550.00
21	A4	50c green	200.00	160.00
22	A4	1p red lil	450.00	275.00
23	A4	1p red lil, *bluish*	*4,000.*	*1,500.*

No. 23 is on a thinner, coarser wove paper than Nos. 19-22.

1863

24	A5	5c orange	75.00	45.00
a.		Star after "Cent"	85.00	50.00
25	A5	10c blue	175.00	20.00
a.		Period after "10"	190.00	25.00
26	A5	20c red	140.00	45.00
a.		Star after "Cent"	160.00	52.50
b.		Transfer of 50c in stone of 20c	*14,000.*	*4,500.*

Bluish Paper.

28	A5	10c blue	100.00	25.00
a.		Period after "10"	110.00	27.50
29	A5	50c green	110.00	40.00
a.		Star after "Cent"	120.00	45.00

Ten varieties of each.

1864 **Wove Paper.**

30	A6	5c orange	40.00	20.00
a.		Tête bêche	350.00	240.00
31	A6	10c blue	35.00	14.00
a.		Period after 10	35.00	14.00
32	A6	20c scarlet	60.00	30.00
33	A6	50c green	50.00	30.00
34	A6	1p red vio	325.00	160.00

Two varieties of each.

Arms of Colombia
A7 A9

A8

1865

35	A7	1c rose	10.00	10.00
a.		bluish pelure paper	14.00	12.50
36	A8	2½c *lilac*	17.50	11.00
37	A9	5c yellow	25.00	14.00
a.		5c org	25.00	14.00
38	A9	10c violet	35.00	7.50
39	A9	20c blue	35.00	10.00
40	A9	50c green	70.00	30.00
41	A9	50c grn (small figures)	47.50	22.50
42	A9	1p vermilion	80.00	15.00
a.		1p rose red	80.00	15.00
b.		Period after "PESO"	90.00	17.50

Ten varieties of each of the 5c, 10c, 20c, and 50c, and six varieties of the 1 peso.
No. 36 was used as a carrier stamp.

A10 A11 A12

A13 A14

A15 A16

1866 **White Wove Paper.**

45	A10	5c orange	20.00	15.00
46	A11	10c lilac	7.00	5.00
a.		Pelure paper	12.50	10.00
47	A12	20c lt bl	20.00	16.50
a.		Pelure paper	37.50	30.00
48	A13	50c green	13.50	13.50
49	A14	1p rose red, *bluish*	60.00	25.00
a.		1p ver	60.00	17.50
51	A15	5p *green*	300.00	175.00
52	A16	10p *vermilion*	265.00	140.00

There are several varieties of the 1 peso having the letters "U", "N", "S" and "O" smaller.

A17

A18 A19

A20 A21

TEN CENTAVOS:
Type I: "B" of "COLOMBIA" over "V" of "CENTAVOS".
Type II: "B" of "COLOMBIA" over "VO" of "CENTAVOS".
ONE PESO:
Type I: Long thin spear heads Diagonal lines in lower part of shield.
Type II: Short thick spear heads. Horizontal and a few diagonal lines in lower part of shield.
Type III: Short thick spear heads. Crossed lines in lower part of shield. Ornaments at each side of circle are broken. (See No. 97.)

1868

53	A17	5c orange	50.00	37.50
54	A18	10c lil (I)	1.65	1.10
a.		10c red vio (I)	1.65	1.10
b.		10c lil (II)	1.65	1.10
c.		10c red vio (II)	1.65	1.10
d.		Printed on both sides	3.50	2.50
55	A19	20c blue	2.00	1.65
56	A20	50c yel grn	2.50	2.10
57	A21	1p ver (II)	3.00	2.25
a.		Tête bêche pair	250.00	225.00
b.		1p rose red (I)	40.00	30.00
c.		1p rose red (II)	3.00	2.25

See also Nos. 83-84, 96-97.

Counterfeits or reprints.
10c. There is a large white dot at the upper left between the circle enclosing the "X" and the ornament below.
50c. There is a shading of dots instead of dashes below the ribbon with motto. There are crossed lines in the lowest section of the shield instead of diagonal or horizontal ones.
1p. The ornaments in the lettered circle are broken. There are crossed lines in the lowest section of the shield.
These counterfeits, or reprints, are on white paper, wove and laid, on colored wove paper and in fancy colors.

A22
Two varieties.

1869-70 **Wove Paper**

59	A22	2½c *violet*	2.50	2.50
a.		Laid paper ('70)	175.00	175.00
b.		Laid batonné paper ('70)	30.00	30.00

Nos. 59, 59a and 59b were used as carrier stamps.
Counterfeits, or reprints, are on magenta paper wove or ribbed.

A23 A24

1870 **Wove Paper.**

62	A23	5c orange	90	90
a.		5c yel	90	90
63	A24	25c *blue*	12.00	12.00

See also No. 89.

In the counterfeits, or reprints, of No. 63, the top of the "2" of "25" does not touch the down stroke. The counterfeits are on paper of various colors.

A25 A26

5 pesos. The ornament at the left of the "C" of "Cinco" cuts into the "C", and the shading of the flag is formed of diagonal lines.
10 pesos. The stars have extra rays between the points, and the central part of the shield has some horizontal lines of shading at each end.

1870 **Surface Colored, Chalky Paper**

64	A25	5p *green*	50.00	57.50
65	A26	10p *vermilion*	62.50	52.50

See also Nos. 77-79, 125-126.

A27

A28 A29

TEN CENTAVOS:
Type I: "S" of "CORREOS" 2¼ mm. high. First "N" of "NACIONALES" small.
Type II: "S" of "CORREOS" 2 mm. high. First "N" of "NACIONALES" wide.

1871-74 **Thin Porous Paper**

66	A27	1c grn ('72)	2.40	2.40
67	A27	1c rose ('73)	2.00	2.00
a.		1c car ('73)	2.25	2.25
68	A28	2c brown	1.10	1.10
a.		2c red brn	1.10	1.10
69	A29	10c vio (I) ('74)	1.35	1.35
a.		10c lil (I) ('74)	1.35	1.35
b.		10c vio (II) ('74)	1.35	1.35
c.		10c lil (II) ('74)	1.35	1.35
d.		Laid paper, as #69 ('72)	80.00	80.00
e.		Laid paper, as "b" ('72)	80.00	80.00

Counterfeits or reprints.
1c. The outer frame of the shield is broken near the upper left corner and the "A" of "Colombia" has no cross-bar.
2c. There are scratches across "DOS" and many white marks around the letters on the large "2".
The counterfeits, or reprints, are on white wove and bluish white laid paper.

Condor
A30

Liberty Head
A31 A32

Wove Paper.

5 pesos, re-drawn: The ornament at the left of the "C" only touches the "C", and the shading of the flag is formed of vertical and diagonal lines.
10 pesos, re-drawn: The stars are distinctly five pointed, and there is no shading in the central part of the shield.

1877

73	A30	5c purple	5.25	1.75
a.		5c lil	5.25	1.75
74	A31	10c bis brn	2.00	1.00
a.		10c red brn	2.00	1.00
b.		10c vio brn	2.00	1.00
75	A32	20c blue	2.50	1.35
a.		20c vio bl	7.50	3.75

77	A26	10p *rose*	67.50	45.00
78	A25	5p *lt grn*, redrawn	47.50	37.50
79	A26	10p *rose*, redrawn	15.00	3.50

Stamps of the issues of 1871-77 are known with private perforations of various gauges, also with sewing machine perforation.

In the counterfeits, or reprints, of the 5 pesos the ornament at the left of the "C" of "Cinco" is separated from the "C" by a black line.

In the counterfeits, or reprints, of the 10 pesos the outer line of the double circle containing "10" is broken at the top, below "OS" of "Unidos", and the vertical lines of shading contained in the double circle are very indistinct. There is a colorless dash below the loop of the "P" of "Pesos".

1876-79 Laid Paper.

80	A30	5c lilac	52.50	52.50
81	A31	10c brown	30.00	12.00
82	A32	20c blue	60.00	30.00
83	A20	50c grn ('79)	70.00	45.00
84	A21	1p pale red (II) ('79)	50.00	16.50

1879 Wove Paper.

89	A24	25c green	27.50	27.50

1881 Blue Wove Paper.

93	A30	5c violet	10.00	6.00
a.		5c lil	10.00	6.00
94	A31	10c brown	5.25	2.25
95	A32	20c blue	4.75	2.75
96	A20	50c yel grn	6.75	5.25
97	A21	1p ver (III)	12.00	7.00

For types of 1p, see note over No. 53.

Reprints of the 10c and 20c are much worn. On the 10c the letters "TAVOS" of "CENTAVOS" often touch. On the 20c the letters "NT" of "VEINTE" touch and the left arm of the "T" is too long. Reprints of the 25c, 50c and 1p have the characteristics previously described. The reprints are on white wove or laid paper, on colored papers, and in fancy colors. Stamps on green paper exist only as reprints.

A34

A35

A36

White Wove Paper.

1 centavo: The period before "UNION" is round and there are rays between the stars and the condors.
2 centavos: The "2" s and "C" s in the corners are placed upright.
5 centavos: The last star at the right almost touches the frame.
10 centavos: The letters of the inscription are thin; there are rays between the stars and the condor.

1881 ***Imperf.***

103	A34	1c green	3.00	3.00
104	A35	2c vermilion	1.00	1.25
a.		2c rose	1.00	1.25
106	A34	5c blue	3.00	1.25
a.		Printed on both sides		
107	A36	10c violet	2.50	1.10
108	A34	20c black	3.00	1.75
		Nos. 103-108 (5)	12.50	8.35

The stamps of this issue are found with perforations of various gauges, also sewing machine perforation, all of which are unofficial.

Liberty Head
A37

A37a

1881 ***Imperf.***

109	A37	1c *green*	2.00	2.50
110	A37	2c *lil rose*	2.00	2.50
111	A37	5c *lilac*	2.40	2.50

Nos. 109 to 111 are found with regular or sewing machine perforation, unofficial.

Reprints:

1c. The top line of the stamp and the top frame extend to the left.

2c. There is a curved line over the scroll below the "AV" of "CENTAVOS".

5c. There are scratches across the "5" in the upper left corner.

All three values were reprinted on the three colors of paper of the originals.

Redrawn.

1 centavo: The period before "UNION" is square and the rays between the stars and the condor have been wholly or partly erased.
2 centavos: The "2" s and "C" s in the corners are placed diagonally.
5 centavos: The last star at the right touches the wing of the condor.
10 centavos: The letters of the inscription are thick; there are no rays under the stars; the last star at the right touches the wing of the condor and this wing touches the frame.

1883 ***Imperf.***

112	A34	1c green	5.25	5.25
113	A37a	2c rose	1.00	1.25
114	A34	5c blue	2.50	1.25
a.		5c ultra	2.50	1.25
b.		Printed on both sides, reverse ultra	30.00	25.00
115	A36	10c violet	2.00	1.65

The stamps of this issue are found with regular or sewing machine perforation, privately applied.

A38

A39

1883 ***Perf. 10½, 12, 13½***

116	A38	1c gray grn, *grn*	1.00	1.00
a.		Imperf., pair	5.00	5.00
117	A39	2c red, *rose*	1.00	1.25
a.		2c org red, rose	1.00	1.25
b.		2c red, *buff*	10.00	10.00
c.		Imperf., pair (#117 or 117a)	5.00	5.00
d.		"DE LOS" in very small caps	10.00	10.00
118	A38	5c bl, *bluish*	1.75	1.75
a.		5c dk bl, *bluish*	1.50	1.25
b.		5c bl	2.50	2.50
c.		Imperf., pair (#118 or 118a)	8.50	8.50
d.		As "b," imperf., pair	12.00	12.00
119	A39	10c org, *yel*	1.25	1.65
a.		"DE LOS" in large caps	62.50	27.50
b.		Imperf., pair	7.50	7.50
120	A39	20c vio, *lil*	1.25	1.60
a.		Imperf., pair	5.00	5.00
122	A38	50c brn, *buff*	1.75	2.75
a.		Perf. 12	2.00	2.75
123	A38	1p cl, *bluish*	4.00	2.65
a.		Imperf., pair	15.00	15.00
		Nos. 116-123 (7)	12.00	12.65

1886 ***Perf. 10½, 11½, 12.***

127	A38	5p brn, *straw*	6.00	6.75
a.		Imperf., pair	35.00	35.00
128	A38	10p *rose*	7.50	6.75
a.		Imperf., pair	35.00	35.00

Republic of Colombia

A40

Simón Bolívar
A41

President Rafael Núñez
A42

1886 ***Perf. 10½ and 13½***

129	A40	1c grn, *grn*	1.25	90
a.		Imperf., pair	7.50	7.50
130	A41	5c bl, *bl*	1.25	50
a.		5c ultra, *bl*	1.25	50
b.		Imperf., pair (#130)	7.50	7.50
131	A42	10c orange	2.75	75
a.		Imperf., pair	7.50	7.50
b.		Pelure paper	3.50	1.00

General Antonio José de Sucre y Alcala
A43

General Antonio Nariño
A44

1887

133	A43	2c org red, *rose*	1.75	1.25
a.		2c org red, *yel*	5.25	5.25
b.		2c org red	7.00	7.00
c.		Imperf., pair (#133)	9.00	9.00
134	A44	20c pur, *grysh*	3.00	1.25
a.		Imperf., pair	9.00	9.00
b.		Pelure paper	3.75	2.50

Impressions of No. 134 on white, blue or greenish blue paper were not regularly issued.

Arms
A45

Nariño
A46

1888

135	A45	50c brn, *buff*	2.00	2.00
a.		Imperf., pair	6.50	6.50
136	A45	1p cl, *bluish*	7.50	2.25
137	A45	1p claret	2.65	1.65
138	A45	5p org brn	7.50	6.00
139	A45	5p black	13.00	9.00
140	A45	10p *rose*	18.50	7.50
		Nos. 135-140 (6)	51.15	28.40

1889

141	A46	20c pur, *grysh*	1.50	1.50
a.		Imperf., pair	7.50	7.50

Impressions on white, blue or greenish blue paper were not regularly issued.

A47

A48

A49

A50

A51

1890-91 ***Perf. 10½, 13½, 11***

142	A47	1c grn, *grn*	1.75	1.50
143	A48	2c org red, *rose*	75	75
144	A49	5c bl, *grnsh bl*	1.00	70
a.		5c dp bl, *bl*	1.00	70
b.		Imperf., pair	6.00	6.00
146	A50	10c brn, *yel*	75	50
147	A51	20c vio, pelure paper	3.00	3.00
		Nos. 142-147 (5)	7.25	6.45

A52

A53

A54

Perf. 10½, 12, 13½, 14 to 15½.

1892 Ordinary Paper.

148	A47	1c red, *yel*	60	50
149	A52	2c red, *rose*	7.50	7.50
150	A52	2c green	35	35
a.		2c yel grn	35	35
151	A49	5c blk, *buff*	3.00	50
152	A50	10c bis brn, *rose*	60	50
153	A53	20c brn, *bl*	75	50
154	A45	50c vio, *vio*	1.00	60
155	A54	1p bl, *grnsh*	1.25	50
156	A45	5p red, *pale rose*	5.25	2.85
157	A45	10p blue	6.75	3.25
a.		Thin, pale rose paper	6.75	3.25
		Nos. 148-157 (10)	27.05	17.05

Nos. 148, 150-155 and 157 exist imperf. Price per pair, $5-$7.50.

A55

A55a

1895–99

158	A55	5c org brn, *pale buff*	75	50
a.		Imperf., pair	6.00	6.00
159	A55	5c red brn, *sal* ('97)	75	50
a.		Imperf., pair	6.00	6.00
160	A53	20c yel brn, *grnsh bl* ('97)	3.75	4.50
160A	A53	20c brn, *buff* ('97)	17.50	12.50
161	A55a	50c red vio, *vio* ('99)	1.50	1.40

Type A55a is a redrawing of type A45. The letters of the inscriptions are slightly larger and the numerals "50" slightly smaller than in type A45.

The 20c brown on white paper is believed to be a chemical changeling.

A56

1899

162	A56	1c red, *yel*	70	50
163	A56	5c red brn, *sal*	60	50
164	A56	10c brn, *lil rose*	2.25	1.60
165	A56	50c bl, *lil*	1.40	1.40

Cartagena Issues.

A57

1899 Blue Overprint. *Imperf.*

167	A57	5c red, *buff*	15.00	15.00
a.		Sewing machine perf.	20.00	20.00
168	A57	10c ultra, *buff*	15.00	15.00
a.		Sewing machine perf.	20.00	20.00

Nos. 168 and 168a differ slightly from the illustration.

A58

A59

A60

A61

Purple Overprint.

1899 *Sewing Machine Perf.*

170	A58	1c brn, *buff*	15.00	15.00
a.		Altered from 10c	25.00	25.00
171	A59	2c blk, *buff*	15.00	15.00
a.		Altered from 10c	25.00	25.00
172	A60	5c mar, *grnsh bl*	20.00	20.00
a.		Perf. 12	20.00	20.00
b.		Without ovpt.	12.50	12.50
173	A61	10c red, *sal*	20.00	20.00
a.		perf. 12	20.00	20.00

Types A58 and A59 illustrate Nos. 170a and 171a, which were made from altered plates of the 10c (No. 168). Nos. 170 and 171 were made from altered plate of the 5c denomination (No. 167), show part of the top flag of the "5" and differ slightly from the illustrations.

Nos. 170–173 exist imperf. Prices about same as perf.

A62

1900 *Imperf.*

Purple Overprint

174	A62	5c red	15.00	15.00
a.		Perf. 12	20.00	20.00

A63 A64

Sewing Machine Perf.

1901 Purple Overprint.

175	A63	1c black	1.00	1.00
a.		Without overprint	2.75	2.75
b.		Double overprint	3.00	3.00
c.		Imperf., pair	2.50	2.50
d.		Inverted overprint	1.50	1.50
176	A64	2c *rose*	1.00	1.00
a.		Imperf., pair	2.50	2.50
b.		Without overprint	2.75	2.75
c.		Double overprint	3.00	3.00

A65 A66

1901 Rose Overprint

177	A65	1c blue	1.00	1.00
a.		Imperf., pair	3.50	3.50
178	A66	2c brown	1.00	1.00
a.		Imperf., pair	3.50	3.50
b.		Without overprint	1.00	1.00

A67

A68

Sewing Machine or Regular Perf. 12, 12½

1902 Magenta Overprint.

179	A67	5c violet	2.00	2.00
a.		Without overprint	2.00	2.00
b.		Double overprint	2.00	2.00
c.		Imperf., pair	4.25	4.25
180	A68	10c yel brn	2.00	2.00
a.		Double overprint	2.00	2.00
b.		Imperf., pair	4.25	4.25
c.		Without overprint	2.00	2.00
d.		Printed on both sides	3.50	3.50

A69

A70

1902 Magenta Overprint

181	A69	5c yel brn	1.50	1.50
a.		Without overprint	1.25	1.25
b.		Imperf., pair	3.50	3.50
182	A69	10c black	1.75	1.75
a.		Without overprint	1.50	1.50
b.		Imperf., pair	8.50	8.50
183	A70	20c maroon	2.50	2.50
b.		Imperf., pair	7.50	7.50

Nos. 181–183 exist tête bêche. Price of 10c and 20c, each $17.50.

Washed copies of Nos. 167–183 are offered as "without overprint."

Barranquilla Issues.

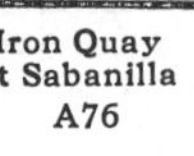

Magdalena River A75

Iron Quay at Sabanilla A76

La Popa Hill A77

1902–03 *Imperf.*

184	A75	2c green	1.10	1.10
185	A75	2c dk bl	1.10	1.10
186	A75	2c rose	21.00	21.00
187	A76	10c scarlet	75	75
188	A76	10c orange	4.75	4.75
189	A76	10c rose	75	75
190	A76	10c maroon	75	75
191	A76	10c claret	75	75
192	A77	20c violet	5.00	5.00
a.		Laid paper		
193	A77	20c dl bl	3.75	3.75
194	A77	20c dl bl, *pink*	50.00	50.00
195	A77	20c car rose	22.50	22.50

Sewing Machine Perf. and Perf. 12.

184a	A75	2c green	7.50	7.50
185a	A75	2c dk bl	4.50	4.50
186a	A75	2c carmine	30.00	30.00
187a	A76	10c scarlet	3.00	3.00
188a	A76	10c orange	15.00	15.00
189a	A76	10c rose	4.75	4.75
190a	A76	10c maroon	4.75	4.75
191a	A76	10c claret	4.75	4.75
192b	A77	20c purple	60	60
c.		20c lil	60	60
193a	A77	20c dl bl	3.25	3.25
194a	A77	20c dl bl, *rose*	50.00	50.00
195b	A77	20c car rose	20.00	20.00

See also Nos. 240–245.

Cruiser "Cartagena" A78

Bolívar A79

General Próspero Pinzón A80

A81

A82

1903-04 *Imperf.*

209	A78	5c blue	1.35	1.35
210	A78	5c bister	3.00	3.00
211	A79	50c yellow	4.50	4.50
212	A79	50c green	4.50	4.50
213	A79	50c scarlet	4.50	4.50
214	A79	50c carmine	4.50	4.50
a.		50c rose	4.50	4.50
215	A79	50c pale brn	3.00	3.00
216	A80	1p yel brn	1.35	1.35
217	A80	1p rose	2.25	2.25
218	A80	1p blue	2.25	2.25
219	A80	1p violet	30.00	30.00
220	A81	5p claret	4.50	4.50
221	A81	5p pale brn	4.50	4.50
222	A81	5p bl grn	4.50	4.50
223	A82	10p pale grn	6.00	6.00
224	A82	10p claret	25.00	25.00
		Nos. 209-224 (16)	105.70	105.70

Nos. 216 and 217 measure 20½x26½mm. and No. 218, 18x24 mm.

Stamps of this issue exist with forged perforations.

Perf. 12.

209a	A78	5c blue	6.00	6.00
210a	A78	5c bister	7.50	7.50
211a	A79	50c yellow	7.50	7.50
b.		50c org	7.50	7.50
212a	A79	50c green	7.50	7.50
213a	A79	50c scarlet	7.50	7.50
214b	A79	50c rose	7.50	7.50
215a	A79	50c pale brn	7.50	7.50
216a	A80	1p yel brn	3.00	3.00
217a	A80	1p rose	4.50	4.50
218a	A80	1p blue	4.50	4.50
219a	A80	1p violet	37.50	37.50
220a	A81	5p claret	11.00	11.00
221a	A81	5p pale brn	12.00	12.00
222a	A81	5p bl grn	12.00	12.00
223a	A82	10p pale grn	13.00	13.00
224a	A82	10p claret	37.50	37.50
		Nos. 209a-224a (16)	186.00	186.00

Imperf.

Laid Paper.

240	A76	10c dk bl, *lil*	4.50	4.50
241	A76	10c dk bl, *bluish*	4.50	4.50
242	A76	10c dk bl, *brn*	4.50	4.50
243	A76	10c dk bl, *sal*	7.50	7.50
244	A76	10c dk bl, *grnsh bl*	6.00	6.00
245	A76	10c dk bl, *dp rose*	4.50	4.50
		Nos. 240-245 (6)	31.50	31.50

Perf. 12.

240a	A76	10c dk bl, *lil*	13.00	13.00
241a	A76	10c dk bl, *bluish*	7.50	7.50
242a	A76	10c dk bl, *brn*	7.50	7.50
243a	A76	10c dk bl, *sal*	45.00	45.00
244a	A76	10c dk bl, *grnsh bl*	20.00	20.00
245a	A76	10c dk bl, *dp rose*	7.50	7.50
		Nos. 240a-245a (6)	100.50	100.50

Medellin Issue.

A83

1902

257	A83	1c grn, *straw*	30	45
a.		Imperf., pair	12.00	12.00
258	A83	2c sal, *rose*	30	45
a.		Imperf., pair	12.00	12.00
259	A83	5c dp bl, *grnsh*	30	45
a.		Imperf., pair	12.00	12.00
260	A83	10c pale brn, *straw*	30	45
a.		Imperf., pair	12.00	12.00
261	A83	20c pur, *rose*	50	60
a.		Imperf., pair	12.00	12.00
262	A83	50c dl rose, *grnsh*	2.00	2.00
a.		Imperf., pair	12.00	12.00
263	A83	1p *yellow*	3.00	3.00
a.		Imperf., pair	32.50	32.50
264	A83	5p sl, *bl*	22.50	22.50
a.		Imperf., pair	65.00	65.00
265	A83	10p dk brn, *rose*	17.50	17.50
a.		Imperf., pair	65.00	65.00
		Nos. 257-265 (9)	46.70	47.40

Regular Issue.

A84

A85

A86

A87

A88

A89

A90

A91

A92

1902 ***Imperf.***

266	A84	2c *rose*	25	25
267	A85	4c red, *grn*	30	30
268	A86	5c grn, *bl*	30	30
269	A87	10c *pink*	30	30
270	A88	20c brn, *buff*	30	30
271	A89	50c dk grn, *rose*	1.00	1.00
272	A90	1p pur, *buff*	45	45
273	A91	5p grn, *bl*	4.25	4.50
274	A92	10p grn, *pale grn*	4.75	4.75
		Nos. 266-274 (9)	11.90	12.15

Sewing Machine Perf.

266a	A84	2c *rose*	75	75
267a	A85	4c red, *grn*	75	75
268a	A86	5c grn, *bl*	90	90
269a	A87	10c *pink*	90	90
270a	A88	20c brn, *buff*	90	90
271a	A89	50c dk grn, *rose*	3.25	2.50
272a	A90	1p pur, *buff*	3.00	3.00
273a	A91	5p grn, *bl*	17.50	17.50
274a	A92	10p grn, *pale grn*	27.50	27.50
		Nos. 266a-274a(9)	55.45	54.70

1903 ***Perf. 12***

266b	A84	2c *rose*	75	75
269b	A87	10c *pink*	1.25	1.25
270b	A88	20c brn, *buff*	1.25	1.25
272b	A90	1p pur, *buff*	3.00	2.50
273b	A91	5p grn, *bl*	22.50	22.50
274b	A92	10p grn, *pale grn*	30.00	30.00
		Nos. 266b-274b (6)	58.75	58.25

1903 ***Imperf.***

284	A85	4c bl, *grn*	30	30
285	A86	5c bl, *bl*	40	40
286	A88	20c bl, *buff*	30	30
288	A89	50c bl, *rose*	1.40	1.40

Sewing Machine Perf.

284a	A85	4c bl, *grn*	90	90
285a	A86	5c bl, *bl*	90	90
286a	A88	20c bl, *buff*	1.10	1.10
288a	A89	50c bl, *rose*	4.50	4.50

Perf. 12

284b	A85	4c bl, *grn*	1.25	1.25
285b	A86	5c bl, *bl*	1.25	1.25
286b	A88	20c bl, *buff*	1.25	1.25
288b	A89	50c bl, *rose*	4.50	4.50

A93

1904 Pelure Paper ***Imperf.***

303	A93	½c yel brn	1.10	1.10
304	A90	1c bl grn	90	90
a.		1c yel grn	1.25	1.25
306	A84	2c blue	90	90
307	A86	5c carmine	1.25	1.25
308	A87	10c violet	90	90
		Nos. 303-308 (5)	5.05	5.05

1904 ***Perf. 13***

303a	A93	½c yel brn	3.00	3.00
304b	A90	1c bl grn	3.75	3.75
c.		1c yel grn	4.50	4.50
306a	A84	2c blue	3.00	3.00

Perf. 12

307a	A86	5c carmine	3.00	3.00
308a	A87	10c violet	3.00	3.00
		Nos. 303a-308a (5)	15.75	15.75

Pres. José Manuel Marroquín

A94 A95 A96

Imprint: "Lit. J. L. Arango Medellin. Col."

1904 Wove Paper ***Perf. 12***

314	A94	½c yellow	90	18
a.		Redrawn	90	18
b.		Imperf., pair	3.75	3.75
315	A94	1c green	75	6
a.		Redrawn	75	6
b.		Imperf. pair	3.00	3.00
316	A94	2c rose	75	10
a.		Redrawn	75	10
b.		Imperf., pair	3.75	3.75
317	A94	5c blue	1.10	18
a.		Redrawn	1.10	18
b.		Imperf., pair	3.75	3.75
318	A94	10c violet	1.50	22
a.		Imperf., pair	4.75	4.75
319	A94	20c black	1.75	30
a.		Redrawn	1.75	30
b.		Imperf., pair	7.50	7.50
320	A95	1p brown	13.00	3.00
a.		Imperf., pair	35.00	35.00
321	A96	5p red & blk, *yel*	45.00	45.00
322	A96	10p bl & blk, *grnsh*	45.00	45.00
		Nos. 314-322 (9)	109.75	94.04

On the redrawn types, the imprint is close to the base of the design instead of being spaced from it. On the redrawn 2c and 5c, the lower end of the vertical white line below "OR" of "CORREOS" forms a hook which turns to the right instead of to the left as in the originals.

See also Nos. 325-330.

A97

A98

1905 ***Imperf.***

323	A97	50p org yel, *pale pink*	80.00	80.00
324	A98	100p dk bl, *dk rose*	75.00	75.00

Imprint: "Lit. Nacional".

Perf. 10, 13, 13½ and Compound.

1908

325	A94	½c orange	90	15
a.		½c yel	90	15
b.		Imperf., pair	2.25	2.25
c.		Without imprint	6.00	6.00
326	A94	1c yel grn	90	6
a.		Without imprint	90	6
d.		Imperf., pair	3.75	3.75
327	A94	2c red	90	6
a.		2c car	90	6
b.		Imperf., pair	3.75	3.75
328	A94	5c blue	65	15
a.		Imperf., pair	6.00	6.00
329	A94	10c violet	12.00	1.00
330	A94	20c gray blk	13.00	70
		Nos. 325-330 (6)	28.35	2.12

The above stamps may be easily distinguished from those of 1904 by the perforation, by the height of the design, 24mm. instead of 23mm., and by the "Lit. Nacional" imprint.

Camilo Torres
A99

Policarpa Salavarrieta
A100

Nariño
A101

Bolívar
A102

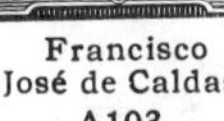
Francisco José de Caldas
A103

Francisco de Paula Santander
A104

Bolívar Demanding Liberation of Slaves
A105

Bolívar Resigning
A106

1910, Aug. **Engraved** ***Perf. 12***

331	A99	½c vio & blk	1.10	70
a.		Center inverted	400.00	400.00
332	A100	1c dp grn	90	70
333	A101	2c scarlet	75	60
334	A102	5c dp bl	1.25	65
335	A103	10c plum	15.00	6.75
336	A104	20c blk brn	17.50	8.00
337	A105	1p dk vio	52.50	25.00
338	A106	10p claret	250.00	200.00
		Nos. 331-338 (8)	339.00	242.40

Colombian independence centenary.

Caldas
A107

Torres
A108

Nariño
A109

Santander
A110

Bolívar
A111

José María Córdoba
A112

Monument to Battle of Boyacá
A113

View of Cartagena
A114

Sucre
A115

Rufino Cuervo
A116

Antonio Ricaurte y Lozano
A117

Coat of Arms
A118

1917 **Engraved.** ***Perf. 14***

339	A107	½c bister	55	15
340	A108	1c green	55	8
341	A109	2c car rose	55	8
342	A110	4c violet	1.20	45
343	A111	5c dl bl	1.75	22
344	A112	10c gray	2.00	22
345	A113	20c red	3.00	30
346	A114	50c carmine	2.25	30
347	A115	1p brt bl	9.00	45
348	A116	2p orange	11.00	75
349	A117	5p gray	22.50	7.50
350	A118	10p dk brn	45.00	10.00
		Nos. 339-350 (12)	99.35	20.50

The 1c, 5c, 10c, 50c, 2p, 5p and 10p also exist perf. 11½ and 11½ compounded with 14.

Lithographed varieties of Nos. 343, 345 and 346 are counterfeits made to defraud the government.

Imperforate copies of Nos. 339-350 are not known to have been regularly issued.

See Nos. 373-374, 400-405.

Nos. 318–319, 329–330 Surcharged in Red

Especie Provisional $ 0.00½

1918 On Issue of 1904.

351	A94	½c on 20c blk	1.40	50
352	A94	3c on 10c vio	2.25	1.00

On Issue of 1908.

353	A94	½c on 20c gray blk	9.00	9.00
354	A94	3c on 10c vio	15.00	5.00

Nos. 351 to 354 inclusive exist with surcharge reading upward or downward. On one stamp in each sheet the letter "S" in "Especie" is omitted. All denominations exist with a small zero before the decimal in the surcharge.

A119

A120

1918 Lithographed. *Perf. 13½.*

358	A119	3c red	75	15
a.		Imperf., pair	6.00	6.00

1920 Engraved. *Perf. 14.*

359	A120	3c red, *org*	45	7
a.		Imperf., pair	4.50	4.50

See also Nos. 371–372.

A121

A122

A123

Perf. 10, 13½ and Compound

1920-21 Lithographed.

360	A121	½c yellow	60	33
361	A121	1c green	1.50	15
362	A121	2c red	75	22
363	A122	3c green	75	22
a.		3c yel grn	75	22
364	A121	5c blue	1.10	30
365	A121	10c violet	4.50	1.50
366	A121	20c dp grn	10.00	4.00
367	A123	50c dk red	10.00	5.25
		Nos. 360-367 (8)	29.20	11.97

The tablet with "PROVISIONAL" was added separately to each design on the various lithographic stones and its position varies slightly on different stamps in the sheet. For some values there were two or more stones, on which the tablet was placed at various angles.

Nos. 360–366 exist imperf.

See also No. 375.

No. 342 Surcharged in Red

PROVICIONAL $003 *a*

PROVISIONAL $0.03 (15mm. wide) *b*

1921

369	A110(a)	3c on 4c vio	1.10	38
a.		Dbl. surcharge	17.50	
370	A110(b)	3c on 4c vio	4.50	2.25

See also No. 377.

Types of 1917–21.

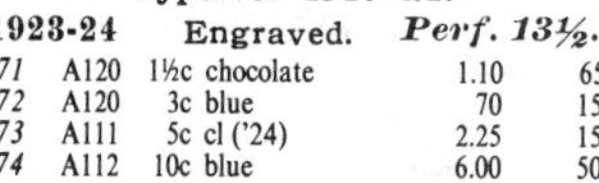

1923-24 Engraved. *Perf. 13½.*

371	A120	1½c chocolate	1.10	65
372	A120	3c blue	70	15
373	A111	5c cl ('24)	2.25	15
374	A112	10c blue	6.00	50

Lithographed.

375	A121	10c dk bl	12.00	7.50
		Nos. 371-375 (5)	22.05	8.95

No. 342 Surcharged in Red

PROVISIONAL $003 (18mm. wide)

1924

377	A110	3c on 4c vio	2.25	1.50
a.		Double surcharge	17.50	
b.		Double surcharge, one inverted	17.50	
c.		With added surch. "3cs." in red		

A124

1924–25 Litho. *Perf. 10, 10x13½*

379	A124	1c red	1.00	35
380	A124	3c dp bl ('25)	1.00	35

Exist imperf. Price, each pair $5.

A125

A126

Black, Red or Green Surcharge and Overprint.

Imprint of Waterlow & Sons.

1925 *Perf. 14, 14½.*

382	A125	1c on 3c bis brn (Bk)	45	15
383	A126	4c vio (R)	55	30
a.		Inverted surch.	10.00	10.00

Imprint of American Bank Note Co.

Perf. 12.

384	A125	1c on 3c bis brn (Bk)	5.00	3.75
a.		Inverted surcharge	15.00	15.00
385	A126	4c vio (G)	60	45
a.		Inverted overprint	8.00	8.00

Correos Provisional

Revenue stamps of basic types A125 and A126 were handstamped as above in violet or blue by the Cali post office in 1925, but were not authorized by the government. Denominations so overprinted are 1c, 2c, 3c, 4c and 5c.

A127

A128

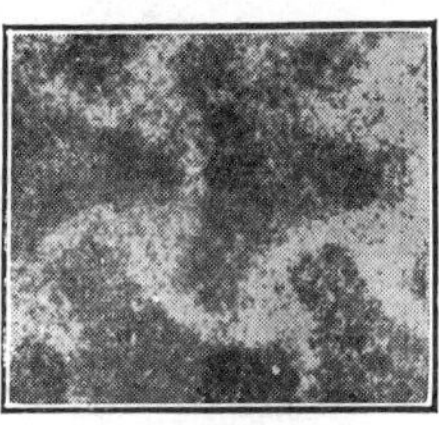
Wmk. 194

Wmkd. Multiple Curvilinear Triangles. (194)

1926 Litho. *Perf. 10, 13½x10*

395	A127	1c gray grn	45	15
396	A128	4c dp bl	45	15

Exist imperf. Price, each pair $4.

Types of 1917 and

Sabana Station A129

Engraved.

1926–29 *Perf. 14* Unwmkd.

400	A110	4c dp bl	60	8
401	A120	8c dk bl	75	15
402	A107	30c ol bis	6.00	90
403	A129	40c brn & yel brn	8.50	1.25
404	A117	5p violet	9.00	75
a.		Perf. 11 ('29)	9.00	1.50
405	A118	10p green	18.50	3.00
a.		Perf. 11 ('29)	37.50	6.00
		Nos. 400-405 (6)	43.35	6.13

Death of Bolívar A130

1930, Dec. 17 *Perf. 12½*

408	A130	4c dk bl & blk	60	45

Issued to commemorate the centenary of the death of Gen. Simón Bolívar. See also Nos. C80–C82.

Nos. 400 and 402 Surcharged in Red or Dark Blue

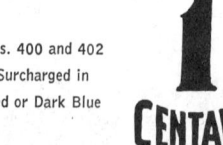

1 CENTAVO

1932, Jan. 20 *Perf. 14*

409	A110	1c on 4c dp bl (R)	45	15
a.		Inverted surcharge	8.00	8.00
410	A107	20c on 30c ol bis (Bl)	9.00	1.00
a.		Inv. surcharge	20.00	
b.		Dbl. surcharge	20.00	

Emerald Mine A131

Oil Wells A132

Coffee Cultivation A133

Platinum Mine A134

Gold Mining A135

Christopher Columbus A136

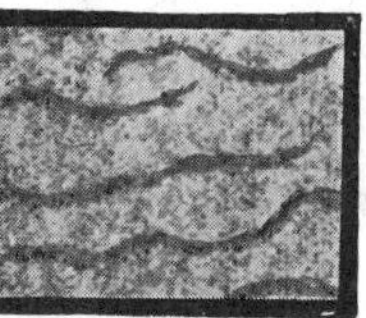
Wmk. 229

Wmkd. Wavy Lines. (229)

Imprint: "Waterlow & Sons Ltd. Londres"

1932 Engraved *Perf. 12½*

411	A131	1c green	75	8
412	A132	2c red	75	8
413	A133	5c brown	70	3
414	A134	8c bl blk	4.50	55
415	A135	10c yellow	4.50	15
416	A136	20c dk bl	7.50	40
		Nos. 411-416 (6)	18.70	1.29

See Nos. 441–442, 464–466a, 517.

Pedro de Heredia A137

Coffee Picking A138

Lithographed.

1934, Jan. 10 *Perf. 11½* Unwmkd.

417	A137	1c dk grn	2.50	90
418	A137	5c chocolate	3.25	75
419	A137	8c dk bl	2.50	90

400th anniversary of Cartagena. See also Nos. C111–C114.

1934, Dec. Engraved *Perf. 12*

420	A138	5c brown	3.25	4

Discus Thrower A139

Post and Telegraph Building A145

Allegory of Olympic Games at Barranquilla—A140

Foot Race—A141

Tennis—A142

Pier at Puerto Colombia—A143

View of the Bay—A144

Designs: 2c, Soccer. 10c, Hurdling. 15c, Athlete in stadium. 18c, Baseball. 24c, Swimming. 50c, View of Barranquilla. 2p, Monument to Flag. 5p, Coat of Arms. 10p, Condor.

1935, Jan. 26 Litho. *Perf. 11½*

421	A139	2c bluish grn & buff	1.25	65
422	A139	4c dp grn	1.25	65
423	A140	5c dk brn & yel	1.50	65
a.		Horizontal pair, imperf. btwn.	275.00	
424	A141	7c dk car	1.75	1.75
425	A142	8c blk & pink	1.75	1.75
426	A141	10c brn & bl	2.85	1.75
427	A143	12c indigo	3.00	2.25
428	A141	15c bl & red brn	4.50	3.50
429	A141	18c dk vio & buff	7.00	6.00
430	A144	20c pur & grn	6.50	5.00
431	A144	24c bluish grn & ultra	7.50	7.00
432	A144	50c ultra & buff	12.50	9.00
433	A145	1p db & bl	110.00	60.00
434	A145	2p dl grn & gray	165.00	110.00
435	A145	5p pur blk & bl	525.00	375.00
436	A145	10p blk & gray	650.00	525.00
		Nos. 421-436 (16)	1,501.35	1,109.95

3rd National Olympic Games, Barranquilla. Counterfeits of 10p exist.

Oil Wells
A155

Gold Mining
A157

Imprint:
"American Bank Note Co."
Engraved

1935, Mar. *Perf. 12* Unwmkd.

437	A155	2c car rose	55	8
439	A157	10c dp org	6.00	15

See also Nos. 468, 470, 498, 516.

No. 347 Surcharged in Black **12 CENTAVOS**

1935, Aug. *Perf. 14*

440	A115	12c on 1p brt bl	2.75	1.35

Types of 1932
Lithographed.
Imprint: "Lit. Nacional Bogotá"

1935-36 *Perf. 11, 11½, 12½*

441	A131	1c lt grn	15	8
a.		Imperf. (pair)	5.00	
442	A133	5c brn ('36)	80	12
a.		Imperf. (pair)	6.00	6.00

Simón Bolívar A159 — Tequendama Falls A160

Wmkd. Wavy Lines. (229)

1937 Engraved *Perf. 12½*

443	A159	1c dp grn	22	8
a.		Perf. 14		
444	A160	12c dp bl	2.25	1.40

See also No. 570.

Soccer Player
A161

Discus Thrower A162 — Runner A163

1937, Jan. 4 Photo. Unwmkd.

445	A161	3c lt grn	1.75	1.25
446	A162	10c car rose	3.00	2.50
447	A163	1p black	45.00	37.50

National Olympic Games, Manizales.

Exposition Palace
A164

Stadium at Barranquilla
A165

Monument to the Colors
A166

1937, Jan. 4

448	A164	5c vio brn	75	45
449	A165	15c blue	5.25	3.75
450	A166	50c org brn	13.00	7.50

Barranquilla National Exposition.

Stamps of 1926-37 Surcharged in Black **1 CENTAVO**

1937-38 *Perf. 12½.* Unwmkd.

452	A161	1c on 3c lt grn	1.10	1.10
a.		Invtd. surcharge	2.50	2.50
453	A120	5c on 8c dk bl	55	40
a.		Invtd. surcharge	2.50	2.50

Wmkd. Wavy Lines. (229)

454	A160	2c on 12c dp bl	55	45
455	A134	5c on 8c bl blk	60	40
a.		Invtd. surcharge	2.25	2.25
456	A160	10c on 12c dp bl ('38)	5.25	90
a.		Dbl. surcharge	12.00	12.00
		Nos. 452-456 (5)	8.05	3.25

Calle del Arco
A168

Entrance to Church of the Rosary
A169

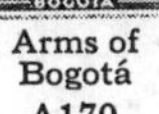

Arms of Bogotá
A170

Gonzálo Jiménez de Quesada
A171

Bochica
A172

Santo Domingo Convent
A173

Mass of the Conquistadors—A174

1938, July 27 *Perf. 12½* Unwmkd.

457	A168	1c yel grn	15	15
458	A169	2c scarlet	15	15
459	A170	5c brn blk	22	15
460	A171	10c brown	45	30
461	A172	15c brt bl	2.25	1.50
462	A173	20c brt red vio	2.25	1.50
463	A174	1p red brn	30.00	22.50
		Nos. 457-463 (7)	35.47	26.25

Bogotá, 400th anniversary.

Types of 1932.
Imprint:
"Litografia Nacional Bogotá".

1938, Dec. 5 Litho. *Perf. 10½, 11*

464	A132	2c rose	1.10	40
465	A135	10c yellow	2.50	45
466	A136	20c dl bl	5.25	1.50
a.		20c dk bl, perf. 12½ ('44)	40.00	4.50

Simón Bolívar
A175

Coffee Picking
A176

Arms of Colombia
A177

Christopher Columbus
A178

Caldas
A179

Sabana Station
A180

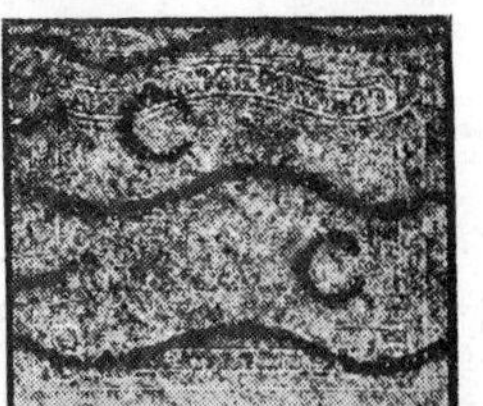

Wmk. 255

Wmkd. Wavy Lines and C Multiple. (255)

Imprint:
"American Bank Note Co."

1939, Mar. 3 Engr. *Perf. 12*

467	A175	1c green	22	3
468	A155	2c car rose	30	3
469	A176	5c dl brn	30	3
470	A157	10c dp org	1.00	5
471	A177	15c dl bl	1.75	30
472	A178	20c vio blk	3.00	30
473	A179	30c ol bis	2.50	45
474	A180	40c bis brn	9.00	2.25
		Nos. 467-474 (8)	18.07	3.44

See also Nos. 497-499, 515, 518, 574.

General Santander
A181

Allegory
A182

General Santander
A183

Statue at Cúcuta
A184

Church at Rosario
A186

Birthplace of Santander
A185

Paya
A187

Bridge at Boyacá
A188

Death of General Santander
A189

Invasion of the Liberators
A190

Perf. 13½x13, 13½x13

Wmkd. Wavy Lines. (229)

1940, May 6 **Engraved**

475	A181	1c ol grn	22	15
476	A182	2c dk car	30	30
477	A183	5c sepia	30	22
478	A184	8c carmine	90	90
479	A185	10c org yel	75	75
480	A186	15c dk bl	2.00	2.00
481	A187	20c green	2.00	2.00
482	A188	50c violet	6.00	3.00
483	A189	1p dp rose	20.00	20.00
484	A190	2p orange	60.00	60.00
		Nos. 475-484 (10)	92.47	89.32

Issued in commemoration of the centenary of the death of General Francisco Santander.

Tobacco Plant
A194

General Santander
A195

Garcia Rovira
A196

R. Galan
A197

Antonio Sucre
A198

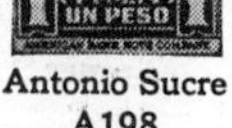
Arms of Palmira
A199

Wmkd.

Wavy Lines and C Multiple. (255)

1940-43 **Engraved.** ***Perf. 12.***

488	A194	8c rose car & grn	1.40	75
489	A195	15c dp bl ('43)	1.40	45
490	A196	20c gray blk ('41)	2.00	55
491	A197	40c brn bis ('41)	2.00	45
492	A198	1p black	6.75	75
		Nos. 488-492 (5)	13.55	2.95

See also Nos. 500, 554.

Lithographed.

1942, July 4 ***Perf. 11*** **Unwmkd.**

493	A199	30c claret	2.25	1.25

Issued to commemorate the 8th National Agricultural Exposition, held at Palmira.

Paradise of Isaacs, Palmira
A200

Signing Treaty of the Wisconsin
A201

1942, July 4

494	A200	50c lt bl grn	3.25	1.40

Issued in honor of the writer, Jorge Isaacs.

1942, Nov. 21 ***Perf. 10½***

495	A201	10c dl org	1.40	75
a.		"2. XI.1902" instead of "21. XI. 1902"	21.00	22.50
b.		Perf. 12	4.50	4.50

Issued in commemoration of the 40th anniversary of the signing of the Treaty of the Wisconsin, November 21, 1902.

No. 470 Surcharged in Black

5 Centavos

1944 ***Perf. 12.*** **Wmk. 255**

496	A157	5c on 10c dp org	30	22

Counterfeits exist of No. 496 with inverted or double surcharge.

Types of 1935–41 and

National Shrine
A202

San Pedro Alejandrino
A203

Engraved.

Imprint:

"Columbian Bank Note Co."

1944–45 ***Perf. 11*** **Unwmkd.**

497	A175	1c green	30	15
498	A155	2c rose	30	15
499	A176	5c dl brn	30	5
500	A196	20c gray blk	3.00	90
501	A202	30c dl ol grn ('45)	1.85	1.00
502	A203	50c rose	1.85	1.10
		Nos. 497-502 (6)	7.60	3.35

No. 499 Surcharged in Black

1 CENTAVO

1944, Oct.

506	A176	1c on 5c dl brn	15	15
507	A176	2c on 5c dl brn	15	15

Nos. 506 and 507 exist with inverted or double surcharge, created by favor.

Flag—A204

Arms—A205

Murillo Toro
A206

Hospital of St. John of God
A207

Virrey Solis
A208

A209

1944, Oct. 10 **Lithographed**

508	A204	2c ultra & bis	40	40
a.		Sheet of 18	12.00	
b.		Imperf., pair	12.50	
509	A205	5c ultra & bis	40	40
a.		Sheet of 22	15.00	
b.		Imperf., pair	12.50	
510	A206	20c blk & bluish grn	90	90
a.		Sheet of 8	12.00	
b.		Imperf., pair	18.50	
511	A207	40c blk & red	4.50	4.50
a.		Sheet of 4	20.00	
512	A208	1p blk & red	10.00	10.00
a.		Sheet of 2	25.00	
		Nos. 508-512 (5)	16.20	16.20

Souvenir Sheet.

Perforated 11x11½ all around, Stamps Imperf.

513	A209	Sheet of five	12.50	12.50

75th anniversary of General Benevolent Association of Cundinamarca. Size of No. 513: 100x87mm.

Nos. 508–513 were printed in composite sheets containing one each of Nos. 508a, 509a, 510a, 511a and 512a, and two of 513. Fifty of these were presented to government officials.

Murillo Toro
A210

San Pedro Alejandrino
A211

1944, Nov. 10 ***Perf. 11***

514	A210	5c lt brn	40	22

Types of 1932–39 and A211.

Imprint:

"Litografia Nacional Bogota".

1944 **Lithographed.** ***Perf. 12½.***

515	A175	1c dp grn	45	30
a.		1c ol grn	45	30
b.		Imperf., pair	3.00	3.00
516	A155	2c dk car	45	30
a.		Imperf., pair	3.00	3.00
517	A135	10c yel org	1.75	75
518	A179	30c gray ol	9.00	6.00
a.		Imperf., pair	37.50	
519	A211	50c rose	9.00	6.00
		Nos. 515-519 (5)	20.65	13.35

No. 469 Overprinted in Green, Blue or Red

Engraved.

1945, July 19 ***Perf. 12*** **Wmk. 255**

520	A176	5c dl brn (G)	25	15
521	A176	5c dl brn (R)	25	15
522	A176	5c dl brn (Bl)	25	15

Portraits are Joseph Stalin, Franklin D. Roosevelt and Winston Churchill.

Clock Tower, Cartagena
A212

1945, Nov. 15

523	A212	50c ol blk	5.75	1.50

Sierra Nevada of Santa Marta
A213

Designs: 30c, Seaplane Tolima. 50c, San Sebastian Fort, Cartagena.

Lithographed.

1945, Dec. 14 ***Perf. 11*** **Unwmkd.**

524	A213	20c lt grn	2.25	1.40
525	A213	30c pale bl	2.25	1.40
526	A213	50c sal pink	2.25	1.40

Issued to commemorate the 25th anniversary of the first airmail service in America, according to the inscription, but earlier services are known to have existed.

No. 442 Surcharged in Black

1 UN CENTAVO

1946, Mar. 8 ***Perf. 11x11½, 12½***

527	A133	1c on 5c brn	15	15
a.		Inverted surcharge	1.25	

Gen. Antonio José de Sucre
A216

Engraved.

1946, Apr. 16 ***Perf. 12*** **Wmk. 255**

Size: 19x26½mm.

528	A216	1c brn & turq grn	22	15
529	A216	2c vio & rose car	22	15

Size: 23x31mm.

530	A216	5c sep & bl	22	15
531	A216	9c dk grn & red	75	60
532	A216	10c ultra & org	75	60

533	A216	20c blk & dp org	75	60
534	A216	30c brn red & grn	75	60
535	A216	40c ol blk & red vio	75	60
536	A216	50c dp brn & vio	1.40	75
		Nos. 528-536 (9)	5.81	4.20

Map of South America
A217

National Observatory
A218

Lithographed.

1946, June 7 *Perf. 11* Unwmkd.

537	A217	15c ultra	75	45
a.		Imperf. (pair)	6.00	

1946, Aug.

538	A218	5c fawn	40	15
a.		Imperf. (pair)	6.00	

See No. 565.

Andrés Bello
A219

Joaquín de Cayzedo y Cuero
A220

Engraved.

1946, Sept. 3 *Perf. 12* Wmk. 255

539	A219	3c sepia	30	22
540	A219	10c orange	60	60
541	A219	15c sl blk	60	60

Issued to commemorate the 80th anniversary of the death of Andrés Bello (1781-1865), poet and educator. See also No. C145.

1946, Sept. 20 *Perf. 12½* Wmk. 229

542	A220	2p bluish grn	6.00	2.00

See also No. 568.

Type of 1945, Overprinted in Black or Green

V JUEGOS C.
A. Y DEL C.
1946

1946, Dec. 6 *Perf. 12* Wmk. 255

543	A212	50c red (Bk)	4.75	4.25
a.		Dbl. overprint	32.50	
544	A212	50c red (G)	4.75	4.25
a.		Dbl. overprint	32.50	

Issued to commemorate the fifth Central American and Caribbean Championship Games.

Coffee
A221

Engraved and Lithographed.

1947, Jan. 10 *Perf. 12½* Wmk. 229

545	A221	5c multi	60	15

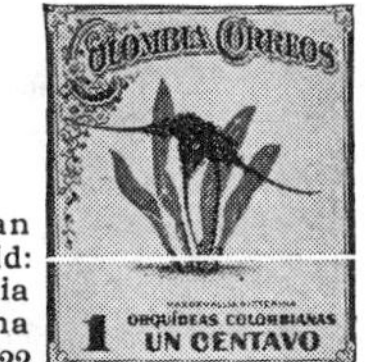

Colombian Orchid: Masdevallia Nycterina
A222

Designs (Orchids): 2c, Miltonia vexillaria. No. 548, Cattleya chocoensis. No. 549, Odontoglossum crispum. No. 550, Cattleya dowiana aurea. 10c, Cattleya labiata trianae.

Engraved and Lithographed.

1947, Feb. 7 *Perf. 12* Wmk. 255

546	A222	1c multi	55	22
547	A222	2c multi	55	22
548	A222	5c multi	1.40	22
549	A222	5c multi	1.40	22
550	A222	5c multi	1.40	22
551	A222	10c multi	2.25	60
		Nos. 546-551 (6)	7.55	1.70

Antonio Nariño
A228

Alberto Urdaneta y Urdaneta
A229

Perf. 12½

1947, May 9 Litho. Unwmkd.

552	A228	5c bl, *grnsh*	30	22
553	A229	10c red brn, *grnsh*	40	30

Issued to commemorate the 4th Pan-American Press Congress, 1946. See also Nos. C146-C147.

Sucre Type of 1940.

Engraved.

1947 *Perf. 12.* Wmk. 255

554	A198	1p violet	3.00	1.00

José Celestino Mutis and José Jerónimo Triana
A230

Miguel A. Caro and Rufino J. Cuervo
A231

1947 *Perf. 12½* Wmk. 229

555	A230	25c ol grn	75	40
556	A231	3p dk pur	5.25	3.75

See also Nos. 567, 569.

Metropolitan Cathedral, Plaza Bolívar, Bogotá
A232

National Capitol
A233

Ministry of Foreign Affairs
A234

A235

1948, Apr. 2

557	A232	5c blk brn	15	10
558	A233	10c orange	60	60
559	A234	15c dk bl	60	60
		Nos. 557-559, C148-C149 (5)	3.25	3.15

Miniature Sheet

Imperf.

560	A235	50c slate	1.75	1.75

Nos. 557-560 commemorate the 9th Pan-American Conference, Bogotá. No. 560 measures 90½x90½mm.

No. RA5A Overprinted in Black

Without Gum.

1948 *Perf. 12½* Unwmkd.

561	PT3	1c yel org	10	8

The letter "C" is the initial of "CORREOS".

Nos. RA33, RA24 and RA25 Overprinted in Black

CORREOS

With Gum.

1948 *Perf. 12.* Wmk. 255

562	PT6	1c olive	8	5
563	PT6	2c green	8	5
564	PT6	20c brown	22	8

Nos. 561-564 exist with inverted and double overprints.

Observatory Type of 1946.

Lithographed

1948, June 30 *Perf. 11* Unwmkd.

565	A218	5c blue	30	8

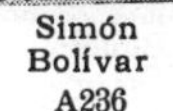

Simón Bolívar
A236

Carlos Martinez Silva
A237

Engraved.

1948, May 29 *Perf. 12* Wmk. 255

566	A236	15c green	60	22

Types of 1946-47.

1948 *Perf. 12½* Unwmkd.

567	A230	25c green	55	15
568	A220	2p dp grn	80	22
569	A231	3p dp red vio	1.50	30

Falls Type of 1937.

1948 Wmk. 229

570	A160	10c red	20	10

Lithographed.

1948, Dec. 21 *Perf. 13½* Unwmkd.

571	A237	40c carmine	60	30

Juan de Dios Carrasquilla
A238

1949, May 20 *Perf. 12½* Wmk. 229

572	A238	5c bister	22	15

Issued to commemorate the 75th anniversary of the foundation of the Colombian Society of Agriculture.

Julio Garavito Armero
A239

Arms of Colombia
A240

Engraved.

1949, Apr. 24 *Perf. 12* Wmk. 229

573	A239	4c green	45	22

Issued to honor Julio Garavito Armero (1865-1920), mathematician.

Coffee Type of 1939.

Imprint: "American Bank Note Co."

1949, Aug. 4 Wmk. 255

574	A176	5c blue	25	5

1949, Oct. 7 *Perf. 13* Unwmkd.

575	A240	15c blue	22	6

Issued to honor the new Constitution. See also Nos. C164-C165.

Shield and Tree
A241

Francisco Javier Cisneros
A242

1949, Oct. 13 *Perf. 12½* Wmk. 229

576	A241	5c olive	22	7

Issued to commemorate the 4th anniversary of Colombia's first Forestry Congress and as propaganda for the government's reforestation program.

1949, Dec. 15 Photo. Unwmkd.

577	A242	50c red vio & yel	1.35	1.00
578	A242	50c grn & vio	1.35	1.00
579	A242	50c brn & lt bl	1.35	1.00

Issued to commemorate the 50th anniversary (in 1948) of the death of Francisco Javier Cisneros.

Masdevallia Chimaera
A243

Odontoglossum Crispum
A244

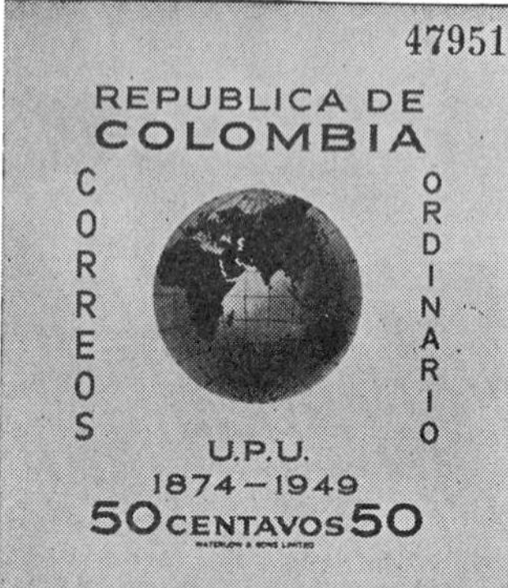

Eastern Hemisphere
A245

Designs: 3c, Cattleya labiata trianae. 4c, Masdevallia nycterina. 5c, Cattleya dowiana aurea. 11c, Miltonia vexillaria. 18c, Santo Domingo post office.

1950, Aug. 22 Photo. *Perf. 13*

580	A243	1c brown	30	15
581	A244	2c violet	30	15
582	A243	3c rose lil	30	15
583	A243	4c emerald	40	15
584	A243	5c red org	1.50	15
585	A244	11c red	1.75	1.50
586	A244	18c ultra	1.75	90
		Nos. 580-586 (7)	6.30	3.15

Miniature Sheet
Imperf.

587	A245	50c org yel	1.50	1.50

Nos. 580-587 commemorate the 75th anniversary (in 1949) of the formation of the Universal Postal Union. No. 587 measures 91x90mm.
See No. C199.

Antonio Baraya
A246

Engraved
1950, Nov. 27 *Perf. 12½* Unwmkd.

588	A246	2c red	15	8

Colombian Farm
A247

1950, Dec. 28 Photo. *Perf. 11½*

589	A247	5c dp car & buff	40	15
590	A247	5c bl grn & gray	40	15
591	A247	5c vio bl & gray	40	15

Issued to publicize rural life.

Arms of Bogotá
A248

Arms of Colombia
A249

Perf. 12x12½
1950, Dec. 28 Engr. Wmkd. 255

592	A248	5p dp grn	3.75	55
593	A249	10p red org	11.00	75

Map and Badge
A250

Guillermo Valencia
A251

Perf. 12½x13
1951, Jan. 30 Photo. Unwmkd.

594	A250	20c red, yel & bl	60	30

Issued to commemorate the 60th anniversary (in 1947) of the formation of the Colombian Society of Engineers.

1951, Oct. 20 Engr. *Perf. 13x13½*

595	A251	25c black	1.40	30

Issued to honor Guillermo Valencia (1873-1943), newspaper founder, governor of Cauca, presidential candidate, author.

No. 468 Overprinted in Black

REVERSION
CONCESION MARES
25 Agosto 1951

1951, Dec. 11 *Perf. 12* Wmk. 255

596	A155	2c car rose	15	6

Issued to publicize the reversion of the Mares oil concession to Colombia.

Nicolas Osorio
A252

Portraits: No. 598, Pompilio Martinez. No. 599, Ezequiel Uriocoechea. No. 600, Jose M. Lombana.

Engraved.
1952, Aug. 6 *Perf. 11½* Unwmkd.
Various Frames.

597	A252	1c dp bl	10	6
598	A252	1c dp bl	10	6
599	A252	1c dp bl	10	6
600	A252	1c dp bl	10	6

Nos. 597-600 were printed in a single sheet containing four panes of twenty-five each, separated by double rows of ornamental tabs. Although inscribed "sobretasa," the stamps were for ordinary postage.

Types of Postal Tax Stamps of 1945-50 and

Communications Building
A253 A253a

1952 *Perf. 12*

601	A253	5c ultra	22	6

Wmk. 255.

602	PT10	20c brown	6.00	30
603	PT6	25c dk gray	7.50	2.25
604	PT10	25c bl grn	75	15
605	A253a	50c org yel	22.50	12.00
606	A253a	1p rose car	2.00	45
607	A253a	2p lil rose	22.50	6.50
608	A253a	2p violet	1.50	70
		Nos. 601-608 (8)	62.97	22.41

Although inscribed "sobretasa," Nos. 601-608 were issued for ordinary postage.

Cathedral of Manizales
A254

Perf. 11½
1952, Oct. 10 Photo. Unwmkd.

609	A254	23c bl & gray blk	40	40

Centenary of city of Manizales.

No. 555 Surcharged in Blue

1ª 19 52
CONFERENCIA
SIDERURGICA
LATINO-AMERICANA.
15

1952, Oct. 30 *Perf. 12½* Wmk. 229

610	A230	15c on 25c ol grn	60	40

Issued to publicize the Latin American Siderurgical Conference, 1952. See also No. C226.

Queen Isabella I and Monument
A255

Engraved
1953, Mar. 10 *Perf. 12½* Unwmkd.

611	A255	23c bl & blk	75	75

Issued to commemorate the fifth centenary of the birth of Queen Isabella I of Spain.

Nos. 606 and 568 Surcharged with New Values in Dark Blue

1953, Oct. 19 Wmk. 255

612	A253a	40c on 1p rose car	1.40	30
613	A220	50c on 2p dp grn	1.40	30

Manuel Ancizar
A256

Portraits: 23c, José Jeronimo Triana. 30c, Manuel Ponce de Leon. 1p, Agustin Codazzi.

Perf. 12½x13
1953, Nov. Engraved Unwmkd.
Frames in Black.

614	A256	14c rose red	60	60
615	A256	23c ultra	45	38
616	A256	30c chocolate	45	22
617	A256	1p emerald	45	22

Issued to commemorate the centenary (in 1950) of the establishment of the Chorographic Commission.
See also Nos. 687, 690, 692.

Murillo Toro and Map
A257

Engraved and Lithographed.
1953, Dec. 12 *Perf. 12* Wmk. 255
Black Surcharge.

618	A257	5c on 5p multi	38	22

Issued to publicize the 2nd National Philatelic Exhibition, Bogotá, December 1953. See also No. C237.

Nos. 609 and 614 Surcharged with New Value or New Value and Ornaments.
Perf. 11½, 12½x13.
1953 Unwmkd.

619	A254	5c on 23c bl & gray blk (C)	55	22
620	A256	5c on 14c blk & rose red (Bk)	55	22

No. 614 surcharged "CINCO" in blue is listed as No. 687.

Symbolical of St. Francis Receiving Christ's Wounds
A258

1954, Apr. 23 Photo. *Perf. 11½*

621	A258	5c sep & grn	38	15

Issued to commemorate the 400th anniversary of the establishment of Colombia's first Franciscan community.

Soldier, Map and Arms
A259

1954, June 13 Engraved *Perf. 13*

622	A259	5c dl bl	22	8

Issued to commemorate the first anniversary of the assumption of the presidency by Gen. Gustavo Rojas Pinilla. See also Nos. C255, 637a.

Sports Emblem
A260

Design: 10c, Stadium and athlete holding arms of Colombia.

1954, July 18 Unwmkd.

623	A260	5c dp bl	45	22
624	A260	10c red	75	1.25

Issued to publicize the 7th National Athletic Games, Cali, July 1954. See also Nos. C256-C257.

History Academy Seal
A261

1954, July 24

625	A261	5c ultra & grn	22	10

Issued to commemorate the 50th anniversary (in 1952) of the Colombian Academy of History.

Convent and Cell of St. Peter Claver
A262

1954, Sept. 9

627	A262	5c dk grn	30	10
a.		Souvenir sheet	2.75	2.75

Issued to commemorate the 300th anniversary of the death of St. Peter Claver.

No. 627a contains one stamp similar to No. 627, but printed in greenish black. Marginal inscriptions in black. Sheet size: 121x129½mm. See also Nos. C258-C258a.

Mercury
A263

1954, Oct. 29

628	A263	5c orange	40	10

Issued to publicize the first International Fair and Exhibition, Bogotá, 1954. See Nos. C259-C260.

Tapestry Madonna
A264

College Cloister—A265

Designs: 10c, Brother Cristobal de Torres. 20c, College chapel and arms.

Perf. 12½x11½, 11½x12½

1954, Dec. 6

629	A264	5c org & blk	45	22
630	A264	10c blue	45	22
631	A265	15c vio brn	55	22
632	A265	20c blk & brn	90	40
a.		Souvenir sheet	4.50	4.50
		Nos. 629-632, C263-C266 (8)	6.65	2.72

Issued to commemorate the 300th anniversary (in 1953) of the founding of the Senior College of Our Lady of the Rosary, Bogota.

No. 632a contains four stamps similar to Nos. 629-632, but printed in different colors: 5c yellow and black, 10c green, 15c dull violet, 20c black and light-blue. Marginal inscriptions in black. Sheet size: 124½x130½mm.

Steel Mill
A266

José Marti
A267

1954, Dec. 12 ***Perf. 12½x13***

633	A266	5c ultra & blk	22	10

Issued to mark the opening of the Paz del Rio steel mill, October 1954. See No. C267.

1955, Jan. 28 ***Perf. 13½x13***

634	A267	5c dp car	15	8

Issued to commemorate the centenary of the birth of José Marti (1853-1895), Cuban patriot. See No. C268.

Arms, Flags and Soldiers Building Bridge
A268

1955, Mar. 23 ***Perf. 12½***

635	A268	10c claret	30	10

Issued to honor Colombian soldiers who served in Korea, 1951-53. See Nos. 637a, C269.

Fleet Emblem
A269

M. S. City of Manizales and New York Skyline
A270

1955, Apr. 12 Unwmkd.

636	A269	15c dp grn	30	10
637	A270	20c violet	30	15
a.		Souvenir sheet	4.50	4.50

Issued to honor the Grand-Colombian Merchant Fleet. See Nos. C270-271a.

No. 637a contains four stamps similar to Nos. 622, 635-637, but printed in different colors: 5c blue, 10c dark carmine, 15c green, 20c purple. Marginal inscriptions in black. Sheet size: 125x131mm.

Hotel Tequendama and Church of San Diego
A271

1955, May 16 Photo. ***Perf. 11½x12***

638	A271	5c blue	15	8

See also No. C273.

Bolivar's Country Estate, Bogotá
A272

1955, Sept. 28 Engr. ***Perf. 12½***

639	A272	5c dp ultra	15	8

Issued to commemorate the 50th anniversary of Rotary International. See No. C274.

Belalcazar, Jiménez de Quesada and Balboa
A273

Caravels and Columbus
A274

Design: 5c, San Martin, Bolivar and Washington.

Engraved and Photogravure.

1955, Oct. 29 ***Perf. 13x12½***

640	A273	2c yel grn & brn	15	10
641	A273	5c brt bl & brn	22	10
642	A274	23c lt ultra & blk	22	22
a.		Souvenir sheet	4.50	4.50
		Nos. 640-642, C275-C280 (9)	13.31	8.52

Issued to publicize the seventh Congress of the Postal Union of the Americas and Spain, Bogota, Oct. 12.-Nov. 9, 1955.

No. 642a contains one each of Nos. 640-642, printed in slightly different shades. It measures 120x132 mm. and is inscribed in black: "Ministerio de Comunicaciones. III Exposicion Filatelica Nacional Bogota 1955."

José Eusebio Caro
A275

1955, Nov. 29 Engr. ***Perf. 13½x13***

643	A275	5c brown	12	6

Issued to commemorate the centenary of the death of José Eusebio Caro (1817-1853), poet. See also No. C281.

Departmental Issue

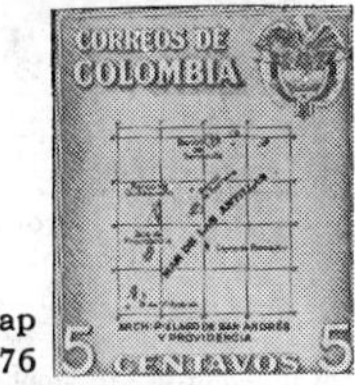

Map
A276

View of San Andres Harbor
A277

Cattle at Waterhole—A278

Designs: 2c, Docks, Atlantico. 3c, "Industry," Antioquia. 4c, Cartagena Harbor, Bolivar. No. 647, Steel Mill, Boyaca. No. 648, Cattle, Cordoba. No. 649, Map. No. 650, San Andres Harbor. No. 651, Cacao picker, Cauca. 10c, Coffee picker, Caldas. 15c, Salt Mine Chapel, Zipaquira, Cundinamarca. 20c, Tropical plants and map, Choco. 23c, Harvester, Huila. 25c, Banana Plantation, Magdalena. 30c, Gold mining, Nariño. 40c, Tobacco plantation, Santander. 50c, Oil wells, North Santander. 60c, Cotton plantation, Tolima. 1p, Sugar industry, Cauca. 3p, Amazon river at Leticia, Amazonas. 5p, Windmills and panoramic view, La Guajira. 10p, Rubber plantation, Vaupes.

Engraved; Engraved and Lithographed.

Perf. 13½x13, 13x13½, 13

1956 Engraved. Unwmkd.

Various Frames.

644	A277	2c car & grn	12	8
645	A276	3c brn vio & blk	12	8

646	A277	4c grn & blk	12	8
647	A276	5c dk brn & bl	15	8
648	A277	5c ol & dk vio brn	35	7
649	A276	5c bl & blk	20	7
650	A277	5c car & grnsh bl	20	7
651	A277	5c ol grn & red brn	22	7
652	A276	10c org & blk	30	6
653	A276	15c ultra & blk	25	10
654	A276	20c dk brn & bl	30	10
655	A277	23c ultra & ver	40	30
656	A277	25c ol grn & blk	40	18
657	A277	30c ultra & brn	20	7
658	A277	40c dl pur & red brn	22	8
659	A277	50c dk grn & blk	30	8
660	A277	60c pale brn & grn	30	8
661	A278	1p mag & grnsh bl	2.00	22
662	A278	2p grn & red brn	2.25	30
663	A278	3p car & blk	2.25	55
664	A278	5p brn & lt ultra	4.50	1.50
665	A276	10p red brn & grn	13.00	5.25
		Nos. 644-665 (22)	28.15	9.47

Nos. 645, 647, 649, 652–654 measure 27x32mm. No. 665 measures 27x37 mm. See also Nos. 681–684, 685, 688–689.

Columbus and Proposed Lighthouse—A279

1956, Oct. 12 Photo. *Perf. 12*

666	A279	3c gray blk	18	10

Issued in honor of Christopher Columbus. See also Nos. C285, C306.

Altar of St. Elizabeth and Tomb of Jimenez de Quesada
A280

1956, Nov. 19 Unwmkd.

667	A280	5c red lil	15	15

Issued to commemorate the 7th centenary of St. Elizabeth of Hungary, patron saint of Sante Fé de Bogotá. See No. C286.

St. Ignatius of Loyola A281 — Javier Pereira A282

1956, Nov. 26 Engr. *Perf. 12½x13*

668	A281	5c blue	22	8

Issued to commemorate the 400th anniversary of the death of St. Ignatius of Loyola. See No. C287.

1956, Dec. 28 *Perf. 12* Unwmkd.

669	A282	5c blue	15	8

Issued to honor 167-year-old Javier Pereira. See No. C288.

Emblem and Dairy Farm
A283

Designs: 2c, Emblem and tractor. 5c, Emblem, coffee and corn.

1957, Mar. 5 Photo. *Perf. 14x13½*

670	A283	1c lt ol grn	10	7
671	A283	2c lt brn	10	7
672	A283	5c lt bl	15	7
		Nos. 670-672, C292-C296 (8)	3.07	2.06

25th anniversary of the Agrarian Savings Bank of Colombia.

Arms of Military Academy and Gen. Rafael Reyes—A284

Design: 10c, Arms and Academy.

1957, July 20 Engr. *Perf. 12½*

673	A284	5c blue	15	7
674	A284	10c orange	15	8
a.		Souv. sheet of 2	12.00	12.00

Issued to commemorate the 50th anniversary of the Colombian Military Academy. See Nos. C299–C300.

No. 674a contains one each of Nos. 673–674 in slightly different shades. It measures 120x131½mm. with marginal inscriptions in black.

Statue of José Matias Delgado
A285

1957, Sept. 16 Photo. *Perf. 12*

675	A285	2c rose brn	10	8

Issued in honor of Jose Matias Delgado, liberator of El Salvador. See No. C301.

Santo Michelena, Marcos V. Crespo, P. Alcantara Herran and UPU Monument—A286

1957, Oct. 10 Unwmkd.

676	A286	5c green	15	15
677	A286	10c gray	15	8

Issued for International Letter Writing Week and the 14th UPU Congress. See Nos. C302–C303.

St. Vincent de Paul and Children
A287

1957, Oct. 18

678	A287	1c dk ol grn	8	7

Issued to commemorate the centenary of the Colombian Society of St. Vincent de Paul. See No. C304.

Fencer
A288

1957, Nov. 22 Photo. *Perf. 12*

679	A288	4c lilac	15	15

Issued to commemorate the third South American Fencing Championship. See No. C305.

Francisco José de Caldas and Hypsometer
A289

1958, May 12 *Perf. 12* Unwmkd.

680	A289	10c black	30	14

Issued for the International Geophysical Year, 1957–58. See Nos. C309–C310.

Departmental Issue.
Type of 1956,
Designs as Before.

1958 Engraved. *Perf. 13*

681	A276	3c ultra & brn	12	8
682	A276	3c ol grn & pur	12	8
683	A276	10c grn & brn	18	7
684	A276	10c dk bl & brn	18	7

Nos. 646, C291, 614, 653, 655, 616, C308, 615 and 611 Surcharged with New Value, and Old Value Obliterated, or Overprinted in Dark Blue or Green.

Perf. 12½, 12½x13, 13.

1958-59 Unwmkd.

685	A277	2c on 4c grn & blk	12	8
686	AP48	5c dp plum & multi ('59)	12	12
687	A256	5c on 14c blk & rose red ("CINCO") ('59)	45	38
688	A276	5c on 15c ultra & blk	12	8
689	A277	5c on 23c ultra & ver (G)	30	30
690	A256	5c on 30c blk & choc	12	8
691	AP40	10c on 25c rose vio	15	7
692	A256	20c on 23c blk & ultra (G) ('59)	30	30
693	A255	20c on 23c bl & blk ('59)	18	14
		Nos. 685-693 (9)	1.86	1.55

On No. 686 the words "Correo Extra Rapido" are obliterated in dark blue.

Father Rafael Almanza and Church of San Diego, Bogota
A290

1958, Oct. 23 Photo. *Perf. 14x13*

695	A290	10c purple	15	5

See also Nos. C313–C314.

Msgr. R. M. Carrasquilla and Church
A291

1959, Jan. 22 *Perf. 14x13*

696	A291	10c dk red brn	15	5

Issued to commemorate the centenary of the birth of Msgr. R. M. Carrasquilla (1857–1930), rector of Our Lady of the Rosary Seminary, Bogotá. See Nos. C315–C316.

Miss Universe 1959
A292

Jorge Eliecer Gaitan
A293

1959, June 26 Photo. *Perf. 11½*

697	A292	10c multi	8	8

Issued to honor Luz Marina Zuluaga, Miss Universe, 1959. See Nos. C317–C318.

Engraved

1959, July 28 *Perf. 12x13½*

698	A293	10c on 3c gray bl (Bl)	22	7
699	A293	30c rose vio	60	30

Issued in honor of Jorge Eliecer Gaitan (1898–1948), lawyer and politician.

No. 698 exists without blue surcharge.

See also Nos. C319–C320.

Gen. Francisco de Paula Santander
A294

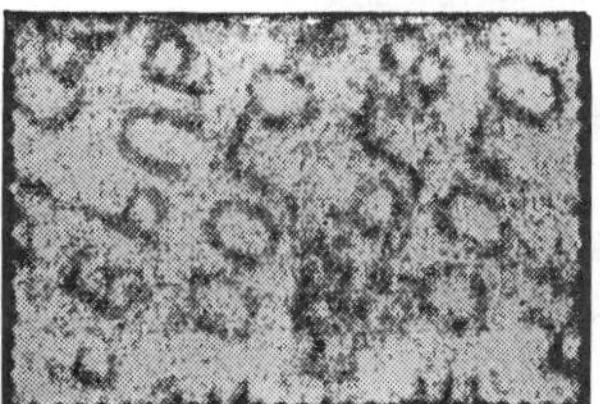
Wmk. 331

Designs: Nos. 701, 703, Simon Bolivar.

Wmkd. "REPUBLICA DE COLOMBIA". (331)

1959 Lithographed *Perf. 12½*

700	A294	5c brn & yel	10	8
701	A294	5c ultra & bl	10	8
702	A294	10c gray & grn	12	8
703	A294	10c gray & red	12	8

See also No. C389.

Capitol, Bogota
A295

1959

704 A295 2c dk bl & red brn 18 12
705 A295 3c blk brn & lil 18 12

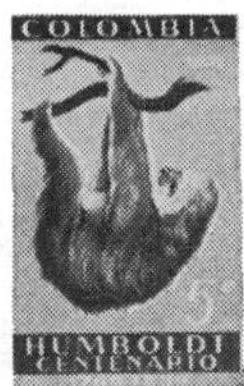

Stamp of 1859 and Mail Transport by Mule
A296

Two-Toed Sloth
A297

Designs (various stamps of 1859 and): 10c, Mail boat on the Magdalena river. 25c, Train.

Photogravure

1959, Dec. 1 ***Perf. 12*** **Unwmkd.**

709 A296 5c org & grn 22 18
710 A296 10c rose cl & bl 22 18
711 A296 15c car rose & grn 45 45
712 A296 25c bl & red brn 45 45
Nos. 709-712, C351-C354 (8) 4.96 3.61

Centenary of Colombian postage stamps.

1960, Feb. 12 ***Perf. 12***

Designs: 10c, Alexander von Humboldt. 20c, Spider monkey.

713 A297 5c grnsh bl & brn 25 10
714 A297 10c blk & dp car 40 5
715 A297 20c cit & gray brn 25 5
Nos. 713-715, C357-C359 (6) 5.75 3.90

Issued to commemorate the centenary of the death of Alexander von Humboldt (1769–1859), German naturalist and geographer.

Anthurium Andreanum
A298

Lincoln Statue, Washington
A299

Flower: 20c, Espeletia grandiflora.

1960, May 10

716 A298 5c multi 22 22
717 A298 20c brn, yel & gray ol 15 12
Nos. 716-717, C360-C370 (13) 15.67 14.95

See also Nos. C420–C425.

Perf. 10½

1960, June 10 **Litho.** **Wmk. 331**

718 A299 20c rose lil & blk 38 30

Issued to commemorate the sesquicentennial of the birth of Abraham Lincoln (1809–1865). See also Nos. C375–C376.

Floredo House, Cradle of the Republic
A300

Arms of Santa Cruz de Mompox
A301

Design: 5c, First coins of Republic.

Perf. 12

1960, July 19 **Photo.** **Unwmkd.**

719 A301 5c grn & ocher 18 12
720 A300 20c ol bis & mar 18 12
721 A301 20c multi 45 22
Nos. 719-721, C377-C385 (12) 7.55 5.94

Issued to commemorate the 150th anniversary of Colombia's independence.

St. Isidro and Farm Animals
A302

Design: 20c, Nativity by Gregorio de Arce Vasquez y Ceballos.

1960, Sept. 26 ***Perf. 12***

722 A302 10c multi 15 12
723 A302 20c multi 22 12

Issued to honor St. Isidro the Farmer, patron saint of the rural people.

See also Nos. 747, C387–C388, C439–C440.

U.N. Headquarters and Emblem
A303

Perf. 11

1960, Oct. 24 **Litho.** **Wmk. 331**

724 A303 20c blk & pink 22 18

Souvenir Sheet

Imperf.

725 A303 50c dk brn, brt grn & blk 3.25 3.25

15th anniversary of the United Nations. No. 725 contains one stamp and has dark brown marginal inscription and black number. Size: 55x48½mm.

Pan-American Highway through Colombia
A304

Alfonso Lopez
A305

Perf. 10½x11

1961, Mar. 7 **Unwmkd.**

726 A304 20c brn & grnsh bl 75 75
Nos. 726, C390-C393 (5) 3.75 3.75

Issued to commemorate the 8th Pan-American Highway Congress, Bogota, May 20–29, 1960.

1961, Mar. 22 **Photo.** ***Perf. 12½***

727 A305 10c brt rose & brn 22 18
728 A305 20c vio & brn 22 18

Issued to honor Alfonso Lopez (1886–1959), President of Colombia.

See Nos. C394–C396.

Cauca River Bridge, Cali
A306

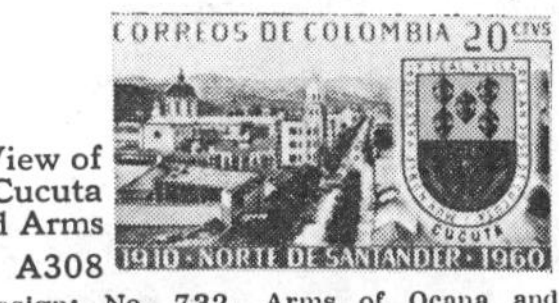

Page from Resolutions of Confederated Cities
A307

1961-62 ***Perf. 12½x13, 13½x13***

729 A306 10c red brn, bl, grn & red ('62) 15 10
730 A307 20c pale brn & blk 22 10
Nos. 729-730, C397-C401 (7) 6.90 5.79

Issued to commemorate the 50th anniversary (in 1960) of the Department of Valle del Cauca.

View of Cucuta and Arms
A308

Design: No. 732, Arms of Ocana and Pamplona.

1961, Aug. 29 ***Perf. 13x13½***

731 A308 20c bl, blk, yel & red 15 6
732 A308 20c ocher, ultra & red 15 6

Issued to commemorate the 50th anniversary (in 1960) of the Department of North Santander. See Nos. C402–C403.

Arms of Popayan
A309

Basketball
A310

Designs: No. 734, Arms of Barranquilla. No. 735, Arms of Bucaramanga.

Perf. 12½x13

1961, Oct. 10 **Unwmkd.**

Arms in Multicolor

733 A309 10c bl & sil 15 7
734 A309 20c bl & yel 15 7
735 A309 20c bl & gold 15 7
Nos. 733-735, C404-C408 (8) 2.98 85

Issued to honor Atlantico Department.

1961, Dec. 16 **Litho.** ***Perf. 13½x14***

Multicolored

736 A310 20c *shown* 15 8
737 A310 20c *Runners* 15 8
738 A310 20c *Boxers* 28 12
739 A310 25c *Soccer* 22 10
Nos. 736-739, C414-C418 (9) 3.70 1.56

4th Bolivarian Games, Barranquilla, 1961.

Colombian Anti-Malaria Emblem
A311

Engineers Society Emblem
A312

Design: 50c, Malaria eradication emblem and mosquito in swamp.

1962, Apr. 12 ***Perf. 12*** **Unwmkd.**

740 A311 20c lt bis & red 22 18
741 A311 50c bis & ultra 30 22
Nos. 740-741, C426-C428 (5) 7.32 7.02

Issued for the World Health Organization drive to eradicate malaria.

1962, June 12 **Photo.** ***Perf. 11½x12***

742 A312 10c multi 30 30
Nos. 742, C429-C432 (5) 3.35 2.91

Issued to commemorate the 75th anniversary of the Colombian Society of Engineers.

Flags of American Nations
A313

Woman Casting Ballot and Statue of Policarpa Salavarrieta
A314

1962, June 28 ***Perf. 13***

Flags in National Colors

743 A313 25c blk & org ver 15 7

Souvenir Sheet

744 A313 2.50p blk & yel 3.50 3.50

Issued to commemorate the 70th anniversary of the founding of the Organization of American States.

No. 744 contains one stamp, black marginal inscription. Size: 45x55mm.

See also No. C433.

Perf. 12x12½

1962, July 20 **Litho.** **Wmk. 229**

745 A314 10c lt bl, gray & blk 12 4

Issued to publicize women's political rights. See also Nos. 752, C434, C448–C450.

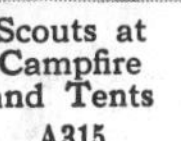

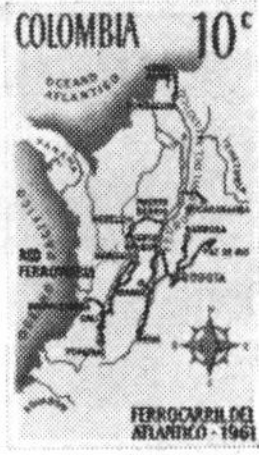

Scouts at Campfire and Tents
A315

Railroad Map of Colombia
A316

Perf. 11½x12

1962, July 28 Photo. Unwmkd.

746 A315 10c brt grnsh bl & brn 45 38
Nos. 746, C435-C438 (5) 7.93 6.68

Issued to commemorate the 30th anniversary of the Colombian Boy Scouts.

St. Isidro Type of 1960 Redrawn

1962, Aug. 28 *Perf. 12*

747 A302 10c pink & multi 15 8

The frame on No. 747 is solid color with white inscription similar to type AP82. See also Nos. C439-C440.

1962, Sept. 28 *Perf. 12½*

748 A316 10c blk, gray, grn & red 22 8
Nos. 748, C441-C444 (5) 7.41 2.54

Issued to publicize the progress of Colombian railroads and to commemorate the completion of the Atlantic Line from Santa Marta to Bogota.

Post Horn
A317

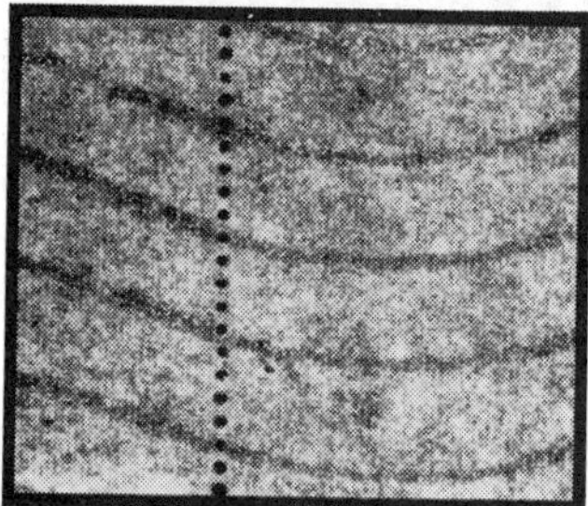

Wmk. 346

Wmkd. Parallel Curved Lines. (346)

1962, Oct. 18 Litho. *Perf. 13½x14*

749 A317 20c gold, dl gray vio & blk 22 7

Issued to commemorate the 50th anniversary of the founding of the Postal Union of the Americas and Spain, UPAE.
See also Nos. C445-C446.

"Virgin of the Rock"
A318

Red Cross Centenary Emblem
A319

1963, Mar. 11 Wmk. 346

750 A318 60c multi 30 8

Issued to commemorate Vatican II, the 21st Ecumenical Council of the Roman Catholic Church. See also No. C447.

1963, May 1 *Perf. 12x12½*

751 A319 5c ol bis & red 15 8

Centenary of International Red Cross.

Women's Rights Type of 1962

1963, July 11 Wmk. 346

752 A314 5c org, gray & blk 6 4

See also Nos. C448-C450.

Manuel Mejia J. and Flag of National Coffee Growers Assn.
A320

Perf. 12½x13

1965, Feb. 10 Engraved Unwmkd.

753 A320 25c rose & blk 30 7

Issued to honor Manuel Mejia J. (1887-1958), banker and manager of the National Coffee Growers Association. See Nos. C464-C466.

Julio Arboleda
A321

1966, Mar. 9 Litho. *Perf. 14x13½*

754 A321 5c lt brn, lt yel grn & blk 5 3

Issued to honor Julio Arboleda (1817-1862), writer, soldier and statesman.

Spanish Galleon, 16th Century
A322

History of Maritime Mail: 15c, Rio Hacha brigantine, 1850. 20c, Uraba canoe. 40c, Magdalena River steamship and barge, 1900. 50c, Modern motor ship and sea gull.

1966, June 16 Photo. Unwmkd.

755 A322 5c org & multi 10 6
756 A322 15c car rose, blk & brn 15 8
757 A322 20c brt grn, org & blk 15 8
758 A322 40c dp bl & multi 30 12
759 A322 50c pale bl & multi 65 35
Nos. 755-759 (5) 1.35 69

Plumed Hogfish
A323

Design: 10p, Bat ray and brittle starfish.

1966, Aug. 25 Photo. *Perf. 12½x13*

760 A323 80c multi 30 15
761 A323 10p multi 6.75 6.75
Nos. 760-761, C481-C483 (5) 21.80 21.40

Arms of Venezuela, Colombia and Chile
A324

1966, Oct. 11 Litho. *Perf. 14x13½*

762 A324 40c yel & multi 15 7

Issued to commemorate the visits of Eduardo Frei and Raul Leoni, presidents of Chile and Venezuela. See Nos. C484-C485.

Camilo Torres, 1766-1816, Lawyer
A325

Portraits: 60c, Jorge Tadeo Lozano (1771-1816), naturalist. 1p, Francisco Antonio Zea (1776-1822), naturalist and politician.

Perf. 13½x14

1967, Jan. 18 Litho. Unwmkd.

763 A325 25c vio & bis 7 5
764 A325 60c dk red brn & bis 15 3
765 A325 1p grn & bis 45 22
Nos. 763-765, C486-C487 (5) 1.20 48

Issued to honor famous men of Colombia.

Map of South America and Arms
A326

1967, Feb. 2 Litho. *Perf. 14x13½*

766 A326 40c multi 22 15
767 A326 60c multi 22 5

Issued to publicize the Declaration of Bogota for cooperation and world peace, signed by Colombia, Chile, Ecuador, Peru and Venezuela. See No. C488.

Monochaetum Orchid and Bee
A327

Orchid: 2p, Passiflora vitifolia and butterfly.

1967, May 23 Litho. *Perf. 14*

768 A327 25c multi 8 6
769 A327 2p multi 1.25 1.25
Nos. 768-769, C489-C491 (5) 3.46 2.23

Issued to commemorate the First National Orchid Exhibition and the Topical Philatelic Flora and Fauna Exhibition, Medellin, Apr. 1967.

Lions Emblem
A328

SENA Emblem
A329

1967, July 12 Litho. *Perf. 13½x14*

770 A328 10p multi 4.50 85

Issued to commemorate the 50th anniversary of Lions International. See No. C492.

Lithographed and Embossed

1967, Sept. 20 Unwmkd.

771 A329 5p gold, brt grn & blk 1.25 22

Issued to commemorate the 10th anniversary of National Apprenticeship Service, SENA. See No. C494.

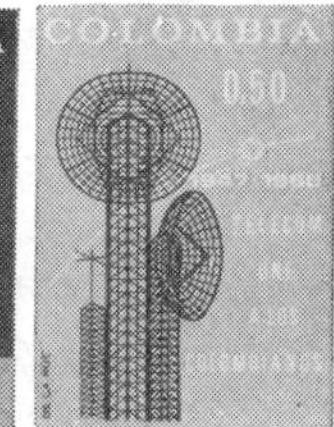

Gold Diadem in Calima Style
A330

Radar Installation
A331

Pre-Columbian Art: 3p, Gold statuette, ornamental globe and bird (horiz.).

Perf. 13½x14, 14x13½

1967, Oct. 13 Photogravure

772 A330 1.60p brt rose lil, gold & brn 90 25
773 A330 3p dk bl, gold & brn 90 40
Nos. 772-773, C495-C497 (5) 15.55 10.23

Issued to commemorate the meeting of the Universal Postal Union Committee on Postal Studies, Bogota, October, 1967.

1968, May 14 Litho. *Perf. 13½x14*

Design: 1p, Map of communications network.

774 A331 50c brt yel grn, blk & org brn 18 7
775 A331 1p multi 35 7

Issued to commemorate the 20th anniversary of the National Telecommunications Service (TELECOM). See Nos. C498-C499.

The Eucharist
A332

St. Augustin, by Gregorio Vasquez
A333

1968, June 6 Litho. *Perf. 13½x14*

776 A332 60c multi 15 5

Issued to publicize the 39th Eucharistic Congress, Bogotá, Aug. 18-25. See Nos. C500-C501.

1968, Aug. 13 Photo. *Perf. 13*

Designs: 60c, The Gathering of Manna, by Gregorio Vasquez. 1p, The Marriage of the Virgin, by Baltazar de Figueroa. 5p, Jeweled monstrance, c. 1700. 10p, Pope Paul VI, painting by Roman Franciscan nuns.

777 A333 25c multi 5 5
778 A333 60c multi 8 5
779 A333 1p multi 15 6
780 A333 5p multi 90 15
781 A333 10p multi 1.50 50
a. Souv. sheet of 2 2.50 1.50
Nos. 777-781, C502-C506 (10) 12.90 5.46

Issued to commemorate the 39th Eucharistic Congress, Bogotá, Aug. 18-25. No. 781a contains two imperf. stamps similar to Nos. 780-781. Black inscription, Congress emblem in crimson and red control number in margin. Size: 90x89½mm.

Pope Paul VI A334

Arms of National University A335

1968, Aug. 22 Litho. *Perf. 13½x14*

782 A334 25c multi 12 7

Issued to commemorate the visit of Pope Paul VI to Colombia, Aug. 22-24. See Nos. C507-C509.

1968, Oct. 29 Litho. *Perf. 13½x14*

783 A335 80c multi 20 3

Issued to commemorate the centenary of the founding of the National University. See No. C510.

Stamp of Antioquia, 1868 A336

Institute Emblem A337

1968, Nov. 20 Litho. *Perf. 12x12½*

784 A336 30c emer & bl 18 5

Souvenir Sheet

785 A336 5p lt ol & bl 3.25 3.25

Issued to commemorate the centenary of the first postage stamps of Antioquia and to publicize the 7th National Philatelic Exhibition, Medellin, Nov. 20-29. No. 785 contains one stamp; vermilion margin with white inscription and blue coat of arms and control number. Size: 59x79mm.

1969, Mar. 5 Litho. *Perf. 13½x14*

786 A337 20c multi 22 8

Issued to commemorate the 25th anniversary (in 1967) of the Inter-American Agricultural Sciences Institute. See No. C511.

Battle of Boyaca (Detail), by José Maria Espinosa—A338

Design: 30c, Army of liberation crossing Pisba Pass, by Francisco Antonio Caro.

1969, July 24 Litho. *Perf. 13½x14*

787 A338 20c gold & multi 12 8
788 A338 30c gold & multi 15 7

Issued to commemorate the sesquicentennial of the fight for independence. See No. C517.

"Poverty" A339

1970, Mar. 1 Litho. *Perf. 14*

789 A339 30c bl & multi 15 8

Issued to publicize the Colombian Institute for Family Welfare and to commemorate the 10th anniversary of the Children's Rights Law.

Greek Mask and Pre-Columbian Symbol of Literary Contest A340

1970, Sept. 12 Litho. *Perf. 14x13½*

790 A340 30c dk brn, red org & ocher 8 5

Issued to publicize the 3rd Latin American Theatrical Festival of the Universities, Manizales, Sept. 12-20.

Colombian Stamps, Envelope and Emblem A341

1970, Sept. 24 Litho. *Perf. 14x13½*

791 A341 2p brt bl & multi 45 7

Issued to publicize Philatelic Week.

Arms of Ibague and Discobolus A342

1970, Oct. 13

792 A342 80c buff, emer & sep 30 7

9th National Games in Ibague.

St. Theresa, by Baltazar de Figueroa A343

1970, Oct. 28 Litho. *Perf. 13½x14*

793 A343 2p multi 60 4

Elevation of St. Theresa (1515-1582), to Doctor of the Church. See No. C568.

Casa Cural A344

1971, May 20 Litho. *Perf. 14x13½*

794 A344 1.10p multi 45 15

Fourth centenary (in 1970) of the founding of Guacari, Valle. See also No. 809.

Dancers and Music, Currulao A345

1971 Litho. *Perf. 13½x14*

Design: 1p, Chicha Maya dancers and music.

795 A345 1p pink & multi 30 8
796 A345 1.10p lt bl & multi 38 8

Souvenir Sheets

Imperf.

797	A345	Sheet of 3, multi	3.75	3.75
a.		2.50p Napanga	50	50
b.		2.50p Joropo	50	50
c.		5p Guabina	1.00	1.00
798	A345	Sheet of 3, multi	3.75	3.75
a.		4p Bambuco	80	80
b.		4p Cumbia	80	80
c.		4p Currulao	80	80

Size of Nos. 797-798: 78x110mm. Issue dates: No. 795, Dec. 20; No. 796, Aug. 5; Nos. 797-798, Aug. 10.

Constitutional Assembly, by Delgado A346

1971, Oct. 2 *Perf. 14*

801 A346 80c multi 22 8

Sequicentennial of Gran Colombian Constitutional Assembly in Rosario del Cucuta. See No. C589.

Arrows Emblem A347

1972, Feb. 24 *Perf. 13½x14*

802 A347 60c blk & gray 45 8

Inter-Governmental Committee on European Migration, 20th anniversary.

Student and World Map A348

1972, Mar. 15 *Perf. 14x13½*

803 A348 1.10p lt grn & brn 30 8

20th anniversary of ICETEX, an organization which furnishes financial help for educational purposes and for technical studies abroad.

U.N. Emblem, Soldier and Frigate A349

1972, Apr. 7

804 A349 1.20p lt bl & multi 30 6

20th anniversary of the Colombian Battalion in Korea.

Mother Francisca Josefa del Castillo A350

Handicraft A351

1972, Apr. 6 *Perf. 13½x14*

805 A350 1.20p brn & multi 30 6

Tercentenary (in 1971) of the birth of Mother Francisca Josefa del Castillo, Poor Clare abbess and writer.

1972, Apr. 11

806 A351 1.10p multi 35 15

Colombian artisans. See Nos. C569-C571.

Maxillaria Triloris A352

Emeralds A353

1972, Apr. 20

807 A352 20p grn & multi 5.25 65

10th National Philatelic Exhibition, Medellin.

1972, June 16 Litho. *Perf. 13½x14*

808 A353 1.10p multi 70 15

Type of 1971

Design: Antonio Nariño House.

1972, June 17 *Perf. 14x13½*

809 A344 1.10p multi 38 7

4th centenary, town of Leyva.

San Andres and Providencia Islands
A354

1972, June 24 ***Perf. 13½x14***

810 A354 60c bl & multi 30 8

Sesquicentennial of annexation by Colombia of San Andres and Providencia Islands.

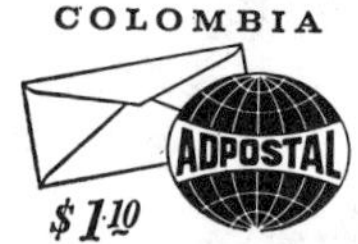

Postal Service Emblem
A355

1972, Nov. 15 Litho. ***Perf. 12½x12***

811 A355 1.10p emerald 22 6

Family
A356

1972, Nov. 23

812 A356 60c orange 22 8

Social progress.

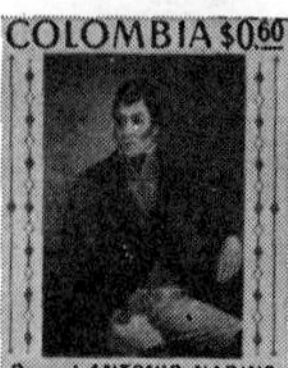

Radio League Emblem
A357

Human Figure, Tamalameque
A358

1973, Apr. 6 Litho. ***Perf. 12x12½***

813 A357 60c lt bl, ultra & red 22 6

40th anniversary of the Colombian Radio Amateurs' League.

1973, June 15 Litho. ***Perf. 13½x14***

Excavated Ceramic Artifacts: 1p, Winged urn, Tairona. 1.10p, Jug, Muisca.

814 A358 60c lt bl & multi 30 15
815 A358 1p org & multi 60 15
816 A358 1.10p vio bl & multi 45 7
Nos. 814-816, C583-C586 (7) 4.10 2.15

Antonio Nariño, by José M. Espinosa
A359

Child
A360

1973, Dec. 13 Litho. ***Perf. 13½x14***

817 A359 60c multi 15 6

Sesquicentennial of the death of General Antonio Nariño (1765–1823).

1973, Dec. 17

818 A360 1.10p multi 22 5

National Campaign for Children's Welfare.

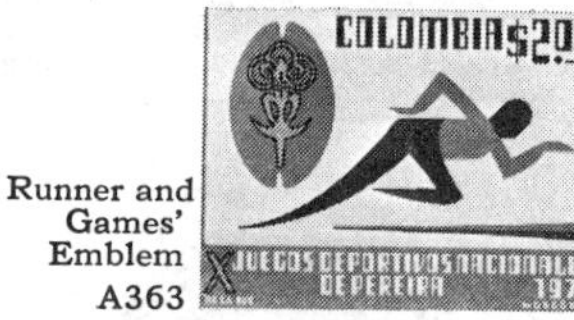

Symbols of Financial Controls
A361

1973, Dec. 20 Litho. ***Perf. 14x13½***

819 A361 80c ultra, ocher & blk 15 8

50th anniversary of Comptroller-general's Office.

Mother Laura Montoya
A362

1974, June 18 Litho. ***Perf. 13½x14***

820 A362 1p multi 30 8

Centenary of the birth of Mother Laura Montoya (1874–1949), founder and Mother Superior of the Missionaries of Mary Immaculata and St. Catherine of Siena.

Runner and Games' Emblem
A363

1974, July 18 Litho. ***Perf. 14x13½***

821 A363 2p ver, yel & brn 30 10

10th National Games, Pereira.

José Rivera
A364

1974, Aug. 3 Litho. ***Perf. 14x13½***

822 A364 10p grn & multi 1.50 18

50th anniversary of the publication of "La Voragine" (The Whirlpool) by José Eustasio Rivera.

Abstract Pattern
A365

Train Emerging from Tunnel
A366

1974, Oct. 24 Litho. ***Perf. 13½x14***

823 A365 1.10p multi 30 8

Centenary of National Insurance Co. See No. C610.

1974, Nov. 27 Litho. ***Perf. 13½x14***

824 A366 1.10p multi 30 8

Centenary of the Antioquia railroad.

Boy, Puppy and Soccer Ball
A367

Design: 1p, Girl with racket and kitten.

1974, Dec. 9

825 A367 80c multi 30 8
826 A367 1p multi 38 15

Christmas 1974.

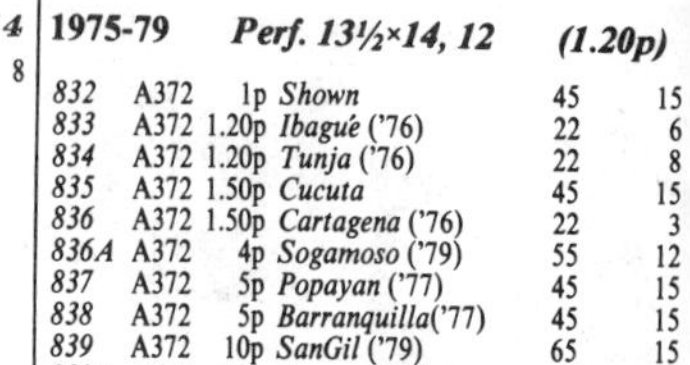

Gold Animal
A368

Design: 1.10p, Gold necklace.

1975, Apr. 11 Litho. ***Perf. 14x13½***

827 A368 80c ultra, gold & brn 30 8
828 A368 1.10p red, gold & brn 30 6

Pre-Columbian Sinu culture artifacts. See Nos. C621–C622.

Guglielmo Marconi
A369

Santa Maria Cathedral
A370

1975, June 2 Litho. ***Perf. 13½x14***

829 A369 3p multi 30 15

Birth centenary of Guglielmo Marconi (1874–1937), Italian electrical engineer and inventor.

1975, July 26

830 A370 80c multi 15 5

400th anniversary of Santa Maria City. See No. C623.

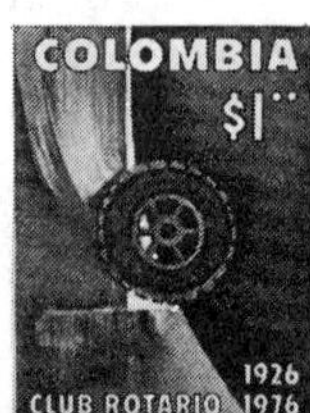

Rafael Nuñez
A371

Arms of Medellin
A372

1975, Sept. 28 Litho. ***Perf. 13½x14***

831 A371 1.10p multi 22 6

Rafael Nuñez (1825–1894), philosopher, poet, political leader, birth sesquicentenary.

1975-79 ***Perf. 13½x14, 12*** ***(1.20p)***

832 A372 1p *Shown* 45 15
833 A372 1.20p *Ibagué* ('76) 22 6
834 A372 1.20p *Tunja* ('76) 22 8
835 A372 1.50p *Cucuta* 45 15
836 A372 1.50p *Cartagena* ('76) 22 3
836A A372 4p *Sogamoso* ('79) 55 12
837 A372 5p *Popayan* ('77) 45 15
838 A372 5p *Barranquilla* ('77) 45 15
839 A372 10p *SanGil* ('79) 65 15
839A A372 10p *Socorro* ('79) 65 15
Nos. 832-839A (10) 4.31 1.19

The 1p commemorates the tercentenary of Medellin; No. 835, the centenary of Cucuta's reconstruction.

No. 827 Surcharged **$ 1.20**

1975 ***Perf. 14x13½***

840 A368 1.20p on 80c multi 15 6

Purace Indians, Cauca
A373

1976, Nov. 10 Litho. ***Perf. 13½x14***

841 A373 1.50p multi 15 5

Callicore
A374

Designs: 5p, Morpho (butterfly). 20p, Anthurium.

1976, Nov. 17 ***Perf. 12***

842 A374 3p multi 45 15
843 A374 5p multi 60 15
844 A374 20p multi 1.75 60

Rotary Emblem
A375

1976, Dec. 3 Litho. ***Perf. 12***

845 A375 1p multi 15 6

Rotary Club of Colombia, 50th anniversary.

Declaration of Independence, by John Trumbull—A376

1976, Dec. 21 Litho. ***Perf. 12***

846 A376 Strip of 3, multi 12.50 13.00
a. 30p, single stamp 3.75 1.75

American Bicentennial. No. 846 printed in sheets of 4 triptychs; black control number in margin showing Bicentennial emblems and personalities of the American Revolution.

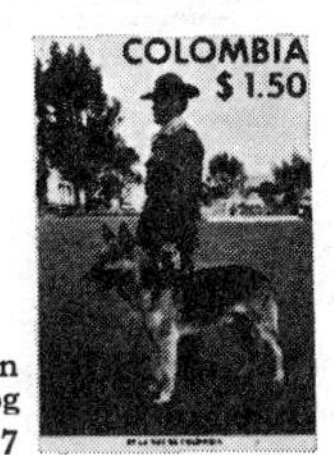

Policeman with Dog
A377

1976, Dec. 29 **Perf. 13½x14**

847 A377 1.50p multi 22 8

Honoring the National Police.

Nos. 831, 834, 847 Surcharged in Light Brown

1977, June Litho. Perf. 13½x14, 12

848 A371 2p on 1.10p multi 30 8
849 A372 2p on 1.20p multi 22 8
850 A377 2p on 1.50p multi 22 8

Souvenir Sheet

Postal Museum, Bogota—A378

1977, July 27 **Litho.** **Perf. 14**

855 A378 25p multi 2.75 2.75

Postal Museum, Bogota. No. 855 contains one stamp (50x40mm.); multicolored margin shows Colombian stamps; black control number. Size: 130x105mm.

Mother and Child
A379

1977–78 **Litho.** **Perf. 12**

856 A379 2p multi 22 3
857 A379 2.50p multi ('78) 75 6

National good nutrition plan.
Issue dates: 2p, Aug. 30. 2.50p, Jan. 26.

COLOMBIA $4.00 Fidel Cano Fundador de El Espectador

Jacana and Eichhornia
A380

Fidel Cano, by Francisco Cano
A381

Design: 20p, Mayan cotinga and pyrostegia venusta.

1977, Sept. 6 **Litho.** **Perf. 14**

858 A380 10p multi 75 30
859 A380 20p multi 1.50 45
Nos. 858-859, C644-C647 (6) 4.20 1.49

1977, Sept. 16 **Perf. 14**

860 A381 4p multi 30 8

90th anniversary of El Espectador, newspaper founded by Fidel Cano.

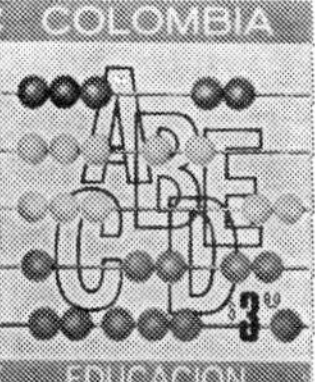

Abacus and Alphabet
A382

COLOMBIA $2.50

Cattleya Triannae
A383

1977, Sept. 16 **Perf. 13½x14**

861 A382 3p multi 22 6

Popular education.

1978, Apr. 18 **Litho.** **Perf. 12**

862 A383 2.50p multi 22 3

1979, May 10 **Litho.** **Perf. 12**

863 A383 3p multi 25 5

Sprinting and Games Emblem
A384

1978, June 27 **Litho.** **Perf. 14**

Multicolored

868 Sheet of 16 18.00 13.00
a. A384 10p *shown* 1.10 30
b. A384 10p *Basketball* 1.10 30
c. A384 10p *Basketball* 1.10 30
d. A384 10p *Boxing* 1.10 30
e. A384 10p *Bicycling* 1.10 30
f. A384 10p *Fencing* 1.10 30
g. A384 10p *Soccer* 1.10 30
h. A384 10p *Gymnastics* 1.10 30
i. A384 10p *Judo* 1.10 30
j. A384 10p *Weight lifting* 1.10 30
k. A384 10p *Wrestling* 1.10 30
l. A384 10p *Swimming* 1.10 30
m. A384 10p *Tennis* 1.10 30
n. A184 10p *Target shooting* 1.10 30
o. A384 10p *Volleyball* 1.10 30
p. A384 10p *Water polo* 1.10 30

13th Central American and Caribbean Games, Medellin. No. 863 has black marginal inscription and control number. Size: 200x160mm.

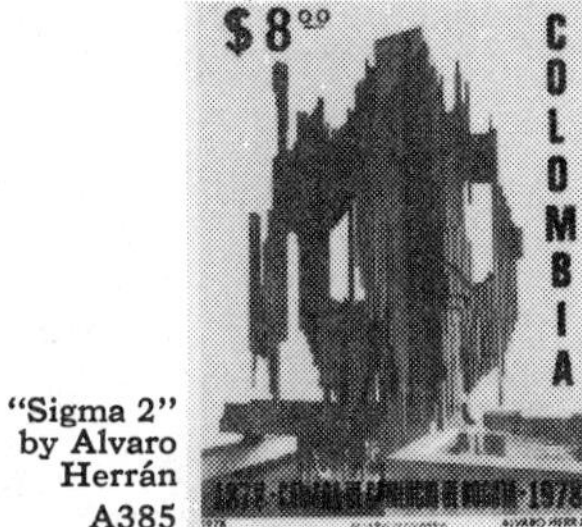

"Sigma 2" by Alvaro Herrán
A385

1978, June 30

869 A385 8p multi 55 30

Chamber of Commerce, Bogota, centenary.

Gen. Tomás Cipriano de Mosquera
A386

1978, Oct. 6 **Litho.** **Perf. 12**

870 A386 6p multi 60 22

Gen. Tomás Cipriano de Mosquera (1778–1878), statesman.

Anthurium Narinenses
A387

1979, July 23 **Perf. 12**

871 A387 3p red & multi 30 8
872 A387 3p pur & multi 30 8
873 A387 3p rose & pur 30 8
874 A387 3p white & multi 30 8

Nos. 871–874 printed in blocks of four, sheets of 100.

Gen. Rafael Uribe, by Acevedo Bernal
A388

1979, Oct. 31 **Litho.** **Perf. 12**

875 A388 8p multi 60 22

Gen. Rafael Uribe, statesman, 60th death anniversary.

Village, by Leonor Alarcon—A389

1979, Nov. 22 **Perf. 14**

876 A389 15p multi 1.25 38

Community Work Boards, 20th anniversary.

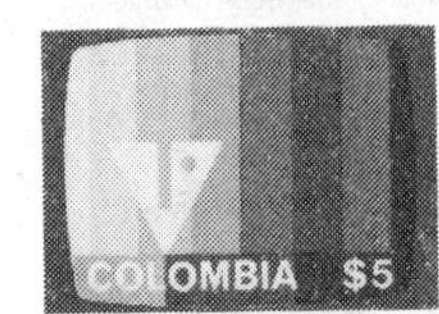

Introduction of Color Television—A390

1980, Mar. 4 **Litho.** **Perf. 14**

877 A390 5p multi 38 12

COLOMBIA $5.00 Feria de Cali · turismo

Bullfight, Arms of Cali—A391

1980, Mar. 25

878 A391 5p multi 38 12

Cali Tourist Festival, Dec. 25, 1979-Jan. 2, 1980.

"Learn to Write"—A392

1980, Apr. 25 **Litho.** **Perf. 12½**

879 Block of 30 9.00 7.50
a. A392 4p, any single 30 8

Each stamp shows letter of alphabet and corresponding animal. Issued in sheets of 90 (30x3).

Villavicencio Festival—A393

Design: 9p, Vallenato festival.

1980 **Litho.** **Perf. 14**

880 A393 5p multi 45 8
881 A393 9p multi 55 15

Issue dates: 5p, July 15; 9p, June 17.

Gustavo Uribe Ramirez and Tree—A394

1980, Aug. 5 **Litho.** **Perf. 12**

882 A394 10p multi 65 22

Gustavo Uribe Ramirez (1893-1968), ecologist.

COLOMBIA $5.00

Narino Palace (Former Presidential Residence)—A395

1980, Sept. 19 **Litho.** **Perf. 14**

883 A396 5p multi 45 15

Monument to First Pioneers of 1819, Armenia—A396

1980, Oct. 14

884 A396 5p multi 38 8

11th National Games, Neiva
A397

Fight against Cancer
A398

1980, Nov. 28 *Perf. 13½x14*
885 A397 5p multi 25 6

1980, Dec. 9
886 A398 10p multi 50 12

Xavier University Law Faculty, 50th Anniversary—A399

1980, Dec. 16 **Litho.** *Perf. 14½*
887 A399 20p multi 1.00 25

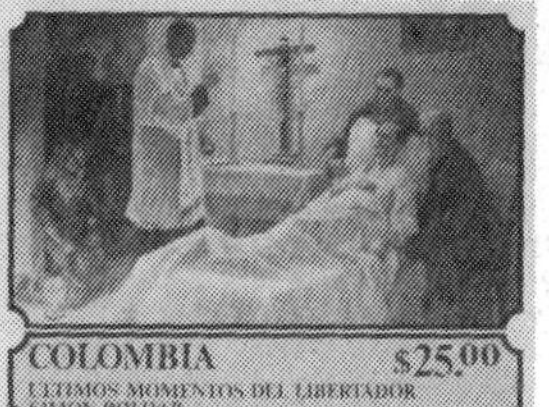

Death of Bolivar—A400

1980, Dec. 17 *Perf. 12*
888 A400 25p multi 1.25 32

Simon Bolivar, death sesquicentennial. See No. C696.

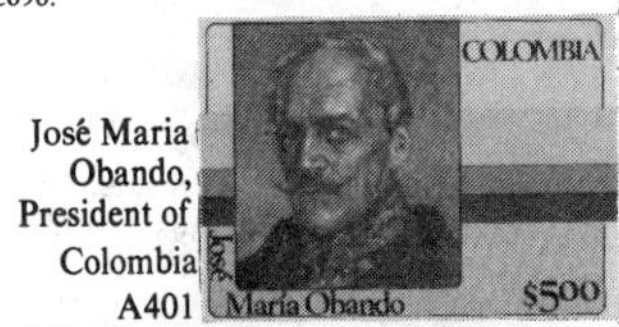

José Maria Obando, President of Colombia
A401

115th Anniv. of Constitution (Former Presidents): No. 889b, Jose Hilario Lopez. No. 889c, Manuel Murillo Toro. No. 889d, Santiago Perez. No. 889e, Rafael Reyes. No. 889f, Carlos E. Restrepo. No. 889g, Jose Vicente Concha. No. 889h, Miguel Abadia Mendez. No. 889i, Eduardo Santos. No. 889j, Mariano Ospina Perez.

1981, June 9 **Litho.** *Perf. 12*
889 Strip of 10 2.25
a-j. A401 5p multi 22 6

President Type of 1981

Designs: No. 890a, Rafael Nunez (1825-1894). No. 890b, Marco Fidel Suarez (1855-1927). No. 890c, Pedro Nel Ospina (1858-1927). No. 890d, Enrique Olaya Herrera (1880-1937). No. 890e, Alfonso Lopez Pumarejo (1886-1959). No. 890f, Aquileo Parra (1825-1900). No. 890g, Santos Gutierrez (1820-1872). No. 890h, Tomas Cipriano de Mosquera (1789-1878). No. 890i, Mariano Ospina Rodriguez. No. 890j, Pedro Alcantara Herran (1800-1872).

1981, Sept. 23 **Litho.** *Perf. 12*
890 Strip of 10 4.50 90
a-j. A401 7p multi 45 6

President Type of 1981

Designs like No. 889.

1981, Aug. 11 **Litho.** *Perf. 12*
891 Strip of 10 10.50 1.50
a-j. A401 7p multi 1.00 12

Girl Sitting on Fence—A407

1982, Feb. 22 **Litho.** *Perf. 12½x12*
898 Strip of 3 2.75 1.35
a. A407 30p shown 90 30
b. A407 30p Girl, basket 90 30
c. A407 30p Boy, wheelbarrow 90 30

President Type of 1981

Designs: a. Simon Bolivar. b. Francisco de Paula Santander. c. Joaquin Mosquera. d. Domingo Caicedo. e. Jose Ignacio de Marquez. f. Roberto Urdaneta Arbelaez. g. Carlos Lozano y Lozano. h. Guillermo Quintero Calderon. i. Jose de Obaldia. j. Juan de Dios Aranzazu.

1982, May 3 *Perf. 12*
899 Strip of 10 2.75 75
a-j. A401 7p multi 28 6

Floral Bouquet
A408

Central Hipotecario Bank, 50th Anniv.
A409

Designs: Various floral arrangements.

1982, July 28
900 Strip of 10 2.25 1.50
a. A408 7p, any single 22 6

1982, July 29 *Perf. 14*
901 A409 9p blk & grn 45 10

St. Thomas Aquinas (1225-1274)—A410

1982, Aug. 6 **Litho.** *Perf. 12*
902 A410 5p multi 15 6

Saint Type of 1982

Paintings by Zurbaran.

1982 **Litho.** *Perf. 12*
903 A410 5p St. Teresa of Avila (1515-1582) 15 6
904 A410 5p St. Francis of Assisi (1182-1226) 15 6

Issue dates: No. 903, Sept. 28; No. 904, Oct. 4.

Arms of Buga City
A411

Gabriel Marquez, 1982 Nobel Prize, Literature
A412

1982 **Litho.** *Perf. 14*
905 A411 10p shown 30 12
906 A411 16p Rionegro 50 20
907 A411 20p Santa Fe de Bogota 1.00 25
908 A411 23p Honda 70 30

1982, Dec. 10 *Perf. 13½x14*
917 A412 7p gray & grn 22 8

See No. C731-C732.

SEMI-POSTAL STAMP

Girl Giving First Aid
SP1

Perf. 13½x14

1966, Apr. 26 Litho. Unwmkd.

B1	SP1	5c +5c multi	8	6

Issued for the Red Cross.

AIR POST STAMPS.

No. 341 Overprinted

1er.
Servicio
Postal
Aereo
6.-18-19

1919 ***Perf. 14.*** **Unwmkd.**

C1	A109	2c car rose	3,000.	1,850.
a.		Numerals "1" with serifs	*7,000.*	*4,000.*

Used for the first experimental flight from Barranquilla to Puerto Colombia, June 18, 1919.

Issued by Compania Colombiana de Navegacion Aerea.

From 1920 to 1932 the internal airmail service of Colombia was handled by the Compania Colombiana de Navegacion Aerea (1920) and the Sociedad Colombo-Alemana de Transportes Aéreos, known familiarly as "SCADTA" (1920-1932). These organizations under government contracts operated and maintained their own post offices, and issued stamps which were the only legal franking for airmail service during this period, both in the internal and international mails. All letters had to bear government stamps as well.

Woman and Boy Watching Plane
AP1

Designs: No. C3, Clouds and small biplane at top. No. C4, Tilted plane viewed close-up from above. No. C5, Flier in plane watching biplane. No. C6, Lighthouse. No. C7, Fuselage and tail of biplane. No. C8, Condor on cliff. No. C9, Plane at rest; pilot foreground. No. C10, Ocean liner.

Lithographed.

1920, Feb. ***Imperf.*** **Unwmkd.**

Without Gum.

C2	AP1	10c grn, red, bl, yel & blk	2,500.	2,000.
C3	AP1	10c bl, red & blk	2,750.	2,000.
C4	AP1	10c yel, red, bl & blk	3,000.	2,000.
C5	AP1	10c bl, red, yel & blk	2,500.	2,000.
C6	AP1	10c bl, grn, red, yel, & blk	2,500.	2,000.
C7	AP1	10c grn, red, bl, red brn & blk	9,000.	3,750.
C8	AP1	10c brn, grn, bl, red & blk	4,000.	2,250.
a.		Without overprint		
C9	AP1	10c grn, bl, red, yel, red brn & blk	2,500.	2,000.
C10	AP1	10c bl, yel, grn, red & blk	4,000.	2,000.

Flier in Plane Watching Biplane
AP2

1920, March

C11	AP2	10c green	120.00	*300.00*

Four other 10c stamps, similar to No. C11, have two designs showing plane, mountains and water. They are printed in deep green or light brown red. Some authorities state that these four were not used regularly.

Issued by Sociedad Colombo-Alemana de Transportes Aereos (SCADTA)

Seaplane over Magdalena River
AP3

1920-21 Lithographed. ***Perf. 12***

C12	AP3	10c yel ('21)	40.00	25.00
C13	AP3	15c bl ('21)	35.00	27.50
C14	AP3	30c blk, *rose*	20.00	10.00
C15	AP3	30c rose ('21)	30.00	20.00
C16	AP3	50c pale grn	30.00	18.50
		Nos. C12-C16 (5)	155.00	101.00

No. C16 Handstamp Surcharged in Violet or Black:
(Illustrations of types "a" to "e" are reduced in size.)

VALOR 10 CENTAVOS
a

VALOR 10 CENTAVOS
b

Valor 10 Céntavos
c

VALOR 30 Ctvos
S.C.A.T.A
d

30¢ 30¢
e

$030
f

$030¢
g

1921

C17	AP3 (a) 10c on 50c		425.00	425.00
C18	AP3 (b) 10c on 50c		425.00	425.00
C19	AP3 (c) 10c on 50c		450.00	450.00
C20	AP3 (b) 30c on 50c		600.00	600.00
C21	AP3 (d) 30c on 50c		600.00	600.00
C22	AP3 (e) 30c on 50c		900.00	500.00
C23	AP3 (f) 30c on 50c		900.00	600.00
C24	AP3 (g) 30c on 50c		725.00	600.00

Plane over Magdalena River
AP4

Plane over Bogota Cathedral
AP5

1921 ***Perf. 11½***

C25	AP4	5c org yel	6.75	6.75
C26	AP4	10c sl grn	2.25	1.50
C27	AP4	15c org brn	2.25	1.60
C28	AP4	20c red brn	3.50	2.25
a.		Imperf. vert., pair	*200.00*	
C29	AP4	30c green	2.75	75
C30	AP4	50c blue	3.50	1.20
C31	AP4	60c vermilion	17.50	11.50
C32	AP5	1p gray blk	20.00	10.00
C33	AP5	2p rose	37.50	22.50
C34	AP5	3p violet	85.00	70.00
C35	AP5	5p ol grn	450.00	450.00
		Nos. C25-C35 (11)	631.00	578.05

Exist imperf.

Nos. C16 and C12 Handstamp Surcharged
(Illustration of type "h" is reduced in size.)

VALOR 20 Ctvs.
h

30 cent.
i

1921-22 ***Perf. 12***

C36	AP3 (h) 20c on 50c		750.00	750.00
C37	AP3 (i) 30c on 10c		450.00	450.00

Seaplane over Magdalena River
AP6

Plane over Bogota Cathedral
AP7

Wmk. 116

Wmkd. Crosses and Circles (116)

1923-28 ***Perf. 14x14½***

C38	AP6	5c org yel	1.00	30
C39	AP6	10c green	1.00	22
C40	AP6	15c carmine	1.00	22
C41	AP6	20c gray	1.00	15
C42	AP6	30c blue	1.00	15
C43	AP6	40c pur ('28)	11.00	6.00
C44	AP6	50c green	2.00	40
C45	AP6	60c brown	2.65	40
C46	AP6	80c ol grn ('28)	45.00	40.00
C47	AP7	1p black	11.00	1.65
C48	AP7	2p red org	21.00	4.50
C49	AP7	3p violet	42.50	25.00
C50	AP7	5p ol grn	72.50	30.00
		Nos. C38-C50 (13)	212.65	108.99

Nos. C41 and C31 Surcharged in Carmine and Dark Blue:

30 30 *j* 30 30 *k*

1923

C51	AP6 (j) 30c on 20c gray (C)		60.00	45.00
C52	AP4 (k) 30c on 60c ver (Bl)		65.00	40.00

Nos. C41-C42 Overprinted in Black

1928 ***Perf. 14x14½*** **Wmk. 116**

C53	AP6	20c gray	75.00	75.00
C54	AP6	30c blue	75.00	75.00

Issued to commemorate the goodwill flight of Lt. Benjamin Mendez from New York to Bogota.

Magdalena River and Tolima Volcano
AP8

Columbus' Ship and Plane
AP9

Wmk. 127

Wmkd. Quatrefoils. (127)

1929, June 1 ***Perf. 14***

C55	AP8	5c yel org	1.00	50
C56	AP8	10c red brn	1.00	40
C57	AP8	15c dp grn	1.00	50
C58	AP8	20c carmine	1.00	22
C59	AP8	30c gray bl	1.00	40
C60	AP8	40c dl vio	1.50	40
C61	AP8	50c dk ol grn	3.00	60
C62	AP8	60c org brn	3.00	60
C63	AP8	80c green	9.00	6.00
C64	AP9	1p blue	12.00	3.00
C65	AP9	2p brn org	18.50	4.75
C66	AP9	3p pale rose vio	37.50	20.00
C67	AP9	5p ol grn	85.00	45.00
		Nos. C55-C67 (13)	174.50	82.37

For International Airmail.

AP10 AP11

1929, June 1 ***Perf. 14*** **Wmk. 127**

C68	AP10	5c yel org	1.50	1.75
C69	AP10	10c red brn	1.00	1.40
C70	AP10	15c dp grn	1.00	1.40

C71	AP10	20c carmine	1.00	1.40
C72	AP10	25c vio bl	1.00	1.40
C73	AP10	30c gray bl	1.00	1.00
C74	AP10	50c dk ol grn	1.20	1.40
C75	AP10	60c brown	3.00	1.40
C76	AP11	1p blue	6.00	6.75
C77	AP11	2p red org	9.00	10.00
C78	AP11	3p violet	100.00	85.00
C79	AP11	5p ol grn	140.00	135.00
		Nos. C68-79 (12)	265.70	247.90

This issue was sold abroad for use on correspondence to be flown from coastal to interior points of Colombia. Cancellations are those of the country of origin rather than Colombia.

Nos. C63, C66 and C64 Surcharged in Black:

10 10
1830 — 1930
m

1830 1930
Simon Bolivar

n

1930, Dec. 15

C80	AP8(m)	10c on 80c grn	6.25	6.25
C81	AP9(n)	20c on 3p pale rose vio	11.00	11.00
C82	AP9(n)	30c on 1p bl	11.00	11.00

Issued to commemorate the centenary of the death of Simon Bolivar (1783-1830).

Colombian Government Issues.

Nos. C55-C67 Overprinted in Black:

CORREO AEREO
o

CORREO AEREO
p

Typographed.

1932, Jan. 1 *Perf. 14* Wmk. 127

C83	AP8(o)	5c yel org	10.00	10.00
C84	AP8(o)	10c red brn	2.25	55
C85	AP8(o)	15c dp grn	2.25	1.25
C86	AP8(o)	20c carmine	2.00	45
C87	AP8(o)	30c gray bl	2.00	60
C88	AP8(o)	40c dl vio	3.00	1.20
C89	AP8(o)	50c dk ol grn	4.00	2.25
C90	AP8(o)	60c org brn	3.00	2.25
C91	AP8(o)	80c green	18.50	12.50
C92	AP9(p)	1p blue	15.00	10.00
C93	AP9(p)	2p brn org	37.50	23.50
C94	AP9(p)	3p pale rose vio	65.00	65.00
C95	AP9(p)	5p ol grn	125.00	135.00
		Nos. C83-C95 (13)	289.50	264.55

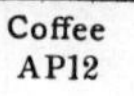

Coffee
AP12

Cattle
AP13

Petroleum
AP14

Bananas
AP15

Gold
AP16

Emerald
AP17

Photogravure.

1932-39 *Perf. 14* Wmk. 127

C96	AP12	5c org & blk brn	90	30
C97	AP13	10c lake & blk	1.25	22
C98	AP14	15c bl grn & vio blk	60	22
C99	AP14	15c ver & vio blk ('39)	4.00	15
C100	AP15	20c car & ol blk	75	8
C101	AP15	20c turq grn & ol blk ('39)	4.75	45
C102	AP12	30c dk bl & blk brn	2.00	22
C103	AP15	40c dk vio & ol bis	1.25	22
C104	AP13	50c dk grn & brnsh blk	4.50	1.50
C105	AP14	60c dk brn & blk vio	1.50	40
C106	AP12	80c grn & blk brn	7.50	2.00
C107	AP16	1p dk bl & ol bis	14.00	1.75
C108	AP16	2p org brn & ol bis	14.00	2.50
C109	AP17	3p dk vio & emer	24.00	7.50
C110	AP17	5p gray blk & emer	67.50	21.00
		Nos. C96-C110 (15)	148.50	38.51

Nos. C104, C106-C108 Surcharged:

1533
CARTAGENA
1933
10 10
a

1533 1933
CARTAGENA
20 centavos 20
b

1934, Jan. 5

C111	AP13(a)	10(c) on 50c	6.00	6.00
C112	AP12(a)	15(c) on 80c	6.00	6.00

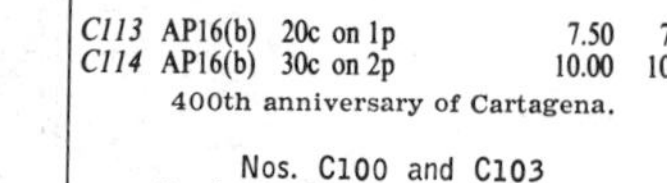

C113	AP16(b)	20c on 1p	7.50	7.50
C114	AP16(b)	30c on 2p	10.00	10.00

400th anniversary of Cartagena.

Nos. C100 and C103 Surcharged in Black or Carmine:

5
cts

15

1939, Jan. 15

C115	AP15	5c on 20c car & ol blk (Bk)	45	30
C116	AP15	5c on 40c dk vio & ol bis (C)	45	30
C117	AP15	15c on 20c car & ol blk (Bk)	2.00	75
a.		Double surcharge	17.50	
b.		Pair, one double surcharge	17.50	
c.		Invtd. surch.	17.50	17.50

No. CF5 Surcharged in Black.

C118	AP15	5c on 20c car & ol blk	90	90

Nos. C102-C103 Surcharged in Black or Red

15
cts

1940, Oct. 20

C119	AP12	15c on 30c dk bl & blk brn	1.00	1.00
a.		Invtd. surch.	17.50	
C120	AP15	15c on 40c dk vio & ol bis (R)	1.75	1.75
a.		Double surcharge	17.50	

Pre-Columbian Monument
AP18

Symbol of Legend of El Dorado
AP19

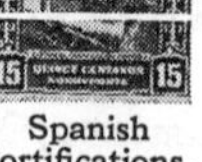

Spanish Fortifications, Cartagena
AP20

Colonial Bogotá
AP21

Proclamation of Independence
AP22

National Library, Bogotá
AP23

Engraved.

1941, Jan. 28 *Perf. 12* Unwmkd.

C121	AP18	5c gray blk	25	12
C122	AP19	10c yel org	25	6
C123	AP20	15c car rose	25	12
C124	AP21	20c yel grn	38	12
a.		Imperf. vert., pair	125.00	
C125	AP18	30c dp bl	50	12
C126	AP19	40c rose lake	70	12
C127	AP20	50c turq grn	70	12
C128	AP21	60c sepia	70	12
C129	AP18	80c ol blk	1.75	55
C130	AP22	1p bl & blk	3.00	70
C131	AP23	2p red org & blk	5.50	1.75
C132	AP22	3p vio & blk	14.00	8.00
C133	AP23	5p lt grn & blk	30.00	20.00
		Nos. C121-C133 (13)	57.98	31.90

See also Nos. C151-C163, C217-C225.

San Sebastian Fort, Cartagena
AP24

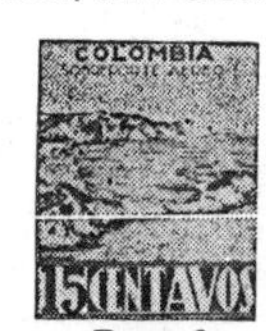

Bay of Santa Marta
AP25

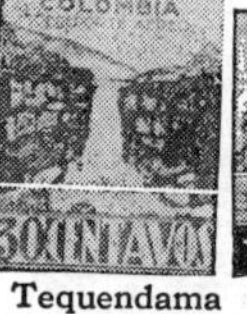

Tequendama Waterfall
AP26

National Capitol, Bogotá
AP27

Lithographed.

1945, Nov. 3 *Perf. 11* Unwmkd.

C134	AP24	5c bl gray	30	15
a.		Imperf., pair	12.00	
C135	AP26	10c yel org	30	15
a.		Imperf., pair	12.00	
C136	AP25	15c rose	30	8
a.		Imperf., pair	12.00	
C137	AP24	20c lt yel grn	45	15
a.		Imperf., pair	12.00	
C138	AP26	30c ultra	50	15
a.		Imperf., pair	12.00	
C139	AP25	40c claret	75	22
a.		Imperf., pair	12.00	
C140	AP24	50c bluish grn	1.00	22
a.		Imperf., pair	12.00	
C141	AP26	60c lt vio brn	2.40	90
a.		Imperf., pair	12.00	
C142	AP25	80c dk sl grn	3.75	1.20
a.		Imperf., pair	15.00	
C143	AP27	1p dk bl	6.00	1.40
a.		Imperf., pair	25.00	
C144	AP27	2p red org	9.00	3.25
a.		Imperf., pair	85.00	
		Nos. C134-C144 (11)	24.75	7.87

Part-perforate varieties exist for all denominations except 80c.

Bello Type of Regular Issue, 1946.

Engraved.

1946, Sept. 3 *Perf. 12* Wmk. 255

C145	A219	5c dp bl	30	22

Issued to commemorate the 80th anniversary of the death of Andrés Bello, poet and educator.

Francisco José de Caldas
AP29

Manuel del Socorro Rodriguez
AP30

Perf. 12½

1947, May 9 Litho. Unwmkd.

No.	Type	Description	Unused	Used
C146	AP29	5c dp bl, *grnsh*	60	45
C147	AP30	10c red org, *grnsh*	75	65

4th Pan-American Press Congress (1946).

Chancellery Patio
AP31

Capitol, Patio Rafael Nunez
AP32

AP33

1948, Apr. 2 Engraved Wmk. 229

No.	Type	Description	Unused	Used
C148	AP31	5c dk brn	15	10
C149	AP32	15c dp bl	1.75	1.75

Miniature Sheet

Imperf.

No.	Type	Description	Unused	Used
C150	AP33	50c brown	1.75	1.75

Nos. C148–C150 commemorate the 9th Pan-American Conference, Bogotá. No. C150 measures 90½x90½mm.

Types of 1941.

1948, July 21 *Perf. 12* Unwmkd.

No.	Type	Description	Unused	Used
C151	AP18	5c org yel	30	7
C152	AP19	10c scarlet	30	7
C153	AP20	15c dp bl	30	5
C154	AP21	20c violet	30	5
C155	AP18	30c yel grn	45	22
C156	AP19	40c gray	60	18
C157	AP20	50c rose lake	75	18
C158	AP21	60c ol gray	75	18
C159	AP18	80c red brn	1.25	22
C160	AP22	1p ol grn & vio brn	2.25	45
C161	AP23	2p dp grn & brt bl	4.00	65
C162	AP22	3p rose car & blk	7.50	5.25
C163	AP23	5p lt brn & turq grn	18.50	9.00
		Nos. C151-C163 (13)	37.25	16.57

"Air Week" 5c Blue

The War and Air Department issued a 5c blue stamp in May, 1949, to publicize Air Week (Semana de Aviacion). The design shows a coat-of-arms, inscribed "FAC," superimposed upon an outline map of Colombia. This stamp had no franking value and its use was optional during May 16-23.

Justice and Liberty
AP34

Wing
AP35

Design: 10c, Liberty holding tablet of laws.

1949, Oct. 7 *Perf. 13* Unwmkd.

No.	Type	Description	Unused	Used
C164	AP34	5c bl grn	15	7
C165	AP34	10c orange	15	7

Issued to honor the new Constitution.

For Domestic Postage.

1950, June 22 Litho. *Perf. 12*

No.	Type	Description	Unused	Used
C166	AP35	5c org yel	45	30
C167	AP35	10c brn red	55	40
C168	AP35	15c lt bl	70	55
C169	AP35	20c lt grn	1.00	65
C170	AP35	30c lil gray	2.00	2.00
C171	AP35	60c chocolate	3.00	3.00

With Network as in Parenthesis.

No.	Type	Description	Unused	Used
C172	AP35	1p gray (buff)	10.00	10.00
C173	AP35	2p bl (pale grn)	25.00	25.00
C174	AP35	5p red brn (red brn)	65.00	65.00
		Nos. C166-C174 (9)	97.70	96.90

No. C172 was issued both with and without network.

Nos. C151–C157 and C160–C163 Overprinted in Black

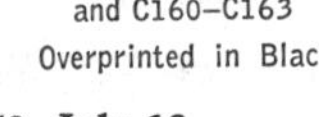

L

1950, July 18

No.	Type	Description	Unused	Used
C175	AP18	5c org yel	30	22
C176	AP19	10c scarlet	30	22
C177	AP20	15c dp bl	30	15
C178	AP21	20c violet	45	22
C179	AP18	30c yel grn	65	22
C180	AP19	40c gray	75	30
C181	AP20	50c rose lake	75	40
C182	AP22	1p ol grn & vio brn	3.25	2.25
C183	AP23	2p dp grn & brt bl	4.50	3.75
C184	AP22	3p rose car & blk	13.00	13.00
C185	AP23	5p lt brn & turq grn	40.00	40.00
		Nos. C175-C185 (11)	64.25	60.73

Nos. C151-C163 Overprinted in Black

1950, July 12

No.	Type	Description	Unused	Used
C186	AP18	5c org yel	30	7
C187	AP19	10c scarlet	30	7
C188	AP20	15c dp bl	30	5
C189	AP21	20c violet	45	7
C190	AP18	30c yel grn	45	7
C191	AP19	40c gray	75	15
C192	AP20	50c rose lake	75	22
C193	AP21	60c ol gray	1.25	22
C194	AP18	80c red brn	2.00	75
C195	AP22	1p ol grn & vio brn	1.20	75
C196	AP23	2p dp grn & brt bl	4.50	1.40
C197	AP22	3p rose car & blk	11.00	9.00
C198	AP23	5p lt brn & turq grn	22.50	21.00
		Nos. C186-C198 (13)	45.75	33.82

On Nos. C175–C198, "L" stands for LANSA, "A" for AVIANCA.

Miniature Sheet

Western Hemisphere
AP36

Imperf.

1950, Aug. 22 Photo. Unwmkd.

No.	Type	Description	Unused	Used
C199	AP36	50c gray	1.40	1.40

Issued to commemorate the 75th anniversary (in 1949) of the formation of the Universal Postal Union.

Types of 1941 Overprinted at Lower Right in Black

L

Engraved.

1951, Sept. 15 *Perf. 12* Unwmkd.

No.	Type	Description	Unused	Used
C200	AP19	40c org yel	2.25	2.25
C201	AP20	50c ultra	2.25	2.25
C202	AP21	60c gray	2.25	2.25
C203	AP18	80c car rose	1.50	1.20
C204	AP22	1p red org & red brn	4.50	3.25
C205	AP23	2p rose car & bl	5.50	4.50
C206	AP22	3p choc & emer	13.00	12.00
C207	AP23	5p org & gray	35.00	35.00
		Nos. C200-C207 (8)	66.25	62.70

Types of 1941 Overprinted at Lower Right in Black

A

1951–54

No.	Type	Description	Unused	Used
C208	AP19	40c org yel	4.00	65
C209	AP20	50c ultra	4.50	90
C210	AP21	60c gray	3.75	75
a.		Overprint centered	2.50	75
C211	AP18	80c car rose	1.25	45
C212	AP22	1p red org & red brn	4.50	55
C213	AP22	1p ol grn & vio brn ('54)	5.00	1.00
C214	AP23	2p rose car & bl	4.50	75
C215	AP22	3p choc & emer	6.50	1.25
C216	AP23	5p org & gray	11.00	3.00
		Nos. C208-C216 (9)	45.00	9.30

All values except the 2p and 3p exist without overprint.

Types of 1941.

1952, May 10 Engraved

No.	Type	Description	Unused	Used
C217	AP18	5c ultra	45	22
C218	AP19	10c ultra	45	22
C219	AP20	15c ultra	45	22
C220	AP21	20c ultra	90	30
C221	AP18	30c ultra	2.00	40
C222	AP18	5c car rose	45	22
C223	AP19	10c car rose	45	22
C224	AP21	20c car rose	90	30
C225	AP18	30c car rose	2.00	45
		Nos. C217-C225 (9)	8.05	2.55

Type of 1941 Surcharged in Blue

1º CONFERENCIA 1952 SIDERURGICA LATINO AMERICANA 70 Ctvos.

1952, Oct. 30

No.	Type	Description	Unused	Used
C226	AP18	70c on 80c car rose	1.75	1.00

Issued to publicize the Latin American Siderurgical Conference, 1952.

Type of Postal Tax Stamps, 1948–50, Nos. 602 and 604 Surcharged or Overprinted in Black

CORREO 5 AEREO

1953 *Perf. 12.* Wmk. 255

No.	Type	Description	Unused	Used
C227	PT10	5c on 8c bl	15	5
C228	PT10	15c on 20c brn	38	8
C229	PT10	15c on 25c bl grn	1.00	10
C230	PT10	25c bl grn	55	8

Many varieties of overprint or surcharge exist on Nos. C227–C231.

No. 570 Overprinted "AEREO" in Blue.

1953, Aug. *Perf. 12½* Wmk. 229

No.	Type	Description	Unused	Used
C231	A160	10c red	22	5

"Extra Rapido"

Stamps inscribed "Extra Rapido" are for use on domestic airmail carried by airlines other than AVIANCA.

No. 585 Surcharged and Overprinted "Extra Rapido" in Dark Blue

CORREO 5 EXTRA RAPIDO 5

1953 *Perf. 13* Unwmkd.

No.	Type	Description	Unused	Used
C232	A244	5c on 11c red	45	45

Capitol and Arms
AP37

Revenue Stamps Overprinted "Correo Extra-Rapido"

Gray Security Paper.

Engraved.

1953 *Perf. 12* Wmk. 255

No.	Type	Description	Unused	Used
C233	AP37	1c on 2c grn	15	6
C234	AP37	50c red org	22	8

AP38

Real Estate Tax Stamps Overprinted "Correo Extra-Rapido" in Black or Carmine

1953

No.	Type	Description	Unused	Used
C235	AP38	5c red org	15	6
C236	AP38	20c brn (C)	22	8

On 20c, overprint is at bottom of stamp and two lines of ornaments cover real estate tax inscription at top.

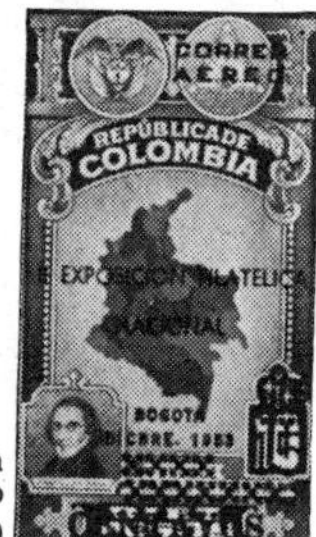

Castillo y Rada and Map
AP39

Real Estate Tax Stamp Surcharged "Correo Aereo, II Exposicion Filatelica Nacional, Bogota Dicbre 1953, 15 Centavos"

Engraved and Lithographed.

1953, Dec. 12

C237 AP39 15c on 10p multi 55 30

Issued to publicize the second National Philatelic Exhibition, Bogota, Dec. 1953.

No. RA45 Overprinted in Black — CORREO EXTRA-RAPIDO

1953

C238 PT10 10c purple 15 6

Galeras Volcano
AP40

Retreat of San Diego
AP41

Designs: 15c (C241), Las Lajas Shrine, Narino. 15c (C242), 50c, Bolivar monument. 20c, 80c, Ruiz mountain, Manizales. 40c, George Isaacs monument, Cali. 60c, Monkey Fountain, Tunja. 1p, Stadium, Medellin. 2p, Pastelillo Fort, Cartagena. 3p, Santo Domingo University gate. 5p, Las Lajas Shrine. 10p, Map of Colombia.

Perf. 13½x13, 13.

1954, Jan. 15 Engraved. Unwmkd.

C239 AP40 5c dp red vio 8 8
C240 AP41 10c black 8 8
C241 AP40 15c red org 22 5
C242 AP40 15c car rose 22 5
C243 AP40 20c brown 30 5
C244 AP40 30c brn org 30 5
C245 AP40 40c blue 30 8
C246 AP40 50c dk vio brn 40 10
C247 AP40 60c dk brn 45 10
C248 AP40 80c red brn 1.10 30

Size: 37x27mm.
Center in Black.

C249 AP41 1p dp bl 2.75 30
C250 AP41 2p dk grn 5.25 45
C251 AP41 3p car rose 9.00 1.40

Size: 38x32mm., 32x38mm.

C252 AP41 5p dk grn & red brn 10.00 3.75
C253 AP40 10p gray grn & red org 12.50 6.75
Nos. C239-C253 (15) 42.95 13.59

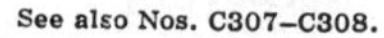
See also Nos. C307–C308.

Condor Carrying Shield
AP42

Inscribed: "Correo Extra-Rapido"
Lithographed.

1954, Apr. 23 ***Perf. 12½.***

C254 AP42 5c lil rose 75 45

Soldier-Map-Arms Type of Regular Issue, 1954.

1954, June 13 Engraved ***Perf. 13***

C255 A259 15c carmine 40 8

Issued to commemorate the first anniversary of the assumption of the presidency by General Rojas Pinilla.
See also No. C271a.

Games Type of Regular Issue, 1954.

Design: 20c, Stadium and Athlete holding arms of Colombia.

1954, July 18

C256 A260 15c chocolate 90 22
C257 A260 20c dp bl grn 1.75 45

7th National Games, Cali, July 1954.

Church of St. Peter Claver, Cartagena
AP45

1954, Sept. 9

C258 AP45 15c brown 45 10
a. Souvenir sheet 2.75 2.75

Issued to commemorate the 300th anniversary of the death of St. Peter Claver.
No. C258a contains one stamp similar to No. C258, but printed in red brown. Marginal inscriptions in black. Sheet size: 120½x127mm.

Mercury Type of Regular Issue, 1954.

1954, Oct. 29

C259 A263 15c dp bl 40 10

Inscribed "Extra Rapido"

C260 A263 50c scarlet 40 10

Issued to publicize the first International Fair and Exhibition, Bogotá, 1954.

Archbishop Manuel José Mosquera
AP47

Inscribed: "Correo Extra Rapido"

1954, Nov. 17

C261 AP47 2c yel grn 15 8

Issued to commemorate the centenary of the death of Archbishop Manuel José Mosquera.

Virgin of Chiquinquira
AP48

Inscribed: "Correo Extra Rapido"
Engraved and Lithographed

1954, Dec. 4

C262 AP48 5c org brn & multi 12 5

See also No. C291.

College Types of Regular Issue, 1954.

Designs: 20c, Brother Cristobal de Torres. 50c, College chapel and arms.

Perf. 12½x11½, 11½x12½

1954, Dec. 6 Engraved **Unwmkd.**

C263 A264 15c org & blk 55 22
C264 A264 20c ultra 75 22
C265 A265 25c dk brn 90 22
C266 A265 50c blk & car 2.10 1.00
a. Souvenir sheet 4.50 4.50

Issued to commemorate the 300th anniversary (in 1953) of the founding of the Senior College of Our Lady of the Rosary, Bogotá.
No. C266a contains four stamps similar to Nos. C263–C266, but printed in different colors: 15c red and black, 20c pale purple, 25c brown, 50c black and olive green. Marginal inscriptions in black. Sheet size: 124½x130½mm.

Steel Mill Type of Regular Issue.

1954, Dec. 12 ***Perf. 12½x13***

C267 A266 20c grn & blk 1.40 90

Issued to mark the opening of the Paz del Rio steel mill, October 1954.

Marti Type of Regular Issue, 1955

1955, Jan. 28 ***Perf. 13½x13***

C268 A267 15c dp grn 40 12

Issued to commemorate the centenary (in 1953) of the birth of José Marti.

Korean Veterans Type of Regular Issue, 1955.

1955, Mar. 23 ***Perf. 12½***

C269 A268 20c dk grn 75 40

Issued to honor Colombian soldiers who served in Korea.

Merchant Fleet Types of Regular Issue, 1955.

1955, Apr. 12 ***Perf. 12½***

C270 A269 25c black 45 12
C271 A270 50c dk grn 75 45
a. Souvenir sheet 4.50 4.50

Issued to honor the Grand-Colombian Merchant Fleet.
No. C271a contains four stamps similar to Nos. C255, C269–C271, but printed in different colors; 15c lilac red, 20c olive, 25c bluish black, 50c bluish green. Marginal inscriptions in black. Sheet size: 125x131mm.

Pres. Marco Fidel Suarez
AP56

Inscribed: "Correo Extra Rapido"

1955, April 23 ***Perf. 13***

C272 AP56 10c dp bl 15 8

Issued to commemorate the centenary of the birth of Marco Fidel Suarez (1855–1927), president in 1918–1921.

Hotel-Church Type of Regular Issue, 1955.

1955, May 16 Photo. *Perf. 11½x12*

C273 A271 15c rose brn 40 7

Rotary Type of Regular Issue, 1955. Engraved.

1955, Oct. 17 *Perf. 13* Unwmkd.

C274 A272 15c dk car rose 40 7

Rotary International, 50th anniversary.

O'Higgins, Santander and Sucre
AP59

Ferdinand the Catholic and Queen Isabella I
AP60

Designs: 2c, Atahualpa, Tisquesuza and Montezuma. 20c, Marti, Hidalgo and Petion. 1p, Artigas, Solano Lopez and Murillo. 2p, Abdon Calderon, Baron de Rio Branco and José de La Mar.

1955, Oct. 12 **Engr. & Photo.**

Inscribed: "Extra Rapido"

C275 AP59 2c dl brn & blk 15 8
C276 AP60 5c dk brn & yel 22 22

Regular Air Post

C277 AP59 15c rose car & blk 40 15
C278 AP59 20c pale brn & blk 45 15
a. Souvenir sheet of 2 4.50 4.50

Inscribed: "Extra Rapido"

C279 AP60 1p ol gray & brn 6.75 4.50
C280 AP60 2p vio & blk 4.75 3.00
Nos. C275-C280 (6) 12.72 8.10

Issued to publicize the 7th Congress of the Postal Union of the Americas and Spain, Bogota, Oct. 12–Nov. 9, 1955.
No. C278a contains one each of Nos. C277–C278 printed in different shades. It measures 120x132mm. with marginal inscription in black: "Ministerio de Comunicaciones. III Exposicion Filatelica Nacional Bogota 1955."

Caro Type of Regular Issue, 1955.

1955, Nov. 29 Engr. *Perf. 13½x13*

C281 A275 15c gray grn 45 15

Issued to commemorate the centenary of the death of José Eusebio Caro, poet.

University of Salamanca
AP62

Inscribed: "Extra Rapido"

1955, Nov. 29 *Perf. 13* Unwmkd.

C282 AP62 20c dk brn 12 8

University of Salamanca, 7th centenary.

Type of Postal Tax Stamp of 1948-50 Surcharged in Black

CORREO
EXTRA-RAPIDO

Engraved.

1956 *Perf. 12* Wmk. 255

C283	PT10	2c on 8c bl	8	5

No. 617 Overprinted in Black

EXTRA-RAPIDO

1956 *Perf. 12½x13* Unwmkd.

C284	A256	1p blk & emer	30	8

Columbus Type of Regular Issue.

1956, Oct. 11 Photo. *Perf. 12*

C285	A279	15c int bl	45	15

Issued in honor of Christopher Columbus. See also No. C306.

St. Elizabeth Type of Regular Issue

1956, Nov. 19

C286	A280	15c red brn	45	22

Issued to commemorate the 7th centenary of St. Elizabeth of Hungary, patron saint of Santa Fé de Bogota.

St. Ignatius Type of Regular Issue

1956, Nov. 26 Engr. *Perf. 12½x13*

C287	A281	5c brown	30	8

Issued to commemorate the 400th anniversary of the death of St. Ignatius of Loyola.

Javier Pereira
AP63

1956, Dec. 28 *Perf. 12* Unwmkd.

C288	AP63	20c rose car	30	8

Issued to honor 167-year-old Javier Pereira.

No. 649 and Type of 1941 Overprinted in Red "EXTRA RAPIDO."

1957 *Perf. 13½x13*

C289	A276	5c bl & blk	22	15

Perf. 12

C290	AP23	5p org & gray	6.75	5.25

The overprint measures 14mm.

Virgin Type of 1954.

Engraved and Lithographed

1957, May 23 *Perf. 13* Unwmkd.

C291	AP48	5c multi	8	6

Bank Type of Regular Issue, 1957.

Designs: C292, 20c, Emblem and dairy farm. 10c, Emblem and tractor. 15c, Emblem, coffee and corn. C293, Emblem, cow, horse and herd.

1957 Photo. *Perf. 14x13½*

C292	A283	5c chocolate	22	10
C293	A283	5c orange	15	10
C294	A283	10c green	70	55
C295	A283	15c black	40	10
C296	A283	20c dl red	1.25	1.00
		Nos. C292-C296 (5)	2.72	1.85

Nos. C292–C296 issued to commemorate the 25th anniversary of the founding of the Agrarian Savings Bank of Colombia.

No. C292 is inscribed "Extra Rapido."

No. C292 issued Mar. 5, others May 23.

Cyclist
AP64

1957, July 6 *Perf. 12* Unwmkd.

C297	AP64	2c brown	15	15
C298	AP64	5c ultra	22	22

Seventh Bicycle Tour of Colombia.

Academy Type of Regular Issue.

Designs: 15c, Coat of arms and Gen. Rafael Reyes. 20c, Coat of arms and Academy.

1957, July 20 Engraved *Perf. 12½*

C299	A284	15c rose car	22	8
C300	A284	20c brown	38	8

Issued to commemorate the 50th anniversary of the Colombian Military Academy.

Delgado Type of Regular Issue, 1957.

1957, Sept. 15 Photo. *Perf. 12*

C301	A285	10c sl bl	22	15

Issued in honor of José Matias Delgado, liberator of El Salvador.

UPU Type of Regular Issue, 1957.

1957, Oct. 10

C302	A286	15c dk red brn	22	18
C303	A286	25c dk bl	25	7

Issued for International Letter Writing Week and the 14th UPU Congress.

St. Vincent de Paul Type of Regular Issue, 1957.

1957, Oct. 18

C304	A287	5c rose brn	25	18

Issued to commemorate the centenary of the Colombian Society of St. Vincent de Paul.

Fencing Type of Regular Issue, 1957.

1957, Nov. 23 *Perf. 12*

C305	A288	20c dk red brn	42	42

Issued to commemorate the third South American Fencing Championship.

Columbus Type of Regular Issue, 1956, Inscribed "Extra Rapido."

1958, Jan. 8 *Perf. 12* Unwmkd.

C306	A279	3c dk grn	10	7

Scenic Type of 1954.

Design: 25c, Las Lajas Shrine.

1958, June 20 Engr. *Perf. 13*

C307	AP40	25c dk bl	40	7
C308	AP40	25c rose vio	40	7

IGY Type of Regular Issue, 1958.

1958, May 12 Photo. *Perf. 12*

C309	A289	25c green	55	8

Inscribed "Extra Rapido."

C310	A289	1p purple	45	12

Nos. C309–C310 issued for the International Geophysical Year, 1957–58.

No. 659 Overprinted "AEREO" in Carmine.

1958, Oct. 16 Engraved *Perf. 13*

C312	A277	50c dk grn & blk	60	15

Almanza Type of Regular Issue, 1958.

1958, Oct. 23 Photo. *Perf. 14x13*

C313	A290	25c dk gray	38	6

Inscribed "Extra Rapido"

C314	A290	10c ol grn	15	5

Carrasquilla Type of Regular Issue, 1959.

1959, Jan. 22 Photo. *Perf. 14x13*

C315	A291	25c car rose	25	8
C316	A291	1p dk bl	75	25

Issued to commemorate the centenary of the birth (in 1857) of Msgr. R. M. Carrasquilla, rector of Our Lady of the Rosary Seminary, Bogota.

Miss Universe Type of Regular Issue, 1959.

1959, June 26 *Perf. 11½* Unwmkd.

C317	A292	1.20p multi	2.00	2.00
C318	A292	5p multi	45.00	45.00

Issued to honor Luz Marina Zuluaga, Miss Universe, 1959.

Gaitan Type of Regular Issue, 1959, Inscribed "Extra Rapido" and Surcharged in Black or Blue.

1959, July 28 Engr. *Perf. 12x13½*

C319	A293	2p on 1p blk	1.00	45
C320	A293	2p on 1p blk (Bl)	1.00	70

Issued in honor of Jorge Eliecer Gaitan, (1898–1948), lawyer and politician.

The 1p black, type A293, exists without surcharge.

No. C247 Surcharged with New Value in Dark Blue; Old Value Obliterated.

1959, Aug. 24 *Perf. 13* Unwmkd.

C321	AP40	50c on 60c dk brn	1.10	55

Regular and Air Post Issues of 1948–1959 Overprinted in Black or Red

UNIFICADO

1959–60

C322	A283	5c orange	40	40
C323	A287	5c rose brn ('60)	45	45
C324	A281	5c brn (R)	55	55
C325	AP41	10c black	22	8
a.		Double ovpt.	3.50	3.50
C326	A160	10c red	65	15
a.		Double ovpt.	2.00	2.00
C328	A284	15c rose car	45	8
a.		Inverted ovpt.	4.50	4.50
C330	AP40	20c brown	22	8
a.		Double ovpt.	2.00	2.00
C331	A284	20c brown	40	40
C332	A288	20c dk red brn ('60)	30	30
C333	AP40	25c rose vio ('60)	28	7
C334	AP40	25c dk bl	28	7
C335	A291	25c car rose	35	15
C336	A290	25c dk gray	28	10
C338	AP40	30c brn org	22	7
C340	AP40	50c on 60c dk brn	55	18
C341	A291	1p dk bl	90	15
a.		Double ovpt.	3.50	3.50
C342	A292	1.20p brn, ultra, car & ol	1.40	1.40
C343	AP41	2p dk grn & blk	1.50	22
C344	AP41	3p car rose & blk	5.25	75
a.		Double ovpt.	12.00	12.00
C345	AP41	5p dk grn & red brn	7.50	1.40
a.		Double ovpt.	12.00	12.00
b.		Invert. ovpt.	12.00	12.00
C346	AP40	10p gray grn & red org	7.50	3.00
		Nos. C322-C346 (21)	29.65	10.05

Issued following agreement between the Colombian government and AVIANCA to unify the air postage used on all mail carried by AVIANCA.

Vertical overprint on Nos. C342 and C346.

Airmail Stamp of 1919 and Planes
AP66

Designs: 60c, No. C349a, C350a, Planes of 1919 and 1959. C349b, C350b, Stamp of 1919 and Planes.

Photogravure.

1959, Dec. 5 *Perf. 12* Unwmkd.

C347	AP66	35c lt bl, blk & red	60	8
C348	AP66	60c yel grn & gray	38	8

Souvenir Sheets.

C349	AP66	Sheet of two	4.50	4.50
a.		1p org & gray	1.00	1.00
b.		1p lil, gray & red	1.00	1.00

Inscribed "Extra Rapido"

1960, May 17

C350	AP66	Sheet of two	4.50	4.50
a.		1.50p red org & gray	1.25	1.25
b.		1.50p ol, gray & rose	1.25	1.25

Nos. C347–C350 issued to commemorate the 40th anniversary of air post service and of the AVIANCA company.

Nos. C349–C350 measure 90x49½mm. with black marginal inscriptions.

Type of Regular Issue, 1959 and

1859 Stamp and Seaplane
AP67

Designs (various stamps of 1859 and): 10c, Map of Colombia. 25c, Pres. Mariano Ospina. 1.20p, Plane over mountains.

1959, Dec. 1 Photo. *Perf. 12*

C351	A296	25c choc & red	55	30
C352	AP67	50c ver & ultra	1.10	60
C353	AP67	1.20p yel grn & car	1.75	1.40

Inscribed "Extra Rapido"

C354	A296	10c lem & vio	22	5

Souvenir Sheet

Tête Bêche 5c Stamps of 1859
AP68

Wmkd. "REPUBLICA DE COLOMBIA". (331)

1959, Dec. 23 Litho. *Imperf.*

C355	AP68	5p bl, *pink*	15.00	15.00

Nos. C351–C355 issued to commemorate the centenary of Colombian postage stamps.

No. C355 contains a tête bêche pair simulating the 5c blue of 1859, No. 2. Sheet sold for 5p. Size: 74½x70mm.

No. C355 exists with inscription "VALOR $5.10" instead of "VALOR $5."

Eldorado Airport, Bogota
AP69

1960, Jan. 5 *Perf. 12½* Wmk. 331

C356	AP69	35c blk & ocher	75	45
C356A	AP69	60c ver & gray	1.10	60

Inscribed "Extra Rapido"

C356B	AP69	1p Prus bl & gray	1.25	60

Ant Bear
AP70

Designs: 1.30p, Armadillo. 1.45p, Parrot fish.

Photogravure

1960, Feb. 12 *Perf. 12* Unwmkd.

C357	AP70	35c sepia	1.10	15
C358	AP70	1.30p rose car & dk brn	2.00	2.00
C359	AP70	1.45p lt bl, bl & yel	1.75	1.75

Issued to commemorate the centenary of the death of Alexander von Humboldt, German naturalist and geographer (1769–1859).

Flower Type of Regular Issue, 1960

Flowers: Nos. C360, C362, C366, Passiflora mollissima. Nos. C361, C364, C367, Odontoglossum luteo purpureum. Nos. C363, C369, Anthurium andreanum. Nos. C365, C370, Stanhopea tigrina. No. C368, Espeletia grandiflora.

1960, May 10 Photo. *Perf. 12*

Flowers in Natural Colors.

C360	A298	5c dk bl	15	12
C361	A298	35c maroon	60	10
C362	A298	60c dk bl	1.10	65
C363	A298	1.45p dk brn	1.25	1.00

Inscribed "Extra Rapido"

C364	A298	5c maroon	15	12
C365	A298	10c brown	15	12
C366	A298	1p dk bl	2.50	2.50
C367	A298	1p maroon	2.50	2.50
C368	A298	1p brown	2.50	2.50
C369	A298	1p brown	2.50	2.50
C370	A298	1p brown	2.50	2.50
		Nos. C360-C370 (11)	15.90	14.61

See also Nos. C420–C425.

Fleeing Family and Uprooted Oak Emblem
AP71

Perf. 10, 11

1960, May 24 Litho. Wmk. 331

C371	AP71	60c bl grn & gray	50	32

Issued to publicize World Refugee Year, July 1, 1959–June 30, 1960.

Souvenir Sheet

Pan-American Highway Through Colombia
AP72

1960, May 28 Lithographed *Imperf.*

C372	AP72	2.50p brn & aqua	6.75	6.75

Issued to commemorate the 8th Pan-American Highway Congress, Bogota, May 20–29.

No. C372 measures 44x54mm. with brown marginal inscription and black control number.

Lincoln Type of Regular Issue.

1960, June 6 *Perf. 10½*

C375	A299	40c dl red brn & blk	1.00	80
C376	A299	60c rose red & blk	45	15

Issued to commemorate the sesquicentennial (in 1959) of the birth of Abraham Lincoln.

Type of Regular Issue and

Joaquin Camacho, Jorge Tadeo Lozano and Jose Miguel Pey
AP73

Designs: No. C378, Arms of Cartagena. 35c, 1.45p, Colombian flag. 60c, Andres Rosillo, Antonio Villavicencio and Joaquin Caicedo. 1p, Manuel de Bernardo Alvarez and Joaquin Gutierrez. 1.20p, Jose Antonio Galan statue. 1.30p, Front page of newspaper La Bagatela, 1811. 1.65p, Antonia Santos, Jose Acevedo y Gomez and Liborio Mejia.

Photogravure

1960, July 20 *Perf. 12* Unwmkd.

C377	AP73	5c lil & brn	18	14
C378	A301	5c dp bl grn & multi	18	14
C379	AP73	35c multi	18	8
C380	AP73	60c red brn & grn	70	22
C381	AP73	1p ver & sl grn	1.00	90
C382	A301	1.20p ultra & ind	1.00	90
C383	AP73	1.30p org & blk	1.00	90
C384	AP73	1.45p multi	1.40	1.10
C385	AP73	1.65p grn & brn	1.10	1.10
		Nos. C377-C385 (9)	6.74	5.48

Souvenir Sheet

Stamps Inscribed "Extra Rapido"

Flag, Coins and Arms of Mompox and Cartagena
AP74

C386	AP74	Sheet of four	4.50	4.50
a.		50c dp cl & multi	85	85
b.		50c grn & multi	85	85
c.		1p brn ol, yel, bl & car	85	85
d.		1p lil & gray	85	85

Nos. C377–C386 issued to commemorate the 150th anniversary of Colombia's independence.

No. C386 measures 90x75mm.

St. Isidro Type of Regular Issue, 1960.

Designs: 35c, No. C388a, St. Isidro and farm animals. No. C388b, Nativity.

Photogravure

1960, Sept. 26 *Perf. 12* Unwmkd.

C387	A302	35c multi	28	12

Souvenir Sheet

Stamps Inscribed "Extra Rapido"

C388	A302	Sheet of two	9.00	9.00
a.		1.50p multi	3.00	3.00
b.		1.50p multi	3.00	3.00

Issued to honor St. Isidro the Farmer, patron saint of the rural people. Black marginal inscription on No. C388. Size: 89½x60mm.

See also Nos. C439–C440.

Type of Regular Issue, 1959

Portrait: 35c, Simon Bolivar.

Perf. 12½

1960, Nov. 23 Litho. Wmk. 331

C389	A294	35c gray	3.75	60

Type of Regular Issue, 1961 (Pan-American Highway)

Perf. 10½x11

1961, Mar. 7 Unwmkd.

C390	A304	10c rose lil & emer	75	75
C391	A304	20c ver & lt bl	75	75
C392	A304	30c blk & emer	75	75

Inscribed "Extra Rapido"

C393	A304	10c dk bl & emer	75	75

Issued to commemorate the 8th Pan-American Highway Congress, Bogota, May 20–29, 1960.

Lopez Type of Regular Issue, 1961

1961, Mar. 22 Photo. *Perf. 12½*

C394	A305	35c bl & brn	60	12

Inscribed "Extra Rapido"

C395	A305	10c emer & brn	22	18

Souvenir Sheet

C396	A305	1p lil & brn	3.75	3.75

Issued to honor Alfonso Lopez (1886–1959), President of Colombia.

No. C396 contains one stamp with margin solidly printed in brown and lilac; colorless inscriptions, and black control number. Size: 60x75mm.

Brother Damian and San Francisco Church, Cali
AP75

Designs: No. 398, Emblem of University del Valle (vert.). 1.30p, Fine Arts School, Cali. 1.45p, Agricultural College, Palmira.

Perf. 13x13½, 13½x13

1961, Aug. 17 Photo. Unwmkd.

C397	AP75	35c vio brn & ol	38	10
C398	AP75	35c ol & grn	38	10
C399	AP75	1.30p sep & pink	90	75
C400	AP75	1.45p multi	90	75

Inscribed: "Extra Rapido"

Design: 10c, View of Cali (vert.).

C401	AP75	10c brn & yel grn	22	14
		Nos. C397-C401 (5)	2.78	1.84

Issued to commemorate the 50th anniversary (in 1960) of the department of Valle del Cauca.

View of Cucuta
AP76

1961, Aug. 29

C402	AP76	35c brn ol & grn	1.00	12

Inscribed: "Extra Rapido"

Design: 10c, Church of the Rosary, Cucuta (vert.).

C403	AP76	10c dk brn & gray grn	22	6

Issued to commemorate the 50th anniversary (in 1960) of the department of North Santander.

Old and New Ships at Barranquilla
AP77

Arms and View of San Gil
AP78

Hotel, Popayan
AP79

Statue of Christ in Procession
AP80

Design: 1.45p, View of Velez.

Perf. 12½x13, 13x12½

1961, Oct. 10 Photo. Unwmkd.

C404	AP77	35c gold & bl	60	7
C405	AP78	35c bl grn, yel & red	55	7
C406	AP79	35c car & brn	60	10
C407	AP78	1.45p brn & grn	60	30

Inscribed: "Extra Rapido."

C408	AP80	10c brn & yel	18	10
		Nos. C404-C408 (5)	2.53	64

Souvenir Sheets

Types of Regular and Air Post Issues

Designs, No. C409: 35c, Barranquilla arms. 40c, Popayan arms. "c," Arms and view of San Gil. "d," Holy Week in Popayan. No. C410: "a," Old and new ships at Barranquilla. "b," Hotel, Popayan. "c," Bucaramanga arms. "d," Holy Week in Popayan.

C409		Sheet of four	6.25	6.25
a.	A309	35c gold & multi	50	50
b.	A309	40c gold & multi	50	50
c.	AP78	1p bl, yel & red	1.10	1.10
d.	AP80	1p car rose & yel	1.10	1.10

Stamps Inscribed: "Extra Rapido."

C410		Sheet of four	6.25	6.25
a.	AP77	50c gold & car rose	85	85
b.	AP79	50c gold & bl	85	85
c.	A309	50c pink & multi	85	85
d.	AP80	50c bl & yel	85	85

Nos. C404–C408 are in honor of the Atlantico Department. Nos. C409–C410 are in honor of the Departments of Atlantico, Cauca and Santander. The sheets have blue marginal inscriptions, black control numbers. Size: 90x75mm.

Nos. 713, 716 and 715 Overprinted and Surcharged AEREO

1961, Sept. *Perf. 12*

C411 A297	5c grnsh bl & brn		10	6
C412 A298	5c multi		12	8
C413 A297	10c on 20c cit & gray brn		12	8

"Aereo" in script on No. C412.
See also Nos. C420–425.

Sports Type of Regular Issue, 1961

Designs: No. C414, Women divers. No. C415, Tennis, mixed doubles. 1.45p, C419b, Baseball. No. C417, Torch bearer. No. C418, C419a, Bolivar statue and flags of six participating nations. No. C419c, Soccer. No. C419d, Basketball.

1961, Dec. 16 Litho. *Perf. 13½x14*

C414	A310	35c ultra, yel & brn	75	7
C415	A310	35c car, yel & brn	75	7
C416	A310	1.45p Prus grn, yel & brn	1.10	90

Inscribed: "Extra Rapido"

C417	A310	10c car lake, yel & brn	15	7
C418	A310	10c ol, yel, bl & red	15	7
		Nos. C414-C418 (5)	2.90	1.18

Souvenir Sheet
Stamps Inscribed: "Extra Rapido."
Imperf.

C419		Sheet of four	6.00	6.00
a.	A310	50c multi	60	60
b.	A310	50c multi	60	60
c.	A310	1p multi	1.20	1.20
d.	A310	1p multi	1.20	1.20

Issued to publicize the 4th Bolivarian Games, Barranquilla, 1961. No. C419 has black marginal inscription and control number. Size: 74x106mm.

Flower Type of 1960

Flowers: 5c, Passiflora mollissima. 10c, Espeletia grandiflora. 20c, 2p, Odontoglossum luteo purpureum. 25c, Stanhopea tigrina. 60c, Anthurium Andreanum.

Photogravure

1962, Jan. 30 *Perf. 12* **Unwmkd.**

Flowers in Natural Colors

C420	A298	5c gray	17	15
C421	A298	10c gray bl	17	15
C422	A298	20c rose lil	22	15
C423	A298	25c citron	55	15
C424	A298	60c lt brn	55	15

Inscribed "Extra Rapido"

C425	A298	2p sal pink	2.25	2.00
		Nos. C420-C425 (6)	3.91	2.75

Anti-Malaria Type of Regular Issue.

Designs: 40c, Colombian anti-malaria emblem. 1p, 1.45p, Malaria eradication emblem and mosquito in swamp.

1962, Apr. 12 Litho. *Perf. 12*

C426	A311	40c yel & red	30	22
C427	A311	1.45p gray & ultra	75	65

Inscribed "Extra Rapido"

C428	A311	1p yel grn & ultra	5.75	5.75

Issued for the World Health Organization drive to eradicate malaria.

Type of Regular Issue, 1962 and

Abelardo Ramos and Engineering School, Cauca
AP81

Designs: 10c, Miguel Triana, Andres A. Arroyo and Monserrate shrine with cable cars. 15c, Diodoro Sanchez and first meeting place of Engineers Society. 2p, Engineers Society emblem.

1962, June 12 Photo. *Perf. 11½x12*

C429	AP81	5c bl & dp rose	15	10
C430	AP81	10c grn & sep	20	15
C431	AP81	15c lil & sep	45	38

Inscribed: "Extra Rapido"

C432	A312	2p blk, yel, red & bl	2.25	2.25

Issued to commemorate the 75th anniversary of the founding of the Colombian Society of Engineers and to publicize the Sixth National Congress of Engineers.

American States Type of 1962.

1962, June 28 Photo. *Perf. 13*

Flags in National Colors

C433	A313	35c blk & bl	50	7

Type of Regular Issue, 1962 (Women's Rights)
Perf. 12x12½

1962, July 20 Litho. Wmk. 229

C434	A314	35c ocher, gray & blk	38	5

Issued to publicize women's political rights. See also Nos. C448–C450.

Scout Type of 1962.

Designs: 15c, No. C438, Scouts at campfire and tents. 40c and No. C437, Girl Scouts.

Perf. 11½x12

1962, July 26 Photo. Unwmkd.

C435	A315	15c brn & rose	38	30
C436	A315	40c dp cl & pink	45	30
C437	A315	1p bl & buff	1.40	45

Inscribed "Extra Rapido"

C438	A315	1p pur & yel	5.25	5.25

Nos. C435 and C438 issued to commemorate the 30th anniversary of the Colombian Boy Scouts. Nos. C436 and C437 commemorate the 25th anniversary of the Girl Scouts.

Nativity by Gregorio Vasquez
AP82

Design: 2p, St. Isidro, similar to type A302.

Inscribed "Extra Rapido"
Photogravure

1962, Aug. 28 *Perf. 12* **Unwmkd.**

C439	AP82	10c gray & multi	15	8
C440	AP82	2p gray & multi	4.50	4.50

See also Nos. C387–C388.

Type of Regular Issue, 1962 and

Pres. Aquileo Parra and Magdalena River Bridge
AP83

Design: 5c, Locomotives of 1854 and 1961. 10c, Railroad map of Colombia.

1962, Sept. 28 Photo. *Perf. 12½*

C441	AP83	5c sep & sl grn	22	8
C442	A316	10c multi	22	8

Engraved

C443	AP83	1p dl pur & brn	1.50	30

Inscribed: "Extra Rapido."

C444	AP83	5p bl, brn & dl grn	5.25	2.00

Issued to publicize the progress of Colombian railroads and to commemorate the completion of the Atlantic Line from Santa Maria to Bogota.

UPAE Type of Regular Issue

Designs: 50c, Map of Americas and carrier pigeon. 60c, Post horn.

Perf. 13½x14

1962, Oct. 18 Litho. Wmk. 346

C445	A317	50c sl grn & gold	45	15
C446	A317	60c gold & plum	30	8

Issued to commemorate the 50th anniversary of the founding of the Postal Union of the Americas and Spain, UPAE.

Pope John XXIII
AP84

1963, Mar. 11

C447	AP84	60c gold, red brn, buff & red	30	8

Issued to commemorate Vatican II, the 21st Ecumenical Council of the Roman Catholic Church.

Type of Regular Issue, 1962 (Women's Rights)

1963–64 *Perf. 12x12½*

C448	A314	5c sal, gray & blk ('64)	6	3
C449	A314	45c pale grn, gray & blk	40	3
C450	A314	45c brt pink, gray & blk	40	3

Games Emblem
AP85

Perf. 13x14

1963, Aug. 12 Wmk. 346

C451	AP85	20c gray & multi	22	7
C452	AP85	80c buff & multi	22	7

Issued to commemorate the South American Athletic Championships (22nd for men, 12th for women), Cali, June 30–July 7.

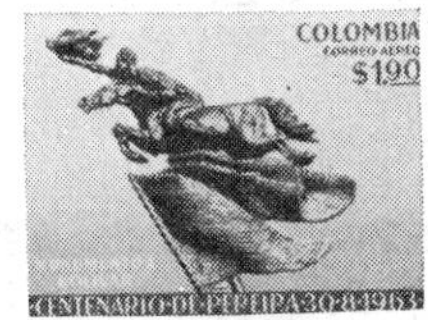

Bolivar Statue by Arenas-Betancourt
AP86

Perf. 14x13½

1963, Aug. 30 Unwmkd.

C453	AP86	1.90p ol bis & bl	38	7

Centenary of the city of Pereira.

Tennis Player
AP87

1963, Oct. 11 *Perf. 13½x14*

C454	AP87	55c multi	15	8

Issued to commemorate the 30th South American Tennis Championships, Medellin, Oct. 3–13.

Pres. John F. Kennedy and Alliance for Progress Emblem
AP88

1963, Dec. 17 Litho. *Perf. 14x13½*

C455	AP88	10c multi	5	3

Issued to honor President John F. Kennedy (1917–1963).

Church of the True Cross, National Pantheon, Bogota
AP89

Design: 2p, Christ of the Martyrs, bell and tomb.

Perf. 13½x14

1964, Mar. 10 Photo. Unwmkd.

C459	AP89	1p multi	38	8
C460	AP89	2p multi	55	30

View of Cartagena
AP90

1964, Mar. 18 Litho. *Perf. 14x13½*

C461	AP90	3p vio, bl, ocher & brn	2.00	75

Issued to commemorate Cartagena's independence in 1811, Simon Bolivar's visit in 1812 and the siege of 1815.

Eleanor Roosevelt
AP91

1964, Nov. 10 Photo. *Perf. 12*

C462	AP91	20c ol & dl red brn	8	8

Issued to honor Eleanor Roosevelt (1884–1962).

Alberto Castilla and Score of "El Bunde"
AP92

1964, Nov. 10 Unwmkd.

C463	AP92	30c ol bis & Prus grn	10	8

Issued to honor the Department of Tolima and Maestro Alberto Castilla (1878–1937) who in 1906 founded the Tolima Conservatory of Music in Ibague.

Mejia Type of Regular Issue

Designs (Mejia portrait and): 45c, Women picking coffee. 5p, Mules carrying coffee bags. 10p, Loading coffee on freighter "Manuel Mejia."

1965, Feb. 10 Engr. *Perf. 12½x13*

C464	A320	45c brn & blk	30	8
C465	A320	5p gray grn & blk	3.00	75
C466	A320	10p ultra & blk	6.00	45

Issued to honor Manuel Mejia J. (1887–1958), banker and manager of the National Coffee Growers Association.

ITU Emblem
AP93

1965, Oct. 25 Photo. *Perf. 12*

C467	AP93	80c Prus bl, lt bl & red	22	8

Issued to commemorate the centenary of the International Telecommunication Union.

Cattleya Truanae
AP94

Pres. Manuel Murillo Toro Statue, Telegraph and Orbits
AP95

1965, Oct. 3 Litho. *Perf. 13½x14*

C468	AP94	20c yel & multi	8	6

Fifth Philatelic Exhibition.

1965, Nov. 1 *Perf. 13½x14, 14x13½*

Design: No. C470, Telegraph and satellites over South America (horiz.).

C469	AP95	60c multi	22	8
C470	AP95	60c multi	22	5

Centenary of the telegraph in Colombia.

Junkers F-13 Seaplane, 1920
AP96

History of Colombian Aviation: 10c, Dornier Wal, 1924. 20c, Dornier Mercur, 1926. 50c, Trimotor Ford, 1932. 60c, De Havilland biplane, 1930. 1p, Douglas DC-4, 1947. 1.40p, Douglas DC-3, 1944. 2.80p, Superconstellation 1049, 1951. 3p, Boeing 720B jet, 1961.

Perf. 14x13½

1965-66 Photo. Unwmkd.

C471	AP96	5c multi	10	7
C472	AP96	10c multi	10	7
C473	AP96	20c multi	18	8
C474	AP96	50c multi	18	8
C475	AP96	60c multi	28	5
C476	AP96	1p multi	45	15
C477	AP96	1.40p multi	60	22
C478	AP96	2.80p multi	1.25	75
C479	AP96	3p multi	1.50	90
		Nos. C471-C479 (9)	4.64	2.37

Issue dates: 5c, 60c, 3p, Dec. 13, 1965; 10c, 1p, 1.40p, July 15, 1966; 20c, 50c, 2.80p, Dec. 14, 1966.

Automobile Club Emblem and Car on Road
AP97

1966, Feb. 16 Litho. *Perf. 14x13½*

C480	AP97	20c multi	8	6

Issued to commemorate the 25th anniversary (in 1965) of the Automobile Club of Colombia.

Fish Type of Regular Issue, 1966.

Fish: 2p, Flying fish. 2.80p, Queen angelfish. 20p, King mackerel.

1966, Aug. 25 Photo. *Perf. 12½x13*

C481	A323	2p multi	75	30
C482	A323	2.80p multi	1.50	1.50
C483	A323	20p multi	12.50	12.50

Coat of Arms Type of Regular Issue, 1966

1966, Oct. 11 Litho. *Perf. 14x13½*

C484	A324	1p ultra & multi	40	10
C485	A324	1.40p red & multi	33	10

Issued to commemorate the visits of Eduardo Frei and Raul Leoni, presidents of Chile and Venezuela.

Portrait Type of Regular Issue

Portraits: 80c, Father Felix Restrepo Mejia, S.J. (1887—1965), theologian and scholar. 1.70p, José Joaquin Casas (1866–1951), educator and diplomat.

Perf. 13½x14

1967, Jan. 18 Litho. Unwmkd.

C486	A325	80c dk bl & bis	15	3
C487	A325	1.70p blk & bis	38	15

Famous men of Colombia.

Declaration of Bogota Type of Regular Issue

1967, Feb. 2 Litho. *Perf. 14x13½*

C488	A326	3p multi	55	22

See note after No. 767.

Orchid Type of Regular Issue

Orchids: 1p, Cattleya dowiana aurea (vert.). 1.20p, Masdevallia coccinea (vert.). 5p, Catasetum macrocarpum and bee.

1967, May 23 Litho. *Perf. 14*

C489	A327	1p multi	60	22
C490	A327	1.20p multi	38	10
C491	A327	5p multi	2.25	60
a.		Souv. sheet of 3	2.50	2.50

Issued to commemorate the First National Orchid Exhibition and the Topical Philatelic Flora and Fauna Exhibition, Medellin, Apr. 1967. No. C491a contains one each of Nos. C489–C491. Gray margin with black inscription and red control number. Size: 99x149mm.

Lions Type of Regular Issue

1967, July 12 Litho. *Perf. 13½x14*

C492	A328	25c multi	22	7

Lions International, 50th anniversary.

"First Caesarean Section" by Grau
AP98

Perf. 14x13½

1967, Sept. 7 Litho. Unwmkd.

C493	AP98	80c multi	15	5

Issued to publicize the 6th Congress of Colombian Surgeons, Bogota, Sept. 25.

SENA Type of Regular Issue

Lithographed and Embossed

1967, Sept. 20 *Perf. 13½x14*

C494	A329	2p gold, ver & blk	75	15

Issued to commemorate the 10th anniversary of National Apprenticeship Service, SENA.

Pre-Columbian Art Type of Regular Issue

Designs: 30c, Bird pectoral. 5p Ornamental pectoral. 20p, Pitcher.

Photogravure

1967, Oct. 13 *Perf. 13½x14*

C495	A330	30c ver, gold & brn	25	8
C496	A330	5p red, gold & brn	2.50	50
a.		Souvenir sheet of 2	2.25	2.25
C497	A330	20p vio, gold & brn	11.00	9.00

Issued to commemorate the meeting of the Universal Postal Union Committee on Postal Studies, Bogota, October, 1967; No. C496a also commemorates the 6th National Philatelic Exhibition. No. C496a contains 2 imperf. stamps in changed colors similar to Nos. C495–C496 (30c has green background and 5 p maroon background). Gray margin with red control number. Size: 92x91mm.

Telecommunications Type of Regular Issue

Designs: 50c, Signal lights. 1p, Early Bird satellite, Southern Cross and radar.

Perf. 13½x14

1968, May 14 Litho. Unwmkd.

C498	A331	50c blk, ver & emer	15	10
C499	A331	1p ultra, yel & gray	28	5

Issued to commemorate the 20th anniversary of the National Telecommunications Service (TELECOM).

Eucharist Type of Regular Issue

1968, June 6 Litho. *Perf. 13½x14*

C500	A332	80c rose lil, red, yel & blk	15	5
C501	A332	3p bl, red, yel & blk	55	15

Issued to publicize the 39th Eucharistic Congress, Bogotá, Aug. 18–25.

Eucharistic Congress Type of Regular Issue

Designs: 80c, The Last Supper, by Gregorio Vasquez (horiz.). 1p, St. Francis Xavier Preaching, by Gregorio Vasquez. 2p, The Dream of the Prophet Elias, by Gregorio Vasquez. 3p, Monstrance, c. 1700. 20p, Pope Paul VI, painting by Roman Franciscan nuns.

1968, Aug. 13 Photo. *Perf. 13*

C502	A333	80c multi	22	5
C503	A333	1p multi	30	5
C504	A333	2p multi	55	15
C505	A333	3p lil & multi	90	15
C506	A333	20p gold & multi	5.75	2.75
		Nos. C502-C506 (5)	7.72	3.15

Issued to commemorate the 39th Eucharistic Congress, Bogotá, Aug. 18–25.

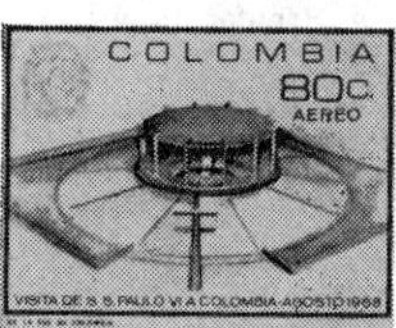

Shrine of the Eucharist, Bogotá
AP99

Designs: 1.20p, Pope Paul VI giving blessing and Papal arms (vert.). 1.80p, Cathedral of Bogotá (vert.).

Perf. 14x13½, 13½x14

1968, Aug. 22 Lithographed

C507	AP99	80c multi	15	7
C508	AP99	1.20p multi	25	15
C509	AP99	1.80p multi	45	22

Visit of Pope Paul VI to Colombia.

Computer Symbols
AP100

1968, Oct. 29 Litho. *Perf. 13½x14*

C510	AP100	20c buff, car & grn	10	5

Issued to commemorate the centenary of the National University and the First Data Processing Congress in 1967 at the University.

Agriculture Institute Type of Regular Issue

1968, Mar. 5 Litho. *Perf. 13½x14*

C511	A337	1p gray & multi	30	8

Issued to commemorate the 25th anniversary (in 1967) of the Inter-American Agricultural Sciences Institute.

Microscope and Pen—AP101

1969, Mar. 24 Litho. *Perf. 14*

C512	AP101	5p blk, yel, ver & pur	1.50	15

Issued to commemorate the 20th anniversary (in 1968) of the University of the Andes.

Alexander von Humboldt and Andes
AP102

1969, May 3 Litho. *Perf. 14x13½*

C513 AP102 1p grn & brn 22 8

Issued to commemorate the bicentenary of the birth of Alexander von Humboldt (1769–1859), German naturalist and traveler.

Map of Colombia, Amphibian Plane and Letter
AP103

Design: 1.50p, No. C516b, Globe, letter, and jet of Avianca airlines.

1969, June 18 Litho. *Perf. 14x13½*

C514 AP103 1p multi 28 6
C515 AP103 1.50p multi 35 15

Souvenir Sheet
Imperf.

C516 AP103 Sheet of 2 4.00 4.00
a. 5p grn & multi 1.00 1.00
b. 5p vio & multi 1.00 1.00

Issued to commemorate the 50th anniversary of the first air post flight in Colombia. No. C516 also publicizes the 8th National Philatelic Exhibition, EXFILBA 69, Barranquilla, June 18–22. No. C516 contains 2 stamps in the designs of the 1p and 1.50p; gray margin with commemorative inscription, coats of arms and red control number. Size: 92x92mm.

Independence Type of Regular Issue

1969, July 24 Litho. *Perf. 13½x14*

Design: 2.30p, Simon Bolivar, José Antonio Anzoategui, Francisco de Paula Santander and victorious army entering Bogotá, Sept. 18, 1819; painting by Ignacio Castillo Cervantes.

C517 A338 2.30p gold & multi 45 22

Issued to commemorate the sesquicentennial of the fight for independence.

Social Security Emblem
AP104

Neurosurgeons' Congress Emblem
AP105

1969, Oct. 29 Litho. *Perf. 13½x14*

C518 AP104 20c emer & blk 15 8

Issued to commemorate the 20th anniversary of the Colombian Institute of Social Security.

1969, Oct. 29

C519 AP105 70c vio, red & yel 30 6

Issued to publicize the 13th Congress of Latin-American Neurosurgeons, Bogotá.

Junkers F-13
AP106

Designs: No. C521, C522b, Globe with airlines from Bogota and Boeing jet. No. C522a, like No. C520.

1969, Nov. 28 Litho. *Perf. 14x13½*

C520 AP106 2p grn & multi 45 15
C521 AP106 3.50p ultra & multi 70 40

Souvenir Sheet
Imperf.

C522 AP106 Sheet of 2 4.00 4.00
a. 3.50p lt grn & multi 75 75
b. 5p ultra & multi 1.10 1.10

Issued to commemorate the 50th anniversary of AVIANCA; No. C522 also publicizes the First Interamerican Philatelic Exhibition, Bogota, Nov. 28–Dec. 7.

No. C522 contains 2 imperf. stamps. Multicolored inscriptions, coat of arms, medals and red control number on light olive margin. Size: 92x90mm.

Child Mailing Letter
AP107

Design: 1.50p, Praying child and gifts.

1969, Dec. 16 Litho. *Perf. 13½x14*

C523 AP107 60c ocher & multi 75 22
C524 AP107 1p multi 75 8
C525 AP107 1.50p multi 90 22

Christmas 1969.

Radar Station and Pre-Columbian Head
AP108

1970, Mar. 25 Litho. *Perf. 14x13½*

C526 AP108 1p dl grn, blk & brick red 45 3

Issued to publicize the opening of the communications satellite earth station at Chocontá in Cundinamarca Province.

Emblem of Colombian Youth Sports Institute
AP109

Art Exhibition Emblem
AP110

Design: 2.30p, Games' emblem (dove and 3 rings).

1970, Apr. 6 Litho. *Perf. 13½x14*

C527 AP109 1.50p dk ol grn, yel & blk 45 30
C528 AP109 2.30p red & multi 60 30

Issued to publicize the 9th National Youth Games, Ibague, July 10–20.

1970, Apr. 30 Litho. *Perf. 13½x14*

C529 AP110 30c multi 15 8

Issued to publicize the 2nd Biennial Art Exhibition, Medellin, May 1–June 14.

Eduardo Santos, Rural and Urban Buildings
AP111

1970, June 18 Litho. *Perf. 14x13½*

C530 AP111 1p grn, yel & blk 30 5

Issued to commemorate the founding (in 1939) of the Territorial Credit Institute.

U.N. Emblem, Scales and Dove
AP112

EXFILCA Emblem
AP113

1970, June 26 *Perf. 13½x14*

C531 AP112 1.50p dk bl, lt bl & yel 30 7

25th anniversary of United Nations.

1970, Nov. Litho. *Perf. 13½x14*

C532 AP113 10p bl, gold & blk 4.25 38

Issued to publicize EXFILCA 70, 2nd Interamerican Philatelic Exhibition. Caracas, Venezuela, Nov. 27–Dec. 6.

Mother Juana Ruperta in Napanga Costume and Music by Efrain Orozco
AP114

Athlete and Games Emblem
AP115

Designs: 1p, Dancers from Eastern Plains and music by Alejandro Wills. No. C535, Guabina man, woman and folk song. No. C536, Bambuco man and woman, and music. No. C537, Man and woman dancing the Cumbia, and music.

1970–71 Litho. *Perf. 13½x14*

C533 AP114 60c dp lil rose & multi 60 12
C534 AP114 1p ultra & multi 55 8
C535 AP114 1.30p bl & multi 55 10
C536 AP114 1.30p emer & multi ('71) 55 10
C537 AP114 1.30p lil & multi ('71) 55 10
Nos. C533-C537 (5) 2.80 50

1971, Mar. 11

Design: 2p, Games emblem.

C542 AP115 1.50p multi 1.10 75
C543 AP115 2p blk, org & grn 1.10 60

6th Pan-American Games, Cali, July 30–Aug. 13.

Gilberto Alzate Avendaño
AP116

1971, Apr. 29 Litho. *Perf. 14x13½*

C544 AP116 1p bl & multi 75 38

Gilberto Alzate Avendaño (1910–1960), journalist and popular leader, 10th anniversary of death.

Commemorative Medal
AP117

Lithographed and Embossed

1971, June 21 *Perf. 14x13½*

C545 AP117 1p sl grn & gold 70 45

Centenary (in 1970) of the Bank of Bogota.

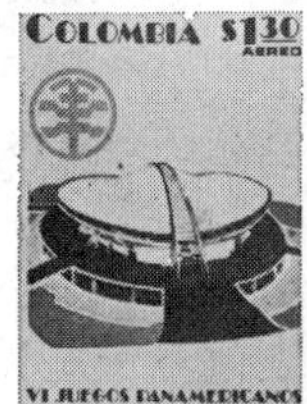

Olympic Center
AP118

Soccer
AP119

Designs (Games Emblem and): Nos. C546–C546c, Olympic Center. No. 547, Soccer. No. C548, Wrestling. No. C549, Bicycling. No. C550, Volleyball. No. C551, Diving (women). No. C552, Fencing. No. C553, Sailing. No. C554, Equestrian. No. C555, Jumping. No. C556, Rowing. No. C557, Cali emblem. No. C558, Basketball (women). No. C559, Stadium. No. C560, Baseball. No. C561, Hockey. No. C562, Weight lifting. No. C563, Medals. No. C564, Boxing. No. C565, Gymnastics (women). No. C566, Sharpshooting.

1971, July 16 Litho. *Perf. 13½x14*

C546 AP118 1.30p yel & multi 1.50 45
a. 1.30p grn & multi 1.50 45
b. 1.30p bl & multi 1.50 45
c. 1.30p car & multi 1.50 45
C547 AP119 1.30p emer & multi 1.50 45
C548 AP119 1.30p lil & multi 1.50 45
C549 AP119 1.30p bl & multi 1.50 45
C550 AP119 1.30p car & multi 1.50 45
C551 AP119 1.30p bl & multi 1.50 45
C552 AP119 1.30p car & multi 1.50 45
C553 AP119 1.30p bl & multi 1.50 45
C554 AP119 1.30p gray & multi 1.50 45
C555 AP119 1.30p grn & multi 1.50 45
C556 AP119 1.30p bl & multi 1.50 45
C557 AP118 1.30p org & multi 1.50 45
C558 AP119 1.30p car & multi 1.50 45
C559 AP118 1.30p lt bl & multi 1.50 45
C560 AP119 1.30p plum & multi 1.50 45
C561 AP119 1.30p yel grn & multi 1.50 45
C562 AP119 1.30p pink & multi 1.50 45

C563	AP118	1.30p dp org & multi	1.50	45
C564	AP119	1.30p plum & multi	1.50	45
C565	AP119	1.30p lil rose & multi	1.50	45
C566	AP119	1.30p grn & multi	1.50	45
a.		Sheet of 25 (Nos. C546-C566)	40.00	17.50

6th Pan American Athletic Games, Cali. First color in listings is color of emblem. No. C546b appears twice in sheet. No. C566a has marginal multicolored inscription commemorating EXFILCALI 71 Philatelic Exhibition.

Battle of Carabobo, by Martin Tovar y Tovar—AP120

1971, Nov. 25 Litho. *Perf. 13½x14*

C567	AP120	1.50p multi	60	38

Sesquicentennial of the Battle of Carabobo.

St. Theresa Type of Regular Issue Overprinted "AEREO"

1972 Lithographed *Perf. 13½x14*

C568	A343	2p multi	45	5

See note after No. 793.

Vendor AP121

Designs: 50c, Woman wearing shawl, and woven shawl. 3p, Fruit vendor (puppet).

1971, Apr. 11 Litho. *Perf. 13½x14*

C569	AP121	50c multi	38	38
C570	AP121	1p multi	30	22
C571	AP121	3p multi	60	38

Colombian artisans.

Mormodes Rolfeanum AP122

1972, Apr. 20 *Perf. 14x13½*

C572	AP122	1.30p multi	50	5

7th World Orchidology Congress, Medellin.

Congo Grande Dancer AP123

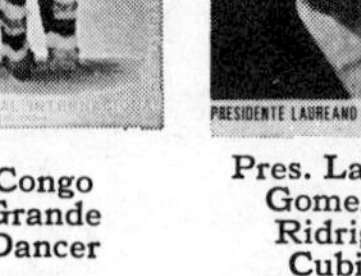

Pres. Laureano Gomez, by Ridriguez Cubillos AP124

1972, June 21 Litho. *Perf. 13½x14*

C573	AP123	1.30p multi	60	7

International Carnival of Barranquilla.

No. C453 Surcharged in Brown **$ 1.30**

1972, Oct. 5 Litho. *Perf. 14x13½*

C574	AP86	1.30p on 1.90p ol bis & bl	1.00	30

1972, Oct. 17 *Perf. 13½x14*

C575	AP124	1.30p multi	22	5

Laureano Gomez (1898–1966), President of Colombia.

1972, Nov. 28

Design: 1.30p, Guillermo León Valencia Muñoz.

C576	AP124	1.30p multi	30	5

Guillermo León Valencia Muñoz (1909–1971), President of Colombia.

Benito Juarez AP125

Rebecca Fountain AP126

1972, Dec. 12 *Perf. 13½x14*

C577	AP125	1.50p multi	38	15

Centenary of the death of Benito Juarez (1806–1872), revolutionary leader and president of Mexico.

1972, Dec. 19 Lithographed

C578	AP126	80c multi	75	45
C579	AP126	1p multi	55	22

"Bucaramanga" AP127

1972, Dec. 22 *Perf. 14x13¼*

C580	AP127	5p multi	1.25	8

350th anniversary of the founding of Bucaramanga.

Xavier University AP128

1973, May 8 Litho. *Perf. 14x13½*

C581	AP128	1.30p lt grn & sep	45	8
C582	AP128	1.50p lt bl & sep	45	8

350th anniversary of the founding of Xavier University in Bogotá.

Ceramic Type of Regular Issue

Excavated Ceramic Artifacts: 1p, Winged urn, Tairona. 1.30p, Woman and child, Sinu. 1.70p, Two-headed figure, Quimbaya. 3.50p, Man, Tumaco.

1973 Lithographed *Perf. 13½x14*

C583	A358	1p multi	1.40	1.40
C584	A358	1.30p multi	75	8
C585	A358	1.70p multi	60	30
C586	A358	3.50p multi	1.25	45

Issue dates: 1p, Oct. 11; others, June 15.

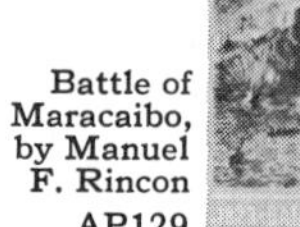

Battle of Maracaibo, by Manuel F. Rincon AP129

1973, July 24 Litho. *Perf. 14x13½*

C587	AP129	10p bl & multi	3.00	22

Battle of Maracaibo, sesquicentennial.

Bank Emblem AP130

1973, Oct. 1 Litho. *Perf. 14x13½*

C588	AP130	2p multi	40	8

50th anniversary of the Bank of the Republic.

No. 801 Overprinted "AEREO"

1973, Oct. 11 *Perf. 14*

C589	A346	80c multi	45	15

Pres. Pedro Nel Ospina, by Coroleano Leudo AP131

Arms of Toro AP132

1973, Nov. 9 *Perf. 13½x14*

C590	AP131	1.50p multi	30	8

50th anniversary of the Ministry of Communications founded under Pres. Ospina.

1973, Dec. 1

C591	AP132	1p multi	22	8

4th centenary of the founding of Toro, Valle del Cauca.

Bolivar, Battle of Bombona AP133

1973, Dec. 7 Litho. *Perf. 14x13½*

C592	AP133	1.30p multi	22	6

Sesquicentennial (in 1972) of the Battle of Bombona.

Nicolaus Copernicus AP134

Andes, Map of South America AP135

1974, Feb. 19 Litho. *Perf. 13½x14*

C593	AP134	2.50p multi	70	30

500th anniversary of the birth of Nicolaus Copernicus (1473–1543), Polish astronomer.

1974, May 11 Litho. *Perf. 14*

C594	AP135	2p multi	45	15

Meeting of Communications Ministers of Members of the Andean Group, Cali, May 7–11, 1974.

Television Set AP136

1974, July 16 Litho. *Perf. 14x13½*

C595	AP136	1.30p org, blk & brn	30	8

20th anniversary of Colombian television and 10th anniversary of INRAVISION, the National Institute of Radio and Television.

Championship Emblem AP137

1974, Aug. 5 Litho. *Perf. 14x13½*

C596	AP137	4.50p multi	55	22

2nd World Swimming Championships, Cali.

Condor—AP138

1974, Aug. 28 *Perf. 14*

C597	AP138	1.50p multi	30	15

Bank of Colombia centenary.

UPU Envelope AP139

1974, Sept. 9 Litho. *Perf. 14*

C598	AP139	20p multi	2.75	60

Centenary of Universal Postal Union.

Symbol of Flight AP140

1974, Sept. *Perf. 12x12½*

C599	AP140	20c olive	8	5

Gen. José Maria Cordoba
AP141

COLOMBIA $1.00 AEREO UPU BERNA-SUIZA 1874-1974

White-tailed Trogon, Letter
AP142

1974, Oct. 14 Litho. *Perf. 13½x14*

C609 AP141 1.30p multi 30 8

Sesquicentennial of the Battles of Junin and Ayacucho.

Insurance Type of 1974

Design: 3p, Abstract pattern.

1974, Oct. 24 Litho. *Perf. 13½x14*

C610 A365 3p multi 45 15

Centenary of National Insurance Company.

Perf. 13½x14, 14x13½

1974, Nov. 14

Designs (UPU Letter and): 1.30p, Keel-billed Toucan (horiz.). 2p, Peruvian cock-of-the-rock (horiz.). 2.50p, Scarlet macaw.

C611 AP142 1p multi 30 12
C612 AP142 1.30p multi 38 5
C613 AP142 2p multi 45 6
C614 AP142 2.50p multi 38 15

Centenary of Universal Postal Union.

Forest No. 1, by Roman Roncancio—AP143

Girl with Thorn in Finger, by Gregorio Vazquez
AP144

Paintings: 3p, Women Fruit Vendors, by Miguel Diaz Vargas (1886–1956). 5p, Annunciation, Santafereña School, 17th–18th centuries.

Perf. 13½x14, 14x13½

1975, Mar. 12 Lithographed

C615 AP143 2p multi 90 7
C616 AP144 3p multi 55 8
C617 AP144 4p multi 65 15
C618 AP144 5p multi 1.00 40

Modern and Colonial Colombian paintings.

Trees and Lake
AP145

Design: 6p, Victoria regia, Amazon River.

1975, Mar. 12 *Perf. 14x13½*

C619 AP145 1p yel & multi 22 8
C620 AP145 6p yel & multi 65 15

Nature conservation of trees and Amazon Region.

Gold Treasure Type of 1975

Designs: 2p, Nose pendant. 10p, Alligator-shaped staff ornament.

1975, Apr. 11 Litho. *Perf. 14x13½*

C621 A368 2p grn, gold & brn 55 8
C622 A368 10p multi 3.00 75

Pre-Columbian Sinu Culture artifacts.

El Rodadero, Santa Maria
AP146

1975, July 26 Litho. *Perf. 14x13½*

C623 AP146 2p multi 30 5

400th anniversary of Santa Maria City.

Maria de J. Paramo
AP147

1975, Aug. 31 Litho. *Perf. 13½x14*

C624 AP147 4p multi 38 8

International Women's Year 1975. Maria de Jesus Paramo de Collazos founded first normal school for women in Bucaramanga in 1875.

"Sugar Cane"
AP148

1976, Mar. 12 Litho. *Perf. 13½x14*

C625 AP148 5p blk & emer 1.25 22

4th Congress of Latin-American and Caribbean sugar-exporting countries, Cali, Mar. 8–12.

View of Bogota—AP149

1976, July 2 Litho. *Perf. 12*

Blue and Multicolored

C626 AP149 10p *shown* 1.50 90
C627 AP149 10p *Barranquilla* 1.50 90
C628 AP149 10p *Cali* 1.50 90
C629 AP149 10p *Medellin* 1.50 90

Habitat, U.N. Conference on Human Settlements, Vancouver, Canada, May 31–June 11. Nos. C626–C629 printed se-tenant in blocks of 4, sheets of 60.

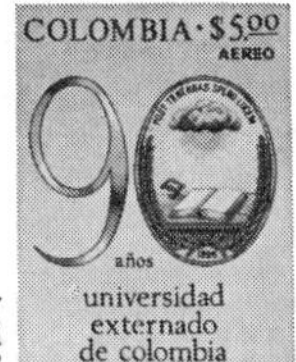

University Emblem and "90"
AP150

1976, Aug. 6 Litho. *Perf. 13½x14*

C630 AP150 5p lt bl & multi 75 15

University of Colombia, 90th anniversary.

Miguel Samper AP151 — Telephone, 1895 AP152

1976, Oct. 29 Litho. *Perf. 13½x14*

C631 AP151 2p multi 30 8

Miguel Samper (1825–1899), economist and writer.

1976, Nov. 2

C632 AP152 3p multi 22 8

Centenary of first telephone call by Alexander Graham Bell, Mar. 10, 1876.

747 Jumbo Jet
AP153

1976, Dec. 3 Litho. *Perf. 12*

C633 AP153 2p multi 22 8

Inauguration of 747 jumbo jet service by Avianca.

Convent, Church and Plaza de San Francisco—AP154

1976, Dec. 29 Litho. *Perf. 14*

C634 AP154 6p multi 75 30

150th anniversary of the Congress of Panama.

Souvenir Sheet

Bank of the Republic Emblem—AP155

1977, June 6 Litho. *Perf. 14*

C635 AP155 25p multi 7.50 7.50

Opening of Philatelic Museum of Medellin under auspices of Banco de la Republica. No. C635 contains one stamp (50x40mm.); multicolored margin shows various orchids; black control number. Size: 130x105mm.

No. C633 Surcharged in Light Brown

1977, June Litho. *Perf. 12*

C636 AP153 3p on 2p multi 22 8

Coffee
AP156

COLOMBIA $10.00 Aereo 50 Años Federación Nacional de Cafeteros

Coffee Grower, Pack Mule
AP157

1977–78 Litho. *Perf. 12½*

C640 AP156 3p multi 22 5
C641 AP156 3.50p multi ('78) 30 5

Colombian coffee.

1977, Aug. 9 Litho. *Perf. 13½x14*

C642 AP157 10p multi 75 10

National Federation of Coffee Growers, 50th anniversary.

Beethoven and 9th Symphony
AP158

AEREO $6.00 COLOMBIA

Games' Emblem
AP159

1977, Aug. 17

C643 AP158 8p multi 75 15

Sesquicentennial of the death of Ludwig van Beethoven (1770–1827).

Bird Type of 1977

Tropical Birds and Plants: No. C644, Woodpecker and meriania. C645, Purple gallinule and water lilies. No. C646, Xipholaena punicea and cochlospermum orinocense. No. C647, Crowned flycatcher and jacaranda copaia.

1977, Sept. 6 Litho. *Perf. 14*

C644 A380 5p multi 60 15
C645 A380 5p multi 60 15
C646 A380 10p multi 75 22
C647 A380 10p multi 75 22

1977, Sept. 9 *Perf. 12x12½*

C648 AP159 6p multi 38 15

13th Central American and Caribbean Games, Medellin, 1978.

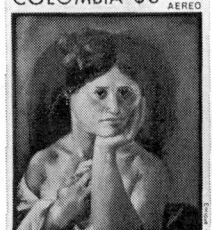

COLOMBIA $8.00 AEREO

La Cayetana, by Enrique Grau
AP160

Design: No. C650, Water Nymphs, by Beatriz Gonzalez.

1977, Sept. 13 ***Perf. 14x13½***

C649 AP160 8p multi 65 22
C650 AP160 8p multi 65 22

Women's suffrage, 20th anniversary.

Judge Francisco Antonio Moreno by, Joaquin Gutierrez
AP161

Design: 25p, Viceroy Manuel de Guirior.

1977, Sept. 13 ***Perf. 12***

C651 AP161 20p multi 1.75 75
C652 AP161 25p multi 2.50 90

Bicentenary of National Library.

Federico Lleras Acosta
AP162

Cauca University Arms
AP163

1977, Sept. 27 **Litho.** ***Perf. 14***

C653 AP162 5p multi 38 15

Dr. Federico Lleras Acosta, veterinarian and bacteriologist; birth centenary.

1977, Oct. 14

C654 AP163 5p multi 45 15

Sesquicentennial of the University of Cauca.

CUDECOM Building, Bogota
AP164

1977, Oct. 14

C655 AP164 1.50p multi 18 6

Colombian Society of Engineers, 90th anniversary.

No. C612 Surcharged with New Value and Bars in Brown

1977, Dec. 3 **Litho.** ***Perf. 14x13½***

C656 AP142 2p on 1.30p multi 45 15

Lost City, Tayrona Culture
AP165

Creator of Energy, by Arenas Betancourt
AP166

1978, Apr. 18 Litho. ***Perf. 12½***

C657 AP165 3.50p multi 30 5

1978, Apr. 25 ***Perf. 12***

C658 AP166 4p bl & multi 38 15

Sesquicentennial of Antioquia University Law School.

Column of the Slaves
AP167

Statue of Catalina, Cartagena
AP168

1978, May 9

C659 AP167 2.50p multi 30 15

Sesquicentennial of Ocaña Convention (meeting of various political groups).

1978, May 30 **Litho.** ***Perf. 12***

C660 AP168 4p blk & lt bl 38 15

Sesquicentennial of University of Cartagena.

Gold Pendant, Tolima
AP169

1978, July 11 **Litho.** ***Perf. 12x12½***

C661 AP169 3.50p multi 30 5

Apotheosis of Spanish Language, by Luis Alberto Acuña—AP170

1978, Aug. 9 ***Perf. 14***

C662 AP170 Strip of 3, multi 6.00 6.75
a. 11p, single stamp 1.50 1.50

Millennium of Spanish language. No. C662 printed in sheets of 15 (3x5). Black control number.

Presidential Guard
AP171

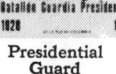

Figure, Muisca Culture
AP172

1978, Aug. 16 ***Perf. 13½x14***

C663 AP171 9p multi 65 45

Presidential Guard Battalion, 50th anniversary.

1978, Sept. 12 **Litho.** ***Perf. 12½***

C664 AP172 3.50p multi 30 5

Apse of Carmelite Church
AP173

1978, Oct. 12 ***Perf. 13***

C665 AP173 30p multi 4.00 85

Souvenir Sheet

Perf. 13½x14

C666 AP173 50p multi 3.75 3.75

ESPAMER '78 Philatelic Exhibition, Bogota, Oct. 12–21. No. C666 contains one stamp; multicolored margin shows enlarged stamp design, ESPAMER emblem and black control number. Size: 125x95mm.

Owl, Gold Ornament, Calima
AP174

Virgin and Child, by Gregorio Vasquez
AP175

1978, Nov. 28 ***Perf. 12½***

C667 AP174 3.50p multi 30 5

1979, May 10 **Litho.** ***Perf. 12½***

C668 AP174 4p multi 30 8

1979, July 17 **Litho.** ***Perf. 12½***

Design: Gold frog, Quimbaya culture.

C669 AP174 5p multi 25 5

1978, Nov. 28 ***Perf. 13½x14***

C671 AP175 2.50p multi 20 8

Christmas 1978.

Bull Ring, Cathedral, Manizales
AP176

1979, Jan. 6 **Litho.** ***Perf. 14***

C672 AP176 7p multi 75 18

Manizales Fair.

Children Playing Hopscotch, and IYC Emblem
AP177

Designs: No. C674, Child at blackboard and UNESCO emblem (horiz.). No. C675, The Paper Collector, by Omar Gordillo, and U.N. emblem.

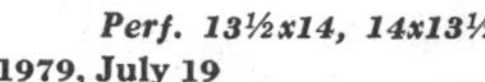
Perf. 13½x14, 14x13½

1979, July 19

C673 AP177 8p multi 55 30
C674 AP177 12p multi 70 30
C675 AP177 12p multi 70 30

International Year of the Child.

Rio Prado Hydroelectric Station
AP178

1979, Aug. 24 ***Perf. 13½x14***

C676 AP178 5p multi 70 15

Tomb, 6th Century—AP179

1979, Sept. 25 **Litho.** ***Perf. 14***

C677 AP179 8p multi 60 30

San Augustin Archaeological Park.

Gonzalo Jimenez de Quesada, by C. Leudo—AP180

1979, Oct. 11 ***Perf. 12***

C678 AP180 20p multi 2.25 90

Gonzalo Jimenez de Quesada (1500-1579), Spanish conquistador.

Hill, Penny Black, Colombia No. 1
AP181

1979, Oct. 23 ***Perf. 13½x14***

C679 AP181 15p multi 1.00 30

Sir Rowland Hill (1795-1879), originator of penny postage.

Amazon Region—AP182

Tourism: 14p, San Fernando Fortress.

1979 **Litho.** ***Perf. 13½×14***

C680	AP182	7p multi	55	22
C681	AP182	14p multi	1.00	60

Issue dates: 7p, Nov. 16; 14p, Nov. 9.

Nativity—AP183

Creche Sculptures: No. C682, Three Kings and soldiers. No. C684, Shepherds.

1979, Nov. 30 ***Perf. 12***

C682	AP183	3p multi	25	15
C683	AP183	3p multi	25	15
C684	AP183	3p multi	25	15

Christmas 1979. Nos. C682-C684 se-tenant in continuous design.

Magdalena Bridge, Avianca Emblem AP184

1979, Dec. 5 ***Perf. 14***

C685	AP184	15p multi	1.00	30

Barranquilla, 350th anniversary; Avianca National Airline, 60th anniversary.

Boy Playing Flute, by Judith Leyster AP185

1980, Feb. 15 ***Perf. 13½x14***

C686	AP185	6p multi	38	15

2nd International Music Competition, Ibague, Dec. 1979.

Gen. Antonio José de Sucre, 150th Death Anniversary—AP186

1980, Feb. 15 **Litho.** ***Perf. 12½x12***

C687	AP186	12p multi	65	22

The Watchman, by Edgar Negret AP187

1980, Feb. 26 ***Perf. 12x12½***

C688	AP187	25p multi	2.00	1.00

Virgin Mary, by Real del Sarte, 1929—AP188

1980, May 23 **Litho.** ***Perf. 14x13½***

C689	AP188	12p multi	55	18

Apparition of the Virgin Mary to Sister Catalina Labouri Gontard, 150th anniversary.

San Gil Produce Market, by Luis Roncancio—AP189

1980, May 27 ***Perf. 13½x14***

C690	AP189	12p multi	60	22

Pres. Enrique Olaya Herrera, by Miguel Diaz Vargas—AP190

1980, Oct. 28 **Litho.** ***Perf. 12***

C691	AP190	20p multi	1.40	50

Enrique Olaya Herrera (1880-1936), president, 1930-1934.

The Boy Fishing in a Bucket—AP191

Christmas 1980 (Christmas Stories by Rafael Pombo): No. C693, The Frog and the Mouse. No. C694, The Seven Lives of the Cat.

1980, Nov. 21 **Litho.** ***Perf. 14½***

C692	AP191	4p multi	30	15
C693	AP191	4p multi	30	15
C694	AP191	4p multi	30	15

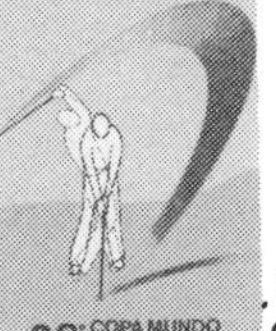

28th World Golf Cup, Cajica—AP192

1980, Dec. 9 **Litho.** ***Perf. 13½x14***

C695	AP192	30p multi	2.00	60

Bolivar Type of 1980

Simon Bolivar Death Sesquicentennial: 6p, Portrait, last words to Colombia (vert.).

1980, Dec. 17 ***Perf. 12***

C696	A400	6p multi	60	15

St. Peter Claver Holding Cross—AP193

1981, Jan. 13 ***Perf. 14½***

C697	AP193	15p multi	75	22

St. Peter Claver (1580-1654), helped American Indians.

Sculptured Bird, San Augustin AP194

Archaeological Finds: No. C699, Funeral chamber, Tierradentro. No. C700, Chamber hallway, Tierradentro. No. C701, Statue of man, San Augustin. Nos. C698-C701 se-tenant.

1981, May 12 **Litho.** ***Perf. 14***

C698	AP194	7p multi	38	10
C699	AP194	7p multi	38	10
C700	AP194	7p multi	38	10
C701	AP194	7p multi	38	10

See Nos. C707-C710.

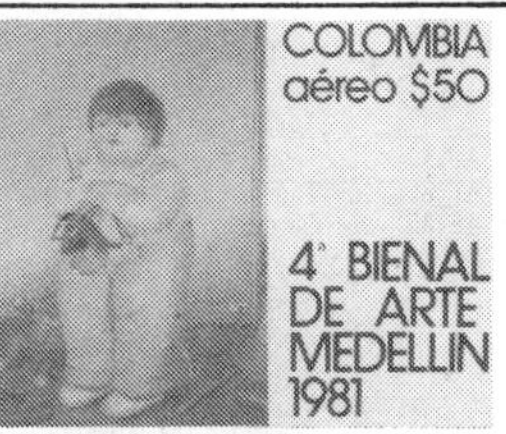

Child with Hobby Horse, by Fernando Botero—AP195

4th Biennial Arts show, Medellin: 20p, Square Abstract, by Omar Rayo. 25p, Flowers, by Alejandro Obregon.

1981, May 15 ***Perf. 12***

C702	AP195	20p multi	1.00	30
C703	AP195	25p multi	1.35	38
C704	AP195	50p multi	2.40	75

8th South American Swimming Championships, Medellin—AP196

1981, June 5

C705	AP196	15p multi	75	22

Santamaria Bull Ring, 50th Anniv.—AP197

1981, June 9 **Litho.** ***Perf. 12***

C706	AP197	30p multi	2.40	65

Archaeological Type of 1981

Quimbaya Culture: Nos. C707-C710 se-tenant.

1981, Sept. 23 **Litho.** ***Perf. 14***

C707	AP194	9p Man	38	10
C708	AP194	9p Seated man	38	10
C709	AP194	9p Seal, print	38	10
C710	AP194	9p Jug	38	10

Tourism Type of 1979

1982		**Litho.**	***Perf. 12***	
C717	AP182	20p Solano Bay	60	12
C718	AP182	20p Tota Lake, Boyaca	60	12
C719	AP182	20p Corrales, Boyaca	60	12

Issue dates: No. C717, June 2; others, June 16.

1982 World Cup—AP200

Designs: Players and team emblems.

1982, June 21		***Perf. 14***	
C720	Sheet of 15	4.00	3.00
a.	AP200 9p any single	28	8

No. C720 has black control number. Size: 181x150mm.

Bogota Gun Club Centenary—AP201

1982, July 16			***Perf. 12***	
C721	AP201	20p multi	60	12

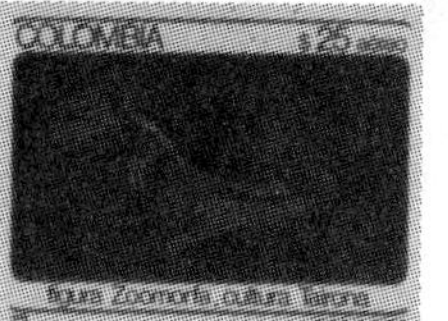

Gold Crocodile Figure, Tairona Culture—AP202

Tairona Culture Exhibit, Gold Museum: Various figures. Nos. C723-C727 vert.

1982, July 28				
C722	AP202	25p lt brn, gold & blk	75	22
C723	AP202	25p brt pink, gold & blk	75	22
C724	AP202	25p grn, gold & blk	75	22
C725	AP202	25p dk bl, gold, & blk	75	22
C726	AP202	25p VIO. gold & blk	75	22
C727	AP202	25p red, gold & blk	75	22
		Nos. C722-C727 (6)	4.50	1.32

Government Buildings, Pereira—AP203

1982, Aug. 4		**Litho.**	***Perf. 12***	
C728	AP203	35p multi	1.10	30

Bi-plane in Flight, by Edgar Antonio Bustos—AP204

1982, Aug. 5			***Perf. 14***	
C729	AP204	18p multi	50	12

American Air Forces Cooperation System.

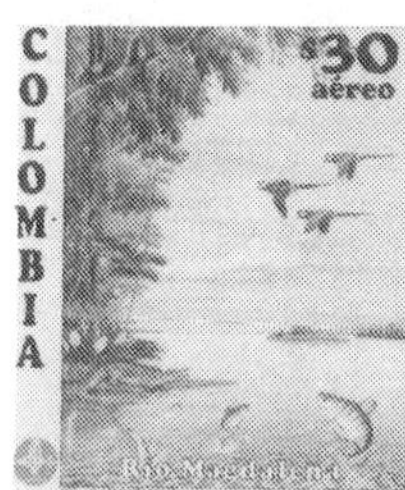

Magdalena River—AP205

1982, Oct. 21		**Litho.**	***Perf. 12***	
C730	AP205	30p multi	90	20

Marquez Type of 1982

1982, Dec. 10			***Perf. 13½x14***	
C731	A412	25p gray & bl	75	18
C732	A412	30p gray & brn	90	20

AIR POST SPECIAL DELIVERY STAMPS

Post Horn and Wings
APSD1

Lithographed

1958, May 19 *Perf. 12* **Unwmkd.**

CE1	APSD1	25c dk bl & red	60	22

Same Overprinted Vertically in Red

1959

CE2	APSD1	25c dk bl & red	75	18

Jet Plane and Envelope
APSD2

1963, Oct. 4 *Perf. 14*

CE3	APSD2	50c red & blk	30	12

Aviation Type of Air Post Issue

History of Colombian Aviation: 80c, Boeing 727 jet, 1966.

Perf. 14x13½

1966, Dec. 14 Photo. **Unwmkd.**

CE4	AP96	80c crim & multi	50	15

AIR POST REGISTRATION STAMPS.

Issued by Sociedad Colombo-Alemana de Transportes Aereos (SCADTA)

No. C41 Overprinted in Red **R**

1923 *Perf. 14x14½* **Wmk. 116**

CF1	AP6	20c gray	4.00	1.50

No. C58 Overprinted in Black **R**

1929 *Perf. 14* **Wmk. 127**

CF2	AP8	20c carmine	5.00	1.50

Same Overprint on No. C71.

CF3	AP10	20c carmine	6.50	6.50

Colombian Government Issues.

Same Overprint on No. C86.

1932

CF4	AP8	20c carmine	10.00	5.75

No. C100 Overprinted **R**

CF5	AP15	20c car & ol blk	6.00	1.75

SPECIAL DELIVERY STAMP.

Special Delivery Messenger
SD1

Engraved.

1917 *Perf. 14.* **Unwmkd.**

E1	SD1	5c gray grn	3.00	4.50

REGISTRATION STAMPS.

R1 R2

Lithographed.

1865 *Imperf.* **Unwmkd.**

F1	R1	5c black	45.00	37.50
F2	R2	5c black	40.00	35.00

R3 R4

1870 White Paper.

Vertical Lines in Background.

F3	R3	5c black	2.25	2.25
F4	R4	5c black	2.25	2.25

Horizontal Lines in Background.

F5	R3	5c black	4.50	4.50
F6	R4	5c black	2.25	2.25

Reprints of Nos. F3 to F6 show either crossed lines or traces of lines in background.

R5

1881 *Imperf.*

F7	R5	10c violet	28.50	30.00
a.		Sewing machine perf.	32.50	35.00
b.		Perf. 11	35.00	37.50

R6

1883 *Perf. 12, 13½*

F8	R6	10c red, *org*	1.75	1.75

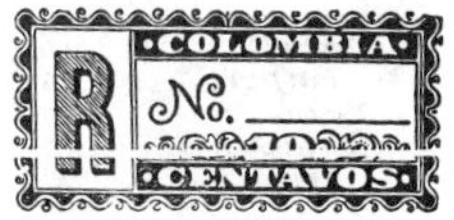

R7

1889-95 *Perf. 12, 13½*

F9	R7	10c red, *grysh*	1.75	1.25
F10	R7	10c red, *yelsh*	1.75	1.25
F11	R7	10c dp brn, *rose buff* ('95)	1.40	75
F12	R7	10c yel brn, *lt buff* ('92)	1.40	75

Nos. F9-F12 exist imperf. Prices same as for perf.

R9

1902 *Imperf.*

F13	R9	20c red brn, *bl*	1.40	1.40
a.		Sewing machine perf.	2.50	2.50
b.		Perf. 12	2.50	2.50

Medellin Issue.

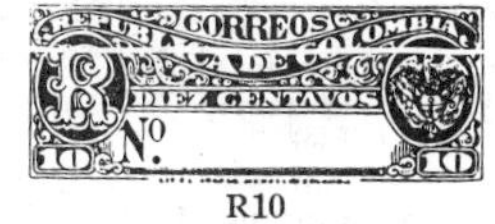

R10

1902 *Perf. 12.*

Wove Paper.

F16	R10	10c blk vio	17.50	17.50
a.		Laid paper	15.00	15.00

Regular Issue.

1903 *Imperf.*

F17	R9	20c bl, *bl*	1.25	1.25
a.		Sewing machine perf.	2.75	2.75
b.		Perf. 12	3.25	3.25

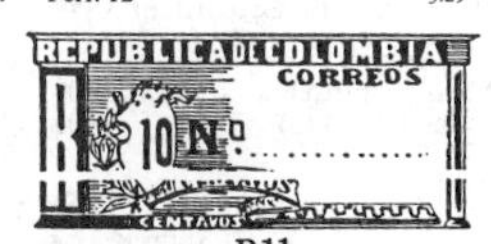

R11

1904 Pelure Paper. *Imperf.*

F19	R11	10c purple	3.00	3.00
a.		Sewing machine perf.	3.00	3.00
b.		Perf. 12	3.00	3.00

R12

Wove Paper.

Imprint: "J. L. Arango".

1904 *Perf. 12*

F20	R12	10c purple	3.00	75
a.		Imperf., pair	9.00	9.00

1909 *Perf. 10, 14, 10x14, 14x10*

Imprint: "Lit. Nacional".

F21	R12	10c purple	3.00	1.00
a.		Imperf., pair	7.50	7.50

Execution at Cartagena in 1816
R13

1910, July 20 Engr. *Perf. 12*

F22	R13	10c red & blk	21.00	*80.00*

Centenary of National Independence.

Pier at Puerto Colombia
R14

Tequendama Falls—R15

Perf. 11, 11½, 14, 11½x14

1917, Aug. 25

F23	R14	4c grn & ultra	1.00	3.00
a.		Center inverted	650.00	650.00
F24	R15	10c dp bl	3.00	75

R16

1925 Lithographed. *Perf. 10x13½*

F25	R16	(10c) blue	3.00	2.00
a.		Imperf., pair	9.00	9.00
b.		Perf. 13½x10	4.50	4.50

ACKNOWLEDGMENT OF RECEIPT STAMPS.

AR1 AR2

Lithographed.

1893 *Perf. 13½.* **Unwmkd.**

H1	AR1	5c ver, *bl*	3.75	3.75

1894 *Perf. 12.*

H2	AR1	5c vermilion	2.00	2.00

1902-03 *Imperf.*

H3	AR2	10c bl, *bl*	60	60
a.		10c bl, *grnsh bl*	60	60
b.		Sewing machine perf.	1.50	1.50
c.		Perf. 12	1.50	1.50

The handstamp "AR" in circle is believed to be a postmark.

AR3 AR4

1904 Pelure Paper *Imperf.*

H12	AR3	5c pale bl	9.00	9.00
a.		Perf. 12	9.00	9.00

No. 307 Overprinted in Black, Green or Volet **A R**

H13	A86	5c carmine	18.50	18.50

1904 *Perf. 12.*

H16	AR4	5c blue	3.75	3.75
a.		Imperf., pair	10.00	10.00

General José Acevedo y Gómez
AR5

1910, July 20 **Engraved**

H17	AR5	5c org & grn	7.50	*17.50*

Centenary of National Independence.

Sabana Station AR6 | Map of Colombia AR7

1917 ***Perf. 14.***

H18	AR6	4c bis brn	2.25	2.75
H19	AR7	5c org brn	2.10	2.10
a.		Imperf., pair	13.50	

LATE FEE STAMPS.

LF1 LF2

Lithographed.

1886 ***Perf. 10½.*** **Unwmkd.**

I1	LF1	2½c *lilac*	2.85	2.00
a.		Imperf., pair	12.00	12.00

1892 ***Perf. 12, 13½.***

I2	LF2	2½c dk bl, *rose*	2.75	2.50
a.		Imperf., pair	10.00	
I3	LF2	2½c ultra, *pink*	2.75	2.50

LF3 LF4

1902 ***Imperf.***

I4	LF3	5c pur, *rose*	65	65
a.		Perf. 12	2.00	2.00

1914 ***Perf. 10, 13½.***

I6	LF4	2c vio brn	3.50	3.50
I7	LF4	5c bl grn	3.50	3.50

Retardo Refardo 1921

Overprints illustrated above are unauthorized and of private origin.

POSTAGE DUE STAMPS.

These are not, strictly speaking, postage due stamps but were issued to cover an additional fee, "Sobreporte", charged on mail to foreign countries with which Colombia had no postal conventions.

D1 D2 D3

Lithographed.

1866 ***Imperf.*** **Unwmkd.**

J1	D1	25c *blue*	37.50	35.00
J2	D2	50c *yellow*	37.50	35.00
J3	D3	1p *rose*	100.00	90.00

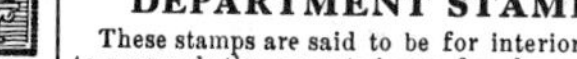

DEPARTMENT STAMPS.

These stamps are said to be for interior postage, to supersede the separate issues for the various departments.

Regular Issues Handstamped in Black, Violet, Blue or Green

Correos Departamentales

a

On Stamps of 1904.

1909 ***Perf. 12.*** **Unwmkd.**

L1	A94	½c yellow	3.00	3.00
a.		Imperf., pair	8.50	8.50
L2	A94	1c yel grn	3.00	3.00
L3	A94	2c red	3.75	3.75
a.		Imperf., pair	14.00	14.00
L4	A94	5c blue	4.50	4.50
L5	A94	10c violet	7.50	7.50
L6	A94	20c black	13.00	13.00
L7	A95	1p brown	24.00	24.00

On Stamp of 1902.

L8	A83	10p dk brn, *rose*	22.50	22.50
		Nos. L1-L8 (8)	81.25	81.25

On Stamps of 1908.

Perf. 10, 13, 13½ and Compound.

L9	A94	½c orange	3.00	3.00
a.		Imperf., pair	6.50	6.50
L10	A94	1c green	4.50	4.50
a.		Without imprint	5.50	5.50
L11	A94	2c red	4.50	4.50
a.		Imperf., pair		
L12	A94	5c blue	4.50	4.50
a.		Imperf., pair	10.00	10.00
L13	A94	10c violet	7.50	7.50

On Tolima Stamp of 1888.

Perf. 10½.

L14	A23	1p red brn	12.00	12.00
		Nos. L9-L14 (6)	36.00	36.00

Regular Issues Handstamped

Correos Depmentales

b

On Stamps of 1904.

Perf. 12.

L15	A94	½c yellow	3.00	3.00
L16	A94	1c yel grn	3.00	3.00
L17	A94	2c red	4.50	4.50
L18	A94	5c blue	4.50	4.50
L19	A94	10c violet	7.50	7.50
L20	A94	20c black	13.00	13.00
L21	A94	1p brown	24.00	24.00
		Nos. L15-L21 (7)	59.50	59.50

On Stamps of 1908.

Perf. 10, 13, 13½.

L22	A94	½c orange	3.00	3.00
L23	A94	1c yel grn	9.00	9.00
L24	A94	2c red	4.50	4.50
a.		Imperf., pair	10.00	10.00
L25	A94	5c lt bl	4.50	4.50

The handstamps on Nos. L1 to L25 are, as usual, found inverted and double.

DEPARTMENT REGISTRATION STAMPS.

Registration Stamps Handstamped like Nos. L1 to L25.

On Registration Stamp of 1904.

1909 ***Perf. 12.*** **Unwmkd.**

LF1	R12(a)	10c purple	25.00	25.00
LF2	R12(b)	10c purple	25.00	25.00

On Registration Stamp of 1909.

Perf. 10, 13.

LF3	R12(a)	10c purple	25.00	25.00
LF4	R12(b)	10c purple	25.00	25.00

Nos. LF1–LF4 exist imperf. Price per pair, $20.

DEPARTMENT ACKNOWLEDGMENT OF RECEIPT STAMPS.

Acknowledgment of Receipt Stamp of 1904 Handstamped like Nos. L1 to L25.

1909 ***Perf. 12.*** **Unwmkd.**

LH1	AR4(a)	5c blue	30.00	30.00
a.		Imperf., pair	45.00	
LH2	AR4(b)	5c blue	30.00	30.00
a.		Imperf., pair	45.00	

Local Stamps for the City of Bogota.

(bō'gō·tä')

A1

Lithographed.

Pelure Paper.

1889 ***Perf. 12*** **Unwmkd.**

LX1	A1	½c black	1.00	1.00
a.		Imperf., pair	5.00	5.00

Impressions on bright blue and blue-gray paper were not regularly issued

A2 A3

White Wove Paper.

1896 ***Perf. 12, 13½***

LX2	A2	½c black	1.00	1.00

1903 ***Imperf.***

LX3	A3	10c *pink*	1.65	1.65
a.		Perf. 12	6.00	6.00

OFFICIAL STAMPS.

Stamps of 1917-1937 Overprinted in Black or Red:

OFICIAL OFICIAL
a *b*

Perf. 11, 12, 13½.

1937 **Unwmkd.**

O1	A131(a)	1c grn (Bk)	15	10
O2	A157(a)	10c dp org (Bk)	22	22
O3	A107(b)	30c ol bis (Bk)	3.00	1.40
O4	A129(b)	40c brn & yel brn (Bk)	1.65	60
O5	A114(b)	50c car (Bk)	1.50	55
O6	A115(b)	1p lt bl (Bk)	4.50	1.85
O7	A116(b)	2p org (Bk)	6.75	3.25
O8	A117(b)	5p gray (Bk)	50.00	15.00
O9	A118(b)	10p dk brn (Bk)	150.00	100.00

Wmkd. Wavy Lines. (229)

Perf. 12½.

O10	A132(a)	2c red (Bk)	22	22
O11	A133(a)	5c brn (Bk)	15	15
O12	A160(a)	12c dp bl (R)	75	30
O13	A136 (b)	20c dk bl (R)	75	40
		Nos. O1-O13 (13)	219.64	124.04

Tall, wrong font "I's" in OFICIAL exist on all stamps with "a" overprint.

POSTAL TAX STAMPS.

"Greatest Mother"
PT1

Lithographed.

1935, May 27 ***Perf. 11½*** **Unwmkd.**

RA1	PT1	5c ol blk & scar	3.00	1.40

This stamp was required on all mail during Red Cross Week in 1935 (May 27–June 3) and in 1936.

Mother and Child
PT2

Perf. 10½, 10½x11.

1937, May 24 **Unwmkd.**

RA2	PT2	5c red	1.00	40

This stamp was required on all mail during Red Cross Week. The tax was for the Red Cross.

Ministry of Posts and Telegraphs Building
PT3 PT4

1939–45 **Litho.** ***Perf. 10½, 12½***

RA3	PT3	¼c dp bl	5	4
RA3A	PT3	¼c dk vio brn ('45)	8	5
RA4	PT3	½c pink	10	5
RA5	PT3	1c violet	55	15
RA5A	PT3	1c yel org ('45)	2.50	90
RA6	PT3	2c pck grn	40	20
RA7	PT3	20c lt brn	1.75	80
		Nos. RA3-RA7 (7)	5.43	2.19

These stamps were obligatory on all mail. The tax was for the construction of the new Communications Building.

The 25c of type PT3 and PT4 were not usable on postal matter.

See also No. 561.

Wmkd. Wavy Lines (229)

1940, Jan. 20 **Engr.** ***Perf. 12½x13***

RA8	PT4	¼c ultra	6	3
RA9	PT4	½c carmine	6	3
RA10	PT4	1c violet	8	3
RA11	PT4	2c bl grn	30	5
RA12	PT4	20c brown	1.25	30
		Nos. RA8-RA12 (5)	1.75	44

See note after No. RA7.

"Protection"
PT5

Wmkd.
Wavy Lines and C Multiple. (255)

1940, Apr. 25 ***Perf. 12***
RA13 PT5 5c rose car 45 22

See also No. RA17.

Postal Tax Stamps of 1939 Surcharged in Black

$ 0,0½
MEDIO CENTAVO

1943 ***Perf. 10½.*** **Unwmkd.**
RA14 PT3 ½c on 1c vio 8 8
a. Inverted surcharge 2.25
RA15 PT3 ½c on 2c pck grn 8 8
RA16 PT3 ½c on 20c lt brn 22 22

Types of 1940.
Imprint:
"Litografia Colombia Bogota S. A."

1944 **Lithographed.** ***Perf. 11.***
RA17 PT5 5c dk rose 45 22

Imprint:
"Lito-Colombia Bogota-Colombia"

RA18 PT4 ¼c ultra 8 6

Ministry of Posts and Telegraphs Building
PT6

Engraved.

1945-48 ***Perf. 12.*** **Wmk. 255**
RA19 PT6 ¼c ultra 5 3
RA20 PT6 ¼c sep ('46) 5 3
RA21 PT6 ½c car rose 5 3
RA22 PT6 ½c dp mag ('46) 5 3
RA23 PT6 1c vio ('46) 5 3
RA23A PT6 1c red org ('46) 5 3
RA24 PT6 2c grn ('46) 8 6
RA25 PT6 20c brn ('46) 1.25 30
a. 20c red brn ('48) 90 15
Nos. RA19-RA25 (8) 1.63 54

These stamps were obligatory on all mail. The surtax was for the construction of the new Communications Building. See also Nos. 603, RA33.

No. 469 Overprinted in Carmine

1946, May 25
RA26 A176 5c dl brn 50 22

The surtax was for the Red Cross.

Ministry of Posts and Telegraphs Building
PT7

Lithographed.

1946 ***Perf. 11*** **Unwmkd.**
RA27 PT7 3c blue 15 8

No. 490 Overprinted in Carmine

SOBRETASA
c

1947 ***Perf. 12*** **Wmk. 255**
RA28 A196 20c gray blk 2.00 1.40

Arms of Colombia and Red Cross
PT8

PT9

Engraved.

1947, Sept. ***Perf. 12½*** **Unwmkd.**
RA29 PT8 5c car lake 22 15

The surtax of Nos. RA29 and RA40 was for the Red Cross. See also No. RA40.

No. 466 Overprinted Type "c" in Carmine.

RA30 A136 20c dk bl 6.00 4.50

Type of 1945.
Engraved.

1947 ***Perf. 12*** **Wmk. 255**
RA33 PT6 1c ol bis 6 4

Lithographed.
Black Surcharge.

1948 ***Perf. 11.*** **Unwmkd.**
RA36 PT9 1c on 5c lt brn 8 5
RA37 PT9 1c on 10c lt vio 8 5
RA38 PT9 1c on 25c red 8 5
RA39 PT9 1c on 50c ultra 8 5

Type of 1947.

1948 ***Perf. 10½***
RA40 PT8 5c vermilion 22 15

Ministry of Posts and Telegraphs Building
PT10

Mother and Child
PT11

Engraved

1948-50 ***Perf. 12*** **Wmk. 255**
RA41 PT10 1c rose car ('49) 4 4
RA42 PT10 2c grn ('50) 8 4
RA43 PT10 3c blue 10 4
RA44 PT10 5c gray 10 6
RA45 PT10 10c purple 30 7
Nos. RA41-RA45 (5) 62 25

A 25c stamp of type PT10 was for use on telegrams, later for regular postage. See Nos. 602, 604.

Lithographed.

1950, May 25 ***Perf. 11*** **Unwmkd.**

Dark Blue Surcharge.

RA46 PT11 5c on 2c gray, red, blk & yel 1.10 45
a. "195" instead of "1950" 2.00 2.00
b. Top bar and "19" of "1950" omit. 2.00 2.00

Marginal perforations omitted, creating 26 straight-edged copies in each sheet of 44. Surtax for Red Cross.

No. 574 Overprinted in Black

SOBRETASA

1950, May 26 ***Perf. 12*** **Wmk. 255**
RA47 A176 5c blue 22 8
a. Inverted ovpt. 1.25

Telegraph Stamp Surcharged in Black.

RA48 A253a 8c on 50c org yel 15 8

Fiscal stamps of type A253a were available for postal use after May 9, 1952. See Nos. 605-608.

Arms and Cross
PT12

Bartolome de Las Casas Aiding Youth
PT13

Engraved.

1951, May ***Perf. 12½*** **Unwmkd.**
RA49 PT12 5c red 30 10
RA50 PT13 5c carmine 30 10

The surtax was for the Red Cross.

No. RA43 Surcharged with New Value in Black.

1951 ***Perf. 12.*** **Wmk. 255**
RA51 PT10 1c on 3c bl 8 5

Type of 1951.
Engraved; Cross Lithographed.

1953 ***Perf. 12½.*** **Unwmkd.**
RA52 PT13 5c grn & car 30 10

The surtax of Nos. RA52-RA60 was for the Red Cross.

No. C254 Overprinted with Cross and Bar in Carmine.

1954
RA53 AP42 5c lil rose 90 55

St. Peter Claver Offering Gifts to Slaves
PT14

Engraved; Cross Typographed

1955, May 2 ***Perf. 13*** **Unwmkd.**
RA54 PT14 5c dp plum & red 30 10

Issued to commemorate the 300th anniversary of the death of St. Peter Claver.

Jean Henri Dunant and Santiago Samper Brush
PT15

Photogravure;
Red Cross and "Cruz Roja" Engraved.

1956, June 1 ***Perf. 13*** **Unwmkd.**
RA55 PT15 5c brn & red 30 10

Nurses and Ambulances
PT16

1958, June 2 **Photo.** ***Perf. 12***
RA56 PT16 5c gray & red 15 8

St. Louisa de Marillac and Church
PT17

Design: No. RA58, Henri Dunant and battle scene.

1960, Sept. 1 **Litho.** ***Perf. 11***
RA57 PT17 5c brn & rose 30 12
RA58 PT17 5c vio bl & rose 30 12

No. RA57 issued to commemorate the 3rd centenary of the Sisters of Charity. No. RA58 issued to commemorate the centenary (in 1959) of the Red Cross idea.

Manuelita de la Cruz
PT18

Red Cross Worker and Patient
PT19

1961, Nov. 2 **Engraved** ***Perf. 13***
RA59 PT18 5c dl pur & red 22 8
RA60 PT18 5c brn & red 22 8

Issued in memory of Red Cross Nurse Manuelita de la Cruz, who died in the line of duty during the floods of 1955. Obligatory on domestic mail for a month.

1965, Apr. 30 **Photo.** ***Perf. 12***
RA61 PT19 5c bl gray & red 8 6

Obligatory on domestic mail during May.

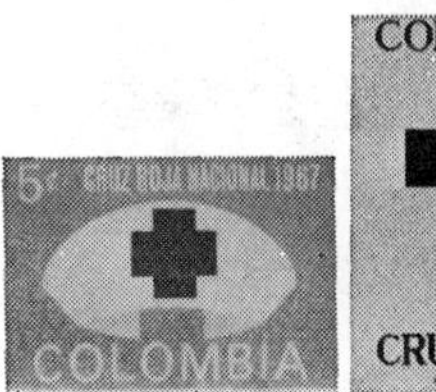

Nurse's Cap
PT20

Red Cross
PT21

1967, June 1 **Litho.** ***Perf. 12***
RA62 PT20 5c brt bl & red 8 6

1969, July 1 **Litho.** ***Perf. 12x12½***
RA63 PT21 5c vio bl & red 8 6

Child Care
PT22

1970, July 1 **Litho.** ***Perf. 12½x12***
RA64 PT22 5c lt bl & red 5 3

Antioquia

(än'tē-ō'kyä)

Originally a State, now a Department of the Republic of Colombia. Until the revolution of 1885, the separate states making up the United States of Colombia were sovereign governments in their own right. On August 4, 1886, the National Council of Bogotá, composed of two delegates from each state, adopted a new constitution which abolished the sovereign rights of states, which then became departments with governors appointed by the President of the Republic. The nine original states represented at the Bogotá Convention retained some of their previous rights, as management of their own finances, and all issued postage stamps until as late as 1904. For Panama's issues, see Panama Nos. 1-30.

Coat of Arms

A1 A2

A3 A4

Lithographed.

Wove Paper.

1868 ***Imperf.*** **Unwmkd.**

1	A1	2½c blue	*600.00*	*400.00*
2	A2	5c green	*450.00*	*300.00*
3	A3	10c lilac	*1,350.*	*525.00*
4	A4	1p red	*350.00*	*275.00*

Reprints of Nos. 1, 3 and 4 are on a bluish white paper and all but No. 3 have scratches across the design.

A5 A6

A7 A8

A9 A10

1869

5	A5	2½c blue	3.00	3.00
6	A6	5c green	3.75	3.75
7	A7	5c green	3.75	3.75
8	A8	10c lilac	5.25	2.00
9	A9	20c brown	5.25	3.75
10	A10	1p rose red	10.00	10.00
a.		1p ver	22.50	22.50

Reprints of Nos. 7, 8 and 10 are on a bluish white paper; reprints of Nos. 5 and 10a on white paper. The 10c blue is believed to be a reprint.

A11

A12 A13

A14 A15

A16 A17

A18

1873

12	A11	1c yel grn	4.50	4.00
a.		1c grn	4.50	4.00
13	A12	5c green	5.25	4.00
14	A13	10c lilac	20.00	20.00
15	A14	20c yel brn	5.25	5.25
a.		20c dk brn	5.25	5.25
16	A15	50c blue	1.75	1.75
17	A16	1p vermilion	3.00	3.00
18	A17	2p *yellow*	7.50	7.50
19	A18	5p *rose*	67.50	60.00

A19 A20

Liberty Head

A21 A22

Pedro Justo Berrio

A23

1875–85

20	A19	1c *grn*, unglazed ('76)	1.50	1.50
a.		Glazed paper	2.25	2.25
b.		1c *lt grn*, laid paper ('85)	3.50	3.00
21	A19	1c blk ('76)	1.10	70
a.		Laid paper	125.00	100.00
22	A19	1c bl grn ('85)	2.25	2.25
23	A19	1c red lil, laid paper ('85)	2.25	2.25
24	A20	2½c blue	2.25	2.25
a.		Pelure paper ('78)	*1,500.*	*1,250.*
25	A21	5c green	15.00	14.00
a.		Laid paper	120.00	80.00
26	A22	5c green	15.00	14.00
a.		Laid paper	120.00	80.00
27	A23	10c lilac	22.50	21.00
a.		Laid paper	120.00	110.00
28	A20	10c vio, pelure paper ('78)	*525.00*	450.00

Arms Liberty

A24 A25

A26 A27

1878–85

29	A24	2½c bl, pelure paper	2.25	2.25
30	A24	2½c grn ('83)	2.25	2.25
a.		Laid paper ('83)	60.00	45.00
31	A24	2½c *buff* ('85)	4.50	4.50
32	A25	5c grn ('83)	2.25	2.25
a.		Pelure paper	24.00	21.00
b.		Laid paper ('82)	30.00	9.00
33	A25	5c vio ('83)	5.25	5.25
a.		5c bl vio ('83)	5.25	5.00
34	A26	10c vio, laid paper ('82)	110.00	45.00
35	A26	10c scar ('83)	2.25	2.25
a.		Tete beche pair	50.00	50.00
36	A27	20c brn ('83)	2.25	2.25
a.		Laid paper ('82)	4.50	4.50

A28 A29

Liberty

A30

1883–85

37	A28	5c brown	4.50	3.25
a.		Laid paper	135.00	75.00
38	A28	5c grn ('85)	90.00	45.00
a.		Laid paper ('85)	100.00	67.50
39	A28	5c yel, laid paper ('85)	4.50	4.50
40	A29	10c bl grn, laid paper	4.50	4.50
41	A29	10c bl, *bl* ('85)	4.50	4.50
42	A29	10c lil, laid paper ('85)	6.00	6.00
a.		Wove paper ('85)	90.00	45.00
43	A30	20c bl, laid paper ('85)	4.50	4.50

Coat of Arms

A31

1886 **Wove Paper.**

55	A31	1c grn, *pink*	65	65
56	A31	2½c *orange*	65	65
57	A31	5c ultra, *buff*	1.75	1.75
a.		5c bl, *buff*	3.00	3.00
58	A31	10c rose, *buff*	85	75
a.		Transfer of 50c in stone of 10c	72.50	72.50
59	A31	20c dk vio, *buff*	1.50	1.50
61	A31	50c yel brn, *buff*	2.75	2.75
62	A31	1p yel, *grn*	4.50	4.50
63	A31	2p grn, *vio*	4.50	4.50

1887-88

64	A31	1c red, *vio*	45	45
65	A31	2½c lil, *pale lil*	65	65
66	A31	5c car, *buff*	75	75
67	A31	5c red, *grn*	2.25	2.25
68	A31	10c brn, *grn*	65	65

Medellin Issue.

A32

A33 A34

1888 **Type-set.**

69	A32	2½c *yellow*	14.00	14.00
70	A33	5c *yellow*	4.50	4.50
71	A34	5c red, *yel*	4.50	4.50

Two varieties of No. 69, six of No. 70 and ten of No. 71.

A35

1889

72	A35	2½c red	4.50	4.50

Ten varieties including "eentavos".

Regular Issue.

Coat of Arms

A36 A37

A38

A39

A40

A41

1889–90 Litho. Perf. 13½

No.	Type	Value	Unused	Used
73	A36	1c *rose*	30	30
74	A36	2½c *blue*	30	30
75	A36	5c *yellow*	38	38
76	A36	10c *green*	38	38
78	A37	20c bl ('90)	1.50	1.50
79	A38	50c vio brn ('90)	3.00	3.00
a.		Transfer of 20c in stone of 50c	90.00	90.00
80	A38	50c grn ('90)	2.50	2.50
81	A39	1p red ('90)	2.25	2.25
82	A40	2p *mag* ('90)	13.00	13.00
83	A41	5p *org red* ('90)	18.50	18.50

Nos. 73–76, 82–83 exist imperf.
The so-called "errors" of Nos. 73 to 76, printed on paper of wrong colors, are essays or, possibly, reprints. They exist perforated and imperforate.
See also No. 96.

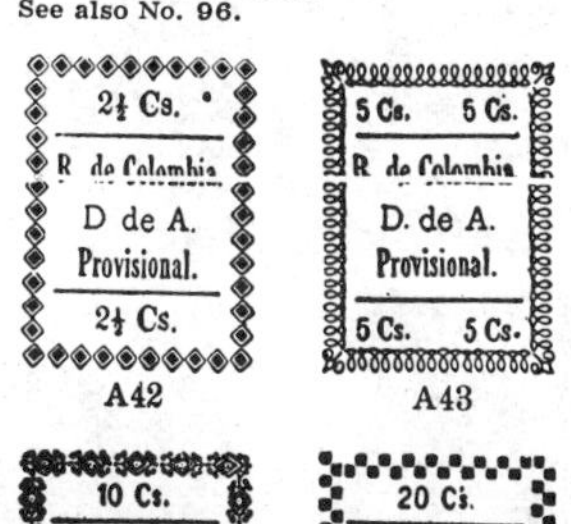
A42 A43

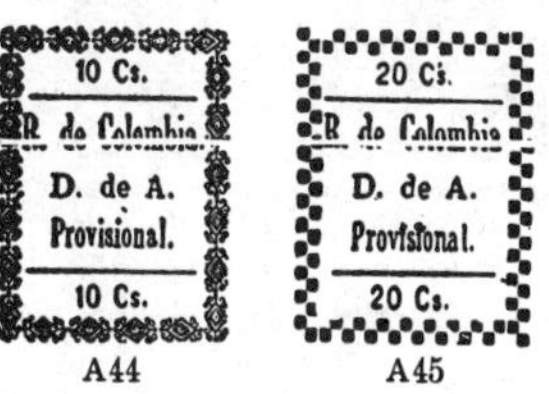
A44 A45

1890 Type-set. Perf. 14.

No.	Type	Value	Unused	Used
84	A42	2½c *buff*	1.75	1.75
85	A43	5c *orange*	1.75	1.75
86	A44	10c *buff*	6.00	6.00
87	A44	10c *rose*	6.75	6.75
88	A45	20c *orange*	6.75	6.75

Twenty varieties of the 5c, ten of each of the other values.

A46 A47

1892 Lithographed Perf. 13½

No.	Type	Value	Unused	Used
89	A46	1c brn, *brnsh*	45	45
90	A46	2½c pur, *lil*	45	45
92	A46	5c *gray*	90	90
a.		Transfer of 2½c in stone of 5c	150.00	

1893

No.	Type	Value	Unused	Used
93	A46	1c blue	30	30
94	A46	2½c green	45	45
95	A46	5c vermilion	30	30
96	A36	10c pale brn	30	30

1896 Perf. 14

No.	Type	Value	Unused	Used
97	A47	2c gray	30	30
98	A47	2c lil rose	30	30
99	A47	2½c brown	30	30
100	A47	2½c stl bl	30	30
101	A47	3c orange	30	30
102	A47	3c ol grn	30	30
103	A47	5c green	30	30
104	A47	5c yel buff	30	30
105	A47	10c brn vio	60	60
106	A47	10c violet	60	60
107	A47	20c brn org	60	60
108	A47	20c blue	1.00	1.00
109	A47	50c gray brn	1.00	1.00
110	A47	50c rose	1.40	1.40
111	A47	1p bl & blk	18.50	18.50
112	A47	1p rose red & blk	18.50	18.50
113	A47	2p org & blk	60.00	60.00
114	A47	2p dk grn & blk	60.00	60.00
115	A47	5p red vio & blk	90.00	90.00
116	A47	5p pur & blk	90.00	90.00

Nos. 115–116 with centers omitted are proofs.

General José María Córdoba
A48

1899 Perf. 11.

No.	Type	Value	Unused	Used
117	A48	½c grnsh bl	7	12
118	A48	1c sl bl	7	12
119	A48	2c sl brn	7	12
120	A48	3c red	7	12
121	A48	4c bis brn	7	12
122	A48	5c green	7	12
123	A48	10c scarlet	7	12
124	A48	20c gray vio	7	12
125	A48	50c ol bis	7	12
126	A48	1p grnsh blk	7	12
127	A48	2p ol gray	7	12
		Nos. 117-127 (11)	77	1.32

Numerous part-perf. and imperf. varieties of Nos. 117-127 exist.

A49

A50 A50a

1901 Type-set Perf. 12

No.	Type	Value	Unused	Used
128	A49	1c red	30	30
129	A50	1c ultra	75	75
130	A50	1c bister	75	75
130A	A50a	1c dl red	75	75
130B	A50a	1c ultra	6.00	6.00

Eight varieties of No. 128, four varieties of Nos. 129–130B.

A51

A52

Atanasio Girardot
A53

Dr. José Félix Restrepo
A54

1902 Lithographed Wove Paper

No.	Type	Value	Unused	Used
131	A51	1c brt rose	22	15
a.		Laid paper	75	75
b.		Imperf., pair	3.00	
132	A51	2c blue	15	15
a.		Transfer of 3c in stone of 2c	6.25	6.25
133	A51	3c green	15	15
a.		Imperf., pair	3.50	
134	A51	4c dl vio	15	15
135	A52	5c rose red	22	22
136	A53	10c rose lil	15	15
a.		Small head	6.25	6.25
b.		10c rose	15	15
137	A53	20c gray grn	22	22
138	A53	30c brt rose	22	22
139	A53	40c blue	22	22
140	A53	50c brn, *yel*	22	22

Laid Paper.

No.	Type	Value	Unused	Used
141	A54	1p pur & blk	90	90
142	A54	2p rose & blk	90	90
143	A54	5p sl bl & blk	1.50	1.50
		Nos. 131-143 (13)	5.22	5.15

1903 Wove Paper.

No.	Type	Value	Unused	Used
143A	A51	1c blue	15	15
144	A51	2c violet	15	15
a.		Imperf.	3.00	

A55

A56

Francisco Antonio Zea
A57

Custodio García Rovira
A58

La Pola (Policarpa Salavarrieta)
A59

J. M. Restrepo
A60

José Fernández Madrid
A61

Juan del Corral
A62

1903–04

No.	Type	Value	Unused	Used
145	A55	4c yel brn	22	22
146	A55	5c blue	22	22
147	A56	10c yellow	22	22
148	A56	20c purple	22	22
149	A56	30c brown	75	75
150	A56	40c green	75	75
151	A56	50c rose	22	22
152	A57	1p ol gray	75	75
153	A58	2p purple	75	75
154	A59	3p dk bl	75	75
155	A60	4p dl red	1.10	1.10
156	A61	5p red brn	1.10	1.10
157	A62	10p scarlet	4.50	4.50
		Nos. 145-157 (13)	11.55	11.55

Nos. 145–146, 151, 153–157 exist imperf. Price by pair, $3 to $4.

Manizales Issue.

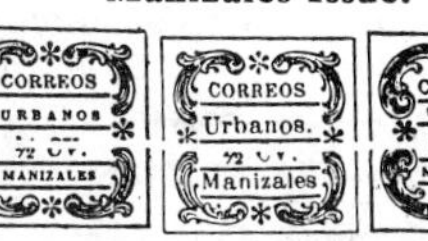

Stamps of these designs are local private post issues.

OFFICIAL STAMPS.

Stamps of 1903–04 with overprint "OFICIAL" were never issued.

REGISTRATION STAMPS.

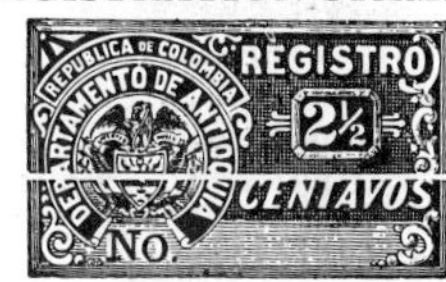
R1

Lithographed.

1896 Perf. 14 Unwmkd.

No.	Type	Value	Unused	Used
F1	R1	2½c rose	1.40	1.40
F2	R1	2½c dl bl	1.40	1.40

Córdoba
R2

R3

1899 Perf. 11

No.	Type	Value	Unused	Used
F3	R2	2½c dl bl	30	30
F4	R3	10c red lil	30	30

R4

1902 Perf. 12

No.	Type	Value	Unused	Used
F5	R4	10c pur, *bl*	38	38
a.		Imperf.		

ACKNOWLEDGMENT OF RECEIPT STAMPS.

AR1

Lithographed.

1902–03 Perf. 12 Unwmkd.

No.	Type	Value	Unused	Used
H1	AR1	5c *rose*	1.10	1.10
H2	AR1	5c sl ('03)	38	38

AR2

Purple Handstamp.

1903 ***Imperf.***

H3	AR2	10c *pink*	21.00	21.00

LATE FEE STAMPS.

Córdoba
LF1

Lithographed.

1899 ***Perf. 11*** **Unwmkd.**

I1	LF1	2½c dk grn	30	30
a.		Imperf., pair	3.50	

LF2 LF3

1901 **Type-set.** ***Perf. 12.***

I2	LF2	2½c red vio	65	65
a.		2½c pur	65	65

1902 **Lithographed**

I3	LF3	2½c violet	22	22

City of Medellin

(mā′thĕ·yēn′)

Stamps of the designs shown were not issued by any governmental agency but by the Sociedad de Mejoras Publicas.

Bolivar

(bō·lē′vär)

Originally a State, now a Department of the Republic of Colombia. (See Antioquia.)

A1

Lithographed.

1863–66 ***Imperf.*** **Unwmkd.**

1	A1	10c green	*850.00*	*500.00*
a.		Five stars below shield	*900.00*	*725.00*
2	A1	10c red ('66)	30.00	30.00
a.		Diagonal half used as 5c on cover		55.00
b.		Five stars below shield	75.00	75.00
3	A1	1p red	10.00	10.00

Fourteen varieties of each.

Coat of Arms

A2 A3

A4 A5

1873

4	A2	5c blue	6.75	6.75
5	A3	10c violet	6.75	6.75
6	A4	20c yel grn	27.50	27.50
7	A5	80c vermilion	60.00	60.00

A6

A7 A8

1874–78

8	A6	5c blue	25.00	25.00
9	A7	5c bl ('78)	7.50	7.50
10	A8	10c vio ('77)	3.75	3.75

Simón Bolívar
A9

Dated "1879".

White Wove Paper.

1879 ***Perf. 12½***

11	A9	5c blue	30	30
a.		Imperf., pair	1.00	
12	A9	10c violet	22	22
13	A9	20c red	30	30
a.		20c grn (error)	12.50	12.50

Bluish Laid Paper.

15	A9	5c blue	30	30
a.		Imperf., pair	2.50	
16	A9	10c violet	2.00	2.00
a.		Imperf., pair	5.00	
17	A9	20c red	40	40
a.		Imperf., pair	2.25	

Stamps of 80c and 1p on white wove paper and 1p on bluish laid paper were prepared but not placed in use.

Dated "1880".

White Wove Paper

1880 ***Perf. 12½***

19	A9	5c blue	30	30
a.		Imperf., pair	2.00	
20	A9	10c violet	40	40
a.		Imperf., pair	2.00	
21	A9	20c red	40	40
a.		20c grn (error)	16.00	16.00
23	A9	80c green	2.75	2.75
24	A9	1p orange	2.75	2.75
a.		Imperf., pair	7.00	

Bluish Laid Paper.

25	A9	5c blue	30	30
a.		Imperf., pair	1.50	
26	A9	10c violet	2.75	2.75
27	A9	20c red	40	40
a.		Imperf., pair	3.50	
28	A9	1p orange	500.00	
a.		Imperf.	*600.00*	

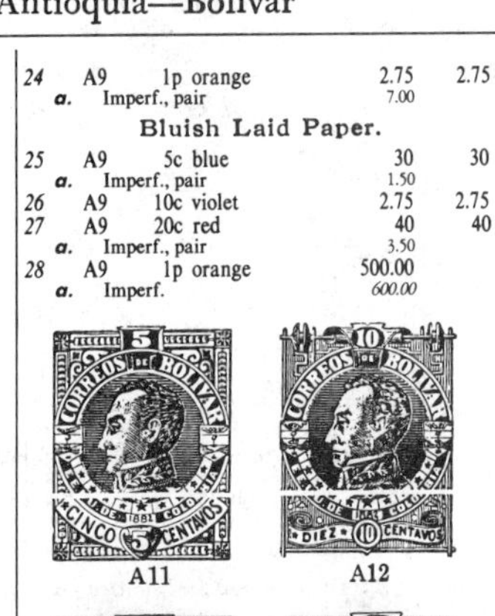

A11 A12

A13 A15

A16

Dated "1882".

White Wove Paper.

1882 ***Perf. 12, 16x12***

29	A11	5c blue	40	40
30	A12	10c lilac	30	30
31	A13	20c red	40	40
33	A15	80c green	80	80
34	A16	1p orange	80	80

Nos. 29, 30 and 34 are known imperforate. They are printer's waste and were not issued through post offices.

Bolívar A17 Bolívar A18

1882 **Engraved** ***Perf. 12***

35	A17	5p bl & rose red	75	75
a.		Imperf., pair	6.00	
b.		Perf. 16	7.50	7.50
c.		Perf. 14	7.50	7.50
36	A17	10p brn & bl	2.00	2.00
a.		Imperf., pair	10.00	
b.		Perf. 16	6.75	6.75
c.		Rouletted	10.00	10.00

Dated "1883".

1883 **Litho.** ***Perf. 12, 16x12***

37	A11	5c blue	22	22
a.		Imperf., pair	1.00	
b.		Perf. 12	2.75	1.25
38	A12	10c lilac	30	30
39	A13	20c red	30	30
41	A15	80c green	40	40
42	A16	1p orange	75	75
a.		Perf. 16x12	2.50	2.50

1884 **Dated "1884"**

43	A11	5c blue	40	40
a.		Perf. 12	11.50	11.50
44	A12	10c lilac	22	22
45	A13	20c red	22	22
a.		Perf. 12	5.25	5.25
47	A15	80c green	30	30
a.		Perf. 12	2.50	2.50
48	A16	1p orange	40	40

1885 **Dated "1885"**

49	A11	5c blue	18	18
50	A12	10c lilac	18	18
51	A13	20c red	18	18
53	A15	80c green	30	30
54	A16	1p orange	40	40

The note after No. 34 will also apply to imperforate stamps of the 1884-85 issues.

1891 ***Perf. 14.***

55	A18	1c black	40	40
56	A18	5c orange	40	40
a.		Imperf., pair	1.00	
57	A18	10c carmine	40	40
58	A18	20c blue	75	75
59	A18	50c green	1.10	1.10
60	A18	1p purple	1.10	1.10
		Nos. 55-60 (6)	4.15	4.15

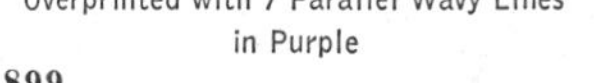

Overprinted with 7 Parallel Wavy Lines in Purple

1899

61	A18	1c black	55.00	55.00

The overprint is a control mark.

Bolívar A19 José Fernández Madrid A20

Manuel Rodriguez Torices A21 José María García de Toledo A22

1903 **Laid Paper** ***Imperf.***

62	A19	50c dk bl, *pink*	75	75
a.		bluish paper	75	75
63	A19	50c sl grn, *pink*	75	75
a.		rose paper	1.10	1.10
b.		grnsh bl paper	2.25	2.25
c.		yel paper	2.75	2.75
d.		brn paper	2.75	2.75
e.		sal paper	6.00	6.00
64	A19	50c pur, *pink*	1.10	1.10
a.		white paper	2.50	2.50
b.		brn paper	2.50	2.50
c.		grnsh bl paper	2.50	2.50
d.		lil paper	2.50	2.50
e.		rose paper	2.25	2.25
f.		yel paper	2.50	2.50
g.		sal paper	4.50	4.50
h.		As "a," wove paper	8.50	8.50
65	A20	1p org, *sal*	75	75
a.		yel paper	4.50	4.50
b.		grnsh bl paper	15.00	15.00
66	A20	1p gray grn, *lil*	1.75	1.75
a.		yel paper	6.75	6.75
b.		sal paper	7.50	7.50
c.		grn paper	7.50	7.50
d.		white wove paper	10.00	
67	A21	5p car rose, *lil*	75	75
a.		brn paper	75	75
b.		yel paper	1.40	1.40
c.		grnsh bl paper	4.50	4.50
d.		bluish paper	6.00	6.00
e.		sal paper	7.50	7.50
f.		rose paper	9.00	9.00
68	A22	10p dk bl, *bluish*	1.50	1.50
a.		grnsh bl paper	1.50	1.50
b.		rose paper	7.50	7.50
c.		sal paper	7.50	7.50
d.		yel paper	7.50	7.50
e.		brn paper	9.00	9.00
f.		lil paper	10.00	10.00
g.		white paper	9.00	9.00

No.	Type	Description	Unused	Used
69	A22	10p pur, *grnsh bl*	4.50	4.50
a.		bluish paper	7.50	7.50
b.		rose paper	6.75	6.75
c.		yel paper	7.50	7.50
d.		brn paper	7.50	7.50

Sewing Machine Perf.

Laid Paper

No.	Type	Description	Unused	Used
70	A19	50c dk bl, *pink*	75	75
a.		bluish paper	75	75
71	A19	50c sl grn, *pink*	1.75	1.75
72	A19	50c pur, *grnsh bl*	2.50	2.50
a.		white paper	2.50	2.50
b.		white wove paper	7.50	
73	A20	1p org, *sal*	1.75	1.75
74	A20	1p gray grn, *lil*	9.00	9.00
a.		yel paper	9.00	9.00
75	A21	5p car rose, *lil*	2.50	2.50
a.		yel paper	1.75	1.75
b.		brn paper	2.50	2.50
c.		bluish paper	5.25	5.25
d.		white wove paper	9.00	
76	A22	10p dk bl, *bluish*	6.75	6.75
a.		grnsh bl paper	4.50	4.50
b.		yel paper	9.00	9.00
c.		As "b," wove paper	10.00	
77	A22	10p pur, *grnsh bl*	6.75	6.75
a.		bluish paper	11.00	11.00
b.		rose paper	8.25	8.25
c.		yel paper	11.00	11.00

José María del Castillo y Rada

A23

Manuel Anguiano

A24

Pantaleón C. Ribón

A25

1904 *Sewing Machine Perf.*

No.	Type	Description	Unused	Used
89	A23	5c black	30	30
a.		Imperf., pair	4.25	4.25
90	A24	10c brown	30	30
a.		Imperf., pair	3.50	3.50
91	A25	20c red	38	38
a.		Imperf., pair	8.00	8.00
92	A25	20c red brn	75	75
a.		Imperf., pair	8.00	8.00

A26

A28

A27

1904 *Imperf.*

No.	Type	Description	Unused	Used
93	A26	½c black	75	75
a.		Tête bêche pair	4.50	4.50
94	A27	1c blue	1.40	1.40
95	A28	2c purple	1.50	1.50

REGISTRATION STAMPS.

Simón Bolívar

R1 R2

Lithographed.

White Wove Paper.

1879 ***Perf. 12½, 16x12.*** **Unwmkd.**

No.	Type	Description	Unused	Used
F1	R1	40c brown	90	90

Bluish Laid Paper.

No.	Type	Description	Unused	Used
F2	R1	40c brown	90	90
a.		Imperf., pair	4.00	

Dated "1880".

1880 White Wove Paper.

No.	Type	Description	Unused	Used
F3	R1	40c brown	40	40

Bluish Laid Paper.

No.	Type	Description	Unused	Used
F4	R1	40c brown	80	80
a.		Imperf., pair	4.50	

Dated "1882" to "1885".

White Wove Paper.

1882–85 ***Perf. 16x12***

No.	Type	Description	Unused	Used
F5	R2	40c brn (1882)	40	40
a.		Perf. 12	22.50	
F6	R2	40c brn (1883)	30	30
a.		Perf. 12	11.50	
F7	R2	40c brn (1884)	30	30
a.		Perf. 12	12.00	
F8	R2	40c brn (1885)	40	40
a.		Perf. 12	3.00	

R3

Laid Paper.

1903 ***Imperf.***

No.	Type	Description	Unused	Used
F9	R3	20c org, *rose*	75	75
a.		sal paper	1.40	1.40
b.		grnsh bl paper	4.50	4.50

Sewing Machine Perf.

No.	Type	Description	Unused	Used
F10	R3	20c org, *rose*	1.50	1.50
a.		sal paper	1.50	1.50
b.		grnsh bl paper	4.50	4.50

R4

1904 Wove Paper

No.	Type	Description	Unused	Used
F11	R4	5c black	4.00	4.00

ACKNOWLEDGMENT OF RECEIPT STAMPS.

AR1

Lithographed

1903 ***Imperf.*** **Unwmkd.**

Laid Paper

No.	Type	Description	Unused	Used
H1	AR1	20c org, *rose*	1.50	1.50
a.		yel paper	1.50	1.50
b.		grnsh bl paper	3.75	3.75
H2	AR1	20c dk bl, *yel*	1.75	1.75
a.		brn paper	1.75	1.75
b.		rose paper	2.00	2.00
c.		sal paper	4.75	4.75
d.		grnsh bl paper	4.50	4.50

Sewing Machine Perf.

No.	Type	Description	Unused	Used
H3	AR1	20c org, *grnsh bl*	7.50	7.50
a.		yel paper	9.00	9.00
H4	AR1	20c dk bl, *yel*	9.00	9.00
a.		lil paper	9.00	

AR2

1904 Wove Paper.

No.	Type	Description	Unused	Used
H5	AR2	2c red	1.40	1.40

LATE FEE STAMPS.

LF1

Lithographed

1903 ***Imperf.*** **Unwmkd.**

Laid Paper.

No.	Type	Description	Unused	Used
I1	LF1	20c car rose, *bluish*	75	75
I2	LF1	20c pur, *bluish*	70	70
a.		rose paper	1.50	1.50
b.		brn paper	1.50	1.50
c.		lil paper	1.75	1.75
d.		yel paper	7.50	7.50

Sewing Machine Perf.

No.	Type	Description	Unused	Used
I3	LF1	20c car rose, *bluish*	75	75
I4	LF1	20c pur, *bluish*	75	75
a.		rose paper	1.50	1.50
b.		lil paper	1.75	1.75
c.		yel paper	7.50	7.50

Boyaca

(bō'yä-kä')

Originally a State, now a Department of the Republic of Colombia. (See Antioquia.)

Diego Mendoza Pérez

A1

Lithographed.

1902 ***Perf. 13½*** **Unwmkd.**

Wove Paper.

No.	Type	Description	Unused	Used
1	A1	5c bl grn	90	90
a.		bluish paper	90.00	90.00
b.		Imperf., pair	13.50	

Laid Paper.

Perf. 12

No.	Type	Description	Unused	Used
2	A1	5c green	100.00	100.00

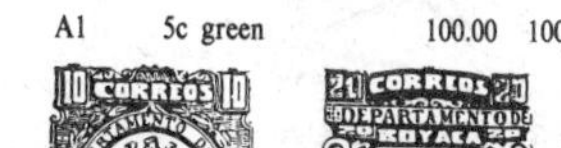

Coat of Arms

A2 A3

General Próspero Pinzón

A4

Numeral of Value

A5

Monument of Battle of Boyacá

A6

President José Manuel Marroquin

A7

1903 Lithographed. ***Imperf.***

No.	Type	Description	Unused	Used
4	A2	10c dk gray	30	30
5	A3	20c red brn	40	40
6	A5	1p red	3.75	3.75
a.		1p cl	4.50	4.50
8	A6	5p *rose*	1.40	1.40
a.		5p *buff*	12.00	12.00
9	A7	10p *buff*	1.40	1.40
a.		10p *rose*	12.00	12.00
b.		Tête bêche pair	18.50	
		Nos. 4-9 (5)	7.25	7.25

Perf. 12.

No.	Type	Description	Unused	Used
10	A2	10c dk gray	30	30
11	A3	20c red brn	45	45
12	A4	50c green	40	40
13	A4	50c dl bl	2.00	2.00
14	A5	1p red	40	40
a.		1p cl	3.75	3.75
16	A6	5p *rose*	1.40	1.40
a.		5p *buff*	12.00	12.00
17	A7	10p *buff*	1.40	1.40
a.		10p *rose*	12.00	12.00
b.		Tête bêche pair	15.00	15.00
		Nos. 10-17 (7)	6.35	6.35

Statue of Bolívar

A8

1904

No.	Type	Description	Unused	Used
18	A8	10c orange	30	30
a.		Imperf., pair	4.50	4.50

Cauca

(kou'kä)

Originally a State, now a Department of the Republic of Colombia. (See Antioquia.)

A1

A2

Handstamped.

1879 (?) ***Imperf.*** **Unwmkd.**

No.	Type	Description	Unused	Used
1	A1	(5c) black	*2,250.*	*2,000.*

1882

No.	Type	Description	Unused	Used
2	A2	5c violet	80.00	80.00
a.		Figure in lower left corner omitted		

A3

A4

1883

No.	Type	Description	Unused	Used
3	A3	(5) violet	25.00	25.00
4	A4	(5) violet	60.00	60.00

A5 A7

1890

5	A5	5c red	75.00	75.00

Nos. 1 to 5 were sanctioned, though not authorized, by the national government.

Imperf., Sewing Machine Perf.

1902 Typeset

8	A7	10c *rose*	2.25	2.25
9	A7	20c *orange*	1.50	1.50

Stamps of this design are believed to be of private origin and without official sanction.

Items inscribed "No hay estampillas" (No stamps available) and others inscribed "Manuel E. Jiménez" are considered by specialists to be receipt labels, not postage stamps.

Cundinamarca

(koon'dē·nä·mär'kä)

Originally a State, now a Department of the Republic of Colombia. (See Antioquia.)

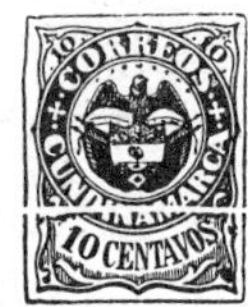

Coat of Arms

A1 A2

Lithographed

1870 ***Imperf.*** **Unwmkd.**

1	A1	5c blue	4.75	4.75
2	A2	10c red	15.00	15.00

The counterfeits, or reprints, show traces of the cuts made to deface the dies.

A3 A4

A5 A6

1877–82

3	A3	10c red ('82)	3.00	3.00
a.		Laid paper ('77)	4.50	4.50

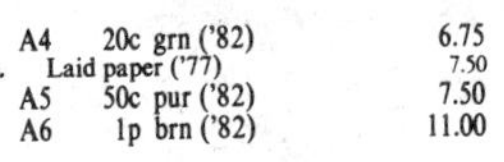

4	A4	20c grn ('82)	6.75	6.75
a.		Laid paper ('77)	7.50	7.50
7	A5	50c pur ('82)	7.50	7.50
8	A6	1p brn ('82)	11.00	11.00

A7

1884

10	A7	5c blue	75	75
11	A7	5c bl (redrawn)	1.50	1.50
a.		Tête bêche pair	75.00	75.00

The redrawn stamp has no period after "COLOMBIA."

A8

CUNDINAMARCA.
CINCUENTA CVOS.

A9

A10

E. U. DE COLOMBIA
E.S. DE CUNDINAMARCA
SELLO PROVISORIO
CORREOS DEL ESTADO
VALE DOS REALES

A11

1883 Typeset

13	A8	10c *yellow*	11.00	11.00
14	A9	50c *rose*	11.00	11.00
15	A10	1p *brown*	30.00	30.00
16	A11	2r *green*	1,600.	

Typeset varieties exist: 4 of the 10c, 2 each of 50c and 1p.

Some experts doubt that No. 16 was issued. The variety without signature and watermarked "flowers" is believed to be a proof. Forgeries exist.

A12

1886 Lithographed.

17	A12	5c blue	75	75
18	A12	10c red	4.50	4.50
19	A12	10c red, *lil*	2.40	2.40
20	A12	20c green	3.75	3.75
a.		20c yel grn	4.50	4.50
21	A12	50c purple	4.50	4.50
22	A12	1p org brn	5.25	5.25

Nos. 17 to 22 have been reprinted. The colors are aniline and differ from those of the original stamps. The impression is coarse and blurred.

A13 A14

Arms

A15 A16

A17 A18

A19 A20

A21

1904 ***Perf. 10½, 12***

23	A13	1c orange	30	30
24	A14	2c gray bl	30	30
25	A15	3c rose	45	45
26	A15	5c ol grn	45	45
27	A16	10c pale brn	45	45
28	A17	15c pink	45	45
29	A18	20c bl, *grn*	45	45
30	A18	20c blue	75	75
31	A19	40c blue	75	75
32	A19	40c bl, *buff*	17.50	17.50
33	A20	50c red vio	75	75
34	A21	1p gray grn	60	60
		Nos. 23-34 (12)	23.20	23.20

Imperf.

23a	A13	1c orange	90	90
24a	A14	2c blue	90	90
b.		2c sl	6.00	6.00
25a	A15	3c rose	90	90
26a	A15	5c ol grn	1.50	1.50
27a	A16	10c pale brn	2.50	2.50
28a	A17	15c pink	45	45
29a	A18	20c bl, *grn*	2.25	2.25
30a	A18	20c blue	2.25	2.25
31a	A19	40c blue	75	75
32a	A19	40c bl, *buff*	17.50	17.50
33a	A20	50c red vio	75	75
34a	A21	1p gray grn	75	75
		Nos. 23a-34a (12)	31.40	31.40

REGISTRATION STAMPS.

R1

1883 ***Imperf.*** **Unwmkd.**

F1	R1	*orange*	15.00	16.50

R2

1904 ***Perf. 12.***

F2	R2	10c bister	1.00	1.00
a.		Imperf.	4.25	4.25

Magdalena

Items inscribed "No hay estampillas" (No stamps available) are considered by specialists to be not postage stamps but receipt labels.

Panama.

Issues of Panama as a state and later Department of Colombia are listed with the Republic of Panama issues (Nos. 1-30).

Santander

(sän'tän·dâr')

Originally a State, now a Department of the Republic of Colombia. (See Antioquia.)

Coat of Arms

A1 A2

Lithographed.

1884 ***Imperf.*** **Unwmkd.**

1	A1	1c blue	30	30
a.		1c gray bl	50	50
2	A2	5c red	50	50
3	A2	10c bluish pur	1.75	1.75
a.		Tête bêche pair		

No. 2 exists unofficially perforated 14.

A3 A4

1886 ***Imperf.***

4	A3	1c blue	90	90
5	A3	5c red	30	30
6	A3	10c red vio	50	50
a.		10c dp vio	50	50
b.		Inscribed "CINCO CENTAVOS"	25.00	25.00

The numerals in the upper corners are omitted on No. 5, while on No. 6 there are no numerals in the side panels. No. 6 exists unofficially perforated 12.

1887

7	A4	1c blue	22	22
a.		1c ultra	1.50	1.50
8	A4	5c red	1.50	1.50
9	A4	10c violet	3.75	3.75

A5

A6

A7

1889 ***Perf. 11½ and 13½.***

10	A5	1c blue	30	30
11	A6	5c red	1.50	1.50
12	A7	10c purple	50	50
a.		Imperf., pair	20.00	

A8

A9

1892 ***Perf. 13½***

13	A8	5c red, *rose buff*	75	75

1895-96

14	A9	5c brown	90	90
15	A9	5c yel grn ('96)	90	90

A10 A11

A12

1899 ***Perf. 10***

16	A10	1c *green*	40	40
17	A11	5c *pink*	40	40
		Perf. 13½.		
18	A12	10c blue	90	90
a.		Perf. 12	1.25	1.25

A13

1903 ***Imperf.***

19	A13	50c red	65	65
a.		50c rose	65	65
b.		"SANTENDER"	3.00	3.00
c.		"Corrcos"	3.00	3.00
d.		"Corceos"	3.00	3.00
e.		Tête bêche pair	6.00	6.00
f.		Pair, one without overprint	3.50	3.50

The overprint "Correos de Departmento Bucaramanga" on the 50c red revenue stamp has been proved to be a cancellation.

A14

A15

Arms Locomotive
A16 A17

A18

A19

A20

1904 ***Imperf.***

22	A14	5c dk grn	30	30
a.		5c yel grn	50	50
24	A15	10c rose	15	15
25	A16	20c brn vio	15	15
26	A17	50c yellow	20	20
27	A18	1p black	20	20
28	A19	5p dk bl	40	40
29	A20	10p carmine	50	50
		Nos. 22-29 (7)	1.90	1.90

1905

30	A14	5c pale bl	50	50
31	A15	10c red brn	50	50
32	A16	20c yel grn	50	50
33	A17	50c red vio	50	50
34	A18	1p dk bl	50	50
35	A19	5p pink	50	50
36	A20	10p red	2.00	2.00
		Nos. 30-36 (7)	5.00	5.00

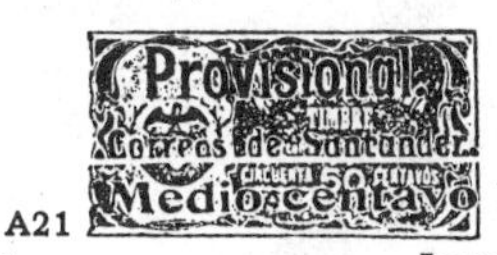

A21

1907 ***Imperf.***

37	A21	½c on 50c rose	65	65

City of Cucuta

(kōō′kōō·tä)

A71 A72

Lithographed.

"Gobierno Provisorio" at Top

1900 ***Perf. 12 Vertically.***

101	A71	1c (ctvo) *bl grn*	4.50	4.50
a.		"cvo."	11.50	11.50
b.		"cvos."	4.50	4.50
c.		"centavo"	5.25	5.25
103	A71	2c black	3.00	3.00
104	A71	5c *pink*	3.00	3.00
a.		Name at side (V)	6.50	6.50
105	A71	10c *pink*	3.00	3.00
a.		Name at side (V)	6.50	6.50
106	A71	20c *yellow*	4.50	4.50
a.		Name at side (G)	9.00	9.00
		Nos. 101-106 (5)	18.00	18.00

"Gobierno Provisional" at Top
Name at Side in Black or Green

108	A72	1c (ctvo.) *bl grn* (Bk)	4.50	4.50
a.		"centavo"	17.50	17.50
109	A72	2c *bl grn* (Bk)	2.50	2.50
110	A72	5c blk (G)	2.50	2.50
a.		"ctvos." smaller	5.00	5.00
112	A72	10c *pink* (Bk)	2.50	2.50
113	A72	20c *yel* (G)	4.50	4.50
		Nos. 108-113 (5)	16.50	16.50

Stamps of these and similar designs on white and yellow paper, with and without surcharges of ½c, 1c or 2c, are believed to have been produced without government authorization.

Tolima

(tō·lē′mä)

Originally a State, now a Department of the Republic of Colombia. (See Antioquia.)

A1

Typeset.

1870 ***Imperf.*** **Unwmkd.**

White Wove Paper.

1	A1	5c black	60.00	32.50
2	A1	10c black	60.00	32.50

Printed from two settings. Setting I, ten types of 5c. Setting II, six types of 5c and four types of 10c.

Blue Laid Batonné Paper.

3	A1	5c black	*750.00*	

Buff Laid Batonné Paper.

4	A1	5c black	120.00	80.00

Blue Wove Paper

5	A1	5c black	67.50	45.00

Blue Vertically Laid Paper.

6	A1	5c black	100.00	70.00
a.		Paper with ruled blue vertical lines		

Blue Horizontally Laid Paper

7	A1	5c black	100.00	70.00

Blue Quadrille Paper.

8	A1	5c black	100.00	90.00

Ten varieties each of Nos. 3-5 and 7; 20 varieties each of Nos. 6 and 8.

Official imitations were made in 1886 from new settings of the type. There are only two varieties of each value. They are printed on blue and white paper, wove, batonné, laid, etc.

A2

A3

A4

A5

Yellowish White Wove Paper.

1871 **Lithographed** ***Imperf.***

9	A2	5c dp brn	2.25	2.25
a.		5c red brn	2.25	2.25
b.		Value reads "CINGO"	37.50	37.50
10	A3	10c blue	6.00	6.00
11	A4	50c green	7.50	7.50
12	A5	1p carmine	12.00	12.00

The 5p stamps, type A2, are bogus varieties made from an altered die of the 5c.

The 10c, 50c and 1 peso stamps have been reprinted on bluish white wove paper. They are from new plates and most copies show traces of fine lines with which the dies had been defaced. Reprints of the 5c have a large cross at the top. The 10c on laid batonné paper is known only as a reprint.

A6

A7

A8

A9

1879 Grayish or White Wove Paper

14	A6	5c yel brn	45	45
a.		5c pur brn	45	45
15	A7	10c blue	50	50
16	A8	50c grn, *bluish*	50	50
a.		White paper	1.50	1.50
17	A9	1p vermilion	2.25	2.25
a.		1p car rose	9.00	9.00

A10

1883 ***Imperf.***

18	A6	5c orange	45	45
19	A7	10c vermilion	90	90
20	A10	20c violet	1.40	1.40

Coat of Arms
A12

1884 ***Imperf.***

23	A12	1c gray	15	15
24	A12	2c rose lil	15	15
a.		2c sl	15	15
25	A12	2½c dl org	15	15
26	A12	5c brown	15	15
27	A12	10c blue	38	38
a.		10c sl	22	22
28	A12	20c lemon	38	38
a.		Laid paper	5.00	5.00
29	A12	25c black	30	30
30	A12	50c green	30	30

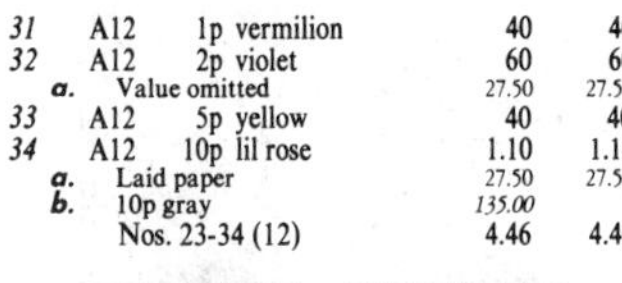

No.	Type	Description	Unused	Used
31	A12	1p vermilion	40	40
32	A12	2p violet	60	60
a.		Value omitted	27.50	27.50
33	A12	5p yellow	40	40
34	A12	10p lil rose	1.10	1.10
a.		Laid paper	27.50	27.50
b.		10p gray	135.00	
		Nos. 23-34 (12)	4.46	4.46

A13

A14

Condor with Long Wings Touching Flagstaffs
A15 A16

1886 Litho. *Perf. 10½, 11*

White Paper

No.	Type	Description	Unused	Used
36	A13	5c brown	1.50	1.50
a.		5c yel brn	1.50	1.50
b.		Imperf., pair	20.00	
37	A14	10c blue	4.50	4.50
a.		Imperf., pair	20.00	
38	A15	50c green	1.75	1.75
a.		Imperf., pair	20.00	

No. 38 has been reprinted in pale gray green, perforated 10½, and No. 39 in bright vermilion, perforated 11½. The impressions show many signs of wear.

Lilac Tinted Paper.

No.	Type	Description	Unused	Used
36c	A13	5c org brn	13.00	13.00
37b	A14	10c blue	13.00	13.00
38b	A15	50c green	9.00	9.00
39	A16	1p vermilion	3.00	3.00
a.		Imperf., pair	30.00	
39b	A16	1p vermilion	7.50	7.50

A17 A18

Condor with Short Wings
A19 A20

1886 White Paper *Perf. 12*

No.	Type	Description	Unused	Used
44	A19	1c gray	7.50	7.50
a.		Imperf., pair	20.00	
45	A17	2c rose lil	8.25	8.25
46	A18	2½c dl org	24.00	24.00
47	A19	5c brown	10.00	10.00
a.		Imperf., pair	32.50	
48	A20	10c blue	10.00	10.00
a.		Imperf., pair	32.50	
49	A20	20c lemon	8.25	8.25
a.		Tête bêche pair	225.00	225.00
50	A20	25c black	7.50	7.50
51	A20	50c green	3.00	3.00
52	A20	1p vermilion	4.50	4.50
a.		Imperf., pair	20.00	
53	A20	2p violet	9.00	9.00
a.		Imperf., pair	25.00	
b.		Tête bêche pair	175.00	175.00
54	A20	5p orange	16.50	16.50
a.		Imperf., pair	40.00	
55	A20	10p lil rose	8.25	8.25
a.		Imperf., pair	20.00	

Condor with Long Wings, Upper Flagstaffs Omitted
A21 A22

1886 *Perf. 12, 12½, 12x11*

No.	Type	Description	Unused	Used
56	A15	2½c dl org	75.00	75.00
a.		Imperf., pair		
b.		Transfer of 5c in stone of 2½c		
c.		Transfer of 10c in stone of 2½c		
57	A21	5c brown	7.50	7.50
a.		Imperf., pair	20.00	
b.		Transfer of 10c in stone of 5c		
c.		As "b," imperf.		
58	A14	10c ultra	13.00	13.00
a.		Imperf., pair	32.50	
b.		Transfer of 5c in stone of 10c		
59	A22	2p red vio	15.00	15.00
a.		Imperf., pair	37.50	
b.		Without numerals in corners, colored background, imperf.	27.50	
c.		As "b," white background	27.50	27.50
60	A22	5p pale org	22.50	22.50
a.		Imperf., pair	55.00	
b.		Bottom label inverted		
c.		Tête bêche pair		
d.		Transfer of 2p in stone of 5p		

Imperf.

No.	Type	Description	Unused	Used
61	A13	1c black	150.00	

No. 56 is similar to type A15, and No. 58 similar to type A14, but both have upper flag-staffs omitted.

A23

1888 *Perf. 10½.*

No.	Type	Description	Unused	Used
62	A23	5c red	15	15
a.		Imperf., pair	3.50	
63	A23	10c green	38	38
a.		Imperf., pair	4.00	
64	A23	50c blue	1.00	1.00
a.		Imperf., pair	6.00	6.00
65	A23	1p red brn	1.75	1.75
a.		Imperf., pair	9.00	

1895 *Perf. 12, 13½*

No.	Type	Description	Unused	Used
66	A23	1c bl, *rose*	30	30
a.		Imperf., pair	9.00	
67	A23	2c grn, *lt grn*	30	30
a.		Imperf., pair	9.00	
68	A23	5c red	15	15
69	A23	10c green	30	30
70	A23	20c bl, *yel*	38	38
a.		Imperf., pair	10.00	
71	A23	1p brown	2.25	2.25
		Nos. 66-71 (6)	3.68	3.68

'No Hay Estampillas'

Items inscribed "No hay estampillas" (No stamps available) are considered by specialists to be not postage stamps but receipt labels.

Honda Issue.

A23a

Black Surcharge.

1896 *Perf. 12*

No.	Type	Description	Unused	Used
78	A23a	1c on 2c grn	45.00	45.00

Excellent counterfeits exist.

Regular Issue.

A24 A25

A26

A27

A28

A29

A30 A31

Sewing Machine or Regular
Perf. 12

1903-04 Lithographed.

No.	Type	Description	Unused	Used
79	A24	4c *green*	30	30
80	A25	10c dl bl	30	30
81	A26	20c orange	60	60
82	A27	50c *rose*	22	22
a.		50c *buff*	22	22
84	A28	1p brown	22	22
85	A29	2p gray	22	22
86	A30	5p red	22	22
a.		Tête bêche pair	6.25	6.25
87	A31	10p *blue*	22	22
a.		10p *lt grn*	22	22
b.		10p *grn glazed*	4.50	4.50
		Nos. 79-87 (8)	6.63	6.63

Imperf.

No.	Type	Description	Unused	Used
79a	A24	4c *green*	30	30
80a	A25	10c dl bl	22	22
81a	A26	20c orange	1.40	1.40
82b	A27	50c *rose*	1.75	1.75
c.		50c *buff*	1.75	1.75
84a	A28	1p brown	22	22
85a	A29	2p gray	22	22
86b	A30	5p red	22	22
c.		Tête bêche pair	6.25	6.25
87c	A31	10p *blue*	2.75	2.75
d.		Tête bêche pair		
e.		10p *lt grn*	4.50	4.50
f.		10p *grn glazed*	22.50	22.50
		Nos. 79a-87c (8)	2.75	2.75

COMORO ISLANDS

LOCATION—In Mozambique Channel between Madagascar and Mozambique.

GOVT.—Republic.

AREA—838 sq. mi.

POP.—262,000 (est. 1974).

CAPITAL—Moroni, Grand Comoro.

The Comoro Archipelago consists of the islands of Mayotte, Anjouan, Grand Comoro (Grande Comore) and Mohéli, which issued their own stamps as French protectorates or colonies in 1897–1914. The archipelago was attached to Madagascar from 1914 to 1946 when it became a separate French Territory. In July, 1975, Anjouan, Grand Comoro and Moheli united to declare independence as the State of Comoro. Mayotte remained French.

100 Centimes = 1 Franc

Anjouan Bay
A2

Comoro Woman Grinding Grain
A3

Moroni Mosque on Grand Comoro
A4

Engraved

1950 *Perf. 13* Unwmkd.

No.	Type	Description	Unused	Used
30	A2	10c blue	15	15
31	A2	50c green	20	20
32	A2	1fr dk ol brn	20	20
33	A3	2fr brt grn	25	25
34	A3	5fr purple	25	25
35	A3	6fr vio brn	35	35
36	A4	7fr red	45	45
37	A4	10fr dk grn	45	45
38	A4	11fr dp ultra	50	50
		Nos. 30-38 (9)	2.80	2.80

Imperforates

Most Comoro Islands stamps exist imperforate in issued and trial colors, and also in small presentation sheets in issued colors.

Military Medal Issue.

Common Design Type

1952 Engraved and Typographed

No.	Type	Description	Unused	Used
39	CD101	15fr multi	25.00	25.00

Mosque of Ouani, Anjouan
A5

Coelacanth
A6

1952–54 Engraved

No.	Type	Description	Unused	Used
40	A5	15fr dk brn	55	55
41	A5	20fr red brn	70	70
42	A6	40fr aqua & ind ('54)	13.50	10.00

FIDES Issue

Common Design Type

1956 *Perf. 13x12½* Unwmkd.

No.	Type	Description	Unused	Used
43	CD103	9fr dp vio	70	50

Human Rights Issue

Common Design Type

1958 Engraved. *Perf. 13*

No.	Type	Description	Unused	Used
44	CD105	20fr ol grn & dk bl	5.50	5.50

Flower Issue

Common Design Type

Design: Colvillea.

1959 Photogravure *Perf. 12½x12*

45	CD104	10fr multi	2.50	1.65

View of Dzaoudzi and Radio Symbol
A8

Design: 25fr, Radio tower and radio waves over Islands.

1960, Dec. 23 Engr. *Perf. 13*

46	A8	20fr mar, vio bl & grn	70	60
47	A8	25fr ultra, brn & grn	85	85

Comoro radio station.

Harpa Conoidalis
A9

Sea Shells: 50c, Cypraecassis rufa. 2fr, Murex ramosus. 5fr, Turbo marmoratus. 20fr, Pterocera scorpio. 25fr, Charonia tritonis.

1962, Jan. 13 Photogravure

Shells in Natural Colors

48	A9	50c lil & brn	30	30
49	A9	1fr yel & red	30	30
50	A9	2fr pale grn & pink	40	40
51	A9	5fr yel & grn	80	80
52	A9	20fr sal & brn	1.85	1.85
53	A9	25fr bis & pink	2.50	2.50
		Nos. 48-53, C5-C6 (8)	21.65	20.15

Wheat Emblem and Globe
A10

1963, Mar. 21 Engr. *Perf. 13*

54	A10	20fr choc & dk grn	2.50	2.25

Issued for the "Freedom from Hunger" campaign of the U.N. Food and Agriculture Organization.

Red Cross Centenary Issue

Common Design Type

1963, Sept. 2 *Perf. 13* Unwmkd.

55	CD113	50fr emer, gray & car	4.00	3.50

Centenary of the International Red Cross.

Human Rights Issue

Common Design Type

1963, Dec. 10 Engraved

56	CD117	15fr dk red & yel grn	4.00	3.50

Common Design Types

pictured in section at front of book.

Tobacco Pouch A13 — **Grand Comoro Canoe** A14

Designs: 4fr, Censer. 10fr, Carved lamp.

1963, Dec. 27 *Perf. 13*

Size: 22x36mm.

57	A13	3fr multi	15	15
58	A13	4fr org, dp cl & sl grn	25	25
59	A13	10fr org brn, dk red brn & grn	50	50
		Nos. 57-59, C8-C9 (5)	6.90	4.60

Philatec Issue

Common Design Type

1964, March 31

60	CD118	50fr dk bl, red & grn	1.65	1.65

1964, Aug. 7 Photo. *Perf. 13x12½*

Design: 30fr, Boutre felucca.

Size: 22x37mm.

61	A14	15fr multi	60	60
62	A14	30fr lt grn & multi	1.00	1.00

See Nos. C10-C11.

Spiny Lobster
A15

Designs: 12fr, Hammerhead shark (horiz.). 20fr, Turtle (horiz.). 25fr, Merou fish.

1965, Dec. 20 Engraved *Perf. 13*

63	A15	1fr grn, lil & ocher	20	20
64	A15	12fr org red, sl & gray	50	40
65	A15	20fr org, red & bl grn	60	50
66	A15	25fr bl grn, dk brn & red	70	60

Hotel Itsandra, Moroni
A16

Design: 15fr, Lake Salé, Grand Comoro.

Photogravure

1966, Dec. 19 *Perf. 12½x13*

67	A16	15fr multi	40	30
68	A16	25fr multi	50	30

See Nos. C18-C19.

Comoro Sunbird
A17

Birds: 10fr, Malachite kingfisher. 15fr, Rothschild's fody. 30fr, Cuckoo-roller.

1967, June 20 Photo. *Perf. 12½x13*

Size: 36x23mm.

69	A17	2fr ocher & multi	60	60
70	A17	10fr lil & multi	80	80
71	A17	15fr yel grn & multi	1.00	1.00
72	A17	30fr pink & multi	1.60	1.60
		Nos. 69-72, C20-C21 (6)	7.85	5.50

WHO Anniversary Issue

Common Design Type

1968, May 4 Engraved *Perf. 13*

73	CD126	40fr grn, vio & dp car	80	70

Issued for the 20th anniversary of the World Health Organization.

Surgeon-fish
A19

Design: 25fr, Imperial angelfish.

1968, Aug. 1 Engraved *Perf. 13*

Size: 36x22mm.

74	A19	20fr vio bl, yel & red brn	40	40
75	A19	25fr Prus bl, dk bl & org	50	50

See Nos. C23-C24.

Human Rights Year Issue

Common Design Type

1968, Aug. 10 Engraved *Perf. 13*

76	CD127	60fr brn, grn & org	1.20	1.20

Msoila Prayer Rug and Praying Man
A20

Designs: Each stamp shows a different prayer position.

1969, Feb. 27 Engraved *Perf. 13*

77	A20	20fr bl grn, rose red & pur	30	25
78	A20	30fr pur, rose red & bl grn	40	35
79	A20	45fr rose red, pur & bl grn	60	50

Vanilla Flower
A21

Design: 15fr, Flower of ylang-ylang tree. 25fr, Poinsettia (country name in upper right corner).

1969–70 Photo. *Perf. 12½x13*

Size: 36x23mm.

80	A21	10fr multi	25	20
81	A21	15fr multi	32	28
82	A21	25fr multi ('70)	50	35
		Nos. 80-82, C26-C28 (6)	6.32	4.68

Issue dates: Nos. 80–81, Mar. 20, 1969. No. 82, Mar. 5, 1970.

ILO Issue

Common Design Type

1969, Nov. 24 Engraved *Perf. 13*

83	CD131	5fr org, emer & gray	25	20

Issued for 50th anniversary of the International Labor Organization.

U.P.U. Headquarters Issue

Common Design Type

1970, May 20 Engraved *Perf. 13*

84	CD133	65fr pur, bl grn & red brn	1.25	80

Chiromani Costume, Anjouan A22 — **Friday Mosque** A23

Design: 25fr, Bouiboui costume, Grand Comoro.

1970, Oct. 30 Photo. *Perf. 12½x13*

85	A22	20fr grn, yel & red	40	32
86	A22	25fr brn, yel & dk bl	50	40

1970, Dec. 18 Engraved *Perf. 13*

87	A23	5fr rose car, grn & grnsh bl	25	15
88	A23	10fr dp lil, grn & vio	32	25
89	A23	40fr cop red, grn & dp brn	55	45

Great White Egret A24 — **Pyrostegia Venusta** A25

Birds: 10fr, Comoro pigeon. 15fr, Green-backed heron. 25fr, Comoro blue pigeon. 35fr, Humblot's flycatcher. 40fr, Allen's gallinule.

Photogravure

1971, March 12 *Perf. 12½x13*

90	A24	5fr multi	20	15
91	A24	10fr yel & multi	28	20
92	A24	15fr bl & multi	30	22
93	A24	25fr org & multi	45	35
94	A24	35fr yel grn & multi	85	60
95	A24	40fr gray & multi	1.00	80
		Nos. 90-95 (6)	3.08	2.32

1971, July 19 Photo. *Perf. 13*

Flowers: 3fr, Dogbane (horiz.). 20fr, Frangipani.

Size: 22x36, 36x22mm.

96	A25	1fr ver & grn	15	15
97	A25	3fr yel, grn & red	25	20
98	A25	20fr ver & grn	70	45
		Nos. 96-98, C37-C38 (5)	3.80	2.30

Lithograph Cone
A26

Sea Shells: 10fr, Pacific lettered cone. 20fr, Aulicus cone. 35fr, Polita nerita. 60fr, Snake-head cowrie.

1971, Oct. 4

99	A26	5fr lt ultra & multi	20	15
100	A26	10fr multi	25	20
101	A26	20fr vio & multi	35	30
102	A26	35fr lt bl & multi	60	45
103	A26	60fr lt vio & multi	80	80
		Nos. 99-103 (5)	2.20	1.90

De Gaulle Issue
Common Design Type

Designs: 20fr, Gen. de Gaulle, 1940. 35fr, Pres. de Gaulle, 1970.

104	CD134	20fr dk car & blk	50	25
105	CD134	35fr dk car & blk	70	55

First anniversary of the death of Charles de Gaulle (1890–1970), president of France.

Louis Pasteur, Slides, Microscope
A27

1972, Aug. 2

106	A27	65fr ind, org, & ol brn	1.00	75

Sesquicentennial of the birth of Louis Pasteur (1822–1895), chemist.

Type of Air Post Issue 1971

Designs: 10fr, View of Goulaivoini. 20fr, Bay, Mitsamiouli. 35fr, Gate and fountain, Foumbouni. 50fr, View of Moroni.

1973, June 28 Photo. ***Perf. 13***

107	AP10	10fr bl & multi	25	20
108	AP10	20fr grn & multi	40	35
109	AP10	35fr bl & multi	70	65
110	AP10	50fr bl & multi	85	75
		Nos. 107-110, C53 (5)	4.45	3.55

Bank of Madagascar and Comoros
A28

Buildings in Moroni: 15fr, Post and Telecommunications Administration. 20fr, Prefecture.

1973, July 10 Photo. ***Perf. 13x12½***

111	A28	5fr multi	12	10
112	A28	15fr multi	22	20
113	A28	20fr multi	40	35

Salimata Hamissi Mosque
A29

Design: 20fr, Zaouiyat Chaduli Mosque (vert.).

Perf. 12½x13, 13x12½

1973, Oct. 20 Photogravure

114	A29	20fr multi	35	30
115	A29	35fr multi	65	60

Cheikh Mausoleum
A30

Design: 50fr, Mausoleum of President Said Mohamed Cheikh (different view).

1974, Mar. 16 Engraved ***Perf. 13***

116	A30	35fr grn, ol brn & blk	55	45
117	A30	50fr grn, ol brn & blk	75	65

Koran Stand, Anjouan
A31

Designs: 15fr, Carved combs (vert.). 20fr, 3-legged table (vert.). 75fr, Sugar press.

1974, May 10 Photo. ***Perf. 12½x13***

118	A31	15fr emer & multi	25	20
119	A31	20fr grn & multi	35	25
120	A31	35fr multi	50	40
121	A31	75fr multi	90	75

UPU Emblem, Symbolic Postmark
A32

1974, Oct. 9 Engr. ***Perf. 13x12½***

122	A32	30fr multi	40	35

Centenary of Universal Postal Union.

Bracelet
A33

Designs: 35fr, Diadem. 120fr, Saber. 135fr, Dagger.

1975, Feb. 28 Engr. ***Perf. 13***

123	A33	20fr multi	35	30
124	A33	35fr grn & multi	55	50
125	A33	120fr bl & multi	1.75	1.50
126	A33	135fr multi	1.85	1.65

Mohani Village, Moheli—A34

Designs: 50fr, Djoezi Village, Moheli. 55fr, Chirazi tombs.

1975, May 26 Photo. ***Perf. 13***

127	A34	30fr vio bl & multi	30	20
128	A34	50fr Prus bl & multi	55	40
129	A34	55fr grn & multi	60	65

Skin Diver Photographing Coelacanth—A35

1975, June 27 Engr. ***Perf. 13***

130	A35	50fr multi	80	60

1975 coelacanth expedition.

State of Comoro

AREA—712 sq. mi.

POP.—216,587 (census 1966).

In 1978 the islands' name became the Federal and Islamic Republic of the Comoros.

Issues of 1971–75 Surcharged and Overprinted with Bars and: "ETAT COMORIEN" in Black, Silver or Red.

Tambourine Player—A36

Design: No. 153, Women dancers and tambourine players.

Printing & Perforations as Before.
A36: Photo., ***Perf. 13***

1975

Multicolored

131	A25	5fr on 1fr	6	6
132	A25	5fr on 3fr	6	6
133	A17	10fr on 2fr	*45*	*45*
134	A28	15fr on 20fr (R)	20	15
135	A29	15fr on 20fr (S)	20	15
136	A33	15fr on 20fr	20	15
137	A31	20fr	28	20
138	A29	25fr on 35fr	35	30
139	A34	30fr	40	35
140	A30	30fr on 35fr	40	35
141	A31	30fr on 35fr	40	35
142	A33	30fr on 35fr	40	35
143	AP10	35fr	45	40
144	SP2	35fr on 35fr+10fr	45	40
145	A24	40fr	55	45
146	A34	50fr	70	60
147	A35	50fr	70	60
148	A34	50fr on 55fr (S)	70	60
149	A31	75fr	1.10	90
150	A26	75fr on 60fr (S)	1.10	90
151	A33	100fr on 120fr	1.40	1.20
152	A36	100fr bl & multi	1.40	1.20
153	A36	100fr on 150fr (S)	1.40	1.20
154	A33	200fr on 135fr	2.80	2.25
155	A32	500fr on 30fr	7.00	6.00
		Nos. 131-155 (25)	*23.15*	*19.62*

Nos. 152–153 exist without overprint or surcharge. No. 155 exists with red surcharge.

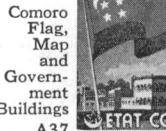

Comoro Flag, Map and Government Buildings
A37

1976, Nov. 18 Litho. ***Perf. 13½***

156	A37	30fr multi	25	15
157	A37	50fr multi	40	25

1st anniversary of independence.

Comoro Flag, UN Headquarters and Emblem
A38

1976, Nov. 25

158	A38	40fr multi	30	20
159	A38	50fr multi	40	25

1st anniversary of United Nations membership.

Islamic Republic

Nos. 156–157 Surcharged and Overprinted with 3 Lines and: "République / Fédérale / et Islamique / des Comores"

1978, July 24 Litho. ***Perf. 13½***

160	A37	30fr multi
161	A37	40fr on 30fr multi
162	A37	50fr multi
163	A37	100fr on 50fr multi

Nos. 160 and 162 were also overprinted to commemorate Queen Elizabeth II coronation anniversary; Capt. James Cook; World Cup Soccer winner; Albrecht Dürer; First powered flight; Railroad anniversary; Voyager I and II; Int. Year of the Child; 1980 Olympic Games; World Cup Soccer, Espana '82.

Italian Ball Game, 18th Century, Modern Soccer—A40

Soccer Cup, Argentina '78 Emblem, Soccer Scene and: 2fr, Ball game, London, 14th century. 3fr, Man and boy with ball, Greece, 5th century B.C. 50fr, Ball game, France, 19th century.

1979 Litho. ***Perf. 13***

Black Surcharge and Overprint

169	A40	1fr on 100fr multi	3	3
170	A40	2fr on 75fr multi	3	3
171	A40	3fr on 30fr multi	3	3
172	A40	50fr multi	50	50
		Nos. 169-172, C96 (5)	2.34	2.34

Otto Lilienthal and Glider—A41

History of Aviation: No. 174, Wright brothers and Flyer A. No. 175, Louis Bleriot and Bleriot XI. 100fr, Claude Dornier and Dornier-Wall hydrofoil.

1979

Black Overprint and Surcharge

173	A41	30fr multi	22	22
174	A41	50fr multi	60	60
175	A41	50fr on 75fr multi	70	70
176	A41	100fr multi	1.25	1.25

Papilio Dardanus Cenea
A42

Butterflies: 15fr, Papilio dardanus. 30fr, Chrysiridia croesus. 50fr, Precis octavia. 75fr, Bunaea alcinoe.

1979

Black Overprint and Surcharge

177	A42	5fr on 20fr multi	5	5
178	A42	15fr multi	15	15
179	A42	30fr multi	35	35
180	A42	50fr multi	60	60
181	A42	75fr multi	1.00	1.00
		Nos. 177-181 (5)	2.15	2.15

For Nos. 169–181 without overprint see "For the Record."

Gallinule
A43

Birds: 30fr, Kingfisher. No. 184, Bee-eater. No. 185, Flycatcher. 200fr, Sunbird.

1979 Litho. ***Perf. 13***

Black Overprint and Surcharge

182	A43	15fr multi	18	18
183	A43	30fr on 35fr multi	40	40
184	A43	50fr on 20fr multi	60	60
185	A43	50fr on 40fr multi	60	60
186	A43	200fr on 75fr multi	2.50	2.50

Giuseppe Verdi—A44

Composers: 30fr, Johann Sebastian Bach. 40fr, Wolfgang Amadeus Mozart. 50fr, Hector Berlioz.

1979

Black Overprint and Surcharge

187	A44	5fr on 100fr multi	5	5
188	A44	30fr multi	30	30
189	A44	40fr multi	40	40
190	A44	50fr multi	60	60
		Nos. 187-190, C98 (5)	1.90	1.90

For Nos. 182–190, C98 without overprint see "For the Record."

Galileo and Voyager I—A46

Exploration of Solar System: 30fr, Kepler and Voyager II. 40fr, Copernicus and Voyager II. 100fr, Huygens and Voyager II.

1979, Feb. 19

196	A46	20fr multi	10	10
197	A46	30fr multi	22	10
198	A46	40fr multi	32	12
199	A46	100fr multi	70	32
		Nos. 196-199, C99-C100 (6)	5.74	2.44

Philidor, Anderssen, Steinitz and King—A47

Design: 100fr, Chess pieces and board, Venetian chess player.

1979, Feb. 19

200	A47	40fr multi	28	8
201	A47	100fr multi	70	25

Chess Grand Masters. See No. C102.

Satellite and Radar—A48

Design: 100fr, Satellites, earth and radar.

1979, Sept. 15 **Litho.** ***Perf. 13***

Black Overprint

202	A48	75fr multi	75	
203	A48	100fr multi	70	70

See No. C103.

U.N. No. 42, Satellite over Earth—A49

1979, Sept. 15

Black Overprint

204	A49	75fr multi	75	

Innsbruck, Olympic Emblems, Skater
A50

1979, Sept. 15

Black Overprint

205	A50	35fr multi	35	

Philipp Reis, Telephone Operators—A51

1979, Sept. 15

Black Overprint

206	A51	75fr multi	75	

For Nos. 202-206 without overprint see "For the Record."

Charaxes Defulvata
A52

Birds: 50fr, Leptosomus discolor. 75fr, Bee eater.

1979, Apr. 10 Litho. ***Perf. 12½***

207	A52	30fr multi	30	12
208	A52	50fr multi	50	22
209	A52	75fr multi	80	35

Litchi Nuts
A53

1979, June 15 Litho. ***Perf. 12½***

Fruit: 70fr, Papayas. 100fr, Avocados. 125fr, Bananas.

210	A53	60fr multi	60
211	A53	70fr multi	70
212	A53	100fr multi	1.00
213	A53	125fr multi	1.25

Basketball Players
A54

1979, Aug. 28 Litho. ***Perf. 13***

214	A54	200fr multi	2.00

Indian Ocean Olympics.

Dugout on Beach
A61

Anjouan Puppet
A62

1980, Jan. 4 Litho. ***Perf. 13***

232	A61	60fr multi	60
233	A62	100fr multi	1.00

Sultan Said Ali—A63

1980, Feb. 20 ***Perf. 12½x13***

234	A63	40fr *shown*	40
235	A63	60fr *Sultan Ahmed*	60

Sherlock Holmes, Doyle—A64

1980, Feb. 25 ***Perf. 12½***

236	A64	200fr multi	2.00

Sir Arthur Conan Doyle (1859-1930), writer.

Grand Mosque, Holy Ka'aba, Mecca—A64a

1980, Mar. 12 ***Perf. 13x12½***

237	A64	75fr multi	75

Discovery of Mecca by Mohammed, 1350th anniversary.

Year of the Holy City of Jerusalem—A65

1980, Mar. 12 ***Perf. 13x13½***

238	A65	60fr multi	60

See "Special Notices" at the front of this volume for data on the listing methods of this Catalogue, abbreviations, condition, prices and examination.

Kepler, Copernicus and Pluto—A66

1980, Apr. 30 Litho. *Perf. 12½*

239	A66	400fr multi	3.00	2.25

Discovery of Pluto, 50th anniversary.

Muscle System, Avicenna—A67

1980, Apr. 30 Engraved *Perf. 13*

240	A67	60fr multi	45	35

Avicenna, Arab physician, birth millennium.

Soccer Players—A69

Designs; Various soccer scenes. 60fr, 150fr, 500fr, vert.

1981, Feb. 20 Litho. *Perf. 12½*

241	A69	60fr multi	60
242	A69	75fr multi	75
243	A69	90fr multi	90
244	A69	100fr multi	1.00
245	A69	150fr multi	1.50
		Nos. 241-245 (5)	4.75

Souvenir Sheet

246	A69	500fr multi	5.00

World Cup Soccer 1982. No. 246 has multicolored margin showing emblems. Size: 104x80mm.

Nos. 236-237, 213, and:

Merops Superciliosus—A70

Perf. 12½, 13x12½ (No. 248)

1981, Feb. Litho.

Red, Black or Blue Surcharge

247	A64	15fr on 200fr multi	15
248	A64a	20fr on 75fr multi	20
249	A53	40fr on 125fr (Bk) multi	40
250	A70	60fr on 75fr (Bl) multi	60

Space Exploration: 50fr, Apollo program (vert.). 75fr, 100fr, 500fr, Columbia space shuttle.

1981, July 13 Litho. *Perf. 14*

251	A71	50fr multi	50
252	A71	75fr multi	75
253	A71	100fr multi	1.00
254	A71	450fr multi	4.50

Souvenir Sheet

255	A71	500fr multi	5.00

No. 255 has multicolored margin showing Eugene Sanger (1905-1964), and rockets. Size: 104x79mm.

Prince Charles and Lady Diana, Buckingham Palace—A72

1981, Sept. 1 Litho. *Perf. 14½*

256	A72	125fr shown	1.25
257	A72	200fr Highwood House	2.00
258	A72	450fr Carnarvon Castle	4.50
	a.	Souvenir sheet of 3	7.75

Royal wedding. No. 258a contains Nos. 256-258 in changed colors. Multicolored margin shows flowers, label shows arms of Prince of Wales. Size: 133x98mm.

Flag Type of 1979

1981, Oct. Litho. *Perf. 13*

259	O1	5fr multi	5
260	O1	15fr multi	15
261	O1	25fr multi	25
262	O1	35fr multi	35
263	O1	75fr multi	75
		Nos. 259-263 (5)	1.55

Nos. 239, 243, 212, 233 Surcharged.

1981, Nov. Litho. *Perf. 12½*

264	A66	5fr on 400fr multi	5
265	A69	20fr on 90fr multi	20
266	A53	45fr on 100fr multi	45
267	A62	45fr on 100fr multi	45

75th Anniv. of Grand Prix—A73

Designs: Winners and their Cars.

1981, Dec. 28 Litho. *Perf. 12½*

268	A73	20fr Mercedes, 1914	20
269	A73	50fr Delage, 1925	50
270	A73	75fr Rudi Caracciola, 1926	75
271	A73	90fr Stirling Moss, 1955	90
272	A73	150fr Maserati, 1957	1.50
		Nos. 268-272 (5)	3.85

Souvenir Sheet

Perf. 13

273	A73	500fr Changing wheels, vert.	5.00

No. 273 has multicolored margin continuing design. Size: 107x86mm.

Scouting Year—A74

1982, Jan. 5

274	A74	50fr Climbing rocks	50
275	A74	75fr Boating	75
276	A74	250fr Sailing	2.50
277	A74	350fr Sailing, diff.	3.50

Souvenir Sheet

Perf. 13

278	A74	500fr Baden-Powell	5.00

No. 278 has multicolored margin continuing design. Size: 78x102mm.

21st Birthday of Princess of Wales—A75

Designs: Various portraits of Princess Diana.

1982, July 1 Litho. *Perf. 14*

279	A75	200fr multi	2.00
280	A75	300fr multi	3.00

Souvenir Sheet

281	A75	500fr multi	5.00

No. 281 has multicolored margin showing portrait. Size: 112x81mm.

Johannes von Goethe (1749-1832)—A76

1982, July

282	A76	75fr multi	75
283	A76	350fr multi	3.50

Nos. 256-258a Overprinted in Blue: "NAISSANCE ROYALE 1982"

1982, July 31 *Perf. 14½*

284	A72	125fr multi	1.25
285	A72	200fr multi	2.00
286	A72	450fr multi	4.50
	a.	Souvenir sheet of 3	7.75

Birth of Prince William of Wales, June 21.

Nos. 241-246 Overprinted with Finalists and Score in Red.

1982, Sept. 20 Litho. *Perf. 12½*

287	A69	60fr multi	60
288	A69	75fr multi	75
289	A69	90fr multi	90
290	A69	100fr multi	1.00
291	A69	1.50fr multi	1.50
		Nos. 287-291 (5)	4.75

Souvenir Sheet

292	A69	500fr multi	5.00

Italy's victory in 1982 World Cup.

Paintings by Norman Rockwell—A77

1982, Oct. 11 Litho. *Perf. 14*

293	A77	60fr 1931	60
294	A77	75fr 1925	75
295	A77	100fr 1922	1.00
296	A77	150fr 1919	1.50
297	A77	200fr 1924	2.00
298	A77	300fr 1918	3.00
		Nos. 293-298 (6)	8.85

Sultans of Anjouan—A78

1982, Dec. *Perf. 12½x13, 13x12½*

299	A78	30fr Said Mohamed Sidi, vert.	30
300	A78	60fr Ahmed Abdallah, vert.	60
301	A78	75fr Salim	75
302	A78	300fr Sidi, Abdallah	3.00

SEMI-POSTAL STAMPS

Anti-Malaria Issue

Common Design Type

Perf. 12½x12

1962, Apr. 7 Engraved Unwmkd.

B1	CD108	25fr+5fr brt. pink	1.75	1.75

Issued for the World Health Organization drive to eradicate malaria.

Nurse Feeding Infant
SP1

Mother and Child
SP2

1967, July 3 Engraved *Perf. 13*

B2	SP1	25fr+5fr red, bright green & choc.	90	90

For the Red Cross.

1974, Aug. 10 Engraved *Perf. 13*

B3	SP2	35fr+10fr red & dark brown	45	45

For the Red Cross.

AIR POST STAMPS.

Comoro Village—AP1

Comoro Men and Moroni Mosque
AP2

Design: 200fr, Mosque of Ouani, Anjouan.

Engraved

1950-54 *Perf. 13* Unwmkd.

C1	AP1	50fr grn & red brn	2.25	1.15
C2	AP2	100fr dk brn & red	3.25	1.15
C3	AP1	200fr dk grn, rose brn & pur ('54)	13.50	6.75

Liberation Issue
Common Design Type

1954, June 6

C4	CD102	15fr sep & red	16.50	15.00

10th anniversary of the liberation of France.

Madrepora Fructicosa
AP3

Design: 100fr, Coral, shells and sea anemones.

Photogravure

1962, Jan. 13 *Perf. 12½x13*

C5	AP3	100fr multi	3.00	3.00
C6	AP3	500fr multi	12.50	11.00

Telstar Issue
Common Design Type

1962, Dec. 5 Engraved *Perf. 13*

C7	CD111	25fr dp vio, dl pur & red lil	2.75	1.50

Type of Regular Issue, 1963.

Designs: 65fr, Baskets. 200fr, Pendant.

Engraved

1963, Dec. 27 *Perf. 13* Unwmkd.

Size: 26½x48mm.

C8	A13	65fr car, grn & ocher	2.00	1.20
C9	A13	200fr grnsh bl, rose lake & red	4.00	2.50

Boat Type of Regular Issue

Designs: 50fr, Mayotte pirogue. 85fr, Schooner.

1964, Aug. 7 Photo. *Perf. 13*

Size: 27x48mm.

C10	A14	50fr multi	1.50	60
C11	A14	85fr multi	2.25	1.35

Olympic Torch and Boxers AP4 — Order of Star of Grand Comoro AP5

1964, Oct. 10 Engraved *Perf. 13*

C12	AP4	100fr red brn, dk brn & gray grn	2.50	2.50

18th Olympic Games, Tokyo, Oct. 10-25.

1964, Dec. 10 Photo. *Perf. 13*

C13	AP5	500fr crim, blk, emer & gold	10.00	6.50

ITU Issue
Common Design Type

1965, May 17 Engraved *Perf. 13*

C14	CD120	50fr gray, grnsh bl & ol	8.50	6.50

International Telecommunication Union centenary.

French Satellite A-1 Issue
Common Design Type

Designs: 25fr, Diamant rocket and launching installations. 30fr, A-1 satellite.

1966, Jan. 17 Engraved *Perf. 13*

C15	CD121	25fr dk pur & ultra	2.00	2.00
C16	CD121	30fr dk pur & ultra	2.50	2.50
	a.	Strip of 2 + label	5.00	5.00

Issued to commemorate the launching of France's first satellite, Nov. 26, 1965. No. C16a contains one each of Nos. C15-C16 and dark purple label with commemorative inscription. Each sheet contains 16 triptychs (2x8).

French Satellite D-1 Issue
Common Design Type

1966, May 16 Engraved *Perf. 13*

C17	CD122	30fr dk grn, org & brn	1.75	1.20

Old Gun Battery, Dzaoudzi
AP6

Design: 200fr, Ksar Castle, Mutsamudu (vert.).

1966, Dec. 19 Photo. *Perf. 13*

C18	AP6	50fr multi	1.00	85
C19	AP6	200fr multi	3.50	2.00

Bird Type of Regular Issue

Birds: 75fr, Madagascar paradise flycatchers. 100fr, Blue-cheeked bee eaters.

1967, June 20 Photo. *Perf. 13*

Size: 27x48mm.

C20	A17	75fr yel grn & multi	1.75	65
C21	A17	100fr lt bl & multi	2.10	85

Woman Skier
AP7

1968, Apr. 29 Engraved *Perf. 13*

C22	AP7	70fr brt grn, lt bl & choc	1.20	75

Issued to commemorate the 10th Winter Olympic Games, Grenoble, France, Feb. 6-18, 1968.

Fish Type of Regular Issue

Designs: 50fr, Moorish idol. 90fr, Diagramma lineatus.

1968, Aug. 1 Engraved *Perf. 13*

Size: 47½x27mm.

C23	A19	50fr plum blk & yel	1.00	90
C24	A19	90fr brt grn, yel & gray grn	1.75	1.35

Swimmer, Butterfly Stroke
AP8

1969, Jan. 27 Photo. *Perf. 12½*

C25	AP8	65fr ver, grnsh bl & blk	1.35	1.00

Issued to commemorate the 19th Olympic Games, Mexico City, Oct. 12-27.

Flower Type of Regular Issue, 1969.

Designs: 50fr, Heliconia sp. (vert.). 85fr, Tuberose (vert.). 200fr, Orchid (angraecum eburneum; vert.).

1969, Mar. 20 Photo. *Perf. 13*

Size: 27x48mm.

C26	A21	50fr gray & multi	1.00	75
C27	A21	85fr multi	1.50	1.00
C28	A21	200fr dk red & multi	2.75	2.10

Concorde Issue
Common Design Type

1969, Apr. 17 Engraved

C29	CD129	100fr pur & brn org	7.50	6.00

View of EXPO, Globe and Moon
AP9

Design: 90fr, Geisha, map of Japan and EXPO emblem.

1970, Sept. 13 Photo. *Perf. 13*

C30	AP9	60fr sl & multi	1.20	75
C31	AP9	90fr multi	1.20	75

EXPO '70 International Exposition, Osaka, Japan, Mar. 15-Sept. 13.

Sunset over Mutsamudu
AP10

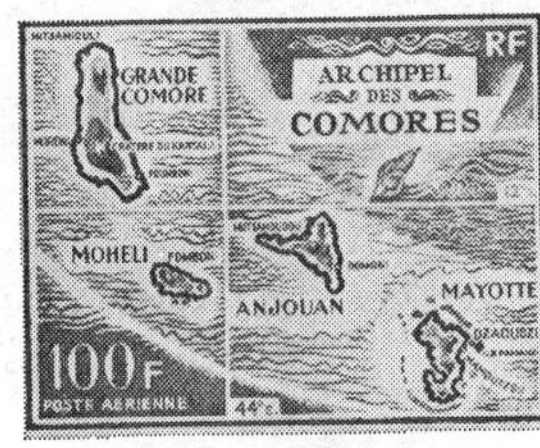

Map of Archipelago
AP11

Designs: 20fr, Sada Village, Mayotte. 65fr, Old Iconi Palace, Grand Comoro. 85fr, Nioumatchoua Island, Mohell.

1971, May 3 Photo. *Perf. 13*

C32	AP10	15fr dk bl & multi	25	10
C33	AP10	20fr multi	45	25
C34	AP10	65fr grn & multi	90	45
C35	AP10	85fr bl & multi	1.10	60

Engraved

C36	AP11	100fr brn red, grn & vio bl	2.00	1.00
		Nos. C32-C36 (5)	4.70	2.40

See Nos. 107-110, C45-C49, C53, C62-C64.

Flower Type of Regular Issue

Flowers: 60fr, Hibiscus schizopetalus. 85fr, Acalypha sanderii.

1971, July 19 Photo. *Perf. 13*

Size: 27x48mm.

C37	A25	60fr grn, ver & yel	1.20	60
C38	A25	85fr grn, red & yel	1.50	90

Mural, Moroni Airport—AP12

Designs: 85fr, Mural in Arrival Hall, Moroni Airport. 100fr, View of Moroni Airport.

1972, Mar. 30 Photo. *Perf. 13*

C39	AP12	65fr gray & multi	60	50
C40	AP12	85fr gray & multi	90	50

Engraved

C41	AP12	100fr brn, bl & sl grn	1.50	75

New airport in Moroni.

Eiffel Tower and Moroni Telephone Exchange—AP13

Design: 75fr, Frenchman and Comoro Islander talking on telephone, radio tower and beacons.

1972, Apr. 24

C42	AP13	35fr dl red & gray	35	20

C43	AP13	75fr dk car, vio & bl	70	35

First radio-telephone connection between France and Comoro Islands.

Underwater Spear-fishing—AP14

1972, July 5 Engraved *Perf. 13*

C44	AP14	70fr vio bl, brt grn & mar	1.10	80

Types of 1971

1972, Nov. 15 Photogravure

Designs: 20fr, Cape Sima. 35fr, Bambao Palace. 40fr, Domoni Palace. 60fr, Gomajou Peninsula. 100fr, Map of Anjouan Island.

C45	AP10	20fr brn & multi	25	20
C46	AP10	35fr dk grn & multi	45	35
C47	AP10	40fr bl & multi	55	40
C48	AP10	60fr grnsh blk & multi	75	60

Engraved

C49	AP11	100fr mar, bl & sl grn	1.50	1.00
		Nos. C45-C49 (5)	3.50	2.55

Pres. Said Mohamed Cheikh AP15

1973, Mar. 16 Photo. *Perf. 13*

C50	AP15	20fr multi	30	25
C51	AP15	35fr multi	50	25

President Said Mohamed Cheikh (1904-1970).

No. C24 Surcharged

120F

Mission Internationale pour l'étude du Cœlacanthe

1973, Apr. 30 Engraved *Perf. 13*

C52	A19	120fr on 90fr multi	1.65	1.25

International Commission for Coelacanth Studies.

Map of Grand Comoro AP16

1973, June 28 Engr. *Perf. 13*

C53	AP16	135fr vio, bl & dk brn	2.25	1.60

See Nos. C65, C68.

Karthala Volcano AP17

1973, July 16 Photo. *Perf. 13x12½*

C54	AP17	120fr multi	1.65	1.25

Eruption of Karthala, Sept. 1972.

Armauer G. Hansen AP18

Design: 150fr, Nicolaus Copernicus.

1973, Sept. 5 Engr. *Perf. 13*

C55	AP18	100fr brn, dk bl & sl grn	1.65	1.25
C56	AP18	150fr grnsh bl, vio bl & choc	2.25	1.50

Centenary of the discovery of the Hansen bacillus, the cause of leprosy (100fr).

500th anniversary of the birth of Nicolaus Copernicus (1473-1543), Polish astronomer (150fr).

Pablo Picasso AP19

1973, Sept. 30 Photogravure

C57	AP19	200fr blk & multi	2.75	2.00

Souvenir Sheet

C58	AP19	100fr blk & multi	1.75	1.75

Pablo Picasso (1881-1973), painter. No. C58 contains one stamp; reddish brown marginal inscription. Size: 100x130mm.

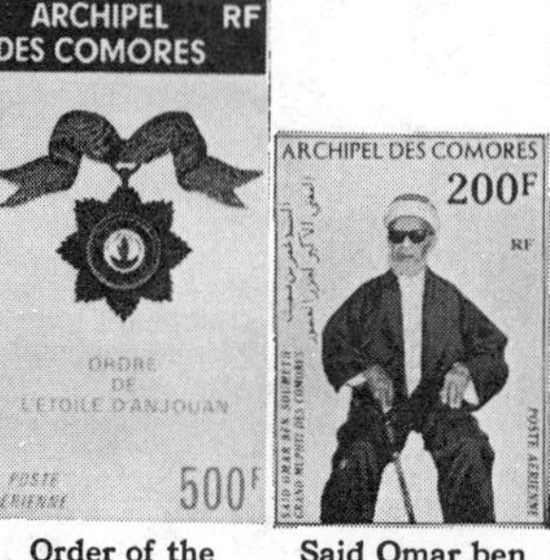

Order of the Star of Anjou AP20

Said Omar ben Soumeth AP21

1974, Jan. 7 Photo. *Perf. 13*

C59	AP20	500fr brn, bl & gold	6.00	5.00

Perf. 13x13½, 13½x13

1974, Jan. 31

Design: 135fr, Grand Mufti Said Omar (horiz.).

C60	AP21	135fr blk & multi	1.60	1.35
C61	AP21	200fr blk & multi	2.75	1.90

Types of 1971-73

1974, Aug. 31 Photo. *Perf. 13*

Designs (Views on Mayotte): 20fr, Moya Beach. 35fr, Chiconi. 90fr, Port Mamutzu. 120fr, Map of Mayotte.

C62	AP10	20fr bl & multi	30	20
C63	AP10	35fr grn & multi	50	40
C64	AP10	90fr multi	1.20	1.00

Engraved

C65	AP16	120fr ultra & grn	1.50	1.20

Jet Take-off—AP22

1975, Jan. 10 Engraved *Perf. 13*

C66	AP22	135fr multi	1.75	1.35

First direct route Moroni-Hahaya-Paris.

Rotary Emblem, Meeting House, Map—AP23

1975, Feb. 23 Photo. *Perf. 13*

C67	AP23	250fr multi	3.25	2.50

Rotary International, 70th anniversary, and Moroni Rotary Club, 10th anniversary.

Map Type of 1973

Design: 230fr, Map of Moheli (horiz.).

1975, May 26 Engr. *Perf. 13*

C68	AP16	230fr ocher, ol grn & bl	3.25	2.50

State of Comoro

Issues of 1968-75 Surcharged and Overprinted with Bars and: "ETAT COMORIEN" in Black, Silver, Red or Orange.

Printing and Perforations as Before.

1975

Multicolored

C69	AP10	10fr on 20fr #C62	12	8
C70	AP15	20fr (S)	28	18
C71	AP10	30fr on 35fr (R) #C63	40	30
C72	AP15	35fr (S)	45	35
C73	AP10	40fr (O)	55	38
C74	A19	50fr	70	45
C75	A25	75fr on 60fr	1.10	70
C76	AP10	75fr on 60fr	1.10	70
C77	AP10	75fr on 65fr (O)	1.10	70
C78	AP14	75fr on 70fr	1.10	70
C79	AP11	100fr #C36	1.40	90
C80	AP11	100fr #C49	1.40	90
C81	AP18	100fr	1.40	90
C82	AP10	100fr on 85fr (O)	1.40	90
C83	A25	100fr on 85fr	1.40	90
C84	AP10	100fr on 90fr	1.40	90
C85	AP21	100fr on 135fr (S)	1.40	90
C86	AP22	100fr on 135fr	1.40	90
C87	AP19	200fr (S)	2.80	1.85
C88	AP21	200fr (S)	2.80	1.85
C89	AP17	200fr on 120fr	2.80	1.85
C90	AP16	200fr on 120fr	2.80	1.85
C91	AP16	200fr on 135fr	2.80	1.85
C92	AP16	200fr on 230fr	2.80	1.85
C93	AP18	400fr on 150fr	5.60	3.75
C94	AP23	400fr on 250fr	5.60	3.75
C95	AP20	500fr	7.00	4.75
		Nos. C69-C95 (27)	53.10	35.09

Surcharged Soccer Type of 1979

Design: 200fr, English soccer game, 19th century, Soccer Cup, Argentina '78 emblem.

1979 Litho. *Perf. 13*

Black Overprint

C96	A40	200fr multi	1.75	1.75

Aviation Type of 1979

Design: 200fr, Charles Lindbergh and Spirit of St. Louis.

1979

Black Overprint

C97	A41	200fr multi	1.75	1.75

For Nos. C96-C97 without overprint see "For the Record."

Composer Type of 1979

Design: 50fr, Peter I. Tchaikovsky.

1979 Litho. *Perf. 13*

Black Surcharge

C98	A44	50fr on 200fr multi	55	55

Space Type of 1979

Exploration of Solar System: 200fr, William Herschel and Voyager II. 400fr, Urbain Leverrier and Voyager II. 500fr, Voyagers I and II, symbolic solar system.

1979, Feb. 19

C99	A46	200fr multi	1.40	55
C100	A46	400fr multi	3.00	1.25

Souvenir Sheet

C101	A46	500fr multi	4.00	1.75

No. C101 has multicolored margin showing symbolic design. Size: 130x80mm.

Chess Masters Type of 1979

Chess Grand Masters Alekhine, Spassky, Fischer, and bishop.

1979, Feb. 19

C102	A47	500fr multi	3.50	1.60

Satellite Type of 1979

Design: 200fr, Satellite (diff.), operator and radar.

1979, Sept. 15 Litho. *Perf. 13*

Black Overprint

C103	A48	200fr multi	2.00	

Gymnasts, Olympic Emblems, Fair Poster-AP24

1979, Sept. 15 Litho. *Perf. 13*

Black Overprint

C104	AP25	250fr multi	2.50	

Unused Prices

Catalogue prices for unused stamps through 1960 are for hinged copies in fine condition.

Never-hinged unused stamps issued before 1961 often sell above Catalogue prices. Current never-hinged prices for various countries will be found in the Scott StampMarket Update.

Leonid Brezhnev, Pres. Ford, Astronauts AP25

Design: 200 fr emblem & earth

Black Overprint

1979, Sept. 15.

C105	AP25	100fr multi	1.00	
C106	AP25	200fr multi	2.00	

For Nos. C103-C106 without overprint see "For the Record."

Rotary Emblem, Landscape AP26

1979, July 31 ***Perf. 13x12½***

C107	AP26	400fr multi.	4.00	

Rotary International.

IYC Emblem, Mother and Child AP27

1979, July 31 Litho. ***Perf. 13x13½***

C108	AP27	250fr multi.	2.50	

International Year of the Child. See No. CB1.

Dimadjou Dispensary, Map of Southern Africa, Emblem—AP28

1980, Feb. 23 **Litho.** ***Perf. 12½***

C109	AP28	100fr *shown*	75	55
C110	AP28	260fr *Globe, Concorde, emblem*	2.00	1.25

Rotary International, 75th anniversary and Moroni Rotary Club, 15th anniversary (100fr).

First Transatlantic Flight, 50th Anniversary—AP29

1980, May 30 **Litho.** ***Perf. 13***

C111	AP29	200fr multi	1.50	1.10

No. C111 Surcharged in Blue

1981, Feb. **Litho.** ***Perf. 13***

C112	AP29	30fr on 200fr multi	30	

The Dove and the Rainbow, by Picasso—AP30

Picasso Birth Centenary: 70fr, Still Life on a Sideboard. 150fr, Studio with Plaster Head. 250fr, Bowl and Pot (vert.). 500fr, The Red Tablecloth.

1981, June 30 **Litho.** ***Perf. 12½***

C113	AP30	40fr multi	40	
C114	AP30	70fr multi	70	
C115	AP30	150fr multi	1.50	
C116	AP30	250fr multi	2.50	
C117	AP30	500fr multi	5.00	
		Nos. C113-C117 (5)	10.10	

Nos. C114, C109-C110, CB1 Surcharged.

1981, Nov. **Litho.** ***Perf. 12½, 13***

C118	AP30	10fr on 70fr multi	10	
C119	AP28	10fr on 100fr multi	10	
C120	AP28	50fr on 260fr multi	50	
C121	AP27	50fr on 200+80fr multi	50	

AIR POST SEMI-POSTAL STAMP

Type of Air Post 1979

Design: IYC emblem, mother and son.

1979, July 31 Litho. ***Perf. 13½x13***

CB1	AP27	200fr +30fr multi	1.75	1.75

International Year of the Child.

POSTAGE DUE STAMPS

Anjouan Mosque D1

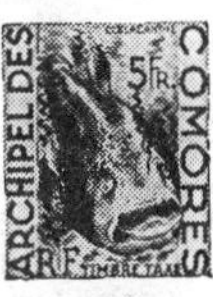

Coelacanth D2

Engraved.

1950 ***Perf. 14x13.*** **Unwmkd.**

J1	D1	50c dp grn	32	32
J2	D1	1fr blk brn	32	32

1954

J3	D2	5fr dk brn & grn	35	35
J4	D2	10fr gray & red brn	55	55
J5	D2	20fr ind & bl	70	70

Hibiscus D3

Designs: 2fr, 15fr, 40fr, 50fr, vertical.

1977, Nov. 19 **Litho.** ***Perf. 13½***

Multicolored

J6	D3	1fr *shown*	3	3
J7	D3	2fr *Pineapple*	3	3
J8	D3	5fr *White butterfly*	6	6
J9	D3	10fr *Chameleon*	10	6
J10	D3	15fr *Blooming banana*	12	8
J11	D3	20fr *Orchids*	15	10
J12	D3	30fr *Allamanda cathartica*	25	15
J13	D3	40r *Cashews*	35	20
J14	D3	50fr *Custard apple*	40	20
J15	D3	100fr *Breadfruit*	80	40
J16	D3	200fr *Vanilla*	1.60	80
J17	D3	500fr *Ylang ylang*	4.00	2.00
		Nos. J6-J17 (12)	7.89	4.11

OFFICIAL STAMPS

Comoro Flag O1

Perf. 13x12½

1979-80 **Litho.** **Unwmkd.**

O1	O1	5fr multi	5	5
O2	O1	10fr multi	10	10
O3	O1	20fr multi	20	10
O4	O1	30fr multi	30	10
O5	O1	40fr multi	40	20
O6	O1	60fr multi ('80)	60	40
O7	O1	100fr multi	1.00	50
		Nos. O1-O7 (7)	2.65	1.45

Pres. Said Mohamed Cheikh (1904-1970)-O2

1980

O8	O2	100fr multi	1.00	60
O9	O2	400fr multi	3.25	2.25

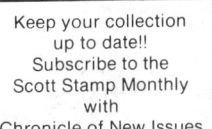

CONGO DEMOCRATIC REPUBLIC

(kŏng′ gō)

LOCATION — Central Africa.

GOVT.—Republic.

AREA—895,348 sq. mi. (estimated).

POP.—22,480,000 (est. 1971).

CAPITAL—Kinshasa (Leopoldville).

Congo was an independent state, founded by Leopold II of Belgium, until 1908 when it was annexed to Belgium as a colony. Congo became an independent republic in 1960. The name was changed to Republic of Zaire, Oct. 28, 1971. See Zaire in Vol. IV for later issues.

100 Centimes = 1 Franc
100 Sengi = 1 Li-Kuta,
100 Ma-Kuta = 1 Zaire (1967)

Belgian Congo Flower Issue of 1952–53 Overprinted or Surcharged **CONGO**

1960, June 6 Photo. ***Perf. 11½***

Flowers in Natural Colors

Size: 21x25½mm.

Granite Paper

No.	Type	Description	Unused	Used
323	A86	10c dp plum & ocher	6	6
324	A86	10c on 15c red & yel grn	10	10
a.		"Congo" ovpt. omitted	10.00	10.00
325	A86	20c grn & gray	6	6
326	A86	40c grn & sal	6	5
327	A86	50c on 60c bl grn & pink	10	10
328	A86	50c on 75c dp plum & gray	10	10
329	A86	1fr car & yel	6	5
330	A86	1.50fr vio & ap grn	8	5
331	A86	2fr ol grn & buff	12	6
332	A86	3fr ol grn & pink	20	8
333	A86	4fr choc & lil	25	20
334	A86	5fr dp plum & lt bl grn	25	10
335	A86	6.50fr dk car & lil	35	10
336	A86	8fr grn & lt yel	50	20
337	A86	10fr dp plum & pale ol	70	20
338	A86	20fr vio bl & dl sal	1.50	55

Overprinted **CONGO**

Size: 22x32mm.

No.	Type	Description	Unused	Used
339	A86	50fr dp plum & gray bl	8.00	3.75
340	A86	100fr grn & buff	14.00	6.50
		Nos. 323-340 (18)	26.49	12.31

Belgian Congo Animal Issue, Nos. 306–317, Overprinted or Surcharged in Red, Blue, Black or Brown **CONGO**

No.	Type	Description	Unused	Used
341	A92	10c bl & brn (R)	6	6
342	A93	20c red org & sl (Bl)	6	6
343	A92	40c brn & bl (Bk)	6	6
344	A93	50c brt ultra, red & sep (R)	5	5
345	A92	1fr brn, grn & blk (Br)	6	5
346	A93	1.50fr blk & org yel (R)	8	6
347	A92	2fr crim, blk & brn (Bl)	10	5
348	A93	3.50fr on 3fr blk, gray & lil rose (Bk)	18	7
349	A92	5fr brn, dk brn & brt grn (Br)	25	10
350	A93	6.50fr bl, brn & org yel (R)	28	10
351	A92	8fr org brn, ol bis & lil (Br)	32	25
352	A93	10fr multi (R)	45	20
		Nos. 341-352 (12)	1.95	1.11

Same Overprint on Belgian Congo No. 318.

1960

No.	Type	Description	Unused	Used
353	A94	50c gldn brn, ocher & red brn	60	60

Same Overprint and Surcharge of New Value on Belgian Congo Nos. 321–322.

Inscription in French

No.	Type	Description	Unused	Used
354	A95	3.50fr on 3fr gray & red	60	50

Inscription in Flemish

No.	Type	Description	Unused	Used
355	A95	3.50fr on 3fr gray & red	60	50

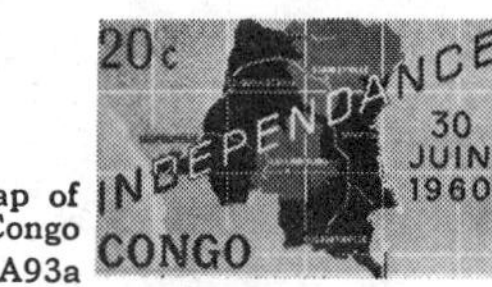

Map of Congo
A93a

1960 **Photogravure** ***Perf. 11½***

No.	Type	Description	Unused	Used
356	A93a	20c brown	8	5
357	A93a	50c rose red	8	3
358	A93a	1fr green	8	6
359	A93a	1.50fr red brn	12	5
360	A93a	2fr rose car	15	5
361	A93a	3.50fr lilac	17	8
362	A93a	5fr brt bl	23	10
363	A93a	6.50fr gray	30	12
364	A93a	10fr orange	50	25
365	A93a	20fr ultra	75	38
		Nos. 356-365 (10)	2.46	1.17

Issued to commemorate Congo's Independence.

Flag, People and Broken Chain
A94

1961 ***Perf. 11½*** **Unwmkd.**

Flag in Blue and Yellow

No.	Type	Description	Unused	Used
366	A94	2fr rose vio	10	6
367	A94	3.50fr vermilion	12	10
368	A94	6.50fr yel brn	25	12
369	A94	10fr brt grn	38	20
370	A94	20fr car rose	65	45
		Nos. 366-370 (5)	1.50	93

Issued to commemorate the signing of the Independence Agreement by Belgium, Jan. 4, 1959.

Nos. 356–365 Overprinted in Blue, Black or Red: "Conference Coquilhatville Avril Mai 1961"

1961

No.	Type	Description	Unused	Used
371	A93a	20c brn (Bl)	70	70
372	A93a	50c rose red (Bk)	70	70
373	A93a	1fr grn (R)	70	70
374	A93a	1.50fr red brn (Bl)	70	70
375	A93a	2fr rose car (Bk)	70	70
376	A93a	3.50fr lil (Bl)	70	70
377	A93a	5fr brt bl (R)	70	70
378	A93a	6.50fr gray (R)	70	70
379	A93a	10fr org (Bk)	70	70
380	A93a	20fr ultra (R)	70	70
		Nos. 371-380 (10)	7.00	7.00

Issued to commemorate the Coquilhatville Conference April–May, 1961.

Pres. Joseph Kasavubu
A95

Kasavubu and Map of Congo
A96

Design: 10fr, 20fr, 50fr, 100fr, Kasavubu in uniform and map.

Photogravure

1961, June 30 ***Perf. 11½*** **Unwmkd.**

Portrait and Inscription in Dark Brown

No.	Type	Description	Unused	Used
381	A95	10c yellow	8	8
382	A95	20c dp rose	8	8
383	A95	40c bl grn	8	8
384	A95	50c salmon	8	8
385	A95	1fr lilac	12	8
386	A95	1.50fr lt brn	15	8
387	A95	2fr brt grn	15	8
388	A96	3.50fr rose pink	20	8
389	A96	5fr gray	2.00	18
390	A96	6.50fr ultra	45	8
391	A96	8fr olive	50	15
392	A95	10fr lt vio	1.20	15
393	A95	20fr orange	1.20	18
394	A95	50fr lt bl	2.00	45
395	A95	100fr ap grn	3.00	75
		Nos. 381-395 (15)	11.29	2.58

First anniversary of independence.

Nos. 381–387, 389 and 392 Overprinted: "REOUVERTURE du PARLEMENT JUILLET 1961"

1961

Portrait and Inscription in Dark Brown

No.	Type	Description	Unused	Used
396	A95	10c yellow	10	8
397	A95	20c dp rose	10	8
398	A95	40c bl grn	10	8
399	A95	50c salmon	42	30
400	A95	1fr lilac	42	30
401	A95	1.50fr lt brn	1.25	1.00
402	A95	2fr brt grn	1.25	1.00
403	A96	5fr gray	1.25	1.00
404	A95	10fr lt vio	1.40	1.25
		Nos. 396-404 (9)	6.29	5.09

Issued to commemorate the re-opening of the Congolese parliament, July, 1961.

Dag Hammarskjold and Map of Africa with Congo
A97

Malaria Eradication Emblem and Mosquito
A98

1962, Jan. 20 **Photo.** ***Perf. 11½***

Gray Background

No.	Type	Description	Unused	Used
405	A97	10c dk brn	5	5
406	A97	20c Prus bl	5	5
407	A97	30c brown	7	7
408	A97	40c dk bl	7	7
409	A97	50c brn red	10	10
410	A97	3fr ol grn	2.90	1.90
411	A97	6.50fr dk vio	85	55
412	A97	8fr red brn	95	70
		Nos. 405-412 (8)	5.04	3.49

Souvenir Sheets

Imperf.

No.	Type	Description	Unused	Used
413	A97	25fr blk brn	4.50	4.50
a.		Ovpt. in grn	1.65	1.65

Nos. 405–413 issued in memory of Dag Hammarskjold, Secretary General of the United Nations, 1953–61.

No. 413 contains one stamp and has gold marginal inscription. Size: 65x90mm.

No 413a is overprinted "30 Juin 1962" on stamp and "2eme Anniversaire de l'Independance" on sheet margin. Issued June 30, 1962.

1962, June 15 **Granite Paper**

No.	Type	Description	Unused	Used
414	A98	1.50fr yel, blk & dk red	8	8
415	A98	2fr yel grn, brn & bl grn	42	20
416	A98	6.50fr ultra, blk & mar	20	15

Issued for the World Health Organization drive to eradicate malaria.

Nos. 405–412 Overprinted in Blue, Purple, Black or Carmine: *"Paix, Travail, Austerite ..,* C. ADOULA 11 juillet 1962"

1962, Oct. 15

Gray Background

No.	Type	Description	Unused	Used
417	A97	10c dk brn (Bl)	7	3
418	A97	20c Prus bl (P)	7	3
419	A97	30c brn (Bk)	7	3
420	A97	40c dk bl (C)	7	3
421	A97	50c brn red (Bl)	1.75	75
422	A97	3fr ol grn (P)	22	7
423	A97	6.50fr dk vio (Bk)	30	12
424	A97	8fr red brn (C)	42	20
		Nos. 417-424 (8)	2.97	1.26

Reorganization of Adoula administration.

Canceled to Order

Starting in 1963, prices in the used column are for "canceled to order" stamps. Postally used copies sell for much more.

A99

1963, Jan. 28 **Engr.** ***Perf. 10½x13***

No.	Type	Description	Unused	Used
425	A99	2fr dl pur	1.40	1.50
426	A99	4fr red	10	8
427	A99	7fr dk bl	15	10
428	A99	20fr sl grn	30	20

Issued to commemorate Congo's first participation at the U.P.U. Congress, New Delhi, March, 1963.

Shoebill
A100

Birds: 10c, Pelicans. 20c, Crested guinea fowl (horiz.). 30c, Openbill. 40c, White-bellied storks (horiz.). 2fr, Marabou. 3fr, Greater flamingos (horiz.). 4fr, Congolese peacock. 5fr, Hartlaub ducks (horiz.). 6fr, Secretary bird. 7fr, Black-casqued hornbill (horiz.). 8fr, Sacred ibis and nest. 10fr, Crowned crane (horiz.). 20fr, Saddle-bill stork (horiz.).

Photogravure

1963 ***Perf. 11½*** **Unwmkd.**

No.	Type	Description	Unused	Used
429	A100	10c pink, ultra & ocher	5	3
430	A100	20c rose red, bl & blk	5	3
431	A100	30c grn, ocher & blk	5	3

432	A100	40c gray, org & blk	5	3
433	A100	1fr brn, emer & gray	5	3
434	A100	2fr gray, red & ind	1.75	50
435	A100	3fr ol grn, blk & rose	8	5
436	A100	4fr car rose, vio bl & grn	8	5
437	A100	5fr lake, lt bl & blk	10	5
438	A100	6fr pur, yel & blk	1.75	50
439	A100	7fr bl grn, blk & ind	15	5
440	A100	8fr yel, org & blk	18	5
441	A100	10fr bl, blk & rose	22	8
442	A100	20fr cit, red & blk	45	10
		Nos. 429-442 (14)	5.01	1.58

Cinchona Ledgeriana — A101

Red Cross Nurse — A102

Designs: 10c, 30c, 5fr, Strophanthus sarmentosus.

Perf. 12½x13½, 13½x12½

1963, May 25 Engr. Unwmkd.

Cross in Red

443	A101	10c vio & dl grn	5	5
444	A101	20c mag & bl	5	5
445	A101	30c grn & org	5	5
446	A101	40c bl & vio	6	6
447	A101	5fr ol & rose cl	12	5
448	A101	7fr org & blk	12	5
449	A102	9fr gray ol & red	18	8
450	A102	20fr pur & red	1.75	1.00
		Nos. 443-450 (8)	2.38	1.39

International Red Cross centenary.

A souvenir sheet of three contains imperf. 5fr, 7fr, and 20fr stamps similar to Nos. 447, 448 and 450, but in changed colors. Marginal inscriptions in violet. Size: 109x75mm. Price $15.

Men Joining Hands and Map of Congo—A103

1963, June 29 Photo. *Perf. 11½*

451	A103	4fr multi	1.25	45
452	A103	5fr multi	10	5
453	A103	9fr multi	20	8
454	A103	12fr multi	28	12

Issued to celebrate national reconciliation.

Bulldozer and Kabambare Sewer, Leopoldville—A104

Designs: 30c, 5fr, 12fr, Excavator and blueprint. 50c, 9fr, Building Ituri road.

1963, July 1 Engraved Unwmkd.

455	A104	20c multi	3	3
456	A104	30c multi	3	3
457	A104	50c multi	3	3
458	A104	3fr multi	1.25	50
459	A104	5fr multi	10	5
460	A104	9fr multi	18	10
461	A104	12fr multi	22	15
		Nos. 455-461 (7)	1.84	89

Issued to publicize aid to Congo by the European Economic Community.

Leopoldville Airport N'Djili

A105

Design: 5fr, 7fr, 50fr, Tail assembly and airport.

1963, Nov. 30 Photo. *Perf. 11½*

462	A105	2fr gray, yel & red brn	5	4
463	A105	5fr mag, vio & yel	8	8
464	A105	6fr bl, yel & dk brn	1.25	55
465	A105	7fr multi	35	22
466	A105	30fr lil, yel & ol	55	38
467	A105	50fr multi	60	40
		Nos. 462-467 (6)	2.88	1.67

Issued to publicize Air Congo.

Nos. 425–428 Overprinted with Silver Frame on Three Sides and Black Inscription: "15e anniversaire/10 DECEMBRE 1948/DROITS DE L'HOMME/ 10 DECEMBRE 1963"

Engraved and Typographed

1963, Dec. 10 *Perf. 10½x13*

468	A99	2fr dl pur	6	6
469	A99	4fr red	8	8
470	A99	7fr dk bl	28	28
471	A99	20fr sl grn	30	30

15th anniversary of Universal Declaration of Human Rights.

Nos. 468–471 exist with side date panels transposed ("1963" at left, "1948" at right). Price, each $5.

Laboratory Technician and Atomic Emblem—A106

Designs: 1.50fr, 60fr, University. 8fr, 75fr, First African nuclear reactor. 25fr, 100fr, University and crest.

1964, Feb. 1 Photo. *Perf. 14x12½*

472	A106	50c multi	8	8
473	A106	1.50fr multi	8	8
474	A106	8fr multi	2.75	2.50
475	A106	25fr multi	25	20
476	A106	30fr multi	30	25
477	A106	60fr multi	55	45
478	A106	75fr multi	75	70
479	A106	100fr multi	1.00	85
a.		Souv. sheet of 3	4.00	4.00
		Nos. 472-479 (8)	5.76	5.11

10th anniversary of Lovanium University, Leopoldville.

No. 479a contains 3 imperf. multicolored stamps: 20fr, design as 50c; 30fr, as 8fr; 100fr. Size: 141x70mm.

Belgian Congo Issues of 1952–59 Overprinted "REPUBLIQUE DU CONGO" and Surcharged in Black on Overprinted Metallic Panels.

1964 *Perf. 11½*

480	A93	1fr on 20c red org & sl (#307)	8	8
481	A86	2fr on 1.50fr multi (#273)	2.10	1.50
482	A93	5fr on 6.50fr multi (#315)	32	20
483	A86	8fr on 6.50fr multi (#278)	40	25

Republic Issues of 1960–61 Surcharged in Black on Overprinted Metallic Rectangles or Ovals.

484	A86	1fr on 6.50fr multi (#335)	8	8
485	A93	1fr on 20c red org & sl (#342)	8	8
486	A86	2fr on 1.50fr multi (#330)	8	8
487	A95	3fr on 20c dp rose & dk brn (#382)	25	20
488	A95	4fr on 40c bl grn & dk brn (#383)	25	20
489	A93	5fr on 6.50fr multi ("Congo" red) (#350)	33	20
a.		"Congo" black	33	20
490	A93a	6fr on 6.50fr gray (#363)	33	22
491	A93a	7fr on 20c brn (#356)	50	28
		Nos. 480-491 (12)	4.80	3.37

Pole Vault A107

Sports: 7fr, 20fr, Javelin (vert.). 8fr, 100fr, Hurdling.

Photogravure

1964, July 13 *Perf. 11½* Unwmkd.

Granite Paper

492	A107	5fr gray, dk brn & car	6	5
493	A107	7fr rose, vio & emer	1.20	55
494	A107	8fr org, yel, red brn & vio bl	10	5
495	A107	10fr bl, vio brn & mag	10	5
496	A107	20fr gray grn, red brn & ver	25	10
497	A107	100fr lil, dk brn & grn	1.20	30
a.		Souv. sheet of 3	6.00	6.00
		Nos. 492-497 (6)	2.91	1.10

Issued to commemorate the 18th Olympic Games, Tokyo, Oct. 10–25. No. 497a contains 3 imperf. stamps (20fr orange & dark brown, pole vault; 30fr citron and dark brown, hurdling; 100fr dull green and dark brown, javelin). Dark brown marginal inscription and dull green Olympic rings. Size: 134x85mm. Sheet issued Sept. 10.

National Palace, Leopoldville

A108

1964, Sept. 15 Granite Paper

498	A108	50c lil rose & bl	3	3
499	A108	1fr bl & lil rose	3	3
500	A108	2fr brn red & vio	3	3
501	A108	3fr emer & red	4	3
502	A108	4fr org & vio bl	4	3
503	A108	5fr gray vio & emer	4	3
504	A108	6fr sep & org	8	3
505	A108	7fr gray ol & red brn	8	3
506	A108	8fr rose red & vio bl	2.85	50
507	A108	9fr vio bl & rose red	7	3
508	A108	10fr brn ol & grn	10	3
509	A108	20fr bl & brn org	15	3
510	A108	30fr dk car rose & grn	22	7
511	A108	40fr ultra & dk car rose	33	7
512	A108	50fr brn org & grn	45	7
513	A108	100fr sl & ver	95	15
		Nos. 498-513 (16)	5.49	1.19

Pres. John F. Kennedy—A109

1964, Dec. 8 Photo. *Perf. 13½*

514	A109	5fr dk bl & blk	8	3
515	A109	6fr rose cl & blk	8	3
516	A109	9fr brn & blk	10	3
517	A109	30fr pur & blk	42	7
518	A109	40fr dl grn & blk	2.85	85
519	A109	60fr red brn & blk	70	30
		Nos. 514-519 (6)	4.23	1.31

Souvenir Sheet

520	A109	150fr blk & mar	3.00	3.00

Issued in memory of Pres. John F. Kennedy (1917–63). No. 520 contains one stamp, black marginal inscription. Size: 64x76mm.

Rocket and Unisphere A110

Basketball A111

Engraved and Typographed

1965, March 1 *Perf. 12* Unwmkd.

521	A110	50c lil & blk	4	3
522	A110	1.50fr bl & lil	4	3
523	A110	2fr red brn & brt grn	4	3
524	A110	10fr brt grn & dk red	1.00	60
525	A110	18fr vio bl & brn	15	8
526	A110	27fr rose red & grn	33	12
527	A110	40fr gray & org	50	18
		Nos. 521-527 (7)	2.10	1.07

New York World's Fair, 1964–65.

1965, Apr. Photo. *Perf. 13½*

Designs: 6fr, 40fr, Soccer (horiz.). 15fr, 60fr, Volleyball.

528	A111	5fr blk, grnsh bl & ocher	4	3
529	A111	6fr blk, bl gray & crim	8	5
530	A111	15fr blk, org & yel grn	12	10
531	A111	24fr blk, rose lil & brt grn	30	10
532	A111	40fr blk, brt grn & ultra	1.75	60
533	A111	60fr blk, bl & red lil	55	20
		Nos. 528-533 (6)	2.84	1.08

First African Games, Leopoldville, Mar. 31–Apr. 7, 1965.

Earth and Satellites

A112

Designs: 9fr, 15fr, 20fr, 40fr, Satellites at left, globe at right.

Perf. 14x14½

1965, June 28 Photo. Unwmkd.

No.	Type	Value & Colors	Unused	Used
534	A112	6fr blk, sal & vio	8	3
535	A112	9fr blk, lt grn & gray	8	3
536	A112	12fr org, gray & blk	10	7
537	A112	15fr grn, ultra & blk	13	7
538	A112	18fr blk, lt grn & gray	1.50	42
539	A112	20fr blk, sal & vio	22	8
540	A112	30fr grn, ultra & blk	33	10
541	A112	40fr org, gray & blk	45	15
		Nos. 534-541 (8)	2.89	95

Issued to commemorate the centenary of the International Telecommunication Union.

Congolese Paratrooper and Parachutes
A113

1965, July 5 ***Perf. 13x14***

No.	Type	Value & Colors	Unused	Used
542	A113	5fr brt bl & brn	5	3
543	A113	6fr org & brn	5	3
544	A113	7fr bl grn & brn	60	28
545	A113	9fr brt pink & brn	10	8
546	A113	18fr lem & brn	18	10
		Nos. 542-546 (5)	98	52

Fifth anniversary of independence.

Soldiers Giving First Aid
A115

The Army Serving the Country: 7fr, Bridge building. 9fr, Feeding child. 19fr, Maintenance of telegraph lines. 20fr, House building. 30fr, Soldier and flag. (19fr, 20fr, 30fr, vertical.)

Perf. 12½x13, 13x12½

1965, Nov. 17

No.	Type	Value & Colors	Unused	Used
553	A115	5fr sal, brn & red	8	3
554	A115	7fr yel & grn	8	3
555	A115	9fr ol & brn	10	3
556	A115	19fr brt grn & brn	90	55
557	A115	20fr lt bl & brn	25	8
558	A115	30fr multi	35	10
		Nos. 553-558 (6)	1.76	82

See also Nos. 582–586.

Matadi Harbor and ICY Emblem
A114

Designs (ICY Emblem and): 8fr, 25fr, Katanga mines. 9fr, 60fr, Tshopo Dam, Stanleyville.

1965, Oct. 25 Photo. ***Perf. 13x14***

No.	Type	Value & Colors	Unused	Used
547	A114	6fr ultra, blk & yel	8	3
548	A114	8fr org red, blk & bl	10	3
549	A114	9fr bl grn, blk & brn org	10	3
550	A114	12fr car rose, blk & gray	1.15	45
551	A114	25fr ol, blk & rose red	27	12
552	A114	60fr gray, blk & org	55	15
		Nos. 547-552 (6)	2.25	81

International Cooperation Year, 1965.

Nos. 551–552 Overprinted with U.N. Emblem and "6e Journée Météorologique Mondiale / 23.3.66." on Metallic Strip

1966, Mar. 23 Photo. ***Perf. 13x14***

No.	Type	Value & Colors	Unused	Used
559	A114	25fr ol & blk	1.10	55
560	A114	60fr gray & blk	1.10	80

6th World Meteorological Day.

Woman's Head and Goat
A116

Designs: 10fr, Sculptured heads. 12fr, Sitting figure and two heads (vert.). 53fr, Figure with earrings and kneeling woman with bowl (vert.).

Perf. 11½x13, 13x11½

1966, Apr. 23 Litho. Unwmkd.

No.	Type	Value & Colors	Unused	Used
561	A116	10fr red, blk & gray	12	12
562	A116	12fr grn, blk & bl	15	15
563	A116	15fr dp bl, blk & lil	18	18
564	A116	53fr dp rose, blk & vio bl	1.50	1.25

Issued to commemorate the International Negro Arts Festival, Dakar, Senegal, Apr. 1–24.

Pres. Joseph Desiré Mobutu and Fishing Industry
A117

Pres. Mobutu and: 4fr, Pyrethrum harvest. 6fr, Building industry. 8fr, Winnowing rice. 10fr, Cotton harvest. 12fr, Banana harvest. 15fr, Cacao harvest. 24fr, Pineapple harvest.

1966, May 1 Photo. ***Perf. 11½***

No.	Type	Value & Colors	Unused	Used
565	A117	2fr dk brn & dk bl	6	6
566	A117	4fr dk brn & org	6	6
567	A117	6fr dk brn & ol	95	85
568	A117	8fr dk brn & brt grnsh bl	7	7
569	A117	10fr dk brn & brn red	10	10
570	A117	12fr dk brn & vio	12	10
571	A117	15fr dk brn & lt ol grn	12	10
572	A117	24fr dk brn & lil rose	30	20
		Nos. 565-572 (8)	1.78	1.54

Souvenir Sheet

Design: Pres. Mobutu without cap, and men rolling up sleeves.

Perf. 11x11½

No.	Type	Value & Colors	Unused	Used
573	A117	Sheet of 4	1.10	1.10
a.		15fr red, blk & ultra	25	25

Issued to honor Lt. Gen. Joseph Desiré Mobutu, President of Congo, and to publicize the "Back to Work" campaign. No. 573 contains four stamps and flag of Congo in margin. Size: 127x94½mm.

Nos. 510–513 Overprinted

1966, June 13 ***Perf. 11½***

No.	Type	Value & Colors	Unused	Used
574	A108	30fr dk car rose & grn	1.00	1.00
575	A108	40fr ultra & dk car rose	1.00	1.00
576	A108	50fr brn org & grn	1.10	1.10
577	A108	100fr sl & ver	1.10	1.10

Issued to commemorate the inauguration of World Health Organization Headquarters, Geneva.

Soccer Player
A118

Designs: 30fr, Two soccer players. 50fr, Three soccer players. 60fr, Jules Rimet Cup, soccer ball and globe.

1966, July 25 Photo. ***Perf. 14***

No.	Type	Value & Colors	Unused	Used
578	A118	10fr ocher, vio & brt grn	10	10
579	A118	30fr brt rose lil, vio & ap grn	35	25
580	A118	50fr ap grn, Prus bl & tan	1.25	1.20
581	A118	60fr brt grn, dk brn & gold	65	55

Issued to commemorate the World Cup Soccer Championship, Wembley, England, July 11–30.

Army Type of 1965

The Army Serving the Country: 2fr, Soldiers giving first aid. 6fr, Feeding child. 10fr, House building (vert.). 18fr, Bridge building. 24fr, Soldier and flag (vert.).

1966, Aug. 8 ***Perf. 12½x13, 13x12½***

No.	Type	Value & Colors	Unused	Used
582	A115	2fr ver, ind & red	5	3
583	A115	6fr ultra & red brn	8	8
584	A115	10fr yel grn & red brn	60	55
585	A115	18fr car rose & vio	15	10
586	A115	24fr multi	25	20
		Nos. 582-586 (5)	1.13	96

Nos. 578–581 Overprinted in Black, Carmine or Green: "FINALE / ANGLETERRE-ALLEMAGNE / 4-2"

1966, Nov. 14 Photo. ***Perf. 14***

No.	Type	Value & Colors	Unused	Used
587	A118	10fr multi (B or C)	22	22
588	A118	30fr multi (B or G)	70	60
589	A118	50fr multi (B or C)	1.10	90
590	A118	60fr multi (B or C)	1.25	1.00

Issued to commemorate England's victory in the World Soccer Cup Championship. The two colors of the overprint alternate in the sheets.

Souvenir Sheets

Pres. John F. Kennedy—A119

1966, Dec. 28 Engraved ***Perf. 13***

No.	Type	Value & Colors	Unused	Used
591	A119	150fr brown	4.50	4.50
592	A119	150fr slate	4.50	4.50

Issued in memory of Pres. John F. Kennedy. No. 591 has slate green, No. 592 deep orange marginal design. Two imperf. sheets exist: 150fr brown with violet blue margin and 150fr slate with lilac margin. Size: 65x76mm. Price $4.25 each.

Nos. 498–503 Surcharged in Black, Red or Maroon

5 K

4e Sommet OUA
KINSHASA
du 11 au 14 - 9 - 67

1967, Sept. 11 Photo. ***Perf. 11½***

No.	Type	Value & Colors	Unused	Used
593	A108	1k on 2fr brn red & vio	8	5
a.		Inverted overprint	9.00	
594	A108	3k on 5fr gray vio & emer	15	10
595	A108	5k on 4fr org & vio bl	25	18
596	A108	6.60k on 1fr bl & lil rose (R)	33	25
a.		Inverted overprint	6.50	
597	A108	9.60k on 50c lil rose & bl	55	40
a.		Inverted overprint	6.50	
598	A108	9.80k on 3fr emer & red (M)	75	55
		Nos. 593-598 (6)	2.11	1.53

Souvenir Sheet

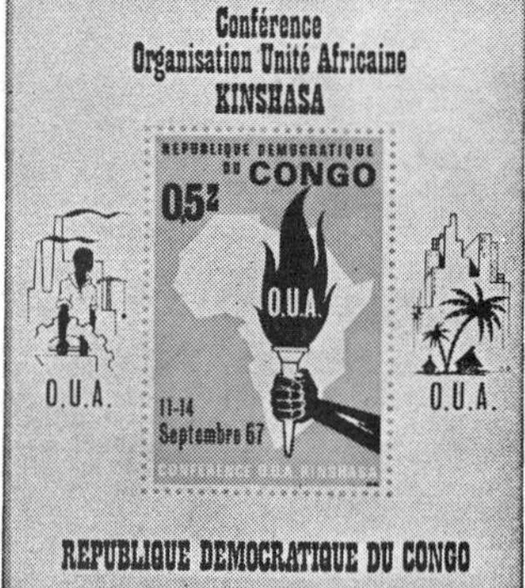

Map of Africa, Torch—A120

No.	Type	Value & Colors	Unused	Used
599	A120	50k grnsh bl, blk & red	2.50	2.50

Issued to commemorate the 4th meeting of the Organization for African Unity, Kinshasa (Leopoldville), Sept. 9–11. No. 599 has black marginal inscription and design in black and red. Size: 76x90mm.

Souvenir Sheet

Horn Blower and EXPO Emblem
A121

1967, Sept. 28 Engr. ***Perf. 11½***

No.	Type	Value & Colors	Unused	Used
600	A121	50k dk brn	2.85	2.85

Issued to commemorate EXPO '67, International Exhibition, Montreal, Apr. 28–Oct. 27, 1967. No. 600 has ultramarine and orange marginal inscription. Size: 90x75mm.

Nos. 565-566 and 582 Overprinted: "NOUVELLE CONSTITUTION 1967" and Surcharged with New Value on Metallic Panel in Magenta or Brown.

Perf. 11½, 12½x13

1967, Oct. 9 Photogravure

601 A117 4k on 2fr dk brn & dk bl (M) 25 20
602 A115 5k on 2fr ver, ind & red (B) 30 25
603 A117 21k on 4fr dk brn & org (M) 1.35 1.00

Issued to commemorate the promulgation of the Constitution, June 4, 1967.

Nos. 528 and 530 Surcharged with New Value and Overprinted: "Iere Jeux Congolais / 25/6 au 2/7/1967 / Kinshasa"

1967, Oct. 16 Photo. *Perf. 13½*

604 A111 1k on 5fr multi 12 12
605 A111 9.60k on 15fr multi 75 75

Issued to commemorate the First Congolese Games, Kinshasa, June 25–July 2, 1967.

No. 465 Surcharged with New Value and Overprinted: "Ier VOL BAC / ONE ELEVEN / 14/5/67"

1967, Oct. 16 *Perf. 11½*

606 A105 9.60k on 7fr multi 1.00 25

Issued to commemorate the first flight of the BAC 111 in the service of Air Congo, May 14, 1967.

Nos. 547 and 549 Surcharged in Red or Black: "JOURNEE MONDIALE / DE L'ENFANCE / 8-10-67"

1968, Feb. 10 Photo. *Perf. 13x14*

607 A114 1k on 6fr ultra, blk & yel (R) 12 12
608 A114 9k on 9fr bl grn, blk & brn org (B) 75 75

Issued for International Children's Day. The surcharge is on a rectangle printed in metallic ink.

Nos. 498, 504 and 501 Surcharged in Blue or Red: "Année Internationale / du Tourisme 24-10-1967"

1968, Feb. 10 *Perf. 11½*

609 A108 5k on 50c lil rose & bl (Bl) 27 27
610 A108 10k on 6fr sep & org (R) 60 60
611 A108 15k on 3fr emer & red (R) 85 85

Issued for International Tourist Year. The surcharge is on a rectangle printed in metallic ink.

Nos. 500, 498 and 502 Surcharged in Black, Violet Blue or Gold

1968, July Photo. *Perf. 11½*

612 A108 1k on 2fr brn red & vio 7 7
613 A108 2k on 50c lil rose & bl (VBl) 15 15
614 A108 2k on 50c lil rose & bl (G) 15 15
615 A108 9.60k on 4fr org & vio bl 60 60

The surcharge on No. 612 consists of a black rectangle and new denomination in upper right corner; the surcharge on No. 613 has a violet blue rectangle with denomination printed in white on it; on No. 614 the rectangle is gold and the denomination black; on No. 615 the rectangle is black and the denomination white.

No. 565 Surcharged in White on Black Rectangle.

1968, Oct. Photo. *Perf. 11½*

616 A117 10k on 2fr dk brn & dk bl 60 12

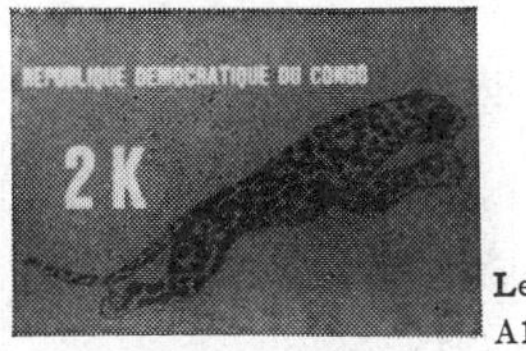

Leopard
A122

1968, Nov. 5 Litho. *Perf. 10½*

617 A122 2k brt grnsh bl & blk 12 5
618 A122 9.60k red & blk 60 15

Mobutu Type of 1966 Surcharged

1968, Dec. 20 Photo. *Perf. 11½*

619 A117 15s on 2fr sep & brt bl 5 5
620 A117 1k on 6fr sep & brn 5 5
621 A117 3k on 10fr sep & emer 15 12
622 A117 5k on 12fr sep & org 25 18
623 A117 20k on 15fr sep & brt grn 1.00 75
624 A117 50k on 24fr sep & brt lil 2.75 1.85
Nos. 619-624 (6) 4.25 3.00

Human Rights Flame
A123

1968, Dec. 30 *Perf. 12½x13*

625 A123 2k lt ultra & brt grn 12 4
626 A123 9.60k grn & dp car 55 35
627 A123 10k brt lil & brn 55 35
628 A123 40k org brn & pur 2.10 1.50

International Human Rights Year.

Type of 1968 Overprinted in Gold

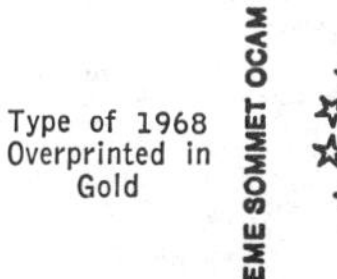

1969, Jan. 27 Photo. *Perf. 12½x13*

629 A123 2k ap grn & red brn 12 6
630 A123 9.60k rose & emer 55 35
631 A123 10k gray & ultra 55 35
632 A123 40k grnsh bl & pur 2.10 1.50

Issued to publicize the 4th summit meeting of OCAM (Organisation Communitée Afrique et Malgache), Kinshasa, Jan. 27.

Kinshasa Fair Emblem and Cotton Boll—A124

Designs (Fair Emblem and): 6k, Copper. 9.60k, Coffee. 9.80k, Diamond. 11.60k, Oil palm fruits.

1969, May 2 Photo. *Perf. 12½x13*

633 A124 2k brt pur, gold & red lil 12 5
634 A124 6k grn, gold & bl grn 35 35
635 A124 9.60k brn, gold & lt brn 55 25
636 A124 9.80k ultra & gold 55 50
637 A124 11.60k hn brn, gold & brn 70 70
Nos. 633-637 (5) 2.27 1.85

Kinshasa Fair, Limete, June 30–July 21.

Fair Entrance, Emblem—A125

Designs (Fair Emblem and): 3k, Gecomin Mining Co. Pavilion. 10k, Administration Building. 25k, Pavilion of the Organization for African Unity.

1969, June 30 Photo. *Perf. 11½*

Granite Paper

638 A125 2k brt rose lil & gold 10 10
639 A125 3k bl & gold 15 15
640 A125 10k lt ol grn & gold 50 40
641 A125 25k cop red & gold 1.15 1.00

Kinshasa Fair, Limete, June 30–July 21.

Congo Arms
A126

Pres. Mobutu
A127

1969, July-Sept. Litho. *Perf. 14*

642 A126 10s org & blk 3 3
643 A126 15s ultra & blk 3 3
644 A126 30s brt grn & blk 3 3
645 A126 60s brt rose lil & blk 3 3
646 A126 90s dp bis & blk 3 3

Perf. 13

647 A127 1k sky bl & multi 3 3
648 A127 2k org & multi 6 4
649 A127 3k multi 9 6
650 A127 5k brt rose & multi 15 13
651 A127 6k ultra & multi 20 15
652 A127 9.60k multi 35 20
653 A127 10k lt lil & multi 50 25
654 A127 20k yel & multi 1.10 50
655 A127 50k multi 2.75 1.20
656 A127 100k fawn & multi 5.00 2.25
Nos. 642-656 (15) 10.38 4.96

Well Driller, by Oscar Bonnevalle
A128

Paintings: 4k, Preparation of cocoa, by Jean Van Noten. 8k, Dock workers, by Constantin Meunier. 10k, Poultry shop, by Henri Evenepoel. 15k, Steel industry, by Constantin Meunier.

Perf. 13x14, 14x13 (8k)

1969, Dec. 15 Lithographed

Size: 41x41mm.

657 A128 3k multi 20 17
658 A128 4k multi 25 20

Size: 28x41mm.

659 A128 8k multi 40 35

Size: 41x41mm.

660 A128 10k multi 65 50
661 A128 15k multi 1.25 75
Nos. 657-661 (5) 2.75 1.97

Issued to commemorate the 50th anniversary of the International Labor Organization.

Souvenir Sheet

Adoration of the Kings, by Rubens
A129

1969, Dec. Engraved *Perf. 13*

662 A129 50k red lil 2.50 2.50

Issued for Christmas 1969. No. 662 has blue and red lilac marginal inscription. Size: 85x85mm.

Pres. Mobutu, Map and Flag of Congo
A130

1970, June 30 Litho. *Perf. 13½x13*

663 A130 10s multi 3 3
664 A130 90s pur & multi 3 3
665 A130 1k brn & multi 3 3
666 A130 2k multi 9 5
667 A130 7k multi 38 23
668 A130 10k multi 55 35
669 A130 20k multi 1.10 75
Nos. 663-669 (7) 2.21 1.47

10th anniversary of independence.

Issues of 1964-1966 Surcharged

0,20 K

Perf. 11½, 12½x13, 13x12½

1970, Sept. 24 Photogravure

670 A108 10s on 1fr bl & lil rose (#499) 8 6
671 A108 20s on 2fr brn red & vio (#500) 8 6
672 A117 20s on 2fr dk brn & dk bl (#565) 15 12
673 A108 30s on 3fr emer & red (#501) 8 6
674 A108 40s on 4fr org & vio bl (#502) 10 8
675 A117 40s on 4fr dk brn & org (#566) 15 12
676 A108 60s on 7fr gray ol & red brn (#505) 1.10 80
677 A108 90s on 9fr vio bl & rose red (#507) 1.10 80
678 A115 90s on 9fr ol & brn (#555) 15 12
679 A115 1k on 7fr yel & grn (#554) 15 12
680 A108 1k on 6fr sep & org (#504) 15 12
681 A117 1k on 12fr dk brn & vio (#570) 1.10 80
682 A117 2k on 24fr dk brn & lil rose (#572) 15 12

No.	Type	Description	Unused	Used
683	A115	2k on 24fr multi (#586)	15	12
684	A108	3k on 30fr dk car rose & grn (#510)	1.10	80
685	A108	4k on 40fr ultra & dk car rose (#511)	15	12
686	A108	5k on 50fr brn org & grn (#512)	2.85	2.00
687	A108	10k on 100fr sl & ver (#513)	1.10	75
		Nos. 670-687 (18)	9.89	7.17

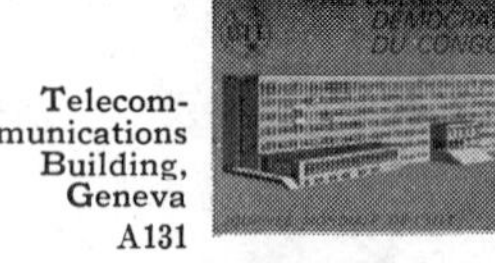

Telecommunications Building, Geneva
A131

Designs: 2k, 6.60k, U.P.U. Headquarters, Bern. 9.80k, 10k, 11k, U.N. Headquarters, New York.

1970, Oct. 24 Photo. *Perf. 11½*

No.	Type	Description	Unused	Used
688	A131	1k pink & grn	5	3
689	A131	2k org & grn	10	5
690	A131	6.60k grnsh bl & rose car	35	18
691	A131	9.60k yel & vio bl	45	25
692	A131	9.80k lt ultra & brn	45	25
693	A131	10k lt pur & brn	45	28
694	A131	11k rose & brn	55	32
		Nos. 688-694 (7)	2.40	1.36

Issued for International Telecommunications Day (1k, 9.60k); Inauguration of new Universal Postal Union Headquarters, Bern (2k, 6.60k); 25th anniversary of United Nations (9.80k, 10k, 11k).

Pres. Mobutu, Congolese Flag and Arch—A132

1970, Nov. 24 Litho. *Perf. 13*

No.	Type	Description	Unused	Used
695	A132	2k yel & multi	12	8
696	A132	10k bl & multi	60	40
697	A132	20k red & multi	1.25	85

Fifth anniversary of new government.

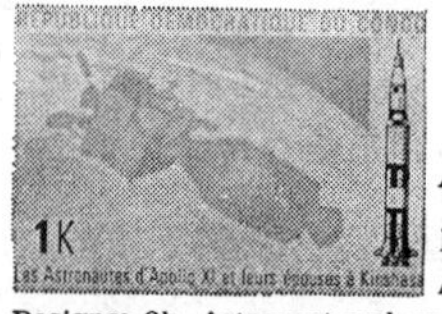

Apollo 11 in Flight
A133

Designs: 2k, Astronaut and spacecraft on moon. 7k, Pres. Mobutu decorating astronauts' wives. 10k, Pres. Mobutu with Neil A. Armstrong, Col. Edwin E. Aldrin, Jr. and Lt. Col. Michael Collins. 30k, Armstrong, Aldrin and Collins in space suits.

1970, Dec. 24 *Perf. 13x13½*

No.	Type	Description	Unused	Used
698	A133	1k bl & blk	5	3
699	A133	2k brt pur & blk	12	8
700	A133	7k dl org & blk	45	30
701	A133	10k rose red & blk	50	40
702	A133	30k grn & blk	1.50	1.10
		Nos. 698-702 (5)	2.62	1.91

Visit of U.S. Apollo 11 astronauts and their wives to Kinshasa.

Metopodontus 4 Savagei—A134

Designs: Various insects of Congo.

1971, Jan. 25 Photo. *Perf. 11½*

No.	Type	Description	Unused	Used
703	A134	10s dl rose & multi	3	3
704	A134	50s gray & multi	3	3
705	A134	90s multi	8	5
706	A134	1k cit & multi	8	5
707	A134	2k gray grn & multi	12	8
708	A134	3k lt vio & multi	22	15
709	A134	5k bl & multi	60	40
710	A134	10k multi	1.00	65
711	A134	30k grn & multi	2.85	1.75
712	A134	40k ocher & multi	3.75	2.50
		Nos. 703-712 (10)	8.76	5.69

Colotis Protomedia—A135

Designs: Various butterflies and moths of Congo.

1971, Feb. 24

No.	Type	Description	Unused	Used
713	A135	10s lt ultra & multi	3	3
714	A135	20s choc & multi	3	3
715	A135	70s dp org & multi	8	5
716	A135	1k vio bl & multi	8	5
717	A135	3k multi	22	15
718	A135	5k dk grn & multi	50	30
719	A135	10k multi	80	50
720	A135	15k emer & multi	1.35	85
721	A135	25k yel & multi	2.00	1.25
722	A135	40k multi	3.50	2.10
		Nos. 713-722 (10)	8.59	5.31

U.N. Emblem, Racial Unity
A136

1971, March 21 Photo. *Perf. 11½*

No.	Type	Description	Unused	Used
723	A136	1k lt grn & multi	5	3
724	A136	4k gray & multi	17	10
725	A136	5k lt lil & multi	27	15
726	A136	10k lt bl & multi	50	30

International year against racial discrimination.

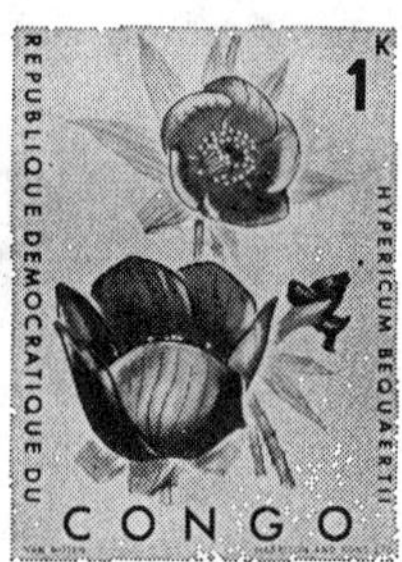

Hypericum Bequaertii
A137

Flowers: 4k, Dissotis brazzae. 20k, Begonia wollastonii. 25k, Cassia alata.

1971, May 24 Litho. *Perf. 14*

No.	Type	Description	Unused	Used
727	A137	1k multi	5	3
728	A137	4k multi	30	18
729	A137	20k multi	1.25	50
730	A137	25k multi	1.65	1.00

Obelisk at N'sele, Pres. Mobutu
A138

1971, May 20 Photo. *Perf. 11½*

No.	Type	Description	Unused	Used
731	A138	4k gold & multi	22	15

4th anniversary of the People's Revolutionary Movement.

Radar Station
A139

Designs: 1k, Waves. 6k, Map of Africa with telecommunications network.

1971, June 25 Photo. *Perf. 11½*

No.	Type	Description	Unused	Used
732	A139	1k rose & multi	5	3
733	A139	3k yel & multi	18	10
734	A139	6k lt bl & multi	40	25

Issued for 3rd World Telecommunications Day, May 17 (1k); opening of satellite telecommunications ground station, Kinshasa, June 30 (3k); Pan-African telecommunication system (6k).

Grass Monkeys
A140

Designs: 20s, Moustached monkeys (vert.). 70s, De Brazza's monkeys. 1k, Yellow baboons. 3k, Pygmy chimpanzee (vert.). 5k, Mangabeys (vert.). 10k, Owl-faced monkeys. 15k, Diana monkeys. 25k, Black-and-white colobus (vert.). 40k, L'Hoest's monkeys (vert.).

1971, Aug.

No.	Type	Description	Unused	Used
735	A140	10s vio & multi	10	3
736	A140	20s lt bl & multi	10	3
737	A140	70s ocher & multi	12	3
738	A140	1k gray & multi	12	3
739	A140	3k rose & multi	25	7
740	A140	5k brn & multi	55	12
741	A140	10k multi	1.00	25
742	A140	15k multi	1.75	50
743	A140	25k brt bl & multi	3.00	75
744	A140	40k red & multi	3.75	1.00
		Nos. 735-744 (10)	10.74	2.81

Hotel Inter-Continental, Kinshasa
A141

1971, Oct. 2 Photogravure *Perf. 13*

No.	Type	Description	Unused	Used
745	A141	2k sil & multi	10	4
746	A141	12k gold & multi	65	25

Man Reading
A142

Designs: 2.50k, Open book and abacus. 7k, Five letters surrounding symbolic head.

1971, Oct. 24

No.	Type	Description	Unused	Used
747	A142	50s gold, red brn, blk & yel	5	3
748	A142	2.50k gold, blk, dk red & tan	15	6
749	A142	7k gold, grn, yel & blk	65	25

Fight against illiteracy.

Succeeding issues are listed in Vol. IV under Zaire.

SEMI-POSTAL STAMPS

Women Carrying Food, Wheat Emblem, and Tractor
SP22

1963, Mar. 21 Photo. *Perf. 14x13*

No.	Type	Description	Unused	Used
B48	SP22	5fr +2fr lil, vio & dk bl	18	12
B49	SP22	9fr +4fr ocher, gray & dk grn	45	25
B50	SP22	12fr +6fr bl, dk bl & vio	50	35
B51	SP22	20fr +10fr red, grn & gray	2.50	2.35

Issued for the "Freedom from Hunger" campaign of the U.N. Food and Agriculture Organization.

CONGO PEOPLE'S REPUBLIC

(ex-French)

LOCATION—West Africa at equator.
GOVT.—Republic.
AREA—132,046 sq. mi.
POP.—1,440,000 (est. 1977).
CAPITAL—Brazzaville.

The former French colony of Middle Congo became a member state of the French Community Nov. 28, 1958, and achieved independence Aug. 15, 1960. For some years before 1958, the colony was joined with three other French territories to form French Equatorial Africa. Issues of Middle Congo (1907–1933) are listed under that heading.

100 Centimes = 1 Franc

Allegory of New Republic
A7

Engraved.

1959 *Perf. 13* Unwmkd.

No.	Type	Description	Unused	Used
89	A7	25fr brn, dp cl, org & ol	45	10

Issued to commemorate the first anniversary of the proclamation of the Republic.

Imperforates

Most stamps of the Republic of the Congo exist imperforate in issued and trial colors, and also in small presentation sheets in issued colors.

C.C.T.A. Issue
Common Design Type

1960 ***Perf. 13*** **Unwmkd.**
90 CD106 50fr dl grn & plum 90 80

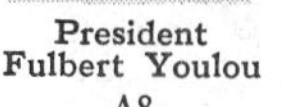

President Fulbert Youlou — A8
Flag, Map and U.N. Emblem — A9

1960
91 A8 15fr grn, blk & car 25 17
92 A8 85fr ind & car 1.10 50

1961, March 11 ***Perf. 13***
Flag in Green, Yellow & Red
93 A9 5fr vio brn & dk bl 10 6
94 A9 20fr org & dk bl 30 22
95 A9 100fr grn & dk bl 1.50 1.35

Congo's admission to United Nations.

Rainbow Runner
A10

Designs (fish): 50c, 3fr, Rainbow runner. 1fr, 2fr, Sloan's viperfish. 5fr, Hatchet fish. 10fr, A deep-sea fish.

1961, Nov. 28 **Engraved**
96 A10 50c brn, ol grn & sal 6 6
97 A10 1fr bl grn & sep 6 6
98 A10 2fr ultra, sep & dk grn 10 10
99 A10 3fr dk bl, grn & sal 10 10
100 A10 5fr red brn, grn & blk 20 15
101 A10 10fr bl & red brn 25 18
Nos. 96-101 (6) 77 65

Brazzaville Market
A11

1962, March 23 ***Perf. 13*** **Unwmkd.**
102 A11 20fr blk, red & grn 25 12

Common Design Types

pictured in section at front of book.

Abidjan Games Issue
Common Design Type

Designs: 20fr, Boxing. 50fr, Running, finish line.

1962, July 21 Photo. ***Perf. 12½x12***
103 CD109 20fr car, brt pink, brn & blk 28 20
104 CD109 50fr car, brt pink, brn & blk 60 45

See No. C7.

African-Malgache Union Issue
Common Design Type

1962, Sept. 8
105 CD110 30fr vio, bluish grn, red & gold 55 55

Waves Around Globe
A11a

Design: 100fr, Orbit patterns around globe.

1963, Sept. 19 ***Perf. 12½***
106 A11a 25fr org, grn & ultra 40 30
107 A11a 100fr lt red brn, bl & plum 1.40 1.10

Issued to publicize space communications.

King Makoko's Collar
A12

Design: 15fr, Kébékébé mask.

Engraved

1963, Oct. 21 ***Perf. 13*** **Unwmkd.**
108 A12 10fr blk & ol bis 15 10
109 A12 15fr brn, blk, bl, yel & red 25 12

UNESCO Emblem, Scales and Tree—A12a

1963, Dec. 10 ***Perf. 13*** **Unwmkd.**
110 A12a 25fr grn, dk bl & brn 35 25

Issued to commemorate the 15th anniversary of the Universal Declaration of Human Rights.

Barograph and WMO Emblem
A12b

1964, Mar. 23 **Engraved**
111 A12b 50fr grn, red brn & ultra 65 65

Fourth World Meteorological Day.

Mechanic with Machine
A13

1964, Apr. 8
112 A13 20fr grnsh bl, mag & dk brn 32 20

Training of technicians.

Corn and Tools
A14

1964, Apr. 24 ***Perf. 13*** **Unwmkd.**
113 A14 80fr brn, grn & brn car 95 50

Importance of manual labor.

Diaboua Ballet
A15

Kébékébé Dance — A16
Carved Figure — A17

1964, May 8 **Engraved**
114 A15 30fr multi 50 30
115 A16 60fr multi 90 60

1964, May 22
116 A17 50fr brn red & sep 65 50

Classroom
A18

1964, May 26
117 A18 25fr dk brn, red & bl 32 20

Issued to publicize education.

Type of Air Post Issue, 1963, Inscribed: "Ier ANNIVERSAIRE DE LA REVOLUTION/ FETE NATIONALE/15 AOUT 1964"

1964, Aug. 15 Photo. ***Perf. 13x12***
118 AP5 20fr lt bl, red, ocher, dk brn & grn 27 15

Issued to commemorate the first anniversary of the revolution and the National Feast Day, Aug. 15.

Fire Squid
A19

Design: 15fr, Johnson's deep-sea angler (fish).

1964, Oct. 20 **Engraved** ***Perf. 13***
119 A19 2fr ver, lt grn & brn 10 8
120 A19 15fr vio, lt ol grn & dp cl 35 20

Cooperation Issue
Common Design Type

1964, Nov. 7 ***Perf. 13*** **Unwmkd.**
121 CD119 25fr car, brt grn & dk brn 35 25

Communications Emblems
A20

1965, Jan. 1 Litho. ***Perf. 12½x13***
122 A20 25fr ol, red brn & blk 40 25

Issued to commemorate the establishment of the national postal administration.

Sitatunga — A21
Dancer on Stilts — A22

Design: 20fr, Elephant (horiz.).

1965, Mar. 15 **Engraved** ***Perf. 13***
123 A21 15fr redsh brn, dl grn & bl 30 15
124 A21 20fr blk, dp bl & sl grn 30 15
125 A22 85fr lil & multi 1.15 90

Pres. Alphonse Massamba-Debat
A23

1965–66 Photo. ***Perf. 12x12½***
126 A23 20fr dk brn, grn & yel 25 15

127 A23 25fr brn, bl grn, emer & blk ('66) 32 15
128 A23 30fr brn, bl grn, org & blk ('66) 40 20

Soccer Player
A24

Designs: 25fr, Games' emblem (map of Africa and runners). 50fr, Field ball player. 85fr, Runner. 100fr, Bicyclist.

1965, July 17 Photo. *Perf. 12½*

Size: 28x28mm.

129 A24 25fr blk, red, yel & grn 32 20

Size: 34x34mm.

130 A24 40fr yel grn & multi 60 40
131 A24 50fr red & multi 65 40
132 A24 85fr blk & multi 1.10 70
133 A24 100fr yel & multi 1.35 85
a. Min. sheet of 5 4.75 4.75
Nos. 129-133 (5) 4.02 2.55

Issued to commemorate the First African Games, Brazzaville, July 18–25. No. 133a contains one each of Nos. 129–133. Size: 136½x169mm.

Arms of Congo
A25

1965, Nov. 15 Litho. *Perf. 12½x13*

134 A25 20fr multi 28 15

Cooperative Village
A26

Design: 30fr, Gymnastic drill team with streamers.

1966, Feb. 18 *Perf. 12½x13*

135 A26 25fr multi 28 15
136 A26 30fr multi 40 25

Sculptured Mask
A27

Designs: 30fr, Weaver, painting. 85fr, String instrument, painting (horiz.).

Perf. 13x12½, 12½x13

1966, Apr. 9 Photogravure

137 A27 30fr multi 40 20
138 A27 85fr multi 1.10 65
139 A27 90fr multi 1.25 70

Issued to publicize the International Negro Arts Festival, Dakar, Senegal, Apr. 1–24.

Men and Clocks
A28

1966, Apr. 15 *Perf. 12½x12*

140 A28 70fr pale brn, ocher & dk brn 1.10 45

Issued to publicize the introduction of the shorter work day (less lunch time, earlier quitting time).

WHO Headquarters, Geneva
A29

1966, May 3 Photo. *Perf. 12½x13*

141 A29 50fr org yel, vio & bl 40 25

Issued to commemorate the inauguration of the World Health Organization Headquarters, Geneva.

Church of St. Peter Claver
A30

Women's Basketball
A31

1966, June 15 Photo. *Perf. 13x12½*

142 A30 70fr multi 1.10 45

1966, July 15 Engraved *Perf. 13*

Sport: 1fr, Women's volleyball (horiz.). 3fr, Women's field ball (horiz.). 5fr, Athletes of various races. 10fr, Torch bearer. 15fr, Soccer and gold medal of First African Games.

143 A31 1fr ultra, choc & ol 6 6
144 A31 2fr choc, grn & bl 8 6
145 A31 3fr dk grn, dk car & choc 10 8
146 A31 5fr sl, emer & choc 12 10
147 A31 10fr dl bl, dk grn & vio 25 12
148 A31 15fr vio, car & choc 30 18
Nos. 143-148 (6) 91 60

Jules Rimet Cup and Globe
A32

1966, July 15 Photo. *Perf. 12½x12*

149 A32 30fr brt red, gold, blk & bl 50 27

Issued to commemorate the 8th World Soccer Cup Championship, Wembley, England, July 11–30.

Savorgnan de Brazza School
A33

1966, Sept. 15 Photo. *Perf. 12½x12*

150 A33 30fr dk pur, grn, yel & blk 40 20

Pointe-Noire Railroad Station
A34

1966, Oct. 15 Engraved *Perf. 13*

151 A34 60fr grn, red & brn 85 35

Student with Microscope
A35

Balumbu Mask
A36

1966, Nov. 28 Engraved *Perf. 13*

152 A35 90fr brn, grn & ind 1.20 75

Issued to commemorate the 20th anniversary of UNESCO (United Nations Educational, Scientific and Cultural Organization).

1966, Dec. 12 Engraved *Perf. 13*

Masks: 10fr, Kuyu. 15fr, Bakwélé. 20fr, Batéké.

153 A36 5fr car rose & dk brn 12 8
154 A36 10fr Prus bl & brn 20 12
155 A36 15fr sep, dl org & dk bl 25 13
156 A36 20fr dp bl & multi 28 15

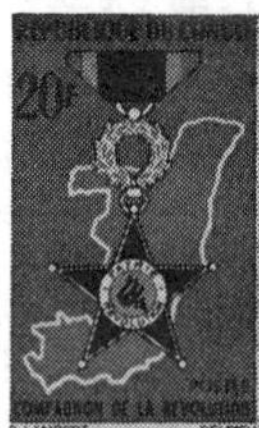

Order of the Revolution and Map
A37

Learning the Alphabet
A38

Design: 45fr, Harvesting and loading sugar cane, and sugar mill.

Perf. 12x12½, 12½x12

1967, March 15 Photogravure

157 A37 20fr org & multi 28 15
158 A38 25fr blk, ocher & dk car 32 20
159 A38 45fr blk, yel grn & lt bl 55 28

Issued to honor the members of the Order of the Revolution (20fr); to publicize the literacy campaign (25fr); to publicize sugar production (45fr).

Mahatma Gandhi
A39

Fruit Vendor
A40

1967, Apr. 21 Engraved *Perf. 13*

160 A39 90fr bl & blk 1.10 60

Issued in memory of Mohandas K. Gandhi (1869–1948), Hindu nationalist leader.

1967, June Photo. *Perf. 13x12½*

Dolls: 5fr, "Elegant Lady." 25fr, Woman pounding saka-saka. 30fr, Mother and child.

161 A40 5fr gold & multi 12 12
162 A40 10fr yel grn & multi 20 15
163 A40 25fr lt ultra & multi 32 20
164 A40 30fr multi 40 25

ITY Emblem, Village and Waterfall
A41

1967, July 5 Engraved *Perf. 13*

165 A41 60fr rose cl, org & ol grn 80 50

Issued for International Tourist Year, 1967.

Symbols of Cooperation
A42

Arms of Brazzaville
A43

Europafrica Issue, 1967

1967, July 20 Photo. *Perf. 12x12½*

166 A42 50fr multi 65 32

1967, Aug. 15 Litho. *Perf. 12½x13*

167 A43 30fr yel & multi 45 20

Fourth anniversary of the revolution.

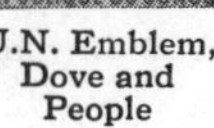

U.N. Emblem, Dove and People
A44

Boy and UNICEF Emblem
A45

1967, Oct. 24 Photo. *Perf. 13x12½*

168 A44 90fr bl, dk brn, red brn & yel 1.35 70

Issued for United Nations Day, Oct. 24.

1967, Dec. 11 Engraved *Perf. 13*

169	A45	90fr mar, blk & ultra	1.20	65

Issued to commemorate the 21st anniversary of UNICEF (United Nations International Children's Emergency Fund).

Albert Luthuli, Dove and Globe A46

1968, Jan. 29 Engr. *Perf. 13*

170	A46	30fr brt grn & ol bis	40	25

Issued in memory of Albert Luthuli (1899–1967) of South Africa, winner of 1960 Nobel Peace Prize.

Arms of Pointe Noire A47

1968, Feb. 20 Litho. *Perf. 12½x13*

171	A47	10fr brt pink & multi	15	12

Motherhood A48

Mayombe Viaduct A49

1968, May 25 Engraved *Perf. 13*

172	A48	15fr dk car rose, sky bl & blk	25	15

Issued for Mother's Day.

1968, June 24

173	A49	45fr mar, sl grn & bl	50	25

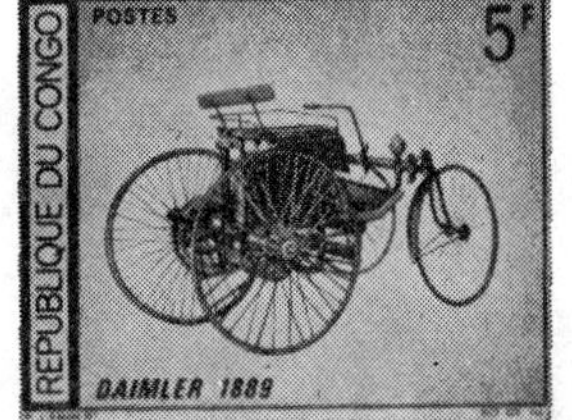

Daimler, 1889—A50

Antique Cars: 20fr, Berliet, 1897. 60fr, Peugeot, 1898. 80fr, Renault, 1900. 85fr, Fiat, 1902.

1968, July 29 Photo. *Perf. 13x12½*

174	A50	5fr ocher & multi	15	15
175	A50	20fr multi	30	25
176	A50	60fr cit & multi	85	45
177	A50	80fr multi	1.10	60
178	A50	85fr multi	1.20	70
		Nos. 174-178 (5)	3.60	2.15

Tanker, Refinery and Map of Area Served—A50a

1968, July 30 *Perf. 12½*

179	A50a	30fr multi	40	18

Issued to commemorate the opening of the Port Gentil (Gabon) Refinery, June 12, 1968.

U.N. Emblem and Tree of Life A51

1968, Nov. 28 Engraved *Perf. 13*

180	A51	25fr dk grn, red & dp lil	40	18

Issued for the 20th anniversary of the World Health Organization.

Development Bank Issue
Common Design Type

1969, Sept. 10 Engraved *Perf. 13*

181	CD130	25fr car rose, grn & ocher	35	15
182	CD130	30fr bl, grn & ocher	40	15

Issued to commemorate the 5th anniversary of the African Development Bank.

Bicycle A52

Designs (Bicycles and Motorcycles): 75fr, Hirondelle. 80fr, Folding bicycle. 85fr, Peugeot. 100fr, Excelsior Manxman. 150fr, Norton. 200fr, Brough Superior "Old Bill." 300fr, Matchless and N.L.G.-J.A.P.S.

1969, Oct. 6 Engraved *Perf. 13*

183	A52	50fr dk ol, org & rose lil	65	32
184	A52	75fr org, rose lake & blk	95	40
185	A52	80fr lil, bl & sl grn	1.00	45
186	A52	85fr dk ol, gray & bl grn	1.10	55
187	A52	100fr blk, vio bl, dk brn & car	1.25	65
188	A52	150fr blk, red brn & brn ol	1.60	90
189	A52	200fr bl grn, sl grn & brt rose lil	2.60	1.10
190	A52	300fr blk, brt rose lil & grn	3.50	1.90
		Nos. 183-190 (8)	12.65	6.27

Mayombe Train and Tourist Year Emblem A53

Design: 40fr, Train and Mbamba Tunnel (vert.).

Perf. 13x12½, 12½x13

1969, Oct. 20 Photogravure

191	A53	40fr multi	55	27
192	A53	60fr multi	70	32

Issued for African Tourist Year.

Loutete Cement Works A54

Designs (Loutete Cement Works): 15fr, Mixing tower (vert.). 25fr, Cable transport (vert.). 30fr, General view of plant.

1969, Dec. 10 Engraved *Perf. 13*

193	A54	10fr dk gray, rose cl & dk ol	13	8
194	A54	15fr Prus bl, red brn & pur	18	13
195	A54	25fr mar, brn & Prus bl	32	18
196	A54	30fr vio brn, ultra & blk	35	22
a.		Min. sheet of 4	1.25	1.25

Issued to publicize the cement factory at Loutete. No. 196a contains one each of Nos. 193–196. Size: 170x100mm.

ASECNA ISSUE
Common Design Type

1969, Dec. 12

197	CD132	100fr dl brn	1.35	65

Pineapple Harvest and ILO Emblem A55

Design: 30fr, Worker at lathe and ILO emblem.

1969, Dec. 20 Engraved *Perf. 13*

198	A55	25fr bl, ol & brn	32	18
199	A55	30fr rose red, choc & sl	35	22

Issued to commemorate the 50th anniversary of the International Labor Organization.

SOTEXCO Textile Plant, Kinsoundi A56

Designs: 20fr, Women in spinnery. 25fr, Hand-printing textiles. 30fr, Checking woven cloth.

1970, Jan. 20

200	A56	15fr grn, blk & lil	18	13
201	A56	20fr plum, car & sl grn	22	13
202	A56	25fr bl, sl & brn	32	18
203	A56	30fr gray, car rose & brn	40	18

Hotel Cosmos, Brazzaville A57

1970, Jan. 30

204	A57	90fr sl grn, bl & red brn	1.00	45

Linzolo Church A58

Diosso Gorge A59

Design: 90fr, Foulakari waterfall.

1970 Engraved *Perf. 13*

205	A58	25fr multi	32	18
206	A59	70fr multi	80	35
207	A59	90fr multi	1.10	45

Issue dates: 25fr, Feb. 10; others, Feb. 25.

Volvaria Esculenta A60

Mushrooms: 10fr, Termitomyces entolomoides. 15fr, Termitomyces microcarpus. 25fr, Termitomyces aurantiacus. 30fr, Termitomyces mammiformis. 50fr, Tremella fuciformis.

1970, Mar. 31 Photo. *Perf. 13*

208	A60	5fr Prus bl & multi	13	8
209	A60	10fr brt car rose & multi	15	12
210	A60	15fr vio bl & multi	25	18
211	A60	25fr dk grn & multi	45	22
212	A60	30fr pur & multi	50	27
213	A60	50fr brt bl & multi	70	45
		Nos. 208-213 (6)	2.18	1.32

Laying Coaxial Cable A61

Design: 30fr, Full view of rail car; 3 cable layers on railway roadbed.

1970, Apr. 30 Engraved *Perf. 13*

214	A61	25fr dk brn & multi	32	18
215	A61	30fr brn & multi	40	22

Issued to publicize the laying of the coaxial cable linking Brazzaville and Pointe Noire.

U.P.U. Headquarters Issue
Common Design Type

1970, May 20

216	CD133	30fr dk pur, gray & mag	45	22

Mother Feeding Child
A62

Dag Hammarskjold and U.N. Emblem
A63

Design: 90fr, Mother nursing infant.

1970, May 30 **Photogravure**

217	A62	85fr vio bl & multi	1.00	55
218	A62	90fr lil & multi	1.10	60

Issued for Mother's Day.

1970, June 20 **Engraved** ***Perf. 13***

Designs (U.N. Emblem and): No. 220, Trygve Lie (horiz.). No. 221, U Thant (horiz.).

219	A63	100fr scar, dk red & dk pur	1.25	75
220	A63	100fr dk red, ultra & ind	1.25	75
221	A63	100fr grn, emer & dk red	1.25	75
a.		Souvenir sheet of 3	4.25	4.25

Issued to commemorate the 25th anniversary of the United Nations and to honor its Secretaries General. No. 221a contains one each of Nos. 219–221; U.N. emblem and scarlet inscriptions in margin. Size: 129½x100mm.

Brillantaisia Vogeliana
A64

Sternotomis Variabilis
A65

Designs (Plants and Beetles): 2fr, Plectranthus decurrens. 3fr, Myrianthemum mirabile. 5fr, Connarus griffonianus. 15fr, Chelorrhina polyphemus. 20fr, Metopodontus savagei.

Perf. 12½x12, 12x12½

1970, June 30 **Photogravure**

222	A64	1fr dk grn & multi	5	3
223	A64	2fr multi	8	5
224	A64	3fr ind & multi	10	6
225	A64	5fr lem & multi	12	10
226	A65	10fr lil & multi	15	12
227	A65	15fr org & multi	22	12
228	A65	20fr multi	27	18
		Nos. 222-228 (7)	99	66

Stegosaurus
A66

Prehistoric Fauna: 20fr, Dinotherium (vert.). 60fr, Brachiosaurus (vert.). 80fr, Arsinoitherium.

1970, July 20

229	A66	15fr dl grn, ocher & red brn	25	15
230	A66	20fr lt bl & multi	30	20
231	A66	60fr lt bl & multi	75	28
232	A66	80fr lt bl & multi	1.10	50

Mikado 141, 1932
A67

Locomotives: 60fr, Steam locomotive 130+032, 1947. 75fr, Alsthom BB 1100, 1962. 85fr, Diesel BB BB 302, 1969.

1970, Aug. 20 **Engraved** ***Perf. 13***

233	A67	40fr mag, bl grn & blk	60	30
234	A67	60fr blk, bl & grn	80	40
235	A67	75fr red, bl & blk	1.00	45
236	A67	85fr car, sl grn & ocher	1.25	55

Cogniauxia Padolaena
A68

Green Night Adder
A69

Tropical Flowers: 2fr, Celosia cristata. 5fr, Plumeria acutifolia. 10fr, Bauhinia variegata. 15fr, Poinsettia. 20fr, Thunbergia grandiflora.

1971, Feb. 10 **Photo.** ***Perf. 12x12½***

237	A68	1fr lil & multi	8	7
238	A68	2fr yel & multi	8	7
239	A68	5fr ultra & multi	12	8
240	A68	10fr yel & multi	20	13
241	A68	15fr multi	32	18
242	A68	20fr dk red & multi	40	18
		Nos. 237-242 (6)	1.20	71

Perf. 12x12½, 12½x12

1971, June 26 **Photogravure**

Reptiles: 10fr, African Egg-eating snake (horiz.). 15fr, Flap-necked chameleon. 20fr, Nile crocodile (horiz.). 25fr, Rock python (horiz.). 30fr, Gaboon viper. 40fr, Brown house snake (horiz.). 45fr, Jameson's mamba.

243	A69	5fr multi	8	8
244	A69	10fr multi	15	12
245	A69	15fr multi	25	15
246	A69	20fr red & multi	32	25
247	A69	25fr grn & multi	40	32
248	A69	30fr multi	50	40
249	A69	40fr bis & multi	50	45
250	A69	45fr multi	65	50
		Nos. 243-250 (8)	2.85	2.27

Pseudimbrasia Deyrollei—A70

Caterpillars: 15fr, Bunaea alcinoe (vert.). 20fr, Epiphora vacuna ploetzi. 25fr, Imbrasia eblis. 30fr, Imbrasia dione (vert.). 40fr, Holocera angulata.

1971, July 3 ***Perf. 13***

251	A70	10fr ver, blk & grn	20	15
252	A70	15fr multi	25	20
253	A70	20fr yel grn, blk & ocher	32	28
254	A70	25fr multi	40	32
255	A70	30fr red, blk & yel	50	40
256	A70	40fr bl, blk & org	75	55
		Nos. 251-256 (6)	2.42	1.90

Cymothoe Sangaris
A71

Butterflies and Moths: 40fr, Papilio dardanus (vert.). 75fr, Iolaus timon. 90fr, Papilio phorcas (vert.). 100fr, Euchloron megaera.

Perf. 12½x12, 12x12½

1971, Oct. 15

257	A71	30fr yel & multi	50	32
258	A71	40fr grn & multi	65	45
259	A71	75fr multi	1.10	65
260	A71	90fr multi	1.35	90
261	A71	100fr ultra & multi	1.75	1.25
		Nos. 257-261 (5)	5.35	3.57

Black and White Men Working Together
A72

1971, Oct. 30 ***Perf. 13x12½***

262	A72	50fr org & multi	50	25

International Year Against Racial Discrimination.

REPUBLIQUE POPULAIRE DU CONGO
30F

Nos. 214–215 Surcharged

INAUGURATION
DE LA LIAISON COAXIALE
18-11-71

1971, Nov. 18 **Engraved** ***Perf. 13***

263	A61	30fr on 25fr multi	40	25
264	A61	40fr on 30fr multi	50	32

Inauguration of cable service between Brazzaville and Pointe Noire. Words of surcharge arranged differently on No. 264.

Map of Congo
A73

1971, Dec. 31 **Photo.** ***Perf. 12½x13***

265	A73	30fr bl & multi	35	25
266	A73	40fr yel grn & multi	40	20
267	A73	100fr gray & multi	1.10	55

"Labor, Democracy, Peace."

Lion
A74

Animals: 2fr, African elephants. 3fr, Leopard. 4fr, Hippopotamus. 5fr, Gorilla (vert.). 20fr, Potto. 30fr, De Brazza's monkey. 40fr, Pygmy chimpanzee (vert.).

1972, Jan. 31 **Engraved** ***Perf. 13***

268	A74	1fr grn & multi	5	5
269	A74	2fr dk red & multi	5	5
270	A74	3fr red brn & multi	10	8
271	A74	4fr vio & multi	10	8
272	A74	5fr brn & multi	12	12
273	A74	20fr org & multi	32	25
274	A74	30fr ocher & multi	50	28
275	A74	40fr Prus bl & multi	65	45
		Nos. 268-275 (8)	1.89	1.36

WHO Emblem
A75

Design: 50fr, WHO emblem (horiz.).

Perf. 12½x13, 13x12½

1973, June 30 **Typographed**

276	A75	40fr grn & multi	32	15
277	A75	50fr multi	40	20

World Health Organization, 25th anniversary.

Kronenbourg Brewery
A76

Designs (Brewery Trademark and): 40fr, Laboratory. 75fr, Vats and controls. 85fr, Automatic control room. 100fr, Pressure room. 250fr, Bottling plant.

1973, July 15 **Engr.** ***Perf. 13***

278	A76	30fr red & multi	25	15
279	A76	40fr red & multi	32	22
280	A76	75fr red & multi	55	32
281	A76	85fr red & multi	80	40
282	A76	100fr red & multi	1.10	60
283	A76	250fr red & multi	2.10	1.10
		Nos. 278-283 (6)	5.12	2.79

Kronenbourg Brewery, Brazzaville.

Golwe Locomotive, 1935
A77

Locomotives: 40fr, Diesel, 1935. 75fr, Diesel Whithcomb, 1946. 85fr, Diesel CC200.

1973, Aug. 1 **Engr.** ***Perf. 13***

284	A77	30fr ind & multi	40	25
285	A77	40fr vio bl & multi	50	25
286	A77	75fr multi	90	40
287	A77	85fr multi	1.00	50

No. 225 Surcharged with New Value, 2 Bars, and Overprinted in Ultramarine: "SECHERESSE SOLIDARITE AFRICAINE"

1973, Aug. 16 **Photo.** ***Perf. 12½x12***

288	A64	100fr on 5fr multi	80	55

African solidarity in drought emergency.

African Postal Union Issue

Common Design Type

1973, Sept. 12 **Engr.** ***Perf. 13***

289	CD137 100fr bl grn, vio & brn	75	40

Bees, Beehive, Honeycomb
A78

1973, Dec. 10 **Engraved** ***Perf. 13***

290	A78	30fr sl grn, dk red & bl	27	18
291	A78	40fr sl bl, sl grn & lt grn	35	18

"Work and economy."

Family, UN and FAO Emblems
A79

Designs: 40fr, Grain, UN and FAO emblems. 100fr, Grain, UN and FAO emblems (vert.).

1973, Dec. 10

292	A79	30fr dk car & dk brn	27	10
293	A79	40fr dk grn, yel & ind	35	15
294	A79	100fr grn, brn & org	80	50

World Food Program, 10th anniversary.

Amilcar Cabral, Cattle and Child
A80

1974, July 15 Engraved *Perf. 13*

295	A80	100fr multi	75	50

First death anniversary of Amilcar Cabral (1924–1973), leader of anti-Portuguese guerrilla activity in Portuguese Guinea.

Félix Eboué, Cross of Lorraine
A81

1974, Aug. 31 Litho. *Perf. 13*

296	A81	30fr bl & multi	25	15
297	A81	40fr brt pink & multi	35	20

Félix A. Eboué (1884–1944), Governor of Chad, first colonial governor to join Free French in WWII, 30th death anniversary.

Pineapples
A82

1974, Nov. 12

Multicolored

298	A82	30fr *shown*	25	15
299	A82	30fr *Bananas*	25	15
300	A82	30fr *Safous*	25	15
301	A82	40fr *Avocados*	35	20
302	A82	40fr *Mangos*	35	20
303	A82	40fr *Papaya*	35	20
304	A82	40fr *Oranges*	35	20
		Nos. 298-304 (7)	2.15	1.25

Charles de Gaulle and Conference Building—A83

1974, Nov. 25 Engraved *Perf. 13*

305	A83	100fr multi	75	50

Brazzaville Conference, 25th anniversary.

George Stephenson and Various Locomotives—A84

1974, Dec. 15

306	A84	75fr sl grn & ol	55	35

George Stephenson (1781–1848), English inventor and railroad founder.

UDEAC Issue

Presidents and Flags of Cameroun, CAR, Congo, Gabon and Meeting Center—A84a

1974, Dec. 8 Photogravure *Perf. 13*

307	A84a	40fr gold & multi	35	20

See note after Cameroun No. 595.
See No. C195.

Irish Setter
A85

Designs: Dogs.

1974, Dec. 15 Photo. *Perf. 13x13½*

Multicolored

308	A85	30fr *shown*	35	18
309	A85	40fr *Borzoi*	45	22
310	A85	75fr *Pointer*	75	35
311	A85	100fr *Great Dane*	1.00	55

1974, Dec. 15

Designs: Cats.

312	A85	30fr *Havana chestnut*	35	15
313	A85	40fr *Red Persian*	45	18
314	A85	75fr *Blue British*	75	35
315	A85	100fr *African serval*	1.00	55

Labor Party Flags and People
A86

Design: 40fr, Hands holding flowers and tools.

1974, Dec. 31 Engr. *Perf. 13x12½*

316	A86	30fr red & multi	25	12
317	A86	40fr red & multi	35	18

5th anniversary of Congolese Labor Party and of introduction of red flag.

Symbols of Development—A87

U Thant and UN Headquarters—A88

Paul G. Hoffman and UN Emblem
A89

Perf. 13x12½, 12½x13

1975, Feb. 28 Lithographed

318	A87	40fr multi	32	18
319	A88	50fr lt bl & multi	35	22
320	A89	50fr yel & multi	35	22

National economic development.

Map of China and Mao Tse-tung—A90

1975, Mar. 9 Engraved *Perf. 13*

321	A90	75fr multi	60	40

25th anniversary of the People's Republic of China.

Woman Breaking Bonds, Women's Activities, Map of Congo
A91

1975, June 20 Litho. *Perf. 12½*

322	A91	40fr gold & multi	40	20

Revolutionary Union of Congolese Women, URFC, 10th anniversary.

CARA Soccer Team—A92

Design: 40fr, Team captain and manager receiving trophy (vert.).

1975, July 15 Litho. *Perf. 12½*

323	A92	30fr multi	27	18
324	A92	40fr multi	35	22

CARA team, winners of African Soccer Cup 1974.

Citroen, 1935—A93

Designs: Early autombiles.

1975, July 17 *Perf. 12*

Multicolored

325	A93	30fr *shown*	25	20
326	A93	40fr *Alfa Romeo, 1911*	35	20
327	A93	50fr *Rolls Royce, 1926*	40	30
328	A93	75fr *Duryea, 1893*	60	45

Tipoye Transport—A94

Design: 40fr, Dugout canoe.

1975, Aug. 5

329	A94	30fr multi	22	13
330	A94	40fr multi	32	18

Traditional means of transportation.

Raising Red Flag—A95

Design: 40fr, National Conference.

1975, Aug. 15

331	A95	30fr multi	25	20
332	A95	40fr multi	35	20

2nd anniversary of installation of popular power (30fr) and 3rd anniversary of National Conference (40fr).

The only foreign revenue stamps listed in this Catalogue are those authorized for prepayment of postage.

Line Fishing A96 — Woman Pounding "Foufou" A97

Traditional Fishing: 30fr, Trap fishing (horiz.). 60fr, Spear fishing. 90fr, Net fishing (horiz.).

1975, Aug. 31 Litho. *Perf. 12*

333	A96	30fr multi	25	20
334	A96	40fr multi	35	20
335	A96	60fr multi	50	30
336	A96	90fr multi	70	50

1975, Sept. 5

Household Tasks: No. 338, Woman chopping wood. 40fr, Woman preparing manioc (horiz.).

337	A97	30fr multi	25	15
338	A97	30fr multi	25	15
339	A97	40fr multi	35	20

Esanga A98

Musical Instruments: 40fr, Kalakwa. 60fr, Likembe. 75fr, Ngongui.

1975, Sept. 20 *Perf. 12½*

340	A98	30fr blk & brn	25	15
341	A98	40fr org & multi	35	20
342	A98	60fr grn & multi	50	35
343	A98	75fr multi	60	40

Dzeke (Congolese) Shell Money A99

Ancient Money: No. 346, like No. 344. Nos. 345, 347, Okengo, Congolese, iron bar. 40fr, Gallic coin, c. 60 B.C. 50fr, Roman denarius, 37 B.C. 60fr, Danubian coin, 2nd century B.C. 85fr, Greek stater, 4th century B.C.

1975–76 Engr. *Perf. 13*

344	A99	30fr red & multi	25	20
345	A99	30fr vio & multi	25	20
346	A99	35fr ol & multi	30	20
347	A99	35fr dk car rose & multi	30	20
348	A99	40fr Prus bl & brn	35	20
349	A99	50fr Prus bl & ol	40	25
350	A99	60fr dk grn & brn	50	35
351	A99	85fr mag & sl grn	65	40
		Nos. 344-351 (8)	3.00	2.00

Nos. 346–347 inscribed "1976" and issued Mar. 1976; others issued Oct. 5, 1975.

Moschops—A100

Pre-historic Animals: 75fr, Tyrannosaurus. 95fr, Cryptocleidus. 100fr, Stegosaurus.

1975, Oct. 15 Litho. *Perf. 13*

352	A100	55fr multi	45	30
353	A100	75fr multi	60	35
354	A100	95fr multi	75	50
355	A100	100fr multi	80	55

Albert Schweitzer A101

1975, Oct. 15 Engraved

356	A101	75fr ol, brn & red	60	40

Albert Schweitzer (1875–1965), medical missionary, birth centenary.

Alexander Fleming A102

Designs: No. 358, André Marie Ampère. No. 359, Clement Ader.

1975, Nov. 15 Engr. *Perf. 13*

357	A102	60fr brn, grn & blk	50	30
358	A102	95fr blk, red & grn	75	55
359	A102	95fr red, bl & ind	75	55

Alexander Fleming (1881–1955), developer of penicillin, 20th death anniversary; André Marie Ampère (1775–1836), physicist, bicentenary of birth; Clement Ader (1841–1925), aviation pioneer, 50th death anniversary.

U.N. Emblem "ONU" and "30"—A103

1975, Dec. 20 Engr. *Perf. 13*

360	A103	95fr car, ultra & grn	75	55

United Nations, 30th anniversary.

Women's Broken Chain—A104

Design: 60fr, Equality between man and woman, globe, IWY emblem.

1975, Dec. 20 Litho. *Perf. 12½*

361	A104	35fr mag, ocher & gray	30	20
362	A104	60fr ultra, brn & blk	50	35

International Women's Year, 1975.

Pres. Marien Ngouabi, Flag and Workers—A105

Echo of the P.C.T. A106

Perf. 12½x12, 13x12½

1975, Dec. 31 Lithographed

363	A105	30fr multi	25	15
364	A106	35fr multi	30	15

6th anniversary of the Congolese Labor Party (P.C.T.). See No. C215.

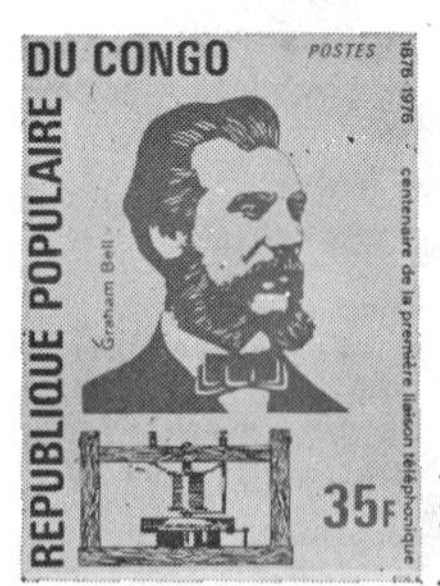

A.G. Bell and 1876 Telephone A107

1976, Apr. 25 Litho. *Perf. 12½x13*

365	A107	35fr yel, brn & org brn	30	20

Centenary of first telephone call by Alexander Graham Bell, Mar. 10, 1876. See No. C229.

Women Selling Fruit and Vegetables A108

Design: 60fr, Market scene.

1976, Sept. 19 Litho. *Perf. 12½x13*

366	A108	35fr multi	30	20
367	A108	60fr multi	50	30

Congolese Coiffure A109

Designs: Various women's hair styles.

1976, Oct. 10 Litho. *Perf. 13*

368	A109	35fr multi	30	20
369	A109	60fr multi	50	35
370	A109	95fr multi	75	50
371	A109	100fr multi	80	55

Pole Vault, Map of Central Africa A110

Design: 95fr, Long jump and map of Central Africa.

1976, Oct. 25 *Perf. 12½*

372	A110	60fr yel & multi	50	35
373	A110	95fr yel & multi	75	55

Gold medalists, 1st Central African Games, Yaoundé, July 27–30, 1975. See Nos. C230–C231.

Antelope A111

1976, Oct. 27 Litho. *Perf. 12½*

Multicolored

Size: 36x36mm.

374	A111	5fr *shown*	5	4
375	A111	10fr *Buffalos*	10	5
376	A111	15fr *Hippopotamus*	10	7
377	A111	20fr *Wart hog*	15	10
378	A111	25fr *Elephants*	20	13
		Nos. 374-378 (5)	60	39

1976, Dec. 8

Designs: Birds.

Multicolored

Size: 26x36mm.

379	A111	5fr *Saddle-bill storks*	5	4

Size: 36x36mm.

380	A111	10fr *Malachite kingfisher*	10	8
381	A111	20fr *Crowned cranes*	15	12

Bicycling, Map of Participants A112 — Heliotrope A113

1976, Dec. 21 Photo. *Perf. 12½x13*

Designs (Map and): 60fr, Fieldball. 80fr, Running. 95fr, Soccer.

382 A112 35fr multi 30 20
383 A112 60fr multi 50 35
384 A112 80fr multi 65 50
385 A112 95fr multi 75 55

First Central African Games, Libreville, Gabon, June–July 1976.

1976, Dec. 23 Photo. *Perf. 12½x13*

Flowers: 5fr, Water lilies. 15fr, Bird-of-paradise flower.

386 A113 5fr multi 5 4
387 A113 10fr multi 10 5
388 A113 15fr multi 15 10

Torch and Olive Branches A114

1976, Dec. 25 Litho. *Perf. 12½x13*

389 A114 35fr multi 20 30

National Pioneer Movement.

The Spirit of '76—A115

Designs: 125fr, Pulling down George III statue. 150fr, Battle of Princeton. 175fr, Generals of Revolutionary War. 200fr, Burgoyne's surrender at Saratoga. 500fr, Battle of Lexington.

1976, Dec. 29 Litho. *Perf. 14*

390 A115 100fr multi 1.00 38
391 A115 125fr multi 1.25 50
392 A115 150fr multi 1.35 55
393 A115 175fr multi 1.65 75
394 A115 200fr multi 1.85 85
Nos. 390-394 (5) 7.10 3.03

Souvenir Sheet

395 A115 500fr multi 4.75 2.00

American Bicentennial.

No. 395 has green and blue margin, black marginal inscription. Size: 114x72 mm.

Dugout Canoe Race A116

Design: 60fr, 2-man dugout canoes.

1977, Mar. 27 Litho. *Perf. 13x13½*

396 A116 35fr multi 30 20
397 A116 60fr multi 50 35

Dugout canoe races on Congo River.

Lilan Goua A117

Fresh-water Fish: 15fr, Liko ko. 25fr, Liyan ga. 35fr, Mbessi. 60fr, Mongandza.

1977, June 15 Litho. *Perf. 12½*

398 A117 10fr multi 10 7
399 A117 15fr multi 15 10
400 A117 25fr multi 20 15
401 A117 35fr multi 30 20
402 A117 60fr multi 50 35
Nos. 398-402 (5) 1.25 87

Traditional Headdress—A118

Design: 60fr, Leopard cap.

1977, June 30 Litho. *Perf. 12½*

403 A118 35fr multi 30 20
404 A118 60fr multi 50 35

See Nos. C234-C235.

Bondjo Wrestling A119

Designs: 40fr, 50fr, Bondjo wrestling (different). 40fr, horiz.

1977, July 15

405 A119 25fr multi 20 15
406 A119 40fr multi 30 25
407 A119 50fr multi 40 30

"Schwaben" LZ 10, 1911 A120

Zeppelins: 60fr, "Viktoria Luise." LZ 11, 1913. 100fr, LZ 120. 200fr, LZ 127. 300fr, "Graf Zeppelin II" LZ 130.

1977, Aug. 5 Litho. *Perf. 11*

408 A120 40fr multi 35 18
409 A120 60fr multi 60 30
410 A120 100fr multi 95 35
411 A120 200fr multi 1.90 80
412 A120 300fr multi 3.00 1.20
Nos. 408-412 (5) 6.80 2.83

History of the Zeppelin. Exist imperf. See No. C236.

Coat of Arms and Rising Sun A121

1977, Aug. 15

413 A121 40fr multi 30 25

14th anniversary of the revolution.

Victor Hugo and The Hunchback of Notre Dame—A122

Designs (Hugo and): 60fr, Les Miserables. 100fr, Les Travailleurs de la Mer (octopus).

1977, Aug. 20 Engr. *Perf. 13*

414 A122 35fr multi 30 20
415 A122 60fr multi 50 35
416 A122 100fr multi 80 60

Victor Hugo (1802–1885), French novelist.

Mao Tse-tung A123

Lithographed; Gold Embossed

1977, Sept. 9 *Perf. 12x12½*

417 A123 400fr red & gold 3.25 2.50

Chairman Mao Tse-tung (1893–1976), Chinese Communist leader, first death anniversary.

Peter Paul Rubens A124

1977, Sept. 20 Gold Embossed

418 A124 600fr gold & lt bl 4.75 4.00

Peter Paul Rubens (1577–1640), painter.

Child Leading Blind Woman Across Street A125

1977, Oct. 22 Litho. *Perf. 12½x13*

419 A125 35fr multi 30 20

World Health Day: To see is life.

Paul Kamba and Records A126

1977, Oct. 29

420 A126 100fr multi 80 6

Paul Kamba (1912–1950), musician.

Trajan Vuia and Flying Machine A127

Designs: 75fr, Louis Bleriot and plane. 100fr, Roland Garros and plane. 200fr, Charles Lindbergh and Spirit of St. Louis. 300fr, Tupolev Tu-144. 500fr, Lindbergh and Spirit of St. Louis over ship in Atlantic.

1977, Nov. 18 Litho. *Perf. 14*

421 A127 60fr multi 60 35
422 A127 75fr multi 70 42
423 A127 100fr multi 95 42
424 A127 200fr multi 1.90 90
425 A127 300fr multi 3.00 1.40
Nos. 421-425 (5) 7.15 3.49

Souvenir Sheet

426 A127 500fr multi 4.00 1.85

History of aviation. No. 426 has multicolored margin showing Spirit of St. Louis at Orly Airport, Paris. Size: 117x91mm.

Elizabeth II and Prince Philip A128

Design: 300fr, Elizabeth II wearing Crown.

1977, Dec. 21

427 A128 250fr multi 2.40 1.30
428 A128 300fr multi 3.00 1.40

25th anniversary of the reign of Queen Elizabeth II. See No. C239.

King Baudouin A129

Design: No. 430, Charles de Gaulle.

1977, Dec. 21

429	A129	200fr multi	1.90	95
430	A129	200fr multi	1.90	95

King Baudouin of Belgium and Charles de Gaulle, president of France.

Ambete Sculpture A130

Design: 85fr, Babembe sculpture.

1978, Feb. 18 Engr. *Perf. 13*

431	A130	35fr lt brn & multi	30	20
432	A130	85fr lt grn & multi	70	50

Congolese art.

St. Simon, by Rubens A131

Rubens Paintings: 140fr, Duke of Lerma. 200fr, Madonna and Saints. 300fr, Rubens and his Wife Helena Fourment. 500fr, Farm at Laeken.

1978, Mar. 7 Litho. *Perf. 13½x14*

433	A131	60fr gold & multi	60	25
434	A131	140fr gold & multi	1.35	45
435	A131	200fr gold & multi	1.90	70
436	A131	300fr gold & multi	3.00	1.00

Souvenir Sheet

437	A131	500fr gold & multi	4.75	2.00

Peter Paul Rubens (1577–1640), 400th birth anniversary. No. 437 contains one stamp; multicolored margin shows entire painting. Size: 106x123mm.

Pres. Ngouabi and Microphones A132

Designs: 60fr, Ngouabi at his desk (horiz.). 100fr, Portrait.

Perf. 12½x13, 13x12½

1978, Mar. 18 Lithographed

438	A132	35fr multi	30	20
439	A132	60fr multi	50	35
440	A132	100fr multi	80	60

Pres. Marien Ngouabi, first death anniversary.

Ferenc Puskas and Argentina '78 Emblem—A133

Players and Emblem: 75fr, Giacinto Facchetti. 100fr, Bobby Moore. 200fr, Raymond Kopa. 300fr, Pelé. 500fr, Franz Beckenbauer.

1978, Apr. 4 *Perf. 14x13½*

441	A133	60fr multi	60	33
442	A133	75fr multi	70	40
443	A133	100fr multi	90	45
444	A133	200fr multi	2.00	95
445	A133	300fr multi	2.85	1.35
		Nos. 441-445 (5)	7.05	3.48

Souvenir Sheet

446	A133	500fr multi	4.75	2.00

11th World Cup Soccer Championship, Argentina, June 1–25. No. 446 has light and dark blue margin showing soccer ball and net. Size: 136x100mm.

Pearl S. Buck and Chinese Women A134

Designs: 75fr, Fridtjof Nansen, refugees and Nansen passport. 100fr, Henri Bergson, book and flame. 200fr, Alexander Fleming and Petri dish. 300fr, Gerhart Hauptmann and book. 500fr, Henri Dunant and Red Cross Station.

1978, Apr. 29

447	A134	60fr multi	60	33
448	A134	75fr multi	70	40
449	A134	100fr multi	90	45
450	A134	200fr multi	2.00	95
451	A134	300fr multi	2.85	1.35
		Nos. 447-451 (5)	7.05	3.48

Souvenir Sheet

452	A134	500fr multi	4.75	2.00

Nobel Prize winners. No. 452 has multicolored margin with head of Alfred Nobel and inscribed "Nobel." Size: 119x81mm.

African Buffalos A135

Animals and Wildlife Fund Emblem: 35fr, Okapi (vert.). 85fr, Rhinoceros. 150fr, Chimpanzee (vert.). 200fr, Hippopotamus. 300fr, Buffon's kob (vert.).

1978 *Perf. 14½*

453	A135	35fr multi	35	25
454	A135	60fr multi	60	30
455	A135	85fr multi	80	42
456	A135	150fr multi	1.40	60
457	A135	200fr multi	2.00	85
458	A135	300fr multi	2.85	1.25
		Nos. 453-458 (6)	8.00	3.67

Endangered animals.

Issue dates: 35fr, Aug. 11. Others, July 11.

Emblem, Young People, Gun and Fist A136

1978, July 28 *Perf. 12½*

459	A136	35fr multi	30	20

11th World Youth Festival, Havana, July 28–Aug. 5.

Pyramids and Camels—A137

Seven Wonders of the Ancient World: 50fr, Hanging Gardens of Babylon. 60fr, Statue of Zeus, Olympia. 95fr, Colossus of Rhodes. 125fr, Mausoleum of Halicarnassus. 150fr, Temple of Artemis, Ephesus. 200fr, Lighthouse, Alexandria. 300fr, Map of Eastern Mediterranean showing locations. (50fr, 60fr, 95fr, 125fr, 200fr, vertical.)

1978, Aug. 12 Litho. *Perf. 14*

460	A137	35fr multi	35	18
461	A137	50fr multi	50	25
462	A137	60fr multi	60	30
463	A137	95fr multi	90	45
464	A137	125fr multi	1.20	55
465	A137	150fr multi	1.50	70
466	A137	200fr multi	1.90	85
467	A137	300fr multi	3.00	1.20
		Nos. 460-467 (8)	9.95	4.48

Nos. 427–428 Overprinted in Silver:
"ANNIVERSAIRE DU COURONNEMENT 1953–1978"

1978, Sept. Litho. *Perf. 14*

468	A128	250fr multi	2.00	75
469	A128	300fr multi	2.40	1.00

25th anniversary of coronation of Queen Elizabeth II. See No. C244.

Kwame N'Krumah and Map of Africa—A138

1978, Sept. 23 Litho. *Perf. 13x12½*

470	A138	60fr multi	50	25

Kwame N'Krumah (1909–1972), president of Ghana.

Wild Boar Hunt—A139

Designs: 50fr, Fish smoking. 60fr, Hunter with spears and dog (vert.).

1978 Litho. *Perf. 12*

471	A139	35fr multi	35	25
472	A139	50fr multi	50	35
473	A139	60fr multi	60	40

Local hunting and fishing.

Issue dates: 35fr, 60fr, Oct. 5; 50fr, Oct. 10.

View of Kalchreut, by Dürer—A140

Paintings by Dürer: 150fr, Elspeth Tucher (vert.). 250fr, "The Great Piece of Turf" (vert.). 350fr, Self-portrait (vert.).

1978, Nov. 23 Litho. *Perf. 14*

474	A140	65fr multi	65	42
475	A140	150fr multi	1.50	1.05
476	A140	250fr multi	2.50	1.75
477	A140	350fr multi	3.50	2.50

Albrecht Dürer (1471–1528), German painter.

Basketmaker A141

Productive Labor: 90fr, Woodcarver. 140fr, Women hoeing field.

1978, Nov. 18 Litho. *Perf. 12½*

Size: 25x36mm.

478	A141	85fr multi	85	60
479	A141	90fr multi	90	62

Size: 27x48mm.

Perf. 12

480	A141	140fr multi	1.40	1.00

Nos. 441–446 Overprinted in Silver:

a. "1962 VAINQUEUR:BRESIL"
b. "1966 VAINQUEUR: / GRANDE BRETAGNE"
c. "1970 VAINQUEUR: / BRESIL"
d. "1974 VAINQUEUR: / ALLEMAGNE (RFA)"
e. "1978 VAINQUEUR /: ARGENTINE"
f. "ARGENTINE–PAYS BAS 3–1 / 25 juin 1978"

1978, Nov. *Perf. 14x13½*

481	A133 (a)	60fr multi	60	40
482	A133 (b)	75fr multi	75	50
483	A133 (c)	100fr multi	1.00	70
484	A133 (d)	200fr multi	2.00	1.40
485	A133 (e)	300fr multi	3.00	2.10
		Nos. 481-485(5)	7.35	5.10

Souvenir Sheet

486	A133 (f)	500fr multi	5.25	

Winners, World Soccer Cup Championships 1962–1978.

Heart and Charts A142

1978, Dec. 16 Engr. *Perf. 13*

487 A142 100fr multi 1.00 70

Fight against hypertension.

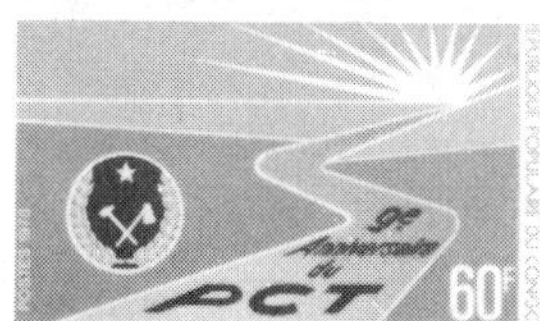

Party Emblem and Road—A143

1978, Dec. 31 Litho. *Perf. 12½x12*

488 A143 60fr multi 60 40

Congolese Labor Party, 9th anniversary.

Capt. Cook, Polynesians and House—A144

Designs: 150fr, Island scene. 250fr, Polynesian longboats. 350fr, Capt. Cook's ships off Hawaii.

1979, Jan. *Perf. 14½*

489 A144 65fr multi 55 42
490 A144 150fr multi 1.50 1.05
491 A144 250fr multi 2.50 1.75
492 A144 350fr multi 3.50 2.50

Capt. James Cook (1728–1779), 250th birth anniversary.

Pres. Marien Ngouabi A145

1979, Mar. 18 Litho. *Perf. 12*

493 A145 35fr multi 35 22
494 A145 60fr multi 60 40

2nd anniversary of assassination of President Ngouabi.

"1979," IYC Emblem, Child A146

1979, Apr. 30 Litho. *Perf. 12½x13*

495 A146 45fr multi 45 30
496 A146 75fr multi 75 50

International Year of the Child.

Pottery Vases and Solanum—A147

Design: 150fr, Mail runner, Concorde, train, UPU emblem, envelope.

1979, June 8 Litho. *Perf. 13*

497 A147 60fr multi 60 35

Engraved

498 A147 150fr multi 1.50 90

Philexafrique II, Libreville, Gabon, June 8–17. Nos. 497, 498 each printed in sheets of 10 with 5 labels showing exhibition emblem.

Rowland Hill, Diesel Locomotive, Germany No. 78—A148

Designs (Rowland Hill and): 100fr, Old steam locomotive and France No. B10. 200fr, Diesel locomotive and US No. 245. 300fr, Steam locomotive and England-Australia First Aerialpost vignette, 1919. 500fr, Electric train, Concorde and Middle Congo No. 75.

1979, June *Perf. 14*

499 A148 65fr multi 65 42
500 A148 100fr multi 1.00 70
501 A148 200fr multi 2.00 1.40
502 A148 300fr multi 3.00 2.10

Souvenir Sheet

503 A148 500fr multi 5.25

Sir Rowland Hill (1795–1879), originator of penny postage. No. 503 has multicolored margin showing locomotive and 19th century woman posting letter in pillar box. Size: 102x77mm.

Salvador Allende, Flags, Demonstrators—A149

1979, July 21 Litho. *Perf. 12½*

504 A149 100fr multi 1.00 70

Salvador Allende, president of Chile.

Old Man Telling Stories—A150

1979, July 28

505 A150 45fr multi 45 30

Story telling as education.

Handball Players A151

Designs: 75fr, Players and ball (vert.). 250fr, Pres. Ngouabi, cup on map of Africa, player.

1979, July 31 Litho. *Perf. 12½*

Size: 40x30mm, 30x40mm

506 A151 45fr multi 45 30
507 A151 75fr multi 75 50

Size: 22x40mm *Perf. 12x12½*

508 A151 250fr multi 2.50 1.75

Marien Ngouabi Handball Cup.

Map and Flag of Congo A152

1979, Aug. 15

509 A152 50fr multi 50 35

16th anniversary of revolution.

Souvenir Sheet

Virgin and Child, by Dürer A153

1979, Aug. 13 *Perf. 13½*

510 A153 500fr red brn & lt grn 5.25

Albrecht Dürer (1471–1528), German engraver and painter. No. 510 has light green and red brown margin showing entire etching. Size: 90x115mm.

Bach and Contemporary Instruments A155

1979, Sept. 10 *Perf. 13½*

Design: No. 512, Albert Einstein, astronauts on moon.

511 A155 200fr multi 2.00 1.40
512 A155 200fr multi 2.00 1.40

Yoro Fishing Port—A156

1979, Sept. 26 Litho. *Perf. 12½*

Multicolored

513 A156 45fr *shown* 45 30
514 A156 75fr *Port at night* 75 50

Moukoukoulou Dam—A157

1979, Oct. 5 *Perf. 12½×12*

515 A157 20fr multi 20 14
516 A157 45fr multi 45 30

Emblem, Control Tower, Jets—A158

1979, Dec. 12 Litho. *Perf. 12½*

517 A158 100fr multi 1.00 75

ASCENA (Air Safety Board), 20th anniversary.

Congolese Labor Party, 10th Anniversary—A159

1979, Dec. 31

518 A159 45fr multi 45 14

Post Office, 15th Anniversary A160

1980, Mar. 30 Litho. *Perf. 12½*

519 A160 45fr multi 45 34
520 A160 95fr multi 95 70

Visit of Pope John Paul II—A161

1980, May 5

521 A161 100fr multi 80 40

Rotary International, 75th Anniversary—A162

1980, May 10 Litho. *Perf. 12½*

522 A162 150fr multi 1.20 60

Pointe Noire Foundry—A163

1980, June 18 **Litho.** ***Perf. 12½***

523	A163	30fr *shown*	24	12
524	A163	35fr *Different view*	28	14

Claude Chappe, Tower—A164

1980, June 21 **Litho.** ***Perf. 12½***

525	A164	200fr multi	1.60	80

Claude Chappe (1763-1805), French engineer.

Mossaka Harbor—A165

1980, June 23

532	A165	45fr *shown*	36	18
533	A165	90fr *Different view*	72	35

Papilio Dardanus (Front and Back) A167

Human Rights Emblem, People A169

July 31st Hospital—A168

1980, July 12 **Litho.** ***Perf. 12½***

534	A167	5fr *shown*	3	3
535	A167	15fr *Kalima aethiops*	12	6
536	A167	20fr *Papilio demodocus*	16	8
537	A167	60fr *Euphaedra*	48	24
538	A167	90fr *Hypolimnas misippus*	72	36
		Nos. 534-538 (5)	1.51	77

Souvenir Sheet

539	A167	300fr *Charaxes smaragdalis*	2.50

Nos. 539 has multicolored margin showing butterflies. Size: 120x80mm.

1980, July 31

540	A168	45fr multi	36	18

1980, Aug. 2

541	A169	350fr *shown*	2.80	1.40
542	A169	500fr *Man breaking chain*	4.00	4.00

Human Rights Convention, 32nd anniversary.

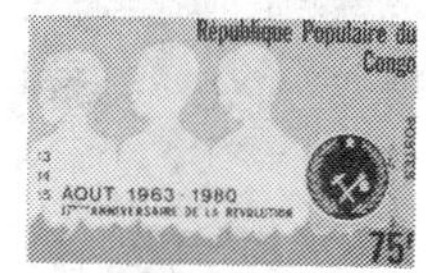

Citizens and Congolese Arms—A170

1980, Aug. 15 ***Perf. 12½***

543	A170	75fr *shown*	60	30
544	A170	95fr *Dove on flag, fists, vert.*	75	38
545	A170	150fr *Dove holding Congolese arms*	1.20	60

August 13-15th Revolution, 17th anniversary.

Coffee and Cocoa Trees on Map of Congo—A171

Coffee and Cocoa Day: 95fr, Branches, map of Congo.

1980, Aug. 18 ***Perf. 13½x13***

546	A171	45fr multi	35	18
547	A171	95fr multi	75	38

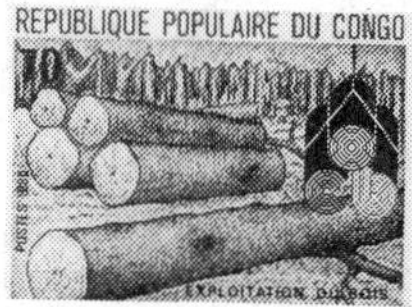

Logging—A172

1980, Aug. 28

548	A172	70fr *shown*	56	28
549	A172	75fr *Wood transport*	60	30

President Neto A173

Lark A174

1980, Sept. 11

550	A173	100fr multi	80	40

1980, Sept. 17

Designs: Birds.

551	A174	45fr multi, horiz.	36	18
552	A174	75fr multi, horiz.	60	30
553	A174	90fr multi, horiz.	72	36
554	A174	150fr multi	1.20	60
555	A174	200fr multi	1.60	80
556	A174	250fr multi	2.00	1.00
a.		Souvenir sheet of 6	6.50	
		Nos. 551-556 (6)	6.48	3.24

No. 556a contains Nos. 551-556. Lilac marginal inscription. Size: 148x105mm.

World Tourism Conference, Manila, Sept. 27—A175

1980, Sept. 27 **Litho.** ***Perf. 13½x13***

557	A175	100fr multi	80	40

First Day of School Term—A176

1980, Oct. 2 **Photo.** ***Perf. 13***

558	A176	50fr multi	40	20

First House in Brazzaville—A177

Brazzaville Centenary: 65fr, First native village. 75fr, Old Town Hall, 1912. 150fr, View from bank of Bacongo, 1912. 200fr, Meeting of explorer Savorgnan de Brazza and chief Makoko, 1880.

1980, Oct. 3 **Litho.** ***Perf. 12½***

559	A177	45fr multi	36	18
560	A177	65fr multi	52	26
561	A177	75fr multi	60	30
562	A177	150fr multi	1.20	60
563	A177	200fr multi	1.60	80
		Nos. 559-563 (5)	4.28	2.14

Boys on Bank of Congo River—A178

1980, Oct. 30

564	A178	80fr *shown*	65	32
565	A178	150fr *Djoue Bridge*	1.20	60

Revolutionary Stadium and Athletes—A179

1980, Nov. 20 ***Perf. 13x12½***

566	A179	60fr multi	50	25

Rebuilt Railroad Bridge over Congo River—A180

1980, Nov. 29 ***Perf. 13x13½***

567	A180	75fr multi	60	30

Mangoes, Loudima Fruit Packing Station—A181

1980, Dec. 2 ***Perf. 13***

568	A181	10fr *shown*	8	4
569	A181	25fr *Oranges*	20	10
570	A181	40fr *Citrons*	32	16
571	A181	85fr *Mandarins*	70	35

African Postal Union, 5th Anniversary—A182

1980, Dec. 24 ***Perf. 13½***

572	A182	100fr multi	80	40

Moungouni Earth Satellite Station—A183

1980, Dec. 30 ***Perf. 12½***

573	A183	75fr multi	60	30

Hertzian Wave Communication, Brazzaville—A184

1980, Dec. 30 ***Perf. 12½x12***

574	A184	150fr multi	1.20	60

1980 African Soccer Champion Team—A185

1981, Jan. 26 Litho. ***Perf. 12½x13, 13x12½***

575	A185	100fr Receiving cup, vert.	80	40
576	A185	150fr shown	1.20	60

Pres. Denis Sassou-Nguesso—A186

1981, Feb. 5 Litho. ***Perf. 12½***

577	A186	45fr multi	36	18
578	A186	75fr multi	60	30
579	A186	100fr multi	80	40

Columbia Space Shuttle Orbiting Earth A187

Space Conquest: 100fr, Luna 17, 1970. 200fr, 300fr, 500fr, Columbia space shuttle, 1981.

1981, May 4 Litho. ***Perf. 14x13½***

580	A187	100fr multi	80	40
581	A187	150fr multi	1.20	60
582	A187	200fr multi	1.60	80
583	A187	300fr multi	2.40	1.20

Souvenir Sheet

584	A187	500fr multi	4.00	2.00

No. 584 has multicolored margin showing space shuttle orbiting earth. Size: 104x79mm.

Fight Against Apartheid A188

Twin Palm Tree of Louingui A189

1981, May 5 Litho. ***Perf. 12½***

585	A188	100fr dp bl	80	40

1981, May 22 ***Perf. 12x12½***

586	A189	75fr multi	60	30

13th World Telecommunications Day—A190

1981, June 6 ***Perf. 12½***

587	A190	120fr multi	95	45

Rubber Extraction—A191

1981, June 27 ***Perf. 13***

588	A191	50fr shown	40	20
589	A191	70fr Sap draining	55	25

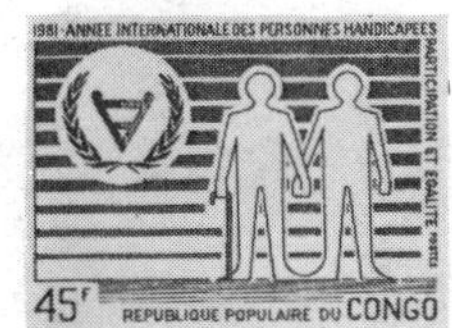
Intl. Year of the Disabled—A192

1981, June 29 **Engr.**

590	A192	45fr multi	36	18

See No. B7.

The Studio, by Picasso (1881-1973)—A193

1981, July 4 ***Perf. 12½***

591	A193	100fr shown	80	40
592	A193	150fr Landscape	1.20	60
593	A193	200fr Cannes Studio	1.60	80
594	A193	300fr Still Life	2.40	1.20
595	A193	500fr Still Life, diff.	4.00	2.00
		Nos. 591-595 (5)	10.00	5.00

Bird Trap—A194

Designs: Animal traps. 10fr vert.

1981, July

596	A194	5fr multi	3	3
597	A194	10fr multi	8	4
598	A194	15fr multi	12	6
599	A194	20fr multi	16	8
600	A194	30fr multi	24	12
601	A194	35fr multi	28	15
		Nos. 596-601 (6)	91	48

Mausoleum of King Maloango—A195

1981, July 4 Litho. ***Perf. 12½***

602	A195	75fr shown	60	30
603	A195	150fr Mausoleum, portrait	1.20	60

Prince Charles and Lady Diana, Coach—A196

Designs: Couple and coaches.

1981, Sept. 1 Litho. ***Perf. 14½***

604	A196	100fr multi	80	40
605	A196	200fr multi	1.60	80
606	A196	300fr multi	2.40	1.20

Souvenir Sheet

607	A196	400fr multi	3.25	1.75

Royal wedding. No. 607 has multicolored margin showing arms of Prince of Wales. Size: 104x78mm.

World Food Day—A197

1981, Oct. 16 Litho. ***Perf. 13½x13***

608	A197	150fr multi	1.20	60

12th World UPU Day—A198

1981, Oct. 24 Engr. ***Perf. 13x12½***

609	A198	90fr multi	72	35

Royal Guard A199

1981, Oct. 31 Litho. ***Perf. 12½x13***

610	A199	45fr multi	35	18

Eradication of Manioc Beetle A200

Natl. Red Cross A201

1981, Nov. 18 Litho. ***Perf. 12½***

611	A200	75fr multi	60	30

1981, Nov. 18 ***Perf. 13***

612	A201	10fr Bandaging patient	8	4
613	A201	35fr Treating child	28	15
614	A201	60fr Drawing well water	50	25

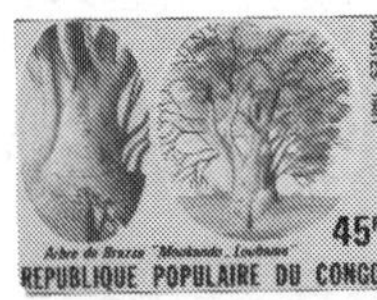
Giant Baobab ("Tree of Savorgnan de Brazza")—A202

1981, Dec. 19 Litho. ***Perf. 13***

615	A202	45fr multi	35	18
616	A202	65fr multi	60	30

Fetish Figure A203

Designs: Various carved figures.

1981, Dec. 19 ***Perf. 13x12½***

617	A203	15fr multi	12	6
618	A203	25fr multi	20	10
619	A203	45fr multi	35	18
620	A203	50fr multi	40	20
621	A203	60fr multi	50	25
		Nos. 617-621 (5)	1.57	79

Caves of Bangou—A204

1981, Dec. 29 ***Perf. 13x13½***

622	A204	20fr multi	16	8
623	A204	25fr multi	20	10

King Makoko and His Queen, Ivory Sculptures by R. Engongodzo—A205

1982, Feb. 27 Litho. ***Perf. 13½x13, 13x13½***

624	A205	25fr Woman, vert.	20	10
625	A205	35fr Woman, diff., vert.	28	14
626	A205	100fr shown	80	40

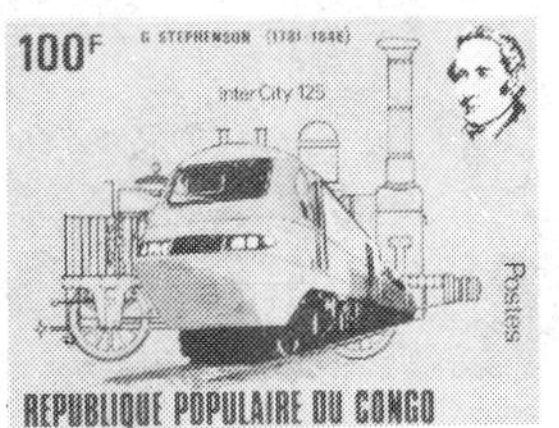

George Stephenson (1781-1848) and Inter City 125, Gt. Britain—A206

Locomotives: 150fr, Sinkansen Bullet Train, Japan. 200fr, Advanced Passenger Train, Gt. Britain. 300fr, TGV-001, France.

1982, Mar. 2 Litho. ***Perf. 12½***

627	A206	100fr multi	80	40
628	A206	150fr multi	1.20	60
629	A206	200fr multi	1.60	80
630	A206	300fr multi	2.40	1.20

Scouting Year—A207

1982, Apr. 13 Litho. ***Perf. 13***

631	A207	100fr Looking through binoculars	80	40
632	A207	150fr Reading map	1.20	60
633	A207	200fr Helping woman	1.60	80
634	A207	300fr Crossing rope bridge	2.40	1.25

Souvenir Sheet

635	A207	500fr Hiking, horiz.	4.00	2.00

No. 635 has multicolored margin continuing design. Size: 96x71mm.

Franklin Roosevelt (1882-1945)—A208

1982, June 12 Litho. ***Perf. 13***

636	A208	150fr shown	1.20	60
637	A208	250fr Washington (1732-1799)	2.00	1.00
638	A208	350fr Goethe (1749-1832)	2.80	1.40

21st Birthday of Princess Diana, July 1—A209

1982, June 12 ***Perf. 14***

639	A209	200fr Candles	1.60	80
640	A209	300fr "21"	2.40	1.25

Souvenir Sheet

641	A209	500fr Diana	4.00	2.00

No. 641 has multicolored margin showing rose. Size: 112x80mm.

5-Year Plan, 1982-1986—A210

1982, June 19 ***Perf. 13x12½, 12½x13***

642	A210	60fr Road construction	50	25
643	A210	100fr Communications, vert	80	40
644	A210	125fr Operating room equipment, vert.	1.00	50
645	A210	150fr Hydroelectric power, vert.	1.20	60

ITU Plenipotentiary Conference, Nairobi—A211

1982, June 26 ***Perf. 13***

646	A211	300fr multi	2.40	1.25

Nos. 604-607 Overprinted in Blue: "NAISSANCE ROYALE 1982"

1982, July 30 ***Perf. 14½***

647	A196	100fr multi	80	40
648	A196	200fr multi	1.60	80
649	A196	300fr multi	2.40	1.25

Souvenir Sheet

650	A196	400fr multi	3.25	1.75

Birth of Prince William of Wales, June 21.

Nutrition Campaign—A212

1982, July 24 Litho. ***Perf. 12½***

651	A212	100fr multi	80	40

WHO African Headquarters, Brazzaville—A213

1982, July 24 Litho. ***Perf. 12½***

652	A213	125fr multi	1.00	50

TB Bacillus Centenary—A214

1982, Aug. 7 ***Perf. 12½x12***

653	A214	250fr Koch, bacillus	2.00	1.00

Pres. Sassou-Nguesso and 1980 Simba Prize—A215

1982, Oct. 20 Litho. ***Perf. 13***

654	A215	100fr multi	80	40

Turtles—A216

Various turtles and tortoises.

1982, Dec. 1

655	A216	30fr multi	24	12
656	A216	45fr multi	35	18
657	A216	55fr multi	45	22

Boy Gathering Coconuts—A217

Nest in Tree Trunk—A218

1982, Dec. 11

658	A217	100fr multi	80	40

1982, Dec. 29 ***Perf. 12½***

659	A218	40fr shown	32	16
660	A218	75fr Nests in palm tree	60	30
661	A218	100fr Woven nest on thron branch	80	40

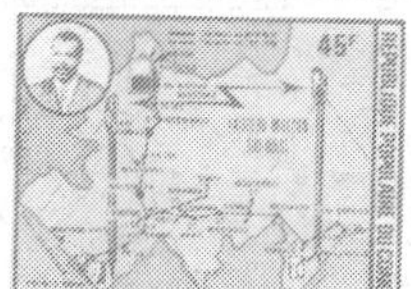

Hertzian Wave Communication Network—A219

1982, Dec. 30

662	A219	45fr multi	35	18
663	A219	60fr multi	50	25
664	A219	95fr multi	75	40

30th Anniv. of Customs Cooperation Council—A220

1983, Jan. 26 Litho. ***Perf. 12½x13***

665	A220	100fr Headquarters	80	40

Mausoleum of Pres. Marien Ngouabi—A221

1983, Feb. 8 ***Perf. 13***

666	A221	60fr multi	50	25
667	A221	80fr multi	65	32

Ironsmiths—A222

1983 ***Perf. 12½***

668	A222	45fr shown	35	18
669	A222	150fr Weaver, vert.	1.20	62

Issue dates: 45fr, Mar. 5; 150fr, Feb. 24

Carved Chess Pieces, by R. Engongonzo—A223

Various pieces.

1983, Feb. 26 ***Perf. 13***

670	A223	40fr multi	32	15
671	A223	60fr multi	50	25
672	A223	95fr multi	75	38

SEMI-POSTAL STAMPS.

Anti-Malaria Issue

Common Design Type

Engraved

1962, Apr. 7 ***Perf. 12½x12***

B3 CD108 25fr +5fr bis 65 65

Issued for the World Health Organization drive to eradicate malaria.

Freedom from Hunger Issue

Common Design Type

1963, Mar. 21 ***Perf. 13*** **Unwmkd.**

B4 CD112 25fr +5fr vio bl, bl grn & brn 60 60

AIR POST STAMPS

Olympic Games Issue

French Equatorial Africa No. C37 Surcharged in Red Like Chad No. C1.

Engraved

1960 ***Perf. 13*** **Unwmkd.**

C1 AP8 250fr on 500fr grnsh blk, blk & sl 5.50 5.50

Issued to commemorate the 17th Olympic Games, Rome, Aug. 25–Sept. 11.

Helicrysum Mechowiam—AP1

Flowers: 200fr, Cogniauxia podolaena. 500fr, Thesium tencio.

1961, Sept. 28 Engraved ***Perf. 13***

C2	AP1	100fr grn, lil & yel	1.35	95
C3	AP1	200fr bl grn, yel & brn	2.65	1.20
C4	AP1	500fr brn red, yel & sl grn	6.00	2.65

Air Afrique Issue

Common Design Type

1961, Nov. 25 ***Perf. 13*** **Unwmkd.**

C5 CD107 50fr lil rose, sl grn & grn 60 50

Founding of Air Afrique.

Loading Timber, Pointe-Noire Harbor—AP2

1962, June 8 Photo. ***Perf. 12½x12***

C6 AP2 50fr multi 60 50

Issued to commemorate the opening of the International Fair and Exhibition, Pointe-Noire, June 8–11.

Abidjan Games Issue

Basketball AP3

1962, July 21 ***Perf. 12x12½***

C7 AP3 100fr multi 1.35 95

Costus Spectabilis AP4

Design: 250fr, Mountain acanthus.

1963 ***Perf. 13*** **Unwmkd.**

C8	AP4	100fr multi	1.35	80
C9	AP4	250fr multi	3.50	1.85

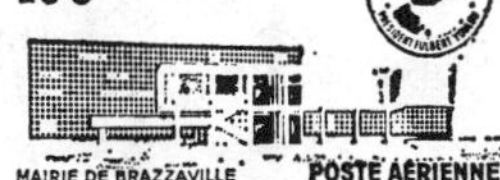

Brazzaville City Hall and Pres. Fulbert Youlou AP4a

1963, Aug. Photo. ***Perf. 13x12***

C10 AP4a 100fr multi 60.00 60.00

African Postal Union Issue

Common Design Type

1963, Sept. 8 ***Perf. 12½***

C13 CD114 85fr pur, ocher & red 95 65

Air Afrique Issue, 1963

Common Design Type

Photogravure

1963, Nov. 19 ***Perf. 13x12*** **Unwmkd.**

C14 CD115 50fr multi 65 50

Liberty Place, Brazzaville—AP5

1963, Nov. 28

C15 AP5 25fr multi 32 25

See also No. 118.

Europafrica Issue

Common Design Type

1963, Nov. 30 ***Perf. 12x13***

C16 CD116 50fr gray, yel & dk brn 80 55

Timber Industry—AP6

1964, May 12 Engraved ***Perf. 13***

C17 AP6 100fr grn, brn red & blk 1.20 70

Chiefs of State Issue

Map and Presidents of Chad, Congo, Gabon and CAR AP6a

1964, June 23 Photo. ***Perf. 12½***

C18 AP6a 100fr multi 1.25 70

See note after Central African Republic No. C19.

Europafrica Issue, 1964

Sunburst, Wheat, Cogwheel and Globe AP7

1964, July 20 ***Perf. 12x13***

C19 AP7 50fr yel, Prus bl & mar 65 40

See note after Cameroun No. 402.

Hammer Thrower, Olympic Flame and Stadium—AP8

Designs (Olympic flame, stadium) and: 50fr, Weight lifter (vert.). 100fr, Badminton (vert.). 200fr, High jump.

1964, July 30 ***Perf. 13*** Engraved

C20	AP8	25fr vio bl, org & red brn	32	15
C21	AP8	50fr yel grn, org & red lil	65	45
C22	AP8	100fr sl grn, org & red brn	1.25	95
C23	AP8	200fr crim, org & dp grn	2.50	1.90
a.		Min. sheet of 4	5.50	5.50

Issued for the 18th Olympic Games, Tokyo, Oct. 10–25, 1964. No. C23a contains one each of Nos. C20–C23. Size: 191x99mm.

Communications Symbols AP8a

1964, Nov. 2 **Litho.** ***Perf. 12½x13***

C24 AP8a 25fr dl rose & dk brn 40 30

See note after Chad No. C19.

Town Hall, Brazzaville—AP9

1965, Jan. 30 Photo. ***Perf. 12½***

C25 AP9 100fr multi 1.20 65

Coupling Hooks—AP10

1965, Feb. 27 Photo. ***Perf. 13x12***

C26 AP10 50fr multi 65 40

Economic Europe-Africa Association.

Breguet Dial Telegraph, ITU Emblem and Telstar AP11

1965, May 17 Engraved ***Perf. 13***

C27 AP11 100fr dk bl, ocher & brn 1.35 80

Issued to commemorate the centenary of the International Telecommunication Union.

Pope John XXIII and St. Peter's Cathedral—AP12

Perf. 12½x13

1965, June 26 Photo. Unwmkd.

C28	AP12	100fr gldn brn & multi	1.20	90

Issued in memory of Pope John XXIII (1881–1963).

Pres. John F. Kennedy AP13 — Log Rolling AP14

Portraits: 25fr on 50fr, Patrice Lumumba, premier of Congo Republic (ex-Belgian). 50fr, Sir Winston Churchill. 80fr, Barthélémy Boganda, premier of Central African Republic.

1965, June 25–26 *Perf. 12½*

C29	AP13	25fr on 50fr dk brn & red	40	40
a.		Surch. omitted	22.50	22.50
C30	AP13	50fr dk brn & yel grn	90	90
C31	AP13	80fr dk brn & bl	1.20	1.20
C32	AP13	100fr dk brn & org yel	1.50	1.50
a.		Min. sheet of 4	6.00	6.00

Issued to honor famous statesmen. No. C32a contains one each of Nos. C29–C32. Size: 106x143 mm.

A second miniature sheet contains one each of Nos. C29a, C30–C32. Price, $30.

1965, Aug. 14 Engraved *Perf. 13*

C33	AP14	50fr grn, brn & red brn	75	40

Issued to publicize national unity.

World Map and Symbols of Agriculture and Industry
AP15

1965, Oct. 18 Engraved *Perf. 13*

C34	AP15	50fr dk bl, blk, brn & org	75	50

International Cooperation Year, 1965.

Abraham Lincoln—AP16

1965, Dec. 15 Photo. *Perf. 13*

C35	AP16	90fr pink & multi	1.10	65

Centenary of death of Abraham Lincoln.

Charles de Gaulle, Torch and Map of Africa—AP17

1966, Feb. 28 Engraved *Perf. 13*

C36	AP17	500fr dk red, dk grn & dk red brn	15.00	12.50

Issued to commemorate the 22nd anniversary of the Brazzaville Conference.

D-1 Satellite over Brazzaville Space Tracking Station AP18 — Grain, Atom Symbol and Map of Africa and Europe AP19

1966, May 15 Engraved *Perf. 13*

C37	AP18	150fr blk, dl red & bl grn	1.85	95

1966, July 20 Photo. *Perf. 12x13*

C38	AP19	50fr multi	80	50

See note after Gabon No. C46.

Pres. Massamba-Debat and President's Palace
AP20

Designs: 30fr, Robespierre and storming of the Bastille. 50fr, Lenin and storming of the Winter Palace.

1966, Aug. 15 Photo. *Perf. 12x12½*

C39	AP20	25fr multi	28	15
C40	AP20	30fr multi	35	15
C41	AP20	50fr multi	60	28
a.		Souv. sheet of 3	1.50	1.50

Issued to commemorate the 3rd anniversary of the revolution. No. C41a contains one each of Nos. C39–C41. Black marginal inscription and control number. Size: 131½x160mm.

Air Afrique Issue, 1966

Common Design Type

1966, Aug. 31 Photo. *Perf. 13*

C42	CD123	30fr lil, lem & blk	45	20

Issued to commemorate the introduction of DC-8F planes by Air Afrique.

Dr. Albert Schweitzer
AP21

1966, Sept. 4 Photo. *Perf. 12½*

C43	AP21	100fr red, blk, bl & lil	1.25	80

Issued to honor Dr. Albert Schweitzer (1875–1965), medical missionary.

Crab, Microscope and Pagoda
AP22

1966, Dec. 26 Photo. *Perf. 13*

C44	AP22	100fr multi	1.20	65

Issued to commemorate the 9th International Anticancer Congress, Tokyo, Oct. 23–29.

Social Weaver
AP23

Birds: 75fr, European Bee-eater. 100fr, Lilac-breasted roller. 150fr, Regal sunbird. 200fr, Crowned cranes. 250fr, Secretary bird. 300fr, Knysna touraco.

1967 Photogravure *Perf. 13*

C45	AP23	50fr multi	1.00	40
C46	AP23	75fr multi	1.35	55
C47	AP23	100fr multi	1.65	80
C48	AP23	150fr multi	2.00	1.10
C49	AP23	200fr multi	2.65	1.35
C50	AP23	250fr multi	3.50	1.75
C51	AP23	300fr multi	4.00	2.25
		Nos. C45-C51 (7)	16.15	8.20

Issue dates: Nos. C45–C47, Feb. 13. Others, June 20.

Shackled Hands
AP24

1967, May 24 Photo. *Perf. 12½x13*

C52	AP24	500fr multi	7.00	3.00

Issued for African Liberation Day.

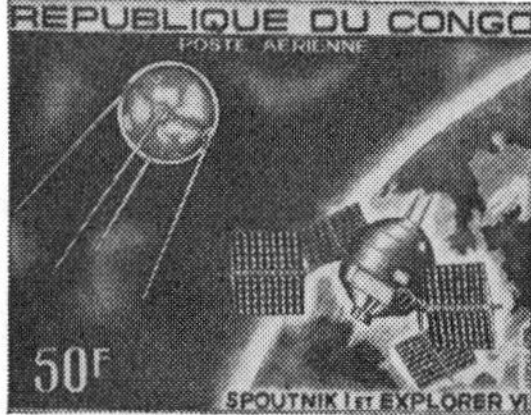

Sputnik 1, Explorer 6 and Earth
AP25

Space Craft: 75fr, Ranger 6, Lunik 2 and moon. 100fr, Mars 1, Mariner 4 and Mars. 200fr, Gemini, Vostok and earth.

1967, Aug. 1 Engr. *Perf. 13*

C53	AP25	50fr pur, bl & org brn	60	32
C54	AP25	75fr dk car & gray	90	50
C55	AP25	100fr red brn, Prus bl & ultra	1.25	80
C56	AP25	200fr car lake, org & bl	2.50	1.60

Space explorations.

African Postal Union Issue, 1967

Common Design Type

1967, Sept. 9 Engraved *Perf. 13*

C57	CD124	100fr ver, ol & emer	1.20	70

Boy Scouts, Tents and Jamboree Emblem—AP26

Design: 70c, Borah Peak, Idaho; tents, Scout sign and Jamboree emblem.

1967, Sept. 29

C58	AP26	50fr brt bl, brn org & red brn	55	28
C59	AP26	70fr dl bl, sl grn & red brn	80	40

Issued to commemorate the 12th Boy Scout World Jamboree, Farragut State Park, Idaho, Aug. 1–9.

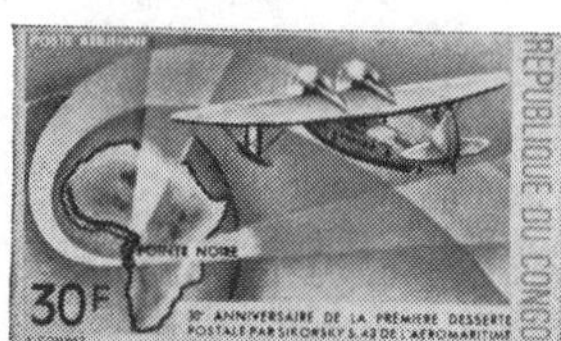

Sikorsky S-43 and Map of Africa
AP27

1967, Oct. 2 Photo. *Perf. 13*

C60	AP27	30fr multi	45	25

Issued to commemorate the 30th anniversary of the first airmail connection by Aeromaritime Lines from Casablanca to Pointe-Noire.

Men of Four Races Dancing on Globe
AP28

1968, Feb 8 Engraved *Perf. 13*

C61 AP28 70fr dk brn, ultra & emer 90 50

Friendship among peoples.

The Oath of the Horatii, by Jacques Louis David—AP29

Paintings: 25fr, On the Barricades, by Delacroix. No. C63, Grandfather and Grandson, by Ghirlandajo (vert.). No. C64, The Demolition of the Bastille, by Hubert Robert. 200fr, Negro Woman Arranging Peonies, by Jean F. Bazille.

Perf. 12x12½, 12½x12

1968 Photogravure

C62	AP29	25fr multi	32	12
C63	AP29	30fr multi	50	32
C64	AP29	30fr multi	35	20
C65	AP29	100fr multi	1.35	80
C66	AP29	200fr multi	3.00	1.75
		Nos. C62-C66 (5)	5.52	3.19

Issue dates: Nos. C62, C64, Aug. 15. Nos. C63, C65-C66, Mar. 20.

See also Nos. C78-C81, C111-C115.

Early Automobile Type of Regular Issue

Designs: 150fr, Ford, 1915. 200fr, Citroën, 1922.

1968, July 29 Photo. *Perf. 13x12½*

C67	A50	150fr multi	2.00	1.00
C68	A50	200fr lil & multi	2.50	1.35

Europafrica Issue

Square Knot
AP30

1968, July 20 Photo. *Perf. 13*

C69 AP30 50fr multi 55 25

Issued to commemorate the 5th anniversary of the economic agreement between the European Economic Community and the African and Malgache Union.

Martin Luther King, Jr.
AP31

Robert F. Kennedy
AP32

1968, Aug. 5 *Perf. 12½*

C70 AP31 50fr lt grn, Prus grn & blk 55 25

Issued in memory of the Rev. Dr. Martin Luther King, Jr. (1929-1968), American civil rights leader.

1968, Sept. 30 Photo. *Perf. 13x12½*

C71 AP32 50fr dp car, ap grn & blk 65 32

Issued in memory of Robert F. Kennedy (1925-68), U.S. Senator and Attorney General.

Running
AP33

Olympic Rings and: 20fr, Soccer (vert.). 60fr, Boxing (vert.). 85fr, High Jump.

1968, Dec. 27 Engraved *Perf. 13*

C72	AP33	5fr emer, brt bl & choc	7	5
C73	AP33	20fr dk bl, brn & dk grn	25	12
C74	AP33	60fr mar, brt grn & choc	75	40
C75	AP33	85fr blk, car rose & choc	1.00	50

Issued to commemorate the 19th Olympic Games, Mexico City, Oct. 12-27.

PHILEXAFRIQUE Issue

G. De Gueidan, by Nicolas de Largillière
AP34

1968, Dec. 30 Photo. *Perf. 12½*

C76 AP34 100fr pink & multi 1.30 1.10

Issued to publicize PHILEXAFRIQUE, Philatelic Exhibition, in Abidjan, Feb. 14-23. Printed with alternating pink label.

See also Nos. C89-C93.

2nd PHILEXAFRIQUE Issue

Common Design Type

Design: 50fr, Middle Congo No. 72 and Pointe-Noire harbor.

1969, Feb. 14 Engraved *Perf. 13*

C77 CD128 50fr car rose, sl grn & bis brn 75 65

Issued to commemorate the opening of PHILEXAFRIQUE, Abidjan, Feb. 14.

Painting Type of 1968.

Paintings: 25fr, Battle of Rivoli, by Carle Vernet. 50fr, Battle of Marengo, by Jacques Augustin Pajou. 75fr, Battle of Friedland, by Horace Vernet. 100fr, Battle of Jena, by Charles Thevenin.

1969, May 20 Photo. *Perf. 12x12½*

C78	AP29	25fr vio bl & multi	40	25
C79	AP29	50fr cop red & multi	75	50
C80	AP29	75fr grn & multi	1.10	50
C81	AP29	100fr brn & multi	1.60	80

Bicentenary of birth of Napoleon I.

Ernesto Ché Guevara
AP35

1969, June 10 Photo. *Perf. 12½*

C82 AP35 90fr brn, org & blk 1.10 55

Issued in memory of Ernesto Ché Guevara (1928-1967), Cuban revolutionist.

Doll, Train and Space Toy
AP36

1969, June 20 Engraved *Perf. 13*

C83 AP36 100fr mag, org & gray 1.20 65

Issued to publicize the International Toy Fair, Nuremberg, Germany.

Europafrica Issue, 1969

Ribbon Tied Around Bar
AP37

1969, Aug. 5 Photo. *Perf. 13x12*

C84 AP37 50fr bl grn, lil & blk 50 30

See note after Chad No. C11.

Armstrong, Aldrin and Collins
AP38

Painter, Poto-Poto School
AP39

Souvenir Sheet

Design: No. C85b, Blast-off from Moon.

Embossed on Gold Foil

1969, Sept. 15 *Imperf.*

C85	AP38	Sheet of 2	20.00	20.00
a.		1000fr gold	9.00	9.00
b.		1000fr gold	9.00	9.00

See note after Algeria No. 427. No. C85 contains one each of Nos. C85a and C85b with simulated perforations. Size: 65x52mm.

1970, Feb. 20 Engraved *Perf. 13*

Designs: 150fr, Sculpture lesson (man, infant and sculpture). 200fr, Potter working on vase.

C86	AP39	100fr multi	1.10	50
C87	AP39	150fr multi	1.60	80
C88	AP39	200fr multi	1.85	1.25

Painting Type (Philexafrique) of 1968

Paintings: 150fr, Child with Cherries, by John Russell. 200fr, Erasmus, by Hans Holbein the Younger. 250fr, "Silence" (head), by Bernardino Luini. 300fr, Scene from the Massacre of Scio, by Delacroix. 500fr, The Capture of Constantinople by the Crusaders, by Delacroix.

1970 Photogravure *Perf. 12½*

C89	AP34	150fr lil & multi	2.00	95
C90	AP34	200fr multi	2.40	1.20
C91	AP34	250fr brn & multi	2.65	1.50
C92	AP34	300fr multi	3.75	1.75
C93	AP34	500fr brn & multi	5.25	2.65
		Nos. C89-C93 (5)	16.05	8.05

Aurichalcite
AP40

Design: 15fr, Dioptase.

1970, Mar. 20

C94	AP40	100fr multi	1.10	55
C95	AP40	150fr multi	1.75	80

Lenin
AP41

Karl Marx
AP42

Design: 75fr, Lenin, seated.

1970, June 25 Photo. *Perf. 12½*

C96	AP41	45fr grn, org & brn	50	20
C97	AP41	75fr vio bl, brn lake & dp cl	75	35

Issued to commemorate the centenary of the birth of Lenin (1870-1924), Russian communist leader.

1970, July 10 Engr. *Perf. 13*

Design: No. C99, Friedrich Engels.

C98	AP42	50fr emer, dk brn & dk red	55	28
C99	AP42	50fr ultra, dk brn & dk red	55	28

Issued in memory of Karl Marx (1818-1883) and Friedrich Engels (1820-1895), German socialist writers.

Otto Lilienthal's Glider, 1891
AP43

Designs: 50fr, "Spirit of St. Louis," Lindbergh's first transatlantic solo flight, 1927. 70fr, Sputnik 1, first satellite in space. 90fr, First man on the moon, Apollo 11, 1969.

1970, Sept. 5 Engraved *Perf. 13*

C100	AP43	45fr dp car, bl & ol bis	55	28
C101	AP43	50fr emer, sl grn & brn	55	32
C102	AP43	70fr brt bl, ol bis & dp car	80	40
C103	AP43	90fr brn, bl & ol gray	1.10	55

Forerunners of space exploration.

Saint on Horseback
AP44

Marilyn Monroe and New York
AP45

Designs from Stained Glass Windows, Brazzaville Cathedral: 150fr, Saint with staff. 250fr, The Elevation of the Host, from rose window.

1970, Dec. 10 Photo. *Perf. 12½*

C104	AP44	100fr dk vio bl & multi	1.10	55
C105	AP44	150fr dk vio bl & multi	1.75	90
C106	AP44	250fr dk vio bl & multi	3.00	1.60
a.		Souvenir sheet of 3	6.00	6.00

Christmas 1970. No. C106a contains one each of Nos. C104-C106. Black marginal inscription. Size: 150x115mm.

1971, Mar. 16 Engraved *Perf. 13*

Portraits: 150fr, Martine Carol and Paris. 200fr, Erich von Stroheim and Vienna. 250fr, Sergei Eisenstein and Moscow.

C107	AP45	100fr brt grn, red brn & ultra	1.00	40
C108	AP45	150fr brn, brt lil & ultra	1.60	60
C109	AP45	200fr choc & ultra	2.00	90
C110	AP45	250fr brt grn, brn vio & ultra	2.40	1.00

History of motion pictures.

Painting Type of 1968

Paintings: 100fr, Christ Carrying Cross, by Paolo Veronese. 150fr, Christ on the Cross, Burgundian School, 1500 (vert.). 200fr, Descent from the Cross, by Rogier van der Weyden. 250fr, Christ Laid in the Tomb, Flemish School, 1500 (vert.). 500fr, Resurrection, by Hans Memling (vert.).

1971, April 26 Photogravure *Perf. 13*

C111	AP29	100fr grn & multi	1.00	50
C112	AP29	150fr grn & multi	1.40	65
C113	AP29	200fr grn & multi	2.00	1.00
C114	AP29	250fr grn & multi	2.40	1.20
C115	AP29	500fr grn & multi	4.75	2.40
		Nos. C111-C115 (5)	11.55	5.75

Easter 1971.

Examination

The Catalogue editors cannot undertake to appraise, identify or pass upon genuineness or condition of stamps.

Map of Africa and Telecommunications System—AP46

1971, June 18 Photo. *Perf. 12½*

C116	AP46	70fr bl, gray & dk brn	65	32
C117	AP46	85fr bl, lil rose & dk brn	75	40
C118	AP46	90fr grn, yel & dk brn	80	45

Pan-African telecommunications system.

Globe and Waves—AP47

1971, June 19

C119	AP47	65fr lt bl & multi	60	27

3rd World Telecommunications Day.

Japanese Mask and Play
AP48

Olympic Torch and Rings
AP49

Design: 150fr, Japanese and African women, symbolic leaves.

1971, June 28 Engr. *Perf. 13*

C120	AP48	75fr lil, blk & mag	80	40
C121	AP48	150fr dk brn, brn red & red lil	1.50	80

PHILATOKYO '71 International Stamp Exhibition, Tokyo, Apr. 20-30.

1971, July 20 Engraved *Perf. 13*

Design: 350fr, Olympic rings and various sports (horiz.).

C122	AP49	150fr brt rose lil, org & sl grn	1.60	90
C123	AP49	350fr bis, brt grn & vio	3.75	1.75

Pre-Olympic Year, 1971.

Scout Emblem, Japanese Dragon and African Carved Canoe—AP50

Designs (Boy Scout Emblem and): 90fr, Japanese mask and African boy (vert.). 100fr, Japanese woman and African drummer (vert.). 250fr, Congolese mask.

1971, Aug. 25

C124	AP50	85fr brt rose lil, Prus bl & brn	1.00	45
C125	AP50	90fr dk car, brn & vio	1.10	50
C126	AP50	100fr ol gray, rose mag & brt grn	1.25	60
C127	AP50	250fr brt grn, choc & car	3.00	1.40

13th Boy Scout World Jamboree, Asagiri Plain, Japan, Aug. 2-10.

Olympic Rings and Running—AP51

Designs (Olympic Rings and): 85fr, Hurdles. 90fr, Weight lifting, boxing, discus, running, javelin. 100fr, Wrestling. 150fr, Boxing.

1971, Sept. 30

C128	AP51	75fr plum, bl & dk brn	70	32
C129	AP51	85fr scar, sl & dk brn	75	35
C130	AP51	90fr vio bl & dk brn	85	45
C131	AP51	100fr brn & sl	1.00	50
C132	AP51	150fr grn, red & dk brn	1.60	80
		Nos. C128-C132 (5)	4.90	2.42

75th anniversary of the first modern Olympic Games.

Congo No. C36 and de Gaulle
AP52

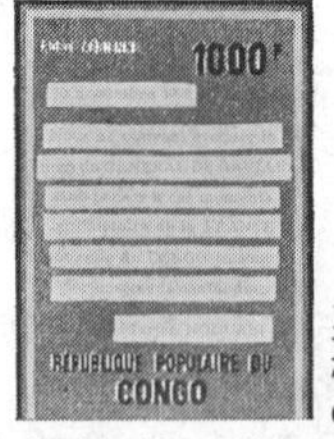

Pres. Marien Ngouabi's Tribute to de Gaulle—AP53

Design: No. C135, Charles de Gaulle.

1971, Nov. 9

C133	AP52	500fr sl grn & multi	6.50	6.50

Lithographed; Gold Embossed
Perf. 12½

C134	AP53	1000fr gold, grn & red	12.00	12.00
C135	AP53	1000fr gold, grn & red	12.00	12.00

Charles de Gaulle (1890-1970), president of France. Nos. C134-C135 printed se-tenant.

African Postal Union Issue, 1971
Common Design Type

Design: 100fr, Allegory of Congo Republic (woman) and UAMPT Building, Brazzaville.

1971, Nov. 13 Photo. *Perf. 13x13½*

C136	CD135	100fr bl & multi	1.10	55

Flag of Congo Republic and "Revolution"—AP54

1971, Nov. 30

C137	AP54	100fr red & multi	1.00	50

8th anniversary of revolution.

Workers and Flag—AP55

Design: 40fr, Flag of Congo Republic and sun.

1971, Dec 31 Photo. *Perf. 13x12½*

C138	AP55	30fr multi	25	12
C139	AP55	40fr red & multi	35	20

2nd anniversary of founding of Congolese Labor Party (No. C138), and adoption of red flag (No. C139).

Book Year Emblem
AP56

1972, June 3 Litho. *Perf. 12½*

C140	AP56	50fr red, grn & yel	40	20

International Book Year 1972.

Congolese Soccer Team—AP57

Design: No. C142, Captain of winning team and cup (vert.).

1973, Feb. 22 Photogravure *Perf. 13*

C141	AP57	100fr ultra, red & blk	1.10	65
C142	AP57	100fr red, yel & blk	1.10	65

Girl Holding Bird, Environment Emblem
AP58

1973, Mar. 5 **Engraved**

C143	AP58	85fr org, sl grn & bl	65	40

U.N. Conference on Human Environment, Stockholm, Sweden, June 5–16, 1972.

Miles Davis
AP59

Designs: 140fr, Ella Fitzgerald. 160fr, Count Basie. 175fr, John Coltrane.

1973, Mar. 5 **Photo.** ***Perf. 13x13½***

C144	AP59	125fr multi	1.00	50
C145	AP59	140fr multi	1.10	55
C146	AP59	160fr multi	1.30	65
C147	AP59	175fr multi	1.50	75

Black American jazz musicians.

Olympic Rings, Hurdling—AP60

Designs (Olympic Rings and): 150fr, Pole vault (vert.). 250fr, Wrestling.

1973, Mar. 15 **Engraved** ***Perf. 13***

C148	AP60	100fr lil rose & vio	1.00	50
C149	AP60	150fr emer & vio	1.50	75
C150	AP60	250fr bl & mag	2.50	1.35

20th Olympic Games, Munich, Aug. 26–Sept. 11, 1972.

Refinery and Storage Tanks, Djéno—AP61

Designs: 230fr, Off-shore drilling platform (vert.). 240fr, Workers assembling drill (vert.). 260fr, Off-shore drilling installation.

1973, Mar. 20

C151	AP61	180fr red, bl & ind	1.60	80
C152	AP61	230fr red, bl & blk	2.00	1.00
C153	AP61	240fr red, ind & brn	2.25	1.20
C154	AP61	260fr red, bl & blk	2.60	1.40

Oil installations, Pointe-Noire.

Astronauts, Landing Module and Lunar Rover on Moon—AP62

1973, Mar. 31

C155	AP62	250fr multi	2.50	1.50

Apollo 17 U.S. moon mission, Dec. 7–19, 1972.

ITU Emblem, Symbols of Communications
AP63

1973, May 24 **Engr.** ***Perf. 13***

C156	AP63	120fr multi	80	40

5th International Telecommunications Day.

White Horse, by Delacroix—AP64

Designs: Paintings by Eugene Delacroix.

1973, June 30 **Photo.** ***Perf. 13***

Multicolored

C157	AP64	150fr *shown*	1.35	1.35
C158	AP64	250fr *Lion sleeping*	2.25	1.90
C159	AP64	300fr *Lion and tiger*	2.75	2.25

See Nos. C169–C171.

Copernicus and Heliocentric System—AP65

1973, June 30 **Engraved**

C160	AP65	50fr multi	45	35

500th anniversary of the birth of Nicolaus Copernicus (1473–1543), Polish astronomer.

Plane, Ship, Rocket, Village, Sun and Clouds—AP66

1973, July

C161	AP66	50fr red & multi	40	28

Centenary of international meteorological cooperation.

Pres. Marien N'Gouabi
AP67

1973, Aug. 12 **Photo.** ***Perf. 13***

C162	AP67	30fr multi	25	10
C163	AP67	40fr aqua & multi	32	15
C164	AP67	75fr red & multi	65	32

10th anniversary of independence.

Stamps, Album, African Woman
AP68

Designs: 40fr, No. C167, Stamps in shape of map of Congo, album, globe. No. C168, Like 30fr.

1973, Aug. 12

C165	AP68	30fr pur & multi	25	12
C166	AP68	40fr multi	32	15
C167	AP68	100fr dk brn & multi	75	55
C168	AP68	100fr ocher & multi	75	55

Nos. C165 and C168 commemorate the 10th anniversary of the revolution, Nos. C166–C167 the International Philatelic Exhibition, Brazzaville.

Painting Type of 1973 Inscribed "EUROPAFRIQUE"

Designs: Details from "Earth and Paradise," by Jan Brueghel, the Elder.

1973, Oct. 10 **Photo.** ***Perf. 13***

Multicolored

C169	AP64	100fr *Spotted hyena*	1.00	75
C170	AP64	100fr *Leopard and lion*	1.00	75
C171	AP64	100fr *Elephant and creatures*	1.00	75

U.S. and Russian Spacecraft Docking—AP69

Design: 80fr, US and USSR spacecraft docked in space and emblems of 1975 joint space mission.

1973, Oct. 15 **Engraved** ***Perf. 13***

C172	AP69	40fr bl, red & brn	35	20
C173	AP69	80fr red, grn & bl	65	40

Planned joint United States and Soviet space missions.

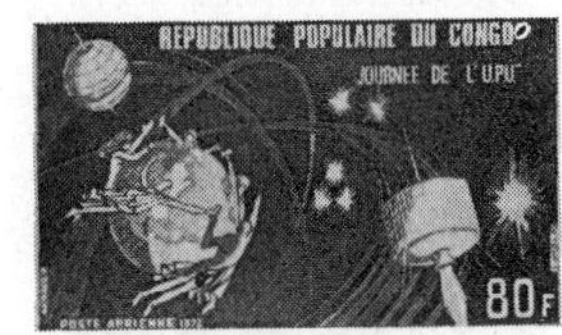

UPU Monument, Satellites, Big Dipper—AP70

1973, Nov. 20 **Engraved** ***Perf. 13***

C174	AP70	80fr vio bl & lt bl	65	35

Universal Postal Union Day.

Astronauts Working in Space—AP71

Design: 40fr, Spacecraft and Skylab docking in space.

1973, Nov. 30

C175	AP71	30fr ultra, sl grn & choc	25	15
C176	AP71	40fr mag, org & sl grn	35	25

Skylab, first space laboratory.

Goalkeeper, Soccer
AP72

Design: 100fr, Soccer player kicking ball.

1973, Dec. 20

C177	AP72	40fr sl grn, sep & brn	32	25
C178	AP72	100fr pur, red & sl grn	1.00	55

World Soccer Cup, Munich, 1974.

John F. Kennedy
AP73

1973. Dec. 20 **Photo.** ***Perf. 12½***

C179	AP73	150fr ultra, gold & blk	1.20	75

10th anniversary of the death of Pres. John F. Kennedy (1917–1963).

Runners
AP74

Flag over Map of Congo
AP75

1973, Dec. 20 **Engraved** ***Perf. 13***

C180	AP74	40fr sl grn, red & brn	32	25
C181	AP74	100fr red, sl grn, & brn	1.00	55

2nd African Games, Lagos, Nigeria.

1973, Dec. 31 **Photogravure**

C182	AP75	40fr dp grn & multi	32	20

4th anniversary of Congolese Labor Party and of the Congo Red Flag.

Soccer and Games Emblem
AP76

1974, June 20 Photo. ***Perf. 13***

C183	AP76	250fr multi	2.00	1.30

World Cup Soccer Championship, Munich, June 13–July 7.

Astronauts Yuri A. Gagarin and Alan B. Shepard—AP77

Designs: 30fr, Space, globe, Russian and American flags with names of astronauts who perished in space. 100fr, Alexei Leonov and Neil A. Armstrong in space and on moon.

1974, June 30 **Engraved** ***Perf. 13***

C184	AP77	30fr red, ultra & brn	25	15
C185	AP77	40fr red, bl & brn	35	20
C186	AP77	100fr car, grn & brn	1.00	60

Soccer Game Superimposed on Ball
AP78

Link-up Emblem, Stages of Link-up
AP79

1974, July 31 Photo. ***Perf. 13***

C187	AP78	250fr multi	2.00	1.30

Germany's victory in World Cup Soccer Championship.

1974, Aug. 8 **Engraved** ***Perf. 13***

Design: 300fr, Spacecraft docking over globe (horiz.).

C188	AP79	200fr pur, bl & red	1.60	1.20
C189	AP79	300fr multi	2.40	1.60

Russo-American space cooperation.

Symbols of Communications, UPU Emblem—AP80

1974, Aug. 10

C190	AP80	500fr blk & red	4.00	2.75

Centenary of Universal Postal Union.

Lenin and Pendulum Trace Pattern—AP81

1974, Sept. 16 **Engraved** ***Perf. 13***

C191	AP81	150fr multi	1.20	80

50th death anniversary of Lenin (1870–1924).

Churchill and Order of the Garter
AP82

Marconi and Wireless Telegraph
AP83

1974, Oct. 1 **Litho.** ***Perf. 13***

C192	AP82	200fr lt grn & multi	1.60	1.00
C193	AP83	200fr lt ultra & multi	1.60	1.00

Birth centenaries of Sir Winston Churchill (1874–1965), statesman; and of Guglielmo Marconi (1874–1937), Italian electrical engineer and inventor.

No. C190 Surcharged in Violet Blue with New Value, 2 Bars and: "9 OCTOBRE 1974"

1974, Oct. 9

C194	AP80	300fr on 500fr multi	2.40	1.60

Universal Postal Union Day.

UDEAC Issue

Presidents and Flags of Cameroun, CAR, Gabon and Congo—AP83a

1974, Dec. 8 **Photogravure** ***Perf. 13***

C195	AP83a	100fr gold & multi	80	60

See note after Cameroun No. 595.

Regatta at Argenteuil, by Monet—AP84

Impressionist Paintings: 40fr, Seated Dancer, by Degas. 50fr, Girl on Swing, by Renoir. 75fr, Girl with Straw Hat, by Renoir. All vertical.

1974, Dec. 15

C196	AP84	30fr gold & multi	35	25
C197	AP84	40fr gold & multi	40	30
C198	AP84	50fr gold & multi	65	50
C199	AP84	75fr gold & multi	70	55

National Fair
AP85

1974, Dec. 20

C200	AP85	30fr multi	25	15

National Fair, Aug. 24–Sept. 8.

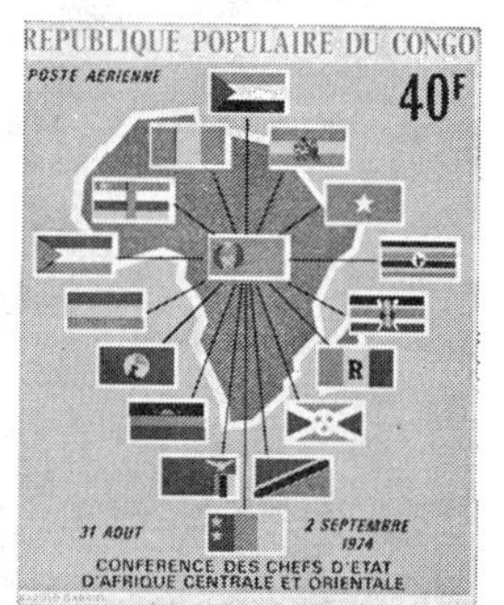

Flags of Participating Nations, Map of Africa—AP86

1974, Dec. 20 ***Perf. 13***

C201	AP86	40fr ultra & multi	40	25

Conference of Chiefs of State of Central and East Africa, Brazzaville, Aug. 31–Sept. 2.

"Five Weeks in a Balloon," by Jules Verne
AP87

Design: 50fr, "Around the World in 80 Days," by Jules Verne.

1975, June 30 **Litho.** ***Perf. 12½***

C202	AP87	40fr multi	35	20
C203	AP87	50fr multi	40	25

Jules Verne (1828–1905), French science fiction writer, 70th death anniversary.

Paris-Brussels Train, 1890—AP88

Design: 75fr, Santa Fe, 1880.

1975, June 30

C204	AP88	50fr ocher & multi	40	25
C205	AP88	75fr lt bl & multi	60	35

Soyuz and Apollo-Soyuz Emblem
AP89

Design: 100fr, Apollo and emblem.

1975, July 20 **Litho.** ***Perf. 12½***

C206	AP89	95fr org, blk & mag	75	50
C207	AP89	100fr vio, bl & blk	80	60

Apollo Soyuz space test project (Russo-American space cooperation), launching July 15; link-up, July 17.

Bicycling and Montreal Olympic Emblem—AP90

Designs (Montreal Olympic Emblem and): 40fr, Boxing (vert.). 50fr, Basketball (vert.). 95fr, High jump. 100fr, Javelin. 150fr, Running.

Perf. 12½x13, 13x12½

1975, Oct. 30 **Photogravure**

C208	AP90	40fr multi	35	20
C209	AP90	50fr red & multi	40	25
C210	AP90	85fr bl & multi	70	50
C211	AP90	95fr org & multi	75	55
C212	AP90	100fr multi	80	60
C213	AP90	150fr multi	1.20	90
		Nos. C208-C213 (6)	4.20	3.00

Pre-Olympic Year 1975.

Map of Africa, Sports and Flags
AP91

Workers and Flag
AP92

1975, Dec. 20 **Litho.** ***Perf. 12½***

C214	AP91	30fr multi	25	15

10th anniversary of first African Games, Brazzaville.

1975, Dec. 31 **Litho.** ***Perf. 12½***

C215	AP92	60fr multi	50	30

6th anniversary of the Congolese Labor Party (P.C.T.).

Alphonse Fondere—AP93

Historic Ships: 5fr, like 30fr. 40fr, Hamburg, 1839. 15fr, 50fr, Gomer, 1831. 20fr, 60fr, Great Eastern, 1858. 95fr, J.M. White II, 1878.

1976 Engraved Perf. 13

C216	AP93	5fr multi	5	3
C217	AP93	10fr multi	8	6
C218	AP93	15fr multi	12	8
C219	AP93	20fr multi	17	12
C220	AP93	30fr multi	25	15
C221	AP93	40fr multi	30	25
C222	AP93	50fr multi	40	30
C223	AP93	60fr multi	50	35
C224	AP93	95fr multi	75	55
		Nos. C216-C224 (9)	2.62	1.89

Issue dates: Nos. C216–C219, May. Nos. C220–C224, Mar. 7.

Europafrica Issue 1976

Peasant Family, by Louis Le Nain
AP94

Paintings: 80fr, Boy with Top, by Jean B. Chardin. 95fr, Venus and Aeneas, by Nicolas Poussin. 100fr, The Rape of the Sabine Women, by Jacques Louis David.

1976, Mar. 20 Litho. Perf. 12½

C225	AP94	60fr gold & multi	50	30
C226	AP94	80fr gold & multi	65	45
C227	AP94	95fr gold & multi	75	55
C228	AP94	100fr gold & multi	80	60

Nos. C225–C228 printed in sheets of 8 stamps and horizontal gutter with commemorative inscription. Black control number in margin.

Telephone Type of 1976

1976, Apr. 25 Litho. Perf. 12½x13

C229	A107	60fr pink, mar & crim	50	35

Centenary of first telephone call by Alexander Graham Bell, Mar. 10, 1876.

Sports Type of 1976

Designs: 150fr, Runner and map of Central Africa. 200fr, Discus and map.

1976, Oct. 25 Perf. 12½

C230	A110	150fr multi	1.20	90
C231	A110	200fr multi	1.60	1.10

Gold medalists, 1st Central African Games, Yaoundé, July 27–30, 1975.

Map of Africa, Flag and OAU Headquarters
AP95

1976, Dec. 16 Typo. Perf. 13x14

C232	AP95	60fr multi	50	35

13th anniversary of the Organization for African Unity.

Europafrica Issue

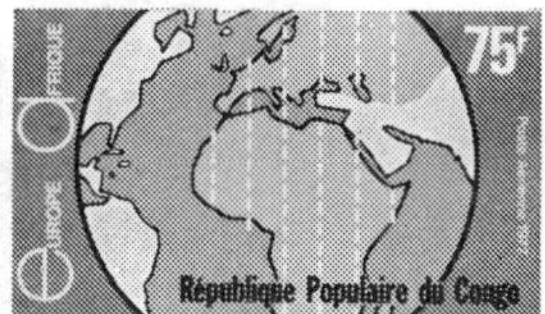

Map of Europe and Africa—AP96

1977, June 28 Litho. Perf. 13

C233	AP96	75fr multi	60	50

Headdress Type of 1977

1977, June 30 Perf. 12½

Designs: 250fr, Two straw caps. 300fr, Beaded cap.

C234	A118	250fr multi	2.00	1.50
C235	A118	300fr multi	2.40	1.80

Zeppelin Type of 1977

Souvenir Sheet

Design: 500fr, LZ 127 over U.S. Capitol.

1977, Aug. 5 Litho. Perf. 11

C236	A120	500fr multi	4.75	2.00

History of the Zeppelin.

No. C236 has multicolored margin showing parts of two Zeppelins. Size: 105x92mm. Exists imperf.

Checkerboard
AP97

1977, Aug. 20 Engr. Perf. 13

C237	AP97	60fr red & blk	50	35

Lomé Convention on General Agreement on Tariffs and Trade (GATT).

Newton, Intelsat Satellite and Classical "Planets"—AP98

1977, Aug. 25

C238	AP98	140fr multi	1.10	90

Isaac Newton (1642–1727), natural philosopher and mathematician, 250th death anniversary.

Elizabeth II Type of 1977

Souvenir Sheet

Design: 500fr, Royal family on balcony.

1977, Dec. 21 Litho. Perf. 14

C239	A128	500fr multi	4.75	2.00

25th anniversary of the reign of Queen Elizabeth II.

Mallard
AP99

Birds: 75fr, Purple heron (vert.). 150fr, Reed warbler (vert.). 240fr, Hoopoe (vert.).

Perf. 13x12½, 12½x13

1978, May 22

C240	AP99	65fr multi	50	25
C241	AP99	75fr multi	60	30
C242	AP99	150fr multi	1.20	65
C243	AP99	240fr multi	1.90	1.00

Souvenir Sheet

No. C239 Overprinted in Silver: "ANNIVERSAIRE DU / COURONNEMENT / 1953–1978"

1978, Sept. Litho. Perf. 14

C244	A128	500fr multi	4.00	1.85

25th anniversary of coronation of Queen Elizabeth II. Size: 111x92mm.

Philexafrique II—Essen Issue

Common Design Types

Designs: No. C245, Leopard and Congo No. C243. No. C246, Eagle and Wurttemberg No. 1.

1978, Nov. 1 Litho. Perf. 12½

C245	CD138	100fr multi	1.00	60
C246	CD139	100fr multi	1.00	60

Nos. C245–C246 printed se-tenant.

Map of Africa Satellites
AP100

1978, Nov. 25 Engr. Perf. 13

C247	AP100	100fr multi	1.00	60

Pan-African Telecommunications Network, PANAFEL.

Map of Africa and People
AP101

1979, Aug. 2 Litho. Perf. 12½

C248	AP101	45fr multi	45	30
C249	AP101	75fr multi	75	50

5th Conference of Panafrican Youth Movement, Brazzaville, Aug. 2–7.

REPUBLIQUE POPULAIRE DU CONGO

Abala Peasant Woman
AP102

1979, Aug. 20

C250	AP102	150fr multi	1.50	90

Nos. C173, C206-C207, C186, C189 Overprinted "ALUNISSAGE APOLLO XI / JUILLET 1969" and Emblem

Perf. 13, 12½

1979, Nov. 5 Engr., Litho.

C251	AP69	80fr multi	80	52
C252	AP89	95fr multi	95	62
C253	AP89	100fr multi	1.00	65
C254	AP77	100fr multi	1.00	65
C255	AP79	300fr multi	3.00	2.00
		Nos. C251-C255 (5)	6.75	4.44

Apollo 11 moon landing, 10th anniversary.

Runner, Olympic Rings—AP103

Pre-Olympic Year: 100fr, Boxing. 200fr, Fencing (vert.). 300fr, Soccer. 500fr, Moscow '80 emblem (vert.).

1979 Litho. Perf. 13½

C256	AP103	65fr multi	52	26
C257	AP103	100fr multi	80	40
C258	AP103	200fr multi	1.60	80
C259	AP103	300fr multi	2.40	1.20
C260	AP103	500fr multi	4.00	2.00
		Nos. C256-C260 (5)	9.32	4.66

Cross-Country Skiing—AP104

Lake Placid '80 Emblem and: 60fr, Slalom. 200fr, Ski jump, 350fr, Downhill skiing (horiz.). 500fr, Woman skier.

1979, Dec Perf. 14½

Size: 24×42, 42×24mm.

C261	AP104	40fr multi	40	28
C262	AP104	60fr multi	60	42
C263	AP104	200fr multi	2.00	1.40
C264	AP104	350fr multi	3.50	2.50

Size: 31½×46½mm. Perf. 14

C265	AP104	500fr multi	5.00	3.50
		Nos. C261-C265 (5)	11.50	8.10

13th Winter Olympic Games, Lake Placid, N.Y., Feb. 12-24, 1980.

Overprinted with names of winners

1980, Apr. 28

C266	AP104	40fr multi (a)	32	16
C267	AP104	60fr multi (b)	48	24
C268	AP104	200fr multi (c)	1.60	80
C269	AP104	350fr multi (d)	2.80	1.40
C270	AP104	500fr multi (e)	4.00	2.00
		Nos. C266-C270 (5)	9.20	4.60

Long Jump, Olympic Rings—AP105

Olympic rings and long jump scenes. Nos. C266, C268-C269 vert.

1980, May 2 Litho. Perf. 14½

C271	AP105	75fr multi	60	30
C272	AP105	150fr multi	1.20	60
C273	AP105	250fr multi	2.00	1.00
C274	AP105	350fr multi	2.80	1.40

Souvenir Sheet

C275	AP105	500fr multi	4.00	2.00

22nd Summer Olympic Games, Moscow, July 19-Aug. 3. No. C275 has multicolored margin showing Kremlin and runners. Size: 104x78mm.

Stadium, Mascot, Madrid Club Emblem—AP106

Stadium, Mascot and Club Emblem: 75fr, Zaragoza. 100fr, Madrid Athletic Club. 150fr, Valencia. 175fr, Spain. 250fr, Barcelona.

1980, June 23 Litho. *Perf. 14x13½*

C276	AP106	60fr multi	48	24
C277	AP106	75fr multi	60	30
C278	AP106	100fr multi	80	40
C279	AP106	150fr multi	1.20	60
C280	AP106	175fr multi	1.40	70
		Nos. C276-C280 (5)	4.48	2.24

Souvenir Sheet

C281	AP106	250fr multi	2.00	1.00

World Soccer Cup 1982. No. C281 has multicolored margin showing mascot. Size: 104½x79mm.

Adoration of the Shepherds—AP107

Rembrandt Paintings: 100fr, The Burial. 200fr, Christ at Emmaus. 300fr, Annunciation (vert.). 500fr, Crucifixion (vert.).

1980, July 4 *Perf. 12½*

C282	AP107	65fr multi	52	26
C283	AP107	100fr multi	80	40
C284	AP107	200fr multi	1.60	80
C285	AP107	300fr multi	2.40	1.20
C286	AP107	500fr multi	4.00	2.00
		Nos. C282-C286 (5)	9.32	4.66

Albert Camus (1913-1960), Writer—AP108

Design: 150fr, Jacques Offenbach (1819-1880), composer (vert.).

1980, July 5 Engraved *Perf. 13*

C287	AP108	100fr multi	80	40
C288	AP108	150fr multi	1.20	60

Raffia Dancing Skirts—AP109

Traditional Dancing Costumes: 300fr, Tam-tam dancers (vert.). 350fr, Masks.

1980, Aug. 6 Litho. *Perf. 13½*

C289	AP109	250fr multi	2.00	1.00
C290	AP109	300fr multi	2.40	1.20
C291	AP109	350fr multi	2.80	1.40

Nos. C271-C275 Overprinted with Winner and Country

1980, Nov. 14 Litho. *Perf. 14½*

C292	AP105	75fr multi	60	30
C293	AP105	150fr multi	1.20	60
C294	AP105	250fr multi	2.00	1.00
C295	AP105	350fr multi	2.80	1.40

Souvenir Sheet

C296	AP105	500fr multi	4.00	2.00

1350th Anniv. of Mohamed's Death at Medina—AP110

1982, July 17 Litho. *Perf. 13*

C297	AP110	400fr Medina Mosque minaret	3.25	1.60

Nos. C276-C281 Overprinted with Finalists and/or Scores in Black on Silver.

1982, Oct. 7 Litho. *Perf. 14x13½*

C298	AP106	60fr multi	50	25
C299	AP106	75fr multi	60	30
C300	AP106	100fr multi	80	40
C301	AP106	150fr multi	1.20	60
C302	AP106	175fr multi	1.40	70
		Nos. C298-C302 (5)	4.50	2.25

Souvenir Sheet

C303	AP106	250fr multi	2.00	1.00

30th Anniv. of Amelia Earhart's Transatlantic Flight—AP111

1982, Dec. 4 Engr. *Perf. 13*

C304	AP111	150fr multi	1.20	60

AIR POST SEMI-POSTAL STAMPS

Hathor Pillar
SPAP1

Engraved

1964, March 9 ***Perf. 13*** **Unwmkd.**

No.	Type	Description	Unused	Used
CB1	SPAP1	10fr+5fr violet & chestnut	28	20
CB2	"	25fr+5fr orange brn. & slate green	45	35
CB3	"	50fr+5fr slate green & brown red	80	70

Issued to publicize the UNESCO world campaign to save historic monuments in Nubia.

POSTAGE DUE STAMPS

Messenger—D6

Early Transportation: 1fr, Litter. 2fr, Canoe. 5fr, Bicyclist. 10fr, Steam locomotive. 25fr, Seaplane.

Engraved

1961, Dec. 4 ***Perf. 11*** **Unwmkd.**

No.	Type	Description	Unused	Used
J34	D6	50c ultra., olive bistre & red	5	5
J35	"	1fr red brown, red & green	5	5
J36	"	2fr green, ultra., & brown	8	8
J37	"	5fr purple & gray brown	12	12
J38	D6	10fr blue, green & chocolate	28	28
J39	"	25fr blue, dk. green & dk. brown	65	65

The two types of each value in Nos. J34–J45 (early and modern transportation) were printed tête bêche, se-tenant at the base.

MH. 1521 Broussard Plane—D7

Modern transportation: 1fr, Land Rover. 2fr, River boat transporting barge. 5fr, Trailer-truck. 10fr, Diesel locomotive. 25fr, Boeing 707 jet plane.

No.	Type	Description	Unused	Used
J40	D7	50c ultra., olive bistre & red	5	5
J41	"	1fr red & green	5	5
J42	"	2fr ultra., green, & brown	8	8
J43	"	5fr purple & gray brown	12	12
J44	"	10fr dark green & chocolate	28	28
J45	"	25fr blue, dk. green & sepia	65	65
		Nos. J34–J45 (12)	2.46	2.46

See note following No. J39.

Flowers
D8

Flowers: 2fr, Phaeomeria magnifica. 5fr, Millettia laurentii. 10fr, Tuberose. 15fr, Pyrostegia venusta. 20fr, Hibiscus.

1971, Mar. 25 Photo. ***Perf. 12x12½***

No.	Type	Description	Unused	Used
J46	D8	1fr multicolored	5	5
J47	"	2fr "	8	8
J48	"	5fr pink & multi.	10	10
J49	"	10fr dk. grn. & multi.	12	12
J50	"	15fr multicolored	25	25
J51	"	20fr "	40	40
		Nos. J46–J51 (6)	1.00	1.00

OFFICIAL STAMPS

Coat of Arms
O1

Typographed

1968–70 ***Perf. 14x13*** **Unwmkd.**

No.	Type	Description	Unused	Used
O1	O1	1fr multi. ('70)	5	3
O2	"	2fr " ('70)	5	5
O3	"	5fr " ('70)	10	8
O4	"	10fr " ('70)	30	18
O5	"	25fr emerald & multi.	25	10
O6	"	30fr red & multi.	30	10
O7	"	50fr multi. ('70)	90	45
O8	"	85fr " ('70)	1.60	90
O9	"	100fr " ('70)	2.00	1.10
O10	"	200fr " ('70)	3.00	2.25
		Nos. O1–O10 (10)	8.55	5.24

CORFU

(kôr·fōō'; kôr'fū)

LOCATION—An island in the Ionian Sea opposite the Greek-Albanian border.

GOVT.—A department of Greece.

AREA—245 sq. mi.

POP.—114,620 (1938).

CAPITAL—Corfu.

In 1923 Italy occupied Corfu (Kerkyra) during a controversy with Greece over the assassination of an Italian official in Epirus. Italy again occupied Corfu in 1941–43.

100 Centesimi = 1 Lira

100 Lepta = 1 Drachma

Issued under Italian Occupation

Italian Stamps of 1901-23 Overprinted **CORFÙ**

1923, Sept. 20 ***Perf. 14*** **Wmk. 140**

No.	Type	Description	Unused	Used
N1	A48	5c green	45	50
N2	A48	10c claret	45	50
N3	A48	15c slate	45	50
N4	A50	20c brn org	45	50
N5	A49	30c org brn	45	50
N6	A49	50c violet	45	50
N7	A49	60c blue	45	50
N8	A46	1 l brn & grn	45	50
		Nos. N1-N8 (8)	3.60	4.00

Italian Stamps of 1901-23 Surcharged **CORFÙ Lepta 25**

1923, Sept. 24

No.	Type	Description	Unused	Used
N9	A48	25 l on 10c cl	2.50	90
N10	A49	60 l on 25c bl	2.00	
N11	A49	70 l on 30c org brn	2.00	
N12	A49	1.20d on 50c vio	2.10	90
N13	A46	2.40d on 1 l brn & grn	2.10	90
N14	A46	4.75d on 2 l grn & org	2.00	

Nos. 10, 11 and 14 were not placed in use.

Issue for Corfu and Paxos.

Nos. N15–N34, NC1–NC12, NJ1–NJ11 and NRA1–NRA3 have been extensively counterfeited, some with forged cancellations.

Stamps of Greece, 1937-38, Overprinted in Black **CORFU**

Perf. 12x13½, 12½x12, 13½x12.

1941, June 5 **Wmk. 252**

No.	Type	Description	Unused	Used
N15	A69	5 l brn red & bl	3.00	3.00
N16	A70	10 l bl & brn red (On 397)	1.00	1.00
N17	A70	10 l bl & brn red (On 413)	52.50	30.00
N18	A71	20 l blk & grn	1.00	1.00
N19	A72	40 l grn & blk	1.50	1.50
N20	A73	50 l brn & blk	4.00	4.00
N21	A74	80 l ind & yel brn	2.00	2.00
N22	A67	1d green	2.00	2.00
N23	A84	1.50d green	12.00	12.00
N24	A75	2d ultra	1.50	1.00
N25	A67	3d red brn	2.00	2.00
N26	A76	5d red	2.00	2.00
N27	A77	6d ol brn	3.50	3.00
N28	A78	7d dk brn	6.00	5.00
N29	A67	8d dp bl	4.00	4.00
N30	A79	10d red brn	135.00	60.00
N31	A80	15d green	10.00	9.00
N32	A81	25d dk bl	8.00	8.00
N33	A84	30d org brn	25.00	22.50
N34	A67	100d car lake	52.50	45.00
		Nos. N15-N34 (20)	328.50	218.00

AIR POST STAMPS.

Greece Nos. C37 and C26 to C35, Overprinted **CORFU**

Perf. 12½x13, 13x12½, 13½x12½.

1941, June 5 **Unwmkd.**

No.	Type	Description	Unused	Used
NC1	D3	50 l dk brn	4.00	4.00
NC2	AP16	1d red	150.00	75.00
NC3	AP17	2d gray bl	5.00	5.00
NC4	AP18	5d violet	5.00	5.00
NC5	AP19	7d dp ultra	5.00	5.00
NC6	AP20	10d bis brn (On C26)	165.00	72.50
NC7	AP20	10d brn org (On C35)	17.50	10.00
NC8	AP21	25d rose	30.00	20.00
NC9	AP22	30d dk grn	42.50	37.50
NC10	AP23	50d violet	32.50	30.00
a.		Double overprint		300.00
NC11	AP24	100d brown	*1,100.*	*500.00*

On No. C36.

Serrate Roulette 13½.

No.	Type	Description	Unused	Used
NC12	D3	50 l vio brn	25.00	20.00
a.		On C36a		

POSTAGE DUE STAMPS.

Postage Due Stamps of Greece, 1913-35 Overprinted **CORFU**

1941, June 5 **Unwmkd.**

Serrate Roulette 13½.

No.	Type	Description	Unused	Used
NJ1	D3	10 l carmine	1.75	1.75
NJ2	D3	25 l ultra	2.00	2.00
NJ3	D3	80 l lil brn	275.00	90.00

Perf. 12½x13, 13½x12½.

No.	Type	Description	Unused	Used
NJ4	D3	1d lt bl (On J80)	*900.00*	*275.00*
NJ5	D3	2d lt red	3.00	2.00
NJ6	D3	5d gray	10.00	9.00
NJ7	D3	10d gray grn	6.00	6.00
NJ8	D3	15d red brn	6.00	6.00
NJ9	D3	25d lt red	6.00	6.00
NJ10	D3	50d orange	8.00	8.00
NJ11	D3	100d sl grn	300.00	175.00

POSTAL TAX STAMPS.

Greece Nos. RA61 to RA63, Overprinted **CORFU**

Perf. 13½x12

1941, June 5 **Unwmkd.**

No.	Type	Description	Unused	Used
NRA1	PT7	10 l brt rose, *pale rose*	1.50	1.50
NRA2	PT7	50 l gray grn, *pale grn*	1.50	1.00
NRA3	PT7	1d dl bl, *lt bl*	7.50	7.00

Stamps overprinted "CORFU" were replaced by Italian stamps overprinted "Isole Jonie." (See Ionian Islands.)

COSTA RICA

(kŏs'tȧ rē'kȧ)

LOCATION—In Central America between Nicaragua and Panama.

GOVT.—Republic.

AREA—19,653 sq. mi.

POP.—2,010,000 (est. 1976).

CAPITAL—San José.

8 Reales = 100 Centavos = 1 Peso

100 Centimos = 1 Colón (1900)

Coat of Arms

A1

Engraved.

1863 ***Perf. 12*** **Unwmkd.**

No.	Type	Description	Unused	Used
1	A1	½r blue	75	1.25
a.		½r lt bl	75	1.25
b.		Horiz. pair, imperf. btwn.	100.00	
c.		Vert. pair, imperf. btwn.		
2	A1	2r scarlet	1.50	2.25
3	A1	4r green	10.00	10.00
4	A1	1p orange	25.00	25.00

The ½r was printed from two plates. The second is in light blue with little or no sky over the mountains.

Imperforate copies of Nos. 1–2 are corner copies from poorly perforated sheets.

Nos. 1–3 Surcharged in Red or Black:

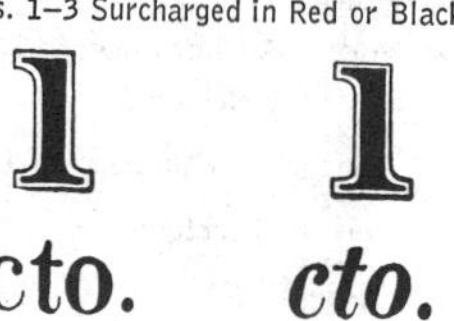

a b

2 cts. 5 cts. U.P.U.

c d

20 CTS U.P.U.

e

1881–82

Red or Black Surcharge.

No.	Type	Description	Unused	Used
7	A1 (a)	1c on ½r bl ('82)	3.00	*12.50*
8	A1 (b)	1c on ½r bl ('82)	12.50	*22.50*
9	A1 (c)	2c on ½r bl	2.50	6.00
a.		Double surch.		
b.		"Cts."		
12	A1 (c)	5c on ½r bl	7.50	12.50
a.		Double surch.		
13	A1 (d)	5c on ½r bl ('82)	100.00	85.00
14	A1 (d)	10c on 2r scar (Bk) ('82)	60.00	60.00
15	A1 (e)	20c on 4r grn ('82)	150.00	100.00

The ½r stamps surcharged "DOS CTS" were never placed in use, and are said to have been surcharged to a dealer's order.

Counterfeits exist of surcharges on Nos. 7–15.

Gen. Prospero Fernández

A6

President Bernardo Soto Alfaro

A7

1883, Jan. 1

No.	Type	Description	Unused	Used
16	A6	1c green	1.00	60
17	A6	2c carmine	90	70
18	A6	5c bl vio	3.00	60
19	A6	10c orange	30.00	6.00
20	A6	40c blue	1.25	90
		Nos. 16-20 (5)	36.15	8.80

Unused copies of 40c usually lack gum.

1887

No.	Type	Description	Unused	Used
21	A7	5c bl vio	6.00	60
22	A7	10c orange	2.25	85

A8 A9

1889 Black Overprint.

No.	Type	Description	Unused	Used
23	A8	1c rose	3.00	1.10
24	A9	5c brown	2.25	1.10

President Soto Alfaro

A10 A11

A12 A13

A14 A15

A16 A17

A18 A19

1889 ***Perf. 14–16 & Compound***

No.	Type	Description	Unused	Used
25	A10	1c brown	40	50
a.		Horiz. pair, imperf. vert	30.00	
b.		Imperf. pair	35.00	
c.		Horiz. or vert. pair, imperf. between	50.00	
26	A11	2c dk grn	30	50
a.		Imperf., pair	25.00	
b.		Vert. pair, imperf. horiz.	30.00	
c.		Horiz. pair, imperf. btwn.	30.00	
27	A12	5c orange	60	30
a.		Imperf., pair	60.00	
b.		Horiz. pair, imperf. btwn.	40.00	
28	A13	10c red brn	50	40
a.		Vert. or horiz. pair, imperf. btwn.	40.00	
29	A14	20c yel grn	35	30
a.		Vert. pair, imperf. horiz.	30.00	
b.		Horizontal pair, imperf. btwn.	30.00	
30	A15	50c rose red	1.25	1.10
31	A16	1p blue	1.75	1.75
32	A17	2p dl vio	12.00	12.00
a.		2p sl	12.50	12.50

33	A18	5p ol grn	45.00	30.00
34	A19	10p black	80.00	60.00
		Nos. 25-34 (10)	142.15	106.85

Arms of Costa Rica
A20 A21

A22 A23

A24 A25

A26 A27

A28 A29

1892 *Perf. 12-15 & Compound*

35	A20	1c grnsh bl	35	50
36	A21	2c yellow	35	50
37	A22	5c red lil	35	20
a.		5c vio	12.00	40
38	A23	10c lt grn	90	40
a.		Horiz. pair, imperf. btwn.	60.00	
39	A24	20c scarlet	7.50	35
a.		Horiz. pair, imperf. btwn.		40.00
40	A25	50c gray bl	6.50	6.00
41	A26	1p grn, *yel*	1.50	1.10
42	A27	2p rose red, *pale lil*	3.50	1.50
a.		2p brn red, *lil*	3.50	1.50
43	A28	5p dk bl, *bl*	3.50	1.50
44	A29	10p brn, *pale buff*	7.00	5.50
a.		10p brn, *yel*	7.00	5.50
		Nos. 35-44 (10)	31.45	17.55

Imperfs. of Nos. 35–44 are proofs.

Statue of Juan Santamaría
A30

Juan Mora Fernández
A31

View of Port Limón
A32

Braulio Carillo ("Branlio" on stamp)
A33

National Theater
A34

José M. Castro
A35

Birris Bridge
A36

Juan Rafael Mora
A37

Jesús Jiménez
A38

Coat of Arms
A39

1901, Jan. *Perf. 12-15½*

45	A30	1c grn & blk	60	15
46	A31	2c ver & blk	75	25
47	A32	5c gray bl & blk	50	20
a.		Vert. pair, imperf. btwn.		125.00
48	A33	10c ocher & blk	1.50	25
49	A34	20c lake & blk	4.50	25
a.		Vert. pair, imperf. btwn.	125.00	
50	A35	50c dl lil & dk bl	4.50	1.50
51	A36	1col ol bis & blk	20.00	3.50
52	A37	2col car rose & dk grn	11.00	2.00
53	A38	5col brn & blk	20.00	2.50
54	A39	10col yel grn & brn red	25.00	3.00
		Nos. 45-54 (10)	88.35	13.60

The 2c exists with center inverted.

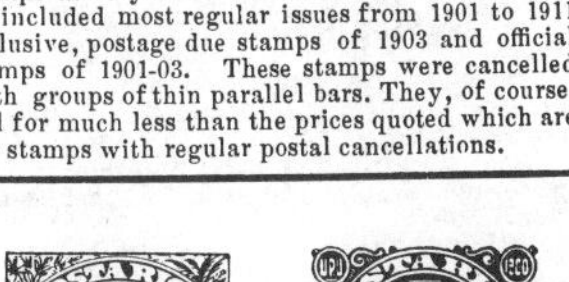

Remainders

In 1914 the government sold a large quantity of stamps at very much less than face value. The lot included most regular issues from 1901 to 1911 inclusive, postage due stamps of 1903 and official stamps of 1901-03. These stamps were cancelled with groups of thin parallel bars. They, of course, sell for much less than the prices quoted which are for stamps with regular postal cancellations.

José M. Cañas
A40

Julián Volio
A41

Eusebio Figueroa Oreamuno
A42

1903 *Perf. 13½, 14, 15*

55	A40	4c red vio & blk	1.75	1.10
56	A41	6c ol grn & blk	6.00	3.00
57	A42	25c gray lil & brn	12.50	30

No. 49 Surcharged in Black: UN CENTIMO

1905

58	A34	1c on 20c lake & blk	75	75
a.		Inverted surcharge	5.00	5.00
b.		Diagonal surcharge	75	75

Specimens surcharged in other colors are proofs.

Statue of Juan Santamaria
A43

Juan Mora Fernández
A44

José M. Cañas
A45

Mauro Fernández
A46

Braulio Carrillo
A47

Julián Volio
A48

Eusebio Figueroa Oreamuno
A49

José M. Castro
A50

Jesús Jiménez
A51

Juan Rafael Mora
A52

1907 *Perf. 11x14* **Unwmkd.**

59	A43	1c red brn & ind	75	30
60	A44	2c yel grn & blk	1.25	30
a.		Perf. 14	1.25	30
61	A45	4c car & ind	6.00	3.00
a.		Perf. 14	175.00	30.00
62	A46	5c yel & dl bl perf 14	90	30
a.		Perf. 11x14	5.00	60
63	A47	10c bl & blk	1.25	60
a.		Perf. 14	1.25	60
64	A48	20c ol grn & blk	7.50	3.50
a.		Perf. 14	7.50	3.00
65	A49	25c gray lil & blk, perf. 14	3.00	1.25
a.		Perf. 11x14	30.00	6.50
66	A50	50c red lil & bl	37.50	11.00
a.		Perf. 14	65.00	17.50
67	A51	1col brn & blk	17.50	11.00
a.		Perf. 14	25.00	13.50
68	A52	2col cl & grn	75.00	40.00
a.		Perf. 14	110.00	55.00
		Nos. 59-68 (10)	150.65	71.25

Imperforate copies of the above set are either proofs or from unfinished sheets, which were placed on the market in London. The 1c, 2c, 5c, 20c, 50c, 1 col. and 2 col. exist with center inverted. Price, 5c, $300; others each $500.

Nos. 59–68 exist with papermaker's watermark.

Statue of Juan Santamaria
A53

Juan Mora Fernández
A54

José M. Cañas
A55

Mauro Fernández
A56

Braulio Carrillo
A57

Julián Volio
A58

Eusebio Figueroa Oreamuno
A59

Jesús Jiménez
A60

1910 *Perf. 12.*

69	A53	1c brown	12	10
70	A54	2c dp grn	30	15
71	A55	4c scarlet	30	15
72	A56	5c orange	30	10
73	A57	10c dp bl	20	10
74	A58	20c ol grn	30	25
75	A59	25c dp vio	3.00	75
76	A60	1col dk brn	60	75
		Nos. 69-76 (8)	5.12	2.35

Nos. 69a–73a and 72b–72c ("Cafe" ovpts.) are listed after No. 111.

No. 60a Overprinted in Red *1911*

1911 *Perf. 14*

77	A44	2c yel grn & blk	1.75	1.10
a.		Inverted overprint	7.00	7.00
b.		Double overprint, both inverted	60.00	

Stamps of 1901-07 Overprinted in Red or Black

* 1911 *

78 A30 1c grn & blk (R) 75 50
a. Black overprint 50.00 25.00
b. Inverted overprint
79 A43 1c red brn & ind (Bk) 90 50
a. Inverted overprint 6.00 5.00
b. Double overprint 7.00 7.00
80 A44 2c yel grn & blk (Bk) 90 50
a. Inverted overprint 3.00 3.00
b. Double overprint, one as on No. 77 27.50 27.50
c. Double overprint, one inverted 17.50 17.50
d. Pair, one stamp No. 77 35.00 25.00
e. Perf. 11x14 1.75 50

Habilitado

No. 55 Overprinted in Black

1911

81 A40 4c red vio & blk 1.50 1.00

Habilitado

Stamps of 1907 Overprinted in Blue, Black or Rose

1911

Perf. 14

82 A46 5c yel & bl (Bl) 60 25
a. "Habilitada" 4.50 3.50
b. "2911" 8.00 4.50
c. Roman "I" in "1911" 2.75 2.00
d. Double overprint 6.00 4.50
e. Inverted overprint 8.00 5.50
f. Black overprint 11.00 3.00
g. Triple overprint 8.00
h. Imperf. horizontally (pair) 55.00
83 A47 10c bl & blk (Bk) 2.75 2.00
a. Roman "I" in "1911" 8.00 5.50
c. Double overprint 27.50 16.50
d. Perf. 11x14 1.75 1.00
84 A47 10c bl & blk (R), perf. 11x14 8.00 8.00
a. Roman "I" in "1911" 22.50 20.00
c. Perf. 14 27.50 16.50

Many counterfeits of overprint exist.

A61

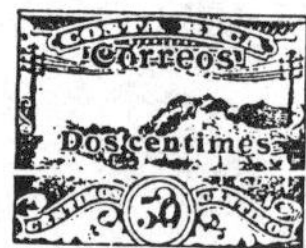

A62

A63

Telegraph Stamps Surcharged in Rose, Blue or Black.

1911 ***Perf. 12, 14, 14x11.***

86 A61 1c on 10c bl (R) 30 20
a. "Coereos" 11.00 8.00
b. Inverted surcharge
87 A61 1c on 10c bl (Bk) 110.00 80.00
a. "Coereos"
88 A61 1c on 25c vio (Bk) 30 20
a. "Coereos" 11.00 8.00
b. Pair, one without surcharge 27.50
c. Double surcharge 11.00
e. Double surcharge, one inverted 16.50
89 A61 1c on 50c red brn (Bl) 60 60
a. Inverted surcharge 7.00 7.00
b. Double surcharge 6.00
90 A61 1c on 1 col brn (R) 60 60
91 A61 1c on 5 col red (Bl) 1.10 85
92 A61 1c on 10 col dk brn (R) 1.35 1.10
93 A62 2c on 5c brn org (Bk) 4.50 3.25
a. Inverted surcharge 11.00 5.50
b. "Correos" inverted 22.50
c. Double surcharge 11.00
94 A62 2c on 10c bl (R) 80.00 52.50
a. Perf. 14 135.00 80.00
b. "Correos" inverted 165.00
c. AS "b," perf. 14 550.00
95 A62 2c on 50c cl (Bk) 60 75
a. Inverted surcharge 5.50 4.50
b. Double surcharge 16.50
96 A62 2c on 1 col brn (Bk) 1.10 1.10
a. Inverted surcharge 16.50
b. Double surcharge 22.50
97 A62 2c on 2 col car (Bk) 85 85
a. Inverted surcharge 10.00 7.00
b. "Correos" inverted 11.00 8.00
c. Double surcharge
d. Perf. 14 16.50 11.00
98 A62 2c on 5 col grn (Bk) 1.10 1.10
a. Inverted surcharge 11.00 8.00
b. "Correos" inverted 22.50 6.00
99 A62 2c on 10 col mar (Bk) 1.35 1.10
a. "Correos" inverted 22.50
100 A63 5c on 5c org (Bl) 60 25
a. Double surcharge 8.50 5.50
b. Inverted surcharge 8.50 5.50
c. Pair, one without surcharge 25.00
Nos. 86-100 (15) 203.75 143.70

Counterfeits exist of Nos. 87, 94 and all minor varieties.

Nos. 93–99 exist with papermaker's watermark.

Coffee Plantation—A64

1921, June 17 Litho. *Perf. 11½*

103 A64 5c bl & blk 1.50 1.25
a. Tête bêche pair 3.25 3.25
b. Imperf., pair 15.00
c. As "a," imperf. 40.00

Centenary of coffee raising in Costa Rica.

Liberty with Torch of Freedom
A65

1921 Typographed. *Perf. 11*

104 A65 5c violet 85 50
a. Imperf. 30.00

Centenary of Central American independence.

Juan Mora and Julio Acosta—A66

1921, Sept. 15 *Perf. 11½*

105 A66 2c org & blk 2.00 1.50
106 A66 3c grn & blk 2.00 1.50
107 A66 6c scar & blk 2.50 1.75
108 A66 15c dk bl & blk 6.00 5.00
109 A66 30c org brn & blk 10.00 9.00
Nos. 105-109 (5) 22.50 18.75

Centenary of Central American independence. Issue requested by Costa Rican Philatelic Society. Authorized by decree calling for 2,000 of 30c and 5,000 each of other values. Many more were printed illegally including imperforates, color changes and inverted centers.

Each sheet of 20 (4x5) contains 5 tête-bêche pairs.

Simón Bolívar
A67

1921 Engraved. *Perf. 12.*

110 A67 15c dp vio 40 20
110a A67 15c dp vio (G) 2.00 1.50
Nos. 69a-110a (6) 2.00 1.50

No. 104 Overprinted

CORREOS

1922

1922 ***Perf. 11***

111 A65 5c violet 60 40
a. Inverted overprint 5.00
b. Double overprint 10.00

Stamps of 1910–1921 Overprinted in Blue, Red, Black or Gold

CAFE DE COSTA RICA

1922 ***Perf. 12***

69a A53 1c brn (Bl) 15 10
70a A54 2c dp grn (R) 20 15
71a A55 4c scarlet 25 20
72a A56 5c orange 40 25

Inverted overprints occur on all values. Counterfeits exist.

No. 72 Overprinted with Double-Lined Circle, Inscribed: "Compre Ud. Cafe de Costa Rica"

1923

72b A56 5c orange 35 25
c. "VD." for "UD." 50.00 50.00
73a A57 10c dp bl (R) 50 40

Jesús Jiménez
A68

1923, June 18 Litho. *Perf. 11½*

112 A68 2c brown 20 20
113 A68 4c green 25 20
114 A68 5c blue 50 20
115 A68 20c carmine 30 30
116 A68 1col violet 50 50
Nos. 112-116 (5) 3.25 2.50

Issued to commemorate the centenary of the birth of President Jesús Jiménez (1823–1898).

Nos. 112 to 116 exist imperforate but were not regularly issued in that condition.

National Monument
A70

Harvesting Coffee
A71

Banana Growing
A73

General Post Office
A74

Columbus Soliciting Aid of Isabella
A75

Christopher Columbus
A76

Columbus at Cariari
A77

Map of Costa Rica
A78

Manuel M. Gutiérrez
A79

1923–26 Engraved *Perf. 12*

117 A70 1c violet 10 10
118 A71 2c yellow 30 20
119 A73 4c dp grn 60 50
120 A74 5c lt bl 1.00 15
121 A74 5c yel grn ('26) 30 10
122 A75 10c red brn 1.25 25

123	A75	10c car rose ('26)	40	10
124	A76	12c car rose	3.00	2.00
125	A77	20c dp bl	4.00	1.35
126	A78	40c orange	7.50	2.50
127	A79	1col ol grn	2.00	60
		Nos. 117-127 (11)	20.45	7.85

See also Nos. 151–156.

Rodrigo Arias Maldonado
A80

1924 *Perf. 12½.*

128	A80	2c dk grn	15	10
a.		Perf. 14	25	10

See No. 162.

Map of Guanacaste
A81

Mission at Nicoya
A82

1924 Lithographed. *Perf. 12.*

129	A81	1c car rose	50	30
130	A81	2c violet	50	30
131	A81	5c green	50	30
132	A81	10c orange	3.50	75
133	A82	15c lt bl	1.10	65
134	A82	20c gray blk	1.75	1.10
135	A82	25c lt brn	2.50	2.00
		Nos. 129-135 (7)	10.35	5.40

Centenary of annexation of Province of Guanacaste to Costa Rica.
Exist imperf. Price, set, $40.

1925

Stamps of 1923 Surcharged:

a

b

136	A74 (a)	3c on 5c lt bl	30	25
137	A75 (a)	6c on 10c red brn	40	40
138	A78 (a)	30c on 40c org	75	60
139	A79 (b)	45c on 1 col ol grn	1.25	75
a.		Double surcharge	25.00	

No. 124 Surcharged

=10 10=

1926

140	A76	10c on 12c car rose	1.50	50

College of San Luis, Cartago
A83

Chapui Asylum, San José
A84

Normal School, Heredia
A85

Ruins of Ujarrás
A86

Engraved

1926 *Perf. 12½.* **Unwmkd.**

143	A83	3c ultra	25	20
144	A84	6c dk brn	40	30
145	A85	30c dp org	90	40
146	A86	45c blk vio	2.00	1.25

No. 124 Surcharged in Black:

1928, Jan. 7 *Perf. 12*

147	A76	10c on 12c car rose	10.00	7.50

Issued in honor of Col. Charles A. Lindbergh during his Good Will Tour of Central America.
The surcharge has been counterfeited.

No. 110 Surcharged 5 5

1928

148	A67	5(c) on 15c dp vio	25	15
a.		Inverted surcharge	25.00	

Type I
A88

CORREOS 5 CENTIMOS — Type II

CORREOS 5 CENTIMOS — Type III

CORREOS 5 CENTIMOS — Type IV

CORREOS 5 CENTIMOS — Type V

Surcharge Typographed (I–V) and (V) Lithographed.

1929 *Perf. 12½*

149	A88	5c on 2 col car (I)	12	12
a.		Type II	12	12
b.		Type III	12	12
c.		Type IV	12	12
d.		Type V	12	12

Telegraph Stamp Surcharged for Postage as in 1929, Surcharge Lithographed.

1929

150	A88	13c on 40c dp grn	15	10
a.		Inverted surcharge	1.25	1.00

Excellent counterfeits exist of No. 150a.

Types of 1923–26 Issues Dated "1929"

Imprint of Waterlow & Sons.

1930 Size: 26x21½mm. *Perf. 12½*

151	A70	1c dk vio	10	8
155	A74	5c green	10	8
156	A75	10c car rose	50	8

Juan Rafael Mora
A89

1931

157	A89	13c car rose	35	25

Seal of Costa Rica Philatelic Society ("Octubre 12 de 1932")
A90

1932, Oct. 12 *Perf. 12*

158	A90	3c orange	25	25
159	A90	5c dk grn	35	35
160	A90	10c car rose	40	40
161	A90	20c dk bl	50	50

Issued to commemorate the Philatelic Exhibition of Oct. 12, 1932. See also Nos. 179–183.

Maldonado Type of 1924.

1934 *Perf. 12½*

162	A80	3c dk grn	10	8

Red Cross Nurse—A91

1935, May 31 *Perf. 12*

163	A91	10c rose car	50	25

Issued in commemoration of the 50th anniversary of the founding of the Costa Rican Red Cross Society.

Air View of Cartago—A92

Miraculous Statuette and View of Cathedral
A93

Vision of 1635
A94

1935, Aug. *Perf. 12½*

164	A92	5c green	25	15
165	A93	10c carmine	50	25
166	A92	30c orange	75	35
167	A94	45c dk vio	1.75	60
168	A93	50c bl blk	3.00	1.25
		Nos. 164-168 (5)	6.25	2.60

Issued to commemorate the tercentenary of the Patron Saint, Our Lady of the Angels, of Costa Rica.

Map of Cocos Island
A95

1936, Jan. 29 *Perf. 14, 11½* **(25c)**

169	A95	4c ocher	35	15
170	A95	8c dk vio	45	25
171	A95	25c orange	50	25
172	A95	35c brn vio	75	25
173	A95	40c brown	1.00	35
174	A95	50c yellow	1.00	50
175	A95	2col yel grn	10.00	4.00
176	A95	5col green	27.50	15.00
		Nos. 169-176 (8)	41.55	20.75

Exist imperf. Price, set, $35.

Map of Cocos Island and Ships of Columbus
A96

1936, Dec. 5 *Perf. 12*

177	A96	5c green	20	6
178	A96	10c car rose	20	6

Seal of Costa Rica Philatelic Society ("Diciembre 1937")—A97

1937

179	A97	2c dk brn	20	20
180	A97	3c black	20	20
181	A97	5c green	25	20
182	A97	10c org red	30	25

Souvenir Sheet.

Imperf.

183	A97	Sheet of four	80	80
a.		2c dk brn	15	15
b.		3c blk	15	15
c.		5c grn	15	15
d.		10c org red	15	15

Issued to commemorate the Philatelic Exhibition, December, 1937. Size of No. 183: 168x101mm.

Purple Guaria Orchid, National Flower—A98

Tuna
A99

Native with Donkey Carrying Bananas
A101

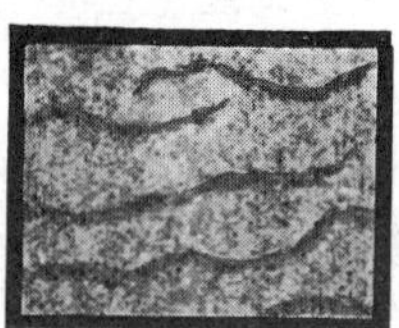

Wmk. 229

Designs: 3c, Cacao pod. 10c, Coffee harvesting.

Wmkd. Wavy Lines. (229)

1937–38 ***Perf. 12½***

184	A98	1c grn & vio ('38)	25	15
185	A98	3c choc ('38)	25	15

Perf. 12

Unwmkd.

186	A99	2c ol gray	30	20
187	A101	5c dk grn	35	15
188	A101	10c car rose	50	30
		Nos. 184-188 (5)	1.65	95

Nos 184–188 were issued to commemorate the National Exposition.

No. 125 Overprinted in Black **1938**

1938 ***Perf. 12.*** **Unwmkd.**

189	A77	20c dp bl	50	25

No. 146 Surcharged in Red:

a

b

c *d*

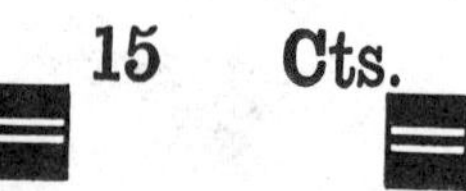

e

1940 ***Perf. 12½.***

190	A86 (a)	15c on 45c blk vio	40	30
190A	A86 (b)	15c on 45c blk vio	40	30
190B	A86 (c)	15c on 45c blk vio	40	30
190C	A86 (d)	15c on 45c blk vio	40	30
190D	A86 (e)	15c on 45c blk vio	30	25
		Nos. 190-190D (5)	1.90	1.45

Allegory—A103

Overprinted "Dia Panamericano de la Salud / 2·Diciembre 1940" and Arc in Black

1940, Dec. 2 **Engraved** ***Perf. 12***

191	A103	5c green	30	20
192	A103	10c rose car	35	25
193	A103	20c dp bl	75	30
194	A103	40c brown	1.25	1.00
195	A103	55c org yel	3.00	1.25
		Nos. 191-195 (5)	5.65	3.00

Pan-American Health Day. See Nos. C46–C54.

Exist without overprint.

Stamps of 1936 Surcharged in Black:

15
CENTIMOS
15

1941 ***Perf. 14, 11½***

196	A95	15c on 25c org	35	30
197	A95	15c on 35c brn vio	35	30
198	A95	15c on 40c brn	35	30
199	A95	15c on 2 col yel grn	35	30
200	A95	15c on 5 col grn	60	55
		Nos. 196-200 (5)	2.00	1.75

Nos. 196–200 exist with surcharge inverted. Price, $5 a set.

National Stadium—A104

Engraved; Flags Typographed in National Colors

1941, May 8 ***Perf. 12½***

201	A104	5c green	1.25	35
a.		Flags omitted	75.00	
202	A104	10c orange	1.00	35
203	A104	15c car rose	1.50	50
204	A104	25c dk bl	2.50	70
205	A104	40c chestnut	6.00	2.00
206	A104	50c purple	8.00	2.50
207	A104	75c red org	15.00	5.00
208	A104	1col dk car	25.00	10.00
		Nos. 201-208 (8)	60.25	21.40

Issued to commemorate the Caribbean and Central American Soccer Championship. See also Nos. C57–C66, C121–C123.

No. 157 Surcharged in Black **5 Céntimos 5**

1941 ***Perf. 12***

209	A89	5c on 13c car rose	12	8

Cleto González Viquez
A105

1941-45 **Engraved.** ***Perf. 12½.***

210	A105	3c dp org	12	10
210A	A105	3c dp plum ('43)	12	10
210B	A105	3c car ('45)	12	10
211	A105	5c dp vio (*José Rodriguez*)	15	12
211A	A105	5c brn blk ('43)	12	12
		Nos. 210-211A (5)	63	54

See also No. 256.

Old University of Costa Rica
A106

New National University
A107

1941, Aug. 26 ***Perf. 12***

212	A106	5c green	40	15
213	A107	10c yel org	45	15
214	A106	15c lil rose	60	15
215	A107	25c dl bl	90	35
216	A106	50c fawn	3.00	2.00
		Nos. 212-216 (5)	5.35	2.80

National University, founded in 1940. See Nos. C74–C80.

Nos. 144, 189 Surcharged in Black or Red

15 CENTIMOS 15

1942 ***Perf. 12½, 12***

217	A84	5c on 6c dk brn	25	20
218	A77	15c on 20c dp bl (R)	35	25

Torch of Freedom, "Victory" and Flags of American Nations
A108

Juan Mora Fernández
A109

1942, Sept. 25 ***Perf. 12***

219	A108	5c rose	30	15
220	A108	5c yel grn	30	15
221	A108	5c purple	30	15
222	A108	5c dp bl	30	15
223	A108	5c red org	30	15
		Nos. 219-223 (5)	1.50	75

1943–47 **Engraved**

Designs: 2c, Bruno Carranza. 3c, Tomas Guardia. 5c, Manuel Aguilar. 15c, Francisco Morazan. 25c, Jose M. Alfaro. 50c, Francisco M. Oreamuno. 1col, Jose M. Castro. 2col, Juan Rafael Mora.

224	A109	1c red lil	6	5
225	A109	2c black	6	6
226	A109	3c dp bl	6	6
227	A109	5c brt bl grn	12	8
a.		5c brt grn ('47)	12	10
228	A109	15c scarlet	15	6
229	A109	25c brt ultra	35	20
230	A109	50c dp vio	1.00	75
231	A109	1col blk brn	3.00	1.50
232	A109	2col dp org	5.00	3.50
		Nos. 224-232 (9)	9.80	6.26

See also Nos. C81–C91A, C124–C127, C179–C181.

View of San Ramón
A118

1944, Jan. 19

233	A118	5c dk grn	15	10
234	A118	10c orange	20	10
235	A118	15c rose pink	30	12
236	A118	40c gray blk	1.30	75
237	A118	50c dp bl	2.00	1.25
		Nos. 233-237 (5)	3.95	2.32

Issued to commemorate the 100th anniversary of the founding of the City of San Ramón. See also Nos. C94–C102.

Nos. 220–223 Overprinted in Red or Black

La entrevista de los Presidentes De la Guardia y Picado contribuirá a afianzar la unidad Continental. 18 setiembre 1944

1944, Sept. 18

238	A108	5c yel grn (Bk)	15	12
239	A108	5c pur (R)	15	12
240	A108	5c dp bl (R)	15	12
241	A108	5c red org (Bk)	15	12

Issued to commemorate the amicable settlement of a boundary dispute with Panama. This overprint also exists on No. 219.

Mauro Fernández
A119

Engraved.

1945, July 21 ***Perf. 14*** **Unwmkd.**

242	A119	20c dp grn	25	15

Issued to commemorate the centenary of the birth of Mauro Fernandez (1844–1905), statesman.

Coffee Harvesting
A120

1945, Oct. 9 ***Perf. 12***

243	A120	5c dk grn & blk	15	8
244	A120	10c org & blk	25	12
245	A120	20c car rose & blk	30	20

No. 242 Surcharged in Red Brown.

1946 ***Perf. 14.*** **Unwmkd.**

246	A119	15c on 20c dp grn	20	12

No. 080 Overprinted in Red **CORREOS 1947**

1947, Mar. 19 ***Perf. 12***

247	A96	5c green	15	10

Cervantes
A121

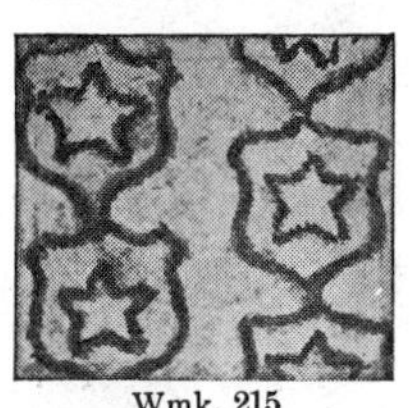

Wmk. 215

Wmkd. Small Star in Shield, Multiple. (215)

1947, Nov. 10 Engraved Perf. 14

249	A121	30c dp bl	30	15
250	A121	55c dp car	50	35

Issued to commemorate the 400th anniversary of the birth of Miguel de Cervantes Saavedra, novelist, playwright and poet.

Franklin D. Roosevelt
A122

1947, Aug. 26 Perf. 12 Unwmkd.

251	A122	5c brt grn	10	10
252	A122	10c car rose	15	12
253	A122	15c ultra	20	18
254	A122	25c org red	25	25
255	A122	50c lilac	50	35
		Nos. 251-255, C160-C167 (13)	9.50	8.95

Small Portrait Type of 1941.

1948 Perf. 12½.

256	A105	3c dp ultra (*Bishop Bernardo A. Thiel*)	10	8

Old University of Costa Rica
A123

1953, June 25 Litho. Perf. 12

Black Surcharge.

257	A123	5c on 10c grn	12	6

Revenue Stamp Surcharged in Red or Blue

A124

Engraved.

1955-56 Perf. 12 Unwmkd.

258	A124	5c on 2c emer (R)	8	6
259	A124	15c on 2c emer (Bl)	18	8
260	A124	15c on 2c emer (R) ('56)	18	8
		Nos. 258-260, C341-C344 (7)	1.59	1.17

Justo A. Facio
A125

Anglo-Costa Rican Bank
A126

1960, Apr. 20 Photo. Perf. 13½

261	A125	10c brn red	8	6

Centenary of the birth (in 1859) of Prof. Justo A. Facio. Exists imperf.

Nos. RA12-RA15 Surcharged in Red — 1963 10 CENTIMOS

1963, Mar.

262	PT3	10c on 5c dk car	25	20
263	PT3	10c on 5c sep	25	20
264	PT3	10c on 5c dl grn	25	20
265	PT3	10c on 5c bl	25	20

1963 Perf. 13½ Unwmkd.

266	A126	10c gray	8	6

Centenary of the Anglo-Costa Rican Bank.

Arms of San José
A127

Alberto M. Brenes Mora
A128

Coats of Arms: 35c, Cartago. 50c, Heredia. 55c, Alajuela. 65c, Guanacaste. 1col, Puntarenas. 2col, Limon.

Lithographed

1969, Sept. 14 Perf. 14x13½

267	A127	15c multi	6	4
268	A127	35c multi	15	10
269	A127	50c gray & multi	20	10
270	A127	55c buff & multi	25	20
271	A127	65c multi	35	25
272	A127	1col pink & multi	60	25
273	A127	2col multi	1.00	50
		Nos. 267-273 (7)	2.61	1.44

1976, March 1 Litho. Perf. 10½

274	A128	1col vio bl	25	20
		Nos. 274, C653-C657 (6)	3.53	2.71

Prof. Alberto Manuel Brenes Mora, botanist, birth centenary.

Map of Costa Rica, Reader with Book
A129

1978, July 17 Litho. Perf. 13½

275	A129	50c multi	12	10

National five-year literacy plan.

SEMI-POSTAL STAMPS.

No. 72 Surcharged in Red

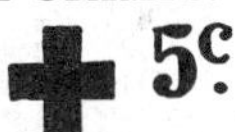

1922 Perf. 12. Unwmkd.

B1	A56	5c +5c org	75	40

Issued for the benefit of the Costa Rican Red Cross Society. In 1928, owing to a temporary shortage of the ordinary 5c stamp, No. B1 was placed on sale as a regular 5c stamp, the surtax being disregarded.

Discus Thrower
SP1

Trophy
SP2

Parthenon
SP3

1924 Lithographed Imperf.

B2	SP1	5c dk grn	3.00	4.00
B3	SP2	10c carmine	3.00	4.00
B4	SP3	20c dk bl	7.00	6.00
a.		Tête bêche pair	15.00	17.50

Perf. 12.

B5	SP1	5c dk grn	3.00	4.00
B6	SP2	10c carmine	3.00	4.00
B7	SP3	20c dk bl	6.00	7.00
a.		Tête bêche pair	15.00	17.50
		Nos. B2-B7 (6)	25.00	29.00

These stamps were sold at a premium of 10c each, to help defray the expenses of athletic games held at San José in December, 1924.

AIR POST STAMPS.

Airplane
AP1

Engraved

1926, June 4 Perf. 12½ Unwmkd.

C1	AP1	20c ultra	2.00	50

No. 123 Overprinted — CORREO AEREO

1930, Mar. 14 Perf. 12

C2	A75	10c car rose	65	20

AP3

1930–32 Perf. 12½

C3	AP3	5c on 10c dk brn ('32)	25	10
a.		Inverted surcharge	6.00	
C4	AP3	20c on 50c ultra	25	20
C5	AP3	40c on 50c ultra	50	20

Telegraph Stamp Overprinted — Correo Aereo

1930, Mar. 19

C6	AP3	1col orange	1.25	30

No. 079 Surcharged in Red

1930, Mar. 11

C7	O7	8c on 1col lil & blk	75	60
C8	O7	20c on 1col lil & blk	1.00	75
C9	O7	40c on 1col lil & blk	2.00	1.50
C10	O7	1col on 1col lil & blk	3.00	2.00

AP6

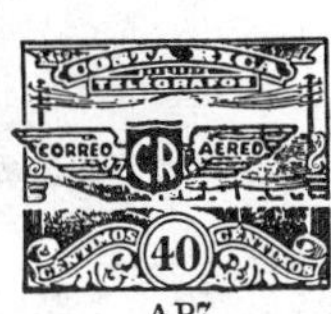

AP7

Red Surcharge on Revenue Stamps

1931–32 Perf. 12

C11	AP6	2col on 2col gray grn	27.50	15.00
C12	AP6	3col on 5col lil brn	27.50	15.00
C13	AP6	5col on 10col gray blk	27.50	15.00

There were two printings of this issue which were practically identical in the colors of the stamps and the surcharges.

Nos. C11 and C13 have the date "1929" on the stamp, No. C12 has "1930".

Black Overprint on Telegraph Stamp

1932, Mar. 8 Perf. 12½

C14	AP7	40c green	2.50	50
a.		Inverted ovpt.	20.00	

Mail Plane about to Land
AP8

Allegory of Flight
AP9

1934, Mar. 14 Perf. 12

C15	AP8	5c green	25	10
C16	AP8	10c car rose	25	8
C17	AP8	15c chocolate	60	15
C18	AP8	20c dp bl	65	12
C19	AP8	25c dp org	85	10
C20	AP8	40c ol blk	1.50	12
C21	AP8	50c gray blk	1.00	25
C22	AP8	60c org yel	2.00	30
C23	AP8	75c dl vio	3.00	60
C24	AP9	1col dp rose	2.25	15
C25	AP9	2col lt bl	2.50	50
C26	AP9	5col black	6.50	4.00
C27	AP9	10col red brn	11.00	7.50
		Nos. C15-C27 (13)	32.35	13.97

Stamps Nos. C15 to C27 with holes punched through were for use of government officials.

See also Nos. C216–C219.

Airplane over Poás Volcano
AP10

1937, Feb. 10

C28	AP10	1c black	12	10
C29	AP10	2c brown	12	10
C30	AP10	3c dk vio	12	10

First Fair of Costa Rica.

Puntarenas
AP11

National Bank
AP12

Perf. 12, 12½

1937, Dec. 15 **Unwmkd.**

C31	AP11	2c blk gray	8	8
C32	AP11	5c green	15	12
C33	AP11	20c dp bl	50	40
C34	AP11	1.40col ol brn	5.00	4.00

Wmkd. Wavy Lines. (229)

1938, Jan. 11 *Perf. 12½*

C35	AP12	1c purple	8	6
C36	AP12	3c red org	10	6
C37	AP12	10c car rose	20	15
C38	AP12	75c brown	3.00	3.00

Nos. C31 to C38 were issued to commemorate the National Products Exposition held at San José in December, 1937.

Airport Administration Building, La Sabana—AP13

1940, May 2 **Engraved** **Unwmkd.**

C39	AP13	5c green	15	10
C40	AP13	10c rose pink	20	15
C41	AP13	25c lt bl	25	20
C42	AP13	35c red brn	45	45
C43	AP13	60c red org	70	70
C44	AP13	85c violet	2.00	1.75
C45	AP13	2.35col turq grn	11.00	11.00
		Nos. C39-C45 (7)	14.75	14.35

Issued to commemorate the opening of the International Airport at La Sabana.

Duran Sanatorium
AP14

Overprinted "Dia Panamericano de la Salud / 2-Diciembre 1940" and Bar in Black

1940, Dec. 2 *Perf. 12*

C46	AP14	10c scarlet	20	15
C47	AP14	15c purple	25	25
C48	AP14	25c lt bl	45	40
C49	AP14	35c bis brn	70	65
C50	AP14	60c pck grn	90	90
C51	AP14	75c olive	2.00	2.25
C52	AP14	1.35col red org	9.00	9.00
C53	AP14	5col sepia	35.00	40.00
C54	AP14	10col red lil	65.00	75.00
		Nos. C46-C54 (9)	113.50	128.60

Pan-American Health Day. Exist without overprint. Few copies of C53–C54 were sold for postal purposes, nearly all having been obtained by philatelic speculators.

No. 174 Surcharged in Black or Blue

AEREO
Aviación Panamericana
Dic. 17 1940
15 CENTIMOS 15

1940, Dec. 17 *Perf. 14*

C55	A95	15c on 50c yel (Bk)	75	75
C56	A95	30c on 50c yel (Bl)	75	75

Issued in commemoration of Pan-American Aviation Day, proclaimed by President F. D. Roosevelt.

The 15c surch. exists on #171, price $40.

International Soccer Game at National Stadium—AP15

1941, May 8 *Perf. 12*

C57	AP15	15c red	1.25	25
C58	AP15	30c dp ultra	1.50	40
C59	AP15	40c red brn	1.50	60
C60	AP15	50c purple	2.00	1.35
C61	AP15	60c brt grn	2.50	1.50
C62	AP15	75c yel org	4.00	2.25
C63	AP15	1col dl vio	7.50	6.00
C64	AP15	1.40col rose	15.00	14.00
C65	AP15	2col bl grn	30.00	27.50
C66	AP15	5col black	65.00	65.00
		Nos. C57-C66 (10)	130.25	118.85

Issued to commemorate the Caribbean and Central American Soccer Championship. See also Nos. C121–C123.

Air Post Stamps of 1934 Overprinted or Surcharged in Black

Mayo 1941
Tratado Limítrofe
Costa Rica - Panamá

with New Values and Bars.

1941, June 2

C67	AP8	5c on 20c dp bl	30	25
C68	AP8	15c on 20c dp bl	40	30
C69	AP8	40c on 75c dl vio	60	40
C70	AP9	65c on 1col dp rose	1.10	90
C71	AP9	1.40col on 2col lt bl	5.50	4.50
C72	AP9	5col black	20.00	16.50
C73	AP9	10col red brn	22.50	22.50
		Nos. C67-C73 (7)	50.40	45.35

Issued in commemoration of the settlement of the Costa Rica-Panama border dispute.

Nos. C67–C73 are found with hyphen omitted in overprint.

University Types of Regular Issue, 1941.

1941, Aug. 26 *Perf. 12*

C74	A107	15c salmon	40	20
C75	A106	30c lt bl	60	25
C76	A107	40c orange	70	50
C77	A106	60c turq grn	85	75
C78	A107	1col violet	3.50	2.75
C79	A106	2col black	8.50	6.50
C80	A107	5col sepia	27.50	22.50
		Nos. C74-C80 (7)	42.05	33.45

National University, founded in 1940.

Portrait Type of Regular Issue, 1943–47.

Designs: 40c, Manuel Aguilar. No. C83, Francisco Morazan. No. C83A, Jose R. De Gallegos. 50c, Jose M. Alfaro. 60c, Francisco M. Oreamuno. 65c, Jose M. Castro. 85c, Juan Rafael Mora. 1col, Jose M. Montealegre. 1.05col, Braulio Carrillo. 1.15col, Jesus Jimenez. 1.40 col, Bruno Carranza. 2col, Tomas Guardia.

1943-45 **Engraved.**

C81	A109	10c rose pink	15	8
C82	A109	40c blue	35	12
C82A	A109	40c car rose ('45)	35	20
C83	A109	45c magenta	50	40
C83A	A109	45c blk ('45)	30	18
C84	A109	50c turq grn	2.00	30
C84A	A109	50c red org ('45)	45	30
C85	A109	60c brt ultra	65	25
C85A	A109	60c brt grn ('45)	30	20
C86	A109	65c scarlet	1.00	40
C86A	A109	65c brt ultra ('45)	35	30
C87	A109	85c dp org	1.25	55
C87A	A109	85c dl pur ('45)	1.65	70
C88	A109	1col black	1.75	35
C88A	A109	1col scar ('45)	75	30
C88B	A109	1.05col bis brn ('45)	90	60
C89	A109	1.15col red brn	2.25	1.85
C89A	A109	1.15col grn ('45)	3.25	1.25
C90	A109	1.40col dp vio	3.50	2.50
C90A	A109	1.40col org yel ('45)	2.00	1.75
C91	A109	2col black	5.50	1.25
C91A	A109	2col ol grn ('45)	1.75	50
		Nos. C81-C91A (22)	30.95	14.33

See also Nos. C124–C127, C179–C181.

Nos. C26-C27 Overprinted in Red or Blue

Legislacion Social
15 Setiembre 1943

1943, Sept. 16

C92	AP9	5col blk (R)	5.00	4.00
C93	AP9	10col red brn (Bl)	10.00	7.50

Mercury and Plane
AP31

1944, Jan. 19

C94	AP31	10c red org	25	20
C95	AP31	15c dk car	30	20
C96	AP31	40c brt ultra	50	40
C97	AP31	45c dp red lil	60	50
C98	AP31	60c turq grn	85	75
C99	AP31	1col dk red brn	1.75	1.50
C100	AP31	1.40col gray blk	10.00	9.00
C101	AP31	5col violet	27.50	27.50
C102	AP31	10col black	50.00	50.00
		Nos. C94-C102 (9)	91.75	90.05

Issued to commemorate the 100th anniversary of the founding of the City of San Ramón.

Very few copies of the 5col or 10col stamps were sold for postal purposes, nearly all having been obtained by philatelic speculators.

No. CO10 With Additional Overprint in Black **1944**

1944, Nov. 22

C103	AP9	1col dp rose	1.00	60
a.		Blue ovpt.	50.00	

Nos. CO1-13 Overprinted in Carmine or Black **1945**

1945, Jan. 12 *Perf. 12* **Unwmkd.**

C104	AP8	5c green	1.00	1.00
C105	AP8	10c car rose (Bk)	1.00	1.00
C106	AP8	15c chocolate	1.00	1.00
C107	AP8	20c dp bl	60	60
C108	AP8	25c dp org (Bk)	1.00	1.00
C109	AP8	40c ol blk	60	60
C110	AP8	50c gray blk	1.00	1.00
C111	AP8	60c org yel (Bk)	1.50	60
C112	AP8	75c dl vio	1.25	1.00
C113	AP9	1col dp rose (Bk)	1.25	60
C114	AP9	2col lt bl	8.00	8.00
C115	AP9	5col black	10.00	10.00
C116	AP9	10col red brn (Bk)	15.00	15.00
		Nos. C104-C116 (13)	43.20	41.40

AP32

Telegraph Stamps Overprinted in Black or Carmine.

Perf. 12½

1945, Feb. 28 **Unwmkd.**

C117	AP32	40c grn (C)	25	12
C118	AP32	50c ultra (C)	30	12
C119	AP32	1col org (Bk)	65	40

Florence Nightingale and Edith Cavell—AP33

1945 **Engraved.**

C120	AP33	1col blk & car	75	50

Issued to commemorate the 60th anniversary of the Costa Rican Red Cross Society.

Soccer Type of 1941.

Inscribed: "Febrero 1946."

1946, May 13 *Perf. 12*

C121	AP15	25c green	1.50	1.10
C122	AP15	30c dl yel	1.50	1.10
C123	AP15	55c dp bl	1.75	1.10

Portrait Type of 1943–47.

Designs: 25c, Aniceto Esquivel. 30c, Vicente Herrera. 55c, Prospero Fernandez. 75c, Bernardo Soto.

1946, May 12

C124	A109	25c blue	20	12
C125	A109	30c red brn	25	20
C126	A109	55c plum	40	30
C127	A109	75c bl grn	60	40

Hospital of St. John of God
AP38

1946, June 24 *Perf. 12½* **Unwmkd.**

Center in Black.

C128	AP38	5c yel grn	10	10
C129	AP38	10c dk brn	10	10
C130	AP38	15c carmine	10	10
C131	AP38	25c dk bl	20	20
C132	AP38	30c dp org	40	30
C133	AP38	40c ol grn	20	20
C134	AP38	50c violet	35	35
C135	AP38	60c dk sl grn	75	70
C136	AP38	75c brown	60	50
a.		Horiz. pair, imperf. btwn.	100.00	
C137	AP38	1col blue	75	40
C138	AP38	2col brn org	1.10	90
C139	AP38	3col dk vio brn	2.75	2.75
C140	AP38	5col yellow	3.50	3.50
		Nos. C128-C140 (13)	10.90	10.10

Rafael Iglesias
AP39

Designs: 3col, Ascensión Esquivel. 5col, Cleto González Víquez. 10col, Ricardo Jiménez Oreamuno.

Wmkd.
Small Star in Shield, Multiple. (215)

1947, Jan. 15 Engraved *Perf. 14*
Center in Black.

C141	AP39	2col blue	1.50	1.10
C142	AP39	3col dp car	2.25	1.50
C143	AP39	5col dk grn	3.50	2.25
C144	AP39	10col orange	6.50	4.00

Nos. C121 to C123 Surcharged in Black

Habilitado para
₡ 0.15
Decreto Nº 16 de
28 de abril de 1947

1947, May 5 *Perf. 12* Unwmkd.

C145	AP15	15c on 25c grn	1.25	1.10
C146	AP15	15c on 30c dl yel	1.25	1.10
C147	AP15	15c on 55c dp bl	1.25	1.10

Nos. C145-C147 exist with inverted surcharge; No. C145 with double surcharge, one inverted.

Columbus in Cariarí
AP43

1947, May 19 Engr. *Perf. 12½*
Center in Black.

C148	AP43	25c green	30	18
C149	AP43	30c dp ultra	30	18
C150	AP43	40c red org	40	20
C151	AP43	45c violet	50	35
C152	AP43	50c brt car	60	30
C153	AP43	65c brn org	1.50	1.00
		Nos. C148-C153 (6)	3.60	2.21

Nos. C84A, C85A, C127, C88A, and C88B Surcharged with New Value in Black or Red.

1947, June 3 *Perf. 12*

C154	A109	15c on 50c red org	25	25
C155	A109	15c on 60c brt grn (R)	25	25
C156	A109	15c on 75c bl grn (R)	25	25
C157	A109	15c on 1col scar	30	30
C158	A109	15c on 1.05col bis brn	25	25
		Nos. C154-C158 (5)	1.30	1.30

Early Steam Locomotive
AP44

Engraved
1947, Nov. 10 *Perf. 12½* Unwmkd.

C159	AP44	35c bl grn & blk	1.00	50

Issued to commemorate the 50th anniversary of the electric railroad to the Pacific coast.

Roosevelt Type of Regular Issue.

1947, Aug. 26 *Perf. 12*

C160	A122	15c green	12	10
C161	A122	30c car rose	18	15
C162	A122	45c red brn	35	35
C163	A122	65c org yel	40	40
C164	A122	75c blue	50	40
C165	A122	1col ol grn	75	70
C166	A122	2col black	2.00	1.85
C167	A122	5col scarlet	4.00	4.00
		Nos. C160-C167 (8)	8.30	7.95

National Theater
AP46

Rafael Iglesias
AP47

1948, Jan. 26 *Perf. 12½*
Center in Black.

C168	AP46	15c brt ultra	20	15
C169	AP46	20c red	25	20
C170	AP47	35c dk grn	35	30
C171	AP46	45c purple	50	35
C172	AP46	50c carmine	50	35
C173	AP46	75c red vio	1.00	1.00
C174	AP46	1col olive	1.85	1.50
C175	AP46	2col red brn	3.00	2.25
C176	AP47	5col org yel	5.00	4.25
C177	AP47	10col brt bl	11.00	8.50
		Nos. C168-C177 (10)	23.65	18.85

50th anniversary of National Theater.

No. C150 Surcharged in Carmine

HABILITADO
PARA
₡ 0.35

1948, Apr. 21

C178	AP43	35c on 40c red org & blk	45	45

Exists with surcharge inverted.

Portrait Type of 1943–47.

Designs: 5c, Salvador Lara. 15c, Carlos Duran.

1948 Engraved *Perf. 12*

C179	A109	5c sepia	15	6
C180	A109	10c ol brn	15	10
C181	A109	15c violet	12	10

Nos. C88B, C120, C89A and C90A Surcharged in Carmine or Black

1824-1949
125 Aniversario
de la Anexión
Guanacaste
₡ 0.55

Perf. 12½, 12

1949, Aug. 28 Unwmkd.

C182	A109	35c on 1.05col bis brn	25	20
C183	AP33	50c on 1col blk & car	40	35
a.		2nd & 3rd lines both read "125 Aniversario"	7.50	7.50
C184	A109	55c on 1.15col grn	65	55
C185	A109	55c on 1.40col org yel (Bk)	65	50

Issued to commemorate the 125th anniversary of the annexation of the province of Guanacaste.

Overprint differs on No. C183, with "Guanacaste" in capitals, and lower case "a" in "Anexión."

The variety "l" for "i" in "Anexion" is found on Nos. C182, C184 and C185.

Symbols of U.P.U.
AP48

1950, Jan. 11 Photo. *Perf. 11½*

C186	AP48	15c lil rose	20	10
C187	AP48	25c chlky bl	25	10
C188	AP48	1col gray grn	50	20

Issued to commemorate the 75th anniversary of the formation of the Universal Postal Union.

Battle of El Tejar, Cartago
AP49

Occupation of Limón
AP50

Bull (Cattle Raising)
AP51

Designs: 25c, Lucha ranch. 35c, Trenches of San Isidro Battalion. 55c and 75c, Observation post. 80c and 1col, Dr. Carlos Luis Valverde.

Inscribed: "Guerra de Liberacion Nacional 1948."

Engraved; Center Photogravure.

1950, July 20 *Perf. 12½*
Center in Black.

C189	AP49	15c brt car	20	10
C190	AP50	20c dl grn	30	20
C191	AP49	25c dl bl	35	25
C192	AP49	35c chestnut	40	25
C193	AP49	55c lilac	80	35
C194	AP49	75c red org	1.25	50
C195	AP50	80c gray	1.25	75
C196	AP50	1col org yel	1.75	85
		Nos. C189-C196 (8)	6.30	3.25

Issued to commemorate the second anniversary of the War for National Liberation.

Inscribed: "Feria Nacional Agricola Ganadera e Industrial Cartago 1950."

1950, July 27

Designs: 1c, 10c, 2col, Bull. 2c, 30c and 3col, Tuna fishing. 3c and 65c, Pineapple. 5c, 50c and 5col, Bananas. 45c, 80c and 10col, Coffee picker.

Center in Black.

C197	AP51	1c brt grn	10	8
C198	AP51	2c brt bl	10	8
C199	AP51	3c chocolate	10	8
C200	AP51	5c dp ultra	10	8
C201	AP51	10c green	15	8
C202	AP51	30c purple	30	18
C203	AP51	45c vermilion	35	25
C204	AP51	50c bl gray	50	15
C205	AP51	65c dk bl	60	35
C206	AP51	80c dp rose	1.25	1.00
C207	AP51	2col org yel	3.50	2.75
C208	AP51	3col blue	5.00	4.00
C209	AP51	5col carmine	10.00	10.00
C210	AP51	10col dp cl	12.50	11.00
		Nos. C197-C210 (14)	34.55	30.08

Issued to publicize the National Agricultural, Livestock and Industrial Fair, Cartago, 1950.

Queen Isabella I and Caravels of Columbus
AP52

Engraved.

1952, Mar. 4 *Perf. 13* Unwmkd.

C211	AP52	15c carmine	10	10
C212	AP52	20c orange	15	15
C213	AP52	25c ultra	20	10
C214	AP52	55c dp grn	50	40
C215	AP52	2col violet	1.50	75
		Nos. C211-C215 (5)	2.45	1.50

Issued to commemorate the 500th anniversary of the birth of Queen Isabella I of Spain.

Mail Plane Type of 1934.

1952-53 *Perf. 12.*

C216	AP8	5c blue	12	8
C217	AP8	10c green	15	8
C218	AP8	15c car rose ('53)	18	8
C219	AP8	35c purple	50	15

Nos. C149-C151, C153 Surcharged in Red: "HABILITADO PARA CINCO CENTIMOS 1953"

1953, Apr. 24 *Perf. 12½*
Center in Black.

C220	AP43	5c on 30c dp ultra	1.25	1.10
C221	AP43	5c on 40c red org	10	10
C222	AP43	5c on 45c vio	10	10
C223	AP43	5c on 65c brn org	30	25

Nos. C161-C163 Surcharged in Black

1953, Apr. 11 *Perf. 12*

C224	A122	15c on 30c car rose	25	20
C225	A122	15c on 45c red brn	25	15
C226	A122	15c on 65c org yel	25	15

Refinery of Vegetable Oils and Fats
AP53

Industries: 10c, Pottery. 15c, Sugar. 20c, Soap. 25c, Lumber. 30c, Matches. 35c, Textiles. 40c, Leather. 45c, Tobacco. 50c, Preserving. 55c, Canning. 60c, General. 65c, Metals. 75c, Pharmaceuticals. 1col, Paper. 2col, Rubber. 3col, Airplane maintenance. 5col, Marble. 10col, Beer.

Engraved; Center Photogravure

1954 *Perf. 13x12½* Unwmkd.
Center in Black

C227	AP53	5c red	10	6
C228	AP53	10c dk bl	15	6
C229	AP53	15c green	12	6
C230	AP53	20c violet	15	10
C231	AP53	25c magenta	15	10
C232	AP53	30c purple	45	30
C233	AP53	35c red vio	25	12
C234	AP53	40c black	40	25
C235	AP53	45c dk grn	75	35
C236	AP53	50c vio brn	50	15
C237	AP53	55c yellow	35	12
C238	AP53	60c brown	90	50
C239	AP53	65c carmine	1.10	75
C240	AP53	75c violet	1.65	65
C241	AP53	1col blue	50	30
a.		Imperf., pair	100.00	
C242	AP53	2col rose pink	1.50	90
C243	AP53	3col ol grn	2.25	1.50
C244	AP53	5col black	3.50	1.25
C245	AP53	10col yellow	10.00	7.50
		Nos. C227-C245 (19)	24.77	15.02

See also Nos. C252–C255A.

Globe and Rotary Emblem AP54 — Map of Costa Rica AP55

Designs: 25c, Hand protecting boy. 40c, 2col, Hospital. 45c, Globe and palm leaves. 60c, Lighthouse.

1956, Feb. 7 Engraved. *Perf. 12*

C246 AP54 10c green 15 6
C247 AP54 25c dk bl 20 18
C248 AP54 40c dk brn 50 40
C249 AP54 45c brt red 35 30
C250 AP54 60c dk red vio 40 35
C251 AP54 2col yel org 1.00 70
Nos. C246-C251 (6) 2.60 1.99

Issued to commemorate the 50th anniversary of Rotary International (in 1955).

Industries Type of 1954
Engraved; Center Photogravure

Designs: 80c, Pharmaceuticals. Other designs as in 1954.

1956–59 Center in Black *Perf. 12*

C252 AP53 5c ultra 20 6
C253 AP53 10c vio bl 20 6
C254 AP53 15c org yel 20 6
C255 AP53 75c red org 40 25

Perf. 13x12½

C255A AP53 80c pur & gray ('59) 70 60
Nos. C252-C255A (5) 1.70 1.03

1957, June 21 Engr. *Perf. 13½x13*

Designs: 10c, Map of Guanacaste. 15c, Inn. 20c, House of Santa Rosa. 25c, Gen. Jose Manuel Quiros. 30c, Old Presidential Palace. 35c, Joaquin Bernardo Calvo. 40c, Luis Molina. 45c, Gen. Jose Joaquin Mora. 50c, Gen. Jose Maria Canas. 55c, Juan Santamaria monument. 60c, National monument. 65c, Antonio Vallerriestra. 70c, Ramon Castilla y Marquesado. 75c, San Carlos fortress. 80c, Francisco Maria Oreamuno. 1col, Pres. Juan Rafael Mora.

C256 AP55 5c lt bl 8 6
C257 AP55 10c green 12 8
C258 AP55 15c dp org 10 8
C259 AP55 20c lt brn 20 12
C260 AP55 25c vio bl 20 15
C261 AP55 30c violet 30 20
C262 AP55 35c car rose 30 20
C263 AP55 40c slate 30 20
C264 AP55 45c rose red 35 25
C265 AP55 50c ultra 35 25
C266 AP55 55c ocher 60 25
C267 AP55 60c brt car 45 35
C268 AP55 65c carmine 50 35
C269 AP55 70c org yel 65 45
C270 AP55 75c emerald 60 40
C271 AP55 80c dk brn 70 50
C272 AP55 1col black 75 50
Nos. C256-C272 (17) 6.55 4.39

Centenary of War of 1856–57.

Cleto Gonzalez Viquez AP56 — Highway and Gonzalez Viquez AP57

Designs: 10c, Ricardo Jimenez Oreamuno. 20c, Puntarenas wharf and Jimenez. 35c, Post and Telegraph Bldg. and Jimenez. 55c, Pipeline and Gonzalez Viquez. 80c, National Library and Gonzalez Viquez. 1col, Electric train and Jimenez. 2col, Gonzales and Jimenez.

1959 Engraved. *Perf. 13½*

C274 AP56 5c car & ultra 6 6
C275 AP56 10c red & gray 6 6

Perf. 13½x13

C276 AP57 15c dk bl grn & blk 6 6
C277 AP57 20c car & brn 15 10
C278 AP57 35c rose lil & bl 20 15
C279 AP57 55c ol & vio 40 30
C280 AP57 80c ultra 60 50
C281 AP57 1col org & mar 60 45
C282 AP57 2col gray & mar 1.50 1.25
Nos. C274-C282 (9) 3.63 2.93

Soccer AP58

Designs: Various soccer scenes.

Photogravure.

1960, March 7 *Perf. 13½* Unwmkd.

C283 AP58 10c black 10 8
C284 AP58 25c ultra 20 15
C285 AP58 35c red org 25 20
C286 AP58 50c red brn 30 25
C287 AP58 85c Prus grn 1.00 75
C288 AP58 5col dp cl 3.25 3.25
Nos. C283-C288 (6) 5.10 4.68

Souvenir Sheet.
Imperf.

C289 AP58 2col blue 1.50 1.50

3rd Pan-American Soccer Games, San José, March, 1960.

Nos. C283–C288 exist imperf.

No. C289 measures 137x80mm. with black marginal inscription.

WRY Uprooted Oak Emblem AP59

1960, Apr. 7 *Perf. 11½* Unwmkd.
Granite Paper

C290 AP59 35c vio bl, blk & yel 30 25
C291 AP59 85c blk & brt pink 60 50

Issued to publicize World Refugee Year, July 1, 1959–June 30, 1960.

Banner and "OEA" AP60

Designs: 35c, "OEA" in oval. 55c, Clasped hands. 2col, "OEA" and map of Americas. 5col, Flags forming bird. 10col, Map of Costa Rica, flags and "OEA."

1960, Aug. 15 Litho. *Perf. 10*

C292 AP60 25c blk & multi 20 15
a. Multi. impression sideways 30.00
C293 AP60 35c multi 50 45
a. Pair, imperf. between 60.00
C294 AP60 55c multi 75 60
C295 AP60 5col multi 4.50 4.00
C296 AP60 10col blk & multi 7.50 6.00
Nos. C292-C296 (5) 13.45 11.20

Souvenir Sheet
Imperf.

C297 AP60 2col multi 3.25 3.25

Nos. C292–C297 issued to commemorate the Pan-American Conference, San Jose, Aug. 15.

No. C297 measures 124x76½mm. with flags of American nations forming border.

St. Louisa de Marillac and Orphanage—AP61

St. Vincent de Paul AP62

Designs: 25c, St. Vincent and old seminary. 50c, St. Louisa and sickroom. 1col, St. Vincent and new seminary.

1960, Oct. 26 Engr. *Perf. 14x13½*

C298 AP61 10c green 10 10
C299 AP61 25c carmine 10 10
C300 AP61 50c dk bl 35 25
C301 AP61 1col brn org 60 50
C302 AP62 5col brown 3.00 2.50
Nos. C298-C302 (5) 4.15 3.45

Issued to commemorate the 300th anniversary of the deaths of St. Vincent de Paul (1581?–1660) and St. Louisa de Marillac (1591–1660). Exist imperf.

Runner—AP63

Sports: 2c, Woman swimmer. 3c, Bicyclist. 4c, Weight lifter. 5c, Woman tennis player. 10c, Boxers. 25c, Soccer player. 85c, Basketball player. 1col, Baseball batter. 5col, Romulus and Remus statue. 10col, Pistol marksman.

Perf. 13½x14

1960, Dec. 14 Photo. Unwmkd.
Designs in Black

C303 AP63 1c brt yel 5 5
C304 AP63 2c lt ultra 5 5
C305 AP63 3c dp rose 5 5
C306 AP63 4c yellow 5 5
C307 AP63 5c brt yel grn 5 5
C308 AP63 10c pink 8 8
C309 AP63 25c lt bl grn 15 15
C310 AP63 85c lilac 1.50 1.25
C311 AP63 1col gray 1.75 1.50
C312 AP63 10col lt vio 15.00 12.00
Nos. C303-C312 (10) 18.73 15.23

Souvenir Sheets
Perf. 14x13½, Imperf.

C313 AP63 5col multi 5.50 5.50

17th Olympic Games, Rome, Aug. 25–Sept. 11.

No. C313 has gold marginal inscription. Size: 100x65mm.

Nos. C303–C312 exist imperf.

No. C255 Surcharged and Overprinted in Blue or Ultramarine:

"XV Campeonato Mundial de Beisbol de Aficionados"

Engraved and Photogravure

1961, Apr. 21 *Perf. 12*
Center in Black

C314 AP53 25c on 75c red org (Bl) 30 12
C315 AP53 75c red org (U) 85 35

15th Amateur Baseball Championships.

Alberto Brenes C. AP64 — Miguel Obregon AP65

Portraits: No. C317, Manuel Aguilar. No. C318, Agustin Gutierrez L. No. C319, Vicente Herrera.

1961, June 12 Photo. *Perf. 12*

C316 AP64 10c dp cl 10 10
C317 AP64 10c blue 10 10
C318 AP64 25c brt vio 20 15
C319 AP64 25c gray 20 15

First Continental Congress of Lawyers, San José, June 11–15. Exist imperf.

See also Nos. C330–C333.

1961, July 19 Litho. *Perf. 13½*

C320 AP65 10c Prus grn 8 8

Birth centenary of Prof. Miguel Obregon L. Exists imperf.

U.N. Food and Agriculture Organization AP66

United Nations Organizations: 20c, World Health Organization. 25c, Int. Labor Organization. 30c, Int. Telecommunication Union. 35c, World Meteorological Organization. 45c, UNESCO. 85c, Int. Civil Aviation Organization. 5col, "United Nations" holding the world. 10col, Int. Bank for Reconstruction and Development.

Engraved

1961, Oct. 24 *Perf. 11½* Unwmkd.

C321 AP66 10c lt grn 12 12
C322 AP66 20c orange 25 20
C323 AP66 25c Prus grn 30 25
C324 AP66 30c dk bl 30 25
C325 AP66 35c car rose 1.40 35
C326 AP66 45c violet 50 30
C327 AP66 85c blue 1.10 85
C328 AP66 10col dk sl grn 8.00 6.50
Nos. C321-C328 (8) 11.97 8.82

Souvenir Sheet
Imperf.

C329 AP66 5col ultra 4.50 4.50

Nos. C321–C329 issued for United Nations Day, Oct. 24.

No. C329 contains one imperf. stamp and has ultramarine border and marginal inscription. Size: 100x65mm.

Portrait Type of 1961

Portraits: No. C330, Dr. José Maria Soto Alfaro. No. C331, Dr. Elias Rojas Roman. No. C332, Dr. Andres Saenz Llorente. No. C333, Dr. Juan José Ulloa Giralt.

1961 Photogravure *Perf. 13½*

C330 AP64 10c bl grn 8 8
C331 AP64 10c violet 10 8

C332	AP64	25c dk gray	20	12
C333	AP64	25c dp cl	20	12

Issued to commemorate the ninth Congress of Physicians of Central America and Panama.

Nos. C229, C236 and C280 Surcharged in Black, Orange or Red.

Engraved; Center Photogravure.

1962 ***Perf. 13x12½, 13½x13***

C334	AP53	10c ("10") on 15c grn & blk	10	10
C334A	AP53	10c ("c0.10") on 15c grn & blk (R)	10	10
C335	AP53	25c on 15c grn & blk	20	12
C336	AP53	35c on 50c vio brn & blk (O)	30	20

Engraved

C337	AP57	85c on 80c ultra (R)	85	65
		Nos. C334-C337 (5)	1.55	1.17

Nos. C324 and C282 Overprinted in Red: "II CONVENCION FILATELICA CENTROAMERICANA SETIEMBRE 1962"

1962, Sept. 12 ***Perf. 11½, 13½x13***

C338	AP66	30c dk bl	65	50
C339	AP57	2col gray & mar	2.00	1.40

Issued to commemorate the second Central American Philatelic Convention.

Revenue Stamp Surcharged with New Values and "CORREO AEREO" in Red

1962 **Engraved** ***Perf. 12***

C341	A124	25c on 2c emer	12	10
C342	A124	35c on 2c emer	20	15
C343	A124	45c on 2c emer	35	30
C344	A124	85c on 2c emer	65	55

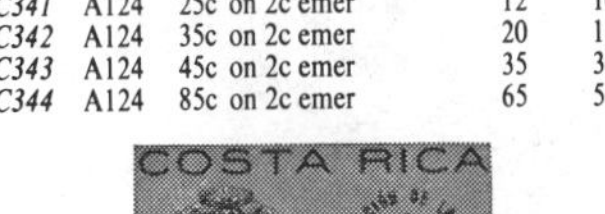

Arms and Malaria Eradication Emblem

AP67

1963, Feb. 14 **Photo.** ***Perf. 11½***

C345	AP67	25c brt rose	20	12
C346	AP67	35c brn org	25	20
C347	AP67	45c ultra	40	30
C348	AP67	85c bl grn	65	55
C349	AP67	1col dk bl	85	70
		Nos. C345-C349 (5)	2.35	1.87

Issued for the World Health Organization drive to eradicate malaria.

Central American Tapir

AP68

Designs: 5c, Paca. 25c, Jaguar. 30c, Ocelot. 35c, Whitetail deer. 40c, Manatee. 85c, White-throated capuchin monkey. 5col, White-lipped peccary.

Photogravure

1963, May ***Perf. 13½*** **Unwmkd.**

C354	AP68	5c yel ol & brn	8	8
C355	AP68	10c org & sl	8	8
C356	AP68	25c bl & yel	20	10
C357	AP68	30c lt yel grn & brn	35	30
C358	AP68	35c bis & red brn	50	25
C359	AP68	40c emer & sl bl	60	40
C360	AP68	85c grn & blk	90	60
C361	AP68	5col gray grn & choc	5.00	4.00
		Nos. C354-C361 (8)	7.71	5.81

Stamp of 1863 and Packet "William Le Lacheur"

AP69

Issue of 1863 and: 2col, Recaredo Bonilla Carrillo, Postmaster, 1862-63. 3col, Burros, overland mail transport, 1839. 10col, Burro railway car.

1963, June 26 **Lithographed**

C362	AP69	25c dl rose & chlky bl	10	8
C363	AP69	2col gray bl & org	1.75	1.25
C364	AP69	3col bis & emer	3.00	2.25
C365	AP69	10col dl grn & ocher	9.00	6.00

Centenary of Costa Rica's stamps.

Souvenir Sheets

Stamps of 1863 and San José Postmark—AP70

Perf. 13½, Imperf.

1963, June 26 **Unwmkd.**

C366	AP70	5col bl, red, grn & org	5.00	5.00

Issued to commemorate the centenary of Costa Rica's stamps. Orange marginal inscription. Size of stamp: 29x50mm. Size of sheet: 60x100mm.

In 1968 copies of No. C366 were overprinted "2-4 Agosto 1968" and "III Exposicion Filatelica Nacional / 'Costa Rica 68'." Price $5.

Animal Type of 1963 Surcharged in Red

Designs: 10c on 1c, Little anteater. 25c on 2c, Gray fox. 35c on 3c, Armadillo. 85c on 4c, Great anteater.

1963, Sept. 14 **Photo.** ***Perf. 13½***

C367	AP68	10c on 1c brt grn & org brn	10	8
C368	AP68	25c on 2c org yel & ol grn	15	8
C369	AP68	35c on 3c bluish grn & brn	18	12
C370	AP68	85c on 4c dp rose & dk brn	45	25

No. C370 exists without surcharge. Price, $50.

President John F. Kennedy

AP71

Ancestral Figure

AP72

Portraits—Presidents: 25c, Francisco J. Orlich, Costa Rica. 30c, Julio A. Rivera, El Salvador. 35c, Miguel Ydigoras F., Guatemala. 85c, Dr. Ramon Villeda M., Honduras. 1col, Luis A. Somoza, Nicaragua. 3col, Roberto F. Chiari, Panama.

1963, Dec. 7 ***Perf. 14*** **Unwmkd.**

Portraits in Black Brown

C371	AP71	25c vio brn	15	10
C372	AP71	30c brt lil rose	20	15
C373	AP71	35c ocher	25	20
C374	AP71	85c gray bl	60	40
C375	AP71	1col org brn	60	45
C376	AP71	3col lt ol grn	3.00	2.00
C377	AP71	5col gray	4.00	3.00
		Nos. C371-C377 (7)	8.80	6.30

Issued to commemorate the meeting of Central American Presidents with Pres. John F. Kennedy, San José, March 18-20, 1963.

1963-64 **Photo.** ***Perf. 12***

Ancient Art: 5c, Dog (horiz.). 10c, Ornamental stool (horiz.). 25c, Male figure. 30c, Ceremonial dancer. 35c, Ceramic vase. 50c, Frog. 55c, Bell. 75c, Six-limbed figure. 85c, Seated man. 90c, Bird-shaped jug. 1col, Twin human beaker (horiz.). 2col, Alligator (horiz.). 3col, Twin-tailed lizard. 5col, Figure under arch. 10col, Polished stone figure.

C378	AP72	5c lt yel grn & Prus grn	5	5
C379	AP72	10c buff & dk grn	6	6
C380	AP72	25c rose & dk brn	12	9
C381	AP72	30c ocher & Prus grn ('64)	15	8
C382	AP72	35c sal & sl grn	18	12
C383	AP72	45c lt bl & dk brn	20	12
C384	AP72	50c dl bl & dk brn	25	18
C385	AP72	55c yel grn & dk brn	30	18
C386	AP72	75c ocher & dk red brn	30	20
C387	AP72	85c yel & red brn	85	55
C388	AP72	90c cit & red brn	1.10	55
C389	AP72	1col lt bl & dk brn	60	35
C390	AP72	2col buff & dk grn	1.00	65
C391	AP72	3col yel grn & dk brn	1.75	1.10
C392	AP72	5col cit & sep	3.00	2.00
C393	AP72	10col rose lil & sl grn	5.00	4.50
		Nos. C378-C393 (16)	14.91	10.78

Flags of Central American States

AP73

Alfredo Gonzalez F.

AP74

Central American Independence Issue

1964 ***Perf. 14***

C394	AP73	30c bl, gray, red & blk	50	40

Nos. C381, C394 and C387 Surcharged ₡ 0.05

1964, Oct. ***Perf. 12, 14***

C395	AP72	5c on 30c ocher & Prus grn	6	6
C396	AP73	15c on 30c bl, gray, red & blk	6	6
C397	AP72	15c on 85c yel & red brn	10	6

No. C388 Surcharged: "C 0.15 / CONFERENCIA POSTAL / DE PARIS—1864"

1964 ***Perf. 12***

C398	AP72	15c on 90c cit & red brn	12	8

Paris Postal Conference.

1965, June **Photo.** ***Perf. 12***

C399	AP74	35c dk bl grn	15	10

Issued to commemorate the 50th anniversary of the National Bank and to honor Alfredo Gonzalez F., first governor of the bank.

No. C390 Overprinted: "75 ANIVERSARIO / ASILO CHAPUI / 1890 - 1965"

1965, Aug. 14 ***Perf. 12*** **Unwmkd.**

C400	AP72	2col buff & dk grn	90	65

Issued to commemorate the 75th anniversary of Chapui Asylum, San José.

Girl, FAO Emblem and Hands Holding Grain

AP75

Church of Nicoya

AP76

Designs (FAO Emblem and): 15c, Map of Costa Rica and silos (horiz.). 50c, World population chart and children. 1 col, Plane over map of Costa Rica (horiz.).

1965 **Lithographed** ***Perf. 14***

C401	AP75	15c lt brn & blk	10	8
C402	AP75	35c blk & yel	20	15
C403	AP75	50c ultra & dk grn	30	20
C404	AP75	1col grn, blk & sil	50	30

Issued for the "Freedom from Hunger" campaign of the U.N. Food and Agriculture Organization.

1965, Dec. 20 ***Perf. 13½x14***

Designs: 5c, Leonidas Briceno B. 15c, Scroll dated "25 de Julio de 1964." 35c, Map of Guanacaste and Nicoya peninsula. 50c, Dancing couple. 1col, Map showing local products.

C405	AP76	5c red brn & blk	5	5
C406	AP76	10c bl & gray	5	5
C407	AP76	15c bis & sl	6	6
C408	AP76	35c bl & sl	15	10
C409	AP76	50c gray & vio bl	25	15
C410	AP76	1col buff & sl	60	40
		Nos. C405-C410 (6)	1.16	81

Acquisition of the Nicoya territory.

Runner and Olympic Rings

AP77

Pres. Kennedy Speaking in San José Cathedral

AP78

1965, Dec. 23 ***Perf. 13x13½***

Olympic Rings and Emblem: 10c, Bicyclists. 40c, Judo. 65c, Basketball. 80c, Soccer. 1col, Hands holding torches, and Mt. Fuji.

C411	AP77	5c bis & multi	6	6
C412	AP77	10c lt lil & multi	6	6

C413	AP77	40c multi	20	15
C414	AP77	65c lem & multi	35	20
C415	AP77	80c tan & multi	50	30
C416	AP77	1col multi	65	40
a.		Souv. sheet of 2	2.25	2.25
		Nos. C411-C416 (6)	1.82	1.17

Issued to commemorate the 18th Olympic Games, Tokyo, Oct. 10–25, 1964. No. C416a contains two 1col stamps, one like No. C416, the other with gray background replacing yellow orange. Dark brown marginal inscription and red control number. Size: 68x93mm. Sheet also exists imperf.

Perf. 13½x13, 13x13½

1965, Dec. 23 Litho. Unwmkd.

Designs: 45c, Friendship 7 capsule circling globe, and Kennedy (horiz.). 85c, Kennedy and John, Jr. 1col, Curtis-Lee Mansion and flame from Kennedy grave, Arlington, Va.

C417	AP78	45c brt bl & lil	25	20
C418	AP78	55c org & brt bl	35	25
C419	AP78	85c gray, dk brn & red brn	55	35
C420	AP78	1col multi	50	40
a.		Souv. sheet of 2	1.50	1.50

Issued in memory of President John F. Kennedy (1917–63). No. C420a contains two 1col stamps, one like No. C420, the other with green background replacing dark blue. Dark gray marginal inscription and red control number. Size: 68x93mm. Sheet also exists imperf.

Firemen with Hoses

AP79

Designs: 5c, Fire engine "Knox" (horiz.). 10c, 1866 fire pump. 35c, Fireman's badge. 50c, Emblem and flags of Confederation of Central American Fire Brigades.

1965, March 12 Litho. *Perf. 11*

C421	AP79	5c blk & red	5	5
C422	AP79	10c bis & red	6	5
C423	AP79	15c blk, red brn & red	8	6
C424	AP79	35c blk & yel	18	10
C425	AP79	50c dk bl & red	30	15
		Nos. C421-C425 (5)	67	41

Centenary of San José Fire Brigade.

Nos. C381, C383, C386 and C418–C419 Surcharged

C0.15
a

C 0.50
b

1966 Photogravure *Perf. 12*

C426	AP72(a)	15c on 30c ocher & Prus grn	10	8
C427	AP72(a)	15c on 45c lt bl & dk brn	10	8
C428	AP72(a)	35c on 75c ocher & dk red brn	20	12

Perf. 13x13½

Lithographed

C429	AP78(a)	35c on 55c org & brt bl	20	12
C430	AP78(b)	50c on 85c multi	35	20
		Nos. C426-C430 (5)	95	60

Revenue Stamps (Basic Type of A124) Surcharged

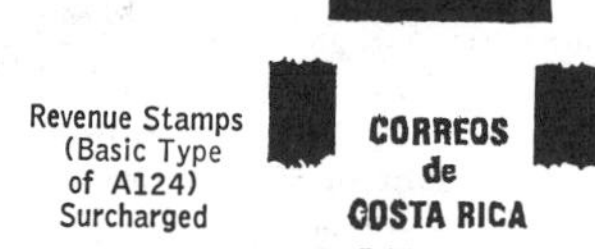

1966, Dec. Engraved *Perf. 12*

C431	A124	15c on 5c bl	10	6
C432	A124	35c on 10c cl	22	12
C433	A124	50c on 20c rose red	35	20

Central Bank of Costa Rica

AP80

1967, Mar. Litho. *Perf. 11*

C434	AP80	5c brt grn	7	5
C435	AP80	15c brown	10	6
C436	AP80	35c scarlet	20	12

Power Lines

AP81

Telecommunications Building, San Pedro

AP82

Designs: 15c, Telephone Central. 25c, La Garita Dam. 35c, Rio Mache Reservoir. 50c, Cachi Dam.

1967, Apr. 24 Litho. *Perf. 11*

C437	AP81	5c dk gray	7	5
C438	AP82	10c brt rose	7	5
C439	AP81	15c brn org	8	6
C440	AP82	25c brt ultra	13	8
C441	AP82	35c brt grn	20	10
C442	AP82	50c red brn	35	20
		Nos. C437-C442 (6)	90	54

Electrification program.

Chondrorhyncha Aromatica

AP83

Institute Emblem

AP84

Orchids: 10c, Miltonia endresii. 15c, Stanhopea cirrhata. 25c, Trichopilia suavis. 35c, Odontoglossum schlieperianum. 50c, Cattleya skinneri. 1col, Cattleya dowiana. 2col, Odontoglossum chiriquense.

1967, June 15 Engr. *Perf. 13x13½*

Orchids in Natural Colors

C443	AP83	5c multi	6	6
C444	AP83	10c ol & multi	12	6
C445	AP83	15c multi	12	8
C446	AP83	25c multi	20	15
C447	AP83	35c dl vio & multi	30	20
C448	AP83	50c brn & multi	35	25
C449	AP83	1col vio & multi	65	50
C450	AP83	2col dk ol bis & multi	1.50	1.00
		Nos. C443-C450 (8)	3.30	2.30

Issued for the University Library.

1967, Oct. 6 Litho. *Perf. 13x13½*

C451	AP84	50c vio bl, lt bl & bl	20	18

Issued to commemorate the 25th anniversary of the Inter-American Agriculture Institute.

Church of Solitude

AP85

LACSA Emblem

AP86

Costa Rican Churches: 10c, Basilica of Santo Domingo, Heredia. 15c, Cathedral of Tilaran. 25c, Cathedral of Alajuela. 30c, Mercy Church. 35c, Basilica of Our Lady of Angels. 40c, Church of St. Raphael, Heredia. 45c, Ujarras ruins. 50c, Ruins of parish church, Cartago. 55c, Cathedral of San José. 65c, Parish church, Puntarenas. 75c, Church of Orosi. 80c, Cathedral of St. Isidro, the General. 85c, St. Ramon Church. 90c, Church of the Abandonned. 1col, Coronado Church. 2col, Church of St. Teresita. 3col, Parish Church, Heredia. 5col, Carmelite Church. 10col, Limon Cathedral.

1967, Dec. 15 Engr. *Perf. 12½*

C452	AP85	5c green	4	4
C453	AP85	10c blue	5	5
C454	AP85	15c lilac	6	6
C455	AP85	25c dl yel	10	8
C456	AP85	30c org brn	12	10
C457	AP85	35c lt bl	15	12
C458	AP85	40c dp org	15	12
C459	AP85	45c dl bl grn	16	15
C460	AP85	50c olive	18	18
C461	AP85	55c brown	20	18
C462	AP85	65c car rose	25	20
C463	AP85	75c sepia	27	25
C464	AP85	80c yellow	35	30
C465	AP85	85c vio blk	40	30
C466	AP85	90c emerald	50	40
C467	AP85	1col slate	35	35
C468	AP85	3col brt grn	90	65
C469	AP85	3col orange	2.50	1.00
C470	AP85	5col vio bl	3.00	1.50
C471	AP85	10col carmine	4.00	3.25
		Nos. C452-C471 (20)	13.73	9.28

See Nos. C561–C576.

Perf. 13x13½, 13½x13

1967, Dec. 12 Litho. & Engraved

Design: 45c, LACSA emblem and jet (horiz.). 50c, Decorated wheel and anniversary emblem.

C472	AP86	40c ultra, grnsh bl & gold	15	15
C473	AP86	45c blk, pale grn, ultra & gold	18	15
C474	AP86	50c bl & multi	20	18

Issued to commemorate the 20th anniversary (in 1966) of Lineas Aereas Costaricenses, LACSA, Costa Rican Airlines.

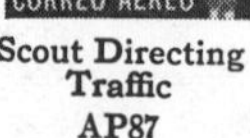

Scout Directing Traffic

AP87

Runner

AP88

Designs: 25c, Campfire under palm tree. 35c, Flag of Costa Rica, Scout flag and emblem. 50c, Encampment (horiz.). 65c, Photograph of first Scout troop (horiz.).

Lithographed and Engraved

1968, Mar. 15 *Perf. 13*

C475	AP87	15c lt bl, blk & lt brn	12	8
C476	AP87	25c lt ultra, vio bl & org	20	12
C477	AP87	35c bl & multi	30	20
C478	AP87	50c multi	35	25
C479	AP87	65c sal, dk bl & brn	50	30
		Nos. C475-C479 (5)	1.47	95

Costa Rican Boy Scouts, 50th anniversary.

1968 Lithographed *Perf. 10x11*

Sports: 40c, Women's running. 55c, Boxing. 65c, Bicycling. 75c, Weight lifting. 1col, High diving. 3col, Rifle shooting.

C481	AP88	30c multi	15	10
C482	AP88	40c multi	25	15
C483	AP88	55c multi	35	25
C484	AP88	65c lil & multi	45	25
C485	AP88	75c multi	45	25
C486	AP88	1col multi	50	35
C487	AP88	3col multi	2.25	1.25
		Nos. C481-C487 (7)	4.40	2.60

Issued to commemorate the 19th Olympic Games, Mexico City, Oct. 12–27.

Philatelic Exhibition Emblem

AP89

1969, June 5 Litho. *Perf. 11x10*

C488	AP89	35c multi	15	10
C489	AP89	40c pink & multi	18	12
C490	AP89	50c lt bl & multi	22	15
C491	AP89	2col multi	80	60

Issued to publicize the 4th National Philatelic Exhibition, San José, June 5–8.

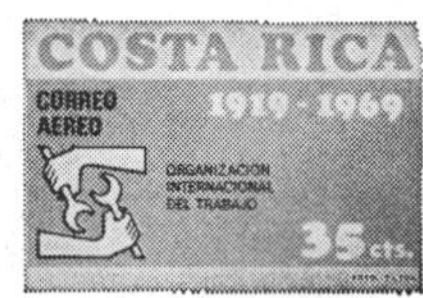

ILO Emblem

AP90

1969, Oct. 29 Litho. *Perf. 10*

C492	AP90	35c bl grn & blk	18	10
C493	AP90	50c scar & blk	27	15

Issued to commemorate the 50th anniversary of the International Labor Organization.

Soccer—AP91

Designs: 65c, Soccer ball, map of North and Central America. 85c, Soccer player. 1 col, Two players in action.

1969, Nov. 23 Litho. *Perf. 11x10*

C494	AP91	65c gray & multi	30	20
C495	AP91	75c multi	30	20
C496	AP91	85c multi	38	25
C497	AP91	1col pink & multi	45	30

Issued to publicize the 4th Soccer Championships (CONCACAF), Nov. 23–Dec. 7.

Stylized Crab—AP92

1970, May 14 Litho. *Perf. 12½*

C498	AP92	10c blk & lil rose	3	3
C499	AP92	15c blk & yel	5	5
C500	AP92	50c blk & brn org	12	10
C501	AP92	1.10col blk & emer	27	20

Issued to publicize the 10th Inter-American Cancer Congress, May 22–29.

Costa Rica No. 124, Magnifying Glass and Stamps AP93

Design: 2col, Father and son with stamps and album.

1970, Sept. 14 Litho. *Perf. 11*

C502	AP93	1col ultra, brn & car rose	30	20
C503	AP93	2col blk, pink & ultra	60	50

The 5th National Philatelic Exhibition.

EXPO Emblem and Costa Rican Cart—AP94

Designs (EXPO Emblem and): 10c, Japanese floral arrangement (vert.). 35c, Pavilion and Tower of the Sun. 40c, Japanese tea ceremony. 45c, Woman picking coffee (vert.). 55c, Earth seen from moon (vert.).

1970, Oct. 22 Litho. *Perf. 13x13½*

C504	AP94	10c multi	6	4
C505	AP94	15c grn & multi	9	6
C506	AP94	35c bl & multi	15	10
C507	AP94	40c gray & multi	20	12
C508	AP94	45c multi	20	15
C509	AP94	55c blk & multi	20	15
		Nos. C504-C509 (6)	90	62

Issued to commemorate EXPO '70 International Exhibition, Osaka, Japan, March 15–Sept. 13.

Escazu Valley, by Margarita Bertheau—AP95

Paintings: 25c, "Irazu," by Rafael A. Garcia (vert.). 80c, Shore landscape, by Teodorico Quiros. 1col, "The Other Face," by Cesar Valverde. 2.50col, Mother and Child, by Luis Daell (vert.).

1970, Nov. 4 Litho. *Perf. 12½*

C510	AP95	25c multi	12	7
C511	AP95	45c multi	12	10
C512	AP95	80c multi	25	15
C513	AP95	1col multi	25	20
C514	AP95	2.50col multi	60	50
		Nos. C510-C514 (5)	1.34	1.02

Arms of Costa Rica, 1964 AP96

Various Coats of Arms, dated: 10c, Nov. 27, 1906. 15c, Sept. 29, 1848. 25c, April 21, 1840. 35c, Nov. 22, 1824. 50c, Nov. 2, 1824. 1col, March 6, 1824. 2col, May 10, 1823.

1971, Feb. 10 Litho. *Perf.14x13½*

C515	AP96	5c buff & multi	3	3
C516	AP96	10c multi	4	3
C517	AP96	15c yel & multi	6	5
C518	AP96	25c pink & multi	9	7
C519	AP96	35c multi	15	10
C520	AP96	50c rose & multi	15	10
C521	AP96	1col beige & multi	25	15
C522	AP96	2col multi	50	30
		Nos. C515-C522 (8)	1.27	83

National Theater AP97

1971, Apr. Litho. *Perf. 11*

C523	AP97	2col plum	50	40

Organization of American States meeting.

José Matias Delgado, Manuel José Arce AP98

Flag of Costa Rica AP99

Independence Leaders: 10c, Miguel Larreinaga and Manuel Antonio de la Cerda, Nicaragua. 15c, José Cecilio del Valle, Dionisio de Herrera, Honduras. 35c, Pablo Alvarado and Florencio del Castillo, Costa Rica. 50c, Antonio Larrazabal and Pedro Molina, Guatemala. 2col, Costa Rica coat of arms.

1971, Sept. 14 *Perf. 13*

C524	AP98	5c multi	3	3
C525	AP98	10c multi	4	3
C526	AP98	15c gray, brn & blk	6	5
C527	AP98	35c multi	15	12
C528	AP98	50c multi	15	12
C529	AP99	1col multi	25	15
C530	AP99	2col multi	50	40
		Nos. C524-C530 (7)	1.18	90

Sesquicentennial of Central American independence.

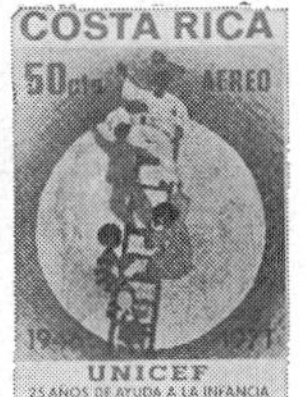

Soccer Federation Emblem AP100 — Children of the World AP101

1971, Dec.

C531	AP100	50c multi	15	10
C532	AP100	60c multi	15	10

50th anniversary of Soccer Federation of Costa Rica.

1972, Jan. 11 *Perf. 12½*

C533	AP101	50c multi	15	10
C534	AP101	1.10col red & multi	30	25

25th anniversary (in 1971) of the United Nations International Children's Fund (UNICEF).

Tree of Guanacaste AP102

Designs: 40c, Hermitage, Liberia. 55c, Petroglyphs, Rincón Brujo. 60c, Painted head, sculpture from Curubandé (vert.).

1972, Feb. 28 *Perf. 11*

C535	AP102	20c brn, ol & brt grn	10	7
C536	AP102	40c brn & ol	15	10
C537	AP102	55c blk & brn	15	12
C538	AP102	60c blk, buff & ver	20	15

Bicentenary of the founding of the city of Liberia, Guanacaste.

Farm and Family AP103 — Inter-American Exhibitions AP104

Designs: 45c, Cattle, dairy products and meat (horiz.). 50c, Kneeling figure with plant. 10col, Farmer and map of Americas.

1972, June 30 Litho. *Perf. 12½*

C539	AP103	20c multi	10	7
C540	AP103	45c multi	15	10
C541	AP103	50c dp yel, grn & blk	15	10
C542	AP103	10col brn, org & blk	2.50	1.50

30th anniversary of the Inter-American Institute of Agricultural Sciences.

1972, Aug. 26 Litho. *Perf. 13*

C543	AP104	50c org & brn	15	10
C544	AP104	2col bl & vio	50	40

4th Interamerican Philatelic Exhibition, EXFILBRA, Rio de Janeiro, Aug. 26–Sept. 2.

First Book Printed in Costa Rica AP105

Design: 50c, 5col, National Library (horiz.).

1972, Dec. 7 Litho. *Perf. 12½*

C545	AP105	20c brt bl	8	7
C546	AP105	50c gold & multi	15	10
C547	AP105	75c multi	20	15
C548	AP105	5col multi	1.25	1.00

International Book Year 1972.

Road to Irazú Volcano AP106

1972–73 *Perf. 11x11½, 11½x11*

Multicolored

C549	AP106	5c *like 20c*	3	3
C550	AP106	15c *Coco-Culebra Bay*	7	4
C551	AP106	20c *shown*	10	7
C552	AP106	25c *like 15c*	10	8
C553	AP106	40c *Manuel Antonio Beach*	15	10
C554	AP106	45c *Tourist Office emblem*	15	12
C555	AP106	50c *Lindora Lake*	15	12
C556	AP106	60c *San Jose P.O. (vert.)*	20	15
C557	AP106	80c *like 40c*	25	20
C558	AP106	90c *like 45c*	25	20
C559	AP106	1col *like 50c*	25	20
C560	AP106	2col *like 60c*	50	40
		Nos. C549-C560 (12)	2.20	1.71

Tourism year of the Americas.

Issue dates: 20c, 25c, 80c, 90c, 1col and 2col, Dec. 26, 1972. Others, Mar. 21, 1973.

Church Type of 1967

Designs as Before

1973, July 16 Engr. *Perf. 12½*

C561	AP85	5c sl grn	6	4
C562	AP85	10c olive	7	5
C563	AP85	15c orange	8	6
C564	AP85	25c brown	10	8
C565	AP85	30c rose cl	10	8
C566	AP85	35c violet	12	10
C567	AP85	40c brt grn	12	10
C568	AP85	45c dl yel	15	10
C569	AP85	50c rose mag	15	10
C570	AP85	55c blue	15	12
C571	AP85	65c black	20	15
C572	AP85	75c rose red	20	15
C573	AP85	80c yel grn	20	15
C574	AP85	85c lilac	25	20
C575	AP85	90c brt pink	25	20
C576	AP85	1col dk bl	25	20
		Nos. C561-C576 (16)	2.45	1.88

Human Rights Flame AP107 — OAS Emblem AP108

1973 Photogravure *Perf. 10½*

C577	AP107	50c blk & red	15	10

25th anniversary of the Universal Declaration of Human Rights.

1973, Dec. 17 Litho. *Perf. 10½*

C578	AP108	20c dk bl & dp car	10	5

25th anniversary of the Organization of American States.

Joaquin Vargas Calvo
AP109

AP110

1974, Jan. 14

Multicolored

C579	AP109	20c *shown*	10	6
C580	AP109	20c *Alejandro Monestel*	10	6
C581	AP109	20c *Julio Mata*	10	6
C582	AP109	60c *Julio Fonseca*	20	15
C583	AP109	2col *Rafael A. Chaves*	50	35
C584	AP109	5col *Manuel M. Gutierrez*	1.25	1.00
		Nos. C579-C584 (6)	2.25	1.68

Costa Rican composers honored by the National Symphony Orchestra.

Revenue Stamps Overprinted "Habilitado para Correo Aereo"

1974, Apr. 5 Engraved *Perf. 12*

C585	AP110	50c brown	15	10
C586	AP110	1col violet	25	15
C587	AP110	2col orange	50	30
C588	AP110	5col olive	1.25	1.00

Telephone Building, San Pedro
AP111

EXFILMEX 74 Emblem
AP112

Designs: 65c, Rio Macho Control (horiz.). 85c, Turbines, Rio Macho Center. 1.25col, Cachi Dam and reservoir (horiz.). 2col, I.C.E. Headquarters.

1974, July 30 Litho. *Perf. 10½*

C589	AP111	50c gold & multi	15	10
C590	AP111	65c gold & multi	20	12
C591	AP111	85c gold & multi	25	15
C592	AP111	1.25col gold & multi	30	20
C593	AP111	2col gold & multi	50	30
		Nos. C589-C593 (5)	1.40	87

25th anniversary of Costa Rican Electrical Institute (I.C.E.).

1974, Aug. 22 *Perf. 13*

C594	AP112	65c green	20	15
C595	AP112	3col lil rose	75	50

5th Inter-American Philatelic Exhibition, EXFILMEX-74 UPU, Mexico City, Oct. 26–Nov. 3.

Map of Costa Rica, 4-S Emblem
AP113

Design: 50c, Young harvesters and 4-S emblem.

1974, Oct. 7 Litho. *Perf. 12x11*

C596	AP113	20c brt grn	10	5
C597	AP113	50c multi	15	10

25th anniversary of 4-S Clubs of Costa Rica (similar to US 4-H Clubs).

Roberto Brenes Mesen
AP114

"Life Insurance"
AP115

Designs: 85c, "Love and Death," manuscript (horiz.). 5col, Hands of writer.

1974, Oct. 14 Litho. *Perf. 10½*

C598	AP114	20c blk & brn	10	5
C599	AP114	85c blk & red	25	20
C600	AP114	5col blk & red brn	1.25	1.00

Birth centenary of Roberto Brenes Mesen, educator and writer.

1974, Oct. 30 *Perf. 14*

Designs: 20c, Ricardo Jiménez Oreamuno and Tomás Soley Güell (horiz.). 50c, Harvest Insurance (hand holding shovel; horiz.). 85c, Maritime insurance (hand holding paper boat). 1.25col, INS emblem. 2col, Workers rehabilitation (arm with crutch). 2.50col, Workers' Compensation (hand holding wrench). 20col, Fire insurance (hands protecting house).

C601	AP115	20c multi	9	5
C602	AP115	50c multi	15	10
C603	AP115	65c multi	15	10
C604	AP115	85c multi	20	15
C605	AP115	1.25col multi	30	20
C606	AP115	2col multi	50	30
C607	AP115	2.50col multi	65	50
C608	AP115	20col multi	5.00	4.00
		Nos. C601-C608 (8)	7.04	5.40

Costa Rican Insurance Institute (Instituto Nacional de Seguros, INS), 50th anniversary.

WPY Emblem
AP116

Oscar J. Pinto F.
AP117

1974, Nov. 13 Litho. *Perf. 11x11½*

C609	AP116	2col vio bl & red	50	30

World Population Year.

1974, Dec. 2 *Perf. 13*

Designs: 50c, Alberto Montes de Oca D., champion sharpshooter. 1col, Eduardo Garnier, sports promoter. O. J. Pinto, introducer of soccer.

C610	AP117	20c gray & dk bl	9	5
C611	AP117	50c gray & dk bl	15	10
C612	AP117	1col gray & dk bl	25	15

First Central American Olympic Games, held in Guatemala, 1973.

Mormodes Buccinator
AP118

Masdevallia Ephippium
AP119

Designs: Orchids.

1975, Mar. 7 Litho. *Perf. 10½, 13½*

Multicolored

C613	AP118	25c *shown*	6	5
C614	AP118	25c *Gongora claviodora*	6	5
C615	AP119	25c *shown*	6	5
C616	AP119	25c *Encyclia spondiadum*	6	5
C617	AP118	65c *Lycaste skinnery alba*	20	15
C618	AP118	65c *Peristeria elata*	20	15
C619	AP119	65c *Miltonia roezelii*	20	15
C620	AP119	65c *Brassavola digbyana*	20	15
C621	AP118	80c *Epidendrum mirabile*	25	20
C622	AP118	80c *Barkeria lindleyana*	25	20
C623	AP119	80c *Cattleya skinneri*	25	20
C624	AP119	80c *Sobralia macrantha*	25	20
C625	AP118	1.40col *Lycaste cruenta*	35	25
C626	AP118	1.40col *Oncidium obryzatum*	35	25
C627	AP119	1.40col *Gongora armeniaca*	35	25
C628	AP119	1.40col *Sievekingia suavis*	35	25

Perf. 13½

C629	AP118	1.75col *Hexisea imbricata*	45	30
C630	AP118	2.15col *Warcewiczella discolor*	55	30
C631	AP119	2.50col *Oncidium kramerianum*	65	50
C632	AP119	3.25col *Cattleya dowiana*	85	60
		Nos. C613-C632 (20)	5.94	4.30

5th National Flower Exhibition.

Stamps of same denominations printed se-tenant. Nos. C613–C628 were printed in both perforations on two different papers: dull finish and shiny. Nos. C629–C632 were printed on shiny paper.

Radio Club Emblem
AP120

Members' Flags and Emblem
AP121

Design: 2col, Federation emblem.

1975, Apr. 16 Litho. *Perf. 13½*

C633	AP120	1col blk & red lil	25	15
C634	AP121	1.10col multi	30	20
C635	AP120	2col blk & bl	50	30

16th Central American Radio Amateurs' Convention, San José, May 2–4.

A little time given to study of the arrangement of the Scott Catalogue can make it easier to use effectively.

Nicoya Beach
AP122

Designs: 75c, Driving cattle. 1col, Colonial Church, Nicoya. 3col, Savannah riders (vert.).

1975, Aug. 1 Litho. *Perf. 13½*

C636	AP122	25c gray & multi	6	5
C637	AP122	75c gray & multi	20	20
C638	AP122	1col gray & multi	25	15
C639	AP122	3col gray & multi	75	60

Sesquicentennial of annexation of Nicoya District.

Costa Rica No. 158
AP123

Designs (Type A90 of 1932): No. C641, No. 159. No. C642, No. 160. No. C643, No. 161.

1975, Aug. 14 Litho. *Perf. 12*

C640	AP123	2.20col blk & org	60	50
C641	AP123	2.20col blk & dk grn	60	50
C642	AP123	2.20col blk & car rose	60	50
C643	AP123	2.20col blk & dk bl	60	50

6th National Philatelic Exhibition, San José, Aug. 14–17. Nos. C640–C643 printed se-tenant.

IWY Emblem
AP124

1975, Oct. Litho. *Perf. 10½*

C644	AP124	40c vio bl & red	10	8
C645	AP124	1.25col blk & ultra	30	20

International Women's Year 1975.

U.N. Emblem
AP125

Designs: 60c, U.N. General Assembly (horiz.). 1.20col, U.N. Headquarters, New York.

1975, Oct. 24 *Perf. 12*

C646	AP125	10c bl & blk	4	3
C647	AP125	60c multi	15	12
C648	AP125	1.20col multi	30	20

30th anniversary of the United Nations.

The Visitation, by Jorge Gallardo
AP126

'20–30' Club Emblem
AP127

Paintings by Jorge Gallardo: 1col, Nativity and Star. 5col, St. Joseph in his Workshop, Virgin and Child.

1975, Nov. ***Perf. 10½***

C649	AP126	50c multi	15	10
C650	AP126	1col multi	25	15
C651	AP126	5col multi	1.25	1.00

Christmas 1975.

1976, Jan. 16 **Litho.** ***Perf. 12***

C652	AP127	1col multi	25	15

'20–30' Club of Costa Rica, 20th anniversary.

Quercus Brenessi Trel
AP128

"Literary Development"
AP129

Plants: 30c, Maxillaria albertii schecht. 55c, Calathea brenesii standl. 2col, Brenesia costaricensis schlecht. 10col, Philodendron brenesii standl.

1976, March 1 ***Perf. 10½***

C653	AP128	5c multi	3	3
C654	AP128	30c multi	10	6
C655	AP128	55c multi	15	12
C656	AP128	2col tan & multi	50	30
C657	AP128	10col multi	2.50	2.00
		Nos. C653-C657 (5)	3.28	2.51

Prof. Alberto Manuel Brenes Mora, botanist, birth centenary.

1976, Apr. 9 **Litho.** ***Perf. 16***

Designs: 1.10col, Man holding book, stylized. 5col, Costa Rican flag emanating from book (horiz.).

C658	AP129	15c multi	6	4
C659	AP129	1.10col multi	25	20
C660	AP129	5col multi	1.25	1.00

Publishing in Costa Rica.

Post-rider, 1839
AP130

Costa Rica No. 13, Post Office
AP131

Designs: 65c, Costa Rica No. 14 and Post Office. 85c, Costa Rica No. 15 and Post Office. 2col, UPU Monument, Bern (vert.).

1976, May 24 ***Perf. 10½***

C661	AP130	20c ap grn & blk	8	5
C662	AP131	50c bis & multi	15	10
C663	AP131	65c multi	20	15
C664	AP131	85c multi	25	20
C665	AP130	2col blk & lt bl	50	40
		Nos. C661-C665 (5)	1.18	90

Centenary of Universal Postal Union (in 1974).

Nos. C662–C664 exist without the surcharges on reproductions of Nos. 13–15.

Telephones, 1876 and 1976
AP132

Designs: 2col, Wall telephone. 5col, Alexander Graham Bell.

1976, June 28

C666	AP132	1.60col lt bl & blk	40	30
C667	AP132	2col multi	50	30
C668	AP132	5col yel & blk	1.25	1.00

Centenary of first telephone call by Alexander Graham Bell, Mar. 10, 1876.

Inverted Center Stamp of 1901 and Association Emblems—AP133

1976, Nov. 11 **Litho.** ***Perf. 10½***

C669	AP133	50c multi	15	10
C670	AP133	1col multi	25	15
C671	AP133	2col multi	50	30

Souvenir Sheet

Design: 5col, 1901 stamp between Costa Rican Philatelic Society and Interamerican Philatelic Federation emblems.

Perf. 12, Imperf.

C672	AP133	5col multi	1.25	1.25

7th National Philatelic Exhibition and 9th Plenary Assembly of the Interamerican Philatelic Federation (FIAF), San José, Nov. 1976. No. C672 has black marginal inscription. Size: 75x60mm.

"Seeing Eye" and Map of Costa Rica
AP134

Amadeo Quiros Blanco
AP135

1976, Nov. 22 ***Perf. 16***

C673	AP134	35c blk & bl	10	8
C674	AP135	2col multi	50	30

General Audit Office, 25th anniversary.

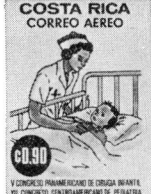

Nurse Attending Child
AP136

LACSA Circling Globe
AP137

Design: 1.10col, National Children's Hospital (horiz.).

1976, Nov. 29

C675	AP136	90c multi	25	20
C676	AP136	1.10col multi	30	25

5th Panamerican Congress of Pediatric Surgery and 12th Congress of Pediatrics.

1976, Dec. 1 ***Perf. 10½***

Designs: 1.20col, Route map. 3col, LACSA emblem and Costa Rican flag.

C677	AP137	1col multi	25	15
C678	AP137	1.20col multi	30	20
C679	AP137	3col multi	75	50

Costa Rican Air Lines (LACSA), 30th anniversary.

Boston Tea Party
AP138

Designs: 5col, Declaration of Independence. 10col, Ringing Liberty Bell to announce Independence (vert.).

1976, Dec. 24

C681	AP138	5col multi	1.25	1.00
C682	AP138	10col multi	2.50	2.00

American Bicentennial.

Tree of Guanacaste
AP139

Felipe J. Alvarado
AP140

Designs (Rotary Emblem and): 60c, Dr. Paul Blanco Cervantes Hospital (horiz.). 3col, Map of Costa Rica (horiz.). 10col, Paul Harris.

1977, Mar. 31 **Litho.** ***Perf. 16***

C683	AP139	40c vio bl & multi	10	8
C684	AP140	50c blk & multi	15	10
C685	AP139	60c vio bl & multi	15	15
C686	AP139	3col vio bl & multi	75	60
C687	AP140	10col blk & multi	2.50	2.00
		Nos. C683-C687 (5)	3.65	2.93

Rotary Club of San José, 50th anniversary.

Boruca Cloth
AP141

Design: 1.50col, Painted wood ornament.

1977, Feb. 22

C688	AP141	75c multi	20	15
C689	AP141	1.50col multi	40	20

National Artisan and Small Industry Program.

Juana Pereira
AP142

Alonso de Anguciana de Gamboa
AP143

Designs: 1col, First Church of Our Lady of the Angels (horiz.). 1.10col, Our Lady of the Angels (gold sculpture). 1.25col, Crown of Our Lady of the Angels.

1977, June 6 **Litho.** ***Perf. 10½***

C690	AP142	50c multi	15	10
C691	AP142	1col multi	25	15
C692	AP142	1.10col multi	30	20
C693	AP142	1.25col multi	35	25

50th anniversary of the coronation of Our Lady of the Angels, patron saint of Costa Rica.

1977, July 4 **Litho.** ***Perf. 10½***

Designs: 75c, Church of Esparza. 1col, Statue of Our Lady of Candlemas. 2col, Statue of Diego de Artieda y Chirino.

C694	AP143	35c multi	10	8
C695	AP143	75c multi	20	15
C696	AP143	1col multi	25	15
C697	AP143	2col multi	50	40

400th anniversary of the founding of Esparza.

CARE Emblem and Child
AP144

Design: 1col, CARE emblem and soybeans (horiz.).

1977, Sept. 14 **Litho.** ***Perf. 16***

C698	AP144	80c multi	20	15
C699	AP144	1col multi	25	15

20th anniversary of CARE (relief organization) in Costa Rica.

Institute's Emblem
AP145

First Map of Americas, 1540
AP146

1977, Oct. 21 Litho. *Perf. 16*

C700	AP145	50c blk & multi	15	10
C701	AP146	1.40col blk & multi	35	30

Hispanic Cultural Institute of Costa Rica, 25th anniversary.

Mercy Church, by Ricardo Ulloa B.
AP147

Health Ministry Emblem
AP148

Paintings: 1col, Christ, by Floria Pinto de Herrero. 5col, St. Francis and the Birds, by Louisa Gonzalez Y Saenz.

1977, Nov. 9 Litho. *Perf. 10½*

C702	AP147	50c multi	15	10
C703	AP147	1col multi	25	15
C704	AP147	5col multi	1.25	1.00

1977, Nov. 16 *Perf. 16*

C705	AP148	1.40col multi	35	30

Creation of Ministry of Health.

Picnic
AP149

José de San Martin
AP150

Designs: 50c, Weaver. 2col, Beach scene. 5col, Fruit and vegetable market. 10col, Swans on lake.

1978, Mar. 21 Litho. *Perf. 10½*

C706	AP149	50c blk & multi	15	10
C707	AP149	1col blk & multi	25	15
C708	AP149	2col blk & multi	50	30
C709	AP149	5col blk & multi	1.25	1.00
C710	AP149	10col blk & multi	2.50	2.00
		Nos. C706-C710 (5)	4.65	3.55

Conference of Latin American Tourist Organizations.

1978, Aug. 7 Litho. *Perf. 10½*

C711	AP150	5col multi	1.25	1.00

Gen. José de San Martin (1778-1850), soldier and statesman, fought for South American independence.

Geographical Institute Emblem
AP151

University Federation Emblem
AP152

1978, Aug. 28 Litho. *Perf. 12½*

C712	AP151	5col multi	1.20	90

Pan-American Geography and History Institute, 50th anniversary.

1978, Sept. 18 *Perf. 11*

C713	AP152	80c ultra	20	15

Central American University Federation, 30th anniversary.

Emblems
AP153

1978, Oct. 24 *Perf. 16*

C714	AP153	2col aqua, blk & gold	48	35

6th Interamerican Philatelic Exhibition, Argentina 78, Buenos Aires, Oct. 1978.

Nos. C629-C631 Overprinted: "50 Aniversario del / primer vuelo de PAN AM / en Costa Rica / 1928-1978"

1978, Nov. 1 Litho. *Perf. 13½*

C715	AP118	1.75col multi	42	30
C716	AP118	2.15col multi	50	38
C717	AP119	2.50col multi	60	45

First Pan Am flight in Costa Rica, 50th anniversary.

Nos. C629-C631 Overprinted: "50 Aniversario de la / visita de Lindbergh a / Costa Rica 1928-1978"

1978, Nov. 1

C718	AP118	1.75col multi	42	30
C719	AP118	2.15col multi	50	38
C720	AP119	2.50col multi	60	45

50th anniversary of Lindbergh's visit to Costa Rica.

Nos. C603 and C607 Surcharged with New Value, 4 Bars and: "Centenario del / Asilo Carlos / Maria Ulloa / 1878-1978"

1978, Nov. 8 *Perf. 14*

C721	AP115	50c on 65c multi	12	10
C722	AP115	2col on 2.50col multi	48	35

Asilo Carlos Maria Ulloa, birth centenary.

No. C617-C620, C630-C631 Surcharged with New Value and 4 Bars.

1978, Nov. 13 Litho. *Perf. 10½, 13½*

C723	AP118	50c on 65c	12	10
C724	AP118	50c on 65c	12	10
C725	AP119	50c on 65c	12	10
C726	AP119	50c on 65c	12	10
C727	AP118	1.20col on 2.15col	30	20
C728	AP119	2col on 2.50col	48	35
		Nos. C723-C728 (6)	1.26	95

Nos. C723-C726 printed se-tenant.

Star over Map of Costa Rica
AP154

"Flying Men", Chorotega
AP155

1978, Nov. 13 *Perf. 10½*

C729	AP154	50c bl & blk	12	10
C730	AP154	1col rose lil & blk	24	18
C731	AP154	5col org & blk	1.20	85

Christmas 1978. Nos. C729-C731 printed in sheets of 100 and se-tenant in sheets of 15 (3x5).

1978, Nov. 20 *Perf. 11½*

Designs: 1.20col, Oviedo giving his History of Indies to Duke of Calabria (horiz.). 10col, Lord of Oviedo's coat of arms.

C732	AP155	85c multi	20	15
C733	AP155	1.20col blk & lt bl	30	20
C734	AP155	10col multi	2.40	1.75

500th birth anniversary of Gonzalo Fernandez de Oviedo, first chronicler of Spanish Indies.

Mgr. Domingo Rivas
AP156

San José Cathedral
AP157

1978, Dec. 6 *Perf. 16*

C735	AP156	1col blk & ind	24	18

Perf. 13½

C736	AP157	20col multi	4.80	3.50

Centenary of the Cathedral of San José.

View of Coco Island
AP158

Designs: 2.10, 3, 5 col, various views of Coco Island. 10col, Installation of memorial plaque, people and flag. 5, 10col (vert.).

1979, Apr. 30 Litho. *Perf. 10½*

C737	AP158	90c multi	22	15
C738	AP158	2.10col multi	50	35
C739	AP158	3col multi	72	55
C740	AP158	5col multi	1.20	90
C741	AP158	10col multi	2.40	1.80
a.		Souvenir sheet of 3	5.25	5.25
		Nos. C737-C741 (5)	5.04	3.75

Visit of Pres. Rodrigo Carazo Odio to Coco Island, June 24, 1978, in the interest of national defense. No. C741a contains Nos. C737-C741. Multicolored margin shows map of Costa Rica. Size: 140x103mm.

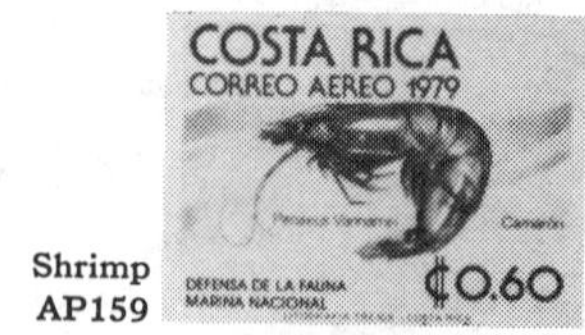

Shrimp
AP159

Designs: 85c, Mahogany snapper. 1.80col, Corvina. 3col, Crayfish. 10col, Tuna.

1979, May 14 Litho. *Perf. 13½*

C742	AP159	60c multi	15	10
C743	AP159	85c multi	20	15
C744	AP159	1.80col multi	45	32
C745	AP159	3col multi	72	55
C746	AP159	10col multi	2.40	1.80
		Nos. C742-C746 (5)	3.92	2.92

Marine life protection.

Hungry Nestlings, IYC Emblem
AP160

1979, May 24 *Perf. 11*

C747	AP160	1col multi	25	18
C748	AP160	2col multi	50	35
C749	AP160	20col multi	4.80	3.60

International Year of the Child.

Microwave Transmitters, Mt. Irazu
AP161

1979, June 28 Litho. *Perf. 14*

Design: 1col, Arenal Dam (horiz.).

C750	AP161	1col multi	25	18
C751	AP161	5col multi	1.25	90

Costa Rican Electricity Institute, 30th anniversary.

Costa Rica No. 1 and Rowland Hill
AP162

Design: 10col, Penny Black and Hill.

1979, July 16 *Perf. 13*

C752	AP162	5col lil rose & bl gray	1.25	18
C753	AP162	10col dl bl & blk	1.25	90

Sir Rowland Hill (1795-1879), originator of penny postage.

Poverty, by Juan Ramon Bonilla
AP163

Sculptures: 60c, Hope, by Hernan Gonzalez. 2.10col, Cattle, by Victor M. Bermudez (horiz.). 5col, Bust of Clorito Picado, by Juan Rafael Chacon. 20col, Mother and Child, by Francisco Zuniga.

1979, July 16 Litho. *Perf. 12*

C754	AP163	60c multi	15	10
C755	AP163	1col multi	25	18
C756	AP163	2.10col multi	45	32
C757	AP163	5col multi	1.25	90
C758	AP163	20col multi	5.00	1.80
		Nos. C754-C758 (5)	7.10	3.30

National Sculpture Contest.

Danaus Plexippus
AP164

Butterflies: 1col, Phoebis philea. 1.80col, Rothschildia. 2.10col, Prepona omphale. 2.60col, Marpesia marcella. 4.05col, Morpho cypris.

1979, Aug. 31 Litho. *Perf. 13½*

C759	AP164	60c multi	15	10
C760	AP164	1col multi	25	18
C761	AP164	1.80col multi	45	32
C762	AP164	2.10col multi	52	38
C763	AP164	2.60col multi	65	48
C764	AP164	4.05col multi	1.00	75
		Nos. C759-C764 (6)	3.02	2.21

SOS Emblem, Houses AP165

Children's Drawings: 5col, 5.50col, Landscapes (diff.).

1979, Sept. 18

C765	AP165	2.50col multi	62	45
C766	AP165	5col multi	1.25	90
C767	AP165	5.50col multi	1.35	1.00

SOS Children's Villages, 30th anniversary.

José Joaquin Rodriguez Z.—AP166

Presidents of Costa Rica: 60c, Rafael Iglesias C. 85c, Ascension Esquivel Ibarra. 1col, Cleto Gonzalez Viquez. 2col, Ricardo Jimenez Oreamuno.

1979, Oct. 8 Litho. *Perf. 13½*

C768	AP166	10c dk bl	5	3
C769	AP166	60c dl pur	15	10
C770	AP166	85c red org	20	15
C771	AP166	1col red org	25	18
C772	AP166	2col brown	50	35
		Nos. C768-C772 (5)	1.15	81

Nos. C768-C772 printed in sheets of 100 and se-tenant in sheets of 25 (5x5).

See Nos. C790-C794.

Holy Family, Creche—AP167

1979, Nov. 16 Litho. *Perf. 12½*

C773	AP167	1col multi	25	18
C774	AP167	1.60col multi	42	30

Christmas 1979.

Reforestation—AP168

1980, Jan. 14 Litho. *Perf. 11*

C775	AP168	1 col multi	25	18
C776	AP168	3.40 col multi	85	62

Anatomy Lesson, by Rembrandt—AP169

1980, Feb. 7 Litho. *Perf. 10½*

C777	AP169	10col multi	2.50	1.80

Legal medicine teaching in Costa Rica, 50th anniversary.

Rotary International, 75th Anniversary—AP170

1980, Feb. 26 *Perf. 16*

C778	AP170	2.10col multi	52	38
C779	AP170	5col multi	1.25	90

Gulf of Nicoya, Satellite Photo—AP171

1980, Mar. 10 Litho. *Perf. 12½*

C780	AP171	2.10 col *Puerto Limon*	52	38
C781	AP171	5 col *shown*	1.25	90

14th International Symposium on Remote Sensing of the Environment, San José, Apr. 23-30.

Soccer, Moscow '80 Emblem—AP172

1980, Apr. 16 Litho. *Perf. 10½*

C782	AP172	1col *shown*	25	18
C783	AP172	3col *Bicycling*	75	55
C784	AP172	4.05col *Baseball*	1.00	75
C785	AP172	20col *Swimming*	5.00	3.50

22nd Summer Olympic Games, Moscow, July 19-Aug. 3.

Poas Volcano—AP173

1980, May 14 Litho. *Perf. 10½*

C786	AP173	1 col *shown*	25	18
C787	AP173	2.50col *Cahuita Beach*	65	45

National Parks Service, 10th anniversary.

José Maria Zeledon Brenes, Score—AP174

Design: 10col, Manuel Maria Gutierrez.

1980, June 25 Litho. *Perf. 12½*

C788	AP174	1col multi	25	18
C789	AP174	10col multi	2.50	1.80

National anthem composed by Brenes (words) and Gutierrez (music).

President Type of 1979

Presidents of Costa Rica: 1col, Alfredo Gonzalez F. 1.60col, Federico Tinoco G. 1.80col, Francisco Aguilar B. 2.10col, Julio Acosta G. 3col, Leon Cortes C.

1980, Aug. 14 Litho. *Perf. 11*

C790	AP166	1col dk red	25	18
C791	AP166	1.60col sl bl	40	28
C792	AP166	1.80col brown	45	30
C793	AP166	2.10col dl grn	52	38
C794	AP166	3col dk pur	75	55
		Nos. C790-C794 (5)	2.37	1.69

8th National Philatelic Exhibition AP175

Fruits AP176

1980, Sept. 11 *Perf. 13½*

C795	AP175	5col multi	1.25	90
C796	AP175	20col multi	5.00	3.60

1980, Sept. 24 *Perf. 10½*

C797	AP176	10c *shown*	3	3
C798	AP176	60c *Cacao*	15	10
C799	AP176	1col *Coffee*	25	18
C800	AP176	2.10col *Bananas*	52	38
C801	AP176	3.40col *Flowers*	85	60
C802	AP176	5col *Sugar cane*	1.25	90
		Nos. C797-C802 (6)	3.05	2.19

Giant Tree, by Jorge Carvajal

AP177

Virgin and Child, by Raphael

AP178

Paintings: 2.10col, Secret Look, by Rolando Cubero. 2.45col, Consuelo, by Fernando Carballo. 3col, Volcano, by Lola Fernandez. 4.05col, attending Mass, by Francisco Amighetti.

1980, Oct. 22 Litho. *Perf. 10½*

C803	AP177	1col multi	25	18
C804	AP177	2.10 col multi	52	38

Size: 28x30mm.

C805	AP177	2.45col multi	62	45

Size: 22x36mm.

C806	AP177	3col multi	75	55
C807	AP177	4.05col multi	1.00	75
		Nos. C803-C807 (5)	3.14	2.31

1980, Nov. 11 *Perf. 13½*

Christmas 1980: 10col, Virgin and Child and St. John, by Raphael.

C808	AP178	1col multi	25	18
C809	AP178	10col multi	2.50	1.80

Juan Santamaria International Airport—AP179

1980, Dec. 11 Litho. *Perf. 10½*
Sizes: 30x30mm., 31x25mm. (1.30 col), 25x32mm. (2.60 col)

C810	AP179	1col *Caldera Harbor*	25	18
C811	AP179	1.30 col *shown*	32	24
C812	AP179	2.10 col *Rio Frio Railroad Bridge*	52	38
C813	AP179	2.60 col *Highway to Colon*	65	48
C814	AP179	5col *Huetar post office*	1.25	90
		Nos. C810-C814 (5)	2.99	2.18

Paying your taxes means progress.

Repertorio Americano Cover, J. Garcia Monge and Signature—AP180

1981, Jan. 2 Litho. *Perf. 10½*

C815	AP180	1.60col multi	40	30
C816	AP180	3col multi	75	55

Birth centenary of J. Garcia Monge, founder of Repertorio Americano journal.

Arms of Aserri (Site of Cornea Bank) AP181

Harpia Harpyja AP182

1981, Jan. 28 Litho. *Perf. 13½*

C817	AP181	1 col shown	25	18
C818	AP181	1.80 co col Eye	45	32
C819	AP181	5 col Rojas	1.25	90

Establishment of human cornea bank, founded by Abelardo Rojas.

1981 *Perf. 11*

C820	AP182	2.10 col shown	52	38
C821	AP182	2.50 col Ara macao	62	45
C822	AP182	3 col Felis concolor	75	55
C823	AP182	5.50 col Ateles geoffrovi	1.40	1.05

Medical and Surgical Clinic—AP183

1981, Apr. 8 **Litho.** ***Perf. 10½***

C824	AP183	5c shown	3	3
C825	AP183	10c Physiology class	3	3
C826	AP183	50c Medical school, A. Chavarria (1st dean)	5	3
C827	AP183	1.30 col Music school	14	8
C828	AP183	3.40 col Carlos Monge Alfaro Library	35	25
C829	AP183	4.05 col R.F. Brenes, rector (1952-1961), vert.	45	30
		Nos. C824-C829 (6)	1.05	72

University of Costa Rica, 40th anniversary.

Mail Transport by Horse—AP184

1981, May 6 **Litho.** ***Perf. 10½***

C830	AP184	1 col shown	25	18
C831	AP184	2.10 col Train, 1857	52	38
C832	AP184	10 col Mail carriers, 1858	2.50	1.75

Heinrich von Stephan (1831-1897), founder of UPU.

13th World Telecommunications Day—AP185

1981, May 18 ***Perf. 11***

C833	AP185	5 col multi	1.25	90
C834	AP185	25 col multi	6.25	4.50

Bishop Bernardo Thiel AP186

Juan Santamaria AP187

1981, June 8 **Litho.** ***Perf. 10½***

C835		Strip of 5, stained glass windows	60	45
a.	AP186	1 col Sts. Peter & Paul	12	8
b.	AP186	1 col St. Vincent de Paul	12	8
c.	AP186	1 col Death of St. Joseph	12	8
d.	AP186	1 col Archangel Michael	12	8
e.	AP186	1 col Holy Family	12	8
C836	AP186	2 col shown	24	16

Consecration of Bernardo Augusto Thiel as Bishop of San Jose.

1981, June 26 ***Perf. 13½***

C837	AP187	1 col shown	12	8
C838	AP187	2.45 col Alajuela Cathedral, horiz.	30	20

Alajuela province.

Potters—AP188

1981, July 10 **Litho.** ***Perf. 10½***

C839	AP188	15c shown	3	3
C840	AP188	1.60 col Bricklayers	20	12
C841	AP188	1.80 col Farmers	22	14
C842	AP188	2.50 col Fishermen	30	18
C843	AP188	3 col Nurse, patient	36	24
C844	AP188	5 col Children, traffic policeman	60	40
		Nos. C839-C844 (6)	1.71	1.11

Model of New Natl. Archives—AP189

Natl. Archives Centenary: 1.40col, Leon Fernandez Bonilla, founder (vert.). 2col, Arms (vert.). 3col, St. Thomas University, former headquarters.

1981, Aug. 24 **Litho.** **Perf 13½**

C845	AP189	1.40col multi	18	12
C846	AP189	2col multi	24	16
C847	AP189	3col multi	36	24
C848	AP189	3.50col multi	42	28

Men Reaching for Sun, Map—AP190

1981, Sept. 9 **Litho.** ***Perf. 11***

C849	AP190	1 col Man in wheelchair, stairs, vert.	12	8
C850	AP190	2.60 col Man reaching for scale, vert.	32	20
C851	AP190	10 col shown	1.20	80

Intl. Year of the Disabled.

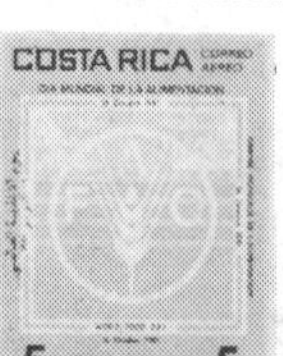

World Food Day AP191

1981, Oct. 16 **Litho.** ***Perf. 10½***

C852	AP191	5 col multi	60	40
C853	AP191	10 col multi	1.20	80

President Type of 1979

President of Costa Rica: 1 col, Rafael A. Calderon Guardia, 1940. 2 col, Teodoro Picado Michalski, 1944. 3 col, José Figueres Ferrer, 1953. 5 col, Otilio Ulate Blanco, 1949. 10 col, Mario Echandi Jimenez, 1958.

1981, Dec. 7 **Litho.** ***Perf. 13½***

C854	AP166	1 col pink	12	8
C855	AP166	2 col orange	24	16
C856	AP166	3 col green	36	24
C857	AP166	5 col dk bl	60	40
C858	AP166	10 col blue	1.20	80
		Nos. C854-C858 (5)	2.52	1.68

Bar Assoc. of Costa Rica Centenary (1981) AP192

1982, Mar. 22 **Litho.** ***Perf. 13½***

C859	AP192	1 col Emblem, horiz.	12	6
C860	AP192	2 col E. Figueroa, 1st pres.	24	10
C861	AP192	20 col Bar building, horiz.	2.40	1.10

National Progress AP193

1982 ***Perf. 10½***

C862	AP193	95c Housing	10	5
C863	AP193	1.15 col Agricultural fair	12	6
C864	AP193	1.45 col Education	18	8
C865	AP193	1.65 col Drinkable water	20	10
C866	AP193	1.80 col Rural medical care	22	12
C867	AP193	2.10 col Recreational areas	25	14
C868	AP193	2.35 col Natl. Theater Square	28	15
C869	AP193	2.60 col Communications	30	16
C870	AP193	3 col Electric railroad	36	18
C871	AP193	4.05 col Irrigation	48	24
		Nos. C862-C871 (10)	2.49	1.28

Issue dates: 1.80 col, 2.10 col, 2.60 col, 3 col, 4.05 col, May 5; others, June 16.

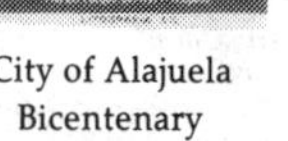

City of Alajuela Bicentenary AP194

Perez Zeledon County, 50th Anniv. (1981) AP195

Designs: 5 col, Central Park Fountain. 10 col, Juan Santamaria Historical and Cultural Museum (horiz.). 15 col, Church of Christ of Esquipulas. 20 col, Monsignor Esteban Lorenzo de Tristan, 25 col, Father Juan Manuel Lopez del Corral.

1982, Aug. 9

C872	AP194	5 col multi	60	30
C873	AP194	10 col multi	1.20	50
C874	AP194	15 col multi	1.80	80
C875	AP194	20 col multi	2.40	1.00
C876	AP194	25 col multi	3.00	1.25
		Nos. C872-C876 (5)	9.00	3.85

1982, Aug. 30

Designs: 10c, Saint's Stone. 50c, Monument to Mothers. 1 col, Pedro Perz Zeledon. 1.25 col, St. Isidro Labrador Church. 3.50 col, Municipal Building (horiz.). 4.25 col, Arms.

C877	AP195	10c multi	3	3
C878	AP195	50c multi	6	3
C879	AP195	1 col multi	12	6
C880	AP195	1.25 col multi	15	6
C881	AP195	3.50 col multi	42	20
C882	AP195	4.25 col multi	50	24
		Nos. C877-C882 (6)	1.28	62

Nos. C695 and C813 Surcharged.

1982, Oct. 28 **Litho.** ***Perf. 10½***

C883	AP143	3col on 75c multi	36	18
C884	AP179	5col on 2.6col multi	60	30

Nos. C640-C643 Surcharged and Overprinted: "IX EXPOSICION FILATELICA—1982."

1982, Oct. 28 ***Perf. 12***

C885	AP123	8.40col on 2.20col #C640	1.00	50
C886	AP123	8.40col on 2.20col #C641	1.00	50
C887	AP123	8.40col on 2.20col #C642	1.00	50
C888	AP123	8.40col on 2.20col #C643	1.00	50
C889	AP123	9.70col on 2.20col #C640	1.20	60
C890	AP123	9.70col on 2.20col #C641	1.20	60
C891	AP123	9.70col on 2.20col #C642	1.20	60
C892	AP123	9.70col on 2.20col #C643	1.20	60
		Nos. C885-C892 (8)	8.80	4.40

9th Natl. Stamp Exhibition.

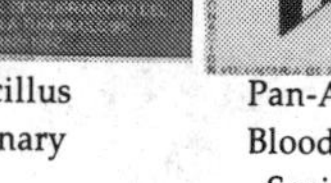

TB Bacillus Centenary AP196

Pan-American Blood Donors' Society, 7th Congress AP197

1982, Nov. 19 ***Perf. 13½***

C893	AP196	1.50col Koch	18	10
C894	AP196	3col Koch, slide	36	18
C895	AP196	3.30col Health Ministry	40	20

1982, Nov. 25 ***Perf. 11***

C896	AP197	30col Natl. Blood Assoc. emblem	3.60	1.80
C897	AP197	50col Congress emblem	6.00	3.00

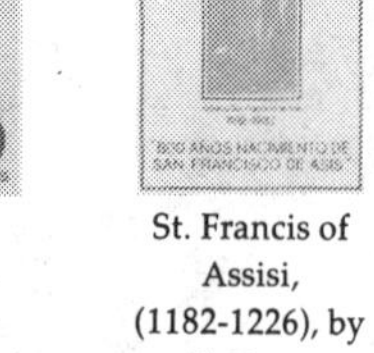

Inter-Governmental Migration Committee, 30th Anniv. AP198

St. Francis of Assisi, (1182-1226), by El Greco AP199

1982, Dec. 13 **Litho.** ***Perf. 10½***

C898	AP198	8.40col Emblem, horiz.	50	25
C899	AP198	9.70col Emblem, diff.	60	30
C900	AP198	11.70col Handshake, horiz.	75	35
C901	AP198	13.05col Emblem, diff., horiz.	80	40

1983, Jan. 3 ***Perf. 16***

C902	AP199	4.80col shown	30	10
C903	AP199	7.40col Portrait, diff.	45	15

Visit of Pope John Paul II—AP200

1983, Mar. 1 **Litho.** ***Perf.***

C904	AP200	5col multi	35	12
C905	AP200	10col multi	70	25
C906	AP200	15col multi	1.05	40

AIR POST SPECIAL DELIVERY STAMPS

U.P.U. Headquarters and Monument, Bern
APSD1

Perf. 10x11

1970, May 20 Litho. Unwmkd.

CE1	APSD1	35c multi	18	10
CE2	APSD1	60c multi	30	15

Issued to commemorate the opening of the new Universal Postal Union Headquarters in Bern. The red and black label attached to the 60c is inscribed "EXPRES". Prices are for stamps with label attached.

Stamps with labels removed were used for regular airmail.

AIR POST OFFICIAL STAMPS.

Air Post Stamps of 1934
Overprinted in Red **OFICIAL**

1934 *Perf. 12.* Unwmkd.

CO1	AP8	5c green	35	35
CO2	AP8	10c car rose	35	35
CO3	AP8	15c chocolate	60	60
CO4	AP8	20c dp bl	90	90
CO5	AP8	25c dp org	90	90
CO6	AP8	40c ol blk	1.00	1.00
CO7	AP8	50c gray blk	1.00	1.00
CO8	AP8	60c org yel	1.25	1.25
CO9	AP8	75c dl vio	1.25	1.25
CO10	AP9	1col dp rose	1.75	1.75
CO11	AP9	2col lt bl	6.00	6.00
CO12	AP9	5col black	11.00	11.00
CO13	AP9	10col red brn	13.00	13.00
		Nos. CO1-CO13 (13)	39.35	39.35

SPECIAL DELIVERY STAMPS

Winged Letter
SD1

Unwmkd.

1972, Mar. 20 Litho. *Perf. 11*

E1	SD1	75c brn & red	25	20
E2	SD1	1.50col bl & red	50	35

1973 *Perf. 11x12*

E3	SD1	75c grn & red	25	20

1973, Nov. 5 Litho. *Perf. 11x11½*

E4	SD1	75c lil & org	25	20

Concorde
SD2

1976, May 17 Litho. *Perf. 16*

E5	SD2	1col ver & multi	25	20

Concorde
SD3

1979, June 15 Litho. *Perf. 12½*

E6	SD3	2col multi	50	35

Concorde—SD4

1980, Dec. 18 Litho. *Perf. 12½*

E7	SD4	2col multi	50	35

1982, Dec. 20 Litho. *Perf. 11*

E8	SD4	4col multi	50	25

POSTAGE DUE STAMPS.

D1 D2

Engraved

1903 *Perf. 14* Unwmkd.

Numerals in Black.

J1	D1	5c sl bl	7.50	1.35
J2	D1	10c brn org	7.50	1.00
J3	D1	15c yel grn	2.75	2.75
J4	D1	20c carmine	3.25	2.50
J5	D1	25c sl gray	4.00	2.75
J6	D1	30c brown	6.50	3.75
J7	D1	40c ol bis	6.50	3.75
J8	D1	50c red vio	6.50	3.25
		Nos. J1-J8 (8)	44.50	21.10

1915 Lithographed. *Perf. 12.*

J9	D2	2c orange	12	12
J10	D2	4c dk bl	12	12
J11	D2	8c gray grn	50	50
J12	D2	10c violet	20	20
J13	D2	20c brown	25	25
		Nos. J9-J13 (5)	1.19	1.19

OFFICIAL STAMPS.

Official stamps normally were not canceled when affixed to official mail in the 19th century. Occasionally they were canceled in a foreign country of destination. Used prices are for used stamps without cancellation or favor-canceled specimens.

Regular Issues Overprinted.

Overprinted in Red, Black, Blue or Green **Oficial**

1883-85 *Perf. 12.* Unwmkd.

O1	A6	1c grn (R)	1.10	1.10
O2	A6	1c grn (Bk)	1.20	1.20
O3	A6	2c car (Bk)	1.60	1.60
O4	A6	2c car (Bl)	1.80	1.80
O5	A6	5c bl vio (R)	4.25	4.25
O6	A6	10c org (G)	5.50	5.50
O7	A6	40c bl (R)	5.50	5.50
		Nos. O1-O7 (7)	20.95	20.95

Overprinted **OFICIAL**

1886

O8	A6	1c grn (Bk)	1.50	1.50
O9	A6	2c car (Bk)	2.50	2.50
O10	A6	5c bl vio (R)	17.50	17.50
O11	A6	10c org (Bk)	17.50	17.50

Overprinted **OFICIAL**

O12	A6	1c grn (Bk)	1.20	1.20
O13	A6	2c car (Bk)	1.80	1.80
O14	A6	5c bl vio (R)	13.50	13.50
O15	A6	10c org (Bk)	13.50	13.50

Nos. O8–O11 and O12–O15 exist se-tenant in vertical pairs. Price, each $75.

Overprinted in Black **Oficial**

O16	A6	5c bl vio	37.50	35.00
O17	A6	10c orange	150.00	75.00

Overprinted **OFICIAL.**

1887

O18	A6	1c green	75	75
a.		"OFICAL"	10.00	10.00
b.		Without period	90	90
O19	A6	2c carmine	70	70
a.		"OFICAL"	6.00	6.00
b.		Without period	90	90
O21	A6	10c orange	4.25	4.25
a.		"OFICAL"	6.50	6.50
b.		Without period	5.00	
c.		Double overprint	10.00	
d.		"OFICAL" doubled		
O22	A7	5c bl vio	2.75	2.75
a.		"OFICAL"	5.00	
b.		Without period	3.60	3.60
O23	A7	10c orange	70	70
a.		"OFICAL"	3.75	3.75
b.		Without period	1.25	
c.		Double overprint	12.50	
O24	A6	40c blue	70	70
a.		"OFICAL"	4.50	4.50
		Nos. O18-O24 (6)	9.85	9.85

Issues of 1889–1901 Overprinted **OFICIAL**

1889 *Perf. 14, 15.*

O25	A10	1c brown	30	30
O26	A11	2c dk grn	30	30
O27	A12	5c orange	30	30
O28	A13	10c red brn	30	30
O29	A14	20c yel grn	30	30
O30	A15	50c rose red	1.50	1.50
		Nos. O25-O30 (6)	3.00	3.00

1892

O31	A20	1c grnsh bl	35	35
O32	A21	2c yellow	35	35
O33	A22	5c violet	35	35
O34	A23	10c lt grn	1.50	1.50
O35	A24	20c scarlet	25	22
O36	A25	50c gray bl	70	70
		Nos. O31-O36 (6)	3.50	3.47

1901–02

O37	A30	1c grn & blk	55	55
O38	A31	2c ver & blk	55	55
O39	A32	5c gray bl & blk	55	55
O40	A33	10c ocher & blk	90	90
O41	A34	20c lake & blk	1.20	1.20
O42	A35	50c lil & dk bl	4.25	4.25
O43	A36	1col ol bis & blk	10.00	10.00
		Nos. O37-O43 (7)	18.00	18.00

No. 46 Overprinted in Green **PROVISORIO OFICIAL**

1903

O44	A31	2c ver & blk	3.50	3.50
b.		"PROVISIORO"	6.00	6.00
d.		Inverted overprint	6.00	6.00
f.		Same as "b" inverted	12.00	12.00

Regular Issue of 1903 Overprinted **OFICIAL**

1903 *Perf. 14, 12½x14.*

O45	A40	4c red vio & blk	1.75	1.75
O46	A41	6c ol grn & blk	2.00	2.00
O47	A42	25c gray lil & brn	9.00	5.00

Regular Issue of 1907 Overprinted **OFICIAL**

1908 *Perf. 14, 11x14.*

O48	A43	1c red brn & ind	12	12
O49	A44	2c yel grn & blk	12	12
O50	A45	4c car & ind	15	15
O51	A46	5c yel & dl bl	20	20
O52	A47	10c bl & blk	1.25	1.25
O53	A49	25c gray lil & blk	25	25
O54	A50	50c red lil & bl	40	40
O55	A51	1col brn & blk	1.00	1.00
		Nos. O48-O55 (8)	3.49	3.49

The 5c, 10c and 25c exist with inverted overprint, the 4c with double impression of head.

Imperf. examples of Nos. O49 and O53 were found in 1970.

Regular Issue of 1910 Overprinted in Black **OFICIAL 15 VI·1917**

1917

O56	A56	5c orange	30	30
a.		Inverted overprint	3.50	3.50
O57	A57	10c dp bl	25	25
a.		Inverted overprint		

O2

1920 Red Surcharge. *Perf. 12.*

O58	O2	15c on 20c ol grn	50	50

O3

O4

O5

O6

1921 Black Surcharge. *Perf. 12, 14.*

O59	O3	10c on 5c org	50	40
a.		"10 CTS." invert.	22.50	
O60	O4	4c car & ind	45	45
a.		"1291" for "1921"	15.00	
O61	O5	6c on 1c red brn & ind	50	50
O62	O6	20c on 25c gray lil & blk	50	50

Overprinted like No. O60.

O63	A50	50c red lil & bl	2.50	2.50
O64	A51	1col brn & blk	4.50	4.50
		Nos. O59-O64 (6)	8.95	8.85

Nos. O60 to O64 exist with date and new values inverted, often in pairs with the normal varieties. These may be printer's waste but probably were deliberately made.

Regular Issue of 1923 Overprinted **OFICIAL**

1923 *Perf. 11½.*

O65	A68	2c brown	30	30
O66	A68	4c green	15	15
O67	A68	5c blue	30	30
O68	A68	20c carmine	20	20
O69	A68	1col violet	40	40
		Nos. O65-O69 (5)	1.35	1.35

Nos. O65 to O69 exist imperforate but were not regularly issued in that condition.

O7

Engraved

1926 *Perf. 12½* **Unwmkd.**

O70	O7	2c ultra & blk	6	6
O71	O7	3c mag & blk	6	6
O72	O7	4c lt bl & blk	8	8
O73	O7	5c grn & blk	8	8
O74	O7	6c ocher & blk	8	8
O75	O7	10c rose red & blk	8	8
O76	O7	20c ol grn & blk	8	8
O77	O7	30c red org & blk	15	15
O78	O7	45c brn & blk	20	20
O79	O7	1col lil & blk	30	30
		Nos. O70-O79 (10)	1.17	1.17

Regular Issue of 1936 Overprinted in Black **OFICIAL**

1936 *Perf. 12.* **Unwmkd.**

O80	A96	5c green	8	8
O81	A96	10c car rose	8	8

Type of 1926.

1937 *Perf. 12½.*

O82	O7	2c vio & blk	8	8
O83	O7	3c bis brn & blk	8	8
O84	O7	4c rose car & blk	8	8
O85	O7	5c ol grn & blk	8	
O86	O7	8c blk brn & blk	10	
O87	O7	10c rose lake & blk	10	
O88	O7	20c ind & blk	12	12
O89	O7	40c red org & blk	25	25
O90	O7	55c dk vio & blk	35	
O91	O7	1col brn vio & blk	30	30
O92	O7	2col gray bl & blk	60	60
O93	O7	5col dl yel & blk	3.00	3.00
O94	O7	10col bl & blk	20.00	20.00
		Nos. O82-O94 (13)	25.14	

Nine stamps of this series exist with perforated star (2c, 3c, 4c, 20c, 40c, 1col, 2col, 5col, 10col). These were issued to officials for postal purposes. Unpunched copies were sold to collectors but had no franking power. Prices for unused are for unpunched.

POSTAL TAX STAMPS

Most postal tax issues were to benefit the Children's Village and were obligatory on all mail during December.

No. C198 Surcharged in Red: "Sello de Navidad Pro-Ciudad de Los Niños 5 5"

Engraved; Center Photogravure.

1958 *Perf. 12½* **Unwmkd.**

RA1	AP51	5c on 2c brt bl & blk	15	6

Similar Surcharge in Green on Type of 1954.

Design: Like No. C228, pottery.

Perf. 12

RA2	AP53	5c on 10c dk bl & blk	40	8
a.		Inverted surch.		

Father Edward J. Flanagan
PT1

Father Peralta
PT2

Paintings: No. RA4, Boy by El Greco. No. RA5, Boy by Jose Ribera. No. RA6, Girl by Amadeo Modigliani.

Photogravure.

1959, Nov. 25 *Perf. 13½* **Unwmkd.**

RA3	PT1	5c green	30	8
RA4	PT1	5c dl gray vio	30	8
RA5	PT1	5c olive	30	8
RA6	PT1	5c lil rose	30	8

Exist imperf.

1960 Lithographed *Perf. 14*

Designs: No. RA8, Girl by Renoir. No. RA9, Boys with cups by Velazquez. No. RA10, Singing children, sculpture by F. Zuñiga.

RA7	PT2	5c chocolate	60	8
RA8	PT2	5c dp org	60	8
RA9	PT2	5c plum	60	8
RA10	PT2	5c grysh bl	60	8

Exist imperf.

No. C229 Surcharged "Sello de Navidad Pro-Ciudad de los Niños 5 5"

Engraved; Center Photogravure

1961 *Perf. 13x12½*

RA11	AP53	5c on 15c grn & blk	25	8

Nicolas, Son of Rubens
PT3

Boys in Workshop
PT4

Designs: No. RA13, Madonna by Bellini. RA14, Angel playing stringed instrument by Melozzo. RA15, Msgr. Rubén Odio H.

1962 Photogravure *Perf. 13½*

RA12	PT3	5c dk car	60	8
RA13	PT3	5c sepia	60	8
RA14	PT3	5c dl grn	60	8
RA15	PT3	5c blue	60	8

Type of 1962, Inscribed "1963" Designs as before

Designs: No. RA16, Rubens' son Nicolas. No. RA17, Madonna, Bellini. No. RA18, Angel, Melozzo. No. RA19, Msgr. Rubén Odio H.

1963 Photogravure *Perf. 13½*

RA16	PT3	5c sepia	35	8
RA17	PT3	5c ultra	35	8
RA18	PT3	5c dk car	35	8
RA19	PT3	5c black	35	8

1964 Lithographed *Perf. 12½*

Designs: No. RA21, Two playing boys. No. RA22, Teacher and children. No. RA23, Priest with boys.

RA20	PT4	5c brt grn	30	8
RA21	PT4	5c rose lil	30	8
RA22	PT4	5c blue	30	8
RA23	PT4	5c brown	30	8

Brother Casiano de Madrid
PT5

Christmas Ornaments
PT6

Designs: No. RA25, National Children's Hospital. No. RA26, Poinsettia. No. RA27, Santa Claus with children (diamond).

1965, Dec. 10 Litho. *Perf. 10*

RA24	PT5	5c red brn	20	8
RA25	PT5	5c green	20	8
RA26	PT5	5c red	20	8
RA27	PT5	5c ultra	20	8

1966 Lithographed *Perf. 11*

Designs: No. RA29, Angel. No. RA30, Church. No. RA31, Reindeer.

RA28	PT6	5c red	20	8
RA29	PT6	5c lt ultra	20	8
RA30	PT6	5c brt grn	20	8
RA31	PT6	5c brown	20	8

General Post Office, San José
PT7

1967, March Litho. *Perf. 11*

RA32	PT7	10c blue	10	6

No. RA32 was issued as a postal tax stamp to be used by organizations normally allowed free postage. On Dec. 15, 1972, it was authorized for use as an ordinary postage stamp.

Madonna and Child
PT8

Star of Bethlehem, Mother and Child
PT9

1967 Lithographed *Perf. 11*

RA33	PT8	5c ol grn	15	5
RA34	PT8	5c dp lil rose	15	5
RA35	PT8	5c brt bl	15	5
RA36	PT8	5c grnsh bl	15	5

1968, Dec. Litho. *Perf. 12½*

RA37	PT9	5c gray	15	5
RA38	PT9	5c rose red	15	5
RA39	PT9	5c dk rose brn	15	5
RA40	PT9	5c bis brn	15	5

Madonna and Child
PT10

1969, Dec. Lithographed *Perf. 12½*

RA41 PT10	5c	dk bl	3	3
RA42 PT10	5c	orange	3	3
RA43 PT10	5c	brn red	3	3
RA44 PT10	5c	bl grn	3	3

Christ Child and Star
PT11

1970, Dec. Litho. *Perf. 12½*

RA45 PT11	5c	brt pur	3	3
RA46 PT11	5c	lil rose	3	3
RA47 PT11	5c	olive	3	3
RA48 PT11	5c	ocher	3	3

Christ Child and "PAX"
PT12

Madonna and Child
PT13

1971, Nov. 29

RA49 PT12	10c	dk bl	7	3
RA50 PT12	10c	orange	7	3
RA51 PT12	10c	brown	7	3
RA52 PT12	10c	green	7	3

1972, Nov. 30 *Perf. 11x11½*

RA53 PT13	10c	dk bl	7	3
RA54 PT13	10c	brt red	7	3
RA55 PT13	10c	lilac	7	3
RA56 PT13	10c	green	7	3

Madonna and Child
PT14

Boys Eating Cake, by Murillo
PT15

1973, Nov. 30 Litho. *Perf. 12½*

RA57 PT14	10c	purple	7	3
RA58 PT14	10c	car rose	7	3
RA59 PT14	10c	gray	7	3
RA60 PT14	10c	org brn	7	3

1974, Nov. 25 *Perf. 13*

Paintings: No. RA62, Virgin and Child, with St. John, by Raphael. No. RA63, Maternity, by Juan R. Bonilla. No. RA64, Praying Child, by Reynolds.

RA61 PT15	10c	brt pink	6	3
RA62 PT15	10c	rose lil	6	3
RA63 PT15	10c	dk gray	6	3
RA64 PT15	10c	vio bl	6	3

"Happy, Dreams, by Sonia Romero
PT16

Virgin and Child, by Hans Memling
PT17

Paintings: No. RA66, Virgin with Carnation, by Leonardo da Vinci. No. RA67, Children with Tortoise, by Francisco Amighetti. No. RA68, Boy with Pigeon, by Picasso.

1975, Nov. 25 Litho. *Perf. 10½*

RA65 PT16	10c	gray	5	3
RA66 PT16	10c	red lil	5	3
RA67 PT16	10c	org brn	5	3
RA68 PT16	10c	brt bl	5	3

Obligatory on all mail during December.

1976, Nov. 24 Litho. *Perf. 10½*

Paintings: No. RA70, Boy with Sombrero, by Auguste Renoir. No. RA71, Meditation (Boy), by Floria Pinto de Herrero. No. RA72, Gaston de Mezerville (boy), by Lolita Zeller de Peralta.

RA69 PT17	10c	rose lil	3	3
RA70 PT17	10c	rose car	3	3
RA71 PT17	10c	gray	3	3
RA72 PT17	10c	vio bl	3	3

Obligatory on all mail during December.

Boy's Head, by Amparo Cruz
PT18

Boy with Kite
PT19

Paintings: No. RA74, Girl's head, by Rubens. No. RA75, Girl and infant, by Cristina Fournier. No. RA76, Mariano Goya, by Goya.

1977, Nov. Litho. *Perf. 10½*

RA73 PT18	10c	gray ol	3	3
RA74 PT18	10c	rose red	3	3
RA75 PT18	10c	brt ultra	3	3
RA76 PT18	10c	brt rose lil	3	3

Obligatory on all mail during December.

1978, Nov. 20 Litho. *Perf. 12½*

Designs: No. RA77, like No. RA76. Nos. RA78–RA79, Girl flying kite.

RA77 PT19	10c	magenta	3	3
RA78 PT19	10c	slate	3	3
RA79 PT19	10c	lilac	3	3
RA80 PT19	10c	vio bl	3	3

Obligatory on all mail during December.

Boy Leaning on Tree—PT20

1979, Nov. 19 Litho. *Perf. 12½*

RA81 PT20	10c	blue	5	3
RA82 PT20	10c	orange	5	3
RA83 PT20	10c	magenta	5	3
RA84 PT20	10c	green	5	3

Obligatory on all mail during December.

Boy on Swing—PT21

1980, Nov. 18 Litho. *Perf. 12½*

RA85 PT21	10c	brt bl	5	3
RA86 PT21	10c	brt yel	5	3
RA87 PT21	10c	crim rose	5	3
RA88 PT21	10c	brt grn	5	3

Obligatory on all mail during December.

Boy Riding Toy Car—PT22

1981, Nov. 19 Litho. *Perf. 11*

RA89 PT22	10c	blue	4	3
RA90 PT22	10c	green	4	3
RA91 PT22	10c	red	4	3
RA92 PT22	10c	orange	4	3

Obligatory on all mail during December.

Youth Running Machine—PT23

1982, Nov. 19 Litho. *Perf. 10½*

RA93 PT23	10c	red	4	3
RA94 PT23	10c	gray	4	3
RA95 PT23	10c	purple	4	3
RA96 PT23	10c	grnsh bl	4	3

Obligatory on all mail during December.

Guanacaste

(gwä'nä·käs'tä)

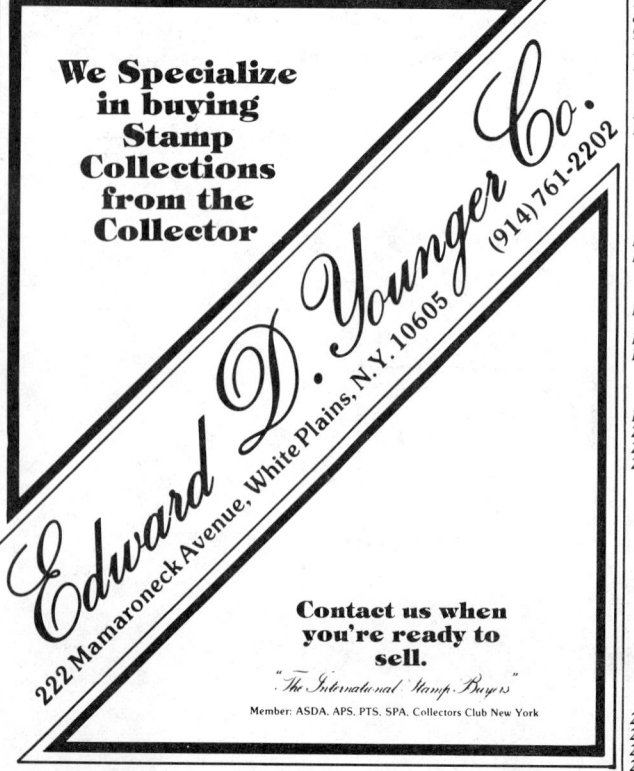

(A province of Costa Rica)

LOCATION—On northwestern coast of Central America.

AREA—4,000 sq. mi. (approx.).

POP.—69,531 (estimated).

CAPITAL—Liberia.

Residents of Guanacaste were allowed to buy Costa Rican stamps, overprinted "Guanacaste," at a discount from face value because of the province's isolation and climate, which makes it difficult to keep mint stamps. Use was restricted to the province.

Counterfeits of most Guanacaste overprints are plentiful.

On Issue of 1883.

Overprinted Horizontally in Black **Guanacaste** 16mm.

1885 *Perf. 12* **Unwmkd.**

No.	Type	Description	Unused	Used
1	A6	1c green	4.00	4.00
a.		"Gnanacaste"	60.00	
2	A6	2C carmine	4.00	3.00
a.		"Gnanacaste"	50.00	
3	A6	10c orange	12.00	12.00
a.		"Gnanacaste"	75.00	

Same Overprint in Red.

No.	Type	Description	Unused	Used
4	A6	1c green	4.00	4.00
a.		"Gnanacaste"	45.00	
b.		Overprinted in blk & red	125.00	
5	A6	5c bl vio	12.50	2.75
a.		"Gnanacaste"	75.00	
6	A6	40c blue	20.00	20.00

Overprinted Horizontally in Black **Guanacaste** 17½mm.

No.	Type	Description	Unused	Used
7	A6	1c green	7.50	6.00
8	A6	2c carmine	7.50	6.00
9	A6	5c bl vio	17.50	3.00
10	A6	10c orange	13.50	8.50
11	A6	40c blue	40.00	40.00

Same Overprint in Red.

No.	Type	Description	Unused	Used
12	A6	5c bl vio	40.00	12.50
13	A6	40c blue	*1,000.*	

Overprinted Horizontally in Black **Guanacaste** 18½mm.

No.	Type	Description	Unused	Used
14	A6	2c carmine	8.00	6.00
15	A6	10c orange	40.00	30.00

Same Overprint in Red.

No.	Type	Description	Unused	Used
16	A6	1c green	7.00	6.00
a.		Double overprint, one in blk	150.00	
17	A6	5c bl vio	32.50	7.00
18	A6	40c blue	50.00	50.00

Same Overprint, Vertically in Black.

No.	Type	Description	Unused	Used
19	A6	1c green	*1,000.*	*1,000.*
20	A6	2c carmine	600.00	600.00
21	A6	5c bl vio	175.00	80.00
22	A6	10c orange	50.00	50.00

Guanacaste (e) GUANACASTE (f) GUANACASTE (g) GUANACASTE (h) GUANACASTE (i)

Overprinted Type e, Vertically.

No.	Type	Description	Unused	Used
23	A6	1c green	100.00	100.00
24	A6	2c carmine	110.00	110.00
25	A6	5c bl vio	125.00	62.50
26	A6	10c orange	65.00	60.00

Overprinted Type f, Vertically.

No.	Type	Description	Unused	Used
27	A6	1c green	175.00	175.00
28	A6	2c carmine	175.00	175.00
29	A6	5c bl vio	200.00	85.00
30	A6	10c orange	75.00	75.00

Overprinted Type g, Vertically.

No.	Type	Description	Unused	Used
31	A6	1c green	300.00	300.00
32	A6	2c carmine	300.00	300.00
33	A6	5c bl vio	300.00	150.00
34	A6	10c orange	150.00	150.00

Overprinted Type h, Vertically.

No.	Type	Description	Unused	Used
35	A6	1c green	150.00	150.00
36	A6	2c carmine	90.00	90.00
37	A6	5c bl vio	175.00	85.00
38	A6	10c orange	40.00	40.00

The authenticity of Costa Rica Nos. 16-19 with overprint "i" has not been established.

On Issues of 1883–87

1888–89

Overprinted Horizontally in Black **Guanacaste**

No.	Type	Description	Unused	Used
42	A7	5c bl vio	20.00	3.00
a.		"Gnanacaste"		

Overprinted Horizontally in Black **Guanacaste**

No.	Type	Description	Unused	Used
43	A7	5c bl vio	17.50	3.00

Overprinted Horizontally in Black **Guanacaste**

No.	Type	Description	Unused	Used
44	A6	2c carmine	2.00	2.00
45	A7	10c orange	2.00	2.00
a.		Invtd. ovpt.		

On Issue of 1889.

Overprinted Type b, Horizontally.

1889

No.	Type	Description	Unused	Used
47	A8	2c blue	30.00	30.00

Vertically

No.	Type	Description	Unused	Used
48	A8	2c bl (c)	150.00	150.00
49	A8	2c bl (e)	75.00	75.00
51	A8	2c bl (f)	90.00	90.00
52	A8	2c bl (g)	300.00	300.00
54	A8	2c bl (h)	135.00	135.00

Dangerous counterfeits exist of Nos. 1–54.

On Nos. 25–33

Overprinted Horizontally in Black **GUANACASTE**

1890 *Perf. 14 and 15*

No.	Type	Description	Unused	Used
55	A10	1c brown	10.00	4.00
56	A11	2c dk grn	4.00	2.50
57	A12	5c orange	6.00	2.50
58	A13	10c red brn	6.00	3.00
59	A14	20c yel grn	1.50	1.50
60	A15	50c rose red	2.50	2.50
a.		"GUAGACASTE"	85.00	
61	A16	1p blue	3.50	3.50
a.		"GUAGACASTE"	85.00	85.00
62	A17	2p violet	6.00	6.00
a.		"GUAGACASTE"	85.00	85.00
63	A18	5p ol grn	35.00	35.00
a.		"GUAGACASTE"	85.00	85.00
		Nos. 55-63 (9)	74.50	60.50

Overprinted Horizontally in Black **GUANACASTE**

No.	Type	Description	Unused	Used
64	A10	1c brown	1.25	1.25
a.		Vert. pair, imperf. btwn.		
65	A11	2c dk grn	1.25	1.25
66	A12	5c orange	1.25	1.25
67	A13	10c red brn	1.25	1.25

CRETE

(krēt)

LOCATION — An island in the Mediterranean Sea south of Greece.

GOVT.—A department of Greece.

AREA—3,235 sq. mi.

POP.—336,150 (1913).

CAPITAL—Canea.

Formerly Crete was a province of Turkey. After an extended period of civil wars, France, Great Britain, Italy and Russia intervened and declaring Crete an autonomy, placed it under the administration of Prince George of Greece as High Commissioner. In October, 1908, the Cretan Assembly voted for union with Greece and in 1913 the union was formally effected.

40 Paras = 1 Piaster
4 Metallik = 1 Grosion (1899)
100 Lepta = 1 Drachma (1900)

Issued Under Joint Administration of France, Great Britain, Italy and Russia

British Sphere of Administration. District of Heraklion (Candia).

A1

A2

Handstamped

1898 ***Imperf.*** **Unwmkd.**

1	A1	20pa violet	650.00	350.00

1898 Lithographed ***Perf. 11½***

2	A2	10pa blue	11.00	15.00
a.		Horizontal pair, imperf. between		
b.		Imperf., pair	225.00	
3	A2	20pa green	11.00	15.00
a.		Imperf., pair	225.00	

1899

4	A2	10pa brown	11.00	15.00
a.		Horizontal pair, imperf. between		
b.		Imperf., pair	225.00	
5	A2	20pa rose	11.00	15.00
a.		Imperf., pair	225.00	

Counterfeits exist of Nos. 1–5.

Reprints exist of Nos. 2–5.

Russian Sphere of Administration. District of Rethymnon.

Coat of Arms

A3 A4

1899 Handstamped ***Imperf.***

10	A3	1m green	9.00	6.50
11	A3	2m black	9.00	6.50
12	A3	2m rose	60.00	50.00
13	A4	1m blue	25.00	17.50

Nos. 10–13 exist on both wove and laid papers. Counterfeits exist.

Poseidon's Trident

A5 A5a

1899 Lithographed ***Perf. 11½***

With Control Mark Overprinted in Violet.

Without Stars at Sides.

14	A5	1m orange	27.50	25.00
15	A5	2m orange	27.50	25.00
16	A5	1gr orange	27.50	25.00
17	A5	1m green	27.50	25.00
18	A5	2m green	27.50	25.00
19	A5	1gr green	27.50	25.00
20	A5	1m yellow	27.50	25.00
21	A5	2m yellow	27.50	25.00
22	A5	1gr yellow	27.50	25.00
23	A5	1m rose	27.50	25.00
24	A5	2m rose	27.50	25.00
25	A5	1gr rose	27.50	25.00
26	A5	1m violet	27.50	25.00
27	A5	2m violet	27.50	25.00
28	A5	1gr violet	27.50	25.00
29	A5	1m blue	27.50	25.00
30	A5	2m blue	27.50	25.00
31	A5	1gr blue	27.50	25.00
32	A5	1m black	650.00	550.00
33	A5	2m black	650.00	550.00
34	A5	1gr black	650.00	550.00

With Stars at Sides.

35	A5a	1m blue	11.00	10.00
36	A5a	2m blue	11.00	10.00
37	A5a	1gr blue	11.00	10.00
38	A5a	1m rose	11.00	10.00
39	A5a	2m rose	11.00	10.00
40	A5a	1gr rose	11.00	10.00
41	A5a	1m green	11.00	10.00
42	A5a	2m green	11.00	10.00
43	A5a	1gr green	11.00	10.00
44	A5a	1m violet	11.00	10.00
45	A5a	2m violet	11.00	10.00
46	A5a	1gr violet	11.00	10.00
		Nos. 35-46 (12)	132.00	120.00

Nearly all of Nos. 14 to 46 may be found without control mark, with double control marks and in various colors.

Counterfeits exist of Nos. 14–46.

Issued by the Cretan Government.

Hermes

A6

Hera

A7

Prince George of Greece

A8

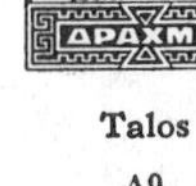

Talos

A9

Minos

A10

St. George and the Dragon

A11

1900, Mar. 1 Engraved ***Perf. 14***

50	A6	1 l vio brn	60	15
51	A7	5 l green	1.25	25
52	A8	10 l red	1.60	15
53	A7	20 l car rose	6.50	2.00

Overprinted ΠΡΟΣΩΡΙΝΟΝ

Red Overprint.

54	A8	25 l blue	4.25	1.60
55	A6	50 l lilac	5.25	2.75
56	A9	1d gray vio	8.00	4.50
57	A10	2d brown	16.50	12.00
58	A11	5d grn & blk	60.00	60.00
		Nos. 54-58 (5)	94.00	80.85

Black Overprint.

59	A8	25 l blue	5.00	1.50
60	A6	50 l lilac	5.50	2.75
61	A9	1d gray vio	8.00	4.50
a.		Inverted overprint	350.00	350.00
62	A10	2d brown	16.50	10.00
63	A11	5d grn & blk	60.00	60.00
		Nos. 59-63 (5)	95.00	78.75

1901 Without Overprint.

64	A6	1 l bister	50	50
65	A7	20 l orange	3.25	60
66	A8	25 l blue	13.50	1.65
67	A6	50 l lilac	16.50	8.50
68	A6	50 l ultra	5.00	5.00
69	A9	1d gray vio	32.50	16.50
70	A10	2d brown	16.50	10.00
71	A11	5d grn & blk	27.50	22.50
		Nos. 64-71 (8)	115.25	65.25

No. 64 is a revenue stamp that was used for postage for a short time. Unused, it can only be considered as a revenue.

Types A6 to A8 in olive yellow, and types A9 to A11 in olive yellow and black are revenue stamps.

No. 66 Overprinted in Black ΠΡΟΣΩΡΙΝΟΝ

1901

72	A8	25 l blue	16.50	2.00
a.		First letter of overprint inverted	125.00	125.00

No. 65 Surcharged in Black 5 5

1904, Dec.

73	A7	5 l on 20 l org	3.25	1.25
a.		Without "5" at right	8.50	8.50

Mycenaean Seal

A12

Britomartis (Cortyna Coin)

A13

Prince George

A14

Kydon and Dog (Cydonia Coin)

A15

Triton (Itanos Coin)

A16

Ariadne (Knossos Coin)

A17

Zeus as Bull Abducting Europa (Cortyna Coin)

A18

Palace of Minos Ruins, Knossos

A19

Arkadi Monastery and Mt. Ida

A20

1905, Feb. 15

74	A12	2 l dl vio	1.00	40
75	A13	5 l yel grn	3.00	35
76	A14	10 l red	3.75	50
77	A15	20 l bl grn	8.00	1.50
78	A16	25 l ultra	6.00	85
79	A17	50 l yel brn	6.50	6.25
80	A18	1d rose car & dp brn	75.00	60.00
81	A19	3d org & blk	37.50	27.50
82	A20	5d ol grn & blk	28.50	25.00
		Nos. 74-82 (9)	169.25	122.35

The so-called revolutionary stamps of 1905 were issued for sale to collectors and, so far as can be ascertained, were of no postal value whatever.

A. T. A. Zaimis

A21

Prince George Landing at Suda

A22

1907, Aug. 28

83	A21	25 l bl & blk	16.50	2.25
84	A22	1d grn & blk	16.00	12.50

Commemorative of the administration under a High Commissioner.

Stamps of 1900-1907 Overprinted in Black **ΕΛΛΑΣ**

1908, Sept. 21

85	A6	1 l vio brn	20	20
86	A12	2 l dl vio	60	40
87	A13	5 l yel grn	1.65	30
88	A8	10 l red	1.65	50
89	A15	20 l bl grn	2.50	1.00
90	A21	25 l bl & blk	8.50	3.25
91	A17	50 l yel brn	8.00	6.25
92	A18	1d rose car & dp brn	85.00	72.50
93	A10	2d brown	8.50	7.25
94	A19	3d org & blk	37.50	35.00
95	A20	5d ol grn & blk	32.50	30.00
		Nos. 85-95 (11)	186.60	156.65

This overprint exists inverted and double, as well as with incorrect, reversed, misplaced and omitted letters. Similar errors are found on the Postage Due and Official stamps with this overprint.

Hermes by Praxiteles A23

1908

96	A23	10 l brn red	3.00	85
a.		Pair, one without overprint	8.00	
b.		Inverted overprint	6.00	
c.		Double overprint	6.00	

Nos. 96 and 114 were not regularly issued without overprint.

No. 53 Surcharged ΕΛΛΑΣ ΠΡΟΣΟΡΙΝΟΝ 5 5

1909

97	A7	5 l on 20 l car rose	125.00	125.00

Forgeries exist of No. 97.

On No. 65

98	A7	5 l on 20 l org	65	55
a.		Inverted surcharge		

Overprinted on Nos. 64, J1 ΕΛΛΑΣ ΠΡΟΣΟΡΙΝΟΝ

99	A6	1 l bister	65	50
100	D1	1 l red	65	50

No. J4 Surcharged ΕΛΛΑΣ 2 ΠΡΟΣΩΡΙΝΟΝ

101	D1	2 l on 20 l red	1.25	1.25
a.		Double surcharge	7.50	
b.		Inverted surcharge	7.50	
c.		Second letter of surch. "D" instead of "P"	30.00	30.00

No. J4 Surcharged ΕΛΛΑΣ 2 ΠΡΟΣΩΡΙΝΟΝ

102	D1	2 l on 20 l red	65	55

Overprinted in Black:

ΕΛΛΑΣ *a*

ΕΛΛΑΣ *b*

ΕΛΛΑΣ *c*

103	A23(a)	10 l brn red	4.50	60
a.		Inverted overprint	30.00	
104	A15(a)	20 l bl grn	5.00	1.00
105	A21(c)	25 l bl & blk	10.00	5.00
106	A17(a)	50 l yel brn	6.50	5.00
107	A22(b)	1d grn & blk	17.50	14.00
108	A10(a)	2d brown	13.50	12.00
109	A19(b)	3d org & blk	100.00	70.00
110	A20(b)	5d ol grn & blk	32.50	30.00
		Nos. 103-110 (8)	189.50	137.60

Stamps of 1900-08 Overprinted in Red or Black ΕΛΛΑΣ *d*

1909-10

111	A6	1 l vio brn	20	20
112	A12	2 l dl vio	65	30
113	A13	5 l yel grn	35	20
114	A23	10 l brn red (Bk)	70	20
115	A15	20 l bl grn	5.00	50
116	A16	25 l ultra	5.00	60
117	A17	50 l yel brn	7.50	5.00
118	A18	1d rose car & dp brn (Bk)	120.00	95.00
119	A19	3d org & blk	50.00	45.00
120	A20	5d ol grn & blk	75.00	57.50
		Nos. 111-120 (10)	264.40	204.50

POSTAGE DUE STAMPS.

D1

Lithographed.

1901 *Perf. 14* Unwmkd.

J1	D1	1 l red	1.10	85
J2	D1	5 l red	2.25	2.00
J3	D1	10 l red	3.25	2.50
J4	D1	20 l red	4.50	2.75
J5	D1	40 l red	6.75	6.75
J6	D1	50 l red	5.50	5.00
J7	D1	1d red	47.50	35.00
J8	D1	2d red	11.00	8.50
		Nos. J1-J8 (8)	81.85	63.35

Surcharged in Black Ι ΔΡΑΧΜΗ

1901

J9	D1	1d on 1d red	15.00	12.50

Overprinted ΕΛΛΑΣ

1908

J10	D1	1 l red	1.00	1.10
a.		Inverted overprint	4.00	4.00
J11	D1	5 l red	3.00	2.50
J12	D1	10 l red	4.00	2.25
J13	D1	20 l red	5.50	5.50
J14	D1	40 l red	8.50	5.50
J15	D1	50 l red	8.50	5.00
J16	D1	1d red	165.00	165.00
J17	D1	1d on 1d red	12.50	8.00
J18	D1	2d red	30.00	17.50
		Nos. J10-J18 (9)	238.00	212.35

Counterfeits of No. J16 exist.

Overprinted ΕΛΛΑΣ

1910

J19	D1	1 l red	65	65
J20	D1	5 l red	2.25	2.25
J21	D1	10 l red	1.65	1.65
J22	D1	20 l red	7.50	6.50
J23	D1	40 l red	5.00	5.00
J24	D1	50 l red	6.50	5.50
J25	D1	1d red	40.00	32.50
J26	D1	2d red	25.00	21.00
		Nos. J19-J26 (8)	88.55	75.05

OFFICIAL STAMPS.

O1

O2

Perf. 14

1908, Jan. 14 Litho. Unwmkd.

O1	O1	10 l dl cl	27.50	3.50
O2	O2	30 l blue	32.50	3.75

Nos. O1-O2 exist imperf.

Overprinted ΕΛΛΑΣ

O3	O1	10 l dl cl	25.00	3.50
a.		Inverted overprint	25.00	
O4	O2	30 l blue	35.00	3.50
a.		Inverted overprint	25.00	

1910

Overprinted ΕΛΛΑΣ

O5	O1	10 l dl cl	2.10	1.00
O6	O2	30 l blue	2.10	1.00

CROATIA

(krō-ā'shĭȧ ; shȧ)

LOCATION—Southeastern Europe.
GOVT.—Independent state.
AREA—44,453 sq. mi.
POP.—7,000,000 (approx.).
CAPITAL—Zagreb.

The Independent Croatian State of 1941–45 became part of the Jugoslav Federation in 1945.

100 Paras = 1 Dinar
100 Banica = 1 Kuna

Jugoslavia Nos. 143 to 148B Overprinted in Black NEZAVISNA DRŽAVA HRVATSKA IIIIII

Typographed.

1941, Apr. 12 *Perf. 12½* Unwmkd.

1	A16	50p orange	1.25	1.50
2	A16	1d yel grn	1.25	1.50
3	A16	1.50d red	1.25	1.25
4	A16	2d dp mag	1.25	1.25
5	A16	3d dl red brn	3.50	3.75
6	A16	4d ultra	3.50	3.75
7	A16	5d dk bl	3.50	3.75
8	A16	5.50d dk vio brn	3.50	3.75
		Nos. 1-8 (8)	19.00	20.50

The overprint exists inverted on Nos. 1–6; double on Nos. 2, 3 and 5.

Jugoslavia Nos. 142 to 154 Overprinted in Black NEZAVISNA DRŽAVA HRVATSKA

1941, Apr. 21

9	A16	25p black	25	25
10	A16	50p orange	25	25
11	A16	1d yel grn	25	25
12	A16	1.50d red	25	25
13	A16	2d dp mag	25	25
14	A16	3d dl red brn	25	25
15	A16	4d ultra	25	25
16	A16	5d dk bl	70	70
17	A16	5.50d dk vio brn	80	80
18	A16	6d sl bl	80	80
19	A16	8d sepia	80	80
20	A16	12d brt vio	80	80
21	A16	16d dl vio	2.00	2.00
22	A16	20d blue	2.50	2.50
23	A16	30d brt pink	3.00	3.00
		Nos. 9-23 (15)	13.15	13.15

The overprint exists inverted on Nos. 9–11, 17 and 20; double on Nos. 9, 12 and 17.

Jugoslavia Nos. 147, 148 Surcharged in Black

1941, May 16

24	A16	1d on 3d dl red brn	25	30
25	A16	2d on 4d ultra	20	20

The overprint exists inverted and double on Nos. 24–25.

Postage Due Stamps of Jugoslavia, Nos. J28, J30 to J32, Overprinted in Black NEZAVISNA DRŽAVA HRVATSKA

1941, May 17

26	D4	50p violet	25	25
27	D4	2d dp bl	35	35
28	D4	5d orange	50	50
29	D4	10d chocolate	50	50

Counterfeit overprints on Nos. 1-29 are plentiful.

Imperforates

Nearly all Croatian stamps, from No. 30 through 80, B3 through B76, J6 through J25, O1 through O24 and RA1 through RA7 exist imperforate.

Ozalj Castle
A1

Designs: 50b, City of Jajce. 75b, Old Warasdin. 1k, Velebit Mountains. 1.50k, Zelanjak. 2k, Zagreb Cathedral. 3k, Osjek Cathedral. 4k, Drina River. No. 38, Konjica. No. 39, Zemun. 6k, Dubrovnik. 7k, Sava River. 8k, Sarajevo. 10k, Plitvice. 12k, Klis Fortress, Split. 20k, Hvar. 30k, Syrmia. 50k, Senj. 100k, Banjaluka (without "F.I.").

Photogravure.

1941-43 *Perf. 11.* Unwmkd.

Ordinary Paper.

30	A1	25b henna	3	3
a.		Tête bêche pair	25	25
31	A1	50b sl bl	3	3
a.		Tête bêche pair	25	25
32	A1	75b dk ol grn	3	3
33	A1	1k Prus grn	3	3
a.		Tête bêche pair	45	45
34	A1	1.50k dp grn	3	3
a.		Tête bêche pair	45	45
35	A1	2k car lake	3	3
a.		Tête bêche pair	30	30
36	A1	3k brn red	3	3
37	A1	4k dp ultra	3	3
a.		Tête bêche pair	30	30
38	A1	5k black	75	20
a.		Tête bêche pair	2.50	2.50
39	A1	5k blue	7	5
40	A1	6k lt ol brn	7	5
a.		Tête bêche pair	30	30
41	A1	7k org red	7	5
a.		Tête bêche pair	35	35

No.	Type	Value / Color	Unused	Used
42	A1	8k chestnut	20	10
a.		Tête bêche pair	90	75
43	A1	10k dk plum	25	5
a.		Tête bêche pair	60	60
44	A1	12k ol brn	35	10
45	A1	20k gldn brn	25	5
a.		Tête bêche pair	85	15
46	A1	30k blk brn	35	10
a.		Tête bêche pair	1.25	1.25
47	A1	50k dk sl grn	75	30
a.		Tête bêche pair	5.25	5.25
48	A1	100k violet	1.25	1.25
		Nos. 30-48 (19)	4.60	2.54

Nos. 31, 35 and 43 exist on thin to pelure paper. Shades of all values exist.

Types of 1941 Overprinted in Brown or Green

1941-1942 10-IV

1942, Apr. 9

No.	Type	Value / Color	Unused	Used
49	A1	2k dk brn	20	15
50	A1	5k dk car	25	20
51	A1	10k dk bl grn (G)	30	25

First anniversary of Croatian independence.

Banjaluka
("F.I." at upper right)
A20

1942, June 13

No.	Type	Value / Color	Unused	Used
52	A20	100k violet	2.00	2.50

Banjaluka Philatelic Exhibition.

No. 35 Surcharged in Red Brown with New Value and Bar.

1942, June 23

No.	Type	Value / Color	Unused	Used
53	A1	25b on 2k car lake	10	10
a.		Tête bêche pair	55	55

Trakoscan Castle
A21

Catherine Zrinski
A23

Design: 12.50k, Citadel of Veliki Tabor.

1943

Pelure Paper

No.	Type	Value / Color	Unused	Used
54	A21	3.50k brn car	40	40
55	A21	12.50k vio blk	40	40

No. 54 exists on ordinary paper.

1943, June 7 Engr. *Perf. 12½*

Designs: 2k, Fran Krsto Frankopan. 3.50k, Peter Zrinski.

Various Frames.

No.	Type	Value / Color	Unused	Used
56	A23	1k dk bl	12	12
57	A23	2k dk ol grn	12	12
58	A23	3.50k dk red	18	18

Rugjer Boscovich
A26

Ante Pavelich
A27

1943, Dec. 13 *Perf. 11*

No.	Type	Value / Color	Unused	Used
59	A26	3.50k cop red	20	20
60	A26	12.50k dk vio brn	30	30

Issued to honor Rugjer Boscovich (1711-1787), Serbo-Croat mathematician and physicist.

1943-44 Litho. *Perf. 12½, 14*

No.	Type	Value / Color	Unused	Used
61	A27	25b org ver	3	3
62	A27	50b Prus bl	3	3
63	A27	75b ol grn	4	3
64	A27	1k lt grn	4	3
65	A27	1.50k dl gray vio	4	4
66	A27	2k rose lake	4	4
67	A27	3k rose brn	4	4
68	A27	3.50k brt bl	4	4
a.		3.50k dk bl, perf. 11½	1.25	1.25
69	A27	4k brt red vio	4	4
70	A27	5k ultra	4	4
71	A27	8k org brn	4	4
72	A27	9k rose pink	6	6
73	A27	10k vio brn	8	8
74	A27	12k dk ol bis	8	8
75	A27	12.50k gray blk	8	8
76	A27	18k dl brn	10	10
77	A27	32k dk brn	10	10
78	A27	50k grnsh bl	20	20
79	A27	70k orange	30	30
80	A27	100k violet	65	65
		Nos. 61-80 (20)	2.07	2.05

Nos. 61 and 63 measure 20½x26mm. Nos. 62 and 64-80 measure 22x27½mm.

Issue dates: 2k, 1943; No. 68a, June 13, 1943, Pavelich's birthday; others, 1944.

"Labor Day 1945"
A28

1945 Photogravure. *Perf. 11½*

No.	Type	Value / Color	Unused	Used
81	A28	3.50k red brn	30	40

SEMI-POSTAL STAMPS.

Types of Jugoslavia, 1941, Overprinted in Gold "NEZAVISNA / DRZAVA / HRVATSKA"

Engraved.

1941, May 10 *Perf. 11½* Unwmkd.

No.	Type	Value / Color	Unused	Used
B1	SP80	1.50d +1.50d bl blk	10.00	12.50
B2	SP81	4d +3d choc	10.00	12.50

Five thousand sets of Jugoslavia Nos. 142-154 were overprinted "NEZAVISNA DRZAVA HRVATSKA 10. IV. 1941" and small shield in red or blue, in 1941. Sold for double face value. Price, set, $175.

Costume of Sinj, Dalmatia
SP1

Soldiers with Arms of the Axis States
SP4

Designs (Costumes): 2k+2k, Travnik, Bosnia. 4k+4k, Turopolje, Croatia.

1941, Oct. 12 Photo. *Perf. 10½x10*

No.	Type	Value / Color	Unused	Used
B3	SP1	1.50k +1.50k Prus bl & red	20	20
B4	SP1	2k +2k ol brn & red	30	30
B5	SP1	4k +4k brn lake & red	70	70

The surtax aided the Croatian Red Cross. Sheets of 20 stamps and 5 labels.

1941, Dec. 3 *Perf. 11*

No.	Type	Value / Color	Unused	Used
B6	SP4	4k +2k bl	1.50	1.50

The surtax was used for Croatian Volunteers in the East.

Model Plane
SP5

Model Plane
SP6

Designs: 3k+3k, Boy with model plane. 4k+4k, Model seaplane in flight.

1942, Mar. 25

No.	Type	Value / Color	Unused	Used
B7	SP5	2k +2k sep	25	25
B8	SP6	2.50k +2.50k dl grn	35	35
B9	SP5	3k +3k brn car	40	40
B10	SP6	4k +4k dp bl	65	65

The surtax aided the society of Croatian Wings (Hrvatska Krila).

Nos. B7-B10 were issued in sheets of 25 and in sheets of 24 plus label.

Souvenir Sheets.

SP9

Perf. 11.

No.	Type	Value / Color	Unused	Used
B11	SP9	Sheet of two	12.50	15.00
a.		2k+8k brn car	2.50	2.50
b.		3k+12k dp bl	2.50	2.50

Imperf.

No.	Type	Value / Color	Unused	Used
B12	SP9	Sheet of two	12.50	15.00
a.		2k+8k dp bl	2.50	2.50
b.		3k+12k brn car	2.50	2.50

The sheets measure 125x110mm.

To commemorate the Aviation Exposition of Zagreb. The surtax aided "Croatian Wings."

Nos. B11 and B12 exist with colors of stamps and inscriptions transposed.

Boy Trumpeters
SP10

Mother and Child
SP12

Triumphal Arch
SP11

1942, July 5 *Perf. 11½*

No.	Type	Value / Color	Unused	Used
B13	SP10	3k +1k lake	50	50
B14	SP11	4k +2k dk brn	50	50
B15	SP12	5k +5k dp bl grn	50	50

The surtax was for national welfare. Sheets of 25.

Matthew Gubec
SP13

Ante Starcevich
SP14

SP15

1942, Nov. 22 *Perf. 14½*

No.	Type	Value / Color	Unused	Used
B16	SP13	3k +6k dk red	20	20
B17	SP14	4k +7k sep	20	20

Souvenir Sheets

Perf. 12, Imperf.

No.	Type	Value / Color	Unused	Used
B18	SP15	5k +20k dl bl	8.50	10.00

Issued to commemorate the heroes of Senj, May 9, 1937. Nos. B16-B17 were printed in sheets of 16 plus 9 labels, each bearing a hero's name. Size of No. B18: 80x95mm. The surtax aided the National Youth Society.

Sestine Peasant
SP16

Designs: 3k+1k, Slavonian peasant. 4k+2k, Bosnian peasant. 10k+5k, Dalmatian peasant. 13k+6k, Sestine peasant.

1942, Oct. 4 *Perf. 11½*

No.	Type	Value / Color	Unused	Used
B20	SP16	1.50k +50b org brn & red	50	50
B21	SP16	3k +1k dl pur & red	50	50
B22	SP16	4k +2k dp bl & red	50	50
B23	SP16	10k +5k dk ol bis & red	85	85
B24	SP16	13k +6k rose lake & red	1.75	1.75
		Nos. B20-B24 (5)	4.10	4.10

The surtax aided the Croatian Red Cross. Issued in sheets of 24 stamps plus label.

Croatian Labor Corpsman
SP20

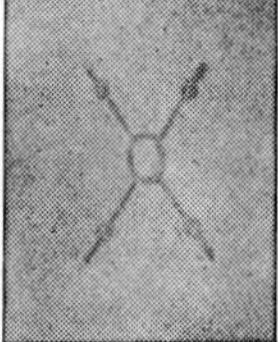

Wmk. 278

Designs: 3k+3k, Corpsman with wheelbarrow. 7k+4k, Corpsman plowing.

Wmkd.

Network Connecting Circles. (278)

1943, Jan. 17 *Perf. 11*

No.	Type	Value / Color	Unused	Used
B25	SP20	2(k) +1(k) ol gray & sep	1.00	1.00

B26	SP20	3(k) +3(k) brn & sep	1.00	1.00
B27	SP20	7(k) +4(k) gray bl & sep	1.00	1.00

The surtax aided the State Labor Service (Drzavna Radna Sluzba). Issued in sheets of 9.

Arms of Zagreb and "Golden Bull"
SP23

1943, Mar. 23 **Unwmkd.**

B28	SP23	3.50k (+6.50k) bril ultra	1.25	1.25

700th anniversary of Zagreb's "Golden Bull," a Magna Carta of civic rights and privileges granted to the city in 1242 by King Bela because the Croats annihilated Tartar hordes at Grobnik.
Issued in sheets of 8 with marginal inscriptions.

Ante Pavelich
SP24

1943, Apr. 10 ***Perf. 14***

B29	SP24	5k +3k cop red	12	12
B30	SP24	7k +5k dk grn	15	15

Surtax aided the National Youth Society.
Issued in sheets of 100, and in miniature sheets of 16 stamps and 9 labels.

Souvenir Sheets.

SP25

1943, May 17 ***Perf. 12, Imperf.***

B31	SP25	12k +8k dp ultra	6.00	6.00

The sheets measure 79x94mm.

Sailor at Sea of Azov
SP26

Designs: 2k+1k, Flier at Sevastopol and Rzhev. 3.50k+1.50k, Infantrymen at Stalingrad. 9k+4.50k, Panzer Division at Don River.

1943, July 1 ***Perf. 11***

B33	SP26	1k +50b grn	12	12
B34	SP26	2k +1k dk red	12	12
B35	SP26	3.50k +1.50k dk bl	12	12
B36	SP26	9k +4.50k chnt	12	12

Issued to honor the Croatian Legion which fought with the Germans in Russia.

Souvenir Sheets.

SP30

Perf. 11, Imperf.

B37	SP30	Sheet of four	1.00	1.00
a.		1k+50b dk bl	15	15
b.		2k+1k grn	15	15
c.		3.50k+1.50k dk red brn	15	15
d.		9k+4.50k bluish blk	15	15

The sheets measure 105x90mm. The surtax aided the Croatian Legion.

St. Mary's Church and Cistercian Cloister, Zagreb, in 1650
SP31

1943, Sept. 12 **Engr.** ***Perf. 14½***

B39	SP31	18k +9k dl gray vio	1.25	1.25

Souvenir Sheet.
Perf. 12½.

B40	SP31	18k +9k blk brn	4.75	5.50

Nos. B39–B40 were issued in connection with the Croatian Philatelic Society Exhibition at Zagreb. Size of No. B40: 100x131 mm.

No. B39 Overprinted in Red **HRVATSKO MORE 8. IX. 1943.**

1943, Sept. 12

B41	SP31	18k +9k dl gray vio	3.50	4.00

Return to Croatia of the Dalmatian and Croatian coasts.

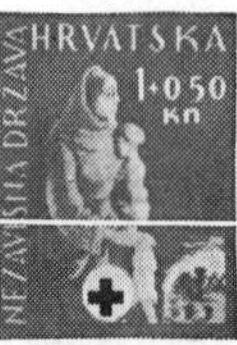

Mother and Children
SP33

Nurse and Patient
SP34

1943, Oct. 3 **Litho.** ***Perf. 11***

B42	SP33	1k +50b bl grn & red	15	15
B43	SP33	2k +1k bril car & red	15	15
B44	SP33	3.50k +1.50k brt bl & red	15	15
B45	SP34	8k +3k red brn & red	15	15
B46	SP34	9k +4k yel grn & red	15	15
B47	SP33	10k +5k dp vio & red	25	25
B48	SP34	12k +6k brt ultra & red	25	25
B49	SP33	12.50k +6k dk brn & red	25	25
B50	SP34	18k +8k brn org & red	75	75
B51	SP34	32k +12k dk gray & red	1.25	1.25
		Nos. B42-B51 (10)	3.50	3.50

The surtax aided the Croatian Red Cross.

Post Horn and Arms
SP35

Carrier Pigeon and Plane
SP36

Mercury
SP37

Winged Wheel
SP38

1944, Feb. 3

B52	SP35	7k +3.50(k) ol bis & red	15	15
B53	SP36	16k +8(k) bl & dk bl	20	20
B54	SP37	24k +12(k) red & rose red	30	30
B55	SP38	32k +16k gray & red	45	45

The surtax benefited communications and railway employees. Sheets of 9.

St. Sebastian
SP39

Statue of Ancient Croatian King
SP41

War Invalids
SP40

Death of King Peter Svacic, 1097
SP42

1944, Feb. 15

B56	SP39	7k +3.50(k) org red & rose car	20	20
B57	SP40	16k +8k yel grn & dk grn	30	30
B58	SP41	24k +12(k) yel brn & red	35	35
B59	SP42	32k +16k bl & dk bl	45	45

The surtax aided wounded war victims.
Issued in sheets of eight stamps, with marginal inscriptions and a central label picturing St. Sebastian.

Black Legion in Combat
SP43

Guarding the Drina
SP44

Jure Francetich
SP45

1944, May 22 **Photo.** ***Imperf.***

B60	SP43	3.50(k) +1.50k brn red	5	3
B61	SP44	12.50(k) +6.50k sl bl	6	4
B62	SP45	18(k) +9k ol brn	10	10

Third anniversary of Croatian independence.
The surtax aided the National Youth Society. Sheets of 20.

Perf. 14½.

B63	SP45	12.50(k) +287.50k int blk	2.75	4.00

Issued to commemorate Jure Francetich.

Labor Corpsmen Marching
SP46

Corpsman Digging
SP47

Designs: 18k+9k, Officer instructing corpsman. 32k+16k, Pavelich reviewing Labor Corps.

Perf. 11, 12½, 14½.

1944, Aug. 20 **Engraved**

B65	SP46	3.50(k) +1(k) dk red	10	10
B66	SP47	12.50(k) +6(k) sep	12	12
B67	SP47	18(k) +9(k) dk bl	12	12

368	SP47	32(k) +16(k) gray grn	15	15

The surtax aided the State Labor Service (Drzavna Radna Sluzba).
Issued in sheets of 8 plus label.

Souvenir Sheet.

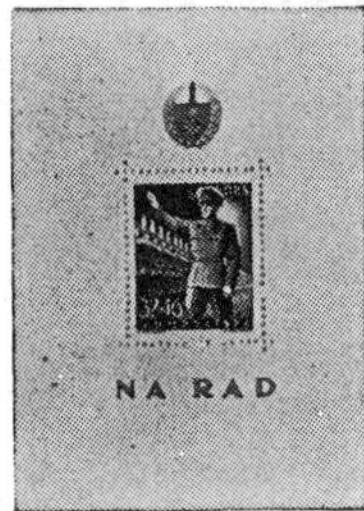

SP50

Perf. 12½.

369	SP50	32(k) +16(k) dk brn, *cr*	2.00	3.00

The sheet measures 72x99mm. The surtax aided the State Labor Service.

Palm Leaf
SP51

Lithographed.

1944, Nov. 12 ***Perf. 11***

370	SP51	2k +1k dl grn & red	10	10
371	SP51	3.50k +1.50k car lake & red	12	12
372	SP51	12.50k +6k ind & red	18	20

The surtax aided the Croatian Red Cross. Sheets of 16.

Men of Storm Division
SP52

Designs: 70k+70k, Soldiers of Storm Division in action. 100k+100k, Storm Division emblem.

Lithographed

1944 ***Perf. 11*** **Unwmkd.**

373	SP52	50k +50k brick red	50.00	60.00
374	SP52	70k +70k sep	50.00	60.00
375	SP52	100k +100k chlky bl, pale bl & dp bl	50.00	60.00

The surtax aided the First Croatian Storm Division. Sheets of 20.

Souvenir Sheet.

SP54

B76	SP54	Sheet of three	600.00	*850.00*
a.		50k+50k brick red		
b.		70k+70k sep		
c.		100k+100k chlky bl, pale bl & dp bl		

Nos. B76a to B76c are inscribed "O. A." in brick red at right below design. The sheet measures 216x132mm. The surtax aided the First Croatian Storm Division. Counterfeits exist.

Postman
SP55

Telephone Line Repairman
SP56

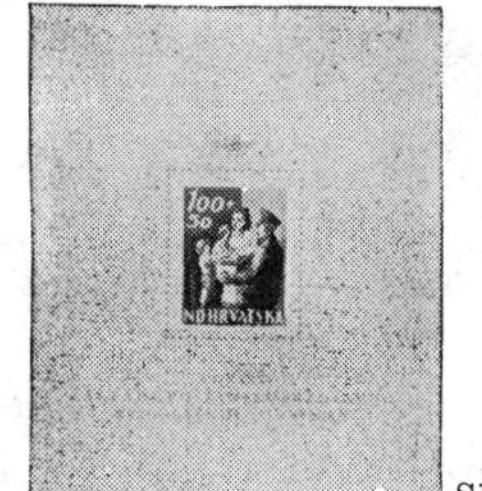

SP59

Designs; 24k+12k, Switchboard operator. 50k+25k, Postman delivering parcel.

1945 Photogravure.

B77	SP55	3.50(k) +1.50(k) sl gray	10	10
B78	SP56	12.50(k) +6(k) brn car	12	12
B79	SP56	24(k) +12(k) dk grn	15	15
B80	SP56	50(k) +25(k) brn vio	25	25

Sheets of eight.

Souvenir Sheet.

B81	SP59	100(k) +50(k) dp brn	2.25	3.00

The surtax on Nos. B77–B81 aided employees of the P.T.T. Size of No. B81: 100x120mm.

POSTAGE DUE STAMPS.

Jugoslavia Nos. J28–J32 Overprinted in Black

NEZAVISNA DRZAVA HRVATSKA

1941, Apr. 26 ***Perf. 12½*** **Unwmkd.**

J1	D4	50p violet	25	25
a.		50p rose vio	6.00	4.00
J2	D4	1d dp mag	25	25
J3	D4	2d dp bl	10.00	10.00
J4	D4	5d orange	75	75
J5	D4	10d chocolate	3.00	3.00
		Nos. J1-J5 (5)	14.25	14.25

The overprint on the 50p exists inverted. Counterfeit overprints exist.

Numeral of Value
D1 D2

1941, Sept. 12 **Litho.** ***Perf. 11***

J6	D1	50b car lake	15	15
J7	D1	1K car lake	15	15
J8	D1	2K car lake	25	25
J9	D1	5K car lake	35	35
J10	D1	10K car lake	60	60
		Nos. J6-J10 (5)	1.50	1.50

Size: 24x24 mm.

1943 ***Perf. 11½, 12x12½, 12½***

J11	D2	50b lt bl & gray	4	4
J12	D2	1k lt bl & gray	4	4
J13	D2	2k lt bl & gray	6	6
J14	D2	4k lt bl & gray	15	15
J15	D2	5k lt bl & gray	18	18
J16	D2	6k lt bl & gray	15	15
J17	D2	10k bl & ind	20	20
J18	D2	15k bl & ind	20	20
J19	D2	20k bl & ind	75	75
		Nos. J11-J19 (9)	1.77	1.77

Size: 25x24¼ mm.

1942, July 30 ***Perf. 10½, 11½***

J20	D2	50b lt bl & gray	15	15
J21	D2	1k lt bl & gray	12	12
J22	D2	2k lt bl & gray	25	25
J23	D2	5k lt bl & gray	25	25
J24	D2	10k lt bl & bl	50	50
J25	D2	20k lt bl & bl	90	90
		Nos. J20-J25 (6)	2.17	2.17

OFFICIAL STAMPS.

Croatian Coat of Arms
O1 O2

Lithographed.

1942–43 ***Perf. 10½, 11½*** **Unwmkd.**

Ordinary Paper

O1	O1	25b rose lake	3	3
O2	O1	50b sl blk	7	3
O3	O1	75b gray grn	4	3
O4	O1	1k org brn	3	3
O5	O1	2k turq bl	4	3
O6	O1	3k vermilion	3	3
O7	O1	4k brn vio	4	3
O8	O1	5k ultra	6	3
a.		Thin paper	7.50	7.50
O9	O1	6k brt vio	4	3
O10	O1	10k lt grn	3	3
O11	O1	12k brn rose	15	15
O12	O1	20k dk bl	20	12
O13	O2	30k brn vio & gray	14	8
O14	O2	40k vio blk & gray	25	25
O15	O2	50k brn lake & gray	75	75
O16	O2	100k blk & pink	75	75
		Nos. O1-O16 (16)	2.65	2.40

1943–44 **Thin Paper** ***Perf. 11½***

O17	O1	25b claret	8	8
O18	O1	50b gray	8	8
O19	O1	75b dl grn	8	8
O20	O1	1k org brn	8	8
O21	O1	2k sl bl	8	8
O22	O1	3.50k car rose	8	8
a.		Ordinary paper	8.00	8.00
O23	O1	6k brt red vio	8	8
O24	O1	12.50k dp org	4.00	4.00
a.		Ordinary paper	3.75	3.75
		Nos. O17-O24 (8)	4.56	4.56

POSTAL TAX STAMPS

Nurse and Soldier
PT1

Wounded Soldier
PT2

Lithographed.

1942, Oct. 4 ***Perf. 11*** **Unwmkd.**

RA1	PT1	1k ol grn & red	20	20

The tax aided the Croatian Red Cross. Issued in sheets of 24 plus label.

1943, Oct. 3

RA2	PT2	2k bl & red	30	30

The tax aided the Croatian Red Cross.

Ruins
PT3

Wounded Soldier
PT4

1944, Jan. 1 **Photo.** ***Perf. 12***

RA3	PT3	1k dk sl grn	6	6
RA4	PT4	2k car lake	6	6
RA5	PT4	5k black	8	8
RA6	PT4	10k dp bl	25	30
RA7	PT4	20k brown	50	60
		Nos. RA3-RA7 (5)	95	1.10

CUBA

(kū'bȧ)

LOCATION—The largest island of the West Indies; south of Florida.

GOVT.—Former Spanish possession.

AREA—44,206 sq. mi.

POP.—6,743,000 (est. 1960).

CAPITAL—Havana.

Formerly a Spanish possession, Cuba made several unsuccessful attempts to gain her freedom, which finally led to the intervention of the United States in 1898. In that year under the Treaty of Paris, Spain relinquished the island to the U. S. in trust for its inhabitants. In 1902 a republic was established and the Cuban Congress took over the government from the military authorities.

8 Reales Plata = 1 Peso
100 Centesimos = 1 Escudo or Peseta (1867)
1000 Milesimas = 100 Centavos = 1 Peso

Pen cancellations are common on the earlier stamps of Cuba. Stamps so cancelled sell for very much less than those with postmark cancellations.

Issued under Spanish Dominion

Used also in Puerto Rico: Nos. 1–4, 9–14, 18–21, 32–34, 35A–37, 39–41, 43–45, 47–49, 51–53.

Used only in Puerto Rico: Nos. 55–57.

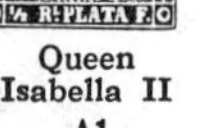

Queen Isabella II
A1

Wmk. 104

Blue Paper.
Wmkd. Loops. (104)

1855 **Typographed** ***Imperf.***

1 A1 ½r p bl grn 35.00 2.50
2 A1 1r p gray grn 35.00 2.50
3 A1 2r p car 125.00 12.50
4 A1 2r p org red 150.00 12.50

Nos. 2–3 also used in Philippines.

Nos. 3–4 Surcharged **Y ¼**

1855–56

5 A1 ¼r p on 2r p car 800.00 200.00
6 A1 ¼r p on 2r p org red 800.00 300.00

Surcharged **Y ¼**

7 A1 ¼r p on 2r p car 600.00 100.00
a. Without fraction bar 350.00
8 A1 ¼r p on 2r p org red 800.00 200.00
a. Without fraction bar 500.00

The "Y¼" surcharge met the "Ynterior" rate for delivery within the city of Havana.

Wmk. 105

Rough Yellowish Paper.
1856 Wmkd. Crossed Lines. (105)

9 A1 ½r p on grnsh bl 6.50 1.25
10 A1 1r p grn 375.00 15.00
a. 1r p emer 400.00 20.00
11 A1 2r p org red 250.00 17.50

White Smooth Paper.

1857 **Unwmkd.**

12 A1 ½r p bl 5.00 60
13 A1 1r p gray grn 5.00 60
a. 1r p pale yel grn 7.00 1.50
14 A1 2r p dl rose 12.00 3.50

Surcharged **Y¼**

1860

15 A1 ¼r p on 2r p dl rose 200.00 75.00
a. 1 of ¼ inverted 250.00 140.00

Queen Isabella II
A2 A3

1862–64 ***Imperf.***

16 A2 ¼r p blk 25.00 12.00
17 A3 ¼r p *buff* ('64) 25.00 10.00
18 A3 ½r p grn ('64) 5.00 1.00
19 A3 ½r p grn, *pale rose* ('64) 12.00 4.00
20 A3 1r p bl, *sal* ('64) 5.00 1.20
a. Diagonal half used as ½r on cover 85.00
21 A3 2r p ver, *buff* ('64) 35.00 10.00

No. 17 Overprinted in Black **66**

1866

22 A3 ¼r p *buff* 75.00 25.00

A5 A6

1866

23 A5 5c dl vio 60.00 27.50
24 A5 10c blue 3.00 1.50
25 A5 20c green 2.50 1.50
26 A5 40c rose 15.00 11.00

Stamps Dated "1867".

1867 ***Perf. 14.***

27 A5 5c dl vio 40.00 12.00
28 A5 10c blue 7.00 1.50
a. Imperf., pair 45.00 9.00
29 A5 20c green 7.00 1.50
a. Imperf., pair 65.00 100.00
30 A5 40c rose 15.00 10.00

Stamps Dated "1868".

1868

31 A6 5c dl vio 25.00 10.00
32 A6 10c blue 5.00 2.00
a. Diagonal half used as 5c on cover 85.00
33 A6 20c green 9.00 3.75
a. Diagonal half used as 10c on cover 125.00
34 A6 40c rose 17.50 9.00

Nos. 31 to 34 Overprinted in Black

HABILITADO
POR LA
NACION.
e

1868

35 A6 5c dl vio 45.00 22.50
35A A6 10c blue 45.00 22.50
36 A6 20c green 45.00 22.50
37 A6 40c rose 45.00 22.50

Stamps Dated "1869".

1869

38 A6 5c rose 45.00 15.00
39 A6 10c red brn 5.00 2.50
a. Diagonal half used as 5c on cover 65.00
40 A6 20c orange 9.00 3.00
41 A6 40c dl vio 40.00 10.00

Nos. 38–41 Overprinted type "e".

42 A6 5c rose 140.00 40.00
43 A6 10c red brn 60.00 22.50
44 A6 20c orange 45.00 30.00
45 A6 40c dl vio 70.00 30.00

"España"
A8 A9

1870 ***Perf. 14***

46 A8 5c blue 150.00 40.00
47 A8 10c green 3.50 90
a. Diagonal half used as 5c on cover 90.00
48 A8 20c red brn 3.50 90
a. Diagonal half used as 10c on cover 90.00
49 A8 40c rose 150.00 30.00

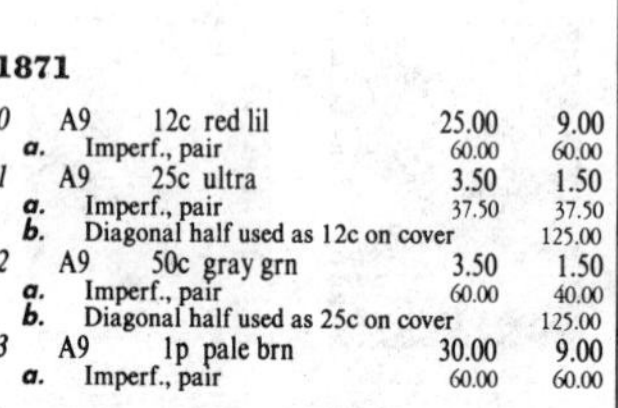

1871

50 A9 12c red lil 25.00 9.00
a. Imperf., pair 60.00 60.00
51 A9 25c ultra 3.50 1.50
a. Imperf., pair 37.50 37.50
b. Diagonal half used as 12c on cover 125.00
52 A9 50c gray grn 3.50 1.50
a. Imperf., pair 60.00 40.00
b. Diagonal half used as 25c on cover 125.00
53 A9 1p pale brn 30.00 9.00
a. Imperf., pair 60.00 60.00

King Amadeo
A10

1873 ***Perf. 14.***

54 A10 12½c dk grn 40.00 15.00
55 A10 25c gray 3.00 1.50
a. Diagonal half used as 12½c on cover 75.00
56 A10 50c brown 1.75 1.50
a. Imperf., pair 50.00 50.00
b. Half used as 25c on cover 75.00
57 A10 1p red brn 240.00 50.00
a. Diagonal half used as 50c on cover 175.00

Issues for Cuba Only

"España" Coat of Arms
A11 A12

1874

58 A11 12½c brown 15.00 7.50
59 A11 25c ultra 1.50 1.00
a. Diagonal half used as 12½c on cover 75.00
60 A11 50c dp vio 2.25 1.00
61 A11 50c gray 2.25 1.00
a. Diagonal half used as 25c on cover 75.00
62 A11 1p carmine 100.00 35.00
a. Imperf., pair 225.00 225.00

1875

63 A12 12½c lt vio 1.75 75
a. Imperf., pair 55.00
64 A12 25c ultra 90 60
a. Imperf., pair 55.00
b. Diagonal half used as 12½c on cover 75.00
65 A12 50c bl grn 90 60
a. Imperf., pair 55.00
b. Diagonal half used as 25c on cover 45.00
66 A12 1p brown 12.00 6.00
a. 1p dk brn 12.00 6.00
b. Half used as 50c on cover 85.00

King Alfonso XII
A13 A14

1876

67 A13 12½c green 3.00 60
68 A13 25c gray 1.25 50
a. Diagonal half used as 12½c on cover 75.00
69 A13 50c ultra 1.25 60
a. Imperf., pair 17.50
70 A13 1p black 12.00 5.00
a. Imperf., pair 40.00

1877

71 A14 10c lt grn 40.00 25.00
72 A14 12½c gray 9.00 1.50
a. Imperf., pair 27.50
73 A14 25c dk grn 70 50
a. Imperf., pair 27.50
74 A14 50c black 70 50
a. Imperf., pair 27.50
b. Half used as 25c on cover 75.00
75 A14 1p brown 25.00 15.00
Nos. 71-75 (5) 75.40 42.50

Stamps Dated "1878".

1878

76 A14 5c blue 60 5
a. Imperf., pair 27.50
77 A14 10c black 60.00 35.0
a. Imperf., pair 175.00
78 A14 12½c brn bis 3.50 1.5
a. 12½c gray bis 2.50 1.2
b. Imperf., pair 27.50
79 A14 25c dp grn 50 2
a. Imperf., pair 27.50
b. Diagonal half used as 12½c on cover 60.0
80 A14 50c dk bl grn 50 2
a. Imperf., pair 27.50
81 A14 1p carmine 12.00 7.0
a. Imperf., pair 55.00
Nos. 76-81 (6) 77.10 44.5

Stamps Dated "1879"

1879

82 A14 5c sl blk 90 5
83 A14 10c orange 125.00 75.0
84 A14 12½c rose 90 5
85 A14 25c ultra 70 5
a. Diagonal half used as 12½c on cover 75.0
b. Imperf., pair 55.00 40.0
86 A14 50c gray 60 4
a. Diagonal half used as 25c on cover 75.0
87 A17 1p ol bis 27.50 15.0
Nos. 82-87 (6) 155.60 91.9

A15

A16

A17

1880

88 A15 5c green 50 15
89 A15 10c lake 75.00 40.00
90 A15 12½c gray 50 15
91 A15 25c gray bl 50 15
a. Diagonal half used as 12½c on cover 75.00
92 A15 50c brown 50 20
a. Half used as 25c on cover 75.00
93 A15 1p yel brn 9.00 3.50
Nos. 88-93 (6) 86.00 44.15

1881

94 A16 1c green 50 15
95 A16 2c lake 35.00 20.00
96 A16 2½c ol bis 90 40
97 A16 5c gray bl 50 15
98 A16 10c yel brn 50 15
99 A16 20c dk brn 9.00 7.00
Nos. 94-99 (6) 46.40 27.85

1882

100 A17 1c green 60 40
101 A17 2c lake 3.50 40
102 A17 2½c dk brn 8.00 2.50
103 A17 5c gray bl 3.50 90
a. Diagonal half used as 2½c on cover 75.00
104 A17 10c ol bis 60 15
105 A17 20c red brn 85.00 35.00
Nos. 100-105 (6) 101.20 39.35

See Nos. 121–131.

Issue of 1882
Surcharged or Overprinted in Black, Blue or Red:

a

b

c

d

e

1883

106	A17 (a)	5 on 5c gray bl (R)	2.25	1.25
a.	Triple surcharge			
b.	Double surcharge		4.00	4.00
c.	Inverted surcharge		3.00	3.00
d.	Without "5" in surcharge		9.00	9.00
e.	Double surcharge, types "a" and "d"			
107	A17 (a)	10 on 10c ol bis (Bl)	2.50	1.50
a.	Inverted surcharge			
b.	Double surcharge		4.00	
108	A17 (a)	20 on 20c red brn (Bk)	27.50	22.50
a.	"10" instead of "20"		65.00	65.00
b.	Double surcharge			
109	A17 (b)	5 on 5c gray bl (R)	2.50	1.25
a.	Inverted surcharge		3.50	3.50
b.	Double surcharge		5.00	
110	A17 (b)	10 on 10c ol bis (Bl)	3.50	1.75
a.	Inverted surcharge		4.50	4.50
b.	Double surcharge			
111	A17 (b)	20 on 20c red brn (Bk)	27.50	22.50
a.	Double surcharge			
b.	Double surcharge, types "b" and "c"			
112	A17 (c)	5 on 5c gray bl (R)	2.50	1.50
a.	Inverted surcharge			
b.	Double surcharge, types "c" and "d"		6.00	
113	A17 (c)	10 on 10c ol bis (Bl)	6.00	2.50
a.	Inverted surcharge			
b.	Double surcharge			
114	A17 (c)	20 on 20c red brn (Bk)	40.00	22.50
a.	"10" instead of "20"		110.00	110.00
b.	Double surcharge			
c.	Double surcharge, types "a" and "c"			
115	A17 (d)	5 on 5c gray bl (R)	2.50	1.50
a.	Inverted surcharge		3.50	3.50
b.	Double surcharge			
116	A17 (d)	10 on 10c ol bis (Bl)	6.00	2.50
a.	Inverted surcharge			
b.	Double surcharge			
117	A17 (d)	20 on 20c red brn (Bk)	65.00	32.50
a.	Double surcharge, types "a" and "d"			
118	A17 (e)	5c gray bl (R)	3.50	2.00
a.	Double overprint		6.00	
119	A17 (e)	10c ol bis (Bl)	6.00	5.00
a.	Double overprint			
120	A17 (e)	20c red brn (Bk)	70.00	37.50
a.	Double overprint			
	Nos. 106-120 (15)		267.25	158.25

No. 120 has been reprinted. The overprint is handstamped instead of being press printed.

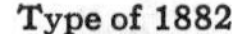
Type of 1882

1882

1st retouch

2d retouch

The differences between the stamps of 1882 and the various retouches are as follows:

Original state: The medallion is surrounded by a heavy line of color of nearly even thickness, touching the horizontal line below the word "Cuba" (or "Filipinas", as the case may be); the opening in the hair above the temple is narrow and pointed.

First retouch: The line around the medallion is thin, except at the upper right, and does not touch the horizontal line above it; the opening in the hair is slightly wider and a trifle rounded; the lock of hair above the forehead is shaped like a broad "V" and ends in a point; there is a faint white line below it, which is not found on the stamps in the original state. Owing to wear of the plate the shape of the lock of hair and the width of the white line below it vary.

Second retouch: The opening in the hair forms a semi-circle; the lock above the forehead is nearly straight, having only a slight wave, and the white line is much broader than before.

1883-86

121	A17	1c grn, 2nd retouch	2.00	25
122	A17	2½c ol bis	50	15
124	A17	2½c violet	50	15
a.	2½c red lil ('85)		60	25
b.	2½c ultra		150.00	70.00
125	A17	5c gray bl, 1st retouch	2.00	15
126	A17	5c gray bl, 2nd retouch	5.00	1.50
a.	Diagonal half used as 2½c on cover			35.00
127	A17	10c brn, 1st retouch	2.50	75
a.	Diagonal half used as 5c on cover			35.00
128	A17	20c ol bis	17.50	4.00
	Nos. 121-128 (7)		30.00	6.95

1888

129	A17	2½c red brn	4.00	1.50
130	A17	10c blue	2.25	1.00
a.	Diagonal half used as 5c on cover			35.00
131	A17	20c brnsh gray	17.50	6.00

King Alfonso XIII
A18 A19

1890-97

132	A18	1c gray brn	13.50	6.00
133	A18	1c ol gray ('91)	10.00	1.25
134	A18	1c ultra ('94)	3.50	50
a.	Imperf., pair		75.00	
135	A18	1c dk vio ('96)	1.75	25
136	A18	2c sl bl	6.00	1.50
137	A18	2c lil brn ('91)	1.75	50
138	A18	2c rose ('94)	20.00	3.00
a.	Imperf., pair		90.00	
139	A18	2c cl ('96)	7.50	90
140	A18	2½c emerald	10.00	2.25
141	A18	2½c sal ('91)	25.00	6.00
142	A18	2½c lil ('94)	2.25	35
a.	Imperf., pair		90.00	
143	A18	2½c rose ('96)	1.00	20
144	A18	5c ol gray	1.00	75
145	A18	5c emer ('91)	1.25	60
a.	Imperf., pair		60.00	
146	A18	5c sl bl ('96)	50	20
147	A18	10c brn vio	2.50	90
148	A18	10c cl ('91)	1.75	60
a.	Imperf., pair		60.00	
149	A18	10c emer ('96)	3.50	25
150	A18	20c dk vio	1.00	75
151	A18	20c ultra ('91)	11.00	6.00
152	A18	20c red brn ('94)	20.00	6.00
a.	Imperf. pair		150.00	
153	A18	20c vio ('96)	20.00	7.00
154	A18	40c org brn ('97)	40.00	15.00
155	A18	80c lil brn ('97)	50.00	20.00
	Nos. 132-155 (24)		254.75	80.75

1898

156	A19	1m org brn	25	20
157	A19	2m org brn	25	20
158	A19	3m org brn	25	20
159	A19	4m org brn	5.00	1.75
160	A19	5m org brn	25	20
161	A19	1c blk vio	25	20
162	A19	2c dk bl grn	25	20
163	A19	3c dk brn	25	20
164	A19	4c orange	13.50	3.50
165	A19	5c car rose	1.25	25
a.	Imperf., pair		55.00	
166	A19	6c dk bl	25	20
a.	Imperf., pair		55.00	
167	A19	8c gray brn	1.25	50
168	A19	10c vermilion	1.25	50
169	A19	15c sl grn	5.50	50
170	A19	20c maroon	75	25
171	A19	40c dk lil	3.00	50
172	A19	60c black	3.00	50
173	A19	80c red brn	17.50	10.00
174	A19	1p yel grn	17.50	10.00
175	A19	2p sl bl	25.00	10.00
	Nos. 156-175 (20)		96.50	39.85

Issued under Administration of the United States.

Puerto Principe Issue.

Issues of Cuba of 1898 and 1896 Surcharged:

HABILITADO 1 cent. — a
HABILITADO 1 cents. — b
HABILITADO 2 cents. — c
HABILITADO 2 cents. — d
HABILITADO 3 cents. — e
HABILITADO 3 cents. — f
HABILITADO 5 cents. — g
HABILITADO 5 cents. — h
HABILITADO 5 cents. — i
HABILITADO 5 cents. — j
HABILITADO 3 cents. — k
HABILITADO 3 cents. — l
HABILITADO 10 cents. — m

Types a, c, d, e, f, g and h are 17½mm. high, the others are 19½mm. high.

Black Surcharge
On Nos. 156, 157, 158 and 160.

1898-99

176	(a)	1c on 1m org brn	50.00	35.00
a.	Inverted surcharge			
177	(b)	1c on 1m org brn	40.00	30.00
a.	Broken figure "I"		75.00	60.00
b.	Inverted surcharge			200.00
d.	Same as "a", inverted			250.00
178	(c)	2c on 2m org brn	20.00	15.00
a.	Inverted surcharge		250.00	50.00
179	(d)	2c on 2m org brn	40.00	25.00
a.	Inverted surcharge		350.00	100.00
179B	(k)	3c on 1m org brn	375.00	150.00
c.	Double surcharge		1,500.	750.00
179D	(l)	3c on 1m org brn	1,500.	600.00
e.	Double surcharge			
179F	(e)	3c on 2m org brn		*2,000.*
179G	(f)	3c on 2m org brn		*2,500.*
180	(e)	3c on 3m org brn	25.00	20.00
a.	Inverted surcharge			100.00
181	(f)	3c on 3m org brn	75.00	50.00
a.	Inverted surcharge			300.00
182	(g)	5c on 1m org brn	700.00	175.00
a.	Inverted surcharge			500.00
183	(h)	5c on 1m org brn	1,500.	400.00
a.	Inverted surcharge			700.00
184	(g)	5c on 2m org brn	750.00	200.00
185	(h)	5c on 2m org brn	1,500.	400.00
186	(g)	5c on 3m org brn		150.00
a.	Inverted surcharge			700.00
187	(h)	5c on 3m org brn		400.00
a.	Inverted surcharge			1,000.
188	(g)	5c on 5m org brn	65.00	50.00
a.	Inverted surcharge		400.00	175.00
b.	Double surcharge			
189	(h)	5c on 5m org brn	350.00	225.00
a.	Inverted surcharge			400.00
b.	Double surcharge			
189C	(i)	5c on 5m org brn		*4,000.*

Black Surcharge on No. P25.

190	(g)	5c on ½m bl grn	250.00	75.00
a.	Inverted surcharge		500.00	150.00
b.	Pair, one without surcharge			*450.00*
191	(h)	5c on ½m bl grn	300.00	90.00
a.	Inverted surcharge			200.00

No.	Type	Description	Unused	Used
192	(i)	5c on ½m bl grn	550.00	200.00
a.		Double surcharge, one diagonal		3,000.
193	(j)	5c on ½m bl grn	700.00	300.00

Red Surcharge on No. 161.

No.	Type	Description	Unused	Used
196	(k)	3c on 1c blk vio	60.00	25.00
a.		Inverted surcharge		200.00
197	(l)	3c on 1c blk vio	125.00	45.00
a.		Inverted surcharge		300.00
198	(i)	5c on 1c blk vio	20.00	20.00
a.		Inverted surcharge		100.00
b.		Vertical surcharge		2,000.
c.		Double surcharge	400.00	600.00
d.		Double inverted surcharge		
199	(j)	5c on 1c blk vio	50.00	40.00
a.		Inverted surcharge		250.00
b.		Vertical surcharge		2,000.
c.		Double surcharge	1,000.	600.00
200	(m)	10c on 1c blk vio	20.00	50.00
a.		Broken figure "I"	40.00	100.00

Black Surcharge on Nos. P26 - P30.

No.	Type	Description	Unused	Used
201	(k)	3c on 1m bl grn	300.00	200.00
a.		Inverted surcharge		400.00
b.		"EENTS"	550.00	400.00
c.		Same as "b", inverted		850.00
202	(l)	3c on 1m bl grn	500.00	400.00
a.		Inverted surcharge		850.00
203	(k)	3c on 2m bl grn	850.00	250.00
a.		"EENTS"	1,200.	450.00
b.		Inverted surcharge		600.00
c.		Same as "a", inverted		750.00
204	(l)	3c on 2m bl grn	1,000.	450.00
a.		Inverted surcharge		750.00
205	(k)	3c on 3m bl grn	900.00	250.00
a.		Inverted surcharge		500.00
b.		"EENTS"	1,200.	375.00
c.		Same as "b", inverted		700.00
206	(l)	3c on 3m bl grn	1,200.	375.00
a.		Invtd. surch.		700.00
211	(i)	5c on 1m bl grn		1,400.
a.		"EENTS"		2,000.
212	(j)	5c on 1m bl grn		2,000.
213	(i)	5c on 2m bl grn		1,250.
a.		"EENTS"		1,750.
214	(j)	5c on 2m bl grn		1,750.
215	(i)	5c on 3m bl grn		500.00
a.		"EENTS"		900.00
216	(j)	5c on 3m bl grn		900.00
217	(i)	5c on 4m bl grn	2,000.	500.00
a.		"EENTS"	2,500.	1,200.
b.		Inverted surcharge		900.00
c.		Same as "a", inverted		1,400.
218	(j)	5c on 4m bl grn		1,100.
a.		Invtd. surch.		1,400.
219	(i)	5c on 8m bl grn	2,500.	1,000.
a.		Inverted surcharge		1,500.
b.		"EENTS"		2,000.
c.		Same as "b", inverted		2,500.
220	(j)	5c on 8m bl grn		2,000.
a.		Invtd. surch.		2,500.

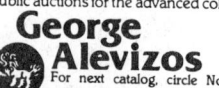

United States Nos. 279a, 267, 279B, 268, 281a, 282C and 283a Surcharged in Black

CUBA
1 c.
de PESO.

Wmkd. USPS (191)

1899 *Perf. 12.*

No.	Type	Description	Unused	Used
221	A87	1c on 1c yel grn	4.00	50
a.		Vertical surcharge		
222	A88	2c on 2c car	4.00	40
a.		2c on 2c red	5.00	40
b.		"CUPA"	100.00	100.00
c.		Invtd. surch.	1,750.	1,500.
223	A88	2½c on 2c red	3.00	50
a.		2½c on 2c car	3.50	2.00
224	A89	3c on 3c pur	8.50	1.25
a.		Period between "B" and "A"	27.50	27.50
225	A91	5c on 5c bl	8.50	1.25
a.		"CUPA"	50.00	40.00
226	A94	10c on 10c brn, type I	22.50	7.50
b.		"CUBA" omitted	1,750.	
226A	A94	10c on 10c brn, type II	4,000.	
		Nos. 221-226 (6)	50.50	11.40

The 2½c was sold and used as a 2c stamp.
Excellent counterfeits of this and the preceding issue exist, especially inverted and double surcharges.

Issues of the Republic under U. S. Military Rule.

Statue of Columbus
A20

Royal Palms
A21

"Cuba"
A22

Ocean Liner
A23

Cane Field
A24

Wmkd. U S—C. (191C)

1899 **Engraved** *Perf. 12*

No.	Type	Description	Unused	Used
227	A20	1c yel grn	3.00	15
228	A21	2c carmine	3.00	15
a.		2c scar	3.00	15
b.		Booklet pane of 6	1,500.	
229	A22	3c purple	3.00	25
230	A23	5c blue	4.50	30
231	A24	10c brown	10.00	75
		Nos. 227-231 (5)	23.50	1.60

Issues of the Republic

No. 229 Surcharged in Carmine

1902, Sept. 30

No.	Type	Description	Unused	Used
232	A22	1c on 3c pur	1.50	75
a.		Inverted surcharge	20.00	20.00
b.		Surcharge sideways (numeral horizontal)		
c.		Double surcharge	30.00	30.00

Counterfeits of the errors are plentiful.

Re-engraved.

The re-engraved stamps of 1905-07 may be distinguished from the issue of 1899 as follows:

ORIGINAL — RE-ENGRAVED

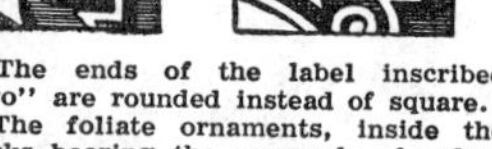

1c: The ends of the label inscribed "Centavo" are rounded instead of square.
2c: The foliate ornaments, inside the oval disks bearing the numerals of value, have been removed.
5c: Two lines forming a right angle have been added in the upper corners of the label bearing the word "Cuba".
10c: A small ball has been added to each of the square ends of the label bearing the word "Cuba".

1905 *Perf. 12* **Unwmkd.**

No.	Type	Description	Unused	Used
233	A20	1c green	2.25	15
234	A21	2c rose	1.50	15
a.		Bklt. pane of 6	125.00	
236	A23	5c blue	37.50	1.50
237	A24	10c brown	4.00	60

Maj. Gen. Antonio Maceo
A26

1907

No.	Type	Description	Unused	Used
238	A26	50c gray bl & blk	1.50	90

Bartolomé Masó
A27

Máximo Gómez
A28

Julio Sanguily
A29

Ignacio Agramonte
A30

Calixto García
A31

José M. Rodriquez y Rodriquez (Mayia)
A32

Carlos Roloff
A33

1910, Feb. 1

No.	Type	Description	Unused	Used
239	A27	1c grn & vio	1.10	10
a.		Center inverted	175.00	175.00
240	A28	2c car & grn	2.25	10
a.		Center inverted	700.00	750.00
241	A29	3c vio & bl	1.50	25
242	A30	5c bl & grn	20.00	1.00
243	A31	8c ol & vio	1.50	40
244	A32	10c brn & bl	8.00	85
a.		Center inverted	1,000.	
245	A26	50c vio & blk	2.25	60
246	A33	1p sl & blk	10.00	5.00
		Nos. 239-246 (8)	46.60	8.30

1911-13

No.	Type	Description	Unused	Used
247	A27	1c green	75	10
248	A28	2c car rose	1.00	8
a.		Bklt. pane of 6 ('13)	55.00	
250	A30	5c ultra	2.25	10
251	A31	8c ol grn & blk	1.50	75
252	A33	1p black	7.00	2.50
		Nos. 247-252 (5)	12.50	3.53

Map of Cuba
A34

1914–15

No.	Type	Description	Unused	Used
253	A34	1c green	75	6
a.		Booklet pane of 6	60.00	
254	A34	2c car rose	75	5
a.		Booklet pane of 6	60.00	
255	A34	2c red ('15)	1.50	5
a.		Booklet pane of 6	60.00	
256	A34	3c violet	5.00	50
257	A34	5c blue	7.00	25
258	A34	8c ol grn	6.00	1.00
259	A34	10c brown	10.00	50
260	A34	10c ol grn ('15)	12.00	75
261	A34	50c orange	70.00	15.00
262	A34	1p gray	90.00	30.00
		Nos. 253-262 (10)	203.00	48.16

Imperf. pairs, price each $500.

Gertrudis Gómez de Avellaneda
A34a

1914

263	A34a	5c blue	15.00	6.00

Issued to commemorate the centenary of the birth of the Cuban poetess, Gertrudis Gómez de Avellaneda (1814–1873).

José Martí
A35

Máximo Gómez
A36

José de la Luz Caballero
A37

Calixto García
A38

Ignacio Agramonte
A39

Tomás Estrada Palma
A40

José A. Saco
A41

Antonio Maceo
A42

Carlos Manuel de Céspedes
A43

1917–18 ***Perf. 12.*** **Unwmkd.**

264	A35	1c bl grn	1.00	5
a.		Booklet pane of 6	25.00	
b.		Booklet pane of 30	175.00	
265	A36	2c rose	75	5
a.		Booklet pane of 6	35.00	
b.		Booklet pane of 30	175.00	
266	A36	2c lt red ('18)	75	5
a.		Booklet pane of 6	35.00	
267	A37	3c violet	1.25	5
a.		Imperf., pair	275.00	
b.		Booklet pane of 6	30.00	
268	A38	5c dp bl	2.50	6
269	A39	8c red brn	6.00	15
270	A40	10c yel brn	3.00	10
271	A41	20c gray grn	12.00	1.00
272	A42	50c dl rose	14.00	1.00
273	A43	1p black	14.00	1.00
		Nos. 264-273 (10)	55.25	3.51

Wmk. 106

Wmkd. Star. (106)

1925-28 ***Perf. 12.***

274	A35	1c bl grn	1.75	6
a.		Booklet pane of 30	250.00	
275	A36	2c brt rose	1.50	5
a.		Booklet pane of 6	50.00	
b.		Booklet pane of 30	250.00	
276	A38	5c dp bl	3.00	10
277	A39	8c red brn ('28)	6.00	50
278	A40	10c yel brn ('27)	7.00	60
279	A41	20c ol grn	11.00	1.00
		Nos. 274-279 (6)	30.25	2.31

1926 ***Imperf.***

280	A35	1c bl grn	2.75	1.75
281	A36	2c brt rose	2.50	1.50
282	A38	5c dp bl	4.00	3.00

See also Nos. 304-310.

Arms of Republic
A44

1927, May 20 ***Perf. 12*** **Unwmkd.**

283	A44	25c violet	12.50	6.00

25th anniversary of the Republic.

Tomás Estrada Palma
A45

Designs: 2c, Gen. Gerardo Machado. 5c, Morro Castle. 8c, Havana Railway Station. 10c, Presidential Palace. 13c, Tobacco Plantation. 20c, Treasury Building. 30c, Sugar Mill. 50c, Havana Cathedral. 1p, Galician Clubhouse, Havana.

1928, Jan. 2 **Wmk. 106**

284	A45	1c dp grn	60	40
285	A45	2c brt rose	60	40
286	A45	5c dp bl	1.75	60
287	A45	8c lt red brn	2.75	1.50
288	A45	10c bis brn	1.50	1.00
289	A45	13c orange	2.25	1.00
290	A45	20c ol grn	2.75	1.25
291	A45	30c dk vio	5.00	1.00
292	A45	50c car rose	8.00	3.50
293	A45	1p gray blk	16.00	8.00
		Nos. 284-293 (10)	41.20	18.65

Sixth Pan-American Conference.

Capitol, Havana
A55

1929, May 18

294	A55	1c green	50	40
295	A55	2c car rose	50	35
296	A55	5c blue	75	50
297	A55	10c bis brn	1.50	60
298	A55	20c violet	5.00	2.50
		Nos. 294-298 (5)	8.25	4.35

Opening of the Capitol, Havana.

Hurdler
A56

1930, Mar. 15 **Engraved**

299	A56	1c green	1.00	50
300	A56	2c carmine	1.00	50
301	A56	5c dp bl	1.50	50
302	A56	10c bis brn	2.25	1.00
303	A56	20c violet	10.00	5.00
		Nos. 299-303 (5)	15.75	7.50

Issued to commemorate the second Central American Athletic Games.

Types of 1917 Portrait Issue.
Flat Plate Printing.
Engraved

1930–45 ***Perf. 10*** **Wmk. 106**

304	A35	1c bl grn	1.10	25
a.		Booklet pane of 6	30.00	
b.		Booklet pane of 30		
305	A36	2c brt rose	175.00	90.00
a.		Booklet pane of 6	1,200.	
305B	A37	3c dk rose vio ('42)	4.50	60
c.		Booklet pane of 6	40.00	
306	A38	5c dk bl	5.00	40
306A	A39	8c red brn ('45)	5.00	50
307	A40	10c brown	5.00	50
a.		10c yel brn ('35)	7.00	1.00
307B	A41	20c ol grn ('41)	8.00	1.00
		Nos. 304-307B (7)	203.60	93.25

Nos. 305 and 305B were printed for booklet panes and all copies have straight edges.

Rotary Press Printing.

308	A35	1c bl grn	1.75	25
309	A36	2c brt rose	1.75	25
a.		Booklet pane of 50		
310	A37	3c violet	2.50	25
a.		3c dl vio ('38)	1.75	25
b.		3c rose vio ('41)	1.75	25
c.		Bklt. pane of 50		

The flat plate stamps measure 18½x21½mm.; those from the rotary press, 19x22mm.

The Mangos of Baragua
A57

War Memorial
A61

Battle of Mal Tiempo
A58

Battle of Coliseo
A59

Maceo, Gómez and Zayas
A60

Wmk. 229

Wmkd. Wavy Lines. (229)

1933, Apr. 23 **Photo.** ***Perf. 12½***

312	A57	3c dk brn	1.00	25
313	A58	5c dk bl	1.00	50
314	A59	10c emerald	3.00	50
315	A60	13c red	3.00	1.25
316	A61	20c black	6.00	4.00
		Nos. 312-316 (5)	14.00	6.50

Issued in commemoration of the War of Independence and the dedication of the "Soldado Invasor" monument.

Types of 1917 Issues with Carmine or Black Overprint Reading Up or Down

GOBIERNO
REVOLUCIONARIO
4-9-1933

Rotary Press Printing.
Engraved

1933, Dec. 23 ***Perf. 10*** **Wmk. 106**

317	A35	1c bl grn (C)	1.00	35

With Additional Surcharge of New Value and Bars.

318	A37	2c on 3c vio (Bk)	1.00	35

Nos. 317–318 commemorate the establishment of a revolutionary junta.

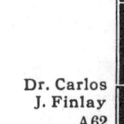

Dr. Carlos J. Finlay
A62

Engraved.

1934, Dec. 3 ***Perf. 10*** **Wmk. 106**

319	A62	2c dk car	1.00	30
320	A62	5c dk bl	2.25	75

Issued to commemorate the centenary of the birth of Dr. Carlos J. Finlay (1833–1915), physician-biologist who found that a mosquito transmitted yellow fever.

Pres. José Miguel Gómez
A63

Gómez Monument
A64

1936, May ***Perf. 10***

322	A63	1c green	60	30
323	A64	2c carmine	1.50	30

Issued in commemoration of the unveiling of a monument to Gen. José Miguel Gómez, ex-president.

Matanzas Issue.

Map of Cuba
A65

Designs: 2c, Map of Free Zone. 4c, S. S. "Rex" in Matanzas Bay. 5c, Ships in Matanzas Bay. 8c, Caves of Bellamar. 10c, Valley of Yumuri. 20c, Yumuri River. 50c, Ships Leaving Port.

Photogravure.

Wmkd. Wavy Lines. (229)

1936, May 5 ***Perf. 12½***

324	A65	1c bl grn	40	25
325	A65	2c red	60	30
326	A65	4c claret	1.25	40
327	A65	5c ultra	1.10	40
328	A65	8c org brn	2.50	1.00
329	A65	10c emerald	2.00	1.00
330	A65	20c brown	5.00	3.50
331	A65	50c slate	8.00	5.00
		Nos. 324-331, C18-C21, CE1, E8 (14)	48.10	27.10

Exist imperf. Price 20% more.

"Peace and Work"
A73

Máximo Gómez Monument
A74

"Independence"
A76

Torch
A75

"Messenger of Peace"
A77

1936, Nov. 18 ***Perf. 12½***

332	A73	1c emerald	50	25
333	A74	2c crimson	60	20
334	A75	4c maroon	75	25
335	A76	5c ultra	2.50	85
336	A77	8c dk grn	4.00	1.75
		Nos. 332-336, C22-C23, E9 (8)	19.85	7.80

Maj. Gen. Máximo Gómez, birth centenary.

Sugar Cane
A78

Primitive Sugar Mill
A79

Modern Sugar Mill
A80

Wmkd. Star. (106)

1937, Oct. 2 **Engraved** ***Perf. 10***

337	A78	1c yel grn	1.00	50
338	A79	2c red	70	30
339	A80	5c brt bl	1.00	60

Issued in commemoration of the 400th anniversary of the sugar cane industry in Cuba.

Argentine Emblem
A81

Mountain Scene (Bolivia)
A82

Arms of Brazil
A83

Canadian Scene
A84

Camilo Henriquez (Chile)
A85

Gen, Francisco de Paula Santander (Colombia)
A86

National Monument (Costa Rica)
A87

Autograph of José Marti (Cuba)
A88

Columbus Lighthouse (Dominican Republic)
A89

Juan Montalvo (Ecuador)
A90

Abraham Lincoln (United States)
A91

Quetzal and Scroll (Guatemala)
A92

Arms of Haiti
A93

Francisco Morazán (Honduras)
A94

Fleet of Columbus
A95

Engraved.

1937, Oct. 13 ***Perf. 10*** **Wmk. 106**

340	A81	1c dp grn	50	50
341	A82	1c green	50	50
342	A83	2c carmine	50	50
343	A84	2c carmine	50	50
344	A85	3c violet	1.50	1.50
345	A86	3c violet	1.50	1.50
346	A87	4c bis brn	1.75	1.75
347	A88	4c bis brn	3.00	3.00
348	A89	5c blue	1.50	1.50
349	A90	5c blue	1.50	1.50
350	A91	8c citron	7.50	7.50
351	A92	8c citron	2.50	2.50
352	A93	10c maroon	2.50	2.50
353	A94	10c maroon	2.50	2.50
354	A95	25c rose lil	25.00	25.00
		Nos. 340-354, C24-C29, E10-E11 (23)	106.75	99.75

Nos. 340 to 354 were sold by the Cuban Post Office for three days, Oct. 13-15, during which no other stamps were sold. They were postally valid for the full face value. Proceeds from their three-day sale above 30,000 pesos were paid by the Cuban Post Office Department to the Association of American Writers and Artists. Remainders were overprinted "SVP" (Without Postal Value).

No. 283 Surcharged in Green

1837 1937
PRIMER CENTENARIO
FERROCARRIL EN CUBA

1937, Nov. 19 ***Perf. 12*** **Unwmkd.**

355	A44	10c on 25c vio	9.00	3.00

Centenary of Cuban railroads.

Ciboney Indian and Cigar
A96

Cigar and Globe
A97

Tobacco Plant and Cigars
A98

Wmkd. Star. (106)

1939, Aug. 28 **Engraved** ***Perf. 10***

356	A96	1c yel grn	25	5
357	A97	2c red	50	5
358	A98	5c brt ultra	1.00	20

General Calixto García
A99 A100

1939, Nov. 6 ***Perf. 10, Imperf.***

359	A99	2c dk red	60	20
360	A100	5c dp bl	1.20	60

Birth centenary of General Garcia.

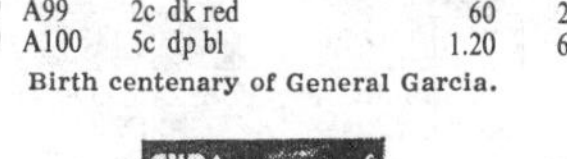

Gonzalo de Quesada
A101

1940, Apr. 30 **Engraved** ***Perf. 10***

361	A101	2c rose red	1.00	50

Pan American Union, 50th anniversary.

Rotary Club Emblem, Cuban Flag and Tobacco Plant
A102

Lions Emblem, Cuban Flag and Royal Palms
A103

1940, May 18 ***Perf. 10*** **Wmk. 106**

362	A102	2c rose red	2.00	1.00

Issued in commemoration of the Rotary International Convention held at Havana.

1940, July 23

363	A103	2c org ver	2.00	1.00

Lions International Convention, Havana.

Dr. Nicolás J. Gutiérrez
A104

1940, Oct. 28

364	A104	2c org ver	1.20	50
365	A104	5c blue	1.50	60
a.		Sheet of four, imperf., unwmkd.	5.00	5.00
b.		As "a," blk overprint ('51)	6.00	6.00

Issued in commemoration of the 100th anniversary of the publication of the first Cuban Medical Review, "El Repertorio Medico Habanero".

No. 365a measures 127x177mm. and contains two each of Nos. 364 and 365 imperforate, and upper and lower marginal inscriptions. The sheet sold for 25c.

In 1951 Nos. 365a was overprinted in black: "50 Aniversario Descubrimiento Agente Transmisor • de la Fiebre Amarilla por el Dr. Carlos J. Finlay • Honor a los Martires de la Ciencia 1901 1951." The overprint is illustrated over No. C43A, but does not include the plane and "Correo Aereo."

Major General Guillermo Moncada
A105

Moncada Riding into Battle
A106

1941, June 25

366	A105	3c dk brn, *buff*	1.20	40
367	A106	5c brt bl	1.50	75

Issued in commemoration of the centenary of the birth of Maj. Gen. Guillermo Moncada (1841-96).

Globe Showing Western Hemisphere
A107

Maceo, Bolívar, Juárez, Lincoln and Arms of Cuba
A108

Tree of Fraternity, Havana
A110

"Labor: Wealth of America"
A109

Statue of Liberty
A111

Perf. 10, Imperf.

1942, Feb. 23 **Wmk. 106**

368	A107	1c emerald	40	12
369	A108	3c org brn	50	15
370	A109	5c blue	90	30
371	A110	10c red vio	2.00	75
372	A111	13c red	2.50	1.25
		Nos. 368-372 (5)	6.30	2.57

Issued to publicize the spirit of Democracy in the Americas.

The imperforate varieties are without gum.

Ignacio Agramonte Loynaz
A112

Rescue of Sanguily by Agramonte
A113

1942, Apr. 10 ***Perf. 10***

373	A112	3c bis brn	90	50
374	A113	5c brt bl, *bluish*	1.75	70

Issued in commemoration of the 100th anniversary of the birth of Ignacio Agramonte Loynaz, patriot.

"Unmask the Fifth Columnists"
A114

" Be Careful, The Fifth Column is Spying on You"
A115

" Destroy it. The Fifth Column is like a Serpent"
A116

" Fulfill your Patriotic Duty by Destroying the Fifth Column"
A117

" Don't be Afraid of the Fifth Column. Attack it"
A118

1943, July 5

375	A114	1c dk bl grn	40	18
376	A115	3c red	60	20
377	A116	5c brt bl	70	20
378	A117	10c dl brn	1.75	60
379	A118	13c dl rose vio	3.50	1.75
		Nos. 375-379 (5)	6.95	2.93

General Eloy Alfaro and Flags of Cuba and Ecuador
A119

1943, Sept. 20

380	A119	3c green	1.25	40

Issued to commemorate the 100th anniversary of the birth of General Eloy Alfaro of Ecuador.

Retirement Security
A120

1943, Nov. 8 ***Perf. 10*** **Wmk. 106**

381	A120	1c yel grn	75	30
382	A120	3c vermilion	90	30
383	A120	5c brt bl	1.00	50

1944, Mar. 18

384	A120	1c brt yel grn	75	30
385	A120	3c salmon	90	30
386	A120	5c lt bl	1.50	75

Half the proceeds from the sale of Nos. 381-386 were used for the Communications Ministry Employees' Retirement Fund.

Portrait of Columbus
A121

Bartolomé de Las Casas
A122

First Statue of Columbus at Cárdenas
A123

Discovery of Tobacco
A124

Columbus Sights Land
A125

1944, May 19

387	A121	1c dk yel grn	30	20
388	A122	3c brown	50	20
389	A123	5c brt bl	70	30
390	A124	10c dk vio	1.75	1.00
391	A125	13c dk red	3.50	1.75
		Nos. 387-391, C36-C37 (7)	9.00	4.15

Issued to commemorate the 450th anniversary of the discovery of America.

Major General Carlos Roloff
A126

Map of the Americas and First Brazilian Postage Stamps
A127

1944, Aug. 21

392	A126	3c violet	75	35

Issued to commemorate the 100th anniversary of the birth of Maj. Gen. Carlos Roloff.

1944, Dec. 20 **Engraved**

393	A127	3c brn org	1.75	75

Issued to commemorate the centenary of the first postage stamps of the Americas, issued by Brazil in 1843.

Seal of the Society
A128

Luis de las Casas and
Luis Maria Penalver
A129

1945, Oct. 5 *Perf. 10* Wmk. 106

394 A128 1c yel grn 30 20
395 A129 2c scarlet 45 20

Issued to commemorate the sesquicentenary of the founding of the Economic Society of Friends of the Country.

Aged Couple—A130

1945, Dec. 27

396 A130 1c dk yel grn 25 10
397 A130 2c scarlet 40 15
398 A130 5c cob bl 75 35

1946, Mar. 26

399 A130 1c brt yel grn 50 25
400 A130 2c sal pink 40 25
401 A130 5c lt bl 60 50

See note after No. 386.

Gabriel de la Concepcion Valdés
Plácido)—A131

1946, Feb. 5

402 A131 2c scarlet 90 30

Issued to commemorate the centenary of the death of the poet Gabriel de la Concepcion Valdés.

Manuel
Marquez Sterling
A132

Globe
and Cross
A133

1946, Apr. 30

403 A132 2c scarlet 90 40

Issued to commemorate the third anniversary of the founding of the Manuel Marquez Sterling Professional School of Journalism.

1946, July 4 Engraved

404 A133 2c scar, *pink* 85 40

Issued in honor of the 80th anniversary of the International Red Cross.

Cow and Milkmaid
A134

Franklin D. Roosevelt
A135

1947, Feb. 20 *Perf. 10* Wmk. 106

405 A134 2c scarlet 75 30

Issued to commemorate the 1947 National Livestock Exposition.

1947, Apr. 12

406 A135 2c vermilion 50 25

Issued to commemorate the second anniversary of the death of Franklin D. Roosevelt.

Antonio Oms Sarret
and Aged Couple
A136

1947, Oct. 20

407 A136 1c dp yel grn 20 15
408 A136 2c scarlet 35 15
409 A136 5c lt bl 75 40

See note after No. 386.

Marta Abreu
Arenabio
de Estevez
A137

"Charity"
A138

Marta Abreu
Monument,
Santa Clara
A139

" Patriotism "
A140

1947, Nov. 29

410 A137 1c dp yel grn 40 25
411 A138 2c scarlet 60 20
412 A139 5c brt bl 1.00 50
413 A140 10c dk vio 2.00 1.00

Issued to commemorate the centenary of the birth of Marta Abreu Arenabio de Estevez, philanthropist and humanitarian.

Armauer Hansen—A141

1948, Apr. 9

414 A141 2c rose car 75 30

International Leprosy Congress, Havana.

Mother and Child
A142

1948, Oct. 15 Engraved

415 A142 1c yel grn 30 20
416 A142 2c scarlet 40 20
417 A142 5c brt bl 85 40

See note after No. 386.

Death of
José Martí
A143

Martí
Rowing to Shore
A144

Engraved.

1948, Nov. 10 *Perf. 10* Wmk. 106

418 A143 2c scarlet 35 20
419 A144 5c brt bl 80 35

Issued to commemorate (in 1945) the 50th anniversary of the death of José Martí, patriot.

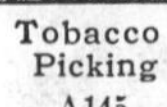

Tobacco
Picking
A145

Liberty Carrying
Flag and Cigars
A146

Cigar and Arms of Cuba
A147

1948, Dec. 6

Size: 22½x26mm.

420 A145 1c green 15 5
421 A146 2c rose car 25 10
422 A147 5c brt bl 35 15

Cuba's tobacco industry.
See Nos. 445–447.

Equestrian Statue
of Gen. Antonio Maceo
A148

Sword Salute to Maceo
A149

Designs: 2c, Portrait of Maceo. 5c, Mausoleum, El Cacahual. 10c, East to West invasion. 20c, Battle of Peralejo. 50c, Declaration of Baragua. 1p, Death of Maceo at San Pedro.

1948, Dec. 15 *Perf. 12½* Wmk. 229

423 A148 1c bl grn 15 10
424 A148 2c red 25 8
425 A148 5c blue 50 25
426 A149 8c blk & brn 75 50
427 A149 10c brn & bl grn 75 35
428 A149 20c bl & car 3.00 1.50
429 A149 50c car & ultra 5.00 3.50
430 A149 1p blk & vio 10.00 5.00
Nos. 423-430 (8) 20.40 11.28

Issued to commemorate the centenary (in 1945) of the birth of General Antonio Maceo.

Symbol of
Pharmacy
A150

Morro
Lighthouse
A151

1948, Dec. 28 *Perf. 10*

431 A150 2c rose car 75 30

Issued to commemorate the First Pan-American Congress of Pharmacy, Havana, December 1948.

1949, Jan. 17 *Perf. 12½* Wmk. 229

432 A151 2c carmine 50 25

Issued to commemorate the centenary (in 1944) of the erection of the Morro Lighthouse.

Jagua Castle, Cienfuegos
A152

1949, Jan. 27 *Perf. 10* Wmk. 106

433 A152 1c yel grn 40 20
434 A152 2c rose red 80 40

Issued to commemorate the 200th anniversary of the construction of Jagua Castle and the centenary of the publication of the first newspaper in Cienfuegos.

Manuel Sanguily y Garritt A153 — Map of Isle of Pines A154

1949, Mar. 31

435	A153	2c rose red	35	20
436	A153	5c blue	75	40

Issued to commemorate the centenary of the birth of Manuel Sanguily y Garritt (1848–1925), cabinet member, editor, author.

1949, Apr. 26

437	A154	5c blue	75	35

Issued to commemorate the 20th anniversary of the recognition of Cuban ownership of the Isle of Pines.

Ismael Cespedes A155

1949, Sept. 28

438	A155	1c yel grn	35	20
439	A155	2c scarlet	35	20
440	A155	5c brt bl	80	40

See note after No. 386.

Gen. Enrique Collazo A156 — Enrique José Varona A157

1950, Feb. 28 Engraved *Perf. 10*

441	A156	2c scarlet	40	20
442	A156	5c brt bl	80	35

Issued to commemorate the centenary (in 1948) of the birth of General Enrique Collazo.

1950, Feb. 28

443	A157	2c scarlet	40	20
444	A157	5c brt bl	80	40

Issued to commemorate the centenary of the birth of Enrique José Varona, writer and patriot.

Tobacco Types of 1948.

1950, June 20 Re-engraved

Size: 21 x 25 mm.

445	A145	1c green	40	10
446	A146	2c rose red	40	10
447	A147	5c blue	60	35

The re-engraved stamps show slight differences in many minor details.

No. 446 Overprinted in Black

BANCO NACIONAL DE CUBA INAUGURACION 27 ABRIL 1950

1950, Apr. 27

448	A146	2c rose red	75	35

Issued to commemorate the opening of the National Bank of Cuba, April 27, 1950.

Re-engraved Tobacco Types of 1950 Overprinted in Carmine

U.P.U 1874 1949

1950, May 18

449	A145	1c yel grn	25	15
450	A146	2c lil rose	40	20
451	A147	5c lt bl	75	25

75th anniversary (in 1949) of Universal Postal Union.

No. 451 exists with surcharge inverted.

Manuel Balanzategui, Antonio L. Pausa and Train Wreck A158 — Fernando Figueredo A159

1950, Sept. 21 Engraved

452	A158	1c yel grn	35	20
453	A158	2c scarlet	35	20
454	A158	5c brt bl	75	40

1951, Mar. 17 *Perf. 10* Wmk. 106

455	A159	1c green	40	15
456	A159	2c scarlet	40	15
457	A159	5c brt bl	75	30

Three-fourths of the proceeds from the sale of these stamps were used for the Communication Ministry Employees' Retirement Fund.

See Nos. 474, C51–C56, E15.

Miguel Teurbe Tolón and Flag A160 — Narciso Lopez A161

Emilia Teurbe Tolón Sewing Flag A162 — Cuban Flag A163

Engraved and Lithographed.

1951, July 3 *Perf. 13* Wmk. 229

458	A160	1c Prus grn, ultra & red	40	20
459	A161	2c red & gray blk	60	25
460	A162	5c ultra & red	1.25	50
461	A163	10c rose vio, bl & red	2.00	75
		Nos. 458-461, C41-C43, E13 (8)	15.50	4.70

Centenary of adoption of Cuba's flag.

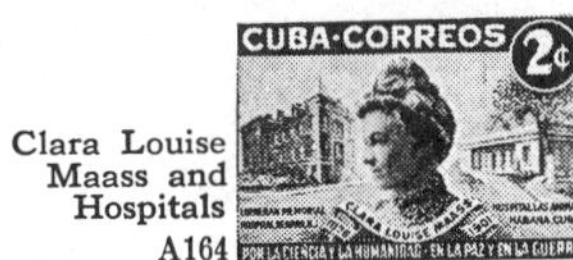

Clara Louise Maass and Hospitals A164

Hospitals: Lutheran Memorial, Newark, N.J. and Las Animas, Havana.

Engraved.

1951, Aug. 24 *Perf. 10* Wmk. 106

462	A164	2c scarlet	90	40

Issued to commemorate the 75th anniversary of the birth of Clara Louise Maass, (1876–1901), American nurse and martyr in yellow fever fight.

Airmail Type and

José Raul Capablanca—A165

Capablanca Club, Havana A166

Design: 2c, Capablanca making "The Exact Play."

Perf. 13

1951, Nov. 1 Photo. Wmk. 229

463	A165	1c bl grn & org	3.50	75
464	AP27	2c rose car & dk brn	4.00	1.50
465	A166	5c blk & dp ultra	8.00	2.50
		Nos. 463-465, C44-C46, E14 (7)	52.00	14.50

Jose Raul Capablanca, World Chess titlist (1921). Imperf., set of 7 pairs, $1,500.

Antonio Guiteras Holmes A167

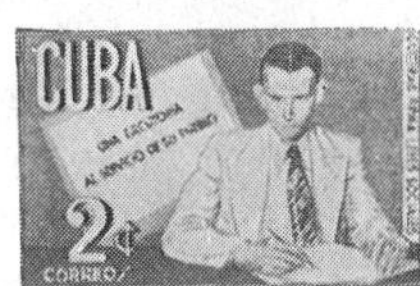

Guiteras Preparing Social Legislation A168

Fort of the Morrillo A169

Engraved.

1951, Oct. 22 *Perf. 10* Wmk. 106

466	A167	1c yel grn	35	15
467	A168	2c rose car	60	20
468	A169	5c dp bl	1.00	30
		Nos. 466-468, C47-C49 (6)	6.70	2.55

Issued to commemorate the 16th anniversary of the Action of the Morrillo and to honor Antonio Guiteras Holmes, who was killed there.

Souvenir sheets containing stamps similar to Nos. 466-468, but in different colors, are listed as Nos. C49a-C49b.

Poinsettia A170 — Maj. Gen. José Maceo A171

1951, Dec. 1 Engr. and Typo.

469	A170	1c grn & car	3.00	50
470	A170	2c rose car & grn	3.50	75

See note after No. 457. See also Nos. 498–499.

1952, Feb. 6 Engraved

471	A171	2c yel brn	40	20
472	A171	5c indigo	90	30

Issued to commemorate the centenary of the birth of Major General José Maceo.

See note after No. C49.

Queen Isabella I A172 — Receipt of Autonomy A173

1952, Feb. 22

473	A172	2c brt red	60	20

Issued to commemorate the 500th anniversary of the birth of Queen Isabella I of Spain.

Souvenir sheets containing 2c stamps of type A172 are listed as Nos. C50a–C50b.

Type of 1951 Surcharged in Green.

1952, Mar. 18

474	A159	10c on 2c yel brn	1.25	50

Engraved.

1952, May 27 *Perf. 12½* Wmk. 106

Designs: 2c, Tomas Estrada Palma and Luis Estevez Romero. 5c, Barnet, Finlay, Guiteras and Nuñez. 8c, Capitol. 20c, Map, Central Highway. 50c, Sugar Mill.

Centers in Black.

475	A173	1c dk grn	40	10
476	A173	2c dk car	50	10
477	A173	5c dk bl	60	20
478	A173	8c dk brn car	1.00	25
479	A173	20c dk ol grn	2.50	75
480	A173	50c dp org	5.00	1.50
		Nos. 475-480, C57-C60, E16 (11)	18.25	5.65

Issued to commemorate the 50th anniversary of the foundation of the Republic of Cuba.

Hands Holding Coffee Beans A174

Designs: 2c, Map and man picking coffee beans. 5c, Farmer with pan of beans.

1952, Aug. 22 *Perf. 13½* Wmk. 229

481	A174	1c green	40	18
482	A174	2c rose red	75	30
483	A174	5c dk vio bl & aqua	1.00	40

Bicentenary of coffee cultivation.

Col. Charles Hernandes y Sandrino
A175

Alonso Alvarez de la Campa
A176

1952, Oct. 7 *Perf. 10* Wmk. 106

484 A175 1c yel grn 35 20
485 A175 2c scarlet 65 15
486 A175 5c blue 75 25
487 A175 8c black 2.00 60
488 A175 10c brn red 2.00 60
489 A175 20c brown 7.50 5.00
Nos. 484-489, C63-C72, E17 (17) 47.75 24.55

See note after No. 457.

Frame Engraved; Center Typographed in Black.

1952, Nov. 27

Portraits: 2c, Carlos A. Latorre. 3c, Anacleto Bermudez. 5c, Eladio G. Toledo. 8c, Angel Laborde. 10c, Jose M. Medina. 13c, Pascual Rodriguez. 20c, Carlos Verdugo.

490 A176 1c green 25 10
491 A176 2c carmine 50 25
492 A176 3c purple 60 25
493 A176 5c blue 60 25
494 A176 8c bis brn 1.25 60
495 A176 10c org brn 1.00 50
496 A176 13c lil rose 2.00 75
497 A176 20c ol grn 3.00 1.25
Nos. 490-497, C73-C74 (10) 12.85 5.55

Issued to commemorate the 81st anniversary of the execution of eight medical students.

Christmas Type of 1951
Dated "1952-1953."
Frame Engraved; Center Typographed.
Centers: Tree.

1952, Dec. 1

498 A170 1c yel grn & car 4.00 1.25
499 A170 3c vio & dk grn 4.00 1.25

Birthplace of José Marti
A177

Marti at St. Lazarus Quarry
A178

Designs: No. 501, Court martial. No. 502, Martiano house, Havana. No. 504, El Abra ranch, Isle of Pines. No. 505, Symbols, "Marti the Poet." No. 506, Marti and Bolivar statue, Caracas. No. 507, At desk in New York. No. 508, House where revolutionary party was formed. No. 509, First issue of "Patria."

1953 Engraved. *Perf. 10.*

500 A177 1c dk grn & red brn 20 10
501 A177 1c dk grn & red brn 20 8
502 A177 3c pur & brn 40 10
503 A178 3c pur & brn 40 8
504 A177 5c dp bl & dk brn 60 25
505 A178 5c ultra & brn 60 25
506 A178 10c red brn & blk 1.50 50
507 A178 10c dk brn & blk 1.50 50
508 A178 13c dk ol grn & dk brn 2.50 1.00
509 A177 13c dk ol grn & brn 2.50 1.25
Nos. 500-509, C79-C89 (21) 29.00 10.95

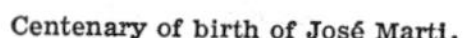
Centenary of birth of José Marti.

Rafael Montoro Valdez
A179

Francisco Carrera Justiz
A180

1953, Mar. 5

510 A179 3c dk vio 50 20

Issued to commemorate the centenary of the birth of Rafael Montoro Valdez, statesman.

1953, Mar. 9

511 A180 3c rose red 50 20

Issued to honor Francisco Carrera Justiz, educator and statesman.

No. 446 Surcharged with New Value.

1953, June 16

512 A146 3c on 2c rose red 40 15

Board of Accounts Bldg., Havana
A181

1953, Nov. 3 Engraved

513 A181 3c blue 40 15

Issued to publicize the First International Congress of Boards of Accounts, Havana, November 2-9, 1953. See also Nos. C90-C91.

Miguel Coyula Llaguno
A182

Communications Association Flag
A183

Designs: 3c, 8c, Enrique Calleja Hensell. 10c, Antonio Ginard Rojas.

1954 Dated 1953.

514 A182 1c green 25 8
515 A182 3c rose red 25 10
516 A183 5c blue 1.00 20
517 A182 8c brn car 1.50 50
518 A182 10c brown 2.50 75
Nos. 514-518, C92-C95, E19 (10) 19.35 9.13

Nos. 515 and 517 show the same portrait, but inscriptions are arranged differently.
See note after No. 457.

José Marti
A184

Maximo Gomez
A184a

Portraits: 3c, José de la Luz Caballero. 4c, Miguel Aldama. 5c, Calixto Garcia. 8c, Ignacio Agramont. 10c, Tomas Estrada Palma. 13c, Carlos J. Finlay. 14c, Serafin Sanchez. 20c, José Antonio Saco. 50c, Antonio Maceo. 1p, Carlos Manuel de Cespedes.

1954-56 *Perf. 10.* Wmk. 106

519 A184 1c green 25 5
520 A184a 2c rose car 25 5
521 A184 3c violet 25 5
521A A184 4c red lil ('55) 30 6
522 A184a 5c sl bl 35 8
523 A184a 8c car lake 50 10
524 A184 10c sepia 50 10
525 A184 13c org red 75 15
525A A184a 14c gray ('56) 1.00 15
526 A184 20c olive 1.50 25
527 A184a 50c org yel 2.50 50
528 A184a 1p orange 5.00 75
Nos. 519-528 (12) 13.15 2.29

In 1962 the Castro government re-issued Nos. 519-520 in changed colors. On the 2c, "1833" is replaced by "?".

Maj. Gen. José M. Rodriguez
A185

Design: 5c, Gen. Rodriguez on horseback.

1954, June 8 Engraved *Perf. 12½*
Center in Dark Brown

529 A185 2c dk car 50 20
530 A185 5c dp bl 1.00 40

Issued to commemorate the centenary of the birth of Maj. Gen. José Maria Rodriguez (in 1851).

Gen. Batista Sanatorium
A186

1954, Sept. 21 *Perf. 10* Wmk. 106

531 A186 3c dp bl 50 20

See also No. C107.

Santa Claus
A187

Maria Luisa Dolz
A188

1954, Dec. 15

532 A187 2c dk grn & car 4.00 75
533 A187 4c car & dk grn 3.50 75
Christmas 1954.

1954, Dec. 23

534 A188 4c dp bl 50 20

Issued to commemorate the centenary of the birth of Maria Luisa Dolz, educator and defender of women's rights. See also No. C108.

Cuban Flag and Scouts Saluting
A189

1954, Dec. 27 *Perf. 12½*

535 A189 4c dk grn 75 30

Issued to publicize the national patrol encampment of the Boy Scouts of Cuba.

Rotary Emblem and Paul P. Harris
A190

1955, Feb. 23 Engraved Wmk. 106

536 A190 4c blue 75 20

Rotary International, 50th anniversary. See also No. C109.

Maj. Gen. Francisco Carrillo
A191

Portrait: 5c, Gen. Carrillo standing.

1955, Mar. 8 *Perf. 10*

537 A191 2c brt red & dk bl 40 15
538 A191 5c dk bl & dk brn 75 25

Issued to commemorate the centenary of the birth of Maj. Gen. Francisco Carrillo (1851-1926).

Stamp of 1885 and Convent of San Francisco—A192

Designs (including 1855 stamp): 4c, Volanta carriage. 10c, Havana, 19th century. 14c, Captain general's residence.

1955, Apr. *Perf. 12½*

539 A192 2c lil rose & dk grnsh bl 75 25
540 A192 4c ocher & dk grn 1.00 25
541 A192 10c ultra & dk red 2.25 1.25
542 A192 14c grn & dp org 5.50 1.50
Nos. 539-542, C110-C113 (8) 17.80 7.10

Issued to commemorate the centenary of Cuba's first postage stamps.

Maj. Gen. Mario G. Menocal
A193

Gen. Emilio Nuñez
A194

Portraits: 10c, J. G. O. Gomez. 14c, A. Sanchez de Bustamente.

1955, June 22

543 A193 2c dk grn 50 6
544 A194 4c lil rose 60 8
545 A193 10c dp bl 1.00 40
546 A194 14c gray vio 2.00 60
Nos. 543-546, C114-C116, E20 (8) 14.10 6.54

See note after No. 457.

Turkey
A195

Gen. Emilio Nuñez
A196

1955, Dec. 15 Engraved

547 A195 2c sl grn & dk car 3.75 75

548 A195 4c rose lake & brt grn 3.75 60

Christmas 1955.

1955, Dec. 27

549 A196 4c claret 50 20

Issued to commemorate the centenary of the birth of Gen. Emilio Nuñez, Cuban revolutionary hero. See also Nos. C127–C128.

Francisco Cagigal de la Vega (1695–1777)
A197

Julian del Casal
A198

1956, Mar. 27 ***Perf. 12½***

552 A197 4c rose brn & sl bl 50 20

Issued to commemorate the bicentenary of the Cuban post. See also No. C129.

1956, May 2

Portraits: 4c, Luisa Perez de Zambrana. 10c, Juan Clemente Zenea. 14c, José Joaquin Palma.

Portraits in Black.

553	A198	2c green	40	10
554	A198	4c rose lil	50	12
555	A198	10c blue	1.00	25
556	A198	14c violet	1.25	35
		Nos. 553-556, C131-C133, E21 (8)	9.65	3.32

See note after No. 457.

Victor Muñoz
A199

Masonic Temple, Havana
A200

1956, May 13

557 A199 4c brn & grn 50 20

Issued in honor of Victor Muñoz (1873–1922), founder of Mother's Day in Cuba. See also No. C134.

1956, June 5

558 A200 4c blue 60 20

See also No. C135.

Virgin of Charity, El Cobre
A201

"The Cry of Yara"
A202

1956, Sept. 8 ***Perf. 12½***

559 A201 4c brt bl & yel 75 20

Issued in honor of Our Lady of Charity of Cobre, patroness of Cuba. See also No. C149.

1956, Oct. 10

560 A202 4c dk grn & brn 50 20

Issued to commemorate Cuba's independence from Spain.

Raimundo G. Menocal
A203

The Three Wise Men
A204

1956, Dec. 3 ***Perf. 12½*** **Wmk. 106**

561 A203 4c dk brn 50 20

Issued to commemorate the centenary of the birth of Prof. Raimundo G. Menocal, physician.

1956, Dec. 1

562 A204 2c red & sl grn 4.00 1.00
563 A204 4c sl grn & red 4.00 75

Christmas 1956.

Martin Morua Delgado
A205

Boy Scouts at Campfire
A206

1957, Jan. 30

564 A205 4c dk grn 50 20

Issued to commemorate the centenary of the birth of Martin Morua Delgado, patriot.

1957, Feb. 22 ***Perf. 12½*** **Wmk. 106**

565 A206 4c sl grn & red 90 35

Issued to commemorate the centenary of the birth of Lord Baden-Powell, founder of the Boy Scouts. See also No. C152.

"The Blind," by M. Vega
A207

Paintings: 4c, "The Art Critics" by M. Melero. 10c, "Volanta in Storm" by A. Menocal. 14c, "The Convalescent" by L. Romañach.

1957, Mar. **Engraved** ***Perf. 12½***

Side and Lower Inscriptions in Dark Brown.

566	A207	2c ol grn	40	25
567	A207	4c org red	50	30
568	A207	10c ol grn	75	50
569	A207	14c ultra	1.00	50
		Nos. 566-569, C153-C155, E22 (8)	9.60	3.85

See note after No. 457.

Emblem of Philatelic Club of Cuba
A208

Juan F. Steegers
A209

1957, Apr. 24

570 A208 4c ocher, bl & red 60 20

Issued for Stamp Day, Apr. 24, and the National Philatelic Exhibition. See No. C156.

1957, Apr. 30

571 A209 4c blue 50 20

Issued in honor of the centenary of the birth of Juan Francisco Steegers y Perera (1856–1921), dactyloscopy pioneer. See No. C157.

Victoria Bru Sanchez
A210

Joaquin de Aguero in Battle of Jucaral
A211

1957, June 3 ***Perf. 12½*** **Wmk. 106**

572 A210 4c indigo 50 20

1957, July 4

573 A211 4c dk grn 50 20

Issued to honor Joaquin de Aguero, Cuban freedom fighter and patriot. See No. C162.

Boy, Dogs and Cat
A212

Col. Rafael Manduley del Rio
A213

1957, July 17

574 A212 4c Prus grn 75 30

Issued in honor of Mrs. Jeanette Ryder, founder of the Humane Society of Cuba. See Nos. C163–C163a.

1957, July 31

575 A213 4c Prus grn 50 15

Issued to honor Col. Manduley del Rio, patriot, on the centenary of his birth (in 1856).

Palace of Justice
A214

1957, Sept. 2 **Engraved** ***Perf. 12½***

576 A214 4c bl gray 50 20

Issued to commemorate the opening of the new Palace of Justice in Havana. See also No. C165.

Generals of the Liberation
A215

1957, Sept. 26

577	A215	4c dl grn & red brn	50	20
578	A215	4c dl bl & red brn	50	20
579	A215	4c rose & brn	50	20
580	A215	4c org yel & brn	50	20
581	A215	4c lt vio & brn	50	20
		Nos. 577-581 (5)	2.50	1.00

Issued to commemorate the Generals of the army of liberation.

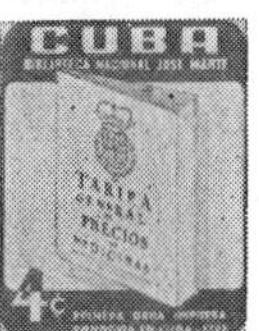

First Publication Printed in Cuba
A216

Patio
A217

1957, Oct. 18 ***Perf. 12½*** **Wmk. 106**

582 A216 4c sl bl 50 15

Issued to publicize the José Marti National Library. See Nos. C167–C168.

1957, Nov. 19

583 A217 4c red brn & grn 50 15

Issued to commemorate the centenary of the first Cuban Normal School. See also Nos. C173–C174.

Trinidad, Founded 1514
A218

Fortifications, Havana, 1611
A219

Views: 10c, Padre Pico street, Santiago de Cuba. 14c, Church of Our Lady, Camaguey.

1957, Dec. 17 **Engraved** ***Perf. 12½***

584	A218	2c brn & ind	35	6
585	A219	4c sl grn & brn	50	5
586	A219	10c sep & red	1.50	50
587	A219	14c grn & dk red	1.25	25
		Nos. 584-587, C175-C177, E23 (8)	8.85	2.81

See note after No. 457.

Nativity
A220

1957, Dec. 20

Center Multicolored.

588 A220 2c dk brn 3.50 1.00
589 A220 4c dk sl grn 3.50 75

Christmas 1957.

Dayton Hedges and Ariguanabo Textile Factory
A221

1958, Jan. 30 *Perf. 12½* Wmk. 106

590	A221	4c blue	50	15

Issued to honor Dayton Hedges, founder of Cuba's textile industry. See No. C178.

Dr. Francisco Dominguez Roldan A222 — José Ignacio Rivero y Alonso A223

1958, Feb. 21

591	A222	4c green	50	15

Issued to honor Dr. Francisco Dominguez Roldan (1864–1942), who introduced radiotherapy and physiotherapy to Cuba.

1958, Apr. 1

592	A223	4c lt ol grn	50	15

Issued in honor of José Ignacio Rivero y Alonso, editor of Diario de la Marina, 1919–1944. See also No. C179.

Map of Cuba and Mail Route, 1756 A224

1958, Apr. 24 *Perf. 12½*

593	A224	4c dk grn, aqua & buff	60	20

Issued for Stamp Day, Apr. 24 and the National Philatelic Exhibition. See No. C180.

Maj. Gen. José Miguel Gomez A225 — Nicolas Ruiz Espadero A226

1958, June 6 *Perf. 12½* Wmk. 106

594	A225	4c slate	50	15

Issued in honor of Maj. Gen. José Miguel Gomez, President of Cuba, 1909–13. See No. C181.

1958, June 27 *Perf. 12½*

Musicians: 4c, Ignacio Cervantes. 10c, José White. 14c, Brindis de Salas.

Indigo Emblem

595	A226	2c brown	50	10
596	A226	4c dk gray	50	20
597	A226	10c ol grn	75	25
598	A226	14c red	1.00	35

Physicians: 2c, Tomas Romay Chacon. 4c, Angel Arturo Aballi. 10c, Fernando Gonzalez del Valle. 14c, Vicente Antonio de Castro.

Green Emblem

599	A226	2c brown	60	10
600	A226	4c gray	1.00	35
601	A226	10c dk car	75	30
602	A226	14c dk bl	1.00	40

Lawyers: 2c, Jose Maria Garcia Montes. 4c, Jose A. Gonzalez Lanuza. 10c, Juan B. Hernandez Barreiro. 14c, Pedro Gonzalez Llorente.

Red Emblem

603	A226	2c sepia	50	10
604	A226	4c gray	75	35
605	A226	10c ol grn	85	25
606	A226	14c sl bl	1.00	35
		Nos. 595-606 (12)	9.20	3.10

Carlos de la Torre A227

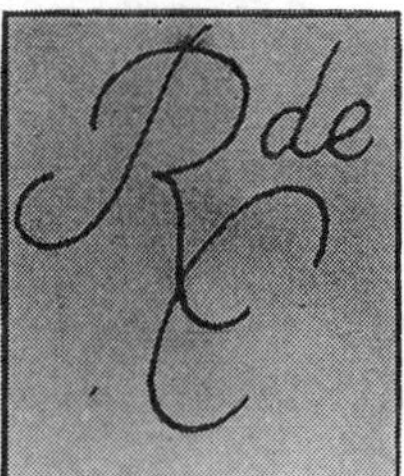

Wmk. 321

Wmkd. "R de C" (321)

1958, Aug. 29 Engraved *Perf. 12½*

607	A227	4c vio bl	60	20

Issued to commemorate the centenary of the birth of Dr. Carlos de la Torre y Huerta (1858–1950), naturalist. See also Nos. C182–C184.

Poey's "Memorias" Title Page A228 — Felipe Poey A229

1958, Sept. 26 Wmk. 106

608	A228	2c blk & lt vio	35	15
609	A229	4c brn blk	45	15
		Nos. 608-609, C185-C191, E26-E27 (11)	47.30	18.05

Issued in honor of Felipe Poey (1799–1891), naturalist.

Theodore Roosevelt A230 — Cattleyopsis Lindenii Orchid A231

1958, Oct. 27 *Perf. 12½*

610	A230	4c gray grn	60	15

Issued to commemorate the centenary of the birth of Theodore Roosevelt. See No. C192.

Engraved & Photogravure

1958, Dec. 16 *Perf. 12½* Wmk. 321

Design: 4c, Oncidium Guibertianum Orchid.

611	A231	2c multi	3.50	1.00
612	A231	4c multi	4.00	1.00

Christmas 1958.

Flag and Revolutionary A232 — Gen. Adolfo Flor Crombet A233

Engraved and Lithographed.

1959, Jan. 28 Wmk. 321

613	A232	2c car rose & gray	30	15

Day of Liberation, Jan. 1, 1959.

1959, Mar. 18 Engr. Wmk. 106

614	A233	4c sl grn	40	15

Issued in honor of General Adolfo Flor Crombet (1848-1895).

Maria Teresa Garcia Montes A234 — Carlos Manuel de Cespedes A235

1959, Nov. 11 *Perf. 12½*

615	A234	4c brown	40	15

Issued to honor Maria Teresa Garcia Montes (1880–1930), founder of the Musical Arts Society. See No. C198.

1959, Oct. 10 *Perf. 12½* Wmk. 106

Presidents: No. 617, Salvador Cisneros Betancourt. No. 618, Manuel de Jesus Calvar. No. 619, Bartolomé Maso. No. 620, Juan B. Spotorno. No. 621, Tomas Estrada Palma. No. 622, Francisco Javier de Céspedes. No. 623, Vicente Garcia.

616	A235	2c sl bl	40	10
617	A235	2c green	40	10
618	A235	2c dp vio	40	10
619	A235	2c org brn	40	10
620	A235	4c dk car	50	20
621	A235	4c dp brn	50	20
622	A235	4c dk gray	50	20
623	A235	4c dk vio	50	20
		Nos. 616-623(8)	3.60	1.20

Issued to honor former Cuban presidents.

No. B3 Surcharged in Red: "HABILITADO PARA / 2¢"

1960 Lithographed. Wmk. 321

624	SP2	2c on 2c+1c car & ultra	50	15

See also No. C199.

Rebel Attack on Moncada Barracks A236

Designs: 2c, Rebels disembarking from "Granma." 10c, Battle of the Uvero. 12c, Map of Cuba and rebel ("The Invasion").

Wmkd. Interlacing Lines (320)

1960, Jan. 28 Engr. *Perf. 12½*

625	A236	1c gray ol, bl & ver	20	15
626	A236	2c bl, gray ol & brn	25	20
627	A236	10c bl, gray ol & red	50	20
628	A236	12c brt bl, brn & grn	75	30
		Nos. 625-628, C200-C202 (7)	6.70	2.85

First anniversary of revolution.

Stamps of 1956-59 Surcharged with New Value in Carmine or Silver

1960, Feb. 3

629	A226	1c on 4c dk gray & ind	40	10
630	A226	1c on 4c gray & grn	60	25
631	A226	1c on 4c gray & red	40	10
632	A227	1c on 4c vio bl	40	10
633	A231	1c on 4c multi (S)	1.00	50
634	A233	1c on 4c sl grn	35	10
635	A234	1c on 4c brn	40	10
636	A184a	2c on 14c gray	50	15
		Nos. 629-636, C203-C204 (10)	5.55	2.00

Tomas Estrada Palma Statue, Havana A237 — Sailboats A238

Statues: 2c, Mambi Victorioso (Battle of San Juan Hill), Santiago de Cuba. 10c, Marta Abreo de Estevez. 12c, Ignacio Agramonte, Camaguey.

Engraved

1960, Mar. 28 *Perf. 12½* Wmk. 321

637	A237	1c brn & dk bl	20	8
638	A237	2c grn & red	30	8
639	A237	10c choc & red	75	25
640	A237	12c gray ol & vio	1.00	40
		Nos. 637-640, C206-C208 (7)	6.10	2.31

See note after No. 386

Nos. 521A, 522 and 525 Surcharged "HABILITADO / PARA / 2¢" in Violet Blue, Red or Black.

1960 *Perf. 10* Wmk. 106

641	A184	2c on 4c red lil (VB)	50	15
642	A184a	2c on 5c sl bl (R)	60	15
643	A184	2c on 13c org red	75	35

No. 307B Surcharged "HABILITADO / 10¢"

644	A41	10c on 20c ol grn	50	20

Perf. 12½

1960, Sept. 22 Engr. Wmk. 321

Design: 2c, Marksman.

645	A238	1c lt vio	30	20
646	A238	2c orange	50	20

Issued to commemorate the 17th Olympic Games, Rome, Aug. 25–Sept. 11.

For souvenir sheet see No. C213a.

Camilo Cienfuegos and View of Escolar—A239

1960, Oct. 27 Litho. Unwmkd.

647	A239	2c brn, bl, grn & red	25	10

Issued to commemorate the first anniversary of the death of Camilo Cienfuegos, revolutionary hero.

Morning Glory—A240

Tobacco and Christmas Hymn
A241

1960 Lithographed *Perf. 12½*

Flowers in Natural Colors

648	A240	1c red	1.00	50
649	A241	1c blk & red (*Tobacco*)	1.25	75
650	A241	1c blk & red (*Mariposa*)	1.25	75
651	A241	1c blk & red (*Guaiacum*)	1.25	75
652	A241	1c blk & red (*Coffee*)	1.25	75
a.		Block of four (1 each, #649-652)	6.50	
653	A240	2c ultra	1.25	75
654	A241	2c blk & ultra (*Tobacco*)	3.50	2.00
655	A241	2c blk & ultra (*Mariposa*)	3.50	2.00
656	A241	2c blk & ultra (*Guaiacum*)	3.50	2.00
657	A241	2c blk & ultra (*Coffee*)	3.50	2.00
a.		Block of four (1 each, #654-657)	17.50	
658	A240	10c ocher	4.00	2.00
659	A241	10c blk & ocher (*Tobacco*)	10.00	5.00
660	A241	10c blk & ocher (*Mariposa*)	10.00	5.00
661	A241	10c blk & ocher (*Guaiacum*)	10.00	5.00
662	A241	10c blk & ocher (*Coffee*)	10.00	5.00
a.		Block of four (1 each, #659-662)	50.00	
		Nos. 648-662 (15)	65.25	34.25

Issued for Christmas 1960.

Nos. 648–662 were printed in three sheets of 25. Nine stamps of type A240 form a center cross; stamps of type A241 form a block of four in each corner with the musical bars joined in an oval around the floral designs.

"Public Capital for Economic Benefit"
A242

Designs: 2c, Chart and symbols of agriculture and industry. 6c, Cogwheels.

Photogravure

1961, Jan. 10 *Perf. 11½* Unwmkd.

663	A242	1c yel, blk & org	20	5
664	A242	2c bl, blk & red	20	5
665	A242	6c yel, red org & blk	50	25
		Nos. 663-665, C215-C218 (7)	4.40	2.25

Issued to publicize the conference of underdeveloped countries, Havana.

Jesus Menéndez and Sugar Cane
A243

1961, Jan. 22 Litho. *Perf. 12½*

666	A243	2c dk grn & brn	20	10

Jesus Menéndez, leader in sugar industry.

Same Overprinted in Red:
"PRIMERO DE MAYO 1961
ESTAMOS VENCIENDO"

1961, May 2

667	A243	2c dk grn & brn	60	40

Issued for May Day, 1961.

Dove and U.N. Emblem
A244

1961, Apr. 12 Litho. *Perf. 12½*

668	A244	2c red brn & yel grn	30	10
669	A244	10c emer & rose lil	50	20
a.		Souvenir sheet	2.00	

Issued to commemorate the 15th anniversary (in 1960) of the United Nations.

See also Nos. C222–C223.

No. 669a contains one each of Nos. 668–669, imperf. with red brown marginal inscription. Size: 107x65mm.

Maceo Stamp of 1907 and 1902 Simulated Cancel
A245

Designs: 1c, Revolutionary 10c stamp of 1874 and 1868 "cancel." 10c, Stamp of 1959 (No. 613) and "cancel."

1961, Apr. 24 Unwmkd.

670	A245	1c dl rose & dk grn	35	25
671	A245	2c sal & dk grn	35	25
672	A245	10c pale grn, car rose & blk	75	40

Issued for Stamp Day, Apr. 24.

Hand Releasing Dove
A246

1961, July 26 *Perf. 12½*

673	A246	2c blk, red, yel & gray	30	10

Issued to commemorate the 26th of July (1953) movement, Castro's revolt against Fulgencio Batista.

Burelage on back consisting of wavy lines and diagonal rows of "CUBA CORREOS" in pale salmon.

Importation Prohibited

Cuban stamps issued after No. 673 have not been listed because the embargo on trade with Cuba, proclaimed Feb. 7, 1962, by President Kennedy, prohibits the importation from any country of stamps of Cuban origin, used or unused.

SEMI-POSTAL STAMPS.

Pierre and Marie Curie
SP1

Wmkd. Star. (106)

1938, Nov. 23 Engraved *Perf. 10*

B1	SP1	2c + 1c sal	3.50	1.25
B2	SP1	5c + 1c dp ultra	3.50	1.50

Issued in commemoration of the 40th anniversary of the discovery of radium by Pierre and Marie Curie. The surtax was for the benefit of the International Union for the Control of Cancer.

"Agriculture" Supporting "Industry"
SP2

Perf. 12½

1959, May 7 Litho. Wmk. 321

B3	SP2	2c + 1c car & ultra	35	15

Agricultural reforms. See Nos. 624, CB1.

Nurse—SP3

Perf. 12½, Imperf.

1959, Sept. 22 Wmk. 229

B4	SP3	2c + 1c crim rose	30	15

AIR POST STAMPS.

Seaplane over Havana Harbor
AP1

Wmkd. Star. (106)

1927, Nov. 1 Engraved *Perf. 12*

C1	AP1	5c dk bl	5.00	20

Type of 1927 Issue Overprinted

LINDBERGH
FEBRERO 1928

1928, Feb. 8

C2	AP1	5c car rose	2.50	1.25

No. 283 Surcharged in Red

CORREO AEREO NACIONAL

10¢ 10¢

1930, Oct. 27 Unwmkd.

C3	A44	10c on 25c vio	2.50	1.25

Airplane and Coast of Cuba
AP3

For Foreign Postage.

1931, Feb. 26 *Perf. 10* Wmk. 106

C4	AP3	5c green	50	5
C5	AP3	10c dk bl	50	5
C6	AP3	15c rose	1.00	30
C7	AP3	20c brown	1.00	6
C8	AP3	30c dk vio	1.50	20
C9	AP3	40c dp org	3.50	40
C10	AP3	50c ol grn	4.00	40
C11	AP3	1p black	6.00	1.00
		Nos. C4-C11 (8)	18.00	2.46

See also No. C40.

Airplane
AP4

For Domestic Postage.

1931-46

C12	AP4	5c rose vio ('32)	40	6
a.		5c brn vio ('36)	40	6
C13	AP4	10c gray blk	40	5
C14	AP4	20c car rose	3.00	85
C14A	AP4	20c rose pink ('46)	1.25	20
C15	AP4	50c dk bl	5.00	85
		Nos. C12-C15 (5)	10.05	2.01

See also No. C130.

Type of 1931 Surcharged in Black

PRIMER TREN AEREO
INTERNACIONAL. 1935
O'Meara y du Pont +10cts.

1935, Apr. 24 *Perf. 10*

C16	AP3	10c + 10c red	7.50	6.00

Imperf.

C17	AP3	10c + 10c red	30.00	30.00

Matanzas Issue.

Air View of Matanzas
AP5

Designs: 10c, Airship "Macon." 20c, Airplane "The Four Winds." 50c, Air View of Fort San Severino.

Photogravure.

Wmkd. Wavy Lines. (229)

1936, May 5 *Perf. 12½*

C18	AP5	5c violet	75	50
C19	AP5	10c yel org	1.50	75
C20	AP5	20c green	5.00	3.00
C21	AP5	50c grnsh sl	9.00	6.00

Exist imperf. Price 20% more.

"Lightning"
AP9

Allegory of Flight
AP10

1936, Nov. 18

C22	AP9	5c violet	3.00	75
C23	AP10	10c org brn	3.50	1.25

Issued in commemoration of the centenary of the birth of Major General Máximo Gómez.

Flat Arch (Panama)
AP11

Carlos Antonio López (Paraguay)
AP12

Inca Gate, Cuzco (Peru)
AP13

Atlacatl (Salvador)
AP14

José Enrique Rodó (Uruguay)
AP15

Simón Bolívar (Venezuela)
AP16

Engraved.

1937, Oct. 13 *Perf. 10* Wmk. 106

C24	AP11	5c red	6.00	5.00
C25	AP12	5c red	6.00	5.00
C26	AP13	10c blue	7.00	6.00
C27	AP14	10c blue	7.00	6.00
C28	AP15	20c green	8.00	7.50
C29	AP16	20c green	8.00	7.50
		Nos. C24-C29 (6)	42.00	37.00

Issued for the benefit of the Association of American Writers and Artists. See note after No. 354.

Type of 1927 Overprinted in Black

1913 1938

ROSILLO

Key West-Habana

1938, May Wmk. 106

C30	AP1	5c dk org	5.00	1.50

Issued in commemoration of the first airplane flight from Key West to Havana, made by Domingo Rosillo, 1913.

Type of 1931–32 Overprinted

EXPERIMENTO DEL COHETE Postal AÑO DE 1939

1939, Oct. 15

C31	AP4	10c emerald	25.00	7.50

Issued in connection with an experimental postal rocket flight held at Havana.

Sir Rowland Hill, Map of Cuba and First Stamps of Britain, Spanish Cuba and Republic of Cuba
AP17

1940, Nov. 28 Engr. Wmk. 106

C32	AP17	10c brown	5.00	2.00

Souvenir Sheet
Imperf.
Unwmkd.

C33	AP17	10c lt brn, sheet of four	12.50	10.00
a.		Single stamp	2.80	2.00

Centenary of the first postage stamp. Sheet measures 128x178mm. Sheet sold for 60c.

No. C33 exists with each of the four stamps overprinted in black: "Exposicion de la ACNU/24 de Octubre de 1951/Dia de las Naciones" and "Historia de la Aviacion" in lower margin.

Price, $70.

Poet José Heredia and Palms
AP18

Heredia and Niagara Falls
AP19

1940, Dec. 30 Wmk. 106

C34	AP18	5c emerald	2.00	1.00
C35	AP19	10c grnsh sl	3.50	1.50

Issued to commemorate the centenary of the death of José Maria Heredia y Campuzano (1803–1839), poet and patriot.

First Cuban Land Sighted by Columbus
AP20

Columbus Lighthouse
AP21

1944, May 19

C36	AP20	5c ol grn	75	20
C37	AP21	10c sl blk	1.50	50

Issued to commemorate the 450th anniversary of the discovery of America.

Conference of La Mejorana (Meceo, Gomez and Marti)
AP22

1948, May 21 *Perf. 12½* Wmk. 229

C38	AP22	8c org yel & blk	2.00	75

Issued to commemorate the 50th anniversary of the start of the War of 1895.

Souvenir Sheet.
No. C33 Overprinted in Ultramarine

1948, May 21 *Imperf.* Unwmkd.

C39	AP17	10c lt brn, sheet of four	8.00	7.00

The overprint is applied in the center of the four stamps, so that a portion falls on each.

Issued in honor of the American Air Mail Society Convention, Havana, May 21 to 23, 1948. The sheets sold for 60c each.

Type of 1931.

1948, June 15 *Perf. 10* Wmk. 106

C40	AP3	8c org brn	1.50	20

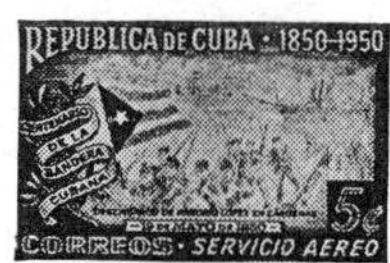

Narciso Lopez Landing at Cárdenas
AP23

Flag on Cuban Fort
AP24

Flag on Morro Castle, Havana
AP25

Engraved and Lithographed.

1951, July 3 *Perf. 13* Wmk. 229

C41	AP23	5c ol grn, ultra & red	1.25	25
C42	AP24	8c red brn, bl & red	2.00	25
C43	AP25	25c gray blk, bl & red	3.00	1.50

Centenary of adoption of Cuba's flag.

Souvenir Sheet.
No. 365a Overprinted in Green.

CORREO AEREO

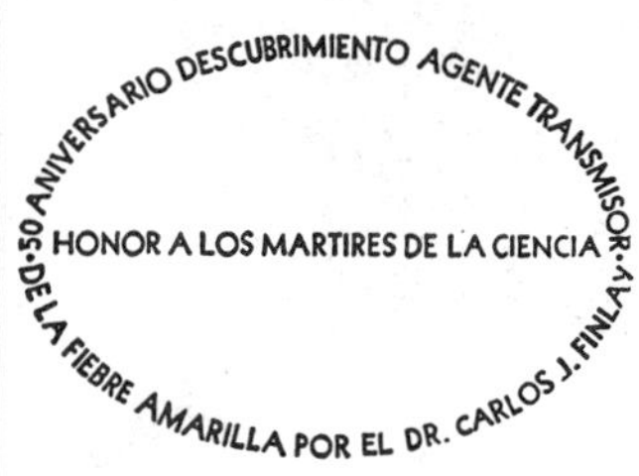

1901 1951

(Reduced Illustration of Overprint)

1951, Aug. 24 *Imperf.* Unwmkd.

C43A	Sheet of four	6.00	5.00

Issued to commemorate the 50th anniversary of the discovery of the cause of yellow fever by Dr. Carlos J. Finlay, and to honor the martyrs of science.

No. C43A measures 127x177 mm. and contains two each of Nos. 364 and 365 imperforate, with upper and lower marginal inscriptions.

Resignation Play of Dr. Lasker
AP26

Capablanca Making "The Exact Play"
AP27

Design: 25c, Capablanca.

Photogravure.

1951, Nov. 1 *Perf. 13* Wmk. 229

C44	AP26	5c bl grn & yel	5.00	1.00
C45	AP27	8c ultra & cl	7.50	1.25
C46	A165	25c brn & dk brn	15.00	4.00

Issued to commemorate the 30th anniversary of the winning of the World Chess title by José Raul Capablanca.

Morrillo Types of Regular Issue, 1951.
Engraved.

1951, Nov. 22 *Perf. 10* Wmk. 106

C47	A167	5c violet	1.00	15
C48	A168	8c dp grn	1.25	25
C49	A169	25c dk brn	2.50	1.50
a.		Souvenir sheet of 6, blk brn, perf. 13	25.00	25.00
b.		Souvenir sheet of 6, grn, imperf.	90.00	90.00

Issued to commemorate the 16th anniversary of the Action of the Morrillo and to honor Antonio Guiteras Holmes who was killed there.

Nos. C49a and C49b contain one each of the 1c, 2c and 5c of types A167-A169 and of the 5c, 8c and 25c airmail stamps of types A167-A169. Marginal inscriptions are typographed in black; coat of arms engraved in color of stamps (black brown or green). Sheets are unwatermarked and measure 124x133mm

Isabella Type of Regular Issue, 1952

1952, Feb. 22

C50	A172	25c purple	3.00	1.00
a.		Souvenir sheet of 2, perf. 11	12.50	10.00
b.		Souvenir sheet of 2, imperf.	15.00	15.00

Issued to commemorate the 500th anniversary of the birth of Queen Isabella I of Spain.

Nos. C50a and C50b contain one each of a 2c of type A172 and a 25c air-mail stamp of type A172. In No. C50a, the 2c and marginal inscriptions are brown carmine; the 25c, dark blue. In No. C50b, the 2c and marginal inscriptions are dark blue; the 25c, brown carmine. Sheets measure 108x108mm.

Type of Regular Issue of 1951 Surcharged in Various Colors

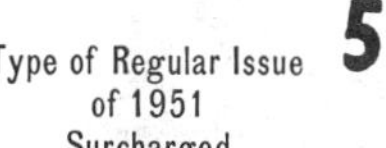

1952, Mar. 18

C51	A159	5c on 2c yel brn	50	15
C52	A159	8c on 2c yel brn (C)	1.00	10
C53	A159	10c on 2c yel brn (Bl)	1.00	15
C54	A159	25c on 2c yel brn (V)	1.50	1.00
C55	A159	50c on 2c yel brn (C)	5.00	2.00
C56	A159	1p on 2c yel brn (Bl)	12.50	7.50
		Nos. C51-C56 (6)	21.50	10.90

Country School AP32

Entrance, University of Havana AP33

Designs: 10c, Presidential Mansion. 25c, Banknote.

Engraved.

1952, May 27 *Perf. 12½* Wmk. 106

Centers Various Shades of Green.

C57	AP32	5c dk pur	50	10
C58	AP33	8c dk red	75	15
C59	AP32	10c dp bl	1.50	25
C60	AP32	25c dk vio brn	2.50	1.25

Issued to commemorate the 50th anniversary of the foundation of the Republic of Cuba.

Plane and Map AP34

Agustín Parlá AP35

Engraved

1952, July 22 *Perf. 10*

C61	AP34	8c black	1.25	50
a.		Souvenir sheet, 8c dp bl	6.00	6.00
b.		Souvenir sheet, 8c dp grn	6.00	6.00
C62	AP35	25c ultra	3.50	1.50
a.		Souvenir sheet, 25c dp bl	6.00	6.00
b.		Souvenir sheet, 25c dp grn	6.00	6.00

Issued to commemorate the 30th anniversary of the Key West-Mariel flight of Agustin Parla.

The four souvenir sheets are perf. 11, measure 107x95mm. and have marginal inscriptions in the same color as the stamp.

Col. Charles Hernandes y Sandrino AP36

1952, Oct. 7

C63	AP36	5c orange	75	15
C64	AP36	8c brt yel grn	75	10
C65	AP36	10c dk brn	1.00	25
C66	AP36	15c dk Prus grn	2.00	75
C67	AP36	20c aqua	2.50	1.00
C68	AP36	25c crimson	2.00	1.00
C69	AP36	30c dk vio bl	5.00	2.50
C70	AP36	45c rose lil	5.00	3.50
C71	AP36	50c indigo	3.00	2.50
C72	AP36	1p bister	10.00	5.00
		Nos. C63-C72 (10)	32.00	16.75

Three-fourths of the proceeds from the sale of Nos. C63–C72 were used for the Communications Ministry Employees' Retirement Fund.

Entrance, University of Havana AP37

F. V. Dominguez, M. Estebanez and F. Capdevila—AP38

Engraved; Centers Typographed.

1952, Nov. 27

C73	AP37	5c ind & dk bl	90	35
C74	AP38	25c org & dk grn	2.75	1.25

Issued to commemorate the 81st anniversary of the execution of eight medical students.

AP39

Lockheed Constellation Airliners AP40

1953, May 22 Engraved.

C75	AP39	8c org brn	50	6
C76	AP39	15c scarlet	2.00	30

Typographed and Engraved

C77	AP40	2p dp grn & dk brn	30.00	12.50
C78	AP40	5p bl & dk brn	40.00	20.00

See also Nos. C120-C121.

Page of Manifesto of Montecristi AP42

House of Maximo Gomez AP43

Designs: No. C79, Marti in Kingston, Jamaica. No. C80, With Workers in Tampa, Florida. No. C83, Marti addressing liberating army. No. C84, Portrait. No. C85, Dos Rios obelisk. No. C86, Marti's first tomb. No. C87, Present tomb. No. C88, Monument in Havana. No. C89, Martian forge.

1953 Engraved *Perf. 10*

C79	AP42	5c dk car & blk	30	12
C80	AP43	5c dk grn & blk	30	12
C81	AP43	8c dk grn & blk	75	15
C82	AP42	8c dk grn & blk	75	15
C83	AP43	10c dk bl & dk car	1.50	40
C84	AP42	10c dk bl & dk car	1.50	40
C85	AP42	15c vio & gray	1.25	75
C86	AP42	15c vio & gray	1.25	75
C87	AP42	25c brn & car	3.00	1.00
C88	AP42	25c brn & car	3.00	1.00
C89	AP43	50c yel & bl	5.00	2.00
		Nos. C79-C89 (11)	18.60	6.84

Issued to commemorate the centenary of the birth of José Martí.

Board of Accounts Building AP44

Design: 25c, Plane above Board of Accounts Bldg.

1953, Nov. 3

C90	AP44	8c rose car	1.00	25
C91	AP44	25c dk gray grn	2.00	1.00

Issued to publicize the First International Congress of Boards of Account, Havana, November 2–9, 1953.

Miguel Coyula Llaguno AP45

Antonio Ginard Rojas AP46

Designs: 10c, Gregorio Hernandez Saez. 1p, Communications Association Flag.

1954

C92	AP45	5c dk bl	50	15
C93	AP46	8c red vio	60	25
C94	AP46	10c orange	1.25	35
C95	AP45	1p black	8.50	6.00

See note after No. C72.

Four-engine Plane and Cane Field AP47

Plane and Harvesters Cutting Cane AP48

Designs in Lower Triangle: 10c, Tractor pulling loaded wagons. 15c, Train of sugar cane. 20c, Modern mill. 25c, Evaporators. 30, Sacks of sugar. 40c, Loading sugar on ship. 45c, Ox cart. 50c, Primitive sugar mill. 1p, Alvaro Reinoso.

1954, Apr. 27 Engraved

C96	AP47	5c yel grn	60	10
C97	AP48	8c brown	1.25	8
C98	AP48	10c dk grn	1.50	15
C99	AP48	15c hn brn	75	35
C100	AP48	20c blue	1.00	50
C101	AP48	25c scarlet	1.50	50
C102	AP48	30c lil rose	2.50	75
C103	AP48	40c dp bl	3.00	1.00
C104	AP48	45c violet	6.00	2.00
C105	AP48	50c brt bl	4.00	1.25
C106	AP47	1p dk gray bl	8.00	2.50
		Nos. C96-C106 (11)	30.10	9.18

Sanatorium Type of Regular Issue, 1954.

1954, Sept. 21 *Perf. 10* Wmk. 106

C107	A186	9c dp grn	1.00	50

Dolz Type of Regular Issue, 1954.

1954, Dec. 23

C108	A188	12c carmine	1.00	50

Issued to commemorate the centenary of the birth of Maria Luisa Dolz, educator and defender of women's rights.

Rotary Type of Regular Issue, 1955.

1955, Feb. 23

C109	A190	12c carmine	1.25	40

Issued to commemorate the 50th anniversary of the founding of Rotary International.

Stamps of 1855 and 1905, Palace of Fine Arts AP52

Designs (including 2 stamps): 12c, Plaza de la Fraternidad. 24c, View of Havana. 30c, Plaza de la Republica.

1955, Apr. 24 *Perf. 12½*

C110	AP52	8c dk grnsh bl & grn	1.25	50
C111	AP52	12c dk ol grn & red	1.50	35
C112	AP52	24c dk red & ultra	1.75	1.00
C113	AP52	30c dp org & brn	3.75	2.00

Issued to commemorate the centenary of Cuba's first postage stamps.

Mariel Bay—AP53

Views: 12c, Varadero beach. 1p, Vinales valley.

1955, June 22 Wmk. 106

C114	AP53	8c dk car & dk grn	75	30
C115	AP53	12c dk ocher & brt bl	1.00	25
C116	AP53	1p dk grn & ocher	6.00	4.00

See note after No. C72.

Map of Crocier's 1914 Flight
AP54

Design: 30c, Jaime Gonzalez Crocier in plane.

1955, July 4 ***Perf. 10***

C117	AP54	12c red & dk grn	60	20
C118	AP54	30c dk grn & mag	2.25	60

Issued to honor Jaime Gonzalez Crocier, aviation pioneer, on the 35th anniversary of his death.

Cuban Museum, Tampa, Fla.
AP55

1955, July 1 Engr. *Perf. 12½*

C119	AP55	12c red & dk brn	1.10	35

Issued to commemorate the centenary of Tampa's incorporation as a town.

Lockheed Type of 1953
Typographed and Engraved

1955, Sept. 21 Wmk. 106

C120	AP40	2p bl & ol grn	17.50	8.50
C121	AP40	5p dp rose & ol grn	37.50	16.50

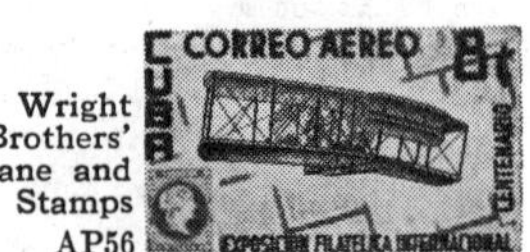

Wright Brothers' Plane and Stamps
AP56

Designs: 12c, Spirit of St. Louis. 24c, Graf Zeppelin. 30c, Constellation passenger plane. 50c, Convair jet fighter.

Engraved and Photogravure.

1955, Nov. 12 *Perf. 12½* Wmk. 106

Inscription and Plane in Black.

C122	AP56	8c car & bl	90	30
C123	AP56	12c yel grn & car	2.00	60
C124	AP56	24c vio & car	3.50	1.50
C125	AP56	30c bl & red org	5.00	3.00
C126	AP56	50c ol grn & red org	7.50	3.50
a.		Souvenir sheet of 5	35.00	35.00
		Nos. C122-C126 (5)	18.90	8.90

Issued to commemorate the International Centenary Philatelic Exhibition in Havana, Nov. 12–19, 1955.

No. C126a is printed on thick paper and measures 140x178mm. It contains one each of Nos. C122–C126 with the background of each stamp printed in a different color from the perforated stamps. The sheet is inscribed in black "Republica de Cuba. Souvenir. Exposition Filatelica Internacional Centenario 1955" and "XXXII Convencion de la American Airmail Society."

"Three Friends" and Gen. Emilio Nuñez
AP57

Design: 12c, Landing on the Cuban Coast.

1955, Dec. 27 Engraved Unwmkd.

C127	AP57	8c ultra & dk car	1.00	40
C128	AP57	12c grn & dk red brn	1.50	50

Issued to commemorate the centenary of the birth of Gen. Emilio Nuñez, Cuban revolutionary hero.

Post Type of Regular Issue, 1956.

Design: 12c, Bishop P. A. Morell de Santa Cruz (1694–1768).

1956, March 27 Wmk. 106

C129	A197	12c dk brn & grn	90	30

Bicentenary of the Cuban post.

Plane Type of 1931–46.

1956 Engraved *Perf. 10*

C130	AP4	50c grnsh bl	2.00	1.00

Portrait Type of Regular Issue, 1956.

1956, May 2 *Perf. 12½*

Portraits: 8c, Gen. Julio Sanguily. 12c, Gen. José Maria Aguirre. 30c, Col. Ernesto Ponts Sterling.

Portraits in Black.

C131	A198	8c brown	75	20
C132	A198	12c dl yel	1.25	20
C133	A198	30c indigo	2.25	1.50

See note after No. C72.

Mother and Child
AP60

Masonic Temple Havana
AP61

1956, May 13 *Perf. 12½* Wmk. 106

C134	AP60	12c ultra & red	80	25

Issued in honor of Mother's Day 1956.

1956, June 5

C135	AP61	12c ol grn	60	20

Pigeon
AP62

Gundlach Hawk
AP63

Birds: 8c, Wood duck. 19c, Herring gulls. 24c, White pelicans. 29c, Common merganser. 30c, Quail. 50c, Herons (great white, great blue and Wurdemann's). 1p, Northern caracara. 2p, Middle American jacana. 5p, Ivory-billed woodpecker.

1956

C136	AP62	8c blue	50	15
C137	AP62	12c dk bl	7.00	10
C138	AP63	14c green	1.50	25
C139	AP63	19c redsh brn	1.00	50
C140	AP63	24c lil rose	1.25	50
C141	AP62	29c green	1.75	50
C142	AP62	30c dk ol bis	2.00	75
C143	AP63	50c sl blk	4.00	1.00
C144	AP63	1p dk car rose	6.00	2.00
C145	AP62	2p rose vio	12.50	4.00
C146	AP63	5p brt red	30.00	8.00
		Nos. C136-C146 (11)	67.50	17.75

See also No. C205.

Type of 1956 Surcharged

Inauguración
Edificio Club
Filatélico de la
República de Cuba
Julio 13 de 1956.

8¢

Design: 24c, White pelicans.

1956, July 13

C147	AP63	8c on 24c dp org	1.00	35

Issued to commemorate the opening of the new building of the Cuba Philatelic Club, Havana, July 14, 1956.

Hubert de Blanck
AP64

Church of Our Lady of Charity
AP65

1956, July 6

C148	AP64	12c ultra	90	25

Issued to commemorate the centenary of the birth of Hubert de Blanck (1856–1932), composer.

1956, Sept. 8

C149	AP65	12c grn & car	90	40
a.		Souvenir sheet of 2, imperf.	9.00	8.00

Issued in honor of Our Lady of Charity of Cobre, patroness of Cuba.

No. C149a contains one each of Nos. 559 and C149 with bright blue marginal inscription and coat of arms. Size: 76x77mm. No. C149a exists with yellow of No. 559 omitted.

Benjamin Franklin
AP66

1956, Oct. 5 Engr. *Perf. 12½*

C150	AP66	12c red brn	1.00	40

Issued to commemorate the 250th anniversary of the birth of Benjamin Franklin.

Type of 1956 Surcharged in Blue

Design: 2p, Middle American jacana.

1956, Oct. 26 Wmk. 106

C151	AP62	12c on 2p dk gray	1.50	75

Issued in honor of the 12th Inter-American Press Association Conference, Havana.

Lord Baden-Powell
AP67

1957, Feb. 22

C152	AP67	12c slate	1.50	35

Issued to commemorate the centenary of the birth of Lord Baden-Powell, founder of the Boy Scouts.

Hanabanilla Waterfall
AP68

Designs: 12c, Sierra de Cubitas. 30c, Puerto Boniato.

1957, March 29

C153	AP68	8c bl & red	75	20
C154	AP68	12c grn & red	1.20	25
C155	AP68	30c ol grn & dk pur	2.00	1.00

See note after No. 457.

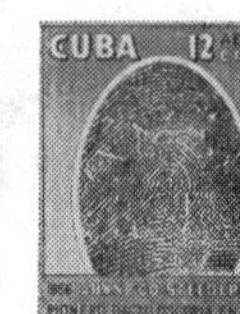

Philatelic Club, Havana
AP69

Fingerprint
AP70

1957, Apr. 24 *Perf. 12½* Wmk. 106

C156	AP69	12c yel, grn & brn	1.00	25

Issued for Stamp Day, Apr. 24, and the National Philatelic Exhibition.

1957, Apr. 30

C157	AP70	12c cl brn	90	20

Issued in honor of the centenary of the birth (in 1856) of Juan Francisco Steegers y Perera, dactyloscopy pioneer.

Baseball Player
AP71

Designs: 12c, Ballerina. 24c, Girl diver. 30c, Boxers.

1957, May 17 *Perf. 12½* Wmk. 106

C158	AP71	8c ol grn & brn	75	35
C159	AP71	12c pale vio & brn	1.50	40
C160	AP71	24c brt bl & brn	2.50	1.00
C161	AP71	30c org & brn	3.00	1.50

Issued to honor young Cuban athletes.

Joaquin de Aguero AP72 · Jeanette Ryder AP73

1957, July 4

C162	AP72	12c indigo	90	25

Issued to honor Joaquin de Aguero, Cuban freedom fighter and patriot.

1957, July 17

C163	AP73	12c dk red brn	90	35
a.		Se-tenant with No. 574	2.00	1.00

Printed in sheets of 40, containing alternate copies of Nos. 574 and C163 to honor Mrs. Jeanette Ryder, founder of the Humane Society of Cuba.

José M. de Heredia y Girard AP74 · John Robert Gregg AP75

1957, Aug. 16 Engr. Wmk. 106

C164	AP74	8c dk bl vio	50	25

Issued in honor of the poet José Maria de Heredia y Girard (1842–1905), Cuban-born French poet.

Justice Type of Regular Issue, 1957.

1957, Sept. 2 *Perf. 12½*

C165	A214	12c green	90	50

Opening of Palace of Justice, Havana.

1957, Oct. 1

C166	AP75	12c dk grn	80	35

Issued to commemorate the 90th anniversary of the birth of John Robert Gregg, inventor of the Gregg shorthand system.

D. Figarola Caneda AP76

José Marti National Library AP77

1957, Oct. 18 *Perf. 12½* Wmk. 106

C167	AP76	8c ultra	50	20
C168	AP77	12c chocolate	90	25

Issued to publicize the José Marti National Library.

Map of Cuba and U. N. Emblem AP78

1957, Oct. 24

C169	AP78	8c dk grn & brn	75	25
C170	AP78	12c car rose & grn	1.00	50
C171	AP78	30c ind & brt pink	2.50	1.00

Issued for United Nations Day, 1957.

Map of Cuba and Florida AP79

1957, Oct. 28

C172	AP79	12c dk red brn & bl	85	40

Issued to commemorate the 30th anniversary of airmail service from Key West to Havana.

Type of Regular Issue, 1957 and

Stairway and Bell Tower AP80

Design: 12c, Facade of Normal School.

1957, Nov. 19 Engraved. *Perf. 12½*

C173	A217	12c ind & ocher	85	20
C174	AP80	30c dk car & gray	1.25	60

Issued to commemorate the centenary of the first Cuban Normal School.

View Types of Regular Issue, 1957.

Views: 8c, El Viso Fort, El Caney. 12c, Sancti Spiritus Church. 30c, Concordia Bridge, Matanzas.

1957, Dec. 17 *Perf. 12½*

C175	A218	8c dk gray & red	75	25
C176	A219	12c brn & gray	1.00	25
C177	A218	30c red brn & bl gray	1.50	85

See note after No. C72.

Hedges Types of Regular Issue, 1958.

Design: 8c, Dayton Hedges and Matanzas rayon factory.

1958, Jan. 30 *Perf. 12½* Wmk. 106

C178	A221	8c green	80	40

Issued to honor Dayton Hedges, founder of Cuba's textile industry.

Diario de la Marina Building AP81

1958, April 1

C179	AP81	29c black	3.00	2.00

Issued in honor of Jose Ignacio Rivero y Alonso, editor of the newspaper, Diario de la Marina.

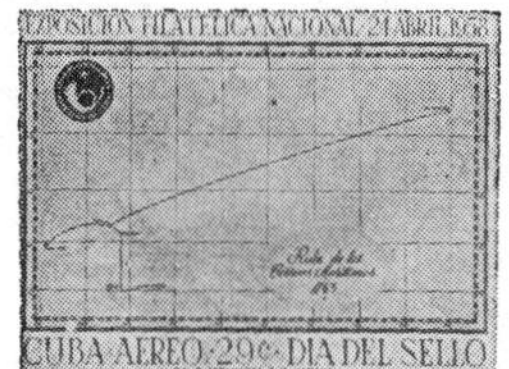

Map Showing Sea Mail Route, 1765 AP82

1958, Apr. 24 *Perf. 12½* Wmk. 106

C180	AP82	29c dk bl aqua & buff	2.25	1.25

Issued for Stamp Day, Apr. 24, and the National Philatelic Exhibition.

Gen. Gomez in Battle AP83

Snail (Polymita Picta) AP84

1958, June 6 Engraved

C181	AP83	12c sl grn	70	25

Issued in honor of Maj. Gen. José Miguel Gomez, President of Cuba, 1909-13.

1958, Aug. 29 *Perf. 12½* Wmk. 321

Fossils: 12c, Megalocnus Rodens. 30c, Ammonite.

C182	AP84	8c gray, red & yel	1.50	75
C183	AP84	12c brn, *yel grn*	2.50	1.25
C184	AP84	30c grn, *pink*	3.50	1.75

Issued to commemorate the centenary of the birth of Dr. Carlos de la Torre, naturalist.

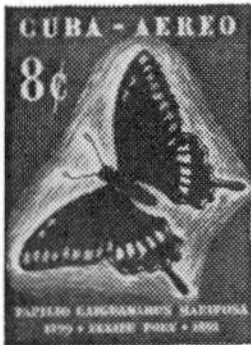

Papilio Caiguanabus AP85

Cuban Sea Bass AP86

Designs: 12c, Teria gundlachia. 14c, Teria ebriola. 19c, Nathalis felicia. 29c, Butter Hamlet. 30c, Tattler.

1958, Sept. 26 *Perf. 12½* Wmk. 106

C185	AP85	8c multi	1.75	50
C186	AP85	12c emer, blk & org	2.00	50
C187	AP85	14c multi	3.00	75
C188	AP85	19c bl, blk & yel	3.75	1.00
C189	AP86	24c multi	4.50	1.00
C190	AP86	29c blk, brn & ultra	7.00	1.25
C191	AP86	30c blk, yel grn & sep	8.00	1.75
		Nos. C185-C191 (7)	30.00	6.75

Issued in honor of Felipe Poey (1799–1891), naturalist.

Battle of San Juan Hill, 1898 AP87

Engraved.

1958, Oct. 27 *Perf. 12½* Wmk. 106

C192	AP87	12c blk brn	90	30

Birth centenary of Theodore Roosevelt.

UNESCO Building, Paris AP88

Design: 30c, "UNESCO" and map of Cuba.

1958, Nov. 7

C193	AP88	12c dk sl grn	1.00	40
C194	AP88	30c dp ultra	2.25	1.35

Issued to commemorate the opening of UNESCO (U. N. Educational, Scientific and Cultural Organization) Headquarters in Paris, Nov. 3.

Postal Notice of 1765 AP89

Musical Arts Building AP90

Design: 30c, Administrative postal book of St. Cristobal, Havana, 1765.

1959, Apr. 24 *Perf. 12½* Wmk. 321

C195	AP89	12c Prus bl & sep	75	25
C196	AP89	30c sep & Prus bl	1.25	85

Issued for Stamp Day, Apr. 24, and the National Philatelic Exhibition.

Type of 1956 Surcharged with New Value, Bar and "ASTA" Emblem in Dark Blue.

1959, Oct. 17 *Perf. 12½* Wmk. 321

C197	AP63	12c on 1p emer	1.00	40

Issued to publicize the meeting of the American Society of Travel Agents, Oct. 17-23.

Engraved.

1959, Nov. 11 *Perf. 12½* Wmk. 106

C198	AP90	12c yel grn	90	25

Issued to commemorate the 40th anniversary of the Musical Arts Society.

No. CB1 Surcharged in Red: "HABILITADO PARA / 12c"

Engraved and Lithographed

1960 *Perf. 12½* Wmk. 321

C199	SPAP1	12c on 12c+3c car & grn	1.50	75

Type of Regular Issue, 1960.

Designs: 8c, Battle of Santa Clara. 12c, Rebel forces entering Havana. 29c, Banknote changing hands ("Clandestine activities in the cities").

Engraved.

1960, Jan. 28 *Perf. 12½* Wmk. 320

C200	A236	8c bl, gray ol & sal	1.00	25
C201	A236	12c gray ol & ocher	1.50	25
C202	A236	29c gray & car	2.50	1.50

First anniversary of the revolution.

Nos. C9 and C104 Surcharged "12c" in Red

1960, Feb. 3 Wmk. 106

C203	AP3	12c on 40c dp org	75	30
C204	AP48	12c on 45c vio	75	30

Pigeon Type of 1956.

1960, Feb. 12 Wmk. 321

C205	AP62	12c brt bl grn	50	10

Statue Type of Regular Issue, 1960.

Statues: 8c, José Marti, Matanzas. 12c, Heroes of the Cacarajicara, Pinar del Rio. 30c, Cosme de la Torriente, Isle of Pines. (horiz.).

1960, March 28 *Perf. 12½*

C206	A237	8c gray & car	60	25
C207	A237	12c bl & car	1.00	25
C208	A237	30c vio & brn	2.25	1.00

See note after No. 386.

Type of 1956 and No. C33 Overprinted in Dark Blue

1960, Apr. 24 Perf. 12½ Wmk. 321

C209	AP62	8c org yel	30	20
C210	AP62	12c cerise	50	20

Souvenir Sheet

C211	AP17	Sheet of four	12.00	12.00

Nos. C209-C211 issued for Stamp Day, Apr. 24, 1960, and to publicize the National Philatelic Exhibition.

No. C211 has added marginal inscription in dark blue commemorating the centenary of the ¼r on 2r (No. 15).

Type of Olympic Games Issue, 1960.

Designs: 8c, Boxer. 12c, Runner.

Engraved

1960, Sept. 22 Perf. 12½ Wmk. 321

C212	A238	8c ultra	40	20
C213	A238	12c car rose	60	40
a.		Souvenir sheet of 4	3.50	

Issued to commemorate the 17th Olympic Games, Rome, Aug. 25–Sept. 11. No. C213a contains one each imperf. of types of Nos. 645-646 and Nos. C212-C213 in dark blue. Red marginal inscription. Size: 78x90mm.

Airmail Stamp of 1930 and Flight Symbols of 1930, 1960

AP91

1960, Oct. 30 Litho. Unwmkd.

C214	AP91	8c multi	2.50	1.50

Issued to commemorate the 30th anniversary of national air mail service.

Sword and Sheaf of Wheat

AP92

Designs: 12c, Two workers (horiz.). 30c, Three maps (horiz.). 50c, Hand inscribed "Peace" in 5 languages.

Granite Paper

1961, Jan. 10 Photo. Perf. 11½

C215	AP92	8c multi	30	20
C216	AP92	12c multi	45	20
C217	AP92	30c blk & red	1.25	50
C218	AP92	50c blk, bl & red	1.50	1.00

Issued to publicize the Conference of Underdeveloped Countries, Havana.

José Marti and "Declaration of Havana"

AP93

Background in Spanish, English or French

1961, Jan. 28 Litho. Perf. 12½

C219	AP93	8c pale grn, blk & red	1.00	60
C220	AP93	12c org yel, blk & pale vio	1.50	1.00
C221	AP93	30c pale bl, blk & pale brn	2.50	1.50
a.		Souvenir sheet of 3	7.50	7.50
		Nos. C219-C221 (9)	15.00	9.30

Declaration of Havana, Sept. 1, 1960.

Sheets of 25 are imprinted in margin "E" for Spanish, "I" for English or "F" for French.

No. C221a contains one each of Nos. C219-C221, imperf. The 8c has background in Spanish, the 12c in English and the 30c in French. Black marginal inscription. Size: 102x79mm.

U.N. Type of 1961.

1961, Apr. 12 Perf. 12½ Unwmkd.

C222	A244	8c dp car & yel	30	10
C223	A244	12c brt ultra & org	60	30
a.		Souvenir sheet of 2	2.00	

Issued to commemorate the 15th anniversary (in 1960) of the United Nations.

No. C223a contains one each of Nos. C222-C223, imperf. with marginal bright ultramarine inscription. Size: 107x65mm.

AIR POST SEMI-POSTAL STAMP

Farm Couple and Factory

SPAP1

Engraved and Lithographed

1959, May 7 Perf. 12½ Wmk. 321

CB1	SPAP1	12c +3c car & grn	1.50	60

Agricultural reforms. See also No. C199.

AIR POST SPECIAL DELIVERY STAMP.

Matanzas Issue.

Matanzas Harbor

APSD1

Photogravure.

Wmkd. Wavy Lines. (229)

1936, May 5 Perf. 12½

CE1	APSD1	15c lt bl	5.00	2.50

Exists imperf. Price $4.75 unused, $2.50 used.

See "Special Notices" at the front of this volume for data on the listing methods of this Catalogue, abbreviations, condition, prices and examination.

SPECIAL DELIVERY STAMPS

Issued under Administration of the United States.

U.S. No. E5 Surcharged in Red

CUBA. 10c. de PESO

Wmkd. USPS (191)

1899 Perf. 12

E1	SD3	10c on 10c bl	100.00	80.00
a.		No period after "CUBA"	275.00	275.00

Issues of the Republic under U. S. Military Rule.

Special Delivery Messenger

SD2

Engraved.

Inscribed: "Immediata".

1899 Wmkd. U S—C (191C)

E2	SD2	10c orange	45.00	10.00

Issues of the Republic

Inscribed: "Inmediata".

Wmkd. U S-C (191C)

1902 Perf. 12.

E3	SD2	10c orange	1.25	60

J. B. Zayas

SD3

1910 Unwmkd.

E4	SD3	10c org & bl	8.00	2.50
a.		Center inverted	750.00	

Airplane and Morro Castle

SD4

1914, Feb. 24 Perf. 12

E5	SD4	10c dk bl	15.00	1.00

1927 Wmkd. Star. (106)

E6	SD4	10c dp bl	12.00	35

1935 Perf. 10.

E7	SD4	10c blue	12.00	30

Matanzas Issue.

Mercury

SD5

Photogravure.

Wmkd. Wavy Lines. (229)

1936, May 5 Perf. 12½

E8	SD5	10c dp cl	6.00	2.50

Exists imperf. Price $4.25 unused, $1 used.

"Triumph of the Revolution"

SD6

1936, Nov. 18

E9	SD6	10c red org	5.00	2.50

Issued in commemoration of the centenary of the birth of Maj. Gen. Máximo Gómez (1836-1905).

Temple of Quetzalcoatl (Mexico)

SD7

Ruben Dario (Nicaragua)

SD8

Engraved

1937, Oct. 13 Perf. 10 Wmk. 106

E10	SD7	10c dp org	6.00	5.00
E11	SD8	10c dp org	6.00	5.00

Issued for the benefit of the Association of American Writers and Artists. See note after No. 354.

Letter and Symbols of Transportation

SD9

1945, Oct. 30

E12	SD9	10c ol brn	2.00	20

Governor's Building, Cárdenas

SD10

Engraved and Lithographed.

1951, July 3 Perf. 13 Wmk. 229

E13	SD10	10c hn brn, ultra & red	5.00	1.00

Issued to commemorate the centenary of the adoption of Cuba's flag.

Chess Type of Regular Issue, 1951

1951, Nov. 1 Photogravure

E14	A166	10c dk grn & rose brn	9.00	3.50

Issued to commemorate the 30th anniversary of the winning of the World Chess title by José Raul Capablanca.

Type of Regular Issue of 1951 Surcharged in Red Violet

10¢ E. ESPECIAL

Engraved.

1952, Mar. 18 Perf. 10 Wmk. 106

E15	A159	10c on 2c yel brn	2.25	75

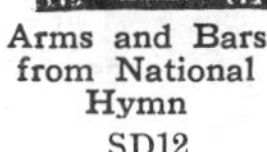

Arms and Bars from National Hymn
SD12

Roseate Tern
SD13

1952, May 27 *Perf. 12½*

E16	SD12	10c dp org & bl	3.00	1.00

Issued to commemorate the 50th anniversary of the founding of the Republic of Cuba.

Type of Air Post Stamps of 1952 Inscribed: "Entrega Especial"

1952, Oct. 7 *Perf. 10*

E17	AP36	10c pale ol grn	2.50	1.00

Three-fourths of the proceeds from the sale of No. E17 were used for the Communications Ministry Employees' Retirement Fund.

1953, July 28

E18	SD13	10c blue	2.50	60

Gregorio Hernandez Saez
SD14

Felix Varela
SD15

1954, Feb. 23

E19	SD14	10c ol grn	3.00	75

1955, June 22 *Perf. 12½*

E20	SD15	10c brn car	2.25	85

See note after No. E17.

Portrait Type of Regular Issue, 1956 Inscribed: "Entrega Especial"

Portrait: 10c, Jose Jacinto Milanes.

1956, May 2 **Wmk. 106**

E21	A18	10c dk car rose & blk	2.25	60

See note after No. E17.

Painting Type of Regular Issue, 1957, Inscribed: "Entrega Especial"

Painting: 10c, "Yesterday" by E. Garcia Cabrera.

1957, Mar. 15 Engraved *Perf. 12½*

E22	A207	10c dk brn & turq bl	3.00	85

See note after No. E17.

View Type of Regular Issue, 1957, Inscribed: "Entrega Especial."

View: 10c, Independence square, Pino del Rio.

1957, Dec. 17

E23	A218	10c dk pur & brn	2.00	60

See note after No. E17.

View in Havana and Messenger
SD16

1958, Jan. 10 **Engraved**

E24	SD16	10c blue	1.50	50
E25	SD16	20c green	2.00	60

See also Nos. E28, E31.

Fish Type of Air Post Issue, 1958, Inscribed "Entrega Especial."

Fish: 10c, Blackfish snapper. 20c, Mosquitofish.

1958, Sept. 26 *Perf. 12½* **Wmk. 106**

E26	AP86	10c blk, bl, pink & yel	4.00	2.00
E27	AP86	20c blk, ultra & pink	12.50	9.00

See note after No. C191.

Messenger Type of 1958

1960 *Perf. 12½* **Wmk. 321**

E28	SD16	10c brt vio	1.50	40

Plane Type of Air Post Issue, of 1931–46, Surcharged in Black or Red: "HABILITADO ENTREGA ESPECIAL 10¢"

1960 *Perf. 10* **Wmk. 106**

E29	AP4	10c on 20c car rose	1.25	50
E30	AP4	10c on 50c grnsh bl (R)	1.00	50

Messenger Type of 1958

1961, June 28 *Perf. 12½* **Wmk. 321**

E31	SD16	10c orange	1.50	50

POSTAGE DUE STAMPS

Issued under Administration of the United States

Postage Due Stamps of the United States Nos. J38, J39, J41 and J42 Surcharged in Black Like Regular Issue of Same Date.

Wmkd. USPS (191)

1899 *Perf. 12.*

J1	D2	1c on 1c dp cl	22.50	3.50
J2	D2	2c on 2c dp cl	20.00	3.50
a.		Inverted surcharge		2,000.
J3	D2	5c on 5c dp cl	22.50	2.50
a.		"CUPA"	175.00	160.00
J4	D2	10c on 10c dp cl	20.00	1.25

Issues of the Republic.

D1

Engraved

1914 *Perf. 12* **Unwmkd.**

J5	D1	1c car rose	4.00	1.00
J6	D1	2c car rose	5.00	1.00
J7	D1	5c car rose	10.00	2.00

1927–28

J8	D1	1c rose red	4.00	1.00
J9	D1	2c rose red	5.00	1.00
J10	D1	5c rose red	9.00	1.50

NEWSPAPER STAMPS.

Issued under Spanish Dominion.

N1

N2

Typographed

1888 *Perf. 14* **Unwmkd.**

P1	N1	½m black	25	25
P2	N1	1m black	30	30
P3	N1	2m black	30	30
P4	N1	3m black	2.00	1.00
P5	N1	4m black	2.50	1.75
P6	N1	8m black	10.00	7.50
		Nos. P1-P6 (6)	15.35	11.10

1890

P7	N2	½m red brn	75	60
P8	N2	1m red brn	75	60
P9	N2	2m red brn	1.25	85
P10	N2	3m red brn	1.50	1.00
P11	N2	4m red brn	10.00	5.00
P12	N2	8m red brn	10.00	5.00
		Nos. P7-P12 (6)	24.25	13.05

1892

P13	N2	½m violet	25	25
P14	N2	1m violet	25	25
P15	N2	2m violet	25	25
P16	N2	3m violet	1.50	25
P17	N2	4m violet	5.00	1.50
P18	N2	8m violet	10.00	2.50
		Nos. P13-P18 (6)	17.25	5.00

1894

P19	N2	½m rose	25	25
a.		Imperf., pair	30.00	
P20	N2	1m rose	75	25
P21	N2	2m rose	75	25
P22	N2	3m rose	2.50	1.00
P23	N2	4m rose	3.50	1.25
P24	N2	8m rose	7.00	3.00
		Nos. P19-P24 (6)	14.75	6.00

1896

P25	N2	½m bl grn	25	25
P26	N2	1m bl grn	25	25
P27	N2	2m bl grn	25	25
P28	N2	3m bl grn	3.50	1.25
P29	N2	4m bl grn	7.00	6.00
P30	N2	8m bl grn	12.00	8.00
		Nos. P25-P30 (6)	23.25	16.00

POSTAL TAX STAMPS.

Mother and Child
PT1

Nurse with Child
PT2

Wmkd. Star. (106)

1938, Dec. 1 Engraved *Perf. 10*

RA1	PT1	1c brt grn	35	10

The tax benefited the National Council of Tuberculosis fund for children's hospitals. Obligatory on all mail during December and January. This note applies also to Nos. RA2–4, RA7–10, RA12–15, RA17–21.

1939, Dec. 1

RA2	PT2	1c org ver	35	10

"Health" Protecting Children
PT3

Mother and Child
PT4

1940, Dec. 1

RA3	PT3	1c dp bl	35	10

1941, Dec. 1

RA4	PT4	1c ol bis	50	10

Victory
PT5

1942–44

RA5	PT5	½c orange	35	10
RA6	PT5	½c gray ('44)	40	10

Issue dates: No. RA5, July 1, 1942. No. RA6, Oct. 3, 1944.

Type of 1941 Overprinted in Black "1942"

1942, Dec. 1

RA7	PT4	1c salmon	60	20
a.		Inverted ovpt.	60.00	30.00

"Health" Protecting Children
PT6

Mother and Child
PT7

1943, Dec. 1

RA8	PT6	1c brown	35	10

1949, Dec. 9

RA9	PT7	1c blue	35	10

Type of 1949 Inscribed: "1950."

1950, Dec. 1 **Engraved**

RA10	PT7	1c rose red	35	10

Model of Proposed Communications Building
PT8

Woman Holding Child Aloft
PT9

1951, June 5 *Perf. 10* **Wmk. 106**

RA11	PT8	1c violet	50	5

The tax was to help build a new Communications Building. This note applies also to Nos. RA16, RA34, RA43.

1951, Dec. 1

RA12	PT9	1c vio bl	35	5
RA13	PT9	1c brn car	35	5
RA14	PT9	1c ol bis	35	5
RA15	PT9	1c dp grn	35	5

Proposed Communications Building
PT10

Child
PT11

1952, Feb. 8

RA16	PT10	1c dk bl	20	5

See also Nos. RA34, RA43.

1952, Dec. 1

RA17	PT11	1c rose car	50	5
RA18	PT11	1c yel grn	50	5
RA19	PT11	1c blue	50	5
RA20	PT11	1c orange	50	5

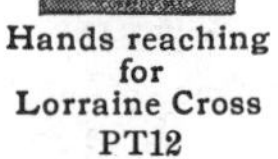

Hands reaching for Lorraine Cross
PT12

Child's Head and Lorraine Cross
PT13

1953, Dec. 1 *Perf. 9½*

RA21	PT12	1c rose car	35	5

1954, Nov. 1 *Perf. 9½x10*

RA22	PT13	1c rose red	35	5
RA23	PT13	1c violet	35	5
RA24	PT13	1c brt bl	35	5
RA25	PT13	1c emerald	35	5

The tax benefited the National Council of Tuberculosis fund for children's hospitals. Obligatory on all mail during November, December, January and February. This note applies also to Nos. RA26–33, RA35–42.

Rose and Watering Can
PT14

Child and Protective Hands
PT15

1955, Nov. 1

RA26	PT14	1c red org	50	10
RA27	PT14	1c red lil	50	10
RA28	PT14	1c brt bl	50	10
RA29	PT14	1c org yel	50	10

1956, Nov. 1

RA30	PT15	1c rose red	35	5
RA31	PT15	1c yel brn	35	5
RA32	PT15	1c brt bl	35	5
RA33	PT15	1c emerald	35	5

Building Type of 1952

1957, Jan. 18 *Perf. 10*

RA34	PT10	1c rose red	20	5

Mother and Child by Silvia Arrojo Fernandez
PT16

National Council of Tuberculosis
PT17

Engraved.

1957, Nov. 1 *Perf. 10* **Wmk. 321**

RA35	PT16	1c dl rose	50	5
RA36	PT16	1c brt bl	50	5
RA37	PT16	1c gray	50	5
RA38	PT16	1c emerald	50	5

1958

RA39	PT17	1c rose red	25	5
RA40	PT17	1c red brn	25	5
RA41	PT17	1c gray	25	5
RA42	PT17	1c emerald	25	5

Building Type of 1952

1958 **Wmk. 321**

RA43	PT10	1c rose red	20	5

CURACAO

(See Netherlands Antilles.)

CYRENAICA

(sĭr'ē·nā'ĭ·kȧ)

LOCATION — In northern Africa bordering on the Mediterranean Sea.

GOVT.—Former Italian colony.

AREA—75,340 sq. mi.

POP.—225,000 (approx. 1934).

CAPITAL—Bengasi (Benghazi).

Cyrenaica was incorporated in the kingdom of Libya in 1951.

100 Centesimi = 1 Lira
1000 Milliemes = 1 Pound (1950)

Propaganda of the Faith Issue.

Italy Nos. 143-146 Overprinted

CIRENAICA

Wmkd. Crowns. (140)

1923 *Perf. 14*

1	A68	20c ol grn & brn org	2.40	3.75
2	A68	30c cl & brn org	2.40	3.75
3	A68	50c vio & brn org	2.10	3.25
4	A68	1 l bl & brn org	2.10	3.25

Fascisti Issue.

Italy Nos. 159-164 Overprinted CIRENAICA in Red or Black.

1923 *Perf. 14* **Unwmkd.**

5	A69	10c dk grn (R)	1.75	2.25
6	A69	30c dk vio (R)	1.75	2.25
7	A69	50c brn car	1.75	2.25

Wmkd. Crowns. (140)

8	A70	1 l blue	1.75	2.25
9	A70	2 l brown	1.75	2.25
10	A71	5 l blk & bl (R)	3.50	6.75
		Nos. 5-10 (6)	12.25	18.00

Manzoni Issue.

Italy Nos. 165-170 Overprinted in Red CIRENAICA

1924 *Perf. 14.*

11	A72	10c brn red & blk	60	1.50
a.		Vertical overprint	200.00	
12	A72	15c bl grn & blk	60	1.50
a.		Vertical ovpt.	200.00	
13	A72	30c blk & sl	60	1.50
a.		Dbl. ovpt., vert.	200.00	225.00
14	A72	50c org brn & blk	60	1.50
a.		Vertical ovpt.	250.00	
15	A72	1 l bl & blk	12.00	25.00
a.		Double overprint	200.00	225.00
16	A72	5 l vio & blk	240.00	525.00
		Nos. 11-16 (6)	254.40	556.00

On Nos. 15 and 16 the overprint is placed vertically at the left side.

Victor Emmanuel Issue.

Italy Nos. 175-177 Overprinted CIRENAICA

1925–26 *Perf. 11* **Unwmkd.**

17	A78	60c brn car	30	60
18	A78	1 l dk bl	30	60
19	A78	1.25 l dk bl ('26)	90	2.00
a.		Perf. 13½	50.00	85.00

Saint Francis of Assisi Issue.

Italian Stamps of 1926 Overprinted CIRENAICA

1926 *Perf. 14* **Wmk. 140**

20	A79	20c gray grn	60	90
21	A80	40c dk vio	60	90
22	A81	60c red brn	60	90

Overprinted in Red Cirenaica

Unwmkd.

23	A82	1.25 l dk bl, perf. 11	60	90
24	A83	5 l +2.50 l ol grn	4.00	6.25
		Nos. 20-24 (5)	6.40	9.85

Volta Issue.

Type of Italy 1927, Overprinted Cirenaica

1927 *Perf. 14.* **Wmkd. Crown. (140)**

25	A84	20c purple	8.00	7.00
26	A84	50c dp org	1.35	2.40
27	A84	1.25 l brt bl	2.00	5.50

No. 25 exists with overprint omitted. Price $75.

Monte Cassino Issue.

Types of 1929 Issue of Italy, Overprinted in Red or Blue CIRENAICA

1929

28	A96	20c dk grn (R)	1.25	2.00
29	A96	25c red org (Bl)	1.25	2.00
30	A98	50c +10c crim (Bl)	1.25	2.00
31	A98	75c +15c ol brn (R)	1.25	2.00
32	A96	1.25 l +25c dk vio (R)	4.75	6.50
33	A98	5 l +1 l saph (R)	4.75	6.50

Overprinted in Red Cirenaica

Unwmkd.

34	A100	10 l +2 l gray brn	4.75	6.50
		Nos. 28-34 (7)	19.25	27.50

Royal Wedding Issue.

Type of Italian Stamps of 1930 Overprinted CIRENAICA

1930 **Wmkd. Crowns. (140)**

35	A101	20c yel grn	90	1.10
36	A101	50c +10c dp org	90	1.25
37	A101	1.25 l +25c rose red	1.20	1.85

No. 35 exists with overprint omitted. Price $750.

Ferrucci Issue.

Types of Italian Stamps of 1930, Overprinted in Red or Blue Cirenaica

1930

38	A102	20c vio (R)	60	60
39	A103	25c dk grn (R)	60	60
40	A103	50c blk (R)	60	60
41	A103	1.25 l dp bl (R)	60	60
42	A104	5 l +2 l dp car (Bl)	3.00	3.00
		Nos. 38-42 (5)	5.40	5.40

Virgil Issue.

Types of Italian Stamps of 1930 Overprinted in Red or Blue

CIRENAICA

1930

43	A106	15c vio blk (R)	18	30
44	A106	20c org brn (Bl)	18	30
45	A106	25c dk grn (R)	18	30
46	A106	30c lt brn (Bl)	18	30
47	A106	50c dl vio (R)	18	30
48	A106	75c rose red	18	30
49	A106	1.25 l gray bl (R)	18	30

Unwmkd.

50	A106	5 l +1.50 l dk vio (R)	2.50	4.00
51	A106	10 l +2.50 l ol brn (Bl)	2.50	4.00
		Nos. 43-51 (9)	6.26	10.10

Saint Anthony of Padua Issue.

Types of Italian Stamps of 1931 Overprinted in Blue or Red CIRENAICA

1931 **Wmkd. Crowns. (140)**

52	A116	20c brn (Bl)	35	60
53	A116	25c grn (R)	35	60
54	A118	30c gray brn (Bl)	35	60
55	A118	50c dl vio (Bl)	35	60
56	A120	1.25 l sl bl (R)	35	60

Overprinted in Red or Black Cirenaica

Unwmkd.

57	A121	75c blk (R)	35	60
58	A122	5 l +2.50 l dk brn (Bk)	4.25	6.25
		Nos. 52-58 (7)	6.35	9.85

Carabineer
A1

1934 Photogravure **Wmk. 140**

59	A1	5c dk ol grn & brn	1.75	3.25
60	A1	10c brn & blk	1.75	3.25
61	A1	20c scar & ind	1.75	3.25
62	A1	50c pur & brn	1.75	3.25
63	A1	60c org brn & ind	1.75	3.25
64	A1	1.25 l dk bl & grn	1.75	3.25
		Nos. 59-64 (6)	10.50	19.50

Issued to commemorate the 2nd Colonial Art Exhibition held at Naples. See also Nos. C24–C29.

Autonomous State

Senussi Warrior
A2 A3

Engraved.

1950 *Perf. 12½* **Unwmkd.**

65	A2	1m dk brn	10	12
66	A2	2m rose car	10	12
67	A2	3m orange	10	12
68	A2	4m dk grn	90	1.20
69	A2	5m gray	12	18
70	A2	8m red org	18	25
71	A2	10m purple	22	25
72	A2	12m red	22	25
73	A2	20m dp bl	22	30
74	A3	50m choc & ultra	1.65	1.75
75	A3	100m bl blk & car rose	7.50	8.50
76	A3	200m vio & pur	10.00	12.00
77	A3	500m dk grn & org	30.00	35.00
		Nos. 65-77 (13)	51.31	60.04

SEMI-POSTAL STAMPS

Many issues of Italy and Italian Colonies include one or more semipostal denominations. To avoid splitting sets, these issues are generally listed as regular postage unless all values carry a surtax.

Holy Year Issue.

Italian Semi-Postal Stamps of 1924 Overprinted in Black or Red

CIRENAICA

1925 *Perf. 12* **Wmk. 140**

B1	SP4	20c +10c dk grn & brn	75	1.50
B2	SP4	30c +15c dk brn & brn	75	1.50
B3	SP4	50c +25c vio & brn	75	1.50
a.		Overprint inverted		
B4	SP4	60c +30c dp rose & brn	75	1.50
B5	SP8	1 l +50c dp bl & vio (R)	1.50	2.25
B6	SP8	5 l +2.50 l org brn & vio (R)	2.00	3.00
		Nos. B1-B6 (6)	6.50	11.25

Colonial Institute Issue.

"Peace" Substituting Spade for Sword—SP1

1926 **Typographed.** ***Perf. 14.***

B7	SP1	5c +5c brn	18	42
B8	SP1	10c +5c ol grn	18	42
B9	SP1	20c +5c bl grn	18	42
B10	SP1	40c +5c brn red	18	42
B11	SP1	60c +5c org	18	42
B12	SP1	1l +5c bl	18	22
		Nos. B7-B12 (6)	1.08	2.32

Surtax for Italian Colonial Institute.

Types of Italian Semi-Postal Stamps of 1926 Overprinted **CIRENAICA**

1927 ***Perf. 11.*** **Unwmkd.**

B13	SP10	40c +20c dk brn & blk	1.00	1.75
B14	SP10	60c +30c brn red & ol brn	1.00	1.75
B15	SP10	1.25l +60c dp bl & blk	1.00	1.75
B16	SP10	5l +2.50l dk grn & blk	1.50	3.75

The surtax on these stamps was for the charitable work of the Voluntary Militia for Italian National Defense.

Allegory of Fascism and Victory SP2

1928 ***Perf. 14.*** **Wmk. 140**

B17	SP2	20c +5c bl grn	65	1.25
B18	SP2	30c +5c red	65	1.25
B19	SP2	50c +10c pur	65	1.25
B20	SP2	1.25l +20c dk bl	65	1.25

Issued to commemorate the 46th anniversary of the Societa Africana d'Italia. The surtax aided that society.

Types of Italian Semi-Postal Stamps of 1926 Overprinted **CIRENAICA**

1929 ***Perf. 11.*** **Unwmkd.**

B21	SP10	30c +10c red & blk	1.00	1.75
B22	SP10	50c +20c vio & blk	1.00	1.75
B23	SP10	1.25l +50c brn & bl	1.50	2.75
B24	SP10	5l +2l ol grn & blk	1.50	2.75

The surtax on Nos. B21–B24 was for the charitable work of the Voluntary Militia for Italian National Defense.

Types of Italian Semi-Postal Stamps of 1926 Overprinted in Black or Red **CIRENAICA**

1930 ***Perf. 14.***

B25	SP10	30c +10c dk grn & bl grn (Bk)	1.75	2.50
B26	SP10	50c +10c dk grn & vio (R)	1.75	2.50
B27	SP10	1.25l +30c ol brn & red brn (R)	2.40	3.75
B28	SP10	5l +1.50l ind & grn (R)	12.50	17.50

The surtax on these stamps was for the charitable work of the Voluntary Militia for Italian National Defense.

Sower SP3

1930 **Photogravure** **Wmk. 140**

B29	SP3	50c +20c ol brn	1.00	1.75
B30	SP3	1.25l +20c dp bl	1.00	1.75
B31	SP3	1.75l +20c grn	1.00	1.75
B32	SP3	2.55l +50c pur	1.75	2.75
B33	SP3	5l +1l dp car	1.75	2.75
		Nos. B29-B33 (5)	6.50	10.75

Issued in commemoration of the 25th anniversary of the Italian Colonial Agricultural Institute.

The surtax was for the aid of that institution.

AIR POST STAMPS.

> Prices for cancelled Air Post stamps of Cyrenaica are for "cancelled to order" copies. Postally used sell for much more.

Air Post Stamps of Tripolitania, 1931, Overprinted in Blue **Cirenaica**

1932 ***Perf. 14.*** **Wmk. 140**

C1	AP1	50c rose car	40	18
C2	AP1	60c dp org	1.00	1.35
C3	AP1	80c dl vio	1.00	1.50

Air Post Stamps of Tripolitania, 1931, Overprinted in Blue **CIRENAICA**

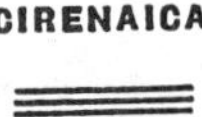

1932

C4	AP1	50c rose car	25	25
C5	AP1	80c dl vio	1.50	2.50

This overprint was also applied to the 60c, Tripolitania No. C9. The overprinted stamp was never used in Cyrenaica, but was sold at Rome in 1943 by the Postmaster General for the Italian Colonies. Price $15.

Arab on Camel AP2

Airplane in Flight AP3

1932 **Photogravure.**

C6	AP2	50c purple	80	12
C7	AP2	75c brn rose	80	1.25
C8	AP2	80c dp bl	80	1.25
C9	AP3	1l black	50	12
C10	AP3	2l green	60	75
C11	AP3	5l dp car	1.50	1.85
		Nos. C6-C11 (6)	5.00	5.34

Graf Zeppelin Issue.

Zeppelin and Clouds forming Pegasus AP4

Zeppelin and Ancient Galley AP5

Zeppelin and Giant Bowman AP6

1933, Apr. 15

C12	AP4	3l dk brn	10.00	10.00
C13	AP5	5l purple	10.00	10.00
C14	AP6	10l dp grn	10.00	10.00
C15	AP5	12l dp bl	10.00	10.00
C16	AP4	15l carmine	10.00	10.00
C17	AP6	20l black	10.00	10.00
		Nos. C12-C17 (6)	60.00	60.00

North Atlantic Cruise Issue.

Airplane Squadron and Constellations AP7

1933, June 1

C18	AP7	19.75l grn & dp bl	25.00	25.00
C19	AP7	44.75l red & ind	25.00	25.00

Type of 1932 Overprinted and Surcharged

1934, Jan. 20

C20	AP3	2l on 5l org brn	2.75	2.75
C21	AP3	3l on 5l yel grn	2.75	2.75
C22	AP3	5l ocher	2.75	2.75
C23	AP3	10l on 5l rose	2.75	2.75

For use on mail to be carried on a special flight from Rome to Buenos Aires.

Transport Plane AP8

Venus of Cyrene AP9

1934, Oct. 9

C24	AP8	25c sl bl & org red	1.75	3.00
C25	AP8	50c dk grn & ind	1.75	3.00
C26	AP8	75c dk brn & org red	1.75	3.00
a.		Imperf.	300.00	
C27	AP9	80c org brn & ol grn	1.75	3.00
C28	AP9	1l scar & ol grn	1.75	3.00
C29	AP9	2l dk bl & brn	1.75	3.00
		Nos. C24-C29 (6)	10.50	18.00

Issued in commemoration of the Second Colonial Arts Exhibition held at Naples.

AIR POST SEMI-POSTAL STAMPS.

King Victor Emmanuel III SPAP1

Photogravure.

1934 ***Perf. 14.*** **Wmk. 104**

CB1	SPAP1	25c +10c gray grn	1.00	1.00
CB2	SPAP1	50c +10c brn	1.00	1.00
CB3	SPAP1	75c +15c rose red	1.00	1.00
CB4	SPAP1	80c +15c brn blk	1.00	1.00
CB5	SPAP1	1l +20c red brn	1.00	1.00
CB6	SPAP1	2l +20c brt bl	1.00	1.00
CB7	SPAP1	3l +25c pur	12.00	12.00
CB8	SPAP1	5l +25c org	12.00	12.00
CB9	SPAP1	10l +30c dp vio	12.00	12.00
CB10	SPAP1	25l +2l dp grn	12.00	12.00
		Nos. CB1-CB10 (10)	54.00	54.00

Issued in commemoration of the 65th birthday of King Victor Emmanuel III and the non-stop flight from Rome to Mogadiscio.

AIR POST SEMI-POSTAL OFFICIAL STAMP.

Type of Air Post Semi-Postal Stamps, 1934, Overprinted Crown and "SERVIZIO DI STATO" in Black.

1934, Nov. 5 ***Perf. 14*** **Wmk. 140**

CBO1	SPAP1	25l +2l cop red	*1,750.*

POSTAGE DUE STAMPS

D1

Engraved

1950 ***Perf. 12½*** **Unwmkd.**

J1	D1	2m dk brn	22.50	27.50
J2	D1	4m dp grn	22.50	27.50
J3	D1	8m scarlet	22.50	27.50
J4	D1	10m vermilion	22.50	27.50
J5	D1	20m org yel	22.50	27.50
J6	D1	40m dp bl	22.50	27.50
J7	D1	100m dk gray	22.50	27.50
		Nos. J1-J7 (7)	157.50	192.50

CZECHOSLOVAKIA

(chěk'ô-slô-vä'kǐ-ȧ)

LOCATION—Central Europe.

GOVT.—Republic.

AREA—49,355 sq. mi.

POP.—15,030,000 (est. 1976).

CAPITAL—Prague.

The Czechoslovakian Republic consists of Bohemia, Moravia and Silesia, Slovakia and Ruthenia (Carpatho-Ukraine). In March, 1939, a German protectorate was established over Bohemia and Moravia, as well as over Slovakia which had meanwhile declared its independence. Ruthenia was incorporated in the territory of Hungary. These territories were returned to the Czechoslovak Republic in 1945, except for Ruthenia which was ceded to Russia. Czechoslovakia became a federal state on Jan. 2, 1969.

100 Haleru = 1 Koruna

Stamps of Austria overprinted "Ceskoslovenska Republika", lion and "Cesko Slovensky Stat", "Provisorni Ceskoslovenska Vlada" and Arms, and "Ceskoslovenska Statni Posta" and Arms were made privately. A few of them were passed through the post but all have been pronounced unofficial and unauthorized by the Postmaster General.

During the occupation of part of Northern Hungary by the Czechoslovak forces, stamps of Hungary were overprinted "Cesko Slovenska Posta", "Ceskoslovenska Statni Posta" and Arms, and "Slovenska Posta" and Arms. These stamps were never officially issued though copies have passed the post.

Hradcany at Prague
A1

Typographed.

1918–19 ***Imperf.*** **Unwmkd.**

1	A1	3(h) red vio	5	5
2	A1	5(h) yel grn	5	5
3	A1	10(h) rose	3	3
4	A1	20(h) bluish grn	6	3
5	A1	25(h) dp bl	25	3
a.		25(h) ultra	30.00	
6	A1	30(h) bister	30	3
7	A1	40(h) red org	30	3
8	A1	100(h) brown	70	4
9	A1	200(h) ultra	1.25	4
10	A1	400(h) purple	2.00	20

On the 3(h) to 40(h) the words "Posta Ceskoslovenska" are in white on a colored background; on the higher values the words are in color on a white background.

See Nos. 368, 1554, 1600.

Perf. 11½, 13½

13	A1	5(h) yel grn	15	3
a.		Perf. 11½x10½	1.20	30
14	A1	10(h) rose	25	10
15	A1	20(h) bluish grn	20	5
a.		Perf. 13½	1.00	40
16	A1	25(h) dp bl	30	5
a.		Perf. 11½	1.25	40
20	A1	200(h) ultra	1.50	10
		Nos. 1-10, 13-16, 20 (15)	7.39	86

All values of this issue exist with various private perforations and copies have been used on letters.

The 3, 30, 40, 100 and 400h formerly listed are now known to have been privately perforated.

A2

Type II. Sun behind cathedral. Colorless foliage in foreground.

Type III. Without sun. Shaded foliage in foreground.

Type IV. No foliage in foreground. Positions of buildings changed. Letters redrawn.

1919 ***Imperf.***

23	A2	1(h) dk brn (II)	4	3
25	A2	5(h) bl grn (IV)	20	5
27	A2	15(h) red (IV)	25	15
29	A2	25(h) dl vio (IV)	25	3
30	A2	50(h) dl vio (II)	35	3
31	A2	50(h) dk bl (IV)	35	3
32	A2	60(h) org (III)	90	15
33	A2	75(h) sl (IV)	50	5
34	A2	80(h) ol grn (III)	1.00	3
36	A2	120(h) gray blk (IV)	1.25	20
38	A2	300(h) dk grn (III)	4.00	20
39	A2	500(h) red brn (IV)	4.00	20
40	A2	1000(h) vio (III)	10.00	1.25
a.		1000(h) bluish vio	30.00	2.50
		Nos. 23-40 (13)	23.09	2.40

1919-20

Perf. 11½, 13½, 13½x11½.

41	A2	1(h) dk brn (II)	4	3
42	A2	5(h) bl grn (IV), perf. 13½	15	3
a.		Perf. 11½	12.50	7.50
43	A2	10(h) yel grn (IV)	10	3
a.		Imperf.	45.00	40.00
b.		Perf. 11½	10.00	45
44	A2	15(h) red (IV)	15	3
a.		Perf. 11½x10½	25.00	2.75
b.		Perf. 11½x13½	40.00	10.00
c.		Perf. 13½x10½	75.00	15.00
45	A2	20(h) rose (IV)	20	3
a.		Imperf.	150.00	125.00
46	A2	25(h) dl vio (IV), perf. 11½	60	3
a.		Perf. 11½x10½	3.50	40
b.		Perf. 13½x10½	20.00	10.00
47	A2	30(h) red vio (IV)	20	4
a.		Imperf.	225.00	175.00
b.		Perf. 14x13½	275.00	35.00
c.		30(h) dp vio	20	8
d.		As "c," perf. 14x13½	275.00	35.00
e.		As "c," imperf.	200.00	175.00
50	A2	60(h) org (III)	50	15
a.		Perf. 14x13½	15.00	10.00
53	A2	120(h) gray blk (IV)	7.00	1.70
		Nos. 41-53 (9)	8.94	2.07

Nos. 43a, 45a and 47a were imperforate by accident and not issued in quantities as were Nos. 23 to 40.

Rouletted stamps of the preceding issues are said to have been made by a postmaster in a branch post office at Prague, or by private firms, but without authority from the Post Office Department.

The 50, 75, 80, 300, 500 and 1000h have been privately perforated.

Unlisted color varieties of types A1 and A2 were not officially released, and some are printer's waste.

Pres. Thomas Garrigue Masaryk
A4

1920 ***Perf. 13½***

61	A4	125(h) gray bl	1.75	10
a.		125(h) ultra	35.00	25.00
b.		Imperf. (gray bl)	25.00	
c.		As "a," imperf.	75.00	
62	A4	500(h) sl, *grysh*	6.00	2.00
a.		Imperf.	30.00	
63	A4	1000(h) blk brn, *brnsh*	11.00	5.00
a.		Imperf.	40.00	

Carrier Pigeon with Letter
A5

Czechoslovakia Breaking Chains to Freedom
A6

Hussite Priest
A7

Agriculture and Science
A8

1920 ***Perf. 14***

65	A5	5(h) dk bl	3	3
a.		Perf. 13½	75.00	20.00
b.		Imperf.	3.75	
66	A5	10(h) bl grn	4	3
a.		Perf. 13½	60.00	25.00
b.		Imperf.	3.75	
67	A5	15(h) red brn	10	3
a.		Imperf.	3.75	
68	A6	20(h) rose	5	3
a.		Imperf.	3.00	
69	A6	25(h) lil brn	8	5
a.		Imperf.	3.00	
70	A6	30(h) red vio	10	3
a.		Imperf.	3.00	
71	A6	40(h) red brn	20	3
a.		Tête bêche pair	3.50	1.75
b.		Perf. 13½	60	20
c.		Imperf.	3.00	
72	A6	50(h) carmine	40	3
a.		Imperf.	3.00	
73	A6	60(h) dk bl	50	3
a.		Tête bêche pair	9.00	5.00
b.		Perf. 13½	4.00	35
c.		Imperf.	2.00	

Photogravure.

74	A7	80(h) purple	50	15
a.		Imperf.	5.00	
75	A7	90(h) blk brn	60	30
a.		Imperf.	5.00	

Typographed ***Perf. 14***

76	A8	100(h) dk grn	80	3
a.		Imperf.	4.50	
77	A8	200(h) violet	1.50	3
a.		Imperf.	4.50	
78	A8	300(h) vermilion	3.25	3
a.		Perf. 14x13½	10.00	30
b.		Imperf.	4.50	
79	A8	400(h) brown	10.00	80
a.		Imperf.	30.00	
80	A8	500(h) dp grn	11.00	80
a.		Perf. 14x13½	80.00	7.50
b.		Imperf.	30.00	
81	A8	600(h) dp vio	13.00	80
a.		Perf. 14x13½	225.00	7.50
b.		Imperf.	30.00	
		Nos. 65-81 (17)	42.15	3.23

No. 69 has background of horizontal lines.

1920–25 ***Perf. 14***

82	A5	5(h) violet	5	3
a.		Tête bêche pair	2.50	1.75
b.		Perf. 13½	25	20
c.		Imperf.	3.50	
83	A5	10(h) ol bis	5	3
a.		Tête bêche pair	3.00	2.00
b.		Perf. 13½	50	15
c.		Imperf.	3.50	
84	A5	20(h) dp org	10	6
a.		Tête bêche pair	40.00	15.00
b.		Perf. 13½	7.50	1.00
c.		Imperf.	4.50	
85	A5	25(h) bl grn	20	5
a.		Imperf.	8.00	
86	A5	30(h) dp vio ('25)	3.00	6
87	A6	50(h) yel grn	50	3
a.		Tête bêche pair	50.00	25.00
b.		Perf. 13½	17.50	3.25
c.		Imperf.	27.50	
88	A6	100(h) dk brn	80	3
a.		Perf. 13½	35.00	25
b.		Imperf.	2.00	
89	A6	150(h) rose	6.00	1.00
a.		Perf. 13½	90.00	1.50
90	A6	185(h) orange	2.00	20
a.		Imperf.	7.00	
91	A6	250(h) dk grn	6.00	30
a.		Imperf.	16.50	
		Nos. 82-91 (10)	18.70	1.79

Type of 1920 Issue Redrawn.

Type I. Rib of leaf below "O" of POSTA is straight and extends to tip. White triangle above book is entirely at left of twig. "P" has a stubby, abnormal appendage.

Type II. Rib is extremely bent; does not reach tip. Triangle extends at right of twig. "P" like Type I.

Type III. Rib of top left leaf is broken in two. Triangle like Type II. "P" has no appendage.

1923 ***Perf. 14, 14x13½***

92	A8	100(h) red, *yel*, III, perf. 14x13½	2.50	3
a.		Type I, perf. 14	2.50	5
b.		Type I, perf. 14x13½	4.00	3
c.		Type II, perf. 14	3.00	3
d.		Type II, perf. 14x13½	3.75	3
e.		Type III, perf. 14	20.00	4
93	A8	200(h) bl, *yel*, II, perf. 14	10.00	10
a.		Type II, perf. 14x13½	15.00	20
b.		Type III, perf. 14	13.50	25
c.		Type III, perf. 14x13½	65.00	40
94	A8	300(h) vio, *yel*, I, perf. 14	10.00	5
a.		Type II, perf. 14	60.00	20
b.		Type II, perf. 14x13½	125.00	30
c.		Type III, perf. 14x13½	12.00	4
d.		Type III, perf. 14	35.00	20

President Masaryk
A9 A10

Wmk. 107
(Vertical)

Perf. 14x13½, 13½

Wmkd. Linden Leaves. (107)

1925 Size: 19½x23mm. Photo.

95	A9	40h brn org	2.00	5
96	A9	50h ol grn	3.50	3
97	A9	60h red vio	4.00	3

Distinctive Marks of the Engravings.

I, II, III: Background of horizontal lines in top and bottom tablets. Inscriptions in Roman letters with serifs.

IV: Crossed horizontal and vertical lines in the tablets. Inscriptions in Antique letters without serifs.

I, II, IV: Shading of crossed diagonal lines on the shoulder at the right.

III. Shading of single lines only.

I: "T" of "Posta" over middle of "V" of "Ceskoslovenska". Three short horizontal lines in lower part of "A" of "Ceskoslovenska".

II: "T" over right arm of "V". One short line in "A".

III: "T" as in II. Blank space in lower part of "A".

IV: "T" over left arm of "V".

Engraved.

I. First Engraving.

Wmkd. Horizontally. (107)

Size: 19¾x22½mm.

98	A10	1k carmine	1.75	10
99	A10	2k dp bl	3.50	25

100	A10	3k brown	10.00	90
101	A10	5k bl grn	3.00	60

Wmkd. Vertically. (107)

Size: 19¼x23mm.

101A	A10	1k carmine	175.00	6.00
101B	A10	2k dp bl	225.00	20.00
101C	A10	3k brown	600.00	22.50
101D	A10	5k bl grn	6.00	1.50

II. Second Engraving.

Wmkd. Horizontally. (107)

Size: 19x21½mm.

102	A10	1k carmine	75.00	40
103	A10	2k dp bl	7.50	20
104	A10	3k brown	8.00	50

III. Third Engraving

Size: 19-19½x21½-22mm.

Perf. 10.

105	A10	1k car rose	2.25	3
a.		Perf. 14	20.00	10

IV. Fourth Engraving.

Size: 19-19½x21½-22mm.

1926 ***Perf. 10, 14.***

106	A10	1k car rose	1.75	3
108	A10	3k brown	8.50	6

See also No. 130.

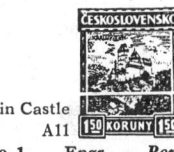

Karlstein Castle
A11

1926, June 1 **Engr.** ***Perf. 10***

109	A11	1.20k red vio	1.50	75
110	A11	1.50k car rose	1.25	5
111	A11	2.50k dk bl	5.00	60

See also Nos. 133, 135.

Karlstein Castle
A12

Pernstein Castle
A13

Orava Castle
A14

Masaryk
A15

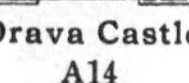

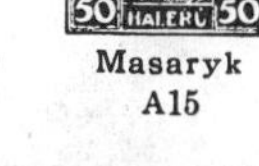

Strahov Monastery
A16

Hradčany at Prague
A17

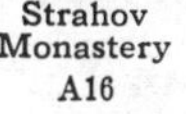

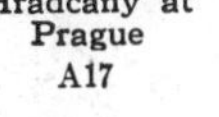

Great Tatra
A18

1926–27 **Engraved** **Wmk. 107**

114	A13	30h gray grn	2.50	20
115	A14	40h red brn	1.00	10
116	A15	50h dp grn	1.00	10
117	A15	60h red vio, *lil*	1.25	4
118	A16	1.20k red vio	7.00	2.50

Perf. 13½

119	A17	2k blue	2.00	10
a.		2k ultra	5.00	50
120	A17	3k dp red	4.00	10
121	A18	4k brn vio ('27)	7.00	60
122	A18	5k dk grn ('27)	30.00	4.50
		Nos. 114-122 (9)	55.75	8.24

No. 116 exists in two types. The one with short, straight mustache at left sells for several times as much as that with longer wavy mustache.

See also Nos. 137–140.

Coil Stamps.

Perf. 10 Vertically.

123	A12	20h brick red	1.50	50
a.		Vert. pair, imperf. horiz.	175.00	
124	A13	30h gray grn	1.00	25
a.		Vert. pair, imperf. horiz.	175.00	
125	A15	50h dp grn	50	12

See also No. 141.

1927-31 ***Perf. 10.*** **Unwmkd.**

126	A13	30h gray grn	40	3
127	A14	40h dp brn	1.25	3
128	A15	50h dp grn	25	3
129	A15	60h red vio	1.10	3
130	A10	1k car rose	8.00	10
131	A15	1k dp red	50	4
132	A16	1.20k red vio	70	4
133	A11	1.50k car ('29)	1.00	5
134	A13	2k dp grn ('29)	80	3
135	A11	2.50k dk bl	10.00	35
136	A14	3k red brn ('31)	1.00	5
		Nos. 126-136 (11)	25.00	78

No. 130 exists in two types. The one with longer mustache at left sells for several times as much as that with the short mustache.

1927–28 ***Perf. 13½***

137	A17	2k ultra	2.00	10
138	A17	3k dp red ('28)	4.00	10
139	A18	4k brn vio ('28)	12.00	1.50
140	A18	5k dk grn ('28)	12.00	60

Coil Stamp.

1927 ***Perf. 10 Vertically***

141	A12	20h brick red	75	20

Hradec Castle
A19

Town Hall, Levoča
A20

Telephone Exchange, Prague
A21

Town of Jasina
A22

Hluboka Castle
A23

Pilgrims' House at Velehrad
A24

Brno Cathedral
A25

Great Tatra
A26

Masaryk
A27

Old City Square, Prague
A28

1928, Oct. 22 ***Perf. 13½***

142	A19	30h black	10	5
143	A20	40h red brn	15	6
144	A21	50h dk grn	25	5
145	A22	60h org red	25	5
146	A23	1k carmine	40	4
147	A24	1.20k brn vio	80	40
148	A25	2k ultra	90	30
149	A26	2.50k dk bl	2.25	1.75
150	A27	3k dk brn	1.75	30
151	A28	5k dp vio	3.50	2.50
		Nos. 142-151 (10)	10.35	5.50

Issued in commemoration of the tenth anniversary of Czechoslovakian independence.

Coat of Arms
A29

1929–37 ***Perf. 10***

152	A29	5h dk ultra ('31)	5	3
153	A29	10h bis brn ('31)	5	3
154	A29	20h red	5	3
155	A29	25h green	8	3
156	A29	30h red vio	8	3
157	A29	40h dk brn ('37)	35	3
a.		40h red brn ('37)	1.00	6

Coil Stamp.

Perf. 10 Vertically.

158	A29	20h red	30	3
		Nos. 152-158 (7)	96	21

St. Wenceslas
A30

Founding St. Vitus' Cathedral
A31

Design: 3k, 5k, St. Wenceslas martyred.

1929, May 14 ***Perf. 13½***

159	A30	50h gray grn	50	10
160	A30	60h sl vio	70	10
161	A31	2k dl bl	1.75	50
162	A30	3k brown	2.00	20
163	A30	5k brn vio	10.00	3.75
		Nos. 159-163 (5)	14.95	4.65

Millenary of the death of St. Wenceslas.

Statue of St. Wenceslas and National Museum, Prague
A33

1929 ***Perf. 10***

164	A33	2.50k dp bl	85	3

Brno Cathedral
A34

Tatra Mountain Scene
A35

Design: 5k, Old City Square, Prague.

1929, Oct. 15 ***Perf. 13½***

165	A34	3k red brn	4.00	12
166	A35	4k indigo	8.00	85
167	A35	5k gray grn	10.00	50

See also No. 183.

A37

Type I

Type II

Two types of 50h:

I. A white space exists across the bottom of the vignette between the coat, shirt and tie and the "HALERU" frame panel.

II. An extra frame line has been added just above the "HALERU" panel which finishes off the coat and tie shading evenly.

1930, Jan. 2 ***Perf. 10***

168	A37	50h myr grn (II)	25	3
a.		Type I	1.25	4
169	A37	60h brn vio	1.10	3
170	A37	1k brn red	50	3

See also No. 234.

Coil Stamp.

1931 ***Perf. 10 Vertically***

171	A37	1k brn red	2.00	1.00

President Masaryk
A38

St. Nicholas' Church, Prague
A39

1930, Mar. 1 ***Perf. 13½***

175	A38	2k gray grn	1.25	35
176	A38	3k red brn	2.00	35
177	A38	5k sl bl	6.00	2.00
178	A38	10k gray blk	12.50	6.00

Eightieth birthday of President Masaryk.

1931, May 15

183	A39	10k blk vio	12.00	3.50

Krivoklat Castle
A40

Krumlov Castle
A42

Design: 4k, Orlik Castle.

1932, Jan. 2 ***Perf. 10***

184	A40	3.50k violet	3.50	1.25
185	A40	4k dp bl	3.50	45
186	A42	5k gray grn	3.50	45

Miroslav Tyrš
A43 A44

1932, Mar. 16

187	A43	50h yel grn	75	4
188	A43	1k brn car	1.00	4
189	A44	2k dk bl	10.00	35
190	A44	3k red brn	17.50	40

Issued to commemorate the centenary of the birth of Miroslav Tyrš (1832–1884), founder of the Sokol movement, and in connection with the 9th Sokol Congress.

Tyrš
A45

1933, Feb. 1

191	A45	60h dl vio	30	3

First Christian Church at Nitra
A46 A47

1933, June 20

192	A46	50h yel grn	50	5
193	A47	1k car rose	4.50	15

Issued in commemoration of Prince Pribina who introduced Christianity into Slovakia and founded there the first Christian church in A. D. 833.

All gutter pairs are vertical.

Friedrich Smetana
A48

1934, Mar. 26 **Engr.** ***Perf. 10***

194	A48	50h yel grn	50	3

Issued to commemorate the 50th anniversary of the death of Friedrich Smetana, Czech composer and pianist.

Consecration of Legion Colors at Kiev, Sept. 21, 1914
A49

Ensign Heyduk with Colors
A51

Legionnaires
A52

Design: 1k, Legion receiving battle flag at Bayonne.

1934, Aug. 15 ***Perf. 10***

195	A49	50h green	30	6
196	A49	1k rose lake	40	5
197	A51	2k dp bl	2.25	40
198	A52	3k red brn	4.50	40

Issued in commemoration of the 20th anniversary of the Czechoslovakian Legion which fought in World War I.

Antonin Dvořák
A53

1934, Nov. 22

199	A53	50h green	40	3

Issued to commemorate the 30th anniversary of the death of Antonin Dvorák, (1841–1904), composer.

Pastoral Scene
A54

1934, Dec. 17 ***Perf. 10***

200	A54	1k claret	70	10
a.		Souvenir sheet of 15	350.00	350.00
b.		As "a," single stamp	10.00	9.00
201	A54	2k blue	2.50	50
a.		Souvenir sheet of 15	1,100.	1,100.
b.		As "a," single stamp	37.50	32.50

Issued in commemoration of the centenary of the National Anthem.

Nos. 200a & 201a were issued in special souvenir sheets of 15 stamps each on thick paper, darker shades, perf. 13½, no gum. Words and music of the anthem at top and bottom of sheet. Forgeries exist.

President Masaryk
A55 A56

1935, Mar. 1

202	A55	50h grn, *buff*	10	3
203	A55	1k cl, *buff*	15	3
204	A56	2k gray bl, *buff*	2.25	15
205	A56	3k brn, *buff*	3.50	20

85th birthday of President Masaryk.

See No. 235.

Monument to Czech Heroes at Arras, France—A57

1935, May 4

206	A57	1k rose	50	3
207	A57	2k dl bl	2.00	30

20th anniversary of the Battle of Arras.

General Milan Stefánik
A58

Sts. Cyril and Methodius
A59

1935, May 18

208	A58	50h green	20	3

1935, June 22

209	A59	50h green	15	6
210	A59	1k claret	50	5
211	A59	2k dp bl	1.75	50

Issued in commemoration of the millenary of the arrival in Moravia of the Apostles Cyril and Methodius.

Masaryk
A60

Statue of Macha, Prague
A61

1935, Oct. 20 ***Perf. 12½***

212	A60	1k rose lake	10	3

No. 212 exists imperforate. See No. 256.

1936, Apr. 30

213	A61	50h dp grn	20	6
214	A61	1k rose lake	40	6

Issued to commemorate the centenary of the death of Karel Hynek Macha (1810–1836), Bohemian poet.

Jan Amos Komensky
A61a

President Eduard Beneš
A62

Gen. Milan Stefánik
A63

1936

215	A61a	40h dk bl	10	3
216	A62	50h dl grn	10	3
217	A63	60h dl vio	10	3

See Nos. 252 and 255.

Castle Palanok near Mukacevo
A64

Town of Banska Bystrica
A65

Castle at Zvikov
A66

Ruins of Castle at Strecno
A67

Castle at Cesky Raj
A68

Palace at Slavkov (Austerlitz)
A69

Statue of King George at Podebrad
A70

Town Square at Olomouc
A71

Castle Ruins at Bratislava
A72

1936, Aug. 1

218	A64	1.20k rose lil	10	4
219	A65	1.50k carmine	10	3
220	A66	2k dk bl grn	13	3
221	A67	2.50k dk bl	12	3
222	A68	3k brown	20	6
223	A69	3.50k dk vio	1.75	50
224	A70	4k dk vio	75	8
225	A71	5k green	50	8
226	A72	10k blue	2.00	50
		Nos. 218-226 (9)	5.65	1.35

President Beneš
A73

Soldiers of the Czech Legion
A74

1937, Apr. 26 ***Perf. 12½*** **Unwmkd.**

227	A73	50h dp grn	10	3

1937, June 15

228	A74	50h dp grn	20	5
229	A74	1k rose lake	35	6

Issued in commemoration of the 20th anniversary of the Battle of Zborov.

Cathedral at Prague
A75

Jan Evangelista Purkyne
A76

1937, July 1

230	A75	2k green	75	15
231	A75	2.50k blue	1.25	35

Issued in commemoration of the 16th anniversary of the founding of the "Little Entente."

1937, Sept. 2

232	A76	50h sl grn	20	5
233	A76	1k dl rose	25	5

Issued in commemoration of the 150th anniversary of the birth of Jan Evangelista Purkyne, Czech physiologist.

Masaryk Types of 1930–35.

1937, Sept. *Perf. 12½*

234	A37	50h black	20	3

With date "14.IX. 1937" in design.

235	A56	2k black	45	15

Issued in commemoration of the death of former President Thomas G. Masaryk on Sept. 14, 1937.

International Labor Bureau Issue.

Stamps of 1936-37 Overprinted in Violet or Black **B.I.T.1937**

1937, Oct. 6 *Perf. 12½*

236	A73	50h dp grn (Bk)	40	30
237	A65	1.50k car (V)	50	30
238	A66	2k dp grn (V)	60	55

Bratislava Philatelic Exhibition Issue.

Souvenir Sheet.

A77

1937, Oct. 24 *Perf. 12½*

239	A77	Sheet of two	1.40	1.40
a.		50h dk bl	50	50
b.		1k brn car	50	50

The sheet measures 149x110mm. The stamps show a view of Poprad Lake (50h) and the tomb of General Milan Stefanik (1k).

No. 239 overprinted "Libération de la Tchéchoslovaquie, 28-X-1945" etc., was sold at a philatelic exhibition in Brussels, Belgium.

St. Barbara's Church, Kutna Hora
A79

Peregrine Falcon, Sokol Emblem
A80

1937, Dec. 4

240	A79	1.60k ol grn	15	4

1938, Jan. 21

241	A80	50h dp grn	40	5
242	A80	1k rose lake	60	8

Issued in commemoration of the 10th International Sokol Games. Imperforate copies of No. 242 are essays. Nos. 241-242 se-tenant with labels sell slightly higher.

Legionnaires
A81

Legionnaires
A82

Legionnaire
A83

1938

243	A81	50h dp grn	15	4
244	A82	50h dp grn	15	5
245	A83	50h dp grn	15	5

Issued to commemorate the 20th anniversary of the Battles of Bachmac, Vouziers and Doss Alto. Nos. 243-245 with label se-tenant sell for more.

Jindrich Fügner, Co-Founder of Sokol Movement
A84

1938, June 18 *Perf. 12½*

246	A84	50h dp grn	10	5
247	A84	1k rose lake	20	4
248	A84	2k sl bl	70	6

Issued to commemorate the 10th Sokol Summer Games. Nos. 246-248 se-tenant with labels sell slightly higher.

View of Pilsen
A85

Cathedral of Kosice
A86

1938, June 24

249	A85	50h dp grn	15	3

Issued in connection with the Provincial Economic Council meeting at Pilsen.

1938, July 15 *Perf. 12½*

250	A86	50h dp grn	15	4

Issued in connection with the Kosice Cultural Exhibition.

Prague Philatelic Exhibition Issue.

Souvenir Sheet.

Vysehrad Castle—Hradcany
A87

1938, June 26 *Perf. 12½*

251	A87	Sheet of two	5.50	5.50
a.		50h dk bl	2.00	2.00
b.		1k dp car	2.00	2.00

Issued in sheets measuring 148½x105mm.

Stefánik Type of 1936.

1938, Nov. 21

252	A63	50h dp grn	10	3

Allegory of the Republic
A89

1938, Dec. 19 **Unwmkd.**

253	A89	2k lt ultra	35	20
254	A89	3k pale brn	75	25

Issued in commemoration of the 20th anniversary of Independence.

"Wir sind frei!"

Stamps of Czechoslovakia, 1918-37, overprinted with a swastika in black or red and "Wir sind frei!" were issued locally and unofficially in 1938 as Czech authorities were evacuating and German authorities arriving. They appeared in the towns of Asch, Karlsbad, Reichenberg - Maffersdorf, Rumburg, etc.

The overprint, sometimes including a surcharge or the town name (as in Karlsbad), exists on many values of postage, air post, semi-postal, postage due and newspaper stamps.

Stefánik Type of 1936.

1939 Engraved *Perf. 12½*

255	A63	60h dk bl	15.00	20.00

Used exclusively in Slovakia.

Masaryk Type of 1935 with hyphen in Cesko - Slovensko.

1939, Apr. 23

256	A60	1k rose lake	15	3

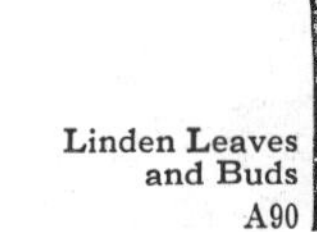

Linden Leaves and Buds
A90

1945 Photogravure. *Perf. 14.*

256A	A90	10(h) black	3	3
257	A90	30(h) yel brn	3	3
258	A90	50(h) dk grn	3	3
258A	A90	60(h) dk bl	3	3

Engraved.
(Buds Open.)
Perf. 12½.

259	A90	60(h) blue	3	3
259A	A90	80(h) org ver	6	5
260	A90	1.20(k) rose	4	3
261	A90	3(k) vio brn	5	3
262	A90	5(k) green	5	3
		Nos. 256A-262(9)	35	29

Thomas G. Masaryk
A91

Coat of Arms
A92

1945-46 Photogravure. *Perf. 12.*

262A	A91	5h dl vio ('46)	8	6
262B	A91	10h org yel ('46)	8	6
262C	A91	20h dk brn ('46)	6	5
263	A91	50h brt grn	10	5
264	A91	1k org red	12	6
265	A91	2k chlky bl	30	20
		Nos. 262A-265 (6)	74	48

1945 *Imperf.*

266	A92	50h ol gray	5	3
267	A92	1k brt red vio	5	3
268	A92	1.50k dk car	6	3
269	A92	2k dp bl	8	3
269A	A92	2.40k hn brn	30	20
270	A92	3k brown	6	5
270A	A92	4k dk sl grn	10	5
271	A92	6k vio bl	30	6
271A	A92	10k sepia	45	10
		Nos. 266-271A (9)	1.45	58

Nos. 266 to 271A exist in two printings. Stamps of the first printing are on thin, hard paper in sheets of 100; those of the second printing on thick, soft wove paper in sheets of 200.

Staff Captain Ridky (British Army)
A93

Dr. Miroslav Novak (French Army)
A94

Captain Otakar Jaros (Russian Army)
A95

Staff Captain Stanislav Zimprich (Foreign Legion)
A96

Second Lieutenant Jiri Kral (French Air Force)
A97

Josef Gabcik (Parachutist)
A98

Staff Captain Alois Vasatko (Royal Air Force)
A99

Private Frantisek Adamek (British Colonial Service)
A100

Engraved

1945, Aug. 18 ***Perf. 11½x12½***

No.	Type	Denomination	Unused	Used
272	A93	5h int bl	3	3
273	A94	10h dk brn	3	3
274	A95	20h brick red	3	3
275	A96	25h rose red	4	3
276	A97	30h purple	10	5
277	A98	40h sepia	5	4
278	A99	50h dk ol	5	4
279	A100	60h violet	15	6
280	A93	1k carmine	5	3
281	A94	1.50k lake	6	4
282	A95	2k ultra	8	3
283	A96	2.50k dp vio	10	5
284	A97	3k sepia	10	5
285	A98	4k rose lil	15	6
286	A99	5k myr grn	27	8
287	A100	10k brt ultra	80	20
		Nos. 272-287 (16)	2.09	85

Flags of Russia, Great Britain, United States and Czechoslovakia
A101

View of Banská Bystrica
A102

Patriot Welcoming Russian Soldier, Turciansky
A103

Ruins of Castle at Sklabina
A104

Czech Patriot, Strecno
A105

1945, Aug. 29 Photo. ***Perf. 10***

No.	Type	Denomination	Unused	Used
288	A101	1.50k brt car	10	8
289	A102	2k brt bl	10	10
290	A103	4k dk brn	40	25
291	A104	4.50k purple	40	25
292	A105	5k dp grn	1.00	50
a.		Souv. card of 5, imperf.	40.00	45.00
		Nos. 288-292 (5)	2.00	1.18

National uprising against the Germans.

No. 292a contains one each of Nos. 288-292 with multicolored marginal design, on thin cardboard, ungummed. Size: 148x210mm. Sold for 50k.

General Milan Stefánik
A106

President Eduard Benes
A107

Thomas G. Masaryk
A108

1945-46 Engraved ***Perf. 12, 12½***

No.	Type	Denomination	Unused	Used
293	A106	30h rose vio	3	3
294	A107	60h blue	10	3
295	A108	1.20(k) car rose	12	3
295A	A108	1.20k rose lil ('46)	10	3
296	A106	2.40(k) rose	12	3
297	A107	3k red vio	24	3
297A	A108	4k dk bl ('46)	15	3
298	A108	5k Prus grn	24	3
299	A107	7k gray	30	3
300	A106	10k gray bl	70	3
300A	A106	20k sep ('46)	1.50	10
		Nos. 293-300A (11)	3.60	40

See also No. 325.

1945 Photogravure. ***Perf. 14.***

No.	Type	Denomination	Unused	Used
301	A108	50h brown	3	3
302	A106	80h dk grn	3	3
303	A107	1.60(k) ol grn	10	3
304	A108	15k red vio	90	5

Kozina and Chod Castle, Taus
A109

Red Army Soldier
A110

Engraved.

1945, Nov. 28 ***Perf. 12½***

No.	Type	Denomination	Unused	Used
305	A109	2.40k rose car	25	20
306	A109	4k blue	30	20

Issued to commemorate the 250th anniversary of the death of Jan Sladky Kozina, peasant leader.

1945, Mar. 26 Litho. ***Imperf.***

No.	Type	Denomination	Unused	Used
307	A110	2k crim rose	60	60
308	A110	5k sl blk	2.25	2.25
309	A110	6k ultra	60	60

Souvenir Sheet.

A111

1945, July 16

Gray Burelage

No.	Type	Denomination	Unused	Used
310	A111	Sheet of three	3.00	3.00
a.		2k crim rose	40	40
b.		5k sl blk	40	40
c.		6k ultra	40	40

Return of President Benes, April, 1945. Size: 137x120mm.

Clasped Hands
A112

Karel Havlícek Borovsky
A113

1945 ***Rouletted 12½***

No.	Type	Denomination	Unused	Used
311	A112	1.50k brn red	3.75	3.75
312	A112	9k red org	90	90
313	A112	13k org brn	1.25	1.25
314	A112	20k blue	3.25	3.25

1946, July 5 Engraved

No.	Type	Denomination	Unused	Used
315	A113	1.20(k) gray blk	25	20

Issued to commemorate the 90th anniversary of the death of Karel Havlicek Borovsky (1821-1856), editor and writer.

Old Town Hall, Brno
A114

Hodonin Square
A115

Perf. 12½x12, 12x12½.

1946, Aug. 3 Engraved **Unwmkd.**

No.	Type	Denomination	Unused	Used
316	A114	2.40(k) dp rose	30	20
317	A115	7.40(k) dl vio	50	10

President Eduard Benes
A116

1946, Oct. 28

No.	Type	Denomination	Unused	Used
318	A116	60h indigo	4	3
319	A116	1.60k dl grn	6	3
320	A116	3k red lil	10	3
321	A116	8k sepia	40	3

Flag and Symbols
A117

Saint Adalbert
A118

1947, Jan. 1 ***Perf. 12½***

No.	Type	Denomination	Unused	Used
322	A117	1.20(k) Prus grn	20	4
323	A117	2.40(k) dp rose	20	3
324	A117	4(k) dp bl	50	15

Issued to publicize Czechoslovakia's two-year reconstruction and rehabilitation program.

Stefanik Type of 1945.

1947, Nov. 5

No.	Type	Denomination	Unused	Used
325	A106	1k red org	10	3

1947, Apr. 23

No.	Type	Denomination	Unused	Used
326	A118	1.60(k) gray	70	50
327	A118	2.40(k) rose car	1.25	90
328	A118	5(k) bl grn	1.00	60

Issued to commemorate the 950th anniversary of the death of Saint Adalbert, Bishop of Prague.

Grief
A119

Allegorical Figure
A120

1947, June 10 Engraved

No.	Type	Denomination	Unused	Used
329	A119	1.20(k) black	40	20
330	A119	1.60(k) sl blk	40	20
331	A120	2.40(k) brn vio	60	40

Destruction of Lidice, 5th anniversary.

World Federation of Youth Symbol
A121

Thomas G. Masaryk
A122

1947, July 20

No.	Type	Denomination	Unused	Used
332	A121	1.20(k) vio brn	50	20
333	A121	4k slate	55	25

Issued to commemorate the World Youth Festival held in Prague, July 20th to August 17, 1947.

1947, Sept. 14

No.	Type	Denomination	Unused	Used
334	A122	1.20(k) gray blk, *buff*	30	15
335	A122	4k bl blk, *cr*	70	20

Death of T. G. Masaryk, 10th anniversary.

Msgr. Stefan Moyses
A123

1947, Oct. 24

No.	Type	Denomination	Unused	Used
336	A123	1.20k rose vio	25	10
337	A123	4k dp bl	50	10

Issued to commemorate the 150th anniversary of the birth of Stefan Moyses, first Slovakian chairman of the Slavic movement.

"Freedom from Social Oppression"
A124

1947, Oct. 26 Photo. ***Perf. 14***

No.	Type	Denomination	Unused	Used
338	A124	2.40k brt car	30	20
339	A124	4k brt ultra	60	20

Issued to commemorate the 30th anniversary of the Russian revolution of October, 1917.

President Eduard Benes
A125

"Czechoslovakia" Greeting Sokol Marchers
A126

1948, Feb. 15 Photogravure

Size: 17½x21½mm.

No.	Type	Denomination	Unused	Used
340	A125	1.50(k) brown	6	3

Size: 19x23mm.

No.	Type	Denomination	Unused	Used
341	A125	2k dp plum	10	3
342	A125	5k brt ultra	25	3

1948, Mar. 7 Engr. ***Perf. 12½***

No.	Type	Denomination	Unused	Used
343	A126	1.50(k) brown	15	6
344	A126	3k rose car	15	6
345	A126	5k blue	50	8

The 11th Sokol Congress.

King Charles IV
A127

St. Wenceslas and King Charles IV
A128

1948, Apr. 7

346 A127 1.50(k) blk brn 15 5
347 A128 2(k) dk brn 20 5
348 A128 3(k) brn red 25 12
349 A127 5(k) dk bl 60 20

Issued to commemorate the 600th anniversary of the foundation of Charles University, Prague.

Czech Peasants in Revolt
A129

Jindrich Vanicek
A130

Photogravure.

1948, May 14 *Perf. 14* Unwmkd.

350 A129 1.50k dk ol brn 15 6

Centenary of abolition of serfdom.

1948, June 10 Engraved *Perf. 12½*

Designs: 1.50k, 2k, Josef Scheiner.

351 A130 1k dk grn 15 5
352 A130 1.50k sepia 15 5
353 A130 2k gray bl 35 8
354 A130 3k claret 50 12

11th Sokol Congress, Prague, 1948.

Frantisek Palacky and F. L. Rieger
A131

Miloslav Josef Hurban
A132

1948, June 20 Unwmkd.

355 A131 1.50k gray 20 8
356 A131 3k brn car 30 8

Issued to commemorate the centenary of the Constituent Assembly at Kromeriz.

1948, Aug. 27 *Perf. 12½*

Designs: 3k, Ludwig Stur. 5k, Michael M. Hodza.

357 A132 1.50(k) dk brn 15 8
358 A132 3(k) car lake 25 8
359 A132 5(k) indigo 45 20

Centenary of 1848 insurrection against Hungary.

Eduard Benes
A133

Czechoslovak Family
A134

1948, Sept. 28

360 A133 8k black 30 10

Issued in tribute to President Eduard Benes, 1884–1948.

1948, Oct. 28 *Perf. 12½x12*

361 A134 1.50k dp bl 10 10
362 A134 3k rose car 30 18

Issued to commemorate the 30th anniversary of Czechoslovakia's Independence.

Pres. Klement Gottwald
A135

Gottwald and Presidential Flag
A136

1948–49 *Perf. 12½.*

Size: 18½x23½mm.

363 A135 1.50(k) dk brn 10 3
364 A135 3(k) car rose 25 3
a. 3(k) rose brn 30 3
365 A135 5(k) gray bl 25 3

Size: 23½x29mm.

366 A135 20(k) purple 1.25 15

See also Nos. 373, 564, 600-604.

Souvenir Sheet.

1948, Nov. 23 *Imperf.* Unwmkd.

367 A136 30k rose brn 4.00 3.00

52nd birthday of Pres. Klement Gottwald (1896–1953). Size: 67x98½mm.

Souvenir Sheet.

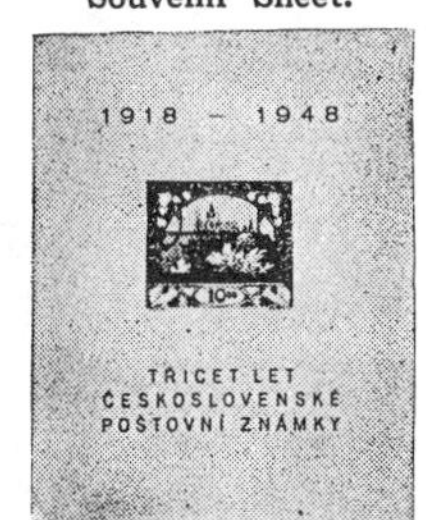

Hradcany Castle
A137

1948, Dec. 18

368 A137 10k dk bl vio 1.25 1.00

30th anniversary of first Czechoslovak postage stamp. Size: 79x90½mm.

Czechoslovak and Russian Workmen Shaking Hands
A138

Lenin
A139

1948, Dec. 12 *Perf. 12½*

369 A138 3k rose car 24 12

Issued to commemorate the fifth anniversary of the treaty of alliance between Czechoslovakia and Russia.

1949, Jan. 21 Engraved *Perf. 12½*

370 A139 1.50(k) vio brn 30 12
371 A139 5(k) dp bl 50 20

25th anniversary of the death of Lenin.

Gottwald Type of 1948
Inscribed: "UNOR 1948" and

Gottwald Addressing Meeting
A140

1949, Feb. 25 Photo. *Perf. 14*

372 A140 3k red brn 15 4

Engraved
Perf. 12½
Size: 23½x29mm.

373 A135 10k dp grn 65 20

Nos. 372 and 373 were issued to commemorate the first anniversary of Klement Gottwald's speech announcing the appointment of a new government.

P. O. Hviezdoslav
A141

Stagecoach and Train
A142

Designs (Writers): 80h, V. Vancura. 1k, J. Sverma. 2k, Julius Fucik. 4k, Jiri Wolker. 8k, Alois Jirasek.

1949 Photogravure. *Perf. 14.*

374 A141 50h vio brn 5 3
375 A141 80h scarlet 8 3
376 A141 1k dk ol grn 8 3
377 A141 2k brt bl 40 3

Engraved
Perf. 12½

378 A141 4k vio brn 40 3
379 A141 8k brn blk 45 3
Nos. 374-379 (6) 1.46 18

1949, May 20

Designs: 5k, Postrider and post bus. 13k, Sailing ship and plane.

380 A142 3k brn car 4.00 3.00
381 A142 5k dp bl 1.00 60
382 A142 13k dp grn 2.00 90

Issued to commemorate the 75th anniversary of the formation of the Universal Postal Union.

Reaping
A143

Communist Emblem and Workers
A144

Workman, Symbol of Industry
A145

Perf. 12½x12, 12x12½.

1949, May 24 Unwmkd.

383 A143 1.50k dp grn 50 35
384 A144 3k brn car 30 20
385 A145 5k dp bl 75 35

No. 384 commemorates the ninth meeting of the Communist Party of Czechoslovakia, May 25, 1949.

Friedrich Smetana and National Theater, Prague
A146

Aleksander Pushkin
A147

1949, June 4 *Perf. 12½x12*

386 A146 1.50k dl grn 35 10
387 A146 5k dp bl 75 30

Issued to commemorate the 125th anniversary of the birth of Friedrich Smetana, composer.

1949, June 6 *Perf. 12x12½*

388 A147 2k ol gray 30 20

Issued to commemorate the 150th anniversary of the birth of Aleksander S. Pushkin.

Frederic Chopin and Conservatory, Warsaw
A148

1949, June 24 *Perf. 12½x12*

389 A148 3k dk red 50 30
390 A148 8k vio brn 1.00 60

Issued to commemorate the centenary of the death of Frederic F. Chopin.

Globe and Ribbon
A149

Zvolen Castle
A150

1949, Aug. 20 *Perf. 12½x12*

391 A149 1.50k vio brn 35 30
392 A149 5k ultra 75 50

Issued to publicize the 50th Prague Sample Fair, September 11–18, 1949.

Starting in 1949, commemorative stamps which are priced in italics were issued in smaller quantities than those in the balance of the set and sold at prices higher than face value.

1949, Aug. 28 *Perf. 12½*

393 A150 10k rose lake 1.00 5

Early Miners
A151

Miner of Today
A152

Design: 5k, Mining Machine.

1949, Sept. 11 *Perf. 12½x12, 12½*

394 A151 1.50k sepia 1.25 90
395 A152 3k car rose 5.00 1.50
396 A151 5k dp bl *5.50* *1.75*

Issued to commemorate the 700th anniversary of the Czechoslovak mining industry and the 150th anniversary of the miner's laws.

Construction Workers A153 — Joseph V. Stalin A154

Design: 2k, Machinist.

1949, Dec. 11 *Perf. 12½*

397 A153 1k dk grn 3.50 1.00
398 A153 2k vio brn 2.00 60

2nd Trade Union Congress, Prague, 1949.

Cream Paper.

1949, Dec. 21 **Unwmkd.**

Design: 3k, Stalin facing left.

399 A154 1.50k grnsh gray 1.00 60
400 A154 3k claret 4.00 1.25

70th birthday of Joseph V. Stalin.

Skier A155 — Efficiency Badge A156

Engraved, 3k Photogravure

1950, Feb. 15 *Perf. 12½, 13½*

401 A155 1.50k gray bl 2.50 75
402 A156 3k vio brn, *cr* 3.00 1.20
403 A155 5k ultra 3.50 1.75

Issued to publicize the 51st Ski Championship for the Tatra cup, Feb. 15–26, 1950.

Vladimir V. Mayakovsky A157

1950, Apr. 14 **Engr.** *Perf. 12½*

404 A157 1.50k dk brn 3.00 1.00
405 A157 3k brn red 3.00 1.00

Issued to commemorate the 20th anniversary of the death of V. V. Mayakovsky, poet.

See also Nos. 414–417, 422–423, 432–433, 464–465, 477–478.

Soviet Tank Soldier and Hradcany A158

Designs: 2k, Hero of Labor medal. 3k, Two workers (militiamen) and Town Hall, Prague. 5k, Text of government program and heraldic lion.

1950, May 5

406 A158 1.50k gray grn 35 25
407 A158 2k dk brn 1.10 75
408 A158 3k brn red 40 25
409 A158 5k dk bl 65 20

Issued on the occasion of the fifth anniversary of the Czechoslovak People's Democratic Republic.

Factory and Young Couple with Tools—A159

Designs: 2k, Steam shovel. 3k, Farmer and farm scene. 5k, Three workers leaving factory.

1950, May 9 **Engraved**

410 A159 1.50k dk grn 1.00 60
411 A159 2k dk brn 1.60 1.00
412 A159 3k rose red 50 25
413 A159 5k dp bl 70 25

Canceled to Order

The government philatelic department started about 1950 to sell canceled sets of new issues. Prices in the second ("used") column are for these canceled-to-order stamps. Postally used copies are worth more.

Portrait Type of 1950

Design: S. K. Neumann.

1950, June 5 *Perf. 12½* **Unwmkd.**

414 A157 1.50k dp bl 25 12
415 A157 3k vio brn 1.00 90

Issued to commemorate the 75th anniversary of the birth of Stanislav Kostka Neumann (1875–1947), journalist and poet.

1950, June 21

Design: Bozena Nemcova.

416 A157 1.50k dp bl 1.25 90
417 A157 7k dk brn 40 20

Issued to commemorate the 130th anniversary of the birth of Bozena Nemcova (1820–1862), writer.

Liberation of Colonies A160

Designs: 2k, Allegory, Fight for Peace. 3k, Group of Students. 5k, Marching Students with flags.

1950, Aug. 14

418 A160 1.50k dk grn 15 5
419 A160 2k sepia 1.25 60
420 A160 3k rose car 25 15
421 A160 5k ultra 60 25

Issued to publicize the 2nd International Students World Congress, Prague, August 12–24, 1950.

Portrait Type of 1950.

Design: Zdenek Fibich.

1950, Oct. 15

422 A157 3k rose brn 1.00 70
423 A157 8k gray grn 40 20

Issued to commemorate the centenary of the birth of Zdenek Fibich, musician.

Miner, Soldier and Farmer A161

Czech and Soviet Soldiers—A162

1950, Oct. 6

424 A161 1.50k slate 75 60
425 A162 3k car rose 40 20

Issued to publicize Czech Army Day.

Prague Castle, 16th Century A163

Prague, 1493 A164

Designs: 3k, Prague, 1606. 5k, Prague, 1794.

1950, Oct. 21 *Perf. 14*

426 A163 1.50k black 3.50 2.00
427 A164 2k chocolate 3.50 2.00
428 A164 3k brn car 3.50 2.00
429 A164 5k gray 3.50 2.00
a. Block of 4 20.00 12.50

Sheets arranged in blocks of four containing one of Nos. 426 to 429. See Nos. 434–435.

Communications Symbols A165

1950, Oct. 25 *Perf. 12½*

430 A165 1.50k chocolate 12 5
431 A165 3k brn car 60 30

Issued to commemorate first anniversary of the foundation of the International League of P.T.T. Employees.

Portrait Type of 1950.

Design: J. Gregor Tajovsky.

1950, Oct. 26

432 A157 1.50k brown 1.00 50
433 A157 5k dp bl 1.00 60

Issued to commemorate the 10th anniversary of the death of J. Gregor Tajovsky (1874–1940), Slovakian writer.

Scenic Type of 1950.

Design: Prague, 1950.

1950, Oct. 28

434 A164 1.50k indigo 35 20
a. Souvenir sheet of 4, imperf. 8.00 8.00
435 A164 3k brn car 85 75

No. 434a measures 121x100 mm. and contains four copies of No. 434, imperforate, with carmine inscription in top margin.

Czech and Soviet Steel Workers A166

1950, Nov. 4 **Unwmkd.**

436 A166 1.50k chocolate 40 20
437 A166 5k dp bl 85 75

Issued to publicize the 2nd meeting of the Union of Czechoslovak-Soviet Friendship.

Dove by Picasso A167

1951, Jan. 20 Photo. *Perf. 14*

438 A167 2k dp bl 4.00 2.50
439 A167 3k rose brn 3.00 2.00

Issued to commemorate the first Czechoslovak Congress of Fighters for Peace, held in Prague.

Julius Fucik A168

1951, Feb. 17 **Engr.** *Perf. 12½*

440 A168 1.50k gray 70 35
441 A168 5k gray bl 1.50 1.00

Drop Hammer A169 — Installing Gear A170

1951, Feb. 24

442 A169 1.50k gray blk 10 5
443 A170 3k vio brn 15 6
444 A169 4k gray bl 75 50

Women Machinists A171 — Apprentice Miners A172

Designs: 3k, Woman tractor operator. 5k, Women of different races.

1951, Mar. 8 Photo. *Perf. 14*

445 A171 1.50k ol brn 30 10
446 A171 3k brn car 1.25 75
447 A171 5k blue 50 20

International Women's Day, Mar. 8.

1951, Apr. 12 **Engr.** *Perf. 12½*

448 A172 1.50k gray 50 30
449 A172 3k red brn 20 8

Plowing A173

Collective Cattle Breeding
A174

1951, Apr. 28 Photo. *Perf. 14*

450	A173	1.50k brown	65	50
451	A174	2k dk grn	*85*	*80*

Tatra Mountain Recreation Center—A175

Mountain Recreation Centers: 2k, Beskydy (Biskids). 3k, Krkonose (Carpathians).

1951, May 5 Engr. *Perf. 12½*

Inscribed: "ROH."

452	A175	1.50k dp grn	25	8
453	A175	2k dk brn	*75*	*60*
454	A175	3k rose brn	25	8

Issued to publicize the summer opening of trade union recreation centers.

Klement Gottwald and Joseph Stalin
A176

Factory Militiaman
A177

Red Army Soldier and Partisan
A178

Marx, Engels, Lenin and Stalin
A179

1951 *Perf. 12½* Unwmkd.

455	A176	1.50k ol gray	70	30
456	A177	2k red brn	30	8
457	A178	3k rose brn	50	8
458	A176	5k dp bl	*3.00*	*2.00*
459	A179	8k gray	1.00	30
		Nos. 455-459 (5)	*5.50*	*2.76*

Issued to commemorate the 30th anniversary of the founding of the Czechoslovak Communist Party.

Antonin Dvorák
A180

Design: 1.50k, 3k, Friedrich Smetana.

1951, May 30

460	A180	1k redsh brn	20	8
461	A180	1.50k ol gray	*70*	*40*
462	A180	2k dk redsh brn	*1.00*	*60*
463	A180	3k rose brn	20	8

International Music Festival, Prague.

Portrait Type of 1950.

1951, June 21

Portrait: Bohumir Smeral (facing right).

464	A157	1.50k dk gray	*55*	*45*
465	A157	3k rose brn	40	15

Issued to commemorate the 10th anniversary of the death of Bohumir Smeral, political leader.

Gymnast on Rings
A181

Designs: 1.50k, Discus Thrower. 3k, Soccer. 5k, Skier.

1951, June 21

466	A181	1k dk grn	80	45
467	A181	1.50k dk brn	80	45
468	A181	3k brn car	1.40	45
469	A181	5k dp bl	*3.00*	*1.50*

Issued to honor the 9th Congress of the Czechoslovak Sokol Federation.

Scene from "Fall of Berlin"
A182

Scene from "The Great Citizen"
A183

1951, July 14

470	A182	80h rose brn	35	25
471	A183	1.50k dk gray	45	35
472	A182	4k gray bl	*1.50*	*1.10*

Issued on the occasion of the International Film Festival, Karlovy Vary, July 14–29, 1951.

Alois Jirásek
A184

"Fables and Fate"
A185

Design: 4k, Scene from "Reign of Tabor."

1951, Aug. 23 Engr. *Perf. 12½*

473	A184	1.50k gray	25	12
474	A184	5k dk bl	*2.00*	*1.50*
		Photo. ***Perf. 14***		
475	A185	3k dk red	35	20
476	A185	4k dk brn	50	25

Issued to commemorate the centenary of the birth of Alois Jirásek, author.

Portrait Type of 1950.

Design: Josef Hybes.

1951, July 21 Engraved

477	A157	1.50k chocolate	20	8
478	A157	2k rose brn	*90*	*50*

Issued to commemorate the centenary of the birth of Josef Hybes (1850–1921), co-founder of Czech Communist Party.

"Ostrava Region"
A186

Mining Iron Ore
A187

1951, Sept. 9

479	A186	1.50k dk brn	12	4
480	A187	3k rose brn	15	3
481	A186	5k dp bl	*1.20*	*75*

Miner's Day, Sept. 9, 1951.

Soldiers on Parade
A188

Designs: 1k, Gunner and field gun. 1.50k, Klement Gottwald. 3k, Tankman and tank. 5k, Aviators.

Photo. (80h, 5k), Engr.

Perf. 14 (80h, 5k), 12½

1951, Oct. 6

Inscribed: "Den CS Armady 1951."

482	A188	80h ol brn	18	15
483	A188	1k dk ol grn	30	25
484	A188	1.50k sepia	40	25
485	A188	3k claret	60	25
486	A188	5k blue	*1.50*	*1.10*
		Nos. 482-486 (5)	*2.98*	*2.00*

Issued to publicize Army Day, Oct. 6, 1951.

Joseph Stalin and Klement Gottwald
A189

Lenin, Stalin and Soldiers
A190

1951, Nov. 3 Engraved *Perf. 12½*

487	A189	1.50k sepia	12	6
488	A190	3k red brn	12	4
489	A189	4k dp bl	*90*	*65*

Issued to publicize the month of Czechoslovak-Soviet friendship, 1951.

Peter Jilemnicky
A191

Ladislav Zapotocky
A192

1951, Dec. 5 Unwmkd.

491	A191	1.50k redsh brn	30	20
492	A191	2k dl bl	*65*	*55*

Issued to commemorate the 50th anniversary of the birth of Peter Jilemnicky (1901–1949), writer.

1952, Jan. 12 *Perf. 11½*

493	A192	1.50k brn red	10	3
494	A192	4k gray	*60*	*45*

Issued to commemorate the centenary of the birth of Ladislav Zapotocky, Bohemian socialist pioneer.

Jan Kollar
A193

Lenin and Lenin Hall
A194

1952, Jan. 30 *Perf. 11½* Unwmkd.

495	A193	3k dk car	10	3
496	A193	5k vio bl	*85*	*65*

Issued to commemorate the centenary of the death of Jan Kollar (1793–1852), poet.

1952, Jan. 30 *Perf. 12½*

497	A194	1.50k rose car	15	3
498	A194	5k dp bl	*75*	*50*

Issued to commemorate the 40th anniversary of the Sixth All-Russian Party Conference.

Emil Holub and African
A195

Klement Gottwald Metallurgical Plant
A196

1952, Feb. 21 *Perf. 11½*

499	A195	3k red brn	40	25
500	A195	5k gray	*1.75*	*1.50*

Issued to commemorate the 50th anniversary of the death of Emil Holub, explorer.

1952, Feb. 25 Photo. *Perf. 14*

Designs: 2k, Foundry. 3k, Chemical plant.

501	A196	1.50k sepia	12	8
502	A196	2k red brn	*1.25*	*95*
503	A196	3k scarlet	20	4

Student, Soldier and Worker
A197

Youths of Three Races
A198

1952, Mar. 21 ***Perf. 14*** **Unwmkd.**

504	A197	1.50k blue	12	6
505	A198	2k ol blk	25	15
506	A197	3k lake	*1.00*	*80*

International Youth Day, Mar. 25, 1952.

Similar to Type of 1951.

Portrait: Otakar Sevcik.

1952, Mar. 22 Engr. ***Perf. 12½***

507	A184	2k choc, *cr*	*50*	*45*
508	A184	3k rose brn, *cr*	15	6

Issued to commemorate the centenary of the birth of Otakar Sevcik, violinist.

Jan A. Komensky
A199

Industrial and Farm Women
A200

1952, Mar. 28 **Cream Paper**

509	A199	1.50k dk brn	*1.35*	*75*
510	A199	11k dk bl	40	10

Issued to commemorate the 360th anniversary of the birth of Jan Amos Komensky (Comenius), teacher and philosopher.

1952, Mar. 8 **Cream Paper**

511	A200	1.50k dp bl	*1.25*	*70*

International Women's Day Mar. 8, 1952.

Woman and Children
A201

Antifascist
A202

1952, Apr. 12 **Cream Paper**

512	A201	2k chocolate	*90*	*65*
513	A201	3k dp cl	18	8

Issued to publicize the International Conference for the Protection of Children, Vienna, April 12-16, 1952.

1952, Apr. 11 Photo. ***Perf. 14***

514	A202	1.50k red brn	12	3
515	A202	2k ultra	*75*	*55*

Issued to publicize the Day of International Solidarity of Fighters against Fascism, April 11, 1952.

Harvester
A203

Design: 3k, Tractor and Seeders.

1952, Apr. 30

516	A203	1.50k dp bl	*80*	*65*
517	A203	2k brown	35	20
518	A203	3k brn red	35	20

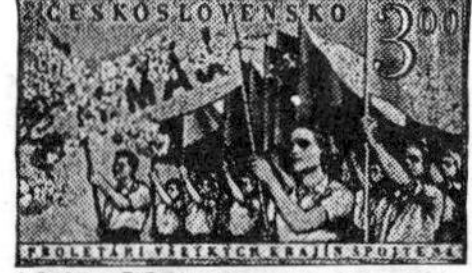

Youths Carrying Flags
A204

1952, May 1

519	A204	3k brn red	70	40
520	A204	4k dk red brn	*90*	*60*

Issued to publicize Labor Day, May 1, 1952.

Crowd Cheering Soviet Soldiers
A205

1952, May 9

521	A205	1.50k dk red	60	40
522	A205	5k dp bl	*1.25*	*95*

Liberation of Czechoslovakia from German occupation, 7th anniversary.

Children
A206

J. V. Myslbek
A207

Design: 3k, "Pioneer" teaching children.

1952, May 31 Engr. ***Perf. 12½***

Cream Paper.

523	A206	1.50k dk brn	10	3
524	A206	2k Prus grn	*80*	*60*
525	A206	3k rose brn	12	4

International Children's Day May 31, 1952.

1952, June 2

Design: 8k, Allegory, "Music."

526	A207	1.50k red brn	18	4
527	A207	2k dk brn	*1.25*	*90*
528	A207	8k gray grn	30	5

Issued to commemorate the 30th anniversary of the death of Joseph V. Myslbek (1848–1922), sculptor.

Beethoven
A208

House of Artists
A209

1952, June 7 ***Perf. 11½*** **Unwmkd.**

529	A208	1.50k sepia	50	40
530	A209	3k red brn	50	40
531	A208	5k indigo	*1.50*	*1.00*

International Music Festival, Prague, 1952.

Lidice, Symbol of a New Life
A210

1952, June 10 ***Perf. 12½***

532	A210	1.50k dk vio brn	20	6
533	A210	5k dk bl	*85*	*55*

Destruction of Lidice, 10th anniversary.

Jan Hus
A211

Bethlehem Chapel
A212

1952, July 5

534	A211	1.50k brown	10	4
535	A212	3k red brn	15	3
536	A211	5k black	*1.10*	*85*

Issued to commemorate the 550th anniversary of the installation of Jan Hus as pastor of Bethlehem Chapel, Prague.

Doctor Examining Patient
A213

Design: 2k, Doctor, Nurse, Mother and child.

1952, July 31

537	A213	1.50k dk brn	*1.00*	*50*
538	A213	2k bl vio	10	4
539	A213	3k rose brn	25	5

Czechoslovakia's Unified Health Service.

Relay Race—A214

Designs: 2k, Canoeing. 3k, Cycling. 4k, Hockey.

1952, Aug. 2 ***Perf. 11½***

540	A214	1.50k dk brn	80	45
541	A214	2k grnsh blk	*1.40*	*1.00*
542	A214	3k red brn	80	45
543	A214	4k dp bl	*3.00*	*2.00*

Issued to publicize Czechoslovakia's Unified Physical Education program.

F. L. Celakovski
A215

Mikulas Ales
A216

1952, Aug. 5 ***Perf. 12½***

544	A215	1.50k dk brn	10	3
545	A215	2k dk grn	*80*	*45*

Issued to commemorate the centenary of the death of Frantisek L. Celakovski, poet and writer.

Perf. 11x11½

1952, Aug. 30 Engraved Unwmkd.

546	A216	1.50k dk gray grn	40	20
547	A216	6k red brn	*2.50*	*1.75*

Birth centenary of Mikulas Ales, painter.

17th Century Mining Towers
A217

Jan Zizka
A218

Designs: 1.50k, Coal Excavator. 2k, Peter Bezruc mine. 3k, Automatic coaling crane.

1952, Sept. 14 ***Perf. 12½***

548	A217	1k sepia	*1.00*	*75*
549	A217	1.50k dk bl	10	5
550	A217	2k ol gray	20	6
551	A217	3k vio brn	25	5

Issued to publicize Miners' Day, Sept. 14, 1952. No. 550 also commemorates the 85th anniversary of the birth of Peter Bezruc (Vladimir Vasek), poet.

1952, Oct. 5 Engraved ***Perf. 11½***

Designs: 2k, Fraternization with Russians. 3k, Marching with flag.

Inscribed: ". . . . Armady 1952,"

552	A218	1.50k rose lake	10	3
553	A218	2k ol bis	20	4
554	A218	3k dk car rose	20	6
555	A218	4k gray	*1.75*	*90*

Issued to publicize Army Day, Oct. 5, 1952.

Souvenir Sheet.

Statues to Bulgarian Partisans and to Soviet Army—A219

1952, Oct. 18 ***Perf. 12½*** **Unwmkd.**

556	A219	Sheet of two	55.00	15.00
a.		2k dp car	15.00	4.00
b.		3k ultra	15.00	4.00

Issued to commemorate the National Philatelic Exhibition, Bratislava, Oct. 18–Nov. 2, 1952.

Danube River, Bratislava
A220

1952, Oct. 18

557	A220	1.50k dk brn	25	10

National Philatelic Exhibition, Bratislava.

Conference with Lenin and Stalin
A221

Worker and Nurse Holding Dove and Olive Branch
A222

1952, Nov. 7

558	A221	2k brn blk	*70*	*55*
559	A221	3k carmine	30	6

Issued to commemorate the 35th anniversary of the Russian Revolution and to publicize Czechoslovak-Soviet friendship.

1952, Nov. 15 Photo. ***Perf. 14***

560	A222	2k brown	*70*	*60*
561	A222	3k red	15	3

Issued to publicize the first State Congress of the Czechoslovak Red Cross.

Matej Louda, Hussite Leader, Painted by Mikulas Ales
A223

Design: 3k, Dragon-killer Trutnov, painted by Ales.

1952, Nov. 18 Engraved *Perf. 11½*

562 A223 2k red brn 30 4
563 A223 3k grnsh gray 40 12

Issued to commemorate the centenary of the birth of Mikulas Ales, painter.

Gottwald Type of 1948–49.
Size: 19x24mm.

1952, June 2 *Perf. 12½* Unwmkd.

564 A135 1k dk grn 10 3

"Peace" Flags A224 — Dove by Picasso A225

1952, Dec. 12 Photo. *Perf. 14*

565 A224 3k red brn 15 3
566 A224 4k dp bl *80* *70*

Issued to publicize the Congress of Nations for Peace, Vienna, Dec. 12–19, 1952.

1953, Jan. 17

Design: 4k, Czech Family.

567 A225 1.50k dk brn 10 3
568 A225 4k sl bl *60* *40*

2nd Czechoslovak Peace Congress.

Smetana Museum
A226

Design: 4k, Jirásek Museum.

1953, Feb. 10 Engraved *Perf. 11½*

569 A226 1.50k dk vio brn 10 3
570 A226 4k dk gray *1.00* *75*

Issued to commemorate the 75th anniversary of the birth of Prof. Zdenek Nejedly.

Martin Kukucin A227 — Jaroslav Vrchlicky A228

Designs: 2k, Karel Jaromir Erben. 3k, Vaclav Matej Kramerius. 5k, Josef Dobrovsky.

1953, Feb. 28

571 A227 1k gray 5 3
572 A228 1.50k olive 10 3
573 A228 2k rose lake 8 4
574 A228 3k lt brn 20 5
575 A228 5k sl bl *1.50* *1.50*
Nos. 571-575 (5) *1.93* *1.65*

Issued to honor Czech writers and poets: 1k, 25th anniversary of death of Kukucin. 1.50k, birth centenary of Vrchlicky. 2k, centenary of completion of "Kytice" by Erben. 3k, birth bicentenary of Kramerius. 5k, birth bicentenary of Dobrovsky.

Militia
A229

Klement Gottwald
A230

Design: 8k, Portraits of Stalin and Gottwald and Peoples Assembly.

Perf. 13½x14

1953, Feb. 25 Photo. Unwmkd.

576 A229 1.50k dp bl 10 3
577 A230 3k red 20 3
578 A229 8k dk brn *1.40* *1.00*

Issued to commemorate the 5th anniversary of the defeat of the attempt to reinstate capitalism.

Book and Torch
A231

Design: 3k, Bedrich Vaclavek.

1953, Mar. 5 Engraved *Perf. 11½*

579 A231 1k sepia *80* *60*
580 A231 3k org brn 30 12

Issued to commemorate the 10th anniversary of the death of Bedrich Vaclavek (1897–1943), socialist writer.

Stalin Type of 1949.
Inscribed "21 XII 1879 - 5 III 1953."

1953, Mar. 12

581 A154 1.50k black 25 15

Death of Joseph Stalin, Mar. 5, 1953.

Mother and Child A232 — Girl Revolutionist A233

1953, Mar. 8

582 A232 1.50k ultra 10 3
583 A233 2k brn red *50* *40*

International Women's Day.

Klement Gottwald
A234

1953, Mar. 19

584 A234 1.50k black 12 6
585 A234 3k black 12 5

Souvenir Sheet.
Imperf.

586 A234 5k black 2.50 1.50

No. 586 measures 68x97 mm., with marginal inscriptions and laurel branch.

Nos. 584-586 commemorate the death of President Klement Gottwald, March 14, 1953.

Josef Pecka, Ladislav Zapotocky and Josef Hybes—A236

1953, Apr. 7 *Perf. 11½* Unwmkd.

587 A236 2k lt vio brn 15 5

Issued to commemorate the 75th anniversary of the first congress of the Czech Social Democratic Party.

Cyclists
A237

1953, Apr. 29

588 A237 3k dp bl 60 30

Issued to commemorate the 6th International Peace Bicycle Race, Prague-Berlin-Warsaw.

Medal of "May 1, 1890"
A238

Designs: 1.50k, Lenin and Stalin. 3k, May Day Parade. 8k, Marx and Engels.

Engraved and Photogravure.

1953, Apr. 30 *Perf. 11½x11, 14*

Inscribed: "1 MAJ 1953"

589 A238 1k chocolate *1.50* *1.35*
590 A238 1.50k dk gray 6 3
591 A238 3k car lake 10 3
592 A238 8k dk gray grn 25 10

Issued to publicize Labor Day, May 1, 1953.

Sowing Grain
A239

Design: 7k, Reaper.

1953, May 8 Photo. *Perf. 14*

593 A239 1.50k brown 50 5
594 A239 7k dp grn *1.50* *1.40*

Issued to publicize the socialization of the village.

Dam A240 — Welder A241

Design: 3k, Iron works.

1953, May 8 *Perf. 11½*

595 A240 1.50k gray *80* *45*
596 A241 2k bl gray 10 3
597 A240 3k red brn 10 3

Josef Slavik A242 — Leos Janacek A243

1953, June 19

598 A242 75h dp gray bl *50* *8*
599 A243 1.60k dk brn 1.25 8

Issued on the occasion of the International Music Festival, Prague, 1953.

Gottwald Type of 1948–49.

1953 *Perf. 12½, 11½*

600 A135 15h yel grn 30 3
601 A135 20h dk vio brn 40 3
602 A135 1k purple 1.10 3
603 A135 3k brn car 15 3
604 A135 3k gray 1.30 3
Nos. 600-604 (5) 3.25 15

Nos. 600-604 vary slightly in size. Nos. 600 and 602 are perf. 12½; Nos. 601, 603-604 are perf. 11½.

Pres. Antonin Zapotocky
A244

1953, June 19 Photo. *Perf. 14*

605 A244 30h vio bl 85 3
606 A244 60h cerise 60 3

Julius Fucik A245 — Book and Carnation A246

1953, Sept. 8 Engraved *Perf. 12½*

607 A245 40h dk vio brn 30 3
608 A246 60h pink *65* *35*

Issued to commemorate the 10th anniversary of the death of Julius Fucik, Communist leader executed by the Nazis.

Miner and Flag
A247

Design: 60h, Oil field and workers.

1953, Sept. 10 *Perf. 11½*

609 A247 30h gray 25 3
610 A247 60h brn vio *60* *40*

Issued to publicize Miner's Day, Sept. 10, 1953.

Volleyball Game A248 — Motorcyclist A249

Design: 60h, Woman throwing javelin.

1953, Sept. 15

611	A248	30h brn red	3.50	1.65
612	A249	40h dk vio brn	3.50	1.25
613	A248	60h rose vio	3.50	1.25

Hussite Warrior
A250

Pres. Antonin Zapotocky
A251

Designs: 60h, Soldier presenting arms. 1k, Red army soldiers.

Inscribed: "Den CS Armady 1953."

1953, Oct. 8

614	A250	30h brown	20	3
615	A250	60h rose lake	40	4
616	A250	1k brn red	1.10	1.00

Issued to publicize Army Day, Oct. 3, 1953.

1953 *Perf. 11½, 12½.* Unwmkd.

617	A251	30h vio bl	50	3
618	A251	60h car rose	60	3

No. 617 is perf. 11½ and measures 19x23 mm. No. 618 is perf. 12½ and measures 18½x23½.

See also No. 780.

Charles Bridge and Prague Castle
A252

Korean and Czech Girls
A253

1953, Aug. 15 Engraved *Perf. 11½*

619	A252	5k gray	2.75	8

1953, Oct. 11 *Perf. 11x11½*

620	A253	30h dk brn	5.00	1.50

Issued to demonstrate Czechoslovakia's friendship with Korea.

Flags, Hradcany Castle and Kremlin
A254

Designs: 60h, Lomonosov University, Moscow. 1.20k, Lenin Ship Canal.

1953, Nov. 7

621	A254	30h dk gray	2.00	1.10
622	A254	60h dk brn	2.25	1.00
623	A254	1.20k ultra	3.25	2.00

Issued to publicize the month of Czechoslovak-Soviet friendship.

Emmy Destinn, Opera Singer
A255

National Theater, Prague
A256

Portrait: 2k, Eduard Vojan, actor.

1953, Nov. 18 *Perf. 14*

624	A255	30h bl blk	80	45
625	A256	60h brown	60	6
626	A255	2k sepia	2.50	1.00

Issued to commemorate the 70th anniversary of the founding of the National Theater.

Josef Manes
A257

Vaclav Hollar
A258

1953, Nov. 28 *Perf. 11x11½*

627	A257	60h brn car	50	8
628	A257	1.20k dp bl	1.50	85

Issued to honor Josef Manes, painter.

1953, Dec. 5

Portrait: 1.20k, Head framed, facing right.

629	A258	30h brn blk	25	8
630	A258	1.20k dk brn	1.25	75

Issued to honor Vaclav Hollar, artist and etcher.

Leo N. Tolstoi
A259

1953, Dec. 29 Unwmkd.

631	A259	60h dk grn	50	15
632	A259	1k chocolate	1.50	85

Issued to commemorate the 125th anniversary of the birth of Leo N. Tolstoi.

Locomotive
A260

Design: 1k, Plane loading mail.

Engraved, Center Photogravure.

1953, Dec. 29 *Perf. 11½x11*

633	A260	60h brn org & gray vio	50	8
634	A260	1k org brn & brt bl	2.00	1.25

Lenin
A261

Lenin Museum, Prague
A262

1954, Jan. 21 Engraved *Perf. 11½*

635	A261	30h dk brn	50	20
636	A262	1.40k chocolate	1.50	1.40

Issued to commemorate the 30th anniversary of the death of Lenin.

Klement Gottwald
A263

Design: 2.40k, Revolutionist with flag.

Perf. 11x11½, 14x13½.

1954, Feb. 18

637	A263	60h dk brn	50	5
638	A263	2.40k rose lake	3.50	2.00

Issued to commemorate the 25th anniversary of the fifth congress of the Communist Party in Czechoslovakia.

Gottwald Mausoleum, Prague
A264

Gottwald and Stalin
A265

Design: 1.20k, Lenin & Stalin mausoleum, Moscow.

1954, Mar. 5 *Perf. 11½, 14x13½*

639	A264	30h ol brn	35	7
640	A265	60h dp ultra	50	12
641	A264	120k rose brn	1.50	1.35

Issued to commemorate the first anniversary of the deaths of Joseph V. Stalin and Klement Gottwald.

Two Runners
A266

Group of Hikers
A267

Design: 1k, Woman swimmer.

1954, Apr. 24 *Perf. 11½*

642	A266	30h dk brn	2.50	1.00
643	A267	80h dk grn	5.50	5.00
644	A266	1k dk vio bl	3.00	1.00

Nurse
A268

Designs: 15h, Construction worker. 40h, Postwoman. 45h, Ironworker. 50h, Soldier. 75h, Lathe operator. 80h, Textile worker. 1k, Farm woman. 1.20k, Scientist and microscope. 1.60k, Miner. 2k, Physician and baby. 2.40k, Engineer. 3k, Chemist.

Perf. 12½x12, 11½x11.

1954

645	A268	15h dk grn	15	3
646	A268	20h lt vio	20	3
647	A268	40h dk brn	30	3
648	A268	45h dk gray bl	25	3
649	A268	50h dk gray grn	40	3
650	A268	75h dp bl	35	3
651	A268	80h vio brn	40	3
652	A268	1k green	60	3
653	A268	1.20k dk vio bl	45	3
654	A268	1.60k brn blk	1.00	3
655	A268	2k org brn	1.25	3
656	A268	2.40k vio bl	1.10	3
657	A268	3k carmine	1.50	5
		Nos. 645-657 (13)	7.95	41

Antonin Dvorák
A269

Prokop Divis
A270

Portraits: 40h, Leos Janacek. 60h, Bedrich Smetana.

1954, May 22 *Perf. 11x11½*

658	A269	30h vio brn	1.75	25
659	A269	40h brick red	2.25	25
660	A269	60h dk bl	1.35	18

Issued to publicize the "Year of Czech Music," 1954.

1954, June 15

661	A270	30h gray	18	3
662	A270	75h vio brn	1.10	65

Issued to commemorate the 200th anniversary of the invention of a lightning conductor by Prokop Divis.

Slovak Insurrectionist
A271

Anton P. Chekhov
A272

Design: 1.20k, Partisan woman.

1954, Aug. 28 *Perf. 11½*

663	A271	30h brn org	15	3
664	A271	1.20k dk bl	1.10	90

Issued to commemorate the 10th anniversary of the Slovak national uprising.

1954, Sept. 24

665	A272	30h dl gray grn	15	4
666	A272	45h dl gray brn	1.10	95

Issued to commemorate the 50th anniversary of the death of Anton P. Chekhov, writer.

Soviet Representative Giving Agricultural Instruction
A273

Designs: 60h, Soviet industrial instruction. 2k, Dancers (cultural collaboration).

1954, Nov. 6 *Perf. 11½x11*

667	A273	30h yel brn	13	3
668	A273	60h dk bl	40	4
669	A273	2k vermilion	1.60	1.50

Issued to publicize the month of Czechoslovak-Soviet friendship.

Jan Neruda
A274

Portraits: 60h, Janko Jesensky. 1.60k, Jiri Wolker.

1954, Nov. 25 ***Perf. 11x11½***

No.	Type	Denomination	Unused	Used
670	A274	30h dk bl	1.25	5
671	A274	60h dl red	*2.00*	*70*
672	A274	1.60k sepia	1.25	30

Issued to honor Czechoslovak poets.

View of Telc
A275

Views: 60h, Levoca. 3k, Ceske Budejovice.

Engraved and Photogravure

1954, Dec. 10

No.	Type	Denomination	Unused	Used
673	A275	30h blk & bis	50	4
674	A275	60h brn & bis	50	4
675	A275	3k blk & bis	*2.50*	*2.25*

Pres. Antonin Zapotocky
A276

Attacking Soldiers
A278

1954, Dec. 18 Engraved ***Perf. 11½***

No.	Type	Denomination	Unused	Used
676	A276	30h blk brn	50	14
677	A276	60h dk bl	40	14

Souvenir Sheet

Imperf.

No.	Type	Denomination	Unused	Used
678	A276	2k dp cl	7.00	3.75

No. 678 measures 65 x 99½ mm., with arms and quotation in dark blue on sheet margins.

Nos. 676-678 commemorate the 70th birthday of President Antonin Zapotocky.

See also Nos. 829-831

1954, Oct. 3 ***Perf. 11½***

Design: 2k, Soldier holding child.

No.	Type	Denomination	Unused	Used
679	A278	60h dk grn	25	3
680	A278	2k dk brn	*1.60*	*1.40*

Issued to publicize Army Day, October 6, 1954.

Woman Holding Torch
A279

Comenius University Building
A280

Design: 45h, Ski jumper.

1955, Jan. 20 Engraved

No.	Type	Denomination	Unused	Used
681	A279	30h red	2.50	35

Engraved and Photogravure.

No.	Type	Denomination	Unused	Used
682	A279	45h blk & bl	2.50	25

Issued to publicize the First National Spartacist Games, 1955.

1955, Jan. 28 Engraved ***Perf. 11½***

Design: 75h, Jan A. Komensky medal.

No.	Type	Denomination	Unused	Used
683	A280	60h dp grn	40	3
684	A280	75h chocolate	*1.00*	*70*

Issued to commemorate the 35th anniversary of the founding of Comenius University, Bratislava.

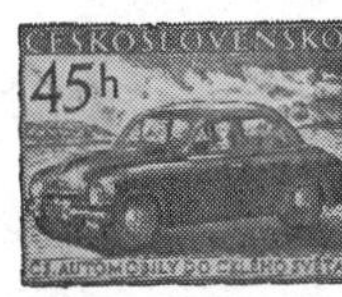

Czechoslovak Automobile—A281

Designs: 60h, Textile worker. 75h, Lathe operator.

1955, Mar. 15 **Unwmkd.**

No.	Type	Denomination	Unused	Used
685	A281	45h dl grn	70	45
686	A281	60h dk vio bl	35	4
687	A281	75h sepia	65	4

Woman Decorating Soviet Soldier
A282

Stalin Memorial, Prague
A283

Designs: 35h, Tankman with flowers. 60h, Children greeting soldier.

1955, May 5 Engraved ***Perf. 11½***

No.	Type	Denomination	Unused	Used
688	A282	30h blue	20	3
689	A282	35h dk brn	*90*	*60*
690	A282	60h cerise	55	3

Photogravure.

No.	Type	Denomination	Unused	Used
691	A283	60h sepia	55	3

Issued to commemorate the 10th anniversary of Czechoslovakia's liberation.

Music and Spring
A284

Foundry Worker
A285

Design: 1k, Woman with lyre.

Engraved and Photogravure

1955, May 12

No.	Type	Denomination	Unused	Used
692	A284	30h blk & pale bl	40	7
693	A284	1k blk & pale rose	*1.25*	*1.25*

Issued on the occasion of the International Music Festival, Prague, 1955.

1955, May 12 **Engraved**

Design: 45h, Farm workers.

No.	Type	Denomination	Unused	Used
694	A285	30h violet	10	3
695	A285	45h green	*80*	*60*

Issued to publicize the third congress of the Trade Union Revolutionary Movement.

Woman Athlete
A286

Jakub Arbes
A287

Designs: 60h, Dancing couple. 1.60k, Athlete.

1955, June 21

No.	Type	Denomination	Unused	Used
696	A286	20h vio bl	*70*	*60*
697	A286	60h green	40	6
698	A286	1.60k red	1.00	30

Issued to publicize the first National Spartacist Games, Prague, June-July, 1955.

1955

Portraits: 30h, Jan Stursa. 40h, Elena Maro-thy-Soltesova. 60h, Josef Vaclav Sladek. 75h, Alexander Stepanovic Popov. 1.40k, Jan Holly. 1.60k, Pavel Josef Safarik.

No.	Type	Denomination	Unused	Used
699	A287	20h brown	25	3
700	A287	30h black	25	3
701	A287	40h gray grn	45	7
702	A287	60h black	25	3
703	A287	75h claret	*1.75*	*85*
704	A287	1.40k blk, *cr*	60	16
705	A287	1.60k dk bl	75	10
		Nos. 699-705 (7)	*4.30*	*1.27*

Issued to commemorate various anniversaries of prominent Slavs.

Girl and Boy of Two Races
A288

Costume of Ocova, Slovakia
A289

1955, July 20

No.	Type	Denomination	Unused	Used
706	A288	60h vio bl	40	4

Issued to commemorate the fifth World Festival of Youth in Warsaw, July 31–August 14, 1955.

1955, July 25

Regional Costumes: 75h, Detva man, Slovakia. 1.60k, Chodsko man, Bohemia. 2k, Hana woman, Moravia.

Frame and Outlines in Brown

No.	Type	Denomination	Unused	Used
707	A289	60h org & rose	*9.00*	*6.00*
708	A289	75h org & lil	*4.00*	*3.00*
709	A289	1.60k bl & org	*7.00*	*6.00*
710	A289	2k yel & rose	*10.00*	*7.00*

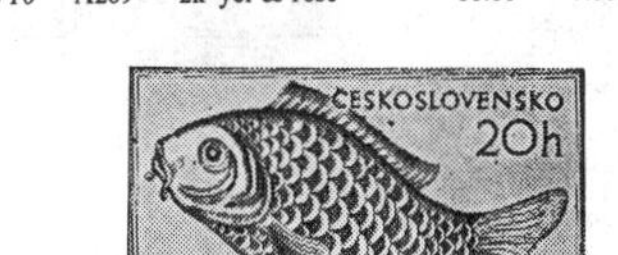

Carp
A290

Designs: 30h, Beetle. 35h, Gray Partridge. 1.40k, Butterfly. 1.50k, Hare.

1955, Aug. 8 **Engr. & Photo.**

No.	Type	Denomination	Unused	Used
711	A290	20h sep & lt bl	80	4
712	A290	30h sep & pink	60	4
713	A290	35h sep & buff	70	10
714	A290	1.40k sep & cr	*3.00*	*2.00*
715	A290	1.50k sep & lt grn	1.40	35
		Nos. 711-715 (5)	*6.50*	*2.53*

Tabor
A291

Designs: 45h, Prachatice. 60h, Jindrichuv Hradec.

1955, Aug. 26 **Engraved**

No.	Type	Denomination	Unused	Used
716	A291	30h vio brn	12	3
717	A291	45h rose car	*80*	*60*
718	A291	60h sage grn	25	4

Issued to publicize the architectural beauty of the towns of Southern Bohemia.

Souvenir Sheet.

Various Views of Prague—A292

Perf. 14x13½

1955, Sept. 10 **Engraved**

No.	Type	Denomination	Unused	Used
719	A292	Sheet of five	25.00	25.00
a.		30h gray blk	3.00	3.00
b.		45h gray blk	3.00	3.00
c.		60h rose lake	3.00	3.00
d.		75h rose lake	3.00	3.00
e.		1.60k gray blk	3.00	3.00

Issued to commemorate the International Philatelic Exhibition, Prague, Sept. 10–25, 1955. Size: 145x110mm.

Exists imperf., price $55.

Motorcyclists
A293

Workers, Soldier and Pioneer
A294

1955, Aug. 28

No.	Type	Denomination	Unused	Used
720	A293	60h vio brn	3.50	40

Issued to commemorate the 30th International Motorcycle Races at Gottwaldov, Sept. 13-18, 1955.

1955, Oct. 6 ***Perf. 11½*** **Unwmkd.**

Design: 60h, Tanks and planes.

No.	Type	Denomination	Unused	Used
721	A294	30h vio brn	20	4
722	A294	60h slate	*1.50*	*1.35*

Army Day, Oct. 6.

Hans Christian Andersen
A295

Portraits: 40h, Friedrich von Schiller. 60h, Adam Mickiewicz. 75h, Walt Whitman.

1955, Oct. 27

No.	Type	Denomination	Unused	Used
723	A295	30h brn red	20	8
724	A295	40h dk bl	*1.25*	*90*
725	A295	60h dp cl	30	8
726	A295	75h grnsh blk	40	8

Issued in honor of these four poets and to mark the 100th anniversary of the publication of Walt Whitman's "Leaves of Grass".

Railroad Bridge
A296

Designs: 30h, Train crossing bridge. 60h, Train approaching tunnel. 1.60k, Miners' housing project.

Inscribed: "Stavba Socialismu."

1955, Dec. 15

727	A296	20h dl grn	15	15
728	A296	30h vio brn	15	6
729	A296	60h slate	30	4
730	A296	1.60k car rose	80	10

Issued to publicize socialist public works.

Hydroelectric Plant A297

Jewelry A298

Designs: 10h, Miner with drill. 25h, Building construction. 30h, Harvester. 60h, Metallurgical plant.

Inscribed:

"Druhy Petilety Plan 1956–1960."

1956, Feb. 20 ***Perf. 11½x11***

731	A297	5h vio brn	15	3
732	A297	10h gray blk	18	3
733	A297	25h dk car rose	40	3
734	A297	30h green	20	3
735	A297	60h vio bl	25	4
		Nos. 731-735 (5)	1.18	16

Second Five Year Plan.

1956, Mar. 17 ***Perf. 11x11½***

Designs: 45h, Glassware. 60h, Ceramics. 75h, Textiles.

736	A298	30h gray grn	50	3
737	A298	45h dk bl	*5.00*	*2.75*
738	A298	60h claret	35	3
739	A298	75h gray	45	5

Products of Czechoslovakian industries.

Karlovy Vary (Karlsbad) A299

"We Serve our People" A300

Various Spas: 45h, Marianske Lazne (Marienbad). 75h, Piestany. 1.20k, Tatry Vysne Ruzbachy (Tatra Mountains).

1956, Mar. 17

740	A299	30h ol grn	75	4
741	A299	45h brown	80	20
742	A299	75h claret	*7.00*	*4.25*
743	A299	1.20k ultra	75	20

Issued to publicize Czechoslovakian spas.

1956, Apr. 9 Photo. ***Perf. 11x11½***

Designs: 60h, Russian War Memorial, Berlin. 1(k), Tank crewman with standard.

744	A300	30h ol brn	20	5
745	A300	60h car rose	25	3
746	A300	1k ultra	*5.25*	*4.00*

Issued to publicize the exhibition: "The Construction and Defense of our Country," Prague, April,'56.

Cyclists A301

Girl Basketball Players A302

Athletes and Olympic Rings A303

Engraved and Photogravure.

1956, Apr. 25 ***Perf. 11½*** **Unwmkd.**

747	A301	30h grn & lt bl	1.75	30
748	A302	45h dk bl & car	1.25	25
749	A303	75h brn & lem	1.25	25

Issued to publicize the following: Ninth International Peace Cycling Race, Warsaw-Berlin-Prague, May 1-15, 1956 (No. 747). Fifth European Womens' Basketball Championship (No. 748). Summer Olympics, Melbourne, Nov. 22 - Dec. 8, 1956 (No. 749).

Mozart A304

Home Guard A305

Designs: 45h, Josef Myslivecek. 60h, Jiri Benda. 1k, Bertramka House, Prague. 1.40k, Xaver Dusek (1731–1799) and wife Josepha. 1.60k, Nostic Theater, Prague.

1956, May 12 **Engraved**

Design in Gray Black.

750	A304	30h bister	35	18
751	A304	45h gray grn	*11.50*	*8.00*
752	A304	60h pale rose lil	45	4
753	A304	1k salmon	50	4
754	A304	1.40k lt bl	1.00	30
755	A304	1.60k lemon	60	10
		Nos. 750-755 (6)	*14.40*	*8.66*

Issued to commemorate the 200th anniversary of the birth of Wolfgang Amadeus Mozart and to publicize the International Music Festival in Prague.

1956, May 25

756	A305	60h vio bl	40	4

Issued to commemorate the first meeting of the Home Guard, Prague, May 25-27, 1956.

Josef Kajetan Tyl A306

River Patrol A307

Portraits: 20h, Ludovit Stur. 30h, Frana Sramek. 1.40k, Karel Havlicek Borovsky.

1956, June 23

757	A306	20h dl pur	30	6
758	A306	30h blue	30	3
759	A306	60h black	30	4
760	A306	1.40k claret	*2.50*	*1.60*

Issued to honor various Czechoslovakian writers. See also Nos. 781–784, 873–876.

1956, July 8 ***Perf. 11x11½***

Design: 60h, Guard and dog.

761	A307	30h ultra	70	30
762	A307	60h green	20	4

Issued to honor men of Frontier Guard.

Type of 1956 and

Steeplechase—A308

1956, Sept. 8 ***Perf. 11½*** **Unwmkd.**

763	A308	60h ind & bis	1.35	35
764	A308	80h brn vio & vio	1.00	15
765	A303	1.20k sl & org	1.00	25

Issued to publicize: Steeplechase, Pardubice, 1956 (No. 763). Marathon race, Kosice, 1956 (No. 764). Olympic Games, Melbourne, Nov. 22–Dec. 8 (No. 765).

Woman Gathering Grapes A309

Fishermen—A310

Designs: 35h, Women gathering hops. 95h, Logging.

1956, Sept. 20 **Engraved**

766	A309	30h brn lake	30	3
767	A309	35h gray grn	30	12
768	A310	80h dk bl	30	5
769	A310	95h chocolate	*1.50*	*1.35*

Issued to publicize natural resources.

Locomotive, 1846 A311

Locomotive, 1855 A312

Locomotives: 40h, 1945. 45h, 1952. 60h, 1955. 1k, 1954.

1956, Nov. 9 ***Perf. 11½*** **Unwmkd.**

770	A311	10h brown	1.40	5
771	A312	30h gray	80	3
772	A312	40h green	2.00	10
773	A312	45h brn car	*11.00*	*8.00*
774	A312	60h indigo	80	4
775	A312	1k ultra	1.00	8
		Nos. 770-775 (6)	*17.00*	*8.30*

Issued to commemorate the European Timetable Conference at Prague, Nov. 9–13.

Costume of Moravia A313

Regional Costumes (women): 1.20k, Blata, Bohemia. 1.40k, Cicmany, Slovakia. 1.60k, Novohradsko, Slovakia.

1956, Dec. 15 ***Perf. 13½***

776	A313	30h brn, ultra & car	1.50	45
777	A313	1.20k brn, car & ultra	1.50	45
778	A313	1.40k brn, ocher & ver	*5.50*	*2.25*
779	A313	1.60k brn, car & grn	1.50	45

See also Nos. 832-835.

Zapotocky Type of 1953.

1956, Oct. 7 ***Perf. 12½*** **Unwmkd.**

780	A251	30h blue	30	3

Portrait Type of 1956.

1957, Jan. 18 Engraved ***Perf. 11½***

Portraits: 15h, Ivan Olbracht. 20h, Karel Toman. 30h, F. X. Salda. 1.60k, Terezia Vansova.

Cream Paper.

781	A306	15h dk red brn	30	5
782	A306	20h dk grn	15	5
783	A306	30h dk brn	15	4
784	A306	1.60k dk bl	65	12

Issued in honor of Czechoslovakian writers.

Kolin Cathedral A315

Views: No. 786, Banska Stiavnica. No. 787, Uherske Hradiste. No. 788, Karlstein. No. 789, Charles Bridge, Prague. 1.25k, Moravska Trebova.

1957, Feb. 23

785	A315	30h dk bl gray	15	3
786	A315	30h rose vio	20	3
787	A315	60h dp rose	20	3
788	A315	60h gray grn	20	3
789	A315	60h brown	20	3
790	A315	1.25k gray	*1.75*	*1.25*
		Nos. 785-790 (6)	*2.70*	*1.40*

Issued to commemorate anniversaries of various towns and landmarks.

Komensky Mausoleum, Naarden
A316

Jan A. Komensky (Comenius)
A317

Farm Woman
A318

Old Prints: 40h, Komensky teaching. 1k, Sun, moon, stars and earth.

***Perf. 11½x11, 14* (A317)**

1957, Mar. 28 Engraved Unwmkd.

791	A316	30h pale brn	20	8
792	A316	40h dk grn	20	8
793	A317	60h chocolate	*1.40*	*80*
794	A316	1k car rose	45	15

Issued to commemorate the 300th anniversary of the publication of "Didactica Opera Omnia" by J. A. Komensky (Comenius). No. 793 issued in sheets of four.

1957, Mar. 22 ***Perf. 11½***

795	A318	30h lt bl grn	35	10

Issued to publicize the 3rd Congress of Agricultural Cooperatives.

Cyclists—A319

Woman Archer—A320

Boxers
A321

Rescue Team—A322

Perf. 11½x11, 11x11½

1957, Apr. 30

796	A319	30h sep & ultra	30	3
797	A319	60h dl grn & bis	*2.50*	*1.60*
798	A320	60h gray & emer	30	4
799	A321	60h sep & org	30	4
800	A322	60h vio & choc	30	4
		Nos. 796-800 (5)	*3.70*	*1.75*

Issued to publicize: 10th International Peace Cycling Race, Prague-Berlin-Warsaw (Nos. 796–797). International Archery Championships (No. 798). European Boxing Championships, Prague (No. 799). Mountain Climbing Rescue Service (No. 800).

Jan V. Stamic
A323

Musicians: No. 802, Ferdinand Laub. No. 803, Frantisek Ondricek. No. 804, Josef B. Foerster. No. 805, Vitezslav Novak. No. 806, Josef Suk.

1957, May 12 ***Perf. 11½***

801	A323	60h purple	20	4
802	A323	60h black	20	4
803	A323	60h sl bl	20	4
804	A323	60h brown	20	4
805	A323	60h dl red brn	20	4
806	A323	60h bl grn	20	4
		Nos. 801-806 (6)	1.20	24

Spring Music Festival, Prague.

Josef Bozek
A324

School of Engineering
A325

Portraits: 60h, F. J. Gerstner. 1k, R. Skuhersky.

1957, May 25

807	A324	30h bluish blk	10	3
808	A324	60h gray brn	20	3
809	A324	1k rose lake	40	10
810	A325	1.40k bl vio	75	10

Issued to commemorate the 250th anniversary of the School of Engineering in Prague.

Pioneer and Philatelic Symbols
A326

Design: 60h, Girl and carrier pigeon.

Engraved and Photogravure.

1957, June 8 ***Perf. 11½***

811	A326	30h ol grn & org	60	10

Engraved ***Perf. 13½***

812	A326	60h brn & vio bl	*1.75*	*1.60*

Youth Philatelic Exhibition, Pardubice.

"Grief"
A327

Motorcyclists
A328

Design: 60h, Rose, symbol of new life.

1957, June 10

813	A327	30h black	25	4
814	A327	60h blk & rose red	*75*	*35*

Destruction of Lidice, 15th anniversary.

1957, July 5 ***Perf. 11½***

815	A328	60h dk gray & bl	60	8

32nd International Motorcycle Race.

Karel Klic
A329

Josef Ressel
A330

1957, July 5

816	A329	30h gray blk	15	3
817	A330	60h vio bl	25	4

Issued to honor Karel Klic, inventor of photogravure, and Josef Ressel, inventor of the ship screw.

Chamois
A331

Gentian
A332

Designs: 30h, Brown bear. 60h, Edelweiss. 1.25k, Tatra Mountains.

1957, Aug. 28 Engr. ***Perf. 11½***

Inscribed: "Tatransky Narodny Park."

818	A331	20h emer & brnsh gray	60	35
819	A331	30h lt bl & brn	30	3
820	A332	40h gldn brn & vio bl	45	4
821	A332	60h yel & grn	35	5
822	A332	1.25k ol grn & bis	*2.50*	*2.25*
		Nos. 818-822 (5)	*4.20*	*2.72*

Issued to publicize the Tatra Mountains National Park. No. 822 measures 48x28½ mm.

"Marycka Magdonova"
A333

Man Holding Banner of Trade Union Congress
A334

Engraved and Photogravure

1957, Sept. 15 ***Perf. 11½*** **Unwmkd.**

823	A333	60h blk & dl red	35	3

Issued to commemorate the 90th birthday of Petr Bezruc, poet and author of "Marycka Magdonova."

1957, Sept. 28 Engraved

824	A334	75h rose red	35	9

Issued to publicize the fourth International Trade Union Congress, Leipzig, Oct. 4–15.

Television Transmitter and Antennas
A335

Design: 60h, Family watching television.

1957, Oct. 19 Engraved ***Perf. 11½***

825	A335	40h dk bl & car	15	3
826	A335	60h redsh brn & emer	20	4

Issued to publicize the television industry.

Worker, Globe and Lenin
A336

Design: 60h, Worker, factory, hammer and sickle.

1957, Nov. 7 ***Perf. 12x11½***

827	A336	30h claret	12	6
828	A336	60h gray bl	25	6

Russian Revolution, 40th anniversary.

Zapotocky Type of 1954 dated: 19 XII 1884 - 13 XI 1957

1957, Nov. 18 ***Perf. 11½*** **Unwmkd.**

829	A276	30h black	15	3
830	A276	60h black	25	3

Souvenir Sheet

Imperf.

831	A276	2k black	1.25	75

Issued to commemorate the death of Pres. Antonin Zapotocky.

No. 831 measures 69x99½mm. Olive branch below stamp; no marginal inscription.

Costume Type of 1956.

Regional Costumes: 45h, Pilsen woman, Bohemia. 75h, Slovacko man, Moravia. 1.25k, Hana woman, Moravia. 1.95k, Teshinsko woman, Silesia.

1957, Dec. 18 Engraved ***Perf. 13½***

832	A313	45h brn, bl & dk red	2.25	90
833	A313	75h dk brn, red & grn	1.75	75

834	A313	1.25k dk brn, scar & ocher	1.75	35
835	A313	1.95k sep, bl & ver	*5.00*	*1.75*

Radio Telescope and Observatory
A337

Meteorological Station in High Tatra
A338

Design: 75h, Sputnik 2 over Earth.

1957, Dec. 20 ***Perf. 11½***

836	A337	30h vio brn & yel	1.75	75
837	A338	45h sep & lt bl	75	45
838	A337	75h cl & bl	3.25	1.25

International Geophysical Year, 1957–58. No. 838 also commemorates the launching of Sputnik 2, Nov. 3, 1957.

Girl Skater
A339

Litomysl Castle
A340

Designs: 40h, Canoeing. 60h, Volleyball. 80h, Parachutist. 1.60k, Soccer.

1958, Jan. 25 Engr. ***Perf. 11½x12***

839	A339	30h rose vio	65	20
840	A339	40h blue	30	4
841	A339	60h redsh brn	35	4
842	A339	80h vio bl	*2.25*	*85*
843	A339	1.60k brt grn	70	12
		Nos. 839-843 (5)	*4.25*	*1.25*

Issued to publicize various sports championship events in 1958.

1958, Feb. 10 ***Perf. 11½***

Design: 60h, Bethlehem Chapel.

844	A340	30h green	10	3
845	A340	60h redsh brn	20	4

Issued to commemorate the 80th anniversary of the birth of Zdenek Nejedly, restorer of Bethlehem Chapel.

Giant Excavator
A341

Jewelry
A342

Peace Dove and: 60h, Soldiers, flame and banner (horiz.). 1.60k, Harvester and rainbow (horiz.).

1958, Feb. 25

846	A341	30h gray vio & yel	15	3
847	A341	60h gray brn & car	30	4
848	A341	1.60k grn & dl yel	90	10

Issued to commemorate the 10th anniversary of the "Victorious February."

Engraved and Photogravure

1958 ***Perf. 11½*** **Unwmkd.**

Designs: 45h, Dolls. 60h, Textiles. 75h, Kaplan turbine. 1.20k, Glass.

849	A342	30h rose car & bl	15	3
850	A342	45h rose red & pale lil	20	3
851	A342	60h vio & aqua	25	3
852	A342	75h ultra & sal	*2.25*	*60*
853	A342	1.20k bl grn & pink	60	6
		Nos. 849-853 (5)	*3.45*	*75*

Issued for the Universal and International Exposition at Brussels.

King George of Podebrad
A343

Design: 60h, View of Prague, 1628.

1958, May 19 **Engraved**

854	A343	30h car rose	20	3
855	A343	60h vio bl	30	3

Issued to publicize the National Archives Exhibition, Prague, May 15–Aug. 15.

"Towards the Stars"
A344

Women of Three Races
A345

Boy, Girl and Globes
A346

1958, May 26

856	A344	30h car rose	60	30
857	A345	45h rose vio	20	12
858	A346	60h blue	25	5

Issued to publicize the following: The Society for Dissemination of Political and Cultural Knowledge (No. 856). The 4th Congress of the International Democratic Women's Federation (No. 857). The First World Trade Union Conference of Working Youths, held in Prague, July 14–20 (No. 858).

Grain, Hammer and Sickle
A347

Atomic Reactor—A348

Design: 45h, Map of Czechoslovakia, hammer and sickle.

1958, May 26

859	A347	30h dl red	10	3
860	A347	45h green	15	3
861	A348	60h dk bl	25	4

Issued to commemorate the 11th Congress of the Czech Communist Party and the 15th anniversary of the Russo-Czechoslovakian Treaty.

Karlovy Vary—A349

Various Spas: 40h, Podebrady. 60h, Marianske Lazne. 80h, Luhacovice. 1.20k, Strbske Pleso. 1.60k, Trencianske Teplice.

1958, June 25

862	A349	30h rose cl	10	3
863	A349	40h redsh brn	12	3
864	A349	60h gray grn	18	3
865	A349	80h sepia	25	3
866	A349	1.20k vio bl	40	4
867	A349	1.60k lt vio	*2.00*	*1.25*
		Nos. 862-867 (6)	*3.05*	*1.41*

Telephone Operator
A350

Pres. Antonin Novotny
A351

Design: 45h, Radio transmitter.

1958, June 20

868	A350	30h blk & brn org	25	3
869	A350	45h blk & lt grn	35	12

Issued to commemorate the Conference of Postal Ministers of Communist Countries, Prague, June 30–July 9.

1958–59 ***Perf. 12½, 11½***

870	A351	30h brt vio bl	10	3
870A	A351	30h lt vio ('59)	20	3
871	A351	60h car rose	25	3

Redrawn.

Perf. 11½

871A	A351	60h rose red ('59)	20	3

On No. 871 the top of the "6" turns down; on No. 871A it is open.

Czechoslovak Pavilion, Brussels
A352

1958, July 15 **Photo. & Engraved**

872	A352	1.95k lt bl & bis brn	1.10	18

Issued to mark Czechoslovakia Week at the Universal and International Exhibition at Brussels.

Portrait Type of 1956.

Portraits: 30h, Julius Fucik. 45h, G. K. Zechenter 60h, Karel Capek. 1.40k, Svatopluk Cech.

1958, Aug. 20 Engr. ***Perf. 11½***

873	A306	30h rose red	10	3
874	A306	45h violet	*1.50*	*50*
875	A306	60h dk bl gray	18	3
876	A306	1.40k gray	40	15

Death anniversaries of four famous Czechs.

The Artist and the Muse
A353

1958, Aug. 20 ***Perf. 14***

877	A353	1.60k black	2.50	1.10

Issued to commemorate the 85th birthday of Max Svabinsky, artist and engraver.

Children's Hospital, Brno—A354

Designs: 60h, New Town Hall, Brno. 1k, St. Thomas Church. 1.60k, View of Brno.

1958, Sept. 6 ***Perf. 11½*** **Unwmkd.**

Size: 40x23mm.

878	A354	30h violet	10	3
879	A354	60h rose red	20	3
880	A354	1k brown	40	12

Perf. 14

Size: 50x28mm.

881	A354	1.60k dk sl grn	*2.50*	*2.00*

Issued to commemorate the National Philatelic Exhibition, Brno, Sept. 9, 1958.

No. 881 sold for 3.10k, including entrance ticket to exhibition. Issued in sheets of four.

Lepiota Procera
A355

Children on Beach
A356

1958, Oct. 6 ***Perf. 14***

Mushrooms: 40h, Boletus edulis. 60h, Krombholzia rufescens. 1.40k, Amanita muscaria L. 1.60k, Armillariella mellea.

882	A355	30h dk brn, grn & buff	30	15
883	A355	40h vio brn & brn org	30	20
884	A355	60h blk, red & buff	45	20
885	A355	1.40k brn, scar & grn	60	30
886	A355	1.60k blk, red brn & ol	*2.75*	*1.50*
		Nos. 882-886 (5)	*4.40*	*2.35*

1958, Oct. 24 *Perf. 14* Unwmkd.

Designs: 45h, Mother, child and bird. 60h, Skier.

887	A356	30h bl, yel & red	18	3
888	A356	45h ultra & car	30	4
889	A356	60h brn, bl & yel	35	10

Issued to commemorate the opening of UNESCO (U.N. Educational, Scientific and Cultural Organization) Headquarters in Paris, Nov. 3.

Bozek's Steam Car of 1815
A357

Designs: 45h, "Präsident" car of 1897. 60h, "Skoda" sports car. 80h, "Tatra" sedan. 1k, "Autocar Skoda" bus. 1.25k, Trucks.

Engraved and Photogravure.

1958, Dec. 1 *Perf. 11½x11*

890	A357	30h vio blk & buff	30	3
891	A357	45h ol & lt ol grn	30	3
892	A357	60h ol gray & sal	30	3
893	A357	80h cl & bl grn	45	15
894	A357	1k brn & lt yel grn	60	20
895	A357	1.25k grn & buff	*2.75*	*80*
		Nos. 890-895 (6)	*4.70*	*1.24*

Issued to honor the automobile industry.

Stamp of 1918 and Allegory
A358

1958, Dec. 18 Engr. *Perf. 11x11½*

896	A358	60h dk bl gray	35	5

Issued to commemorate the 40th anniversary of the first Czechoslovakian postage stamp.

Ice Hockey—A359

Sports: 30h, Girl throwing javelin. 60h, Ice hockey. 1k, Hurdling. 1.60k, Rowing. 2k, High jump.

1959, Feb. 14 *Perf. 11½x11*

897	A359	20h dk brn & gray	30	3
898	A359	30h red brn & org brn	30	3
899	A359	60h dk bl & pale grn	18	3
900	A359	1k mar & cit	50	4
901	A359	1.60k dl vio & lt bl	55	10
902	A359	2k red brn & lt bl	*2.25*	*1.25*
		Nos. 897-902 (6)	*4.08*	*1.48*

Congress Emblem
A360

"Equality of All Races"
A361

Design: 60h, Industrial and agricultural workers and emblem.

1959, Feb. 27 *Perf. 11½*

903	A360	30h mar & lt bl	15	3
904	A360	60h dk bl & yel	20	3

Issued to commemorate the 4th Agricultural Co-operative Congress in Prague.

1959, Mar. 23

Designs: 1k, "Peace." 2k, Mother and Child: "Freedom for Colonial People."

905	A361	60h gray grn	30	5
906	A361	1k gray	35	6
907	A361	2k dk gray bl	*2.00*	*60*

Issued to commemorate the 10th anniversary of the signing of the Universal Declaration of Human Rights.

Girl Holding Doll
A362

Frederic Joliot Curie
A363

Engraved and Photogravure.

Designs: 40h, Pioneer studying map. 60h, Pioneer with radio. 80h, Girl pioneer planting tree.

1959, Mar. 28

908	A362	30h vio bl & yel	15	3
909	A362	40h ind & ultra	20	3
910	A362	60h blk & lil	20	3
911	A362	80h brn & lt grn	40	12

10th anniversary of the Pioneer organization.

1959, Apr. 17 Engraved

912	A363	60h sepia	90	20

Issued to honor Frederic Joliot Curie and the 10th anniversary of the World Peace Movement.

"Reaching for the Moon"
A364

Town Hall Pilsen
A365

1959, Apr. 17

913	A364	30h vio bl	1.00	25

Issued to publicize the Second Congress of the Czechoslovak Association for the Propagation of Political and Cultural knowledge.

1959, May 2

Designs: 60h, Part of steam condenser turbine. 1k, St. Bartholomew's Church, Pilsen. 1.60k, Part of lathe.

914	A365	30h lt brn	10	3
915	A365	60h vio & lt grn	20	4
916	A365	1k vio bl	65	15
917	A365	1.60k blk & yel	*2.00*	*1.00*

Issued to publicize the 2nd Pilsen Stamp Exhibition in connection with the centenary of the Skoda (Lenin) armament works.

Factory and Emblem
A366

Design: 60h, Dam.

Inscribed: "IV Vseodborovy sjezd, 1959."

1959, May 13

918	A366	30h rose & yel	12	3
919	A366	60h ol gray & bl	25	4

4th Trade Union Congress.

Zvolen Castle—A367

1959, June 13

920	A367	60h gray ol & yel	35	5

Regional Stamp Exhibition, Zvolen, 1959.

Frantisek Benda
A368

Aurel Stodola
A369

Portraits: 30h, Vaclav Kliment Klicpera. 60h, Karel V. Rais. 80h, Antonin Slavicek. 1k, Peter Bezruc.

1959, June 22 *Perf. 11½x11*

921	A368	15h vio bl	5	3
922	A368	30h org brn	10	3
923	A369	40h dl grn	15	3
924	A369	60h dl red brn	25	4
925	A369	80h dl vio	30	6
926	A368	1k dk brn	50	6
		Nos. 921-926 (6)	1.35	25

View of the Fair Grounds
A370

Designs: 60h, Fair emblem and world map. 1.60k, Pavilion "Z."

Inscribed: "Mezinarodni Veletrh Brne 6.-20.IX. 1959."

Engraved and Photogravure.

1959, July 20 *Perf. 11½* Unwmkd.

927	A370	30h lil & yel	12	3
928	A370	60h dl bl	25	3
929	A370	1.60k dk bl & bis	60	12

International Fair at Brno, Sept. 6–20.

Revolutionist and Flag—A371

Slovakian Fighter
A372

Design: 1.60k, Linden leaves, sun and factory.

Engraved.

1959, Aug. 29 *Perf. 11½* Unwmkd.

930	A371	30h blk & rose	15	3
931	A372	60h car rose	25	3
932	A371	1.60k dk bl & yel	65	6

Issued to commemorate the 15th anniversary of the national Slovakian revolution and the 40th anniversary of the Slovakian Soviet Republic.

Alpine Marmots—A373

Animals: 40h, Bison. 60h, Lynx (vert.). 1k, Wolf. 1.60k, Red deer.

Engraved and Photogravure.

1959, Sept. 25

933	A373	30h blk & gray	30	3
934	A373	40h dk brn & bluish grn	45	8
935	A373	60h brn red & yel	35	3
936	A373	1k ol brn & bl	*2.50*	*95*
937	A373	1.60k red brn & pink	75	15
		Nos. 933-937 (5)	*4.35*	*1.24*

Issued to commemorate the 10th anniversary of the establishment of the Tatra National Park.

Lunik 2 Hitting Moon and Russian Flag—A374

1959, Sept. 23 *Perf. 11½*

938	A374	60h dk red & lt ultra	90	20

Issued to commemorate the landing of the Soviet rocket on the moon, Sept. 13, 1959.

Stamp Printing Works, Peking
A375

1959, Oct. 1

939	A375	30h pale grn & red	15	3

Issued to commemorate 10 years of Czechoslovakian - Chinese friendship.

Haydn
A376

Great Spotted Woodpecker
A377

Design: 3k, Charles Darwin.

1959, Oct. 16 Engr. *Perf. 11½*

940	A376	60h vio blk	35	5
941	A376	3k dk red brn	*1.50*	*85*

150th anniversary of death of Franz Joseph Haydn, Austrian composer, and 150th anniversary of birth of Charles Darwin, English naturalist.

1959, Nov. 16 *Perf. 14*

Birds: 30h, Blue tits. 40h, Nuthatch. 60th, Golden oriole. 80h, Goldfinch. 1k, Bullfinch. 1.20k, European kingfisher.

942	A377	20h multi	30	12
943	A377	30h multi	20	12
944	A377	40h multi	*2.50*	*1.00*
945	A377	60h multi	40	10
946	A377	80h multi	40	20
947	A377	1k multi	50	20
948	A377	1.20k multi	60	40
		Nos. 942-948 (7)	*4.90*	*2.14*

Nikola Tesla—A378

Designs: 30h, Alexander S. Popov. 35h, Edouard Branly. 60h, Guglielmo Marconi. 1k, Heinrich Hertz. 2k, Edwin Howard Armstrong and research tower, Alpine, N. J.

Engraved and Photogravure.

1959, Dec. 7 *Perf. 11½*

949	A378	25h blk & pink	*70*	*20*
950	A378	30h blk & org	15	4
951	A378	35h blk & lt vio	18	4
952	A378	60h blk & bl	20	4
953	A378	1k blk & lt grn	30	6
954	A378	2k blk & bis	*1.75*	*60*
		Nos. 949-954 (6)	*3.28*	*98*

Issued to honor inventors in the fields of telegraphy and radio.

Gymnast
A379

Designs: 60h, Skier. 1.60k, Handball players.

Engraved and Photogravure.

1960, Jan. 20 *Perf. 11½*

955	A379	30h sal pink & brn	40	15
956	A379	60h lt bl & blk	50	15
957	A379	1.60k bis & brn	1.10	20

2nd Winter Spartacist Games.

1960, June 15 Unwmkd.

Designs: 30h, Two girls in "Red Ball" drill. 60h, Gymnast with stick. 1k, Three girls with hoops.

958	A379	30h lt grn & rose cl	20	3
959	A379	60h pink & blk	50	10
960	A379	1k ocher & vio bl	70	15

Issued to commemorate the 2nd Summer Spartacist Games, Prague, June 23–July 3.

River Dredge Boat
A380

Ships; 60h, River tug. 1k, Tourist steamer. 1.20k, Cargo ship "Lidice."

1960, Feb. 22 *Perf. 11½*

961	A380	30h sl grn & sal	20	3
962	A380	60h mar & pale bl	40	3
963	A380	1k dk vio & yel	60	4
964	A380	1.20k lil & pale grn	*80*	*30*

Ice Hockey Players—A381

Design: 1.80k, Figure skaters.

1960, Feb. 27

965	A381	60h sep & lt bl	60	20
966	A381	1.80k blk & lt grn	*4.00*	*3.00*

Issued to commemorate the 8th Olympic Winter Games, Squaw Valley, Calif., Feb. 18-29, 1960.

1960, June 15 Unwmkd.

Designs: 1k, Running. 1.80k, Women's gymnastics. 2k, Rowing.

967	A381	1k blk & org	60	20
968	A381	1.80k blk & sal pink	1.00	40
969	A381	2k blk & bl	*2.50*	*1.25*

Issued to commemorate the 17th Olympic Games, Rome, Aug. 25–Sept. 11.

Trencin Castle
A382

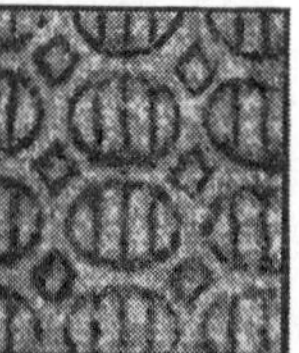

Wmk. 341

Castles: 10h, Bezdez. 20h, Kost. 30h, Pernstein. 40h, Kremnica. 50h, Krivoklát castle. 60h, Karlstein. 1k, Smolenice. 1.60k, Kokorin.

1960-63 Engraved *Perf. 11½*

970	A382	5h gray vio	5	3
971	A382	10h black	5	3
972	A382	20h brn org	10	3
973	A382	30h green	15	3
974	A382	40h brown	20	3
974A	A382	50h blk ('63)	20	3
975	A382	60h rose red	25	3
976	A382	1k lilac	40	3
977	A382	1.60k dk bl	70	3
		Nos. 970-977 (9)	2.10	27

Wmkd. Striped Ovals (341)

1961, Oct.

977A	A382	30h green	1.50	70

Lenin
A383

Soldier Holding Child
A384

1960, Apr. 22 Unwmkd.

978	A383	60h gray ol	45	15

90th anniversary of the birth of Lenin.

1960, May 5

Designs: No. 980, Child eating pie. No. 981, Soldier helping concentration camp victim. No. 982, Welder and factory (horiz.). No. 983, Tractor driver and farm (horiz.).

Engraved and Photogravure

979	A384	30h mar & lt bl	20	3
980	A384	30h dl red	20	3
981	A384	30h grn & dl bl	20	3
982	A384	60h dk bl & buff	35	3
983	A384	60h redsh brn & yel grn	40	3
		Nos. 979-983 (5)	1.35	15

15th anniversary of liberation.

Steelworker—A385

Design: 60h, Farm woman and child.

1960, May 24

984	A385	30h mar & gray	12	3
985	A385	60h grn & pale bl	25	3

Issued to publicize the 1960 parliamentary elections.

Red Cross Nurse Holding Dove—A386

Fire Fighters
A387

1960, May 26 Unwmkd.

986	A386	30h brn car & bl	20	3
987	A387	60h dk bl & pink	35	3

Issued to commemorate the 3rd Congress of the Czechoslovakian Red Cross (No. 986), and the 2nd Fire Fighters' Congress (No. 987).

Hand of Philatelist with Tongs and Two Stamps
A388

Design: 1k, Globe and 1937 Bratislava stamp (shown in miniature on 60h).

Engraved and Photogravure

1960, July 11 *Perf. 11½*

988	A388	60h blk & dl yel	35	3
989	A388	1k blk & bl	65	5

Issued to publicize the National Stamp Exhibition, Bratislava, Sept. 24–Oct. 9.

See Nos. C49–C50.

Stalin Mine, Ostrava-Hermanovice
A390

Viktorin Cornelius, Lawyer
A391

Designs: 20h, Power station, Hodonin. 30h, Gottwald iron works, Kuncice. 40h, Harvester. 60h, Oil refinery.

1960, July 25

992	A390	10h blk & pale grn	8	3
993	A390	20h mar & lt bl	12	3
994	A390	30h ind & pink	12	3
995	A390	40h grn & pale lil	20	3
996	A390	60h dk bl & yel	30	3
		Nos. 992-996 (5)	82	15

Issued to publicize the new five-year plan.

1960, Aug. 23 Engraved

Portraits: 20h, Karel Matej Capek-Chod, writer. 30h, Hana Kvapilova, actress. 40h, Oskar Nedbal, composer. 60h, Otakar Ostrcil, composer.

997	A391	10h black	15	3
998	A391	20h red brn	18	3
999	A391	30h rose red	20	3
1000	A391	40h dl grn	30	3
1001	A391	60h gray vio	35	4
		Nos. 997-1001 (5)	1.18	16

See also Nos. 1037–41.

Skoda Sports Plane Flying Upside Down
A392

1960, Aug. 28 Engr. & Photo.

1002	A392	60h vio bl & bl	60	7

Issued to commemorate the first aerobatic world championships, Bratislava.

Constitution and "Czechoslovakia"
A393

1960, Sept. 18

1003	A393	30h vio bl & pink	15	3

Issued to commemorate the proclamation of the new socialist constitution.

Workers Reading Newspaper
A394

Man Holding Newspaper
A395

1960, Sept. 18

1004	A394	30h sl & ver	12	3
1005	A395	60h blk & rose	24	3

Issued for the Day of the Czechoslovak Press, Sept. 21, 1960, and to commemorate the 40th anniversary of the Rudé Právo paper.

Globes and Laurel—A396

1960, Sept. 18 Engraved

1006	A396	30h dk bl & bis	15	3

Issued to commemorate the 15th anniversary of the World Federation of Trade Unions.

Black-crowned Night Heron
A397

Doronicum Clusii (Thistle)
A398

Birds: 30h, Great crested grebe. 40h, Lapwing. 60h, Gray heron. 1k, Graylag goose (horiz.). 1.60k, Mallard (horiz.).

Engraved and Photogravure

1960, Oct. 24 ***Perf. 11½*** **Unwmkd.**

Designs in Black

1007	A397	25h pale vio bl	20	5
1008	A397	30h pale cit	40	6
1009	A397	40h pale bl	25	6
1010	A397	60h pink	40	10
1011	A397	1k pale yel	50	20
1012	A397	1.60k lt vio	*2.75*	*1.10*
		Nos. 1007-1012 (6)	*4.50*	*1.57*

1960, Nov. 21 Engraved ***Perf. 14***

Flowers: 30h, Cyclamen. 40h, Primrose. 60h, Hen-and-chickens. 1k, Gentian. 2k, Pasqueflower.

1013	A398	20h blk, yel & grn	9	3
1014	A398	30h blk, car rose & grn	15	3
1015	A398	40h blk, yel & grn	20	3

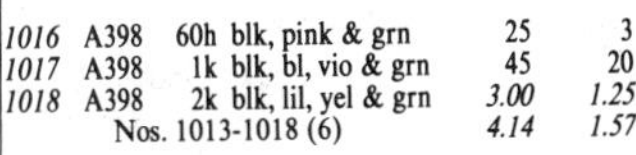

1016	A398	60h blk, pink & grn	25	3
1017	A398	1k blk, bl, vio & grn	45	20
1018	A398	2k blk, lil, yel & grn	*3.00*	*1.25*
		Nos. 1013-1018 (6)	*4.14*	*1.57*

Alfons Mucha
A399

1960, Dec. 18 Engr. ***Perf. 11½x12***

1019	A399	60h dk bl gray	30	3

Issued for the Day of the Czechoslovak Postage Stamp and to commemorate the centenary of the birth of Alfons Mucha, designer of the first Czechoslovakian stamp (Type A1).

Rolling-mill Control Bridge
A400

Athletes with Flags
A401

Designs: 30h, Turbo generator. 60h, Ditch-digging machine.

1961, Jan. 20 ***Perf. 11½*** **Unwmkd.**

1020	A400	20h blue	20	3
1021	A400	30h rose	25	3
1022	A400	60h brt grn	40	3

Third Five-Year Plan.

Perf. 11x11½, 11½x11

1961, Feb. 20 Engr. & Photo.

Designs: No. 1024, Motorcycle race (horiz.). 40h, Sculling (horiz.). 60h, Ice skater. 1k, Rugby. 1.20k, Soccer. 1.60k, Long-distance runners.

1023	A401	30h rose red & bl	15	3
1024	A401	30h dk bl & car	15	3
1025	A401	40h dk gray & car	40	4
1026	A401	60h lil & bl	35	3
1027	A401	1k ultra & yel	45	10
1028	A401	1.20k grn & buff	65	20
1029	A401	1.60k sep & sal	*2.00*	*1.00*
		Nos. 1023-1029 (7)	*4.15*	*1.43*

Various sports events.

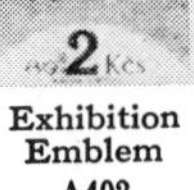

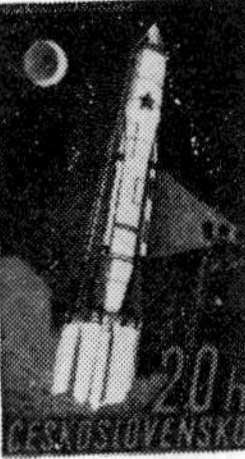

Exhibition Emblem
A402

Rocket Launching
A403

1961, Mar. 6 Engraved ***Perf. 11½***

1030	A402	2k dk bl & red	2.50	8

Issued to publicize the "Praga 1962" International Stamp Exhibition, Prague, Sept. 1962.

1961, Mar. 6 Engr. & Photo.

Designs: 30h, Sputnik III (horiz.). 40h, As 20h, but inscribed "Start Kosmicke Rakety k Venusi—12.II.1961". 60h, Sputnik I (horiz.). 1.60k, Interplanetary station (horiz.). 2k, Similar to type A404, without commemorative inscription.

1031	A403	20h vio & pink	40	3
1032	A403	30h dk grn & buff	15	3
1033	A403	40h dk red & yel grn	20	3
1034	A403	60h vio & buff	40	4
1035	A403	1.60k dk bl & pale grn	95	20
1036	A403	2k mar & pale bl	*2.50*	*1.35*
		Nos. 1031-1036 (6)	*4.60*	*1.68*

Issued to publicize Soviet space research.

Portrait Type of 1960

Portraits: No. 1037, Jindrich Mosna. No. 1038, Pavol Orszagh Hviezdoslav. No. 1039, Alois Mrstik. No. 1040, Joza Uprka. No. 1041, Josef Hora.

1961, March 27 ***Perf. 11½***

1037	A391	60h green	25	3
1038	A391	60h dk bl	25	3
a.		"ORSZACH" instead of "ORSZAGH"	75	18
1039	A391	60h dl cl	25	3
1040	A391	60h gray	25	3
1041	A391	60h sepia	25	3
		Nos. 1037-1041 (5)	1.25	15

Man Flying into Space
A404

1961, Apr. 13 Engraved and Photo.

1042	A404	60h car & pale bl	50	4
1043	A404	3k ultra & yel	*2.50*	*80*

Issued to commemorate the first man in space, Yuri A. Gagarin, Apr. 12, 1961. See also No. 1036.

Flute Player
A405

Blast Furnace and Mine, Kladno
A406

Designs: No. 1045, Dancer. 60h, Lyre player.

1961, Apr. 24 Engraved

1044	A405	30h brn blk	35	3
1045	A405	30h brn red	35	3
1046	A405	60h vio bl	35	4

Issued to commemorate the 150th anniversary of the Prague Conservatory of Music.

1961, Apr. 24

1047	A406	3k dl red	1.25	3

Marching Workers
A407

Woman with Hammer and Sickle
A408

Klement Gottwald Museum
A409

Designs: No. 1050, Lenin Museum. No. 1051, Crowd with flags. No. 1053, Man saluting Red Star.

1961, May 10

1048	A407	30h dl vio	10	3
1049	A409	30h dk bl	10	3
1050	A409	30h redsh brn	10	3
1051	A407	60h vermilion	25	4
1052	A408	60h dk grn	25	4
1053	A408	60h carmine	25	4
		Nos. 1048-1053 (6)	1.05	21

Czech Communist Party, 40th anniversary.

Puppet
A410

Designs: Various Puppets.

Engraved and Photogravure

1961, June 20 ***Perf. 11½*** **Unwmkd.**

1054	A410	30h ver & yel	15	3
1055	A410	40h sep & bluish grn	15	3
1056	A410	60h vio bl & sal	25	3
1057	A410	1k grn & lt bl	40	6
1058	A410	1.60k mar & pale vio	*1.75*	*45*
		Nos. 1054-1058 (5)	*2.70*	*60*

Woman, Map of Africa and Flag of Czechoslovakia
A411

1961, June 26

1059	A411	60h red & bl	35	3

Issued to publicize the friendship between the people of Africa and Czechoslovakia.

Map of Europe and Fair Emblem

A412

Designs (Fair emblem and): 60h Horizontal boring machine (vert.). 1k, Scientists' meeting and nuclear physics emblem.

Engraved and Photogravure

1961, Aug. 14 ***Perf. 11½***

1060 A412 30h dk bl & pale grn 15 4
1061 A412 60h grn & pink 25 3
1062 A412 1k vio brn & lt bl 40 6

Issued to publicize the International Trade Fair, Brno, Sept. 10–24.

Sugar Beet, Cup of Coffee and Bags of Sugar — **A413**

Charles Bridge, St. Nicholas Church and Hradcany — **A414**

Designs: 30h, Clover. 40h, Wheat. 60h, Hops. 1.40k, Corn. 2k, Potatoes.

1961, Sept. 18 ***Perf. 11½*** **Unwmkd.**

1063 A413 20h sl & lil 8 3
1064 A413 30h pale cl & bis 9 3
1065 A413 40h brn & org 12 3
1066 A413 60h sl grn & bis 18 3
1067 A413 1.40k brn & fawn 45 6
1068 A413 2k dl vio & bl 2.25 75
Nos. 1063-1068 (6) 3.17 93

1961, Sept. 25

1069 A414 60h vio bl & car 1.25 5

Issued to commemorate the 26th session of the Governor's Council of the Red Cross Societies League, Prague.

Orlik Dam and Kaplan Turbine

A415

Designs: 30h, View of Prague, flags and stamps. 40h, Hluboká Castle, river and fish. 60h, Karlovy Vary and cup. 1k, Pilsen and beer bottle. 1.20k, North Bohemia landscape and vase. 1.60k, Tatra mountains, boots, ice pick and rope. 2k, Ironworks, Ostrava Kuncice and pulley. 3k, Brno and ball bearing. 4k, Bratislava and grapes. 5k, Prague and flags.

Engraved and Photogravure

1961 ***Perf. 11½*** **Unwmkd.**

Size: 41x23mm.

1070 A415 20h gray & bl 50 45
1071 A415 30h vio bl & red 20 15
1072 A415 40h dk bl & lt grn 45 40
1073 A415 60h dk bl & yel 45 40
1074 A415 1k mar & grn 80 45
1075 A415 1.20k grn & pink 1.10 65
1076 A415 1.60k brn & vio bl 1.25 65
1077 A415 2k blk & ocher 1.75 1.35
1078 A415 3k ultra & yel 2.25 1.75
1079 A415 4k pur & sal 3.50 2.75

Engraved

Perf. 13½

Size: 50x29mm.

1080 A415 5k multi 20.00 17.50
Nos. 1070-1080 (11) 32.25 26.50

Issued to publicize the "PRAGA 1962 World Exhibition of Postage Stamps," Aug. 18–Sept. 2, 1962. No. 1080 was printed in sheet of four with marginal inscription.

Globe

A416

Engraved and Photogravure

1961, Nov. 27 ***Perf. 11½***

1081 A416 60h red & ultra 40 10

Issued to publicize the Fifth World Congress of Trade Unions, Moscow, Dec. 4–16.

Orange Tip Butterfly — **A417**

Bicyclists — **A418**

Designs (butterflies): 20h, Zerynthia hypsipyle Sch. 30h, Apollo. 40h, Swallowtail. 60h, Peacock. 80h, Mourning cloak (Camberwell beauty). 1k, Underwing (moth). 1.60k, Red admiral. 2k, Brimstone (sulphur).

1961, Nov. 27 **Engraved**

Brown Frame and Inscriptions

1082 A417 15h bl, org & yel 10 6
1083 A417 20h bl, yel & red 10 10
1084 A417 30h bl, car & grn 15 10
1085 A417 40h bl, ocher & car 30 10
1086 A417 60h bl, red brn & yel 40 12
1087 A417 80h bl, yel, brn & grn 60 25
1088 A417 1k pale brn, pink & bl 70 35
1089 A417 1.60k multi 90 55
1090 A417 2k bl, yel & red 4.50 1.75
Nos. 1082-1090 (9) 7.75 3.38

Printed in sheets of ten.

Engraved and Photogravure

1962, Feb. 5 ***Perf. 11½*** **Unwmkd.**

Sports: 40h, Woman gymnast. 60h, Figure skaters. 1k, Woman bowler. 1.20k, Goalkeeper, soccer. 1.60k, Discus thrower.

1091 A418 30h blk & vio bl 10 3
1092 A418 40h blk & yel 15 3
1093 A418 60h sl & grnsh bl 20 3
1094 A418 1k blk & pink 50 8
1095 A428 1.20k blk & grn 60 15
1096 A418 1.60k blk & dl grn 2.00 1.00
Nos. 1091-1096 (6) 3.55 1.32

Various 1962 sports events.

No. 1095 does not have the commemorative inscription.

Karel Kovarovic

A419

Frantisek Zaviska and Karel Petr

A420

Designs: 20h, Frantisek Skroup. 30h, Bozena Nemcova. 60h, View of Prague and staff of Aesculapius. 1.60k, Ladislav Celakovsky. 1.80k, Miloslav Valouch and Juraj Hronec.

1962, Feb. 26 **Engraved**

1097 A419 10h red brn 5 3
1098 A419 20h vio bl 8 3
1099 A419 30h brown 12 3
1100 A420 40h claret 15 6
1101 A419 60h black 25 4
1102 A419 1.60k sl grn 60 4
1103 A420 1.80k dk bl 65 10
Nos. 1097-1103 (7) 1.90 33

Various cultural personalities and events.

Miner and Flag—A421

1962, Mar. 19 **Engr. & Photo.**

1104 A421 60h ind & rose 35 3

Issued to commemorate the 30th anniversary of the miners' strike at Most.

"Man Conquering Space"

A422

Soviet Spaceship Vostok 2—A423

Designs: 40h, Launching of Soviet space rocket. 80h, Multi-stage automatic rocket. 1k, Automatic station on moon. 1.60k, Television satellite.

1962, Mar. 26 **Engr. & Photo.**

1105 A422 30h dk red & lt bl 12 3
1106 A422 40h dk bl & sal 18 3
1107 A423 60h dk bl & pink 30 4
1108 A423 80h rose vio & lt grn 35 5
1109 A422 1k ind & cit 45 10
1110 A423 1.60k grn & buff 2.50 1.10
Nos. 1105-1110 (6) 3.90 1.35

Issued to publicize space research.

Polar Bear

A424

Zoo Animals: 30h, Chimpanzee. 60h, Camel. 1k, African and Indian elephants (horiz.). 1.40k, Leopard (horiz.). 1.60k, Przewalski horse (horiz.).

1962, Apr. 24 ***Perf. 11½*** **Unwmkd.**

Design and Inscriptions in Black

1111 A424 20h grnsh bl 6 3
1112 A424 30h violet 9 3
1113 A424 60h orange 20 4
1114 A424 1k green 45 5
1115 A424 1.40k car rose 70 20
1116 A424 1.60k lt brn 2.75 1.00
Nos. 1111-1116 (6) 4.25 1.35

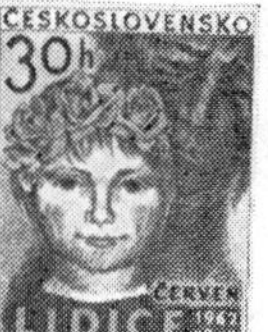

Child and Grieving Mother — **A425**

Klary's Fountain, Teplice — **A426**

Design: 60h, Flowers growing from ruins of Ležáky.

1962, June 9 **Engr. and Photo.**

1118 A425 30h blk & red 18 3
1119 A425 60h blk & dl bl 40 3

Issued to commemorate the 20th anniversary of the destruction of Lidice and Ležáky by the Nazis.

1962, June 9

1120 A426 60h dl grn & yel 35 3

Issued to commemorate the 1,200th anniversary of the discovery of the medicinal springs of Teplice.

Malaria Eradication Emblem, Cross and Dove — **A427**

Soccer Goalkeeper — **A428**

Design: 3k, Dove and malaria eradication emblem.

1962, June 18 **Engr. & Photo.**

1121 A427 60h blk & crim 30 4
1122 A427 3k dk bl & yel 2.25 80

Issued for the World Health Organization drive to eradicate malaria.

1962, June 20 ***Perf. 11½*** **Unwmkd.**

1123	A428	1.60k grn & yel	1.10	18

Issued to commemorate Czechoslovakia's participation in the World Cup Soccer Championship, Chile, May 30–June 17. See No. 1095.

Soldier in Swimming Relay Race
A429

"Agriculture"
A430

1962, July 20

Designs: 40h, Soldier hurdling. 60h, Soccer player. 1k, Soldier with rifle in relay race.

1124	A429	30h grn & lt ultra	10	3
1125	A429	40h dk pur & yel	12	3
1126	A429	60h brn & grn	25	4
1127	A429	1k dk bl & sal pink	60	15

Issued to publicize the 2nd Summer Spartacist Games of Friendly Armies, Prague, September, 1962.

1962 Engraved ***Perf. 13½***

Designs: 60h, Astronaut in capsule. 80h, Boy with flute (horiz.). 1k, Workers of three races (horiz.). 1.40k, Children dancing around tree. 1.60k, Flying bird (horiz.). 5k, View of Prague (horiz.).

1128	A430	30h multi	1.00	90
1129	A430	60h multi	90	90
a.		Miniature sheet of 8	*13.00*	*13.00*
1130	A430	80h multi	1.25	1.25
1131	A430	1k multi	2.25	2.25
1132	A430	1.40k multi	2.25	2.25
1133	A430	1.60k multi	*6.00*	*4.00*
		Nos. 1128-1133 (6)	*13.65*	*11.55*

Souvenir Sheet

1134	A430	5k multi	*12.50*	*12.50*
a.		Imperf.	*55.00*	*55.00*

Issued to commemorate the "PRAGA 1962 World Exhibition of Postage Stamps," Aug. 18–Sept. 2, 1962. No. 1133 also commemorates FIP Day, Sept. 1 (Federation Internationale de Philatelie.) Printed in sheets of 10.

No. 1129a contains four stamps each of Nos. 1128–29 and two labels arranged in two rows of two se-tenant pairs of Nos. 1128–29 with a label between. Size: 170x107mm. Sold for 5k, only with ticket.

No. 1134 contains one large stamp (51x30mm). Black marginal inscription. Size of sheet: 95x74mm. Sold only with ticket.

Children in Day Nursery and Factory
A431

Sailboat and Trade Union Rest Home, Zinkovy
A432

Engraved and Photogravure

1962, Oct. 29 ***Perf. 11½*** **Unwmkd.**

1135	A431	30h blk & lt bl	12	3
1136	A432	60h brn & yel	25	3

Cruiser "Aurora"
A433

1962, Nov. 7

1137	A433	30h blk & gray bl	12	3
1138	A433	60h blk & pink	22	3

Issued to commemorate the 45th anniversary of the Russian October revolution.

Cosmonaut and Worker
A434

Lenin
A435

1962, Nov. 7

1139	A434	30h dk red & bl	12	3
1140	A435	60h blk & dp rose	22	3

40th anniversary of the U.S.S.R.

Symbolic Crane—A436

Designs: 40h, Agricultural products (vert.). 60h, Factories.

1962, Dec. 4

1141	A436	30h dk red & yel	10	3
1142	A436	40h gray bl & yel	20	3
1143	A436	60h blk & dp rose	45	15

Issued to commemorate the 12th Congress of the Communist Party of Czechoslovakia.

Ground Beetle
A437

Table Tennis
A438

Beetles: 30h, Cardinal beetle. 60h, Stag beetle (vert.). 1k, Great water beetle. 1.60k, Alpine longicorn (vert.). 2k, Ground beetle (vert.).

1962, Dec. 15 Engraved ***Perf. 14***

1144	A437	20h multi	15	3
1145	A437	30h multi	15	3
1146	A437	60h multi	25	5
1147	A437	1k multi	40	20
1148	A437	1.60k multi	1.50	50
1149	A437	2k multi	*3.50*	*1.50*
		Nos. 1144-1149 (6)	*5.95*	*2.31*

Engraved and Photogravure

1963, Jan. ***Perf. 11½***

Sports: 60h, Bicyclist. 80h, Skier. 1k, Motorcyclist. 1.20k, Weight lifter. 1.60k, Hurdler.

1150	A438	30h blk & dp grn	20	3
1151	A438	60h blk & org	25	3
1152	A438	80h blk & ultra	35	10
1153	A438	1k blk & vio	45	25
1154	A438	1.20k blk & pale brn	60	45
1155	A438	1.60k blk & car	1.00	45
		Nos. 1150-1155 (6)	2.85	1.31

Various 1963 sports events.

Industrial Plant, Laurel and Star
A439

Symbol of Child Welfare Home
A440

Industrial Plant and Symbol of Growth
A441

1963, Feb. 25 ***Perf. 11½*** **Unwmkd.**

1156	A439	30h car & lt bl	10	3
1157	A440	60h blk & car	25	3
1158	A441	60h blk & red	25	3

Issued to commemorate the 15th anniversary of the "Victorious February" and to publicize the 5th Trade Union Congress.

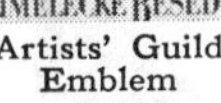

Artists' Guild Emblem
A442

Juraj Jánosik
A443

Eduard Urx
A444

National Theater, Prague
A445

Designs: No. 1163, Woman reading to children. No. 1164, Juraj Pálkovic. 1.60k, Max Svabinsky.

Engr. & Photo.; Engr. (A444)

1963, Mar. 25 ***Perf. 11½*** **Unwmkd.**

1159	A442	20h blk & Prus bl	5	3
1160	A443	30h car & lt bl	10	3
1161	A444	30h carmine	10	3
1162	A445	60h dl red brn & lt bl	20	3
1163	A444	60h green	20	3
1164	A444	60h black	30	3
1165	A444	1.60k brown	60	6
		Nos. 1159-1165 (7)	1.55	24

Various cultural personalities and events.

Boy and Girl with Flag
A446

Television Transmitter
A447

Engraved and Photogravure

1963, Apr. 18 ***Perf. 11½***

1166	A446	30h sl & rose red	18	3

The 4th Congress of Czechoslovak Youth.

1963, Apr. 25

Design: 40h, Television camera, mast and set (horiz.).

1167	A447	40h buff & sl	15	3
1168	A447	60h dk red & lt bl	25	3

Czechoslovak television, 10th anniversary.

Rocket to the Sun
A448

Designs: 50h, Rockets and Sputniks leaving Earth. 60h, Spacecraft to and from Moon. 1k, 3k, Interplanetary station and Mars 1. 1.60k, Atomic rocket and Jupiter. 2k, Rocket returning from Saturn.

1963, Apr. 25

1169	A448	30h red brn & buff	12	3
1170	A448	50h sl & bluish grn	20	6
1171	A448	60h dk grn & yel	30	3
1172	A448	1k dk gray & sal	50	10
1173	A448	1.60k gray brn & lt grn	80	20
1174	A448	2k dk pur & yel	*2.75*	*1.00*
		Nos. 1169-1174 (6)	*4.67*	*1.42*

Souvenir Sheet

Imperf.

1175	A448	3k Prus grn & org red	*4.00*	*4.00*

No. 1175 issued to commemorate the first Space Research Exhibition, Prague, Apr., 1963. Prussian green and red orange marginal inscription and design. Size: 85x70 mm.

Studio and Radio
A449

Design: 1k, Globe inscribed "Peace" and aerial mast (vert.).

Engraved and Photogravure

1963, May 18 ***Perf. 11½*** **Unwmkd.**

1176	A449	30h choc & pale grn	15	3
1177	A449	1k bluish grn & lil	35	3

40th anniversary of Czechoslovak radio.

Tupolev Tu-104B Turbojet
A450

Design: 1.80k, Ilyushin Il-18 Moskva.

1963, May 25

1178 A450 80h vio & lt bl 35 3
1179 A450 1.80k dk bl & lt grn 90 3

40th anniversary of Czechoslovak airlines.

Ninth Century Ring and Map of Moravian Settlements
A451

Woman Singing
A452

Design: 1.60k, Falconer, 9th century silver disk.

1963, May 25

1180 A451 30h lt grn & blk 15 3
1181 A451 1.60k dl yel & blk 60 3

1100th anniversary of Moravian empire.

1963, May 25 **Engraved**

1182 A452 30h brt red 45 3

Issued to commemorate the 60th anniversary of the founding of the Moravian Teachers' Singing Club.

Kromeriz Castle and Barley
A453

Centenary Emblem, Nurse and Playing Child
A454

Engraved and Photogravure

1963, June 20 *Perf. 11½* Unwmkd.

1183 A453 30h sl grn & yel 45 3

Issued to publicize the National Agricultural Exhibition and to commemorate the 700th anniversary of Kromeriz.

1963, June 20

1184 A454 30h dk gray & car 45 3

Centenary of the International Red Cross.

Bee, Honeycomb and Emblem
A455

Liberec Fair Emblem
A456

1963, June 20

1185 A455 1k brn & yel 45 4

Issued to publicize the 19th International Beekeepers Congress, Apimondia, 1963.

1963, July 13

1186 A456 30h blk & dp rose 45 3

Liberec Consumer Goods Fair.

Town Hall, Brno
A457

Cave, Moravian Karst
A458

1963, July 29

Design: 60h, Town Hall tower, Brno.

1187 A457 30h lt bl & mar 10 3
1188 A457 60h pink & dk bl 20 3

International Trade Fair, Brno.

1963, July 29

Designs: No. 1190, Trout, Hornad Valley. 60h, Great Hawk Gorge. 80h, Macocha mountains.

1189 A458 30h brn & lt bl 35 3
1190 A458 30h dk bl & dl grn 40 3
1191 A458 60h grn & bl 35 3
1192 A458 80h sep & pink 35 8

Blast Furnace
A459

Engraved and Photogravure

1963, Aug. 15 *Perf. 11½* Unwmkd.

1193 A459 60h blk & bluish grn 35 3

Issued to publicize the 30th International Congress of Iron Founders, Prague.

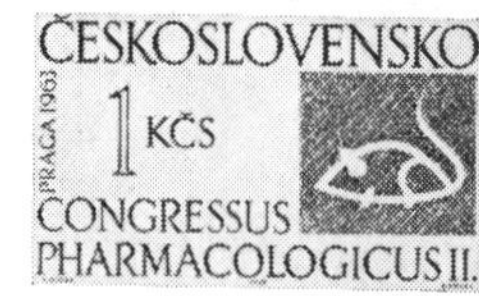

White Mouse—A460

1963, Aug. 15

1194 A460 1k blk & car 45 3

Issued to publicize the second International Pharmacological Congress, Prague.

Farm Machinery for Underfed Nations
A461

Wooden Toys
A462

1963, Aug. 15 **Engraved**

1195 A461 1.60k black 75 4

Issued for the "Freedom from Hunger" campaign of the U.N. Food and Agriculture Organization.

1963, Sept. 2 Engraved *Perf. 13½*

Folk Art (Inscribed "UNESCO"): 80h, Cock and flowers. 1k, Flowers in vase. 1.20k, Janosik, Slovak hero. 1.60k, Stag. 2k, Postilion.

1196 A462 60h red & vio bl 20 10
1197 A462 80h multi 30 12
1198 A462 1k multi 40 18
1199 A462 1.20k multi 50 20
1200 A462 1.60k multi 60 30
1201 A462 2k multi *3.50* *1.00*
Nos. 1196-1201 (6) *5.50* *1.90*

Sheets of 10.

Canoeing
A463

Tree and Star
A464

Sports: 40h, Volleyball. 60h, Wrestling. 80h, Basketball. 1k, Boxing. 1.60k, Gymnastics.

Engraved and Photogravure

1963, Oct. 26 ***Perf. 11½***

1202 A463 30h ind & grn 10 3
1203 A463 40h red brn & lt bl 15 3
1204 A463 60h brn red & yel 20 5
1205 A463 80h dk pur & dp org 35 12
1206 A463 1k ultra & dp rose 40 12
1207 A463 1.60k vio bl & ultra *3.00* *1.00*
Nos. 1202-1207 (6) *4.20* *1.35*

1964 Olympic Games, Tokyo.

1963, Dec. 11 *Perf. 11½* Unwmkd.

Design: 60h, Star, hammer and sickle.

1208 A464 30h bis brn & lt bl 10 3
1209 A464 60h car & gray 20 3

Issued to commemorate the 20th anniversary of the Russo-Czechoslovakian Treaty.

Atom Diagrams Surrounding Head
A465

Chamois
A466

1963, Dec. 12 **Engraved**

1210 A465 60h dk pur 45 3

Issued to publicize the 3rd Congress of the Association for the Propagation of Scientific Knowledge.

1963, Dec. 14 ***Perf. 14***

Animals: 40h, Alpine ibex. 60h, Mouflon. 1.20k, Roe deer. 1.60k, Fallow deer. 2k, Red deer.

1211 A466 30h multi 60 15
1212 A466 40h multi 70 25
1213 A466 60h brn, yel & grn 90 30
1214 A466 1.20k multi 95 30
1215 A466 1.60k multi 1.50 60
1216 A466 2k multi *5.00* *2.75*
Nos. 1211-1216 (6) *9.65* *4.35*

Figure Skating
A467

Ice Hockey
A468

Designs: 80h, Skiing (horiz.). 1k, Field ball player.

Engraved and Photogravure

1964, Jan. 20 *Perf. 11½* Unwmkd.

1217 A467 30h vio bl & yel 20 3
1218 A467 80h dk bl & org 50 5
1219 A467 1k brn & lil 55 20

Issued to commemorate the International University Games (30h and 80h) and the World Field Ball Championships (1k).

1964, Jan. 20

Designs: 1.80k, Toboggan. 2k, Ski jump.

1220 A468 1k pur & pale grn 75 45
1221 A468 1.80k sl grn & bl gray 1.15 1.00
1222 A468 2k dk bl & pale grn *4.00* *3.50*

Issued to commemorate the 9th Winter Olympic Games, Innsbruck, Jan. 29–Feb. 9, 1964.

Magura Rest Home, High Tatra
A469

Design: 80h, Slovak National Insurrection Rest Home, Low Tatra.

1964, Feb. 19 *Perf. 11½* Unwmkd.

1223 A469 60h grn & yel 25 3
1224 A469 80h vio bl & pink 30 3

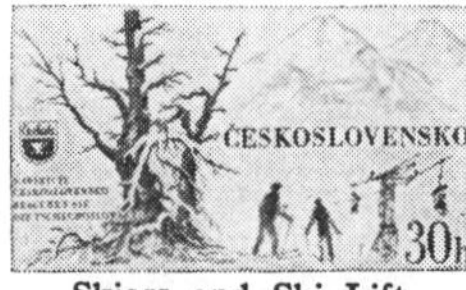

Skiers and Ski Lift
A470

Designs: 60h, Automobile camp, Telč. 1k, Fishing, Spis Castle. 1.80k, Lake and boats, Český Krumlov.

1964, Feb. 19 **Engr. & Photo.**

1225 A470 30h dk vio brn & bl 15 3
1226 A470 60h sl & car 25 3
1227 A470 1k brn & ol 50 4
1228 A470 1.80k sl grn & org 75 15

Moses, Day and Night by Michelangelo
A471

Designs: 60h, "A Midsummer Night's Dream," by Shakespeare. 1k, Man, telescope and heaven (vert.). 1.60k, King George of Podebrad (1420–71).

1964, March 20

1229 A471 40h blk & yel grn 20 3
1230 A471 60h sl & car 20 3
1231 A471 1k blk & lt bl 35 5
1232 A471 1.60k blk & yel 75 15

Issued to commemorate the following: 400th anniversary of the death of Michelangelo (40h); 400th anniversary of the birth of Shakespeare (60h); 400th anniversary of the birth of Galileo (1k); 500th anniversary of the pacifist efforts of King George of Podebrad (1.60k).

Yuri A. Gagarin—A472

Astronauts: 60h, German Titov. 80h, John H. Glenn, Jr. 1k, Scott M. Carpenter (vert.). 1.20k, Pavel R. Popovich and Andrian G. Nikolayev. 1.40k, Walter M. Schirra (vert.). 1.60k, Gordon L. Cooper (vert.). 2k, Valentina Tereshkova and Valeri Bykovski (vert.).

Engraved and Photogravure

1964, Apr. 27 *Perf. 11½* Unwmkd.

Yellow Paper

1233 A472 30h blk & vio bl 60 10
1234 A472 60h dk grn & dk car 30 10
1235 A472 80h dk car & vio 35 10
1236 A472 1k ultra & rose vio 45 15
1237 A472 1.20k ver & ol gray 1.00 25
1238 A472 1.40k blk & dl grn 1.20 40
1239 A472 1.60k pale pur & Prus grn *4.00* *1.75*
1240 A472 2k dk bl & red 1.75 80
Nos. 1233-1240 (8) *9.65* *3.65*

World's first 10 astronauts.

Creeping Bellflower
A473

Film 'Flower' and Karlovy Vary Colonnade
A474

Flowers: 80h, Musk thistle. 1k, Chicory. 1.20k, Yellow iris. 1.60k, Gentian. 2k, Corn poppy.

1964, June 15 Engraved *Perf. 14*

1241 A473 60h dk grn, lil & org 1.50 30
1242 A473 80h blk, grn & red lil 1.50 30
1243 A473 1k vio bl, grn & pink 1.50 40
1244 A473 1.20k blk, yel & grn 1.50 40
1245 A473 1.60k vio & grn 1.50 40
1246 A473 2k vio, red & grn *7.50* *2.25*
Nos. 1241-1246 (6) *15.00* *4.05*

Engraved and Photogravure

1964, June 20 *Perf. 13½* Unwmkd.

1247 A474 60h blk, bl & car 1.25 10

Issued to commemorate the 14th International Film Festival at Karlovy Vary, July 4–19.

Silesian Coat of Arms
A475

Young Miner of 1764
A476

1964, June 20 *Perf. 11½*

1248 A475 30h blk & yel 35 3

Issued to commemorate the 150th anniversary of the Silesian Museum, Opava.

1964, June 20

1249 A476 60h sep & lt grn 35 3

Issued to commemorate the bicentenary of the Mining School at Banska Stiavnica.

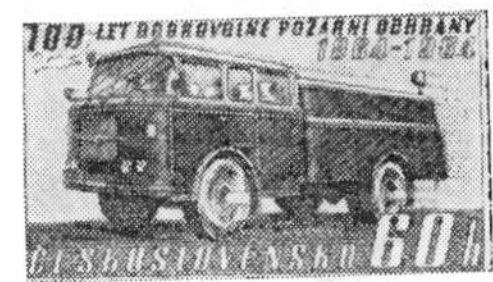

Skoda Fire Engine
A477

1964, June 20

1250 A477 60h car rose & lt bl 35 3

Issued to commemorate the centenary of voluntary fire brigades in Bohemia.

Gulls, Hradcany Castle, Red Cross
A478

Human Heart
A479

1964, July 10

1251 A478 60h car & bluish gray 35 3

Issued to commemorate the 4th Czechoslovak Red Cross Congress at Prague.

1964, July 10

1252 A479 1.60k ultra & car 80 5

Issued to commemorate the 4th European Cardiological Congress at Prague.

Partisans, Girl and Factories
A480

Battle Scene, 1944
A481

Design: 60h, Partisans and flame.

Engraved and Photogravure

1964, Aug. 17 *Perf. 11½* Unwmkd.

1253 A480 30h brn & red 10 3
1254 A480 60h dk bl & red 22 3
1255 A481 60h blk & red 22 3

Issued to commemorate the 20th anniversary of the Slovak National Uprising; No. 1255 commemorates the 20th anniversary of the Battles of Dukla Pass.

Hradcany at Prague
A482

Discus Thrower and Pole Vaulter
A483

Design: 5k, Charles Bridge and Hradcany.

1964, Aug. 30 *Perf. 11½x12*

1256 A482 60h blk & red 75 10

Souvenir Sheet

Engraved *Imperf.*

1257 A482 5k dp cl 2.25 2.00

Millenium of the Hradcany, Prague.
No. 1257 measures 76x98mm.; stamp size: 30x50mm.

Engraved and Photogravure

1964, Sept. 2 *Perf. 13½*

Designs: 60h, Bicycling (horiz.). 1k, Soccer. 1.20k, Rowing. 1.60k, Swimming (horiz.). 2.80k, Weight lifting (horiz.).

1258 A483 60h multi 30 12
1259 A483 80h multi 40 12
1260 A483 1k multi 50 18
1261 A483 1.20k multi 60 25
1262 A483 1.60k multi 1.00 50
1263 A483 2.80k multi *4.50* *2.50*
Nos. 1258-1263 (6) *7.30* *3.67*

Issued to commemorate the 18th Olympic Games, Tokyo, Oct. 10–25. Sheets of 10.

Miniature Sheet

Space Ship Voskhod I, Astronauts and Globe—A484

Engraved and Photogravure

1964, Nov. 12 *Perf. 11½* Unwmkd.

1264 A484 3k dk bl & dl lil, *buff* 6.50 4.50

Issued to commemorate the Russian three-manned space flight of Vladimir M. Komarov, Boris B. Yegorov and Konstantin Feoktistov, Oct. 12–13. No. 1264 contains one stamp. Size of stamp: 49x30 mm.; size of sheet: 92x66mm.

Steam Engine and Atomic Power Plant
A485

Diesel Engine "CKD Praha"
A486

1964, Nov. 16 Engraved

1265 A485 30h dl red brn 15 3

Engraved and Photogravure

1266 A486 60h grn & sal 25 3

Issued to publicize traditions and development of engineering; No. 1265 commemorates the 150th anniversary of the First Brno Engineering Works, No. 1266 honors the engineering concern CKD Praha.

European Redstart
A487

Birds: 60h, Green woodpecker. 80h, Hawfinch. 1k, Black woodpecker. 1.20k, European robin. 1.60k, European roller.

1964, Nov. 16 Litho. *Perf. 10½*

1267 A487 30h multi 15 3
1268 A487 60h blk & multi 30 3
1269 A487 80h multi 35 8
1270 A487 1k multi 45 18
1271 A487 1.20k lt vio bl & blk 50 25
1272 A487 1.60k yel & blk 80 60
Nos. 1267-1272 (6) 2.55 1.17

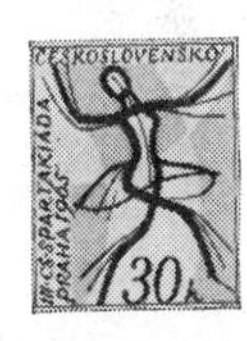

Dancer
A488

"In the Sun" Pre-school Children
A489

Designs: 60h, "Over the Obstacles," teenagers. 1k, "Movement and Beauty," woman flag twirler. 1.60k, Runners at start.

Engraved and Photogravure

1965 *Perf. 11½* Unwmkd.

1273 A488 30h red & lt bl 15 3

Perf. 11½x12

1274 A489 30h vio bl & car 10 3
1275 A489 60h brn & ultra 20 3
1276 A489 1k blk & yel 40 6
1277 A489 1.60k mar & gray 65 30
Nos. 1273-1277 (5) 1.50 45

Issued to publicize the Third National Spartacist Games. Issue dates: No. 1273, Jan. 3. Nos. 1274–1277, May 24.

Mountain Rescue Service
A490

Arms and View, Beroun
A491

1965, Jan. 15 *Perf. 11½* Unwmkd.

Designs: No. 1279, Woman gymnast. No. 1280, Bicyclists. No. 1281, Women hurdlers.

1278 A490 60h vio & bl 30 4

1279	A490	60h mar & ocher	30	4
1280	A490	60h blk & car	30	4
1281	A490	60h grn & yel	30	4

Issued to publicize: Mountain Rescue Service (No. 1278); First World Championship in Artistic Gymnastics, Prague, December 1965 (No. 1279); World Championship in Indoor Bicycling, Prague, Oct., 1965 (No. 1280); "Universiada 1965," Brno (No. 1281).

1965, Feb. 15 Engr. and Photo.

Designs: No. 1283, Town Square, Domazlice. No. 1284, Old and new buildings, Frydek-Mystek. No. 1285, Arms and view, Lipnik. No. 1286, Fortified wall, City Hall and Arms, Policka. No. 1287, View and hops, Zatek. No. 1288, Small fortress and rose, Terezin.

1282	A491	30h vio bl & lt bl	20	3
1283	A491	30h dl pur & yel	20	3
1284	A491	30h sl & gray	20	3
1285	A491	30h grn & bis	20	3
1286	A491	30h brn & tan	20	3
1287	A491	30h dk bl & cit	20	3
1288	A491	30h blk & rose	20	3
		Nos. 1282-1288 (7)	1.40	21

Nos. 1282–87 commemorate the 700th anniversary of the founding of various Bohemian towns; No. 1288 commemorates the 20th anniversary of the liberation of the Theresienstadt (Terezin) concentration camp.

Sun's Corona—A492

Space Research: 30h, Sun. 60h, Exploration of the Moon. 1k, Twin space craft (vert.). 1.40k, Space station. 1.60k, Exploration of Mars (vert.). 2k, USSR and USA Meteorological collaboration.

Perf. 12x11½, 11½x12

1965, Mar. 15 Engr. & Photo.

1289	A492	20h rose & red lil	10	3
1290	A492	30h rose red & yel	12	3
1291	A492	60h bluish blk & yel	22	3
1292	A492	1k pur & pale bl	35	9
1293	A492	1.40k blk & sal	50	14
1294	A492	1.60k blk & pink	65	35
1295	A492	2k bluish blk & lt bl	*1.40*	*1.25*
		Nos. 1289-1295 (7)	*3.34*	*1.92*

Issued to publicize space research; Nos. 1289–1290 also commemorate the International Quiet Sun Year, 1964–65.

Frantisek Ventura, Equestrian; Amsterdam, 1928
A493

Czechoslovakian Olympic Victories: 30h, Discus, Paris, 1900. 60h, Running, Helsinki, 1952. 1k, Weight lifting, Los Angeles, 1932. 1.40k, Gymnastics, Berlin, 1936. 1.60k, Double sculling, Rome, 1960. 2k, Women's gymnastics, Tokyo, 1964.

1965, Apr. 16 ***Perf. 11½x12***

1296	A493	20h choc & gold	10	3
1297	A493	30h ind & emer	12	3
1298	A493	60h ultra & gold	22	4
1299	A493	1k red brn & gold	45	15
1300	A493	1.40k dk sl grn & gold	90	50
1301	A493	1.60k blk & gold	1.00	55
1302	A493	2k mar & gold	1.20	60
		Nos. 1296-1302 (7)	3.99	1.90

Astronauts Virgil Grissom and John Young—A494

Designs: No. 1304, Alexei Leonov floating in space. No. 1305, Launching pad at Cape Kennedy, U.S.A. No. 1306, Leonov leaving space ship.

1965, Apr. 17 ***Perf. 11x11½***

1303	A494	60h sl bl & lil rose	25	18
1304	A494	60h vio blk & bl	25	18
1305	A494	3k sl bl & lil rose	1.75	1.25
1306	A494	3k vio blk & bl	1.75	1.25

Issued to honor American and Soviet astronauts. Printed in sheets of 25; one sheet contains 20 No. 1303 and 5 No. 1305, the other sheet contains 20 No. 1304 and 5 No. 1306.

Russian Soldier, View of Prague and Guerrilla Fighters—A495

Designs: No. 1308, Blast furnace, workers and tank. 60h, Worker and factory. 1k, Worker and new constructions. 1.60k, Woman farmer, new farm buildings and machinery.

1965, May 5 Engraved ***Perf. 13½***

1307	A495	30h dk red, blk & ol	12	3
1308	A495	30h multi	12	3
1309	A495	60h vio bl, red & blk	25	4
1310	A495	1k dp org, blk & brn	40	10
1311	A495	1.60k yel, red & blk	65	20
		Nos. 1307-1311 (5)	1.54	40

Issued to commemorate the 20th anniversary of liberation from the Nazis.

Slovakian Kopov Dog—A496

Dogs: 40h, German shepherd. 60h, Czech hunting dog with pheasant. 1k, Poodle. 1.60k, Czech terrier. 2k, Afghan hound.

1965, June 10 ***Perf. 12x11½***

1312	A496	30h blk & red org	15	3
1313	A496	40h blk & yel	20	3
1314	A496	60h blk & ver	25	4
1315	A496	1k blk & dk car rose	50	8
1316	A496	1.60k blk & org	90	18
1317	A496	2k blk & org	1.50	75
		Nos. 1312-1317 (6)	3.50	1.11

Issued to publicize the World Dog Show at Brno and the International Dog Breeders Congress, Prague.

U.N. Headquarters Building, N.Y.
A497

Designs: 60h, U.N. Emblem and inscription. 1.60k, ICY emblem.

1965, June 24 ***Perf. 12x11½***

1318	A497	60h dk red brn & yel	25	4
1319	A497	1k ultra & lt bl	40	7
1320	A497	1.60k gold & dk red	75	35

Issued to commemorate the 20th anniversary of the United Nations and for the International Cooperation Year, 1965.

Trade Union Emblem
A498

1965, June 24 Engraved

1321	A498	60h dk red & ultra	35	3

Issued to commemorate the 20th anniversary of the International Trade Union Federation.

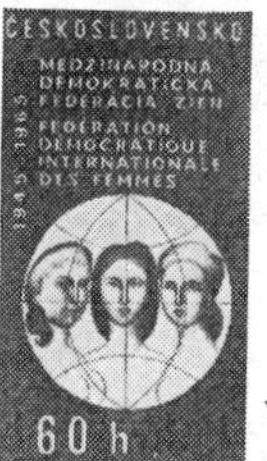

Women and Globe
A499

1965, June 24 ***Perf. 11½x12***

1322	A499	60h vio bl	35	3

Issued to commemorate the 20th anniversary of the International Women's Federation.

Children's House (Burgraves' Palace), Hradcany
A500

Matthias Tower
A501

1965, June 25 ***Perf. 11½***

1323	A500	30h sl grn	20	3
1324	A501	60h dk brn	40	3

Issued to publicize the Hradcany, Prague.

Marx and Lenin
A502

1965, July 1 Engraved and Photo.

1325	A502	60h car rose & gold	30	3

Issued to commemorate the 6th conference of Postal Ministers of Communist Countries, Peking, June 21–July 15.

Joseph Navratil
A503

Jan Hus
A504

Gregor Johann Mendel
A505

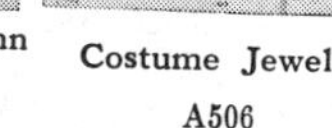

Costume Jewelry
A506

Bohuslav Martinu
A507

ITU Emblem and Communication Symbols
A509

Seated Woman and University of Bratislava
A508

Macromolecular Symposium Emblem
A510

Design: No. 1327, Ludwig Stur (diff. frame).

Engraved and Photogravure

1965 ***Perf. 11½*** **Unwmkd.**

1326	A503	30h blk & fawn	18	3
1327	A503	30h blk & dl grn	20	3
1328	A504	60h blk & crim	35	3
1329	A505	60h vio bl & red	35	3
1330	A506	60h pur & gold	35	3
1331	A507	60h blk & org	35	3
1332	A508	60h brn, *yel*	35	3
1333	A509	1k org & bl	50	4
1334	A510	1k blk & dp org	50	5
		Nos. 1326-1334 (9)	3.13	30

No. 1326 commemorates the centenary of the death of Josef Navratil (1798–1865), painter; No. 1327, the sesquicentennial of the birth of Ludwig Stur (1815–56), Slovak author and historian; No. 1328 commemorates the 550th anniversary of the death of Jan Hus, religious reformer; No. 1329, the centenary of publication of Mendel's laws of inheritance; No. 1330 publicizes the "Jablonec 1965" costume jewelry exhibition; No. 1331, the 75th anniversary of the birth of Bohuslav Martinu (1890–1959), composer; No. 1332, the 500th anniversary of the founding of the University of Bratislava as Academia Istropolitana; No. 1333, the centenary of the International Telecommunication Union; No. 1334, the International Symposium on Macromolecular Chemistry, Prague, Sept. 1–8.

"Young Woman at her Toilette," by Titian
A512

Help for Flood Victims
A513

Rescue of Flood Victims
A514

Miniature Sheet

1965, Aug. 12

1336	A512	5k multi	3.25	2.75

Issued to publicize the Hradcany Art Gallery. No. 1336 contains one stamp; size of sheet: 75x97mm.

1965, Sept. 6 Engraved

1337	A513	30h vio bl	15	7

Engraved and Photogravure

1338	A514	2k dk ol grn & ol	90	65

Help for Danube flood victims in Slovakia.

Dotterel
A515

Mountain Birds: 60h, Wall creeper (vert.). 1.20k, Lesser redpoll. 1.40k, Golden eagle (vert.). 1.60k, Ring ouzel. 2k, Eurasian nutcracker (vert.).

1965, Sept. 20 Litho. *Perf. 11*

1339	A515	30h multi	12	3
1340	A515	60h multi	25	3
1341	A515	1.20k multi	60	10
1342	A515	1.40k multi	70	20
1343	A515	1.60k multi	80	25
1344	A515	2k multi	1.10	1.00
		Nos. 1339-1344 (6)	3.57	1.61

Levoca
A516

Coltsfoot
A517

Views of Towns: 10h, Jindrichuv Hradec. 20h, Nitra. 30h, Kosice. 40h, Hradec Králové. 50h, Telc. 60h, Ostrava. 1k, Olomouc. 1.20k, Ceske Budejovice. 1.60k, Cheb. 2k, Brno. 3k, Bratislava. 5k, Prague.

Engraved and Photogravure

1965–66 *Perf. 11½x12*

Size: 23x19mm.

1345	A516	5h blk & yel	3	3
1346	A516	10h ultra & ol bis	6	3
1347	A516	20h blk & lt bl	8	3
1348	A516	30h vio bl & lt grn	12	3
1348A	A516	40h dk brn & lt bl ('66)	15	3
1348B	A516	50h blk & ocher ('66)	20	3
1348C	A516	60h red & gray ('66)	25	3
1348D	A516	1k pur & pale grn ('66)	45	3

Perf. 11½x11

Size: 30x23mm.

1349	A516	1.20k sl & lt bl	55	4
1350	A516	1.60k ind & yel	70	3
1351	A516	2k sl grn & pale yel	90	5
1352	A516	3k brn & yel	1.35	6
1353	A516	5k blk & pink	2.50	11
		Nos. 1345-1353 (13)	7.34	53

1965, Dec. 3 Engraved *Perf. 14*

Medicinal Plants: 60h, Meadow saffron. 80h, Corn poppy. 1k, Foxglove. 1.20k, Arnica. 1.60k, Cornflower. 2k, Dog rose.

1354	A517	30h multi	15	8
1355	A517	60h multi	25	12
1356	A517	80h multi	30	15
1357	A517	1k multi	55	20
1358	A517	1.20k multi	75	25
1359	A517	1.60k multi	1.00	40
1360	A517	2k multi	*4.00*	*2.00*
		Nos. 1354-1360 (7)	*7.00*	*3.20*

Strip of "Stamps"—A518

Engraved and Photogravure

1965, Dec. 18 *Perf. 11½*

1361	A518	1k dk red & gold	3.00	2.50

Issued for Stamp Day, 1965.

Romain Rolland
A519

Symbolic Musical Instruments and Names of Composers
A520

Portraits: No. 1362, Stanislav Sucharda. No. 1363, Ignac Josef Pesina. No. 1365, Donatello.

1966, Feb. 14 Engraved *Perf. 11½*

1362	A519	30h dp grn	10	3
1363	A519	30h vio bl	10	3
1364	A519	60h rose lake	22	3
1365	A519	60h brown	22	3

Issued to commemorate the following: No. 1362, centenary of birth of Stanislav Sucharda (1866–1916), sculptor; No. 1363, bicentenary of birth of Ignac Josef Pesina (1766–1808), veterinarian. No. 1364, centenary of birth of Romain Rolland (1866–1944), French writer; No. 1365, 500th anniversary of death of Donatello (1386–1466), Italian sculptor.

1966, Feb. 15 Engr. and Photo.

1366	A520	30h blk & gold	55	20

Issued to commemorate the 70th anniversary of the Czech Philharmonic Orchestra.

Figure Skating Pair—A521

Designs: No. 1368, Man skater. No. 1369, Volleyball player, spiking (vert.). 1k, Volleyball player, saving (vert.). 1.60k, Woman skater. 2k, Figure skating pair.

1966, Feb. 17

1367	A521	30h dk car rose	15	3
1368	A521	60h green	30	4
1369	A521	60h car & buff	30	4
1370	A521	1k vio & lt bl	45	5
1371	A521	1.60k brn & yel	60	9
1372	A521	2k bl & grnsh bl	*2.50*	*80*
		Nos. 1367-1372 (6)	*4.30*	*1.05*

Nos. 1367–68 and 1371–72 commemorate the European Figure Skating Championships, Bratislava; Nos. 1369–70 commemorate the World Volleyball Championships.

Souvenir Sheet

Girl Dancing—A522

1966, Mar. 21 Engraved *Imperf.*

1373	A522	3k sl bl, red & bl	1.75	1.75

Issued to commemorate the centenary of the opera "The Bartered Bride" by Bedrich Smetana. Opening chorus "Why shouldn't we be happy. ." in margin. Size: 85x105mm.

"Ajax" 1841
A523

Locomotives: 30h, "Karlstejn" 1865. 60h, Steam engine, 1946. 1k, Steam engine with tender, 1946. 1.60k, Electric locomotive, 1964. 2k, Diesel locomotive, 1964.

1966, March 21 *Perf. 11½x11*

Buff Paper

1374	A523	20h sepia	10	3
1375	A523	30h dl vio	12	3
1376	A523	60h dl pur	30	3
1377	A523	1k dk bl	40	7
1378	A523	1.60k dk bl grn	70	30
1379	A523	2k dk red	*4.00*	*1.10*
		Nos. 1374-1379 (6)	*5.62*	*1.56*

European Perch
A524

Fish: 30h, Brown trout (vert.). 1k, Carp. 1.20k, Northern pike. 1.40k, Grayling. 1.60k, Eel.

Perf. 13x13½, 13½x13

1966, Apr. 22 Litho. **Unwmkd.**

1380	A524	30h multi	15	3
1381	A524	60h multi	25	3
1382	A524	1k multi	40	5
1383	A524	1.20k multi	50	15
1384	A524	1.40k multi	60	25
1385	A524	1.60k multi	*3.75*	*1.50*
		Nos. 1380-1385 (6)	*5.65*	*2.01*

Issued to publicize the International Fishing Championships, Svit, Sept. 3–5.

WHO Headquarters, Geneva
A525

Engraved and Photogravure

1966, Apr. 25 *Perf. 12x11½*

1386	A525	1k dk bl & lt bl	45	10

Issued to commemorate the inauguration of the World Health Organization Headquarters, Geneva.

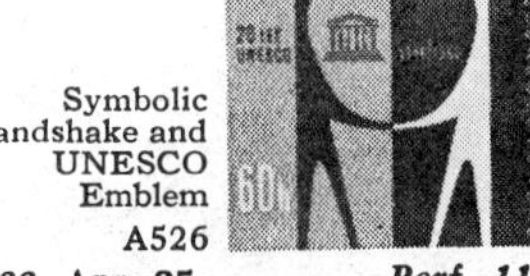

Symbolic Handshake and UNESCO Emblem
A526

1966, Apr. 25 *Perf. 11½*

1387	A526	60h bis & ol gray	25	5

Issued to commemorate the 20th anniversary of UNESCO (U.N. Educational, Scientific and Cultural Organization).

Prague Castle Issue

Belvedere Palace and St. Vitus' Cathedral
A527

Crown of St. Wenceslas, 1346
A528

Design: 60h, Madonna, altarpiece from St. George's Church.

1966, May 9 Engraved *Perf. 11½*

1388	A527	30h dk bl	25	3

Engraved and Photogravure

1389	A527	60h blk & yel bis	55	10

Souvenir Sheet

Engraved

1390	A528	5k multi	3.00	3.00

See also Nos. 1537–1539.

Tiger Swallowtail
A529

Butterflies and Moths: 60h, Clouded sulphur. 80h, European purple emperor. 1k, Apollo. 1.20k, Burnet moth. 2k, Tiger moth.

1966, May 23 Engraved *Perf. 14*

1391	A529	30h multi	10	8
1392	A529	60h multi	25	10
1393	A529	80h multi	35	12
1394	A529	1k multi	40	15
1395	A529	1.20k multi	60	20
1396	A529	2k multi	*3.75*	*1.50*
		Nos. 1391-1396 (6)	*5.45*	*2.15*

Sheets of ten.

Flags of Russia and Czechoslovakia
A530

Designs: 60h, Rays surrounding hammer and sickle "sun." 1.60k, Girl's head and stars.

Engraved and Photogravure

1966, May 31 *Perf. 11½*

1397	A530	30h dk bl & crim	12	3
1398	A530	60h dk bl & red	25	5
1399	A530	1.60k red & dk bl	70	15

Issued to commemorate the 13th Congress of the Communist Party of Czechoslovakia.

Dakota Chief
A531

Designs: 20h, Indians, canoe and tepee (horiz.). 30h, Tomahawk. 40h, Haida totem poles. 60h, Kachina, good spirit of the Hopis. 1k, Indian on horseback hunting buffalo (horiz.). 1.20k, Calumet, Dakota peace pipe.

1966, June 20 Engr. & Photo.

Size: 23x40mm.

1400	A531	20h vio bl & dp org	10	5
1401	A531	30h blk & dl org	10	5
1402	A531	40h blk & lt bl	10	8
1403	A531	60h grn & yel	30	10
1404	A531	1k pur & emer	40	20
1405	A531	1.20k vio bl & rose lil	60	40

Engraved

Perf. 14

Size: 23x37mm.

1406	A531	1.40k multi	*2.25*	*75*
		Nos. 1400-1406 (7)	*3.85*	*1.63*

Issued to commemorate the centenary of the Náprstek Ethnographic Museum, Prague, and in connection with "The Indians of North America" exhibition.

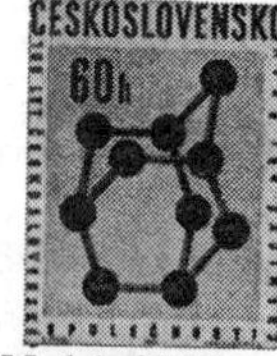

Model of Molecule
A532

Engraved and Photogravure

1966, July 4 *Perf. 11½* Unwmkd.

1407	A532	60h blk & lt bl	30	3

Issued to commemorate the centenary of the Czechoslovak Chemical Society.

"Guernica" by Pablo Picasso
A533

1966, July 5

Size: 75x30mm.

1408	A533	60h blk & pale bl	2.00	2.00

30th anniversary of International Brigade in Spanish Civil War.

Sheets of 15 stamps and 5 labels inscribed "Picasso-Guernica 1937."

Pantheon, Bratislava
A534

Designs: No. 1410, Devin Castle and Ludwig Stur. No. 1411, View of Nachod. No. 1412, State Science Library, Olomouc.

1966, July 25 Engraved

1409	A534	30h dl pur	10	3
1410	A534	60h dk bl	25	3
1411	A534	60h green	25	3
1412	A534	60h sepia	25	3

No. 1409 publicizes the Russian War Memorial, Bratislava; No. 1410, the 9th century Devin Castle as symbol of Slovak nationalism; No. 1411 commemorates the 700th anniversary of the founding of Nachod; No. 1412, the 400th anniversary of the State Science Library, Olomouc.

Atom Symbol and Sun
A535

Engraved and Photogravure

1966, Aug. 29 *Perf. 11½*

1413	A535	60h blk & red	30	3

Issued to publicize Jachýmov (Joachimsthal), where pitchblende was first discovered, "cradle of the atomic age."

Brno Fair Emblem
A536

Olympia Coin and Olympic Rings
A537

1966, Aug. 29

1414	A536	60h blk & red	30	3

8th International Trade Fair, Brno.

1966, Aug. 29

Design: 1k, Olympic flame, Czechoslovak flag and Olympic rings.

1415	A537	60h blk & gold	30	4
1416	A537	1k dk bl & red	55	30

Issued to commemorate the 70th anniversary of the Olympic Committee.

Missile Carrier, Tank and Jet Plane
A538

1966, Aug. 31

1417	A538	60h blk & ap grn	35	5

Issued to commemorate the maneuvers of the armies of the Warsaw Pact countries.

Mercury
A539

Designs: 30h, Moravian silver thaler, 1620, reverse and obverse (vert.). 1.60k, Old and new buildings of Brno State Theater. 5k, International Trade Fair Administration Tower and postmark (vert.).

1966, Sept. 10

1418	A539	30h dk red & blk	30	4
1419	A539	60h org & blk	30	4
1420	A539	1.60k blk & brt grn	75	35

Souvenir Sheet

1421	A539	5k multi	3.25	3.25

Issued to publicize the Brno Philatelic Exhibition, Sept. 11–25. No. 1421 contains one stamp (size: 30x40mm.). Marginal black inscription and exhibition emblem. Size: 73½x100mm.

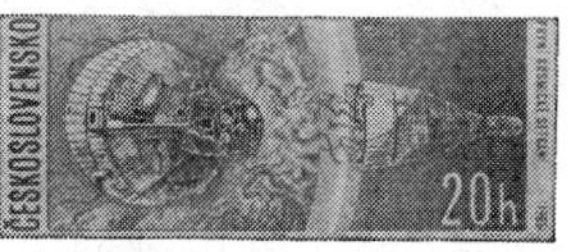

First Meeting in Orbit—A540

Designs: 30h, Photograph of far side of Moon and Russian satellite. 60h, Photograph of Mars and Mariner 4. 80h, Soft landing on Moon. 1k, Satellite, laser beam and binary code. 1.20k, Telstar over Earth and receiving station.

Engraved and Photogravure

1966, Sept. 26 *Perf. 11½*

1422	A540	20h vio & lt grn	10	3
1423	A540	30h blk & sal pink	15	3
1424	A540	60h sl & lil	25	4
1425	A540	80h dk pur & lt bl	40	20
1426	A540	1k blk & vio	50	25
1427	A540	1.20k red & bl	*2.00*	*75*
		Nos. 1422-1427 (6)	*3.40*	*1.30*

Issued to publicize American and Russian achievements in space research.

Badger
A541

Game Animals: 40h, Red deer (vert.). 60h, Lynx. 80h, Hare. 1k, Red fox. 1.20k, Brown bear (vert.). 2k, Wild boar.

1966, Nov. 28 Litho. *Perf. 13½*

1428	A541	30h multi	12	4
1429	A541	40h multi	18	4
1430	A541	60h multi	25	4
1431	A541	80h multi (*europaens*)	35	12
a.		80h multi (*europaeus*)	2.00	2.00
1432	A541	1K multi	50	20
1433	A541	1.20k multi	60	25
1434	A541	2k multi	*4.00*	*2.00*
		Nos. 1428-1434 (7)	*6.00*	*2.69*

The sheet of 50 of the 80h contains 40 with misspelling "europaens" and 10 with "europaeus."

"Spring" by Vaclav Hollar, 1607–77
A542

Paintings: No. 1436, Portrait of Mrs. F. Wussin, by Jan Kupecký (1667–1740). No. 1437, Snow Owl by Karel Purkyne (1834–1868). No. 1438, Tulips by Vaclav Spála (1885–1964). No. 1439, Recruit by Ludovít Fulla (1902–).

1966, Dec. 8 Engraved *Perf. 14*

1435	A542	1k black	3.50	3.50
1436	A542	1k multi	3.50	3.50
1437	A542	1k multi	3.50	3.50
1438	A542	1k multi	3.50	3.50
1439	A542	1k multi	*12.00*	*12.00*
		Nos. 1435-1439 (5)	*26.00*	*26.00*

Printed in sheets of 4 stamps and 2 labels. The labels in sheet of No. 1435 are inscribed "Vaclav Hollar 1607–1677" in fancy frame. Other labels are blank.

See also No. 1484.

Symbolic Bird—A543

Engraved and Photogravure

1966, Dec. 17 *Perf. 11½*

1440	A543	1k dp bl & yel	85	75

Issued for Stamp Day.

Youth
A544

1967, Jan. 16 *Perf. 11½*

1441	A544	30h ver & lt bl	15	4

Issued to publicize the 5th Congress of the Czechoslovak Youth Organization.

Symbolic Flower and Machinery
A545

1967, Jan. 16 Engr. & Photo.

1442	A545	30h car & yel	15	4

6th Trade Union Congress, Prague.

Parents with Dead Child
A545a

1967, Jan. 16 *Perf. 11½*

1442A	A545a	60h blk & sal	30	6

Issued to publicize "Peace and Freedom in Viet Nam."

View of Jihlava and Tourist Year Emblem—A546

Views and Tourist Year Emblem: 40h, Spielberg Castle and churches, Brno. 1.20k, Danube, castle and churches, Bratislava. 1.60k, Vlatava River bridges, Hradcany and churches, Prague.

1967, Feb. 13 Engraved *Perf. 11½*

Size: 40x23mm.

1443	A546	30h brn vio	12	4
1444	A546	40h maroon	18	4

Size: 75x30mm.

1445	A546	1.20k vio bl	65	20
1446	A546	1.60k black	*1.60*	*60*

International Tourist Year, 1967.

Black-tailed Godwit
A547

Birds: 40h, Shoveler (horiz.). 60h, Purple heron. 80h, Penduline tit. 1k, Avocet. 1.40k, Black stork. 1.60k, Tufted duck (horiz.).

1967, Feb. 20 Litho. *Perf. 13½*

1447	A547	30h multi	10	4
1448	A547	40h multi	12	5
1449	A547	60h multi	20	4
1450	A547	80h multi	30	10
1451	A547	1k multi	40	12
1452	A547	1.40k multi	70	35
1453	A547	1.60k multi	*2.50*	*1.20*
		Nos. 1447-1453 (7)	*4.32*	*1.90*

Solar Research and Satellite
A548

Space Research: 40h, Space craft, rocket and construction of station. 60h, Man on moon and orientation system. 1k, Exploration of solar system and rocket. 1.20k, Lunar satellites and moon photograph. 1.60k, Planned lunar architecture and moon landing.

Engraved and Photogravure

1967, March 24 *Perf. 11½*

1454	A548	30h yel & dk red	12	4
1455	A548	40h vio bl & blk	15	4
1456	A548	60h lil & grn	25	5
1457	A548	1k brt pink & sl	45	12
1458	A548	1.20k lt vio & blk	65	20
1459	A548	1.60k brn lake & blk	*2.00*	*60*
		Nos. 1454-1459 (6)	*3.62*	*1.05*

Gothic Painting, by Master Theodoric
A549

Designs: 40h, "Burning of Master Hus," from Litomerice Hymnal. 60h, Modern glass sculpture. 80h, "The Shepherdess and the Chimney Sweep," Andersen fairy tale, painting by J. Trnka. 1k, Section of pressure vessel from atomic power station. 1.20k, Three ceramic figurines, by P. Rada. 3k, Montreal skyline and EXPO '67 emblem.

1967, Apr. 10 Engraved *Perf. 14*

Size: 37x23mm.

1460	A549	30h multi	15	5
1461	A549	40h multi	20	10
1462	A549	60h multi	30	15
1463	A549	80h multi	45	20
1464	A549	1k multi	50	30
1465	A549	1.20k multi	*1.50*	*60*
		Nos. 1460-1465 (6)	*3.10*	*1.40*

Souvenir Sheet

Perf. 11½

Size: 40x30mm.

1466	A549	3k multi	2.25	2.25

Issued to commemorate EXPO '67, International Exhibition, Montreal, Apr. 28–Oct. 27, 1967. No. 1466 contains one stamp with drawing of the Czechoslovakian pavilion in the margin. Size of sheet: 96x74mm.

Canoe Race
A550

Women Playing Field Ball
A551

Designs: No. 1468, Wheels, dove and emblems of Warsaw, Berlin, Prague. 1.60k, Canoe slalom.

Perf. 12x11½, 11½x12

1967, Apr. 17 Engr. and Photo.

1467	A550	60h blk & brt bl	20	8
1468	A550	60h blk & sal	20	8
1469	A551	60h blk & grnsh bl	20	8
1470	A551	1.60k blk & brt vio	*1.75*	*70*

Issued to commemorate the following: No. 1467, 5th International Wild-Water Canoeing Championships; No. 1468, 20th Warsaw-Berlin-Prague Bicycle Race; No. 1469, Women's Field Ball Championships; No. 1470, 10th International Water Slalom Championships.

"Golden Street"
A552

Designs: 60h, Interior of Hall of King Wenceslas. 5k, St. Matthew, from illuminated manuscript, 11th century.

1967, May 9 *Perf. 11½x11*

1471	A552	30h rose cl	20	3
1472	A552	60h bluish blk	45	15

Souvenir Sheet

Perf. 11½

1473	A552	5k multi	3.50	3.50

Issued to publicize the Castle of Prague. No. 1473 contains one stamp with Latin marginal inscription in gold. Size: 75x95 mm.

Stylized Lyre with Flowers
A553

Old-New Synagogue, Prague
A554

Engraved and Photogravure

1967, May 10 *Perf. 11½*

1474	A553	60h dl pur & brt grn	35	6

Prague Music Festival.

1967, May 22 *Perf. 11½*

Designs: 30h, Detail from Torah curtain, 1593. 60h, Prague Printer's emblem, 1530. 1k, Mikulov jug, 1804. 1.40k, Memorial for Concentration Camp Victims 1939–45, Pincas Synagogue (menorah and tablet). 1.60k, Tombstone of David Gans, 1613.

1475	A554	30h dl red & lt bl	45	8
1476	A554	60h blk & lt grn	60	8
1477	A554	1k dk bl & rose lil	90	18
1478	A554	1.20k dk brn & mar	1.25	45
1479	A554	1.40k blk & yel	1.50	60
1480	A554	1.60k grn & yel	*3.75*	*1.60*
		Nos. 1475-1480 (6)	*8.45*	*2.99*

Issued to show Jewish relics. The items shown on the 30h, 60h and 1k are from the State Jewish Museum, Prague.

"Lidice"
A555

Prague Architecture
A556

1967, June 9 *Perf. 11½* Unwmkd.

1481	A555	30h blk & brt rose	20	3

Issued to commemorate the 25th anniversary of the destruction of Lidice by the Nazis.

1967, June 10 Engr. & Photo.

1482	A556	1k blk & gold	45	18

Issued to publicize the 9th Congress of the International Union of Architects, Prague.

Petr Bezruc
A557

1967, June 21

1483	A557	60h dl rose & blk	25	5

Issued to commemorate the centenary of the birth of Petr Bezruc, poet and writer.

Painting Type of 1966

Design: 2k, Henri Rousseau (1844–1910), self-portrait.

1967, June 22 Engr. *Perf. 11½*

1484	A542	2k multi	2.00	1.40

Issued to publicize Praga 68, World Stamp Exhibition, Prague, June 22–July 7, 1968. Printed in sheets of 4 stamps (2x2), separated by horizontal gutter with commemorative inscription and picture of National Gallery, site of Praga 68.

View of Skalitz
A558

Designs: No. 1486, Mining tower and church steeple, Pribram. No. 1487, Hands holding book and view of Presov.

1967, Aug. 21 Engr. *Perf. 11½*

1485	A558	30h vio bl	10	4
1486	A558	30h sl grn	10	4
1487	A558	30h claret	10	4

Issued to commemorate anniversaries of the towns of Skalitz, Pribram and Presov.

Colonnade and Spring, Karlovy Vary and Communications Emblem
A559

1967, Aug. 21 Engr. and Photo.

1488	A559	30h vio bl & gold	35	5

Issued to commemorate the 5th Sports and Cultural Festival of the Employees of the Ministry of Communications, Karlovy Vary.

Ondrejov Conservatory and Galaxy
A560

1967, Aug. 22 Engraved

1489	A560	60h vio bl, rose lil & sil	75	20

Issued to commemorate the 13th International Congress of the Astronomic Union.

Orchid
A561

Flowers from the Botanical Gardens: 30h, Cobaea scandens. 40h, Lycaste deppei. 60h, Glottiphyllum davisii. 1k, Anthurium. 1.20k, Rhodocactus. 1.40k, Moth orchid.

1967, Aug. 30 Litho. *Perf. 12½*

1490	A561	20h multi	8	3
1491	A561	30h pink & multi	12	3
1492	A561	40h multi	25	4
1493	A561	60h lt bl & multi	25	4
1494	A561	1k multi	55	15
1495	A561	1.20k lt yel & multi	95	18
1496	A561	1.40k multi	*2.75*	*90*
		Nos. 1490-1496 (7)	*4.95*	*1.37*

Red Squirrel
A562

Animals from the Tatra National Park: 60h, Wild cat. 1k, Ermine. 1.20k, Dormouse. 1.40k, Hedgehog. 1.60k, Pine marten.

Engraved and Photogravure

1967, Sept. 25 ***Perf. 11½***

1497	A562	30h blk, yel & org	15	3
1498	A562	60h blk & buff	30	6
1499	A562	1k blk & lt bl	50	15
1500	A562	1.20k brn, pale grn & yel	55	18
1501	A562	1.40k blk, pink & yel	70	20
1502	A562	1.60k blk, org & yel	*3.75*	*1.50*
		Nos. 1497-1502 (6)	*5.95*	*2.12*

Rockets and Weapons
A563

1967, Oct. 6 Engraved ***Perf. 11½***

1503	A563	30h sl grn	30	5

Day of the Czechoslovak People's Army.

Cruiser "Aurora" Firing at Winter Palace—A564

Designs: 60h, Hammer and sickle emblems and Red Star (vert.). 1k, Hands reaching for hammer and sickle (vert.).

Engraved and Photogravure

1967, Nov. 7

1504	A564	30h blk & dk car	10	3
1505	A564	60h blk & dk car	20	4
1506	A564	1k blk & dk car	35	10

Issued to commemorate the 50th anniversary of the Russian October Revolution.

The Conjurer, by Frantisek Tichy
A565

Paintings: 80h, Don Quixote, by Cyprian Majernik. 1k, Promenade in the Park, by Norbert Grund. 1.20k, Self-portrait, by Peter J. Brandl. 1.60k, Saints from Jan of Jeren Epitaph, by Czech Master of 1395.

1967, Nov. 13 Engr. ***Perf. 11½***

1507	A565	60h multi	45	40
1508	A565	80h multi	60	50
1509	A565	1k multi	80	75
1510	A565	1.20k multi	95	80
1511	A565	1.60k multi	*4.75*	*4.25*
		Nos. 1507-1511 (5)	*7.55*	*6.70*

Sheets of 4. See Nos. 1589-1593, 1658-1662, 1711-1715, 1779-1783, 1847-1851, 1908-1913, 2043-2047, 2090-2093, 2147-2151, 2335-2339.

Pres. Antonin Novotny
A566

1967, Dec. 9 Engraved ***Perf. 11½***

1512	A566	2k bl gray	75	4
1513	A566	3k brown	1.10	6

Czechoslovakia Nos. 65, 71 and 81 of 1920—A567

1967, Dec. 18

1514	A567	1k mar & sil	1.25	1.10

Issued for Stamp Day.

Symbolic Flag and Dates
A568

1968, Jan. 15 Engr. ***Perf. 11½***

1515	A568	30h red, dk bl & ultra	35	15

50th anniversary of Czechoslovakia.

Figure Skating and Olympic Rings
A569

Designs (Olympic Rings and): 1k, Ski course. 1.60k, Toboggan chute. 2k, Ice hockey.

1968, Jan. 29 Engr. and Photo.

1516	A569	60h blk, yel & ocher	30	7
1517	A569	1k ol grn, lt bl & lem	40	18
1518	A569	1.60k blk, lil & bl grn	70	25
1519	A569	2k blk, ap grn & lt bl	*2.50*	*75*

Issued to publicize the 10th Winter Olympic Games, Grenoble, France, Feb. 6–18.

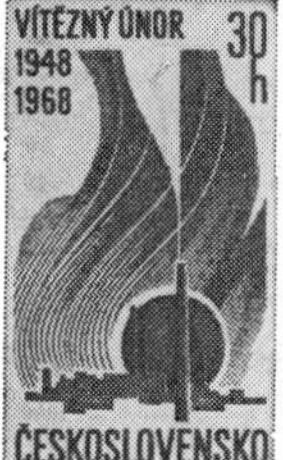

Factories and Rising Sun
A570

Design: 60h, Workers and banner.

Engraved and Photogravure

1968, Feb. 25 ***Perf. 11½x12***

1520	A570	30h car & dk bl	10	4
1521	A570	60h car & dk bl	25	5

20th anniversary of February Revolution.

Map of Battle of Sokolow
A571

Human Rights Flame
A572

Engraved and Photogravure

1968, Mar. 8 ***Perf. 11½***

1522	A571	30h blk, brt bl & car	35	5

Engraved

1523	A572	1k rose car	55	15

No. 1522 commemorates the 25th anniversary of the Battle of Sokolow, Mar. 8, 1943, against the German Army; No. 1523 commemorates the International Human Rights Year.

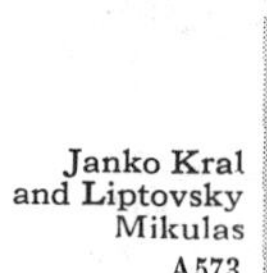

Janko Kral and Liptovsky Mikulas
A573

Karl Marx
A574

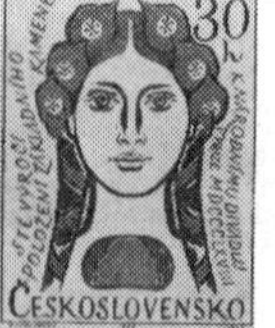

Girl's Head
A575

Arms and Allegory
A576

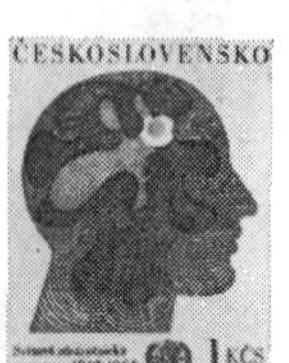

Head
A577

1968, Mar. 25 Engraved

1524	A573	30h green	20	3
1525	A574	30h claret	20	3

Engraved and Photogravure

1526	A575	30h dk red & gold	20	3
1527	A576	30h dk bl & dp org	20	3
1528	A577	1k multi	1.10	35
		Nos. 1524-1528 (5)	1.90	47

Issued to commemorate the following: The writer Janko Kral and the Slovak town Liptovsky Mikulas (No. 1524); 150th anniversary of the birth of Karl Marx (No. 1525); centenary of the cornerstone laying of the Prague National Theater (No. 1526); 150th anniversary of the Prague National Museum (No. 1527); 20th anniversary of the World Health Organization (1k).

Symbolic Radio Waves
A578

Design: No. 1530, Symbolic television screens.

Engraved and Photogravure

1968, Apr. 29 ***Perf. 11½***

1529	A578	30h blk, car & vio bl	15	6
1530	A578	30h blk, car & vio bl	15	6

Issued to commemorate the 45th anniversary of Czechoslovak broadcasting (No. 1529), and the 15th anniversary of television (No. 1530).

Olympic Rings, Mexican Sculpture and Gymnast
A579

Olympic Rings and: 40h, Runner and "The Sanctification of Quetzalcoatl." 60h, Netball and Mexican ornaments. 1k, Czechoslovak and Mexican Olympic emblems and carved altar. 1.60k, Soccer and ornaments. 2k, View of Hradcany, weather vane and key.

1968, Apr. 30

1531	A579	30h blk, bl & car	10	3
1532	A579	40h multi	20	4
1533	A579	60h multi	30	4
1534	A579	1k multi	45	15
1535	A579	1.60k multi	65	20
1536	A579	2k blk & multi	*2.50*	*80*
		Nos. 1531-1536 (6)	*4.20*	*1.26*

Issued to publicize the 19th Olympic Games, Mexico City, Oct. 12–27.

Prague Castle Types of 1966

Designs: 30h, Tombstone of Bretislav I. 60h, Romanesque door knocker, St. Wenceslas Chapel. 5k, Head of St. Peter, mosaic from Golden Gate of St. Vitus Cathedral.

Photogravure and Engraved

1968, May 9 ***Perf. 11½***

1537	A527	30h multi	20	3
1538	A527	60h blk, red & cit	35	4

Souvenir Sheet

Engraved

1539	A528	5k multi	4.50	4.50

No. 1539 contains one stamp, black ornament in margin. Size: 75x94mm.

Pres. Ludvik Svoboda
A580

1968–70 Engraved *Perf. 11½*

No.	Type	Description	Unused	Used
1540	A580	30h ultra	10	3
1540A	A580	50h grn ('70)	25	3
1541	A580	60h maroon	20	3
1541A	A580	1k rose car ('70)	55	8

Shades exist of No. 1541A.

"Business," Sculpture by Otto Gutfreund
A581

Cabaret Performer, by František Kupka
A582

Photo. & Engr.; Engr. (2k)

1968, June 5

Designs (The New Prague): 40h, Broadcasting Corporation Building. 60h, New Parliament. 1.40k, Tapestry by Jan Bauch "Prague 1787." 3k, Presidential standard.

No.	Type	Description	Unused	Used
1542	A581	30h blk & multi	9	3
1543	A581	40h blk & multi	15	3
1544	A581	60h dk brn & multi	30	7
1545	A581	1.40k dk brn & multi	65	18
1546	A582	2k ind & multi	*2.25*	*2.25*
1547	A581	3k blk & multi	1.25	95
		Nos. 1542-1547 (6)	*4.69*	*3.51*

1968, June 21 *Perf. 11½*

Designs (The Old Prague): 30h, St. George's Basilica. 60h, Renaissance fountain. 1k, Villa America-Dvorak Museum, 18th Century building. 1.60k, Emblem from the House of Three Violins, 18th century. 2k, Josefina, by Josef Manes. 3k, Emblem of Prague, 1475.

No.	Type	Description	Unused	Used
1548	A581	30h grn, gray & yel	9	3
1549	A581	60h dk vio, ap grn & gold	25	4
1550	A581	1k blk, lt bl & pink	50	12
1551	A581	1.60k sl grn & multi	65	20
1552	A582	2k brn & multi	*1.75*	*1.50*
1553	A581	3k blk, yel, bl & pink	1.35	65
		Nos. 1548-1553 (6)	*4.59*	*2.54*

Nos. 1542–1553 issued to publicize the Praga 68 Philatelic Exhibition. Nos. 1542–1545, 1547–1551 and 1553 issued in sheets of 15 stamps and 15 labels with Praga 68 emblem and inscription. Nos. 1546 and 1552 issued in sheets of 4 (2x2) with one horizontal label between top and bottom rows showing Praga 68 emblem.

Souvenir Sheet

View of Prague and Emblems
A583

Engraved and Photogravure

1968, June 22 *Imperf.*

No.	Type	Description	Unused	Used
1554	A583	10k multi	7.50	6.00

Issued for Praga 68 and to commemorate the 50th anniversary of Czechoslovak postage stamps. Type of 1918 issue and commemorative inscription in margin. Size: 75½x110mm. Sold only together with a 5k admission ticket to the Praga 68 philatelic Exhibition.

Madonna with the Rose Garlands, by Dürer
A584

1968, July 6 *Perf. 11½*

No.	Type	Description	Unused	Used
1555	A584	5k multi	4.50	3.50

Issued to commemorate FIP Day, July 6 (Féderation Internationale de Philatélie). Issued in sheets of 4 (2x2) with one horizontal label between, showing Praga 68 emblem.

Stage-coach on Rails
A585

Design: 1k, Steam and electric locomotives.

1968, Aug. 6 Engr. & Photo.

No.	Type	Description	Unused	Used
1556	A585	60h multi	55	20
1557	A585	1k multi	75	20

No. 1556 commemorates the 140th anniversary of the horse-drawn railroad České-Budějovice to Linz; No. 1557 commemorates the centenary of the České-Budějovice to Plzeň railroad.

Fanciful "S"
A586

1968, Aug. 7 *Perf. 11½*

No.	Type	Description	Unused	Used
1558	A586	30h vio bl & car	20	3

Issued to commemorate the 6th International Slavonic Congress in Prague.

Ardspach Rocks and Ammonite
A587

Designs: 60h, Basalt formation and frog skeleton fossil. 80h, Rocks, basalt veins and polished agate. 1k, Pelecypoda (fossil shell) and Belanske Tatra mountains. 1.60k, Trilobite and Barrande rock formation.

1968, Aug. 8

No.	Type	Description	Unused	Used
1559	A587	30h blk & cit	12	3
1560	A587	60h blk & rose cl	30	7
1561	A587	80h blk, lt vio & pink	35	10
1562	A587	1k blk & lt bl	45	17
1563	A587	1.60k blk & bis	*2.50*	*1.00*
		Nos. 1559-1563 (5)	*3.72*	*1.37*

Issued to publicize the 23rd International Geological Congress, Prague, Aug. 8–Sept. 3.

Raising Slovak Flag
A588

Design: 60h, Slovak partisans, and mountain.

1968, Sept. 9 Engraved *Perf. 11½*

No.	Type	Description	Unused	Used
1564	A588	30h ultra	10	3
1565	A588	60h red	20	5

No. 1564 honors the Slovak National Council, No. 1565 commemorates the 120th anniversary of the Slovak national uprising.

Flowerpot, by Jiri Schlessinger (age 10)
A589

Drawings by Children in Terezin Concentration Camp: 30h, Jew and Guard, by Jiri Beutler (age 10). 60h, Butterflies, by Kitty Brunnerova (age 11).

Engraved and Photogravure

1968, Sept. 30 *Perf. 11½*

Size: 30x23mm.

No.	Type	Description	Unused	Used
1566	A589	30h blk, buff & rose lil	12	5
1567	A589	60h blk & multi	25	8

Perf. 12x11½

Size: 41x23mm.

No.	Type	Description	Unused	Used
1568	A589	1k blk & multi	40	18

30th anniversary of Munich Pact.

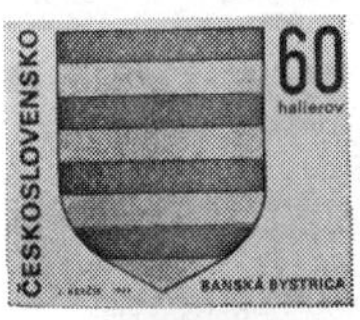

Arms of Banská Bystrica
A590

Arms of Prague
A591

Arms of Regional Capitals: No. 1570, Bratislava. No. 1571, Brno. No. 1572, České Budějovice. No. 1573, Hradec Králové. No. 1574, Košice. No. 1575, Ostrava (horse). No. 1576, Plzeň. No. 1577, Ustí nad Labem.

1968, Oct. 21 *Perf. 11½*

No.	Type	Description	Unused	Used
1569	A590	60h blk, red & sil	25	8
1570	A590	60h blk, red, sil & ultra	25	8
1571	A590	60h blk, red & sil	25	8
1572	A590	60h blk, red, sil & gold	25	8
1573	A590	60h blk, red, sil & gold	25	8
1574	A590	60h blk, bl, red & gold	25	8
1575	A590	60h blk, bl, yel & red	25	8
1576	A590	60h blk, emer, red & gold	25	8
1577	A590	60h blk, red, sil & gold	25	8

Perf. 11½x12

No.	Type	Description	Unused	Used
1578	A591	1k multi	50	45
		Nos. 1569-1578 (10)	2.75	1.17

No. 1578 issued in sheets of 10. See also Nos. 1652–1657, 1742–1747, 1886–1888, 2000–2001.

Flag and Linden Leaves
A592

Bohemian Lion Breaking Chains (Type SP1 of 1919)

A593

Design: 60h, Map of Czechoslovakia, linden leaves, Hradcany in Prague and Castle in Bratislava.

1968, Oct. 28 *Perf. 12x11½*

1579	A592	30h dp bl & mag	20	3
1580	A592	60h blk, gold, red & ultra	25	5

Souvenir Sheet

Engraved *Perf. 11½x12*

1581	A593	5k red	2.50	2.50

Issued to commemorate the 50th anniversary of the founding of Czechoslovakia. No. 1581 has violet blue marginal inscription and red ornament. Size: 75x100mm.

Ernest Hemingway (1899–1961) Cinderlad

A594 A595

Caricatures: 30h, Karel Capek (1890–1938), writer. 40h, George Bernard Shaw (1856–1950), writer. 60h, Maxim Gorki (1868–1930), writer. 1k, Pablo Picasso (1881–1973), painter. 1.20k, Taikan Yokoyama (1868–1958), painter. 1.40k, Charlie Chaplin (1889–1977), actor.

Engraved and Photogravure

1968, Nov. 18 *Perf. 11½x12*

1582	A594	20h blk, org & red	6	3
1583	A594	30h blk & multi	15	3
1584	A594	40h blk, lil & car	15	4
1585	A594	60h blk, sky bl & grn	18	5
1586	A594	1k blk, brn & yel	45	10
1587	A594	1.20k blk, dp car & vio	50	18
1588	A594	1.40k blk, brn & dp org	*2.50*	*85*
		Nos. 1582-1588 (7)	*3.99*	*1.28*

Issued to honor cultural personalities of the 20th century and UNESCO (United Nations Educational, Scientific and Cultural Organization). See Nos. 1628–1633.

Painting Type of 1967

Czechoslovakian Art: 60h, Cleopatra II, by Jan Zrzavy (1890–). 80h, Black Lake (man and horse), by Jan Preisler (1872–1918). 1.20k, Giovanni Francisci as a Volunteer, by Peter Michal Bohun (1822–1879). 1.60k, Princess Hyacinth, by Alfons Mucha (1860–1939). 3k, Madonna and Child, woodcarving, 1518, by Master Paul of Levoca.

1968, Nov. 29 Engraved *Perf. 11½*

1589	A565	60h multi	35	30
1590	A565	80h multi	55	50
1591	A565	1.20k multi	90	80
1592	A565	1.60k multi	1.25	1.10
1593	A565	3k multi	*5.25*	*4.25*
		Nos. 1589-1593 (5)	*8.30*	*6.95*

Sheets of 4.

1968, Dec. 18 Engr. and Photo.

Slovak Fairy Tales: 60h, The Proud Lady. 80h, The Ruling Knight. 1k, Good Day, Little Bench. 1.20k, The Spellbound Castle. 1.80k, The Miraculous Hunter. The designs are from illustrations by Ludovit Fulla for "Slovak Stories."

1594	A595	30h multi	9	5
1595	A595	60h multi	22	7
1596	A595	80h multi	30	10
1597	A595	1k multi	35	13
1598	A595	1.20k multi	50	15
1599	A595	1.80k multi	*2.00*	*1.00*
		Nos. 1594-1599 (6)	*3.46*	*1.50*

Czechoslovakia Nos. 2 and 3

A596

1968, Dec. 18

1600	A596	1k vio bl & gold	1.10	1.00

Issued to commemorate the 50th anniversary of Czechoslovakian postage stamps.

Crescent, Cross and Lion and Sun Emblems ILO Emblem

A597 A598

Design: 60h, 12 crosses in circles forming large cross.

Engraved and Photogravure

1969, Jan. 31 *Perf. 11½*

1601	A597	60h blk, red & gold	25	5
1602	A597	1k blk, ultra & red	45	12

No. 1601 commemorates the 50th anniversary of the Czechoslovak Red Cross; No. 1602 commemorates the 50th anniversary of the League of Red Cross Societies.

1969, Jan. 31

1603	A598	1k blk & gray	35	12

Issued to commemorate the 50th anniversary of the International Labor Organization.

Cheb Pistol

A599

Historical Firearms: 40h, Italian pistol with Dutch decorations, c. 1600. 60h, Wheellock rifle from Matej Kubik workshop c. 1720. 1k, Flintlock pistol, Devieuxe workshop, Liege, c. 1760. 1.40k, Duelling pistols, from Lebeda workshop, Prague, c. 1835. 1.60k, Derringer pistols, U.S.A., c. 1865.

1969, Feb. 18

1604	A599	30h blk & multi	9	3
1605	A599	40h blk & multi	15	4
1606	A599	60h blk & multi	20	6
1607	A599	1k blk & multi	45	10
1608	A599	1.40k blk & multi	70	25
1609	A599	1.60k blk & multi	*2.00*	*85*
		Nos. 1604-1609 (6)	*3.59*	*1.33*

Bratislava Castle, Muse and Book

A600

Designs: No. 1611, Science symbols and emblem (Brno University). No. 1612, Harp, laurel and musicians' names. No. 1613, Theatrical scene. No. 1614, Arms of Slovakia, banner and blossoms. No. 1615, School, outstretched hands and woman with linden leaves.

1969, Mar. 24 Engr. *Perf. 11½*

1610	A600	60h vio bl	25	6

Engraved and Photogravure

1611	A600	60h blk, gold & sl	25	6
1612	A600	60h gold, bl, blk & red	25	6
1613	A600	60h blk & rose red	25	6
1614	A600	60h rose red, sil & bl	25	6
1615	A600	60h blk & gold	25	6
		Nos. 1610-1615 (6)	1.50	36

Nos. 1610–1614 issued to commemorate the 50th anniversary of: Komensky University in Bratislava (#1610); Brno University (#1611); Brno Conservatory of Music (#1612); Slovak National Theater (#1613); Slovak Soviet Republic (#1614); No. 1615 commemorates the centenary of the Zniev Gymnasium (academic high school).

Baldachin-top Car and Four-seat Coupé of 1900–1905—A601

Designs: 1.60k, Laurin & Klement Voiturette, 1907, and L & K touring car with American top, 1907. 1.80k, First Prague bus, 1907, and sectionalized Skoda bus, 1967.

1969, Mar. 25

1616	A601	30h blk, lil & lt grn	12	3
1617	A601	1.60k blk, org brn & lt bl	65	20
1618	A601	1.80k multi	*2.00*	*1.25*

Peace, by Ladislav Guderna

A602

Engraved and Photogravure

1969, Apr. 21 *Perf. 11*

1619	A602	1.60k multi	80	55

Issued to commemorate the 20th anniversary of the Peace Movement. Issued in sheets of 15 stamps and 5 tabs.

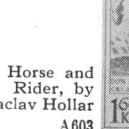

Horse and Rider, by Vaclav Hollar

A603

Old Engravings of Horses: 30h, Prancing Stallion, by Hendrik Goltzius (horiz.). 80h, Groom Leading Horse, by Matthäus Merian (horiz.). 1.80k, Horse and Soldier, by Albrecht Dürer. 2.40k, Groom and Horse, by Johann E. Ridinger.

1969, Apr. 24 *Perf. 11x11½, 11½x11*

Yellowish Paper

1620	A603	30h dk brn	9	3
1621	A603	80h vio brn	30	10
1622	A603	1.60k slate	65	20
1623	A603	1.80k sepia	80	30
1624	A603	2.40k multi	*2.25*	*75*
		Nos. 1620-1624 (5)	*4.09*	*1.38*

M. R. Stefánik as Astronomy Professor and French General

A604

1969, May 4 Engraved *Perf. 11½*

1625	A604	60h rose cl	35	10

Issued to commemorate the 50th anniversary of the death of Gen. Milan R. Stefánik.

St. Wenceslas Pressing Wine, Mural by the Master of Litomerice

A605

Design: No. 1627, Coronation banner of the Estates, 1723, with St. Wenceslas and coats of arms of Bohemia and Czech Crown lands.

1969, May 9 Engraved *Perf. 11½*

1626	A605	3k multi	2.00	1.75
1627	A605	3k multi	2.00	1.75

Issued to publicize the art treasures of the Castle of Prague. See Nos. 1689–1690.

Caricature Type of 1968

Caricatures: 30h, Pavol Orszagh Hviezdoslav (1849–1921), Slovak writer. 40h, Gilbert K. Chesterton (1874–1936), English writer. 60h, Vladimir Mayakovski (1893–1930), Russian poet. 1k, Henri Matisse (1869–1954), French painter. 1.80k, Ales Hrdlicka (1869–1943), Czech-born American anthropologist. 2k, Franz Kafka (1883–1924), Austrian writer.

Engraved and Photogravure

1969, June 17 *Perf. 11½x12*

1628	A594	30h blk, red & bl	9	5

1629	A594	40h blk, bl & lt vio	12	6
1630	A594	60h blk, rose & yel	18	8
1631	A594	1k blk & multi	45	12
1632	A594	1.80k blk, ultra & ocher	75	23
1633	A594	2k blk, yel & brt grn	1.75	50
		Nos. 1628-1633 (6)	3.34	1.04

Issued to honor cultural personalities of the 20th century and UNESCO.

"Music," by Alfons Mucha
A606

Paintings by Mucha: 60h, "Painting." 1k, "Dance." 2.40k, "Ruby" and "Amethyst."

1969, July 14 Perf. 11½x11

Size: 30x49mm.

1634	A606	30h blk & multi	9	3
1635	A606	60h blk & multi	18	8
1636	A606	1k blk & multi	35	12

Size: 39x51mm.

1637	A606	2.40k blk & multi	2.00	1.75

Issued to commemorate the 30th anniversary of the death of Alfons Mucha (1860–1930), painter and stamp designer (Type A1).

Pres. Svoboda and Partisans
A607

Design: No. 1639, Slovak fighters and mourners.

Engraved and Photogravure

1969, Aug. 29 Perf. 11

1638	A607	30h ol grn & red, *yel*	12	3
1639	A607	30h vio bl & red, *yel*	12	3

Issued to commemorate the 25th anniversary of the Slovak uprising and of the Battle of Dukla.

Tatra Mountain Stream and Gentians
A608

Designs: 60h, Various views in Tatra Mountains. No. 1644, Mountain pass and gentians. No. 1645, Houses, Krivan Mountain and autumn crocuses.

1969, Sept. 8 Engraved Perf. 11

Size: 71x33mm.

1640	A608	60h gray	35	6
1641	A608	60h dk bl	35	6
1642	A608	60h dl gray vio	35	6

Perf. 11½

Size: 40x23mm.

1643	A608	1.60k multi	75	25
1644	A608	1.60k multi	1.50	60
1645	A608	1.60k multi	75	25
		Nos. 1640-1645(6)	4.05	1.28

Issued to commemorate the 20th anniversary of the creation of the Tatra Mountains National Park. Nos. 1640–1642 are printed in sheets of 15 (3x5) with 5 labels showing mountain plants. Nos. 1643–1645 issued in sheets of 10.

Bronze Belt Ornaments
A609

Archaeological Treasures from Bohemia and Moravia: 30h, Gilt ornament with 6 masks. 1k, Jeweled earrings. 1.80k, Front and back of lead cross with Greek inscription. 2k, Gilt strap ornament with human figure.

Engraved and Photogravure

1969, Sept. 30 Perf. 11½x11

1646	A609	20h gold & multi	6	5
1647	A609	30h gold & multi	10	5
1648	A609	1k red & multi	40	16
1649	A609	1.80k dl org & multi	80	30
1650	A609	2k gold & multi	1.50	50
		Nos. 1646-1650 (5)	2.86	1.06

"Mail Circling the World"
A610

1969, Oct. 1 Engraved Perf. 12

1651	A610	3.20k multi	1.50	75

Issued to commemorate the 16th Universal Postal Union Congress, Tokyo, Oct. 1–Nov. 14. Issued in sheets of 4.

Coat of Arms Type of 1968

Engraved and Photogravure

1969, Oct. 25 Perf. 11½

Multicolored

1652	A590	50h *Bardejov*	25	8
1653	A590	50h *Hranice*	25	8
1654	A590	50h *Kezmarok*	25	8
1655	A590	50h *Krnov*	25	8
1656	A590	50h *Litomerice*	25	8
1657	A590	50h *Manetin*	25	8
		Nos. 1652-1657 (6)	1.50	48

Painting Type of 1968

Designs: 60h, Requiem, 1944, by Frantisek Muzika. 1k, Resurrection, 1380, by the Master of the Trebon Altar. 1.60k, Crucifixion, 1950, by Vincent Hloznik. 1.80k, Girl with Doll, 1863, by Julius Bencur. 2.20k, St. Jerome, 1357–67, by Master Theodorik.

Engraved and Photogravure

1969, Nov. 25 Perf. 11½

1658	A565	60h multi	30	25
1659	A565	1k multi	50	45
1660	A565	1.60k multi	75	65
1661	A565	1.80k multi	1.10	1.00
1662	A565	2.20k multi	2.50	2.25
		Nos. 1658-1662 (5)	5.15	4.60

Sheets of 4.

Symbolic Sheet of Stamps—A611

1969, Dec. 18 Perf. 11½x12

1663	A611	1k dk brn, ultra & gold	50	45

Issued for Stamp Day 1969.

Ski Jump—A612

Designs: 60h, Long distance skier. 1k, Ski jump and slope. 1.60k, Woman skier.

Engraved and Photogravure

1970, Jan. 6 Perf. 11½

1664	A612	50h multi	15	5
1665	A612	60h multi	18	5
1666	A612	1k multi	40	15
1667	A612	1.60k multi	1.25	45

Issued to publicize the International Ski Championships "Tatra 1970."

Ludwig van Beethoven (1770–1827)
A613

Portraits: No. 1669, Friedrich Engels (1820–1895), German socialist. No. 1670, Maximilian Hell (1720–1792), Slovakian Jesuit and astronomer. No. 1671, Lenin (1870–1924), Russian Communist leader. No. 1672, Josef Manes (1820–1871), Czech painter. No. 1673, John Amos Comenius (1592–1670), theologian and educator.

1970, Feb. 17 Engr. Perf. 11x11½

1668	A613	40h black	15	6
1669	A613	40h dl red	15	6
1670	A613	40h yel brn	15	6
1671	A613	40h dl red	15	6
1672	A613	40h brown	15	6
1673	A613	40h black	15	6
		Nos. 1668-1673 (6)	90	36

Issued to commemorate the anniversaries of the birth of Beethoven, Engels, Hell, Lenin and Manes, the 300th anniversary of the death of Comenius, and to honor UNESCO.

Bells
A614

Designs: 80h, Machine tools and lathe. 1k, Folklore masks. 1.60k, Angel and Three Wise Men, 17th century icon from Koniec. 2k, View of Orlik Castle, 1787, by F. K. Wolf. 3k, "Passing through Koshu down to Mishima" from Hokusai's 36 Views of Fuji.

Engraved and Photogravure

1970, Mar. 13 Perf. 11½x11

Size: 40x23mm.

1674	A614	50h multi	20	3
1675	A614	80h multi	30	5
1676	A614	1k multi	40	6

Size: 50x40mm.

Perf. 11½

1677	A614	1.60k multi	75	40
1678	A614	2k multi	1.00	50
1679	A614	3k multi	2.50	2.00
		Nos. 1674-1679 (6)	5.15	3.04

Issued to publicize EXPO '70 International Exhibition, Osaka, Japan, March 15–Sept. 13, 1970. Nos. 1674–1676 issued in sheets of 50, Nos. 1677–1679 in sheets of 4.

Kosice Townhall, Laurel and Czechoslovak Arms
A615

1970, Apr. 5 Perf. 11

1680	A615	60h sl, ver & gold	50	6

Issued to commemorate the 25th anniversary of the government's Kosice Program.

"The Remarkable Horse" by Josef Lada
A616

Lenin
A617

Paintings by Josef Lada: 60h, Autumn, 1955 (horiz.). 1.80k, "The Water Sprite." 2.40k, Children in Winter, 1943 (horiz.).

1970, Apr. 21 Perf. 11½

1681	A616	60h blk & multi	25	10
1682	A616	1k blk & multi	40	15
1683	A616	1.80k blk & multi	75	25
1684	A616	2.40k blk & multi	1.75	1.00

1970, Apr. 22 Engr. & Photo.

Design: 60h, Lenin without cap, facing left.

1685	A617	30h dk red & gold	12	3
1686	A617	60h blk & gold	30	6

Issued to commemorate the centenary of the birth of Lenin (1870–1924), Russian communist leader.

Fighters on the Barricades
A618

Design: No. 1688, Lilac, Russian tank and castle.

Engraved and Photogravure

1970, May 5 Perf. 11x11½

1687	A618	30h dl pur, gold & bl	20	6
1688	A618	30h dl grn, gold & red	20	6

No. 1687 commemorates the 25th anniversary of the Prague uprising and No. 1688 the 25th anniversary of the liberation of Czechoslovakia from the Germans.

Prague Castle Art Type of 1969

Designs: No. 1689, Bust of St. Vitus, 1486. No. 1690, Hermes and Athena, by Bartholomy Springer (1546–1611), mural from White Tower.

1970, May 7 Engr. *Perf. 11½*

1689	A605	3k mar & multi	1.75	1.50
1690	A605	3k lt bl & multi	1.75	1.50

Issued to publicize art treasures of the Castle of Prague.

Compass Rose, U.N. Headquarters and Famous Buildings of the World
A619

Engraved and Photogravure

1970, June 26 *Perf. 11*

1691	A619	1k blk & multi	45	30

Issued to commemorate the 25th anniversary of the United Nations. Issued in sheets of 15 (3x5) and 5 labels showing U.N. emblem.

Cannon from 30 Years' War and Baron Munchhausen
A620

Historical Cannons: 60h, Cannon from Hussite war and St. Barbara. 1.20k, Cannon from Prussian-Austrian war, and legendary cannoneer Javurek. 1.80k, Early 20th century cannon and spaceship "La Colombiad" (Jules Verne). 2.40k, World War I cannon and "Good Soldier Schweik."

1970, Aug. 31 *Perf. 11½*

1692	A620	30h blk & multi	9	3
1693	A620	60h blk & multi	18	5
1694	A620	1.20k blk & multi	36	10
1695	A620	1.80k blk & multi	75	22
1696	A620	2.40k blk & multi	*1.75*	*75*
		Nos. 1692-1696 (5)	*3.13*	*1.15*

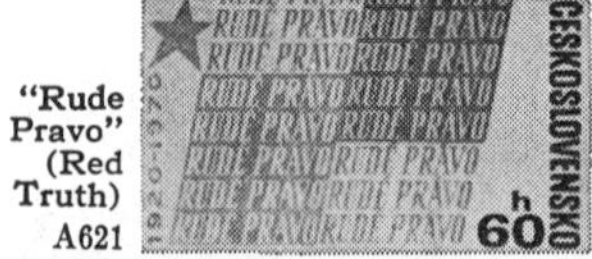

"Rude Pravo" (Red Truth)
A621

1970, Sept. 21 *Perf. 11½x11*

1697	A621	60h car gold & blk	25	5

Issued to commemorate the 50th anniversary of the Rude Pravo newspaper.

"Great Sun" House Sign and Old Town Tower Bridge, Prague
A622

Designs: 60h, "Blue Lion" and Town Hall Tower, Brno. 1k, Gothic corner stone and Town Hall Tower, Bratislava. 1.40k, Coat of Arms and Gothic Tower, Bratislava, and medallion. 1.60k, Moravian Eagle and Gothic Town Hall Tower, Brno. 1.80k, "Black Sun" and "Green Frog" house signs and New Town Hall, Prague.

Engr. & Photo.

1970, Sept. 23 *Perf. 11x11½*

1698	A622	40h blk & multi	12	6
1699	A622	60h blk & multi	18	10
1700	A622	1k blk & multi	35	16
1701	A622	1.40k blk & multi	*1.50*	*75*
1702	A622	1.60k blk & multi	60	24
1703	A622	1.80k blk & multi	75	28
		Nos. 1698-1703 (6)	*3.50*	*1.59*

Germany–Uruguay Semifinal Soccer Match—A623

Designs: 20h, Sundisk Games' emblem and flags of participating nations. 60h, England-Czechoslovakia match and coats of arms. 1k, Romania-Czechoslovakia match and coats of arms. 1.20k, Brazil-Italy, final match and emblems. 1.80k, Brazil-Czechoslovakia match and emblems.

1970, Oct. 29 *Perf. 11½*

1704	A623	20h blk & multi	6	3
1705	A623	40h blk & multi	12	4
1706	A623	60h blk & multi	18	5
1707	A623	1k blk & multi	40	6
1708	A623	1.20k blk & multi	45	15
1709	A623	1.80k blk & multi	*1.50*	*55*
		Nos. 1704-1709 (6)	*2.71*	*88*

Issued to commemorate the 9th World Soccer Championships for the Jules Rimet Cup, Mexico City, May 30–June 21.

Congress Emblem
A624

1970, Nov. 9 Engr. & Photo.

1710	A624	30h blk, gold, ultra & red	30	3

Congress of the Czechoslovak Socialist Youth Federation.

Painting Type of 1967

Paintings: 1k, Seated Mother, by Mikulas Galanda. 1.20k, Bridesmaid, by Karel Svolinsky. 1.40k, Walk by Night, 1944, by Frantisek Hudecek. 1.80k, Banska Bystrica Market, by Dominik Skutecky. 2.40k, Adoration of the Kings, from the Vysehrad Codex, 1085.

1970, Nov. 27 Engr. *Perf. 11½*

1711	A565	1k multi	40	35
1712	A565	1.20k multi	55	50
1713	A565	1.40k multi	75	65
1714	A565	1.80k multi	1.00	80
1715	A565	2.40k multi	*2.50*	*2.25*
		Nos. 1711-1715 (5)	*5.20*	*4.55*

Sheets of 4.

Radar
A625

Designs: 40h, Interkosmos 3, geophysical satellite. 60h, Molniya meteorological satellite. 1k, Astronaut and Vostok satellite. No. 1720, Interkosmos 4, solar research satellite. No. 1720A, Space satellite (Sputnik) over city. 1.60k, Two-stage rocket on launching pad.

Engraved and Photogravure

1970–71 *Perf. 11*

1716	A625	20h blk & multi	15	3
1717	A625	40h blk & multi	15	4
1718	A625	60h blk & multi	20	5
1719	A625	1k blk & multi	40	6
1720	A625	1.20k blk & multi	50	15
1720A	A625	1.20k blk & multi ('71)	55	15
1721	A625	1.60k blk & multi	*1.25*	*50*
		Nos. 1716-1721 (7)	*3.20*	*98*

Issued to publicize "Interkosmos," the collaboration of communist countries in various phases of space research. Issue dates: No. 1720A, Nov. 15, 1971; others, Nov. 30, 1970.

Face of Christ on Veronica's Veil
A626

Slovak Ikons, 16th–18th Centuries: 60h, Adam and Eve in the Garden (vert.). 2k, St. George and the Dragon. 2.80k, St. Michael (vert.).

1970, Dec. 17 Engraved *Perf. 11½*

Cream Paper

1722	A626	60h multi	25	22
1723	A626	1k multi	40	35
1724	A626	2k multi	80	70
1725	A626	2.80k multi	*2.50*	*2.25*

Sheets of 4.

Carrier Pigeon Type of 1920
A627

Engr. & Photo.

1970, Dec. 18 *Perf. 11x11½*

1726	A627	1k red, blk & yel grn	45	40

Stamp Day.

Song of the Barricades, 1938, by Karel Stika
A628

Designs (Czech and Slovak Graphic Art): 50h, Fruit Grower's Barge, 1941, by Cyril Bouda. 60h, Moon (woman) Searching for Lilies of the Valley, 1913, by Jan Zrzavy. 1k, At the Edge of Town (working man and woman), 1931, by Koloman Sokol. 1.60k, Summer, 1641, by Vaclav Hollar. 2k, Gamekeeper and Shepherd of Orava Castle, 1847, by Peter M. Bohun.

Engraved (40h, 60h, 1k); Engraved and Photogravure (others)

1971, Jan. 28 *Perf. 11½*

1727	A628	40h brown	12	6
1728	A628	50h blk & multi	15	8
1729	A628	60h slate	18	10
1730	A628	1k black	40	16
1731	A628	1.60k blk & buff	65	24
1732	A628	2k blk & multi	*1.75*	*50*
		Nos. 1727-1732 (6)	*3.25*	*1.14*

Saris Church A629 Bell Tower, Hronsek—A630

Designs: 1k, Roofs and folk art, Horácko. 2.40k, House, Jicinsko. 3k, House and folk art, Cechy-Melnicko. 3.60k, Chrudimsko Church. 5k, Watch Tower, Cesky-Nachod. 5.40k, Baroque house, Posumavi. 6k, Cottage, Orava. 9k, Cottage, Turnovsko. 10k, Old houses, Liptov. 14k, House and wayside bell stand. 20k, Houses, Slovensko-Cicmany.

Perf. 11½x11, 11x11½

1971–72 Engr. and Photo.

1733	A630	1k blk & multi	40	4
1734	A629	1.60k blk, dk grn & vio	65	6
1735	A630	2k blk & multi	80	4
1736	A629	2.40k blk & multi	95	6
1736A	A630	3k blk & multi ('72)	1.20	8
1737	A629	3.60k blk & multi	1.50	6
1737A	A630	5k blk & multi ('72)	1.75	12
1738	A629	5.40k blk & multi	1.75	6
1739	A630	6k blk & multi	2.10	9
1740	A630	9k blk & multi	3.00	30
1740A	A629	10k blk & multi ('72)	3.75	30
1741	A629	14k blk & multi	5.00	25
1741A	A629	20k blk & multi ('72)	7.50	90
		Nos. 1733-1741A (13)	30.35	2.36

Nos. 1736A, 1738, 1740 are horizontal.

Coat of Arms Type of 1968

1971, Feb. 26 *Perf. 11½*

Multicolored

1742	A590	60h *Zilina*	25	8
1743	A590	60h *Levoca*	25	8
1744	A590	60h *Ceska Trebova*	25	8
1745	A590	60h *Uhersky Brod*	25	8
1746	A590	60h *Trutnov*	25	8
1747	A590	60h *Karltovy*	25	8
		Nos. 1742-1747 (6)	1.50	48

"Fight of the Communards and Rise of the International"—A631

Design: No. 1749, World fight against racial discrimination, and "UNESCO."

1971, March 18 *Perf. 11*

1748	A631	1k multi	50	25
1749	A631	1k multi	50	25

No. 1748 commemorates the centenary of the Paris Commune. No. 1749 publicizes the Year against Racial Discrimination. Issued in sheets of 15 stamps and 5 labels.

Edelweiss, Mountaineering Map and Equipment
A632

Engraved and Photogravure

1971, Apr. 27 *Perf. 11½x11*

1750	A632	30h multi	20	3

50th anniversary of Slovak Alpine Club.

Singer
A633

1971, Apr. 27 *Perf. 11½*

1751	A633	30h multi	20	3

50th anniversary of Slovak Teachers' Choir.

Abbess' Crosier, 16th Century
A634

Design: No. 1753, Allegory of Music, 16th century mural.

1971, May 9

1752	A634	3k gold & multi	1.75	1.60
1753	A634	3k blk, dk brn & buff	1.75	1.60

Art treasures of the Castle of Prague. Sheets of 4. See also Nos. 1817-1818, 1884-1885, 1937-1938, 2040-2041, 2081-2082, 2114-2115, 2176-2177, 2238-2239, 2329-2330.

Lenin
A635

Designs: 40h, Hammer and sickle allegory. 60h, Raised fists. 1k, Star, hammer and sickle.

1971, May 14 *Perf. 11*

1754	A635	30h blk, red & gold	15	3
1755	A635	40h blk, ultra, red & gold	20	4
1756	A635	60h blk, ultra, red & gold	30	5
1757	A635	1k blk, ultra, red & gold	55	10

50th anniversary of the Czechoslovak Communist Party.

Star, Hammer-Sickle Emblems
A636

Design: 60h, Hammer-sickle emblem, fist and people (vert.).

Perf. 11½x11, 11x11½

1971, May 24 Engr. & Photo.

1758	A636	30h blk, red, gold & yel	15	3
1759	A636	60h blk, red, gold & bl	30	8

14th Congress of Communist Party of Czechoslovakia.

Ring-necked Pheasant
A637

Designs: 60h, Rainbow trout. 80h, Mouflon. 1k, Chamois. 2k, Stag. 2.60k, Wild boar.

1971, Aug. 17 *Perf. 11½x11*

1760	A637	20h org & multi	6	4
1761	A637	60h lt bl & multi	18	6
1762	A637	80h yel & multi	24	6
1763	A637	1k lt grn & multi	30	10
1764	A637	2k lil & multi	75	30
1765	A637	2.60k bis & multi	*3.00*	*1.00*
		Nos. 1760-1765 (6)	*4.53*	*1.56*

World Hunting Exhibition, Budapest, Aug. 27–30.

Diesel Locomotive
A638

Gymnasts and Banners
A639

1971, Sept. 2 *Perf. 11x11½*

1766	A638	30h lt bl, blk & red	9	3

Centenary of CKD, Prague Machine Foundry.

1971, Sept. 2 *Perf. 11½x11*

1767	A639	30h red brn, gold & ultra	9	3

50th anniversary of Workers' Physical Exercise Federation.

Road Intersections and Bridge
A640

1971, Sept. 2 Engr. & Photo.

1768	A640	1k blk, gold, red & bl	45	20

14th World Highways and Bridges Congress. Sheets of 25 stamps and 25 labels printed se-tenant with continuous design.

Chinese Fairytale, by Eva Bednarova
A641

Designs: 1k, Tiger and other animals, by Mirko Hanak. 1.60k, The Miraculous Bamboo Shoot, by Yasuo Segawa (horiz.).

Perf. 11½x11, 11x11½

1971, Sept. 10

1769	A641	60h multi	30	10
1770	A641	1k multi	60	20
1771	A641	1.60k multi	1.40	60

Bratislava BIB 71 biennial exhibition of illustrations for children's books.

Apothecary Jars and Coltsfoot
A642

Designs: 60h, Jars and dog rose. 1k, Scales and adonis vernalis. 1.20k, Mortars and valerian. 1.80k, Retorts and chicory. 2.40k, Mill, mortar and henbane.

1971, Sept. 20 *Perf. 11½x11*

Yellow Paper

1772	A642	30h multi	9	5
1773	A642	60h multi	18	8
1774	A642	1k multi	35	12
1775	A642	1.20k multi	50	16
1776	A642	1.80k multi	85	30
1777	A642	2.40k multi	*1.60*	*50*
		Nos. 1772-1777 (6)	*3.57*	*1.21*

International Pharmaceutical Congress.

Painting Type of 1967

Paintings: 1k, "Waiting" (woman's head), 1967, by Imro Weiner-Král. 1.20k, Resurrection, by Master of Vyssi Brod, 14th century. 1.40k, Woman with Pitcher, by Milos Bazovsky. 1.80k, Veruna Cudova (in folk costume), by Josef Mánes. 2.40k, Detail from "Feast of the Rose Garlands," by Albrecht Dürer.

1971, Nov. 27 *Perf. 11½*

1779	A565	1k multi	40	35
1780	A565	1.20k multi	50	45
1781	A565	1.40k multi	60	55
1782	A565	1.80k multi	90	80
1783	A565	2.40k multi	*2.25*	*2.00*
		Nos. 1779-1783 (5)	*4.65*	*4.15*

Sheets of 4.

Workers Revolt in Krompachy, by Julius Nemcik—A643

1971, Nov. 28 *Perf. 11x11½*

1784	A643	60h multi	35	10

History of the Czechoslovak Communist Party.

Wooden Dolls and Birds
A644

Folk Art and UNICEF Emblem: 80h, Jug handles, carved. 1k, Horseback rider. 1.60k, Shepherd carrying lamb. 2k, Easter eggs and rattle. 3k, "Zbojnik," folk hero.

1971, Dec. 11 *Perf. 11½*

1785	A644	60h multi	25	5
1786	A644	80h multi	35	8
1787	A644	1k multi	50	12
1788	A644	1.60k multi	75	20
1789	A644	2k multi	1.50	55
1790	A644	3k multi	2.25	75
		Nos. 1785-1790 (6)	5.60	1.75

25th anniversary of the United Nations International Children's Fund (UNICEF).

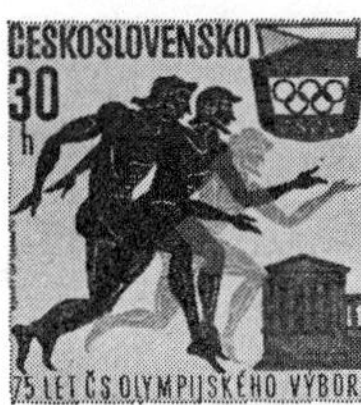

Runners, Parthenon, Czechoslovak Olympic Emblem
A645

Designs: 40h, Women's high jump, Olympic emblem and plan for Prague Stadium. 1.60k, Cross-country skiers, Sapporo '72 emblem and ski jump in High Tatras. 2.60k, Discus thrower, Discobolus and St. Vitus Cathedral.

1971, Dec. 16 Engr. & Photo.

1791	A645	30h multi	10	6
1792	A645	40h multi	13	9
1793	A645	1.60k multi	60	45
1794	A645	2.60k multi	1.50	60

75th anniversary of Czechoslovak Olympic Committee (30h, 2.60k); 20th Summer Olympic Games, Munich, Aug. 26–Sept. 10, 1972 (40h); 11th Winter Olympic Games, Sapporo, Japan, Feb. 3–13, 1972 (1.60k).

Post Horns and Lion—A646

1971, Dec. 17 *Perf. 11x11½*

1795	A646	1k blk, gold, car & bl	55	30

Stamp Day.

Figure Skating
A647

"Ležáky"
A648

Designs (Olympic Emblems and): 50h, Ski jump. 1k, Ice hockey. 1.60k, Sledding, women's.

1972, Jan. 13 *Perf. 11½*

1796	A647	40h pur, org & red	13	8
1797	A647	50h dk bl, org & red	17	8
1798	A647	1k mag, org & red	40	18
1799	A647	1.60k bl grn, org & red	*1.50*	*50*

11th Winter Olympic Games, Sapporo, Japan, Feb. 3–13.

1972, Feb. 16 Engr. & Photo.

Designs: No. 1801, Boy's head behind barbed wire (horiz.). No. 1802, Hand rising from ruins. No. 1803, Soldier and banner (horiz.).

1800	A648	30h blk, dl org & red	15	3
1801	A648	30h blk & brn org	15	3
1802	A648	60h blk, yel & red	25	5
1803	A648	60h sl grn & multi	25	5

30th anniversary of: destruction of Ležáky (No. 1800) and Lidice (1802); Terezin concentration camp (No. 1801); Czechoslovak Army unit in Russia (No. 1803).

Book Year Emblem
A649

Steam and Diesel Locomotives
A650

1972, Mar. 17 *Perf. 11½x11*

1804	A649	1k blk & org brn	40	10

International Book Year 1972.

1972, Mar. 17 *Perf. 11½x11*

1805 A650 30h multi 25 3

Centenary of the Kosice-Bohumin railroad.

"Pasture," by Vojtech Sedlacek
A651

Designs: 50h, Dressage, by Frantisek Tichy. 60th, Otakara Kubina, by Vaclav Fiala. 1k, The Three Kings, by Ernest Zmetak. 1.60k, Woman Dressing, by Ludovit Fulla.

Photogravure and Engraved

1972, Mar. 27 *Perf. 11½x11*

1806 A651 40h multi 13 5
1807 A651 50h multi 17 6
1808 A651 60h multi 30 8
1809 A651 1k multi 45 20
1810 A651 1.60k multi *1.40* *1.25*
Nos. 1806-1810 (5) *2.45* *1.64*

Czech and Slovak graphic art. 1.60k issued in sheets of 4. See also Nos. 1859–1862, 1921–1924.

Ice Hockey
A652

Design: 1k, Two players.

1972, Apr. 7 *Perf. 11*

1811 A652 60h blk & multi 20 7
1812 A652 1k blk & multi 40 20

World and European Ice Hockey Championships, Prague.

Bicycling, Olympic Rings and Emblem
A653

1972, Apr. 7 **Multicolored**

1813 A653 50h *shown* 20 6
1814 A653 1.60k *Diving* 60 15
1815 A653 1.80k *Canoeing* 75 20
1816 A653 2k *Gymnast* *1.50* *75*

20th Olympic Games, Munich, Aug. 26–Sept. 11.

Prague Castle Art Type of 1971

Designs: No. 1817, Adam and Eve, column capital, St. Vitus Cathedral. No. 1818, Czech coat of arms (lion), c. 1500.

1972, May 9 *Perf. 11½*

1817 A634 3k blk & multi *3.00* *2.50*
1818 A634 3k blk, red, sil & gold 1.75 1.50

Art treasures of Castle of Prague. Sheets of 4.

Andrej Sladkovic (1820–1872), Poet
A654

Portraits: No. 1820, Janko Kral (1822–1876), poet. No. 1821, Ludmilla Podjavorinska (1872–1951), writer. No. 1822, Antonin Hudecek (1872–1941), painter. No. 1823, Frantisek Bilek (1872–1941), sculptor. No. 1824, Jan Preisler (1872–1918), painter.

Engraved and Photogravure

1972, June 14 *Perf. 11*

1819 A654 40h pur, ol & bl 20 8
1820 A654 40h dk grn, bl & yel 20 8
1821 A654 40h blk & multi 20 8
1822 A654 40h brn, grn & bl 20 8
1823 A654 40h choc, grn & org 20 8
1824 A654 40h grn, sl & dp org 20 8
Nos. 1819-1824 (6) 1.20 48

Men with Banners
A655

1972, June 14 *Perf. 11x11½*

1825 A655 30h dk vio bl, red & yel 10 3

8th Trade Union Congress, Prague.

Art Forms of Wire
A656

Ornamental Wirework: 60h, Plane and rosette. 80h, Four-headed dragon and ornament. 1k, Locomotive and loops. 2.60k, Tray and owl.

1972, Aug. 28 *Perf. 11½x11*

1826 A656 20h sal & multi 7 5
1827 A656 60h multi 20 8
1828 A656 80h pink & multi 30 10
1829 A656 1k multi 40 18
1830 A656 2.60k rose & multi *1.75* *60*
Nos. 1826-1830 (5) *2.72* *1.01*

"Jiskra"
A657

Engraved and Photogravure

1972, Sept. 27 *Perf. 11½x11*

Size: 40x22mm.

Multicolored Design on Blue Paper

1831 A657 50h *shown* 17 5
1832 A657 60h *"Mir"* 20 5
1833 A657 80h *"Republika"* 26 6

Size: 48x29mm.

Perf. 11x11½

1834 A657 1k *"Kosice"* 33 10
1835 A657 1.60k *"Dukla"* 53 16
1836 A657 2k *"Kladno"* *2.00* *85*
Nos. 1831-1836 (6) *3.49* *1.27*

Czechoslovak sea-going vessels.

Hussar, 18th Century Tile
A658

1972, Oct. 24 *Perf. 11½x11*

Multicolored

1837 A658 30h *shown* 10 6
1838 A658 60h *Janissary* 20 8
1839 A658 80h *St. Martin* 30 10
1840 A658 1.60k *St. George* 75 15
1841 A658 1.80k *Nobleman's guard* 95 20
1842 A658 2.20k *Slovakian horseman* *2.00* *1.00*
Nos. 1837-1842 (6) *4.30* *1.59*

Horsemen from 18th–19th century tiles or enamel paintings on glass.

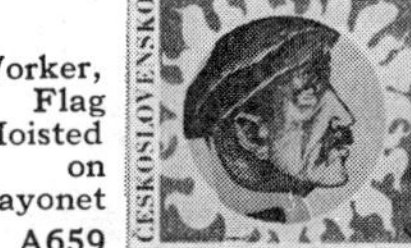

Worker, Flag Hoisted on Bayonet
A659

Star, Hammer and Sickle
A660

1972, Nov. 7 *Perf. 11x11½*

1843 A659 30h gold & multi 12 6
1844 A660 60h rose car & gold 24 8

55th anniversary of the Russian October Revolution (30h); 50th anniversary of the Soviet Union (60h).

Nos. 1811–1812 Overprinted in Violet Blue or Black

CSSR

MAJSTROM

SVETA

1972 *Perf. 11*

1845 A652 60h multi (VBl) 7.50 7.50
1846 A652 1k multi (Bk) 7.50 7.50

Czechoslovakia's victorious ice hockey team. The overprint on the 60h is in Czech and reads ČSSR/MISTREM/SVĚTA; the overprint on the 1k (shown) is in Slovak.

Painting Type of 1967

Designs: 1k, "Nosegay" (nudes and flowers), by Max Svabinsky. 1.20k, Struggle of St. Ladislas with Kuman nomad, anonymous, 14th century. 1.40k, Lady with Fur Hat, by Vaclav Hollar. 1.80k, Midsummer Night's Dream, 1962, by Josef Liesler. 2.40k, Pablo Picasso, self-portrait.

1972, Nov. 27 **Photo. & Engr.**

1847 A565 1k multi 45 40
1848 A565 1.20k multi 60 55
1849 A565 1.40k blk & cr 90 80
1850 A565 1.80k multi 1.10 1.00
1851 A565 2.40k multi *3.00* *2.75*
Nos. 1847-1851 (5) *6.05* *5.50*

Sheets of 4.

Goldfinch
A661

Songbirds: 60h, Warbler feeding young cuckoo. 80h, Cuckoo. 1k, Black-billed magpie. 1.60k, Bullfinch. 3k, Song thrush.

1972, Dec. 15

Size: 30x48½mm.

1852 A661 60h yel & multi 24 10
1853 A661 80h multi 32 14
1854 A661 1k lt bl & multi 40 16

Engraved

Size: 30x23mm.

1855 A661 1.60k multi 75 12
1856 A661 2k multi 95 30
1857 A661 3k multi *2.50* *90*
Nos. 1852-1857 (6) *5.16* *1.72*

Post Horn and Allegory—A662

1972, Dec. 18 **Photo. & Engr.**

1858 A662 1k blk, red lil & gold 50 45

Stamp Day.

Art Type of 1972

1973, Jan. 25 *Perf. 11½x11*

Designs: 30h, Flowers in Window, by Jaroslav Grus. 60h, Quest for Happiness, by Josef Balaz. 1.60k, Balloon, by Kamil Lhotak. 1.80k, Woman with Viola, by Richard Wiesner.

1859 A651 30h multi 12 5
1860 A651 60h multi 24 10
1861 A651 1.60k multi 64 15
1862 A651 1.80k multi *1.50* *70*

Czech and Slovak graphic art.

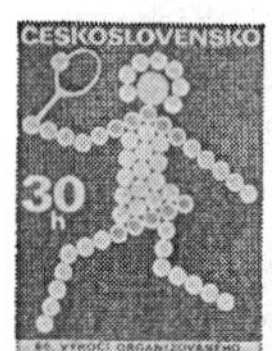

Tennis Player
A663

Figure Skater
A664

Torch and Star
A665

1973, Feb. 22 *Perf. 11*

1863 A663 30h vio & multi 12 5
1864 A664 60h blk & multi 24 10
1865 A665 1k multi 40 18

80th anniversary of the tennis organization in Czechoslovakia (30h); World figure skating championships, Bratislava (60h); 3rd summer army Spartakiad of socialist countries (1k).

Star and Factories
A666

Workers' Militia, Emblem and Flag
A667

1973, Feb. 23 Photo. & Engr.

1866	A666	30h multi	12	5
1867	A667	60h multi	24	10

25th anniversary of the Communist revolution in Czechoslovakia and of the Militia.

Capt. Jan Nalepka, Major Antonin Sochor and Laurel—A668

Designs (Torch and): 40h, Evzen Rosicky, Mirko Nespor and ivy leaves. 60h, Vlado Clementis, Karol Smidke and linden leaves. 80h, Jan Osoha, Josef Molak and oak leaves. 1k, Marie Kuderikova, Jozka Jaburkova and rose. 1.60k, Vaclav Sinkule, Eduard Urx and palm leaf.

1973, Mar. 20 *Perf. 11½x11*

Yellow Paper

1868	A668	30h blk, ver & gold	12	5
1869	A668	40h blk, ver & grn	16	7
1870	A668	60h blk, ver & gold	24	10
1871	A668	80h blk, ver & gold	32	14
1872	A668	1k blk, ver & grn	45	18
1873	A668	1.60k blk, ver & sil	*1.00*	*28*
		Nos. 1868-1873 (6)	*2.29*	*82*

Fighters against and victims of Fascism and Nazism during German Occupation.

Virgil I. Grissom, Edward H. White, Roger B. Chaffee—A669

Designs: 20h, Soviet planetary station "Vebera." 30h, "Intercosmos" station. 40h, Lunokhod on moon. 3.60k, Vladimir M. Komarov, Georgi T. Dobrovolsky, Vladislav N. Volkov, Victor I. Patsayev. 5k, Yuri A. Gagarin.

Photogravure and Engraved

1973, Apr. 12 *Perf. 11½x11*

Size: 40x22mm.

1874	A669	20h multi	8	3
1875	A669	30h multi	12	5
1876	A669	40h multi	16	7

Engraved *Perf. 11½*

Size: 49x30mm.

1877	A669	3k multi	1.35	75
1878	A669	3.60k multi	2.25	1.50
1879	A669	5k multi	*4.00*	*3.50*
		Nos. 1874-1879 (6)	*7.96*	*5.90*

In memory of American and Russian astronauts.

Radio
A670

Telephone and Map of Czechoslovakia
A671

Television
A672

1973, May 1 *Perf. 11½x11*

1880	A670	30h blk & multi	12	5
1881	A671	30h lt bl, pink & blk	12	5
1882	A672	30h dp bl & multi	12	5

Czechoslovak anniversaries: 50 years of broadcasting (No. 1880); 20 years of telephone service to all communities (No. 1881); 20 years of television (No. 1882).

Coat of Arms and Linden Branch
A673

1973, May 9 *Perf. 11x11½*

1883	A673	60h red & multi	24	10

25th anniversary of the Constitution of May 9.

Prague Castle Art Type of 1971

Designs: No. 1884, Royal Legate, 14th century. No. 1885, Seal of King Charles IV, 1351.

1973, May 9 *Perf. 11½*

1884	A634	3k bl & multi	1.75	1.75
1885	A634	3k gold, grn & dk brn	1.50	1.50

Art treasures of Castle of Prague. Sheets of 4.

Coat of Arms Type of 1968

1973, June 20

Multicolored

1886	A590	60h *Mikulov*	24	15
1887	A590	60h *Zlutice*	24	15
1888	A590	60h *Smolenice*	24	15

Coats of arms of Czechoslovakian cities.

Heraldic Colors of Olomouc and Moravia
A674

Anthurium
A675

1973, Aug. 23 Photo. & Engr.

1889	A674	30h multi	15	8

400th anniversary of University of Olomouc.

1973, Aug. 23 *Perf. 11½*

Sizes: 60h, 1k, 2k, 30x50mm.; 1.60k, 1.80k, 3.60k, 23x39mm.

Multicolored

1890	A675	60h *Tulips*	30	25
1891	A675	1k *Rose*	40	35
1892	A675	1.60k *shown*	70	35
1893	A675	1.80k *Iris*	90	75
1894	A675	2k *Chrysanthemum*	*2.50*	*2.25*
1895	A675	3.60k *Cymbidium*	1.60	1.35
		Nos. 1890-1895 (6)	*6.40*	*5.30*

Flower Show, Olomouc, Aug. 18–Sept. 2. 60h, 1k, 2k issued in sheets of 4, others in sheets of 10.

Irish Setter
A676

Designs: Hunting dogs.

1973, Sept. 5

Multicolored

1896	A676	20h *shown*	7	3
1897	A676	30h *Czech terrier*	12	5
1898	A676	40h *Bavarian hunting dog*	20	7
1899	A676	60h *German pointer*	35	12
1900	A676	1k *Cocker spaniel*	50	20
1901	A676	1.60k *Dachshund*	*1.50*	*35*
		Nos. 1896-1901 (6)	*2.74*	*82*

50th anniversary of the Czechoslovak United Hunting Organization.

St. John, the Baptist, by Svabinsky
A677

Works by Max Svabinsky: 60h, "August Noon" (woman). 80h, "Marriage of True Minds" (artist and muse). 1k, "Paradise Sonata I" (Adam dreaming of Eve). 2.60k, Last Judgment, stained glass window, St. Vitus Cathedral.

1973, Sept. 17 Litho. & Engr.

1902	A677	20h blk & pale grn	7	5
1903	A677	60h blk & buff	24	12

Engraved

1904	A677	80h black	45	28
1905	A677	1k sl grn	60	50
1906	A677	2.60k multi	*2.25*	*2.00*
		Nos. 1902-1906 (5)	*3.61*	*2.95*

Centenary of the birth of Max Svabinsky (1873–1962), artist and stamp designer. 20h and 60h issued in sheets of 25; 80h and 1k se-tenant in sheets of 4 checkerwise; 2.60k in sheets of 4.

Trade Union Emblem
A678

1973, Oct. 15 Photo. & Engr.

1907	A678	1k red, bl & yel	45	18

8th Congress of the World Federation of Trade Unions, Varna, Bulgaria.

Painting Type of 1967

Designs: 1k, Boy from Martinique, by Antonin Pelc. 1.20k, "Fortitude" (mountaineer), by Martin Benka. 1.80k, Rembrandt, self-portrait. 2k, Pierrot, by Bohumil Kubista. 2.40k, Ilona Kubinyiova, by Peter M. Bohun. 3.60k, Virgin and Child (Veveri Madonna), c. 1350.

Photogravure and Engraved

1973, Nov. 27 *Perf. 11½*

1908	A565	1k multi, vio bl inscriptions	*1.75*	*1.60*
a.		1k multi, blk inscriptions	*5.00*	*4.50*
1909	A565	1.20k multi	*2.00*	*1.75*
1910	A565	1.80k multi	75	65
1911	A565	2k multi	80	70
1912	A565	2.40k multi	96	85
1913	A565	3.60k multi	1.45	1.30
		Nos. 1908-1913 (6)	*7.71*	*6.85*

Sheets of 4. Nos. 1910–1913 printed se-tenant with gold and black inscription on gutter.

Central background bluish gray on No. 1908, light bluish green on No. 1908a.

Postilion—A679

1973, Dec. 18

1914	A679	1k gold & multi	45	30

Stamp Day 1974 and 55th anniversary of Czechoslovak postage stamps. Printed with 2 labels showing telephone and telegraph.

"CSSR"
A680

Friedrich Smetana
A681

Pablo Neruda, Chilean Flag
A682

Comecon Building, Moscow
A683

1974, Jan. 1

1915	A680	30h red, gold & ultra	12	3

5th anniversary of Federal Government in the Czechoslovak Socialist Republic.

1974, Jan. 4 *Perf. 11x11½*

Design: No. 1917, Josef Suk.

1916	A681	60h blk, bl & yel	24	12
1917	A681	60h grn & multi	24	12
1918	A682	60h bl, blk & red	24	12

Sesquicentennial of the birth of Friedrich Smetana (1824–1884), composer; centenary of the birth of Josef Suk (1874–1935), composer, and in memory of Pablo Neruda (Neftali Ricardo Reyes, 1904–1973), Chilean poet.

1974, Jan. 23

1919	A683	1k gold, red & vio bl	40	16

25th anniversary of the Council of Mutual Economic Assistance (COMECON).

Symbols of Postal Service—A684

1974, Feb. 20 ***Perf. 11½***

1920	A684	3.60k multi	1.85	60

BRNO '74 National Stamp Exhibition, Brno, June 8–23.

Art Type of 1972

Designs: 60h, Tulips 1973, by Josef Broz. 1k, Structures 1961 (poppy and building), by Orest Dubay. 1.60k, Bird and flowers (Golden Sun-Glowing Day), by Adolf Zabransky. 1.80k, Artificial flowers, by Frantisek Gross.

1974, Feb. 21 ***Perf. 11½x11***

1921	A651	60h multi	24	10
1922	A651	1k multi	50	20
1923	A651	1.60k multi	75	24
1924	A651	1.80k multi	1.25	40

Czech and Slovak graphic art.

Oskar Benes and Vaclav Prochazka A685

Portraits: 40h, Milos Uher and Anton Sedlacek. 60h, Jan Hajecek and Marie Sedlackova. 80h, Jan Sverma and Albin Grznar. 1k, Jaroslav Neliba and Alois Hovorka. 1.60k, Ladislav Exnar and Ludovit Kukorelli.

Photogravure and Engraved

1974, Mar. 21 ***Perf. 11½x11***

1925	A685	30h ind & multi	12	3
1926	A685	40h ind & multi	16	6
1927	A685	60h ind & multi	24	8
1928	A685	80h ind & multi	32	10
1929	A685	1k ind & multi	40	14
1930	A685	1.60k ind & multi	1.00	35
		Nos. 1925-1930(6)	2.24	76

Partisan commanders and fighters.

"Water, the Source of Energy" A686

Symbolic Designs: 1k, Importance of water for agriculture. 1.20k, Study of the oceans. 1.60k, "Hydrological Decade." 2k, Struggle for unpolluted water.

1974, Apr. 25 **Engr.** ***Perf. 11½***

1931	A686	60h multi	24	24
1932	A686	1k multi	40	40
1933	A686	1.20k multi	60	60
1934	A686	1.60k multi	90	90
1935	A686	2k multi	1.25	1.20
		Nos. 1931-1935 (5)	3.39	3.34

Hydrological Decade (UNESCO), 1965–1974. Sheets of 4.

Allegory Holding "Molniya," and Ground Station A687

Sousaphone A688

1974, Apr. 30 **Photo. & Engr.**

1936	A687	30h vio bl & multi	20	6

"Intersputnik," first satellite communications ground station in Czechoslovakia.

Prague Castle Art Type of 1971

Designs: No. 1937, Golden Cock, 17th century locket. No. 1938, Glass monstrance, 1840.

1974, May 9 **Engr.** ***Perf. 11½***

1937	A634	3k gold & multi	1.75	1.60
1938	A634	3k blk & multi	1.75	1.60

Art treasures of Castle of Prague. Sheets of 4.

Photogravure and Engraved

1974, May 12 ***Perf. 11x11½***

Multicolored

1939	A688	20h *shown*	8	4
1940	A688	30h *Bagpipe*	12	8
1941	A688	40h *Violin, by Martin Benka*	16	12
1942	A688	1k *Pyramid piano*	40	18
1943	A688	1.60k *Tenor quinton, 1754*	90	30
		Nos. 1939-1943 (5)	1.66	72

Prague and Bratislava Music Festivals. The 1.60k also commemorates 25th anniversary of Slovak Philharmonic Orchestra.

Child A689

Photogravure and Engraved

1974, June 1 ***Perf. 11½***

1944	A689	60h multi	30	12

Children's Day. Design is from illustration for children's book by Adolf Zabransky.

Globe, People and Exhibition Emblems A690

Design: 6k, Rays and emblems symbolizing "Oneness and Mutuality."

1974, June 1

1945	A690	30h multi	12	6
1946	A690	6k multi	2.75	1.20

BRNO 74 National Stamp Exhibition, Brno, June 8–23. Sheets of 16 stamps and 14 labels.

Resistance Fighter A691

Actress Holding Tragedy and Comedy Masks A692

Photogravure and Engraved

1974, Aug. 29 ***Perf. 11½***

1947	A691	30h multi	12	6

Slovak National Uprising, 30th anniversary.

1974, Aug. 29

1948	A692	30h red, sil & blk	12	6

Bratislava Academy of Music and Drama, 25th anniversary.

Slovak Girl with Flower A693

1974, Aug. 29

1949	A693	30h multi	12	6

SLUK, Slovak folksong and dance ensemble, 25th anniversary.

Hero and Leander A694

Design: 2.40k, Hero watching Leander swim the Hellespont. No. 1952, Leander reaching shore. No. 1953, Hero mourning over Leander's body. No. 1954, Hermione, Leander's sister. No. 1955, Mourning Cupid. Designs are from 17th century English tapestries in Bratislava Council Palace.

1974–76 **Photo. & Engr.**

1950	A694	2k multi	1.70	1.50
1951	A694	2.40k multi	1.70	1.50
1952	A694	3k multi	1.75	1.50
1953	A694	3k multi	1.75	1.60
1954	A694	3.60k multi	2.00	1.75
1955	A694	3.60k multi	1.60	1.40
		Nos. 1950-1955 (6)	10.50	9.25

Issue dates: Nos. 1950–1951, Sept. 25, 1974. Nos. 1952, 1954, Aug. 29, 1975. Nos. 1953, 1955, May 9, 1976.

Soldier Standing Guard, Target, 1840 A695

Painted Folk-art Targets: 60h, Landscape with Pierrot and flags, 1828. 1k, Diana crowning champion marksman, 1832. 1.60k, Still life with guitar, 1839. 2.40k, Salvo and stag in flight, 1834. 3k, Turk and giraffe, 1831.

1974, Sept. 26 ***Perf. 11½***

Size: 30x50mm.

1956	A695	30h blk & multi	12	6
1957	A695	60h blk & multi	24	12
1958	A695	1k blk & multi	40	20

Engraved ***Perf. 12***

Size: 40x50mm.

1959	A695	1.60k grn & multi	80	55
1960	A695	2.40k sep & multi	1.25	1.00
1961	A695	3k multi	1.75	1.50
		Nos. 1956-1961 (6)	4.56	3.43

UPU Emblem and Postilion—A696

Designs (UPU Emblem and): 40h, Mail coach. 60h, Railroad mail coach, 1851. 80h, Early mail truck. 1k, Czechoslovak Airlines mail plane. 1.60k, Radar.

Photogravure and Engraved

1974, Oct. 9 ***Perf. 11½***

1962	A696	30h multi	12	6
1963	A696	40h multi	16	8
1964	A696	60h multi	24	12
1965	A696	80h multi	35	16
1966	A696	1k multi	45	20
1967	A696	1.60k multi	80	32
		Nos. 1962-1967 (6)	2.12	94

Centenary of Universal Postal Union.

Post Horn, Old Town Bridge Tower A697

Sealed Letter A698

Stylized Bird A699

ČESKOSLOVENSKO h PSČ 30

Postal Code Symbol A699a

Designs: 40h, Postilion. No. 1971, Carrier pigeon. No. 1979, Map of Czechoslovakia with postal code numbers.

Photogravure and Engraved

1974, Oct. 31 ***Perf. 11½x11***

1968	A697	20h multi	8	5
1969	A698	30h brn, bl & red	12	5
1970	A697	40h multi	16	5
1971	A698	60h bl, yel & red	24	5

Coil Stamps

1975–76 **Photogravure** ***Perf. 14***

1976	A699	30h brt bl	10	3
1977	A699	60h carmine	20	3
1978	A699a	30h emer ('76)	10	3
1979	A699a	60h scar ('76)	20	3

Nos. 1976–1979 have black control number on back of every fifth stamp.

Ludvik Kuba, Self-portrait, 1941
A700

Paintings: 1.20k, Violinist Frantisek Ondricek, by Vaclav Brozik. 1.60k, Vase with Flowers, by Otakar Kubin. 1.80k, Woman with Pitcher, by Janko Alexy. 2.40k, Bacchanalia, c. 1635, by Karel Skreta.

1974, Nov. 27 Engraved Perf. 11½

1980	A700	1k multi	40	40
1981	A700	1.20k multi	60	48
1982	A700	1.60k multi	80	70
1983	A700	1.80k multi	1.00	90
1984	A700	2.40k multi	1.25	1.00
		Nos. 1980-1984 (5)	4.05	3.48

Czech and Slovak art. Sheets of 4.
See Nos. 2209-2211.

Post Horn—A701

Photogravure and Engraved

1974, Dec. 18 Perf. 11x11½

1985	A701	1k multi	50	30

Stamp Day.

Still-life with Hare, by Hollar
A702

Designs: 1k, The Lion and the Mouse, by Vaclav Hollar. 1.60k, Deer Hunt, by Philip Galle. 1.80k, Grand Hunt, by Jacques Callot.

Lithographed and Engraved

1975, Feb. 26 Perf. 11½x11

1988	A702	60h blk & buff	24	6
1989	A702	1k blk & buff	40	10
1990	A702	1.60k blk & yel	75	30
1991	A702	1.80k blk & buff	1.00	60

Hunting scenes from old engravings.

Guns Pointing at Family
A703

Young Woman and Globe
A704

Designs: 1k, Women and building on fire. 1.20k, People and roses. All designs include names of destroyed villages.

Photogravure and Engraved

1975, Feb. 26 Perf. 11

1992	A703	60h multi	30	6
1993	A703	1k multi	50	15
1994	A703	1.20k multi	48	18

Destruction of 14 villages by the Nazis, 30th anniversary.

1975, Mar. 7 Perf. 11½x11

1995	A704	30h red & multi	15	3

International Women's Year 1975.

Little Queens, Moravian Folk Custom
A705

Folk Customs: 1k, Straw masks (animal heads and blackened faces), Slovak. 1.40k, The Tale of Maid Dorothea (executioner, girl, king and devil). 2k, Drowning of Morena, symbol of death and winter.

1975, Mar. 26 Engr. Perf. 11½

1996	A705	60h blk & multi	60	25
1997	A705	1k blk & multi	50	45
1998	A705	1.40k blk & multi	60	55
1999	A705	2k blk & multi	1.00	90

Sheets of four.

Coat of Arms Type of 1968

Photogravure & Engraved

1975, Apr. 17 Perf. 11½

Multicolored

2000	A590	60h *Nymburk*	24	8
2001	A590	60h *Znojmo*	24	8

Coats of arms of Czechoslovakian cities.

Czech May Uprising—A706

Liberation by Soviet Army—A707

Czechoslovak-Russian Friendship—A708

1975, May 9 Photo. & Engr.

2002	A706	1k multi	40	15

Engraved

2003	A707	1k multi	40	15

Photogravure and Engraved

2004	A708	1k multi	40	15

30th anniversary of the May uprising of the Czech people and of liberation by the Soviet Army; 5th anniversary of the Czechoslovak-Soviet Treaty of Friendship, Cooperation and Mutual Aid.

Adolescents' Exercises—A709

Designs: 60h, Children's exercises. 1k, Men's and women's exercises.

Photogravure and Engraved

1975, June 15 Perf. 12x11½

2005	A709	30h lil & multi	12	3
2006	A709	60h multi	26	8
2007	A709	1k vio & multi	44	15

Spartakiad 1975, Prague, June 26–29. Nos. 2005–2007 each issued in sheets of 30 stamps and 40 labels, showing different Spartakiad emblems.

Datrioides Microlepis and Sea Horse—A710

Tropical Fish (Aquarium): 1k, Beta splendens regan and pterophyllum scalare. 1.20k, Carassius auratus. 1.60k, Amphiprion percula and chaetodon sp. 2k, Pomacanthodes semicirculatus, pomocanthus maculosus and paracanthorus hepatus.

1975, June 27 Perf. 11½

2008	A710	60h multi	26	8
2009	A710	1k multi	50	10
2010	A710	1.20k multi	65	25
2011	A710	1.60k multi	95	45
2012	A710	2k multi	1.10	50
		Nos. 2008-2012 (5)	3.46	1.38

Pelicans, by Nikita Charushin
A711

Book Illustrations: 30h, The Dreamer, by Lieselotte Schwarz. 40h, Hero on horseback, by Val Muntenau. 60h, Peacock, by Klaus Ensikat. 80h, Man on horseback, by Robert Dubravec.

1975, Sept. 5

2013	A711	20h multi	10	6
2014	A711	30h multi	12	8
2015	A711	40h multi	15	10
2016	A711	60h multi	26	12
2017	A711	80h multi	40	20
		Nos. 2013-2017 (5)	1.03	56

Bratislava BIB 75 biennial exhibition of illustrations for children's books.

Nos. 2013–2017 issued in sheets of 25 stamps and 15 labels with designs and inscriptions in various languages.

Strakonice, 1951
A712

Designs: Motorcycles.

Photogravure and Engraved

1975, Sept. 29 Perf. 11½

Multicolored

2018	A712	20h *shown*	8	3
2019	A712	40h *Jawa 250, 1945*	15	5
2020	A712	60h *Jawa 175, 1935*	24	8
2021	A712	1k *ITAR, 1921*	44	25
2022	A712	1.20k *ORION, 1903*	65	30
2023	A712	1.80k *Laurin & Klement, 1898*	90	35
		Nos. 2018-2023 (6)	2.46	1.06

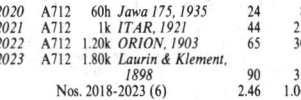

Study of Short-wave Solar Radiation
A713

Soyuz-Apollo Link-up in Space
A714

Designs: 60h, Study of aurora borealis and Oréol satellite. 1k, Study of ionosphere and cosmic radiation. 2k, Copernicus, radio map of the sun and satellite.

1975, Sept. 30

2024	A713	30h multi	12	5
2025	A713	60h yel, rose red & vio	24	8
2026	A713	1k bl, yel & vio	44	20
2027	A713	2k red, vio & yel	1.00	50

Engraved

2028	A714	5k vio & multi	2.75	2.50
		Nos. 2024-2028 (5)	4.55	3.33

International cooperation in space research. No. 2028 issued in sheets of 4.

The design of No. 2026 appears to be inverted.

Slovnaft, Petrochemical Plant—A715

Designs: 60h, Atomic power station. 1k, Construction of Prague subway. 1.20k, Construction of Friendship pipeline. 1.40k, Combine harvesters. 1.60k, Apartment house construction.

1975, Oct. 28 Photo. & Engr.

2029	A715	30h multi	12	5
2030	A715	60h multi	24	8
2031	A715	1k multi	44	10
2032	A715	1.20k multi	65	12
2033	A715	1.40k multi	70	30
2034	A715	1.60k multi	90	35
		Nos. 2029-2034 (6)	3.05	1.00

Socialist construction, 30th anniversary. Nos. 2029–2034 printed se-tenant with labels.

Pres. Gustav Husak
A716

1975, Oct. 28 Engraved

2035	A716	30h ultra	12	3
2036	A716	60h rose red	24	3

Prague Castle Art Type of 1971

Designs: 3k, Gold earring, 9th century. 3.60k, Arms of Premysl Dynasty and Bohemia from lid of leather case containing Bohemian crown, 14th century.

1975, Oct. 29

2040	A634	3k blk, grn, pur & gold	1.60	1.40
2041	A634	3.60k red & multi	1.75	1.50

Art treasures of Castle of Prague. Sheets of 4.

Miniature Sheet

Ludvik Svoboda, Road Map, Buzuluk to Prague, Carnations—A717

1975, Nov. 25

2042	A717	10k multi	15.00	15.00

Pres. Ludvik Svoboda, 80th birthday. Size of No. 2042: 75x95mm. (stamp size: 40x55mm.).

Exists imperf., price $50.

Art Type of 1967

Paintings: 1k, "May 1975" (Woman and doves for 30th anniversary of peace), by Zdenek Sklenar. 1.40k, Woman in national costume, by Eugen Nevan. 1.80k, "Liberation of Prague," by Alena Cermakova (horiz.). 2.40k, "Fire 1938" (woman raising fist), by Josef Capek. 3.40k, Old Prague, 1828, by Vincenc Morstadt.

1975, Nov. 27 Engr. *Perf. 11½*

2043	A565	1k blk, buff & brn	44	40
2044	A565	1.40k multi	70	60
2045	A565	1.80k multi	1.00	80
2046	A565	2.40k multi	1.25	1.00
2047	A565	3.40k multi	1.70	1.70
		Nos. 2043-2047 (5)	5.09	4.50

Sheets of 4.

Carrier Pigeon—A718

Photogravure and Engraved

1975, Dec. 18 *Perf. 11½*

2048	A718	1k red & multi	50	20

Stamp Day 1975.

Frantisek Halas A719

Wilhelm Pieck A720

Frantisek Lexa A721

Jindrich Jindrich A722

Ivan Krasko A723

Photogravure and Engraved

1976, Feb. 25 *Perf. 11½*

2049	A719	60h multi	24	8
2050	A720	60h multi	24	8
2051	A721	60h multi	24	8
2052	A722	60h multi	24	8
2053	A723	60h multi	24	8
		Nos. 2049-2053 (5)	1.20	40

Anniversaries: Frantisek Halas (1901–1949), poet (No. 2049); Wilhelm Pieck (1876–1960), president of German Democratic Republic (No. 2050); Frantisek Lexa (1876–1960), professor of Egyptology (No. 2051); Jindrich Jindrich (1876–1967), composer and writer (No. 2052); Ivan Krasko (1876–1958), Slovak poet (No. 2053). No. 2051 printed in sheets of 10, others in sheets of 50.

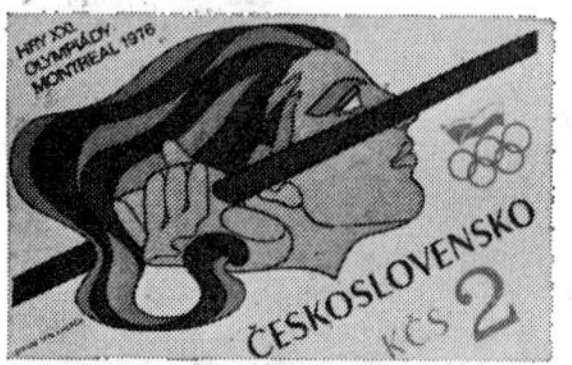

Ski Jump, Olympic Emblem A724

Designs (Winter Olympic Games Emblem and): 1.40k, Figure skating, women's. 1.60k, Ice hockey.

Photogravure and Engraved

1976, Mar. 22 *Perf. 12x11½*

2054	A724	1k gold & multi	44	15
2055	A724	1.40k gold & multi	60	25
2056	A724	1.60k gold & multi	70	30

12th Winter Olympic Games, Innsbruck, Austria, Feb. 4–15.

Javelin and Olympic Rings—A725

Designs (Olympic Rings and): 3k, Relay race. 3.60k, Shot put.

1976, Mar. 22 *Perf. 11½*

2057	A725	2k multi	90	35
2058	A725	3k multi	1.30	50
2059	A725	3.60k multi	1.60	60

21st Olympic Games, Montreal, Canada, July 17–Aug. 1.

Table Tennis A726

1976, Mar. 22 *Perf. 11x12*

2060	A726	1k multi	44	20

European Table Tennis Championship, Prague, Mar. 26–Apr. 4.

Symbolic of Communist Party A727

Worker, Derrick, Emblem A728

1976, Apr. 12 *Perf. 11x12*

2061	A727	30h gold & multi	12	4
2062	A728	60h gold & multi	24	8

15th Congress of the Communist Party of Czechoslovakia.

Radio Prague Orchestra A729

Dancer, Violin, Tragic Mask A730

Actors A731

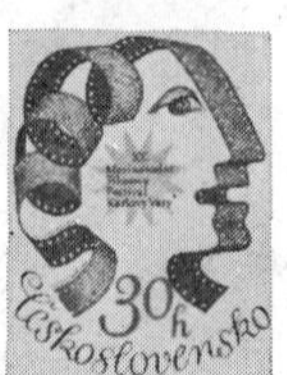

Folk Dancers A732

Film Festival—A733

1976, Apr. 26 *Perf. 11½*

2063	A729	20h gold & multi	8	3
2064	A730	20h pink & multi	8	3
2065	A731	20h lt bl & multi	8	3
2066	A732	30h blk & multi	12	4
2067	A733	30h vio bl, rose & grn	12	4
		Nos. 2063-2067 (5)	48	17

Commemorating: Czechoslovak Radio Symphony Orchestra, Prague, 50th anniversary (No. 2063); Academy of Music and Dramatic Art, Prague, 50th anniversary (No. 2064); Nova Scena Theater Company, Bratislava, 30th anniversary (No. 2065); International Folk Song and Dance Festival, Straznice, 30th anniversary (No. 2066); 20th International Film Festival, Karlovy Vary (No. 2067).

Hammer and Sickle

A734 A735

Design: 6k, Hammer and sickle (horiz.).

1976, May 14

2068	A734	30h gold, red & dk bl	20	4
2069	A735	60h gold, red & dp car	45	15

Souvenir Sheet

2070	A735	6k red & multi	2.60	2.60

Czechoslovak Communist Party, 55th anniversary. No. 2070 contains one stamp (50x30mm.); violet blue marginal inscription and gold emblem. Size: 99x90mm.

Ships in Storm, by Frans Huys (1522–1562) A736

Old Engravings of Ships: 60h, by Václav Hollar (1607–1677). 1k, by Regnier Nooms Zeeman (1623–1668). 2k, by François Chereau (1680–1729).

Photogravure and Engraved

1976, July 21 *Perf. 11x11½*

2071	A736	40h buff & blk	16	6
2072	A736	60h gray, buff & blk	24	8
2073	A736	1k lt grn, buff & blk	44	15
2074	A736	2k lt bl, buff & blk	88	35

"UNESCO" A737

1976, July 30 *Perf. 11½*

2075	A737	2k gray & multi	88	45

30th anniversary of UNESCO. Sheets of 10.

Souvenir Sheet

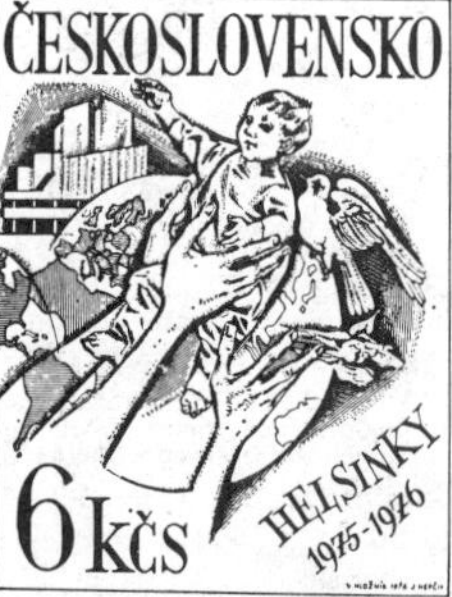

Hands Holding Infant, Globe and Dove A738

1976, July 30

2076	A738	6k, sheet of 2, multi	10.00	10.00

European Security and Cooperation Conference, Helsinki, Finland, 2nd anniversary. No. 2076 contains 2 stamps, marginal inscription and ornamental designs in blue and black. Size: 115x165mm.

Merino Ram A739

Couple Smoking, WHO Emblem and Skull A740

Designs: 40h, Bern-Hana milk cow. 1.60k, Kladruby stallion Generalissimus XXVII.

Photogravure and Engraved

1976, Aug. 28 ***Perf. 11½x12***

2077	A739	30h multi	12	4
2078	A739	40h multi	16	5
2079	A739	1.60k multi	70	25

Bountiful Earth Exhibition, Ceske Budejovice, Aug. 28–Sept. 12.

1976, Sept. 7 ***Perf. 12x11½***

2080	A740	2k multi	88	50

Fight against smoking, World Health Organization drive against drug addiction. Printed in sheets of 10 (2x5) with WHO emblems and inscription in margin.

Prague Castle Art Type of 1971

Designs: 3k, View of Prague Castle, by F. Hoogenberghe, 1572. 3.60k, Faun and Satyr, sculptured panel, 16th century.

1976, Oct. 22 **Engr.** ***Perf. 11½***

2081	A634	3k multi	1.30	1.15
2082	A634	3.60k multi	1.55	1.40

Art treasures of Castle of Prague.

Guernica 1937, by Imro Weiner-Kral A741

1976, Oct. 22

2083	A741	5k multi	2.25	90

40th anniversary of the International Brigade in Spain.

Zebras A472

Designs: 20h, Elephants (vert.). 30h, Cheetah. 40h, Giraffes (vert.). 60h, Rhinoceros. 3k, Bongos (vert.).

Photogravure and Engraved

Perf. 11½x11, 11x11½

1976, Nov. 3

2084	A742	10h multi	4	3
2085	A742	20h multi	8	3
2086	A742	30h multi	12	4
2087	A742	40h multi	16	5
2088	A742	60h multi	24	8
2089	A742	3k multi	1.30	45
		Nos. 2084-2089 (6)	1.94	68

African animals in Dvur Kralove Zoo.

Art Type of 1967

Paintings of Flowers: 1k, by Peter Matejka. 1.40k, by Cyril Bouda. 2k, by Jan Breughel. 3.60k, J. Rudolf Bys.

1976, Nov. 27 **Engr.** ***Perf. 11½***

2090	A565	1k multi	60	55
2091	A565	1.40k multi	85	80
2092	A565	2k multi	1.35	1.10
2093	A565	3.60k multi	2.00	1.85

Sheets of 4. Emblem and name of Praga 1978 on horizontal gutter.

Postrider, 17th Century, and Satellites—A743

1976, Dec. 18 **Photo. & Engr.**

2094	A743	1k multi	44	20

Stamp Day 1976.

Ice Hockey A744

Arms of Vranov A745

Designs: 1k, Biathlon. 1.60k, Ski jump. 2k, Downhill skiing.

Photogravure and Engraved

1977, Feb. 11 ***Perf. 11½***

2095	A744	60h multi	24	8
2096	A744	1k multi	44	12
2097	A744	1.60k multi	68	22
2098	A744	2k multi	88	35

6th Winter Spartakiad of Socialist Countries' Armies.

1977, Feb. 20

Designs: Coats of Arms of Czechoslovak towns.

Multicolored

2099	A745	60h *shown*	24	8
2100	A745	60h *Kralupy & Vltavou*	24	8
2101	A745	60h *Jicin*	24	8
2102	A745	60h *Valasske Mezirici*	24	8

See Nos. 2297-2300.

Window, Michna Palace A746

Prague Renaissance Windows: 30h, Michna Palace. 40h, Thun Palace. 60h, Archbishop's Palace, Hradcany. 5k, St. Nicholas Church.

1977, Mar. 10

2103	A746	20h multi	8	3
2104	A746	30h multi	12	4
2105	A746	40h multi	16	5
2106	A746	60h multi	24	8
2107	A746	5k multi	2.20	1.00
		Nos. 2103-2107 (5)	2.80	1.20

PRAGA 1978 International Philatelic Exhibition, Prague, Sept. 8–17, 1978.

Children, Auxiliary Police A747

Photogravure and Engraved

1977, Apr. 21 ***Perf. 11½***

2108	A747	60h multi	24	8

Auxiliary Police, 25th anniversary.

Warsaw, Polish Flag, Bicyclists A748

Congress Emblem A749

Designs: 60h, Berlin, DDR flag, bicyclists. 1k, Prague, Czechoslovakian flag, victorious bicyclist. 1.40k, Bicyclists on highways, modern views of Berlin, Prague and Warsaw.

1977, May 7

2109	A748	30h multi	12	4
2110	A748	60h multi	30	15
2111	A748	1k multi	44	15
2112	A748	1.40k multi	60	30

30th International Bicycle Peace Race Warsaw-Prague-Berlin.

Photogravure and Engraved

1977, May 25 ***Perf. 11½***

2113	A749	30h car, red & gold	12	4

9th Trade Union Congress, Prague 1977.

Prague Castle Art Type of 1971

Designs: 3k, Onyx footed bowl, 1350. 3.60k, Bronze horse, 1619.

1977, June 7 **Engraved**

2114	A634	3k multi	1.30	1.20
2115	A634	3.60k multi	1.60	1.50

Art treasures of Castle of Prague. Sheets of 4.

French Postrider, 19th Century, PRAGA '78 Emblem A750

Postal Uniforms: 1k, Austrian, 1838. 2k, Austrian, late 18th century. 3.60k, Germany, early 18th century.

1977, June 8 **Photo. & Engr.**

2116	A750	60h multi	24	8
2117	A750	1k multi	44	15
2118	A750	2k multi	88	30
2119	A750	3.60k multi	1.50	65

PRAGA 1978 International Philatelic Exhibition, Prague, Sept. 8–17, 1978.

Nos. 2116–2119 issued in sheets of 50 and sheets of 4 with 4 labels and horizontal gutter.

Coffeepots, Porcelain Mark A751

Mlada Boleslav Costume A752

Czechoslovak Porcelain and Porcelain Marks: 30h, Urn. 40h, Vase. 60h, Cup and saucer, jugs. 1k, Candlestick and plate. 3k, Cup and saucer, coffeepot.

1977, June 15

2120	A751	20h multi	8	3
2121	A751	30h multi	12	4
2122	A751	40h multi	16	6
2123	A751	60h multi	24	8
2124	A751	1k multi	44	15
2125	A751	3k multi	1.30	45
		Nos. 2120-2125 (6)	2.34	81

1977, Aug. 31 **Engraved** ***Perf. 11½***

PRAGA Emblem and Folk Costumes from: 1.60k, Vazek. 3.60k, Zavadka. 5k, Belkovice.

2126	A752	1k multi	44	40
2127	A752	1.60k multi	68	60
2128	A752	3.60k multi	1.55	1.40
2129	A752	5k multi	2.20	2.00

Issued in sheets of 10 and in sheets of 8 plus 2 labels showing PRAGA '78 emblem.

Old Woman, Devil and Spinner, by Viera Bombova A753

Book Illustrations: 60h, Bear and tiger, by Genadij Pavlisin. 1k, Coach drawn by 4 horses (Hans Christian Andersen), by Ulf Lovgren. 2k, Bear and flamingos (Lewis Carroll), by Nicole Claveloux. 3k, King with keys, and toys, by Jiri Trnka.

1977, Sept. 9 **Photo. & Engr.**

2130	A753	40h multi	16	6
2131	A753	60h multi	24	8
2132	A753	1k multi	44	15
2133	A753	2k multi	88	30
2134	A753	3k multi	1.30	45
		Nos. 2130-2134 (5)	3.02	1.04

Prize-winning designs, 6th biennial exhibition of illustrations for children's books, Bratislava.

Globe, Violin, Doves, View of Prague A754

Photogravure and Engraved

1977, Sept. 28 ***Perf. 11½***

2135	A754	60h multi	24	8

Congress of International Music Council of UNESCO, Prague and Bratislava.

Souvenir Sheets

"For a Europe of Peace" A755

Designs: 1.60k, "For a Europe of Co-operation." 2.40k, "For a Europe of Social Progress."

1977, Oct. 3 **Multicolored**

2136	A755	60h, Sheet of 2	55	50
2137	A755	1.60k, Sheet of 2	1.50	1.35
2138	A755	2.40k, Sheet of 2	2.25	2.00

2nd European Security and Cooperation Conference, Belgrade. Nos. 2136–2138 each contain 2 stamps and 2 blue on buff inscriptions and ornaments. Size: 130x 80mm.

S. P. Koroljov, Sputnik I Emblem
A756

Sailors, Cruiser Aurora
A757

Designs: 30h, Yuri A. Gagarin and Vostok I. 40h, Alexei Leonov. 1k, Neil A. Armstrong and footprint on moon. 1.60k, Construction of orbital space station.

1977, Oct. 4

2139	A756	20h multi	8	3
2140	A756	30h multi	12	5
2141	A756	40h multi	16	6
2142	A756	1k multi	44	15
2143	A756	1.60k multi	68	25
		Nos. 2139-2143 (5)	1.48	54

Space research, 20th anniversary of first earth satellite.

1977, Nov. 7

2144	A757	30h multi	12	4

60th anniversary of Russian October Revolution.

"Russia" Arms of USSR, Kremlin
A758

"Science"
A759

1977, Nov. 7

2145	A758	30h multi	12	4

55th anniversary of the Union of Soviet Socialist Republics (USSR).

1977, Nov. 17

2146	A759	3k multi	1.35	55

Czechoslovak Academy of Science, 25th anniversary.

Art Type of 1967

Paintings: 2k, "Fear" (woman), by Jan Murdoch. 2.40k, Jan Francisci, portrait by Peter M. Bohun. 2.60k, Vaclav Hollar, self-portrait, 1647. 3k, Young Woman, 1528, by Lucas Cranach. 5k, Cleopatra, by Rubens.

1977, Nov. 27 **Engr.** ***Perf. 11½***

2147	A565	2k multi	88	80
2148	A565	2.40k multi	1.00	90
2149	A565	2.60k multi	1.15	1.00
2150	A565	3k multi	1.30	1.15
2151	A565	5k multi	2.20	2.00
		Nos. 2147-2151 (5)	6.53	5.85

Sheets of 4.

View of Bratislava, by Georg Hoefnagel—A760

Design: 3.60k, Arms of Bratislava, 1436.

1977, Dec. 6

2152	A760	3k multi	1.30	1.15
2153	A760	3.60k multi	1.55	1.40

Sheets of 4. See Nos. 2174-2175, 2270-2271, 2331-2332, 2364-2365.

Stamp Pattern and Post Horn—A761

1977, Dec. 18 **Photo. & Engr.**

2154	A761	1k multi	45	15

Stamp Day.

Zdenek Nejedly
A762

Karl Marx
A763

Photogravure and Engraved

1978, Feb. 10 ***Perf. 11½***

2155	A762	30h multi	12	4
2156	A763	40h multi	16	6

Zdenek Nejedly (1878–1962), musicologist and historian; Karl Marx (1818–1883), political philosopher.

Civilians Greeting Guardsmen
A764

Intellectual, Farm Woman and Steel Worker, Flag—A765

1978, Feb. 25

2157	A764	1k gold & multi	45	15
2158	A765	1k gold & multi	45	15

30th anniversary of "Victorious February" (No. 2157), and National Front (No. 2158). See Note after 2190.

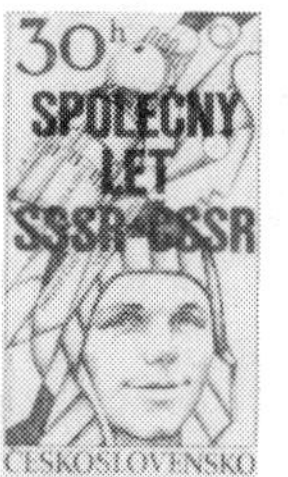

Yuri A. Gagarin and Vostok I
A766

10k Coin, 1964, and 25k Coin, 1965
A767

Design: 30h, 3.60k, like No. 2140.

Engr.; Overprint Photogravure (Blue and carmine on 30h, green and lilac rose on 3.60k)

1978, Mar. 2 ***Perf. 11½x12***

2159	A766	30h dk red	85	65
2160	A766	3.60k vio bl	8.50	6.50

Capt. V. Remek, first Czechoslovakian cosmonaut on Russian spaceship Soyuz 28, Mar. 2–9.

1978, Mar. 14 **Photo. & Engr.**

Designs: 40h, Medal for Culture, 1972. 1.40k, Charles University medal, 1948. 3k, Ferdinand I medal, 1568. 5k, Gold florin, 1335.

2161	A767	20h sil & multi	8	3
2162	A767	40h sil & multi	16	6
2163	A767	1.40k gold & multi	60	15
2164	A767	3k gold & multi	1.35	55
2165	A767	5k gold & multi	2.20	1.00
		Nos. 2161-2165 (5)	4.39	1.79

650th anniversary of Kremnica Mint.

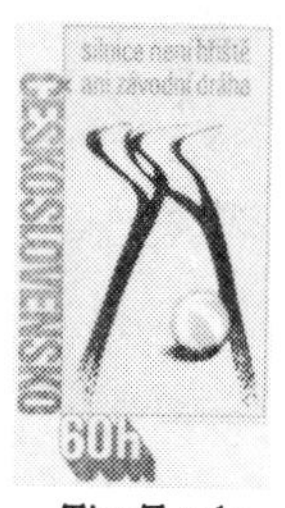

Tire Tracks and Ball
A768

Congress Emblem
A769

1978, Mar. 15

2166	A768	60h multi	24	8

Road safety.

Photogravure and Engraved

1978, Apr. 16 ***Perf. 11½***

2167	A769	1k multi	45	15

9th World Trade Union Congress, Prague 1978.

Shot Put and Praha '78 Emblem
A770

Designs: 1k, Pole vault. 3.60k, Women runners.

1978, Apr. 26

2168	A770	40h multi	16	6
2169	A770	1k multi	45	15
2170	A770	3.60k multi	1.55	38

5th European Athletic Championships, Prague 1978.

Ice Hockey—A771

Designs: 30h, Hockey. 2k, Ice hockey play.

1978, Apr. 26

2171	A771	30h multi	12	4
2172	A771	60h multi	25	15
2173	A771	2k multi	90	20

5th European Ice Hockey Championships and 70th anniversary of Bandy hockey.

Bratislava Type of 1977

Designs: 3k, Bratislava, 1955, by Orest Dubay. 3.60k, Fishpound Square, Bratislava, 1955, by Imro Weiner-Kral.

1978, May 9 **Engr.** ***Perf. 11½***

2174	A760	3k multi	1.30	1.15
2175	A760	3.60k multi	1.55	1.40

Sheets of 4.

Prague Castle Art Type of 1971

Designs: 3k, King Ottokar II, detail from tomb. 3.60k, Charles IV, detail from votiv panel by Jan Ocka.

1978, May 9

2176	A634	3k multi	1.30	1.15
2177	A634	3.60k multi	1.55	1.40

Art treasures of Castle of Prague. Sheets of 4.

Ministry of Post, Prague
A772

Photogravure and Engraved

1978, May 29 ***Perf. 12x11½***

2178	A772	60h multi	25	8

14th session of permanent COMECOM Commission (Ministers of Post and Telecommunications of Socialist Countries).

Palacky Bridge
A773

Prague Bridges and PRAGA '78 Emblem: 40h, Railroad bridge. 1k, Bridge of May 1. 2k, Manes Bridge. 3k, Svatopluk Cech Bridge. 5.40k, Charles Bridge.

1978, May 30

2179	A773	20h blk & multi	8	3
2180	A773	40h blk & multi	16	6
2181	A773	1k blk & multi	45	15
2182	A773	2k blk & multi	90	25
2183	A773	3k blk & multi	1.30	35
2184	A773	5.40k blk & multi	2.35	1.05
		Nos. 2179-2184 (6)	5.24	1.89

PRAGA 1978 International Philatelic Exhibition, Prague, Sept. 8–17.

St. Peter and Apostles, Clock Tower, and Emblem
A774

Town Hall Clock, Prague, by Josef Manes, and PRAGA '78 Emblem: 1k, Astronomical clock. 2k, Prague's coat of arms. 3k, Grape harvest (September). 3.60k, Libra. 10k, Arms surrounded by zodiac signs and scenes symbolic of 12 months (horiz.). 2k, 3k, 3.60k show details from design of 10k.

1978, June 20 *Perf. 11½x11*

2185	A774	40h multi	16	6
2186	A774	1k multi	45	15
2187	A774	2k multi	90	30
2188	A774	3k multi	1.30	35
2189	A774	3.60k multi	1.55	60
		Nos. 2185-2189 (5)	4.36	1.46

Souvenir Sheet

Perf. 12x12

2190	A774	10k multi	8.00	8.00

PRAGA'78 Intl. Philatelic Exhibition, Prague, Sept. 8-17. No. 1290 contains one stamp (50x40mm.): margin shows black clock tower, red inscription. Size: 90x125mm. Sheet exists imperf.

A non-valid souvenir sheet contains 4 imperf. copies of No. 2157. Blue marginal inscriptions, red PRAGA emblems. Sold only with PRAGA ticket.

Folk Dancers
A775

Photogravure and Engraved

1978, July 7 *Perf. 11½x12*

2191	A775	30h multi	12	5

25th Folklore Festival, Vychodna.

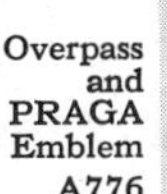

Overpass and PRAGA Emblem
A776

Designs (PRAGA Emblem and): 1k, 2k, Modern office buildings (diff.). 6k, Old and new Prague. 20k, Charles Bridge and Old Town, by Vincent Morstadt, 1828.

1978 *Perf. 12x11½*

2192	A776	60h blk & multi	25	8
2193	A776	1k blk & multi	45	15
2194	A776	2k blk & multi	90	30
2195	A776	6k blk & multi	2.60	75

Souvenir Sheet

Engraved

2196	A776	20k multi	9.50	9.00

PRAGA 1978 International Philatelic Exhibition, Prague, Sept. 8–17. No. 2196 also commemorates 60th anniversary of Czechoslovak postage stamps. Size of No. 2196: 95x76mm. (stamp 61x45mm.).

Issue dates: Nos. 2192–2195, Sept. 8; No. 2196, Sept. 10.

Souvenir Sheet

Apollo's Companion, by Titian
A777

Design: No. 2197b, King Midas. Stamps show details from "Apollo Flaying Marsya" by Titian.

1978, Sept. 12 *Perf. 11½*

2197		Sheet of 2	9.50	9.00
a.	A777	10k multi	4.50	4.00
b.	A777	10k multi	4.50	4.00

Titian (1488–1576), Venetian painter. Margin of No. 2197 shows painting from which stamp designs were taken, black inscription and red PRAGA emblem. Size: 109x165mm. No. 2197 with dark blue marginal inscription "FIP" was sold only with entrance ticket to PRAGA Philatelic Exhibition.

Exhibition Hall
A778

Photogravure and Engraved

1978, Sept. 13 *Perf. 11½x11*

2198	A778	30h multi	12	5

22nd International Engineering Fair, Brno.

Postal Newspaper Service
A779

TV Screen, Headquarters and Logo
A780

Newspaper, Microphone
A781

Photogravure and Engraved

1978, Sept. 21 *Perf. 11½*

2199	A779	30h multi	12	5
2200	A780	30h multi	12	5
2201	A781	30h multi	12	5

25th anniversaries: Postal News Service (No. 2199); Day of the Press (No. 2200); Broadcasting and Television Day (No. 2201).

Sulky Race
A782

Pardubice Steeplechase: 10h, Falling horses and jockeys at fence. 30h, Race. 40h, Horses passing post. 1.60k, Hurdling. 4.40k, Winner.

1978, Oct. 6 *Perf. 12x11½*

2202	A782	10h multi	4	3
2203	A782	20h multi	8	3
2204	A782	30h multi	12	5
2205	A782	40h multi	16	6
2206	A782	1.60k multi	70	25
2207	A782	4.40k multi	2.00	50
		Nos. 2202-2207 (6)	3.10	92

Woman Holding Arms of Czechoslovakia
A783

Photogravure and Engraved

1978, Oct. 28 *Perf. 11½*

2208	A783	60h multi	25	10

60th anniversary of independence.

Art Type of 1974

Paintings: 2.40k, Flowers, by Jakub Bohdan (1660–1724). 3k, The Dream of Salas, by Ludovit Fulla (1902–) (horiz.). 3.60k, Apostle with Censer, Master of the Spissko Capitals (c. 1480–1490).

1978, Nov. 27 **Engraved**

2209	A700	2.40k multi	1.05	90
2210	A700	3k multi	1.30	1.15
2211	A700	3.60k multi	1.60	1.40

Slovak National Gallery, 30th anniversary.

Musicians, by Jan Könyves
A784

Slovak Ceramics: 30h, Janosik on Horseback, by Jozef Franko. 40h, Woman in Folk Costume by Michal Polasko. 1k, Three Girls Singing, by Ignac Bizmayer. 1.60k, Janosik Dancing, by Ferdis Kostka.

Photogravure and Engraved

1978, Dec. 5 *Perf. 11½x12*

2212	A784	20h multi	8	3
2213	A784	30h multi	12	5
2214	A784	40k multi	16	6
2215	A784	1k multi	45	10
2216	A784	1.60k multi	70	18
		Nos. 2212-2216 (5)	1.51	42

Alfons Mucha and his Design for 1918 Issue—A785

1978, Dec. 18 *Perf. 11½*

2217	A785	1k multi	45	10

60th Stamp Day.

COMECON Building, Moscow
A786

Photogravure and Engraved

1979, Jan. 1 *Perf. 11½*

2218	A786	1k multi	45	10

Council for Mutual Economic Aid (COMECON), 30th anniversary.

Woman's Head and Grain
A787

Woman, Workers, Child, Doves
A788

1979, Jan. 1

2219	A787	30h multi	12	5
2220	A788	60h multi	25	8

Czechoslovakian Federation, 10th anniversary (30h); United Agricultural Production Association, 30th anniversary (60h).

Soyuz 28, Rockets and Capsule
A789

Designs: 60h, Astronauts Aleksei Gubarev and Vladimir Remek on launching pad (vert.). 1.60k, Soviet astronauts J. Romanenko and G. Grecko, Salyut 6 and recovery ship. 2k, Salyut-Soyuz orbital complex, post office in space and Czechoslovakia No. 2153. 4k, Soyuz 28, crew after landing and trajectory map (vert.). 10k, Gubarev and Remek, Intercosmos emblem, arms of Czechoslovakia and USSR.

1979, Mar. 2

2221	A789	30h multi	12	5
2222	A789	60h multi	25	8
2223	A789	1.60k multi	70	18
2224	A789	2k multi	90	20
2225	A789	4k multi	1.80	40
		Nos. 2221-2225 (5)	3.77	91

Souvenir Sheet

2226	A789	10k multi	5.00	3.00

First anniversary of joint Czechoslovak-Soviet space flight. Size of No. 2226: 76x93mm. (stamp 39x55mm.). No. 2226 exists imperf.

Alpine Bellflowers
A790

Stylized Satellite, Dial, Tape
A791

Mountain Flowers: 20h, Crocus. 30h, Pinks. 40h, Alpine hawkweed. 3k, Larkspur.

Photogravure and Engraved

1979, Mar. 23 *Perf. 11½*

2227	A790	10h multi	5	3
2228	A790	20h multi	8	3
2229	A790	30h multi	12	5
2230	A790	40h multi	16	6
2231	A790	3k multi	1.25	30
		Nos. 2227-2231 (5)	1.66	47

Mountain Rescue Service, 25th anniversary.

1979, Apr. 2

2232	A791	10h multi	5	3

Telecommunications research, 30th anniversary.

Artist and Model, Dove, Bratislava Castle—A792

Cog Wheels, Transformer and Student—A793

Musical Instruments, Bratislava Castle—A794

Pioneer Scarf, IYC Emblem—A795

Red Star, Man, Child and Doves A796

1979, Apr. 2

2233	A792	20h multi	8	3
2234	A793	20h multi	8	3
2235	A794	30h multi	12	5
2236	A795	30h multi	12	5
2237	A796	60h multi	25	10
		Nos. 2233-2237 (5)	65	26

Fine Arts Academy, Bratislava, 30th anniversary; Slovak Technical University, 40th anniversary; Radio Symphony Orchestra, Bratislava, 30th anniversary; Young Pioneers, 30th anniversary and International Year of the Child; Peace Movement, 30th anniversary.

Prague Castle Art Type of 1971

Designs: 3k, Burial crown of King Ottokar II. 3.60k, Portrait of Mrs. Reitmayer, by Karel Purkyne.

Photogravure and Engraved

1979, May 9 *Perf. 11½*

2238	A634	3k multi	1.25	1.10
2239	A634	3.60k multi	1.50	1.35

Arms of Vlachovo Brezi, 1538 A797

Animals in Heraldry: 60h, Jesenik, 1509 (bear and eagle). 1.20k, Vysoke Myto, 1471 (St. George slaying dragon). 1.80k, Martin, 1854 (St. Martin giving coat to beggar). 2k, Zebrak, 1674 (mythological beast).

1979, May 25 *Perf. 11½x12*

2240	A797	30h multi	12	5
2241	A797	60h multi	25	10
2242	A797	1.20k multi	50	20
2243	A797	1.80k multi	75	25
2244	A797	2k multi	85	25
		Nos. 2240-2244 (5)	2.47	85

Forest, Thriving and Destroyed A798

Designs: 1.80k, Water. 3.60k, City. 4k, Cattle. All designs show good and bad environment, separated by exclamation point; Man and Biosphere emblem.

1979, June 22 **Engr.** *Perf. 11½*

2245	A798	60h multi	25	10
2246	A798	1.80k multi	75	25
2247	A798	3.60k multi	1.50	50
2248	A798	4k multi	1.70	60

Man and Biosphere Program of UNESCO.

Blast Furnace A799

Photogravure and Engraved

1979, Aug. 29 *Perf. 11x11½*

2249	A799	30h multi	12	5

Slovak National Uprising, 35th anniversary.

Frog and Goat—A800

Book Illustrations (IYC Emblem and): 40h, Knight on horseback. 60h, Maidens. 1k, Boy with sled following rooster. 3k, King riding flying beast.

1979, Aug. 30 *Perf. 11½x11*

2250	A800	20h multi	8	3
2251	A800	40h multi	16	6
2252	A800	60h multi	25	10
2253	A800	1k multi	45	18
2254	A800	3k multi	1.25	45
		Nos. 2250-2254 (5)	2.19	82

Prize-winning designs, 7th biennial exhibition of illustrations for children's books, Bratislava; International Year of the Child. Printed with labels showing story characters.

"Bone Shaker" Bicycles, 1870—A801

1979, Sept. 14 *Perf. 12x11½*

Bicycles from: 20h, 1978. 40h, 1910. 60h, 1886. 3.60k, 1820.

2255	A801	20h multi	8	3
2256	A801	40h multi	16	6
2257	A801	60h multi	25	10
2258	A801	2k multi	90	30
2259	A801	3.60k multi	1.50	50
		Nos. 2255-2259 (5)	2.89	99

Bracket Clock, 18th Century—A802

Designs: 18th century clocks.

Photogravure and Engraved

1979, Oct. 1 *Perf. 11½*

2260	A802	40h multi	16	6
2261	A802	60h multi	25	10
2262	A802	80h multi	32	12
2263	A802	1k multi	45	15
2264	A802	2k multi	90	30
		Nos. 2260-2264 (5)	2.08	73

Art Type of 1967

Paintings: 1.60k, Sunday by the River, by Alois Moravec. 2k, Self-portrait, by Gustav Mally. 3k, Self-portrait, by Ilia Yefimovic Repin. 3.60k, Horseback Rider, by Jan Bauch. 5k, Dancing Peasants, by Albrecht Dürer.

1979, Nov. 27 **Engraved** *Perf. 12*

2265	A565	1.60k multi	72	24
2266	A565	2k multi	90	30
2267	A565	3k multi	1.35	45
2268	A565	3.60k multi	1.60	55
2269	A565	5k multi	2.25	75
		Nos. 2265-2269 (5)	6.82	2.29

Bratislava Type of 1977

Designs: 3k, Bratislava Castle on the Danube, by L. Janscha, 1787. 3.60k, Bratislava Castle, stone engraving by Wolf, 1815.

1979, Dec. 5

2270	A760	3k multi	1.35	45
2271	A760	3.60k multi	1.62	55

Stamp Day—A803

Engraved and Photogravure

1979, Dec. 18 *Perf. 11½×12*

2272	A803	1k multi	45	15

Numeral—A804

1979-80 **Photo.** *Perf. 11½×12*

2273	A804	50h red ('79)	22	8
2274	A804	1k brn ('79)	45	15
2275	A804	2k grn ('80)	90	30
2276	A804	3k lake ('80)	1.35	45

Runners and Dove—A805

1980, Jan. 29 Engr. & Photo. *Perf. 12x11½*

2289	A805	50h multi	22	8

50th International Peace Marathon, Kosice, Oct. 4.

Downhill Skiing—A806

1980, Jan. 29 *Perf. 11½x12*

2290	A806	1k *shown*	45	15
2291	A806	2k *Speed skating*	90	30
2292	A806	3k *Four-man bobsled*	1.35	45

13th Winter Olympic Games, Lake Placid, N.Y., Feb. 12-24.

Basketball—A807

1980, Jan. 29 *Perf. 11½*

2293	A807	40h *shown*	18	6
2294	A807	1k *Swimming*	45	15
2295	A807	2k *Hurdles*	90	30
2296	A807	3.60k *Fencing*	1.60	55

22nd Olympic Games, Moscow, July 19-Aug. 3.

Arms Type of 1977

1980, Feb. 20 **Photo. & Engr.** *Perf. 11½*

2297	A745	50h *Bystrice Nad Pernstejnem*	22	8
2298	A745	50h *Kunstat*	22	8
2299	A745	50h *Rozmital Pod Tremsinem*	22	8
2300	A745	50h *Zlata Idka*	22	8

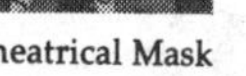

Theatrical Mask A808

Slovak National Theater, Actors A809

1980, Mar. 1

2301	A808	50h multi	22	8
2302	A809	1k multi	45	15

50th Jiraskuv Hronov Theatrical Ensemble Review; Slovak National Theater, Bratislava, 60th anniversary.

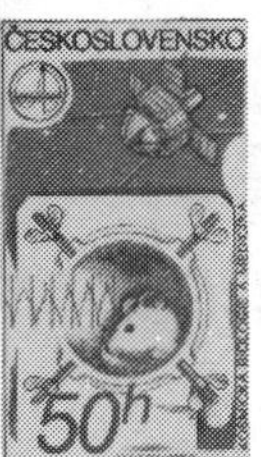
Mouse in Space, Satellite A810

Police Corps Banner, Emblem A811

Intercosmos: 1k, Weather map, satellite. 1.60k, Intersputnik television transmission. 4k, Camera, satellite. 5k, Czech satellite station, 1978 (horiz.). 10k, Intercosmos emblem (horiz.).

1980, Apr. 12 *Perf. 11½x12, 12x11½*

2303	A810	50h multi	22	8
2304	A810	1k multi	45	15
2305	A810	1.60k multi	72	22
2306	A810	4k multi	1.80	60
2307	A810	5k multi	2.25	75
		Nos. 2303-2307 (5)	5.44	1.80

Souvenir Sheet

2308	A810	10k multi	4.50	1.50

Intercosmos cooperative space program. No. 2308 has multicolored margin showing emblems, flags of participating countries. Size: 75½x94mm.

1980, Apr. 17 *Perf. 11½*

2309	A811	50h multi	22	8

National Police Corps, 35th anniversary.

Lenin's 110th Birth Anniversary—A812

Design: No. 2311, Engel's 160th birth anniversary.

1980, Apr. 22

2310	A812	1k tan & brn	45	15
2311	A812	1k lt grn & brn	45	15

Old and Modern Prague, Czech Flag, Bouquet—A813

Boy Writing "Peace"—A814

Pact Members' Flags, Dove—A815

Czech and Soviet Arms, Prague and Moscow Views—A816

1980, May 6 *Perf. 12x11½*

2312	A813	50h multi	22	8
2313	A814	1k multi	45	15
2314	A815	1k multi	45	15
2315	A816	1k multi	45	15

Liberation by Soviet army, 35th anniv.; Soviet victory in WWII, 35th anniv.; Signing of Warsaw Pact (Bulgaria, Czechoslovakia, German Democratic Rep., Hungary, Poland, Romania, USSR), 25th anniv.; Czechoslovak-Soviet Treaty of Friendship, Cooperation and Mutual Aid, 10th anniv.

Souvenir Sheet

United Nations, 35th Anniversary—A817

1980, June 3 **Engraved** *Perf. 12*

2316	A817	4k sheet of 2	3.75	3.00

No. 2316 contains 2 stamps, marginal inscription and symbols of peace and destruction. Size: 111x165½mm.

Athletes Parading Banners in Strahov Stadium, Prague, Spartakiad Emblem—A818

1980, June 3 Photo. & Engr. *Perf. 12x11½*

2317	A818	50h *shown*	22	8
2318	A818	1k *Gymnast*, vert.	45	15

Spartakiad 1980, Prague, June 26-29.

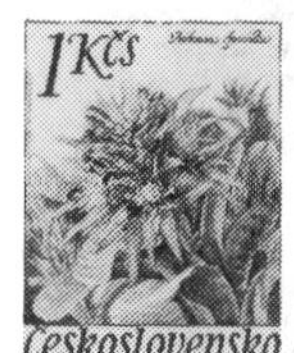
Aechmea Fasciata—A819

1980, Aug. 13 **Photo. & Engr.** *Perf. 12*

2319	A819	50h *Gerbera Jamesonii*	22	8
2320	A819	1k *Aechmea fasciata*	45	15
2321	A819	2k *Strelitzia reginae*	90	30
2322	A819	4k *Paphiopedilum*	1.80	60

Olomouc and Bratislava Flower Shows.

Chad Girl, Embroidery—A820

Designs: Folktale character embroideries.

Photogravure & Engraved

1980, Sept. 24 *Perf. 11½x12*

2323	A820	50h *shown*	22	8
2324	A820	1k *Punch and dog*	45	15
2325	A820	2k *Dandy and Posy*	90	30
2326	A820	4k *Lion and moon*	1.80	60
2327	A820	5k *Wallachian dance*	2.25	75
		Nos. 2323-2327 (5)	5.62	1.88

National Census—A821

Photogravure & Engraved

1980, Sept. 24 *Perf. 12x11½*

2328	A821	1k multi	45	15

Prague Castle Type of 1971

Designs: 3k, Old Palace gateway. 4k, Armorial lion, 16th century.

1980, Oct. 28 *Perf. 12*

2329	A634	3k multi	1.35	45
2330	A634	4k multi	1.80	60

Bratislava Type of 1977

Designs: 3k, View across the Danube, by J. Eder, 1810. 4k, The Old Royal Bridge, by J.A. Lantz, 1820.

1980, Oct. 28

2331	A760	3k multi	1.35	45
2332	A760	4k multi	1.80	60

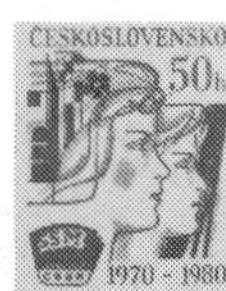
10th Anniversay of Socialist Youth Federation—A822

1980, Nov. 9 *Perf. 12x11½*

2333	A822	50h multi	22	8

No. 2137 Overprinted in Red: 3. / MEZINARODNI VELETRH ZNZMEK / ESSEN '80

1980, Nov. 18

2334	A755	1.60k multi	*15.00*	*15.00*

Czechoslovak Day / ESSEN '80, 3rd International Stamp Exhibition, No. 2334 has overprinted red marginal inscription.

Art Type of 1967

Designs: 1k, Pavel Jozef Safarik, by Jozef B. Klemens. 2k, Peasant Revolt mosaic, Anna Podzemma. 3k, St. Lucia, 14th century statue. 4k, Waste Heaps, by Jan Zrzavy (horiz.). 5k, Labor, sculpture by Jan Stursa.

1980, Nov. 27 **Engraved** *Perf. 12*

2335	A565	1k multi	45	15
2336	A565	2k multi	90	30
2337	A565	3k multi	1.35	45
2338	A565	4k multi	1.80	60
2339	A565	5k multi	2.25	75
		Nos. 2335-2339 (5)	6.75	2.25

Stamp Day—A823

Photogravure & Engraved

1980, Dec. 18 *Perf. 11½x12*

2340	A823	1k multi	45	15

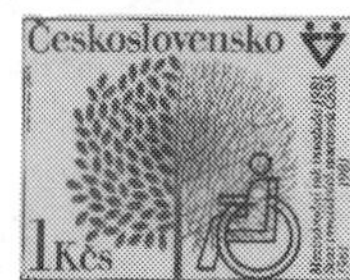
7th Five-year Plan, 1981-1985—A824

1981, Jan. 1 **Photo. & Engr.** *Perf. 11½*

2341	A824	50h multi	22	8

International Year of the Disabled—A825

1981, Feb. 24

2342	A825	1k multi	45	15

Landau, 1800—A826

1981, Feb. 25 *Perf. 12x11½*

2343	A826	50h shown	22	8
2344	A826	1k Mail coach, 1830	45	15
2345	A826	3.60k Mail sled, 1840	1.65	55
2346	A826	5k 4-horse mail coach, 1860	2.25	75
2347	A826	7k Open carriage, 1840	3.15	1.05
a.		Sheet of 4	13.00	5.00
		Nos. 2343-2347 (5)	7.72	2.58

WIPA '81 Intl. Philatelic Exhibition, Vienna, Austria, May 22-31. No. 2347a has multicolored margin showing exhibition emblems. Size: 150x106mm. Issued May 10.

Wolfgang Amadeus Mozart—A827

Famous Men: No. 2348, Joesph Hlavka (1831-1908). No. 2349, Juraj Hronec (1881-1959). No. 2350, Jan Sverma (1901-1944). No. 2351, Mikulas Schneider-Trnavsky (1881-1958). No. 2352, B. Bolzano (1781-1848). No. 2353, Dimitri Shostakovich (1906-1975), composer. No. 2354, George Bernard Shaw (1856-1950), playwright.

1981, Mar. 10 Photo. & Engr. *Perf. 11½*

2348	A827	50h multi	22	8
2349	A827	50h multi	22	8
2350	A827	50h multi	22	8
2351	A827	50h multi	22	8
2352	A827	1k multi	45	15
2353	A827	1k multi	45	15
2354	A827	1k multi	45	15
2355	A827	1k multi	45	15
		Nos. 2348-2355 (8)	2.68	92

Souvenir Sheet

Yuri Gagarin—A828

1981, Apr. 5 *Perf. 12*

2356		Sheet of 2	5.50	2.00
a.	A828 6k		2.70	90

20th anniversary of first manned space flight. Margin shows satellites orbiting earth, intercosmos emblem and flags. Size: 108½x166mm.

Workers and Banner—A829

1981, Apr. 6 *Perf. 12x11½*

2357	A829	50h shown	22	8
2358	A829	1k Hands holding banner	45	15
2359	A829	4k Worker holding banner, vert.	1.80	60

Czechoslovakian Communist Party, 60th anniversary.

Congress Emblem, View of Prague—A830

1981, Apr. 6

2360	A830	50h shown	22	8
2361	A830	1k Bratislava	45	15

16th Communist Party Congress.

Agriculture Museum, 90th Anniv.
A831

Natl. Assembly Elections
A832

1981, May 14 *Perf. 11½x12*

2362	A831	1k multi	45	15

1981, June 1

2363	A832	50h multi	22	8

Bratislava Type of 1977

Designs: 3k, Bratislava Castle, by G.B. Probst, 1760. 4k, Grassalkovic Palace, by C. Bschor, 1815.

1981, June 10 *Perf. 12*

2364	A760	3k multi	1.35	45
2365	A760	4k multi	1.80	60

Uran and Red October Hotels—A833

Successes of Socialist Achievements Exhibition: 1k, Brno-Bratislava Highway, Jihlava. 2k, Nuclear power station, Jaslovske Bohunice.

1981, June 10 *Perf. 12x11½*

2366	A833	80h multi	36	12
2367	A833	1k multi	45	15
2368	A833	2k multi	90	30

Border Defense Units, 30th Anniv.
A834

Civil Defense, 30th Anniv.
A835

Army Cooperation, 30th Anniv.—A836

Rysy Youth Mountain Climbing Contest—A837

1981, July 11 Photo. & Engr. *Perf. 11½*

2369	A834	40h multi	18	6
2370	A835	50h multi	22	8
2371	A836	1k multi	45	15
2372	A837	3.60k multi	1.65	55

30th Natl. Festival of Amateur Puppet Ensembles—A838

1981, July 2 Photo. & Engr. *Perf. 11½*

2373	A838	2k Punch and Devil	90	30

Souvenir Sheet

Guernica, by Pablo Picasso—A839

1981, July 2 Engr. *Perf. 11½x12*

2374	A839	10k multi	4.50	1.50

Picasso's birth centenary; 45th anniv. of Intl. Brigades in Spain. No. 2374 has multicolored margin showing Picasso drawings. Size: 90x76mm.

Cat Holding Flower, by Etienne Delessert—A840

8th Biennial Exhibition of Children's Book Illustrations (Designs by): 50h, Albin Brunovsky (vert.). 1k, Adolf Born. 2k, Vive Tolli. 10k, Suekichi Akaba.

1981, Sept. 5 Photo. & Engr. *Perf. 11½*

2375	A840	50h multi	22	8
2376	A840	1k multi	45	15
2377	A840	2k multi	90	30
2378	A840	4k multi	1.80	60
2379	A840	10k multi	4.50	1.50
		Nos. 2375-2379 (5)	7.87	2.63

Prague Zoo, 50th Anniv.—A841

1981, Sept. 28 Photo. & Engr. *Perf. 11½x12*

2380	A841	50h Gorillas	22	8
2381	A841	1k Lions	45	15
2382	A841	7k Przewalski's horses	3.15	1.05

Anti-smoking Campaign—A842

1981, Oct. 27 Photo. & Engr. *Perf. 12*

2383	A842	4k multi	1.80	60

No. 2383 se-tenant with label.

Prague Castle Type of 1971

Designs: 3k, Carved dragon, Palais Lobkovitz, 16th cent. 4k, St. Vitus Cathedral, by J. Sember and G. Dobler, 19th cent.

1981, Oct. 28

2384	A634	3k multi	1.35	45
2385	A634	4k multi	1.80	60

Art Type of 1967

Designs: 1k, View of Prague, by Vaclav Hollar (1607-1677). 2k, Czechoslovak Academy medallion, engraved by Otakar Spaniel (1881-1955). 3k, Jihoceska Vysivka, by Zdenek Sklenar (b. 1910). 4k, Still Life, by A.M. Gerasimov (1881-1963). 5k, Standing Woman, by Pablo Picasso (1881-1973).

1981, Nov. 27 Engr. *Perf. 12*

2386	A565	1k multi	45	15
2387	A565	2k multi	90	30
2388	A565	3k multi	1.35	45
2389	A656	4k multi	1.80	60
2390	A565	5k multi	2.25	75
		Nos. 2386-2390 (5)	6.75	2.25

Stamp Day—A843

1981, Dec. 18 Photo. & Engr. *Perf. 11½x12*

2391	A843	1k Engraver Eduard Karel	45	15

Russian Workers' Party, Prague Congress, 70th Anniv.—A844

1982, Jan. 18 Photo. & Engr. *Perf. 12*

2392		Sheet of 4	3.75	1.25
a.	A844 2k Lenin		90	30

No. 2392 has red and dark blue margin showing Congress building. Size: 108x83mm.

1982 World Cup Soccer—A845

Designs: Various soccer players.

1982, Jan. 29 *Perf. 12x11½*

2393	A845	1k multi	45	15
2394	A845	3.60k multi	1.65	55
2395	A845	4k multi	1.80	60

10th World Trade Union Congress, Havana
A846

Arms of Hrob
A847

1982, Feb. 10 *Perf. 11½*

2396	A846	1k multi	45	15

1982, Feb. 10 *Perf. 12x11½*

Arms of various cities.

2397	A847	50h shown	22	8
2398	A847	50h Nove Mesto Nad Metuji	22	8
2399	A847	50h Trencin	22	8
2400	A847	50h Mlada Boleslav	22	8

50th Anniv. of the Great Strike at Most—A848

1982, Mar. 23 Photo. & Engr. *Perf. 11½*

2401	A848	1k multi	45	15

60th Intl. Railway Union Congress—A849

1982, Mar. 23 Photo. & Engr. *Perf. 12x11½*

2402	A849	6k Steam locomotive, 1922, electric, 1982	2.75	90

10th Workers' Congress, Prague
A850

George Dimitrov (1882-1947) First Bulgarian Prime Minister
A851

1982, Apr. 15

2403	A850	1k multi	45	15

1982, May 1

2404	A851	50h multi	22	8

The Muse Euterpe Playing a Flute, by Crispin de Passe (1565-1637)
A852

10th Lidice Intl. Children's Drawing Contest
A853

Engravings: 50h, The Lute Player, by Jacob de Gheyn (1565-1629). 1k, Woman Flautist, by Adriaen Collaert (1560-1618). 2k, Musicians in a Hostel, by Rembrandt (1606-1669). 3k, Hurdy-gurdy Player, by Jacques Callot (1594-1635).

1982, May 18 *Perf. 11½x12*

2405	A852	40h multi	18	6
2406	A852	50h multi	22	8
2407	A852	1k multi	45	15
2408	A852	2k multi	90	30
2409	A852	3k multi	1.35	45
		Nos. 2405-2409 (5)	3.10	1.04

1982, May 18

2410	A853	2k multi	90	30

Issued in sheets of 6.

40th Anniv. of Destruction of Lidice and Lezaky—A854

1982, June 4 *Perf. 11½*

2411	A854	1k Girl, rose	45	15
2412	A854	1k Hands, barbed wire	45	15

U.N. Disarmament Conference—A855

1982, June 4 *Perf. 12*

2413		Sheet of 2	5.50	2.00
a.		A855 6k Woman holding doves	2.75	90

Souvenir Sheet

2nd UN Conference on Peaceful Uses of Outer Space, Vienna, Aug. 9-21—A856

1982, Aug. 9 **Photo. & Engr.** *Perf. 12*

2414	A856	5k Sheet of 2	4.50	1.50

No. 2414 contains 2 stamps, marginal inscription, space themes. Size: 165x108mm.

Krivoklat Castle—A857

1982, Aug. 31 *Perf. 12x11½*

2415	A857	50h shown	22	8
2416	A857	1k Statues (Krivoklat)	45	15
2417	A857	2k Nitra Castle	90	30
2418	A857	3k Pottery, lock (Nitra)	1.35	45
a.		Souvenir Sheet of 4	3.00	1.00

No. 2418a contains Nos. 2415-2418. Size: 106x126mm.

50th Anniv. of Zizkov Hill Natl. Monument—A858

1982, Sept. 16

2419	A858	1k multi	45	15

Prague Castle Type of 1971

Designs: 3k, St. George and the Dragon, 1373. 4k, Tomb of King Vratislav I, 10th cent.

1982, Sept. 28 *Perf. 12*

2420	A634	3k multi	1.35	45
2421	A634	4k multi	1.80	60

Bratislava Type of 1977

Designs: 3k, Paddle steamer, Parnik, 1818. 4k, View from Bridge, 19th cent.

1982, Sept. 29

2422	A760	3k multi	1.35	45
2423	A760	4k multi	1.80	60

European Danube Commission—A859

1982, Sept. 29 *Perf. 11½x12*

2424	A859	3k Steamer, Bratislava Bridge	1.35	45
a.		Souvenir sheet of 4	6.50	2.00
2425	A859	3.60k Ferry, Budapest	1.65	55
a.		Souvenir sheet of 4	6.75	2.25

Nos. 2424a-2425a have multicolored margins showing flags and river map. Size: 129x127mm.

16th Communist Party Congress—A860

1982, Oct. 28 *Perf. 12x11½*

2426	A860	20h Agriculture	10	3
2427	A860	1k Industry	45	15
2428	A860	3k Engineering	1.35	45

30th Anniv. of Academy of Sciences—A861

1982, Oct. 29 *Perf. 11½*

2429	A861	6k Emblem	2.75	90

65th Anniv. of October Revolution—A862

Design: 1k, 60th anniv. of USSR.

1982, Nov. 7 *Perf. 12x11½*

2430	A862	50h multi	22	8
2431	A862	1k multi	45	15

Jaroslav Hasek, Writer, Sculpture by Josef Malejovsky—A863

Sculptures: 2k, Jan Zrzavy, freedom fighter, by Jan Simota. 4.40k, Leos Janacek, composer, by Milos Axman. 6k, Martin Kukucin, freedom fighter, by Jan Kulich. 7k, Peaceful Work, by Rudolf Pribis.

Photo. & Engr.

1982, Nov. 26 *Perf. 11½x12*

2432	A863	1k multi	45	15
2433	A863	2k multi	90	30
2434	A863	4.40k multi	2.00	68
2435	A863	6k multi	2.75	90
2436	A863	7k multi	3.25	1.05
		Nos. 2432-2436 (5)	9.35	3.08

Art Type of 1967

Paintings: 1k, Revolution in Spain, by Josef Sima (1891-1971). 2k, Woman Dressing, by Rudolf Kremlicka (1886-1932). 3k, The Girl Bride, by Dezider Milly (1906-1971). 4k, Performers, by Jan Zelibsky (b. 1907). 5k, The Complaint of the Birds, by Emil Filla (1882-1953).

1982, Nov. 27 *Perf. 12*

2437	A565	1k multi	45	15
2438	A565	2k multi	90	30
2439	A565	3k multi	1.35	45
2440	A565	4k multi	1.80	60
2441	A565	5k multi	2.25	75
		Nos. 2437-2441 (5)	6.75	2.25

SEMI-POSTAL STAMPS.

Nos. B1–B123 were sold, in sets only, at 1½ times face value at the Philatelists' Window of the Prague P.O. for charity benefit. They were available for ordinary postage.

The overprints of Nos. B1–B123 have been well forged.

Austrian Stamps of 1916-18 Overprinted in Black or Blue

POŠTA ČESKOSLOVENSKÁ 1919

a

1919 *Perf. 12½.*

B1	A37	3h brt vio	10	10
B2	A37	5h lt grn	10	10
B3	A37	6h dp org (Bl)	40	40
B4	A37	6h dp org (Bk)	*1,400.*	*1,400.*
B5	A37	10h magenta	60	60
B6	A37	12h lt bl	60	60
B7	A42	15h dl red	5	5
B8	A42	20h dk grn	8	8
a.		20h grn	100.00	75.00
B9	A42	25h blue	20	20
B10	A42	30h dl vio	20	20
B11	A39	40h ol grn	25	25
B12	A39	50h dk grn	20	20
B13	A39	60h dp bl	30	30
B14	A39	80h org brn	20	20
B15	A39	90h red vio	55	55
B16	A39	1k car, *yel* (Bl)	40	40
B17	A39	1k car, *yel* (Bk)	125.00	125.00
B18	A40	2k lt bl	2.25	2.25
B18A	A40	2k dk bl	*3,500.*	*3,000.*
B19	A40	3k car rose	50.00	30.00
B19A	A40	3k claret	1,200.	1,100.
B20	A40	4k yel grn	12.00	9.00
B20A	A40	4k dp grn	50.00	35.00
B21	A40	10k violet	325.00	250.00
B21A	A40	10k dp vio	525.00	325.00

The used price of No. B18A is for copies which have only a Czechoslovakian cancellation. Some of the copies of Austria No. 160 which were officially overprinted with type "a" and sold by the post office, had previously been used and lightly canceled with Austrian cancellations. These canceled-before-overprinting copies, which were postally valid, sell for about one-fourth as much.

Granite Paper.

B22	A40	2k lt bl	2.25	2.25
B23	A40	3k car rose	8.50	8.00
B24	A40	4k yel grn		
B25	A40	10k dp vio		

Excellent counterfeits of Nos. B1–B25 exist.

Austrian Newspaper Stamps Overprinted

POŠTA ČESKOSLOVENSKÁ 1919

b

Imperf.

On Stamp of 1908.

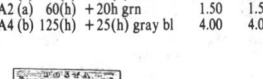

B26	N8	10h carmine	2,000.	2,000.

On Stamps of 1916.

B27	N9	2h brown	10	10
B28	N9	4h green	20	20
B29	N9	6h dp bl	20	20
B30	N9	10h orange	3.50	3.00
B31	N9	30h claret	1.75	1.25
		Nos. B27-B31 (5)	5.75	4.75

Austrian Special Handling Stamps Overprinted in Blue or Black.

Stamps of 1916 Overprinted

POŠTA ČESKOSLOVENSKÁ 1919

c

Perf. 12½.

B32	SH1	2h cl, *yel* (Bl)	30.00	27.50
B33	SH1	5h dp grn, *yel*	*1,400.*	*1,000.*

Stamps of 1917 Overprinted

POŠTA ČESKOSLOVENSKÁ 1919

d

B34	SH2	2h cl, *yel* (Bl)	20	20
a.		Vert. pair, imperf. btwn.	*250.00*	
B35	SH2	2h cl, *yel* (Bk)	75.00	50.00
B36	SH2	5h grn, *yel* (Bk)	20	20

Austrian Air Post Stamps, Nos. C1–C3, Overprinted Type "c" Diagonally.

B37	A40	1.50k on 2k lil	250.00	175.00
B38	A40	2.50k on 3k ocher	250.00	175.00
B39	A40	4k gray	1,000.	800.00

1919

Austrian Postage Due Stamps of 1908–13 Overprinted Type "b".

B40	D3	2h carmine	*4,500.*	*4,000.*
B41	D3	4h carmine	25.00	17.50
B42	D3	6h carmine	15.00	8.00
B43	D3	14h carmine	80.00	55.00
B44	D3	25h carmine	60.00	40.00
B45	D3	30h carmine	600.00	550.00
B46	D3	50h carmine	1,200.	1,100.

Austria Nos. J49–J56 Overprinted Type "b".

B47	D4	5h rose red	10	10
B48	D4	10h rose red	15	15
B49	D4	15h rose red	15	15
B50	D4	20h rose red	2.00	2.00
B51	D4	25h rose red	1.25	1.25
B52	D4	30h rose red	50	50
B53	D4	40h rose red	1.60	1.60
B54	D4	50h rose red	425.00	375.00

Austria Nos. J57–J59 Overprinted Type "a".

B55	D5	1k ultra	7.00	6.50
B56	D5	5k ultra	50.00	45.00
B57	D5	10k ultra	400.00	375.00

Austria Nos. J47–J48, J60–J63 Overprinted Type "c" Diagonally.

B58	A22	1h gray	20.00	17.50
B59	A23	15h on 2h vio	150.00	150.00
B60	A38	10h on 24h bl	120.00	120.00
B61	A38	15h on 36h vio	1.00	1.00
B62	A38	20h on 54h org	120.00	120.00
B63	A38	50h on 42h choc	1.00	1.00

Hungarian Stamps Overprinted Type "b".

Wmkd. Double Cross. (137)

1919 *Perf. 15.*

On Stamps of 1913-16.

B64	A4	1f slate	1,500.	1,500.
B65	A4	2f yellow	3.50	3.00
B66	A4	3f orange	40.00	40.00
B67	A4	6f ol grn	4.00	3.50
B68	A4	50f lake, *bl*	2.00	1.50
B69	A4	60f grn, *sal*	50.00	40.00
B70	A4	70f red brn, *grn*	1,500.	1,500.

On Stamps of 1916.

B71	A8	10f rose	275.00	275.00
B72	A8	15f violet	150.00	150.00

On Stamps of 1916-18.

B73	A9	2f brn org	15	15
B74	A9	3f red lil	20	20
B75	A9	5f green	10	10
B76	A9	6f grnsh bl	70	70
B77	A9	10f rose red	1.75	1.75
B78	A9	15f violet	30	25
B79	A9	20f gray brn	7.50	7.50
B80	A9	25f dl bl	1.00	75
B81	A9	35f brown	6.50	6.50
B82	A9	40f ol grn	1.75	1.75

Overprinted Type "d".

B83	A10	50f red vio & lil	1.00	80
B84	A10	75f brt bl & pale bl	80	80
B85	A10	80f yel grn & pale grn	1.50	1.50
B86	A10	1k red brn & cl	2.00	2.00
B87	A10	2k ol brn & bis	7.00	7.00
B88	A10	3k dk vio & ind	45.00	40.00
B89	A10	5k dk brn & lt brn	160.00	125.00
B90	A10	10k vio brn & vio	1,200.	1,100.

Overprinted Type "b".

On Stamps of 1918.

B91	A11	10f scarlet	25	25
B92	A11	20f dk brn	25	25
B93	A11	25f dp bl	2.00	1.00
B94	A12	40f ol grn	2.25	1.75
B95	A12	50f lilac	45.00	40.00

On Stamps of 1919.

B96	A13	10f red	7.50	7.50
B97	A13	20f dk brn	*4,000.*	*4,000.*

Same Overprint

On Hungarian Newspaper Stamp of 1914.

Imperf.

B98	N5	(2f) orange	15	15

Same Overprint

On Hungarian Special Delivery Stamp.

Perf. 15.

B99	SD1	2f gray grn & red	15	15

Same Overprint

On Hungarian Semi-Postal Stamps.

B100	SP3	10f +2f rose red	60	60
B101	SP4	15f +2f vio	1.00	1.00
B102	SP5	40f +2f brn car	3.00	3.00
		Nos. B98-B102 (5)	4.90	4.90

Hungarian Postage Due Stamps of 1903–18 Overprinted Type "b".

Wmkd. Crown in Circle. (135)

1919 *Perf. 11½, 12.*

B103	D1	50f grn & blk	*750.00*	*750.00*

Wmkd. Crown. (136, 136a)

Perf. 11½, 12, 15.

B104	D1	1f grn & blk	*700.00*	*700.00*
B105	D1	2f grn & blk	*400.00*	*400.00*
B106	D1	12f grn & blk	*3,000.*	*3,000.*
B107	D1	50f grn & blk	225.00	225.00

Wmkd. Double Cross. (137)

Perf. 15.

On Stamps of 1914.

B110	D1	1f grn & blk	400.00	400.00
B111	D1	2f grn & blk	300.00	300.00
B112	D1	5f grn & blk	750.00	750.00
B113	D1	12f grn & blk	*1,350.*	*1,350.*
B114	D1	50f grn & blk	225.00	225.00

On Stamps of 1915-18.

B115	D1	1f grn & red	200.00	200.00
B116	D1	2f grn & red	1.00	1.00
B117	D1	5f grn & red	10.00	10.00
B118	D1	6f grn & red	2.00	2.00
B119	D1	10f grn & red	80	80
a.		Pair, one without overprint		
B120	D1	12f grn & red	2.75	2.75
B121	D1	15f grn & red	7.25	7.25
B122	D1	20f grn & red	1.50	1.50
B123	D1	30f grn & red	55.00	55.00
		Nos. B115-B123 (9)	280.30	280.30

POSTA ČESKOSLOVENSKÁ

Bohemian Lion Breaking its Chains SP1

Mother and Child SP2

1919 **Typographed.** **Unwmkd.**

Perf. 11½, 13½ and Compound.

Pinkish Paper.

B124	SP1	15(h) gray grn	5	5
B125	SP1	25(h) dk brn	5	5
a.		25(h) lt brn	3.50	
B126	SP1	50(h) dk bl	5	5

Photogravure.

Yellowish Paper.

B127	SP2	75(h) slate	5	5
B128	SP2	100(h) brn vio	5	5
B129	SP2	120(h) vio, *yel*	5	5
		Nos. B124-B129 (6)	30	30

Nos. B124–B129 honor the Czecho-Slovak Legion. Nos. B124–B126 commemorate the first anniversary of Czechoslovak independence. Nos. B127–B129 were sold for the benefit of Legionnaires' orphans. Imperforates exist.

See No. 1581.

Regular Issues of Czechoslovakia Surcharged in Red:

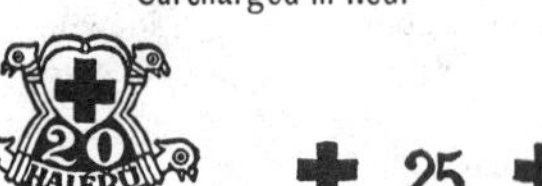

a b

1920 *Perf. 13½.*

B130	A1 (a)	40(h) +20(h) bis	1.50	1.50
B131	A2 (a)	60(h) +20h grn	1.50	1.50
B132	A4 (b)	125(h) +25(h) gray bl	4.00	4.00

President Masaryk SP3

Wmkd. Linden Leaves. (107)

1923 **Engraved** *Perf. 13½x14½*

B133	SP3	50(h) gray grn	1.25	75
B134	SP3	100(h) carmine	2.50	1.25
B135	SP3	200(h) blue	11.00	7.50
B136	SP3	300(h) dk brn	12.00	7.50

Issued in commemoration of the fifth anniversary of the Republic.

The monogram "CSP" (Ceskoslovenska Posta) is printed on top of the gum in brown on the back of each stamp. These stamps were sold at double their face values, the excess being given to the Red Cross and other charitable organizations.

International Olympic Congress Issue.

1925

Semi-Postal Stamps of 1923 Overprinted in Blue or Red

CONGRES OLYMP. INTERNAT. PRAHA1925

B137	SP3	50(h) gray grn (Bl)	12.00	9.00
B138	SP3	100(h) car (Bl)	20.00	15.00
B139	SP3	200(h) bl (R)	125.00	100.00

These stamps were sold at double their face values, the excess being divided between a fund for post office clerks and the Olympic Games Committee.

Sokol Issue.

1926

Semi-Postal Stamps of 1923 Overprinted in Blue or Red

VIII. SLET VŠESOKOLSKÝ
PRAHA 1926

B140	SP3	50 (h) gray grn (Bl)	7.50	6.50
B141	SP3	100 (h) car (Bl)	9.00	7.50
B142	SP3	200 (h) bl (R)	42.50	30.00
a.		Double overprint		
B143	SP3	300 (h) dk brn (R)	75.00	52.50

These stamps were sold at double their face values, the excess being given to the Congress of Sokols, June, 1926.

Midwife Presenting Newborn Child to its Father; after a Painting by Josef Manes

SP4 SP5

Engraved.

1936 ***Perf. 12½*** **Unwmkd.**

B144	SP4	50h +50h grn	60	60
B145	SP5	1k +50h cl	1.00	1.00
B146	SP4	2k +50h bl	2.50	2.50

"Lullaby" by Stanislav Sucharda

SP6 SP7

1937 ***Perf. 12½.***

B147	SP6	50h +50h dl grn	50	50
B148	SP6	1k +50h rose lake	1.00	1.00
B149	SP7	2k +1k dl bl	2.00	2.00

President Masaryk and Little Girl in Native Costume
SP8

1938 ***Perf. 12½***

B150	SP8	50h +50h dp grn	60	60
B151	SP8	1k +50h rose lake	70	70

Souvenir Sheet.
Imperf.

B152	SP8	2k +3k blk	4.50	4.50

No. B152 measures 72x90mm. with marginal inscriptions of "TGM" and Masaryk's signature.

Issued to commemorate the 88th anniversary of the birth of President Masaryk (1850–1937).

Souvenir Sheet.

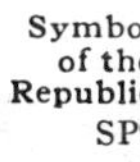

Symbol of the Republic
SP9

1938 ***Perf. 12½***

B153	SP9	2k (+8k) dk bl, sheet	4.50	4.50

Issued in sheets measuring 79x90mm. The surtax was devoted to national relief for refugees.

"Republic" and Congress Emblem — SP10
St. George Slaying the Dragon — SP11

1945 Engraved

B154	SP10	1.50(k) +1.50(k) car rose	20	10
B155	SP10	2.50(k) +2.50(k) bl	25	10

Issued to commemorate the Students' World Congress at Prague, Nov. 17, 1945.

1946

B156	SP11	2.40k +2.60k car rose	25	15
B157	SP11	4k +6k bl	50	25

Souvenir Sheet.
Imperf.

B158	SP11	4k +6k bl	1.00	1.00

No. B158 measures 70x90mm., with marginal inscriptions: "Pravda Vitezi Kveten 1945 1946." Nos. B156–B158 commemorate the 1st anniversary of Czechoslovakia's liberation. The surtax aided World War II orphans.

Souvenir Sheet.

SP13

1946, Aug. 3 ***Imperf.***

B159	SP13	2.40k rose brn	75	75

Issued for the Brno National Stamp Exhibition, August, 1946.

The sheet measures 70x89mm. It was sold for 10k.

"You Went Away"
SP14

"You Remained Ours"
SP15

"You Came Back"
SP16

1946, Oct. 28 Photo. ***Perf. 14***

B160	SP14	1.60k +1.40k red brn	30	30
B161	SP15	2.40k +2.60k scar	45	45
B162	SP16	4k +4k dp bl	75	75

The surtax was for repatriated Slovaks.

Barefoot Boy — SP17
Woman and Child — SP18

Designs: 2k+1k, Mother and child. 3k+1k, Little girl.

Engraved.

1948, Dec. 18 ***Perf. 12½*** **Unwmkd.**

B163	SP17	1.50(k) +1(k) rose lil	25	8
B164	SP17	2(k) +1(k) dp bl	25	8
B165	SP17	3(k) +1(k) rose car	35	30

The surtax was for child welfare.

Labels alternate with stamps in sheets of Nos. B163–B165.

Inscribed: "Detem 1949."

1949, Dec. 18 ***Perf. 12½***

Design: 3k+1k, Man lifting child.

B166	SP18	1.50k +50h gray	4.50	1.75
B167	SP18	3k +1k cl	5.50	2.25

The surtax was for child welfare.

Dove Carrying Olive Branch
SP19 SP20

1949, Dec. 18

B168	SP19	1.50k +50h cl	4.50	1.75
B169	SP20	3k +1k rose red	4.50	1.75

The surtax was for the Red Cross.

AIR POST STAMPS.

Stamps of 1918-19 Surcharged in Red, Blue or Green:

14 Kč

1920 ***Imperf.*** **Unwmkd.**

C1	A1	14k on 200(h) ultra (R)	17.50	17.50
a.		Inverted surcharge	70.00	
C2	A2	24k on 500(h) red brn (Bl)	50.00	50.00
a.		Inverted surcharge	100.00	
C3	A2	28k on 1000 (h) vio (G)	45.00	45.00
a.		Inverted surcharge	100.00	
b.		Double surch.	100.00	

Perf. 14, 14x13½

C4	A1	14k on 200 (h) ultra (R)	35.00	35.00
a.		Perf. 14 x 13½	70.00	70.00
C5	A2	24k on 500 (h) red brn (Bl)	90.00	90.00
a.		Perf. 14 x 13½	110.00	110.00
C6	A2	28k on 1000(h) vio (G)	52.50	52.50
a.		Inverted surcharge	110.00	110.00
b.		Perf. 14	*400.00*	*400.00*

Excellent counterfeits of the overprint are known.

Stamps of 1920 Surcharged in Black or Violet:

50

1922, June 15

C7	A8	50(h) on 100(h) dl grn (Bk)	2.50	2.50
a.		Inverted surcharge	50.00	
b.		Double surcharge	45.00	
C8	A8	100(h) on 200(h) vio (Bk)	3.50	3.50
a.		Inverted surcharge	50.00	
C9	A8	250(h) on 400(h) brn (V)	9.00	9.00
a.		Inverted surcharge	50.00	

Fokker Monoplane — AP3
Smolik S 19 — AP4

Smolik S 19—AP5

Fokker over Prague—AP6

Engraved.

1930, Dec. 16 ***Perf. 13½***

C10	AP3	50(h) dp grn	20	20
a.		Perf. 12	3.00	3.00
C11	AP3	1k dp red	30	30
a.		Perf. 12	30.00	30.00
b.		Perf. 12 x 13½	4.50	4.50
C12	AP4	2k dk grn	70	60
a.		Perf. 12	22.50	22.50
b.		Perf. 13½ x 12	15.00	15.00
C13	AP4	3k red vio	2.00	1.50
C14	AP5	4k indigo	1.25	1.00
a.		Perf. 12	9.00	9.00
C15	AP5	5k red brn	1.75	1.50
a.		Perf. 12	*750.00*	
C16	AP6	10k vio bl	5.50	5.25
a.		10k ultra	9.00	9.00
C17	AP6	20k gray vio	6.00	5.00
a.		Perf. 12	6.00	4.50
b.		Perf. 13½x12	*600.00*	
		Nos. C10-C17 (8)	17.70	15.35

Two types exist of the 50h, 1k and 2k, and three types of the 3k, differing chiefly in the size of the printed area. A "no hill at left" variety of the 3k exists.

Imperforate copies of Nos. C10 to C17 are proofs.

Type of 1930 with hyphen in Cesko - Slovensko.

1939, Apr. 22 *Perf. 13½*

C18	AP3	30h rose lil	10	7

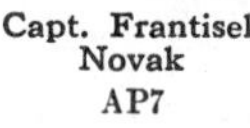

Capt. Frantisek Novak
AP7

Plane over Bratislava Castle
AP8

Plane over Charles Bridge Prague
AP9

1946–47 *Perf. 12½*

C19	AP7	1.50k rose red	15	8
C20	AP7	5.50k dk gray bl	40	9
C21	AP7	9k sep ('47)	1.00	6
C22	AP8	10k dl grn	80	12
C23	AP7	16k violet	1.25	30
C24	AP8	20k lt bl	1.50	60
C25	AP9	24k dk bl, *cr*	1.40	2.00
C26	AP9	24k rose lake	2.25	65
C27	AP9	50k dk gray bl	4.50	1.50
		Nos. C19-C27 (9)	13.25	5.40

No. C25 was issued June 12, 1946, for use on the first Prague-New York flight.

Nos. C19 to C24, C26 and C27 Surcharged with New Value and Bars in Various Colors.

1949, Sept. 1 *Perf. 12½*

C28	AP7	1k on 1.50k rose red (Bl)	12	10
C29	AP7	3k on 5.50k dk gray bl (C)	18	12
C30	AP7	6k on 9k sep (Br)	30	20
C31	AP7	7.50k on 16k vio (C)	60	20
C32	AP8	8k on 10k dl grn (G)	75	35
C33	AP8	12.50k on 20k lt bl (Bl)	1.00	35
C34	AP9	15k on 24k rose lake (Bl)	2.00	50
C35	AP9	30k on 50k dk gray bl (Bl)	2.50	75
		Nos. C28-C35 (8)	7.45	2.57

Karlovy Vary (Karlsbad)
AP10

Designs: 10k, Piestany. 15k, Marienbad. 20k, Sliac.

1951, Apr. 2 **Engraved** *Perf. 13½*

C36	AP10	6k sage grn	1.50	60
C37	AP10	10k dp plum	1.75	75
C38	AP10	15k dp ultra	3.00	1.00
C39	AP10	20k sepia	*10.00*	*2.50*

View of Cesky Krumlov
AP11

Views: 1.55k, Olomouc. 2.35k, Banska Bystrica. 2.75k, Bratislava. 10k, Prague.

Perf. 11½

1955, Feb. 20 (10k) and Mar. 28

Cream Paper

C40	AP11	80h ol grn	1.25	8
C41	AP11	1.55k vio brn	1.00	15
C42	AP11	2.35k vio bl	2.00	25
C43	AP11	2.75k rose brn	2.50	1.00
C44	AP11	10k indigo	4.50	1.25
		Nos. C40-C44 (5)	11.25	2.73

Airline: Moscow-Prague-Paris
AP12

Design: 2.35k, Airline: Prague-Cairo-Beirut-Damascus.

Engraved and Photogravure.

1957, Oct. 15 *Perf. 11½* **Unwmkd.**

C45	AP12	75h ultra & rose	65	10
C46	AP12	2.35k ultra & org yel	1.20	20

Planes at First Czech Aviation School, Pardubice
AP13

Design: 1.80k, Jan Kasper and flight of first Czech plane, 1909.

1959, Oct. 15

C47	AP13	1k gray & yel	40	8
C48	AP13	1.80k blk & pale bl	80	12

Issued to commemorate the 50th anniversary of Jan Kasper's first flight Aug. 25, 1909, at Pardubice.

Mail Coach, Plane and Arms of Bratislava
AP14

Design: 2.80k, Helicopter over Bratislava.

Engraved and Photogravure

1960, Sept. 24 *Perf. 11½* **Unwmkd.**

C49	AP14	1.60k dk bl & gray	*2.50*	*1.50*
C50	AP14	2.80k grn & buff	*4.00*	*2.00*

Issued to publicize the National Stamp Exhibition, Bratislava, Sept. 24–Oct. 9.

Prague Hails Gagarin
AP15

Design: 1.80k, Gagarin, rocket and dove.

1961, June 22

C51	AP15	60h gray & car	25	5
C52	AP15	1.80k gray & bl	1.10	25

No. C51 commemorates Maj. Gagarin's visit to Prague, Apr. 28–29; No. C52 commemorates the first man in space, Yuri A. Gagarin, Apr. 12, 1961.

Dove and Nest of Eggs
AP16

Designs ("PRAGA" emblem and): 1.40k, Dove. 2.80k, Symbolic flower with five petals. 4.20k, Five leaves.

1962, May 14 **Engraved** *Perf. 14*

C53	AP16	80h multi	75	60
C54	AP16	1.40k blk, dk red & bl	1.50	1.25
C55	AP16	2.80k multi	2.25	1.75
C56	AP16	4.20k multi	3.75	3.50

Issued to publicize the "PRAGA 1962" World Exhibition of Postage Stamps, Aug. 18–Sept. 2, 1962.

Vostok 5 and Lt. Col. Valeri Bykovski—AP17

Design: 2.80k, Vostok VI and Lt. Valentina Tereshkova.

1963, June 26

C57	AP17	80h sl bl & pink	45	15
C58	AP17	2.80k dl red brn & lt bl	1.10	35

Issued to commemorate the space flights of Valeri Bykovski, June 14–19, and Valentina Tereshkova, first woman astronaut, June 16–19, 1963.

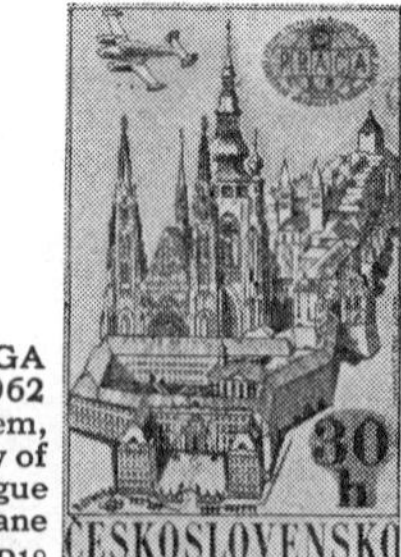

PRAGA 1962 Emblem, View of Prague and Plane
AP18

Designs: 60h, Istanbul '63 (Hagia Sophia). 1k, Philatec Paris 1964 (Ile de la Cité.) 1.40k, WIPA 1965 (Belvedere Palace, Vienna). 1.60k, SIPEX 1966 (Capitol, Washington). 2k, Amphilex '67 (harbor and old town, Amsterdam). 5k, PRAGA 1968 (View of Prague).

Engraved and Photogravure

1967, Oct. 30 *Perf. 11½*

Size: 30x50mm.

C59	AP18	30h choc, yel & rose	10	5
C60	AP18	60h dk grn, yel & lil	25	15
C61	AP18	1k blk, brick red & lt bl	40	20
C62	AP18	1.40k vio, yel & dp org	55	28
C63	AP18	1.60k ind, tan & lil	65	45
C64	AP18	2k dk grn, org & red	90	60

Size: 40x50mm.

C65	AP18	5k multi	*3.00*	*2.75*
		Nos. C59-C65 (7)	*5.85*	*4.48*

Issued to publicize the PRAGA 1968 World Stamp Exhibition, Prague, June 22–July 7, 1968. No. C59–C64 issued in sheets of 15 stamps and 15 bilingual labels. No. C65 issued in sheets of 4 stamps and one center label with commemorative inscription and airplane design.

Glider L-13
AP19

Airplanes: 60h, Sports plane L-40. 80h, Aero taxi L-200. 1k, Crop-spraying plane Z-37. 1.60k, Aerobatics trainer Z-526. 2k, Jet trainer L-29.

1967, Dec. 11 **Engr. and Photo.**

C66	AP19	30h multi	10	4
C67	AP19	60h multi	22	7
C68	AP19	80h multi	30	10
C69	AP19	1k multi	36	12
C70	AP19	1.60k multi	60	20
C71	AP19	2k multi	*1.50*	*60*
		Nos. C66-C71 (6)	*3.08*	*1.13*

Charles Bridge, Prague, and Balloon
AP20

Astronaut, Moon and Manhattan
AP21

Designs: 1k, Belvedere, fountain and early plane. 2k, Hradcany, Prague, and airship.

1968, Feb. 5 *Perf. 11½* **Unwmkd.**

C72	AP20	60h multi	30	15
C73	AP20	1k multi	45	20
C74	AP20	2k multi	75	35

Issued to publicize the PRAGA 1968 World Stamp Exhibition, Prague, June 22–July 7, 1968.

1969, July 21 **Engr. and Photo.**

Design: 3k, Lunar landing module and J. F. Kennedy Airport, New York.

C75	AP21	60h blk, vio, yel & sil	35	10
C76	AP21	3k blk, bl, ocher & sil	1.65	75

Issued to commemorate man's first landing on the moon, July 20, 1969, U. S. astronauts Neil A. Armstrong and Col. Edwin E. Aldrin, Jr., with Lieut. Col. Michael Collins piloting Apollo 11.

Nos. C75–C76 printed with label inscribed with names of astronauts and European date of moon landing.

TU-104A over Bitov Castle
AP22

Designs: 60h, IL-62 over Bezdez Castle. 1.40k, TU-134A over Orava Castle. 1.90k, IL-18 over Veveri Castle. 2.40k, IL-14 over Pernstejn Castle. 3.60k, TU-154 over Trencin Castle.

1973, Oct. 24 **Engr.** ***Perf. 11½***

C77	AP22	30h multi	12	3
C78	AP22	60h multi	24	8
C79	AP22	1.40k multi	55	15
C80	AP22	1.90k multi	75	22
C81	AP22	2.40k multi	*2.00*	*50*
C82	AP22	3.60k multi	1.50	45
		Nos. C77-C82 (6)	*5.16*	*1.43*

50 years of Czechoslovakian aviation.

Old Water Tower and Manes Hall—AP23

Designs (Praga 1978 Emblem, Plane Silhouette and): 1.60k, Congress Hall. 2k, Powder Tower (vert.). 2.40k, Charles Bridge and Old Bridge Tower. 4k, Old Town Hall on Old Town Square (vert.). 6k, Prague Castle and St. Vitus Cathedral (vert.).

Engraved and Photogravure

1976, June 23 ***Perf. 11½***

C83	AP23	60h ind & multi	24	8
C84	AP23	1.60k ind & multi	68	18
C85	AP23	2k ind & multi	90	30
C86	AP23	2.40k ind & multi	1.00	35
C87	AP23	4k ind & multi	1.75	45
C88	AP23	6k ind & multi	2.50	80
		Nos. C83-C88 (6)	7.07	2.16

PRAGA 1978 International Philatelic Exhibition, Prague, Sept. 8–17, 1978.

Zeppelin, 1909 and 1928
AP24

Designs (PRAGA '78 Emblem and): 1k, Ader, 1890, L'Eole and Dunn, 1914. 1.60k, Jeffries-Blanchard balloon, 1785. 2k, Otto Lilienthal's glider, 1896. 4.40k, Jan Kaspar's plane, Pardubice, 1911.

Photogravure and Engraved

1977, Sept. 15 ***Perf. 11½***

C89	AP24	60h multi	24	8
C90	AP24	1k multi	44	10
C91	AP24	1.60k multi	68	18
C92	AP24	2k multi	88	30
C93	AP24	4.40k multi	1.95	65
		Nos. C89-C93 (5)	4.19	1.31

History of aviation.

SPECIAL DELIVERY STAMPS.

Doves
SD1

Typographed.

1919-20 ***Imperf.*** **Unwmkd.**

E1	SD1	2(h) red vio, *yel*	5	5
E2	SD1	5(h) yel grn, *yel*	5	5
E3	SD1	10(h) red brn, *yel* ('20)	60	45

1921 White Paper.

E1a	SD1	2(h) red vio	6.00
E2a	SD1	5(h) yel grn	5.00
E3a	SD1	10(h) red brn	100.00

It is doubted that Nos. E1a-E3a were regularly issued.

PERSONAL DELIVERY STAMPS.

PD1

Design: No. EX2, "D" in each corner.

Photogravure

1937 ***Perf. 13½*** **Unwmkd.**

EX1	PD1	50h blue	30	30
EX2	PD1	50h carmine	30	30

PD3

1946 ***Perf. 13½***

EX3	PD3	2k dp bl	25	20

POSTAGE DUE STAMPS.

D1 D2

Typographed.

1918-20 ***Imperf.*** **Unwmkd.**

J1	D1	5(h) dp bis	3	3
J2	D1	10(h) dp bis	4	3
J3	D1	15(h) dp bis	6	3
J4	D1	20(h) dp bis	6	3
J5	D1	25(h) dp bis	25	8
J6	D1	30(h) dp bis	6	3
J7	D1	40(h) dp bis	60	20
J8	D1	50(h) dp bis	45	3
J9	D1	100(h) blk brn	60	3
J10	D1	250(h) orange	11.50	1.00
J11	D1	400(h) scarlet	11.50	1.00
J12	D1	500(h) gray grn	2.75	10
J13	D1	1000(h) purple	4.00	6
J14	D1	2000(h) dk bl	20.00	20
		Nos. J1-J14 (14)	51.90	2.85

1922 Blue Surcharge

J15	D2	20(h) on 3(h) red vio	40	15
J16	D2	50(h) on 75(h) sl	75	4
J17	D2	60(h) on 80(h) ol grn	50	10
J18	D2	100(h) on 80(h) ol grn	50	4
J19	D2	200(h) on 400(h) pur	1.35	10
		Nos. J15-J19 (5)	3.50	43

1923-26 Violet Surcharge.

J20	D2	10(h) on 3(h) red vio	6	4
J21	D2	20(h) on 3(h) red vio	6	4
J22	D2	30(h) on 3(h) red vio	13	5
J23	D2	40(h) on 3(h) red vio	20	3
J24	D2	50(h) on 75(h) sl	1.00	5
J25	D2	60(h) on 50(h) dk vio ('26)	1.75	90
J26	D2	60(h) on 50(h) dk bl ('26)	1.75	90
J27	D2	60(h) on 75(h) sl	80	6
J28	D2	100(h) on 80(h) ol grn	40.00	8
J29	D2	100(h) on 120(h) gray blk	1.25	4
J30	D2	100(h) on 400(h) pur ('26)	60	6
J31	D2	100(h) on 1000(h) dp vio ('26)	1.40	10
		Nos. J20-J31 (12)	49.00	2.35

Nos. J15, J19, J20, J22, J23 and J30 were surcharged on stamps of type A1; others of the groups J15 to J31 were surcharged on stamps of type A2.

Postage Due Stamp of 1918-20 Surcharged in Violet **50**

1924

J32	D1	50(h) on 400(h) scar	1.25	10
J33	D1	60(h) on 400(h) scar	3.50	40
J34	D1	100(h) on 400(h) scar	2.50	10

Postage Due Stamps of 1918-20 Surcharged with New Values in Violet as in 1924.

1925

J35	D1	10(h) on 5(h) bis	6	6
J36	D1	20(h) on 5(h) bis	6	6
J37	D1	30(h) on 15(h) bis	20	10
J38	D1	40(h) on 15(h) bis	25	4
J39	D1	50(h) on 250(h) org	1.25	10
J40	D1	60(h) on 250(h) org	1.75	25
J41	D1	100(h) on 250(h) org	3.50	15
		Nos. J35-J41 (7)	7.07	76

Stamps of 1918-19 Surcharged with New Values in Violet as in 1922.

1926 ***Perf. 14, 11½***

J42	D2	30(h) on 15(h) red	40	8
J43	D2	40(h) on 15(h) red	35	8

D3 D4

Violet Surcharge.

1926 ***Perf. 14***

J44	D3	30(h) on 100(h) dk grn	10	3
J45	D3	40(h) on 200(h) vio	15	3
J46	D3	40(h) on 300(h) ver	65	15
a.		Perf. 14x13½		30.00
J47	D3	50(h) on 500(h) dp grn	50	3
a.		Perf. 14x13½	2.50	
J48	D3	60(h) on 400(h) brn	1.00	10
J49	D3	100(h) on 600(h) dp vio	2.50	10
a.		Perf. 14x13½	25.00	1.00
		Nos. J44-J49 (6)	4.90	44

1927 Violet Surcharge.

J50	D4	100(h) dk brn	60	5
a.		Perf. 13½	*225.00*	10.00

Surcharged with New Value in Violet.

1927

J51	D4	40(h) on 185(h) org	15	3
J52	D4	50(h) on 20(h) car	30	4
a.		50(h) on 50(h) car (error)		*8,000.*
J53	D4	50(h) on 150(h) rose	30	4
a.		Perf. 13½	9.00	1.50
J54	D4	60(h) on 25(h) brn	40	25
J55	D4	60(h) on 185(h) org	40	4
J56	D4	100(h) on 25(h) brn	50	4
		Nos. J50-J56 (7)	2.65	49

No. J52a is known only used.

No. J12 Surcharged in Violet **200**

1927 ***Imperf.***

J57	D1	200(h) on 500(h) gray grn	3.50	1.75

D5 D6

1928 ***Perf. 14x13½.***

J58	D5	5h dk red	5	3
J59	D5	10h dk red	5	3
J60	D5	20h dk red	6	3
J61	D5	30h dk red	6	3
J62	D5	40h dk red	6	3
J63	D5	50h dk red	5	3
J64	D5	60h dk red	5	3
J65	D5	1k ultra	25	3
J66	D5	2k ultra	50	3
J67	D5	5k ultra	90	3
J68	D5	10k ultra	2.00	4
J69	D5	20k ultra	4.00	6
		Nos. J58-J69 (12)	8.03	40

1946-48 **Photogravure** ***Perf. 14***

J70	D6	10h dk bl	4	3
J71	D6	20h dk bl	6	3
J72	D6	50h dk bl	10	3
J73	D6	1k car rose	25	3
J74	D6	1.20k car rose	50	3
J75	D6	1.50k car rose ('48)	60	3
J76	D6	1.60k car rose	70	3
J77	D6	2k car rose ('48)	75	3
J78	D6	2.40k car rose	1.00	3
J79	D6	3k car rose	1.25	3
J80	D6	5k car rose	2.25	3
J81	D6	6k car rose ('48)	2.50	3
		Nos. J70-J81 (12)	10.00	36

D7 D8

1954-55 Engraved ***Perf. 12½, 11½***

J82	D7	5h gray grn ('55)	3	3
J83	D7	10h gray grn ('55)	4	3
J84	D7	30h gray grn	10	3
J85	D7	50h gray grn ('55)	15	3
J86	D7	60h gray grn ('55)	18	3
J87	D7	95h gray grn	40	3
J88	D8	1k violet	40	3
J89	D8	1.20k vio ('55)	40	3
J90	D8	1.50k violet	80	3
J91	D8	1.60k vio ('55)	80	3
J92	D8	2k violet	1.50	3
J93	D8	3k violet	1.50	3
J94	D8	5k vio ('55)	2.50	15
		Nos. J82-J94 (13)	8.80	51

Perf. 11½ stamps are from a 1963 printing which lacks the 95h, 1.60k, and 2k.

Stylized Flower
D9

Designs: Various stylized flowers.

Engraved and Photogravure

1971-72 ***Perf. 11½***

J95	D9	10h vio bl & pink ('72)	8	3
J96	D9	20h vio & lt bl ('72)	10	3
J97	D9	30h emer & lil rose ('72)	10	3
J98	D9	60h pur & emer ('72)	20	3
J99	D9	80h org & vio bl ('72)	27	3

J100	D9	1k dk red & emer ('72)	50	3
J101	D9	1.20k grn & org ('72)	40	3
J102	D9	2k bl & red ('72)	80	4
J103	D9	3k blk & yel ('72)	95	10
J104	D9	4k brn & ultra ('72)	1.60	8
J105	D9	5.40k red & lil	2.00	25
J106	D9	6k brick red & org ('72)	2.75	35
		Nos. J95-J106 (12)	9.75	1.03

OFFICIAL STAMPS.

Coat of Arms
O1

Lithographed.

1945 ***Perf. 10½x10.*** **Unwmkd.**

O1	O1	50h dp sl grn	6	5
O2	O1	1k dp bl vio	8	5
O3	O1	1.20k plum	20	20
O4	O1	1.50k crim rose	10	4
O5	O1	2.50k brt ultra	20	20
O6	O1	5k dk vio brn	30	30
O7	O1	8k rose pink	50	50
		Nos. O1-O7 (7)	1.44	1.34

Redrawn.

1947 **Photogravure.** ***Perf. 14.***

O8	O1	60h red	3	3
O9	O1	80h dl ol grn	3	3
O10	O1	1k dk lil gray	4	3
O11	O1	1.20k dp plum	8	3
O12	O1	2.40k dk car rose	12	6
O13	O1	4k brt ultra	25	20
O14	O1	5k dk vio brn	30	25
O15	O1	7.40k purple	50	40
		Nos. O8-O15 (8)	1.35	1.03

There are many minor changes in design, size of numerals, etc., of the redrawn stamps.

NEWSPAPER STAMPS.

Windhover
N1

Typographed.

1918-20 ***Imperf.*** **Unwmkd.**

P1	N1	2(h) gray grn	3	3
P2	N1	5(h) grn ('20)	3	3
a.		5(h) dk grn	30	8
P3	N1	6(h) red	40	40
P4	N1	10(h) dl vio	3	3
P5	N1	20(h) blue	6	3
P6	N1	30(h) gray brn	15	3
P7	N1	50(h) org ('20)	30	10
P8	N1	100(h) red brn ('20)	40	15
		Nos. P1-P8 (8)	1.40	80

Nos. P1 to P8 exist privately perforated.

Stamps of 1918–19 Surcharged in Violet

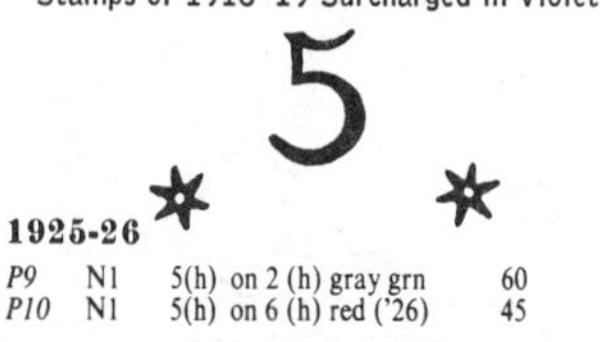

1925-26

P9	N1	5(h) on 2 (h) gray grn	60	30
P10	N1	5(h) on 6 (h) red ('26)	45	30

Special Delivery Stamps of 1918-20 Overprinted in Violet NOVINY

1926

P11	SD1	5(h) ap grn, *yel*	25	20
a.		5(h) dl grn, *yel*	50	30
P12	SD1	10(h) red brn, *yel*	15	10

With Additional Surcharge of New Value.

P13	SD1	5(h) on 2(h) red vio, *yel*	15	3

Newspaper Stamps of 1918-19 Overprinted in Violet **O.T.**

1934

P14	N1	10(h) dl vio	5	3
P15	N1	20(h) blue	5	5
P16	N1	30(h) gray brn	15	10

Overprinted for use by commercial firms only.

Carrier Pigeon
N2

1937 ***Imperf.***

P17	N2	2h bis brn	3	3
P18	N2	5h dl bl	3	3
P19	N2	7h red org	3	3
P20	N2	9h emerald	3	3
P21	N2	10h hn brn	3	3
P22	N2	12h ultra	5	5
P23	N2	20h dk grn	5	5
P24	N2	50h dk brn	5	5
P25	N2	1k ol gray	10	5
		Nos. P17-P25 (9)	40	35

Bratislava Philatelic Exhibition Issue.

Souvenir Sheet.

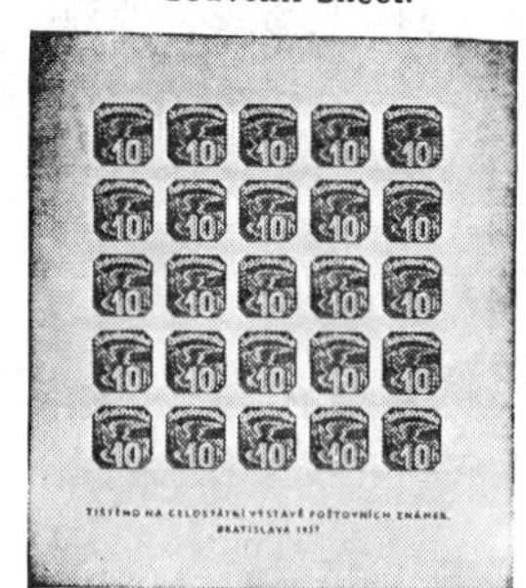

N3

1937 ***Imperf.***

P26	N3	10h hn brn, sheet of 25	2.50	2.50

Issued in sheets measuring 150x165mm.

Newspaper Delivery Boy
N4

Typographed.

1945 ***Imperf.*** **Unwmkd.**

P27	N4	5h dl bl	3	3
P28	N4	10h red	3	3
P29	N4	15h emerald	3	3
P30	N4	20h dk sl grn	3	3
P31	N4	25h brt red vio	3	3
P32	N4	30h ocher	3	3
P33	N4	40h red org	3	3
P34	N4	50h brn red	6	3
P35	N4	1k sl gray	10	4
P36	N4	5k dp vio bl	18	10
		Nos. P27-P36 (10)	55	38

Czechoslovak Legion Post

The Czechoslovak Legion in Siberia issued these stamps for use on its mail and that of local residents. Forgeries exist.

Urn and Cathedral at Irkutsk
A1

Armored Railroad Car
A2

Sentinel
A3

Lion of Bohemia
A4

1919 **Lithographed.** ***Perf. 11½.***

1	A1	25(k) carmine	16.50
a.		Imperf.	15.00
2	A2	50(k) yel grn	16.50
a.		Imperf.	15.00
3	A3	1 (r) red brn	32.50
a.		Imperf.	30.00

Originals of Nos. 1–3 and 1a–3a have yellowish gum. Ungummed remainders, which were given a white gum, exist imperforate and perforated 11½ and 14. Price per set, $3.

Embossed.

Perce en Arc in Blue.

4	A4	(25k) bl & rose	2.00

Two types: (I) Six points on star-like mace head at right of goblet; large saber handle; measures 19¾ x 24¾ mm. (II) Five points on mace head; small saber handle; measures 20 x 25mm.

1920 No. 4 Overprinted **1920**

5	A4	(25k) bl & rose	7.00

Both types of No. 4 received overprint.

No. 5 Surcharged with New Values in Green **2**

6	A4	2(k) bl & rose	35.00
7	A4	3(k) bl & rose	35.00
8	A4	5(k) bl & rose	35.00
9	A4	10(k) bl & rose	35.00
10	A4	15(k) bl & rose	35.00
11	A4	25(k) bl & rose	35.00
12	A4	35(k) bl & rose	35.00
13	A4	50(k) bl & rose	35.00
14	A4	1r bl & rose	35.00
		Nos. 6-14 (9)	315.00

BOHEMIA AND MORAVIA

(bô-hē'mĭ-ȧ & mô-rā'vĭ-ȧ)

German Protectorate.

Stamps of Czechoslovakia, 1928-39, Overprinted in Black

BÖHMEN u. MÄHREN
ČECHY a MORAVA

Perf. 10, 12½, 12x12½.

1939, July 15 **Unwmkd.**

No.	Type	Denom. & Color	Unused	Used
1	A29	5h dk ultra	12	18
2	A29	10h brown	12	18
3	A29	20h red	12	18
4	A29	25h green	12	18
5	A29	30h red vio	12	18
6	A61a	40h dk bl	3.00	3.50
7	A85	50h dp grn	12	18
8	A63	60h dl vio	3.00	3.50
9	A60	1k rose lake (212)	45	75
10	A60	1k rose lake (256)	45	75
11	A64	1.20k rose lil	3.50	4.50
12	A65	1.50k carmine	2.00	2.75
13	A79	1.60k ol grn	2.00	2.75
a.		"Mähnen"	35.00	40.00
14	A66	2k dk bl grn	1.75	1.75
15	A67	2.50k dk bl	3.50	3.50
16	A68	3k brown	3.75	3.75
17	A70	4k dk vio	4.00	4.00
18	A71	5k green	4.50	4.50
19	A72	10k blue	5.75	6.50
		Nos. 1-19 (19)	38.37	43.58

The size of the overprint varies with the size of the stamps, Nos. 1 to 10 measure 17½x15½mm., Nos. 11 to 16 measure 19x18mm., Nos. 17 and 19 measure 28x17½ and No. 18 measures 23½x23mm.

Linden Leaves and Closed Buds
A1

1939–41 **Photogravure** ***Perf. 14***

No.	Type	Denom. & Color	Unused	Used
20	A1	5h dk bl	3	3
21	A1	10h blk brn	3	3
22	A1	20h crimson	3	3
23	A1	25h dk bl grn	13	15
24	A1	30h dp plum	5	10
24A	A1	30h gldn brn ('41)	4	3
25	A1	40h org ('40)	10	5
26	A1	50h sl grn ('40)	4	3
		Nos. 20-26 (8)	45	45

See also Nos. 49–51.

Castle at Zvikov
A2

Karlstein Castle
A3

St. Barbara's Church, Kutna Hora
A4

Cathedral at Prague
A5

Brno Cathedral
A6

Town Square, Olomouc
A7

1939 **Engraved.** ***Perf. 12½.***

No.	Type	Denom. & Color	Unused	Used
27	A2	40h dk bl	5	4
28	A3	50h dk bl grn	4	3
29	A4	60h dl vio	4	4
30	A5	1k dp rose	4	3
31	A6	1.20k rose lil	35	35
32	A6	1.50k rose car	8	4
33	A7	2k dk bl grn	25	6
34	A7	2.50k dk bl	15	6
		Nos. 27-34 (8)	1.00	65

No. 31 measures 23½x29½mm., while No. 42 measures 18½x23mm.

Zlin—A8

Iron Works at Moravská Ostrava
A9

Prague
A10

1939–40

No.	Type	Denom. & Color	Unused	Used
35	A8	3k dl rose vio	10	5
36	A9	4k sl ('40)	10	5
37	A10	5k green	1.00	15
38	A10	10k lt ultra	60	40
39	A10	20k yel brn	1.20	1.00
		Nos. 35-39 (5)	3.00	1.65

Types of 1939 and

Neuhaus
A11

Lainsitz Bridge near Bechyne
A14

Pernstein Castle
A12

Samson Fountain Budweis
A15

Pardubice Castle
A13

Kromeriz
A16

Wallenstein Palace, Prague
A17

1940 **Engraved.** ***Perf. 12½***

No.	Type	Denom. & Color	Unused	Used
40	A11	50h dk bl grn	10	8
41	A12	80h dp bl	10	8
42	A6	1.20k vio brn	35	8
43	A13	2k gray grn	10	4
44	A14	5k dk bl grn	10	5
45	A15	6k brn vio	15	15
46	A16	8k sl grn	15	15
47	A17	10k blue	60	15
48	A10	20k sepia	1.35	80
		Nos. 40-48 (9)	3.00	1.58

No. 42 measures 18½x23mm.; No. 31, 23½x29½mm.

Types of 1939–40.

1941

No.	Type	Denom. & Color	Unused	Used
49	A1	60h violet	5	4
50	A1	80h red org	6	5
51	A1	1k brown	6	3
52	A5	1.20k rose red	5	3
53	A4	1.50k lil rose	8	4
53A	A13	2k lt bl	8	10
53B	A6	2.50k ultra	12	10
53C	A12	3k olive	15	6
		Nos. 49-53C (8)	65	45

Nos. 49–51 show buds open. Nos. 52 and 53B measure 18¾x23½mm. and have no inscriptions below design.

Antonin Dvorák
A18

1941, Aug. 25 **Engr.** ***Perf. 12½***

No.	Type	Denom. & Color	Unused	Used
54	A18	60h dl lil	10	15
55	A18	1.20k sepia	20	30

Birth centenary of Antonin Dvorák (1841–1904), composer.

Labels alternate with stamps in sheets of Nos. 54–55.

Farming Scene
A19

Factories
A20

1941, Sept. 7 **Photo.** ***Perf. 13½***

No.	Type	Denom. & Color	Unused	Used
56	A19	30h dk red brn	4	6
57	A19	60h dk grn	4	10
58	A20	1.20k dk plum	10	20
59	A20	2.50k sapphire	15	28

Issued to publicize the Prague Fair.

Nos. 52 and 53B Overprinted in Blue or Red

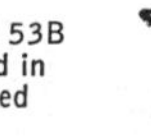

1942, Mar. 15 ***Perf. 12½***

No.	Type	Denom. & Color	Unused	Used
60	A5	1.20k rose red (Bl)	25	35
61	A6	2.50k ultra (R)	40	35

Issued to commemorate the third anniversary of the Protectorate of Bohemia and Moravia.

Adolf Hitler
A21

17th Century Messenger
A22

1942 **Photogravure.** ***Perf. 14.***

Size: 17½x21½mm.

No.	Type	Denom. & Color	Unused	Used
62	A21	10(h) gray blk	3	3
63	A21	30(h) bis brn	3	3
64	A21	40(h) sl bl	3	3
65	A21	50(h) sl grn	3	3
66	A21	60(h) purple	3	3
67	A21	80(h) org ver	4	4

Engraved.

Perf. 12½

Size: 18x21mm.

No.	Type	Denom. & Color	Unused	Used
68	A21	1k dl brn	5	4
69	A21	1.20(k) carmine	5	3
70	A21	1.50(k) claret	5	3
71	A21	1.60(k) Prus grn	5	5
72	A21	2k lt bl	5	4
73	A21	2.40(k) fawn	6	12

Size: 18½x24mm.

No.	Type	Denom. & Color	Unused	Used
74	A21	2.50(k) ultra	5	4
75	A21	3k ol grn	6	4
76	A21	4k brt red vio	6	4
77	A21	5k myr grn	8	4
78	A21	6k cl brn	8	6
79	A21	8k indigo	12	8

Size: 23½x29¾mm.

No.	Type	Denom. & Color	Unused	Used
80	A21	10k dk gray grn	15	10
81	A21	20k gray vio	20	20
82	A21	30k red	60	65
83	A21	50k dp bl	80	90
		Nos. 62-83 (22)	2.70	2.65

1943, Jan. 10 **Photo.** ***Perf. 13½***

No.	Type	Denom. & Color	Unused	Used
84	A22	60(h) dk rose vio	5	5

Stamp Day.

Scene from "Die Meistersinger"—A23

Richard Wagner
A24

Scene from "Siegfried"
A25

1943, May 22

No.	Type	Denom. & Color	Unused	Used
85	A23	60(h) violet	5	4
86	A24	1.20(k) car rose	6	8
87	A25	2.50(k) dp ultra	6	10

130th anniversary of the birth of Richard Wagner (1813–1883).

St. Vitus' Cathedral, Prague
A26

Adolf Hitler
A27

1944, Nov. 21 Engr. *Perf. 12½*

88	A26	1.50(k) dl rose brn	4	8
89	A26	2.50(k) dl lil bl	5	15

1944

90	A27	4.20(k) green	20	25

SEMI-POSTAL STAMPS.

Nurse and Wounded Soldier
SP1

Red Cross Nurse and Patient
SP2

Perf. 13½

1940, June 29 Photo. Unwmkd.

B1	SP1	60h +40h ind	55	55
B2	SP1	1.20k +80h dp plum	65	65

Surtax for German Red Cross.
Labels alternate with stamps in sheets of Nos. B1–B2.

1941, Apr. 20

B3	SP2	60h +40h ind	20	30
B4	SP2	1.20k +80h dp plum	20	40

Surtax for German Red Cross.
Labels alternate with stamps in sheets of Nos. B3–B4.

Old Theater, Prague
SP3

Wolfgang Amadeus Mozart
SP4

1941, Oct. 26

B5	SP3	30h +30h brn	5	5
B6	SP3	60h +60h Prus grn	10	10
B7	SP4	1.20k +1.20k scar	10	10
B8	SP4	2.50k +2.50k dk bl	20	30

150th anniversary of Mozart's death.
Labels alternate with stamps in sheets of Nos. B5–B8. The labels with Nos. B5–B6 show two bars of Mozart's opera "Don Giovanni." Those with Nos. B7–B8 show Mozart's piano.

Adolf Hitler
SP5

Nurse and Soldier
SP6

1942, Apr. 20 Engr. *Perf. 12½*

B9	SP5	30(h) +20(h) dl brn vio	4	4
B10	SP5	60(h) +40(h) dl grn	4	4
B11	SP5	1.20(k) +80(h) dp cl	6	6
B12	SP5	2.50(k) +1.50(k) dl bl	10	16

Issued to commemorate Hitler's 53rd birthday.

1942, Sept. 4 *Perf. 13½*

B13	SP6	60h +40h dp bl	7	7
B14	SP6	1.20(k) +80(h) dp plum	8	8

The surtax aided the German Red Cross.

Emperor Charles IV
SP7

Peter Parler
SP8

John the Blind, King of Bohemia
SP9

Adolf Hitler
SP10

1943, Jan. 29

B15	SP7	60(h) +40(h) vio	6	5
B16	SP8	1.20(k) +80(h) car	8	6
B17	SP9	2.50(k) +1.50(k) vio bl	12	14

The surtax was for the benefit of the German wartime winter relief.

1943, Apr. 20 Engr. *Perf. 12½*

B18	SP10	60(h) +1.40(k) dl vio	8	8
B19	SP10	1.20(k) +3.80(k) car	10	12

Issued to commemorate Hitler's 54th birthday.

Deathmask of Reinhard Heydrich
SP11

Eagle and Red Cross
SP12

1943, May 28 Photo. *Perf. 13½*

B20	SP11	60(h) +4.40(h) blk	25	25

No. B20 exists in a miniature sheet containing a single copy. It was given to officials attending Heydrich's funeral.

1943, Sept. 16 *Perf. 13*

B21	SP12	1.20(k) +8.80(k) blk & car	7	10

The surtax aided the German Red Cross.

Native Costumes
SP13

Nazi Emblem and Arms of Bohemia, Moravia
SP14

1944, Mar. 15 *Perf. 13½*

B22	SP13	1.20(k) +3.80(k) rose lake	10	10
B23	SP14	4.20(k) +10.80(k) gldn brn	10	10
B24	SP13	10k +20k saph	15	20

Fifth anniversary of protectorate.

Adolf Hitler
SP15

Friedrich Smetana
SP16

1944, Apr. 20

B25	SP15	60(h) +1.40(k) ol blk	4	5
B26	SP15	1.20(k) +3.80(k) sl grn	6	10

1944, May 12 Engr. *Perf. 12½*

B27	SP16	60(h) +1.40(k) dk gray grn	4	6
B28	SP16	1.20(k) +3.80(k) brn car	10	15

Issued to commemorate the 60th anniversary of the death of Friedrich Smetana (1824-84), Czech composer and pianist.

PERSONAL DELIVERY STAMPS.

PD1

Photogravure.

1939–40 *Perf. 13½* Unwmkd.

EX1	PD1	50h ind & bl ('40)	55	60
EX2	PD1	50h car & rose	55	60

POSTAGE DUE STAMPS.

D1

Typographed.

1939–40 *Perf. 14* Unwmkd.

J1	D1	5h dk car	6	6
J2	D1	10h dk car	6	6
J3	D1	20h dk car	6	6
J4	D1	30h dk car	6	6
J5	D1	40h dk car	9	9
J6	D1	50h dk car	9	9
J7	D1	60h dk car	9	9
J8	D1	80h dk car	9	9
J9	D1	1k brt ultra	15	20
J10	D1	1.20k brt ultra ('40)	18	25
J11	D1	2k brt ultra	35	45
J12	D1	5k brt ultra	35	45
J13	D1	10k brt ultra	75	1.00
J14	D1	20k brt ultra	2.00	2.25
		Nos. J1-J14 (14)	4.38	5.20

OFFICIAL STAMPS.

Numeral
O1

Eagle
O2

Typographed.

1941, Jan. 1 *Perf. 14* Unwmkd.

O1	O1	30h ocher	3	3
O2	O1	40h indigo	3	3
O3	O1	50h emerald	3	3
O4	O1	60h sl grn	3	3
O5	O1	80h org red	20	15
O6	O1	1k red brn	5	3
O7	O1	1.20k carmine	6	5
O8	O1	1.50k dp plum	15	15
O9	O1	2k brt bl	15	15
O10	O1	3k olive	15	15
O11	O1	4k red vio	25	25
O12	O1	5k org yel	55	55
		Nos. O1-O12 (12)	1.68	1.60

1943, Feb. 15

O13	O2	30(h) bister	3	3
O14	O2	40(h) indigo	3	3
O15	O2	50(h) yel grn	3	3
O16	O2	60(h) dp vio	3	3
O17	O2	80(h) org red	3	3
O18	O2	1k chocolate	3	4
O19	O2	1.20(k) carmine	3	3
O20	O2	1.50(k) brn red	4	6
O21	O2	2k lt bl	6	6
O22	O2	3k olive	6	6
O23	O2	4k red vio	8	8
O24	O2	5k dk grn	15	12
		Nos. O13-O24 (12)	60	60

NEWSPAPER STAMPS.

N1

N2

Carrier Pigeon

Typographed.

1939 *Imperf.* Unwmkd.

P1	N1	2h ocher	3	3
P2	N1	5h ultra	3	3
P3	N1	7h red org	3	3
P4	N1	9h emerald	3	3
P5	N1	10h hn brn	4	3
P6	N1	12h dk ultra	5	5
P7	N1	20h dk grn	6	10
P8	N1	50h red brn	8	15
P9	N1	1k grnsh gray	30	35
		Nos. P1-P9 (9)	65	80

1940

No. P5 Overprinted in Black **GD-OT**

P10	N1	10h hn brn	15	25

Overprinted for use by commercial firms.

1943, Feb. 15

P11	N2	2(h) ocher	3	3
P12	N2	5(h) lt bl	3	3
P13	N2	7(h) red org	3	3
P14	N2	9(h) emerald	3	3
P15	N2	10(h) hn brn	3	3
P16	N2	12(h) dk ultra	3	3
P17	N2	20(h) dk grn	4	3
P18	N2	50(h) red brn	4	6
P19	N2	1k sl grn	4	8
		Nos. P11-P19 (9)	30	35

Helpful notes abound in the "Information for Collectors" section at the front of this volume.

CARPATHO-UKRAINE

(kär·pä'thō-ū'krān)

A former province of Czechoslovakia known as Ruthenia, which in 1938 became an autonomous Czechoslovak state as a result of the Munich Agreement. On Mar. 16, 1939, it was incorporated in the Kingdom of Hungary.

100 Haleru = 1 Koruna

View of Jasina
A1

Perf. 12½

1939, Mar. 15 Engr. Unwmkd.

1	A1	3k ultra	2.75	*12.00*

Issued in commemoration of the inauguration of the Carpatho-Ukraine Diet, March 2, 1939.

SLOVAKIA

(slō·vä'kĭ·ȧ)

LOCATION—Central Europe.

GOVT.—Nominally independent republic.

AREA—14,848 sq. mi.

POP.—2,450,000.

CAPITAL—Bratislava.

Formerly a province of Czechoslovakia, Slovakia declared its independence in March, 1939. A treaty was immediately concluded with Germany guaranteeing Slovakian independence but providing for German "protection" for 25 years.

In 1945 the republic ended and Slovakia again became a part of Czechoslovakia.

100 Halierov = 1 Koruna

Czechoslovakia No. 226 Surcharged in Orange Red

Otvorenie slovenského snemu 18. I. 1939

300 h

1939, Jan. 18 *Perf. 12½* Unwmkd.

1	A72	300h on 10k bl	75	*2.75*

Issued to commemorate the opening of the Slovakian Parliament.

Stamps of Czechoslovakia, 1928-39, Overprinted in Red or Blue ***Slovenský štát 1939***

1939 *Perf. 10, 12½, 12x12½*

2	A29	5h dk ultra (R)	75	75
3	A29	10h brn (R)	9	9
4	A29	20h red (Bl)	5	5
5	A29	25h grn (R)	1.50	1.50
6	A29	30h red vio (bl)	5	5
7	A61a	40h dk bl (R)	14	14
8	A73	50h dp grn (R)	5	5
9	A63	50h dp grn (R)	5	5
10	A63	60h dl vio (R)	9	9
11	A63	60h dk bl (R)	8.50	8.50
12	A60	1k rose lake (bl) (On No. 212)	5	5

Overprinted Diagonally.

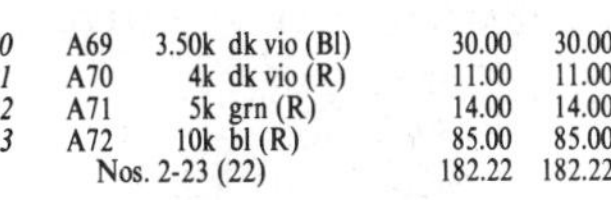

13	A64	1.20k rose lil (Bl)	20	20
14	A65	1.50k car (Bl)	20	20
15	A79	1.60k ol grn (Bl)	2.25	2.25
16	A66	2k dk bl grn (R)	2.25	2.25
17	A67	2.50k dk bl (R)	50	50
18	A68	3k brn (R)	50	50
19	A69	3.50k dk vio (R)	25.00	25.00
20	A69	3.50k dk vio (Bl)	30.00	30.00
21	A70	4k dk vio (R)	11.00	11.00
22	A71	5k grn (R)	14.00	14.00
23	A72	10k bl (R)	85.00	85.00
		Nos. 2-23 (22)	182.22	182.22

Excellent counterfeit overprints exist.

Andrej Hlinka
A1 A2

Overprinted in Red or Blue.

Photogravure.

1939, Apr. *Perf. 12½* Unwmkd.

24	A1	50h dk grn (R)	85	30
a.		Perf. 10½	2.00	1.00
b.		Perf. 10½x12½	4.00	3.25
25	A1	1k dk car rose (Bl)	1.50	50
a.		Perf. 10½	40.00	
b.		Perf. 10½x12½	10.00	6.00

1939 *Perf. 12½* Unwmkd.

26	A2	5h brt ultra	30	45
27	A2	10h ol grn	60	45
a.		Perf. 10½x12½	20.00	4.75
b.		Perf. 10½	20.00	6.00
28	A2	20h org red	60	45
a.		Imperf.	35	35
29	A2	30h dp vio	60	45
a.		Imperf.	55	55
b.		Perf. 10½x12½	4.00	2.50
c.		Perf. 10½	7.25	6.00
30	A2	50h dk grn	60	45
31	A2	1k dk car rose	90	30
32	A2	2.50k brt bl	50	20
33	A2	3k blk brn	2.00	20
		Nos. 26-33 (8)	6.10	2.95

On Nos. 32 and 33 a pearl frame surrounds the medallion. See Nos. 55–57, 69.

General Stefánik and Memorial Tomb
A3

Rev. Josef Murgas and Radio Towers
A4

1939, May *Perf. 12½*

Size: 25x20mm.

34	A3	40h dk bl	55
35	A3	60h sl grn	55
36	A3	1k gray vio	55

Size: 30x23¾ mm.

37	A3	2k bl vio & sep	55

Prepared to commemorate the 20th anniversary of the death of Gen. Milan Stefánik, but not issued.

1939 Unwmkd.

38	A4	60h purple	15	10
39	A4	1.20k sl blk	45	20

Issued in commemoration of the 10th anniversary of the death of Rev. Josef Murgas. See No. 65.

Girl Weaving
A5

Woodcutter
A6

Girl at Spring
A7

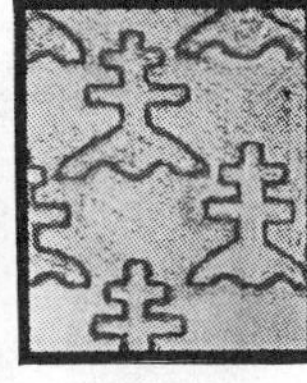

Wmk. 263

Wmkd. Double-Barred Cross Multiple. (263)

1939–44 *Perf. 12½*

40	A5	2k dk bl grn	5.00	45
41	A6	4k cop brn	65	18
42	A7	5k org red	1.00	45
a.		Perf. 10 ('44)	75	50

Dr. Josef Tiso
A8

Presidential Residence
A9

1939–44 *Perf. 12½* Wmk. 263

43	A8	50h sl grn	15	4
43A	A8	70h dk red brn ('42)	15	4
b.		Perf. 10½ ('44)	15	4

See also No. 88.

1940, Mar. 14

44	A9	10k dp bl	1.00	75

Tatra Mountains
A10

Krivan Peak
A11

Edelweiss in the Tatra Mountains
A12

Chamois
A13

Church at Javorina
A14

1940–43 *Perf. 12½* Wmk. 263

Size: 17x21mm.

45	A10	5h dk ol grn	30	5
46	A11	10h dp brn	18	5
47	A12	20h bl blk	18	5
48	A13	25h ol brn	18	5
49	A14	30h chnt brn	18	5
a.		Perf. 10½ ('43)	18	5
		Nos. 45-49 (5)	1.02	25

See Nos. 84–87, 103–107.

Hlinka Type of 1939

1940–42 *Perf. 12½* Wmk. 263

55	A2	1k dk car rose	60	30
56	A2	2.50k brt bl ('42)	45	20
a.		Perf. 10½	45	20
57	A2	3k blk brn ('41)	45	20
a.		Perf. 10½	45	20

On Nos. 56 and 57 a pearl frame surrounds the medallion.

Stiavnica
A15

Lietava
A16

Spissky Hrad
A17

Bojnice
A18

1941 *Perf. 12½*

58	A15	1.20(k) rose lake	5	4
59	A16	1.50(k) rose pink	6	4
60	A17	1.60(k) ryl bl	8	4
61	A18	2k dk gray grn	6	4

Slovakian Castles.

S. M. Daxner and Stefan Moyses
A19

Andrej Hlinka
A20

1941, May 26 Photo. Wmk. 263

62	A19	50h ol grn	1.50	1.50
63	A19	1k sl bl	6.00	6.00
64	A19	2k black	6.00	6.00

Issued in commemoration of the 80th anniversary of the Memorandum of the Slovak Nation.

Murgas Type of 1939

1941 Wmk. 263

65	A4	60h purple	20	10

1942

69	A20	1.30k dk pur	25	5

Post Horn and Miniature Stamp
A21

Philatelist
A22

Philatelist—A23

1942, May 23

70	A21	30h dk grn	1.00	1.25
71	A22	70h dk car rose	1.00	1.25
72	A23	80h purple	1.00	1.25
73	A21	1.30k dk brn	1.00	1.25

Issued to commemorate the National Philatelic Exhibition at Bratislava.

On No. 70 the miniature stamp bears the coat-of-arms of Bratislava; on No. 73 it shows the National arms of Slovakia.

St. Stephen's Cathedral, Vienna
A24

1942, Oct. 12 ***Perf. 14***

74	A24	70h bl grn	90	90
75	A24	1.30k ol grn	90	90
76	A24	2k sapphire	2.00	2.50

Issued to commemorate the European Postal Congress held in Vienna.

Slovakian Educational Society
A25

1942, Dec. 14

77	A25	70h black	10	10
78	A25	1k rose red	20	25
79	A25	1.30k sapphire	15	20
80	A25	2k chnt brn	20	25
81	A25	3k dk grn	30	30
82	A25	4k dl pur	45	40
		Nos. 77-82 (6)	1.40	1.50

Slovakian Educational Society, 150th anniversary.

Andrej Hlinka
A26

1943 **Wmk. 263**

83	A26	1.30k brt ultra	15	10

See also Nos. 93-94A.

Types of 1939–40

1943 ***Perf. 12½.*** **Unwmkd.**

Size: 17x21mm.

84	A11	10h dp brn	15	10
85	A12	20h bl blk	25	20
86	A13	25h ol brn	30	30
87	A14	30h chnt brn	30	30
88	A8	70h dk red brn	30	15
		Nos. 84-88 (5)	1.30	1.05

Presov Church
A27

Locomotive
A28

Railway Tunnel
A29

Viaduct
A30

1943, Sept. 5 ***Perf. 14***

89	A27	70h dk rose vio	35	35
90	A28	80h sapphire	35	35
91	A29	1.30k black	35	35
92	A30	2k dk vio brn	75	75

Issued to commemorate the inauguration of the new railroad line between Presov and Strazske.

Hlinka Type of 1943 and

Ludwig Stur
A31

Martin Razus
A32

1944 **Unwmkd.**

93	A31	80h sl grn	10	10
94	A32	1k brn red	18	18
94A	A26	1.30k brt ultra	45	30

Prince Pribina
A33

Designs: 70h, Prince Mojmir. 80h, Prince Ratislav. 1.30k, King Svatopluk. 2k, Prince Kocel. 3k, Prince Mojmir II. 5k, Prince Svatopluk II. 10k, Prince Braslav.

1944, Mar. 14

95	A33	50h dk grn	10	10
96	A33	70h lil rose	10	10
97	A33	80h red brn	10	10
98	A33	1.30k brt ultra	10	10
99	A33	2k Prus bl	20	20
100	A33	3k dk brn	30	30
101	A33	5k violet	60	60
102	A33	10k black	1.50	1.75
		Nos. 95-102 (8)	3.00	3.25

Scenic Types of 1940

Size: 18x23mm.

1944, Apr. 1 ***Perf. 14***

103	A11	10h brt car	20	20
104	A12	20h brt bl	20	20
105	A13	25h brn red	20	20
106	A14	30h red vio	20	20
107	A10	50h dp grn	20	20
		Nos. 103-107 (5)	1.00	1.00

Issued to honor the 5th anniversary of Slovakia's independence.

Symbolic of National Protection
A41

President Josef Tiso
A42

1944, Oct. 6 **Wmk. 263**

108	A41	2k green	40	40
109	A41	3.80k red vio	45	45

1945 **Unwmkd.**

110	A42	1k orange	55	48
111	A42	1.50k brown	20	9
112	A42	2k green	25	9
113	A42	4k rose red	60	50
114	A42	5k sapphire	60	50

Wmk. 263

115	A42	10k red vio	60	50
		Nos. 110-115 (6)	2.80	2.16

To commemorate the sixth anniversary of the Republic of Slovakia's declaration of independence, March 14, 1939.

SEMI-POSTAL STAMPS.

Josef Tiso
SP1

Perf. 12½

1939, Nov. 6 **Photo.** **Wmk. 263**

B1	SP1	2.50k +2.50k ryl bl	2.50	2.50

The surtax was used for Child Welfare.

Medical Corpsman and Wounded Soldier
SP2

1941, Nov. 10

B2	SP2	50h +50h dl grn	30	45
B3	SP2	1k +1k rose lake	45	60
B4	SP2	2k +1k brt bl	1.00	1.10

Mother and Child
SP3

Soldier and Hlinka Youth
SP4

1941, Dec. 10

B5	SP3	50h +50h dl grn	40	40
B6	SP3	1k +1k brn	50	50
B7	SP3	2k +1k vio	70	75

The surtax was for the benefit of child welfare.

1942, Mar. 14

B8	SP4	70h +1k brn org	30	35
B9	SP4	1.30k +1k brt bl	40	50
B10	SP4	2k +1k rose red	1.10	1.25

The surtax aided the Hlinka Youth Society "Hlinkova Mladez."

National Costumes

SP5 SP6 SP7

1943 ***Perf. 14.***

B11	SP5	50h +50h dk sl grn	20	25
B12	SP6	70h +1k dp car	20	25
B13	SP7	80h +2k dk bl	40	50

The surtax was for the benefit of children, the Red Cross and winter relief of the Slovakian popular party.

Infantrymen
SP8

Aviator—SP9

Tank and Gun Crew
SP10

1943, July 28

B14	SP8	70h +2k rose brn	45	50
B15	SP9	1.30k +2k saph	60	70
B16	SP10	2k +2k ol grn	90	1.00

The surtax was for soldiers' welfare.

"The Slovak Language Is Our Life"— L. Stur
SP11

Slovakian National Museum
SP12

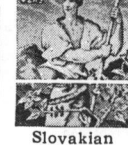

Slovakian Foundation
SP13

Slovakian Peasant
SP14

1943, Oct. 16

B17	SP11	30h +1k brn red	20	20
B18	SP12	70h +1k sl grn	70	70
B19	SP13	80h +2k sl bl	20	20
B20	SP14	1.30k +2k dl brn	20	20

The surtax was for the benefit of Slovakian cultural institutions.

Soccer Player
SP15

Skier
SP16

Diver
SP17

Relay Race
SP18

1944, Apr. 30 **Unwmkd.**

B21	SP15	70h +70h sl grn	75	80
B22	SP16	1k +1k vio	75	80
B23	SP17	1.30k +1.30k Prus bl	75	80
B24	SP18	2k +2k chnt brn	75	80

Symbolic of National Protection
SP19

Children
SP20

1944, Oct. 6 **Wmk. 263**

B25	SP19	70h +4h saph	90	1.00
B26	SP19	1.30k +4k red brn	90	1.00

The surtax was for the benefit of social institutions.

1944, Dec. 18

B27	SP20	2k +4k lt bl	1.75	2.00
a.		Sheet of 8 + Label	25.00	35.00

The surtax was to aid social work for Slovak youth.

AIR POST STAMPS.

Planes over Tatra Mountains
AP1 AP2

Perf. 12½

1939, Nov. 20 **Photo.** **Unwmkd.**

C1	AP1	30h violet	20	20
C2	AP1	50h dk grn	20	20
C3	AP1	1k vermilion	25	25
C4	AP2	2l grnsh blk	50	50
C5	AP2	3k dk brn	70	70
C6	AP2	4k sl bl	1.50	1.50
		Nos. C1-C6 (6)	3.35	3.35

See also No. C10.

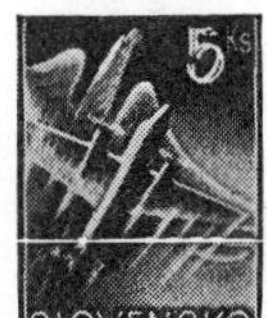

Plane in Flight
AP3

Perf. 12½

1940, Nov. 30 **Wmk. 263**

C7	AP3	5k dk vio brn	45	60
C8	AP3	10k gray blk	45	60
C9	AP3	20k myr grn	90	1.25

Type of 1939.

1944, Sept. 15 **Wmk. 263**

C10	AP1	1k vermilion	50	50

PERSONAL DELIVERY STAMPS

PD1

Photogravure.

1940 ***Imperf.*** **Wmk. 263**

EX1	PD1	50h ind & bl	60	75
EX2	PD1	50h car & rose	60	75

POSTAGE DUE STAMPS.

D1

Letter, Post Horn
D2

Photogravure.

1939 ***Perf. 12½*** **Unwmkd.**

J1	D1	5h brt bl	35	50
J2	D1	10h brt bl	35	50
J3	D1	20h brt bl	35	50
J4	D1	30h brt bl	1.00	75
J5	D1	40h brt bl	1.00	70
J6	D1	50h brt bl	1.75	70
J7	D1	60h brt bl	1.25	70
J8	D1	1k dk car	12.00	7.00
J9	D1	2k dk car	13.50	2.50
J10	D1	5k dk car	4.50	2.50
J11	D1	10k dk car	25.00	7.00
J12	D1	20k dk car	14.00	8.75
		Nos. J1-J12 (12)	75.05	32.10

1940-41 **Wmk. 263**

J13	D1	5h brt bl ('41)	50	50
J14	D1	10h brt bl ('41)	25	25
J15	D1	20h brt bl ('41)	25	25
J16	D1	30h brt bl ('41)	4.25	4.25
J17	D1	40h brt bl ('41)	50	50
J18	D1	50h brt bl ('41)	85	85
J19	D1	60h brt bl	85	85
J20	D1	1k dk car ('41)	1.00	1.00
J21	D1	2k dk car ('41)	6.00	6.00
J22	D1	5k dk car ('41)	2.50	2.50
J23	D1	10k dk car ('41)	2.75	2.75
		Nos. J13-J23 (11)	19.70	19.70

1942 ***Perf. 14.*** **Unwmkd.**

J24	D2	10h dp brn	7	10
J25	D2	20h dp brn	7	17
J26	D2	40h dp brn	14	17
J27	D2	50h dp brn	85	17
J28	D2	60h dp brn	17	17
J29	D2	80h dp brn	17	17
J30	D2	1k rose red	20	20
J31	D2	1.10k rose red	50	50
J32	D2	1.30k rose red	28	17
J33	D2	1.60k rose red	35	17
J34	D2	2k rose red	50	17
J35	D2	2.60k rose red	90	90
J36	D2	3.50k rose red	2.00	2.00
J37	D2	5k rose red	2.00	2.00
J38	D2	10k rose red	2.50	2.50
		Nos. J24-J38 (15)	10.70	9.56

NEWSPAPER STAMPS.

Newspaper Stamps of Czechoslovakia, 1937, Overprinted in Red or Blue

1939
SLOVENSKÝ ŠTÁT

1939, Apr. ***Imperf.*** **Unwmkd.**

P1	N2	2h bis brn (Bl)	30	30
P2	N2	5h dl bl (R)	30	30
P3	N2	7h red org (Bl)	30	30
P4	N2	9h emer (R)	30	30
P5	N2	10h hn brn (Bl)	30	30
P6	N2	12h ultra (R)	30	30
P7	N2	20h dk grn (R)	60	60
P8	N2	50h dk brn (Bl)	2.00	2.00
P9	N2	1k grnsh gray (R)	9.00	9.00
		Nos. P1-P9 (9)	13.40	13.40

Excellent counterfeits exist of Nos. P1 to P9.

Arms of Slovakia
N1

Type Block "N" (for "Noviny"—Newspaper)
N2

1939 Typographed.

P10	N1	2h ocher	12	10
P11	N1	5h ultra	25	15
P12	N1	7h red org	25	15
P13	N1	9h emerald	25	15
P14	N1	10h hn brn	30	15
P15	N1	12h dk ultra	25	15
P16	N1	20h dk grn	30	20
P17	N1	50h red brn	40	20
P18	N1	1k grnsh gray	30	25
		Nos.P10-P18 (9)	2.42	1.50

1940-41 **Wmk. 263**

P20	N1	5h ultra	15	10
P23	N1	10h hn brn	12	14
P24	N1	15h brt pur ('41)	12	14
P25	N1	20h dk grn	35	25
P26	N1	25h lt bl ('41)	35	20
P27	N1	40h red org ('41)	35	20
P28	N1	50h chocolate	40	20
P29	N1	1k grnsh gray ('41)	45	35
P30	N1	2k emer ('41)	70	50
		Nos. P20-P30 (9)	2.99	2.08

1943 Photogravure. **Unwmkd.**

P31	N2	10h green	20	20
P32	N2	15h dk brn	20	20
P33	N2	20h ultra	20	20
P34	N2	50h rose red	20	20
P35	N2	1k sl grn	35	35
P36	N2	2k int bl	75	75
		Nos. P31-P36 (6)	1.90	1.90

DAHOMEY

(dä·hō′mā)

LOCATION—West coast of Africa.
GOVT.—Republic.
AREA—43,483 sq. mi.
POP.—3,030,000 (est. 1974).
CAPITAL—Porto-Novo.

Formerly a native kingdom including Benin, Dahomey was annexed by France in 1894. It became part of the colonial administrative unit of French West Africa in 1895. Stamps of French West Africa superseded those of Dahomey in 1945. The Republic of Dahomey was proclaimed Dec. 4, 1958.

The republic changed its name to the People's Republic of Benin on Nov. 30, 1975. See Benin for stamps issued after that date.

100 Centimes = 1 Franc

Navigation and Commerce
A1

Perf. 14x13½.

1899–1905 **Typo.** **Unwmkd.**

Name of Colony in Blue or Carmine.

1	A1	1c *lil bl* ('01)	45	45
2	A1	2c brn, *buff* ('04)	60	60
3	A1	4c cl, *lav*('04)	90	90
4	A1	5c yel grn ('04)	1.85	1.85
5	A1	10c red ('01)	1.60	90
6	A1	15c gray ('01)	1.10	60
7	A1	20c red, *grn*('04)	7.25	6.75
8	A1	25c *rose* ('99)	6.25	3.75
9	A1	25c bl ('01)	6.50	5.00
10	A1	30c brn *bis*('04)	7.25	6.50
11	A1	40c red *straw* ('04)	8.00	7.25
12	A1	50c brn, *az* (name in red) ('01)	8.50	5.50
12A	A1	50c brn, *az* (name in bl) ('05)	15.00	11.00
13	A1	75c dp vio, *org* ('04)	40.00	32.50
14	A1	1fr brnz grn, *straw* ('04)	17.50	15.00
15	A1	2fr vio, *rose* ('04)	50.00	40.00
16	A1	5fr red lil, *lav* ('04)	67.50	57.50
		Nos. 1-16 (17)	240.25	196.05

Gen. Louis Faidherbe
A2

Oil Palm
A3

Dr. Noel Eugène Ballay
A4

1906–07 ***Perf. 13½x14.***

Name of Colony in Red or Blue.

17	A2	1c slate	45	45
18	A2	2c chocolate	45	45
19	A2	4c choc, *gray bl*	95	85
20	A2	5c green	3.50	80
21	A2	10c car (B)	6.75	90
22	A3	20c *azure*	6.00	4.00
23	A3	25c bl, *pnksh*	8.00	4.25
24	A3	30c choc, *pnksh*	6.75	4.25
25	A3	35c *yellow*	42.50	5.50
26	A3	45c choc, *grnsh* ('07)	6.75	5.50
27	A3	50c dp vio	8.00	5.75
28	A3	75c bl, *org*	8.00	6.50
29	A4	1fr blk, *az*	9.00	6.75
30	A4	2fr bl, *pink*	55.00	55.00
31	A4	5fr car, *straw*(B)	45.00	40.00
		Nos. 17-31 (15)	207.10	140.95

Stamps of 1901-05 Surcharged in Black or Carmine

05 10
a *b*

1912 ***Perf. 14x13½.***

32	(a)	5c on 2c brn, *buff*	35	35
33	(a)	5c on 4c cl, *lav*(C)	45	45
a.		Double surcharge	100.00	
34	(a)	5c on 15c gray (C)	45	45
35	(a)	5c on 20c red, *grn*	45	45
36	(a)	5c on 25c bl (C)	45	45
a.		Inverted surcharge	85.00	
37	(a)	5c on 30c brn, *bis* (C)	65	65
38	(b)	10c on 40c red, *straw*	45	45
a.		Inverted surcharge	135.00	
39	(b)	10c on 50c brn, *az*, name in bl (C)	60	60
40	(b)	10c on 50c brn, *az*, name in red (C)	525.00	600.00
41	(b)	10c on 75c vio, *org*	2.75	2.75
		Nos. 32-39, 41 (9)	6.60	6.60

Two spacings between the surcharged numerals are found on Nos. 32 to 41.

Man Climbing Oil Palm
A5

1913–39 ***Perf. 13½x14.***

No.	Type	Description	Unused	Used
42	A5	1c vio & blk	3	3
43	A5	2c choc & rose	5	5
44	A5	4c blk & brn	5	5
45	A5	5c yel grn & bl grn	12	12
46	A5	5c vio brn & vio ('22)	6	6
47	A5	10c org red & rose	38	28
48	A5	10c yel grn & bl grn ('22)	12	12
49	A5	10c red & ol ('25)	6	6
50	A5	15c brn org & dk vio ('17)	12	12
51	A5	20c gray & choc	12	6
52	A5	20c bluish grn & grn ('26)	5	5
53	A5	20c mag & blk ('27)	6	6
54	A5	25c ultra & dp bl	45	32
55	A5	25c vio brn & org ('22)	18	18
56	A5	30c choc & vio	80	70
57	A5	30c red org & rose ('22)	60	60
58	A5	30c yel & vio ('25)	8	8
59	A5	30c dl grn & grn ('27)	12	12
60	A5	35c brn & blk	40	30
61	A5	35c bl grn & grn ('38)	12	12
62	A5	40c blk & red org	15	12
63	A5	45c gray & ultra	15	15
64	A5	50c choc & brn	1.60	1.40
65	A5	50c ultra & bl ('22)	30	30
66	A5	50c brn red & bl ('26)	6	6
67	A5	55c gray grn & choc ('38)	12	12
68	A5	60c vio, *pnksh* ('25)	8	8
69	A5	65c yel brn & ol grn ('26)	28	28
70	A5	75c bl & vio	28	22
71	A5	80c hn brn & ultra ('38)	12	12
72	A5	85c dk bl & ver ('26)	40	40
73	A5	90c rose & brn red ('30)	30	30
74	A5	90c yel bis & red org ('39)	30	22
75	A5	1fr bl grn & blk	45	32
76	A5	1fr dk bl & ultra ('26)	45	45
77	A5	1fr yel brn & lt red ('28)	55	38
78	A5	1fr dk red & red org ('38)	38	28
79	A5	1.10fr vio & bis ('28)	85	85
80	A5	1.25fr dp bl & dk brn ('33)	8.50	3.25
81	A5	1.50fr dk bl & lt bl ('30)	38	30
82	A5	1.75fr dk brn & dp buff ('33)	1.20	75
83	A5	1.75fr ind & ultra ('38)	30	18
84	A5	2fr yel org & choc	45	38
85	A5	3fr red vio ('30)	75	65
86	A5	5fr vio & dp bl	90	70
		Nos. 42-86 (45)	23.27	15.74

The 1c gray and yellow green and 5c dull red and black are Togo Nos. 193a, 196a.

Common Design Types

pictured in section at front of book.

Type of 1913 Surcharged

60 60

1922–25

No.	Type	Description	Unused	Used
87	A5	60c on 75c vio, *pnksh*	30	30
a.		Double surcharge	27.50	
88	A5	65c on 15c brn org & dk vio ('25)	45	45
89	A5	85c on 15c brn org & dk vio ('25)	45	45

Stamps and Type of 1913–39 Surcharged with New Value and Bars.

1924–27

No.	Type	Description	Unused	Used
90	A5	25c on 2fr org & choc	30	30
91	A5	90c on 75c cer & brn red ('27)	60	60
92	A5	1.25fr on 1fr dk bl & ultra (R) ('26)	22	22
93	A5	1.50fr on 1fr dk bl & grnsh bl ('27)	75	75
94	A5	3fr on 5fr olvn & dp org ('27)	3.75	3.75
95	A5	10fr on 5fr bl vio & red brn ('27)	3.00	3.00
96	A5	20fr on 5fr ver & dl grn ('27)	3.00	3.00
		Nos. 90-96 (7)	11.62	11.62

Colonial Exposition Issue.

Common Design Types

1931 **Engraved.** ***Perf. 12½.***

Name of Country in Black.

No.	Type	Description	Unused	Used
97	CD70	40c dp grn	2.25	2.25
98	CD71	50c violet	2.25	2.25
99	CD72	90c red org	2.25	2.25
100	CD73	1.50fr dl bl	2.25	2.25

Paris International Exposition Issue.

Common Design Types

1937 **Engraved.** ***Perf. 13.***

No.	Type	Description	Unused	Used
101	CD74	20c dp vio	50	50
102	CD75	30c dk grn	55	55
103	CD76	40c car rose	55	55
104	CD77	50c dk brn	55	55
105	CD78	90c red	50	50
106	CD79	1.50fr ultra	50	50
		Nos. 101-106 (6)	3.15	3.15

Souvenir Sheet.

Imperf.

No.	Type	Description	Unused	Used
107	CD77	3fr dp bl & blk	2.25	2.25

Size of No. 107: 118x99mm.

Caillié Issue.

Common Design Type

1939, Apr. 5 Engr. ***Perf. 12½x12***

No.	Type	Description	Unused	Used
108	CD81	90c org brn & org	60	60
109	CD81	2fr brt vio	60	60
110	CD81	2.25fr ultra & dk bl	70	70

New York World's Fair Issue.

Common Design Type

1939 **Engraved.**

No.	Type	Description	Unused	Used
111	CD82	1.25fr car lake	40	40
112	CD82	2.25fr ultra	40	40

Man Poling a Canoe
A7

Pile House
A8

Sailboat on Lake Nokoué
A9

Dahomey Warrior
A10

1941 ***Perf. 13.***

No.	Type	Description	Unused	Used
113	A7	2c scarlet	6	6
114	A7	3c dp bl	6	6
115	A7	5c brn vio	18	18
116	A7	10c green	12	12
117	A7	15c black	5	5
118	A8	20c vio brn	5	5
119	A8	30c dk vio	12	12
120	A8	40c scarlet	30	30
121	A8	50c sl grn	30	30
122	A8	60c black	10	10
123	A8	70c brt red vio	12	12
124	A9	80c brn blk	22	22
125	A9	1fr violet	30	30
126	A9	1.30fr brn vio	38	38
127	A9	1.40fr green	45	45
128	A9	1.50fr brt rose	45	45
129	A9	2fr brn org	55	55
130	A10	2.50fr dk bl	45	45
131	A10	3fr scarlet	55	55
132	A10	5fr sl grn	40	40
133	A10	10fr vio brn	65	90
134	A10	20fr black	90	90
		Nos. 113-134 (22)	6.76	7.01

Stamps of type A8 without "RF" were issued in 1944 by the Vichy Government, but were not placed on sale in the colony.

Pile House and Marshal Pétain
A11

1941 ***Perf. 12½x12.***

No.	Type	Description	Unused	Used
135	A11	1fr green	32	
136	A11	2.50fr blue	32	

Republic

Village Ganvié—A12

Engraved

1960, Mar. 1 ***Perf. 12*** **Unwmkd.**

No.	Type	Description	Unused	Used
137	A12	25fr dk bl, brn & red	40	10

Imperforates

Most Dahomey stamps from 1960 onward exist imperforate in issued and trial colors, and also in small presentation sheets in issued colors.

C.C.T.A. Issue

Common Design Type

1960, May 16

No.	Type	Description	Unused	Used
138	CD106	5fr rose lil & ultra	40	35

Issued to commemorate the 10th anniversary of the Commission for Technical Co-operation in Africa South of the Sahara (C.C.T.A.).

Emblem of the Entente
A13

Prime Minister Hubert Maga
A14

Council of the Entente Issue

1960, May 29 Photo. ***Perf. 13x13½***

No.	Type	Description	Unused	Used
139	A13	25fr multi	60	50

Issued to commemorate the first anniversary of the Council of the Entente (Dahomey, Ivory Coast, Niger and Upper Volta).

1960, Aug. **Engraved** ***Perf. 13***

No.	Type	Description	Unused	Used
140	A14	85fr dp cl & blk	1.20	35

Issued on the occasion of Dahomey's proclamation of independence, Aug. 1, 1960.

Weaver
A15

Doves, U.N. Building and Emblem
A16

Designs: 2fr, 10fr, Wood sculptor. 3fr, 15fr, Fisherman and net (horiz.). 4fr, 20fr, Potter (horiz.).

1961, Feb. 17 **Engraved** ***Perf. 13***

No.	Type	Description	Unused	Used
141	A15	1fr rose, org & red lil	6	3
142	A15	2fr bis brn & choc	5	3
143	A15	3fr grn & org	8	6
144	A15	4fr ol bis & cl	12	10
145	A15	6fr rose, lt vio & ver	12	10
146	A15	10fr bl & grn	25	12
147	A15	15fr red lil & vio	27	18
148	A15	20fr bluish vio & Prus bl	40	25
		Nos. 141-148 (8)	1.35	87

No. 140 Surcharged with New Value, Bars and: "Président de la République"

1961, Aug. 1

No.	Type	Description	Unused	Used
149	A14	100fr on 85fr dp cl & blk	1.60	1.50

First anniversary of Independence.

1961, Sept. 20 ***Perf. 13*** **Unwmkd.**

No.	Type	Description	Unused	Used
150	A16	5fr multi	30	20
151	A16	60fr multi	90	80

Issued to commemorate the first anniversary of Dahomey's admission to the United Nations. See No. C16 and souvenir sheet No. C16a.

No. 137 Overprinted:
"JEUX SPORTIFS D'ABIDJAN
24 AU 31 DECEMBRE 1961"

1961, Dec. 24

152	A12	25fr dk bl, brn & red	50	40

Abidjan Games, Dec. 24–31.

Interior of Burned-out Fort Ouidah and Wrecked Car—A17

1962, July 31 Photo. ***Perf. 12½***

153	A17	30fr multi	45	20
154	A17	60fr multi	90	50

Issued to commemorate the first anniversary of the evacuation of Fort Ouidah by the Portuguese, and its occupation by Dahomey.

African and Malgache Union Issue

Common Design Type

1962, Sept. 8 ***Perf. 12½x12***

155	CD110	30fr red lil, bluish grn, red & gold	70	30

Issued to commemorate the first anniversary of the African and Malgache Union.

Red Cross Nurses and Map
A18

Engraved

1962, Oct. 5 ***Perf. 13*** **Unwmkd.**

156	A18	5fr bl, choc & red	10	5
157	A18	20fr bl, dk grn & red	30	25
158	A18	25fr bl, brn & red	40	30
159	A18	30fr bl, blk & red	50	30

Ganvié Woman in Canoe
A19

Peuhl Herdsman and Cattle
A20

Designs: 3fr, 65fr, Bariba chief of Nikki. 15fr, 50fr, Ouidah witch doctor, rock python. 20fr, 30fr, Nessoukoué women carrying vases on heads, Abomey. 25fr, 40fr, Dahomey girl. 60fr, Peuhl herdsman and cattle. 85fr, Ganvié woman in canoe.

1963, Feb. 18 ***Perf. 13*** **Unwmkd.**

160	A19	2fr grnsh bl & vio	5	5
161	A19	3fr bl & blk	6	5
162	A20	5fr brn, blk & grn	10	6
163	A19	15fr brn, bl grn & red brn	25	15
164	A19	20fr grn, blk & car	30	20
165	A20	25fr dk brn, bl & bl grn	35	15
166	A19	30fr brn org, choc & mag	45	20
167	A20	40fr choc, grn & brt bl	60	30
168	A19	50fr blk, grn, brn & red brn	75	35
169	A20	60fr choc, org red & ol	85	40
170	A19	65fr org brn & choc	90	50
171	A19	85fr brt bl & choc	1.25	75
		Nos. 160-171 (12)	5.91	3.16

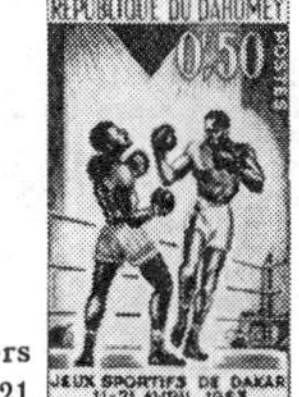

Boxers
A21

Designs: 1fr, 20fr, Soccer goalkeeper (horiz.). 2fr, 5fr, Runners.

1963, Apr. 11 **Engraved**

172	A21	50c grn & bl	4	4
173	A21	1fr ol, blk & brn	5	5
174	A21	2fr ol, bl & brn	6	6
175	A21	5fr brn, crim & blk	10	8
176	A21	15fr dk vio & brn	25	20
177	A21	20fr multi	40	30
		Nos. 172-177 (6)	90	73

Friendship Games, Dakar, Apr. 11–21.

President's Palace, Cotonou
A22

1963, Aug. 1 Photo. ***Perf. 12½x12***

178	A22	25fr multi	40	25

Third anniversary of independence.

Gen. Toussaint L'Ouverture
A23

U.N. Emblem, Flame and "15"
A24

1963, Nov. 18 ***Perf. 12x13*** **Unwmkd.**

179	A23	25fr multi	40	25
180	A23	30fr multi	45	30
181	A23	100fr ultra, brn & red	1.50	1.00

Issued to honor Pierre Dominique Toussaint L'Ouverture (1743–1803), Haitian general, statesman and descendant of the kings of Allada (Dahomey).

1963, Dec. 10 ***Perf. 12***

182	A24	4fr multi	8	8
183	A24	6fr multi	10	8
184	A24	25fr multi	40	30

Issued to commemorate the 15th anniversary of the Universal Declaration of Human Rights.

Somba Dance
A25

Regional Dances: 3fr, Nago dance, Pobe-Ketou (horiz.). 10fr, Dance of the baton. 15fr, Nago dance, Ouidah (horiz.). 25fr, Dance of the Sakpatassi. 30fr, Dance of the Nessouhouessi (horiz.).

1964, Aug. 8 Engraved ***Perf. 13***

185	A25	2fr red, emer & blk	4	3
186	A25	3fr dl red, bl & grn	6	4
187	A25	10fr pur, blk & red	15	10
188	A25	15fr mag, blk & grn	25	15
189	A25	25fr Prus bl, brn & org	40	25
190	A25	30fr dk red, choc & org	45	35
		Nos. 185-190 (6)	1.35	92

Runner
A26

Design: 85fr, Bicyclist.

1964, Oct. 20 Photo. ***Perf. 11***

191	A26	60fr lt brn & grn	75	55
192	A26	85fr vio bl & red lil	1.25	90

18th Olympic Games, Tokyo, Oct. 10–25.

Cooperation Issue

Common Design Type

1964, Nov. 7 Engraved ***Perf. 13***

193	CD119	25fr org, vio & dk brn	40	25

UNICEF Emblem, Mother and Child
A27

IQSY Emblem and Apollo Satellite
A28

Design: 25fr, Mother holding child in her arms.

1964, Dec. 11 ***Perf. 13*** **Unwmkd.**

194	A27	20fr yel grn, dk red & blk	30	25
195	A27	25fr bl, dk red & blk	40	25

Issued for the 18th anniversary of the United Nations International Children's Emergency Fund (UNICEF).

1964, Dec. 22 Photo. ***Perf. 13x12½***

Design: 100fr, IQSY emblem and Nimbus weather satellite.

196	A28	25fr grn & lt yel	50	20
197	A28	100fr dp plum & yel	1.50	90

International Quiet Sun Year, 1964–65.

Abomey Tapestry
A29

Designs (Abomey tapestries): 25fr, Warrior and fight scenes. 50fr, Birds and warriors (horiz.). 85fr, Animals, ship and plants (horiz.).

1965, Apr. 12 Photo. ***Perf. 12½***

198	A29	20fr multi	30	20
199	A29	25fr multi	40	30
200	A29	50fr multi	75	50
201	A29	85fr multi	1.25	90
a.		Min. sheet of 4	2.75	2.75

Issued to publicize the local rug weaving industry. No. 201a contains one each of Nos. 198–201. Size: 194x100mm.

Baudot Telegraph Distributor and Ader Telephone
A30

1965, May 17 Engraved ***Perf. 13***

202	A30	100fr lil, org & blk	1.50	60

Issued to commemorate the centenary of the International Telecommunication Union.

Cotonou Harbor—A31

Design: 100fr, Cotonou Harbor, denomination at left.

1965, Aug. 1 Photo. ***Perf. 12½***

203	A31	25fr multi	45	25
204	A31	100fr multi	1.65	1.00

Issued to commemorate the opening of Cotonou Harbor. Nos. 203–204 printed se-tenant show a panoramic view of the harbor.

Cybium Tritor
A32

Fish: 25fr, Dentex filosus. 30fr, Atlantic sailfish. 50fr, Blackish tripletail.

1965, Sept. 20 Engraved ***Perf. 13***

205	A32	10fr blk & brt bl	15	12
206	A32	25fr brt bl, org & blk	40	30
207	A32	30fr vio bl & grnsh bl	45	30
208	A32	50fr blk, gray bl & org	75	50

Independence Monument
A33

1965, Oct. 28 Photo. *Perf. 12x12½*

209	A33	25fr gray, blk & red	40	20
210	A33	30fr lt ultra, blk & red	45	25

October 28 Revolution, 2nd anniversary.

No. 165 Surcharged

1 F

1965, Nov. Engraved *Perf. 13*

211	A20	1fr on 25fr dk brn, bl & bl grn	8	6

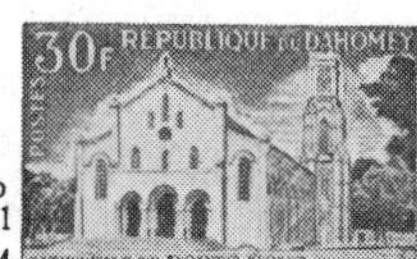

Porto Novo Cathedral
A34

Designs: 50fr, Ouidah Pro-Cathedral (vert.). 70fr, Cotonou Cathedral.

1966, March 21 Engraved *Perf. 13*

212	A34	30fr Prus bl, vio brn & grn	45	30
213	A34	50fr vio brn, Prus bl & brn	75	45
214	A34	70fr grn, Prus bl & vio brn	1.10	65

Jewelry
A35

Designs: 30fr, Architecture. 50fr, Musician. 70fr, Crucifixion, sculpture.

1966, Apr. 4 Engr. *Perf. 13*

215	A35	15fr dl red brn & blk	25	15
216	A35	30fr dk brn, ultra & brn red	45	25
217	A35	50fr brt bl & dk brn	75	40
218	A35	70fr red brn & blk	1.10	65

Issued to commemorate the International Negro Arts Festival, Dakar, Senegal, Apr. 1–24.

Nos. 203–204 Surcharged

ACCORD DE COOPERATION

FRANCE - DAHOMEY

5e Anniversaire - 24 Avril 1966

15 F

1966, Apr. 24 Photo. *Perf. 12½*

219	A31	15fr on 25fr multi	25	15
220	A31	15fr on 100fr multi	25	15

Issued to commemorate the fifth anniversary of the Cooperation Agreement between France and Dahomey.

WHO Headquarters from the East
A36

1966, May 3 *Perf. 12½x13*

Size: 35x22½mm.

221	A36	30fr multi	45	30

Issued to commemorate the inauguration of the World Health Organization Headquarters, Geneva. See No. C32.

Boy Scout Signaling
A37

Designs: 10fr, Patrol standard with pennant (vert.). 30fr, Campfire and map of Dahomey (vert.). 50fr, Scouts building foot bridge.

1966, Oct. 17 Engraved *Perf. 13*

222	A37	5fr dk brn, ocher & red	10	4
223	A37	10fr blk, grn & rose cl	15	6
224	A37	30fr org, red brn & pur	40	25
225	A37	50fr vio bl, grn & dk brn	70	40
a.		Minature sheet of 4	1.65	1.65

No. 225a contains one each of Nos. 222–225. Size: 168x94mm.

Clappertonia Ficifolia
A38

Lions Emblem, Dancing Children and Bird
A39

Flowers: 3fr, Hewittia sublobata. 5fr, Butterfly pea. 10fr, Water lily. 15fr, Commelina forskalaei. 30fr, Eremomastax speciosa.

1967, Feb. 20 Photo. *Perf. 12x12½*

226	A38	1fr multi	8	5
227	A38	3fr multi	12	5
228	A38	5fr multi	15	8
229	A38	10fr multi	25	10
230	A38	15fr multi	30	18
231	A38	30fr multi	60	30
		Nos. 226-231 (6)	1.50	76

Nos. 170–171 Surcharged with New Value and Heavy Bar

1967, Mar. 1 Engraved *Perf. 13*

232	A19	30fr on 65fr org brn & choc	45	35
a.		Double surch.	18.50	
233	A19	30fr on 85fr brt bl & choc	45	35
a.		Double surch.	27.50	
b.		Invtd. surch.	27.50	

1967, March 20

234	A39	100fr dl vio, dp bl & grn	1.60	50

50th anniversary of Lions International.

EXPO '67 "Man in the City" Pavilion
A40

Design: 70fr, "The New Africa" exhibit.

1967, June 12 Engraved *Perf. 13*

235	A40	30fr grn & choc	45	20
236	A40	70fr grn & brn red	1.00	65

Issued to commemorate EXPO '67, International Exhibition, Montreal, Apr. 28–Oct. 27, 1967. See No. C57 and miniature sheet No. C57a.

Europafrica Issue, 1967

Trade (Blood) Circulation, Map of Europe and Africa
A41

1967, July 20 Photo. *Perf. 12x12½*

237	A41	30fr multi	40	20
238	A41	45fr multi	65	25

Scouts Climbing Mountain, Jamboree Emblem
A42

Design: 70fr, Jamboree emblem and Scouts launching canoe.

1967, Aug. 7 Engraved *Perf. 13*

239	A42	30fr brt bl, red brn & sl	45	20
240	A42	70fr brt bl, sl grn & dk brn	1.00	65

Issued to commemorate the 12th Boy Scout World Jamboree, Farragut State Park, Idaho, Aug. 1–9. For souvenir sheet see No. C59a.

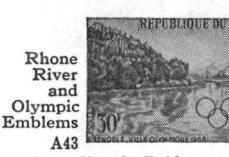

Rhone River and Olympic Emblems
A43

Designs (Olympic Emblems and): 45fr, View of Grenoble (vert.). 100fr, Rhone Bridge, Grenoble, and Pierre de Coubertin.

1967, Sept. 2 Engraved *Perf. 13*

241	A43	30fr bis, dp bl & grn	50	20
242	A43	45fr ultra, grn & brn	85	25
243	A43	100fr choc, grn & brt bl	1.65	90
a.		Miniature sheet of 3	3.25	3.25

Issued to publicize the 10th Winter Olympic Games, Grenoble, Feb. 6–18, 1968. No. 243a contains one each of Nos. 241–243. Size: 129x100mm.

Monetary Union Issue

Common Design Type

1967, Nov. 4 Engraved *Perf. 13*

244	CD125	30fr grn, dk car & dk brn	45	25

Issued to commemorate the 5th anniversary of the West African Monetary Union.

Cape Buffalo
A45

Animals from the Pendjari Reservation: 30fr, Lion. 45fr, Buffon's kob. 70fr, African slender-snouted crocodile. 100fr, Hippopotamus.

1968, Mar. 18 Photo. *Perf. 12½x13*

245	A45	15fr multi	25	15
246	A45	30fr pur & multi	45	20
247	A45	45fr bl & multi	70	30
248	A45	70fr multi	1.00	45
249	A45	100fr multi	1.50	80
		Nos. 245-249 (5)	3.90	1.90

WHO Emblem
A46

1968, Apr. 22 Engraved *Perf. 13*

250	A46	30fr dk bl, red brn & brt bl	45	20
251	A46	70fr multi	1.00	55

Issued to commemorate the 20th anniversary of the World Health Organization.

Leopard
A47

Animals: 5fr, Warthog. 60fr, Spotted hyena. 75fr, Anubius baboon. 90fr, Hartebeest.

1969, Feb. 10 Photo. *Perf. 12½x12*

252	A47	5fr dk brn & multi	8	5
253	A47	30fr dp ultra & multi	45	20
254	A47	60fr dk grn & multi	90	40
255	A47	75fr dk bl & multi	1.10	55
256	A47	90fr dk grn & multi	1.35	70
		Nos. 252-256 (5)	3.88	1.90

Heads, Symbols of Agriculture and Science, and Globe
A48

1969, Mar. 10 Engraved *Perf. 13*

257	A48	30fr org & multi	45	20
258	A48	70fr mar & multi	1.00	50

Issued to commemorate the 50th anniversary of the International Labor Organization.

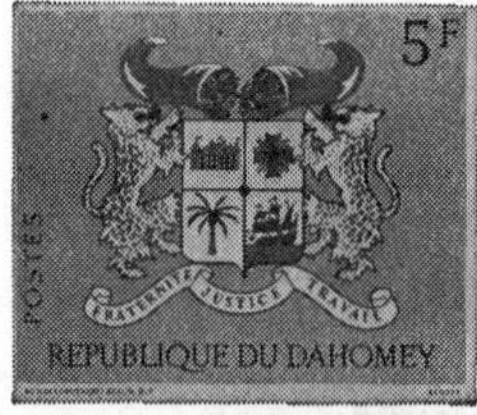

Arms of Dahomey
A49

1969, June 30 Litho. *Perf. 13½x13*

259	A49	5fr yel & multi	8	6
260	A49	30fr org red & multi	40	25

See also No. C101.

Development Bank Issue

Cornucopia and Bank Emblem
A50

1969, Sept. 10 Photo. ***Perf. 13***

261 A50 30fr blk, grn & ocher 50 25

Issued to commemorate the 5th anniversary of the African Development Bank.

Europafrica Issue

Ambary (Kenaf) Industry, Cotonou
A51

Design: 45fr, Cotton industry, Parakou.

1969, Sept. 22 Litho. ***Perf. 14***

262 A51 30fr multi 40 25
263 A51 45fr multi 60 30

See Nos. C105–C105a.

Sakpata Dance and Tourist Year Emblem
A52

Dances and Tourist Year Emblem: 30fr, Guelede dance. 45fr, Sato dance.

1969, Dec. 15 Litho. ***Perf. 14***

264 A52 10fr multi 20 10
265 A52 30fr multi 45 20
266 A52 45fr multi 65 35

See No. C108.

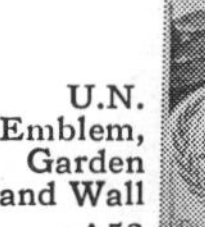

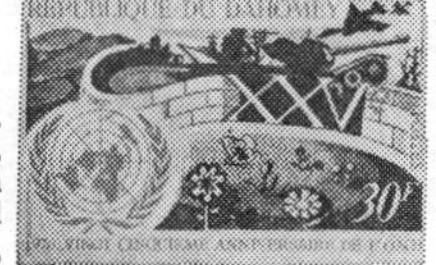

U.N. Emblem, Garden and Wall
A53

1970, Apr. 6 Engraved ***Perf. 13***

267 A53 30fr ultra, red org & sl 45 20
268 A53 40fr ultra, brn & sl grn 60 30

25th anniversary of the United Nations.

ASECNA Issue

Common Design Type

1970, June 1 Engraved ***Perf. 13***

269 CD132 40fr red & pur 60 35

Mt. Fuji, EXPO '70 Emblem, Monorail Train
A54

1970, June 15 Litho. ***Perf. 13½x14***

270 A54 5fr grn, red & vio bl 12 8

Issued to publicize EXPO '70 International Exhibition, Osaka, Japan, Mar. 15–Sept. 13, 1970. See Nos. C124–C125.

Alkemy, King of Ardres
A55

Designs: 40fr, Sailing ships "La Justice" and "La Concorde," Ardres, 1670. 50fr, Matheo Lopes, ambassador of the King of Ardres and his coat of arms. 200fr, Louis XIV and fleur-de-lis.

1970, July 6 Engraved ***Perf. 13***

271 A55 40fr brt grn, ultra & brn 65 22
272 A55 50fr dk car, choc & emer 75 27
273 A55 70fr gray, lem & choc 1.00 40
274 A55 200fr Prus bl, dk car & choc 2.75 1.20

Issued to commemorate the 300th anniversary of the mission from the King of Ardres to the King of France, and of the audience with Louis XIV on Dec. 19, 1670.

Star of the Order of Independence
A56

Bariba Warrior
A57

1970, Aug. 1 Photo. ***Perf. 12***

275 A56 30fr multi 35 20
276 A56 40fr multi 50 25

The 10th anniversary of independence.

1970, Aug. 24 ***Perf. 12½x13***

Designs: 2fr, 50fr, Two horsemen. 10fr, 70fr, Horseman facing left.

277 A57 1fr yel & multi 6 3
278 A57 2fr gray grn & multi 8 6
279 A57 10fr bl & multi 15 10
280 A57 40fr yel grn & multi 55 30
281 A57 50fr gold & multi 65 30
282 A57 70fr lil rose & multi 1.00 50
Nos. 277-282 (6) 2.49 1.29

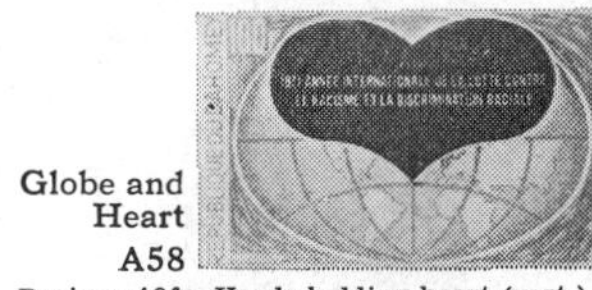

Globe and Heart
A58

Design: 40fr, Hands holding heart (vert.).

1971, June 7 Engraved ***Perf. 13***

283 A58 40fr red, grn & dk brn 50 30
284 A58 100fr grn, red & bl 1.10 60

International year against racial discrimination.

Ancestral Figures and Lottery Ticket
A59

King Behanzin's Emblem (1889–1894)
A60

1971, June 24 Litho. ***Perf. 14***

285 A59 35fr multi 40 20
286 A59 40fr multi 50 25

4th anniversary of the National Lottery.

Photo.; Litho. (25fr, 135fr)

1971–72 ***Perf. 12½***

Emblems of the Kings of Abomey: 25fr, Agoliagbo (1894–1900). 35fr, Ganyehoussou (1620–1645), bird and cup (horiz.). 100fr, Guezo (1818–1858), bull, tree and birds. 135fr, Ouegbadja (1645–1685) (horiz.). 140fr, Glèle (1858–1889), lion and sword (horiz.)

287 A60 25fr multi ('72) 30 15
288 A60 35fr grn & multi 45 20
289 A60 40fr grn & multi 50 25
290 A60 100fr red & multi 1.25 45
291 A60 135fr multi ('72) 1.40 70
292 A60 140fr brn & multi 1.75 85
Nos. 287-292 (6) 5.65 2.60

Issue dates: 25fr, 135fr, July 17, 1972. Others, Aug. 3, 1971.

Kabuki Actor, Long-distance Skiing
A61

Brahms and "Soir d'été"
A62

1972, Feb. Engraved ***Perf. 13***

293 A61 35fr dk car, brn & bl grn 50 25

11th Winter Olympic Games, Sapporo, Japan, Feb. 3–13. See No. C153.

No. 268 Surcharged

1972

294 A53 35fr on 40fr multi 45 25

1972, June 29 Engraved ***Perf. 13***

Design: 65fr, Brahms, woman at piano and music (horiz.).

295 A62 30fr red brn, blk & lil 40 25
296 A62 65fr red brn, blk & lil 80 50

75th anniversary of the death of Johannes Brahms (1833–1897), German composer.

The Hare and The Tortoise, by La Fontaine—A63

Fables: 35fr, The Fox and The Stork (vert.). 40fr, The Cat, The Weasel and Rabbit.

1972, Aug. 28 Engr. ***Perf. 13***

297 A63 10fr multi 15 10
298 A63 35fr dk red & multi 45 25
299 A63 40fr ultra & multi 50 30

Jean de La Fontaine (1621–1695), French fabulist.

West African Monetary Union Issue

Common Design Type

1972, Nov. 2 Engraved ***Perf. 13***

300 CD136 40fr choc, ocher & gray 40 25

10th anniversary of West African Monetary Union.

Dr. Hansen, Microscope, Bacilli
A65

Design: 85 fr, Portrait of Dr. Hansen.

1973, May 14 Engr. ***Perf. 13***

301 A65 35fr ultra, vio brn & brn 30 20
302 A65 85fr yel grn, bis & ver 75 50

Centenary of the discovery by Dr. Armauer G. Hansen of the Hansen bacillus, the cause of leprosy.

Arms of Dahomey
A66

1973, June 25 Photo. ***Perf. 13***

303 A66 5fr ultra & multi 8 5
304 A66 35fr ocher & multi 30 15
305 A66 40fr red org & multi 35 17

INTERPOL Emblem and Spiderweb
A67

Design: 50fr, INTERPOL emblem and communications symbols (vert.).

1973, July Engraved

306 A67 35fr ver, grn & brn 35 20
307 A67 50fr grn, brn & red 50 30

50th anniversary of International Criminal Police Organization (INTERPOL).

Education in Hygiene and Nutrition
A68

Design: 100fr, Prenatal examination and care, WHO emblem.

1973, Aug. 2 Photo. ***Perf. 12½x13***

308 A68 35fr multi 35 15
309 A68 100fr multi 85 50

World Health Organization, 25th anniversary.

No. 248 Surcharged with New Value, 2 Bars, and Overprinted in Red: "SECHERESSE SOLIDARITE AFRICAINE"

1973, Aug. 16

310 A45 100fr on 70fr multi 1.20 65

African solidarity in drought emergency.

African Postal Union Issue

Common Design Type

1973, Sept. 12 Engraved ***Perf. 13***

311 CD137 100fr red, pur & blk 1.00 55

Epinephelus Aeneus—A69

Fish: 15fr, Drepane africana. 35fr, Pragus ehrenbergi.

1973, Sept. 18

312	A69	5fr sl bl & ind	12	7
313	A69	15fr blk & brt bl	12	10
314	A69	35fr emer, ocher & sep	30	15

Chameleon A70

Design: 40fr, Emblem over map of Dahomey (vert.).

1973, Nov. 30 Photo. *Perf. 13*

315	A70	35fr ol & multi	35	20
316	A70	40fr multi	40	30

1st anniversary of the Oct. 26 revolution.

The Chameleon in the Tree—A71

Designs: 5fr, The elephant, the hen and the dog (vert.). 10fr, The sparrowhawk and the dog (vert.). 25fr, The chameleon in the tree. 40fr, The eagle, the viper and the hen.

1974, Feb. 14 Photo. *Perf. 13*

317	A71	5fr emer & multi	8	5
318	A71	10fr sl bl & multi	10	7
319	A71	25fr sl bl & multi	20	15
320	A71	40fr lt bl & multi	35	17

Folktales of Dahomey.

German Shepherd—A72

1974, Apr. 25 Photo. *Perf. 13*

Multicolored

321	A72	40fr *shown*	35	20
322	A72	50fr *Boxer*	40	25
323	A72	100fr *Saluki*	85	60

Council Issue

Map and Flags of Members A73

1974, May 29 Photo. *Perf. 13x12½*

324	A73	40fr bl & multi	35	20

15th anniversary of the Council of Accord.

Locomotive 232, 1911—A74

Designs: Locomotives.

1974, Sept. 2 Photo. *Perf. 13x12½*

Multicolored

325	A74	35fr *shown*	30	20
326	A74	40fr *Freight, 1877*	35	20
327	A74	100fr *Crampton, 1849*	85	60
328	A74	200fr *Stephenson, 1846*	1.65	1.25

Globe, Money, People in Bank A75

1974, Oct. 31 Engraved *Perf. 13*

329	A75	35fr multi	35	20

World Savings Day.

Dompago Dance, Hissi Tribe A76

Flags of Dahomey and Nigeria over Africa A77

Folk Dances: 25fr, Fetish Dance, Vaudou-Tchinan. 40fr, Bamboo Dance, Agbehoun. 100fr, Somba Dance, Sandoua (horiz.).

1975, Aug. 4 Litho. *Perf. 12*

330	A76	10fr yel & multi	12	6
331	A76	25fr dk grn & multi	20	12
332	A76	40fr red & multi	32	22
333	A76	100fr multi	85	50

1975, Aug. 11 Photo. *Perf. 12½x13*

Design: 100fr, Arrows connecting maps of Dahomey and Nigeria (horiz.).

334	A77	65fr multi	55	35
335	A77	100fr grn & multi	85	55

Year of intensified cooperation between Dahomey and Nigeria.

Map, Pylons, Emblem—A78

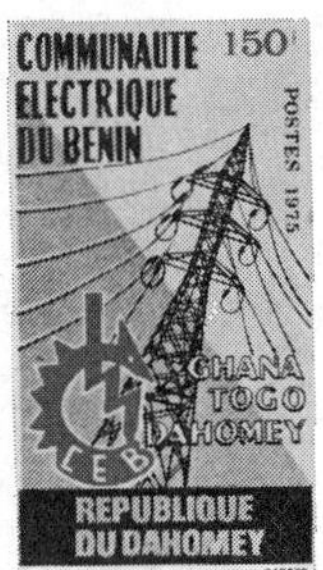

Benin Electric Community Emblem and Pylon A79

1975, Aug. 18

336	A78	40fr multi	35	25
337	A79	150fr multi	1.25	85

Benin Electric Community and Ghana-Togo-Dahomey cooperation.

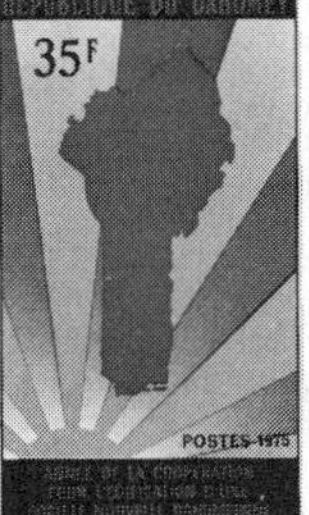

Map of Dahomey, Rising Sun A80

Albert Schweitzer, Nurse, Patient A81

1975, Aug. 25 Photo. *Perf. 12½x13*

338	A80	35fr multi	28	15

Cooperation Year for the creation of a new Dahoman society.

1975, Sept. 22 Engr. *Perf. 13*

339	A81	200fr ol, grn & red brn	1.65	1.10

Birth centenary of Albert Schweitzer (1875–1965), medical missionary and musician.

Woman Speaking on Telephone, IWY Emblem A82

Design: 150fr, International Women's Year emblem and linked rings.

1975, Oct. 20 Engr. *Perf. 12½x13*

340	A82	50fr Prus bl & lil	40	25
341	A82	150fr emer, brn & org	1.25	65

International Women's Year 1975.

Later issues are listed under Benin.

SEMI-POSTAL STAMPS.

Regular Issue of 1913 Surcharged in Red

1915 *Perf. 14x13½.* Unwmkd.

B1	A5	10c +5c org red & rose	55	40

Curie Issue
Common Design Type

1938 *Perf. 13*

B2	CD80	1.75fr +50c brt ultra	4.50	4.50

French Revolution Issue
Common Design Type

Name and Value Typo. in Black.

1939 Photogravure.

B3	CD83	45(c) +25(c) grn	3.50	3.50
B4	CD83	70(c) +30(c) brn	3.50	3.50
B5	CD83	90(c) +35(c) red org	3.50	3.50
B6	CD83	1.25fr +1fr rose pink	3.50	3.50
B7	CD83	2.25fr +2fr bl	3.50	3.50
		Nos. B3-B7 (5)	17.50	17.50

Postage Stamps of 1913-38 Surcharged in Black

SECOURS + 1 fr. NATIONAL

1941 *Perf. 13½x14.*

B8	A5	50c +1fr brn red & bl	60	60
B9	A5	80c +2fr hn brn & ultra	2.50	2.50
B10	A5	1.50fr +2fr dk bl & lt bl	3.25	3.25
B11	A5	2fr +3fr yel org & choc	3.25	3.25

Common Design Type and

Radio Operator
SP1

Senegalese Artillerymen
SP2

1941 Photogravure. *Perf. 13½.*

B12	SP1	1fr +1fr red	55
B13	CD86	1.50fr +3fr cl	55
B14	SP2	2.50fr +1fr bl	55

The surtax was for the defense of the colonies.

Stamps of type A11 surcharged "OEUVRES COLONIALES" and new values were issued in 1944 by the Vichy Government, but were not placed on sale in the colony.

Republic

Anti-Malaria Issue
Common Design Type

1962, Apr. 7 Engr. *Perf. 12½x12*

B15	CD108	25fr +5fr org brn	70	70

Issued for the World Health Organization drive to eradicate malaria.

Freedom from Hunger Issue
Common Design Type

1963, Mar. 21 *Perf. 13* Unwmkd.

B16	CD112	25fr +5fr ol, brn red & brn	70	70

AIR POST STAMPS.

Common Design Type
Engraved.

1940 *Perf. 12½* Unwmkd.

C1	CD85	1.90fr ultra	12	12
C2	CD85	2.90fr dk red	15	15
C3	CD85	4.50fr dk gray grn	32	32
C4	CD85	4.90fr yel bis	40	40
C5	CD85	6.90fr dp org	60	60
		Nos. C1-C5 (5)	1.59	1.59

Common Design Types

1942

C6	CD88	50c car & bl	12	
C7	CD88	1fr brn & blk	15	
C8	CD88	2fr dk grn & red brn	17	
C9	CD88	3fr dk bl & scar	38	
C10	CD88	5fr vio & brn red	30	

Frame Engr., Center Typo.

C11	CD89	10fr ultra, ind & org	38	
C12	CD89	20fr rose car, mag & gray blk	40	
C13	CD89	50fr yel grn, dl grn & dp bl	80	1.25
		Nos. C6-C13 (8)	2.70	

There is doubt whether Nos. C6-C12 were officially placed in use.

Republic

Somba House—AP4

Design: 500fr, Royal Court of Abomey.

Engraved

1960, Apr. 1 *Perf. 13* Unwmkd.

C14	AP4	100fr ind, ocher & vio brn	1.50	45
C15	AP4	500fr bis brn, brn red & dk grn	7.00	1.25

Type of Regular Issue, 1961.

1961, Sept. 20

C16	A16	200fr multi	3.25	2.75
	a.	Souvenir sheet of three	4.75	4.75

Issued to commemorate the first anniversary of Dahomey's admission to the United Nations. No. C16a contains one each of Nos. 150-151 and C16. Bistre marginal inscription. Size: 129x85mm.

Air Afrique Issue
Common Design Type

1962, Feb. 17 *Perf. 13*

C17	CD107	25fr ultra, blk & org brn	55	45

Issued to commemorate the founding of Air Afrique (African Airlines).

Palace of the African and Malgache Union, Cotonou
AP5

1963, July 27 Photo. *Perf. 13x12*

C18	AP5	250fr dk & lt bl, ocher & grn	3.50	2.00

Issued to commemorate the assembly of chiefs of state of the African and Malgache Union held at Cotonou in July.

African Postal Union Issue
Common Design Type

1963, Sept. 8 *Perf. 12½* Unwmkd.

C19	CD114	25fr brt bl, ocher & red	45	30

See note after Cameroun No. C47.

Boeing 707—AP6

Designs (Boeing 707): 200fr, On the ground. 300fr, Over Cotonou airport. 500fr, In the air.

1963, Oct. 25 Engraved *Perf. 13*

C20	AP6	100fr dk pur, grn & bis	1.25	40
C21	AP6	200fr vio, brn org & grn	2.50	1.25
C22	AP6	300fr bl, red brn & brt grn	3.50	1.75
C23	AP6	500fr brn org, dk brn & yel grn	6.00	2.50

Priests Carrying Funerary Boat, Isis Temple, Philae
AP7

1964, March 9 *Perf. 13* Unwmkd.

C24	AP7	25fr vio bl & brn	70	50

Issued to publicize the UNESCO world campaign to save historic monuments in Nubia.

Weather Map and Symbols
AP8

1965, Mar. 23 Photo. *Perf. 12½*

C25	AP8	50fr multi	80	50

Fifth World Meteorological Day.

ICY Emblem and Men of Various Races—AP9

1965, June 26 Engraved *Perf. 13*

C26	AP9	25fr dl pur, mar & grn	40	20
C27	AP9	85fr dp bl, mar & sl grn	1.25	80

International Cooperation Year, 1965.

Winston Churchill
AP10

1965, June 15 Photo. *Perf. 12½*

C28	AP10	100fr multi	1.65	1.25

Issued in memory of Sir Winston Churchill (1874-1965), statesman and World War II leader.

Abraham Lincoln—AP11

1965, July 15 *Perf. 13*

C29	AP11	100fr multi	1.65	1.25

Centenary of death of Abraham Lincoln.

John F. Kennedy and Arms of Dahomey
AP12

1965, Nov. 22 Photo. *Perf. 12½*

C30	AP12	100fr dp grn & blk	1.65	1.25

Issued in memory of President John F. Kennedy (1917-63).

Dr. Albert Schweitzer and Patients
AP13

1966, Jan. 17 Photo. *Perf. 12½*

C31	AP13	100fr multi	1.65	1.25

Issued in memory of Dr. Albert Schweitzer (1875-1965), medical missionary, theologian and musician.

WHO Type of Regular Issue

Design: 100fr, WHO Headquarters from the West.

1966, May 3 *Perf. 13* Unwmkd.

Size: 47x28mm.

C32	A36	100fr ultra, yel & blk	1.65	1.00

Issued to commemorate the inauguration of the World Health Organization Headquarters, Geneva.

Pygmy Goose
AP14

Broad-billed Rollers
AP15

Birds: 100fr, Firey-breasted bush-shrike. 250fr, Emerald cuckoos. 500fr, Emerald starling.

1966–67 ***Perf. 12½***

C33	AP14	50fr multi	1.00	40
C34	AP14	100fr multi	1.75	65
C35	AP15	200fr multi ('67)	3.25	1.35
C36	AP15	250fr multi ('67)	4.00	1.85
C37	AP14	500fr multi	7.00	3.50
		Nos. C33-C37 (5)	17.00	7.75

Issue dates: 50fr, 100fr, 500fr, June 13, 1966. Others, Jan. 20, 1967.

Industrial Symbols
AP16

1966, July 21 **Photo.** ***Perf. 12x13***

C38	AP16	100fr multi	1.50	90

3rd anniversary of agreement between European Economic Community and the African and Malagache Union.

Pope Paul VI and St. Peter's, Rome—AP17

Pope Paul VI and U.N. General Assembly
AP18

Design: 70fr, Pope Paul VI and view of New York City.

1966, Aug. 22 **Engraved** ***Perf. 13***

C39	AP17	50fr brt grn, rose car & org brn	85	40
C40	AAP17	70fr dk bl, sl grn & lake	1.25	60
C41	AP18	100fr dk grn, brn vio & sl bl	1.85	1.00
a.		Min. sheet of 3	4.00	4.00

Issued to commemorate Pope Paul's appeal for peace before the U.N. General Assembly, Oct. 4, 1965. No. C41a contains one each of Nos. C39–C41. Size: 178x100mm.

Air Afrique Issue, 1966
Common Design Type

1966, Aug. 31 **Photo.** ***Perf. 12½***

C42	CD123	30fr dk vio, blk & gray	50	25

Issued to commemorate the introduction of DC-8F planes by Air Afrique.

"Science"—AP20

Designs: 45fr, "Art" (carved female statue, vert.). 100fr, "Education" (book and letters).

1966, Nov. 4 **Engraved** ***Perf. 13***

C43	AP20	30fr mag, ultra & vio brn	40	25
C44	AP20	45fr mar & grn	70	40
C45	AP20	100fr blk, mar & brt bl	1.50	90
a.		Min. sheet of 3	3.50	3.50

Issued to commemorate the 20th anniversary of UNESCO (United Nations Educational, Scientific and Cultural Organization). No. C45a contains one each of Nos. C43–C45 Size: 169x100mm.

Madonna by Alessio Baldovinetti
AP21

Designs: 50fr, Nativity after 15th century Beaune tapestry. 100fr, Adoration of the Shepherds, by José Ribera.

1966, Dec. 25 **Photo.** ***Perf. 12½x12***

C46	AP21	50fr multi	2.25	1.35
C47	AP21	100fr multi	4.00	2.75
C48	AP21	200fr multi	6.75	5.00

Christmas 1966.

See Nos. C95–C96, C109–C115.

1967, Apr. 10 ***Perf. 12½x12***

Paintings by Ingres: No. C49, Self-portrait, 1804. No. C50, Oedipus and the Sphinx.

C49	AP21	100fr multi	2.00	1.50
C50	AP21	100fr multi	2.00	1.50

Issued to commemorate the centenary of the death of Jean Auguste Dominique Ingres (1780–1867), French painter.

Three-master Suzanne—AP22

Windjammers: 45fr, Three-master Esmeralda (vert.). 80fr, Schooner Marie Alice (vert.). 100fr, Four-master Antonin.

1967, May 8 ***Perf. 13***

C51	AP22	30fr multi	50	25
C52	AP22	45fr multi	70	45
C53	AP22	80fr multi	1.20	60
C54	AP22	100fr multi	1.50	85

Nos. C29-C30 Surcharged

29 MAI 1967
50e Anniversaire
de la naissance
de
John F. Kennedy

125F

1967, May 29 **Photo.** ***Perf. 13, 12½***

C55	AP11	125fr on 100fr multi	2.00	1.00
a.		Surch. invtd.	22.50	
C56	AP12	125fr on 100fr dp grn & blk	2.00	1.00
a.		Surch. invtd.	25.00	

Issued to commemorate the 50th anniversary of the birth of President John F. Kennedy.

EXPO '67 "Man In Space" Pavilion
AP23

1967, June 12 **Engraved** ***Perf. 13***

C57	AP23	100fr dl red & Prus bl	1.50	85
a.		Min. sheet of 3	3.25	3.25

Issued to commemorate EXPO '67, International Exhibition, Montreal, Apr. 28–Oct. 27, 1967. No. C57a contains one each of Nos. 235–236 and C57. Size: 149x100mm.

Europafrica Issue, 1967

Konrad Adenauer, by Oscar Kokoschká
AP24

1967, July 19 **Photo.** ***Perf. 12½x12***

C58	AP24	70fr multi	1.25	90
a.		Souv. sheet of 4	5.00	5.00

Issued in memory of Konrad Adenauer (1876–1967), chancellor of West Germany (1949–1963). No. C58a contains 4 No. C58. Dark gray marginal inscription. Size: 140x158mm.

Jamboree Emblem, Ropes and World Map
AP25

1967, Aug. 7 **Engr.** ***Perf. 13***

C59	AP25	100fr lil, sl grn & dp bl	1.50	90
a.		Souv. sheet of 3	3.75	3.50

Issued to commemorate the 12th Boy Scout World Jamboree, Farragut State Park, Idaho, Aug. 1–9. No. C59a contains one each of Nos. 239–240 and C59. Bright blue marginal inscription. Size: 149x100mm.

No. C48 Surcharged in Red

150F

RICCIONE
12-29
Août
1967

1967, Aug. 12 **Photo.** ***Perf. 12½x12***

C60	AP21	150fr on 200fr multi	2.50	2.00
a.		"150F" omitted	110.00	110.00

Issued to publicize the Riccione, Italy, Stamp Exhibition.

African Postal Union Issue, 1967
Common Design Type

1967, Sept. 9 **Engraved** ***Perf. 13***

C61	CD124	100fr red, brt lil & emer	1.50	1.00

Charles de Gaulle
AP26

1967, Nov. 21 **Photo.** ***Perf. 12½x13***

C62	AP26	100fr multi	2.50	2.00
a.		Souv. sheet of 4	10.00	10.00

Issued to honor Pres. Charles de Gaulle of France on the occasion of Pres. Christophe Soglo's state visit to Paris, Nov. 1967. No. C62a contains 4 No. C62. Black marginal inscription. Size: 140x161 mm.

Madonna, by Matthias Grunewald
AP27

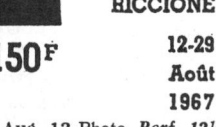

Paintings: 50fr, Holy Family by the Master of St. Sebastian (horiz.). 100fr, Adoration of the Magi by Ulrich Apt the Elder. 200fr, Annunciation, by Matthias Grunewald.

1967, Dec. 11 Photo. *Perf. 12½*

C63	AP27	30fr multi	35	25
C64	AP27	50fr multi	70	40
C65	AP27	100fr multi	1.50	90
C66	AP27	200fr multi	3.00	1.40

Christmas 1967.

Venus de Milo and Mariner 5

AP28

Gutenberg Monument, Strasbourg Cathedral

AP29

Design: No. C68, Venus de Milo and Venus 4 Rocket.

1968, Feb. 17 Photo. *Perf. 13*

C67	AP28	70fr grnsh bl & multi	1.25	60
C68	AP28	70fr dp bl & multi	1.25	60
a.		Souv. sheet of 2	2.50	2.50

Issued to commemorate the explorations of the planet Venus, Oct. 18–19, 1967. No. C68a contains one each of Nos. C67–C68. Black marginal inscription. Size: 106x96mm.

1968, May 20 Litho. *Perf. 14x13½*

Design: 100fr, Gutenberg Monument, Mainz, and Gutenberg press.

C69	AP29	45fr grn & org	70	35
C70	AP29	100fr dk & lt bl	1.35	65
a.		Souv. sheet of 2	2.25	2.25

Issued to commemorate the 500th anniversary of the death of Johann Gutenberg, inventor of printing from movable type. No. C70a contains one each of Nos. C69–C70. Marginal inscription in green and dark blue. Size: 130x100mm.

Martin Luther King, Jr. AP30

Designs: 30fr, "We must meet hate with creative love" in French, English and German. 100fr, Full-face portrait.

Perf. 12½, 13½x13

1968, June 17 Photogravure

Size: 26x46mm.

C71	AP30	30fr red brn, yel & blk	40	20

Size: 26x37mm.

C72	AP30	55fr multi	70	40
C73	AP30	100fr multi	1.25	65
a.		Min. sheet of 3	2.75	2.75

Issued in memory of the Rev. Dr. Martin Luther King, Jr. (1929–1968), American civil rights leader. No. C73a contains one each of Nos. C71–C73. Size: 150x 114mm.

Robert Schuman—AP31

Designs: 45fr, Alcide de Gasperi. 70fr, Konrad Adenauer.

1968, July 20 Photo. *Perf. 13*

C74	AP31	30fr dp yel, blk & grn	40	20
C75	AP31	45fr org, dk brn & ol	60	30
C76	AP31	70fr multi	1.00	45

Issued to commemorate the 5th anniversary of the economic agreement between the European Economic Community and the African and Malgache Union.

Battle of Montebello, by Henri Philippoteaux

AP32

Paintings: 45fr, 2nd Zouave Regiment at Magenta, by Riballier. 70fr, Battle of Magenta, by Louis Eugène Charpentier. 100fr, Battle of Solferino, by Charpentier.

1968, Aug. 12 *Perf. 12½x12*

C77	AP32	30fr multi	45	20
C78	AP32	45fr multi	70	30
C79	AP32	70fr multi	1.00	50
C80	AP32	100fr multi	1.50	75

Issued for the Red Cross.

Mail Truck in Village—AP33

Designs: 45fr, Mail truck stopping at rural post office. 55fr, Mail truck at river bank. 70fr, Mail truck and train.

1968, Oct. 7 Photo. *Perf. 13x12½*

C81	AP33	30fr multi	30	20
C82	AP33	45fr multi	60	30
C83	AP33	55fr multi	70	40
C84	AP33	70fr multi	85	50

Aztec Stadium, Mexico City

AP34

Designs (Olympic Rings and); 45fr, Ball player, Mayan sculpture (vert.). 70fr, Wrestler, sculpture from Uxpanapan (vert.). 150fr, Olympic Stadium, Mexico City.

1968, Nov. 20 Engraved *Perf. 13*

C85	AP34	30fr dp cl & sl grn	45	20
C86	AP34	45fr ultra & dk rose brn	60	25
C87	AP34	70fr sl grn & dk brn	90	40
C88	AP34	150fr dk car & dk brn	2.10	1.00
a.		Min. sheet of 4	4.50	4.50

Issued to commemorate the 19th Olympic Games, Mexico City, Oct. 12–27.

No. C88a contains one each of Nos. C85–C88. It is folded down the vertical gutter separating Nos. C85–C86 se-tenant at left and Nos. C87–C88 se-tenant at right. Size: 235x102mm.

The Annunciation, by Foujita

AP35

Paintings by Foujita: 30fr, Nativity (horiz.). 100fr, The Virgin and Child. 200fr, The Baptism of Christ.

Perf. 12x12½, 12½x12

1968, Nov. 25 Photogravure

C89	AP35	30fr multi	50	20
C90	AP35	70fr multi	90	45
C91	AP35	100fr multi	1.50	65
C92	AP35	200fr multi	3.00	1.35

Christmas 1968.

PHILEXAFRIQUE Issue

Painting: 100fr, Diderot, by Louis Michel Vanloo.

1968, Dec. 16 *Perf. 12½x12*

C93	AP35	100fr multi	1.50	1.00

Issued to publicize PHILEXAFRIQUE, Philatelic Exhibition in Abidjan, Feb. 14–23. Printed with alternating bluish violet label.

2nd PHILEXAFRIQUE Issue

Common Design Type

Design: 50fr, Dahomey No. 119 and aerial view of Cotonou.

1969, Feb. 14 Engraved *Perf. 13*

C94	CD128	50fr bl, brn & pur	75	60

Issued to commemorate the opening of PHILEXAFRIQUE, Feb. 14.

Type of Painting (Christmas) Issue, 1966

Paintings: No. C95, Virgin of the Rocks, by Leonardo da Vinci. No. C96, Virgin with the Scales, by Cesare da Sesto.

1969, Mar. 17 Photo. *Perf. 12½x12*

C95	AP21	100fr vio & multi	1.35	65
C96	AP21	100fr grn & multi	1.35	65

Issued to commemorate the 450th anniversary of the death of Leonardo da Vinci (1452–1519).

General Bonaparte, by Jacques Louis David

AP36

Paintings: 60fr, Napoleon I in 1809, by Robert J. Lefevre. 75fr, Napoleon on the Battlefield of Eylau, by Antoine Jean Gros (horiz.). 200fr, Gen. Bonaparte at Arcole, by Gros.

1969, Apr. 14 Photo. *Perf. 12½x12*

C97	AP36	30fr multi	1.20	85
C98	AP36	60fr multi	1.75	1.25
C99	AP36	75fr multi	2.50	1.65
C100	AP36	200fr multi	5.50	3.25

Bicentenary of the birth of Napoleon I.

Arms Type of Regular Issue, 1969

1969, June 30 Litho. *Perf. 13½x13*

C101	A49	50fr multi	60	30

Apollo 8 Trip Around the Moon

AP37

Embossed on Gold Foil

1969, July *Die-cut Perf. 10½*

C102	AP37	1000fr gold	15.00	15.00

Issued to commemorate the U.S. Apollo 8 mission, which put the first men into orbit around the moon, Dec. 21–27, 1968.

ALUNISSAGE
APOLLO XI
JUILLET 1969

Nos. C67–C68 Surcharged

= 125F

1969, Aug. 1 Photo. *Perf. 13*

C103	AP28	125fr on 70fr grnsh bl & multi	2.00	1.00
C104	AP28	125fr on 70fr dp bl & multi	2.00	1.00

Issued to commemorate man's first landing on the moon, July 20, 1969; U. S. astronauts Neil A. Armstrong and Col. Edwin E. Aldrin, Jr., with Lieut. Col. Michael Collins piloting Apollo 11.

Europafrica Issue

Type of Regular Issue, 1969

Design: 100fr, Oil palm industry, Cotonou.

1969, Sept. 22 Litho. *Perf. 14*

C105	A51	100fr multi	1.25	65
a.		Souv. sheet of 3	2.25	2.25

No. C105a contains one each of Nos. 262–263 and C105. Black marginal inscription. Size: 107½x148mm.

Dahomey Rotary Emblem

AP38

1969, Sept. 25 *Perf. 14x13½*

C106	AP38	50fr multi	75	40

No. C33 Surcharged

1969, Nov. 15 Photo. ***Perf. 12½***

C107 AP14 10fr on 50fr multi 12 6

Dance Type of Regular Issue

Design: 70fr, Teke dance and Tourist Year emblem.

1969, Dec. 15 Litho. ***Perf. 14***

C108 A52 70fr multi 90 40

Painting Type of 1966

Paintings: 30fr, Annunciation, by Vrancke van der Stockt. 45fr, Nativity, Swabian School (horiz.). 110fr, Madonna and Child, by the Master of the Gold Brocade. 200fr, Adoration of the Kings, Antwerp School.

Perf. 12½x12, 12x12½

1969, Dec. 20

C109 AP21 30fr multi 50 35
C110 AP21 45fr red & multi 75 50
C111 AP21 110fr multi 2.00 1.20
C112 AP21 200fr multi 3.50 2.25

Christmas 1969.

1969, Dec. 27 ***Perf. 12½x12***

Paintings: No. C113, The Artist's Studio (detail), by Gustave Courbet. No. C114, Self-portrait with Gold Chain, by Rembrandt. 150fr, Hendrickje Stoffels, by Rembrandt.

C113 AP21 100fr red & multi 1.25 75
C114 AP21 100fr grn & multi 1.25 75
C115 AP21 150fr multi 2.00 1.00

Franklin D. Roosevelt AP39 **Astronauts, Rocket and U.S. Flag AP40**

1970, Feb. Photo. ***Perf. 12½***

C116 AP39 100fr ultra, yel grn & blk 1.25 50

Issued to commemorate the 25th anniversary of the death of Pres. Franklin Delano Roosevelt (1882–1945).

1970, Mar. 9 Photo. ***Perf. 12½***

Designs: 50fr, Astronauts riding rocket through space. 70fr, Astronauts in landing module approaching moon. 110fr, Astronauts planting U.S. flag on moon.

C117 AP40 30fr multi 40 25

Souvenir Sheet

C118 AP40 Sheet of 4 3.50 3.50
a. 50fr vio bl & multi 60 60
b. 70fr vio bl & multi 85 85
c. 110fr vio bl & multi 1.25 1.25

See note after No. C104. No. C118 contains one each of Nos. C117, C118a, C118b and C118c; violet blue marginal inscription in French, German and English. Size: 120x157mm.

Walt Whitman and Dahoman Huts AP41

1970, Apr. 30 Engraved ***Perf. 13***

C119 AP41 100fr Prus bl, brn & emer 1.25 50

Issued to honor Walt Whitman (1818–1892), American poet.

No. C117 Surcharged in Silver with New Value, Heavy Bar and:

"APOLLO XIII / SOLIDARITE / SPATIALE / INTERNATIONALE"

1970, May 15 Photo. ***Perf. 12½***

C120 AP40 40fr on 30fr multi 65 65

The flight of Apollo 13.

Soccer Players and Globe—AP42

Designs: 50fr, Goalkeeper catching ball. 200fr, Players kicking ball.

1970, May 19

C121 AP42 40fr multi 60 35
C122 AP42 50fr multi 70 40
C123 AP42 200fr multi 3.00 1.40

Issued to publicize the 9th World Soccer Championships for the Jules Rimet Cup, Mexico City, May 30–June 21, 1970.

EXPO '70 Type of Regular Issue

Designs (EXPO '70 Emblems and): 70fr, Dahomey pavilion. 120fr, Mt. Fuji, temple and torii.

1970, June 15 Litho. ***Perf. 13½x14***

C124 A54 70fr yel, red & dk vio 85 40
C125 A54 120fr yel, red & grn 1.50 75

Issued to publicize EXPO '70 International Exhibition Osaka, Japan, Mar. 15–Sept. 13, 1970.

No. C123 Surcharged with New Value and Overprinted:

"Bresil-Italie / 4–1"

1970, July 13 Photo. ***Perf. 12½***

C126 AP42 100fr on 200fr multi 1.50 65

Issued to commemorate Brazil's victory in the 9th World Soccer Championships, Mexico City.

Mercury, Map of Africa and Europe AP43 **Ludwig van Beethoven AP44**

Europafrica Issue, 1970

1970, July 20 Photo. ***Perf. 12x13***

C127 AP43 40fr multi 50 30
C128 AP43 70fr multi 85 40

1970, Sept. 21 Litho. ***Perf. 14x13½***

C129 AP44 90fr brt bl & vio blk 1.25 50
C130 AP44 110fr yel grn & dk brn 1.35 70

Issued to commemorate the bicentenary of the birth of Ludwig van Beethoven (1770–1827), composer.

Symbols of Learning
AP45

1970, Nov. 6 Photo. ***Perf. 12½***

C131 AP45 100fr multi 1.25 50

Issued to commemorate the laying of the foundation stone for the University at Calavi.

Annunciation, Rhenish School, c.1340
AP46

Paintings of Rhenish School, circa 1340: 70fr, Nativity. 110fr, Adoration of the Kings. 200fr, Presentation at the Temple.

1970, Nov. 9 ***Perf. 12½x12***

C132 AP46 40fr gold & multi 50 25
C133 AP46 70fr gold & multi 90 35
C134 AP46 110fr gold & multi 1.35 60
C135 AP46 200fr gold & multi 2.75 1.10

Christmas 1970.

Charles de Gaulle, Arc de Triomphe and Flag
AP47

Design: 500fr, de Gaulle as old man and Notre Dame Cathedral, Paris.

1971, March 15 Photo. ***Perf. 12½***

C136 AP47 40fr multi 60 30
C137 AP47 500fr multi 6.00 3.00

In memory of Gen. Charles de Gaulle (1890–1970), President of France.

L' Indifférent, by Watteau
AP48

Painting: No. C139, Woman playing stringed instrument, by Watteau.

1971, May 3 Photo. ***Perf. 13***

C138 AP48 100fr red brn & multi 1.20 80
C139 AP48 100fr red brn & multi 1.20 80

250th death anniversary of Jean Antoine Watteau (1684–1721), French painter.

1971, May 29 Photo. ***Perf. 13***

Dürer Paintings: 100fr, Self-portrait, 1498. 200fr, Self-portrait, 1500.

C140 AP48 100fr bl grn & multi 1.20 80
C141 AP48 200fr dk grn & multi 2.75 1.60

500th anniversary of the birth of Albrecht Dürer (1471–1528), German painter and engraver. See Nos. C151–C152, C174–C175.

Johannes Kepler and Diagram
AP49

Designs: 200fr, Kepler, trajectories, satellite and rocket.

1971, July 12 Engraved ***Perf. 13***

C142 AP49 40fr brt rose lil, blk & vio bl 50 25
C143 AP49 200fr red, blk & dk bl 2.75 1.20

400th anniversary of the birth of Johannes Kepler (1571–1630), German astronomer.

Europafrica Issue

Jet Plane, Maps of Europe and Africa—AP50

Designs: 100fr, Ocean liner, maps of Europe and Africa.

1971, July 19 Photo. ***Perf. 12½x12***

C144 AP50 50fr blk, lt bl & org 60 30
C145 AP50 100fr multi 1.20 60

African Postal Union Issue, 1971
Common Design Type

Design: 100fr, Dahomey coat of arms and UAMPT building, Brazzaville, Congo.

1971, Nov. 13 ***Perf. 13x13½***

C146 CD135 100fr bl & multi 1.20 60

Flight into Egypt, by Van Dyke
AP51

Paintings: 40fr, Adoration of the Shepherds, by the Master of the Hausbuch, c. 1500 (vert.). 70fr, Adoration of the Kings, by Holbein the Elder (vert.). 200fr, The Birth of Christ, by Dürer.

1971, Nov. 22 ***Perf. 13***

C147 AP51 40fr gold & multi 50 25
C148 AP51 70fr gold & multi 90 45

C149 AP51 100fr gold & multi 1.20 50
C150 AP51 200fr gold & multi 2.40 1.20

Christmas 1971.

Painting Type of 1971 Inscribed: "25e ANNIVERSAIRE DE L'UNICEF"

Paintings: 40fr, Prince Balthazar, by Velasquez. 100fr, Infanta Margarita Maria, by Velázquez.

1971, Dec. 11

C151 AP48 40fr gold & multi 50 30
C152 AP48 100fr gold & multi 1.20 50

25th anniversary of the United Nations International Children's Fund (UNICEF).

Olympic Games Type of Regular Issue

Design: 150fr, Sapporo '72 emblem, ski jump and stork flying.

1972, Feb. Engraved *Perf. 13*

C153 A61 150fr brn, dp rose lil & bl 2.00 1.00

11th Winter Olympic Games, Sapporo, Japan, Feb. 3–13.

Boy Scout and Scout Flag
AP52

Designs: 40fr, Scout playing marimba. 100fr, Scouts doing farm work.

1972, Mar. 19 Photo. *Perf. 13*

Size: 26x35mm.

C154 AP52 35fr multi 30 20
C155 AP52 40fr multi 50 25

Size: 26x46mm.

C156 AP52 100fr yel & multi 1.20 60
a. Souvenir sheet of 3 2.25 2.25

World Boy Scout Seminar, Cotonou, March 1972. No. C156a contains Nos. C154–C156 with perf. 12½. Red marginal inscription and black control number. Size: 150x115mm.

Workers Training Institute and Friedrich Naumann—AP53

Design: 250fr, Workers Training Institute and Pres. Theodor Heuss of Germany.

1972, Mar. 29 Photo. *Perf. 13x12*

C157 AP53 100fr brt rose, blk & vio 1.10 55
C158 AP53 250fr bl, blk & vio 3.00 1.25

Laying of foundation stone for National Workers Training Institute.

Mosaic Floor, St. Mark's, Venice—AP54

12th Century Mosaics from St. Mark's Basilica: 40fr, Roosters carrying fox on a pole. 65fr, Noah sending out dove.

1972, Apr. 10 *Perf. 13*

C159 AP54 35fr gold & multi 50 30
C160 AP54 40fr gold & multi 60 40
C161 AP54 65fr gold & multi 90 60

UNESCO campaign to save Venice.

Neapolitan and Dahoman Dancers
AP55

1972, May 3 *Perf. 13½x13*

C162 AP55 100fr multi 1.20 70

12th Philatelic Exhibition, Naples.

Running, German Eagle, Olympic Rings
AP56

Designs (Olympic Rings and): 85fr, High jump and Glyptothek, Munich. 150fr, Shot put and Propylaeum, Munich.

1972, June 12 Engraved *Perf. 13*

C163 AP56 20fr ultra, grn & brn 25 15
C164 AP56 85fr brn, grn & ultra 90 40
C165 AP56 150fr grn, brn & ultra 1.75 90
a. Miniature sheet of 3 3.50 3.50

20th Olympic Games, Munich, Aug. 26–Sept. 10. No. C165a contains one each of Nos. C163–C165. Size: 130x99mm.

Louis Blériot and his Plane—AP57

1972, June 26

C166 AP57 100fr vio, cl & brt bl 1.20 65

Birth centenary of Louis Blériot (1872–1936), French aviation pioneer.

Adam, by Lucas Cranach
AP58

Design: 200fr, Eve, by Lucas Cranach.

1972, Oct. 24 Photogravure

C167 AP58 150fr multi 2.00 1.00
C168 AP58 200fr multi 2.50 1.10

500th anniversary of the birth of Lucas Cranach (1472–1553), German painter.

Pauline Borghese, by Canova
AP59

1972, Nov. 8

C169 AP59 250fr multi 3.00 1.50

Sesquicentennial of the death of Antonio Canova (1757–1822), Italian sculptor.

Nos. C163–C165 Overprinted:

a. 5.00m.–10.00m. / VIREN / 2 MEDAILLES D'OR
b. HAUTEUR DAMES / MEYFARTH / MEDAILLE D'OR
c. POIDS / KOMAR / MEDAILLE D'OR

1972, Nov. 13 Engraved *Perf. 13*

C170 AP56 (a) 20fr multi 30 20
C171 AP56 (b) 85fr multi 1.00 50
C172 AP56 (c) 150fr multi 2.00 1.10
a. Miniature sheet of 3 3.75 3.75

Gold medal winners in 20th Olympic Games: Lasse Viren, Finland, 5,000m. and 10,000m. races (20fr); Ulrike Meyfarth, Germany, women's high jump (85fr); Wladyslaw Komar, Poland, shot put (150fr).

Louis Pasteur
AP60

1972, Nov. 30

C173 AP60 100fr brt grn, lil & brn 1.20 65

Sesquicentennial of the birth of Louis Pasteur (1822–1895), chemist and bacteriologist.

Painting Type of 1971

Paintings by Georges de La Tour: 35fr, Vielle player. 150fr, The Newborn (horiz.).

1972, Dec. 11 Photogravure

C174 AP48 35fr multi 42 20
C175 AP48 150fr multi 2.00 1.10

320th death anniversary of Georges de La Tour (1593–1652), French painter.

Annunciation, School of Agnolo Gaddi
AP61

Paintings: 125fr, Nativity, by Simone dei Crocifissi. 140fr, Adoration of the Shepherds, by Giovanni di Pietro. 250fr, Adoration of the Kings, by Giotto.

1972, Dec. 15

C176 AP61 35fr gold & multi 40 20
C177 AP61 125fr gold & multi 1.20 60
C178 AP61 140fr gold & multi 1.60 80
C179 AP61 250fr gold & multi 2.60 1.50

Christmas 1972. See Nos. C195–C198, C218, C223, C225–C226.

Statue of St. Teresa, Basilica of Lisieux—AP62

Design: 100fr, St. Teresa, roses, and globe (vert.).

1973, May 14 Photo. *Perf. 13*

C180 AP62 40fr blk, gold & lt ultra 40 25
C181 AP62 100fr gold & multi 1.00 55

Centenary of the birth of St. Teresa of Lisieux (Therese Martin, 1873–97), Carmelite nun.

Scouts, African Scout Emblem—AP63

Designs (African Scout Emblem and): 20fr, Lord Baden-Powell (vert.). 40fr, Scouts building bridge.

1973, July 2 Engraved *Perf. 13*

C182 AP63 15fr bl, grn & choc 15 10
C183 AP63 20fr ol & Prus bl 20 15
C184 AP63 40fr grn, Prus bl & brn 40 20
a. Souvenir sheet of 3 85 85

24th Boy Scout World Conference, Nairobi, Kenya, July 16–21. No. C184a contains 3 stamps similar to Nos. C182–C184 in changed colors (15fr in ultramarine, slate green and chocolate; 20fr in chocolate, ultramarine and indigo; 40fr in slate green, indigo and chocolate). Ultramarine marginal inscription and border. Size: 180x100 mm.

Copernicus, Venera and Mariner Satellites—AP64

Design: 125fr, Copernicus, sun, earth and moon (vert.).

1973, Aug. 20 Engr. *Perf. 13*

C185 AP64 65fr blk, dk brn & org 80 45
C186 AP64 125fr bl, sl grn & pur 1.25 65

500th anniversary of the birth of Nicolaus Copernicus (1473–1543), Polish astronomer.

Head and City Hall, Brussels
AP64a

1973, Sept. 17 Engraved *Perf. 13*

C187	AP64a	100fr blk, Prus bl & dk grn	90	60

African Weeks, Brussels, Sept. 15–30, 1973.

WMO Emblem, World Weather Map—AP65

1973, Sept. 25

C188	AP65	100fr ol grn & lt brn	1.00	60

Centenary of international meteorological cooperation.

Europafrica Issue

"EUROPAFRIQUE"—AP66

Design: 40fr, similar to 35fr.

1973, Oct. 1 Engraved *Perf. 13*

C189	AP66	35fr multi	35	20
C190	AP66	40fr bl, sep & ultra	40	30

John F. Kennedy AP67

1973, Oct. 18

C191	AP67	200fr bl grn, vio & sl grn	2.00	1.20
a.		Souvenir sheet	2.50	2.50

10th anniversary of the death of President John F. Kennedy (1917–1963). No. C191a contains one stamp in changed colors (bright blue, magenta & brown). Magenta marginal inscription and border. Size: 140x109mm.

Soccer—AP68

Designs: 40fr, Two soccer players. 100fr, Three soccer players.

1973, Nov. 19 Engr. *Perf. 13*

C192	AP68	35fr multi	30	20
C193	AP68	40fr multi	40	25
C194	AP68	100fr multi	90	65

World Soccer Cup, Munich 1974.

Painting Type of 1972

Designs: 35fr, Annunciation, by Dirk Bouts. 100fr, Nativity, by Giotto. 150fr, Adoration of the Kings, by Botticelli. 200fr, Adoration of the Shepherds, by Jacopo Bassano (horiz.).

1973, Dec. 20 Photo. *Perf. 13*

C195	AP61	35fr gold & multi	35	25
C196	AP61	100fr gold & multi	1.00	60
C197	AP61	150fr gold & multi	1.50	1.00
C198	AP61	200fr gold & multi	2.00	1.30

Christmas 1973.

No. C188 Surcharged in Violet with New Value and: "OPERATION SKYLAB / 1973–1974"

1974, Feb. 4 Engraved *Perf. 13*

C199	AP65	200fr on 100fr multi	1.75	1.25

Skylab U.S. space missions, 1973–74.

Skiers, Snowflake, Olympic Rings AP69

1974, Feb. 25 Engraved *Perf. 13*

C200	AP69	100fr vio bl, brn & brt bl	90	65

50th anniversary of first Winter Olympic Games, Chamonix, France.

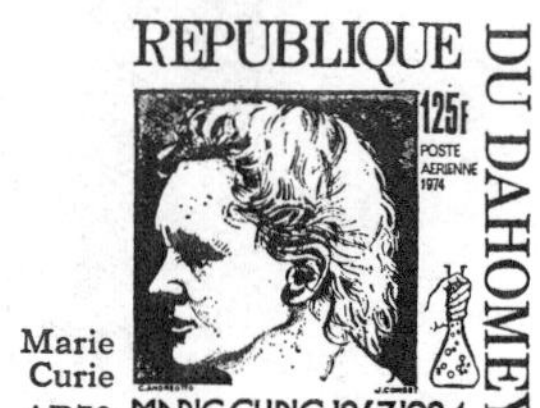

Marie Curie AP70

Designs: 50fr, Lenin. 150fr, Churchill.

1974, June 7 Engr. *Perf. 13*

C201	AP70	50fr dk red & brt lil	45	30
C202	AP70	125fr ol & dl red	1.10	75
C203	AP70	150fr brt lil & Prus bl	1.35	90

50th anniversary of the death of Lenin (50fr); 40th anniversary of the death of Marie Sklodowska Curie (125fr); centenary of the birth of Winston Churchill (150fr).

Bishop, Persian, 18th Century AP71

Frederic Chopin AP72

Design: 200fr, Queen, Siamese chess piece, 19th century.

1974, June 14 Photo. *Perf. 12½x13*

C204	AP71	50fr org & multi	50	35
C205	AP71	200fr brt grn & multi	1.75	1.25

21st Chess Olympiad, Nice, June 6–30, 1974.

1974, June 24 Engr. *Perf. 13*

Design: No. C207, Ludwig van Beethoven.

C206	AP72	150fr blk & cop red	1.25	90
C207	AP72	150fr blk & cop red	1.25	90

Famous musicians, Frederic Chopin (1810–1849) and Ludwig van Beethoven (1770–1827).

Astronaut on Moon, and Earth AP73

1974, July 10 Engraved *Perf. 13*

C208	AP73	150fr multi	1.25	1.00

5th anniversary of the first moon walk.

Nos. C182–C183 Surcharged and Overprinted in Black or Red: "XIe JAMBOREE PANARABE DE BATROUN-LIBAN"

1974, July 19

C209	AP63	100fr on 15fr multi	75	45
C210	AP63	140fr on 20fr multi (R)	1.20	75

11th Pan-Arab Jamboree, Batrun, Lebanon, Aug. 1974. Overprint includes 2 bars over old denomination; 2-line overprint on No. C209, 3 lines on No. C210.

Nos. C193–C194 Overprinted and Surcharged with New Value and Two Bars: "R F A 2 / HOLLANDE 1"

1974, July 26 Engraved *Perf. 13*

C211	AP68	100fr on 40fr	80	35
C212	AP68	150fr on 100fr	1.20	55

World Cup Soccer Championship, 1974, victory of German Federal Republic.

Earth and UPU Emblem—AP74

Designs (UPU Emblem and): 65fr, Concorde in flight. 125fr, French railroad car, c. 1860. 200fr, African drummer and Renault mail truck, pre-1939.

1974, Aug. 5 Engraved *Perf. 13*

C213	AP74	35fr rose cl & vio	30	10
C214	AP74	65fr Prus grn & cl	60	20
C215	AP74	125fr multi	1.10	42
C216	AP74	200fr multi	1.75	70

Centenary of Universal Postal Union.

Painting Type of 1972 and

Lion of Belfort by Frederic A. Bartholdi—AP75

Painting: 250fr, Girl with Falcon, by Philippe de Champaigne.

1974, Aug. 20 Engraved *Perf. 13*

C217	AP75	100fr rose brn	1.00	35
C218	AP61	250fr multi	2.50	1.00

Rhamphorhynchus—AP76

Prehistoric Animals: 150fr, Stegosaurus. 200fr, Tyrannosaurus.

1974, Sept. 23 Photogravure

C219	AP76	35fr multi	30	12
C220	AP76	150fr multi	1.20	55
C221	AP76	200fr multi	1.50	70

Europafrica Issue

Globe, Cogwheel, Emblem—AP77

1974, Dec. 20 Typo. *Perf. 13*

C222	AP77	250fr red & multi	2.50	1.00

Printed tête bêche in sheets of 10.

Christmas Type of 1972 and

Nativity, by Martin Schongauer AP78

Paintings: 35fr, Annunciation, by Schongauer. 100fr, Virgin in Rose Arbor, by Schongauer. 250fr, Virgin and Child, with St. John the Baptist, by Botticelli.

1974, Dec. 23 Photo. *Perf. 13*

C223	AP61	35fr gold & multi	30	15
C224	AP78	40fr gold & multi	40	25
C225	AP61	100fr gold & multi	1.00	35
C226	AP61	250fr gold & multi	2.50	1.00

Apollo and Soyuz Spacecraft AP79

Designs: 200fr, American and Russian flags, rocket take-off. 500fr, Apollo-Soyuz link-up.

1975, July 16 Litho. *Perf. 12½*

C227	AP79	35fr multi	30	15
C228	AP79	200fr vio bl, red & bl	1.60	70
C229	AP79	500fr vio bl, ind & red	4.00	2.25

Apollo Soyuz space test project (Russo-American cooperation); launching July 15; link-up, July 17.

Nos. C227–C228 Surcharged in Silver or Black: "RENCONTRE / APOLLO-SOYOUZ / 17 Juil. 1975"

1975, July 17 Litho. Perf. 12½

C230	AP79	100fr on 35fr (S)	80	35
C231	AP79	300fr on 200fr	2.40	1.00

Apollo-Soyuz link-up in space, July 17, 1975.

ARPHILA Emblem, "Stamps" and Head of Ceres—AP80

1975, Aug. 22 Engr. Perf. 13

C232	AP80	100fr blk, bl & lil	90	35

ARPHILA 75, International Philatelic Exhibition, Paris, June 6–16.

Holy Family, by Michelangelo AP81 — Infantry and Stars AP82

Europafrica Issue

1975, Sept. 29 Litho. Perf. 12

C233	AP81	300fr gold & multi	2.75	1.00

1975, Nov. 18 Engr. Perf. 13

Designs (Stars and): 135fr, Drummers and fifer. 300fr, Artillery with cannon. 500fr, Cavalry.

C234	AP82	75fr grn car & pur	60	25
C235	AP82	135fr bl, mag & sep	1.10	45
C236	AP82	300fr vio bl, ver & choc	2.40	1.00
C237	AP82	500fr ver, dk grn & brn	4.00	1.75

American bicentennial.

Diving and Olympic Rings AP83

Design: 250fr, Soccer and Olympic rings.

1975, Nov. 24

C238	AP83	40fr vio, grnsh bl & ol brn	35	15
C239	AP83	250fr red, emer & brn	2.00	90

Pre-Olympic Year 1975.

AIR POST SEMI-POSTAL STAMPS.

V1

V2

V3

V4

Stamps of the preceding designs were issued in 1942 by the Vichy Government, but were not placed in use in the colony.

AIR POST PARCEL POST STAMPS

Nos. C20–C23, C14 Surcharged in Black or Red

300F

COLIS POSTAUX

1967–69 Engraved Perf. 13

CQ1	AP6	200fr on 200fr multi	4.50	3.25
CQ2	AP6	300fr on 100fr multi	5.50	4.50
CQ3	AP6	500fr on 300fr multi	9.00	6.25
CQ4	AP6	1000fr on 500fr multi	20.00	16.50
CQ5	AP4	5000fr on 100fr multi (R) ('69)	80.00	80.00
		Nos. CQ1-CQ5 (5)	119.00	110.50

On No. CQ5, "Colis Postaux" is at top, bar at right.

POSTAGE DUE STAMPS.

Dahomey Natives D1 — Numeral of Value D2

Typographed.

1906 Perf. 14x13½. Unwmkd.

J1	D1	5c grn, *grnsh*	1.10	1.10
J2	D1	10c red brn	2.00	2.00
J3	D1	15c dk bl	3.75	3.75
J4	D1	20c *yellow*	2.35	2.35
J5	D1	30c red, *straw*	3.25	3.25
J6	D1	50c violet	10.00	10.00
J7	D1	60c *buff*	5.50	5.50
J8	D1	1fr *pinkish*	15.00	15.00
		Nos. J1-J8 (8)	42.95	42.95

1914

J9	D2	5c green	6	6
J10	D2	10c rose	12	12
J11	D2	15c gray	18	18
J12	D2	20c brown	32	32
J13	D2	30c blue	35	35
J14	D2	50c black	50	50
J15	D2	60c orange	70	70
J16	D2	1fr violet	70	70
		Nos. J9-J16 (8)	2.93	2.93

1927

Type of 1914 Issue Surcharged **2F.**

J17	D2	2fr on 1fr lil rose	1.35	1.35
J18	D2	3fr on 1fr org brn	1.75	1.75

Carved Mask D3

1941 Engraved Perf. 14x13

J19	D3	5c black	6	6
J20	D3	10c lil rose	6	6
J21	D3	15c dk bl	6	6
J22	D3	20c brt yel grn	12	12
J23	D3	30c orange	18	18
J24	D3	50c vio brn	32	32
J25	D3	60c sl grn	35	35
J26	D3	1fr rose red	45	45
J27	D3	2fr yellow	45	45
J28	D3	3fr dk pur	60	60
		Nos. J19-J28 (10)	2.65	2.65

Stamps of type D3 with value numerals replacing "RF" at upper left corner were issued in 1943-44 by the Vichy Government, but were not placed on sale in the colony.

Republic

Panther and Man—D4

Perf. 14x13½

1963, July 22 Typo. Unwmkd.

J29	D4	1fr grn & rose cl	5	5
J30	D4	2fr brn & emer	8	8
J31	D4	5fr org & vio bl	15	15
J32	D4	10fr mag & blk	35	35
J33	D4	20fr vio bl & org	40	40
		Nos. J29-J33 (5)	1.03	1.03

Mail Boat—D5

Designs: No. J35, Heliograph. No. J36, Morse receiver. No. J37, Mailman on bicycle. No. J38, Early telephone. No. J39, Autorail. No. J40, Mail truck. No. J41, Radio tower. No. J42, DC-8F jet plane. No. J43, Early Bird communications satellite.

1967, Oct. 24 Engraved Perf. 11

J34	D5	1fr brn, dl pur & bl	10	10
J35	D5	1fr dl pur, brn & bl	10	10
J36	D5	3fr dk brn, dk grn & org	15	15
J37	D5	3fr dk grn, dk brn & org	15	15
J38	D5	5fr ol bis, lil & bl	22	22
J39	D5	5fr lil, ol bis & bl	22	22
J40	D5	10fr brn org, vio & grn	38	38
J41	D5	10fr vio, brn org & grn	38	38
J42	D5	30fr Prus bl, mar & vio	70	70
J43	D5	30fr vio, Prus bl & mar	70	70
		Nos. J34-J43 (10)	3.10	3.10

The two designs of each value in Nos. J34–J43 were printed tête bêche, se-tenant at the base.

PARCEL POST STAMPS

COLIS POSTAUX

Nos. 141–146 and 148 Surcharged

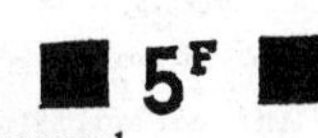

Engraved

1967, Jan. Perf. 13 Unwmkd.

Q1	A15	5fr on 1fr multi	15	15
Q2	A15	10fr on 2fr multi	30	30
Q3	A15	20fr on 6fr multi	45	45
Q4	A15	25fr on 3fr multi	60	60
Q5	A15	30fr on 4fr multi	70	70
Q6	A15	50fr on 10fr multi	1.10	1.10
a.		"20" instead of "50"	70.00	
Q7	A15	100fr on 20fr multi	2.25	2.25
		Nos. Q1-Q7 (7)	5.55	5.55

The surcharge is arranged to fit the shape of the stamp.

No. Q6a occurred once on the sheet of the 50fr on 10fr.

DALMATIA

(dăl·mā′shĭ·ȧ; -shȧ)

LOCATION — A promontory in the northwestern part of the Balkan Peninsula, together with several small islands in the Adriatic Sea.

GOVT.—Part of the former Austro-Hungarian crownland of the same name.

AREA—113 sq. mi.

POP.—18,719 (1921).

CAPITAL—Zara.

Stamps were issued during Italian occupation. This territory was subsequently annexed by Italy.

100 Centesimi = 1 Corona = 1 Lira

Issued under Italian Occupation.

Italy No. 87 Surcharged **una corona**

Wmkd. Crown. (140)

1919, May 1 *Perf. 14*

No.	Type	Description	Unused	Used
1	A46	1cor on 1 l brn & grn	55	70

Italian Stamps of 1906-08 Surcharged **5 centesimi di corona** *a*

1921–22

No.	Type	Description	Unused	Used
2	A48	5c on 5c grn	15	15
3	A48	10c on 10c cl	15	15
4	A49	25c on 25c bl ('22)	45	65
5	A49	50c on 50c vio ('22)	60	75

Italian Stamps of 1901-10 Surcharged **1 corona** *b*

No.	Type	Description	Unused	Used
6	A46	1cor on 1 l brn & grn ('22)	75	90
7	A46	5cor on 5 l bl & rose ('22)	5.25	6.75
8	A51	10cor on 10 l gray grn & red ('22)	8.50	12.00
		Nos. 1-8 (8)	16.40	22.05

Surcharges similar to these but differing in style or arrangement of type were used in Austria under Italian occupation.

SPECIAL DELIVERY STAMPS.

Italian Special Delivery Stamp No. E1 Surcharged **25 centesimi di corona**

Wmkd. Crowns. (140)

1921 *Perf. 14*

No.	Type	Description	Unused	Used
E1	SD1	25c on 25c rose red	38	45
a.		Double surcharge	13.50	13.50

Italian Special Delivery Stamp Surcharged **LIRE 1,20 DI CORONA**

1922

No.	Type	Description	Unused	Used
E2	SD2	1.20 l on 1.20 l bl & rose	27.50	

No. E2 was not placed in use.

POSTAGE DUE STAMPS.

Italian Postage Due Stamps Surcharged types "a" or "b"

Wmkd. Crown. (140)

1922 *Perf. 14.*

No.	Type	Description	Unused	Used
J1	D3 (a)	50c on 50c buff & mag	50	70
J2	D3 (b)	1cor on 1 l bl & red	80	1.00
J3	D3 (b)	2cor on 2 l bl & red	3.75	4.75
J4	D3 (b)	5cor on 5 l bl & red	4.75	6.75

DANISH WEST INDIES

LOCATION—A group of islands in the West Indies, lying east of Puerto Rico.

GOVT.—A former Danish colony.

AREA—132 sq. mi.

POP.—27,086 (1911).

CAPITAL—Charlotte Amalie.

The United States bought these islands in 1917 and they became the U. S. Virgin Islands, using U. S. stamps and currency.

100 Cents = 1 Dollar
100 Bits = 1 Franc (1905)

Coat of Arms
A1

Wmk. 111

Yellowish Paper.
Yellow Wavy-line Burelage, UL to LR
Wmkd. Small Crown (111)

1856 **Typographed** *Imperf.*

No.	Type	Description	Unused	Used
1	A1	3c dk car, brn gum	170.00	170.00
a.		3c dk car, yel gum	250.00	250.00
b.		3c dk car, white gum	1,100.	

No. 2 was reprinted in carmine, unwatermarked, in 1930. Price $120.

A second (1942) reprint in rose carmine, unwatermarked, has printed on the back across each horizontal row: "Nytryk 1942, G. A. Hagemann: Danmarks og Dansk Vestindiens diens Freimaerker, Bind 2." Price $60.

White Paper
Yellow Wavy-line Burelage, UR to LL

1866

No.	Type	Description	Unused	Used
2	A1	3c rose	75.00	70.00

1873 *Perf. 12½*

No.	Type	Description	Unused	Used
3	A1	3c rose	150.00	170.00

Without Burelage.

No.	Type	Description	Unused	Used
4	A1	4c dl bl	275.00	350.00
a.		Imperf., (pair)	950.00	1,200.
b.		Horiz. pair, imperf. vert.	750.00	900.00

No. 4 was reprinted in 1930 in ultramarine, unwatermarked and imperf. Price $120.

A second (1942) reprint of No. 4 in blue, unwatermarked and imperf., has printing on the back like the 1942 reprint of No. 1. Price $60.

Numeral of Value
A2

NORMAL FRAME

INVERTED FRAME

The arabesques in the corners have a main stem and a branch. When the frame is in normal position, in the upper left corner the branch leaves the main stem half way between two little leaflets. In the lower right corner the branch starts at the foot of the second leaflet. When the frame is inverted the corner designs are, of course, transposed.

Wmk. 112

White Wove Paper, Varying from Thin to Thick.

Perf. 14x13½

1874-96 **Wmkd. Crown. (112)**

No.	Type	Description	Unused	Used
5	A2	1c grn & brn red	25.00	22.50
a.		1c grn & rose lil	37.50	30.00
b.		1c grn & red vio	37.50	30.00
c.		1c grn & vio	80.00	80.00
e.		Inverted frame	25.00	22.50
6	A2	3c bl & car	27.50	17.00
d.		Imperf., pair	600.00	
e.		Inverted frame	27.50	16.00
7	A2	4c brn & dl bl	20.00	20.00
b.		4c brn & ultra	225.00	160.00
c.		Diagonal half used as 2c on cover		225.00
d.		Inverted frame	750.00	550.00
8	A2	5c grn & gray	32.50	20.00
b.		Inverted frame	32.50	20.00
9	A2	7c lil & org	30.00	70.00
a.		7c lil & yel	70.00	80.00
b.		Inverted frame	60.00	90.00
10	A2	10c bl & brn	32.50	20.00
b.		Period between "t" & "s" of "cents"	40.00	27.50
c.		Inverted frame	30.00	20.00
11	A2	12c red lil & yel grn	35.00	42.50
a.		12c lil & dp grn	80.00	65.00
12	A2	14c lil & grn	625.00	750.00
a.		Inverted frame	1,700.	1,900.
13	A2	50c violet	120.00	140.00
a.		50c gray vio	150.00	170.00

Nos. 9 and 13 Surcharged in Black

1 CENT *a* **10 CENTS 1895** *b*

1887–95

No.	Type	Description	Unused	Used
14	A2 (a)	1c on 7c lil & org	75.00	100.00
a.		1c on 7c lil & yel	120.00	140.00
b.		Double surcharge	250.00	300.00
c.		Inverted surcharge	110.00	120.00
d.		Triple surcharge		
e.		Pair, one without surch.		
15	A2 (b)	10c on 50c vio ('95)	30.00	35.00

Type of 1873

1896–1901 *Perf. 13*

No.	Type	Description	Unused	Used
16	A2	1c grn & red vio ('98)	13.00	13.00
a.		Normal frame	300.00	300.00
17	A2	3c bl & lake ('98)	13.00	13.00
a.		Normal frame	260.00	260.00
18	A2	4c bis & dl bl ('01)	13.00	13.00
a.		Diagonal half used as 2c on cover		40.00
b.		Inverted frame	60.00	60.00
19	A2	5c grn & gray	42.50	37.50
a.		Normal frame	600.00	600.00
20	A2	10c bl & brn ('01)	85.00	100.00
a.		Inverted frame	900.00	1,400.
b.		Period between "t" and "s" of "cents"	95.00	110.00
		Nos. 16-20 (5)	166.50	176.50

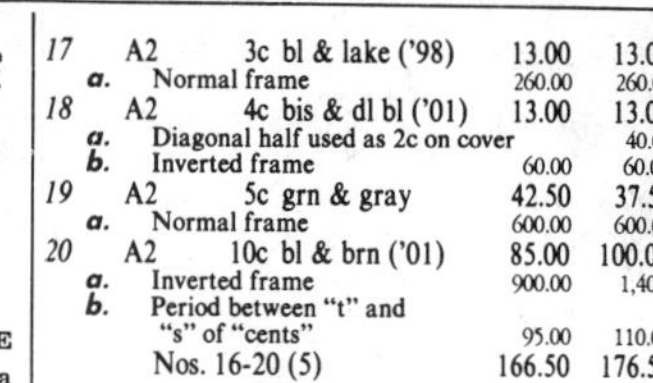

Arms
A5

1900

No.	Type	Description	Unused	Used
21	A5	1c lt grn	2.50	2.50
22	A5	5c lt bl	13.00	13.00

See also Nos. 29–30.

Nos. 6, 17, 20 Surcharged:

2 CENTS 1902 *c* **8 Cents 1902** *d*

Surcharge "c" in Black

1902 *Perf. 14x13½*

No.	Type	Description	Unused	Used
23	A2	2c on 3c bl & car	450.00	500.00
a.		"2" in date with straight tail	475.00	525.00
b.		Normal frame	1,250.	

Perf. 13

No.	Type	Description	Unused	Used
24	A2	2c on 3c bl & lake	10.00	12.00
a.		"2" in date with straight tail	11.00	13.00
b.		Dated "1901"	400.00	450.00
c.		Normal frame	225.00	275.00
d.		Dark grn surch.	1,400.	
e.		As "d" & "a"	1,500.	
f.		As "d" & "c"		
25	A2	8c on 10c bl & brn	25.00	35.00
a.		"2" with straight tail	27.50	37.50
b.		On No. 20b	30.00	40.00
c.		Inverted frame	325.00	350.00

Surcharge "d" in Black

No.	Type	Description	Unused	Used
27	A2	2c on 3c bl & lake	12.50	17.50
a.		Normal frame	275.00	300.00
28	A2	8c on 10c bl & brn	11.00	11.00
a.		On No. 20b	16.00	16.00
b.		Inverted frame	275.00	275.00

Wmk. 113

1903 **Wmkd. Crown (113)**

No.	Type	Description	Unused	Used
29	A5	2c carmine	13.00	13.00
30	A5	8c brown	27.50	32.50

King Christian IX
A8

St. Thomas Harbor
A9

1905		Typographed		Perf. 13
31	A8	5b green	7.50	4.00
32	A8	10b red	7.50	4.00
33	A8	20b grn & bl	15.00	15.00
34	A8	25b ultra	15.00	15.00
35	A8	40b red & gray	12.50	12.50
36	A8	50b yel & gray	12.50	15.00

Frame Typo., Center Engraved
Wmkd. Two Crowns. (113)
Perf. 12

37	A9	1fr grn & bl	20.00	30.00
38	A9	2fr org red & brn	42.50	60.00
39	A9	5fr yel & brn	110.00	250.00
		Nos. 31-39 (9)	242.50	405.50

Nos. 18, 22, 30 Surcharged in Black

5
BIT
1905

Wmkd. Crown. (112)

1905				Perf. 13
40	A2	5b on 4c bis & dl bl	22.50	45.00
a.		Inverted frame	42.50	60.00
41	A5	5b on 5c lt bl	14.00	27.50

Wmkd. Crown. (113)

42	A5	5b on 8c brn	14.00	27.50

King Frederik VIII
A10

Frame Typo., Center Engraved

1908		Perf. 13		Wmk. 113
43	A10	5b green	2.50	1.30
44	A10	10b red	2.50	1.30
45	A10	15b vio & brn	5.00	5.00
46	A10	20b grn & bl	37.50	20.00
47	A10	25b bl & dk bl	3.25	2.00
48	A10	30b cl & sl	62.50	37.50
49	A10	40b ver & gray	6.50	8.00
50	A10	50b yel & brn	7.00	10.00
		Nos. 43-50 (8)	126.75	85.10

King Christian X
A11

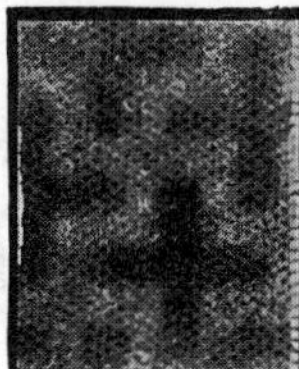

Wmk. 114

Wmkd. Multiple Crosses. (114)

1915–17				Perf. 14x14½
51	A11	5b yel grn	3.00	6.00
52	A11	10b red	3.00	52.50
53	A11	15b lil & red brn	3.00	52.50
54	A11	20b grn & bl	3.00	52.50
55	A11	25b bl & dk bl	3.00	12.00
56	A11	30b cl & blk	3.00	52.50
57	A11	40b org & blk	3.00	52.50
58	A11	50b yel & brn	3.00	52.50
		Nos. 51-58 (8)	24.00	333.00

Forged and favor cancellations exist.

POSTAGE DUE STAMPS.

Royal Cipher, "Christian 9 Rex"
D1

Lithographed

1902		Perf. 11½		Unwmkd.
J1	D1	1c dk bl	8.00	14.00
J2	D1	4c dk bl	12.50	17.50
J3	D1	6c dk bl	32.50	52.50
J4	D1	10c dk bl	25.00	35.00

There are five types of each value. On the 4c they may be distinguished by differences in the figures "4"; on the other values the differences are minute.

It was not the custom to cancel these stamps. Copies without gum have probably been used.

Counterfeits of Nos. J1–J4 exist.

D2

1905–13				Perf. 13
J5	D2	5b red & gray	6.50	8.00
J6	D2	20b red & gray	14.00	20.00
J7	D2	30b red & gray	8.50	13.00
J8	D2	50b red & gray	12.50	18.00
a.		Perf. 14x14½ ('13)	20.00	80.00
b.		Perf. 11½	275.00	

All values of this issue are known imperforate, but were not regularly issued.

Counterfeits of Nos. J5–J8 exist.

Danish West Indies stamps were replaced by those of the United States in 1917, after the U.S. bought the islands.

DANZIG

(dăn[t]'sĭg ; dăn'zĭg)

LOCATION—In northern Europe bordering on the Baltic Sea.

GOVT.—Former free city and state.

AREA—754 sq. mi.

POP.— 407,000 (approx. 1939).

CAPITAL—Danzig.

Established as a "Free City and State" under the protection of the League of Nations in 1920, Danzig was seized by Germany in 1939. It became a Polish province in 1945.

100 Pfennig = 1 Gulden (1923)
100 Pfennig = 1 Mark

Used Prices of 1920–23

are for favor-canceled stamps unless otherwise noted. Postally used copies bring higher prices.

German Stamps of 1906-20 Overprinted in Black

Danzig

Wmkd. Lozenges. (125)

1920		Perf. 14, 14½, 15x14½		
1	A16	5pf green	20	18
2	A16	10pf car rose	20	18
3	A22	15pf vio brn	20	18
4	A16	20pf bl vio	20	18
5	A16	30pf org & blk, *buff*	20	18
6	A16	40pf car rose	20	18
7	A16	50pf pur & blk, *buff*	20	18
8	A17	1m red	70	60
9	A17	1.25m green	70	60
10	A17	1.50m yel brn	85	85
11	A21	2m blue	1.40	1.40
a.		Double ovpt.	1,000.	
12	A21	2.50m lil rose	1.75	3.00
13	A19	3m blk vio	4.75	6.50
14	A16	4m blk & rose	4.50	5.00
15	A20	5m sl & car	1.75	1.75
a.		Center inverted	6,000.	
b.		Invtd. ovpt.		9,000.
		Nos. 1-15 (15)	17.80	20.96

The 5pf brown, 10pf orange and 40pf lake and black with this overprint were not regularly issued. Price for trio, $850.

"Germania"
A1

German Stamps of 1906-20 Surcharged in Violet, Red, Green or Brown.

1920				
19	A1	5pf on 30pf org & blk, *buff* (V)	12	12
20	A1	10pf on 20pf bl vio (R)	12	12
a.		Double surch.	175.00	175.00
21	A1	25pf on 30pf org & blk, *buff* (G)	12	12
a.		Inverted surcharge	175.00	175.00
22	A1	60pf on 30pf org & blk, *buff* (Br)	55	55
a.		Double surch.	175.00	200.00
23	A1	80pf on 30pf org & blk, *buff* (V)	55	55

A2

A3

A4

A5

A6

A7

Surcharged in Black, Red, Blue or Green

Gray Burelage with Points Up.

25	A2	1m on 30pf org & blk, *buff* (Bk)	75	1.40
a.		Pair, one without surcharge		
26	A3	1¼m on 3pf brn (R)	75	1.40
27	A4	2m on 35pf red brn (Bl)	1.00	1.40
d.		Surch. omitted	100.00	100.00
28	A5	3m on 7½pf org (G)	1.00	1.40
29	A6	5m on 2pf gray (R)	1.00	1.40
30	A7	10m on 7½pf org (Bk)	3.00	7.25

Gray Burelage with Points Down.

26a	A3	1¼m on 3pf brn	27.50	27.50
27a	A4	2m on 35pf red brn	350.00	275.00
28a	A5	3m on 7½pf org	10.00	12.00
29a	A6	5m on 2pf gray	10.00	20.00
30a	A7	10m on 7½pf org	5.00	7.25

Violet Burelage with Points Up.

25b	A2	1m on 30pf org & blk, *buff*	30.00	40.00
26b	A3	1 ¼m on 3pf brn	4.00	6.00
27b	A4	2m on 35pf red brn	12.50	17.50
28b	A5	3m on 7½pf org	1.50	1.60
29b	A6	5m on 2pf gray	1.50	1.60
30b	A7	10m on 7½pf org	1.50	1.60

Violet Burelage with Points Down.

25c	A2	1m on 30pf org & blk, *buff*	1.10	1.50
26c	A3	1¼m on 3pf brn	4.00	7.25
27c	A4	2m on 35pf red brn	14.00	25.00
28c	A5	3m on 7½pf org	40.00	55.00
29c	A6	5m on 2pf gray	4.50	5.50
30c	A7	10m on 7½pf org	14.00	22.00

Excellent counterfeits of the surcharges are known.

German Stamps of 1906-20 Overprinted in Blue

1920				
31	A22	2pf gray	130.00	200.00
32	A22	2½pf gray	190.00	300.00
33	A16	3pf brown	11.00	17.50
a.		Dbl. overprint	75.00	75.00
34	A16	5pf green	25	25
a.		Dbl. overprint	50.00	50.00
35	A22	7½pf orange	40.00	50.00
36	A16	10pf carmine	4.00	4.75
a.		Dbl. overprint	100.00	
37	A22	15pf dk vio	40	45
a.		"Danzig" omitted	25.00	
b.		Dbl. overprint	50.00	
38	A16	20pf bl vio	40	45

Overprinted in Carmine or Blue.

39	A16	25pf org & blk, *yel*	40	45
40	A16	30pf org & blk, *buff*	65.00	75.00
42	A16	40pf lake & blk	1.50	2.00
a.		Inverted overprint		
b.		Double ovpt.		
43	A16	50pf pur & blk, *buff*	210.00	300.00
44	A16	60pf mag (Bl)	3,000.	3,000.
45	A16	75pf grn & blk	40	45
46	A16	80pf lake & blk, *rose*	2.75	3.75
47	A17	1m carmine	1,150.	1,150.

Overprinted in Carmine

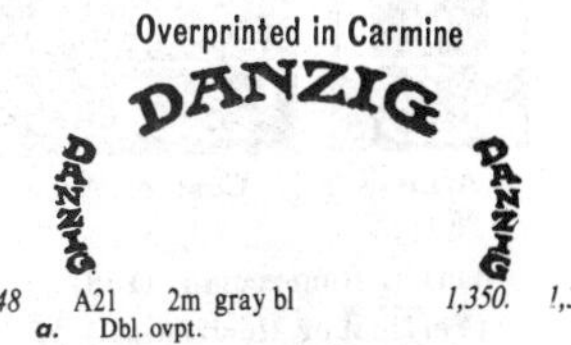

48	A21	2m gray bl	1,350.	1,350.
a.		Dbl. ovpt.		

Counterfeit overprints of Nos. 31 to 48 exist.

Nos. 44, 47 and 48 were issued in small quantities and usually affixed directly to the mail by the postal clerk.

Hanseatic Trading Ship
A8 A9

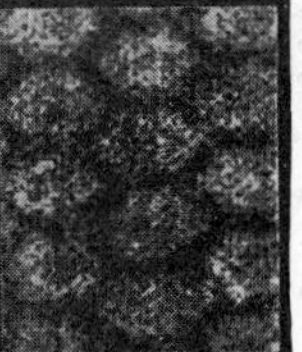

Wmk. 108

Serrate Roulette 13½.

Wmkd. Honeycomb. (108)

1921, Jan. 31 Typographed

49 A8 5(pf) brn & vio 40 40
50 A8 10(pf) org & dk vio 40 40
51 A8 25(pf) grn & car rose 80 80
52 A8 40(pf) car rose 3.25 3.25
53 A8 80(pf) ultra 50 50
54 A9 1m car rose & blk 1.60 1.75
55 A9 2m dk bl & dk grn 5.00 6.00
56 A9 3m blk & grnsh bl 1.60 2.50
57 A9 5m ind & rose red 1.60 2.50
58 A9 10m dk grn & brn org 3.00 6.00
Nos. 49-58 (10) 18.15 24.10

Issued in commemoration of the Constitution.

Nos. 49 and 50 with center in red instead of violet and Nos. 49, 50 and 54 with center inverted are probably proofs. All values of this issue exist imperforate but are not known to have been regularly issued in that condition.

1921, Mar. 11 *Perf. 14*

59 A8 25(pf) grn & car rose 90 90
60 A8 40(pf) car rose 1.00 1.00
61 A8 80(pf) ultra 6.00 6.00

No. 45 Surcharged in Black

A10

1921, May 6 **Wmk. 125**

62 A10 60pf on 75pf grn & blk 60 60
a. Double surcharge 90.00 90.00

Arms
A11

Coat of Arms
A12

Wmkd. Honeycomb. (108)

(Vertical or Horizontal.)

1921-22 *Perf. 14*

63 A11 5(pf) orange 25 25
64 A11 10(pf) dk brn 16 16
65 A11 15(pf) green 16 16
66 A11 20(pf) slate 16 16
67 A11 25(pf) dk grn 20 20
68 A11 30(pf) bl & car 25 30
a. Center inverted 40.00
69 A11 40pf grn & car 16 16
a. Center inverted 40.00
70 A11 50pf dk grn & car 16 16
71 A11 60pf carmine 16 30
72 A11 80pf blk & car 25 40

Paper With Faint Gray Network.

73 A11 1m org & car 16 16
a. Center inverted 40.00
74 A11 1.20m bl vio 1.40 1.40
75 A11 2m gray & car 3.25 3.25
76 A11 3m vio & car 9.50 11.00

Serrate Roulette 13½

77 A12 5m grn, red & blk 1.50 2.00
78 A12 9m rose, red & org ('22) 3.75 5.50
79 A12 10m ultra, red & blk 1.50 2.00
80 A12 20m red & blk 1.50 2.00
Nos. 63-80 (18) 24.47 29.56

In this and succeeding issues the mark values usually have the face of the paper covered with a gray network. This network is often very faint and occasionally is omitted.

Nos. 64, 66, 69-76 exist imperf. Price, each $15.

See Nos. 81-93, 99-105.

Type of 1921 and

Coat of Arms
A13 A13a

1922 *Perf. 14* **Wmk. 108**

81 A11 75(pf) dp vio 12 15
82 A11 80(pf) green 12 15
83 A11 1.25m vio & car 12 15
84 A11 1.50m sl gray 20 20
85 A11 2m car rose 12 15
86 A11 2.40m dk brn & car 1.10 1.25
87 A11 3m car lake 20 22
88 A11 4m dk bl 1.10 1.25
89 A11 5m dp grn 16 20
90 A11 6m car lake 12 17
a. 6m car rose, wmk. 109 horiz. (error) 2,500.
91 A11 8m lt bl 40 60
92 A11 10m orange 16 20
93 A11 20m org brn 16 22
94 A13 50m gold & car 1.75 3.00
a. 50m gold & red 10.00 12.00
95 A13a 100m metallic grn & red 3.25 4.75
Nos. 81-95 (15) 9.08 12.66

No. 95 has buff instead of gray network.

Nos. 81-83, 85-86, 88 exist imperf. Price, each $15.

Nos. 94-95 exist imperf. Price, each $45.

Nos. 87, 88 and 91 Surcharged in Black or Carmine

l

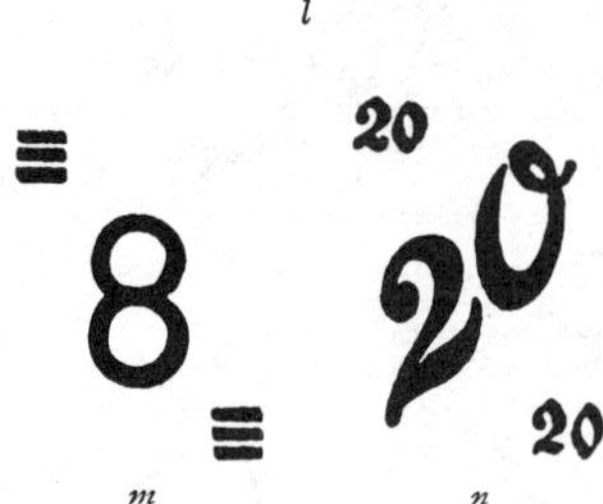

m n

1922

96 A11 (l) 6m on 3m car lake 18 20
a. Dbl. surch.
97 A11 (m) 8m on 4m dk bl 25 45
a. Dbl. surch. 85.00 85.00
98 A11 (n) 20m on 8m lt bl (C) 30 40

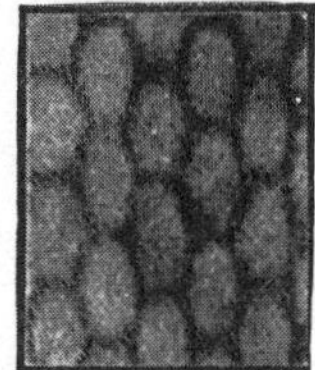

Wmk. 109

Wmkd. Webbing. (109)

(Vertical or Horizontal.)

1922-23 *Perf. 14*

99 A11 4m dk bl 20 30
100 A11 5m dk grn 20 30
102 A11 10m orange 20 30
103 A11 20m org brn 20 30

Paper Without Network.

104 A11 40m pale bl 20 24
105 A11 80m red 20 24
Nos. 99-105 (6) 1.20 1.68

Nos. 104-105 exist imperf. Price, each $15.

Coat of Arms
A15 A15a

Coat of Arms
A16

1923 *Perf. 14*

Paper With Gray Network.

106 A15 50m pale bl & red 20 30
107 A15a 100m dk grn & red 20 30
108 A15a 150m vio & red 20 30
109 A16 250m vio & red 25 30
110 A16 500m gray blk & red 25 30
111 A16 1000m brn & red 25 30
112 A16 5000m sil & red 1.60 4.00

Paper Without Network.

113 A15 50m pale bl 20 24
114 A15a 100m dp grn 20 24
115 A15 200m orange 20 24
Nos. 106-115 (10) 3.55 6.52

Nos. 109-112 exist imperf. Price, each $22.50.

Nos. 113-115 exist imperf. Price, each $15.

A17

1923 *Perf. 14*

Paper With Gray Network.

117 A17 250m vio & red 20 24
118 A17 300m bl grn & red 15 25
119 A17 500m gray & red 20 24
120 A17 1000m brn & red 20 24
121 A17 3000m vio & red 20 24
123 A16 10,000m org & red 50 50
124 A16 20,000m pale bl & red 60 70
125 A16 50,000m grn & red 50 70
Nos. 117-125 (8) 2.55 3.11

Nos. 117-125 exist imperf. Price, each $15.

Surcharged in Red

100 000

1923, Aug. 14

126 A16 100,000m on 20,000m pale bl & red 1.35 4.50

1923 *Perf. 14*

Paper Without Network.

127 A17 1000m brown 20 25
129 A17 5000m rose 20 25
131 A17 20,000m pale bl 20 25
132 A17 50,000m green 20 25

Paper With Gray Network.

133 A17 100,000m dp bl 20 25
134 A17 250,000m violet 20 25
135 A17 500,000m slate 20 25
Nos. 127-135 (7) 1.40 1.75

Nos. 126-135 exist imperf.

Abbreviations.

th=(tausend) thousand

mil=million

Stamps of Preceding Issues Surcharged

100 Tausend

1923 *Perf. 14*

Paper Without Network.

137 A15 40th m on 200m org 80 *1.50*
a. Double surcharge 85.00
138 A15 100th m on 200m org 80 *1.50*
139 A15 250th m on 200m org 8.50 *11.50*
140 A15a 400th m on 100m dp grn 50 60
141 A17 500th m on 50,000m grn 50 60
142 A17 1 mil m on 10,000m org 4.00 *7.50*

The surcharges on Nos. 140 to 142 differ in details from those on Nos. 137 to 139.

Type of 1923 Surcharged

10 Millionen

Paper With Gray Network.

143 A16 10 mil m on 1,000,000m org 60 50
Nos. 137-143 (7) 15.70 *23.70*

Nos. 142-143 exist imperf. Price, each $15.

Type of 1923 Surcharged

1 Million

Perf. 14.

Paper Without Network.

144 A17 1 mil m on 10,000m rose 30 40
145 A17 2 mil m on 10,000m rose 30 40
146 A17 3 mil m on 10,000m rose 30 40
147 A17 5 mil m on 10,000m rose 30 40
b. Dbl. surch. 85.00
148 A17 10 mil m on 10,000m gray lil 45 45
149 A17 20 mil m on 10,000m gray lil 45 45
150 A17 25 mil m on 10,000m gray lil 40 45
151 A17 40 mil m on 10,000m gray lil 40 45
a. Double surcharge 75.00
152 A17 50 mil m on 10,000m gray lil 40 45

Type of 1923 Surcharged in Red

300
Millionen

153 A17 100 mil m on 10,000m gray lil 40 45
154 A17 300 mil m on 10,000m gray lil 40 45
155 A17 500 mil m on 10,000m gray lil 40 45
Nos. 144-155 (12) 4.50 5.20

Nos. 144–147 exist imperf. Price, each $15.
Nos. 153–155 exist imperf. Price, each $17.50.

Types of 1923 Surcharged

10
Pfennige

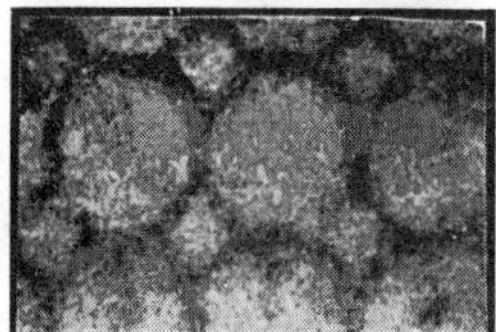

Wmk. 110

Wmkd. Octagons. (110)

1923 ***Perf. 14***

156 A15 5pf on 50m rose 85 60
157 A15 10pf on 50m rose 85 65
158 A15a 20pf on 100m rose 85 75
159 A15 25pf on 50m rose 8.00 12.50
160 A15 30pf on 50m rose 4.75 3.00
161 A15a 40pf on 100m rose 3.50 3.50
162 A15a 50pf on 100m rose 5.00 4.00
163 A15a 75pf on 100m rose 13.50 20.00

◇◇◇◇◇

Type of 1923 Surcharged

2
Gulden

164 A16 1g on 1 mil m rose 8.00 9.00
165 A16 2g on 1 mil m rose 20.00 25.00
166 A16 3g on 1 mil m rose 50.00 60.00
167 A16 5g on 1 mil m rose 50.00 65.00
Nos. 156-167 (12) 165.30 203.95

Coat of Arms
A19

Wmkd. Webbing. (109)

1924–37 ***Perf. 14***

168 A19 3(pf) brn, *yelsh* ('36) 2.00 1.00
a. 3(pf) dp brn, *white* ('27) 3.50 1.00
170 A19 5(pf) org, *yelsh* ('36) 4.00 30
a. White paper 5.00 25
b. Bklt. pane of 10
c. Tête bêche pair 400.00
d. Syncopated perf., #170 ('37) 15.00 12.50
e. Syncopated perf., #170a ('32) 25.00 12.50
171 A19 7(pf) yel grn ('33) 1.75 2.00
172 A19 8(pf) yel grn ('37) 3.50 5.00
173 A19 10(pf) grn, *yelsh* ('36) 6.50 30
a. White paper 7.50 25
b. Bklt. pane of 10
c. 10(pf) bl grn, *yelsh* ('37) 7.00 50
d. Tête bêche pair 400.00
e. Syncopated perf., #173 ('37) 25.00 14.00
f. Syncopated perf., #173a ('32) 32.50 17.50
g. Syncopated perf., #173c ('37) 12.50 17.50
175 A19 15(pf) gray 3.00 50
176 A19 15(pf) red, *yelsh* ('36) 3.25 15
a. White paper ('25) 3.25 15
b. Bklt. pane of 10
177 A19 20(pf) car & red 3.00 25
178 A19 20(pf) gray ('35) 2.50 2.25
179 A19 25(pf) sl & red 19.00 1.00
180 A19 25(pf) car ('35) 20.00 1.25
181 A19 30(pf) grn & red 10.00 35
182 A19 30(pf) dk vio ('35) 2.25 3.50
183 A19 35(pf) ultra ('25) 1.50 75
184 A19 40(pf) dk bl & bl 8.50 35
185 A19 40(pf) yel brn & red ('35) 10.00 16.00
186 A19 40(pf) dk bl ('35) 2.00 2.00
a. Imperf. 45.00
187 A19 50(pf) bl & red 10.00 5.00
a. Yellowish paper ('36) 11.00 6.00
188 A19 55(pf) plum & scar ('37) 5.50 10.00
189 A19 60(pf) dk grn & red ('35) 9.00 17.50
190 A19 70(pf) yel grn & red ('35) 3.00 4.00
191 A19 75(pf) vio & red 5.00 4.00
a. Yellowish paper ('36) 3.75 5.00
192 A19 80(pf) dk org brn & red ('35) 4.00 6.00
Nos. 168-192 (23) 139.25 83.45

The 5pf and 10pf with syncopated perforations (Netherlands type C) are coils.
See also Nos. 225–232.

Oliva Castle and Cathedral
A20

St. Mary's Church
A23

Council Chamber on the Langenmarkt
A24

Wmk. 125

Designs: 2g, Mottlau River and Krantor. 3g, View of Zoppot.

Wmkd. Lozenges. (125)

1924–32 **Engraved.** ***Perf. 14.***

193 A20 1g yel grn & blk 37.50 32.50
Parcel post cancel 17.50
194 A20 1g org & gray blk ('25) 24.00 2.00
a. 1g red org & blk ('32) 32.50 7.50
Parcel post cancel 1.25
195 A20 2g red vio & blk 70.00 60.00
Parcel post cancel 45.00
196 A20 2g rose & blk ('25) 3.00 3.50
Parcel post cancel 2.50
197 A20 3g dk bl & blk 5.00 5.00
Parcel post cancel 3.00
198 A23 5g brn red & blk 5.00 5.00
Parcel post cancel 3.00
199 A24 10g dk brn & blk 40.00 50.00
Parcel post cancel 30.00
Nos. 193-199 (7) 184.50 158.00

See also No. 233.

Stamps of 1924-25 Overprinted in Black, Violet or Red

1920
15. November
1930

Wmkd. Webbing. (109)

1930, Nov. 15 **Typographed**

200 A19 5(pf) orange 3.00 3.00
201 A19 10(pf) yel grn (V) 5.00 4.50
202 A19 15(pf) red 7.00 6.00
203 A19 20(pf) car & red 3.50 3.50
204 A19 25(pf) sl & red 6.00 5.00
205 A19 30(pf) grn & red 14.00 17.50
206 A19 35(pf) ultra (R) 55.00 60.00
207 A19 40(pf) dk bl & bl (R) 16.50 20.00
208 A19 50(pf) dp bl & red 55.00 60.00
209 A19 75(pf) vio & red 55.00 60.00

Wmkd. Lozenges. (125)
Engraved.

210 A20 1g org & blk (R) 55.00 60.00
Nos. 200-210 (11) 275.00 299.50

10th anniversary of the Free State. Counterfeits exist.

Nos. 171 and 183 Surcharged in Red Blue or Green:

w x

1934-36

211 A19 (w) 6(pf) on 7(pf) yel grn (R) 1.50 2.00
212 A19 (w) 8(pf) on 7(pf) yel grn (Bl) ('35) 3.50 4.00
213 A19 (w) 8(pf) on 7(pf) yel grn (R) ('36) 2.25 2.50
214 A19 (w) 8(pf) on 7(pf) yel grn (G) ('36) 1.50 3.00
215 A19 (x) 30(pf) on 35(pf) ultra (Bl) 16.00 20.00
Nos. 211-215 (5) 24.75 31.50

Bathing Beach, Brösen
A25

View of Brösen Beach
A26

War Memorial at Brösen
A27

Skyline of Danzig
A28

Wmkd. Webbing. (109)

1936, June 23 **Typo.** ***Perf. 14***

216 A25 10pf dp grn 1.00 1.25
217 A26 25pf rose red 1.25 2.00
218 A27 40pf brt bl 2.50 2.50

Village of Brösen, 125th anniversary. Exist imperf. Price of set, $110.

1937, Mar. 27

219 A28 10(pf) dk bl 1.00 1.75
220 A28 15(pf) vio brn 1.75 2.00

Air Defense League.

Danzig Philatelic Exhibition Issue.
Souvenir Sheet.

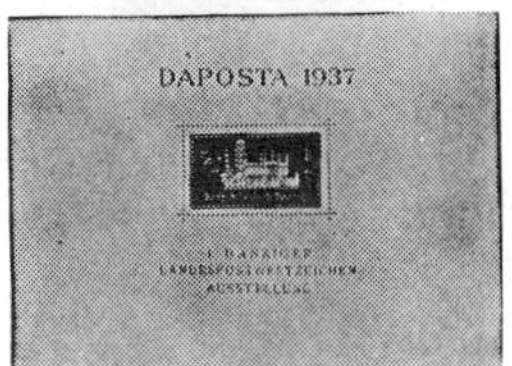

St. Mary's Church
A29

1937, June 6 ***Perf. 14*** **Wmk. 109**

221 A29 50pf dk grn 2.00 4.00

Issued for the Danzig Philatelic Exhibition, June 6–8, 1937. Sheet measures 149x104mm.

Arthur Schopenhauer
A30 A31

Design: 40(pf), Full-face portrait, white hair.

Perf. 14

1938, Feb. 22 **Photo.** **Unwmkd.**

222 A30 15(pf) dl bl 2.00 2.50
223 A31 25(pf) sepia 5.00 5.50
224 A31 40(pf) org ver 2.50 2.75

Issued in commemoration of the 150th anniversary of the birth of Schopenhauer.

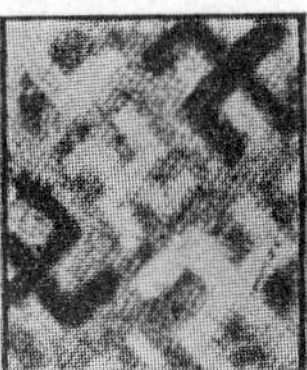

Wmk. 237

Type of 1924-35.
Wmkd. Swastikas. (237)

1938–39 Typographed *Perf. 14*

225	A19	3(pf) brown	1.00	*5.00*
226	A19	5(pf) orange	1.00	1.00
a.		Booklet pane of 10		
b.		Syncopated perf.	2.00	4.75
227	A19	8(pf) yel grn	6.00	*12.00*
228	A19	10(pf) bl grn	1.00	1.00
a.		Booklet pane of 10		
b.		Syncopated perf.	3.00	6.00
229	A19	15(pf) scarlet	2.75	4.75
a.		Booklet pane of 10		
230	A19	25(pf) carmine	2.75	4.75
231	A19	40(pf) dk bl	2.75	4.75
232	A19	50(pf) brt bl & red ('39)	2.75	4.75

Engraved.

233	A20	1g red org & blk	6.00	9.50
		Nos. 225-233 (9)	26.00	*47.50*

No. 233 measures 32½x21¼mm; No. 194, 31x21mm.

Nos. 226b and 228b are coils with Netherlands type C perforation.

Knights in Tournament, 1500
A33

French Leaving Danzig, 1814
A35

Designs: 10(pf), Signing of Danzig-Sweden neutrality treaty, 1630. 25(pf), Battle of Weichselmünde, 1577.

Photogravure.

1939, Jan. 7 *Perf. 14* Unwmkd.

234	A33	5(pf) dk grn	1.00	2.00
235	A33	10(pf) cop brn	1.25	2.50
236	A35	15(pf) sl blk	1.50	3.00
237	A35	25(pf) brn vio	2.00	3.50

Stamp Day.

Scientists Issue.

Gregor Mendel
A37

Designs: 15(pf), Dr. Robert Koch. 25(pf), Wilhelm Roentgen.

1939, Apr. 29 Photo. *Perf. 13x14*

238	A37	10(pf) cop brn	70	80
239	A37	15(pf) indigo	90	1.10
240	A37	25(pf) dk ol grn	1.25	2.00

Issued in honor of the achievements of Mendel, Koch and Roentgen.

Issued under German Administration

Stamps of Danzig, 1925-39, Surcharged in Black:

Rpf 4 Deutsches Reich Rpf 4
a

4 Rpf Deutsches Reich 4 Rpf
b

1 Reichsmark

Deutsches Reich
c

Wmkd. Webbing. (109)

1939 *Perf. 14.*

241	A19(b)	4rpf on 35(pf) ultra	1.75	1.75
242	A19(b)	12rpf on 7(pf) yel grn	2.00	2.00
243	A19(a)	20rpf gray	6.00	6.00

Wmkd. Swastikas. (237)

244	A19(a)	3rpf brown	1.75	1.75
245	A19(a)	5rpf orange	1.75	1.75
246	A19(a)	8rpf yel grn	3.00	3.00
247	A19(a)	10rpf bl grn	3.50	3.50
248	A19(a)	15rpf scarlet	4.25	4.25
249	A19(a)	25rpf carmine	4.75	4.75
250	A19(a)	30rpf dk vio	3.25	3.25
251	A19(a)	40rpf dk bl	4.75	4.75
252	A19(a)	50rpf brt bl & red	7.00	7.00
253	A20(c)	1rm on 1g red org & blk	30.00	30.00

Wmkd. Lozenges. (125)

254	A20(c)	2rm on 2g rose & blk	35.00	35.00
		Nos. 241-254 (14)	108.75	108.75

Nos. 241 to 254 were valid throughout Germany.

SEMI-POSTAL STAMPS.

St. George and Dragon
SP1

Wmkd. Honeycomb. (108)
Size: 19x22 mm.

1921, Oct. 16 Typo. *Perf. 14*

B1	SP1	30pf +30pf grn & org	75	75
B2	SP1	60pf +60pf rose & org	2.00	2.00

Size: 25x30 mm.
Serrate Roulette 13½.

B3	SP1	1.20m +1.20m dk bl & org	3.50	3.50

Aged Pensioner
SP2

Wmkd. Webbing. (109)
Paper With Gray Network.

1923, Mar. *Perf. 14*

B4	SP2	50m +20m lake	30	40
B5	SP2	100m +30m red vio	30	40

Philatelic Exhibition Issue.

Neptune Fountain
SP3

Various Frames.

1929, July 7 Engr. Unwmkd.

B6	SP3	10(pf) yel grn & gray	3.75	4.00
B7	SP3	15(pf) car & gray	3.75	4.00
B8	SP3	25(pf) ultra & gray	12.50	10.00
a.		25(pf) vio bl & blk	72.50	80.00

These stamps were sold exclusively at the Danzig Philatelic Exhibition, June 7th to 14th, 1929. They were sold at double their face values, the excess being for the aid of the exhibition.

Regular Issue of 1924-25 Surcharged in Black

5 W. H. W.

1934, Jan. 15 Wmk. 109

B9	A19	5(pf) +5(pf) org	16.00	16.00
B10	A19	10(pf) +5(pf) yel grn	37.50	37.50
B11	A19	15(pf) +5(pf) car	22.50	22.50

Surtax for winter welfare. Counterfeits exist.

Stock Tower SP4 George Hall SP6

City Gate, 16th Century
SP5

1935, Dec. 16 Typo. *Perf. 14*

B12	SP4	5(pf) +5pf org	1.00	1.00
B13	SP5	10(pf) +5pf grn	1.25	1.50
B14	SP6	15(pf) +10pf scar	2.50	3.00

Surtax for winter welfare.

Milk Can Tower
SP7

Frauentor
SP8

Krantor
SP9

Langgarter Gate
SP10

High Gate
SP11

1936, Nov. 25

B15	SP7	10pf +5pf dk bl	1.50	2.00
a.		Imperf.	75.00	
B16	SP8	15pf +5pf dl grn	1.50	2.00
B17	SP9	25pf +10pf red brn	1.75	2.50
B18	SP10	40pf +20pf brn & red brn	2.50	4.00
B19	SP11	50pf +20pf bl & dk bl	3.50	5.50
		Nos. B15-B19 (5)	10.75	16.00

Surtax for winter welfare.

SP12

SP13

1937, Oct. 30

B20	SP12	25(pf) +25(pf) dk car	4.00	5.50
B21	SP13	40(pf) +40(pf) bl & red	4.00	5.50
a.		Souvenir sheet of two	20.00	25.00

Founding of Danzig community at Magdeburg.

No. B21a contains one each of Nos. B20-B21 with marginal inscriptions including "1937." Size: 146x105mm.

Madonna
SP14

Mercury
SP15

Weather Vane, Town Hall
SP16

Neptune Fountain
SP17

St. George and Dragon
SP18

1937, Dec. 13

B23	SP14	5pf +5pf brt vio	3.25	3.50
B24	SP15	10pf +10pf dk brn	3.75	4.75
B25	SP16	15pf +5pf bl & yel brn	4.75	5.50
B26	SP17	25pf +10pf bl grn & grn	5.50	6.50
B27	SP18	40pf +25pf brt car & bl	9.00	9.50
		Nos. B23-B27 (5)	26.25	29.75

Surtax for winter welfare. Designs are from frieze of the Artushof.

"Peter von Danzig" Yacht Race
SP19

Ships: 10+5pf, Dredger Fu Shing. 15+10pf, S. S. Columbus. 25+10pf, S. S. City of Danzig. 40+15pf, Peter von Danzig, 1472.

1938, Nov. 28 Photo. Unwmkd.

B28	SP19	5(pf) +5(pf) dk bl grn	1.75	2.00
B29	SP19	10(pf) +5(pf) gldn brn	2.50	2.75
B30	SP19	15(pf) +10(pf) ol grn	2.75	3.25
B31	SP19	25(pf) +10(pf) ind	3.50	4.00
B32	SP19	40(pf) +15(pf) vio brn	4.25	4.75
		Nos. B28-B32 (5)	14.75	16.75

Surtax for winter welfare.

AIR POST STAMPS.

AP1 AP2

No. 6 Surcharged in Blue or Carmine.

Wmkd. Lozenges. (125)

1920, Sept. 29 ***Perf. 14***

C1	AP1	40(pf) on 40pf car rose	2.25	2.75
a.		Double surcharge	250.00	250.00
C2	AP1	60(pf) on 40pf car rose (C)	2.25	2.75
a.		Double surcharge	250.00	250.00
C3	A2	1m on 40pf car rose	2.25	2.75

Plane faces left on No. C2.

Plane over Danzig
AP3 AP4

Wmkd. Honeycomb. (108)

1921-22 Typographed. ***Perf. 14.***

C4	AP3	40(pf) bl grn	40	50
C5	AP3	60(pf) dk vio	40	50
C6	AP3	1m carmine	40	50
C7	AP3	2m org brn	40	50

Serrate Roulette 13½.

Size: 34½x23mm.

C8	AP4	5m vio bl	1.25	1.40
C9	AP4	10m dp grn ('22)	2.50	3.00
		Nos. C4-C49 (6)	5.35	6.40

Nos. C4–C9 exist imperf. Price, each $45.

Wmkd. Webbing. (109)

1923 ***Perf. 14.***

C10	AP3	40(pf) bl grn	50	*1.50*
C11	AP3	60(pf) dk vio	50	*1.50*
a.		Double impression	75.00	
C12	AP3	1m carmine	50	*1.50*
C13	AP3	2m org brn	50	*1.50*
C14	AP3	25m pale bl	50	50

Serrate Roulette 13½.

Size: 34½x23mm.

C15	AP4	5m vio bl	50	55
C16	AP4	10m dp grn	50	55

Paper With Gray Network.

C17	AP4	20m org brn	50	55

Size: 40x23mm.

C18	AP4	50m orange	50	55
C19	AP4	100m red	50	55
C20	AP4	250m dk brn	50	55
C21	AP4	500m car rose	50	55
		Nos. C10-C21 (12)	6.00	*10.35*

Nos. C14, C18–C21 exist imperf. Price, each $35.

Post Horn and Airplanes
AP5

1923, Oct. 18 ***Perf. 14***

Paper Without Network.

C22	AP5	250,000m scarlet	50	1.25
C23	AP5	500,000m scarlet	50	1.25

Exist imperf. Price, each $27.50.

Surcharged **2 Millionen**

C24	AP5	2mil m on 100,000m scar	50	1.00
C25	AP5	5mil m on 50,000m scar	50	1.00
b.		Cliché of 10,000m in sheet of 50,000m	20.00	40.00

Exist imperf. Price, each $45.

Nos. C24 and C25 were not regularly issued without surcharge, although copies have been passed through the post. Price, uncanceled, each $7.50.

Plane over Danzig
AP6 AP7

1924

C26	AP6	10(pf) vermilion	22.50	3.75
C27	AP6	20(pf) car rose	2.25	1.75
C28	AP6	40(pf) ol brn	5.00	2.50
C29	AP6	1g dp grn	5.00	2.50
C30	AP7	2½g vio brn	37.50	37.50
		Nos. C26-C30 (5)	72.25	48.00

Nos. C26–C30 exist imperf. Price of Nos. C26–C29 $45 each; No. C30, $110.

Regular Issue of 1924 Surcharged in Various Colors

10 ▬▬ 10
Luftpost-Ausstellung
1932

1932 Wmkd. Lozenges. (125)

C31	A20	10(pf) on 1g yel grn & blk (G)	13.50	12.50
C32	A20	15(pf) on 2g red vio & blk (V)	13.50	12.50
C33	A20	20(pf) on 3g dk bl & blk (Bl)	13.50	12.50
C34	A23	25(pf) on 5g brn red & blk (R)	13.50	12.50
C35	A24	30(pf) on 10g dk brn & blk (Br)	13.50	12.50
		Nos. C31-C35 (5)	67.50	62.50

Issued in connection with the International Air Post Exhibition of 1932. The surcharges were variously arranged to suit the shapes and designs of the stamps. The stamps were sold at double their surcharged values, the excess being donated to the exhibition funds.

Airplane
AP8 AP9

1935 Wmkd. Webbing. (109)

C36	AP8	10pf scarlet	2.50	50
C37	AP8	15pf yellow	3.25	1.75
C38	AP8	25pf dk grn	2.50	1.75
C39	AP8	50pf gray bl	10.00	8.75
C40	AP9	1g magenta	6.00	*12.00*
		Nos. C36-C40 (5)	24.25	*24.75*

See also Nos. C42–C45.

Souvenir Sheet

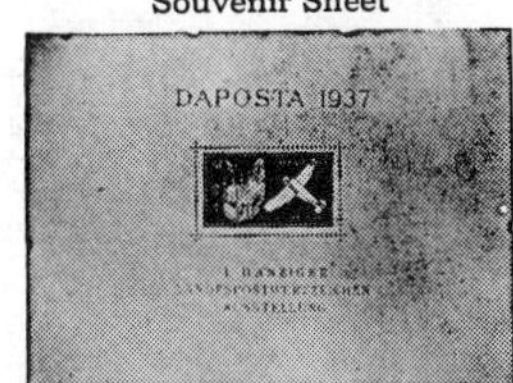

St. Mary's Church—AP10

1937, June 6 ***Perf. 14***

C41	AP10	50pf dk bl	2.00	4.00

Issued for the Danzig Philatelic Exhibition, June 6–8, 1937. Size: 149x104mm.

Type of 1935.

1938–39 Wmkd. Swastikas. (237)

C42	AP8	10pf scarlet	2.25	6.00
C43	AP8	15pf yel ('39)	2.25	6.50
C44	AP8	25pf dk grn	2.25	6.50
C45	AP8	50pf gray bl ('39)	7.25	15.00

POSTAGE DUE STAMPS.

Danzig Coat of Arms
D1 D2

Wmkd. Honeycomb. (108)

1921-22 Typographed. ***Perf. 14***

Paper Without Network.

J1	D1	10(pf) dp vio	40	45
J2	D1	20(pf) dp vio	40	45
J3	D1	40(pf) dp vio	40	45
J4	D1	60(pf) dp vio	40	45
J5	D1	75(pf) dp vio ('22)	40	45
J6	D1	80(pf) dp vio	40	45
J7	D1	120(pf) dp vio	40	45
J8	D1	200(pf) dp vio ('22)	1.00	1.00
J9	D1	240(pf) dp vio	1.00	1.00
J10	D1	300(pf) dp vio ('22)	1.00	1.00
J11	D1	400(pf) dp vio	1.00	1.00
J12	D1	500(pf) dp vio	1.00	1.00
J13	D1	800(pf) dp vio ('22)	1.00	1.00
J14	D1	20m dp vio ('22)	1.00	1.00
		Nos. J1-J14 (14)	9.80	10.15

Nos. J1–J14 exist imperf. Price, each $13.50.

1923 Wmkd. Webbing. (109)

J15	D1	100(pf) dp vio	50	55
J16	D1	200(pf) dp vio	3.00	3.00
J17	D1	300(pf) dp vio	50	55
J18	D1	400(pf) dp vio	50	55
J19	D1	500(pf) dp vio	50	55
J20	D1	800(pf) dp vio	70	75
J21	D1	10m dp vio	50	55
J22	D1	20m dp vio	50	55
J23	D1	50m dp vio	50	55

Paper With Gray Network.

J24	D1	100m dp vio	40	45
J25	D1	500m dp vio	40	45
		Nos. J15-J25 (11)	8.00	8.50

Nos. J22–J25 exist imperf. Price, each $11.50.

Nos. J22–J23 and type of 1923 Surcharged

10000

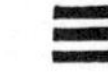

1923, Oct. 1

Paper Without Network.

J26	D1	5000(m) on 50m	40	45
J27	D1	10,000(m) on 20m	40	45
J28	D1	50,000(m) on 500m	40	45
J29	D1	100,000(m) on 20m	1.00	1.10

On No. J26 the numerals of the surcharge are all of the larger size.

A 1000(m) on 100m deep violet was prepared but not issued. Price, $110.

Nos. J26–J28 exist imperf. Price, each $22.50.

1923–28 Wmkd. Octagons. (110)

J30	D2	5(pf) bl & blk	1.00	60
J31	D2	10(pf) bl & blk	1.00	40
J32	D2	15(pf) bl & blk	1.00	80
J33	D2	20(pf) bl & blk	1.75	1.40
J34	D2	30(pf) bl & blk	10.00	85
J35	D2	40(pf) bl & blk	2.50	2.00
J36	D2	50(pf) bl & blk	2.50	60
J37	D2	60(pf) bl & blk	16.00	16.00
J38	D2	100(pf) bl & blk	16.00	6.50
J39	D2	3g bl & car	10.00	20.00
a.		"Guldeu" instead of "Gulden"	450.00	
		Nos. J30-J39 (10)	61.75	49.15

Used prices of Nos. J30–J39 are for postally used copies.

Postage Due Stamps of 1923 Issue Surcharged in Red **5**

1932, Dec. 20

J40 D2 5(pf) on 40(pf) bl & blk 3.00 4.75
J41 D2 10(pf) on 60(pf) bl & blk 50.00 6.00
J42 D2 20(pf) on 100(pf) bl & blk 3.25 5.00

Type of 1923.
Wmkd. Swastikas. (237)

1938-39 *Perf. 14.*

J43 D2 10(pf) bl & blk ('39) 1.60 *10.00*
J44 D2 30(pf) bl & blk 2.50 *15.00*
J45 D2 40(pf) bl & blk ('39) 7.25 *30.00*
J46 D2 60(pf) bl & blk ('39) 9.00 *30.00*
J47 D2 100(pf) bl & blk 11.00 *30.00*
Nos. J43-J47 (5) 31.35 *115.00*

OFFICIAL STAMPS.

Regular Issues of 1921–22 Overprinted **D M** *a*

Wmkd. Honeycomb. (108)

1921-22 *Perf. 14x14½.*

O1 A11 5(pf) orange 30 30
O2 A11 10(pf) dk brn 20 25
a. Invtd. ovpt. 75.00
O3 A11 15(pf) green 20 25
O4 A11 20(pf) slate 20 25
O5 A11 25(pf) dk grn 20 25
O6 A11 30(pf) bl & car 50 60
O7 A11 40(pf) grn & car 25 30
O8 A11 50(pf) dk grn & car 25 30
O9 A11 60(pf) carmine 25 30
O10 A11 75(pf) dp vio ('22) 25 30
O11 A11 80(pf) blk & car 1.25 1.50
O12 A11 80(pf) grn ('22) 25 30

Paper With Faint Gray Network

O14 A11 1m org & car 20 30
O15 A11 1.20m bl vio 1.25 1.50
O16 A11 1.25m vio & car ('22) 25 30
O17 A11 1.50m sl gray ('22) 25 25
O18 A11 2m gray & car 18.00 18.00
a. Invtd. ovpt.
O19 A11 2m car rose ('22) 25 30
O20 A11 2.40m dk brn & car ('22) 1.85 2.25
O21 A11 3m vio & car 13.50 14.50
O22 A11 3m car lake ('22) 25 25
O23 A11 4m dk bl ('22) 1.85 2.25
O24 A11 5m dp grn ('22) 25 25
O25 A11 6m car lake ('22) 25 25
O26 A11 10m org ('22) 25 25
O27 A11 20m org brn ('22) 25 25
Nos. O1-O27 (26) 42.75 45.80

Double overprints exist on Nos. O1–O2, O5–O7, O10 and O12. Price, each $17.50.

Same Overprint on No. 96

O28 A11 6m on 3m car lake 25 50
a. Inverted overprint 30.00

No. 77 Overprinted ***D M***

1922 ***Serrate Roulette 13½***

O29 A12 5m grn, red & blk 4.75 5.50

Nos. 99–103, 106–107 Overprinted Type "a"

Wmkd. Webbing. (109)

1923 ***Perf. 14***

O30 A11 4m dk bl 25 25
O31 A11 5m dk grn 25 40
O32 A11 10m orange 25 25
O33 A11 20m org brn 25 25
O34 A15 50m pale bl & red 25 25
O35 A15a 100m dk grn & red 25 25

Nos. 113–115, 118–120 Overprinted Type "a"

O36 A15 50m pale bl 25 30
a. Inverted overprint 30.00
O37 A15a 100m dk grn 25 25
O38 A15 200m orange 25 25
a. Inverted overprint 30.00

Paper With Gray Network.

O39 A17 300m bl grn & red 25 25
O40 A17 500m gray & red 25 30
O41 A17 1000m brn & red 25 30
Nos. O30-O41 (12) 3.00 3.30

Regular Issue of 1924-25 Overprinted *Dienst-marke*

1924-25 *Perf. 14x14½*

O42 A19 5(pf) orange 2.50 1.50
O43 A19 10(pf) yel grn 2.50 1.50
O44 A19 15(pf) gray 2.50 1.50
O45 A19 15(pf) red ('25) 22.50 9.00
O46 A19 20(pf) car & red 2.50 1.50
O47 A19 25(pf) sl & red 24.00 22.50
O48 A19 30(pf) grn & red 3.50 2.75
O49 A19 35(pf) ultra ('25) 50.00 45.00
O50 A19 40(pf) dk bl & dl bl 7.25 7.25
O51 A19 50(pf) dp bl & red 22.50 22.50
O52 A19 75(pf) vio & red 45.00 *70.00*
Nos. O42-O52 (11) 184.75 *185.00*

Double overprints exist on Nos. O42–O44, O47, O50–O52. Price, each $65.

DENMARK

(děn'märk)

LOCATION—Denmark occupies the northern part of a peninsula which separates the North and Baltic Seas, and includes the surrounding islands.

GOVT.—Kingdom.

AREA—16,629 sq. mi.

POP.—5,150,000 (est. 1975).

CAPITAL—Copenhagen.

96 Skilling = 1 Rigsbank Daler
100 Ore = 1 Krone (1875)

> Prices of early Denmark stamps vary according to condition. Quotations for Nos. 1–15 are for fine copies. Very fine to superb specimens sell at much higher prices, and inferior or poor copies sell at reduced prices, depending on the condition of the individual specimen.

Numeral and Inscription of Value
A1

Royal Emblems
A2

Wmk. 111

Wmkd. Small Crown. (111)

1851 Typographed. ***Imperf.***

With Yellow Brown Burelage.

1 A1 2rs blue *4,000.* 1,600.
a. First printing *6,750.* *3,000.*
2 A2 4rs brown 750.00 47.50
a. First printing 900.00 60.00
b. 4rs yel brn 1,000. 75.00

The first printing of Nos. 1 and 2 had the burelage printed from a copper plate, giving a clear impression with the lines in slight relief. The subsequent impressions had the burelage typographed, with the lines fainter and not rising above the surface of the paper.

Nos. 1-2 were reprinted in 1885 and 1901 on heavy yellowish paper, unwatermarked and imperforate, with a brown burelage. No. 1 was also reprinted without burelage, on both yellowish and white paper. Price for least costly reprint of No. 1, $40.

No. 2 was reprinted in 1951 in 10 shades with "Colour Specimen 1951" printed on the back. It was also reprinted in 1961 in 2 shades without burelage and with "Farve Nytryk 1961" printed on the back. Price for least costly reprint of No. 2, $8.50.

Dotting in Spandrels
A3

Wavy Lines in Spandrels
A4

1854–57

3 A3 2s bl ('55) 130.00 60.00
4 A3 4s brown 250.00 13.00
a. 4s yel brn 250.00 13.00
5 A3 8s grn ('57) 525.00 80.00
a. 8s yel grn 525.00 80.00
6 A3 16s gray lil ('57) 650.00 190.00

1858-62

7 A4 4s brown 70.00 8.00
a. 4s yel brn 70.00 8.00
b. Wmk. 112 ('62) 70.00 10.00
8 A4 8s green 525.00 100.00

Nos. 2 to 8 inclusive are known with unofficial perforation 12 or 13, and Nos. 4, 5, 7 and 8 with unofficial roulette 9½.

Nos. 3, 6-8 were reprinted in 1885 on heavy yellowish paper, unwatermarked, imperforate and without burelage. Nos. 4-5 were reprinted in 1924 on white paper, unwatermarked, imperforate, gummed and without burelage. Price for No. 3, $9; Nos. 4-5, each $85; No. 6, $15; Nos. 7-8, each $7.50.

Wmk. 112

Wmkd. Crown. (112)

1863 ***Rouletted 11***

9 A4 4s brown 110.00 22.50
a. 4s dp brn 110.00 22.50
10 A3 16s violet 1,200. 800.00

Royal Emblems
A5

1864-68 ***Perf. 13.***

11 A5 2s bl ('65) 100.00 47.50
a. Imperf., (pair) 250.00 300.00
b. Perf. 12½ 325.00 225.00
12 A5 3s red vio ('65) 120.00 80.00
a. Imperf., (pair) 300.00
b. Perf. 12½ 375.00 300.00
13 A5 4s red 80.00 8.00
a. Imperf., (pair) 180.00 300.00
14 A5 8s bis ('68) 500.00 100.00
a. Imperf., (pair) 900.00
b. Perf. 12½ 525.00 250.00
15 A5 16s ol grn 550.00 125.00
a. Imperf., (pair) 1,200.
b. Perf. 12½ 1,250. 900.00

Nos. 11-15 were reprinted in 1886 on heavy yellowish paper, unwatermarked, imperforate and without gum. The reprints of all values except the 4s were printed in two vertical rows of six, inverted with respect to each other, so that horizontal pairs are always tête bêche. Price $8 each.

Nos. 13 and 15 were reprinted in 1942 with printing on the back across each horizontal row: "Nytryk 1942. G. A. Hagemann: Danmarks og Vestindiens Frimaerker, Bind 2." Price, $50 each.

A6

NORMAL FRAME

INVERTED FRAME

The arabesques in the corners have a main stem and a branch. When the frame is in normal position, in the upper left corner the branch leaves the main stem half way between two little leaflets. In the lower right corner the branch starts at the foot of the second leaflet. When the frame is inverted the corner designs are, of course, transposed.

1870–71 ***Perf. 14x13½*** **Wmk. 112**

Paper Varying from Thin to Thick.

16 A6 2s gray & ultra ('71) 100.00 35.00
a. 2s gray & bl 90.00 32.50
b. Imperf., (pair) 275.00
c. Inverted frame 1,000. 600.00
17 A6 3s gray & brt lil ('71) 170.00 90.00
a. Imperf., (pair) 325.00
b. Inverted frame 1,700. 1,300.
18 A6 4s gray & car 100.00 15.00
a. Imperf., (pair) 275.00
b. Inverted frame 900.00 150.00
19 A6 8s gray & brn ('71) 250.00 80.00
a. Imperf., (pair) 450.00
b. Inverted frame 1,400. 900.00
20 A6 16s gray & grn ('71) 325.00 170.00
a. Imperf., (pair) 675.00
b. Inverted frame 1,700. 1,400.

Perf. 12½.

21 A6 2s gray & bl ('71) 2,000. 2,250.
22 A6 4s gray & car 240.00 100.00
24 A6 48s brn & lil 700.00 250.00
a. Imperf., (pair) 1,200.
b. Inverted frame 2,500. 1,700.

Nos. 16-20, 24 were reprinted in 1886 on thin white paper, unwatermarked, imperforate and without gum. These were printed in sheets of 10 in which 1 stamp has the normal frame (price $22.50 each and 9 the inverted (price $9 each; No. 24, $12).

1875–79 ***Perf. 14x13½.***

25 A6 3ö gray bl & gray 13.00 9.00
a. First "A" of "DANMARK" missing 70.00 100.00
b. Imperf.
c. Inverted frame 13.00 9.00

No.	Type	Description	Unused	Used
26	A6	4ø sl & bl	11.00	25
a.		4ø gray & bl	11.00	25
b.		4ø sl & ultra	50.00	7.00
c.		4ø gray & ultra	50.00	7.00
d.		Imperf., (pair)	250.00	
e.		Inverted frame	13.00	25
27	A6	5ø rose & bl ('79)	42.50	50.00
a.		Ball of lower curve of large "5" missing	170.00	275.00
b.		Inverted frame	1,000.	1,700.
28	A6	8ø sl & car	14.00	25
a.		8ø gray & car	40.00	1.70
b.		Imperf., (pair)	275.00	
c.		Inverted frame	15.00	25
29	A6	12ø sl & dl lake	13.00	3.00
a.		12ø gray & brt lil	50.00	11.00
b.		12ø gray & dl mag	13.00	3.00
c.		Inverted frame	13.00	3.50
30	A6	16ø sl & brn	60.00	3.00
a.		16ø lt gray & brn	80.00	13.00
b.		Inverted frame	50.00	3.00
31	A6	20ø rose & gray	65.00	13.00
a.		20ø car & gray	65.00	13.00
b.		Inverted frame	65.00	13.00
32	A6	25ø gray & grn	65.00	17.50
a.		Inverted frame	90.00	40.00
33	A6	50ø brn & vio	72.50	25.00
a.		50ø brn & bl vio	450.00	80.00
b.		Inverted frame	72.50	25.00
34	A6	100ø gray & org ('77)	110.00	27.50
a.		Imperf., (pair)	450.00	
b.		Inverted frame	160.00	60.00

The stamps of this issue on thin semi-transparent paper are far scarcer than those on thicker paper.

See also Nos. 41-42, 44, 46-47, 50-52.

Arms

A7

Two types of numerals in corners:

1882

Small Corner Numerals.

No.	Type	Description	Unused	Used
35	A7	5ø green	150.00	70.00
37	A7	20ø blue	160.00	40.00

1884-85

Larger Corner Numerals.

No.	Type	Description	Unused	Used
38	A7	5ø green	13.00	2.25
a.		Imperf.		
39	A7	10ø car ('85)	14.00	1.20
a.		Small numerals in corners	550.00	550.00
b.		Imperf., pair	250.00	
c.		Pair, Nos. 39,39a	625.00	750.00
40	A7	20ø blue	20.00	1.20
a.		Pair, Nos. 37, 40	500.00	700.00
b.		Imperf., pair	2,500.	

Stamps with large corner numerals have white line around crown and lower oval touches frame.

The plate of the 10 ore, No. 39, was damaged and three clichés in the bottom row were replaced by clichés for post cards, which had small numerals in the corners, making the variety No. 39a.

Two clichés with small numerals were inserted in the plate of No. 40.

Wmkd. Crown. (112)

1895-1901 — *Perf. 13.*

No.	Type	Description	Unused	Used
41	A6	3ø bl & gray	10.00	3.50
b.		Inverted frame	12.00	3.75
42	A6	4ø sl & bl ('96)	6.00	20
a.		Inverted frame	6.00	20
43	A7	5ø green	10.00	1.10
44	A6	8ø sl & car	6.00	20
a.		Inverted frame	6.00	20
45	A7	10ø rose car	12.50	1.00
46	A6	12ø sl & dl lake	6.00	2.50
a.		Inverted frame	14.00	3.00
47	A6	16ø sl & brn	25.00	5.00
a.		Inverted frame	27.50	5.00
48	A7	20ø blue	12.50	2.00
49	A7	24ø brn ('01)	17.50	5.00
50	A6	25ø gray & grn ('98)	60.00	11.00
a.		Inverted frame	55.00	18.00
51	A6	50ø brn & vio ('97)	55.00	20.00
a.		Inverted frame	75.00	30.00

1902-04 — Wmkd. Crown. (113)

No.	Type	Description	Unused	Used
41c	A6	3ø bl & gray	3.75	3.00
d.		Invtd. frame	60.00	40.00
42b	A6	4ø sl & bl	20.00	10.00
c.		Invtd. frame	80.00	47.50
43a	A7	5ø green	2.75	25
44d	A6	8ø sl & car	475.00	400.00
45a	A7	10ø rose car	2.75	25
48a	A7	20ø blue	11.00	2.00
50b	A6	25ø gray & grn	12.50	5.00
c.		Invtd. frame	85.00	27.50
51b	A6	50ø brn & vio	35.00	12.50
c.		Invtd. frame	170.00	85.00
52	A6	100ø sl & org	65.00	22.50
a.		Inverted frame	65.00	25.00
52b	A6	100ø sl & org	30.00	12.50
c.		Invtd. frame	200.00	90.00

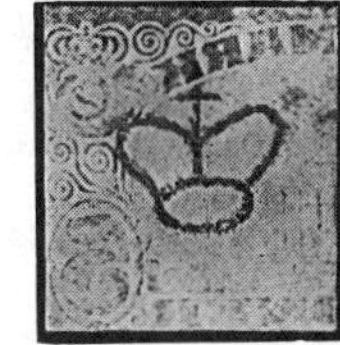

Wmk. 113

1902 — Wmkd. Crown. (113)

No.	Type	Description	Unused	Used
53	A7	1ø orange	1.00	60
a.		Imperf., pair	250.00	
54	A7	15ø lilac	12.50	75
a.		Imperf., pair		

Nos. 44d, 44, 49 Surcharged:

4 ØRE — *a*

15 15 ØRE — *b*

1904-12 — Wmkd. Crown. (113)

No.	Type	Description	Unused	Used
55	A6(a)	4ø on 8ø sl & car	4.00	4.00
a.		Wmk. 112 ('12)	35.00	60.00
b.		As "a", inverted frame		

Wmkd. Crown. (112)

No.	Type	Description	Unused	Used
56	A7(b)	15ø on 24ø brn	5.50	5.50
a.		Short "15" at right	40.00	60.00

Numeral of Value

A10

King Christian IX

A11

King Frederik VIII

A12

Wmkd. Crown. (113)

1905-17 — Typographed. *Perf. 13.*

No.	Type	Description	Unused	Used
57	A10	1ø org ('06)	2.25	30
58	A10	2ø carmine	2.25	20
a.		Perf. 14x14½ ('17)	5.00	5.00
59	A10	3ø gray	5.00	45
60	A10	4ø dl bl	5.00	20
a.		Perf. 14x14½ ('17)	16.00	16.00
61	A10	5ø dp grn ('12)	5.00	15
62	A10	10ø dp rose ('12)	6.00	15
63	A10	15ø lilac	16.00	50
64	A10	20ø dk bl ('12)	42.50	1.25
		Nos. 57-64 (8)	84.00	3.20

The three wavy lines in design A10 are symbolical of the three waters which separate the principal Danish islands.

See also Nos. 85-96.

1904-05 — Engraved.

No.	Type	Description	Unused	Used
65	A11	10ø scarlet	5.50	20
66	A11	20ø blue	20.00	1.25
67	A11	25ø brn ('05)	20.00	3.25
68	A11	50ø dl vio ('05)	47.50	45.00
69	A11	100ø ocher ('05)	40.00	40.00
		Nos. 65-69 (5)	133.00	89.70

1905-06 — Re-engraved.

No.	Type	Description	Unused	Used
70	A11	5ø green	5.00	20
71	A11	10ø scar ('06)	15.00	25

The re-engraved stamps are much clearer than the originals, and the decoration on the king's left breast has been removed.

1907-12

No.	Type	Description	Unused	Used
72	A12	5ø green	1.25	12
a.		Imperf.		
73	A12	10ø red	2.75	8
a.		Imperf.		
74	A12	20ø indigo	6.50	60
a.		20ø brt bl ('11)	9.00	90
75	A12	25ø ol brn	12.50	60
76	A12	35ø dp org ('12)	10.00	5.50
77	A12	50ø claret	40.00	5.50
78	A12	100ø bis brn	80.00	3.50
		Nos.72-78 (7)	153.00	15.90

Nos. 47, 31 and O9 Surcharged:

35 ØRE — *c*

35 ØRE FRIMÆRKE — *d*

Dark Blue Surcharge.

1912 — Wmkd. Crown. (112) — *Perf. 13.*

No.	Type	Description	Unused	Used
79	A6(c)	35ø on 16ø sl & brn	20.00	35.00
a.		Inverted frame	250.00	325.00

Perf. 14x13½.

No.	Type	Description	Unused	Used
80	A6(c)	35ø on 20ø rose & gray	16.00	25.00
a.		Inverted frame	75.00	100.00

Black Surcharge.

No.	Type	Description	Unused	Used
81	O1(d)	35ø on 32ø grn	30.00	50.00

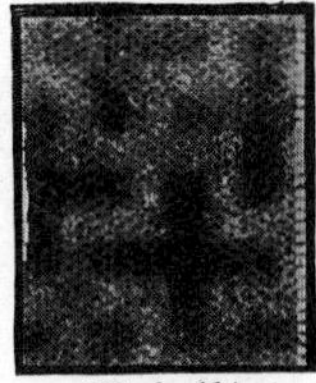

General Post Office, Copenhagen

A15

Wmkd. Two Crowns. (113)

1912 — Engraved — *Perf. 13*

No.	Type	Description	Unused	Used
82	A15	5k dk red	500.00	150.00

See No. 135.

Wmk. 114

Wmkd. Multiple Crosses. (114)

1913-30 — Typo. — *Perf. 14x14½*

No.	Type	Description	Unused	Used
85	A10	1ø dp org ('14)	60	30
a.		Booklet pane of 4, (2 No. 85, 2 No. 91 + 2 labels)	16.00	
86	A10	2ø car ('13)	80	15
a.		Imperf., (pair)	225.00	400.00
b.		Booklet pane, 4+2 labels	16.00	
87	A10	3ø gray ('13)	2.00	20
88	A10	4ø bl ('13)	4.50	12
a.		Half used as 2ø on cover		1,000.
89	A10	5ø dk brn ('21)	1.25	10
a.		Imperf., pair	275.00	
b.		Booklet pane, 4+2 labels	11.00	
90	A10	5ø lt grn ('30)	2.00	12
a.		Booklet pane, 4+2 labels	12.00	
b.		Booklet pane of 50		
91	A10	7ø ap grn ('26)	2.50	18
a.		Booklet pane, 4+2 labels	14.00	
92	A10	7ø dk vio ('30)	7.00	1.75
93	A10	8ø gray ('21)	5.50	1.00
94	A10	10ø grn ('21)	1.00	8
a.		Imperf., (pair)	350.00	
b.		Booklet pane, 4+2 labels	25.00	
95	A10	10ø bis brn ('30)	1.50	12
a.		Booklet pane, 4+2 labels	15.00	
b.		Booklet pane of 50		
96	A10	12ø vio ('26)	9.00	1.75
		Nos. 85-96 (12)	37.65	5.87

Unused Prices through 1960 are for hinged copies in fine condition.

No. 88a was used with No. 97 in Faroe Islands Jan. 3-23, 1919.

King Christian X

A16 A17

1913-28 — Typo. — *Perf. 14x14½*

No.	Type	Description	Unused	Used
97	A16	5ø green	1.50	6
a.		Booklet pane of 4	20.00	
98	A16	7ø org ('18)	4.00	60
99	A16	8ø dk gray ('20)	7.00	2.25
100	A16	10ø red	1.75	6
a.		Imperf., (pair)	350.00	
b.		Booklet pane of 4	20.00	
101	A16	12ø gray grn ('18)	12.50	10.00
102	A16	15ø violet	2.25	6
103	A16	20ø dp bl	8.50	50
104	A16	20ø brn ('21)	1.25	6
105	A16	20ø red ('26)	3.00	20
106	A16	25ø dk brn	11.00	50
107	A16	25ø brn & blk ('20)	45.00	3.75
108	A16	25ø red ('22)	4.50	70
109	A16	25ø yel grn ('25)	3.75	50
110	A16	27ø ver & blk ('18)	45.00	47.50
111	A16	30ø grn & blk ('18)	11.00	1.50
112	A16	30ø org ('21)	3.50	80
113	A16	30ø dk bl ('25)	3.75	60
114	A16	35ø orange	11.00	1.50
115	A16	35ø yel & blk ('19)	10.00	1.25
116	A16	40ø vio & blk ('18)	10.00	1.25
117	A16	40ø gray bl & blk ('20)	22.50	3.25
118	A16	40ø dk bl ('22)	6.00	1.50
119	A16	40ø org ('25)	3.50	55
120	A16	50ø claret	22.50	3.00
121	A16	50ø cl & blk ('19)	52.50	1.25
122	A16	50ø lt gray ('22)	6.50	20
a.		50ø dk gray ('21)	30.00	1.25
123	A16	60ø brn & bl ('19)	22.50	1.75
a.		60ø brn & ultra ('19)	75.00	8.50
124	A16	60ø grn bl ('21)	9.00	80
125	A16	70ø brn & grn ('20)	16.00	1.10
126	A16	80ø bl grn ('15)	52.50	20.00
127	A16	90ø brn & red ('20)	16.00	1.25
128	A16	1k brn & bl ('22)	35.00	1.25
129	A16	2k gray & cl ('25)	75.00	10.00
130	A16	5k vio & brn ('27)	12.50	7.50
131	A16	10k ver & yel grn ('28)	375.00	80.00
		Nos. 97-131 (35)	927.25	207.04

No. 97 surcharged "2 ORE" is Faroe Islands No. 1.

Nos. 87 and 98, 89 and 94, 89 and 104, 90 and 95, 97 and 103, 100 and 102 exist se-tenant in coils for use in vending machines.

1913-20 — Engraved

No.	Type	Description	Unused	Used
132	A17	1k yel brn	90.00	70
133	A17	2k gray	110.00	5.50
134	A17	5k pur ('20)	22.50	8.00

G.P.O. Type of 1912
Engraved

1915 ***Perf. 14x14½*** **Wmk. 114**

135	A15	5k dk red ('15)	600.00	150.00

Nos. 46 and O10 Surcharged in Black

DANMARK 80 ØRE POSTFRIM.

e

Typographed
Perf. 13

1915 **Wmkd. Crown. (112)**

136	A6 (c)	80ø on 12ø sl & dl lake	45.00	75.00
a.		Invtd. frame	425.00	675.00
137	O1 (e)	80ø on 8ø car	50.00	90.00
a.		"POSTERIM"	80.00	150.00

POSTFRIM.

Newspaper Stamps Surcharged

ØRE 27 ØRE

DANMARK

On Issue of 1907.

1918 ***Perf. 13*** **Wmkd. Crown. (113)**

138	N1	27ø on 1ø ol	150.00	250.00
139	N1	27ø on 5ø bl	150.00	250.00
140	N1	27ø on 7ø car	150.00	250.00
141	N1	27ø on 10ø dp lil	150.00	250.00
142	N1	27ø on 68ø yel brn	11.00	22.50
143	N1	27ø on 5k rose & yel grn	9.00	15.00
144	N1	27ø on 10k bis & bl	12.50	25.00
		Nos. 138-144 (7)	632.50	1,062.50

On Issue of 1914–15.
Wmkd. Multiple Crosses. (114)
Perf. 14x14½.

145	N1	27ø on 1ø ol gray	6.00	9.00
146	N1	27ø on 5ø bl	12.50	22.50
147	N1	27ø on 7ø rose	6.00	8.00
148	N1	27ø on 8ø grn	8.00	12.50
149	N1	27ø on 10ø dp lil	6.00	8.00
150	N1	27ø on 20ø grn	7.00	9.00
151	N1	27ø on 29ø org yel	6.00	8.00
152	N1	27ø on 38ø org	52.50	72.50
153	N1	27ø on 41ø yel brn	11.00	27.50
154	N1	27ø on 1k bl grn & mar	5.00	5.00
		Nos. 145-154 (10)	120.00	182.00

Kronborg Castle
A20

Sonderborg Castle
A21

Roskilde Cathedral
A22

Perf. 14½x14, 14x14½

1920, Oct. 5 **Typographed**

156	A20	10ø red	6.00	50
157	A21	20ø slate	6.00	50
158	A22	40ø dk brn	20.00	8.00

This issue was to commemorate the reunion of Northern Schleswig with Denmark.

1921

159	A20	10ø green	6.00	50
160	A22	40ø dk bl	42.50	9.00

Stamps of 1918 Surcharged in Blue

8 8

1921-22

161	A16	8ø on 7ø org ('22)	3.25	2.50
162	A16	8ø on 12ø gray grn	5.00	5.00

No. 87 Surcharged

8

1921

163	A10	8ø on 3ø gray	3.25	2.75

King Christian X
A23

King Christian IV
A24

A25

A26

1924, Dec. 1 ***Perf. 14x14½.***

164	A23	10ø green	6.00	2.00
165	A24	10ø green	6.00	2.00
166	A25	10ø green	6.00	2.00
167	A26	10ø green	6.00	2.00
168	A23	15ø violet	6.00	2.00
169	A24	15ø violet	6.00	2.00
170	A25	15ø violet	6.00	2.00
171	A26	15ø violet	6.00	2.00
172	A23	20ø dk brn	6.00	2.00
173	A24	20ø dk brn	6.00	2.00
174	A25	20ø dk brn	6.00	2.00
175	A26	20ø dk brn	6.00	2.00
		3 Blocks of 4, #164-175	120.00	100.00
		Nos. 164-175 (12)	72.00	24.00

Issued to commemorate the 300th anniversary of the Danish postal service.

The sheets of each value are composed of stamps of types A23, A24, A25 and A26, arranged in groups of four as illustrated.

Stamps of 1921-22 Surcharged:

20 20 *k* 20 20 *l*

1926

176	A16 (k)	20ø on 30ø org	7.00	8.50
177	A16 (l)	20ø on 40ø dk bl	9.00	12.00

A27

A28

1926, Mar. 11 ***Perf. 14x14½.***

178	A27	10ø dl grn	1.50	15
179	A28	20ø dk red	2.00	15
180	A28	30ø dk bl	10.00	90

Issued in commemoration of the 75th anniversary of the introduction of postage stamps in Denmark.

Stamps of 1913-26 Surcharged in Blue or Black

7 *m* 7 7 *n*

1926-27 ***Perf. 14x14½.***

181	A10 (m)	7ø on 8ø gray (Bl)	2.75	3.25
182	A16 (n)	7ø on 27ø ver & blk	9.00	12.50
183	A16 (n)	7ø on 20ø red ('27)	1.10	70
184	A16 (n)	12ø on 15ø vio	5.00	5.50

Surcharged on Official Stamps of 1914–23.

185	O1 (e)	7ø on 1ø org	6.00	8.00
186	O1 (e)	7ø on 3ø gray	12.00	20.00
187	O1 (e)	7ø on 4ø bl	5.00	10.00
188	O1 (e)	7ø on 5ø grn	80.00	110.00
189	O1 (e)	7ø on 10ø grn	6.50	8.50
190	O1 (e)	7ø on 15ø vio	5.00	7.50
191	O1 (e)	7ø on 20ø ind	22.50	32.50
a.		Double surcharge	500.00	
		Nos. 181-191 (11)	154.85	218.45

Caravel
A30

King Christian X
A31

1927 **Typographed.** ***Perf. 14x14½.***

192	A30	15ø red	4.75	6
193	A30	20ø gray	6.50	50
194	A30	25ø lt bl	1.00	10
195	A30	30ø ocher	1.00	10
196	A30	35ø red brn	8.00	15
197	A30	40ø yel grn	8.00	15
		Nos. 192-197 (6)	29.25	1.41

See also Nos. 232–238J.

1930, Sept. 26

210	A31	5ø ap grn	2.50	10
a.		Booklet pane, 4 + 2 labels	25.00	
211	A31	7ø violet	8.00	3.00
212	A31	8ø dk gray	35.00	10.00
213	A31	10ø yel brn	6.50	30
a.		Booklet pane, 4 + 2 labels	35.00	
214	A31	15ø red	6.50	30
215	A31	20ø lt gray	30.00	3.00
216	A31	25ø lt bl	12.00	40
217	A31	30ø yel buff	12.00	1.10
218	A31	35ø red brn	12.00	3.00
219	A31	40ø dp grn	12.00	1.10
		Nos. 210-219 (10)	136.50	22.30

60th birthday of King Christian X.

Wavy Lines and Numeral of Value
A32

Type of 1905–12 Issue.
Engraved, Redrawn

1933–40 ***Perf. 13*** **Unwmkd.**

220	A32	1ø gray blk	5	3
221	A32	2ø scarlet	10	5
222	A32	4ø blue	50	15
223	A32	5ø yel grn	1.75	15
a.		5ø gray grn	27.50	30.00
b.		Tête bêche pair	15.00	15.00
c.		Booklet pane of 4	8.00	
d.		Booklet pane of 4, (1 No. 223a & 3 No. B6)	32.50	
224	A32	5ø rose lake ('38)	3	3
a.		Booklet pane of 4	25	
b.		Booklet pane of 10	75	
224C	A32	6ø org ('40)	40	6
225	A32	7ø violet	3.00	25
226	A32	7ø yel grn ('38)	2.50	30
226A	A32	7ø lt brn ('40)	40	15
227	A32	8ø gray	1.00	15
227A	A32	8ø yel grn ('40)	45	10
228	A32	10ø yel org	17.50	6
a.		Tête bêche pair	40.00	25.00
b.		Booklet pane of 4	87.50	
229	A32	10ø lt brn ('37)	12.50	10
a.		Booklet pane of 4	62.50	
b.		Booklet pane of 4, (1 No. 229 & 3 No. B7)	35.00	
230	A32	10ø vio ('38)	80	3
a.		Booklet pane of 4	4.00	
b.		Bklt. pane of 4, (2 No. 230 & 2 No. B10)	5.00	
		Nos. 220-230 (14)	40.98	1.61

The stamps of 1905–12 were typographed. They had a solid background with groups of small hearts below the heraldic lions in the upper corners and below "DA" and "RK" of "DANMARK". The numerals of value were enclosed in single-lined ovals.

The 1933–40 stamps are line-engraved and have a background of crossed lines. The hearts have been removed and the numerals of value are now in double-lined ovals. Two types exist of some values.

The 1ø, No. 220, was issued on fluorescent paper in 1969.

No. 230 with wide margins is from booklet pane No. 230b.

Of the tête bêche pairs, those with gutters are twice as plentiful. Prices are for the less costly.

Surcharges of 20, 50 and 60øre on Nos. 220, 224 and 224C are listed as Faroe Islands Nos. 2–3, 5–6.

See also Nos. 318, 333, 382, 416, 437–437A, 493–498.

Certain Tête Bêche

pairs of 1938–55 issues which reached the market in 1971, and were not regularly issued, are not listed. This group comprises 24 different major-number vertical pairs of types A32, A47, A61 and SP3 (13 with gutters, 11 without), and pairs of some minor numbers and shades. They were removed from booklet pane sheets.

Type of 1927 Issue.

1933–34 **Engraved.** ***Perf. 13***

Type I.

Type I—Two columns of squares between sail and left frame line.

232	A30	20ø gray	15.00	20
233	A30	25ø blue	65.00	8.00
234	A30	25ø brn ('34)	37.50	15
235	A30	30ø org yel	3.00	1.25
236	A30	30ø bl ('34)	2.75	15
237	A30	35ø violet	1.80	35
238	A30	40ø yel grn	4.00	18
		Nos. 232-238 (7)	129.05	10.28

Type II.

Type II—One column of squares between sail and left frame line.

1933-40

238A	A30	15ø dp red	4.00	6
k.		Booklet pane of 4	20.00	
l.		Booklet pane of 4, (1 No. 238A, 3 No. B8)	45.00	
238B	A30	15ø yel grn ('40)	12.00	10
238C	A30	20ø gray blk ('39)	6.50	15
238D	A30	20ø red ('40)	1.60	5
238E	A30	25ø dp brn ('39)	1.60	10
238F	A30	30ø bl ('39)	5.50	20
238G	A30	30ø org ('40)	1.25	10
238H	A30	35ø vio ('40)	2.25	45
238I	A30	40ø yel grn ('39)	17.00	50
238J	A30	40ø bl ('40)	2.00	12
		Nos. 238A-238J (10)	53.70	1.83

Nos. 232–238J, engraved, have cross-hatched background. Nos. 192–197, typographed, have solid background.

No. 238A surcharged 20ore is listed as Faroe Islands No. 4.

King Christian X
A33

1934–41 ***Perf. 13***

239	A33	50ø gray	2.50	15
240	A33	60ø bl grn	4.25	35
240A	A33	75ø dk bl ('41)	1.50	20
241	A33	1k lt brn	6.50	10
242	A33	2k dl red	13.00	1.00
243	A33	5k violet	22.50	5.00
		Nos. 239-243 (6)	50.25	6.80

Nos. 233, 235 Surcharged in Black

4

1934, June 9

244	A30	4ø on 25ø bl	65	35
245	A30	10ø on 30ø org yel	5.50	2.50

"The Ugly Duckling"
A34

Hans Christian Andersen
A35

"The Little Mermaid"
A36

1935, Oct. 4 *Perf. 13*

No.	Type	Description	Unused	Used
246	A34	5ø lt grn	6.00	12
a.		Tête bêche pair	22.50	11.00
b.		Bklt. pane of 4	27.50	
247	A35	7ø dl vio	5.00	1.00
248	A36	10ø orange	9.00	15
a.		Tête bêche pair	25.00	17.00
b.		Bklt. pane of 4	50.00	
249	A35	15ø red	25.00	10
a.		Tête bêche pair	55.00	27.50
b.		Bklt. pane of 4	125.00	
250	A35	20ø gray	20.00	1.00
251	A35	30ø dl bl	6.00	50
		Nos. 246-251 (6)	71.00	2.87

Issued to commemorate the centenary of the publication of the earliest installment of Hans Christian Andersen's "Fairy Tales."

Note on tête bêche pair prices after No. 230 applies to Nos. 246a, 248a and 249a.

Nikolai Church
A37

Hans Tausen
A38

Ribe Cathedral
A39

1936 *Perf. 13*

No.	Type	Description	Unused	Used
252	A37	5ø green	4.00	30
a.		Bklt. pane of 4	20.00	
253	A37	7ø violet	3.50	1.10
254	A38	10ø lt brn	4.00	10
a.		Bklt. pane of 4	20.00	
255	A38	15ø dl rose	7.00	10
256	A39	30ø blue	25.00	90
		Nos. 252-256 (5)	43.50	2.50

Issued in commemoration of the 400th anniversary of the Church Reformation in Denmark.

No. 229 Overprinted in Blue

K.P.K.
17.-26. SEPT.
19 37

1937, Sept. 17

No.	Type	Description	Unused	Used
257	A32	10ø lt brn	4.50	4.50

Issued in commemoration of the Jubilee Exhibition held by the Copenhagen Philatelic Club on the occasion of their 50th anniversary. The stamps were on sale at the Exhibition only, each holder of a ticket of admission (1kr.) being entitled to purchase 20 stamps at face value, and each holder of a season ticket (5kr.) being entitled to purchase 100 stamps.

Yacht and Summer Palace, Marselisborg
A40

King Christian X in Streets of Copenhagen
A41

Equestrian Statue of King Frederik V and Amalienborg Palace
A42

1937, May 15 *Perf. 13*

No.	Type	Description	Unused	Used
258	A40	5ø green	3.50	35
a.		Bklt. pane of 4	17.50	
259	A41	10ø brown	3.50	18
a.		Bklt. pane of 4	17.50	
260	A42	15ø scarlet	3.50	18
a.		Bklt. pane of 4	20.00	
261	A41	30ø blue	25.00	2.00

Issued in commemoration of the 25th anniversary of the accession to the throne of King Christian X.

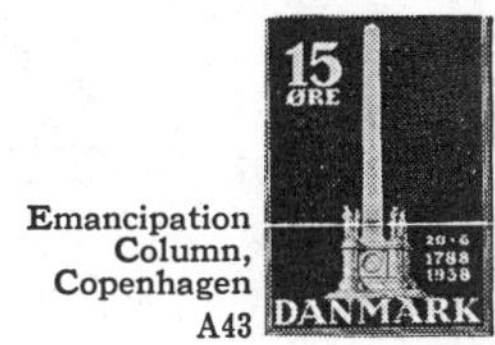
Emancipation Column, Copenhagen
A43

1938, June 20 *Perf. 13*

No.	Type	Description	Unused	Used
262	A43	15ø scarlet	1.25	20

Issued to commemorate the 150th anniversary of the abolition of serfdom in Denmark.

No. 223 Overprinted in Red on Alternate Stamps

D.F.U.
FRIM-UDST.
19 38

1938, Sept. 2

No.	Type	Description	Unused	Used
263	A32	5ø yel grn (pair)	7.50	8.00

10th Danish Philatelic Exhibition.

Bertel Thorvaldsen
A44

Statue of Jason
A45

1938, Nov. 17 Engr. *Perf. 13*

No.	Type	Description	Unused	Used
264	A44	5ø rose lake	1.00	15
265	A45	10ø purple	1.00	12
266	A44	30ø dk bl	4.25	55

The return to Denmark in 1838 of Bertel Thorvaldsen, Danish sculptor.

Stamps of 1933-39 Surcharged with New Values in Black:

6 (a) 15 (b) 20 (c)

1940

No.	Type	Description	Unused	Used
267	A32 (a)	6ø on 7ø yel grn	35	35
268	A32 (a)	6ø on 8ø gray	30	20
269	A30 (b)	15ø on 40ø yel grn (On No. 238)	4.00	4.50
270	A30 (b)	15ø on 40ø yel grn (On No. 238I)	2.25	1.75
271	A30 (c)	20ø on 15ø dp red	1.75	15
272	A30 (b)	40ø on 30ø bl (On No. 238F)	2.00	35
		Nos. 267-272 (6)	10.65	7.30

Bering's Ship
A46

1941, Nov. 27 Engr. *Perf. 13*

No.	Type	Description	Unused	Used
277	A46	10ø dk vio	60	20
278	A46	20ø red brn	1.25	40
279	A46	40ø dk bl	80	50

Issued in commemoration of the 200th anniversary of the death of Vitus Bering, explorer.

King Christian X
A47

1942-46 *Perf. 13* **Unwmkd.**

No.	Type	Description	Unused	Used
280	A47	10ø violet	25	3
281	A47	15ø yel grn	60	6
282	A47	20ø red	60	3
283	A47	25ø brn ('43)	75	6
284	A47	30ø org ('43)	75	10
285	A47	35ø brt red vio ('44)	75	20
286	A47	40ø bl ('43)	75	10
286A	A47	45ø ol brn ('46)	1.25	20
286B	A47	50ø gray ('45)	1.50	10
287	A47	60ø bluish grn ('44)	1.25	10
287A	A47	75ø dk bl ('46)	1.50	20
		Nos. 280-287A (11)	9.95	1.18

Round Tower
A48

Condor Plane
A49

1942, Nov. 27

No.	Type	Description	Unused	Used
288	A48	10ø violet	25	20

Issued to commemorate the 300th anniversary of the Round Tower, Copenhagen.

1943, Oct. 29

No.	Type	Description	Unused	Used
289	A49	20ø red	30	20

Issued to commemorate the 25th anniversary of the Danish Aviation Company (Det Danske Luftfartsselskab).

Ejby Church
A50

Designs: 15ø, Oesterlars Church. 20ø, Hvidbjerg Church.

1944 Engraved. *Perf. 13*

No.	Type	Description	Unused	Used
290	A50	10ø violet	25	20
291	A50	15ø yel grn	70	70
292	A50	20ø red	25	20

Ole Roemer
A53

King Christian X
A54

1944, Sept. 25

No.	Type	Description	Unused	Used
293	A53	20ø hn brn	40	20

Issued to commemorate the 300th anniversary of the birth of Ole Roemer, astronomer.

1945, Sept. 26

No.	Type	Description	Unused	Used
294	A54	10ø lilac	20	10
295	A54	20ø red	40	10
296	A54	40ø dp bl	90	25

75th birthday of King Christian X.

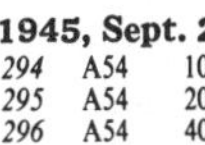

Small State Seal
A55

Tycho Brahe
A56

1946-47 *Perf. 13* **Unwmkd.**

No.	Type	Description	Unused	Used
297	A55	1k brown	80	5
298	A55	2k red ('47)	80	5
299	A55	5k dl bl	2.00	6

Nos. 297-299 issued on ordinary and fluorescent paper.

See also Nos. 395-400, 441A-444D, 499-506, 629-650.

1946, Dec. 14 **Engraved**

No.	Type	Description	Unused	Used
300	A56	20(ø) dk red	30	10

Issued to commemorate the 400th anniversary of the birth of Tycho Brahe, astronomer.

First Danish Locomotive
A57

Modern Steam Locomotive
A58

Diesel Locomotive
A59

1947, June 27

No.	Type	Description	Unused	Used
301	A57	15(ø) stl bl	50	30
302	A58	20(ø) red	50	20
303	A59	40(ø) dp bl	1.50	85

Issued to commemorate the centenary of the inauguration of the Danish State Railways.

Jacob C. Jacobsen
A60

King Frederik IX
A61

1947, Nov. 10 *Perf. 13*

No.	Type	Description	Unused	Used
304	A60	20(ø) dk red	45	20

Issued to commemorate the 60th anniversary of the death of Jacob Christian Jacobsen, founder of the Glyptothek Art Museum, Copenhagen.

1948-50 *Perf. 13* **Unwmkd.**

Three types among 15ø, 20ø, 30ø:

I. Background of horizontal lines. No outline at left for cheek and ear. King's uniform textured in strong lines.

II. Background of vertical and horizontal lines. Contour of cheek and ear at left. Uniform same.

III. Background and facial contour lines as in II. Uniform lines double and thinner.

No.	Type	Description	Unused	Used
306	A61	15(ø) grn (II)	2.25	6
a.		Type III ('49)	1.50	6

307	A61	20(ö) dk red (I)	1.25	6
a.		Type III ('49)	1.25	6
308	A61	25(ö) lt brn	1.75	10
309	A61	30(ö) org (II)	18.00	15
a.		Type III ('50)	18.00	15
310	A61	40(ö) dl bl ('49)	5.00	60
311	A61	45(ö) ol ('50)	1.50	10
312	A61	50(ö) gray ('49)	2.00	10
313	A61	60(ö) grnsh bl ('50)	2.50	10
314	A61	75(ö) lil rose ('50)	1.50	10
		Nos. 306-314 (9)	35.75	1.37

See also Nos. 319-326, 334-341, 354.

Legislative Assembly, 1849
A62

Symbol of U.P.U.
A63

1949, June 5

315	A62	20(ö) red brn	50	15

Issued to commemorate the centenary of the adoption of the Danish constitution.

1949, Oct. 9

316	A63	40ö dl bl	1.25	85

Issued to commemorate the 75th anniversary of the formation of the Universal Postal Union.

Kalundborg Radio Station and Masts
A64

1950, Apr. 1 **Engr.** ***Perf. 13***

317	A64	20ö brn red	60	25

Issued to commemorate the 25th anniversary of radio broadcasting in Denmark.

Types of 1933-50.

1950–51 ***Perf. 13*** **Unwmkd.**

318	A32	10ö green	4	3
319	A61	15(ö) lilac	90	3
b.		15(ö) gray lil	2.75	3
320	A61	20(ö) lt brn	50	3
321	A61	25(ö) dk red	4.50	3
322	A61	35(ö) gray grn ('51)	1.20	15
323	A61	40(ö) gray	1.20	6
324	A61	50(ö) dk bl	3.25	20
325	A61	55(ö) brn ('51)	22.50	3.50
326	A61	70(ö) dp grn	3.75	10
		Nos. 318-326 (9)	37.84	4.13

Warship of 1701
A65

Hans Christian Oersted
A66

1951, Feb. 26 **Engr.** ***Perf. 13***

327	A65	25(ö) dk red	1.10	25
328	A65	50(ö) dp bl	5.50	1.75

Issued to commemorate the 250th anniversary of the foundation of the Naval Officers' College.

1951, Mar. 9 **Unwmkd.**

329	A66	50(ö) blue	2.25	75

Issued to commemorate the centenary of the death of Hans Christian Oersted, physicist.

Post Chaise ("Ball Post")
A67

Marine Rescue
A68

1951, Apr. 1 ***Perf. 13***

330	A67	15(ö) purple	1.75	25
331	A67	25(ö) hn brn	1.75	25

Issued to commemorate the centenary of Denmark's first postage stamp.

1952, Mar. 26

332	A68	25(ö) red brn	80	30

Issued to commemorate the centenary of the foundation of the Danish Lifesaving Service.

Types of 1933-50.

1952–53 ***Perf. 13***

333	A32	12(ö) lt yel grn	50	3
334	A61	25(ö) lt bl	1.60	25
335	A61	30(ö) brn red	1.00	3
336	A61	50(ö) aqua ('53)	80	6
337	A61	60(ö) dp bl ('53)	1.00	6
338	A61	65(ö) gray ('53)	1.00	10
339	A61	80(ö) org ('53)	1.00	6
340	A61	90(ö) ol ('53)	4.00	6
341	A61	95(ö) red org ('53)	1.75	35
		Nos. 333-341 (9)	12.65	1.00

Jelling Runic Stone
A69

Designs: 15(ö), Vikings' camp, Trelleborg. 20(ö), Church of Kalundborg. 30(ö), Nyborg castle. 60(ö), Goose tower, Vordinborg.

1953–56 ***Perf. 13***

342	A69	10(ö) dp grn	15	5
343	A69	15(ö) lt rose vio	15	5
344	A69	20(ö) brown	20	8
345	A69	30(ö) red ('54)	25	8
346	A69	60(ö) dp bl ('54)	70	20

Designs: 10(ö), Manor house, Spottrup. 15(ö), Hammershus castle ruins. 20(ö), Copenhagen stock exchange. 30(ö), Statue of Frederik V, Amalienborg. 60(ö), Soldier statue at Fredericia.

347	A69	10(ö) grn ('54)	15	5
348	A69	15(ö) lil ('55)	15	5
349	A69	20(ö) brn ('55)	20	8
350	A69	30(ö) red ('55)	25	8
351	A69	60(ö) dp bl ('56)	1.10	20
		Nos. 342-351 (10)	3.30	92

Nos. 342-351 were issued to commemorate the 1000th anniversary of the Kingdom of Denmark. Each stamp represents a different century.

Telegraph Equipment of 1854
A70

King Frederik V
A71

1954, Feb. 2 ***Perf. 13***

352	A70	30(ö) red brn	80	15

Issued to commemorate the centenary of the telegraph in Denmark.

1954, Mar. 31

353	A71	30(ö) dk red	1.00	12

Issued to commemorate the 200th anniversary of the founding of the Royal Academy of Fine Arts.

Type of 1948-50

1955, Apr. 27

354	A61	25(ö) lilac	40	5

Nos. 224C and 226A Surcharged with New Value in Black. Nos. 307 and 321 Surcharged with New Value and 4 Bars.

1955–56

355	A32	5ö on 6ö org	20	20
356	A32	5ö on 7ö lt brn	20	20
357	A61	30(ö) on 20(ö) dk red (I)	40	10
a.		Type III	70	15
b.		Double surch.	550.00	550.00
358	A61	30(ö) on 25(ö) dk red ('56)	90	6
a.		Double surch.		

Sören Kierkegaard—A72

Ellehammer's Plane—A73

1955, Nov. 11 **Unwmkd.**

359	A72	30(ö) dk red	60	12

Issued to commemorate the 100th anniversary of the death of Sören Kierkegaard, philosopher and theologian.

1956, Sept. 12 **Engraved**

360	A73	30ö dl red	90	12

Issued to commemorate the 50th anniversary of the first flight made by Jacob Christian Hansen Ellehammer in a heavier-than-air craft.

Northern Countries Issue.

Whooper Swans
A74

1956, Oct. 30 ***Perf. 13***

361	A74	30ö rose red	5.00	35
362	A74	60ö ultra	2.50	1.25

Issued to emphasize the close bonds among the northern countries: Denmark, Finland, Iceland, Norway and Sweden.

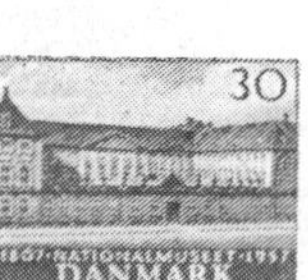

Prince's Palace
A75

Harvester
A76

Design: 60ö, Sun God's Chariot.

1957, May 15 **Unwmkd.**

363	A75	30ö dl red	2.25	25
364	A75	60ö dk bl	1.50	60

Issued to commemorate the 150th anniversary of the National Museum.

1958, Sept. 4 **Engr.** ***Perf. 13***

365	A76	30ö fawn	40	12

Centenary of the Royal Veterinary and Agricultural College.

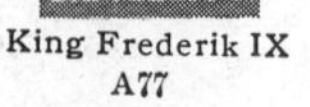

King Frederik IX
A77

Ballet Dancer
A78

1959, Mar. 11

366	A77	30ö rose red	1.00	8
367	A77	35ö rose lil	75	65
368	A77	60ö ultra	75	25

King Frederik's 60th birthday.

1959, May 16

369	A78	35ö rose lil	40	20

Issued to publicize the Danish Ballet and Music Festival, May 17–31. See also Nos. 401, 422.

No. 319 Surcharged

1960, Apr. 7

370	A61	30ö on 15ö pur	40	20

Issued to publicize World Refugee Year, July 1, 1959–June 30, 1960.

Seeder and Farm
A79

Designs: 30ö, Harvester combine. 60ö, Plow.

1960, Apr. 28 **Engr.** ***Perf. 13***

371	A79	12ö green	20	20
372	A79	30ö dl red	20	20
373	A79	60ö dk bl	85	35

King Frederik IX and Queen Ingrid
A80

1960, May 24 **Unwmkd.**

374	A80	30ö dl red	1.00	20
375	A80	60ö blue	80	30

Issued to commemorate the 25th anniversary of the marriage of King Frederik IX and Queen Ingrid.

Bascule Light
A81

Niels R. Finsen
A82

1960, June 8 **Engraved**

376	A81	30ö dl red	45	15

Issued to commemorate the 400th anniversary of the Lighthouse Service.

1960, Aug. 1 ***Perf. 13***

377	A82	30ö dk red	45	15

Issued to commemorate the centenary of the birth of Dr. Niels R. Finsen, physician and scientist.

Nursing Mother
A83

DC-8 Airliner
A84

1960, Aug. 16 **Unwmkd.**

378	A83	60ø ultra	1.00	35

Issued to commemorate the 10th meeting of the regional committee for Europe of the World Health Organization, Copenhagen, Aug. 16–20.

Europa Issue, 1960

Common Design Type

1960, Sept. 19 ***Perf. 13***

Size: 28x21mm.

379	CD3	60ø ultra	1.25	35

SAS Issue

1961, Feb. 24

380	A84	60ø ultra	1.00	25

Issued to commemorate the 10th anniversary of the Scandinavian Airlines System, SAS.

Landscape
A85

Frederik IX
A86

1961, Apr. 21 ***Perf. 13***

381	A85	30ø cop brn	35	8

Issued to commemorate the 50th anniversary of Denmark's Society of Nature Lovers.

Fluorescent Paper

as well as ordinary paper, was used in printing many definitive and commemorative stamps, starting in 1962. These include No. 220; the 15, 20, 25, 30, 35 (Nos. 386 and 387), 50 and 60ø, 1.20k, 1.50k and 25k definitives of following set, and Nos. 297–299, 318, 318a–b, 333, 380, 401–427, 429–435, 438–439, 493, 543, 548, B30.

Only fluorescent paper was used for Nos. 436–437, 437A and 440 onward; in semi-postals from B31 onward.

1961–63 **Engraved** ***Perf. 13***

382	A32	15ø grn ('63)	30	3
383	A86	20ø brown	80	5
384	A86	25ø brn ('63)	30	3
385	A86	30ø rose red	1.00	3
386	A86	35ø ol grn	1.20	50
387	A86	35ø rose red ('63)	40	3
388	A86	40ø gray	1.25	5
389	A86	50ø aqua	1.00	6
390	A86	60ø ultra	1.25	10
391	A86	70ø green	2.25	20
392	A86	80ø red org	2.50	10
393	A86	90ø ol bis	6.50	20
394	A86	95ø cl ('63)	1.25	60
		Nos. 382-394 (13)	20.00	1.98

See also Nos. 417–419, 438–441.

State Seal Type of 1946–47

1962–65

395	A55	1.10k lil ('65)	5.00	1.00
396	A55	1.20k gray	4.00	8
397	A55	1.25k orange	4.00	12
398	A55	1.30k grn ('65)	5.00	70
399	A55	1.50k red lil	2.00	6
400	A55	25k yel grn	7.50	50
		Nos. 395-400 (6)	27.50	2.46

Dancer Type of 1959

Inscribed "15-31 MAJ"

1962, Apr. 26

401	A78	60ø ultra	70	25

Issued to publicize the Danish Ballet and Music Festival, May 15–31. No. 369 is dated "17-31 MAJ."

Old Mill
A87

M.S. Selandia
A88

1962, May 10 ***Perf. 13*** **Unwmkd.**

402	A87	10ø red brn	15	10

Issued to commemorate the centenary of the abolition of mill monopolies.

1962, June 14 **Engraved**

403	A88	60ø dk bl	3.50	3.25

Issued to commemorate the 50th anniversary of M.S. Selandia, the first Diesel ship.

Violin Scroll, Leaves, Lights and Balloon—A89

1962, Aug. 31

404	A89	35ø rose vio	30	10

Issued to commemorate the 150th anniversary of the birth of Georg Carstensen, founder of Tivoli amusement park, Copenhagen.

Cliffs on Möen Island
A90

Germinating Wheat
A91

1962, Nov. 22

405	A90	20ø pale brn	15	5

Issued to publicize preservation of natural treasures and landmarks.

1963, Mar. 21 **Engraved**

406	A91	35ø fawn	30	8

Issued for the "Freedom from Hunger" campaign of the U.N. Food and Agriculture Organization.

Railroad Wheel, Tire Tracks, Waves and Swallow
A92

Sailing Vessel, Coach, Postilions and Globe
A93

1963, May 14 ***Perf. 13*** **Unwmkd.**

407	A92	15ø green	20	10

Issued to commemorate the inauguration of the "Bird Flight Line" railroad link between Denmark and Germany.

1963, May 27

408	A93	60ø dk bl	80	20

Issued to commemorate the centenary of the first International Postal Conference, Paris, 1863.

Niels Bohr and Atom Diagram
A94

Early Public School Drawn on Slate
A95

1963, Nov. 21 **Engraved**

409	A94	35ø red brn	45	10
410	A94	60ø dk bl	90	20

Issued to commemorate the 50th anniversary of Prof. Niels Bohr's (1885–1962) atom theory.

1964, June 19 ***Perf. 13*** **Unwmkd.**

411	A95	35ø red brn	30	6

Issued to commemorate the 150th anniversary of the royal decrees for the public school system.

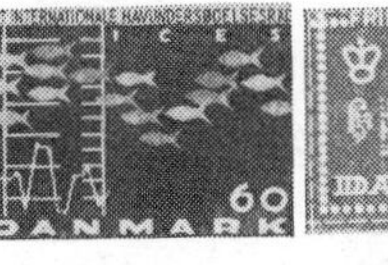

Fish and Chart
A96

Danish Watermarks and Perforations
A97

1964, Sept. 7 **Engraved**

412	A96	60ø vio bl	60	15

Issued to commemorate the Conference of the International Council for the Exploration of the Sea, Copenhagen.

1964, Oct. 10 ***Perf. 13***

413	A97	35ø pink	35	8

Issued for the 25th anniversary of Stamp Day and to publicize the Odense Stamp Exhibition, Oct. 10–11.

Landscape
A98

Calculator, Ledger and Inkwell
A99

1964, Nov. 12 **Engraved**

414	A98	25ø brown	20	6

Issued to publicize preservation of natural treasures and landmarks.

1965, Mar. 8 **Unwmkd.**

415	A99	15ø lt ol grn	15	6

Issued to commemorate the centenary of the first Business School in Denmark.

Types of 1933 and 1961

1965, May 15 **Engraved** ***Perf. 13***

416	A32	25ø ap grn	35	3
417	A86	40ø brown	35	3
418	A86	50ø rose red	45	3
419	A86	80ø ultra	1.25	10

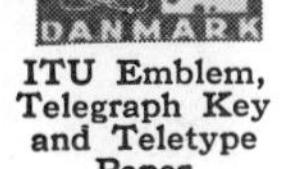

ITU Emblem, Telegraph Key and Teletype Paper
A100

Carl Nielsen
A101

1965, May 17

420	A100	80ø dk bl	60	15

Issued to commemorate the centenary of the International Telecommunication Union.

1965, June 9 **Engraved**

421	A101	50ø brn red	30	10

Issued to commemorate the centenary of the birth of Carl Nielsen (1865–1931), composer.

Dancer Type of 1959

Inscribed "15-31 MAJ"

1965, Sept. 23

422	A78	50ø rose red	40	15

Issued to publicize the Danish Ballet and Music Festival, May 15–31.

Bogo Windmill
A102

Mylius Dalgas Surveying Wasteland
A103

1965, Nov. 10 **Engraved** ***Perf. 13***

423	A102	40ø brown	30	10

Issued to publicize the preservation of natural treasures and landmarks.

1966, Feb. 24

424	A103	25ø ol grn	20	10

Issued to commemorate the centenary of the Danish Heath Society (reclamation of wastelands), founded by Enrico Mylius Dalgas.

Christen Kold
A104

1966, March 29 ***Perf. 13***

425	A104	50ø dl red	40	10

Issued to commemorate the 150th anniversary of the birth of Christen Kold (1816–70), educator.

Poorhouse, Copenhagen
A105

Holte Allée, Bregentved
A106

Dolmen (Grave) in Jutland
A107

1966 **Unwmkd.**

426	A105	50ø dl red	40	10
427	A106	80ø dk bl	1.00	20
428	A107	1.50k dk sl grn	1.50	25

Nos. 426–428 issued to publicize preservation of national treasures and ancient monuments. Issue dates: 50ø, May 12; 80ø, June 16; 1.50k, Nov. 24.

Georg Jensen by Ejnar Nielsen
A108

Music Bar and Instruments
A109

1966, Aug. 31 **Engr.** ***Perf. 13***

429	A108	80ø dk bl	1.00	20

Issued to commemorate the centenary of the birth of Georg Jensen, silversmith.

1967, Jan. 9

430	A109	50ö dk red	40	6

Issued to commemorate the centenary of the Royal Danish Academy of Music.

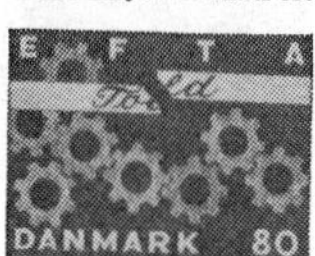

Cogwheels, and Broken Customs Duty Ribbon
A110

1967, Mar. 2

431	A110	80ö dk bl	1.10	25

Issued to publicize the European Free Trade Association. Industrial tariffs were abolished Dec. 31, 1966, among EFTA members: Austria, Denmark, Finland, Great Britain, Norway, Portugal, Sweden and Switzerland.

Windmill and Medieval Fortress
A111

Designs: 40ö, Ship's rigging and baroque house front. 50ö, Old Town Hall. 80ö, New building construction.

1967 Engraved *Perf. 13*

432	A111	25ö green	60	20
433	A111	40ö sepia	50	25
434	A111	50ö red brn	50	12
435	A111	80ö dk bl	1.50	35

The 800th anniversary of Copenhagen.
Issue dates: Nos. 432–433, Apr. 6; Nos. 434–435, May 11.

Princess Margrethe and Prince Henri
A112

1967, June 10

436	A112	50ö red	60	10

Issued to commemorate the marriage of Crown Princess Margrethe and Prince Henri de Monpezat.

Types of 1933–1961

1967–71 Engraved *Perf. 13*

437	A32	30ö dk grn	25	4
437A	A32	40ö org ('71)	35	8
438	A86	50ö brown	1.25	6
439	A86	60ö rose red	1.25	5
440	A86	80ö green	1.00	5
441	A86	90ö ultra	1.40	10
441A	A55	1.20k Prus grn ('71)	2.50	20
442	A55	2.20k orange	5.50	10
443	A55	2.80k gray	4.50	20
444	A55	2.90k rose vio	5.50	20
444A	A55	3k dk sl grn ('69)	1.10	10
444B	A55	3.10k plum ('70)	5.00	20
444C	A55	4k gray ('69)	1.50	10
444D	A55	4.10k ol ('70)	5.00	20
		Nos. 437-444D (14)	36.10	1.68

Issue dates: Nos. 437–441, June 30, 1967; Nos. 442–443, July 8, 1967; No. 444, Apr. 29, 1968; Nos. 444A, 444C, Aug. 28, 1969; Nos. 444B, 444D, Aug. 27, 1970; Nos. 437A, 441A, June 24, 1971.

Hans Christian Sonne
A113

Cross-anchor and Porpoise
A114

1967, Sept. 21

445	A113	60ö red	40	10

Issued to commemorate the 150th anniversary of the birth of Hans Christian Sonne, pioneer of the cooperative movement in Denmark.

1967, Nov. 9 Engraved *Perf. 13*

446	A114	90ö dk bl	1.00	40

Issued to commemorate the centenary of the Danish Seamen's Church in Foreign Ports.

Esbjerg Harbor
A115

Koldinghus
A116

1968, Apr. 24

447	A115	30ö dk yel grn	25	6

Centenary of Esbjerg Harbor.

1968, June 13

448	A116	60ö cop red	30	6

700th anniversary of Koldinghus Castle.

Shipbuilding Industry
A117

Sower
A118

Designs: 50ö, Chemical industry. 60ö, Electric power. 90ö, Engineering.

1968, Oct. 24 Engraved *Perf. 13*

449	A117	30ö green	25	20
450	A117	50ö brown	30	10
451	A117	60ö red brn	40	10
452	A117	90ö dk bl	70	40

Issued to publicize Danish industries.

1969, Jan. 29

453	A118	30ö gray grn	20	8

Issued to commemorate the 200th anniversary of the Royal Agricultural Society of Denmark.

Five Ancient Ships
A119

Frederik IX
A120

Nordic Cooperation Issue

1969, Feb. 28 Engraved *Perf. 13*

454	A119	60ö brn red	1.75	25
455	A119	90ö blue	2.50	1.00

Issued to commemorate the 50th anniversary of the Nordic Society and to commemorate the centenary of postal cooperation among the northern countries: Denmark, Finland, Iceland, Norway and Sweden. The design is taken from a coin found at the site of Birka, an ancient Swedish town.

1969, Mar. 11

456	A120	50ö sepia	35	10
457	A120	60ö dl red	35	10

70th birthday of King Frederik IX.

Europa Issue, 1969
Common Design Type

1969, Apr. 28
Size: 28x20mm.

458	CD12	90ö chlky bl	1.25	60

Kronborg Castle
A121

Danish Flag
A122

1969, May 22 Engraved *Perf. 13*

459	A121	50ö brown	25	10

Issued to commemorate the 50th anniversary of the association of Danes living abroad.

1969, June 12

460	A122	60ö bluish blk, red & gray	50	10

Issued to commemorate the 750th anniversary of the fall of the Dannebrog (Danish flag) from heaven.

Martin Andersen Nexø
A123

Niels Stensen
A124

1969, Aug. 28

461	A123	80ö dp grn	60	15

Issued to commemorate the centenary of the birth of Martin Andersen Nexø (1869–1954), novelist.

1969, Sept. 25

462	A124	1k dp brn	65	15

Issued to commemorate the 300th anniversary of the publication of Niels Stensen's geological work "On Solid Bodies."

Abstract Design
A125

Symbolic Design
A126

1969, Nov. 10 Engraved *Perf. 13*

463	A125	60ö rose, red & ultra	40	10

1969, Nov. 20

464	A126	30ö ol grn	25	10

Issued to commemorate the centenary of the birth of Valdemar Poulsen (1869–1942), electrical engineer and inventor.

Post Office Bank
A127

School Safety Patrol
A128

1970, Jan. 15 Engraved *Perf. 13*

465	A127	60ö dk red & org	40	10

Issued to commemorate the 50th anniversary of post office banking service.

1970, Feb. 19

466	A128	50ö brown	40	10

Issued to publicize road safety.

Candle in Window
A129

Deer
A130

1970, May 4 Engraved *Perf. 13*

467	A129	50ö sl, dl bl & yel	40	10

Issued to commemorate the 25th anniversary of liberation from the Germans.

1970, May 28

468	A130	60ö yel grn, red & brn	40	10

Tercentenary of Jaegersborg Deer Park.

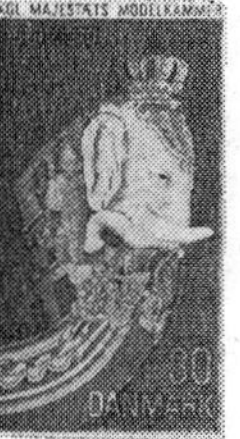

Elephant Figurehead, 1741
A131

"The Homecoming" by Povl Christensen
A132

1970, June 15 *Perf. 11½*

469	A131	30ö multi	30	15

Royal Naval Museum, tercentenary.

1970, June 15 *Perf. 13*

470	A132	60ö org, dl vio & ol grn	40	10

Issued to commemorate the 50th anniversary of the union of North Schleswig and Denmark.

Electromagnet
A133

1970, Aug. 13 Engraved

471	A133	80ö gray grn	65	12

Issued to commemorate the 150th anniversary of Hans Christian Oersted's discovery of electromagnetism.

Bronze Age Ship
A134

Ships: 50ö, Viking shipbuilding, from Bayeux tapestry. 60ö, Thuroe schooner with topgallant. 90ö, Tanker.

1970, Sept. 24

472	A134	30ö ocher & brn	40	25
473	A134	50ö brn red & rose brn	40	20
474	A134	60ö gray ol & red brn	70	20
475	A134	90ö bl grn & ultra	1.25	1.00

U.N. Emblem
A135

1970, Oct. 22 Engraved *Perf. 13*

476	A135	90ø bl, grn & red	1.00	70

25th anniversary of the United Nations.

Bertel Thorvaldsen
A136

Mathilde Fibiger
A137

1970, Nov. 19

477	A136	2k sl bl	1.25	25

Issued to commemorate the bicentenary of the birth of Bertel Thorvaldsen (1768–1844), sculptor.

1971, Feb. 25

478	A137	80ø ol grn	60	12

Danish Women's Association centenary.

Refugees
A138

Hans Egede
A139

1971, March 26 Engr. *Perf. 13*

479	A138	50ø brown	40	15
480	A138	60ø brn red	60	10

Joint northern campaign for the benefit of refugees.

1971, May 27

481	A139	1k brown	70	15

250th anniversary of arrival of Hans Egede in Greenland and beginning of its colonization.

Swimming
A140

Designs: 50ø, Gymnastics. 60ø, Soccer. 90ø, Sailing.

1971, Oct. 14

482	A140	30ø bl & grn	40	25
483	A140	50ø dk red & brn	40	15
484	A140	60ø gray, yel & dk bl	60	15
485	A140	90ø ultra, pale grn & vio	1.00	40

Georg Brandes
A141

1971, Nov. 11 Engr. *Perf. 13*

486	A141	90ø dk bl	70	25

Centenary of first lectures given by Georg Brandes (1842–1927), writer and literary critic.

Sugar Production
A142

1972, Jan. 27

487	A142	80ø sl grn	60	15

Centenary of Danish sugar production.

King Frederik IX
A143

1972, Mar. 11 Engr. *Perf. 13*

488	A143	60ø red brn	45	10

In memory of King Frederik IX (1899–1972).

Abstract Design
A144

1972, Mar. 11

489	A144	1.20k brt rose lil, bl gray & brn	1.00	60

Centenary of the Danish Meteorological Institute.

Nikolai F. S. Grundtvig
A145

Locomotive, 1847, Ferry, Travelers
A146

1972, May 4 Engraved *Perf. 13*

490	A145	1k sepia	70	30

Centenary of the death of Nikolai Frederik Severin Grundtvig (1783–1872), theologian and poet.

1972, June 26

491	A146	70ø rose red	60	20

125th anniversary of Danish State Railways.

Rebild Hills
A147

"Tinker Turned Politician"
A148

1972, June 26

492	A147	1k bl, sl grn & mar	70	25

Types of 1933–46

1972–78 Engraved *Perf. 13*

493	A32	20ø sl bl ('74)	7	3
494	A32	50ø sep ('74)	18	3
495	A32	60ø ap grn ('76)	1.25	3
496	A32	60ø gray ('78)	22	3
497	A32	70ø red	1.25	3
498	A32	70ø ap grn ('77)	25	8
499	A55	2.50k orange	2.00	15
500	A55	2.80k ol ('75)	1.00	30
501	A55	3.50k lilac	2.50	10
502	A55	4.50k olive	4.00	10
503	A55	6k vio blk ('76)	2.10	30
504	A55	7k red lil ('78)	2.50	40
505	A55	9k brn ol ('77)	3.25	40
506	A55	10k lem ('76)	3.50	40
		Nos. 493-506 (14)	24.07	2.38

1972, Sept. 14

507	A148	70ø dk red	35	10

250th anniversary of the comedies of Ludvig Holberg (1684–1754) on the Danish stage.

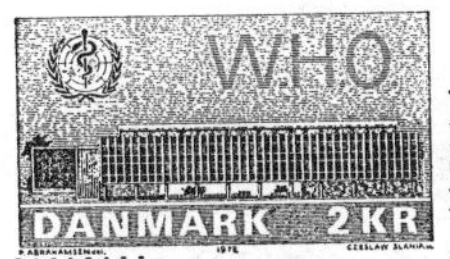

WHO Building, Copenhagen
A149

1972, Sept. 14

508	A149	2k bl, blk & lt red brn	1.25	50

Opening of World Health Organization Building, Copenhagen.

Bridge Across Little Belt
A150

Aeroskobing House c. 1740
A151

Designs (Diagrams): 60ø, Hanstholm Harbor. 70ø, Lim Fjord Tunnel. 90ø, Knudshoved Harbor.

1972, Oct. 19 Engraved *Perf. 13*

509	A150	40ø dk grn	35	20
510	A150	60ø dk brn	60	10
511	A150	70ø dk red	60	10
512	A150	90ø dk bl grn	75	35

Highway engineering.

1972, Nov. 23

Danish Architecture: 60ø, East Bornholm farmhouse, 17th century (horiz.). 70ø, House, Christianshavn, c. 1710. 1.20k, Hvide Sande farmhouse, c. 1810 (horiz.).

Size: 20x28mm., 27x20mm.

513	A151	40ø red, brn & blk	60	25
514	A151	60ø blk, vio bl & grn	60	25

Size: 18x37mm., 36x20mm.

515	A151	70ø red, dk red & blk	70	18
516	A151	1.20k dk brn, red & grn	1.00	40

Johannes V. Jensen
A152

Guard Rails and Cogwheels
A153

1973, Feb. 22 Engraved *Perf. 13*

517	A152	90ø green	60	15

Centenary of the birth of Johannes Vilhelm Jensen (1873–1950), lyric poet and novelist.

1973, Mar. 22

518	A153	50ø sepia	30	15

Centenary of first Danish Factory Act for labor protection.

P. C. Abildgaard
A154

Rhododendron
A155

1973, Mar. 22

519	A154	1k dl bl	70	30

Bicentenary of Royal Veterinary College, Christianshaven, founded by Prof. P. C. Abildgaard.

1973, Apr. 26

Design: 70ø, Dronningen of Denmark rose.

520	A155	60ø brn, grn & vio	70	20
521	A155	70ø dk red, rose & grn	70	20

Centenary of the founding of the Horticultural Society of Denmark.

Nordic Cooperation Issue 1973

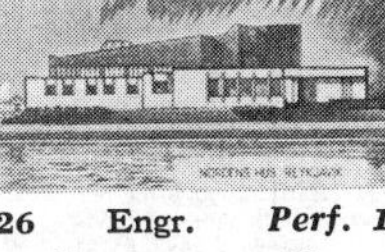

Nordic House, Reykjavik
A156

1973, June 26 Engr. *Perf. 13*

522	A156	70ø multi	75	30
523	A156	1k multi	3.00	75

A century of postal cooperation among Denmark, Finland, Iceland, Norway and Sweden, and in connection with the Nordic Postal Conference, Reykjavik.

Sextant, Stella Nova and Cassiopeia
A157

St. Mark, from 11th Century Book of Dalby
A158

1973, Oct. 18 Engraved *Perf. 13*

524	A157	2k dk bl	1.00	30

400th anniversary of the publication of "De Nova Stella," by Tycho Brahe.

1973, Oct. 18 Photo. *Perf. 14x14½*

525	A158	120ø buff & multi	1.25	80

300th anniversary of Royal Library.

Devil and Gossips, Fanefjord Church, 1480
A159

Frescoes: No. 527, Queen Esther and King Ahasuerus, Tirsted Church, c.1400. No. 528, Miraculous Harvest, Jetsmark Church, c.1474. No. 529, Jesus carrying cross, and wearing crown of thorns, Biersted Church, c.1400. No. 530, Creation of Eve, Fanefjord Church, c.1480.

1973, Nov. 28 Engr. *Perf. 13*

Cream Paper

526	A159	70ø dk red, yel & grn	1.50	50
527	A159	70ø dk red, yel & grn	1.50	50
528	A159	70ø dk red, yel & grn	1.50	50

529	A159	70ö dk red, yel & grn	1.50	50
530	A159	70ö dk red, yel & grn	1.50	50
a.		Booklet pane of 10	45.00	
		Nos. 526-530 (5)	7.50	2.50

Nos. 526–530 printed se-tenant in sheets of 50 (5x10). No. 530a contains 2 each of Nos. 526–530.

Blood Donors
A160

Queen Margrethe
A161

1974, Jan. 24

531	A160	90ö pur & red	60	20

"Blood Saves Lives."

1974–78 Engraved Perf. 13

532	A161	60ö brown	40	10
533	A161	60ö orange	40	3
534	A161	70ö red	40	3
535	A161	70ö dk brn	40	3
536	A161	80ö green	40	15
537	A161	80ö dp brn ('76)	40	3
538	A161	90ö red lil	40	4
539	A161	90ö dl red	60	3
540	A161	90ö sl grn ('76)	40	3
541	A161	100ö dp ultra	50	5
542	A161	100ö gray ('75)	40	5
543	A161	100ö red ('76)	40	5
544	A161	100ö brn ('77)	35	5
a.		Bklt. pane of 5 (#544, #494, 2 #493, #318)	2.25	
545	A161	110ö org ('78)	40	5
546	A161	120ö slate	45	6
547	A161	120ö red ('77)	45	6
548	A161	130ö ultra ('75)	1.25	50
549	A161	150ö vio bl ('78)	50	40
550	A161	180ö sl grn ('77)	65	10

Pantomime Theater
A162

1974, May 16

552	A162	100ö indigo	70	20

Centenary of the Pantomime Theater, Tivoli.

Hverringe
A163

Views: 60ö, Norre Lyndelse, Carl Nielsen's childhood home. 70ö, Odense, Hans Chr. Andersen's childhood home. 90ö, Hesselagergaard (vert.). 120ö, Hindsholm.

1974, June 20 Engr. Perf. 13

553	A163	50ö brn & multi	70	30
554	A163	60ö sl grn & multi	60	35
555	A163	70ö red brn & multi	60	35
556	A163	90ö dk grn & mar	1.00	15
557	A163	120ö red org & dk grn	1.10	35
		Nos. 553-557 (5)	4.00	1.50

Emblem, Runner with Map
A164

Iris
A165

Design: 80ö, Compass.

1974, Aug. 22 Engr. Perf. 13

558	A164	70ö dk bl & brn	60	40
559	A164	80ö brn & vio bl	60	40

World Orienteering Championships 1974.

1974, Sept. 19

Design: 120ö, Purple orchid.

560	A165	90ö brn, vio bl & sl grn	60	20
561	A165	120ö ind, lil & sl grn	1.10	40

Copenhagen Botanical Garden centenary.

Mailman, 1624, and Postilion, 1780
A166

Carrier Pigeon
A167

Design: 90ö, Balloon and sailing ships.

1974, Oct. 9 Engraved Perf. 13

562	A166	70ö lem & dk brn	60	40
563	A166	90ö dl grn & sep	75	20
564	A167	120ö dk bl	1.00	35

350th anniversary of Danish Post Office (70ö, 90ö) and centenary of Universal Postal Union (120ö).

Souvenir Sheet

Ferslew's Essays, 1849 and 1852—A168

Engr. & Photo.

1975, Feb. 27 Perf. 13

565	A168	Sheet of 4, multi	7.00	7.50
a.		70ö *Coat of arms*	1.60	1.70
b.		80ö *King Frederik VII*	1.60	1.70
c.		90ö *King Frederik VII*	1.60	1.70
d.		100ö *Mercury*	1.60	1.70

HAFNIA 76 International Stamp Exhibition, Copenhagen, Aug. 20–29, 1976. Size of No. 565: 68x93mm. Sold for 5k.

See No. 585.

Early Radio Equipment
A169

Flora Danica Plate
A170

1975, Mar. 20 Engr. Perf. 13

566	A169	90ö dl red	65	18

Danish broadcasting, 50th anniversary.

1975, May 22

Danish China: 90ö, Flora Danica tureen. 130ö, Vase and tea caddy, blue fluted china.

567	A170	50ö sl grn	70	18
568	A170	90ö brn red	1.25	15
569	A170	130ö vio bl	1.25	1.00

Church of Moravian Brethren, Christiansfeld
A171

Designs: 120ö, Kongsgaard farmhouse, Lejre. 150ö, Anna Queenstraede, Helsingor (vert.).

1975, June 19

570	A171	70ö sepia	40	40
571	A171	120ö ol grn	1.75	40
572	A171	150ö vio blk	80	20

European Architectural Heritage Year 1975.

Hans Christian Andersen
A172

Watchman's Square, Abenra
A173

Designs: 70ö, Numbskull Jack, drawing by Vilh. Pedersen. 130ö, The Marshking's Daughter, drawing by L. Frohlich.

1975, Aug. 28 Engr. Perf. 13

573	A172	70ö brn & blk	1.00	60
574	A172	90ö brn red & dk brn	1.75	20
575	A172	130ö bl blk & sep	1.50	1.25

Hans Christian Andersen (1805–1875), writer, death centenary.

1975, Sept. 25

Designs: 90ö, Haderslev Cathedral (vert.). 100ö, Mögeltönder Polder. 120ö, Mouth of Vidaaen at Höjer Floodgates.

576	A173	70ö multi	60	40
577	A173	90ö multi	70	20
578	A173	100ö multi	70	20
579	A173	120ö multi	1.00	35

European Kingfisher
A174

Designs: 70ö, Hedgehog. 90ö, Cats. 130ö, Avocets. 200ö, Otter.

1975, Oct. 23 Engr. Perf. 13

580	A174	50ö vio blk	70	25
581	A174	70ö black	70	25
582	A174	90ö brown	70	20
583	A174	130ö bluish blk	1.25	1.10
584	A174	200ö brn blk	1.10	32
		Nos. 580-584 (5)	4.45	2.12

Protected animals, and for the centenary of the Danish Society for the Prevention of Cruelty to Animals (90ö).

Souvenir Sheet

HAFNIA Type of 1974

1975, Nov. 20 Engr. & Photo.

585	A168	Sheet of 4, multi	4.50	5.00
a.		50ö buff & brn No. 2	1.00	1.15
b.		70ö buff, brn & bl, No. 1	1.00	1.15
c.		90ö buff, bl & brn, No. 11	1.00	1.15
d.		130ö ol, brn & buff, No. 19	1.00	1.15

HAFNIA 76 International Stamp Exhibition, Copenhagen, Aug. 20–29, 1976. Size of No. 585: 68x93mm. Sold for 5k.

Copenhagen, Center
A175

View from Round Tower
A176

Copenhagen, Views: 100ö, Central Station, interior. 130ö, Harbor.

1976, Mar. 25 Engr. Perf. 12½

586	A175	60ö multi	60	25
587	A176	80ö multi	70	25
588	A176	100ö multi	35	10
589	A175	130ö multi	1.50	1.10

Postilion, by Otto Bache
A177

Emil Chr. Hansen, Physiologist, in Laboratory
A178

1976, June 17 Engr. Perf. 12½

590	A177	130ö multi	2.00	2.00

Souvenir Sheet

591	A177	130ö multi	10.00	11.00

HAFNIA 76 International Stamp Exhibition, Copenhagen, Aug. 20–29. No. 591 contains one stamp similar to No. 590 with design continuous into sheet margin. Sheet shows painting "A String of Horses Outside an Inn" of which No. 590 shows a detail. Black marginal inscription and HAFNIA emblem. Size: 103x81mm. Sheet sold for 15k including exhibition ticket.

1976, Sept. 23 Engr. Perf. 13

592	A178	100ö org red	35	10

Carlsberg Foundation (art and science), centenary.

Glass Blower Molding Glass
A179

Five Water Lilies
A180

Danish Glass Production: 80ö, Finished glass removed from pipe. 130ö, Glass cut off from foot. 150ö, Glass blown up in mold.

1976, Nov. 18 Engr. Perf. 13

593	A179	60ö slate	22	15
594	A179	80ö dk brn	30	20
595	A179	130ö dk bl	90	90
596	A179	150ö red brn	52	20

Photogravure and Engraved

1977, Feb. 2 Perf. 12½

597	A180	100ö brt grn & multi	60	35
598	A180	130ö ultra & multi	2.50	2.25

Nordic countries cooperation for protection of the environment and 25th Session of Nordic Council, Helsinki, Feb. 19.

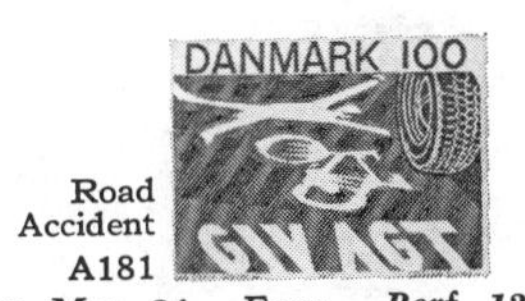

Road Accident
A181

1977, Mar. 24 Engr. *Perf. 12½*

599 A181 100ö brn red 40 10

Road Safety Traffic Act, May 1, 1977.

Europa Issue 1977

Allinge
A182

Design: 1.30k, View, Ringsted.

1977, May 2 Engr. *Perf. 12½*

600 A182 1k dl red 85 30
601 A182 1.30k dk bl 3.00 2.50

Kongeåen
A183

Landscapes, Southern Jutland: 90ö, Skallingen. 150ö, Tørskind. 200ö, Jelling.

1977, June 30 Engr. *Perf. 12½*

602 A183 60ö multi 70 60
603 A183 90ö multi 32 15
604 A183 150ö multi 55 20
605 A183 200ö multi 70 30

See Nos. 616-619, 655-658.

Hammers and Horseshoes
A184

Globe Flower
A185

Designs: 1k, Chisel, square and plane. 1.30k, Trowel, ceiling brush and folding ruler.

1977, Sept. 22 Engr. *Perf. 12½*

606 A184 80ö dk brn 30 25
607 A184 1k red 35 15
608 A184 1.30k vio bl 1.10 50

Danish crafts.

1977, Nov. 17 Engr. *Perf. 12½*

Design: 1.50k, Cnidium dubium.

609 A185 1k multi 60 20
610 A185 1.50k multi 1.10 70

Endangered flora.

Handball
A186

1978, Jan. 19 *Perf. 12½*

611 A186 1.20k red 42 16

Men's World Handball Championships.

Christian IV, Frederiksborg Castle
A187

Frederiksborg Museum
A188

1978, Mar. 16

612 A187 1.20k brn red 42 16
613 A188 1.80k black 65 30

Frederiksborg Museum, centenary.

Europa Issue

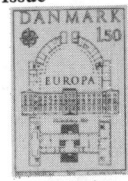

Jens Bang's House, Aalborg
A189

Frederiksborg Castle, Ground Plan and Elevation
A190

1978, May 11 Engr. *Perf. 12½*

614 A189 1.20k red 42 16
615 A190 1.50k dk bl & vio bl 1.25 70

Landscape Type of 1977

Landscapes, Central Jutland: 70ö, Kongenshus Memorial Park. 120ö, Post Office, Old Town in Aarhus. 150ö, Lignite fields, Soby. 180ö, Church wall, Stadil Church.

1978, June 15 Engr. *Perf. 12½*

616 A183 70ö multi 35 30
617 A183 120ö multi 42 16
618 A183 150ö multi 60 50
619 A183 180ö multi 65 25

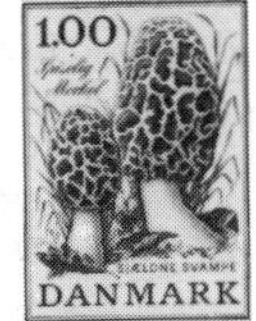

Boats in Harbor
A191

Edible Morel
A192

Designs: 1k, Eel traps. 1.80k, Boats in berth. 2.50k, Drying nets.

1978, Sept. 7 Engr. *Perf. 12½*

620 A191 70ö ol gray 28 12
621 A191 1k redsh brn 40 15
622 A191 1.80k slate 72 25
623 A191 2.50k sepia 1.00 40

Danish fishing industry.

1978, Nov. 16 Engr. *Perf. 12½*

Design: 1.20k, Satan's mushroom.

624 A192 1k sepia 45 25
625 A192 1.20k dl red 48 16

Telephones
A193

1979, Jan. 25 Engr. *Perf. 12½*

626 A193 1.20k dl red 48 16

Centenary of Danish telephone.

University Seal
A194

Pentagram: University Faculties
A195

1979, Apr. 5 Engr. *Perf. 12½*

627 A194 1.30k vermilion 52 20
628 A195 1.60k dk vio bl 80 70

University of Copenhagen, 500th anniversary.

Types of 1933–1974

1979-81 Engr. *Perf. 13*

629 A32 80o green 32 3
630 A161 90o slate 36 3
631 A32 100o dp grn ('81) 40 15
632 A161 110o brown 45 5
a. Bklt. pane of 5 (#493-494, #632, 2 #318) ('79) 1.00
633 A161 120o bluish blk ('81) 48 20
634 A161 130o red 52 6
635 A161 130o brn ('81) 52 20
636 A161 140o red org ('80) 70 8
637 A161 150o red org ('81) 60 22
638 A161 160o ultra 65 8
639 A161 160o red ('81) 65 25
a. Bklt. pane of 14 (2 each #318, 635, 639, 8 #494) 4.00
640 A161 180o ultra ('80) 70 8
641 A161 210o gray ('80) 85 30
642 A161 230o ol grn ('81) 90 35
643 A161 250o bl grn ('81) 1.00 38
644 A55 2.80k dl grn 1.10 40
645 A55 3.30k brn red ('81) 1.35 45
646 A55 4.30k brn red ('80) 1.75 60
647 A55 4.70k rose lil ('81) 1.90 70
648 A55 8k orange 2.75 60
649 A55 12k red brn ('81) 4.00 1.80
Nos. 629-649 (21) 21.95 7.01

Europa Issue 1979

Mail Cart, 1785
A196

Design: 1.60k, Morse key and amplifier.

1979, May 10 *Perf. 12½*

651 A196 1.30k red 52 20
652 A196 1.60k dk bl 75 65

Gripping Beast Pendant
A197

Viking Art: 2k, Key with gripping beast design.

1979, June 14 Engr. *Perf. 13*

653 A197 1.10k sepia 45 30
654 A197 2k grnsh gray 80 30

Landscape Type of 1977

Landscapes, Northern Jutland: 80ö, Mols Bjerge. 90ö, Orslev Kloster. 200ö, Trans. 280ö, Bovbjerg.

1979, Sept. 6 Engr. *Perf. 12½*

655 A183 80ö multi 32 20
656 A183 90ö multi 36 20
657 A183 200ö multi 80 30
658 A183 280ö multi 1.00 45

Adam Oehlenschläger—A198

1979, Oct, 4 Engraved *Perf. 13*

659 A198 1.30k dk car 52 20

Adam Oehlenschläger (1799-1850), poet and dramatist.

Score, Violin, Dancing Couple
A199

Ballerina
A200

1979, Nov. 8 Engraved *Perf. 13×12½*

660 A199 1.10k brown 45 18
661 A200 1.60k ultra 65 25

Jacob Gade (b. 1879), composer; August Bournoville (1805-1879), ballet master.

Royal Mail Guards' Office, Copenhagen, 1779—A201

1980, Feb. 14 Engraved *Perf. 13*

662 A201 1.30k brn red 52 20

National Postal Service, 200th anniversary.

Symbols of Occupation, Health and Education—A202

1980, May 5 Engraved *Perf. 13*

663 A202 1.60k dk bl 65 50

World Conference of the U.N. Decade for Women, Copenhagen, July 14-30.

Europa Issue 1980

Karen Blixen (1855-1962), Writer—A203

Design: 1.60k, August Krogh (1874-1949), physiologist.

1980, May 5

664 A203 1.30k red 52 20
665 A203 1.60k blue 70 60

Landscape Type of 1977

Landscapes, Northern Jutland: 80ø, Viking ship burial grounds, Lindholm Hoje/ 110ø, Lighthouse, Skagen (vert.). 200ø, Borglum Monastery. 280ø, Fishing boats, Vorupor Beach.

1980, June 19 **Engraved** ***Perf. 13***

666	A183	80ø	multi	35	25
667	A183	110ø	multi	45	25
668	A183	200ø	multi	80	30
669	A183	280ø	multi	1.00	50

Nordic Cooperation Issue

Silver Tankard, by Borchardt Rollufse, 1641—A204

1980, Sept. 9 **Engr.** ***Perf. 13***

670	A204	1.30k	*shown*	52	20
671	A204	1.80k	*Bishop's bowl, Copenhagen faience, 18th century*	70	60

Frisian Sceat Facsimile, Obverse and Reverse, 9th Century—A205

Coins: 1.40k, Silver coin of King Valdemar the Great and Absalon, 1157-1182. 1.80k, Gold current ducat of King Christian VII, 1781.

1980, Oct. 9 **Engraved** ***Perf. 13***

672	A205	1.30k	red & redsh brn	52	20
673	A205	1.40k	ol gray & sl grn	55	22
674	A205	1.80k	dk bl & sl bl	70	50

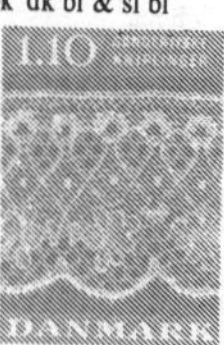

Tonder Lace Pattern, North Schleswig—A206

Designs: Tonder lace patterns.

1980, Nov. 13 **Engraved** ***Perf. 13***

675	A206	1.10k	brown	45	18
676	A206	1.30k	brn red	52	20
677	A206	2k	ol gray	80	30

Nyboder Development, Copenhagen, 350th Anniversary—A207

Design: 1.30k, View of Nyboder (diff.).

1981, Mar. 19

678	A207	1.30k	dp org & ocher	52	20
679	A207	1.60k	dp org & ocher	65	25

Tilting at a Barrel on Shrovetide A208

Design: 2k, Midsummer's Eve bonfire.

1981, May 4 **Engr.** ***Perf. 13***

680	A208	1.60k	brn red	65	25
681	A208	2k	dk bl	80	45

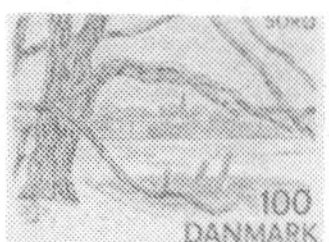

Soro Lake and Academy, Zealand—A209

Designs: Views of Zealand.

1981, June 18 **Engr.** ***Perf. 13***

682	A209	100o	shown	40	15
683	A209	150o	Poet N. Gruntvig's home, Udby	60	22
684	A209	160o	K. Munk's home, Opager	65	25
685	A209	200o	Gronsund	80	30
686	A209	230o	Bornholm Isld.	90	35
			Nos. 682-686 (5)	3.35	1.27

European Urban Renaissance Year A210

1981, Sept. 10 **Engr.** ***Perf. 12½x13***

687	A210	1.60k	dl red	65	25

Type of 1933

1981

688	A32	30ø	orange	12	5
689	A32	40ø	purple	16	6

Ellehammer's 18-horsepower Biplane, 1906—A211

1981, Oct. 8 **Engr.** ***Perf. 13***

696	A211	1k	shown	40	15
697	A211	1.30k	R-1 Fokker CV reconnaissance plane, 1926	52	20
698	A211	1.60k	Bellanca J-300, 1931	65	25
699	A211	2.30k	DC-7C, 1957	90	35

Queen Margrethe II, 10th Anniv. of Accession A212

1982, Jan. 14

705	A212	1.60k	dl red	65	25
706	A212	1.60k	dk ol grn ('82)	50	18
707	A212	1.80k	sep ('82)	55	20
708	A212	2k	dl red ('82)	60	25
709	A212	2.30k	vio ('82)	70	30
712	A212	2.70k	dk bl ('82)	80	35

Issue dates: 1.80k, 2k, 2.70k, May 13; others, Aug. 26.

World Figure Skating Championships—A213

1982, Feb. 25

721	A213	2k	dk bl	80	30

Customs Service Centenary—A214

1982, Feb. 25 **Engr.** ***Perf. 12½***

722	A214	1.60k	Revenue schooner Argus	50	18

Europa Issue, 1982—A215

1982, May 3 **Engr.** ***Perf. 12½***

723	A215	2k	Abolition of adscription, 1788	60	40
724	A215	2.70k	Women's voting right, 1915	85	55

Butter Churn, Barn, Hjedding A216

Records Office, 400th Anniv. A217

1982, June 10 **Engr.** ***Perf. 13***

725	A216	1.80k	brown	55	35

Cooperative dairy farming centenary.

1982, June 10

726	A217	2.70k	green	85	55

Steen Steensen Blicher (1782-1848), Poet, by J.V. Gertner—A218

1982, Aug. 26 **Engr.** ***Perf. 13***

727	A218	2k	brn red	60	25

Robert Storm Petersen (1882-1949), Cartoonist A219

Printing in Denmark, 500th Anniv. A220

Characters: 1.50k, Three little men and the number man. 2k, Peter and Ping the penguin (horiz.).

1982, Sept. 23 **Engr.** ***Perf. 12½***

728	A219	1.50k	dk bl & red	45	16
729	A219	2k	red & ol grn	60	25

1982, Sept. 23

730	A220	1.80k	Press, text, ink balls	55	20

500th Anniv. of University Library—A221

1982, Nov. 4

731	A221	2.70k	Library seal	80	35

World Communications Year—A222

1983, Jan. 27 **Engr.** ***Perf.***

732	A222	2k	multi	60	25

Amusement Park, 400th Anniv. A223

Badminton Championship A224

1983, Feb. 24

733	A223	2k	multi	60	25

1983, Feb. 24

734	A224	2.70k	multi	82	34

Nordic Cooperation Issue—A225

1983, Mar. 24 ***Perf. 13***

735	A225	2.50k	Egeskov Castle	75	30
736	A225	3.50k	Troll Church, North Jutland	1.05	45

SEMI-POSTAL STAMPS.

Nos. 159, 157 Surcharged in Red **+ 5 +**

Wmkd. Multiple Crosses. (114)

1921, June 17 *Perf. 14½x14*

B1 A20 10ø +5ø grn 30.00 35.00
B2 A21 20ø +10ø sl 35.00 42.50

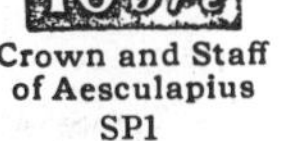

Crown and Staff of Aesculapius SP1

Dybbol Mill SP2

1929, Aug. 1 **Engraved**

B3 SP1 10ø yel grn 7.00 7.00
a. Bklt. pane of 2 22.50
B4 SP1 15ø brick red 7.00 7.00
a. Bklt. pane of 2 22.50
B5 SP1 25ø dp bl 32.50 32.50
a. Bklt. pane of 2 100.00

These stamps were sold at a premium of 5 öre each for benefit of the Danish Cancer Committee.

1937, Jan. 20 *Perf. 13* **Unwmkd.**

B6 SP2 5(ø) +5(ø) grn 1.20 1.20
B7 SP2 10(ø) +5(ø) lt brn 5.00 5.00
B8 SP2 15(ø) +5(ø) car 5.00 5.00

The surtax was for a fund in memory of H. P. Hanssen, statesman.

Nos. 223a and B6, Nos. 229 and B7, Nos. 238A and B8 are found se-tenant in booklets. For booklet panes, see Nos. 223d, 229b and 238e.

Queen Alexandrine SP3

Princesses Ingrid and Margrethe SP4

1939–41 *Perf. 13*

B9 SP3 5ø +3ø rose lake & red ('40) 40 40
a. Booklet pane of 4 2.00 2.00
B10 SP3 10ø +5ø dk vio & red 50 35
B11 SP3 15ø +5ø scar & red 80 80

The surtax was for the Danish Red Cross.

Nos. 230 and B10 have been issued se-tenant in booklets. See No. 230b. In this pane No. 230 measures 23½x31mm. from perf. to perf.

1941-43

B12 SP4 10(ø) +5(ø) dk vio 40 40
a. Bklt. pane of 10 15.00
B13 SP4 20(ø) +5(ø) red ('43) 40 40

The surtax was for the Children's Charity Fund.

No. 288 Surcharged in Red

1944, May 11

B14 A48 10ø +5ø vio 30 30
a. Bklt. pane of 10 14.00

The surtax was for the Danish Red Cross.

Symbols of Freedom SP5

Explosions at Rail Junction SP6

Danish Flag SP7

Princess Anne-Marie SP8

1947, May 4 **Engr.** *Perf. 13*

B15 SP5 15(ø) +5(ø) grn 50 50
B16 SP6 20(ø) +5(ø) dk red 75 75
B17 SP7 40(ø) +5(ø) dp bl 1.25 1.25

Issued in memory of the Danish struggle for liberty and the liberation of Denmark. The surtax was for the Liberty Fund.

1950, Oct. 19 **Unwmkd.**

B18 SP8 25ø +5ø rose brn 1.00 1.00

The surtax was for the National Children's Welfare Association.

S. S. Jutlandia SP9

1951, Sept. 13 *Perf. 13*

B19 SP9 25(ø) +5(ø) red 1.25 1.25

The surtax was for the Red Cross.

No. 335 Surcharged in Black **NL + 10**

1953, Feb. 13

B20 A61 30(ø) +10(ø) brn red 2.50 2.50

The surtax was for flood relief in the Netherlands.

Stone Memorial SP10

1953, Mar. 26 *Perf. 13*

B21 SP10 30(ø) +5(ø) dk red 2.25 2.25

The surtax was for cultural work of the Danish Border Union.

Nos. B15 and B16 Surcharged with New Value and Ornamental Screen in Black

1955, Feb. 17

B22 SP5 20(ø) +5(ø) on 15(ø) +5(ø) grn 2.25 2.25
B23 SP6 30(ø) +5(ø) on 20(ø) +5(ø) dk red 2.25 2.25

The surtax was for the Liberty Fund.

No. 341 Surcharged

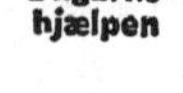

1957, Mar. 25

B24 A61 30ø +5ø on 95ø red org 1.00 1.00

The surtax went to the Danish Red Cross for aid to Hungary.

No. 335 Surcharged: "Gronlandsfonden + 10"

1959, Feb. 23

B25 A61 30ø +10ø brn red 2.00 2.00

The surtax was for the Greenland Fund.

Globe Encircled by Red Cross Flags SP11

Queen Ingrid SP12

1959, June 24 **Engr.** *Perf. 13*

B26 SP11 30ø +5ø rose red 85 65
B27 SP11 60ø +5ø lt ultra & car 1.50 1.25

Issued to commemorate the centenary of the International Red Cross idea. The surtax was for the Red Cross. Crosses photogravure on No. B27.

1960, Oct. 25 **Unwmkd.**

B28 SP12 30ø +10ø dk red 1.50 1.30

Issued to commemorate Queen Ingrid's 25th anniversary as a Girl Scout. The surtax was for the Scouts' fund for needy and sick children.

African Mother and Child SP13

Healthy and Crippled Hands SP14

1962, May 24

B29 SP13 30ø +10ø dk red 1.50 1.50

Issued to aid underdeveloped countries.

1963, June 24 *Perf. 13*

B30 SP14 35ø +10ø dk red 2.00 2.00

The surtax was for the benefit of the Cripples' Foundation.

Old Bridge at Danish-German Border SP15

1964, May 28 **Engraved**

B31 SP15 35ø +10ø hn brn 1.50 1.50

The surtax was for the Danish Border Union.

Princesses Margrethe, Benedikte and Anne-Marie SP16

Happy Child SP17

1964, Aug. 24

B32 SP16 35ø +10ø dl red 1.50 1.50
B33 SP16 60ø +10ø dk bl & red 1.75 1.75

The surtax was for the Red Cross.

1965, Oct. 21 **Engr.** *Perf. 13*

B34 SP17 50ø +10ø brick red 85 85

The surtax was for the National Children's Welfare Association.

"Red Cross" in 32 Languages and Red Cross, Red Lion and Sun, and Red Crescent Emblems SP18

1966, Jan. 20 **Engraved** *Perf. 13*

B35 SP18 50ø +10ø red 90 90

Engraved and Photogravure

B36 SP18 80ø +10ø dk bl & red 2.00 2.00

The surtax was for the Red Cross.

"Refugees 66" SP19

Symbolic Rose SP20

1966, Oct. 24 **Engraved** *Perf. 13*

B37 SP19 40ø +10ø sep 1.50 1.50
B38 SP19 50ø +10ø rose red 1.50 1.50
B39 SP19 80ø +10ø bl 2.75 2.75

The surtax was for aid to refugees.

1967, Oct. 12

B40 SP20 60ø +10ø brn red 90 90

The surcharge was for the Salvation Army.

Two Greenland Boys in Round Tower SP21

1968, Sept. 12 **Engraved** *Perf. 13*

B41 SP21 60ø +10ø dk red 1.30 1.30

The surtax was for child welfare work in Greenland.

Princess Margrethe and Prince Henrik with Prince Frederik SP22

1969, Dec. 11

B42	SP22	50ø +10ø brn & red	1.25	1.25
B43	SP22	60ø +10ø brn red & red	1.25	1.25

The surtax was for the Danish Red Cross.

Child Seeking Help
SP23

1970, Mar. 13

B44	SP23	60ø +10ø brn red	85	85

Surtax for "Save the Children Fund."

Child
SP24

1971, Apr. 29 Engraved *Perf. 13*

B45	SP24	60ø +10ø cop red	85	85

Surtax was for the National Children's Welfare Association.

Marsh Marigold
SP25

1972, Aug. 17

B46	SP25	70ø +10ø grn & yel	85	85

Centenary of the Society and Home for the Disabled.

Heimaey Town and Volcano
SP26

1973, Oct. 17 Engraved *Perf. 13*

B47	SP26	70ø +20ø vio bl & red	1.00	1.00

The surtax was for the victims of the eruption of Heimaey Volcano, Jan. 23, 1973.

Queen Margrethe, IWY Emblem
SP27

1975, Mar. 20 Engr. *Perf. 13*

B48	SP27	90ø +20ø red & buff	1.30	1.30

International Women's Year 1975. Surtax was for a foundation to benefit women primarily in Greenland and Faroe Islands.

Skuldelev I
SP28

Ships: 90ø+20ø, Thingvalla, emigrant steamer. 100ø+20ø, Liner Frederick VIII, c. 1930. 130ø+20ø, Three-master Danmark.

1976, Jan. 22 Engr. *Perf. 13*

B49	SP28	70 +20ø ol brn	1.50	1.50
B50	SP28	90 +20ø brick red	1.50	1.50
B51	SP28	100 +20ø ol grn	1.50	1.50
B52	SP28	130 +20ø vio bl	1.50	1.50

Bicentenary of American Declaration of Independence.

People and Red Cross
SP29

Invalid in Wheelchair
SP30

1976, Feb. 26 Engr. *Perf. 13*

B53	SP29	100ø +20ø red & blk	75	75
B54	SP29	130ø +20ø bl, red & blk	1.00	1.00

Centenary of Danish Red Cross.

1976, May 6 Engr. *Perf. 13*

B55	SP30	100ø +20ø ver & blk	75	75

The surtax was for the Foundation to Aid the Disabled.

Mother and Child
SP31

Anti-Cancer Campaign
SP32

1977, Mar. 24 Engr. *Perf. 12½*

B56	SP31	1k +20ø multi	75	75

Danish Society for the Mentally Handicapped, 25th anniversary. Surtax was for the Society.

1978, Oct. 12 Engr. *Perf. 13*

B57	SP32	120ø +20ø red	75	75

Danish Anti-Cancer Campaign, 50th anniversary. Surtax was for campaign.

Child and IYC Emblem
SP33

1979, Jan. 25 Engr. *Perf. 12½*

B58	SP33	1.20k +20ø red & brn	85	85

International Year of the Child.

Foundation for the Disabled, 25th Anniversary—SP34

1980, Apr. 10 Engraved *Perf. 13*

B59	SP34	130ø +20ø brn red	60	60

Children Playing Ball—SP35

1981, Feb. 5 Engraved *Perf. 12½x13*

B60	SP35	1.60k +20ø brn red	70	40

Surtax was for child welfare.

AIR POST STAMPS.

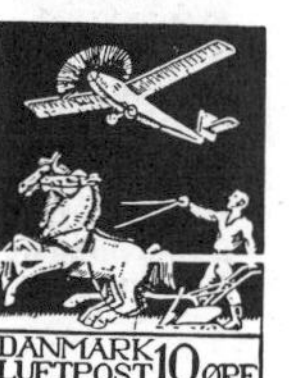

Airplane and Plowman
AP1

Towers of Copenhagen
AP2

Wmkd. Multiple Crosses. (114)

1925–29 Typo. *Perf. 12x12½*

C1	AP1	10ø yel grn	22.50	25.00
C2	AP1	15ø vio ('26)	45.00	50.00
C3	AP1	25ø scarlet	40.00	45.00
C4	AP1	50ø lt gray ('29)	110.00	125.00
C5	AP1	1k choc ('29)	100.00	110.00
		Nos. C1-C5 (5)	317.50	355.00

Perf. 13

1934, June 9 Engr. Unwmkd.

C6	AP2	10ø orange	1.50	1.50
C7	AP2	15ø red	6.00	6.00
C8	AP2	20ø Prus bl	6.00	6.00
C9	AP2	50ø ol blk	6.00	6.00
C10	AP2	1k brown	20.00	20.00
		Nos. C6-C10 (5)	39.50	39.50

LATE FEE STAMPS

Numeral
LF1

Coat of Arms
LF2

Wmkd. Multiple Crosses. (114)

1923 Typographed *Perf. 14x14½*

I1	LF1	10ø green	7.50	1.50
a.		Double ovpt.		

No. I1 was, at first, not a postage stamp but represented a tax for the services of the post office clerks in filling out postal forms and writing addresses. In 1923 it was put into use as a Late Fee stamp.

1926–31

I2	LF2	10ø green	3.25	60
I3	LF2	10ø brn ('31)	2.75	60

Engraved

1934 *Perf. 13* Unwmkd.

I4	LF2	5ø green	40	15
I5	LF2	10ø orange	40	20

POSTAGE DUE STAMPS.

Regular Issues of 1913-20 Overprinted **PORTO**

Wmkd. Multiple Crosses. (114)

1921, May 1 *Perf. 14x14½*

J1	A10	1ø dp org	2.00	1.50
J2	A16	5ø green	2.50	1.60
J3	A16	7ø orange	3.00	2.50
J4	A16	10ø red	15.00	8.00
J5	A16	20ø dp bl	7.00	3.25
J6	A16	25ø brn & blk	13.00	2.25
J7	A16	50ø cl & blk	7.00	1.50
		Nos. J1-J7 (7)	49.50	20.60

Same Overprint in Dark Blue On Military Stamp of 1917

1921, Nov. 23

J8	A16	10ø red	7.00	4.50
a.		"S" inverted	130.00	130.00

Numeral of Value
D1

Typographed (Solid Panel).

1921-30 *Perf. 14x14½.*

J9	D1	1ø org ('22)	60	45
J10	D1	4ø bl ('25)	1.75	1.60
J11	D1	5ø brn ('22)	1.00	80
J12	D1	5ø lt grn ('30)	80	45
J13	D1	7ø ap grn ('27)	13.00	13.00
J14	D1	7ø dk vio ('30)	17.50	17.50
J15	D1	10ø yel grn ('22)	1.00	45
J16	D1	10ø lt brn ('30)	90	35
J17	D1	20ø grnsh bl ('21)	1.50	75
a.		Double impression	1,600.	
J18	D1	20ø gray ('30)	2.00	85
J19	D1	25ø scar ('23)	2.50	75
J20	D1	25ø vio ('26)	2.50	1.00
J21	D1	25ø lt bl ('30)	4.00	2.50
J22	D1	1k dk bl ('21)	27.50	6.00
J23	D1	1k brn & dk bl ('25)	12.50	3.00
J24	D1	5k pur ('25)	20.00	7.00
		Nos. J9-J24 (16)	109.05	56.45

Engraved (Lined Panel).

1934–55 *Perf. 13* Unwmkd.

J25	D1	1ø slate	18	10
J26	D1	2ø carmine	18	10
J27	D1	5ø yel grn	18	6
J28	D1	6ø dk ol ('41)	45	12
J29	D1	8ø mag ('50)	2.75	3.00
J30	D1	10ø orange	18	6
J31	D1	12ø dp ultra ('55)	45	40
J32	D1	15ø vio ('37)	75	10
J33	D1	20ø gray	75	10
J34	D1	25ø blue	60	18
J35	D1	30ø grn ('53)	60	18
J36	D1	40ø cl ('49)	75	18
J37	D1	1k brown	1.00	18
		Nos. J25-J37 (13)	8.82	4.76

No. 96 Surcharged in Black **PORTO 15**

1934 *Perf. 14x14½* Wmk. 114

J38	A10	15ø on 12ø vio	2.50	75

MILITARY STAMPS.

Nos. 97 and 100 Overprinted in Blue **S F**

Wmkd. Multiple Crosses. (114)

1917 *Perf. 14x14½.*

M1	A16	5ø green	18.00	25.00
a.		'S' inverted	200.00	225.00
M2	A16	10ø red	15.00	18.00
a.		'S' inverted	120.00	130.00

The letters "S F" are the initials of "Soldater Frimaerke" (Soldier's Stamp).

OFFICIAL STAMPS.

Small State Seal
O1

Wmkd. Crown. (112)

1871 Typographed *Perf. 14x13½*

O1	O1	2s blue	100.00	75.00
a.		2s ultra	100.00	75.00
b.		Imperf., pair	250.00	
O2	O1	4s carmine	55.00	14.00
a.		Imperf., pair	250.00	
O3	O1	16s green	250.00	175.00
a.		Imperf., pair	350.00	

Perf. 12½.

O4	O1	4s carmine	3,250.	325.00
O5	O1	16s green	325.00	250.00

Nos. O1, O2 and O3 were reprinted in 1886 upon white wove paper, unwatermarked and imperforate. Price $9 each.

1875 *Perf. 14x13½.*

O6	O1	3ø violet	3.00	9.00
O7	O1	4ø grnsh bl	4.00	2.25
O8	O1	8ø carmine	3.25	80
a.		Imperf., pair		
O9	O1	32ø green	32.50	25.00

1899-02 *Perf. 13.*

O9A	O1	3ø red lil ('02)	4.00	4.00
c.		Imperf., pair	375.00	
O9B	O1	4ø blue	1.50	1.50
O10	O1	8ø carmine	16.00	13.00

1902-06 Wmkd. Crown. (113)

O11	O1	1ø orange	2.50	2.50
O12	O1	3ø red lil ('06)	1.00	1.00
O13	O1	4ø bl ('03)	1.50	1.50
O14	O1	5ø green	1.10	35
O15	O1	10ø carmine	1.50	80
		Nos. O11-O15 (5)	7.60	6.15

Wmkd. Multiple Crosses. (114)

1914-23 *Perf. 14x14½.*

O16	O1	1ø orange	1.75	1.50
O17	O1	3ø gray ('18)	5.00	5.00
O18	O1	4ø bl ('16)	32.50	27.50
O19	O1	5ø grn ('15)	1.00	35
O20	O1	5ø choc ('23)	4.50	8.00
O21	O1	10ø red ('17)	3.50	1.25
O22	O1	10ø grn ('21)	1.50	90
O23	O1	15ø vio ('19)	27.50	25.00
O24	O1	20ø ind ('20)	10.00	6.00
		Nos. O16-O24 (9)	87.25	75.50

The use of Official stamps was discontinued April 1, 1924.

NEWSPAPER STAMPS.

Numeral of Value

N1

Wmkd. Crown. (113)

1907 Typographed *Perf. 13*

P1	N1	1ø olive	4.00	1.50
P2	N1	5ø blue	17.50	10.00
P3	N1	7ø carmine	6.00	40
P4	N1	10ø dp lil	11.00	2.00
P5	N1	20ø green	11.00	65
P6	N1	38ø orange	16.00	70
P7	N1	68ø yel brn	25.00	11.00
P8	N1	1k bl grn & cl	11.00	90
P9	N1	5k rose & yel grn	75.00	16.00
P10	N1	10k bis & bl	80.00	14.00
		Nos. P1-P10 (10)	256.50	57.15

Wmkd. Multiple Crosses. (114)

1914-15 *Perf. 14x14½.*

P11	N1	1ø ol gray	4.00	50
P12	N1	5ø blue	14.00	4.50
P13	N1	7ø rose	10.00	60
P14	N1	8ø grn ('15)	12.00	60
P15	N1	10ø dp lil	12.00	60
P16	N1	20ø green	130.00	1.25
a.		Imperf., pair	550.00	
P17	N1	29ø org yel ('15)	16.00	1.10
P18	N1	38ø orange	2,500.	125.00
P19	N1	41ø yel brn ('15)	16.00	80
P20	N1	1k bl grn & mar	25.00	65
		Nos. P11 P17, P19-P20 (9)	239.00	10.60

PARCEL POST STAMPS.

These stamps were for use on postal packets sent by the Esbjerg-Fanö Ferry Service.

Regular Issues of 1913-30 Overprinted

POSTFÆRGE

Wmkd. Multiple Crosses. (114)

1919-41 *Perf. 14x14½.*

Q1	A10	10ø grn ('22)	16.00	11.00
Q2	A10	10ø bis brn ('30)	14.00	6.00
Q3	A16	10ø red	50.00	50.00
a.		"POSFFAERGE"	180.00	225.00
Q4	A16	15ø violet	20.00	20.00
a.		"POSFFAERGE'	160.00	175.00
Q5	A16	30ø org ('22)	14.00	12.00
Q6	A16	30ø dk bl ('26)	4.00	4.00
Q7	A16	50ø cl & blk ('20)	175.00	175.00
Q8	A16	50ø lt gray ('22)	22.50	6.50
a.		50ø dk gray ('22)	100.00	100.00
Q9	A16	1k brn & bl ('24)	55.00	15.00
Q9A	A16	5k vio & brn ('41)	4.00	3.50
Q10	A16	10k ver & grn ('30)	100.00	100.00

Engraved.

Q11	A17	1k yel brn	130.00	130.00
a.		"POSFFAERGE"	1,250.	1,400.
		Nos. Q1-Q11 (12)	474.50	403.00

1927-30

Q12	A30	15ø red ('27)	22.50	10.00
Q13	A30	30ø ocher ('27)	22.50	12.00
Q14	A30	40ø yel grn ('30)	16.00	6.50

Overprinted on Regular Issues of 1933-40.

1936-42 *Perf. 13* **Unwmkd.**

Q15	A32	5ø rose lake ('42)	20	20
Q16	A32	10ø yel org	32.50	27.50
Q17	A32	10ø lt brn ('38)	1.75	1.75
Q18	A32	10ø pur ('39)	35	35
Q19	A30	15ø dp red	1.25	90
Q20	A30	30ø bl, I	7.00	4.75
Q21	A30	30ø bl, II ('40)	10.00	11.00
Q22	A30	30ø org, II ('42)	1.00	90
Q23	A30	40ø yel grn, I	7.00	4.75
Q24	A30	40ø yel grn, II ('40)	10.00	11.00
Q25	A30	40ø bl, II ('42)	1.00	1.00
Q26	A33	50ø gray	2.00	1.75
Q27	A33	1k lt brn	1.50	1.25
		Nos. Q15-Q27 (13)	75.55	67.10

Overprinted on Nos. 284, 286 and 286B

1945

Q28	A47	30ø orange	2.00	1.50
Q29	A47	40ø blue	1.75	1.50
Q30	A47	50ø gray	2.00	1.50

Overprinted on Nos. 318, 309, 310, 312 and 297.

1949-53

Q31	A32	10ø grn ('53)	35	35
Q32	A61	30ø orange	2.50	1.50
Q33	A61	40ø dl bl	2.50	1.50
Q34	A61	50ø gray ('50)	7.50	3.25
Q35	A55	1k brn ('50)	2.00	1.10
		Nos. Q31-Q35 (5)	14.85	7.70

Overprinted on Nos. 335, 323, 336, 326 and 397.

1955-65

Q36	A61	30ø brn red	1.20	1.10
Q37	A61	40ø gray	1.00	1.00
Q38	A61	50ø aqua	1.25	1.25
Q39	A61	70ø dp grn	1.25	1.10
Q40	A55	1.25k org ('65)	7.00	7.50
		Nos. Q36-Q40 (5)	11.70	11.95

Overprinted on Nos. 417 and 419.

1967 Engraved *Perf. 13*

Q41	A86	40ø brown	1.00	1.00
Q42	A86	80ø ultra	1.00	1.00

Nos. 224, 438, 441, 297-299 Overprinted

POSTFÆRGE

1967-74 Engraved *Perf. 13*

Q43	A32	5ø rose lake	20	20
Q44	A86	50ø brn ('74)	80	80
Q45	A86	90ø ultra ('70)	1.25	1.25
Q46	A55	1k brown	1.75	1.50
Q47	A55	2k red ('72)	2.25	2.25
Q48	A55	5k dl bl ('72)	4.00	4.00
		Nos. Q43-Q48 (6)	10.25	10.00

Nos. Q44-Q45, Q47-Q48 are on fluorescent paper.

Overprinted on No. 544

1975, Feb. 27

Q49	A161	100ø dp ultra	1.25	1.25

DIEGO-SUAREZ

(dyā'gō swä'rās)

LOCATION—A town at the northern end of Madagascar.

GOVT.—Former French colony.

POP.—12,237.

From 1885 to 1896 Diégo-Suarez, (Antsirane), a French naval base, was a separate colony and issued its own stamps. These were succeeded by stamps of Madagascar.

100 Centimes = 1 Franc

Stamps of French Colonies Handstamp Surcharged in Violet

1890 ***Perf. 14x13½.*** **Unwmkd.**

No.	Type	Description	Unused	Used
1	A9	15c on 1c *bl*	140.00	40.00
2	A9	15c on 5c grn, *grnsh*	325.00	40.00
3	A9	15c on 10c *lav*	140.00	40.00
4	A9	15c on 20c red, *grn*	325.00	40.00
5	A9	15c on 25c *rose*	60.00	22.50

This surcharge is found inverted, double, etc. Counterfeits exist.

Ship Flying French Flag

A2

Symbolical of Union of France and Madagascar

A3 A4

France

A5

1890 **Lithographed.** ***Imperf.***

No.	Type	Description	Unused	Used
6	A2	1c black	575.00	160.00
7	A3	5c black	525.00	120.00
8	A4	15c black	140.00	45.00
9	A5	25c black	150.00	67.50

A6

1891

No.	Type	Description	Unused	Used
10	A6	5c black	125.00	50.00

Excellent counterfeits exist of Nos. 6 to 10.

Stamps of French Colonies Surcharged in Red or Black:

a b

1892 ***Perf. 14x13½***

No.	Type	Description	Unused	Used
11	A9 (a)	5c on 10c *lav* (R)	110.00	50.00
a.		Inverted surcharge	225.00	175.00
12	A9 (b)	5c on 20c red, *grn*	90.00	35.00
a.		Inverted surcharge	225.00	175.00

Stamps of French Colonies Overprinted in Black or Red

c

1892

No.	Type	Description	Unused	Used
13	A9	1c bl (R)	14.00	8.00
a.		Inverted overprint	90.00	70.00
14	A9	2c brn, *buff*	14.00	8.00
a.		Inverted overprint	90.00	70.00
15	A9	4c cl, *lav*	22.50	16.50
16	A9	5c grn, *grnsh*	45.00	35.00
a.		Inverted overprint	90.00	62.50
17	A9	10c *lavender*	16.50	12.50
a.		Inverted overprint	90.00	70.00
18	A9	15c *blue*	14.00	9.00
19	A9	20c red, *grn*	16.50	11.00
20	A9	25c *rose*	12.50	7.50
a.		Inverted overprint	90.00	70.00
21	A9	30c brn, *bis* (R)	675.00	525.00
a.		Inverted overprint		850.00
22	A9	35c *yellow*	675.00	525.00
a.		Inverted overprint		850.00
23	A9	75c car, *rose*	32.50	21.00
24	A9	1fr brnz grn, *straw* (R)	32.50	21.00
a.		Double overprint	110.00	85.00

Navigation and Commerce

A10 A11

1892 **Typographed.**

Name of Colony in Blue or Carmine.

No.	Type	Description	Unused	Used
25	A10	1c *blue*	1.00	1.00
26	A10	2c brn, *buff*	1.25	1.10
27	A10	4c cl, *lav*	1.00	1.00
28	A10	5c grn, *grnsh*	2.25	1.75
29	A10	10c *lavender*	3.50	2.00
30	A10	15c bl, quadrille paper	4.50	3.50
31	A10	20c red, *grn*	7.50	6.00
32	A10	25c *rose*	6.75	5.50
33	A10	30c brn, *bis*	7.50	6.25
34	A10	40c red, *straw*	9.50	8.00
35	A10	50c car, *rose*	22.50	11.00
36	A10	75c vio, *org*	18.50	13.50
37	A10	1fr brnz grn, *straw*	27.50	20.00
		Nos. 25-37 (13)	113.25	80.60

1894

No.	Type	Description	Unused	Used
38	A11	1c *blue*	45	45
39	A11	2c brn, *buff*	1.10	90
40	A11	4c cl, *lav*	1.10	90
41	A11	5c grn, *grnsh*	2.10	1.75
42	A11	10c *lavender*	2.25	2.00
43	A11	15c bl, quadrille paper	2.25	2.00
44	A11	20c red, *grn*	5.00	3.50
45	A11	25c *rose*	3.50	2.25
46	A11	30c brn, *bis*	3.75	2.25
47	A11	40c red, *straw*	3.75	2.25
48	A11	50c car, *rose*	5.50	4.00
49	A11	75c vio, *org*	4.00	2.25
50	A11	1fr brnz grn, *straw*	8.00	6.00
		Nos. 38-50 (13)	42.75	30.50

Bisected stamps of type A11 are mentioned in note after Madagascar No. 62.

POSTAGE DUE STAMPS.

D1

D2

Lithographed.

1891 ***Imperf.*** **Unwmkd.**

No.	Type	Description	Unused	Used
J1	D1	5c violet	75.00	27.50
J2	D2	50c black	75.00	27.50

Excellent counterfeits exist of Nos. J1 and J2.

Postage Due Stamps of French Colonies Overprinted Type "c" in Black

1892

No.	Type	Description	Unused	Used
J3	D1	1c black	60.00	32.50
J4	D1	2c black	60.00	32.50
a.		Inverted overprint	210.00	160.00
J5	D1	3c black	60.00	35.00
J6	D1	4c black	60.00	35.00
J7	D1	5c black	60.00	35.00
J8	D1	10c black	16.50	13.50
a.		Inverted overprint	210.00	160.00
J9	D1	15c black	16.50	13.50
a.		Double overprint	325.00	275.00
J10	D1	20c black	100.00	67.50
J11	D1	30c black	52.50	35.00
a.		Inverted overprint	210.00	160.00
J12	D1	60c black	725.00	400.00
J13	D1	1fr brown	1,150.	675.00

DJIBOUTI

(jē'bōō'tē')

LOCATION—East Africa.

GOVT.—Republic.

AREA—8,800 sq. mi.

POP.—300,000 (est. 1977).

CAPITAL—Djibouti.

The French Territory of the Afars and Issas became the Republic of Djibouti June 27, 1977. For 1894–1902 issues with "Djibouti" or "DJ", see Somali Coast.

Afars and Issas Issues of 1972–1977 Overprinted and Surcharged with Bars and "REPUBLIQUE DE DJIBOUTI" in Black, Dark Green, Blue or Brown

Printing and Perforations as Before

1977

Multicolored

No.	Type	Description	Unused	Used
439	A63	1fr on 4fr (#358;B)	5	5
440	A81	2fr on 5fr (#433;B)	5	5
441	A75	5fr on 20fr (#421;B)	15	15
442	A70	8fr (#380;B)	22	22
443	A71	20fr (#387;DG)	45	45
444	A81	30fr (#434;B)	60	60
445	A71	40fr (#388;DG)	75	75
446	A71	45fr (#389;Bl)	90	90
447	A78	45fr (#428;B)	90	90
448	A72	50fr (#394;B)	1.10	1.10
449	A71	60fr (#391;Br)	1.25	1.25
450	A79	70fr (#430;B)	1.40	1.40
451	A81	70fr (#435;B)	1.40	1.40
452	A74	100fr (#418;B)	1.75	1.75
453	A72	150fr (#399;B)	2.75	2.75
454	A76	200fr (#422;B)	3.50	3.50
455	A80	200fr (#432;B)	3.50	3.50
456	A74	300fr (#419;B)	5.50	5.50
		Nos. 439-456, C106-C108 (21)	33.42	31.32

Map and Flag of Djibouti

A83

Water Pipe

A84

Design: 65fr, Map and flag of Djibouti, map of Africa (horiz.).

1977, June 27 **Litho.** ***Perf. 12½***

No.	Type	Description	Unused	Used
457	A83	45fr multi	50	40
458	A83	65fr multi	75	55

Independence, June 27.

1977, July 4

Designs: 10fr, Headrest (horiz.). 25fr, Pitcher.

No.	Type	Description	Unused	Used
459	A84	10fr multi	10	8
460	A84	20fr multi	20	15
461	A84	25fr multi	30	22

Ostrich

A85

Design: 100fr, Weaver.

1977, Aug. 11 **Litho.** ***Perf. 12½***

No.	Type	Description	Unused	Used
462	A85	90fr multi	1.00	75
463	A85	100fr multi	1.10	85

Snail

A86

Designs: 15fr, Fiddler crab. 50fr, Klipspringers. 70fr, Green turtle. 80fr, Priacanthus hamrur (fish). 150fr, Dolphinfish.

1977 **Litho.** ***Perf. 12½***

No.	Type	Description	Unused	Used
464	A86	15fr multi	15	10
465	A86	45fr multi	50	40
466	A86	50fr multi	55	40
467	A86	70fr multi	85	60
468	A86	80fr multi	90	70
469	A86	150fr multi	1.75	1.25
		Nos. 464-469 (6)	4.70	3.45

Issue dates: 45fr, 70fr, 80fr, Sept. 14. Others, Dec. 5.

Pres. Hassan Gouled Aptidon and Djibouti Flag

A87

1978, Feb. 12 **Litho.** ***Perf. 13***

No.	Type	Description	Unused	Used
470	A87	65fr multi	75	50

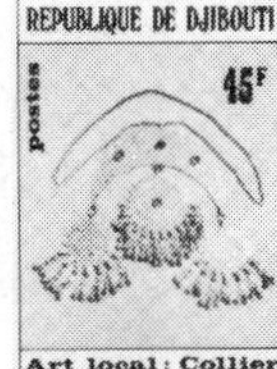
Charaxes Hansali A88 — Necklace A89

Butterflies: 20fr, Colias electo. 25fr, Acraea chilo. 150fr, Junonia hierta.

1978, Mar. 13 Litho. Perf. 12½x13

471	A88	5fr multi	5	4
472	A88	20fr multi	20	15
473	A88	25fr multi	30	22
474	A88	150fr multi	1.75	1.25

1978, May 29 Litho. Perf. 12½x13

Design: 55fr, Necklace (different).

475	A89	45fr pink & multi	50	35
476	A89	55fr bl & multi	60	40

Bougainvillea A90

Flowers: 35fr, Hibiscus schizopetalus. 250fr, Caesalpinia pulcherrima.

1978, July 10 Photo. Perf. 12½x13

477	A90	15fr multi	18	15
478	A90	35fr multi	40	30
479	A90	250fr multi	2.75	2.25

Charonia Nodifera—A91

Sea Shell: 80fr, Charonia variegata.

1978, Oct. 9 Litho. Perf. 13

480	A91	10fr multi	15	10
481	A91	80fr multi	1.20	80

Chaetodon A92

Fish: 30fr, Yellow surgeonfish. 40fr, Harlequinfish.

1978, Nov. 20 Litho. Perf. 13x12½

482	A92	8fr multi	12	8
483	A92	30fr multi	45	30
484	A92	40fr multi	60	40

Alsthom BB 1201 at Dock—A93

Locomotives: 55fr, Steam locomotive 231. 60fr, Steam locomotive 130 and map of route. 75fr, Diesel.

1979, Jan. 29 Litho. Perf. 13

485	A93	40fr multi	60	40
486	A93	55fr multi	82	55
487	A93	60fr multi	90	60
488	A93	75fr multi	1.12	75

Djibouti-Addis Ababa railroad.

Children and IYC Emblem—A94

Design: 200fr, Mother and child, IYC emblem.

1979, Feb. 26 Litho. Perf. 13

489	A94	20fr multi	30	20
490	A94	200fr multi	3.00	2.00

International Year of the Child.

Plane over Ardoukoba Volcano—A95

Design: 30fr, Helicopter over Ardoukoba Volcano (vert.).

1979, Mar. 19

491	A95	30fr multi	45	30
492	A95	90fr multi	1.35	90

Rowland Hill, Postal Clerks, No. C109—A96

Designs: 100fr, Somali Coast No. 22, Djibouti No. 457, letters, Rowland Hill. 150fr, Letters hoisted onto ship, smoke signals, Rowland Hill.

1979, Apr. 17 Litho. Perf. 13x12½

493	A96	25fr multi	38	25
494	A96	100fr multi	1.50	1.00
495	A96	150fr multi	2.25	1.50

Sir Rowland Hill (1795–1879), originator of penny postage.

View of Djibouti, Bird and Local Woman—A97

Design: 80fr, Map and flag of Djibouti, UPU emblem, Concorde, train and mail runner.

1979, June 8 Litho. Perf. 13x12½

496	A97	55fr multi	82	55
497	A97	80fr multi	1.20	80

Philexafrique II, Libreville, Gabon, June 8–17. Nos. 496, 497 each printed in sheets of 10 with 5 labels showing exhibition emblem.

Solanacea A98

Flowers: 2fr, Opuntia (vert.). 15fr, Trichodesma. 45fr, Acacia etbaica. 50fr, Thunbergia alata (vert.).

Perf. 13x13½, 13½x13

1979, June 18

498	A98	2fr multi	3	3
499	A98	8fr multi	12	8
500	A98	15fr multi	22	15
501	A98	45fr multi	68	45
502	A98	50fr multi	75	50
		Nos. 498-502 (5)	1.80	1.21

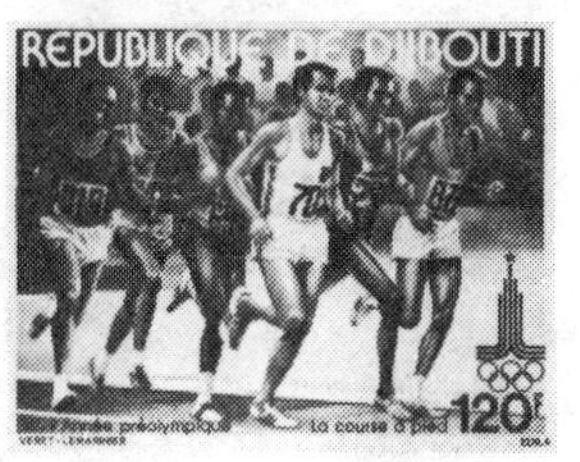
Running—A99

Olympic Emblem and: 70fr, Basketball 200fr, Soccer (horiz.).

Perf. 12½×13, 13×12½

1979, Oct. 22 Litho.

503	A99	70fr multi	1.05	70
504	A99	120fr multi	1.80	1.20
505	A99	200fr multi	3.00	2.00

Pre-Olympic Year.

Cypraecassis Rufa—A100

Shells: 40fr, Lambis chiragra arthritica. 300fr, Harpa connaidalis.

1979, Dec. 22 Litho. Perf. 13

506	A100	10fr multi	15	10
507	A100	40fr multi	60	40
508	A100	300fr multi	4.50	3.00

Rotary International, 75th Anniversary—A101

1980, Feb. 19 Litho. Perf. 13x12½

509	A101	90fr multi	1.35	90

See "Special Notices" at the front of this volume for data on the listing methods of this Catalogue, abbreviations, condition, prices and examination.

Lions Club of Djibouti—A102

1980, Feb. 19

510	A102	100fr multi	1.50	1.00

Colotis Danae—A103

1980, Mar. 17 Perf. 13x13½

511	A103	5fr *shown*	8	5
512	A103	55fr *Danaus chrysippus*	82	55

Chess Players, Knight—A104

Chess Federation Creation: 75fr, Chess Game, Florence, 1493.

1980, June 9 Litho. Perf. 13

513	A104	20fr multi	30	20
514	A104	75fr multi	1.10	75

Cribraria—A105

1980, Aug. 12 Litho. Perf. 13

515	A105	15fr *shown*	25	15
516	A105	85fr *Nautilius pompilius*	1.40	85

Alexander Fleming, Discoverer of Penicillin—A106

Design: 130fr, Jules Verne, French science fiction writer; earth, moon and spacecraft.

1980, Sept. 1

517	A106	20fr multi	30	20
518	A106	130fr multi	2.00	1.30

Capt. Cook and Endeavor—A107

Capt James Cook Death Bicentenary: 90fr, Ships and Maps of voyages.

1980, Nov. 20 **Litho.** ***Perf. 13***

519	A107	55fr multi	82	55
520	A107	90fr multi	1.35	90

Souvenir sheets of 1 exist, perf. 12½x12.

Angel Fish—A108

1981, Apr. 13 **Litho.** ***Perf. 12½***

521	A108	25fr shown	38	25
522	A108	55fr Moorish idol	82	55
523	A108	70fr Scad	1.05	70

13th World Telecommunications Day—A109

1981, May 17 **Litho.** ***Perf. 13***

524	A109	140fr multi	2.10	1.40

Type 231 Steam Locomotive, Germany, 1958 and Amtrak, US, 1980—A110

Locomotives: 55fr, Stephenson and his Rocket, Djibouti Railways 230 engine. 65fr, Type TGV, France, Type 962, Japan.

1981, June 9 **Litho.** ***Perf. 13***

525	A110	40fr multi	60	40
526	A110	55fr multi	80	55
527	A110	65fr multi	95	65

Radio Amateurs Club—A111

1981, June 25

528	A111	250fr multi	3.75	2.50

Prince Charles and Lady Diana—A112

1981, June 29

529	A112	180fr shown	2.75	1.80
530	A112	200fr Couple, diff.	3.00	2.00

Royal Wedding.

Lord Nelson and Victory—A113

1981, July 6 **Litho.** ***Perf. 13x12½***

531	A113	100fr multi	1.50	1.00
532	A113	175fr multi	2.60	1.75

Lord Horatio Nelson (1758-1805).

Scout Tending Campfire—A114

1981, July 16 **Litho.** ***Perf. 13***

533	A114	60fr shown	90	60
534	A114	105fr Scout giving sign	1.60	1.05

28th World Scouting Conference, Dakar, Aug. (60fr); 4th Pan-African Scouting Conference, Abidjan, Aug. (105fr).

Pawn and Queen, Swedish Bone Chess Pieces, 13th Cent.—A115

1981, Oct. 15 **Litho.** ***Perf. 13***

535	A115	50fr shown	75	50
536	A115	130fr Pawn, knight, Chinese, 19th cent., vert.	1.90	1.30

Sheraton Hotel Opening—A116

1981, Nov. 15 **Litho.** ***Perf. 13x12½***

537	A116	75fr multi	1.10	75

Acacia Mellifera—A117

1981, Dec. 21 ***Perf. 13***

538	A117	10fr Clitoria ternatea, vert.	15	10
539	A117	30fr shown	45	30
540	A117	35fr Punica granatum	50	35
541	A117	45fr Malvaceous plant, vert.	70	45

Nos. 535-536 Overprinted with Winners' Names.

1981, Dec. **Litho.** ***Perf. 13***

542	A115	50fr multi	75	50
543	A115	130fr multi	1.90	1.30

World Chess Championship.

1982 World Chess Championship A117a

14th World Telecommunications Day A118

1982, Apr. 8 **Litho.** ***Perf. 13***

545	A117	125fr Ivory bishop	1.90	1.25
546	A117	175fr Queen, pawn, 19th cent.	2.60	1.75

1982, May 17

547	A118	150fr multi	2.25	1.50

Bus and Jeep—A119

1982, July 27 **Litho.** ***Perf. 13***

548	A119	20fr shown	30	20
549	A119	25fr Dhow, ferry	38	25
550	A119	55fr Train, jet	80	45

Shells from the Red Sea—A120

1982, Nov. 20 **Litho.** ***Perf. 12½***

551	A120	10fr Cypraea erythraeensis	15	10
552	A120	15fr Conus sumatrensis	22	15
553	A120	25fr Cypraea pulchra	38	25
554	A120	30fr Conus inscriptus	45	30
555	A120	70fr Casmaria ponderosa	1.05	70
556	A120	150fr Cypraea exusta	2.25	1.50
		Nos. 551-556 (6)	4.50	3.00

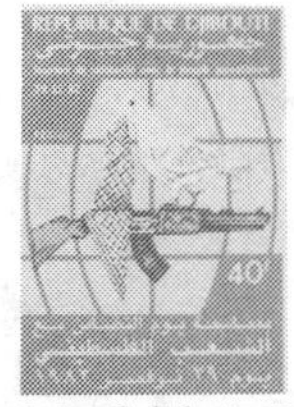

Intl. Palestinian Solidarity Day—A121

1982, Nov. 29 **Litho.** ***Perf. 13***

557	A121	40fr multi	60	40

AIR POST STAMPS

Afars and Issas Nos. C104-C105, C103 Overprinted with Bars and "REPUBLIQUE DE DJIBOUTI" in Brown or Black

1977 Engraved *Perf. 13*

C106	AP37	55fr multi (Br)	60	45
C107	AP37	75fr multi	85	65

Litho. *Perf. 12*

C108	AP36	500fr multi	5.75	4.00

Map of Djibouti, Dove, UN Emblem—AP38

1977, Oct. 19 Photo. *Perf. 13*

C109	AP38	300fr multi	3.50	2.25

Djibouti's admission to the United Nations.

Marcel Brochet MB 101, 1955—AP39

Designs: 85fr, Tiger Moth, 1960. 200fr, Rallye-Commodore, 1973.

1978, Feb. 27 Litho. *Perf. 13*

C110	AP39	60fr multi	65	45
C111	AP39	85fr multi	90	60
C112	AP39	200fr multi	2.25	1.50

Djibouti Aero Club.

Old Man, by Rubens AP40

Design: 500fr, Hippopotamus Hunt, by Rubens (horiz.).

1978, Apr. 24 Photo. *Perf. 13*

C113	AP40	50fr multi	55	40
C114	AP40	500fr multi	5.50	4.00

Peter Paul Rubens (1577-1640), 400th birth anniversary.

Player Holding Soccer Cup AP41

Design: 300fr, Soccer player, map of South America with Argentina, Cup and emblem.

1978, June 20 Litho. *Perf. 13*

C115	AP41	100fr multi	1.10	75
C116	AP41	300fr multi	3.25	2.50

11th World Cup Soccer Championship, Argentina, June 1-25.

Nos. C115-C116 Overprinted:
a. ARGENTINE / CHAMPION 1978
b. ARGENTINE / HOLLANDE / 3-1

1978, Aug. 20 Litho. *Perf. 13*

C117	AP41(a)	100fmulti	1.10	75
C118	AP41(b)	300fmulti	3.25	2.50

Argentina's victory in 1978 Soccer Championship.

Tahitian Women, by Gauguin—AP42

Young Hare, by Dürer AP43

Perf. 13x12½, 12½x13

1978, Sept. 25 Lithographed

C119	AP42	100fr multi	1.10	75
C120	AP43	250fr multi	2.75	2.00

Paul Gauguin (1848-1903) and Albrecht Dürer (1471-1528), painters.

Philexafrique II—Essen Issue

Common Design Types

Designs: No. C121, Lynx and Djibouti No. 456. No. C122, Jay and Brunswick No. 3.

1978, Dec. 13 Litho. *Perf. 13x12½*

C121	CD138	90fr multi	1.00	70
C122	CD139	90fr multi	1.00	70

Nos. C121-C122 printed se-tenant.

UPU Emblem, Map of Djibouti, Dove AP44

1978, Dec. 18 Engr. *Perf. 13*

C123	AP44	200fr multi	3.00	2.00

Centenary of Congress of Paris.

Common Design Types pictured in section at front of book.

Junkers JU-52 and Dewoitine D-338—AP45

Powered Flight, 75th Anniversary: 250fr, Potez P63-11, 1941 and Supermarine Spitfire HF-VII, 1942. 500fr, Concorde, 1969 and Sikorsky S-40 "American Clipper," 1931.

1979, May 21 Litho. *Perf. 13x12½*

C124	AP45	140fr multi	2.10	1.40
C125	AP45	250fr multi	3.75	2.50
C126	AP45	500fr multi	7.50	5.00

The Laundress, by Honore Daumier AP46

1979, July 10 Litho. *Perf. 12½x13*

C127	AP46	500fr multi	7.50	5.00

Olympic Emblem, Skis, Sleds—AP47

1980, Jan. 21 Litho. *Perf. 13*

C128	AP47	150fr multi	2.25	1.50

13th Winter Olympic Games, Lake Placid, N.Y., Feb. 12-24.

Cathedral of the Archangel, Basketball, Moscow '80 Emblem—AP48

1980, Apr. 10 Litho. *Perf. 13*

C129	AP48	60fr *shown*	90	60
C130	AP48	120fr *Lomonossov Univ., Moscow, Soccer*	1.80	1.20
C131	AP48	250fr *Cathedral of the Annunciation, Running*	3.75	2.50

22nd Summer Olympic Games, Moscow, July 18-Aug. 3.

Air Djibouti, 1st Anniversary—AP49

1980, Mar. 29 Litho. *Perf. 13x12½*

C132	AP49	400fr multi	6.00	4.00

No. C128 Surcharged in Black and Blue or Purple:

80fr. A.M. MOSER-PROEL / AUTRICHE / DESCENTE DAMES / MEDAILLE D'OR

200fr. HEIDEN / USA / 5 MEDAILLES D'OR / PATINAGE DE VITESSE

1980, Apr. 5 Litho. *Perf. 13*

C133	AP47	80fr on 150fr multi	1.20	80
C134	AP47	200fr on 150fr multi (P)	3.00	2.00

Apollo 11 Moon Landing, 10th Anniversary—AP50

Space Conquests: 300fr, Apollo-Soyuz space project, 5th anniversary.

1980, May 8

C135	AP50	200fr multi	3.00	2.00
C136	AP50	300fr multi	4.50	3.00

Satellite Earth Station Inauguration—AP51

1980, July 3 Litho. *Perf. 13*

C137	AP51	500fr multi	7.50	5.00

Graf Zeppelin—AP52

1980, Oct. 2 Litho. *Perf. 13*

C138	AP52	100fr *shown*	1.50	1.00
C139	AP52	150fr *Ferdinand von Zeppelin, blimp*	2.25	1.50

Zeppelin flight, 80th anniversary.

Voyager Passing Saturn—AP53

1980, Dec. 21 **Litho.** ***Perf. 13***

C140	AP53	250fr multi	3.75	2.50

Soccer Players—AP54

World Cup Soccer Preliminary Games: 200fr, Players (diff.).

1981, Jan. 14

C141	AP54	80fr multi	1.20	80
C142	AP54	200fr multi	3.00	2.00

European—African Economic Convention—AP55

1981, Feb. 10 **Litho.** ***Perf. 13***

C143	AP55	100fr multi	1.50	1.00

5th Anniversary of Viking I Take-off to Mars—AP56

20th Anniversary of Various Space Flights: 75fr, Vostok I, Yuri Gagarin (vert.). 150fr, Freedom 7, Alan B. Shepard (vert.).

1981, Mar. 9 **Litho.** ***Perf. 13***

C144	AP56	75fr multi	1.10	75
C145	AP56	120fr multi	1.80	1.20
C146	AP56	150fr multi	2.25	1.50

Football Players, by Picasso (1881-1973)—AP57

Design: 400fr Man Wearing a Turban, by Rembrandt (1606-1669) (vert.).

1981, Aug. 3 **Litho.** ***Perf. 13x12½, 12½x13***

C147	AP57	300fr multi	4.50	3.00
C148	AP57	400fr multi	6.00	4.50

Columbia Space Shuttle—AP58

1981, Sept. 24 **Litho.** ***Perf. 13***

C149	AP58	90fr Shuttle, diff., vert.	1.35	90
C150	AP58	120fr shown	1.80	1.20

Nos. C149-C150 Overprinted in Brown with Astronauts' Names and Dates.

1981, Nov. 12 **Litho.** ***Perf. 13***

C151	AP58	90fr multi	1.35	90
C152	AP58	120fr multi	1.80	1.20

1982 World Cup Soccer—AP59

Designs: Various soccer players.

1982, Jan. 20

C153	AP59	110fr multi	1.65	1.10
C154	AP59	220fr multi	3.30	2.25

Space Anniversaries—AP60

Designs: 40fr, Luna 9 moon landing, 15th (vert.). 60fr, John Glenn's flight, 20th (vert.). 180fr, Viking I Mars landing, 5th.

1982, Feb. 15

C155	AP60	40fr multi	60	40
C156	AP60	60fr multi	90	60
C157	AP60	180fr multi	2.75	1.80

21 Birthday of Princess Diana of Wales—AP61

1982, Apr. 29 **Litho.** ***Perf. 12½x13***

C158	AP61	120fr Portrait	1.80	1.25
C159	AP61	180fr Portrait, diff.	2.75	1.80

No. 489, Boy Examining Collection—AP62

1982, May 10 ***Perf. 13x12½***

C160	AP62	80fr shown	1.25	80
C161	AP62	140fr No. 495	2.10	1.40

PHILEXFRANCE '82 Stamp Exhibition, Paris, June 11-21. Nos. C160-C161 se-tenant with label showing show emblem, dates.

1350th Anniv. of Mohamed's Death at Medina—AP63

1982, June 8 **Litho.** ***Perf. 13***

C162	AP63	500fr Medina Mosque	7.50	5.00

Scouting Year—AP64

1982, June 28

C163	AP64	95fr Baden-Powell	1.50	1.00
C164	AP64	200fr Camp, scouts	3.00	2.00

2nd UN Conference on Peaceful Uses of Outer Space, Vienna, Aug. 9-21—AP65

1982, Aug. 19

C165	AP65	350fr multi	5.25	3.50

Nos. C153-C154 Overprinted with Winner's Name and Scores.

1982, July 21 **Litho.** ***Perf. 13***

C166	AP59	110fr multi	1.65	1.10
C167	AP59	220fr multi	3.25	2.25

Italy's victory in 1982 World Cup.

Nos. C158-C159 Overprinted in Blue or Red with Date, Name, and Title.

1982, Aug. 9 ***Perf. 12½x13***

C168	AP61	120fr multi	1.75	1.25
C169	AP61	180fr multi (R)	2.75	1.80

Birth of Prince William of Wales, June 21.

Franklin D. Roosevelt (1882-1945)—AP66

1982, Oct. 7 **Litho.** ***Perf.***

C170	AP66	115fr shown	1.75	1.15
C171	AP66	250fr George Washington	3.75	2.50

Manned Flight Bicentenary AP67

Pre-olympic Year AP68

1983, Jan. 20 **Litho.** ***Perf. 13***

C172	AP67	35fr Montgolfiere, 1783	48	32
C173	AP67	45fr Giffard, Paris Exposition, 1878	68	42
C174	AP67	120fr Double Eagle II, 1978	1.75	1.25

1983, Feb. 15

C175	AP68	75fr Volleyball	1.15	75
C176	AP68	125fr Wind surfing	1.85	1.25

DOMINICAN REPUBLIC

(dô·mĭn′ĭ·kăn rē·pŭb′lĭk)

LOCATION — The republic comprises about two-thirds of the island of Hispaniola in the West Indies.

GOVT.—Republic.

AREA—18,700 sq. mi.

POP.—5,000,000 (est. 1977).

CAPITAL—Santo Domingo (formerly Ciudad Trujillo).

8 Reales = 1 Peso
100 Centavos = 1 Peso (1880)
100 Centimos = 1 Franco (1883)
100 Centavos = 1 Peso (1885)

> Prices of early Dominican Republic stamps vary according to condition. Quotations for Nos. 1–31 are for fine copies. Very fine to superb specimens sell at much higher prices, and inferior or poor copies sell at reduced prices, depending on the condition of the individual specimen.

Coat of Arms
A1 A2

Typographed

1865 *Imperf.* **Unwmkd.**

Wove Paper.

No.	Type	Description	Unused	Used
1	A1	½r *rose*	350.00	350.00
2	A1	1r *dp grn*	800.00	800.00

Twelve varieties of each.

Laid Paper.

No.	Type	Description	Unused	Used
3	A2	½r *pale grn*	550.00	500.00
4	A2	1r *straw*	1,300.	1,200.

Twelve varieties of the ½r, ten varieties of the 1r.

A3 A4

1866 **Laid Paper** **Unwmkd.**

No.	Type	Description	Unused	Used
5	A3	½r *straw*	200.00	150.00
6	A3	1r *pale grn*	800.00	800.00
7	A4	1r *pale grn*	175.00	150.00

Nos. 5–8 have 21 varieties (sheets of 21).

Wmk. 115

Wmkd. Diamonds. (115)

No.	Type	Description	Unused	Used
8	A3	1r *pale grn*	*2,250.*	*2,250.*

1866–67 **Wove Paper.** **Unwmkd.**

No.	Type	Description	Unused	Used
9	A3	½r *rose* ('67)	55.00	55.00
10	A3	1r *pale grn*	100.00	85.00
a.		Inscription double, top and bottom	*400.00*	*400.00*
11	A3	1r *bl* ('67)	45.00	35.00
a.		1r *lt bl* ('67)	45.00	35.00
b.		No space between "Un" and "real"	275.00	225.00
c.		Without inscription at top & bottom	400.00	350.00
d.		Inscription invtd., top & bottom		

1867-71 **Pelure Paper.**

No.	Type	Description	Unused	Used
13	A3	½r *rose*	115.00	90.00
15	A3	½r *lav* ('68)	200.00	200.00
a.		Without inscription at top and bottom		650.00
b.		Double inscriptions, one inverted		*550.00*
16	A3	½r *grnsh gray* ('68)	200.00	200.00
18	A3	½r *ol* ('69)	*2,500.*	*2,500.*
23	A3	1r *lavender*	175.00	175.00
24	A4	1r *rose* ('68)	175.00	175.00
25	A4	1r *mag* ('69)	*1,200.*	*1,200.*
26	A4	1r *sal* ('71)	175.00	175.00

1870-73 **Ordinary Paper.**

No.	Type	Description	Unused	Used
27	A3	½r *magenta*	900.00	900.00
28	A3	½r bl, *rose* (blk inscription) ('71)	65.00	35.00
a.		Blue inscription	600.00	600.00
b.		Without inscription at top and bottom		
29	A3	½r *yel* ('73)	40.00	27.50
a.		Without inscription at top and bottom	500.00	500.00
30	A4	1r *vio* ('73)	30.00	27.50
a.		Without inscription at top and bottom	600.00	600.00
31	A4	1r *dk grn*	80.00	65.00

Nos. 9–31 have 21 varieties (sheets of 21). Nos. 29 and 30 are known pin-perforated, unofficially.

Bisects are known of several of the early 1r stamps.

Coat of Arms
A5 A6

1879 ***Perf. 12½x13***

No.	Type	Description	Unused	Used
32	A5	½r violet	2.50	2.00
a.		Imperf., pair	10.00	10.00
b.		Horiz. pair, imperf. vert.	22.50	
33	A5	½r vio, *bluish*	2.50	2.00
a.		Imperf., pair	10.00	8.00
34	A5	1r carmine	2.50	2.00
a.		Imperf., pair	10.00	8.00
b.		Perf. 13	8.00	8.00
c.		Perf. 13x12½	9.00	9.00
35	A5	1r car, *sal*	2.50	2.00
a.		Imperf., pair	10.00	10.00

In 1891 15 stamps of 1879–83 were surcharged "U P U," new values and crossed diagonal lines.

Rouletted in Color

1880 **Typographed**

No.	Type	Description	Unused	Used
36	A6	1c green	1.50	1.00
a.		Broken "T"	10.00	8.00
b.		Laid paper	50.00	50.00
37	A6	2c red	1.00	75
a.		Pelure paper	40.00	40.00
b.		Laid paper	40.00	40.00
38	A6	5c blue	1.25	75
39	A6	10c rose	3.00	1.00
40	A6	20c brown	2.00	1.00
41	A6	25c violet	2.50	1.25
42	A6	50c orange	2.75	1.75
43	A6	75c ultra	5.00	2.75
a.		Laid paper	35.00	35.00
44	A6	1p gold	7.00	4.50
a.		Laid paper	50.00	50.00
b.		Double impression	40.00	40.00
		Nos. 36-44 (9)	26.00	14.75

1881 **Network Covering Stamp.**

No.	Type	Description	Unused	Used
45	A6	1c green	1.00	60
a.		Broken "T"	6.00	5.00
46	A6	2c red	1.00	60
47	A6	5c blue	1.25	60
48	A6	10c rose	1.50	75
49	A6	20c brown	1.50	90
50	A6	25c violet	2.00	1.00
51	A6	50c orange	2.00	1.00
52	A6	75c ultra	6.50	3.50
53	A6	1p gold	8.25	5.50
		Nos. 45-53 (9)	25.00	14.45

Preceding Issues Surcharged with Value in New Currency:

5 céntimos.
a

5 céntimos
b

5 céntimos.
c

1 franco.
d

1 Franco.
e

1 franco
f

1 franco, 25 céntimos.
g

5 francos.
h

5 francos
i

1883 **Without Network.**

No.	Type	Description	Unused	Used
54	(a)	5c on 1c grn	2.25	1.50
a.		Broken "T" in "CENTAVO"	9.00	9.00
b.		Inverted surcharge	20.00	20.00
c.		Surcharged "25 céntimos"	60.00	60.00
d.		Surcharged "10 céntimos"	30.00	30.00
55	(b)	5c on 1c grn	17.50	7.00
a.		Broken "T" in "CENTAVO"	30.00	30.00
b.		Double surch.	125.00	
c.		Inverted surcharge	70.00	70.00
56	(c)	5c on 1c grn	12.50	6.00
a.		Broken "T" in "CENTAVO"	30.00	30.00
b.		Surcharged "10 céntimos"	35.00	35.00
c.		Surcharged "25 céntimos"	40.00	40.00
57	(a)	10c on 2c red	5.50	4.00
a.		Inverted surcharge	30.00	30.00
d.		Surcharged "5 céntimos"	60.00	60.00
e.		Surcharged "25 céntimos"	90.00	90.00
58	(c)	10c on 2c red	5.50	4.00
a.		"Céntimso"		
b.		Inverted surcharge	50.00	50.00
c.		Surcharged "25 céntimos"	75.00	75.00
d.		"10" omitted	75.00	
59	(a)	25c on 5c bl	6.50	4.50
a.		Surcharged "5 céntimos"	60.00	
b.		Surcharged "10 céntimos"	60.00	60.00
c.		Surcharged "50 céntimos"	90.00	90.00
d.		Inverted surcharge	45.00	45.00
60	(c)	25c on 5c bl	6.50	3.50
a.		Inverted surcharge	55.00	45.00
b.		Surcharged "10 céntimos"	55.00	45.00
e.		"25" omitted	100.00	
f.		Surcharged on back		100.00
61	(a)	50c on 10c rose	20.00	10.00
a.		Inverted surcharge	55.00	50.00
62	(c)	50c on 10c rose	32.50	17.50
a.		Inverted surcharge	60.00	60.00
63	(d)	1fr on 20c brn	17.50	12.50
64	(e)	1fr on 20c brn	22.50	13.00
a.		Comma after "Franco,"	30.00	30.00
65	(f)	1fr on 20c brn	22.50	14.00
a.		Inverted surcharge		100.00
66	(g)	1fr25c on 25c vio	22.50	16.00
a.		Inverted surcharge	75.00	75.00
67	(g)	2fr50c on 50c org	15.00	12.00
a.		Inverted surcharge	45.00	35.00
68	(g)	3fr75c on 75c ultra	25.00	20.00
b.		Inverted surcharge	60.00	60.00
c.		Laid paper	75.00	75.00
70	(i)	5fr on 1p gold	550.00	500.00
a.		"s" of "francos" inverted	750.00	750.00

With Network.

No.	Type	Description	Unused	Used
71	(a)	5c on 1c grn	3.75	3.00
a.		Broken "T" in "CENTAVO"	7.50	7.50
b.		Inverted surcharge	25.00	25.00
c.		Double surch.	22.50	20.00
d.		Surcharged "25 céntimos"	45.00	45.00
e.		"5" omitted	90.00	90.00
72	(b)	5c on 1c grn	17.50	7.50
a.		Broken "T" in "CENTAVO"	40.00	17.50
b.		Inverted surcharge	45.00	45.00
73	(c)	5c on 1c grn	22.50	8.50
a.		Broken "T" in "CENTAVO"	30.00	15.00
b.		Surcharged "10 céntimos"	45.00	30.00
c.		Surcharged "25 céntimos"	75.00	
74	(a)	10c on 2c red	4.50	3.00
a.		Surcharged "5 céntimos"	60.00	50.00
b.		Surcharged "25 céntimos"	90.00	90.00
c.		"10" omitted	75.00	
75	(c)	10c on 2c red	3.50	2.00
a.		Inverted surcharge	30.00	17.50
76	(a)	25c on 5c bl	8.00	4.00
a.		Surcharged "10 céntimos"	100.00	
b.		Surcharged "5 céntimos"	75.00	
c.		Surcharged "50 céntimos"	90.00	
77	(c)	25c on 5c bl	65.00	32.50
a.		Inverted surcharge		
b.		Surcharged on back		
78	(a)	50c on 10c rose	25.00	7.00
a.		Inverted surcharge	30.00	17.50
b.		Surcharged "25 c'‡ntimos"	75.00	
79	(c)	50c on 10c rose	27.50	8.00
a.		Inverted surcharge	60.00	
80	(d)	1fr on 20c brn	14.00	11.00
81	(e)	1fr on 20c brn	16.00	13.00
a.		Comma after "Franco,"	45.00	45.00
b.		Inverted surcharge	90.00	
82	(f)	1fr on 20c brn	22.50	16.50
83	(g)	1fr25c on 25c vio	40.00	30.00
a.		Inverted surcharge	75.00	
84	(g)	2fr50c on 50c org	25.00	16.50
a.		Inverted surcharge	45.00	35.00
85	(g)	3fr75c on 75c ultra	40.00	35.00
86	(h)	5fr on 1p gold	150.00	150.00
a.		Inverted surcharge		
87	(i)	5fr on 1p gold	175.00	175.00

Many minor varieties exist in Nos. 54– 87: accent on "i" of "centimos"; "5" with straight top; "1" with straight serif.

Coat of Arms
A7 A7a

1885–91 **Engraved** ***Perf. 12***

No.	Type	Description	Unused	Used
88	A7	1c green	1.00	60
89	A7	2c vermilion	1.00	60
90	A7	5c blue	1.50	60
91	A7a	10c orange	2.50	75
92	A7a	20c dk brn	2.50	1.00
93	A7a	50c vio ('91)	8.00	6.00
94	A7	1p car ('91)	20.00	12.00
95	A7	2p red brn ('91)	25.00	14.00
		Nos. 88-95 (8)	61.50	35.55

Nos. 93, 94 and 95 were issued without gum.

Imperf. varieties are proofs.

Coat of Arms
A8

1895–97 ***Perf. 12½x14***

No.	Design	Description	Unused	Used
96	A8	1c green	1.50	60
a.		Perf. 14 ('97)	1.75	70
97	A8	2c org red	1.50	60
a.		Perf. 14 ('97)	6.00	90
98	A8	5c blue	1.50	60
a.		Perf. 14 ('97)	1.75	1.00
99	A8	10c orange	2.00	1.25
a.		Perf. 14 ('97)	2.50	1.50

Nos. 96 to 99 are known imperforate but were not issued in this condition.

Columbus Mausoleum Issue.

Voyage of Diego Méndez from Jamaica—A9

Enriquillo's Revolt
A10

Sarcophagus of Columbus
A11

"Española" Guarding Remains of Columbus
A12

Toscanelli Replying to Columbus
A13

Bartolomé de las Casas Defending Indians
A14

Columbus at Salamanca
A15

Columbus' Mausoleum
A16

1899, Feb. 27 Litho. ***Perf. 11½***

No.	Design	Description	Unused	Used
100	A9	1c brn vio	6.00	5.00
a.		Imperf., pair	17.50	
102	A10	2c rose red	2.00	1.00
a.		Imperf., pair	6.00	
103	A11	5c blue	2.25	1.00
a.		Imperf., pair	7.00	
104	A12	10c orange	5.00	1.75
a.		Tête bêche pair	60.00	60.00
b.		Imperf. pair	10.00	
105	A13	20c brown	8.50	5.50
a.		Imperf. pair	17.50	
106	A14	50c yel grn	8.50	6.00
a.		Tête bêche pair	80.00	80.00
b.		Imperf. pair	22.50	
c.		as "a," imperf.	150.00	
107	A15	1p gray bl	20.00	15.00
a.		Imperf. pair	50.00	
108	A16	2p bis brn	40.00	40.00
a.		Imperf. pair	85.00	

1900, Jan.

No.	Design	Description	Unused	Used
109	A11	¼c black	1.00	1.00
a.		Imperf. pair	3.00	3.50
110	A15	½c black	1.00	1.00
b.		Imperf. pair	3.00	3.50
110A	A9	1c gray grn	1.00	75
c.		Imperf. pair	5.00	
		Nos. 100-110A (11)	95.25	78.00

Nos. 100–110A were issued to raise funds for a Columbus mausoleum.

Map of Hispaniola
A17

Coat of Arms
A18

1900, Oct. 21 ***Perf. 14*** **Unwmkd.**

No.	Design	Description	Unused	Used
111	A17	¼c dk bl	90	60
112	A17	½c rose	90	60
113	A17	1c ol grn	90	60
114	A17	2c dp grn	90	60
115	A17	5c red brn	90	60
a.		Vertical pair, imperf. between	25.00	

Perf. 12.

No.	Design	Description	Unused	Used
116	A17	10c orange	90	60
117	A17	20c lilac	4.00	3.00
a.		20c rose (error)	8.00	8.00
118	A17	50c black	3.50	3.00
119	A17	1p brown	4.00	3.00
		Nos. 111-119 (9)	16.90	12.60

Several varieties in design are known in this issue. They were deliberately made. Counterfeits of Nos. 111–119 abound.

1901–06 Typographed ***Perf. 14***

No.	Design	Description	Unused	Used
120	A18	½c car & vio	90	50
121	A18	½c blk & org ('05)	1.50	85
122	A18	½c grn & blk ('06)	1.00	35
123	A18	1c ol grn & vio	90	25
124	A18	1c blk & ultra ('05)	1.75	75
125	A18	1c car & blk ('06)	90	40
126	A18	2c dp grn & vio	85	25
127	A18	2c blk & vio ('05)	1.75	60
128	A18	2c org brn & blk ('06)	90	20
129	A18	5c org brn & vio	90	30
130	A18	5c blk & cl ('05)	2.25	1.00
131	A18	5c bl & blk ('06)	1.00	40
132	A18	10c org & vio	1.50	50
133	A18	10c blk & grn ('05)	4.00	2.00
134	A18	10c red vio & blk ('06)	1.25	50
135	A18	20c brn vio & vio	2.75	1.00
136	A18	20c blk & ol ('05)	12.50	7.00
137	A18	20c ol grn & blk ('06)	7.00	3.50
138	A18	50c gray blk & vio	9.00	5.50
139	A18	50c blk & red brn ('05)	40.00	22.50
140	A18	50c brn & blk ('06)	7.00	6.00
141	A18	1p brn & vio	17.50	10.00
142	A18	1p blk & gray ('05)	225.00	225.00
143	A18	1p vio & blk ('06)	17.50	10.00
		Nos. 120-143 (24)	359.60	299.35

Issue dates: Nov. 15, 1901, May 11, 1905, Aug. 17, 1906.
See also Nos. 172–176.

Francisco Sánchez
A19

Juan Pablo Duarte
A20

Ramón Mella
A21

Ft. Santo Domingo
A22

1902, Feb. 25 **Engraved** ***Perf. 12***

No.	Design	Description	Unused	Used
144	A19	1c dk grn & blk	35	35
a.		Center inverted	3.50	
145	A20	2c scar & blk	35	35
a.		Center inverted	3.50	
146	A20	5c bl & blk	35	35
a.		Center inverted	3.50	
147	A19	10c org & blk	35	35
148	A21	12c pur & blk	35	35
a.		Center inverted	3.50	
149	A21	20c rose & blk	50	50
a.		Center inverted	3.50	
150	A22	50c brn & blk	75	75
a.		Center inverted	3.50	
		Nos. 144-150 (7)	3.00	3.00

400th anniversary of Santo Domingo. Imperforate varieties of Nos. 144 to 150 were never sold to the public.

Nos. 138, 141 Surcharged in Black

2
dos cts

1904, Aug.

No.	Design	Description	Unused	Used
151	A18	2c on 50c blk & vio	8.00	6.50
a.		Inverted surcharge	17.50	17.50
152	A18	2c on 1p brn & vio	11.00	8.00
a.		Inverted surcharge	15.00	15.00
b.		"2" omitted	50.00	50.00
c.		As "b," inverted	90.00	90.00
153	A18	5c on 50c blk & vio	3.00	2.50
a.		Inverted surcharge	7.50	7.50
154	A18	5c on 1p brn & vio	4.50	3.50
a.		Inverted surcharge	7.50	7.50
155	A18	10c on 50c blk & vio	7.00	6.00
a.		Inverted surcharge	15.00	15.00
156	A18	10c on 1p brn & vio	7.00	6.00
a.		Inverted surcharge	10.00	8.50
		Nos. 151-156 (6)	40.50	32.50

Official Stamps of 1902 Overprinted

16 de Agosto
1904

Red Overprint.

1904, Aug. 16

No.	Design	Description	Unused	Used
157	O1	5c dk bl & blk	4.50	3.25
a.		Inverted overprint	7.00	6.00

Black Overprint.

No.	Design	Description	Unused	Used
158	O1	2c scar & blk	7.50	4.50
a.		Inverted overprint	8.00	7.00
159	O1	5c dk bl & blk	750.00	750.00
160	O1	10c yel grn & blk	7.00	5.00
a.		Inverted overprint	14.00	14.00

Surcharged

16 de Agosto
1 1904 1

No.	Design	Description	Unused	Used
161	O1	1c on 20c yel & blk	5.00	4.00
a.		Inverted surcharge	7.50	6.50

Nos. J1–J2 Surcharged or Overprinted

REPUBLICA
DOMINICANA
1
CENTAVOS
CORREOS

Surcharged "CENTAVOS".

1904-05 Black Surcharge.

No.	Design	Description	Unused	Used
162	D1	1c on 2c ol gray	100.00	100.00
a.		"entavos"		
b.		"Dominican"	225.00	225.00
c.		"Centavo"	225.00	225.00

Carmine Surcharge or Overprint.

No.	Design	Description	Unused	Used
163	D1	1c on 2c ol gray	2.75	1.25
a.		Inverted surcharge	3.50	3.00
b.		"Domihicana"	14.00	14.00
c.		Same as "b," inverted	37.50	37.50
d.		"Dominican"	12.50	12.50
e.		"Centavos" omitted	35.00	35.00
g.		"entavos"	30.00	
163F	D1	1c on 4c ol gray	27.50	7.00
164	D1	2c ol gray	1.00	50
a.		"Domihicana"	9.00	9.00
b.		Inverted overprint	2.50	2.50
c.		Same as "a," inverted	20.00	20.00
d.		"Dominican"	6.00	6.00
e.		"Centavo" omitted	12.00	8.00
f.		"entavos"	10.00	10.00
g.		Same as "f," inverted	30.00	30.00
h.		Same as "d," inverted	30.00	30.00

Surcharged "CENTAVO".

No.	Design	Description	Unused	Used
165	D1	1c on 4c ol gray	1.00	75
a.		"Domihicana"	10.00	10.00
c.		Inverted surcharge	2.50	2.50
d.		"1" omitted	2.50	2.50
e.		Same as "a," invtd.	35.00	35.00
f.		Same as "d," invtd.	50.00	50.00
g.		Double surcharge	35.00	35.00

No. 92 Surcharged in Red

DOS
1905
CENTAVOS

1905, Apr. 4

No.	Design	Description	Unused	Used
166	A7a	2c on 20c dk brn	7.50	6.00
a.		Inverted surcharge	17.50	17.50
167	A7a	5c on 20c dk brn	3.25	2.00
a.		Inverted surcharge	20.00	20.00
b.		Double surcharge	30.00	30.00
168	A7a	10c on 20c dk brn	7.50	6.00

Nos. 166–168 exist with inverted "A" for "V" in "CENTAVOS" in surcharge.

Nos. J2, J4, J3 Surcharged:

REPUBLICA DOMINICANA. UN centavo.

REPUBLICA DOMINICANA. DOS centavos.

1906, Jan. 16 ***Perf. 14***

Red Surcharge.

No.	Design	Description	Unused	Used
169	D1	1c on 4c ol gray	1.00	60
a.		Inverted surcharge	15.00	15.00

1906, May 1

Black Surcharge.

No.	Type	Description	Unused	Used
170	D1	1c on 10c ol gray	1.25	60
a.		Inverted surcharge	15.00	15.00
b.		Double surcharge	20.00	20.00
c.		'OMINICANA'	25.00	25.00
171	D1	2c on 5c ol gray	1.25	60
a.		Inverted surcharge	15.00	15.00

The varieties small "C" or small "A" in "REPUBLICA" are found on Nos. 169, 170 and 171.

Arms Type of 1901–06.

Wmk. 116

Wmkd. Crosses and Circles. (116)

1907-10

No.	Type	Description	Unused	Used
172	A18	½c grn & blk ('08)	80	25
173	A18	1c car & blk	80	20
174	A18	2c org brn & blk	80	20
175	A18	5c bl & blk	90	30
176	A18	10c red vio & blk ('10)	6.50	1.25
		Nos. 172-176 (5)	9.80	2.20

No. 06 Overprinted in Red: **HABILITADO 1911**

Perf. 13½x14, 13½x13

1911, July 11

No.	Type	Description	Unused	Used
177	O2	2c scar & blk	1.50	75
a.		'HABILITAOO'	12.50	8.50
b.		Inverted overprint	30.00	
c.		Double overprint	30.00	

Coat of Arms A23

Juan Pablo Duarte A24

1911-13 ***Perf. 14.***

Center in Black

No.	Type	Description	Unused	Used
178	A23	½c org ('13)	35	20
179	A23	1c green	35	15
180	A23	2c carmine	35	15
181	A23	5c gray bl ('13)	75	20
182	A23	10c red vio	1.50	60
183	A23	20c ol grn	8.00	5.00
184	A23	50c yel brn ('12)	3.50	3.00
185	A23	1p vio ('12)	6.00	3.50
		Nos. 178-185 (8)	20.80	12.80

See Nos. 230–232.

1914, Apr. 13 ***Perf. 13x14***

Background Red, White and Blue.

No.	Type	Description	Unused	Used
186	A24	½c org & blk	70	55
187	A24	1c grn & blk	70	55
188	A24	2c rose & blk	70	55
189	A24	5c sl & blk	85	60
190	A24	10c mag & blk	1.25	75
191	A24	20c ol grn & blk	3.00	2.50
192	A24	50c brn & blk	4.00	3.50
193	A24	1p dl lil & blk	6.00	4.50
		Nos. 186-193 (8)	17.20	13.50

To commemorate the centenary of the birth of Juan Pablo Duarte (1813–1876), patriot and revolutionary.

Official Stamps of 1909–12 Surcharged in Violet or Overprinted in Red:

Habilitado 1915 MEDIO CENTAVO (a) — Habilitado 1915 (b)

1915, Feb. ***Perf. 13½x13, 13½x14***

No.	Type	Description	Unused	Used
194	O2 (a)	½c on 20c org & blk	75	50
a.		Inverted surcharge	7.50	
b.		Double surcharge	11.00	
c.		'Habilitado' omitted	6.00	
195	O2 (b)	1c bl grn & blk	1.00	35
a.		Inverted overprint	7.50	
b.		Double overprint	9.00	
c.		Overprinted '1915' only	17.50	
196	O2 (b)	2c scar & blk	1.00	35
a.		Inverted overprint	6.00	
b.		Double overprint	10.00	
c.		Overprinted '1915' only	12.50	
d.		'1915' double		
197	O2 (b)	5c dk bl & blk	1.25	35
a.		Inverted overprint	9.00	
b.		Double overprint	11.00	
c.		Double overprint, one inverted	35.00	
d.		Overprinted '1915' only	12.00	
198	O2 (b)	10c yel grn & blk	3.00	2.50
a.		Inverted overprint	9.00	
199	O2 (b)	20c org & blk	10.00	8.00
a.		'Habilitado' omitted		
		Nos. 194-199 (6)	17.00	12.05

Nos. 194, 196–198 are known with both perforations. Nos. 195 and 199 are only perf. 13½x13.

The variety capital "I" for "1" in "Habilitado" occurs once in each sheet in all denominations.

A25

Type of 1911–13 Redrawn Overprinted "1915" in Red. Lithographed.

1915 ***Perf. 11½*** **Unwmkd.**

TWO CENTAVOS:

Type I. "DOS" in small letters.

Type II. "DOS" in larger letters with white dot at each end of the word.

No.	Type	Description	Unused	Used
200	A25	½c vio & blk	85	25
a.		Imperf., pair	6.00	
201	A25	1c yel brn & blk	85	12
a.		Imperf., pair	7.00	
b.		Vert. pair, imperf. horiz.	13.50	
c.		Horiz. pair, imperf. vert.	13.50	
202	A25	2c ol grn & blk (I)	3.00	35
a.		Imperf., pair	7.50	
203	A25	2c ol grn & blk (II)	6.00	25
a.		Center omitted	125.00	
b.		Frame omitted	125.00	
c.		Imperf., pair	7.50	
d.		Horiz. pair, imperf. vert.	12.50	
204	A25	5c mag & blk	3.00	35
a.		Pair, one without overprint	70.00	
b.		Imperf., pair	7.50	
205	A25	10c gray bl & blk	3.00	50
a.		Imperf., pair	9.00	
b.		Horiz. pair, imperf. vert.	50.00	
206	A25	20c rose red & blk	8.00	1.75
a.		Imperf., pair	15.00	
207	A25	50c grn & blk	9.00	4.00
a.		Imperf., pair	30.00	
208	A25	1p org & blk	17.50	8.00
a.		Imperf., pair	50.00	
		Nos. 200-208 (9)	51.20	15.57

Type of 1915 Overprinted "1916" in Red.

1916

No.	Type	Description	Unused	Used
209	A25	½c vio & blk	1.00	15
a.		Imperf., pair	30.00	
210	A25	1c grn & blk	2.00	15
a.		Imperf., pair	30.00	

Type of 1915 Overprinted "1917" in Red.

1917-19

No.	Type	Description	Unused	Used
213	A25	½c red lil & blk	1.50	40
a.		Horizontal pair, imperf. between	60.00	60.00
214	A25	1c yel grn & blk	1.50	10
215	A25	2c ol grn & blk	1.25	10
a.		Imperf., pair	40.00	
216	A25	5c mag & blk	11.00	1.00

Type of 1915 Overprinted "1919" in Red

1919

No.	Type	Description	Unused	Used
219	A25	2c ol grn & blk	6.00	15

Type of 1915 Overprinted "1920" in Red.

1920-27

No.	Type	Description	Unused	Used
220	A25	½c lil rose & blk	70	30
a.		Horizontal pair, imperf. between	35.00	35.00
b.		Inverted overprint		
c.		Double overprint		
d.		Double overprint, one inverted		
221	A25	1c yel grn & blk	70	12
a.		Overprint omitted	90.00	
222	A25	2c ol grn & blk	70	8
a.		Vertical pair, imperf. between	40.00	
223	A25	5c dp rose & blk	7.00	70
224	A25	10c bl & blk	4.00	30
225	A25	20c rose red & blk ('27)	7.00	70
226	A25	50c grn & blk ('27)	60.00	15.00
		Nos. 220-226 (7)	80.10	17.20

Type of 1915 Overprinted "1921" in Red.

1921

No.	Type	Description	Unused	Used
227	A25	1c yel grn & blk	1.75	40
a.		Horizontal pair, imperf. between	50.00	50.00
b.		Imperf., pair	50.00	50.00
228	A25	2c ol grn & blk	3.50	45

Redrawn Design of 1915 without Overprint

1922

No.	Type	Description	Unused	Used
230	A25	1c green	1.00	15
231	A25	2c car (II)	1.50	15
232	A25	5c blue	3.00	35

Arms of Dominican Republic A26 A27

Second Redrawing.

TEN CENTAVOS:

Type I. Numerals 2 mm. high. "DIEZ" in thick letters with large white dot at each end.

Type II. Numerals 3 mm. high. "DIEZ" in thin letters with white dot with colored center at each end.

1924-27

No.	Type	Description	Unused	Used
233	A26	1c green	70	10
a.		Vertical pair, imperf. between	50.00	50.00
234	A26	2c red	85	10
235	A26	5c blue	85	12
236	A26	10c pale bl & blk (I) ('26)	10.00	2.00
236A	A26	10c pale bl & blk (II)	25.00	1.00
236B	A26	50c gray grn & blk ('26)	50.00	30.00
237	A26	1p org & blk ('27)	17.50	12.50
		Nos. 233-237 (7)	104.90	45.82

In the second redrawing the shield has a flat top and the design differs in many details from the stamps of 1911–13 and 1915–22.

1927

No.	Type	Description	Unused	Used
238	A27	½c lil rose & blk	40	10

Exhibition Pavilion A28

1927 ***Perf. 12.*** **Unwmkd.**

No.	Type	Description	Unused	Used
239	A28	2c carmine	1.00	60
240	A28	5c ultra	1.25	60

Issued to commemorate the National and West Indian Exhibition at Santiago de los Caballeros.

Ruins of Columbus' Fortress A29

1928

No.	Type	Description	Unused	Used
241	A29	½c lil rose	65	35
242	A29	1c dp grn	60	15
a.		Horizontal pair, imperf. between	25.00	
243	A29	2c red	60	15
244	A29	5c dk bl	1.50	40
245	A29	10c lt bl	1.50	40
246	A29	20c rose	2.75	60
247	A29	50c yel grn	12.50	7.00
248	A29	1p org yel	22.50	15.00
		Nos. 241-248 (8)	42.60	24.05

Reprints exist of 1c, 2c and 10c.

Horacio Vasquez A30

Convent of San Ignacio de Loyola A31

1929

No.	Type	Description	Unused	Used
249	A30	½c dl rose	60	30
a.		Imperf., pair	15.00	
250	A30	1c gray grn	60	20
a.		Imperf., pair	15.00	
251	A30	2c red	70	20
a.		Imperf., pair	12.00	
252	A30	5c dk ultra	1.25	35
a.		Imperf., pair	17.50	

No.	Type	Description	Unused	Used
253	A30	10c pale bl	1.75	50
		Nos. 249-253 (5)	4.90	1.55

Issued in commemoration of the signing of the "Frontier" treaty between the Dominican Republic and Haiti.

1930, May 1 *Perf. 11½*

No.	Type	Description	Unused	Used
254	A31	½c red brn	75	60
a.		Imperf., pair	60.00	60.00
255	A31	1c dp grn	70	15
256	A31	2c vermilion	70	15
257	A31	5c dp bl	1.75	50
258	A31	10c lt bl	3.50	1.25
		Nos. 254-258 (5)	7.40	2.65

Cathedral of Santo Domingo, First Church in America
A32

1931 *Perf. 12.*

No.	Type	Description	Unused	Used
260	A32	1c dp grn	75	20
a.		Imperf., pair	65.00	
261	A32	2c scarlet	75	20
a.		Imperf., pair	65.00	
262	A32	3c violet	85	15
263	A32	7c dk bl	2.00	30
264	A32	8c bister	3.50	1.00
265	A32	10c lt bl	4.50	1.25
a.		Imperf., pair	50.00	
		Nos. 260-265 (6)	12.35	3.10

Overprinted or Surcharged in Black.

1932, Dec. 20 *Perf. 12*

Cross in Red

No.	Type	Description	Unused	Used
265B	A32a	1c yel grn	75	60
265C	A32a	3c on 2c vio	1.00	70
265D	A32a	5c blue	3.00	2.00
265E	A32a	7c on 10c turq bl	3.50	3.00

Proceeds of sale given to Red Cross. Valid Dec. 20. to Jan. 5, 1933.

Fernando Arturo de Merino As Archbishop
A33

As President
A34

Cathedral of Santo Domingo
A36

1933, Feb. 27 **Engraved** *Perf. 14*

No.	Type	Description	Unused	Used
266	A35	½c lt vio	35	35
267	A33	1c yel grn	40	20
268	A34	2c lt red	1.00	85
269	A33	3c dp vio	50	20
270	A35	5c dk bl	65	30
271	A34	7c ultra	1.35	50
272	A35	8c dk grn	1.75	1.00
273	A33	10c org yel	1.50	40
274	A34	20c car rose	3.25	2.00
275	A36	50c lemon	13.00	8.00
276	A36	1p dk brn	32.50	20.00
		Nos. 266-276 (11)	56.25	33.80

Issued in commemoration of the centenary of the birth of Fernando Arturo de Meriño (1833–1906)

Tower of Homage, Ozama Fortress
A37

1932 **Lithographed** *Perf. 12*

No.	Type	Description	Unused	Used
278	A37	1c green	50	20
279	A37	3c violet	75	10

Issue dates: 1c, July 2; 3c, June 22.

"CORREOS" added at left.

1933, May 28

No.	Type	Description	Unused	Used
283	A37	1c dk grn	60	20

President Rafael L. Trujillo
A38 A39

1933, Aug. 16 **Engraved** *Perf. 14*

No.	Type	Description	Unused	Used
286	A38	1c yel grn & blk	75	40
287	A39	3c dp vio & blk	85	25
288	A38	7c ultra & blk	2.50	85

Commemorating the 42nd anniversary of the birth of President Rafael Leonidas Trujillo Molina.

San Rafael Bridge
A40

1934 **Lithographed.** *Perf. 12.*

No.	Type	Description	Unused	Used
289	A40	½c dl vio	80	35
290	A40	1c dk grn	1.10	25
291	A40	3c violet	1.75	12

Opening of San Rafael Bridge.

Trujillo Bridge
A41

1934

No.	Type	Description	Unused	Used
292	A41	½c red brn	75	25
293	A41	1c green	1.10	12
294	A41	3c purple	1.50	15

Issued in commemoration of the opening of the General Trujillo Bridge near Ciudad Trujillo.

Ramfis Bridge
A42

1935, Apr. 6

No.	Type	Description	Unused	Used
295	A42	1c green	65	12
296	A42	3c yel brn	70	12
297	A42	5c brn vio	1.50	75
298	A42	10c rose	3.00	1.50

Issued in commemoration of the opening of the Ramfis Bridge over the Higuamo River.

President Trujillo—A43

A44

A45

1935 *Perf. 11*

No.	Type	Description	Unused	Used
299	A43	3c yel brn	45	25
300	A44	5c org red, bl, red & bis	55	15
301	A45	7c ultra, bl, red & brn	80	15
302	A44	10c red vio, bl, red & bis	1.25	15

Issued in commemoration of the ratification of a treaty setting the frontier between Dominican Republic and Haiti.

National Palace—A46

1935, Apr. 1 *Perf. 11½*

No.	Type	Description	Unused	Used
303	A46	25c yel org	3.00	25

Issued for obligatory use on all mail addressed to the president and cabinet ministers.

Post Office, Santiago
A47

1936

No.	Type	Description	Unused	Used
304	A47	½c brt vio	45	30
305	A47	1c green	45	12

Issue dates: ½c, Jan. 14; 1c, Jan. 4.

George Washington Ave., Ciudad Trujillo
A48

1936, Feb. 22

No.	Type	Description	Unused	Used
306	A48	½c brn & vio brn	50	40
a.		Imperf., pair	50.00	
307	A48	2c car & brn	50	30
308	A48	3c yel org & red brn	90	25
309	A48	7c ultra, bl & brn	1.25	75
a.		Imperf., pair	50.00	

Issued in commemoration of the dedication of George Washington Avenue, Ciudad Trujillo.

José Nuñez de Cáceres
A49

Felix M. del Monte
A55

Proposed National Library
A56

Designs: 1c, Gen. Gregorio Luperon. 2c, Emiliano Tejera. 3c, President Trujillo. 5c, Jose Reyes. 7c, Gen. Antonio Duverge. 25c, Francisco J. Peynado. 30c, Salome Urena. 50c, Gen. Jose M. Cabral. 1p, Manuel de Jesus Galvan. 2p, Gaston F. Deligne.

Engraved.

1936 *Perf. 13½, 14.* **Unwmkd.**

No.	Type	Description	Unused	Used
310	A49	½c dl vio	40	25
311	A49	1c dk grn	30	15
312	A49	2c carmine	30	20
313	A49	3c violet	35	10
314	A49	5c dp ultra	60	35
315	A49	7c sl bl	1.00	75
316	A55	10c orange	1.25	45
317	A56	20c ol grn	5.00	2.75
318	A55	25c gray vio	5.00	3.00
319	A55	30c scarlet	7.50	4.25
320	A55	50c blk brn	9.00	4.25
321	A55	1p black	22.50	20.00
322	A55	2p yel brn	60.00	55.00
		Nos. 310-322 (13)	113.20	91.50

The funds derived from the sale of these stamps were returned to the National Treasury Fund for the erection of a building for the National Library and Archives.

Issue dates: 3c, 7c, Mar. 18; others, May 22.

President Trujillo and Obelisk
A62

1937, Jan. 11 **Litho.** *Perf. 11½*

No.	Type	Description	Unused	Used
323	A62	1c green	30	10
324	A62	3c violet	60	15
325	A62	7c bl & turq bl	1.75	90

Issued in commemoration of the first anniversary of naming Ciudad Trujillo.

Discus Thrower and Flag
A63

1937, Aug. 14

Flag in Red and Blue.

326	A63	1c dk grn	10.00	1.00
327	A63	3c violet	12.50	75
328	A63	7c dk bl	22.50	4.00

Issued in commemoration of the First National Olympic Games, August 16, 1937.

Symbolical of Peace, Labor and Progress—A64

1937, Sept. 18 ***Perf. 12***

329	A64	3c purple	50	12

"8th Year of the Benefactor."

Monument to Father F. X. Billini
A65

1937, Dec. 29

330	A65	½c dp org	25	12
331	A65	5c purple	70	25

Issued in commemoration of the centenary of the birth of Father Francisco Xavier Billini (1837–1890).

Globe and Torch of Liberty
A66

1938, Feb. 22 ***Perf. 11½***

332	A66	1c green	45	10
333	A66	3c purple	70	10
334	A66	10c orange	1.25	30

Issued in commemoration of the 150th anniversary of the Constitution of the United States of America.

Pledge of Trinitarians, City Gate and National Flag
A67

1938, July 16 ***Perf. 12***

335	A67	1c grn, red & dk bl	60	30
336	A67	3c pur, red & bl	75	25
337	A67	10c org, red & bl	1.50	70

Issued in commemoration of the Trinitarians and patriots, Francisco Del Rosario Sanchez, Ramon Matias Mella and Juan Pablo Duarte, who helped free their country from foreign domination.

Seal of the University of Santo Domingo
A68

1938, Oct. 28

338	A68	½c orange	40	25
339	A68	1c dp grn & lt grn	50	15
340	A68	3c pur & pale vio	60	15
341	A68	7c dp bl & lt bl	1.25	60

Issued in commemoration of the fourth centenary of the founding of the University of Santo Domingo, on October 28, 1538.

Trylon and Perisphere, Flag and Proposed Columbus Lighthouse—A69

1939, Apr. 30 Litho. ***Perf. 12***

Flag in Blue and Red.

342	A69	½c red org & org	50	20
343	A69	1c grn & lt grn	55	20
344	A69	3c pur & pale vio	60	18
345	A69	10c org & yel	1.75	70
		Nos. 342-345, C33 (5)	5.15	2.13

New York World's Fair.

José Trujillo Valdez
A70

1939 Typographed

346	A70	½c blk & pale gray	40	25
347	A70	1c blk & yel grn	50	15
348	A70	3c blk & yel brn	60	15
349	A70	7c blk & dp ultra	1.25	75
350	A70	10c blk & brt red vio	2.25	60
		Nos. 346-350 (5)	5.00	1.90

Issued in commemoration of the fourth anniversary of the death of José Trujillo Valdez (1863–1935), father of President Trujillo Molina.

Map of the Americas and Flags of 21 American Republics
A71

Sir Rowland Hill
A72

1940, Apr. 14 Litho. ***Perf. 11½***

Flags in National Colors

351	A71	1c dp grn	40	15
352	A71	2c carmine	55	25
353	A71	3c red vio	80	10
354	A71	10c orange	1.60	30
355	A71	1p chestnut	22.50	15.00
		Nos. 351-355 (5)	25.85	15.80

Issued in commemoration of the 50th anniversary of the founding of the Pan American Union.

1940, May 6 ***Perf. 12***

356	A72	3c brt red vio & rose lil	10.00	60
357	A72	7c dk bl & lt bl	18.00	2.25

Centenary of first postage stamp.

Julia Molina Trujillo—A73

1940, May 26

358	A73	1c grn, lt grn & dk grn	45	12
359	A73	2c brt red, buff & dp rose	60	25
360	A73	3c org, dl org & brn org	75	12
361	A73	7c bl, pale bl & dk bl	1.75	65

Issued in commemoration of Mother's Day.

Map of Caribbean
A74

1940, June 6 ***Perf. 11½***

362	A74	3c brt car & pale rose	60	15
363	A74	7c dk bl & lt bl	1.25	25
364	A74	1p yel grn & pale grn	12.50	6.50

Issued in commemoration of the second Inter-American Caribbean Conference held at Ciudad Trujillo, May 31 to June 6.

Marion Military Hospital
A75

1940, Dec. 24

365	A75	½c chnt & fawn	40	30

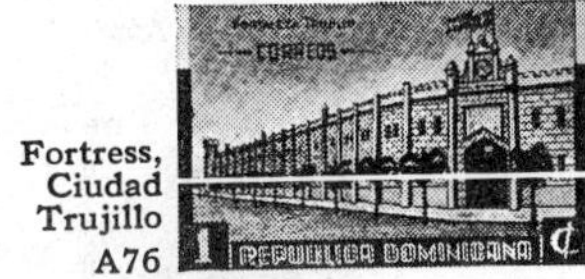

Fortress, Ciudad Trujillo
A76

Statue of Columbus, Ciudad Trujillo
A77

1941

366	A76	1c dk grn & lt grn	20	8
367	A77	2c brt red & rose	25	12
368	A77	10c org brn & buff	85	15

Issue dates: 1c, Mar. 27; others, Apr. 7.

Sánchez, Duarte, Mella and Trujillo—A78

1941, May 16

369	A78	3c brt red lil & red vio	35	12
370	A78	4c brt red, crim & pale rose	45	15
371	A78	13c dk bl & lt bl	1.00	30
372	A78	15c org brn & buff	3.00	1.25
373	A78	17c lt bl, bl & pale bl	3.00	1.35
374	A78	1p org, yel brn & pale org	11.00	5.00
375	A78	2p lt gray & pale gray	22.50	11.00
		Nos. 369-375 (7)	41.30	19.17

Issued in commemoration of the Trujillo-Hull Treaty signed September 24, 1940 and effective April 1, 1941.

Bastion of February
A79

1941, Oct. 20

376	A79	5c brt bl & lt bl	80	30

School, Torch of Knowledge, Pres. Trujillo—A80

1941

377	A80	½c chnt & fawn	30	12
378	A80	1c dk grn & lt grn	40	15

Education campaign.
Issue dates: ½c, Dec. 12, 1c, Dec. 2.

Reserve Bank of Dominican Republic
A81

1942 **Unwmkd.**

379	A81	5c lt brn & buff	60	15
380	A81	17c dp bl & lt bl	1.50	60

Issued to commemorate the founding of the Reserve Bank, October 24, 1941.

Representation of Transportation
A82

1942, Aug. 15

381	A82	3c dk brn, grn yel & lt bl	70	10
382	A82	15c pur, grn, yel & lt bl	1.75	60

Issued in commemoration of the 8th anniversary of the Day of Posts and Telegraph.

Virgin of Altagracia
A83

1942, Aug. 15

383	A83	½c gray & pale gray	1.25	15
384	A83	1c dp grn & lt grn	2.50	10
385	A83	3c brt red lil & lil	11.00	10
386	A83	5c dk vio brn & vio brn	3.50	15
387	A83	10c rose pink & pink	10.00	40
388	A83	15c dp bl & lt bl	11.00	50
		Nos. 383-388 (6)	39.25	1.40

Issued to commemorate the 20th anniversary of the coronation of Our Lady of Altagracia.

Bananas
A84

Cows
A85

1942-43

389	A84	3c dk brn & grn ('43)	70	15
390	A84	4c ver & blk ('43)	75	30
391	A85	5c dp bl & cop brn	65	15
392	A85	15c dk pur & bl grn	1.25	55

Emblems of Dominican and Trujillista Parties
A86

1943, Jan.

393	A86	3c orange	55	10
394	A86	4c dk red	75	20
395	A86	13c brt red lil	1.60	30
396	A86	1p lt bl	7.50	2.75

Issued in commemoration of the reelection of President Rafael Trujillo Molina, May 16, 1942.

Model Market, Ciudad Trujillo
A87

1944

397	A87	2c dk brn & buff	25	15

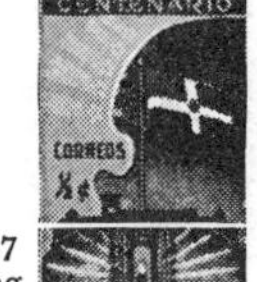

Bastion of Feb. 27 and National Flag
A88

1944, Feb. 27 **Unwmkd.**

Flag in Dark Blue and Carmine.

398	A88	½c ocher	12	10
399	A88	1c yel grn	12	8
400	A88	2c scarlet	20	12
401	A88	3c brt red vio	25	10
402	A88	5c yel org	30	15
403	A88	7c brt bl	40	30
404	A88	10c org brn	60	45
405	A88	20c ol grn	1.00	70
406	A88	50c lt bl	3.00	2.00
		Nos. 398-406, C46-C48 (12)	10.84	6.82

Souvenir Sheet.

Imperf.

407		Sheet of 12, multi	150.00	150.00
a.		Single stamp	5.00	5.00

Centenary of Independence.

No. 407 contains one each of Nos. 398-406, C46-C48 with simulated perforations. Inscribed in brown: "Serie Conmemorativa del Centenario de la Republica 27 de Febrero." Size: 141x205mm.

Battlefield and Nurse with Child
A90

1944, Aug. 1

408	A90	1c dk bl grn, buff & car	25	10
a.		Vertical pair, imperf. between	15.00	
b.		Horiz. pair, imperf. vert.	15.00	
409	A90	2c dk brn, buff & car	50	15
410	A90	3c brt bl, buff & car	50	10
411	A90	10c rose car, buff & car	1.00	25

Issued to honor the 80th anniversary of the International Red Cross.

Municipal Building, San Cristóbal
A91

Emblem of Communications
A92

Lithographed.

1945, Jan. 10 ***Perf. 12*** **Unwmkd.**

412	A91	½c bl & lt bl	10	10
413	A91	1c dk grn & grn	15	8
414	A91	2c red org & org	15	10
415	A91	3c dk brn & brn	20	12
416	A91	10c ultra & gray bl	70	20
		Nos. 412-416 (5)	1.30	60

Centenary of the constitution.

1945, Sept. 1

Center in Dark Blue and Carmine.

417	A92	3c orange	20	8
418	A92	20c yel grn	1.20	30
419	A92	50c lt bl	2.50	90
		Nos. 417-419, C53-C56 (7)	5.90	2.38

Palace of Justice, Ciudad Trujillo
A93

1946 ***Perf. 11½.***

420	A93	3c dk red brn & buff	30	10

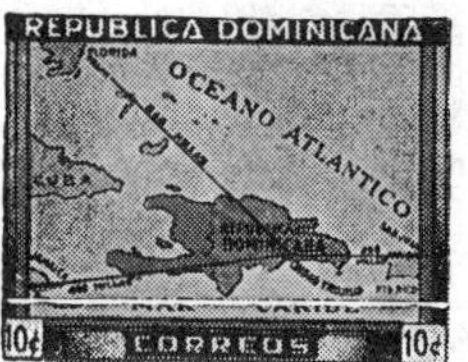

Map of Hispaniola
A94

1946, Aug. 4 ***Perf. 12***

421	A94	10c rose brn, yel, lil, bl, red & grn	60	25

Issued to commemorate the 450th anniversary of the founding of Santo Domingo. See also Nos. C62-C63.

Waterfall of Jimenoa—A95

1946-47

Center Multicolored

422	A95	1c yel grn ('47)	20	8
423	A95	2c car ('47)	20	10
424	A95	3c dp bl	25	8
425	A95	13c red vio ('47)	70	40
426	A95	20c choc ('47)	1.50	40
427	A95	50c org ('47)	2.75	1.50
		Nos. 422-427, C64-C67 (10)	10.85	6.36

Executive Palace
A96

1948, Feb. 27

428	A96	1c yel grn	12	8
429	A96	3c dp bl	18	8

See also Nos. C68-C69.

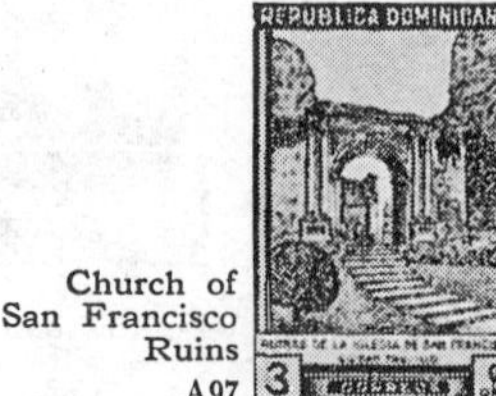

Church of San Francisco Ruins
A97

1949, Apr. 13 ***Perf. 11½***

430	A97	1c dk grn & pale grn	15	6
431	A97	3c dp bl & pale bl	20	8
		Nos. 430-431, C70-C73 (6)	2.55	1.46

Gen. Pedro Santana
A98

Pigeon and Globe
A99

1949, Aug. 10

432	A98	3c dp bl & bl	25	10

Issued to commemorate the centenary of the Battle of Las Carreras. See No. C74.

1949, Sept. 15

Center and Inscriptions in Brown.

433	A99	1c grn & pale grn	18	12
434	A99	2c yel grn & yel	22	8
435	A99	5c bl & pale bl	30	10
436	A99	7c dk vio bl & pale bl	65	25

Issued to commemorate the 75th anniversary of the formation of the Universal Postal Union.

Hotel Jimani—A100

Hotels: 1c, 2c, Hamaca. 5c, Montana. 15c, San Cristobal. 20c, Maguana.

1950-52

437	A100	½c org brn & buff	10	8
438	A100	1c dp grn & grn ('51)	15	8
439	A100	2c red org & sal ('52)	15	8
440	A100	5c bl & lt bl	30	8
441	A100	15c dp org & yel	65	12
442	A100	20c lil & rose lil	1.25	20
443	A100	1p choc & yel	5.00	2.00
		Nos. 437-443, C75-C76 (9)	10.75	5.01

The ½c, 15c and 20c exist imperf.

Ruins of Church and Hospital of San Nicolas de Bari
A101

School of Medicine
A102

Queen Isabella I
A103

1950, Oct. 2

444 A101 2c dk grn & rose brn 30 10
445 A102 5c vio bl & org brn 40 12

18th Pan-American Health Conference. Exist imperf. See No. C77.

1951, Oct. 12

446 A103 5c dk bl & red brn 35 15

500th anniversary of the birth of Queen Isabella I of Spain. Exists imperf.

Dr. Salvador B. Gautier Hospital A104

1952, Aug.

447 A104 1c dk grn 12 6
448 A104 2c red 18 6
449 A104 5c vio bl 35 10
Nos. 447-449, C78-C79 (5) 3.50 2.52

Columbus Lighthouse and Flags of 21 Republics A105

1953, Jan. 6 Engraved *Perf. 13*

450 A105 2c dk grn 20 6
451 A105 5c dp bl 30 8
452 A105 10c dp car 50 30
Nos. 450-452, C80-C86 (10) 9.15 6.69

Miniature sheet containing Nos. 450–452 and C80–C86 is listed as No. C86a.

Treasury Building, Ciudad Trujillo A106

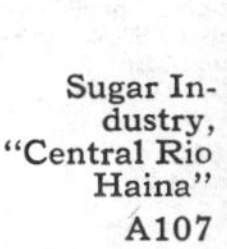

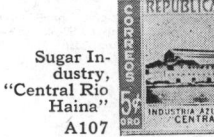

Sugar Industry, "Central Rio Haina" A107

1953 Lithographed. *Perf. 11½.*

453 A106 ½c brown 8 6
454 A106 2c dk bl 10 8
455 A107 5c bl & vio brn 20 8
456 A106 15c orange 75 25

José Marti A108

Monument to the Peace of Trujillo A109

1954 *Perf. 12½.*

457 A108 10c dp bl & dk brn 45 18

Centenary of the birth of José Marti (1853–1895), Cuban patriot.

1954, May 25

458 A109 2c green 8 6
459 A109 7c blue 25 8
460 A109 20c orange 80 15

See also No. 493.

Rotary Emblem A110

1955, Feb. 23 *Perf. 12*

461 A110 7c dp bl 60 25

50th anniversary, Rotary International. See No. C90.

Gen. Rafael L. Trujillo A111

Designs: 4c, Trujillo in civilian clothes. 7c, Trujillo statue. 10c, Symbols of culture and prosperity.

1955, May 16 Engr. *Perf. 13½x13*

462 A111 2c red 10 6
463 A111 4c lt ol grn 15 8
464 A111 7c indigo 25 12
465 A111 10c brown 50 20
Nos. 462-465, C91-C93 (7) 3.15 1.58

25th anniversary of the Trujillo era.

General Rafael L. Trujillo A112

Angelita Trujillo A113

1955, Dec. 20 *Perf. 13* Unwmkd.

466 A112 7c dp cl 35 12
467 A112 10c dk bl 55 18

See also No. C94.

1955, Dec. 20 Litho. *Perf. 12½*

468 A113 10c bl & ultra 55 18

Nos. 466–468 were issued to publicize the International Fair of Peace and Brotherhood in Ciudad Trujillo, Dec. 1955.

Airport A114

1956, Apr. 6 *Perf. 12½*

469 A114 1c brown 12 8
470 A114 2c red org 18 8

Issued to commemorate the third Caribbean conference of the International Civil Aviation Organization. See No. C95.

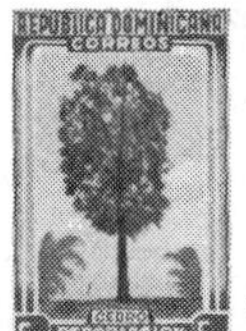

Cedar A115

See also No. 493.

1956, Dec. 8 *Perf. 11½x12*

471 A115 5c car rose & grn 30 10
472 A115 6c red vio & grn 35 15

Issued to publicize the reforestation program. See No. C96.

Fair Emblem A116

Fanny Blankers-Koen, Netherlands A117

1957, Jan. 10 *Perf. 12½*

473 A116 7c bl, lt brn & ver 35 15

Issued to publicize the 2nd International Livestock Show, Ciudad Trujillo, Jan. 10–20, 1957. Exists imperf.

Engraved & Lithographed

1957, Jan. 24 *Perf. 11½*

Olympic Winners and Flags: 2c, Jesse Owens, United States. 3c, Kee Chung Sohn, Japan. 5c, Lord Burghley, England. 7c, Bob Mathias, United States.

Flags in National Colors.

474 A117 1c brn, lt bl, vio & mar 10 10
475 A117 2c dk brn, lt bl & vio 15 15
476 A117 3c red lil & red 25 20
477 A117 5c red org & vio 35 25
478 A117 7c grn & vio 50 35
Nos. 474-478, C97-C99 (8) 2.70 2.40

To commemorate the 16th Olympic Games, Melbourne, Nov. 22–Dec. 8, 1956. Exist imperf.

Miniature sheets of 5 exist, perf. and imperf., containing one each of Nos. 474–478. Sheets measure 169 x 86 mm. and have no marginal inscriptions. Price, 2 sheets, perf. and imperf., $6.

Lars Hall, Sweden, Pentathlon A118

Olympic Winners and Flags: 2c, Betty Cuthbert, Australia, 100 & 200 meter dash. 3c, Egil Danielsen, Norway, javelin. 5c, Alain Mimoun, France, marathon. 7c, Norman Read, New Zealand, 50 km. walk.

Perf. 13½

1957, July 18 Photo. Unwmkd.

Flags in National Colors.

479 A118 1c brn & brt bl 10 8
480 A118 2c org ver & dk bl 10 10
481 A118 3c dk bl 15 12
482 A118 5c ol & dk bl 25 18
483 A118 7c rose brn & dk bl 40 25
Nos. 479-483, C100-C102 (8) 2.15 1.88

Issued in honor of the 1956 Olympic winners. Exist imperf.

Miniature sheets of 8 exist, perf. and imperf., containing one each of Nos. 479–483 and C100–C102. The center label in these sheets is printed in two forms: Olympic gold medal or Olympic flag. Sheets measure 140x140mm. Price, 4 sheets, perf. and imperf., medal and flag, $18.

A third set of similar miniature sheets (perf. and imperf.) with center label showing an incorrect version of the Dominican Republic flag (colors transposed) was printed. These sheets are said to have been briefly sold on the first day, then withdrawn as the misprint was discovered.

Price, 2 sheets, perf. & imperf., $125.

Gerald Ouellette, Canada, Small Bore Rifle, Prone—A119

Ron Delaney, Ireland, 1,500 Meter Run—A120

Olympic Winners and Flags: 3c, Tenley Albright, United States, figure skating. 5c, Joaquin Capilla, Mexico, platform diving. 7c, Ercole Baldini, Italy, individual road race (cycling).

Engraved and Lithographed

1957, Nov. 12 *Perf. 13½*

Flags in National Colors

484 A119 1c red brn 10 10
485 A120 2c gray brn 10 12
486 A119 3c violet 15 15
487 A120 5c red org 25 18
488 A119 7c Prus grn 30 30
Nos. 484-488, C103-C105 (8) 2.15 2.05

Issued in honor of the 1956 Olympic winners. Exist imperf.

Miniature sheets of 5 exist, perf. and imperf., containing one each of Nos. 484–488. Sheets have no marginal inscriptions. Price, 2 sheets, perf. and imperf., $5.50.

Mahogany Flower A121

1957-58 Lithographed *Perf. 12½*

489 A121 2c grn & mar 12 8

Perf. 12

490 A121 4c lil & rose ('58) 18 12
491 A121 7c ultra & gray grn 35 12
492 A121 25c brn & org ('58) 85 35

Sizes: No. 489, 25x29¼mm.; Nos. 490–492, 24x28¾mm. In 1959, the 2c was reissued in size 24¼x28½mm. with slightly different tones of green and maroon.

Issue dates: 2c, Oct. 24; 7c, Nov. 6; 4c and 25c, Apr. 7, 1958.

Type of 1954, Redrawn

Perf. 12x11½

1957, June 12 **Unwmkd.**

493 A109 7c brt bl 50 18

On No. 493 the "$" is smaller, the shading of the sky and steps stronger and the letters in "Correos" shorter and bolder.

Cervantes, Globe and Book
A122

1958, Apr. 23 Litho. ***Perf. 12½***

494 A122 4c yel grn 15 6
495 A122 7c red lil 20 10
496 A122 10c lt ol brn 35 15

Fourth Book Fair, Apr. 23-28. Exist imperf.

Gen. Rafael L. Trujillo
A123

1958, Aug. 16 ***Perf. 12***

497 A123 2c red lil & yel 6 6
498 A123 4c grn & yel 15 8
499 A123 7c brn & yel 25 12
a. Souv. sheet of 3 90 75

Issued to commemorate the 25th anniversary of Gen. Trujillo's designation as "Benefactor of his country."

No. 499a measures 152x101mm and contains one each of Nos. 497-499, imperf. Brown marginal inscription.

S. S. Rhadames
A124

1958, Oct. 27 ***Perf. 12½***

500 A124 7c brt bl 40 18

Day of the Dominican Merchant Marine. Exists imperf.

Shozo Sasahara, Japan, Featherweight Wrestling
A125

Olympic Winners and Flags: 1c, Gillian Sheen, England, fencing (vert.). 2c, Milton Campbell, United States, decathlon (vert.). 5c, Madeleine Berthod, Switzerland, downhill skiing. 7c, Murray Rose, Australia, 400 & 1,500 meter freestyle.

1958, Oct. 30 Photo. ***Perf. 13½***

Flags in National Colors

501 A125 1c rose, ind & ultra 10 10
502 A125 2c brn & bl 10 10
503 A125 3c gray, vio, blk & buff 20 22
504 A125 5c rose, dk bl, brn & red 30 28
505 A125 7c lt brn, dk bl & red 35 30
Nos. 501-505, C106-C108 (8) 2.35 2.30

To honor 1956 Olympic winners. Exist imperf.

Miniature sheets of 5 exist, perf. and imperf. containing one each of Nos. 501-505. Size: 140x119½mm. Price, 2 sheets, perf. and imperf., $3.

Globe and Symbolic Fire
A126

1958, Nov. 3 Litho. ***Perf. 11½***

506 A126 7c bl & dp car 25 15

Issued to commemorate the opening of UNESCO (U. N. Educational, Scientific and Cultural Organization) Headquarters in Paris, Nov. 3.

Dominican Republic Pavilion, Brussels Fair
A127

1958, Dec. 9 ***Perf. 12½*** **Unwmkd.**

507 A127 7c bl grn 30 15

Issued for the Universal and International Exposition at Brussels. See Nos. C109-C110a.

Gen. Trujillo Placing Wreath on Altar of the Nation
A128

1959, July 10 ***Perf. 12***

508 A128 9c brn, grn, red & gold 30 15
a. Souv. sheet 60 60

Issued to commemorate the 29th anniversary of the Trujillo regime.

No. 508a contains one 9c, imperf. Size: 141x90mm.

Lt. Leonidas Rhadames Trujillo, Team Captain
A129

Jamaican Polo Team
A130

Design: 10c, Lt. Trujillo on polo pony.

1959, May 15

509 A129 2c violet 18 12
510 A130 7c yel brn 45 25
511 A130 10c green 50 35

Jamaica-Dominican Republic polo match at Ciudad Trujillo.

See also No. C111.

Symbolical of Census
A131

1959, Aug. 15 Litho. ***Perf. 12½***

Flag in Ultramarine and Red.

512 A131 1c bl & blk 12 10
513 A131 9c grn & blk 30 25
514 A131 13c org & blk 50 35

Issued to publicize the 1960 census.

Trujillo Stadium
A132

1959, Aug. 27

515 A132 9c grn & gray 50 30

Issued to publicize the 3rd Pan American Games Chicago, Aug. 27-Sept. 7.

Charles V
A133

1959, Oct. 12 ***Perf. 12*** **Unwmkd.**

516 A133 5c brt pink 20 10
517 A133 9c vio bl 30 15

Issued to commemorate the 400th anniversary of the death of Charles V (1500-1558), Holy Roman Emperor.

Rhadames Bridge
A134

Designs: 1c and No. 520, Different view of bridge.

1959-60 Lithographed. ***Perf. 12***

518 A134 1c grn & gray ('60) 12 10
519 A134 2c ultra & gray 20 12
520 A134 2c red & gray ('60) 20 10
521 A134 5c brn & dl red brn 30 18

Issue dates: No. 519, Oct. 22; 5c, Nov. 30; 1c and No. 520, Feb. 6, 1960.

Sosua Refugee Settlement and WRY Emblem—A135

1960, Apr. 7 ***Perf. 12½***

Center in Gray

522 A135 5c red brn & yel grn 15 10
523 A135 9c car & lt bl 30 15
524 A135 13c org & grn 40 25
Nos. 522-524, C113-C114 (5) 2.05 1.50

Issued to publicize World Refugee Year, July 1, 1959-June 30, 1960.

Sholam Takhti, Iran, Lightweight Wrestling—A136

Olympic Winners: 2c, Mauru Furukawa, Japan, 200 meter breast stroke. 3c, Mildred McDaniel, U.S.A., high jump. 5c, Terence Spinks, England, featherweight boxing. 7c, Carlo Pavesi, Italy, fencing.

Perf. 13½

1960, Sept. 14 Photo. **Unwmkd.**

Flags in National Colors

525 A136 1c red, yel grn & blk 6 8
526 A136 2c org, grnsh bl & brn 10 12
527 A136 3c hn brn & bl 12 14
528 A136 5c brn & ultra 20 18
529 A136 7c grn, bl & rose brn 20 22
Nos. 525-529, C115-C117 (8) 1.83 1.89

Issued to commemorate the 17th Olympic Games, Rome, Aug. 25-Sept. 11. Exist imperf.

Miniature sheets of 5 exist, perf. and imperf., containing one each of Nos. 525-529, and a Dominican Republic flag in national colors. Sheet size: 160x121mm.

Price, 2 sheets, perf. & imperf., $4.

Post Office, Ciudad Trujillo
A137

1960, Aug. 26 Litho. ***Perf. 11½x12***

530 A137 2c ultra & gray 15 10

Exists imperf.

REPUBLICA DOMINICANA
9¢
CORREOS
FERIA AGROPECUARIA E INDUSTRIAL SAN JUAN DE LA MAGUANA

Cattle—A138

1960, Aug. 30

531 A138 9c car & gray 35 18

Issued to publicize the Agricultural and Industrial Fair, San Juan de la Maguana.

Nos. 518, 490-491, 453, 427 Surcharged in Red, Black or Blue

HABILITADO PARA 2¢

1960-61 ***Perf. 12***

536 A134 2c on 1c grn & gray (R) 20 10
537 A121 9c on 4c lil & rose 70 15
a. Inverted surcharge 35.00
538 A121 9c on 7c ultra & gray grn (R) ('61) 70 20
539 A106 36c on ½c brn ('61) 2.25 1.00
a. Inverted surcharge 30.00
540 A95 1p on 50c multi (Bl) ('61) 5.00 2.75
Nos. 536-540 (5) 8.85 4.20

Trujillo Memorial
A139

Coffee and Cacao
A140

1961 ***Perf. 11½*** **Unwmkd.**

548 A139 1c brown 12 5
549 A139 2c green 15 5
550 A139 4c rose lil 60 50
551 A139 5c lt bl 35 12
552 A139 9c red org 45 30
Nos. 548-552 (5) 1.67 1.02

Issued in memory of Gen. Rafael L. Trujillo (1891-1961).

1961, Dec. 30 **Litho.** ***Perf. 12½***

553 A140 1c bl grn 5 5
554 A140 2c org brn 8 5
555 A140 4c violet 15 8
556 A140 5c blue 15 8
557 A140 9c gray 35 8
Nos. 553-557, C118-C119 (7) 2.03 1.59

Exist imperf.

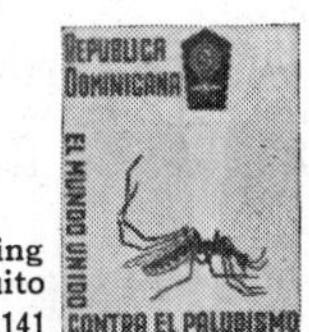

Dagger Pointing at Mosquito
A141

1962, Apr. 29 **Photo.** ***Perf. 12***

558 A141 10c brt pink & red lil 25 18
559 A141 20c pale brn & brn 50 45
560 A141 25c pale grn & yel grn 65 50
Nos. 558-560, B39-B40, C120-C121, CB24-CB25 (9) 4.60 4.13

Issued for the World Health Organization drive to eradicate malaria.

Broken Fetters and Laurel
A142

"Justice" and Map of Dominican Republic
A143

Farm, Factory and Flag
A144

Design: 20c, Flag, torch and inscription.

1962, May 30 **Litho.** ***Perf. 12½***

561 A142 1c grn, yel, ultra & red 12 8
562 A143 9c bis ultra & red 40 18
563 A142 20c lt bl, ultra & red 70 35
a. Souv. sheet of 3 1.75 1.75
564 A143 1p lil, ultra & red 4.00 2.50
Nos. 561-564, C122-C123 (6) 7.12 4.41

First anniversary of end of Trujillo era. Exist imperf.

No. 563a contains one each of Nos. 561-563, imperf. with ultramarine inscription on pink background. Size: 154x91mm.

1962, May 22

565 A144 1c ultra, red & grn 5 4
566 A144 2c ultra & red 10 5
567 A144 3c ultra, red & brn 12 6
568 A144 5c ultra, red & bl 20 8
569 A144 15c ultra, red & org 40 20
Nos. 565-569 (5) 87 43

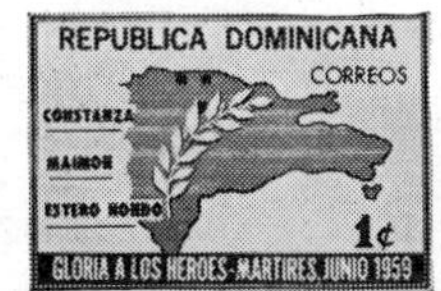

Map and Laurel
A145

1962, June 14 **Lithographed**

570 A145 1c black 35 20

Issued to honor the martyrs of June 1959 revolution.

Western Hemisphere and Carrier Pigeon
A146

Archbishop Adolfo Alejandro Nouel
A147

1962, Oct. 23 ***Perf. 12½*** **Unwmkd.**

571 A146 2c rose red 12 6
572 A146 9c orange 35 18
573 A146 14c bl grn 40 30
Nos. 571-573, C124-C125 (5) 2.07 1.44

Issued to commemorate the 50th anniversary of the founding of the Postal Union of the Americas and Spain, UPAE.

1962, Dec. 18

574 A147 2c bl grn & dl bl 8 5
575 A147 9c org & red brn 35 18
576 A147 13c mar & vio brn 45 30
Nos. 574-576, C126-C127 (5) 2.13 1.48

Issued to commemorate the centenary of the birth of Archbishop Adolfo Alejandro Nouel, President of Dominican Republic in 1911.

Globe, Banner and Emblems
A148

1963, Apr. 15 ***Perf. 11½*** **Unwmkd.**

Banner in Dark Blue & Red

577 A148 2c green 10 5
578 A148 5c brt rose lil 25 10
579 A148 9c orange 40 18
Nos. 577-579, B41-B43 (6) 1.29 84

Issued for the "Freedom from Hunger" campaign of the U.N. Food and Agriculture Organization.

Juan Pablo Duarte
A149

Designs: 7c, Francisco Sanchez. 9c, Ramon Mella.

1963, July 7 **Litho.** ***Perf. 12x11½***

580 A149 2c ultra 6 5
581 A149 7c dl grn 18 18
582 A149 9c red lil 25 20

Issued to commemorate the 120th anniversary of separation from Haiti. See also No. C128.

Ulises F. Espaillat, Benigno F. de Rojas and Pedro F. Bono
A150

Designs: 4c, Generals Santiago Rodriguez, José Cabrera and Benito Moncion. 5c, Capotillo monument. 9c, Generals Gaspar Polanco, Gregorio Luperon and José A. Salcedo.

1963, Aug. 16 ***Perf. 11½*** **Unwmkd.**

583 A150 2c green 8 5
584 A150 4c red org 12 10
585 A150 5c brown 15 12
586 A150 9c brt bl 25 20
a. Souv. sheet of 4 1.50 1.50

Issued to commemorate the centenary of the Restoration. No. 586a contains 4 imperf. stamps similar to Nos. 583-586. Brown marginal inscription. Size: 229x 106½mm.

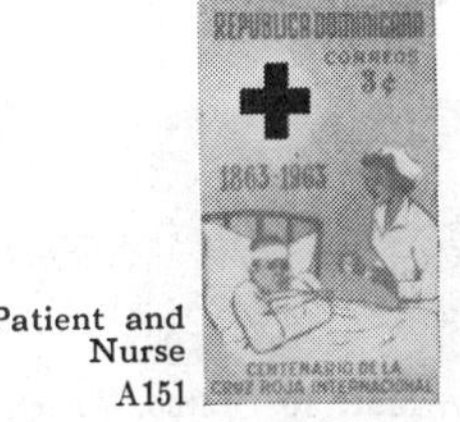

Patient and Nurse
A151

1963, Oct. 25 ***Perf. 12½*** **Unwmkd.**

587 A151 3c gray & car 12 12
588 A151 6c emer & red 25 15

Centenary of International Red Cross. Exist imperf. See No. C129.

Scales, Globe and UNESCO Emblem
A152

1963, Dec. 10 **Lithographed**

589 A152 6c pink & dp pink 18 12
590 A152 50c lt grn & grn 1.10 85

Universal Declaration of Human Rights, 15th anniversary. Exist imperf. See also Nos. C130-C131.

Ramses II Battling the Hittites (from Abu Simbel)—A153

Design: 6c, Two heads of Ramses II.

1964, March 8 ***Perf. 12½*** **Unwmkd.**

591 A153 3c pale pink & ver 10 8
592 A153 6c pale bl & ultra 20 15
593 A153 9c pale rose & red brn 30 20
Nos 591-593, C132-C133 (5) 1.35 1.03

Issued to publicize the UNESCO world campaign to save historic monuments in Nubia.

Maximo Gomez
A154

Palm Chat
A155

1964, Apr. 30 **Lithographed**

594 A154 2c lt bl & bl 6 6
595 A154 6c dl pink & dl cl 18 12

Issued to commemorate the bicentenary of the founding of the town of Bani.

1964, June 8 ***Perf. 12½*** **Unwmkd.**

Design: 6c, Hispaniolan parrot.

Size: 27x37½mm.

596 A155 3c ultra, brn & yel 15 12
597 A155 6c gray & multi 30 18

See also Nos. 602-604, C134.

Rocket Leaving Earth
A156

Designs: 1c, Launching of rocket (vert.). 3c, Space capsule orbiting earth. 6c, As 2c.

1964, July 28 **Lithographed**

598 A156 1c sky bl 10 8
599 A156 2c emerald 15 10
600 A156 3c blue 20 15
601 A156 6c sky bl 35 18
Nos. 598-601, C135-C136 (6) 1.70 1.11

Issued to commemorate the conquest of space.

Bird Type of 1964

Designs: 1c, Narrow-billed tody. 2c, Hispaniolan emerald hummingbird. 6c, Hispaniolan trogon.

1964, Nov. 7 *Perf. 11½*

Size: 26x37mm.

Birds in Natural Colors

602	A155	1c brt pink	10	9
603	A155	2c dk brn	12	9
604	A155	6c blue	25	18

Universal Postal Union and United Nations Emblems
A157

1964, Dec. 5 Litho. *Perf. 12½*

605	A157	1c red	7	5
606	A157	4c green	18	10
607	A157	5c orange	20	12

Issued to commemorate the 15th Universal Postal Union Congress, Vienna, Austria, May–June 1964. See also No. C138.

International Cooperation Year Emblem—A158

1965, Feb. 16 *Perf. 12½* **Unwmkd.**

608	A158	2c lt bl & ultra	6	5
609	A158	3c emer & dk grn	8	6
610	A158	6c sal pink & red	18	10

Issued to publicize the United Nations International Cooperation Year. See No. C139.

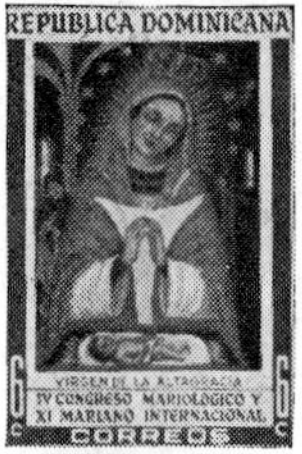

Virgin of Altagracia A159 — Flags of 21 American Nations A160

Design: 2c, Hands holding lily.

1965, Mar. 18 *Perf. 12½* **Unwmkd.**

611	A159	2c grn, emer & dp rose	12	8
612	A159	6c multi	50	40

Issued to commemorate the Fourth Mariological Congress and the Eleventh International Marian Congress. No. 612 exists imperf. See No. C140.

1965, Apr. 14 Litho. *Perf. 11½*

613	A160	2c brn, yel & multi	6	5
614	A160	6c red lil & multi	18	12

Organization of American States.

Stamp of 1865 (No. 1)
A161

1965, Dec. 28 Litho. *Perf. 12½*

615	A161	1c pink, buff & blk	8	6
616	A161	2c bl, buff & blk	10	7
617	A161	6c emer, buff & blk	20	15
a.		Souv. sheet of 2	1.75	1.75
		Nos. 615-617, C142-C143 (5)	1.13	93

Issued to commemorate the centenary of the first Dominican postage stamps. No. 617a shows replicas of Nos. 1–2. Bright blue marginal inscription. Size: 100x65 mm. Sold for 50c.

WHO Headquarters, Geneva
A162

1966, May 21 Litho. *Perf. 12½*

618	A162	6c blue	18	10
619	A162	10c red lil	30	18

Issued to commemorate the inauguration of World Health Organization Headquarters, Geneva.

Man Holding Map of Republic
A163

1966, May 23

620	A163	2c blk & brt grn	6	4
621	A163	6c blk & dp org	18	10

Issued to publicize the general elections, June 1, 1966.

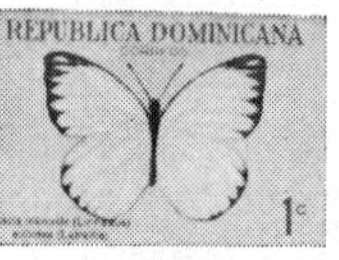

Ascia Monuste A164 — National Altar A165

1966 Lithographed *Perf. 12½*

Various Butterflies in Natural Colors

Size: 31x21mm.

622	A164	1c bl & vio bl	6	6
623	A164	2c lt grn & brt grn	10	10
624	A164	3c lt gray & gray	15	15
625	A164	6c pink & mag	25	25
626	A164	8c buff & brn	40	40
		Nos. 622-626, C146-C148 (8)	6.46	4.26

Issue dates: 1c, Sept. 7; 3c, Sept. 11; others, Nov. 8.

1967, Jan. 18 Litho. *Perf. 11½*

627	A165	1c brt bl	3	3
628	A165	2c car rose	4	4
629	A165	3c emerald	6	5
630	A165	4c gray	8	6
631	A165	5c org yel	10	8
632	A165	6c orange	12	10
		Nos. 627-632, C149-C151 (9)	1.33	1.06

Map of Republic and Emblem
A166

1967, Mar. 30 Litho. *Perf. 12½*

633	A166	2c yel, bl & blk	7	5
634	A166	6c org, bl & blk	20	10
635	A166	10c emer, bl & blk	35	18

Development Year, 1967.

Rook and Knight
A167

1967, June 23 Litho. *Perf. 12½*

636	A167	25c multi	80	60

Issued to commemorate the 5th Central American Chess Championships, Santo Domingo. See also Nos. C152–C152a.

Alliance for Progress A168 — Institute Emblem A169

1967, Sept. 16 Litho. *Perf. 12½*

637	A168	1c brt grn	4	4

Issued to commemorate the 6th anniversary of the Alliance for Progress. See Nos. C153–C154.

1967, Oct. 7

638	A169	3c brt grn	9	7
639	A169	6c sal pink	18	12

Issued to commemorate the 25th anniversary of the Inter-American Agriculture Institute. See also No. C155.

Globe and Satellite
A170

1968, June 15 Typo. *Perf. 12*

640	A170	6c blk & multi	30	25

Issued to commemorate World Meteorological Day, Mar. 23. See Nos. C156–C157.

Boxers
A171

1968, June 29

641	A171	6c rose red & dp cl	25	20

Issued to commemorate the fight between Carlos Ortiz, Puerto Rico, and Teo Cruz, Dominican Republic, for the World Lightweight Boxing Championship. See Nos. C158–C159.

Lions Emblem
A172

1968, Aug. 9 Litho. *Perf. 11½*

642	A172	6c brn & multi	20	12

Issued to commemorate the 50th anniversary (in 1967) of Lions International. See No. C160.

Wrestling and Olympic Emblem
A173

Designs (Olympic Emblem and): 6c, Running. 25c, Boxing.

1968, Nov. 12 Litho. *Perf. 11½*

643	A173	1c sky bl & multi	10	8
644	A173	6c pale grn & multi	25	15
645	A173	25c pale lil & multi	1.00	55
		Nos. 643-645, C161-C162 (5)	2.80	2.13

Issued to commemorate the 19th Olympic Games, Mexico City, Oct. 12–27.

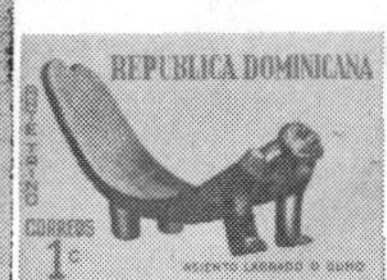

Map of Americas and House A174 — Stool in Human Form A175

1969, Jan. 25 Litho. *Perf. 12½*

646	A174	6c brt bl, lt bl & grn	20	12

Issued to publicize the 7th Inter-American Conference for Savings and Loans, Santo Domingo, Jan. 25–31. See No. C163.

1969, Jan. 31 Litho. *Perf. 12½*

Taino Art: 2c, Wood carved mother figure (vert.). 3c, Face carved on 3-cornered stone. 4c, Stone hatchet (vert.). 5c, Clay pot.

647	A175	1c yel, org & blk	6	5
648	A175	2c lt grn, grn & blk	8	6
649	A175	3c cit, ol & brt grn	12	10
650	A175	4c lt lil, lil & brt grn	18	15
651	A175	5c yel, org & brn	20	18
		Nos. 647-651, C164-C166 (8)	1.69	1.21

Taino art flourished in the West Indies at the time of Columbus.

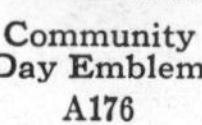

Community Day Emblem A176 — COTAL Emblem A177

Headquarters Building and COTAL Emblem
A178

1969, Mar. 25 Litho. *Perf. 12½*

652	A176	6c dl grn & gold	20	10

Issued for Community Development Day, March 22.

1969, May 25 Litho. *Perf. 12½*

Design: 2c, Boy and COTAL emblem.

653	A177	1c lt & dk bl & red	3	3
654	A177	2c emer & dk grn	6	4
655	A178	6c ver & pink	18	10

Issued to publicize the 12th Congress of the Confederation of Latin American Tourist Organizations (COTAL), Santo Domingo, May 25–29.
See No. C167.

ILO Emblem A179 Sliding into Base A180

1969, June 27 Litho. *Perf. 12½*

656	A179	6c lt grnsh bl, grnsh bl & blk	40	10

Issued to commemorate the 50th anniversary of the International Labor Organization. See No. C168.

1969, Aug. 15 Litho. *Perf. 12½*

Designs: 1c, Catching a fly ball. 2c, View of Cibao Stadium (horiz.).

Size: 21x31mm. (1c, 3c); 43x30mm. (2c).

657	A180	1c grn & gray	10	6
658	A180	2c grn & lt grn	12	10
659	A180	3c pur & red brn	15	12
		Nos. 657-659, C169-C171 (6)	4.07	2.71

Issued to publicize the 17th World Amateur Baseball Championships, Santo Domingo.

Las Damas Dam
A181

Tavera Dam—A182

Designs: 2c, Las Damas hydroelectric station (vert.). 6c, Arroyo Hondo substation.

1969 Lithographed *Perf. 12*

660	A181	2c grn & multi	6	4
661	A181	3c dk bl & multi	9	5
662	A181	6c brt rose lil	18	10
663	A182	6c multi	18	10
		Nos. 660-663, C172-C173 (6)	1.11	59

Issued to publicize the national electrification plan.
Issue dates: Nos. 660–662, Sept. 15. No. 663, Oct. 15.

Juan Pablo Duarte A183 Map of Republic, People, Census Emblem A184

1970, Jan. 26 Litho. *Perf. 12*

664	A183	1c emer & dk grn	5	3
665	A183	2c sal pink & dp car	6	4
666	A183	3c brt pink & plum	9	5
667	A183	6c bl & vio bl	18	10
		Nos. 664-667, C174 (5)	68	40

Issued for Duarte Day in memory of Juan Pablo Duarte (1813–1876), liberator.

1970, Feb. 6 *Perf. 11*

Design: 6c, Census emblem and inscription.

668	A184	5c emer & blk	15	8
669	A184	6c ultra & bl	18	10

Census of 1970. See No. C175.

Abelardo Rodriguez Urdaneta
A185

"One of Many"
A186

1970, Feb. 20 Litho. *Perf. 12½*

670	A185	3c ultra	9	6
671	A186	6c grn & yel grn	18	10

Issued to honor Abelardo Rodriguez Urdaneta, sculptor. See No. C176.

Masonic Symbols
A187

1970, Mar. 2

672	A187	6c green	18	10

Issued to publicize the 8th Inter-American Masonic Conference, Santo Domingo, Mar. 1–7. See No. C177.

Communications Satellite—A188

1970, May 25 Litho. *Perf. 12½*

673	A188	20c ol & gray	75	45

Issued for World Telecommunications Day. See No. C178.

U.P.U. Headquarters, Bern
A189

1970, June 5 *Perf. 11*

674	A189	6c gray & brn	18	10

Issued to commemorate the inauguration of the new Universal Postal Union Headquarters in Bern. See No. C179.

Education Year Emblem A190 Pedro Alejandrino Pina A191

1970, June 26 Litho. *Perf. 12½*

675	A190	4c rose lil	12	6

Issued for International Education Year, 1970. See No. C180.

1970, Aug. 24 Litho. *Perf. 12½*

676	A191	6c lt red brn & blk	18	10

Issued to commemorate the 150th anniversary of the birth and the centenary of the death of Pedro Alejandrino Pina (1820–70), author.

Children Reading
A192

1970, Oct. 12 Litho. *Perf. 12½*

677	A192	5c dl grn	15	8

Issued to publicize the First World Exhibition of Books and Culture Festival, Santo Domingo, Oct. 11–Dec. 11. See Nos. C181–C182.

Virgin of Altagracia A193 Manuel Rodriguez Objio A194

1971, Jan. 20 Litho. *Perf. 12½*

678	A193	3c multi	15	10

Inauguration of the Basilica of Our Lady of Altagracia. See No. C184.

1971, June 18 Litho. *Perf. 11*

679	A194	6c lt bl	18	10

Centenary of the death of Manuel Rodriguez Objio (1838–1871), poet.

Boxing and Canoeing
A195

Design: 5c, Basketball.

1971, Sept. 10

680	A195	2c brn & org	10	8
681	A195	5c brn & lt grn	20	12

2nd National Games. See No. C186.

Goat and Fruit
A196

Designs: 2c, Cow and goose. 3c, Cacao and horse. 6c, Bananas, coffee and pig.

1971, Sept. 29 *Perf. 12½*

682	A196	1c brn & multi	3	3
683	A196	2c plum & multi	6	4
684	A196	3c grn & multi	9	8
685	A196	6c bl & multi	18	12
		Nos. 682-685, C187 (5)	96	72

6th National agriculture and livestock census.

José Nuñez de Cáceres—A197 Shepherds and Star—A198

1971, Dec. 1 *Perf. 11*

686	A197	6c lt bl, lil & dk bl	18	10

Sesquicentennial of first national independence. See No. C188.

1971, Dec. 10 *Perf. 12½*

687	A198	6c bl, brn & yel	20	12

Christmas 1971. See No. C189.

UNICEF Emblem, Child on Beach
A199

1971, Dec. 14 Litho. *Perf. 11*

688 A199 6c gray bl & multi 18 10

25th anniversary of the United Nations International Children's Fund (UNICEF). See No. C190.

Book Year Emblem
A200

Taino Mask
A201

1972, Jan. 25 *Perf. 12½*

689 A200 1c grn, ultra & red 4 4
690 A200 2c brn, ultra & red 6 4

International Book Year 1972. See No. C191.

1972, May 10 Litho. *Perf. 11*

Taino Art: 4c, Ladle and amulet. 6c, Human figure.

691 A201 2c pink & multi 6 4
692 A201 4c blk, bl & ocher 12 6
693 A201 6c gray & multi 18 10
Nos. 691-693, C194-C196 (6) 1.51 82

Taino art. See note after No. 651.

Globe
A202

1972, May 17 *Perf. 12½*

694 A202 6c bl & multi 18 10

4th World Telecommunications Day. See No. C197.

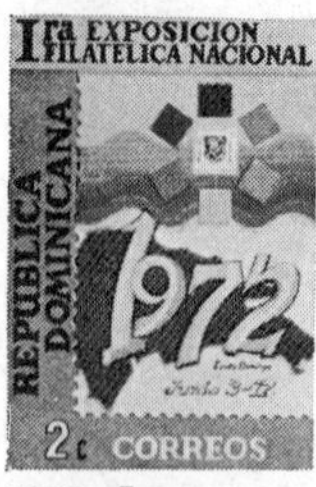

"1972," Stamps and Map of Dominican Republic
A203

1972, June 3

695 A203 2c grn & multi 6 4

First National Philatelic Exhibition, Santo Domingo, June 3–17. See No. C198.

Basketball
A204

1972, Aug. 25 Litho. *Perf. 12½*

696 A204 2c bl & multi 12 10

20th Olympic Games, Munich, Aug. 26–Sept. 11. See No. C199.

Club Emblem
A205

1972, Sept. 29 Litho. *Perf. 10½*

697 A205 1c lt grn & multi 3 3

50th anniversary of the Club Activo 20–30 Internacional. See No. C200.

Emilio A. Morel
A206

1972, Oct. 20 *Perf. 12½*

698 A206 6c brt pink & multi 18 10

Emilio A. Morel (1884–1958), poet and journalist. See No. C201.

Central Bank Building
A207

Design: 5c, One peso note.

1972, Oct. 23

699 A207 1c blk & multi 3 3
700 A207 5c red, blk & grn 15 8

25th anniversary of Central Bank. See No. C202.

Holy Family
A208

Poinsettia
A209

1972, Nov. 21

701 A208 2c rose lil, pur & gold 8 6
702 A209 6c red & multi 20 12

Christmas 1972. See No. C203.

Mail Box and Student
A210

1972, Dec. 15

703 A210 2c rose red 6 3
704 A210 6c blue 18 10
705 A210 10c emerald 30 15

Publicity for correspondence schools.

Tavera Dam
A211

1973, Feb. 26 Litho. *Perf. 12½*

706 A211 10c multi 30 15

Inauguration of the Tavera Dam.

Various Sports—A212

1973, Mar. 30 *Perf. 13½x13*

707 A212 2c brn, yel & grn, block of 4 50 30
a. Upper left 10 5
b. Upper right 10 5
c. Lower left 10 5
d. Lower right 10 5
708 A212 25c dk grn & yel grn, block of 4 4.00 2.00
a. Upper left 80 40
b. Upper right 80 40
c. Lower left 80 40
d. Lower right 80 40
Nos. 707-708, C204-C205 (4 blocks of 4) 7.50 4.10

Publicity for the 12th Central American and Caribbean Games, Santo Domingo, Summer 1974.

Christ Carrying the Cross
A213

Design: 6c, Belfry of Church of Our Lady of Carmen (vert.).

1973, Apr. 18 Litho. *Perf. 10½*

709 A213 2c multi 10 6
710 A213 6c multi 20 15

Holy Week, 1973. See No. C206.

WMO Emblem, Weather Satellite, "Weather"
A214

Mask, Cibao
A215

1973, Aug. 10 Litho. *Perf. 13½x13*

711 A214 6c mag & multi 18 12

Centenary of international meteorological cooperation. See No. C208.

1973, Oct. 12 Litho. *Perf. 10½*

Multicolored

712 A215 1c *Maguey drum* (horiz.) 3 3
713 A215 2c *Carved amber* (horiz.) 6 4
714 A215 4c *shown* 12 8
715 A215 6c *Pottery* 18 12
Nos. 712-715, C210-C211 (6) 90 62

Opening of Museum of Mankind in Santo Domingo.

Nativity
A216

Design: 6c, Stained glass window (vert.).

Perf. 13½x13, 13x13½

1973, Nov. 26

716 A216 2c blk, bl & yel 8 6
717 A216 6c rose & multi 20 15

Christmas 1973. See No. C212. No. 717 exists imperf.

Dominican Scout Emblem
A217

Design: 5c, Scouts and flag.

1973, Dec. 7 Lithographed *Perf. 12*

Size: 35x35mm.

718 A217 1c ultra & multi 3 3

Size: 26x36mm.

719 A217 5c blk & multi 15 10

50th anniversary of Dominican Republic Boy Scouts. See No. C213.

Sports Palace, Basketball Players
A218

Design: 6c, Bicyclist and race track.

1974, Feb. 25 Litho. *Perf. 13½*

720 A218 2c red brn & multi 8 6
721 A218 6c yel & multi 20 15

12th Central American and Caribbean Games, Santo Domingo, 1974. See Nos. C214–C215.

Bell Tower, Cathedral of Santo Domingo
A219

Mater Dolorosa
A220

1974, June 27 Litho. *Perf. 13½*

722 A219 2c multi 8 6
723 A220 6c multi 20 15

Holy Week 1974. See No. C216.

Francisco del Rosario Sanchez Bridge—A221

1974, July 12 *Perf. 12*

724	A221	6c multi	18	12

See No. C217.

Map, Emblem and Patient A222

Design: 5c, Map of Dominican Republic, diabetics' emblem and pancreas.

1974, Aug. 22 Litho. *Perf. 13*

725	A222	4c bl & multi	12	8
726	A222	5c yel grn & multi	12	10

Fight against diabetes. See Nos. C218–C219.

Train and UPU Emblem A223

Design: 6c, Mail coach and UPU emblem.

1974, Oct. 9 Litho. *Perf. 13¼*

727	A223	2c bl & multi	6	4
728	A223	6c brn & multi	18	12

Centenary of Universal Postal Union. See Nos. C220–C221a.

Golfers A224

Design: 2c, Championship emblem and badge of Dominican Golf Association (horiz.).

Perf. 13x13½, 13½x13

1974, Oct. 24

729	A224	2c yel & blk	8	6
730	A224	6c bl & multi	20	15

World Amateur Golf Championships. See Nos. C222–C223.

Christmas Decorations A225

Virgin and Child A226

1974, Dec. 3 Litho. *Perf. 12*

731	A225	2c multi	8	6
732	A226	6c multi	20	15

Christmas 1974. See No. C224.

Tomatoes, FAO Emblem A227

1974, Dec. 5

Multicolored

733	A227	2c *shown*	6	4
734	A227	3c *Avocados*	9	6
735	A227	5c *Coconuts*	15	10

World Food Program, 10th anniversary. See No. C225.

Fernando A. Defillo A228

Tower, Our Lady of the Rosary Convent A229

1975, Feb. 14 Litho. *Perf. 13½x13*

736	A228	1c dl brn	3	3
737	A228	6c dl grn	18	12

Dr. Fernando A. Defillo (1874–1949), physician.

1975, Mar. 26 Litho. *Perf. 13½*

Design: 2c, Jesus saying "I am the Resurrection and the Life."

738	A229	2c brn & multi	6	4
739	A229	6c multi	18	12

Holy Week 1975. See No. C226.

Hands (Steel Beams) with Symbols of Agriculture, Industry A230

1975, May 19 Litho. *Perf. 10½x10*

740	A230	6c dl bl & multi	18	12

16th Assembly of the Governors of the International Development Bank, Santo Domingo, May 1975. See No. C228.

Satellite Tracking Station A231

1975, June 21 Litho. *Perf. 13½*

741	A231	5c multi	15	10

Opening of first earth satellite tracking station in Dominican Republic. See No. C229.

Apollo A232

Design: 4c, Soyuz.

1975, July 24

Size: 35x25mm.

742	A232	1c bl & multi	3	3
743	A232	4c vio bl & multi	12	8

Apollo Soyuz space test project (Russo-American cooperation), launching July 15; link-up, July 17. See No. C230.

Father Rafael C. Castellanos A233

1975, Aug. 6 Litho. *Perf. 12*

744	A233	6c brn & buff	18	12

Father Rafael C. Castellanos (1875–1934), first Apostolic Administrator in Dominican Republic, birth centenary.

Women and Men Around IWY Emblem A234

1975, Aug. 6 *Perf. 13*

745	A234	3c org & multi	9	6

International Women's Year 1975.

Guacanagarix A235

Basketball A236

Indian Chiefs: 2c, Guarionex. 3c, Caonabo. 4c, Bohechio. 5c, Cayacoa. 6c, Anacona (woman). 9c, Hatuey.

1975, Sept. 27 Litho. *Perf. 12*

746	A235	1c yel & multi	3	3
747	A235	2c sal & multi	6	4
748	A235	3c vio bl & multi	9	6
749	A235	4c grn & multi	12	8
750	A235	5c bl & multi	15	10
751	A235	6c vio & multi	18	12
752	A235	9c rose & multi	27	18
		Nos. 746-752, C231-C233 (10)	1.65	1.11

1975, Oct. 24 Litho. *Perf. 12*

Design: 6c, Baseball and Games' emblem.

753	A236	2c pink & multi	8	6
754	A236	6c org & multi	20	15

7th Pan-American Games, Mexico City, Oct. 13–26. See Nos. C234–C235.

Carolers A237

Design: 6c, Dominican nativity with farmers and shepherds.

1975, Dec. 12 Litho. *Perf. 13x13½*

755	A237	2c yel & multi	6	4
756	A237	6c bl & multi	18	12

Christmas 1975. See No. C236.

Abudefdul Marginatus—A238

1976, Jan. 23 Litho. *Perf. 13*

Multicolored

757	A238	10c *shown*	30	20
758	A238	10c *Snakefish*	30	20
759	A238	10c *Squirrelfish*	30	20
760	A238	10c *Angelfish*	30	20
761	A238	10c *Porgy*	30	20
		Nos. 757-761 (5)	1.50	1.00

Nos. 757–761 printed se-tenant.

Ascension, by J. Priego A239

"Separacion Dominicana" and Adm. Cambiaso A240

Design: 2c, Mary Magdalene, by Enrique Godoy.

1976, Apr. 14 Litho. *Perf. 13½*

762	A239	2c bl & multi	8	6
763	A239	6c yel & multi	20	10

Holy Week 1976. See No. C238.

1976, Apr. 15 *Perf. 13½x13*

764	A240	20c multi	60	40

Naval Battle off Tortuga, Apr. 15, 1844.

Maps of US and Dominican Republic A241

Design: 9c, Maps within cogwheels.

1976, May 29 Litho. *Perf. 13½*

765	A241	6c vio bl & multi	18	8
766	A241	9c vio bl & multi	28	12

American Bicentennial. See Nos. C239–C240.

Flags of Dominican Republic and Spain
A242

1976, May 31

767 A242 6c multi 50 8

Visit of King Juan Carlos I and Queen Sofia of Spain. See No. C241.

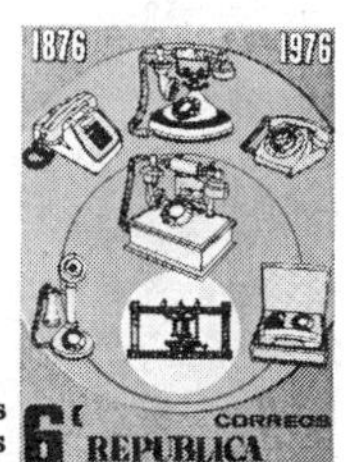

Various Telephones
A243

1976, July 15 ***Perf. 12x12½***

768 A243 6c multi 18 8

Centenary of first telephone call by Alexander Graham Bell, Mar. 10, 1876. See No. C242.

Vision of Duarte, by Luis Desangles
A244

Juan Pablo Duarte, by Rhadames Mejia
A245

1976, July 20 Litho. *Perf. 13x13½*

769 A244 2c multi 6 3

Perf. 13½

770 A245 6c multi 18 8

Juan Pablo Duarte, liberation hero, death centenary. See Nos. C243–C244.

Fire Hydrant
A246

Design: 6c, Firemen's emblem.

1976, Sept. 13 Litho. *Perf. 12*

771 A246 4c multi 12 6
772 A246 6c multi 18 8

Honoring firemen. Nos. 771–772 inscribed "Corrreos". See No. C245.

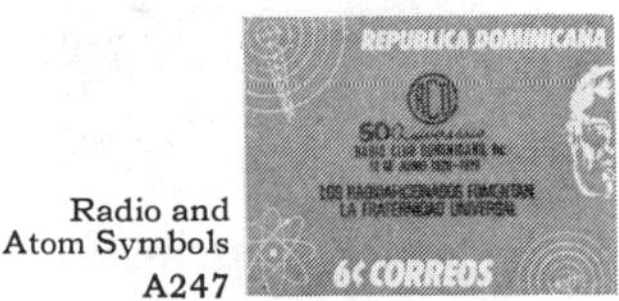

Radio and Atom Symbols
A247

1976, Oct. 8 Lithographed *Perf. 13½*

773 A247 6c red & blk 18 8

Dominican Radio Club, 50th anniversary. See No. C246.

Spain, Central and South America, Galleon
A248

1976, Oct. 22 Litho. *Perf. 13½*

774 A248 6c multi 18 8

Spanish heritage. See No. C247.

Boxing and Montreal Emblem
A249

Design: 3c, Weight lifting.

1976, Oct. 22 *Perf. 12*

775 A249 2c bl & multi 6 3
776 A249 3c multi 9 4

21st Olympic Games, Montreal, Canada, July 17–Aug. 1. See Nos. C248–C249.

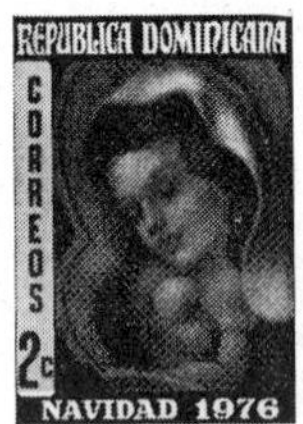

Virgin and Child
A250

Three Kings
A251

1976, Dec. 8 Litho. *Perf. 13½*

777 A250 2c multi 6 3
778 A251 6c multi 18 12

Christmas 1976. See No. C250.

Cable Car and Beach Scenes
A252

1977, Jan. 7

779 A252 6c multi 18 12

Tourist publicity. See Nos. C251–C253.

Championship Emblem
A253

1977, Mar. 4 Litho. *Perf. 13½*

780 A253 3c rose & multi 10 6
781 A253 5c yel & multi 15 10

10th Central American and Caribbean Children's and Young People's Swimming Championships, Santo Domingo. See Nos. C254–C255.

Christ Carrying Cross
A254

Design: 6c, Head with crown of thorns.

1977, Apr. 18 Litho. *Perf. 13½x13*

782 A254 2c multi 6 3
783 A254 6c blk & rose 18 8

Holy Week 1977. See No. C256.

Doves, Lions Emblem
A255

1977, May 6 *Perf. 13½x13*

784 A255 2c lt bl & multi 6 3
785 A255 6c sal & multi 18 8

12th annual Dominican Republic Lions Convention. See No. C257.

Battle Scene
A256

1977, June 15 Litho. *Perf. 13x13½*

786 A256 20c multi 60 40

Dominican Navy.

Water Lily
A257

Designs: 4c, "Flor de Mayo" (orchid). 6c, Sebesten.

1977, Aug. 19 Litho. *Perf. 12*

787 A257 2c multi 6 3
788 A257 4c multi 12 6
789 A257 6c multi 18 8
Nos. 787-789,C259-C260 (5) 1.57 97

National Botanical Garden.

Chart and Computers
A258

1977 Litho. *Perf. 13*

790 A258 6c multi 18 8

7th 'nteramerican Statistics Conference. See No. C261.

Solenodon Paradoxus
A259

Design: 20c, Iguana and Congress emblem.

1977, Dec. 29 Litho. *Perf. 13*

791 A259 6c multi 18 8
792 A259 20c multi 60 40

8th Pan-American Veterinary and Zootechnical Congress. See Nos. C262–C263.

Main Gate, Casa del Cordon, 1503
A260

Crown of Thorns, Tools at the Cross
A261

1978, Jan. 19 *Perf. 13x13½*

Size: 26x36mm.

793 A260 6c multi 18 8

Spanish heritage. See No. C264.

1978, Mar. 21 Litho. *Perf. 12*

Design: 6c, Head of Jesus with crown of thorns.

Size: 22x33mm.

794 A261 2c multi 6 3
795 A261 6c slate 18 8

Holy Week 1978. See Nos. C265–C266.

Cardinal Octavio A. Beras Rojas
A262

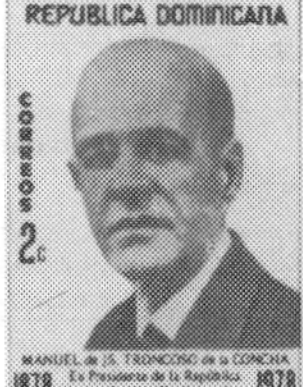

Pres. Manuel de Troncoso
A263

1978, May 5 Litho. *Perf. 13*

796 A262 6c multi 18 8

First Cardinal from Dominican Republic, consecrated May 24, 1976. See No. C268.

1978, June 12 Litho. *Perf. 13½*

797 A263 2c blk, rose & brn 6 3
798 A263 6c blk, gray & brn 18 8

Manuel de Jesus Troncoso de la Concha (1878–1955), president of Dominican Republic 1940–1942.

Father Juan N. Zegri y Moreno
A264

1978, July 11 Litho. *Perf. 13x13½*

799 A264 6c multi 18 8

Congregation of the Merciful Sisters of Charity, centenary. See No. C273.

Boxing and Games' Emblem
A265

Design: 6c, Weight lifting.

1978, July 21 *Perf. 12*

800 A265 2c multi 6 3
801 A265 6c multi 18 8

13th Central American and Caribbean Games, Medellin, Colombia. See Nos. C274–C275.

Sun over Landscape
A266

Ships of Columbus, Map of Dominican Republic
A267

Design: 6c, Sun over beach and boat.

1978, Sept. 12 Litho. *Perf. 12*

802 A266 2c multi 6 3
803 A266 6c multi 18 8

Tourist publicity. See Nos. C280–C281.

1978, Oct. 12 Litho. *Perf. 13½*

804 A267 2c multi 6 3

Spanish heritage. See No. C282.

Dove, Lamp, Poinsettia
A268

Design: 6c, Dominican family and star (vert.).

1978, Dec. 5 Litho. *Perf. 12*

805 A268 2c multi 6 3
806 A268 6c multi 18 8

Christmas 1978. See No. C284.

Starving Child, ICY Emblem
A269

1979, Feb. 26 Litho. *Perf. 12*

807 A269 2c org & blk 6 3

International Year of the Child. See Nos. C287–C289.

Crucifixion
A270

Design: 3c, Jesus carrying cross (horiz.).

1979, Apr. 9 Litho. *Perf. 13½*

808 A270 2c multi 6 3
809 A270 3c multi 10 4

Holy Week. See No. C290.

Stigmaphyllon Periplocifolium
A271

1979, May 17 Litho. *Perf. 12*

810 A271 50c multi 1.50 1.00

"Dr. Rafael M. Moscoso" National Botanical Garden. See Nos. C293–C295.

Heart, Diseased Blood Vessel
A272

Design: 1p, Cardiology Institute and heart.

1979, June 2 Litho. *Perf. 13½*

811 A272 3c multi 10 4
812 A272 1p multi 3.00 2.00

Dominican Cardiology Institute. See No. C296.

Baseball, Games' Emblem
A273

Design: 3c, Bicycling and Games' emblem (vert.).

1979, June 20

813 A273 2c multi 6 3
814 A273 3c multi 10 4

8th Pan American Games, Puerto Rico, June 30–July 15. See No. C297.

Soccer
A274

Thomas A. Edison
A275

Design: 25c, Swimming (horiz.).

1979, Aug. 8 Litho. *Perf. 12*

815 A274 2c multi 6 3
816 A274 25c multi 75 50

Third National Games. See No. C298.

1979, Aug. 27 *Perf. 13½*

817 A275 25c multi 75 50

Centenary of invention of electric light. See No. C300.

Hand Holding Electric Plug
A276

Design: 6c, Filling automobile gas tank.

1979, Aug. 30

818 A276 2c multi 6 3
819 A276 6c multi 18 12

Energy conservation.

Parrot—A277

Birds: 6c, Temnotrogon roseigaster.

1979, Sept. 9 Litho. *Perf. 12*

820 A277 2c multi 6 3
821 A277 6c multi 18 12
Nos. 820-821, C301-C303 (5) 2.09 1.39

Lions Emblem, Map of Dominican Republic—A278

1979, Nov. 13 Litho. *Perf. 12*

822 A278 20c multi 60 30

Lions International Club of Dominican Republic, 10th anniversary. See No. C304.

Holy Family—A279

1979, Dec. 18 Litho. *Perf. 12*

823 A279 2c multi 6 3

Christmas 1979. See No. C305.

See "Special Notices" at the front of this volume for data on the listing methods of this Catalogue, abbreviations, condition, prices and examination.

Jesus Carrying Cross—A280

1980, Mar. 27 Litho. *Perf. 12*

824 A280 3c multi 10 4

Holy Week. See Nos. C306-C307.

Cacao Harvest (Agriculture Year)—A281

1980, May 15 Litho. *Perf. 13½*

825 A281 1c *shown* 3 3
826 A281 2c *Coffee* 6 3
827 A281 3c *Plantain* 10 4
828 A281 4c *Sugar cane* 12 8
829 A281 5c *Corn* 15 10
Nos. 825-829 (5) 46 28

Cotuf Gold Mine, Pueblo Viejo, Flag of Dominican Republic—A282

1980, July 8 Litho. *Perf. 13½*

830 A282 6c multi 18 12

Nationalization of gold mining. See Nos. C310-C311.

Blind Man's Buff—A283

1980, July 21 *Perf. 12*

831 A283 3c *shown* 10 4
832 A283 4c *Marbles* 12 8
833 A283 5c *Drawing in sand* 15 10
834 A283 6c *Hopscotch* 18 12

Iguana—A284

1980, Aug. 30 Litho. *Perf. 12*

835 A284 20c multi 60 40
Nos. 835, C313-C316 (5) 3.15 2.09

Dance, by Jaime Colson—A285

Litho.

1980, Sept. 23 *Perf. 13x13½, 13½x13*

836	A285	3c *shown*	10	4
837	A285	50c *Woman, by Gilberto Hernandez Ortega,* vert.	1.50	1.00

See Nos. C318-C319.

Three Kings—A286

1980, Dec. 5 **Litho.** *Perf. 13½*

838	A286	3c *shown*	10	4
839	A286	6c *Carolers*	18	12

Christmas 1980. See No. C327.

Salcedo Province Centenary—A287

1981, Jan. 14 **Litho.** *Perf. 13½*

840	A287	6c multi	18	12

See No. C328.

Juan Pablo Duarte—A288

1981, Feb. 6 **Litho.** *Perf. 12*

841	A288	2c sep & dp bis	6	4

Juan Pablo Duarte, liberation hero, 105th anniversary of death.

Gymnast A289

Mother Mazzarello A290

1981, Mar. 31 **Litho.** *Perf. 13½*

842	A289	1c shown	3	3
843	A289	2c Running	6	4
844	A289	3c Pole vault	10	6
845	A289	6c Boxing	18	12
		Nos. 842-845, C331 (5)	67	45

5th National Games. See No. C331.

1981, Apr. 14 *Perf. 12*

846	A290	6c multi	18	12

Mother Maria Mazzarello (1837-1881), founder of Daughters of Mary.

Pedro Henriquez Urena, Historian (1884-1946) A291

1981, May 18 **Litho.** *Perf. 13½*

847	A291	6c gray vio & lt gray	18	12

Forest Conservation A292

1981, June 30 **Litho.** *Perf. 12*

848	A292	2c shown	6	4
849	A292	6c River, forest	18	12

Family in House, Census Emblem—A293

1981, Aug. 14 **Litho.** *Perf. 12*

850	A293	3c shown	10	6
851	A293	6c Farmer	18	12

1981 natl. population and housing census.

Christmas 1981—A294

1981, Dec. 23 **Litho.** *Perf. 13½*

852	A294	2c Bells	6	4
853	A294	3c Poinsettia	10	6

See No. C353

Juan Pablo Duarte—A295

1982, Jan. 29 **Litho.** *Perf. 13½*

854	A295	2c bl & pale bl	6	4

National Elections—A296

Designs: Voters casting votes. 3c, 6c vert.

1982, Mar. 30 **Litho.** *Perf. 13½*

855	A296	2c multi	6	4
856	A296	3c multi	10	6
857	A296	6c multi	20	12

A297

Emilio Prud'Homme (1856-1932), Composer A298

Designs: Various forms of energy.

1982, May 10 **Litho.** *Perf. 12*

858	A297	1c multi	3	3
859	A297	2c multi	6	4
860	A297	3c multi	10	6
861	A297	4c multi	12	8
862	A297	5c multi	16	12
863	A297	6c multi	20	12
		Nos. 858-863 (6)	67	45

1982, Aug. 2 *Perf. 12x12½*

864	A298	6c multi	20	12

Pres. Antonio Guzman Fernandez (1911-1982)—A299

1982, Aug. 4 *Perf. 13x13½*

865	A299	6c multi	20	12

14th Central American and Caribbean Games—A300

1982, Aug. 13 *Perf. 12*

866	A300	3c Baseball	10	6

See Nos. C368-C370. Exist imperf.

San Pedro de Macoris Province Centenary—A301

1982, Aug. 26 *Perf. 13*

867	A301	1c Wagon	3	3
868	A301	2c Stained-glass window	6	4
869	A301	5c Views	16	10

Size of 1c, 5c, 42x29mm. See No. C375.

St. Teresa of Jesus of Avila (1515-1582)—A302

1982, Nov. 17 **Litho.** *Perf. 13½*

870	A302	6c multi	20	12

Christmas 1982 A303

Environmental Protection A304

Various Christmas balls.

1982, Dec. 8

871	A303	6c multi	20	12

See No. C380.

1982, Dec. 15 *Perf. 12*

872	A304	2c Bird	6	4
873	A304	3c Water	10	6
874	A304	6c Forest	20	12
875	A304	20c Fish	60	40

SEMI-POSTAL STAMPS

Nos. 474-478
Surcharged in Red

+2¢

Engraved and Lithographed.

1957, Feb. 8 *Perf. 11½* Unwmkd.

Flags in National Colors

B1	A117	1c +2c brn, lt bl, vio & mar	10	10
B2	A117	2c +2c dk brn, lt bl & vio	10	10
B3	A117	3c +2c red lil & red	15	15
B4	A117	5c +2c red org & vio	25	25
B5	A117	7c +2c grn & vio	35	35
		Nos. B1-B5, CB1-CB3 (8)	2.50	2.50

The surtax was to aid Hungarian refugees. A similar 25c surcharge was applied to the miniature sheets described in the footnote following No. 478. Price, 2 sheets, perf. and imperf., $17.50.

Nos. 479-483
Surcharged in
Red Orange

1957, Sept. 9 Photo. *Perf. 13½*

Flags in National Colors

B6	A118	1c +2c brn & brt bl	20	20
B7	A118	2c +2c org ver & dk bl	30	25
B8	A118	3c +2c dk bl	35	35
B9	A118	5c +2c ol & dk bl	50	35
B10	A118	7c +2c rose brn & dk bl	60	45
		Nos. B6-B10, CB4-CB6 (8)	4.10	3.70

Issued to commemorate the centenary of the birth of Lord Baden Powell and the 50th anniversary of the Scout Movement. The surtax was for the Dominican Republic Boy Scouts.

A similar 5c surcharge was applied to the miniature sheets described in the footnote following No. 483. Price, 4 sheets, perf. and imperf., medal and flag, $35.

Types of Olympic Regular Issue, 1957,
Surcharged in Carmine

REFUGIADOS REFUGIADOS
a *b*

1958, May 26 Engr. & Litho.

Flags in National Colors

Pink Paper

B11	A119(a)	1c +2c red brn	25	25
B12	A119(b)	1c +2c red brn	25	25
B13	A120(a)	2c +2c gray brn	30	30
B14	A120(b)	2c +2c gray brn	30	30
B15	A119(a)	3c +2c vio	30	30
B16	A119(b)	3c +2c vio	30	30
B17	A120(a)	5c +2c red org	40	40
B18	A120(b)	5c +2c red org	40	40
B19	A119(a)	7c +2c Prus grn	50	50
B20	A119(b)	7c +2c Prus grn	50	50
		Nos. B11-B20, CB7-CB12 (16)	6.50	6.50

The surtax was for the United Nations Relief and Works Agency for Palestine Refugees.

A similar 5c surcharge, plus marginal United Nations emblem and "UNRWA," was applied to the miniature sheets described in the footnote following No. 488. Price, 4 sheets, perf. and imperf., $30.

Nos. 501-505
Surcharged

Perf. 13½

1959, Apr. 13 Photo. Unwmkd.

Flags in National Colors

B21	A125	1c +2c rose, ind & ultra	35	35
B22	A125	2c +2c brn & bl	45	45
B23	A125	3c +2c gray, vio, blk & buff	50	50
B24	A125	5c +2c rose, dk bl, brn & red	60	60
B25	A125	7c +2c lt brn, dk bl & red	65	65
		Nos. B21-B25, CB13-CB15 (8)	5.80	5.80

International Geophysical Year, 1957-58.

A similar 5c surcharge was applied to the miniature sheets described in the footnote following No. 505. Price, 2 sheets, perf. and imperf., $22.50.

Type of 1957
Surcharged in Red

Engraved and Lithographed

1959, Sept. 10 *Imperf.* Unwmkd.

Flags in National Colors

B26	A117	1c +2c brn, lt bl, vio & mar	20	20
B27	A117	2c +2c dk brn, lt bl & vio	20	20
B28	A117	3c +2c red lil & red	25	25
B29	A117	5c +2c red org & vio	30	30
B30	A117	7c +2c grn & vio	40	40
		Nos. B26-B30, CB16-CB18 (8)	3.10	3.10

3rd Pan American Games, Chicago, Aug. 27-Sept. 7, 1959.

World Refugee Year Issue

Nos. 522-524
Surcharged in Red

1960, Apr. 7 Litho. *Perf. 12½*

Center in Gray

B31	A135	5c +5c red brn & yel grn	25	25
B32	A135	9c +5c car & lt bl	30	30
B33	A135	13c +5c org & grn	60	60
		Nos. B31-B33, CB19-CB20 (5)	2.00	2.00

Issued to publicize World Refugee Year, July 1, 1959-June 30, 1960. The surtax was for aid to refugees.

Souvenir sheets exist perf. and imperf., containing one each of Nos. B31-B33 and CB19-CB20. Size: 152x99mm. Black marginal inscription. Price, 2 sheets, perf. and imperf., $10.

Nos. 525-529 Surcharged:
"XV ANIVERSARIO DE LA
UNESCO +2c"

1962, Jan. 8 Photo. *Perf. 13½*

Flags in National Colors

B34	A136	1c +2c red, yel grn & blk	8	8
B35	A136	2c +2c org, grnsh bl & brn	10	10
B36	A136	3c +2c hn brn & bl	12	12
B37	A136	5c +2c brn & ultra	18	18
B38	A136	7c +2c grn, bl & rose brn	20	20
		Nos. B34-B38, CB21-CB23 (8)	2.08	2.08

Issued to commemorate the 15th anniversary (in 1961) of UNESCO (U.N. Educational, Scientific and Cultural Organization).

A similar 5c surcharge was applied to the miniature sheets described in the footnote following No. 529. Price, 2 sheets, perf. and imperf., $7.50.

Anti-Malaria Type of Regular Issue, 1962

1962, Apr. 29 Litho. *Perf. 12*

B39	A141	10c +2c brt pink & red lil	30	25
B40	A141	20c +2c pale brn & brn	50	40

Issued for the World Health Organization drive to eradicate malaria.

Type of Regular Issue, 1963

1963, Apr. 15 *Perf. 11½* Unwmkd.

Banner in Dark Blue & Red

B41	A148	2c +1c grn	6	6
B42	A148	5c +2c brt rose lil	18	15
B43	A148	9c +2c org	30	30

Issued for the "Freedom from Hunger" campaign of the U.N. Food and Agriculture organization. A souvenir sheet contains three imperf. stamps similar to Nos. B41-B43. Dark blue marginal inscription. Size: 172x102mm. Price, $1.25.

Nos. 591-593
Surcharged

1964, March 8 *Perf. 12½*

B44	A153	3c +2c pale pink & ver	20	20
B45	A153	6c +2c pale bl & ultra	25	25
B46	A153	9c +2c pale rose & red brn	40	40
		Nos. B44-B46, CB26-CB27 (5)	1.50	1.50

Issued to publicize the UNESCO world campaign to save historic monuments in Nubia.

Nos. 622-626
Surcharged

PRO DAMNIFICADOS CICLON INES

1966, Dec. 9 Litho. *Perf. 12½*

Size: 31x21mm.

B47	A164	1c +2c multi	20	10
B48	A164	2c +2c multi	25	15
B49	A164	3c +2c multi	25	15
B50	A164	6c +4c multi	40	35
B51	A164	8c +4c multi	50	45
		Nos. B47-B51, CB28-CB30 (8)	6.35	5.95

The surtax was for victims of hurricane Inez.

AIR POST STAMPS

Map of Hispaniola—AP1

Perf. 11½

1928, May 31 Litho. Unwmkd.

C1	AP1	10c dp ultra	7.00	4.00

1930

C2	AP1	10c ocher	5.00	4.00
a.		Vertical pair imperf. between	*1,000.*	
C3	AP1	15c scarlet	10.00	5.50
C4	AP1	20c dl grn	4.50	85
C5	AP1	30c violet	10.00	6.50

Nos. C2 to C5 have only "CENTAVOS" in lower panel. Dates of issue: 10c, 20c, Jan. 24; 15c, 30c, Feb. 14.

1930

C6	AP1	10c lt bl	2.50	1.00
C7	AP1	15c bl grn	5.00	1.50
C8	AP1	20c yel brn	5.50	75
a.		Imperf. vertically (pair)	500.00	
C9	AP1	30c chocolate	9.00	2.50

Dates of issue: 10c, 15c, 20c, Sept.; 30c, Oct.

Batwing Sundial Erected in 1753
AP2

1931-33 *Perf. 12*

C10	AP2	10c carmine	5.50	85
C11	AP2	10c lt bl ('32)	2.25	75
C12	AP2	10c dk grn ('33)	9.00	3.50
C13	AP2	15c rose lil	4.00	75
C14	AP2	20c dk bl	8.00	2.25
a.		Numerals reading up at left and down at right	8.50	3.25
b.		Imperf., pair	400.00	
C15	AP2	30c green	3.50	50
C16	AP2	50c red brn	9.00	1.00
C17	AP2	1p dp org	15.00	3.50
		Nos. C10-C17 (8)	56.25	13.10

Issue dates: Aug. 16, 1931; July 2, 1932; May 28, 1933.

Airplane and Ozama Fortress
AP3

1933, Nov. 20

C18	AP3	10c dk bl	4.50	75

Airplane and Trujillo Bridge
AP4

1934, Sept. 20

C19	AP4	10c dk bl	4.00	75

Symbolic of Flight
AP5

1935, Apr. 29

C20	AP5	10c lt bl & dk bl	3.00	65

AP6

1936, Feb. 11 *Perf. 11½*

C21	AP6	10c dk bl & turq bl	3.50	65

Allegory of Flight
AP7

1936, Oct. 17

C22	AP7	10c dk bl, bl & turq bl	3.25	50

Macoris Airport
AP8

1937, Oct. 22

C23	AP8	10c green	1.50	20

Fleet of Columbus
AP9

Air Fleet
AP10

Proposed Columbus Lighthouse
AP11

1937, Nov. 9 ***Perf. 12***

C24	AP9	10c rose red	2.50	1.50
C25	AP10	15c purple	2.00	1.00
C26	AP11	20c dk bl & lt bl	2.00	1.00
C27	AP10	25c red vio	3.00	1.25
C28	AP11	30c yel grn	2.75	1.00
C29	AP10	50c brown	5.50	1.50
C30	AP11	75c dk ol grn	14.00	14.00
C31	AP9	1p orange	9.00	3.00
		Nos. C24-C31 (8)	40.75	24.25

Issued in commemoration of the goodwill flight to all American countries by the planes "Colon", "Pinta", "Niña" and "Santa Maria".

Pan American Clipper
AP12

1938, July 30

C32	AP12	10c green	1.50	20

Trylon and Perisphere, Plane and Proposed Columbus Lighthouse—AP13

1939, Apr. 30

C33	AP13	10c grn & lt grn	1.75	85

New York World's Fair.

Airplane
AP14

1939, Oct. 18

C34	AP14	10c grn & dp grn	2.00	30
a.		Pair, imperf. between	*700.00*	

Proposed Columbus Lighthouse, Plane and Caravels—AP15

Christopher Columbus and Proposed Lighthouse
AP16

Proposed Lighthouse
AP17

Christopher Columbus
AP18

Caravel—AP19

1940, Oct. 12

C35	AP15	10c saph & lt bl	75	75
C36	AP16	15c org brn & brn	1.15	1.00
C37	AP17	20c rose red & red	1.15	1.00
C38	AP18	25c brt red lil & red vio	1.15	50
C39	AP19	50c grn & lt grn	2.25	2.00
		Nos. C35-C39 (5)	6.45	5.25

Discovery of America by Columbus and proposed Columbus memorial lighthouse in Dominican Republic.

Posts and Telegraph Building, San Cristobal
AP20

1941, Feb. 21

C40	AP20	10c brt red lil & pale lil rose	65	25

Globe, Wing and Letter
AP21

1942, Feb. 13

C41	AP21	10c dk vio brn	80	8
C42	AP21	75c dp org	5.00	3.00

Plane
AP22

1943, Sept. 1

C43	AP22	10c brt red lil	60	12
C44	AP22	20c dp bl & bl	70	18
C45	AP22	25c yel ol	8.00	4.00

Plane, Flag, Coat of Arms and Torch of Liberty
AP23

1944, Feb. 27 ***Perf. 11½***

Flag in Gray, Dark Blue, Carmine

C46	AP23	10c multi	60	12
C47	AP23	20c multi	75	20
C48	AP23	1p multi	3.50	2.50

Centenary of Independence. See No. 407 for souvenir sheet listing.

Communications Building, Ciudad Trujillo
AP24

1944, Nov. 12 **Litho.** ***Perf. 12***

C49	AP24	9c yel grn & bl	30	15
C50	AP24	13c dl brn & rose car	35	10
C51	AP24	25c org & dl red	60	15
b.		Vert. pair, imperf. between	75.00	
C52	AP24	30c blk & ultra	1.25	1.10

Twenty booklets of 100 (25 panes of 4) of the 25c were issued. Single panes are unknown to experts.

Emblem of Communications
AP25

1945, Sept. 1

Center in Dark Blue and Carmine.

C53	AP25	7c dp yel grn	30	35
C54	AP25	12c red org	35	25
C55	AP25	13c dp bl	45	20
C56	AP25	25c org brn	90	30

AP26

Flags and National Anthem
AP27

Lithographed.

1946, Feb. 27 ***Perf. 12*** **Unwmkd.**

Center in Dark Blue, Deep Carmine and Black.

C57	AP26	10c carmine	70	60
C58	AP26	15c blue	1.50	1.00
C59	AP26	20c chocolate	1.75	1.00
C60	AP26	35c orange	2.00	1.00
C61	AP27	1p grn, yel grn & cit	20.00	15.00
		Nos. C57-C61 (5)	25.95	18.60

Nos. C57–C61 exist imperf.

Map of Hispaniola
AP28

1946, Aug. 4

C62	AP28	10c multi	50	20
C63	AP28	13c multi	85	20

See note after No. 421.

Waterfall of Jimenoa
AP29

1947, Mar. 18 Lithographed

Center Multicolored.

C64	AP29	18c lt bl	75	75
C65	AP29	23c carmine	1.00	85
C66	AP29	50c red vio	1.50	70
C67	AP29	75c chocolate	2.00	1.50

Executive Palace
AP30

1948, Feb. 27

C68	AP30	37c org brn	1.25	1.00
C69	AP30	1p org yel	3.50	2.50

Church of San Francisco Ruins
AP31

Las Carreras Monument
AP32

1949 *Perf. 11½* Unwmkd.

C70	AP31	7c ol grn & pale ol grn	20	15
C71	AP31	10c org brn & buff	25	12
C72	AP31	15c brt rose & pale pink	75	35
C73	AP31	20c grn & pale grn	1.00	70

Issue dates: 10c, Apr. 4; others, Apr. 13.

1949, Aug. 10

C74	AP32	10c red & pink	35	8

Issued to commemorate the centenary of the Battle of Las Carreras.

Hotel Montana
AP33

Design: 37c, Hotel San Cristobal.

1950, Sept.

C75	AP33	12c dk bl & bl	40	12
C76	AP33	37c car & pink	2.75	2.25

Map, Plane and Caduceus
AP34

1950, Oct. 2

C77	AP34	12c org brn & yel	60	15

The 13th Pan-American Health Conference. Exists imperf.

Dr. Salvador B. Gautier Hospital
AP35

1952, Aug.

C78	AP35	23c dp bl	85	80
C79	AP35	29c carmine	2.00	1.50

Columbus Lighthouse and Plane
AP36

Ano Mariano Initials in Monogram
AP37

1953. Jan. 6 Engraved *Perf. 13*

C80	AP36	12c ocher	35	25
C81	AP36	14c dk bl	40	35
C82	AP36	20c blk brn	75	60
C83	AP36	23c dp plum	80	65
C84	AP36	25c dk bl	85	70
C85	AP36	29c dp grn	1.00	70
C86	AP36	1p red brn	4.00	3.00
a.		Miniature sheet of 10	12.00	12.00
		Nos. C80-C86 (7)	8.15	6.25

No. C86a is lithographed and contains one each of Nos. 450–452 and C80–C86, in slightly different shades. Sheet measures 190x130mm. and is imperf. with simulated perforations printed in dark blue. No marginal inscriptions.

A miniature sheet similar to No. C86a, but measuring 200x163mm. and in folder, exists. Price, $60.

1954, Aug. 21 Litho. *Perf. 11½*

C87	AP37	8c claret	25	15
C88	AP37	11c blue	35	10
C89	AP37	33c brn org	1.00	65

Marian Year. Nos. C87–C89 exist imperf.

Rotary Type of Regular Issue, 1955.

1955, Feb. 23 *Perf. 12*

C90	A110	11c rose red	40	20

Rotary International, 50th anniversary.

Flags
AP39

Portraits of General Hector B. Trujillo: 25c, In civilian clothes. 33c, In uniform.

Engraved.

1955, May 16 *Perf. 13½x13*

C91	AP39	11c bl, yel & car	45	12
C92	AP39	25c rose vio	70	40
C93	AP39	33c org brn	1.00	60

The center of No. C91 is lithographed. Issued to commemorate the 25th anniversary of the inauguration of the Trujillo era.

Fair Type of Regular Issue, 1955

1955, Dec. 20 *Perf. 13* Unwmkd.

C94	A112	11c vermilion	40	12

Issued to publicize the International Fair of Peace and Brotherhood in Ciudad Trujillo, Dec. 1955.

ICAO Type of Regular Issue, 1956.

1956, Apr. 6 Litho. *Perf. 12½*

C95	A114	11c ultra	35	12

Issued to commemorate the third Caribbean conference of the International Civil Aviation Organization.

Tree Type of Regular Issue, 1956.

Design: 13c, Mahogany tree.

1956, Dec. 8 Litho. *Perf. 11½x12*

C96	A115	13c org & grn	45	18

Issued to publicize the reforestation program.

Type of Regular Issue, 1957.

Olympic Winners and Flags: 11c, Paavo Nurmi, Finland. 16c, Ugo Frigerio, Italy. 17c, Mildred Didrikson ("Didrickson" on stamp), United States.

Engraved and Lithographed.

1957, Jan. 24 *Perf. 11½* Unwmkd.

Flags in National Colors

C97	A117	11c ultra & red org	30	30
C98	A117	16c car & lt grn	45	45
C99	A117	17c blk, vio & red	60	60

Issued to commemorate the 16th Olympic Games, Melbourne, Nov. 22–Dec. 8, 1956. Exist imperf.

Souvenir sheets of 3 exist, perf. and imperf., containing one each of Nos. C97–C99. Sheets measure 169x86mm., with Olympic flag and motto on left margin.

Price, 2 sheets, perf. & imperf., $7.

Type of Regular Issue, 1957.

Olympic Winners and Flags: 11c, Robert Morrow, United States, 100 & 200 meter dash. 16c, Chris Brasher, England, steeplechase. 17c, A. Ferreira Da Silva, Brazil, hop, step and jump.

1957, July 18 Photo. *Perf. 13½*

Flags in National Colors

C100	A118	11c yel grn & dk bl	30	30
C101	A118	16c lil & dk bl	40	40
C102	A118	17c brn & bl grn	45	45

1956 Olympic winners. Exist imperf.

See note on miniature sheets following No. 483.

Types of Regular Issue, 1957.

Olympic Winners and Flags: 11c, Hans Winkler, Germany, individual jumping. 16c, Alfred Oerter, United States, discus throw. 17c, Shirley Strickland, Australia, 800 meter hurdles.

Engraved and Lithographed.

Flags in National Colors

1957, Nov. 12 *Perf. 13½* Unwmkd.

C103	A119	11c ultra	30	25
C104	A120	16c rose car	45	45
C105	A119	17c claret	50	50

1956 Olympic winners. Exist imperf.

Miniature sheets of 3 exist, perf. and imperf., containing one each of Nos. C103–C105. Sheets have no marginal inscriptions. Price, 2 sheets, perf. and imperf., $5.50.

Type of Regular Issue, 1958.

Olympic Winners and Flags: 11c, Charles Jenkins, 400 & 800 meter run, and Thomas Courtney, 1,600 meter relay, United States. 16c, Field hockey team, India. 17c, Yachting team, Sweden.

Photogravure.

1958, Oct. 30 *Perf. 13½* Unwmkd.

Flags in National Colors

C106	A125	11c bl; ol & brn	35	35
C107	A125	16c lt grn, org & dk bl	45	45
C108	A125	17c ver, bl & yel	50	50

1956 Olympic winners. Exist imperf.

Miniature sheets of 3 exist, perf. and imperf., containing one each of Nos. C106–C108. Size: 140x78½mm. Price, 2 sheets, perf. and imperf., $3.

Fair Type of Regular Issue, 1958.

1958, Dec. 9 Litho. *Perf. 12½*

C109	A127	9c gray	30	20
C110	A127	25c lt vio	75	45
a.		Souvenir sheet of 3, imperf.	2.25	1.75

No. C110a contains one each of Nos. C109-C110 and 507 and measures 137x72½mm. Black marginal inscription.

Issued for the Universal and International Exposition at Brussels.

Polo Type of Regular Issue, 1959

Design: 11c, Dominican polo team.

1959, May 15 *Perf. 12*

C111	A130	11c orange	45	40

Jamaica-Dominican Republic polo match at Ciudad Trujillo.

"San Cristobal" Plane
AP42

Lithographed.

1960, Feb. 25 *Perf. 11½* Unwmkd.

C112	AP42	13c org, bl, grn & gray	45	25

Dominican Civil Aviation.

Children and WRY Emblem
AP43

1960, Apr. 7 *Perf. 12½*

C113	AP43	10c plum, gray & grn	55	45
C114	AP43	13c gray & grn	65	55

Issued to publicize World Refugee Year, July 1, 1959–June 30, 1960.

Olympic Type of Regular Issue.

Olympic Winners: 11c, Pat McCormick, U.S.A., diving. 16c, Mithat Bayrack, Turkey, welterweight wrestling. 17c, Ursula Happe, Germany, 200 meter breast stroke.

Photogravure

1960, Sept. 14 *Perf. 13½*

Flags in National Colors

C115	A136	11c bl, gray & brn	30	30
C116	A136	16c red, brn & ol	40	40
C117	A136	17c blk, bl & ocher	45	45

Issued to commemorate the 17th Olympic Games, Rome, Aug. 25–Sept. 11. Exist imperf.

Miniature sheets of 3 exist, perf. and imperf., containing one each of Nos. C115–C117, with no marginal inscription. Size: 160x76mm. Price, 2 sheets, perf. and imperf., $3.75.

Coffee-Cacao Type of Regular Issue, 1961

1961, Dec. 30 Litho. *Perf. 12½*

C118	A140	13c org ver	40	40
C119	A140	33c brt yel	85	85

Exist imperf.

Anti-Malaria Type of Regular Issue, 1962

1962, Apr. 29 *Perf. 12* Unwmkd.

C120	A141	13c pink & red	35	30

C121 A141 33c org & dp org 75 75

Issued for the World Health Organization drive to eradicate malaria.

Type of Regular Issue, 1962.

Designs: 13c, Broken fetters and laurel. 50c, Flag, torch and inscription.

1962, May 30 ***Perf. 12½***

C122 A142 13c brn, yel, ol, ultra & red 40 30
C123 A142 50c rose lil, ultra & red 1.50 1.00

First anniversary, end of Trujillo era. No. C122 exists imperf.

UPAE Type of Regular Issue, 1962

1962, Oct. 23 ***Perf. 12½***

C124 A146 13c brt bl 50 30
C125 A146 22c dl red brn 70 60

Issued to commemorate the 50th anniversary of the founding of the Postal Union of the Americas and Spain, UPAE. Exist imperf.

Nouel Type of Regular Issue, 1962

Design: Frame altered with rosary and cross surrounding portrait.

1962, Dec. 18

C126 A147 13c bl & pale bl 50 30
C127 A147 25c vio & pale vio 75 65
a. Souv. sheet 1.25 1.25

Birth centenary of Archbishop Adolfo Alejandro Nouel, president of Republic in 1911. Exist imperf.

No. C127a contains one each of Nos. C126–C127 imperf. Pale violet margin with blue inscription. Size: 153x93mm.

Sanchez, Duarte, Mella
AP44

1963, July 7 **Litho.** ***Perf. 11½x12***

C128 AP44 15c orange 40 30

Issued to commemorate the 120th anniversary of separation from Haiti.

World Map
AP45

1963, Oct. 25 ***Perf. 12½*** **Unwmkd.**

C129 AP45 10c gray & car 40 35

Centenary of International Red Cross. Exists imperf.

Human Rights Type of Regular Issue, 1963

1963, Dec. 10 **Lithographed**

C130 A152 7c fawn & red brn 30 25
C131 A152 10c lt bl & bl 35 25

15th anniversary, Universal Declaration of Human Rights. Exist imperf.

Ramses II Battling the Hittites (from Abu Simbel)
AP46

1964, March 8 ***Perf. 12½***

C132 AP46 10c brt vio 35 25
C133 AP46 13c yellow 40 35

UNESCO world campaign to save historic monuments in Nubia. Exist imperf.

Striated Woodpecker—AP47

1964, June 8 **Lithographed**

C134 AP47 10c multi 40 30

Type of Space Issue, 1964

Designs: 7c, Rocket leaving earth. 10c, Space capsule orbiting earth.

1964, July 28 ***Perf. 12½*** **Unwmkd.**

C135 A156 7c brt grn 40 25
C136 A156 10c vio bl 50 35
a. Souv. sheet 5.00 5.00

Issued to commemorate the conquest of space.

No. C136a contains 7c and 10c stamps similar to Nos. C135–C136 with gray border, violet blue inscription and simulated perforation. Size: 149x82mm.

Pres. John F. Kennedy
AP48

1964, Nov. 22 ***Perf. 11½***

C137 AP48 10c buff & dk brn 50 35

Issued in memory of President John F. Kennedy (1917–63). Sheets of 10 (5x2) with brown marginal inscription and date and sheets of 50.

U.P.U. Type of Regular Issue

1964, Dec. 5 **Litho.** ***Perf. 12½***

C138 A157 7c blue 20 18

Issued to commemorate the 15th Universal Postal Union Congress, Vienna, Austria, May–June, 1964.

ICY Type of Regular Issue, 1965

1965, Feb. 16 ***Perf. 12½*** **Unwmkd.**

C139 A158 10c lil & vio 35 30

Issued to publicize the United Nations International Cooperation Year.

Basilica of Our Lady of Altagracia
AP49

1965, Mar. 18 ***Perf. 12½*** **Unwmkd.**

C140 AP49 10c multi 50 35

Issued to commemorate the Fourth Mariological Congress and the Eleventh International Marian Congress.

Abraham Lincoln
AP50

1965, Apr. 15 **Litho.** ***Perf. 12½***

C141 AP50 17c brt bl 50 35

Issued to commemorate the centenary of the death of Abraham Lincoln.

Stamp Centenary Type of Regular Issue, 1965

Design: Stamp of 1865, (No. 2).

1965, Dec. 28 **Litho.** ***Perf. 12½***

C142 A161 7c vio, lt grn & blk 35 30
C143 A161 10c yel, lt grn & blk 40 35

Issued to commemorate the centenary of the first Dominican postage stamps.

ITU Emblem, Old and New Communication Equipment
AP51

1966, Apr. 6 **Litho.** ***Perf. 12½***

C144 AP51 28c pink & car 80 60
C145 AP51 45c brt grn & grn 1.25 1.00

Issued to commemorate the centenary (in 1965) of the International Telecommunication Union.

Butterfly Type of Regular Issue

1966, Nov. 8 **Litho.** ***Perf. 12½***

Various Butterflies in Natural Colors

Size: 35x24mm.

C146 A164 10c lt vio & vio 50 30
C147 A164 50c org & dp org 2.00 1.25
C148 A164 75c pink & rose red 3.00 1.75

Altar Type of Regular Issue

1967, Jan. 18 **Litho.** ***Perf. 11½***

C149 A165 7c lt ol grn 20 15
C150 A165 10c lilac 25 20
C151 A165 20c yel brn 45 35

Chess Type of Regular Issue

Design: 10c, Pawn and Bishop.

1967, June 23 **Litho.** ***Perf. 12½***

C152 A167 10c ol, lt ol & blk 50 35
a. Souv. sheet 1.25 1.25

Issued to commemorate the 5th Central American Chess Championships, Santo Domingo. No. C152a contains 2 imperf. stamps similar to Nos. 636 and C152. Gray chessboard design in margin with map of Dominican Republic and black inscription. Size: 117x76mm.

Alliance for Progress Type of Regular Issue

1967, Sept. 16 **Litho.** ***Perf. 12½***

C153 A168 8c gray 22 15
C154 A168 10c blue 28 18

Alliance for Progress, 6th anniversary.

Cornucopia and Emblem
AP52

Latin American Flags
AP53

1967, Oct. 7

C155 AP52 12c multi 30 20

Issued to commemorate the 25th anniversary of the Inter-American Agriculture Institute.

Satellite Type of Regular Issue

1968, June 15 **Typo.** ***Perf. 12***

C156 A170 10c dp bl & multi 40 30
C157 A170 15c pur & multi 55 40

World Meteorological Day, Mar. 23.

Boxing Type of Regular Issue

Designs: Two views of boxing match.

1968, June 29

C158 A171 7c org yel & grn 25 15
C159 A171 10c gray & bl 35 20

See note after No. 641.

Lions Type of Regular Issue

1968, Aug. 9 **Litho.** ***Perf. 11½***

C160 A172 10c ultra & multi 35 20

Issued to commemorate the 50th anniversary (in 1967) of Lions International.

Olympic Type of Regular Issue

Designs (Olympic Emblem and): 10c, Weight lifting. 33c, Pistol shooting.

1968, Nov. 12 **Litho.** ***Perf. 11½***

C161 A173 10c buff & multi 35 35
C162 A173 33c pink & multi 1.10 1.00

Issued to commemorate the 19th Olympic Games, Mexico City, Oct. 12–27.

1969, Jan. 25 **Litho.** ***Perf. 12½***

C163 AP53 10c pink & multi 30 18

Issued to publicize the 7th Inter-American Savings and Loan Conference, Santo Domingo, Jan. 25–31.

Taino Art Type of Regular Issue

Taino Art: 7c, Various spatulas with human heads (vert.). 10c, Female torso forming drinking vessel. 20c, Vase with human head (vert.).

1969, Jan. 31 **Litho.** ***Perf. 12½***

C164 A175 7c lt bl, bl & lem 20 12
C165 A175 10c pink, ver & brn 35 20
C166 A175 20c yel, org & brn 50 35

COTAL Type of Regular Issue

Design: 10c, Airport of the Americas and COTAL emblem.

1969, May 25 **Litho.** ***Perf. 12½***

C167 A178 10c brn & pale fawn 25 18

See note after No. 655.

ILO Type of Regular Issue

1969, June 27 **Litho.** ***Perf. 12½***

C168 A179 10c rose, red & blk 25 18

Issued to commemorate the 50th anniversary of the International Labor Organization.

Baseball Type of Regular Issue

Designs: 7c, Bleachers, Tetelo Vargas Stadium (horiz.). 10c, Batter, catcher and umpire. 1p, Quisqueya Stadium (horiz.).

1969, Aug. 15 **Litho.** ***Perf. 12½***

Size: 43x30mm. (7c, 1p); 21x31mm. (10c).

C169 A180 7c mag & org 30 18
C170 A180 10c mar & rose red 40 25
C171 A180 1p vio bl & brn 3.00 2.00

Issued to publicize the 17th World Amateur Baseball Championships.

Electrification Types of Regular Issue

Design: No. C172, Rio Haina steam plant. No. C173, Valdesa Dam.

1969 **Lithographed** ***Perf. 12***

C172 A181 10c org ver 30 15
C173 A182 10c multi 30 15

Issued to publicize the national electrification plan.

Issue dates: No C172, Sept. 15; No. C173, Oct. 15.

Duarte Type of Regular Issue

1970, Jan. 26 **Litho.** ***Perf. 12***

C174 A183 10c brn & dk brn 30 18

Issued for Duarte Day in memory of Juan Pablo Duarte (1813–1876), liberator.

Census Type of Regular Issue

Design: 10c, Buildings and census emblem.

1970, Feb. 6 **Perf. 11**

C175 A184 10c lt bl & multi 35 25

Issued to publicize the 1970 census.

Sculpture Type of Regular Issue

Design: 10c, The Prisoner, by Abelardo Rodriguez Urdaneta (vert.).

1970, Feb. 20 **Litho.** **Perf. 12½**

C176 A186 10c bluish gray 30 20

Issued to honor Abelardo Rodriguez Urdaneta, sculptor.

Masonic Type of Regular Issue

1970, Mar. 2

C177 A187 10c brown 25 18

The 8th Inter-American Masonic Conference, Santo Domingo, Mar. 1–7.

Satellite Type of Regular Issue

1970, May 25 **Litho.** **Perf. 12½**

C178 A188 7c bl & gray 25 20

World Telecommunications Day.

U.P.U. Type of Regular Issue

1970, June 5 **Perf. 11**

C179 A189 10c yel & brn 20 18

Inauguration of new Universal Postal Union headquarters, Bern.

Education Year Type of Regular Issue

1970, June 26 **Litho.** **Perf. 12½**

C180 A190 15c brt pink 30 25

International Education Year, 1970.

Dancers
AP54

Album, Globe and Emblem
AP55

Design: 10c, U.N. emblem and wheel.

1970, Oct. 12 **Litho.** **Perf. 12½**

C181 AP54 7c bl & multi 20 12
C182 AP54 10c pink & multi 30 18

Issued to publicize the First World Exhibition of Books and Culture Festival, Santo Domingo, Oct. 11–Dec. 11.

1970, Oct. 26 **Litho.** **Perf. 11**

C183 AP55 10c multi 30 20

Issued to publicize EXFILCA 70, 2nd Interamerican Philatelic Exhibition, Caracas, Venezuela, Nov. 27–Dec. 6.

Basilica of Our Lady of Altagracia
AP56

1971, Jan. 20 **Litho.** **Perf. 12½**

C184 AP56 17c multi 55 35

Inauguration of the Basilica of Our Lady of Altagracia.

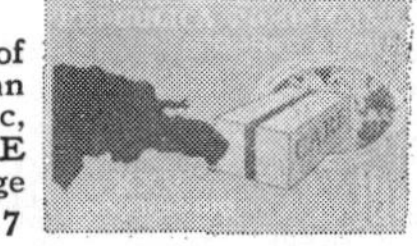

Map of Dominican Republic, CARE Package
AP57

1971, May 28 **Litho.** **Perf. 12½**

C185 AP57 10c bl & grn 25 18

25th anniversary of CARE, a U.S.-Canadian Cooperative for American Relief Everywhere.

Sports Type of Regular Issue

Design: 7c, Volleyball.

1971, Sept. 10 **Perf. 11**

C186 A195 7c lil & gray 25 15

2nd National Games.

Animal Type of Regular Issue

Design: 25c, Cock and grain.

1971, Sept. 29 **Perf. 12½**

C187 A196 25c blk & multi 60 45

6th National agriculture and livestock census.

Independence Type of Regular Issue

Design: 10c, Dominican-Colombian flag of 1821.

1971, Dec. 1 **Perf. 11**

C188 A197 10c vio bl, yel & red 25 18

Sesquicentennial of first national independence.

Christmas Type of Regular Issue

Design: 10c, Bell, 1493.

1971, Dec. 10 **Perf. 12½**

C189 A198 10c red, grn & yel 25 18

Christmas 1971.

UNICEF Type of Regular Issue

Design: 15c, UNICEF emblem and child on beach.

1971, Dec. **Perf. 11**

C190 A199 15c multi 35 27

25th anniversary of the United Nations International Children's Fund (UNICEF).

Book Year Type of Regular Issue

1972, Jan. 25 **Litho.** **Perf. 12½**

C191 A200 12c lil, dk bl & red 30 22

International Book Year 1972.

Magnifying Glass over Peru on Map of Americas
AP58

"Your Heart is your Health"
AP59

1972, Mar. 7 **Litho.** **Perf. 12**

C192 AP58 10c bl & multi 35 25

EXFILIMA '71, 3rd Inter-American Philatelic Exposition, Lima, Peru, Nov. 6–14, 1971.

1972, Apr. 27 **Litho.** **Perf. 11**

C193 AP59 7c red & multi 20 12

World Health Day.

Taino Art Type of 1972

Taino Art: 8c, Ritual vessel showing human figures. 10c, Trumpet (shell). 25c, Carved vomiting spoons. All horiz.

1972, May 10 **Litho.** **Perf. 11**

C194 A201 8c multi 20 12
C195 A201 10c lt bl & multi 30 15
C196 A201 25c multi 65 35

Telecommunications Type of Regular Issue

1972, May 17 **Perf. 12½**

C197 A202 21c yel & multi 50 30

4th World Telecommunications Day.

Exhibition Type of Regular Issue

1972, June 3

C198 A203 33c org & multi 90 50

First National Philatelic Exhibition, Santo Domingo, June 3–17.

Olympic Type of Regular Issue.

Design: 33c, Running.

1972, Aug. 25 **Litho.** **Perf. 12½**

C199 A204 33c yel & multi 1.00 60

20th Olympic Games, Munich, Aug. 26–Sept. 11.

Club Type of Regular Issue

1972, Sept. 29 **Litho.** **Perf. 10½**

C200 A205 20c bl & multi 50 30

50th anniversary of the Club Activo 20–30 Internacional.

Morel Type of Regular Issue

1972, Oct. 20 **Litho.** **Perf. 12½**

C201 A206 10c multi 25 15

Emilio A. Morel (1884–1958), poet and journalist.

Bank Type of Regular Issue

Design: 25c, Silver coin, 1947, and entrance to the Mint.

1972, Oct. 23

C202 A207 25c ocher & multi 60 35

25th anniversary of the Central Bank.

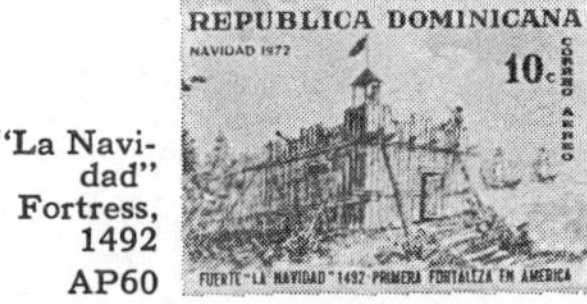

"La Navidad" Fortress, 1492
AP60

1972, Nov. 21 **Litho.** **Perf. 12½**

C203 AP60 10c multi 20 14

Christmas 1972.

Sports Type of Regular Issue

Designs: Various sports.

1973, Mar. 30 **Litho.** **Perf. 13½x13**

C204 A212 8c blk & lt bl, block of 4 1.25 80
a. Upper left 25 15
b. Upper right 25 15
c. Lower left 25 15
d. Lower right 25 15
C205 A212 10c dk bl & lil rose, block of 4 1.75 1.00
a. Upper left 35 20
b. Upper right 35 20
c. Lower left 35 20
d. Lower right 35 20

Publicity for the 12th Central American and Caribbean Games, Santo Domingo, Summer 1974.

Easter Type 1973

Design: 10c, Belfry of Church of Our Lady of Help.

1973, Apr. 18 **Litho.** **Perf. 10½**

C206 A213 10c multi 30 15

Holy Week 1973.

North and South America on Globe
AP61

1973, May 29 **Litho.** **Perf. 12**

C207 AP61 7c multi 21 15

Pan-American Health Organization, 70th anniversary (in 1972).

WMO Type of Regular Issue

1973, Aug. 10 **Litho.** **Perf. 13½x13**

C208 A214 7c grn & multi 21 15

Centenary of international meteorological cooperation.

INTERPOL Emblem Police Scientist
AP62

1973, Sept. 28 **Litho.** **Perf. 10½**

C209 AP62 10c vio bl, bl & emer 30 20

50th anniversary of International Criminal Police Organization.

Handicraft Type of Regular Issue

1973, Oct. 12

Multicolored

C210 A215 7c *Sailing ship, mosaic* 21 15
C211 A215 10c *Maracas rattlesif (horiz.)* 30 20

Opening of Museum of Mankind in Santo Domingo.

Christmas Type of Regular Issue

Design: 10c, Angels adoring Christ Child.

1973, Nov. 26 **Litho.** **Perf. 13½x13**

C212 A216 10c multi 30 20

Christmas 1973.

Scout Type of Regular Issue

Design: 21c, Scouts cooking and Lord Baden-Powell.

1973, Dec. 7 **Litho.** **Perf. 12**

C213 A217 21c red & multi 63 42

50th anniversary of Dominican Republic Boy Scouts.

Sport Type of Regular Issue

Designs: 10c, Olympic swimming pool and diver. 25c, Olympic Stadium, soccer and discus.

1974, Feb. 25 **Litho.** **Perf. 13½**

C214 A218 10c bl & multi 30 20
C215 A218 25c multi 75 50

12th Central American and Caribbean Games, Santo Domingo, 1974.

The Last Supper
AP63

1974, June 27 **Litho.** **Perf. 13½**

C216 AP63 10c multi 30 20

Holy Week 1974.

Bridge Type of 1974

Design: 10c, Higuamo Bridge.

1974, July 12 **Perf. 12**

C217 A221 10c multi 30 20

Diabetes Type of 1974

Designs (Map of Dominican Republic, Diabetics' Emblem and): 7c, Kidney. 33c, Eye and heart.

1974, Aug. 22 **Litho.** **Perf. 13**

C218 A222 7c yel & multi 22 15
C219 A222 33c lt bl & multi 1.00 65

Fight against diabetes.

UPU Type of 1974

Designs (UPU Emblem and): 7c, Ships. 33c, Jet.

1974, Oct. 9 Litho. *Perf. 13½*

C220	A223	7c grn & multi	22	15
C221	A223	33c red & multi	1.00	35
a.		Souvenir sheet of 4	1.75	1.75

Centenary of Universal Postal Union. No. C221a contains one each of Nos. 727-728 and C220-C221 forming continuous design. Red marginal inscription. Size: 120x91mm.

Golfers and Championship Emblem AP64

Design: 20c, Golfer and Golf Association emblem.

1974, Oct. 24 Litho. *Perf. 13x13½*

C222	AP64	10c grn & multi	35	25
C223	AP64	20c grn & multi	65	45

World Amateur Golf Championships.

Hand Holding Dove AP65

1974, Dec. 3 Litho. *Perf. 12*

C224	AP65	10c multi	30	20

Christmas 1974.

FAO Type of 1974

Design: 10c, Bee, beehive and barrel of honey.

1974, Dec. 5

C225	A227	10c multi	30	20

World Food Program, 10th anniversary.

Chrismon, Lamb, Candle and Palm AP66

Spain No. 1, España 75 Emblem AP67

1975, Mar. 26 Litho. *Perf. 13½*

C226	AP66	10c gold & multi	30	20

Holy Week 1975.

1975, Apr. 10

C227	AP67	12c red, yel & blk	36	25

España 75, International Philatelic Exhibition, Madrid, Apr. 4-13.

Development Bank Type of 1975

1975, May 19 Litho. *Perf. 10½x10*

C228	A230	10c rose car & multi	30	20

16th Assembly of the Governors of the International Development Bank, Santo Domingo, May 1975.

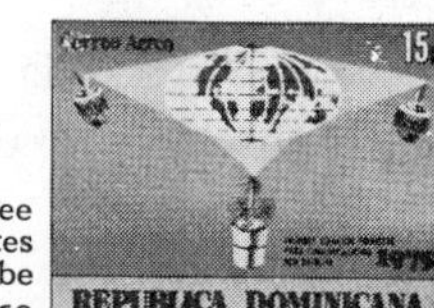

Three Satellites and Globe AP68

1975, June 21 Litho. *Perf. 13½*

C229	AP68	15c multi	45	30

Opening of first earth satellite tracking station in Dominican Republic.

Apollo Type of 1975

Design: 2p, Apollo-Soyuz link-up over earth.

1975, July 24 *Perf. 13*

Size: 42x28mm.

C230	A232	2p multi	5.00	3.00

Apollo Soyuz space test project (Russo-American cooperation), launching July 15; link-up, July 17.

Indian Chief Type of 1975

Designs: 7c, Mayobanex. 8c, Cotubanama and Juan de Esquivel. 10c, Enriquillo and Mencia.

1975, Sept. 27 Litho. *Perf. 12*

C231	A235	7c lt grn & multi	21	14
C232	A235	8c org & multi	24	16
C233	A235	10c gray & multi	30	20

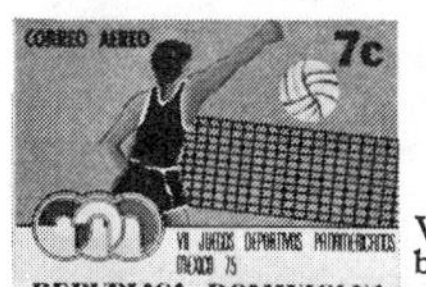

Volleyball AP69

Design: 10c, Weight lifting and Games' emblem.

1975, Oct. 24 Litho. *Perf. 12*

C234	AP69	7c bl & multi	25	20
C235	AP69	10c multi	35	25

7th Pan-American Games, Mexico City, Oct. 13-26.

Christmas Type of 1975

Design: 10c, Dove and peace message.

1975, Dec. 12 Litho. *Perf. 13x13½*

C236	A237	10c yel & multi	30	20

Christmas 1975.

Valdesia Dam—AP70

1976, Jan. 26 Litho. *Perf. 13*

C237	AP70	10c multi	30	20

Holy Week Type 1976

Design: 10c, Crucifixion, by Eliezer Castillo.

1976, Apr. 14 Litho. *Perf. 13½*

C238	A239	10c multi	30	20

Holy Week 1976.

Bicentennial Type of 1976 and

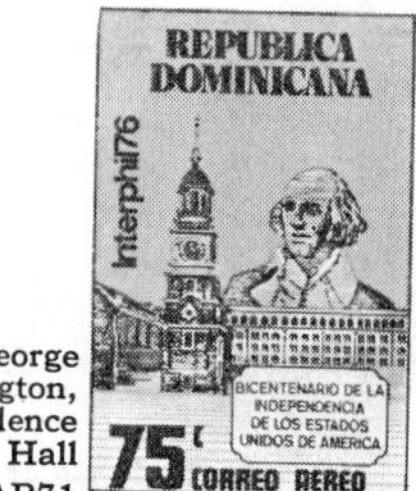

George Washington, Independence Hall AP71

Design: 10c, Hands holding maps of US and Dominican Republic.

1976, May 29 Litho. *Perf. 13½*

C239	A241	10c vio bl, grn & blk	30	20
C240	AP71	75c blk & org	2.25	1.50

American Bicentennial; No. C240 also for Interphil 76 International Philatelic Exhibition, Philadelphia, Pa., May 29-June 6.

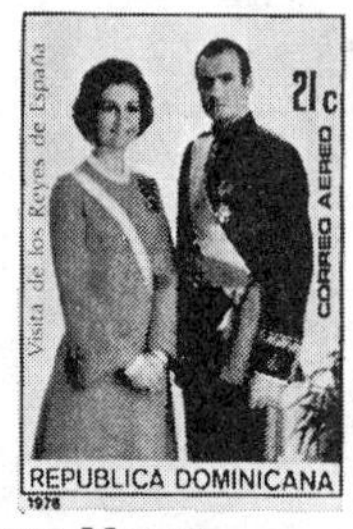

King Juan Carlos I and Queen Sofia AP72

1976, May 31

C241	AP72	21c multi	1.50	50

Visit of King Juan Carlos I and Queen Sofia of Spain.

Telephone Type of 1976

Design: 10c, Alexander Graham Bell and telephones, 1876 and 1976.

1976

C242	A243	10c multi	30	20

Centenary of first telephone call by Alexander Graham Bell, Mar. 10, 1876.

Duarte Types of 1976

Designs: 10c, Scroll with Duarte letter and Dominican flag. 33c, Duarte leaving for Exile, by E. Godoy.

1976, July 20 Litho. *Perf. 13½*

C243	A245	10c bl & multi	30	20

Perf. 13x13½

C244	A244	33c brn & multi	1.00	65

Juan Pablo Duarte, liberation hero, death centenary.

Fire Engine AP73

1976, Sept. 13 Litho. *Perf. 12*

C245	AP73	10c multi	30	20

Honoring firemen.

Radio Club Type of 1976

1976, Oct. 8 Lithographed *Perf. 13½*

C246	A247	10c bl & blk	30	20

Dominican Radio Club, 50th anniversary.

Various People AP74

1976, Oct. 15 Litho. *Perf. 13½*

C247	AP74	21c multi	65	42

Spanish heritage.

Olympic Games Type of 1976

Design (Montreal Olympic Games Emblem and): 10c, Running. 25c, Basketball.

1976, Oct. 22 *Perf. 12*

C248	A249	10c ocher & multi	30	20
C249	A249	25c grn & multi	75	50

21st Olympic Games, Montreal, Canada, July 17-Aug. 1.

Christmas Type of 1976

Design: 10c, Angel with bells.

1976, Dec. 8 Litho. *Perf. 13½*

C250	A251	10c multi	30	20

Tourist Activities AP75

Designs: 12c, Angling and hotel. 25c, Horseback riding and waterfall (vert.).

1977, Jan. 7

Size: 36x36mm.

C251	AP75	10c multi	30	20

Size: 34x25½, 25½x34mm.

C252	AP75	12c multi	36	25
C253	AP75	25c multi	75	50

Tourist publicity.

Championship Type of 1977

1977, Mar. 4 Litho. *Perf. 13½*

C254	A253	10c yel grn & multi	30	20
C255	A253	25c lt brn & multi	75	50

10th Central American and Caribbean Children's and Young People's Swimming Championships, Santo Domingo.

Holy Week Type 1977

Design: 10c, Belfry and open book.

1977, Apr. 15 Litho. *Perf. 13½x13*

C256	A254	10c multi	30	20

Holy Week 1977.

Lions Type of 1977

1977, May 6 *Perf. 13½x13*

C257	A255	7c lt grn & multi	21	15

12th annual Dominican Republic Lions Convention.

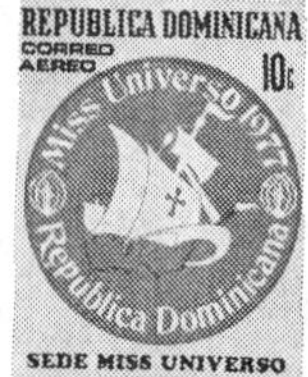

Caravel under Sail AP76

1977, July 16 Litho. *Perf. 13*

C258	AP76	10c multi	30	20

Miss Universe Contest, held in Dominican Republic.

Melon Cactus AP77

Design: 33c, Coccothrinax (tree).

1977, Aug. 19 Litho. *Perf. 12*

C259	AP77	7c multi	21	15
C260	AP77	33c multi	1.00	65

National Botanical Garden.

Chart and Factories
AP78

1977 Litho. *Perf. 13x13½*

C261 AP78 28c multi 85 55

7th Interamerican Statistics Conference.

Animal Type of 1977

Designs (Congress Emblem and): 10c, "Dorado," red Roman stud bull. 25c, Flamingo (vert.).

1977, Dec. 29 Litho. *Perf. 13*

C262 A259 10c multi 30 20
C263 A259 25c multi 75 50

8th Pan-American Veterinary and Zootechnical Congress.

Spanish Heritage Type of 1978

Design: 21c, Window, Casa del Tostado, 16th century.

1978, Jan. 19 *Perf. 13x13½*

Size: 28x41mm.

C264 A260 21c multi 65 42

Holy Week Type, 1978

Designs: 7c, Facade, Santo Domingo Cathedral. 10c, Facade of Dominican Convent.

1978, Mar. 21 Litho. *Perf. 12*

Size: 27x36mm.

C265 A261 7c multi 22 14
C266 A261 10c multi 30 20

Holy Week 1978.

Schooner Duarte
AP79

1978, Apr. 15 Litho. *Perf. 13½*

C267 AP79 7c multi 22 14

Dominican naval forces training ship.

Cardinal Type of 1978

1978, May 5 Litho. *Perf. 13*

C268 A262 10c multi 30 20

Octavio A. Beras Rojas, first Cardinal from Dominican Republic.

Antenna
AP80

1978, May 17 Litho. *Perf. 13½*

C269 AP80 25c sil & multi 75 50

10th World Telecommunications Day.

No. C1 and Map
AP81

1978, June 6

C270 AP81 10c multi 30 20

50th anniversary of first Dominican Republic airmail stamp.

Globe, Soccer Ball, Emblem
AP82

Crown, Cross and Rosary Emblem
AP83

Design: 33c, Soccer field, Argentina '78 emblem and globe.

1978, June 29

C271 AP82 12c multi 36 25
C272 AP82 33c multi 1.00 65

11th World Cup Soccer Championship, Argentina, June 1–25.

1978, July 11 *Perf. 13x13½*

C273 AP83 21c multi 62 42

Congregation of the Merciful Sisters of Charity, centenary.

Sports Type of 1978

Designs (Games' Emblem and): 7c, Baseball (vert.). 10c, Soccer (vert.).

1978, July 21 Litho. *Perf. 13½*

C274 A265 7c multi 22 14
C275 A265 10c multi 30 20

13th Central American and Caribbean Games, Medellin, Colombia.

Wright Brothers and Glider, 1902
AP84

Designs: 7c, Diagrams of Flyer I and jet (vert.). 13c, Diagram of air flow over wing. 45c, Flyer I over world map.

1978, Aug. 8 *Perf. 12*

C276 AP84 7c multi 22 14
C277 AP84 10c multi 40 20
C278 AP84 13c multi 50 25
C279 AP84 45c multi 1.50 90

75th anniversary of first powered flight.

Tourist Type of 1978

Designs: 7c, Sun and musical instruments. 10c, Sun and plane over Santo Domingo.

1978, Sept. 12 Litho. *Perf. 12*

C280 A266 7c multi 22 14
C281 A266 10c multi 30 20

Tourist publicity.

People and Globe
AP85

1978, Oct. 12 Litho. *Perf. 13½*

C282 AP85 21c multi 65 22

Spanish heritage.

Dominican Republic and UN Flags
AP86

1978, Oct. 23 *Perf. 12*

C283 AP86 33c multi 1.00 35

33rd anniversary of the United Nations.

Statue of the Virgin
AP87

1978, Dec. 5 Litho. *Perf. 12*

C284 AP87 10c multi 30 20

Christmas 1978.

Pope John Paul II
AP88

1979, Jan. 25 Litho. *Perf. 13½*

C285 AP88 10c multi 1.00 30

Visit of Pope John Paul II to the Dominican Republic, Jan. 25–26.

Map of Beata Island
AP89

1979, Jan. 25 *Perf. 12*

C286 AP89 10c multi 30 20

First expedition of radio amateurs to Beata Island.

Year of the Child Type, 1979

Designs (ICY Emblem and): 7c, Children reading book. 10c, Symbolic head and protective hands. 33c, Hands and jars.

1979, Feb. 26

C287 A269 7c multi 20 14
C288 A269 10c multi 30 20
C289 A269 33c multi 1.00 65

International Year of the Child.

Pope John Paul II Giving Benediction
AP90

Adm. Juan Bautista Cambiaso
AP91

1979, Apr. 9 Litho. *Perf. 13½*

C290 AP90 10c multi 30 20

Holy Week.

1979, Apr. 14 *Perf. 12*

C291 AP91 10c multi 30 20

135th anniversary of the Battle of Tortuguero.

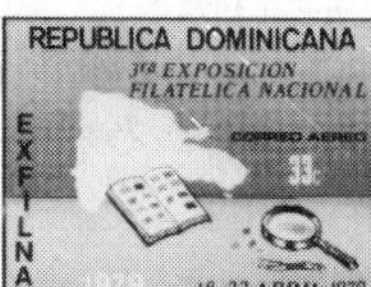

Map of Dominican Rep., Album, Magnifier
AP92

1979, Apr. 18

C292 AP92 33c multi 1.00 65

EXFILNA, 3rd National Philatelic Exhibition, Apr. 18–22.

Flower Type of 1979

Designs: 7c, Passionflower. 10c, Isidorea pungens. 13c, Calotropis procera.

1979, May 17 Litho. *Perf. 12*

C293 A271 7c multi 20 14
C294 A271 10c multi 30 20
C295 A271 13c multi 40 25

"Dr. Rafael M. Moscoso" National Botanical Garden.

Cardiology Type, 1979

Design: 10c, Figure of man showing blood circulation (vert.).

1979, June 2 Litho. *Perf. 13½*

C296 A272 10c multi 30 20

Dominican Cardiology Institute.

Sports Type of 1979

Design: 7c, Runner and Games' emblem (vert.).

1979, June 20

C297 A273 7c multi 20 14

8th Pan American Games, Puerto Rico, June 30–July 15.

Soccer Type of 1979

Design: 10c, Tennis (vert.).

1979, Aug. 8 Litho. *Perf. 12*

C298 A273 10c multi 30 20

Third National Games.

Rowland Hill, Dominican Republic No. 1
AP93

1979, Aug. 21 *Perf. 13½*

C299 AP93 2p multi 6.00 1.50

Sir Rowland Hill (1795–1879), originator of penny postage.

Electric Light Type of 1979

Design: 10c, "100" and light bulb (horiz).

1979, Aug. 27 *Perf. 13½*

C300 A275 10c multi 30 20

Centenary of invention of electric light.

Bird Type of 1979

Birds: 7c, Phaenicophilus palmarum. 10c, Calyptophilus frugivorus tertius. 45c, Icterus dominicensis.

1979, Sept. 9 Litho. *Perf. 12*

C301 A277 7c multi 20 14
C302 A277 10c multi 30 20
C303 A277 45c multi 1.35 90

Lion Type of 1979

Design: 10c, Melvin Jones, organization founder.

1979, Nov. 13 **Litho.** ***Perf. 12***

C304 A278 10c multi 30 15

Lions International Club of Dominican Republic, 10th anniversary.

Christmas Type of 1979

Christmas 1979: 10c, Three Kings riding camels.

1979, Dec. 18 **Litho.** ***Perf. 12***

C305 A279 10c multi 30 20

Holy Week Type of 1980

Holy Week: 7c, Crucifixion. 10c, Resurrection.

1980, Mar. 27 **Litho.** ***Perf. 12***

C306 A280 7c multi 20 14
C307 A280 10c multi 30 20

Navy Day—AP94

1980, Apr. 15 **Litho.** ***Perf. 13½***

C308 AP94 21c multi 65 45

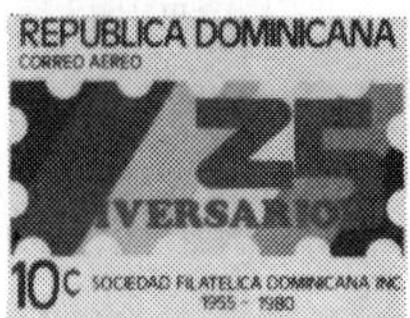

Dominican Philatelic Society, 25th Anniversary—AP95

1980, Apr. 18

C309 AP95 10c multi 30 20

Gold Type of 1980

1980, July 8 **Litho.** ***Perf. 13½***

C310 A282 10c *Drag line mining* 30 20
C311 A282 33c *Mine* 1.00 65

Nationalization of gold mining.

Tourism Secretariat Emblem—AP96

1980, Aug. 26 **Litho.** ***Perf. 13½***

C312 10c *shown* 30 20
C313 33c *Conference emblem* 1.00 65

World Tourism Conference, Manila, Sept. 27.

Iguana Type of 1980

1980, Aug. 30 ***Perf. 12***

C314 A284 7c *American crocodile* 20 14
C315 A284 10c *Cuban rat* 30 20
C316 A284 25c *Manatee* 75 50
C317 A284 45c *Turtle* 1.35 85

Painting Type of 1980

1980, Sept. 23 **Litho.** ***Perf. 13½x13***

C318 A285 10c *Abstract, by Paul Guidicelli*, vert. 30 20
C319 A285 17c *Farmer, by Yoryi Morel*, vert. 50 35

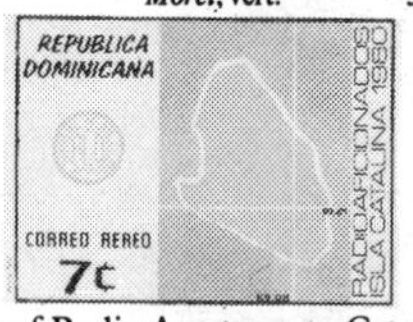

Visit of Radio Amateurs to Catalina Island — AP97

1980, Oct. 3

C320 AP97 7c multi 22 14

Rotary International, 75th Anniversary—AP98

1980, Oct. 23 **Litho.** ***Perf. 12***

C321 AP98 10c *Globe, emblem*, vert. 30 20
C322 AP98 33c *shown* 1.00 65

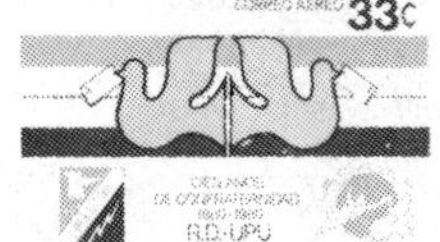

Carrier Pigeons, UPU Emblem—AP99

1980, Oct. 31 ***Perf. 13½***

C323 AP99 33c *shown* 1.00 65
C324 AP99 45c *Pigeons*, diff. 1.35 85
C325 AP99 50c *Pigeon, stamp* 1.50 1.00

Souvenir Sheet
Imperf.

C326 AP99 1.10p *UPU emblem* 3.25 3.00

Universal Postal Union membership centenary. No. C326 contains one stamp (48½x31mm); brown marginal inscription. Size: 102½x70mm.

Christmas Type of 1980

1980, Dec. 5 **Litho.** ***Perf. 13½***

C327 A286 10c *Holy Family* 30 20

Christmas 1980.

Salcedo Type of 1981

Design: Map and arms of Salcedo.

1981, Jan. 14 **Litho.** ***Perf. 13½***

C328 A287 10c multi 30 20

Industrial Symbols, Seminar Emblem—AP100

1981, Feb. 18 **Litho.** **Perf 13½**

C329 AP100 10c shown 30 20
C330 AP100 33c Seminar emblem 1.00 65

CODIA Chemical Engineering Seminar.

National Games Type of 1981

1981, Mar. 31 **Litho.** ***Perf. 13½***

C331 A289 10c Baseball 30 20

Admiral Juan Alejandro Acosta—AP101

1981, Apr. 15

C332 AP101 10c multi 30 20

Battle of Tortuguero anniversary.

13th World Telecommunications Day—AP102

1981, May 16 **Litho.** ***Perf. 12***

C333 AP102 10c multi 30 20

Heinrich von Stephan AP103

Worker in Wheelchair AP104

1981, July 15 **Litho.** ***Perf. 13½***

C334 AP103 33c tan & lt red brn 1.00 65

Birth sesquicentennial of Universal Postal Union founder.

1981, July 24

C335 AP104 7c Stylized people 22 14
C336 AP104 33c shown 1.00 65

Intl. Year of the Disabled.

EXPURIDOM '81 Intl. Stamp Show, Santo Domingo, July 31—Aug. 2 AP105

1981, July 31

C337 AP105 7c multi 22 14

Bullet Holes in Target, Competition Emblem—AP106

1981, Aug. 12

C338 AP106 10c shown 30 20
C339 AP106 15c Riflemen 45 30
C340 AP106 25c Pistol shooting 75 50

2nd World Sharpshooting Championship.

Exports—AP107

1981, Oct. 16 **Litho.** ***Perf. 12***

C341 AP107 7c Jewelry 22 14
C342 AP107 10c Handicrafts 30 20
C343 AP107 11c Fruit 34 22
C344 AP107 17c Vegetables 52 34

World Food Day—AP108

1981, Oct. 16 **Litho.** ***Perf. 13½***

C345 AP108 10c Fruits 30 20
C346 AP108 50c Vegetables 1.50 1.00

5th Natl. Games—AP109

1981, Dec. 5 **Litho.** ***Perf. 13½***

C347 AP109 10c Javelin, vert. 30 20
C348 AP109 50c Cycling 1.50 1.00

Orchids—AP110

1981, Dec. 14

C349 AP110 7c Encyclia cochleata 22 14
C350 AP110 10c Broughtonia domingensis 30 20
C351 AP110 25c Encyclia truncata 75 50
C352 AP110 75c Elleanthus capitatus 2.25 1.50

Christmas Type of 1981

1981, Dec. 23

C353 A294 10c Dove, sun 30 20

Battle of Tortuguero Anniv.—AP111

1982, Apr. 15 Litho. perf. 13½

C354	AP111	10c Naval Academy, cadets	30	20

1982 World Cup Soccer
AP112

American Air Forces Cooperation System
AP113

Designs: Various soccer players.

1982, Apr. 19

C355	AP112	10c multi	30	20
C356	AP112	21c multi	65	42
C357	AP112	33c multi	1.00	65

1982, Apr. 12 ***Perf. 12***

C358	AP113	10c multi	30	20

Scouting Year—AP114

1982, Apr. 30 Litho. ***Perf. 13½***

C359	AP114	10c Baden-Powell, vert.	30	20
C360	AP114	15c Globe	45	30
C361	AP114	25c Baden-Powell, scout, vert.	75	50

Dancers
AP115

Espamer '82 Emblem
AP116

1982, June 1 Litho. ***Perf. 13½***

C362	AP115	7c Emblem	22	14
C363	AP115	10c Cathedral, Casa del Tostado, Santo Domingo	30	20
C364	AP115	33c shown	1.00	65

Tourist Org. of the Americas, 25th Congress (COTAL '82), Santo Domingo.

1982, July 5

Espamer '82 Intl. Stamp Exhibition, San Juan, Oct. 12-17: Symbolic stamps. 7c, 13c horiz.

C365	AP116	7c multi	22	14
C366	AP116	13c multi	40	25
C367	AP116	50c multi	1.50	1.00

Sports Type of 1982

1982, Aug. 13 ***Perf. 12***

C368	A300	10c Basketball	30	20
C369	A300	13c Boxing	40	25
C370	A300	25c Gymnast	75	50

Harbor, by Alejandro Bonilla—AP117

Paintings: 10c, Portrait of a Woman, by Leopoldo Navarro. 45c, Amelia Francasci, by Luis Desangles. 2p, Portrait, by Abelardo Rodriguez Urdaneta. 10c, 45c, 2p vert.

1982, Aug. 20 ***Perf. 13***

C371	AP117	7c multi	22	14
C372	AP117	10c multi	30	20
C373	AP117	45c multi	1.35	90
C374	AP117	2p multi	6.00	4.00

San Pedro de Macoris Type of 1982

1982, Aug. 26

Size: 42x29mm.

C375	A301	7c Lake	22	14

35th Anniv. of Central Bank—AP118

1982 Litho. ***Perf. 13½x13***

C376	AP118	10c multi	30	20

490th Anniv. of Discovery of America—AP119

1982, Oct. 7 Litho. ***Perf. 13½***

C377	AP119	7c Map	22	14
C378	AP119	10c Santa Maria, vert.	30	20
C379	AP119	21c Colombus, vert.	65	42

Christmas Type of 1982

1982, Dec. 8

C380	A303	10c multi	30	20

AIR POST SEMI-POSTAL STAMPS

Nos. C97-C99 Surcharged in Red

Engraved and Lithographed.

1957, Feb. 8 *Perf. 11½* **Unwmkd.**

Flags in National Colors

CB1	A117	11c +2c ultra & red org	40	40
CB2	A117	16c +2c car & lt grn	55	55
CB3	A117	17c +2c blk, vio & red	60	60

The surtax was to aid Hungarian refugees. A similar 25c surcharge was applied to the souvenir sheets described in the footnote following No. C99. Price, 2 sheets, perf. and imperf., $17.50.

Nos. C100-C102 Surcharged in Red Orange

1957, Sept. 9 Photo. *Perf. 13½*

Flags in National Colors

CB4	A118	11c +2c yel grn & dk bl	60	55
CB5	A118	16c +2c lil & dk bl	75	75
CB6	A118	17c +2c brn & bl grn	80	80

See note after No. B10.

A similar 5c surcharge was applied to the miniature sheets described in the footnote following No. 483. Price, 4 sheets, Perf. & imperf., medal and flag, $40.

Types of Olympic Air Post Stamps, 1957, Surcharged in Carmine

+2¢ +2¢

REFUGIADOS REFUGIADOS

a *b*

Engraved and Lithographed

1958, May 26 *Perf. 13½*

Flags in National Colors

Pink Paper

CB7	A119(a)	11c +2c ultra	40	40
CB8	A119(b)	11c +2c ultra	40	40
CB9	A120(a)	16c +2c rose car	50	50
CB10	A120(b)	16c +2c rose car	50	50
CB11	A119(a)	17c +2c cl	60	60
CB12	A119(b)	17c +2c cl	60	60
		Nos. CB7-CB12 (6)	3.00	3.00

The surtax was for the United Nations Relief and Works Agency for Palestine Refugees.

A similar 5c surcharge, plus marginal United Nations emblem and "UNRWA," was applied to the miniature sheets described in the footnote following No. C105. Price, 4 sheets, perf. and imperf., $30.

Nos. C106-C108 Surcharged

Photogravure.

1959, Apr. 13 *Perf. 13½* **Unwmkd.**

Flags in National Colors

CB13	A125	11c +2c bl, ol & brn	75	75
CB14	A125	16c +2c lt grn, org & dk bl	1.00	1.00
CB15	A125	17c +2c ver bl & yel	1.50	1.50

Issued for the International Geophysical Year.

A similar 5c surcharge was applied to the miniature sheets described in the footnote following No. C108. Price, 2 sheets, perf. and imperf., $25.

Type of Regular Issue 1957 Surcharged in Red

Engraved and Lithographed

1959, Sept. 10 *Imperf.*

Flags in National Colors

CB16	A117	11c +2c ultra & red org	50	50
CB17	A117	16c +2c car & lt grn	60	60
CB18	A117	17c +2c blk, vio & red	65	65

Issued for the 3rd Pan American Games, Chicago, Aug. 27-Sept. 7, 1959.

World Refugee Year Issue.

Nos. C113-C114 Surcharged in Red

1960, Apr. 7 Litho. *Perf. 12½*

CB19	AP43	10c+5c plum, gray & green	40	40
CB20	"	13c+5c gray & green	45	45

For souvenir sheets see note after No. B33.

Nos. C115-C117 Surcharged: "XV ANIVERSARIO DE LA UNESCO +2c"

Photogravure

1962, Jan. 8 *Perf. 13½* **Unwmkd.**

Flags in National Colors

CB21	A136	11c+2c blue, gray & brown	35	35
CB22	"	16c+2c red, brown & olive	50	50
CB23	"	17c+2c black, blue & ochre	55	55

See note after No. B38.

A similar 5c surcharge was applied to the miniature sheets described in the footnote following No. C117. Price, 2 sheets, perf. and imperf., $7.50.

Anti-Malaria Type of Regular Issue, 1962.

1962, Apr. 29 Litho. *Perf. 12*

CB24	A141	13c+2c pink & red	40	40
CB25	"	33c+2c orange & deep orange	90	90

Issued for the World Health Organization drive to eradicate malaria. Souvenir sheets exist, perf. and imperf. containing one each of Nos. B39-B40, CB24-CB25 and a 25c+2c pale green and yellow green. Dark brown marginal inscription. Size: 169x102mm.

Nos. C132-C133 Surcharged

1964, March 8

CB26	AP46	10c+2c brt. vio.	30	30
CB27	"	13c+2c yellow	35	35

Issued to publicize the UNESCO world campaign to save historic monuments in Nubia.

Nos. C146-C148 Surcharged Like Semi-Postal Issue B47-B51

1966, Dec. 9 Litho. *Perf. 12½*

Size: 35x24mm.

CB28	A164	10c +5c multi	50	50
CB29	A164	50c +10c multi	1.75	1.75
CB30	A164	75c +10c multi	2.50	2.50

Surtax for victims of hurricane Inez.

AIR POST OFFICIAL STAMPS.

OAP1

Typographed.

Blue Overprint.

1930, Dec. 3 *Perf. 12* **Unwmkd.**

CO1	OAP1	10c light blue	17.50	15.00
		a. Pair, one without overprint	*1,500.*	
CO2	"	20c orange	17.50	15.00

SPECIAL DELIVERY STAMPS.

Biplane

SD1

Lithographed.

1920 *Perf. 11½.* **Unwmkd.**

E1	SD1	10c dp ultra	7.00	1.50
	a.	Imperf., pair		

Special Delivery Messenger

SD2

1925

E2	SD2	10c dk bl	15.00	3.00

SD3

1927

E3	SD3	10c red brn	7.50	1.50
	a.	"E EXPRESO" at top	70.00	60.00

Type of 1927.

Redrawn.

1941

E4	SD3	10c yel grn	3.00	1.00
E5	SD3	10c dk bl grn	2.00	75

The redrawn design differs slightly from SD3.

Issue dates: E4, Mar. 27; E5, Aug. 7.

Emblem of Communications

SD4

1945, Sept. 1 *Perf. 12*

E6	SD4	10c rose carmine, carmine & dark blue	65	30

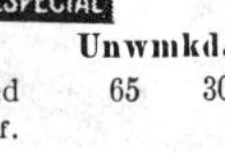

1950 Lithographed. **Unwmkd.**

E7	SD5	10c multicolored	65	30

Exists imperf.

Modern Communications System

SD6

1956, Aug. 18 *Perf. 11½*

E8	SD6	25c green	1.00	50

Carrier Pigeon

SD7

1967 Lithographed *Perf. 11½*

E9	SD7	25c light blue	90	40

Carrier Pigeon, Globe

SD8

1978, Aug. 2 Litho. *Perf. 13½*

E10	SD8	25c multicolored	75	40

ENTREGA ESPECIAL 25¢ REPUBLICA DOMINICANA CORREOS 1979

Messenger and Plane—SD9

1979, Nov. 30 *Perf. 13½*

E11	SD9	25c multi	75	50

INSURED LETTER STAMPS.

Merino Issue of 1933 Surcharged in Red or Black

PRIMA
VALORES DECLARADOS
SERVICIO INTERIOR
8
CENTAVOS

1935, Feb. 1 *Perf. 14.* Unwmkd.

No.	Type	Description	Unused	Used
G1	A34	8c on 7c ultra	50	25
a.		Invtd. surcharge	25.00	
G2	A33	15c on 10c org yel	50	20
a.		Invtd. surcharge	25.00	
G3	A35	30c on 8c dk grn	2.00	75
G4	A34	45c on 20c car rose (Bk)	3.00	1.00
G5	A36	70c on 50c lem	7.00	1.50
		Nos. G1-G5 (5)	13.00	3.70

Merino Issue of 1933 Surcharged in Red

PRIMA
VALORES DECLARADOS
SERVICIO INTERIOR
8
CENTAVOS

1940

No.	Type	Description	Unused	Used
G6	A35	8c on ½c lt vio	2.00	1.50
G7	A34	8c on 7c ultra	2.00	1.50

Coat of Arms
IL1

1940–45 Lithographed. *Perf. 11½*

Arms in Black

No.	Type	Description	Unused	Used
G8	IL1	8c brn red	1.00	10
a.		8c dk red, no shading on inner frame	1.00	12
G9	IL1	15c dp org ('45)	1.50	20
G10	IL1	30c dk grn ('41)	2.50	20
a.		30c yel grn	2.00	20
G11	IL1	45c ultra ('44)	2.50	50
G12	IL1	70c ol brn ('44)	3.00	45
		Nos. G8-G12 (5)	10.50	1.45

Redrawn Type of 1940-45.

1952–53 Arms in Black.

No.	Type	Description	Unused	Used
G13	IL1	8c car lake ('53)	70	30
G14	IL1	15c red org ('53)	1.30	45
G15	IL1	70c dp brn car	5.00	1.50

Larger and bolder numerals on 8c and 15c. Smaller and bolder "70." There are many other minor differences in the design.

1954 Type of 1940-45

Arms in Black, 15x16mm.

No.	Type	Description	Unused	Used
G16	IL1	10c carmine	75	20

Coat of Arms
IL2

Lithographed.

1955–69 *Perf. 11½* Unwmkd.

Arms in Black, 13½x11½mm.

No.	Type	Description	Unused	Used
G17	IL2	10c car rose	50	12
G18	IL2	15c red org ('56)	2.00	1.50
G19	IL2	20c red org ('58)	85	45
a.		20c org ('69)	1.25	45
b.		20c org, retouched ('69)	2.50	1.25
G20	IL2	30c dk grn ('55)	1.25	25
G21	IL2	40c dk grn ('58)	1.75	1.00
a.		40c lt yel grn ('62)	1.75	75
G22	IL2	45c ultra ('56)	3.50	1.50
G23	IL2	70c dp brn car ('56)	3.50	2.00
		Nos. G17-G23 (7)	13.35	6.82

On No. G19b the horizontal shading lines of shield are omitted.

Type of 1940–45
Second Redrawing

1963 *Perf. 12½*

Arms in Black, 17x16mm.

No.	Type	Description	Unused	Used
G24	IL1	10c red org	60	40
G25	IL1	20c orange	80	70

Third Redrawing

1966 Lithographed *Perf. 12½*

Arms in Black, 14x14mm.

No.	Type	Description	Unused	Used
G26	IL1	10c violet	50	30
G27	IL1	40c orange	2.00	1.25

Type of 1955–62

1968 Lithographed *Perf. 11½*

Arms in Black, 13½x11½mm.

No.	Type	Description	Unused	Used
G28	IL2	20c red	1.00	60
G29	IL2	60c yellow	2.25	1.50

1973–76 Lithographed *Perf. 12½*

Arms in Black, 11x11mm.

No.	Type	Description	Unused	Used
G30	IL2	10c car rose ('76)	50	30
G31	IL2	20c yellow	1.00	75
G32	IL2	20c org ('76)	1.00	50
G33	IL2	40c yel grn	2.00	1.25
a.		40c grn ('76)	1.20	60
G34	IL2	70c blue	2.25	1.50

1973 *Perf. 11½*

Arms in Black, 13½x11½mm.

No.	Type	Description	Unused	Used
G35	IL2	10c dk vio	1.00	35

1978, Aug. 9 *Perf. 10½*

Arms in Black, 11x11mm.

No.	Type	Description	Unused	Used
G36	IL2	10c rose mag	50	20
G37	IL2	40c brt grn	1.50	75

POSTAGE DUE STAMPS.

Numeral of Value
D1

Typographed.

1901	*Perf. 14.*		Unwmkd.	
J1	D1	2 (c) ol gray	60	15
J2	D1	4 (c) ol gray	75	20
J3	D1	5 (c) ol gray	1.50	30
J4	D1	10 (c) ol gray	2.50	75

Wmkd. Crosses and Circles. (116)

1909				
J5	D1	2 (c) ol gray	75	25
J6	D1	4 (c) ol gray	75	35
J7	D1	6 (c) ol gray	2.00	75
J8	D1	10 (c) ol gray	4.00	2.00

1913				
J9	D1	2 (c) ol grn	50	15
J10	D1	4 (c) ol grn	60	20
J11	D1	6 (c) ol grn	75	25
J12	D1	10 (c) ol grn	1.00	45

Lithographed.

1922	*Perf. 11½.*		Unwmkd.	
J13	D1	1 (c) ol grn	60	50

Numeral of Value
D2 D3

1942				
J14	D2	1c dk red & pale pink	20	10
J15	D2	2c dk bl & pale bl	20	15
J16	D2	4c dk grn & pale grn	20	20
J17	D2	6c brn & buff	30	25
J18	D2	8c yel org & pale yel	40	30
J19	D2	10c mag & pale pink	50	40
		Nos. J14-J19 (6)	1.80	1.40

1959

Size: 20½x25mm.

J20	D2	2c dk bl	1.00	75

1960-66 Lithographed *Perf. 11½*
Size: 21x25½mm.

J21	D3	1c dk car rose	1.00	1.00
J22	D3	2c dk bl ('66)	1.00	1.00
J23	D3	4c green	2.50	2.50

OFFICIAL STAMPS.

Bastion of February 27
O1

Lithographed

1902, Feb. 25	*Perf. 12*		Unwmkd.	
O1	O1	2c scar & blk	40	20
O2	O1	5c dk bl & blk	60	25
O3	O1	10c yel grn & blk	70	40
O4	O1	20c yel & blk	85	50
a.		Imperf., pair	12.50	

Bastion of February 27
O2

Columbus Lighthouse
O3

Wmkd. Crosses and Circles. (116)

Typographed

1909-12	*Perf. 13½x13,*		*13½x14*	
O5	O2	1c bl grn & blk	20	20
O6	O2	2c scar & blk	25	25
O7	O2	5c dk bl & blk	40	30
O8	O2	10c yel grn & blk ('12)	85	60
O9	O2	20c org & blk ('12)	1.50	85
		Nos. O5-O9 (5)	3.20	2.20

The 2c and 5c are found in both perforations; 1c and 20c only perf. 13½x13; 10c only perf. 13½x14.

1928	*Perf. 12.*		Unwmkd.	
O10	O3	1c green	10	8
O11	O3	2c red	15	15
O12	O3	5c ultra	25	25
O13	O3	10c lt bl	35	35
O14	O3	20c orange	50	50
		Nos. O10-O14 (5)	1.35	1.33

Proposed Columbus Lighthouse
O4

1937	Lithographed.		*Perf. 11½.*	
O15	O4	3c dk pur	40	15
O16	O4	7c ind & bl	50	35
O17	O4	10c org yel	70	50

Proposed Columbus Lighthouse
O5

1939-41				
O18	O5	1c dp grn & lt grn	10	6
O19	O5	2c crim & pale pink	12	8
O20	O5	3c pur & lt vio	15	8
O21	O5	5c dk bl & lt bl ('40)	35	18
O21A	O5	5c lt bl ('41)	80	20
O22	O5	7c brt bl & lt bl ('41)	40	15
O23	O5	10c yel org & pale org ('41)	60	25
O24	O5	20c brn org & buff ('41)	1.50	40
O25	O5	50c brt red lil & pale lil ('41)	3.00	1.25
		Nos. O18-O25 (9)	7.02	2.65

Type of 1939.
Redrawn.

1950				
O26	O5	50c dp car & rose	1.75	1.00

The numerals "50" measure 3mm., and are close to left and right frames; numerals measure 4mm. on No. O25. There are other minor differences.

Denominations in "Centavos Oro."

1950				
O27	O5	5c lt bl	25	10
O28	O5	10c yel & pale yel	50	20
O29	O5	20c dl org brn & buff	75	45

Letters of top inscription are 1½mm. high.

Type of 1939-41.
Second Redrawing.
Denominations in "Centavos Oro."

1958	*Perf. 11½*		Unwmkd.	
O30	O5	7c bl & lt bl	20	10
O31	O5	20c yel brn & buff	50	35
O32	O5	50c red lil & brt pink	1.25	85

The letters of top inscription are 2mm. high, the trees at base of monument have been redrawn, etc. On No. O32 the numerals are similar to No. O26.

POSTAL TAX STAMPS.

Santo Domingo after Hurricane
PT1

Hurricane's Effect on Capital
PT2

Lithographed.

1930, Dec.	*Perf. 12.*		Unwmkd.	
RA1	PT1	1c grn & rose	25	15
a.		Tête Bêche pair	2.50	2.50
RA2	PT1	2c red rose	30	25
a.		Tête Bêche pair	2.50	2.00
RA3	PT2	5c ultra & rose	50	25
a.		Tête Bêche pair	3.00	3.00
RA4	PT2	10c yel & rose	60	50
a.		Tête Bêche pair	3.00	3.00
		Imperf.		
RA5	PT1	1c grn & rose	50	30
a.		Tête Bêche pair	2.50	2.50
RA6	PT1	2c red & rose	60	35
a.		Tête Bêche pair	2.50	2.50
RA7	PT2	5c ultra & rose	75	60
a.		Tête Bêche pair	3.00	3.00
RA8	PT2	10c yel & rose	1.00	80
a.		Tête Bêche pair	3.00	3.00
		Nos. RA1-RA8 (8)	4.50	3.20

Dr. Martos Sanatorium
PT3

Nurse and Child
PT4

1944, Apr. 1	Litho.		*Perf. 11½*	
RA9	PT3	1c dp bl, sl bl & red	25	1

1947, Apr. 1			Unwmkd.	
RA10	PT4	1c dp bl, pale bl & car	25	1

Sanatorium of the Holy Help
PT5

1949, Apr. 1				
RA11	PT5	1c dp bl, pale bl & car	25	1

Youth Holding Banner
PT6

"Suffer Little Children to Come Unto Me"
PT7

1950, Apr. 1			*Perf. 11½*	
RA12	PT6	1c dp bl, pale bl & car	30	1

1950, Dec. 1			*Perf. 12, 12½*	
		Size: 22½ x 32mm.		
RA13	PT7	1c lt bl & pale bl	40	15

Vertical line centering side borders merges into dots toward the bottom. See also Nos. RA13A, RA17, RA19, RA26, RA32, RA35.

The tax was for child welfare.

1951, Dec. 1		Redrawn		
RA13A	PT7	1c lt bl & pale bl	1.25	25

In the redrawn stamp, the standing child, a blonde in No. RA13, is changed to a brunette; more foliage has been added above child's head and to branches showing in upper right corner. Vertical dashes in side borders.

Tuberculosis Sanatorium, Santiago—PT8

1952, Apr. 1	Litho.		*Perf. 11½*	
RA14	PT8	1c lt bl & car	25	15

Sword, Serpent and Crab
PT9

1953, Feb. 1	*Perf. 12.*		Unwmkd.	
RA15	PT9	1c carmine	30	15

The tax was for the Dominican League Against Cancer. See also Nos. RA18, RA21, RA43, RA46, RA51, RA56, RA61, RA67, RA72, RA76, RA82, RA88.

Tuberculosis Dispensary for Children—PT10

1953, Apr. 1 Litho. *Perf. 12½*

RA16 PT10 1c dp bl, pale bl & red 25 15

Jesus Type of 1950 Second Redrawing

1953, Dec. 1 *Perf. 11½*

Size: 22x31mm.

RA17 PT7 1c blue 50 15

Solid shading in sky reduced to a few scattered dots. Girl's left arm indicated. Rough white dots in side borders.

Cancer Type of 1952

1954, Oct. 1 Redrawn *Perf. 12½*

RA18 PT9 1c rose car 25 12
a. 1c red org ('61) 50 15
b. 1c car ('70) 60 25

Upper right serif of numeral "1" eliminated; diagonal line added through "C" and period removed; sword extended, placing top on a line with top of "1." Dots of background screen arranged diagonally. Many other differences.

The tax was for the Dominican League Against Cancer. No. RA18a exists imperf.

On No. RA18b background screen eliminates white outline of crab.

Jesus Type of 1950

1954, Dec. 1 Third Redrawing

Size: 23x32¾mm.

RA19 PT7 1c brt bl 30 15

Center completely screened. Girl's left hand shown, resting on Jesus' knee. Tiny white horizontal rectangles in side borders.

Lorraine Cross as Bell Clapper PT11

1955, Apr. 1 Litho. *Perf. 11½x12*

RA20 PT11 1c blk, yel & red 25 12

Cancer Type of 1952. Second Redrawing.

1956, Oct. 1 *Perf. 12½*

RA21 PT9 1c carmine 35 15
a. 1c red org ('64) 1.50 75

Similar to No. RA18, but dots of background screen arranged in vertical and horizontal rows. Outlines of central device, lettering and frame clearly delineated. "C" of "¢" smaller. Upper claw in solid color.

TB Dispensary Type of 1953

1954, Apr. 1 Redrawn

RA22 PT10 1c bl & red 25 15
a. Red (cross) omitted 60.00

No. RA22 has third color omitted; clouds added; bolder letters and numerals.

Angelita Trujillo PT12 — Lorraine Cross PT13

1955, Dec. 1 *Perf. 12½* Unwmkd.

RA23 PT12 1c violet 25 15

The tax was for child welfare.

1956, Apr. 1 Litho. *Perf. 11½*

RA24 PT13 1c blk, grn, lem & red 25 12

The tax was for the Anti-Tuberculosis League. Inscribed: B.C.G. (Bacillus Calmette-Guerin).

Children PT14 — Lorraine Cross PT15

1957, Apr. 1

RA25 PT14 1c red, blk, yel, grn & bl 25 12

Jesus Type of 1950 Fourth Redrawing.

1956, Dec. 1 *Perf. 12* Unwmkd.

Size: 21¾x31¼mm.

RA26 PT7 1c blue 25 12

Thin white lines around numeral boxes. Girl's bouquet touches Jesus' sleeve. Tiny white squares or rectangles in side borders. Foliage at either side of "Era de Trujillo" panel.

1958, Apr. 1 Litho. *Perf. 12½*

RA27 PT15 1c brn car & red 20 12

Type of 1958 Inscribed "1959"

1959, Apr. 1

RA28 PT15 1c brn car & red 20 12

Lorraine Cross PT16 — Lorraine Cross PT17

1960, Apr. 1 Litho. *Perf. 12*

RA29 PT16 1c bl, pale yel & red 30 20

The tax was for the Anti-Tuberculosis League.

1961, Apr. 1 *Perf. 11½* Unwmkd.

RA30 PT17 1c bl & red 15 12

The tax was for the Anti-Tuberculosis League.

Maria de los Angeles M. de Trujillo and Housing Project PT18

1961, Aug. 1 Lithographed *Perf. 12*

RA31 PT18 1c car rose 30 12

The tax was for aid to the needy. Nos. RA31–RA33 exist imperf.

Jesus Type of 1950 Fifth Redrawing

1961, Dec. 1 *Perf. 12½* Unwmkd.

RA32 PT7 1c blue 25 15

No. RA32 is similar to No. RA19, but "Era de Trujillo" has been replaced by a solid color panel.

Type of 1961 Dated "1962."

1962, Apr. 1 *Perf. 12½*

RA33 PT17 1c bl & red 15 12

The tax was for the Anti-Tuberculosis League.

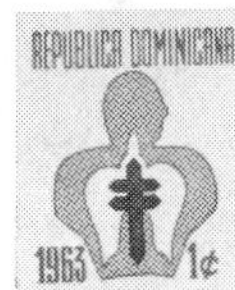

Man's Chest and Lorraine Cross PT19 — Hibiscus PT20

1963, Apr. 1 *Perf. 12x11½*

RA34 PT19 1c ultra & red 25 12

Jesus Type of 1950 Sixth Redrawing

1963, Dec. 1 *Perf. 11½*

Size: 21¾x32mm.

RA35 PT7 1c blue 20 12
a. 1c dp bl ('64) 20 12

No. RA35 is similar to No. RA26, but "Era de Trujillo" panel has been omitted.

1966, Apr. 1 Litho. *Perf. 11½*

RA36 PT20 1c emer & car 20 12

The tax was for the Anti-Tuberculosis League.

Domingoa Nodosa PT21 — Civil Defense Emblem PT22

1967, Apr. 1 Litho. *Perf. 12½*

RA37 PT21 1c lil & red 15 12

The tax was for the Anti-Tuberculosis League.

1967, July 1 Litho. *Rouletted 13*

RA38 PT22 1c multi 25 18

The tax was for the Civil Defense Organization.

Boy, School and Yule Bells PT23 — Hand Holding Invalid PT24

1967, Dec. 1 Litho. *Perf. 12½*

RA39 PT23 1c rose red & pink 35 12

1968 *Perf. 11*

RA40 PT23 1c vermilion 40 18

No. RA40 has screened background; No. RA39, smooth background.

The tax was for child welfare.

See Nos. RA49A, RA52, RA57, RA62, RA68, RA73, RA77, RA81.

1968, Mar. 19 Litho. *Perf. 12½*

RA41 PT24 1c grn & yel 15 8
a. 1c ol grn & dp yel, perf. 11½x12 ('69) 15 8

The tax was for the rehabilitation of the handicapped. See Nos. RA47, RA50, RA54.

Dogbane PT25 — Schoolyard and Torch PT26

1968, Apr. 25 Litho. *Perf. 12½*

RA42 PT25 1c emer, yel & red 8 4

The tax was for the Anti-Tuberculosis League. See Nos. RA45, RA49.

Redrawn Cancer Type of 1955

1968, Oct. 1 Litho. *Perf. 12*

RA43 PT9 1c emerald 15 8

The tax was for the Dominican League against Cancer.

1969, Feb. 1 Litho. *Perf. 12½*

RA44 PT26 1c lt bl 8 4

Issued for Education Year 1969.

Flower Type of 1968

Design: No. RA45, Violets.

1969, Apr. 25 Litho. *Perf. 12½*

RA45 PT25 1c emer, lil & red 12 8

The tax was for the Anti-Tuberculosis League.

Redrawn Cancer Type of 1955

1969, Oct. 1 Litho. *Perf. 11*

RA46 PT9 1c brt rose lil 15 5

The tax was for the Dominican League against Cancer.

Invalid Type of 1968

1970, Mar. 2 *Perf. 12½*

RA47 PT24 1c blue 18 12

The tax was for the rehabilitation of the handicapped.

Book, Sun and Education Year Emblem PT27 — Communications Emblem PT28

1970, Feb. 6 *Perf. 11*

RA48 PT27 1c brt pink 8 4

International Education Year.

Flower Type of 1968

Design: 1c, Eleanthus capitatus; cross in upper left corner, denomination in lower right.

1970, Apr. 30 *Perf. 11*

RA49 PT25 1c emer, red & yel 15 8

Tax for Anti-Tuberculosis League.

Boy Type of 1967

1970, Dec. 1 *Perf. 12½*

RA49A PT23 1c orange 30 20

1971, Jan. 2 Litho. *Perf. 11*

Size: 17½x20½mm.

RA49B PT28 1c vio bl & red (white frame) 20 10

Tax was for Postal and Telegraph Communications School.

See Nos. RA53, RA58, RA63, RA69, RA78.

Invalid Type of 1968

1971, Mar. 1 Litho. *Perf. 11*

RA50 PT24 1c brt. rose lilac 15 8

Tax was for rehabilitation of the handicapped.

Cancer Type of 1952
Third Redrawing

1971, Oct. 1 *Perf. 11½*

RA51 PT9 1c dp. yellow green 18 10

Background of No. RA51 appears white and design stands out. No. RA43 has greenish background and design appears faint. Numeral "1" on No. RA51 is 3½mm. high, on No. RA43 it is 3mm.

Boy Type of 1967

1971, Dec. 1 Litho. *Perf. 11*

RA52 PT23 1c green 35 10

Communications Type of 1971

1972, Jan. 3 Litho. *Perf. 12½*

Size: 19x22mm.

RA53 PT28 1c dk bl & red (bl frame) 20 8

Tax was for the Postal and Telegraph Communications School.

Invalid Type of 1968

1972, Mar. 1 Litho. *Perf. 11½*

RA54 PT24 1c brown 15 10

Orchid
PT29

1972, Apr. 2 *Perf. 11*

RA55 PT29 1c lt. green, red & yellow 20 10

Tax was for the Anti-Tuberculosis League.

Redrawn Cancer Type of 1954–58

1972, Oct. 2 *Perf. 12½*

RA56 PT9 1c orange 18 10

Tax was for Dominican League against Cancer.

Boy Type of 1967

1972, Dec. 1 *Perf. 12*

RA57 PT23 1c violet 15 10

Tax was for child welfare.

Communications Type of 1971

1973, Jan. 2 *Perf. 10½*

Size: 19x22mm.

RA58 PT28 1c dark blue & red (red frame) 10 8

Tax was for Postal and Telegraph Communications School.

Invalid
PT30

Hibiscus
PT31

1973, Mar. 1 Litho. *Perf. 12½*

Size: 21x25mm.

RA59 PT30 1c olive 15 8

Tax was for the Dominican Rehabilitation Association. See Nos. RA66, RA70, RA74, RA79, RA86.

1973, Apr. 17 Litho. *Perf. 10½*

RA60 PT31 1c multicolored 15 8

Tax was for Anti-Tuberculosis League. Exists imperf.

Cancer Type of 1952 Redrawn and "1973" Added

1973, Oct. 1 *Perf. 13½*

RA61 PT9 1c ol grn 10 8

Tax was for Dominican League Against Cancer.

Boy Type of 1967

1973, Dec. 1 Litho. *Perf. 13x13½*

RA62 PT23 1c blue 18 12

Communications Type of 1971

1973, Nov. 3 *Perf. 10½*

Size: 19x22mm.

RA63 PT28 1c bl & red (lt grn frame) 10 6

Tax was for Postal and Telegraph Communications School. Exists imperf.

Invalid Type of 1972

1974, Mar. 1 Litho. *Perf. 10½*

Size: 22x27½mm.

RA66 PT30 1c lt ultra 18 15

See note after No. RA59.

Cancer Type of 1952 Redrawn and "1974" Added

1974, Oct. 1 *Perf. 12*

RA67 PT9 1c orange 15 8

Tax was for Dominican League Against Cancer.

Boy Type of 1967

1974, Dec. 2 Litho. *Perf. 11½*

RA68 PT23 1c dk. brn. & buff 15 8

Communications Type of 1971

1974, Nov. 13 *Perf. 10½*

RA69 PT28 1c blue & red (yel. frame) 15 8

Invalid Type of 1972 Dated "1975"

1975, Mar. 1 *Perf. 13½x13*

Size: 21x32mm.

RA70 PT30 1c olive brown 15 8

Tax was for the Dominican Rehabilitation Association.

Catteeyopsis Rosea
PT32

Oncidium Colochilum
PT33

1975, Apr. 1 *Perf. 12*

RA71 PT32 1c blue & multi. 15 8

Tax was for Anti-Tuberculosis League.

Cancer Type of 1952 Redrawn and "1975" Added

1975, Oct. 1 Litho. *Perf. 12*

RA72 PT9 1c violet blue 15 8

Tax was for Dominican League Against Cancer. Exists imperf.

Boy Type of 1967

1975, Dec. 1 Litho. *Perf. 12*

RA73 PT23 1c red orange 15 8

Tax was for child welfare.

Invalid Type of 1973 Dated "1976"

1976, Mar. 1 Litho. *Perf. 12*

Size: 21x31mm.

RA74 PT30 1c ultramarine 15 8

Tax was for Dominican Rehabilitation Association.

1976, Apr. 6 *Perf. 13x13½*

RA75 PT33 1c green & multi. 15 8

Tax was for Anti-Tuberculosis League. See No. RA80, RA84.

Cancer Type of 1952 Redrawn and "1976" Added

1976, Oct. 1 Litho. *Perf. 13½*

RA76 PT9 1c green 15 8

Tax was for Dominican League Against Cancer.

Boy Type of 1967

1976, Dec. 1 Litho. *Perf. 13½*

RA77 PT23 1c purple 15 8

Tax was for child welfare.

Communications Type of 1971

1977, Jan. 7 Litho. *Perf. 10½*

Size: 19x22mm.

RA78 PT28 1c blue & red (lilac frame) 15 8

Tax was for Postal and Telegraph Communications School.

Invalid Type of 1973 Dated "1977"

1977, Mar. 11 *Perf. 12*

Size: 21x31mm.

RA79 PT30 1c ultramarine 15 8

Tax was for Dominican Rehabilitation Association.

Orchid Type of 1976 Dated "1977"

Orchid: Oncidium variegatum.

1977, Apr. 22 Litho. *Perf. 13½*

RA80 PT33 1c multicolored 15 8

Tax was for Anti-Tuberculosis League.

Boy Type of 1967

1977, Dec. 27 Litho. *Perf. 12*

RA81 PT23 1c emerald 15 8

Tax was for child welfare.

Cancer Type of 1952 Redrawn and "1977" Added

1978, Oct. 2 Litho. *Perf. 13½*

RA82 PT9 1c lilac rose 15 8

Tax was for Dominican League Against Cancer.

Mother, Child and Holly
PT34

University Seal
PT35

1978, Dec. 1 Litho. *Perf. 13½*

RA83 PT34 1c green 15 8

Tax was for child welfare.

See No. RA89.

Orchid Type of 1973 Dated "1978"

Flower: Yellow alder.

1978 Litho. *Perf. 13½*

RA84 PT33 1c light blue & multicolored 15 8

Tax was for Anti-Tuberculosis League.

1979, Feb. 10 Litho. *Perf. 13½*

RA85 PT35 2c ultra & gray 15

450th anniversary of University of Santo Domingo.

Invalid Type of 1973 Dated "1978"

1979, Mar. 1 Litho. *Perf. 12*

RA86 PT30 1c emerald 8

Tax was for Dominican Rehabilitation Association.

Invalid —PT36

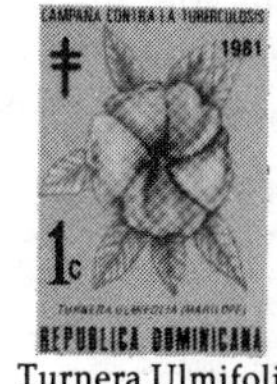

Turnera Ulmifolia (Marilope)—PT37

1980, Feb. 28 Litho. *Perf. 13½*

RA87 PT36 1c ol & cit 8 3

Cancer Type of 1952 Redrawn and "1980" Added

1980

RA88 PT9 1c vio & dk pur 8 3

Mother and Child Type of 1978 Inscribed 1980.

1980 Litho. *Perf. 13½*

RA89 PT34 1c brt bl 8 3

1981, Apr. 15 Litho. *Perf. 12*

RA90 PT37 1c multi 8 3

Tax was for Anti-Tuberculosis League.

POSTAL TAX AIR POST STAMPS.

HABILITADO PARA
CORREO AEREO

Postal Tax Stamps Surcharged in Red or Gold

+5

930, Dec. 3 ***Perf. 12*** **Unwmkd.**

AC1 PT2	5c +5c blk & rose (R)	22.50	22.50
a.	Tête bêche pair	175.00	
b.	"Habilitado Para" missing	75.00	
AC2 PT2	10c +10c blk & rose (R)	22.50	22.50
a.	Tête bêche pair	175.00	
b.	"Habilitado Para" missing	75.00	
c.	Gold surch.	225.00	225.00
d.	As "c," tête bêche pair	750.00	
e.	As "c," "Habilitado Para" missing	400.00	

Nos. RAC1–RAC2 were on sale only on Dec. 3, 1930.

AC4 PT2	5c +5c ultra & rose (R)	10.00	10.00
a.	Tête bêche pair	75.00	
b.	Inverted surcharge	70.00	
c.	Tête bêche pair, inverted surcharge	1,000.	
d.	Pair, one without surcharge	300.00	
e.	"Habilitado Para" missing	25.00	
AC5 PT2	10c +10c yel & rose (G)	7.50	7.50
a.	Tête bêche pair	70.00	
b.	"Habilitado Para" missing	30.00	

Imperf.

AC6 PT2	5c +5c ultra & rose (R)	10.00	10.00
a.	Tête bêche pair	85.00	
b.	"Habilitado Para" missing	30.00	
AC7 PT2	10c +10c yel & rose (G)	10.00	10.00
a.	Tête bêche pair	85.00	
b.	"Habilitado Para" missing	30.00	

It was obligatory to use Nos. RA1 to RA8 and RAC1 and RAC7 on all postal matter, in amounts equal to the ordinary postage.

This surtax was for the aid of sufferers from the hurricane of Sept. 3rd, 1930.

No. 261 Overprinted in Green

CORREO AEREO INTERNO

1933, Oct. 11

AC8 A32	2c scarlet	60	45
a.	Double overprint	15.00	
b.	Pair, one without ovpt.	500.00	

By official decree a copy of this stamp, in addition to the regular postage, had to be used on every letter, etc., sent by the internal air post service.

DUTCH INDIES

(See Netherlands Indies.)

DUTCH NEW GUINEA

(See Netherlands New Guinea.)

EASTERN RUMELIA

(ēs′tẽrn rōō·mē′lĭ·ȧ ; -mēl′yȧ)

(South Bulgaria)

LOCATION—In southern Bulgaria.

GOVT.—A former autonomous unit of the Turkish Empire.

CAPITAL—Philippopolis (Plovdiv).

In 1885 the province of Eastern Rumelia revolted against Turkish rule and united with Bulgaria, adopting the new name of South Bulgaria. This union was assured by the Treaty of Bucharest in 1886, following the war between Serbia and Bulgaria.

40 Paras = 1 Piastre

Counterfeits of all overprints are plentiful.

A1

A2

A3

Stamps of Turkey, 1876-84, Overprinted in Blue.

1880		Perf. 13½	Unwmkd.	
1	A1	½pi on 20pa yel grn	35.00	35.00
2	A1	2pi on 2pi yel brn		
3	A2	10pa blk & rose	40.00	
4	A2	20pa vio & grn	37.50	37.50
5	A2	1pi blk & bl		
6	A2	2pi blk & buff	75.00	75.00
7	A2	5pi red & bl	250.00	250.00
8	A3	10pa blk & red lil	25.00	

Nos. 2, 3, 5 and 8 were not placed in use.

Inverted and double overprints of all values exist.

Same, with Extra Overprint "R. O."

9	A3	10pa blk & red lil	40.00	40.00

Crescent and Turkish Inscriptions of Value

A4

1881	Typographed		Perf. 13½	
10	A4	5pa blk & ol	2.00	60
11	A4	10pa blk & grn	7.00	60
12	A4	20pa blk & rose	30	60
13	A4	1pi blk & bl	3.00	2.50
14	A4	5pi rose & bl	25.00	35.00

Tête bêche pairs, imperforates and all perf. 11½ copies of Nos. 10 to 14 were not placed in use, and were found only in the remainder stock. This is true also of a 10pa cliché in the 20pa plate, and of a cliché of Turkey No. 63 in the 1pi plate.

1884		Perf. 11½, 13½		
15	A4	5pa lil & pale lil	20	20
16	A4	10pa grn & pale grn	10	20
17	A4	20pa car & pale rose	20	
18	A4	1pi bl & pale bl	20	
19	A4	5pi brn & pale brn	150.00	

No. 17–19 were not placed in use.

Nos. 15 to 19 imperf. are from the remainder stock.

South Bulgaria.

Counterfeits of all overprints are plentiful.

Nos. 10 to 14 Overprinted in Two Types:

a

b

Type a: Four toes on each foot.
Type b: Three toes on each foot.

1885		Perf. 13½.	Unwmkd.	
		Blue Overprint.		
20	A4	5pa blk & ol	100.00	100.00
21	A4	10pa blk & grn	350.00	350.00
22	A4	20pa blk & rose	100.00	100.00
23	A4	1pi blk & bl	20.00	22.50
24	A4	5pi rose & bl	300.00	325.00
		Black Overprint.		
25	A4	1pi blk & bl	16.50	20.00
26	A4	5pi rose & bl	400.00	400.00

Same Overprint on Nos. 15 to 17.

Perf. 11½, 13½

		Blue Overprint.		
27	A4	5pa lil & pale lil, perf. 11½	9.00	14.00
a.		Perf. 13½	22.50	27.50
28	A4	10pa grn & pale grn	9.00	14.00
29	A4	20pa car & pale rose	80.00	90.00
		Black Overprint.		
30	A4	5pa lil & pale lil	16.00	20.00
31	A4	10pa grn & pale grn	16.00	20.00
32	A4	20pa car & pale rose	14.00	20.00

Nos. 10 to 14 Handstamped in Black in Two Types:

a

b

Type a: First letter at top circular.
Type b: First letter at top oval.

1885		Perf. 13½		
33	A4	5pa blk & ol	300.00	
34	A4	10pa blk & grn	300.00	
35	A4	20pa blk & rose	55.00	65.00
36	A4	1pi blk & bl	40.00	45.00
a.		On Turkey No. 63 (error)		
37	A4	5pi rose & bl	500.00	600.00

Same Handstamp in Black on Nos. 15 to 17.

Perf. 11½, 13½.

38	A4	5pa lil & pale lil, perf. 13½	11.00	11.00
a.		Perf. 11½	100.00	125.00
39	A4	10pa grn & pale grn	10.00	11.00
40	A4	20pa car & pale rose	10.00	15.00

Nos. 20 to 40 exist with inverted and double handstamps. Overprints in unlisted colors are proofs.

The stamps of South Bulgaria were superseded in 1886 by those of Bulgaria.

EASTERN SILESIA

(ēs′tẽrn sĭ·lē′shĭ·ȧ ; -shȧ)

LOCATION—In central Europe.

GOVT.—Former Austrian crownland.

AREA—1,987 sq. mi.

POP.—680,422 (estimated 1920).

CAPITAL—Troppau.

After World War I, this territory was occupied by Czechoslovakia and eventually was divided between Poland and Czechoslovakia, the dividing line running through Teschen.

100 Heller = 1 Krone
100 Fennigi = 1 Marka

Plebiscite Issues.

Stamps of Czechoslovakia 1918-20, Overprinted in Black, Blue, Violet or Red **SO 1920**

1920		Imperf.	Unwmkd.	
1	A2	1(h) dk brn	35	35
2	A1	3(h) red vio	20	20
3	A2	5(h) bl grn	37.50	32.50
4	A2	15(h) red	16.50	11.00
5	A1	20(h) bl grn	20	20
6	A2	25(h) dl vio	1.25	75
7	A1	30(h) bis (R)	25	20
8	A1	40(h) red org	30	20
9	A2	50(h) dl vio	50	40
10	A2	50(h) dk bl	1.75	1.50
11	A2	60(h) org (Bl)	1.25	1.00
12	A2	75(h) sl (R)	50	50
13	A2	80(h) ol grn (R)	50	50
14	A1	100(h) brown	60	50
15	A2	120(h) gray blk (R)	3.00	1.75
16	A1	200(h) ultra (R)	1.60	1.50
17	A2	300(h) grn (R)	2.50	2.25
18	A1	400(h) pur (R)	2.00	1.75
20	A2	500(h) red brn (Bl)	10.00	8.00
a.		Black overprint	17.50	17.50
21	A2	1000(h) vio (Bl)	12.50	10.00
a.		Black ovpt.	175.00	175.00
		Nos. 1-21 (20)	93.25	75.05

Perf. 11½, 14

22	A2	1(h) dk brn	5	5
23	A2	5(h) bl grn	10	10
24	A2	10(h) yel grn	10	10
a.		Imperf.	400.00	400.00
25	A2	15(h) red	15	15
26	A2	20(h) rose	30	30
a.		Imperf.	500.00	500.00
27	A2	25(h) dl vio	30	30
28	A2	30(h) red vio (Bl)	40	40
29	A2	60(h) org (Bl)	50	50
30	A1	200(h) ultra (R)	5.00	4.50
		Nos. 22-30 (9)	6.90	6.40

The letters "S. O." are the initials of "Silésie Orientale".

Forged cancellations are found on Nos. 1-30.

Overprinted **19 SO 20**

31	A4	500(h) sl, *grysh* (C)	100.00
32	A4	1000(h) blk brn, *brnsh* (V)	100.00

Excellent counterfeits of this overprint exist.

Stamps of Poland, 1919, Overprinted **S. O. 1920.**

1920			Perf. 11½	
41	A10	5f green	10	10
42	A10	10f red brn	10	10
43	A10	15f lt red	10	10
44	A11	25f ol grn	10	10
45	A11	50f bl grn	10	10

Overprinted **S. O. 1920.**

46	A17	1k dp grn	10	10
47	A17	1.50k brown	10	10
48	A17	2k dk bl	10	10
49	A18	2.50k dl vio	10	10
50	A19	5k sl bl	10	10
		Nos. 41-50 (10)	1.00	1.00

SPECIAL DELIVERY STAMPS.

Czechoslovakia Special Delivery Stamps Overprinted **S O 19 20**

1920		Imperf.	Unwmkd.	
		Blue Overprint.		
E1	SD1	2(h) red vio, *yel*	15	15
a.		Black overprint	1.25	1.25
E2	SD1	5(h) yel grn, *yel*	15	15
a.		Black overprint	7.50	7.50

POSTAGE DUE STAMPS.

Czechoslovakia Postage Due Stamps Overprinted In Blue or Red **SO 1920**

1920		Imperf.	Unwmkd.	
J1	D1	5(h) dp bis (Bl)	15	20
a.		Black ovpt.	65.00	70.00
J2	D1	10(h) dp bis	15	20
J3	D1	15(h) dp bis	15	20
J4	D1	20(h) dp bis	15	20
J5	D1	25(h) dp bis	15	20
J6	D1	30(h) dp bis	25	40
J7	D1	40(h) dp bis	45	50
J8	D1	50(h) dp bis	75	1.00
J9	D1	100(h) blk brn (R)	75	1.00
J10	D1	500(h) gray grn (R)	5.00	5.25
J11	D1	1000(h) pur (R)	10.00	11.50
		Nos. J1-J11 (11)	17.95	20.65

Forged cancellations exist.

NEWSPAPER STAMPS.

Czechoslovakia Newspaper Stamps Overprinted in Black **SO 1920**

1920		Imperf.	Unwmkd.	
P1	N1	2(h) gray grn	10	10
P2	N1	6(h) red	10	10
P3	N1	10(h) dl vio	45	45
P4	N1	20(h) blue	45	45
P5	N1	30(h) gray brn	45	45
		Nos. P1-P5 (5)	1.55	1.55

ECUADOR

(ĕk'wȧ·dôr)

LOCATION — On the northwest coast of South America, bordering on the Pacific Ocean.

GOVT.—Republic.

AREA—116,270 sq. mi. (approx.).

POP.—7,560,000 (est. 1977).

CAPITAL—Quito.

The Republic of Ecuador was so constituted on May 11, 1830, after the Civil War which separated the original members of the Republic of Colombia, founded by Simón Bolívar, by uniting the Presidency of Quito with the Viceroyalty of New Granada, and the Captaincy of Venezuela. The Presidency of Quito became the Republic of Ecuador.

8 Reales = 1 Peso
100 Centavos = 1 Sucre (1881)

Coat of Arms
A1 A2

Typographed.
Quadrille Paper.

1865 ***Imperf.*** **Unwmkd.**

1	A1	1r yellow	30.00	20.00

1865–66 **Wove paper**

2	A1	½r ultra	13.00	10.00
a.		½r gray bl	13.00	10.00
b.		Batonne paper	25.00	17.50
c.		Blue paper	125.00	90.00
3	A1	1r buff	18.00	13.00
a.		1r org buff	22.50	15.00
4	A1	1r yellow	13.00	10.00
a.		1r ol yel	18.00	13.00
b.		Laid paper	125.00	90.00
c.		Diagonal half used as ½r on cover		200.00
d.		Batonne paper	25.00	20.00
5	A1	1r green	180.00	45.00
a.		Diagonal half used as ½r on cover		200.00
6	A2	4r red ('66)	240.00	110.00
a.		4r red brn	240.00	110.00
b.		Arms in circle	240.00	110.00
c.		Printed on both sides	500.00	
d.		Half used as 2r on cover		1,000.

Letter paper embossed with arms of Ecuador was used in printing a number of sheets of Nos. 2, 4–6.

Papermakers' watermarks are known on No. 2 ("Bath" and crown) and No. 4 ("Rolland Freres").

On the 4r the oval holding the coat of arms is usually 13½–14mm. wide, but on about one-fifth of the stamps in the sheet it is 15–15½mm. wide, almost a circle.

The 2r, 8r and 12r, type A1, are bogus.

Proofs of the ½r, type A1, are known in black and green.

An essay of type A2 shows the condor's head facing right.

1871–72 **Blue-surface Paper**

7	A1	½r ultra	22.50	16.00
8	A1	1r yellow	130.00	50.00

Reprints of types A1 and A2 differ in color from originals, have a different sheet makeup and lack gum. Type A1 reprints usually have a double frame-line at left. All stamps on blue paper with horizontal blue lines are reprints.

Coat of Arms
A3 A4

Lithographed

1872 **White Paper** ***Perf. 11***

9	A3	½r blue	15.00	3.00
10	A4	1r yellow	17.50	5.00
11	A3	1p rose	3.00	*10.00*

The 1r surcharged 4c is fraudulent.

Coat of Arms
A5 A6

A7 A8

A9 A10

1881, Nov. 1 **Engraved** ***Perf. 12***

12	A5	1c yel brn	10	10
13	A6	2c lake	15	15
14	A7	5c blue	3.00	50
15	A8	10c orange	15	15
16	A9	20c gray vio	20	20
17	A10	50c bl grn	40	*1.20*
		Nos. 12-17 (6)	4.00	*2.30*

The 1c surcharged 3c, and 20c surcharged 5c are fraudulent.

No. 17 Surcharged in Black

DIEZ
CENTAVOS

1883, April

18	A10	10c on 50c bl grn	20.00	17.50
a.		Double surcharge		

A12 A13

A14 A15

1887

19	A12	1c bl grn	30	15
20	A13	2c vermilion	50	15
21	A14	5c blue	1.50	30
22	A15	80c ol grn	3.00	*7.50*

President Juan Flores
A16

1892

23	A16	1c orange	15	10
24	A16	2c dk brn	15	10
25	A16	5c vermilion	15	10
26	A16	10c green	15	10
27	A16	20c red brn	15	10
28	A16	50c maroon	15	*40*
29	A16	1s blue	25	*1.00*
30	A16	5s purple	75	*1.50*
		Nos. 23-30 (8)	1.90	*3.40*

The issues of 1892, 1894, 1895 and 1896 were printed by the Hamilton Bank Note Co., New York, to the order of N. F. Seebeck, who held a contract for stamps with the government of Ecuador.

No. 30 in green is said to be an essay or color trial.

Nos. 29 and 30 Surcharged in Black

1893

Surcharge Measures 25½x2½ mm.

31	A16	5c on 1s bl	2.25	2.00
32	A16	5c on 5s pur	6.50	5.00
a.		Double surcharge		

Surcharge Measures 24x2¼ mm.

33	A16	5c on 1s bl	1.75	1.50
a.		Double surcharge, one inverted		
34	A16	5c on 5s pur	7.50	6.00
a.		Double surcharge, one inverted		

Nos. 28–30 Surcharged in Black

35	A16	5c on 50c mar	75	65
a.		Inverted surch.	2.50	
36	A16	5c on 1s bl	1.25	1.00
37	A16	5c on 5s pur	6.00	5.00

President Juan Flores A19 — President Vicente Rocafuerte A20

38	A19	5c on 5s lake	1.00	75

It is stated that No. 38 was used exclusively as a postage stamp and not for telegrams.

1894 **Dated 1894.** ***Perf. 12.***

Various Frames

39	A20	1c blue	30	30
40	A20	2c yel brn	30	30
41	A20	5c green	30	30
b.		Perf. 14	4.00	1.50
42	A20	10c vermilion	50	40
43	A20	20c black	75	50
44	A20	50c orange	4.00	1.50
45	A20	1s carmine	6.00	3.00
46	A20	5s dk bl	8.00	6.00
		Nos. 39-46 (8)	20.15	12.30

1895 **Same, Dated "1895".**

47	A20	1c blue	60	50
48	A20	2c yel brn	60	50
49	A20	5c green	50	35
50	A20	10c vermilion	50	30
51	A20	20c black	75	65
52	A20	50c orange	2.50	1.25
53	A20	1s carmine	12.50	5.00
54	A20	5s dk bl	6.00	2.50
		Nos. 47-54 (8)	23.95	11.05

Reprints of the 2c, 10c, 50c, 1s and 5s of the 1894–95 issues are generally on thick paper. Original issues are on thin to medium thick paper. To distinguish reprints from originals, a comparison of paper thickness, paper color, gum, printing clarity and direction of paper weave is necessary. Price 10 cents each.

Coat of Arms
A21 A22

A23 A24

A25 A26

A27 A28

Wmk. 117

1896 **Wmkd. Liberty Cap. (117)**

55	A21	1c dk grn	50	45
56	A22	2c red	50	20
57	A23	5c blue	50	20
58	A24	10c bis brn	40	*50*
59	A25	20c orange	70	*1.00*
60	A26	50c dk bl	1.25	*2.00*
61	A27	1s yel brn	2.50	*2.50*
62	A28	5s violet	5.00	*4.00*
		Nos. 55-62 (8)	11.35	*10.85*

Unwmkd.

62A	A21	1c dk grn	60	20
62B	A22	2c red	60	20
62C	A23	5c blue	60	20
62D	A24	10c bis brn	50	*1.00*
62E	A25	20c orange	3.75	*4.00*
62F	A26	50c dk bl	50	*2.00*
62G	A27	1s yel brn	3.50	*6.00*
62H	A28	5s violet	3.75	*4.00*
		Nos. 62A-62H (8)	13.80	*17.60*

Reprints of Nos. 55-62H are on very thick paper, with paper weave direction vertical. Price 10 cents each.

Vicente Roca, Diego Noboa and José Olmedo
A28a

General Juan Francisco Elizalde
A28b

Lithographed

1896, Oct. 9 ***Perf. 11½*** **Unwmkd.**

No.	Type	Description	Unused	Used
63	A28a	1c rose	50	50
64	A28b	2c blue	50	50
65	A28a	5c green	60	60
66	A28b	10c ocher	60	60
67	A28a	20c red	75	1.25
68	A28b	50c violet	1.00	2.00
69	A28a	1s orange	2.00	2.50
		Nos. 63-69 (7)	5.95	7.95

Issued in commemoration of the success of the Liberal Party in 1845 and 1895.

Coat of Arms
A29 A30

Black Surcharge.

1896, Nov. ***Perf. 12***

No.	Type	Description	Unused	Used
70	A29	1c on 1c ver, '1893-1894'	60	40
a.		Inverted surcharge	1.75	1.50
b.		Double surcharge	6.00	5.00
71	A29	2c on 2c bl, "1893-1894"	1.50	1.25
a.		Invtd. surcharge	3.00	2.50
72	A29	5c on 10c org, "1887-1888"	60	40
a.		Inverted surcharge	1.50	1.25
b.		Double surcharge	3.50	3.00
c.		Surcharged "2cts"	75	60
d.		"1893-1894"	4.00	3.50
73	A29	10c on 4c brn, '1887-1888'	1.00	75
a.		Inverted surcharge	1.50	1.25
b.		Double surcharge	3.00	2.50
c.		Double surcharge, one inverted		
d.		Surcharged "1 cto"	2.25	2.00
e.		"1891-1892"	12.50	10.00

Similar surcharges of type A29 include: Dated "1887–1888"—1c on 1c blue green, 1c on 2c red, 1c on 4c brown, 1c on 10c yellow; 2c on 2c red, 2c on 10c yellow; 10c on 1c green. Dated "1891–1892"—1c on 1c blue green, 1c on 4c brown. Dated "1893–1894"—2c on 10c yellow; 10c on 1c vermilion, 10c on 10s black.

Wmkd. Liberty Cap. (117)

Surcharge in Black or Red

1896, Oct.

No.	Type	Description	Unused	Used
74	A30	5c on 20c org	12.50	9.00
76	A30	10c on 50c dk bl (R)	11.00	9.00
a.		Double surcharge		

The surcharge is diagonal, horizontal, or vertical.

Overprinted

On Issue of 1894.

1897 **Unwmkd.**

No.	Type	Description	Unused	Used
77	A20	1c blue	1.50	1.00
78	A20	2c yel brn	1.25	65
79	A20	5c green	60	40
80	A20	10c vermilion	1.75	1.25
81	A20	20c black	2.00	1.50
82	A20	50c orange	4.50	1.25
83	A20	1s carmine	13.00	3.00
84	A20	5s dk bl	55.00	40.00
		Nos.77-84 (8)	79.60	49.05

On Issue of 1895.

No.	Type	Description	Unused	Used
85	A20	1c blue	4.00	3.50
86	A20	2c yel brn	1.50	1.25
87	A20	5c green	1.25	75
88	A20	10c vermilion	4.50	4.00
89	A20	20c black	1.25	1.25
90	A20	50c orange	22.50	9.00
91	A20	1s carmine	10.00	5.00
92	A20	5s dk bl	10.00	8.00
		Nos. 85-92 (8)	55.00	32.75

Overprinted

On Issue of 1894.

No.	Type	Description	Unused	Used
93	A20	1c blue	1.00	60
94	A20	2c yel brn	75	50
95	A20	5c green	40	20
96	A20	10c vermilion	2.25	1.25
97	A20	20c black	2.50	1.25
98	A20	50c orange	4.50	1.75
99	A20	1s carmine	8.00	4.50
100	A20	5s dk bl	55.00	45.00
		Nos. 93-100 (8)	74.40	55.05

On Issue of 1895.

No.	Type	Description	Unused	Used
101	A20	1c blue	2.25	80
102	A20	2c yel brn	1.00	80
103	A20	5c green	1.25	70
104	A20	10c vermilion	4.00	2.50
105	A20	20c black	3.50	80
106	A20	50c orange	1.30	85
107	A20	1s carmine	6.00	4.00
108	A20	5s dk bl	7.00	5.00
		Nos. 101-108 (8)	26.30	15.45

Overprints on Nos. 77–108 are to be found reading upward from left to right and downward from left to right, as well as inverted.

Overprinted **1897 Y 1898**

1897 On Issue of 1894.

No.	Type	Description	Unused	Used
109	A20	10c vermilion	55.00	50.00

On Issue of 1895.

No.	Type	Description	Unused	Used
110	A20	2c yel brn	45.00	40.00
111	A20	1s carmine	55.00	50.00
112	A20	5s dk bl	55.00	40.00

Nos. 56, 59 Overprinted

1897, June **Wmk. 117**

No.	Type	Description	Unused	Used
113	A22	2c red	45.00	40.00
114	A25	20c orange	50.00	45.00

Many forged overprints on Nos. 77–114 exist, made on original stamps and reprints.

Same Overprint on Stamps or Types of 1896.

1897 ***Perf. 11½.*** **Unwmkd.**

No.	Type	Description	Unused	Used
115	A28a	1c rose	1.75	1.50
116	A28b	2c blue	1.50	1.25
117	A28b	10c ocher	1.50	1.25
118	A28a	1s yellow	4.50	4.00

No. 63 Overprinted

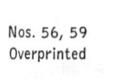

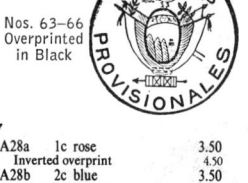

1897

No.	Type	Description	Unused	Used
119	A28a	1c rose	90	75

Nos. 63–66 Overprinted in Black

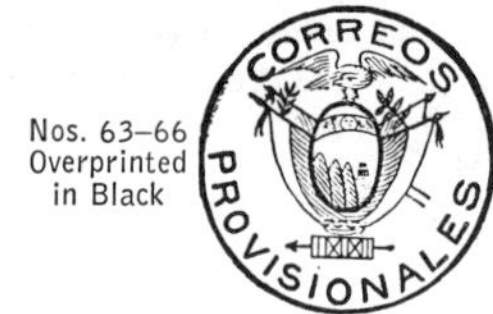

1897

No.	Type	Description	Unused	Used
122	A28a	1c rose	3.50	3.00
a.		Inverted overprint	4.50	4.00
123	A28b	2c blue	3.50	3.00
a.		Inverted overprint	4.50	4.00
124	A28a	5c green	3.50	3.00
a.		Inverted overprint	4.50	4.00
125	A28b	10c ocher	3.50	3.00
a.		Double overprint	8.00	7.00
b.		Inverted overprint	4.00	4.00

The 20c, 50c and 1s with this overprint in black and all values of the issue overprinted in blue are reprints.

Coat of Arms
A33

1897, June 23 **Engr.** ***Perf. 14–16***

No.	Type	Description	Unused	Used
127	A33	1c dk yel grn	15	15
128	A33	2c org red	20	15
129	A33	5c lake	20	20
130	A33	10c dk brn	20	25
131	A33	20c yellow	40	60
132	A33	50c dl bl	40	1.00
133	A33	1s gray	50	1.25
134	A33	5s dk lil	75	1.75
		Nos. 127-134 (8)	2.80	5.35

A34

A35

1899, May

No.	Type	Description	Unused	Used
135	A34	1c on 2c org red	2.25	75
136	A35	5c on 10c brn	1.75	50
a.		Double surcharge		

Luis Vargas Torres
A36

Abdón Calderón
A37

Juan Montalvo
A38

José Mejia
A39

Santa Cruz y Espejo
A40

Pedro Carbo
A41

José Joaquín Olmedo
A42

Pedro Moncayo
A43

1899 ***Perf. 12½–16***

No.	Type	Description	Unused	Used
137	A36	1c gray bl & blk	20	12
a.		Imperf. vertically		
138	A37	2c brn lil & blk	20	10
139	A38	5c lake & blk	25	12
140	A39	10c vio & blk	25	10
141	A40	20c grn & blk	25	12
142	A41	50c lil rose & blk	1.00	60
143	A42	1s ocher & blk	4.00	2.00
144	A43	5s lil & blk	7.50	5.00
		Nos. 137-144 (8)	13.65	8.16

1901

No.	Type	Description	Unused	Used
145	A36	1c scar & blk	15	10
146	A37	2c grn & blk	20	10
147	A38	5c gray lil & blk	20	10
148	A39	10c dp bl & blk	20	15
149	A40	20c gray & blk	25	15
150	A41	50c lt bl & blk	1.00	75
151	A42	1s brn & blk	4.00	2.50
152	A43	5s gray blk & blk	6.00	5.00
		Nos. 145-152 (8)	12.00	8.85

In July, 1902, following the theft of a quantity of stamps during a fire at Guayaquil, the Government authorized the governors of the provinces to handstamp their stocks. Many varieties of these handstamps exist.

Other control marks were used in 1907.

A44

Surcharged on Revenue Stamp Dated 1901-1902.

1903-06 ***Perf. 14, 15.***

No.	Type	Description	Unused	Used
153	A44	1c on 5c gray lil ('06)	30	25
154	A44	1c on 20c gray ('06)	4.50	3.00
155	A44	1c on 25c yel	60	25
a.		Double surcharge		
156	A44	1c on 1s bl ('06)	35.00	22.50
157	A44	3c on 5c gray lil ('06)	4.50	2.50
158	A44	3c on 20c gray ('06)	11.00	7.50
159	A44	3c on 25c yel ('06)	11.00	7.50
159A	A44	3c on 1s bl ('06)	1.25	1.00
		Nos. 153-159A (8)	68.15	44.50

Counterfeits are plentiful. See Nos. 191–197.

Capt. Abdón Calderón
A45 A46

1904, July 31 ***Perf. 12***

No.	Type	Description	Unused	Used
160	A45	1c red & blk	35	30
161	A45	2c bl & blk	35	30
162	A46	5c yel & blk	1.50	1.00
163	A45	10c red & blk	3.00	1.00
164	A45	20c bl & blk	7.50	2.50
165	A46	50c yel & blk	60.00	40.00
		Nos. 160-165 (6)	72.70	45.10

Issued in commemoration of the centenary of the birth of Abdón Calderón, 1804–1904.

President Vicente Roca
A47

President Diego Noboa
A48

President Francisco Robles
A49

President José M. Urvina
A50

President García Moreno
A51

President Jerónimo Carrión
A52

President Javier Espinoza
A53

President Antonio Borrero
A54

1907, July *Perf. 14, 15*

166	A47	1c red & blk	25	15
167	A48	2c pale bl & blk	35	20
168	A49	3c org & blk	50	20
169	A50	5c lil rose & blk	60	15
170	A51	10c dp bl & blk	2.00	25
171	A52	20c yel grn & blk	2.30	30
172	A53	50c vio & blk	5.00	75
173	A54	1s grn & blk	7.50	2.00
		Nos. 166-173 (8)	18.50	4.00

The stamps of the 1907 issue frequently have control marks similar to those found on the 1899 and 1901 issues. These marks were applied to distinguish the stamps issued in the various provinces and to serve as a check on local officials.

Locomotive
A55

García Moreno
A56

Gen. Eloy Alfaro
A57

Abelardo Moncayo
A58

Archer Harman
A59

James Sivewright
A60

Mt. Chimborazo
A61

1908

174	A55	1c red brn	75	75
175	A56	2c bl & blk	1.25	1.00
176	A57	5c cl & blk	2.50	2.00
177	A58	10c ocher & blk	1.50	1.25
178	A59	20c grn & blk	1.50	1.50
179	A60	50c gray & blk	1.50	1.50
180	A61	1s black	3.00	3.00
		Nos. 174-180 (7)	12.00	11.00

Issued in commemoration of the opening of the Guayaquil-Quito Railway.

José Mejía Vallejo
A62

Francisco J. E. Santa Cruz y Espejo
A63

Francisco Ascásubi
A64

Juan Salinas
A65

Juan Pío de Montúfar
A66

Carlos de Montúfar
A67

Juan de Dios Morales
A68

Manuel R. de Quiroga
A69

Principal Exposition Building
A70

1909 *Perf. 12.*

181	A62	1c green	25	40
182	A63	2c blue	25	40
183	A64	3c orange	25	50
184	A65	5c claret	25	50
185	A66	10c yel brn	30	50
186	A67	20c gray	30	75
187	A68	50c vermilion	30	75
188	A69	1s ol grn	30	1.00
189	A70	5s violet	1.00	2.00
		Nos. 181-189 (9)	3.20	6.80

National Exposition of 1909.

Surcharged CINCO CENTAVOS

1909

190	A68	5c on 50c ver	85	75

Revenue Stamps Surcharged as in 1903.

1910 *Perf. 14, 15*

Stamps Dated 1905-1906.

191	A44	1c on 5c grn	1.25	1.00
192	A44	5c on 20c bl	4.50	1.25
193	A44	5c on 25c vio	7.00	2.25

Stamps Dated 1907-1908.

194	A44	1c on 5c grn	30	15
195	A44	5c on 20c bl	8.00	6.00
196	A44	5c on 25c vio	30	25

Stamp Dated 1909—1910

197	A44	5c on 20c bl	*40.00*	*35.00*

President Roca
A71

President Noboa
A72

President Robles
A73

President Urvina
A74

President Moreno
A75

President Borrero
A76

1911-28 *Perf. 12.*

198	A71	1c scar & blk	15	8
199	A71	1c org ('16)	15	8
200	A71	1c lt bl ('25)	15	8
201	A72	2c bl & blk	35	8
202	A72	2c grn ('16)	15	8
203	A72	2c dk vio ('25)	15	8
204	A73	3c org & blk ('13)	1.25	35
205	A73	3c blk ('15)	15	8
206	A74	5c scar & blk	60	8
207	A74	5c vio ('15)	25	8
208	A74	5c rose ('25)	25	8
209	A74	5c dk brn ('28)	30	8
210	A75	10c dp bl & blk	1.00	8
211	A75	10c dp bl ('15)	1.00	20
212	A75	10c yel grn ('25)	25	8
213	A75	10c blk ('28)	75	10
214	A76	1s grn & blk	5.00	1.50
215	A76	1s org & blk ('27)	3.00	30
		Nos. 198-215 (18)	14.90	3.49

A77

1912 *Perf. 14, 15*

216	A77	1c on 1s grn	60	60
217	A77	2c on 2s car	90	90
218	A77	2c on 5s dl bl	90	90
219	A77	2c on 10s yel	2.00	1.50
a.		Inverted surcharge	4.00	3.50

No. 216 exists with narrow "V" and small "U" in "UN" and Nos. 217, 218 and 219 with "D" with serifs or small "O" in "DOS".

Enrique Váldez
A78

Jerónimo Carrión
A79

Javier Espinoza
A80

1915-17 *Perf. 12*

220	A78	4c red & blk	20	8
221	A79	20c grn & blk ('17)	2.00	25
222	A80	50c dp vio & blk	3.50	50

Olmedo
A86

Monument to "Fathers of the Country"
A95

Laurel Wreath and Star
A104

Designs: 2c, Rafael Ximena. 3c, Roca. 4c, Luis F. Viviero. 5c, Luis Febres Cordero. 6c, Francisco Lavayen. 7c, Jorge Antonio de Elizalde. 8c, Baltazar Garcia. 9c, Jose de Antepara. 15c, Luis Urdaneta. 20c, Jose M. Villamil. 30c, Miguel Letamendi. 40c, Gregorio Escobedo. 50c, Gen. Antonio Jose de Sucre. 60c, Juan Illingworth. 70c, Roca. 80c, Rocafuerte. 1s, Simon Bolivar.

1920

223	A86	1c yel grn	25	10
224	A86	2c carmine	20	15
225	A86	3c yel brn	20	15
226	A86	4c myr grn	35	20
227	A86	5c pale bl	35	10
228	A86	6c red org	50	40
229	A86	7c brown	1.25	75
230	A86	8c ap grn	75	50
231	A86	9c lake	2.25	1.50
232	A95	10c lt bl	1.00	20
233	A86	15c dk gray	1.25	50
234	A86	20c dk vio	1.25	25
235	A86	30c brt vio	2.25	1.25
236	A86	40c dk brn	3.00	2.00
237	A86	50c dk grn	2.50	50
238	A86	60c dk bl	4.00	2.25
239	A86	70c gray	7.00	5.00
240	A86	80c org yel	6.00	5.00
241	A104	90c green	7.00	5.00
242	A86	1s pale bl	12.50	8.00
		Nos. 223-242 (20)	53.85	33.80

Nos. 223 to 242 were issued in commemoration of the centenary of the independence of Guayaquil.

Postal Tax Stamp of 1924 Overprinted

POSTAL

1925

259	PT6	20c bis brn	1.50	50

Stamps of 1915–25 Overprinted in Black or Red (Upright or Inverted)

QUITO 1926 ESMERALDAS

1926

260	A71	1c lt bl	3.00	2.50
261	A72	2c dk vio	3.00	2.50
262	A73	3c blk (R)	3.00	2.50
263	A86	4c myr grn	3.00	2.50
264	A74	5c rose	3.00	2.50
265	A75	10c yel grn	3.00	2.50
		Nos. 260-265 (6)	18.00	15.00

Quito-Esmeraldas railway opening.

Postal Tax Stamps of 1920-24 Overprinted

POSTAL

1927

266	PT6	1c ol grn	15	8
a.		"POSTAI"	2.00	1.25
b.		Double overprint	2.00	1.25
c.		Inverted overprint	2.00	1.25
267	PT6	2c dp grn	15	8
a.		"POSTAI"	2.00	1.25
b.		Double overprint	2.00	1.25
268	PT6	20c bis brn	1.00	15
a.		"POSTAI"	12.50	7.50

Quito Post Office
A109

1927, June

269	A109	5c orange	20	10
270	A109	10c dk grn	25	15
271	A109	20c violet	50	25

Opening of new Quito P.O.

Postal Tax Stamp of 1924 Overprinted **POSTAL** in Dark Blue.

1928

273	PT6	20c bis brn	30	10
a.		Double overprint, one inverted	2.00	1.00

A110

Nos. 235, 239–240 Overprinted in Red Brown and Surcharged in Dark Blue.

1928, July 8

274	A110	10c on 30c vio	3.00	3.00
a.		Surch. invtd.		
275	A110	50c on 70c gray	4.00	4.00
276	A110	1s on 80c org yel	5.00	5.00
a.		Surch. invtd.		

Quito-Cayambe railway opening.

Stamps of 1920 Surcharged

ASAMBLEA NCNAL. 1928 5 CTVOS.

1928, Oct. 9

277	A86	1c on 1c yel grn	11.00	10.00
278	A86	1c on 2c car	20	15
279	A86	2c on 3c yel brn	1.25	1.00
a.		Double surcharge, one reading up	6.00	6.00
280	A86	2c on 4c myr grn	90	75
281	A86	2c on 5c lt bl	50	35
a.		Double surcharge	6.00	6.00
282	A86	2c on 7c brn	15.00	12.50
283	A86	5c on 6c red org	25	20
a.		"5 ctvos." omitted	20.00	20.00
284	A86	10c on 7c brn	75	60
285	A86	20c on 8c ap grn	25	20
a.		Double surcharge		
286	A95	40c on 10c bl	3.50	3.00
287	A86	40c on 15c dk gray	60	50
288	A86	50c on 20c dk vio	10.00	9.00
289	A86	1s on 40c dk brn	2.25	2.00
290	A86	5s on 50c dk grn	3.00	2.25
291	A86	10s on 60c dk bl	12.00	9.00

With Additional Surcharge in Red

0.10

292	A86	10c on 2c on 7c brn	20	20
a.		Red surcharge double	6.00	6.00
		Nos. 277-292 (16)	61.65	51.70

National Assembly of 1928.
Counterfeit overprints exist of Nos. 277–291.

A111

A112

Surcharged in Various Colors

1928, Oct. 31 *Perf. 14*

293	A111	5c on 20c gray lil (Bk)	1.25	1.00
294	A111	10c on 20c gray lil (R)	1.25	1.00
295	A111	20c on 1s grn (O)	1.25	1.00
296	A111	50c on 1s grn (Bl)	1.50	75
297	A111	1s on 1s grn (V)	2.00	1.00
298	A111	5s on 2s red (G)	6.00	5.00
299	A111	10s on 2s red (Br)	7.50	7.50
a.		Black surcharge	8.00	8.00
		Nos. 293-299 (7)	20.75	17.25

Quito-Otavalo railway opening.

Postal Tax Stamp of 1924 Overprinted in Red **POSTAL**

1929 *Perf. 12.*

302	PT6	2c dp grn	10	10

There are two types of overprint on No. 302 differing slightly.

1929 Red Overprint.

303	A112	1c dk bl	10	10
a.		Overprint reading down	10	10

See also Nos. 586–587.

Plowing
A113

Cultivating Cacao
A114

Cacao Pod
A115

Growing Tobacco
A116

Exportation of Fruits
A117

Landscape—A118

Loading Sugar Cane
A119

Scene in Quito
A120

Scene in Quito
A121

Olmedo
A122

Sucre
A123

Bolívar
A124

Monument to Simón Bolívar
A125

1930, Aug. 1 *Perf. 12½*

No.	Type	Description	Unused	Used
04	A113	1c yel & car	20	10
05	A114	2c yel & grn	20	10
06	A115	5c dp grn & vio brn	25	15
07	A116	6c yel & red	30	25
08	A117	10c org & ol grn	35	15
09	A118	16c red & yel grn	50	40
10	A119	20c ultra & yel	50	18
11	A120	40c org & sep	60	18
12	A121	50c org & sep	75	18
13	A122	1s dp grn & blk	2.50	25
14	A123	2s dk bl & blk	5.00	50
15	A124	5s dk vio & blk	9.00	75
16	A125	10s car rose & blk	25.00	6.00
		Nos. 304-316 (13)	45.15	9.19

Centenary of founding of republic.

A126 A127

1933 Red Overprint. *Perf. 15.*

No.	Type	Description	Unused	Used
17	A126	10c ol brn	25	15

Blue Overprint.

No.	Type	Description	Unused	Used
18	A127	10c ol brn	25	10
a.		Inverted overprint	5.00	5.00

Nos. 307, 309 Surcharged in Black

1933 *Perf. 12½*

No.	Type	Description	Unused	Used
19	A116	5c on 6c yel & red	30	15
20	A118	10c on 16c red & yel grn	40	15
a.		Inverted ovpt.	4.00	4.00

Landscape A128 Mt. Chimborazo A129

1934-45 *Perf. 12.*

No.	Type	Description	Unused	Used
321	A128	5c violet	15	8
322	A128	5c blue	15	8
323	A128	5c dk brn	15	8
323A	A128	5c sl blk ('45)	15	8
324	A128	10c rose	15	8
325	A128	10c dk grn	15	8
326	A128	10c brown	15	8
327	A128	10c orange	15	8
328	A128	10c ol grn	15	8
329	A128	10c gray blk ('35)	20	8
329A	A128	10c red lil ('44)	15	8

Perf. 14.

No.	Type	Description	Unused	Used
330	A129	1s car rose	1.50	60
		Nos. 321-330 (12)	3.20	1.48

Stamps of 1930 Surcharged or Overprinted in various colors similar to:

INAUGURACION MONUMENTO A BOLIVAR

QUITO, 24 DE JULIO DE 1935

1935 *Perf. 12½.*

No.	Type	Description	Unused	Used
331	A116	5c on 6c yel & red (Bl)	30	15
332	A116	10c on 6c yel & red (G)	35	15
333	A119	20c ultra & yel (R)	40	20
334	A120	40c org & sep (G)	50	30
335	A121	50c org & sep (G)	70	50
336	A124	1s on 5s dk vio & blk (Gold)	2.00	90
337	A124	2s on 5s dk vio & blk (Gold)	3.00	1.35
338	A125	5s on 10s car rose & blk (Bl)	5.00	3.25
		Nos. 331-338, C35-C38 (12)	36.25	30.80

Unveiling of a monument to Bolivar at Quito, July 24, 1935.

The five-stamp Sociedad Colombista Panamericana series of 1935 and five air-mail stamps of a similar design are not recognized by this Catalogue as having been issued primarily for postal purposes.

Telegraph Stamp Overprinted Diagonally in Red **POSTAL**

1935 *Perf. 14½*

No.	Type	Description	Unused	Used
339	A126	10c ol brn	12	8

Map of Galápagos Islands A130 Galapagos Land Iguana A131

Galápagos Tortoise A132 Charles R. Darwin A133

Columbus A134 Island Scene A135

1936 *Perf. 14.*

No.	Type	Description	Unused	Used
340	A130	2c black	25	10
341	A131	5c ol grn	35	15
342	A132	10c brown	60	15
343	A133	20c dk vio	60	20
344	A134	1s dk car	1.25	50
345	A135	2s dk bl	2.25	1.00
		Nos. 340-345 (6)	5.30	2.10

Issued to commemorate the centenary of the visit of Charles Darwin to the Galápagos Islands, September 17, 1835.

Tobacco Stamp Overprinted in Black

P O S T A L

1936 *Rouletted 7.*

No.	Type	Description	Unused	Used
346	PT7	1c rose red	12	8
a.		Horiz. pair, imperf. vertical		
b.		Double surcharge		

No. 346 is similar to type PT7 but does not include "CASA CORREOS".

Louis Godin, Charles M. de la Condamine and Pierre Bouguer
A136

Portraits: 5c, 20c, Antonio Ulloa, La Condamine and Jorge Juan.

1936 Engraved. *Perf. 12½*

No.	Type	Description	Unused	Used
347	A136	2c dp bl	8	8
348	A136	5c dk grn	10	8
349	A136	10c dp org	12	8
350	A136	20c violet	30	15
351	A136	50c dk red	60	35
		Nos. 347-351, C39-C42 (9)	3.10	1.46

Bicentenary of Geodesical Mission to Quito.

Independence Monument
A137

1936 *Perf. 13½x14.*

No.	Type	Description	Unused	Used
352	A137	2c green	1.75	30
353	A137	5c dk vio	1.75	30
354	A137	10c car rose	1.75	35
355	A137	20c black	1.75	50
356	A137	50c blue	3.00	1.50
357	A137	1s dk red	3.50	1.75
		Nos. 352-357, C43-C50 (14)	45.50	36.45

Issued to commemorate the first International Philatelic Exhibition at Quito.

Coat of Arms
A138

Overprint in Black or Red

1937 *Perf. 12½*

No.	Type	Description	Unused	Used
359	A138	5c ol grn	25	10
360	A138	10c dk bl (R)	25	10

Andean Landscape A139 Atahualpa, the Last Inca A140

Hat Weavers A141 Coast Landscape A142

Gold Washing
A143

1937, Aug. 19 *Perf. 11½*

No.	Type	Description	Unused	Used
361	A139	2c green	15	8
362	A140	5c dp rose	20	8
363	A141	10c blue	25	5
364	A142	20c dp rose	60	25
365	A143	1s ol grn	85	35
		Nos. 361-365 (5)	2.05	81

"Liberty" Carrying Flag of Ecuador
A144

Engraved and Lithographed

1938, Feb. 22 *Perf. 12*

Center Multicolored

No.	Type	Description	Unused	Used
366	A144	2c blue	25	10
367	A144	5c violet	35	10
368	A144	10c black	40	10
369	A144	20c brown	50	15
370	A144	50c black	75	18
371	A144	1s ol blk	1.25	35
372	A144	2s dk brn	2.50	50
		Nos. 366-372, C57-C63 (14)	12.50	3.08

U.S. Constitution, 150th anniversary.

Winged Figure Holding Globe A145 Cactus and Winged Wheel A146

"Communications"
A147

"Construction"
A148

Engraved.

1938, Oct. 30 ***Perf. 13, 13x13½***

373	A145	10c brt ultra	15	6
374	A146	50c dp red vio	25	12
375	A147	1s cop red	50	10
376	A148	2s dk grn	75	10

Progress of Ecuador Exhibition.

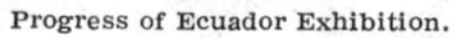

Parade of Athletes
A149

Runner
A150

Basketball
A151

Wrestlers
A152

Diver
A153

1939, Mar. ***Perf. 12***

377	A149	5c car rose	3.00	50
378	A150	10c dp bl	3.50	60
379	A151	50c gray ol	4.00	75
380	A152	1s dl vio	7.50	75
381	A153	2s dl ol grn	10.00	1.00
		Nos. 377-381, C65-C69 (10)	54.75	5.75

First Bolivarian Games (1938), La Paz.

Dolores Mission
A154

Trylon and Perisphere
A155

1939, June 16 ***Perf. 12½x13***

382	A154	2c bl grn	6	6
383	A154	5c rose red	10	6
384	A154	10c ultra	15	6
385	A154	50c yel brn	40	25
386	A154	1s black	70	25
387	A154	2s purple	1.20	25
		Nos. 382-387, C73-C79 (13)	4.43	1.83

Golden Gate International Exposition.

1939, June 30

388	A155	2c lt ol grn	10	8
389	A155	5c red org	15	8
390	A155	10c ultra	20	10
391	A155	50c sl gray	60	20
392	A155	1s rose car	90	25
393	A155	2s blk brn	1.50	30
		Nos. 388-393, C80-C86 (13)	5.66	1.90

New York World's Fair.

Flags of the 21 American Republics
A156

Francisco J. E. Santa Cruz y Espejo
A157

1940 ***Perf. 12.***

394	A156	5c dp rose & blk	15	10
395	A156	10c dk bl & blk	20	10
396	A156	50c Prus grn & blk	50	15
397	A156	1s dp vio & blk	75	30
		Nos. 394-397, C87-C90 (8)	4.70	1.75

Pan American Union, 50th anniversary.

1941, Dec. 15

398	A157	30c blue	35	10
399	A157	1s red org	75	20

Issued to commemorate the Exposition of Journalism held under the auspices of the National Newspaper Men's Union. See Nos. C91-C92.

Francisco de Orellana
A158

Gonzalo Pizarro
A159

View of Guayaquil—A160

View of Quito—A161

1942, Jan. 30

400	A158	10c sepia	20	10
401	A159	40c dp rose	40	10
402	A160	1s violet	60	20
403	A161	2s dk bl	1.00	40
		Nos. 400-403, C93-C96 (8)	6.60	2.43

Issued to commemorate the 400th anniversary of the discovery and exploration of the Amazon River by Francisco de Orellana.

Remigio Crespo Toral
A162

Alfredo Baquerizo Moreno
A163

1942 ***Perf. 13½***

404	A162	10c green	10	6
405	A162	50c brown	25	10

See also No. C97.

1942

406	A163	10c green	10	6

Mt. Chimborazo
A164

1942–47 ***Perf. 12***

407	A164	30c red brn	20	8
407A	A164	30c lt bl ('43)	20	8
407B	A164	30c red org ('44)	20	8
407C	A164	30c grn ('47)	20	8

View of Guayaquil
A165

1942–44

408	A165	20c red	15	10
408A	A165	20c dp bl ('44)	15	10

Gen. Eloy Alfaro
A166

Devil's Nose
A167

Designs: 30c, Military College. 1s, Montecristi, Alfaro's birthplace.

1942

409	A166	10c dk rose & blk	20	8
410	A167	20c ol blk & red brn	20	10
411	A167	30c ol gray & grn	30	12
412	A167	1s sl & sal	60	25
		Nos. 409-412, C98-C101 (8)	6.30	3.45

Issued to commemorate the centenary of the birth of President Alfaro (1842–1903).

Nos. 370–372
Overprinted in Red Brown

BIENVENIDO — WALLACE

Abril 15 — 1943

1943, Apr. 15 ***Perf. 11½***

413	A144	50c multi	60	60
414	A144	1s multi	1.25	1.25
415	A144	2s multi	1.75	1.75
		Nos. 413-415, C102-C104 (6)	9.35	6.40

Visit of Vice-President Henry A. Wallace of the United States.

"30 Centavos"
A170

Black Surcharge.

1943 ***Perf. 12½***

416	A170	30c on 50c red brn	20	1
a.		Without bars	20	1

Map Showing United States and Ecuador
A171

1943, Oct. 9 ***Perf. 12***

417	A171	10c dl vio	30	25
418	A171	20c red brn	30	25
419	A171	30c orange	40	30
420	A171	50c ol grn	50	30
421	A171	1s dp vio	60	50
422	A171	10s ol bis	6.00	3.50
		Nos. 417-422, C114-C118 (11)	19.95	14.35

Issued to commemorate the good will tour of President Arroyo del Rio in 1942.

1944, Feb. 7

423	A171	10c yel grn	20	15
424	A171	20c rose pink	25	20
425	A171	30c dk gray brn	30	25
426	A171	50c dp red lil	50	35
427	A171	1s ol gray	60	50
428	A171	10s red org	6.00	4.00
		Nos.423-428, C119-C123 (11)	13.95	9.90

No. 385
Surcharged in Black

30
Centavos

1944 ***Perf. 12½x13*** **Unwmkd.**

429	A154	30c on 50c yel brn	25	10

Archbishop Federico González Suárez
A172

Government Palace, Quito
A173

1944 ***Perf. 12***

430	A172	10c dp bl	15	8
431	A172	20c green	20	8
432	A172	30c dk vio brn	30	6
433	A172	1s dl vio	60	20
		Nos. 430-433, C124-C127 (8)	5.75	3.22

Birth centenary of Archbishop Federico Gonzalez Suarez.

Air Post Stamps
Nos. C76 and C83
Surcharged in Black

POSTAL
30
Centavos

1944 ***Perf. 12½x13***

434	AP15	30c on 50c rose vio	25	12
435	AP16	30c on 50c sl grn	25	12

Nos. 382 and 388
Surcharged in Black

CINCO
Centavos

1944–45

436	A154	5c on 2c bl grn	15	12
a.		Double surcharge		
437	A155	5c on 2c lt ol grn ('45)	15	12

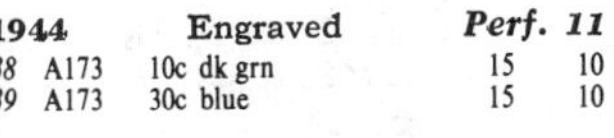

1944 Engraved *Perf. 11*

38	A173	10c dk grn	15	10
39	A173	30c blue	15	10

Symbol of the Red Cross
A174

1945, Apr. 25 *Perf. 12*

Cross in Rose.

440	A174	30c bis brn	75	25
441	A174	1s red brn	90	30
442	A174	5s turq grn	2.00	1.00
443	A174	10s scarlet	5.00	3.00
		Nos. 440-443, C131-C134 (8)	19.65	12.55

International Red Cross, 80th anniversary.

Nos. 370 to 372
Overprinted in Dark Blue and Gold

LOOR A CHILE
OCTUBRE 2 1945

1945, Oct. 2 *Perf. 11½*

Center Multicolored.

444	A144	50c black	40	25
a.		Double overprint		
445	A144	1s ol blk	60	35
446	A144	2s dk brn	1.20	75
		Nos. 444-446, C139-C141 (6)	4.65	3.70

Visit of Pres. Juan Antonio Rios of Chile.

General Antonio José de Sucre
A175

1945, Nov. 14 Engraved *Perf. 12*

447	A175	10c olive	6	6
448	A175	20c red brn	12	10
449	A175	40c ol gray	15	12
450	A175	1s dk grn	30	25
451	A175	2s sepia	70	40
		Nos. 447-451, C142-C146 (10)	5.93	3.88

150th anniversary of birth of Gen. Antonio José de Sucre.

No. 438 Surcharged in Blue

VEINTE
CENTAVOS

1945 *Perf. 11*

452	A173	20c on 10c dk grn	15	10
a.		Fancy bar omitted		

Map of Pan-American Highway and Arms of Loja
A176

1946, Apr. 22 Engraved *Perf. 12*

453	A176	20c red brn	12	8
454	A176	30c brt grn	18	12
455	A176	1s brt ultra	25	25
456	A176	5s dp red lil	1.50	1.00
457	A176	10s scarlet	3.25	2.50
		Nos. 453-457, C147-C151 (10)	10.75	6.95

Torch of Democracy
A177

Popular Suffrage
A178

Flag of Ecuador
A179

Pres. José M. Velasco Ibarra
A180

1946, Aug. 9 *Perf. 12½* Unwmkd.

458	A177	5c dk bl	8	6
459	A178	10c Prus grn	12	6
460	A179	20c carmine	30	15
461	A180	30c chocolate	50	20
		Nos. 458-461, C152-C155 (8)	2.80	1.47

Issued to commemorate the 2nd anniversary of the Revolution of May 28, 1944.

"30 Ctvs."
A181
Black Surcharge.

1946

462	A181	30c on 50c red brn	15	15

Nos. CO13-CO14
With Additional Overprint in Black

POSTAL

1946 *Perf. 11½*

463	AP7	10c chestnut	10	10
464	AP7	20c ol blk	15	15

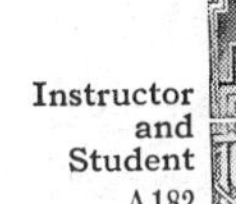

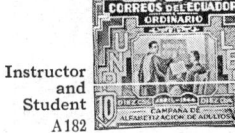

Instructor and Student
A182

1946, Sept. 16 *Perf. 12½*

465	A182	10c dp bl	20	10
466	A182	20c chocolate	20	10
467	A182	30c dk grn	25	15
468	A182	50c bluish blk	50	20
469	A182	1s dk red	75	25
470	A182	10s dk vio	5.00	1.25
		Nos. 465-470, C156-C160 (11)	14.50	5.05

Campaign for adult education.

Mariana de Jesus Paredes y Flores
A183

Urn
A184

1946, Nov. 28

471	A183	10c blk brn	25	12
472	A183	20c green	25	12
473	A183	30c purple	35	20
474	A184	1s rose brn	75	50
		Nos. 471-474, C161-C164 (8)	5.65	3.87

Issued to commemorate the 300th anniversary of the death of the Blessed Mariana de Jesus Paredes y Flores.

Pres. Vicente Rocafuerte
A185

Jesuits' Church Quito
A186

F.J.E. de Santa Cruz y Espejo
A187

1947, Nov. 27 *Perf. 12*

475	A185	5c redsh brn	10	8
476	A185	10c sepia	10	8
477	A185	15c gray blk	15	8
478	A186	20c redsh brn	25	8
479	A186	30c red vio	25	10
480	A186	40c brt ultra	35	20
481	A187	45c dk sl grn	40	20
482	A187	50c ol blk	50	25
483	A187	80c org red	60	20
		Nos. 475-483, C165-C171 (16)	4.70	2.27

Type of 1946,
Overprinted "POSTAL" in Black but
Without Additional Surcharge.

1948 Engraved.

484	A181	10c orange	75	10

Andrés Bello
A188

Flagship of Columbus
A189

1948, Apr. 21 *Perf. 13*

485	A188	20c lt bl	25	12
486	A188	30c rose car	35	15
487	A188	40c bl grn	40	20
488	A188	1s blk brn	75	25
		Nos. 485-488, C172-C174 (7)	3.15	1.57

83rd anniversary of the death of Andrés Bello (1781-1865), educator.

No. 480
Overprinted
in Black

CONFERENCIA
ECONOMICA
GRANCOLOMBIANA
MAYO 24 DE 1.948

1948, May 24 *Perf. 12*

489	A186	40c brt ultra	25	20

See also No. C175.

1948 *Perf. 14*

490	A189	10c dk bl grn	15	6
491	A189	20c brown	25	8
492	A189	30c dk pur	30	8
493	A189	50c dp cl	40	10
494	A189	1s ultra	50	15
495	A189	5s carmine	1.75	35
		Nos. 490-495, C176-C180 (11)	8.00	2.92

Issued to publicize the proposed Columbus Memorial Lighthouse near Ciudad Trujillo. Dominican Republic.

No. 483
Overprinted
in Blue

Feria Nacional
1948
ECUADOR
de hoy y del
MAÑANA

1948 *Perf. 12*

"MANANA" Reading Down.

496	A187	80c org red	40	35

Issued to publicize the National Fair of Today and Tomorrrow, 1948. See No. C181.

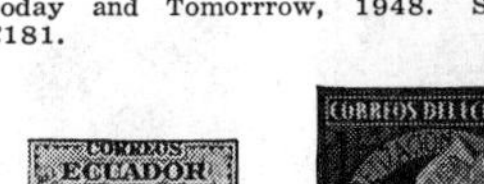

Telegrafo I in Flight
A190

Book and Pen
A191

1948 Engraved. *Perf. 12½*

497	A190	30c red org	25	8
498	A190	40c rose lil	25	8
499	A190	60c vio bl	25	10
500	A190	1s brn red	35	12
501	A190	3s brown	1.00	30
502	A190	5s gray blk	1.25	45
		Nos. 497-502, C182-C187 (12)	7.00	4.13

25th anniversary (in 1945) of the first postal flight in Ecuador.

1948, Oct. 12 Perf. 14 Unwmkd.

503	A191	10c dp cl	10	6
504	A191	20c brown	15	8
505	A191	30c dk grn	20	10
506	A191	50c red	25	12
507	A191	1s purple	35	15
508	A191	1s dl bl	3.50	50
		Nos. 503-508, C188-C192 (11)	8.25	3.31

Campaign for adult education.

Franklin D. Roosevelt and Two of "Four Freedoms"
A192 A193

1948, Oct. 24 Perf. 12½

509	A192	10c rose brn & gray	20	15
510	A192	20c brn ol & bl	25	15
511	A193	30c ol bis & car rose	40	20
512	A193	40c red vio & sep	50	20
513	A193	1s org brn & car	60	40
		Nos. 509-513, C193-C197 (10)	5.05	2.70

Issued in tribute to Franklin D. Roosevelt (1882–1945).

Maldonado and Map
A194

Riobamba Aqueduct
A195

Maldonado on Bank of Riobamba
A196

Pedro V. Maldonado
A197

1948, Nov. 17 Engraved Unwmkd.

514	A194	5c gray blk & ver	25	8
515	A195	10c car & gray blk	30	8
516	A196	30c bis brn & ultra	40	12
517	A195	40c sage grn & vio	50	12
518	A194	50c grn & car	60	15
519	A197	1s brn & sl bl	75	20
		Nos. 514-519, C198-C201 (10)	4.80	1.75

Bicentenary of the death of Pedro Vicente Maldonado, geographer.

A198

Miguel de Cervantes Saavedra
A199

1949, May 2 Perf. 12½x12

520	A198	30c dk car rose & dp ultra	20	12
521	A199	60c bis & brn vio	40	20
522	A198	1s grn & rose car	60	25
523	A199	2s gray blk & red brn	1.50	40
524	A198	5s choc & aqua	2.50	75
		Nos. 520-524, C202-C206 (10)	11.25	3.42

Issued to commemorate the 400th anniversary of the birth of Miguel de Cervantes Saavedra, novelist, playwright and poet.

No. 480 Surcharged in Carmine

II CONGRESO
Junio 1949
0.10
Eucarístico Ncl.

1949, June 15 Perf. 12

525	A186	10c on 40c brt ultra	25	10
526	A186	20c on 40c brt ultra	35	15
	a.	Double surcharge		
527	A186	30c on 40c brt ultra	40	20
		Nos. 525-527, C207-C209 (6)	1.75	1.20

Issued to commemorate the Second National Eucharistic Congress, Quito, June, 1949.

No. 526 exists se-tenant with No. 527

Monument on Equator
A200

Arms of Ecuador
R1

1949, June Engr. Perf. 12½x12

528	A200	10c dp plum	30	12

No. 542 Surcharged in Black and Carmine

0.30
75 ANIVERSARIO
U. P. U.

1949 Perf. 12x12½

529	A203	10c on 50c grn	20	15
530	A203	20c on 50c grn	30	15
531	A203	30c on 50c grn	50	15
		Nos.529-531, C210-C213 (7)	4.35	2.55

Universal Postal Union, 75th anniversary.

Consular Service Stamps Surcharged in Black

POSTAL
20 ctvs.

1949 Perf. 12

532	R1	20c on 25c red brn	12	8
533	R1	30c on 50c gray	12	8

Nos. RA49A and RA55 Overprinted in Black

POSTAL
a

1950 Perf. 12. Unwmkd.

534	PT18	5c green	12	8
535	PT21	5c blue	12	8

Overprint 15 mm. on No. 534.

Nos. 528 and 517 to 519 Overprinted or Surcharged
ALFABETIZACION
in Black or Carmine.

1950, Feb. 10 Perf. 12½x12

536	A200	10c dp plum	12	12

Perf. 12½

537	A195	20c on 40c sage grn & vio	15	15
538	A195	30c on 40c sage grn & vio	20	20
539	A194	50c grn & car	25	20
540	A197	1s brn & sl bl (C)	35	20

No. C220 Overprinted Type "a" in Carmine.
Perf. 11
Overprint 15 mm. long.

541	AP28	10s violet	2.50	1.00
		Nos. 536-541, C216-C220 (11)	7.92	4.07

Nos. 536 to 541 were issued to publicize adult education.

San Pablo Lake
A203

Perf. 12x12½

1950, May Engraved Unwmkd.

542	A203	50c green	30	20

Consular Service Stamp Surcharged "CORREOS" and New Value Vertically in Black.

1950 Perf. 12

544	R1	30c on 50c gray	20	8

Coat of Arms
R2

Consular Service Stamps Overprinted or Surcharged in Black.

POSTAL 20 Ctvs. 20
b

POSTAL
c

CORREOS
d

50 ctvs.
POSTAL
e

1951 Perf. 12. Unwmkd.

545	R1 (b)	5c on 10c car rose	10	8
546	R1 (c)	10c car rose	15	8
547	R1 (d)	10c car rose	15	8
548	R1 (b)	20c on 25c red brn	15	8
549	R1 (b)	30c on 50c gray	20	8
550	R2 (b)	40c on 25c bl	25	10
551	R2 (e)	50c on 25c bl	30	10
		Nos. 545-551 (7)	1.30	60

Surcharge on No. 545 expressed: "5 ctvs." Small (lower case) "c" in "ctvs." on No. 550.

Consular Service Stamps Surcharged in Black

CAMPAÑA
Alfabetización
20 Ctvs. 20

1951

552	R2	20c on 25c bl	25	10
553	R2	30c on 25c bl	25	15

Adult education. See Nos. C225-C226.

Consular Service Stamp Surcharged Type "e" in Black.

1951

554	R2	"$0,30" on 50c car rose	25	15

Reliquary of St. Mariana and Vatican
A204

Perf. 12½x12

1952, Feb. Engraved Unwmkd.

555	A204	10c emer & red brn	15	8
556	A204	20c dp bl & pur	20	12
557	A204	30c car & bl grn	35	15
		Nos. 555-557, C227-C230 (7)	3.20	1.23

Issued to publicize the canonization of Mariana de Jesus Paredes y Flores.

Presidents Galo Plaza and Harry Truman
A205

Design: 2s, Pres. Plaza addressing U. S. Congress.

1952, Mar. 26 ***Perf. 12***

558 A205 1s rose car & gray blk 50 25
559 A205 2s dl bl & sep 1.00 35

Issued to commemorate the 1951 visit of Pres. Galo Plaza y Lasso to the United States. See Nos. C231-C232.

R3

Fiscal Stamps Surcharged or Overprinted Type "c" Horizontally in Carmine or Black.

Engraved.

1952 ***Perf. 12.*** **Unwmkd.**

560 R3 20c on 30c dp bl (C) 12 6
561 R3 30c dp bl 15 6

Diagonal Overprint.

562 A138 50c purple 20 6

Pres. José M. Urvina, Slave and "Liberty"
A206

Lithographed.

1952 ***Hyphen-hole Perf. 7x6½***

563 A206 20c red & grn 25 6
564 A206 30c red & vio bl 30 8
565 A206 50c bl & car 50 10
Nos. 563-565, C236-C239 (7) 6.05 1.74

Centenary of abolition of slavery in Ecuador. Counterfeits exist.

Consular Service Stamps Surcharged in Black

POSTAL
10
Centavos
f

1952-53 ***Perf. 12.*** **Unwmkd.**

566 R1 10c on 20s bl ('53) 12 8
567 R1 20c on 10s gray ('53) 15 8
568 R1 20c on 20s bl 15 8
569 R1 30c on 10s gray ('53) 20 8
570 R1 30c on 20s bl 20 8
Nos. 566-570 (5) 82 40

Similar surcharges of 60c and 90c on the 20s blue are said to be bogus.

Teacher and Students
A207

New Citizens Voting
A208

Designs: 10c, Instructor with student. 30c, Teaching the alphabet.

1953, Apr. 13 **Engraved**

571 A207 5c lt bl 25 6
572 A207 10c dk car rose 30 6
573 A208 20c brt brn org 40 8
574 A208 30c dp red lil 60 10
Nos. 571-574, C240-C241 (6) 3.55 60

1952 adult education campaign.

A209 **Cuicocha Lagoon**
A210

Black Surcharge.

1953

575 A209 40c on 50c pur 50 25

1953 **Engraved.** ***Perf. 13x12½.***

Designs: 10c, Equatorial Line monument. 20c, Quininde countryside. 30c, Tomebamba river. 40c, La Chilintosa rock. 50c, Iliniza Mountains.

Frames in Black.

576 A210 5c brt bl 6 6
577 A210 10c brt grn 6 6
578 A210 20c purple 10 10
579 A210 30c brown 10 10
580 A210 40c orange 15 15
581 A210 50c dp car 40 15
Nos. 576-581 (6) 87 62

Carlos Maria Cardinal de la Torre and Arches
A211

1954, Jan. **Photo.** ***Perf. 8½***

582 A211 30c blk & ver 20 8
583 A211 50c blk & rose lil 25 10
Nos. 582-583, C253-C255 (5) 1.55 78

Issued to commemorate the first anniversary of the elevation of Archbishop de la Torre to Cardinal.

Queen Isabella I
A212

1954, Apr. 22

584 A212 30c blk & gray 25 10
585 A212 50c blk brn & yel 30 15
Nos. 584-585, C256-C260 (7) 2.15 1.53

Issued to commemorate the 500th anniversary of the birth of Queen Isabella I (1451-1504) of Spain.

Type of 1929; "POSTAL" Overprint Larger, No Letterspacing.

1954-55 ***Perf. 12*** **Unwmkd.**

586 A112 5c ol grn ('55) 20 8
587 A112 10c orange 25 8

The normal overprint on Nos. 586-587 reads up. It also exists reading down.

Indian Messenger
A213

Products of Ecuador
A214

1954, Aug. 2 **Litho.** ***Perf. 11***

588 A213 30c dk brn 20 15

Issued to publicize the Day of the Postal Employee. See also No. C263.

1954, Sept. 24 **Photogravure**

589 A214 10c orange 10 6
590 A214 20c vermilion 15 6
591 A214 30c rose pink 20 6
592 A214 40c dk gray grn 30 10
593 A214 50c yel brn 40 12
Nos. 589-593 (5) 1.15 40

José Abel Castillo
A215

Babahoyo River Los Rios
A216

Perf. 11½x11

1955, Oct. 19 **Engraved** **Unwmkd.**

594 A215 30c ol bis 15 15
595 A215 5c dk gray 20 15
Nos. 594-595, C282-C286 (7) 3.35 1.76

Issued to commemorate the 30th anniversary of the first flight of the "Telegrafo I" and to honor José Abel Castillo, aviation pioneer.

1955-56 **Photogravure** ***Perf. 13***

Designs: 5c, Palms, Esmeraldas. 10c, Fishermen, Manabi. 30c, Guayaquil, Guayas. 50c, Pital River, El Oro. 70c, Cactus, Galapagos Isls. 80c, Orchids, Napo-Pastaza. 1s, Aguacate Mission, Zamora-Chinchipe. 2s, Jibaro Indian, Morona-Santiago.

596 A216 5c yel grn ('56) 10 10
597 A216 10c bl ('56) 12 10
598 A216 20c brown 15 10
599 A216 30c dk gray 15 10
600 A216 30c bl grn 20 10
601 A216 70c ol ('56) 25 10
602 A216 80c dp vio ('56) 60 12
603 A216 1s org ('56) 40 15
604 A216 2s rose red ('56) 75 25
Nos. 596-604 (9) 2.72 1.12

See also Nos. 620-630, 670, C288-C297, C310-C311.

Brother Juan Adam Schwarz, S. J.
A217

1956, Aug. 27 **Engraved** ***Perf. 13½***

605 A217 5c yel grn 6 6
606 A217 10c org red 8 6
607 A217 20c lt vio 10 6
608 A217 30c dk grn 10 6
609 A217 40c blue 12 6
610 A217 50c dp ultra 20 6
611 A217 70c orange 30 8
Nos. 605-611, C302-C305 (11) 2.36 1.59

Issued to commemorate the bicentennial of printing in Ecuador and in honor of Brother Juan Adam Schwarz, S.J.

Andres Hurtado de Mendoza
A218

Gil Ramirez Davalos
A219

Designs: 20c, Brother Vincent Solano.

1957, Apr. 7 ***Perf. 12*** **Unwmkd.**

612 A218 5c dk bl, *pink* 10 5
613 A219 10c grn, *grnsh* 15 5
614 A218 20c choc, *buff* 20 5
a. Souvenir sheet of 4 60 60
Nos. 612-614, C312-C314 (6) 1.10 53

Issued to commemorate the fourth centenary of the founding of Cuenca.

No. 614a contains two 5c gray and two 20c brown red stamps in designs similar to Nos. 612 and 614. It was printed on white ungummed paper, is imperf. and is inscribed "II Exposicion Filatelica Nacional, Cuenca, 11 al 20 de Abril de 1957." Size: 140x120mm.

Francisco Marcos, Gen. Pedro Alcantara Herran and Santos Michelena
A220

1957, Sept. 5 **Engr.** ***Perf. 14½x14***

615 A220 40c yellow 15 5
616 A220 50c ultra 20 6
617 A220 2s dk red 60 25

7th Postal Congress of the Americas and Spain (in 1955).

Souvenir Sheets

Various Railroad Scenes
A221

Lithographed.

1957 *Perf. 10½x11*

618	A221	Sheet of five 20c	1.00	1.00
619	A221	Sheet of five 30c	60	50

Issued to commemorate the opening of the Quito-Ibarra-San Lorenzo railroad.

Nos. 618–619 measure 118x110mm. with ultramarine inscriptions and contain 2 orange yellow, 1 ultramarine and 2 carmine stamps, each in a different design.

Scenic Type of 1955–56.

Designs as before, except: 40c, Cactus, Galapagos Islands. No. 629, San Pablo, Imbabura.

1957-58 Photogravure. *Perf. 13*

620	A216	5c lt bl	15	8
621	A216	10c brown	15	8
622	A216	20c crim rose	15	8
623	A216	20c yel grn	15	8
624	A216	30c rose red	15	8
625	A216	40c chlky bl	50	8
626	A216	50c lt vio	15	8
627	A216	90c brt ultra	50	8
628	A216	1s dk brn	25	10
629	A216	1s gray blk ('58)	25	10
630	A216	2s brown	60	20
		Nos. 620-630 (11)	3.00	1.04

Blue and Yellow Macaw
A222

Birds: 20c, Red-breasted toucan. 30c, Condor. 40c, Black-tailed and sword-tailed hummingbirds.

Perf. 13½x13

1958, Jan. 7 Litho. **Unwmkd.**

Birds in Natural Colors.

634	A222	10c red brn	25	8
635	A222	20c dk gray	25	10
636	A222	30c brt yel grn	50	12
637	A222	40c red org	50	15

Carlos Sanz de Santamaria
A223

Richard M. Nixon and Flags
A224

Design: No. 640, Dr. Ramon Villeda Morales and flags. 2.20s, José Carlos de Macedo Soares and horizontal flags.

1958 *Perf. 12*

Flags in Red, Blue, Yellow & Green.

638	A223	1.80s dl vio	60	20
639	A224	2s dk grn	60	25
640	A224	2s dk brn	60	20
641	A223	2.20s blk brn	60	25

No. 638 commemorates the visit of Colombia's Foreign Minister Dr. Carlos Sanz de Santamaria to Ecuador.

No. 639 commemorates the visit of U. S. Vice President Richard M. Nixon to Ecuador, May 9-10.

No. 640 commemorates the visit of President Ramon Villeda Morales of Honduras.

No. 641 commemorates the visit of Brazil's Foreign Minister José Carlos de Macedo Soares to Ecuador. See Nos. C419–C421.

Locomotive of 1908
A225

Garcia Moreno, Jose Caamano, L. Plaza and Eloi Alfaro
A226

Design: 50c, Diesel locomotive.

Perf. 13½x14, 14

1958, Aug. 9 Photo. **Unwmkd.**

642	A225	30c brn blk	15	6
643	A225	50c dk car	25	10
644	A226	5s dk brn	1.00	70

Issued to commemorate the 50th anniversary of the Guayaquil-Quito railroad.

Cardinal
A227

Birds: 30c, Andean cock-of-the-rock. 50c, Glossy cowbird. 60c, Red-fronted Amazon.

1958 Lithographed. *Perf. 13½x13*

Birds in Natural Colors.

645	A227	20c bluish grn, blk & red	15	10
646	A227	30c buff, blk & brt bl	18	10
647	A227	50c org, blk & grn	25	12
648	A227	60c pale rose, blk & bluish grn	30	15

UNESCO Building and Eiffel Tower, Paris
A228

1958, Nov. 3 Engraved *Perf. 12½*

649	A228	80c brown	35	20

Issued to commemorate the opening of UNESCO (U. N. Educational, Scientific and Cultural Organization) Headquarters in Paris, Nov. 3.

Globe and Satellites
A229

Virgin of Quito
A230

1958, Dec. 20 Photo. *Perf. 14x13½*

650	A229	1.80s dk bl	1.50	60

Issued to commemorate the International Geophysical Year, 1957–58.

1959, Sept. 8 *Perf. 13* **Unwmkd.**

651	A230	5c ol grn	10	8
652	A230	10c yel brn	10	8
653	A230	20c purple	10	8
654	A230	30c ultra	15	8
655	A230	80c dk car rose	20	10
		Nos. 651-655 (5)	65	42

See also No. C290.

Uprooted Oak Emblem
A231

1960, Apr. 7 Litho. *Perf. 14x13*

656	A231	80c rose car & grn	25	15

Issued to publicize World Refugee Year, July 1, 1959–June 30, 1960.

Great Anteater and Arms
A232

Animals: 40c, Tapir and map. 80c, Spectacled bear and arms. 1s, Puma and map.

1960, May 14 Photo. *Perf. 13*

657	A232	20c org, grn & blk	10	10
658	A232	40c yel grn, bl grn & brn	20	10
659	A232	80c bl, blk & red brn	35	20
660	A232	1s Prus bl, plum & ocher	60	30

Issued to commemorate the 4th centenary of the founding of the city of Baeza.

See also Nos. 676–679.

Hotel Quito
A233

Designs: No. 662, Dormitory, Catholic University. No. 663, Dormitory, Central University. No. 664, Airport, Quito. No. 665, Overpass on Highway to Quito. No. 666, Security Bank. No. 667, Ministry of Foreign Affairs. No. 668, Government Palace. No. 669, Legislative Palace.

Perf. 11x11½

1960, Aug. 8 Engraved **Unwmkd.**

661	A233	1s dk pur & redsh brn	20	15
662	A233	1s dk bl & brn	20	15
663	A233	1s blk & red	20	15
664	A233	1s dk bl & ultra	20	15
665	A233	1s dk pur & dk car rose	20	15
666	A233	1s blk & ol bis	20	15
667	A233	1s dk pur & turq	20	15
668	A233	1s dk bl & grn	20	15
669	A233	1s blk & vio	20	15
		Nos. 661-669 (9)	1.80	1.35

11th Inter-American Conference, Quito.

Souvenir Sheet

Type of Regular Issue, 1955–56.

Design: Orchids, Napo-Pastaza.

1960 Photogravure *Perf. 13*

Yellow Paper.

670	A216	Sheet of two	40	40
a.		80c dp vio	15	15
b.		90c dp grn	15	15

Issued to commemorate the 25th anniversary of Asociacion Filatelica Ecuatoriana. Marginal inscription in silver. Size: 85x55mm. Exists with silver inscription omitted.

"Freedom of Expression"
A234

Manabi Bridge
A235

Designs: 10c, "Freedom to vote." 20c, "Freedom to work." 30c, Coins, "Monetary stability."

1960, Aug. 29 Litho. *Perf. 13*

671	A234	5c dk bl	8	8
672	A234	10c lt vio	8	8
673	A234	20c orange	12	8
674	A234	30c bluish grn	15	8
675	A235	40c brn & bluish grn	20	8
		Nos. 671-675 (5)	63	40

Issued to publicize the achievements of President Camilo Ponce Enriquez. See Nos. C370–C374.

Animal Type of 1960.

Animals: 10c, Collared peccary. 20c, Kinkajou. 80c, Jaguars. 1s, Mountain coati.

Photogravure

1961, July 13 *Perf. 13* **Unwmkd.**

676	A232	10c grn, rose red & blk	10	5
677	A232	20c vio, grnsh bl & brn	15	7
678	A232	80c red org, dl yel & blk	30	12
679	A232	1s brn, brt grn & org	45	20

Issued to commemorate the 400th anniversary of the founding of the city of Tena.

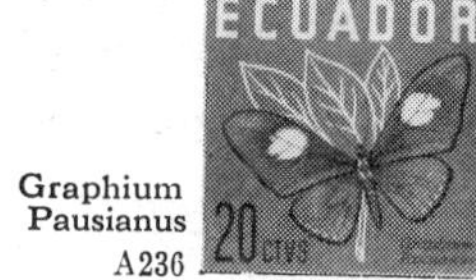

Graphium Pausianus
A236

Butterflies: 30c, Papilio torquatus leptalea. 50c, Graphium molops molops. 80c, Battus lycidas.

1961, July 13 Litho. *Perf. 13½*

680	A236	20c pink & multi	10	5
681	A236	30c lt ultra & multi	15	6
682	A236	50c org & multi	20	10
683	A236	80c bl grn & multi	30	15

See also Nos. 711–713.

Galapagos Islands Nos. L1–L3 Overprinted in Black or Red

1961

Estación de Biología Marítima de Galápagos

XXXXXXXXXXXX

1961, Oct. 31 Photo. *Perf. 12*

684	A1	20c dk brn	25	10
685	A2	50c violet	25	10
686	A1	1s dk ol grn (R)	50	20
		Nos. 684-686, C389-C391 (6)	2.70	1.65

Establishment of maritime biological stations on Galapagos Islands by UNESCO. Overprint arranged differently on 20c, 1s. See Nos. C389-C391.

Daniel Enrique Proano School
A237

Designs: 60c, Loja-Zamora highway (vert.). 80c, Aguirre Abad College, Guayaquil. 1s, Army quarters, Quito.

Perf. 11x11½, 11½x11

1962, Jan. 10 Engr. Unwmkd.

687	A237	50c dl bl & blk	10	5
688	A237	60c ol grn & blk	15	8
689	A237	80c org red & blk	25	10
690	A237	1s rose lake & blk	30	12

Pres. Arosemena, Flags of Ecuador, U.S.
A238

Protection for The Family
A239

Designs (Arosemena and): 10c, Flags of Ecuador. 20c, Flags of Ecuador and Panama.

1963, July 1 Litho. *Perf. 14*

691	A238	10c buff & multi	10	5
692	A238	20c multi	15	5
693	A238	60c multi	20	6
		Nos. 691-693, C409-C411 (6)	2.05	96

Issued to commemorate Pres. Carlos J. Arosemena's friendship trip, July 1962.

1963, July 9 *Perf. 14* Unwmkd.

694	A239	10c ultra, red, gray & blk	15	8

Issued to commemorate the 25th anniversary of Social Insurance. See No. C413.

No. 655 Overprinted or Surcharged in Black or Blue

1961 DIA DEL EMPLEADO POSTAL 10

1963 Photogravure *Perf. 13*

695	A230	10c on 80c dk car rose	5	5
696	A230	20c on 80c dk car rose	10	8
697	A230	50c on 80c dk car rose	12	10
698	A230	60c on 80c dk car rose (Bl)	20	12
699	A230	80c dk car rose	30	15
		Nos. 695-699 (5)	77	50

Nos. 661-669 Surcharged 0,10 XXXXX

1964, Apr. 20 Engr. *Perf. 11x11½*

700	A233	10c on 1s dk pur & redsh brn	8	4
701	A233	10c on 1s dk pur & turq	8	4
702	A233	20c on 1s dk bl & brn	10	4
703	A233	20c on 1s dk bl & grn	10	4
704	A233	30c on 1s dk pur & dk car rose	15	5
705	A233	40c on 1s blk & ol bis	15	5
706	A233	60c on 1s blk & red	20	10
707	A233	80c on 1s dk bl & ultra	30	15
708	A233	80c on 1s blk & vio	30	15
		Nos. 700-708 (9)	1.46	66

No. 656 Overprinted in Black or Light Ultramarine 1961

1964 Lithographed *Perf. 14x13*

709	A231	80c rose car & grn	2.50	75

Butterfly Type of 1961

Butterflies: Same as on Nos. 680, 682–683.

1964, June Litho. *Perf. 13½*

711	A236	20c brt grn & multi	8	8
712	A236	50c sal pink & multi	12	8
713	A236	80c lt red brn & multi	20	10

Alliance for Progress Emblem, Agriculture and Industry
A240

Designs: 50c, Emblem, gear wheels, mountain and seashore. 80c, Emblem, banana worker, fish, factory and ship.

1964, Aug. 26 *Perf. 12* Unwmkd.

715	A240	40c bis brn & vio	15	8
716	A240	50c red org & blk	25	10
717	A240	80c bl & dk brn	30	20

Issued to publicize the Alliance for Progress which aims to stimulate economic growth and raise living standards in Latin America.

No. 650 Overprinted in Red FARO DE COLON

1964 Photogravure *Perf. 14x13½*

718	A229	1.80s dk bl	2.75	1.50

No. 656 Overprinted

(Reduced Size)
Overprint covers four stamps

1964, July Litho. *Perf. 14x13*

719	A231	80c rose car & grn (block of 4)	3.25	1.50

Organization of American States.

World Map and Banana Tree
A241

1964, Oct. 26 *Perf. 12½x12*

720	A241	50c dk brn, gray & gray ol	8	6
721	A241	80c blk, org & gray ol	12	8

Issued to publicize the Banana Conference, Oct.–Nov. 1964. See Nos. C427–C428a.

King Philip II of Spain and Map of Upper Amazon River
A242

Designs (Map and): 20c, Juan de Salinas de Loyola. 30c, Hernando de Santillan.

1964, Dec. 6 Litho. *Perf. 13½*

722	A242	10c rose, blk & buff	10	6
723	A242	20c bl grn, blk & buff	15	8
724	A242	30c bl, blk & buff	15	8

Issued to commemorate the 4th centenary of the establishment of the Royal High Court in Quito.

Pole Vaulting
A243

1964, Dec. 16 *Perf. 14x13½*

725	A243	80c vio bl, yel grn & brn	20	10

Issued to commemorate the 18th Olympic Games, Tokyo, Oct. 10–25. See also Nos. C432–C434.

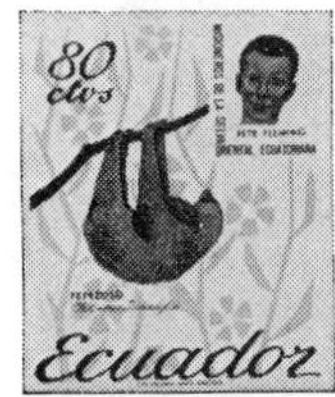

Peter Fleming and Two-toed Sloth
A244

Designs: 20c, James Elliot and armadillo. 30c, T. Edward McCully, Jr., and squirrel. 40c, Roger Youderian and deer. 60c, Nathaniel (Nate) Saint and plane over Napo River.

1965 *Perf. 13½* Unwmkd.

726	A244	20c emer & multi	6	5
727	A244	30c yel & multi	8	5
728	A244	40c lil & multi	10	8
729	A244	60c multi	15	10
730	A244	80c multi	20	12
		Nos. 726-730 (5)	59	40

Issued in memory of five American Protestant missionaries, killed by the Auca Indians, Jan. 8, 1956. Issue dates: 80c, May 11; others, July 8.

Juan B. Vázquez and Benigno Malo College
A245

1965, June 6 Litho. *Perf. 14*

731	A245	20c blk, yel & vio bl	5	5
732	A245	60c blk, red, yel & vio bl	10	8
733	A245	80c blk, emer, yel & vio bl	15	10

Issued to commemorate the centenary (in 1964) of the founding of Benigno Malo National College.

National Anthem, Juan Leon Mera and Antonio Neumane
A246

1965, Aug. 10 Litho. *Perf. 13½*

734	A246	50c pink & blk	8	6
735	A246	80c lt grn & blk	12	10
736	A246	5s bis & blk	60	45
737	A246	10s lt ultra & blk	1.10	90

Issued to commemorate the centenary of the national anthem. The name of the poet Juan Leon Mera is misspelled on the stamps.

Torch and Athletes (Shot Put, Discus, Javelin and Hammer Throw)
A247

Torch and Athletes: 50c, 1s, Runners. 60c, 1.50s, Soccer.

1965, Nov. 20 *Perf. 12x12½*

738	A247	40c org, gold, & blk	6	6
739	A247	50c org ver, gold & blk	10	8
740	A247	60c bl, gold & blk	12	10
741	A247	80c brt yel grn, gold & blk	15	12
742	A247	1s lt vio, gold & blk	20	15
743	A247	1.50s brt pink, gold & blk	25	20
		Nos. 738-743, C435-C440 (12)	3.18	2.69

Issued to publicize the 5th Bolivarian Games, held at Guayaquil and Quito.

Stamps of 1865
A248

1965, Dec. 30 Litho. *Perf. 13½*

Stamps of 1865 in Yellow, Ultramarine & Green

744	A248	80c rose red	20	15
745	A248	1.30s rose lil	30	15
746	A248	2s chocolate	40	20
747	A248	4s black	70	35
a.		Souv. sheet of 4	1.75	1.75

Issued to commemorate the centenary of Ecuadorian postage stamps. No. 747a contains four imperf. stamps similar to Nos. 744–747. Dark blue marginal inscription and black control number. Size: 140x125 mm.

Pavonine Quetzal

A249

Bust of Peñaherrera, Central University, Quito

A250

Birds: 50c, Blue-crowned motmot. 60c, Paradise tanager. 80c, Wire-tailed manakin.

1966, June 17 Litho. *Perf. 13½*

Birds in Natural Colors

748	A249	40c dl rose & blk	10	8
749	A249	50c sal & blk	10	8
750	A249	60c lt ocher & blk	15	10
751	A249	80c lt bl & blk	15	10
		Nos. 748-751, C441-C448 (12)	3.05	2.51

Various Surcharges on Issues of 1956-66

1967-68

752	AP72	30c on 1.10s multi (C337)	10	5
753	AP66	40c on 1.70s yel brn (C292)	10	5
754	A247	40c on 3.50s lt vio, gold & blk (C438)	10	5
755	A246	50c on 5s bis & blk (736) ('68)	12	5
756	A247	80c on 1.50s brt pink, gold & blk (743)	20	8
757	A249	80c on 2.50s lt yel grn & multi (C445)	20	8
758	A249	1s on 4s gray & multi (C447)	20	10
759	AP66	1.30s on 1.90s ol (C293)	30	20
760	A246	2s on 10s lt ultra & blk (737) ('68)	50	20
		Nos. 752-760, C449-C450 (11)	2.02	1.02

The surcharge on Nos. 754-755, 757 and 759-760 includes "Resello." The obliteration of old denomination and arrangement of surcharges differ on each stamp.

Perf. 12x12½, 12½x12

1967, Dec. 29 Lithographed

Designs: 50c, Law books. 80c, Open book and laurel (horiz.).

761	A250	50c brt grn & blk	10	8
762	A250	60c rose & blk	10	8
763	A250	80c rose lil & blk	10	8
		Nos. 761-763, C451-C452 (5)	65	51

Issued to commemorate the centenary (in 1964) of the birth of Dr. Victor Manuel Peñaherrera (1864-1932), author of the civil and criminal codes of Ecuador.

Otto Arosemena Gomez

A251

Lions Emblem

A252

1968, May 9 Litho. *Perf. 13½x14*

Design: 1s, Page from the Constitution.

764	A251	80c lil & multi	8	6
765	A251	1s multi	10	8

First anniversary of the administration of Pres. Otto Arosemena Gomez. See Nos. C453-C454.

1968, May 24 Litho. *Perf. 13½x14*

766	A252	80c multi	10	10
767	A252	1.30s multi	20	15
768	A252	2s pink & multi	30	20
a.		Souv. sheet of 1	4.00	4.00

Issued to commemorate the 50th anniversary (in 1967) of Lions International.

No. 768a contains one 5s stamp (size: 39x49mm.). Violet blue marginal inscriptions and red control numbers. Size: 71x104mm. Exists imperf.

Nos. C331 and C326 Surcharged in Violet and Dark Blue

RESELLO

$ 0,40

a

$ 0,50

RESELLO

b

1969, Jan. 10 *Perf. 11½, 14x13½*

769	AP79 (a)	40c on 1.30s grn & brn red (V)	6	6
770	AP76 (b)	50c on 1.30s dk grn & lt brn (DBl)	10	10

Type of 1958 Surcharged and Overprinted in Plum and Black

RESELLO $ 0,50

Design: Ignacio Luis Arcaya, Foreign Minister of Venezuela.

1969, Mar. Litho. *Perf. 12*

Flags in Red, Blue and Yellow.

771	A223	50c on 2s sep	8	5
772	A223	80c on 2s sep	12	8
773	A223	1s on 2s sep	15	10
774	A223	2s sepia	25	20
		Nos. 771-774, C455-C457 (7)	98	74

Nos. 771-774 were not issued without overprint. The obliteration of old denomination on No. 772 is a small square around a star. Overprint is plum, except for the black small coat of arms on right flag.

Map of Ecuador and Oriental Region

A253

Surcharge Typographed in Dark Blue, Red Brown, Black or Lilac

1969 Lithographed *Perf. 14*

775	A253	20c on 30c multi (DBl)	6	5
776	A253	40c on 30c multi (RBr)	6	6
777	A253	50c on 30c multi (DBl)	8	8
778	A253	60c on 30c multi (DBl)	10	10
779	A253	80c on 30c multi (Bk)	12	12
780	A253	1s on 30c multi (L)	15	15
781	A253	1.30s on 30c multi (Bk)	20	15
782	A253	1.50s on 30c multi (Bk)	25	20
783	A256	2s on 30c multi (DBl)	35	25
784	A256	3s on 30c multi (DBl)	50	35
785	A256	4s on 30c multi (Bk)	35	20
786	A256	5s on 30c multi (Bk)	40	30
		Nos. 775-786 (12)	2.62	2.01

Nos. 775-786 were not issued without surcharge.

M. L. King, John and Robert Kennedy

A254

Thecla Coronata

A255

1969-70 Typographed *Perf. 12½*

787	A254	4s blk, bl, grn & buff	50	20

Perf. 13½

788	A254	4s blk, lt bl & grn ('70)	50	20

In memory of John F. Kennedy, Robert F. Kennedy and Martin Luther King, Jr.

1970 Lithographed *Perf. 12½*

Butterflies: 20c, Papilio zabreus. 30c, Heliconius chestertoni. 40c, Papilio pausanias. 50c, Pereute leucodrosime. 60c, Metamorpha dido. 80c, Morpho cypris. 1s, Catagramma astarte.

789	A255	10c buff & multi	10	8
790	A255	20c lt grn & multi	10	8
791	A255	30c pink & multi	10	8
792	A255	40c lt bl & multi	10	8
793	A255	50c gold & multi	10	8
794	A255	60c sal & multi	10	8
795	A255	80c sil & multi	15	8
796	A255	1s lt grn & multi	15	10
		Nos. 789-796, C461-C462 (10)	1.18	89

Same, White Background

1970 *Perf. 13½*

797	A255	10c multi	5	5
798	A255	20c multi	5	5
799	A255	30c multi	5	5
800	A255	40c multi	6	5
801	A255	50c multi	8	5
802	A255	60c multi	10	8
803	A255	80c multi	10	8
804	A255	1s multi	15	10
		Nos. 797-804, C463-C464 (10)	92	74

Surcharged Revenue Stamps

A256 A257

1970, June 16 Litho. *Perf. 14*

Red Surcharge

805	A256	1s on 1s lt bl	15	5
806	A256	1.30s on 1s lt bl	20	8
807	A256	1.50s on 1s lt bl	25	10
808	A256	2s on 1s lt bl	30	12
809	A256	5s on 1s lt bl	60	25
810	A256	10s on 1s lt bl	1.25	50
		Nos. 805-810 (6)	2.75	1.10

1970 Typographed *Perf. 12*

Black Surcharge

811	A257	60c on 1s vio	10	8
812	A257	80c on 1s vio	10	8
813	A257	1s on 1s vio	15	8
814	A257	1.10s on 1s vio	15	8
815	A257	1.30s on 1s vio	15	8
816	A257	1.50s on 1s vio	20	8
817	A257	2s on 1s vio	25	8
818	A257	2.20s on 1s vio	40	
819	A257	3s on 1s vio	50	
		Nos. 811-819 (9)	2.00	

1970

820	A257	1.10s on 2s grn	15	1
821	A257	1.30s on 2s grn	20	
822	A257	1.50s on 2s grn	20	1
823	A257	2s on 2s grn	25	
824	A257	3.40s on 2s grn	50	1
825	A257	5s on 2s grn	75	2
826	A257	10s on 2s grn	1.25	3
827	A257	20s on 2s grn	2.50	5
828	A257	50s on 2s grn	6.00	1.2
		Nos. 820-828 (9)	11.80	2.7

1970

829	A257	3s on 5s bl	40	
830	A257	5s on 5s bl	75	1
831	A257	10s on 40s org	1.00	2

Arms of Zamora Chinchipe

A258

Flags of Ecuador and Chile

A259

Design: 1s, Arms and flag of Esmeraldas.

1971 Lithographed *Perf. 10½*

832	A258	50c pale yel & multi	5	3
833	A258	1s sal & multi	10	8
		Nos. 832-833, C465-C469 (7)	2.28	1.76

1971, Sept. *Perf. 12½*

840	A259	1.30s blk & multi	13	10

Visit of Pres. Salvador Allende of Chile, Aug. 24. See Nos. C481-C482.

Ismael Pérez Pazmiño

A260

1971, Sept. 16 *Perf. 12x11½*

841	A260	1s grn & multi	10	8

50th anniversary of "El Universo," newspaper founded by Ismael Pérez Pazmiño. See Nos. C485-C486.

CARE Package

A261

Flags of Ecuador and Argentina

A262

1971-72 *Perf. 12½*

842	A261	30c lil ('72)	5	5
843	A261	40c emer ('72)	5	5
844	A261	50c blue	8	6
845	A261	60c carmine	8	6
846	A261	80c lt brn ('72)	10	6
		Nos. 842-846 (5)	36	28

25th anniversary of CARE, a U.S.-Canadian Cooperative for American Relief Everywhere.

1972 *Perf. 11½*

847	A262	1s blk & multi	10	8

Visit of Lt. Gen. Alejandro Agustin Lanusse, president of Argentina, Jan. 25. See Nos. C491-C492.

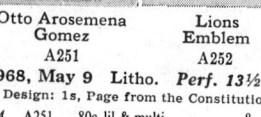

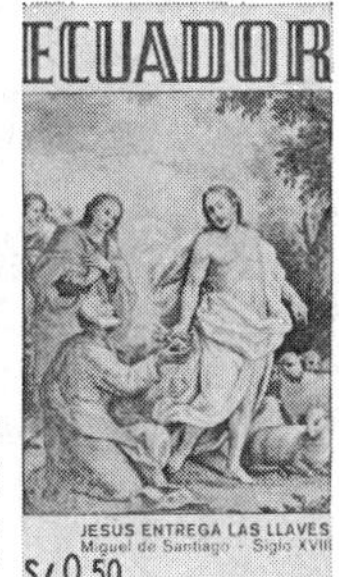

Jesus Giving Keys to St. Peter, by Miguel de Santiago
A263

Ecuadorian Paintings: 1.10s, Virgin of Mercy, Quito School. 2s, Virgin Mary, by Manuel Samaniego.

1972, Apr. 24 Litho. *Perf. 14x13½*

848	A263	50c blk & multi	8	5
849	A263	1.10s blk & multi	12	10
850	A263	2s blk & multi	25	20
a.		Souv. sheet of 3	50	50
		Nos. 848-850, C494-C495 (5)	1.75	1.45

No. 850a contains 3 imperf. stamps similar to Nos. 848–850. Blue marginal inscription. Size: 129x110mm.

1972, May 4

Ecuadorian Statues: 50c, Our Lady of Sorrow, by Caspicara. 1.10s, Nativity. Quito School (horiz.). 2s, Virgin of Quito, anonymous.

851	A263	50c blk & multi	8	3
852	A263	1.10s blk & multi	15	10
853	A263	2s blk & multi	25	15
a.		Souv. sheet of 3	50	50
		Nos. 851-853, C496-C497 (5)	1.78	1.28

Letters of "Ecuador" 3mm. high on Nos. 851–853, 7mm. high on Nos. 848–850. No. 853a contains 3 imperf. stamps similar to Nos. 851–853. Blue marginal inscription. Size. 129x110mm.

Gen. Juan Ignacio Pareja
A264

Designs: 40c, Juan José Flores. 50c, Leon de Febres Cordero. 60c, Ignacio Torres. 70c, Francisco de Paula Santander. 1s, José M. Cordova.

1972, May 24 *Perf. 12½*

854	A264	30c bl & multi	3	3
855	A264	40c bl & multi	4	3
856	A264	50c bl & multi	5	4
857	A264	60c bl & multi	10	5
858	A264	70c bl & multi	10	5
859	A264	1s bl & multi	15	10
		Nos. 854-859, C498-C503 (12)	4.80	3.60

Sesquicentennial of the Battle of Pichincha and the liberation of Quito.

Woman Wearing Poncho
A265

Designs: 3s, Striped poncho. 5s, Embroidered poncho. 10s, Metal vase.

1972, July Photo. *Perf. 13*

860	A265	2s multi	25	15
861	A265	3s multi	35	25
862	A265	5s multi	60	20
863	A265	10s dp bl & multi	1.25	50
a.		Souvenir sheet of 4	2.50	2.50
		Nos. 860-863, C504-C507 (8)	4.45	2.65

Handicraft of Ecuador. No. 863a contains 4 imperf. stamps similar to Nos. 860–863. Gray green marginal inscription and ornament. Black control number. Size 104x164mm.

Sucre Statue, Santo Domingo
A266

Radar Station
A267

Wmk. 367

Wmkd. Liberty Cap, Emblem and Inscription (367)

1972, Dec. 6 Litho. *Perf. 11½*

Designs: 1.80s, San Agustin Convent. 2.30s, Plaza de la Independencia. 2.50s, Bolivar statue, La Alameda. 4.75s, Chapel door.

864	A266	1.20s yel & multi	15	10
865	A266	1.80s yel & multi	20	15
866	A266	2.30s yel & multi	30	20
867	A266	2.50s yel & multi	40	25
868	A266	4.75s yel & multi	60	30
		Nos. 864-868, C518-C524 (12)	5.80	4.28

Sesquicentennial of the Battle of Pichincha.

1973, Apr. 5 Litho. *Perf. 11½*

869	A267	1s multi	30	15

Inauguration of earth telecommunications station, Oct. 19, 1972.

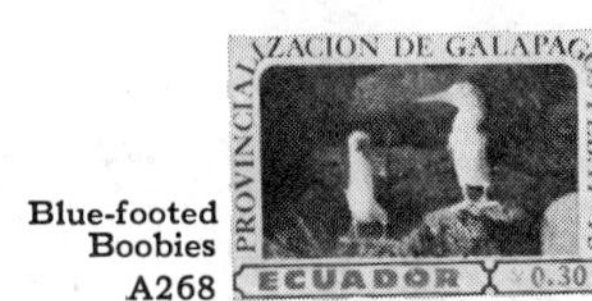

Blue-footed Boobies
A268

1973 Lithographed *Perf. 11½x12*

Multicolored

870	A268	30c *shown*	10	5
871	A268	40c *Blue-faced booby*	10	5
872	A268	50c *Oyster-catcher*	15	6
873	A268	60c *California sea lions*	15	10
874	A268	70c *Galapagos giant tortoise*	20	10
875	A268	1s *California sea lion*	25	15
		Nos. 870-875, C527-C528 (8)	1.49	78

Elevation of Galapagos Islands to a province of Ecuador.
Issue dates: 50c, Oct. 3; others Aug. 16.

Black-chinned Mountain Tanager
A269

Birds of Ecuador: 2s, Moriche oriole. 3s, Toucan barbet (vert.). 5s, Masked crimson tanager (vert.). 10s, Blue-necked tanager (vert.).

Perf. 11x11½, 11½x11

1973, Dec. 6 Litho. Unwmkd.

876	A269	1s brick red & multi	20	10
877	A269	2s lt bl & multi	35	15
878	A269	3s lt grn & multi	35	20
879	A269	5s pale lil & multi	85	35
880	A269	10s pale yel grn & multi	1.75	75
		Nos. 876-880 (5)	3.50	1.55

Two souvenir sheets exist: one contains 2 imperf. stamps similar to Nos. 876–877 with yellow margin and black inscription; the other 3 stamps similar to Nos. 878–880; gray margin and black inscription including "Aereo." Both sheets dated "1972." Size: 143x84mm.

Marco T. Varea, Botanist
A270

Portraits: 60c, Pio Jaramillo Alvarado, writer. 70c, Prof. Luciano Andrade M. No. 883, Marco T. Varea, botanist. No. 884, Dr. Juan Modesto Carbo Noboa, medical researcher. No. 885, Alfredo J. Valenzuela. No. 886, Capt. Edmundo Chiriboga G. 1.20s, Francisco Campos R., scientist. 1.80s, Luis Vernaza Lazarte, philanthropist.

1974 *Perf. 12x11½* Unwmkd.

881	A270	60c crim rose	10	5
882	A270	70c lilac	12	6
883	A270	1s ultra	15	8
884	A270	1s orange	15	8
885	A270	1s emerald	15	8
886	A270	1s brown	15	8
887	A270	1.20s ap grn	20	10
889	A270	1.80s lt bl	30	15
		Nos. 881-889 (8)	1.32	68

Arcade
A271

Designs: 30c, Monastery, entrance. 40c, Church. 50c, View of Church through gate (vert.). 60c, Chapel (vert.). 70c, Church and cemetery (vert.).

Perf. 11½x12, 12x11½

1975, Feb. 4 Lithographed

896	A271	20c yel & multi	5	5
897	A271	30c yel & multi	5	5
898	A271	40c yel & multi	10	5
899	A271	50c yel & multi	10	5
900	A271	60c yel & multi	15	5
901	A271	70c yel & multi	15	10
		Nos. 896-901 (6)	60	35

Colonial Monastery, Tilipulo, Cotopaxi Province.

Angel Polibio Chaves, Founder of Bolivar Province
A272

Portrait: No. 903, Emilio Estrada Ycaza (1916–1961), archeologist.

1975 Litho. *Perf. 12x11½*

902	A272	80c vio bl & lt bl	15	10
903	A272	80c ver & pink	15	10

Issue dates: No. 902, Feb. 21; No. 903, Mar. 25.

R. Rodriguez Palacios and A. Duran Quintero
A273

"Woman of Action"
A274

1975, Apr. 1 Litho. *Perf. 12x11½*

910	A273	1s multi	15	10

Meeting of the Ministers for Public Works of Ecuador and Colombia, July 27, 1973.

See Nos. C547–C548.

1975, June

Design: No. 912, 1s, "Woman of Peace."

911	A274	1s yel & multi	15	10
912	A274	1s bl & multi	15	10

International Women's Year 1975.

Planes, Soldier and Ship
A275

1975, July 9 *Perf. 11½x12*

913	A275	2s multi	35	20

Three years of National Revolutionary Government.

Hurdling
A276

Designs: Modern sports drawn Inca style.

1975, Sept. 11 Litho. *Perf. 11½*

914	A276	20c *shown*	5	5
915	A276	20c *Chess*	5	5
916	A276	30c *Basketball*	5	5
917	A276	30c *Boxing*	5	5
918	A276	40c *Bicycling*	8	5
919	A276	40c *Steeplechase*	8	5
920	A276	50c *Soccer*	8	5
921	A276	50c *Fencing*	8	5
922	A276	60c *Golf*	10	5
923	A276	60c *Vaulting*	10	5
924	A276	70c *Judo (standing)*	12	5
925	A276	70c *Wrestling*	12	5
926	A276	80c *Swimming*	15	8
927	A276	80c *Weight lifting*	15	8

928 A276 1s *Table Tennis* 15 10
929 A276 1s *Paddle ball* 15 10
Nos. 914-929, C554-C558 (21) 3.25 1.80

3rd Ecuadorian Games.

Genciana A277

Designs: Ecuadorian plants.

Perf. 12x11½, 11½x12

1975, Nov. 18 Lithographed

Multicolored

930 A277 20c *Orchid* (vert.) 3 3
931 A277 30c *shown* 4 3
932 A277 40c *Bromeliaceae cactacceae (vert.)* 5 3
933 A277 50c *Orchid* 6 3
934 A277 60c *Orchid* 7 4
935 A277 80c *Flowering cactus* 10 5
936 A277 1s *Orchid* 12 6
Nos. 930-936, C559-C563 (12) 2.31 1.19

Venus, Chorrera Culture
A278

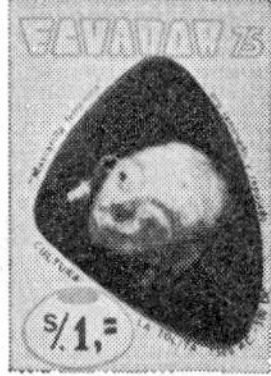

Female Mask, Tolita Culture
A279

Designs: 30c, Venus, Valdivia Culture. 40c, Seated man, Chorrera Culture. 50c, Man with poncho, Panzaleo Culture (late). 60c, Mythical head, Cashaloma Culture. 80c, Musician, Tolita Culture. No. 943, Chief Priest, Manteña Culture. No. 945, Ornament, Tolita Culture. No. 946, Angry mask, Tolita Culture.

1976, Feb. 12 Litho. *Perf. 11½*

937 A278 20c multi 5 3
938 A278 30c multi 5 3
939 A278 40c multi 6 3
940 A278 50c multi 8 3
941 A278 60c multi 8 4
942 A278 80c multi 12 5
943 A278 1s multi 15 6
944 A279 1s multi 15 6
945 A279 1s multi 15 6
946 A279 1s multi 15 6
Nos. 937-946, C568-C572 (15) 2.88 1.37

Archaeological artifacts.

Strawberries
A280

Carlos Amable Ortiz (1859–1937)
A281

1976, Mar. 30

947 A280 1s bl & multi 15 6

25th Flower and Fruit Festival, Ambato. See Nos. C573–C574.

1976, Mar. 15 Litho. *Perf. 11½*

Portraits: No. 949, Sixto Maria Duran (1875–1947). No. 950, Segundo Cueva Celi (1901–1969). No. 951, Cristobal Ojeda Davila (1910–1952). No. 952, Luis Alberto Valencia (1918–1970).

948 A281 1s ver & multi 15 6
949 A281 1s org & multi 15 6
950 A281 1s lt grn & multi 15 6
951 A281 1s bl & multi 15 6
952 A281 1s lt brn & multi 15 6
Nos. 948-952 (5) 75 30

Ecuadorian composers and musicians.

Institute Emblem
A282

1977, Aug. 15 Litho. *Perf. 11½x12*

953 A282 2s multi 24 12

11th General Assembly of Pan-American Institute of Geography and History, Quito, Aug. 15–30. See Nos. C597–C597a.

Hands Holding Rotary Emblem
A283

José Peralta
A284

1977, Aug. 31 Litho. *Perf. 12*

954 A283 1s multi 12 6
955 A283 2s multi 24 12

Souvenir Sheets

Imperf.

956 A283 5s multi 70 50
957 A283 10s multi 1.40 75

Rotary Club of Guayaquil, 50th anniversary. Nos. 956–957 have black control numbers. Size: 90x115mm.

1977 Litho. *Perf. 11½*

Design: 2.40s, Peralta statue.

958 A284 1.80s multi 22 10
959 A284 2.40s multi 28 14

José Peralta (1855–1937), writer, 40th death anniversary. See No. C609.

Blue-faced Booby
A285

Galapagos Birds: 1.80s, Red-footed booby. 2.40s, Blue-footed boobies. 3.40s, Gull. 4.40s, Galapagos hawk. 5.40s, Map of Galapagos Islands and boobies (vert.).

Perf. 11½x12, 12x11½

1977, Nov. 29 Lithographed

960 A285 1.20s multi 14 6
961 A285 1.80s multi 22 10
962 A285 2.40s multi 28 14
963 A285 3.40s multi 40 20
964 A285 4.40s multi 52 25
965 A285 5.40s multi 65 28
Nos. 960-965 (6) 2.21 1.03

Dr. Corral Moscoso Hospital, Cuenca
A286

1978, Apr. 12 Litho. *Perf. 11½x12*

966 A286 3s multi 36 18

Inauguration (in 1977) of Dr. Vicente Corral Moscoso Regional Hospital, Cuenca. See Nos. C613–C614.

Surveyor Plane over Ecuador
A287

Latin-American Lions Emblem
A288

1978, Apr. 12 Litho. *Perf. 11½*

967 A287 6s multi 72 35

Military Geographical Institute, 50th anniversary. See Nos. C619–C620.

1978

968 A288 3s multi 36 18
969 A288 4.20s multi 50 25

7th meeting of Latin American Lions, Jan. 25–29. See Nos. C621–C623.

70th Anniversary Emblem
A289

1978, Sept. Litho. *Perf. 11½*

970 A289 4.20s gray & multi 50 25

70th anniversary of Filanbanco (Philanthropic Bank). See No. C626.

Goalmouth and Net—A290

Designs: 1.80s, "Gauchito" and Games emblem (vert.). 4.40s, "Gauchito" (vert.).

1978, Nov. 1 Litho. *Perf. 12*

971 A290 1.20s multi 14 6
972 A290 1.80s multi 22 10
973 A290 4.40s multi 52 25
Nos. 971-973, C627-C629 (6) 3.13 1.53

11th World Cup Soccer Championship, Argentina, June 1–25.

Symbols for Male and Female
A291

1979, Feb. 15 Litho. *Perf. 12x11½*

974 A291 3.40s multi 40 20

Inter-American Women's Commission, 50th anniversary.

Emblem
A292

1979, June 21 Litho. *Perf. 11½x12*

975 A292 4.40s multi 52 25
976 A293 5.40s multi 65 28

Ecuadorian Mortgage Bank, 16th anniversary.

Street Scene, Quito
A293

Unwmkd.

1979, Aug. 3 Litho. *Perf. 12x11½*

977 A293 3.40s multi 40 20

National heritage: Quito and Galapagos Islands. See Nos. C651–C653.

Jose Joaquin de Olmedo (1780-1847), Physician
A294

Chief Enriquillo, Dominican Republic
A295

1980, Apr. 29 Litho. *Perf. 12x11½*

978 A294 3s multi 36 18
979 A294 5s multi 60 30

First President of Free State of Guayaquil, 1820. See No. C662.

1980, May 12

Indo-American Tribal Chiefs: 3.40s, Guaycaypuro, Venezuela. No. 982, Abayuba, Uruguay. No. 983, Atlacatl, Salvador.

980 A295 3s multi 36 18
981 A295 3.40s multi 40 20
982 A295 5s multi 60 30
983 A295 5s multi 60 30
Nos. 980-983, C663-C678 (20) 25.46 12.78

King Juan Carlos and Queen Sofia, Visit to Ecuador—A296

1980, May 18 *Perf. 11½x12*

984 A296 3.40s multi 40 20

See No. C679.

Cofan Indian, Napo Province—A297

1980, June 10 **Litho.** ***Perf. 12x11½***

985 A297 3s *shown* 36 16
986 A297 3.40s *Zuleta woman, Imbabura* 40 20
987 A297 5s *Chota woman, Imbabura* 60 30
Nos. 985-987, C681-C684 (7) 6.41 3.18

Basilica, Our Lady of Mercy Church, Quito—A298

1980, July 7 **Litho.** ***Perf. 11½***

988 A298 3.40s *shown* 40 20
989 A298 3.40s *Basilica balcony, vert.* 40 20
Nos. 988-989, C685-C691 (9) 9.40 4.69

Souvenir Sheet

990 A298 5s multi 75 50

Virgin of Mercy, patron saint of Ecuadorian armed forces. No. 990 contains designs of Nos. C686, C690, 989; black control number. Size: 91x116mm.

Olympic Torch and Rings—A299

1980, July 19 ***Perf. 12x11½***

991 A299 5s multi 60 30
992 A299 7.60s multi 90 45

Souvenir Sheet
Imperf.

993 A299 30s multi 3.60 1.80

22nd Summer Olympic Games, Moscow, July 19-Aug. 3. See Nos. C695-C696.

No. 993 contains vignettes in designs of Nos. 991 and C695, black control number. Size: 116x90mm.

Coronation of Virgin of Cisne, 50th Anniversary—A300

1980 **Litho.** ***Perf. 11½***

994 A300 1.20s *shown* 15 6
995 A300 3.40s *Different statue* 42 20

J.J. Olmeda, Father de Velasco, Flags of Ecuador and Riobamba, Constitution—A301

1980, Sept. 20 **Litho.** ***Perf. 11½***

996 A301 3.40s multi 42 20
997 A301 5s multi 62 30

Souvenir Sheet
Imperf.

998 A301 30s multi 3.75 1.75

Constitutional Assembly of Riobamba sesquicentennial. No. 998 contains vignettes in designs of Nos. 996-997, black control number. Size: 116x90mm. See Nos. C700-C702.

First Lady Mrs. Aguilera—A302

Wmk. 367

1980, Oct. 9 **Litho.** ***Perf. 12x11½***

999 A302 1.20s multi 15 6
1000 A302 3.40s multi 42 20

Democratic government, 1st anniversary. See Nos. C703-C705.

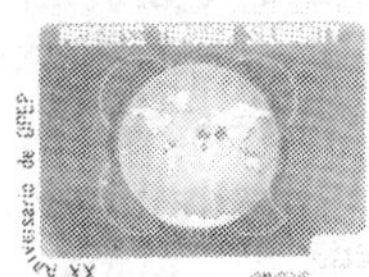

OPEC Emblem—A303

1980, Nov. 8 ***Perf. 11½x12***

1001 A303 3.40s multi 42 20

20th anniversary of OPEC. See No. C706.

Decorative Hedges, Capitol Gardens, Carchi—A304

1980, Nov. 21 ***Perf. 13***

1002 A304 3s multi 36 16

Carchi province centennial. See Nos. C707-C708.

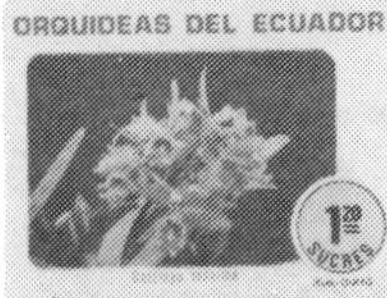

Cattleya Maxima—A305

Designs: Orchids.

1980, Nov. 22 ***Perf. 11½x12***

1003 A305 1.20s *shown* 15 6
1004 A305 3s *Comparattia speciosa* 36 16
1005 A305 3.40s *Cattleya iricolor* 42 20
Nos. 1003-1005, C708-C711 (7) 21.03 10.47

Souvenir Sheet
Imperf.

1006 A305 20s multi 2.50 1.25

No. 1006 contains vignettes in desings of Nos. 1003-1005; black control number. Size: 115x90mm.

Pope John Paul II and Children—A306

1007 A306 3.40s multi 42 20

Christmas 1980/visit of Pope John Paul II. See Nos. C715-C716.

Carlos and Jorge Ortega, Editors of El Comercio—A307

El Comercio Newspaper, 75th Anniversary: 3.40s, Editors Cesar and Carlos Jacome.

1981, Jan. 6

1008 A307 2s multi 24 10
1009 A307 3.40s multi 42 20

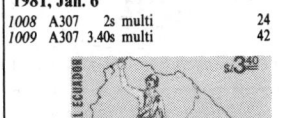

Soldier on Map of Ecuador—A308

National Defense (Map of Ecuador and): No. 1011, Pres. Roldos.

1981, Mar. 10 **Litho.** ***Perf. 13***

1010 A308 3.40s multi 42 20
1011 A308 3.40s multi 42 20

Theodore E. Gildred and Ecuador I A309

1981, Mar. 31 **Litho.** ***Perf. 13***

1012 A309 2s lt bl & blk 24 10

Ecuador-U.S. flight, 50th anniv.

Octavio Cordero Palacios (1870-1930), Humanist—A310

1981, Apr. 10

1013 A310 2s multi 24 10

Radio Station HCJB 50th Anniv.—A311

1981 **Litho.** ***Perf. 13***

1014 A311 2s multi 24 10

See Nos. C721-C722.

Virgin of Dolorosa—A312

1981, Apr.30 **Litho.** ***Perf. 12***

1015 A312 2s shown 24 10
1016 A312 2s San Gabriel College Church 24 10

Miracle of the painting of the Virgin of Dolorosa at San Gabriel College, 75th anniv.

Dr. Rafael Mendoza Aviles Bridge Inauguration—A313

1981, July 25 ***Perf. 13***

1017 A313 2s multi 24 10

World Food Day—A314

1981, Dec. 31 **Litho.** ***Perf. 13½x13***

1018 A314 5s multi 60 25

See No. C728.

Transnave Shipping Co. 10th Anniv. A315

Intl. Year of the Disabled A316

1982, Jan. 21 **Litho.** ***Perf. 13***

1019 A315 3.50s Freighter Isla Salango 45 22

1982, Feb. 25

1020 A316 3.40s Man in wheelchair 42 20

See Nos. C729-C730.

Arch
A317

Juan Montalvo Birth Sesquicentennial
A318

1982, May **Litho.** ***Perf. 13***

1021	A317	2s shown	24	10
1022	A317	3s Houses	36	15

Souvenir Sheet

1023		Sheet of 4 18th cent. map of Quito	3.00	1.25
a.-d.	A317	6s multi	72	30

QUITEX '82, 4th Natl. Stamp Exhibition, Quito, Apr. 16-22. No. 1023 contains 4 stamps (48x31mm., perf. 12½); black control number, inscription. Size: 109x89mm.

1982

1024	A318	2s Portrait	24	10
1025	A318	3s Mausoleum	36	15

See No. C731.

American Air Forces Cooperation System
A319

4th World Swimming Champ., Guayaquil
A320

1982

1026	A319	5s Emblem	60	25

1982, July 30

1027	A320	1.80s Stadium	22	10
1028	A320	3.40s Water polo	42	20

See Nos. C732-C733.

Juan L. Mera (1832-?), Writer, by Victor Mideros—A321

1982, Dec. **Litho.** ***Perf. 13***

1029	A321	5.40s shown	65	26
1030	A321	6s Statue	72	30

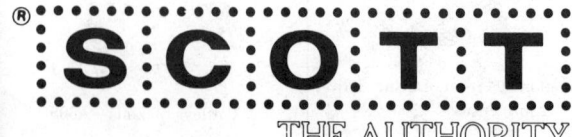

SEMI-POSTAL STAMPS.

Nos. 423-428
Surcharged in Carmine or Blue:

Hospital
Méndez + $ 0,50

1944, May 9 *Perf. 12* **Unwmkd.**

B1	A171	10c +10c yel grn (C)	50	35
B2	A171	20c +20c rose pink	50	40
B3	A171	30c +20c dk gray brn	50	50
B4	A171	50c +20c dp red lil	1.00	75
B5	A171	1s +50c ol gray (C)	1.50	1.25
B6	A171	10s +2s red org	6.00	3.50
		Nos. B1-B6 (6)	10.00	6.75

The surtax aided Mendez Hospital.

AIR POST STAMPS.

In 1928–30, the internal airmail service of Ecuador was handled by the Sociedad Colombo-Alemana de Transportes Aereos ("SCADTA") under government sanction. During this period SCADTA issued stamps which were the only legal franking for airmail service except that handled under contract with Pan American-Grace Airways. SCADTA issues are Nos. C1–C6, C16–C25.

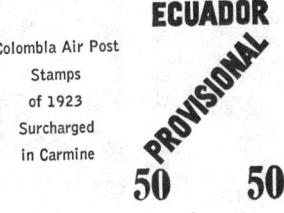

Colombia Air Post Stamps of 1923 Surcharged in Carmine

ECUADOR
PROVISIONAL
50 50

"Provisional" at 45° Angle.

Perf. 14x14½

1928, Aug. 28 **Wmk. 116**

C1	AP6	50c on 10c grn	150.00	100.00
C2	AP6	75c on 15c car	300.00	200.00
C3	AP6	1s on 20c gray	100.00	60.00
C4	AP6	1½s on 30c bl	85.00	50.00
C5	AP6	3s on 60c brn	150.00	75.00
		Nos. C1-C5 (5)	785.00	485.00

"Provisional" at 41° Angle.

1929, Mar. 20

C1a	AP6	50c on 10c grn	165.00	150.00
C2a	AP6	75c on 15c car	200.00	175.00
C3a	AP6	1s on 20c gray	165.00	175.00

Same with "Cts." Between Surcharged Numerals

C6	AP6	50c on 10c grn	*1,250.*	*1,000.*

A 75c on 15c carmine with "Cts." between the surcharged numerals exists. There is no evidence that it was regularly issued or used.

Plane over River Guayas
AP1

Engraved.

1929, May 5 *Perf. 12* **Unwmkd.**

C8	AP1	2c black	20	10
C9	AP1	5c car rose	20	10
C10	AP1	10c dp brn	25	6
C11	AP1	20c dk vio	40	8
C12	AP1	50c dp grn	1.25	35
C13	AP1	1s dk bl	3.50	1.75
C14	AP1	5s org yel	10.00	5.00
C15	AP1	10s org red	65.00	60.00
		Nos. C8-C15 (8)	80.80	67.44

Issued to commemorate the establishing of commercial air service in Ecuador. The stamps were available for all forms of postal service and were largely used for franking ordinary letters.

Nos. C13–C15 show numerals in color on white background. Counterfeits of No. C15 exist.

See Nos. C26–C31.

Quito Cathedral
AP2

Mount Chimborazo
AP3

Lithographed.

1929, Apr. 1 *Perf. 14* **Wmk. 127**

C16	AP2	50c red brn	2.50	2.50
C17	AP2	75c green	2.50	2.50
C18	AP2	1s rose	3.50	2.50
C19	AP2	1½s gray bl	3.50	3.00
C20	AP2	2s violet	12.50	10.00
C21	AP2	3s brown	12.50	10.00
C22	AP3	5s lt bl	40.00	30.00
C23	AP3	10s lt red	85.00	65.00
C24	AP3	15s violet	150.00	125.00
C25	AP3	25s ol grn	200.00	150.00
		Nos. C16-C25 (10)	512.00	400.50

Plane Type of 1929

Engraved.

1930-44 *Perf. 12.* **Unwmkd.**

C26	AP1	1s car lake	3.50	50
C27	AP1	1s grn ('44)	60	12
C28	AP1	5s ol grn	5.00	4.00
C29	AP1	5s pur ('44)	1.25	12
C30	AP1	10s black	15.00	5.00
C31	AP1	10s brt ultra ('44)	2.25	12
		Nos. C26-C31 (6)	27.60	9.86

Nos. C26–C31 show numerals in color on white background.

Overprinted in Various Colors.

AP4

1930, June 4

C32	AP4	1s car lake (Bk)	15.00	15.00
a.		Double overprint (R Br + Bk)	85.00	
C33	AP4	5s ol grn (Bl)	15.00	15.00
C34	AP4	10s blk (R Br)	15.00	15.00

Issued to commemorate the flight of Capt. Benjamin Mendez from Bogota to Quito, bearing a crown of flowers for the tomb of Grand Marshal Sucre.

Air Post Official Stamps of 1929–30
Overprinted in Various Colors

INAUGURACION
MONUMENTO
A BOLIVAR
QUITO, 24 DE
JULIO DE 1935

or Surcharged Similarly
in Upper & Lower Case

1935, July 24

C35	AP1	50c dp grn (Bl)	6.00	6.00
C36	AP1	50c ol brn (R)	6.00	6.00
C37	AP1	1s on 5s ol grn (Bk)	6.00	6.00
a.		Double surcharge	100.00	
C38	AP1	2s on 10s blk (R)	6.00	6.00

Issued to commemorate the unveiling of a monument to Bolivar at Quito, July 24th, 1935.

Geodesical Mission Issue

Nos. 349-351
Overprinted
in Blue or Black

AÉREO

1936, July 3 *Perf. 12½*

C39	A136	10c dp org (Bl)	30	10
C40	A136	20c vio (Bk)	30	10
C41	A136	50c dk red (Bl)	50	12

Charles M. de la Condamine and Pedro Maldonado
AP5

C42	AP5	70c black	80	40

Bicentenary of Geodesical Mission visit to Quito.

Philatelic Exhibition Issue

Type of Regular Issue
Overprinted

"AEREA"

1936, Oct. 20 *Perf. 13½x14*

C43	A137	2c rose	5.00	5.00
C44	A137	5c brn org	5.00	5.00
C45	A137	10c brown	5.00	5.00
C46	A137	20c ultra	5.00	5.00
C47	A137	50c red vio	5.00	5.00
C48	A137	1s green	5.00	5.00
		Nos. C43-C48 (6)	30.00	30.00

Condor and Plane—AP6

Perf. 13½

C49	AP6	70c org brn	1.00	75
C50	AP6	1s dl vio	1.00	1.00

Nos. C43–C50 were issued to commemorate the first International Philatelic Exhibition at Quito.

Condor over "El Altar"
AP7

1937-46 *Perf. 11½, 12*

C51	AP7	10c chestnut	10	5
C52	AP7	20c ol blk	20	6
C53	AP7	40c rose car ('46)	20	6
C54	AP7	70c blk brn	25	15
C55	AP7	1s gray blk	35	25
C56	AP7	2s dk vio	90	35
		Nos. C51-C56 (6)	2.00	92

Issue dates: 40c, Oct. 7, 1946; others, Aug. 19, 1937.

Portrait of Washington, American Eagle and Flags
AP8

Engraved and Lithographed.

1938, Feb. 9 *Perf. 12*

Center Multicolored.

C57	AP8	2c brown	20	10
C58	AP8	5c black	20	10
C59	AP8	10c brown	25	10
C60	AP8	20c dk bl	50	10
C61	AP8	50c violet	85	20
C62	AP8	1s black	1.50	25
C63	AP8	2s violet	3.00	75
		Nos. C57-C63 (7)	6.50	1.60

Issued in commemoration of the 150th anniversary of the Constitution of the United States of America.

In 1947, Nos. C61 to C63 were overprinted in dark blue: "Primero la Patria!" and plane. These revolutionary propaganda stamps were later renounced by decree.

No. RA35
Surcharged in Red

AEREO
SEDTA
0,65

1938, Nov. 16 *Perf. 13½*

C64	PT12	65c on 3c ultra	15	10

A national airmail concession was given to the Sociedad Ecuatoriano de Transportes Aereos (SEDTA)) in July, 1938. No. RA35 was surcharged for SEDTA postal requirements. SEDTA operated through 1940.

Army Horseman
AP9

Woman Runner
AP10

Tennis
AP11

Boxing
AP12

Olympic Fire
AP13

1939, Mar. **Engraved** *Perf. 12*

C65	AP9	5c lt grn	1.00	15
C66	AP10	10c salmon	1.25	25
C67	AP11	50c redsh brn	6.00	25
C68	AP12	1s blk brn	7.50	50
C69	AP13	2s rose car	11.00	1.00
		Nos. C65-C69 (5)	26.75	2.15

First Bolivarian Games (1938), La Paz.

Plane over Chimborazo
AP14

1939, May 1 *Perf. 13x12½*

C70	AP14	1s yel brn	30	15
C71	AP14	2s rose vio	60	15
C72	AP14	5s black	1.65	15

Golden Gate Bridge and Mountain Peak
AP15

Empire State Building and Mountain Peak
AP16

1939 *Perf. 12½x13*

C73	AP15	2c black		6	6
C74	AP15	5c rose red		6	6
C75	AP15	10c indigo		10	8
C76	AP15	50c rose vio		15	15
C77	AP15	1s chocolate		20	15
C78	AP15	2s yel brn		40	15
C79	AP15	5s emerald		85	25
		Nos. C73-C79 (7)		1.82	90

Golden Gate International Exposition.

1939

C80	AP16	2c brn org	8	8
C81	AP16	5c dk car	8	8
C82	AP16	10c indigo	10	8
C83	AP16	50c sl grn	15	10
C84	AP16	1s dp org	30	10
C85	AP16	2s dk red vio	50	25
C86	AP16	5s dk gray	1.00	20
		Nos. C80-C86 (7)	2.21	89

New York World's Fair.

Map of the Americas and Airplane
AP17

Francisco J. E. Santa Cruz y Espejo
AP18

1940, July 9

C87	AP17	10c red org & bl	25	10
C88	AP17	70c sep & bl	35	10
C89	AP17	1s cop brn & bl	50	15
C90	AP17	10s blk & bl	2.00	75

Pan American Union, 50th anniversary.

1941, Dec. 15

C91	AP18	3s rose car	1.50	20
C92	AP18	10s yel org	3.00	40

See note after No. 399.

Old Map of South America Showing Amazon River
AP19

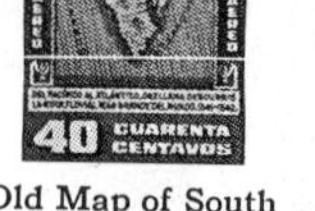
Panoramic View of Amazon River
AP20

Designs: 70c, Gonzalo de Pineda. 5s, Painting of the expedition.

1942, Jan. 30

C93	AP19	40c blk & buff	50	18
C94	AP19	70c olive	90	15
C95	AP20	2s dk grn	1.00	40
C96	AP19	5s rose	2.00	90

See note after No. 403.

Remigio Crespo Toral
AP21

1942, Sept. 1 *Perf. 13½*

C97	AP21	10c dl vio	40	10

Gen. Eloy Alfaro
AP22

Devil's Nose
AP23

Designs: 3s, Military College. 5s, Montecristi, Alfaro's birthplace.

1943, Feb. 16 *Perf. 12*

C98	AP22	70c dk rose & blk	60	30
C99	AP23	1s ol blk & red brn	90	60
C100	AP23	3s ol gray & grn	1.25	90
C101	AP23	5s sl & sal	2.25	1.15

Issued to commemorate the centenary of the birth of President Alfaro (1842-1903).

Nos. C61-C63 Overprinted in Red Brown

BIENVENIDO — WALLACE

Abril 15 — 1943

1943, Apr. 15 *Perf. 11½*

Center Multicolored.

C102	AP8	50c violet	1.50	70
C103	AP8	1s black	1.75	85
C104	AP8	2s violet	2.50	1.25

Issued to commemorate the visit of Vice-President Henry A. Wallace of the United States.

Nos. 374-376 Overprinted "AEREO LOOR A BOLIVIA JUNIO 11—1943" (like Nos. C111-C113).

1943, June 11 *Perf. 13*

C105	A146	50c dp red vio	25	25
C106	A147	1s cop red	50	35
C107	A148	2s dk grn	75	50

Issued to commemorate the visit of President Enrique Penaranda of Bolivia.
Vertical overprints on Nos. C105-C106.

Nos. 374-376 Overprinted "AEREO LOOR A PARAGUAY JULIO 5—1943" (like Nos. C111-C113).

1943, July 5

C108	A146	50c dp red vio	25	25
a.		Double ovpt.	40.00	
C109	A147	1s cop red	50	35
C110	A148	2s dk grn	75	40

Issued to commemorate the visit of President Higinio Morinigo of Paraguay.
Vertical overprints on Nos. C108-C109.

Nos. 374-376 Overprinted in Black

AEREO

LOOR A VENEZUELA

JULIO 23 — 1943

1943, July 23

C111	A146	50c dp red vio	25	25
C112	A147	1s cop red	50	40
C113	A148	2s dk grn	75	40

Issued to commemorate the visit of President Isaias Medina Angarita of Venezuela.
Vertical overprint on Nos. C111-C112.
See also Nos. C105-C110.

President Arroyo del Rio Addressing U.S. Congress
AP26

1943, Oct. 9 *Perf. 12*

C114	AP26	50c dk brn	60	50
C115	AP26	70c brt rose	75	75
C116	AP26	3s dk bl	1.00	75
C117	AP26	5s dk grn	2.00	1.25
C118	AP26	10s ol blk	7.50	6.00
		Nos. C114-C118 (5)	11.85	9.25

Issued to commemorate the good will tour of President Arroyo del Rio in 1942.

1944, Feb. 7

C119	AP26	50c dp red lil	60	45
C120	AP26	70c red brn	1.00	50
C121	AP26	3s turq grn	1.00	50
C122	AP26	5s brt ultra	1.50	1.25
C123	AP26	10s scarlet	2.00	1.75
		Nos. C119-C123 (5)	6.10	4.45

Church of San Francisco, Quito
AP27

1944, Feb. 13

C124	AP27	70c turq grn	75	50
C125	AP27	1s olive	75	50
C126	AP27	3s red org	1.25	80
C127	AP27	5s car rose	1.75	1.00

See note after No. 433.

Government Palace, Quito
AP28

1944 **Engraved** *Perf. 11*

C128	AP28	3s orange	60	15
C129	AP28	5s dk brn	90	15
C130	AP28	10s dk red	2.00	20

See also No. C221.

Symbol of the Red Cross
AP29

1945, Apr. 25 *Perf. 12* **Unwmkd.**

Cross in Rose.

C131	AP29	2s dp bl	1.00	1.00
C132	AP29	3s green	1.50	1.00
C133	AP29	5s dk vio	2.50	1.50
C134	AP29	10s car rose	6.00	4.50

Issued to commemorate the 80th anniversary of the founding of the International Red Cross.

No. RA55 Surcharged in Black

AEREO
40
Ctvs.

1945, June 8

C135	PT21	40c on 5c bl	25	15
a.		Double surcharge	10.00	

Counterfeits exist.

Nos. C128 to C130 Overprinted in Green

V
SETIEMBRE 5
1945

1945, Sept. 6 *Perf. 11*

C136	AP28	3s orange	75	75
a.		Inverted ovpt.	30.00	
b.		Double ovpt.	30.00	
C137	AP28	5s dk brn	1.00	1.00
C138	AP28	10s dk red	3.00	3.00

Nos. C61-C63 Overprinted in Dark Blue and Gold

LOOR A CHILE
OCTUBRE 2 1945

1945, Oct. 2 *Perf. 12*

Center Multicolored.

C139	AP8	50c violet	75	75
C140	AP8	1s black	85	80
C141	AP8	2s violet	85	80

Visit of Pres. Juan Antonio Rios of Chile.

Monument to Liberty
AP30

Map of Pan-American Highway and Arms of Cuenca
AP31

1945, Nov. 14 **Engraved.**

C142	AP30	30c blue	25	15
C143	AP30	40c rose car	35	15
C144	AP30	1s dl vio	75	40
C145	AP30	3s gray blk	1.25	1.00
C146	AP30	5s pur brn	2.00	1.25
		Nos. C142-C146 (5)	4.60	2.95

Issued to commemorate the 150th anniversary of the birth of General Antonio José de Sucre.

1946, Apr. 22 **Unwmkd.**

C147	AP31	1s car rose	50	45
C148	AP31	2s violet	70	60
C149	AP31	3s turq grn	1.00	55
C150	AP31	5s red org	1.25	75
C151	AP31	10s dk bl	2.00	65
		Nos. C147-C151 (5)	5.45	3.00

Revolution Types of Regular Issue

1946, Aug. 9 *Perf. 12½*

C152	A177	40c dp cl	10	10
C153	A178	1s sepia	25	10
C154	A179	2s indigo	60	25
C155	A180	3s ol grn	85	55

Issued to commemorate the 2nd anniversary of the Revolution of May 28, 1944.

National Union of Periodicals, Initials and Quill Pen
AP36

1946, Sept. 16

C156	AP36	50c dl pur	50	35
C157	AP36	70c dk grn	60	40
C158	AP36	3s red	1.00	50
C159	AP36	5s indigo	1.50	75
C160	AP36	10s chocolate	4.00	1.00
		Nos. C156-C160 (5)	7.60	3.00

Issued to publicize a campaign for adult education.

The Blessed Mariana Teaching Children
AP37

"Lily of Quito"
AP38

1946, Nov. 28 **Unwmkd.**

C161	AP37	40c chocolate	45	15
C162	AP37	60c dp bl	55	50
C163	AP38	3s org yel	1.10	1.00
C164	AP38	5s green	1.85	1.25

Issued to commemorate the 300th anniversary of the death of the Blessed Mariana de Jesus Paredes y Flores.

Juan de Velasco
AP39

Riobamba Irrigation Canal
AP40

1947, Nov. 27 ***Perf. 12***

C165	AP39	60c dk grn	15	8
C166	AP39	70c purple	20	8
C167	AP39	1s blk brn	20	6
C168	AP39	1.10s car rose	20	18
C169	AP40	1.30s dp bl	25	20
C170	AP40	1.90s ol bis	50	25
C171	AP40	2s ol grn	50	15
		Nos. C165-C171 (7)	2.00	1.00

Andrés Bello
AP41

Christopher Columbus
AP42

1948, Apr. 21 ***Perf. 13***

C172	AP41	60c magenta	30	15
C173	AP41	1.30s dk bl grn	60	35
C174	AP41	1.90s dk rose car	50	35

No. C166 Overprinted in Black

CONFERENCIA
ECONOMICA
GRANCOLOMBIANA
MAYO 24 DE 1.948

1948, May 24 ***Perf. 12***

C175	AP39	70c purple	65	45

1948, May 26 ***Perf. 14***

C176	AP42	50c ol grn	20	20
C177	AP42	70c rose car	30	30
C178	AP42	3c ultra	65	60
C179	AP42	5s brown	1.25	50
C180	AP42	10s dp vio	2.25	50
		Nos. C176-C180 (5)	4.65	2.10

See note after No. 495.

No. C169 Overprinted in Carmine

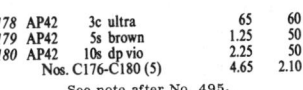

Feria Nacional
1948
ECUADOR de hoy y del MAÑANA

1948, Aug. 26 ***Perf. 12*** **Unwmkd.**

C181	AP40	1.30s dp bl	60	45

Issued to publicize the National Fair of Today and Tomorrow, 1948.

Elia Liut and Telegrafo I
AP43

Teacher and Pupils
AP44

1948, Sept. 10 ***Perf. 12½***

C182	AP43	60c rose red	40	35
C183	AP43	1s green	45	40
C184	AP43	1.30s dp cl	45	45
C185	AP43	1.90s dp vio	50	45
C186	AP43	2s dk brn	60	55
C187	AP43	5s blue	1.25	80
		Nos. C182-C187 (6)	3.65	3.00

Issued to commemorate the 25th anniversary (in 1945) of the first postal flight in Ecuador.

1948, Oct. 12 ***Perf. 14***

C188	AP44	50c violet	40	35
C189	AP44	70c dp bl	40	35
C190	AP44	3s dk grn	60	55
C191	AP44	5s red	80	40
C192	AP44	10s brown	1.50	65
		Nos. C188-C192 (5)	3.70	2.30

Campaign for adult education.

Franklin D. Roosevelt and Two of "Four Freedoms"
AP45 AP46

1948, Oct. 24 ***Perf. 12½***

C193	AP45	60c emer & org brn	20	20
C194	AP45	1s car rose & sl	25	25
C195	AP46	1.50s grn & red brn	40	35
C196	AP46	2s red & blk	90	40
C197	AP46	5s ultra & blk	1.35	40
		Nos. C193-C197 (5)	3.10	1.60

Issued in tribute to Franklin D. Roosevelt, 1882–1945.

Maldonado Types of Regular Issue

1948, Nov. 17

C198	A196	60c dp org & rose car	40	15
C199	A197	90c red & gray blk	40	15
C200	A196	1.30s pur & dp org	60	35
C201	A197	2s dp bl & dl grn	60	35

See note after No. 519.

Juan Montalvo and Cervantes
AP47

Don Quixote
AP48

1949, May 2 **Engr.** ***Perf. 12½x12***

C202	AP47	1.30s ol brn & ultra	60	50
C203	AP48	1.90s grn & rose car	60	40
C204	AP47	3s vio & org brn	60	40
C205	AP48	5s red & gray blk	1.75	20
C206	AP47	10s red lil & aqua	2.50	20
		Nos. C202-C206 (5)	6.05	1.70

Issued to commemorate the 400th anniversary of the birth of Miguel de Cervantes Saavedra, novelist, playwright and poet, and the 60th anniversary of the death of Juan Montalvo (1832–1889), Ecuadorean writer.

No. C168 Surcharged in Blue

II CONGRESO
Junio 1949
Eucarístico Ncl.
50 —— 50

1949, June 15 ***Perf. 12***

C207	AP39	50c on 1.10s car rose	20	20
C208	AP39	60c on 1.10s car rose	25	25
C209	AP39	90c on 1.10s car rose	30	30

Issued to commemorate the Second Eucharistic Congress, Quito, June 1949.

No. C128 Surcharged in Black

75 Aniversario
* U. P. U. *
60 centavos 60

1949, Oct. 11 ***Perf. 11***

C210	AP28	60c on 3s org	60	50
a.		Double surcharge	20.00	
C211	AP28	90c on 3s org	55	35
C212	AP28	1s on 3s org	70	55
C213	AP28	2s on 3s org	1.50	70

"SUCRE(S)" in capitals on Nos. C212-C213.
Issued to commemorate the 75th anniversary of the formation of the Universal Postal Union.

AP49

Black Surcharge.

1950 ***Perf. 12*** **Unwmkd.**

C214	AP49	60c on 50c gray	20	8
a.		Double surcharge	20.00	

No. C170 Surcharged with New Value in Black.

C215	AP40	90c on 1.90s ol bis	50	18

Nos. C168, C128-C129 and Type of 1944 Surcharged or Overprinted **ALFABETIZACION** in Black or Carmine.

1950, Feb. 10 ***Perf. 12***

C216	AP39	50c on 1.10s car rose	25	20
C217	AP39	70c on 1.10s car rose	30	25

Perf. 11

C218	AP28	3s orange	70	60
C219	AP28	5s dk brn (C)	1.10	70
C220	AP28	10s vio (C)	2.00	45
		Nos. C216-C220 (5)	4.35	2.20

Issued to publicize adult education.

Govt. Palace Type of 1944

1950, May 15 **Engr.** ***Perf. 11***

C221	AP28	10s violet	1.25	10

No. C169 Surcharged with New Value in Black.

1950 ***Perf. 12***

C222	AP40	90c on 1.30s dp bl	30	10

See No. C235.

Nos. C128-C129 Overprinted in Black

20.000 Cruce
Línea Ecuatorial
PANAGRA
26-Julio-1951

1951, July 28 ***Perf. 11*** **Unwmkd.**

C223	AP28	3s orange	80	80
C224	AP28	5s dk brn	1.35	1.10

Issued to commemorate the 20,000th crossing of the equator by Pan American-Grace Airways planes.

Nos. C202-C203 Surcharged in Black

CAMPANA

Alfabetización
60 Ctvs. 60
a

CAMPAÑA
ALFABETIZACION
1,00 Sucre 1,00
b

1951 ***Perf. 12½x12*** **Unwmkd.**

C225	AP47 (a)	60c on 1.30s ol brn & ultra	35	15

C226	AP48 (b)	1s on 1.90s grn & rose car	35	15
a.		Inverted surcharge	17.50	

Issued to publicize adult education.

St. Mariana de Jesus
AP50

1952, Feb. 15 Engraved.

C227	AP50	60c plum & aqua	55	25
C228	AP50	90c dk grn & lt ultra	60	20
C229	AP50	1s car & dk grn	65	25
C230	AP50	2s ind & rose lil	70	18

Issued to publicize the canonization of Mariana de Jesus Paredes y Flores.

Presidents
Galo Plaza and Harry Truman
AP51

Design: 5s, Pres. Plaza addressing U. S. Congress.

1952, Mar. 26 ***Perf. 12***

C231	AP51	3s lil & bl grn	75	60
C232	AP51	5s red brn & ol gray	1.50	1.25
a.		Souvenir sheet	4.00	4.00

No. C232a measures 126 x 61 mm., and contains one each of Nos. C231 and C232, with marginal inscriptions in lilac and red brown.

Issued to commemorate the 1951 visit of Pres. Galo Plaza y Lasso to the United States.

Consular Service Stamps Surcharged "AEREO" and New Value in Black.

1952 ***Perf. 12*** **Unwmkd.**

C233	R2	60c on 1s grn	15	8
C234	R2	1s on 1s grn	20	10

Type R2 illustrated above No. 545.

No. C169 Surcharged with New Value in Carmine.

C235	AP40	90c on 1.30s dp bl	15	8

See No. C222.

Pres. José M. Urvina and Allegory of Freedom
AP52

Torch of Knowledge
AP53

Hyphen-hole Perf. 7x6½

1952, Nov. 18 **Lithographed.**

C236	AP52	60c rose red & bl	1.25	45
C237	AP52	90c lil & red	1.25	50
C238	AP52	1s org & grn	1.25	25
C239	AP52	2s red brn & bl	1.25	30

Centenary of abolition of slavery in Ecuador. Counterfeits exist.

Engraved.

Design: 2s, Aged couple studying alphabet.

1953, Apr. 13 ***Perf. 12*** **Unwmkd.**

C240	AP53	1s dk bl	75	15
C241	AP53	2s red org	1.25	15

1952 adult education campaign.

Globe Showing Part of Western Hemisphere
AP54

1953, June 5 ***Perf. 12½x12***

C242	AP54	60c org yel	40	40
C243	AP54	90c dk bl	50	40
C244	AP54	3s carmine	1.00	60

Issued to publicize the crossing of the equator by the Pan-American highway.

Consular Service Stamps Surcharged in Black

AEREO 1 SUCRE *a*

1 SUCRE AEREO *b*

1953-54 ***Perf. 12.***

C245	R1 (a)	60c on 2s brn	30	10
C246	R2 (a)	60c on 5s sep ('54)	30	10
C247	R2 (a)	70c on 5s sep ('54)	35	15
C248	R2 (a)	90c on 50c car rose ('54)	50	10
C249	R1 (b)	1s on 2s brn	50	15
C250	R1 (a)	1s on 2s brn ('54)	50	10
C251	R1 (a)	2s on 2s brn ('54)	60	25
C252	R1 (a)	3s on 5s vio ('54)	1.00	30
		Nos. C245-C252 (8)	4.05	1.25

The surcharge reads upward on Nos. C250-C252.

Carlos Maria Cardinal de la Torre
AP55

Queen Isabella I
AP56

1954, Jan. 13 Photo. ***Perf. 8½.***

Center in Black.

C253	AP55	60c rose lil	25	10
C254	AP55	90c green	35	15
C255	AP55	3s orange	50	35

Issued to commemorate the first anniversary of the elevation of Archbishop de la Torre to Cardinal.

1954, April 22

C256	AP56	60c dk grn & grn	12	12
C257	AP56	90c lil rose	18	18
C258	AP56	1s blk & pale lil	20	18
C259	AP56	2s blk brn & pale bl	35	30
C260	AP56	5s blk brn & buff	75	50
		Nos. C256-C260 (5)	1.60	1.28

See note after No. 585.

Post Office, Guayaquil—AP57

Engraved.

1954, May 19 ***Perf. 12½x12.***

Black Surcharge

C261	AP57	80c on 20c red	30	20
C262	AP57	1s on 20c red	40	20

Issued to commemorate the 25th anniversary of Pan American-Grace Airways' operation in Ecuador.

Plane, Gateway and Wheel
AP58

Lithographed

1954, Aug. 2 ***Perf. 11*** **Unwmkd.**

C263	AP58	80c blue	20	15

Issued to publicize the Day of the Postal Employee.

San Pablo Lagoon
AP59

1954, Sept. 24 **Photogravure**

C264	AP59	60c orange	10	6
C265	AP59	70c rose pink	15	6
C266	AP59	90c dp grn	20	8
C267	AP59	1s dk gray grn	25	8
C268	AP59	2s blue	40	12
C269	AP59	3s yel brn	50	20
		Nos. C264-C269 (6)	1.60	60

Glorification of Abdon Calderon Garaicoa
AP60

Capt. Calderon
AP61

1954, Oct. 1

C270	AP60	80c rose pink	35	18
C271	AP61	90c blue	35	18

Issued to commemorate the 150th anniversary of the birth of Capt. Abdon Calderon Garaicoa.

El Cebollar College
AP62

Brother Miguel Instructing Boys
AP63

Designs: 90c, Francisco Febres Cordero (Brother Miguel). 2.50s, Tomb of Brother Miguel. 3s, Monument to Brother Miguel.

1954, Dec. 3 ***Perf. 11*** **Unwmkd.**

C272	AP62	70c dk grn	15	10
C273	AP63	80c dk brn	20	10
C274	AP63	90c dk gray bl	20	10
C275	AP63	2.50s indigo	35	30
C276	AP62	3s lil rose	60	50
		Nos. C272-C276 (5)	1.50	1.10

Issued to commemorate the centenary of the birth of Francisco Febres Cordero (Brother Miguel).

No. C221 Surcharged in Various Colors

E. M. P. 1955

$ 1,00

1955, May 25

C277	AP28	1s on 10s vio (Bk)	35	15
C278	AP28	1.70s on 10s vio (C)	50	20
C279	AP28	4.20s on 10s vio (Br)	1.00	75

Denomination in larger type on No. C279.

Issued to publicize the National Exhibition of Daily Periodicals.

"La Rotonda," Guayaquil, and Rotary Emblem
AP64

Design: 90c, Eugenio Espejo hospital, Quito, and Rotary emblem.

1955, July 9 Engraved ***Perf. 12½***

C280	AP64	80c dk brn	50	40
C281	AP64	90c dk grn	50	45

Issued to commemorate the 50th anniversary of the founding of Rotary International.

José Abel Castillo
AP65

Design:
2s, 5s, José Abel Castillo and Map of Ecuador.

1955, Oct. 19 ***Perf. 11x11½***

C282	AP65	60c chocolate	50	18
C283	AP65	90c lt ol grn	50	18
C284	AP65	1s lilac	50	15
C285	AP65	2s vermilion	50	25
C286	AP65	5s ultra	1.00	70
		Nos. C282-C286 (5)	3.00	1.46

See note after No. 595.

No. C29 Surcharged in Black.

1
X SUCRE X

1955, Oct. 24 *Perf. 12*

C287	AP1	1s on 5s pur	35	30

A similar surcharge on No. C29, set in two lines with letters 5mm. high and no X's or black-out line of squares, was privately applied.

San Pablo, Imbabura
AP66

Designs: 50s, Rumichaca Caves. 1.30s, Virgin of Quito. 1.50s, Cotopaxi Volcano. 1.70s, Tungurahua Volcano, Tungurahua. 1.90s, Guanacos. 2.40s, Mat market. 2.50s, Ruins at Incapirca. 4.20s, El Carmen, Cuenca, Azuay. 4.80s, Santo Domingo Church.

1956, Jan. 2 Photo. *Perf. 13*

C288	AP66	50c sl bl	40	10
C289	AP66	1s ultra	40	12
C290	AP66	1.30s crimson	45	18
C291	AP66	1.50s dp grn	35	12
C292	AP66	1.70s yel brn	25	15
C293	AP66	1.90s olive	40	35
C294	AP66	2.40s red org	45	35
C295	AP66	2.50s violet	45	35
C296	AP66	4.20s black	60	50
C297	AP66	4.80s yel org	75	65
		Nos. C288-C297 (10)	4.50	2.87

See also Nos. C310-C311.

Honorato Vazquez
AP67

Title Page of First Book
AP68

1956, May 28 Engraved

Various Portraits.

C298	AP67	1s yel grn	25	15
C299	AP67	1.50s red	35	25
C300	AP67	1.70s brt bl	30	25
C301	AP67	1.90s sl bl	35	25

Birth centenary (in 1955) of Honorato Vazquez, statesman.

1956, Aug. 27 *Perf. 13½* **Unwmkd.**

C302	AP68	1s black	20	15
C303	AP68	1.70s sl bl	25	20
C304	AP68	2s blk brn	40	30
C305	AP68	3s redsh brn	55	50

Bicentenary of printing in Ecuador.

Hands Reaching for U.N. Emblem
AP69

1956, Oct. 24 *Perf. 14*

C307	AP69	1.70s red org	75	30

Issued to commemorate the tenth anniversary of the United Nations (in 1955).
See also No. C319.

Coat of Arms and Basketball Player
AP70

Designs: 1.70s, Map of South America with flags and girl basketball players.

Photogravure.

1956, Dec. 28 *Perf. 14½x14*

C308	AP70	1s red lil	30	15
C309	AP70	1.70s dp grn	55	25

Issued to commemorate the 6th South American Women's Basketball Championship, August 1956.

Scenic Type of 1956.

1957, Jan. 2 *Perf. 13*

C310	AP66	50c bl grn	30	12
C311	AP66	1s orange	40	20

Type of Regular Issue, 1957

Designs: 50c, Map of Cuenca, 16th century. 80c, Cathedral of Cuenca. 1s, Modern City Hall.

Photogravure.

1957, Apr. 7 *Perf. 12* **Unwmkd.**

C312	A219	50c brn, *cr*	15	8
a.		Souvenir sheet of 4	1.00	1.00
C313	A219	80c red, *bluish*	20	18
C314	A219	1s pur, *yel*	30	12
a.		Souvenir sheet of 3	1.50	1.50

Issued to commemorate the fourth centenary of the founding of Cuenca.

No. C312a contains four imperf. 50c stamps similar to No. 613, but inscribed "AEREO" and printed in green. The sheet measures 140x120mm. and is printed on white ungummed paper. It is inscribed "IV Reunion de Consulta de la Comision del Instituto Panamericano de Geografia e Historia, Cuenca 4 al 12 de Abril de 1957."

No. C314a contains three imperf. stamps in designs similar to Nos. C312–C314, but with colors changed to orange (50c), brown (80c), violet (1s). The sheet measures 140x120mm. and is printed on white ungummed paper. It is inscribed "III Congreso de Ingenieros y Arquitectos del Ecuador, Cuenca, 6 al 9 de Abril de 1957."

Gabriela Mistral
AP71

Arms of Espejo, Carchi
AP72

Lithographed.

1957, Sept. 18 *Perf. 14* **Unwmkd.**

C315	AP71	2s lt bl, blk & red	40	25

Issued to honor Gabriela Mistral (1889–1957), Chilean poet and educator.
See also Nos. C406–C407.

Province of Carchi.

1957, Nov. 16 *Perf. 14½x13½*

Arms of Cantons: 2s, Montufar. 4.20s, Tulcan.

Coat of Arms Multicolored.

C316	AP72	1s carmine	25	15
C317	AP72	2s black	35	20
C318	AP72	4.20s ultra	75	55

See also Nos. C334–C337, C355–C364, C392–C395.

Redrawn U.N. Type of 1956.

1957, Dec. 10 Engraved. *Perf. 14*

C319	AP69	2s grnsh bl	60	50

Issued to honor the United Nations. Dates, as on No. C307, are omitted; inscribed: "Homenaje a las Naciones Unidas."

Mater Dolorosa, San Gabriel College
AP73

Rafael Maria Arizaga
AP74

Design: Nos. C321 & 1s, Door of San Gabriel College, Quito.

1958, Apr. 27 Engraved. *Perf. 14*

C320	AP73	30c rose cl, *dp rose*	25	15
C321	AP73	30c rose cl, *dp rose*	25	15
C322	AP73	1s dk bl, *lt bl*	25	15
C323	AP73	1.70s dk bl, *lt bl*	30	25

Issued to commemorate tbe 50th anniversary of the miracle of San Gabriel College, Quito.
Issued in 2 sheets of 50. One sheet contains alternate copies of Nos. C320-C321, the other Nos. C322-C323.

1958, July 21 Lithographed

C324	AP74	1s multi	20	15

Issued to commemorate the centenary of the birth of Rafael Maria Arizaga (1858–1933), writer.
See also Nos. C343, C350, C412.

Daule River Bridge
AP75

Engraved.

1958, July 25 *Perf. 13½x14*

C325	AP75	1.30s green	30	20

Issued to commemorate the opening of the River Daule bridge in Guayas province.
See also Nos. C367–C369.

Basketball Player
AP76

Symbolical of the Eucharist
AP77

Photogravure

1958, Sept. 1 *Perf. 14x13½*

C326	AP76	1.30s dk grn & lt brn	60	50

South American basketball championships.

1958, Sept. 25 Litho. **Unwmkd.**

Design: 60c, Cathedral of Guayaquil.

C327	AP77	10c vio & buff	10	10
C328	AP77	60c org & vio brn	15	12
C329	AP77	1s brn & lt bl	25	15

Souvenir Sheet

Symbolical of the Eucharist
AP78

Perf. 13½x14

C330	AP78	Sheet of four	1.00	1.00
a.		40c dk bl (any position)	20	20

Nos. C327-C330 issued to commemorate the 3rd National Eucharistic Congress.
No. C330 measures 115 x 88¾mm.

Stamps of 1865 and 1920
AP79

Designs: 2s, Stamps of 1920 and 1948. 4.20s, Municipal museum and library.

Photogravure.

1958, Oct. 8 *Perf. 11½* **Unwmkd.**

Granite Paper

C331	AP79	1.30s grn & brn red	35	30
C332	AP79	2s bl & vio	60	40
C333	AP79	4.20s dk brn	1.10	80

Issued to publicize the National Philatelic Exposition (EXFIGUA), Guayaquil, Oct. 4-14.

Coat of Arms Type of 1957.

Province of Imbabura.

Arms of Cantons: 50c, Cotacachi. 60c, Antonio Ante. 80c, Otalvo. 1.10s, Ibarra.

Lithographed.

1958, Nov. 9 *Perf. 14½x13½*

Coats of Arms Multicolored.

C334	AP72	50c blk & red	10	10
C335	AP72	60c blk, bl & red	15	10
C336	AP72	80c blk & yel	20	10
C337	AP72	1.10s blk & red	30	15

Charles V
AP80

Paul Rivet
AP81

Engraved & Photogravure

Perf. 14x13½

1958, Dec. 12 **Unwmkd.**

C338	AP80	2s brn red & dk brn	40	25
C339	AP80	4.20s dk gray & red brn	75	60

Issued to commemorate the 400th anniversary of the death of Charles V, Holy Roman Emperor.

1958, Dec. 29 Photo. *Perf. 11½*

Granite Paper.

C340	AP81	1s brown	20	15

Issued in honor of Paul Rivet (1876–1958), French anthropologist.

1959, May 6

Portrait: 2s, Alexander von Humboldt.

C341 AP81 2s slate 30 15

Issued to commemorate the centenary of the death of Alexander von Humboldt, German naturalist and geographer.

Front Page of "El Telegrafo"
AP82

1959, Feb. Litho. *Perf. 13½*

C342 AP82 1.30s bl grn & blk 30 20

Issued to commemorate the 75th anniversary of Ecuador's oldest newspaper.

Portrait Type of 1958

Portrait: José Luis Tamayo.

1959, June 26 *Perf. 14* Unwmkd.

Portrait Multicolored.

C343 AP74 1.30s lt grn, bl & sal 30 18

Issued to commemorate the centenary of the birth of José Luis Tamayo (1858–1947), lawyer.

El Sagrario and House of Manuela Canizares
AP83

Condor
AP84

Designs: 80c, Hall at San Agustin. 1s, First words of the constitutional act. 2s, Entrance to Cuartel Real. 4.20s, Allegory of Liberty.

Photogravure.

1959, Aug. 28 *Perf. 14* Unwmkd.

C344 AP83 20c ultra & lt brn 10 6
C345 AP83 80c brt bl & dp org 15 8
C346 AP83 1s dk red & dk ol 20 12
C347 AP84 1.30s brt bl & org 35 15
C348 AP84 2s ultra & org brn 35 20
C349 AP84 4.20s scar & brt bl 75 55
Nos. C344-C349 (6) 1.90 1.16

Sesquicentennial of the revolution.

Portrait Type of 1958

Portrait: 1s, Alfredo Baquerizo Moreno.

1959, Sept. 26 Litho. *Perf. 14*

C350 AP74 1s gray, red & sal 18 12

Issued to commemorate the centenary of the birth of Alfredo Baquerizo Moreno (1859–1951), statesman.

Pope Pius XII
AP85

1959, Oct. 9 *Perf. 14½* Unwmkd.

C351 AP85 1.30s multi 40 35

Issued in memory of Pope Pius XII.

Flags of Argentina, Bolivia, Brazil, Guatemala, Haiti, Mexico and Peru
AP86

Flags of: 80c, Chile, Costa Rica, Cuba, Dominican Republic, Panama, Paraguay, United States. 1.30s, Colombia, Ecuador, Honduras, Nicaragua, Salvador, Uruguay, Venezuela.

1959, Oct. 12 *Perf. 13½.*

C352 AP86 50c multi 20 10
C353 AP86 80c yel, red & bl 25 18
C354 AP86 1.30s multi 35 25

Organization of American States.

Coat of Arms Type of 1957
Province of Pichincha.

Arms of Cantons: 10c, Rumiñahui. 40c, Pedro Moncayo. 1s, Mejia. 1.30s, Cayambe. 4.20s, Quito.

Lithographed.

1959–60 *Perf. 14½x13½* Unwmkd.

Coat of Arms Multicolored.

C355 AP72 10c blk & dk red ('60) 6 6
C356 AP72 40c blk & yel 10 6
C357 AP72 1s blk & brn ('60) 15 10
C358 AP72 1.30s blk & grn ('60) 25 15
C359 AP72 4.20s blk & org 60 50
Nos. C355-C359 (5) 1.16 87

Province of Cotopaxi.

Arms of Cantons: 40c, Pangua. 60c, Pujili. 70c, Saquisili. 1s, Salcedo. 1.30s, Latacunga.

1960

Coat of Arms Multicolored

C360 AP72 40c blk & car 6 6
C361 AP72 60c blk & bl 15 8
C362 AP72 70c blk & turq 25 10
C363 AP72 1s blk & red org 30 12
C364 AP72 1.30s blk & org 35 15
Nos. C360-C364 (5) 1.11 51

Flags of American Nations
AP87

1960, Feb. 23 *Perf. 13x12½*

C365 AP87 1.30s multi 20 15
C366 AP87 2s multi 30 25

Issued to commemorate the 11th Inter-American Conference, Feb. 1960.

Bridge Type of 1958.

Bridges: No. C367, Juntas. No. C368, Saracay. 2s, Railroad bridge, Ambato.

1960 Lithographed *Perf. 13½*

C367 AP75 1.30s chocolate 20 15

Photo. *Perf. 12½*

C368 AP75 1.30s emerald 20 10
C369 AP75 2s brown 35 20

Building of three new bridges.

Bahia-Chone Road
AP88

Pres. Camilo Ponce Enriquez
AP89

Designs: 4.20s, Public Works Building, Cuenca. 5s, El Coca airport. 10s, New Harbor, Guayaquil.

1960, Aug. Litho. *Perf. 14*

C370 AP88 1.30s blk & dl yel 25 15
C371 AP88 4.20s rose car & lt grn 50 50
C372 AP88 5s dk brn & yel 75 60
C373 AP88 10s dk bl & bl 1.50 1.25

Perf. 11x11½

C374 AP89 2s org brn & blk 2.50 50
Nos. C370-C374 (5) 5.50 3.00

Nos. C370–C374 issued to publicize the achievements of Pres. Camilo Ponce Enriquez (1956–1960).

Issue dates: Nos. C370–C373, Aug. 24. No. C374, Aug. 31.

Red Cross Building, Quito and Henri Dunant—AP90

1960, Oct. 5 *Perf. 13x14* Unwmkd.

C375 AP90 2s rose vio & car 50 25

Centenary (in 1959) of Red Cross idea.

El Belen Church, Quito
AP91

1961, Jan. 14 *Perf. 12½*

C376 AP91 3s multi 65 35

Issued to commemorate Ecuador's participation in the 1960 Barcelona Philatelic Congress.

Map of Ecuador and Amazon River System
AP92

1961, Feb. 27 Litho. *Perf. 10½*

C377 AP92 80c sal, cl & grn 25 20
C378 AP92 1.30s gray, sl & grn 30 25
C379 AP92 2s beige, red & grn 40 30

Issued to commemorate Amazon Week, and the 132nd anniversary of the Battle of Tarqui against Peru.

Juan Montalvo, Juan Leon Mera, Juan Benigno Vela
AP93

Hugo Ortiz G.
AP94

1961, Apr. 13 *Perf. 13* Unwmkd.

C380 AP93 1.30s sal & blk 35 15

Centenary of Tungurahua province.

1961, May 25 *Perf. 14x14½*

Design: No. C382, Ortiz monument.

C381 AP94 1.30s grnsh bl, blk & yel 25 15
C382 AP94 1.30s grnsh bl, pur, ol & brn 25 15

Issued in memory of Lieutenant Hugo Ortiz G., killed in battle Aug. 2, 1941.

Condor and Airplane Stamp of 1936
AP95

Designs: 1.30s, Map of South America and stamp of 1865. 2s, Bolivar monument stamp of 1930.

Perf. 10½

1961, May 25 Litho. Unwmkd.

Size: 41x28mm.

C383 AP95 80c org & vio 35 20

Size: 41x34mm.

C384 AP95 1.30s bl, yel, ol & car 50 30

Size: 40½x37mm.

C385 AP95 2s car rose & blk 60 40

Issued to publicize the Third National Philatelic Exhibition, Quito, May 25–June 3, 1961.

Arms of Los Rios and Egret
AP96

1961, May 27 ***Perf. 14½x13½***

Coat of Arms Multicolored

C386 AP96 2s bl & blk 50 35

Centenary (in 1960) of Los Rios province.

Gabriel Garcia Moreno **Remigio Crespo Toral**
AP97 **AP98**

1961, Sept. 24 ***Perf. 12*** **Unwmkd.**

C387 AP97 1s bl, brn & buff 25 15

Issued to commemorate the centenary of the restoration of national integrity.

1961, Nov. 3 ***Perf. 14*** **Unwmkd.**

C388 AP98 50c multi 15 15

Issued to commemorate the centenary of the birth of Remigio Crespo Toral, poet laureate of Ecuador.

Galapagos Islands Nos. LC1-LC3 Overprinted in Black or Red: "Estacion de Biologia Maritima de Galapagos" and "UNESCO 1961" (Similarly to Nos. 684-686).

1961, Oct. 31 **Photo.** ***Perf. 12***

C389 A1 1s dp bl 40 30
a. "de Galapagos" on top line 1.50 1.50
C390 A1 1.80s rose vio 50 30
a. UNESCO emblem omitted 1.00 1.00
C391 A1 4.20s blk (R) 80 65

Issued to commemorate the establishment of maritime biological stations on Galapagos Islands by UNESCO.

Coat of Arms Type of 1957.
Province of Tungurahua.

Arms of Cantons: 50c, Pillaro. 1s, Pelileo. 1.30s, Baños. 2s, Ambato.

Perf. 14½x13½

1962, Mar. 30 **Litho.** **Unwmkd.**

Coats of Arms Multicolored

C392 AP72 50c black 15 6
C393 AP72 1s black 20 12
C394 AP72 1.30s black 30 15
C395 AP72 2s black 40 25

Pres. Arosemena and Prince Philip, Arms of Ecuador and Great Britain and Equator Monument
AP99

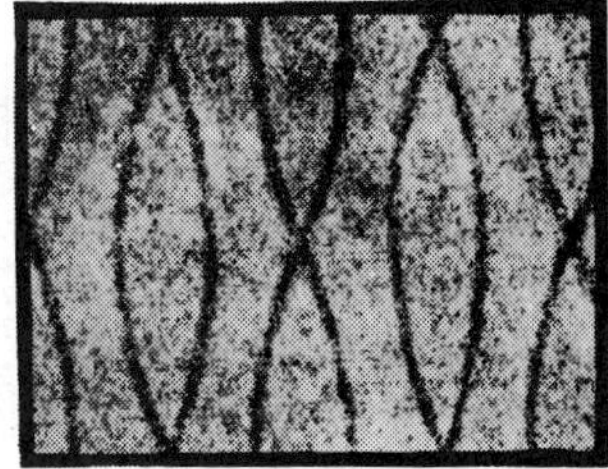

Wmk. 340

Wmkd. Alternating Interlaced Wavy Lines. (340)

1962, Feb. 17 ***Perf. 14x13½***

C396 AP99 1.30s bl, sep, red & yel 25 20
C397 AP99 2s multi 35 25

Issued to commemorate the visit of Prince Philip, Duke of Edinburgh, to Ecuador, Feb. 17–20, 1962.

Mountain Farming
AP100

Lithographed

1963, Mar. 21 ***Perf. 12½*** **Unwmkd.**

C398 AP100 30c emer, yel & blk 15 10
C399 AP100 3s dl red, grn & org 60 40
C400 AP100 4.20s bl, blk & yel 75 50

Issued for the "Freedom from Hunger" campaign of the U.N. Food and Agriculture Organization.

Mosquito and Malaria Eradication Emblem
AP101

1963, Apr. 17 ***Perf. 12½*** **Unwmkd.**

C401 AP101 50c dl yel, car rose & blk 10 10
C402 AP101 80c brt grn, car rose & blk 15 12
C403 AP101 2s brt pink, dp cl & blk 35 35

Issued for the World Health Organization drive to eradicate malaria.

Stagecoach and Jet Plane
AP102

1963, May 7 **Lithographed**

C404 AP102 2s org & car rose 50 25
C405 AP102 4.20s cl & ultra 75 50

Issued to commemorate the centenary of the first International Postal Conference, Paris, 1863.

Type of 1957 Inscribed "Islas Galapagos," Surcharged with New Value and Overprinted "Ecuador" in Black or Red.

1963, June 19 ***Perf. 14*** **Unwmkd.**

C406 AP71 5s on 2s gray, dk bl & red 60 50
C407 AP71 10s on 2s gray, dk bl & red (R) 1.20 1.00

The basic 2s exists without surcharge and overprint. No. C407 exists with "ECUADOR" omitted, and with both "ECUADOR" and "10 SUCRES" double.

No. C375 Overprinted: "1863-1963/Centenario/de la Fundación/de la Cruz Roja/Internacional"

Photogravure

1963, June 21 ***Perf. 13x14***

C408 AP90 2s rose vio & car 40 30

Issued to commemorate the centenary of the founding of the International Red Cross.

Type of Regular Issue, 1963.

Designs (Arosemena and): 70c, Flags of Ecuador. 2s, Flags of Ecuador and Panama. 4s, Flags of Ecuador and U.S.

1963, July 1 **Lithographed** ***Perf. 14***

C409 A238 70c pale bl & multi 20 10
C410 A238 2s pink & multi 40 20
C411 A238 4s lt bl & multi 1.00 50

Issued to commemorate Pres. Arosemena's friendship trip, July 1962.

Portrait Type of 1958

Portrait: 2s, Dr. Mariano Cueva.

Lithographed

1963, July 4 ***Perf. 14*** **Unwmkd.**

C412 AP74 2s lt grn & multi 35 20

Issued to commemorate the 150th anniversary of the birth of Dr. Mariano Cueva (1812–1882).

Social Insurance Symbol **Mother and Child**
AP103 **AP104**

1963, July 9 **Lithographed**

C413 AP103 10s brn, bl, gray & ocher 1.00 90

12th anniversary of Social Insurance.

1963, July 28 ***Perf. 12½***

C414 AP104 1.30s org, dk bl & blk 30 20
C415 AP104 5s gray, red & brn 70 50

Issued to publicize the 7th Pan-American and South American Pediatrics Congresses, Quito.

Simon Bolivar Airport, Guayaquil
AP105

1963, July 25 ***Perf. 14***

C416 AP105 60c gray 15 8
C417 AP105 70c dl grn 20 10
C418 AP105 5s brn vio 65 45

Issued to commemorate the opening of Simon Bolivar Airport, Guayaquil, July 15, 1962.

Nos. 638, 640-641 Overprinted "AEREO"

1964 ***Perf. 12***

Flags in National Colors

C419 A223 1.80s dl vio 60 50
C420 A224 2s dk brn 60 50
C421 A223 2.20s blk brn 60 50

On 1.80s and 2.20s, "AEREO" is vertical, reading down.

No. 650 Overprinted in Gold: "FARO DE COLON / AEREO"

1964 **Photo.** ***Perf. 14x13½***

C422 A229 1.80s dk bl 3.00 2.00

Nos. C352-C354 Overprinted **1961**

1964 **Lithographed** ***Perf. 13½***

C423 AP86 50c bl & multi 75 40
C424 AP86 80c yel & multi 75 40
C425 AP86 1.30s pale grn & multi 75 40

No. C307 Overprinted: "DECLARACION / DERECHOS HUMANOS / 1964 / XV-ANIV"

Engraved

1964, Sept. 29 ***Perf. 14*** **Unwmkd.**

C426 AP69 1.70s red org 50 30

Issued to commemorate the 15th anniversary (in 1963) of the Universal Declaration of Human Rights.

Banana Type of Regular Issue

1964, Oct. 26 **Litho.** ***Perf. 12½x12***

C427 A241 4.20s blk, bis & gray ol 50 45
C428 A241 10s blk, scar & gray ol 1.00 85
a. Souv. sheet of 4 2.00 2.00

Issued to publicize the Banana Conference, Oct.–Nov. 1964. No. C428a contains four imperf. stamps similar to Nos. 720-721 and C427-C428. Pale blue margin with black inscription and red control number. Size: 120x95mm.

John F. Kennedy, Flag-draped Coffin and John Jr.
AP106

1964, Nov. 22 **Litho.** ***Perf. 14***

C429 AP106 4.20s multi 1.00 80
C430 AP106 5s multi 1.25 1.00
C431 AP106 10s multi 2.00 1.50
a. Souv. sheet of 3 7.50 7.50

Issued in memory of President John F. Kennedy (1917–63).

No. C431a contains stamps similar to Nos. C429-C431, imperf. Pale lilac margin with brown and white inscriptions. Red control number. Size: 114x130mm.

Olympic Type of Regular Issue

Designs: 1.30s, Gymnast (vert.). 1.80s, Hurdler. 2s, Basketball.

Perf. 13½x14, 14x13½

1964, Dec. 16 **Unwmkd.**

C432 A243 1.30s vio bl, ver & brn 30 20
C433 A243 1.80s vio bl & multi 35 25

C434	A243	2s red & multi	45	30
a.		Souv. sheet of 4	4.00	4.00

18th Olympic Games, Tokyo, Oct. 10–25.

No. C434a contains stamps similar to Nos. 725 and C432–C434, imperf. Pale olive margin with black and white inscriptions and red control number. Size: 139x107mm.

Sports Type of Regular Issue, 1965

Torch and Athletes: 2s, 3s, Diver, gymnast, wrestlers and weight lifter. 2.50s, 4s, Bicyclists. 3.50s, 5s, Jumpers.

1965, Nov. 20 Litho. *Perf. 12x12½*

C435	A247	2s bl, gold & blk	25	18
C436	A247	2.50s org, gold & blk	30	25
C437	A247	3s brt pink, gold & blk	35	30
C438	A247	3.50s lt vio, gold & bl	40	35
C439	A247	4s brt yel grn, gold & blk	45	40
C440	A247	5s red org, gold & blk	55	50
a.		Souv. sheet of 12	5.00	5.00
		Nos. C435-C440 (6)	2.30	1.98

Issued to commemorate the 5th Bolivarian Games, held at Guayaquil and Quito. No. C440a contains 12 imperf. stamps similar to Nos. 738–743 and C435–C440. Black and red inscriptions. Size: 215x129mm.

Bird Type of Regular Issue

Birds: 1s, Yellow grosbeak. 1.30s, Black-headed parrot. 1.50s, Scarlet tanager. 2s, Sapphire quail-dove. 2.50s, Violet-tailed sylph. 3s, Lemon-throated barbet. 4s, Yellow-tailed oriole. 10s, Collared puffbird.

1966, June 17 Litho. *Perf. 13½*

Birds in Natural Colors

C441	A249	1s lt red brn & blk	10	8
C442	A249	1.30s pink & blk	15	10
C443	A249	1.50s pale grn & blk	15	12
C444	A249	2s sal & blk	20	15
C445	A249	2.50s lt yel grn & blk	25	20
C446	A249	3s sal & blk	30	25
C447	A249	4s gray & blk	40	35
C448	A249	10s beige & blk	1.00	90
		Nos. C441-C448 (8)	2.55	2.15

Nos. C436 and C443 Surcharged

1967

C449	A247	80c on 2.50s org, gold & blk	10	8
C450	A249	80c on 1.50s multi	10	8

Old denomination on No. C449 is obliterated with heavy bar; the surcharge on No. C450 includes "Resello" and an ornament over old denomination.

Peñaherrera Monument, Quito
AP107

Design: 2s, Peñaherrera statue.

1967, Dec. 29 Litho. *Perf. 12x12½*

C451	AP107	1.30s blk & org	15	12
C452	AP107	2s blk & lt ultra	20	15

See note after No. 763.

Arosemena Type of Regular Issue, 1968

Designs: 1.30s, Inauguration of Pres. Arosemena. 2s, Pres. Arosemena speaking in Punta del Este.

1968, May 9 Litho. *Perf. 13½x14*

C453	A251	1.30s multi	15	12
C454	A251	2s multi	20	18

First anniversary of administration of Pres. Otto Arosemena Gomez.

No. C448 Surcharged in Plum, Dark Blue or Green

RESELLO

$ 0,80

1969, Jan. 9 Litho. *Perf. 13½*

Bird in Natural Colors

C455	A249	80c on 10s beige (P)	8	8
C456	A249	1s on 10s beige (DBl)	10	10
C457	A249	2s on 10s beige (G)	20	18

"Operation Friendship"
AP108

1969-70 Typo. *Perf. 13½*

C458	AP108	2s yel, blk, red & lt bl	20	18
a.		Perf. 12½	20	18
C459	AP108	2s bl, blk, car & yel ('70)	20	18

Friendship campaign. Medallion background on Nos. C458 and C458a is blue; on No. C459, yellow.

No. 639 Surcharged in Gold "S/. 5 AEREO" and Bar

1969, Nov. 25 Litho. *Perf. 12*

C460	A224	5s on 2s multi	1.75	1.00

Butterfly Type of Regular Issue

Butterflies: 1.30s, Morpho peleides. 1.50s, Anartia amathea.

1970 Lithographed *Perf. 12½*

C461	A255	1.30s multi	13	11
C462	A255	1.50s pink & multi	15	12

Same, White Background

1970 *Perf. 13½*

C463	A255	1.30s multi	13	11
C464	A255	1.50s multi	15	12

Arms Type of Regular Issue

Provincial Arms and Flags: 1.30s, El Oro. 2s, Loja. 3s, Manabi. 5s, Pichincha. 10s, Guayas.

1971 Lithographed *Perf. 10½*

C465	A258	1.30s pink & multi	13	10
C466	A258	2s multi	20	15
C467	A258	3s multi	30	25
C468	A258	5s multi	50	40
C469	A258	10s multi	1.00	75
		Nos. C465-C469 (5)	2.13	1.65

Presentation of the Virgin
AP109

Pres. Allende and Chilean Flag
AP110

Art of Quito: 1.50s, Blessed Anne at Prayer. 2s, St. Theresa de Jesus. 2.50s, Altar of Carmen (horiz.). 3s, Descent from the Cross. 4s, Christ of St. Mariana de Jesus. 5s, Shrine of St. Anthony. 10s, Cross of San Diego.

1971 *Perf. 11½*

Inscriptions in Black

C473	AP109	1.30s multi	20	10
C474	AP109	1.50s multi	25	12
C475	AP109	2s multi	35	15
C476	AP109	2.50s multi	40	20
C477	AP109	3s multi	50	25
C478	AP109	4s multi	75	30
C479	AP109	5s multi	75	40
C480	AP109	10s multi	1.50	75
		Nos. C473-C480 (8)	4.70	2.27

Design: 2.10s, Pres. José M. Velasco Ibarra of Ecuador, Pres. Salvador Allende of Chile and national flags.

1971, Aug. 24 *Perf. 12½*

C481	AP110	2s multi	20	15
C482	AP110	2.10s multi	21	16

Visit of Pres. Salvador Allende of Chile, Aug. 24.

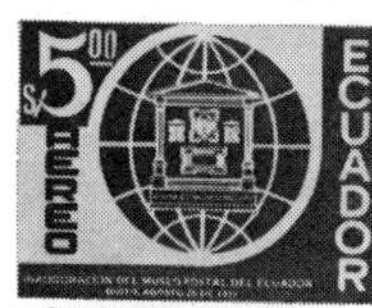

Globe and Emblem
AP111

1971

C483	AP111	5s black	75	40
C484	AP111	5.50s dl pur & blk	75	45

Opening of Postal Museum, Aug. 24, 1971.

Pazmiño Type of Regular Issue

1971, Sept. 16 *Perf. 12x11½*

C485	A260	1.50s grn & multi	15	12
C486	A260	2.50s grn & multi	25	20

50th anniversary of "El Universo," newspaper founded by Ismael Pérez Pazmiño.

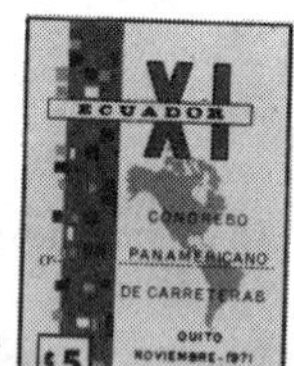

Map of Americas
AP112

Designs: 10s, Converging roads and map. 20s, Map of Americas and Equator. 50s, Mountain road and monument on Equator.

1971 *Perf. 11½*

C487	AP112	5s org & multi	75	45
C488	AP112	10s org & blk	1.50	90
C489	AP112	20s blk, bl & brt rose	2.50	1.80
C490	AP112	50s bl, blk & gray	6.00	4.00

11th Pan-American Road Congress.
Issue dates: 5s, 10s, 50s, Nov. 15; 20s, Nov. 22.

Arms of Ecuador and Argentina
AP113

Design: 5s, Presidents José M. Velasco Ibarra and Alejandro Agustin Lanusse.

1972

C491	AP113	3s blk & multi	30	27
C492	AP113	5s blk & multi	50	40

Visit of Lt. Gen. Alejandro Agustin Lanusse, president of Argentina, Jan. 25.

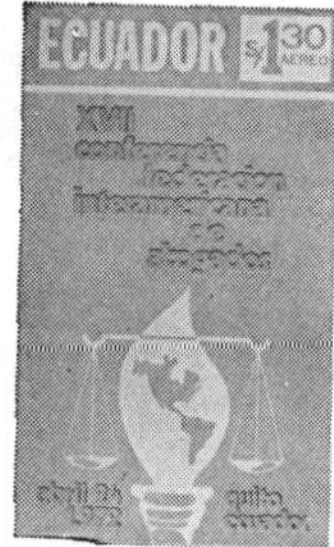

Flame, Scales, Map of Americas
AP114

1972, Apr. 24 Litho. *Perf. 12½*

C493	AP114	1.30s bl & red	13	10

17th Conference of the Interamerican Federation of Lawyers, Quito, Apr. 24.

Religious Paintings Type of Regular Issue

Ecuadorian Paintings: 3s, Virgin of the Flowers, by Miguel de Santiago. 10s, Virgin of the Rosary, by Quito School.

1972, Apr. 24 *Perf. 14x13½*

C494	A263	3s blk & multi	30	25
C495	A263	10s blk & multi	1.00	75
a.		Souv. sheet of 2	1.40	1.40

No. C495a contains one each of Nos. C494–C495. Blue marginal inscription. Size: 98x110½mm. Exists imperf.

1972, May 4

Ecuadorian Statues: 3s, St. Dominic, Quito School. 10s, St. Rosa of Lima, by Bernardo de Legarda.

C496	A263	3s blk & multi	30	25
C497	A263	10s blk & multi	1.00	75
a.		Souv. sheet of 2	1.40	1.40

No. C497a contains one each of Nos. C496–C497. Blue marginal inscription. Size: 98x110½mm. Exists imperf. Letters of "Ecuador" 3mm. high on Nos. C496–C497, 7mm. high on Nos. C494–C495.

Portrait Type of Regular Issue

Designs (Generals, from Paintings): 1.30s, José María Saenz. 3s, Tomás Wright. 4s, Antonio Farfan. 5s, Antonio José de Sucre. 10s, Simon Bolivar. 20s, Arms of Ecuador.

1972, May 24

C498	A264	1.30s bl & multi	13	10
C499	A264	3s bl & multi	30	25
C500	A264	4s bl & multi	40	30
C501	A264	5s bl & multi	50	40
C502	A264	10s bl & multi	1.00	75
C503	A264	20s bl & multi	2.00	1.50
		Nos. C498-C503 (6)	4.33	3.30

Sesquicentennial of the Battle of Pichincha and the liberation of Quito.

Artisan Type of Regular Issue

Designs: 2s, Woman wearing flowered poncho. 3s, Striped poncho. 5s, Poncho with roses. 10s, Gold sunburst sculpture.

1972, July Photo. *Perf. 13*

C504	A265	2s multi	20	15
C505	A265	3s multi	30	25
C506	A265	5s multi	50	40
C507	A265	10s org red & multi	1.00	75
a.		Souvenir sheet of 4	2.25	2.25

Handicraft of Ecuador. No. C507a contains one each of Nos. C504–C507. Pale claret marginal inscription and ornament. Black control number. Size 104x164mm.

Epidendrum Orchid
AP115

1972 Photogravure *Perf. 12½*

Multicolored; Flowers in Natural Colors

C508 AP115 4s *shown* 50 30
C509 AP115 6s *Canna* 75 45
C510 AP115 10s *Jimson weed* 1.25 75
a. Souv. sheet of 3 3.00 3.00

No. C510a contains one each of Nos. C508–C510. Blue marginal inscription and ornaments. Black control number. Size: 166x106mm. Exists imperf.

Oil Drilling Towers
AP116

Coat of Arms
AP117

1972, Oct. 17 Litho. *Perf. 11½*

C511 AP116 1.30s bl & multi 20 10

Ecuadorian oil industry.

1972, Nov. 18 Litho. *Perf. 11½*

Arms Multicolored

C512 AP117 2s black 25 15
C513 AP117 3s black 40 25
C514 AP117 4s black 50 30
C515 AP117 4.50s black 50 35
C516 AP117 6.30s black 1.00 50
C517 AP117 6.90s black 1.00 55
Nos. C512-C517 (6) 3.65 2.10

Pichincha Type of Regular Issue

Designs: 2.40s, Corridor, San Agustin. 4.50s, La Merced Convent. 5.50s, Column base. 6.30s, Chapter Hall, San Agustin. 6.90s, Interior, San Agustin. 7.40s, Crucifixion, Cantuña Chapel. 7.90s, Decorated ceiling, San Agustin.

1972, Dec. 6 Wmk. 367

C518 A266 2.40s yel & multi 25 18
C519 A266 4.50s yel & multi 45 35
C520 A266 5.50s yel & multi 55 45
C521 A266 6.30s yel & multi 65 50
C522 A266 6.90s yel & multi 70 55
C523 A266 7.40s yel & multi 75 60
C524 A266 7.90s yel & multi 80 65
Nos. C518-C524 (7) 4.15 3.28

Sesquicentennial of the Battle of Pichincha.

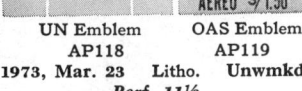

UN Emblem
AP118

OAS Emblem
AP119

1973, Mar. 23 Litho. Unwmkd.

Perf. 11½

C525 AP118 1.30s lt bl & blk 30 15

25th anniversary of the Economic Committee for Latin America (CEPAL).

Wmk. 367

1973, Apr. 14 Litho. *Perf. 11½*

C526 AP119 1.50s multi 27 14
a. Unwatermarked

Day of the Americas and "Philately for Peace."

Bird Type of Regular Issue

1973 *Perf. 11½x11* Unwmkd.

C527 A268 1.30s *Blue-footed booby* 24 12
C528 A268 3s *Brown pelican* 30 15

Elevation of Galapagos Islands to a province of Ecuador.

Presidents Lara and Caldera
AP120

1973, June 15 Wmk. 367

C529 AP120 3s multi 55 28

Visit of Pres. Rafael Caldera of Venezuela, Feb. 5–7.

Silver Coin, 1934
AP121

Globe, OPEC Emblem, Oil Derrick
AP122

Ecuadorian Coins: 10s, Silver coin, obverse. 50s, Gold coin, 1928.

Perf. 14

1973, Dec. 14 Photo. Unwmkd.

C530 AP121 5s multi 50 25
C531 AP121 10s multi 1.00 50
C532 AP121 50s multi 5.00 2.50
a. Souvenir sheet of 3 6.75 6.75

No. C532a contains one each of Nos. C530–C532; light blue margin with gold and black inscription, coat of arms and control numbers. Dated "1972." Size: 115x88mm. Exists imperf.

A gold marginal overprint was applied in 1974 to No. C532a (perf. and imperf.): "X Campeonato Mundial de Football / Munich—1974".

A carmine overprint was applied in 1974 to No. C532a (perf. and imperf.): "Seminario de Telecommunicaciones Rurales, / Septiembre—1974 / Quito—Ecuador" and ITU emblem.

1974, June 15 Litho. *Perf. 11½*

C533 AP122 2s multi 24 12

Meeting of Organization of Oil Exporting Countries, Quito, June 15–24.

Ecuadorian Flag, UPU Emblem
AP123

1974, July 15 Litho. *Perf. 11½*

C534 AP123 1.30s multi 20 15

Centenary of Universal Postal Union.

Teodoro Wolf
AP124

Capt. Edmundo Chiriboga
AP125

1974 Lithographed *Perf. 12x11½*

C535 AP124 1.30s blk & ultra 15 8
C536 AP125 1.50s gray 18 8

Teodoro Wolf, geographer; Edmundo Chiriboga, national hero. Issue dates, No. C535, Nov. 29; No. C536, Dec. 4.

Congress Emblem
AP126

1974, Dec. 8 Litho. *Perf. 11½x12*

C537 AP126 5s bl & multi 60 30

8th Inter-American Postmasters' Congress, Quito.

Map of Americas and Coat of Arms
AP127

Manuel J. Calle, Journalist
AP128

1975, Feb. 1 *Perf. 12x11½*

C538 AP127 3s bl & multi 35 18

EXFIGUA Stamp Exhibition and 5th General Assembly of Federacion Inter-Americana de Filatelia, Guayaquil, Nov. 1973.

1975 *Perf. 12x11½*

Portraits: No. C540, Leopoldo Benites V., president of U.N. General Assembly, 1973–74; No. C541, Adofo H. Simmonds G. (1892–1969), journalists; No. C542, Juan de Dios Martinez Mera, President of Ecuador, birth centenary.

C539 AP128 5s lil rose 60 30
C540 AP128 5s gray 60 30
C541 AP128 5s violet 60 30
C542 AP128 5s blk & rose red 60 30

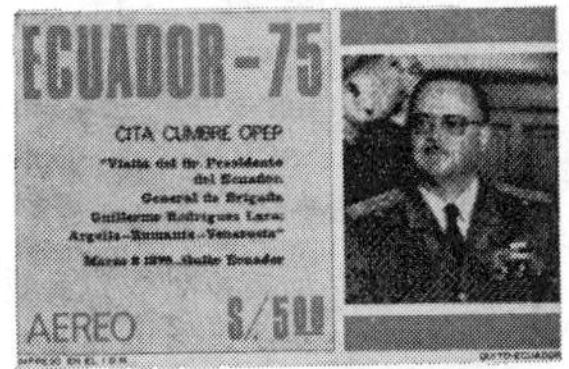

Pres. Guillermo Rodriguez Lara—AP129

1975 *Perf. 12* Unwmkd.

C546 AP129 5s ver & blk 75 30

State visit of Pres. Guillermo Rodriguez Lara to Algeria, Romania and Venezuela.

Meeting Type of 1975

Designs: 1.50s, Rafael Rodriguez Palacio and Argelino Duran Quintero meeting at border in Ruichacha. 2s, Signing border agreement.

1975, Apr. 1 Litho. *Perf. 12x11½*

C547 A273 1.50s multi 18 10
C548 A273 2s multi 24 12

Meeting of the Ministers for Public Works of Ecuador and Colombia, July 27, 1973.

Sacred Heart (Painting)
AP130

Quito Cathedral
AP131

Design: 2s, Monstrance.

1975, Apr. 28 Litho. *Perf. 12x11½*

C549 AP130 1.30s yel & multi 20 8
C550 AP130 2s bl & multi 30 12
C551 AP131 3s multi 40 18

3rd Bolivarian Eucharistic Congress, Quito, June 9–16, 1974.

J. Delgado Panchana with Trophy
AP132

J. Delgado Panchana Swimming
AP133

Perf. 12x11½, 11½x12

1975, June 12 Unwmkd.

C552 AP132 1.30s bl & multi 25 8
C553 AP133 3s blk & multi 50 18

Jorge Delgado Panchana. South American swimming champion, 1971 and 1974.

Sports Type of 1975

1975, Sept. 11 Litho. *Perf. 11½*

C554 A276 1.30s *Tennis* 15 8
C555 A276 2s *Target shooting* 24 12
C556 A276 2.80s *Volleyball* 34 16
C557 A276 3s *Raft with sails* 36 18
C558 A276 5s *Mask* 60 30
Nos. C554-C558 (5) 1.69 84

3rd Ecuadorian Games.

Flower Type of 1975

1975, Nov. 18 Litho. *Perf. 11½x12*

C559 A277 1.30s *Pitcairnia pungens* 16 8
C560 A277 2s *Scarlet sage* 24 12
C561 A277 3s *Amaryllis* 36 18
C562 A277 4s *Opuntia quitense* 48 24
C563 A277 5s *Amaryllis* 60 30
Nos. C559-C563 (5) 1.84 92

Tail Assemblies and Emblem
AP134

Planes over Map of Ecuador
AP135

1975, Dec. 17 Litho. *Perf. 11½*

C564	AP134	1.30s bl & multi	20	8
C565	AP135	3s multi	45	18

TAME, Military Transport Airline, 13th anniversary.

Benalcázar Statue
AP136

1976, Feb. 6 Litho. *Perf. 11½*

C566	AP136	2s multi	30	12
C567	AP136	3s multi	50	18

Sebastián de Benalcázar (1495–1550), Spanish conquistador, founder of Quito.

Archaeology Type of 1975

Designs: 1.30s, Seated man, Carchi Culture. 2s, Funerary urn, Tuncahuan Culture. 3s, Priest, Bahia de Caraquez Culture. 4s, Snail's shell, Cuasmal Culture. 5s, Bowl supported by figurines, Guangala Culture.

1976, Feb. 12 Litho. *Perf. 11½*

C568	A278	1.30s multi	16	8
C569	A278	2s multi	24	12
C570	A278	3s multi	36	18
C571	A278	4s multi	48	24
C572	A278	5s multi	60	30
		Nos. C568-C572 (5)	1.84	92

Archaeological artifacts.

Fruit Type of 1976

Designs: 2s, Apples. 5s, Rose.

1976, Mar. 30

C573	A280	2s bl & multi	24	12
C574	A280	5s bl & multi	60	30

25th Flower and Fruit Festival, Ambato.

Lufthansa Jet
AP137

1976, June 25 Litho. *Perf. 12*

C575	AP137	10s bl & multi	1.20	75

Lufthansa, 50th anniversary.

An imperf. 20s miniature sheet exists, similar to No. C575 enlarged, with overprinted black bar covering line below "Lufthansa." Size: 90x115mm.

Projected Post Office, Quito
AP138

Fruit Peddler
AP139

1976, Aug. 10 Litho. *Perf. 12*

C576	AP138	5s blk & multi	60	30

Design for new General Post Office, Quito.

1976, July 25

Designs: No. C578, Longshoreman. No. C579, Cerros del Carmen and Santa Ana, hills of Guayaquil (horiz.). No. C580, Sebastián de Belalcázar. No. C581, Francisco de Orellana. No. C582, Chief Guayas and his wife Quila.

C577	AP139	1.30s red & multi	16	8
C578	AP139	1.30s red & multi	16	8
C579	AP139	1.30s red & multi	16	8
C580	AP139	2s red & multi	24	12
C581	AP139	2s red & multi	24	12
C582	AP139	2s red & multi	24	12
		Nos. C577-C582 (6)	1.20	60

Founding of Quayaquil, 441st anniversary.

Emblem and Laurel
AP140

1976, Aug. 9

C583	AP140	1.30s yel & multi	16	8

Bolivarian Society of Ecuador, 50th anniversary.

Western Hemisphere and Equator Monument
AP141

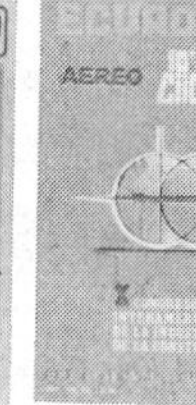

Congress Emblem
AP142

1976, Sept. 6

C584	AP141	2s multi	24	12

Souvenir Sheet

Imperf.

C585	AP141	5s multi	*3.00*	*3.00*

3rd Conference of Pan-American Transport Ministers, Quito, Sept. 6–11. No. C585 contains design similar to No. C584 with black denomination and red control number in margin. Size: 95x114mm.

1976, Sept. 27 Litho. *Perf. 11½*

C586	AP142	1.30s bl & multi	16	8
C587	AP142	3s bl & multi	36	18

Souvenir Sheet

Imperf.

C588	AP142	10s bl & multi	1.50	1.50

10th Inter-American Congress of the Construction Industry, Quito, Sept. 27–30. No. C588 has black control number. Size: 89x115mm.

George Washington
AP143

Design: 5s, Naval battle, Sept. 23, 1779, in which the Bonhomme Richard, commanded by John Paul Jones, defeated and captured the Serapis, British man-of-war, off Yorkshire coast (horiz.).

1976, Oct. 18 Litho. *Perf. 12*

C589	AP143	3s blk & multi	65	18
C590	AP143	5s red brn & yel	85	30

American Bicentennial.

Dr. Hideyo Noguchi
AP144

Luis Cordero
AP145

1976 Litho. *Perf. 11½*

C591	AP144	3s yel & multi	36	18

Dr. Hideyo Noguchi (1876–1928), bacteriologist (at Rockefeller Institute), birth centenary. A 10s imperf. miniature sheet in same design exists with red control number and without "Aereo." Size: 95x114 mm.

1976, Dec. Litho. *Perf. 11½*

C592	AP145	2s multi	24	12

Luis Cordero (1833–1912), president of Ecuador.

Mariuxi Febres Cordero
AP146

1976, Dec. *Perf. 11½*

C593	AP146	3s multi	36	18

Mariuxi Febres Cordero, South American swimming champion.

Flags and Monument
AP147

1976, Nov. 9 *Perf. 12*

C594	AP147	3s multi	36	18

Miniature Sheet

Imperf.

C595	AP147	5s multi	70	70

2nd Meeting of the Agriculture Ministers of the Andean Countries, Quito, Nov. 8–10. No. C595 has red control number. Size: 95x115mm.

See "Special Notices" at the front of this volume for data on the listing methods of this Catalogue, abbreviations, condition, prices and examination.

Sister Catalina
AP148

Congress Hall, Quito
AP149

1977, June 17 Litho. *Perf. 12x11½*

C596	AP148	1.30s blk & pale sal	16	8

Sister Catalina de Jesus Herrera (1717–1795), writer.

1977, Aug. 15 Litho. *Perf. 12x11½*

C597	AP149	5s multi	60	30
a.		10s souvenir sheet	1.30	

11th General Assembly of Pan-American Institute of Geography and History, Quito, Aug. 15–30. No. C597a contains the designs of types A282 and AP149 without denominations and with simulated perforations; black and blue inscriptions, black control number. Size: 90x115mm.

Pres. Alfonso López Michelsen, Flag of Colombia—AP150

Designs: 5s, Pres. López M. of Colombia, Pres. Alfredo Povedo B. of Ecuador and aide. 7s, as 5s (vert.). 9s, 10s, Presidents with aides.

1977 *Perf. 12*

C598	AP150	2.60s multi	50	15
C599	AP150	5s multi	85	30
C600	AP150	7s multi	85	42
C601	AP150	9s multi	1.10	55

Imperf.

C602	AP150	10s multi	1.30	

Meeting of the Presidents of Ecuador and Colombia and Declaration of Putumayo, Feb. 25, 1977. Nos. C598–C602 are overprinted in multiple fluorescent, colorless rows: INSTITUTO GEOGRAFICO MILITAR GOBIERNO DEL ECUADOR. No. C602 has black control number. Size: 115x91mm.

Ceramic Figure, Tolita Culture
AP151

Designs: 9s, Divine Shepherdess, sculpture by Bernardo de Legarda. 11s, The Fruit Seller, sculpture by Legarda. 20s, Sun God, pre-Columbian gold mask.

1977, Aug. 24 *Perf. 12*

C603	AP151	7s gold & multi	85	42
C604	AP151	9s gold & multi	1.10	55
C605	AP151	11s gold & multi	1.32	68

Souvenir Sheet
Gold Embossed *Imperf.*

C606 AP151 20s vio, bl, blk & gold 2.60

Central Bank of Ecuador, 50th anniversary. No. C606 has black control number. Size: 89x115mm. Nos. C603–C605 overprinted like Nos. C598–C602.

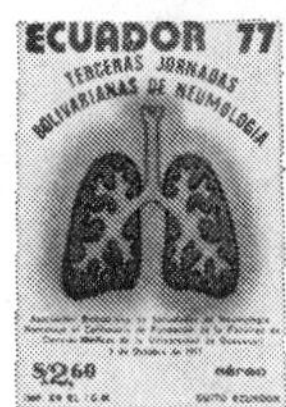

Lungs
AP152

Brother Miguel, St. Peter's, Rome
AP153

1977, Oct. 5 Litho. *Perf. 12x11½*

C607 AP152 2.60s multi 32 15

3rd Congress of the Bolivarian Pneumonic Society and centenary of the founding of the medical faculty of the University of Guayaquil.

1977

C608 AP153 2.60s multi 32 15

Beatification of Brother Miguel.

Peralta Type of 1977

Design: 2.60s, Titles of works by Peralta and his bookmark.

1977 ***Perf. 11½***

C609 A284 2.60s multi 32 15

José Peralta (1855–1937), writer, 40th death anniversary.

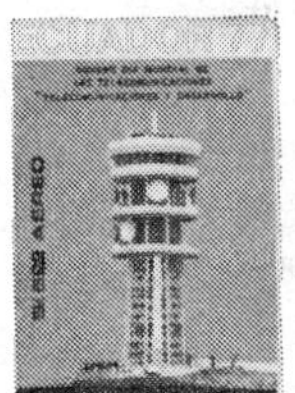

Broadcast Tower
AP154

Remigio Romero y Cordero
AP155

1977, Dec. 2 Litho. *Perf. 12x11½*

C610 AP154 5s multi 60 30

9th World Telecommunications Day.

1978, Mar. 2 Litho. *Perf. 12½x11½*

C611 AP155 3s multi 36 18
C612 AP155 10.60s multi 1.25 60

Imperf.

C612A AP155 10s multi 1.20 65

Remigio Romero y Cordero (1895–1967), poet.

No. C612A contains a vignette similar to Nos. C611–C612, poem and black control number. Size: 90x114mm.

Dr. Vicente Corral Moscoso
AP156

Faces
AP157

Design: 5s, Hospital emblem with Caduceus.

1978, Apr. 12 Litho. *Imperf.*

C613 AP156 5s multi 75 35

Perf. 12x11½

C614 APP156 7.60s multi 90 45

Inauguration (in 1977) of Dr. Vicente Corral Moscoso Regional Hospital, Cuenca.

No. C613 has black control number. Size: 89x114mm.

1978, Mar. 17

Designs: 9s, Emblems and flags of Ecuador. 10s, 11s, Hands reaching for light.

C615 AP157 7s multi 85 42
C616 AP157 9s multi 1.10 55
C617 AP157 11s multi 1.35 65

Imperf.

C618 AP157 10s multi 1.20 65

Ecuadorian Social Security Institute, 50th anniversary.

No. C618 has black control number. Size: 89x114mm.

Geographical Institute Type of 1978

Design: 7.60s, Plane over map of Ecuador with mountains.

1978, Apr. 12 Litho. *Perf. 11½*

C619 A287 7.60s multi 90 45

Imperf.

C620 A287 10s multi 1.20 65

Military Geographical Institute, 50th anniversary. No. C620 contains 2 vignettes with simulated perforations in designs of Nos. 967 and C619, Institute emblem, black control number. Size: 115x89mm.

Lions Type of 1978

1978 ***Perf. 11½***

C621 A288 5s multi 60 30
C622 A288 6.20s multi 75 38

Imperf.

C623 A288 10s multi 1.20 65

7th meeting of Latin American Lions, Jan. 25–29. No. C623 contains a vignette similar to Nos. C621–C622, inscriptions and black control number. Size: 115x90mm.

San Martin
AP158

1978, Apr. 13 Litho. *Perf. 12*

C624 AP158 10.60s multi 1.30 65

Imperf.

C625 AP158 10s multi 1.20 65

Gen. José de San Martin (1778–1850), soldier and statesman. No. C625 contains a vignette similar to No. C624, inscriptions and black control number. Size: 115x 90mm.

Bank Type of 1978

Design: 5s, Bank emblem.

1978, Sept. Litho. *Perf. 11½*

C626 A289 5s gray & multi 60 30

70th anniversary of Filanbanco (Philanthropic Bank).

Soccer Type of 1978

Designs: 2.60s, "Gauchito" and Games' emblem. 5s, "Gauchito." 7s, Soccer ball. 9s, Games' emblem (vert.). 10s, Games' emblem.

1978, Nov. 1 ***Perf. 12***

C627 A290 2.60s multi 30 15
C628 A290 7s multi 85 42
C629 A290 9s multi 1.10 55

Imperf.

C630 A290 5s blk & bl 60 30
C631 A290 10s blk & bl 1.20 65

11th World Cup Soccer Championship, Argentina, June 1–25. Nos. C630–C631 have black control numbers. Size: 115x 90mm.

Bernardo O'Higgins
AP159

Old Men of Vilcabamba
AP160

1978, Nov. 11 Litho. *Perf. 12x11½*

C632 AP159 10.60s multi 1.30 65

Imperf.

C633 AP159 10s multi 1.20 65

Gen. Bernardo O'Higgins (1778–1842), Chilean soldier and statesman. No. C633 contains a vignette similar to No. C632, inscriptions and black control number. Size: 115x90mm.

1978, Nov. 11 ***Perf. 12x11½***

C634 AP160 5s multi 60 30

Vilcabamba, valley of longevity.

Hubert H. Humphrey
AP161

Virgin and Child
AP162

1978, Nov. 27 Litho. *Perf. 12x11½*

C635 AP161 5s multi 60 30

Hubert H. Humphrey (1911–1978), Vice President of the U.S.

1978

Children's Drawings: 4.60s, Holy Family. 6.20s, Candle and children.

C636 AP162 2.20s multi 26 12
C637 AP162 4.60s multi 55 28
C638 AP162 6.20s multi 75 38

Christmas 1978.

Village, by Anibal Villacis
AP163

Ecuadorian Painters: No. C640, Mountain Village, by Gilberto Almeida. No. C641, Bay, by Roura Oxandaberro. No. C642, Abstract, by Luis Molinari. No. C643, Statue, by Oswaldo Viteri. No. C644, Tools, by Enrique Tabara.

1978, Dec. 9 ***Perf. 12***

C639 AP163 5s multi 60 30
C640 AP163 5s multi 60 30
C641 AP163 5s multi 60 30
C642 AP163 5s multi 60 30
C643 AP163 5s multi 60 30
C644 AP163 5s multi 60 30
Nos. C639-C644 (6) 3.60 1.80

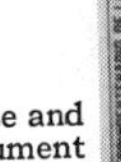

House and Monument
AP164

Design: 3.40s, Monument (vert.).

1979, Feb. 27 Litho. *Perf. 12*

C645 AP164 2.40s multi 30 15
C646 AP164 3.40s multi 40 18

Imperf.

C647 AP164 10s multi 1.20

Sesquicentennial of Battle of Portete and Tarqui. No. C647 contains vignettes similar to Nos. C645–C646; inscriptions and black control number. Size: 115x90mm.

Fish and Ship
AP165

Flags of Ecuador and U.S.
AP166

Designs: 7s, Map of Ecuador and Galapagos showing territorial waters (horiz.). 9s, Map of South America with west-coast territorial waters.

Perf. 12x11½, 11½x12

1979, July 23 Litho. Wmk. 367

C648 AP165 5s multi 60 30
C649 AP165 7s multi 80 40
C650 AP165 9s multi 1.05 50

Declaration of 200-mile territorial limit, 25th anniversary.

1979, Aug. 3 ***Perf. 12x11½***

Designs: 10.60s, Bells in Quito clock tower (horiz.). 13.60s, Aerial view of Galapagos coast.

C651 A293 10.60s multi 1.30 65
C652 A293 13.60s multi 1.65 85

Souvenir Sheet
Imperf. **Unwmkd.**

C653 A293 10s multi 1.20 65

National heritage: Quito and Galapagos Islands. No. C653 contains vignettes similar to Nos. 977, C651–C652; black control number, black and blue inscriptions. Size: 115x90mm.

1979, Aug. *Perf. 11½x12* Wmk. 367

C654 AP166 7.60s multi 85 45
C655 AP166 10.60s multi 1.30 65

Souvenir Sheet
Imperf. **Unwmkd.**

C656 AP166 10s multi 1.20 65

5th anniversary of Ecuador–U.S. Chamber of Commerce. No. C656 contains vignettes similar to Nos. C654–C655; black control number and marginal inscription. Size: 115x90mm.

Smiling Girl, IYC Emblem
AP167

1979, Sept. 7 Litho. *Perf. 12x11½*

C657 AP167 10s multi 1.20 60

International Year of the Child.

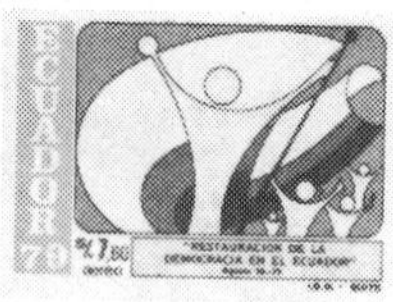

Citizens and Flag of Ecuador—AP168

Design: 10.60s, Pres. Jaime Roldas Aguilera, flag of Ecuador (vert.).

Unwmkd.

1979, Sept. 27 Litho. *Perf. 11½*

C658 AP168 7.60s multi 92 50

Wmk. 367

C659 AP168 10.60s multi 1.25 60

Restoration of democracy to Ecuador.

Ecuador Coat of Arms, Olympic Rings and Eagle—AP169

1979, Nov. 23 Litho. *Perf. 12×11½*

C660 AP169 28s multi 3.35 1.65

5th National Games, Cuenca.

CIESPAL Building, Quito—AP170

1979, Dec. 26 *Perf. 11½×12½*

C661 AP170 10s multi 1.20 60

Opening of Ecuadorian Institute of Engineers building.

Olmedo Type of 1980

1980, Apr. 29 Litho. *Perf. 12x11½*

C662 A294 10s multi 1.20 60

Tribal Chief Type of 1980

1980, May 12

Indo-American Tribal Chiefs: No. C663, Cuauhtemoc, Mexico. No. C664, Lempira, Honduras No. C665, Nicaragua. No. C666, Lambaré, Paraguay. No. C667, Urraca, Panama. No. C668, Anacoana, Haiti No. C669, Caupolican, Chile. No. C670, Tacun-Uman, Guatemala. No. C671, Calarca, Colombia. No. C672. Garabito, Costa Rica. No. C673, Hatuey, Cuba. No. C674, Cmarao, Brazil. No. C675, Tehuelche, Argentina. No.C676, Tupaj Katri, Bolivia. 17.80s, Sequoya, U.S. 22.80s, Ruminahui, Ecuador.

C663 A295 7.60s multi 90 45
C664 A295 7.60s multi 90 45
C665 A295 7.60s multi 90 45
C666 A295 10s multi 1.20 60
C667 A295 10s multi 1.20 60
C668 A295 10.60s multi 1.30 65
C669 A295 10.60s multi 1.30 65
C670 A295 10.60s multi 1.30 65
C671 A295 12.80s multi 1.55 78
C672 A295 12.80s multi 1.55 78
C673 A295 12.80s multi 1.55 78
C674 A295 13.60s multi 1.65 82
C675 A295 13.60s multi 1.65 82
C676 A295 13.60s multi 1.65 82
C677 A295 17.80s multi 2.15 1.10
C678 A295 22.80s multi 2.75 1.40
Nos. C663-C678 (16) 23.50 11.80

Royal Visit Type of 1980

1980, May 18 *Perf. 11½x12*

C679 A296 10.60s multi 1.30 65

Pichincha Provincial Development Council Building AP171

1980, June 1 *Perf. 12x11½*

C680 AP171 10.60s multi 1.30 65

Progress in Pichincha Province.

Indian Type of 1980

1980, June 10 Litho. *Perf. 12x11½*

C681 A297 7.60s *Salasaca boy, Tungurahua* 90 45
C682 A297 10s *Amula woman, Chimborazo* 1.20 60
C683 A297 10.60s *Canar woman, Canar* 1.30 65
C684 A297 13.60s *Colorado Indian, Pichincha* 1.65 82

Virgin of Mercy Type of 1980

1980, July 7 Litho. *Perf. 11½*

C685 A298 7.60s *Cupola, cloisters* 90 45
C686 A298 7.60s *Gold screen* 90 45
C687 A298 7.60s *Quito from basilica tower* 90 45
C688 A298 10.60s *Retable* 1.30 65
C689 A298 10.60s *Pulpit* 1.30 65
C690 A298 13.60s *Cupola* 1.65 82
C691 A298 13.60s *Statue of Virgin* 1.65 82
Nos. C685-C691 (7) 8.60 4.29

Virgin of Mercy, patron saint of Ecuadorian armed forces.

U.P.U. Monument AP172

Marshal Sucre, by Marco Sales AP173

Design: 17.80s, Mail box, 1880.

1980, July 7 *Perf. 12*

C692 AP172 10.60s multi 1.30 65
C693 AP172 17.80s multi 2.15 1.10

Souvenir Sheet

C694 AP172 25s multi 3.50 1.75

Universal Postal Union membership centenary. No. C694 contains designs of C692 and C693 (horiz.), perf. 11½. Black control number. Size: 116x91mm.

Olympic Type of 1980.

Design: 10.60s, 13.60s, Moscow '80 emblem, Olympic rings.

1980, July 19 *Perf. 12x11½*

C695 A299 10.60s multi 1.30 65
C696 A299 13.60s multi 1.65 82

Souvenir Sheet

Imperf.

C697 A299 30s multi 3.60 1.80

22nd Summer Olympic Games, Moscow, July 19-Aug. 3.

No. C697 contains vignettes in designs of Nos. 991 and C695, black control number. Size: 116x90mm.

1980

C698 AP173 10.60s multi 1.30 65

Marshal Antonio Jose de Sucre, death sesquicentennial.

Rotary International, 75th Anniversary—AP174

1980, Aug. 4 *Perf. 11½*

C699 AP174 10s multi 1.25 60

Riobamba Type of 1980

Design: 7.60s, 10.60s, Monstrance, Riobamba Cathedral (vert.).

1980, Sept. 20 Litho. *Perf. 11½*

C700 A301 7.60s multi 90 45
C701 A301 10.60s multi 1.30 65

Souvenir Sheet

Imperf.

C702 A301 30s multi 3.75 1.75

Constitutional Assembly of Riobamba sesquicentennial. No. C702 contains vignettes in designs of Nos. 996-997, black control number. Size: 116x90mm.

Democracy Type of 1980

Designs: 7.60s, 10.60s, Pres. Aguilera and voter.

Wmk. 367

1980, Oct. 9 Litho. *Perf. 12x11½*

C703 A302 7.60s multi 90 45
C704 A302 10.60s multi 1.30 65

Souvenir Sheet

Imperf.

C705 A302 15s multi 2.00 1.00

No. C705 contains vignettes in designs of Nos. 999 and C703; control number.

OPEC Type of 1980

20th Anniversary of OPEC: 7.60s, Men holding OPEC emblem (vert.).

1980, Nov. 8 *Perf. 11½x12*

C706 A303 7.60s multi 90 45

Carchi Province Type of 1980

Designs: 10.60s, Governor's Palace (vert.). 17.80s, Victory Museum, Central Square (vert.).

1980, Nov. 21 *Perf. 13*

C707 A304 10.60s multi 1.30 65
C708 A304 17.80s multi 2.15 1.10

Orchid Type of 1980

1980, Nov. 22 *Perf. 12x11½, 11½x12*

C709 A305 7.60s *Anguloa uniflora* 90 45
C710 A305 10.60s *Scuticaria salesiana* 1.20 60
C711 A305 50s *Helcia sanguinolenta, vert.* 6.00 3.00
C712 A305 100s *Anguloa virginalis* 12.00 6.00

Souvenir Sheet

Imperf.

C713 A305 20s multi 2.50 1.25
C714 A305 20s multi 2.50 1.25

Nos. C713-C714 contain vignettes in designs of Nos. C709-C710 and C711-C712 respectively; blue control numbers: 115 x 90 mm.

Christmas Type of 1980

Designs: 7.60s, Pope blessing crowd (vert.). 10.60s, Portrait (vert.).

1980, Dec. 27 *Perf. 12*

C715 A306 7.60s multi 90 45
C716 A306 10.60s multi 1.30 65

Isidro Cueva AP175

Simon Bolivar, by Marco Salas AP176

1980, Nov. 20 *Perf. 13*

C717 AP175 18.20s multi 2.20 1.10

Dr. Isidro Ayora Cueva, former president, birth centenary.

1980, Dec. 17 *Perf. 11½*

C718 AP176 13.60s multi 1.65 82

Simon Bolivar death sesquicentennial.

Turtle, Galapagos Islands—AP177

Design: 100s, Oldest Ecuadorian mail box, 1793 (vert.).

1981, Feb. 12 Litho. *Perf. 13*

C719 AP177 50s multi 6.00 3.00
C720 AP177 100s multi 12.00 6.00

HCJB Type of 1981

1981 Litho. *Perf. 13*

C721 A311 7.60s Emblem, horiz. 90 45
C722 A311 10.60s Emblem, diff. 1.30 65

Soccer Players AP178

1981, July 8

C723 AP178 7.60s Emblem 90 45
C724 AP178 10.60s shown 1.30 65
C725 AP178 13.60s World Cup 1.65 80

Souvenir Sheets

C726 AP178 20s multi 2.50 1.25
C727 AP178 20s multi 2.50 1.25

1982 World Cup Soccer Championship. Nos. C726-C727 contain vignettes in designs of Nos. C723 and C724 respectively; black control numbers. Size: 115x90mm.

World Food Day Type of 1981

1981, Dec. 31 Litho. *Perf. 13x13½*

C728 A314 10s Farming, vert. 1.20 50

IYD Type of 1982

1982, Feb. 25 Litho. *Perf. 13*

C729 A316 7.60s Emblem 90 45
C730 A316 10.60s Man with crutch 1.30 65

Montalvo Type of 1982

1982 Litho. *Perf. 13*

C731 A318 5s Home, horiz. 60 25

Swimming Type of 1982

1982, July 30

C732	A320	10.20s Emblem, vert.	1.25	55
C733	A320	14.20s Diving, vert.	1.70	70

AIR POST SEMI-POSTAL STAMPS.

Nos. C119-C123 Surcharged in Blue or Red:

Hospital

Méndez + $ 0,50

1944, May 9 ***Perf. 12*** **Unwmkd.**

CB1	AP26	50c +50c dp red lil		5.00	5.00
CB2	AP26	70c +30c red brn		5.00	5.00
CB3	AP26	3s +50c turq grn (R)		5.00	5.00
CB4	AP26	5s +1s brt ultra (R)		5.00	5.00
CB5	AP26	10s +2s scar		5.00	5.00
		Nos. CB1-CB5 (5)		25.00	25.00

The surtax aided Mendez Hospital.

AIR POST REGISTRATION STAMPS.

Issued by Sociedad Colombo-Alemana de Transportes Aereos (SCADTA)

Nos. C3 and C3a Overprinted "R" in Carmine.

1928-29 ***Perf. 14x14½*** **Wmk. 116**

CF1	AP6	1s on 20c gray (#C3)	200.00	175.00
a.		1s on 20c gray (C3a) ('29)	225.00	200.00

No. C18 Overprinted "R" in Black.

1929, Apr. 1 ***Perf. 14*** **Wmk. 127**

CF2	AP2	1s rose	90.00	75.00

AIR POST OFFICIAL STAMPS.

in Red or Black **OFICIAL**

1929, May ***Perf. 12*** **Unwmkd.**

CO1	AP1	2c blk (R)	60	60
CO2	AP1	5c car rose	60	60
CO3	AP1	10c dp brn	60	60
CO4	AP1	20c dk vio	60	60
CO5	AP1	50c dp grn	2.00	1.50
CO6	AP1	1s dk bl	2.00	1.75
a.		Invtd. ovpt.	375.00	
CO7	AP1	5s org yel	7.50	7.50
CO8	AP1	10s org red	165.00	135.00
		Nos. CO1-CO8 (8)	178.90	148.15

Establishment of commercial air service in Ecuador.

Counterfeits of No. CO8 exist.

1930, Jan. 9

CO9	AP1	50c ol brn	1.50	1.35
CO10	AP1	1s car lake	2.50	2.00
CO11	AP1	5s ol grn	5.00	5.00
CO12	AP1	10s black	10.00	10.00

Air Post Stamps of 1937 Overprinted in Black **OFICIAL**

1937, Aug. 19 ***Perf. 11½***

CO13	AP7	10c chestnut	25	20
CO14	AP7	20c ol blk	35	20
CO15	AP7	70c blk brn	35	20
CO16	AP7	1s gray blk	50	20
CO17	AP7	2s dk vio	60	40
		Nos.CO13-CO17 (5)	2.05	1.20

No. C79 Overprinted in Black **OFICIAL**

1940, Aug. 1 ***Perf. 12½x13***

CO18	AP15	5s emerald	1.25	90

Nos. C352-C354 Overprinted: "1961 oficial"

1964 ***Perf. 13½***

CO19	AP86	50c bl & multi	1.00	1.00
CO20	A86	80c yel & multi	1.00	1.00
CO21	A86	1.30s pale grn & multi	1.00	1.00

SPECIAL DELIVERY STAMPS.

SD1

1928 ***Perf. 12.*** **Unwmkd.**

E1	SD1	2c on 2c bl	3.00	*5.00*
E2	SD1	5c on 2c bl	2.50	*5.00*
E3	SD1	10c on 2c bl	3.00	*3.00*
a.		10 CTVOS inverted	10.00	*15.00*
E4	SD1	20c on 2c bl	4.00	*5.00*
E5	SD1	50c on 2c bl	4.00	*5.00*
		Nos. E1-E5 (5)	16.50	*23.00*

No. RA49A Surcharged in Red

EXPRESO 20 Ctvs.

1945

E6	PT18	20c on 5c grn	25	10

LATE FEE STAMP.

No. RA49A Surcharged in Black

U. H. 10 Ctvs.

1945 ***Perf. 12.*** **Unwmkd.**

I1	PT18	10c on 5c grn	15	12

POSTAGE DUE STAMPS.

Numeral D1

Coat of Arms D2

Wmkd. Liberty Cap. (117)

1896 **Engraved** ***Perf. 12***

J1	D1	1c bl grn	1.25	2.00
J2	D1	2c bl grn	40	1.00
J3	D1	5c bl grn	1.25	1.25
J4	D1	10c bl grn	85	1.50
J5	D1	20c bl grn	35	*2.00*
J6	D1	50c bl grn	30	*2.50*
J7	D1	100c bl grn	60	*5.00*
		Nos. J1-J7 (5)	5.00	*15.25*

Reprints are on very thick paper with distinct watermark and vertical paper-weave direction. Price 5c each.

Unwmkd.

J8	D1	1c bl grn	1.75	*4.00*
J9	D1	2c bl grn	1.75	*4.00*
J10	D1	5c bl grn	1.75	*4.00*
J11	D1	10c bl grn	1.75	*4.00*
J12	D1	20c bl grn	2.25	*5.00*
J13	D1	50c bl grn	3.00	*7.00*
J14	D1	100c bl grn	4.00	*10.00*
		Nos. J8-J14 (7)	16.25	*38.00*

1929

J15	D2	5c dp bl	15	8
J16	D2	10c org yel	20	12
J17	D2	20c red	30	25

Numeral D3

Lithographed

1958, Nov. ***Perf. 13½*** **Unwmkd.**

J18	D3	10c brt lil	5	3
J19	D3	50c emerald	10	6
J20	D3	1s maroon	20	15
J21	D3	2s red	30	25

OFFICIAL STAMPS.

Regular Issues of 1881 and 1887
Handstamped in Black

OFICIAL

1886 ***Perf. 12*** **Unwmkd.**

O1	A5	1c yel brn	50	50
O2	A6	2c lake	75	75
O3	A7	5c blue	1.25	1.25
O4	A8	10c orange	1.00	1.00
O5	A9	20c gray vio	1.00	1.00
O6	A10	50c bl grn	4.00	3.50
		Nos. O1-O6 (6)	8.50	8.00

1887

O7	A12	1c green	75	75
O8	A13	2c vermilion	75	75
O9	A14	5c blue	1.00	1.00
O10	A15	80c ol grn	4.00	3.00

Nos. O1 to O10 are known with red handstamp but these are believed to be speculative.

The overprint on the 1886-87 issues is handstamped and is found in various positions.

Flores
O1

Arms
O1a

1892 Carmine Overprint.

O11	O1	1c ultra	12	25
O12	O1	2c ultra	12	25
O13	O1	5c ultra	12	25
O14	O1	10c ultra	12	20
O15	O1	20c ultra	12	10
O16	O1	50c ultra	12	50
O17	O1	1s ultra	40	50
		Nos. O11-O17 (7)	1.12	2.05

1894

O18	O1a	1c sl grn (R)	2.50
O19	O1a	2c lake (Bk)	2.50

Nos. O18 and O19 were not placed in use.

Rocafuerte
O2

Dated 1894.

1894 Carmine Overprint

O20	O2	1c gray blk	25	50
O21	O2	2c gray blk	25	25
O22	O2	5c gray blk	25	25
O23	O2	10c gray blk	10	20
O24	O2	20c gray blk	30	25
O25	O2	50c gray blk	1.50	1.50
O26	O2	1s gray blk	2.00	2.00
		Nos. O20-O26 (7)	4.65	4.95

Dated 1895

1895 Carmine Overprint.

O27	O2	1c gray blk	2.25	2.25
O28	O2	2c gray blk	3.00	3.00
O29	O2	5c gray blk	50	50
O30	O2	10c gray blk	3.00	3.00
O31	O2	20c gray blk	5.00	5.00
O32	O2	50c gray blk	*12.50*	*12.50*
O33	O2	1s gray blk	1.50	1.50
		Nos. O27-O33 (7)	*27.75*	*27.75*

Reprints of 1894-95 issues are on very thick paper with paper weave found both horizontal and vertical for all denominations. Generally they are blacker than originals.

Overprinted FRANQUEO OFICIAL in Carmine.

1896 **Wmkd. Liberty Cap. (117)**

O34	A21	1c ol bis	35	35
O35	A22	2c ol bis	35	35
O36	A23	5c ol bis	35	35
O37	A24	10c ol bis	35	35
O38	A25	20c ol bis	35	35
O39	A26	50c ol bis	35	35
O40	A27	1s ol bis	1.00	75
O41	A28	5s ol bis	1.75	1.65
		Nos. O34-O41 (8)	4.85	4.50

Reprints of Nos. O34-O41 are on thick paper with vertical paper weave direction.

Unwmkd.

O42	A21	1c ol bis	1.00	1.00
O43	A22	2c ol bis	1.00	1.00
O44	A23	5c ol bis	1.00	70
O45	A24	10c ol bis	75	60
O46	A25	20c ol bis	1.00	1.00
O47	A26	50c ol bis	1.00	1.50
O48	A27	1s ol bis	2.00	1.25
O49	A28	5s ol bis	3.00	2.25
		Nos. O42-O49 (8)	10.75	9.30

Reprints of Nos. O42-O49 all have overprint in black. Price 3c each.

Issue of 1894
Overprinted 1897 1898

1897-98

O50	O2	1c gray blk	*5.00*	*5.00*
O51	O2	2c gray blk	*6.00*	*6.00*
O52	O2	5c gray blk	*50.00*	*50.00*
O53	O2	10c gray blk	*6.00*	*6.00*
O54	O2	20c gray blk	*2.75*	*1.75*
O55	O2	50c gray blk	*10.00*	*10.00*
O56	O2	1s gray blk	*15.00*	*15.00*
		Nos. O50-O56 (7)	*94.75*	*93.75*

Issue of 1894
Overprinted 1897 1898

O57	O2	1c gray blk	*1.50*	*1.50*
O58	O2	2c gray blk	*3.50*	*1.25*
O59	O2	5c gray blk	*6.00*	*6.00*
O60	O2	10c gray blk	*50.00*	*50.00*
O61	O2	20c gray blk	*1.50*	*1.50*
O62	O2	50c gray blk	*6.00*	*5.00*
O63	O2	1s gray blk	*65.00*	*65.00*
		Nos. O57-O63 (7)	*133.50*	*130.25*

Issue of 1894
Overprinted 1897 Y 1898

O64	O2	1c gray blk	*8.00*	*8.00*
O65	O2	2c gray blk	*8.00*	*8.00*
O66	O2	5c gray blk	*8.00*	*8.00*
O67	O2	10c gray blk	*8.00*	*8.00*
O68	O2	20c gray blk	*8.00*	*8.00*
O69	O2	50c gray blk	*8.00*	*8.00*
O70	O2	1s gray blk	*8.00*	*8.00*
		Nos. O64-O70 (7)	*56.00*	*56.00*

Issue of 1895
Overprinted in Black 1897 1898

O71	O2	1c gray blk	*3.00*	*3.00*
O72	O2	2c gray blk	*2.00*	*2.00*
O73	O2	5c gray blk	*3.00*	*3.00*
O74	O2	10c gray blk	*3.00*	*3.00*
O75	O2	20c gray blk	*5.00*	*5.00*
O76	O2	50c gray blk	*22.50*	
O77	O2	1s gray blk	*45.00*	*45.00*
		Nos. O71-O77 (7)	*83.50*	

Issue of 1895
Overprinted 1897 1898

O78	O2	1c gray blk	*1.25*	*1.25*
O79	O2	2c gray blk	*90*	*90*
O80	O2	5c gray blk	*2.50*	*2.50*
O81	O2	10c gray blk	*90*	*90*
O82	O2	20c gray blk	*1.00*	*60*
O83	O2	50c gray blk	*2.00*	*75*
O84	O2	1s gray blk	*7.50*	*7.50*
		Nos. O78-O84 (7)	*16.05*	*14.40*

Issue of 1895
Overprinted 1897 Y 1898

O85	O2	1c gray blk	*40.00*	*40.00*
O86	O2	2c gray blk	*1.25*	*1.25*
O87	O2	5c gray blk	*95*	*75*
O88	O2	10c gray blk	*35.00*	*35.00*
O89	O2	20c gray blk	*60.00*	*60.00*
O90	O2	50c gray blk	*15.00*	*15.00*
O91	O2	1s gray blk	*75.00*	*75.00*
		Nos. O85-O91 (7)	*227.20*	*227.00*

Many forged overprints of Nos. O50-O91 exist, made on the original stamps and reprints.

O3

Black Surcharge.

1898-99 ***Perf. 15, 16***

O92	O3	5c on 50c lil	30	30
a.		Inverted surcharge	1.50	1.50
O93	O3	10c on 20s org	85	85
a.		Double surcharge	2.25	2.25
O94	O3	10c on 50c lil	*75.00*	*75.00*
O95	O3	20c on 50c lil	2.50	2.50
O96	O3	20c on 50s grn	2.25	2.25
		Nos. O92-O96 (5)	*80.90*	*80.90*

Green Surcharge.

O97	O3	5c on 50c lil	1.25	1.25
a.		Double surcharge	2.00	
b.		Double surcharge, blk and grn	6.50	
c.		Same as 'b', blk surcharge inverted	2.00	

1899 Red Surcharge.

O98	O3	5c on 50c lil	1.25	1.25
a.		Double surcharge	2.00	
b.		Double surcharge, blk and red	2.50	
O99	O3	20c on 50s grn	2.50	2.50
a.		Inverted surcharge	5.00	
b.		Double surcharge, red and blk	8.00	

Similar Surcharge.
Value in Words in Two Lines.
Black Surcharge.

O100	O3	1c on 5c bl	*27.50*

Red Surcharge

O101	O3	2c on 5c bl	*40.00*
O102	O3	4c on 20c bl	*35.00*

Types of Regular Issue of 1899
Overprinted in Black
OFICIAL

1899 ***Perf. 14, 15***

O103	A37	2c org & blk	40	1.00
O104	A39	10c org & blk	40	1.00
O105	A40	20c org & blk	30	1.50
O106	A41	50c org & blk	30	2.00

OFICIAL

The above overprint was applied to remainders of the postage stamps of 1904 with the idea of increasing their salability. They were never regularly in use as official stamps.

Regular Issue of
1911-13 Overprinted
in Black
OFICIAL

1913 ***Perf. 12.***

O107	A71	1c scar & blk	75	75
O108	A72	2c bl & blk	75	75
O109	A73	3c org & blk	40	35
O110	A74	5c scar & blk	1.00	75
O111	A75	10c bl & blk	1.00	30
		Nos. O107-O111 (5)	3.90	2.90

Regular Issue of
1911-13
Overprinted
OFICIAL

Overprint 22x3½ mm.

1916-17

O112	A72	2c bl & blk	7.50	7.50
O113	A74	5c scar & blk	7.50	7.50
O114	A75	10c bl & blk	4.50	4.50

Overprint 25x4 mm.

O115	A71	1c scar & blk	75	75
O116	A72	2c bl & blk	1.00	1.00
a.		Invtd. ovpt.	1.50	1.50
O117	A73	3c org & blk	60	60
O118	A74	5c scar & blk	1.00	1.00
O119	A75	10c bl & blk	1.00	50
		Nos. O115-O119 (5)	4.35	3.85

Same Overprint
On Regular Issue of 1915-17.

O120	A71	1c orange	30	30
O121	A72	2c green	30	30
O122	A73	3c black	50	40
O123	A78	4c red & blk	50	50
a.		Invtd. ovpt.	1.00	
O124	A74	5c violet	30	25
O125	A75	10c blue	55	55
O126	A79	20c grn & blk	3.50	3.50
		Nos. O120-O126 (7)	5.95	5.80

Regular Issues
of 1911-17
Overprinted in
Black or Red
OFICIAL

O127	A71	1c orange	20	15
O128	A72	2c green	20	20
O129	A73	3c blk (Bk)	15	10
O130	A73	3c blk (R)	20	20
a.		Inverted overprint		
O131	A78	4c red & blk	20	10
O132	A74	5c violet	35	20
O133	A75	10c bl & blk	1.00	50
O134	A75	10c blue	20	20
O135	A79	20c grn & blk	1.00	40
		Nos. O127-O135 (9)	3.50	2.05

Regular Issue of 1920
Overprinted OFICIAL

1920

O136	A86	1c green	15	15
a.		Inverted overprint	2.00	2.00
O137	A86	2c carmine	12	12
O138	A86	3c yel brn	15	15
O139	A86	4c dk grn	20	20
a.		Inverted overprint	2.00	3.00
O140	A86	5c blue	20	20
O141	A86	6c orange	15	15
O142	A86	7c brown	20	20
O143	A86	8c yel grn	25	25

O144	A86	9c red	35	35
O145	A95	10c blue	20	20
O146	A86	15c gray	1.00	1.00
O147	A86	20c dp vio	1.25	1.10
O148	A86	30c violet	1.40	1.20
O149	A86	40c dk brn	2.00	1.00
O150	A86	50c dk grn	1.25	1.25
O151	A86	60c dk bl	1.50	1.50
O152	A86	70c gray	1.50	1.50
O153	A86	80c yellow	1.75	1.75
O154	A104	90c green	2.00	2.00
O155	A86	1s blue	3.00	3.00
		Nos. O136-O155 (20)	18.62	17.27

Nos. O136 to O155 were issued in commemoration of the centenary of the independence of Guayaquil.

Stamps of 1911 Overprinted **OFICIAL**

1922

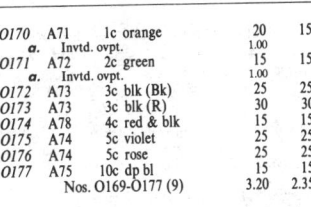

O156	A71	1c scar & blk	75	30
O157	A72	2c bl & blk	35	30

Revenue Stamps of 1919-1920 Overprinted like Nos. O156 and O157

1924

O158	PT3	1c dk bl	40	30
O159	PT3	2c green	2.00	1.25

Regular Issues of 1911-17 Overprinted **OFICIAL**

1924

O160	A71	1c orange	1.50	1.50
a.		Inverted overprint	2.50	

Overprinted in Black or Red **OFICIAL**

O161	A72	2c green	10	10
O162	A73	3c blk (R)	12	12
O163	A78	4c red & blk	25	25
O164	A74	5c violet	30	15
O165	A75	10c dp bl	25	20
O166	A76	1s grn & blk	85	85
		Nos. O160-O166 (7)	3.37	3.17

No. O106 with Additional Overprint **Acuerdo No 4.228**

1924 *Perf. 14, 15*

O167	A41	50c org & blk	1.00	1.00

Nos. O160 to O167 inclusive exist with inverted overprint.

No. 199 Overprinted **OFICIAL**

1924 *Perf. 12*

O168	A71	1c orange	1.00	1.00

Regular Issues of 1911-25 Overprinted **OFICIAL**

1925

O169	A71	1c scar & blk	1.50	70
a.		Invtd. ovpt.	1.50	
O170	A71	1c orange	20	15
a.		Invtd. ovpt.	1.00	
O171	A72	2c green	15	15
a.		Invtd. ovpt.	1.00	
O172	A73	3c blk (Bk)	25	25
O173	A73	3c blk (R)	30	30
O174	A78	4c red & blk	15	15
O175	A74	5c violet	25	25
O176	A74	5c rose	25	25
O177	A75	10c dp bl	15	15
		Nos. O169-O177 (9)	3.20	2.35

Regular Issues of 1916-25 Overprinted Vertically Up or Down **OFICIAL**

1927, Oct.

O178	A71	1c orange	15	15
O179	A86	2c carmine	15	12
O180	A86	3c yel brn	15	12
O181	A86	4c myr grn	15	12
O182	A86	5c pale bl	15	15
O183	A75	10c yel grn	15	12
		Nos. O178-O183 (6)	90	78

Regular Issues of 1920-27 Overprinted **OFICIAL**

1928

O184	A71	1c lt bl	15	12
O185	A86	2c carmine	15	12
O186	A86	3c yel brn	15	15
a.		Invtd. ovpt.	1.00	
O187	A86	4c myr grn	15	15
O188	A86	5c lt bl	15	15
O189	A75	10c yel grn	15	15
O190	A109	20c violet	15	15
a.		Ovpt. reading up	1.00	
		Nos. O184-O190 (7)	1.05	99

The overprint is placed vertically reading down on No. O190.

Regular Issue of 1936 Overprinted in Black **OFICIAL**

1936 *Perf. 14.*

O191	A131	5c ol grn	8	6
O192	A132	10c brown	10	12
O193	A133	20c dk vio	12	10
O194	A134	1s dk car	30	25
O195	A135	2s dk bl	50	40
		Nos. O191-O195 (5)	1.10	93

Regular Postage Stamps of 1937 Overprinted in Black **OFICIAL**

1937 *Perf. 11½*

O196	A139	2c green	5	5
O197	A140	5c dp rose	10	10
O198	A141	10c blue	10	10
O199	A142	20c dp rose	10	10
O200	A143	1s ol grn	25	20
		Nos. O196-O200 (5)	60	55

Tobacco Stamp, Overprinted in Black **CORRESPONDENCIA OFICIAL**

1946 *Rouletted.* **Unwmkd.**

O201	PT7	1c rose red	6	6

Communications Building, Quito
O4

Lithographed.

1947 *Perf. 11* **Unwmkd.**

O202	O4	30c brown	15	15
O203	O4	30c grnsh bl	15	10
a.		Imperf., pair		
O204	O4	30c purple	15	10

Nos. O202 to O204 overprinted "Primero la Patria!" and plane in dark blue are said to be essays.

No. 719 with Additional Diagonal Overprint: ***oficial***

1964 *Perf. 14x13*

O205	A231	80c rose car & grn (block of 4)	3.00	3.00

The "OEA" overprint covers four stamps, the "oficial" overprint is applied to every stamp.

A set of 20 imperforate items in the above Roosevelt design, some overprinted with the initials of various government ministries, was released in 1949. Later that year a set of eight miniature sheets, bearing the same design plus a marginal inscription, "Presidencia (or Vicepresidencia) de la Republica," and a frame-line were released. In the editors' opinion, information justifying the listing of these issues has not been received.

POSTAL TAX STAMPS.

Roca
PT1

1920 *Perf. 12.* **Unwmkd.**

RA1	PT1	1c orange	35	15

PT2

PT3

RA2	PT2	1c red & bl	25	15
a.		"de" inverted	2.00	2.00
b.		Double overprint	2.00	60
c.		Inverted overprint	2.00	60
RA3	PT3	1c dp bl	30	10
a.		Inverted ovpt.	1.25	1.00
b.		Double ovpt.	1.25	1.00

PT4

PT5

Red or Black Surcharge or Overprint.

Stamp Dated 1911-1912

RA4	PT4	20c dp bl	27.50	12.00

Stamp Dated 1913-1914.

RA5	PT4	20c dp bl (R)	1.50	50

Stamp Dated 1917-1918.

RA6	PT4	20c ol grn (R)	2.00	75
a.		Dated 1919-20	9.00	
RA7	PT5	1c on 2c grn	30	12

Stamp Dated 1911-1912.

RA8	PT5	1c on 5c grn	25	10
a.		Double surcharge		

Stamp Dated 1913-1914.

RA9	PT5	1c on 5c grn	2.50	50
a.		Double surcharge	3.00	2.00

On Nos. RA7, RA8 and RA9 the surcharge is found reading upward or downward.

Post Office
PT6

1920-24 **Engraved.**

RA10	PT6	1c ol grn	15	10
RA11	PT6	2c dp grn	20	10
RA12	PT6	20c bis brn ('24)	75	20
RA13	PT6	2s violet	3.00	3.00
RA14	PT6	5s blue	5.00	5.00
		Nos. RA10-RA14 (5)	9.10	8.40

Revenue Stamps of 1917-18 Surcharged Vertically in Red reading up or down **Casa de Correos VEINTE CTS. 1921—1922**

1921-22

RA15	PT5	20c on 1c dk bl	20.00	3.00
RA16	PT5	20c on 2c grn	20.00	3.00

No. RA12 Surcharged in Green **DOS CENTAVOS — 2 —**

1924

RA17	PT6	2c on 20c bis brn	20	10
a.		Invtd. surch.	2.00	2.00
b.		Dbl. surch.	3.00	3.00

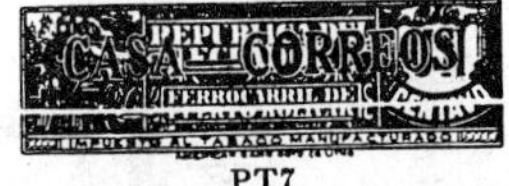

PT7

1924 *Rouletted 7*

RA18	PT7	1c rose red	25	15
a.		Inverted overprint	1.50	

Similar Design, Eagle at left

Perf. 12

RA19	PT7	2c blue	30	12
a.		Inverted overprint	1.50	1.00

PT8

Inscribed "Timbre Fiscal".

1924

RA20	PT8	1c yellow	1.00	75
RA21	PT8	2c dk bl	40	20

Inscribed "Region Oriental".

RA22	PT8	1c yellow	35	15
RA23	PT8	2c dk bl	35	30

Overprint on No. RA22 reads down or up.

Revenue Stamp Overprinted in Blue **CASA de Correos y Telegrafos de Guayaguil**

1934

RA24	2c green	15	10
a.	Blue overprint inverted	2.00	1.50
b.	Blue overprint double, one inverted	2.50	1.50

Postage Stamp of 1930 Overprinted in Red

Perf. 12½.

RA25 A119 20c ultra & yel 25 20

Telegraph Stamp Overprinted in Red, like No. RA24, and Surcharged diagonally in Black

1934 *Perf. 14*

RA26 2c on 10c ol brn 20 15
 a. Double surcharge 2.00

Overprint Blue, Surcharge Red.

RA27 2c on 10c ol brn 25 15

PT9

PT10

1934–36 *Perf. 12.*

RA28 PT9 2c green 15 10
 a. Both overprints in red ('36) 15 10

Postal Tax stamp of 1920–24, overprinted in red "POSTAL" has been again overprinted "CASA de Correos y Teleg. de Guayaquil" in black.

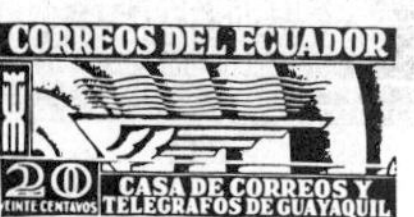

Symbols of Post and Telegraph Service
PT11

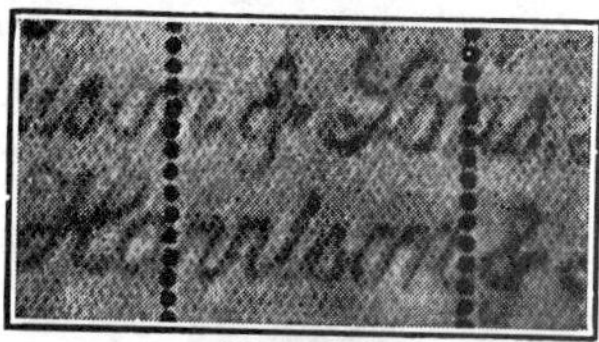
Wmk. 233

Photogravure.
Wmkd.
"Harrison & Sons, London" in Script Letters. (233)

1934 *Perf. 14½x14.*

RA29 PT10 2c yel grn 15 10

Issued to pay a postal tax of 2c for the rebuilding of the General Post Office at Guayaquil.

1935

RA30 PT11 20c claret 15 10

Issued to pay a postal tax of 20c for the rebuilding of the General Post Office at Guayaquil.

No. RA29 Surcharged in Red and Overprinted in Black

3 ctvs,
Seguro Social del Campesino Quito, 16 de Otbre-1935

1935

RA31 PT10 3c on 2c yel grn 15 10
 a. Double surcharge

Issued for the Social and Rural Workers' Insurance Fund.

Tobacco Stamp Surcharged in Black

Seguro Social 3
del Campesino ctvs

1936 *Rouletted 7.* **Unwmkd.**

RA32 PT7 3c on 1c rose red 15 10
 a. Lines of words reversed 18 12
 b. Imperf. vertically (pair)

Issued for the Social and Rural Workers' Insurance Fund.

No. 310 Overprinted in Black

Casa de Correos y Telégrafos de Guayaquil

1936 *Perf. 12½*

RA33 A119 20c ultra & yel 15 8
 a. Double overprint

Tobacco Stamp Surcharged in Black

SEGURO SOCIAL 3
DEL CAMPESINO ctvs.

1936 *Rouletted 7*

RA34 PT7 3c on 1c rose red 15 10

Issued for the Social and Rural Workers' Insurance Fund.

PT12

PT13

Worker

1936 Engraved *Perf. 13½*

RA35 PT12 3c ultra 10 5

Issued for the Social and Rural Workers' Insurance Fund.

Surcharged in Black.

1936

RA36 PT13 5c on 3c ultra 15 12

This combines the 2c for the rebuilding of the post office with the 3c for the Social and Rural Workers' Insurance Fund.

National Defense Issue.

Tobacco Stamp, Surcharged in Black.

TIMBRE PATRIOTICO
DIEZ CENTAVOS

1936 *Rouletted 7.*

RA37 PT7 10c on 1c rose 20 12
 a. Double surch.

Symbolical of Defense
PT14

1937–42 *Perf. 13½*

RA38 PT14 10c dp bl 20 10

A 1s violet and 2s green exist in type PT14.

PT15

Overprinted or Surcharged in Black.

1937–42 Engr. & Typo. *Perf. 13½*

RA39 PT15 5c lt brn & red 20 10
 d. Invert. ovpt. 3.50

Perf. 12, 11½.

RA39A PT15 20c on 5c rose pink & red ('42) 7.50
RA39B PT15 20c on 1s yel brn & red ('42) 7.50
RA39C PT15 20c on 2s grn & red ('42) 7.50

A 50c dark blue and red exists in type PT15.

5 5

No. RA38 Surcharged in Red

POSTAL ADICIONAL

1937 Engraved *Perf. 12½*

RA40 PT14 5c on 10c dp bl 25 12

Map of Ecuador
PT16

1938 *Perf. 14x13½.*

RA41 PT16 5c car rose 18 10

Issued for the Social and Rural Workers' Insurance Fund.

No. C42 Surcharged in Red

20 20
CASA DE CORREOS Y TELEGRAFOS DE GUAYAQUIL
20 20

1938 *Perf. 12½.*

RA42 AP5 20c on 70c blk 30 10

No. 307 Surcharged in Red

CAMPAÑA CONTRA EL CANCER

5 5

1938

RA43 A116 5c on 6c yel & red 15 6

This stamp was obligatory on all mail from Nov. 23rd to 30th, 1938. The tax was for the International Union for the Control of Cancer.

Tobacco Stamp, Surcharged in Black

POSTAL ADICIONAL
CINCO CENTAVOS

1939 *Rouletted.*

RA44 PT7 5c on 1c rose 12 10
 a. Double surcharge
 b. Triple surcharge

Tobacco Stamp, Surcharged in Blue

CASAS DE CORREOS Y TELEGRAFOS CINCO CENTAVOS

1940

RA45 PT7 5c on 1c rose red 15 10
 a. Double surcharge 1.00 1.00

No. 370 Surcharged in Carmine

CASA DE CORREOS y TELEGRAFOS DE GUAYAQUIL

20 20

1940 *Perf. 11½.*

RA46 A144 20c on 50c blk & multi 15 12
 a. Double surcharge, one inverted

Tobacco Stamp, Surcharged in Black

TIMBRE PATRIOTICO
VEINTE CENTAVOS

1940 *Rouletted*

RA47 PT7 20c on 1c rose red 15 7

Farmer Plowing
PT17

Communication Symbols
PT18

1940 *Perf. 13x13½.*

RA48 PT17 5c car rose 25 10

1940-43 *Perf. 12.*

RA49 PT18 5c cop brn 15 10
RA49A PT18 5c grn ('43) 15 10

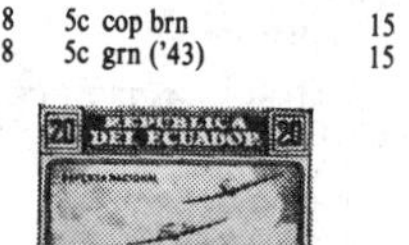

Pursuit Planes
PT19

1941 *Perf. 11½x13*

RA50 PT19 20c ultra 25 6

The tax was used for national defense.

Warrior Shielding Women
PT20

1942–46 Engraved *Perf. 12*

RA51 PT20 20c dk bl 25 10
RA51A PT20 40c blk brn ('46) 25 10

The tax was used for national defense.

A 20c carmine, 20c brown and 30c gray exist lithographed in type PT20.

No. 370 Surcharged in Carmine

CASA DE CORREOS y TELEGRAFOS DE GUAYAQUIL

VEINTE CENTAVOS

1942 *Perf. 11½*

RA52 A144 20c on 50c blk & multi 25 15
 a. Double surch. 2.50

No. RA35 Surcharged in Red

ADICIONAL
CINCO
CENTAVOS

1943 ***Perf. 13½.***

RA53 PT12	5c on 3c ultra	10	4

No. RA53 with Additional Surcharge in Black

5 Centavos
CASA DE
CORREOS
DE GQUIL.
y

1943

RA54 PT12	5c on 5c on 3c ultra	10	4

Peons
PT21

1943 ***Perf. 12***

RA55 PT21	5c blue	20	10

The tax was for farm workers.

Revenue Stamp (as No. RA64) Overprinted in Black

TIMBRE
PATRIOTICO

1943 ***Perf. 12½***

RA56	20c red org	6.00	35

Revenue Stamp (as No. RA64) Surcharged in Black

TIMBRE PATRIOTICO
VEINTE CENTAVOS

1943 ***Perf. 12***

RA57	20c on 10c org	55	10
a.	Double surch.		

Coat of Arms
PT22

1943 ***Perf. 12½***

RA58 PT22	20c org red	12	10

The tax was for national defense.

No. RA58 Surcharged in Black

30
Centavos

1944

RA59 PT22	30c on 20c org red	15	10
a.	Double surcharge		

Consular Service Stamps Surcharged in Black

TIMBRE
ESCOLAR
20 ctvs. 20

1951 ***Perf. 12.*** **Unwmkd.**

RA60 R1	20c on 1s red	15	8
RA61 R1	20c on 2s brn	15	8
RA62 R1	20c on 5s vio	15	8

Teacher and Pupils in Schoolyard
PT23

PT24

1952 **Engraved.** ***Perf. 13***

RA63 PT23	20c bl grn	15	8

Revenue Stamp Overprinted "PATRIOTICO / SANITARIO"

1952 ***Perf. 12***

RA64 PT24	40(c) ol grn	20	10

Woman Holding Flag
PT25

PT26

1953 ***Perf. 12½.***

RA65 PT25	40c ultra	30	10

Telegraph Stamp Surcharged "ESCOLAR 20 Centavos" in Black

1954 ***Perf. 13.*** **Unwmkd.**

RA66 PT26	20c on 30c red brn	30	12

Revenue Stamps Surcharged or Overprinted Horizontally in Black "PRO TURISMO 1954"

1954 ***Perf. 12*** **Unwmkd.**

RA67 R2	10c on 25c bl	25	10
RA68 R3	10c on 50c org red	25	10
RA69 R3	10c carmine	25	10

PT27

Telegraph Stamp Surcharged "Pro-Turismo 1954 10 ctvs. 10" in Black

1954 ***Perf. 13***

RA70 PT27	10c on 30c red brn	35	12

Revenue Stamp Overprinted in Black

ESCOLAR

1954 ***Perf. 12***

RA71 R3	20c ol blk	35	12

Consular Service Stamp Surcharged in Black

0,20 0,20
ESCOLAR
Veinte centavos

1954

RA72 R1	20c on 10s gray	35	12

Young Student at Desk
PT28

Globe, Ship and Plane
PT29

Imprint:
"Heraclio Fournier.—Vitoria"

1954 **Photo.** ***Perf. 11***

RA73 PT28	20c rose pink	35	12

See also No. RA76.

1954 **Engraved** ***Perf. 12***

RA74 PT29	10c dp mag	35	12

Soldier Kissing Flag
PT30

1955 **Photogravure.** ***Perf. 11***

RA75 PT30	40c blue	35	12

See also No. RA77.

Types of 1954-55 Redrawn.
Imprint:
"Thomas de la Rue & Co. Ltd."

1957 ***Perf. 13*** **Unwmkd.**

RA76 PT28	20c rose pink	15	8
	Perf. 14x14½		
RA77 PT30	40c blue	40	20

No. RA77 is inscribed "Republica del Ecuador."

AIR POST POSTAL TAX STAMPS.

No. 438 Surcharged in Black or Carmine

FOMENTO-AERO-
COMUNICACIONES
20 Ctvs.

1945 ***Perf. 11.*** **Unwmkd.**

RAC1 A173	20c on 10c dk grn	35	15
a.	Pair, one without surch.	45.00	
RAC2 A173	20c on 10c dk grn (C)	35	15

Obligatory on letters and parcel post carried on planes in the domestic service.

Liberty, Mercury and Planes
PTAP1

1946 **Engraved.** ***Perf. 12.***

RAC3 PTAP1	20c org brn	25	15

Galapagos Islands
(Columbus Archipelago)

Issued for use in the Galapagos Islands, a province of Ecuador, but were commonly used throughout the country.

Sea Lions
A1

Map
A2

Design: 1s, Marine iguana.

Photogravure.

1957, July 15 ***Perf. 12*** **Unwmkd.**

L1	A1	20c dk brn	30	15
L2	A2	50c violet	20	15
L3	A1	1s dl ol grn	80	40

Issued to commemorate the 125th anniversary of Ecuador's possession of the Galapagos Islands, and to publicize the islands.

AIR POST STAMPS

Type of Regular Issue, 1957.

Designs: 1s, Santa Cruz Island. 1.80s, Map of Galapagos archipelago. 4.20s, Galapagos giant tortoise.

Photogravure.

1957, July 19 ***Perf. 12*** **Unwmkd.**

LC1	A1	1s dp bl	25	15
LC2	A1	1.80s rose vio	50	25
LC3	A1	4.20s black	1.25	60

Issued to commemorate the 125th anniversary of Ecuador's possession of the Galapagos Islands and to publicize the islands.

Redrawn Type of Ecuador, 1956

1959, Jan. 3 **Engraved.** ***Perf. 14***

LC4 AP69	2s lt ol grn	75	50

Issued to honor the United Nations.
See note after No. C407.

EGYPT

(ē'jĭpt)

LOCATION—In northern Africa, bordering on the Mediterranean and the Red Sea.

GOVT.—Republic.

AREA—386,198 sq. mi.

POP.—38,740,000 (est. 1977).

CAPITAL—Cairo.

Modern Egypt was a part of Turkey until 1914 when a British Protectorate was declared over the country and the Khedive was deposed in favor of Hussein Kamil under the title of Sultan. In 1922 the protectorate ended and the reigning sultan was declared king of the new monarchy. Egypt became a republic on June 18, 1953. Egypt merged with Syria in 1958 to form the United Arab Republic. Syria left this union in 1961. In 1971 Egypt took the name of Arab Republic of Egypt.

40 Paras = 1 Piastre
1000 Milliemes = 100 Piastres = 1 Pound (1888)
1000 Milliemes = 1 Pound

Turkish Suzerainty

Turkish Inscriptions
A1

A2 A3

A4 A5

A6 A7

Wmk. 118

Surcharged in Black

Wmkd. Pyramid and Star. (118)

Perf. 12½

1866, Jan. 1 Lithographed

No.	Type	Description	Unused	Used
1	A1	5pa sl grn	25.00	25.00
a.		Imperf. pair	275.00	
b.		Pair, imperf. btwn.	350.00	
c.		Perf. 12½x13	50.00	50.00
d.		Perf. 13	350.00	450.00
2	A2	10pa brown	45.00	30.00
a.		Imperf. pair	250.00	
b.		Pair, imperf. btwn.	250.00	
c.		Perf. 13	250.00	
d.		Perf. 12½x15	325.00	350.00
3	A3	20pa blue	70.00	35.00
a.		Imperf. pair	350.00	
b.		Pair, imperf. btwn.		
c.		Perf. 12½x13	125.00	125.00
d.		Perf. 13	600.00	350.00
4	A4	2pi yellow	80.00	40.00
a.		Imperf.	125.00	75.00
b.		Imperf. vert or horiz. pair	350.00	350.00
c.		Perf. 12½x15	150.00	
d.		Diagonal half used as 1 pi on cover		1,500.
e.		Perf. 12½x13, 13x12½	120.00	50.00
5	A5	5pi rose	250.00	200.00
a.		Imperf.	300.00	300.00
b.		Imperf. vert. or horiz. pair	1,000.	
d.		Inscription of 10 pi, imperf.	500.00	
e.		Perf. 12½x13, 13x12½	300.00	300.00
f.		As "d" perf. 12½x15	600.00	600.00
6	A6	10pi sl bl	275.00	250.00
a.		Imperf.	275.00	275.00
b.		Pair, imperf. btwn.	2,000.	
c.		Perf. 12½x13, 13x12½	500.00	500.00
d.		Perf. 13	2,000.	

Unwmkd.

Typographed

No.	Type	Description	Unused	Used
7	A7	1pi rose lil	50.00	5.00
a.		Imperf.	100.00	
b.		Pair, imperf. vert.	275.00	
c.		Perf. 12½x13, 13x12½	100.00	35.00
d.		Perf. 13	350.00	200.00

Single imperforates of types A1–A10 are sometimes simulated by trimming wide-margined copies of perforated stamps.

Proofs of Nos. 1–7 are on smooth white paper, unwatermarked and imperforate. Proofs of No. 7 are on thinner paper than No. 7a.

Sphinx and Pyramid
A8

Wmk. 119

Wmkd. Crescent and Star. (119)

1867 Litho. *Perf. 15x12½*

No.	Type	Description	Unused	Used
8	A8	5pa orange	12.00	10.00
a.		Imperf.	50.00	50.00
b.		Imperf. vert. or horiz. pair	200.00	
9	A8	10pa lilac	35.00	10.00
a.		10pa vio	30.00	10.00
b.		Half used as 5pa on newspaper piece		600.00
11	A8	20pa bl grn	35.00	15.00
a.		20pa yel grn	40.00	15.00
13	A8	1pi rose red	5.00	1.25
a.		Imperf.	60.00	
b.		Pair, imperf. btwn.	200.00	
c.		Half used as 20pa on cover		700.00
d.		Rouletted	50.00	
14	A8	2pi blue	70.00	12.00
a.		Imperf.	150.00	
b.		Imperf. vert., pair		
c.		Diagonal half used as 1pi on cover		
d.		Perf. 12½	300.00	
15	A8	5pi brown	250.00	150.00

There are four types of each value, so placed that any block of four contains all four types.

A9

A10

Typographed by the Government at Boulac

Clear Impressions.
Thick Opaque Paper.

Perf. 12½x13½, Clean-cut.

1872 Wmk. 119

No.	Type	Description	Unused	Used
19	A9	5pa brown	8.00	4.50
20	A9	10pa lilac	8.00	3.00
21	A9	20pa blue	25.00	3.50
22	A9	1pi rose red	25.00	60
h.		Half used as 20pa on cover		300.00
23	A9	2pi dl yel	50.00	5.00
24	A9	2½pi dl vio	45.00	5.00
25	A9	5pi green	200.00	30.00
j.		Tête bêche pair		

Perf. 13½, Clean-cut.

No.	Type	Description	Unused	Used
19a	A9	5pa brown	20.00	12.00
20a	A9	10pa dl lil	8.00	3.00
21a	A9	20pa blue	45.00	15.00
22a	A9	1pi rose red	50.00	2.75
23a	A9	2pi dl yel	20.00	3.50
24a	A9	2½pi dl vio	800.00	250.00
25a	A9	5pi green	300.00	75.00

Lithographed

No.	Type	Description	Unused	Used
21m	A9	20pa bl, perf. 12½x13½	120.00	40.00
21n	A9	20pa bl, perf. 13½	200.00	75.00
21p	A9	20pa bl, imperf.	200.00	
22m	A9	1pi rose red, perf. 12½x13½	250.00	3.00
22n	A9	1pi rose red, perf. 13½		5.00

Typographed

Blurred Impressions.
Thinner Paper.

Wmkd. Crescent and Star. (119)

1874-75 *Perf. 12½, Rough.*

No.	Type	Description	Unused	Used
26	A10	5pa brn ('75)	6.00	2.50
e.		Imperforate		40.00
f.		Imperforate horiz., pair	150.00	150.00
g.		Tête bêche pair	50.00	50.00
20b	A9	10pa gray lil	6.00	3.00
g.		Tête bêche pair	200.00	200.00
21b	A9	20pa gray bl	40.00	3.00
k.		Half used as 10pa on cover		400.00
22b	A9	1pi vermilion	4.00	85
f.		Imperforate	8.00	7.00
g.		Tête bêche pair	75.00	75.00
23b	A9	2pi yellow	30.00	4.00
j.		Tête bêche pair	500.00	500.00
24b	A9	2½pi dp vio	5.00	2.50
e.		Imperforate	22.50	22.50
f.		Tête bêche pair	400.00	400.00
25b	A9	5pi yel grn	35.00	10.00
e.		Imperforate	25.00	

No. 26f normally occurs tête-bêche.

Perf. 13½x12½, Rough.

No.	Type	Description	Unused	Used
26c	A10	5pa brown	4.00	2.50
j.		Tête bêche pair	35.00	35.00
20c	A9	10pa gray lil	6.00	2.50
j.		Tête bêche pair	200.00	200.00
21c	A9	20pa gray bl	4.00	2.75
h.		Pair, imperf. between	250.00	
22c	A9	1pi vermilion	11.00	1.00
j.		Tête bêche pair	300.00	300.00
23c	A9	2pi yellow	5.00	4.00
g.		Tête bêche pair	400.00	400.00
k.		Half used as 1pi on cover		850.00

Perf. 12½x13½, Rough.

No.	Type	Description	Unused	Used
23d	A9	2pi yel ('75)	16.50	5.00
h.		Tête bêche pair		
24d	A9	2½pi dp vio ('75)	15.00	9.00
j.		Tête bêche pair	700.00	700.00
25d	A9	5pi yel grn ('75)	250.00	150.00

Stamp of 1872-75 Surcharged in Black

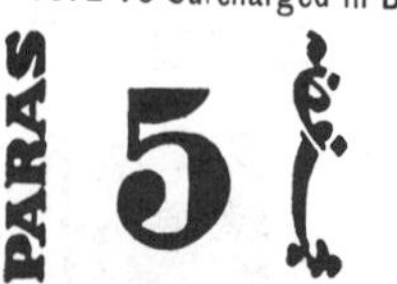

Perf. 12½, 12½x13½, Rough

1879, Jan. 1

No.	Type	Description	Unused	Used
27	A9	5pa on 2½pi dl vio	6.00	6.00
a.		Imperf.	35.00	35.00
b.		Tête bêche pair	2,000.	2,000.
c.		Inverted surcharge	60.00	60.00
d.		Perf. 12½x13½	6.00	6.50
e.		As "d," tête bêche pair		
f.		As "c," perf. 12½x13½	110.00	110.00
28	A9	10pa on 2½pi dl vio	6.00	6.00
a.		Imperf.		
b.		Tête bêche pair	1,250.	1,250.
c.		Inverted surcharge	70.00	70.00
d.		Perf. 12½x13½	10.00	10.00
e.		As "c," perf. 12½x13½	90.00	90.00

A11

A12

A13

A14

A15

A16

1879-93 Typo. *Perf. 14x13½*

No.	Type	Description	Unused	Used
29	A11	5pa brown	25	15
30	A12	10pa violet	25.00	3.00
31	A12	10pa lil rose ('81)	40.00	4.00
32	A12	10pa gray ('82)	10.00	75
33	A12	10pa grn ('84)	20	12
34	A13	20pa ultra	55.00	1.25
35	A13	20pa rose ('84)	7.50	40
36	A14	1pi rose	15.00	25
37	A14	1pi ultra ('84)	2.00	10
38	A15	2pi org yel	13.50	35
39	A15	2pi org brn	10.00	35
40	A16	5pi green	75.00	5.50
41	A16	5pi gray ('84)	9.00	40
		Nos. 29-41 (13)	262.45	16.62

Imperf. examples of Nos. 29–31, 35–38 and 40 are proofs.

A17

1884, Feb. 1

No.	Type	Description	Unused	Used
42	A17	20pa on 5pi grn	10.00	1.00
a.		Inverted surcharge	40.00	35.00

A18

A19

A20

1888

No.	Type	Description	Unused	Used
43	A18	1m brown	25	5
44	A19	2m green	50	6
45	A20	5m car rose	1.00	5

Imperf. examples of Nos. 43–45 are proofs.

A21

A22

1889-93

46	A21	3m mar ('92)	2.50	80
47	A21	3m org ('93)	1.25	15
48	A22	10pi purple	21.00	50

Nos. 37, 39, 41, 43 to 45, 47 and 48 exist on both ordinary and chalky paper.

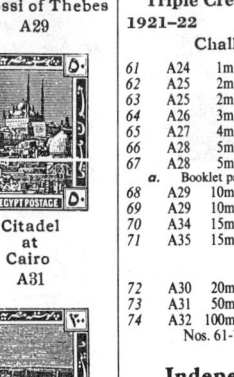

A23

1906 Chalk-surfaced Paper.

49	A23	4m brn red	1.50	60

Boats on Nile A24 — Cleopatra A25

Ras-el-Tin Palace A26 — Giza Pyramids A27

Sphinx A28 — Colossi of Thebes A29

Pylon of Karnak and Temple of Khonsu A30 — Citadel at Cairo A31

Rock Temple of Abu Simbel A32 — Aswan Dam A33

Perf. 13½x14

1914, Jan. 8 Wmk. 119

Chalk-surfaced Paper

50	A24	1m ol brn	12	8
51	A25	2m dp grn	30	12
52	A26	3m orange	50	15
53	A27	4m red	1.00	50
54	A28	5m lake	60	4
a.		Bklt. pane of 6		
55	A29	10m dk bl	1.25	8
		Perf. 14		
56	A30	20m ol grn	3.00	15
57	A31	50m red vio	5.00	50
58	A32	100m black	10.00	50
59	A33	200m plum	25.00	85
		Nos. 50-59 (10)	46.77	2.97

All values of this issue exist imperforate on both watermarked and unwatermarked paper but are not known to have been issued in that condition.

See also Nos. 61-72.

British Protectorate

No. 52 Surcharged

2 Milliemes ملليمان

1915, Oct. 15

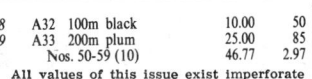

60	A26	2m on 3m org	60	50
a.		Inverted surcharge	150.00	150.00

Scenic Types of 1914 and

Statue of Ramses II

A34 — A35

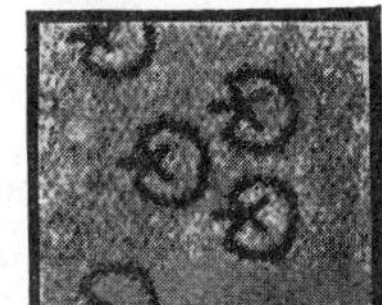

Wmk. 120

Wmkd. Triple Crescent and Star. (120)

1921-22 *Perf. 13½x14*

Chalk-surfaced Paper

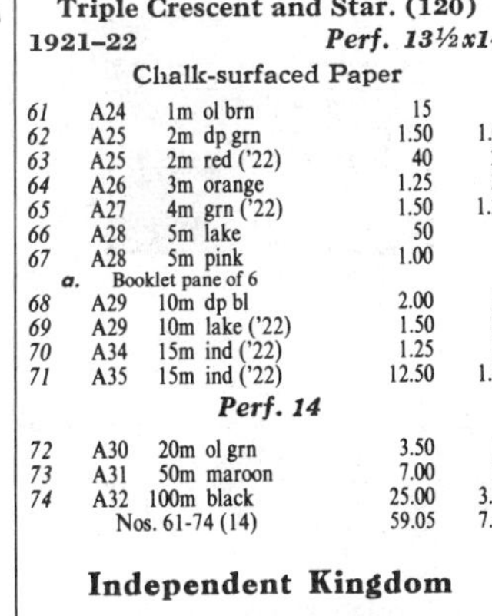

61	A24	1m ol brn	15	7
62	A25	2m dp grn	1.50	1.00
63	A25	2m red ('22)	40	20
64	A26	3m orange	1.25	35
65	A27	4m grn ('22)	1.50	1.25
66	A28	5m lake	50	6
67	A28	5m pink	1.00	6
a.		Booklet pane of 6		
68	A29	10m dp bl	2.00	10
69	A29	10m lake ('22)	1.50	25
70	A34	15m ind ('22)	1.25	15
71	A35	15m ind ('22)	12.50	1.00
		Perf. 14		
72	A30	20m ol grn	3.50	15
73	A31	50m maroon	7.00	30
74	A32	100m black	25.00	3.00
		Nos. 61-74 (14)	59.05	7.94

Independent Kingdom

Stamps of 1921-22 Overprinted

المملكة المصرية ١٥ مارس ١٩٢٢

1922, Oct. 10

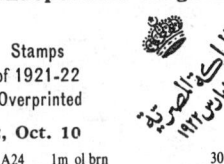

78	A24	1m ol brn	30	15
a.		Inverted overprint	60.00	60.00
b.		Double overprint	75.00	75.00
79	A25	2m red	50	10
a.		Double overprint	50.00	50.00
80	A26	3m orange	1.00	50
81	A27	4m green	75	50
a.		Double ovpt.	100.00	
b.		Inverted ovpt.		
82	A28	5m pink	60	5
83	A29	10m lake	1.00	6
84	A34	15m indigo	2.50	10
85	A35	15m indigo	1.25	25
		Perf. 14		
86	A30	20m ol grn	2.25	20
a.		Inverted overprint	150.00	150.00
b.		Double overprint	125.00	125.00
87	A31	50m maroon	3.00	20
a.		Inverted overprint	400.00	400.00
b.		Double overprint		
88	A32	100m black	10.00	60
a.		Inverted overprint	225.00	225.00
b.		Double overprint	225.00	225.00
		Nos. 78-88 (11)	23.15	2.71

Same Overprint on Nos. 58-59

Wmkd. Crescent and Star (119)

90	A32	100m black	67.50	40.00
91	A33	200m plum	10.00	60
a.		Inverted overprint		350.00

Nos. 78-91 were issued to commemorate the proclamation of the Egyptian monarchy.

The overprint signifies "The Egyptian Kingdom, March 15, 1922". It exists in four types, one lithographed and three typographed on Nos 78-87, but lithographed only on Nos. 88-91.

King Fuad

A36 — A37

Wmkd. Triple Crescent and Star. (120)

Size 18x22½ mm.

1923-24 Photo. *Perf. 13½*

92	A36	1m orange	10	6
93	A36	2m black	15	6
94	A36	3m brown	50	18
a.		Imperf., pair	225.00	
95	A36	4m yel grn	50	15
96	A36	5m org brn	15	4
a.		Imperf., pair	30.00	
97	A36	10m rose	35	5
98	A36	15m ultra	50	5
a.		Imperf., pair	225.00	
		Perf. 14		
		Size 22x28 mm.		
99	A36	20m dk grn	1.25	10
100	A36	50m myr grn	4.00	10
101	A36	100m red vio	7.50	25
102	A36	200m vio ('24)	14.00	1.00
a.		Imperf., pair	375.00	
103	A37	£1 ultra & dk vio ('24)	100.00	10.00
a.		Imperf., pair	900.00	
		Nos. 92-103 (12)	129.00	12.04

Thoth Carving Name of King Fuad

A38

1925, Apr. Litho. *Perf. 11*

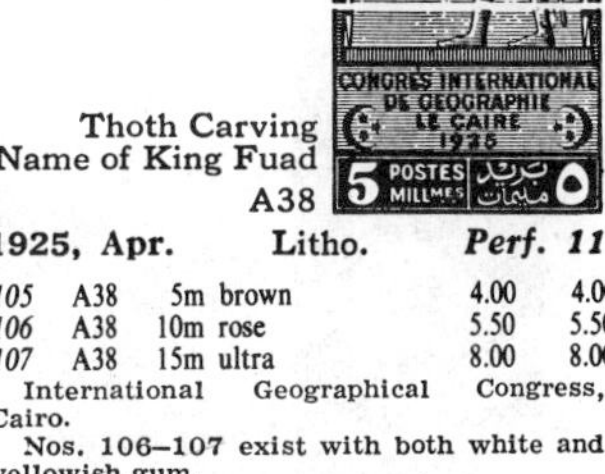

105	A38	5m brown	4.00	4.00
106	A38	10m rose	5.50	5.50
107	A38	15m ultra	8.00	8.00

International Geographical Congress, Cairo.

Nos. 106-107 exist with both white and yellowish gum.

Oxen Plowing

A39

Wmk. 195

Wmkd. Multiple Crown and Arabic F. (195)

1926 *Perf. 13x13½*

108	A39	5m lt brn	1.00	70
109	A39	10m brt rose	1.00	70
110	A39	15m dp bl	1.00	70
111	A39	50m Prus grn	5.00	4.00
112	A39	100m brn vio	11.00	7.00
113	A39	200m brt vio	15.00	12.00
		Nos. 108-113 (6)	34.00	25.10

Issued to commemorate the 12th Agricultural and Industrial Exhibition at Gezira. "F" in watermark stands for Fuad.

King Fuad

A40

Perf. 14x14½

1926, Apr. 2 Photo. Wmk. 120

114	A40	50pi brn vio & red vio	70.00	13.00

58th birthday of King Fuad.

Nos. 111-113 Surcharged

5 MILLIEMES

Perf. 13x13½

1926, Aug. 24 Wmk. 195

115	A39	5m on 50m Prus grn	1.50	1.25
116	A39	10m on 100m brn vio	1.50	1.25
117	A39	15m on 200m brt vio	1.50	1.25
a.		Dbl. surcharge	150.00	

Ship of Hatshepsut—A41

1926, Dec. 9 Litho. *Perf. 13x13½*

118	A41	5m brn & blk	2.00	1.00
119	A41	10m dp red & blk	2.50	1.25
120	A41	15m dp bl & blk	2.50	1.25

International Navigation Congress, Cairo.

Nos. 118–120, 114 Overprinted

PORT FOUAD
a

PORT FOUAD
b

1926, Dec. 21

121	A41 (a)	5m brn & blk	90.00	70.00
122	A41 (a)	10m dp red & blk	90.00	70.00
123	A41 (a)	15m dp bl & blk	90.00	70.00

***Perf. 14x14½* Wmk. 120**

124	A40 (b)	50pi brn vio & red vio	1,200.	1,000.

Inauguration of Port Fuad opposite Port Said.

Nos. 121–123 have a block over "Le Caire" at lower left.

Forgeries of Nos. 121–124 exist.

Branch of Cotton
A42

Perf. 13x13½

1927, Jan. 25 Wmk. 195

125	A42	5m dk brn & sl grn	1.00	1.00
126	A42	10m dp red & sl grn	2.50	1.50
127	A42	15m dp bl & sl grn	2.50	1.50

International Cotton Congress, Cairo.

King Fuad
A43 A44

A45

A46

Photogravure.

1927–37 *Perf. 13x13½* Wmk. 195

128	A43	1m orange	10	4
129	A43	2m black	15	4
130	A43	3m ol brn	15	8
131	A43	3m dp grn ('30)	25	6
132	A43	4m yel grn	45	15
133	A43	4m brn ('30)	50	20
134	A43	4m dp grn ('34)	75	18
135	A43	5m dk red brn ('29)	25	3
a.		Booklet pane of 6		
b.		5m chnt	30	3
136	A43	10m dk red ('29)	60	3
a.		10m org red	90	6
b.		Booklet pane of 6		
137	A43	10m pur ('34)	1.30	8
138	A43	13m car rose ('32)	50	12
139	A43	15m ultra	1.00	4
a.		Booklet pane of 6		
140	A43	15m dk vio ('34)	2.00	5
141	A43	20m ultra ('34)	3.50	8

Early printings of Nos. 128, 129, 130, 132, 135, 136 and 139 were from plates with screen of vertical dots in the vignette; later printings show screen of diagonal dots.

Perf. 13½x14

142	A44	20m ol grn	1.00	5
143	A44	20m ultra ('32)	2.25	6
144	A44	40m ol brn ('32)	1.25	6
145	A44	50m Prus grn	1.00	3
a.		50m grnsh bl	1.50	3
146	A4	100m brn vio	4.00	6
a.		100m cl	4.00	8
147	A44	200m dp vio	5.00	25

Printings of Nos. 142, 145 and 146, made in 1929 and later, were from new plates with stronger mpressions and darker colors.

Lithographed; Center Photogravure.
Perf. 13x13½

148	A45	500m choc & Prus bl ('32)	40.00	5.00
a.		Entirely photogravure	50.00	8.00
149	A46	£1 dk grn & org brn ('37)	50.00	5.00
a.		Entirely photogravure	50.00	5.00
		Nos. 128-149 (22)	116.00	11.69

Statue of Amenhotep, Son of Hapu
A47

1927, Dec. 29 Photo. *Perf. 13½x13*

150	A47	5m org brn	45	40
151	A47	10m cop red	85	55
152	A47	15m dp bl	1.00	65

Statistical Congress, Cairo.

Imhotep
A48

Mohammed Ali Pasha
A49

1928, Dec. 15

153	A48	5m org brn	75	35
154	A49	10m cop red	75	35

Issued to commemorate the International Congress of Medicine at Cairo and the centenary of the Faculty of Medicine at Cairo.

Prince Farouk
A50

1929, Feb. 11 Lithographed

155	A50	5m choc & gray	1.00	1.00
156	A50	10m dl red & gray	2.00	1.00
157	A50	15m ultra & gray	2.00	1.00
158	A50	20m Prus bl & gray	2.00	1.00

Ninth birthday of Prince Farouk.

1929

155a	A50	5m choc & blk	100.00	100.00
156a	A50	10m dl red & brn	100.00	100.00
157a	A50	15m ultra & brn	100.00	100.00
158a	A50	20m Prus bl & brn	100.00	100.00

Nos. 155a to 158a are trial color proofs. They were sent to the Universal Postal Union, but were never placed on sale to the public, although some are known used.

Tomb Fresco at El-Bersheh
A51

1931, Feb. 15 *Perf. 13x13½*

163	A51	5m brown	70	60
164	A51	10m cop red	1.50	60
165	A51	15m dk bl	2.00	75

Issued to commemorate the 14th Agricultural and Industrial Exhibition, Cairo.

Nos. 114 and 103 Surcharged with Bars and

MILLS 50 ملیما ٥٠
a

MILLS 100 ملیم ١٠٠
b

1932 *Perf. 14x14½* Wmk. 120

166	A40	50m on 50pi brn vio & red vio	5.00	1.25

Perf. 14

167	A37	100m on £1 ultra & dk vio	125.00	100.00

Locomotive of 1852
A52

Designs (Locomotives): 13m, Of 1859. 15m, Of 1862. 20m, Of 1932.

Perf. 13x13½

1933, Jan. 19 Litho. Wmk. 195

168	A52	5m brn & blk	2.50	1.50
169	A52	13m dl red & blk	10.00	7.50
170	A52	15m pur & blk	10.00	7.50
171	A52	2m dp bl & blk	10.00	7.50

International Railroad Congress, Heliopolis.

Commercial Passenger Airplane
A56

Dornier Do-X—A57

Graf Zeppelin
A58

1933, Dec. 20 Photogravure

172	A56	5m brown	3.25	1.50
173	A56	10m brt vio	8.00	6.00
174	A57	13m brn car	10.00	6.00
175	A57	15m violet	8.00	6.00
176	A58	20m blue	15.00	12.50
		Nos. 172-176 (5)	44.25	32.00

International Aviation Congress, Cairo.

Khedive Ismail Pasha
A59 A60

1934, Feb. 1 *Perf. 13½*

177	A59	1m dp org	15	15
178	A59	2m black	20	15
179	A59	3m brown	20	20
180	A59	4m bl grn	30	30
181	A59	5m red brn	30	15
182	A59	10m violet	60	25
183	A59	13m cop red	90	60
184	A59	15m dl vio	70	25
185	A59	20m ultra	1.00	40
186	A59	50m Prus bl	3.00	40
187	A59	100m ol grn	6.50	60
188	A59	200m dp vio	20.00	3.00

Perf. 13½x13

189	A60	50pi brown	90.00	42.50
190	A60	£1 Prus bl	160.00	65.00
		Nos. 177-190 (14)	283.85	113.95

10th Congress of Universal Postal Union, Cairo.

King Fuad
A61

1936-37 *Perf. 13½*

191	A61	1m dl org	12	4
192	A61	2m black	25	4
193	A61	4m dk grn	30	10
194	A61	5m chestnut	25	3
a.		Booklet pane of 6		
195	A61	10m pur ('37)	1.00	10
196	A61	15m brn vio	1.50	8
197	A61	20m sapphire	2.00	10
		Nos. 191-197 (7)	5.42	49

Entrance to Agricultural Building
A62

Agricultural Building
A63

Design: 15m, 20m, Industrial Building.

1936, Feb. 15 *Perf. 13½x13*

198	A62	5m brown	55	50

Perf. 13x13½

199	A63	10m violet	80	75
200	A63	13m cop red	1.50	1.00
201	A63	15m dk vio	1.00	75
202	A63	20m blue	2.00	2.00
		Nos. 198-202 (5)	5.85	5.00

Issued to commemorate the 15th Agricultural and Industrial Exhibition, Cairo.

Signing of Treaty—A65

1936, Dec. 22 *Perf. 11*

203	A65	5m brown	50	40
204	A65	15m dk vio	75	50
205	A65	20m sapphire	1.50	70

Signing of Anglo-Egyptian Treaty, Aug. 26, 1936.

King Farouk
A66

Medal for Montreux Conference
A67

1937-44 *Perf. 13x13½* **Wmk. 195**

206	A66	1m brn org	4	3
207	A66	2m vermilion	5	4
208	A66	3m brown	5	3
209	A66	4m green	10	5
210	A66	5m red brn	10	3
a.		Booklet pane of 6	75	
211	A66	6m lt yel grn ('40)	20	3
a.		Booklet pane of 6	1.00	
212	A66	10m purple	20	3
a.		Booklet pane of 6	3.00	
213	A66	13m rose car	20	12
214	A66	15m dk vio brn	25	3
a.		Booklet pane of 6	3.00	
215	A66	20m blue	30	3
216	A66	20m lil gray ('44)	35	6
		Nos. 206-216 (11)	1.84	48

1937, Oct. 15 *Perf. 13½x13*

217	A67	5m red brn	35	30
218	A67	15m dk vio	65	50
219	A67	20m sapphire	75	60

Issued in commemoration of the International Treaty signed at Montreux, Switzerland, under which foreign privileges in Egypt were to end in 1949.

Eye of Ré
A68

1937, Dec. 8 *Perf. 13x13½*

220	A68	5m brown	60	55
221	A68	15m dk vio	1.00	60
222	A68	20m sapphire	1.40	60

15th Ophthalmological Congress, Cairo, December, 1937.

King Farouk, Queen Farida—A69

1938, Jan. 20 *Perf. 11*

223	A69	5m red brn	3.50	2.50

Royal wedding of King Farouk and Farida Zulficar.

Inscribed: "11 Fevrier 1938"

1938, Feb. 11

224	A69	£1 grn & sep	100.00	100.00

King Farouk's 18th birthday.

Cotton Picker
A70

1938, Jan. 26 *Perf. 13½x13*

225	A70	5m red brn	65	60
226	A70	15m dk vio	2.00	1.25
227	A70	20m sapphire	1.50	1.00

Issued to commemorate the 18th International Cotton Congress at Cairo.

Pyramids of Giza and Colossus of Thebes—A71

1938, Feb. 1 *Perf. 13x13½*

228	A71	5m red brn	80	75
229	A71	15m dk vio	1.50	1.00
230	A71	20m sapphire	2.00	1.00

International Telecommunication Conference, Cairo.

Branch of Hydnocarpus—A72

1938, Mar. 21 *Perf. 13x13½*

231	A72	5m red brn	85	50
232	A72	15m dk vio	1.50	70
233	A72	20m sapphire	1.50	70

International Leprosy Congress, Cairo.

King Farouk and Pyramids
A73

King Farouk
A74 A75

Backgrounds: 40m, Hussan Mosque. 50m, Cairo Citadel. 100m, Aswan Dam. 200m, Cairo University.

1939-46 **Photo.** *Perf. 14x13½*

234	A73	30m gray	35	3
a.		30m sl gray	30	3
234B	A73	30m ol grn ('46)	35	4
235	A73	40m dk brn	50	3
236	A73	50m Prus grn	55	3
237	A73	100m brn vio	80	4
238	A73	200m dk vio	2.00	8

Perf. 13½x13

239	A74	50pi grn & sep	4.50	50
240	A75	£1 dp bl & dk brn	9.00	70
		Nos. 234-240 (8)	18.05	1.45

For £1 with A77 portrait, see No. 269D. See Nos. 267-269D.

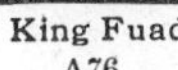

King Fuad
A76

King Farouk
A77

1944, Apr. 28 *Perf. 13½x13*

241	A76	10m dk vio	20	20

Issued to commemorate the eighth anniversary of the death of King Fuad.

1944-50 *Perf. 13x13½* **Wmk. 195**

242	A77	1m yel brn ('45)	6	3
243	A77	2m red org ('45)	6	3
244	A77	3m sep ('46)	20	15
245	A77	4m dp grn ('45)	25	20
a.		Booklet pane of 6		
246	A77	5m red brn ('46)	10	3
247	A77	10m dp vio	18	3
b.		Booklet pane of 6		
247A	A77	13m rose red ('50)	60	25
248	A77	15m dk vio ('45)	20	3
249	A77	17m ol grn	25	8
250	A77	20m dk gray ('45)	30	6
251	A77	22m dp bl ('45)	40	10
a.		Booklet pane of 6		
		Nos. 242-251 (11)	2.60	99

King Farouk
A78

Khedive Ismail Pasha
A79

1945, Feb. 10 *Perf. 13½x13*

252	A78	10m dp vio	20	20

25th birthday of King Farouk.

1945, Mar. 2 **Photogravure**

253	A79	10m dk ol	20	20

50th anniversary of death of Khedive Ismail Pasha.

Flags of Arab Nations
A80

1945, July 29

254	A80	10m violet	12	12
255	A80	22m dp yel grn	30	30

League of Arab Nations Conference, Cairo, Mar. 22, 1945.

Flags of Egypt and Saudi Arabia
A81

Perf. 13x13½

1946, Jan. 10 **Wmk. 195**

256	A81	10m dp yel grn	15	15

Visit of King Ibn Saud, Jan., 1946.

Citadel, Cairo
A82

1946, Aug. 9

257	A82	10m yel brn & dp yel grn	25	25

Withdrawal of British troops from Cairo Citadel, Aug. 9, 1946.

King Farouk and Inchas Palace, Cairo
A83

Portraits: 2m, Prince Abdullah, Yemen. 3m, Pres. Bechara el-Khoury, Lebanon. 4m, King Abdul Aziz ibn Saud, Saudi Arabia. 5m, King Faisal II, Iraq. 10m, Amir Abdullah ibn Hussein, Jordan. 15m, Pres. Shukri el Kouatly, Syria.

1946, Nov. 9

258	A83	1m dp yel grn	8	8
259	A83	2m sepia	8	8
260	A83	3m dp bl	10	10
261	A83	4m brn org	12	12
262	A83	5m brn red	15	15
263	A83	10m dk gray	18	18
264	A83	15m dp vio	20	20
		No. 258-264 (7)	91	91

Issued to commemorate the Arab League Congress at Cairo, May 28, 1946.

Parliament Building, Cairo
A84

1947, Apr. 7 **Photogravure**

265	A84	10m green	18	18

Issued to commemorate the 36th conference of the Interparliamentary Union, April, 1947.

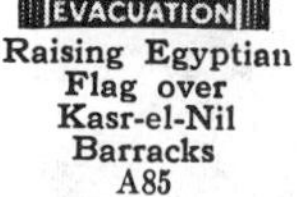

Raising Egyptian Flag over Kasr-el-Nil Barracks
A85

King Farouk
A85a

1947, May 6 ***Perf. 13½x13***

266	A85	10m dp plum & yel grn	15	15

Issued to commemorate the withdrawal of British troops from the Nile Delta.

Farouk Types 1939 Redrawn

1947–51 ***Perf. 14x31½*** **Wmk. 195**

267	A73	30m ol grn	30	3
268	A73	40m dk brn	40	4
269	A73	50m Prus grn ('48)	55	5
269A	A73	100m dk brn vio ('49)	1.65	8
269B	A73	200m dk vio ('49)	5.00	20

Perf. 13½13

269C	A85a	50pi grn & sep ('51)	12.00	3.75
269D	A75	£1 dp bl & dk brn ('50)	30.00	2.00
		Nos. 267-269D (7)	49.90	6.15

The king faces slightly to the left and clouds have been added in the sky on Nos. 267–269B. Backgrounds as in 1939–46 issue. Portrait on £1 as on type A77.

Field and Branch of Cotton
A86

Map and Infantry Column
A87

Perf. 13½x13

1948, Apr. 1 **Wmk. 195**

270	A86	10m ol grn	30	25

Issued to commemorate the International Cotton Congress held at Cairo in April, 1948.

1948, June 15 ***Perf. 11½x11***

271	A87	10m green	35	35

Arrival of Egyptian troops at Gaza, May 15, 1948.

Ibrahim Pasha
A88

1948, Nov. 10 ***Perf. 13x13½***

272	A88	10m brn red & dp grn	25	25

Issued to commemorate the centenary of the death of Ibrahim Pasha (1789–1848).

Statue, "The Nile"
A89

Protection of Industry and Agriculture
A90

Perf. 13x13½

1949, Mar. 1 **Photo.** **Wmk. 195**

273	A89	1m dk grn	10	10
274	A89	10m purple	20	20
275	A89	17m crimson	25	25
276	A89	22m dp bl	30	30

Perf. 11½x11

277	A90	30m dk brn	40	40
		Nos. 273-277 (5)	1.25	1.25

Souvenir Sheets.
Photogravure and Lithographed.
Imperf.

278	A89	Sheet of 4	1.25	1.25
a.		1m red brn	25	25
b.		10m dk brn	25	25
c.		17m brn org	25	25
d.		22m dk Prus grn	25	25
279	A90	Sheet of 2	1.75	1.75
a.		10m vio gray	75	75
b.		30m red org	75	75

Nos. 273–279 were issued to publicize the 16th Agricultural and Industrial Exposition, Cairo.

No. 278 has frame and marginal inscriptions in dark green. Size: 127x104½ mm.

No. 279 has frame and marginal inscriptions in dark violet. Size: 108x123 mm.

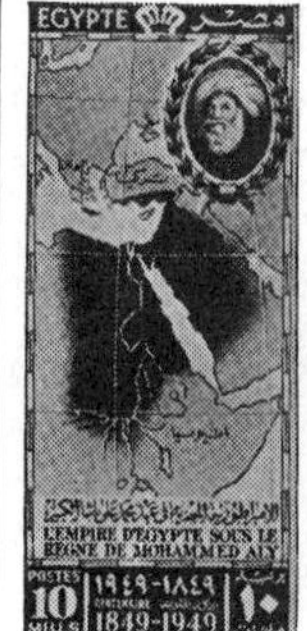

Mohammed Ali and Map
A93

Globe
A94

Perf. 11½x11

1949, Aug. 2 **Photo.** **Wmk. 195**

280	A93	10m org brn & grn	25	25

Centenary of death of Mohammed Ali.

1949, Oct. 9 ***Perf. 13½x13***

281	A94	10m rose brn	35	30
282	A94	22m violet	60	50
283	A94	30m dl bl	80	70

75th anniversary of the formation of the Universal Postal Union.

Scales of Justice
A95

1949, Oct. 14 ***Perf. 13x13½***

284	A95	10m dp ol grn	20	20

Issued to commemorate the end of the Mixed Judiciary System, Oct. 14, 1949.

Desert Scene
A96

1950, Dec. 27

285	A96	10m vio & red brn	25	25

Issued to commemorate the opening of the Fuad I Institute of the Desert.

Fuad I University
A97

1950, Dec. 27

286	A97	22m dp grn & cl	35	35

Issued to commemorate the 25th anniversary of the founding of Fuad I University.

Globe and Khedive Ismail Pasha
A98

1950, Dec. 27

287	A98	30m cl & dp grn	40	40

75th anniversary of Royal Geographic Society of Egypt.

Picking Cotton
A99

1951, Feb. 24

290	A99	10m ol grn	20	20

International Cotton Congress, 1951.

King Farouk and Queen Narriman
A100

1951, May 6 **Photo.** ***Perf. 11x11½***

291	A100	10m grn & red brn	1.00	1.00
a.		Souvenir sheet	1.35	1.35

Issued to commemorate the marriage of King Farouk and Narriman Sadek, May 6, 1951.

No. 291a was issued in sheets measuring 129x112 mm., with ornamental border and inscriptions in gray and black.

Stadium Entrance
A101

Arms of Alexandria and Olympic Emblem
A102

King Farouk
A103

1951, Oct. 5 ***Perf. 13x13½, 13½x13***

292	A101	10m brown	50	50
293	A102	22m dp grn	90	90
294	A103	30m bl & dp grn	1.00	1.00
a.		Souvenir sheet	5.00	5.00

Issued to publicize the first Mediterranean Games, Alexandria, Oct. 5–20, 1951.

No. 294a measures 189x117mm., and contains one each of Nos. 292–294 with ornamental frame and background in buff.

Winged Figure and Map
A105

Designs: 22m, King Farouk and Map. 30m, King Farouk and Flag.

Dated "16 Oct. 1951."

1952, Feb. 11 ***Perf. 13½x13***

296	A105	10m dp grn	50	50
297	A105	22m plum & dp grn	90	90
298	A105	30m grn & brn	1.00	1.00
a.		Souvenir sheet	5.00	5.00

Issued to commemorate the abrogation of the Anglo-Egyptian treaty.

No. 298a measures 134 x 113mm., and contains one each of Nos. 296 to 298, with ornamental border and Arabic inscriptions in gray.

Stamps of 1937-51 Overprinted in Various Colors

ملك مصر والسودان
١٦ اكتوبر سنة ١٩٥١

Perf. 13x13½

1952, Jan. 17 **Wmk. 195**

299	A77	1m yel brn	10	8
300	A77	2m red org (Bl)	10	8
301	A66	3m brn (Bl)	12	10
302	A77	4m dp grn (RV)	12	8
303	A66	6m lt yel grn (RV)	30	15
304	A77	10m dp vio (C)	20	4
305	A77	13m rose red (Bl)	25	15
306	A77	15m dk vio (C)	60	22
307	A77	17m ol grn (C)	90	15
308	A77	20m dk gray (RV)	1.00	15
309	A77	22m dp bl (C)	1.50	80

No. 244, the 3m sepia, exists with this overprint but was not regularly issued or used.

Same Overprint, 24½mm. Wide on Nos. 267 to 269B.

Perf. 14x13½

310	A73	30m ol grn	55	8
a.		Dark bl overprint	35	6

311	A73	40m dk brn (G)	50	18
312	A73	50m Prus grn (C)	65	10
313	A73	100m dk brn vio (C)	1.00	25
314	A73	200m dk vio (C)	2.50	30

Same Overprint, 19mm. Wide, on Nos. 269C–269D.

Perf. 13½x13.

315	A85a	50pi grn & sep (C)	12.00	3.50
316	A75	£1 dp bl & dk brn (Bl)	25.00	3.75
		Nos. 299-316 (18)	47.39	10.16

The overprint translates: King of Egypt and the Sudan, Oct. 16, 1951.

Egyptian Flag
A106

Perf. 13½x13

1952, May 6 Photo. Wmk. 195

317	A106	10m org yel, dp bl & dp grn	25	25
a.		Souvenir sheet	85	85

Issued to commemorate the birth of Crown Prince Ahmed Fuad, January 16, 1952.

No. 317a measures 115½ x 137½mm., with ornamental border and Arabic inscriptions in deep blue, salmon and green.

"Dawn of New Era"
A107

Symbolical of Egypt Freed
A108

Designs: 10m, "Egypt" with raised sword. 22m, Citizens marching with flag.

Perf. 13x13½, 13½x13

1952, Nov. 23

Dated: "23 Juillet 1952."

318	A107	4m dp grn & org	10	10
319	A107	10m dp grn & cop brn	15	15
320	A108	17m brn org & dp grn	25	25
321	A108	22m choc & dp grn	35	35

Change of government, July 23, 1952.

Republic

Farmer
A109

Soldier
A110

Mosque of Sultan Hassan
A111

Queen Nefertiti
A112

1953–56 ***Perf. 13x13½***

322	A109	1m red brn	5	3
323	A109	2m dk lil	6	4
324	A109	3m brt bl	6	4
325	A109	4m dk grn	6	4
326	A110	10m dk brn (*"Defence"*)	12	6
327	A110	10m dk brn (*"Defense"*)	8	3
328	A110	15m gray	15	3
329	A110	17m dk grnsh bl	18	6
330	A110	20m purple	18	6

Perf. 13½.

331	A111	30m dl grn	20	4
332	A111	32m brt bl	25	10
333	A111	35m vio ('55)	50	5
334	A111	37m gldn brn ('56)	60	8
335	A111	40m red brn	30	4
336	A111	50m vio brn	45	5
337	A112	100m hn brn	75	10
338	A112	200m dk grnsh bl	1.25	20
339	A112	500m purple	5.00	90
340	A112	£1 dk grn, blk & red	9.00	70
		Nos. 332-340 (19)	19.24	2.65

Nos. 327–330 are inscribed "Defense." See No. 490.

Nos. 206, 208 and 211 Overprinted in Black with Three Bars to Obliterate Portrait.

1953 ***Perf. 13x13½***

342	A66	1m brn org	2.25	2.25
343	A66	3m brown	8	6
344	A66	6m lt yel grn	8	6

Same Overprint on Stamps of 1939–51

Perf. 13x13½, 13½x13.

345	A77	1m yel brn	6	6
346	A77	2m red org	6	6
347	A77	3m sepia	6	6
348	A77	4m dp grn	8	6
349	A77	10m dp vio	12	10
350	A77	13m rose red	18	15
351	A77	15m dk vio	18	10
352	A77	17m ol grn	20	15
353	A77	20m dk gray	25	12
354	A77	22m dp bl	30	25
355	A73	30m ol grn (#267)	35	18
356	A73	50m Prus grn (#269)	50	20
357	A73	100m dk brn vio (#269A)	75	25
358	A73	200m dk vio (#269B)	2.50	35
359	A85a	50pi grn & sep	6.00	1.00
360	A75	£1 dp bl & dk brn (#269D)	15.00	1.35
		Nos. 345-360 (16)	26.59	4.44

Same Overprint on Nos. 299-309, 311 and 314.

360A	A77	1m yel brn	1.50	1.50
360B	A77	2m red org	25	20
360C	A66	3m brown	1.50	1.50
360D	A77	4m dp grn	1.50	1.50
360E	A66	6m lt yel grn	2.00	1.50
361	A77	10m dp vio	1.00	1.00
362	A77	13m rose red	50	30
362A	A77	15m dk vio	6.00	6.00
362B	A77	17m ol grn	6.00	6.00
362C	A77	20m dk gray	6.00	6.00
362D	A77	22m dp bl	22.50	22.50
363	A73	40m dk brn	60	35
364	A73	200m dk vio	2.50	50
		Nos. 360A-364 (13)	51.85	48.85

Practically all values of Nos. 342-364 exist with double overprint.

Symbols of Electronic Progress
A113

1953, Nov. 23 Photo. ***Perf. 13x13½***

365	A113	10m brt bl	25	25

Electronics Exposition, Cairo, Nov. 23.

Crowd Acclaiming the Republic
A114

Farmer
A115

Design: 30m, Crowd, flag and eagle.

Perf. 13½x13

1954, June 18 Wmk. 195

366	A114	10m brown	15	15
367	A114	30m dp bl	35	35

Issued to commemorate the first anniversary of the proclamation of the republic.

1954-55 ***Perf. 13x13½.***

368	A115	1m red brn	5	3
369	A115	2m dk lil	5	3
370	A115	3m brt bl	6	4
371	A115	4m dk grn ('55)	6	6
372	A115	5m dp car ('55)	12	8
		Nos. 368-372 (5)	34	24

Paul P. Harris and Rotary Emblem
A118

Design: 35m, Globe, wings and Rotary emblem.

Perf. 13½x13

1955, Feb. 23 Wmk. 195

378	A118	10m claret	30	15
379	A118	35m blue	60	40

Issued to commemorate the 50th anniversary of the founding of Rotary International.

Nos. 375-377 Overprinted مؤتمر البريد العربي القاهرة ١٩٥٥/٣/١٥

1955, Nov. 1

381	A117	5m yel brn	10	10
382	A117	10m green	20	20
383	A117	37m violet	55	55

Issued to commemorate the Arab Postal Union Congress held at Cairo, March 15, 1955.

Map of Africa and Asia, Olive Branch and Rings
A119

Globe, Torch, Dove and Olive Branch
A120

Perf. 13x13½, 13½x13

1956, July 29

384	A119	10m chnt & grn	20	15
385	A120	35m org yel & dl pur	45	40

Afro-Asian Festival, Cairo, July, 1956.

Map of Suez Canal and Ship
A121

Queen Nefertiti
A122

Egyptian Flag and Map
A116

Globe
A117

Design: 35m, Bugler, soldier and map.

1954, Nov. 4 ***Perf. 13½x13***

373	A116	10m rose vio & grn	15	15
374	A116	35m ver, blk & bl grn	50	50

Issued to commemorate the agreement of Oct. 19, 1954, with Great Britain for the evacuation of the Suez Canal zone by British troops.

Arab Postal Union Issue.

1955, Jan. 1

375	A117	5m yel brn	10	10
376	A117	10m green	20	20
377	A117	37m violet	60	60

Issued to commemorate the founding of the Arab Postal Union, July 1, 1954.

Perf. 11½x11

1956, Sept. 26 **Wmk. 195**

386 A121 10m bl & buff 30 25

Nationalization of the Suez Canal, July 26, 1956. See also No. 393.

1956, Oct. 15 ***Perf. 13½x13***

387 A122 10m dk grn 45 45

Issued to publicize the International Museum Week (UNESCO), Oct. 8-14.

Egyptians Defending Port Said
A123

1956, Dec. 20 Litho. ***Perf. 11x11½***

388 A123 10m brn vio 25 20

Issued in honor of the defenders of Port Said.

No. 388 Overprinted in Carmine Rose — الجلاء ٢٢/١٢/٥٦ EVACUATION 22·12·56

1957, Jan. 14

389 A123 10m brn vio 25 20

Issued to commemorate the evacuation of Port Said by British and French troops, Dec. 22, 1956.

Old and New Trains
A124

1957, Jan. 30 Photo. ***Perf. 13x13½***

390 A124 10m red vio & gray 18 15

Issued to commemorate the 100th anniversary of the Egyptian Railway System (in 1956).

Mother and Children
A125

1957, Mar. 21

391 A125 10m crimson 18 15

Mother's Day, 1957.

Battle Scene
A126

Perf. 13x13½

1957, Mar. 28 **Wmk. 195**

392 A126 10m brt bl 15 15

Issued to commemorate the 150th anniversary of the victory over the British at Rosetta.

Type of 1956;
New Inscriptions in English

1957, Apr. 15 ***Perf. 11½x11***

393 A121 100m bl & yel grn 80 65

Issued to commemorate the reopening of the Suez Canal.

No. 393 is inscribed: "Nationalisation of Suez Canal Co. Guarantees Freedom of Navigation" and "Reopening 1957".

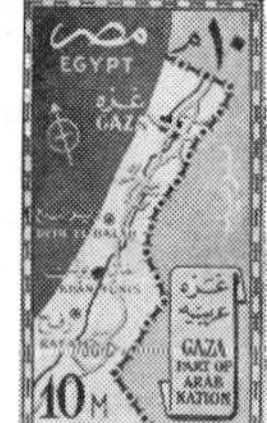

Map of Gaza Strip
A127

Perf. 13½x13

1957, May 4 **Photo.** **Wmk. 195**

394 A127 10m Prus bl 20 18

"Gaza Part of Arab Nation."

Al Azhar University
A128

1957, Apr. 27 ***Perf. 13x13½***

New Arabic Date in Red.

395 A128 10m brt vio 15 15
396 A128 15m vio brn 20 20
397 A128 20m dk gray 25 25

Millenary of Al Azhar University, Cairo.

Shepheard's Hotel, Cairo
A129

Gate, Palace and Eagle
A130

Perf. 13½x13

1957, July 20 **Wmk. 195**

398 A129 10m brt vio 15 12

Reopening of Shepheard's Hotel, Cairo.

Wmk. 315

Wmkd. Multiple Eagle (315)

1957, July 22 ***Perf. 11½x11***

399 A130 10m yel & brn 15 12

First meeting of New National Assembly.

Amasis I in Battle of Avaris, 1580 B. C.—A131

Designs: No. 401, Sultan Saladin, Hitteen, 1187 A. D. No. 402, Louis IX of France in chains, Mansourah, 1250 (vertical). No. 403, Map of Middle East, Ein Galout, 1260. No. 404, Port Said, 1956.

Inscribed:
"Egypt Tomb of Aggressors 1957"

Perf. 13x13½, 13½x13

1957, July 26

400 A131 10m car rose 18 10
401 A131 10m dk ol grn 18 10
402 A131 10m brn vio 18 10
403 A131 10m grnsh bl 18 10
404 A131 10m yel brn 18 10
Nos. 400-404 (5) 90 50

No. 400 exists with Wmk. 195.

Ahmed Arabi Speaking to the Khedive—A132

Perf. 13x13½

1957, Sept. 16 **Wmk. 315**

405 A132 10m dp vio 15 12

75th anniversary of Arabi Revolution.

Hafez Ibrahim
A133

Portrait: No. 407, Ahmed Shawky.

1957, Oct. 14 ***Perf. 13½x13***

406 A133 10m dl red brn 15 12
407 A133 10m ol grn 15 12

Nos. 406–407 are printed se-tenant in sheets of 50. Issued to commemorate the 25th anniversary of the deaths of Hafez Ibrahim and Ahmed Shawky, poets.

MiG and Ilyushin Planes—A134

Design: No. 409, Viscount plane.

1957, Dec. 19 ***Perf. 13x13½***

408 A134 10m ultra 15 12
409 A134 10m green 15 12

Issued to commemorate the 25th anniversaries of the Egyptian Air Force and of Misrair, the Egyptian airline. Nos. 408–409 printed se-tenant.

Pyramids, Dove and Globe—A135

1957, Dec. 26 **Photo.** **Wmk. 315**

410 A135 5m brn org 10 8
411 A135 10m green 15 12
412 A135 15m brt vio 20 20

Issued to publicize the Afro-Asian Peoples Conference, Cairo, Dec. 26–Jan. 2.

Farmer's Wife
A136

Ramses II
A137

1957-58 ***Perf. 13½*** **Wmk. 315**

413 A136 1m bl grn ('58) 5 5
414 A137 10m violet 12 8

"Industry"
A138

Wmk. 318

Wmkd.
Multiple Eagle and "Misr" (318)

1958

415 A136 1m lt bl grn 5 4
416 A138 5m brown 6 4
417 A137 10m violet 12 4

See also Nos. 438–444, 474–488.

Cyclists
A139

Mustafa Kamel
A140

Perf. 13½x13

1958, Jan. 12 **Wmk. 315**

418 A139 10m lt red brn 18 15

Issued to publicize the fifth International Bicycle Race, Egypt, Jan. 12–26.

1958, Feb. 10 **Photo.** **Wmk. 318**

419 A140 10m bl gray 18 15

Issued to commemorate the 50th anniversary of the death of Mustafa Kamel, orator and politician.

United Arab Republic

Linked Maps of Egypt and Syria
A141

Cotton
A142

Perf. 11½x11

1958, Mar. 22 **Wmk. 318**

436	A141	10m yel & grn	15	12

Birth of United Arab Republic. See No. C90.

1958, Apr. 5 ***Perf. 13½x13***

437	A142	10m Prus bl	15	12

Issued for the International Fair for Egyptian Cotton, April, 1958.

Types of 1957–58 Inscribed "U.A.R. EGYPT" and

Princess Nofret
A143

Designs: 1m, Farmer's wife. 2m, Ibn-Tulun's Mosque. 4m, 14th century glass lamp (design lacks "1963" of A217). 5m. "Industry" (factories and cogwheel). 10m, Ramses II. 35m, "Commerce" (eagle, ship and cargo).

1958 ***Perf. 13½x14***

438	A136	1m crimson	5	3
439	A138	2m blue	5	4
440	A143	3m dk red brn	5	3
441	A217	4m green	5	3
442	A138	5m brown	6	4
443	A137	10m violet	12	3
444	A138	35m lt ultra	80	5
		Nos. 438-444 (7)	1.18	25

See Nos. 474–488, 532–535.

Qasim Amin
A144

Doves, Broken Chain and Globe
A145

1958, Apr. 23 ***Perf. 13½x13***

445	A144	10m dp bl	18	12

50th anniversary of the death of Qasim Amin, author of "Emancipation of Women."

1958, June 18

446	A145	10m violet	15	10

Issued on the fifth anniversary of the republic to publicize the struggle of peoples and individuals for freedom.

Cement Industry
A146

Industries: No. 448, Textile. No. 449, Iron & steel. No. 450, Petroleum (Oil). No. 451, Electricity and fertilizers.

Perf. 13½x13

1958, July 23 **Photo.** **Wmk. 318**

447	A146	10m red brn	15	10
448	A146	10m bl grn	15	10
449	A146	10m brt red	15	10
450	A146	10m ol grn	15	10
451	A146	10m dk bl	15	10
		Nos. 447-451 (5)	75	50

Nos. 447–451 are printed in one sheet of 25 in vertical rows of five.

Souvenir Sheet

U. A. R. Flag—A147

1958, July 23 ***Imperf.***

452	A147	50m grn, dp car & blk	10.00	10.00

No. 452 measures 80½x75½mm. with black marginal inscription. Nos. 447–452 issued on the 6th anniversary of the Revolution of July 23, 1952.

Sayed Darwich
A148

Hand Holding Torch, Broken Chain and Flag
A149

1958, Sept. 15 ***Perf. 13½x13***

453	A148	10m vio brn	12	10

Issued to commemorate the 35th anniversary of the death of Sayed Darwich, Arab composer.

1958, Oct. 14 **Photo.** **Wmk. 318**

454	A149	10m car rose	12	10

Establishment of the Republic of Iraq.

Maps and Cogwheels
A150

1958, Dec. 8 ***Perf. 13x13½***

455	A150	10m blue	18	10

Issued to publicize the Economic Conference of Afro-Asian Countries, Cairo, Dec. 8.

Overprinted in Red in English and Arabic in 3 Lines: "Industrial and Agricultural Production Fair."

1958, Dec. 9

456	A150	10m lt red brn	18	10

Issued to publicize the Industrial and Agricultural Production Fair, Cairo, Dec. 9.

Dr. Mahmoud Azmy and U.N. Emblem—A151

1958, Dec. 10

457	A151	10m dl vio	20	15
458	A151	35m green	55	45

Tenth anniversary of the signing of the Universal Declaration of Human Rights.

University Building, Sphinx, "Education" and God Thoth
A152

1958, Dec. 21 **Photo.** **Wmk. 318**

459	A152	10m grnsh blk	12	10

50th anniversary of Cairo University.

الجمهورية العربية المتحدة ═

٥٥

No. 337 Surcharged

UAR
═
55

1959, Jan. 20 ***Perf. 13½*** **Wmk. 195**

460	A112	55m on 100m hn brn	45	30

Emblem
A153

1959, Feb. 2 ***Perf. 13x13½***

461	A153	10m lt ol grn	12	10

Afro-Asian Youth Conference, Cairo, Feb. 2.

Arms of U.A.R.
A154

Perf. 13½x13

1959, Feb. 22 **Photo.** **Wmk. 318**

462	A154	10m grn, blk & red	12	10

First anniversary, United Arab Republic.

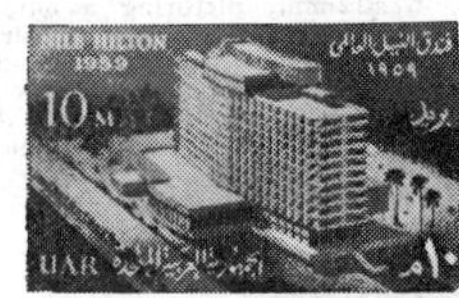

Nile Hilton Hotel
A155

1959, Feb. 22 ***Perf. 13x13½***

463	A155	10m dk gray	12	10

Opening of the Nile Hilton Hotel, Cairo.

Globe, Radio and Telegraph—A156

1959, Mar. 1

464	A156	10m violet	12	10

Arab Union of Telecommunications.

United Arab States Issue

Flags of U. A. R. and Yemen
A157

1959, Mar. 8

465	A157	10m sl grn, car & blk	12	10

First anniversary of United Arab States.

Oil Derrick and Pipe Line
A158

Perf. 13½x13

1959, Apr. 16 **Litho.** **Wmk. 318**

466	A158	10m lt bl & dk bl	12	8

First Arab Petroleum Congress, Cairo.

Railroad
A159

Designs: No. 468, Bus on highway. No. 469, River barge. No. 470, Ocean liner. No. 471, Telecommunications on map. No. 472, Stamp printing building, Heliopolis.

1959, July 23 **Photo.** ***Perf. 13x13½***

Frame in Gray.

467	A159	10m maroon	7	7
468	A159	10m green	7	7
469	A159	10m violet	7	7
470	A159	10m dk bl	8	8
471	A159	10m dl pur	8	8

472	A159	10m scarlet	8	8
		Nos. 467-472 (6)	45	45

An imperf. souvenir sheet, issued with this set, commemorates the seventh anniversary of the Egyptian revolution of 1952. The sheet carries a single 50m green and red stamp, 57x32mm., picturing a ship, train, plane and motorcycle mail carrier. Marginal Arabic inscriptions in black; size: 80x74mm. The government printed 140,000 of this sheet and sold it only if the buyer also bought five sets of Nos. 467-472.

Globe, Swallows and Map
A160

1959, Aug. 8 ***Perf. 13½x13***

473	A160	10m maroon	10	8

Issued to commemorate the convention of the Association of Arab Emigrants in the United States.

Types of 1953-58 without "Egypt" and

St. Simon's Gate, Bosra, Syria
A161

Wmk. 328

Designs: 1m, Farmer's wife. 2m, Ibn-Tulun's Mosque. 3m, Princess Nofret. 4m, 14th century glass lamp (design lacks "1963" of A217). 5m, "Industry" (factories and cogwheel). 10m, Ramses II. 15m, Omayyad Mosque, Damascus. 20m, Lotus vase, Tutankhamen treasure. 35m, Eagle, ship and cargo. 40m, Scribe statue. 45m, Saladin's citadel, Aleppo. 55m, Eagle, cotton and wheat. 60m, Dam and factory. 100m, Eagle, hand, cotton and grain. 200m, Palmyra ruins, Syria. 500m, Queen Nefertiti, inscribed "UAR" (no ovpt.).

Wmkd. U A R. (328)

Photogravure.

1959-60 ***Perf. 13½x14, 14x13½.***

474	A136	1m vermilion	3	3
475	A138	2m dp bl ('60)	4	4
476	A143	3m maroon	4	4
477	A217	4m grn ('60)	4	4
478	A138	5m blk ('60)	5	4
479	A137	10m dk ol grn	10	3
480	A138	15m dp cl	15	4
481	A138	20m crim ('60)	20	5
482	A161	30m brn vio	30	6
483	A138	35m lt vio bl ('60)	40	6
484	A143	40m sepia	60	8
485	A161	45m lil gray ('60)	1.00	8
486	A138	55m brt bl grn	1.00	8
487	A138	60m dp pur ('60)	60	8
488	A138	100m org & sl grn ('60)	2.00	10
489	A161	200m lt bl & mar	3.50	10
490	A112	500m dk gray & red ('60)	6.00	30
		Nos. 474-490 (17)	16.05	1.25

Shield and Cogwheel
A162

Perf. 13½x13

1959, Oct. 20 Photo. **Wmk. 328**

491	A162	10m brt car rose	12	8

Issued for Army Day, 1959.

Cairo Museum—A163

1959, Nov. 18 ***Perf. 13x13½***

492	A163	10m ol gray	12	8

Centenary of Cairo museum.

Abu Simbel Temple of Ramses II
A164

1959, Dec. 22 ***Perf. 11x11½***

493	A164	10m lt red brn, *pnksh*	25	20

Issued as propaganda to save historic monuments in Nubia threatened by the construction of Aswan High Dam.

Postrider, 12th century
A165

1960, Jan. 2 ***Perf. 13x13½***

494	A165	10m dk bl	12	8

Issued for Post Day, Jan. 2.

Hydroelectric Power Station, Aswan Dam—A166

1960, Jan. 9

495	A166	10m vio blk	15	8

Issued to commemorate the inauguration of the Aswan Dam hydroelectric power station, Jan. 9.

Arabic and English Description of Aswan High Dam—A167

Architect's Drawing of Aswan High Dam—A168

1960, Jan. 9 ***Perf. 11x11½***

496	A167	10m claret	15	8
497	A168	35m claret	45	25

Issued to commemorate the start of work on the Aswan High Dam. Nos. 496-497 printed se-tenant vertically in sheet.

Symbols of Agriculture and Industry
A169

Arms and Flag
A170

1960, Jan. 16 ***Perf. 13½x13***

498	A169	10m gray grn & sl grn	12	8

Industrial and Agricultural Fair, Cairo.

1960, Feb. 22 Photo. **Wmk. 328**

499	A170	10m grn, blk & red	12	8

Issued to commemorate the 2nd anniversary of the proclamation of the United Arab Republic.

No. 340 Overprinted "UAR" in English and Arabic in Red

1960 ***Perf. 13½*** **Wmk. 195**

500	A112	£1 dk grn, blk & red	10.00	1.00
a.		Double ovpt.	*50.00*	

"Art"
A171

Perf. 13½x13

1960, Mar. 1 **Wmk. 328**

501	A171	10m brown	12	8

Issued to publicize the 3rd Biennial Exhibition of Fine Arts in Alexandria.

Arab League Center, Cairo—A172

1960, Mar. 22 Photo. ***Perf. 13x13½***

502	A172	10m dl grn & blk	12	8

Opening of Arab League Center and Arab Postal Museum, Cairo.

Refugees Pointing to Map of Palestine—A173

1960, Apr. 7

503	A173	10m org ver	10	8
504	A173	35m Prus bl	35	30

Issued to publicize World Refugee Year, July 1, 1959-June 30, 1960.

Weight Lifter
A174

Stadium, Cairo—A175

Sports: No. 506, Basketball. No. 507, Soccer. No. 508, Fencing. No. 509, Rowing. 30m, Steeplechase (horiz.). 35m, Swimming (horiz.)

Perf. 13½x13

1960, July 23 Photo. **Wmk. 328**

505	A174	5m gray	5	5
506	A174	5m brown	5	5
507	A174	5m dp cl	10	5
508	A174	10m brt car	15	5
509	A174	10m gray grn	15	5
510	A174	30m purple	35	15
511	A174	35m dk bl	45	20
		Nos. 505-511 (7)	1.30	60

Souvenir Sheet

Imperf.

512	A175	100m car & brn	1.25	75

Nos. 505-511 issued to commemorate the 17th Olympic Games, Rome, Aug. 25-Sept. 11.

Nos. 505-509 are printed in one sheet of 25 in vertical rows of five.

No. 512 measures 80x75mm. with black marginal inscription.

Dove and U.N. Emblem
A176

Design: 35m, Lights surrounding U.N. emblem (horiz.).

Perf. 13½x13

1960, Oct. 24 **Wmk. 328**

513	A176	10m purple	10	8
514	A176	35m brt rose	30	25

15th anniversary of United Nations.

Abu Simbel Temple of Queen Nefertari—A177

Perf. 11x11½

1960, Nov. 14 **Photo.** **Wmk. 328**

515	A177	10m ocher, *buff*	25	20

Issued as propaganda to save historic monuments in Nubia and in connection with the UNESCO meeting, Paris, Nov. 14.

Model Post Office A178

1961, Jan. 2 ***Perf. 13x13½***

516	A178	10m brt car rose	12	8

Issued for Post Day, Jan. 2.

Eagle, Fasces and Victory Wreath A179 **Wheat and Globe Surrounded by Flags A180**

1961, Feb. 22 ***Perf. 13½x13***

517	A179	10m dl vio	12	8

3rd anniversary of United Arab Republic.

1961, March 21 **Wmk. 328**

518	A180	10m vermilion	12	8

Issued to publicize the International Agricultural Exhibition, Cairo, March 21–April 20.

Patrice Lumumba and Map A181 **Reading Braille and WHO Emblem A182**

1961, March 30 ***Perf. 13½x13***

519	A181	10m black	12	8

Issued for Africa Day, Apr. 15 and to commemorate the 3rd Conference of Independent African States, Cairo, March 25–31.

1961, Apr. 6 **Photogravure**

520	A182	10m red brn	12	8

World Health Organization Day. See No. B21.

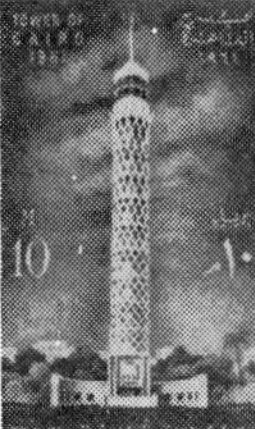

Tower of Cairo A183 **Arab Woman and Son, Palestine Map A184**

1961, Apr. 11 ***Perf. 13½x13***

521	A183	10m grnsh bl	12	8

Issued to commemorate the opening of the 600-foot Tower of Cairo, on island of Gizireh. See also No. C95.

1961, May 15 **Wmk. 328**

522	A184	10m brt grn	15	8

Issued for Palestine Day.

Symbols of Industry and Electricity A185

Chart and Workers—A186

Designs: No. 524, New buildings and family. No. 525, Ship, train, bus and radio. No. 526, Dam, cotton and field. No. 527, Hand holding candle and family.

Photogravure

1961, July 23 ***Perf. 13x13½***

523	A185	10m dp car	8	3
524	A185	10m brt bl	8	3
525	A185	10m dk vio brn	8	3
526	A185	35m dk grn	28	5
527	A185	35m brt pur	28	6
		Nos. 523-527 (5)	80	20

Souvenir Sheet

Imperf.

528	A186	100m red brn	1.25	1.25

Nos. 523–528 issued to commemorate the ninth anniversary of the revolution. No. 528 has pale brown border with black inscription. Size: 82x75mm.

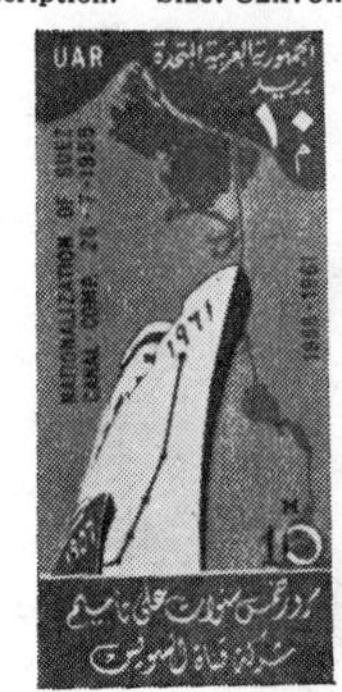

Map of Suez Canal and Ships A187

Perf. 11½x11

1961, July 26 **Unwmkd.**

529	A187	10m olive	12	8

Fifth anniversary of the nationalization of the Suez Canal Company.

Various Enterprises of Misr Bank A188

Perf. 13x13½

1961, Aug. 22 **Wmk. 328**

530	A188	10m red brn, *pnksh*	12	8

The 41st anniversary of Misr Bank.

Flag, Ship's Wheel and Battleship A189

1961, Aug. 29 **Photo.** ***Perf. 13½x13***

531	A189	10m dp bl	12	8

Issued for Navy Day.

Eagle of Saladin over Cairo A190 **U.N. Emblem, Book, Cogwheel and Corn A191**

Type A143 of 1958 Redrawn and Type A190

1961, Aug. 31 ***Perf. 11½*** **Unwmkd.**

Designs: 1m, Farmer's wife. 4m, 14th century glass lamp. 35m, "Commerce."

532	A143	1m blue	3	3
533	A143	4m olive	5	3
534	A190	10m purple	10	3
535	A143	35m sl bl	30	6

Smaller of two Arabic inscriptions in new positions: 1m, at right above Egyptian numeral; 4m, upward to spot beside waist of lamp; 35m, upper left corner below "UAR." On 4m, "UAR" is 2mm. deep instead of 1mm. "Egypt" omitted as in 1959–60.

Perf. 13½x13

1961, Oct. 24 **Photo.** **Wmk. 328**

Design: 35m, Globe and cogwheel (horiz.).

536	A191	10m blk & ocher	10	8
537	A191	35m bl grn & brn	30	25

Issued to honor the United Nations' Technical Assistance Program and to commemorate the 16th anniversary of the United Nations.

Trajan's Kiosk, Philae—A192

1961, Nov. 4 ***Perf. 11½*** **Unwmkd.**

Size: 60x27mm.

538	A192	10m dp vio bl	25	20

Issued to commemorate the 15th anniversary of UNESCO, and to publicize UNESCO's help in safeguarding the monuments of Nubia.

Palette, Brushes and Map of Mediterranean A193 **Atom and Educational Symbols A194**

1961, Dec. 14 ***Perf. 13½*** **Wmk. 328**

539	A193	10m dk red brn	12	8

Issued to publicize the 4th Biennial Exhibition of Fine Arts in Alexandria.

1961, Dec. 18

540	A194	10m dl pur	12	8

Issued to publicize Education Day.

Arms of U.A.R. A195

1961, Dec. 23 ***Perf. 11½*** **Unwmkd.**

541	A195	10m brt pink, brt grn & blk	12	8

Issued to commemorate Victory Day.

Sphinx at Giza A196

1961, Dec. 27 ***Perf. 11x11½***

542	A196	10m black	12	8

Issued to publicize the "Sound and Light" Project, the installation of floodlights and sound equipment at the site of the Pyramids and Sphinx.

Post Office Printing Plant, Nasser City—A197

1962, Jan. 2 Photo. ***Perf. 11½x11***

543	A197	10m dk brn	12	8

Issued for Post Day, Jan. 2.

Map of Africa, King Mohammed V of Morocco and Flags
A198

1962, Jan. 4 ***Perf. 11x11½***

544	A198	10m indigo	12	8

Issued to commemorate the first anniversary of the African Charter, Casablanca.

Girl Scout Saluting and Emblem
A199

Perf. 13x13½

1962, Feb. 22 **Wmk. 328**

545	A199	10m brt bl	15	10

Egyptian Girl Scouts' 25th anniversary.

Arab Refugees, Flag and Map
A200

Mother and Child
A201

1962, March 7 ***Perf. 13½x13***

546	A200	10m dk sl grn	12	8

Issued to commemorate the 5th anniversary of the liberation of the Gaza Strip.

1962, March 21 Photogravure

547	A201	10m dk vio brn	12	8

Issued for Arab Mother's Day, March 21.

Map of Africa and Post Horn
A202

1962, Apr. 23 **Wmk. 328**

548	A202	10m crim & ocher	12	8
549	A202	50m dp bl & ocher	40	30

Establishment of African Postal Union.

Cadets on Parade and Academy Emblem—A203

1962, June 18 ***Perf. 13x13½***

550	A203	10m green	12	8

Issued to commemorate the 150th anniversary of the Egyptian Military Academy.

Malaria Eradication Emblem
A204

Theodor Bilharz
A205

1962, June 20 ***Perf. 13½x13***

551	A204	10m dk brn & red	12	8
552	A204	35m dk grn & bl	30	28

Issued for the World Health Organization drive to eradicate malaria.

1962, June 24 ***Perf. 11x11½***

553	A205	10m brn org	12	8

Issued to commemorate the centenary of the death of Dr. Theodor Bilharz (1825-1862), German physician who first described bilharziasis, an endemic disease in Egypt.

Patrice Lumumba and Map of Africa
A206

Hand on Charter
A207

Wmk. 342

Watermarked Coat of Arms, Multiple (342)

1962, July 1 **Photogravure**

554	A206	10m rose & red	12	8

Issued in memory of Patrice Lumumba (1925-61), Premier of Congo.

1962, July 10 ***Perf. 11x11½***

555	A207	10m brt bl & dk brn	12	8

Proclamation of the National Charter.

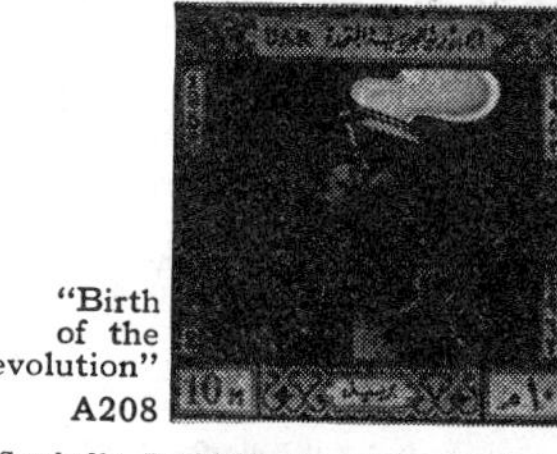

"Birth of the Revolution"
A208

Symbolic Designs: No. 557, Proclamation (Scroll and book). No. 558, Agricultural Reform (Farm and crescent). No. 559, Bandung Conference (Dove, globe and olive branch). No. 560, Birth of UAR (Eagle and flag). No. 561, Industrialization (cogwheel, factory, ship and bus). No. 562, Aswan High Dam. No. 563, Social Revolution (Modern buildings and emblem). 100m, Arms of UAR, emblems of Afro-Asian and African countries and United Nations emblem.

1962, July 23 ***Perf. 11½***

556	A208	10m brn, dk red brn & pink	15	8
557	A208	10m dk bl & sep	15	8
558	A208	10m sep & brt bl	15	8
559	A208	10m ol & dk ultra	15	8
560	A208	10m grn, blk & red	15	8
561	A208	10m brn org & ind	15	8
562	A208	10m brn org & vio blk	15	8
563	A208	10m org & blk	15	9
		Nos. 556-563 (8)	1.20	65

Souvenir Sheets

Perf. 11½, Imperf.

564	A208	100m grn, pink, red & blk	1.25	1.00

Issued to commemorate the tenth anniversary of the revolution. No 564 contains one stamp; green marginal inscription. Size: 71x79mm.

Mahmoud Moukhtar, Museum and Sculpture—A209

1962, July 24 ***Perf. 11½x11***

565	A209	10m lt vio bl & ol	10	8

Issued to commemorate the opening of the Moukhtar Museum, Island of Gezireh. The sculpture is "La Vestale de Secrets" by Moukhtar.

Flag of Algeria and Map of Africa Showing Algeria
A210

1962, Aug. 15 ***Perf. 11x11½***

566	A210	10m multi	12	8

Algeria's independence, July 1, 1962.

Rocket, Arms of U.A.R. and Atom Symbol
A211

1962, Sept. 1 Photo. **Wmk. 342**

567	A211	10m brt grn, red & blk	12	8

Launching of U.A.R. rockets.

Rifle and Target—A212

Map of Africa, Table Tennis Paddle, Net and Ball—A213

1962, Sept. 18 ***Perf. 11½***

568	A212	5m grn, blk & red	5	5
569	A213	5m grn, blk & red	6	5
570	A212	10m bis, bl & dk grn	12	10
571	A213	10m bis, bl & dk grn	12	10
572	A212	35m dp ultra, red & blk	40	30
573	A213	35m dp ultra, red & blk	40	30
		Nos. 568-573 (6)	1.15	90

Issued to commemorate the 38th World Shooting Championships and the First African Table Tennis Tournament. Types A212 and A213 are printed se-tenant at the base in sheets of 70.

Dag Hammarskjold and U.N. Emblem—A214

Perf. 11½x11

1962, Oct. 24 Photo. **Wmk. 342**

Portrait in Slate Blue

574	A214	5m dp lil	5	4
575	A214	10m olive	12	8
576	A214	35m dp ultra	30	30

Issued to honor Dag Hammarskjold, Secretary General of the United Nations, 1953-61, and to commemorate the 17th anniversary of the United Nations.

Condition is the all-important factor of price. Prices quoted are for stamps in fine condition.

Queen Nefertari Crowned by Isis and Hathor
A215

1962, Oct. 31 ***Perf. 11½***

577	A215	10m bl & ocher	15	15

Issued to publicize the UNESCO campaign to safeguard the monuments of Nubia.

Jet Trainer, Hawker Hart Biplane and College Emblem
A216

1962. Nov. 2 ***Perf. 11½x11***

578	A216	10m bl, dk bl & crim	12	8

25th anniversary of Air Force College.

14th Century Glass Lamp and "1963"
A217

Yemen Flag and Hand with Torch
A218

1963, Feb. 20 ***Perf. 11x11½***

579	A217	4m dk brn, grn & car	6	4

Issued for use on greeting cards. See also nos. 441, 477.

1963, Mar. 14 Photo. Wmk. 342

580	A218	10m ol & brt car	10	8

Establishment of Yemen Arab Republic.

Tennis Player, Pyramids and Globe
A219

Perf. 11½x11

1963, Mar. 20 **Unwmkd.**

581	A219	10m gray, blk & brn	10	8

Issued to commemorate the International Lawn Tennis Championships, Cairo.

Cow, U.N. and F.A.O. Emblems
A220

Designs: 10m, Corn, wheat and emblems (vert.). 35m, Wheat, corn and emblems.

Perf. 11½x11, 11x11½

1963, Mar. 21 **Wmk. 342**

582	A220	5m vio & dp org	5	4
583	A220	10m ultra & yel	10	8
584	A220	35m bl, yel & blk	30	28

Issued for the "Freedom from Hunger" campaign of the U.N. Food and Agriculture Organization.

Centenary Emblem
A221

Design: 35m, Globe and emblem.

Perf. 11x11½

1963, May 8 **Unwmkd.**

585	A221	10m lt bl, red & mar	10	8
586	A221	35m lt bl & red	30	25

Centenary of the Red Cross.

Arab Socialist Union Emblem
A222

Design: 50m, Tools, torch and symbol of National Charter.

Photogravure

1963, July 23 ***Perf. 11½*** **Wmk. 342**

587	A222	10m sl & rose pink	10	8

Souvenir Sheets

Perf. 11½, Imperf.

588	A222	50m vio bl & org yel	1.00	1.00

Issued to commemorate the 11th anniversary of the revolution and to publicize the Arab Socialist Union. No. 588 contains one stamp, violet blue marginal inscription. Size: 69x80mm.

Television Station, Cairo, and Screen
A223

1963, Aug. 1 ***Perf. 11½x11***

589	A223	10m dk bl & yel	10	8

Issued to publicize the 2nd International Television Festival, Alexandria, Sept. 1–10.

Queen Nefertari
A224

Swimmer and Map of Suez Canal
A225

Designs: 10m, Great Hypostyle Hall, Abu Simbel. 35m, Ramses in moonlight.

Photogravure

1963, Oct. 1 ***Perf. 11*** **Wmk. 342**

Size: 25x42mm. (5m, 35m); 28x61mm. (10m)

590	A224	5m brt vio bl & yel	5	4
591	A224	10m gray, blk & red org	10	8
592	A224	35m org yel & blk	30	28

Issued to publicize the UNESCO world campaign to save historic monuments in Nubia.

1963, Oct. 15

593	A225	10m bl & sal rose	10	8

Issued to commemorate the International Suez Canal Swimming Championship.

Ministry of Agriculture—A226

Perf. 11½x11

1963, Nov. 20 **Wmk. 342**

594	A226	10m multi	10	8

Issued to commemorate the 50th anniversary of the Ministry of Agriculture.

Modern Building and Map of Africa and Asia—A227

1963, Dec. 7

595	A227	10m multi	10	8

Afro-Asian Housing Congress, Dec. 7–12.

Scales, Globe, UN Emblem—A228

1963, Dec. 10

596	A228	5m dk grn & yel	8	4
597	A228	10m bl, gray & blk	15	8
598	A228	35m rose red, pink & red	40	28

Issued to commemorate the 15th anniversary of the Universal Declaration of Human Rights.

Sculpture, Arms of Alexandria and Palette with Flags
A229

1963, Dec. 12 ***Perf. 11x11½***

599	A229	10m pale bl, dk bl & brn	10	8

Issued to publicize the 5th Biennial Exhibition of Fine Arts in Alexandria.

Lion and Nile Hilton Hotel
A230

Vase, 13th Century
A231

Pharaoh Userkaf (5th Dynasty)
A232

Designs: 1m, Vase, 14th century. 2m, Ivory headrest. 3m, Pharaonic calcite boat. 4m, Minaret and gate. 5m, Nile and Aswan High Dam. 10m, Eagle of Saladin over pyramids. 15m, Window, Ibn Tulun's mosque. No 608, Mitwalli Gate, Cairo. 35m, Nefertari. 40m, Tower Hotel. 55m, Sultan Hassan's Mosque. 60m, Courtyard, Al Azhar University. 200m, Head of Ramses II. 500m, Funerary mask of Tutankhamen.

Photogravure

1964–67 ***Perf. 11*** **Unwmkd.**

Size: Nos. 608, 612, 19x24mm.; others, 24x29mm.

600	A231	1m cit & ultra	5	3
601	A230	2m mag & bis	10	5
602	A230	3m sal, org & bl	10	5
603	A235	4m ocher, blk & ultra	25	10
604	A230	5m brn & brt bl	10	10
a.		5m brn & dk bl	10	10
605	A231	10m grn, dk brn & lt brn	10	10
606	A230	15m ultra & yel	10	8
607	A230	20m brn org & blk	15	8
608	A231	20m lt ol grn ('67)	25	8
609	A231	30m yel & brn	35	10
610	A231	35m sal, ocher & ultra	30	10
611	A231	40m ultra & yel	35	10
612	A231	55m brt red lil ('67)	50	20
613	A231	60m grnsh bl & yel brn	45	20

Wmk. 342

614	A232	100m dk vio brn & sl	1.50	25
615	A232	200m bluish blk & yel brn	3.50	50
616	A232	500m ultra & dp org	6.00	1.00
		Nos. 600-616 (17)	14.15	3.12

Nos. 603 and N107 lack the vertically arranged dates which appear at lower right on No. 619.

HSN Commission Emblem
A233

Perf. 11x11½

1964, Jan. 10 **Wmk. 342**

617 A233 10m dl bl, dk bl & yel 10 5

Issued to commemorate the first conference of the Commission of Health, Sanitation and Nutrition.

Arab League Emblem—A234

1964, Jan. 13 ***Perf. 11***

618 A234 10m brt grn & blk 10 5

Issued to commemorate the first meeting of the Heads of State of the Arab League, Cairo, January.

Minaret at Night
A235

1964 ***Perf. 11*** **Unwmkd.**

619 A235 4m emer, blk & red 8 3

Issued for use on greeting cards. See also No. 603.

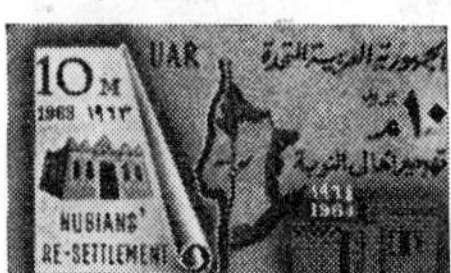

Old and New Dwellings and Map of Nubia—A236

Perf. 11½x11

1964, Feb. 27 Photo. Wmk. 342

620 A236 10m dl vio & yel 10 8

Resettlement of Nubian population.

Map of Africa and Asia and Train
A237

1964, March 21

621 A237 10m dl bl, dk bl & yel 8 8

Asian Railway Conference, Cairo, Mar. 21.

Ikhnaton and Nefertiti with Children
A238

1964, Mar. 21 ***Perf. 11x11½***

622 A238 10m dk brn & ultra 8 8

Issued for Arab Mother's Day, March 21.

Arab Postal Union Emblem
A239

World Health Organization Emblem
A240

1964, Apr. 1 **Photo.** **Wmk. 342**

623 A239 10m org brn & bl, *sal* 8 8

Issued to commemorate the 10th anniversary of the Permanent Office of the Arab Postal Union.

1964, Apr. 7

624 A240 10m dk bl & red 8 8

World Health Day (Anti-Tuberculosis).

Statue of Liberty, World's Fair Pavilion and Pyramids
A241

1964, Apr. 22 ***Perf. 11½x11***

625 A241 10m brt grn & ol, *grysh* 8 8

New York World's Fair, 1964-65.

Nile and Aswan High Dam
A242

1964, May 15 ***Perf. 11½*** **Unwmkd.**

626 A242 10m blk & bl 8 8

The diversion of the Nile.

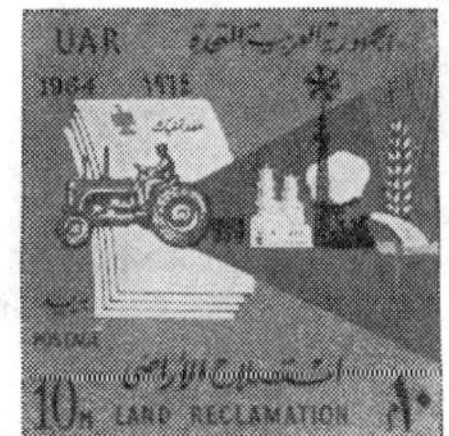

"Land Reclamation"—A243

Design: No. 628, "Electricity," Aswan High Dam hydroelectric station.

1964, July 23 ***Perf. 11½***

627 A243 10m yel & emer 8 8
628 A243 10m grn & blk 8 8

Issued to publicize land reclamation and hydroelectric power due to the Aswan High Dam.

An imperf. souvenir sheet, issued July 23, contains two 50m black and blue stamps showing Aswan High Dam before and after diversion of the Nile. Black portrait of President Nasser and blue inscription in margin. Size of stamps: 42x26 mm.; size of sheet: 104x81mm. Price $2.25.

Map of Africa and 34 Flags
A244

1964, July 17 **Photogravure**

629 A244 10m brn, brt bl & blk 8 8

Issued to commemorate the Assembly of Heads of State and Government of the Organization for African Unity at Cairo in July.

Jamboree Emblem—A245

Design: No. 631, Emblem of Air Scouts.

1964, Aug. 28 ***Perf. 11½*** **Unwmkd.**

630 A245 10m red, grn & blk 12 8
631 A245 10m grn & red 12 8

The 6th Pan Arab Jamboree, Alexandria.

Flag of Algeria—A246

1964, Sept. 5 ***Perf. 11½x11***

Flags in Original Colors

632 A246 10m grn (*Algeria*) 20 10
633 A246 10m grn (*Iraq*) 20 10
634 A246 10m grn (*Jordan*) 20 10
635 A246 10m grn (*Kuwait*) 20 10
636 A246 10m grn (*Lebanon*) 20 10
637 A246 10m grn (*Libya*) 20 10
638 A246 10m grn (*Morocco*) 20 10
639 A246 10m grn (*Saudi Arabia*) 20 10
640 A246 10m bl (*Sudan*) 20 10
641 A246 10m grn (*Syria*) 20 10
642 A246 10m grn (*Tunisia*) 20 10
643 A246 10m grn (*Egypt*) 20 10
644 A246 10m grn (*Yemen*) 20 10
Nos. 632-644 (13) 2.60 1.30

Issued to commemorate the second meeting of the Heads of State of the Arab League, Alexandria, Sept. 1964.

World Map, Dove, Olive Branches and Pyramids—A247

1964, Oct. 5 ***Perf. 11½***

645 A247 10m sl bl & yel 8 8

Issued to commemorate the Conference of Heads of State of Non-Aligned Countries, Cairo, Oct. 1964.

Pharaonic Athletes—A248

Designs from ancient decorations: 10m, Four athletes (vert.). 35m, Wrestlers (vert.). 50m, Pharaoh in chariot hunting.

Perf. 11½x11, 11x11½

1964, Oct. 10 **Photo.** **Unwmkd.**

Sizes: 39x22mm., 22x39mm.

646 A248 5m lt grn & org 4 4
647 A248 10m sl bl & lt brn 8 8
648 A248 35m dl vio & lt brn 38 35

Size: 58x24mm.

649 A248 50m ultra & brn org 40 40

18th Olympic Games Tokyo, Oct. 10-25.

Emblem, Map of Africa and Asia
A249

Map of Africa, Communication Symbols
A250

1964, Oct. 10 ***Perf. 11x11½***

650 A249 10m vio & yel 8 8

First Afro-Asian Medical Congress.

1964, Oct. 24

651 A250 10m grn & blk 8 8

Issued to commemorate the Pan-African and Malagasy Posts and Telecommunications Congress, Cairo, Oct. 24-Nov. 6.

Horus and Facade of Nefertari Temple, Abu Simbel—A251

Ramses II
A252

Designs: 35m, A god holding rope of life, Abu Simbel. 50m, Isis of Kalabsha (horiz.).

1964, Oct. 24 ***Perf. 11½, 11x11½***

652	A251	5m grnsh bl & yel brn	10	4
653	A252	10m sep & brt yel	20	5
654	A251	35m brn org & ind	60	35

Souvenir Sheet
Imperf.

655	A252	50m ol & vio blk	75	75

Issued to publicize the "Save the Monuments of Nubia" campaign. No. 655 contains one horizontal stamp; violet black and olive marginal inscription. Size: 106x63mm.

Emblems of Cooperation, Rural Handicraft and Women's Work
A253

Perf. 11½x11

1964, Dec. 8 Photo. Unwmkd.

656	A253	10m yel & dk bl	8	8

Issued to commemorate the 25th anniversary of the Ministry of Social Affairs.

United Nations and UNESCO Emblems, Pyramids
A254

Minaret, Mardani Mosque
A255

1964, Dec. 24 ***Perf. 11x11½***

657	A254	10m ultra & yel	8	8

Issued for UNESCO Day.

1965, Jan. 20 Photo. ***Perf. 11***

658	A255	4m bl & dk brn	3	3

Issued for use on greeting cards.

Police Emblem over City
A256

Oil Derrick and Emblem
A257

Perf. 11x11½

1965, Jan. 25 Wmk. 342

659	A256	10m blk & yel	8	8

Issued for Police Day.

1965, Mar. 16 Photogravure

660	A257	10m dk brn & yel	8	8

Issued to publicize the 5th Arab Petroleum Congress and the 2nd Arab Petroleum Exhibition.

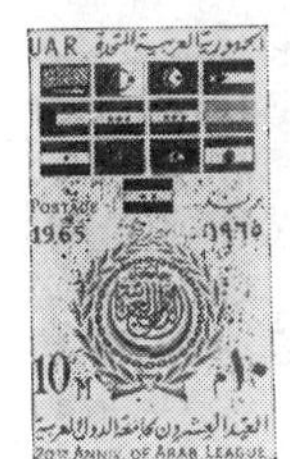

Flags and Emblem of the Arab League
A258

Red Crescent and WHO Emblem
A259

Design: 20m, Arab League emblem (horiz.).

1965, Mar. 22 Wmk. 342

661	A258	10m grn, red & blk	15	15
662	A258	20m ultra & brn	16	15

20th anniversary of the Arab League.

1965, Apr. 7 Photogravure

663	A259	10m bl & crim	8	8

Issued to commemorate World Health Day (Smallpox: Constant Alert).

Dagger in Map of Palestine
A260

1965, Apr. 9 ***Perf. 11x11½***

664	A260	10m blk & red	8	8

Deir Yassin massacre, Apr. 9, 1948.

ITU Emblem, Old and New Communication Equipment
A261

1965, May 17 ***Perf. 11½x11***

665	A261	5m vio blk & yel	4	4
666	A261	10m red & yel	8	5
667	A261	35m dk bl, ultra & yel	28	25

Issued to commemorate the centenary of the International Telecommunication Union.

Library Aflame and Lamp
A262

1965, June 7 Photo. Wmk. 342

668	A262	10m blk, grn & red	8	5

Issued to commemorate the burning of the Library of Algiers, June 7, 1962.

Sheik Mohammed Abdo
A263

1965, July 11 ***Perf. 11x11½***

669	A263	10m Prus bl & bis brn	6	5

Issued to commemorate the 60th anniversary of the death of Mohammed Abdo (1850-1905), Mufti of Egypt.

Pouring Ladle (Heavy Industry)
A264

President Gamal Abdel Nasser and Emblems of Arab League, African Unity Organization, Afro-Asian Countries and United Nations
A265

1965, July 23 ***Perf. 11½***

Designs: No. 670, Search for off-shore oil. No. 672, Housing, construction in Nassar City (diamond shaped).

670	A264	10m ind & lt bl	10	10
671	A264	10m brn & yel	10	10
672	A264	10m yel brn & blk	10	10
673	A265	100m lt grn & blk	1.75	1.75

13th anniversary of the revolution.

The 100m was printed in sheets of six, consisting of two singles and two vertical pairs. Margins and gutters contain multiple UAR coat of arms in light green. Size: 240x330mm.

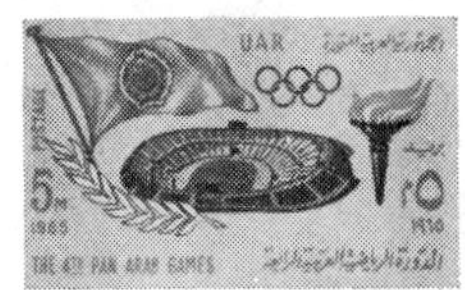

4th Pan Arab Games Emblem
A266

Map and Emblems of Previous Games
A267

Designs: No. 675, Swimmers Zeitun and Abd el Gelil and arms of Alexandria. 35m, Race horse "Saadoon."

Perf. 11½x11; 11½ (#676)

1965, Sept. 2 Photo. Wmk. 342

674	A266	5m bl & red	3	3
675	A266	10m dp bl & dk brn	15	10
676	A267	10m org brn & dp bl	15	10
677	A266	35m grn & brn	28	25

Issued to publicize the 4th Pan Arab Games, Cairo, Sept. 2-11. No. 675 commemorates the long-distance swimming competition at Alexandria, a part of the Games.

Map of Arab Countries, Emblem of Arab League and Broken Chain—A268

1965, Sept. 13 Photo. ***Perf. 11½***

678	A268	10m brn & yel	6	5

Issued to commemorate the Third Arab Summit Conference, Casablanca, Sept. 13.

Land Forces Emblem and Sun
A269

Perf. 11x11½

1965, Oct. 20 **Wmk. 342**

679	A269	10m bis brn & blk	6	5

Issued for Land Forces Day.

Map of Africa, Torch and Olive Branches—A270

1965, Oct. 21 ***Perf. 11½***

680	A270	10m dl pur & car rose	6	5

Issued to commemorate the Assembly of Heads of State of the Organization for African Unity.

Ramses II, Abu Simbel, and ICY Emblem
A271

Pillars, Philae, and U.N. Emblem
A272

Designs: 35m, Two Ramses II statues, Abu Simbel and UNESCO emblem. 50m, Cartouche of Ramses II and ICY emblem (horiz.).

Photogravure

1965, Oct. 24 ***Perf. 11½*** **Wmk. 342**

681	A271	5m yel & sl grn	10	10
682	A272	10m bl & blk	35	15
683	A271	35m dk vio & yel	75	25

Souvenir Sheet

Imperf.

684	A272	50m brt ultra & dk brn	1.25	1.00

Issued to publicize the international cooperation in saving the Nubian monuments. No. 684 also commemorates the 20th anniversary of the United Nations. No. 684 contains one stamp (42x25m.) and has marginal inscription in bright ultramarine and dark brown. Size: 105x63mm.

Al-Maqrizi, Buildings and Books
A273

Perf. 11½x11

1965, Nov. 20 **Photo.** **Wmk. 342**

685	A273	10m ol & dk sl grn	6	5

Issued to commemorate the 600th anniversary of the birth of Ahmed Al-Maqrizi (1365–1442), historian.

Flag of U.A.R., Arms of Alexandria and Art Symbols—A274

1965, Dec. 16 ***Perf. 11x11½***

686	A274	10m multi	6	5

Issued to publicize the 6th Biennial Exhibition of Fine Arts in Alexandria, Dec. 16, 1965–March 31, 1966.

Parchment Letter, Carrier Pigeon and Postrider—A275

1966, Jan. 2 ***Perf. 11½*** **Wmk. 342**

687	A275	10m multi	10	10

Post Day, Jan. 2. See Nos. CB1–CB2.

Lamp and Arch
A276

Exhibition Poster
A277

1966, Jan. 10 ***Perf. 11*** **Unwmkd.**

688	A276	4m vio & dp org	3	3

Issued for use on greeting cards.

Perf. 11x11½

1966, Jan. 27 **Wmk. 342**

689	A277	10m lt bl & blk	6	5

Industrial Exhibition, Jan. 29–Feb.

Arab League Emblem
A278

Printed Page and Torch
A279

1966, March 22 **Photo.** **Wmk. 342**

690	A278	10m brt yel & pur	6	5

Arab Publicity Week, March 22–28.

1966, March 25 ***Perf. 11x11½***

691	A279	10m dp org & sl bl	6	5

Centenary of the national press.

Traffic Signal at Night
A280

Hands Holding Torch, Flags of U.A.R. and Iraq
A281

1966, May 4 **Photo.** **Wmk. 342**

692	A280	10m grn & red	6	5

Issued for Traffic Day.

1966. May 26 ***Perf. 11x11½***

693	A281	10m dp cl, rose red & brt grn	6	5

Friendship between U.A.R. and Iraq.

Workers and U.N. Emblem
A282

Perf. 11½x11

1966, June 1 **Photo.** **Wmk. 342**

694	A282	5m bl grn & blk	3	3
695	A282	10m brt rose lil & grn	6	5
696	A282	35m org & blk	28	25

Issued to commemorate the 50th session of the International Labor Organization.

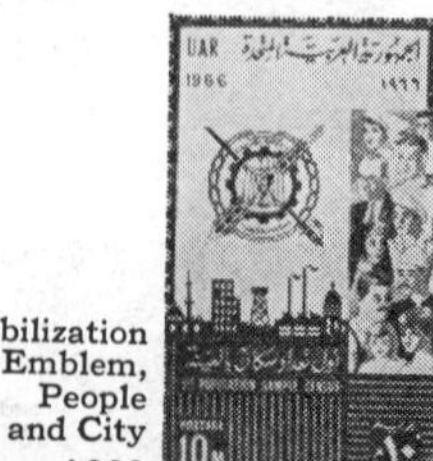

Mobilization Dept. Emblem, People and City
A283

1966, June 30 ***Perf. 11x11½***

697	A283	10m dl pur & brn	6	5

Population sample, May 31–June 16.

"Salah el Din," Crane and Cogwheel
A284

Present-day Basket Dance and Pharaonic Dance—A285

Designs: No. 699, Transfer of first stones of Abu Simbel. No. 700, Development of Sinai (map of Red Sea area and Sinai Peninsula). No. 701, El Maadi Hospital and nurse with patient.

Perf. 11½

1966, July 23 **Photo.** **Wmk. 342**

698	A284	10m org & multi	10	10
699	A284	10m brt grn & multi	10	10
700	A284	10m yel & multi	10	10
701	A284	10m lt bl & multi	10	10

Souvenir Sheet

Imperf.

702	A285	100m multi	1.00	1.00

Issued to commemorate the 14th anniversary of the revolution. No. 702 contains one stamp. Size: 115x67mm.

Suez Canal Headquarters, Ships and Map of Canal—A286

1966, July 26 ***Perf. 11½***

703	A286	10m bl & crim	15	10

Issued to commemorate the 10th anniversary of the nationalization of the Suez Canal.

Cotton, Farmers with Plow and Tractor
A287

Designs: 10m, Rice. 35m, Onions.

Perf. 11½x11

1966, Sept. 9 **Photo.** **Wmk. 342**

704	A287	5m pur & lt bl	3	3
705	A287	10m emer & yel brn	10	10
706	A287	35m bl & org	28	25

Issued for Farmer's Day.

WHO Headquarters, Geneva
A288

Designs: 10m, U.N. refugee emblem. 35m, UNICEF emblem.

Perf. 11½x11

1966, Oct. 24 Wmk. 342

707	A288	5m ol & brt pur	3	3
708	A288	10m org & brt pur	10	10
709	A288	35m lt bl & brt pur	28	25

21st anniversary of the United Nations.

World Map and Festival Emblem
A289

1966, Nov. 8 Photogravure

710	A289	10m brt pur & yel	6	5

Issued to publicize the 5th International Television Festival, Nov. 1–10.

Arms of UAR, Rocket and Pylon
A290

1966, Dec. 23 *Perf. 11½* Wmk. 342

711	A290	10m brt grn & car rose	10	10

Issued for Victory Day.

Jackal
A291

Design: 35m, Alabaster head from Tutankhamen treasure.

1967, Jan. 2 Photogravure

712	A291	10m sl, yel & brn	25	20
713	A291	35m bl, dk vio & ocher	45	45

Issued for Post Day, Jan. 2.

Carnations
A292

Workers Planting Tree
A293

1967, Jan. 10 *Perf. 11* Unwmkd.

714	A292	4m cit & pur	5	3

Issued for use on greeting cards.

Perf. 11x11½

1967, Mar. 15 Wmk. 342

715	A293	10m brt grn & blk vio	8	5

Issued to publicize the Tree Festival.

Gamal el-Dine el-Afaghani and Arab League Emblem
A294

1967, Mar. 22 Photo. Wmk. 342

716	A294	10m dp grn & dk brn	8	5

Arab Publicity Week, March 22–28.

Census Emblem, Man, Woman and Factory—A295

1967, Apr. 23 *Perf. 11½x11*

717	A295	10m blk & dp org	8	5

First industrial census.

Brickmaking Fresco, Tomb of Rekhmire, Thebes, 1504–1450 B.C.—A296

1967, May 1 Photo. Wmk. 342

718	A296	10m ol & org	8	5

Issued for Labor Day, 1967.

Ramses II and Queen Nefertari
A297

Design: 35m, Shooting geese, frieze from tomb of Atet at Meidum, c. 2724 B. C.

Perf. 11½x11

1967, June 7 Photo. Wmk. 342

719	A297	10m multi	25	20
720	A297	35m dk grn & org	45	45
		Nos. 719-720, C113-C115 (5)	3.20	1.85

Issued for International Tourist Year, 1967.

President Nasser, Crowd and Map of Palestine
A298

1967, June 22 *Perf. 11½*

721	A298	10m dp org, yel & ol	45	30

Issued to publicize Arab solidarity for "the defense of Palestine."

Souvenir Sheet

National Products—A299

1967, July 23 *Imperf.* Wmk. 342

722	A299	100m multi	90	90

Issued to commemorate the 15th anniversary of the revolution. No. 722 contains one stamp with yellow, green and brown margin. Size: 111½x66mm.

Salama Higazi
A300

Perf. 11x11½

1967, Oct. 14 Photo. Wmk. 342

723	A300	20m brn & dk bl	12	8

Issued to commemorate the 50th anniversary of the death of Salama Higazi, pioneer of Egyptian lyric stage.

Stag on Ceramic Disk
A301

Design: 55m, Apse showing Christ in Glory, Madonna and Saints, Coptic Museum, and UNESCO Emblem.

1967, Oct. 24 *Perf. 11½*

724	A301	20m dl rose & dk bl	12	8
725	A301	55m dk sl grn & yel	45	25

Issued to commemorate the 22nd anniversary of the United Nations. See No. C117.

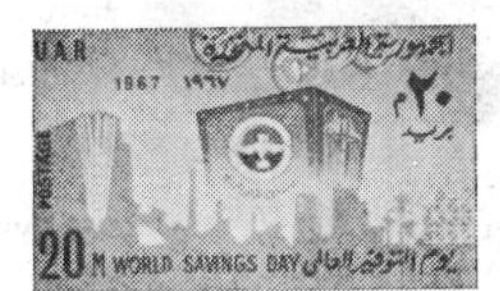

Savings Bank and Postal Authority Emblems—A302

1967, Oct. 31 *Perf. 11½x11*

726	A302	20m sal pink & dk bl	12	8

International Savings Day.

Rose
A303

Photogravure

1967, Dec. 15 *Perf. 11* Unwmkd.

727	A303	5m grn & rose lil	5	3

Issued for use on greeting cards.

Pharaonic Dress
A304

Aswan High Dam and Power Lines
A305

Designs: Various pharaonic dresses from temple decorations.

Perf 11x11½

1968, Jan. 2 Wmk. 342

728	A304	20m brn, grn & buff	25	10
729	A304	55m lt grn, yel & sep	75	25
730	A304	80m dk brn, bl & brt rose	1.25	50

Issued for Post Day, Jan. 2.

1968, Jan. 9

731	A305	20m yel, bl & dk brn	10	8

Issued to commemorate the first electricity generated by the Aswan Hydroelectric Station.

Alabaster Vessel, Tutankhamen Treasure
A306

Girl, Moon and Paint Brushes
A308

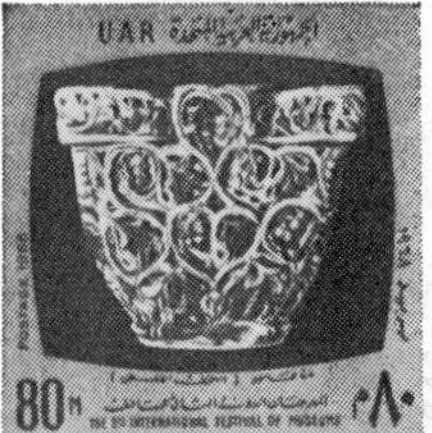

Capital of Coptic Limestone Pillar
A307

Perf. 11x11½, 11½

1968, Jan. 20 Photo. Wmk. 342

732	A306	20m dk ultra, yel & brn	15	10
733	A307	80m lt grn, dk pur & ol grn	40	35

2nd International Festival of Museums.

1968, Feb. 15 ***Perf. 11x11½***

734	A308	20m brt bl & blk	10	8

Issued to publicize the 7th Biennial Exhibition of Fine Arts, Alexandria, Feb. 15.

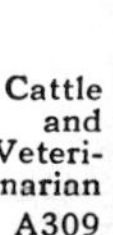

Cattle and Veterinarian A309

Perf. 11½x11

1968, May 4 Photo. **Wmk. 342**

735	A309	20m brn, yel & grn	10	8

8th Arab Veterinary Congress, Cairo.

Human Rights Flame A310

Perf. 11x11½

1968, July 1 Photo. **Wmk. 342**

736	A310	20m cit, crim & grn	12	8
737	A310	60m sky bl, crim & grn	36	30

International Human Rights Year, 1968.

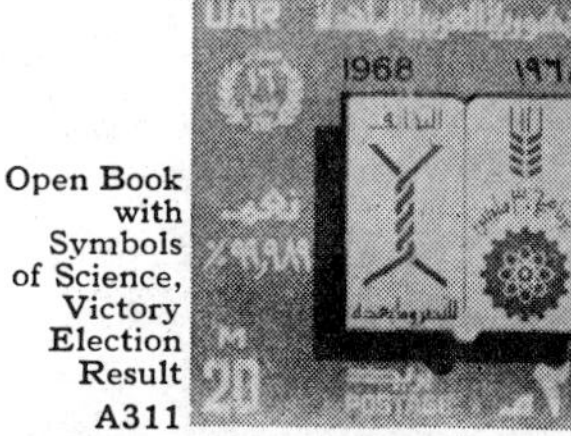

Open Book with Symbols of Science, Victory Election Result A311

Workers, Cogwheel with Coat of Arms and Open Book A312

1968, July 23 ***Perf. 11½***

738	A311	20m rose red & sl grn	12	8

Souvenir Sheet

Imperf.

739	A312	10m lt grn, org & pur	1.00	1.00

16th anniversary of the revolution.
No. 739 has orange marginal inscription and the ornaments. Size: 116x68mm.

Imhotep and WHO Emblem—A313

Design: No. 741, Avicenna and WHO emblem.

Perf. 11½x11

1968, Sept. 1 Photo. **Wmk. 342**

740	A313	20m bl, yel & brn	30	10
741	A313	20m yel, bl & brn	30	10

Issued to commemorate the 20th anniversary of the World Health Organization. Nos. 740–741 printed in checkerboard sheets of 50 (5x10).

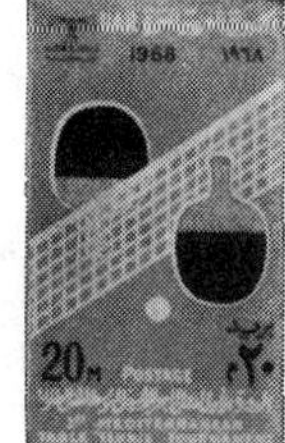

Table Tennis A314

Perf. 11x11½

1968, Sept. 20 Photo. **Wmk. 342**

742	A314	20m lt grn & dk brn	12	8

First Mediterranean Table Tennis Tournament, Alexandria, Sept. 20–27.

Factories and Fair Emblem A315

1968, Oct. 20 ***Perf. 11½*** **Wmk. 342**

743	A315	20m bl gray, red & sl bl	12	8

Cairo International Industrial Fair.

Temples of Philae—A316

Refugees, Map of Palestine, Refugee Year Emblem A317

Design: 55m, Temple at Philae and UNESCO emblem.

1968, Oct. 24 **Photogravure**

744	A316	20m multi	12	8
745	A317	30m multi	25	20
746	A317	55m lt bl, yel & blk	50	26

Issued for United Nations Day, Oct. 24.

Egyptian Boy Scout Emblem A318

1968, Nov. 1

747	A318	10m dl org & vio bl	6	4

50th anniversary of Egyptian Boy Scouts.

Pharaonic Sports A319

Design: 30m, Pharaonic sports (different).

1968, Nov. 1

748	A319	20m pale ol, pale sal & blk	12	8
749	A319	30m pale bl, buff & pur	18	15

Issued to commemorate the 19th Olympic Games, Mexico City, Oct. 12–27.

Aly Moubarak A320

Lotus A321

1968, Nov. 9 ***Perf. 11½***

750	A320	20m grn, brn & bis	25	8

Issued to honor Aly Moubarak (1823–1893), founder of the modern educational system in Egypt.

1968, Dec. 11 Photo. **Wmk. 342**

751	A321	5m brt bl, grn & yel	10	3

Issued for use on greeting cards.

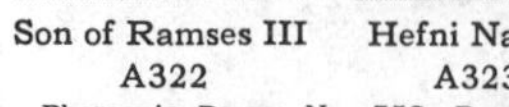

Son of Ramses III A322

Hefni Nassef A323

Pharaonic Dress: No. 753, Ramses III. No. 754, Girl carrying basket on her head. 55m, Queen of the New Empire in transparent dress.

1969, Jan. 2 Photo. ***Perf. 11½***

752	A322	5m bl & multi	20	5
753	A322	20m bl & multi	25	10
754	A322	20m bl & multi	30	15
755	A322	55m bl & multi	70	35

Issued for Post Day, Jan. 2.

Perf. 11x11½

1969, Mar. 2 Photo. **Wmk. 342**

Portrait: No. 757, Mohammed Farid.

756	A323	20m pur & brn	30	10
757	A323	20m emer & brn	30	10

Issued to commemorate the 50th anniversaries of the death of Hefni Nassef (1860–1919) writer and government worker, and of Mohammed Farid (1867–1919), lawyer and Speaker of the Nationalist Party. Nos. 756–757 printed se-tenant in sheets of 50 (10x5).

Teacher and Children A324

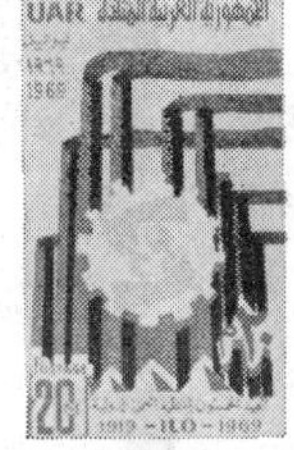

ILO Emblem and Factory Chimneys A325

1969, Mar. 2 ***Perf. 11x11½***

758	A324	20m multi	25	8

Arab Teacher's Day.

1969, Apr. 11 Photo. **Wmk. 342**

759	A325	20m brn, ultra & car	25	8

Issued to commemorate the 50th anniversary of the International Labor Organization.

Flag of Algeria, Africa Day and Tourist Year Emblems—A326

Wmk. 342

1969, May 25 Litho. ***Perf. 11½x11***

Flags in Original Colors

760	A326	10m grn (*Algeria*)	20	12
761	A326	10m grn (*Botswana*)	20	12
762	A326	10m grn (*Burundi*)	20	12
763	A326	10m grn (*Cameroun*)	20	12
764	A326	10m bl (*Cent. Afr. Rep.*)	20	12
765	A326	10m bl (*Chad*)	20	12
766	A326	10m bl (*Congo, ex-Belgian*)	20	12
767	A326	10m grn (*Congo, ex-French*)	20	12
768	A326	10m grn (*Dahomey*)	20	12
769	A326	10m bl (*Equatorial Guinea*)	20	12
770	A326	10m bl (*Ethiopia*)	20	12
771	A326	10m bl (*Gabon*)	20	12
772	A326	10m grn (*Gambia*)	20	12
773	A326	10m grn (*Ghana*)	20	12
774	A326	10m grn (*Guinea*)	20	12
775	A326	10m grn (*Ivory Coast*)	20	12
776	A326	10m grn (*Kenya*)	20	12
777	A326	10m grn (*Lesotho*)	20	12
778	A326	10m bl (*Liberia*)	20	12
779	A326	10m grn (*Libya*)	20	12
780	A326	10m grn (*Malagasy*)	20	12
781	A326	10m grn (*Malawi*)	20	12
782	A326	10m grn (*Mali*)	20	12
783	A326	10m grn (*Mauritania*)	20	12
784	A326	10m bl (*Mauritius*)	20	12
785	A326	10m grn (*Morocco*)	20	12
786	A326	10m grn (*Niger*)	20	12
787	A326	10m grn (*Nigeria*)	20	12
788	A326	10m grn (*Rwanda*)	20	12
789	A326	10m grn (*Senegal*)	20	12
790	A326	10m grn (*Sierra Leone*)	20	12
791	A326	10m grn (*Somalia*)	20	12
792	A326	10m bl (*Sudan*)	20	12

793 A326 10m vio (*Swaziland*) 20 12
794 A326 10m bl (*Tanzania*) 20 12
795 A326 10m grn (*Togo*) 20 12
796 A326 10m grn (*Tunisia*) 20 12
797 A326 10m blk (*Uganda*) 20 12
798 A326 10m grn (*Egypt*) 20 12
799 A326 10m grn (*Upper Volta*) 20 12
800 A326 10m bl (*Zambia*) 20 12
Nos. 760-800 (41) 8.20 4.92

Year of African Tourism, 1969.

El Fetouh Gate, Cairo
A327

Sculptures from the Egyptian Museum, Cairo—A328

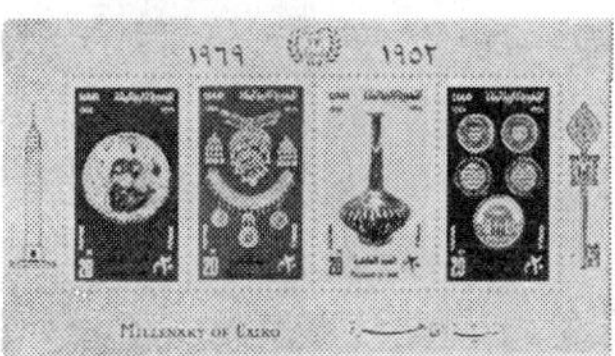

Millenary of Cairo—A329

Designs: No. 802, Al Azhar University. No. 803, The Citadel. No. 805, Sculptures, Coptic Museum. No. 806, Glass plate and vase, Fatimid dynasty, Islamic Museum. No. 807a, Islamic coin. No. 807b, Fatimist era jewelry. No. 807c, Copper vase. No. 807d, Coins and plaque.

Perf. 11½x11

1969, July 23 Photo. Wmk. 342

801 A327 10m dk brn & multi 10 4
802 A327 10m grn & multi 10 4
803 A327 10m bl & multi 10 4

Perf. 11½

804 A328 20m yel grn & multi 25 10
805 A328 20m dp ultra & multi 25 10
806 A328 20m brn & multi 25 10
Nos. 801-806 (6) 1.05 42

Souvenir Sheet

807 A329 Souv. sheet of 4 1.25 1.25
a. 20m dk bl & multi 18 12
b. 20m lil & multi 18 12
c. 20m yel & multi 18 12
d. 20m dk grn & multi 18 12

Issued to commemorate the millenium of the founding of Cairo. No. 807 has pale lilac margin and dark blue inscription. Size: 128x70mm.

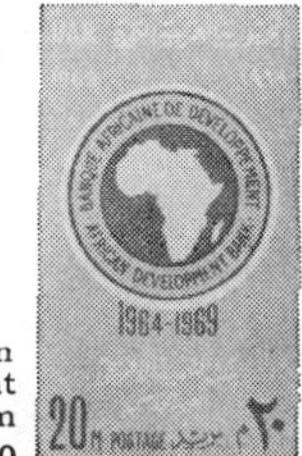

African Development Bank Emblem
A330

Perf. 11x11½

1969, Sept. 10 Photo. Wmk. 342

808 A330 20m emer, yel & vio 25 8

Issued to publicize the 5th anniversary of the African Development Bank.

Pharaonic Boat and UN Emblem
A331

Temple of Philae Inundated and UNESCO Emblem
A332

Design: 5m, King and Queen from Abu Simbel Temple and UNESCO Emblem (size: 21x38mm.).

Perf. 11x11½, 11½x11

1969, Oct. 24 Photo. Wmk. 342

809 A332 5m brn & multi 5 3
810 A331 20m yel & ultra 25 8

Perf. 11½

811 A332 55m yel & multi 45 22

Issued for United Nations Day.

Ships of 1869 and 1967 and Maps of Africa and Suez Canal—A333

1969, Nov. 15 ***Perf. 11½x11***

812 A333 20m lt bl & multi 25 8

Centenary of the Suez Canal.

Cairo Opera House and Performance of Aida—A334

1969, Nov. 15

813 A334 20m multi 25 8

Centenary of the Cairo Opera House.

Crowd with Egyptian and Revolutionary Flags—A335

1969, Nov. 15 ***Perf. 11½x11***

814 A335 20m brt grn, dl lil & red 25 8

Revolution of 1919.

Ancient Arithmetic and Computer Cards—A336

Perf. 11½x11

1969, Dec. 17 Photo. Wmk. 342

815 A336 20m multi 25 8

Issued to publicize the International Congress for Scientific Accounting, Cairo, Dec. 17–19.

Poinsettia
A337

Sakkara Step Pyramid
A338

El Fetouh Gate, Cairo
A339

Fountain, Sultan Hassan Mosque, Cairo
A340

King Khafre (Ruled c. 2850 B.C.)
A341

1969, Dec. 24 ***Perf. 11*** **Unwmkd.**

816 A337 5m yel, grn & car 3 3

Issued for use on greeting cards.

Photo.; Engr. (20m, 55m)

Unwmkd.; Wmk. 342 (20m, £1)

1969–70 ***Perf. 11***

Designs: 5m, Al Azhar Mosque. 10m, Luxor Temple. 50m, Qaitbay Fort, Alexandria.

817 A338 1m multi ('70) 3 3
818 A338 5m multi ('70) 3 3
819 A338 10m multi ('70) 6 4
820 A339 20m dk brn 40 8
821 A338 50m multi ('70) 30 20
822 A340 55m sl grn 75 22

Perf. 11½

Photo. and Engr.

823 A341 £1 org & sl grn ('70) 7.00 4.00
Nos. 817-823 (7) 8.57 4.60

See Nos. 889–891, 893–897, 899, 901–902, 904.

Veiled Women, by Mahmoud Said
A342

Perf. 11x11½

1970, Jan. 2 Photo. Wmk. 342

Size: 45x89mm.

824 A342 100m bl & multi 1.75 45

Post Day, Jan. 2. Sheet of 8 with two panes of 4.

Parliament, Scales, Globe and Laurel—A343

1970, Feb. 2 ***Perf. 11½x11***

825 A343 20m bl, vio bl & ocher 25 8

Issued to publicize the International Conference of Parliamentarians on the Middle East Crisis, Cairo, Feb. 2–5.

Map of Arab League Countries, Flag and Emblem—A344

Perf. 11½x11

1970, Mar. 22 Photo. Wmk. 342

826 A344 30m brn org, grn & dk pur 25 12

Issued to commemorate the 25th anniversary of the Arab League. See No. B42.

Mena House and Sheraton Hotel
A345

1970, Mar. 23

827 A345 20m ol, org & bl 25 8

Issued to commemorate the centenary of Mena House and the inauguration of the Cairo Sheraton Hotel.

Manufacture of Medicine—A346

1970, Apr. 20

828	A346	20m brn, yel & bl	25	8

Issued to commemorate the 30th anniversary of the production of medicines in Egypt.

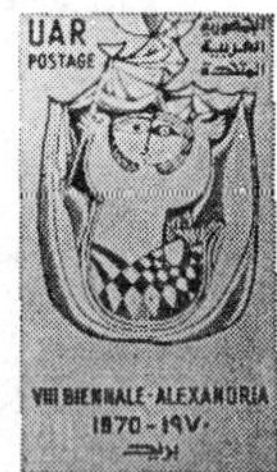

Mermaid
A347

1970, Apr. 20 ***Perf. 11x11½***

829	A347	20m org, blk & ultra	25	8

Issued to publicize the 8th Biennial Exhibition of Fine Arts, Alexandria, March 12.

Misr Bank and Talaat Harb
A348

ITU Emblem
A349

1970, May 7 Photo. **Wmk. 342**

830	A348	20m multi	25	8

50th anniversary of Misr Bank.

1970, May 17 ***Perf. 11x11½***

831	A349	20m dk brn, yel & dl bl	25	8

World Telecommunications Day.

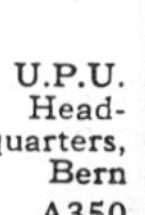

U.P.U. Headquarters, Bern
A350

1970, May 20 ***Perf. 11½x11***

832	A350	20m multi	25	8

Issued to commemorate the inauguration of the new Universal Postal Union Headquarters in Bern. See No. C128.

Basketball Player and Map of Africa
A351

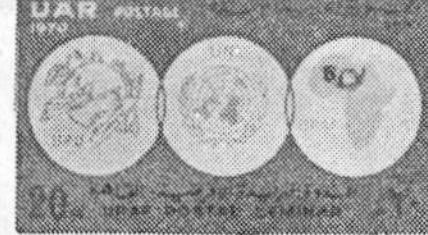

U.P.U., U.N. and U.P.A.F. Emblems
A352

Designs: No. 834, Soccer player, map of Africa and cup (horiz.).

Perf. 11x11½, 11½x11

1970, May 25 Photo. **Wmk. 342**

833	A351	20m lt bl, yel & brn	25	8
834	A351	20m yel & multi	25	8
835	A352	20m ocher, grn & blk	25	8

Issued for Africa Day. No. 833 also commemorates the 5th African basketball championship for men; No. 834 the annual African Soccer championship and No. 835 publicizes the African Postal Union seminar.

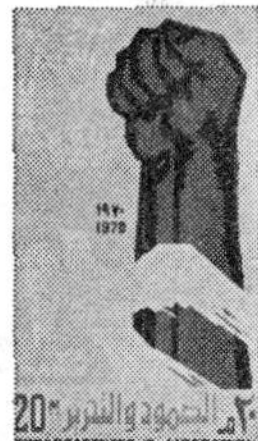

Fist and Freed Bird
A353

1970, July 23 Photo. ***Perf. 11***

836	A353	20m lt grn, org & blk	25	8

Souvenir Sheet

Imperf.

837	A353	100m lt bl, dp org & blk	1.00	45

Issued to commemorate the 18th anniversary of the revolution. No. 837 contains one stamp; U.N. emblem, Scales of Justice and orange commemorative inscription in margin. Size: 110x70mm.

Al Aqsa Mosque on Fire—A354

1970, Aug. 21 ***Perf. 11*** **Wmk. 342**

838	A354	20m multi	25	8
839	A354	60m brt bl & multi	50	24

First anniversary of the burning of Al Aqsa Mosque, Jerusalem.

Standardization Emblems
A355

1970, Oct. 14 ***Perf. 11*** **Wmk. 342**

840	A355	20m yel, ultra & grn	25	8

Issued to commemorate World Standards Day and the 25th anniversary of the International Standardization Organization, ISO.

U.N. Emblem, Scales and Dove
A356

Temple at Philae
A357

Child, Education Year and U.N. Emblems
A358

Designs: 10m, U.N. emblem. No. 845, Second Temple at Philae (denomination at left).

Perf. 11 (5m), 11½ (others)

1970, Oct. 24 Photo. **Wmk. 342**

841	A356	5m lt bl, rose lil & sl	10	10
842	A357	10m yel, brn & lt bl	15	10
843	A358	20m sl & multi	25	15
844	A357	55m brn, bl & ocher	45	25
845	A357	55m brn, bl & ocher	45	25
		Strip of 3 (#842,844-845)	1.05	60
		Nos. 841-845, B43 (6)	1.90	1.05

Issued to commemorate the 25th anniversary of the United Nations. No. 843 also commemorates International Education Year; Nos. 842, 844-845 commemorate the work of UNESCO in saving the Temples of Philae; Nos. 842, 844-845 printed se-tenant in sheets of 35 (15 No. 842 and 10 each Nos. 844-845). Nos. 844-845 show continuous picture of the Temples at Philae.

Gamal Abdel Nasser
A359

1970, Nov. 6 ***Perf. 11*** **Wmk. 342**

846	A359	5m sky bl & blk	8	3
847	A359	20m gray grn & blk	25	8

Issued in memory of Gamal Abdel Nasser (1918-1970), President of Egypt. See Nos. C129-C130.

Medical Association Building
A360

Designs: No. 849, Old and new National Library. No. 850, Egyptian Credo (Nasser quotation). No. 851, Engineering Society, old and new buildings. No. 852, Government Printing Offices, old and new buildings.

1970, Dec. 20 Photo. ***Perf. 11***

848	A360	20m yel, grn & brn	25	8
849	A360	20m grn & multi	25	8
850	A360	20m lt bl & brn	25	8
851	A360	20m bl, yel & brn	25	8
852	A360	20m bl, yel & brn	25	8
		Nos. 848-852 (5)	1.25	40

Nos. 848-852 printed se-tenant in sheets of 50 (5x10) commemorate: 50th anniversary of Egyptian Medical Association (No. 848); centenary of National Library (No. 849); Egyptian Engineering Association (No. 851) sesquicentennial of Government Printing Offices (No. 852).

Map and Flags of UAR, Libya, Sudan
A361

1970, Dec. 27 ***Perf. 11½***

853	A361	20m lt grn, car & blk	25	8

Signing of the Charter of Tripoli affirming the unity of UAR, Libya and the Sudan, Dec. 27, 1970.

Qalawun Minaret
A362

Designs (Minarets): 10m, As Saleh. 20m, Isna. 55m, Al Hakim.

1971, Jan. 2 ***Perf. 11*** **Wmk. 342**

854	A362	5m grn & multi	5	3
855	A362	10m grn & multi	15	4
856	A362	20m grn & multi	25	8
857	A362	55m grn & multi	55	20
		Strip of 4 (#854-857) + label	1.00	35

Post Day, 1971. Nos. 854-857 printed se-tenant in sheets of 40 stamps and 10 blue and yellow labels.

See Nos. 905-908, 932-935.

Gamal Abdel Nasser
A363

Photogravure and Engraved

1971 ***Perf. 11½*** **Wmk. 342**

858	A363	200m brn vio & dk bl	2.50	1.00
859	A363	500m bl & blk	6.00	2.75

Souvenir Sheet

Design: Portrait facing right.

Imperf.

860	A363	Sheet of 2	6.00	3.75
	a.	100m lt grn & blk	3.00	1.00
	b.	200m bl & blk	2.25	1.75

No. 860 commemorates inauguration of the Aswan High Dam, which is shown in margin. Green and blue marginal inscription. Size: 134x79mm.

Issue dates: No. 860, Jan. 15; Nos. 858-859, Feb. 1.

See No. 903.

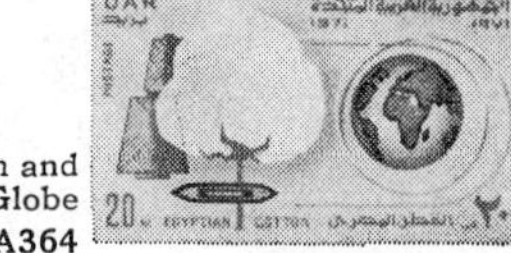

Cotton and Globe
A364

1971, Mar. 6 Photo. *Perf. 11½x11*

861 A364 20m lt grn, bl & brn 25 10

Egyptian cotton.

Arab Countries, and Arab Postal Union Emblem
A365

1971, Mar. 6 Wmk. 342

862 A365 20m lt bl, org & sl grn 25 10

9th Arab Postal Congress, Cairo, March 6–25. See No. C131.

Cairo Fair Emblem
A366

1971, Mar. 6 *Perf. 11x11½*

863 A366 20m plum, blk & org 25 10

Cairo International Fair, March 2–23.

Nesy Ra, Apers Papyrus and WHO Emblem—A367

Perf. 11½x11

1971, Apr. 30 Photo. Wmk. 342

864 A367 20m yel bis & pur 25 10

World Health Organization Day.

Gamal Abdel Nasser
A368

1971, May 1 *Perf. 11*

865 A368 20m pur & bl gray 12 8
866 A368 55m bl & pur 33 20

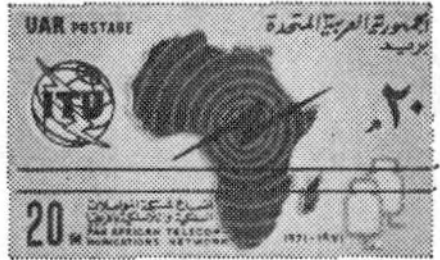

Map of Africa, Telecommunications Symbols
A369

1971, May 17 *Perf. 11½x11*

867 A369 20m bl & multi 25 10

Pan-African telecommunications system.

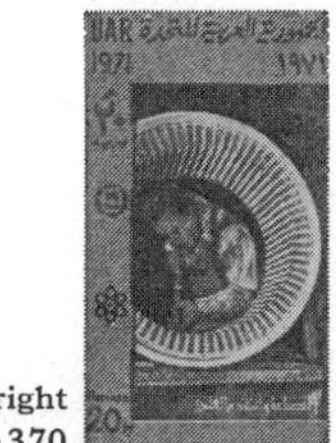

Wheelwright
A370

Hand Holding Wheat and Laurel
A371

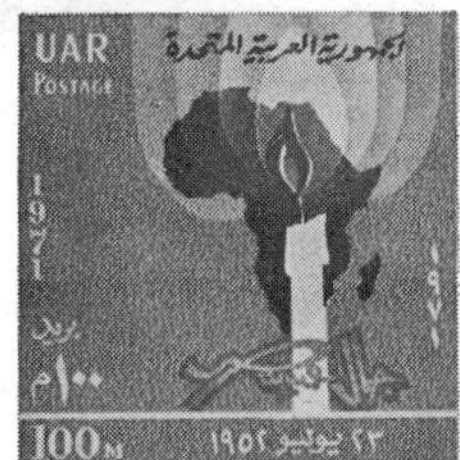

Candle Lighting Africa—A372

Perf. 11x11½

1971, July 23 Photo. Wmk. 342

868 A370 20m yel & multi 25 8
869 A371 20m tan, grn & ocher 25 8

Souvenir Sheet

Imperf.

870 A372 100m bl & multi 1.00 60

19th anniversary of the July Revolution. No. 870 contains one stamp with simulated perforations in gold and with blue marginal inscription. Portrait of Pres. Nasser in margin. Size: 115x70mm.

Arab Postal Union Emblem
A373

1971, Aug. 3 *Perf. 11½*

871 A373 20m blk, yel & grn 25 8

25th anniversary of the Conference of Sofar, Lebanon, establishing the Arab Postal Union. See No. C135.

Arab Republic of Egypt

Three Links
A374

Perf. 11½x11

1971, Sept. 28 Photo. Wmk. 342

872 A374 20m gray, org brn & blk 25 10

Confederation of Arab Republics (Egypt, Syria and Libya). See No. C136.

Gamal Abdel Nasser
A375

Blood Donation
A376

1971, Sept. 28 *Perf. 11x11½*

873 A375 5m sl grn & vio brn 3 3
874 A375 20m vio brn & ultra 12 8
875 A375 30m ultra & brn 18 12
876 A375 55m brn & emer 33 20

First anniversary of the death of President Gamal Abdel Nasser.

1971, Oct. 24

877 A376 20m grn & car 25 8

"Blood Saves Lives."

Princess Nursing Child, UNICEF Emblem
A377

Submerged Pillar, Philae, UNESCO Emblem
A379

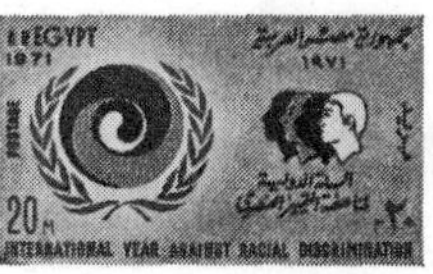

Equality Year Emblem
A378

Perf. 11x11½, 11½x11

1971, Oct. 24 Photo. Wmk. 342

878 A377 5m buff, blk & org brn 5 3
879 A378 20m red brn, grn, yel & blk 25 8
880 A379 55m blk, lt bl, yel & brn 50 20

United Nations Day. No. 878 honors U.N. International Children's Fund; No. 879 for International Year Against Racial Discrimination; No. 880 honors U.N. Educational, Scientific and Cultural Organization. See No. C137.

Postal Traffic Center, Alexandria
A380

1971, Oct. 31 *Perf. 11½x11*

881 A380 20m bl & bis 25 8

Opening of Postal Traffic Center in Alexandria.

Sunflower
A381

Abdalla El Nadim
A382

1971, Nov. 13 *Perf. 11*

882 A381 5m lt bl & multi 10 5

For use on greeting cards.

1971, Nov. 14 *Perf. 11x11½*

883 A382 20m grn & brn 25 10

Abdalla El Nadim (1845–1896), journalist, publisher, connected with Orabi Revolution.

Section of Earth's Crust, Map of Africa on Globe
A383

1971, Nov. 27 *Perf. 11½x11*

884 A383 20m ultra, yel & brn 25 10

75th anniversary of Egyptian Geological Survey and International Conference, Nov. 27–Dec. 1.

Postal Union Emblem, Letter and Dove
A384

Design: 55m, African Postal Union emblem and letter.

1971, Dec. 2

885 A384 5m multi 5 3
886 A384 20m ol, blk & org 25 8
887 A384 55m red, blk & bl 50 20

10th anniversary of African Postal Union. See No. C138.

Money and Safe Deposit Box
A385

1971, Dec. 23 *Perf. 11½*

888 A385 20m rose, brn & grn 25 8

70th anniversary of Postal Savings Bank.

Types of 1969–70, 1971 Inscribed "A. R. Egypt" and

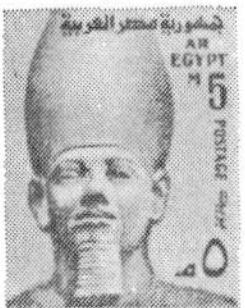

Ramses II
A385a

Designs as before and: No. 894, King Citi I. No. 897, Queen Nefertari. No. 900, Sphinx and Middle Pyramid. 100m, Cairo Mosque. 200m, Head of Pharaoh Userkaf.

Unwmkd., Wmk. 342 (#892A, 901-904)
1972-76 Photo. *Perf. 11*

No.	Type	Description	Unused	Used
889	A338	1m multi	3	3
890	A338	1m dk brn ('73)	3	3
891	A338	5m multi	3	3
892	A385a	5m ol ('73)	3	3
892A	A385a	5m bis ('76)	3	3
893	A338	10m multi	7	5
894	A338	10m lt brn ('73)	5	3
895	A339	20m olive	40	20
896	A339	20m pur ('73)	10	3
897	A338	50m multi	33	22
898	A385a	50m dl bl ('73)	25	15
899	A340	55m red lil	36	24
900	A340	55m grn ('74)	75	40
901	A339	100m lt bl, dp org & blk	50	35

Perf. 11½

Photogravure and Engraved

No.	Type	Description	Unused	Used
902	A341	200m yel grn & brn	1.00	70
903	A363	500m bl & choc	2.30	1.50
904	A341	£1 org & sl grn	4.60	3.50
		Nos. 889-904 (17)	10.86	7.52

Minaret Type of 1971

Designs: 5m, West Minaret, Nasser Mosque. 20m, East Minaret, Nasser Mosque. 30m, Minaret, Al Gawli Mosque. 55m, Minaret, Ibn Tulun Mosque.

Photogravure

1972, Jan. 2 *Perf. 11* Wmk. 342

No.	Type	Description	Unused	Used
905	A362	5m dk grn & multi	3	3
906	A362	20m dk grn & multi	14	9
907	A362	30m dk grn & multi	20	14
908	A362	55m dk grn & multi	36	25
		Strip of 4 (#905-908) + label	73	51

Post Day, 1972. Nos. 905–908 printed se-tenant in sheets of 40 stamps and 10 blue and yellow labels.

Police Emblem and Activities
A386

1972, Jan. 25 *Perf. 11½*

No.	Type	Description	Unused	Used
909	A386	20m dl bl, brn & yel	25	9

Police Day 1972.

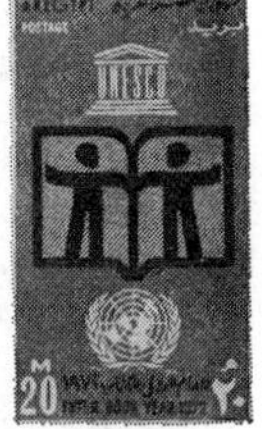

UNESCO, U.N. and Book Year Emblems
A387

1972, Jan. 25 *Perf. 11x11½*

No.	Type	Description	Unused	Used
910	A387	20m lt yel grn, vio bl & yel	25	9

International Book Year 1972.

Alexandria Biennale
A388

1972, Feb. 15 *Perf. 11½* Wmk. 342

No.	Type	Description	Unused	Used
911	A388	20m blk, brt rose & yel	14	9

9th Biennial Exhibition of Fine Arts, Alexandria, March, 1972.

Fair Emblem
A389

Abdel Moniem Riad
390

1972, March 5 *Perf. 11x11½*

No.	Type	Description	Unused	Used
912	A389	20m bl, org & yel grn	25	9

International Cairo Fair.

1972, Mar. 21 Photo. Wmk. 342

No.	Type	Description	Unused	Used
913	A390	20m bl & brn	25	9

In memory of Brig. Gen. Abdel Moniem Riad (1919–1969), military hero.

Bird Feeding Young
A391

1972, Mar. 21 *Perf. 11½*

No.	Type	Description	Unused	Used
914	A391	20m yel & multi	25	9

Mother's Day.

Tutankhamen
A392

Design: 55m, Back of chair with king's name and symbols of eternity.

1972, May 22 Unwmkd.

No.	Type	Description	Unused	Used
915	A392	20m gray, blk & ocher	50	20
916	A392	55m pur & yel	1.00	30

50th anniversary of the discovery of the tomb of Tutankhamen by Howard Carter and Lord Carnarvon. See Nos. C142–C144.

Queen Nefertiti
A393

Perf. 11½

1972, May 22 Photo. Wmk. 342

No.	Type	Description	Unused	Used
917	A393	20m red, blk & gold	10	7

50th anniversary of the Society of the Friends of Art.

Map of Africa
A394

1972, May 25 *Perf. 11x11½*

No.	Type	Description	Unused	Used
918	A394	20m pur, bl & brn	25	7

Africa Day.

Atom Symbol, "Faith and Science"
A395

Design: No. 920, Egyptian coat of arms.

1972, July 23 *Perf. 11½*

No.	Type	Description	Unused	Used
919	A395	20m bl, cl & blk	15	7
920	A395	20m ol grn, gold & blk	15	7

20th anniversary of the revolution.

Boxing, Olympic and Motion Emblems—A396

Designs (Olympic and Motion Emblems and): 10m, Wrestling. 20m, Basketball.

1972, Aug. 17 *Perf. 11½x11*

No.	Type	Description	Unused	Used
921	A396	5m bl & multi	3	3
922	A396	10m yel & multi	5	4
923	A396	20m ver & multi	10	7
		Nos. 921-923, C149-C152 (7)	1.01	66

20th Olympic Games, Munich, Aug. 26–Sept. 11.

Flag of Confederation of Arab Republics—A397

1972, Sept. 1 *Perf. 11½* Wmk. 342

No.	Type	Description	Unused	Used
924	A397	20m car, bis & blk	15	7

First anniversary of Confederation of Arab Republics.

Red Crescent, TB and UN Emblems
A398

Heart and WHO Emblem
A399

Refugees, UNRWA Emblem, Map of Palestine—A400

Design: 55m, Inundated Temple of Philae, UNESCO emblem.

1972, Oct. 24 Photo. *Perf. 11x11½*

No.	Type	Description	Unused	Used
925	A398	10m brn org, red & bl	5	3

Perf. 11½

No.	Type	Description	Unused	Used
926	A399	20m grn, yel & blk	10	7

Perf. 11

No.	Type	Description	Unused	Used
927	A400	30m lt bl, pur & lt brn	15	10

Perf. 11½

No.	Type	Description	Unused	Used
928	A399	55m brn, gold & bluish gray	27	18

United Nations Day. No. 925 commemorates the 14th Regional Tuberculosis Conference, Cairo, 1972; No. 926 is for World Health Month; No. 927 publicizes aid to refugees and No. 928 the U.N. campaign to save the Temples at Philae.

Morning Glory
A401

1972, Oct. 24 *Perf. 11*

No.	Type	Description	Unused	Used
929	A401	10m yel, lil & grn	5	3

For use on greeting cards.

"Seeing Eye"
A402

1972, Nov. 30 *Perf. 11½*

No.	Type	Description	Unused	Used
930	A402	20m multi	15	7

Social Work Day.

Sculling Race, View of Luxor—A403

1972, Dec. 17 *Perf. 11* Wmk. 342

No.	Type	Description	Unused	Used
931	A403	20m bl & brn	10	7

Third Nile International Rowing Festival, Dec. 1972.

Minaret Type of 1971

Minarets: 10m, Al Maridani, 1338. 20m, Bashtak, 1337. 30m, Qusun, 1330. 55m, Al Gashankir, 1306.

1973, Jan. 2

Frame in Brt. Yel. Green

932	A362	10m multi	5	3
933	A362	20m multi	10	7
934	A362	30m multi	15	10
935	A362	55m multi	27	18
		Strip of 4 (#932-935) + Label	57	38

Post Day, 1973. Nos. 932–935 printed se-tenant in sheets of 40 stamps and 10 yellow and green labels.

Cairo Fair Emblem
A404

Perf. 11½x11

1973, Mar. 21 Photo. Wmk. 342

936	A404	20m gray & multi	10	7

International Cairo Fair.

Family
A405

1973, Mar. 21 *Perf. 11x11½*

937	A405	20m multi	10	7

Family planning.

Sania Girls' School and Hoda Sharawi
A406

Perf. 11½x11

1973, July 15 Photo. Wmk. 342

938	A406	20m ultra, grn & brn	10	7

Centenary of education for girls and 50th anniversary of the Egyptian Women's Union, founded by Hoda Sharawi.

Rifaa el Tahtawi
A407

1973, July 15 *Perf. 11x11½*

939	A407	20m brt grn, ol & brn	10	7

Centenary of the death of Rifaa el Tahtawi, champion of democracy and principal of language school.

Omar Makram
A408

Abdel Rahman al Gabarti, Historian
A409

"Reconstruction and Battle"—A410

Design: No. 941, Mohamed Korayem, martyr.

1973, July 23

940	A408	20m yel grn, bl & brn	10	7
941	A408	20m lt grn, bl & brn	10	7
942	A409	20m ocher & brn	10	7

Souvenir Sheet

Imperf.

943	A410	110m gold, bl & blk	1.00	1.00

21st anniversary of the revolution establishing the republic. No. 943 contains one stamp and has gold marginal inscription. Size: 97x102mm.

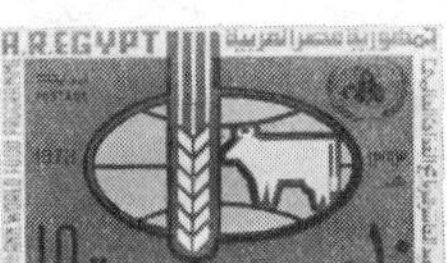

Grain, Cow, FAO Emblem
A411

Perf. 11½x11

1973, Oct. 24 Wmk. 342

944	A411	10m brn, dk bl & yel grn	5	4

10th anniversary of the World Food Organization.

Inundated Temples at Philae
A412

1973, Oct. 24 *Perf. 11½*

945	A412	55m bl, pur & org	40	18

UNESCO campaign to save the temples at Philae.

Bank Building
A413

1973, Oct. 24

946	A413	20m brn org, grn & blk	10	8

75th anniversary of the National Bank of Egypt.

Rose
A414

1973, Oct. 24 *Perf. 11*

947	A414	10m bl & multi	5	3

For use on greeting cards.

Human Rights Flame
A415

Taha Hussein
A416

Perf. 11x11½

1973, Dec. 8 Photo. Wmk. 342

948	A415	20m yel grn, dk bl & car	10	8

25th anniversary of the Universal Declaration of Human Rights.

1973, Dec. 10

949	A416	20m dk bl, brn & emer	10	8

In memory of Dr. Taha Hussein (1893–1973), "Father of Education" in Egypt, writer, philosopher.

Pres. Sadat, Flag and Battle of Oct. 6—A417

1973, Dec. 23 *Perf. 11x11½*

950	A417	20m yel, blk & red	1.00	60

Crossing of Suez Canal by Egyptian forces, Oct. 6, 1973.

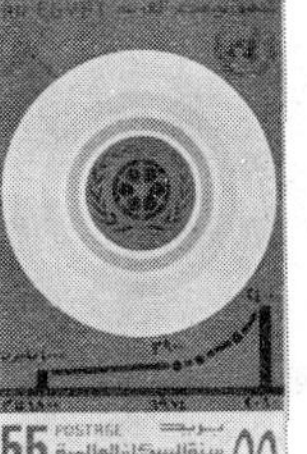

WPY Emblem and Chart
A418

Cairo Fair Emblem
A419

1974, Mar. 21 *Perf. 11* **Wmk. 342**

951	A418	55m org, grn & dk bl	28	18

World Population Year.

1974, Mar. 21 Photogravure

952	A419	20m bl & multi	15	8

Cairo International Fair.

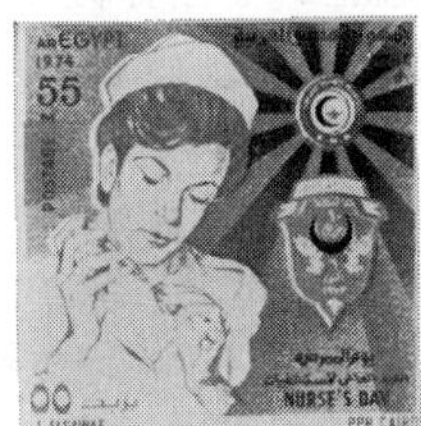

Nurse and Medal of Angels of Ramadan 10
A420

1974, May 15 *Perf. 11½*

953	A420	55m multi	28	18

Nurses' and World Hospital Day.

Workers, Relief Carving from Queen Tee's Tomb, Sakhara—A421

1974, May 15 *Perf. 11*

954	A421	20m yel, bl & brn	15	8

Workers' Day.

Pres. Sadat, Troops Crossing Suez Canal
A422

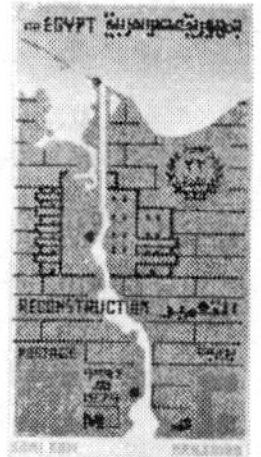

"Reconstruction," Map of Suez Canal and New Building
A423

Sheet of Aluminum
A424

Design: 110m, Pres. Sadat's "October Working Paper," symbols of science and development.

1974, July 23 Photo. ***Perf. 11x11½***

955	A422	20m multi	10	8
956	A423	20m bl, gold & blk	10	8

Perf. 11½

957	A424	20m plum & sil	10	8

Souvenir Sheet

Imperf.

958	A424	110m grn & multi	55	55

22nd anniversary of the revolution establishing the republic and for the end of the October War. No. 958 contains one stamp (52x59mm.). Gold and green marginal inscription. Size: 72½x108mm.

Pres. Sadat and Flag—A425

Perf. 11x11½

1974, Oct. 6 **Wmk. 342**

959	A425	20m yel, blk & red	50	20

First anniversary of Battle of Oct. 6.

Palette and Brushes
A426

1974, Oct. 6 ***Perf. 11½***

960	A426	30m pur, yel & blk	15	12

6th Exhibition of Plastic Art.

Teachers and Pupils
A427

1974, Oct. 6 ***Perf. 11x11½***

961	A427	20m multi	10	8

Teachers' Day.

Souvenir Sheet

UPU Monument, Bern—A428

1974, Oct. 6 ***Imperf.***

962	A428	110m gold & multi	1.00	1.00

Centenary of Universal Postal Union. No. 962 contains one stamp, yellow green marginal inscription. Size: 75x100mm.

Emblems, Cogwheel and Calipers—A429

Refugee Camp under Attack and UN Refugee Organization Emblem
A430

Child and UNICEF Emblem
A431

Temple of Philae
A432

1974, Oct. 24 ***Perf. 11½, 11x11½***

963	A429	10m blk, bl & yel	5	4
964	A430	20m dp org, bl & blk	10	8
965	A431	30m grn, bl & brn	15	12
966	A432	55m blk, bl & yel	35	18

United Nations Day. World Standards Day (10m); Palestinian refugee repatriation (20m); Family Planning (30m); Campaign to save Temple of Philae (55m).

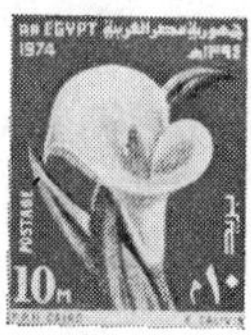

Calla Lily
A433

1974, Nov. 7 ***Perf. 11***

967	A433	10m ultra & multi	5	4

For use on greeting cards.

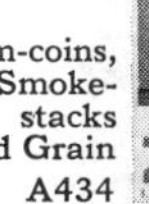

10m-coins, Smoke-stacks and Grain
A434

1974, Nov. 7 ***Perf. 11½x11***

968	A434	20m yel grn, dk bl & sil	10	8

International Savings Day.

Organization Emblem and Medical Services
A435

1974, Nov. 7 ***Perf. 11½***

969	A435	30m vio, red & gold	15	12

Health Insurance Organization, 10th anniversary.

Mustafa Lutfy El Manfalouty
A436

Abbas Mahmoud El Akkad
A437

Perf. 11x11½

1974, Dec. 8 Photo. Wmk. 342

970	A436	20m bl blk & brn	15	8
971	A437	20m brn & bl blk	15	8

Arab writers; Mustafa Lutfy El Manfalouty (1876–1924) and Abbas Mahmoud El Akkad (1889–1964). Nos. 970–971 printed se-tenant in sheets of 50.

Goddess Maat Facing God Thoth—A438

Fish-shaped Vase—A439

Pharaonic Golden Vase
A440

Sign of Life, Mirror
A441

Perf. 11½

1975, Jan. 2 Photo. Wmk. 342

972	A438	20m sil & multi	20	10
973	A439	30m multi	25	15
974	A440	55m multi	35	25
975	A441	110m bl & multi	75	50

Post Day 1975. Egyptian art works from 12th–5th centuries B.C.

Om Kolthoum
A442

Perf. 11½

1975, Mar. 3 Photo. Unwmkd.

976	A442	20m brown	20	12

In memory of Om Kolthoum, singer.

Crescent, Globe, Al Aqsa and Kaaba
A443

Cairo Fair Emblem
A444

1975, Mar. 25

977	A443	20m multi	10	8

Mohammed's Birthday.

Perf. 11x11½

1975, Mar. 25 **Wmk. 342**

978	A444	20m multi	10	8

International Cairo Fair.

Kasr El Ainy Hospital WHO Emblem A445

Perf. 11½x11

1975, May 7 Photo. Wmk. 342

979 A445 20m dk brn & bl 10 8

World Health Organization Day.

Children Reading Book A446

Children and Line Graph A447

1975, May 7 *Perf. 11x11½*

980 A446 20m multi 10 8
981 A447 20m multi 10 8

Science Day.

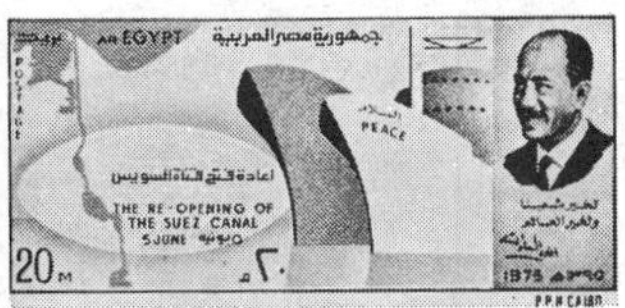

Suez Canal, Globe, Ships, Pres. Sadat—A448

1975, June 5 *Perf. 11½*

982 A448 20m bl, brn & blk 35 20

Reopening of the Suez Canal, June 5. See Nos. C166-C167.

Belmabgoknis Flowers A449

1975, July 30 Photo. Wmk. 342

983 A449 10m grn & bl 5 3

For use on greeting cards.

Sphinx and Pyramids Illuminated A450

Rural Electrification A451

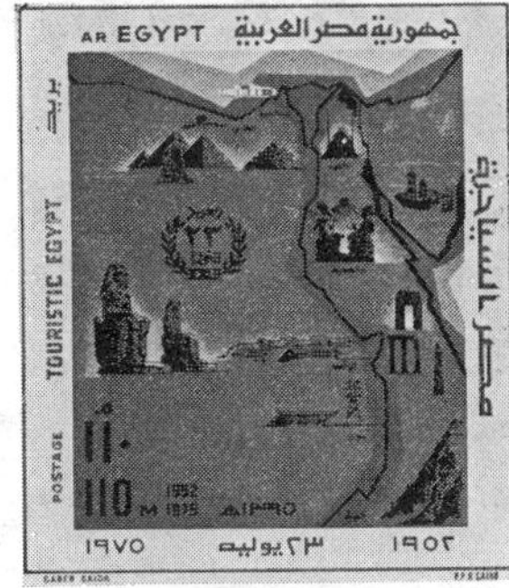

Map of Egypt with Tourist Sites—A452

1975, July 23

984 A450 20m blk, org & grn 15 8
985 A451 20m dk bl & brn 15 8

Perf. 11

986 A452 110m multi 1.00 1.00

23rd anniversary of the revolution establishing the republic. No. 986 printed in sheets of 6 (2x3). Size: 71x80mm.

Volleyball A453

1975, Aug. 2 Photo. *Perf. 11x11½*

Orange & Green

987 A453 20m *shown* 10 8
988 A453 20m *Running* 10 8
989 A453 20m *Torch and flag bearers* 10 8
990 A453 20m *Basketball* 10 8
991 A453 20m *Soccer* 10 8
Nos. 987-991 (5) 50 40

6th Arab School Tournament. Nos. 987-991 printed se-tenant in sheets of 50.

Egyptian Flag and Tanks A454

Perf. 11½

1975 Photo. Unwmkd.

992 A454 20m multi 10 8

Two-line Arabic Inscription in Bottom Panel, "M" over "20"

992A A454 20m multi 10 8

No. 992 commemorates 2nd anniversary of Battle of Oct. 6, "The Spark;" No. 992A, the International Symposium on War of October 1973, Cairo University, Oct. 27-31.
Issue dates: No. 992, Oct. 6. No. 992A, Oct. 24.

Arrows Pointing to Fluke, and Emblems A455

Submerged Wall and Sculpture, UNESCO Emblem A456

Perf. 11x11½

1975, Oct. 24 Wmk. 342

993 A455 20m multi 10 8
994 A456 55m multi 75 30

United Nations Day. 20m publicizes International Conference on Schistosomiasis (Bilharziasis); 55m commemorates UNESCO help in saving temples at Philae. See Nos. C169-C170.

Pharaonic Gate, University Emblem A457

Al Biruni A458

1975, Nov. 15 Photo. Wmk. 342

995 A457 20m multi 10 8

Ain Shams University, 25th anniversary.

1975, Dec. 23 Photo. *Perf. 11x11½*

Designs: No. 997, Al Farabi and lute. No. 998, Al Kanady, book and compass.

996 A458 20m bl, brn & grn 10 8
997 A458 20m bl, brn & grn 10 8
998 A458 20m bl, brn & grn 10 8

Arab philosophers.

Ibex (Prow) A459

Designs (from Tutankhamen's Tomb): 30m, Lioness. 55m, Cow's head (Goddess Hawthor). 110m, Hippopotamus' head (God Horus).

1976, Jan. 2 *Perf. 11½* Unwmkd.

999 A459 20m multi 25 15

Wmk. 342

1000 A459 30m brn, gold & ultra 50 30
1001 A459 55m multi 50 35
1002 A459 110m multi 1.00 75

Post Day 1976.

Lake, Aswan Dam, Industry and Agriculture—A460

Perf. 11½x11

1976, Jan. 27 Photo. Wmk. 342

1003 A460 20m multi 10 8

Filling of lake formed by Aswan High Dam.

Fair Emblem A461

Commemorative Medal A462

1976, Mar. 15 *Perf. 11x11½*

1004 A461 20m org & pur 10 8

9th International Cairo Fair, Mar. 8-27.

1976, Mar. 15 Wmk. 342

1005 A462 20m ol, yel & blk 10 8

11th Biennial Exhibition of Fine Arts, Alexandria.

Hands Shielding Invalid A463

1976, Apr. 7 Photo. *Perf. 11½*

1006 A463 20m dk grn, lt grn & yel 10 8

Founding of Faithfulness and Hope Society.

Eye and WHO Emblem A464

1976, Apr. 7

1007 A464 20m dk brn, yel & grn 10 8

World Health Day: "Foresight prevents blindness."

Pres. Sadat, Legal Department Emblem A465

Perf. 11½x11

1976, May 15 Photo. Wmk. 342

1008 A465 20m ol & multi 10 8

Centenary of State Legal Department.

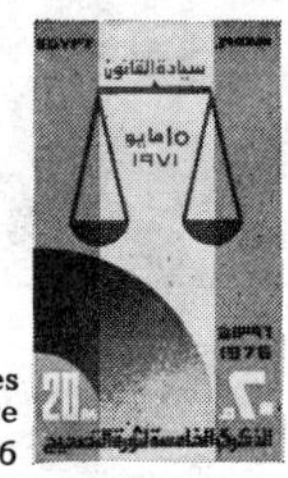

Scales of Justice
A466

1976, May 15 ***Perf. 11x11½***

1009 A466 20m car, blk & grn 10 8

5th anniversary of Rectification Movement.

Al-Ahram Front Page, First Issue
A467

Perf. 11½x11

1976, June 25 Photo. **Wmk. 342**

1010 A467 20m bis & multi 10 8

Centenary of Al-Ahram newspaper.

World Map, Pres. Sadat and Emblems—A468

1976, July 23 ***Perf. 11x11½***

1011 A468 20m bl, blk & yel 10 8

Souvenir Sheet

Imperf.

1012 A468 110m bl, blk & yel 1.00 75

24th anniversary of the revolution. No. 1012 shows design of No. 1011 enlarged to fill entire area. Size: 85x76mm.

Scarborough Lily
A469

1976, Sept. 10 Photo. ***Perf. 11***

1013 A469 10m multi 5 4

For use on greeting cards.

Reconstruction of Sinai by Irrigation—A470

Abu Redice Oil Wells and Refinery
A471

Unknown Soldier, Memorial Pyramid for October War—A472

1976, Oct. 6 ***Perf. 11x11½***

1014 A470 20m multi 10 8
1015 A471 20m multi 10 8
1016 A472 110m grn, bl & blk 1.00 1.00

October War (crossing of Suez Canal), 3rd anniversary. Size of No. 1016: 65x77 mm.

Papyrus with Children's Animal Story—A473

Al Aqsa Mosque, Palestinian Refugees
A474

Designs: 55m, Isis, from Philae Temple, UNESCO emblem (vert.). 110m, UNESCO emblem and "30".

Perf. 11½, 11½x11

1976, Oct. 24 Photo. **Wmk. 342**

1017 A473 20m dk bl, bis & brn 10 8
1018 A474 30m brn, grn & blk 15 12
1019 A473 55m dk bl & bis 28 18
1020 A474 110m lt grn, vio bl & red 1.00 35

30th anniversary of UNESCO.

Census Chart
A475

1976, Nov. 22 Photo. ***Perf. 11½x11***

1021 A475 20m multi 10 8

10th General Population and Housing Census.

Nile and Commemorative Medal—A476

Ikhnaton
A477

1976, Nov. 22 ***Perf. 11x11½***

1022 A476 20m grn & brn 10 8

Geographical Society of Egypt, centenary (in 1975).

1977, Jan. 2 Photo. ***Perf. 11x11½***

Designs: 30m, Ikhnaton's daughter. 55m, Nefertiti, Ikhnaton's wife. 110m, Ikhnaton, front view.

1023 A477 20m multi 20 15
1024 A477 30m multi 25 20
1025 A477 55m multi 50 30
1026 A477 110m multi 1.00 75

Post Day 1977.

Policeman, Emblem and Emergency Car—A478

Wmk. 342

1977, Feb. 25 Photo. ***Perf. 11½x11***

1027 A478 20m multi 20 8

Police Day.

Map of Africa, Arab League Emblem
A479

1977, Mar. 7 ***Perf. 11x11½***

1028 A479 55m multi 28 18

First Afro-Arab Summit Conference, Cairo.

Fair Emblem, Pharaonic Ship—A480

1977, Mar. 7 ***Perf. 11½x11***

1029 A480 20m grn, blk & red 20 8

10th International Cairo Fair.

King Faisal
A481

1977, Mar. 22 Photo. ***Perf. 11x11½***

1030 A481 20m ind & brn 10 8

King Faisal Ben Abdel-Aziz Al Saud of Saudi Arabia (1906–1975).

Healthy and Crippled Children
A482

1977, Apr. 12 **Wmk. 342**

1031 A482 20m multi 10 8

National campaign to fight poliomyelitis.

APU Emblem, Members' Flags
A483

1977, Apr. 12 ***Perf. 11½***

1032 A483 20m bl & multi 10 8
1033 A483 30m gray & multi 15 12

25th anniversary of Arab Postal Union (APU).

Children's Village
A484

Perf. 11½x11

1977, May 7 Photo. **Wmk. 342**

1034 A484 20m multi 10 8
1035 A484 55m multi 28 18

Inauguration of Children's Village, Cairo.

Loom, Spindle and Factory
A485

1977, May 7

1036 A485 20m multi 10 8

Egyptian Spinning and Weaving Company, El Mehalla el Kobra, 50th anniversary.

Satellite, Globe, ITU Emblem
A486

1977, May 17 ***Perf. 11x11½***

1037 A486 110m dk bl & multi 1.00 75

World Telecommunications Day.

Flag and "25" A487

Egyptian Flag and Eagle—A488

Wmk. 342

1977, July 23 Photo. *Perf. 11½x11*

1038 A487 20m sil, car & blk 20 8

Perf. 11x11½

1039 A488 110m multi 75 35

25th anniversary of July 23rd Revolution. No. 1039 printed in sheets of six. Size: 75x83mm.

Saad Zaghloul A489

Archbishop Capucci, Map of Palestine A490

Perf. 11x11½

1977, Aug. 23 Photo. Wmk. 342

1040 A489 20m dk grn & dk brn 20 8

Saad Zaghloul, leader of 1919 Revolution, 50th death anniversary.

1977, Sept. 1

1041 A490 45m emer & bl 45 18

Palestinian Archbishop Hilarion Capucci, jailed by Israel in 1974.

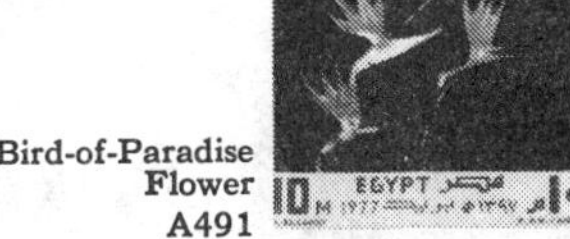

Bird-of-Paradise Flower A491

1977, Sept. 3

1042 A491 10m multi 10 4

For use on greeting cards.

Proclamation Greening the Land A492

Wmk. 342

1977, Sept. 25 Photo. *Perf. 11x11½*

1043 A492 20m multi 20 8

Agrarian Reform Law, 25th anniversary.

Soldier, Tanks, Medal of Oct. 6 A493

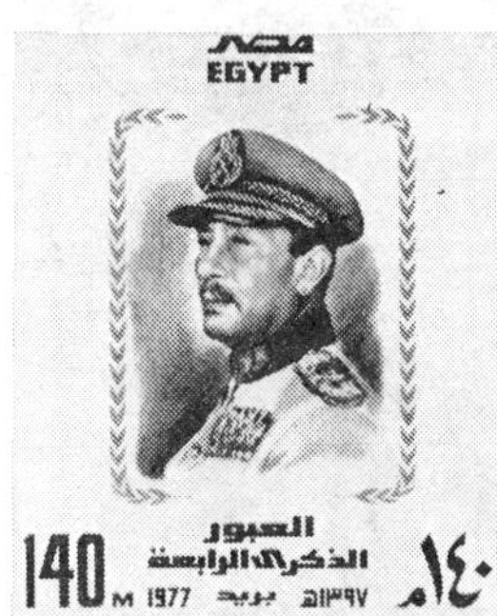

Anwar El Sadat—A494

1977, Oct. 6 *Perf. 11½x11*

1044 A493 20m multi 20 8

Unwmkd. *Perf. 11*

1045 A494 140m dk brn, gold & red 1.40 1.40

Crossing of Suez Canal, 4th anniversary. No. 1045 printed in sheets of 16.

Refugees Looking at Al Aqsa Mosque A495

Goddess Taueret and Spirit of Flight (Horus) A496

Mural Relief, Temple of Philae A497

Wmk. 342

1977, Oct. 24 Photo. *Perf. 11*

1046 A495 45m grn, red & blk 22 16
1047 A496 55m dp bl & yel 28 18
1048 A497 140m ol bis & dk brn 70 48

United Nations Day.

Electric Trains, First Egyptian Locomotive A498

1977, Oct. 22

1049 A498 20m multi 10 8

125th anniversary of Egyptian railroads.

Film and Eye A499

1977, Nov. 16 *Perf. 11½x11*

1050 A499 20m gray, blk & gold 10 8

50th anniversary of Egyptian cinema.

Natural Gas Well and Refinery A500

1977, Nov. 17 Photogravure

1051 A500 20m multi 10 8

National Oil Festival, celebrating the acquisition of Sinai oil wells.

Pres. Sadat and Dome of the Rock—A501

Wmk. 342

1977, Dec. 31 Photo. *Perf. 11½x11*

1052 A501 20m grn, brn & blk 10 8
1053 A501 140m grn, blk & brn 70 48

Pres. Sadat's peace mission to Israel.

Ramses II A502

Design: 45m, Queen Nefertari, bas-relief.

1978, Jan. 2 *Perf. 11½*

1054 A502 20m grn, blk & gold 10 8
1055 A502 45m org, blk & ol 22 16

Post Day 1978.

Water Wheels, Fayum A503

Flying Duck, from Floor in Ikhnaton's Palace—A504

Designs: 5m, Birdhouse, 10m, Statue of Horus. 20m, Al Rifa'i Mosque, Cairo. 50m, Monastery, Wadi al-Natrun. 55m, Ruins of Edfu Temple. 70m, Bridge of Oct. 6. 85m, Medum pyramid. 100m, Facade, El Morsi Mosque, Alexandria. 200m, Column, Alexandria, and Sphinx. 500m, Arabian stallion.

Wmk. 342

1978-79 *Perf. 11½*

1056	A503	1m	sl bl	3	3
1057	A503	5m	bis brn	3	3
1058	A503	10m	brt grn	5	3
1059	A503	20m	dk brn	10	8
1059A	A503	30m	sepia	15	15
1060	A503	50m	brt bl	25	15
1061	A503	55m	olive	28	18
1062	A503	70m	ol ('79)	35	20
1062A	A503	80m	like #1062	40	40
1063	A503	85m	dp pur	42	30
1064	A503	100m	brown	50	40
1065	A503	200m	bl & ind	1.00	80
1066	A504	500m	multi	2.50	
1067	A504	£1	multi	5.00	
	Nos. 1056-1067 (12)			11.06	

Issue dates: 500m, £1, Feb. 27. Others, July 23, 70m, Aug. 22, 1979.

Fair Emblem and Wheat A505

1978, Mar. 15 *Perf. 11½*

1072 A505 20m multi 10 8

11th Cairo International Fair, Mar. 11–25.

Emblem, Kasr El Ainy School A506

1978, Mar. 18 *Perf. 11½x11*

1073 A506 20m lt bl, blk & gold 10 8

Kasr El Ainy School of Medicine, 150th anniversary.

Soldiers and Emblem A507

Youssef El Sebai A508

1978, Mar. 30 ***Perf. 11x11½***

1074 A507 20m multi 10 8
1075 A508 20m bis brn 10 8

Nos. 1069-1070 printed se-tenant.

Youssef El Sebai, newspaper editor, assassinated on Cyprus and in memory of the commandos killed in raid on Cyprus.

Biennale Medal, Statue for Entrance to Port Said
A509

1978, Apr. 1 ***Perf. 11½***

1076 A509 20m bl, grn & blk 10 8

12th Biennial Exhibition of Fine Arts, Alexandria.

Child with Smallpox, UN Emblem
A510

1978, Apr. 7 **Photo.** ***Perf. 11½***

1077 A510 20m multi 10 8

Eradication of smallpox.

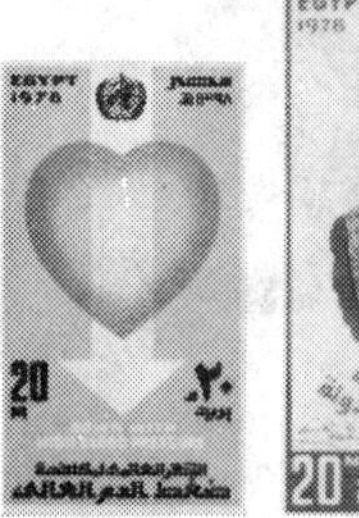

Heart and Arrow, UN Emblem
A511

Anwar El Sadat
A512

1978, Apr. 7 **Wmk. 342**

1078 A511 20m multi 10 8

Fight against hypertension.

1978, May 15 Photo. ***Perf. 11½x11***

1079 A512 20m grn, brn & gold 10 8

7th anniversary of Rectification Movement.

Social Security Emblem—A513

1978, May 16 ***Perf. 11***

1080 A513 20m lt grn & dk brn 10 8

General Organization of Insurance and Pensions (Social Security), 25th anniversary.

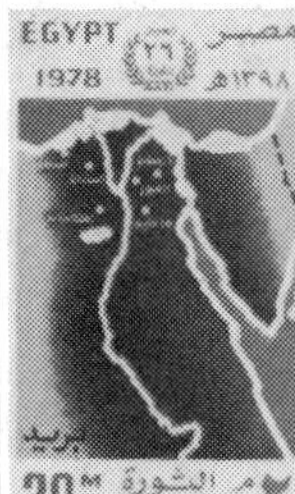

New Cities on Map of Egypt
A514

Map of Egypt and Sudan, Wheat
A515

Wmk. 342

1978, July 23 **Photo.** ***Perf. 11½***

1081 A514 20m multi 10 8
1082 A515 45m multi 22 16

26th anniversary of July 23rd revolution.

Symbols of Egyptian Ministries
A516

1978, Aug. 28 Photo. ***Perf. 11½x11***

1083 A516 20m multi 10 8

Centenary of Egyptian Ministerial System.

Pres. Nasser and "Spirit of Egypt" Showing Way—A517

1978, Oct. 6 **Photo.** ***Perf. 11x11½***

1084 A517 20m multi 10 8

Crossing of Suez Canal, 5th anniversary.

Human Rights Emblem
A518

Dove and Human Rights Emblem
A520

Kobet al Sakra Mosque, Refugee Camp
A519

Design: 55m, Temple at Biga and UNESCO emblem (horiz.).

Perf. 11, 11½ (45m)

1978, Oct. 24 **Photo.** **Wmk. 342**

1085 A518 20m multi 10 8
1086 A519 45m multi 22 16
1087 A518 55m multi 28 18
1088 A520 140m multi 70 48

United Nations Day.

Pilgrims, Mt. Arafat and Holy Kaaba—A521

1978, Nov. 7 **Photo.** ***Perf. 11***

1089 A521 45m multi 22 16

Pilgrimage to Mecca.

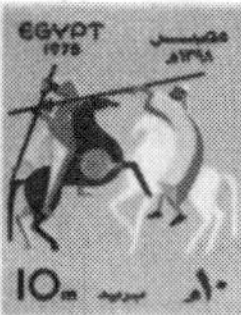

Tahtib Horse Dance
A522

1978, Nov. 7

1090 A522 10m multi 5 4
1091 A522 20m multi 10 8

U.N. Emblem, Globe and Grain
A523

1978, Nov. 11 **Photo** ***Perf. 11½***

1092 A523 20m grn, dk bl & yel 10 8

Technical Cooperation Among Developing Countries Conference, Buenos Aires, Argentina, Sept. 1978.

Pipes, Map and Emblem of Sumed Pipeline—A524

1978, Nov. 11

1093 A524 20m brn, bl & yel 10 8

Inauguration of Sumed pipeline from Suez to Alexandria, 1st anniversary.

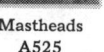

Mastheads
A525

Abu el Walid
A526

1978, Dec. 24 ***Perf. 11x11½***

1094 A525 20m brn & blk 10 8

150th anniversary of the newspaper El Wakea el Masriya.

1978, Dec. 24

1095 A526 45m brt grn & ind 22 18

800th death anniversary of Abu el Walid ibn Rashid.

Helwan Observatory and Sky—A527

1978, Dec. 30 **Wmk. 342**

1096 A527 20m multi 10 8

Helwan Observatory, 75th anniversary.

Second Daughter of Ramses II
A528

Ramses Statues, Abu Simbel, and Cartouches
A529

1979, Jan. 2 **Photo.** ***Perf. 11***

1097 A528 20m brn & yel 10 8

Perf. 11½x11

1098 A529 140m multi 70 48

Post Day 1978.

Book, Reader and Globe
A530

Wmk. 342

1979, Feb. 1 Photo. ***Perf. 11½x11***

1099 A530 20m yel grn & brn 10 10

Cairo 11th International Book Fair.

Wheat, Globe, Fair Emblem—A531

Perf. 11x11½

1979, Mar. 17 Photo. **Unwmkd.**

1100 A531 20m bl, org & blk 10 10

12th Cairo International Fair, March–Apr.

Skull, Poppy, Agency Emblem—A532

1979, Mar. 20 ***Perf. 11***

1101 A532 70m multi 35 35

Anti-Narcotics General Administration, 50th anniversary.

Isis Holding Horus
A533

1979, Mar. 21

1102 A533 140m multi 70 70

Mother's Day.

World Map and Book—A534

Perf. 11x11½

1979, Mar. 22 **Wmk. 342**

1103 A534 45m yel, bl & brn 22 22

Cultural achievements of the Arabs.

Pres. Sadat's Signature, Peace Doves
A535

Wmk. 342

1979, Mar. 31 Photo. ***Perf. 11½***

1104 A535 70m brt grn & red 35 35
1105 A535 140m yel grn & red 70 70

Signing of Peace Treaty between Egypt and Israel, Mar. 26.

1979, May 26 Photo. ***Perf. 11½***

1106 A535 20m yel & dk brn 10 10

Return of Al Arish to Egypt.

Honey-comb with Food Symbols
A536

1979, May 15

1107 A636 20m multi 10 10

8th anniversary of movement to establish food security.

Coins, 1959, 1979
A537

Photogravure

Perf. 11½x11

1979, June 1 **Wmk. 342**

1108 A537 20m yel & gray 10 10

25th anniversary of the Egyptian Mint.

Egypt No. 1104 under Magnifying Glass—A538

1979, June 1 ***Perf. 11***

1109 A538 20m grn, blk & brn 10 10

Philatelic Society of Egypt, 50th anniversary.

See "Special Notices" at the front of this volume for data on the listing methods of this Catalogue, abbreviations, condition, prices and examination.

Book, Atom Symbol, Rising Sun
A539

"23 July," "Revolution" and "Peace"—A540

Perf. 11½x11

1979, July 23 **Wmk. 342**

1110 A539 20m multi 10 10

Miniature Sheet

Imperf.

1111 A540 140m multi 70 70

27th anniversary of July 23rd revolution. Size of No. 1111: 50x62mm.

Musicians
A541

1979, Aug. 22 ***Perf. 11½***

1112 A541 10m multi 5 6

For use on greeting cards.

Dove over Map of Suez Canal
A542

Wmk. 342

1979, Oct. 6 Photo. ***Perf. 11½***

1113 A542 20m bl & brn 10 10

Crossing of Suez Canal, 6th anniversary.

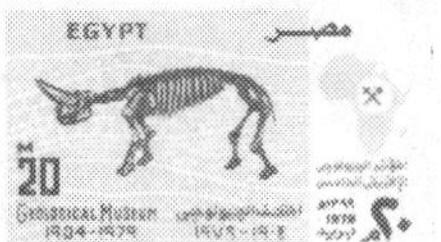

Dinosaur Skeleton, Map of Africa
A543

Wmk. 342

1979, Oct. 9 Photo. ***Perf. 11½x11***

1114 A543 20m multi 10 10

Egyptian Geological Museum, 75th anniversary.

T Square on Drawing Board—A544

1979, Oct. 11 ***Perf. 11***

1115 A544 20m multi 10 10

Engineers Day.

Human Rights Emblem Over Globe
A545

Boy Balancing IYC Emblem
A546

Unwmkd.

1979, Oct. 24 Photo. ***Perf. 11½***

1116 A545 45m multi 22 22
1117 A546 140m multi 70 70

United Nations Day and International Year of the Child.

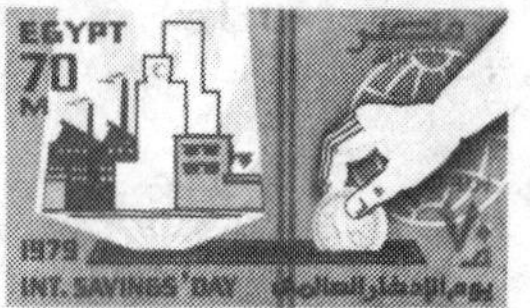

International Savings Day—A547

1979, Oct. 31

1118 A547 70m multi 35 35

Shooting Championship Emblem
A548

1979, Nov. 16

1119 A548 20m multi 10 10

20th International Military Shooting Championship, Cairo.

International Palestinian Solidarity Day
A549

1979, Nov. 29 ***Perf. 11×11½***

1120	A549	140m multi	70	70

Dove Holding Grain, Rotary Emblem, Globe—A550

1979, Dec. 3 **Photo.** ***Perf. 11½***

1121	A550	45m multi	22	22

Rotary International, 75th anniversary; Cairo Rotary Club, 50th anniversary.

Arms Factories, 25th Anniversary
A551

Wmk. 342

1979, Dec. 23 **Photo.** ***Perf. 11½×11***

1122	A551	20m lt ol grn & brn	10	10

Aly El Garem (1881-1949)
A552

Pharaonic Capital
A553

Poets: No. 1124, Mahmoud Samy El Baroudy (1839-1904).

1979, Dec. 25 ***Perf. 11×11½***

1123	A552	20m dk brn & yel brn	10	10
1124	A552	20m brn & dk brn	10	10

Nos. 1123-1124 printed se-tenant.

1980, Jan. 2 **Unwmkd.** ***Perf. 11½***

Post Day: Various Pharaonic capitals. Printed se-tenant.

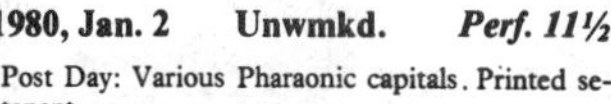

1125	A553	20m multi	10	10
1126	A553	45m multi	22	22
1127	A553	70m multi	35	35
1128	A553	140m multi	70	70

Golden Goddess of Writing, Fair Emblem
A554

Exhibition Catalogue and Medal
A555

1980, Feb. 2 **Photo.** ***Perf. 11½***

1129	A554	20m multi	10	10

12th Cairo International Book Fair, Jan. 24-Feb. 4.

1980, Feb. 2

1130	A555	20m multi	10	10

13th Biennial Exhibition of Fine Arts, Alexandria.

13th Cairo International Fair—A556

1980, Mar. 8 **Photo.** ***Perf. 11x11½***

1131	A556	20m multi	10	10

Kiosk of Trajan—A557

1980, Mar. 10 ***Perf. 11½***

1132		Strip of 4 plus label	1.40	1.40
a.		A557 70m, single stamp	35	35

UNESCO campaign to save Nubian monuments, 20th anniversary. Shown on stamps are Temples of Philae, Kalabsha, Korasy.

Physicians' Day—A558

1980, Mar. 18 ***Perf. 11x11½***

1133	A558	20m multi	10	10

Rectification Movement, 9th Anniversary—A559

Wmk. 342

1980, May 15 **Photo.** ***Perf. 11½x11***

1134	A559	20m multi	10	10

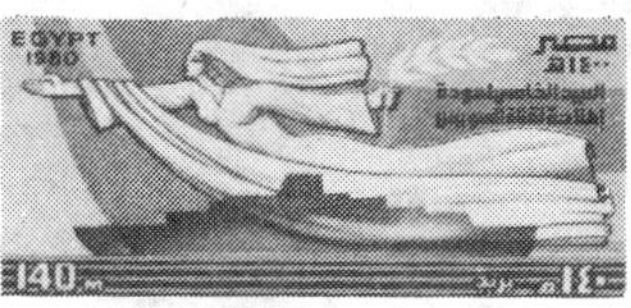

Re-opening of Suez Canal, 5th Anniversary—A560

1980, June 5 ***Perf. 11½***

1135	A560	140m multi	70	70

Prevention of Cruelty to Animals Week—A561

1980, June 5

1136	A561	20m lt yel grn & gray	10	10

Industry Day—A562

Wmk. 342

1980, July 12 **Photo.** ***Perf. 11½x11***

1137	A562	20m multi	10	10

Leaf with Text—A563

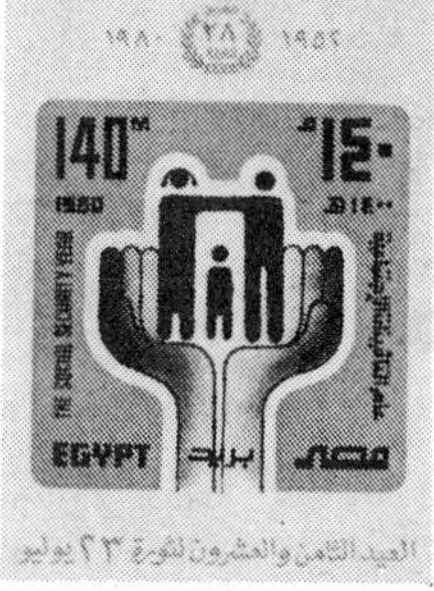

Family Protection Emblem—A564

1980, July 23 ***Perf. 11½***

1138	A563	20m multi	10	10

Souvenir Sheet
Imperf.

1139	A564	140m multi	75	75

July 23rd Revolution, 28th anniversary; Social Security Year. Size of No. 1139: 51x67mm.

Erksous Seller and Nakrazan Player—A565

Photo.

1980, Aug. 8 ***Perf. 11½*** ***Unwmkd.***

1140	A565	10m multi	5	5

For use on greeting cards.

7th Anniversary of Suez Canal Crossing—A566

1980, Oct. 6 **Litho.**

1141	A566	20m multi	10	10

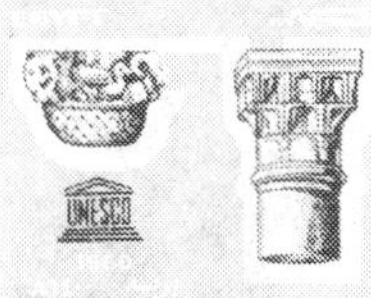

Islamic and Coptic Columns—A567

International Telecommunications Union Emblem—A568

Wmk. 342

1980, Oct. 24 **Photo.** ***Perf. 11½***

1142 A567 70m multi 35 35
1143 A568 140m multi 70 70

United Nations Day. Campaign to save Egyptian monuments (70m), International Telecommunications Day (140m).

Hegira (Pilgrimage Year)—A569

1980, Nov. 9 **Litho.** ***Perf. 11x11½***

1144 A569 45m multi 22 22

Opening of Suez Canal Third Branch—A570

Wmk. 342

980, Dec. 16 **Photo.** ***Perf. 11½x11***

1145 A570 70m multi 35 35

Mustafa Sadek El-Rafai (1880-1927), Writer—A571

Famous Men: No. 1147, Ali Mustafa Mousharafa (1898-1950), mathematician, No. 1148, Ali Ibraham (1880-1947), physician. Nos. 1146-1148 se-tenant.

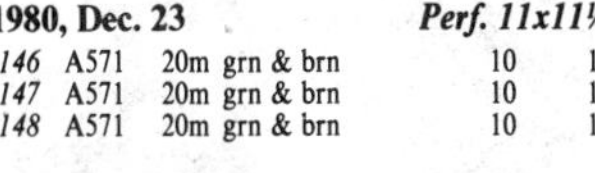

1980, Dec. 23 ***Perf. 11x11½***

1146 A571 20m grn & brn 10 10
1147 A571 20m grn & brn 10 10
1148 A571 20m grn & brn 10 10

Ladybug Scarab Emblem A572

Heinrich von Stephan, UPU A573

Unwmkd.

1981, Jan. 2 **Photo.** ***Perf. 11½***

1149 A572 70m *shown* 35 35
1150 A572 70m *Scarab, reverse* 35 35

Post Day.

1981, Jan. 7 **Wmk. 342** ***Perf. 11x11½***

1151 A573 140m grnsh bl & dk brn 70 70

Heinrich von Stephan (1831-1897), founder of Universal Postal Union, birth sesquicentennial.

13th Cairo International Book Fair—A574

1981, Feb. 1 ***Perf. 11½x11***

1152 A574 20m multi 10 10

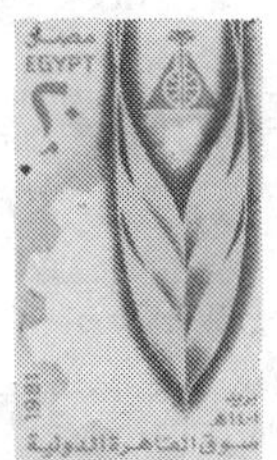

14th Cairo International Fair, Mar. 14-28—A575

Wmk. 342

1981, Mar. 14 **Photo.** ***Perf. 11x11½***

1153 A575 20m multi 10 10

Rural Electrification Authority, 10th Anniversary—A576

1981, Mar. 18

1154 A576 20m multi 10 10

Veterans' Day—A577

1981, Mar. 26

1155 A577 20m multi 10 10

International Dentistry Conference, Cairo—A578

Wmk. 342

1981, Apr. 14 **Photo.** ***Perf. 11x11½***

1156 A578 20m red & ol 10 10

Trade Union Emblem A579

Nurses' Day A580

Wmk. 342

1981, May 1 **Photo.** ***Perf. 11x11½***

1157 A579 20m brt bl & dk brn 10 10

International Confederation of Arab Trade Unions, 25th anniv.

1981, May 12

1158 A580 20m multi 10 10

Irrigation Equipment (Electrification Movement) A581

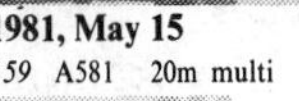

1981, May 15 ***Perf. 11½***

1159 A581 20m multi 10 10

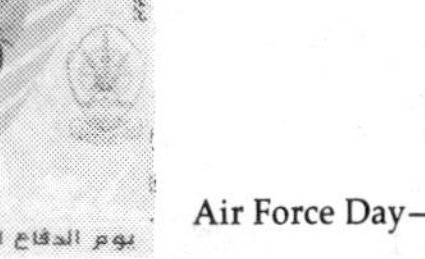

Air Force Day—A582

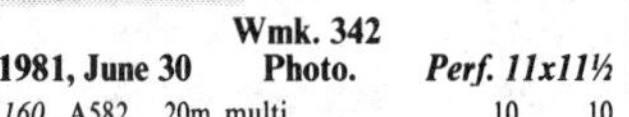

Wmk. 342

1981, June 30 **Photo.** ***Perf. 11x11½***

1160 A582 20m multi 10 10

Flag Surrounding Map of Suez Canal—A583

Wmk. 342

1981, July 23 **Photo.** ***Perf. 11½***

1161 A583 10m multi 5 5
1162 A583 20m Emblems 10 10

July 23rd Revolution, 29th anniv.; Social Defense Year.

1981 Feasts—A584

Wmk. 342

1981, July 29 **Photo.** ***Perf. 11***

1163 A584 10m multi 5 5

Kemal Ataturk—A585

1981, Aug. 10 ***Perf. 11x11½***

1164 A585 140m dk grn & brn 70 70

Arabi Pasha, Leader of Egyptian Force A586

Athlete, Pyramids, Sphinx A587

Wmk. 342

1981, Sept. 9 **Photo.** ***Perf. 11x11½***

1165 A586 20m dk grn & brn 10 10

Orabi Revolution centenary.

1981, Sept. 14

1166 A587 45m multi 22 22

World Muscular Athletics Championships, Cairo.

Ministry of Industry and Mineral Resources, 25th Anniv.—A588

Wmk. 342

1981, Sept. 26 Photo. *Perf. 11x11½*
1167 A588 45m multi 22 22

20th Intl. Occupational Health Congress, Cairo—A589

1981, Sept. 28 *Perf. 11½x11*
1168 A589 20m multi 10 10

8th Anniv. of Suez Canal Crossing—A590

1981, Oct. 6
1169 A590 20m multi 10 10

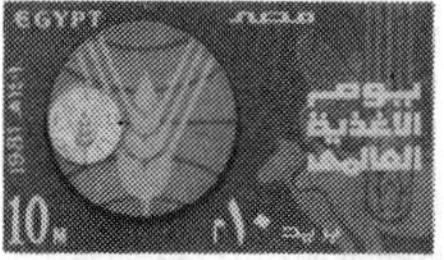

World Food Day—A591

13th World Telecommunications Day
A592

Intl. Year of the Disabled
A593

Fight Against Apartheid—A594

Wmk. 342

1981, Oct. 24 Photo. *Perf. 11½x11, 11x11½*
1170 A591 10m multi 5 5
1171 A592 20m multi 10 10
1172 A593 45m multi 22 22
1173 A594 230m multi 1.15 1.15

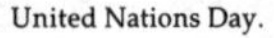
United Nations Day.

Pres. Anwar El-Sadat (1917-1981)—A595

1981, Nov. 14 Unwkd. *Perf. 11x11½*
1174 A595 30m multi 15 15
1175 A595 230m multi 1.15 1.15

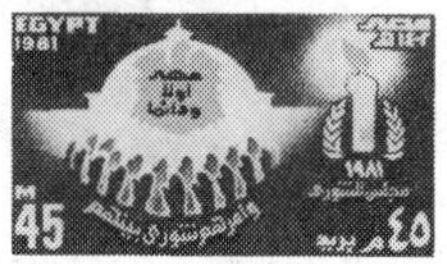

Establishment of Shura Family Council—A596

Wmk. 342

1981, Dec. 12 Photo. *Perf. 11½x11*
1176 A596 45m pur & yel 22 22

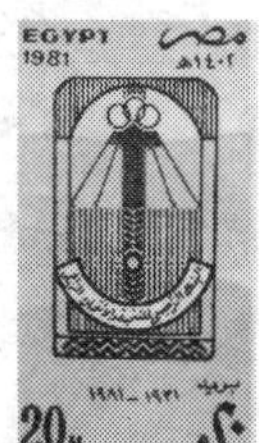

Agricultural Credit and Development Bank, 50th Anniv.—A597

1981, Dec. 15 *Perf. 11x11½*
1177 A597 20m multi 10 10

Famous Men Type of 1980

Designs: 30m, Ali el-Ghayati (1885-1956), journalist. 60m, Omar Ebn sl-Fared (1181-1234), Sufi poet. Nos. 1178-1179 se-tenant.

Wmk. 342

1981, Dec. 21 Photo. *Perf. 11x11½*
1178 A571 30m grn & brn 15 15
1179 A571 60m grn & brn 30 30

20th Anniv. of African Postal Union—A598

1981, Dec. 21 *Perf. 11½x11*
1180 A598 60m multi 30 30

14th Cairo Intl. Book Fair

A599

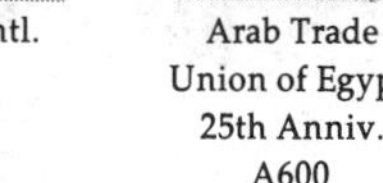

Arab Trade Union of Egypt, 25th Anniv.
A600

1982, Jan. 28
1181 A599 3p brn & Yel 15 15

1982, Jan. 30
1182 A600 3p multi 15 15

Khartoum Branch of Cairo University, 25th Anniv.—A601

1982, Mar. 4 Wmk. 342 *Perf. 11½x11*
1183 A601 6p bl & grn 30 30

15th Cairo Intl. Fair—A602

1982, Mar. 13 *Perf. 11x11½*
1184 A602 3p multi 15 15

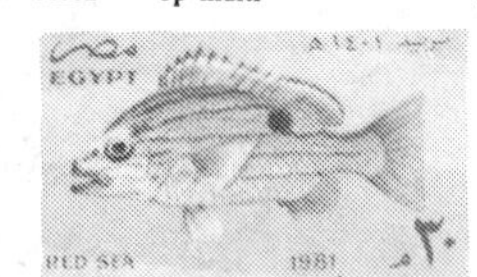

50th Anniv. of Al-Ghardaka Marine Biological Station—A603

Fish of the Red Sea. Nos. 1185-1188 se-tenant in continuous design.

1982, Apr. 24 Litho. *Perf. 11½x11*
1185 A603 10m Blue-banded sea perch 5 5
1186 A603 30m Lined butterfly fish 15 15
1187 A603 60m Batfish 30 30
1188 A603 230m Blue-spotted boxfish 1.15 1.15

Liberation of the Sinai—A604

1982, Apr. 25 Photo. *Perf. 11x11½*
1189 A604 3p multi 15 15

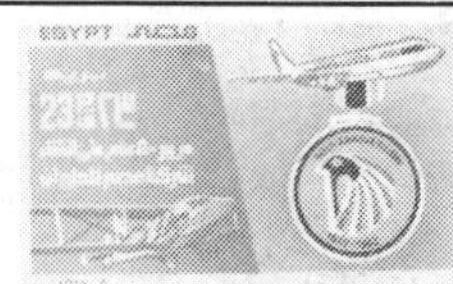

50th Anniv. of Egypt Air—A605

1982, May 7 Photo. *Perf. 11½x11*
1190 A605 23p multi 1.15 1.15

Minaret—A606

Souvenir Sheet

Al Azhar Mosque—A607

Wmk. 342

1982, June 28 Photo. *Perf. 11x11½*
1191 Strip of 4 plus label 1.25 1.25
a. A606 6p, any single multi 30 30

Unwmkd. Imperf.
1192 A607 23p multi 1.25 1.25

Al Azhar Mosque millennium. Size of No. 1192: 61x60mm.

Dove—A608

Flower in Natl. Colors—A609

Wmk. 342

1982, July 23 Photo. *Perf. 11x11½*
1193 A608 3p multi 15 15

Souvenir Sheet

Imperf.
1194 A609 23p multi 1.25 1.25

30th anniv. of July 23rd Revolution. Size of No. 1194: 55x74mm.

World Tourism Day—A610

Wmk. 342

1982, Sept. 27 Photo. *Perf. 11½x11*

1195 A610 23p Sphinx, pyramid of Cheops, St. Catherine's Tower 1.25 1.25

10th Anniv. of Suez Canal Crossing—A611

1982, Oct. 6

1196 A611 3p Memorial, map.15 15

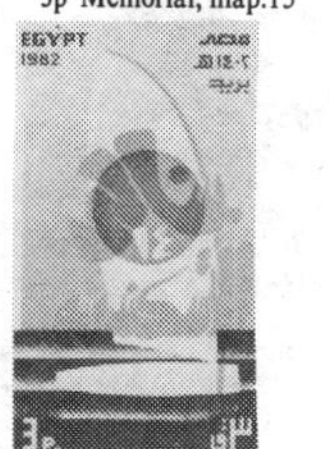

Biennale of Alexandria Art Exhibition—A612

1982, Oct. 17 *Perf. 11x11½*

1197 A612 3p multi 15 15

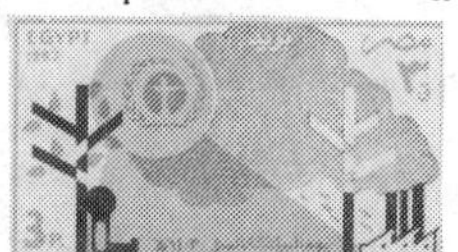

10th Anniv. of UN Conference on Human Environment—A613

2nd UN Conference on Peaceful Uses of Outer Space, Vienna, Aug. 9-21—A614

Scouting Year—A615

TB Bacillus Centenary—A616

1982, Oct. 24 *Perf. 11½x11, 11½ (A615)*

1198 A613 3p multi 15 15
1199 A614 6p multi 30 30
1200 A615 6p multi 30 30
1201 A616 8p multi 40 40

United Nations Day.

50th Anniv. of Air Force—A617

1982, Nov. 2 *Perf. 11½x11*

1202 A617 3p Jet, plane 15 15

Ahmed Chawki (1868-1932) and Hafez Ibrahim (1871-1932), Poets—A618

Wmk. 342

1982, Nov. 25 Photo. *Perf. 11½x11*

1203 A618 6p multi 30 30

Natl. Research Center, 25th Anniv.—A619

1982, Dec. 12 Photo. *Perf. 11x11½*

1204 A619 3p red & bl 15 15

50th Anniv. of Arab Language Society—A620

1982, Dec. 25 *Perf. 11½x11*

1205 A620 6p multi 30 30

Year of the Aged A621 — Post Day A622

1982, Dec. 25 *Perf. 11x11½*

1206 A621 23p multi 1.15 1.15

1983, Jan. 2 *Perf. 11½*

1207 A622 3p multi 15 15

15th Cairo Intl. Book Fair—A623

Wmk. 342

1983, Jan. 25 Photo. *Perf. 11x11½*

1208 A623 3p bl & red 15 15

Police Day—A624

1983, Jan. 25 *Perf. 11½x11*

1209 A624 3p multi 15 15

16th Cairo Intl. Fair A625 — 5th UN African Map Conference, Cairo A626

Wmk. 342

1983, Mar. 2 Photo. *Perf. 11x11½*

1210 A625 3p multi 15 15

1983, Mar. 2

1211 A626 3p lt grn & bl 15 15

African Ministers of Transport, Communications and Planning, 3rd Conference—A627

1983, Mar. 8 *Perf. 11½x11*

1212 A627 23p grn & bl 1.15 1.15

Victory in African Soccer Cup—A628

1983, Mar. 20 *Perf. 11x11½*

1213 A628 3p Heading 15 15
1214 A628 3p Kick 15 15

SEMI-POSTAL STAMPS.

Princess Ferial
SP1

Wmkd. Multiple Crown and Arabic F. (195)

1940, May 17 Photo. *Perf. 13½x14*

B1	SP1	5m +5m cop brn	50	45

No. B1 Overprinted in Green **1943** ١٩٤٣

1943, Nov. 17

B2	SP1	5m +5m cop brn	5.00	4.00
a.		Arabic date "1493"	160.00	160.00

The surtax on Nos. B1 and B2 was for the children's fund.

First Postage Stamp of Egypt
SP2

Khedive Ismail Pasha
SP3

Designs: 17m+17m, King Fuad. 22m+22m, King Farouk.

Perf. 13x13½

1946, Feb. 28 Wmk. 195

B3	SP2	1m +1m gray	10	10
B4	SP3	10m +10m vio	15	15
B5	SP3	17m +17m brn	25	25
B6	SP3	22m +22m yel grn	30	30
a.		Souvenir sheet, perf. 8½	35.00	30.00
b.		As "a," imperf.	35.00	30.00

Issued to commemorate the 80th anniversary of Egypt's first postage stamp.

Nos. B6a and B6b measure 129x171mm. and contain one each of Nos. B3 to B6, with inscriptions in top and bottom margins.

Goddess Hathor, King Men-kau-Re (Mycerinus) and Jackal-headed Goddess
SP7

Ramesseum, Thebes—SP8

Queen Nefertiti
SP9

Funerary Mask of King Tutankhamen
SP10

Perf. 13½x13

1947, Mar. 9 Wmk. 195

B9	SP7	5m +5m sl	25	25
B10	SP8	15m +15m dp bl	50	40
B11	SP9	30m +30m hn brn	70	70
B12	SP10	50m +50m brn	1.00	1.00

Issued to commemorate the International Exposition of Contemporary Art, Cairo.

Boy Scout Emblem
SP11

Scout Emblems: 20m+10m, Sea Scouts. 35m+15m, Air Explorers.

Photogravure.

1956, July 25 *Perf. 13½x13*

B13	SP11	10m +10m grn	35	30
B14	SP11	20m +10m ultra	50	45
B15	SP11	35m +15m bl	70	65

Issued to commemorate the 2nd Arab Scout Jamboree, Alexandria-Aboukir, 1956.

Souvenir sheets, perf. and imperf., contain one each of Nos. B13-B15. Size: 118×158mm. Price $400 each.

Ambulance
SP12

1957, May 13 *Perf. 13x13½*

B16	SP12	10m +5m rose red	20	18

Issued to commemorate the 50th anniversary of the Public Aid Society.

United Arab Republic

Eye and Map of Africa, Europe and Asia
SP13

Postal Emblem
SP14

Perf. 13½x13

1958, Mar. 1 Photo. Wmk. 318

B17	SP13	10m +5m org	60	60

Issued to commemorate the First Afro-Asian Congress of Ophthalmology, Cairo.

The surtax was for centers to aid the blind.

1959, Jan. 2

B18	SP14	10m +5m bl grn, red & blk	15	12

Issued for Post Day, Jan. 2. The surtax went to the social fund for postal employees.

Children and U. N. Emblem
SP15

Arab League Building, Cairo, and Emblem
SP16

1959, Oct. 24 Wmk. 328

B19	SP15	10m +5m brn lake	20	12
B20	SP15	35m +10m dk bl	40	35

Issued for International Children's Day and to honor UNICEF.

Braille Type of Regular Issue, 1961.

1961, Apr. 6 *Perf. 13½x13*

B21	A182	35m +15m yel & brn	50	50

World Health Organization Day.

1962, Mar. 22 Photo. Wmk. 328

B22	SP16	10m +5m gray	25	25

Arab Publicity Week, Mar. 22–28.

Postal Emblem
SP17

Stamp of 1866—SP18

1963, Jan. 2 *Perf. 11½* Wmk. 342

B23	SP17	20m +10m brt grn, red & blk	50	50
B24	SP18	40m +20m blk & brn org	75	75
B25	SP18	40m +20m brn org & blk	75	75

Issued for Post Day, Jan. 2 and to publicize the 1966 exhibition of the Federation International de Philatelie. Nos. B24–B25 printed se-tenant.

Arms of U.A.R. and Pyramids
SP19

1964, Jan. 2 *Perf. 11* Wmk. 342

B26	SP19	10m +5m org yel & grn	1.00	75
B27	SP19	80m +40m grnsh bl & blk	2.00	1.50
B28	SP19	115m +55m org brn & blk	2.50	2.00

Issued for Post Day. Jan. 2.

Type of 1963 and

Postal Emblem—SP20

Designs: No. B30, Emblem of Postal Secondary School. 80m+40m, Postal emblem, gearwheel and laurel wreath.

Photogravure

1965, Jan. 2 *Perf. 11½* Unwmkd.

B29	SP20	10m +5m lt grn & car	12	12
B30	SP20	10m +5m ultra, car & blk	12	12
B31	SP18	80m +40m rose, brt grn & blk	95	95

Issued for Post Day, Jan. 2. No. B31 also publicizes the Stamp Centenary Exhibition.

Souvenir Sheet

Stamps of Egypt, 1866—SP21

1966, Jan. 2 *Imperf.* Wmk. 342

B32	SP21	140m +60m blk, sl bl & rose	2.00	2.00

Issued for Post Day, 1966, and to commemorate the centenary of the first Egyptian postage stamps. Size: 105x62mm.

Pharaonic "Mediator"
SP22

Design: 115m+40, Pharaonic guard.

1967, Jan. 2 *Perf. 11½* Wmk. 342

B33	SP22	80m +20m multi	1.25	1.00
B34	SP22	115m +40m multi	2.50	1.50

Issued for Post Day, Jan. 2.

Grand Canal, Doges' Palace, Venice, and Santa Maria del Fiore, Florence—SP23

Design: 115m+30m, Piazetta and Campanile, Venice, and Palazzo Vecchio, Florence.

Perf. 11½x11

1967, Dec. 9 Photo. Wmk. 342

B35	SP23	80m +20m grn, yel & brn	65	65
B36	SP23	115m +30m ol, yel & sl bl	1.00	1.00

The surtax was to help save the cultural monuments of Venice and Florence, damaged in the 1966 floods.

Boy and Girl SP24

Emblem and Flags of Arab League SP25

Design: No. B38, Five children and arch.

Perf. 11

1968, Dec. 11 Photo. Wmk. 342

B37	SP24	20m +10m car, bl & lt brn	18	18
B38	SP24	20m +10m vio bl, sep & lt grn	18	18

Issued for Children's Day and to commemorate the 22nd anniversary of UNICEF (United Nations Children's Fund).

1969, Mar. 22 *Perf. 11x11½*

B39	SP25	20m +10m multi	35	18

Arab Publicity Week, March 22–28.

Refugee Family SP26

Perf. 11½

1969, Oct. 24 Photo. Wmk. 342

B40	SP26	30m +10m multi	35	18

Issued for United Nations Day.

Men of Three Races, Human Rights Emblem SP27

1970, Mar. 21 *Perf. 11½x11*

B41	SP27	20m +10m multi	25	18

Issued to publicize the International Day for the Elimination of Racial Discrimination.

Arab League Type of Regular Issue

1970, Mar. 22 Wmk. 342

B42	A344	20m +10m bl, grn & brn	25	18

25th anniversary of Arab League.

Map of Palestine and Refugees SP28

Perf. 11½x11

1970, Oct. 24 Photo. Wmk. 342

B43	SP28	20m +10m multi	50	20

Issued to commemorate the 25th anniversary of the United Nations and to draw attention to the plight of the Palestinian refugees.

Arab Republic of Egypt

Blind Girl, WHO and Society Emblems SP29

1973, Oct. 24 Photo. *Perf. 11x11½*

B44	SP29	20m +10m bl & gold	25	15

25th anniversary of the World Health Organization and for the Light and Hope Society, which educates and helps blind girls.

Map of Africa, OAU Emblem SP30

Social Work Day Emblem SP31

Perf. 11x11½

1973, Dec. 8 Photo. Wmk. 342

B45	SP30	55m +20m multi	1.50	1.50

10th anniversary of the Organization for African Unity.

1973, Dec. 8

B46	SP31	20m +10m multi	25	15

Social Work Day.

Jehane al Sadat Consoling Wounded Man—SP32

1974, Mar. 21 *Perf. 11* Wmk. 342

B47	SP32	20m +10m multi	15	15

Faithfulness and Hope Society.

AIR POST STAMPS.

Mail Plane in Flight AP1

Wmkd. Multiple Crown and Arabic F. (195)

Photogravure.

1926, Mar. 10 *Perf. 13x13½.*

C1	AP1	27m dp vio	12.00	8.00

1929, July 17

C2	AP1	27m org brn	4.00	3.00

Zeppelin Issue.

No. C2 Surcharged in Blue or Violet

GRAF ZEPPELIN AVRIL 1931 50 جراف زبلين ابريل ١٩٣١ ٥٠

1931, Apr. 6

C3	AP1	50m on 27m org brn (Bl)	35.00	30.00
a.		"1951" instead of "1931"	50.00	50.00
C4	AP1	100m on 27m org brn (V)	35.00	30.00

Airplane over Giza Pyramids AP2

1933–38 Lithographed *Perf. 13x13½*

C5	AP2	1m org & blk	10	8
C6	AP2	2m gray & blk	1.00	55
C7	AP2	2m org red & blk ('38)	80	75
C8	AP2	3m ol brn & blk	20	20
C9	AP2	4m grn & blk	50	45
C10	AP2	5m dp brn & blk	35	10
C11	AP2	6m dk grn & blk	70	65
C12	AP2	7m dk bl & blk	45	45
C13	AP2	8m vio & blk	25	15
C14	AP2	9m dp red & blk	80	80
C15	AP2	10m vio & brn	50	15
C16	AP2	20m dk grn & brn	35	10
C17	AP2	30m dl bl & brn	50	20
C18	AP2	40m dp red & brn	10.00	20
C19	AP2	50m org & brn	7.25	20
C20	AP2	60m gray & brn	2.75	20
C21	AP2	70m dk bl & bl grn	1.50	20
C22	AP2	80m ol brn & bl grn	1.50	20
C23	AP2	90m org & bl grn	2.50	20
C24	AP2	100m vio & bl grn	3.00	25
C25	AP2	200m dp red & bl grn	6.00	50
		Nos. C5-C25 (21)	41.00	6.58

Type of 1933.

1941–43 Photogravure

C34	AP2	5m cop brn ('43)	15	12
C35	AP2	10m violet	40	20
C36	AP2	25m dk vio brn ('43)	40	20
C37	AP2	30m green	50	20

No. C37 Overprinted in Black

مؤتمر الملاحة الجوية الدولى للشرق الأوسط

Le Caire 1946 - ١٩٤٦ القاهرة

1946, Oct. 1

C38	AP2	30m green	40	20
a.		Double overprint	125.00	125.00
b.		Inverted overprint	150.00	150.00

Issued to commemorate the Middle East International Air Navigation Congress, Cairo, October 1946.

King Farouk, Delta Dam and DC-3 Plane—AP3

Perf. 13x13½

1947, Feb. 19 Photo. Wmk. 195

C39	AP3	2m red org	10	4
C40	AP3	3m dk brn	10	10
C41	AP3	5m red brn	10	10
C42	AP3	7m dp yel org	12	12
C43	AP3	8m green	15	10
C44	AP3	10m violet	15	8
C45	AP3	20m brt bl	25	15
C46	AP3	30m brn vio	35	18
C47	AP3	40m car rose	50	20
C48	AP3	50m Prus grn	60	25
C49	AP3	100m ol grn	1.00	45
C50	AP3	200m dk gray	2.00	1.25
		Nos. C39-C50 (12)	5.42	3.02

Nos. C49 and C50 Surcharged in Black

Mills. 13 مليم ١٣

S.A.I.D.E.

23-8-1948 ١٩٤٨

1948, Aug. 23

C51	AP3	13m on 100m ol grn	45	45
C52	AP3	22m on 200m dk gray	55	55
a.		Date omitted		

Issued to commemorate the inaugural flights of "Services Aeriens Internationaux d'Egypte" from Cairo to Athens and Rome, August 23, 1948.

Nos. C39 to C50 Overprinted in Various Colors

ملك مصر والسودان ١٦ اكتوبر سنة ١٩٥١

Overprint 27mm. Wide.

1952, Jan. *Perf. 13x13½* Wmk. 195

C53	AP3	2m red org (Bl)	8	8
C54	AP3	3m dk brn (RV)	10	10
C55	AP3	5m red brn	12	10
C56	AP3	7m dp yel org (Bl)	25	25
C57	AP3	8m grn (RV)	18	18
C58	AP3	10m vio (G)	25	25
C59	AP3	20m brt bl (RV)	1.25	1.00
C60	AP3	30m brn vio (G)	50	40
C61	AP3	40m car rose	1.65	80
C62	AP3	50m Prus grn (RV)	1.00	1.00
C63	AP3	100m ol grn	2.00	1.85
C64	AP3	200m dk gray (RV)	3.25	3.25
		Nos. C53-C64 (12)	10.63	9.26

See note after No. 316.

Delta Dam and Douglas DC-3 AP4

1953 Photogravure.

C65 AP4	5m red brn	10	8
C66 AP4	15m ol grn	18	15

Nos. C39-C49 Overprinted in Black with Three Bars to Obliterate Portrait.

1953

C67 AP3	2m red org	20	20
C68 AP3	3m dk brn	40	40
C69 AP3	5m red brn	10	10
C70 AP3	7m dp yel org	15	15
C71 AP3	8m green	20	20
C72 AP3	10m violet	6.00	6.00
C73 AP3	20m brt bl	25	20
C74 AP3	30m brn vio	40	35
C75 AP3	40m car rose	45	45
C76 AP3	50m Prus grn	60	55
C77 AP3	100m ol grn	1.00	1.00
C77A AP3	200m gray	15.00	15.00
	Nos. C67-C77A (12)	24.75	24.60

Nos. C53-C64 Overprinted in Black with Three Bars to Obliterate Portrait.

1953

C78 AP3	2m red org	8	8
C79 AP3	3m dk brn	12	12
C80 AP3	5m red brn	8	8
C81 AP3	7m dp yel org	3.00	3.00
C82 AP3	8m green	18	18
C83 AP3	10m violet	25	25
C84 AP3	20m brt bl	15.00	15.00
C85 AP3	30m brn vio	35	35
C86 AP3	40m car rose	15.00	15.00
C87 AP3	50m Prus grn	50	45
C88 AP3	100m ol grn	75	75
C89 AP3	200m dk gray	2.00	1.75
	Nos. C78-C89 (12)	37.31	37.01

Practically all values of Nos. C67-C89 exist with double overprint.

United Arab Republic

Type of Regular Issue

Perf. 11½x11

1958, March 22 Photo. Wmk. 318

C90 A141	15m ultra & red brn	20	20

Birth of United Arab Republic.

Pyramids at Giza AP5

Al Azhar University AP6

Designs: 15m, Colossi of Memnon, Thebes. 90m, St. Catherine Monastery, Mt. Sinai.

1959-60 *Perf. 13x13½* Wmk. 328

C91 AP5	5m brt red	5	5
C92 AP5	15m dk dl vio	15	15
C93 A6	60m dk grn	50	50
C94 AP5	90m brn car ('60)	1.00	40

Nos. C91-C93 exist imperf. See also Nos. C101, C105.

Type of Regular Issue, Redrawn (Tower of Cairo)

1961, May 1 *Perf. 13½x13*

C95 A183	50m brt bl	40	35

Top inscription has been replaced by two airplanes.

Weather Vane, Anemometer and U.N. World Meteorological Organization Emblem—AP7

Perf. 11½x11

1962, Mar. 23 Photo. Unwmkd.

C96 AP7	60m yel & dp bl	50	50

2nd World Meteorological Day, Mar. 23.

Patrice Lumumba and Map of Africa AP8

Perf. 13½x13

1962, July 1 Wmk. 328

C97 AP8	35m multi	30	30

Issued in memory of Patrice Lumumba (1925-61), Premier of Congo.

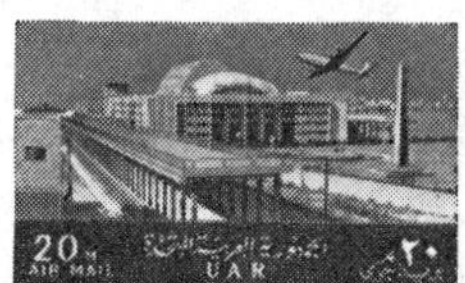

Maritime Station, Alexandria AP9

Designs: 30m, International Airport, Cairo. 40m, Railroad Station, Luxor.

1963, Mar. 18 *Perf. 13x13½*

C98 AP9	20m dk brn	16	12
C99 AP9	30m car rose	25	20
C100 AP9	40m black	35	30

Type of 1959-60 and

Temple of Queen Nefertari, Abu Simbel—AP10

Arch and Tower of Cairo AP11

Designs: 80m, Al Azhar University seen through arch. 140m, Ramses II, Abu Simbel.

Perf. 11½x11, 11x11½

1963, Oct. 24 Photo. Wmk. 342

C101 AP6	80m vio blk & brt bl	3.00	50
C102 AP10	115m brn & yel	95	70
C103 AP10	140m pale vio, blk & org red	1.15	90

Unwmkd.

C104 AP11	50m yel brn & brt bl ('64)	50	40
C105 AP6	80m vio bl & lt bl ('65)	2.50	50

Weather Vane, Anemometer and WMO Emblem—AP12

Perf. 11½x11

1965, Mar. 23 Wmk. 342

C106 AP12	80m dk bl & rose lil	65	50

Fifth World Meteorological Day.

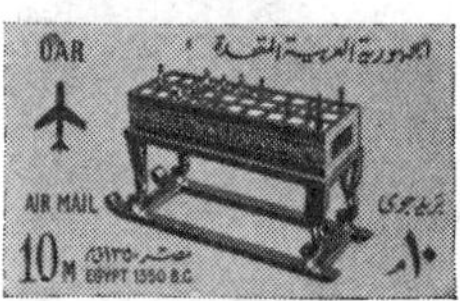

Game Board from Tomb of Tutankhamen—AP13

1965, July 1 Photo. Unwmkd.

C107 AP13	10m yel & dk bl	6	5

Temples at Abu Simbel—AP14

1966, Apr. 28 *Perf. 11½* Wmk. 342

C108 A14	20m multi	12	10
C109 A14	80m multi	48	35

Issued to commemorate the transfer of the temples of Abu Simbel to a hilltop, 1963-66.

Scout Camp and Jamboree Emblem—AP15

1966, Aug. 10 *Perf. 11½x11*

C110 AP15	20m ol & rose	12	10

Issued to commemorate the 7th Pan-Arab Boy Scout Jamboree, Good Daim, Libya, Aug. 12.

St. Catherine Monastery, Mt. Sinai AP16

1966, Nov. 30 Photo. Wmk. 342

C111 AP16	80m multi	48	35

Issued to commemorate the 1400th anniversary of St. Catherine Monastery, Sinai.

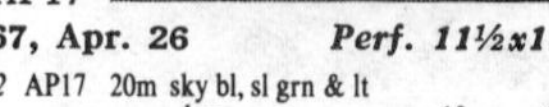

Cairo Airport AP17

1967, Apr. 26 *Perf. 11½x11*

C112 AP17	20m sky bl, sl grn & lt brn	12	10

Hotel El Alamein and Map of Nile Delta AP18

Designs: 80m, The Virgin's Tree, Virgin Mary and Child. 115m, Fishing in the Red Sea.

1967, June 7 *Perf. 11½* Wmk. 342

C113 AP18	20m dl pur, sl grn & dl org	20	10
C114 AP18	80m bl & multi	80	35
C115 AP18	115m brn, org & bl	1.50	75

Issued for International Tourist Year, 1967.

Oil Derricks, Map of Egypt—AP19

1967, July 23 Photogravure

C116 AP19	50m org & bluish blk	30	26

15th anniversary of the revolution.

Type of Regular Issue, 1967

Design: 80m, Back of Tutankhamen's throne and UNESCO emblem.

1967, Oct. 24 *Perf. 11½* Wmk. 342

C117 A301	80m bl & yel	48	35

22nd anniversary of the United Nations.

Koran—AP20

1968, Mar. 25 *Perf. 11½* Wmk. 342

C118 AP20	30m lil, bl & yel	50	15
C119 AP20	80m lil, bl & yel	1.00	35

Issued to commemorate the 1400th anniversary of the Koran. Nos. C118-C119 are printed in miniature sheets of 4 containing 2 each of Nos. C118-C119, decorative border and gutters. Size: 240x158 mm.

St. Mark and St. Mark's Cathedral—AP21

1968, June 25 *Perf. 11½* Wmk. 342

C120 AP21	80m brt grn, dk brn & dp car	48	35

Issued to commemorate the 1900th anniversary of the martyrdom of St. Mark and to commemorate the consecration of St. Mark's Cathedral, Cairo.

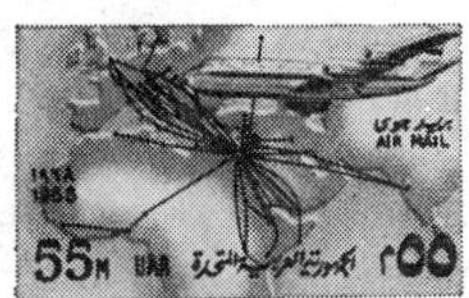

Map of United Arab Airlines and Boeing 707—AP22

Design: No. C122, Ilyushin 18 and routes of United Arab Airlines.

1968-69 Photo. *Perf. 11½x11*

C121 AP22 55m bl, ocher & car 33 26
C122 AP22 55m bl, yel & vio blk ('69) 33 26

Issued to commemorate the first flights of a Boeing 707 (No. C121) and an Ilyushin 18 (No. C122) for United Arab Airlines.

Mahatma Gandhi, Arms of India and UAR AP23 — **Imam El Boukhary AP24**

1969, Sept. 10 *Perf. 11x11½*

C123 AP23 80m lt bl, ocher & brn 65 35

Issued to commemorate the centenary of the birth of Mohandas K. Gandhi (1869-1948), leader in India's fight for independence.

1969, Dec. 27 Photo. Wmk. 342

C124 AP24 30m lt ol & dk brn 18 15

Issued to commemorate the 1100th anniversary of the death of the Imam El Boukhary (824-870), philosopher and writer.

Azzahir Beybars Mosque AP25

1969, Dec. 27 Engr. *Perf. 11½x11*

C125 AP25 30m red lil 18 15

700th anniversary of the founding of the Azzahir Beybars Mosque, Cairo.

Lenin AP26

Perf. 11x11½

1970, Apr. 22 Photo. Wmk. 342

C126 AP26 80m lt grn & brn 48 35

Issued to commemorate the centenary of the birth of Lenin (1870-1924).

Phantom Fighters and Destroyed Factory—AP27

1970, May 1 *Perf. 11½x11*

C127 AP27 80m yel, grn & dk vio brn 75 35

Issued to commemorate the destruction of the Abu-Zaabal factory by Israeli planes.

U.P.U. Type of Regular Issue

1970, May 20 Photo. Wmk. 342

C128 A350 80m multi 48 35

Issued to commemorate the inauguration of the new Universal Postal Union Headquarters in Bern.

Nasser and Burial Mosque AP28

1970, Nov. 6 *Perf. 11* Wmk. 342

C129 AP28 30m ol & blk 18 15
C130 AP28 80m brn & blk 48 35

Issued in memory of Gamal Abdel Nasser (1918-1970), President of Egypt.

Postal Congress Type of Regular Issue

Perf. 11½x11

1971, Mar. 6 Photo. Wmk. 342

C131 A365 30m lt ol, org & sl grn 18 15

9th Arab Postal Congress, Cairo, March 6-25.

Nasser, El Rifaei and Sultan Hussein Mosques—AP29

Designs: 85m, Nasser and Ramses Square, Cairo. 110m, Nasser, Sphinx and pyramids.

Perf. 11½x11

1971, July 1 Photo. Wmk. 342

C132 AP29 30m multi 50 15
C133 AP29 85m multi 1.25 35
C134 AP29 110m multi 1.75 50

APU Type of Regular Issue

1971, Aug. 3 *Perf. 11½* Wmk. 342

C135 A373 30m brn, yel & Bl 18 15

25th anniversary of the Conference of Sofar, Lebanon, establishing the Arab Postal Union.

Arab Republic of Egypt

Confederation Type of Regular Issue

Perf. 11½x11

1971, Sept. 28 Photo. Wmk. 342

C136 A374 30m gray, sl grn & dk pur 18 12

Confederation of Arab Republics (Egypt, Syria and Libya).

Al Aqsa Mosque and Woman AP30

Perf. 11½

1971, Oct. 24 Photo. Wmk. 342

C137 AP30 30m bl, yel, brn & grn 18 12

25th anniversary of the United Nations (in 1970) and for the return of Palestinian refugees.

Postal Union Type of Regular Issue

Design: 30m, African Postal Union emblem and letter.

1971, Dec. 2 *Perf. 11½x11*

C138 A384 30m grn, blk & bl 18 12

10th anniversary of African Postal Union.

Aida, Triumphal March AP31

1971, Dec. 23 *Perf. 11½* Wmk. 342

C139 AP31 110m dk brn, yel & sl grn 70 40

Centenary of the first performance of the opera Aida, by Giuseppe Verdi.

Globe, Glider, Rocket Club Emblem AP32 — **St. Catherine's Monastery on Fire AP33**

1972, Feb. 11 *Perf. 11x11½*

C140 AP32 30m bl, ocher & yel 18 12

International Aerospace Education Conference, Cairo, Jan. 11-13.

Perf. 11½x11

1972, Feb. 15 Unwmkd.

C141 AP33 110m dp car, org & blk 70 40

The burning of St. Catherine's Monastery in Sinai Desert, Nov. 30, 1971.

Tutankhamen in Garden AP34

Tutankhamen, from 2nd Sarcophagus—AP35

Design: No. C143, Ankhesenamun.

1972, May 22 Photo. *Perf. 11½*

C142 AP34 110m brn org, bl & grn 1.00 35
C143 AP34 110m brn org, bl & grn 1.00 35

Souvenir Sheet

Imperf.

C144 AP35 200m gold & multi 3.50 3.50

50th anniversary of the discovery of the tomb of Tutankhamen. Nos. C142-C143 printed se-tenant in sheets of 50. The continuous design is from a painted ivory plaque on lid of a coffer.

No. C144 has blue inscription and gold scarab ornaments in margin. Size: 97x102 mm.

Souvenir Sheet

Flag of Confederation of Arab Republics—AP36

1972, July 23 Photo. *Imperf.*

C145 AP36 110m gold, dp car & blk 1.00 1.00

20th anniversary of the revolution. No. C145 has gold commemorative inscription and black portraits of Presidents Nasser and Anwar El Sadat in margin. Size: 107x69 mm.

Temples at Abu Simbel
AP37

Designs: 30m, Al Azhar Mosque and St. George's Church. 110m, Pyramids at Giza.

1972 ***Perf. 11½x11*** **Wmk. 342**

C146	AP37	30m bl brn & buff	15	10
C147	AP37	85m bl, brn & ocher	45	30
C148	AP37	110m multi	56	32

Issue dates: Nos. C146, C148, Nov. 22; No. C147, Aug. 1.

Olympic Type of Regular Issue

Designs (Olympic and Motion Emblems and): No. C149, Handball. No. C150, Weight lifting. 50m, Swimming. 55m, Gymnastics. All vertical.

1972, Aug. 17 ***Perf. 11x11½***

C149	A396	30m multi	15	10
C150	A396	30m yel & multi	15	10
C151	A396	50m bl & multi	25	16
C152	A396	55m multi	28	16

Champollion, Rosetta Stone, Hieroglyphics—AP38

1972, Oct. 16

C153	AP38	110m gold, grn & blk	1.25	50

Sesquicentennial of the deciphering of Egyptian hieroglyphics by Jean-François Champollion.

World Map, Telephone, Radar, ITU Emblem—AP39

1973, Mar. 21 **Photo.** ***Perf. 11***

C154	AP39	30m lt bl, dk bl & blk	15	10

5th World Telecommunications Day.

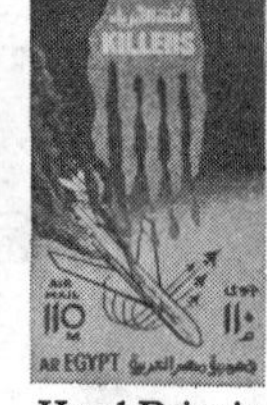

Karnak Temple, Luxor
AP40

Hand Dripping Blood and Falling Plane
AP41

1973, Mar. 21

C155	AP40	110m dp ultra, blk & rose	1.00	70

Sound and light at Karnak.

1973, May 1 ***Perf. 11x11½***

C156	AP41	110m multi	1.50	75

Israeli attack on Libyan civilian plane, Feb. 1973.

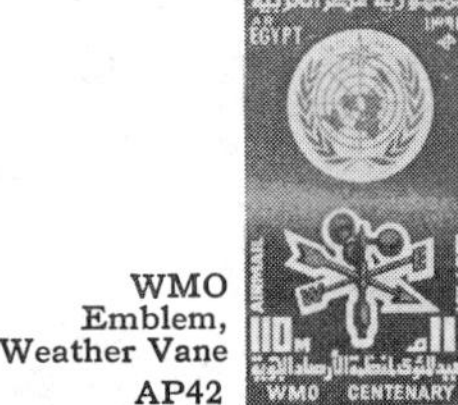

WMO Emblem, Weather Vane
AP42

1973, Oct. 24 ***Perf. 11x11½***

C157	AP42	110m bl, gold & pur	1.00	50

Centenary of international meteorological cooperation.

Refugees, Map of Palestine
AP43

1973, Oct. 24 ***Perf. 11½***

C158	AP43	30m dk brn, yel & bl	35	25

Plight of Palestinian refugees.

INTERPOL Emblem
AP44

Postal and UPU Emblems
AP45

Perf. 11x11½

1973, Dec. 8 **Photo.** **Wmk. 342**

C159	AP44	110m blk & multi	55	28

50th anniversary of the International Criminal Police Organization.

1974, Jan. 2 ***Perf. 11*** **Unwmkd.**

Designs (UPU Emblems and): 30m, Arab Postal Union emblem. 55m, African Postal Union emblem. 110m, Universal Postal Union emblem.

Size: 26x46½mm.

C160	AP45	20m gray, red & blk	10	8
C161	AP45	30m sal, blk & pur	15	10
C162	AP45	55m emer, blk & brt mag	70	25

Size: 37x37½mm. ***Perf. 11½***

C163	AP45	110m lt bl, blk & gold	1.00	50

Post Day 1974.

Solar Bark of Khufu (Cheops)
AP46

Photogravure

1974, Mar. 21 ***Perf. 11½*** **Wmk. 342**

C164	AP46	110m bl, gold & brn	1.00	50

Solar Bark Museum.

Hotel Meridien
AP47

1974, Oct. 6 ***Perf. 11½x11***

C165	AP47	110m multi	1.00	50

Opening of Hotel Meridien, Cairo.

Suez Canal Type of 1975

1975, June 5 ***Perf. 11½***

C166	A448	30m bl, yel grn & ind	40	25
C167	A448	110m ind & bl	1.25	50

Reopening of the Suez Canal, June 5.

Irrigation Commission Emblem
AP48

1975, July 20

C168	AP48	110m org & dk grn	1.00	50

9th International Congress on Irrigation and Drainage, Moscow, and 25th anniversary of the International Commission on Irrigation and Drainage.

Refugees and UNWRA Emblem—AP49

Woman and IWY Emblem
AP50

Perf. 11x11½

1975, Oct. 24 **Photo.** **Wmk. 342**

C169	AP49	30m multi	15	12

Unwmkd.

C170	AP50	110m ol, org & blk	1.00	50

United Nations Day. 30m publicizes U.N. help for refugees; 110m is for International Women's Year 1975.

Step Pyramid, Sakhara, and Entrance Gate
AP51

Designs: 45m, Plane over Giza Pyramids. 140m, Plane over boats on Nile.

Perf. 11½x11

1977, Nov. 15 **Photo.** **Wmk. 342**

C171	AP51	45m yel & brn	22	16
C171A	AP51	60m olive	30	30
C172	AP51	115m bl & brn	60	30
C173	AP51	140m bl & pur	70	48

Flyer and U.N. ICAO Emblem
AP52

Wmk. 342

1978, Dec. 30 **Photo.** ***Perf. 11x11½***

C174	AP52	140m bl, blk & brn	70	55

75th anniversary of 1st powered flight.

Seeing Eye Medallion—AP53

Wmk. 342

1981, Oct. 1 **Photo.** ***Perf. 11½x11***

C175	AP53	230m multi	1.15	60

Hilton Ramses Hotel Opening—AP54

Wmk. 342

1982, Mar. 15 **Photo.** ***Perf. 11x11½***

C176	AP54	18½p multi	10	5

AIR POST SEMI-POSTAL STAMPS

United Arab Republic

Pharaonic Mail Carriers and Papyrus Plants
SPAP1

Design: 115m+55m, Jet plane, world map and stamp of Egypt, 1926 (No. C1).

Photogravure

1966, Jan. 2 Perf. 11½ Wmk. 342

CB1	SPAP1 80m +40m yel, grn, brn, lil & bl		80	70
CB2	SPAP1 115m +55m bl, yel & lil		1.00	85

Issued for Post Day, Jan. 2. Nos. CB1–CB2 printed se-tenant in sheets of 28.

SPECIAL DELIVERY STAMPS.

Motor-cycle Postman
SD1

Wmkd.
Multiple Crown and Arabic F. (195)

1926, Nov. 28 Photo. Perf. 13x13½

E1	SD1	20m dk grn	6.50	2.00

1929, Sept.

E2	SD1	20m brn red & blk	75	40

Inscribed "Postes Expres."

1943–44 Lithographed

E3	SD1	26m brn red & gray blk	1.00	90
E4	SD1	40m dl brn & pale gray ('44)	75	30

No. E4 Overprinted in Black ملك مصر والسودان ١٦ اكتوبر سنة ١٩٥١

Overprint 27mm. Wide.

1952, Jan.

E5	SD1	40m dl brn & pale gray	60	45

See note after No. 316.

POSTAGE DUE STAMPS.

D1 D2

Wmkd. Crescent and Star. (119)

1884, Jan. 1 Litho. Perf. 10½

J1	D1	10pa red	10.00	2.00
a.		Imperf. vert., pair	125.00	
J2	D1	20pa red	18.00	4.00
J3	D1	1pi red	32.50	7.50
J4	D1	2pi red	50.00	4.00
J5	D1	5pi red	10.00	7.50

1886, Aug. 1 Unwmkd.

J6	D1	10pa red	3.00	1.00
a.		Imperf. vert., pair	75.00	60.00
J7	D1	20pa red	75.00	10.00
J8	D1	1pi red	2.50	1.00
J9	D1	2pi red	2.50	50

1888, Jan. 1 Perf. 11½

J10	D2	2m green	1.50	75
a.		Horiz. pair, imperf. between	75.00	
J11	D2	5m rose red	2.50	75
J12	D2	1pi blue	25.00	8.50
J13	D2	2pi yellow	17.50	3.50
J14	D2	5pi gray	75.00	50.00
a.		Period after 'PIASTRES'	100.00	75.00
		Nos. J10-J14 (5)	121.50	63.50

Excellent counterfeits of J1 to J14 are plentiful. There are four types of each of Nos. J1 to J14, so placed that any block of four contains all four types.

D3 D4

Typographed.

1889 Perf. 14x13½ Wmk. 119

J15	D3	2m green	75	10
a.		Half used as 1m on cover		5.00
J16	D3	4m maroon	50	8
J17	D3	1pi ultra	85	8
J18	D3	2pi orange	1.25	25

Nos. J15–J18 exist on both ordinary and chalky paper. Imperf. examples of Nos. J15–J17 are proofs.

Black Surcharge.

1898

J19	D4	3m on 2pi org	30	25
a.		Inverted surch.	30.00	30.00
b.		Double surcharge	100.00	100.00
c.		Pair, one without surcharge	175.00	

There are two types of this surcharge. In one type, the spacing between the last two Arabic characters at the right is 2mm. In the other type, this spacing is 3mm., and there is an added sign on top of the second character from the right.

D5 D6

Wmkd.
Triple Crescent and Star. (120)

1921 Perf. 14x13½

J20	D5	2m green	40	35
J21	D5	4m vermilion	1.50	75
J22	D6	10m dp bl	1.50	1.00

1921-22

J23	D5	2m vermilion	30	15
J24	D5	4m green	30	15
J25	D6	10m lake ('22)	40	10

Nos. J18, J23–J25 Overprinted

1922, Oct. 10 Wmk. 119

J26	D3	2pi orange	4.00	1.00
a.		Ovpt. right side up	8.00	5.00

Wmk. 120

J27	D5	2m vermilion	35	25
J28	D5	4m green	60	50
J29	D6	10m lake	1.00	60

Overprint on Nos. J26–J29 is inverted.

Arabic Numeral
D7

Wmkd.
Multiple Crown and Arabic F. (195)

1927–56 Lithographed Perf. 13x13½

Size: 18x22½ mm.

J30	D7	2m slate	25	15
J31	D7	2m org ('38)	25	15
J32	D7	4m green	40	15
J33	D7	4m ol brn ('32)	80	20
J34	D7	5m brown	80	30
J35	D7	6m gray grn ('41)	50	20
J36	D7	8m brn vio	50	25
J37	D7	10m brick red ('29)	65	25
a.		10m dp red	75	35
J38	D7	12m rose lake ('41)	75	25
J38A	D7	20m dk red ('56)	1.50	75

Perf. 13½x14

Size: 22x28 mm.

J39	D7	30m purple	3.50	1.50
		Nos. J30-J39 (11)	9.90	4.15

Postage Due Stamps and Type of 1927 Overprinted in Various Colors ملك مصر والسودان ١٦ اكتوبر سنة ١٩٥١

1952, Jan. 16 Perf. 13x13½

J40	D7	2m org (Bl)	15	15
J41	D7	4m green	30	30
J42	D7	6m gray grn (RV)	35	35
J43	D7	8m brn vio (Bl)	40	35
J44	D7	10m dl rose (Bl)	75	35
a.		10m brn red (Bk)	65	40
J45	D7	12m rose lake (Bl)	50	30

Perf. 14

J46	D7	30m pur (C)	1.50	55
		Nos. J40-J46 (7)	3.95	2.35

See note after No. 316.

United Arab Republic

1960 Perf. 13x13½ Wmk. 318

Size: 18x22½ mm.

J47	D7	2m orange	45	15
J48	D7	4m lt grn	55	20
J49	D7	6m green	75	25
J50	D7	8m brn vio	55	35
J51	D7	12m rose brn	1.00	50
J52	D7	20m dl rose brn	1.50	50

Perf. 14

Size: 22x28 mm.

J53	D7	30m violet	5.00	1.00
		Nos. J47-J53 (7)	9.80	2.95

1962 Perf. 13x13½ Wmk. 328

Size: 18x22½mm.

J54	D7	2m salmon	15	10
J55	D7	4m lt grn	25	10
J56	D7	10m red brn	50	15
J57	D7	12m rose brn	80	60
J58	D7	20m dl rose brn	1.65	1.00

Perf. 14

Size: 22x28mm.

J59	D7	30m lt vio	2.00	1.75
		Nos. J54-J59 (6)	5.35	3.70

D8

Photogravure

1965 Perf. 11 Unwmkd.

J60	D8	2m org & vio blk	10	10
J61	D8	8m lt bl & dk bl	15	15
J62	D8	10m yel & emer	15	15
J63	D8	20m lt bl & vio blk	20	15
J64	D8	40m org & emer	35	20
		Nos. J60-J64 (5)	95	75

A little time given to study of the arrangement of the Scott Catalogue can make it easier to use effectively.

MILITARY STAMPS

From November 1, 1932 to February 29, 1936 members of the British Forces in Egypt were permitted to send letters to Great Britain at reduced rates. Special seals were used in place of Egyptian stamps. These seals were replaced by special stamps March 1, 1936.

Fuad Type of 1927.
Inscribed "Army Post".
Wmkd.
Multiple Crown and Arabic F. (195)

1936, Mar. 1 Photo. Perf. 13½x14

M1	A44	3m green	50	15
M2	A44	10m carmine	1.50	30

King Farouk
M1

1939, Dec. 16 Perf. 13x13½

M3	M1	3m green	50	3.00
M4	M1	10m car rose	1.50	20

United Arab Republic

Arms of UAR and Military Emblems
M2

Perf. 11x11½

1971, Apr. 15 Photo. Wmk. 342

M5	M2	10m purple	10	10

OFFICIAL STAMPS.

O1

Wmkd. Crescent and Star. (119)

1893, Jan. 1 Typo. Perf. 14x13½

O1	O1	org brn	30	15

No. O1 exists on ordinary and chalky paper.
Imperf. examples of No. O1 are proofs.

Regular Issues of 1884-93 Overprinted O.H.H.S. اميري

1907

O2	A18	1m brown	15	6
O3	A19	2m green	20	6
a.		Double ovpt.		
O4	A21	3m orange	20	6
O5	A20	5m car rose	35	4
O6	A14	1pi ultra	50	6
O7	A16	5pi gray	3.00	20
		Nos. O2-O7 (6)	4.40	48

Imperf. examples of Nos. O2–O3, O5–O7 are proofs.

1913 Overprinted O.H.H.S.

O8	A20	5m car rose	30	15
a.		Inverted overprint	100.00	50.00
b.		No period after "S"	6.50	3.50

Regular Issues Overprinted O.H.H.S. اميرى

1914–15 On Issues of 1888–1906

O9	A19	2m green	30	20
a.		Inverted ovpt.	20.00	20.00
b.		Dbl. ovpt.	250.00	250.00
c.		No period after "S"	6.00	6.00

No.	Type	Description	Unused	Used
O10	A23	4m brn red	30	20
a.		Inverted ovpt.	140.00	110.00

On Issue of 1914.

No.	Type	Description	Unused	Used
O11	A24	1m ol brn	20	12
a.		No period after "S"	2.50	2.50
O12	A26	3m orange	25	15
a.		No period after "S"	5.00	5.00
O13	A28	5m lake	30	8
a.		No period after "S"	4.00	4.00
b.		Two periods after "S"	4.00	4.00
		Nos. O9-O13 (5)	1.35	75

Regular Issues Overprinted

O.H.H.S. أميري

On Issues of 1888–1906

1915, Oct.

No.	Type	Description	Unused	Used
O14	A19	2m green	20	12
a.		Inverted overprint	10.00	10.00
b.		Double overprint	15.00	
O15	A23	4m brn red	35	15

On Issue of 1914.

No.	Type	Description	Unused	Used
O16	A28	5m lake	35	18
a.		Pair, one without ovpt.	200.00	

On Issue of 1921-22.

1922 Wmk. 120

No.	Type	Description	Unused	Used
O17	A24	1m ol brn	4.00	1.50
a.		Two periods after "S"	300.00	
O18	A25	2m red	4.00	1.50
O19	A26	3m orange	90.00	75.00
O20	A28	5m pink	4.00	1.50
a.		Double ovpt.	100.00	

Regular Issues of 1921-22 Overprinted

O.H.E.M.S. الحكومة المصرية

1922

No.	Type	Description	Unused	Used
O21	A24	1m ol brn	35	25
a.		Two periods after "S"	35.00	
O22	A25	2m red	40	30
O23	A26	3m orange	1.25	80
O24	A27	4m green	2.00	1.50
a.		Two periods after "H" none after "S"	100.00	100.00
O25	A28	5m pink	60	25
a.		Two periods after "H" none after "S"	50.00	50.00
O26	A29	10m dp bl	1.50	1.00
O27	A34	15m indigo	1.75	1.25
O28	A35	15m indigo	80.00	60.00
a.		Two periods after "H" none after "S"	300.00	300.00
O29	A31	50m maroon	6.00	3.75
		Nos. O21-O29 (9)	93.85	69.10

1923

No.	Type	Description	Unused	Used
O30	A29	10m lake	1.75	1.25
a.		Two periods after "H" none after "S"	75.00	75.00

Regular Issue of 1923 Overprinted in Black or Red

أميري

1924 *Perf. 13½x14*

No.	Type	Description	Unused	Used
O31	A36	1m orange	60	20
O32	A36	2m gray (R)	75	45
O33	A36	3m brown	2.00	70
O34	A36	4m yel grn	2.50	1.00
O35	A36	5m org brn	75	30
O36	A36	10m rose	2.25	45
O37	A36	15m ultra	2.50	75

Perf. 14

No.	Type	Description	Unused	Used
O38	A36	50m myr grn	6.00	1.75
		Nos. O31-O38 (8)	17.35	5.60

O2 O3

Wmkd. Multiple Crown and Arabic F. (195)

1926–35 Litho. *Perf. 13x13½*

Size 18½x22mm.

No.	Type	Description	Unused	Used
O39	O2	1m lt org	6	6
O40	O2	2m black	6	6
O41	O2	3m ol brn	8	8
O42	O2	4m lt grn	10	8
O43	O2	5m brown	15	6
O44	O2	10m dl red	50	8
O45	O2	10m brt vio ('34)	25	8
O46	O2	15m dp bl	60	10
O47	O2	15m brn vio ('34)	30	8
O48	O2	20m dp bl ('35)	40	10

Perf. 13½

Size 22½x27½ mm.

No.	Type	Description	Unused	Used
O49	O2	20m ol grn	1.00	20
O50	O2	50m myr grn	1.00	15
		Nos. O39-O50 (12)	4.50	1.13

1938, Dec. Size 22½x19mm.

No.	Type	Description	Unused	Used
O51	O3	1m orange	4	4
O52	O3	2m red	6	6
O53	O3	3m ol brn	8	8
O54	O3	4m yel grn	10	8
O55	O3	5m brown	10	6
O56	O3	10m brt vio	12	8
O57	O3	15m rose vio	18	10
O58	O3	20m blue	20	12

Perf. 14x13½.

Size 26½x22 mm.

No.	Type	Description	Unused	Used
O59	O3	50m myr grn	40	15
		Nos. O51-O59 (9)	1.28	77

Nos. O51 to O59 Overprinted in Various Colors

ملك مصر والسودان ١٦ اكتوبر سنة ١٩٥١

Overprint 19mm. Wide.

1952, Jan. *Perf. 13x13½*

No.	Type	Description	Unused	Used
O60	O3	1m org (Br)	4	4
O61	O3	2m red	4	4
O62	O3	3m ol brn (Bl)	5	5
O63	O3	4m yel grn (Bl)	5	5
O64	O3	5m brn (Bl)	8	8
O65	O3	10m brt vio (Bl)	10	8
O66	O3	15m rose vio (Bl)	15	12
O67	O3	20m blue	20	20

Overprint 24½mm. Wide.

Perf. 14x13½.

No.	Type	Description	Unused	Used
O68	O3	50m myr grn (RV)	50	45
		Nos. O60-O68 (9)	1.21	1.11

See note after No. 316.

United Arab Republic

Numeral O4

Arms of U.A.R. O5

Perf. 13x13½

1959 Lithographed Wmk. 318

No.	Type	Description	Unused	Used
O69	O4	10m brn vio	45	8
O70	O4	35m chlky bl	90	12

1962–63 Wmk. 328

No.	Type	Description	Unused	Used
O71	O4	1m org ('63)	3	3
O72	O4	4m yel grn ('63)	3	3
O73	O4	5m brown	4	4
O74	O4	10m dk brn	4	4
O75	O4	35m dk bl	26	26
O76	O4	50m green	40	40
O77	O4	100m vio ('63)	80	40
O78	O4	200m rose red ('63)	1.60	80
O79	O4	500m gray ('63)	4.00	2.00
		Nos. O71-O79 (9)	7.20	4.00

Photogravure

1966–68 *Perf. 11½x11* **Unwmkd.**

No.	Type	Description	Unused	Used
O80	O5	1m ultra	3	3
O81	O5	4m brown	3	3
O82	O5	5m olive	3	3
O83	O5	10m brn blk	5	5
O84	O5	20m magenta	10	10
O85	O5	35m dk pur	18	18
O86	O5	50m orange	25	25
O87	O5	55m dk pur	28	28

Wmk. 342

No.	Type	Description	Unused	Used
O88	O5	100m brt grn & brick red	50	40
O89	O5	200m bl & brick red	1.00	75
O90	O5	500m ol & brick red	2.50	2.00
		Nos. O80-O90 (11)	4.95	4.10

1969 Wmk. 342

No.	Type	Description	Unused	Used
O91	O5	10m magenta	6	6

Arab Republic of Egypt

Arms of Egypt O6

Perf. 11

1972, June 30 Photo. Wmk. 342

No.	Type	Description	Unused	Used
O92	O6	1m blk & vio bl	3	3
a.		1m blk & lt bl ('75)	3	3
O93	O6	10m blk & car	5	5
a.		10m blk & rose red ('76)	5	5
O94	O6	20m blk & ol	10	10
O95	O6	50m blk & org	25	25
O96	O6	55m blk & pur	27	27
		Nos. O92-O96 (5)	70	70

1973

No.	Type	Description	Unused	Used
O97	O6	20m lil & sep	10	10
a.		20m pur & lt brn ('76)	10	10
O98	O6	70m brn, blk & grn ('79)	35	35

1982 Photo. *Perf. 11*

No.	Type	Description	Unused	Used
O99	O6	30m pur & brn	15	15
O100	O6	60m blk & org	30	30
O101	O6	80m blk & grn	40	40

Issue dates: 30m, Feb. 12; 60m, Feb. 24; 80m, Feb. 18.

OCCUPATION STAMPS

For Use in Palestine.

فلسطين

Nos. 208, 211 and 213 Overprinted in Green or Black

PALESTINE

a

Perf. 13x13½

1948, May 15 Wmk. 195

No.	Type	Description	Unused	Used
N1	A66	3m brown	12	12
N2	A66	6m lt yel grn (Bk)	15	15
N3	A66	13m rose car	18	18

Same Overprint in Red, Green or Black on Stamps of Egypt, 1939–46.

Perf. 13x13½, 13½x13

No.	Type	Description	Unused	Used
N4	A77	1m yel brn (G)	12	12
N5	A77	2m red org (G)	12	12
N6	A77	4m dp grn	12	12
N7	A77	5m red brn (Bk)	15	15
N8	A77	10m dp vio	18	18
N9	A77	15m dk vio	18	18
N10	A77	17m ol grn	20	20
N11	A77	20m dk gray	25	25
N12	A77	22m dp bl	30	30
N13	A74	50pi grn & sep	5.00	4.00
N14	A75	£1 dp bl & dk brn	10.00	8.00

The two lines of the overprint are more widely separated on Nos. N13 and N14.

Nos. 267–269, 237 and 238 Overprinted in Red

فلسطين

PALESTINE

b

Perf. 14x13½.

No.	Type	Description	Unused	Used
N15	A73	30m ol grn	35	35
N16	A73	40m dk brn	45	45
N17	A73	50m Prus grn	60	60
N18	A73	100m brn vio	1.75	1.75
N19	A73	200m dk vio	3.50	3.50
		Nos. N1-N19 (19)	23.72	20.72

Overprint arranged to fit size of stamps.

Nos. N1-N19 Overprinted in Black with Three Bars to Obliterate Portrait

Perf. 13x13½, 13½x13, 14x13½

1953 Wmk. 195

No.	Type	Description	Unused	Used
N20	A77	1m yel brn	5	5
N21	A77	2m red org	5	5
N22	A66	3m brown	8	8
N23	A77	4m dp grn	8	8
N24	A77	5m red brn	10	10
N25	A66	6m lt yel grn	12	12
N26	A77	10m dp vio	15	15
N27	A66	13m rose car	20	20
N28	A77	15m dk vio	20	20
N29	A77	17m ol grn	25	25
N30	A77	20m dk gray	30	30
N31	A77	22m dp bl	35	35
N32	A73	30m ol grn	45	45
N33	A73	40m dk brn	60	60
N34	A73	50m Prus grn	90	90
N35	A73	100m brn vio	2.00	2.00
N36	A73	200m dk vio	4.00	4.00
N37	A74	50pi grn & sep	10.00	10.00
N38	A75	£1 dp bl & dk brn	15.00	15.00
		Nos. N20-N38 (19)	34.88	34.88

Regular Issue of 1953–55 Overprinted Type "a" in Blue or Red

1954-55 *Perf. 13x13½*

No.	Type	Description	Unused	Used
N39	A115	1m red brn	4	4
N40	A115	2m dk lil	5	5
N41	A115	3m brt bl (R)	6	6
N42	A115	4m dk grn (R)	8	8
N43	A115	5m dp car	10	10
N44	A110	10m dk brn	12	12
N45	A110	15m gray (R)	15	15

N46	A110	17m dk grnsh bl (R)	15	15
N47	A110	20m pur (R) ('54)	18	18

فلسطين

Nos. 331–333 and 335–340 Overprinted in Blue or Red

PALESTINE
c

1955-56 ***Perf. 13½.***

N48	A111	30m dl grn (R)	20	20
N49	A111	32m brt bl (R)	25	25
N50	A111	35m vio (R)	25	25
N51	A111	40m red brn	40	40
N52	A111	50m vio brn	45	45
N53	A112	100m hn brn	1.00	1.00
N54	A112	200m dk grnsh bl (R)	2.25	2.25
N55	A112	500m pur (R)	5.00	5.00
N56	A112	£1 dk grn, blk & red (R) ('56)	10.00	10.00
		Nos. N39-N56 (18)	20.73	20.73

Type of 1957 Overprinted in Red

فلسطين
PALESTINE
d

1957 ***Perf. 13½x13*** **Wmk. 195**

N57	A127	10m bl grn	1.00	1.00

Nos. 414-417 Overprinted Type "d" in Red.

1957-58 ***Perf. 13½*** **Wmk. 315**

N58	A137	10m violet	15	15

Wmk. 318

N59	A136	1m lt bl grn ('58)	6	6
N60	A138	5m brn ('58)	8	8
N61	A137	10m vio ('58)	15	15

United Arab Republic

Nos. 438–444 Overprinted Type "d" in Red or Green

Photogravure.

1958 ***Perf. 13½x14*** **Wmk. 318**

N62	A136	1m crimson	5	5
N63	A137	2m blue	5	5
N64	A143	3m dk red brn (G)	5	5
N65	A217	4m green	6	6
N66	A138	5m brown	10	10
N67	A137	10m violet	10	10
N68	A137	35m lt ultra	40	40
		Nos. N62-N68 (7)	81	81

Same Overprint in Red on Freedom Struggle Type of 1958

1958 ***Perf. 13½x13***

N69	A145	10m dk brn	1.00	1.00

Same Overprint in Green on Declaration of Human Rights Type of 1958.

1958 ***Perf. 13x13½***

N70	A151	10m rose vio	1.00	1.00
N71	A151	35m red brn	1.50	1.50

No. 460 Overprinted Type "d" in Green

1959 ***Perf. 13½*** **Wmk. 195**

N72	A112	55m on 100m hn brn	75	75

"PALESTINE" Added in English and Arabic to Stamps of Egypt

World Refugee Year Type

1960 ***Perf. 13x13½*** **Wmk. 328**

N73	A173	10m org brn	10	10
N74	A173	35m dk bl gray	30	30

Type of Regular Issue 1959–60

1960 ***Perf. 13½x14***

N75	A136	1m brn org	5	5
N76	A217	4m ol gray	5	5
N77	A138	5m dk dl pur	6	6
N78	A137	10m dk ol grn	12	12

Palestine Day Type

1961, May 15 ***Perf. 13½x13***

N79	A184	10m purple	12	12

WHO Day Type

1961 ***Perf. 13½x13*** **Wmk. 328**

N80	A182	10m blue	15	15

U.N.T.A.P. Type

1961, Oct. 24

N81	A191	10m dk bl & org	10	10
N82	A191	35m ver & blk	30	30

Education Day Type

1961, Dec. 18 Photo. ***Perf. 13½***

N83	A194	10m red brn	10	10

Victory Day Type

1961, Dec. 23 ***Perf. 11½*** **Unwmkd.**

N84	A195	10m brn org & brn	12	12

Gaza Strip Type

Perf. 13½x13

1962, March 7 **Wmk. 328**

N85	A200	10m red brn	10	10

Arab Publicity Week Type

1962, March 22 ***Perf. 13½x13***

N86	SP16	10m dk pur	10	10

Anti-Malaria Type

1962, June 20 **Photogravure**

N87	A204	10m brn & dk car rose	10	10
N88	A204	35m blk & yel	30	30

Hammarskjold Type

Perf. 11½x11

1962, Oct. 24 **Wmk. 342**

Portrait in Slate Blue

N89	A214	5m brt rose	6	6
N90	A214	10m brown	15	15
N91	A214	35m blue	35	35

Lamp Type of Regular Issue

Perf. 11x11½

1963, Feb. 20 **Unwmkd.**

N92	A217	4m dk brn, org & ultra	6	6

"Freedom from Hunger" Type

Perf. 11½x11, 11x11½

1963, Mar. 21 **Wmk. 342**

N93	A220	5m lt grn & dp org	5	5
N94	A220	10m ol & yel	8	8
N95	A220	35m dl pur, yel & blk	28	28

Red Cross Centenary Type

Designs: 10m, Centenary emblem, bottom panel added. 35m, Globe and emblem, top and bottom panels added.

Perf. 11x11½

1963, May 8 **Unwmkd.**

N96	A221	10m dk bl & crim	8	8
N97	A221	35m crim & dk bl	28	28

"Save Abu Simbel" Type, 1963

1963, Oct. 15 ***Perf. 11*** **Wmk. 342**

N98	A224	5m blk & yel	5	5
N99	A224	10m gray, blk & yel	8	8
N100	A224	35m org yel & vio	28	28

Human Rights Type, 1963

1963, Dec. 10 Photo. ***Perf. 11½x11***

N101	A228	5m dk brn & yel	5	5
N102	A228	10m dp cl, gray & blk	8	8
N103	A228	35m lt grn, pale grn & blk	28	28

Types of Regular Issue, 1964

1964 ***Perf. 11*** **Unwmkd.**

N104	A231	1m cit & lt vio	5	5
N105	A230	2m org & sl	5	5
N106	A230	3m bl & ocher	5	5
N107	A235	4m ol gray, ol, brn & rose	5	5
N108	A230	5m rose & brt bl	10	10
a.		5m rose & dk bl	1.00	1.00
N109	A231	10m ol, rose & brn	8	8
N110	A230	15m lil & yel	20	20
N111	A230	20m brn blk & ol	10	10
N112	A231	30m dp org & ind	15	15
N113	A231	35m buff, ocher & emer	18	18
N114	A231	40m ultra & emer	20	20
N115	A231	60m grnsh bl & brn org	40	40

Wmk. 342

N116	A232	100m bluish blk & yel brn	50	50
		Nos. N104-N116 (13)	2.11	2.11

Arab League Council Type, 1964

1964, Jan. 13 **Photogravure**

N117	A234	10m ol & blk	5	5

Minaret Type, 1964

1964 ***Perf. 11*** **Unwmkd.**

N118	A235	4m ol, red brn & red	5	5

Arab Postal Union Type, 1964

1964, Apr. 1 ***Perf. 11*** **Wmk. 342**

N119	A239	10m emer & ultra, *lt grn*	8	8

WHO Type, 1964

1964, Apr. 7

N120	A240	10m vio blk & red	8	8

Minaret Type, 1965

1965, Jan. 20 ***Perf. 11*** **Unwmkd.**

N121	A255	4m grn & dk brn	6	6

Arab League Type, 1965

1965, Mar. 22 ***Perf. 11*** **Wmk. 342**

N122	A258	10m grn, red & blk	8	8
N123	A258	20m grn & brn	16	16

World Health Day Type, 1965

1965, Apr. 7 ***Perf. 11*** **Wmk. 342**

N124	A259	10m brt grn & crim	8	8

Massacre Type, 1965

1965, Apr. 9 **Photogravure**

N125	A260	10m sl bl & red	12	12

ITU Type, 1965

1965, May 17 ***Perf. 11*** **Wmk. 342**

N126	A261	5m sl grn, sl bl & yel	5	5
N127	A261	10m car, rose red & gray	8	8
N128	A261	35m vio bl, ultra & yel	28	28

United Nations Type, 1966

Designs: 5m, WHO Headquarters Building, Geneva. 10m, U.N. Refugee emblem. 35m, UNICEF emblem.

1966, Oct. 24 ***Perf. 11*** **Wmk. 342**

N129	A288	5m rose & brt pur	5	5
N130	A288	10m yel brn & brt pur	6	6
N131	A288	35m brt grn & brt pur	28	28

Victory Day Type, 1966

Photogravure

1966, Dec. 23 ***Perf. 11½*** **Wmk. 342**

N132	A290	10m ol & car rose	6	6

Arab Publicity Week Type, 1967

Perf. 11x11½

1967, Mar. 22 Photo. **Wmk. 342**

N133	A294	10m vio bl & brn	6	6

Labor Day Type, 1967

Perf. 11½x11

1967, May 1 Photo. **Wmk. 342**

N134	A296	10m ol & sep	6	6

OCCUPATION AIR POST STAMPS.

Nos. C39–C50 Overprinted Type "b" in Black, Carmine or Red.

Perf. 13x13½

1948, May 15 **Wmk. 195**

NC1	AP3	2m red org (Bk)	12	12
NC2	AP3	3m dk brn (C)	12	12
NC3	AP3	5m red brn (Bk)	12	12
NC4	AP3	7m dp yel org (Bk)	15	15
NC5	AP3	8m grn (C)	15	15
NC6	AP3	10m violet	18	18
NC7	AP3	20m brt bl	25	25
NC8	AP3	30m brn vio (Bk)	35	35
NC9	AP3	40m car rose (Bk)	50	50
NC10	AP3	50m Prus grn	75	75
NC11	AP3	100m ol grn	1.25	1.25
NC12	AP3	200m dk gray	2.50	2.50
		Nos. NC1-NC12 (12)	6.44	6.44

Nos. NC1-NC12 Overprinted in Black with Three Bars to Obliterate Portrait

1953

NC13	AP3	2m red org	75	75
NC14	AP3	3m dk brn	15	15
NC15	AP3	5m red brn	3.00	3.00
NC16	AP3	7m dp yel org	30	30
NC17	AP3	8m green	60	60
NC18	AP3	10m violet	25	25
NC19	AP3	20m brt bl	40	40
NC20	AP3	30m brn vio	35	35
NC21	AP3	40m car rose	45	45
NC22	AP3	50m Prus grn	75	75
NC23	AP3	100m ol grn	3.00	3.00
NC24	AP3	200m dk gray	2.25	2.25
		Nos. NC13-NC24 (12)	12.25	12.25

Nos. NC1-NC3, NC6, NC10, NC11 with Additional Overprint in Various Colors

ملك مصر والسودان
١٦ اكتوبر سنة ١٩٥١

Overprinted in Black with Three Bars to Obliterate Portrait

NC25	AP3	2m red org (Bk+Bl)	10	10
NC26	AP3	3m dk brn (Bk+RV)	2.00	2.00
NC27	AP3	5m red brn (Bk)	12	10
NC28	AP3	10m vio (R+G)	2.50	2.50
NC29	AP3	50m Prus grn (R+RV)	1.50	1.50
NC30	AP3	100m ol grn (R+Bk)	8.50	8.50
		Nos. NC25-NC30 (6)	14.72	14.70

Nos. C65-C66 Overprinted Type "b" in Black or Red

1955 ***Perf. 13x13½*** **Wmk. 195**

NC31	AP4	5m red brn	75	75
NC32	AP4	15m ol grn (R)	1.00	1.00

United Arab Republic

"PALESTINE" Added in Arabic and English to Air Post Stamps.

Type of 1963

Perf. 11½x11

1963, Oct. 24 Photo. **Wmk. 342**

NC33	AP6	80m blk & brt bl	1.00	65
NC34	AP10	115m blk & yel	1.50	95
NC35	AP10	140m bl, ultra & org red	2.00	1.15

Cairo Tower Type, 1964

Perf. 11x11½

1964, Nov. 2 **Unwmkd.**

NC36	AP11	50m dl vio & lt bl	40	40

World Meteorological Day Type

1965, Mar. 23 ***Perf. 11*** **Wmk. 342**

NC37	AP12	80m dk bl & org	65	65

Type of Regular Issue, 1965
(Game Board)

1965, July 1 Photo. *Perf. 11*

NC38	AP13	10m brn org & brt grn	6	6

OCCUPATION SPECIAL DELIVERY STAMP.

No. E4 Overprinted Type "b" in Carmine.

1948 *Perf. 13x13½.* Wmk. 195

NE1	SD1	40m dl brn & pale gray	45	45

OCCUPATION POSTAGE DUE STAMPS.

Postage Due Stamps of Egypt, 1927-41, Overprinted Type "a" in Black or Rose.

1948 *Perf. 13x13½.* Wmk. 195

NJ1	D7	2m orange	5	5
NJ2	D7	4m grn (R)	5	5
NJ3	D7	6m gray grn	6	6
NJ4	D7	8m brn vio	8	8
NJ5	D7	10m brick red	10	10
NJ6	D7	12m rose lake	12	12

Overprinted Type "b" in Red.
Perf. 14.
Size: 22x28mm.

NJ7	D7	30m purple	30	30
		Nos. NJ1-NJ7 (7)	76	76

ELOBEY, ANNOBON AND CORISCO

(å·lō'bå, än'ō·bōn' & kō·ris'kō)

LOCATION — A group of islands near the Guinea Coast of western Africa.

GOVT. — Spanish colonial possessions administered as part of the Continental Guinea District. A second district under the same governor-general included Fernando Po.

AREA—13¾ sq. mi.

POP.—2,950 (estimated 1910).

CAPITAL—Santa Isabel.

100 Centimos = 1 Peseta

King Alfonso XIII
A1

Typographed.

Control Numbers on Back

1903 *Perf. 14* Unwmkd.

1	A1	¼c carmine	60	30
2	A1	½c dk vio	60	30
3	A1	1c black	60	30
4	A1	2c red	60	30
5	A1	3c dk grn	60	30
6	A1	4c dk bl grn	60	30
7	A1	5c violet	60	30
8	A1	10c rose lake	1.25	85
9	A1	15c org buff	3.50	85
10	A1	25c dk bl	6.00	2.50
11	A1	50c red brn	8.50	3.50
12	A1	75c blk brn	8.50	4.75
13	A1	1p org red	12.00	7.00
14	A1	2p chocolate	32.50	18.50
15	A1	3p dp ol grn	47.50	22.50
16	A1	4p claret	100.00	32.50
17	A1	5p bl grn	120.00	32.50
18	A1	10p dl bl	225.00	47.50
		Nos. 1-18 (18)	568.95	175.05

Same as A1, Dated "1905".

1905 Control Numbers on Back

19	A1	1c carmine	1.25	35
20	A1	2c dp vio	5.50	35
21	A1	3c black	1.25	35
22	A1	4c dl red	1.25	35
23	A1	5c dp grn	1.25	35
24	A1	10c bl grn	4.25	55
25	A1	15c violet	5.50	2.50
26	A1	25c rose lake	5.50	2.50
27	A1	50c org buff	9.50	3.25
28	A1	75c dk bl	9.50	3.25
29	A1	1p red brn	18.00	8.00
30	A1	2p blk brn	19.00	11.00
31	A1	3p org red	19.00	11.00
32	A1	4p dk brn	135.00	45.00
33	A1	5p brnz grn	135.00	45.00
34	A1	10p claret	375.00	125.00
		Nos. 19-34 (16)	745.75	258.80

Nos. 19–22 Surcharged in Black or Red

1906
10 CÉNTS.

1906

35	A1	10c on 1c rose (Bk)	11.00	6.75
	a.	Inverted surcharge	11.00	6.75
	b.	Value omitted	30.00	16.00
	c.	Frame omitted	16.00	8.00
	d.	Double surcharge	11.00	6.75
	e.	Surcharged "15 cents"	32.50	16.00
	f.	Surcharged "25 cents"	45.00	22.00
	g.	Surcharged "50 cents"	45.00	22.50
	h.	"1906" omitted	17.00	8.00
36	A1	15c on 2c dp vio (R)	11.00	6.75
	a.	Frame omitted	12.00	6.50
	b.	Surcharged "25 cents"	16.00	9.50
	c.	Inverted surcharge	11.00	6.75
	d.	Double surcharge	11.00	6.75
36E	A1	15c on 2c dp vio (Bk)	16.00	9.50
37	A1	25c on 3c blk (R)	11.00	6.75
	a.	Inverted surcharge	11.00	6.75
	b.	Double surcharge	11.00	6.75
	c.	Surcharged "15 cents"	16.00	9.50
	d.	Surcharged "50 cents"	22.50	11.00
37E	A1	25c on 3c blk (Bk)	16.00	9.50
	f.	Inverted surcharge	16.00	9.50
	g.	Surcharged "15 cents"	16.00	11.00
	h.	Surcharged "10 cents"	22.50	9.50
38	A1	50c on 4c red (Bk)	11.00	6.75
	a.	Inverted surcharge	11.00	6.75
	b.	Value omitted	37.50	18.50
	c.	Frame omitted	16.50	8.00
	e.	Double surcharge	11.00	6.75
	f.	"1906" omitted	16.50	8.00
	g.	Surcharged "10 cents"	32.50	16.00
	h.	Surcharged "25 cents"	32.50	16.00
		Nos. 35-38 (6)	76.00	46.00

Eight other surcharges were prepared but not issued: 10c on 50c, 75c, 1p, 2p and 3p; 15c on 50c and 5p; 50c on 5c.

King Alfonso XIII
A2

1907 Control Numbers on Back

39	A2	1c dk vio	60	50
40	A2	2c black	60	50
41	A2	3c red org	60	50
42	A2	4c dk grn	60	50
43	A2	5c bl grn	60	50
44	A2	10c violet	6.75	2.75
45	A2	15c carmine	2.50	90
46	A2	25c orange	2.50	90
47	A2	50c blue	2.50	90
48	A2	75c brown	7.25	1.50
49	A2	1p blk brn	12.00	2.75
50	A2	2p org red	16.00	4.25
51	A2	3p dk brn	16.00	4.25
52	A2	4p brnz grn	16.00	4.25
53	A2	5p claret	24.00	4.25
54	A2	10p rose	57.50	12.00
		Nos. 39-54 (16)	166.00	41.20

Stamps of 1907 Surcharged

HABILITADO
PARA
05 CTMS

1908-09 Black Surcharge.

55	A2	5c on 3c red org ('09)	3.25	1.50
56	A2	5c on 4c dk grn ('09)	3.25	1.50
57	A2	5c on 10c vio	6.75	6.00
58	A2	25c on 10c vio	30.00	16.00

1910 Red Surcharge.

59	A2	5c on 1c dk vio	3.25	1.50
60	A2	5c on 2c blk	3.25	1.50

Nos. 55–60 exist with surcharge inverted (price each $10 unused, $7.50 used); with double surcharge, one black, one red (price $15 each); with "PARA" omitted (price each $15 unused, $7.50 used).

The same 5c surcharge was also applied to Nos. 45–54, but these were not issued. Price $10 each.

In 1909, stamps of Spanish Guinea replaced those of Elobey, Annobon and Corisco.

1909
CORREOS
10 cen de peseta

Revenue stamps surcharged as above were unauthorized although some were postally used.

EPIRUS

(ĕ·pī'rŭs)

LOCATION—Southeastern Europe comprising parts of Greece and Albania.

This territory formerly belonged to Turkey but is now divided between Greece and Albania. The northern part of the Greek section, now a part of Albania, set up a provisional government during 1912–13 and issued postage stamps but it collapsed in 1916, following Greek occupation. The name "Epirus" is taken from the Greek word meaning "Mainland."

100 Lepta = 1 Drachma

Chimarra Issue.

Double-headed Eagle, Skull and Crossbones
A1

Handstamped. Without Gum.

1914 (Feb.) *Imperf.* Unwmkd.

Control Mark in Blue.

1	A1	1 l blk & bl		
2	A1	5 l bl & red		
3	A1	10 l red & blk		
4	A1	25 l bl & red		
		Nos. 1-4 (4)	*475.00*	*350.00*

All values exist without control mark. This mark is a solid blue oval, about 12x8 mm., containing the colorless Greek letters "ΣΠ," the first two letters of Spiromilios, the Chimarra commander.

All four exist with value inverted and the 1, 5 and 10 l with value double.

Some students question the official character of this issue. Counterfeits are plentiful.

Provisional Government Issues

Infantryman with Rifle
A2 A3

Serrate Roulette 13½

1914 (March) Lithographed

5	A2	1 l orange	75	75
6	A2	5 l green	50	50
7	A3	10 l carmine	50	50
8	A3	25 l dp bl	50	50
9	A2	50 l brown	2.00	2.00
10	A2	1d violet	3.00	3.00
11	A2	2d blue	20.00	17.50
12	A2	5d gray grn	16.00	12.00
		Nos. 5-12 (8)	43.25	36.75

Turkish stamps surcharged "Epirus Autonomous" and new values in Greek were on sale for a few days in Argyrokastron (Gjinokaster).

Flag of Epirus
A5

1914 (Aug.)

15	A5	1 l brn & bl	65	65
16	A5	5 l grn & bl	65	65
17	A5	10 l rose red & bl	90	90
18	A5	25 l dk bl & bl	1.25	1.25
19	A5	50 l vio & bl	1.25	1.25
20	A5	1d car & bl	6.00	6.00
21	A5	2d org & bl	1.25	1.25
22	A5	5d dk grn & bl	6.00	6.00
		Nos. 15-22 (8)	17.95	17.95

Koritsa Issue.

A7

1914

26	A7	25 l dk bl & bl	4.00	4.50
27	A7	50 l vio & bl	7.00	8.00

Chimarra Issue.

1911-23 Issues of Greece Overprinted

ΕΛΛΗΝΙΚΗ
1914
ΧΕΙΜΑΡΡΑ

1914 (Aug.)

34	A24	1 l green	5.25	4.50
35	A25	2 l carmine	5.25	4.50
36	A24	3 l vermilion	5.25	4.50
37	A26	5 l green	7.50	5.25
38	A24	10 l carmine	11.00	8.50
39	A25	20 l slate	15.00	12.50
40	A25	25 l blue	21.00	17.50
41	A26	50 l vio brn	25.00	22.50
		Nos. 34-41 (8)	95.25	79.75

The 2 l and 3 l are engraved stamps of the 1911–21 issue, the others are lithographed stamps of the 1912–23 issue.

Overprint reads: "Greek Chimarra 1914".

Stamps of this issue are with or without a black monogram (S.S., for S. Spiromilios) in manuscript. Counterfeits are plentiful.

Foreign postal stationery (stamped envelopes, postal cards and air letter sheets) lies beyond the scope of this Catalogue which is limited to adhesive postage stamps.

Stamps of the following designs were not regularly issued for postal purposes in the opinion of the editors.

Three varieties, 1914

Six varieties, 1914

Seven varieties, 1914.

Fifteen varieties, 1914.

Four varieties, 1920.

OCCUPATION STAMPS.

Issued under Greek Occupation.

Greek Occupation Stamps of 1913 Overprinted Horizontally

Β. ΗΠΕΙΡΟΣ

Serrate Roulette 13½.

1914-15 Black Overprint. **Unwmkd.**

N1	O1	1 l brown	1.20	1.20
N2	O2	2 l red	1.20	1.20
b.		2 l rose	2.40	2.40
N4	O2	3 l orange	1.20	1.20
N5	O1	5 l green	2.40	1.60
N6	O1	10 l rose red	3.25	2.25
N7	O1	20 l violet	5.25	5.25
N8	O2	25 l pale bl	5.75	5.75
N9	O1	30 l gray grn	20.00	17.50
N10	O2	40 l indigo	20.00	17.50
N11	O1	50 l dk bl	20.00	17.50
N12	O2	1d vio brn	62.50	55.00
		Nos. N1-N12 (11)	142.75	125.95

The overprint exists double on 4 denominations (1 l, 2 l red, 3 l and 1d); inverted on 7 (1 l, 2 l red, 3 l, 5 l, 10 l, 20 l and 1d). Prices twice or triple normal copies.

Red Overprint.

N1a	1 l brown	4.00
N2a	2 l red	4.00
N4a	3 l orange	4.00
N5a	5 l green	4.00

Nos. N1a–N5a were not issued. Exist canceled.

Regular Issues of Greece, 1911–23, Overprinted

Β. ΗΠΕΙΡΟΣ

On Issue of 1911-21

1916 Engraved.

N17	A24	3 l vermilion	2.00	2.00
N18	A26	30 l car rose	30.00	30.00
N19	A27	1d ultra	52.50	52.50
N20	A27	2d vermilion	60.00	55.00
N21	A27	3d car rose	67.50	67.50
N22	A27	5d ultra	175.00	175.00
a.		Double overprint	175.00	175.00
		Nos. N17-N22 (6)	387.00	382.00

On Issue of 1912-23.

1916 Lithographed

N23	A24	1 l green	2.00	2.00
N24	A25	2 l carmine	2.00	2.00
N25	A24	3 l vermilion	2.00	2.00
N26	A26	5 l green	2.00	2.00
N27	A24	10 l carmine	2.00	2.25
N28	A25	20 l slate	5.75	5.75
N29	A25	25 l blue	6.00	6.00
N30	A26	30 l rose	10.50	10.50
N31	A25	40 l indigo	10.50	10.50
N32	A26	50 l vio brn	10.50	10.50
		Nos. N23-N32 (10)	53.25	53.50

In each sheet there are two varieties in the overprint: the "I" in "Epirus" omitted and an inverted "L" in place of the first letter of the word.

Counterfeits exist of Nos. N1–N32.

Postage stamps issued in 1940–41, during Greek occupation, are listed under Greece.

EQUATORIAL GUINEA

LOCATION—Gulf of Guinea, West Africa.

GOVT.—Republic.

AREA—10,832 sq. mi.

POP.—310,000 (est. 1974).

CAPITAL—Malabo.

The Spanish provinces Fernando Po and Rio Muni united and became independent as the Republic of Equatorial Guinea, Oct. 12, 1968.

100 Centimos = 1 Peseta

Clasped Hands and Laurel

A1

Pres. Francisco Macias Nguema

A2

Photogravure

1968, Oct. 12 ***Perf. 13*** **Unwmkd.**

1	A1	1p dp bl, gold & sep	8	8
2	A1	1.50p dk grn, gold & brn	8	8
3	A1	6p cop red, gold & brn	30	15

Issued to commemorate the attainment of independence, Oct. 12, 1968.

1970, Jan. 27 ***Perf. 13x12½***

4	A2	50c dl org, brn & crim	8	8
5	A2	1p pink, grn & lil	8	8
6	A2	1.50p pale ol, brn & bl grn	8	8
7	A2	2p buff, grn & ol	10	8
8	A2	2.50p pale grn, dk grn & dk bl	15	8
9	A2	10p bis, Prus bl & vio brn	1.50	15
10	A2	25p gray, blk & brn	2.65	40
		Nos. 4-10 (7)	4.64	95

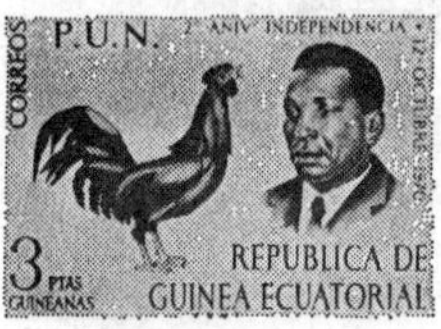

Pres. Macias Nguema and Cock

A3

1971, Apr. Photogravure ***Perf. 13***

11	A3	3p lt bl & multi	10	10
12	A3	5p buff & multi	30	10
13	A3	10p pale lil & multi	50	15
14	A3	25p pale grn & multi	90	50

2nd anniversary of independence, Oct. 12, 1970.

Torch, Bow and Arrows—A4

1972 Photogravure ***Perf. 11½***

15	A4	50p ocher & multi	2.50	75

"3rd Triumphal Year."

SPECIAL DELIVERY STAMPS

Archer with Crossbow—SD1

1971, Oct. 12 Photo. ***Perf. 12½x13***

E1	SD1	4p bl & multi	22	10
E2	SD1	8p rose & multi	40	15

3rd anniversary of independence.

ERITREA

(ĕr'ē-trā'ä)

LOCATION—In northeast Africa, bordering on the Red Sea.

GOVT.—Former Italian Colony.

AREA—15,754 sq. mi. (1936).

POP.—600,573 (1931).

CAPITAL—Asmara.

Eritrea was incorporated as a State of Italian East Africa in 1936.

100 Centesimi = 1 Lira

Stamps of Italy Overprinted

Colonia Eritrea

a

b

Wmk. 140

Wmkd. Crown (140)

1892 ***Perf. 14.***

Overprinted Type "a" in Black.

1	A6	1c brnz grn	1.40	45
a.		Invtd. overprint	175.00	120.00
b.		Double ovpt.	325.00	
2	A7	2c org brn	45	30
a.		Invtd. overprint	300.00	185.00
b.		Double ovpt.	325.00	
3	A33	5c green	15.00	1.50
a.		Invtd. overprint	*2,250.*	*1,250.*

Overprinted Type "b" in Black.

4	A17	10c claret	7.25	90
5	A17	20c orange	45.00	1.00
6	A17	25c blue	135.00	6.50
7	A25	40c brown	2.25	2.25
8	A26	45c sl grn	2.50	2.50
9	A27	60c violet	2.75	3.00
10	A28	1 l brn & yel	4.50	4.50
11	A38	5 l bl & rose	120.00	57.50

1895-99

Overprinted type "a" in Black.

12	A39	1c brn ('99)	2.75	3.50
13	A40	2c org brn ('99)	35	42
14	A41	5c green	35	30
a.		Inverted ovpt.	*400.00*	*1,000.*

Overprinted type "b" in Black.

15	A34	10c cl ('98)	55	45
16	A35	20c orange	65	60
17	A36	25c blue	1.00	90
18	A37	45c ol grn	2.75	3.50

Overprinted type "a" in Black.

1903–28

19	A42	1c brown	12	12
a.		Inverted ovpt.	18.50	18.50
20	A43	2c org brn	12	12
21	A44	5c bl grn	10.00	25
22	A45	10c claret	12.00	25
23	A45	20c orange	30	28
24	A45	25c blue	65.00	3.50
a.		Double ovpt.	90.00	100.00
25	A45	40c brown	47.50	3.50
26	A45	45c ol grn	65	65
27	A45	50c violet	42.50	3.50
28	A46	75c dk red & rose ('28)	4.25	1.25
29	A46	1 l brn & grn	60	25
30	A46	1.25 l bl & ultra ('28)	3.25	60
31	A46	2 l dk grn & org ('25)	3.75	4.50
32	A46	2.50 l dk grn & org ('28)	17.50	4.00
33	A46	5 l bl & rose	7.25	2.75
		Nos. 19-33 (15)	214.79	25.52

Surcharged in Black

Colonia Eritrea
C. 15

1905

34	A45	15c on 20c org	3.50	50

Overprinted type "a" in Black

1908-28

35	A48	5c green	12	18
36	A48	10c cl ('09)	12	18
37	A48	15c sl ('20)	90	45
38	A49	20c grn ('25)	90	90
39	A49	20c lil brn ('28)	60	60
40	A49	25c bl ('09)	30	18
41	A49	30c gray ('25)	90	90
42	A49	40c brn ('16)	6.00	3.50
43	A49	50c vio ('16)	60	25
44	A49	60c brn car ('18)	1.60	2.25
45	A49	60c brn org ('28)	20.00	27.50
46	A51	10 l gray grn & red ('16)	90.00	125.00
		Nos. 35-46 (12)	122.04	161.89

See also No. 53.

Government Building at Massaua

A1 A2

Engraved.

1910–29 ***Perf. 13½*** **Unwmkd.**

47	A1	15c slate	40.00	2.00
a.		Perf. 11 ('29)	20.00	13.50
48	A2	25c dk bl	55	60
a.		Perf. 12		

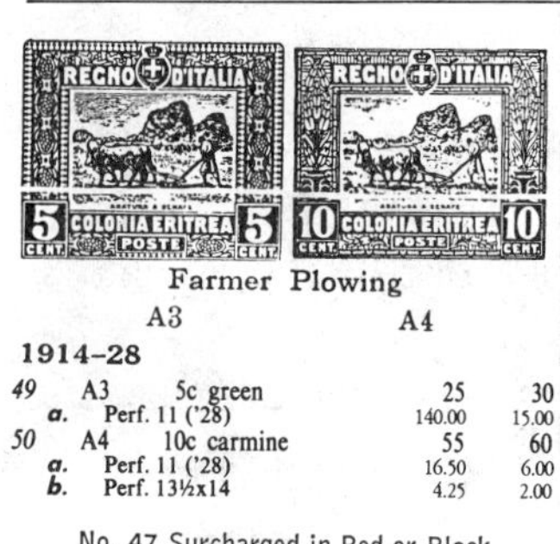

Farmer Plowing
A3 A4

1914-28

49	A3	5c green	25	30
a.		Perf. 11 ('28)	140.00	15.00
50	A4	10c carmine	55	60
a.		Perf. 11 ('28)	16.50	6.00
b.		Perf. 13½x14	4.25	2.00

No. 47 Surcharged in Red or Black

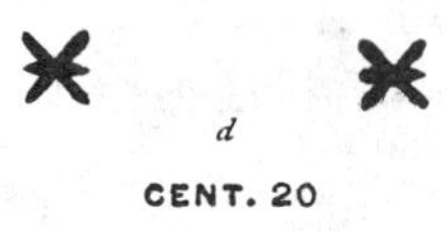

Cent. 5

d

CENT. 20

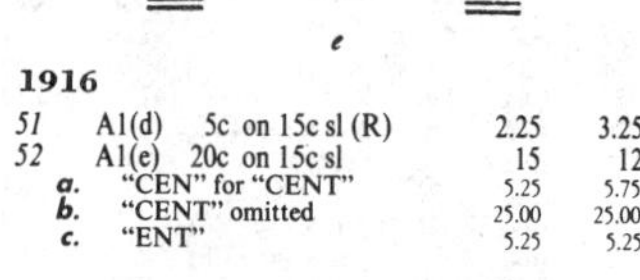

e

1916

51	A1(d)	5c on 15c sl (R)	2.25	3.25
52	A1(e)	20c on 15c sl	15	12
a.		"CEN" for "CENT"	5.25	5.75
b.		"CENT" omitted	25.00	25.00
c.		"ENT"	5.25	5.25

Italy No. 113 Overprinted in Black ERITREA
f

1921 *Perf. 14.* **Wmk. 140**

53	A50	20c brn org	60	75

Victory Issue.

Italian Victory Stamps of 1921 Overprinted type "f" 13mm. long.

1922

54	A64	5c ol grn	30	60
55	A64	10c red	30	60
56	A64	15c sl grn	40	1.00
57	A64	25c ultra	65	1.00

Somalia Nos. 10-16 Overprinted ERITREA
g

In Black and Bars over Original Values,

1922 **Wmkd. Crowns. (140)**

58	A1	2c on 1b brn	1.50	2.10
59	A1	5c on 2b bl grn	1.50	1.85
60	A2	10c on 1a cl	1.50	60
61	A2	15c on 2a brn org	1.50	90
62	A2	25c on 2½a bl	1.50	90
63	A2	50c on 5a yel	2.00	1.50
a.		"ERITREA" double		200.00
64	A2	1 l on 10a Ll	2.50	3.00
a.		"ERITREA" double	120.00	135.00
		Nos. 58-64 (7)	12.00	10.85

See Nos. 81-87.

Propagation of the Faith Issue.

Italy Nos. 143-146 Overprinted ERITREA

1923

65	A68	20c ol grn & brn org	2.00	3.75
66	A68	30c cl & brn org	2.00	3.75
67	A68	50c vio & brn org	1.75	3.00
68	A68	1 l bl & brn org	1.75	3.00

Fascisti Issue.

Italy Nos. 159-164 Overprinted in Red or Black

ERITREA
j

1923 *Perf. 14* **Unwmkd.**

69	A69	10c dk grn (R)	1.50	2.00
70	A69	30c dk vio (R)	1.50	2.00
71	A69	50c brn car	1.50	2.00

Wmkd. Crowns. (140)

72	A70	1 l blue	1.50	2.00
73	A70	2 l brown	1.50	2.00
74	A71	5 l blk & bl (R)	3.00	6.75
		Nos. 69-74 (6)	10.50	16.75

Manzoni Issue.

Italy Nos. 165-170 Overprinted ERITREA in Red.

1924 *Perf. 14.*

75	A72	10c brn red & blk	50	1.50
76	A72	15c bl grn & blk	50	1.50
77	A72	30c blk & sl	50	1.50
78	A72	50c org brn & blk	50	1.50
79	A72	1 l bl & blk	10.00	25.00
80	A72	5 l vio & blk	225.00	500.00
		Nos. 75-80 (6)	237.00	531.00

On Nos. 79 and 80 the overprint is placed vertically at the left side.

Somalia Nos. 10-16 Overprinted type "g" in Blue or Red.

1924

Bars over Original Values.

81	A1	2c on 1b brn	3.75	4.25
82	A1	5c on 2b bl grn (R)	2.40	3.25
83	A2	10c on 1a rose red	1.25	1.50
84	A2	15c on 2a brn org	1.25	1.50
a.		Pair, one without "ERITREA"	325.00	
85	A2	25c on 2½a bl (R)	1.25	1.50
a.		Double surch.	135.00	
86	A2	50c on 5a yel	3.00	1.50
87	A2	1 l on 10a lil (R)	4.00	5.25
		Nos. 81-87 (7)	16.90	18.75

Stamps of Italy, 1901-08 Overprinted type "j" in Black.

1924

88	A42	1c brown	90	1.75
a.		Inverted ovpt.	60.00	
89	A43	2c org brn	38	60
90	A48	5c green	90	90

Victor Emmanuel Issue.

Italy Nos. 175-177 Overprinted ERITREA
k

1925-26 *Perf. 11* **Unwmkd.**

91	A78	60c brn car	25	60
a.		Perf. 13½	1.25	2.50
92	A78	1 l dk bl	25	60
a.		Perf. 13½	7,500.	1,500.

Perf. 13½

93	A78	1.25 l dk bl ('26)	40	90
a.		Perf. 11	90	1.85

Saint Francis of Assisi Issue.

Italian Stamps of 1926 Overprinted

ERITREA

1926 *Perf. 14* **Wmk. 140**

94	A79	20c gray grn	45	90
95	A80	40c dk vio	45	90
96	A81	60c red vio	45	90

Overprinted in Red **Eritrea**

Perf. 11 **Unwmkd.**

97	A82	1.25 l dk bl	45	90

Perf. 14

98	A83	5 l + 2.50 l ol grn	3.75	5.75
		Nos. 94-98 (5)	5.55	9.35

Italian Stamps of 1926 Overprinted type "f" in Black.

1926 *Perf. 14.* **Wmk. 140**

99	A46	75c dk red & rose	3.75	1.25
a.		Double ovpt.	65.00	
100	A46	1.25 l bl & ultra	3.00	60
101	A46	2.50 l dk grn & org	18.50	4.25

Volta Issue.

Type of Italy, 1927, Overprinted Eritrea
o

1927

102	A84	20c purple	2.00	3.75
103	103	50c dp org	2.00	2.50
a.		Double overprint	16.50	
104	A84	1.25 l brt bl	4.00	6.25

Italian Stamps of 1925-28 Overprinted type "a" in Black.

1928-29

105	A86	7½c lt brn ('29)	3.75	6.00
106	A86	50c brt vio	3.75	5.25

Italian Stamps of 1927-28 Overprinted type "f."

1928-29

107	A86	50c brt vio	7.50	10.00

Perf. 11. **Unwmkd.**

107A	A85	1.75 l dp brn	6.25	3.00

Italy No. 192 Overprinted type "o."

1928 *Perf. 14* **Wmk. 140**

108	A85	50c brn & sl	1.25	45

Monte Cassino Issue.

Types of 1929 Issue of Italy Overprinted in Red or Blue ERITREA

1929 *Perf. 14.*

109	A96	20c dk grn (R)	1.25	1.85
110	A96	25c red org (Bl)	1.25	1.85
111	A98	50c + 10c crim (Bl)	1.25	1.85
112	A98	75c + 15c ol brn (R)	1.25	1.85
113	A96	1.25 l + 25c dl vio (R)	4.75	6.75
114	A98	5 l + 1 l saph (R)	4.75	6.75

Overprinted in Red **Eritrea**

Unwmkd.

115	A100	10 l + 2 l gray brn	4.75	6.75
		Nos. 109-115 (7)	19.25	27.65

Royal Wedding Issue.

Type of Italian Stamps of 1930 Overprinted ERITREA

1930 **Wmk. 140**

116	A101	20c yel grn	70	1.10
117	A101	50c + 10c dp org	70	1.25
118	A101	1.25 l + 25c rose red	1.00	1.75

Lancer
A5

Scene in Massaua
A6

Designs: 2c, 35c, Lancer. 5c, 10c, Postman. 15c, Lineman. 25c, Askari (infantryman). 2 l, Railroad viaduct. 5 l, Asmara Deghe Selam. 10 l, Camels.

Lithographed

1930 *Perf. 14* **Wmk. 140**

119	A5	2c brt bl & blk	40	35
120	A5	5c dk vio & blk	40	35
121	A5	10c yel brn & blk	40	30
122	A5	15c dk grn & blk	40	30
123	A5	25c gray grn & blk	40	22
124	A5	35c red brn & blk	1.00	1.15
125	A6	1 l dk bl & blk	27	22
126	A6	2 l choc & blk	2.50	3.25
127	A6	5 l ol grn & blk	3.50	5.00
128	A6	10 l dl bl & blk	4.00	6.00
		Nos. 119-128 (10)	13.27	17.14

Ferrucci Issue.

Types of Italian Stamps of 1930 Overprinted type "f" in Red or Blue.

1930

129	A102	20c vio (R)	45	60
130	A103	25c dk grn (R)	45	60
131	A103	50c blk (R)	45	60
132	A103	1.25 l dp bl (R)	45	60
133	A104	5 l dp car (Bl)	2.25	3.00
		Nos. 129-133 (5)	4.05	5.40

Virgil Issue.

Types of Italian Stamps of 1930 Overprinted in Red or Blue

ERITREA

1930 **Photogravure.**

134	A106	15c vio blk	12	30
135	A106	20c org brn	12	30
136	A106	25c dk grn	12	30
137	A106	30c lt brn	12	30
138	A106	50c dl vio	12	30
139	A106	75c rose red	12	30
140	A106	1.25 l gray bl	12	30

Engraved.

Unwmkd.

141	A106	5 l + 1.50 l dk vio	2.25	3.75
142	A106	10 l + 2.50 l ol brn	2.25	3.75
		Nos. 134-142 (9)	5.34	9.60

Saint Anthony of Padua Issue.

Types of Italian Stamps of 1931 Overprinted type "f" in Blue, Red or Black

1931 **Photogravure.** **Wmk. 140**

143	A116	20c brn (Bl)	30	60
144	A116	25c grn (R)	30	60
145	A118	30c gray brn (Bl)	30	60
146	A118	50c dl vio (Bl)	30	60
147	A120	1.25 l sl bl (R)	30	60

Engraved.

Unwmkd.

148	A121	75c blk (R)	30	60
149	A122	5 l + 2.50 l dk brn (Bk)	3.75	6.00
		Nos. 143-149 (7)	5.55	9.60

King Victor Emmanuel III
A13

1931 **Photo.** **Wmkd. Crown. (140)**

150	A13	7½c ol brn	30	40
151	A13	20c sl bl & car	20	12
152	A13	30c ol grn & brn vio	25	12
153	A13	40c bl & yel grn	25	12
154	A13	50c bis brn & ol	10	12
155	A13	75c car rose	45	12
156	A13	1.25 l vio & ind	80	12
157	A13	2.50 l dl grn	1.50	50
		Nos. 150-157 (8)	3.85	1.62

Camel
A14

Temple Ruins
A18

Designs: 2c, 10, Camel. 5c, 15c, Shark fishery. 25c, Baobab tree. 35c, Pastoral scene. 2 l, African elephant. 5 l, Eritrean man. 10 l, Eritrean woman.

1934 Photo. Wmkd. Crowns. (140)

158	A14	2c dp bl	30	30
159	A14	5c black	30	25
160	A14	10c brown	30	18
161	A14	15c org brn	50	30
162	A14	25c gray grn	30	12
163	A14	35c purple	1.00	1.15
164	A18	1 l dk bl gray	22	12
165	A14	2 l ol blk	3.00	70
166	A18	5 l car rose	2.25	70
167	A18	10 l red org	3.00	90
		Nos. 158-167 (10)	11.17	4.72

Abruzzi Issue.

Types of 1934 Issue Overprinted in Black or Red

ONORANZE AL DUCA DEGLI ABRUZZI

1934

168	A14	10c dl bl (R)	3.00	2.50
169	A14	15c blue	3.00	2.50
170	A14	35c grn (R)	1.25	2.50
171	A18	1 l cop red	1.25	2.50
172	A14	2 l rose red	4.50	4.25
173	A18	5 l pur (R)	2.50	4.25
174	A18	10 l ol grn (R)	2.50	4.25
		Nos. 168-174 (7)	18.00	22.75

Grant's Gazelle
A22

1934 Photogravure

175	A22	5c ol grn & brn	1.75	3.25
176	A22	10c yel brn & blk	1.75	3.25
177	A22	20c scar & ind	1.75	3.25
178	A22	50c dk vio & brn	1.75	3.25
179	A22	60c org brn & ind	1.75	3.25
180	A22	1.25 l dk bl & grn	1.75	3.25
		Nos. 175-180 (6)	10.50	19.50

Second Colonial Arts Exhibition, Naples. See also Nos. C1–C6.

SEMI-POSTAL STAMPS.

Many issues of Italy and Italian Colonies include one or more semipostal denominations. To avoid splitting sets, these issues are generally listed as regular postage, airmail, etc., unless all values carry a surtax.

Italy Nos. B1–B3 Overprinted type "f."

1915-16 *Perf. 14.* Wmk. 140

B1	SP1	10c +5c rose	60	1.25
a.		"EPITREA"	3.25	3.50
b.		Inverted ovpt.	150.00	150.00
B2	SP2	15c +5c sl	3.00	4.50
B3	SP2	20c +5c org	1.25	1.75
a.		"EPITREA"	6.50	6.50
b.		Inverted overprint	37.50	37.50
c.		Pair, one without ovpt.		700.00

No. B2 Surcharged **20**

1916

B4	SP2	20c on 15c+5c sl	3.00	4.50
a.		"EPITREA"	18.50	18.50
b.		Pair, one without overprint	210.00	

Counterfeits exist of the minor varieties of Nos. B1, B3–B4.

Holy Year Issue.

Italy Nos. B20–B25 Overprinted in Black or Red

ERITREA

1925 *Perf. 12*

B5	SP4	20c +10c dk grn & brn	70	1.50
B6	SP4	30c +15c dk brn & brn	70	1.50
a.		Double overprint		
B7	SP4	50c +25c vio & brn	70	1.50
B8	SP4	60c +30c dp rose & brn	70	1.50
a.		Inverted overprint		
B9	SP8	1 l +50c dp bl & vio (R)	1.35	2.50
B10	SP8	5 l +2.50 l org brn & vio (R)	1.85	3.00
		Nos. B5-B10 (6)	6.00	11.50

Colonial Institute Issue.

"Peace" Substituting Spade for Sword
SP1

1926 Typographed *Perf. 14*

B11	SP1	5c +5c brn	18	45
B12	SP1	10c +5c ol grn	18	45
B13	SP1	20c +5c bl grn	18	45
B14	SP1	40c +5c brn red	18	45
B15	SP1	60c +5c org	18	45
B16	SP1	1 l +5c bl	18	45
		Nos. B11-B16 (6)	1.08	2.70

The surtax of 5c on each stamp was for the Italian Colonial Institute.

Types of Italian Semi-Postal Stamps of 1926 Overprinted type "k."

1927 *Perf. 11½* Unwmkd.

B17	SP10	40c +20c dk brn & blk	90	1.85
B18	SP10	60c +30c brn red & ol brn	90	1.85
B19	SP10	1.25 l +60c dp bl & blk	90	1.85
B20	SP10	5 l +2.50 l dk grn & blk	1.35	3.75

The surtax on these stamps was for the charitable work of the Voluntary Militia for Italian National Defense.

Fascism and Victory
SP2

Typographed.

1928 *Perf. 14.* Wmk. 140

B21	SP2	20c +5c bl grn	60	1.25
B22	SP2	30c +5c red	60	1.25
B23	SP2	50c +10c pur	60	1.25
B24	SP2	1.25 l + 20c dk bl	60	1.25

The surtax was for the Society Africana d'Italia, whose 46th anniversary was commemorated by the issue.

Types of Italian Semi-Postal Stamps of 1928 Overprinted type "f."

1929 *Perf. 11.* Unwmkd.

B25	SP10	30c +10c red & blk	90	1.85
B26	SP10	50c +20c vio & blk	90	1.85
B27	SP10	1.25 l +50c brn & bl	1.40	2.65
B28	SP10	5 l +2 l ol grn & blk	1.40	2.65

The surtax was for the charitable work of the Voluntary Militia for Italian National Defense.

Types of Italian Semi-Postal Stamps of 1929 Overprinted type "f" in Black or Red.

1930 *Perf. 14.*

B29	SP10	30c +10c dk grn & bl grn (Bk)	1.85	2.50
B30	SP10	50c +10c dk grn & vio (R)	1.85	2.50
B31	SP10	1.25 l +30c ol brn & red brn (R)	2.25	3.75
B32	SP10	5 l +1.50 l ind & grn (R)	12.50	18.50

The surtax was for the charitable work of the Voluntary Militia for Italian National Defense.

Agriculture
SP3

1930 Photogravure Wmk. 140

B33	SP3	50c +20c ol brn	1.00	1.85
B34	SP3	1.25 l +20c dp bl	1.00	1.85
B35	SP3	1.75 l +20c grn	1.00	1.85
B36	SP3	2.55 l +50c pur	1.75	2.75
B37	SP3	5 l +1 l dp car	1.75	2.75
		Nos. B33-37 (5)	6.50	11.05

Italian Colonial Agricultural Institute, 25th anniversary. The surtax aided that institution.

AIR POST STAMPS

Desert Scene—AP1

Design: 80c, 1 l, 2 l, Plane and globe.

Wmkd. Crowns. (140)

1934 Photogravure. *Perf. 14.*

C1	AP1	25c sl bl & org red	1.75	3.25
C2	AP1	50c grn & ind	1.75	3.25
C3	AP1	75c brn & org red	1.75	3.25
C4	AP1	80c org brn & ol grn	1.75	3.25
C5	AP1	1 l scar & ol grn	1.75	3.25
C6	AP1	2 l dk bl & brn	1.75	3.25
		Nos. C1-C6 (6)	10.50	19.50

Second Colonial Arts Exhibition, Naples.

Plowing
AP3

Plane and Cacti
AP6

Designs: 25c, 1.50 l, Plowing. 50c, 2 l, Plane over mountain pass. 60c, 5 l, Plane and trees. 75c, 10 l, Plane and cacti. 1 l, 3 l, Bridge.

1936 Photogravure.

C7	AP3	25c dp grn	22	35
C8	AP3	50c dk brn	18	22
C9	AP3	60c brn org	65	1.00
C10	AP6	75c org brn	45	28
C11	AP3	1 l dp bl	12	18
C12	AP3	1.50 l purple	30	30
C13	AP3	2 l gray bl	45	30
C14	AP3	3 l cop red	8.00	3.50
C15	AP3	5 l green	4.00	90
C16	AP6	10 l rose red	12.00	1.15
		Nos. C7-C16 (10)	26.37	8.18

AIR POST SEMI-POSTAL STAMPS.

King Victor Emmanuel III
SPAP1

Photogravure.

1934 *Perf. 14* Wmk. 140

CB1	SPAP1	25c +10c gray grn	1.50	1.50
CB2	SPAP1	50c +10c brn	1.50	1.50
CB3	SPAP1	75c +15c rose red	1.50	1.50
CB4	SPAP1	80c +15c blk brn	1.50	1.50
CB5	SPAP1	1 l +20c red brn	1.50	1.50
CB6	SPAP1	2 l +20c brt bl	1.50	1.50
CB7	SPAP1	3 l +25c pur	13.00	13.00
CB8	SPAP1	5 l +25c org	13.00	13.00
CB9	SPAP1	10 l +30c dp vio	13.00	13.00
CB10	SPAP1	25 l +2 l dp grn	13.00	13.00
		Nos. CB1-CB10 (10)	61.00	61.00

Issued in commemoration of the 65th birthday of King Victor Emmanuel III and the nonstop flight from Rome to Mogadiscio. Used prices are for stamps canceled to order.

AIR POST SEMI-POSTAL OFFICIAL STAMP.

Type of Air Post Semi-Postal Stamps, 1934, Overprinted Crown and "SERVIZIO DI STATO" in Black.

1934 *Perf. 14.* Wmk. 140

CBO1	SPAP1	25 l +2 l cop red	*1,750.*	

SPECIAL DELIVERY STAMPS.

Special Delivery Stamps of Italy, Overprinted type "a."

1907 *Perf. 14* Wmk. 140

E1	SD1	25c rose red	3.00	3.50
a.		Double ovpt.		

1909

E2	SD2	30c bl & rose	27.50	27.50

1920

E3	SD1	50c dl red	90	1.25

"Italia"
SD1

1924 Engraved. Unwmkd.

No.	Type	Description	Unused	Used
E4	SD1	60c dk red & brn	2.50	3.50
a.		Perf. 13½	3.00	4.50
E5	SD1	2 l dk bl & red	3.75	4.75

Nos. E4 and E5 Surcharged in Dark Blue or Red:

70 ٧٠

v

2,50 ٢,٥٠

w

1926

No.	Type	Description	Unused	Used
E6	SD1	(v) 70c on 60c dk red & brn (Bl)	2.50	3.50
E7	SD1	(w) 2.50l on 2 l dk bl & red (R)	3.75	4.75

Type of 1924 Surcharged in Blue or Black:

LIRE 1,25 ١,٢٥

1927–35 Perf. 11

No.	Type	Description	Unused	Used
E8	SD1	1.25 l on 60c dk red & brn (Bl)	2.10	35
a.		Perf. 14 (Bl) ('35)	60.00	3.50
b.		Perf. 11 (Bk) ('35)	210.00	6.00
c.		Perf. 14 (Bk) ('35)	2,100.	140.00

AUTHORIZED DELIVERY STAMP.

Authorized Delivery Stamp of Italy, No. EY2, Overprinted Type "f" in Black.

1939–41 Perf. 14 Wmk. 140

No.	Type	Description	Unused	Used
EY1	AD2	10c dk brn ('41)	25	
a.		10c redsh brn	20.00	32.50

On No. EY1a, which was used in Eritrea, the overprint hits the figures "10." On No. EY1, which was sold in Rome, the overprint falls above the 10's.

POSTAGE DUE STAMPS.

Postage Due Stamps of Italy Overprinted type "a" at Top

1903 Perf. 14 Wmk. 140

No.	Type	Description	Unused	Used
J1	D3	5c buff & mag	4.50	6.00
a.		Double overprint	45.00	
J2	D3	10c buff & mag	1.75	2.40
J3	D3	20c buff & mag	1.75	2.40
J4	D3	30c buff & mag	2.75	3.50
J5	D3	40c buff & mag	7.25	9.50
J6	D3	50c buff & mag	8.00	11.00
J7	D3	60c buff & mag	3.00	4.75
J8	D3	1 l bl & mag	3.00	1.25
J9	D3	2 l bl & mag	4.50	7.25
J10	D3	5 l bl & mag	30.00	42.50
J11	D3	10 l bl & mag	550.00	47.50

Same with Overprint at Bottom

1920–22

No.	Type	Description	Unused	Used
J1b	D3	5c buff & mag	25	42
c.		Numeral and ovpt. inverted	27.50	
J2a	D3	10c buff & mag	50	60
J3a	D3	20c buff & mag	60.00	42.50
J4a	D3	30c buff & mag	5.00	4.75
J5a	D3	40c buff & mag	3.00	3.00
J6a	D3	50c buff & mag	3.00	3.00
J7a	D3	60c buff & mag	5.00	6.00
J8a	D3	1 l bl & mag	7.50	8.50
J9a	D3	2 l bl & mag	500.00	325.00
J10a	D3	5 l bl & mag	40.00	42.50
J11a	D3	10 l bl & mag	3.00	4.25

1903 Wmk. 140

No.	Type	Description	Unused	Used
J12	D4	50 l yellow	120.00	42.50
J13	D4	100 l blue	47.50	12.00

1927

No.	Type	Description	Unused	Used
J14	D3	60c buff & brn	10.00	15.00

Postage Due Stamps of Italy, 1934, Overprinted type "j" in Black.

1934

No.	Type	Description	Unused	Used
J15	D6	5c brown	25	38
J16	D6	10c blue	25	38
J17	D6	20c rose red	50	60
a.		Inverted ovpt.	85.00	
J18	D6	25c green	50	60
J19	D6	30c red org	50	75
J20	D6	40c blk brn	50	75
J21	D6	50c violet	50	30
J22	D6	60c black	75	1.25
J23	D7	1 l red org	75	60
J24	D7	2 l green	12.50	17.50
J25	D7	5 l violet	14.00	18.50
J26	D7	10 l blue	14.00	18.50
J27	D7	20 l car rose	17.50	23.50
		Nos. J15-J27 (13)	62.50	83.61

PARCEL POST STAMPS.

These stamps were used by affixing them to the way bill so that one half remained on it following the parcel, the other half staying on the receipt given the sender. Most used halves are right halves. Complete stamps were obtainable canceled, probably to order. Both unused and used prices are for complete stamps.

Parcel Post Stamps of Italy, 1914-17, Overprinted type "j" in Black on Each Half.

1916 Perf. 13½. Wmk. 140

No.	Type	Description	Unused	Used
Q1	PP2	5c brown	30.00	42.50
Q2	PP2	10c dp bl	1,500.	1,600.
Q3	PP2	25c red	40.00	55.00
Q4	PP2	50c orange	7.25	12.00
Q5	PP2	1 l violet	7.25	12.00
Q6	PP2	2 l green	4.75	7.25
Q7	PP2	3 l bister	52.50	72.50
Q8	PP2	4 l slate	52.50	72.50

Halves Used

Q1, Q7-Q8	2.00
Q2	30.00
Q3	1.00
Q4	25
Q5-Q6	30

Overprinted type "f" on Each Half.

1917-24

No.	Type	Description	Unused	Used
Q9	PP2	5c brown	60	90
Q10	PP2	10c dp bl	40	60
Q11	PP2	20c black	40	60
Q12	PP2	25c red	40	60
Q13	PP2	50c orange	60	90
Q14	PP2	1 l violet	60	90
Q15	PP2	2 l green	60	90
Q16	PP2	3 l bister	1.00	1.50
Q17	PP2	4 l slate	1.50	2.10
Q18	PP2	10 l rose lil ('24)	18.00	24.00
Q19	PP2	12 l red brn ('24)	45.00	65.00
Q20	PP2	15 l ol grn ('24)	45.00	65.00
Q21	PP2	20 l brn vio ('24)	45.00	65.00
		Nos. Q9-Q21 (13)	159.10	228.00

Halves Used

Q9-Q16	10
Q17	12
Q18	40
Q19	75
Q20	1.25
Q21	2.00

Parcel Post Stamps of Italy, 1927-39, Overprinted type "f" on Each Half.

1927–37

No.	Type	Description	Unused	Used
Q21A	PP3	10c dp bl ('37)	2,250.	165.00
Q22	PP3	25c red ('37)	185.00	3.75
Q23	PP3	30c ultra ('29)	18	38
Q24	PP3	50c org ('36)	185.00	3.75
Q25	PP3	60c red ('29)	18	38
Q26	PP3	1 l brn vio ('36)	90.00	1.50
a.		1 l lil	100.00	1.50
Q27	PP3	2 l grn ('36)	25.00	2.10
Q28	PP3	3 l bister	30	1.10
Q29	PP3	4 l gray	45	1.50
Q30	PP3	10 l rose lil ('36)	60.00	67.50
Q31	PP3	20 l lil brn ('36)	75.00	85.00
		Nos. Q22-Q31 (10)	621.11	166.96

Halves Used

Q21A	8.00
Q22-Q25, Q27-Q28	20
Q26, Q26a, Q27	30
Q30	75
Q31	1.50

ESTONIA

(ĕs·tō'nĭ·ȧ)

LOCATION—In Northern Europe, bordering on the Baltic Sea and the Gulf of Finland.

GOVT.—Former independent republic.

AREA—18,353 sq. mi.

POP.—1,126,413 (1940).

CAPITAL—Tallinn.

Formerly a part of Russia, Estonia declared its independence in 1918. In 1940 it was incorporated in the Union of Soviet Socialist Republics.

100 Kopecks = 1 Ruble
100 Penni = 1 Mark (1919)
100 Sents = 1 Kroon (1928)

A1

A2

Lithographed.

1918–19 Imperf. Unwmkd.

No.	Type	Description	Unused	Used
1	A1	5k pale red	50	50
2	A1	15k brt bl	50	50
a.		Perf. 11½	20.00	20.00
3	A2	35p gray brn ('19)	1.00	1.00
a.		Printed on both sides	100.00	
4	A2	70p ol grn ('19)	1.50	1.50

Nos. 1–4 exist privately perforated.

Russian Stamps of 1909-17 Handstamped in Violet or Black

Eesti Post

1919 Perf. 14, 14½x15, 13½.

No.	Type	Description	Unused	Used
8	A14	1k orange	2,500.	2,500.
9	A14	2k green	25.00	25.00
10	A14	3k red	32.50	32.50
11	A14	5k claret	32.50	32.50
12	A15	10k dk bl (Bk)	32.50	32.50
13	A15	10k dk bl	60.00	60.00
14	A14	10k on 7k lt bl (Bk)	400.00	400.00
15	A11	15k red brn & bl	32.50	32.50
16	A11	25k grn & vio	32.50	32.50
17	A11	35k red brn & grn	1,200.	1,200.
18	A8	50k vio & grn	90.00	90.00
19	A9	1r pale brn, brn & org	150.00	150.00
20	A13	10r scar, yel & gray	2,750.	2,750.

Imperf.

No.	Type	Description	Unused	Used
21	A14	1k orange	30.00	30.00
22	A14	2k green	400.00	400.00
23	A14	3k red	55.00	55.00
24	A9	1r pale brn, brn & red org	300.00	300.00
25	A12	3½r mar & grn	400.00	400.00
26	A13	5r dk bl, grn & pale bl	500.00	500.00

This overprint has been extensively counterfeited.

No. 20 is always creased.

Gulls
A3

1919, May 13 Imperf.

No.	Type	Description	Unused	Used
27	A3	5p yellow	1.50	75

A4 A5

A6

A7

Viking Ship
A8

1919–20 Perf. 11½

No.	Type	Description	Unused	Used
28	A4	10p green	35	35

Imperf.

No.	Type	Description	Unused	Used
29	A4	5p orange	10	10
30	A4	10p green	10	10
31	A5	15p rose	20	20
32	A6	35p blue	40	40
33	A7	70p dl vio ('20)	40	40
34	A8	1m bl & blk brn	1.00	50
a.		Gray granite paper ('20)	60	35
35	A8	5m yel & blk	1.75	75
a.		Gray granite paper ('20)	60	45
b.		Inverted center (white paper)	400.00	400.00
36	A8	15m yel grn & vio ('20)	3.00	85
37	A8	25m ultra & blk brn ('20)	4.50	2.50
		Nos. 28-37 (10)	11.80	6.15

See also Nos. 76–77.

Skyline of Tallinn
A9

1920–24 Imperf. Pelure Paper

No.	Type	Description	Unused	Used
39	A9	25p green	30	10
40	A9	25p yel ('24)	50	20
41	A9	35p rose	40	10
42	A9	50p grn ('21)	30	10
43	A9	1m vermilion	85	15
44	A9	2m blue	75	20
45	A9	2m ultra	40	15
46	A9	2.50m blue	90	20
		Nos. 39-46 (8)	4.40	1.20

Nos. 39 to 46 with sewing machine perforation are unofficial.

Stamps of 1919-20 Surcharged

1 Mk. 2 Mk.

a b

1920 Imperf.

No.	Type	Description	Unused	Used
55	A5	1m on 15p rose	25	20

56	A9	1m on 35p rose	25	20
57	A7	2m on 70p dl vio	50	25

Weaver A10 Blacksmith A11

1922–23 Typographed. *Imperf.*

58	A10	½m org ('23)	2.00	2.00
59	A10	1m brn ('23)	2.50	2.00
60	A10	2m yel grn	2.50	2.00
61	A10	2½m claret	2.50	2.00
62	A11	5m rose	3.50	2.50
63	A11	9m red ('23)	8.00	5.00
64	A11	10m dp bl	4.50	2.50
		Nos. 58-64 (7)	25.50	18.00

1922-25 *Perf. 14.*

65	A10	½m org ('23)	75	10
66	A10	1m brn ('23)	1.50	10
67	A10	2m yel grn	2.00	10
68	A10	2½m claret	2.50	10
69	A10	3m bl grn ('24)	2.00	10
70	A11	5m rose	3.00	10
71	A11	9m red ('23)	2.50	1.10
72	A11	10m dp bl	3.00	10
73	A11	12m red ('25)	4.50	1.75
74	A11	15m plum ('25)	4.00	50
75	A11	20m ultra ('25)	10.00	30
		Nos. 65-75 (11)	35.75	4.35

See also No. 89.

Viking Ship Type of 1920.

1922, June 8 *Perf. 14x13½*

76	A8	15m yel grn & vio	5.00	35
77	A8	25m ultra & blk brn	7.50	2.00

Map of Estonia A13

1923–24

Paper with Lilac Network.

78	A13	100m ol grn & bl	17.50	1.00

Paper with Buff Network.

79	A13	300m brn & bl ('24)	35.00	5.00

National Theater, Tallinn A14

1924, Dec. 9 *Perf. 14x13½.*

Paper with Blue Network.

81	A14	30m vio & blk	7.50	3.00

Paper with Rose Network.

82	A14	70m car rose & blk	12.50	3.50

Vanemuine Theater, Tartu A15

1927, Oct. 25

Paper with Lilac Network.

83	A15	40m dp bl & ol brn	6.00	1.25

Stamps of 1922–25 Surcharged in New Currency in Red or Black

1918 24/II 1928 S. S.

1928 *Perf. 14.*

84	A10	2s yel grn	1.00	20
85	A11	5s rose red	1.00	15
86	A11	10s dp bl	1.25	15
a.		Imperf., pair	400.00	400.00
87	A11	15s plum	4.00	50
88	A11	20s ultra	2.00	60
		Nos. 84-88 (5)	9.25	1.60

10th anniversary of independence.

3rd Philatelic Exhibition Issue

Blacksmith Type of 1922–23.

1928, July 6

89	A11	10m gray	4.50	2.25
a.		Imperf., pair		

Sold only at Tallinn Philatelic Exhibition.

Arms A16

Paper with Network as in Parenthesis.

1928-35 *Perf. 14, 14½x14.*

90	A16	1s dk gray (bl)	40	10
91	A16	2s yel grn (org)	45	10
92	A16	4s grn (brn) ('29)	80	10
93	A16	5s red (grn)	45	10
a.		5 feet on lowest lion	15.00	10.00
b.		Booklet pane of 6		
94	A16	8s vio (buff) ('29)	2.00	10
95	A16	10s lt bl (lil)	1.75	10
a.		Booklet pane of 6		
96	A16	12s crim (grn)	3.00	10
97	A16	15s yel (bl)	3.00	10
98	A16	15s car (gray) ('35)	10.00	1.25
99	A16	20s sl bl (red)	3.00	10
100	A16	25s red vio (grn) ('29)	7.50	20
101	A16	25s bl (brn) ('35)	15.00	1.25
102	A16	40s red org (bl) ('29)	7.00	40
103	A16	60s gray (brn) ('29)	7.50	45
104	A16	80s brn (bl) ('29)	10.00	1.00
		Nos.90-104 (15)	71.85	5.45

A 1940 printing of the 1s is on thick, gray-toned laid paper. Price, $3.

Types of 1924 Issues Surcharged:

KROON 1 KROON
a

2 KROONI 2
b

3 KROONI 3
c

1930, Sept. 1 *Perf. 14x13½.*

Paper with Green Network.

105	A14	1k on 70m car & blk	7.00	5.00

Paper with Rose Network.

106	A13	2k on 300m brn & bl	13.00	6.00

Paper with Blue Network.

107	A13	3k on 300m brn & bl	30.00	20.00

University Observatory A17

University of Tartu A18

Paper with Network as in Parenthesis.

1932, June 1 *Perf. 14.*

108	A17	5s red (yel)	6.00	45
109	A18	10s lt bl (lil)	1.60	10
110	A17	12s car (bl)	7.50	1.50
111	A18	20s dk bl (grn)	7.50	25

University of Tartu tercentenary.

Narva Falls A19 Ancient Bard Playing Harp A20

1933, Apr. 1 Photo. *Perf. 14x13½.*

112	A19	1k gray blk	6.00	60

See also No. 149.

Paper with Network as in Parenthesis.

1933, May 29 Typo. *Perf. 14*

113	A20	2s grn (org)	3.00	30
114	A20	5s red (grn)	4.00	30
115	A20	10s bl (lil)	5.00	20

Tenth National Singing Festival.

Woman Harvester A21 President Konstantin Päts A22

1935, Mar. 1 Engr. *Perf. 13½.*

116	A21	3k blk brn	90	90

1936-40 Typographed. *Perf. 14.*

117	A22	1s chocolate	45	12
118	A22	2s yel grn	45	10
119	A22	3s dp org ('40)	6.00	5.00
120	A22	4s rose vio	1.00	10
121	A22	5s lt bl grn	1.00	10
122	A22	6s rose lake	75	10
123	A22	6s dp grn ('40)	30.00	25.00
124	A22	10s grnsh bl	1.00	10
125	A22	15s crim rose ('37)	2.00	20
126	A22	15s dp bl ('40)	6.50	20
127	A22	18s dp car ('39)	22.50	7.00
128	A22	20s brt vio	1.75	10
129	A22	25s dk bl ('38)	7.50	15
130	A22	30s bis ('38)	8.00	25
131	A22	30s ultra ('39)	10.00	1.00
132	A22	50s org brn	7.00	50
133	A22	60s brt pink	12.00	1.50
		Nos. 117-133(17)	117.90	41.52

St. Brigitta Convent Entrance A23

Ruins of Convent, Pirita River A24

Front View of Convent A25

Seal of Convent A26

Paper with Network as in Parenthesis.

1936, June 10 *Perf. 13½.*

134	A23	5s grn (buff)	50	20
135	A24	10s bl (lil)	75	20
136	A25	15s red (org)	1.00	1.50
137	A26	25s ultra (brn)	1.50	2.00

St. Brigitta Convent, 500th anniversary.

Harbor at Tallinn A27

1938, Apr. 11 Engraved *Perf. 14*

138	A27	2k blue	75	1.50

Friedrich R. Faehlmann A28

Friedrich R. Kreutzwald A29

1938 Typographed. *Perf. 13½.*

139	A28	5s dk grn	50	50
140	A29	10s dp brn	1.00	1.00
141	A29	15s dk car	1.25	1.25
142	A28	25s ultra	2.25	2.25
a.		Sheet of four	10.00	17.50

Society of Estonian Scholars centenary.

No. 142a contains one each of Nos. 139–142, with inscription in top margin. Size: 89x138mm.

Hospital at Pärnu A30

Seashore Hotel A31

1939, June 20 Typographed

144	A30	5s dk grn	75	30
145	A31	10s dp red vio	75	35
146	A30	18s dk car	2.75	2.75
147	A31	30s dp bl	3.25	3.00
a.		Sheet of four	17.50	40.00

Centenary of health resort and baths at Pärnu.

No. 147a contains one each of Nos. 144–147, with inscription at left. Size: 137x 90mm.

Narva Falls Type of 1933.

1940, Apr. 15 Engraved

149	A19	1k sl grn	75	2.00

The sky consists of heavy horizontal lines and the background consists of horizontal and vertical lines.

Carrier Pigeon and Plane A32

1940, July 30 — Typographed

150 A32	3s red org		20	15
151 A32	10s purple		20	10
152 A32	15s rose brn		25	10
153 A32	30s dk bl		2.00	1.25

Centenary of the first postage stamp.

SEMI-POSTAL STAMPS.

Assisting Wounded Soldier
SP1

Offering Aid to Wounded Hero
SP2

Lithographed

1920, June *Imperf.* **Unwmkd.**

B1 SP1	35p +10p red & ol grn	30	35
B2 SP2	70p +15p dp bl & brn	30	35

Surcharged ⁑ 2 Mk ⁑

1920

B3 SP1	1m on 35p+10p red & ol grn	50	50
B4 SP2	2m on 70p+15p dp bl & brn	50	50

Nurse and Wounded Soldier
SP3

1921, Aug. 1 *Imperf.*

B5 SP3	2½ (3½)m org, brn & car	75	1.10
B6 SP3	5 (7)m ultra, brn & car	75	1.10

1922, Apr. 26 *Perf. 13½x14*

B7 SP3	2½ (3½)m org, brn & car	1.25	1.65
a.	Vert. pair, imperf. horiz.	12.50	17.50
B8 SP3	5 (7)m ultra, brn & car	1.25	1.65
a.	Vert. pair, imperf. horiz.	12.50	17.50

Nos. B5–B8 Overprinted — Aita hädalist.

1923 *Imperf.*

B9 SP3	2½ (3½)m	25.00	32.50
B10 SP3	5 (7)m	30.00	37.50

Perf. 13½x14.

B11 SP3	2½ (3½)m	32.50	40.00
a.	Vert. pair, imperf. horiz.	125.00	175.00
B12 SP3	5 (7)m	35.00	42.50
a.	Vert. pair, imperf. horiz.	125.00	175.00

Excellent forgeries are plentiful.

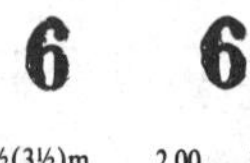

Nos. B7 and B8 Surcharged

5 5

6 6

1926, June 15

B13 SP3	5 (6)m on 2½(3½)m	2.00	1.75
a.	Vert. pair, imperf. horiz.	12.50	17.50
B14 SP3	10 (12)m on 5(7)m	2.50	2.00
a.	Vert. pair, imperf. horiz.	12.50	17.50

Nos. B5–B14 had the franking value of the lower figure. They were sold for the higher figure, the excess going to the Red Cross Society.

Kuressaare Castle
SP4

Tartu Cathedral
SP5

Parliament Building, Tallinn
SP6

Narva Fortress
SP7

View of Tallinn
SP8

Wmk. 207

Reduced illustration. Watermark covers a large part of sheet.

Laid Paper.

Wmkd. Arms of Finland in the Sheet. (207)

1927, Nov. 19 Typo. *Perf. 14½x14*

B15 SP4	5m +5m bl grn & ol, *grysh*	45	75
B16 SP5	10m +10m dp bl & brn, *cr*	45	75
B17 SP6	12m +12m rose red & ol grn, *bluish*	45	75

Perf. 14x13½

B18 SP7	20m +20m bl & choc, *gray*	70	1.25
B19 SP8	40m +40m org brn & sl, *buff*	90	1.25
	Nos. B15-B19 (5)	2.95	4.75

The money derived from the surtax was donated to the Committee for the commemoration of War for Liberation.

Red Cross Issue.

Symbolical of Succor to Injured
SP9

Symbolical of "Light of Hope"
SP10

1931, Aug. 1 *Perf. 13½* **Unwmkd.**

B20 SP9	2s +3s grn & car	6.00	6.00
B21 SP10	5s +3s red & car	6.00	6.00
B22 SP10	10s +3s lt bl & car	6.00	6.00
B23 SP9	20s +3s dk bl & car	12.00	12.00

Nurse and Child
SP11

Lorraine Cross and Flower
SP13

Taagepera Sanatorium
SP12

Paper with Network as in Parenthesis.

1933, Oct. 1 *Perf. 14, 14½.*

B24 SP11	5s +3s ver (grn)	7.50	7.50
B25 SP12	10s +3s lt bl & red (vio)	7.50	7.50
B26 SP13	12s +3s rose & red (grn)	7.50	7.50
B27 SP12	20s +3s dk bl & red (org)	12.50	12.50

The surtax was for a fund to combat tuberculosis.

Arms of Narva
SP14

Arms of Pärnu
SP15

Arms of Tartu
SP16

Arms of Tallinn
SP17

Paper with Network as in Parenthesis.

1936, Feb. 1 *Perf. 13½*

B28 SP14	10s +10s grn & ultra (gray)	4.00	5.00
B29 SP15	15s +15s car & bl (gray)	5.00	6.00
B30 SP16	25s +25s gray bl & red (brn)	6.00	7.00
B31 SP17	50s +50s blk & dl org (ol)	15.00	22.50

Arms of Paide
SP18

Arms of Rakvere
SP19

Arms of Valga
SP20

Arms of Viljandi
SP21

Paper with Network as in Parenthesis.

1937, Jan. 2

B32 SP18	10s +10s grn (gray)	4.00	5.00
B33 SP19	15s +15s red brn (gray)	4.00	5.00
B34 SP20	25s +25s dk bl (lil)	6.00	7.50
B35 SP21	50s +50s dk vio (gray)	12.50	20.00

Arms of Baltiski
SP22

Arms of Vöru
SP23

Arms of Haapsalu
SP24

Arms of Kuressaare
SP25

Designs are the armorial bearings of various cities.

1938, Jan. 21

Paper with Gray Network.

B36 SP22	10s +10s dk brn	3.50	4.50
B37 SP23	15s +15s car & grn	4.00	5.00
B38 SP24	25s +25s dk bl & car	6.00	7.00
B39 SP25	50s +50s blk & org yel	12.50	17.50
a.	Sheet of four	27.50	37.50

No. B39a measures 106x150 mm. and contains one each of Nos. B36 to B39, with marginal inscriptions. Issued in connection with the annual Charity Ball held at Tallinn, January 2, 1938.

Arms of Viljandi SP27

Arms of Pärnu SP28

Arms of Tartu SP29

Arms of Harju SP30

Designs are the armorial bearings of various districts.

1939, Jan. 10

Paper with Gray Network.

B41	SP27	10s +10s dk bl grn	4.00	5.00
B42	SP28	15s +15s car	4.00	5.00
B43	SP29	25s +25s dk bl	6.00	7.00
B44	SP30	50s +50s brn lake	12.50	25.00
a.		Sheet of four	37.50	50.00

No. B44a measures 90x138mm., and contains one each of Nos. B41 to B44, with marginal inscriptions.

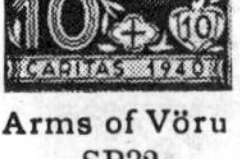

Arms of Võru SP32

Arms of Järva SP33

Arms of Lääne SP34

Arms of Saare SP35

Paper with Gray Network.

1940, Jan. 2 Typo. *Perf. 13½*

B46	SP32	10s +10s dp grn & ultra	3.00	4.50
B47	SP33	15s +15s dk car & ultra	3.00	4.50
B48	SP34	25s +25s dk bl & scar	4.00	7.50
B49	SP35	50s +50s ocher & ultra	7.50	20.00

AIR POST STAMPS.

Airplane AP1

Typographed.

1920, Mar. 13 *Imperf.* **Unwmkd.**

C1	AP1	5m yel, bl & blk	2.25	2.50

No. C1 Overprinted "1923" in Red.

1923, Oct. 1

C2	AP1	5m multi	7.00	9.00

No. C1 Surcharged in Red

1923, Oct. 1

C3	AP1	15m on 5m multi	10.00	12.00

Pairs of No. C1 Surcharged in Black or Red

45 Marka

1923

1923, Oct.

C4	AP1	10m on 5m+5m (B)	10.00	12.50
C5	AP1	20m on 5m+5m (R)	22.50	30.00
C6	AP1	45m on 5m+5m (R)	75.00	90.00

Rough Perf. 11½.

C7	AP1	10m on 5m+5m (B)	*200.00*	*250.00*
C8	AP1	20m on 5m+5m (R)	*100.00*	*150.00*

The pairs comprising Nos. C7 and C8 are imperforate between. Forged surcharges and perforations abound.

Monoplane in Flight—AP2

Designs: Various views of planes in flight.

1924, Feb. 12 *Imperf.*

C9	AP2	5m yel & blk	2.00	2.50
C10	AP2	10m bl & blk	2.00	2.50
C11	AP2	15m red & blk	2.00	2.50
C12	AP2	20m grn & blk	2.00	2.50
C13	AP2	45m vio & blk	2.00	3.00
		Nos. C9-C13 (5)	10.00	13.00

The paper is covered with a faint network in pale shades of the frame colors. There are four varieties of the frames and five of the pictures.

1925, July 15 *Perf. 13½.*

C14	AP2	5m yel & blk	1.50	2.00
C15	AP2	10m bl & blk	1.50	2.00
C16	AP2	15m red & blk	1.50	2.00
C17	AP2	20m grn & blk	1.50	2.00
C18	AP2	45m vio & blk	1.50	2.50
		Nos. C14-C18 (5)	7.50	10.50

Counterfeits of Nos. C1 to C18 are plentiful.

OCCUPATION STAMPS.

Issued under German Occupation.

For Use in Tartu (Dorpat)

Russian Stamps of 1909-12 Surcharged

20 Pfg.

1918 *Perf. 14x14½* **Unwmkd.**

N1	A15	20pf on 10k dk bl	27.50	35.00
N2	A8	40pf on 20k bl & car	30.00	35.00

Forged overprints exist.

Estonian Arms and Swastika OS1

Perf. 11½

1941, Aug. Typo. **Unwmkd.**

N3	OS1	15k brown	9.00	10.00
N4	OS1	20k green	9.00	10.00
N5	OS1	30k dk bl	12.00	10.00

Exist imperf. Price $60.

Nos. N3–N5 were issued on both ordinary paper with colorless gum and thick chalky paper with yellow gum. Same prices.

SEMI-POSTAL STAMPS

Mountain Tower, Tallinn OSP1

Designs: 20k+20k, Stone Bridge, Tartu (horiz.). 30k+30k, Narva Castle (horiz.). 50k+50k, Tallinn view (horiz.). 60k+60k, Tartu University. 100k+100k, Narva Castle, close view.

Paper with Gray Network

Perf. 11½

1941, Sept. 29 Photo. **Unwmkd.**

NB1	OSP1	5k +15k dk brn	35	*1.50*
NB2	OSP1	20k +20k red lil	35	*1.50*
NB3	OSP1	30k +30k dk bl	35	*1.50*
NB4	OSP1	50k +50k bluish grn	35	*1.50*
NB5	OSP1	60k +60k car	60	*2.00*
NB6	OSP1	100k +100k gray	1.50	*2.50*
		Nos. NB1-NB6 (6)	3.50	*10.50*

Nos. NB1–NB6 exist imperf. Price, set unused $14, used $30.

A miniature sheet containing one each of Nos. NB1–NB6, imperf., exists in various colors. It was not postally valid.

ETHIOPIA

(ē'thĭ·ō'pĭ·ȧ)

(Abyssinia)

LOCATION—In northeastern Africa.

GOVT.—Former monarchy.

AREA—398,350 sq. mi.

POP.—28,930,000 (est. 1977).

CAPITAL—Addis Ababa.

16 Guerche = 1 Menelik Dollar
or 1 Maria Theresa Dollar
100 Centimes = 1 Franc (1905)
40 Paras = 1 Piastre (1908)
16 Mehalek = 1 Thaler or Talari (1928)
100 Centimes = 1 Thaler (1936)
100 Cents = 1 Ethiopian Dollar (1946)
100 Cents = 1 Birr (1978)

Excellent forgeries of Nos. 1–86 exist.

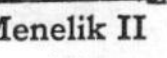

Menelik II A1

Lion of Judah A2

Typographed

1894 *Perf. 14x13½* **Unwmkd.**

1	A1	¼g green	2.00	2.00
2	A1	½g red	1.35	1.35
3	A1	1g blue	1.35	1.35
4	A1	2g dk brn	1.35	1.35
5	A2	4g lil brn	1.35	1.35
6	A2	8g violet	1.35	1.35
7	A2	16g black	1.65	1.65
		Nos. 1-7 (7)	10.40	10.40

For 4g, 8g and 16g stamps of type A1, see Nos. J3a, J4a, and J7a.

Nos. 1–7 Handstamped in Violet, Blue or Black

Ethiopie

1901

8	A1	¼g green	7.00	7.00
9	A1	½g red	7.00	7.00
10	A1	1g blue	7.00	7.00
11	A1	2g dk brn	7.00	7.00
12	A2	4g lil brn	10.00	10.00
13	A2	8g violet	12.50	12.50
14	A2	16g black	14.00	14.00
		Nos.8-14 (7)	64.50	64.50

Two types of overprint on Nos. 8–14: 9½mm. and 8½mm. wide.

Handstamped in Violet, Blue or Black

ቦስጣ።

1902

15	A1	¼g green	4.50	4.50
16	A1	½g red	4.50	4.50
17	A1	1g blue	6.75	6.75
18	A1	2g dk brn	6.75	6.75
19	A2	4g lil brn	11.00	11.00
20	A2	8g violet	15.00	15.00
21	A2	16g black	27.50	27.50
		Nos. 15-21 (7)	76.00	76.00

The handstamp reads "Bosta" (Post).

Handstamped in Violet, Blue or Black

መልክት።

1903

22	A1	¼g green	4.50	4.50
a.		On stamp No. 15		
23	A1	½g red	4.50	4.50
24	A1	1g blue	6.75	6.75
a.		On stamp No. 17		
25	A1	2g dk brn	9.00	9.00
26	A2	4g lil brn	9.00	9.00
27	A2	8g violet	20.00	20.00
28	A2	16g black	27.50	27.50
		Nos. 22-28 (7)	81.25	81.25

The handstamp reads "Malekt." (Message).

Handstamped in Violet or Blue

ምልክት

1904

36	A1	¼g green	9.00	9.00
37	A1	½g red	9.00	9.00
38	A1	1g blue	11.00	11.00
39	A1	2g dk brn	14.00	14.00
40	A2	4g lil brn	18.00	18.00
41	A2	8g violet	30.00	30.00
42	A2	16g black	45.00	45.00
		Nos. 36-42 (7)	136.00	136.00

The handstamp reads "Malekt." (Message).

Preceding Issues Surcharged with New Values in French Currency in Blue, Violet, Rose or Black:

05 *a*   1,60 *b*

1905

On Nos. 1 to 7.

43	A1 (a)	5c on ¼g grn	5.75	5.75
44	A1 (a)	10c on ½g red	5.75	5.75
45	A1 (a)	20c on 1g bl	5.75	5.75
46	A1 (a)	40c on 2g dk brn	7.50	7.50
47	A2 (a)	80c on 4g lil brn	12.00	12.00
48	A2 (b)	1.60fr on 8g vio	15.00	15.00
49	A2 (b)	3.20fr on 16g blk	22.50	22.50
		Nos. 43-49 (7)	74.25	74.25

On No. 8.

50	A1 (a)	5c on ¼g grn	67.50	67.50

On Nos. 15 to 20.

51	A1 (a)	5c on ¼g grn	12.50	12.50
51B	A1 (a)	10c on ½g red	*225.00*	*225.00*
51C	A1 (a)	20c on 1g bl	*16.50*	
51D	A1 (a)	40c on 2g dk brn	*55.00*	

No.	Type	Description	Unused	Used
51E	A2 (a)	80c on 4g lil brn	*80.00*	
51F	A2 (b)	1.60fr on 8g vio	*110.00*	

On Nos. 22, 24 & 26.

No.	Type	Description	Unused	Used
52	A1 (a)	5c on ¼g grn	30.00	30.00
52B	A1 (a)	20c on 1g bl	*40.00*	
52D	A2 (a)	80c on 4g lil brn	*110.00*	

On No. 36.

No.	Type	Description	Unused	Used
53	A1 (a)	5c on ¼g grn	27.50	27.50

The status of Nos. 51C–51F, 52B–52D is questioned.

5%m — *c*

5 centimes. — *d*

On No. 2.

No.	Type	Description	Unused	Used
54	A1 (c)	5c on half of ½g red	3.25	3.25

On Nos. 15 & 21.

No.	Type	Description	Unused	Used
54B	A1(c)	5c on ¼g grn	42.50	42.50
55	A2(d)	5c on 16g blk	85.00	85.00

On No. 28.

No.	Type	Description	Unused	Used
56	A2(d)	5c on 16g blk	85.00	85.00

The overprints and surcharges on Nos. 8 to 56 inclusive were handstamped, the work being very roughly done. Apparently any color of ink that was at hand was used. It is not at all improbable that other varieties may exist.

As is usual with handstamped overprints and surcharges there are many inverted and double.

Surcharged with New Values in Various Colors and ምኒልክ in Violet.

1906, Jan. 1

No.	Type	Description	Unused	Used
57	A1	5c on ¼g grn	5.50	5.50
58	A1	10c on ½g red	7.00	7.00
59	A1	20c on 1g bl	7.00	7.00
60	A1	40c on 2g dk brn	7.00	7.00
61	A2	80c on 4g lil brn	8.25	8.25
62	A2	1.60fr on 8g vio	11.00	11.00
63	A2	3.20fr on 16g blk	30.00	30.00
		Nos. 57-63 (7)	75.75	75.75

Two types of the 4-character overprint ("Menelik"): 15x3½mm. and 16½x4½ mm.

Surcharged with New Values and ምኒልክ፡፡ in Violet.

1906, July 1

No.	Type	Description	Unused	Used
64	A1	5c on ¼g grn	5.50	5.50
a.		Surcharged "20"	35.00	35.00
65	A1	10c on ½g red	5.50	5.50
66	A1	20c on 1g bl	8.25	8.25
67	A1	40c on 2g dk brn	8.25	8.25
68	A2	80c on 4g lil brn	11.00	11.00
69	A2	1.60fr on 8g vio	11.00	13.00
70	A2	3.20fr on 16g blk	30.00	35.00
		Nos. 64-70 (7)	79.50	86.50

The control overprint reads "Menelik."

Surcharged in Violet:

☆1/2☆ — *e*

✱ 1. ✱ — *f*

1907, July 1

No.	Type	Description	Unused	Used
71	A1(e)	¼ on ¼g grn	5.50	5.50
72	A1(e)	½ on ½g red	5.50	5.00
73	A1(f)	1 on 1g bl	6.75	6.75
74	A1(f)	2 on 2g dk brn	8.25	8.25
a.		Surcharged "40"	42.50	
75	A2(f)	4 on 4g lil brn	8.25	8.25
a.		Surcharged "80"	42.50	
76	A2(f)	8 on 8g vio	15.00	15.00
77	A2(f)	16 on 16g blk	22.50	22.50
		Nos. 71-77 (7)	71.75	71.25

Nos. 71–72 are also found with stars farther away from figures.

The control overprint reads "Dagmawi" ("Second"), meaning Emperor Menelik II.

Nos. 2, 23 Surcharged in Blue

1 PIASTRE

1908, Mar. 25

No.	Type	Description	Unused	Used
78	A1	1pi on ½g red (#2)	5.50	5.50
79	A1	1pi on ½g red (#23)	*200.00*	*200.00*

The surcharges on Nos. 57 to 79 are handstamped and are found double, inverted, etc.

Surcharged in Black

1/4 piastre

1908, Nov. 1

No.	Type	Description	Unused	Used
80	A1	¼p on ¼g grn	1.00	1.00
81	A1	½p on ½g red	1.00	1.00
82	A1	1p on 1g bl	1.75	1.75
83	A1	2p on 2g dk brn	2.50	2.50
84	A2	4p on 4g lil brn	3.50	3.50
85	A2	8p on 8g vio	8.25	8.25
86	A2	16p on 16g blk	15.00	15.00
		Nos. 80-86 (7)	33.00	33.00

Surcharges on Nos. 80–85 are found double, inverted, etc.

King Solomon's Throne
A3

Menelik in Native Costume
A4

Menelik in Royal Dress
A5

1909, Mar. 27 *Perf. 11½*

No.	Type	Description	Unused	Used
87	A3	¼g bl grn	60	50
88	A3	½g rose	60	50
89	A3	1g grn & org	2.50	1.25
90	A4	2g blue	2.50	1.50
91	A4	4g grn & car	3.75	3.00
92	A5	8g ver & dp grn	6.25	4.50
93	A5	16g ver & car	9.00	7.50
		Nos. 87-93 (7)	25.20	18.75

Nos. 1–7 Handstamped and Surcharged in ms.

AFF EXCEP FAUTE TIMB

1911, Oct. 1 *Perf. 14x13½*

No.	Type	Description	Unused	Used
94	A1	¼g on ¼g grn	75.00	35.00
95	A1	½g on ½g red	75.00	35.00
96	A1	1g on 1g bl	75.00	35.00
97	A1	2g on 2g dk brn	75.00	35.00
98	A2	4g on 4g lil brn	75.00	35.00
99	A2	8g on 8g vio	75.00	35.00
100	A2	16g on 16g blk	75.00	35.00
		Nos. 94-100 (7)	525.00	245.00

Nos. 94–100 are provisionals used at Dire-Dawa for 5 days. The overprint is abbreviated from "Affranchissement Exceptionnel Faute Timbres" (Special Franking Lacking Stamps). Nos. 94–100 exist without ms. surcharge. Forgeries exist.

Stamps of 1909 Handstamped in Violet or Black:

g

11-2-1917

h

1917, Mar. 30 *Perf. 11½*

No.	Type	Description	Unused	Used
101	A3(g)	¼g bl grn (V)	2.75	2.75
102	A3(g)	½g rose (V)	2.75	2.75
104	A4(h)	2g bl (Bk)	3.25	3.25
105	A4(h)	4g grn & car (Bk)	6.00	6.00
106	A5(h)	8g ver & dp grn (Bk)	10.00	10.00
107	A5(h)	16g ver & car (Bk)	18.00	18.00
		Nos. 101-107 (6)	42.75	42.75

Coronation of Empress Zauditu.

Nos. 101–107 exist with overprint inverted and Nos. 101–106 with it double.

Stamps of 1909 Overprinted in Blue, Black or Red:

11/2/1917 — *i*

11/2/1917 — *j*

1917, Apr. 5

No.	Type	Description	Unused	Used
108	A3(i)	¼g Bl grn (bl)	25	25
109	A3(i)	½g rose (Bl)	25	25
110	A3(i)	1g grn & org (Bl)	1.75	1.75
111	A4(i)	2g bl (R)	55.00	60.00
112	A4(j)	2g bl (Bk)	30	25
113	A4(j)	4g grn & car (Bl)	75	75
a.		Black ovpt.	10.00	10.00
114	A5(j)	8g ver & dp grn (Bl)	60	60
115	A5(j)	16g ver & car (Bl)	1.00	1.00
		Nos. 108-115 (8)	59.90	64.85

Coronation of Empress Zauditu.

Nos. 108–115 all exist with double overprint and inverted overprint. Nos. 108, 112, 113, 114 and 115 exist with double overprint, one inverted, and various combinations.

Preceding Issue with Additional Surcharge

1/4 — *k* 1/2 — *l* 1 — *m* 2 — *n*

1917, May 28

No.	Type	Description	Unused	Used
116	A5(k)	¼g on 8g ver & dp grn	2.50	2.50
117	A5(l)	½g on 8g ver & dp grn	2.50	2.50
118	A5(m)	1g on 16g ver & car	6.50	6.50
119	A5(n)	2g on 16g ver & car	6.50	6.50

Nos. 116 to 119 all exist with the numerals double and inverted and No. 116 with the Amharic surcharge double.

Sommering's Gazelle
A6

Ras Tafari
A9

Cathedral of St. George—A12

Empress Waizeri Zauditu
A18

Designs: ¼g, Giraffes. ½g, Leopard. 2g, Ras Tafari. 4g, Regent Tafari. 8g, White rhinoceros. 12g, Somali ostriches. 1t, African elephant. 2t, Water buffalo. 3t, Lions. 5t, 10t, Empress Zauditu.

1919, June 16 Typo. *Perf. 11½.*

No.	Type	Description	Unused	Used
120	A6	⅛g vio & brn	10	6
121	A6	¼g bl grn & db	10	6
122	A6	½g scar & ol grn	10	6
123	A9	1g rose lil & gray grn	8	5
124	A9	2g dp ultra & fawn	8	6
125	A9	4g turq bl & org	10	10
126	A12	6g lt bl & org	10	10
127	A12	8g ol grn & blk brn	25	12
128	A12	12g red vio & gray	40	20
129	A12	1t rose & gray blk	70	30
130	A12	2t blk & brn	1.75	1.10
131	A12	3t grn & dp org	2.00	1.40
132	A18	4t brn & lil rose	2.25	2.00
133	A18	5t car & gray	3.00	3.00
134	A18	10t gray grn & bis	6.00	4.00
		Nos. 120-134 (15)	17.01	12.61

Reprints differ slightly in color from originals. Reprints exist imperf. and some values with inverted centers. Price for set, unused or canceled, $1.50.

No. 132 Surcharged in Blue

፬ ግርሽ ።
4guerches

1919, Oct.

No.	Type	Description	Unused	Used
135	A18	4g on 4t brn & lil rose	90	90

The Amharic surcharge indicates the new value and, therefore, varies on Nos. 135 to 154. There are numerous defective letters and figures, several types of the "2" of "½," the errors "guerhce," "gnerche," etc.

Stamps of 1919 Surcharged

አንድ ፡
ግርሽ ።
1 guerche

1921–22

No.	Type	Description	Unused	Used
136	A6	½g on ⅛g vio & brn ('22)	50	50
137	A6	1g on ¼g grn & db	50	50
138	A9	2g on 1g lil brn & gray grn ('22)	75	75
139	A18	2g on 4t brn & lil rose ('22)	25.00	25.00
140	A6	2½g on ½g scar & ol grn	75	75
141	A9	4g on 2g ultra & fawn ('22)	75	75
		Nos. 136-141 (6)	28.25	28.25

Stamps and Type of 1919 Surcharged

፩ ግርሽ ፡
1 guerche

1925–28

No.	Type	Description	Unused	Used
142	A12	½g on 1t rose & gray blk ('26)	75	75
a.		Without colon ('28)	10.00	10.00
143	A18	½g on 5t car & gray ('26)	40	40
144	A12	1g on 6g bl & org	40	40
145	A12	1g on 12g lil & gray	62.50	62.50
146	A12	1g on 3t grn & org ('26)	15.00	15.00
147	A18	1g on 10t gray grn & bis ('26)	50	50
		Nos. 142-147 (6)	79.55	79.55

On No. 142 the surcharge is at the left side of the stamp, reading upward. On No. 142a it is at the right, reading downward. The two surcharges are from different, though similar, settings. On No. 146 the surcharge is at the right, reading upward. See note following No. 154.

There are also many irregularly produced settings in imitation of Nos. 136–154 which differ slightly from the originals.

Type of 1919 Surcharged

፩ ግርሽ ፡

= 1 guerche =

1926

No.	Type	Description	Unused	Used
147A	A12	1g on 12g lil & gray	50.00	50.00
b.		Vertical bars at lower right corner	57.50	

Stamps of 1919 Surcharged

አንድ ፡ ግርሽ ፡

1 guerche 

1926

No.	Type	Description	Unused	Used
148	A12	½g on 8g ol grn & blk brn	1.00	1.00
149	A12	1g on 6g bl & org	21.00	21.00
150	A12	1g on 12g lil & gray	62.50	62.50

Stamps of 1919 Surcharged

የግርሽ ፡ አላድ ፡

1/2 guerche 

1927

No.	Type	Description	Unused	Used
151	A12	½g on 8g ol grn & blk brn	75	75
152	A12	1g on 6g bl & org	30.00	30.00
153	A12	1g on 12g lil & gray	90	90
154	A12	1g on 3t grn & org	62.50	62.50

Many varieties of surcharge, such as double, inverted, lines transposed or omitted, and inverted "2" in "½," exist on Nos. 136-154.

Ras Tafari
A22

Empress Zauditu
A23

1928, Sept. 5 Typo. *Perf. 13½x14*

No.	Type	Description	Unused	Used
155	A22	⅛m org & lt bl	50	40
156	A23	¼m ind & red org	30	30
157	A22	½m gray grn & blk	50	40
158	A23	1m dk car & blk	30	25
159	A22	2m dk bl & blk	30	25
160	A23	4m yel & ol	30	25
161	A22	8m vio & ol	80	60
162	A23	1t org brn & vio	1.00	80
163	A22	2t grn & bis	1.40	1.40
164	A23	3t choc & grn	2.00	1.50
		Nos. 155-164 (10)	7.40	6.15

፲፱፻፳

Preceding Issue Overprinted in Black, Violet or Red

ፖ፡ ቴ፡ ቴ፡፡
የተመረቀበት፡
ቀን፡ መታሰቢያ፡

1928, Sept. 1

No.	Type	Description	Unused	Used
165	A22	⅛m org & lt bl (Bk)	1.00	1.00
166	A23	¼m ind & red org (V)	1.00	1.00
167	A22	½m gray grn & blk (V)	1.00	1.00
168	A23	1m dk car & blk (V)	1.00	1.00
169	A22	2m dk bl & blk (R)	1.00	1.00
170	A23	4m yel & ol (Bk)	1.00	1.00
171	A22	8m vio & ol (R)	1.00	1.00
172	A23	1t org brn & vio (Bk)	1.00	1.00
173	A22	2t grn & bis (R)	1.50	1.50
174	A23	3t choc & grn (R)	2.00	2.00
		Nos. 165-174 (10)	11.50	11.50

Opening of General Post Office, Addis Ababa.

Stamps of 1928 Issue Handstamped in Violet, Red or Black

ንጉሥ፡ ተፈሪ፡
NEGOUS TEFERI

1928, Oct. 7

No.	Type	Description	Unused	Used
175	A22	⅛m org & lt bl (V)	1.00	1.00
176	A23	½m gray grn & blk (R)	1.00	1.00
177	A22	2m dk bl & blk (R)	1.00	1.00
178	A22	8m vio & ol (Bk)	1.00	1.00
179	A22	2t grn & bis (V)	1.00	1.00
		Nos. 175-179 (5)	5.00	5.00

Crowning of Regent Tafari Makonen as Negus on Oct. 7, 1928.

Nos. 175–177 exist with overprint vertical.

Stamps of 1928 Overprinted in Red or Green

ቀዳማዊ
ኃይለ ሥላሴ
መጋቢት ጽ፭ ቀን
፲፱፻፳፪

HAYLE SELASSIE 1er
3 Avril 1930

1930, Apr. 3

No.	Type	Description	Unused	Used
180	A22	⅛m org & lt bl (R)	20	15
181	A23	¼m ind & red org (G)	25	20
182	A22	½m gray grn & blk (R)	20	15
183	A23	1m dk car & blk (G)	25	20
184	A22	2m dk bl & blk (R)	25	20
185	A23	4m yel & ol (R)	40	30
186	A22	8m vio & ol (R)	75	75
187	A23	1t org brn & vio (R)	1.75	1.75
188	A22	2t grn & bis (R)	2.25	2.25
189	A23	3t choc & grn (R)	3.00	3.00
		Nos. 180-189 (10)	9.30	8.95

Issued in commemoration of the proclamation of the Negus Tafari as King of Kings of Abyssinia under the name "Haile Selassie I."

A similar overprint, set in four vertical lines, was printed on all denominations of the 1928 issue. It was not considered satisfactory and was rejected. The trial impressions were not placed on sale to the public, but some copies reached private hands and have been passed through the post.

Stamps of 1928 Overprinted in Red or Olive Brown

ቀዳማዊ ፡
ኃይለ ፡ ሥላሴ ፡
መጋቢት፡ጽ፭፡ቀን፡
፲፱፻፳፪

HAILE SELASSIE 1er
3 Avril 1930

1930, Apr. 3

No.	Type	Description	Unused	Used
190	A22	⅛m org & lt bl	25	20
191	A23	¼m ind & red org (OB)	25	25
192	A22	½m gray grn & blk	25	20
193	A23	1m dk car & blk (OB)	25	25
194	A22	2m dk bl & blk	25	25
195	A23	4m yel & ol	50	50
196	A22	8m vio & ol	75	75
197	A23	1t org brn & vio	1.75	1.75
198	A22	2t grn & bis	2.25	2.25
199	A23	3t choc & grn	3.00	3.00
		Nos. 190-199 (10)	9.50	9.40

Issued in commemoration of the proclamation of the Negus Tafari as Emperor Haile Selassie I.

All stamps of this series exist with "H" of "HAILE" omitted.

Stamps of 1928 Handstamped in Violet or Red

ሥላሴ፡
፳፫
ጥቅምት፡
፲፱፻፳፫

1930, Nov. 2

No.	Type	Description	Unused	Used
200	A22	⅛m org & lt bl (V)	30	25
201	A23	¼m ind & red org (V)	30	25
202	A22	½M gray grn & blk (R)	30	25
203	A23	1m dk car & blk (V)	30	25
204	A22	2m dk bl & blk (R)	30	25
205	A23	4m yel & ol (V)	30	25
206	A22	8m vio & ol (V or R)	75	75
207	A23	1t org brn & vio (V)	1.00	1.00
208	A22	2t grn & bis (V or R)	1.50	1.50
209	A23	3t choc & grn (V or R)	2.25	2.25
		Nos. 200-209 (10)	7.30	7.00

Issued in commemoration of the coronation of the Emperor Haile Selassie I, November 2nd, 1930.

Haile Selassie Coronation Monument, Symbols of Empire
A24

1930, Nov. Engraved *Perf. 12½*

No.	Type	Description	Unused	Used
210	A24	1g orange	20	20
211	A24	2g ultra	20	20
212	A24	4g violet	20	20
213	A24	8g dl grn	35	30
214	A24	1t brown	50	50
215	A24	3t green	75	75
216	A24	5t red brn	75	75
		Nos. 210-216 (7)	2.95	2.90

Coronation of Emperor Haile Selassie I.

Reprints of Nos. 210 to 216 exist. Paper is thinner and gum whiter than the originals. Price 7c each.

Stamps of 1928 Surcharged in Green, Red or Blue

የመሐለቅ ጃተኛ

1/8 Mehalek

የመሐለቅ ግማሽ — Type I

የመሐለቅ ሩብ — Type II

1931, Mar. 20 *Perf. 13½x14.*

No.	Type	Description	Unused	Used
217	A23	⅛m on 1m dk car & blk (G)	30	30
218	A22	⅛m on 2m dk bl & blk (R)	30	30

219 A23 ⅛m on 4m yel & ol (G) 30 30
220 A23 ¼m on 1m dk car & blk (Bl) 30 30
221 A22 ¼m on 2m dk bl & blk (R) 75 75
222 A23 ¼m on 4m yel & ol (G) 75 75
225 A23 ½m on 1m dk car & blk (Bl) 75 75
226 A22 ½m on 2m dk bl & blk (R) 75 75
227 A23 ½m on 4m yel & ol (G) (II) 75 75
a. ½m on 4m yel & ol (I) 7.50 7.50
228 A23 ½m on 3t choc & grn (R) 6.00 6.00
230 A22 1m on 2m dk bl & blk (R) 1.00 1.00
Nos. 217-230 (11) 11.95 11.95

The ½m on 1/8m orange and light blue and ½m on ¼m indigo and red orange were clandestinely printed and never sold at the post office.

No. 230 with double surcharge in red and blue is a color trial.

Ras Makonnen
A25

Empress Menen
A27

View of Hawash River and Railroad Bridge—A26

Designs: 2g, 8g, Haile Selassie I (profile). 4g, 1t, Statue of Menelik II. 3t, Empress Menen (full face). 5t, Haile Selassie I (full face).

Perf. 12½, 12x12½, 12½x12.

1931, June 27 Engraved

232 A25 ⅛g red 15 15
233 A26 ¼g ol grn 15 15
234 A25 ½g dk vio 20 15
235 A27 1g red org 20 20
236 A27 2g ultra 25 25
237 A25 4g violet 35 35
238 A27 8g bl grn 1.10 1.10
239 A25 1t chocolate 2.00 2.00
240 A27 3t yel grn 3.25 3.25
241 A27 5t red brn 5.00 5.00
Nos. 232-241 (10) 12.65 12.60

Reprints of Nos. 232 to 241 are on thinner and whiter paper than the originals. Price 5c each.

Stamps of 1931 Surcharged in Blue or Carmine similar to cut

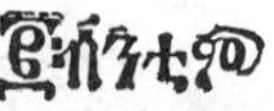

1936 *Perf. 12x12½, 12½x12.*

242 A25 1c on ⅛g red 1.10 75
243 A26 2c on ¼g ol grn (C) 1.10 75
244 A25 3c on ½g dk vio 1.10 85
245 A27 5c on 1g red org 2.00 1.25
246 A27 10c on 2g ultra (C) 2.50 1.50
Nos. 242-246 (5) 7.80 5.10

Haile Selassie I
A32 A33

Lithographed

1942, Mar. 23 *Perf. 14x13½*

247 A32 4c lt bl grn, ind & blk 50 40
248 A32 10c rose, ind & blk 1.50 85
249 A32 20c dp ultra, ind & blk 3.00 1.25

1942-43 Unwmkd.

250 A33 4c lt bl grn & ind 30 20
251 A33 8c yel org & ind 40 20
252 A33 10c rose & ind 55 30
253 A33 12c dl vio & ind 65 35
254 A33 20c dp ultra & ind 1.00 50
255 A33 25c dl grn & ind ('43) 1.50 75
256 A33 50c dl brn & ind ('43) 2.25 1.25
257 A33 60c lil & ind ('43) 3.00 1.75
Nos. 250-257 (8) 9.65 5.30

ኦቤሊስክ ፡
OBELISK
3 Nov. 1943

Nos. 250-254 Surcharged in Black or Brown

፴
3

1943, Nov. 3

258 A33 5c on 4c lt bl grn & ind 27.50 27.50
259 A33 10c on 8c yel org & ind 27.50 27.50
260 A33 15c on 10c rose & ind 27.50 27.50
261 A33 20c on 12c dl vio & ind (Br) 27.50 27.50
262 A33 30c on 20c dp ultra & ind (Br) 27.50 27.50
Nos. 258-262 (5) 137.50 137.50

Restoration of the Obelisk in Myazzia Place, Addis Ababa, and the 14th anniversary of the coronation of Emperor Haile Selassie I.

On No. 262, "3" is surcharged on "2" of "20" to make "30."

Palace of Menelik II
A34

Menelik II
A35

Statue
A36

Designs: 50c, Mausoleum. 65c, Menelik II (with scepter).

1944, Dec. 31 Litho. *Perf. 10½*

263 A34 5c green 1.25 75
264 A35 10c red lil 1.75 1.00
265 A36 20c dp bl 3.00 2.00
266 A34 50c dl pur 3.50 2.00
267 A35 65c bis brn 6.00 3.00
Nos. 263-267 (5) 15.50 8.75

Issued to commemorate the centenary of the birth of Emperor Menelik II, August 18, 1844.

Unissued Semi-Postal Stamps Overprinted in Carmine:

ድ ል

Nurse and Baby
A39

Various Designs Inscribed "Croix Rouge".

1945, Aug. 7 Photo. *Perf. 11½*

268 A39 5c brt grn 60 60
269 A39 10c brt red 60 60
270 A39 25c brt bl 60 60
271 A39 50c dk yel brn 3.00 2.50
272 A39 1t brt vio 5.00 4.00
Nos. 268-272 (5) 9.80 8.30

Nos. 268 to 272 without overprint were ordered printed in Switzerland before Ethiopia fell to the invading Italians, so were not delivered to Addis Ababa. After that country's liberation, the set was overprinted "V" and issued for ordinary postage. These stamps exist without overprint, but were not so issued. Price $1.25.

See Nos. B36-B40.

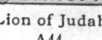

Lion of Judah
A44

Menelik II
A45

Mail Transport, Old and New
A46

Designs: 50c, Old Post Office, Addis Ababa. 70c, Menelik II and Haile Selassie I.

1947, Apr. 18 Engraved *Perf. 13*

273 A44 10c yel org 1.50 60
274 A45 20c dp bl 2.00 75
275 A46 30c org brn 3.00 1.25
276 A46 50c dk sl grn 7.00 2.50
277 A46 70c red vio 12.50 5.00
Nos. 273-277 (5) 26.00 10.10

Issued to commemorate the 50th anniversary of Ethiopia's postal system.

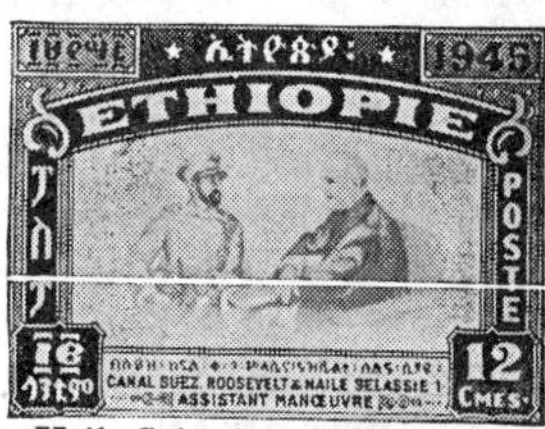
Haile Selassie and Franklin D. Roosevelt—A49

Design: 65c, Roosevelt and U. S. Flags.

Engraved and Photogravure.

1947, May 23 *Perf. 12½* Unwmkd.

278 A49 12c car lake & bl grn 50 25
279 A49 25c dk bl & rose 1.00 50
280 A49 65c blk, red & dp bl 2.00 1.25
Nos. 278-280, C21-C22 (5) 18.00 14.00

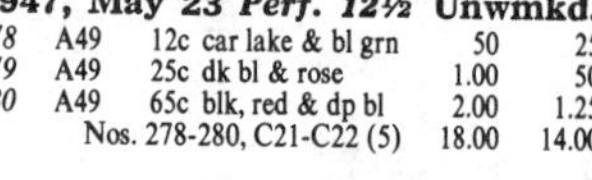

Negus Sahle Selassie—A50

Negus Sahle Selassie
A52

Design: 30c, View of Ankober.

1947, May 1 Engraved *Perf. 13*

281 A50 20c dp bl 1.50 75
282 A50 30c dk pur 2.50 1.00
283 A52 $1 dp grn 6.00 3.00

150th anniversary of Selassie dynasty.

No. 255 Surcharged in Orange

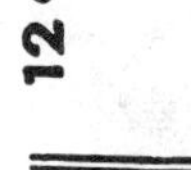

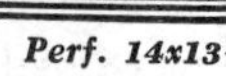

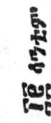

1947, July 14 *Perf. 14x13½*

284 A33 12c on 25c dl grn & ind 30.00 30.00

Amba Alaguie—A53

Wmk. 282

Designs: 2c, Trinity Church. 4c, Debra Sina. 5c, Mecan, near Achanguie. 8c, Lake Tana. 12c, 15c, Parliament Building, Addis Ababa. 20c, Aiba, near Mai Cheo. 30c, Bahr Bridge over Blue Nile. 60c, 70c, Canoe on Lake Tana. $1, Omo Falls. $3, Mt. Alamata. $5, Ras Dashan Mountains.

Wmkd.
Ethiopian Star and Amharic Characters, Multiple. (282)

1947-53 Engraved *Perf. 13x13½*

285	A53	1c rose vio	10	5
286	A53	2c bl vio	15	8
287	A53	4c green	25	12
288	A53	5c dk grn	25	12
289	A53	8c dp org	40	20
290	A53	12c red	50	20
290A	A53	15c dk ol brn ('53)	45	20
291	A53	20c blue	75	30
292	A53	30c org brn	1.25	40
292A	A53	60c red ('51)	1.50	70
293	A53	70c rose lil	2.50	65
294	A53	$1 dk car rose	5.00	75
295	A53	$3 brt bl	12.00	2.50
296	A53	$5 olive	17.50	4.50
		Nos. 285-296 (14)	42.60	10.77

Issue dates: 15c, May 25, 1953; 60c, Feb. 10, 1951; others, Aug. 23, 1947.

Empress Waizero Menen and Emperor Haile Selassie I
A54

1949, May 5 *Perf. 13* Wmk. 282

297	A54	20c blue	1.00	50
298	A54	30c yel org	1.00	65
299	A54	50c purple	2.50	1.25
300	A54	80c green	3.00	1.50
301	A54	$1 red	5.50	2.50
		Nos. 297-301 (5)	13.00	6.40

Central ornaments differ on each denomination.

Issued to commemorate the eighth anniversary of Ethiopia's liberation from Italian occupation.

Dejach Balcha Hospital—A55

Abuna Petros
A56

Designs: 20c, Haile Selassie raising flag. 30c, Lion of Judah statue. 50c, Empress Waizero Menen, Haile Selassie and building.

Perf. 13x13½, 13½x13.

1950, Nov. 2 Engr. Wmk. 282

302	A55	5c purple	60	30
303	A56	10c dp plum	1.50	60
304	A56	20c dp car	2.00	75
305	A56	30c green	3.50	1.50
306	A55	50c dp bl	6.00	3.00
		Nos. 302-306 (5)	13.60	6.15

Issued to commemorate the 20th anniversary of the coronation of Emperor Haile Selassie and Empress Menen.

Abbaye Bridge
A57

1951, Jan. 1 *Perf. 14* Unwmkd.

308	A57	5c dk grn & dk brn	3.00	30
309	A57	10c dp org & blk	4.00	35
310	A57	15c dp bl & org brn	6.00	50
311	A57	30c ol & lil rose	10.00	65
312	A57	60c brn & dp bl	15.00	1.50
313	A57	80c pur & grn	20.00	2.25
		Nos. 308-313 (6)	58.00	5.55

Issued to commemorate the opening of the Abbaye Bridge over the Blue Nile.

Tomb of Ras Makonnen
A58

1951, Mar. 2

Center in Black.

314	A58	5c dk grn	1.50	25
315	A58	10c dp ultra	1.50	35
316	A58	15c blue	2.00	35
317	A58	30c claret	5.00	1.35
318	A58	80c rose car	7.00	2.00
319	A58	$1 org brn	8.00	2.00
		Nos. 314-319 (6)	25.00	6.30

55th anniversary of the Battle of Adwa.

Emperor Haile Selassie I
A59

1952, July 23 *Perf. 13½*

320	A59	5c dk grn	35	20
321	A59	10c red org	60	25
322	A59	15c black	85	35
323	A59	25c ultra	1.25	35
324	A59	30c violet	1.50	60
325	A59	50c rose red	2.25	85
326	A59	65c chocolate	3.75	1.50
		Nos. 320-326 (7)	10.55	4.10

60th birthday of Haile Selassie I.

Open Road to Sea
A60

Designs: 25c, 50c, Road and broken chain. 65c, Map. 80c, Allegory: Reunion. $1, Haile Selassie raising flag. $2, Ethiopian flag and seascape. $3, Haile Selassie addressing League of Nations.

Engraved.

1952, Sept. 11 *Perf. 13* Wmk. 282

327	A60	15c brn car	1.00	35
328	A60	25c red brn	1.25	55
329	A60	30c yel brn	2.00	85
330	A60	50c purple	2.75	1.10
331	A60	65c gray	4.00	1.40
332	A60	80c bl grn	5.00	1.75
333	A60	$1 rose car	10.00	2.50
334	A60	$2 dp bl	17.50	4.00
335	A60	$3 magenta	32.50	7.50
		Nos. 327-335 (9)	76.00	20.00

Issued to celebrate Ethiopia's federation with Eritrea, effected Sept. 11, 1952.

Haile Selassie and New Ethiopian Port
A61

Design: 15c, 30c, Haile Selassie on deck of ship.

1953, Oct. 4

337	A61	10c red & dk brn	1.50	75
338	A61	15c bl & dk grn	1.75	75
339	A61	25c org & dk brn	2.75	1.25
340	A61	30c red brn & dk grn	5.00	1.50
341	A61	50c pur & dk brn	9.00	3.25
		Nos. 337-341 (5)	20.00	7.50

Issued to commemorate the first anniversary of the federation of Ethiopia and Eritrea.

Princess Tsahai at a Sickbed
A62

Perf. 13x13½

1955, July 8 Engr. Wmk. 282

Cross Typographed in Red

342	A62	15c choc & ultra	1.25	50
343	A62	20c grn & org	1.75	60
344	A62	30c ultra & grn	3.00	75

Issued to commemorate the 20th anniversary of the founding of the Ethiopian Red Cross.

Promulgating the Constitution
A63

Bishops' Consecration by Archbishop
A64

Designs: 25c, Kagnew Battalion. 35c, Reunion with the Motherland. 50c, "Progress." 65c, Empress Waizero Menen and Emperor Haile Selassie I.

Engraved.

1955, Nov. 3 *Perf. 12½* Unwmkd.

345	A63	5c grn & choc	50	25
346	A64	20c car & grn	1.10	35
347	A64	25c mag & gray	1.50	50
348	A63	35c brn & red org	2.00	65
349	A64	50c dk brn & ultra	3.00	1.00
350	A64	65c vio & car	4.25	1.50
		Nos. 345-350 (6)	12.35	4.25

Issued to commemorate the silver jubilee of the coronation of Emperor Haile Selassie I and Empress Waizero Menen.

Emperor Haile Selassie and Fair Emblem
A65

1955, Nov. 5 Wmk. 282

351	A65	5c grn & ol grn	60	15
352	A65	10c car & dp ultra	90	25
353	A65	15c vio blk & grn	1.25	35
354	A65	50c mag & red brn	1.75	90

Silver Jubilee Fair, Addis Ababa.

Nos. 291 and 292A Overprinted

የዓለም ስደተኞች ዓመት፣
World Refugee Year
1959-1960

1960, Apr. 7 *Perf. 13x13½*

355	A53	20c blue	50	35
356	A53	60c red	1.00	65

Issued to publicize World Refugee Year, July 1, 1959–June 30, 1960.

Map of Africa, "Liberty" and Haile Selassie
A66

Emperor Haile Selassie
A67

Perf. 13½

1960, June 14 Engr. Unwmkd.

357	A66	20c org & grn	75	75
358	A66	80c org & vio	1.75	75
359	A66	$1 org & mar	2.00	1.00

Issued to commemorate the 2nd Conference of Independent African States at Tunis. Issued in sheets of 10.

1960, Nov. 2 *Perf. 14* Wmk. 282

360	A67	10c brn & bl	50	25
361	A67	25c vio & emer	1.00	35
362	A67	50c dk bl & org yel	1.75	1.25
363	A67	65c sl grn & sal pink	2.50	1.25
364	A67	$1 ind & rose vio	3.50	1.75
		Nos. 360-364 (5)	9.25	4.85

Issued to commemorate the 30th anniversary of the coronation of Emperor Haile Selassie I.

Africa Hall, U.N. Economic Commission for Africa

A68

1961, Apr. 15 ***Perf. 14*** **Wmk. 282**

365	A68	80c ultra	1.25	65

Issued for Africa Freedom Day, Apr. 15. Issued in sheets of 10.

Map of Ethiopia, Olive Branch and Emperor Haile Selassie I

A69

1961, May 5 ***Perf. 13x13½***

366	A69	20c green	30	20
367	A69	30c vio bl	45	30
368	A69	$1 brown	1.75	80

Issued to commemorate the 20th anniversary of Ethiopia's liberation from Italian occupation.

African Wild Ass

A70

Designs: 15c, Eland. 25c, Elephant. 35c, Giraffe. 50c, Beisa. $1, Lion.

1961, June 16 ***Perf. 14*** **Wmk. 282**

369	A70	5c blk & emer	18	5
370	A70	15c red brn & grn	30	5
371	A70	25c sep & emer	40	15
372	A70	35c lt red brn & grn	50	20
373	A70	50c brn red & emer	65	45
374	A70	$1 red brn & grn	2.25	1.25
		Nos. 369-374 (6)	4.28	2.15

Issued in sheets of 10.

Emperor Haile Selassie I and Empress Waizero Menen

A71

1961, July 27 ***Perf. 11*** **Unwmkd.**

375	A71	10c green	60	30
376	A71	50c vio bl	1.10	65
377	A71	$1 car rose	2.00	1.25

Issued to commemorate the golden wedding anniversary of the Emperor and Empress.

Warlike Horsemanship (Guks)

A72

Designs: 15c, Hockey. 20c, Bicycling. 30c, Soccer. 50c, Marathon runner, Olympic winner, 1960.

Photogravure and Engraved

1962, Jan. 14 ***Perf. 12x11½***

378	A72	10c yel grn & car	18	5
379	A72	15c pink & dk brn	25	8
380	A72	20c red & blk	35	12
381	A72	30c ultra & dl pur	55	20
382	A72	50c yel & grn	1.10	30
		Nos. 378-382 (5)	2.43	75

Issued to commemorate the Third Africa Football (soccer) Cup, Addis Ababa, Jan. 14–22.

Malaria Eradication Emblem, World Map and Mosquito

A73

Engraved

1962, Apr. 7 ***Perf. 13½*** **Wmk. 282**

383	A73	15c black	25	12
384	A73	30c purple	50	35
385	A73	60c red brn	1.25	75

Issued for the World Health Organization drive to eradicate malaria.

Abyssinian Ground Hornbill

A74

Birds: 15c, Abyssinian roller. 30c, Bateleur (vert.). 50c, Double-toothed barbet (vert.). $1, Didric cuckoo.

Photogravure

1962, May 5 ***Perf. 11½*** **Unwmkd.**

Granite Paper

386	A74	5c multi	30	10
387	A74	15c emer, brn & ultra	60	20
388	A74	30c lt brn, blk & red	1.10	30
389	A74	50c multi	2.25	85
390	A74	$1 multi	4.00	1.50
		Nos. 386-390 (5)	8.25	2.95

See also Nos. C77–C81, C97–C101, C107–C111.

Assab Hospital

A75

Designs: 15c, School at Assab. 20c, Church at Massawa. 50c, Mosque at Massava. 60c, Assab port.

Engraved

1962, Sept. 11 ***Perf. 13½*** **Wmk. 282**

391	A75	3c purple	20	4
392	A75	15c dk bl	25	12
393	A75	20c green	30	14
394	A75	50c brown	75	35
395	A75	60c car rose	1.10	50
		Nos. 391-395 (5)	2.60	1.15

Issued to commemorate the tenth anniversary of the Federation of Ethiopia and Eritrea.

King Bazen, Madonna and Stars over Bethlehem—A76

Designs: 15c, Ezana, obelisks and temple. 20c, Kaleb and sailing fleet. 50c, Lalibela, rock-church and frescoes (vert.). 60c, Yekuno Amlak and priests preaching in village. 75c, Zara Yacob and procession around tree. $1, Lebna Dengel and tournament.

Photogravure

1962, Nov. 2 ***Perf. 14½*** **Unwmkd.**

396	A76	10c multi	20	10
397	A76	15c multi	30	10
398	A76	20c multi	35	15
399	A76	50c multi	70	25
400	A76	60c multi	75	40
401	A76	75c multi	1.25	60
402	A76	$1 multi	1.75	1.10
		Nos. 396-402 (7)	5.30	2.70

Issued on the 32nd anniversary of the coronation of Emperor Haile Selassie I and to commemorate ancient kings and saints.

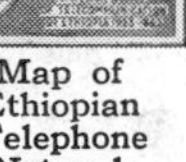

Map of Ethiopian Telephone Network

A77

Wheat Emblem

A78

Designs: 50c, Radio mast and waves. 60c, Telegraph pole and rising sun.

Perf. 13½x14

1963, Jan. 1 **Engraved** **Wmk. 282**

403	A77	10c dk red	50	15
404	A77	50c ultra	1.25	55
405	A77	60c brown	1.50	60

Issued to commemorate the 10th anniversary of the Imperial Board of Telecommunications.

1963, Mar. 21 ***Perf. 13½*** **Unwmkd.**

406	A78	5c dp rose	12	6
407	A78	10c rose car	18	10
408	A78	15c vio bl	30	15
409	A78	30c emerald	45	30

Issued for the "Freedom from Hunger" campaign of the U.N. Food and Agriculture Organization.

Abuna Salama

A79

Queen of Sheba

A80

Spiritual Leaders: 15c, Abuna Aregawi. 30c, Abuna Tekle Haimanot. 40c. Yared. 60c, Zara Yacob.

1964, Jan. 3 ***Perf. 13½*** **Unwmkd.**

410	A79	10c blue	25	10
411	A79	15c dk grn	35	15
412	A79	30c brn red	60	35
413	A79	40c dk bl	1.00	60
414	A79	60c brown	1.50	1.10
		Nos. 410-414 (5)	3.70	2.30

1964, March 2 **Photo.** ***Perf. 11½***

Ethiopian Queens: 15c, Helen. 50c, Seble Wongel. 60c, Mentiwab. 80c, Taitu, consort of Menelik II.

Granite Paper

415	A80	10c multi	50	15
416	A80	15c multi	60	20
417	A80	50c multi	1.25	55
418	A80	60c multi	2.00	85
419	A80	80c multi	2.50	1.25
		Nos. 415-419 (5)	6.85	3.00

Priest Teaching Alphabet to Children

A81

Eleanor Roosevelt

A82

Designs: 10c, Classroom. 15c, Woman learning to read (vert.). 40c, Students in chemistry laboratory (vert.). 60c, Graduation procession (vert.).

1964, June 1 ***Perf. 11½*** **Unwmkd.**

Granite Paper

420	A81	5c brown	15	7
421	A81	10c emerald	15	10
422	A81	15c rose vio	20	14
423	A81	40c vio bl	60	25
424	A81	60c dk pur	1.00	50
		Nos. 420-424 (5)	2.10	1.06

Issued to publicize education.

1964, Oct. 11 **Photogravure**

Granite Paper

Portrait in Slate Blue

425	A82	10c yel bis	15	8
426	A82	60c org brn	80	50
427	A82	80c grn & gold	1.00	70

Issued to honor Eleanor Roosevelt (1884–1962).

King Serse Dengel and View of Gondar, 1563

A83

Ethiopian Leaders: 10c, King Fasiladas and Gondar in 1632. 20c, King Yassu the Great and Gondar in 1682. 25c, Emperor Theodore II and map of Ethiopia. 60c, Emperor John IV and Battle of Gura, 1876. 80c, Emperor Menelik II and Battle of Adwa, 1896.

1964, Dec. 12 **Photo.** ***Perf. 14½x14***

428	A83	5c multi	10	4
429	A83	10c multi	15	6
430	A83	20c multi	30	15
431	A83	25c multi	50	20
432	A83	60c multi	1.00	55
433	A83	80c multi	1.25	75
		Nos. 428-433(6)	3.30	1.75

Ethiopian Rose

A84

Flowers: 10c, Kosso tree. 25c, St.-John's-wort. 35c, Parrot's-beak. 60c, Maskal daisy.

1965, Mar. 30 ***Perf. 12x13½***

434	A84	5c multi	10	5
435	A84	10c multi	15	5
436	A84	25c multi	50	15
437	A84	35c multi	90	30
438	A84	60c grn, yel & org	1.25	50
		Nos. 434-438 (5)	2.90	1.05

ITU Emblem, Old and New Communication Symbols
A85

Perf. 13½x14½

1965, May 17 Litho. Unwmkd.

439	A85	5c bl, ind & yel	15	6
440	A85	10c bl, ind & org	25	10
441	A85	60c bl, ind & lil rose	90	50

Issued to commemorate the centenary of the International Telecommunication Union.

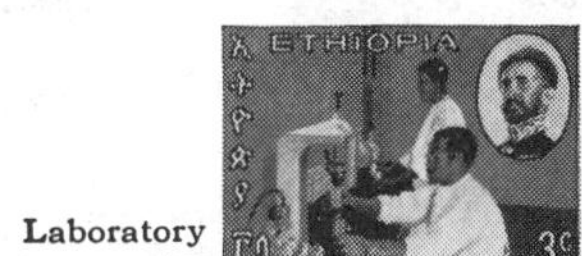

Laboratory
A86

Designs: 5c, Textile spinning mill. 10c, Sugar factory. 20c, Mountain road. 25c, Autobus. 30c, Diesel locomotive and bridge. 35c, Railroad station, Addis Ababa.

1965, July 19 Photo. *Perf. 11½*

Granite Paper

Portrait in Black

442	A86	3c sepia	8	3
443	A86	5c dl pur & buff	10	5
444	A86	10c blk & gray	12	5
445	A86	20c grn & pale yel	25	10
446	A86	25c dk brn & yel	35	15
447	A86	30c mar & gray	55	25
448	A86	35c dk bl & gray	65	35
		Nos. 442-448 (7)	2.10	98

ICY Emblem
A87

1965, Oct. 24 *Perf. 11½* Unwmkd.

Granite Paper

449	A87	10c bl & red brn	20	10
450	A87	50c dp bl & red brn	75	40
451	A87	80c vio bl & red brn	1.00	60

International Cooperation Year, 1965.

National Bank Emblem
A88

Designs: 10c, Commercial Bank emblem. 60c, National and Commercial Bank buildings.

1965, Nov. 2 Photo. *Perf. 13*

452	A88	10c dp car, blk & ind	35	10
453	A88	30c ultra, blk & ind	65	30
454	A88	60c blk, yel & ind	95	50

Issued to publicize the National and Commercial Banks of Ethiopia.

"Light and Peace" Press Building
A89

1966, Apr. 5 Engraved *Perf. 13*

455	A89	5c pink & blk	8	4
456	A89	15c lt yel grn & blk	35	12
457	A89	30c org yel & blk	60	30

Issued to commemorate the opening of the "Light and Peace" Printing Press building.

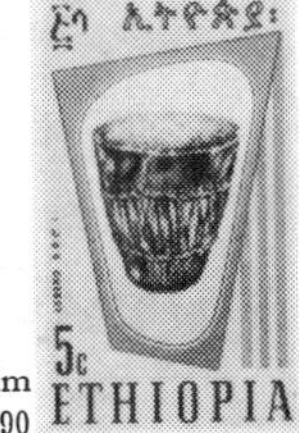

Kebero Drum
A90

Musical Instruments: 10c, Begena harp. 35c, Mesenko guitar. 50c, Krar lyre. 60c, Washent flutes.

1966, Sept. 9 Photo. *Perf. 13½*

458	A90	5c brt grn & blk	10	5
459	A90	10c dl bl & blk	15	8
460	A90	35c org & blk	55	25
461	A90	50c yel & blk	80	35
462	A90	60c rose car & blk	1.00	60
		Nos. 458-462 (5)	2.60	1.33

Emperor Haile Selassie—A91

1966, Nov. 1 *Perf. 12* Unwmkd.

463	A91	10c blk, gold & grn	15	5
464	A91	15c blk, gold & dp car	30	10
465	A91	40c blk & gold	90	60

Issued to commemorate 50 years of leadership of Emperor Haile Selassie.

UNESCO Emblem and Map of Africa
A92

Lithographed

1966, Nov. 30 *Perf. 13½* Wmk. 282

466	A92	15c bl car & blk	35	10
467	A92	60c ol, brn & dk bl	90	45

Issued to commemorate the 20th anniversary of UNESCO (United Nations Educational, Scientific and Cultural Organization).

WHO Headquarters, Geneva
A93

1966, Nov. 30

468	A93	5c ol, ultra & brn	20	5
469	A93	40c brn, pur & emer	65	35

Issued to commemorate the opening of World Health Organization Headquarters, Geneva.

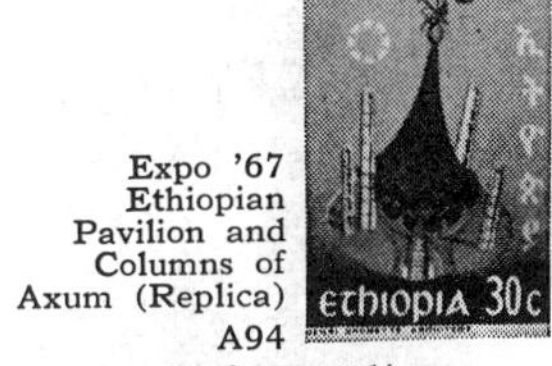

Expo '67 Ethiopian Pavilion and Columns of Axum (Replica)
A94

Perf. 12x13½

1967, May 2 Photo. Unwmkd.

470	A94	30c brt bl & multi	60	25
471	A94	45c multi	75	35
472	A94	80c gray & multi	1.50	60

Issued to commemorate EXPO '67, International Exhibition, Montreal, Apr. 28–Oct. 27, 1967.

Diesel Train and Map—A95

1967, June 7 Photo. *Perf. 12*

473	A95	15c multi	35	15
474	A95	30c multi	75	30
475	A95	50c multi	1.25	35

Issued to commemorate the 50th anniversary of the Djibouti-Addis Ababa railroad.

Papilionidae Aethiops
A96

Various Butterflies.

Perf. 13½x13

1967, June 30 Photo. Unwmkd.

476	A96	5c buff & multi	10	5
477	A96	10c lil & multi	25	6
478	A96	20c multi	50	15
479	A96	35c bl & multi	1.00	35
480	A96	40c multi	1.25	40
		Nos. 476-480 (5)	3.10	1.01

Emperor Haile Selassie and Lion of Judah
A97

1967, July 21 *Perf. 11½*

Granite Paper

481	A97	10c dk brn, emer & gold	25	12
482	A97	15c dk brn, yel & gold	40	15
483	A97	$1 dk brn, red & gold	1.75	75

Souvenir Sheet

484	A97	$1 dk brn, pur & gold	4.00	3.75

Issued to commemorate the 75th birthday of Emperor Haile Selassie. No. 484 contains one stamp; brown marginal inscription. Size 120x75mm.

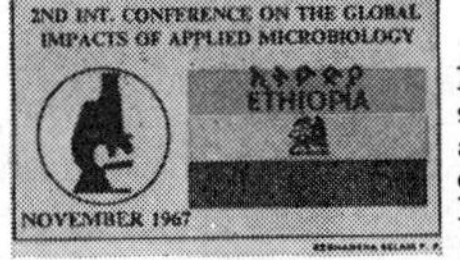

Microscope and Ethiopian Flag
A98

1967, Nov. 6 Litho. *Perf. 13*

Flag in Grn., Yel., Red & Blk.

485	A98	5c blue	15	5
486	A98	30c ocher	50	25
487	A98	$1 violet	1.75	80

Issued to commemorate the 2nd International Conference on the Global Impact of Applied Microbiology, Addis Ababa, Nov. 6–12.

Wall Painting from Debre Berhan Selassie Church, Gondar, 17th Century—A99

Designs (ITY Emblem and): 25c, Votive throne from Atsbe Dera, 4th Century B.C. (vert.). 35c, Prehistoric cave painting, Harar Province. 50c, Prehistoric stone tools, Melke Kontoure (vert.).

1967, Nov. 20 Photo. *Perf. 14½*

488	A99	15c multi	50	20
489	A99	25c yel grn, buff & blk	70	30
490	A99	35c grn, brn & blk	80	50
491	A99	50c yel & blk	1.00	75

International Tourist Year, 1967.

Processional Bronze Cross, Biet-Maryam Church
A100

Emperor Theodore
A101

Crosses of Lalibela: 10c, Processional copper cross. 15c, Copper cross, Biet-Maryam church. 20c, Lalibela-style cross. 50c, Chiseled copper cross, Madhani Alem church.

1967, Dec. 7 Photo. *Perf. 14½*

Crosses in Silver

492	A100	5c yel & blk	8	4
493	A100	10c red org & blk	15	6
494	A100	15c vio & blk	25	10
495	A100	20c brt rose & blk	30	15
496	A100	50c org yel & blk	1.10	50
		Nos. 492-496 (5)	1.88	85

Perf. 14x13½

1968, Apr. 18 Litho. Unwmkd.

Designs: 20c, Emperor Theodore and lions (horiz.). 50c, Imperial crown.

497	A101	10c lt vio, ocher & brn	15	6
498	A101	20c lil, brn & dk vio	35	15
499	A101	50c dk grn, org & rose cl	1.00	40

Issued to commemorate the centenary of the death of the Emperor Theodore (1818?–1868).

Human Rights Flame
A102

1968, May 31 ***Perf. 14½*** **Unwmkd.**

500	A102	15c pink, red & blk	30	30
501	A102	$1 lt bl, brt bl & blk	1.50	1.50

International Human Rights Year, 1968.

Shah Riza Pahlavi, Emperor and Flags—A103

1968, June 3 **Litho.** ***Perf. 13½***

502	A103	5c multi	12	12
503	A103	15c multi	25	25
504	A103	30c multi	85	85

Issued to commemorate the visit of Shah Mohammed Riza Pahlavi of Iran.

Emperor Haile Selassie Appealing to League of Nations, 1935

A104

Designs: 35c, African Unity Building and map of Africa. $1, World map, symbolizing international relations.

1968, July 22 **Photo.** ***Perf. 14x13½***

505	A104	15c bl, red, blk & gold	25	25
506	A104	35c blk, emer, red & gold	55	55
507	A104	$1 dk bl, lil, blk & gold	1.75	1.75

Ethiopia's struggle for peace.

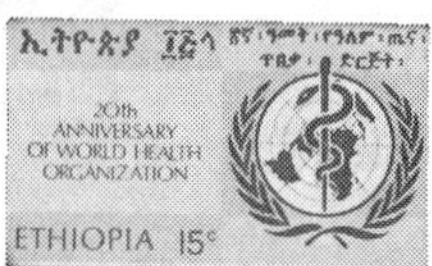

WHO Emblem

A105

Perf. 14x13½

1968, Aug. 30 **Litho.** **Unwmkd.**

508	A105	15c brt grn & blk	25	25
509	A105	60c red lil & blk	90	90

Issued to commemorate the 20th anniversary of the World Health Organization.

Running

A106

Designs: 15c, Soccer. 20c, Boxing. 40c, Basketball. 50c, Bicycling.

1968, Oct. 12 ***Perf. 11½***

510	A106	10c lt grn & multi	15	15
511	A106	15c brt vio & multi	25	25
512	A106	20c bl & multi	30	30
513	A106	40c multi	60	60
514	A106	50c beige & multi	90	90
		Nos. 510-514 (5)	2.20	2.20

Issued to commemorate the 19th Olympic Games, Mexico City, Oct. 12–27.

Arrussi Woman

A107

Regional Costumes: 15c, Man from Gemu Gefa. 20c, Gojam man. 30c, Kefa man. 35c, Harer woman. 50c, Ilubabor grass coat. 60c, Woman from Eritrea.

Perf. 13½x13

1968, Dec. 10 **Photo.** **Unwmkd.**

515	A107	5c sil & multi	7	7
516	A107	15c sil & multi	15	15
517	A107	20c sil & multi	20	20
518	A107	30c sil & multi	30	30
519	A107	35c sil & multi	35	35
520	A107	50c sil & multi	60	60
521	A107	60c sil & multi	85	85
		Nos. 515-521 (7)	2.52	2.52

See Nos. 575–581.

Message Stick and Amharic Postal Emblem—A108

1969, Mar. 10 **Litho.** ***Perf. 14***

522	A108	10c emer, blk & brn	20	20
523	A108	15c yel, blk & brn	30	30
524	A108	35c multi	75	75

Issued to commemorate the 75th anniversary of Ethiopian postal service.

ILO Emblem

A109

1969, Apr. 11 **Litho.** ***Perf. 14½***

525	A109	15c org & blk	30	30
526	A109	60c emer & blk	1.25	1.25

Issued to commemorate the 50th anniversary of the International Labor Organization.

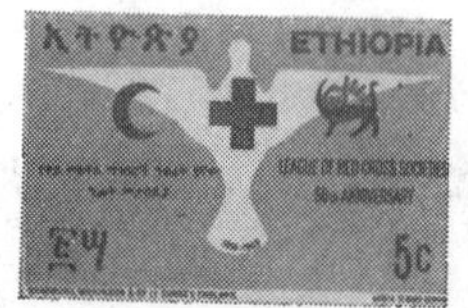

Dove, Red Cross, Crescent, Lion and Sun Emblems—A110

1969, May 8 ***Perf. 13*** **Wmk. 282**

527	A110	5c lt ultra, blk & red	8	8
528	A110	15c lt ultra, grn & red	30	30
529	A110	30c lt ultra, vio bl & red	60	60

Issued to commemorate the 50th anniversary of the League of Red Cross Societies.

Endybis Silver Coin, 3rd Century

A111

Ancient Ethiopian Coins: 10c, Gold coin of Ezana, 4th century. 15c, Gold coin of Kaleb, 6th century. 30c, Bronze coin of Armah, 7th century. 40c, Bronze coin of Wazena, 7th century. 50c, Silver coin of Gersem, 8th century.

1969, June 19 **Photo.** ***Perf. 14½***

530	A111	5c ultra, blk & sil	10	10
531	A111	10c brt red, blk & gold	18	18
532	A111	15c brn, blk & gold	30	30
533	A111	30c dp car, blk & brnz	60	60
534	A111	40c dk grn, blk & brnz	70	70
535	A111	50c dp vio, blk & sil	90	90
		Nos. 530-535 (6)	2.78	2.78

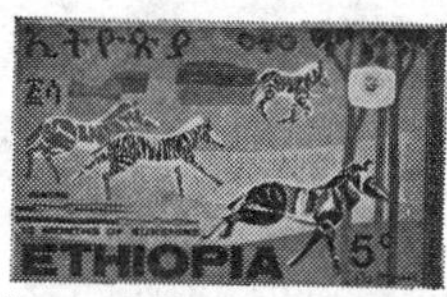

Zebras and Tourist Year Emblem

A112

Designs: 10c, Camping. 15c, Fishing. 20c, Water skiing. 25c, Mountaineering (vert.).

Perf. 13x13½, 13½x13

1969, Aug. 29 **Litho.** **Unwmkd.**

536	A112	5c multi	10	10
537	A112	10c multi	15	15
538	A112	15c multi	25	25
539	A112	20c multi	40	40
540	A112	25c multi	50	50
		Nos. 536-540 (5)	1.40	1.40

International Year of African Tourism.

Stylized Bird and U.N. Emblem

A113

Designs: 30c, Stylized flowers, U.N. and peace emblems (vert.). 60c, Stylized bird, U.N. emblem and plane.

1969, Oct. 24 ***Perf. 11½*** **Unwmkd.**

541	A113	10c lt bl & multi	15	15
542	A113	30c lt bl & multi	45	45
543	A113	60c lt bl & multi	1.00	1.00

25th anniversary of the United Nations.

See "Special Notices" at the front of this volume for data on the listing methods of this Catalogue, abbreviations, condition, prices and examination.

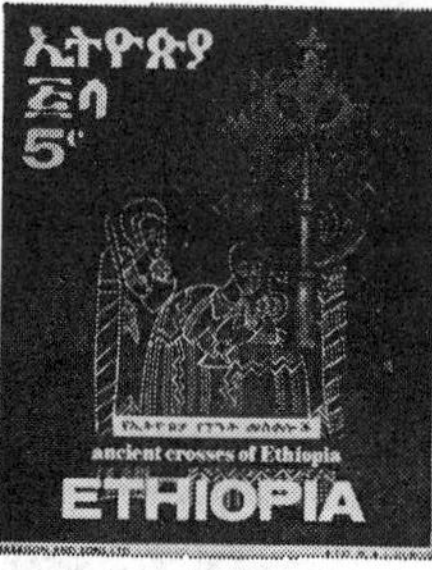

Ancient Cross and Holy Family

A114

Designs: Various ancient crosses.

Photogravure

1969, Dec. 10 ***Perf. 14½x13½***

544	A114	5c blk, yel & dk bl	10	10
545	A114	10c blk & yel	15	15
546	A114	25c blk, yel & grn	50	50
547	A114	60c blk & ocher	1.25	1.25

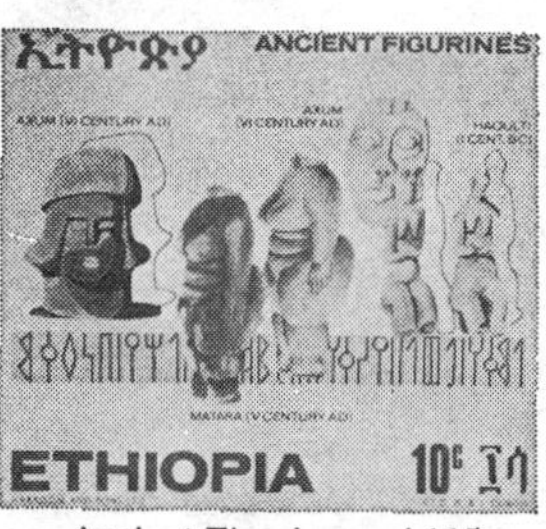

Ancient Figurines—A115

Ancient Ethiopian Pottery: 20c, Vases, Yeha period, 4th–3rd centuries B.C. 25c, Vases and jugs, Axum, 4th–6th centuries A.D. 35c, Bird-shaped jug and jugs, Matara, 4th–6th centuries A.D. 60c, Decorated pottery, Adulis, 6th–7th centuries A.D.

1970, Feb. 6 **Photo.** ***Perf. 14½***

548	A115	10c blk & multi	15	15
549	A115	20c blk & multi	30	30
550	A115	25c blk & multi	35	35
551	A115	35c blk & multi	60	60
552	A115	60c blk & multi	1.10	1.10
		Nos. 548-552 (5)	2.50	2.50

Medhane Alem Church—A116

Rock Churches of Lalibela, 12th–13th Centuries: 10c, Bieta Emmanuel. 15c, The four Rock Churches of Lalibela. 20c, Bieta Mariam. 50c, Bieta Giorgis.

1970, Apr. 15 ***Perf. 13*** **Unwmkd.**

553	A116	5c brn & multi	8	8
554	A116	10c brn & multi	15	15
555	A116	15c brn & multi	30	30
556	A116	20c brn & multi	50	50
557	A116	50c brn & multi	1.15	1.15
		Nos. 553-557 (5)	2.18	2.18

Sailfish Tang

A117

Tropical Fish: 10c, Undulate triggerfish. 15c, Orange butterflyfish. 25c, Butterflyfish. 50c, Imperial Angelfish.

1970, June 19 **Photo.** ***Perf. 12½***

558	A117	5c multi	10	10

559	A117	10c multi	15	15
560	A117	15c multi	25	25
561	A117	25c multi	60	60
562	A117	50c multi	1.25	1.25
		Nos. 558-562 (5)	2.35	2.35

Education Year Emblem
A118

1970, Aug. 14 *Perf. 13½* Unwmkd.

563	A118	10c multi	15	15
564	A118	20c gold, ultra & emer	35	35
565	A118	50c gold, emer & org	85	85

Issued for International Education Year.

Map of Africa
A119

Designs: 30c, Flag of Organization of African Unity. 40c, OAU Headquarters, Addis Ababa.

1970, Sept. 21 Photo. *Perf. 13½*

566	A119	20c multi	27	27
567	A119	30c multi	40	40
568	A119	40c grn & multi	75	75

Organization of African Unity.

Emperor Haile Selassie
A120

1970, Oct. 30 *Perf. 14½* Unwmkd.

569	A120	15c Prus bl & multi	18	18
570	A120	50c multi	65	65
571	A120	60c multi	1.25	1.25

Issued to commemorate the 40th anniversary of the coronation of Emperor Haile Selassie I.

Posts, Telecommunications and G.P.O. Buildings—A121

1970, Dec. 30 Litho. *Perf. 13½*

572	A121	10c ver & multi	18	18
573	A121	50c brn & multi	1.00	1.00
574	A121	80c multi	1.25	1.25

Opening of new Posts, Telecommunications and General Post Office buildings.

Costume Type of 1968

Regional Costumes: 5c, Warrior from Begemedir and Semain. 10c, Woman from Bale. 15c, Warrior from Wolega. 20c, Woman from Showa. 25c, Man from Sidamo. 40c, Woman from Tigre. 50c, Man from Wello.

1971, Feb. 17 Photo. *Perf. 11½*

Granite Paper

575	A107	5c gold & multi	8	8
576	A107	10c gold & multi	15	15
577	A107	15c gold & multi	25	25
578	A107	20c gold & multi	30	30
579	A107	25c gold & multi	40	40
580	A107	40c gold & multi	50	50
581	A107	50c gold & multi	1.00	1.00
		Nos. 575-581 (7)	2.68	2.68

Plane's Tail with Emblem
A122

Designs: 10c, Ethiopian scenes. 20c, Nose of Boeing 707. 60c, Pilots in cockpit, and engine. 80c, Globe with routes shown.

1971, Apr. 8 *Perf. 14½x14*

582	A122	5c multi	8	8
583	A122	10c multi	15	15
584	A122	20c multi	30	30
585	A122	60c multi	1.00	1.00
586	A122	80c multi	1.35	1.35
		Nos. 582-586 (5)	2.88	2.88

Ethiopian Airlines, 25th anniversary.

Fountain of Life, 15th Century Gospel Book
A123

Ethiopian Paintings: 10c, King David, 15th century manuscript. 25c, St. George, 17th century painting on canvas. 50c, King Lalibela, 18th century painting on wood. 60c, Yared singing before King Kaleb, mural in Axum Cathedral, 18th century.

1971, June 15 Photo. *Perf. 11½*

Granite Paper

587	A123	5c tan & multi	8	8
588	A123	10c pale sal & multi	15	15
589	A123	25c lem & multi	30	30
590	A123	50c yel & multi	80	80
591	A123	60c gray & multi	1.25	1.25
		Nos. 587-591 (5)	2.58	2.58

Black and White Heads, Globes
A124

Designs: 60c, Black and white hand holding globe. 80c, Four races, globes.

1971, Aug. 31 Unwmkd.

592	A124	10c org, red brn & blk	20	20
593	A124	60c grn, bl & blk	75	75
594	A124	80c bl, org, yel & blk	1.25	1.25

International Year Against Racial Discrimination.

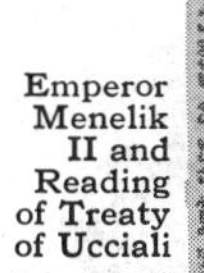

Emperor Menelik II and Reading of Treaty of Ucciali
A125

Contemporary Paintings: 30c, Menelik II on horseback gathering the tribes. 50c, Ethiopians and Italians in Battle of Adwa. 60c, Menelik II at head of his army.

1971, Oct. 20 Litho. *Perf. 13½*

595	A125	10c multi	20	20
596	A125	30c multi	50	50
597	A125	50c multi	75	75
598	A125	60c multi	1.25	1.25

75th anniversary of victory of Adwa over the Italians, March 1, 1896.

Haile Selassie Broadcasting and Map of Ethiopia
A126

Designs: 5c, Two telephones, 1897, Menelik II and Ras Makonnen. 30c, Ethiopians around television set. 40c, Telephone microwave circuits. 60c, Map of Africa on globe and telephone dial.

1971, Nov. 2

599	A126	5c brn & multi	6	6
600	A126	10c yel & multi	12	12
601	A126	30c vio bl & multi	40	40
602	A126	40c blk & multi	55	55
603	A126	60c vio bl & multi	1.10	1.10
		Nos. 599-603 (5)	2.23	2.23

75th anniversary of telecommunications in Ethiopia.

UNICEF Emblem, Mother and Child
A127

Designs (UNICEF Emblem and): 10c, Children drinking milk. 15c, Man holding sick child. 30c, Kindergarten class. 50c, Father and son.

1971, Dec. 15 Unwmkd.

604	A127	5c yel & multi	8	8
605	A127	10c pale brn & multi	15	15
606	A127	15c rose & multi	22	22
607	A127	30c vio & multi	45	45
608	A127	50c grn & multi	75	75
		Nos. 604-608 (5)	1.65	1.65

25th anniversary of the United Nations International Children's Fund (UNICEF).

Nos. 445-448 Overprinted

U.N. SECURITY COUNCIL
FIRST MEETING
IN AFRICA 1972

1972, Jan. 28 Photo. *Perf. 11*

Portrait in Black

609	A86	20c grn & pale yel	30	30
610	A86	25c dk brn & yel	45	45
611	A86	30c mar & gray	65	65
612	A86	35c dk bl & gray	80	80

First meeting of U.N. Security Council in Africa.

River Boat on Lake Haik—A128

1972, Feb. 7 Litho. *Perf. 11½*

Granite Paper; Multicolored

613	A128	10c *shown*	15	15
614	A128	20c *Boats on Lake Abaya*	30	30
615	A128	30c *on Lake Tana*	60	60
616	A128	60c *on Baro River*	1.25	1.25

Proclamation of Cyrus the Great
A129

1972, Mar. 28 Photo. *Perf. 14x14½*

617	A129	10c red & multi	15	15
618	A129	60c emer & multi	90	90
619	A129	80c gray & multi	1.25	1.25

2500th anniversary of the founding of the Persian empire by Cyrus the Great.

Houses, Sidamo Province
A130

Ethiopian Architecture: 10c, Tigre Province. 20c, Eritrea Province. 40c, Addis Ababa. 80c, Shoa Province.

1972, Apr. 11 Litho. *Perf. 13½*

620	A130	5c blk & multi	8	8
621	A130	10c blk, gray & brn	15	15
622	A130	20c blk & multi	30	30
623	A130	40c blk, bl grn & brn	60	60
624	A130	80c blk, brn & red brn	1.35	1.35
		Nos. 620-624 (5)	2.48	2.48

Hands Holding Map of Ethiopia
A131

Designs: 10c, Hands shielding Ethiopians. 25c, Map of Africa, hands reaching for African Unity emblem. 50c, Brown and white hands clasped, U.N. emblem. 60c, Hands protecting dove. Each denomination shows different portrait of the Emperor.

Perf. 14½x14

1972, July 21 Litho. Unwmkd.

625	A131	5c scar & multi	7	7
626	A131	10c ultra & multi	13	13
627	A131	25c vio bl & multi	33	33
628	A131	50c lt bl & multi	65	65

629	A131	60c brn & multi	80	80
		Nos. 625-629 (5)	1.98	1.98

80th birthday of Emperor Haile Selassie.

Running, Flags of Mexico, Japan, Italy
A132

1972, Aug. 25 ***Perf. 13½x13***

Multicolored

630	A132	10c *shown*	13	13
631	A132	30c *Soccer*	40	40
632	A132	50c *Bicycling*	80	80
633	A132	60c *Boxing*	1.10	1.10

20th Olympic Games, Munich, Germany, Aug. 26–Sept. 11.

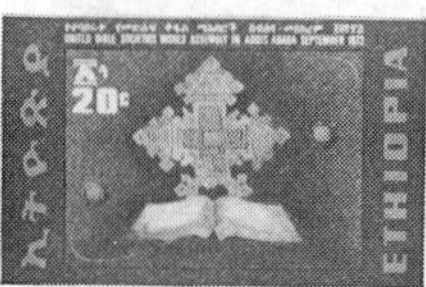

Open Bible, Cross and Orbit
A133

Designs: 50c, First and 1972 headquarters of the British and Foreign Bible Society (vert.). 80c, First Amharic Bible.

1972, Sept. 25 Photo. ***Perf. 13½***

634	A133	20c dp red & multi	27	27
635	A133	50c dp red & multi	65	65
636	A133	80c dp red & multi	1.25	1.25

United Bible Societies World Assembly, Addis Ababa, Sept. 1972.

Security Council Meeting
A134

Designs: 60c, Building where Security Council met. 80c, Map of Africa with flags of participating members.

1972, Nov. 1 Litho. ***Perf. 13½***

637	A134	10c lt bl & vio bl	13	13
638	A134	60c multi	75	75
639	A134	80c multi	1.50	1.50

First United Nations Security Council meeting, Addis Ababa, Jan. 28–Feb. 4, 1972.

Fish in Polluted Sea
A135

Designs: 30c, Fisherman, beacon, family. 80c, Polluted seashore.

1973, Feb. 23 Photo. ***Perf. 13½***

640	A135	20c gold & multi	30	30
641	A135	30c gold & multi	45	45
642	A135	80c gold & multi	1.25	1.25

World message from the sea, Ethiopian anti-pollution campaign.

INTERPOL and Ethiopian Police Emblems
A136

Designs: 50c, INTERPOL emblem and General Secretariat, Paris. 60c, INTERPOL emblem.

1973, Mar. 20 Photo. ***Perf. 13½***

643	A136	40c dl org & blk	65	65
644	A136	50c bl, blk & yel	85	85
645	A136	60c dk car & blk	1.00	1.00

50th anniversary of International Criminal Police Organization (INTERPOL).

Virgin of Emperor Zara Yaqob
A137

Ethiopian Art: 15c, Crucifixion, Zara Yaqob period. 30c, Virgin and Child, from Entoto Mariam Church. 40c, Christ, contemporary mosaic. 80c, The Evangelists, contemporary bas-relief.

1973, May 15 Photo. ***Perf. 11½***

Granite Paper

646	A137	5c brn & multi	7	7
647	A137	15c dp bl & multi	20	20
648	A137	30c gray grn & multi	55	55
649	A137	40c multi	60	60
650	A137	80c sl & multi	1.50	1.50
		Nos. 646-650 (5)	2.92	2.92

Free African States in 1963 and 1973
A138

Designs (Map of Africa and): 10c, Flags of OAU members. 20c, Symbols of progress. 40c, Dove and people. 80c, Emblems of various UN agencies.

1973 May 25 ***Perf. 14½x14***

651	A138	5c red & multi	8	8
652	A138	10c ol gray & multi	17	17
653	A138	20c grn & multi	33	33
654	A138	40c sep & multi	65	65
655	A138	80c lt bl & multi	1.75	1.75
		Nos. 651-655 (5)	2.98	2.98

Organization for African Unity, 10th anniversary.

Scouts Saluting Ethiopian and Scout Flags
A139

Designs: 15c, Road and road sign. 30c, Girl Scout reading to old man. 40c, Scout and disabled people. 60c, Ethiopian Boy Scout.

1973, July 10 Photo. ***Perf. 11½***

Granite Paper

656	A139	5c bl & multi	7	7
657	A139	15c lt grn & multi	20	20
658	A139	30c yel & multi	42	42
659	A139	40c crim & multi	60	60
660	A139	60c vio & multi	1.10	1.10
		Nos. 656-660 (5)	2.39	2.39

24th Boy Scout World Conference, Nairobi, Kenya, July 16–21.

WMO Emblem
A140

Designs: 50c, WMO emblem and anemometer. 60c, Weather satellite over earth, and WMO emblem.

1973, Sept. 4 Photo. ***Perf. 13½***

661	A140	40c blk, bl & dl bl	55	55
662	A140	50c dl bl & blk	65	65
663	A140	60c dl bl & multi	1.00	1.00

Centenary of international meteorological cooperation.

Prince Makonnen, Duke of Harer
A141

Human Rights Flame
A142

Designs: 5c, Old wall of Harer. 20c, Operating room. 40c, Boy Scouts learning first aid, and hospital. 80c, Prince Makonnen and hospital.

1973, Nov. 1 ***Perf. 14½*** **Unwmkd.**

664	A141	5c gray & multi	5	5
665	A141	10c red brn & multi	10	10
666	A141	20c grn & multi	30	30
667	A141	40c brn red & multi	65	65
668	A141	80c ultra & multi	1.35	1.35
		Nos. 664-668 (5)	2.45	2.45

Opening of Prince Makonnen Memorial Hospital.

Perf. 11½

1973, Nov. 16 Photo. **Unwmkd.**

Granite Paper

669	A142	40c yel, gold & dk grn	60	60
670	A142	50c lt grn, gold & dk grn	75	75
671	A142	60c org, gold & dk grn	1.00	1.00

25th anniversary of the Universal Declaration of Human Rights.

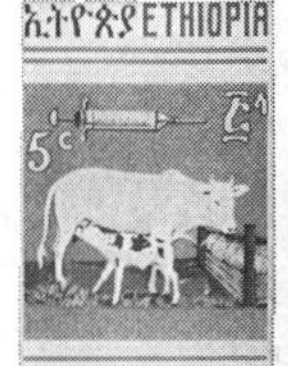

Emperor Haile Selassie
A143

1973, Nov. 5 Photo. ***Perf. 11½***

672	A143	5c yel & multi	5	3
673	A143	10c brt bl & multi	12	5
674	A143	15c grn & multi	18	7
675	A143	20c dl yel & multi	25	10
676	A143	25c multi	30	13
677	A143	30c multi	35	15
678	A143	35c multi	42	17
679	A143	40c ultra & multi	48	20
680	A143	45c multi	55	22
681	A143	50c org & multi	60	25
682	A143	55c mag & multi	75	50
683	A143	60c multi	90	65
684	A143	70c red org & multi	1.00	70
685	A143	90c brt vio & multi	1.20	85
686	A143	$1 multi	1.60	1.10
687	A143	$2 org & multi	3.00	2.00
688	A143	$3 multi	4.50	3.00
689	A143	$5 multi	7.50	5.00
		Nos. 672-689 (18)	23.75	15.17

Wicker Furniture
A144

Designs: Various wicker baskets, wall hangings, dinnerware.

1974, Jan. 31 Photo. ***Perf. 11½***

Granite Paper

690	A144	5c vio bl & multi	5	5
691	A144	10c vio bl & multi	10	10
692	A144	30c vio bl & multi	30	30
693	A144	50c vio bl & multi	60	60
694	A144	60c vio bl & multi	75	75
		Nos. 690-694 (5)	1.80	1.80

Cow, Calf, Syringe
A145

Designs: 15c, Inoculation of cattle. 20c, Bullock and syringe. 50c, Laboratory technician, cow's head, syringe. 60c, Map of Ethiopia, cattle, syringe.

1974, Feb. 20 Litho. ***Perf. 13½x13***

695	A145	5c sep & multi	5	5
696	A145	15c ultra & multi	15	15
697	A145	20c ultra & multi	20	20
698	A145	50c org & multi	75	75
699	A145	60c gold & multi	1.00	1.00
		Nos. 695-699 (5)	2.15	2.15

Campaign against cattle plague.

Umbrella Makers
A146

Designs: 30c, Weaving. 50c, Child care. 60c, Foundation headquarters.

1974, Apr. 17 Photo. ***Perf. 14½***

700	A146	10c lt lil & multi	10	10
701	A146	30c multi	30	30
702	A146	50c multi	60	60
703	A146	60c bl & multi	75	75

20th anniversary of Haile Selassie I Foundation.

Ceremonial Robe
A147

Designs: Ceremonial robes.

1974, June 26 Lithographed ***Perf. 13***

704	A147	15c multi	15	15
705	A147	25c ocher & multi	25	25
706	A147	35c grn & multi	50	50
707	A147	40c lt brn & multi	60	60
708	A147	60c gray & multi	85	85
		Nos. 704-708 (5)	2.35	2.35

World Population Statistics
A148

Designs: 50c, "Larger families—lower living standard." 60c, Rising population graph.

1974, Aug. 19 Photo. *Perf. 14½*

709	A148	40c yel & multi	50	50
710	A148	50c vio & multi	60	60
711	A148	60c grn & multi	75	75

World Population Year 1974.

UPU Emblem, Letter Carrier's Staff A149 — Celebration Around "Damara" Pillar A150

Designs (UPU Emblem and): 50c, Letters and flags. 60c, Globe. 70c, Headquarters, Bern.

1974, Oct. 9 Photo. *Perf. 11½*

Granite Paper

712	A149	15c yel & multi	15	15
713	A149	50c multi	60	60
714	A149	60c ultra & multi	75	75
715	A149	70c multi	85	85

Centenary of Universal Postal Union.

1974, Dec. 17 Photo. *Perf. 14x14½*

Designs: 5c, Site of Gishen Mariam Monastery. 20c, Cross and festivities. 80c, Torch (Chibos) Parade.

716	A150	5c yel & multi	5	5
717	A150	10c yel & multi	10	10
718	A150	20c yel & multi	25	25
719	A150	80c yel & multi	1.00	1.00

Meskel Festival, Sept. 26–27, commemorating the finding in the 4th century of the True Cross, of which a fragment is kept at Gishen Mariam Monastery in Wollo Province.

Precis Clelia A151 — Adoration of the Kings A152

Butterflies: 25c, Charaxes achaemenes. 45c, Papilio dardanus. 50c, Charaxes druceanus. 60c, Papilio demodocus.

1975, Feb. 18 Photo. *Perf. 12x12½*

720	A151	10c sil & multi	10	10
721	A151	25c gold & multi	25	25
722	A151	45c pur & multi	65	65
723	A151	50c grn & multi	85	85
724	A151	60c brt bl & multi	1.00	1.00
		Nos. 720-724 (5)	2.85	2.85

1975, Apr. 23 Photo. *Perf. 11½*

Designs: 10c, Baptism of Jesus. 15c, Jesus teaching in the Temple. 30c, Jesus giving sight to the blind. 40c, Crucifixion. 80c, Resurrection.

Granite Paper

725	A152	5c brn & multi	5	5
726	A152	10c blk & multi	10	10
727	A152	15c dk brn & multi	15	15
728	A152	30c dk brn & multi	30	30
729	A152	40c blk & multi	60	60
730	A152	80c sl & multi	1.10	1.10
		Nos. 725-730 (6)	2.30	2.30

Murals from Ethiopian churches.

Warthog A153

Designs: Wild animals.

1975, May 27 Photo. *Perf. 11½*

Multicolored; Granite Paper

731	A153	5c *shown*	5	5
732	A153	10c *Aardvark*	10	10
733	A153	20c *Semien wolf*	20	20
734	A153	40c *Gelada baboon*	50	50
735	A153	80c *Civet*	1.10	1.10
		Nos. 731-735 (5)	1.95	1.95

"Peace," Dove, Globe, IWY Emblem A154

Designs (IWY Emblem and): 50c, Symbols of development. 90c, Equality between men and women.

1975, June 30 Litho. *Perf. 14x14½*

736	A154	40c bl & blk	50	50
737	A154	50c sal & multi	60	60
738	A154	90c multi	1.25	1.25

International Women's Year 1975.

Postal Museum A155

Designs: Various interior views of Postal Museum.

1975, Aug. 19 Photo. *Perf. 13x12½*

739	A155	10c ocher & multi	10	10
740	A155	30c pink & multi	30	30
741	A155	60c multi	75	75
742	A155	70c lt grn & multi	85	85

Ethiopian National Postal Museum, opening.

Map of Ethiopia and Sun A156

1975, Sept. 11 Photo. *Perf. 11½*

Granite Paper

743	A156	5c lil & multi	5	5
744	A156	10c ultra & multi	10	10
745	A156	25c brn & multi	25	25
746	A156	50c yel & multi	60	60
747	A156	90c brt grn & multi	1.10	1.10
		Nos. 743-747 (5)	2.10	2.10

1st anniversary of Ethiopia Tikdem (Socialism).

U.N. Emblem A157

1975, Oct. 24 Photo. *Perf. 11½*

748	A157	40c lil & multi	50	50
749	A157	50c multi	60	60
750	A157	90c bl & multi	1.10	1.10

United Nations, 30th anniversary.

Ilubabor Hair Style A158 — Delphinium Wellbyi A159

Regional Hair Styles: 15c, Arusi. 20c, Eritrea. 30c, Bale. 35c, Kefa. 50c, Begemdir. 60c, Shewa.

1975, Dec. 15 Photo. *Perf. 11½*

751	A158	5c multi	5	5
752	A158	15c multi	15	15
753	A158	20c multi	25	25
754	A158	30c multi	35	35
755	A158	35c multi	50	50
756	A158	50c multi	60	60
757	A158	60c multi	75	75
		Nos. 751-757 (7)	2.65	2.65

See Nos. 832–838.

1976, Jan. 15 Photo. *Perf. 11½*

Flowers: 10c, Plectocephalus varians. 20c, Brachystelma asmarensis (horiz.). 40c, Ceropegia inflata. 80c, Erythrina brucei.

758	A159	5c multi	5	5
759	A159	10c multi	10	10
760	A159	20c multi	25	25
761	A159	40c multi	50	50
762	A159	80c multi	1.00	1.00
		Nos. 758-762 (5)	1.90	1.90

Goalkeeper, Map of Africa, Games' Emblem A160

Designs: Various scenes from soccer, map of Africa and ball.

1976, Feb. 27 Photo. *Perf. 14½*

763	A160	5c org & multi	5	5
764	A160	10c yel & multi	10	10
765	A160	25c lil & multi	30	30
766	A160	50c grn & multi	60	60
767	A160	90c brt grn & multi	1.10	1.10
		Nos. 763-767 (5)	2.15	2.15

10th African Cup of Nations, Addis Ababa and Dire Dawa, Feb. 29–Mar. 14.

Telephones, 1876 and 1976 A161 — Ethiopian Jewelry A162

Designs: 60c, Alexander Graham Bell. 90c, Transmission tower.

1976, Mar. 10 Litho. *Perf. 12x13½*

768	A161	30c lt ocher & multi	35	35
769	A161	60c emer & multi	75	75
770	A161	90c ver, blk & buff	1.10	1.10

Centenary of first telephone call by Alexander Graham Bell, Mar. 10, 1876.

Granite Paper

1976, May 14 Photo. *Perf. 11½*

Designs: Women wearing various kinds of Ethiopian jewelry.

771	A162	5c bl & multi	5	5
772	A162	10c plum & multi	10	10
773	A162	20c gray & multi	30	30
774	A162	40c grn & multi	60	60
775	A162	80c org & multi	1.10	1.10
		Nos. 771-775 (5)	2.15	2.15

Boxing A163 — Hands Holding Map of Ethiopia A164

Designs (Montreal Olympic Emblem and): 80c, Runner and maple leaf. 90c, Bicycling.

1976, July 15 Litho. *Perf. 12½x12*

776	A163	10c multi	10	10
777	A163	80c brt red, blk & grn	1.00	1.00
778	A163	90c brt red & multi	1.10	1.10

21st Olympic Games, Montreal, Canada, July 17–Aug. 1.

1976, Aug. 5 Photo. *Perf. 14½*

779	A164	5c rose & multi	5	5
780	A164	10c ol & multi	10	10
781	A164	25c org & multi	25	25
782	A164	50c multi	60	60
783	A164	90c dk bl & multi	1.10	1.10
		Nos. 779-783 (5)	2.10	2.10

Development through cooperation.

Revolution Emblem: Eye and Map A165

1976, Sept. 9 Photo. *Perf. 13½*

784	A165	5c multi	5	5
785	A165	10c multi	10	10
786	A165	25c multi	25	25
787	A165	50c yel & multi	60	60
788	A165	90c grn & multi	1.10	1.10
		Nos. 784-788 (5)	2.10	2.10

2nd anniversary of the revolution (Tikdem).

Sunburst Around Crest A166 — Plane Over Man with Donkey A167

1976, Sept. 13 Photo. *Perf. 11½*

789	A166	5c grn gold & blk	5	3
790	A166	10c org, gold & blk	10	5
791	A166	15c grnsh bl, gold & blk	15	8
792	A166	20c lil, gold & blk	20	10
793	A166	25c brt grn, gold & blk	25	12
794	A166	30c car, gold & blk	30	15
795	A166	35c yel, gold & blk	35	18

796	A166	40c ol, gold & blk	40	20
797	A166	45c brt grn, gold & blk	45	22
798	A166	50c car rose, gold & blk	50	25
799	A166	55c ultra, gold & blk	55	28
800	A166	60c fawn, gold & blk	60	30
801	A166	70c rose, gold & blk	70	35
802	A166	90c bl, gold & blk	90	45
803	A166	$1 dl grn, gold & blk	1.00	50
804	A166	$2 gray, gold & blk	2.00	1.00
805	A166	$3 brn vio, gold & blk	3.00	1.50
806	A166	$5 sl bl, gold & blk	5.00	2.50
		Nos. 789-806 (18)	16.50	8.26

1976, Oct. 28 Litho. *Perf. 12x12½*

Designs: 10c, Globe showing routes. 25c, Crew and passengers forming star. 50c, Propeller and jet engine. 90c, Airplanes surrounding map of Ethiopia.

807	A167	5c dl bl & multi	5	5
808	A167	10c lil & multi	10	10
809	A167	25c multi	25	25
810	A167	50c org & multi	50	50
811	A167	90c ol & multi	90	90
		Nos. 807-811 (5)	1.80	1.80

Ethiopian Airlines, 30th anniversary.

Tortoises

A168

Hand Holding Makeshift Hammer

A169

Reptiles: 20c, Chameleon. 30c, Python. 40c, Monitor lizard. 80c, Nile crocodiles.

1976, Dec. 15 Photo. *Perf. 14½*

812	A168	10c multi	10	10
813	A168	20c multi	20	20
814	A168	30c multi	30	30
815	A168	40c multi	40	40
816	A168	80c multi	80	80
		Nos. 812-816 (5)	1.80	1.80

1977, Jan. 20 Litho. *Perf. 12½*

Designs: 5c, Hands holding bowl and plane dropping food. 45c, Infant with empty bowl, and bank note. 60c, Map of affected area, footprints and tire tracks. 80c, Film strip, camera and Ethiopian sitting between eggshells.

817	A169	5c multi	5	5
818	A169	10c multi	10	10
819	A169	45c multi	45	45
820	A169	60c multi	60	60
821	A169	80c multi	80	80
		Nos. 817-821 (5)	2.00	2.00

Ethiopian Relief and Rehabilitation Commission for drought and disaster areas.

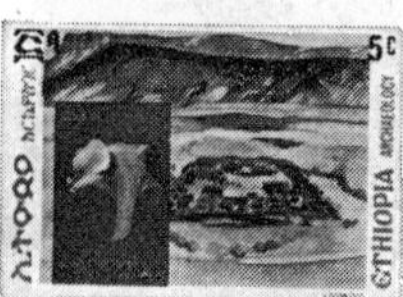

Elephant and Ruins, Axum, 7th Century

A170

Designs: 10c, Ibex and temple, 5th century, B.C., Yeha. 25c, Megalithic dolmen and pottery, Sourre Kabanawa. 50c, Awash Valley, stone axe, Acheulean period. 80c, Omo Valley, hominid jawbone.

1977, Mar. 15 Photo. *Perf. 13½*

822	A170	5c gold & multi	5	5
823	A170	10c gold & multi	10	10
824	A170	25c gold & multi	25	25
825	A170	50c gold & multi	50	50
826	A170	80c gold & multi	80	80
		Nos. 822-826 (5)	1.70	1.70

Archaeological sites and finds in Ethiopia.

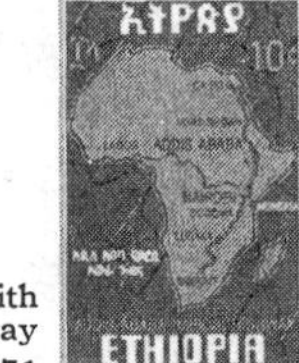

Map of Africa with Trans-East Highway

A171

1977, Mar. 30 *Perf. 14*

827	A171	10c gold & multi	10	10
828	A171	20c gold & multi	20	20
829	A171	40c gold & multi	40	40
830	A171	50c gold & multi	50	50
831	A171	60c gold & multi	60	60
		Nos. 827-831 (5)	1.80	1.80

Addis Ababa to Nairobi Highway and projected highways to Cairo, Egypt, and Gaborone, Botswana.

Hairstyle Type of 1975

Regional Hairstyles: 5c, Wollega. 10c, Gojjam. 15c, Tigre. 20c, Harrar. 25c, Gemu Gofa. 40c, Sidamo. 50c, Wollo.

1977, Apr. 28 Photo. *Perf. 11½*

832	A158	5c multi	5	5
833	A158	10c multi	10	10
834	A158	15c multi	15	15
835	A158	20c multi	20	20
836	A158	25c multi	25	25
837	A158	40c multi	45	45
838	A158	50c multi	60	60
		Nos. 832-838 (7)	1.80	1.80

Addis Ababa

A172

Towns of Ethiopia: 10c, Asmara. 25c, Harer. 50c, Jima. 90c, Dese.

1977, June 20 Photo. *Perf. 14½*

839	A172	5c sil & multi	5	5
840	A172	10c sil & multi	10	10
841	A172	25c sil & multi	25	25
842	A172	50c sil & multi	50	50
843	A172	90c sil & multi	90	90
		Nos. 839-843 (5)	1.80	1.80

Terebratula Abyssinica

A173

Fractured Imperial Crown

A174

Fossil Shells: 10c, Terebratula subalata. 25c, Cuculloea lefeburiaua. 50c, Ostrea plicatissima. 90c, Trigonia cousobrina.

1977, Aug. 15 Photo. *Perf. 14x13½*

844	A173	5c multi	5	5
845	A173	10c multi	10	10
846	A173	25c multi	25	25
847	A173	50c multi	50	50
848	A173	90c multi	90	90
		Nos. 844-848 (5)	1.80	1.80

1977, Sept. 9 Litho. *Perf. 15*

Designs: 10c, Symbol of the Revolution (spade, axe, torch). 25c, Warriors, hammer and sickle, map of Ethiopia. 60c, Soldier, farmer and map. 80c, Map and emblem of revolutionary government.

849	A174	5c multi	5	5
850	A174	10c multi	10	10
851	A174	25c multi	25	25
852	A174	60c multi	60	60
853	A174	80c multi	80	80
		Nos. 849-853 (5)	1.80	1.80

Third anniversary of the revolution.

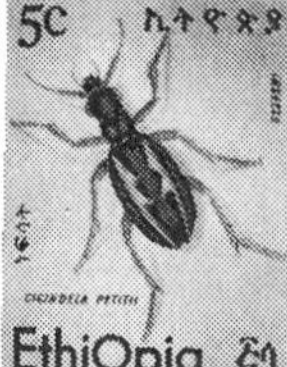

Cicindela Petitii

A175

Lenin, Globe, Map of Ethiopia and Emblem

A176

Insects: 10c, Heliocopris dillonii. 25c, Poekilocerus vignaudii. 50c, Pepsis heros. 90c, Pepsis dedjaz.

1977, Sept. 30 Photo. *Perf. 14x13½*

854	A175	5c multi	5	5
855	A175	10c multi	10	10
856	A175	25c multi	25	25
857	A175	50c multi	50	50
858	A175	90c multi	90	90
		Nos. 854-858 (5)	1.80	1.80

1977, Nov. 15 Litho. *Perf. 12*

859	A176	5c org & multi	5	5
860	A176	10c multi	10	10
861	A176	25c sal & multi	25	25
862	A176	50c lt bl & multi	50	50
863	A176	90c yel & multi	90	90
		Nos. 859-863 (5)	1.80	1.80

60th anniversary of Russian October Revolution.

Chondrostoma Dilloni

A177

Salt-water Fish: 10c, Ostracion cubicus. 25c, Serranus summana. 50c, Serranus luti. 90c, Tetraodon maculatus.

1978, Jan. 20 Litho. *Perf. 15½*

864	A177	5c multi	5	5
865	A177	10c multi	10	10
866	A177	25c multi	25	25
867	A177	50c multi	50	50
868	A177	90c multi	90	90
		Nos. 864-868 (5)	1.80	1.80

Cattle

A178

Domestic Animals: 10c, Mules. 25c, Goats. 50c, Dromedaries. 90c, Horses.

1978, Mar. 27 Litho. *Perf. 13½x14*

869	A178	5c yel & multi	5	5
870	A178	10c multi	10	10
871	A178	25c grn & multi	25	25
872	A178	50c ver & multi	50	50
873	A178	90c ultra & multi	90	90
		Nos. 869-873 (5)	1.80	1.80

Foreign postal stationery (stamped envelopes, postal cards and air letter sheets) lies beyond the scope of this Catalogue which is limited to adhesive postage stamps.

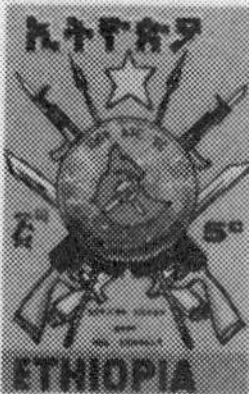

Weapons and Shield, Map of Ethiopia

A179

Bronze Ibex, 5th Century B.C.

A180

Designs: (Map of Ethiopia and): 10c, Civilian fighters. 25c, Map of Africa. 60c, Soldiers. 80c, Red Cross nurse and wounded man.

1978, May Litho. *Perf. 15½*

874	A179	5c multi	5	5
875	A179	10c multi	10	10
876	A179	25c multi	25	25
877	A179	60c multi	60	60
878	A179	80c multi	80	80
		Nos. 874-878 (5)	1.80	1.80

"Call of the Motherland."

1978, June 21 Litho. *Perf. 15½*

Ancient Bronzes: 10c, Lion, Yeha, 5th century B.C. (horiz.). 25c, Lamp with ibex attacked by dog, Matara, 1st century B.C. 50c, Goat, Axum, 3rd century A.D. (horiz.). 90c, Ax, chisel and sickle, Yeha, 5th–4th centuries B.C.

879	A180	5c multi	5	5
880	A180	10c multi	10	10
881	A180	25c multi	25	25
882	A180	50c multi	50	50
883	A180	90c multi	90	90
		Nos. 879-883 (5)	1.80	1.80

Globe and Argentina '78 Emblem

A181

Designs (Argentina '78 Emblem and): 20c, Soccer player kicking ball. 30c, Two players embracing, net and ball. 55c, World map and ball. 70c, Soccer field (vert.).

Perf. 14x13½, 13½x14

1978, July 19 Lithographed

884	A181	5c multi	5	5
885	A181	20c multi	20	20
886	A181	30c multi	30	30
887	A181	55c multi	55	55
888	A181	70c multi	70	70
		Nos. 884-888 (5)	1.80	1.80

11th World Cup Soccer Championship, Argentina, June 1–25.

Map of Africa, Oppressed African

A182

Designs (Map of Africa and): 10c, Policeman pointing gun. 25c, Sniper with gun. 60c, African caught in net. 80c, Head of free man.

1978, Aug. 25 *Perf. 12½x13½*

889	A182	5c multi	5	5
890	A182	10c multi	10	10
891	A182	25c multi	25	25
892	A182	60c multi	60	60
893	A182	80c multi	80	80
		Nos. 889-893 (5)	1.80	1.80

Namibia Day.

Soldiers, Guerrilla and Jets
A183

Design: $1, People looking toward sun, crushing snake, flags.

1978, Sept. 8 Photo. *Perf. 14*

894	A183	80c multi	80	80
895	A183	1b multi	1.00	1.00

4th anniversary of revolution.

Hand and Globe with Tools
A184

Designs: 15c, Symbols of energy, communications, education, medicine, agriculture and industry. 25c, Cogwheels and world map. 60c, Globe and hands passing wrench. 70c, Flying geese and turtle over globe.

1978, Nov. 10 Litho. *Perf. 12x12½*

896	A184	10c multi	10	10
897	A184	15c multi	15	15
898	A184	25c multi	25	25
899	A184	60c multi	60	60
900	A184	70c multi	70	70
		Nos. 896-900 (5)	1.80	1.80

Technical Cooperation Among Developing Countries Conference, Buenos Aires, Argentina, Sept. 1978.

Human Rights Emblem
A185

1978, Dec. 7 Photo. *Perf. 12½x13½*

901	A185	5c multi	5	5
902	A185	15c multi	15	15
903	A185	25c multi	25	25
904	A185	35c multi	35	35
905	A185	1b multi	1.00	1.00
		Nos. 901-905 (5)	1.80	1.80

Declaration of Human Rights, 30th anniversary.

Broken Chain, Anti-Apartheid Emblem
A186

Stele from Osole
A187

1978, Dec. 28 Litho. *Perf. 12½x12*

906	A186	5c multi	5	5
907	A186	20c multi	20	20
908	A186	30c multi	30	30
909	A186	55c multi	55	55
910	A186	70c multi	70	70
		Nos. 906-910 (5)	1.80	1.80

Anti-Apartheid Year.

1979, Jan. 25 *Perf. 14*

Ancient Carved Stones, Soddo Region: 10c, Anthropomorphous stele, Gorashino. 25c, Leaning stone, Wado. 60c, Round stones, Ambeut. 80c, Bas-relief, Tiya.

911	A187	5c multi	5	5
912	A187	10c multi	10	10
913	A187	25c multi	25	25
914	A187	60c multi	60	60
915	A187	80c multi	80	80
		Nos. 911-915 (5)	1.80	1.80

Cotton and Shemma Valley
A188

Shemma Industry: 10c, Women spinning cotton yarn. 20c, Man reeling cotton. 65c, Weaver. 80c, Cotton garments.

1979, Mar. 15 Litho. *Perf. 15½*

916	A188	5c multi	5	5
917	A188	10c multi	10	10
918	A188	20c multi	20	20
919	A188	65c multi	65	65
920	A188	80c multi	80	80
		Nos. 916-920 (5)	1.80	1.80

"Grar" Tree
A189

Designs: Ethiopian trees.

1979, Apr. 26 Photo. *Perf. 13½x14*

921	A189	5c multi	5	5
922	A189	10c multi	10	10
923	A189	25c multi	25	25
924	A189	50c multi	50	50
925	A189	90c multi	90	90
		Nos. 921-925 (5)	1.80	1.80

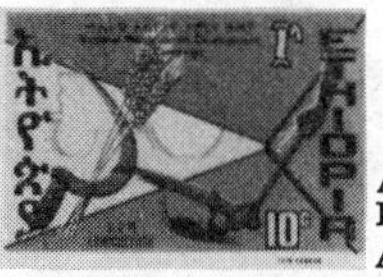

Agricultural Development
A190

Revolutionary Development Campaign: 15c, Industry. 25c, Transportation and communication. 60c, Education and health. 70c, Commerce.

1979, July 3 Litho. *Perf. 12x12½*

926	A190	10c multi	10	10
927	A190	15c multi	15	15
928	A190	25c multi	25	25
929	A190	60c multi	60	60
930	A190	70c multi	70	70
		Nos. 926-930 (5)	1.80	1.80

IYC Emblem
A191

Designs: 15c, Adults leading children. 25c, Adult helping child. 60c, IYC emblem surrounded by children. 70c, Adult and children embracing.

Perf. 12x12½

1979, Aug. 16 Lithographed

931	A191	10c multi	10	10
932	A191	15c multi	15	15
933	A191	25c multi	25	25
934	A191	60c multi	60	60
935	A191	70c multi	70	70
		Nos. 931-935 (5)	1.80	1.80

International Year of the Child.

Guerrilla Fighters—A192

Designs: 15c, Soldiers. 25c, Map of Africa within cogwheel and star. 60c, Students with book and torch. 70c, Family, hammer and sickle emblem.

1979, Sept. 11 Photo. *Perf. 14*

936	A192	10c multi	10	10
937	A192	15c multi	15	15
938	A192	25c multi	25	25
939	A192	60c multi	60	60
940	A192	70c multi	70	70
		Nos. 936-940 (5)	1.80	1.80

Fifth anniversary of revolution.

Telephone Receiver
A193

Telecom Emblem and: 5c, Symbolic waves. 35c, Satellite beaming to earth. 45c, Dish antenna. 65c, Television cameraman.

1979, Sept. Photo. *Perf. 11½*

941	A193	5c multi	5	5
942	A193	30c multi	30	30
943	A193	35c multi	35	35
944	A193	45c multi	45	45
945	A193	65c multi	65	65
		Nos. 941-945 (5)	1.80	1.80

3rd World Telecommunications Exhibition, Geneva, Sept. 20–26.

Incense Container—A194

1979, Nov. 15 Litho. *Perf. 15*

946	A194	5c *shown*	5	5
947	A194	10c *Vase*	10	10
948	A194	25c *Earthenware cover*	25	25
949	A194	60c *Milk container*	60	60
950	A194	80c *Storage container*	80	80
		Nos. 946-950 (5)	1.80	1.80

Wooden Grain Bowl
A195

Lappet-faced Vulture
A196

1980, Jan. Litho. *Perf. 13½×13*

Multicolored

951	A195	5c *shown*	5	5
952	A195	30c *Chair, stool*	30	30
953	A195	35c *Mortar, pestle*	35	35
954	A195	45c *Buckets*	45	45
955	A195	65c *Storage jars*	65	65
		Nos. 951-955 (5)	1.80	1.80

1980, Feb. 12 *Perf. 13½×14*

Birds of Prey: 15c, Long-crested hawk eagle. 25c, Secretary bird. 60c, Abyssinian long-eared owl. 70c, Lanner falcon.

956	A196	10c multi	10	10
957	A196	15c multi	15	15
958	A196	25c multi	25	25
959	A196	60c multi	60	60
960	A196	70c multi	70	70
		Nos. 956-960 (5)	1.80	1.80

Fight Against Cigarette Smoking
A197

1980, Apr. 7 Photo. *Perf. 13x13½*

961	A197	20c *shown*	20	20
962	A197	60c *Cigarette*	60	60
963	A197	1b *Respiratory system*	1.00	1.00

"110" and Lenin House Museum
A198

110th Birthday of Lenin (Paintings): 15c, In hiding. 20c, As a young man. 40c, Returning to Russia. $1, Speaking on the Goelro Plan.

1980, Apr. 22 Litho. *Perf. 12×12½*

964	A198	5c multi	5	5
965	A198	15c multi	15	15
966	A198	20c multi	20	20
967	A198	40c multi	40	40
968	A198	1b multi	1.00	1.00
		Nos. 964-968 (5)	1.80	1.80

Grévy's Zebras—A199

1980, June 10 Litho. *Perf. 12½x12*

969	A199	10c *shown*	10	10
970	A199	15c *Gazelles*	15	15
971	A199	25c *Wild hunting dogs*	25	25
972	A199	60c *Swayne's hartebeests*	60	60
973	A199	70c *Cheetahs*	70	70
		Nos. 969-973 (5)	1.80	1.80

Runner, Moscow '80 Emblem—A200

1980, July 19 **Photo.** ***Perf. 11½×12***

974	A200	30c *shown*	30	30
975	A200	70c *Gymnast*	70	70
976	A200	80c *Boxing*	80	80

22nd Summer Olympic Games, Moscow, July 19-Aug.3.

Taking off Blindfold—A201

1980, Sept. 11 **Photo.** ***Perf. 14x13½***

977	A201	30c *shown*	30	30
978	A201	40c *Revolutionary*	40	40
979	A201	50c *Woman breaking chain*	50	50
980	A201	70c *Russian and Ethiopian flags*	70	70

6th anniversary of revolution.

Bamboo Food Basket—A202

1980, Oct. 23 **Litho.** ***Perf. 14***

981	A202	5c *shown*	5	5
982	A202	15c *Hand basket*	15	15
983	A202	25c *Stool*	25	25
984	A202	35c *Fruit basket*	35	35
985	A202	1b *Lamp shade*	1.00	1.00
		Nos. 981-985 (5)	1.80	1.80

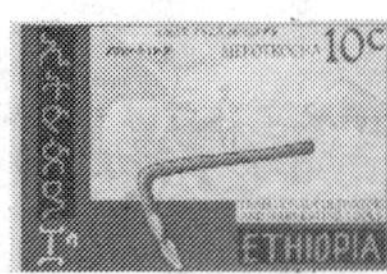

Mekotkocha (Used in Weeding)—A203

Traditional Harvesting Tools: 15c, Layda (grain separater). 40c, Mensh (fork). 45c, Medekdekia (soil turner). 70c, Plow and yoke.

1980, Dec. 18 **Litho.** ***Perf. 12½x12***

986	A203	10c multi	10	10
987	A203	15c multi	15	15
988	A203	40c multi	40	40
989	A203	45c multi	45	45
990	A203	70c multi	70	70
		Nos. 986-990 (5)	1.80	1.80

Baro River Bridge Opening—A204

1981, Feb. 28 **Photo.** ***Perf.13½ x 13***

991	A204	15c *Canoes and ferry*	15	15
992	A204	65c *Bridge construction*	65	65
993	A204	1b *shown*	1.00	1.00

Simion National Park—A205

World Heritage Year: 5c, Wawel Castle, Poland. 15c, Quito Cathedral, Ecuador. 20c, Old Slave Quarters, Goree Island, Senegal. 30c, Mesa Verde Indian village, U.S. $1, L'Anse aux Meadows excavation, Canada.

1981, Mar. 10 Photo. ***Perf. 11x11½, 11½x11***

994	A205	5c multi	5	5
995	A205	15c multi	15	15
996	A205	20c multi	20	20
997	A205	30c multi	30	30
998	A205	80c multi	80	80
999	A205	1b multi	1.00	1.00

1981, June 16 **Photo.**

Designs: 10c, Biet Medhami Alem Church, Ethiopia. 15c, Nahenni National Park, Canada. 20c, Yellowstone River Lower Falls, U.S. 30c, Aachen Cathedral, Germany. 80c, Kicker Rock, San Cristobal Island, Ecuador. 1b, The Lizak corridor, Holy Cross Chapel, Cracow, Poland (vert.).

1000	A205	10c multi	10	10
1001	A205	15c multi	15	15
1002	A205	20c multi	20	20
1003	A205	30c multi	30	30
1004	A205	80c multi	80	80
1005	A205	1b multi	1.00	1.00
		Nos. 994-1005 (12)	5.05	5.05

Ancient Drinking Vessel A206

1981, May 5 **Litho.** ***Perf. 12½x12***

1006	A206	20c shown	20	20
1007	A206	25c Spice container	25	25
1008	A206	35c Jug	35	35
1009	A206	40c Cooking pot holder	40	40
1010	A206	60c Animal figurine	60	60
		Nos. 1006-1010 (5)	1.80	1.80

Intl. Year of the Disabled A207

7th Anniv. of Revolution A208

1981, July 16 **Photo.** ***Perf. 11½x12***

1011	A207	5c Prostheses	5	5
1012	A207	15c Boys writing	15	15
1013	A207	20c Activities	20	20
1014	A207	40c Knitting	40	40
1015	A207	1b Weaving	1.00	1.00
		Nos. 1011-1015 (5)	1.80	1.80

1981, Sept. 10 ***Perf. 14***

1016	A208	20c Children's Center	20	20
1017	A208	60c Heroes' Center	60	60
1018	A208	1b Serto Ader (state newspaper)	1.00	1.00

World Food Day—A209

1981, Oct. 15 **Litho.** ***Perf. 13½x12½***

1019	A209	5c Wheat airlift	5	5
1020	A209	15c Plowing	15	15
1021	A209	20c Malnutrition	20	20
1022	A209	40c Agriculture education	40	40
1023	A209	1b Cattle, corn	1.00	1.00
		Nos. 1019-1023 (5)	1.80	1.80

Ancient Bronze Type of 1978

1981, Dec. 15 **Litho.** ***Perf. 14x13½***

1024	A180	15c Pitcher	15	15
1025	A180	45c Tsenatsil (musical instrument)	45	45
1026	A180	50c Pitcher, diff.	50	50
1027	A180	70c Pot	70	70

Horn Artifacts—A210

1982, Feb. 18 **Photo.** ***Perf. 12x12½***

1028	A210	10c Tobacco containers	10	10
1029	A210	15c Cup	15	15
1030	A210	40c Container, diff.	40	40
1031	A210	45c Goblet	45	45
1032	A210	70c Spoons	70	70
		Nos. 1028-1032 (5)	9.05	1.80

Coffee Cultivation—A211

1982, Apr. 20 **Photo.** ***Perf 13½***

1033	A211	5c Plants	5	5
1034	A211	15c Bushes	15	15
1035	A211	25c Mature bushes	25	25
1036	A211	35c Picking beans	35	35
1037	A211	1b Drinking coffee	1.00	1.00
		Nos. 1033-1037 (5)	1.80	1.80

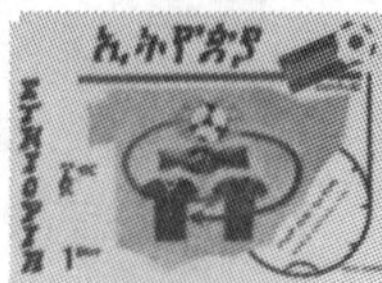

1982 World Cup—A212

1982, June 10 **Litho.** ***Perf. 13½x12½***

1038	A212	5c multi	5	5
1039	A212	15c multi	15	15
1040	A212	20c multi	20	20
1041	A212	40c multi	40	40
1042	A212	1b multi	1.00	1.00
		Nos. 1038-1042 (5)	1.80	1.80

TB Bacillus Centenary A213

8th Anniv. of Revolution A214

1982, July 12 **Litho.** ***Perf. 13½x12½***

1043	A213	15c Cow	15	15
1044	A213	20c Magnifying glass	20	20
1045	A213	30c Koch, microscope	30	30
1046	A213	35c Koch	35	35
1047	A213	80c Man coughing	80	80
		Nos. 1043-1047 (5)	1.80	1.80

1982, Sept. 10 ***Perf. 12½x13½***

Designs: Symbols of justice.

1048	A214	80c multi	80	80
1049	A214	1b multi	1.00	1.00

World Standards Day—A215

1982, Oct. 14 **Litho.** ***Perf. 13½x12½***

1050	A215	5c Hand, foot, square	5	5
1051	A215	15c Scales	15	15
1052	A215	20c Rulers	20	20
1053	A215	40c Weights	40	40
1054	A215	1b Emblem	1.00	1.00
		Nos. 1050-1054 (5)	1.80	1.80

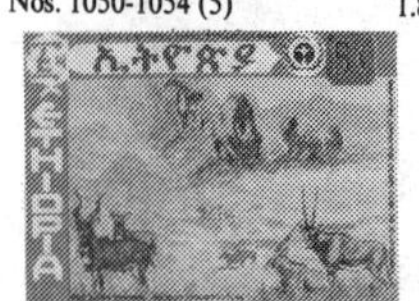

10th Anniv. of UN Conference on Human Environment—A216

1982, Dec. 13 **Litho.** ***Perf.***

1055	A216	5c Wildlife conservation	5	5
1056	A216	15c Environmental health and settlement	15	15
1057	A216	20c Forest protection	20	20
1058	A216	40c Natl. literacy campaign	40	40
1059	A216	1b Soil and water conservation	1.00	1.00
		Nos. 1055-1059 (5)	1.80	1.80

Cave of Sof Omar—A217

Various views.

1983, Feb. 10 **Photo.** ***Perf.***

1060	A217	5c multi	5	5
1061	A217	10c multi	10	10
1062	A217	15c multi	15	15
1063	A217	70c multi	70	70
1064	A217	80c multi	80	80
		Nos. 1060-1064 (5)	1.80	1.80

SEMI-POSTAL STAMPS.

Types of 1931, Overprinted in Red at Upper Left ✚

Perf. 12x12½, 12½x12.

1936, Feb. 25 **Unwmkd.**

B1	A27	1g lt grn	35	30
B2	A27	2g rose	35	30
B3	A25	4g blue	35	30
B4	A27	8g brown	50	50
B5	A25	1t purple	50	50
		Nos. B1-B5 (5)	2.05	1.90

Nos. B1–B5 were sold at twice face value, the surtax going to the Red Cross.

Nos. 289, 290 and 292 to 294 Surcharged in Blue

EXPOSITION 1949 +8c

Perf. 13x13½

1949, June 13 **Wmk. 282**

B6	A53	8c +8c dp org	1.25	1.25
B7	A53	12c +5c red	1.25	1.25
B8	A53	30c +15c org brn	2.50	2.50
B9	A53	70c +70c rose lil	16.50	16.50
B10	A53	$1 +80c dk car rose	20.00	20.00
		Nos. B6-B10 (5)	41.50	41.50

Type A39 Surcharged in Carmine

✚ + 10 ct.

Photogravure.

1950, May 8 *Perf. 11½* **Unwmkd.**

Various Designs

Inscribed "Croix Rouge"

B11	A39	5c +10c brt grn	1.00	1.00
B12	A39	10c +10c brt red	1.50	1.50
B13	A39	25c +10c brt bl	2.50	2.50
B14	A39	50c +10c dk yel brn	7.00	7.00
B15	A39	1t +10c brt vio	11.00	11.00
		Nos. B11-B15 (5)	23.00	23.00

The surtax was for the Red Cross.

Nos. B6-B10 Overprinted in Black

1951

Perf. 13x13½

1951, Nov. 17 **Wmk. 282**

B16	A53	8c +8c dp org	75	75
B17	A53	12c +5c red	75	75
B18	A53	30c +15c org brn	1.10	1.10
B19	A53	70c +70c rose lil	10.00	10.00
B20	A53	$1 +80c dk car rose	15.00	15.00
		Nos. B16-B20 (5)	27.60	27.60

Tree, Staff and Snake SP1

Engraved

1951, Nov. 25 *Perf. 13* **Wmk. 282**

Lower Panel in Red.

B21	SP1	5c +2c dp bl grn	30	15
B22	SP1	10c +3c org	50	25
B23	SP1	15c +3c dp bl	60	40
B24	SP1	30c +5c red	1.35	1.00
B25	SP1	50c +7c red brn	3.00	2.00
B26	SP1	$1 +10c pur	5.25	3.00
		Nos. B21-B26 (6)	11.00	6.80

The surtax was for anti-tuberculosis work.

1958, Dec. 1

Lower Panel in Red

B27	SP1	20c +3c dl pur	40	30
B28	SP1	25c +4c emer	50	35
B29	SP1	35c +5c rose vio	75	40
B30	SP1	60c +7c vio bl	1.50	80
B31	SP1	65c +7c vio	3.00	1.75
B32	SP1	80c +9c car rose	5.00	3.00
		Nos. B27-B32 (6)	11.15	6.60

The surtax was for anti-tuberculosis work.

Nos. B27-B32 were the only stamps on sale from Dec. 1-25, 1958.

Type of Regular Issue, 1955, Surcharged

RED CROSS CENTENARY 1859 1959 +2c

Engraved; Cross Typographed in Red

1959, May 30 **Wmk. 282**

B33	A62	15c +2c ol bis & rose red	60	60
B34	A62	20c +3c vio & emer	75	75
B35	A62	30c +5c rose car & grnsh bl	1.25	1.25

Issued to commemorate the centenary of the International Red Cross idea. The surtax was for the Red Cross.

Type A39 Surcharged

Silver Jubilee 1960 + 5 ct.

Perf. 11½

1960, May 7 **Photo.** **Unwmkd.**

B36	A39	5c +1c brt grn	35	25
B37	A39	10c +2c brt red	50	30
B38	A39	25c +3c brt bl	1.10	75
B39	A39	50c +4c dk yel brn	1.75	1.50
B40	A39	1t +5c brt vio	3.00	2.75
		Nos. B36-B40 (5)	6.70	5.55

25th anniversary of Ethiopian Red Cross.

Crippled Boy on Crutches SP2

Engraved

1963, July 23 *Perf. 13½* **Wmk. 282**

B41	SP2	10c +2c ultra	25	25
B42	SP2	15c +3c red	35	30
B43	SP2	50c +5c brt grn	1.10	1.00
B44	SP2	60c +5c red lil	1.75	1.25

The surtax was to aid the disabled.

AIR POST STAMPS.

Regular Issue of 1928 Handstamped in Violet, Red, Black or Green

Perf. 13½x14

1929, Aug. 17 **Unwmkd.**

C1	A22	⅛m org & lt bl	75	90
C2	A23	¼m ind & red org	75	90
C3	A22	½m gray grn & blk	75	90
C4	A23	1m dk car & blk	75	90
C5	A22	2m dk bl & blk	90	1.10
C6	A23	4m yel & ol	90	1.10
C7	A22	8m vio & ol	90	1.10
C8	A23	1t org brn & vio	1.10	1.10
C9	A22	2t grn & bis	1.50	1.75
C10	A23	3t choc & grn	1.50	1.75
		Nos. C1-C10 (10)	9.80	11.50

The overprint signifies "16 August 1929—Airplane of the Ethiopian Government." The stamps commemorate the arrival at Addis Ababa of the first air mail carried by an airplane of the Ethiopian Government. There are three types of the overprint: (I) 19½mm. high; "colon" at right of bottom word. (II) 20mm. high; same "colon." (III) 19½-mm. high; no "colon." Many errors exist.

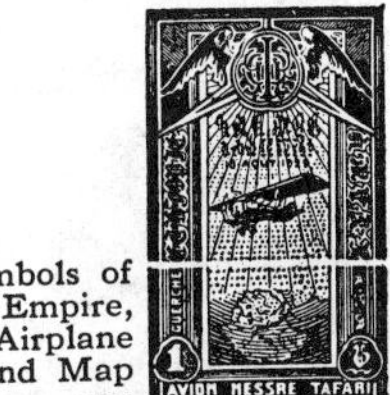

Symbols of Empire, Airplane and Map AP1

931, June 17 **Engr.** *Perf. 12½*

C11	AP1	1g org red	20	30
C12	AP1	2g ultra	25	35
C13	AP1	4g violet	30	50
C14	AP1	8g bl grn	70	1.00
C15	AP1	1t ol brn	1.75	1.25
C16	AP1	2t carmine	3.00	4.50
C17	AP1	3t yel grn	4.50	6.00
		Nos. C11-C17 (7)	10.70	13.90

Nos. C11 to C17 exist imperforate.

Reprints of C11 to C17 exist. Paper is thinner and gum whiter than the originals. Reprints usually sell at about one-tenth of above prices.

Nos. 250, 255 and 257 Surcharged in Black

a: 20 - 4 - 39

b: AERIENNE ETHIOPIENNE REPRISE POSTE 29/12/46 Eth. Doll. 0,50

Perf. 14x13½

1947, Mar. 20 **Unwmkd.**

C18	A33 (a)	12c on 4c lt bl grn & ind	30.00	30.00
C19	A33 (b)	50c on 25c dl grn & ind	30.00	30.00
a.		"26-12-46"	110.00	
C20	A33 (b)	$2 on 60c lil & ind	50.00	50.00
a.		"26-12-46"	110.00	

Resumption of airmail service, Dec. 29, 1946.

Franklin D. Roosevelt AP2

Design: $2, Haile Selassie.

Engraved and Photogravure.

1947, May 23 *Perf. 12½*

C21	AP2	$1 dk pur & sep	6.00	4.50
C22	AP2	$2 car & dp bl	8.50	7.50

Farmer Plowing AP3

Designs: 10c, 25c, Zoquala, extinct volcano. 30c, 35c, Tesissat Falls, Abai River. 65c, 70c, Amba Alaguie. $1, Sacala, source of Nile. $3, Gorgora and Dembia, Lake Tana. $5, Magdala, former capital. $10, Ras Dashan, mountain peak.

Engraved

1947–55 *Perf. 13x13½* **Wmk. 282**

C23	AP3	8c pur brn	25	12
C24	AP3	10c brt grn	25	12
C25	AP3	25c dl pur ('52)	40	20
C26	AP3	30c org yel	60	15
C27	AP3	35c bl ('55)	60	30
C28	AP3	65c pur ('51)	90	50
C29	AP3	70c red	1.50	55
C30	AP3	$1 dp bl	1.75	75
C31	AP3	$3 rose lil	7.50	4.50
C32	AP3	$5 red brn	12.50	6.25
C33	AP3	$10 rose vio	22.50	15.00
		Nos. C23-C33 (11)	48.75	28.44

U. P. U. Monument, Bern—AP4

1950, Apr. 3 *Perf. 12½* **Unwmkd.**

C34	AP4	5c grn & red	30	20
C35	AP4	15c dk sl grn & car	40	30
C36	AP4	25c org yel & grn	50	40
C37	AP4	50c car & ultra	1.25	1.00

Issued to commemorate the 75th anniversary of the formation of the Universal Postal Union.

Convair Plane over Mountains AP5

Engraved and Lithographed

1955, Dec. 30 *Perf. 12½* **Unwmkd.**

Center Multicolored

C38	AP5	10c gray grn	50	30
C39	AP5	15c carmine	60	35
C40	AP5	20c violet	85	50

10th anniversary of Ethiopian Airlines.

Promulgating the Constitution AP6

Perf. 14x13½

1956, July 16 **Engr.** **Wmk. 282**

C41	AP6	10c redsh brn & ultra	35	25

C42	AP6	15c dk car rose & ol grn	50	30
C43	AP6	20c bl & org red	75	50
C44	AP6	25c pur & grn	85	55
C45	AP6	30c dk grn & red brn	1.25	85
		Nos. C41-C45 (5)	3.70	2.45

25th anniversary of the constitution.

Aksum
AP7

Ancient Capitals: 10c, Lalibela. 15c, Gondar. 20c, Mekele. 25c, Ankober.

1957, Feb. 7 ***Perf. 14***

Centers in Green.

C46	AP7	5c red brn	50	25
C47	AP7	10c rose car	50	25
C48	AP7	15c red org	60	30
C49	AP7	20c ultra	85	45
C50	AP7	25c claret	1.25	65
		Nos. C46-C50 (5)	3.70	1.90

Amharic "A"
AP8

Designs: Various Amharic characters and views of Addis Ababa. The characters, arranged by values, spell Addis Ababa.

1957, Feb. 14 **Engraved**

Amharic Letters in Scarlet.

C51	AP8	5c ultra, *sal pink*	15	10
C52	AP8	10c ol grn, *pink*	25	20
C53	AP8	15c dl pur, *yel*	35	20
C54	AP8	20c grn, *buff*	50	30
C55	AP8	25c plum, *pale bl*	80	35
C56	AP8	30c red, *pale grn*	1.00	40
		Nos. C51-C56 (6)	3.05	1.55

70th anniversary of Addis Ababa.

Map, Rock Church at Lalibela and Obelisk—AP9

1958, April 15 ***Perf. 13½*** **Wmk. 282**

C57	AP9	10c green	35	15
C58	AP9	20c rose red	50	30
C59	AP9	30c brt bl	85	35

Issued to commemorate the conference of Independent African States, Accra, April 15–22.

Map of Africa and U. N. Emblem
AP10

1958, Dec. 29 ***Perf. 13***

C60	AP10	5c emerald	25	8
C61	AP10	20c car rose	40	25
C62	AP10	25c ultra	50	40
C63	AP10	50c pale pur	1.00	55

Issued to commemorate the first session of the United Nations Economic Conference for Africa, opened in Addis Ababa Dec. 29.

Nos. C23–29 Overprinted

የአየር ፖስታ ፴ኛ ዓመት
30th Airmail Ann.
1929 - 1959

Perf. 13x13½

1959, Aug. 16 Engraved Wmk. 282

C64	AP3	8c pur brn	30	25
C65	AP3	10c brt grn	40	30
C66	AP3	25c dl pur	60	35
C67	AP3	30c org yel	65	50
C68	AP3	35c blue	85	55
C69	AP3	65c purple	1.25	85
C70	AP3	70c red	1.60	1.10
		Nos. C64-C70 (7)	5.65	3.90

30th anniversary of Ethiopian airmail service.

Ethiopian Soldier and Map of Congo
AP11

Globe with Map of Africa
AP12

Photogravure

1962, July 23 ***Perf. 11½*** **Unwmkd.**

Granite Paper

C71	AP11	15c org, bl, brn & grn	30	15
C72	AP11	50c pur, bl, brn & grn	70	45
C73	AP11	60c red, bl, brn & grn	1.00	50

Issued to commemorate the second anniversary of the Ethiopian contingent of the United Nations forces in the Congo and in honor of the 70th birthday of Emperor Haile Selassie.

1963, May 22 **Granite Paper**

C74	AP12	10c mag & blk	30	15
C75	AP12	40c emer & BK	70	35
C76	AP12	60c bl & blk	1.00	50

Issued to commemorate the conference of African heads of state for African Unity, Addis Ababa.

Bird Type of Regular Issue, 1962

Birds: 10c, Black-headed forest oriole. 15c, Broad-tailed paradise whydah (vert.). 20c, Lammergeier (vert.). 50c, White-checked touraco. 80c, Purple indigo bird.

1963, Sept. 12 ***Perf. 11½***

Granite Paper

C77	A74	10c multi	20	12
C78	A74	15c multi	25	18
C79	A74	20c bl, blk & ocher	45	25
C80	A74	50c lem & multi	75	45
C81	A74	80c ultra, blk & brn	1.50	75
		Nos. C77-C81 (5)	3.15	1.75

Swimming
AP13

Sport: 10c, Basketball (vert.). 15c, Javelin. 80c, Soccer game in stadium.

Perf. 14x13½

1964, Sept. 15 **Litho.** **Unwmkd.**

C82	AP13	5c multi	10	15
C83	AP13	10c multi	15	15
C84	AP13	15c multi	30	30
C85	AP13	80c multi	1.25	60

18th Olympic Games, Tokyo, Oct. 10–25.

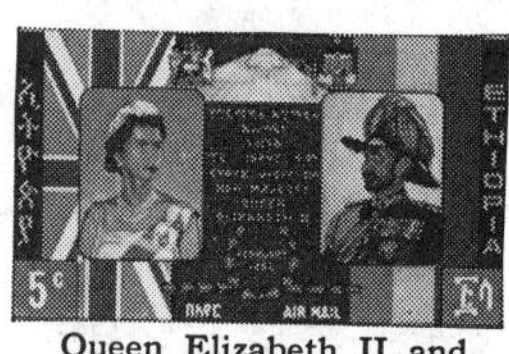

Queen Elizabeth II and Emperor Haile Selassie
AP14

1965, Feb. 1 **Photo.** ***Perf. 11½***

Granite Paper

C86	AP14	5c multi	12	5
C87	AP14	35c multi	50	30
C88	AP14	60c multi	85	50

Issued to commemorate the visit of Queen Elizabeth II of Great Britain, Feb. 1–8.

Koka Dam and Power Plant
AP15

Designs: 15c, Sugar cane field. 50c, Blue Nile bridge. 60c, Gondar castles. 80c, Coffee tree. $1, Cattle at water hole. $3, Camels at well. $5, Ethiopian Air Lines jet plane.

1965, July 19 ***Perf. 11½*** **Unwmkd.**

Granite Paper

Portrait in Black

C89	AP15	15c vio brn & buff	20	15
C90	AP15	40c vio bl & lt bl	50	30
C91	AP15	50c grn & lt bl	60	35
C92	AP15	60c cl & yel	75	45
C93	AP15	80c grn, yel & red	90	50
C94	AP15	$1 brn & lt bl	1.10	60
C95	AP15	$3 cl & pink	3.50	1.65
C96	AP15	$5 ultra & lt bl	7.50	3.00
		Nos. C89-C96 (8)	15.05	7.00

Bird Type of Regular Issue, 1962

Birds: 10c, White-collared kingfisher. 15c, Blue-breasted bee-eater. 25c, African paradise flycatcher. 40c, Village weaver. 60c, White-collared pigeon.

1966, Feb. 15 **Photo.** ***Perf. 11½***

Granite Paper

C97	A74	10c dl yel & multi	20	15
C98	A74	15c lt bl & multi	30	15
C99	A74	25c gray & multi	65	35
C100	A74	40c pink & multi	1.25	50
C101	A74	60c multi	1.50	75
		Nos. C97-C101 (5)	3.90	1.90

Black Rhinoceros—AP16

Animals: 10c, Leopard. 20c, Black-and-white colobus (monkey). 30c, Mountain nyala. 60c, Nubian ibex.

1966, June 20 **Litho.** ***Perf. 13***

C102	AP16	5c dp grn, blk & gray	15	7
C103	AP16	10c grn, blk & ocher	20	10
C104	AP16	20c cit, blk & grn	40	15
C105	AP16	30c yel grn, blk & ocher	60	18
C106	AP16	60c yel grn, blk & dk brn	1.25	30
		Nos. C102-C106 (5)	2.60	80

Bird Type of Regular Issue, 1962

Birds: 10c, Blue-winged goose (vert.). 15c, Yellow-billed duck. 20c, Wattled ibis. 25c, Striped swallow. 40c, Black-winged lovebird (vert.).

1967, Sept. 29 **Photo.** ***Perf. 11½***

Granite Paper

C107	A74	10c lt ultra & multi	20	15
C108	A74	15c grn & multi	25	15
C109	A74	20c yel & multi	30	15
C110	A74	25c sal & multi	50	15
C111	A74	40c pink & multi	1.00	40
		Nos. C107-C111 (5)	2.25	1.00

SPECIAL DELIVERY STAMPS.

Motorcycle Messenger
SD1

Addis Ababa Post Office
SD2

Engraved.

1947, Apr. 24 ***Perf. 13*** **Unwmkd.**

E1	SD1	30c org brn	60	50
E2	SD2	50c blue	2.00	1.50

1954–62 **Wmk. 282**

E3	SD1	30c org brn ('62)	1.00	75
E4	SD2	50c blue	90	50

POSTAGE DUE STAMPS.

Menelik II
D1

Perf. 14x13½

1896, June 10 **Unwmkd.**

Black Overprint.

J1	D1	¼g green	1.00	
J2	D1	½g red	1.00	
J3	D1	4g lil brn	60	
a.		Without overprint	60	
J4	D1	8g violet	60	
a.		Without overprint	60	

Red Overprint.

J5	D1	1g blue	1.00	
J6	D1	2g dk brn	1.00	
J7	D1	16g black	60	
a.		Without overprint	60	
		Nos. J1-J7 (7)	5.80	

Regular Issue of 1894
Handstamped in Various Colors:

T T

a *b*

1905, Jan. 1

J8	A1 (a)	¼g green	10.00	10.00
J9	A1 (a)	½g red	10.00	10.00

J10	A1 (a)	1g blue	10.00	10.00
J11	A1 (a)	2g dk brn	10.00	10.00
J12	A1 (a)	4g lil brn	10.00	10.00
J13	A1 (a)	8g violet	14.00	14.00
J14	A1 (a)	16g black	30.00	30.00
J15	A1 (b)	¼g green	10.00	10.00
J16	A1 (b)	½g red	10.00	10.00
J17	A1 (b)	1g blue	10.00	10.00
J18	A1 (b)	2g dk brn	10.00	10.00
J19	A2 (b)	4g lil brn	10.00	10.00
J20	A2 (b)	8g violet	14.00	14.00
J21	A2 (b)	16g black	30.00	30.00
		Nos. J8-J21 (14)	188.00	188.00

Excellent forgeries of Nos. J8–J42 exist.

Regular Issue of 1894 Handstamped in Blue or Violet

TAXE A PERCEVOIR T

1906, July 1

J22	A1	¼g green	7.50	7.50
J23	A1	½g red	7.50	7.50
J24	A1	1g blue	7.50	7.50
J25	A1	2g dk brn	7.50	7.50
J26	A2	4g lil brn	7.50	7.50
J27	A2	8g violet	11.50	11.50
J28	A2	16g black	17.50	17.50
		Nos. J22-J28 (7)	66.50	66.50

Nos. J22, J24, J25 and J26 exist with inverted overprint, also No. J22 with double overprint.

With Additional Surcharge of Value Handstamped as on Regular Issue of 1907.

1907, July 1

J29	A1(e)	¼ on ¼g grn	12.50	12.50
J30	A1(e)	½ on ½g red	12.50	12.50
J31	A1(f)	1 on 1g bl	12.50	12.50
J32	A1(f)	2 on 2g dk brn	12.50	12.50
J33	A2(f)	4 on 4g lil brn	12.50	12.50
J34	A2(f)	8 on 8g vio	12.50	12.50
J35	A2(f)	16 on 16g blk	20.00	20.00
		Nos. J29-J35 (7)	95.00	95.00

Nos. J30, J31, J32 and J33 exist with inverted surcharge.

Regular Issue of 1894 Handstamped in Black

1908, Dec. 1

J36	A1	¼g green	85	60
J37	A1	½g red	85	60
J38	A1	1g blue	85	60
J39	A1	2g dk brn	1.00	70
J40	A2	4g lil brn	1.40	1.25
J41	A2	8g violet	3.25	3.50
J42	A2	16g black	10.00	10.00
		Nos. J36-J42 (7)	18.20	17.25

Nos. J36 to J42 exist with inverted overprint and Nos. J36, J37, J38 and J40 with double overprint.

Same Handstamp on Regular Issue of 1909.

1912, Dec. 1 *Perf. 11½*

J43	A3	¼g bl grn	75	55
J44	A3	½g rose	1.25	75
J45	A3	1g grn & org	2.75	2.00
J46	A4	2g blue	3.25	2.75
J47	A4	4g grn & car	4.75	3.25
J48	A5	8g ver & dp grn	6.75	5.50
J49	A5	16g ver & car	16.50	13.50
		Nos. J43-J49 (7)	36.00	28.30

Nos. J43 to J49, all exist with inverted overprint.

Same Handstamp on Regular Issue of 1919 in Blue Black

1925–27 *Perf. 11½*

J50	A6	⅛g vio & brn	*20.00*	*20.00*
J51	A6	¼g bl grn & db	*20.00*	*20.00*
J52	A6	½g scar & ol grn	*20.00*	*20.00*
J53	A9	1g rose lil & gray grn	*2.50*	*2.50*
J54	A9	2g dp ultra & fawn	*20.00*	*20.00*

Same Handstamp on Nos. 110 and 112.

1930 (?)

J55	A3(i)	1g grn & org	*20.00*	*20.00*
J56	A4(j)	2g blue	*20.00*	*20.00*

D2

Lithographed.

1951, Apr. 2 *Perf. 11½* **Unwmkd.**

J57	D2	1c emerald	20	10
J58	D2	5c rose red	25	15
J59	D2	10c violet	40	20
J60	D2	20c ocher	60	55
J61	D2	50c brt ultra	1.25	1.10
J62	D2	$1 rose lil	2.25	1.75
		Nos. J57-J62 (6)	4.95	3.85

OCCUPATION STAMPS.

Issued under Italian Occupation.

100 Centesimi = 1 Lira

Victor Emmanuel III

OS1

Emperor Victor Emmanuel

OS2

Wmk. 140

1936 Wmkd. Crowns. (140) *Perf. 14*

N1	OS1	10c org brn	30	30
N2	OS1	20c purple	60	60
N3	OS2	25c dk grn	35	35
N4	OS2	30c dk brn	35	35
N5	OS2	50c rose car	35	35
N6	OS1	75c dp org	65	65
N7	OS1	1.25 l dp bl	1.25	1.25
		Nos. N1-N7 (7)	3.85	3.85

For later issues see Italian East Africa.

The first price column gives the catalogue value of an unused stamp, the second that of a used stamp.

FAR EASTERN REPUBLIC

(fär ēs'tẽrn rē·pŭb'lĭk)

LOCATION—In Siberia east of Lake Baikal.

GOVT.—Republic.

AREA—900,745 sq. mi.

POP.—1,560,000 (approx. 1920)

CAPITAL—Chita.

A short-lived independent government was established here in 1920.

100 Kopecks = 1 Ruble

Vladivostok Issue.

Russian Stamps Surcharged or Overprinted:

DBP

a

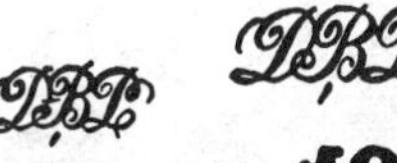

b c

On Stamps of 1909–17.

Perf. 14, 14½x15, 13½.

1920 **Unwmkd.**

2	A14(a)	2k green	12.50	17.50
3	A14(a)	3k red	10.00	12.50
4	A11(b)	3k on 35k red brn & grn	12.50	17.50
5	A15(a)	4k carmine	10.00	12.50
6	A11(b)	4k on 70k brn & org	8.00	8.00
8	A11(b)	7k on 15k red brn & bl	3.50	5.00
a.		Inverted surcharge	45.00	
b.		Pair, one overprinted "DBP" only		
9	A15(a)	10k dk bl	75.00	100.00
a.		Overprint on back	135.00	
10	A12(c)	10k on 3½r mar & lt grn	27.50	32.50
11	A11(a)	14k bl & rose	27.50	32.50
12	A11(a)	15k red brn & bl	12.50	15.00
13	A8(a)	20k bl & car	80.00	100.00
14	A11(b)	20k on 14k bl & rose	8.00	9.00
a.		Surch. on back	55.00	
15	A11(a)	25k grn & vio	16.00	20.00
16	A11(a)	35k red brn & grn	45.00	55.00
17	A8(a)	50k brn vio & grn	15.00	20.00
18	A9(a)	1r pale brn, dk brn & org	350.00	450.00

On Stamps of 1917.

Imperf.

21	A14(a)	1k orange	11.00	12.50
22	A14(a)	2k gray grn	5.00	5.00
23	A14(a)	3k red	15.00	17.50
25	A11(b)	7k on 15k red brn & dp bl	5.00	5.00
a.		Pair, one without surcharge		
b.		Pair, one overprinted "DBP" only		
26	A12(c)	10k on 3½r mar & lt grn	15.00	17.50
27	A9(a)	1r pale brn, brn & red org	17.50	20.00

On Stamps of Siberia 1919.

Perf. 14, 14½x15.

30	A14(a)	35k on 2k grn	6.00	7.50
a.		"DBP" on back	40.00	80.00

Imperf.

31	A14(a)	35k on 2k grn	14.00	15.00
32	A14(a)	70k on 1k org	7.50	9.00

Counterfeit surcharges and overprints abound.

Postal Savings Stamps Surcharged for Postal Use.

A1

Wmk. 171

Wmkd. Diamonds. (171)

Perf. 14½x15.

35	A1(b)	1k on 5k grn, *buff*	15.00	20.00
36	A1(b)	2k on 10k brn, *buff*	20.00	25.00

The letters on these stamps resembling "DBP," are the Russian initials of "Dalni Vostochini Respoublika" (Far Eastern Republic).

Chita Issue.

A2

A2a

Typographed.

1921 *Imperf.* **Unwmkd.**

38	A2	2k gray grn	1.50	1.75
39	A2a	4k rose	1.50	1.75
40	A2	5k claret	2.00	3.00
41	A2a	10k blue	3.00	3.50

Blagoveshchensk Issue.

A3

1921 Lithographed *Imperf.*

42	A3	2r red	5.00	6.00
43	A3	3r dk grn	5.00	6.00
44	A3	5r dk bl	5.00	6.00
a.		Tête bêche pair	50.00	60.00
45	A3	15r dk brn	5.00	6.00
46	A3	30r dk vio	5.00	6.00
a.		Tête bêche pair	50.00	60.00
		Nos. 42-46 (5)	25.00	30.00

Remainders of Nos. 42–46 were canceled in colored crayon or by typographed bars. These sell for half of foregoing prices.

Chita Issue.

A4

A5

1922 Lithographed. *Imperf.*

49	A4	1k orange	1.00	1.75
50	A4	3k dl red	60	1.00
51	A5	4k dp rose & buff	60	1.00
52	A4	5k org brn	1.50	1.00
53	A4	7k lt bl	1.50	3.00
a.		Perf. 11½	1.50	3.00
b.		Rouletted 9	2.50	4.50
c.		Perf. 11½x rouletted	5.00	7.00
54	A5	10k dk bl & red	75	1.50
55	A4	15k dl rose	1.00	1.75
56	A5	20k bl & red	1.00	1.75
57	A5	30k grn & red org	1.25	2.25
58	A5	50k blk & red org	2.00	3.50
		Nos. 49-58 (10)	11.20	18.50

The 4k exists with "4" omitted.

Vladivostok Issue.

Stamps of 1921 Overprinted in Red

1917
7-XI
1922

1922 *Imperf.*

62	A2	2k gray grn	12.50	17.50
a.		Inverted overprint	42.50	
63	A2a	4k rose	12.50	17.50
a.		Inverted overprint	75.00	
b.		Double overprint	60.00	
64	A2	5k claret	15.00	22.50
a.		Inverted overprint	75.00	
b.		Double overprint	60.00	
65	A2a	10k blue	15.00	22.50
a.		Inverted overprint	150.00	

Issued to commemorate the fifth anniversary of the Russian revolution of November, 1917.

Once in the setting the figures "22" of 1922 have the bottom stroke curved instead of straight. Price $15 apiece.

Vladivostok Issue.

Russian Stamps of 1922-23 Surcharged in Black or Red

Д. В.
коп. 1 коп.
ЗОЛОТОМ

1923 *Imperf.*

66	A50	1k on 100r red	60	1.50
a.		Invtd. surch.	55.00	
67	A50	2k on 70r vio	60	1.50
68	A49	5k on 10r bl (R)	60	1.50
69	A50	10k on 50r brn	1.00	2.50
a.		Invtd. surch.	37.50	

Perf. 14½x15.

70	A50	1k on 100r red	1.00	2.50
		Nos. 66-70 (5)	3.80	9.50

OCCUPATION STAMPS.

Issued under Occupation of General Semenov. Chita Issue.

Russian Stamps of 1909-12 Surcharged:

P. 1 P.
a

2p.50к. P. 5 P.
b *c*

1920 *Perf. 14, 14x15½* **Unwmkd.**

N1	A15 (a)	1r on 4k car	30.00	40.00
N2	A8 (b)	2r50k on 20k bl & car	30.00	40.00
N3	A14 (c)	5r on 5k cl	17.50	27.50
a.		Double surch.	35.00	
N4	A11 (a)	10r on 70k brn & org	30.00	40.00

FAROE ISLANDS

(The Faroes)

LOCATION—North Atlantic Ocean.
GOVT.—Self-governing part of Kingdom of Denmark.
AREA—540 sq. mi.
POP.—40,000 (1975).
CAPITAL—Thorshavn.

100 Ore = 1 Krone

Denmark No. 97 Handstamp Surcharged

2
ØRE

1919, Jan. Typo. *Perf. 14x14½*

1	A16	2ö on 5ö grn	1,200.	525.00

Counterfeits of surcharge exist.

Denmark No. 88a, the bisect, was used with Denmark No. 97 in Faroe Islands Jan. 3–23, 1919.

Denmark Nos. 220, 224, 238A, 224C Surcharged in Blue or Black

50 ≡ 50
b

20 |||| 20
c

20
d

1940–41 Engraved *Perf. 13*

2	A32 (b)	20(ö) on 1ö gray blk (Bl) ('41)	95.00	110.00
3	A32 (c)	20(ö) on 5ö rose lake (Bl) ('41)	70.00	35.00
4	A30 (d)	20(ö) on 15ö dp red (Bk)	90.00	20.00
5	A32 (b)	50(ö) on 5ö rose lake (Bk)	350.00	100.00
6	A32 (b)	60(ö) on 6ö org (Bk)	200.00	225.00
		Nos. 2-6 (5)	805.00	490.00

Nos. 2–6 were issued during British administration.

Map of Islands, 1673
A1

Map of North Atlantic, 1573
A2

West Coast, Sandoy
A3

Vidoy and Svinoy, by Eyvindur Mohr
A4

Designs: 50ö, 90ö, like 5ö. 60ö, 80ö, 120ö, like 10ö. 200ö, like 70ö. 250ö, 300ö, View of Streymoy and Vagar. 450ö, Houses, Nes, by Ruth Smith. 500ö, View of Hvitanes and Skalafjordur, by S. Joensen-Mikines.

Perf. 13

1975, Jan. 30 Engr. **Unwmkd.**

7	A1	5ö sepia	3	3
8	A2	10ö emer & dk bl	4	4
9	A1	50ö grysh grn	18	18
10	A2	60ö brn & dk bl	5.00	5.00
11	A3	70ö vio bl & sl grn	5.00	5.00
12	A2	80ö ocher & dk bl	30	30
13	A1	90ö red brn	5.00	5.00
14	A2	120ö brt bl & dk bl	45	45
15	A3	200ö vio bl & sl grn	70	70
16	A3	250ö multi	90	90
17	A3	300ö multi	10.00	7.00

Photo. *Perf. 12½x13*

18	A4	350ö multi	1.25	1.25
19	A4	450ö multi	1.60	1.60
20	A4	500ö multi	1.75	1.75
		Nos. 7-20 (14)	32.20	29.20

Faroe Boat
A5

Faroe Flag
A6

Faroe Mailman
A7

Engr.; Litho. (A6)

1976, Apr. 1 *Perf. 12½x13, 12 (A6)*

21	A5	125ö cop red	4.50	4.00
22	A6	160ö multi	60	60
23	A7	800ö olive	2.50	2.50

Faroe Islands independent Postal service, Apr. 1, 1976.

Motor Fishing Boat
A8

Faroese Fishing Vessels and Map of Islands: 125ö, Inland fishing cutter. 160ö, Modern seine fishing vessel. 600ö, Deep-sea fishing trawler.

1977, Apr. 28 Photo. *Perf. 14½x14*

24	A8	100ö grn & blk	9.00	8.00
25	A8	125ö car & blk	3.00	3.00
26	A8	160ö bl & blk	60	60
27	A8	600ö brn & blk	3.00	3.00

Common Snipe
A9

Birds: 180ö, Oystercatcher. 250ö, Whimbrel.

Photogravure & Engraved

1977, Sept. 29 *Perf. 14½x14*

28	A9	70ö multi	70	70
29	A9	180ö multi	90	90
30	A9	250ö multi	1.20	1.20

See "Special Notices" at the front of this volume for data on the listing methods of this Catalogue, abbreviations, condition, prices and examination.

North Coast, Puffins
A10

FØROYAR 130

Mykines Village
A11

Mykines Island: 140ö, Tilled fields and coast. 150ö, Aerial view. 180ö, Map.

Perf. 13x13½, 13½x13

1978, Jan. 26 Photogravure

Size: 21x28mm., 28x21mm.

31	A10	100ö multi	35	3
32	A11	130ö multi	45	4
33	A11	140ö multi	1.75	1.7
34	A10	150ö multi	52	5

Size: 37x26mm. *Perf. 14½x14*

35	A11	180ö multi	65	6
		Nos. 31-35 (5)	3.72	3.7

Gannets
A12

Old Library
A13

Sea Birds: 180ö, Puffins. 400ö, Guillemots.

Lithographed and Engraved

1978, Apr. 13 *Perf. 12x12½*

36	A12	140ö multi	2.25	2.25
37	A12	180ö multi	2.25	2.25
38	A12	400ö multi	1.40	1.40

1978, Dec. 7 *Perf. 13*

Design: 180ö, New Library.

39	A13	140ö gray grn & lt grn	2.00	2.00
40	A13	180ö brn & buff	1.00	75

Completion of New Library Building.

Girl Guide, Tent and Fire
A14

1978, Dec. 7 Photo. *Perf. 13½*

41	A14	140ö multi	2.50	2.50

Faroese Girl Guides, 50th anniversary.

Ram
A15

Lithographed and Engraved

1979, Mar. 19 *Perf. 12*

42	A15	25k multi	7.50	7.50

Europa Issue 1979

Denmark No. 88a

A16

Design: 180ö, Faroe Islands No. 1.

Lithographed and Engraved

1979, May 7 *Perf. 12½*

43	A16	140o yel & bl	2.50	2.50
44	A16	180o rose, grn & blk	2.50	2.50

Girl Wearing Festive Costume

A17

Children's Drawings and IYC Emblem: 150ö, Fisherman. 200ö, Two friends.

Lithographed and Engraved

1979, Oct. 1 *Perf. 12*

45	A17	110ö multi	45	45
46	A17	150ö multi	55	55
47	A17	200ö multi	75	75

International Year of the Child.

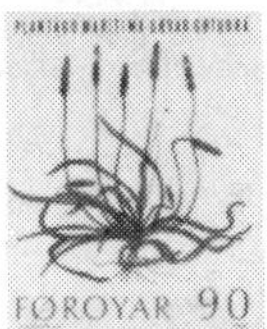

Sea Plantain—A18

1980, Mar. 17 **Photo.** *Perf. 12x11½*

48	A18	90ö *shown*	32	32
49	A18	110ö *Glacier buttercup*	38	38
50	A18	150ö *Purple saxifrage*	52	52
51	A18	200ö *Starry saxifrage*	68	68
52	A18	400ö *Lady's mantle*	1.35	1.35
		Nos. 48-52 (5)	3.25	3.25

Jakob Jakobsen (1864-1918), Linguist — A19

Coat of Arms, Virgin and Child, Gothic Pew Gable — A20

Europa Issue 1980

Design: 200ö, Vensel Ulrich Hammershaimb (1819-1909), theologian, linguist and folklorist.

1980, Oct. 6 **Engr.** *Perf. 11½*

53	A19	150ö dl grn	52	52
54	A19	200ö dl red brn	68	68

1980, Oct. 6 **Photo. & Engr.** *Perf. 13½*

Kirkjubour Pew Gables, 15th Century: 140ö, Norwegian coat of arms, John the Baptist. 150ö, Christ's head, St. Peter. 200ö, Hand in halo, Apostle Paul.

55	A20	110ö multi	38	38
56	A20	140ö multi	48	48
57	A20	150ö multi	52	52
58	A20	200ö multi	68	68

Fishing Boats, Old Torshavn—A21

Designs: Sketches of Old Torshavn by Ingalzur Reyni.

1981, Mar. 2 **Engraved**

59	A21	110ö dk grn	38	38
60	A21	140ö black	48	48
61	A21	150ö dk brn	52	52
62	A21	200ö dk bl	68	68

Europa Issue 1981

The Ring Dance—A22

Design: 200o, The garter dance.

1981, June 1 **Engr.** *Perf. 13x14*

63	A22	150o pale rose & grn	52	52
64	A22	200o pale yel grn & dk brn	68	68

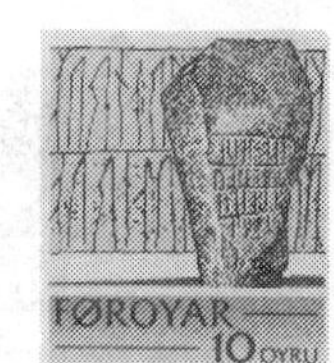

Rune Stones, 800-1000 AD—A23

Historic Writings: 1k, Folksong, 1846. 3k, Sheep Letter excerpt, 1298. 6k, Seal and text, 1533. 10k, Titlepage from Faeroae et Faeroa, by Lucas Jacobson Debes, library.

1981, Oct. 19 **Photo. & Engr.** *Perf. 11½*

65	A23	10o multi	4	4
69	A23	1k multi	34	34
72	A23	3k multi	1.05	1.05
75	A23	6k multi	2.10	2.10
78	A23	10k multi	3.40	3.40
		Nos. 65-80 (5)	6.93	6.93

Europa 1982—A24

1982, Mar. 15 **Engr.** *Perf. 13½*

81	A24	1.50k Viking North Atlantic routes	52	52
82	A24	2k Viking house foundation	70	70

View of Gjogv, by Ingalvur av Reyni—A25

1982, June 7 **Litho.** *Perf. 12½x13*

83	A25	180o shown	65	65
84	A25	220o Hvalvik	75	75
85	A25	250o Kvivik	90	90

Ballad of Harra Paetur and Elinborg—A26

Designs: Scenes from the medieval ballad of chivalry.

1982, Sept. 27 **Litho.**

86	A26	220o multi	75	75
87	A26	250o multi	90	90
88	A26	350o multi	1.20	1.20
89	A26	450o multi	1.60	1.60

Cargo Ships—A27

1983, Feb. 21 **Litho.** *Perf. 14x14½*

90	A27	220o Arcturus, 1856	75	75
91	A27	250o Laura, 1882	90	90
92	A27	700o Thyra, 1866	2.40	2.40

Chessmen, by Pol i Buo (1791-1857)—A28

1983, May 2 **Engr.** *Perf. 13 Vert.*

93	A28	250o King	90	90
94	A28	250o Queen	90	90
a.		Bklt. pane of 6 (3 each #93-94)	5.50	

Nos. 93-94 issued only in booklets.

FERNANDO PO

(fẽr·năn′dō pō′)

LOCATION—An island in the Gulf of Guinea off west Africa.

GOVT.—Province of Spain.

AREA—800 sq. mi.

POP.—62,612 (1960).

CAPITAL—Santa Isabel.

Together with the islands of Elobey, Annobon and Corisco, Fernando Po came under the administration of Spanish Guinea. Postage stamps of Spanish Guinea were used until 1960.

The provinces of Fernando Po and Rio Muni united Oct. 12, 1968, to form the Republic of Equatorial Guinea.

100 Centimos = 1 Escudo = 2.50 Pesetas
100 Centimos = 1 Peseta
1000 Milesimas = 100 Centavos = 1 Peso (1882)

Queen Isabella II A1 — King Alfonso XII A2

Typographed.

1868 *Perf. 14* **Unwmkd.**

1	A1	20c brown	425.00	150.00

Forgeries exist.

1879 **Centimos de Peseta.**

2	A2	5c green	42.50	7.50
3	A2	10c rose	42.50	7.50
4	A2	50c blue	55.00	7.50

1882-89 **Centavos de Peso.**

5	A2	1c green	12.00	3.00
6	A2	2c rose	18.00	5.00
7	A2	5c gray bl	37.50	6.75
8	A2	10c dk brn ('89)	52.50	5.50

Nos. 5–7 Handstamp Surcharged in Blue, Black or Violet

a

1884–95

9	A2	50c on 1c grn ('95)	55.00	12.00
11	A2	50c on 2c rose	24.00	4.50
12	A2	50c on 5c bl ('87)	57.50	14.00

Inverted and double surcharges exist.

King Alfonso XIII A4

1894–97 *Perf. 14*

13	A4	⅛c sl ('96)	20.00	2.75
14	A4	2c rose ('96)	15.00	1.85
15	A4	5c bl grn ('97)	15.00	1.85
16	A4	6c dk vio ('96)	13.00	2.25
17	A4	10c brn vio ('94)	100.00	25.00
18	A4	10c lake ('95)	25.00	5.00
19	A4	10c org brn ('96)	11.00	1.75
20	A4	12½c dk brn ('96)	12.00	2.25
21	A4	20c sl bl ('96)	12.00	2.25
22	A4	25c cl ('96)	20.00	2.25
		Nos. 13-22 (10)	243.00	47.20

Stamps of 1894–97 Handstamped in Blue, Black or Red

b *c*

Type "b" Surcharge

1896–98

23	A4	5c on 2c rose (Bl)	20.00	4.00
24	A4	5c on 10c brn vio (Bl)	60.00	10.00
25	A4	5c on 12½c brn (Bl)	15.00	3.75
a.		Black surcharge	15.00	3.75

Type "c" Surcharge

26	A4	5c on ⅛c sl (Bk)	9.50	4.50
27	A4	5c on 2c rose (Bl)	9.50	4.50
a.		Black surcharge	9.50	4.50
28	A4	5c on 5c grn (R)	55.00	12.00
29	A4	5c on 6c dk vio (R)	9.50	8.00
a.		Violet surcharge	11.00	10.00
30	A4	5c on 10c org brn (Bk)	67.50	15.00
31	A4	5c on 12½c brn (R)	16.50	6.00
32	A4	5c on 20c sl bl (R)	16.00	4.75
33	A4	5c on 25c cl (Bk)	16.00	6.00
a.		Blue surcharge	16.00	6.00

Type "a" Surcharge

1898–99

34	A4	50c on 2c rose (Bl)	26.50	6.00
35	A4	50c on 10c brn vio (Bl)	62.50	16.00
36	A4	50c on 10c lake (Bl)	72.50	16.00
37	A4	50c on 10c org brn (Bl)	62.50	16.00
38	A4	50c on 12½c brn (Bk)	57.50	11.00

The "a" surcharge also exists on 1/8c, 5c and 25c.

Arms
A5 A6

Revenue Stamps Handstamped in Blue

1897–98 *Imperf.*

39	A5	5c on 10c rose	35.00	17.50
40	A6	10c rose	35.00	17.50

A7

Arms—A8

A9

A9a

Revenue Stamps Handstamped in Black or Red

1899 *Imperf.*

41	A7	15c on 10c grn	45.00	25.00
a.		Blue surcharge, vertical	45.00	25.00
42	A8	10c on 25c grn	120.00	80.00
43	A9	15c on 25c grn	180.00	120.00
43A	A9a	15c on 25c grn (R)	*3,500.*	*2,000.*
b.		Black surcharge	*3,500.*	*2,000.*

Surcharge on No. 41 is either horizontal, inverted or vertical.

On No. 42 "CORREOS" is overprinted in red.

King Alfonso XIII A10

1899 *Perf. 14*

44	A10	1m org brn	2.50	60
45	A10	2m org brn	2.50	60
46	A10	3m org brn	2.50	60
47	A10	4m org brn	2.50	60
48	A10	5m org brn	2.50	60
49	A10	1c blk vio	2.50	60
50	A10	2c dk bl grn	2.50	60
51	A10	3c dk brn	2.50	60
52	A10	4c orange	12.00	1.25
53	A10	5c car ros	2.50	60
54	A10	6c dk bl	2.50	60
55	A10	8c gray brn	7.25	60
56	A10	10c vermilion	4.75	60
57	A10	15c sl grn	4.75	60
58	A10	20c maroon	13.00	1.25
59	A10	40c violet	85.00	15.00
60	A10	60c black	85.00	15.00
61	A10	80c red brn	85.00	15.00
62	A10	1p yel grn	300.00	70.00
63	A10	2p sl bl	300.00	70.00
		Nos. 44-63 (20)	921.75	195.30

Nos. 44–63 exist imperf. Price for set, $1,400.

1900 Surcharged type "a",

64	A10	50c on 20c mar	12.00	3.75
a.		Blue surcharge	24.00	7.50

Surcharged type "b".

64B	A10	5c on 20c mar	110.00	8.50

Surcharged type "c".

65	A10	5c on 20c mar	13.00	3.75

Dated "1900"

1900

66	A10	1m black	3.50	60
67	A10	2m black	3.50	60
68	A10	3m black	3.50	60
69	A10	4m black	3.50	60
70	A10	5m black	3.50	60
71	A10	1c green	3.50	60
72	A10	2c violet	3.50	60
73	A10	3c rose	3.50	60
74	A10	4c blk brn	3.50	60
75	A10	5c blue	3.50	60
76	A10	6c orange	3.50	1.50
77	A10	8c brnz grn	3.50	1.50
78	A10	10c claret	3.50	60
79	A10	15c dk vio	3.50	60
80	A10	20c ol brn	3.50	60
81	A10	40c brown	8.00	1.75
82	A10	60c green	18.50	1.75
83	A10	80c dk bl	18.50	3.25
84	A10	1p red brn	100.00	17.50
85	A10	2p orange	150.00	37.50
		Nos. 66-85 (20)	347.50	72.55

Nos. 66–85 exist imperf.

A11 A12

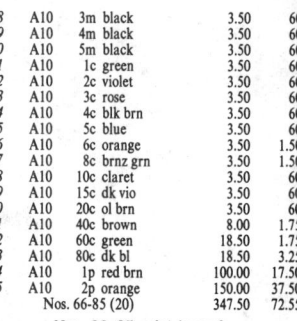

Revenue Stamps Overprinted or Surcharged with Handstamp in Red or Black

1900 *Imperf.*

86	A11	10c bl (R)	45.00	15.00
87	A12	5c on 10c bl	110.00	52.50

Nos. 52 and 80 Surcharged type "a" in Violet or Black.

1900

88	A10	50c on 4c org (V)	18.50	5.25
a.		Green surcharge	30.00	15.00
88B	A10	50c on 20c ol brn	14.00	6.00

A13 A14

1901 *Perf. 14*

89	A13	1c black	2.50	60
90	A13	2c org brn	2.50	60
91	A13	3c dk vio	2.50	60
92	A13	4c lt vio	2.50	60
93	A13	5c org red	1.50	60
94	A13	10c vio brn	1.50	60
95	A13	25c dp bl	1.50	60
96	A13	50c claret	2.50	60
97	A13	75c dk brn	1.75	60
98	A13	1p bl grn	32.50	4.25
99	A13	2p red brn	32.50	6.50
100	A13	3p ol grn	32.50	8.50
101	A13	4p dl red	32.50	8.50
102	A13	5p dk grn	40.00	8.50
103	A13	10p buff	85.00	21.00
		Nos. 89-103 (15)	273.75	62.65

Dated "1902"

1902 **Control Numbers on Back.**

104	A13	5c dk grn	2.50	35
105	A13	10c slate	2.50	35
106	A13	25c claret	6.00	90
107	A13	50c vio brn	15.00	2.50
108	A13	75c lt vio	15.00	2.50
109	A13	1p car rose	17.50	3.50
110	A13	2p ol grn	35.00	8.50
111	A13	5p org red	55.00	19.00
		Nos. 104-111 (8)	148.50	37.60

Nos. 104–111 exist imperf. Price for set, $425.

1903 *Perf. 14*

Control Numbers on Back

112	A14	¼c dk vio	35	25
113	A14	½c black	35	25

114	A14	1c scarlet	35	25
115	A14	2c dk grn	35	25
116	A14	3c bl grn	35	25
117	A14	4c violet	35	25
118	A14	5c rose lake	50	25
119	A14	10c org buff	60	30
120	A14	15c bl grn	2.50	90
121	A14	25c red brn	2.75	1.25
122	A14	50c blk brn	4.50	2.00
123	A14	75c carmine	16.00	3.50
124	A14	1p dk brn	22.50	5.50
125	A14	2p dk ol grn	30.00	7.25
126	A14	3p claret	30.00	7.25
127	A14	4p dk bl	40.00	12.00
128	A14	5p dp dl bl	55.00	14.00
129	A14	10p dl red	115.00	21.00
		Nos. 112-129 (18)	321.45	76.70

Dated "1905"

1905 Control Numbers on Back.

136	A14	1c dp vio	35	30
137	A14	2c black	35	30
138	A14	3c vermilion	35	30
139	A14	4c dp grn	35	30
140	A14	5c bl grn	50	30
141	A14	10c violet	1.50	42
142	A14	15c car lake	1.50	42
143	A14	25c org buff	10.00	1.25
144	A14	50c green	8.00	1.75
145	A14	75c red brn	9.50	5.50
146	A14	1p dp gray brn	10.00	5.50
147	A14	2p carmine	19.00	8.00
148	A14	3p dp brn	30.00	9.50
149	A14	4p brnz grn	35.00	11.00
150	A14	5p claret	55.00	17.50
151	A14	10p dp bl	90.00	25.00
		Nos. 136-151 (16)	271.40	87.34

King Alfonso XIII
A15

1907 Control Numbers on Back.

152	A15	1c bl blk	25	30
153	A15	2c car rose	25	6
154	A15	3c dp vio	25	6
155	A15	4c black	25	6
156	A15	5c org buff	30	25
157	A15	10c maroon	1.50	42
158	A15	15c brnz grn	50	25
159	A15	25c dk brn	20.00	75
160	A15	50c bl grn	30	18
161	A15	75c vermilion	35	18
162	A15	1p dl bl	2.00	42
163	A15	2p brown	8.50	2.75
164	A15	3p lake	8.50	2.75
165	A15	4p violet	8.50	2.75
166	A15	5p blk brn	8.50	2.75
167	A15	10p org brn	8.50	2.75
		Nos. 152-167 (16)	68.45	16.68

No. 157 Handstamp Surcharged in Black or Blue

HABILITADO
PARA
05CTMS

1908

168	A15	5c on 10c mar (Bk)	3.75	2.25
169	A15	5c on 10c mar (Bl)	12.50	6.00

The surcharge on Nos. 168–169 exists inverted, double and otherwise.

Seville-Barcelona Issue of Spain, 1929, Overprinted FERNANDO POO in Blue or Red

1929 *Perf. 11.*

170	A52	5c rose lake	18	18
171	A53	10c grn (R)	18	18
a.		Perf. 14	60	50
172	A50	15c Prus bl (R)	18	18
173	A51	20c pur (R)	18	18
174	A50	25c brt rose	18	18
175	A52	30c blk brn	18	18
176	A53	40c dk bl (R)	35	35
177	A51	50c dp org	60	55
178	A52	1p bl blk (R)	1.75	1.20
179	A53	4p dp rose	8.75	6.75
180	A53	10p brown	11.50	8.50
		Nos. 170-180 (11)	24.03	18.43

Virgin Mary
A16

Photogravure

1960 *Perf. 13x12½* Unwmkd.

181	A16	25c dl gray vio	6	6
182	A16	50c brn ol	6	6
183	A16	75c vio brn	6	6
184	A16	1p org ver	6	6
185	A16	1.50p lt bl grn	6	6
186	A16	2p red lil	6	6
187	A16	3p dk bl	4.00	1.25
188	A16	5p lt red brn	30	6
189	A16	10p lt ol grn	60	18
		Nos. 181-189 (9)	5.26	1.85

Tricorn and Windmill from "The Three-Cornered Hat" by Falla
A17

Manuel de Falla
A18

1960 *Perf. 13x12½, 12½x13*

190	A17	35c sl grn	10	3
191	A18	80c Prus grn	10	4

Issued to honor Manuel de Falla (1876–1946), Spanish composer.

See Nos. B1–B2.

Map of Fernando Po
A19

General Franco
A20

Designs: 70c, Santa Isabel Cathedral.

Perf. 13x12½, 12½x13

1961, Oct. 1 Photo. Unwmkd.

192	A19	25c gray vio	10	3
193	A20	50c ol brn	10	4
194	A19	70c brt grn	10	4
195	A20	1p red org	12	4

Issued to commemorate the 25th anniversary of the nomination of Gen. Francisco Franco as Chief of State.

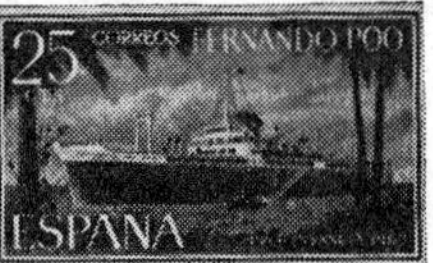

Ocean Liner
A21

Design: 50c, S.S. San Francisco.

1962, July 10 *Perf. 12½x13*

196	A21	25c dl vio	10	3
197	A21	50c gray ol	10	3
198	A21	1p org brn	10	6

Mailman
A22

Mail Transport Symbols
A23

Perf. 13x12½, 12½x13

1962, Nov. 23 Unwmkd.

199	A22	15c dk grn	10	3
200	A23	35c lil rose	10	3
201	A22	1p brown	10	4

Issued for Stamp Day.

Fetish
A24

1963, Jan. 29 *Perf. 13x12½*

202	A24	50c ol gray	10	3
203	A24	1p dp mag	10	4

Issued to help the victims of the Seville flood.

Nuns
A25

Design: 50c, Nun and child (vert.).

Perf. 12½x13, 13x12½

1963, July 6 Photo. Unwmkd.

204	A25	25c brt lil	10	3
205	A25	50c dl grn	10	3
206	A25	1p red org	10	4

Issued for child welfare.

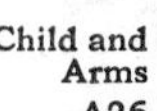

Child and Arms
A26

1963, July 12 *Perf. 12½x13*

207	A26	50c brn ol	4	4
208	A26	1p car rose	6	6

Issued for Barcelona flood relief.

Governor Chacon
A27

Orange Blossoms
A28

Men in Dugout Canoe
A29

1964, Mar. 6 *Perf. 12½x13, 13x12½*

209	A27	25c vio blk	10	3
210	A28	50c dk ol	10	3
211	A27	1p brn red	10	6

Issued for Stamp Day 1963.

1964, June 1 Photo. *Perf. 13x12½*

Design: 50c, Pineapple.

212	A29	25c purple	10	4
213	A28	50c dl ol	10	4
214	A29	1p dp cl	10	5

Issued for child welfare.

Ring-necked Francolin
A30

1964, July 1

Designs: 15c, 70c, 3p, Ring-necked francolin. 25c, 1p, 5p, Two mallards. 50c, 1.50p, 10p, Head of great blue touraco.

215	A30	15c chestnut	4	3
216	A30	25c dl vio	4	3
217	A30	50c dk ol grn	4	3
218	A30	70c green	6	3
219	A30	1p brn org	10	3
220	A30	1.50p grnsh bl	18	6
221	A30	3p vio bl	90	18
222	A30	5p dl pur	2.25	30
223	A30	10p brt grn	3.25	1.25
		Nos. 215-223 (9)	6.86	1.94

The Three Kings
A31

Designs: 50c, 1.50p, Caspar (vert.).

Perf. 13x12½, 12½x13

1964, Nov. 23 Unwmkd.

224	A31	50c green	3	3
225	A31	1p org ver	5	5
226	A31	1.50p dp grn	18	6
227	A31	3p ultra	2.25	1.35

Issued for Stamp Day, 1964.

Boy
A32

Woman Fruit Picker
A33

Design: 1.50p, Girl learning to write, and church.

1964, Mar. 1 Photo. *Perf. 13x12½*

228	A32	50c indigo	3	3
229	A33	1p dk red	6	4
230	A33	1.50p grnsh bl	18	6

Issued to commemorate 25 years of peace.

Plectrocnemia Cruciata
A34

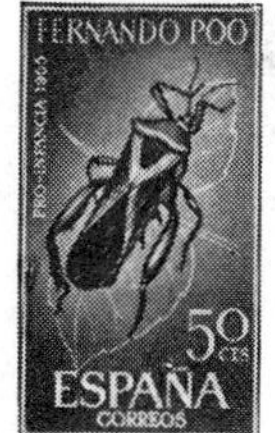

Design: 1p, Metopodontus savagei (horiz.).

Perf. 13x12½, 12½x13

1965, June 1 Photo. Unwmkd.

231	A34	50c sl grn	3	3
232	A34	1p rose red	6	4
233	A34	1.50p Prus bl	18	6

Issued for child welfare.

Pole Vault
A35

Arms of Fernando Po
A36

Perf. 12½x13, 13x12½

1965, Nov. 23 Photo. Unwmkd.

234	A35	50c yel grn	3	3
235	A36	1p brt org brn	6	4
236	A35	1.50p brt bl	18	6

Issued for Stamp Day, 1965.

White and Negro Children Reading
A37

Design: 1.50p, St. Elizabeth of Hungary (vert.).

Perf. 12½x13, 13x12½

1966, June 1 Photo. Unwmkd.

237	A37	50c dk grn	3	3
238	A37	1p brn red	6	4
239	A37	1.50p dk bl	18	6

Issued for child welfare.

White-nosed Monkey
A38

Designs: 40c, 4p, Head of moustached monkey (vert.).

1966, Nov. 23 Photo. *Perf. 13*

240	A38	10c dk bl & yel	3	3
241	A38	40c lt brn, bl & blk	3	3
242	A38	1.50p ol bis, brn org & blk	12	6
243	A38	4p sl grn, brn org & blk	25	18

Issued for Stamp Day, 1966.

Flowers
A39

Designs: 40c, 4p, Six flowers.

1967, June 1 Photo. *Perf. 13*

244	A39	10c brt car & pale grn	3	3
245	A39	40c red brn & org	3	3
246	A39	1.50p red lil & lt red brn	12	6
247	A39	4p dk bl & lt grn	25	18

Issued for child welfare.

Linsang
A40

Designs: 1.50p, Needle-clawed galago (vert.). 3.50p, Fraser's scaly-tailed flying squirrel.

1967, Nov. 23 Photo. *Perf. 13*

248	A40	1p blk & bis	12	6
249	A40	1.50p brn & ol	12	12
250	A40	3.50p rose lake & dl grn	25	25

Issued for Stamp Day 1967.

Stamp of 1868, No. 1, and Arms of San Carlos—A41

Designs: 1.50p, Fernando Po No. 1 and arms of Santa Isabel. 2.50p, Fernando Po No. 1 and arms of Fernando Po.

1968, Feb. 4 Photo. *Perf. 13*

251	A41	1p brt plum & brn org	12	12
252	A41	1.50p dp bl & brn org	12	12
253	A41	2.50p brn & brn org	25	18

Centenary of the first postage stamp.

Zodiac Issue

Libra
A42

Signs of the Zodiac: 1.50p, Leo. 2.50p, Aquarius.

1968, Apr. 25 Photo. *Perf. 13*

254	A42	1p brt mag, *lt yel*	12	12
255	A42	1.50p brn, *pink*	12	12
256	A42	2.50p dk vio, *yel*	25	18

Issued for child welfare.

SEMI-POSTAL STAMPS

Types of Regular Issue, 1960

Designs: 10c+5c, Manuel de Falla. 15c+5c, Dancers from "Love, the Magician."

Perf. 12½x13, 13x12½

1960 Photogravure Unwmkd.

B1	A18	10c +5c mar	10	5
B2	A17	15c +5c dk brn & bis	10	5

The surtax was for child welfare.

Whale
SP1

Design: 20c+5c, 50c+20c, Harpooning whale.

1961 *Perf. 12½x13*

B3	SP1	10c +5c rose brn	6	5
B4	SP1	20c +5c dk sl grn	6	5
B5	SP1	30c +10c ol brn	6	5
B6	SP1	50c +20c dk brn	25	6

Issued for Stamp Day, 1960.

Hand Blessing Woman
SP2

Design: 25c+10c, Boy making sign of the cross, and crucifix.

1961, June 21 *Perf. 13x12½*

B7	SP2	10c +5c rose brn	10	3
B8	SP2	25c +10c gray vio	10	3
B9	SP2	80c +20c dk grn	10	4

The surtax was for child welfare.

Ethiopian Tortoise
SP3

Design: 25c+10c, 1p+10c, Native carriers, palms and shore.

1961, Nov. 23 *Perf. 12½x13*

B10	SP3	10c +5c rose red	10	3
B11	SP3	25c +10c dk pur	10	3
B12	SP3	30c +10c vio brn	10	3
B13	SP3	1p +10c red org	10	4

Issued for Stamp Day 1961.

FEZZAN

(See Libya, Occupation Stamps).

FINLAND

(fĭn'lănd)

(Suomi)

LOCATION—In northern Europe bordering on the Gulfs of Bothnia and Finland.

GOVT.—Republic.

AREA—130,119 sq. mi. (excluding water area).

POP.—4,740,000 (est. 1977).

CAPITAL—Helsinki (Helsingfors).

Finland was a Grand Duchy of the Russian Empire from 1809 until December, 1917, when it declared its independence.

100 Kopecks = 1 Ruble
100 Pennia = 1 Markka (1866)

Issues under Russian Empire.

Prices of early Finland stamps vary according to condition. Quotations for Nos. 1–3B are for fine copies. Used prices are for pen-canceled copies. Very fine to superb specimens sell at much higher prices, and inferior or poor copies sell at reduced prices, depending on the condition of the individual specimen.

Coat of Arms
A1

Typographed.

1856 *Imperf.* Unwmkd.

Small Pearls in Post Horns.

Wove Paper.

1	A1	5k blue	*7,000.*	1,200.
		Pen and town cancellation		1,800.
		Town cancellation		3,000.
	a.	Tête bêche pair		*30,000.*
		As "a," pen and town cancellation		*37,500.*
2	A1	10k rose	7,000.	300.00
		Pen and town cancellation		675.00
		Town canncellation		900.00
	a.	Tête bêche pair		*20,000.*
		As "a," pen and town cancellation		*27,500.*

1858

Wide Vertically Laid Paper

2C	A1	10k rose		1,100.
		Pen and town cancellation		1,600.
		Town cancellation		2,000.
	d.	Tête bêche pair		

The wide vertically laid paper has 13–14 distinct lines per 2 cm. The 10k rose also exists on a narrow laid paper with lines sometimes indistinct. Price, 60 per cent of that for a wide laid paper example.

A 5k blue with small pearls exists on narrow vertically laid paper.

Stamps on diagonally laid paper are envelope cut squares.

Large Pearls in Post Horns.

Wove Paper.

3	A1	5k blue	*6,000.*	1,100.
		Pen and town cancellation		1,500.
		Town cancellation		2,250.
	a.	Tête bêche pair		*30,000.*
		As "a," pen and town cancellation		*37,500.*

1859

Wide Vertically Laid Paper

No.	Type	Description	Unused	Used
3B	A1	5k blue	10,000.	
		Pen and town cancellation	12,500.	

Reprints of Nos. 2 and 3, made in 1862, are on brownish paper, on vertically laid paper, and in tête bêche pairs on normal and vertically laid paper. Reprints of 1871, 1881 and 1893 are on yellowish or white paper. Price for least costly of each, $45.

In 1956, Nos. 2 and 3 were reprinted for the Centenary with post horn watermark and gum. Price, $50 each.

Coat of Arms
A2

Serpentine Roulette 7½, 8

1860

Nos. 4-13, with serpentine roulette, are seldom in perfect condition. Usually some of the "teeth" are missing. In average condition, one or two teeth are gone. Prices are for average specimens. Copies with all teeth intact sell for many times more.

Four types of indentation are noted:

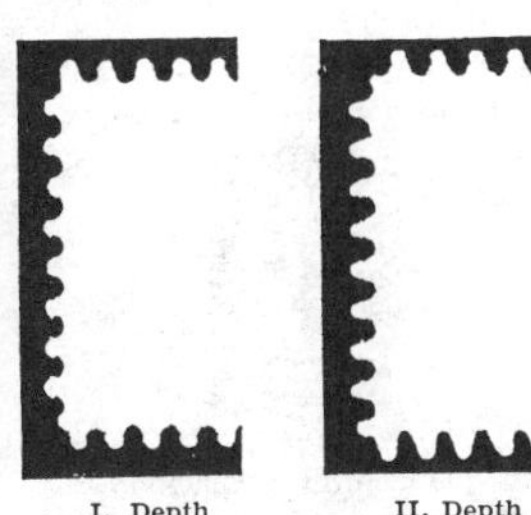

I. Depth 1-1¼mm. II. Depth 1½-1¾mm.

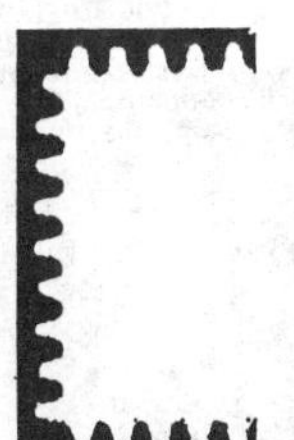

III. Depth 2-2¼mm. IV. Shovel-shaped teeth. Depth 1¼-1½mm.

Wove Paper.

No.	Type	Description	Unused	Used
4	A2	5k bl, *bluish*, roulette I	375.00	75.00
a.		Roulette II	450.00	75.00
b.		Imperf. vert.		
5	A2	10k rose, *pale rose*, roulette I	325.00	32.50
a.		Roulette II	475.00	45.00

A3

A4

1866-74 *Serpentine Roulette*

No.	Type	Description	Unused	Used
6	A3	5p pur brn, *lil*, roulette I ('73)	170.00	50.00
a.		Roulette II		1,400.
b.		5p red brn, *lil*, roulette III ('71)	170.00	50.00
7	A3	8p *grn*, roulette III ('67)	175.00	67.50
a.		Ribbed paper, roulette III ('72)	750.00	175.00
b.		Roulette II ('74)	180.00	67.50
c.		As "b," ribbed paper ('74)	250.00	85.00
d.		Roulette I ('73)	275.00	90.00
e.		As "d," ribbed paper	750.00	210.00
f.		Serp. roulette 10½ ('67)		7,000.
8	A3	10p *yel*, roulette III ('70)	260.00	67.50
a.		10p *buff*, roulette II	375.00	100.00
b.		10p *buff*, roulette I ('73)	325.00	125.00
9	A3	20p bl, *bl*, roulette III	200.00	22.50
a.		Roulette II	200.00	25.00
b.		Roulette I ('73)	400.00	40.00
c.		Roulette IV ('74)	1,100.	500.00
d.		Imperf. horiz.		300.00
e.		Printed on both sides (40p bl on back)		6,500.
10	A3	40p rose, *lil rose*, roulette III	200.00	22.50
a.		Ribbed paper, roulette III ('73)	325.00	40.00
b.		Roulette II	200.00	25.00
c.		As "b," ribbed paper ('73)	275.00	35.00
d.		Roulette I	525.00	42.50
e.		As "d," ribbed paper	375.00	42.50
f.		Roulette IV		1,200.
g.		As "f," ribbed paper		1,500.
h.		Serp. roulette 10½		4,500.
11	A4	1m yel brn, roulette III ('67)	1,000.	400.00
a.		Roulette II	1,800.	575.00
b.		Final "A" of "MARKKA" covered by color spot	1,400.	500.00

Nos. 7f and 10h are also known in compound serpentine roulette 10½ and 7½.

Nos. 4 to 11 were reprinted in 1893 on thick wove paper. Colors differ from originals. Roulette type IV. Price for Nos. 4-10, each $30. Price for No. 11, $42.50.

Thin or Thick Laid Paper.

No.	Type	Description	Unused	Used
12	A3	5p red brn, *lil*, roulette III	160.00	50.00
a.		Roulette II	180.00	60.00
b.		Roulette I	180.00	60.00
d.		5p *buff*, roul. III (error)		6,250.
e.		Tête bêche pair		10,000.
13	A3	10p *buff*, roulette III	275.00	70.00
a.		10p *yel*, roulette II	325.00	80.00
b.		10p *yel*, roulette I	1,200.	185.00
c.		10p red brn, *lil*, roul. III (error)	6,000.	4,000.

A5 A6

1875 *Perf. 14x13½*

No.	Type	Description	Unused	Used
16	A5	32p lake	1,600.	700.00

1875-81 *Perf. 11*

No.	Type	Description	Unused	Used
17	A5	2p gray	50.00	52.50
18	A5	5p orange	140.00	12.00
a.		5p yel	140.00	20.00
19	A5	8p bl grn	170.00	65.00
a.		8p yel grn	180.00	70.00
20	A5	10p brn ('81)	275.00	60.00
21	A5	20p ultra	120.00	2.75
a.		20p bl	120.00	3.00
b.		20p Prus bl	200.00	27.50
c.		Tête bêche pair	3,000.	2,250.
22	A5	25p car ('79)	140.00	13.00
a.		25p rose	160.00	27.50
23	A5	32p carmine	260.00	30.00
a.		32p rose	325.00	45.00
24	A5	1m vio ('77)	425.00	130.00

A souvenir card was issued in 1974 for NORDIA 1975 reproducing a block of four of the unissued "1 MARKKAA" design.

Nos. 19 and 23 were reprinted in 1893, perf. 12½. Price $17.50 each.

1881-83 *Perf. 12½*

No.	Type	Description	Unused	Used
25	A5	2p gray	13.00	14.00
a.		Imperf., pair	150.00	
26	A5	5p orange	40.00	6.00
a.		Tête bêche pair	3,500.	3,000.
b.		Imperf. vert., pair	150.00	150.00
c.		Imperf. horiz., pair		175.00
27	A5	10p brown	90.00	17.50
28	A5	20p ultra	30.00	2.00
a.		20p bl	32.50	2.00
b.		Tête bêche pair	2,250.	1,800.
c.		Imperf., pair	100.00	
29	A5	25p rose	47.50	8.50
a.		25p car	47.50	8.50
b.		Tête bêche pair	4,000.	4,500.
30	A5	1m vio ('82)	260.00	45.00

Nos. 27-29 were reprinted in 1893 in deeper shades, perf. 12½. Price $35 each.

1881 *Perf. 11x12½*

No.	Type	Description	Unused	Used
26d	A5	5p orange	260.00	80.00
27a	A5	10p brown	900.00	250.00
28d	A5	20p ultra	425.00	40.00
28e	A5	20p blue	425.00	40.00
29c	A5	25p rose	350.00	100.00
29d	A5	25p carmine	350.00	100.00
30a	A5	1m violet		1,000.

1881 *Perf. 12½x11*

No.	Type	Description	Unused	Used
26e	A5	5p orange	260.00	80.00
27b	A5	10p brown	900.00	250.00
28f	A5	20p ultra	425.00	40.00
28g	A5	20p blue	425.00	40.00
29e	A5	25p rose	350.00	100.00
29f	A5	25p carmine	350.00	100.00

1885 *Perf. 12½.*

No.	Type	Description	Unused	Used
31	A5	5p emerald	22.50	50
a.		5p yel grn	22.50	50
b.		Tête bêche pair	5,000.	4,250.
32	A5	10p carmine	32.50	3.00
a.		10p rose	32.50	3.00
33	A5	20p orange	27.50	40
a.		20p yel	37.50	3.25
b.		Tête bêche pair	3,250.	2,750.
34	A5	25p ultra	55.00	1.40
a.		25p bl	55.00	1.20
35	A5	1m gray & rose	25.00	16.00
36	A5	5m grn & rose	425.00	325.00
37	A5	10m brn & rose	650.00	550.00

1889-92 *Perf. 12½*

No.	Type	Description	Unused	Used
38	A6	2p sl ('90)	70	70
39	A6	5p grn ('90)	22.50	20
40	A6	10p car ('90)	35.00	40
a.		10p rose ('90)	35.00	40
41	A6	20p org ('92)	27.50	20
a.		20p yel ('90)	35.00	1.40
42	A6	25p ultra ('91)	40.00	40
a.		25p bl	50.00	70
43	A6	1m sl & rose ('92)	7.00	2.75
a.		1m brnsh gray & rose ('90)	40.00	3.75
44	A6	5m grn & rose ('90)	47.50	55.00
45	A6	10m brn & rose ('90)	65.00	80.00

The 2p slate, perf. 14x13, is believed to be an essay.

See also Nos. 60-63.

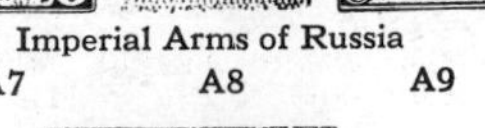

Imperial Arms of Russia
A7 A8 A9

A10

A11

Wmk. 168

Laid Paper.
Wmkd.
Wavy Lines and Letters. (168)

1891-92 *Perf. 14½x15*

No.	Type	Description	Unused	Used
46	A7	1k org yel	5.50	6.50
47	A7	2k green	6.50	8.00
48	A7	3k carmine	8.50	11.00
49	A8	4k rose	12.00	12.00
50	A7	7k dk bl	7.00	2.25
51	A8	10k dk bl	14.00	9.00
52	A9	14k bl & rose	20.00	16.00
53	A8	20k bl & car	15.00	13.00
54	A9	35k vio & grn	27.50	32.50
55	A8	50k vio & grn	27.50	25.00

Perf. 13½.

No.	Type	Description	Unused	Used
56	A10	1r brn & org	90.00	75.00
57	A11	3½r blk & gray	325.00	375.00
a.		3½r blk & yel *(error)*	6,500.	5,500.
58	A11	7r blk & yel	260.00	260.00
		Nos. 46-58 (13)	818.50	845.25

Forgeries of Nos. 57, 57a, 58 exist.

Type of 1889-90.
Wove Paper.

1895-96 *Perf. 14x13* Unwmkd.

No.	Type	Description	Unused	Used
60	A6	5p green	65	15
61	A6	10p rose	65	15
a.		Imperf.	70.00	70.00
62	A6	20p orange	65	15
a.		Imperf.	65.00	65.00
63	A6	25p ultra	1.25	45
a.		25p bl	1.25	45
b.		Imperf.	100.00	100.00

A12

A13

A14

A15

1901 Lithographed *Perf. 14½x15*

Chalky Paper.

64	A12	2p yellow	4.00	2.00
65	A12	5p green	13.00	40
66	A12	10p carmine	20.00	80
67	A12	20p dk bl	32.50	40
68	A14	1m vio & grn	150.00	5.50

Perf. 13½.

69	A15	10m blk & gray	275.00	200.00
		Nos. 64-69 (6)	494.50	209.10

Imperf. sheets of 10p and 20p, stolen during production, were privately perforated 11½ to defraud the P.O. Uncanceled imperfs. of Nos. 65-68 are believed to be proofs.

Types of 1901 Redrawn.

No. 64. No. 70.

2p. On No. 64, the "2" below "II" is shifted slightly leftward. On No. 70, the "2" is centered below "II."

No. 65. No. 71.

5p. On No. 65, the frame lines are very close. On No. 71, a clear white space separates them.

Nos. 66, 67. Nos. 72, 73.

10p, 20p. On Nos. 66-67, the horizontal central background lines are faint and broken. On Nos. 72-73, they are clear and solid, though still thin.

20p. On No. 67, "H" close to "2" with period midway. On No. 73 they are slightly separated with period close to "H".

No. 68. Nos. 74, 74a.

1m. On No. 68, the "1" following "MARKKA" lacks serif at base. On Nos. 74-74a, this "1" has serif.

No. 69. No. 75.

10m. On No. 69, the serifs of "M" and "A" in top and bottom panels do not touch. On No. 75, the serifs join.

1901-14 Typo. *Perf. 14, 14½x15*

Ordinary Paper.

70	A12	2p orange	90	90
a.		Imperf.	325.00	325.00
71	A12	5p green	1.75	20
b.		Imperf.	80.00	80.00
72	A13	10p carmine	70	10
a.		Imperf.	80.00	80.00
b.		Background inverted	17.50	75
73	A12	20p dk bl	60	10
a.		Imperf.	80.00	80.00
74	A14	1m lil & grn, perf. 14 ('14)	1.30	25
a.		1m vio & bl grn, perf. 14½x15 ('02)	8.00	30
b.		Imperf.	100.00	100.00
		Nos. 70-74 (5)	5.25	1.55

Perf. 13½.

75	A15	10m blk & db ('03)	135.00	32.50

A16 A17 A18

1911-16 *Perf. 14, 14½x15*

77	A16	2p orange	12	15
78	A16	5p green	12	6
a.		Imperf.	80.00	65.00
b.		Perf. 14½x15	180.00	25.00
79	A17	10p rose	25	5
a.		Imperf.	60.00	60.00
b.		Perf. 14½x15	1.25	85
80	A16	20p dp bl	30	5
a.		Imperf.	40.00	40.00
81	A18	40p vio & bl	15	10
a.		Perf. 14½x15	1,400.	1,200.
		Nos. 77-81 (5)	94	41

There are three minor types of No. 79.

Perf. 14½

82	A15	10m blk & grnsh gray ('16)	130.00	140.00
a.		Horiz. pair, imperf. vert.	1,000.	

Republic.

Helsinki Issue.

Arms of the Republic A19

Two types of the 40p.
Type I—Thin figures of value.
Type II—Thick figures of value.

Perf. 14, 14½x15

1917-29 Unwmkd.

83	A19	5p green	15	8
84	A19	5p gray ('19)	15	8
85	A19	10p rose	25	8
a.		Imperf.	200.00	200.00
86	A19	10p grn ('19)	1.25	10
a.		Perf. 14½x15		850.00
87	A19	10p lt bl ('21)	15	8
88	A19	20p buff	25	10
89	A19	20p rose ('20)	50	10
90	A19	20p brn ('24)	35	35
91	A19	25p blue	30	10
92	A19	25p lt brn ('19)	18	10
93	A19	30p grn ('23)	40	25
94	A19	40p vio (I)	25	8
a.		Perf. 14½x15	180.00	7.50
95	A19	40p bl grn (II) ('29)	15	35
a.		Type I ('24)	7.00	1.75
96	A19	50p org brn	25	8
97	A19	50p dp bl ('19)	4.00	12
a.		Perf. 14½x15		500.00
98	A19	50p grn ('21)	15	10
99	A19	60p red vio ('21)	30	8
a.		Imperf.	55.00	90.00
100	A19	75p yel ('21)	15	25
101	A19	1m dl rose & blk	12.50	10
102	A19	1m red org ('25)	15	7.00
103	A19	1½m bl grn & red vio ('29)	15	12
104	A19	2m grn & blk ('21)	2.50	30
105	A19	2m dk bl & ind ('22)	1.00	8
106	A19	3m bl & blk ('21)	50.00	18
107	A19	5m red vio & blk	25.00	15
108	A19	10m brn & gray blk, perf. 14	85	65
a.		10m lt brn & blk, perf. 14½x15 ('29)	5.50	110.00
110	A19	25m dl red & yel ('21)	80	12.00
		Nos. 83-108, 110 (27)	102.13	23.06

Copies of a 2½p gray of this type exist. They are proofs from the original die which were distributed through the Universal Postal Union. No plate was made for this denomination.

See also Nos. 127-140, 143-152.

Vasa Issue

A20

1918 Lithographed. *Perf. 11½.*

111	A20	5p green	40	60
112	A20	10p red	35	55
113	A20	30p slate	60	1.40
114	A20	40p brn vio	30	60
115	A20	50p org brn	50	1.40
116	A20	70p gray brn	2.25	7.00
117	A20	1m red & gray	50	80
118	A20	5m red vio & gray	70.00	100.00
		Nos. 111-118 (8)	74.90	112.35

Nos. 111-118 exist imperforate but were not regularly issued in that condition.

Sheet margin copies, perf. on 3 sides, imperf. on margin side, were sold by post office.

Stamps and Type of 1917-29 Surcharged 50 50 50

1919 *Perf. 14*

119	A19	10p on 5p grn	40	30
120	A19	20p on 10p rose	40	30
121	A19	50p on 25p bl	80	30
122	A19	75p on 20p org	20	20

Stamps and Type of 1917-29 Surcharged:

30 P (a) 1½ M (b)

1921

123	A19 (a)	30p on 10p grn	80	15
124	A19 (a)	60p on 40p red vio	4.00	40
125	A19 (a)	90p on 20p rose	15	25
126	A19 (a)	1½m on 50p bl	1.50	20
a.		Thin "2" in "½"	7.00	2.50
b.		Imperf.	120.00	150.00

Wmk. 121

Arms Type of 1917-29.

Wmkd. Multiple Swastika. (121)

1925-29 *Perf. 14, 14½x15*

127	A19	10p ultra ('27)	60	80
128	A19	20p brown	60	80
129	A19	25p brn org ('29)	1.50	22.50
130	A19	30p yel grn	15	25
131	A19	40p bl grn (I)	2.50	10
a.		Type II	3.50	15
132	A19	50p gray grn ('27)	50	15
133	A19	60p red vio	15	20
134	A19	1m dp org	4.25	15
135	A19	1½m bl grn & red vio	8.50	12
136	A19	2m dk bl & ind	40	18
137	A19	3m chlky bl & blk	1.25	20
138	A19	5m red vio & blk	35	15
139	A19	10m lt brn & blk ('27)	4.00	6.50
140	A19	25m dp org & yel ('27)	20.00	200.00
		Nos. 127-140 (14)	44.75	

A21 Wmk. 208

Wmkd. Post Horn. (208)

1927. Dec. 6 Typo. *Perf. 14*

141	A21	1½m dp vio	15	25
142	A21	2m dp bl	40	1.00

Issued in commemoration of the tenth anniversary of Finnish independence.

Arms Type of 1917-29.

Perf. 14½x15

1927-29 Wmk. 208

143	A19	20p lt brn ('29)	1.25	5.50
144	A19	40p bl grn (II) ('28)	15	15
145	A19	50p gray grn ('28)	15	20
146	A19	1m dp org	15	15
a.		Imperf.	120.00	140.00
b.		Perf. 14	1.50	15
147	A19	1½m bl grn & red vio ('28)	3.25	15
a.		Perf. 14	300.00	11.00
148	A19	2m dk bl & ind ('28)	15	30
149	A19	3m chlky bl & blk	15	20
a.		Perf. 14	2.75	2.00
150	A19	5m red vio & blk ('28)	15	20
151	A19	10m lt brn & blk	80	22.50
152	A19	25m brn org & yel	80	55.00
		Nos. 143-152 (10)	7.00	

Philatelic Exhibition Issue.

A22

Overprint in Black

1928, Nov. 10 Litho. Wmk. 208

153	A22	1m dp org	10.00	13.00
154	A22	1½m bl grn & red vio	10.00	13.00

Nos. 153 and 154 were sold exclusively at the Helsinki Philatelic Exhibition, Nov. 10-18, 1928, and were valid only during that period.

S. S. "Bore" Leaving Turku A23

Turku Cathedral A24

Turku Castle A25

Typographed

1929, May 22 *Perf. 14* Wmk. 208

155	A23	1m ol grn	2.00	2.75
156	A24	1½m chocolate	4.00	2.50
157	A25	2m dk gray	60	3.50

Issued to commemorate the 700th anniversary of the founding of the city of Turku (Abo).

A26

1930–46 ***Perf. 14*** **Unwmkd.**

158 A26 5p chocolate 10 10
159 A26 10p dl vio 10 10
160 A26 20p yel grn 25 25
161 A26 25p yel brn 15 10
a. Booklet pane of 4 70
162 A26 40p bl grn 3.50 25
163 A26 50p yellow 60 25
164 A26 50p bl grn ('32) 15 6
a. Booklet pane of 4 70
b. Imperf. 80.00 80.00
165 A26 60p dk gray 25 20
165A A26 75p dp org ('42) 15 10
166 A26 1m red org 60 8
a. Booklet pane of 4 2.75
166B A26 1m yel grn ('42) 40 10
167 A26 1.20m crimson 35 50
168 A26 1.25m yel ('32) 20 6
a. Booklet pane of 4 90
169 A26 1½m red vio 4.50 10
170 A26 1½m car ('32) 20 10
170A A26 1½m sl ('40) 20 8
170B A26 1.75m org yel ('40) 75 15
171 A26 2m indigo 25 15
172 A26 2m dp vio ('32) 12.00 8
173 A26 2m car ('36) 25 8
a. Booklet pane of 4 1.10
173B A26 2m yel org ('42) 40 10
173C A26 2m bl grn ('45) 25 10
174 A26 2½m brt bl ('32) 2.00 15
174A A26 2½m car ('42) 20 8
174B A26 2.75m rose vio ('40) 12 8
175 A26 3m ol blk 30.00 15
a. Double foot on lion *250.00* *100.00*
175B A26 3m car ('45) 30 10
175C A26 3m yel ('45) 30 35
176 A26 3½m brt bl ('36) 6.00 15
176A A26 3½m ol ('42) 20 8
176B A26 4m ol ('45) 50 8
176C A26 4½m saph ('42) 20 20
176D A26 5m saph ('45) 30 10
176E A26 5m pur ('45) 30 15
j. Imperf. 80.00 80.00
176F A26 5m yel ('46) 60 5
k. Imperf. 50.00 25.00
176G A26 6m car ('45) 30 15
m. Imperf. 80.00 80.00
176H A26 8m pur ('46) 20 10
176I A26 10m saph ('45) 1.00 10
Nos. 158-176I (38) 68.12 5.16

See also Nos. 257–262, 270–274, 291–296, 302–304.

Stamps of types A26–A29 overprinted "ITA KARJALA" are listed under Karelia, Nos. N1–N15.

Castle in Savonlinna
A27

Lake Saima
A28

Woodchopper
A29

1930 **Engraved**

177 A27 5m blue 30 6
178 A28 10m gray lil 70.00 3.00
179 A29 25m blk brn 2.00 12

See also Nos. 205 and 305.

Elias Lönnrot
A30

Seal of Finnish Literary Society
A31

1931, Jan. 1 **Typographed**

180 A30 1m ol brn 4.00 3.00
181 A31 1½m dl bl 15.00 3.00

Centenary of Finnish Literary Society.

A32

1931, Feb. 28

182 A32 1½m red 4.50 5.50
183 A32 2m blue 3.00 5.50

75th anniversary of first use of postage stamps in Finland.

Nos. 162-163 Surcharged

50 PEN.

=

1932, Jan.

195 A26 50p on 40p bl grn 1.50 20
196 A26 1.25m on 50p yel 4.00 70

President P. E. Svinhufvud
A33

Alexis Kivi
A34

1931, Dec. 15

197 A33 2m gray bl & blk 2.25 1.75

Issued to commemorate the 70th birthday of President Pehr Eyvind Svinhufvud.

Lake Saima Type of 1930.

1932–43 **Re-engraved**

205 A28 10m red vio ('43) 75 10
a. 10m dk vio 25.00 70

On Nos. 205 and 205a the lines of the islands, the clouds and the foilage are much deeper and stronger than on No. 178.

1934, Oct. 10 **Typographed**

206 A34 2m red vio 2.75 2.00

Issued in commemoration of the centenary of the birth of Alexis Kivi, Finnish poet (1834–1872).

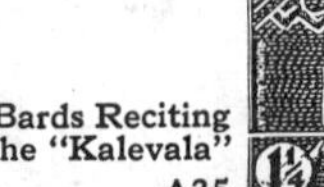

Bards Reciting the "Kalevala"
A35

Goddess Louhi, As Eagle Seizing Magic Mill
A36

Kullervo
A37

1935, Feb. 28 **Engraved**

207 A35 1¼m brn lake 1.50 1.20
208 A36 2m black 3.75 70
209 A37 2½m blue 4.50 1.75

Issued to commemorate the centenary of the publication of the "Kalevala" (Finnish National Epic).

No. 170 Surcharged in Black

2
MARKKAA
=

1937, Feb.

212 A26 2m on 1½m car 5.00 50

Field Marshal Gustaf Mannerheim
A38

Swede-Finn Co-operation in Colonization
A39

1937, June 4 Photo. ***Perf. 14***

213 A38 2m ultra 85 75

Issued in commemoration of the 70th birthday of Field Marshal Baron Carl Gustaf Mannerheim, June 4th, 1937.

1938, June 1

214 A39 3½m dk brn 1.80 1.40

Tercentenary of the colonization of Delaware by Swedes and Finns.

Early Post Office
A40

Designs: 1¼m, Mail delivery in 1700. 2m, Modern mail plane. 3½m, Helsinki post office.

1938, Sept. 6 Photo. ***Perf. 14***

215 A40 50p green 45 45
a. Bklt. pane of 3 7.50
216 A40 1¼m dk bl 1.00 1.00
a. Bklt. pane of 2 10.00
217 A40 2m scarlet 1.75 50
a. Bklt. pane of 2 13.00
218 A40 3½m sl blk 6.00 5.00
a. Bklt. pane of 2 37.50

Issued in commemoration of the 300th anniversary of the Finnish Postal System.

Post Office, Helsinki
A44

1939–42 **Photogravure**

219 A44 4m brn blk 25 15

Engraved

219A A44 7m blk brn ('42) 75 15
219B A44 9m rose lake ('42) 75 15

See also No. 248.

University of Helsinki
A45

1940, May 1 **Photogravure**

220 A45 2m dp bl & bl 80 80

Issued in commemoration of the 300th anniversary of the founding of the University of Helsinki.

Nos. 168 and 173 Surcharged in Black

mk
1:75
=

1940, June 16 **Typographed**

221 A26 1.75m on 1.25m yel 1.00 70
222 A26 2.75m on 2m car 3.25 40

President Kallio Reviewing Military Band
A46

1941, May 24 **Engraved**

223 A46 2.75m black 80 80

Issued in memory of President Kyösti Kallio (1873–1940).

Castle at Viborg
A47

1941, Aug. 30 **Typographed**

224 A47 1.75m yel org 50 60
225 A47 2.75m rose vio 50 60
226 A47 3.50m blue 1.00 1.25

Field Marshal Mannerheim
A48

Wmk. 273

Wmkd. Roses. (273)

1941, Dec. 31 **Engraved** ***Perf. 14***

227 A48 50p dl grn 70 80
228 A48 1.75m dp brn 70 80
229 A48 2m dk red 70 80
230 A48 2.75m dl vio brn 70 80
231 A48 3.50m dp bl 70 80
232 A48 5m sl bl 70 80
Nos. 227-232 (6) 4.20 4.80

President Risto Ryti
A49

233 A49 50p dl grn 50 80
234 A49 1.75m dp brn 60 80
235 A49 2m dk red 60 80
236 A49 2.75m dl vio brn 80 80
237 A49 3.50m dp bl 50 80
238 A49 5m sl bl 50 80
Nos. 233-238 (6) 3.50 4.80

Types A48–A49 overprinted "ITA KARJALA" are listed under Karelia, Nos. N16–N27.

Häme Bridge, Tampere
A50

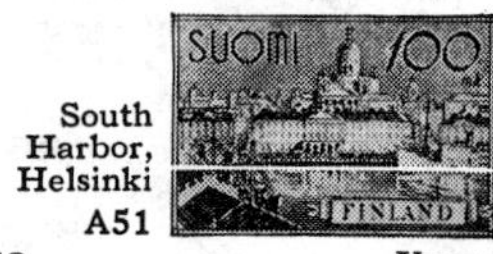

South Harbor, Helsinki
A51

1942 **Unwmkd.**

239	A50	50m dl brn vio	2.00	12
240	A51	100m indigo	2.50	20

See also No. 350.

Altar and Open Bible
A52

17th Century Printer
A53

1942, Oct. 10

241	A52	2.75m dk brn	50	1.00
242	A53	3.50m vio bl	80	1.75

Issued to commemorate the 300th anniversary of the printing of the first Bible in Finnish, 1642.

No. 174B Surcharged in Black

3½mk

1943, Feb. 1

243	A26	3.50m on 2.75m rose vio	15	15

Minna Canth
A54

1944, Mar. 20

244	A54	3.50m dk ol grn	40	50

Issued to commemorate the centenary of the birth of Minna Canth (1844–96), author and playwright.

President P. E. Svinhufvud
A55

K. J. Stahlberg
A56

1944, Aug. 1

245	A55	3.50m black	50	50

Death of President Svinhufvud (1861–1944).

1945, May 16 **Engraved** ***Perf. 14***

246	A56	3.50m brn vio	25	50

80th birthday of Dr. K. J. Stahlberg.

Castle in Savonlinna
A57

Jean Sibelius
A58

1945, Sept. 4

247	A57	15m lil rose	1.25	15
248	A44	20m sepia	1.50	8

For a 35m of type A57, see No. 280.

1945, Dec. 8

249	A58	5m dk sl grn	18	25

80th birthday of Jean Sibelius (1865–1957), composer.

No. 176E Surcharged with New Value and Bars in Black.

1946, Mar. 16

250	A26	8(m) on 5m pur	20	20

Victorious Athletes
A59

Lighthouse at Uto
A60

1946, June 1 **Engraved** ***Perf. 13½***

251	A59	8m brn vio	40	40

Issued to commemorate the 3rd Sports Festival, Helsinki, June 27–30, 1946.

1946, Sept. 19

252	A60	8m dp vio	40	40

Issued to commemorate the 250th anniversary of the Finnish Department of Pilots and Lighthouses.

Post Bus
A61

1946–47 ***Perf. 14*** **Unwmkd.**

253	A61	16m gray blk	40	50
253A	A61	30m gray blk ('47)	1.75	20

Old Town Hall, Porvoo
A62

Cathedral, Porvoo
A63

1946, Dec. 3

254	A62	5m gray blk	30	45
255	A63	8m dp cl	30	45

Issued to commemorate the 600th anniversary of the founding of the city of Porvoo (Borga).

Waterfront, Tammisaari
A64

1946, Dec. 14

256	A64	8m grnsh blk	30	45

Issued to commemorate the 400th anniversary of the founding of the town of Tammisaari (Ekenas).

Lion Type of 1930.

1947 Typographed ***Perf. 14***

257	A26	2½m dk grn	25	8
258	A26	3m sl gray	20	8
259	A26	6m dp org	1.00	12
260	A26	7m carmine	20	10
261	A26	10m purple	3.25	8
262	A26	12m dp bl	1.25	8
		Nos. 257-262 (6)	6.15	54

Pres. Juho K. Paasikivi
A65

Postal Savings Emblem
A66

1947, Mar. 15 **Engraved**

263	A65	10m gray blk	35	35

1947, Apr. 1

264	A66	10m brn vio	35	35

Issued to commemorate the 60th anniversary of the foundation of the Finnish Postal Savings Bank.

Ilmarinen, the Plowman
A67

Girl and Boy Athletes
A68

1947, June 2

265	A67	10m gray blk	35	35

Issued to mark the second year of peace following World War II.

1947, June 2

266	A68	10m brt bl	45	45

Issued to commemorate the Finnish Athletic Festival, Helsingfors, June 29–July 3, 1947.

Wheat and Savings Bank Association Emblem
A69

Sower
A70

1947, Aug. 21

267	A69	10m red brn	35	35

Issued to commemorate the 125th anniversary of the Finnish Savings Bank Association.

1947, Nov. 1

268	A70	10m gray blk	35	35

Issued to commemorate the 50th anniversary of Finnish Agricultural Societies.

Koli Mountain and Lake Pielisjärvi
A71

Statue of Michael Agricola
A72

1947, Nov. 1

269	A71	10m indigo	35	35

Issued to commemorate the 60th anniversary of the Finnish Touring Association.

Lion Type of 1930.

1948 Typographed. ***Perf. 14***

270	A26	3m dk grn	1.50	15
271	A26	6m yel grn	60	30
272	A26	9m carmine	45	8
273	A26	15m dk bl	4.00	8
274	A26	24m brn lake	1.25	20
		Nos. 270-274 (5)	7.80	81

No. 261 Surcharged with New Value and Bars in Black.

1948, Feb. 9

275	A26	12(m) on 10m pur	1.00	18

1948, Oct. 2 **Engraved** ***Perf. 14***

Design: 12m, Agricola translating New Testament.

276	A72	7m rose vio	65	1.50
277	A72	12m gray bl	65	1.50

Issued to commemorate the 400th anniversary of publication of the Finnish translation of the New Testament, by Michael Agricola.

Sveaborg Fortress
A73

Post Rider
A74

1948, Oct. 15

278	A73	12m dp grn	1.25	1.25

Issued to commemorate the 200th anniversary of the construction of Sveaborg Fortress on the Gulf of Finland.

1948, Oct. 27

279	A74	12m green	20.00	25.00

Issued to commemorate the Helsinki Philatelic Exhibition. Sold only at exhibition, for 62m of which 50m was entrance fee.

1949 **Castle Type of 1945.**

280	A57	35m violet	4.50	15

Sawmill and Cellulose Plant
A75

Pine Tree and Globe
A76

Woman with Torch
A77

1949, June 15

281	A75	9m brown	1.75	1.75
282	A76	15m dl grn	1.75	1.75

Issued to publicize the Third World Forestry Congress, Helsinki, July 10–20, 1949.

1949, July 16 Engraved *Perf. 14*

283	A77	5m dl grn	4.00	*12.00*
284	A77	15m red (*Worker*)	4.00	*12.00*

Issued to commemorate the 50th anniversary of the Finnish labor movement.

Harbor of Lappeenranta (Willmanstrand)
A78

Raahe (Brahestad)
A79

1949

285	A78	5m dk bl grn	80	45
286	A79	9m brn car	80	65
287	A78	15m brt bl (*Kristiinan-kaupunki*)	1.20	80

Issued to commemorate the 300th anniversary of the founding of Willmanstrand, Brahestad and Kristinestad (Kristiinankaupunki).

Issue dates: 5m, Aug. 6; 9m, Aug. 13; 15m, July 30.

Technical High School Badge
A80

Hannes Gebhard
A81

1949, Sept. 13

288	A80	15m ultra	80	80

Issued to commemorate the centenary of the founding of the technical school.

1949, Oct. 2

289	A81	15m dl grn	80	80

Issued to commemorate the 50th anniversary of the establishment of Finnish cooperatives.

Finnish Lake Country
A82

1949, Oct. 8

290	A82	15m blue	1.00	1.00

Issued to commemorate the 75th anniversary of the formation of the Universal Postal Union.

Lion Type of 1930

1950 Typographed *Perf. 14.*

291	A26	8m brt grn	65	80
292	A26	9m red org	60	20
293	A26	10m vio brn	4.50	10
294	A26	12m scarlet	65	15
295	A26	15m plum	10.00	10
296	A26	20m dp bl	6.00	10
		Nos. 291-296 (6)	22.40	1.45

Forsell's Map of Old Helsinki
A83

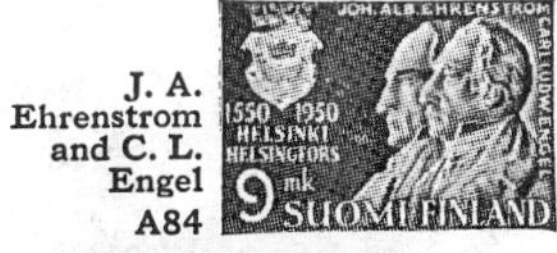

J. A. Ehrenstrom and C. L. Engel
A84

City Hall
A85

1950, June 11 Engraved

297	A83	5m emerald	40	40
298	A84	9m brown	80	80
299	A85	15m dp bl	80	80

Issued to commemorate the 400th anniversary of the founding of Helsinki.

J. K. Paasikivi
A86

View of Kajaani
A87

1950, Nov. 27

300	A86	20m dp ultra	75	30

80th birthday of Pres. J. K. Paasikivi.

1951, July 7 *Perf. 14* Unwmkd.

301	A87	20m red brn	75	50

Tercentenary of Kajaani.

Lion and Chopper Types of 1930

1952 Typographed

302	A26	10m emerald	2.25	15
303	A26	15m red	3.25	12
304	A26	25m blue	3.25	10

Engraved

305	A29	40m blk brn	3.00	12

Arms of Pietarsaari
A88

Rooftops of Vaasa
A89

1952, June 19 *Perf. 14* Unwmkd.

306	A88	25m blue	80	60

Issued to commemorate the 300th anniversary of the founding of Pietarsaari (Jacobstad).

1952, Aug. 3

307	A89	25m brown	80	60

Centenary of the burning of Vaasa.

Chess Symbols
A90

1952, Aug. 10

308	A90	25m gray	1.75	1.75

Issued to publicize the 10th Chess Olympics, Helsinki, Aug. 10–31, 1952.

Torch Bearers
A91

1953, Jan. 27

309	A91	25m blue	80	60

Issued to commemorate the centenary of the temperance movement in Finland.

Air View of Hamina (Fredrikshamn)
A92

Ivar Wilskman
A93

1953, June 20

310	A92	25m dk gray grn	80	60

Tercentenary of Hamina.

1954, Feb. 26

311	A93	25m blue	90	60

Issued to commemorate the centenary of the birth of Prof. Ivar Wilskman, "father of gymnastics in Finland."

Arms of Finland
A94

"In the Outer Archipelago"
A95

1954–59 *Perf. 11½*

312	A94	1m red brn ('55)	60	8
313	A94	2m grn ('55)	60	8
314	A94	3m dp org	60	8
314A	A94	4m gray ('58)	50	8
315	A94	5m vio bl	1.00	8
316	A94	10m bl grn	1.25	5
a.		Bklt. pane of 5 (vert. strip)	18.00	
317	A94	15m rose red	3.50	5
318	A94	15m yel org ('57)	5.00	8
319	A94	20m rose lil	6.00	10
320	A94	20m rose red ('56)	2.50	5
321	A94	25m dp bl	4.00	5
322	A94	25m rose lil ('59)	7.00	8
323	A94	30m lt ultra ('56)	2.50	5
		Nos. 312-323 (13)	35.05	91

See Nos. 398, 400–405A, 457–459, 461A–462, 464–464B.

1954, July 21 *Perf. 14*

324	A95	25m black	80	60

Issued to commemorate the centenary of the birth of Albert Edelfelt, painter.

J. J. Nervander
A96

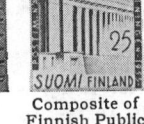

Composite of Finnish Public Buildings
A97

1955, Feb. 23

325	A96	25m blue	1.00	60

Issued to commemorate the 150th anniversary of the birth of J. J. Nervander, astronomer and poet.

1955, Mar. 20 Engraved *Perf. 14*

326	A97	25m gray	17.50	17.50

Sold for 125m, which included the price of admission to the National Postage Stamp Exhibition, Helsinki, March 30 to April 3, 1955.

Bishop Henrik with Foot on Lalli, his Murderer
A98

Conference Hall, Helsinki
A99

Design: 25m, Arrival of Bishop Henrik and monks.

1955, May 19

327	A98	15m rose brn	1.20	60
328	A98	25m green	1.20	60

Issued to commemorate the 800th anniversary of the adoption of Christianity in Finland.

1955, Aug. 25

329	A99	25m bluish grn	1.20	1.00

Issued to commemorate the 44th conference of the Interparliamentarian Union, Helsinki, Aug. 25-31, 1955.

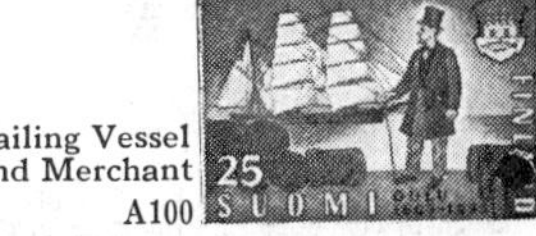

Sailing Vessel and Merchant
A100

1955, Sept. 2

330	A100	25m sepia	1.20	1.00

350th anniversary of founding of Oulu.

Town Hall, Lahti
A101

Radio Sender and Map of Finland
A102

1955, Nov. 1 *Perf. 14x13½*

331	A101	25m vio bl	1.20	1.00

50th anniversary of founding of Lahti.

1955, Dec. 10 *Perf. 14*

Designs: 15m, Otto Nyberg. 25m, Telegraph wires and pines under snow.

Inscribed:

Lennatin 1855-1955 Telegrafen.

332	A102	10m green	1.00	70
333	A102	15m dl vio	1.00	70
334	A102	25m lt ultra	1.00	70

Issued to commemorate the centenary of the telegraph in Finland.

Lighthouse and Porkkala Peninsula
A103

1956, Jan. 26 ***Perf. 14*** **Unwmkd.**

335 A103 25m grnsh bl 1.00 60

Issued to commemorate the return of the Porkkala Region to Finland by Russia, Jan. 1956.

Church at Lammi
A104

Designs: 40m, House of Parliament. 60m, Fortress of Olavinlinna (Olofsborg).

1956–57 ***Perf. 11½***

336 A104 30m gray ol 1.00 15
337 A104 40m dl pur 2.25 15
338 A104 50m gray ol ('57) 4.25 15
338A A104 60m pale pur ('57) 6.00 15

See Nos. 406–408A.

Johan V. Snellman
A105

Gymnast and Athletes
A106

1956, May 12 **Engraved** ***Perf. 14***

339 A105 25m dk vio brn 1.00 60

Issued to commemorate the 150th anniversary of the birth of Johan V. Snellman (1806–1881), statesman.

1956, June 28

340 A106 30m vio bl 1.10 70

Issued to commemorate the Finnish Gymnastic and Sports Games, Helsinki, June 28–July 1, 1956.

A107

Rouletted

1956, July 7 **Typo.** **Wmk. 208**

341 A107 30m dp ultra 3.50 5.50
a. Tête bêche pair 7.00 11.00
b. Pane of 10 37.50 60.00

Issued to publicize the FINLANDIA Philatelic Exhibition, Helsinki, July 7–15, 1956.

Printed in sheets containing four 2x5 panes, with white margins around each group. The stamps in each double row are printed tete-beche, making the position of the watermark differ in the vertical row of each pane of ten.

Sold for 155m, price including entrance ticket to exhibition.

Town Hall at Vasa
A108

Engraved.

1956, Oct. 2 ***Perf. 14*** **Unwmkd.**

342 A108 30m brt bl 1.00 60

350th anniversary of Vasa.

Northern Countries Issue.

Whooper Swans
A108a

1956, Oct. 30 ***Perf. 12½***

343 A108a 20m rose red 5.00 1.50
344 A108a 30m ultra 12.00 1.50

See footnote after Denmark No. 362.

University Clinic, Helsinki
A109

Scout Sign, Emblem and Globe
A110

1956, Dec. 17 ***Perf. 11½***

345 A109 30m dl grn 1.00 60

Issued to commemorate the bicentenary of public health service in Finland.

1957, Feb. 22 ***Perf. 14***

346 A110 30m ultra 1.25 70

50th anniversary of Boy Scouts.

Arms Holding Hammers and Laurel
A111

"Lex" from Seal of Parliament
A112

Design: 20m, Factories and cogwheel.

1957, Apr. 15 **Engraved** ***Perf. 13½***

347 A111 20m dk bl 1.00 60
348 A111 30m carmine 1.00 60

Issued to commemorate the 50th anniversaries of the Central Federation of Finnish Employers (No. 347) and of the Finnish Trade Union Movement (No. 348).

1957, May 23 ***Perf. 14***

349 A112 30m ol gray 1.00 60

Issued to commemorate the 50th anniversary of the Finnish parliament.

Harbor Type of 1942.

1957 ***Perf. 14*** **Unwmkd.**

350 A51 100m grnsh bl 3.00 20

Ida Aalberg
A114

Arms of Finland
A115

1957, Dec. 4 ***Perf. 14***

351 A114 30m vio gray & mar 1.00 60

Issued to commemorate the centenary of the birth of Ida Aalberg, Finnish actress.

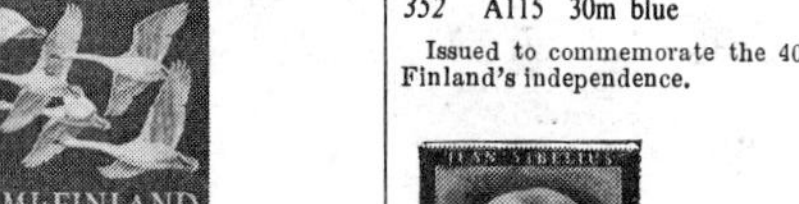

1957, Dec. 6 ***Perf. 11½***

352 A115 30m blue 1.00 60

Issued to commemorate the 40th anniversary of Finland's independence.

Jean Sibelius
A116

Ski Jump
A117

1957, Dec. 8 ***Perf. 14***

353 A116 30m black 1.00 60

Issued in memory of Jean Sibelius (1865–1957), composer.

1958, Feb. 1 **Engraved** ***Perf. 11½***

Design: 30m, Skier (vertical).

354 A117 20m sl grn 1.00 1.00
355 A117 30m blue 1.25 75

Issued to publicize the Nordic championships of the International Ski Federation, Lahti.

"March of the Bjorneborgienses," by Edelfelt
A118

South Harbor, Helsinki
A119

1958, Mar. 8

356 A118 30m vio gray 1.25 70

Issued to commemorate the 400th anniversary of the founding of Pori (Bjorneborg).

1958, June 2 ***Perf. 11½*** **Unwmkd.**

357 A119 100m bluish grn 12.50 15

See No. 410.

Seal of Jyväsky lä Lyceum
A120

1958, Oct. 1 ***Perf. 11½***

358 A120 30m rose car 1.40 70

Issued to commemorate the centenary of the founding of the first Finnish secondary school.

Chrismon and Globe
A121

Diet at Porvoo, 1809
A122

1959, Jan. 19

359 A121 30m dl vio 1.00 60

Issued to commemorate the centenary of the Finnish Missionary Society.

1959, Mar. 22 ***Perf. 11½***

360 A122 30m dk bl gray 1.00 60

Issued to commemorate the 150th anniversary of the inauguration of the Diet at Porvoo.

Saw Cutting Log
A123

Pyhakoski Power Station
A124

Design: 30m, Forest.

1959, May 13 **Engraved**

361 A123 10m redsh brn 80 60
362 A123 30m green 1.00 80

No. 361 commemorates the centenary of the establishment of the first steam sawmill in Finland; No. 362, the centenary of the Department of Forestry.

1959, May 24

363 A124 75m gray 2.00 15

See No. 409.

Oil Lamp
A125

Woman Gymnast
A126

1959, Dec. 19

364 A125 30m blue 1.00 50

Issued to commemorate the centenary of the liberation of the country trade.

1959, Nov. 14 **Unwmkd.**

365 A126 30m rose lil 1.00 50

Issued to honor Finnish women's gymnastics and the centenary of the birth of Elin Oihonna Kallio, pioneer of Finnish women's physical education.

Arms of Six New Towns
A127

1960, Jan. 2 ***Perf. 14***

366 A127 30m lt vio 1.00 50

Issued to commemorate the founding of new towns in Finland: Hyvinkaa, Kouvola, Riihimaki, Rovaniemi, Salo and Seinajoki.

Type of 1860 Issue
A128

Typographed

1960, Mar. 25 ***Rouletted 4½***

367 A128 30m bl & gray 7.50 8.00

Issued to commemorate the centenary of Finland's serpentine roulette stamps, and in connection with HELSINKI 1960, 40th anniversary exhibition of the Federation of Philatelic Societies of Finland, March 25–31. Sold only at the exhibition for 150m including entrance ticket.

Mother and Child, Waiting Crowd and Uprooted Oak Emblem
A129

1960, Apr. 7 Engraved *Perf. 11½*

368	A129	30m rose cl	80	45
369	A129	40m dk bl	80	50

Issued to publicize World Refugee Year, July 1, 1959–June 30, 1960.

Johan Gadolin
A130

Hj. Nortamo
A131

1960, June 4 *Perf. 11½*

370	A130	30m dk brn	1.00	50

Issued to commemorate the bicentennary of the birth of Johan Gadolin, chemist.

1960, June 13 Unwmkd.

371	A131	30m gray grn	1.00	50

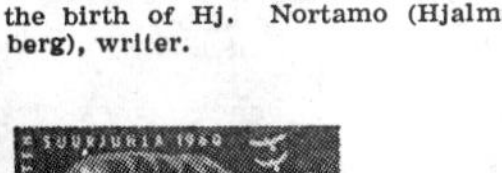

Issued to commemorate the centenary of the birth of Hj. Nortamo (Hjalmar Nordberg), writer.

Symbolic Tree and Cuckoo
A132

1960, June 18

372	A132	30m vermilion	1.00	50

Karelian National Festival, Helsinki, June 18–19.

Geodetic Instrument
A133

Urho Kekkonen
A134

Design: 30m, Aurora borealis and globe.

1960, July 26 *Perf. 13½* Unwmkd.

373	A133	10m bl & pale brn	80	45
374	A133	30m ver & rose car	1.00	60

Issued to publicize the 12th General Assembly of the International Union of Geodesy and Geophysics, Helsinki.

1960, Sept. 3 Engraved *Perf. 11½*

375	A134	30m vio bl	1.00	45

Issued to honor President Urho Kekkonen on his 60th birthday.

Europa Issue, 1960

Common Design Type

1960, Sept. 19 *Perf. 13½*

Size: 30½x21mm.

376	CD3	30m dk bl & Prus bl	65	45
377	CD3	40m dk brn & plum	80	45

A 30m gray similar to No. 376 was printed with simulated perforations in a non-valid souvenir sheet privately released in London for STAMPEX 1961.

Uno Cygnaeus
A135

"Pommern" and Arms of Mariehamn
A136

1960, Oct. 13 *Perf. 11½*

378	A135	30m dl vio	1.00	50

Issued to commemorate the 150th anniversary of the birth of Pastor Uno Cygnaeus, founder of elementary schools.

1961 Feb. 21 *Perf. 11½*

379	A136	30m grnsh bl	1.00	50

Centenary of the founding of Mariehamn.

Lake and Rowboat
A137

Turku Castle
A138

1961 Engraved Unwmkd.

380	A137	5m green	35	10
381	A138	125m sl grn	12.00	40

See also Nos. 399, 411.

Postal Savings Bank Emblem
A139

Symbol of Standardization
A140

1961, May 24

382	A139	30m Prus grn	1.00	50

Issued to commemorate the 75th anniversary of Finland's Postal Savings Bank.

Lithographed

1961, June 5 *Perf. 14x13½*

383	A140	30m dk sl grn & org	1.00	50

Issued to commemorate the meeting of the International Organization for Standardization, ISO, Helsinki, June 5.

Juhani Aho
A141

Engraved

1961, Sept. 11 *Perf. 11½* Unwmkd.

384	A141	30m red brn	1.00	50

Issued to commemorate the centenary of the birth of Juhani Aho (1861–1921), writer.

Various Buildings
A142

1961, Oct. 16 *Perf. 11½*

385	A142	30m slate	1.00	50

Issued to commemorate 150 years of the Central Board of Buildings.

Arvid Jarnefelt
A143

1961, Nov. 16

386	A143	30m dp cl	1.00	50

Issued to commemorate the centenary of the birth of Arvid Jarnefelt, writer.

Bank of Finland
A144

First Finnish Locomotive
A145

1961, Dec. 12 Engraved *Perf. 11½*

387	A144	30m brn vio	1.00	50

150th anniversary of Bank of Finland.

1962, Jan. 31 *Perf. 11½* Unwmkd.

Designs: 30m, Steam locomotive and timber car. 40m, Diesel locomotive and passenger train.

388	A145	10m gray grn	1.00	45
389	A145	30m vio bl	1.25	45
390	A145	40m dl red brn	1.25	60

Centenary of the Finnish State Railways.

Mora Stone
A146

1962, Feb. 15

391	A146	30m gray brn	1.00	50

Issued to commemorate 600 years of political rights of the Finnish people.

Senate Place, Helsinki
A147

1962, Apr. 8 *Perf. 11½* Unwmkd.

392	A147	30m vio brn	1.00	50

Issued to commemorate the sesquicentennial of the proclamation of Helsinki as capital of Finland.

Common Design Types
pictured in section at front of book.

Customs Emblem
A148

Staff of Mercury
A149

1962, Apr. 11

393	A148	30m red	1.00	50

Issued to commemorate the sesquicentennial of the Finnish Board of Customs.

1962, May 21 Engraved

394	A149	30m bluish grn	1.00	50

Issued to commemorate the centenary of the first commercial bank in Finland.

Santeri Alkio
A150

Finnish Labor Emblem and Conveyor Belt
A151

1962, June 17 *Perf. 11½* Unwmkd.

395	A150	30m brn car	1.00	50

Issued to commemorate the centenary of the birth of Santeri Alkio, writer and pioneer of the young people's societies in Finland.

1962, Oct. 19

396	A151	30m chocolate	80	45

National production progress.

Survey Plane and Compass
A152

1962, Nov. 14

397	A152	30m yel grn	1.00	50

Issued to commemorate the 150th anniversary of the Finnish Land Survey Board.

Types of 1954–61 and

Log Floating
A153

Parainen Bridge
A154

Farm on Lake Shore
A155

Ristikallio in Kuusamo—A156

Designs: 40p, House of Parliament. 50p, Church at Lammi. 60p, 65p, Fortress of Olavinlinna. 2.50m, Aerial view of Punkaharju.

1963-67 Engraved *Perf. 11½*

398	A94	5p vio bl	50	6
a.		Booklet pane of 2 (vert. pair)	20.00	
b.		Bklt. pane of 2 (horiz. pair)	20.00	
399	A137	5p green	30	8
400	A94	10p bl grn	50	6
a.		Booklet pane of 2 (vert. pair)	20.00	
401	A94	15p yel org	85	6
402	A94	20p rose red	60	6
a.		Booklet pane of 1	20.00	
b.		Bklt. pane of 3 (2 No. 400, 1 No. 402 + label; horiz. strip)	30.00	
c.		Bklt. pane of 5 (2 No. 398, 2 No. 400, 1 No. 402; horiz. strip)	4.75	
403	A94	25p rose lil	85	6
404	A94	30p lt ultra	4.00	6
404A	A94	30p bl gray ('65)	45	6
405	A94	35p blue	1.00	6
405A	A94	40p ultra ('67)	1.00	6
406	A104	40p dl pur	1.00	10
407	A104	50p gray ol	1.00	10
408	A104	60p pale pur	1.00	10
408A	A104	65p pale pur ('67)	1.00	10
409	A124	75p gray	1.10	10
410	A119	1m bluish grn	55	3
411	A138	1.25m sl grn	1.75	10
412	A153	1.50m dk grnsh gray	1.10	8
413	A154	1.75m blue	1.75	10
414	A155	2m grn ('64)	1.10	8
414A	A155	2.50m ultra & yel ('67)	2.10	25
415	A156	5m dk sl grn ('64)	4.00	60
		Nos. 398-415 (22)	27.50	2.36

Pennia denominations expressed: "0,05", "0,10", etc.

Four stamps of type A94 (5p, 10p, 20p, 25p) come in two types: I. Four vertical lines in "O" of SUOMI. II. Three lines in "O."

See also Nos. 457-464B.

Mother and Child A157

1963, Mar. 21 *Perf. 11½* Unwmkd.

416	A157	40p red brn	1.00	50

Issued for the "Freedom from Hunger" campaign of the U.N. Food and Agriculture Organization.

"Christ Today" A158

Design: 10p, Crown of thorns and medieval cross of consecration.

1963, July 30 Engraved *Perf. 11½*

417	A158	10p maroon	65	30
418	A158	30p dk grn	80	45

Issued to commemorate the 4th assembly of the Lutheran World Federation, Helsinki, July 30-Aug. 8.

Europa Issue, 1963

Common Design Type

1963, Sept. 16

Size: 30x20mm.

419	CD6	40p red lil	1.10	50

Assembly Building, Helsinki A159

1963, Sept. 18

420	A159	30p vio bl	1.00	50

Issued to commemorate the centenary of the Representative Assembly of Finland.

Convair Metropolitan A160

M. A. Castrén A161

Design: 40p, Caravelle jetliner.

1963, Nov. 1

421	A160	35p sl grn	1.00	50
422	A160	40p brt ultra	1.00	50

40th anniversary of Finnish air traffic.

1963, Dec. 2 Unwmkd.

423	A161	35p vio bl	1.00	50

Issued to commemorate the 150th anniversary of the birth of Matthias Alexander Castrén (1813-52), ethnologist and philologist.

Stone Elk's Head, 2000 B.C. A162

Emil Nestor Setälä A163

1964, Feb. 5 Litho. *Perf. 11½*

424	A162	35p ocher & sl grn	1.00	50

Issued to commemorate the centenary of the Finnish Artists' Association. The soapstone sculpture was found at Huittinen.

1964, Feb. 27 Engraved

425	A163	35p dk red brn	1.00	50

Issued to commemorate the centenary of the birth of Emil Nestor Setälä (1864-1946), philologist, minister of education and foreign affairs and chancellor of Abo University.

Staff of Aesculapius A164

1964, June 13 *Perf. 11½* Unwmkd.

426	A164	40p sl grn	1.00	50

Issued to commemorate the 18th General Assembly of the World Medical Association, Helsinki, June 13-19, 1964.

Ice Hockey A165

1965, Jan. 4 Engraved

427	A165	35p dk bl	1.00	50

Issued to publicize the World Ice Hockey Championships, Finland, March 3-14, 1965.

Design from Centenary Medal A166

1965, Feb. 6 *Perf. 11½* Unwmkd.

428	A166	35p ol gray	1.00	50

Issued to commemorate the centenary of communal self-government in Finland.

K. J. Stahlberg and "Lex" by W. Runeberg A167

1965, Mar. 22 Engraved

429	A167	35p brown	1.00	50

Issued to commemorate the centenary of the birth of Kaarlo Juho Stahlberg (1865-1952), first President of Finland.

International Cooperation Year Emblem A168

1965, Apr. 2 Lithographed *Perf. 14*

430	A168	40p bis, dl red, blk & grn	1.00	50

U.N. International Cooperation Year.

"Fratricide" by Gallen-Kallela A169

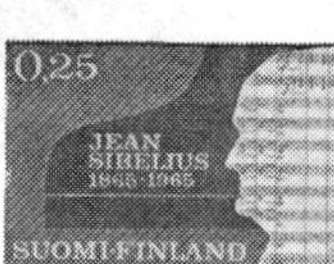

Sibelius, Piano and Score A170

Design: 35p, Girl's Head by Akseli Gallen-Kallela.

1965, Aug. 26 *Perf. 13½x14*

431	A169	25p multi	1.25	65
432	A169	35p multi	1.25	65

Issued to commemorate the centenary of the birth of the painter Akseli Gallen-Kallela.

1965, May 15 Engraved *Perf. 11½*

Design: 35p, Musical score and bird.

433	A170	25p violet	1.10	55
434	A170	35p dl grn	1.10	55

Issued to commemorate the centenary of the birth of Jean Sibelius (1865-1957), composer.

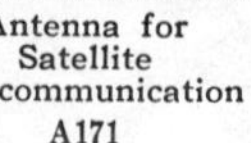

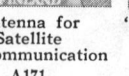

Antenna for Satellite Telecommunication A171

"Winter Day" by Pekka Halonen A172

1965, May 17

435	A171	35p blue	1.00	45

Issued to commemorate the centenary of the International Telecommunication Union.

Perf. 14x13½

1965, Sept. 23 Litho. Unwmkd.

436	A172	35p gold & multi	1.10	45

Issued to commemorate the centenary of the birth of the painter Pekka Halonen.

Europa Issue, 1965

Common Design Type

Engraved and Lithographed

1965, Sept. 27 *Perf. 13½x14*

437	CD8	40p bis, red brn, dk bl & grn	1.10	50

"Growth" A173

Old Post Office A174

1966, May 11 Litho. *Perf. 14*

438	A173	35p vio bl & bl	80	45

Issued to commemorate the centenary of the promulgation of the Elementary School Decree.

1966, June 11 Litho. *Perf. 14*

439	A174	35p ocher, yel, dk bl & blk	7.50	8.00

Issued to commemorate the centenary of the first postage stamps in Finnish currency, and in connection with the NORDIA Stamp Exhibition, Helsinki, June 11-15. The stamp was sold only to buyers of a 1.25m exhibition entrance ticket.

UNESCO Emblem and World Map A175

Finnish Police Emblem A176

Lithographed and Engraved

1966, Oct. 9 *Perf. 14*

440	A175	40p grn, yel, blk & brn org	1.00	45

Issued to commemorate the 20th anniversary of UNESCO (United Nations Educational, Scientific and Cultural Organization).

1966, Oct. 15

441	A176	35p dp ultra, blk & sil	1.00	45

Issued to honor the Finnish police.

Insurance Sesquicentennial Medal A177

Engraved and Photogravure

1966, Oct. 28 *Perf. 14*

442	A177	35p mar, ol & blk	1.00	45

Issued to commemorate the 150th anniversary of the Finnish insurance system.

UNICEF Emblem A178

1966, Nov. 14

443	A178	15p lt ultra, pur & grn	60	40

Issued to publicize the activities of UNICEF (United Nations Children's Emergency Fund).

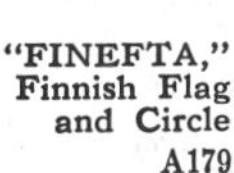

"FINEFTA," Finnish Flag and Circle
A179

1967, Feb. 15 Engraved *Perf. 14*

444	A179	40p ultra	1.00	40

Issued to publicize the European Free Trade Association, EFTA. See note after Denmark No. 431.

Windmill and Arms of Uusikaupunki
A180

Mannerheim Monument by Aimo Tukiainen
A181

Lithographed and Engraved

1967, Apr. 19 *Perf. 14*

445	A180	40p multi	1.00	40

Issued to commemorate the 350th anniversary of Uusikaupunki (Nystad).

1967, June 4 *Perf. 14*

446	A181	40p vio & multi	1.00	40

Issued to commemorate the centenary of the birth of Field Marshal Carl Gustav Emil Mannerheim.

Double Mortise Corner
A182

Watermark of Thomasböle Paper Mill
A183

Lithographed and Photogravure

1967, June 16

447	A182	40p multi	1.00	40

Issued to honor Finnish settlers in Sweden.

Lithographed and Engraved

1967, Sept. 6 *Perf. 14*

448	A183	40p ol & blk	1.00	40

Issued to commemorate the 300th anniversary of the Finnish paper industry.

Martin Luther, by Lucas Cranach
A184

Photogravure and Engraved

1967, Nov. 4 *Perf. 14*

449	A184	40p bis & brn	1.00	40

450th anniversary of the Reformation.

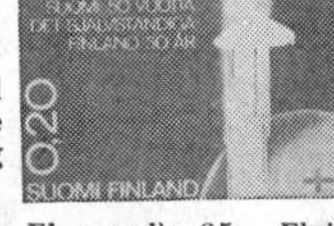

"Wood and Water" Globe and Flag
A185

Designs (Globe, Flag and): 25p, Flying swan. 40p, Ear of wheat.

1967, Dec. 5 *Perf. 11½*

450	A185	20p grn & bl	1.00	40
451	A185	25p ultra & bl	1.00	40
452	A185	40p mag & bl	1.00	40

Issued to commemorate the 50th anniversary of Finland's independence.

Zachris Topelius and Blue Bird
A186

1968, Jan. 14 Litho. *Perf. 14*

453	A186	25p bl & multi	1.00	40

Issued to commemorate the 150th anniversary of the birth of Zachris Topelius (1818–1898), writer and educator.

Skiers and Ski Lift
A187

1968, Feb. 19 Photo. *Perf. 14*

454	A187	25p multi	1.00	40

Issued to publicize Winter Tourism in Finland.

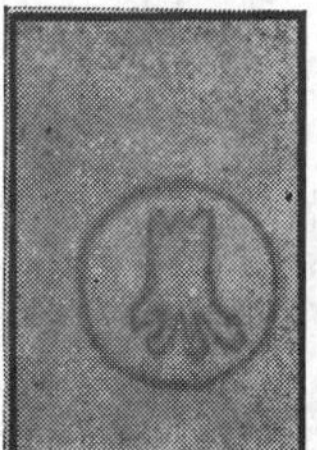
Paper Making, by Hannes Autere
A188

Wmk. 363

Wmkd. Tree Stump (363)

1968, Mar. 12 Lithographed

455	A188	45p dk red, brn & org	1.00	40

Issued to publicize the Finnish paper industry and to commemorate the 150th anniversary of the oldest Finnish paper mill, Tervakoski, whose own watermark was used for this stamp.

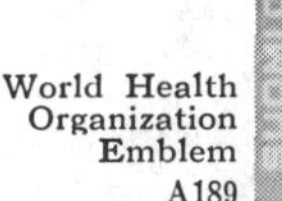

World Health Organization Emblem
A189

Lithographed and Photogravure

1968, Apr. 6 *Perf. 14* Unwmkd.

456	A189	40p red org, dk bl & gold	1.00	40

To honor World Health Organization.

Lion Type of 1954–58 and

Market Place and Mermaid Fountain, Helsinki
A190

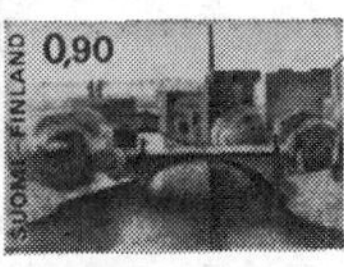

Keuru Wooden Church, 1758
A191

Häme Bridge, Tampere—A192

Finnish Arms from Grave of King Gustav Vasa, 1581
A194

Designs: 25p, Post bus. 30p, Aquarium-Planetarium, Tampere. No. 463, P.O., Tampere. No. 465, National Museum, Helsinki (vert.). No. 467A, like 70p. 1.30m, Helsinki railroad station.

Engr. (type A94); Litho. (#465 & type A190); Engr. & Litho. (others).

Perf. 11½; 12½ (type A190); 14 (#465, 470A); 13½ (#470).

1968–78

457	A94	1p lt red brn	30	5
458	A94	2p gray grn	30	3
459	A94	4p gray	30	5
460	A192	25p multi ('71)	30	6
461	A191	30p multi ('71)	75	15
461A	A94	35p dl org ('74)	70	6
b.		Bklt. pane of 4 (#398, #461A, #400, #464A) + label	2.00	
462	A94	40p org ('73)	55	3
a.		Bklt. pane of 3 (2 #404A, #462) + 2 labels	7.50	
463	A192	40p multi ('73)	1.25	10
464	A94	50p lt ultra ('70)	1.00	3
c.		Bklt. pane of 5 (#401, #403, #464, 2 #398) + 5 labels	6.50	
464A	A94	50p rose lake ('74)	75	3
d.		Bklt. pane of 4 (#400, 2 #402, #464A) + label	2.50	
464B	A94	60p bl ('73)	35	4
465	A191	60p multi ('73)	35	4
466	A190	70p multi ('73)	75	10
467	A191	80p multi ('70)	2.00	10
467A	A190	80p multi ('76)	45	10
468	A192	90p multi	1.50	10
469	A191	1.30m multi ('71)	90	12
470	A194	10m multi ('74)	5.50	60
470A	A194	20m multi ('78)	11.00	2.00
		Nos. 457-470A (19)	29.00	3.79

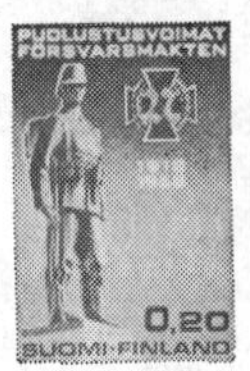

Infantry Monument, Vaasa
A195

Camping Ground
A196

Designs: 25p, War Memorial (cross), Hietaniemi Cemetery. 40p, Soldier, 1968.

1968, June 4 Photo. *Perf. 14*

471	A195	20p lt vio & multi	1.00	35
472	A195	25p lt bl & multi	1.00	35
473	A195	40p org & multi	1.00	35

To honor Finnish national defense.

1968, June 10 Lithographed

474	A196	25p multi	1.00	40

Issued to publicize Finland for summer vacations.

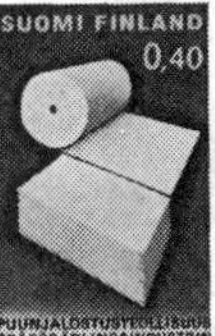

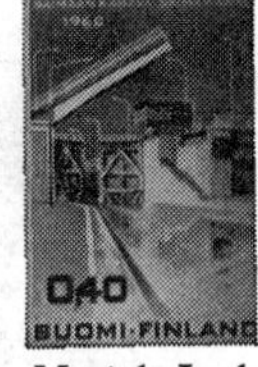

Paper, Pulp and Pine
A197

Mustola Lock, Saima Canal
A198

Lithographed and Embossed

1968, July 2 *Perf. 14* Unwmkd.

475	A197	40p multi	1.00	40

Finnish wood industry.

1968, Aug. 5 Litho. *Perf. 14*

476	A198	40p multi	1.00	40

Opening of the Saima Canal.

Oskar Merikanto and Pipe Organ
A199

1968, Aug. 5 Unwmkd.

477	A199	40p vio, sil & lt brn	1.00	40

Issued to commemorate the centenary of the birth of Oskar Merikanto, composer.

Ships in Harbor and Emblem of Central Chamber of Commerce
A200

Welder
A201

1968, Sept. 13 Litho. *Perf. 14*

478	A200	40p lt bl, brt bl & blk	1.00	40

Issued to publicize economic development and to commemorate the 50th anniversary of the Central Chamber of Commerce of Finland.

1968, Oct. 11 Lithographed *Perf. 14*

479	A201	40p bl & multi	1.00	40

Finnish metal industry.

Lyre, Students' Emblem
A202

Five Ancient Ships
A203

Lithographed and Engraved

1968, Nov. 24 *Perf. 14*

480	A202	40p ultra, vio bl & gold	1.00	40

Issued to publicize the work of the student unions in Finnish social life.

Nordic Cooperation Issue

1968, Feb. 28 Engraved *Perf. 11½*

481	A203	40p lt ultra	1.40	35

See footnote after Denmark No. 455.

Town Hall and Arms of Kemi
A203a

1969, Mar. 5 Photo. ***Perf. 14***

482 A203a 40p multi 1.00 40

Centenary of the town of Kemi.

Europa Issue, 1969
Common Design Type

1969, Apr. 28 Photo. ***Perf. 14***
Size: 30x20mm.

483 CD12 40p dl rose, vio bl & dk bl 2.50 50

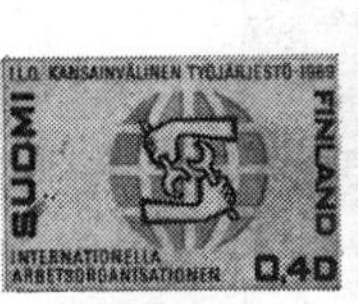

I.L.O. Emblem
A204

Armas Järnefelt
A205

Lithographed and Engraved

1969, June 2 ***Perf. 11½***

484 A204 40p dp rose & vio bl 1.00 35

Issued to commemorate the 50th anniversary of the International Labor Organization.

1969, Aug. 14 Photo. ***Perf. 14***

485 A205 40p multi 1.00 35

Centenary of the birth of Armas Järnefelt (1869–1958), composer and conductor. Portrait on stamp by Vilho Sjöström.

Emblems and Flag
A206

Johannes Linnankoski
A207

1969, Sept. 19 Photo. ***Perf. 14***

486 A206 40p lt bl, blk, grn & lil 1.00 35

Issued to publicize the importance of National and International Fairs in Finnish economy.

1969, Oct. 18 **Lithographed**

487 A207 40p dk brn red & multi 1.00 35

Issued to commemorate the centenary of the birth of Johannes Linnankoski (1869–1913), writer.

Educational Symbols
A208

Lithographed and Engraved

1969, Nov. 24 ***Perf. 11½***

488 A208 40p gray, vio & grn 1.00 35

Centenary of the Central School Board.

DC-8-62 CF Plane and Helsinki Airport
A209

1969, Dec. 22 Photo. ***Perf. 14***

489 A209 25p sky bl & multi 1.00 35

Golden Eagle
A210

1970, Feb. 10 Litho. ***Perf. 14***

490 A210 30p multi 2.00 50

Year of Nature Conservation, 1970.

Swatches in Shape of Factories
A211

1970, Mar. 9 Litho. ***Perf. 14***

491 A211 50p multi 1.00 30

Finnish textile industry.

Molecule Diagram and Factories
A212

UNESCO Emblem and Lenin
A213

Atom Diagram and Laurel
A214

U.N. Emblem and Globe
A215

1970, Mar. 26 Photo. ***Perf. 14***

492 A212 50p multi 1.00 30

Finnish chemical industry.

1970 **Litho. and Engraved**

493 A213 30p gold & multi 1.00 35
494 A214 30p red & multi 1.00 35

Photogravure and Gold Embossed

495 A215 50p bl, vio bl & gold 1.00 35

Issued to commemorate the 25th anniversary of the United Nations. No. 493 also publicizes the UNESCO-sponsored Lenin Symposium, Tampere, Apr. 6–10. No. 494 also publicizes the Nuclear Data Conference of the Atomic Energy Commission, Otaniemi (Helsinki), June 15–19.
Issue dates: No. 493, Apr. 6; No. 494, June 15; No. 495, Oct. 24.

Handicapped Volleyball Player
A216

Meeting of Auroraseura Society
A217

1970, June 27 Litho. ***Perf. 14***

496 A216 50p org, red & blk 1.00 35

Issued to publicize the position of handicapped civilians and war veterans in society and their potential contributions to it.

1970, Aug. 15 Photo. ***Perf. 14***

497 A217 50p multi 1.00 35

Issued to commemorate the 200th anniversary of the Auroraseura Society, dedicated to the study of Finnish history, geography, economy and language. The design of the stamp is after a painting by Eero Jarnefelt.

Uusikaarlepyy Arms, Church and 17th Century Building—A218

Urho Kekkonen, Medal by Aimo Tukiainen
A219

Design: No. 499, Arms of Kokkola, harbor, Sports Palace and 17th century building.

1970 ***Perf. 14***

498 A218 50p multi 1.00 35
499 A218 50p multi 1.00 35

Issued to commemorate the 350th anniversaries of the towns of Uusikaarlepyy and Kokkola. Issue dates: No. 498, Aug. 21; No. 499, Sept. 17.

1970, Sept. 3 **Litho. & Engr.**

500 A219 50p ultra, sil & blk 1.00 30

70th birthday of Pres. Urho Kekkonen.

Globe, Maps of U.S., Finland, U.S.S.R.—A220

Pres. Paasikivi by Essi Renavall
A221

Lithographed and Gold Embossed

1970, Nov. 2

501 A220 50p blk, bl, pink & gold 1.00 30

Issued to publicize the Strategic Arms Limitation Talks (SALT) between the U.S. and U.S.S.R., Helsinki, Nov. 2–Dec. 18.

1970, Nov. 27 Photo. ***Perf. 14***

502 A221 50p gold, brt bl & sl 1.25 30

Centenary of the birth of Juho Kusti Paasikivi (1870–1956), President of Finland.

Cogwheels
A222

1971, Jan. 28 Litho. ***Perf. 14***

503 A222 50p multi 1.00 30

Finnish industry.

Europa Issue, 1971
Common Design Type

1971, May 3 Litho. ***Perf. 14***
Size: 30x20mm.

504 CD14 50p dp rose, yel & blk 2.00 50

Tornio Church
A223

Front Page, January 15, 1771
A224

1971, May 12 Litho. ***Perf. 14***

505 A223 50p multi 1.00 30

350th anniversary of the town of Tornio.

1971, June 1 Litho. ***Perf. 14***

506 A224 50p multi 1.00 30

Bicentenary of the Finnish press.

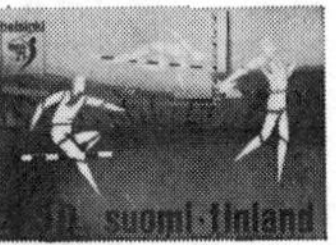

Athletes in Helsinki Stadium
A225

Design: 50p, Running and javelin in Helsinki Stadium.

1971, July 5 Lithographed *Perf. 14*

507 A225 30p multi 1.25 50
508 A225 50p multi 1.25 50

European Athletic Championships.

Sailboats
A226

1971, July 14

509 A226 50p multi 1.25 40

International Lightning Class Championships, Helsinki, July 14–Aug. 1.

Silver Tea Pot, Guild's Emblem, Tools
A227

1971, Aug. 6

510 A227 50p lil & multi 1.00 30

600th anniversary of Finnish goldsmiths' art.

"Plastic Buttons and Houses"
A228

Photogravure and Embossed

1971, Oct. 20 *Perf. 14*

511 A228 50p multi 1.00 30

Finnish plastics industry.

Europa Issue 1972

Common Design Type

1972, May 2 Litho. *Perf. 14*

Size: 20x30mm.

512 CD15 30p dk red & multi 1.50 50

513 CD15 50p lt brn & multi 1.50 50

Finnish National Theater
A229

1972, May 22 Litho. *Perf. 14*

514 A229 50p lt vio & multi 1.00 30

Centenary of the Finnish National Theater, founded by Kaarlo and Emilie Bergbom.

Globe, U.S. and U.S.S.R. Flags
A230

1972, June 2

515 A230 50p multi 1.00 50

Strategic Arms Limitation Talks (SALT), final meeting, Helsinki, Mar. 28–May 26; treaty signed, Moscow, May 26.

Map and Arms of Aland
A231

Training Ship Suomen Joutsen
A232

1972, June 9

516 A231 50p multi 2.50 60

50th anniversary of first Provincial Meeting of Aland.

1972, June 19

517 A232 50p org & multi 1.10 50

Tall Ships' Race 1972, Helsinki, Aug. 20.

Costume from Perni, 12th Century
A233

Circle Surrounding Map of Europe
A234

1972, Nov. 19 Litho. *Perf. 13*

Multicolored

518 A233 50p *shown* 1.25 30

519 A233 50p *Married couple, Tenhola, 18th century* 1.25 30

520 A233 50p *Girl, Nastola, 19th century* 1.25 30

521 A233 50p *Man, Voyni, 19th century* 1.25 30

522 A233 50p *Lapps, Inari, 19th century* 1.25 30

a. Booklet pane of 10 14.00

Nos. 518-522 (5) 6.25 1.50

Regional costumes. Nos. 518–522 printed se-tenant.

No. 522a contains 2 each of Nos. 518–522.

See Nos. 533–537.

1972, Dec. 11 *Perf. 14x13½*

523 A234 50p multi 2.25 50

Preparatory Conference on European Security and Cooperation.

Book, Finnish and Soviet Colors
A235

Litho.; Gold Embossed

1973, Apr. 6 *Perf. 14*

524 A235 60p gold & multi 1.00 30

25th anniversary of the Soviet-Finnish Treaty of Friendship.

Pres. Kyösti Kallio
A236

1973, Apr. 10 Litho. *Perf. 13*

525 A236 60p multi 1.00 30

Centenary of the birth of Kyösti Kallio (1873–1940), president of Finland.

Europa Issue 1973

Common Design Type

1973, Apr. 30 Photo. *Perf. 14*

Size: 31x21mm.

526 CD16 60p bl, brt bl & emer 1.00 30

Nordic Cooperation Issue

Nordic House, Reykjavik
A236a

1973, June 26 Engr. *Perf. 12½*

527 A236a 60p multi 1.50 50

528 A236a 70p multi 1.50 50

A century of postal cooperation among Denmark, Finland, Iceland, Norway and Sweden, and in connection with the Nordic Postal Conference, Reykjavik.

Map of Europe, "EUROPA" as a Maze
A237

Litho., Embossed

1973, July 3 *Perf. 13*

529 A237 70p multi 1.00 30

Conference for European Security and Cooperation, Helsinki, July 1973.

Paddling
A238

Radiosonde, WMO Emblem
A239

1973, July 18 Litho. *Perf. 14*

530 A238 60p multi 1.00 30

Canoeing World Championships, Tampere, July 26–29.

1973, Aug. 6 Litho. *Perf. 14*

531 A239 60p multi 1.00 30

Centenary of international meteorological cooperation.

Eliel Saarinen and Design for Parliament, Helsinki
A240

1973, Aug. 20 *Perf. 12½x13*

532 A240 60p multi 1.00 30

Centenary of the birth of Eliel Saarinen (1873–1950), architect.

Costume Type of 1972

1973, Oct. 10 Litho. *Perf. 13*

Multicolored

533 A233 60p *Woman, Kaukola* 1.50 30

534 A233 60p *Woman, Jaaski* 1.50 30

535 A233 60p *Married couple, Koivisto* 1.50 30

536 A233 60p *Mother and son, Sakyla* 1.50 30

537 A233 60p *Girl, Hainavesi* 1.50 30

Nos. 533-537 (5) 7.50 1.50

Regional costumes. Nos. 533–537 printed se-tenant.

DC10–30 Jet
A241

1973, Nov. 1 Litho. *Perf. 14*

538 A241 60p multi 1.00 30

50th anniversary of regular air service, Finnair.

Santa Claus in Reindeer Sleigh
A242

1973, Nov. 15 Litho. *Perf. 14*

539 A242 30p multi 1.00 25

Christmas 1973.

"The Barber of Seville"
A243

1973, Nov. 21

540 A243 60p multi 1.00 30

Centenary of opera in Finland.

Production of Porcelain Jug
A244

Nurmi, by Waino Aaltonen
A245

1973, Nov. 23

541 A244 60p bl & multi 1.00 30

Finnish porcelain.

1973, Dec. 11

542 A245 60p multi 1.00 30

Paavo Nurmi (1897–1973), runner, Olympic winner, 1920–1924–1928.

Arms, Map and Harbor of Hanko
A246

1974, Jan. 10 Litho. *Perf. 14*

543 A246 60p bl & multi 1.00 30

Centenary of the town of Hanko.

Ice Hockey
A247

1974, Mar. 5 Lithographed *Perf. 14*

544 A247 60p multi 1.00 30

European and World Ice Hockey Championships, held in Finland.

Seagulls (7 Baltic States)
A248

1974, Mar. 18 *Perf. 12½*

545 A248 60p multi 1.00 30

Protection of marine environment of the Baltic Sea.

Goddess of Freedom, by Waino Aaltonen
A249

Ilmari Kianto and Old Pine
A250

Europa Issue, 1974

1974, Apr. 29 Litho. *Perf. 13x12½*

546 A249 70p multi 1.00 30

1974, May 7 *Perf. 13*

547 A250 60p multi 1.00 30

Ilmari Kianto (1874–1970), writer.

Society Emblem, Symbol
A251

Lithographed and Embossed

1974, June 12 *Perf. 13½x14*

548 A251 60p gold & multi 1.00 30

Centenary of Adult Education.

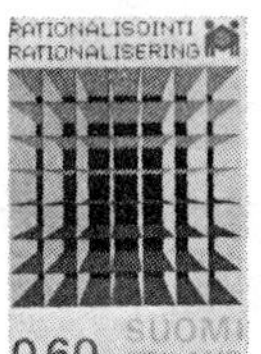

Grid A252 — UPU Emblem A253

1974, June 14 Litho. *Perf. 14x13½*

549 A252 60p multi 1.00 30

Rationalization Year in Finland, dedicated to economic and business improvements.

1974, Oct. 10 Litho. *Perf. 13½x14*

550 A253 60p multi 1.00 30
551 A253 70p multi 1.00 30

Centenary of Universal Postal Union.

Elves Distributing Gifts A254 — Concrete Bridge and Granite Bridge, Aunessilta A255

1974, Nov. 16 Litho. *Perf. 14x13½*

552 A254 35p multi 80 30

Christmas 1974.

Lithographed and Engraved

1974, Dec. 17 *Perf. 14*

553 A255 60p multi 80 30

Royal Finnish Directorate of Roads and Waterways, 175th anniversary.

Coat of Arms, 1581 A256 — Chimneyless Log Sauna A256a

Cheese Frames
A257

Carved Wooden Distaffs A258 — Kirvu Weather Vane A258a

Design: 1.50m, Wood-carved high drinking bowl, 1542.

Perf. 11½; 14 (2m)

1975–79		Engraved		
555	A256	10p red lil ('78)	6	3
a.		Bklt. pane of 4 (#555, 2 #556, #559) + label	60	
b.		Bklt. pane of 5 (2 #555, #557, #563, #564)	2.25	
556	A256	20p ol ('77)	12	3
557	A256	30p car ('77)	18	3
558	A256	40p orange	22	3
559	A256	50p grn ('76)	28	3
560	A256	60p blue	35	3
561	A256	70p sepia	40	3
562	A256	80p dl red & bl grn ('76)	45	3
563	A256	90p vio ('77)	50	3
564	A256	1.10m yel ('79)	60	8
565	A256	1.20m dk bl ('79)	65	10
566	A258	1.50m multi ('76)	85	10
		Lithographed		
567	A256a	2m multi ('77)	1.15	25
		Lithographed and Engraved		
568	A257	2.50m multi ('76)	1.40	25
569	A258	4.50m multi ('76)	2.50	35
570	A258a	5m multi ('77)	2.80	35
		Nos. 555-570 (16)	12.51	1.75

Finland No. 16 A259 — Girl Combing Hair, by Magnus Enckell A260

Lithographed and Typographed

1975, Apr. 26 *Perf. 13*

571 A259 70p multi 4.00 4.00

Nordia 75 Philatelic Exhibition, Helsinki, Apr. 26–May 1. Sold only at exhibition for 3m including entrance ticket.

Europa Issue 1975

Design: 90p, Washerwoman, by Tyko Sallinen (1879–1955).

1975, Apr. 28 Litho. *Perf. 13x12½*

572 A260 70p gray & multi 1.00 40
573 A260 90p tan & multi 1.00 40

Balance of Justice, Sword of Legality A261 — Rescue Boat and Sinking Ship A262

1975, May 7 *Perf. 14*

574 A261 70p vio bl & multi 80 30

Sesquicentennial of State Economy Comptroller's Office.

1975, June 2 Litho. *Perf. 14*

575 A262 70p multi 80 30

12th International Salvage Conference, Finland, stressing importance of coordinating sea, air and communications resources in salvage operations.

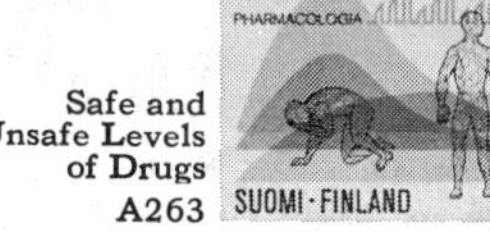

Safe and Unsafe Levels of Drugs
A263

1975, July 21 Litho. *Perf. 14*

576 A263 70p multi 80 30

Importance of pharmacological studies and for the 6th International Pharmacology Congress, Helsinki.

Olavinlinna Castle
A264

1975, July 29 *Perf. 13*

577 A264 70p multi 80 30

500th anniversary of Olavinlinna Castle.

Swallows over Finlandia Hall A265 — "Men and Women Working for Peace" A266

1975, July 30

578 A265 90p multi 1.00 30

European Security and Cooperation Conference, Helsinki, July 30–Aug. 1. (The swallows of the design represent freedom, mobility and continuity.)

1975, Oct. 24 Litho. *Perf. 13x12½*

579 A266 70p multi 80 30

International Women's Year 1975.

"Continuity and Growth" A267 — Boys as Three Kings and Herod A268

1975, Oct. 29 *Perf. 13*

580 A267 70p brn & multi 80 30

Industrial Art and for the centenary of the Finnish Society of Industrial Art.

1975, Nov. 8 *Perf. 14*

581 A268 40p bl & multi 80 25

Christmas 1975.

Top Border of State Debenture
A269

Lithographed and Engraved

1976, Jan. 9 *Perf. 11½*

582 A269 80p multi 80 30

Centenary of State Treasury.

Glider over Lake Region
A270

1976, Jan. 13 Litho. *Perf. 14*

583 A270 80p multi 1.25 40

15th World Glider Championships, Rayskala, June 13–27.

Heikki Klemetti
A271

1976, Feb. 14 Litho. *Perf. 13*

584 A271 80p grn & multi 80 30

Prof. Heikki Klemetti (1876–1953), musician and writer, birth centenary.

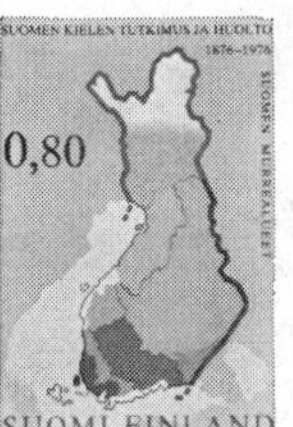

Map with Areas of Different Dialects A272 — Aino Ackté, by Albert Edelfelt A273

1976, Mar. 10 Litho. *Perf. 13*

585 A272 80p multi 80 30

Finnish Language Society, centenary.

1976, Apr. 23

586 A273 70p yel & multi 80 30

Aino Ackté (1876–1944), opera singer, birth centenary.

Europa Issue 1976

Knife from Voyri, Sheath and Belt
A274

1976, May 3 Litho. *Perf. 13*

587 A274 80p vio bl & multi 2.25 50

Radio and Television
A275

1976, Sept. 9 Litho. *Perf. 13*

588 A275 80p multi 80 30

Radio broadcasting in Finland, 50th anniversary.

Christmas Morning Ride to Church
A276

1976, Oct. 23 Litho. *Perf. 14*

589 A276 50p multi 70 30

Christmas 1976.

Turku Chapter Seal (Virgin and Child)
A277

1976, Nov. 1 Litho. *Perf. 12½*

590 A277 80p buff, brn & red 80 30

700th anniversary of the Cathedral Chapter of Turku.

Alvar Aalto, Finlandia Hall, Helsinki
A278

1976, Nov. 4

591 A278 80p multi 80 30

Hugo Alvar Henrik Aalto (1898–1976), architect.

Ice Dancers
A280

Five Water Lilies
A281

1977, Jan. 25 Litho. *Perf. 13*

592 A280 90p multi 80 30

European Figure Skating Championships, Finland, Jan. 25–29.

Photogravure and Engraved

1977, Feb. 2 *Perf. 12½*

593 A281 90p brt grn & multi 1.10 45
594 A281 1m ultra & multi 1.10 45

Nordic countries cooperation for protection of the environment and 25th Session of Nordic Council, Helsinki, Feb. 19.

Icebreaker Rescuing Merchantman
A282

1977, Mar. 2 Litho. *Perf. 13*

595 A282 90p multi 80 30

Winter navigation between Finland and Sweden, centenary.

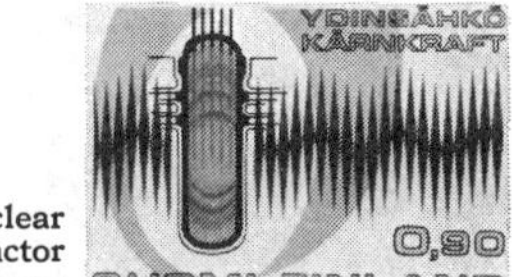

Nuclear Reactor
A283

1977, Mar. 3 *Perf. 12½x13*

596 A283 90p multi 70 30

Opening of nuclear power station on Hästholmen Island.

Europa Issue 1977

Autumn Landscape, Northern Finland
A284

1977, May 2 Litho. *Perf. 12½x13*

597 A284 90p multi 1.10 40

Tree, Birds and Nest
A285

Orthodox Church, Valamo Cloister
A286

1977, May 4 *Perf. 13x12½*

598 A285 90p multi 80 30

75th anniversary of cooperative banks.

1977, May 31 Litho. *Perf. 14*

599 A286 90p multi 80 30

Consecration festival of new Orthodox Church at Valamo Cloister, Heinävesi; 800th anniversary of introduction of orthodoxy in Karelia and of founding of Valamo Cloister.

Paavo Ruotsalainen
A287

1977, July 8 Litho. *Perf. 13*

600 A287 90p multi 80 30

Paavo Ruotsalainen (1777–1852), lay leader of Pietists in Finland.

People Fleeing Fire and Water
A288

Volleyball
A289

1977, Sept. 14 Litho. *Perf. 14*

601 A288 90p multi 70 30

Civil defense for security.

1977, Sept. 15

602 A289 90p multi 90 40

European Women's Volleyball Championships, Finland, Sept. 29–Oct. 2.

Children Bringing Water for Sauna
A290

1977, Oct. 25

603 A290 50p multi 70 25

Christmas 1977.

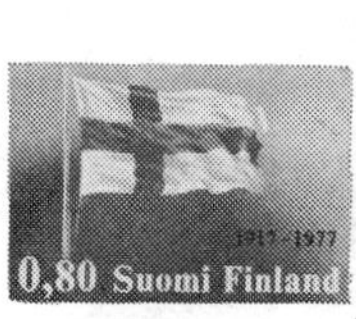

Finnish Flag
A291

Wall Telephone, 1880, New Telephone
A292

1977, Dec. 5 Litho. *Perf. 14*

Size: 31x21mm.

604 A291 80p multi 90 40

Size: 37x25mm. *Perf. 13*

605 A291 1m multi 1.40 40

60th anniversary of Finland's declaration of independence.

1977, Dec. 9 *Perf. 14*

606 A292 1m multi 80 30

Centenary of first telephone in Finland.

Harbor, Sunila Factory, Kotka Arms
A293

1978, Jan. 2 Litho. *Perf. 14*

607 A293 1m multi 80 30

Centenary of founding of Kotka.

Europa Issue 1978

Paimio Sanitarium by Alvar Aalto
A294

Design: 1.20m, Hvittrask studio house, 1902 (horiz.).

1978, May 2 Litho. *Perf. 13*

608 A294 1m multi 2.25 35
609 A294 1.20m multi 5.00 4.50

Rural Bus Service
A295

1978, June 8 Litho. *Perf. 14*

610 A295 1m multi 80 30

Eino Leino and Eagle
A296

1978, July 6 Litho. *Perf. 13*

611 A296 1m multi 80 30

Eino Leino (1878–1926), poet.

Function Theory and Rhythmical Lines
A297

1978, Aug. 15 Litho. *Perf. 14*

612 A297 1m multi 80 30

ICM 78, International Congress of Mathematicians, Helsinki, Aug. 15–23.

Child Feeding Birds
A298

1978, Oct. 23 Litho. *Perf. 14*

613 A298 50p multi 55 25

Christmas 1978.

Child, Flowers, IYC Emblem
A299

1979, Jan. 2 Litho. *Perf. 13*

614 A299 1.10m multi 2.25 35

International Year of the Child.

Runner
A300

1979, Feb. 7 Litho. *Perf. 14*

615 A300 1.10m multi 1.40 40

8th Orienteering World Championships, Finland, Sept. 1–4.

Old School, Hamina, Academy Flag
A301

1979, Mar. 20 Litho. *Perf. 14*

616 A301 1.10m multi 80 30

200th anniversary of Finnish Military Academy.

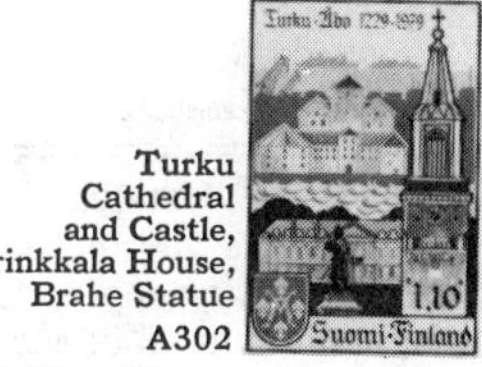

Turku Cathedral and Castle, Prinkkala House, Brahe Statue
A302

1979, Mar. 31

617 A302 1.10m multi 80 30

Streetcar, Helsinki A303

1979, May 2 Litho. *Perf. 14*

618 A303 1.10m multicolored 60 28

Non-polluting urban transportation.

View of Tampere, 1779 A304

View of Tampere, 1979—A305

1979, May 2

619 A304 90p multicolored 50 25

1979, Oct. 1 Litho. *Perf. 13*

620 A305 1.10m multi 60 38

Bicentenary of founding of Tampere.

Europa Issue 1979

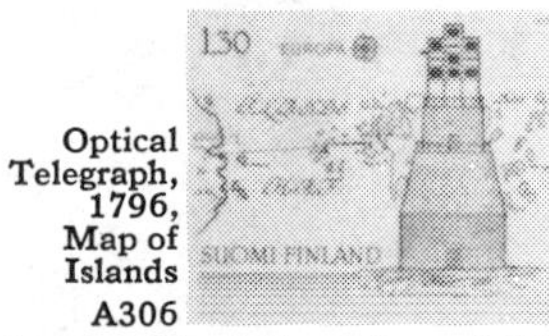

Optical Telegraph, 1796, Map of Islands A306

Design: 1.10m, Letter of Queen Christina to Per Brahe, 1638, establishing postal service (vert.).

1979, May 2 *Perf. 13*

621 A306 1.10m multicolored 60 28
622 " 1.30m " 72 30

Shops and Merchants' Signs—A307

1979, Sept. 26 *Perf. 14*

623 A307 1.10m multi 60 38

Business and industry regulation centenary.

See "Special Notices" at the front of this volume for data on the listing methods of this Catalogue, abbreviations, condition, prices and examination.

Old and New Cars, Street Crossing A308

1979, Oct. 1

624 A308 1.10m multi 60 38

Road safety.

Elves Feeding Horse—A309

1979, Oct. 24

625 A309 60p multi 35 16

Christmas 1979.

Korppi House, Lapinjarvi—A310

Farm houses, First Row: Syrjala House, Tammela, 2 stamps in continuous design; Murtovaara House, Valtimo; Antila House, Lapua. Second row: Lofts, Pohjanmaa; Courtyard gate, Kanajarvi House, Kalvola; Main door, Havuselka House, Kauhajoki; Maki-Rasinpera House and dinner bell tower; Gable and eaves, Rasula Kuortane granary.

1979, Oct. 27 Litho. *Perf. 13*

626 A310 Bklt. pane of 10 6.00
a-j. 1.10m, single stamp 60 38

Type of 1975

Kauhaneva Swamp A315

Hame Castle, Hameenlinna A316

Windmill, Harrstrom

A318

Shuttle, Raanu Designs—A322

Kaspaikka Towel Design

A323

Bridal Rug, Teisko, 1815

A324

Iron-forged Door, Hollola Church A325

Litho. & Engr.: #631, 635A, 639, 641
Litho.: 640, others engr.

Perf. 11½: #632, 634, 635, others perf. 14.

1979-83

631	A315	70p multi	40	18
632	A316	90p brn red	45	25
633	A256	1m red brn	55	35
634	A318	1m bl & red brn	50	32
635	A256	1.30m dk grn	65	40
635A	A315	1.80m Eastern Gulf natl. park	90	60
636	A322	3m multi ('79)	1.65	40
639	A323	6m multi ('80)	3.30	40
640	A324	7m multi	3.85	50
641	A325	8m multi	4.00	75

Coil Stamp

Perf. 12½ Horiz.

642A A318 1m bl & red brn 50 32

Maria Jotuni (1880-1943), Writer A327

1980, Apr. 9 Litho.

643 A327 1.10m multi 60 30

Europa Issue 1980

Frans Eemil Sillanpaa (1888-1964), Writer—A328

Design: 1.30m, Artturi Ilmari Virtanen (1895-1973), chemist (vert.).

1980, Apr. 28 *Perf. 13*

644 A328 1.10m multi 60 30
645 A328 1.30m multi 72 45

Pres. Urho Kekkonen, 80th Birthday—A329

1980, Sept. 3 Litho. *Perf. 13*

646 A329 1.10m multi 60 30

Nordic Cooperation Issue

Back-piece Harness, 19th century—A330

1980, Sept. 9 *Perf. 14*

647 A330 1.10m *shown* 60 30
648 A330 1.30m *Collar harness, vert.* 72 30

Biathlon—A331

1980, Oct. 17 Litho. *Perf. 14*

649 A331 1.10m multi 60 30

World Biathlon Championship, Lahti, Feb. 10-15, 1981.

Pull the Roller, Weighing out the Salt—A332

Christmas 1980 (Traditional Games): 1.10m, Putting out the shoemaker's eye.

1980, Oct. 27

650 A332 60p multi 35 16
651 A332 1.10m multi 60 30

Boxing Match A333 — Glass Blowing A334

1981, Feb. 28 **Litho.** ***Perf. 14***

652 A333 1.10m multi 60 38

European Boxing Championships, Tampere, May 2-10.

1981, Mar. 12

653 A334 1.10m multi 60 38

Glass industry, 300th anniversary.

Mail Boat Furst Menschikoff, 1836—A335

1981, May 6 **Litho. & Engr.** ***Perf. 13***

654 A335 1.10m brn & tan 3.50 3.50

Nordia '81 Stamp Exhibition, Helsinki, May 6-10. Sold only at exhibition for 3m including entrance ticket.

Europa Issue 1981

Rowing to Church—A336

1981, May 18 **Litho.** ***Perf. 13***

655 A336 1.10m shown 60 38
656 A336 1.50m Midsummer's Eve dance 85 52

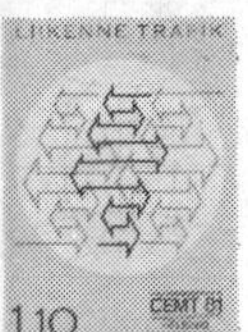

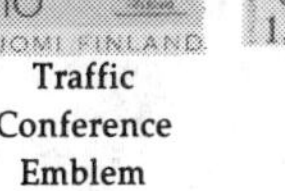

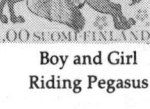

Traffic Conference Emblem A357 — Boy and Girl Riding Pegasus A358

1981, May 26 **Litho.** ***Perf. 14***

657 A357 1.10m multi 60 38

European Conference of Ministers of Transport, May 25-28.

1981, June 11

658 A358 1m multi 55 35

Youth associations centenary.

Intl. Year of the Disabled—A359

1981, Sept. 2 **Litho.** ***Perf. 13***

659 A359 1.10m multi 60 38

Christmas 1981 A360

1981, Oct. 27 **Litho.** ***Perf. 14***

660 A360 70p Children, Christmas tree 40 22
661 A360 1.10m Decorating tree, vert. 60 40

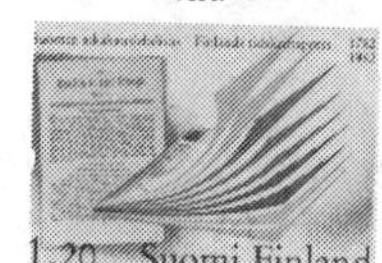

"Om Konsten att Ratt Behaga" First Issue (Periodicals Bicentenary)—A341

1982, Jan. 15

662 A341 1.20m multi 65 40

Multiharju Forest, Seitseminen Natl. Park—A342

1982, Feb. 8

663 A342 1.60m multi 90 60

Kuopio Bicentenary A343 — Score, String Instrument Neck A344

1982, Mar. 4 **Litho.** ***Perf. 14***

664 A343 1.20m multi 65 40

1982, Mar. 11 ***Perf. 13***

665 A344 1.20m multi 65 40

Centenaries of Sibelius Academy of Music and Helsinki Orchestra.

Electric Power Plant Centenary—A345

1982, Mar. 15 ***Perf. 14***

666 A345 1.20m multi 65 40

Gardening—A346

1982, Apr. 16 **Litho.** ***Perf. 14***

667 A346 1.10m multi 50 30

Europa Issue 1982—A347

Designs: 1.20m, Publication of Abckiria (first Finnish book), 1543. (Sculpture of Mikael Agricola, printer, by Oskari Jauhiainen, 1951). 1.50m, Turku Academy, first Finnish university (Turku Academy Inaugural Procession, 1640, after Albert Edelfelt).

1982, Apr. 29 **Litho.** ***Perf. 13x12½***

668 A347 1.20m multi 55 35

Size: 47x31mm. ***Perf. 12½***

669 A347 1.50m multi 70 45

Intl. Monetary Fund and World Bank Emblems—A348

1982, May 12 ***Perf. 14***

670 A348 1.60m multi 72 46

IMF Interim Committee and IMF-WB Joint Development Committee Meeting, Helsinki, May 12-14.

75th Anniv. of Unicameral Parliament—A349

1982, May 25

671 A349 2.40m Future, by Waino Aaltonen, Parliament 1.00 65

House Type of 1979

Manor Houses, First Row: a, Kuitia, Parainen, 1490. b, Louhisaari, Askainen, 1655. c, Frugard, Joroinen, 1780. d, Jokioinen, 1798. e, Moisio, Elimaki, 1820. Second Row: f, Sjundby, Siuntio, 1560. g, Fagervik, Inkoo, 1773. h, Mustio, Karjaa, 1792. i, Fiskars, Pohja, 1818. j, Kotkaniemi, Vihti, 1836.

1982, June 14 **Litho.** ***Perf. 13x13½***

672 A310 Bklt. pane of 10 6.00
a-j. 1.20m, single stamp 60 40

Christmas 1982—A350

1982, Oct. 25

673 A350 90p Feeding forest animals 45 30
674 A350 1.20m Children eating porridge 60 40

Europa 1983—A351

1983, Mar. 24 **Litho.** ***Perf. 14***

675 A351 1.20m Panning for gold 60 40
676 A351 1.30m Kitkajoki River rapids 65 42

World Communications Year—A352

1983, Apr. 9 **Litho.** ***Perf.***

677 A352 1.30m Postal services 65 42
678 A352 1.70m Sound waves, optical cables 85 50

SEMI-POSTAL STAMPS

Arms
SP1 1M+50 P

Typographed.

1922, May 15 ***Perf. 14*** **Unwmkd.**

B1	SP1 1m+50p gray & red		80	*7.00*
a.	Perf. 13x13½		5.00	

Red Cross Standard SP2 — Symbolic SP3 — Ship of Mercy SP4

1930, Feb. 6

B2	SP2	1m +10p red org & red	1.85	*8.00*
B3	SP3	1½m +15p grysh grn & red	1.65	*8.00*
B4	SP4	2m +20p dk bl & red	3.00	*25.00*

The surtax on this and subsequent similar issues was for the benefit of the Red Cross Society of Finland.

Church in Hattula SP5 — SP8

Designs: 1½m+15p, Castle of Hameenlinna. 2m+20p, Fortress of Viipuri.

1931, Jan. 1 **Engraved**

Cross in Red.

B5	SP5	1m +10p gray grn	3.00	*10.00*
B6	SP5	1½m +15p lil brn	9.00	9.00
B7	SP5	2m +20p dl bl	1.85	*15.00*

Typographed.

1931, Oct. 15 ***Rouletted 4, 5***

B8	SP8	1m +4m blk	30.00	37.50

The surtax was to assist the Postal Museum of Finland in purchasing the Richard Granberg collection of entire envelopes.

Helsinki University Library SP9 — Nikolai Church at Helsinki SP10

Design: 2½m+25p, Parliament Building, Helsinki.

1932, Jan. 1 ***Perf. 14***

B9	SP9	1¼m +10p ol bis & red	1.75	*12.50*
B10	SP10	2m +20p dp vio & red	1.00	*6.00*
B11	SP9	2½m +25p lt bl & red	2.00	*25.00*

Bishop Magnus Tawast SP12 — Michael Agricola SP13

Design: 2½m+25p, Isacus Rothovius.

1933, Jan. 20 **Engraved**

B12	SP12	1¼m +10p blk brn & red	2.50	3.50
B13	SP13	2m +20p brn vio & red	75	1.50
B14	SP13	2½m +25p ind & red	1.00	1.50

Evert Horn SP15

Designs: 2m+20p, Torsten Stalhandske. 2½m+25p, Jakob (Lazy Jake) de la Gardie.

1934, Jan. **Cross in Red.**

B15	SP15	1¼m +10p brn	1.00	1.50
B16	SP15	2m +20p gray lil	1.80	3.50
B17	SP15	2½m +25p gray	1.00	2.00

Mathias Calonius SP18 — Robert Henrik Rehbinder SP21

Designs: 2m+20p, Henrik C. Porthan. 2½m+25p, Anders Chydenius.

1935, Jan. 1 **Cross in Red.**

B18	SP18	1¼m +15p brn	75	1.75
B19	SP18	2m +20p gray lil	1.50	2.00
B20	SP18	2½m +25p gray bl	75	1.75

1936, Jan. 1

Designs: 2m+20p, Count Gustaf Mauritz Armfelt. 2½m+25p, Count Arvid Bernard Horn.

Cross in Red.

B21	SP21	1¼m +15p dk brn	75	1.00
B22	SP21	2m +20p vio brn	4.00	4.50
B23	SP21	2½m +25p bl	75	1.50

The "Uusimaa" SP24 — The "Turunmaa" SP25

Design: 3½m+35p, The "Hameenmaa."

1937, Jan. 1 **Cross in Red.**

B24	SP24	1¼m +15p brn	1.00	1.50
B25	SP25	2m +20p brn lake	18.50	4.50
B26	SP24	3½m +35p ind	80	1.80

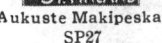

Aukuste Makipeska SP27 — Skiing SP31

Designs: 1¼m+15p, Robert Isidor Orn. 2m+20p, Edward Bergenheim. 3½m+35p, Johan Mauritz Nordenstam.

1938, Jan. 5 **Engraved**

Cross in Red

B27	SP27	50p +5p dk grn	70	1.00
B28	SP27	1¼m +15p dk brn	1.00	1.50
B29	SP27	2m +20p rose lake	9.00	4.50
B30	SP27	3½m +35p dk bl	90	1.50

1938, Jan. 18

Designs: 2+1m, Ski jumper. 3.50+1.50m, Skier.

B31	SP31	1.25m +75p sl grn	6.00	10.00
B32	SP31	2m +1m dk car	6.00	10.00
B33	SP31	3.50m +1.50m dk bl	6.00	10.00

Issued to commemorate the ski championships held at Lahti.

Soldier—SP34

1938, May 16

B34	SP34	2m +½m bl	2.00	2.50

Issued to commemorate the victory of the White Army over the Red Guards. The surtax was for the benefit of the members of the Union of the Finnish Front.

Battlefield at Solferino SP35

1939, Jan. 2 **Cross in Scarlet.**

B35	SP35	50p +5p dk grn	75	1.00
B36	SP35	1¼m +15p dk brn	75	1.00
B37	SP35	2m +20p lake	18.50	5.50
B38	SP35	3½m +35p dk bl	80	1.50

Issued in commemoration of the 75th anniversary of the founding of the International Red Cross Society.

Soldiers with Crossbows SP36 — Arms of Finland SP40

Designs: 1¼m+15p, Cavalryman. 2m+20p, Soldier of Charles XII of Sweden. 3½m+35p, Officer and soldier of War with Russia, 1808–1809.

1940, Jan. 3 **Cross in Red.**

B39	SP36	50p +5p dk grn	70	1.50
B40	SP36	1¼m +15p dk brn	2.00	2.50
B41	SP36	2m +20p lake	2.00	2.50
B42	SP36	3½m +35p dp ultra	2.00	2.50

The surtax aided the Finnish Red Cross.

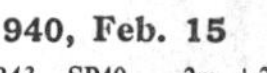

1940, Feb. 15 **Lithographed**

B43	SP40	2m +2m ind	50	1.00

The surtax was given to a fund for the preservation of neutrality.

Mason SP41 — Soldier's Emblem SP45

Designs: 1.75m+15p, Farmer plowing. 2.75m+25p, Mother and child. 3.50m+35p, Finnish flag.

1941, Jan. 2 **Engraved**

Cross in Red.

B44	SP41	50p +5p grn	50	1.10
B45	SP41	1.75m +15p brn	1.25	2.00
B46	SP41	2.75m +25p brn car	6.50	7.00
B47	SP41	3.50m +35p dp ultra	1.25	2.00

See also Nos. B65–B68.

1941, May 24 **Unwmkd.**

B48	SP45	2.75m +25p brt ultra	80	80

The surtax was for the aid of the soldiers who fought in the Russo-Finnish War.

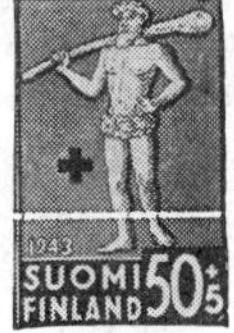

Aaland Arms SP46 — Lapland Arms SP51

Designs: Coats of Arms—1.75m+15p, Nyland. 2.75m+25p, Finland's first arms. 3.50m+35p, Karelia. 4.75m+45p, Satakunta.

1942, Jan. 2 ***Perf. 14***

Cross in Red.

B49	SP46	50p +5p grn	60	60
B50	SP46	1.75m +15p brn	1.25	1.75
B51	SP46	2.75m +25p dk red	1.25	1.75
B52	SP46	3.50m +35p dp ultra	1.25	1.75
B53	SP46	4.75m +45p dk sl grn	1.00	1.75
		Nos. B49-B53 (5)	5.35	7.60

The surtax aided the Finnish Red Cross.

1943, Jan. 6 **Inscribed "1943."**

Designs: Coats of Arms—2m+20p, Hame. 3.50m+35p, Eastern Bothnia. 4.50m+45p, Savo.

Cross in Red.

B54	SP51	50p +5p grn	50	75
B55	SP51	2m +20p brn	60	1.25
B56	SP51	3.50m +35p dk red	60	1.25
B57	SP51	4.50m +45p brt ultra	1.00	2.50

The surtax aided the Finnish Red Cross.

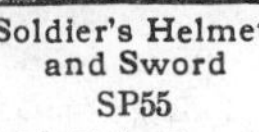

Soldier's Helmet and Sword SP55 — Mother and Children SP56

1943, Feb. 1 ***Perf. 13***

B58	SP55	2m +50p dk brn	50	70
B59	SP56	3.50m +1m brn red	50	70

The surtax was for national welfare.

Red Cross Train
SP57

Designs: 2m+50p, Ambulance. 3.50m+75p, Red Cross Hospital, Helsinki. 4.50m+1m, Hospital plane.

Inscribed "1944"

1944, Jan. 2 ***Perf. 14***

Cross in Red.

B60	SP57	50p +25p grn	25	30
B61	SP57	2m +50p sep	25	40
B62	SP57	3.50m +75p ver	40	40
B63	SP57	4.50m +1m brt ultra	70	1.10

The surtax aided the Finnish Red Cross.

Symbols of Peace SP61 — Wrestling SP62

1944, Dec. 1

B64	SP61	3.50m +1.50m dk red brn	40	40

The surtax was for national welfare.

Types of 1941 Inscribed "1945."
Photogravure and Engraved.

1945, May 2 **Cross in Red.**

B65	SP41	1m +25p grn	20	25
B66	SP41	2m +50p brn	30	50
B67	SP41	3.50m +75p brn car	30	50
B68	SP41	4.50m +1m dp ultra	50	70

The surtax was for the Finnish Red Cross.

1945, Apr. 16 Engraved *Perf. 13½*

Designs: 2+1m, Gymnast. 3.50+1.75m, Runner. 4.50+2.25m, Skier. 7+3.50m, Javelin thrower.

B69	SP62	1m +50p bluish grn	30	60
B70	SP62	2m +1m dp red	30	60
B71	SP62	3.50m +1.75m dl vio	30	60
B72	SP62	4.50m +2.25m ultra	30	60
B73	SP62	7m +3.50m dl brn	50	1.10
		Nos. B69-B73 (5)	1.70	3.50

Fishing SP67 — Nurse and Children SP71

Designs: 3+75p, Churning. 5+1.25m, Reaping. 10+2.50m, Logging.

Engraved; Cross Typo. in Red

1946, Jan. 7

B74	SP67	1m +25p dl grn	50	50
B75	SP67	3m +75p lil brn	30	50
B76	SP67	5m +1.25m rose red	30	50
a.		Red cross omitted	400.00	
B77	SP67	10m +2.50m ultra	50	50

The surtax was for the Finnish Red Cross.

1946, Sept. 2 **Engraved**

Design: 8+2m, Doctor examining infant.

B78	SP71	5m +1m grn	40	60
B79	SP71	8m +2m brn vio	40	60

The surtax was for the prevention of tuberculosis.

Nos. B78 and B79 Surcharged with New Values in Black.

1947, Apr. 1

B80	SP71	6m +1m on 5m +1m grn	40	60
B81	SP71	10m +2m on 8m+2m brn vio	40	60

The surtax was for the prevention of tuberculosis.

Medical Examination of Infants
SP73 — SP74

Designs: 10+2.50m, Infant held by the feet. 12+3m, Mme. Alli Paasikivi and a child. 20+5m, Infant standing.

1947, Sept. 15 **Engraved**

B82	SP73	2.50m +1m grn	40	85
B83	SP74	6m +1.50m dk red	55	1.00
B84	SP74	10m +2.50m red brn	55	1.00
B85	SP73	12m +3m dp bl	1.00	1.20
B86	SP74	20m +5m dk red vio	1.00	1.20
		Nos. B82-B86 (5)	3.50	5.25

The surtax was for the prevention of tuberculosis.

Zachris Topelius
SP78

Designs: 7+2m, Fredrik Pacius. 12+3m, Johan L. Runeberg. 20+5m, Fredrik Cygnaeus.

Engraved; Cross Typo. in Red

1948, May 10 *Perf. 14* Unwmkd.

B87	SP78	3m +1m grn	50	50
B88	SP78	7m +2m rose red	65	65
B89	SP78	12m +3m brt bl	60	1.20
B90	SP78	20m +5m dk vio	80	1.20

The surtax was for the Finnish Red Cross.

Nos. B83, B84 and B86 Surcharged with New Values and Bars in Black.

1948, Sept. 13 Engr. *Perf. 13½*

B91	SP74	7m +2m on 6m+1.50m dk red	1.20	2.00
B92	SP74	15m +3m on 10m+2.50m red brn	80	1.50
B93	SP74	24m +6m on 20m+5m dk red vio	80	1.80

The surtax was for the prevention of tuberculosis.

Tying Birch Boughs SP79 — Wood Anemone SP83

Designs: 9+3m, Bathers in Sauna house. 15+5m, Rural bath house. 30+10m, Cold plunge in lake.

Engraved; Cross Typo. in Red

1949, May 5 ***Perf. 13½x14***

B94	SP79	5m +2m dl grn	60	85
B95	SP79	9m +3m dk car	60	85
B96	SP79	15m +5m dp bl	60	1.10
B97	SP79	30m +10m dk vio brn	1.00	2.00

The surtax was for the Finnish Red Cross.

1949, June 2 **Engraved**

Designs: 9+3m, Wild rose. 15+5m, Coltsfoot.

Inscribed: "1949"

B98	SP83	5m +2m grn	70	1.00
B99	SP83	9m +3m car	80	1.10
B100	SP83	15m +5m ol bis	80	1.10

The surtax was for the prevention of tuberculosis.

Similar to Type of 1949.

Designs: 5+2m, Water lily. 9+3m, Pasqueflower. 15+5m, Bell flower cluster.

1950, Apr. 1 Inscribed: "1950."

B101	SP83	5m +2m emer	2.00	2.00
B102	SP83	9m +3m rose car	90	90
B103	SP83	15m +5m bl	90	90

The surtax was for the prevention of tuberculosis.

Hospital Entrance, Helsinki SP84 — Blood Donor's Medal SP86

Design: 12+3m, Giving blood.

Engraved; Cross Typo. in Red

1951, Mar. 17 *Perf. 14* Unwmkd.

B104	SP84	7m +2m choc	75	90
B105	SP84	12m +3m bl vio	75	90
B106	SP86	20m +5m car	1.75	1.75

The surtax was for the Finnish Red Cross.

Capercaillie
SP87

Designs: 12m+3m, European cranes. 20m+5m, Caspian terns.

1951, Oct. 26 **Engraved**

B107	SP87	7m +2m dk grn	2.00	2.50
B108	SP87	12m +3m rose brn	2.00	2.50
B109	SP87	20m +5m bl	2.00	2.50

The surtax was for the prevention of tuberculosis.

Diver SP88 — Soccer Players SP89

Designs: 20m+3m, Stadum, Helsinki. 25m+4m, Runners.

1951-52

Inscribed: "XV Olympia 1952."

B110	SP88	12m +2m rose car	65	1.00
B111	SP89	15m +2m grn ('52)	65	1.00
B112	SP88	20m +3m dp bl	65	1.00
B113	SP89	25m +4m brn ('52)	65	1.00

Issued to publicize the XV Olympic Games, Helsinki, 1952. The surtax was to help finance the games.

Margin blocks of four of each denomination were cut from regular or perf.-through-margin sheets and pasted by the selvage, overlapping, in a printed folder to create a kind of souvenir booklet. Price $17.50

Field Marshal Mannerheim SP90 — Great Titmouse SP91

Engraved; Cross Typo. in Red

1952, Mar. 4

B114	SP90	10m +2m gray	1.20	1.30
B115	SP90	15m +3m rose vio	1.20	1.30
B116	SP90	25m +5m bl	1.50	2.00

The surtax was for the Red Cross.

1952, Dec. 4 **Engraved**

Designs: 15m+3m, Spotted flycatchers and nest. 25m+5m, Swift.

B117	SP91	10m +2m grn	2.00	2.00
B118	SP91	15m +3m plum	2.00	2.00
B119	SP91	25m +5m dp bl	2.00	2.00

The surtax was for the prevention of tuberculosis.

European Red Squirrel SP92 — Children Receiving Parcel from Welfare Worker SP93

Designs: 15m+3m, Brown bear. 25m+5m, European elk.

Engraved.

1953, Nov. 16 *Perf. 14* Unwmkd.

B120	SP92	10m +2m red brn	2.00	2.00
B121	SP92	15m +3m vio	2.00	2.00
B122	SP92	25m +5m dk grn	2.00	2.00

The surtax was for the prevention of tuberculosis.

Engraved; Cross Typographed in Red

1954, Mar. 8 ***Perf. 11½***

Designs: 15m+3m, Aged woman knitting. 25m+5m, Blind basket-maker and dog.

B123	SP93	10m +2m dk ol grn	1.60	1.60
B124	SP93	15m +3m dk bl	1.60	1.60
B125	SP93	25m +5m dk brn	1.60	1.60

The surtax was for the Finnish Red Cross.

Bumblebees and Dandelions SP94 — European Perch SP95

Designs: 15m+3m, Butterfly. 25m+5m, Dragonfly.

Engraved; Cross Typographed in Red

1954, Dec. 7 *Perf. 14*

B126	SP94	10m +2m brn	1.30	1.30
B127	SP94	15m +3m car	1.50	1.50
B128	SP94	25m +5m bl	1.50	1.50

The surtax was for the prevention of tuberculosis.

Engraved; Cross Typographed in Red

1955, Sept. 26 *Perf. 14*

Designs: 15m+3m, Northern pike. 25m+5m, Atlantic salmon.

B129	SP95	10(m) +2(m) dl grn	1.20	1.20
B130	SP95	15(m) +3(m) vio brn	1.40	1.40
B131	SP95	25(m) +5(m) dk bl	1.40	1.40

The surtax was for the Anti-Tuberculosis Society.

Gen. von Dobeln in Battle of Juthas, 1808
SP96

Waxwing
SP97

Illustrations by Albert Edelfelter from J. L. Runeberg's "Tales of Ensign Stal": 15(m)+3(m), Col. J. Z. Duncker holding flag. 25(m)+5(m), Son of fallen Soldier.

Engraved; Cross Typographed in Red.

1955, Nov. 24

B132	SP96	10(m) +2(m) dp ultra	1.10	1.10
B133	SP96	15(m) +3(m) dk red brn	1.10	1.10
B134	SP96	25(m) +5(m) grn	2.00	2.00

The surtax was for the Red Cross.

Engraved; Cross Typographed in Red.

Birds: 20m+3m, Eagle owl. 30m+5m, Mute swan.

1956, Sept. 25 *Perf. 11½*

B135	SP97	10m +2m dl red brn	1.10	1.10
B136	SP97	20m +3m bl grn	1.40	1.40
B137	SP97	30m +5m bl	1.40	1.40

The surtax was for the Anti-Tuberculosis Society.

Pekka Aulin
SP98

Wolverine (Glutton)
SP99

Portraits: 10m+2m, Leonard von Pfaler. 20m+3m, Gustaf Johansson. 30m+5m, Viktor Magnus von Born.

Engraved; Cross Typographed in Red.

1956, Nov. 26 **Unwmkd.**

B138	SP98	5m +1m grysh grn	85	85
B139	SP98	10m +2m brn	1.10	1.10
B140	SP98	20m +3m mag	1.50	1.50
B141	SP98	30m +5m lt ultra	1.50	1.50

The surtax was for the Red Cross.

Engraved; Cross Typographed in Red

1957, Sept. 5 *Perf. 11½*

Designs: 20m+3m, Lynx. 30m+5m, Reindeer.

B142	SP99	10m +2m dl pur	1.20	1.20
B143	SP99	20m +3m sep	1.50	1.50
B144	SP99	30m +5m dk bl	1.50	1.50

The surtax was for the Anti-Tuberculosis Society. See also Nos. B160–B165.

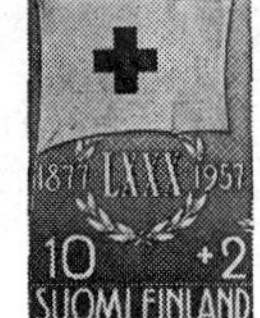

Red Cross Flag
SP100

Raspberry
SP101

1957, Nov. 25 **Engraved** *Perf. 14*

Cross in Red.

B145	SP100	10m +2m ol grn	1.75	1.75
B146	SP100	20m +3m mar	1.75	1.75
B147	SP100	30m +5m dl bl	1.75	1.75

Issued to commemorate the 80th anniversary of the Finnish Red Cross.

Type of 1952.

Flowers: 10m+2m, Lily of the valley. 20m+3m, Red clover. 30m+5m, Hepatica.

Engraved; Cross Typographed in Red

1958, May 5 *Perf. 14* **Unwmkd.**

B148	SP91	10m +2m grn	1.20	1.20
B149	SP91	20m +3m lil rose	1.40	1.40
B150	SP91	30m +5m ultra	1.40	1.40

The surtax was for the Anti-Tuberculosis Society.

Engraved; Cross Typographed in Red.

1958, Nov. 20 *Perf. 11½*

Designs: 20m+3m, Cowberry. 30m+5m, Blueberry.

B151	SP101	10m +2m org	1.20	1.20
B152	SP101	20m +3m red	1.40	1.40
B153	SP101	30m +5m dk bl	1.40	1.40

The surtax was for the Red Cross.

Daisy
SP102

Reindeer
SP103

Designs: 20m+5m, Primrose. 30m+5m, Cornflower.

Engraved; Cross Typographed in Red.

1959, Sept. 7 **Unwmkd.**

B154	SP102	10m +2m grn	2.50	1.75
B155	SP102	20m +3m lt brn	2.75	2.00
B156	SP102	30m +5m bl	2.75	2.00

The surtax was for the Anti-Tuberculosis Society.

Engraved; Cross Typographed in Red

1960, Nov. 24 *Perf. 11½*

Designs: 20m+3m, Lapp and lasso. 30m+5m, Mountains.

B157	SP103	10m +2m dk gray	1.20	1.20
B158	SP103	20m +3m gray vio	1.60	1.60
B159	SP103	30m +5m rose vio	1.60	1.60

The surtax was for the Red Cross.

Animal Type of 1957.

Designs: 10m+2m, Muskrat. 20m+3m, Otter. 30m+5m, Seal.

Engr.; Cross at right, Typo. in Red

1961, Sept. 4

B160	SP99	10m +2m brn car	1.20	1.20
B161	SP99	20m +3m sl bl	1.60	1.60
B162	SP99	30m +5m bl grn	1.60	1.60

The surtax was for the Anti-Tuberculosis Society.

Animal Type of 1957.

Designs: 10m+2m, Hare. 20m+3m, Pine marten. 30m+5m, Ermine.

Engraved; Cross Typographed in Red

1962, Oct. 1

B163	SP99	10m +2m gray	1.20	1.20
B164	SP99	20m +3m dl red brn	1.60	1.60
B165	SP99	30m +5m vio bl	1.60	1.60

The surtax was for the Anti-Tuberculosis Society.

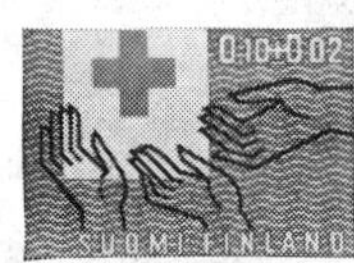

Cross and Outstretched Hands
SP104

Engraved; Cross Typographed in Red

1963, May 8 *Perf. 11½* **Unwmkd.**

B166	SP104	10p +2p red brn	1.10	1.10
B167	SP104	20p +3p vio	1.30	1.30
B168	SP104	30p +5p grn	1.30	1.30

The surtax was for the Red Cross.

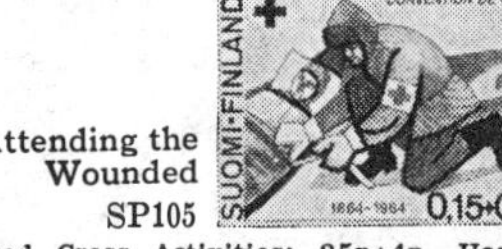

Attending the Wounded
SP105

Red Cross Activities: 25p+4p, Hospital ship. 35p+5p, Prisoner-of-war health examination. 40p+7p, Gift parcel distribution.

Engraved; Cross Typographed in Red

1964, May 26 *Perf. 11½*

B169	SP105	15p +3p vio bl	85	85
B170	SP105	25p +4p grn	1.10	1.10
B171	SP105	35p +5p vio brn	1.10	1.10
B172	SP105	40p +7p dk ol grn	1.10	1.10

The surtax was for the Red Cross.

Finnish Spitz
SP106

Artificial Respiration
SP107

Designs: 25p+4p, Karelian bear dog. 35p+5p, Finnish hunting dog.

Engraved; Cross Typographed in Red

1965, May 10 *Perf. 11½*

B173	AP106	15p +3p org brn	1.20	1.20
B174	AP106	25p +4p blk	1.60	1.60
B175	AP106	35p +5p gray brn	1.60	1.60

Surtax for Anti-Tuberculosis Society.

1966, May 7 Lithographed *Perf. 14*

First Aid: 25p+4p, Skin diver rescuing occupants of submerged car. 35p+5p, Helicopter rescue in winter.

B176	SP107	15p +3p multi	1.10	1.10
B177	SP107	25p +4p multi	1.10	1.10
B178	SP107	35p +5p multi	1.30	1.30

The surtax was for the Red Cross.

Birch
SP108

Horse-drawn Ambulance
SP109

Trees: 25p+4p, Pine. 40p+7p, Spruce.

1967, May 12 **Litho.** *Perf. 14*

B179	SP108	20p +3p multi	1.10	1.1
B180	SP108	25p +4p multi	1.10	1.1
B181	SP108	40p +7p multi	1.10	1.1

Surtax for Anti-Tuberculosis Society. See Nos. B185–B187.

1967, Nov. 24 **Litho.** *Perf. 14*

Designs: 25p+4p, Ambulance, 1967. 40p+7p, Red Cross.

Cross in Red

B182	SP109	20p +3p dl yel, grn & blk	1.10	1.1
B183	SP109	25p +4p vio & blk	1.10	1.1
B184	SP109	40p +7p dk grn, blk & dk bl	1.10	1.1

The surtax was for the Red Cross.

Tree Type of 1967

Trees: 20p+3p, Juniper. 25+4p, Aspen. 40p+7p, Chokecherry.

1969, May 12 **Litho.** *Perf. 14*

B185	SP108	20p +3p multi	1.00	1.00
B186	SP108	25p +4p multi	1.00	1.00
B187	SP108	40p +7p multi	1.00	1.00

Surtax for Anti-Tuberculosis Society.

"On the Lapp's Magic Rock"
SP110

Designs: 30p+6p, Juhani blowing horn on Impivaara Rock (vert.). 50+10p, The Pale Maiden. The designs are from illustrations by Askeli Gallen-Kallelas for "The Seven Brothers" by Aleksis Kivi.

1970, May 8 **Litho.** *Perf. 14*

B188	SP110	25p +5p multi	1.00	1.00
B189	SP110	30p +6p multi	1.00	1.00
B190	SP110	50p +10p multi	1.00	1.00

The surtax was for the Red Cross.

Cutting and Loading Timber
SP111

Designs: 30p+6p, Floating logs downstream. 50p+10p, Sorting logs at sawmill.

1971, Apr. 25 **Litho.** *Perf. 14*

B191	SP111	25p +5p multi	1.00	1.00
B192	SP111	30p +6p multi	1.00	1.00
B193	SP111	50p +10p multi	1.00	1.00

Surtax for Anti-Tuberculosis Society.

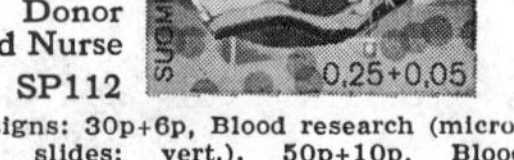

Blood Donor and Nurse
SP112

Designs: 30p+6p, Blood research (microscope, slides; vert.). 50p+10p, Blood transfusion.

1972, Oct. 23

B194	AP112	25p +5p multi	1.00	1.00
B195	AP112	30p +6p multi	1.00	1.00
B196	AP112	50p +10p multi	1.00	1.00

Surtax was for the Red Cross.

Girl with Lamb, by Hugo Simberg
SP113

Paintings: 40p+10p, Summer Evening, by Vilho Sjöström. 60p+15p, Woman at Mountain Fountain, by Juho Rissanen.

1973, Sept. 12 Litho. *Perf. 13x12½*

B197	SP113	30p	+5p multi	1.00	1.00
B198	SP113	40p	+10p multi	1.20	1.20
B199	SP113	60p	+15p multi	1.20	1.20

Surtax was for the Red Cross. Birth centenaries of featured artists.

Morel SP114

Mushrooms: 50p+10p, Chanterelle. 60p+15p, Boletus edulis.

1974, Sept. 24 Litho. *Perf. 12½x13*

B200	SP114	35p	+5p multi	1.00	1.00
B201	SP114	50p	+10p multi	1.20	1.20
B202	SP114	60p	+15p multi	1.20	1.20

Finnish Red Cross.

Echo, by Ellen Thesleff (1869–1954) SP115

Paintings: 60p+15p, Hilda Wiik, by Maria Wiik (1853–1928). 70p+20p, At Home (old woman in chair), by Helene Schjerfbeck (1862–1946).

1975, Sept. 30 Litho. *Perf. 13x12½*

B203	SP115	40p	+10p multi	75	75
B204	SP115	60p	+15p multi	1.00	1.00
B205	SP115	70p	+20p multi	1.00	1.00

Finnish Red Cross. In honor of International Women's Year paintings by women artists were chosen.

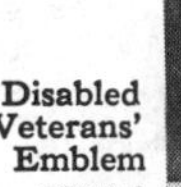

Disabled Veterans' Emblem SP116

Lithographed and Photogravure

1976, Jan. 15 *Perf. 14*

B206	SP116	70p	+30p multi	1.40	1.40

The surtax was for hospitals for disabled war veterans.

Wedding Procession SP117

Designs: 70p+15p, Wedding dance (vert.). 80p+20p, Bride, groom, matron and pastor at wedding dinner.

1976, Sept. 15 Litho. *Perf. 13*

B207	SP117	50p	+10p multi	75	75
B208	SP117	70p	+15p multi	1.00	1.00
B209	SP117	80p	+20p multi	1.00	1.00

Surtax for Anti-Tuberculosis Society.

Disaster Relief SP118

Designs: 80p+15p, Community work. 90p+20p, Blood transfusion service.

1977, Jan. 19 Litho. *Perf. 14*

B210	SP118	50p	+10p multi	75	75
B211	SP118	80p	+15p multi	90	90
B212	SP118	90p	+20p multi	90	90

Finnish Red Cross centenary.

Long-distance Skiing SP119

Design: 1m+50p, Ski jump.

1977, Oct. 5 Litho. *Perf. 13*

B213	SP119	80p	+40p multi	2.25	2.25
B214	SP119	1m	+50p multi	2.25	2.25

Surtax was for World Ski Championships, Lahti, Feb. 17–26, 1978.

Saffron Milkcap SP120

Edible Mushrooms: 80p+15p, Parasol mushrooms (vert.). 1m+20p, Gypsy mushrooms.

1978, Sept. 13 Litho. *Perf. 13*

B215	SP120	50p	+10p multi	75	75
B216	SP120	80p	+15p multi	1.00	1.00
B217	SP120	1m	+20p multi	1.00	1.00

Surtax was for Red Cross.

See Nos. B221-B223.

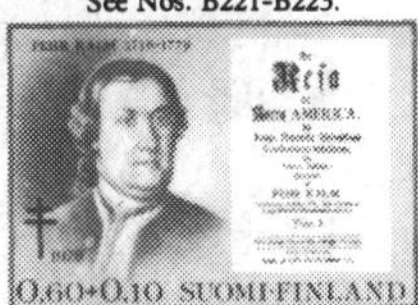

Pehr Kalm, 1716-1779—SP121

Finnish Scientists: 90p + 15p, Title page of Pehr Adrian Gadd's (1727-1797) book (vert.). 1.10m +20p, Petter Forsskal (1732-1763).

Perf. 12½×13, 13×12½

1979, Sept. 26 Litho.

B218	SP121	60p	+10p multi	70	70
B219	SP121	90p	+15p multi	70	70
B220	SP121	1.10m	+20p multi	70	70

Surtax was for the Finnish Anti-Tuberculosis Assocation.

Mushroom Type of 1978

Edible Mushrooms: 60p+10p, Woolly milkcap. 90p+15p, Orange-cap boletus (vert.). 1.10m+20p, Russula paludosa.

1980, Apr. 19 Litho. *Perf. 13*

B221	SP120	60p	+10p multi	40	40
B222	SP120	90p	+15p multi	60	60
B223	SP120	1.10m	+20p multi	70	70

Surtax was for Red Cross.

Fuchsia—SP122

1981, Aug. 24 Litho. *Perf. 13*

B224	SP122	70p	+10p shown	45	45
B225	SP122	1m	+15p African violet	65	40
B226	SP122	1.10m	+20p Geranium	75	75

Surtax was for Red Cross.

Garden Dormouse—SP123

1982, Aug. 16 Litho. *Perf. 13*

B227	SP123	90	+10p shown	50	50
B228	SP123	1.10m	+15p Flying squirrels	65	65
B229	SP123	1.20m	+20p European minks	70	70

Surtax was for Red Cross. No. B228 vert.

AIR POST STAMPS.

No. 178 Overprinted in Red **ZEPPELIN 1930**

1930, Sept. 24 ***Perf. 14*** **Unwmkd.**

C1	A28	10m gray lil	135.00	200.00
a.		1830 for 1930	2,000.	2,250.

Issued Sept. 24, 1930; overprinted expressly for use on mail carried in "Graf Zeppelin" on her return flight from Finland to Germany on Sept. 24, 1930, after which trip the stamps ceased to be valid for postage. Forgeries of Nos. C1 and C1a are almost always on No. 205, rather than No. 178.

Douglas DC-2 AP1

1944 **Engraved**

C2	AP1	3.50m dk brn	50	70

Issued to commemorate the 20th anniversary of Air Transport Service, 1923-43.

Douglas DC-6 Over Winter Landscape AP2

1950, Feb. 13

C3	AP2	300m blue	18.00	7.00

Available also for ordinary postage.

Type of 1950 Redrawn

1958, Jan. 20 ***Perf. 11½***

C4	AP2	300 (m) bl	22.50	1.10

On No. C4 "mk" is omitted.

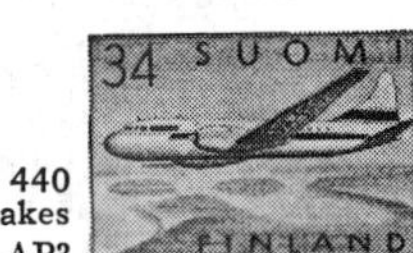

Convair 440 over Lakes AP3

1958, Oct. 31 ***Perf. 11½*** **Unwmkd.**

C5	AP3	34m blue	1.30	55

No. C5 Surcharged with New Value and Bars

1959, Apr. 5

C6	AP3	45m on 34m bl	2.50	2.25

1959, Nov. 2

C7	AP3	45m blue	1.80	60

1963, Feb. 15

C8	AP3	45p blue	90	20

DC-6 Type of 1950

1963, Oct. 10

C9	AP2	3m blue	1.75	35

Convair Type of 1958

1970, July 15

C10	AP3	57p ultra	1.30	45

MILITARY STAMPS.

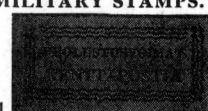

M1

Typographed.

1941, Nov. 1 ***Imperf.*** **Unwmkd.**

M1	M1	(4m) *dk org*	20	60

No. M1 has simulated roulette printed in black.

Type of 1930-46 Overprinted in Black **KENTTÄ-POSTI FÄLTPOST**

1943, Oct. 16 ***Perf. 14***

M2	A26	2m dp org	25	35
M3	A26	3½m grnsh bl	25	35

Post Horn and Sword M2

1943 **Size: 29½x19½mm.**

M4	M2	(2m) green	25	35
M5	M2	(3m) rose vio	25	35

1944 **Size: 20x16mm.**

M6	M2	(2m) green	25	30
M7	M2	(3m) rose vio	25	30

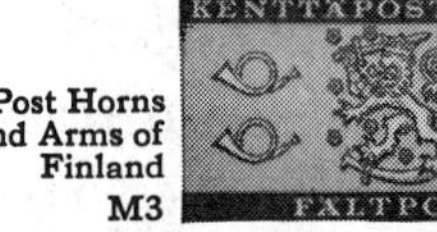

Post Horns and Arms of Finland M3

1963, Sept. 26 **Litho.** ***Perf. 14***

M8	M3	vio bl	*250.00*	*225.00*

Used during maneuvers Sept. 30–Oct. 5, 1963. Valid from Sept. 26.

PARCEL POST STAMPS

AUTOPAKETTI 0025290 1 mk N:o 6 BILPAKET

PP1

Wmkd. Rose & Triangles Multiple

Rouletted 6 on 2 or 3 Sides

1949–50 **Typographed**

Q1	PP1	1m brt grn & blk	1.75	4.50
Q2	PP1	5m red & blk	11.00	14.00
Q3	PP1	20m org & blk	22.50	22.50
Q4	PP1	50m bl & blk ('50)	7.50	8.50
Q5	PP1	100m brn & blk ('50)	7.50	8.50
		Nos. Q1-Q5 (5)	50.25	58.00

Mail Bus PP2

Engraved

1952–58 ***Perf. 14*** **Unwmkd.**

Q6	PP2	5m car rose	2.25	2.25
Q7	PP2	20m orange	4.00	4.00
Q8	PP2	50m bl ('54)	8.00	8.00
Q9	PP2	100m brn ('58)	10.00	10.00

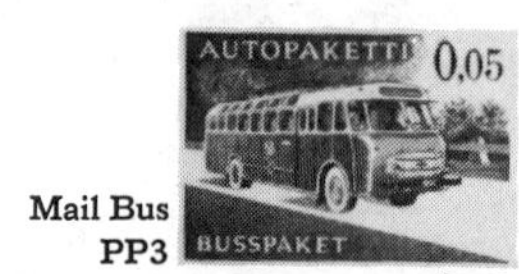

Mail Bus PP3

1963 ***Perf. 12***

Q10	PP3	5p red & blk	2.00	2.00
Q11	PP3	20p org & blk	60	60
Q12	PP3	50p bl & blk	60	60
Q13	PP3	1m brn & blk	60	75

Nos. Q1–Q13 were issued only in booklets: panes of 6 for Nos. Q1–Q5, 10 for Nos. Q6–Q9 and 5 for Nos. Q10–Q13.

Used prices are for regular postal or mail-bus cancels. Pen strokes, cutting or other cancels sell for half as much.

1981 SISU Bus—PP4

1981, Dec. 7 **Photo. & Engr.** ***Perf. 12 Horiz.***

Q14	PP4	50p dk bl & blk	28	20
Q15	PP4	1m dk brn & blk	55	35
Q16	PP4	5m grn & blk	2.75	1.75
Q17	PP4	10m red & blk	5.50	3.50

FIUME

(fyōō′mȧ)

LOCATION—A city and surrounding territory on the Adriatic Sea.

GOVT.—Formerly a part of Italy.

AREA—8 sq. mi.

POP.—44,956 (estimated 1924).

Formerly a port of Hungary, Fiume was claimed by Jugoslavia and Italy following World War I. During the discussion, the poet, Gabriele d'Annunzio, organized his legionnaires and seized Fiume, together with the islands of Arbe, Carnaro and Veglia, in the name of Italy. Jugoslavia recognized Italy's claim and the city was annexed in January, 1924.

100 Filler = 1 Korona
100 Centesimi = 1 Corona (1919)
100 Centesimi = 1 Lira

Hungarian Stamps of 1916-18 Overprinted — FIUME

Wmkd. Double Cross. (137)

1918, Dec. 2 *Perf. 15*

On Stamps of 1916.

White Numerals.

1	A8	10f rose	30.00	10.00
2	A8	15f violet	17.50	6.50

Nos. 1–2 overprints are handstamped.

On Stamps of 1916–18.

Colored Numerals.

3	A9	2f brn org	40	20
4	A9	3f red vio	40	20
5	A9	5f green	40	20
6	A9	6f grnsh bl	40	20
7	A9	10f rose red	30.00	8.00
8	A9	15f violet	40	20
9	A9	20f gray brn	40	20
10	A9	25f dp bl	65	40
11	A9	35f brown	85	60
12	A9	40f ol grn	8.00	2.00

White Numerals

13	A10	50f red vio & lil	80	50
14	A10	75f brt bl & pale bl	2.00	60
15	A10	80f grn & pale grn	80	50
16	A10	1k red brn & cl	8.00	2.00
17	A10	2k ol brn & bis	60	50
18	A10	3k dk vio & ind	4.00	2.00
19	A10	5k dk brn & lt brn	10.00	5.00
20	A10	10k vio brn & vio	90.00	60.00

Inverted or double overprints exist on most of Nos. 4–15.

On Stamps of 1918.

21	A11	10f scarlet	50	25
22	A11	20f dk brn	50	20
23	A12	40f ol grn	6.00	1.50

The overprint on Nos. 3–23 was applied both by press and handstamp. Prices are for the less costly. Prices of Nos. 7, 12, 20 and 23 are for handstamps.

Forgeries of Nos. 1–23 abound.

A1

A2

Postage Due Stamps of Hungary, 1915-20 Overprinted and Surcharged in Black.

1919, Jan.

24	A1	45f on 6f grn & red	2.25	60
25	A1	45f on 20f grn & red	2.25	60

Hungarian Savings Bank Stamp Surcharged in Black.

1919, Jan. 29

26	A2	15f on 10f dk vio	2.25	70

"Italy"
A3

Italian Flag on Clock-Tower in Fiume
A4

"Revolution"
A5

Sailor Raising Italian Flag at Fiume (1918)
A6

Lithographed.

1919 *Perf. 11½* **Unwmkd.**

27	A3	2c dl bl	15	15
28	A3	3c gray brn	15	15
29	A3	5c yel grn	15	15
30	A4	10c rose	15	15
31	A4	15c violet	15	15
32	A4	20c green	15	15
33	A5	25c dk bl	15	15
34	A6	30c dp vio	15	15
35	A5	40c brown	22	22
36	A5	45c orange	15	15
37	A6	50c yel grn	15	15
38	A6	60c claret	15	15
39	A6	1cor brn org	15	15
40	A6	2cor brt bl	22	15
41	A6	3cor org red	22	15
42	A6	5cor dp brn	22	22
43	A6	10cor ol grn	1.50	1.00
		Nos. 27-43 (17)	4.18	3.54

The earlier printings of January and February are on thin grayish paper and in sheets of 70. A March printing is on semi-transparent white paper, also in sheets of 70. An April printing is on white paper of medium thickness and in sheets of 100. Part-perforate examples of most of this series are known.

A7

A8

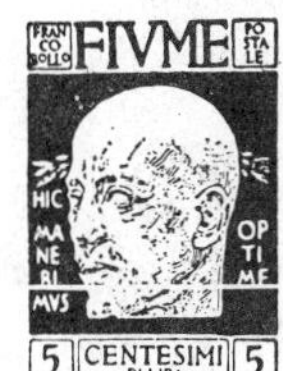

A9

A10

1919, July 28 *Perf. 11½*

46	A7	5c yel grn	15	15
47	A8	10c rose	15	15
48	A9	30c violet	22	15
49	A10	40c yel brn	60	45
50	A10	45c orange	22	15
51	A9	50c yel grn	22	15
52	A9	60c claret	22	15
a.		Perf. 13x12½	25.00	25.00
53	A9	10cor ol grn	1.15	75
a.		Perf. 13x12½	25.00	18.50
b.		Perf. 10½	25.00	18.50
		Nos. 46-53 (8)	2.93	2.10

Five other denominations—25c, 1cor, 2cor, 3cor and 5cor—were not officially issued. Some copies of the 25c are known canceled.

Stamps of 1919 Handstamp Surcharged — FRANCO 5

1919–20

58	A4	5c on 20c grn ('20)	15	15
59	A10	5c on 25c bl	15	15
60	A5	10c on 45c org	15	15
61	A9	15c on 30c vio ('20)	15	15
62	A10	15c on 45c org	15	15
63	A9	15c on 60c cl ('20)	15	15
64	A6	25c on 50c yel grn ('20)	1.00	55
65	A9	25c on 50c yel grn ('20)	15	15
66	A6	55c on 1cor brn org	1.15	60
67	A6	55c on 2cor brt bl	1.15	85
68	A6	55c on 3cor org red	1.20	85
69	A6	55c on 5cor dp brn	1.20	85
70	A9	55c on 10cor ol grn	1.35	1.25
		Nos. 58-70 (13)	8.10	6.00

Semi-Postal Stamps of 1919 Surcharged:

Valore globale Cent. 5
a

Valore globale Cent. 45
b

1919–20

73	SP6(a)	5c on 5c grn	15	15
74	SP6(a)	10c on 10c rose	15	15
75	SP6(a)	15c on 15c gray	15	15
76	SP6(a)	20c on 20c org	15	15
77	SP9(a)	25c on 25c bl ('20)	15	15
78	SP7(b)	45c on 45c ol grn	15	15
79	SP7(b)	60c on 60c rose	15	15
80	SP7(b)	80c on 80c vio	15	15
81	SP7(b)	1cor on 1cor sl	15	15
82	SP8(a)	2cor on 2cor red brn	30	30
83	SP8(a)	3cor on 3cor blk brn	60	60
84	SP8(a)	5cor on 5cor yel brn	90	90
85	SP8(a)	10cor on 10cor dk vio ('20)	30	30
		Nos. 73-85 (13)	3.45	3.45

Double or inverted surcharges, or imperf. varieties, exist on most of Nos. 73–85.

There were three settings of the surcharges on Nos. 73–85 except No. 77 which is known only with one setting.

FIVME POSTA ITALIANE — HIC MANEBIMVS — OPTIME — 5 CENTESIMI DI LIRA 5

Gabriele d'Annunzio
A11

POSTE DI FIUME — XII SETTEMBRE MCMXIX — CENT. 5

Severing the Gordian Knot
A12

Pale Buff Background.

1920, Sept. 12 Typo. *Perf. 11½*

86	A11	5c green	15	15
87	A11	10c carmine	15	15
88	A11	15c dk gray	15	15
89	A11	20c orange	22	15
90	A11	25c dk bl	38	15
91	A11	30c red brn	50	15
92	A11	45c ol gray	60	15
93	A11	50c lilac	60	15
94	A11	55c bister	60	15
95	A11	1 l black	1.20	45
96	A11	2 l red vio	2.75	75
97	A11	3 l dk grn	2.75	1.15
98	A11	5 l brown	2.75	1.15
99	A11	10 l gray vio	3.25	1.65
		Nos. 86-99 (14)	16.05	6.50

Counterfeits of Nos. 86 to 99 are plentiful.

1920, Sept. 12

Designs: 10c, Ancient emblem of Fiume. 20c Head of "Fiume." 25c, Hands holding daggers.

100	A12	5c green	10.00	3.75
101	A12	10c dp rose	2.25	75
102	A12	20c brn org	3.00	75
103	A12	25c dk bl	15.00	6.25

These stamps were issued to mark the anniversary of the occupation of Fiume by d'Annunzio. They were available for franking the correspondence of the legionnaires on the day of issue only, Sept. 12, 1920

Counterfeits of Nos. 100 to 103 are plentiful.

Commemorative Stamps of 1920 Overprinted in Black or Red and New Values — Reggenza Italiana del Carnaro

1920, Nov. 20

104	A12	1c on 5c grn	15	15
105	A12	2c on 25c bl (R)	15	15
106	A12	5c green	15	15
107	A12	10c rose	15	15
108	A12	15c on 10c rose	15	15
109	A12	15c on 20c brn org	15	15
110	A12	15c on 25c bl (R)	22	22
111	A12	20c brn org	15	15
112	A12	25c bl (R)	15	15
113	A12	25c bl (Bk)	37.50	25.00
114	A12	25c on 10c rose	1.50	1.00
115	A12	50c on 20c brn org	15	15
116	A12	55c on 5c grn	10	10
117	A12	1 l on 10c rose	1.85	1.15
118	A12	1 l on 25c bl (R)	165.00	67.50
119	A12	2 l on 5c grn	3.75	1.85
120	A12	5 l on 10c rose	30.00	5.00
121	A12	10 l on 20c brn org	110.00	25.00
		Nos. 104-121 (18)	351.27	128.17

The Fiume Legionnaires of d'Annunzio occupied the islands of Arbe and Veglia in the Gulf of Carnaro from Nov. 13, 1920, until Jan. 5, 1921.

Varieties of overprint or surcharge exist for most of Nos. 104–121.

Same Overprint with **ARBE** at top

1920, Nov. 18

122	A12	5c green	1.25	50
123	A12	10c rose	1.50	75
124	A12	20c brn org	2.25	1.00
125	A12	25c dp bl	7.50	3.50
126	A12	50c on 20c brn org	3.00	1.50
127	A12	55c on 5c grn	3.00	1.50
		Nos. 122-127 (6)	18.50	8.75

The overprint on Nos. 122–125 comes in two widths: 11mm. and 14mm. Prices are for the 11mm. width.

Same Overprint with **VEGLIA** at top.

1920, Nov. 18

128	A12	5c green	1.25	50
129	A12	10c rose	1.50	75
130	A12	20c brn org	2.25	1.00
131	A12	25c dp bl	7.50	3.50
132	A12	50c on 20c brn org	3.00	1.50
133	A12	55c on 5c grn	3.00	1.50
		Nos. 128-133 (6)	18.50	8.75

The overprint on Nos. 128–131 comes in two widths: 17mm. and 19mm. Prices are for the 17mm. width.

Nos. 122–133 exist with double and inverted overprints.

Counterfeits of these overprints exist.

Stamps of 1920 Overprinted — Governo Provvisorio

1921, Feb. 2

Pale Buff Background.

134	A11	5c green	15	15
135	A11	10c carmine	15	15
136	A11	15c dk gray	15	15
137	A11	20c orange	15	15
138	A11	25c dk bl	15	15
139	A11	30c red brn	22	15
140	A11	45c ol gray	22	15
141	A11	50c lilac	22	15
142	A11	55c bister	30	15
143	A11	1 l black	25.00	25.00

144	A11	2 l red vio	1.00	60
145	A11	3 l dk grn	1.85	1.50
146	A11	5 l brown	1.85	60
147	A11	10 l gray vio	2.75	2.50

With Additional Surcharge LIRE UNA

148	A11	1 l on 30c red brn	45	22
		Nos. 134-148 (15)	34.61	31.77

Most of Nos. 134–143, 148 and E10–E11 exist with inverted or double overprint. See Nos. E10–E11.

First Constituent Assembly.

24 - IV - 1921

Semi-Postal Stamps of 1919 Overprinted

1921, Apr. 24

149	SP6	5c bl grn	45	15
150	SP6	10c rose	38	15
151	SP6	15c gray	38	15
152	SP6	20c orange	38	15
153	SP7	45c ol grn	55	30
154	SP7	60c car rose	70	55
155	SP7	80c brt vio	90	70

With Additional Overprint "L".

156	SP7	1 l on 1cor dk sl	1.25	90
157	SP8	2 l on 2cor red brn	4.00	25
158	SP8	3 l on 3cor blk brn	8.50	5.50
159	SP8	5 l on 5cor yel brn	10.00	30
160	SP8	10 l on 10cor dk vio	11.00	8.50
		Nos. 149-160 (12)	38.49	17.60

The overprint exists inverted on several denominations.

Second Constituent Assembly.

"Constitution" Issue of 1921 With Additional Overprint "1922".

1922

161	SP6	5c bl grn	1.25	25
162	SP6	10c rose	15	22
163	SP6	15c gray	2.50	38
164	SP6	20c orange	15	22
165	SP7	45c ol grn	15	22
166	SP7	60c car rose	15	22
167	SP7	80c brt vio	15	22
168	SP7	1 l on 1cor dk sl	15	22
169	SP8	2 l on 2cor red brn	15	22
170	SP8	3 l on 3cor blk brn	22	30
171	SP8	5 l on 5cor yel brn	30	35
		Nos. 161-171 (11)	5.32	2.82

Nos. 161–171 have the overprint in heavier type than Nos. 149–160 and "IV" in Roman instead of sans-serif numerals.

The overprint exists inverted or double on almost all values.

Venetian Ship A16

Roman Arch A17

St. Vitus A18

Rostral Column A19

1923, Mar. 23 *Perf. 11½*

Pale Buff Background.

172	A16	5c bl grn	15	15
173	A16	10c violet	15	15
174	A16	15c brown	15	15
175	A17	20c org red	15	15
176	A17	25c dk gray	15	15
177	A17	30c dk grn	15	15
178	A18	50c dl bl	15	15
179	A18	60c rose	15	15
180	A18	1 l dk bl	15	15
181	A19	2 l vio brn	1.50	38
182	A19	3 l ol bis	10.00	3.75
183	A19	5 l yel brn	3.75	1.10
		Nos. 172-183 (12)	16.60	6.58

Stamps of 1923 Overprinted

REGNO D'ITALIA

1924, Feb. 22

Pale Buff Background.

184	A16	5c bl grn	15	22
185	A16	10c violet	15	22
186	A16	15c brown	15	22
187	A17	20c org red	15	22
188	A17	25c dk gray	15	22
189	A17	30c dk grn	15	22
190	A18	50c dl bl	15	22
191	A18	60c red	15	22
192	A18	1 l dk bl	15	22
193	A19	2 l vio brn	65	65
194	A19	3 l olive	1.25	1.25
195	A19	5 l yel brn	1.65	1.65
		Nos. 184-195 (12)	4.90	5.53

The overprint exists inverted on almost all values.

Stamps of 1923 Overprinted

1924, Mar. 1

Pale Buff Background.

196	A16	5c bl grn	15	22
197	A16	10c violet	15	22
198	A16	15c brown	15	22
199	A17	20c org red	15	22
200	A17	25c dk gray	15	22
201	A17	30c dk grn	15	22
202	A18	50c dl bl	15	22
203	A18	60c red	15	22
204	A18	1 l dk bl	15	22
205	A19	2 l vio brn	45	60
206	A19	3 l olive	60	75
207	A19	5 l yel brn	60	75
		Nos. 196-207 (12)	3.00	4.08

Postage stamps of Fiume were superseded by stamps of Italy.

SEMI-POSTAL STAMPS.

Semi-Postal Stamps of Hungary, 1916-17. Overprinted FIUME

Wmkd. Double Cross. (137)

1918, Dec. 2 *Perf. 15*

B1	SP3	10f +2f rose	90	38
	a.	Inverted overprint	15.00	7.50
B2	SP4	15f +2f dl vio	90	30
	a.	Inverted overprint	11.00	5.00
B3	SP5	40f +2f brn car	1.25	55
	a.	Inverted overprint	11.00	5.00

Examples of Nos. B1–B3 with overprint hand-stamped sell for higher prices.

Statue of Romulus and Remus Being Suckled by Wolf SP6

Venetian Galley SP7

Church of St. Mark's, Venice SP8

Typographed.

1919, May 18 *Perf. 11½* **Unwmkd.**

B4	SP6	5c +5 l bl grn	2.25	1.00
B5	SP6	10c +5 l rose	2.25	1.00
B6	SP6	15c +5 l dk gray	2.25	1.00
B7	SP6	20c +5 l org	2.25	1.00
B8	SP7	45c +5 l ol grn	2.25	1.00
B9	SP7	60c +5 l car rose	2.25	1.00
B10	SP7	80c +5 l brt vio	2.25	1.00
B11	SP7	1cor +5 l dk sl	2.25	1.00
B12	SP8	2cor +5 l red brn	2.25	1.00
B13	SP8	3cor +5 l blk brn	2.25	1.00
B14	SP8	5cor +5 l yel brn	2.25	1.00
B15	SP8	10cor +5 l dk vio	2.25	1.00
		Nos. B4-B15 (12)	27.00	12.00

Nos. B4 to B15 were issued in commemoration of the 200th day of peace. The surtax aided Fiume students in Italy. "Posta di Fiume" is printed on the back of Nos. B4–B16.

Dr. Antonio Grossich SP9

1919, Sept. 20

B16	SP9	25c +2 l bl	22	15

The surtax benefited the Dr. Grossich Foundation.

SPECIAL DELIVERY STAMPS

Special Delivery Stamp of Hungary, 1916, Overprinted FIUME

1918, Dec. 2 *Perf. 15* **Wmk. 137**

E1	SD1	2f gray grn & red	22	15

No. E1 with overprint handstamped sells for more.

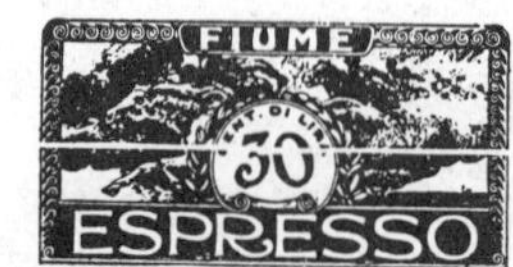

SD3

Typographed.

1920, Sept. 12 *Perf. 11½* **Unwmkd.**

E2	SD3	30c sl bl	60	25
E3	SD3	50c rose	60	25

Nos. 102 and 100 Surcharged

Reggenza Italiana del Carnaro 50 50 ESPRESSO

1920, Nov.

E4	A12	30c on 20c brn org	35.00	10.00
E5	A12	50c on 5c grn	9.00	3.00

Same Surcharge with **A R B E** at top.

E6	A12	30c on 20c brn org	42.50	13.00
E7	A12	50c on 5c grn	18.50	6.25

Overprint on Nos. E6–E7 is 11mm. wide.

Same Surcharge with **V E G L I A** at top.

E8	A12	30c on 20c brn org	42.50	13.00
E9	A12	50c on 5c grn	18.50	6.25

Overprint on Nos. E8–E9 is 17mm. wide.

Nos. E2 and E3 Overprinted

Governo Provvisorio

1921, Feb. 2

E10	SD3	30c sl bl	60	25
E11	SD3	50c rose	60	25

Fiume in 16th Century SD4

1923, Mar. 23 *Perf. 11, 11½.*

E12	SD4	60c rose & buff	25	20
E13	SD4	2 l dk bl & buff	38	42

Stamps of 1923 Overprinted

1924, Feb. 22

E14	SD4	60c car & buff	25	25
E15	SD4	2 l dk bl & buff	38	38

1924, Mar. 1 Overprinted

22 Febbraio 1924

E16	SD4	60c car & buff	25	25
E17	SD4	2 l dk bl & buff	38	38

POSTAGE DUE STAMPS.

Postage Due Stamps of Hungary, 1915–1916, Overprinted FIUME

1918, Dec. *Perf. 15* **Wmk. 137**

J1	D1	6f grn & blk	60.00	15.00
J2	D1	12f grn & blk	52.50	15.00
J3	D1	50f grn & blk	30.00	7.50
J4	D1	1f grn & red	7.50	3.75
J5	D1	2f grn & red	22	15
J6	D1	5f grn & red	3.00	1.15
J7	D1	6f grn & red	22	15
J8	D1	10f grn & red	4.50	2.25
J9	D1	12f grn & red	22	15
J10	D1	15f grn & red	6.00	3.75

11 D1 20f grn & red 30 15
12 D1 30f grn & red 6.00 3.00

The overprint on Nos. J1–J12 was applied both by press and handstamp. Prices are for the less costly. Inverted and double overprints exist. Excellent forgeries exist.

Eagle
D2

Typographed

1919, July 28 *Perf. 11½* **Unwmkd.**

J13 D2 2c brown 15 15
J14 D2 5c brown 15 15

Semi-Postal Stamps of 1919 with Overprint "Valore Globale" Surcharged:

Segnatasse

L. 0.02

a

1921, Mar. 21

J15 SP6 2c on 15c gray 30 30
J16 SP6 4c on 10c rose 15 15
J17 SP9 5c on 25c bl 15 15
J18 SP6 6c on 20c org 15 15
J19 SP6 10c on 20c org 55 45

Surcharged:

Segnatasse

L. 0.20

b

J20 SP7 20c on 45c ol grn 38 38
J21 SP7 30c on 1cor dk sl 38 45
J22 SP7 40c on 80c vio 22 22
J23 SP7 50c on 60c car 30 30
J24 SP7 60c on 45c ol grn 38 38
J25 SP7 80c on 45c ol grn 38 38

Surcharged type "a."

J26 SP8 1 l on 2cor red brn 75 75
Nos. J15-J26 (12) 4.09 4.06

See note below No. 85 regarding settings of "Valore Globale" overprint.

NEWSPAPER STAMPS.

Newspaper Stamp of Hungary, 1914, Overprinted FIUME

1918, Dec. 2 *Imperf.* **Wmk. 137**

P1 N5 (2f) orange 22 15

No. P1 with overprint handstamped sells for more.

Eagle
N1

1919 *Perf. 11½* **Unwmkd.**

P2 N1 2c dp buff 25 25

Re-engraved

P3 N1 2c dp buff 38 38

In the re-engraved stamp the top of the "2" is rounder and broader, the feet of the eagle show clearly and the diamond at bottom has six lines instead of five.

Steamer
N2

1920, Sept. 12

P4 N2 1c gray grn 15 15

No. P4 exists imperf.

See note on FIUME-KUPA Zone, Italian Occupation, after Jugoslavia No. NJ22.

FRANCE

(frăns)

LOCATION—Western Europe.
GOVT.—Republic.
AREA—212,918 sq. mi.
POP.—53,080,000 (est. 1977).
CAPITAL—Paris.

100 Centimes = 1 Franc

> Prices of early French stamps vary according to condition. Quotations for Nos. 1–48 are for fine copies. Very fine to superb specimens sell at much higher prices, and inferior or poor copies sell at reduced prices, depending on the condition of the individual specimen.

Ceres
A1

FORTY CENTIMES.

4 Type I. 4 Type II.

Typographed

1849–50 *Imperf.* **Unwmkd.**

1 A1 10c bis, *yelsh* ('50) 1,200. 300.00
a. 10c dk bis, *yelsh* 1,400. 375.00
b. 10c grnsh bis 2,750. 575.00
c. Tête bêche pr. *50,000.* *10,000.*
2 A1 15c yel grn, *grnsh* ('50) *10,000.* 1,100.
a. 15c grn, *grnsh* *10,000.* 1,100.
b. Tête bêche pair *110,000.*
3 A1 20c blk, *yelsh* 300.00 50.00
a. 20c blk 450.00 65.00
b. 20c blk, *buff* 1,650. 450.00
c. Tête bêche pair 5,250. 4,750.
4 A1 20c dk bl 1,100.
a. 20c bl, *bluish* 1,250.
b. 20c bl, *yelsh* 1,650.
c. Tête bêche pair *27,500.*
6 A1 25c lt bl, *bluish* 3,000. 40.00
a. 25c bl, *bluish* ('50) 3,750. 65.00
b. 25c bl, *yelsh* 3,250. 55.00
c. Tête bêche pr. *100,000.* *8,000.*
7 A1 40c org, *yelsh* (I)('50) 1,750. 500.00
a. 40c org ver, *yelsh* (I) 2,100. 600.00
b. 40c org, *yelsh* (II) *14,000.* *3,500.*
c. Pair, types I and II *20,000.* *6,750.*
8 A1 1fr dl org red *27,500.* *14,500.*
a. 1fr ver, *yelsh* *50,000.* *18,000.*
b. Tête bêche pair *200,000.* *150,000.*
c. 1fr pale ver ("Vervelle") *13,500.*
9 A1 1fr dk car, *yelsh* 5,250. 950.00
a. Tête bêche pair *100,000.* *18,000.*
b. 1fr brn car *9,500.* 1,400.
c. 1fr lt car 5,500. 1,000.

No. 4, which lacks gum, was not issued due to a rate change to 25c after the stamps were prepared.

An ungummed sheet of No. 8c was found in 1895 among the effects of Anatole A. Hulot, the printer. It was sold to Ernest Vervelle, a Parisian dealer, by whose name the stamps are known.

Nos. 1, 4, 6, 7 and 13 are of similar designs and colors to French Colonies Nos. 9, 11, 12, 14, and 8. There are numerous shades of each. They can seldom be correctly allocated except by the cancellations.

See Nos. 329–329e, 612–613, 624.

1862 **Re-issue.**

1d A1 10c bister 285.00
2d A1 15c yel grn 375.00
3d A1 20c blk, *yelsh* 265.00
4d A1 20c blue 265.00
6d A1 25c blue 265.00
7d A1 40c org (I) 300.00
7e A1 40c org (II) *10,000.*
9d A1 1fr pale lake 400.00

The re-issues are in lighter colors and on whiter paper than the originals. An official imitation of the essay, 25c on 20c blue, was made at the same time as the re-issues.

President Louis Napoleon
A2

Emperor Napoleon III
A3

1852

10 A2 10c pale bis, *yelsh* *17,500.* 500.00
a. 10c dk bis, *yelsh* *20,000.* 600.00
11 A2 25c bl, *bluish* 1,850. 50.00

1862 **Re-issue.**

10b A2 10c bister 350.00
11a A2 25c blue 265.00

The re-issues are in lighter colors and on whiter paper than the originals.

1853–60 *Imperf.*

Die I. The curl above the forehead directly below "R" of "EMPIRE" is made up of two lines very close together, often appearing to form a single thick line. There is no shading across the neck.

Die II. The curl is made of two distinct, more widely separated lines. There are lines of shading across the upper neck.

12 A3 1c ol grn, *pale bl* (II) ('60) 110.00 70.00
a. 1c brnz grn, *pale bluish* 120.00 80.00
13 A3 5c grn, *grnsh* (I) ('54) 475.00 70.00
14 A3 10c bis, *yelsh* (I) 325.00 8.00
a. 10c yel, *yelsh* (I) 1,750. 85.00
b. 10c bis brn, *yelsh* (I) 450.00 22.50
c. 10c bis, *yelsh* (II) ('60) 500.00 37.50
15 A3 20c bl, *bluish* (I) ('54) 150.00 1.20
a. 20c dk bl, *bluish* (I) 240.00 2.00
b. 20c mlky bl (I) 300.00 16.00
c. 20c bl, *lil* (I) *3,750.* 100.00
d. 20c bl, *bluish* (II) ('60) 350.00 5.00
e. As "d," tête bêche pair 85,000.
16 A3 20c bl, *grnsh* (I) *4,500.* 200.00
a. 20c bl, *grnsh* (II) *4,500.* 265.00
17 A3 25c bl, *bluish* (I) 1,500. 275.00

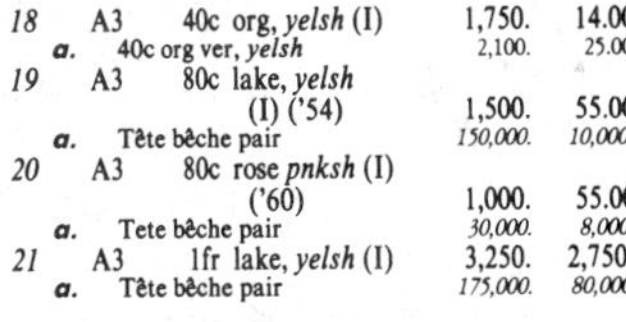

18 A3 40c org, *yelsh* (I) 1,750. 14.00
a. 40c org ver, *yelsh* 2,100. 25.00
19 A3 80c lake, *yelsh* (I) ('54) 1,500. 55.00
a. Tête bêche pair *150,000.* *10,000.*
20 A3 80c rose *pnksh* (I) ('60) 1,000. 55.00
a. Tete bêche pair *30,000.* *8,000.*
21 A3 1fr lake, *yelsh* (I) 3,250. 2,750.
a. Tête bêche pair *175,000.* *80,000.*

Most values of the 1853–60 issue are known unofficially rouletted, pin-perf., perf. 7 and percé en scie.

1862 **Re-issue.**

17c A3 25c bl (I) 250.00
20c A3 80c rose (I) 1,200.
21c A3 1fr lake (I) 1,100.
d. Tête bêche pair *11,000.*

The re-issues are in lighter colors and on whiter paper than the originals.

1862-71 *Perf. 14x13½*

22 A3 1c ol grn, *pale bl* (II) 67.50 37.50
a. 1c brnz grn, *pale bl* (II) 75.00 40.00
23 A3 5c yel grn, *grnsh*(I) 125.00 8.50
a. dp grn, *grnsh* (I) 165.00 11.00
24 A3 5c grn, *pale bl* ('71) (I) 600.00 72.50
25 A3 10c bis, *yelsh* (II) 650.00 4.00
a. 10c yel brn, *yelsh* (II) 675.00 5.50
26 A3 20c bl, *bluish* (II) 135.00 80
a. Tête bêche pair (II) 3,000. 1,100.
27 A3 40c org, *yelsh* (I) 825.00 6.00
28 A3 80c rose, *pnksh* (I) 700.00 40.00
a. 80c brt rose, *pnksh* (I) 850.00 60.00
b. Tête bêche pair (I) *9,500.* *3,500.*

Napoleon III
A4 A5

Napoleon III
A6

1863–70 *Perf. 14x13½*

29 A4 1c brnz grn, *pale bl* ('70) 17.50 12.50
a. 1c ol grn, *pale bl* 22.50 15.00
b. Imperf. 1,300.
30 A4 2c red brn, *yelsh* 52.50 25.00
a. Imperf. 250.00
31 A4 4c gray 125.00 50.00
a. Tête bêche pair *9,000.* *7,000.*
b. Imperf. 200.00
32 A5 10c bis, *yelsh* ('67) 175.00 5.00
a. Imperf. 200.00
33 A5 20c bl, *bluish* ('67) 135.00 1.40
a. Imperf. 350.00
34 A5 30c brn, *yelsh* ('67) 450.00 18.50
a. 30c dk brn, *yelsh* 700.00 35.00
c. Imperf. 200.00
35 A5 40c org, *yelsh* ('68) 525.00 12.00
a. 40c pale org, *yelsh* 550.00 14.00
b. Imperf. 265.00

No.	Design	Description	Unused	Used
36	A5	80c rose, *pnksh* ('68)	475.00	22.50
a.		80c car, *yelsh*	650.00	35.00
b.		Imperf.	575.00	
37	A6	5fr gray lil *lav* ('69)	5,000.	900.00
a.		"5" and "F" omitted		50,000.
b.		Imperf.	8,000.	

No. 33 exists in two types, differing in the size of the dots at either side of POSTES.

On No. 37, the "5" and "F" vary in height from 3¾mm. to 4½mm. All known copies of No. 37a are more or less damaged.

The imperforate varieties of Nos. 29–36 constitute the "Rothschild Issue," said to have been authorized exclusively for the banker to use on his correspondence. Used copies exist.

No. 29 was reprinted in 1887 by authority of Granet, Minister of Posts. The reprints show a yellowish shade under the ultraviolet lamp. Price $850.

Ceres

A7 A8

A9 A10

Type I Type II

A11

Type III

Bordeaux Issue. Lithographed.

On the lithographed stamps, except for type I of the 20c, the shading on the cheek and neck is in lines or dashes, not in dots. On the typographed stamps the shading is in dots.

The 2c, 10c and 20c (types II and III) occur in two or more types. The most easily distinguishable are:

2c—Type A. To the left of and within the top of the left "2" are lines of shading composed of dots.

2c—Type B. These lines of dots are replaced by solid lines.

10c—Type A. The inner frame lines are of the same thickness as all other frame lines.

10c—Type B. The inner frame lines are much thicker than the others.

Three Types of the 20c.

A9—Type I. The inscriptions in the upper and lower labels are small and there is quite a space between the upper label and the circle containing the head. There is also very little shading under the eye and in the neck.

A10—Type II. The inscriptions in the labels are similar to those of the first type, the shading under the eye and in the neck is heavier and the upper label and circle almost touch.

A11—Type III. The inscriptions in the labels are much larger than those of the two preceding types, and are similar to those of the other values of the same type in the set.

1870–71 ***Imperf.***

No.	Design	Description	Unused	Used
38	A7	1c ol grn, *pale bl*	75.00	80.00
a.		1c brnz grn, *pale bl*	100.00	110.00
39	A7	2c red brn, *yelsh* (B)	200.00	225.00
a.		2c brick red, *yelsh* (B)	1,100.	9,000.
b.		2c mar, *yelsh* (B)	1,400.	1,000.
c.		2c choc, *yelsh* (A)	900.00	900.00
40	A7	4c gray	250.00	250.00
41	A8	5c grn, *grnsh*	225.00	135.00
a.		5c yel grn, *grnsh*	250.00	165.00
b.		5c emer, *grnsh*	1,800.	1,000.
42	A8	10c bis, *yelsh* (A)	700.00	60.00
a.		10c bis, *yelsh* (B)	750.00	70.00
43	A9	20c bl, *bluish*(I)	*9,000.*	650.00
a.		20c dk bl, *bluish*(I)	*10,000.*	850.00
44	A10	20c bl, *bluish* (II)	800.00	55.00
a.		20c dk bl, *bluish* (II)	1,050.	110.00
b.		20c ultra, *bluish* (II)	*15,000.*	*3,000.*
45	A11	20c bl, *bluish* (III) ('71)	800.00	17.50
a.		20c ultra, *bluish* (III)	2,000.	750.00
46	A8	30c brn, *yelsh*	375.00	275.00
a.		30c blk brn, *yelsh*	1,500.	800.00
47	A8	40c org, *yelsh*	375.00	125.00
a.		40c yel org, *yelsh*	375.00	125.00
b.		40c red org, *yelsh*	700.00	200.00
c.		40c scar, *yelsh*	*5,250.*	*2,000.*
48	A8	80c rose, *pnksh*	475.00	250.00
a.		80c dl rose, *pnksh*	600.00	275.00

All values of the 1870 issue are known rouletted, pin-perf. and perf. 14, unofficially.

A12

Blue Surcharge

1871 Typographed. ***Perf. 14x13½.***

No.	Design	Description	Unused	Used
49	A12	10(c) on 10c bis	1,400.	

No. 49 was never placed in use. Counterfeits exist.

Ceres

A13 A14

Two types of the 40c as in the 1849–50 issue.

1870–73 Typo. ***Perf. 14x13½***

No.	Design	Description	Unused	Used
50	A7	1c ol grn, *pale bl*	25.00	12.00
a.		1c brnz grn, *pale bl* ('72)	32.50	13.00
51	A7	2c red brn, *yelsh* ('72)	57.50	12.00
52	A7	4c gray ('72)	225.00	32.50
53	A7	5c yel grn, *pale bl*('72)	90.00	7.25
a.		5c grn	100.00	10.00
54	A13	10c bis, *yelsh*	325.00	57.50
a.		Tête bêche pair	3,250.	1,750.
55	A13	10c bis, *rose*('73)	200.00	8.00
a.		Tête bêche pair	2,500.	1,400.
56	A13	15c bis, *yelsh* ('71)	200.00	4.00
a.		Tête bêche pair	*20,000.*	*5,000.*
57	A13	20c dl bl, *bluish*	165.00	6.50
a.		20c brt bl, *bluish*	200.00	10.00
b.		Tête b'‡che pair	2,500.	1,200.
58	A13	25c bl, *bluish* ('71)	70.00	1.00
a.		25c dk bl, *bluish*	80.00	1.20
b.		Tête bêche pair	3,750.	2,000.
59	A13	40c org, *yelsh* (I)	375.00	5.00
a.		40c org yel, *yelsh* (I)	450.00	7.00
b.		40c org, *yelsh* (II)	1,800.	165.00
c.		40c org yel, *yelsh* (II)	1,800.	165.00
d.		Pair, types I and II	*3,250.*	500.00

No. 58 exists in three main plate varieties, differing in one or another of the flower-like corner ornaments.

Nos. 54, 57 and 58 were reprinted imperf. in 1887. See note after No. 37.

1872-75 Larger Numerals.

No.	Design	Description	Unused	Used
60	A14	10c bis, *rose* ('75)	165.00	8.00
a.		Clichê of 15c in plate of 10c	2,750.	3,000.
b.		As"a," se-tenant with #60	*3,750.*	*4,000.*
61	A14	15c bis ('73)	165.00	4.75
62	A14	30c brn, *yelsh*	325.00	5.75
63	A14	80c rose, *pnksh*	400.00	12.00

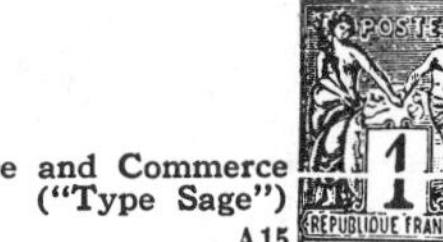

Peace and Commerce ("Type Sage")

A15

Type I. The "N" of "INV" is under the "B" of "REPUBLIQUE".

Type II. The "N" of "INV" is under the "U" of "REPUBLIQUE".

1876-78 Type I.

No.	Design	Description	Unused	Used
64	A15	1c grn, *grnsh*	100.00	50.00
a.		Imperf.	165.00	
65	A15	2c grn, *grnsh*	950.00	250.00
a.		Imperf.	1,000.	
66	A15	4c grn, *grnsh*	85.00	40.00
a.		Imperf.	175.00	
67	A15	5c grn, *grnsh*	400.00	40.00
a.		Imperf.	550.00	
68	A15	10c grn, *grnsh*	525.00	22.50
a.		Imperf.	550.00	
69	A15	15c gray lil, *grysh*	525.00	20.00
a.		Imperf.	550.00	
70	A15	20c red brn, *straw*	375.00	15.00
a.		Imperf.	400.00	
71	A15	20c bl, *bluish*	*11,000.*	
72	A15	25c ultra, *bluish*	*4,000.*	70.00
73	A15	30c brn, *yelsh*	250.00	8.00
a.		Imperf.	275.00	
74	A15	40c red, *straw* ('78)	250.00	30.00
a.		Imperf.	275.00	
75	A15	75c car, *rose*	525.00	11.00
a.		Imperf.	550.00	
76	A15	1fr brnz grn, *straw*	375.00	10.00
a.		Imperf.	450.00	

No. 71 was never put into use.

The reprints of No. 71 are of the second type. They are imperforate or with forged perforation.

1876-77 Type II.

No.	Design	Description	Unused	Used
77	A15	2c grn, *grnsh*	70.00	17.50
78	A15	5c grn, *grnsh*	16.50	30
a.		Imperf.	165.00	
79	A15	10c grn, *grnsh*	850.00	250.00
80	A15	15c gray lil, *grysh*	350.00	1.40
81	A15	25c ultra, *bluish*	300.00	35
a.		25c bl, *bluish*	300.00	55
b.		Pair, types I & II	*25,000.*	*7,500.*
c.		Imperf.	400.00	
82	A15	30c yel brn, *yelsh*	27.50	60
a.		30c brn, *yelsh*	30.00	80
b.		Imperf.	550.00	
83	A15	75c car, *rose* ('77)	1,200.	90.00
84	A15	1fr brnz grn, *straw* ('77)	52.50	5.00
a.		Imperf.	550.00	

1877-80

No.	Design	Description	Unused	Used
86	A15	1c *lil bl*	2.00	55
a.		1c *gray bl*	2.25	70
b.		Imperf.	90.00	
87	A15	1c *Prus bl* ('80)	*6,000.*	*3,000.*
88	A15	2c brn, *straw*	3.00	80
a.		2c brn, *yel*	4.00	1.65
b.		Imperf.	90.00	
89	A15	3c yel, *straw* ('78)	125.00	40.00
a.		Imperf.	150.00	
90	A15	4c cl, *lav*	3.00	1.65
a.		4c vio brn, *lav*	4.50	2.50
b.		Imperf.	90.00	
91	A15	10c *lavender*	25.00	75
a.		10c *rose lil*	27.50	1.00
b.		10c *lil*	27.50	1.00
c.		Imperf.	95.00	
92	A15	15c bl ('78)	15.00	30
a.		Imperf.	110.00	
b.		15c bl, *bluish*	265.00	3.00
93	A15	25c *red* ('78)	575.00	22.50
a.		Imperf.	725.00	
94	A15	35c *yel* ('78)	350.00	30.00
a.		35c *yel org*	375.00	35.00
b.		Imperf.	350.00	
95	A15	40c red, *straw* ('80)	45.00	1.40
a.		Imperf.	265.00	
96	A15	5fr vio, *lav*	400.00	80.00
a.		5fr red lil, *lav*	450.00	90.00
b.		Imperf.	800.00	

1879-90

No.	Design	Description	Unused	Used
97	A15	3c gray, *grysh*('80)	2.00	1.10
a.		Imperf.	90.00	
98	A15	20c red, *yel grn*	25.00	2.35
a.		20c red, *dp grn* ('84)	35.00	4.50
b.		Imperf.	100.00	
99	A15	25c yel, *straw*	200.00	4.00
a.		Imperf.	285.00	
100	A15	25c *pale rose* ('86)	27.50	50
a.		Imperf.	135.00	
101	A15	50c rose, *rose* ('90)	90.00	1.00
a.		50c car, *rose*	95.00	1.00
102	A15	75c dp vio, *org* ('90)	130.00	30.00
a.		75c dp vio, *yel*	140.00	35.00

1892 Quadrille Paper

No.	Design	Description	Unused	Used
103	A15	15c blue	9.00	25
a.		Imperf.	135.00	

1898–1900 Ordinary Paper

No.	Design	Description	Unused	Used
104	A15	5c yel grn	10.00	30
a.		Imperf.	110.00	

Type I.

No.	Design	Description	Unused	Used
105	A15	5c yel grn	7.50	70
a.		Imperf.	200.00	
106	A15	10c *lavender*	12.00	2.00
a.		Imperf.	225.00	
107	A15	50c car, *rose*	95.00	27.50
108	A15	2fr brn, *az* ('00)	80.00	30.00
b.		Imperf.	*2,500.*	

See also No. 226.

Reprints of A15, type II, were made in 1887 and left imperf. See note after No. 37. Price for set of 27, $2,750.

Liberty, Equality and Fraternity

A16

"The Rights of Man"

A17

Liberty and Peace

A18

1900–29 ***Perf. 14x13½***

No.	Design	Description	Unused	Used
109	A16	1c gray	55	5
a.		Imperf.	32.50	
110	A16	2c vio brn	55	5
a.		Imperf.	45.00	
111	A16	3c orange	75	8
a.		3c red	16.50	5.00
b.		Imperf.	35.00	
112	A16	4c yel brn	2.50	60
a.		Imperf.	165.00	
113	A16	5c green	1.20	5
a.		Imperf.	80.00	
b.		Bklt. pane of 10	30.00	
114	A16	7½c lil ('26)	65	40
115	A16	10c lil ('29)	5.25	10
116	A17	10c carmine	27.50	75
a.		Numerals printed separately	30.00	10.00
b.		Imperf., #116 or 116a	275.00	
117	A17	15c orange	9.00	30
a.		Imperf.	190.00	
118	A17	20c brn vio	80.00	8.50
119	A17	25c blue	140.00	1.20
a.		Numerals printed separately	150.00	7.50
b.		Imperf. #119 or 119a	450.00	
120	A17	30c violet	95.00	5.75
121	A18	40c red & pale bl	20.00	50
a.		Imperf.	175.00	
122	A18	45c grn & bl ('06)	27.50	1.10
a.		Imperf.	200.00	

123	A18	50c bis brn & lav	140.00	1.25
a.		Imperf.	300.00	
124	A18	60c vio & ultra ('20)	1.25	38
a.		Imperf.	400.00	
125	A18	1fr cl & ol grn	40.00	32
a.		Imperf.	200.00	
126	A18	2fr gray vio & yel	950.00	62.50
a.		Imperf.	2,750.	
127	A18	2fr org & pale bl ('20)	52.50	32
a.		Imperf.	550.00	
128	A18	3fr vio & bl ('25)	30.00	6.75
129	A18	3fr brt vio & rose ('27)	70.00	1.65
a.		Imperf.	375.00	
130	A18	5fr dk bl & buff	100.00	3.75
a.		Imperf.	900.00	
131	A18	10fr grn & red ('26)	135.00	13.00
132	A18	20fr mag & grn ('26)	240.00	35.00
		Nos. 109-132 (24)	2,169.20	144.35

In the 10c and 25c values, the first printings show the numerals to have been impressed by a second operation, whereas, in later printings, the numerals were inserted in the plates. Two operations were used for all 20c and 30c, and one operation for the 15c.

No. 114 was issued precanceled only. Prices for precanceled stamps in first column are for those which have not been through the post and have original gum. Prices in the second column are for postally used, gumless stamps.

See also No. P7.

Flat Plate & Rotary Press

The following stamps were printed by both flat plate and rotary press: Nos. 109-113, 144-146, 163, 166, 168, 170, 177-178, 185, 192 and P7.

"Rights of Man"—A19

Sower A20

1902

133	A19	10c rose red	30.00	38
a.		Imperf.	225.00	
134	A19	15c pale red	10.00	30
a.		Imperf.	425.00	
135	A19	20c brn vio	105.00	13.00
a.		Imperf.	450.00	
136	A19	25c blue	120.00	1.50
137	A19	30c lilac	275.00	11.00
a.		Imperf.	800.00	
		Nos. 133-137 (5)	540.00	26.18

1903-38

138	A20	10c rose	10.00	6
a.		Imperf.	100.00	
139	A20	15c sl grn	3.25	5
a.		Imperf.	100.00	
b.		Booklet pane of 10	40.00	
140	A20	20c vio brn	85.00	1.20
a.		Imperf.	135.00	
141	A20	25c dl bl	95.00	1.40
a.		Imperf.	150.00	
142	A20	30c violet	210.00	5.75
a.		Imperf.	425.00	
143	A20	45c lt vio ('26)	5.25	70
144	A20	50c dl bl ('21)	30.00	60
a.		Imperf.	65.00	
145	A20	50c gray grn ('26)	5.75	15
a.		Imperf.	100.00	
146	A20	50c ver ('26)	25	5
a.		Booklet pane of 10	7.50	
b.		Imperf.	80.00	
147	A20	50c grnsh bl ('38)	80	5
a.		Imperf.	50.00	
148	A20	60c lt vio ('24)	5.75	90
149	A20	65c rose ('24)	2.25	65
a.		Imperf.	160.00	
150	A20	65c gray grn ('27)	5.25	90
151	A20	75c rose lil ('26)	4.00	20
a.		Imperf.	450.00	
152	A20	80c ver ('26)	57.50	6.75
153	A20	85c ver ('24)	16.00	50
154	A20	1fr dl bl ('26)	7.00	5
		Nos. 138-154 (17)	543.05	19.96

See also Nos. 941, 942A.

Sower, Ground under Feet

A21

Sower, no Ground under Feet

A22

1906

With Ground Under Feet of Figure

155	A21	10c red	4.00	70
a.		Imperf., pair	225.00	

1906–37

TEN AND THIRTY-FIVE CENTIMES.

Type I. Numerals and letters of the inscriptions thin.

Type II. Numerals and letters thicker.

No Ground Under the Feet.

156	A22	1c ol bis ('33)	12	8
157	A22	2c dk grn ('33)	12	6
158	A22	3c ver ('33)	12	6
159	A22	5c green	2.00	5
a.		Imperf., pair	27.50	
b.		Bklt. pane of 10	37.50	
160	A22	5c org ('21)	2.00	7
a.		Bklt. pane of 10	32.50	
161	A22	5c cer ('34)	15	6
162	A22	10c red (II)	2.00	5
a.		Imperf., pair	27.50	
b.		10c red (I) ('06)	11.00	25
c.		Booklet pane of 10 (I)	125.00	
d.		Booklet pane of 10 (II)	75.00	
e.		Booklet pane of 6 (II)	250.00	
163	A22	10c grn (II) ('21)	70	5
a.		10c grn (I) ('27)	30.00	27.50
b.		Booklet pane of 10 (II)	15.00	
c.		Booklet pane of 10 (I)	325.00	
164	A22	10c ultra ('32)	60	7
165	A22	15c red brn ('26)	28	3
a.		Booklet pane of 10	25.00	
166	A22	20c brown	3.75	15
a.		Imperf., pair	52.50	
167	A22	20c red vio ('26)	28	3
a.		Bklt. pane of 10	6.50	
168	A22	25c blue	2.00	12
a.		Bklt. pane of 10	32.50	
b.		Imperf., pair	52.50	
169	A22	25c brn ('27)	20	5
170	A22	30c orange	15.00	80
a.		Imperf., pair	175.00	
171	A22	30c red ('21)	11.00	1.65
172	A22	30c cer ('25)	1.10	10
a.		Booklet pane of 10	11.00	
173	A22	30c lt bl ('25)	2.50	5
a.		Bklt. pane of 10	27.50	
174	A22	30c cop red ('37)	40	10
a.		Booklet pane of 10	7.50	
175	A22	35c vio (II) ('26)	13.50	60
a.		Imperf., pair	175.00	
b.		35c vio (I) ('06)	200.00	5.00
176	A22	35c grn ('37)	90	20
177	A22	40c ol ('25)	1.10	12
b.		Bklt. pane of 10	32.50	
178	A22	40c ver ('26)	2.00	18
a.		Bklt. pane of 10	22.50	
179	A22	40c vio ('27)	2.50	15
180	A22	40c lt ultra ('28)	1.65	12
181	A22	1.05fr ver ('25)	8.75	2.75
182	A22	1.10fr cer ('27)	12.50	1.40
183	A22	1.40fr cer ('26)	20.00	15.00
184	A22	2fr Prus grn ('31)	12.50	40
		Nos. 156-184 (29)	119.72	24.55

The 10c and 35c, type I, were slightly retouched by adding thin white outlines to the sack of grain, the underside of the right arm and the back of the skirt. It is difficult to distinguish the retouches except on clearly-printed copies. The white outlines were made stronger on the stamps of type II.

Stamps of types A16, A18, A20 and A22 were printed in 1916–20 on paper of poor quality, usually grayish and containing bits of fiber. This is called G. C. (Grande Consommation) paper.

Nos. 160, 162b, 163, 175b and 176 also exist imperf.

See also Nos. 241–241b, P8.

Louis Pasteur

A23

1923-26

185	A23	10c green	65	12
a.		Booklet pane of 10	9.00	
186	A23	15c grn ('24)	1.00	12
187	A23	20c grn ('26)	2.25	22
188	A23	30c red	40	20
189	A23	30c grn ('26)	50	12
190	A23	45c red ('24)	1.85	1.00
191	A23	50c blue	3.75	20
192	A23	75c bl ('24)	3.25	35
a.		Imperf., pair	285.00	
193	A23	90c red ('26)	12.00	2.50
194	A23	1fr bl ('25)	20.00	12
195	A23	1.25fr bl ('26)	21.00	5.00
196	A23	1.50fr bl ('26)	6.00	15
		Nos. 185-196 (12)	72.65	10.10

Nos. 185, 188 and 191 were issued to commemorate the centenary of the birth of Pasteur.

No. 125 Overprinted in Blue

CONGRES PHILATELIQUE
DE
BORDEAUX
1923

1923, June 15

197	A18	1fr cl & ol grn	450.00	450.00

Allegory of Olympic Games at Paris

A24

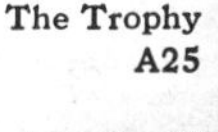

The Trophy

A25

Milo of Crotona

A26

Victorious Athlete

A27

Perf. 14x13½, 13½x14

1924, Apr. 1

198	A24	10c gray grn & yel grn	1.20	35
199	A25	25c rose & dk rose	1.85	22
200	A26	30c brn red & blk	8.50	7.50
201	A27	50c ultra & dk bl	16.00	3.00

8th Olympic Games, Paris. Exist imperf.

Pierre de Ronsard

A28

1924, Oct. 6 *Perf. 14x13½*

219	A28	75c bl, *bluish*	75	60

Issued to commemorate the 400th anniversary of the birth of Pierre de Ronsard, poet (1524-1585).

"Light and Liberty" Allegory—A29

Majolica Vase

A30

Potter Decorating Vase—A31

Terrace of Château—A32

1924-25 *Perf. 14x13½, 13½x14.*

220	A29	10c dk grn & yel ('25)	60	38
221	A30	15c ind & grn ('25)	60	38
a.		Imperf.	125.00	
222	A31	25c vio brn & garnet	65	25
223	A32	25c gray bl & vio ('25)	1.00	50
a.		Imperf.	425.00	
224	A31	75c ind & ultra	2.75	1.25
225	A29	75c dk bl & lt bl ('25)	12.00	4.75
a.		Imperf.	150.00	
		Nos. 220-225 (6)	17.60	7.51

Issued to commemorate the International Exhibition of Decorative Modern Arts at Paris, 1925.

Philatelic Exhibition Issue.

Souvenir Sheet.

A32a

1925, May 2 *Perf. 14x13½*

226	A32a	5fr car (A15, type II) sheet of four	900.00	900.00
a.		Imperf. sheet	4,750.	
b.		Single stamp, perf.	125.00	120.00
c.		Single stamp, imperf.	950.00	

Issued in sheets measuring 140x220 mm.
These were not on sale at post offices but solely at the International Philatelic Exhibition, Paris, May, 1925.

Stamps of 1907–26 Surcharged **=25c**

1926-27

227	A22	25c on 30c lt bl	22	12
228	A22	25c on 35c vio	22	15
a.		Double surcharge	275.00	
229	A20	50c on 60c lt vio ('27)	1.10	30
230	A20	50c on 65c rose ('27)	85	15
231	A23	50c on 75c bl	2.25	25
232	A20	50c on 80c ver ('27)	80	40
233	A20	50c on 85c ver ('27)	1.10	20
234	A22	50c on 1.05fr ver ('27)	1.60	30
235	A23	50c on 1.25fr bl	1.40	25
236	A20	55c on 60c lt vio	150.00	52.50
238	A22	90c on 1.05fr ver	4.00	2.75
240	A22	1.10fr on 1.40fr cer	1.00	35
		Nos. 227-240 (12)	164.54	57.72

No. 236 is known only precanceled. See second note after No. 132.
Nos. 229, 230, 234, 238 and 240 have three bars instead of two. The 55c surcharge has thinner, larger numerals and a rounded "c." Width, including bars, is 17mm., instead of 13mm.

Strasbourg Exhibition Issue.

Souvenir Sheet.

A32b

1927, June 4

241	A32b	Sheet of two	900.00	900.00
a.		5fr lt ultra (A22)	240.00	240.00
b.		10fr car rose (A22)	240.00	240.00

Issued in sheets measuring 111x140mm. Sold at the Strasbourg Philatelic Exhibition as souvenirs.

Marcelin Berthleot
A33

1927, Sept. 7

242	A33	90c dl rose	60	22

Issued to commemorate the centenary of the birth of Marcelin Berthelot (1827–1907), chemist and statesman.

Lafayette, Washington, S. S. Paris and Airplane "Spirit of St. Louis"

A34

1927, Sept. 15

243	A34	90c dl red	80	50
a.		Value omitted	1,100.	
244	A34	1.50fr dp bl	2.00	80
a.		Value omitted	900.00	

Visit of American Legionnaires to France, September, 1927. Exist imperf.

Joan of Arc
A35

1929, Mar.

245	A35	50c dl bl	75	15
a.		Booklet pane of 10	8.50	
b.		Imperf.	125.00	

Issued in commemoration of the 500th anniversary of the relief of Orleans by the French forces led by Joan of Arc.

Le Havre Exhibition Issue.

A36

Blue Overprint.

1929, May 18

246	A36	2fr org & pale bl	575.00	525.00

No. 246 was sold exclusively at the International Philatelic Exhibition, Le Havre, May, 1929. Sold for 7fr, which included a 5fr admission ticket.
Excellent counterfeits of No. 246 exist.

Reims Cathedral
A37

Dies I, II & III. Die IV

Die I Die II Die III

3fr—Die I. The window of the first turret on the left is made of two lines. The horizontal line of the frame surrounding 3F is not continuous.
3fr—Die II. Same as Die I but the line under 3F is continuous.
3fr—Die III. Same as Die II but there is a deeply cut line separating 3 and F.
3fr—Die IV. The window of the first turret on the left is made of three lines.

Mont-Saint-Michel
A38

Die I. Die II.

5fr—Die I. The line at the top of the spire is broken.
5fr—Die II. The line is unbroken.

Port of La Rochelle
A39

Dies I & II. Die III.

10fr—Die I. The top of the "E" of "POSTES" has a serif. The oval of shading inside the "0" of "10 fr" and the outer oval are broken at their bases.
10fr—Die II. The same top has no serif. Interior and exterior of "0" broken as in Die I.
10fr—Die III. Top of "E" has no serif. Interior and exterior of "0" complete.

Pont du Gard, Nimes
A40

Dies I & II.

Die III.

20fr—Die I. Shading of the first complete arch in the left middle tier is made of horizontal lines. Size 36 x 20¾ mm. Perf. 13½.
20fr—Die II. Same, size 35½ x 21 mm. Perf. 11.
20fr—Die III. Shading of same arch is made of three diagonal lines. Thin paper. Perf. 13.

Engraved.

1929–33 *Perf. 11, 13, 13½*

247	A37	3fr dk gray ('30) (I)	100.00	2.75
247A	A37	3fr dk gray ('30) (II)	150.00	4.50
247B	A37	3fr dk gray ('30) (III)	475.00	22.50
248	A37	3fr bluish sl ('31) (IV)	100.00	3.00

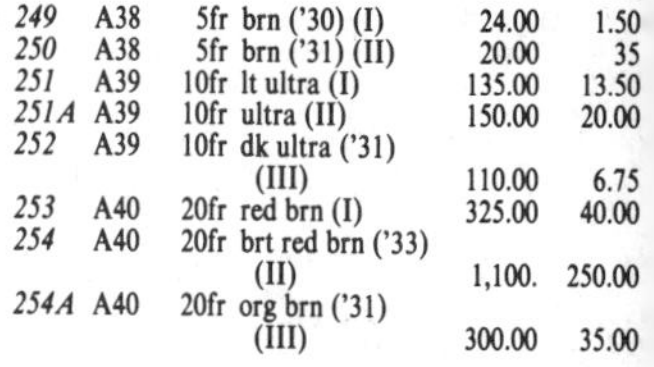

249	A38	5fr brn ('30) (I)	24.00	1.50
250	A38	5fr brn ('31) (II)	20.00	35
251	A39	10fr lt ultra (I)	135.00	13.50
251A	A39	10fr ultra (II)	150.00	20.00
252	A39	10fr dk ultra ('31) (III)	110.00	6.75
253	A40	20fr red brn (I)	325.00	40.00
254	A40	20fr brt red brn ('33) (II)	1,100.	250.00
254A	A40	20fr org brn ('31) (III)	300.00	35.00

View of Algiers
A41

1929, Jan. 1 Typographed

255	A41	50c bl & rose red	2.00	22

Issued in commemoration of the centenary of the first French settlement in Algeria.

Nos. 146 and 196 Overprinted **CONGRÈS DU B. I. T. 1930**

1930, Apr. 23 *Perf. 14x13½*

256	A20	50c vermilion	1.75	1.25
257	A23	1.50fr blue	13.00	11.00

International Labor Bureau, 48th Congress, Paris.

Colonial Exposition Issue.

Fachi Woman
A42

French Colonials
A43

1930–31 Typo. *Perf. 14x13½*

258	A42	15c gray blk	45	15
259	A42	40c dk brn	1.40	12
260	A42	50c dk red	45	5
a.		Booklet pane of 10	10.00	
261	A42	1.50fr dp bl	10.00	25

Photogravure.

Perf. 13½.

262	A43	1.50fr dp bl ('31)	37.50	1.00
		Nos. 258-262 (5)	49.80	1.57

Arc de Triomphe
A44

Peace with Olive Branch
A45

1931 Engraved *Perf. 13*

263	A44	2fr red brn	27.50	35

1932–39 Typo. *Perf. 14x13½*

264	A45	30c dp grn	50	15
265	A45	40c brt vio	32	6
266	A45	45c yel brn	2.00	65
267	A45	50c rose red	15	3
a.		Imperf., pair	75.00	
b.		Booklet pane of 10	7.50	
268	A45	55c dl vio ('37)	65	15
269	A45	60c ocher ('37)	20	15
270	A45	65c vio brn	50	12
271	A45	65c brt ultra ('37)	25	10
a.		Booklet pane of 10	8.50	
272	A45	75c ol grn	20	12
273	A45	80c org ('38)	15	15
274	A45	90c dk red	37.50	1.60
275	A45	90c brt grn ('38)	8	6

276	A45	90c ultra ('38)	80	3
a.		Booklet pane of 10	12.50	
277	A45	1fr orange	1.25	5
278	A45	1fr rose pink ('38)	1.60	12
279	A45	1.25fr brn ol	75.00	2.75
280	A45	1.25fr rose car ('39)	2.25	85
281	A45	1.40fr brt red vio ('39)	6.00	3.50
282	A45	1.50fr dp bl	28	15
283	A45	1.75fr magenta	5.00	15
		Nos. 264-283 (20)	134.68	10.94

The 50c is found in 4 types, differing in the lines below belt and size of "c."

Le Puy-en-Velay—A46

1933 Engraved *Perf. 13*

290	A46	90c rose	3.50	40

Aristide Briand A47

Paul Doumer A48

Victor Hugo A49

1933, Dec. 11 Typo. *Perf. 14x13½*

291	A47	30c bl grn	20.00	8.00
292	A48	75c red vio	25.00	60
293	A49	1.25fr claret	2.25	60

Dove and Olive Branch A50

Joseph Marie Jacquard A51

1934, Feb. 20

294	A50	1.50fr ultra	80.00	14.00

1934, Mar. 14 Engr. *Perf. 14x13*

295	A51	40c blue	2.40	80

Issued to commemorate the centenary of the death of Joseph Marie Jacquard (1752–1834), inventor of an improved loom for figured weaving.

Jacques Cartier A52

1934, July 18 *Perf. 13*

296	A52	75c rose lil	22.50	1.35
297	A52	1.50fr blue	52.50	2.75

Issued to commemorate the 400th anniversary of Carter's discovery of Canada.

No. 279 Surcharged

50c

1934, Nov. *Perf. 14x13½*

298	A45	50c on 1.25fr brn ol	3.75	22

Breton River Scene A53

1935, Feb. Engraved *Perf. 13*

299	A53	2fr bl grn	37.50	45

S. S. Normandie—A54

1935, April

300	A54	1.50fr dk bl	20.00	1.10
a.		1.50fr bl ('36)	75.00	14.00
b.		1.50fr bl grn ('36)	*2,250.*	

Issued in commemoration of the maiden voyage of the transatlantic steamship, the "Normandie".

Benjamin Delessert A55

1935, May 20

301	A55	75c bl grn	24.00	75

Issued in commemoration of the opening of the International Savings Bank Congress, May 20, 1935.

View of St. Trophime at Arles A56

Victor Hugo A57

1935, May 3

302	A56	3.50fr dk brn	35.00	2.25

1935, May 30 *Perf. 14x13*

303	A57	1.25fr magenta	2.75	90

Victor Hugo (1802–1885), 50th anniversary of death.

Cardinal Richelieu A58

Jacques Callot A59

1935, June 12 *Perf. 13*

304	A58	1.50fr dp rose	22.50	1.25

Issued in commemoration of the tercentenary of the founding of the French Academy by Cardinal Richelieu.

1935, Nov. *Perf. 14x13*

305	A59	75c red	13.00	30

Issued in commemoration of the 300th anniversary of the death of Jacques Callot, engraver.

André Marie Ampère A60

1936, Feb. 27 *Perf. 13*

306	A60	75c brown	22.50	85

Issued to commemorate the centenary of the death of André Marie Ampère (1775–1836), scientist. (Portrait by Louis Boilly.)

Windmill at Fontvielle, Immortalized by Daudet—A61

1936, Apr. 27

307	A61	2fr ultra	1.75	22

Issued in commemoration of the 70th anniversary of the publication, in 1866, of Alphonse Daudet's "Lettres de mon Moulin".

Pilâtre de Rozier and his Balloon A62

1936, June 4

308	A62	75c Prus bl	22.50	2.25

Issued in commemoration of the 150th anniversary of the death of Jean Joseph Pilâtre de Rozier, balloonist.

Rouget de Lisle A63

"La Marseillaise" A64

1936, June 27

309	A63	20c Prus grn	1.50	60
310	A64	40c dk brn	5.25	2.00

Centenary of the death of Claude Joseph Rouget de Lisle, composer of "La Marseillaise."

Canadian War Memorial at Vimy Ridge—A65

1936, July 26

311	A65	75c hn brn	10.00	1.50
312	A65	1.50fr dl bl	17.50	7.00

Issued to commemorate the unveiling of the Canadian War Memorial at Vimy Ridge, July 26, 1936.

Jean Léon Jaurès A66

Jean Jaurès A67

1936, July 30

313	A66	40c red brn	2.75	50
314	A67	1.50fr ultra	12.50	1.85

Issued in commemoration of the assassination of Jean Léon Jaurès (1859–1914), socialist and politician.

Herald A68

Allegory of Exposition A69

1936, Sept. 15 Typo. *Perf. 14x13½*

315	A68	20c brt vio	35	22
316	A68	30c Prus grn	2.25	75
317	A68	40c ultra	75	15
318	A68	50c red org	50	8
319	A69	90c carmine	11.50	6.25
320	A69	1.50fr ultra	26.50	1.85
		Nos. 315-320 (6)	41.85	9.30

Publicity for the 1937 Paris Exposition.

"Peace" A70

1936, Oct. 1 Engr. *Perf. 13*

321	A70	1.50fr blue	16.50	1.00

Skiing A71

1937, Jan. 18

322	A71	1.50fr dk bl	10.00	1.00

Issued in commemoration of the International Ski Meet at Chamonix—Mont Blanc.

Pierre Corneille, Portrait by Charles Le Brun A72

1937, Feb. 15

323	A72	75c brn car	1.50	60

Issued to commemorate the 300th anniversary of the publication of "Le Cid."

Paris Exposition Issue.

Exposition Allegory—A73

1937, Mar. 15

324	A73	1.50fr turq bl	1.85	60

Jean Mermoz A74

Memorial to Mermoz A75

1937, Apr. 27

325	A74	30c dk sl grn	60	40
326	A75	3fr dk vio	7.50	3.00
a.		3fr vio	9.00	3.00

Issued in honor of aviator Jean Mermoz (1901–36).

Electric Train A76

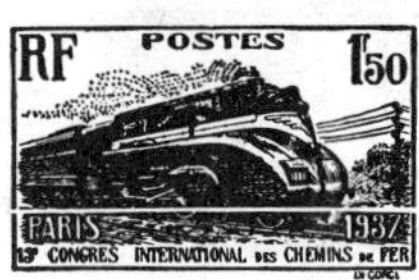

Streamlined Locomotive A77

1937, May 31

327	A76	30c dk grn	1.00	90
328	A77	1.50fr dk ultra	11.00	6.50

13th International Railroad Congress.

International Philatelic Exhibition Issue.
Souvenir Sheet

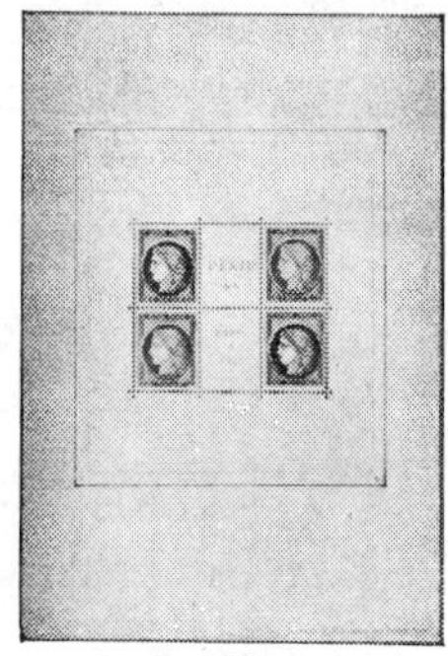

A77a
Ceres Type of 1849–50.

1937, June 18 Typo. *Perf. 14x13½*

329	A77a	Sheet of four (A1)	250.00	250.00
a.		5c ultra & dk brn	50.00	50.00
b.		15c red & rose red	50.00	50.00
c.		30c ultra & rose red	50.00	50.00
d.		50c red & dk brn	50.00	50.00
e.		Imperf. sheet of four	*1,600.*	

Issued in sheets measuring 150x220mm. The sheets were sold only at the exhibition in Paris, a ticket of admission being required for each sheet purchased.

René Descartes, by Frans Hals A78

1937, June Engraved *Perf. 13*

Inscribed: "Discours sur la Méthode."

330	A78	90c cop red	1.35	90

Inscribed "Discours de la Méthode"

331	A78	90c cop red	2.25	90

Issued in commemoration of the third centenary of the publication of "Discours de la Méthode" by René Descartes.

France Congratulating U.S.A. A79

1937, Sept. 17

332	A79	1.75fr ultra	1.65	1.00

Issued to commemorate the 150th anniversary of the Constitution of the United States of America.

No. 277 Surcharged in Red

80c

1937, Oct. *Perf. 14x13½*

333	A45	80c on 1fr org	30	30
a.		Inverted surch.	425.00	

Mountain Road at Iseran A80

1937, Oct. 4 Engraved *Perf. 13*

334	A80	90c dk grn	50	15

Issued in commemoration of the opening of the mountain road at Iseran, Savoy.

Ceres A81

1938–40 Typo. *Perf. 14x13½*

335	A81	1.75fr dk ultra	1.20	18
336	A81	2fr car rose ('39)	30	15
337	A81	2.25fr ultra ('39)	6.50	30
338	A81	2.50fr grn ('39)	2.50	15
339	A81	2.50fr vio bl ('40)	1.00	30
340	A81	3fr rose lil ('39)	1.00	5
		Nos. 335-340 (6)	12.50	1.13

Léon Gambetta A82

1938, Apr. 2 Engraved *Perf. 13*

341	A82	55c dk vio	45	35

Issued in commemoration of the centenary of the birth of Léon Gambetta (1838-1882), lawyer and statesman.

Arc de Triomphe of Orange A82a

Miners A83

Keep and Gate of Vincennes A86

Palace of the Popes, Avignon A84

Medieval Walls of Carcassonne A85

Port of St. Malo—A87

1938

342	A82a	2fr brn blk	1.25	90
343	A83	2.15fr vio brn	1.15	40
344	A84	3fr car brn	9.00	3.25
345	A85	5fr dp ultra	60	22
346	A86	10fr brn, *bl*	2.25	1.25
347	A87	20fr dk bl grn	50.00	17.50
		Nos. 342-347 (6)	64.25	23.52

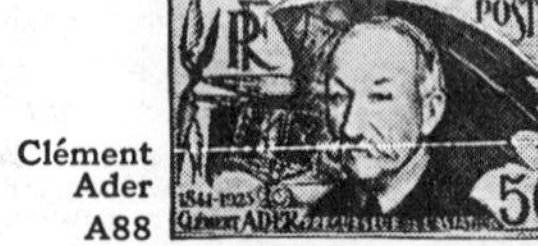

Clément Ader A88

1938, June 16

348	A88	50fr ultra (thin paper)	130.00	75.00
a.		50fr dk ultra (thick paper)	140.00	90.00

Issued in honor of Clément Ader, air pioneer.

Soccer Players A89

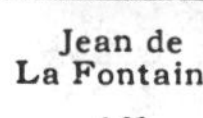

1938, June 1

349	A89	1.75fr dk ultra	10.00	6.00

World Cup Soccer Championship.

Costume of Champagne Region A90

Jean de La Fontaine A91

1938, June 13

350	A90	1.75fr dk ultra	5.00	2.75

Issued in commemoration of the tercentenary of the birth of Dom Pierre Pérignon, discoverer of the champagne process.

1938, July 8

351	A91	55c dk bl grn	65	45

Issued to honor Jean de La Fontaine (1621-1695) the fabulist.

Seal of Friendship and Peace, Victoria Tower and Arc de Triomphe—A92

1938, July 19

352	A92	1.75fr ultra	1.00	80

Issued in honor of the visit of King George VI and Queen Elizabeth of Great Britain to France.

Mercury A93

Paul Cézanne, Self-portrait A95

1938–42 Typo. *Perf. 14x13½*

353	A93	1c dk brn ('39)	5	3
354	A93	2c sl grn ('39)	5	3
355	A93	5c rose	5	3
356	A93	10c ultra	5	3
357	A93	15c red org	4	3
358	A93	15c org brn ('39)	75	15
359	A93	20c red vio	4	3
360	A93	25c bl grn	15	3
361	A93	30c rose red ('39)	5	3
362	A93	40c dk vio ('39)	5	3
363	A93	45c lt grn ('39)	70	35
364	A93	50c dp bl ('39)	4.00	15
365	A93	50c dk grn ('41)	65	15
366	A93	50c grnsh bl ('42)	9	3
367	A93	60c red org ('39)	25	8

368	A93	70c mag ('39)	30	7
369	A93	75c dk org brn ('39)	6.25	1.85
		Nos. 353-369 (17)	13.52	3.10

No. 366 exists imperforate. See also Nos. 455–458.

1939, Mar. 15 Engr. *Perf. 13*

370 A95 2.25fr Prus bl 5.50 2.75

Issued in commemoration of the centenary of the birth of Paul Cézanne (1839–1906), painter.

Georges Clemenceau and Battleship Clemenceau—A96

1939, Apr. 18

371 A96 90c ultra 50 35

Issued to commemorate the laying of the keel of the warship "Clemenceau" January 17, 1939.

Statue of Liberty, French Pavilion, Trylon and Perisphere—A97

1939-40

372	A97	2.25fr ultra	4.50	2.25
373	A97	2.50fr ultra ('40)	3.50	2.75

New York World's Fair.

Joseph Nicéphore Niepce and Louis Jacques Mandé Daguerre A98

1939. Apr. 24

374 A98 2.25fr dk bl 5.50 3.50

Centenary of photography.

Iris A99

Pumping Station at Marly A100

1939-44 Typo. *Perf. 14x13½*

375	A99	80c red brn ('40)	20	12
376	A99	80c yel grn ('44)	8	4
377	A99	1fr green	45	5
378	A99	1fr crim ('40)	10	3
a.		Bklt. pane of 10	5.00	
379	A99	1fr grnsh bl ('44)	10	10
380	A99	1.20fr vio ('44)	6	5
381	A99	1.30fr ultra ('40)	20	12
382	A99	1.50fr red org ('41)	30	15
383	A99	1.50fr hn brn ('44)	6	5
384	A99	2fr vio brn ('44)	8	5
385	A99	2.40fr car rose ('44)	20	20
386	A99	3fr org ('44)	15	10
387	A99	4fr ultra ('44)	20	20
		Nos. 375-387 (13)	2.18	1.26

1939 Engraved. *Perf. 13.*

388 A100 2.25fr brt ultra 7.00 2.75

Issued in commemoration of France's participation in the International Water Exposition at Liège.

St. Gregory of Tours A101

1939, June 10

389 A101 90c red 65 45

Issued to commemorate the 14th centenary of the birth of St. Gregory of Tours, historian and bishop.

"The Oath of the Tennis Court" by Jacques David—A102

1939, June 20

390 A102 90c dp sl grn 70 40

150th anniversary of French Revolution.

Cathedral of Strasbourg A103

1939, June 23

391 A103 70c brn car 70 40

Issued to commemorate the 500th anniversary of the completion of Strasbourg Cathedral.

Porte Chaussée, Verdun—A104

1939, June 23

392 A104 90c blk brn 1.25 90

Issued to commemorate the 23rd anniversary of the Battle of Verdun.

View of Pau A105

1939, Aug. 25

393 A105 90c brt rose, *gray bl* 1.20 60

Maid of Languedoc A106

Bridge at Lyons A107

1939

394	A106	70c blk, *bl*	55	35
395	A107	90c dl brn vio	55	35

Imperforates

Nearly all French stamps issued from 1940 onward exist imperforate. Officially 20 sheets, ranging from 25 to 100 subjects, were left imperforate.

Georges Guynemer A108

1940, Nov. 7

396 A108 50fr ultra 14.50 9.00

Issued in honor of Georges Guynemer (1894-1917), World War I ace.

Stamps of 1938-39 Surcharged in Carmine **1F**

1940-41 *Perf. 14x13½.*

397	A81	1fr on 1.75fr dk ultra	15	15
398	A81	1fr on 2.25fr ultra ('41)	15	15
399	A81	1fr on 2.50fr grn ('41)	35	35

Stamps of 1932-39 Surcharged in Carmine, Red or Black **= 1F**

Perf. 13, 14x13½.

400	A22	30c on 35c grn (C) ('41)	10	10
401	A45	50c on 55c dl vio (C) ('41)	12	12
a.		Invtd. surch.	400.00	
402	A45	50c on 65c brt ultra (C) ('41)	8	8
403	A45	50c on 75c ol grn (C) ('41)	10	10
404	A93	50c on 75c dk org brn (C) ('41)	14	14
405	A45	50c on 80c org (C) ('41)	12	12
406	A45	50c on 90c ultra (C) ('41)	8	8
a.		Invtd. surch.	165.00	
b.		"05" instead of "50"	3,250.	
407	A45	1fr on 1.25fr rose car (Bk) ('41)	25	25
408	A45	1fr on 1.40fr brt red vio (R) ('41)	20	20
a.		Dble. surch.	550.00	
409	A45	1fr on 1.50fr dk bl (C) ('41)	25	25
410	A83	1fr on 2.15fr vio brn (C)	10	10
411	A85	2.50fr on 5fr dp ultra (C) ('41)	22	22
a.		Dble. surch.	185.00	85.00
412	A86	5fr on 10fr brn, *bl* (C) ('41)	2.00	2.00
413	A87	10fr on 20fr dk bl grn (C) ('41)	1.00	1.00
414	A88	20fr on 50fr dk ultra (#348a) (C) ('41)	37.50	37.50
a.		20fr on 50fr ultra, thin paper (#348)	45.00	45.00
		Nos. 400-414 (15)	42.26	42.26

Marshal Pétain A109

Frédéric Mistral A110

1941 *Perf. 13.*

415	A109	40c red brn	55	40
416	A109	80c turq bl	70	50
417	A109	1fr red	25	20
418	A109	2.50fr dp ultra	1.35	90

1941, Feb. 20 *Perf. 14x13*

419 A110 1fr brn lake 20 20

Issued in honor of Frédéric Mistral, poet and Nobel prize winner for literature in 1904.

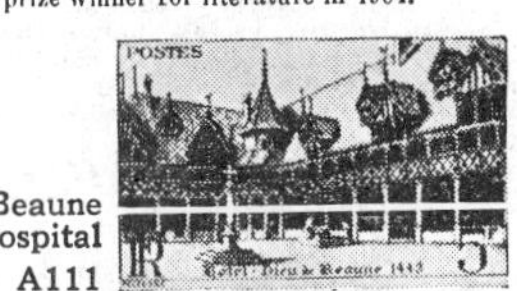

Beaune Hospital A111

View of Angers A112

Ramparts of St. Louis, Aiguesmortes A113

1941

420	A111	5fr brn blk	25	15
421	A112	10fr dk vio	20	10
422	A113	20fr brn blk	65	60

1942

Inscribed "Postes Francaises". Imprint: "FELTESSE" at right.

423 A111 15fr brn lake 35 30

Marshal Pétain A114 A115

Marshal Pétain A116 A117

Marshal Pétain A118

1941–42 Typo. *Perf. 14x13½*

427	A114	20c lil ('42)	5	5
428	A114	30c rose red	5	5
429	A114	40c ultra	15	12
431	A115	50c dp grn	5	5
432	A115	60c vio ('42)	6	6
433	A115	70c saph ('42)	6	6
434	A115	70c org ('42)	8	8
435	A115	80c brown	15	15
436	A115	80c emer ('42)	8	8
437	A115	1fr rose red	6	6
438	A115	1.20fr red brn ('42)	5	5
439	A116	1.50fr rose	6	6
440	A116	1.50fr dl red brn ('42)	5	5
a.		Booklet pane of 10	3.50	
441	A116	2fr bl grn ('42)	5	5
443	A116	2.40fr rose red ('42)	10	6
444	A116	2.50fr ultra	60	30
445	A116	3fr orange	5	5
446	A115	4fr ultra ('42)	8	6
447	A115	4.50fr dk grn ('42)	55	30
		Nos. 427-447 (19)	2.38	1.74

Nos. 431 to 438 measure 16½ x 20¾ mm.

No. 440 was forged by the French Underground ("Defense de la France") and used to frank clandestine journals, etc., from February to June, 1944. The forgeries were ungummed, both perforated 11½ and imperforate, with a back handstamp covering six stamps and including the words: "Atelier des Faux."

1942 Engraved. *Perf. 14x13.*

448	A115	4fr brt ultra	25	12
449	A115	4.50fr dk grn	15	15
450	A117	5fr Prus grn	6	5

Perf. 13

451	A118	50fr black	2.75	2.25

Nos. 448 and 449 measure 18x21½mm.

Jules Massenet A119

Stendhal (Marie Henri Beyle) A120

1942, June 22 *Perf. 14x13*

452	A119	4fr Prus grn	25	20

Issued to commemorate the centenary of the birth of Jules Massenet (1842–1912), composer.

1942, Sept. 14 *Perf. 13*

453	A120	4fr blk brn & org red	40	40

Issued to commemorate the centenary of the death of Stendhal (1783–1842), writer.

André Blondel A121

Town-Hall Belfry, Arras A122

1942, Sept. 14

454	A121	4fr dl bl	35	35

Issued in honor of André Eugène Blondel (1863–1938), physicist.

Mercury Type of 1938–42 Inscribed "Postes Françaises".

1942 *Perf. 14x13½*

455	A93	10c ultra	6	5
456	A93	30c rose red	6	5
457	A93	40c dk vio	10	10
458	A93	50c turq bl	6	5

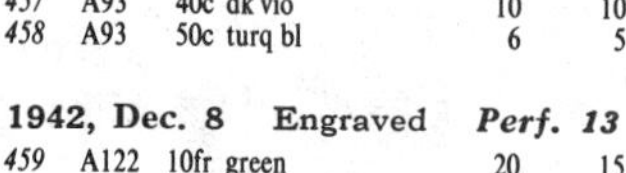

1942, Dec. 8 Engraved *Perf. 13*

459	A122	10fr green	20	15

Coats of Arms.

Lyon A123

Brittany A124

Provence A125

Ile de France A126

1943 Typographed. *Perf. 14x13½*

460	A123	5fr vio bl, org, red org & blk	20	8
461	A124	10fr ocher & blk	30	18
462	A125	15fr vio bl, org, red & blk	2.00	1.40
463	A126	20fr vio bl, org, & dl brn	1.10	90

Antoine Lavoisier A127

1943, July 5 Engr. *Perf. 14x13*

464	A127	4fr ultra	18	18

Issued to commemorate the 200th anniversary of the birth of Lavoisier (1743-94), French scientist.

Lake Lerie and Meije Dauphiné Alps—A128

1943, July 5 *Perf. 13*

465	A128	20fr dl gray grn	55	55

Nicolas Rolin, Guigone de Salins and Hospital of Beaune—A129

1943, July 21

466	A129	4fr blue	30	30

Issued to commemorate the 500th anniversary of the founding of the Hospital of Beaune.

Coats of Arms.

Flanders A130

Languedoc A131

Orléans A132

Normandy A133

1944, Mar. 27 Typo. *Perf. 14x13½*

467	A130	5fr ver, org & blk	15	6
468	A131	10fr brn, blk, dl red & yel	20	18
469	A132	15fr brn, brt ultra & org	70	60
470	A133	20fr ultra, dl red org & blk	90	70

Edouard Branly A134

Early Postal Car A135

1944, Feb. 21 Engraved *Perf. 14x13*

471	A134	4fr ultra	20	15

Issued to commemorate the centenary of the birth of Edouard Branly, electrical inventor.

1944, June 10 *Perf. 13*

472	A135	1.50fr dk bl grn	15	15

Issued to commemorate the centenary of France's traveling postal service.

Chateau de Chenonceaux A136

Claude Chappe A137

1944, June 10

473	A136	15fr lil brn	35	35
a.		15fr blk brn	3.75	1.35
b.		15fr blk	30.00	

1944, Aug. 14 *Perf. 14x13*

474	A137	4fr dk ultra	15	15

Issued to commemorate the 150th anniversary of the invention of an optical telegraph by Claude Chappe (1763–1805).

Gallic Cock A138

Marianne A139

1944 Lithograped *Perf. 12*

477	A138	10c yel grn	6	6
478	A138	30c dk rose vio	10	10
479	A138	40c blue	6	6
480	A138	50c dk red	6	6
481	A139	60c ol brn	10	10
482	A139	70c rose lil	6	6
483	A139	80c yel grn	55	55
484	A139	1fr violet	5	5
485	A139	1.20fr dp car	10	10
486	A139	1.50fr dp bl	8	8
487	A138	2fr indigo	10	10
488	A139	2.40fr red org	90	90
489	A139	3fr dp bl grn	20	20
490	A139	4fr grnsh bl	20	20
491	A139	4.50fr black	15	15
492	A139	5fr vio bl	3.50	3.50
493	A138	10fr violet	3.50	3.50
494	A138	15fr ol brn	3.50	3.50
495	A138	20fr dk sl grn	3.50	3.50
		Nos. 477-495 (19)	16.77	16.77

Nos. 477–495 were issued first in Corsica after the Allied landing, and released in Paris Nov. 15, 1944.

Chateau de Chenonceaux—A140

1944, Oct. 30 Engraved *Perf. 13*

496	A140	25fr black	45	45

Thomas Robert Bugeaud A141

1944, Nov. 20

497	A141	4fr myr grn	18	18

Issued to commemorate the 100th anniversary of the Battle of Isly, August 14th, 1844.

Church of St. Denis A142

1944, Nov. 20

498	A142	2.40fr brn car	15	15

Issued to commemorate the 800th anniversary of the Church of St. Denis.

Type of 1938-42, Overprinted in Black RF Inscribed "Postes Francaises"

1944 *Perf. 14x13½.*

499	A93	10c ultra	5	5
500	A93	30c rose red	5	5
501	A93	40c dk vio	5	5
502	A93	50c grnsh bl	5	5

The overprint "RF" in various forms, with or without Lorraine Cross, was also applied to stamps of the French State at Lyon and fourteen other cities.

French Forces of the Interior and Symbol of Liberation A143

1945, Jan.

503	A143	4fr dk ultra	18	10

Issued to commemorate the Liberation.

Stamps of the above design, and of one incorporating "FRANCE" in the top panel, were printed by photogravure in England during World War II upon order of the Free French Government. They were not issued. There are three values in each design; 25c green, 1fr red, 2.50fr blue. Price: set, above design, $135; set inscribed "FRANCE," $300.

Marianne
A144

Perf. 11½x12½.

1944-45 Engraved Unwmkd.

No.	Type	Value	Color	Unused	Used
05	A144	10c	ultra	4	3
06	A144	30c	bister	4	3
07	A144	40c	indigo	4	3
08	A144	50c	red org	4	3
09	A144	60c	chlky bl	4	3
10	A144	70c	sepia	4	4
11	A144	80c	dp grn	4	3
12	A144	1fr	lilac	4	3
13	A144	1.20fr	dk ol grn	4	4
14	A144	1.50fr	rose ('44)	5	4
15	A144	2fr	dk brn	6	5
16	A144	2.40fr	red	6	6
17	A144	3fr	brt ol grn	6	5
18	A144	4fr	brt ultra	5	5
19	A144	4.50fr	sl gray	12	6
20	A144	5fr	brt org	15	15
21	A144	10fr	yel grn	18	18
22	A144	15fr	lake	35	30
23	A144	20fr	brn org	1.00	60
23A	A144	50fr	dp pur	3.50	2.00
			Nos. 505-523A (20)	5.94	3.83

The 2.40fr exists imperf. in a miniature sheet of 4 which was not issued.

Coat of Arms A145 — Ceres A146 — Marianne A147

1945-47 Typo. *Perf. 14x13½.*

No.	Type	Value	Color	Unused	Used
524	A145	10c	brn blk	5	3
525	A145	30c	dk bl grn	10	10
526	A145	40c	lil rose	10	10
527	A145	50c	vio bl	5	3
528	A146	60c	brt ultra	15	15
530	A146	80c	brt grn	5	3
531	A146	90c	dl grn ('46)	70	40
532	A146	1fr	rose red	5	3
533	A146	1.20fr	brn blk	15	15
534	A146	1.50fr	rose lil	6	6
535	A147	1.50fr	rose pink	12	5
536	A147	2fr	myr grn	5	3
536A	A146	2fr	lt bl grn ('46)	15	10
537	A147	2.40fr	scarlet	25	10
538	A146	2.50fr	brn ('46)	15	10
539	A147	3fr	sepia	8	5
540	A147	3fr	dp rose ('46)	8	5
541	A147	4fr	ultra	12	6
541A	A147	4fr	vio ('46)	12	10
541B	A147	4.50fr	ultra ('47)	10	3
542	A147	5fr	lt grn	12	4
542A	A147	5fr	rose pink ('47)	6	4
543	A147	6fr	brt ultra	25	8
544	A147	6fr	crim rose ('46)	35	5
545	A147	10fr	red org	25	20
546	A147	10fr	ultra ('46)	70	20
547	A147	15fr	brt red vio	2.00	65
			Nos. 524-547 (27)	6.41	3.01

No. 531 is known only precanceled. See second note after No. 132.

Due to a reduction of the domestic postage rate, No. 542A was sold for 4.50fr.

See also Nos. 576 to 580, 594 to 602, 614, 615, 650 to 654.

Engraved.

1945-46 *Perf. 14x13*

No.	Type	Value	Color	Unused	Used
548	A147	4fr	dk bl	15	5
549	A147	10fr	dp bl ('46)	45	15
550	A147	15fr	brt red vio ('46)	3.75	80
551	A147	20fr	bl grn ('46)	90	20
552	A147	25fr	red ('46)	3.75	80
			Nos. 548-552 (5)	9.00	2.00

Marianne
A148

1945 Engraved *Perf. 13*

No.	Type	Value	Color	Unused	Used
553	A148	20fr	dk grn	1.10	50
554	A148	25fr	violet	1.50	80
555	A148	50fr	red brn	1.60	80
556	A148	100fr	brt rose car	5.50	2.50

CFA

French stamps inscribed or surcharged "CFA" and new value are listed under Réunion in Vol. IV.

Arms of Metz A149 — Arms of Strasbourg A150

1945, Mar. 3 *Perf. 14x13*

No.	Type	Value	Color	Unused	Used
557	A149	2.40fr	dl bl	8	8
558	A150	4fr	blk brn	8	8

Liberation of Metz and Strasbourg.

Costumes of Alsace and Lorraine and Cathedrals of Strasbourg and Metz—A151

1945, May 16 *Perf. 13*

No.	Type	Value	Color	Unused	Used
559	A151	4fr	hn brn	15	15

Liberation of Alsace and Lorraine.

World Map Showing French Possessions—A152

1945, Sept. 17

No.	Type	Value	Color	Unused	Used
560	A152	2fr	Prus bl	15	15

No. B193 Surcharged with New Value in Black.

1946 *Perf. 14x13½*

No.	Type	Value	Color	Unused	Used
561	SP147	3fr on 2fr+1fr	red org	5	5

Coats of Arms.

Corsica A153 — Alsace A154

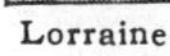

Lorraine A155 — County of Nice A156

Typographed.

1946 *Perf. 14x13½.* Unwmkd.

No.	Type	Value	Color	Unused	Used
562	A153	10c	dp ultra & blk	5	3
563	A154	30c	blk, red org & yel	6	5
564	A155	50c	brn, yel & red	6	5
565	A156	60c	red, ultra & blk	8	6

Reaching for "Peace" A157 — Holding the Dove of Peace A158

1946, July 29 Engraved *Perf. 13*

No.	Type	Value	Color	Unused	Used
566	A157	3fr	Prus grn	10	8
567	A158	10fr	dk bl	18	15

Peace Conference of Paris, 1946.

Vézelay
A159

Luxembourg Palace
A160

Rocamadour
A161

Pointe du Raz, Finistère
A162

1946 *Perf. 13.* Unwmkd.

No.	Type	Value	Color	Unused	Used
568	A159	5fr	rose vio	15	8
569	A160	10fr	dk bl	15	8
570	A161	15fr	dk vio brn	45	10
571	A162	20fr	sl gray	25	6

See also Nos. 591-592.

Globe and Wreath
A163

1946, Nov.

No.	Type	Value	Color	Unused	Used
572	A163	10fr	dk bl	25	25

Issued to honor the general conference of the United Nations Educational, Scientific and Cultural Organization, Paris, 1946.

Cannes
A164

Stanislas Square, Nancy
A165

1946-48 Engraved *Perf. 13*

No.	Type	Value	Color	Unused	Used
573	A164	6fr	rose red	20	12
574	A165	25fr	blk brn	35	8
575	A165	25fr	dk bl ('48)	2.25	65

Ceres & Marianne Types of 1945.

Typographed.

1947 *Perf. 14x13½* Unwmkd.

No.	Type	Value	Color	Unused	Used
576	A146	1.30fr	dl bl	25	15
577	A147	3fr	green	40	10
578	A147	3.50fr	brn red	25	10
579	A147	5fr	blue	18	3
580	A147	6fr	carmine	15	3
			Nos. 576-580 (5)	1.23	41

Colonnade of the Louvre
A166

La Conciergerie, Paris Prison
A167

La Cité, Oldest Section of Paris
A168

Place de la Concorde
A169

1947, May 7 Engraved *Perf. 13*

No.	Type	Value	Color	Unused	Used
581	A166	3.50fr	chocolate	35	35
582	A167	4.50fr	dk sl gray	35	35
583	A168	6fr	red	55	55
584	A169	10fr	brt ultra	55	55

Issued to commemorate the 12th Congress of the Universal Postal Union, Paris, May 7 to July 7, 1947.

Auguste Pavie
A170

François Fénelon
A171

1947, May 30

585	A170 4.50fr sepia		17	17

Issued to commemorate the centenary of the birth of Auguste Pavie, French pioneer in Laos.

1947, July 12

586	A171 4.50fr chocolate		17	17

Issued to honor Francois de Salignac de la Mothe-Fénelon, prelate and writer.

Fleur-de-Lis and Double Carrick Bend
A172

1947, Aug. 2 **Unwmkd.**

587	A172	5fr brown	20	20

Issued to commemorate the 6th World Boy Scout Jamboree held at Moisson, August 9th to 18th, 1947.

Captured Patriot
A173

View of Conques
A174

1947, Nov. 10 **Engraved** ***Perf. 13***

588	A173	5fr sepia	20	20

No. 576 Surcharged in Carmine.

1947, Nov. **Typo.** ***Perf. 14x13½***

589	A146	1fr on 1.30fr dl bl	10	10

1947, Dec. 18 **Engraved** ***Perf. 13***

590	A174	15fr hn brn	35	25

Types of 1946-47.

1948 **Re-engraved.**

591	A160	12fr rose car	25	25
592	A160	15fr brt red	25	25
593	A174	18fr dk bl	35	20

"FRANCE" substituted for inscriptions "RF" and "REPUBLIQUE FRANCAISE."

Marianne Type of 1945.

1948–49 **Typo.** ***Perf. 14x13½***

594	A147	2.50fr brown	2.25	1.25
595	A147	3fr lil rose	20	6
596	A147	4fr lt bl grn	30	6
597	A147	4fr brn org	90	20
598	A147	5fr lt bl grn	35	3
599	A147	8fr blue	30	6
600	A147	10fr brt vio	25	3
601	A147	12fr ultra ('49)	90	6
602	A147	15fr crim rose ('49)	55	3
a.		Bklt. pane of 10	80.00	
		Nos. 594-602 (9)	6.00	1.78

No. 594 known only precanceled. See second note after No. 132.

François René de Chateaubriand
A175

1948, July 3 **Engraved** ***Perf. 13***

603	A175	18fr dk bl	35	30

Issued to commemorate the centenary of the death of Vicomte de Chateaubriand (1768–1848).

Philippe François M. de Hautecloque (Gen. Jacques Leclerc)—A176

1948, July 3

604	A176	6fr gray blk	20	15

See also Nos. 692-692A.

Chaillot Palace
A177

A178

1948, Sept. 21

605	A177	12fr car rose	35	35
606	A178	18fr indigo	40	40

Issued to commemorate the meeting of the United Nations General Assembly, Paris, 1948.

Genissiat Dam
A179

Paul Langevin
A180

1948, Sept. 21

607	A179	12fr car rose	45	40

1948, Nov. 17 ***Perf. 14x13***

Design: 8fr, Jean Perrin.

608	A180	5fr dk brn car	15	12
609	A180	8fr dk grnsh bl	15	12

Issued to commemorate the placing of the ashes of physicists Paul Langevin (1872–1946) and Jean Perrin (1870–1942) in the Pantheon.

No. 544 Surcharged with New Value and Bars in Black.

1949, Jan. ***Perf. 14x13½***

610	A147	5fr on 6fr crim rose	15	7

Arctic Scene
A181

1949, May 2 ***Perf. 13***

611	A181	15fr indigo	45	45

Issued to publicize French polar explorations.

Types of 1849 and 1945.

1949, May 9 **Engraved** ***Imperf.***

612	A1	15fr red	4.50	4.50
a.		Strip of 4 (1 each Nos. 612 to 615) + label	20.00	20.00
613	A1	25fr dp bl	4.50	4.50

Perf. 14x13

614	A147	15fr red	4.50	4.50
615	A147	25fr dp bl	4.50	4.50

Printed in sheets containing a horizontal row of ten each of Nos. 612 to 615, the imperforate and perforated stamps separated by a row of labels.

Nos. 612 to 615 were issued to commemorate the centenary of the first French postage stamps.

Arms of Burgundy
A182

Designs (Arms): 50c, Guyenne (Aquitania). 1fr, Savoy. 2fr, Auvergne. 4fr, Anjou.

1949, May 11 **Typo.** ***Perf. 14x13½***

616	A182	10c bl, red & yel	6	3
617	A182	50c bl, red & yel	8	4
618	A182	1fr brn & red	8	4
619	A182	2fr grn, yel & red	20	4
620	A182	4fr bl, red & yel	40	18
		Nos. 616-620 (5)	82	33

See also Nos. 659–663, 694–699, 733–739, 782–785.

Collegiate Church of St. Barnard and Dauphiné Arms—A183

1949, May 14 **Engraved** ***Perf. 13***

621	A183	12fr red brn	30	25

Issued to commemorate the 600th anniversary of France's acquisition of the Dauphiné region.

U.S. and French Flags, Plane and Steamship—A184

1949, May 14

622	A184	25fr bl & car	55	45

Issued to publicize Franco-American friendship.

Cloister of St. Wandrille Abbey
A185

1949, May 18

623	A185	25fr dp ultra	35	8

See also No. 649.

Type of 1849 Inscribed "1849–1949" in Lower Margin.

1949, June 1

624	A1	10fr brn org	55.00	55.00
a.		Sheet of 10	600.00	600.00

Issued to commemorate the centenary of the first French postage stamp.

No. 624 has wide margins, measuring 40 x 52 mm., from perforation to perforation. Sold for 110 francs which included cost of admission to the Centenary International Exhibition, Paris, June 1949.

Claude Chappe
A186

Jean Racine
A187

Designs: 15fr, François Arago and André M. Ampère. 25fr, Emile Baudot. 50fr, Gen. Gustave A. Ferrié.

Inscribed: "C.I.T.T. PARIS 1949".

1949, June 13 ***Perf. 13*** **Unwmkd.**

625	A186	10fr vermilion	80	70
626	A186	15fr sepia	1.50	80
627	A186	25fr dp cl	3.50	3.00
628	A186	50fr dp bl	5.00	2.75

Issued to publicize the International Telegraph and Telephone Conference, Paris, May–July 1949.

1949

629	A187	12fr sepia	35	35

Issued to commemorate the 250th anniversary of the death of Jean Racine, dramatist.

Abbey of St. Bertrand de Comminges
A188

Meuse Valley, Ardennes
A189

Mt. Gerbier de Jonc, Vivarais
A190

1949 **Engraved.**

630	A188	20fr dk red	35	6
631	A189	40fr Prus grn	4.00	15
632	A190	50fr sepia	1.60	12

A191

1949, Oct. 18

633	A191	15fr dp car	30	25

Issued to commemorate the 50th anniversary of the Assembly of Presidents of Chambers of Commerce of the French Union.

U.P.U. Allegory
A192

1949, Nov. 7

634	A192	5fr dk grn	25	20
635	A192	15fr dp car	45	30
636	A192	25fr dp bl	1.25	1.00

Issued to commemorate the 75th anniversary of the formation of the Universal Postal Union.

Raymond Poincaré
A193

François Rabelais
A195

Charles Péguy and Cathedral at Chartres—A194

1950, May 27 ***Perf. 13*** **Unwmkd.**

637	A193	15fr indigo	35	30

1950, June

638	A194	12fr dk brn	35	35
639	A195	12fr red brn	40	40

Chateau of Chateaudun
A196

1950, Nov. 25

640	A196	8fr choc & bis brn	35	35

Madame Récamier
A197

Marie de Sévigné
A198

1950

641	A197	12fr dk grn	40	40
642	A198	15fr ultra	35	35

Palace of Fontainbleau
A199

1951, Jan. 20

643	A199	12fr dk brn	45	45

Jules Ferry
A200

Jean-Baptiste de la Salle
A202

Hands Holding Shuttle
A201

1951, Mar. 17

644	A200	15fr brt red	60	50

1951, Apr. 9

645	A201	25fr dp ultra	1.10	90

Issued to publicize the International Textile Exposition at Lille, April–May, 1951.

1951, Apr. 28

646	A202	15fr chocolate	40	40

Issued to commemorate the 300th anniversary of the birth of Jean-Baptiste de la Salle, educator and saint.

Map and Anchor
A203

1951, May 12

647	A203	15fr dp ultra	60	50

Issued to commemorate the 50th anniversary of the creation of the French colonial troops.

Vincent d'Indy
A204

1951, May 15

648	A204	25fr dp grn	2.25	1.75

Issued to commemorate the centenary of the birth of Vincent d'Indy, composer.

Abbey Type of 1949.

1951

649	A185	30fr brt bl	4.50	3.75

Marianne Type of 1945–47.

1951 Typographed. ***Perf. 14x13½***

650	A147	5fr dl vio	55	3
651	A147	6fr green	5.00	40
652	A147	12fr red org	80	10
653	A147	15fr ultra	30	6
a.		Booklet pane of 10	15.00	
654	A147	18fr cerise	9.00	70
		Nos. 650-654 (5)	15.65	1.29

Professors Nocard, Bouley and Chauveau; Gate at Lyons School—A205

1951, June 8 Engraved ***Perf. 13***

655	A205	12fr red vio	65	55

Issued to honor Veterinary Medicine.

Gen. Picqué, Cols. Roussin and Villemin; Val de Grace Dome
A206

1951, June 17 **Unwmkd.**

656	A206	15fr red brn	75	50

Issued to honor Military Medicine.

St. Nicholas, by Jean Didier
A207

1951, June 23

657	A207	15fr ind, dp cl & org	60	45

Chateau Bontemps, Arbois
A208

1951, June 23

658	A208	30fr indigo	80	15

Arms Type of 1949

Arms of: 10c, Artois. 50c, Limousin. 1fr, Béarn. 2fr, Touraine. 3fr, Franche-Comté.

1951, June Typo. ***Perf. 14x13½***

659	A182	10c red, vio bl & yel	6	3
660	A182	50c grn, red & blk	15	8
661	A182	1fr bl, red & yel	25	6
662	A182	2fr vio bl, red & yel	60	5
663	A182	3fr red, vio bl & yel	80	20
		Nos. 659-663 (5)	1.86	42

Seal of Paris
A209

Maurice Noguès and Globe
A210

Engraved

1951, July 7 ***Perf. 13*** **Unwmkd.**

664	A209	15fr dp bl, dk brn & red	55	35

Issued to commemorate the 2,000th anniversary of the founding of Paris.

1951, Oct. 13

665	A210	12fr ind & bl	60	45

Issued to honor Maurice Nogues, aviation pioneer.

Charles Baudelaire
A211

Poets: 12fr, Paul Verlaine. 15fr, Arthur Rimbaud.

1951, Oct. 27

666	A211	8fr purple	45	45
667	A211	12fr gray	60	60
668	A211	15fr dp grn	70	70

Georges Clemenceau
A212

1951, Nov. 11

669	A212	15fr blk brn	35	35

Issued to commemorate the centenary of the birth of Georges Clemenceau.

Chateau du Clos, Vougeot
A213

1951, Nov. 17

670	A213	30fr blk brn & brn	2.00	1.10

Chaillot Palace and Eiffel Tower
A214

1951, Nov. 6

671	A214	18fr red	1.00	90
672	A214	30fr dp ultra	1.25	1.10

Issued to publicize the opening of the Geneva Assembly of the United Nations, Paris, Nov. 6, 1951.

Observatory, Pic du Midi
A215

Abbaye aux Hommes, Caen
A216

1951, Dec. 22

673	A215	40fr violet	3.25	15
674	A216	50fr blk brn	2.75	8

Marshal Jean de Lattre de Tassigny—A217

1952, May 8 ***Perf. 13*** **Unwmkd.**

675	A217	15fr vio brn	1.00	45

Issued to honor Marshal Jean de Lattre de Tassigny, 1890–1952.
See also No. 717.

Gate of France, Vaucouleurs
A218

1952, May 11

676 A218 12fr brn blk 2.00 1.25

Flags and Monument at Narvik, Norway
A219

1952, May 28

677 A219 30fr vio bl 3.00 1.75

Issued to commemorate the 12th anniversary of the Battle of Narvik, May 27, 1940.

Chateau de Chambord
A220

1952, May 30

678 A220 20fr dk pur 50 8

Assembly Hall, Strasbourg
A221

1952, May 31

679 A221 30fr dk grn 11.00 6.75

Issued to honor the Council of Europe.

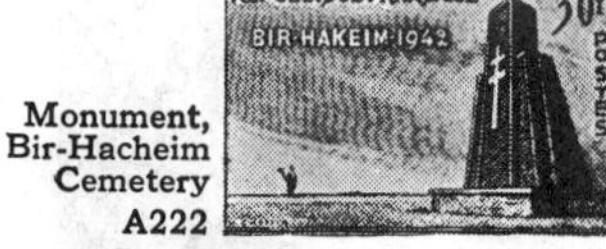

Monument, Bir-Hacheim Cemetery
A222

1952, June 14

680 A222 30fr rose lake 3.25 2.25

Issued to commemorate the 10th anniversary of the defense of Bir-Hacheim.

Abbey of the Holy Cross, Poitiers
A223

1952, June 21

681 A223 15fr brt red 45 40

Issued to commemorate the 14th centenary of the foundation of the Abbey of the Holy Cross at Poitiers.

Leonardo da Vinci, Amboise Chateau and La Signoria, Florence—A224

1952, July 9

682 A224 30fr dp ultra 7.25 4.50

Issued to commemorate the 500th anniversary of the birth of Leonardo da Vinci.

Garabit Viaduct
A225

1952, July 5

683 A225 15fr dk bl 55 45

Sword and Military Medals, 1852-1952
A226

Dr. René Laënnec
A227

1952, July 5

684 A226 15fr choc, grn & yel 55 45

Issued to commemorate the centenary of the creation of the Military Medal.

1952, Nov. 7

685 A227 12fr dk grn 60 50

Versailles Gate, Painted by Utrillo
A228

1952, Dec. 20

686 A228 18fr vio brn 2.00 1.40

Publicity for the restoration of Versailles Palace. See also No. 728.

Mannequin
A229

1953, Apr. 24 ***Perf. 13*** **Unwmkd.**

687 A229 30fr bl blk & rose vio 80 35

Issued to publicize the dressmaking industry of France.

Gargantua of François Rabelais
A230

Célimène from The Misanthrope
A231

Figaro, from the Barber of Seville
A232

Hernani of Victor Hugo
A233

1953

688 A230 6fr dp plum & car 15 10
689 A231 8 fr ind & ultra 15 10
690 A232 12fr vio brn & dk grn 15 10
691 A233 18fr vio brn & blk brn 70 35

Type of 1948
Inscribed "Général Leclerc
Maréchal de France"

1953-54

692 A176 8 fr red brn 70 55
692A A176 12fr dk grn & gray grn ('54) 2.50 1.60

Issued to honor the memory of General Jacques Leclerc.

Map and Cyclists, 1903-1953
A234

1953, July 26

693 A234 12fr red brn, ultra & blk 85 75

Issued to commemorate the 50th anniversary of the inauguration of the Bicycle Tour of France.

Arms Type of 1949.

Coats of Arms: 50c, Picardy. 70c, Gascony. 80c, Berri. 1fr, Poitou. 2fr, Champagne. 3fr, Dauphiné.

1953 Typographed. ***Perf. 14x13½***

694 A182 50c bl, yel & red 30 20
695 A182 70c red, bl & yel 30 20
696 A182 80c bl, red & yel 30 20
697 A182 1fr blk, red & yel 25 6
698 A182 2fr brn, bl & yel 25 6
699 A182 3fr red, bl & yel 50 15
Nos. 694-699 (6) 1.90 87

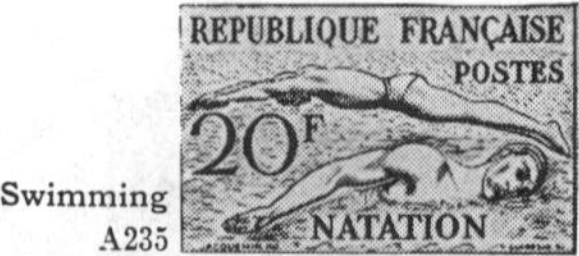

Swimming
A235

Sports: 25fr, Track. 30fr, Fencing. 40fr, Canoe racing. 50fr, Rowing. 75fr, Equestrian.

1953, Nov. 28 **Engr.** ***Perf. 13***

700 A235 20fr car & dk brn 1.50 10
701 A235 25fr dk grn & dk brn 5.25 30
702 A235 30fr ultra & dk brn 1.50 20
703 A235 40fr choc & ind 6.00 20
704 A235 50fr bl grn & dk brn 3.00 15
705 A235 75fr org & cl 27.50 10.50
Nos. 700-705 (6) 44.75 11.45

No. 654 Surcharged
with New Value and Bars in Black.

1954 ***Perf. 14x13½***

706 A147 15fr on 18fr cer 90 15

Farm Woman
A236

Gallic Cock
A237

1954 **Typographed**

707 A236 4fr blue 30 5
708 A236 8fr brn red 6.50 90
709 A237 12fr cerise 4.00 50
710 A237 24fr bl grn 17.50 4.50

Nos. 707-710 are known only precanceled. See also Nos. 833-834, 840-844, 910-913, 939 and 952-955. See second note after No. 132.

Tapestry and Gobelin Workshop
A238

Entrance to Exhibition Park
A239

Designs: 30fr, Book manufacture. 40fr, Porcelain and glassware. 50fr, Jewelry and metalsmith's work. 75fr, Flowers and perfumes.

1954, May 6 **Engr.** ***Perf. 13***

711 A238 25fr red brn car & blk brn 4.50 15
712 A238 30fr dk grn & lil gray 75 6
713 A238 40fr dk brn, vio brn & org brn 1.10 8
714 A238 50fr brt ultra, dl grn & org brn 1.10 6
715 A238 75fr dp car & mag 5.25 45
Nos. 711-715 (5) 12.70 80

1954, May 22

716 A239 15fr bl & dk car 55 45

Issued to commemorate the 50th anniversary of the founding of the Fair of Paris.

De Lattre Type of 1952

1954, June 5

717 A217 12fr vio bl & ind 2.50 1.60

Allied Landings
A240

1954, June 5

718 A240 15fr scar & ultra 60 45

The 10th anniversary of the liberation.

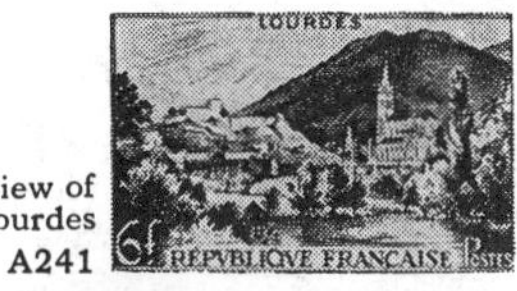

View of Lourdes
A241

Street Corner, Quimper
A242

Views: 8fr, Seine valley, Les Andelys. 10fr, Beach at Royan. 18fr, Cheverny Chateau. 20fr, Beach, Gulf of Ajaccio.

1954

719	A241	6fr ultra, ind & dk grn	30	10
720	A241	8fr brt bl & dk grn	30	10
721	A241	10fr aqua & org brn	30	5
722	A242	12fr rose vio & dk vio	30	5
723	A241	18fr bl, dk grn & ind	1.25	45
724	A241	20fr blk brn, bl grn & red brn	1.25	10
		Nos. 719-724 (6)	3.70	85

See also No. 873.

Abbey Ruins, Jumièges
A243

St. Philibert Abbey, Tournus
A244

1954, June 13

725	A243	12fr vio bl, ind & dk grn	1.50	1.10

13th centenary of Abbey of Jumièges.

1954, June 18

726	A244	30fr ind & bl	9.00	6.00

Issued to publicize the first conference of the International Center of Romance Studies.

View of Stenay
A245

1954, June 26

727	A245	15fr dk brn & org brn	1.00	60

Issued to commemorate the 300th anniversary of the acquisition of Stenay by France.

Versailles Type of 1952

1954, July 10

728	A228	18fr dp bl, ind & vio brn	7.25	4.50

Villandry Chateau
A246

1954, July 17

729	A246	18fr dk bl & dk bl grn	6.25	4.50

Napoleon Awarding Legion of Honor Decoration—A247

1954, Aug. 14

730	A247	12fr scarlet	1.50	90

Issued to commemorate the 150th anniversary of the first Legion of Honor awards at Camp de Boulogne.

Cadets Marching Through Gateway
A248

1954, Aug. 1

731	A248	15fr vio gray, dk bl & car	1.50	90

Issued to commemorate the 150th anniversary of the founding of the Military School of Saint-Cyr.

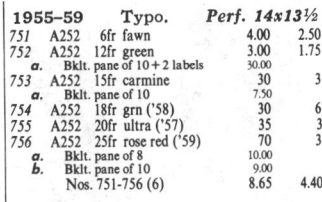

Allegory
A249

Duke de Saint-Simon
A250

1954, Oct. 4

732	A249	30fr ind & choc	9.00	6.00

Issued to publicize the fact that the metric system was first introduced in France.

Arms Type of 1949

Arms: 50c, Maine. 70c, Navarre. 80c, Nivernais. 1fr, Bourbonnais. 2fr, Angoumois. 3fr, Aunis. 5fr, Saintonge.

1954 Typographed. ***Perf. 14x13½***

733	A182	50c multi	15	7
734	A182	70c grn, red & yel	18	14
735	A182	80c bl, red & yel	20	18
736	A182	1fr red, bl & yel	20	6
737	A182	2fr blk, red & yel	7	3
738	A182	3fr brn, red & yel	5	3
739	A182	5fr bl & yel	10	3
		Nos. 733-739 (7)	95	54

1955, Feb. 5 Engr. ***Perf. 13***

740	A250	12fr dk brn & vio brn	1.00	70

Issued to commemorate the 200th anniversary of the death of Louis de Rouvroy, Duke de Saint-Simon (1675–1755).

Allegory and Rotary Emblem
A251

Marianne
A252

1955, Feb. 23

741	A251	30fr vio bl, bl & org	1.00	70

Issued to commemorate the 50th anniversary of the founding of Rotary International.

1955–59 Typo. ***Perf. 14x13½***

751	A252	6fr fawn	4.00	2.50
752	A252	12fr green	3.00	1.75
a.		Bklt. pane of 10+2 labels	30.00	
753	A252	15fr carmine	30	3
a.		Bklt. pane of 10	7.50	
754	A252	18fr grn ('58)	30	6
755	A252	20fr ultra ('57)	35	3
756	A252	25fr rose red ('59)	70	3
a.		Bklt. pane of 8	10.00	
b.		Bklt. pane of 10	9.00	
		Nos. 751-756 (6)	8.65	4.40

No. 751 was issued in coils of 1,000. No. 752 was issued in panes of 10 stamps and two labels with marginal instructions for folding to form a booklet.

Nos. 754–755 are found in two types, distinguished by the numerals. On the 18fr there is no serif at base of "1" on the earlier type.

Philippe Lebon, Inventor of Illuminating Gas—A253

Inventors: 10fr, Barthélemy Thimonnier, sewing machine. 12fr, Nicolas Appert, canned foods. 18fr, Dr. E. H. St. Claire Deville, aluminum. 25fr, Pierre Martin, steel making. 30fr, Bernigaud de Chardonnet, rayon.

1955, Mar. 5 Engraved

757	A253	5fr dk vio bl & bl	1.00	80
758	A253	10fr dk brn & org brn	1.00	80
759	A253	12fr dk grn	1.00	80
760	A253	18fr dk vio bl & ind	3.00	2.25
761	A253	25fr dk brnsh pur & vio	3.00	2.25
762	A253	30fr rose car & scar	3.00	2.25
		Nos. 757-762 (6)	12.00	9.15

St. Stephen Bridge, Limoges
A254

1955, Mar. 26 ***Perf. 13*** **Unwmkd.**

763	A254	12fr yel brn & dk vio brn	1.50	1.00

Gloved Model in Place de la Concorde
A255

1955, Mar. 26

764	A255	25fr blk brn, vio bl & blk	75	15

Issued to publicize French glove manufacturing.

Jean Pierre Claris de Florian
A256

1955, Apr. 2

765	A256	12fr bl grn	80	65

200th anniversary of the birth of Jean Pierre Claris de Florian, fabulist.

Eiffel Tower and Television Antennas
A257

1955, Apr. 16

766	A257	15fr ind & ultra	70	55

Issued to publicize French advancement in television.

Wire Fence and Guard Tower
A258

1955, Apr. 23

767	A258	12fr dk gray bl & brn blk	70	65

Issued to commemorate the 10th anniversary of the liberation of concentration camps.

Electric Train
A259

1955, May 11

768	A259	12fr blk brn & sl bl	1.00	70

Issued to publicize the electrification of the Valenciennes-Thionville railroad line.

Jacquemart of Moulins
A260

1955, May 28

769	A260	12fr blk brn	1.40	90

Jules Verne and Nautilus
A261

1955, June 3

770	A261	30fr indigo	7.25	6.00

Issued to commemorate the 50th anniversary of the death of Jules Verne.

Auguste and Louis Lumière and Motion Picture Projector
A262

1955, June 12

771	A262	30fr rose brn	6.00	5.00

Issued to commemorate the 60th anniversary of the invention of motion pictures.

Jacques Coeur and His Mansion at Bourges
A263

1955, June 18

772	A263	12fr violet	2.75	1.75

Issued to commemorate the 5th centenary of the death of Jacques Coeur (1395?–1456), French merchant.

Corvette "La Capricieuse"
A264

1955, July 9

773	A264	30fr aqua & dk bl	6.25	5.00

Issued to commemorate the centenary of the voyage of La Capricieuse to Canada.

Bordeaux
A265

Designs: 8fr, Marseilles. 10fr, Nice. 12fr, Valentre bridge, Cahors. 18fr, Uzerche. 25fr, Fortifications, Brouage.

1955, Oct. 15

774	A265	6fr car lake	25	8
775	A265	8fr indigo	25	5
776	A265	10fr dp ultra	30	5
777	A265	12fr vio & brn	30	5
778	A265	18fr bluish grn & ind	50	10
779	A265	25fr org brn & red brn	60	5
		Nos. 774-779 (6)	2.20	38

See Nos. 838–839.

Mount Pelée, Martinique
A266

1955, Nov. 1

780	A266	20fr dk & lt pur	80	10

Gérard de Nerval
A267

1955, Nov. 11

781	A267	12fr lake & sep	60	40

Issued to commemorate the centenary of the death of Gérard de Nerval (Labrunie), author.

Arms Type of 1949.

Arms of: 50c, County of Foix. 70c, Marche. 80c, Roussillon. 1fr, Comtat Venaissin.

Perf. 14x13½

1955, Nov. 19 Typo. Unwmkd.

782	A182	50c multi	8	4
783	A182	70c red, bl & yel	8	4
784	A182	80c brn, yel & red	8	4
785	A182	1fr bl, red & yel	8	5

Concentration Camp Victim and Monument
A268

Belfry at Douai
A269

1956, Jan. 14 Engr. *Perf. 13*

786	A268	15fr brn blk & red brn	35	35

No. 786 shows the national memorial for Nazi deportation victims erected at the Natzwiller Struthof concentration camp in Alsace.

1956, Feb. 11

787	A269	15fr ultra & ind	35	35

Col. Emil Driant
A270

1956, Feb. 21

788	A270	15fr dk bl	30	30

Issued to commemorate the 40th anniversary of the death of Col. Emil Driant during the battle of Verdun.

Trench Fighting
A271

1956, Mar. 3

789	A271	30fr ind & dk ol	1.30	1.00

40th anniversary of Battle of Verdun.

Jean Henri Fabre, Entomology
A272

Scientists: 15fr, Charles Tellier, Refrigeration. 18fr, Camille Flammarion, Popular Astronomy. 30fr, Paul Sabatier, Catalytic Chemistry.

1956, Apr. 7

790	A272	12fr vio brn & org brn	70	55
791	A272	15fr vio bl & int blk	1.00	55
792	A272	18fr brt ultra	2.50	1.50
793	A272	30fr Prus grn & dk grn	3.00	2.00

Grand Trianon, Versailles
A273

1956, Apr. 14

794	A273	12fr vio brn & gray grn	1.65	1.10

Symbols of Latin American and French Culture
A274

1956, Apr. 21

795	A274	30fr brn & red brn	2.50	1.60

Issued in recognition of the friendship between France and Latin America.

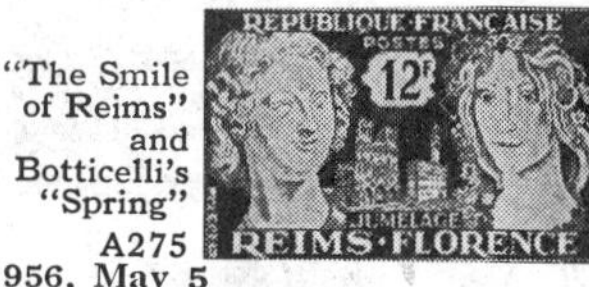

"The Smile of Reims" and Botticelli's "Spring"
A275

1956, May 5

796	A275	12fr blk & grn	1.00	45

Issued to emphasize the cultural and artistic kinship of Reims and Florence.

Leprosarium and Maltese Cross
A276

1956, May 12

797	A276	12fr sep, red brn & red	55	40

Issued in honor of the Knights of Malta.

St. Yves de Treguier
A277

1956, May 19

798	A277	15fr bluish gray & blk	35	30

Issued in honor of St. Yves, patron saint of lawyers.

Marshal Franchet d'Esperey
A278

Miners Monument
A279

1956, May 26

799	A278	30fr dp cl	1.30	90

Issued to commemorate the centenary of the birth of Marshal Louis Franchet d'Esperey.

1956, June 2

800	A279	12fr vio brn	55	45

Issued to commemorate the 100th anniversary of the town Montceau-les-Mines.

Basketball
A280

"Rebuilding Europe"
A281

Sports: 40fr, Pelota (Jai alai). 50fr, Rugby. 75fr, Mountain climbing.

1956, July 7

801	A280	30fr gray vio & blk	75	15
802	A280	40fr brn & vio brn	1.50	25
803	A280	50fr rose vio & vio	1.50	6
804	A280	75fr ind, grn & bl	3.50	1.10

Europa Issue.

Perf. 13½x14

1956, Sept. 15 Typo. Unwmkd.

805	A281	15fr rose & rose lake	1.75	35

Engraved.

Perf. 13

806	A281	30fr lt bl & vio bl	8.00	1.25

Issued to symbolize the cooperation among the six countries comprising the Coal and Steel Community.

No. 805 measures 21x35½mm., No. 806 measures 22x35½mm.

Dam at Donzère-Mondragon
A282

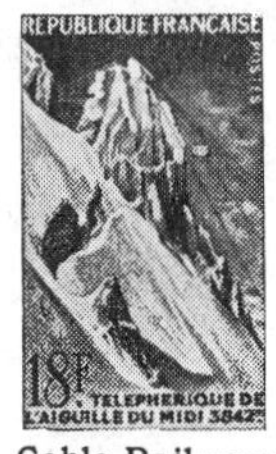

Cable Railway to Pic du Midi
A283

Rhine Port of Strasbourg
A284

1956, Oct. 6 Engraved *Perf. 13*

807	A282	12fr gray vio & vio brn	1.10	80
808	A283	18fr indigo	1.75	1.10
809	A284	30fr ind & dk bl	3.75	1.90

French technical achievements.

Antoine-Augustin Parmentier
A285

1956, Oct. 27

810	A285	12fr brn red & brn	55	35

Issued in honor of A. A. Parmentier, nutrition chemist, who popularized the potato in France.

Petrarch—A286

Portraits: 12fr, J. B. Lully. 15fr, J. J. Rousseau. 18fr, Benjamin Franklin. 20fr, Frederic Chopin. 30fr, Vincent van Gogh.

1956, Nov. 10

811	A286	8fr green	80	60
812	A286	12fr claret	80	60
813	A286	15fr dk red	1.10	80
814	A286	18fr ultra	3.00	2.25
815	A286	20fr brt vio	3.00	1.50
816	A286	30fr brt grnsh bl	4.00	3.00
		Nos. 811-816 (6)	12.70	8.75

Issued in honor of famous men who lived in France.

Pierre de Coubertin and Olympic Stadium—A287

1956, Nov. 24

817	A287	30fr dk bl gray & pur	1.75	1.10

Issued in honor of Baron Pierre de Coubertin, founder of the modern Olympic Games.

Homing Pigeon
A288

1957, Jan. 12

818	A288	15fr dp ultra, ind & red brn	40	35

Victor Schoelcher
A289

1957, Feb. 16 **Engraved**

819	A289	18fr lil rose	40	35

Issued in honor of Victor Schoelcher, who freed the slaves in the French Colonies.

Sèvres Porcelain
A290

1957, Mar. 23 ***Perf. 13*** **Unwmkd.**

820	A290	30fr ultra & vio bl	70	55

Issued to commemorate the the bicentenary of the porcelain works at Sèvres (in 1956).

Gaston Planté and Storage Battery
A291

Designs: 12fr, Antoine Béclère and X-ray apparatus. 18fr, Octave Terrillon, autoclave, microscope and surgical instruments. 30fr, Etienne Oemichen and early helicopter.

1957, Apr. 13

821	A291	8fr gray blk & dp cl	55	55
822	A291	12fr dk bl, blk & emer	55	55
823	A291	18fr rose red & mag	1.75	1.75
824	A291	30fr grn & sl grn	2.50	2.50

Uzès Chateau
A292

1957, Apr. 27

825	A292	12fr sl bl & bis brn	40	30

Jean Moulin
A293

Le Quesnoy
A294

Portraits: 10fr, Honoré d'Estienne d'Orves. 12fr, Robert Keller. 18fr, Pierre Brossolette. 20fr, Jean-Baptiste Lebas.

1957, May 18

826	A293	8fr vio brn	70	55
827	A293	10fr blk & vio bl	60	55
828	A293	12fr brn & sl grn	70	45
829	A293	18fr pur & blk	2.00	1.45
830	A293	20fr Prus bl & dk bl	1.10	60
		Nos. 826-830 (5)	5.10	3.60

Issued in honor of the heroes of the French Underground of World War II.
See also Nos. 879–882, 915–919, 959–963, 990–993.

1957, June 1

831	A294	8fr dk sl grn	20	8

See also No. 837.

Symbols of Justice
A295

1957, June 1

832	A295	12fr sep & ultra	25	25

Issued to commemorate the 150th anniversary of the French Cour des Comptes.

Farm Woman Type of 1954.

1957-59 ***Perf. 14x13½***

833	A236	6fr orange	15	5
833A	A236	10fr brt grn ('59)	95	8
834	A236	12fr red lil	25	12

Nos. 833-834 issued without precancellation.

Symbols of Public Works
A296

1957, June 20 **Engr.** ***Perf. 13***

835	A296	30fr sl grn, brn & ocher	65	55

Brest
A297

1957, July 6

836	A297	12fr gray grn & brn ol	70	55

Scenic Types of 1955, 1957.

Designs; 15fr, Le Quesnoy. 35fr, Bordeaux. 70fr, Valentre bridge, Cahors.

1957, July 19 **Unwmkd.**

837	A294	15fr dk bl grn & sep	20	4
838	A265	35fr dk bl grn & sl grn	1.75	45
839	A265	70fr blk & dl grn	3.50	1.00

Gallic Cock Type of 1954.

1957 **Typo.** ***Perf. 14x13½***

840	A237	5fr ol bis	30	6
841	A237	10fr brt bl	1.00	20
842	A237	15fr plum	2.25	70
843	A237	30fr brt red	4.25	1.25
844	A237	45fr green	35.00	17.50
		Nos. 840-844 (5)	42.80	19.71

Nos. 840–844 are known only precanceled. See second note after No. 132.

Leo Lagrange and Stadium
A298

1957, Aug. 31 **Engr.** ***Perf. 13***

845	A298	18fr lil gray & blk	45	35

Issued to commemorate the International University Games, Paris, Aug. 31-Sept. 8.

"United Europe"
A299

Auguste Comte
A300

1957, Sept. 16

846	A299	20fr red brn & grn	55	15
847	A299	35fr dk brn & bl	1.70	55

Issued to publicize a united Europe for peace and prosperity.

1957, Sept. 14

848	A300	35fr brn red & sep	70	70

Issued to commemorate the centenary of the death of Auguste Comte, mathematician and philosopher.

Roman Amphitheater, Lyon
A301

1957, Oct. 5 ***Perf. 13***

849	A301	20fr brn org & brn vio	45	45

Issued to commemorate the 2,000th anniversary of the founding of Lyon.

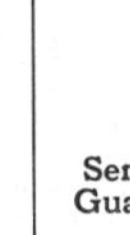

Sens River, Guadeloupe
A302

Beynac-Cazenac, Dordogne
A303

Nicolaus Copernicus
A304

Designs: 10fr, Elysee Palace. 25fr, Chateau de Valencay, Indre. 35fr, Rouen Cathedral. 50fr, Roman Ruins, Saint-Remy. 65fr, Evian-les-Bains.

1957, Oct. 19

850	A302	8fr grn & lt brn	15	8
851	A302	10fr dk ol bis & vio brn	15	5
852	A303	18fr ind & dk brn	25	5
853	A302	25fr bl gray & vio brn	30	8
854	A303	35fr car rose & lake	40	5
855	A302	50fr ol grn & ol bis	60	5
856	A302	65fr dk bl & ind	1.00	10
		Nos. 850-856 (7)	2.85	46

See also Nos. 907–909.

1957, Nov. 9 **Engraved** ***Perf. 13***

Portraits: 10fr, Michelangelo. 12fr, Miguel de Cervantes. 15fr, Rembrandt. 18fr, Isaac Newton. 25fr, Mozart. 35fr, Johann Wolfgang von Goethe.

857	A304	8fr dk brn	75	45
858	A304	10fr dk grn	75	45
859	A304	12fr dk pur	80	50
860	A304	15fr brn & org brn	90	40
861	A304	18fr dp bl	1.75	1.10
862	A304	25fr lil & cl	1.50	65
863	A304	35fr blue	2.00	1.75
		Nos. 857-863 (7)	8.45	5.30

Louis Jacques Thénard
A305

1957, Nov. 30 **Unwmkd.**

864	A305	15fr ol bis & grnsh blk	35	35

Issued to commemorate the centenary of the death of L. J. Thenard, chemist, and the founding of the Charitable Society of the Friends of Science.

Dr. Philippe Pinel A306

Joseph Louis Lagrange A307

Doctors' Portraits: 12fr, Fernand Widal. 15fr, Charles Nicolle. 35fr, René Leriche.

1958, Jan. 25

865 A306 8fr brn ol 1.00 75
866 A306 12fr brt vio bl 1.00 75
867 A306 15fr dp bl 1.50 90
868 A306 35fr black 2.00 1.40

Issued in honor of famous French physicians.

1958, Feb. 15 ***Perf. 13***

Portraits: 12fr, Urbain Jean Joseph Leverrier. 15fr, Jean Bernard Leon Foucault. 35fr, Claude Louis Berthollet.

869 A307 8fr bl grn & vio bl 1.00 75
870 A307 12fr sep & gray 1.10 1.00
871 A307 15fr sl grn & grn 1.75 1.25
872 A307 35fr mar & cop red 2.25 1.50

Issued to honor French scientists.

Lourdes Type of 1954.

1958

873 A241 20fr grnsh bl & ol 45 10

Le Havre A308

Maubeuge A309

Designs: 18fr, Saint-Die. 25fr, Sete.

1958, Mar. 29 Engr. ***Perf. 13***

874 A308 12fr ol grn & car rose 60 60
875 A309 15fr brt pur & brn 75 60
876 A309 18fr ultra & ind 1.00 90
877 A308 25fr dk bl, bl grn & brn 1.35 90

Reconstruction of war-damaged cities.

French Pavilion, Brussels A310

1958, Apr. 12

878 A310 35fr brn, dk grn & bl 45 40

Issued for the Universal and International Exposition at Brussels.

Heroes Type of 1957.

Portraits: 8fr, Jean Cavaillès. 12fr, Fred Scamaroni. 15fr, Simone Michel-Levy. 20fr, Jacques Bingen.

1958, Apr. 19

879 A293 8fr vio & blk 60 45
880 A293 12fr ultra & grn 60 45
881 A293 15fr brn & gray 1.75 1.25
882 A293 20fr ol & ultra 1.50 1.00

Issued in honor of the heroes of the French Underground in World War II.

Bowling A311

Sports: 15fr, Naval joust. 18fr, Archery (vert.). 25fr, Breton wrestling (vert.).

1958, Apr. 26

883 A311 12fr rose & brn 75 55
884 A311 15fr bl, ol gray & grn 1.00 65
885 A311 18fr grn & brn 1.75 1.10
886 A311 25fr brn & ind 2.00 1.50

Senlis Cathedral A312

1958, May 17

887 A312 15fr ultra & ind 45 45

Bayeux Tapestry Horsemen A313

1958, June 21

888 A313 15fr bl & car 55 35

Europa Issue, 1958

Common Design Type

Size: 22x36mm.

1958, Sept. 13 Engraved ***Perf. 13***

889 CD1 20fr rose red 55 15
890 CD1 35fr ultra 90 35

Foix Chateau A314

1958, Oct. 11

891 A314 15fr ultra, grn & ol brn 25 20

Common Design Types pictured in section at front of book.

City Halls, Paris and Rome A315

1958, Oct. 11

892 A315 35fr gray, grnsh bl & rose red 60 45

Issued to publicize the cultural ties between Rome and Paris and the need for European unity.

UNESCO Building, Paris A316

Design: 35fr, Different view of building.

1958, Nov. 1 ***Perf. 13***

893 A316 20fr grnsh bl & ol bis 20 15
894 A316 35fr dk sl grn & red org 20 15

Issued to commemorate the opening of UNESCO (U.N. Educational, Scientific and Cultural Organization) Headquarters in Paris, Nov. 3.

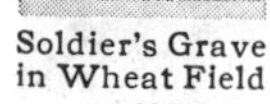

Soldier's Grave in Wheat Field A317

Arms of Marseilles A318

1958, Nov. 11

895 A317 15fr dk grn & ultra 25 20

Issued to commemorate the 40th anniversary of the World War I armistice.

1958–59 Typo. ***Perf. 14x13½***

Arms (Cities): 70c, Lyon. 80c, Toulouse. 1fr, Bordeaux. 2fr, Nice. 3fr, Nantes. 5fr, Lille. 15fr, Algiers.

896 A318 50c dk bl & ultra 5 5
897 A318 70c multi 4 5
898 A318 80c red, bl & yel 5 5
899 A318 1fr dk bl, yel & red 6 4
900 A318 2fr dk bl, red & grn 6 5
901 A318 3fr multi 6 5
902 A318 5fr dk brn & red 6 5
903 A318 15fr multi ('59) 20 6
Nos. 896-903 (8) 58 40

See also Nos. 938, 940, 973, 1040–1042, 1091–1095, 1142–1144.

Arc de Triomphe and Flowers A319

1959, Jan. 17 Engraved ***Perf. 13***

904 A319 15fr brn, bl, grn, cl & red 25 20

Paris Flower Festival.

Symbols of Learning and Medal A320

1959, Jan. 24 ***Perf. 13***

905 A320 20fr lake, blk & vio 25 20

Issued to commemorate the sesquicentennial of the Palm Leaf Medal of the French Academy.

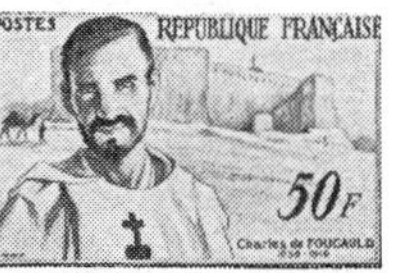

Charles de Foucauld A321

1959, Jan. 31

906 A321 50fr dp brn, bl & mar 80 65

Issued to honor Father Charles de Foucauld, explorer and missionary of the Sahara.

Type of 1957

Designs: 30fr, Elysee Palace. 85fr, Evian-les Bains. 100fr, Sens River, Guadeloupe.

1959, Feb. 10

907 A302 30fr dk sl grn 90 8
908 A302 85fr dp cl 2.75 15
909 A302 100fr dp vio 5.00 15

Gallic Cock Type of 1954.

1959 Typographed. ***Perf. 14x13½***

910 A237 8fr violet 60 6
911 A237 20fr yel grn 2.50 70
912 A237 40fr hn brn 5.50 3.00
913 A237 55fr emerald 24.00 14.00

Nos. 910–913 were issued with precancellation. See second note after No. 132.

Miners' Tools and School A322

1959, Apr. 11 Engr. ***Perf. 13***

914 A322 20fr red, blk & bl 25 20

Issued to commemorate the 175th anniversary of the National Mining School.

Heroes Type of 1957.

Portraits: No. 915, The five martyrs of the Buffon school. No. 916, Yvonne Le Roux. No. 917, Médéric-Védy. No. 918, Louis Martin-Bret. 30fr, Gaston Moutardier.

1959, Apr. 25 Engr. ***Perf. 13***

915 A293 15fr blk & vio 45 35
916 A293 15fr mag & rose vio 55 50
917 A293 20fr grn & grnsh bl 60 50
918 A293 20fr org brn & brn 90 70
919 A293 30fr mag & vio 1.00 70
Nos. 915-919 (5) 3.50 2.75

Dam at Foum el Gherza A323

Marcoule Atomic Center
A324

Designs: 30fr, Oil field at Hassi Messaoud, Sahara. 50fr, C. N. I. T. Building (Centre National des Industries et des Techniques).

1959, May 23

920	A323	15fr ol & grnsh bl	35	25
921	A324	20fr brt car & red brn	55	40
922	A324	30fr dk bl, brn & grn	75	40
923	A323	50fr ol grn & sl bl	1.35	55

Issued to publicize French technical achievements.

Marceline Desbordes-Valmore
A325

1959, June 20

924	A325	30fr bl, brn & grn	35	35

Issued to commemorate the centenary of the death of Marceline Desbordes-Valmore, poet.

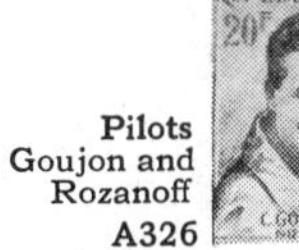

Pilots Goujon and Rozanoff
A326

1959, June 13

925	A326	20fr lt bl & org brn	40	40

Issued in honor of Charles Goujon and Col. Constantin Rozanoff, test pilots.

Tancarville Bridge
A327

1959, Aug. 1 Engr. *Perf. 13*

926	A327	30fr dk bl, brn & ol	35	30

Marianne and Ship of State
A328

Jean Jaures
A329

1959, July Typo. *Perf. 14x13½*

927	A328	25fr blk & red	45	3

See also No. 942.

1959, Sept. 12 Engr. *Perf. 13*

928	A329	50fr chocolate	55	45

Issued to commemorate the centenary of the birth of Jean Jaures, socialist leader.

Europa Issue, 1959

Common Design Type

1959, Sept. 19

Size: 22x36mm

929	CD2	25fr brt grn	55	20
930	CD2	50fr brt vio	90	35

Blood Donors
A330

1959, Oct. 17 Engraved

931	A330	20fr mag & gray	30	25

French-Spanish Handshake
A331

1959, Oct. 24 *Perf. 13*

932	A331	50fr bl, rose car & org	60	45

Issued to commemorate the 300th anniversary of the signing of the Treaty of the Pyrenees.

Polio Victim Holding Crutches
A332

Henri Bergson
A333

1959, Oct. 31

933	A332	20fr dk bl	25	20

Vaccination against poliomyelitis.

1959, Nov. 7

934	A333	50fr lt red brn	55	45

Issued to commemorate the centenary of the birth of Henri Bergson, philosopher.

Avesnes-sur-Helpe
A334

Design: 30fr, Perpignan.

1959, Nov. 14

935	A334	20fr sep & bl	30	20
936	A334	30fr brn, dp cl & bl	35	20

New NATO Headquarters, Paris
A335

1959, Dec. 12

937	A335	50fr grn, brn & ultra	1.10	70

Issued to commemorate the 10th anniversary of the North Atlantic Treaty Organization.

Types of 1958–59 and

Farm Woman
A336

Sower
A337

Designs: 5c, Arms of Lille. 15c, Arms of Algiers. 25c, Marianne and Ship of State.

Typographed.

1960–61 *Perf. 14x13½* Unwmkd.

938	A318	5c dk brn & red	8.00	6
939	A336	10c brt grn	30	3
940	A318	15c red, ultra, yel & grn	30	5
941	A337	20c grnsh bl & car rose	30	3
942	A328	25c ver & ultra	2.25	3
b.		Bklt. pane of 8	24.00	
c.		Bklt. pane of 10	30.00	
942A	A337	30c gray & ultra ('61)	2.25	35
		Nos. 938-942A (6)	13.40	55

Earlier stamps of Farm Woman type (A336), but with no decimals in denominations, are listed as Nos. 707–708, 833–834 (A236). Nos. 938–942A are in the New Franc currency (100 old francs equal 1 New Franc).

Laon Cathedral
A338

Kerrata Gorge
A339

Designs: 30c, Fougères Chateau. 50c, Mosque, Tlemcen. 65c, Sioule Valley. 85c, Chaumont Viaduct. 1fr, Cilaos Church, Reunion.

1960, Jan. 16 Engr. *Perf. 13*

943	A338	15c bl & ind	25	8
944	A338	30c bl, sep & grn	1.00	6
945	A339	45c brt vio & ol gray	75	6
946	A339	50c sl grn & lt cl	80	4
947	A338	65c sl grn, bl & blk brn	85	20
948	A338	85c bl, sep & grn	1.60	10
949	A339	1fr vio bl, bl & grn	1.50	4
		Nos. 943-949 (7)	6.75	58

Pierre de Nolhac
A340

1960, Feb. 13

950	A340	20c blk & gray	45	30

Issued to commemorate the centenary of the birth of Pierre de Nolhac, curator of Versailles and historian.

Museum of Art and Industry, Saint-Etienne
A341

1960, Feb. 20

951	A341	30c brn, car & sl	60	45

Gallic Cock Type of 1954.

1960 Typographed. *Perf. 14x13½*

952	A237	8c violet	90	6
953	A237	20c yel grn	3.75	45
954	A237	40c hn brn	8.50	2.50
955	A237	55c emerald	30.00	15.00

Nos. 952–955 were issued only precanceled. See second note after No. 132.

View of Cannes
A342

1960, Mar. 5 Engr. *Perf. 13*

956	A342	50c red brn & lt grn	1.10	80

Issued to commemorate the meeting of European municipal administrators, Cannes, March, 1960.

Woman of Savoy and Alps
A343

Woman of Nice and Shore
A344

1960 *Perf. 13* Unwmkd.

957	A343	30c sl grn	60	45
958	A344	50c brn, yel & rose	70	50

Issued to commemorate the centenary of the annexation of Nice and Savoy.

Heroes Type of 1957.

Portraits: No. 959, Edmund Debeaumarché. No. 960, Pierre Massé. No. 961, Maurice Ripoche. No. 962, Leonce Vieljeux. 50c, Abbé René Bonpain.

1960, Mar. 26

959	A293	20c bis & blk	2.00	1.25
960	A293	20c pink & rose cl	2.00	1.25
961	A293	30c vio & brt vio	2.00	1.50
962	A293	30c sl bl & brt bl	2.50	2.00
963	A293	50c sl grn & red brn	3.50	2.50
		Nos. 959-963 (5)	12.00	8.50

Issued in honor of the heroes of the French Underground of World War II.

"Education" and Children
A345

1960, May 21 Engraved *Perf. 13*

964	A345	20c rose lil, pur & blk	25	15

Issued to commemorate the 150th anniversary of the first secondary school in Strasbourg.

Blois Chateau
A346

View of La Bourboule
A347

1960, May

965	A346	30c dk bl, sep & grn	75	45
966	A347	50c ol brn, car & grn	90	60

Lorraine Cross
A348

Marianne
A349

1960, June 18

967	A348	20c red brn, dk brn & yel grn	30	25

Issued to commemorate the 20th anniversary of the French Resistance Movement in World War II.

Typographed

1960, June 18 ***Perf. 14x13½***

968	A349	25c lake & gray	20	5
a.		Bklt. pane of 8	5.00	
b.		Bklt. pane of 10	4.50	

Jean Bouin and Stadium
A350

1960, July 9 Engraved ***Perf. 13***

969	A350	20c bl, mag & ol gray	35	20

Issued to commemorate the 17th Olympic Games, Rome, Aug. 25–Sept. 11.

Europa Issue, 1960.

Common Design Type

1960, Sept. 17 ***Perf. 13***

Size: 36x22mm.

970	CD3	25c grn & bluish grn	25	8
971	CD3	50c mar & red lil	45	30

Lisieux Basilica
A351

1960, Sept. 24 ***Perf. 13***

972	A351	15c bl, gray & blk	35	30

Arms Type of 1958–59.

Design: Arms of Oran.

Typographed

1960, Oct. 15 ***Perf. 14x13½***

973	A318	5c red, bl, yel & emer	25	5

Madame de Staël by François Gerard
A352

1960, Oct. 22 Engraved ***Perf. 13***

974	A352	30c dl cl & brn	35	25

Issued to honor Madame de Staël (1766–1817), writer.

Gen. J. B. E. Estienne
A353

1960, Nov. 5

975	A353	15c lt lil & blk	25	25

Issued to commemorate the centenary of the birth of Gen. Jean Baptiste Eugene Estienne.

Marc Sangnier and Youth Hostel at Bierville
A354

1960, Nov. 5

976	A354	20c bl, blk & lil	20	15

Issued to honor Marc Sangnier, founder of the French League for Youth Hostels.

Badge of Order of Liberation
A355

1960, Nov. 14 Engraved ***Perf. 13***

977	A355	20c blk & brt grn	35	25

Order of Liberation, 20th anniversary.

Lapwings
A356

Birds: 30c, Puffin. 45c, European teal. 50c, European bee-eaters.

1960, Nov. 12

978	A356	20c multi	40	25
979	A356	30c multi	40	25
980	A356	45c multi	1.10	80
981	A356	50c multi	90	40

Issued to publicize wildlife protection.

André Honnorat
A357

1960, Nov. 19

982	A357	30c bl, blk & grn	35	20

Issued to honor André Honnorat, statesman, fighter against tuberculosis and founder of the University City of Paris, an international students' community.

St. Barbara and Medieval View of School
A358

1960, Dec. 3 Engraved

983	A358	30c red, bl & ol brn	45	35

Issued to commemorate the 500th anniversary of St. Barbara School, Paris.

"Mediterranean" by Aristide Maillol
A359

Marianne by Cocteau
A360

1961, Feb. 18 ***Perf. 13*** **Unwmkd.**

984	A359	20c car & ind	30	20

Issued to commemorate the centenary of the birth of Aristide Maillol, sculptor.

1961, Feb. 23

985	A360	20c bl & car	20	3

A second type has an extra inverted-V-shaped mark (a blue flag top) at right of hair tip. Price unused $2, used 50 cents.

Paris Airport, Orly
A361

1961, Feb. 25

986	A361	50c blk, dk bl, & bluish grn	55	35

Issued to commemorate the inauguration of new facilities at Orly airport.

George Méliès and Motion Picture Screen
A362

1961, March 11

987	A362	50c pur, ind & ol bis	90	50

Issued to commemorate the centenary of the birth of George Méliès, motion picture pioneer.

Jean Baptiste Henri Lacordaire
A363

1961, Mar. 25 ***Perf. 13***

988	A363	30c lt brn & blk	35	25

Issued to commemorate the centenary of the death of the Dominican monk Lacordaire, orator and liberal Catholic leader.

A364

1961, Mar. 25

989	A364	30c grn, red brn & red	35	30

Introduction of tobacco use into France, fourth centenary. By error stamp portrays Jan Nicquet instead of Jean Nicot.

Heroes Type of 1957.

Portraits: No. 990, Jacques Renouvin. No. 991, Lionel Dubray. No. 992, Paul Gateaud. No. 993, Mère Elisabeth.

1961, Apr. 22

990	A293	20c bl & lil	80	55
991	A293	20c gray grn & bl	80	60
992	A293	30c brn org & blk	1.10	70
993	A293	30c vio & blk	1.50	90

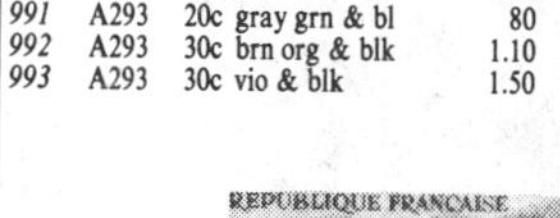

Bagnoles-de-l'Orne
A365

1961, May 6

994	A365	20c ol, ocher, bl & grn	30	25

Dove, Olive Branch and Federation Emblem
A366

1961, May 6

995	A366	50c brt bl, grn & mar	40	30

World Federation of Ex-Service Men.

Deauville in 19th Century
A367

1961, May 13 Engraved

996	A367	50c rose cl	1.10	90

Centenary of Deauville.

La Champmeslé
A368

Mont-Dore, Snowflake and Cable Car
A369

French actors: No. 998, Talma. No. 999, Rachel. No. 1000, Gérard Philipe. No. 1001, Raimu.

1961, June 10 *Perf. 13* Unwmkd.

Dark Carmine Frame

997	A368	20c choc & yel grn	45	30
998	A368	30c brn & crim	55	35
999	A368	30c yel grn & sl grn	55	35
1000	A368	50c ol & choc	80	60
1001	A368	50c bl grn & red brn	80	50
		Nos. 997-1001 (5)	3.15	2.10

Issued to honor great French actors and in connection with the Fifth World Congress of the International Federation of Actors.

1961, July 1

1002	A369	20c org & rose lil	30	25

Pierre Fauchard A370

St. Theobald's Church, Thann A371

1961, July 1

1003	A370	50c dk grn & blk	60	45

Issued to commemorate the bicentenary of the death of Pierre Fauchard, first surgeon dentist.

1961, July 1

1004	A371	20c sl grn, vio & brn	70	45

800th anniversary of Thann.

Europa Issue, 1961

Common Design Type

1961, Sept. 16 *Perf. 13*

Size: 35x22mm.

1005	CD4	25c vermilion	20	10
1006	CD4	50c ultra	40	25

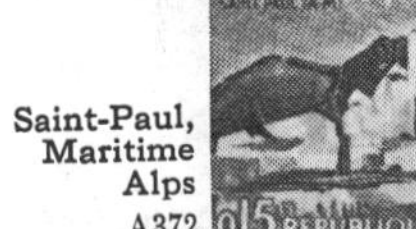

Saint-Paul, Maritime Alps A372

Designs: 30c, Beach and sailboats, Arcachon. 45c, Sully-sur-Loire Chateau. 50c, View of Cognac. 65c, Rance Valley and Dinan. 85c, City hall and Rodin's Burghers, Calais. 1fr, Roman gates of Lodi, Medea, Algeria.

1961, Oct. 9 Engraved *Perf. 13*

1007	A372	15c bl & pur	15	6
1008	A372	30c ultra, sl grn & lt brn	25	10
1009	A372	45c vio bl, red brn & grn	35	5
1010	A372	50c grn, Prus bl & sl	50	5
1011	A372	65c red brn, sl grn & bl	50	10
1012	A372	85c sl grn, sl & red brn	75	15
1013	A372	1fr dk bl, sl & bis	2.00	8
		Nos. 1007-1013 (7)	4.50	59

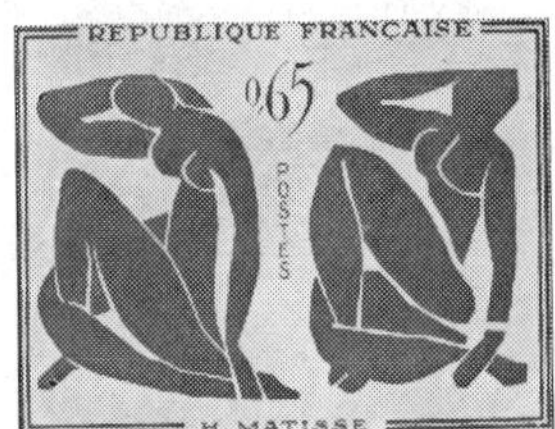

Blue Nudes, by Matisse—A373

Paintings: 50c, "The Messenger," by Braque. 85c, "The Cardplayers," by Cézanne. 1fr, "The 14th July," by Roger de La Fresnaye.

1961, Nov. 10 *Perf. 13x12*

1014	A373	50c dk brn, bl, blk & gray	3.50	2.00
1015	A373	65c grn, vio, & ultra	4.50	3.00
1016	A373	85c blk, brn, red & ol	3.50	2.75
1017	A373	1fr multi	6.25	4.00

Liner France A374

1962, Jan. 11 Engraved *Perf. 13*

1018	A374	30c dk bl, blk & car	45	45

New French liner France.

Skier Going Downhill A375

Maurice Bourdet A376

Design: 50c, Slalom.

1962, Jan. 27 *Perf. 13*

1019	A375	30c ultra & dk vio bl	35	30
1020	A375	50c dk grn, bl & lil	55	35

Issued to publicize the World Ski Championships, Chamonix, Feb. 1962.

1962, Feb. 17

1021	A376	30c slate	30	25

Issued to commemorate the 60th anniversary of the birth of Maurice Bourdet, radio commentator and resistance hero.

Pierre-Fidele Bretonneau A377

1962, Feb. 17

1022	A377	50c brt lil & bl	45	35

Issued to commemorate the centenary of the death of Pierre-Fidele Bretonneau, physician.

Chateau and Bridge, Laval, Mayenne A378

Gallic Cock A379

1962, Feb. 24

1023	A378	20c bis brn & sl grn	30	25

1962–65 *Perf. 13*

1024	A379	25c ultra, car & brn	30	5
a.		Bklt. pane of 4 (horiz. strip)	2.50	
1024B	A379	30c gray grn, red & brn ('65)	1.00	5
c.		Bklt. pane of 5	6.00	
d.		Bklt. pane of 10	12.00	

No. 1024 was also issued on experimental luminescent paper in 1963.

Ramparts of Vannes A380

Dunkirk A381

Paris Beach, Le Touquet A381a

1962 Engraved *Perf. 13*

1025	A380	30c dk bl	60	40
1026	A381	95c grn, bis & red lil	1.25	20
1027	A381a	1fr grn, red brn & bl	60	5

No. 1026 commemorates the 300th anniversary of Dunkirk.

Stage Setting and Globe A382

1962, Mar. 24 Unwmkd.

1028	A382	50c sl grn, ocher & mag	45	40

International Day of the Theater, Mar. 27.

Memorial to Fighting France, Mont Valerien A383

Resistance Heroes' Monument, Vercors A384

Design: 50c, Ile de Sein monument.

1962, Apr. 7

1029	A383	20c ol & sl grn	50	35
1030	A384	30c bluish blk	60	45
1031	A384	50c bl & ind	80	60

Issued to publicize memorials for the French Underground in World War II.

Malaria Eradication Emblem and Swamp A385

Nurses with Child and Hospital A386

1962, Apr. 14 Engraved

1032	A385	50c dk bl & dk red	45	40

Issued for the World Health Organization drive to eradicate malaria.

1962, May 5 *Perf. 13* Unwmkd.

1033	A386	30c bl grn, gray & red brn	25	25

National Hospital Week, May 5–12.

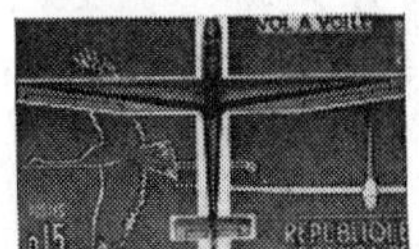

Glider—A387

Design: 20c, Planes showing development of aviation.

1962, May 12

1034	A387	15c org red & brn	20	18
1035	A387	20c lil rose & rose cl	25	18

Issued to publicize sports aviation.

School Emblem
A388

1962, May 19 **Engraved**

1036 A388 50c mar, ocher & dk vio 60 50

Issued to commemorate the centenary of the Watchmaker's School at Besançon.

Louis XIV and Workers Showing Modern Gobelin—A389

1962, May 26 ***Perf. 13*** **Unwmkd.**

1037 A389 50c ol, sl grn & car 55 45

Issued to commemorate the 300th anniversary of the Gobelin tapestry works, Paris.

Blaise Pascal—A390

1962, May 26

1038 A390 50c sl grn & dp org 60 55

Issued to commemorate 300th anniversary of the death of Blaise Pascal (1623–1662), mathematician, scientist and philosopher.

Palace of Justice, Rennes
A391

1962, June 12

1039 A391 30c blk, grysh bl & grn 70 40

Arms Type of 1958–59

Arms: 5c, Amiens. 10c, Troyes. 15c, Nevers.

1962–63 **Typo.** ***Perf. 14x13½***

1040 A318 5c ver, ultra & yel 7 4
1041 A318 10c red, ultra & yel ('63) 5 4
1042 A318 15c ver, ultra & yel 10 4

Phosphor Tagging

In 1970 France began to experiment with luminescence. Phosphor bars have been added to Nos. 1041, 1143, 1231, 1231C, 1292A-1294B, 1494-1498, 1563-1579, etc.

Rose
A392

Design: 30c, Old-fashioned rose.

1962, Sept. 8 **Engraved** ***Perf. 13***

1043 A392 20c ol, grn & brt car 25 20
1044 A392 30c dk sl grn, ol & car 45 35

Europa Issue, 1962
Common Design Type

1962, Sept. 15

Size: 36x22mm.

1045 CD5 25c violet 20 8
1046 CD5 50c hn brn 40 25

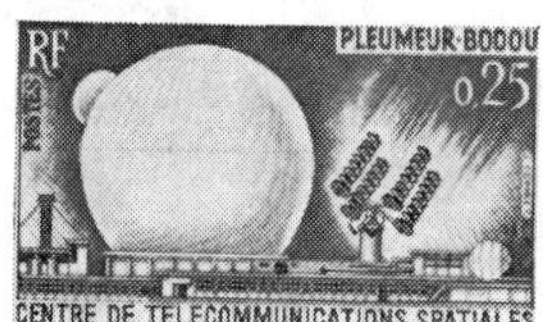

Space Communications Center, Pleumeur-Bodou, France—A394

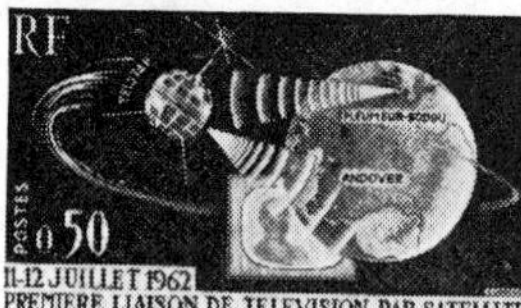

Telstar, Earth and Television Set
A395

1962, Sept. 29 **Engraved** ***Perf. 13***

1047 A394 25c gray, yel & grn 25 15
1048 A395 50c dk bl, grn & ultra 45 35

Issued to commemorate the first television connection of the United States and Europe through the Telstar satellite, July 11–12.

"Bonjour Monsieur Courbet" by Gustave Courbet—A396

Paintings: 65c, "Madame Manet on Blue Sofa," by Edouard Manet. 1fr, "Guards officer on horseback," by Theodore Géricault (vert.).

1962, Nov. 9 ***Perf. 13x12, 12x13***

1049 A396 50c multi 5.00 2.75
1050 A396 65c multi 3.50 2.25
1051 A396 1fr multi 6.00 4.00

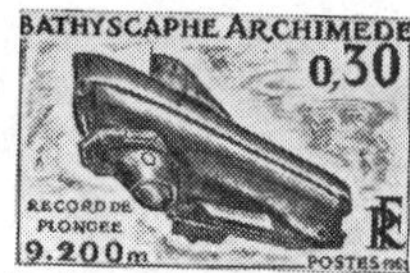

Bathyscaph "Archimede"
A397

1963, Jan. 26 ***Perf. 13*** **Unwmkd.**

1052 A397 30c dk bl & blk 35 30

French deep-sea explorations.

Flowers and Nantes Chateau
A398

1963, Feb. 11

1053 A398 30c vio bl, car & sl grn 35 30

Nantes flower festival.

St. Peter, Window at St. Foy de Conches—A399

Design: 50c, Jacob Wrestling with the Angel, by Delacroix.

1963, Mar. 2 ***Perf. 12x13***

1054 A399 50c multi 4.50 3.00
1055 A399 1fr multi 7.00 5.50

See also Nos. 1076–1077.

Hungry Woman and Wheat Emblem
A400

1963, Mar. 21 **Engraved** ***Perf. 13***

1056 A400 50c sl grn & brn 50 40

Issued for the "Freedom from Hunger" campaign of the U.N. Food and Agriculture Organization.

Cemetery and Memorial, Glières
A401

Design: 50c, Memorial, Ile de la Cité, Paris.

1963, Mar. 23 ***Perf. 13*** **Unwmkd.**

1057 A401 30c dk brn & ol 35 3
1058 A401 50c indigo 40 4

Issued to commemorate the heroes of the resistance against the Nazis.

Beethoven, Birthplace at Bonn and Rhine
A402

Designs: No. 1060, Emile Verhaeren, memorial at Roisin and residence. No. 1061, Giuseppe Mazzini, Marcus Aurelius statue and Via Appia, Rome. No. 1062, Emile Mayrisch, Colpach Chateau and blast furnace, Esch. No. 1063, Hugo de Groot, Palace of Peace, The Hague and St. Agatha Church, Delft.

1963, Apr. 27 ***Perf. 13*** **Unwmkd.**

1059 A402 20c ocher, sl & brt grn 35 35
1060 A402 20c pur, blk & mar 35 35
1061 A402 20c mar, sl & ol 35 35
1062 A402 20c mar, dk brn & ocher 35 35
1063 A402 30c dk brn, vio & ocher 35 35
Nos. 1059-1063 (5) 1.75 1.75

Issued to honor famous men of the European Common Market countries.

Hotel des Postes and Stagecoach, 1863
A403

1963, May 4

1064 A403 50c grysh blk 40 30

Issued to commemorate the first International Postal Conference, Paris, 1863.

Lycée Louis-le-Grand, Belvédère, Panthéon and St. Étienne du Mont Church
A404

1963, May 18

1065 A404 30c sl grn 30 25

Issued to commemorate the 400th anniversary of the Jesuit Clermont secondary school, named after Louis XIV.

St. Peter's Church and Ramparts, Caen
A405

1963, June 1 ***Perf. 13*** **Unwmkd.**

1066 A405 30c gray bl & brn 30 25

Radio Telescope, Nançay—A406

1963, June 8 Engraved

1067	A406	50c dk bl & dk brn	45	30

Amboise Chateau
A407

Saint-Flour
A408

Designs: 50c, Côte d'Azur Varoise. 85c, Vittel. 95c, Moissac.

1963, June 15

1068	A407	30c sl, grn & bis	30	5
1069	A407	50c dk grn, dk bl & hn brn	45	5
1070	A408	60c ultra, dk grn & hn brn	50	15
1071	A407	85c dk grn, yel grn & brn	1.10	15
1072	A408	95c dk brn & blk	90	20
		Nos. 1068-1072 (5)	3.25	60

Water Skiing Slalom
A409

1963, Aug. 31 *Perf. 13* Unwmkd.

1073	A409	30c sl grn, blk & car	30	20

Issued to commemorate the World Water Skiing Championships, Vichy.

Europa Issue, 1963
Common Design Type

1963, Sept. 14

Size: 36x22mm.

1074	CD6	25c red brn	25	18
1075	CD6	50c green	45	24

Type of 1963

Designs: 85c, "The Married Couple of the Eiffel Tower" by Marc Chagall. 95c, "The Fur Merchants," window, Chartres Cathedral.

1963, Nov. 9 Engraved *Perf. 12x13*

1076	A399	85c multi	2.00	1.40
1077	A399	95c multi	1.10	80

Philatec Issue
Common Design Type

1963, Dec. 14 *Perf. 13* Unwmkd.

1078	CD118	25c dk gray, sl grn & dk car	25	6

Radio and Television Center, Paris
A411

1963, Dec. 15 Engraved

1079	A411	20c org brn, sl & ol	20	8

Fire Brigade Insignia, Symbols of Fire, Water and Civilian Defense
A412

1964, Feb. 8 Engraved *Perf. 13*

1082	A412	30c bl, org & red	25	20

Issued to honor the fire brigades and civilian defense corps.

Handicapped Laboratory Technician
A413

1964, Feb. 22 *Perf. 13* Unwmkd.

1083	A413	30c grn, red brn & brn	25	15

Rehabilitation of the handicapped.

John II the Good (1319–64) by Girard d'Orleans
A414

1964, Apr. 25 *Perf. 12x13*

1084	A414	1fr multi	2.75	2.00

The lack of a price for a listed item does not necessarily indicate rarity.

Stamp of 1900 A415 — Mechanized Mail Handling A416

Designs: No. 1086, Stamp of 1900, Type A17. No. 1088, Telecommunications.

1964, May 9 *Perf. 13*

1085	A415	25c bis & dk car	30	30
1086	A415	25c bis & bl	30	30
1087	A416	30c blk, bl & org brn	30	30
1088	A416	30c blk, car rose & bluish grn	30	30
a.		Strip of 4 (1 each Nos. 1085-1088 + label)	1.25	1.25

Printed in sheets of 20 stamps, containing five No. 1088a. The label shows the Philatec emblem in green.

Type of Semi-Postal Issue, 1959 with "25e ANNIVERSAIRE" added

1964, May 9

1089	SP208	25c multi	25	12

25th anniversary, night airmail service.

Madonna and Child from Rose Window of Notre Dame
A417

1964, May 23 *Perf. 12x13*

1090	A417	60c multi	65	60

Issued to commemorate the 800th anniversary of Notre Dame Cathedral, Paris.

Arms Type of 1958–59

Arms: 1c, Niort. 2c, Guéret. 12c, Agen. 18c, Saint-Denis, Réunion. 30c, Paris.

1964–65 Typo. *Perf. 14x13½*

1091	A318	1c vio bl & yel	5	3
1092	A318	2c emer, vio bl & yel	5	3
1093	A318	12c blk, red & yel	10	3
1094	A318	18c multi	18	10
1095	A318	30c vio, bl & red ('65)	25	4
a.		Bklt. pane of 10	7.00	
		Nos. 1091-1095 (5)	63	23

Gallic Coin
A418
Perf. 13½x14

1964–66 Typographed Unwmkd.

1096	A418	10c emer & bis	1.50	12
1097	A418	15c org & bis ('66)	50	12
1098	A418	25c lil & brn	60	20
1099	A418	50c brt bl & brn	1.25	50

Nos. 1096–1099 are known only precanceled. See second note after No. 132. See Nos. 1240–1242, 1315–1318, 1421–1424.

Postrider, Rocket and Radar Equipment—A419

1964, June 5 Engraved *Perf. 13*

1100	A419	1fr brn, dk red & dk bl	27.50	23.50

Sold for 4fr, including 3fr admission to PHILATEC. Issued in sheets of 8 stamps and 8 labels (2x8 subjects with labels in horizontal rows 1, 4, 5, 8; stamps in rows 2, 3, 6, 7). Commemorative inscriptions on side margins.

Caesar's Tower, Provins
A420

Chapel of Notre Dame du Haut, Ronchamp—A421

1964–65

1101	A421	40c sl grn, dk brn & brn ('65)	30	6
1102	A420	70c sl, grn & car	50	6
1103	A421	1.25fr brt bl, sl grn & ol	1.00	40

The 40c was issued in vertical coils in 1971. Every 10th coil stamp has a red control number printed twice on the back.

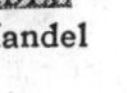

Georges Mandel A422 — Judo A423

1964, July 4 *Perf. 13* Unwmkd.

1104	A422	30c vio brn	25	25

Issued to commemorate the 20th anniversary of the death of Georges Mandel (1885–1944), Cabinet minister, executed by the Nazis.

1964, July 4

1105	A423	50c dk bl & vio brn	45	20

Issued to publicize the 18th Olympic Games, Tokyo, Oct. 10–25, 1964.

Champlevé Enamel from Limoges, 12th Century—A424

Design: No. 1107, The Lady (Claude Le Viste ?) with the Unicorn, 15th century tapestry.

1964 *Perf. 12x13*

1106	A424	1fr multi	2.00	1.35
1107	A424	1fr multi	75	60

No. 1106 shows part of an enamel sepulchral plate portraying Geoffrey IV, Count of Anjou and Le Maine (1113–1151), who was called Geoffrey Plantagenet.

Issue dates: No. 1106, July 4. No. 1107, Oct. 31.

Paris Taxis Carrying Soldiers to Front, 1914 A425

1964, Sept. 5 *Perf. 13* **Unwmkd.**

1108	A425	30c blk, bl & red	35	20

50th anniversary of Battle of the Marne.

Europa Issue, 1964

Common Design Type

1964, Sept. 12 **Engraved**

Size: 22x36mm.

1109	CD7	25c dk car, dp ocher & grn	20	10
1110	CD7	50c vio, yel grn & dk car	35	25

Cooperation Issue

Common Design Type

1964, Nov. 6 *Perf. 13* **Unwmkd.**

1111	CD119	25c red brn, dk brn & dk bl	20	10

Joux Chateau A427

1965, Feb. 6 **Engraved**

1112	A427	1.30fr redsh brn, brn red & dk brn	90	15

"The English Girl from the Star" by Toulouse-Lautrec—A428

St. Paul on the Damascus Road, Window, Cathedral of Sens

A429

Leaving for the Hunt

A430

Apocalypse Tapestry, 14th Century

A431

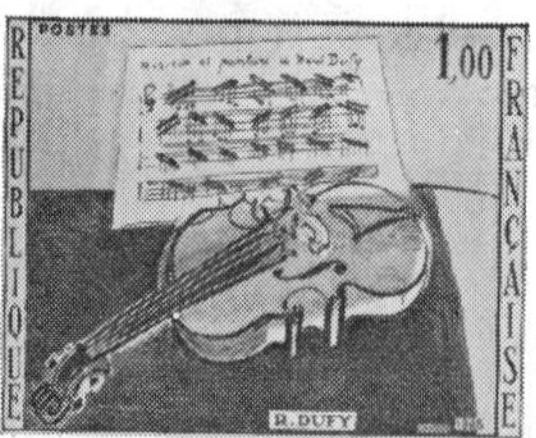

"The Red Violin" by Raoul Dufy

A432

Designs: No. 1115, "August" miniature of Book of Hours of Jean de France, Duc de Berry ("Les Très Riches Heures du Duc de Berry"), painted by Flemish brothers, Pol, Hermant and Jannequin Limbourg, 1411–16. No. 1116, Scene from oldest existing set of French tapestries, showing the Winepress of the Wrath of God (Revelations 14: 19–20).

1965 *Perf. 12x13, 13x12*

1113	A428	1fr multi	55	45
1114	A429	1fr multi	45	40
1115	A430	1fr multi	45	40
1116	A431	1fr multi	45	40
1117	A432	1fr blk, pink & car	45	40
		Nos. 1113-1117 (5)	2.35	2.05

No. 1114 issued to commemorate the 800th anniversary of the Cathedral of Sens.

Dates of issue: No. 1113, Mar. 12. No. 1114, June 5. No. 1115, Sept. 25. No. 1116, Oct. 30. No. 1117, Nov. 6.

Paris Parade of Returning Deportees, 1945 A433

1965, Apr. 1 *Perf. 13* **Unwmkd.**

1118	A433	40c Prus grn	40	30

Issued to commemorate the 20th anniversary of the return of people deported during World War II.

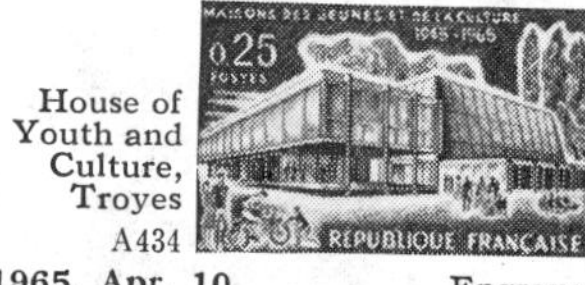

House of Youth and Culture, Troyes A434

1965, Apr. 10 **Engraved**

1119	A434	25c ind, brn & dk grn	35	20

Issued to publicize the 20th anniversary of the establishment of recreational cultural centers for young people.

Woman Carrying Flowers

A435

Flags of France, USA, USSR and Great Britain Crushing Swastika

A436

1965, Apr. 24 *Perf. 13* **Unwmkd.**

1120	A435	60c dk grn, dp org & ver	45	40

Issued to publicize the tourist Campaign of Welcome and Amiability.

1965, May 8

1121	A436	40c blk, car & ultra	35	25

Issued to commemorate the 20th anniversary of victory in World War II.

Telegraph Key, Syncom Satellite and Pleumeur-Bodou Station A437

1965, May 17

1122	A437	60c dk bl, brn & blk	45	40

Issued to commemorate the centenary of the International Telecommunication Union.

Croix de Guerre A438

1965, May 22 **Engraved**

1123	A438	40c red, brn & brt grn	30	2

Issued to commemorate the 50th anniversary of the Croix de Guerre medal.

Cathedral of Bourges A439

Moustiers-Sainte-Marie

A440

Views: 30c, Road and tunnel, Mont Blanc. 60c, Aix-les-Bains, sailboat. 75c, Tarn Gorge, Lozère mountains. 95c, Vendée River, man poling boat, and windmill. 1fr, Prehistoric stone monuments, Carnac.

1965, June–July

1124	A439	30c bl, vio bl & brn vio	30	6
1125	A439	40c gray bl & redsh brn	30	20
1126	A440	50c grn, bl gray & bis	40	6
1127	A439	60c bl & red brn	45	10
1128	A439	75c brn, bl & grn	90	45
1129	A440	95c brn, grn & bl	85	20
1130	A440	1fr gray grn & brn	80	6
		Nos. 1124-1130 (7)	4.00	1.13

No. 1124 was issued July 17 to commemorate the opening of the Mont Blanc Tunnel. No. 1125 (Bourges Cathedral) was issued in connection with the French Philatelic Societies Federation Congress, held at Bourges.

Europa Issue, 1965

Common Design Type

1965, Sept. 25 *Perf. 13*

Size: 36x22mm.

1131	CD8	30c red	25	6
1132	CD8	60c gray	45	35

Planting Seedling

A441

Etienne Régnault, "Le Taureau" and Coast of Reunion

A442

1965, Oct. 2

1133	A441	25c sl grn, yel grn & red brn	25	15

National reforestation campaign.

1965. Oct. 2

1134	A442	30c ind & dk car	25	15

Tercentenary of settlement of Reunion.

Atomic Reactor and Diagram, Symbols of Industry, Agriculture and Medicine
A443

1965, Oct. 9

1135 A443 60c brt bl & blk 45 40

Issued to commemorate the 20th anniversary of the Atomic Energy Commission.

Air Academy and Emblem
A444

1965, Nov. 6 ***Perf. 13***

1136 A444 25c dk bl & grn 25 10

Issued to commemorate the 50th anniversary of the Air Academy, Salon-de-Provence.

French Satellite A-1 Issue
Common Design Type
Design: 60c, A-1 satellite.

1965, Nov. 30 Engraved ***Perf. 13***

1137 CD121 30c Prus bl, brt bl & blk 25 25
1138 CD121 60c blk, Prus bl & brt bl 35 35
a. Strip of 2 + label 65 65

Issued to commemorate the launching of France's first satellite, Nov. 26, 1965. No. 1138a contains one each of Nos. 1137–1138 and bright blue label with commemorative inscription. Each sheet contains 16 triptychs (2x8).

Arms of Auch
A446

Arms (Cities): 20c, Saint-Lô. 25c, Mont-de-Marsan.

Typo.; Photo. (20c)

1966 ***Perf. 14x13; 14 (20c)***

1142 A446 5c bl & red 5 3
1143 A446 20c vio bl, sil, gold & red 20 3
1144 A446 25c red brn & ultra 20 6

The 5c and 20c were issued in sheets and in vertical coils. In the coils, every 10th stamp has a red control number on the back.

French Satellite D-1 Issue
Common Design Type

1966, Feb. 18 Engraved ***Perf. 13***

1148 CD122 60c bl blk, grn & cl 40 35

Launching of the D-1 satellite at Hammaguir, Algeria, Feb. 17, 1966.

Horses from Bronze Vessel of Vix
A448

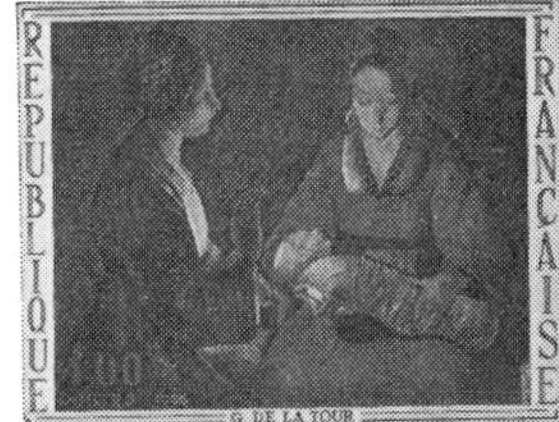

"The Newborn" by Georges de La Tour
A449

The Baptism of Judas (4th Century Bishop of Jerusalem)
A450

"The Moon and the Bull" Tapestry by Jean Lurçat
A451

"Crispin and Scapin" by Honoré Daumier
A452

1966 ***Perf. 13x12, 12x13***

1149 A448 1fr multi 45 40
1150 A449 1fr multi 45 40
1151 A450 1fr multi 45 40
1152 A451 1fr multi 45 40
1153 A452 1fr multi 45 40
Nos. 1149-1153 (5) 2.25 2.00

The design of No. 1149 is a detail from a 6th century B.C. vessel, found in 1953 in a grave near Vix, Cote d'Or.
The design of No. 1151 is from a stained glass window in the 13th century Sainte-Chapelle, Paris.
Issue dates: No. 1149, Mar. 26. No. 1150, June 25. No. 1151, Oct. 22. No. 1152, Nov. 19. No. 1153, Dec. 10.

Chessboard, Knight, Emblems for King and Queen
A453

St. Michael Slaying the Dragon
A455

Rhone Bridge, Pont-Saint-Esprit
A454

1966, Apr. 2 Engraved ***Perf. 13***

1154 A453 60c sep, gray & dk vio bl 60 45

Issued to publicize the Chess Festival.

1966, Apr. 23 ***Perf. 13*** **Unwmkd.**

1155 A454 25c blk & dl bl 20 15

1966, Apr. 30 Litho. and Engr.

1156 A455 25c multi 25 15

Millenium of Mont-Saint-Michel.

Stanislas Leszczynski, Lunéville Chateau
A456

1966, May 6 **Engraved**

1157 A456 25c sl, grn & brn 20 15

Issued to commemorate the 200th anniversary of the reunion of Lorraine and Bar (Barrois) with France.

St. Andrew's and Sèvre River, Niort
A457

1966, May 28 Engraved ***Perf. 13***

1158 A457 40c brt bl, ind & grn 30 25

Bernard Le Bovier de Fontenelle and 1666 Meeting Room
A458

1966, June 4

1159 A458 60c dk car rose & brn 40 30

300th anniversary, Académie des Sciences.

William the Conqueror, Castle and Norman Ships—A459

1966, June 4

1160 A459 60c brn red & dp bl 40 35

900th anniversary of Battle of Hastings.

Tracks, Globe and Eiffel Tower
A460

1966, June 11

1161 A460 60c dk brn, car & dl bl 40 30

19th International Railroad Congress.

Oléron Bridge
A461

1966, June 20

1162 A461 25c Prus bl, brn & bl 20 10

Issued to commemorate the opening of Oléron Bridge, connecting Oléron Island in the Bay of Biscay with the French mainland.

Europa Issue, 1966
Common Design Type

1966, Sept. 24 Engraved ***Perf. 13***
Size: 22x36mm.

1163 CD9 30c Prus bl 20 10
1164 CD9 60c red 40 30

Vercingetorix at Gergovie, 52 B.C.
A462

Bishop Remi Baptizing King Clovis, 496 A.D.
A463

Design: 60c, Charlemagne attending school (page holding book for crowned king).

1966, Nov. 5 *Perf. 13*

1165	A462	40c choc, grn & gray bl	30	20
1166	A463	40c dk red brn & blk	30	20
1167	A463	60c pur, rose car & brn	40	30

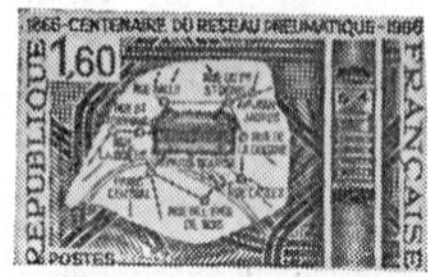

Map of Pneumatic Post and Tube
A464

1966, Nov. 11

1168	A464	1.60fr mar & ind	90	50

Centenary of Paris pneumatic post system.

Val Chateau
A465

1966, Nov. 19 Engraved *Perf. 13*

1169	A465	2.30fr dk bl, sl grn & brn	1.50	15

Rance Power Station
A466

1966, Dec. 3

1170	A466	60c dk bl, sl grn & brn	45	30

Issued to publicize the tidal power station in the estuary of the Rance River on the English Channel.

European Broadcasting Union Emblem
A467

1967, Mar. 4 Engraved *Perf. 13*

1171	A467	40c dk bl & rose brn	30	25

Issued to publicize the 3rd International Congress of the European Broadcasting Union, Paris, March 8–22.

"Father Juniet's Gig" by Henri Rousseau—A468

Francois I by Jean Clouet
A469

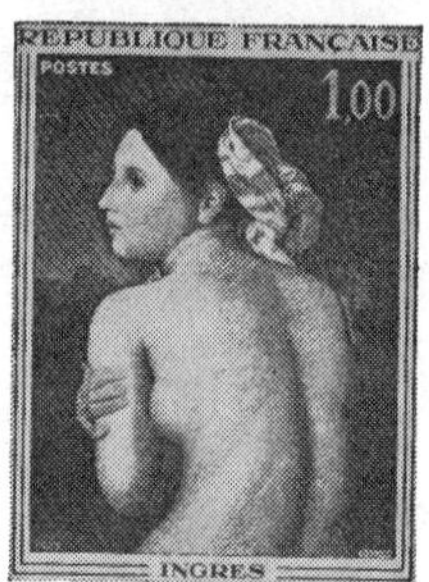

The Bather, by Jean-Dominique Ingres
A470

St. Eloi, the Goldsmith, at Work
A471

1967 Engr. *Perf. 13x12, 12x13*

1172	A468	1fr multi	50	40
1173	A469	1fr multi	50	40
1174	A470	1fr multi	50	40
1175	A471	1fr multi	50	40

The design of No. 1175 is from a 16th century stained glass window in the Church of Sainte Madeleine, Troyes.

Issue dates: No. 1172, Apr. 15. No. 1173, July 1. No. 1174, Sept. 9. No. 1175, Oct. 7.

Snow Crystal and Olympic Rings
A472

1967, Apr. 22 Photogravure *Perf. 13*

1176	A472	60c brt & lt bl & red	45	25

Issued to publicize the 10th Winter Olympic Games, Grenoble, Feb. 6–18, 1968.

French Pavilion, EXPO '67
A473

1967, Apr. 22 **Engraved**

1177	A473	60c dl bl & bl grn	50	25

Issued to commemorate the International Exhibition EXPO '67, Montreal, Apr. 28–Oct. 27, 1967.

Europa Issue, 1967
Common Design Type

1967, Apr. 29

Size: 22x36mm.

1178	CD10	30c bl & gray	20	8
1179	CD10	60c brn & lt bl	40	25

Great Bridge, Bordeaux—A474

1967, May 8

1180	A474	25c ol, blk & brn	25	15

Nungesser, Coli and "L'Oiseau Blanc"
A475

1967, May 8

1181	A475	40c sl, dk & lt brn	30	20

Issued to commemorate the 40th anniversary of the attempted transatlantic flight of Charles Nungesser and François Coli, French aviators.

Goüin House, Tours
A476

1967, May 13 Engraved *Perf. 13*

1182	A476	40c vio bl, red brn & red	30	20

Issued to publicize the Congress of the Federation of French Philatelic Societies in Tours.

Ramon and Alfort Veterinary School
A477

1967, May 27

1183	A477	25c brn, dp bl & yel grn	25	15

Issued to commemorate the 200th anniversary of the Alfort Veterinary School and to honor Professor Gaston Ramon (1886–1963).

Robert Esnault-Pelterie, Diamant Rocket and A-1 Satellite—A478

1967, May 27

1184	A478	60c sl & vio bl	45	30

Issued to honor Robert Esnault-Pelterie (1881–1957), aviation and space expert.

City Hall, Saint-Quentin
A479

Saint-Germain-en-Laye
A480

Views: 60c, Clock Tower, Vire. 75c, Beach, La Baule, Brittany. 95c, Harbor, Boulogne-sur-Mer. 1fr, Rodez Cathedral. 1.50fr, Morlaix; old houses, grotesque carving, viaduct.

1967

1185	A479	50c bl, sl bl & brn	40	6
1186	A479	60c dp bl, sl bl & dk red brn	45	20
1187	A480	70c rose car, red brn & bl	45	5
1188	A480	75c multi	60	35
1189	A480	95c sky bl, lil & sl grn	65	35
1190	A479	1fr ind & bl gray	60	5
1191	A479	1.50fr brt bl, brt grn & red brn	1.00	30
		Nos. 1185-1191 (7)	4.15	1.36

Issue Dates: 1fr, 1.50fr, June 10; 70c, June 17; 50c, 60c, 95c, July 8; 75c, July 24.

Orchids
A481

Cross of Lorraine, Soldiers and Sailors
A483

Scales of Justice, City and Harbor
A482

1967, July 29 Engr. *Perf. 13*

1192 A481 40c dp car, brt pink & pur 30 20

Orleans flower festival.

1967, Sept. 4

1193 A482 60c dk plum, dl bl & ocher 40 25

Issued to publicize the 9th International Accountancy Congress, Paris, Sept. 6–12.

1967, Oct. 7 Engraved *Perf. 13*

1194 A483 25c brn, dp ultra & bl 20 10

Issued to commemorate the 25th anniversary of the Battle of Bir Hacheim.

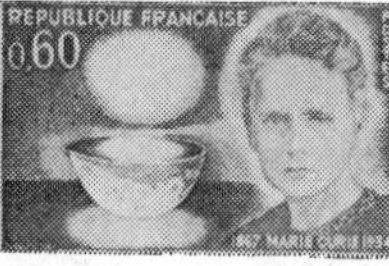

Marie Curie, Bowl Glowing with Radium
A484

1967, Oct. 23 Engr. *Perf. 13*

1195 A484 60c dk bl & ultra 35 30

Issued to commemorate the centenary of the birth of Marie Curie (1867–1934), scientist who discovered radium and polonium, Nobel prize winner for physics and chemistry.

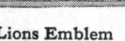

Lions Emblem
A485

Marianne (by Cheffer)
A486

1967, Oct. 28

1196 A485 40c dk car & vio bl 30 20

50th anniversary of Lions International.

1967, Nov. 4 Engraved

1197 A486 25c dk bl 60 20
1198 A486 30c brt lil 70 3
a. Bklt. pane of 5 5.00
b. Bklt. pane of 10 11.00

Coils (vertical) of Nos. 1197 and 1231 show a red number on the back of every 10th stamp.

See Nos. 1230–1231C.

King Philip II (Philip Augustus) at Battle of Bouvines
A487

Designs: No. 1200, Election of Hugh Capet as King (horiz.). 60c, King Louis IX (St. Louis) holding audience for the poor.

1967, Nov. 13 Engraved *Perf. 13*

1199 A487 40c gray & blk 30 20
1200 A487 40c stl bl & ultra 30 20
1201 A487 60c grn & dk red brn 45 25

Commemorative Medal
A488

1968, Jan. 6 Engraved *Perf. 13*

1202 A488 40c dk sl grn & bis 30 20

Issued to commemorate the 50th anniversary of postal checking service.

Various Road Signs
A489

1968, Feb. 24

1203 A489 25c lil, red & dk bl grn 20 15

Issued to publicize road safety.

Prehistoric Paintings, Lascaux Cave—A490

"Arearea" (Merriment) by Paul Gauguin—A491

The Dance, by Emile Antoine Bourdelle
A492

Portrait of the Model, by Auguste Renoir
A493

1968 Engr. *Perf. 13x12, 12x13*

1204 A490 1fr multi 55 45
1205 A491 1fr multi 60 45
1206 A492 1fr car & gray ol 60 45
1207 A493 1fr multi 60 45

Issue dates: No. 1204, Apr. 13. No. 1205, Sept. 21. No. 1206, Oct. 26. No. 1207, Nov. 9.

Audio-visual Institute, Royan
A494

1968, Apr. 13 *Perf. 13*

1208 A494 40c sl grn, brn & Prus bl 25 15

Issued to publicize the 5th Conference for World Cooperation with the theme of teaching living languages by audio-visual means.

Europa Issue, 1968

Common Design Type

1968, Apr. 27

Size: 36x22mm

1209 CD11 30c brt red lil & ocher 20 10
1210 CD11 60c brn & lake 40 30

Alain René Le Sage
A495

1968, May 4

1211 A495 40c bl & rose vio 30 15

Issued to commemorate the 300th anniversary of the birth of Alain René Le Sage (1668–1747), novelist and playwright.

Chateau de Langeais
A496

1968, May 4

1212 A496 60c sl bl, grn & red brn 45 25

Pierre Larousse
A497

1968, May 11 Engraved *Perf. 13*

1213 A497 40c rose vio & brn 30 15

Issued to honor Pierre Larousse (1817–1875), grammarian, lexicographer and encyclopedist.

Gnarled Trunk and Fir Tree
A498

1968, May 18 Engraved *Perf. 13*

1214 A498 25c grnsh bl, brn & grn 25 15

Issued to commemorate the twinning of Rambouillet Forest in France and the Black Forest in Germany.

Map of Papal Enclave, Valréas, and John XXII Receiving Homage—A499

1968, May 25

1215 A499 60c brn, bis brn & pur 45 30

Issued to commemorate the 650th anniversary of the papal enclave at Valréas.

Louis XIV, Arms of France and Flanders
A500

1968, June 29

1216 A500 40c rose car, gray & lem 30 15

Issued to commemorate the 300th anniversary of the Treaty of Aachen which reunited Flanders with France.

Martrou Bridge, Rochefort
A501

1968, July 20

1217 A501 25c sky bl, blk & dk red brn 20 10

Letord Lorraine Bimotor Plane over Map of France—A502

1968, Aug. 17 Engraved *Perf. 13*

1218 A502 25c brt bl, ind & red 20 12

Issued to commemorate the 50th anniversary of the first regularly scheduled air mail route in France from Paris to St. Nazaire.

Tower de Constance, Aigues-Mortes
A503

1968, Aug. 31

1219 A503 25c red brn, sky bl & ol bis 20 10

Bicentenary of the release of Huguenot prisoners from the Tower de Constance, Aigues-Mortes.

Cathedral and Pont Vieux, Beziers
A504

1968, Sept. 7 Engraved *Perf. 13*

1220 A504 40c ind, bis & grn 30 10

"Victory" over White Tower of Salonika
A505

1968, Sept. 28

1221 A505 40c red lil & plum 30 15

Issued to commemorate the 50th anniversary of the armistice on the eastern front in World War I, Sept. 29, 1918.

Louis XV, Arms of France and Corsica
A506

1968, Oct. 5 *Perf. 13*

1222 A506 25c ultra, grn & blk 25 15

Issued to commemorate the 200th anniversary of the return of Corsica to France.

Relay Race
A507

1968, Oct. 12

1223 A507 40c ultra, brt grn & ol brn 35 30

Issued to commemorate the 19th Olympic Games, Mexico City, Oct. 12–27.

Polar Camp with Helicopter, Plane and Snocat Tractor—A508

1968, Oct. 19

1224 A508 40c Prus bl, lt grnsh bl & brn red 35 20

20 years of French Polar expeditions.

Leon Bailby, Paris Opera Staircase and Hospital Beds
A509

"Victory" over Arc de Triomphe and Eternal Flame
A510

1968, Oct. 26

1225 A509 40c ocher & mar 30 20

Issued to publicize the 50th anniversary of the "Little White Beds" children's hospital fund.

1968, Nov. 9 Engraved *Perf. 13*

1226 A510 25c dk car rose & dp bl 20 10

Issued to commemorate the 50th anniversary of the armistice which ended World War I.

Death of Bertrand Du Guesclin at Chateauneuf-de-Randon, 1380
A511

1968, Nov. 16

Designs: No. 1228, King Philip IV (the Fair) and first States-General assembly, 1302 (horiz.). 60c, Joan of Arc leaving Vaucouleurs, 1429.

1227 A511 40c cop red, grn & gray 30 15
1228 A511 40c grn, ultra & brn 30 15
1229 A511 60c vio bl, sl bl & bis 45 25

See also No. 1260.

Marianne Type of 1967

1969–70 Engraved *Perf. 13*

1230 A486 30c green 30 5
a. Bklt. pane of 10 4.00
1231 A486 40c dp car 40 3
a. Bklt. pane of 5 (horiz. strip) 3.25
b. Bklt. pane of 10 5.50
d. With label ('70) 80 40

Typographed *Perf. 14x13*

1231C A486 30c bl grn 25 3

No. 1231d was issued in sheets of 50 with alternating labels showing coat of arms of Perigueux, arranged checkerwise, to commemorate the inauguration of the Perigueux stamp printing plant.

The 40c coil is noted after No. 1198.

Church of Brou, Bourg-en-Bresse
A512

Views: 80c, Vouglans Dam, Jura. 85c, Chateau de Chantilly. 1.15fr, Sailboats in La Trinité-sur-Mer harbor.

1969 Engraved *Perf. 13*

1232 A512 45c ol, bl & red brn 35 7
1233 A512 80c ol bis, brn red & dk brn 60 8
1234 A512 85c sl grn, dl bl & gray 70 40
1235 A512 1.15fr brt bl, gray grn & brn 75 45

"February" Bas-relief from Amiens Cathedral
A513

Philip the Good, by Roger van der Weyden
A514

Sts. Savin and Cyprian before Ladicius, Mural, St. Savin, Vienne—A515

The Circus, by Georges Seurat
A515a

1969 *Perf. 12x13*

1236 A513 1fr dk grn & brn 60 45
1237 A514 1fr multi 60 45
1238 A515 1fr multi 60 45
1239 A515a 1fr multi 60 45

Issue dates: No. 1236, Feb. 22; No. 1237, May 3; No. 1238, June 28; No. 1239, Nov. 8.

Gallic Coin Type of 1964–66

1969 Typographed *Perf. 13½x14*

1240 A418 22c brt grn & vio 80 15
1241 A418 35c red & ultra 1.60 35
1242 A418 70c ultra & red brn 7.00 2.25

Nos. 1240–1242 are known only precanceled. See note after No. 132.

Hautefort Chateau
A516

1969, Apr. 5 Engraved *Perf. 13*

1243 A516 70c bl, sl & bis 50 30

Irises
A517

1969, Apr. 12 Photogravure

1244 A517 45c multi 40 25

Issued to publicize the 3rd International Flower Show, Paris, Apr. 23–Oct. 5.

Europa Issue, 1969

Common Design Type

1969, Apr. 26 Engraved *Perf. 13*

Size: 36x22mm.

1245 CD12 40c car rose 25 7
1246 CD12 70c Prus bl 45 30

Albert Thomas and Thomas Memorial, Geneva
A518

1969, May 10 Engraved *Perf. 13*

1247 A518 70c brn, ol bis & ind 50 25

Issued to commemorate the 50th anniversary of the International Labor Organization and to honor Albert Thomas (1878–1932), director of the ILO 1920–1932.

Garigliano Battle Scene, 1944
A519

1969, May 10

1248 A519 45c blk & vio 40 25

Issued to commemorate the 25th anniversary of the Battle of the Garigliano against the Germans.

Chateau du Marché, Chalons-sur-Marne
A520

Parachutists over Normandy Beach
A521

1969, May 24

1249 A520 45c bis, dl bl & grn 35 20

Federation of French Philatelic Societies, 42nd congress.

1969, May 31

1250 A521 45c dk bl & vio bl 45 25

Issued to commemorate the 25th anniversary of the landing of Special Air Service and Free French commandos in Normandy, June 6, 1944.

Monument of the French Resistance, Mt. Mouchet
A522

1969, June 7

1251 A522 45c dk grn, sl & ind 45 25

Issued to commemorate the 25th anniversary of the battle of Mt. Mouchet between French resistance fighters and the Germans, June 2 and 10, 1944.

French Troops Landing in Provence
A523

1969, Aug. 23 Engraved *Perf. 13*

1252 A523 45c sl & blk brn 45 25

Issued to commemorate the 25th anniversary of the landing of French and American forces in Provence, Aug. 15, 1944.

Russian and French Aviators
A524

1969, Oct. 18 Engraved *Perf. 13*

1253 A524 45c sl, dp bl & car 45 25

Issued to honor the French aviators of the Normandy-Neman Squadron who fought on the Russian Front, 1942–45.

Kayak on Isère River
A525

1969, Aug. 2 Engraved *Perf. 13*

1254 A525 70c org brn, ol & dk bl 55 30

Issued to commemorate the International Canoe and Kayak Championships, Bourg-Saint-Maurice, Savoy, July 31–Aug. 6.

Napoleon as Young Officer and his Birthplace, Ajaccio—A526

1969, Aug. 16

1255 A526 70c brt grnsh bl, ol & rose vio 55 35

Issued to commemorate the 200th anniversary of the birth of Napoleon Bonaparte (1769–1821).

Drops of Water and Diamond
A527

Mediterranean Mouflon
A528

1969, Sept. 27

1256 A527 70c blk, dp bl & brt grn 50 25

European Water Charter.

1969, Oct. 11

1257 A528 45c ol, blk & org brn 40 30

Issued to publicize wildlife protection.

Central School of Arts and Crafts
A529

1969, Oct. 18

1258 A529 70c dk grn, yel grn & org 45 30

Issued to commemorate the inauguration of the Central School of Arts and Crafts at Chatenay-Malabry.

Nuclear Submarine "Le Redoutable"
A530

1969, Oct. 25

1259 A530 70c dp bl, grn & sl grn 50 30

Type of 1968 and

Henri IV and Edict of Nantes
A531

Designs: No. 1260, Pierre Terrail de Bayard wounded at Battle of Brescia (after a painting in Versailles). No. 1262, Louis XI, Charles the Bold and map of France.

1969, Nov. 8 Engraved *Perf. 13*

1260 A511 80c brn, bis & blk 50 25
1261 A531 80c blk & vio bl 50 25
1262 A531 80c ol, dp grn & dk red brn 60 30

"Firecrest" and Alain Gerbault
A532

1970, Jan. 10 Engraved *Perf. 13*

1263 A532 70c ind, brt bl & gray 50 30

Issued to commemorate the 40th anniversary of the completion of Alain Gerbault's trip around the world aboard the "Firecrest," 1923–29.

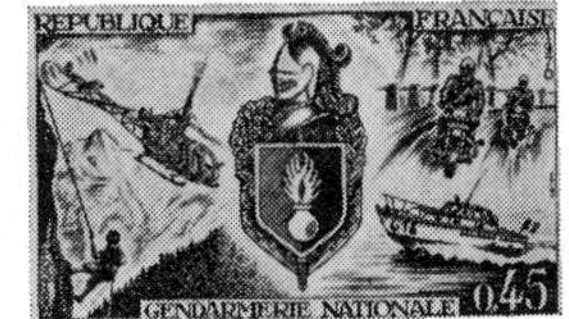

Gendarmery Emblem, Mountain Climber, Helicopter, Motorcyclists and Motorboat—A533

1970, Jan. 31

1264 A533 45c sl grn, dk bl & brn 35 25

Issued to honor the National Gendarmery, founded 1791.

Field Ball Player
A534

1970, Feb. 21 Engraved *Perf. 13*

1265 A534 80c sl grn 55 30

Issued to publicize the 7th International Field Ball Games, Feb. 26–March 8.

Alphonse Juin and Church of the Invalides—A535

1970, Feb. 28

1266 A535 45c gray bl & dk brn 40 25

Issued to honor Marshal Alphonse Pierre Juin (1888–1967), military leader.

Aerotrain
A536

1970, Mar. 7

1267 A536 80c pur & gray 50 30

Issued to publicize the introduction of the aerotrain, which reaches a speed of 320 miles per hour.

Pierre Joseph Pelletier, Joseph Bienaimé Caventou, Quinine Formula and Cell—A537

1970, Mar. 21 Engraved *Perf. 13*

1268 A537 50c sl grn, sky bl & dp car 45 20

Discovery of quinine, 150th anniversary.

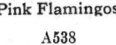

Pink Flamingos
A538

Diamant B Rocket and Radar
A539

1970, Mar. 21

1269	A538	45c ol, gray & pink	40	20

European Nature Conservation Year, 1970.

1970, Mar. 28

1270	A539	45c brt grn	40	25

Issued to publicize the space center in Guyana and the launching of the Diamant B rocket, Mar. 10, 1970.

Europa Issue, 1970
Common Design Type

1970, May 2 Engraved *Perf. 13*
Size: 36x22mm.

1271	CD13	40c dp car	30	10
1272	CD13	80c sky bl	50	30

Annunciation, by Primitive Painter of Savoy, 1480
A540

The Triumph of Flora, by Jean Baptiste Carpeaux—A541

Diana Returning from the Hunt, by François Boucher—A542

Dancer with Bouquet, by Edgar Degas
A543

1970 *Perf. 12x13, 13x12*

1273	A540	1fr multi	70	45
1274	A541	1fr red brn	70	45
1275	A542	1fr multi	70	45
1276	A543	1fr multi	70	45

Issue dates: No. 1273, May 9. No. 1274, July 4. No. 1275, Oct. 10. No. 1276, Nov. 14.

Arms of Lens, Miner's Lamp and Pit Head
A544

1970, May 16 Engraved *Perf 13*

1277	A544	40c scarlet	30	15

Issued to publicize the 43rd National Congress of the Federation of French Philatelic Societies, Lens, May 14–21.

Diamond Rock, Martinique
A545

Haute Provence Observatory and Spiral Nebula
A546

Designs: 95c, Chancelade Abbey, Dordogne. 1fr, Gosier Islet, Guadeloupe.

1970, June 20 Engraved *Perf. 13*

1278	A545	50c sl grn, brt bl & plum	40	10
1279	A545	95c lt ol, car & brn	75	40
1280	A545	1fr sl grn, brt bl & dk car rose	60	8
1281	A546	1.30fr dk bl, vio bl & dk grn	1.10	45

Hand Reaching for Freedom
A547

Handicapped Javelin Thrower
A548

1970, June 27

1282	A547	45c vio bl, bl & bis	35	15

Liberation of concentration camps, 25th anniversary.

1970, June 27

1283	A548	45c rose car, ultra & emer	40	20

Issued to publicize the International Games of the Handicapped, St. Etienne, June 1970.

Pole Vault
A549

1970, Sept. 11 Engraved *Perf. 13*

1284	A549	45c car, bl & ind	40	20

Issued to publicize the First European Junior Athletic Championships, Colombes, Sept. 11–13.

Royal Salt Works, Arc-et-Senans
A550

1970, Sept. 26

1285	A550	80c bl, brn & dk grn	60	30

Issued to publicize the restoration of the 18th century Royal Salt Works buildings, by Claude Nicolas Ledoux (1736–1806) at Arc-et-Senans, for use as a center for studies of all aspects of future human life.

Armand Jean du Plessis, Duc de Richelieu—A551

Designs: No. 1287, Battle of Fontenoy, 1745. No. 1288, Louis XIV and Versailles.

1970, Oct. 17 Engraved *Perf. 13*

1286	A551	45c blk, sl & car rose	35	30
1287	A551	45c org, brn & ind	35	30
1288	A551	45c sl grn, lem & org brn	35	30

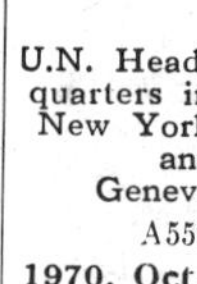

U.N. Headquarters in New York and Geneva
A552

1970, Oct. 24 Engr. *Perf. 13*

1289	A552	80c ol, dp ultra & dk pur	50	35

25th anniversary of the United Nations.

View of Bordeaux and France No. 43—A553

1970, Nov. 7

1290	A553	80c vio bl & gray bl	50	35

Centenary of the Bordeaux issue.

Col. Denfert-Rochereau and Lion of Belfort, by Frederic A. Bartholdi—A554

1970, Nov. 14

1291	A554	45c dk bl, ol & red brn	40	25

Centenary of the siege of Belfort during Franco-Prussian War.

Marianne (by Bequet)
A555

1971–74 Typographed *Perf. 14x13*

1292	A555	45c sky bl	40	6
1292A	A555	60c grn ('74)	1.25	4

Engraved *Perf. 13*

1293	A555	50c rose car	50	4
a.		Bklt. pane of 5 (horiz. strip)	3.50	
b.		Bklt. pane of 10	6.00	
1294	A555	60c grn ('74)	3.25	15
a.		Booklet pane of 10	37.50	
1294B	A555	80c car rose ('74)	75	5
c.		Booklet pane of 5	5.00	
d.		Booklet pane of 10	10.00	

Nos. 1294 and 1294B issued also in vertical coils with control number on back of every 10th stamp.

No. 1293 issued only in booklets and in vertical coils with red control number on back of every 10th stamp.

See Nos. 1494–1498.

St. Matthew, Sculpture from Strasbourg Cathedral
A556

Winnower, by François Millet
A557

The Dreamer, by Georges Rouault
A558

1971 Engraved *Perf. 12x13*

1295	A556	1fr dk red brn	70	45
1296	A557	1fr multi	70	45
1297	A558	1fr multi	70	45

Issue dates: No. 1295, Jan. 23; No. 1296, Apr. 3; No. 1297, June 5.

Figure Skating Pair—A560

1971, Feb. 20 Engraved *Perf. 13*

1299 A560 80c vio bl, sl & aqua 60 40

World Figure Skating Championships, Lyons, Feb. 23–28.

Underwater Exploration A561

1971, March 6

1300 A561 80c bl blk & bl grn 55 30

International Exhibition of Ocean Exploration, Bordeaux, March 9–14.

Cape Horn Clipper "Antoinette" and Solidor Castle, Saint-Malo A562

1971, Apr. 10 Engraved *Perf. 13*

1301 A562 80c bl, pur & sl 50 35

Pyrenean Chamois A563

1971, Apr. 24 Engraved *Perf. 13*

1302 A563 65c bl, dk brn & brn ol 50 25

National Park of Western Pyrenees.

Europa Issue, 1971

Common Design Type and

Santa Maria della Salute, Venice A564

1971, May 8 Engraved *Perf. 13*

1303 A564 50c bl gray & ol bis 40 15

Size: 36x22mm.

1304 CD14 80c rose lil 50 30

Cardinal, Nobleman and Lawyer—A565

Storming of the Bastille—A566

Design: No. 1306, Battle of Valmy.

1971

1305 A565 45c bl, rose red & pur 35 20
1306 A565 45c bl, ol bis & brn red 35 20
1307 A566 65c dk brn, gray bl & mag 50 35

No. 1305 commemorates the opening of the Estates General, May 5, 1789; No. 1306, Battle of Valmy (Sept. 20, 1792) between French and Prussian armies; 65c, Storming of the Bastille, Paris, July 14, 1789.

Issue dates: No. 1305, May 8; No. 1306, Sept. 18; 65c, July 10.

Grenoble A568

1971, May 29 Engraved *Perf. 13*

1308 A568 50c ocher, lil & rose red 30 15

44th National Congress of the Federation of French Philatelic Societies, Grenoble, May 30–31.

"Rural Family Aid" Shedding Light on Village A569

1971, June 5

1309 A569 40c vio, bl & grn 30 15

Aid for rural families.

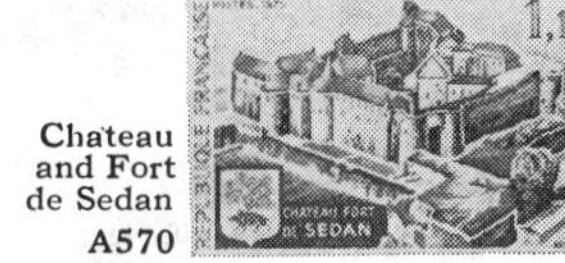

Chateau and Fort de Sedan A570

Pont d'Arc, Ardèche Gorge A571

Views: 60c, Sainte Chapelle, Riom. 65c, Fountain and tower, Dole. 90c, Tower and street, Riquewihr.

1971 Engraved *Perf. 13*

1310 A571 60c blk, grn & bl 35 8
1311 A571 65c lil, ocher & blk 45 8
1312 A571 90c grn, vio brn & red brn 55 15
1313 A570 1.10fr sl grn, Prus bl & brn 75 30
1314 A571 1.40fr sl grn, bl & dk brn 90 25
Nos. 1310-1314 (5) 3.00 86

Issue dates: 60c, June 19; 65c, 90c, July 3; 1.10fr, 1.40fr, June 12.

Gallic Coin Type of 1964–66

1971, July 1 Typo. *Perf. 13½x14*

1315 A418 26c lil & brn 55 15
1316 A418 30c lt brn & brn 1.00 20
1317 A418 45c dl grn & brn 2.25 35
1318 A418 90c red & brn 2.75 65

Nos. 1315–1318 are known only precanceled. See second paragraph after No. 132.

Bourbon Palace A572

1971, Aug. 28 Engraved *Perf. 13*

1319 A572 90c vio bl 60 30

59th Conference of the Interparliamentary Union.

Embroidery and Tool Making A573

1971, Oct. 16

1320 A573 90c brn red, brt lil & cl 65 30

40th anniversary of the first assembly of presidents of artisans' guilds.

Reunion Chameleon A574

1971, Nov. 6 Photo. *Perf. 13*

1321 A574 60c brn, yel, grn & blk 1.25 50

Nature protection.

De Gaulle Issue

Common Design Type and

De Gaulle in Brazzaville, 1944 A576

Designs: No. 1324, De Gaulle entering Paris, 1944. No. 1325, Pres. de Gaulle, 1970.

1971, Nov. 9 Engraved

1322 CD134 50c black 50 20
1323 A576 50c ultra 50 20
1324 A576 50c rose red 50 20
1325 CD134 50c black 50 20
a. Strip of 4 + label 2.75 1.75

First anniversary of the death of Charles de Gaulle (1890–1970). Nos. 1322–1325 printed se-tenant in sheets of 20 containing 5 strips of 4 plus label with Cross of Lorraine and inscription.

Antoine Portal and first Session of Academy—A577

1971, Nov. 13

1326 A577 45c dk pur & mag 35 20

Sesquicentennial of the founding of the National Academy of Medicine; Baron Antoine Portal was first president.

L'Etude, by Jean Honoré Fragonard A578

Women in Garden, by Claude Monet A579

St. Peter Presenting Pierre de Bourbon, by Maitre de Moulins A580

Boats, by André Derain—A581

1972 Engr. *Perf. 12x13, 13x12*

1327	A578	1fr blk & multi	65	45
1328	A579	1fr sl grn & multi	65	45
1329	A580	2fr dk brn & multi	2.75	1.25
1330	A581	2fr yel & multi	4.50	1.35

Issue dates: No. 1327, Jan. 22; No. 1328, June 17; No. 1329, Oct. 14; No. 1330, Dec. 16.

Map of South Indian Ocean, Penguin and Ships
A582

1972, Jan. 29 *Perf. 13*

1331	A582	90c blk, bl & ocher	90	45

Bicentenary of discovery of the Crozet and Kerguelen Islands.

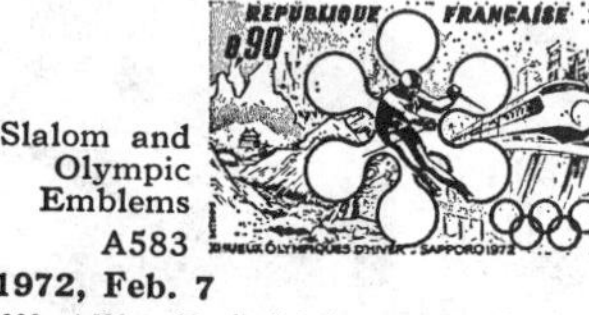

Slalom and Olympic Emblems
A583

1972, Feb. 7

1332	A583	90c dk ol & dp car	75	35

11th Winter Olympic Games, Sapporo, Japan, Feb. 3–13.

Hearts, U.N. Emblem, Caduceus and Pacemaker—A584

1972, Apr. 8 Engr. *Perf. 13*

1333	A584	45c dk car, org & gray	40	25

"Your heart is your health," world health month.

Red Deer, Sologne Plateau
A585

Charlieu Abbey
A585a

Bazoches-du-Morvand Chateau
A586

Saint-Just Cathedral, Narbonne
A587

1972 *Perf. 13*

1334	A585	1fr ocher & red brn	75	15
1335	A585a	1.20fr sl & dl brn	65	20
1336	A586	2fr sl grn, blk & red brn	1.25	15
1337	A587	3.50fr bl, gray ol & car rose	2.00	35

Issue dates: 1fr, Sept. 10; 1.20fr, Apr. 29; 2fr, Sept. 9; 3.50fr, Apr. 8.

Eagle Owl
A588

Design: 60c, Salmon (horiz.).

1972

1338	A588	60c grn, ind & brt bl	1.10	50
1339	A588	65c sl, ol brn & sep	1.10	50

Nature protection. Issue dates: 60c, May 27; 65c, Apr. 15.

Europa Issue 1972

Common Design Type and

Aix-la-Chapelle Cathedral
A589

1972, Apr. 22 Engr. *Perf. 13*

1340	A589	50c yel, vio brn & dk ol	35	10

Photogravure

Size: 22x36mm.

1341	CD15	90c red org & multi	65	20

Bouquet Made of Hearts and Blood Donors' Emblem
A590

Newfoundlander "Côte d'Emeraude"
A591

1972, May 5 Engraved

1342	A590	40c red	30	15

20th anniversary of the Blood Donors Association of Post and Telecommunications Employees.

1972, May 6

1343	A591	90c org, vio bl & sl grn	65	40

Cathedral, Saint-Brieuc
A592

1972, May 20

1344	A592	50c lil rose	35	20

45th Congress of the Federation of French Philatelic Societies, Saint-Brieuc, May 21–22.

Hand Holding Symbol of Postal Code
A593

1972, June 3 Typo. *Perf. 14x13*

1345	A593	30c grn, blk & car	20	10
1346	A593	50c car, blk & yel	30	6

Introduction of postal code system.

Old and New Communications
A594

1972, July 1 Engraved *Perf. 13*

1347	A594	45c sl & vio bl	30	15

21st International Congress of P.T.T. (Post, Telegraph and Telephone) Employees, Paris, July 1–7.

Hurdler and Olympic Rings
A595

1972, July 8

1348	A595	1fr dp ol	75	35

20th Olympic Games, Munich, Aug. 26–Sept. 11.

Hikers and Mt. Aigoual
A596

Bicyclist
A597

1972, July 15 Photo. *Perf. 13*

1349	A596	40c brt rose & multi	2.00	80

International Year of Tourism and 25th anniversary of the National Hikers Association.

1972, July 22 Engraved

1350	A597	1fr gray, brn & lil	2.00	80

World Bicycling Championships, Marseille, July 29–Aug. 2.

"Incroyables and Merveilleuse," 1794
A598

Designs: 60c, Bonaparte at the Arcole Bridge. 65c, Egyptian expedition (soldiers and scientists finding antiquities; pyramids in background).

1972 Engraved *Perf. 13*

1351	A598	45c ol, dk grn & car rose	40	30
1352	A598	60c red, blk & ind	50	30
1353	A598	65c ocher, ultra & choc	50	30

French history. Issue dates: 45c, Oct. 7; 60c, 65c, Nov. 11.

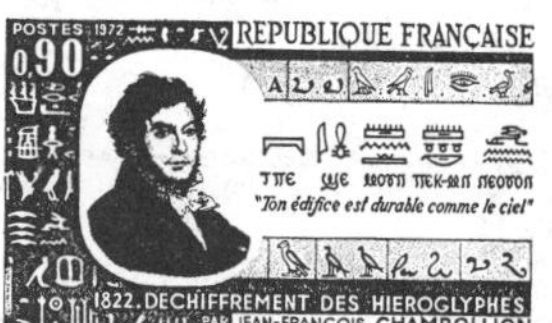

Champollion, Rosetta Stone with Key Inscription—A599

1972, Oct. 14

1354	A599	90c vio bl, brn red & blk	65	35

Sesquicentennial of the deciphering of hieroglyphs by Jean-François Champollion.

St. Teresa, Portal of Notre Dame of Alençon
A600

1973, Jan. 6 Engraved *Perf. 13*

1355	A600	1fr Prus bl & ind	90	30

Centenary of the birth of St. Teresa of Lisieux, the Little Flower (Thérèse Martin, 1873–1897), Carmelite nun.

Anthurium (Martinique)
A601

1973, Jan. 20 Photogravure

1356	A601	50c gray & multi	35	15

Colors of France and Germany Interlaced—A602

1973, Jan. 22

Size: 48x27mm.

1357	A602	50c multi	35	20

10th anniversary of the Franco-German Cooperation Treaty. See Germany No. 1101.

Polish Immigrants—A603

1973, Feb. 3 Engraved *Perf. 13*

1358	A603	40c sl grn, dp car & brn	30	20

50th anniversary of Polish immigration into France, 1921–1923.

Last Supper, St. Austremoine Church, Issoire
A604

Kneeling Woman, by Charles Le Brun
A605

Angel, Wood, Moutier-D'Ahun
A606

Lady Playing Archlute, by Antoine Watteau
A607

1973 Engraved *Perf. 12x13*

1359	A604	2fr brn & multi	2.00	1.00
1360	A605	2fr dk red & yel	2.00	1.00
1361	A606	2fr ol brn & vio brn	2.00	1.00
1362	A607	2fr blk & multi	1.50	1.00

Issue dates: No. 1359, Feb. 10; No. 1360, Apr. 28; No. 1361, May 26; No. 1362, Sept. 22.

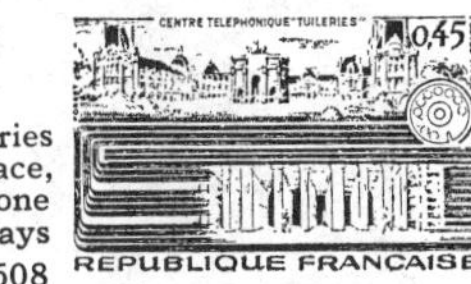

Tuileries Palace, Telephone Relays
A608

Oil Tanker, Francis I Lock
A609

Airbus A300-B
A610

1973

1363	A608	45c ultra, sl grn & bis	45	15
1364	A609	90c plum, blk & bl	60	20
1365	A610	3fr dk grn, bl & blk	2.25	1.25

French technical achievements.
Issue dates: 45c, May 15; 90c, Oct. 27; 3fr, Apr. 7.

Europa Issue 1973

Common Design Type and

City Hall, Brussels, CEPT Emblem
A611

1973, Apr. 14 Engr. *Perf. 13*

1366	A611	50c brt pink & choc	35	15

Photogravure
Size: 36x22mm.

1367	CD16	90c sl grn & multi	65	35

Masonic Lodge Emblem
A612

1973, May 12 Engr. *Perf. 13*

1368	A612	90c mag & vio bl	70	35

Bicentenary of the Free Masons of France.

Guadeloupe Raccoon
A613

White Storks
A614

1973

1369	A613	40c lil, sep & ol	45	30
1370	A614	60c blk, aqua & org red	55	35

Nature protection.
Issue dates: 40c, June 23; 60c, May 12.

Tourist Issue

Doubs Waterfall
A615

Clos-Lucé, Amboise
A617

Palace of Dukes of Burgundy, Dijon
A616

Design: 90c, Gien Chateau.

1973 Engraved *Perf. 13*

1371	A615	60c multi	30	15
1372	A616	65c red & pur	40	20
1373	A616	90c Prus bl, ind & brn	50	20
1374	A617	1fr ocher, bl & sl grn	50	15

Issue dates: 60c, Sept. 8; 65c, May 19; 90c, Aug. 18; 1fr, June 23.

Academy Emblem
A618

1973, May 26

1375	A618	1fr lil, sl grn & red	60	30

50th anniversary of the Academy of Overseas Sciences.

Racing Car and Clocks
A619

1973, June 2

1376	A619	60c dk brn & bl	60	30

50th anniversary of the 24-hour automobile race at Le Mans.

Five-master France II—A620

1973, June 9

1377	A620	90c ultra, Prus bl & ind	60	30

Tower and Square, Toulouse
A621

1973, June 9

1378	A621	50c pur & red brn	35	20

46th Congress of the Federation of French Philatelic Societies, Toulouse, June 9–12.

Dr. Armauer G. Hansen
A622

Ducretet and his Transmission Diagram
A623

1973, Sept. 29 Engraved *Perf. 13*

1379	A622	45c grn, dk ol & ocher	40	15

Centenary of the discovery of the Hansen bacillus, the cause of leprosy.

1973, Oct. 6

1380	A623	1fr yel grn & mag	60	25

75th anniversary of the first transmission of radio signals from the Eiffel Tower to the Pantheon by Eugene Ducretet (1844–1915).

Molière as Sganarelle
A624

1973, Oct. 20

1381	A624	1fr dk red & ol brn	60	30

Tercentenary of the death of Molière (Jean-Baptiste Poquelin; 1622–1673), playwright and actor.

Pierre Bourgoin and Philippe Kieffer
A625

1973, Oct. 27

1382 A625 1fr red, rose cl & vio bl 60 30

Pierre Bourgoin (1907–70), and Philippe Kieffer (1899–1963), heroes of the Free French forces in World War II.

Napoleon, Jean Portalis and Palace of Justice, Paris—A626

Exhibition Halls—A627

The Coronation of Napoleon, by Jean Louis David
A628

1973 Engraved *Perf. 13*

1383 A626 45c bl, choc & gray 30 20
1384 A627 60c ol, sl grn & brn 40 25
1385 A628 1fr sl grn, ol & cl 65 35

History of France. No. 1383 commemorates the preparation of the Code Napoleon; No. 1384, Napoleon's encouragement of industry and No. 1385 his coronation. Issue dates: 45c, Nov. 3; 60c, Nov. 24; 1fr, Nov. 12.

Eternal Flame, Arc de Triomphe
A629

Weather Vane
A630

1973, Nov. 10

1386 A629 40c pur, vio bl & red 30 15

50th anniversary of the Eternal Flame at the Arc de Triomphe, Paris.

1973, Dec. 1

1387 A630 65c ultra, blk & grn 35 25

50th anniversary of the Department of Agriculture.

Human Rights Flame and Man
A631

Postal Museum
A632

1973, Dec. 8 Engraved *Perf. 13*

1388 A631 45c car, org & blk 30 15

25th anniversary of the Universal Declaration of Human Rights.

1973, Dec. 19

1389 A632 50c mar & bis 30 15

Opening of new post and philately museum, Paris.

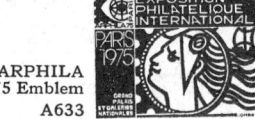

ARPHILA 75 Emblem
A633

1974, Jan. 19 Engraved *Perf. 13*

1390 A633 50c brn, bl & brt lil 35 15

ARPHILA 75 Philatelic Exhibition, Paris, June 1975.

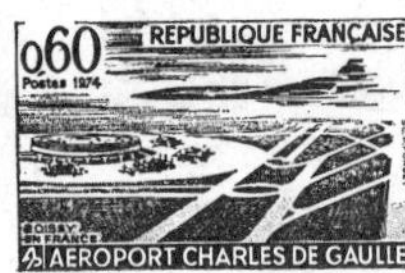

Concorde over Charles de Gaulle Airport
A634

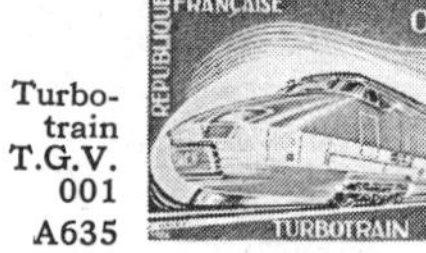

Turbo-train T.G.V. 001
A635

Phenix Nuclear Power Station
A636

1974 Engraved *Perf. 13*

1391 A634 60c pur & ol gray 55 30
1392 A635 60c multi 1.10 45
1393 A636 65c multi 40 25

French technical achievements.
Issue dates: No. 1391, Mar. 18; No. 1392, Aug. 31; 65c, Sept. 21.

Cardinal Richelieu, by Philippe de Champaigne—A637

Painting by Joan Miró—A638

Canal du Loing, by Alfred Sisley
A639

"In Honor of Nicolas Fouquet," Tapestry by Georges Mathieu
A640

Engr.; Photo. (※1395, 1397)

1974 *Perf. 12x13, 13x12*

1394 A637 2fr multi 1.50 1.00
1395 A638 2fr multi 1.50 1.10
1396 A639 2fr multi 1.75 1.10
1397 A640 2fr multi 1.75 1.10

Nos. 1394–1397 are printed in sheets of 25 with alternating labels publicizing "ARPHILA 75," Paris, June 6–16, 1975.
Issue dates: No. 1394, Mar. 23; No. 1395, Sept. 14; No. 1396, Nov. 9; No. 1397, Nov. 16.

French Alps and Gentian
A641

1974, Mar. 30 Engr. *Perf. 13*

1398 A641 65c vio bl & gray 55 35

Centenary of the French Alpine Club.

Europa Issue 1974

"Age of Bronze," by Auguste Rodin
A642

"Air," by Aristide Maillol
A643

1974, Apr. 20 *Perf. 13*

1399 A642 50c brt rose lil & blk 40 15
1400 A643 90c ol & brn 85 35

Sea Rescue—A644

1974, Apr. 27

1401 A644 90c multi 50 20

Reorganized sea rescue organization.

Council Building, View of Strasbourg and Emblem—A645

1974, May 4 Engr. *Perf. 13*

1402 A645 45c ind, bis & bl 30 15

25th anniversary of the Council of Europe.

Tourist Issue

View of Salers
A646

Basilica of St. Nicolas de Porte
A647

Seashell over Corsica
A648

Design: 1.10fr, View of Lot Valley.

1974		Engraved	*Perf. 13*	
1403	A646	65c yel grn & choc	40	20
1404	A646	1.10fr choc & sl grn	60	35
1405	A647	2fr gray & lil	1.10	30
1406	A648	3fr multi	1.50	45

Issue dates: 65c, June 22; 1.10fr, Sept. 7; 2fr, Oct. 12; 3fr, May 11.

Bison
A649

Giant Armadillo of Guyana
A650

1974				
1407	A649	40c bis, choc & bl	40	15
1408	A650	65c sl, ol & grn	40	30

Nature protection.
Issue dates: No. 1407, May 25; No. 1408, Oct. 19.

Americans Landing in Normandy and Arms of Normandy—A651

General Marie-Pierre Koenig
A652

Order of the French Resistance
A653

1974				
1409	A651	45c grn, rose & ind	35	20
1410	A652	1fr multi	60	30
1411	A653	1fr multi	60	30

30th anniversary of the liberation of France from the Nazis. Design of No. 1410 includes diagram of battle of Bir-Hakeim and Free French and Bir-Hakeim memorials.
Issue dates, 45c, June 8; No. 1410, May 25. No. 1411, Nov. 23. See No. B478.

Pfister House, 16th Century, Colmar
A654

1974, June 1				
1412	A654	50c multi	30	10

47th Congress of the Federation of French Philatelic Societies, Colmar, May 30–June 4.

Chess
A655

1974, June 8				
1413	A655	1fr dk brn & multi	80	45

21st Chess Olympiad, Nice, June 6–30.

Facade with Statue of Louis XIV, and 1675 Medal
A656

1974, June 15				
1414	A656	40c ind, bl & brn	30	10

300th anniversary of the founding of the Hotel des Invalides (Home for poor and sick officers and soldiers).

Peacocks Holding Letter, and Globe—A657

1974, Oct. 5		Engraved	*Perf. 13*	
1415	A657	1.20fr ultra, dp grn & dk car	70	50

Centenary of Universal Postal Union.

Copernicus and Heliocentric System—A658

1974, Oct. 12				
1416	A658	1.20fr multi	60	45

500th anniversary of the birth of Nicolaus Copernicus (1473–1543), Polish astronomer.

Tourist Issue

Palace of Justice, Rouen
A659

Saint-Pol-de-Leon
A660

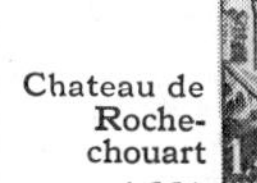

Chateau de Rochechouart
A661

1975		Engraved	*Perf. 13*	
1417	A659	85c multi	55	20
1418	A660	1.20fr bl, bis & choc	60	25
1419	A661	1.40fr brn, ind & grn	75	25

Issue dates: 85c, Jan. 25; 1.20fr, Jan. 18; 1.40fr, Jan. 11.

Snowy Egret
A662

Gallic Coin
A663

1975, Feb. 15		Engraved	*Perf. 13*	
1420	A662	70c brt bl & bis	50	25

Nature protection.

1975, Feb. 16		Typo.	*Perf. 13½x14*	
1421	A663	42c org & mag	1.50	30
1422	A663	48c lt bl & red brn	2.00	30
1423	A663	70c brt pink & red	3.00	60
1424	A663	1.35fr lt grn & brn	3.75	90

Nos. 1421–1424 are known only precanceled. See second note after No. 132. See Nos. 1460–1463, 1487–1490.

The Eye—A664

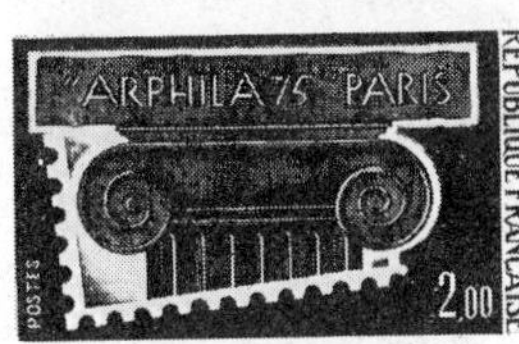

Ionic Capital—A665

Graphic Art—A666

Ceres—A667

1975		Engraved	*Perf. 13*	
1425	A664	1fr red, pur & org	70	25
1426	A665	2fr grn, sl grn & mag	1.10	40
1427	A666	3fr dk car & ol grn	1.50	70
1428	A667	4fr red, sl grn & bis	2.00	90

Souvenir Sheet

1429		Sheet of 4	11.00	11.00
a.	A664	2fr dp car & sl bl	1.50	1.50
b.	A665	3fr brt bl, sl bl & dp car	2.00	2.00
c.	A666	4fr sl bl, brt bl & plum	2.50	2.50
d.	A667	6fr brt bl, sl bl & plum	3.50	3.50

ARPHILA 75, International Philatelic Exhibition, Paris, June 6–16. No. 1429 has ornamental border and commemorative inscription. Size: 150x143mm. Issue dates: 1fr, Mar. 1; 2fr, Mar. 22; 3fr, Apr. 19; 4fr, May 17; souvenir sheet, Apr. 2.

Pres. Georges Pompidou
A668

Paul as Harlequin, by Picasso
A669

1975, Apr. 3		Engraved	*Perf. 13*	
1430	A668	80c blk & gray	45	15

Georges Pompidou (1911–74), President of France, 1969–74.

Europa Issue 1975

1975, Apr. 26 Photo. *Perf. 13*

Design: 1.20fr, Woman on Balcony, by Kees van Dongen (horiz.).

1431	A669	80c multi	60	20
1432	A669	1.20fr multi	80	40

Machines, Globe, Emblem
A670

1975, May 3		Engraved		
1433	A670	1.20fr bl, blk & red	60	35

World Machine Tool Exhibition, Paris, June 17–26.

Senate Assembly Hall
A671

1975, May 24 Engraved *Perf. 13*

1434 A671 1.20fr ol & dk car 60 35

Centenary of the Senate of the Republic.

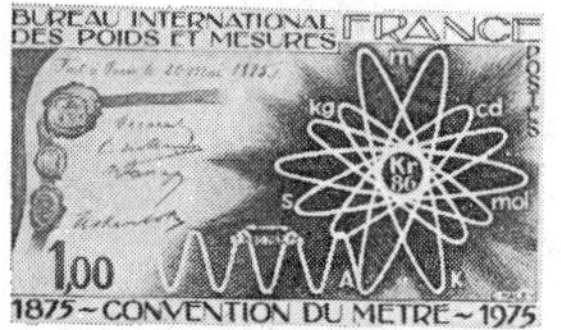

Meter Convention Document, Atom Diagram and Waves—A672

1975, May 31

1435 A672 1fr multi 50 25

Centenary of International Meter Convention, Paris, 1875.

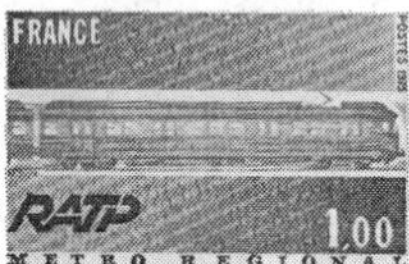

Metro Regional Train
A673

"Gazelle" Helicopter
A674

1975

1436 A673 1fr ind & brt bl 1.00 30
1437 A674 1.30fr vio bl & grn 80 40

French technical achievements.
Issue dates: 1fr, June 21; 1.30fr, May 31.

Youth and Flasks, Symbols of Study and Growth
A675

1975, June 21

1438 A675 70c red pur & blk 40 20

Student Health Foundation.

People's Theater, Bussang, and Maurice Pottecher—A676

1975, Aug. 9 Engraved *Perf. 13*

1439 A676 85c multi 45 30

80th anniversary of the People's Theater at Bussang, founded by Maurice Pottecher.

Regions of France

Central France
A677

Aquitaine
A678

Limousin
A679

Picardy
A680

Burgundy
A681

Loire
A682

Guyana
A683

Auvergne
A684

Poitou-Charentes
A685

Southern Pyrenees—A686

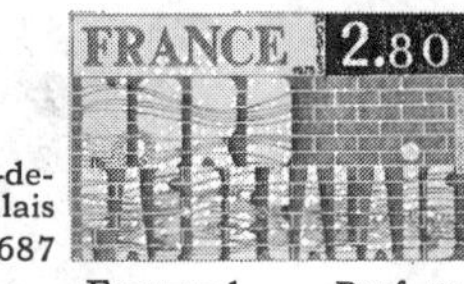

Pas-de-Calais
A687

1975–76 Engraved *Perf. 13*

1440	A677	25c bl & yel grn	30	15
1441	A678	60c multi	35	15
1442	A679	70c multi	55	15
1443	A680	85c bl, grn & org	60	30
1444	A681	1fr red, yel & mar	75	20
1445	A682	1.15fr bl, bis & grn	75	20
1446	A683	1.25fr multi	75	20
1447	A684	1.30fr dk bl & red	75	30
1448	A685	1.90fr sl, ol & Prus bl	1.25	30
1449	A686	2.20fr multi	1.40	55
1450	A687	2.80fr car, bl & blk	2.00	75
		Nos. 1440-1450 (11)	9.45	3.25

Issue dates—1975: 85c, Nov. 15; 1fr, Oct. 25; 1.15fr, Sept. 6; 1.30fr, Oct. 4; 1.90fr, Dec. 6; 2.80fr, Dec. 13. 1976: 25c, Jan. 31; 2.20fr, Jan. 10; 60c, May 22; 70c, May 29; 125fr, Oct. 16.

French Flag, F.-H. Manhes, Jean Verneau, Pierre Kaan
A690

1975, Sept. 27

1453 A690 1fr multi 45 25

Liberation of concentration camps, 30th anniversary. F.-H. Manhes (1889–1959), Jean Verneau (1890–1944) and Pierre Kaan (1903–1945) were French resistance leaders, imprisoned in concentration camps.

Monument, by Joseph Riviere
A691

1975, Oct. 11

1454 A691 70c multi 40 20

Land Mine Demolition Service, 30th anniversary. Monument was erected in Alsace to honor land mine victims.

Symbols of Suburban Living
A692

1975, Oct. 18

1455 A692 1.70fr brn, bl & grn 1.00 55

Creation of new towns.

Women and Rainbow
A693

1975, Nov. 8 Photogravure

1456 A693 1.20fr sil & multi 60 35

International Women's Year 1975.

Saint-Nazaire Bridge
A694

1975, Nov. 8 Engraved

1457 A694 1.40fr bl, ind & grn 85 25

French and Russian Flags
A695

Frigate Melpomene
A696

1975, Nov. 22

1458 A695 1.20fr bl, red & ocher 65 35

Franco-Soviet diplomatic relations, 50th anniversary.

1975, Dec. 6

1459 A696 90c multi 50 30

Gallic Coin Type of 1975

1976, Jan. 1 Typo. *Perf. 13½x14*

1460	A663	50c lt grn & brn	1.20	45
1461	A663	60c lil & brn	2.00	45
1462	A663	90c org & brn	2.25	1.10
1463	A663	1.60fr vio & brn	4.50	3.00

Nos. 1460–1463 are known only precanceled. See second note after No. 132.

Lintel, St. Genis des Fontaines Church—A697

Venus of Brassempouy (Paleolithic)
A698

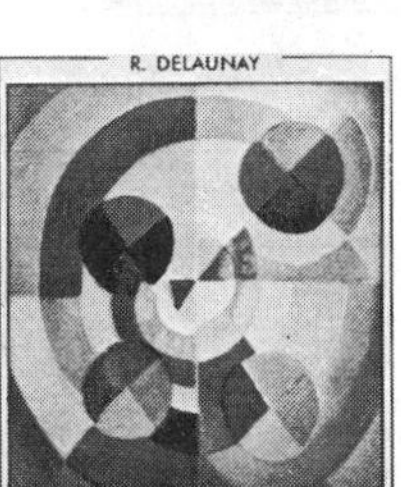

"The Joy of Life," by Robert Delaunay—A699

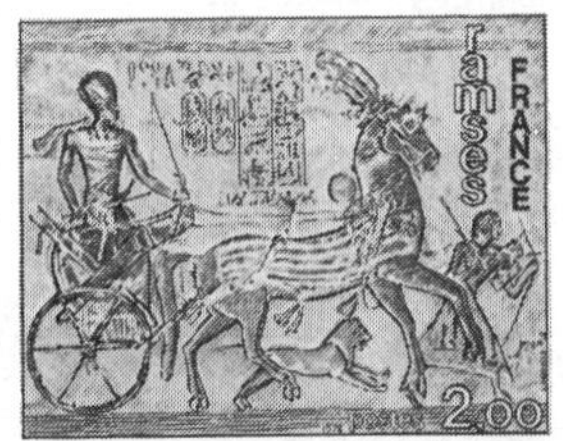

Ramses II, from Abu Simbel Temple, Egypt—A700

Still Life, by Maurice de Vlaminck—A701

1976 Engr. *Perf. 13*

1464 A697 2fr bl & sl bl 1.30 90
1465 A698 2fr dk brn & yel 1.30 90

Photo. *Perf. 12½x13*

1466 A699 2fr multi 1.30 90

Engr. *Perf. 13x12½*

1467 A700 2fr multi 1.10 70

Perf. 13

1468 A701 2fr multi 1.10 70
Nos. 1464-1468 (5) 6.10 4.10

Issue dates: No. 1464, Jan. 24; No. 1465, Mar. 6; No. 1466, July 24; No. 1467, Sept. 4; No. 1468, Dec. 18.

Tourist Issue

Chateau Fort de Bonaguil
A702

Lodève Cathedral
A703

Biarritz
A704

Thiers
A705

Ussel
A706

Chateau de Malmaison
A707

1976 Engraved *Perf. 13*

1469 A702 1fr multi 45 15
1470 A703 1.10fr vio bl 55 20
1471 A704 1.40fr multi 60 25
1472 A705 1.70fr multi 75 20
1473 A706 2fr multi 1.10 25
1474 A707 3fr multi 1.40 35
Nos. 1469-1474 (6) 4.85 1.40

Issue dates: 1fr, 2fr, July 10; 1.10fr, Nov. 13; 1.40fr, Sept. 25; 1.70fr, Oct. 9; 3fr, Apr. 10.

Destroyers, Association Emblem
A708

1976, Apr. 24

1475 A708 1fr vio bl, mag & lem 75 35

Naval Reserve Officers Association, 50th anniversary.

Gate, Rouen
A709

Young Person
A710

1976, Apr. 24

1476 A709 80c ol gray & sal 45 20

49th Congress of the Federation of French Philatelic Societies, Rouen, Apr. 23–May 2.

1976, Apr. 27

1477 A710 60c bl grn, ind & car 45 20

JUVAROUEN 76, International Youth Philatelic Exhibition, Rouen, Apr. 25–May 2.

Europa Issue 1976

Ceramic Pitcher, Strasbourg, 18th Century
A711

Design: 1.20fr, Sevres porcelain plate and CEPT emblem.

1976, May 8 Photo. *Perf. 13*

1478 A711 80c multi 45 25
1479 A711 1.20fr multi 75 35

Count de Vergennes and Benjamin Franklin—A712

1976, May 15 Engr. *Perf. 13*

1480 A712 1.20fr multi 60 45

American Bicentennial.

Battle of Verdun Memorial
A713

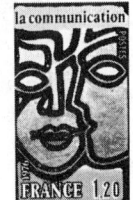

Communication
A714

1976, June 12 Engraved

1481 A713 1fr multi 45 25

Battle of Verdun, 60th anniversary.

1976, June 12 Photogravure

1482 A714 1.20fr multi 55 35

Troncais Forest
A715

Cross of Lorraine
A716

1976, June 19 Engraved

1483 A715 70c grn & multi 40 25

Protection of the environment.

1976, June 19

1484 A716 1fr multi 45 25

Association of Free French, 30th anniversary.

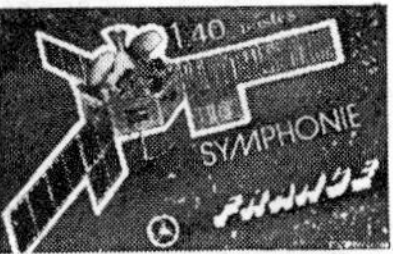

Symphonie Communications Satellite
A717

1976, June 26 Photogravure

1485 A717 1.40fr multi 80 40

French technical achievements.

Gallic Coin Type of 1975

1976, July 1 Typo. *Perf. 13½x14*

1487 A663 52c ver & dk brn 80 30
1488 A663 62c vio & dk brn 1.75 60
1489 A663 95c tan & dk brn 2.00 90
1490 A663 1.70fr dk bl & dk brn 3.75 2.25

Nos. 1487–1490 are known only precanceled. See second note after No. 132.

Paris Summer Festival
A719

1976, July 10 Engraved

1491 A719 1fr multi 55 25

Summer festival in Tuileries Gardens, Paris.

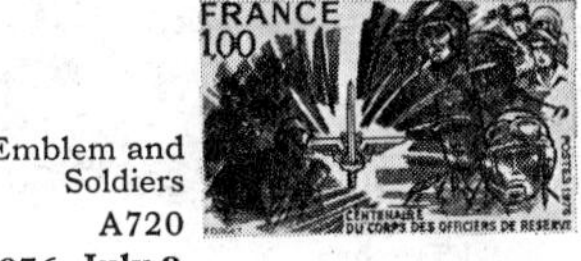

Emblem and Soldiers
A720

1976, July 8

1492 A720 1fr blk, dp bl & mag 50 30

Officers Reserve Corps, centenary.

Sailing
A721

1976, July 17

1493 A721 1.20fr bl, blk & vio 60 30

21st Olympic Games, Montreal, Canada, July 17–Aug. 1.

Marianne Type of 1971–74

1976 Typographed *Perf. 14x13*

1494 A555 80c green 50 4

Engraved *Perf. 13*

1495 A555 80c green 50 4
a. Booklet pane of 10 5.00
1496 A555 1fr car rose 60 5
a. Booklet pane of 5 4.50
b. Booklet pane of 10 8.00

No. 1495 issued in booklets only. "POSTES" 6mm. long on Nos. 1292A and 1494; 4mm. on others.

Nos. 1494 and 1496 were issued untagged in 1977.

Coil Stamps

1976, Aug. 1 Engr. ***Perf. 13 Horiz.***

1497	A555	80c green	60	30
1498	A555	1fr car rose	60	30

Red control number on back of every 10th stamp.

Woman's Head, by Jean Carzou—A722

1976, Sept. 18 Engr. ***Perf. 13x12½***

1499	A722	2fr multi	1.10	70

Old and New Telephones—A723

1976, Sept. 25 Engr. ***Perf. 13***

1500	A723	1fr multi	50	20

Centenary of first telephone call by Alexander Graham Bell, Mar. 10, 1876.

Festival Emblem and Trophy, Pyrenees, Hercules and Pyrène
A724

Police Emblem
A725

1976, Oct. 2

1501	A724	1.40fr multi	70	35

10th International Tourist Film Festival, Tarbes, Oct. 4–10.

1976, Oct. 9 Engr. ***Perf. 13***

1502	A725	1.10fr ultra, red & ol	65	25

National Police, help and protection.

Atomic Particle Accelerator, Diagram—A726

1976, Oct. 22 Photogravure

1503	A726	1.40fr multi	80	35

European Center for Nuclear Research (CERN).

"Exhibitions"
A727

1976, Nov. 20 Engr. ***Perf. 13***

1504	A727	1.50fr multi	75	30

Trade Fairs and Exhibitions.

Abstract Design
A728

1976, Nov. 27 Photogravure

1505	A728	1.10fr multi	60	30

Customs Service.

Atlantic Museum, Port Louis—A729

1976, Dec. 4 Engraved

1506	A729	1.45fr grnsh bl & ol	75	35

Regions of France

Réunion
A730

Martinique
A731

Franche-Comté
A732

Brittany
A733

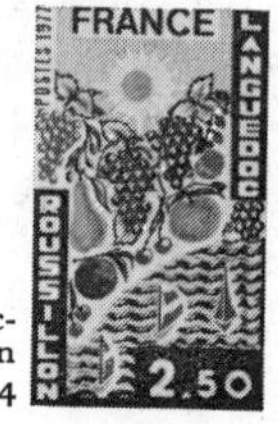

Languedoc-Roussillon
A734

Rhône-Alps
A735

Champagne-Ardennes
A736

Alsace
A737

Photo. (1.45fr, 1.50fr, 2.50fr); Engr.
1977 ***Perf. 13***

1507	A730	1.45fr grn & lil rose	75	25
1508	A731	1.50fr multi	80	25
1509	A732	2.10fr multi	1.10	30
1510	A733	2.40fr multi	1.50	35
1511	A734	2.50fr multi	1.50	40
1512	A735	2.75fr Prus bl	1.75	45
1513	A736	3.20fr multi	2.00	75
1514	A737	3.90fr multi	2.50	90
		Nos. 1507-1514 (8)	11.90	3.65

Issue dates: 1.45fr, Feb. 5; 1.50fr, Jan. 29; 2.10fr, Jan. 8; 2.40fr, Feb. 19; 2.50fr, Jan. 15; 2.75fr, Jan. 22; 3.20fr, Apr. 16; 3.90fr, Feb. 26.

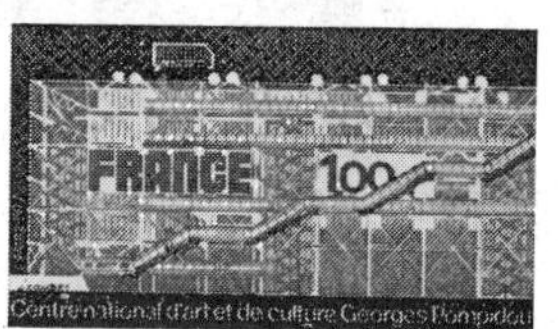

Pompidou Cultural Center—A738

1977, Feb. 5 Engr. ***Perf. 13***

1515	A738	1fr multi	45	15

Inauguration of the Georges Pompidou National Center for Art and Culture, Paris.

Dunkirk Harbor
A739

1977, Feb. 12

1516	A739	50c multi	30	12

Expansion of Dunkirk harbor facilities.

Bridge at Mantes, by Corot—A740

Virgin and Child, by Rubens
A741

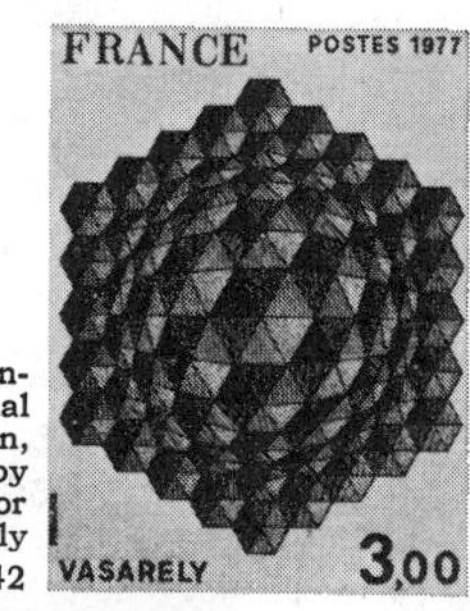

Tridimensional Design, by Victor Vasarely
A742

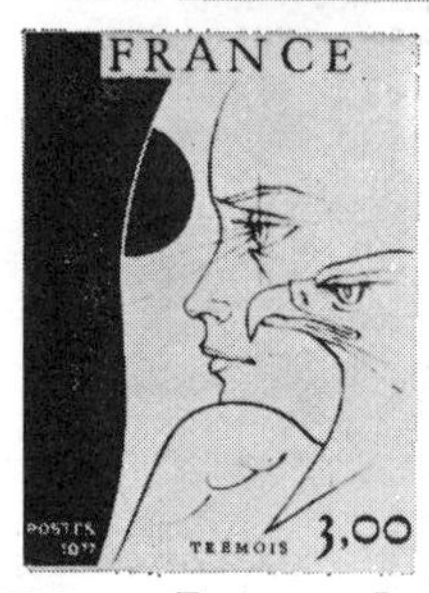

Head and Eagle, by Pierre-Yves Tremois
A743

1977 Engr. ***Perf. 13x12½***

1517	A740	2fr multi	1.00	60

Perf. 12x13

1518	A741	2fr multi	1.10	40

Perf. 12½x13

1519	A742	3fr ultra & sl grn	1.50	70

Photogravure

1520	A743	3fr dk red & blk	1.50	75

Issue dates: No. 1517, Feb. 12; No. 1518, Nov. 5; No. 1519, Apr. 7; No. 1520, Sept. 17.

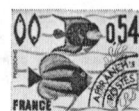

Hand Holding Torch and Sword
A744

Pisces
A745

1977, Mar. 5 Engr. ***Perf. 13***

1521	A744	80c ultra & multi	50	20

"France remembers its dead."

1977–78 Engraved ***Perf. 13***

Zodiac Signs: 58c, Cancer. 61c, Sagittarius. 68c, Taurus. 73c, Aries. 78c, Libra. 1.05fr, Scorpio. 1.15fr, Capricorn. 1.25fr, Leo. 1.85fr, Aquarius. 2fr, Virgo. 2.10fr, Gemini.

1522	A745	54c vio bl	75	35
1523	A745	58c emerald	1.25	45

1524 A745 61c brt bl 65 35
1525 A745 68c dp brn 90 50
1526 A745 73c rose car 2.00 90
1527 A745 78c vermilion 80 50
1528 A745 1.05fr brt lil 2.00 1.10
1529 A745 1.15fr orange 3.00 1.50
1530 A745 1.25fr lt ol grn 1.40 90
1531 A745 1.85fr sl grn 3.25 1.40
1532 A745 2fr bl grn 3.75 2.50
1533 A745 2.10fr lil rose 2.00 1.50
Nos. 1522-1533 (12) 21.75 11.95

Issue dates: 54c, 68c, 1.05fr, 1.85fr, Apr. 1, 1977. Others, 1978.
Nos. 1522-1533 are known only precanceled. See second note after No. 132.

Europa Issue

Village in Provence
A746

Design: 1.40fr, Brittany port.

1977, Apr. 23
1534 A746 1fr multi 50 15
1535 A746 1.40fr multi 75 25

Flowers and Gardening
A747

1977, Apr. 23 Engr. ***Perf. 13***
1536 A747 1.70fr multi 75 35
National Horticulture Society, centenary.

Symbolic Flower
A748

1977, May 7
1537 A748 1.40fr multi 60 30
International Flower Show, Nantes, May 12–23.

Battle of Cambray
A749

1977, May 14
1538 A749 80c multi 45 15
300th anniversary of the capture of Cambray and the incorporation of Cambresis District into France.

Carmes Church, School, Map of France
A750

Modern Constructions
A751

1977, May 14
1539 A750 1.10fr multi 55 25
Catholic Institutes in France.

1977, May 21
1540 A751 1.10fr multi 50 25
European Federation of the Construction Industry.

Annecy Castle
A752

1977, May 28
1541 A752 1fr multi 55 15
Congress of the Federation of French Philatelic Societies, Annecy, May 28–30.

Tourist Issue

Abbey, Pont-à-Mousson
A753

Abbey Tower, Saint-Amand-les-Eaux
A754

Collegiate Church of Dorat
A755

Fontenay Abbey
A756

Bayeux Cathedral
A757

Chateau de Vitré
A758

1977 Engraved ***Perf. 13***
1542 A753 1.25fr multi 55 20
1543 A754 1.40fr multi 65 25
1544 A755 1.45fr multi 65 25
1545 A756 1.50fr multi 75 30
1546 A757 1.90fr blk & yel 80 35
1547 A758 2.40fr blk & yel 1.10 25
Nos. 1542-1547 (6) 4.50 1.60

Issue dates: 1.25fr, Oct. 1; 1.40fr, Sept. 17; 1.45fr, July 16; 1.50fr, June 4; 1.90fr, July 9; 2.40fr, Sept. 24.

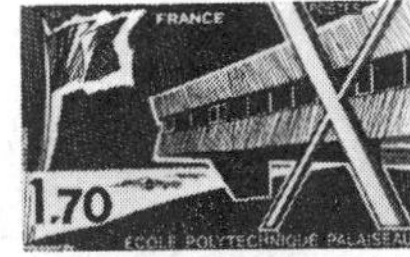

Polytechnic School and "X"
A759

1977, June 4 Engr. ***Perf. 13***
1548 A759 1.70fr multi 80 35
Relocation at Palaiseau of Polytechnic School, founded 1794.

Soccer and Cup—A760

1977, June 11
1549 A760 80c multi 70 30
Soccer Cup of France, 60th anniversary.

De Gaulle Memorial
A761

Stylized Map of France
A762

Photogravure & Embossed

1977, June 18
1550 A761 1fr gold & multi 60 15
5th anniversary of dedication of De Gaulle memorial at Colombey-les-Deux-Eglises.

1977, June 18 Engr. ***Perf. 13***
1551 A762 1.10fr ultra & red 60 25
French Junior Chamber of Commerce.

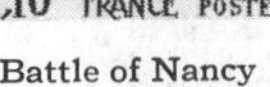

Battle of Nancy
A763

Arms of Burgundy
A764

1977, June 25
1552 A763 1.10fr bl & sl 60 30
Battle of Nancy between the Dukes of Burgundy and Lorraine, 500th anniversary.

1977, July 2
1553 A764 1.25fr ol brn & sl grn 65 30
Annexation of Burgundy by the French Crown, 500th anniversary.

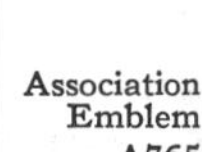

Association Emblem
A765

1977, July 8
1554 A765 1.40fr ultra, ol & red 70 30
French-speaking Parliamentary Association.

Red Cicada
A766

1977, Sept. 10 Photo. ***Perf. 13***
1555 A766 80c multi 45 25
Nature protection.

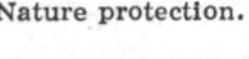

French Handicrafts
A767

1977, Oct. 1 Engraved ***Perf. 13***
1556 A767 1.40fr multi 60 25
French craftsmen.

Industry and Agriculture
A768

1977, Oct. 22
1557 A768 80c brn & ol 40 20
Economic and Social Council, 30th anniversary.

Table Tennis
A769

1977, Dec. 17 Engr. ***Perf. 13***
1558 A769 1.10fr multi 50 25
French Table Tennis Federation, 50th anniversary, and French team, gold medal winner, Birmingham.

Abstract, by Roger Excoffon—A770

1977, Dec. 17 ***Perf. 13x12½***
1559 A770 3fr multi 1.50 75

Sabine, after David
A771

1977–78		**Engraved**		**Perf. 13**	
1560	A771	1c slate		3	3
1561	A771	2c brt vio		3	3
1562	A771	5c sl grn		3	3
1563	A771	10c red brn		5	3
1564	A771	15c Prus bl		8	3
1565	A771	20c brt grn		15	3
1566	A771	30c orange		15	4
1567	A771	50c red lil		25	4
1568	A771	80c green		1.35	4
a.		Bklt. pane of 10		13.50	
1569	A771	80c olive		30	4
1570	A771	1fr red		1.50	5
a.		Bklt. pane of 5		8.00	
b.		Bklt. pane of 10		16.00	
1571	A771	1fr green		60	5
a.		Bklt. pane of 10		6.00	
1572	A771	1.20fr red		60	5
a.		Bklt. pane of 5		3.00	
b.		Bklt. pane of 10		6.00	
1573	A771	1.40fr brt bl		1.50	20
1574	A771	1.70fr grnsh bl		75	20
1575	A771	2fr emerald		75	6
1576	A771	2.10fr lil rose		80	10
1577	A771	3fr dk brn		1.00	35
		Nos. 1560-1577 (18)		9.92	1.40

Coil Stamps

1978			**Perf. 13 Horiz.**	
1578	A771	80c brt grn	1.50	45
1579	A771	1fr brt grn	90	40
1579A	A771	1fr brt red	1.50	45
1579B	A771	1.20fr brt red	90	40

Percheron, by Jacques Birr
A772

Osprey
A773

1978		**Photo.**	**Perf. 13**	
1580	A772	1.70fr multi	90	45
		Engraved		
1581	A773	1.80fr multi	80	25

Nature protection.
Issue dates: 1.70fr, Jan. 7; 1.80fr, Oct. 14.

Examination

The Catalogue editors cannot undertake to appraise, identify or pass upon genuineness or condition of stamps.

Tournament, 1662, Etching
A774

Institut de France and Pont des Arts, Paris, by Bernard Buffet
A776

Horses, by Yves Brayer—A777

1978		**Engr.**	**Perf. 12x13**	
1582	A774	2fr black	1.00	50
		Perf. 13x12		
1584	A776	3fr multi	1.50	50
1585	A777	3fr multi	1.40	60

Issue dates: 2fr, Jan. 14; No. 1584, Feb. 4; No. 1585, Dec. 9.

Communications School and Tower
A778

1978, Jan. 19		**Engr.**	**Perf. 13**	
1586	A778	80c Prus bl	35	15

National Telecommunications School, centenary.

Swedish and French Flags, Map of Saint Barthelemy—A779

1978, Jan. 19				
1587	A779	1.10fr multi	50	25

Centenary of the reunion with France of Saint Barthelemy Island, West Indies.

Regions of France

Ile de France
A780

Tanker, Refinery, Flower, Upper Normandy
A781

Lower Normandy
A782

1978		**Photo.**	**Perf. 13**	
1588	A780	1fr red, bl & blk	65	15
		Engr.		
1589	A781	1.40fr multi	80	25
		Photogravure		
1590	A782	1.70fr multi	90	35

Issue dates. 1fr, Mar. 4; 1.40fr, Jan. 21; 1.70fr, Mar. 31.

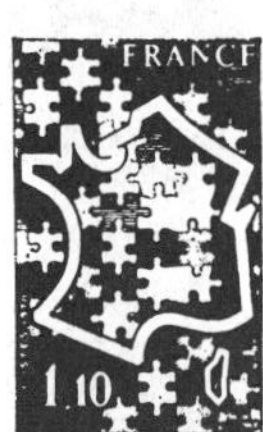

Stylized Map of France
A788

Young Stamp Collector
A789

1978, Feb. 11		**Engr.**	**Perf. 13**	
1596	A788	1.10fr vio & grn	50	15

Program of administrative changes, 15th anniversary.

1978, Feb. 25				
1597	A789	80c multi	35	15

JUVEXNIORT, Youth Philatelic Exhibition, Niort, Feb. 25–March 5.

Tourist Issue

Verdon Gorge
A790

Saint-Saturnin Church
A792

Pont Neuf, Paris
A791

Our Lady of Bec-Hellouin Abbey
A793

Chateau D'Esquelbecq
A794

Aubazine Abbey
A795

Fontevraud Abbey
A796

1978		**Engraved**	**Perf. 13**	
1598	A790	50c multi	25	10
1599	A791	80c multi	40	10
1600	A792	1fr black	45	10
1601	A793	1.10fr multi	50	15
1602	A794	1.10fr multi	45	15
1603	A795	1.25fr car & brn	60	20
1604	A796	1.70fr multi	75	25
		Nos. 1598-1604 (7)	3.40	1.05

Issue dates: 1.25fr, Feb. 18; 50c, Mar. 6; No. 1601, Mar. 26; 80c, May 27; 1fr, June 10; 1.70fr, June 3; No. 1602, June 17.

Fish and Under-water Flora
A797

1978, Apr. 15		**Photo.**	**Perf. 13**	
1605	A797	1.25fr multi	60	30

Port Cros National Park, 15th anniversary.

Flowers, Butterflies and Houses
A798

1978, Apr. 22		**Engr.**	**Perf. 13**	
1606	A798	1.70fr multi	1.50	30

50th anniversary of the beautification of France campaign.

Hands Shielding Source of Heat and Light—A799

1978, Apr. 22

1607 A799 1fr multi 60 15

Energy conservation.

World War I Memorial near Lens A800

Fountain of the Innocents, Paris A801

1978, May 6

1608 A800 2fr lem & mag 1.00 35

Colline Notre Dame de Lorette memorial of World War I.

Europa Issue 1978

Design: 1.40fr, Flower Park Fountain, Paris.

1978, May 6

1609 A801 1fr multi 55 15
1610 A801 1.40fr multi 70 25

Maurois Palace, Troyes A802

1978, May 13

1611 A802 1fr multi 45 15

51st Congress of the Federation of French Philatelic Societies, Troyes, May 13–15.

Roland Garros Tennis Court and Player—A803

1978, May 27

1612 A803 1fr multi 55 15

Roland Garros Tennis Court, 50th anniversary.

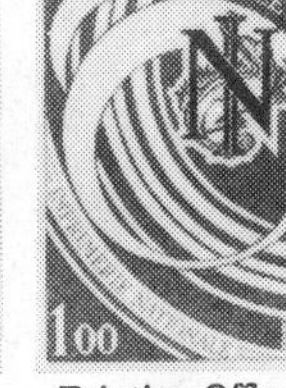

Hand and Plant A804

Printing Office Emblem—A805

1978, Sept. 9 Engr. *Perf. 13*

1613 A804 1.30fr brn, red & grn 60 20

Encouragement of handicrafts.

1978, Sept. 23

1614 A805 1fr multi 45 15

National Printing Office, established 1538.

Fortress, Besançon, and Collegiate Church, Dole A806

Valenciennes and Maubeuge A807

1978

1615 A806 1.20fr multi 60 20
1616 A807 1.20fr multi 60 20

Reunion of Franche-Comté and Valenciennes and Maubeuge with France, 300th anniversary.

Issue dates: No. 1615, Sept. 23, No. 1616, Sept. 30.

Sower Type of 1906–1937 and Academy Emblem A808

Gymnasts, Strasbourg Cathedral, Storks A809

1978, Oct. 7

1617 A808 1fr multi 50 20

Academy of Philately, 50th anniversary.

1978, Oct. 21

1618 A809 1fr multi 55 15

19th World Gymnastics Championships, Strasbourg, Oct. 23–26.

Various Sports A810

Polish Veterans' Monument A811

1978, Oct. 21

1619 A810 1fr multi 60 20

Sports for all.

1978, Nov. 11

1620 A811 1.70fr multi 75 35

Polish veterans of World War II.

Railroad Car and Monument, Compiègne Forest, Rethondes—A812

1978, Nov. 11 Engr. *Perf. 13*

1621 A812 1.20fr indigo 55 15

60th anniversary of World War I armistice.

Handicapped People A813

1978, Nov. 18

1622 A813 1fr multi 45 15

Rehabilitation of the handicapped.

Human Rights Emblem A814

1978, Dec. 9 Engr. *Perf. 13*

1623 A814 1.70fr dk brn & bl 75 30

30th anniversary of Universal Declaration of Human Rights.

Child and IYC Emblem A815

1979, Jan. 6 Engr. *Perf. 13*

1624 A815 1.70fr multi 2.25 60

International Year of the Child.

"Music," 15th Century Miniature A816

1979, Jan. 13 *Perf. 13x12½*

1625 A816 2fr multi 90 35

Diana Taking a Bath, d'Ecouen Castle A817

Church at Auvers-on-Oise, by Vincent Van Gogh—A818

Head of Marianne, by Salvador Dali A819

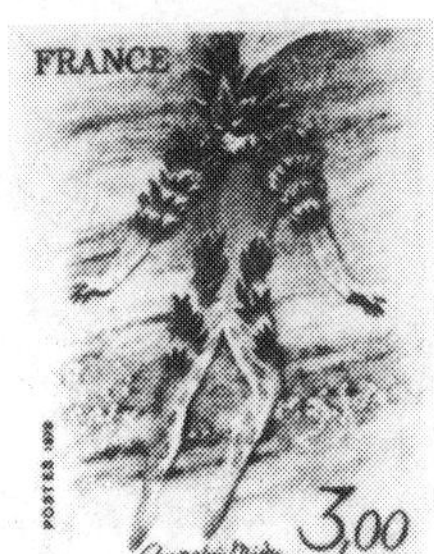

Fire Dancer from The Magic Flute, by Chaplain Midy—A820

1979 Photo. *Perf. 12½x13*

1626 A817 2fr multi 90 45
1627 A818 2fr multi 90 45
1628 A819 3fr multi 1.10 60
1629 A820 3fr multi 1.10 60

Issue dates: No. 1626, Sept. 22; No. 1627, Oct. 27; No. 1628, Nov. 19; No. 1629, Nov. 26.

Orange Agaric
A821

Mushrooms: 83c, Death trumpet. 1.30fr, Olive wood pleurotus. 2.25fr, Cauliflower claveria.

1979, Jan. 15 Engr. *Perf. 13*

1630	A821	64c	orange	50	30
1631	A821	83c	brown	65	40
1632	A821	1.30fr	yel bis	90	60
1633	A821	2.25fr	brn pur	1.40	1.00

Nos. 1630–1633 are known only precanceled. See second note after No. 132.

Victor Segalen
A822

1979, Jan. 20

1634	A822	1.50fr	multi	60	20

Victor Segalen (1878–1919), physician, explorer and writer.

Hibiscus and Palms
A823

1979, Feb. 3

1635	A823	35c	multi	20	10

International Flower Festival, Martinique.

Buddha, Stupas, Temple of Borobudur
A824

1979, Feb. 24

1636	A824	1.80fr	ol & sl grn	75	35

Save the Temple of Borobudur, Java, campaign.

Boy, by Poulbot
A825

1979, Mar. 24 Photogravure

1637	A825	1.20fr	multi	50	20

Francisque Poulbot (1879–1946).

Tourist Issue

Chateau de Maisons, Laffitte
A826

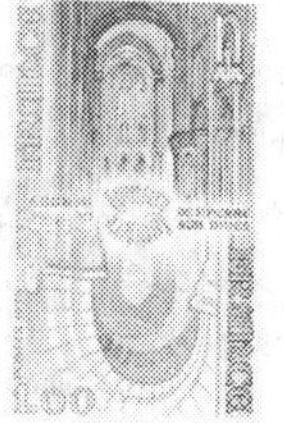

Bernay and St. Pierre sur Dives Abbeys
A827

View of Auray
A827a

Steenvorde Windmill
A828

Wall Painting, Niaux Cave
A829

Royal Palace, Perpignan
A830

1979 Engraved *Perf. 13*

1638	A826	45c	multi	20	6
1639	A827	1fr	multi	40	15
1640	A827a	1fr	multi	40	15
1641	A828	1.20fr	multi	50	20
1642	A829	1.50fr	multi	55	15
1643	A830	1.70fr	multi	70	25
		Nos. 1638-1643 (6)		2.75	96

Issue dates: 45c, Oct. 6; No. 1639, June 16; No. 1640, June 30; 1.20fr, May 12; 1.50fr, July 9; 1.70fr, Apr. 21.

Honey Bee
A831

1979, Mar. 31 Engr. *Perf. 13*

1644	A831	1fr	multi	50	15

Nature protection.

St. Germain des Prés Abbey
A832

1979, Apr. 21

1645	A842	1.40fr	multi	55	25

Europa Issue 1979

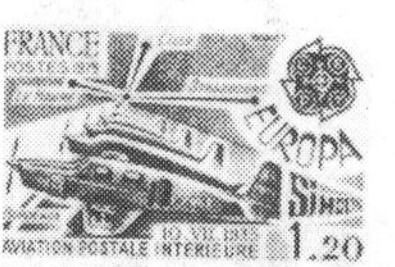

Simoun Mail Monoplanes, 1935, and Map of Mail Routes—A833

Design: 1.70fr, Floating spheres used on Seine during siege of Paris, 1870.

1979, Apr. 28

1646	A843	1.20fr	multi	60	25
1647	A843	1.70fr	multi	75	30

Ship and View of Nantes
A834

1979, May 5 Engr. *Perf. 13*

1648	A884	1.20fr	multi	50	25

52nd National Congress of French Philatelic Societies, Nantes, May 5–7.

Royal Palace, 1789
A835

1979, May 19

1649	A885	1fr	car rose & pur	40	20

European Elections
A836

1979, May 19 Photo. *Perf. 13*

1650	A886	1.20fr	multi	50	15

European Parliament, first direct elections, June 10.

Joan of Arc Monument
A837

1979, May 24 Engraved

1651	A887	1.70fr	brt lil rose	70	25

Joan of Arc, the Maid of Orleans (1412–1431).

Felix Guyon and Catheters
A840

1979, June 23

1652	A840	1.80fr	sep & bl	70	25

Felix Guyon (1831–1920), urologist.

Lantern Tower, La Rochelle
A841

Telecom '79
A842

Towers: 88c, Chartres Cathedral. 1.40fr, Bourges Cathedral. 2.35fr, Amiens Cathedral.

1979, Aug. 13 Engr. *Perf. 13*

1653	A841	68c	vio brn & blk	50	25
1654	A841	88c	ultra & blk	65	35
1655	A841	1.40fr	gray grn & blk	90	75
1656	A841	2.35fr	dl brn & blk	1.40	90

Nos. 1653–1656 are known only precanceled. See second note after No. 132.

See Nos. 1684-1687.

1979, Sept. 22

1657	A842	1.10fr	multi	40	15

3rd World Telecommunications Exhibition.

Sabine Type of 1977–78

1979-81 Engr. *Perf. 13*

1658	A771	40c	('81)	15	5
1659	A771	60c	('81)	20	5
1660	A771	70c	vio bl	30	10
1661	A771	90c	('81)	35	5
1662	A771	1fr	gray ol	30	5
1663	A771	1.10fr	green	90	5
1664	A771	1.20fr	grn ('80)	50	5
1665	A771	1.30fr	rose red	90	5
1666	A771	1.40fr	rose red ('80)	55	5
1667	A771	1.60fr	purple	1.00	10
1668	A771	1.80fr	ocher	75	15
1669	A771	3.50fr	('81)	1.10	5
1670	A771	4fr	('81)	1.25	5
1671	A771	5fr	('81)	1.50	5
		Nos. 1658-1671 (14)		9.75	90

Coil Stamps

1979-80 *Perf. 13 Horiz.*

1674	A771	1.10fr	green	90	30
1675	A771	1.20fr	grn ('80)	55	30
1676	A771	1.30fr	rose red	90	30
1677	A771	1.40fr	rose red ('80)	65	30

Lorraine Region—A845

1979, Nov. 10

1678	A845	2.30fr multi	80	25

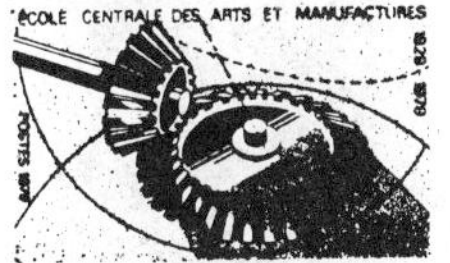

Gears—A847

1979, Nov. 17 *Perf. 13*

1680	A847	1.80fr multi	70	25

anniversary.

Judo Throw—A848

1979, Nov. 24 **Engr.**

1681	A848	1.60fr multi	60	25

World Judo Championships, Paris, Dec.

Violins—A849

1979, Dec. 10

1682	A849	1.30fr multi	50	20

Eurovision—A850

1980, Jan. 12 **Engraved** *Perf. 13×13½*

1683	A850	1.80fr multi	65	30

Tower Type of 1979

Designs: 76c, Chateau d'Angers. 99c, Chateau de Kerjean. 1.60fr, Chateau de Pierrefonds. 2.65fr, Chateau de Tarascon.

1980, Jan. 21 **Engraved**

1684	A841	76c	grnsh bl & blk	35	25
1685	A841	99c	sl grn & blk	50	35
1686	A841	1.60fr	red & blk	80	75
1687	A841	2.65fr	brn org & blk	1.40	90

Nos. 1684-1687 are known only precanceled. See second note after No. 132.

Self-portrait , by Albrecht Dürer, Philexfrance '82 Emblem—A851

Woman Holding Fan, by Ossip Zadkine—A852

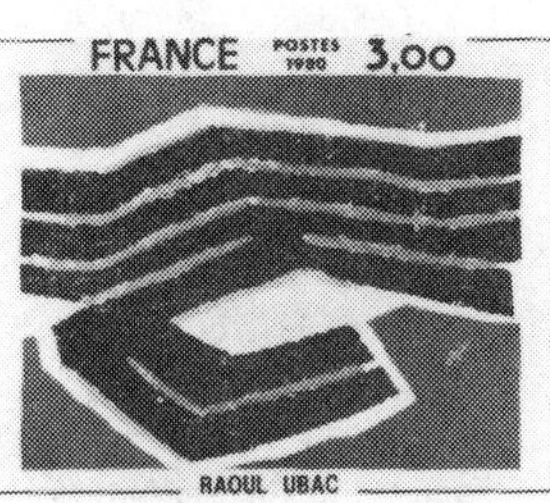

Abstract, by Raoul Ubak—A853

Hommage to J.S. Bach, by Jean Picart Le Doux—A854

Peasant, by Louis Le Nain—A855

Woman with Blue Eyes, by Modigliani—A856

Abstract, by Hans Hartung—A857

Perf. 12½x13, 13x12½

1980 **Engr., Engr. & Photo**

1688	A851	2fr	multi	70	40
1689	A852	3fr	multi	1.10	60
1690	A853	3fr	multi	1.10	60
1691	A854	3fr	multi	1.00	60
1692	A855	3fr	multi	1.00	45
1693	A856	4fr	multi	1.30	45
1694	A857	4fr	ultra & blk	1.25	50
		Nos. 1688-1694 (7)		7.45	3.60

Issue dates: #1688, June 7; #1689, Jan. 19; #1690, Feb. 2; #1691, Sept. 20; #1693, Oct. 26; #1692, Nov. 10; #1694, Dec. 20.

Giants of the North Festival—A858

1980, Feb. 16 *Perf. 13*

1695	A858	1.60fr	55	25

French Cuisine—A859

1980, Feb. 23

1696	A859	90c red & lt brn	35	20

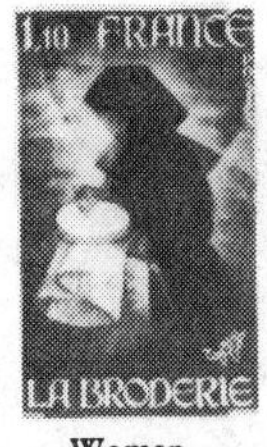

Woman Embroidering A860

Fight Against Cigarette Smoking A861

Photo. & Engr.

1980, Mar. 29 *Perf. 13*

1697	A860	1.10fr multi	45	20

Photo. *Perf. 13*

1980, Apr. 5

1698	A861	1.30fr multi	50	20

Europa Issue

Aristide Briand—A862

Design: 1.80fr, St. Benedict.

1980, Apr. 26 **Engraved** *Perf. 13*

1699	A862	1.30fr red & red brn	50	10
1700	A862	1.80fr multi	65	25

Aristide Briand (1862-1932), prime minister, 1909-1911, 1921-1922; St. Benedict, patron saint of Europe.

Liancourt, College, Map of Northwestern France—A863

1980, May 19 **Engraved** *Perf. 13*

1701	A863	2fr	dk grn & pur	70	30

National College of Arts and Handicrafts (founded by Larochefoucauld Liancourt) bicentenary

Cranes, Town Hall Tower, Dunkirk A864

1980, May 24

1702 A864 1.30fr multi 45 20

53rd National Congress of French Federation of Philatelic Societies, Dunkirk, May 24-26.

Tourist Issue

Cordes A865 — Montauban A867

Chateau de Maintenon—A866

St. Peter's Abbey, Solesmes—A868 — Puy Cathedral A869

1980 **Engraved** ***Perf. 13***

1703	A865 1.50fr multi		55	10
1704	A866 2fr multi		70	10
1705	A867 2.30fr multi		75	10
1706	A868 2.50fr multi		75	10
1707	A869 3.20fr multi		1.10	10
	Nos. 1703-1707 (5)		3.85	50

Issue dates: #1703, Apr. 5; #1704, June 7; #1705, May 7; #1706, Sept. 20; #1707, May 12.

Graellsia Isabellae—A870

1980, May 31 **Photo.**

1708 A870 1.10fr multi 45 16

See "Special Notices" at the front of this volume for data on the listing methods of this Catalogue, abbreviations, condition, prices and examination.

Association Emblem A871 — Marianne, French Architecture A872

1980, June 10 **Photo.**

1709 A871 1.30fr red & bl 45 20

International Public Relations Association, 25th anniversary.

1980, June 21 **Engr.**

1710 A872 1.50fr 50 25

Heritage Year.

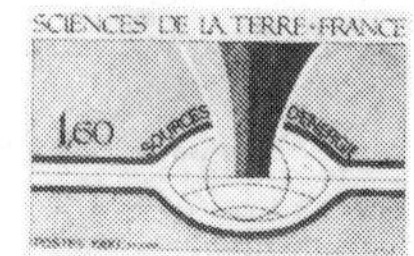

Earth Sciences—A873

1980, July 5

1711 A873 1.60fr 55 30

International Geological Congress.

Rochambeau's Landing—A874

1980, July 15

1712 A874 2.50fr multi 90 45

Rochambeau's landing at Newport, R.I. (American Revolution), bicentenary.

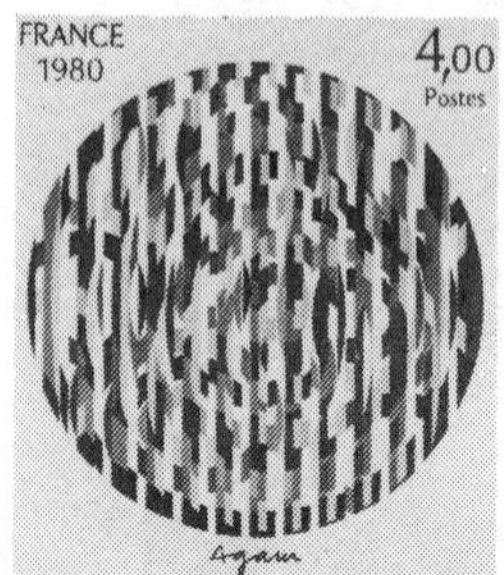

Message of Peace, by Yaacov Agam—A875

1980, Oct. 4 **Photo.** ***Perf. 11½x13***

1713 A875 4fr multi 1.25 60

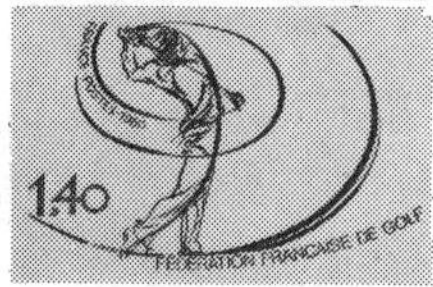

French Golf Federation—A876

1980, Oct. 18 **Engraved**

1714 A876 1.40fr multi 55 20

Comedie Francaise, 300th Anniversary—A877

1980, Oct. 18

1715 A877 2fr multi 70 20

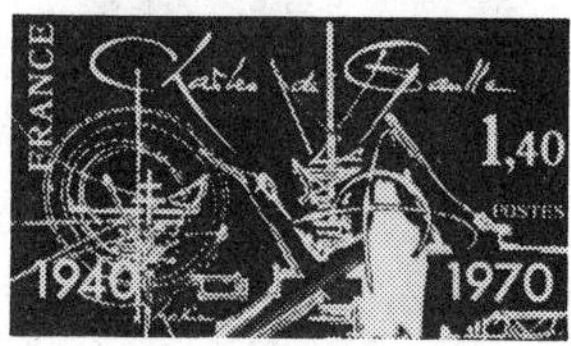

Charles de Gaulle—A878

1980, Nov. 10 **Photo.** ***Perf. 13***

1716 A878 1.40fr multi 55 15

40th anniversary of De Gaulle's appeal of June 18, and 10th anniversary of his death.

Guardsman—A879

1980, Nov. 24 **Engr.** ***Perf. 13***

1717 A879 1.70fr multi 55 25

Rambouillet Chateau—A880

1980, Dec. 6 **Engraved** ***Perf. 13***

1718 A880 2.20fr multi 70 20

Tower Type of 1979

Designs: 88c, Imperial Chapel, Ajaccio. 1.14fr, Astronomical Clock, Besancon. 1.84fr, Coucy Castle ruins. 3.05fr, Font-de-Gaume cave drawing, Les Eyzies de Tayac.

1981, Jan. 11 **Engraved** ***Perf. 13***

1719	A841	88c dp mag & blk	30	20
1720	A841	1.14fr ultra & blk	45	30
1721	A841	1.84fr dk grn & blk	70	45
1722	A841	3.05fr brn red & blk	1.25	80

Nos. 1719-1722 are known only precanceled. See second note after No. 132.

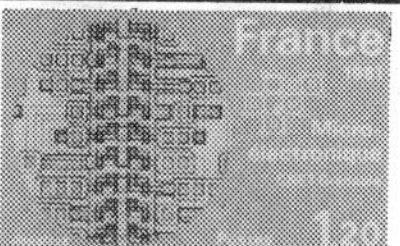

Microelectronics—A881

1981 **Photogravure**

1723	A881 1.20fr shown		40	15
1724	A881 1.20fr Biology		40	15
1725	A881 1.40fr Energy		45	10
1726	A881 1.80fr Marine exploration		60	30
1727	A881 2fr Telemetry		60	20
	Nos. 1723-1727 (5)		2.45	90

Issue dates: No. 1723, Feb. 5; others, Mar. 28.

Abstract, by Albert Gleizes—A882

1981, Feb. 28 ***Perf. 12½x13***

1728 A882 4fr multi 1.25 60

On the Bank of the Chou—A884

1981, Apr. 18 **Engr.** ***Perf. 13x12½***

1729 A883 2fr multi 60 40

Child Watering Smiling Map of France—A884

1981, Mar. 14 **Engraved** ***Perf. 13***

1730 A884 1.40fr multi 45 20

Sully Chateau, Rosny-sur-Seine—A885

1981, Mar. 21

1731 A885 2.50fr multi 75 15

Tourist Issue

Roman Temple, Nimes—A886

1981, Apr. 11 *Perf. 13*

1732 A886 1.70fr multi 55 20

Church of St. Jean, Lyon
A887

St. Anne d'Auray Basilica
A888

1981 Engr. *Perf. 13*

1733 A887 1.40fr dk red & dk brn 45 10
1734 A888 2.20fr bl & blk 70 20

Issue dates: 1.40fr, May 30; 2.20fr, July 4.

Vaucelles Abbey—A889

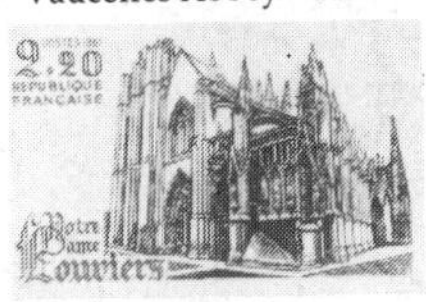

Notre Dame of Louviers—A890

1981

1735 A889 2fr red & blk 55 15
1736 A890 2.20fr red brn & dk brn 70 30

Issue dates: 2fr, Sept. 19; 2.20fr, Sept. 26.

Europa Issue 1981

Bouree—A891

Folkdances: 2fr, Sardane.

1981, May 4 *Perf. 13*

1737 A891 1.40fr multi 45 10
1738 A891 2fr multi 60 15

Bookbinding
A892

Cadets
A893

1981, Apr. 4 *Perf. 13*

1739 A892 1.50fr ol & car rose 45 20

1981, May 16

1740 A893 2.50fr multi 75 25

Military College at St. Maixent centenary.

Man Drawing Geometric Diagram—A894

1981, May 23 **Photo.**

1741 A894 2fr shown 60 40
1742 A894 2fr Faces 60 40

PHILEXFRANCE '82 Stamp Exhibition, Paris, June 11-21, 1982. Nos. 1741-1742 se-tenant with label showing exhibition emblem.

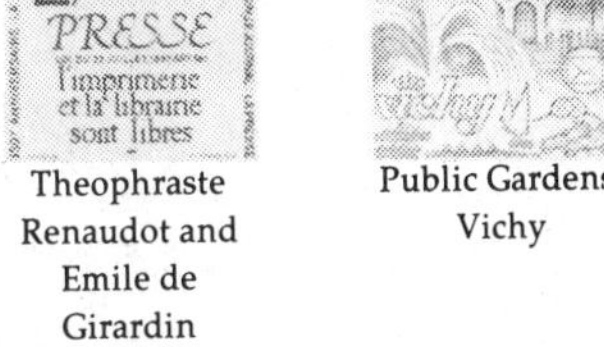

Theophraste Renaudot and Emile de Girardin
A895

Public Gardens, Vichy
A896

1981, May 30 **Engr.**

1743 A895 2.20fr blk & red 70 25

350th anniversary of La Gazette (founded by Renaudot), and death centenary of founder of Le Journal (de Girardin).

1981, June 6

1744 A896 1.40fr multi 45 10

54th National Congress of French Federation of Philatelic Societies, Vichy.

Higher National College for Commercial Studies Centenary—A897

1981, June 20 *Perf. 13*

1745 A897 1.40fr multi 45 15

Sea Shore Conservation—A898

1981, June 20

1746 A898 1.60fr multi 50 20

World Fencing Championship, Clermont-Ferrand, July 2-13—A899

1981, June 27

1747 A899 1.80fr multi 55 20

Sabine, after David—A900

1981, Sept. 1 **Engr.**

1755 A900 1.40fr green 45 10
1756 A900 1.60fr red 55 10
1757 A900 2.30fr blue 75 20

Coil Stamps

1981 Engr. ***Perf. 13 Vert.***

1758 A900 1.40fr green 50 30
1759 A900 1.60fr red 60 20

Highway Safety ("Drink or Drive")—A901

1981, Sept. 5 *Perf. 13*

1768 A901 1.60fr multi 55 10

45th Intl. PEN Club Congress
A902

Jules Ferry, Statesman
A903

1981, Sept *Perf. 13*

1769 A902 2fr multi 60 20

1981, Sept. 28 *Perf. 12½x13*

1770 A903 1.60fr multi 55 15

Free compulsory public school centenary.

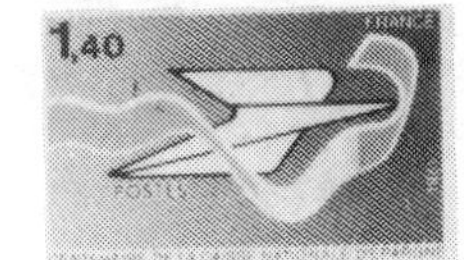

Natl. Savings Bank Centenary—A904

1981, Sept. 21 **Photo.** *Perf. 13*

1771 A904 1.40fr multi 45 20
1772 A904 1.60fr multi 55 15

The Divers, by Edouard Pignon—A905

1981, Oct. 3 *Perf. 13x12½*

1773 A905 4fr multi 1.10 40

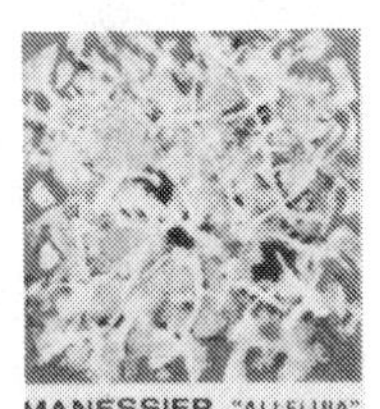

Alleluia, by Alfred Manessier—A906

1981, Dec. 19 **Photo.** *Perf. 12x13*

1774 A906 4fr multi 1.10 40

Tourist Issue

Saint-Emilion—A907

Crest—A908

1981 Engr. *Perf. 13x12½, 13 (2.90fr)*

1775 A907 2.60fr dk red & lt ol grn 70 20
1776 A908 2.90fr dk grn 75 10

Issue dates: #1775, Oct. 10; #1776, Nov. 28.

150th Anniv. of Naval Academy—A909

1981, Oct. 17 *Perf. 13*

1777 A909 1.40fr multi 45 15

St. Hubert Kneeling Before the Stag, 15th Cent. Sculpture A910

1981, Oct. 24

1778	A910	1.60fr multi	55	15

Museum of hunting and nature.

V. Schoelcher, J. Jaures, J. Moulin and the Pantheon—A911

1981, Nov. 2

1779	A911	1.60fr	55	15

Intl. Year of the Disabled—A912

1981, Nov. 7

1780	A912	1.60fr	55	10

Men Leading Cattle, 2nd Cent. Roman Mosaic—A913

1981, Nov. 14 *Perf. 13x12*

1781	A913	2fr multi	60	30

Virgil's birth bimillennium.

Martyrs of Chateaubriant A914

1981, Dec. 12 **Engr.** *Perf. 13*

1782	A914	1.40fr multi	55	20

Liberty, after Delacroix—A915

1982 **Engr.** *Perf. 13*

1783	A915	5c dk grn	3	3
1784	A915	10c dl red	5	3
1785	A915	15c brt rose lil	5	3
1786	A915	20c brt grn	6	3
1787	A915	30c orange	9	3
1788	A915	40c brown	12	3
1789	A915	50c lilac	15	8
1790	A915	60c	20	5
1791	A915	70c	20	5
1791A	A915	80c	25	5
1791B	A915	90c	30	10
1792	A915	1fr ol grn	30	10
1794	A915	1.40fr green	45	10
1795	A915	1.60fr grn ('82)	50	15
1796	A915	1.60fr red	50	10
1797	A915	1.80fr red ('82)	55	15
1798	A915	2fr brt yel grn	60	20
1799	A915	2.30fr blue	70	20
1800	A915	2.60fr bl ('82)	80	20
1801	A915	3fr	90	25
1802	A915	4fr	1.20	30
1803	A915	5fr gray bl	1.50	50

Coil Stamps
Perf. 13 Horiz.

1805	A915	1.40fr green	45	15
1806	A915	1.60fr red	50	15
1807	A915	1.60fr green	50	30
1807A	A915	1.80fr red	55	35

Tourist Issue

St. Pierre and Miquelon A916

Corsica A917

1982, Jan. 9

1808	A916	1.60fr dk bl & blk	50	15
1809	A917	1.90fr bl & red	60	20

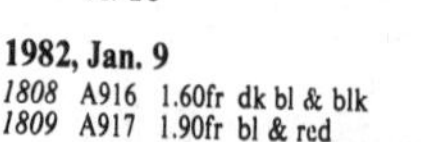

Renaissance Fountain, Aix-en Provence—A918

Collonges-la-Rouge—A919

Castle of Henry IV, Pau—A920

1982 *Perf. 13*

1810	A918	2fr multi	60	20
1811	A919	3fr multi	90	30
1812	A920	3fr multi	90	30

Issue dates, Aix-en-Provence, June 21, Collonges-la-Rouge, July 5, Pau, May 15.

Lille A921

Chateau Ripaille, Haute-Savoie A921a

1982 *Perf. 13x12½*

1813	A921	1.80fr multi	55	15
1813A	A921A	2.90fr multi	90	25

Issue dates: 1.80fr, Oct. 16; 2.90fr, Sept. 4.

Tower Type of 1979

Designs: 97c, Tanlay Castle, Yonne. 1.25fr, Salses Fort, Pyrenees-Orientales. 2.03fr, Montlhery Tower, Essonne. 3.36fr, Castle d'If, Bouches-du-Rhone.

1982, Jan. 11

1814	A841	97c	30	14
1815	A841	1.25fr	35	16
1816	A841	2.03fr	60	32
1817	A841	3.36fr	1.10	45

Nos. 1814-1817 are known only precanceled. See second note after No. 132.

800th Birth Anniv. of St. Francis of Assisi—A922

1982, Feb. 6

1818	A922	2fr blk & bl	60	20

Posts and Mankind A923

Posts and Technology A924

1982, Feb. 13 **Photo.**

1819	A923	2fr multi	60	20
1820	A924	2fr multi	60	20

PHILEXFRANCE '82 Stamp Exhibition, Paris, June 11-21. Nos. 1819-1820 se-tenant.

Souvenir Sheet

Marianne, by Jean Cocteau—A925

1982, June 11

1821		Sheet of 2	10.00	10.00
a.		A925 4fr red & bl		
b.		A925 6fr bl & red		

No. 1821 has gray marginal inscription, show emblem. Size: 100x71mm. Sold only with 20fr show admission ticket.

Scouting Year—A926

1982, Feb. 20 **Engr.**

1822	A926	2.30fr yel grn & blk	70	20

31st Natl. Census A927

Bale-Mulhouse Airport Opening A928

1982, Feb. 27 **Photo.**

1823	A927	1.60fr multi	50	15

1982, Mar. 15 **Engr.** *Perf. 13*

1824	A928	1.90fr multi	60	20

Fight Against Racism A929

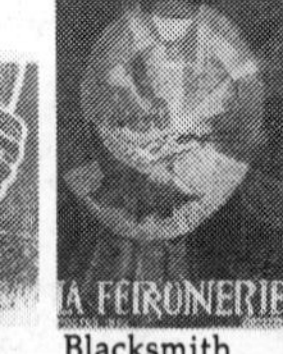

Blacksmith A930

1982, Mar. 20

1825	A929	2.30fr brn & red org	70	20

1982, Apr. 17

1826	A930	1.40fr	45	15

Europa 1982—A931

1982, Apr. 24

1827	A931	1.60fr Treaty of Rome, 1957	50	15
1828	A931	2.30fr Treaty of Verdun, 843	70	20

1982 World Cup—A932

1982, Apr. 28
1829 A932 1.80fr multi 55 15

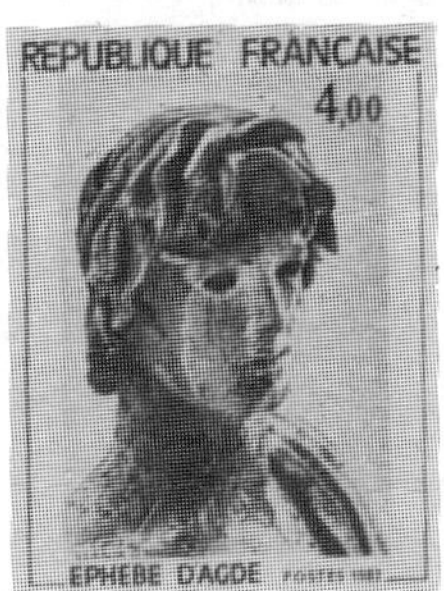

Young Greek Soldier, Hellenic Sculpture, Agude—A933

1982, May 15 ***Perf. 12½x13***
1830 A933 4fr multi 1.20 40

Embarkation for Ostia, by Claude Gellee—A934

The Lacemaker, by Vermeer—A935

Turkish Chamber, by Balthus—A936

1982 **Photo.** ***Perf. 13x12½***
1831 A934 4fr multi 1.20 40
1832 A935 4fr multi 1.20 40
1833 A936 4fr multi 1.20 40

Issue dates: No. 1831, June 19; No. 1832, Sept. 4; No. 1833, Nov. 8.

35th Intl. Film Festival, Cannes A937

Natl. Space Studies Center, 20th Anniv. A938

1982, May 15 **Photo.** ***Perf. 13***
1834 A937 2.30fr multi 70 20

1982, May 15 **Engr.**
1835 A938 2.60fr multi 60 25

Industrialized Countries' Summit Meeting, Versailles, June 4-6—A939

1982, June 4
1836 A939 2.60fr multi 1.30 35

Jules Valles (1832-1885), Writer—A940

1982, June 4 **Engr.** ***Perf. 13***
1837 A940 1.60fr ol grn & dk grn 50 15

Frederic and Irene Curie, Radiation Diagrams—A941

1982, June 26
1838 A941 1.80fr multi 55 15

Electric Street Lighting Centenary—A942

1982, July 10
1839 A942 1.80fr dk bl & vio 55 15

The Family, by Marc Boyan—A943

Photo. & Engr.

1982, Sept. 18 ***Perf. 12½x13***
1840 A943 4fr multi 1.20 40

Natl. Federation of Firemen Centenary A944

Marionettes A945

1982, Sept. 18 **Engr.** ***Perf. 13***
1841 A944 3.30fr red & sep 1.00 30

1982, Sept. 25
1842 A945 1.80fr multi 55 15

Rugby—A946

1982, Oct. 9
1843 A946 1.60fr multi 50 15

Higher Education—A947

1982, Oct. 16
1844 A947 1.80fr red & dk bl 55 15

TB Bacillus Centenary—A948

1982, Nov. 13
1845 A948 2.60fr multi 80 25

St. Teresa of Avila (1515-1582)—A949

1982, Nov. 20
1846 A949 2.10fr multi 65 20

Leon Blum (1872-1950), Politician—A950

1982, Dec. 18 **Engr.** ***Perf. 13***
1847 A950 1.80fr dk brn & brn 55 15

Cavelier de la Salle (1643-1687), Explorer—A951

1982, Dec. 18 ***Perf. 13x12½***
1848 A951 3.25fr multi 1.00 30

Spring—A952

1983, Jan. 17 **Engr.** ***Perf. 13***
1849 A952 1.05fr shown 35 10
1850 A952 1.35fr Summer 40 15
1851 A952 2.19fr Autumn 65 25
1852 A952 3.63fr Winter 1.10 35

Nos. 1849-1852 known only pre-canceled. See second note after No. 132.

Provence—Alpes-Cote d'Azur—A953

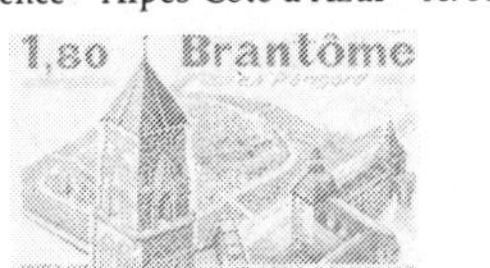

Brantome (Perigord)—A954

Perf. 13, 13x12½

1983 **Photo., Engr.**
1853 A953 1fr multi 30 10
1854 A954 1.80fr multi 55 15

Issue dates: 1fr, Jan. 8; 1.80fr, Feb. 5.

Martin Luther (1483-1546)—A959

1983, Feb. 12 Engr. *Perf. 13*

1859	A959	3.30fr dk brn & tan	1.00	30

Alliance Francaise Centenary—A960

1983, Feb. 19

1860	A960	1.80fr multi	55	15

Danielle Casanova (d. 1942), Resistance Leader—A961

1983, Mar. 8

1861	A961	3fr	90	30

World Communications Year—A962

1983, Mar. 12 Photo. *Perf.*

1862	A962	2.60fr multi	1.30	30

Female Nude, by Raphael—A964

Aurora-Set, by Dewasne—A965

1983 Engr., Photo. *Perf. 13*

1865	A964	4fr multi	2.00	50
1866	A965	4fr multi	2.00	50

Issue dates: No. 1865, Mar. 19; No. 1866, Apr. 9.

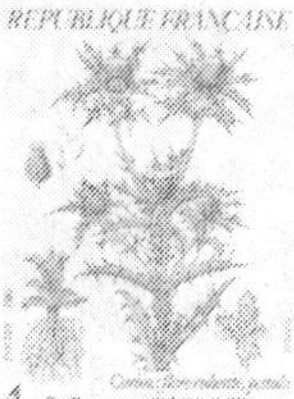

Thistle—A969

1983, Apr. 23 Engr. *Perf. 12½x12*

1870	A969	1fr shown	50	12
1871	A969	2fr Martagon lily	1.00	25
1872	A969	3fr Aster	1.50	40
1873	A969	4fr Aconite	2.00	50

INDEX of Commemorative Issues

SEMI-POSTAL STAMPS.

SP1 SP2

Red Surcharge on No. B1

Typographed

1914 *Perf. 14x13½* **Unwmkd.**

B1	SP1	10c +5c red	6.00	5.25
B2	SP2	10c +5c red	37.50	3.75
a.		Bklt. pane of 10	475.00	

Issue dates: No. B1, Aug. 11; No. B2, Sept. 10.

Widow at Grave SP3 War Orphans SP4

Woman Plowing SP5

"Trench of Bayonets" SP6

Lion of Belfort SP7

"La Marseillaise" SP8

1917-19

B3	SP3	2c +3c vio brn	4.50	4.50
B4	SP4	5c +5c grn ('19)	11.00	7.00
B5	SP5	15c +10c gray grn	22.50	22.50
B6	SP5	25c +15c dp bl	100.00	55.00
B7	SP6	35c +25c sl & vio	150.00	120.00
B8	SP7	50c +50c pale brn & dk brn	240.00	180.00
B9	SP8	1fr +1fr cl & mar	450.00	350.00
B10	SP8	5fr +5fr dp bl & blk	1,800.	1,250.
		Nos. B3-B10 (8)	2,778.	1,989.

Hospital Ship and Field Hospital SP9

1918, Aug.

B11	SP9	15c +5c sl & red	160.00	57.50

Semi-Postal Stamps of 1917-19 Surcharged **+5c**

1922, Sept. 1

B12	SP3	2c +1c vio brn	38	38
B13	SP4	5c +2½c grn	60	60
B14	SP5	15c +5c gray grn	90	90
B15	SP5	25c +5c dp bl	1.75	1.75
B16	SP6	35c +5c sl & vio	11.00	11.00
B17	SP7	50c +10c pale brn & dk brn	15.00	15.00
a.		Pair, one without surcharge		
B18	SP8	1fr +25c cl & mar	27.50	27.50
B19	SP8	5fr +1fr bl & blk	160.00	160.00
		Nos. B12-B19 (8)	217.13	217.13

Style and arrangement of surcharge differs for each denomination.

Types of 1917-19.

1926-27

B20	SP3	2c +1c vio brn	1.10	1.10
B21	SP7	50c +10c ol brn & dk brn	25.00	12.50
B22	SP8	1fr +25c dp rose & red brn	62.50	35.00
B23	SP8	5fr +1fr sl bl & blk	135.00	90.00

Sinking Fund Issues.

Types of Regular Issues of 1903–07 Surcharged in Red or Blue

Caisse d'Amortissement **+10c**

1927, Sept. 26

B24	A22	40c +10c lt bl (R)	6.00	6.00
B25	A20	50c +25c grn (Bl)	9.00	9.00

Type of Regular Issue of 1923 Surcharged in Black

C A **+50c**

B26	A23	1.50fr +50c org	11.00	11.00

Industry and Agriculture SP10

1928, May **Engraved** *Perf. 13½*

B27	SP10	1.50fr +8.50fr dl bl	150.00	150.00
a.		1.50fr+8.50fr bl grn	475.00	475.00

Types of 1903-23 Issues Surcharged as in 1927.

1928, Oct. 1 *Perf. 14x13½*

B28	A22	40c +10c gray lil (R)	11.00	11.00
B29	A20	50c +25c org brn (Bl)	30.00	27.50
B30	A23	1.50fr +50c rose lil (Bk)	42.50	40.00

Types of 1903-23 Issues Surcharged as in 1927.

1929, Oct. 1

B31	A22	40c +10c grn	19.00	17.00
B32	A20	50c +25c lil rose	30.00	27.50
B33	A23	1.50fr +50c chnt	55.00	52.50

"The Smile of Reims" SP11

1930, Mar. 15 **Engraved** *Perf. 13*

B34	SP11	1.50fr +3.50fr red vio	90.00	90.00
a.		Bklt. pane of 4	425.00	425.00

Types of 1903–07 Issues Surcharged

Caisse d'Amortissement **+10c**

1930, Oct. 1 *Perf. 14x13½*

B35	A22	40c +10c cer	22.50	18.00
B36	A20	50c +25c gray brn	40.00	35.00
B37	A22	1.50fr +50c vio	70.00	60.00

Allegory, French Provinces SP12

1931, Mar. 1 *Perf. 13*

B38	SP12	1.50fr +3.50fr grn	150.00	150.00

Types of 1903–07 Issues Surcharged

Caisse d'Amortissement **+10c**

1931, Oct. 1 *Perf. 14x13½*

B39	A22	40c +10c ol grn	37.50	35.00
B40	A20	50c +25c gray vio	110.00	85.00
B41	A22	1.50fr +50c dp red	120.00	100.00

"France" Giving Aid to an Intellectual SP13

Symbolic of Music SP14

1935, Dec. 9 **Engraved** *Perf. 13*

B42	SP13	50c +10c ultra	4.50	2.50
B43	SP14	50c +2fr dl red	62.50	45.00

The surtax was for the aid of distressed and exiled intellectuals.

Statue of Liberty SP15

Children of the Unemployed SP16

1936-37

B44	SP15	50c +25c dk bl ('37)	4.75	3.75
B45	SP15	75c +50c vio	10.00	7.50

The surtax was for the aid of political refugees.

1936, May

B46	SP16	50c +10c cop red	6.75	4.50

The surtax was for the aid of children of the unemployed.

Type of 1935 Semi-Postal Surcharged in Black **+20c**

1936, Nov.

B47	SP14	20c on 50c+2fr dl red	4.50	3.75

Jacques Callot SP17

Anatole France (Jacques Anatole Thibault) SP18

Hector Berlioz SP19

Victor Hugo SP20

Auguste Rodin SP21

Louis Pasteur SP22

1936–37 **Engraved**

B48	SP17	20c +10c brn car	3.50	3.00
B49	SP18	30c +10c emer ('37)	3.75	2.25
B50	SP19	40c +10c emer	3.75	3.00
B51	SP20	50c +10c cop red	5.50	3.00
B52	SP21	90c +10c rose red ('37)	7.50	5.25
B53	SP22	1.50fr +50c dp ultra	25.00	16.50
		Nos. B48-B53 (6)	49.00	33.00

The surtax was used for relief of unemployed intellectuals.

1938

B54	SP18	30c +10c brn car	2.25	2.25
B55	SP17	35c +10c dl grn	3.75	3.00
B56	SP19	55c +10c dl vio	6.75	3.75
B57	SP20	65c +10c ultra	6.75	3.75
B58	SP21	1fr +10c car lake	6.75	3.75
B59	SP22	1.75fr +25c dp bl	13.00	7.50
		Nos. B54-B59 (6)	39.25	24.00

Tug of War
SP23

Foot Race
SP24

Hiking
SP25

1937, June 16

B60	SP23	20c +10c brn	3.00	2.25
B61	SP24	40c +10c red brn	3.00	2.25
B62	SP25	50c +10c blk brn	3.00	2.25

The surtax was for the Recreation Fund of the employees of the Post, Telephone and Telegraph.

Pierre Loti
(Louis Marie Julien Viaud)
SP26

1937, Aug.

B63	SP26	50c +20c rose car	4.00	3.50

The surtax was for the Pierre Loti Monument Fund.

"France" and Infant
SP27

1937–39

B64	SP27	65c +25c brn vio	2.00	1.50
B65	SP27	90c +30c pck bl ('39)	1.50	1.25

The surtax was used for public health work.

Winged Victory of Samothrace
SP28

Jean Charcot
SP29

1937, Aug.

B66	SP28	30c bl grn	100.00	42.50
B67	SP28	55c red	100.00	42.50

On sale at the Louvre for 2.50 fr. The surtax of 1.65 fr. was for the benefit of the Louvre Museum.

1938-39

B68	SP29	65c +35c dk bl grn	1.50	1.50
B69	SP29	90c +35c brt red vio ('39)	9.00	8.00

The surtax was for the benefit of French seamen.

Palace of Versailles
SP30

1938, May 9

B70	SP30	1.75fr +75c dp bl	20.00	16.50

Issued in commemoration of the National Exposition of Painting and Sculpture at Versailles. The surtax was for the benefit of the Versailles Concert Society.

French Soldier
SP31

Monument
SP32

1938, May 16

B71	SP31	55c +70c brn vio	3.75	3.00
B72	SP31	65c +1.10fr pck bl	3.75	3.00

The surtax was for a fund to erect a monument to the glory of the French Infantrymen.

1938, May 25

B73	SP32	55c +45c ver	11.00	8.00

The surtax was for a fund to erect a monument in honor of the Army Medical Corps.

Reims Cathedral
SP33

"France" Welcoming Her Sons
SP34

1938, July 10

B74	SP33	65c +35c ultra	9.00	7.50

Issued to commemorate the completion of the reconstruction of Reims Cathedral, July 10, 1938.

1938, Aug. 8

B75	SP34	65c +60c rose car	5.25	3.75

The surtax was for the benefit of French volunteers repatriated from Spain.

Curie Issue
Common Design Type

1938, Sept. 1

B76	CD80	1.75fr +50c dp ultra	8.00	6.50

Victory Parade Passing Arc de Triomphe
SP36

1938, Oct. 8

B77	SP36	65c +35c brn car	5.00	3.75

20th anniversary of the Armistice.

Student and Nurse—SP37

1938, Dec. 1

B78	SP37	65c +60c pck bl	5.25	3.75

The surtax was for Student Relief.

Blind Man and Radio
SP38

1938, Dec.

B79	SP38	90c +25c brn vio	6.00	4.50

The surtax was used to help provide radios for the blind.

Civilian Facing Firing Squad
SP39

Red Cross Nurse
SP40

1939, Feb. 1

B80	SP39	90c +35c blk brn	6.00	5.00

The surtax was used to erect a monument to civilian victims of World War I.

1939, Mar. 24

B81	SP40	90c +35c dk sl grn, turq bl & red	6.00	4.50

Issued in commemoration of the 75th anniversary of the founding of the International Red Cross Society.

Army Engineer—SP41

1939, Apr. 3

B82	SP41	70c +50c ver	6.50	5.00

Issued in honor of the Army Engineering Corps. The surtax was used to erect a monument to those members who died in World War I.

Ministry of Post, Telegraph and Telephone
SP42

1939, Apr. 8

B83	SP42	90c +35c turq bl	12.00	9.00

The surtax was used to aid orphans of employees of the postal system. Issued to commemorate the opening of the new building for the Ministry of Post, Telegraph and Telephones.

Mother and Child
SP43

Eiffel Tower
SP44

1939, Apr. 24

B84	SP43	90c +35c red	3.00	2.25

The surtax was used to aid children of the unemployed.

1939, May 5

B85	SP44	90c +50c red vio	7.50	5.25

Issued in commemoration of the 50th anniversary of the Eiffel Tower. The surtax was used for celebration festivities.

Puvis de Chavannes
SP45

Claude Debussy
SP46

Honoré de Balzac
SP47

Claude Bernard
SP48

1939–40

B86	SP45	40c	+10c ver	1.50	1.25
B87	SP46	70c	+10c brn vio	1.85	1.65
B87A	SP46	80c	+10c brn vio ('40)	2.00	2.00
B88	SP47	90c	+10c brt red vio	3.00	2.50
B88A	SP47	1fr	+10c brt red vio ('40)	2.00	2.00
B89	SP48	2.25fr	+25c brt ultra	6.00	3.75
B89A	SP48	2.50fr	+25c brt ultra ('40)	2.00	2.00
			Nos. B86-B89A (7)	18.35	15.15

The surtax was used to aid unemployed intellectuals.

Mothers and Children
SP49 SP50

1939, June 15

B90	SP49	70c	+80c bl, grn & vio	3.25	3.00
B91	SP50	90c	+60c dk brn, dl vio & brn	4.00	3.75

The surtax was used to aid France's repopulation campaign.

"The Letter" by Jean Honoré Fragonard
SP51

Statue of Widow and Children
SP52

1939, July 6

B92	SP51	40c	+60c brn, sep & pur	4.00	3.25

The surtax was used for the Postal Museum.

1939, July 20

B93	SP52	70c	+30c brn vio	6.75	5.25

The surtax was for the benefit of French seamen.

French Soldier
SP53

Colonial Trooper
SP54

1940, Feb. 15

B94	SP53	40c	+60c sep	1.25	90
B95	SP54	1fr	+50c turq bl	1.25	90

The surtax was used to assist the families of mobilized men.

World Map Showing French Possessions
SP55

1940, Apr. 15

B96	SP55	1fr	+25c scar	3.00	2.25

Marshal Joseph J .C. Joffre
SP56

Marshal Ferdinand Foch
SP57

Gen. Joseph S. Gallieni
SP58

Woman Plowing
SP59

1940, May 1

B97	SP56	80c	+45c choc	2.00	2.00
B98	SP57	1fr	+50c dk vio	2.50	2.50
B99	SP58	1.50fr	+50c brn red	2.50	2.50
B100	SP59	2.50fr	+50c ind & dl bl	2.75	2.75

The surtax was used for war charities.

Doctor, Nurse, Soldier and Family
SP60

Nurse and Wounded Soldier
SP61

1940, May 12

B101	SP60	80c	+1fr dk grn & red	4.00	3.50
B102	SP61	1fr	+2fr sep & red	4.00	3.50

The surtax was used for the Red Cross.

Nurse with Injured Children
SP62

1940, Nov. 12

B103	SP62	1fr	+2fr sep	75	60

The surtax was used for victims of the war.

Wheat Harvest
SP63

Sowing
SP64

Picking Grapes
SP65

Grazing Cattle
SP66

1940, Dec. 2

B104	SP63	80c	+2fr brn blk	1.65	1.40
B105	SP64	1fr	+2fr chnt	1.65	1.40
B106	SP65	1.50fr	+2fr brt vio	1.65	1.40
B107	SP66	2.50fr	+2fr dp grn	2.00	1.65

The surtax was for national relief.

Prisoners of War
SP67 SP68

1941, Jan. 1

B108	SP67	80c	+5fr dk grn	1.25	1.25
B109	SP68	1fr	+5fr rose brn	1.25	1.25

The surtax was for prisoners of war.

Science Fighting Cancer
SP69

1941, Feb. 20

B110	SP69	2.50fr	+50c sl blk & brn	1.30	1.30

The surtax was used for the control of cancer.

Type of 1941 Surcharged "+10c" in Blue.

1941, Mar. 4

B111	A109	1fr	+10c crim	15	15

Men Hauling Coal
SP70

"France" Aiding Needy Man
SP71

1941

B112	SP70	1fr	+2fr sep	1.00	75
B113	SP71	2.50fr	+7.50fr dk bl	1.75	1.50

The surtax was for Marshal Pétain's National Relief Fund.

Liner Pasteur
SP72

Red Surcharge

1941, July 17

B114	SP72	1fr	+1fr on 70c dk bl grn	15	15

World Map, Mercator Projection
SP73

1941

B115	SP73	1fr	+1fr multi	60	60

Fisherman
SP74

1941, Oct. 23

B116	SP74	1fr +9fr dk bl grn	1.10	1.10

Surtax for benefit of French seamen.

Arms of Various Cities.

Nancy
SP75

Lille
SP76

Rouen
SP77

Bordeaux
SP78

Toulouse
SP79

Clermont-Ferrand
SP80

Marseilles
SP81

Lyon
SP82

Rennes
SP83

Reims
SP84

Montpellier
SP85

Paris
SP86

1941 ***Perf. 14x13.***

B117	SP75	20c +30c brn blk	2.50	2.50
B118	SP76	40c +60c org brn	2.50	2.50
B119	SP77	50c +70c grnsh bl	2.50	2.50
B120	SP78	70c +80c rose vio	2.50	2.50
B121	SP79	80c +1fr dp rose	2.50	2.50
B122	SP80	1fr +1fr blk	2.50	2.50
B123	SP81	1.50fr +2fr dk bl	2.50	2.50
B124	SP82	2fr +2fr dk vio	2.50	2.50
B125	SP83	2.50fr +3fr brt grn	2.50	2.50
B126	SP84	3fr +5fr org brn	2.50	2.50
B127	SP85	5fr +6fr brt ultra	2.50	2.50
B128	SP86	10fr +10fr dk red	2.50	2.50
		Nos. B117-B128 (12)	30.00	30.00

Count de La Pérouse
SP87

1942, Mar. 23 ***Perf. 13***

B129	SP87	2.50fr +7.50fr ultra	85	85

Issued to commemorate the 200th anniversary of the birth of Jean Francois de Galaup de La Pérouse, (1741–1788), French navigator and explorer. The surtax was for National Relief.

Planes over Fields
SP88

1942, Apr. 4

B130	SP88	1.50fr +3.50fr lt vio	40	40

The surtax was for the benefit of French airmen and their families.

Alexis Chabrier
SP89

1942, May 18

B131	SP89	2fr +3fr sep	85	85

Emmanuel Chabrier (1841–1894), composer, birth centenary. The surtax was for works of charity among musicians.

Symbolical of French Colonial Empire
SP90

1942, May 18

B132	SP90	1.50fr +8.50fr blk	75	75

The surtax was for National Relief.

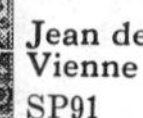

Jean de Vienne
SP91

1942, June 16

B133	SP91	1.50fr +8.50fr sep	85	85

Issued in commemoration of the 600th anniversary of the birth of Jean de Vienne, first admiral of France. The surtax was for the benefit of French seamen.

Type of Regular Issue, 1941 Surcharged in Carmine

+ 50

S N

1942, Sept. 10 ***Perf. 14x13½***

B134	A116	1.50fr +50c brt ultra	15	15

The surtax was for national relief ("Secours National").

Arms of Various Cities.

Chambéry
SP92

La Rochelle
SP93

Poitiers
SP94

Orléans
SP95

Grenoble
SP96

Angers
SP97

Dijon
SP98

Limoges
SP99

Le Havre
SP100

Nantes
SP101

Nice
SP102

St. Etienne
SP103

Engraved.

1942, Oct. ***Perf. 14x13*** **Unwmkd.**

B135	SP92	50c +60c blk	2.50	2.50
B136	SP93	60c +70c grnsh bl	2.50	2.50
B137	SP94	80c +1fr rose	2.50	2.50
B138	SP95	1fr +1.30fr dk grn	2.50	2.50
B139	SP96	1.20fr +1.50fr rose vio	2.50	2.50
B140	SP97	1.50fr +1.80fr sl bl	2.50	2.50
B141	SP98	2fr +2.30fr dp rose	2.50	2.50
B142	SP99	2.40fr +2.80fr sl grn	2.50	2.50
B143	SP100	3fr +3.50fr dp vio	2.50	2.50
B144	SP101	4fr +5fr lt ultra	2.50	2.50
B145	SP102	4.50fr +6fr red	2.50	2.50
B146	SP103	5fr +7fr brt red vio	2.50	2.50
		Nos. B135-B146 (12)	30.00	30.00

The surtax was for national relief.

Tricolor Legion—SP104

1942, Oct. 12 ***Perf. 13***

B147	SP104	1.20 +8.80fr dk bl	4.00	4.00
a.		Vert. strip of 3 (1 each Nos. B147, B148 + albino impression)	11.00	11.00
B148	SP104	1.20 +8.80fr crim	4.00	4.00

These stamps were printed in sheets of 20 stamps and 5 albino impressions arranged: 2 horizontal rows of 5 dark blue stamps, 1 row of 5 albino impressions, and 2 rows of 5 crimson stamps.

Marshal Henri Philippe Pétain
SP105 SP106

1943, Feb. 8

B149	SP105	1fr +10fr rose red	3.00	3.00
a.		Strip of 4 (1 each Nos. B149-B152 + label)	13.00	13.00
B150	SP105	1fr +10fr bl	3.00	3.00
B151	SP106	2fr +12fr rose red	3.00	3.00
B152	SP106	2fr +12fr bl	3.00	3.00

The surtax was for national relief. Printed in sheets of 20, the 10 blue stamps at left, the 10 rose red at right, separated by a vertical row of five white labels bearing a tri-colored battle-ax.

Marshal Pétain
SP107

"Work"
SP108

"Family"
SP109

"State"
SP110

Marshal Pétain
SP111

1943, June 7

No.	Type	Value	Color	Mint	Used
B153	SP107	1.20fr	+1.40fr dl vio	10.00	10.00
a.		Strip of 5 (1 each Nos. B153 to B157)		60.00	60.00
B154	SP108	1.50fr	+2.50fr red	10.00	10.00
B155	SP109	2.40fr	+7fr brn	10.00	10.00
B156	SP110	4fr	+10fr dk vio	10.00	10.00
B157	SP111	5fr	+15fr red brn	10.00	10.00
		Nos. B153-B157 (5)		50.00	50.00

Issued to commemorate Pétain's 87th birthday. The surtax was for national relief.
Printed in sheets of 25 (5x5). Each horizontal strip includes the five values, arranged by denomination.

Civilians Under Air Attack
SP112

Civilians Doing Farm Work
SP113

Prisoner's Family Doing Farm Work
SP114

1943, Aug. 23

No.	Type	Value	Color	Mint	Used
B158	SP112	1.50fr	+3.50fr blk	50	50

Surtax was for bomb victims at Billancourt, Dunkirk, Lorient, Saint-Nazaire.

1943, Sept. 27

No.	Type	Value	Color	Mint	Used
B159	SP113	1.50fr	+8.50fr sep	75	75
B160	SP114	2.40fr	+7.60fr dk grn	75	75

The surtax was for families of war prisoners.

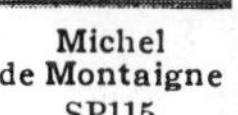

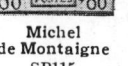

Michel de Montaigne
SP115

Picardy Costume
SP121

Designs: 1.20fr+1.50fr, Francois Clouet. 1.50fr+3fr, Ambrose Paré. 2.40fr+4fr, Chevalier Pierre de Bayard. 4fr+6fr, Duke of Sully. 5fr+10fr, Henri IV.

1943, Oct. 2

No.	Type	Value	Color	Mint	Used
B161	SP115	60c	+80c Prus grn	1.50	1.50
B162	SP115	1.20fr	+1.50fr blk	1.65	1.65
B163	SP115	1.50fr	+3fr dp ultra	1.65	1.65
B164	SP115	2.40fr	+4fr red	1.65	1.65
B165	SP115	4fr	+6fr dl brn red	2.00	2.00
B166	SP115	5fr	+10fr dl grn	2.00	2.00
		Nos. B161-B166 (6)		10.45	10.45

The surtax was for national relief. Issued to honor famous 16th century Frenchmen.

1943, Dec. 27

Designs: 18th Century Costumes: 1.20fr+2fr, Brittany. 1.50fr+4fr, Ile de France. 2.40+5fr, Burgundy. 4fr+6fr, Auvergne. 5fr+7fr, Provence.

No.	Type	Value	Color	Mint	Used
B167	SP121	60c	+1.30fr sep	2.00	2.00
B168	SP121	1.20fr	+2fr lt vio	2.00	2.00
B169	SP121	1.50fr	+4fr turq bl	2.00	2.00
B170	SP121	2.40fr	+5fr rose car	2.00	2.00
B171	SP121	4fr	+6fr chlky bl	2.75	2.75
B172	SP121	5fr	+7fr red	2.75	2.75
		Nos. B167-B172 (6)		13.50	13.50

The surtax was for national relief.

Admiral Tourville
SP127

Charles Gounod
SP128

1944, Feb. 21

No.	Type	Value	Color	Mint	Used
B173	SP127	4fr	+6fr dl red brn	55	55

Issued to commemorate the 300th anniversary of the birth of Admiral Anne-Hilarion de Cotentin Tourville (1642–1701).

1944, Mar. 27 *Perf. 14x13*

No.	Type	Value	Color	Mint	Used
B174	SP128	1.50fr	+3.50fr sep	20	20

Issued to commemorate the 50th anniversary of the death of Charles Gounod, composer (1818–1893).

Marshal Pétain
SP129

Farming
SP130

Industry
SP131

1944, Apr. 24 *Perf. 13*

No.	Type	Value	Color	Mint	Used
B175	SP129	1.50fr	+3.50fr sep	2.75	2.75
B176	SP130	2fr	+3fr dp ultra	60	60
B177	SP131	4fr	+6fr rose red	60	60

Marshal Henri Pétain's 88th birthday.

Modern Streamliner and 19th Century Train
SP132

Molière (Jean-Baptiste Poquelin)
SP133

1944, Aug. 14

No.	Type	Value	Color	Mint	Used
B178	SP132	4fr	+6fr blk	45	45

Issued to commemorate the centenary of the Paris-Rouen, Paris-Orléans railroad.

1944, July 31

Designs: 80c+2.20fr, Jules Hardouin Mansart. 1.20fr+2.80fr, Blaise Pascal. 1.50fr+3.50fr, Louis II of Bourbon. 2fr+4fr, Jean-Baptiste Colbert. 4fr+6fr, Louis XIV.

No.	Type	Value	Color	Mint	Used
B179	SP133	50c	+1.50fr rose car	95	95
B180	SP133	80c	+2.20fr dk grn	95	95
B181	SP133	1.20fr	+2.80fr blk	95	95
B182	SP133	1.50fr	+3.50fr brt ultra	95	95
B183	SP133	2fr	+4fr dl brn red	95	95
B184	SP133	4fr	+6fr red	95	95
		Nos. B179-B184 (6)		5.70	5.70

Noted 17th century Frenchmen.

French Cathedrals.

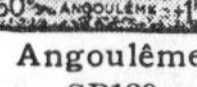

Angoulême
SP139

Chartres
SP140

Amiens
SP141

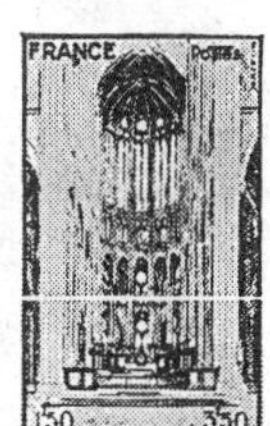

Beauvais
SP142

Albi
SP143

1944, Nov. 20

No.	Type	Value	Color	Mint	Used
B185	SP139	50c	+1.50fr blk	25	25
B186	SP140	80c	+2.20fr rose vio	35	35
B187	SP141	1.20fr	+2.80fr brn car	45	45
B188	SP142	1.50fr	+3.50fr dp bl	55	55
B189	SP143	4fr	+6fr org red	55	55
		Nos. B185-B189 (5)		2.15	2.15

Coat of Arms of Renouard de Villayer
SP144

Sarah Bernhardt
SP145

1944, Dec. 9 **Engraved**

No.	Type	Value	Color	Mint	Used
B190	SP144	1.50fr	+3.50fr dp brn	15	15

Stamp Day.

1945, May 16 ***Perf. 13*** **Unwmkd.**

No.	Type	Value	Color	Mint	Used
B191	SP145	4fr	+1fr dk vio brn	20	20

Issued to commemorate the 100th anniversary of the birth of Sarah Bernhardt, actress.

War Victims
SP146

Tuberculosis Patient
SP147

1945, May 16

No.	Type	Value	Color	Mint	Used
B192	SP146	4fr	+6fr dk vio brn	10	10

The surtax was for war victims of the P.T.T.

1945, May 16 **Typo.** ***Perf. 14x13½***

No.	Type	Value	Color	Mint	Used
B193	SP147	2fr	+1fr red org	5	5

The surtax was for the aid of tuberculosis victims.

Boy and Girl
SP148

Burning of Oradour Church
SP149

1945, July 9 **Engraved** ***Perf. 13***

No.	Type	Value	Color	Mint	Used
B194	SP148	4fr	+2fr Prus grn	15	15

The surtax was used for child welfare.

1945, Oct. 13

No.	Type	Value	Color	Mint	Used
B195	SP149	4fr	+2fr sep	15	15

Destruction of Oradour, June, 1944.

Louis XI and Post Rider
SP150

1945, Oct. 13

B196	SP150	2fr +3fr dp ultra	20	20

Stamp Day.

Ruins of Dunkirk
SP151

Ruins of Rouen—SP152

Ruins of Caen—SP153

Ruins of Saint-Malo
SP154

1945, Nov. 5

B197	SP151	1.50fr +1.50fr red brn	20	20
B198	SP152	2fr +2fr vio	20	20
B199	SP153	2.40fr +2.60fr bl	20	20
B200	SP154	4fr +4fr blk	20	20

The surtax was to aid the suffering residents of Dunkirk, Rouen, Caen and Saint Malo.

Alfred Fournier
SP155

Henri Becquerel
SP156

1946, Feb. 4 Engraved *Perf. 13*

B201	SP155	2fr +3fr red brn	20	20
B202	SP156	2fr +3fr vio	20	20

Issued to raise funds for the fight against veneral disease (B201) and for the struggle against cancer (B202).

No. B202 commemorated the 50th anniversary of the discovery of radio-activity by Henri Becquerel.

See also No. B221.

Church of the Invalides, Paris—SP157

1946, Mar. 11

B203	SP157	4fr +6fr red brn	25	25

The surtax was to aid disabled war veterans.

French Warships
SP158

1946, Apr. 8

B204	SP158	2fr +3fr gray blk	20	20

The surtax was for naval charities.

"The Letter" by Jean Siméon Chardin
SP159

Fouquet de la Varane
SP160

1946, May 25

B205	SP159	2fr +3fr brn red	35	35

The surtax was used for the Postal Museum.

1946, June 29

B206	SP160	3fr +2fr sep	40	40

Stamp Day.

François Villon
SP161

Designs: 3fr+1fr, Jean Fouquet. 4fr+3fr, Philippe de Commynes. 5fr+4fr, Joan of Arc. 6fr+5fr, Jean de Gerson. 10fr+6fr, Charles VII.

1946, Oct. 28

B207	SP161	2fr +1fr dk Prus grn	1.25	1.25
B208	SP161	3fr +1fr dk bl vio	1.25	1.25
B209	SP161	4fr +3fr hn brn	1.25	1.25
B210	SP161	5fr +4fr ultra	1.25	1.25
B211	SP161	6fr +5fr sep	1.25	1.25
B212	SP161	10fr +6fr red	1.25	1.25
		Nos. B207-B212 (6)	7.50	7.50

Church of St. Sernin, Toulouse
SP167

Notre Dame du Port, Clermont-Ferrand
SP168

Cathedral of St. Front, Perigueux
SP169

Cathedral of St. Julien, Le Mans
SP170

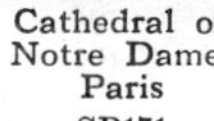

Cathedral of Notre Dame, Paris
SP171

François Michel le Tellier de Louvois
SP172

1947 Engraved

B213	SP167	1fr +1fr car rose	35	35
B214	SP168	3fr +2fr dk bl vio	35	35
B215	SP169	4fr +3fr hn brn	70	70
B216	SP170	6fr +4fr dp bl	1.00	1.00
B217	SP171	10fr +6fr dk gray grn	1.35	1.35
		Nos. B213-B217 (5)	3.75	3.75

1947, Mar. 15

B218	SP172	4.50fr +5.50fr car rose	1.10	1.10

Stamp Day, March 15, 1947.

Submarine Pens, Shipyard and Monument
SP173

1947, Aug. 2

B219	SP173	6fr +4fr bluish blk	20	15

Issued to commemorate the British commando raid on the Nazi U-boat base at St. Nazaire, 1942.

Liberty Highway Marker
SP174

Louis Braille
SP175

1947, Sept. 5

B220	SP174	6fr +4fr dk grn	25	25

The surtax was to help defray maintenance costs of the Liberty Highway.

Fournier Type of 1946

1947, Oct. 20

B221	SP155	2fr +3fr ind	25	25

1948, Jan. 19

B222	SP175	6fr +4fr pur	30	30

Etienne Arago
SP176

Alphonse de Lamartine
SP177

1948, Mar. 6

B223	SP176	6fr +4fr blk brn	40	40

Stamp Day, March 6-7, 1948.

1948, Apr. 5 Engraved *Perf. 13*

Designs: 3fr+2fr, Alexandre A. Ledru-Rollin. 4fr+3fr, Louis Blanc. 5fr+4fr, Albert (Alexandre Martin). 6fr+5fr, Pierre J. Proudhon. 10fr+6fr, Louis Auguste Blanqui. 15fr+7fr, Armand Barbès. 20fr+8fr, Dennis A. Affre.

B224	SP177	1fr +1fr dk grn	1.25	1.25
B225	SP177	3fr +2fr hn brn	1.40	1.40
B226	SP177	4fr +3fr vio brn	1.40	1.40
B227	SP177	5fr +4fr lt bl grn	1.75	1.75
B228	SP177	6fr +5fr ind	1.75	1.75
B229	SP177	10fr +6fr car rose	1.75	1.75
B230	SP177	15fr +7fr sl blk	2.75	2.75
B231	SP177	20fr +8fr pur	3.00	3.00
		Nos. B224-B231 (8)	15.05	15.05

Centenary of the Revolution of 1848.

Dr. Léon Charles Albert Calmette
SP178

1948, June 18

B232	SP178	6fr +4fr dk grnsh bl	25	25

Issued to mark the first International Congress on the Calmette-Guerin bacillus vaccine.

Farmer
SP179

Designs: 5fr+3fr, Fisherman. 8fr+4fr, Miner. 10fr+6fr, Metal worker.

1949, Feb. 14

B233	SP179	3fr +1fr cl	70	45
B234	SP179	5fr +3fr dk bl	70	70
B235	SP179	8fr +4fr ind	80	60
B236	SP179	10fr +6fr dk red	1.10	90

Étienne François de Choiseul and Post Cart
SP180

Baron de la Brède et de Montesquieu
SP181

1949, Mar. 26

B237	SP180	15fr +5fr dk grn	1.25	1.25

Stamp Day, March 26–27, 1949.

1949, Nov. 14

Designs: 8fr+2fr, Voltaire. 10fr+3fr, Antoine Watteau. 12fr+4fr, Georges de Buffon. 15fr+5fr, Joseph F. Dupleix. 25fr+10fr, A. R. J. Turgot.

B238	SP181	5fr +1fr dk grn	3.75	3.75
B239	SP181	8fr +2fr ind	3.75	3.75
B240	SP181	10fr +3fr brn red	3.75	3.75
B241	SP181	12fr +4fr pur	3.75	3.75
B242	SP181	15fr +5fr rose car	5.00	5.00
B243	SP181	25fr +10fr ultra	5.00	5.00
		Nos. B238-B243 (6)	25.00	25.00

"Spring"
SP182

Designs: 8fr+2fr, Summer. 12fr+3fr, Autumn. 15fr+4fr, Winter.

1949, Dec. 19

B244	SP182	5fr +1fr grn	2.00	2.00
B245	SP182	8fr +2fr yel org	2.00	2.00
B246	SP182	12fr +3fr pur	2.50	2.50
B247	SP182	15fr +4fr dp bl	2.50	2.50

Postman
SP183

1950, Mar. 11

B248	SP183	12fr +3fr dp bl	3.75	3.00

Stamp Day, March 11–12, 1950.

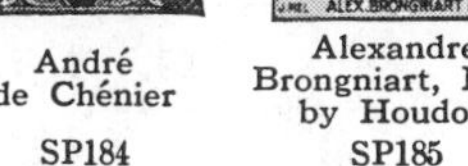

André de Chénier
SP184

Alexandre Brongniart, Bust by Houdon
SP185

Portraits: 8fr+3fr, J. L. David. 10fr+4fr, Lazare Carnot. 12fr+5fr, G. J. Danton. 15fr+6fr, Maximilian Robespierre. 20fr+10fr, Louis Hoche.

1950, July 10 Engraved *Perf. 13*

Frames in Indigo.

B249	SP184	5fr +2fr brn vio	6.75	6.75
B250	SP184	8fr +3fr blk brn	6.75	6.75
B251	SP184	10fr +4fr lake	7.50	7.50
B252	SP184	12fr +5fr red brn	7.50	7.50
B253	SP184	15fr +6fr dk grn	8.50	8.50
B254	SP184	20fr +10fr dk vio bl	8.50	8.50
		Nos. B249-B254 (6)	45.50	45.50

1950, Dec. 22

Design: 15fr–3fr, "L'Amour" by Etienne M. Falconet.

B255	SP185	8fr +2fr ind & car	3.00	3.00
B256	SP185	15fr +3fr red brn & car	3.00	3.00

The surtax was for the Red Cross.

Mail Car Interior
SP186

Alfred de Musset
SP187

1951, Mar. 10 *Perf. 13* Unwmkd.

B257	SP186	12fr +3fr lil gray	3.00	3.00

Stamp Day, March 10–11, 1951.

1951, June 2

Designs: 8fr+2fr, Eugène Delacroix. 10fr+3fr, J.-L. Gay-Lussac. 12fr+4fr, Robert Surcouf. 15fr+5fr, C. M. Talleyrand. 30fr+10fr, Napoleon I.

Frames in Dark Brown.

B258	SP187	5fr +1fr dk grn	6.75	6.75
B259	SP187	8fr +2fr vio brn	7.50	7.50
B260	SP187	10fr +3fr grnsh blk	7.50	7.50
B261	SP187	12fr +4fr dk vio brn	7.50	7.50
B262	SP187	15fr +5fr brn car	7.50	7.50
B263	SP187	30fr +10fr ind	12.00	12.00
		Nos. B258-B263 (6)	48.75	48.75

Child at Prayer by Le Maître de Moulins
SP188

18th Century Child by Quentin de la Tour
SP189

1951, Dec. 15

Cross in Red.

B264	SP188	12fr +3fr dk brn	3.75	3.75
B265	SP189	15fr +5fr dp ultra	3.75	3.75

The surtax was for the Red Cross.

Stagecoach of 1844
SP190

1952, Mar. 8 *Perf. 13*

B266	SP190	12fr +3fr dp grn	3.50	3.50

Stamp Day, March 8, 1952.

Gustave Flaubert
SP191

Portraits: 12fr+3fr, Edouard Manet. 15fr+4fr, Camille Saint-Saens. 18fr+5fr, Henri Poincaré. 20fr+6fr, Georges-Eugene Haussmann. 30fr+7fr, Adolphe Thiers.

1952, Oct. 18

Frames in Dark Brown.

B267	SP191	8fr +2fr ind	6.00	6.00
B268	SP191	12fr +3fr vio bl	6.00	6.00
B269	SP191	15fr +4fr dk grn	6.00	6.00
B270	SP191	18fr +5fr dk brn	6.00	6.00
B271	SP191	20fr +6fr car	6.75	6.75
B272	SP191	30fr +7fr pur	6.75	6.75
		Nos. B267-B272 (6)	37.50	37.50

Cupid from Diana Fountain Versailles
SP192

Design: 15fr+5fr, Similar detail, cupid facing left.

1952, Dec. 13

Cross in Red.

B273	SP192	12fr +3fr dk grn	4.50	4.50
B274	SP192	15fr +5fr ind	4.50	4.50
a.		Bklt. pane of 10	65.00	

The surtax was for the Red Cross.

Count d'Argenson
SP193

St. Bernard
SP194

1953, Mar. 14

B275	SP193	12fr +3fr dp bl	3.00	3.00

Issued to commemorate the Day of the Stamp. The surtax was for the Red Cross.

1953, July 9

Portraits: 12fr+3fr, Olivier de Serres. 15fr+4fr, Jean Philippe Rameau. 18fr+5fr, Gaspard Monge. 20fr+6fr, Jules Michelet. 30fr+7fr, Marshal Hubert Lyautey.

B276	SP194	8fr +2fr ultra	6.00	6.00
B277	SP194	12fr +3fr dk grn	6.00	6.00
B278	SP194	15fr +4fr brn car	7.50	7.50
B279	SP194	18fr +5fr dk bl	7.50	7.50
B280	SP194	20fr +6fr dk pur	7.50	7.50
B281	SP194	30fr +7fr brn	8.50	8.50
		Nos. B276-B281 (6)	43.00	43.00

The surtax was for the Red Cross.

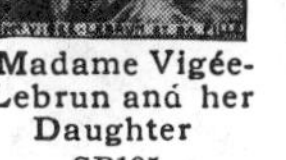

Madame Vigée-Lebrun and her Daughter
SP195

Count Antoine de La Vallette
SP196

Design: 15fr+5fr, "The Return from Baptism," by Louis Le Nain.

1953, Dec. 12

Cross in Red

B282	SP195	12fr +3fr red brn	8.50	8.50
a.		Bklt. pane (4 #B282, 4 #B283 with gutter btwn.)	80.00	
B283	SP195	15fr +5fr ind	10.00	10.00

The surtax was for the Red Cross.

1954, Mar. 20 Engraved *Perf. 13*

B284	SP196	12fr +3fr dp grn & choc	4.50	4.50

Stamp Day, March 20, 1954.

Louis IX
SP197

"The Sick Child," by Eugene Carrière
SP198

Portraits: 15fr+5fr, Jacques Benigne Bossuet. 18fr+6fr, Sadi Carnot. 20fr+7fr, Antoine Bourdelle. 25fr+8fr, Dr. Emile Roux. 30fr+10fr, Paul Valéry.

1954, July 10

B285	SP197	12fr +4fr dp bl	16.50	16.50
B286	SP197	15fr +5fr pur	18.00	18.00
B287	SP197	18fr +6fr dk brn	18.00	18.00
B288	SP197	20fr +7fr crim	22.50	22.50
B289	SP197	25fr +8fr ind	22.50	22.50
B290	SP197	30fr +10fr dp cl	22.50	22.50
		Nos. B285-B290 (6)	120.00	120.00

See also Nos. B303–B308 and B312–B317.

1954, Dec. 18

Design: 15fr+5fr, "Young Girl with Doves," by Jean Baptiste Greuze.

Cross in Red

B291	SP198	12fr +3fr vio gray & ind	9.00	9.00
a.		Bklt. pane (4 #B291, 4 #B292 with gutter btwn.)	80.00	
B292	SP198	15fr +5fr dk brn & org brn	9.00	9.00

No. B291a was issued to commemorate the 90th anniversary of the Red Cross. The gutter between panes is inscribed in red.

The surtax was for the Red Cross.

Balloon Post, 1870
SP199

1955, Mar. 19 ***Perf. 13*** **Unwmkd.**

No.	Type	Description	Unused	Used
B293	SP199	12fr +3fr dk grnsh bl, vio brn & ol grn	6.00	5.00

Stamp Day, March 19–20, 1955.

King Philip II
SP200

Child with Cage by Pigalle
SP201

Portraits: 15fr+6fr, Francois de Malherbé. 18fr+7fr, Sebastien de Vauban. 25fr+8fr, Charles G. de Vergennes. 30fr+9fr, Pierre S. de Laplace. 50fr+15fr, Pierre Auguste Renoir.

1955, June 11

No.	Type	Description	Unused	Used
B294	SP200	12fr +5fr brt pur	15.00	15.00
B295	SP200	15fr +6fr dp bl	15.00	15.00
B296	SP200	18fr +7fr dp grn	15.00	15.00
B297	SP200	25fr +8fr gray	18.00	18.00
B298	SP200	30fr +9fr rose brn	20.00	20.00
B299	SP200	50fr +15fr bl grn	20.00	20.00
		Nos. B294-B299 (6)	103.00	103.00

See also Nos. B321–B326.

1955, Dec. 17

Design: 15fr+5fr, Child with Goose, by Boethus of Chalcedon.

Cross in Red.

No.	Type	Description	Unused	Used
B300	SP201	12fr +3fr cl	5.25	5.25
B301	SP201	15fr +5fr dk bl	5.25	5.25
a.		Booklet pane of 10	67.50	

The surtax was for the Red Cross.

Francois of Taxis
SP202

1956, Mar. 17 **Engraved** ***Perf. 13***

No.	Type	Description	Unused	Used
B302	SP202	12fr +3fr ultra, grn & dk brn	2.25	2.25

Stamp Day, March 17–18, 1956.

Portrait Type of 1954.

Portraits: No. 303, Guillaume Budé. No. B304, Jean Goujon. No. B305, Samuel de Champlain. No. B306, Jean Simeon Chardin. No. B307, Maurice Barrès. No. B308, Maurice Ravel.

1956, June 9 ***Perf. 13***

No.	Type	Description	Unused	Used
B303	SP197	12fr +3fr saph	3.75	3.75
B304	SP197	12fr +3fr lil gray	3.75	3.75
B305	SP197	12fr +3fr brt red	3.75	3.75
B306	SP197	15fr +5fr grn	4.50	4.50
B307	SP197	15fr +5fr vio brn	5.25	5.25
B308	SP197	15fr +5fr dp vio	5.25	5.25
		Nos. B303-B308 (6)	26.25	26.25

Peasant Boy by Le Nain
SP203

Design: 15fr+5fr, Gilles by Watteau.

1956, Dec. 8 **Unwmkd.**

Cross in Red

No.	Type	Description	Unused	Used
B309	SP203	12fr +3fr ol gray	3.50	3.50
a.		Bklt. pane (4 #B309, 4 #B310 with gutter btwn.)	32.50	
B310	SP203	15fr +5fr rose lake	3.50	3.50

The surtax was for the Red Cross.

Genoese Felucca, 1750
SP204

1957, Mar. 16 ***Perf. 13***

No.	Type	Description	Unused	Used
B311	SP204	12fr +3fr bluish gray & brn blk	2.00	1.50

Issued to commemorate the Day of the Stamp, March 16, 1957, and to honor the Maritime Postal Service.

Portrait Type of 1954

1957, June 15

Portraits: No. B312, Jean de Joinville. No. B313, Bernard Palissy. No. B314, Quentin de la Tour. No. B315, Hugues Félicité Robert de Lamennais. No. B316, George Sand. No. B317, Jules Guesde.

No.	Type	Description	Unused	Used
B312	SP197	12fr +3fr ol gray & ol grn	2.75	2.75
B313	SP197	12fr +3fr grnsh blk & grnsh bl	3.00	3.00
B314	SP197	15fr +5fr cl & brt red	3.50	3.50
B315	SP197	15fr +5fr ultra & ind	3.50	3.50
B316	SP197	18fr +7fr grnsh blk & dk grn	4.00	4.00
B317	SP197	18fr +7fr dk vio brn & red brn	4.50	4.50
		Nos. B312-B317 (6)	21.25	21.25

Blind Man and Beggar, Engraving by Jacques Callot
SP205

Design: 20fr+8fr, Women beggars.

1957, Dec. 7 **Engraved** ***Perf. 13***

No.	Type	Description	Unused	Used
B318	SP205	15fr +7fr ultra & red	3.50	3.50
a.		Bklt. pane (4 #B318, 4 #B319 with gutter btwn.)	32.50	
B319	SP205	20fr +8fr dk vio brn & red	3.50	3.50

The surtax was for the Red Cross.

Motorized Mail Distribution
SP206

1958, Mar. 15

No.	Type	Description	Unused	Used
B320	SP206	15fr +5fr ol gray, ol grn & red brn	1.75	1.50

Stamp Day, Mar. 15.

Portrait Type of 1955.

Portraits: No. B321, Joachim du Bellay. No. B322, Jean Bart. No. B323, Denis Diderot. No. B324, Gustave Courbet. 20fr+8fr, J. B. Carpeaux. 35fr+15fr, Toulouse-Lautrec.

1958, June 7 **Engraved** ***Perf. 13***

No.	Type	Description	Unused	Used
B321	SP200	12fr +4fr yel grn	2.25	2.25
B322	SP200	12fr +4fr dk bl	2.25	2.25
B323	SP200	15fr +5fr dl cl	2.25	2.25
B324	SP200	15fr +5fr ultra	2.75	2.75
B325	SP200	20fr +8fr brt red	2.75	2.75
B326	SP200	35fr +15fr grn	3.00	3.00
		Nos. B321-B326 (6)	15.25	15.25

St. Vincent de Paul
SP207

Portrait: 20fr+8fr, J. H. Dunant.

1958, Dec. 6 **Unwmkd.**

Cross in Carmine.

No.	Type	Description	Unused	Used
B327	SP207	15fr +7fr grysh grn	1.40	1.40
a.		Bklt. pane (4 #B327, 4 #B328 with gutter btwn.)	13.00	
B328	SP207	20fr +8fr vio	1.40	1.40

The surtax was for the Red Cross.

Plane Landing at Night
SP208

1959, Mar. 21

No.	Type	Description	Unused	Used
B329	SP208	20fr +5fr sl grn, blk & rose	60	60

Issued for the Day of the Stamp, March 21, and to publicize night air mail service. The surtax was for the Red Cross.

See also No. 1089.

Geoffroi de Villehardouin and Ships
SP209

Designs: No. B331, André Le Nôtre and formal garden. No. B332, Jean Le Rond d'Alembert, books and wheel. No. B333, David d'Angers, statue and building. No. B334, M. F. X. Bichat and torch. No. B335, Frédéric Auguste Bartholdi, Statue of Liberty and Lion of Belfort.

1959, June 13 **Engraved** ***Perf. 13***

No.	Type	Description	Unused	Used
B330	SP209	15fr +5fr vio bl	1.65	1.65
B331	SP209	15fr +5fr dk sl grn	1.65	1.65
B332	SP209	20fr +10fr ol bis	2.00	2.00
B333	SP209	20fr +10fr dk gray	2.00	2.00
B334	SP209	30fr +10fr dk car rose	2.50	2.50
B335	SP209	30fr +10fr org brn	2.50	2.50
		Nos. B330-B335 (6)	12.30	12.30

The surtax was for the Red Cross.

No. 927 Surcharged **FREJUS +5f**

1959, Dec. **Typo.** ***Perf. 14x13½***

No.	Type	Description	Unused	Used
B336	A328	25fr +5fr blk & red	40	40

The surtax was for the flood victims at Frejus.

Charles Michel de l'Épée
SP210

Design: 25fr+10fr, Valentin Hauy.

1959, Dec. 5 **Engraved** ***Perf. 13***

Cross in Carmine

No.	Type	Description	Unused	Used
B337	SP210	20fr +10fr blk & cl	1.25	1.25
a.		Bklt. pane (4 #B337, 4 #B338 with gutter btwn.)	12.00	
B338	SP210	25fr +10fr dk bl & blk	1.25	1.25

The surtax was for the Red Cross.

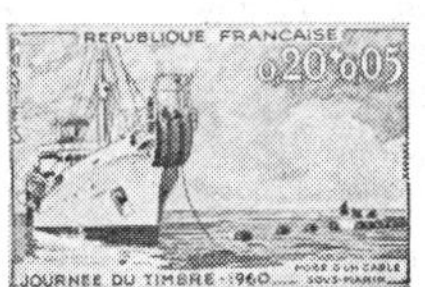

Ship Laying Underwater Cable
SP211

1960, Mar. 12

No.	Type	Description	Unused	Used
B339	SP211	20c +5c grnsh bl & dk bl	1.25	1.25

Issued for the Day of the Stamp. The surtax went to the Red Cross.

Refugee Girl Amid Ruins
SP212

1960, Apr. 7

No.	Type	Description	Unused	Used
B340	SP212	25c +10c grn, brn & ind	40	40

Issued to publicize World Refugee Year, July 1, 1959–June 30, 1960. The surtax was for aid to refugees.

Michel de L'Hospital
SP213

Designs: No. B342, Henri de la Tour D'Auvergne, Viscount of Turenne. No. B343, Nicolas Boileau (Despreaux). No. B344, Jean-Martin Charcot, M.D. No. B345, Georges Bizet. 50c+15c, Edgar Degás.

1960, June 11 **Engraved** ***Perf. 13***

No.	Type	Description	Unused	Used
B341	SP213	10c +5c pur & rose car	2.50	2.50
B342	SP213	20c +10c ol & vio brn	2.75	2.75
B343	SP213	20c +10c Prus grn & dp yel grn	3.50	3.50
B344	SP213	30c +10c rose car & rose red	3.50	3.50

B345 SP213 30c +10c dk bl & vio bl 4.00 4.00
B346 SP213 50c +15c sl bl & gray 4.50 4.50
Nos. B341-B346 (6) 20.75 20.75

The surtax was for the Red Cross. See also Nos. B350-B355.

Staff of the Brotherhood of St. Martin
SP214

Letter Carrier, Paris 1760
SP215

Design: 25c+10c, St. Martin, 16th century wood sculpture.

1960, Dec. 3 *Perf. 13* Unwmkd.

B347 SP214 20c +10c rose cl & red 3.00 3.00
a. Bklt. pane (4 #B347, 4# B348 with gutter btwn.) 27.50
B348 SP214 25c +10c lt ultra & red 3.00 3.00

The surtax was for the Red Cross.

1961, March 18 *Perf. 13*

B349 SP215 20c +5c sl grn, brn & red 1.00 80

Stamp Day. Surtax for Red Cross.

Famous Men Type of 1960

Designs: 15+5c, Bertrand Du Guesclin. B351, Pierre Puget. B352, Charles Coulomb. 30+10c, Antoine Drouot. 45c+10c, Honoré Daumier. 50+15c, Guillaume Apollinaire.

1961, May 20 Engraved

B350 SP213 15c +5c red brn & blk 2.00 2.00
B351 SP213 20c +10c dk grn & lt bl 2.00 2.00
B352 SP213 20c +10c ver & rose car 2.25 2.25
B353 SP213 30c +10c blk & brn org 2.25 2.25
B354 SP213 45c +10c choc & dk grn 3.00 3.00
B355 SP213 50c +15c dk car rose & vio 3.00 3.00
Nos. B350-B355 (6) 14.50 14.50

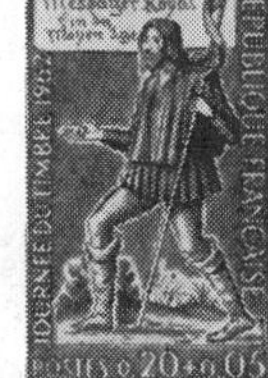

"Love" by Rouault
SP216

Medieval Royal Messenger
SP217

Designs from "Miserere" by Georges Rouault: 25c+10c, "The Blind Consoles the Seeing."

1961, Dec. 2 *Perf. 13*

B356 SP216 20c +10c brn, blk & red 2.25 2.25
a. Bklt. pane (4 #B356, 4 #B357 with gutter btwn.) 20.00
B357 SP216 25c +10c brn, blk & red 2.25 2.25

The surtax was for the Red Cross.

1962, March 17

B358 SP217 20c +5c rose red, bl & sep 75 60

Stamp Day. Surtax for Red Cross.

Denis Papin, Scientist
SP218

Rosalie Fragonard by Fragonard
SP219

Portraits: No. B360, Edme Bouchardon, sculptor. No. B361, Joseph Lakanal, educator. 30c+10c, Gustave Charpentier, composer. 45c+15c, Edouard Estaunié, writer. 50c+20c, Hyacinthe Vincent, physician and bacteriologist.

1962, June 2 Engraved

B359 SP218 15c +5c bluish grn & dk gray 2.75 2.75
B360 SP218 20c +10c cl brn 2.75 2.75
B361 SP218 20c +10c gray & sl 2.75 2.75
B362 SP218 30c +10c brt bl & ind 3.50 3.50
B363 SP218 45c +15c org brn & choc 3.75 3.75
B364 SP218 50c +20c grnsh bl & blk 3.75 3.75
Nos. B359-B364 (6) 19.25 19.25

The surtax was for the Red Cross.

1962, Dec. 8

Design: 25c+10c, Child dressed as Pierrot.

Cross in Red

B365 SP219 20c +10c redsh brn 1.10 1.10
a. Bklt. pane (4 #B365, 4 #B366 with gutter btwn.) 10.00
B366 SP219 25c +10c dl grn 1.10 1.10

The surtax was for the Red Cross.

Jacques Amyot, Classical Scholar
SP220

Portraits: 30c+10c, Pierre de Marivaux, playwright. 50c+20c, Jacques Daviel, surgeon.

1963, Feb. 23 *Perf. 13* Unwmkd.

B367 SP220 20c +10c mar, gray & pur 1.50 1.50
B368 SP220 30c +10c Prus grn & mar 1.50 1.50
B369 SP220 50c +20c ultra, ocher & ol 1.50 1.50

The surtax was for the Red Cross.

Roman Chariot
SP221

1963, March 16 Engraved

B370 SP221 20c +5c brn org & vio brn 35 35

Stamp Day. Surtax for Red Cross.

Étienne Méhul, Composer
SP222

Designs: 30c+10c, Nicolas-Louis Vauquelin, chemist. 50c+20c, Alfred de Vigny, poet.

1963, May 25 *Perf. 13* Unwmkd.

B371 SP222 20c +10c dp bl, dk brn & dp org 1.75 1.75
B372 SP222 30c +10c mag, gray ol & blk 1.50 1.50
B373 SP222 50c +20c sl, blk & brn 2.25 2.25

The surtax was for the Red Cross.

"Child with Grapes" by David d'Angers and Centenary Emblem
SP223

Design: 25c+10c, "The Fifer," by Edouard Manet.

1963, Dec. 9 *Perf. 13* Unwmkd.

B374 SP223 20c +10c blk & red 60 60
a. Bklt. pane (4 #B374, 4 #B375 with gutter btwn.) 6.00
B375 SP223 25c +10c sl grn & red 60 60

Issued to commemorate the centenary of the International and the French Red Cross. The surtax was for the Red Cross.

Post Rider, 18th Century
SP224

1964, March 14 Engraved

B376 SP224 20c +5c Prus grn 30 25
Issued for Stamp Day.

Resistance Memorial by Watkin, Luxembourg Gardens
SP225

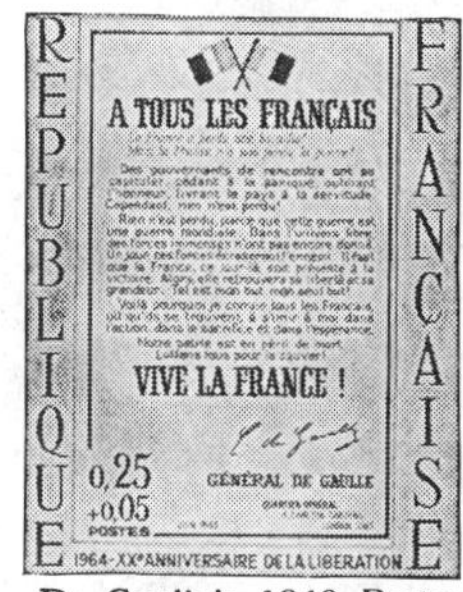

De Gaulle's 1940 Poster "A Tous les Francais"
SP226

Allied Troops Landing in Normandy and Provence—SP227

Designs: 20c+5c, "Deportation," concentration camp with watchtower and barbed wire. No. B380, Street fighting in Paris and Strasbourg.

1964 Engraved *Perf. 13*

B377 SP225 20c +5c sl blk 55 55

Perf. 12x13

B378 SP226 25c +5c dk red, bl, red & blk 85 85

Perf. 13

B379 SP227 30c +5c blk, bl & org brn 55 55
B380 SP227 30c +5c org brn, cl & blk 70 70
B381 SP225 50c +5c dk grn 85 85
Nos. B377-B381 (5) 3.50 3.50

Issued to commemorate the 20th anniversary of liberation from the Nazis.
Issue dates: Nos. B377, B381, Mar. 21; No. B378, June 18; No. B379, June 6; No. B380, Aug. 22.

President René Coty
SP229

Jean Nicolas Corvisart
SP230

Portraits: No. B383, John Calvin. No. B384, Pope Sylvester II (Gerbert).

1964 *Perf. 13* Unwmkd.

B382 SP229 30c +10c dp cl & blk 35 35
B383 SP229 30c +10c dk grn, blk & brn 35 35
B384 SP229 30c +10c sl & cl 35 35

The surtax was for the Red Cross.
Issue dates: No. B382, Apr. 25; No. B383, May 25; No. B384, June 1.

1964, Dec. 12 Engraved

Portrait; 25c+10c, Dominique Larrey.

Cross in Carmine

B385 SP230 20c +10c blk 40 30
a. Bklt. pane (4 #B385, 4 #B386 with gutter btwn.) 4.00
B386 SP230 25c +10c blk 40 30

Issued to honor Jean Nicolas Corvisart (1755-1821), physician of Napoleon I, and Dominique Larrey (1766-1842), Chief Surgeon of the Imperial Armies. The surtax was for the Red Cross.

Paul Dukas, Composer
SP231

Portraits: No. B387, Duke François de La Rochefoucauld, writer. No. B388, Nicolas Poussin, painter. No. B389, Duke Charles of Orléans, poet.

1965, Feb. Engraved *Perf. 13*

B387	SP231	30c +10c org brn & dk bl	50	50
B388	SP231	30c +10c car & dk red brn	50	50
B389	SP231	40c +10c dk red brn, dk red & Prus bl	55	55
B390	SP231	40c +10c dk brn & sl bl	55	55

The surtax was for the Red Cross.
Nos. B387 and B390 were issued Feb. 13; Nos. B388-B389 were issued Feb. 20.

Packet "La Guienne"
SP232

1965, Mar. 29 *Perf. 13* Unwmkd.

B391	SP232	25c +10c ultra, blk & sl grn	50	50

Issued for Stamp Day, 1965. "La Guienne" was used for transatlantic mail service. Surtax was for the Red Cross.

Infant with Spoon by Auguste Renoir
SP233

Design: 30c+10c, Coco Writing (Renoir's daughter Claude).

1965, Dec. 11 Engraved *Perf. 13*

Cross in Carmine

B392	SP233	25c +10c sl	25	25
a.		Bklt. pane (4 #B392, 4 #B393 with gutter btwn.)	3.25	
B393	SP233	30c +10c dl red brn	35	35

The surtax was for the Red Cross.

Francois Mansart and Carnavalet Palace, Paris—SP234

Designs: No. B395, St. Pierre Fourier and Basilica of St. Pierre Fourier, Mirecourt. No. B396, Marcel Proust and St. Hilaire Bridge, Illiers. No. B397, Gabriel Fauré, monument and score of "Penelope." No. B398, Elie Metchnikoff, microscope and Pasteur Institute. No. B399, Hippolyte Taine and birthplace.

1966 Engraved *Perf. 13*

B394	SP234	30c +10c dk red brn & grn	40	40
B395	SP234	30c +10c blk & gray grn	40	40
B396	SP234	30c +10c ind, sep & grn	40	40
B397	SP234	30c +10c bis brn & ind	40	40
B398	SP234	30c +10c blk & dl brn	40	40
B399	SP234	30c +10c grn & ol brn	40	40
		Nos. B394-B399 (6)	2.40	2.40

The surtax was for the Red Cross.
Issue dates: Nos. B394-B396, Feb. 12. Others, June 25.

Engraver Cutting Die and Tools
SP235

1966, March 19 Engraved *Perf. 13*

B400	SP235	25c +10c sl, dk brn & dp org	45	45

Stamp Day. Surtax for Red Cross.

Angel of Victory, Verdun Fortress, Marching Troops
SP236

First Aid on Battlefield, 1859
SP237

1966, May 28 *Perf. 13*

B401	SP236	30c +5c Prus bl, ultra & dk bl	30	30

Victory of Verdun, 50th anniversary.

1966, Dec. 10 Engraved *Perf. 13*

Design: 30c+10c, Nurse giving first aid to child, 1966.

Cross in Carmine

B402	SP237	25c +10c grn	40	40
a.		Bklt pane (4 #B402, 4 # B403 with gutter btwn.)	3.75	
B403	SP237	30c +10c sl	40	40

The surtax was for the Red Cross.

Emile Zola
SP238

Letter Carrier, 1865
SP239

Portraits: No. B405, Beaumarchais (pen name of Pierre Augustin Caron). No. B406, St. Francois de Sales (1567-1622). No. B407, Albert Camus (1913-1960).

1967 Engraved *Perf. 13*

B404	SP238	30c +10c sl bl & bl	40	40
B405	SP238	30c +10c rose brn & lil	40	40
B406	SP238	30c +10c dl vio & pur	40	40
B407	SP238	30c +10c brn & dl cl	40	40

The surtax was for the Red Cross.
Issue dates: Nos. B404-B405, Feb. 4. Others, June 24.

1967, Apr. 8

B408	SP239	25c +10c ind, grn & red	35	35

Issued for Stamp Day.

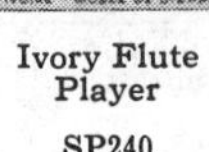

Ivory Flute Player
SP240

Ski Jump and Long Distance Skiing
SP241

Design: 30c+10c, Violin player, ivory carving.

1967, Dec. 16 Engraved *Perf. 13*

Cross in Carmine

B409	SP240	25c +10c dl vio & lt brn	40	40
a.		Bklt. pane (4 #B409, 4 #B410 with gutter btwn.)	3.50	
B410	SP240	30c +10c grn & lt brn	40	40

The surtax was for the Red Cross.

1968, Jan. 27

Designs: 40c+10c, Ice hockey. 60c+20c, Olympic flame and snowflakes. 75c+25c, Woman figure skater. 95c+35c, Slalom.

B411	SP241	30c +10c ver, gray & brn	30	30
B412	SP241	40c +10c lil, lem & brt mag	35	35
B413	SP241	60c +20c dk grn, org & brt vio	45	45
B414	SP241	75c +25c brt pink, yel grn & blk	65	65
B415	SP241	95c +35c bl, brt pink & red brn	80	80
		Nos. B411-B415 (5)	2.55	2.55

Issued for the 10th Winter Olympic Games, Grenoble, Feb. 6-18.

Rural Mailman, 1830
SP242

1968, Mar. 16 Engraved *Perf. 13*

B416	SP242	25c +10c bl gray, ultra & red	30	30

Issued for Stamp Day.

François Couperin, Composer, and Instruments
SP243

Portraits: No. B418, Gen. Louis Desaix de Veygoux (1768-1800) and scene showing his death at the Battle of Marengo, Italy. No. B419, Saint-Pol-Roux (pen name of Paul-Pierre Roux, 1861-1940), Christ on the Cross and ruins of Camaret-sur-Mer. No. B420, Paul Claudel (poet and diplomat, 1868-1955) and Joan of Arc at the stake.

1968 Engraved *Perf. 13*

B417	SP243	30c +10c pur & rose lil	30	30
B418	SP243	30c +10c dk grn & brn	30	30
B419	SP243	30c +10c cop red & ol bis	30	30
B420	SP243	30c +10c dk brn & lil	30	30

Issue dates: Nos. B417-B418, Mar, 23; Nos. B419-B420, July 6.

Spring, by Nicolas Mignard
SP244

Designs (Paintings by Nicolas Mignard): 30c+10c, Fall. No. B423, Summer. No. B424, Winter.

1968-69 Engraved *Perf. 13*

Cross in Carmine

B421	SP244	25c +10c pur & sl bl	35	35
a.		Bklt. pane (4 #B421, 4 #B422 with gutter btwn.)	3.50	
B422	SP244	30c +10c brn & rose car	35	35
B423	SP244	40c +15c dk brn & brn ('69)	45	45
a.		Bklt. pane (4 #B423, 4 #B424 with gutter btwn.)	4.50	
B424	SP244	40c +15c pur & Prus bl ('69)	45	45

The surtax was for the Red Cross.

Mailmen's Omnibus, 1881
SP245

1969, Mar. 15 Engraved *Perf. 13*

B425	SP245	30c +10c brn, grn & blk	30	30

Issued for Stamp Day.

Gen. Francois Marceau
SP246

Portraits: No. B427, Charles Augustin Sainte-Beuve (1804-1869), writer. No. B428, Albert Roussel (1869-1937), musician. No. B429, Marshal Jean Lannes (1769-1809). No. B430, Georges Cuvier (1769-1832), naturalist. No. B431, André Gide, (1869-1951), writer.

1969

B426	SP246	50c +10c brn red	55	55
B427	SP246	50c +10c sl bl	55	55
B428	SP246	50c +10c dp vio bl	55	55
B429	SP246	50c +10c choc	55	55
B430	SP246	50c +10c dp plum	55	55
B431	SP246	50c +10c bl grn	55	55
		Nos. B426-B431 (6)	3.30	3.30

The surtax was for the Red Cross.
Issue dates: Nos. B426-B428, Mar. 24. No. B429, May 10, Nos. B430-B431, May 17.

Gen. Jacques Leclerc, La Madeleine and Battle—SP247

1969, Aug. 23 Engraved *Perf. 13*

B432	SP247	45c +10c sl & ol	55	55

Issued to commemorate the 25th anniversary of the liberation of Paris, Aug. 25, 1944.

Same Inscribed
"Liberation de Strasbourg"

1969, Nov. 22 Engraved *Perf. 13*

B433	SP247	70c +10c brn, choc & ol	70	70

Issued to commemorate the 25th anniversary of the liberation of Strasbourg.

Philibert Delorme, Architect, and Chateau d'Anet—SP248

Designs: No. B435, Louis Le Vau (1612–1670), architect, and Vaux-le-Vicomte Chateau, Paris. No. B436, Prosper Merimée (1803–1870), writer, and Carmen. No. B437, Alexandre Dumas (1820–1870), writer, and Three Musketeers. No. B438, Edouard Branly (1844–1940), physicist, electric circuit and convent of the Carmes, Paris. No. B439, Maurice de Broglie (1875–1960), physicist, and X-ray spectrograph.

1970 Engraved *Perf. 13*

B434	SP248	40c +10c sl grn	55	55
B435	SP248	40c +10c dk car	55	55
B436	SP248	40c +10c Prus bl	55	55
B437	SP248	40c +10c vio bl	55	55
B438	SP248	40c +10c dp brn	55	55
B439	SP248	40c +10c dk gray	55	55
		Nos. B434-B439 (6)	3.30	3.30

The surtax was for the Red Cross.
Issue dates: No. B434–B436, Feb. 14; Nos. B437–B439, Apr. 11.

City Mailman, 1830 SP249 **"Life and Death"** SP250

1970, Mar. 14

B440	SP249	40c +10c blk, ultra & dk car rose	45	40

Issued for Stamp Day.

1970, Apr. 4

B441	SP250	40c +10c brt bl, ol & car rose	40	30

Issued to publicize the fight against cancer in connection with Health Day, Apr. 7.

Marshal de Lattre de Tassigny
SP251

1970, May 8 Engraved *Perf. 13*

B442	SP251	40c +10c sl & vio bl	40	35

Issued to commemorate the 25th anniversary of the entry into Berlin of French troops under Marshal Jean de Lattre de Tassigny, May 8, 1945.

Lord and Lady, Dissay Chapel Fresco
SP252

Design: No. B444, Angel holding whips, from fresco in Dissay Castle Chapel, Vienne, c. 1500.

1970, Dec. 12 Engraved *Perf. 13*

Cross in Carmine

B443	SP252	40c +15c grn	85	75
a.		Bklt. pane (4 #B443, 4 #B444 with gutter btwn.)	9.00	
B444	SP252	40c +15c cop red	85	75

The surtax was for the Red Cross.

Daniel-Francois Auber and "Fra Diavolo" Music
SP253

Designs: No. B446, Gen. Charles Diego Brosset (1898–1944), and Basilica of Fourvière. No. B447, Victor Grignard (1871–1935), chemist, and Nobel Prize medal. No. B448, Henri Farman (1874–1958) and plane. No. B449, Gen. Charles Georges Delestraint (1879–1945) and scroll. No. B450, Jean Eugène Robert-Houdin (1805–1871) and magician's act.

1971 Engraved *Perf. 13*

B445	SP253	50c +10c brn vio & brn	1.25	1.10
B446	SP253	50c +10c dk sl grn & ol gray	1.25	1.10
B447	SP253	50c +10c brn red & ol	1.25	1.10
B448	SP253	50c +10c vio bl & vio	1.25	1.10
B449	SP253	50c +10c pur & cl	1.25	1.10
B450	SP253	50c +10c sl grn & bl grn	1.25	1.10
		Nos. B445-B450 (6)	7.50	6.60

The surtax was for the Red Cross.
Issue dates: Nos. B445–B446, Mar. 6. No. B447, May 8. No. B448, May 29. Nos. B449–B450, Oct. 16.

Army Post Office, 1914–1918
SP254

1971, March 27 Engr. *Perf. 13*

B451	SP254	50c +10c ol, brn & bl	55	45

Stamp Day, 1971.

Girl with Dog, by Greuze **SP255** **Aristide Bergès (1833–1904)** **SP256**

Design: 50c+10c, "The Dead Bird," by Jean-Baptiste Greuze (1725–1805).

1971, Dec. 11

Cross in Carmine

B452	SP255	30c +10c vio bl	75	75
a.		Bklt. pane (4 #B452, 4 #B453 with gutter btwn.)	8.00	
B453	SP255	50c +10c dp car	75	75

The surtax was for the Red Cross.

1972 Engraved *Perf. 13*

Portraits: No. B455, Paul de Chomedey (1612–1676), founder of Montreal, and arms of Neuville-sur-Vanne. No. B456, Edouard Belin (1876–1963), inventor. No. B457, Louis Blériot (1872–1936), aviation pioneer. No. B458, Adm. François Joseph, Count de Grasse (1722–1788), hero of the American Revolution. No. B459, Théophile Gautier (1811–1872), writer.

B454	SP256	50c +10c blk & grn	1.10	1.10
B455	SP256	50c +10c blk & bl	1.10	1.10
B456	SP256	50c +10c blk & lil rose	1.10	1.10
B457	SP256	50c +10c red & blk	1.10	1.10
B458	SP256	50c +10c org & blk	1.50	1.50
B459	SP256	50c +10c blk & brn	1.50	1.50
		Nos. B454-B459 (6)	7.40	7.40

The surtax was for the Red Cross.
Issue dates: Nos. B454–B455, Feb. 19; No. B456, June 24; No. B457, July 1; Nos. B458–B459, Sept. 9.

Rural Mailman, 1894 **SP257** **Nicolas Desgenettes** **SP258**

1972, Mar. 18 Engr. *Perf. 13*

B460	SP257	50c +10c bl, yel & ol gray	55	45

Stamp Day 1972.

1972, Dec. 16 Engraved *Perf. 13*

Designs: 30c+10c, René Nicolas Dufriche, Baron Desgenettes, M.D. (1762–1837). 50c+10c, François Joseph Broussais, M.D. (1772–1838).

B461	SP258	30c +10c sl grn & red	90	75
a.		Bklt. pane (4 #B461, 4 #B462 with gutter btwn.)	8.00	
B462	SP258	50c +10c red	90	75

The surtax was for the Red Cross.

Gaspard de Coligny
SP259

Portraits: No. B463, Gaspard de Coligny (1519–1572), admiral and Huguenot leader. No. B464, Ernest Renan (1823–1892), philologist and historian. No. B465, Alberto Santos Dumont (1873–1932), Brazilian aviator. No. B466, Gabrielle-Sidonie Colette (1873–1954), writer. No. B467, René Duguay-Trouin (1673–1736), naval commander. No. B468, Louis Pasteur (1822–1895), chemist, bacteriologist. No. B469, Tony Garnier (1869–1948), architect.

1973 Engraved *Perf. 13*

B463	SP259	50c +10c multi	1.10	1.00
B464	SP259	50c +10c multi	1.10	1.00
B465	SP259	50c +10c multi	1.10	1.00
B466	SP259	50c +10c multi	1.10	1.00
B467	SP259	50c +10c multi	1.10	1.00
B468	SP259	50c +10c multi	1.20	1.10
B469	SP259	50c +10c multi	1.20	1.10
		Nos. B463-B469 (7)	7.90	7.20

Issue dates: No. B463, Feb. 17; No. B464, Apr. 28; No. B465, May 26; No. B466, June 2; No. B467, June 9; No. B468, Oct. 6; No. B469, Nov. 17.

Mail Coach, 1835
SP260

1973, Mar. 24 Engraved *Perf. 13*

B470	SP260	50c +10c grnsh bl	55	45

Stamp Day, 1973.

Mary Magdalene **SP261** **St. Louis-Marie de Montfort** **SP262**

Design: 50c+10c, Mourning woman. Designs are from 15th century Tomb of Tonnerre.

1973, Dec. 1

B471	SP261	30c +10c sl grn & red	60	60
a.		Bklt. pane (4 # B471, 4 #B472 with gutter btwn.)	5.50	
B472	SP261	50c +10c dk gray & red	75	75

Surtax was for the Red Cross.

1974, Feb. 23 Engraved *Perf. 13*

Portraits: No. B474, Francis Poulenc (1899–1963), composer. No. B475, Jules Barbey d'Aurevilly (1808–1889), writer. No. B476, Jean Giraudoux (1882–1944), writer.

B473	SP262	50c +10c multi	1.50	1.50
B474	SP262	50c +10c multi	1.10	1.10
B475	SP262	80c +15c multi	1.25	1.25
B476	SP262	80c +15c multi	1.25	1.25

Issue dates: No. B473, Mar. 9; No. B474, July 20; Nos. B475–B476, Nov. 16.

Automatically Sorted Letters
SP263

1974, Mar. 9 Engraved *Perf. 13*

B477	SP263	50c +10c multi	40	35

Stamp Day 1974. Automatic letter sorting center, Orleans-la-Source, opened Jan. 30, 1973.

Order of Liberation and 5 Honored Cities—SP264

1974, June 15 Engraved *Perf. 13*

B478	SP264	1fr +10c multi	70	60

30th anniversary of liberation from the Nazis.

"Summer" SP265 "Winter" SP266

Designs: B481, "Spring" (girl on swing). B482, "Fall" (umbrella and rabbits).

1974, Nov. 30 Engr. *Perf. 13*

B479	SP265	60c +15c multi	60	60
a.		Bklt. pane (4 #B479, 4 # B480 with gutter btwn.)	6.00	
B480	SP266	80c +15c multi	75	75

1975, Nov. 29

B481	SP265	60c +15c multi	55	45
a.		Booklet pane (4#B481, 4#B482 with gutter btwn.)	6.00	
B482	SP266	80c +20c multi	75	70

Surtax was for the Red Cross.

Dr. Albert Schweitzer SP267 Edmond Michelet SP268

André Siegfried and Map SP269

Portraits: No. B483, Albert Schweitzer (1875–1965), medical missionary, birth centenary. No. B484, Edmond Michelet (1899–1970), Resistance hero, statesman. No. B485, Robert Schuman (1886–1963), promoter of United Europe. No. B486, Eugene Thomas (1903–1969), minister of PTT. No. B487, André Siegfried (1875–1959), political science professor, writer, birth centenary.

1975 Engraved *Perf. 13*

B483	SP267	80c +20c multi	60	60
B484	SP268	80c +20c bl & ind	60	60
B485	SP268	80c +20c blk & ind	60	60
B486	SP268	80c +20c blk & sl	60	60
B487	SP269	80c +20c blk & bl	70	70
		Nos. B483-B487 (5)	3.10	3.10

Issue dates: No. B483, Jan. 11; No. B484, Feb. 22; No. B485, May 10; No. B486, June 28; No. B487, Nov. 15.

Second Republic Mailman's Badge SP270

1975, Mar. 8 Photogravure

B488	SP270	80c +20c multi	55	50

Stamp Day.

"Sage" Type of 1876 SP271 Marshal A. J. de Moncey SP272

1976, Mar. 13 Engr. *Perf. 13*

B489	SP271	80c +20c blk & lil	60	60

Stamp Day 1976.

1976 Engraved *Perf. 13*

Designs: No. B491, Max Jacob (1876–1944), Dadaist writer, by Picasso. No. B492, Jean Mounet-Sully (1841–1916), actor. No. B493, Gen. Pierre Daumesnil (1776–1832). No. B494, Eugène Fromentin (1820–1876), painter.

B490	SP272	80c +20c multi	70	70
B491	SP272	80c +20c red brn & ol	70	70
B492	SP272	80c +20c multi	70	70
B493	SP272	1fr +20c multi	70	70
B494	SP272	1fr +20c multi	70	70
		Nos. B490-B494 (5)	3.50	3.50

Issue dates: No. B490, May 22; No. B491, July 22. No. B492, Aug. 28; No. B493, Sept. 4; No. B494, Sept. 25.

Anna de Noailles SP273 St. Barbara SP274

1976, Nov. 6 Engr. *Perf. 13*

B495	SP273	1fr +20c multi	70	70

Anna de Noailles (1876–1933), writer and poet.

1976, Nov. 20

Design: 1fr+25c, Cimmerian Sibyl. Sculptures from Brou Cathedral.

Cross in Carmine

B496	SP274	80c +20c vio	75	70
a.		Booklet pane (4 #B496, 4 #B497 with gutter between)	7.75	
B497	SP274	1fr +25c dk brn	90	85

Surtax was for the Red Cross.

Marckolsheim Relay Station Sign SP275

1977, Mar. 26 Engr. *Perf. 13*

B498	SP275	1fr +20c multi	60	60

Stamp Day.

Edouard Herriot, Statesman and Writer SP276 Christmas Figurine, Provence SP277

Designs: No. B500, Abbé Breuil (1877–1961), archaeologist. No. B501, Guillaume de Machault (1305–1377), poet and composer. No. B502, Charles Cros (1842–1888).

1977 Engraved *Perf. 13*

B499	SP276	1fr +20c multi	70	70
B500	SP276	1fr +20c multi	70	70
B501	SP276	1fr +20c multi	70	70
B502	SP276	1fr +20c multi	70	70

Issue dates: No. B499, Oct. 8; No. B500, Oct. 15; No. B501, Nov. 12; No. B502, Dec. 3.

1977, Nov. 26

Design: 1fr+25c, Christmas figurine (woman), Provence.

B503	SP277	80c +20c red & ind	70	70
a.		Booklet pane (4 #B503, 4 #B504 with gutter between)	7.00	
B504	SP277	1fr +25c red & sl grn	85	85

Surtax was for the Red Cross.

Marie Noël, Writer SP278 Mail Collection, 1900 SP279

Designs: No. B506, Georges Bernanos (1888–1948), writer. No. B507, Leo Tolstoi (1828–1910), Russian writer. No. B508, Charles Marie Leconte de Lisle (1818–1894), poet. No. B509, Voltaire (1694–1778) and Jean Jacques Rousseau (1712–1778). No. B510, Claude Bernard (1813–1878), physiologist.

1978 Engraved *Perf. 13*

B505	SP278	1fr +20c multi	60	60
B506	SP278	1fr +20c multi	60	60
B507	SP278	1fr +20c multi	60	60
B508	SP278	1fr +20c multi	60	60
B509	SP278	1fr +20c multi	60	60
B510	SP278	1fr +20c multi	60	60
		Nos. B505-B510 (6)	3.60	3.60

Issue dates: No. B505, Feb. 11; No. B506, Feb. 18; No. B507, Apr. 15; No. B508, Mar. 26; No. B509, July 1; No. B510, Sept. 16.

1978, Apr. 8 Engr. *Perf. 13*

B511	SP279	1fr +20c multi	60	60

Stamp Day 1978.

The Hare and the Tortoise SP280

Design: 1.20fr+30c, The City Rat and the Country Rat.

1978, Dec. 2 Engr. *Perf. 13*

B512	SP280	1fr +25c multi	75	60
a.		Booklet pane (4 #B512,4 #B513 with gutter between)	7.00	
B513	SP280	1.20fr +30c multi	90	75

Surtax was for the Red Cross.

Ladislas Marshal de Berchény (1689–1778) SP281

Design: No. B515, Leon Jouhaux (1879–1954), labor leader. No. B516, Peter Abelard (1079–1142), theologian and writer. No. B517, Georges Courteline (1860–1929), humorist. No. B518, Simone Weil (1909–1943), social philosopher. No. B519, André Malraux (1901–1976), novelist.

1979 Engraved *Perf. 13*

B514	SP281	1.20fr +30c multi	75	75
B515	SP281	1.20fr +30c multi	75	75
B516	SP281	1.20fr +30c multi	75	75
B517	SP281	1.20fr +30c multi	75	75
B518	SP281	1.30fr +30c multi	75	75
B519	SP281	1.30fr +30c multi	75	75
		Nos. B514-B519 (6)	4.50	4.50

Issue dates: Nos. B514, Jan. 13; B515, May 12; B516, June 9; B517, June 25; B518, Nov. 12; B519, Nov. 26.

General Post Office, from 1908 Post Card—SP282

1979, Mar. 10 Engr. *Perf. 13*

B520	SP282	1.20fr +30c multi	60	45

Stamp Day 1979.

Woman, Stained-Glass Window SP283

Stained-glass windows, Church of St. Joan of Arc, Rouen: 1.30fr + 30c, Simon the Magician.

1979, Dec. 1

B521	SP283	1.10fr +30c multi	60	55
a.		Bklt. pane (4# B521, 4# B522 with gutter between)	6.00	
B522	SP283	1.30fr +30c multi	70	60

Surtax was for the Red Cross.

Eugene Viollet le Duc (1814-1879), Architect—SP284

Jean-Marie de Le Mennais (1780-1860), Priest and Educator—SP285

Designs No. B524, Jean Monnet (1888-1979), economist and diplomat. No. B526, Frederic Mistral (1830-1914), poet. No. B527, Saint-John Perse (Alexis Leger, 1887-1975), poet and diplomat. No. B528, Pierre Paul de Riquet (1604-1680), canal builder.

1980 Engr. *Perf. 13*

B523	SP284	1.30fr +30c multi	60	60
B524	SP284	1.30fr +30c multi	60	60
B525	SP285	1.40fr +30c bl	70	60
B526	SP285	1.40fr +30c blk	70	60
B527	SP285	1.40fr +30c multi	70	60
B528	SP284	1.40fr +30c multi	70	60
		Nos. B523-B528 (6)	4.00	3.60

Issue dates: No. B523, Feb. 16; No. B524, Nos. B525-B526, Sept. 6; Nos. B527-B528, Oct. 11.

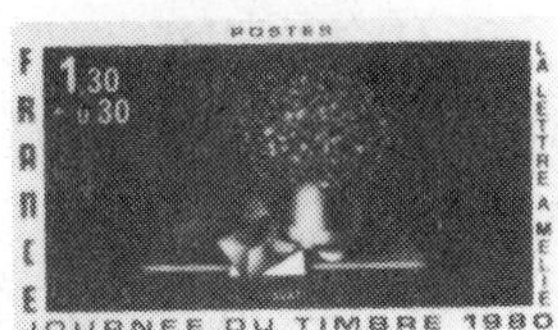

The Letter to Melie, By Avanti, Stamp Day 1980—SP285

1980, Mar. 8 Photo.

B529	SP285	1.30fr +30c multi	60	55

Filling the Granaries, Choir Stall Detail, Amiens Cathedral—SP287

Design: 1.40fr+30c, Grapes from the Promised Land.

1980, Dec. 6 Engraved *Perf. 13*

B530	SP287	1.20fr +30c red & dk red brn	55	45
B531	SP287	1.40fr +30c red & dk red brn	60	55
a.		Bklt. pane (4 #B530, 4 #B531 with gutter between)	6.75	

Sister Anne-Marie Javouhey (1779-1851), Founded Congregation of St. Joseph of Cluny—SP288

Designs: No. B532, Louis Armand (1905-1971), railway engineer. B533, Louis Jouvet (1887-1951), theater director. B534, Marc Boegner (1881-1970), peace worker. No. B536, Jacques Offenbach (1819-1880), composer. No. B537, Pierre Teilhard de Chardin (1881-1955), philosopher.

1981 Engr. *Perf. 13*

B532	SP288	1.20fr +30c multi	55	45
B533	SP288	1.20fr +30c multi	55	45
B534	SP288	1.40fr +30c multi	60	45
B535	SP288	1.40fr+30c brn ol & gray brn	60	45
B536	SP288	1.40fr+30c blk & bluish gray	60	45
B537	SP288	1.40fr +30c multi	60	45
		Nos. B532-B537 (6)	3.50	2.70

Issue dates: #B532, May 23; #B533, June 13; #B534, Nov. 14; #B535, Feb. 7; #B536, Feb. 14; #B537, May 23.

The Love Letter, by Goya—SP289

1981, Mar. 7 *Perf. 13x12½*

B538	SP289	1.40fr +30c multi	60	45

Stamp Day 1981.

Scourges of the Passion—SP290

Guillaume Postel (1510-1581), Theologian—SP291

Stained-glass Windows, Church of the Sacred Heart, Audincourt: 1.60fr+30c, "Peace."

1981, Dec. 5 Photo. *Perf. 13*

B539	SP290	1.40 +30c multi	45	40
B540	SP290	1.60 +30c multi	50	45
a.		Bklt. pane (4 #B539, 4 #B540 with gutter between)	5.00	

1982 Engr. *Perf. 13*

Designs: No. B542, Henri Mondor (1885-1962), physician. No. B545, Robert Debre (1882-1978), writer.

Designs: No. B543, Andre Chantemesse (1851-1919), scientist. No. B546, Gustave Eiffel (1832-1923), engineer.

B541	SP291	1.40fr +30c	55	55
B542	SP291	1.40fr +30c dk brn & dk bl	55	55
B543	SP291	1.60fr +30c multi	60	60
B544	SP291	1.60fr +40c	60	60
B545	SP291	1.60fr +40c dk bl	60	60
B546	SP291	1.80fr +40c multi	65	65

Woman Reading, by Picasso—SP292

1982, Mar. 27

B547	SP292	1.60fr +40c multi	60	60

Stamp Day.

Five Weeks in a Balloon, by Jules Verne—SP293

Design: 20,000 Leagues under the Sea.

1982, Nov 20

B548	SP293	1.60fr +30c multi	60	60
B549	SP293	1.80fr +40c multi	65	65

Surtax was for Red Cross.

Andre Messager (1853-1929)—SP294

Designs: No. B553, Hector Berlioz (1803-1869), composer. No. B551, J.A. Gabriel (1698-1782), architect.

1983 Engr. *Perf. 12½x13*

B550	SP294	1.60fr +30c multi	60	60
B551	SP294	1.60fr +30c multi	60	60
B553	SP294	1.80fr +40c dp lil & blk	65	65

Issue dates: No. B550, Jan. 15; No. B553, Jan. 22.

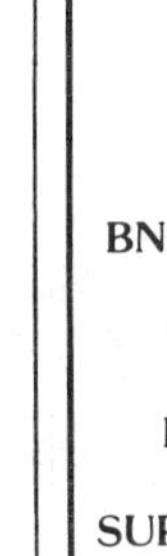

Man Dictating a Letter, by Rembrandt—SP295

Photo. & Engr.

1983, Feb. 26 *Perf. 13x12½*

B556	SP295	1.80fr +40c multi	65	65

Stamp Day.

AIR POST STAMPS.

Nos. 127, 130 Overprinted in Dark Blue or Black

Poste Aérienne

Perf. 14x13½

1927, June 25 **Unwmkd.**

C1	A18	2fr org & bl (DB)	200.00	175.00
C2	A18	5fr dk bl & buff (Bk)	200.00	175.00

These stamps were on sale only at the International Aviation Exhibition at Marseilles, June, 1927. One set could be purchased by each holder of an admission ticket. Excellent counterfeits exist.

Nos. 242, 196 Surcharged **10 Fr.**

1928, Aug. 23

C3	A33	10fr on 90c dl rose	1,750.	1,750.
a.		Inverted surcharge	*10,000.*	*10,000.*
b.		Space between "10" and bars 6½mm	*2,750.*	*2,750.*
C4	A23	10fr on 1.50fr bl	*8,000.*	*8,000.*
a.		Space between "10" and bars 6½mm	*10,000.*	*10,000.*

Nos. C3-C4 received their surcharge in New York by order of the French consul-general. They were for use in paying the 10fr fee for letters leaving the liner Ile de France on a catapulted hydroplane when the ship was one day off the coast of France on its eastward voyage.

The normal space between "10" and bars is 4½mm., but on 10 stamps in each pane of 50 the space is 6½mm. Counterfeits exist.

View of Marseille, Church of Notre Dame at Left
AP1

1930-31 **Engraved** ***Perf. 13***

C5	AP1	1.50fr dp car	20.00	2.00
C6	AP1	1.50fr dk bl ('31)	20.00	1.75
a.		1.50fr ultra	37.50	12.00
b.		With perf. initials (EIPA 30)	550.00	400.00

No. C6a was sold at the International Air Post Exhibition, Paris, Nov. 6-20, 1930, at face value plus 5 francs, the price of admission. Most of the stamps of the first printing were perforated "EIPA30".

Blériot's Monoplane—AP2

1934, Sept. 1 ***Perf. 13***

C7	AP2	2.25fr violet	20.00	5.50

Issued in commemoration of the first flight across the English Channel, by Louis Blériot.

Plane over Paris
AP3

1936

C8	AP3	85c dp grn	3.25	75
C9	AP3	1.50fr blue	9.50	3.75
C10	AP3	2.25fr violet	20.00	5.50
C11	AP3	2.50fr rose	27.50	6.25
C12	AP3	3fr ultra	9.00	55
C13	AP3	3.50fr org brn	65.00	16.00
C14	AP3	50fr emerald	900.00	300.00
a.		50fr dp grn	1,200.	575.00
		Nos. C8-C14 (7)	1,034.25	332.80

Monoplane over Paris—AP4
Paper with Red Network Overprint

1936, July 10 ***Perf. 12½***

C15	AP4	50fr ultra	750.00	250.00

Airplane and Galleon
AP5

Airplane and Globe
AP6

1936, Aug. 17 ***Perf. 13***

C16	AP5	1.50fr dk ultra	13.00	2.25
C17	AP6	10fr Prus grn	350.00	110.00

Issued in commemoration of the 100th air mail flight across the South Atlantic Ocean.

Centaur and Plane
AP7

Iris
AP8

Zeus Carrying Hebe
AP9

Chariot of the Sun
AP10

1946-47 **Engraved** **Unwmkd.**

C18	AP7	40fr dk grn	50	12
C19	AP8	50fr rose pink	50	12
C20	AP9	100fr dk bl ('47)	2.50	40
C21	AP10	200fr red	2.75	60

Ile de la Cité, Paris, and Gull
AP11

1947, May 7

C22	AP11	500fr dk Prus grn	37.50	32.50

Universal Postal Union 12th Congress, Paris, May 7-July 7, 1947.

View of Lille
AP12

Air View of Paris—AP13

Designs: 200fr, Bordeaux. 300fr, Lyon. 500fr, Marseille.

1949-50 ***Perf. 13.*** **Unwmkd.**

C23	AP12	100fr sepia	90	15
C24	AP12	200fr dk bl grn	8.00	80
C25	AP12	300fr purple	16.50	11.00
C26	AP12	500fr brt red	37.50	4.50
C27	AP13	1000fr sep & blk, *bl* ('50)	80.00	20.00
		Nos. C23-C27 (5)	142.90	36.45

Alexander III Bridge and Petit Palais, Paris—AP14

1949, June 13

C28	AP14	100fr brn car	7.50	5.00

Issued to publicize the International Telegraph and Telephone Conference, Paris, May-July 1949.

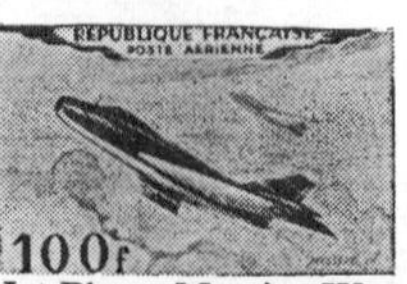

Jet Plane, Mystère IV
AP15

Planes: 200fr, Noratlas. 500fr, Miles Magister. 1000fr, Provence.

1954, Jan. 16

C29	AP15	100fr red brn & bl	1.25	12
C30	AP15	200fr blk brn & vio bl	4.50	15
C31	AP15	500fr car & org	85.00	10.00
C32	AP15	1000fr vio brn, bl grn & ind	100.00	15.00

Maryse Bastié and Plane
AP16

1955, June 4 ***Perf. 13*** **Unwmkd.**

C33	AP16	50fr dp plum & rose pink	7.50	5.00

Issued to honor Maryse Bastié, 1898-1952.

Caravelle—AP17

Designs: 300fr, Morane Saulnier 760 "Paris." 1000fr, Alouette helicopter.

1957-59 **Engraved.** ***Perf. 13***

C34	AP17	300fr sl grn, grnsh bl & sep ('59)	4.00	2.25
C35	AP17	500fr dp ultra & blk	40.00	2.25
C36	AP17	1000fr lil, ol blk & blk ('58)	60.00	22.50

Types of 1954-59.

Planes: 2fr, Noratlas. 3fr, MS760, Paris. 5fr, Caravelle. 10fr, Alouette helicopter.

1960, Jan. 11

C37	AP15	2fr vio bl & ultra	2.00	8
a.		2fr ultra	3.25	25
C38	AP17	3fr sl grn, grnsh bl & sep	1.75	8
C39	AP17	5fr dp ultra & blk	3.00	25
C40	AP17	10fr lil, ol blk & blk	17.00	1.50

Type of 1957-59.

Design: 2fr, Jet plane, Mystère 20.

1965, June 12 **Engraved** ***Perf. 13***

C41	AP17	2fr sl bl & ind	1.25	8

Concorde Issue
Common Design Type

1969, Mar. 2 **Engraved** ***Perf. 13***

C42	CD129	1fr ind & brt bl	1.75	40

Issued to commemorate the first flight of the prototype Concorde plane at Toulouse, March 1, 1969.

Jean Mermoz, Antoine de Saint-Exupéry and Concorde—AP19

1970, Sept. 19 **Engraved** ***Perf. 13***

C43	AP19	20fr bl & ind	5.25	45

Issued to honor Jean Mermoz (1901-1936) and the writer Antoine de Saint-Exupéry (1900-1944), aviators and air mail pioneers.

Balloon, Gare d'Austerlitz, Paris
AP20

1971, Jan. 16 Engraved *Perf. 13*

4 AP20 95c bl, vio bl, org & sl grn 1.10 90

Centenary of the balloon post from besieged Paris, 1870–71.

Didier Daurat, Raymond Vanier and Plane Landing at Night—AP21

1971, Apr. 17 Engraved *Perf. 13*

45 AP21 5fr Prus bl, blk & lt grn 1.50 12

Honoring Didier Daurat (1891–1969) and Raymond Vanier (1895–1965), aviation pioneers.

Hélène Boucher, Maryse Hilsz and Caudron-Renault and Moth-Morane Planes—AP22

Design: 15fr, Henri Guillaumet, Paul Codos, Latécoère 521, Guillaumet's crashed plane in Andes, skyscrapers.

1972–73 Engraved *Perf. 13*

46 AP22 10fr plum, red & sl 3.00 15
47 AP22 15fr dp car, gray & brn ('73) 4.00 45

Hélène Boucher (1908–1934) and Maryse Hilsz (1901–1946), aviation pioneers.
Henri Guillaumet (1902–1940) and Paul Codos (1896–1960), aviation pioneers.
Issue dates: 10fr, June 10, 1972; 15fr, Feb. 24, 1973.

Concorde
AP23

1976, Jan. 10 Engr. *Perf. 13*

C48 AP23 1.70fr brt bl, red & blk 1.00 50

First flight of supersonic jet Concorde from Paris to Rio de Janeiro, Jan. 21.

Planes over the Atlantic, New York-Paris—AP24

1977, June 4 Engr. *Perf. 13*

C49 AP24 1.90fr multi 90 50

First transatlantic flight by Charles A. Lindbergh from New York to Paris, 50th anniversary, and first attempted westbound flight by French aviators Charles Nungesser and Francois Coli.

Plane over Flight Route
AP25

1978, Oct. 14 Engr. *Perf. 13*

C50 AP25 1.50fr multi 65 38

75th anniversary of first airmail route from Villacoublay to Pauillac, Gironde.

Rocket, Concorde, Exhibition Hall
AP26

1979, June 9 Engr. *Perf. 13*

C51 AP26 1.70fr ultra, org & brn 75 30

33rd International Aerospace and Space Show, Le Bourget, June 11–15.

First Nonstop Transatlantic Flight, Paris-New York—AP27

1980, Aug. 30 Engr. *Perf. 13*

C52 AP27 2.50fr vio brn & ultra 80 22

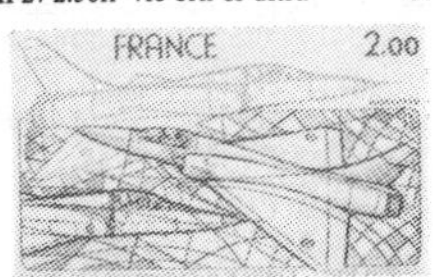

34th Intl. Space and Aeronautics Exhibition, June 5-14—AP28

1981, June 6 Engr. *Perf. 13*

C53 AP28 2fr multi 60 18

Dieudonné Costes and Joseph Le Brix and their Breguet Bi-plane—AP29

1981, Sept. 12 Engr.

C54 AP29 10fr dk brn & red 3.00 1.50

First South Atlantic crossing, Oct. 14-15, 1927.

Seaplane Late-300—AP30

1982, Dec. 4 Engr. *Perf.*

C55 AP30 1.60fr multi 50 30

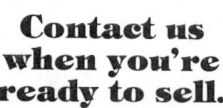

AIR POST SEMI-POSTAL STAMPS.

Antoine de Saint-Exupéry
SPAP1

Col. Jean Dagnaux
SPAP2

Engraved

1948 ***Perf. 13*** **Unwmkd.**

CB1	SPAP1	50fr +30fr vio brn	1.20	1.20
CB2	SPAP2	100fr +70fr dk bl	2.40	2.00

Modern Plane and Ader's "Eole"
SPAP3

1948. Feb.

CB3	SPAP3	40fr +10fr dk bl	1.00	90

Issued to commemorate the 50th anniversary of the flight of Clément Ader's plane, the Eole, in 1897.

POSTAGE DUE STAMPS.

D1

D2

Lithographed

1859–70 ***Imperf.*** **Unwmkd.**

J1	D1	10c black	*8,000.*	200.00
J2	D1	15c blk ('70)	120.00	200.00

In the lithographed stamps the central bar of the "E" of "CENTIMES" is very short, and the accent on "a" slants at an angle of 30°, for the 10c and 17° for the 15c, while on the typographed the central bar of the "E" is almost as wide as the top and bottom bars and the accent on the "a" slants at an angle of 47°.

No. J2 is known rouletted unofficially.

1859-78 Typographed.

J3	D1	10c black	20.00	15.00
J4	D1	15c blk ('63)	22.50	12.50
J5	D1	20c blk ('77)	*1,850.*	
J6	D1	25c blk ('71)	90.00	37.50
J7	D1	30c blk ('78)	150.00	100.00
J8	D1	40c bl ('71)	265.00	350.00
a.		40c ultra	*4,000.*	*5,000.*
b.		40c Prus bl	*1,850.*	
J9	D1	60c yel ('71)	400.00	*1,000.*
J10	D1	60c bl ('78)	50.00	*90.00*
a.		60c dk bl	450.00	550.00
J10B	D1	60c black	*1,850.*	

The 20c and 60c black were never put into use.

Nos. J3, J4, J6, J8 and J9 are known rouletted unofficially and Nos. J4, J6, J7 and J10 pin-perf. unofficially.

1882-92 ***Perf. 14x13½.***

J11	D2	1c black	60	60
J12	D2	2c black	11.00	12.00
J13	D2	3c black	11.00	13.00
J14	D2	4c black	18.50	14.00
J15	D2	5c black	40.00	11.00
J16	D2	10c black	37.50	1.10
J17	D2	15c black	20.00	5.25
J18	D2	20c black	100.00	65.00
J19	D2	30c black	75.00	1.10
J20	D2	40c black	45.00	25.00
J21	D2	50c blk ('92)	225.00	90.00
J22	D2	60c blk ('84)	225.00	27.50
J23	D2	1fr black	275.00	185.00
J24	D2	2fr blk ('84)	525.00	375.00
J25	D2	5fr blk ('84)	1,000.	700.00

Excellent counterfeits exist of Nos. J23-J25.

1884

J26	D2	1fr brown	175.00	55.00
J27	D2	2fr brown	110.00	85.00
J28	D2	5fr brown	200.00	150.00

1893–1941

J29	D2	5c bl ('94)	38	22
J30	D2	10c brown	38	15
J31	D2	15c lt grn ('94)	11.00	90
J32	D2	20c ol grn ('06)	1.75	22
J33	D2	25c rose ('23)	2.75	2.00
J34	D2	30c red ('94)	1.25	8
J35	D2	30c org red ('94)	425.00	60.00
J36	D2	40c rose ('25)	4.75	1.85
J37	D2	45c grn ('24)	3.50	2.25
J38	D2	50c brn vio ('95)	38	15
a.		50c lil	38	15
J39	D2	60c bl grn ('25)	45	25
J40	D2	1fr rose, *straw* ('96)	425.00	300.00
J41	D2	1fr red brn, *straw* ('20)	1.75	15
J42	D2	1fr red brn ('35)	45	18
J43	D2	2fr red org ('10)	150.00	37.50
J44	D2	2fr brt vio ('26)	38	22
J45	D2	3fr mag ('26)	38	22
J45A	D2	5fr red org ('41)	1.25	1.25

D3

D4

1908–25

J46	D3	1c ol grn	60	25
J47	D3	10c violet	60	15
a.		Imperf., pair	175.00	
J48	D3	20c bis ('19)	9.00	38
J49	D3	30c bis ('09)	4.50	30
J50	D3	50c red ('09)	175.00	45.00
J51	D3	60c red ('25)	1.75	90
		Nos. J46-J51 (6)	191.45	46.98

"Recouvrements" stamps were used to recover charges due on undelivered or refused mail which was returned to the sender.

Nos. J49–J50 Surcharged — 20 c.

1917

J52	D3	20c on 30c bis	7.50	2.25
J53	D3	40c on 50c red	7.50	1.75
a.		Double surch.	165.00	

In Jan. 1917 several values of the current issue of postage stamps were handstamped "T" in a triangle and used as postage due stamps.

Recouvrements Stamps of 1908-25 Surcharged — 50

1926

J54	D3	50c on 10c lil	3.00	1.40
J55	D3	60c on 1c ol grn	4.50	2.25
J56	D3	1fr on 60c red	12.00	5.25
J57	D3	2fr on 60c red	12.00	6.00

1927-31

J58	D4	1c ol grn ('28)	1.00	38
J59	D4	10c rose ('31)	1.40	3
J60	D4	30c bister	3.50	1
J61	D4	60c red	2.75	1
J62	D4	1fr violet	10.00	2.2
J63	D4	1fr Prus grn ('31)	11.50	4
J64	D4	2fr blue	37.50	12.5
J65	D4	2fr ol brn ('31)	110.00	14.0
		Nos. J58-J65 (8)	177.65	30.2

Nos. J62 to J65 have the numerals of value double-lined.

Nos. J64, J62 Surcharged in Red or Black — 1F 20

1929

J66	D4	1.20fr on 2fr bl	27.50	4.0
J67	D4	5fr on 1fr vio (Bk)	35.00	5.5

No. J61 Surcharged — UN FRANC

1931

J68	D4	1fr on 60c red	13.00	1.5

Sheaves of Wheat
D5 D6

Typographed.

1943-46 ***Perf. 14x13½.*** **Unwmkd.**

J69	D5	10c sepia	15	10
J70	D5	30c brt red vio	15	12
J71	D5	50c bl grn	15	12
J72	D5	1fr brt ultra	15	12
J73	D5	1.50fr rose red	15	12
J74	D5	2fr turq bl	32	12
J75	D5	3fr brn org	32	12
J76	D5	4fr dp vio ('45)	2.50	1.60
J77	D5	5fr brt pink	40	20
J78	D5	10fr red org ('45)	2.00	65
J79	D5	20fr ol bis ('46)	5.25	1.75
		Nos. J69-J79 (11)	11.54	5.02

Type of 1943.
Inscribed "Timbre Taxe."

1946-53

J80	D5	10c sep ('47)	1.40	1.10
J81	D5	30c brt red vio ('47)	1.00	75
J82	D5	50c bl grn ('47)	5.25	3.25
J83	D5	1fr brt ultra ('47)	15	5
J85	D5	2fr turq bl	15	8
J86	D5	3fr brn org	15	5
J87	D5	4fr dp vio	32	12
J88	D5	5fr brt pink ('47)	32	12
J89	D5	10fr red org ('47)	32	12
J90	D5	20fr ol bis ('47)	1.40	30
J91	D5	50fr dk grn ('50)	6.25	32
J92	D5	100fr dp grn ('53)	40.00	3.50
		Nos. J80-J92 (12)	56.71	9.76

1960 **Typographed.** ***Perf. 14x13½***

J93	D6	5c brt pink	1.40	30
J94	D6	10c red org	1.60	30
J95	D6	20c ol bis	3.25	30
J96	D6	50c dk grn	9.00	1.10
J97	D6	1fr dp grn	35.00	1.25
		Nos. J93-J97 (5)	50.25	3.25

Corn Poppy
D7

Flowers: 5c, Centaury. 10c, Gentian. 20c, Violets. 30c, Forget-me-not. 40c, Columbine. 50c, Clover. 1fr, Soldanel.

1964–71 **Typo.** ***Perf. 14x13½***

J98	D7	5c car rose, red & grn ('65)	5	5
J99	D7	10c car rose, brt bl & grn ('65)	12	5
J100	D7	15c brn, grn & red	12	6
J101	D7	20c dk grn, grn & vio ('71)	12	5

2	D7	30c brn, ultra & grn	14	6
3	D7	40c dk grn, scar & yel ('71)	15	12
4	D7	50c vio bl, car & grn ('65)	18	8
5	D7	1fr vio bl, lil & grn ('65)	38	12
		Nos. J98-J105 (8)	1.26	59

MILITARY STAMPS

Regular Issue Overprinted in Black or Red **F. M.**

901-39 ***Perf. 14x13½*** **Unwmkd.**

	A17	15c org ('01)	65.00	8.00
a.		Inverted overprint	150.00	72.50
b.		Imperf., pair	300.00	
2	A19	15c pale red ('03)	55.00	5.00
3	A20	15c sl grn ('04)	45.00	5.50
a.		No period after "M"	90.00	37.50
b.		Imperf., pair	200.00	
4	A20	10c rose ('06)	30.00	7.00
a.		No period after "M"	75.00	37.50
b.		Imperf., pair	250.00	
5	A22	10c red ('07)	60	20
a.		Inverted overprint	52.50	35.00
b.		Imperf., pair	175.00	
6	A20	50c ver ('29)	3.25	75
a.		No period after "M"	35.00	15.00
b.		Period in front of F	35.00	15.00
7	A45	50c rose red ('34)	1.20	25
a.		No period after "M"	5.00	3.00
b.		Invtd. ovpt.	50.00	30.00
8	A45	65c brt ultra (R) ('38)	35	20
a.		No period after "M"	25.00	18.50
9	A45	90c ultra (R) ('39)	40	30

"F. M." are initials of Franchise Militaire (Military Frank). See No. S1.

M1

Flag—M2

1946-47 **Typographed.**

M10	M1	dk grn	90	45
M11	M1	rose red ('47)	22	5

Nos. M10-M11 were valid also in the French colonies.

1964, July 20 ***Perf. 13x14***

M12	M2	multi	30	22

OFFICIAL STAMPS

For the Council of Europe.

For use only on mail posted in the post office in the Council of Europe Building, Strasbourg.

France No. 854 Overprinted: "CONSEIL DE L'EUROPE."

Engraved.

1958, Jan. 14 ***Perf. 13*** **Unwmkd.**

1O1	A303	35fr car rose & lake	2.25	3.50

Council of Europe Flag O1

1958-59

Flag in Ultramarine.

1O2	O1	8fr red org & brn vio	25	25
1O3	O1	20fr yel & lt brn	50	40
1O4	O1	25fr lil rose & sl grn ('59)	1.00	55
1O5	O1	35fr red	90	80
1O6	O1	50fr lil rose ('59)	1.60	1.60
		Nos. 1O2-1O6 (5)	4.25	3.60

1963, Jan. 3

Flag in Ultramarine

1O7	O1	20c yel & lt brn	1.25	75
1O8	O1	25c lil rose & sl grn	2.25	1.50
1O9	O1	50c lil rose	2.75	2.25

1965-71

Flag in Ultramarine & Yellow

1O10	O1	25c ver, yel & sl grn	1.25	1.00
1O11	O1	30c ver & yel	1.25	1.00
1O12	O1	40c ver, yel & gray ('69)	1.10	1.00
1O13	O1	50c red, yel & grn ('71)	2.00	1.40
1O14	O1	60c ver, yel & vio	1.25	1.00
1O15	O1	70c ver, yel & dk brn ('69)	3.75	3.00
		Nos. 1O10-1O15 (6)	11.85	9.15

Issue dates: 25c, 30c, 60c, Jan. 16, 1965. 50c, Feb. 20, 1971. Others, Mar. 24, 1969.

Type of 1958 Inscribed "FRANCE"

1975-76 **Engraved** ***Perf. 13***

Flag in Ultramarine & Yellow

1O16	O1	60c org, yel & emer	1.10	90
1O17	O1	80c yel & mag	1.85	1.40
1O18	O1	1fr car, yel & gray ol ('76)	3.75	3.00
1O19	O1	1.20fr org, yel & bl	4.50	3.75

Issue dates: 1fr, Oct. 16, 1976. Others, Nov. 22, 1975.

New Council Headquarters, Strasbourg O2

1977, Jan. 22 **Engr.** ***Perf. 13***

1O20	O2	80c car & multi	90	60
1O21	O2	1fr brn & multi	90	60
1O22	O2	1.40fr gray & multi	1.50	1.25

Human Rights Emblem in Upper Left Corner

1978, Oct. 14

1O23	O2	1.20fr red lil & multi	60	55
1O24	O2	1.70fr bl & multi	90	75

30th anniversary of the Universal Declaration of Human Rights.

Council Headquarters Type of 1977

1980, Nov. 24 **Engraved** ***Perf. 13***

1O25	O2	1.40fr olive	55	45
1O26	O2	2fr bl gray	70	60

For the United Nations Educational, Scientific and Cultural Organization

For use only on mail posted in the post office in the UNESCO Building, Paris.

Khmer Buddha and Hermes by Praxiteles O1

Engraved

1961-65 ***Perf. 13*** **Unwmkd.**

2O1	O1	20c dk gray, ol bis & bl	45	38
2O2	O1	25c blk, lake & grn	60	45
2O3	O1	30c choc & bis brn ('65)	1.10	90
2O4	O1	50c blk, red & vio bl	2.50	2.00
2O5	O1	60c grnsh bl, red brn & rose lil ('65)	2.25	2.00
		Nos. 2O1-2O5 (5)	6.90	5.73

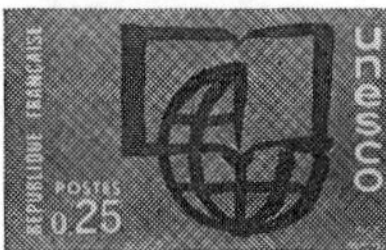

Book and Globe O2

1966, Dec. 17

2O6	O2	25c gray	50	50
2O7	O2	30c dk red	75	75
2O8	O2	60c green	1.35	1.35

20th anniversary of UNESCO.

Human Rights Flame O3

1969-71 **Engraved** ***Perf. 13***

2O9	O3	30c sl grn, red & dp brn	50	50
2O10	O3	40c dk car rose, red & dp brn	75	65
2O11	O3	50c ultra, car & brn ('71)	1.40	1.40
2O12	O3	70c pur, red & sl	4.00	3.50

Universal Declaration of Human Rights.

Type of 1969 Inscribed "FRANCE"

1975, Nov. 15 **Engr.** ***Perf. 13***

2O13	O3	60c grn, red & dk brn	1.10	90
2O14	O3	80c ocher, red & red brn	1.85	1.40
2O15	O3	1.20fr ind, red & brn	4.50	3.75

O4

1976-78 **Engr.** ***Perf. 13***

2O16	O4	80c multi	90	75
2O17	O4	1fr multi	1.00	75
2O18	O4	1.20fr multi ('78)	60	55
2O19	O4	1.40fr multi	1.85	1.50
2O20	O4	1.70fr multi ('78)	90	75
		Nos. 2O16-2O20 (5)	5.25	4.30

Issue dates: 1.20fr, 1.70fr, Oct. 14, 1978. Others, Oct. 23, 1976.

Slave Quarters, Senegal—O5

Designs: 1.40fr, Mohenjo-Daro excavations, Pakistan. 2fr, Sans-Souci Palace, Haiti.

1980, Nov. 17 **Engr.** ***Perf. 13***

2O21	O5	1.20fr multi	45	40
2O22	O5	1.40fr multi	55	50
2O23	O5	2fr multi	70	60

NEWSPAPER STAMPS.

Coat of Arms N1

Typographed.

1868 ***Imperf.*** **Unwmkd.**

P1	N1	2c lilac	250.00	65.00
P2	N1	2c (+2c) bl	500.00	250.00

Perf. 12½.

P3	N1	2c lilac	40.00	21.00
P4	N1	2c (+4c) rose	125.00	85.00
P5	N1	2c (+2c) bl	60.00	32.50
P6	N1	5c lilac	900.00	600.00

Nos. P2, P4, and P5 were sold for face plus an added fiscal charge indicated in parenthesis. Nos. P1, P3 and P6 were used simply as fiscals.

The 2c rose and 5c lilac imperforate and the 5c rose and 5c blue, both imperforate and perforated, were never put into use.

Nos. P1-P6 were reprinted for the 1913 Ghent Exhibition and the 1937 Paris Exhibition (PEXIP).

No. 109 Surcharged in Red **1/2 centime**

1919 ***Perf. 14x13½***

P7	A16	½c on 1c gray	20	15
a.		Inverted surcharge	400.00	250.00

No. 156 Surcharged.

1933

P8	A22	½c on 1c ol bis	50	40

FRANCHISE STAMP.

No. 276 Overprinted "F".

1939 ***Perf. 14x13½*** **Unwmkd.**

S1	A45	90c ultra	2.50	2.50
a.		Period after "F"	25.00	25.00

No. S1 was for the use of Spanish refugee soldiers in France. "F" stands for "Fugitives."

OCCUPATION STAMPS.

Issued under German Occupation.

(Alsace and Lorraine).

O1

Perf. 13½x14.

1870 **Typographed** **Unwmkd.**

Network with Points Up.

N1	O1	1c ol grn	52.50	110.00
N2	O1	2c red brn	100.00	135.00
a.		2c dk brn	125.00	165.00
N3	O1	4c gray	95.00	65.00
N4	O1	5c yel grn	62.50	10.00
N5	O1	10c yel brn	30.00	3.50
a.		10c bis brn	57.50	5.00
b.		Network lem yel	72.50	8.50
N6	O1	20c ultra	67.50	10.00
N7	O1	25c brown	125.00	67.50
a.		25c blk brn	165.00	100.00

There are three varieties of the 4c and two of the 10c, differing in the position of the figures of value, and several other setting varieties.

Network with Points Down.

No.	Type	Description	Unused	Used
N8	O1	1c ol grn	325.00	800.00
N9	O1	2c red brn	150.00	700.00
N10	O1	4c gray	165.00	125.00
N11	O1	5c yel grn	2,500.	325.00
N12	O1	10c bister	80.00	10.00
a.		Network lem yel	275.00	80.00
N13	O1	20c ultra	225.00	115.00
N14	O1	25c brown	500.00	250.00

Official imitations have the network with points downward. The "P" of "Postes" is 2½mm. from the border in the imitations and 3mm. in the originals. The word "Postes" measures 12¾ to 13mm. on the imitations, and from 11 to 12½mm. on the originals.

The imitations are perf. 13½x14½; originals, perf. 13½x14¼.

The stamps for Alsace and Lorraine were replaced by stamps of the German Empire on Jan. 1, 1872.

German Stamps of 1905–16 Surcharged:

3 Cent.
a

b

✻ 1F.25Cent. ✻
c

Wmkd. Lozenges. (125)

1916 *Perf. 14, 14½.*

No.	Type	Description	Unused	Used
N15	A16(a)	3c on 3pf brn	50	50
N16	A16(a)	5c on 5pf grn	50	75
N17	A22(a)	8c onn 7½pf org	60	1.00
N18	A16(a)	10c on 10pf car	50	50
N19	A22(a)	15c on 15pf yel brn	50	50
N20	A16(a)	25c on 20pf bl	75	75
a.		25c on 20pf ultra	75	75
N21	A16(a)	40c on 30pf org & blk, *buff*	1.00	1.00
N22	A16(a)	50c on 40pf lake & blk	1.00	1.25
N23	A16(a)	75c on 60pf mag	3.00	3.50
N24	A16(b)	1fr on 80pf lake & blk, *rose*	4.00	6.00
N25	A17(c)	1fr25c on 1m car	22.50	25.00
a.		Double surcharge	100.00	
N26	A21(c)	2fr50c on 2m gray bl	22.50	20.00
a.		Double surcharge	100.00	
		Nos. N15-N26 (12)	57.35	60.75

These stamps were also used in parts of Belgium occupied by the German forces.

Alsace.

Issued under German Occupation.

Stamps of Germany 1933-36 Overprinted in Black **Elsaß**

Wmkd. Swastikas. (237)

1940 *Perf. 14*

No.	Type	Description	Unused	Used
N27	A64	3(pf) ol bis	30	50
N28	A64	4(pf) dl bl	50	90
N29	A64	5(pf) brt grn	30	50
N30	A64	6(pf) dk grn	30	50
N31	A64	8(pf) vermilion	30	50
N32	A64	10(pf) chocolate	30	1.00
N33	A64	12(pf) dp car	35	65
N34	A64	15(pf) maroon	50	1.10
N35	A64	20(pf) brt bl	50	1.10
N36	A64	25(pf) ultra	70	1.50
N37	A64	30(pf) ol grn	1.25	1.75
N38	A64	40(pf) red vio	1.25	1.75
N39	A64	50(pf) dk grn & blk	1.75	2.25
N40	A64	60(pf) cl & blk	2.00	4.00
N41	A64	80(pf) dk bl & blk	2.25	5.00
N42	A64	100(pf) org & blk	3.25	4.00
		Nos. N27-N42 (16)	15.80	27.00

Lorraine.

Issued under German Occupation.

Stamps of Germany 1933-36

Overprinted in Black **Lothringen**

Wmkd. Swastikas. (237)

1940 *Perf. 14.*

No.	Type	Description	Unused	Used
N43	A64	3(pf) ol bis	30	1.00
N44	A64	4(pf) dl bl	38	1.00
N45	A64	5(pf) brt grn	30	1.00
N46	A64	6(pf) dk grn	30	50
N47	A64	8(pf) vermilion	30	1.00
N48	A64	10(pf) chocolate	30	75
N49	A64	12(pf) dp car	50	75
N50	A64	15(pf) maroon	60	1.25
a.		Inverted surcharge	125.00	
N51	A64	20(pf) brt bl	60	1.40
N52	A64	25(pf) ultra	75	1.40
N53	A64	30(pf) ol grn	85	1.50
N54	A64	40(pf) red vio	85	1.50
N55	A64	50(pf) dk grn & blk	1.60	2.50
N56	A64	60(pf) cl & blk	1.90	3.00
N57	A64	80(pf) dk bl & blk	2.25	3.75
N58	A64	100(pf) org & blk	14.00	12.00
		Nos. N43-N58 (16)	25.28	33.55

Besetztes Gebiet Nordfrankreich

These three words, in a rectangular frame covering two stamps, were handstamped in black on Nos. 267, 367 and 369 and used in the Dunkerque region in July-August, 1940. The German commander of Dunkerque authorized the overprint.

Issued jointly by the Allied Military Government of the United States and Great Britain, for civilian use.

Arc de Triomphe
OS2

Lithographed

1944 *Perf. 11* **Unwmkd.**

No.	Type	Description	Unused	Used
2N1	OS2	5c brt red vio	5	5
2N2	OS2	10c lt gray	5	5
2N3	OS2	25c brown	5	5
2N4	OS2	50c ol bis	5	5
2N5	OS2	1fr pck grn	5	5
2N6	OS2	1.50fr rose pink	6	6
2N7	OS2	2.50fr purple	10	10
2N8	OS2	4fr ultra	12	12
2N9	OS2	5fr black	12	12
2N10	OS2	10fr yel org	14.00	12.00
		Nos. 2N1-2N10 (10)	14.65	12.65

1945

Denominations in Black.

No.	Type	Description	Unused	Used
2N11	OS2	30c orange	6	6
2N12	OS2	40c pale gray	6	6
2N13	OS2	50c ol bis	6	6
2N14	OS2	60c violet	6	6
2N15	OS2	80c emerald	6	6
2N16	OS2	1.20fr brown	12	12
2N17	OS2	1.50fr vermilion	6	6
2N18	OS2	2fr yellow	12	12
2N19	OS2	2.40fr dk rose	12	12
2N20	OS2	3fr brt red vio	12	12
		Nos. 2N11-2N20 (10)	84	84

FRENCH OFFICES ABROAD

OFFICES IN CHINA

Prior to 1923 several of the world powers maintained their own post offices in China for the purpose of sending and receiving overseas mail. French offices were maintained in Canton, Hoi Hao (Hoihow), Kwangchowan (Kouang-tchéou-wan), Mongtseu (Mong-tseu), Packhoi (Pakhoi), Tong King (Tchongking), Yunnan Fou (Yunnanfu).

100 Centimes = 1 Franc
100 Cents = 1 Piastre

Peace and Commerce
A1

Stamps of France
Overprinted in Red or Black.
Perf. 14x13½.

1894–1900 **Unwmkd.**

No.	Type	Description	Unused	Used
1	A1	5c grn, *grnsh* (R)	1.35	1.25
2	A1	5c yel grn, I (R) ('00)	1.65	85
a.		Type II	21.00	10.00
3	A1	10c *lav*, I (R)	3.00	75
a.		Type II	10.00	7.50
4	A1	15c bl (R)	3.00	1.25
5	A1	20c red, *grn*	3.00	1.50
6	A1	25c *rose* (R)	3.00	1.00
7	A1	30c brn, *bis*	2.75	2.25
8	A1	40c red, *straw*	3.50	2.50
9	A1	50c car, *rose*, I	9.00	7.50
a.		Red overprint	25.00	
b.		Type II (Bk)	7.50	5.00
10	A1	75c dp vio, *org*(R)	40.00	32.50
11	A1	1fr brnz grn, *straw*	7.50	2.25
a.		Double overprint	150.00	
12	A1	2fr brn, *az* ('00)	19.00	12.50
12A	A1	5fr red lil, *lav*	37.50	25.00
b.		Red overprint	165.00	

Surcharged in Black **Chine 25**

No.	Type	Description	Unused	Used
13	A1	25c on 1fr brnz, grn, *straw*	37.50	22.50

Surcharged in Red **Chine 2 Cents**

1901

No.	Type	Description	Unused	Used
14	A1	2c on 25c *rose*	700.00	175.00
15	A1	4c on 25c *rose*	600.00	165.00
16	A1	6c on 25c *rose*	650.00	300.00
17	A1	16c on 25c *rose*	200.00	140.00
a.		Black surcharge		4,500.

Stamps of Indo-China Surcharged in Black **CHINE 二之五仙**

1902–04

No.	Type	Description	Unused	Used
18	A3	1c *lil bl*	1.00	85
19	A3	2c brn, *buff*	1.50	1.25
20	A3	4c cl, *lav*	1.25	1.00
21	A3	5c yel grn	1.75	1.25
22	A3	10c red	1.50	1.25
23	A3	15c gray	2.25	2.00
24	A3	20c red, *grn*	3.50	3.00
25	A3	25c *rose*	4.50	3.25
26	A3	25c bl ('04)	3.75	3.00
27	A3	30c brn, *bis*	2.50	2.25
28	A3	40c red, *straw*	11.00	10.50
29	A3	50c car, *rose*	30.00	25.00
30	A3	50c brn, *az* ('04)	5.00	4.00
31	A3	75c vio, *org*	15.00	1
32	A3	1fr brnz grn, *straw*	18.00	1
33	A3	5fr red lil, *lav*	45.00	3
		Nos. 18-33 (16)	147.50	12

The Chinese characters surcharged o Nos. 18–33 are the Chinese equivalents o the French values and therefore differ o each denomination. Another printing o these stamps was made in 1904 which di fers from the first one principally in th size and shape of the letters in "CHINE" particularly the "H" which is much thinne in the second printing. Prices are for th less expensive variety. Many varieties o surcharge exist.

Liberty, Equality and Fraternity
A3

"Rights of Man"
A4

A5

1902-03 **Typographed.**

No.	Type	Description	Unused	Used
34	A3	5c green	85	8
35	A4	10c rose red ('03)	85	8
36	A4	15c pale red	1.35	8
37	A4	20c brn vio ('03)	2.75	2.7
38	A4	25c bl ('03)	2.50	1.
39	A4	30c lil ('03)	2.75	2.7
40	A5	40c red & pale bl	6.25	6.0
41	A5	50c bis brn & lav	7.50	6.5
42	A5	1fr cl & ol grn	10.50	5.5
43	A5	2fr gray vio & yel	25.00	19.0
44	A5	5fr dk bl & buff	40.00	30.0
		Nos. 34-44 (11)	100.30	75.9

Surcharged in Black **5**

1903

No.	Type	Description	Unused	Used
45	A4	5c on 15c pale red	8.00	4.2
a.		Invtd. surcharge	37.50	37.5

Stamps of Indo-China, 1904–06, Surcharged as Nos. 18 to 33 in Black.

1904–05

No.	Type	Description	Unused	Used
46	A4	1c ol grn	85	8
47	A4	2c vio brn, *buff*	85	8
47A	A4	4c cl, *bluish*	700.00	550.0
48	A4	5c dp grn	1.25	1.2
49	A4	10c carmine	1.25	1.2
50	A4	15c org brn, *bl*	1.25	1.2
51	A4	20c red, *grn*	5.50	5.50
52	A4	25c dp bl	3.00	1.65
53	A4	40c *bluish*	2.75	1.75
54	A4	1fr pale grn	250.00	170.00
55	A4	2fr brn, *org*	17.50	12.50
56	A4	10fr org brn, *grn*	100.00	90.00
		Nos. 46-56 (12)	1,084.20	836.85

Many varieties of the surcharge exist on Nos. 46–55.

Stamps of 1902-03 Surcharged in Black **2 CENTS 仙二**

1907

No.	Type	Description	Unused	Used
57	A3	2c on 5c grn	45	45
58	A4	4c on 10c rose red	45	45
a.		Pair, one without surcharge	30.00	
59	A4	6c on 15c pale red	1.00	60
60	A4	8c on 20c brn vio	2.75	2.25
a.		"8" inverted	25.00	25.00
61	A4	10c on 25c bl	35	30
62	A5	20c on 50c bis brn & lav	1.50	1.25
a.		Double surcharge		
b.		Triple surch.	125.00	125.00
63	A5	40c on 1fr cl & ol grn	10.50	6.25

64 A5 2pi on 5fr dk bl & buff 10.50 6.25
a. Double surcharge 700.00 700.00
Nos. 57-64 (8) 27.50 17.80

Stamps of 1902-03 Surcharged in Black — 2 CENTS 分二

1911-22

65 A3 2c on 5c grn 50 30
66 A4 4c on 10c rose red 60 30
67 A4 6c on 15c org 1.10 45
68 A4 8c on 20c brn vio 80 50
69 A4 10c on 25c bl ('21) 90 50
70 A4 20c on 50c bl ('22) 27.50 25.00
71 A5 40c on 1fr cl & ol grn 1.50 1.10

No. 44 Surcharged — 2 $ 圓二

73 A5 $2 on 5fr bl & buff ('22) 100.00 85.00
Nos. 65-73 (8) 132.90 113.15

Types of 1902-03 Surcharged in Black — 2 CENTS 分二

1922

75 A3 1c on 5c org 1.50 85
76 A4 2c on 10c grn 3.00 2.50
77 A4 3c on 15c org 4.50 4.25
78 A4 4c on 20c red brn 6.00 4.25
79 A4 5c on 25c dk vio 3.00 1.65
80 A4 6c on 30c red 6.00 5.00
82 A4 10c on 50c bl 6.00 5.00
83 A5 20c on 1fr cl & ol grn 16.00 14.00
84 A5 40c on 2fr org & pale bl 16.00 14.00
85 A5 $1 on 5fr dk bl & buff 100.00 100.00
Nos. 75-85 (10) 162.00 151.50

POSTAGE DUE STAMPS.

Postage Due Stamps of France Handstamped in Red or Black — Chine

Perf. 14x13½.

1901-07 Unwmkd.

J1 D2 5c lt bl (R) 2.00 1.75
J2 D2 10c choc (R) 4.25 3.50
J3 D2 15c lt grn (R) 4.25 3.50
J4 D2 20c ol grn (R) ('07) 4.50 3.75
J5 D2 30c carmine 6.25 5.50
J6 D2 50c lilac 6.25 5.50
Nos. J1-J6 (6) 27.50 23.50

Stamps of 1894-1900 Handstamped in Carmine — A PERCEVOIR

1903

J7 A1 5c yel grn 1,750. 625.00
a. pur handstamp 1,750. 625.00
b. 5c grn, grnsh 3,750.
J8 A1 10c lavender 3,750. 3,250.
a. pur handstamp 3,750. 3,250.
J9 A1 15c blue 1,650. 550.00
a. pur handstamp 1,650. 550.00
J10 A1 30c brn, bis 1,100. 65.00
a. pur handstamp 1,100. 65.00

Same Handstamp on Stamps of 1902-03 in Carmine

1903

J14 A3 5c green 1,100. 600.00
a. pur handstamp 1,100. 600.00
J15 A4 10c rose red 450.00 100.00
a. pur handstamp 450.00 100.00
J16 A4 15c pale red 500.00 110.00
a. pur handstamp 500.00 110.00

Stamps of 1894-1900 Handstamped in Carmine — A PERCEVOIR

1903

J20 A1 5c yel grn 1,200. 225.00
a. pur handstamp 1,200. 225.00
b. 5c grn, grnsh 3,750.
J21 A1 10c lavender 4,250. 3,300.
a. pur handstamp 4,250. 3,300.
J22 A1 15c blue 750.00 60.00
a. pur handstamp 750.00 60.00
J23 A1 30c brn, bis 325.00 55.00
a. pur handstamp 325.00 55.00

Same Handstamp on Stamps of 1902-03 in Carmine or Purple

1903

J27 A3 5c grn (C) 750.00 400.00
a. pur handstamp 750.00 400.00
J28 A4 10c rose red (C) 225.00 32.50
a. pur handstamp 225.00 32.50
J29 A4 15c pale red (C) 425.00 32.50
a. pur handstamp 425.00 32.50
J30 A4 30c lil (P) 4,250. 3,750.

The handstamps on Nos. J7-J30 are found inverted, double, etc.

The cancellations on these stamps should have dates between Sept. 1, and Nov. 30, 1903, to be genuine.

Postage Due Stamps of France 1893-1910 Surcharged in Black — 2 CENTS 分二

1911

J33 D2 2c on 5c bl 80 65
a. Double surch. 50.00 50.00
J34 D2 4c on 10c choc 70 65
a. Double surch. 50.00 50.00
J35 D2 8c on 20c ol grn 1.00 85
a. Double surch. 50.00 50.00
J36 D2 20c on 50c lil 1.10 85

1922

J37 D2 1c on 5c bl 42.50 37.50
J38 D2 2c on 10c brn 62.50 55.00
J39 D2 4c on 20c ol grn 62.50 55.00
J40 D2 10c on 50c brn vio 62.50 55.00

CANTON

Stamps of Indo-China, 1892-1900, Overprinted in Red — CANTON 州廣

1901 *Perf. 14x13½.* Unwmkd.

1 A3 1c lil bl 95 95
1A A3 2c brn, buff 95 95
2 A3 4c cl, lav 1.25 1.25
2A A3 5c grn, grnsh 350.00 350.00
3 A3 5c yel grn 1.25 1.25
4 A3 10c lavender 2.75 2.75
5 A3 15c bl, quadrille paper 1.75 1.75
6 A3 15c gray 2.75 2.75
a. Dbl. overprint 20.00
7 A3 20c red, grn 5.00 5.00
8 A3 25c rose 5.00 5.00
9 A3 30c brn, bis 10.00 10.00
10 A3 40c red, straw 12.50 12.50
11 A3 50c car, rose 17.50 17.50
12 A3 75c dp vio, org 21.00 21.00
13 A3 1fr brnz grn, straw 17.50 17.50
14 A3 5fr red lil, lav 150.00 150.00
Nos. 1-14 (16) 600.15 600.15

The Chinese characters in the overprint on Nos. 1-14 read "Canton." On Nos. 15-64, they restate the denomination of the basic stamp.

Surcharged in Black — CANTON 仙六

1903-04

15 A3 1c lil bl 1.75 1.75
16 A3 2c brn, buff 1.75 1.75
17 A3 4c cl, lav 1.75 1.75
18 A3 5c yel grn 1.50 1.10
19 A3 10c rose red 1.50 1.10
20 A3 15c gray 2.25 1.75
21 A3 20c red, grn 9.00 8.50
22 A3 25c blue 3.75 2.75
23 A3 25c rose ('04) 3.75 3.00
24 A3 30c brn, bis 11.00 10.00
25 A3 40c red, straw 30.00 25.00
26 A3 50c car, rose 210.00 200.00
27 A3 50c brn, az ('04) 42.50 37.50
28 A3 75c dp vio, org 42.50 37.50
a. "INDO-CHINE" inverted 19,000.
29 A3 1fr brnz grn, straw 37.50 35.00
30 A3 5fr red lil, lav 37.50 37.50
Nos. 15-30 (16) 438.00 405.95

Many varieties of the surcharge exist on Nos. 15-30.

Stamps of Indo-China, 1892-1906, Surcharged in Red or Black — CANTON 花銀八厘

A second printing of the 1906 surcharges of Canton, Hoi Hao, Kwangchowan, Mongtseu, Packhoi, Tong King and Yunnan Fou was made in 1908. The inks are grayish instead of full black and vermilion instead of carmine. Prices are for the cheaper variety which usually is the second printing.

The 4c and 50c of the 1892 issue of Indo-China are known with this surcharge and similarly surcharged for other cities in China. The surcharges on these two stamps are always inverted. It is stated that they were irregularly produced and never issued.

1906

31 A4 1c ol grn (R) 85 85
32 A4 2c vio brn, buff 85 85
33 A4 4c cl, bluish (R) 85 85
34 A4 5c dp grn (R) 1.10 85
35 A4 10c carmine 1.50 1.25
36 A4 15c org brn, bl 1.75 1.75
37 A4 20c red, grn 1.25 1.25
38 A4 25c dp bl 1.25 1.25
39 A4 30c pale brn 2.50 2.25
40 A4 35c yel (R) 1.25 1.00
41 A4 40c bluish (R) 2.75 2.50
42 A4 50c bis brn 3.25 3.00
43 A3 75c dp vio, org (R) 30.00 27.50
44 A4 1fr pale grn 6.25 6.25
45 A4 2fr brn, org (R) 22.50 20.00
46 A3 5fr red lil, lav 42.50 37.50
47 A4 10fr org brn, grn 40.00 40.00
Nos. 31-47 (17) 160.40 148.90

The surcharge exists inverted on 1c, 25c and 1fr.

Stamps of Indo-China, 1907, Surcharged "CANTON", and Chinese Characters, in Red or Blue.

1908

48 A5 1c ol brn & blk 60 50
49 A5 2c brn & blk 60 50
50 A5 4c bl & blk 85 75
51 A5 5c grn & blk 85 75
52 A5 10c red & blk (Bl) 85 75
53 A5 15c vio & blk 1.50 1.50
54 A6 20c vio & blk 1.50 1.50
55 A6 25c bl & blk 1.50 1.50
56 A6 30c brn & blk 3.50 3.25
57 A6 35c ol grn & blk 3.50 3.25
58 A6 40c brn & blk 4.50 4.00
59 A6 50c car & blk (Bl) 6.00 4.25
60 A7 75c ver & blk (Bl) 6.00 5.00
61 A8 1fr car & blk (Bl) 8.00 7.50
62 A9 2fr grn & blk 22.50 20.00
63 A10 5fr bl & blk 25.00 22.50
64 A11 10fr pur & blk 50.00 45.00
Nos. 48-64 (17) 137.25 122.50

Nos. 48-64 Surcharged with New Values in Cents or Piastres in Black, Red or Blue

1919

65 A5 2/5c on 1c 55 50
66 A5 4/5c on 2c 55 50
67 A5 1 3/5c on 4c (R) 60 50
68 A5 2c on 5c 60 50
69 A5 4c on 10c (Bl) 60 50
a. Chinese "2" instead of "4" 10.00 10.00
70 A5 6c on 15c 95 60
71 A6 8c on 20c 95 95
72 A6 10c on 25c 1.25 75
73 A6 12c on 30c 1.25 75
a. Double surcharge 60.00 60.00
74 A6 14c on 35c 1.25 75
a. Closed "4" 4.50 4.50
75 A6 16c on 40c 1.25 95
76 A6 20c on 50c (Bl) 1.25 95
77 A7 30c on 75c (Bl) 1.25 70
78 A8 40c on 1fr (Bl) 5.25 3.50
79 A9 80c on 2fr (R) 5.25 4.50
80 A10 2pi on 5fr (R) 7.00 6.25
81 A11 4pi on 10fr (R) 7.00 6.25
Nos. 65-81 (17) 36.80 29.40

HOI HAO

Stamps of Indo-China Overprinted in Red — HOI HAO 州瓊

1901 *Perf. 14x13½.* Unwmkd.

1 A3 1c lil bl 1.40 1.40
2 A3 2c brn, buff 1.40 1.40
3 A3 4c cl, lav 1.40 1.40
4 A3 5c yel grn 1.40 1.40
5 A3 10c lavender 2.10 2.10
6 A3 15c blue 950.00 450.00
7 A3 15c gray 90 90
8 A3 20c red, grn 7.50 7.50
9 A3 25c rose 3.25 3.00
10 A3 30c brn, bis 12.50 11.00
11 A3 40c red, straw 12.50 11.00
12 A3 50c car, rose 18.00 16.00
13 A3 75c dp vio, org 100.00 92.50
14 A3 1fr brnz grn, straw 400.00 375.00
15 A3 5fr red lil, lav 325.00 300.00
Nos. 1-15 (15) 1,837.35 1,274.60

The Chinese characters in the overprint on Nos. 1-15 read "Hoi Hao." On Nos. 16-66, they restate the denomination of the basic stamp.

Surcharged in Black — HOI HAO 仙六

1903-04

16 A3 1c lil bl 45 45
17 A3 2c brn, buff 45 45
18 A3 4c cl, lav 1.00 1.00
19 A3 5c yel grn 1.00 1.00
20 A3 10c red 1.00 1.00
21 A3 15c gray 90 90
22 A3 20c red, grn 2.50 2.50
23 A3 25c blue 1.40 1.40
24 A3 25c rose ('04) 1.10 1.10
25 A3 30c brn, bis 1.50 1.50
26 A3 40c red, straw 17.50 17.50
27 A3 50c car, rose 20.00 20.00
28 A3 50c brn, az ('04) 62.50 62.50
29 A3 75c dp vio, org 21.00 21.00
a. "INDO-CHINE" inverted 17,500.
30 A3 1fr brnz grn, straw 21.00 21.00
31 A3 5fr red lil, lav 95.00 95.00
Nos. 16-31 (16) 248.30 248.30

Many varieties of the surcharge exist on Nos. 1-31.

Stamps of Indo-China, 1892-1906, Surcharged in Red or Black — HOI HAO 花銀八厘

1906

32 A4 1c ol grn (R) 90 90
33 A4 2c vio brn, buff 90 90
34 A4 4c cl, bluish (R) 1.25 1.25
35 A4 5c dp grn (R) 1.75 1.75
36 A4 10c carmine 1.75 1.75
37 A4 15c org brn, bl 1.85 1.85
38 A4 20c red, grn 2.50 2.50
39 A4 25c dp bl 3.50 3.50
40 A4 30c pale brn 3.50 3.50
41 A4 35c yel (R) 6.00 6.00
42 A4 40c bluish (R) 6.00 6.00
43 A4 50c gray brn 7.00 7.00

44	A3	75c	dp vio, *org* (R)	18.00	18.00
45	A4	1fr	pale grn	19.50	19.50
46	A4	2fr	brn, *org* (R)	19.50	19.50
47	A3	5fr	red lil, *lav*	62.50	62.50
48	A4	10fr	org brn, *grn*	75.00	75.00
			Nos. 32-48 (17)	231.40	231.40

Stamps of Indo-China, 1907, Surcharged "HOI HAO" and Chinese Characters, in Red or Blue.

1908

49	A5	1c	ol brn & blk	45	45
50	A5	2c	brn & blk	45	45
51	A5	4c	bl & blk	60	60
52	A5	5c	grn & blk	1.00	1.00
53	A5	10c	red & blk (Bl)	1.25	1.25
54	A5	15c	vio & blk	2.50	2.50
55	A6	20c	vio & blk	3.25	3.25
56	A6	25c	bl & blk	3.25	3.25
57	A6	30c	brn & blk	3.25	3.25
58	A6	35c	ol grn & blk	3.25	3.25
59	A6	40c	brn & blk	2.50	2.50
61	A6	50c	car & blk (Bl)	3.50	3.50
62	A7	75c	ver & blk (Bl)	4.25	4.25
63	A8	1fr	car & blk (Bl)	9.00	9.00
64	A9	2fr	grn & blk	19.00	19.00
65	A10	5fr	bl & blk	32.50	32.50
66	A11	10fr	pur & blk	50.00	50.00
			Nos. 49-66 (17)	140.00	140.00

Issue of 1908 Surcharged with New Values in Cents or Piastres in Black, Red or Blue.

1919

67	A5	2/5c	on 1c ol brn & blk	50	50
68	A5	4/5c	on 2c yel brn & blk	50	50
69	A5	1 3/5c	on 4c bl & blk (R)	70	70
70	A5	2c	on 5c grn & blk	45	45
71	A5	4c	on 10c red & blk (Bl)	75	75
	a.		Chinese "2" instead of "4"	3.00	3.00
72	A5	6c	on 15c vio & blk	75	75
73	A6	8c	on 20c vio & blk	1.00	1.00
	a.		"S" of "CENTS" omitted	45.00	45.00
74	A6	10c	on 25c bl & blk	2.50	2.50
75	A6	12c	on 30c brn & blk	75	75
76	A6	14c	on 35c ol grn & blk	75	75
	a.		Closed "4"	6.25	6.25
77	A6	16c	on 40c yel brn & blk	75	75
79	A6	20c	on 50c car & blk (Bl)	1.00	1.00
80	A7	30c	on 75c ver & blk (Bl)	1.40	1.40
81	A8	40c	on 1fr car & blk (Bl)	4.00	4.00
82	A9	80c	on 2fr grn & blk (R)	10.50	10.50
83	A10	2pi	on 5fr bl & blk (R)	27.50	27.50
	a.		Triple surcharge of new value	200.00	
84	A11	4pi	on 10fr pur & blk (R)	100.00	100.00
			Nos. 67-84 (17)	153.80	153.80

KWANGCHOWAN

A Chinese Territory leased to France, 1898 to 1945.

Stamps of Indo-China, 1892-1906, Surcharged in Red or Black

Kouang Tchéou-Wan

花銀八厘

1906 ***Perf. 14x13½*** **Unwmkd.**

1	A4	1c	ol grn (R)	1.40	1.40
2	A4	2c	vio brn, *buff*	1.40	1.40
3	A4	4c	cl, *bluish* (R)	2.00	2.00
4	A4	5c	dp grn (R)	2.00	2.00
5	A4	10c	carmine	2.00	2.00
6	A4	15c	org brn, *bl*	4.00	4.00
7	A4	20c	red, *grn*	2.00	2.00
8	A4	25c	dp bl	2.00	2.00
9	A4	30c	pale brn	2.25	2.25
10	A4	35c	*yel* (R)	2.50	2.50
11	A4	40c	*bluish* (R)	2.25	2.25
12	A4	50c	bis brn	9.50	9.50
13	A3	75c	dp vio, *org* (R)	12.50	12.50
14	A4	1fr	pale grn	15.00	15.00
15	A4	2fr	brn, *org* (R)	15.00	15.00
16	A3	5fr	red lil, *lav*	100.00	100.00
17	A4	10fr	org brn, *grn*	125.00	125.00
			Nos. 1-17 (17)	300.80	300.80

Various varieties of the surcharge exist on Nos. 2–10.

Stamps of Indo-China, 1907, Surcharged "KOUANG-TCHEOU" and Value in Chinese in Red or Blue.

1908

18	A5	1c	ol brn & blk	30	30
19	A5	2c	brn & blk	30	30
20	A5	4c	bl & blk	30	30
21	A5	5c	grn & blk	30	30
22	A5	10c	red & blk (Bl)	30	30
23	A5	15c	vio & blk	1.00	1.00
24	A6	20c	vio & blk	1.90	1.90
25	A6	25c	bl & blk	2.25	2.25
26	A6	30c	brn & blk	4.25	4.25
27	A6	35c	ol grn & blk	5.00	5.00
28	A6	40c	brn & blk	5.00	5.00
30	A6	50c	car & blk (Bl)	5.00	5.00
31	A7	75c	ver & blk (Bl)	5.00	5.00
32	A8	1fr	car & blk (Bl)	7.50	7.50
33	A9	2fr	grn & blk	20.00	20.00
34	A10	5fr	bl & blk	30.00	30.00
35	A11	10fr	pur & blk	50.00	50.00
	a.		Double surch.	350.00	350.00
	b.		Triple surch.	350.00	350.00
			Nos. 18-35 (17)	138.40	138.40

The Chinese characters overprinted on Nos. 1 to 35 repeat the denomination of the basic stamp.

Issue of 1908 Surcharged with New Values in Cents or Piastres in Black, Red or Blue.

1919

36	A5	2/5c	on 1c ol grn & blk	30	30
37	A5	4/5c	on 2c yel brn & blk	30	30
38	A5	1 3/5c	on 4c bl & blk (R)	40	30
39	A5	2c	on 5c grn & blk	40	30
	a.		"2 CENTS" inverted	35.00	
40	A5	4c	on 10c red & blk (Bl)	1.25	50
41	A5	6c	on 15c vio & blk	40	25
42	A6	8c	on 20c vio & blk	1.75	1.50
43	A6	10c	on 25c bl & blk	4.25	4.00
44	A6	12c	on 30c brn & blk	75	60
45	A6	14c	on 35c ol grn & blk	1.00	90
	a.		Closed "4"	15.00	12.50
46	A6	16c	on 40c yel brn & blk	65	50
48	A6	20c	on 50c car & blk (Bl)	65	55
49	A7	30c	on 75c ver & blk (Bl)	3.00	3.00
50	A8	40c	on 1fr car & blk (Bl)	3.50	3.00
	a.		"40 CENTS" inverted		
51	A9	80c	on 2fr grn & blk (R)	4.50	3.00
52	A10	2pi	on 5fr bl & blk (R)	85.00	75.00
53	A11	4pi	on 10fr pur & blk (R)	9.50	9.00
			Nos. 36-53 (17)	117.60	103.00

Stamps of Indo-China, 1922-23, Overprinted in Black, Red or Blue KOUANG-TCHEOU

1923

54	A12	1/10c	blk & sal (Bl)	8	8
55	A12	1/5c	dp bl & blk (R)	8	8
	a.		Black ovpt.	45.00	
56	A12	2/5c	ol brn & blk (R)	10	10
57	A12	4/5c	brt rose & blk	15	15
58	A12	1c	yel brn & blk (Bl)	15	15
59	A12	2c	gray grn & blk (R)	40	40
60	A12	3c	vio & blk (R)	40	40
61	A12	4c	org & blk	40	40
62	A12	5c	car & blk	40	40
63	A13	6c	dl red & blk	50	50
64	A13	7c	ol grn & blk	40	40
65	A13	8c	blk (R)	75	75
66	A13	9c	yel & blk	75	75
67	A13	10c	bl & blk	75	75
68	A13	11c	vio & blk	75	75
69	A13	12c	brn & blk	75	75
70	A13	15c	org & blk	95	95
71	A13	20c	bl & blk, *straw* (R)	75	75
72	A13	40c	ver & blk, *bluish* (Bl)	1.50	1.50
73	A13	1pi	bl grn & blk, *grnsh*	4.00	4.00
74	A13	2pi	vio brn & blk, *pnksh* (Bl)	5.00	5.00
			Nos. 54-74 (21)	19.01	19.01

Indo-China Stamps of 1927 Overprinted in Black or Red KOUANG-TCHÉOU

1927

75	A14	1/10c	lt ol grn (R)	6	6
76	A14	1/5c	yellow	8	8
77	A14	2/5c	lt bl (R)	12	12
78	A14	4/5c	dp brn	15	15
79	A14	1c	orange	25	25
80	A14	2c	bl grn (R)	30	30
81	A14	3c	ind (R)	30	30
82	A14	4c	lil rose	30	30
83	A14	5c	dp vio	40	40
84	A15	6c	dp red	40	40
85	A15	7c	lt brn	40	40
86	A15	8c	gray grn (R)	40	40
87	A15	9c	red vio	50	50
88	A15	10c	lt bl (R)	50	50
89	A15	11c	orange	50	50
90	A15	12c	myr grn (R)	50	50
91	A16	15c	dl rose & ol brn	1.00	1.00
92	A16	20c	vio & sl (R)	1.00	1.00
93	A17	25c	org brn & lil rose	1.00	1.00
94	A17	30c	dp bl & ol gray (R)	75	75
95	A18	40c	ver & lt bl	70	70
96	A18	50c	lt grn & sl (R)	75	75
97	A19	1pi	dk bl, blk & yel (R)	1.80	1.80
98	A19	2pi	red, dp bl & org (R)	1.80	1.80
	a.		Double ovpt.	45.00	
			Nos. 75-98 (24)	13.96	13.96

Stamps of Indo-China, 1931-41, Overprinted in Black or Red KOUANG-TCHÉOU

1937–41 ***Perf. 13, 13½***

99	A20	1/10c	Prus bl	5	5
100	A20	1/5c	lake	6	6
101	A20	2/5c	org red	8	8
102	A20	½c	red brn	10	10
103	A20	4/5c	dk vio	10	10
104	A20	1c	blk brn	8	8
105	A20	2c	dk grn	8	8
	a.		Inverted ovpt.	62.50	
106	A21	3c	dk grn	30	30
107	A21	3c	yel brn ('41)	8	8
108	A21	4c	dk bl (R)	40	40
109	A21	4c	dk grn ('41)	15	15
110	A21	4c	yel org ('41)	75	75
111	A21	5c	dp vio	40	40
112	A21	5c	dp grn ('41)	15	15
113	A21	6c	org red	18	18
114	A21	7c	blk (R) ('41)	18	18
115	A21	8c	rose lake ('41)	18	18
116	A21	9c	blk, *yel* (R) ('41)	18	18
	d.		Black ovpt.	4.00	4.00
117	A22	10c	dk bl (R)	50	50
118	A22	10c	ultra, *pink* (R) ('41)	40	40
119	A22	15c	dk bl (R)	25	25
120	A22	18c	bl (R) ('41)	8	8
121	A22	20c	rose	18	18
122	A22	21c	ol grn	18	18
123	A22	22c	grn ('41)	20	20
124	A22	25c	dp vio	1.25	1.25
125	A22	25c	dk bl (R) ('41)	20	20
126	A22	30c	org brn	25	25
127	A23	50c	dk brn	40	40
128	A23	60c	dl vio	40	40
129	A23	70c	lt bl (R) ('41)	25	25
130	A23	1pi	yel grn	70	70
131	A23	2pi	red	70	70
			Nos. 99-131 (33)	9.44	9.44

Colonial Arts Exhibition Issue.

Common Design Type

Souvenir Sheet.

1937 **Engraved.** ***Imperf.***

132	CD79	30c	grn & sep	2.50	2.50

Sheet size: 118x99mm.

New York World's Fair Issue.

Common Design Type

1939 ***Perf. 12½x12*** **Unwmkd.**

133	CD82	13c	car lake	40	40
134	CD82	23c	ultra	40	40

Petain Issue.

Indo-China Nos. 209–209A Overprinted "KOUANG TCHEOU" in Blue or Red.

1941 **Engraved** ***Perf. 12½x12***

135	A27a	10c	car lake (B)	25	
136	A27a	25c	bl (R)	25	

Nos. 135–136 were issued by the Vichy government, and were not placed on sale in Kwangchowan. This is also true of 16 stamps of Indo-China types A20–A23 without "RF" and overprinted "KOUANG-TCHEOU."

SEMI-POSTAL STAMPS.

French Revolution Issue

Common Design Type

Photogravure.

1939 ***Perf. 13.*** **Unwmkd.**

Name and Value Typo. in Black.

B1	CD83	6c	+2c grn	2.75	2.75
B2	CD83	7c	+3c brn	2.75	2.75
B3	CD83	9c	+4c red org	2.75	2.75
B4	CD83	13c	+10c rose pink	2.75	2.75
B5	CD83	23c	+20c bl	2.75	2.75
			Nos. B1-B5 (5)	13.75	13.75

Indo-China Nos. B19A and B19C Overprinted "KOUANG-TCHEOU" in Blue or Red, and Common Design Type

1941 **Photogravure** ***Perf. 13½***

B6	SP1	10c	+10c red (B)	35	
B7	CD86	15c	+30c mar & car	35	
B8	SP2	25c	+10c bl (R)	45	

Nos. B6–B8 were issued by the Vichy government, and were not placed on sale in Kwangchowan.

Nos. 135–136 were surcharged "OEUVRES COLONIALES" and surtax (including change of denomination of the 25c to 5c). These were issued in 1944 by the Vichy government, and not placed on sale in Kwangchowan.

Common Design Types

pictured in section at front of book.

AIR POST SEMI-POSTAL STAMPS.

Stamps of Indo-China types V4, V5 and V6 overprinted "KOUANG - TCHEOU" and type of Cameroons V10 inscribed "KOUANG - TCHEOU" were issued in 1942 by the Vichy Government, but were not placed on sale in the territory.

MONGTSEU
(Mengtsz)

Stamps of Indo-China Surcharged in Black

MONGTZE
仙 六

1903-04 ***Perf. 14x13½.*** **Unwmkd.**

No.	Type	Description	Unused	Used
1	A3	1c *lil bl*	2.75	2.75
2	A3	2c brn, *buff*	2.25	2.25
3	A3	4c cl, *lav*	2.75	2.75
4	A3	5c yel grn	2.50	2.50
5	A3	10c red	3.00	3.00
6	A3	15c gray	4.25	4.25
7	A3	20c red, *grn*	4.00	4.00
7C	A3	25c *rose*	375.00	375.00
8	A3	25c blue	5.00	5.00
9	A3	30c brn, *bis*	4.25	4.25
10	A3	40c red, *straw*	30.00	30.00
11	A3	50c car, *rose*	170.00	170.00
12	A3	50c brn, *az* ('04)	45.00	45.00
13	A3	75c dp vio, *org*	45.00	45.00
a.		"INDO-CHINE" inverted	22,500.	
14	A3	1fr brnz grn, *straw*	45.00	45.00
15	A3	5fr red lil, *lav*	45.00	45.00
		Nos. 1-15 (16)	785.75	785.75

Many varieties of the surcharge exist on Nos. 1–15.

Stamps of Indo-China, 1892–1906, Surcharged in Red or Black

Mong-Tseu
花銀八厘

1906

No.	Type	Description	Unused	Used
16	A4	1c ol grn (R)	90	90
17	A4	2c vio brn, *buff*	90	90
18	A4	4c cl, *bluish*(R)	90	90
19	A4	5c dp grn (R)	90	90
20	A4	10c carmine	1.20	1.20
21	A4	15c org brn, *bl*	1.20	1.20
22	A4	20c red, *grn*	2.25	2.25
23	A4	25c dp bl	2.25	2.25
24	A4	30c pale brn	3.50	3.50
25	A4	35c *yel* (R)	2.50	2.50
26	A4	40c *bluish* (R)	2.50	2.50
27	A4	50c bis brn	10.00	10.00
28	A3	75c dp vio, *org* (R)	20.00	20.00
a.		"INDO-CHINE" inverted	22,500.	
29	A4	1fr pale grn	10.00	10.00
30	A4	2fr brn, *org* (R)	22.50	22.50
31	A3	5fr red lil, *lav*	50.00	50.00
32	A4	10fr org brn, *grn*	70.00	70.00
a.		Chinese characters inverted	950.00	950.00
		Nos. 16-32 (17)	201.50	201.50

Inverted varieties of the surcharge exist on Nos. 19, 22 and 32.

Stamps of Indo-China, 1907, Surcharged "MONGTSEU" and Value in Chinese in Red or Blue.

1908

No.	Type	Description	Unused	Used
33	A5	1c ol brn & blk	40	40
34	A5	2c brn & blk	40	40
35	A5	4c bl & blk	50	50
36	A5	5c grn & blk	75	75
37	A5	10c red & blk (Bl)	1.20	1.20
38	A5	15c vio & blk	1.20	1.20
39	A6	20c vio & blk	2.00	2.00
40	A6	25c bl & blk	2.75	2.75
41	A6	30c brn & blk	1.75	1.75
42	A6	35c ol grn & blk	2.00	2.00
43	A6	40c brn & blk	2.00	2.00
45	A6	50c car & blk (Bl)	2.50	2.50
46	A7	75c ver & blk (Bl)	5.00	5.00
47	A8	1fr car & blk (Bl)	5.00	5.00
48	A9	2fr grn & blk	6.25	6.25
49	A10	5fr bl & blk	55.00	55.00
50	A11	10fr pur & blk	57.50	57.50
		Nos. 33-50 (17)	146.20	146.20

The Chinese characters overprinted on Nos. 1 to 50 repeat the denomination of the basic stamp.

Issue of 1908 Surcharged with New Values in Cents or Piastres in Black, Red or Blue.

1919

No.	Type	Description	Unused	Used
51	A5	⅖c on 1c ol brn & blk	40	40
52	A5	⅘c on 2c yel brn & blk	40	40
53	A5	1⅗c on 4c bl & blk (R)	90	90
54	A5	2c on 5c grn & blk	55	55
55	A5	4c on 10c red & blk (Bl)	1.10	1.10
56	A5	6c on 15c vio & blk	1.10	1.10
57	A6	8c on 20c vio & blk	2.00	2.00
58	A6	10c on 25c bl & blk	1.40	1.40
59	A6	12c on 30c brn & blk	1.40	1.40
60	A6	14c on 35c ol grn & blk	1.40	1.40
a.		Closed "4"	7.00	7.00
61	A6	16c on 40c yel brn & blk	1.75	1.75
63	A6	20c on 50c car & blk (Bl)	1.75	1.75
64	A7	30c on 75c ver & blk (Bl)	1.50	1.50
65	A8	40c on 1fr car & blk (Bl)	3.75	3.75
66	A9	80c on 2fr grn & blk (R)	2.50	2.50
a.		Triple surcharge, one inverted	185.00	185.00
67	A10	2pi on 5fr bl & blk (R)	70.00	70.00
a.		Triple surcharge, one inverted	210.00	210.00
b.		Double surch.	210.00	210.00
68	A11	4pi on 10fr pur & blk (R)	10.50	10.50
		Nos. 51-68 (17)	102.40	102.40

PAKHOI

Stamps of Indo-China Surcharged in Black

PACKHOI
仙 六

1903–04 ***Perf. 14x13½*** **Unwmkd.**

No.	Type	Description	Unused	Used
1	A3	1c *lil bl*	3.50	3.50
2	A3	2c brn, *buff*	3.00	3.00
3	A3	4c cl, *lav*	2.25	2.25
4	A3	5c yel grn	2.25	2.25
5	A3	10c red	2.00	2.00
6	A3	15c gray	2.00	2.00
7	A3	20c red, *grn*	3.50	3.50
8	A3	25c blue	3.50	3.50
9	A3	25c *rose*('04)	2.00	2.00
10	A3	30c brn, *bis*	3.50	3.50
11	A3	40c red, *straw*	27.50	27.50
12	A3	50c car, *rose*	225.00	225.00
13	A3	50c brn, *az* ('04)	30.00	30.00
14	A3	75c dp vio, *org*	32.50	32.50
a.		"INDO-CHINE" inverted	17,500.	
15	A3	1fr brnz grn, *straw*	37.50	37.50
16	A3	5fr red lil, *lav*	62.50	62.50
		Nos. 1-16 (16)	442.50	442.50

Many varieties of the surcharge exist on Nos. 1–16.

Stamps of Indo-China 1892–1906, Surcharged in Red or Black

PAK-HOI
花銀八厘

1906

No.	Type	Description	Unused	Used
17	A4	1c ol grn (R)	90	90
18	A4	2c vio brn, *buff*	90	90
19	A4	4c cl, *bluish* (R)	90	90
20	A4	5c dp grn (R)	90	90
21	A4	10c carmine	90	90
22	A4	15c org brn, *bl*	2.50	2.50
23	A4	20c red, *grn*	1.75	1.75
24	A4	25c dp bl	1.75	1.75
25	A4	30c pale brn	1.75	1.75
26	A4	35c *yel* (R)	1.75	1.75
27	A4	40c *bluish*(R)	1.85	1.85
28	A4	50c bis brn	3.00	3.00
29	A3	75c dp vio, *org* (R)	22.50	22.50
30	A4	1fr pale grn	14.00	14.00
31	A4	2fr brn, *org*(R)	20.00	20.00
32	A3	5fr red lil, *lav*	50.00	50.00
33	A4	10fr org brn, *grn*	60.00	60.00
		Nos. 17-33 (17)	185.35	185.35

Various varieties of the surcharge exist on Nos. 17–24.

Stamps of Indo-China, 1907, Surcharged "PAKHOI" and Value in Chinese in Red or Blue.

1908

No.	Type	Description	Unused	Used
34	A5	1c ol brn & blk	25	25
35	A5	2c brn & blk	30	30
36	A5	4c bl & blk	40	40
37	A5	5c grn & blk	55	55
38	A5	10c red & blk (Bl)	55	55
39	A5	15c vio & blk	90	90
40	A6	20c vio & blk	90	90
41	A6	25c bl & blk	90	90
42	A6	30c brn & blk	1.40	1.40
43	A6	35c ol grn & blk	1.40	1.40
44	A6	40c brn & blk	1.40	1.40
46	A6	50c car & blk (Bl)	1.40	1.40
47	A7	75c ver & blk (Bl)	2.75	2.75
48	A8	1fr car & blk (Bl)	3.50	3.50
49	A9	2fr grn & blk	8.50	8.50
50	A10	5fr bl & blk	45.00	45.00
51	A11	10fr pur & blk	75.00	75.00
		Nos. 34-51 (17)	145.10	145.10

The Chinese characters overprinted on Nos. 1 to 51 repeat the denomination of the basic stamps.

Issue of 1908 Surcharged with New Values in Cents or Piastres in Black, Red or Blue.

1919

No.	Type	Description	Unused	Used
52	A5	⅖c on 1c ol brn & blk	45	45
a.		"PAK-HOI" and Chinese double	70.00	70.00
53	A5	⅘c on 2c yel brn & blk	45	45
54	A5	1⅗c on 4c bl & blk (R)	45	45
55	A5	2c on 5c grn & blk	60	60
56	A5	4c on 10c red & blk (Bl)	1.40	1.40
57	A5	6c on 15c vio & blk	45	45
58	A6	8c on 20c vio & blk	1.40	1.40
59	A6	10c on 25c bl & blk	1.75	1.75
60	A6	12c on 30c brn & blk	90	90
a.		"12 CENTS" double	70.00	70.00
61	A6	14c on 35c ol grn & blk	40	40
a.		Closed "4"	5.00	5.00
62	A6	16c on 40c yel brn & blk	1.00	1.00
64	A6	20c on 50c car & blk (Bl)	80	80
65	A7	30c on 75c ver & blk (Bl)	90	90
66	A8	40c on 1fr car & blk (Bl)	5.00	5.00
67	A9	80c on 2fr grn & blk (R)	1.90	1.90
68	A10	2pi on 5fr bl & blk (R)	5.00	5.00
69	A11	4pi on 10fr pur & blk (R)	10.00	10.00
		Nos. 52-69 (17)	32.85	32.85

TCHONGKING
(Chungking)

Stamps of Indo-China Surcharged in Black

TCHONGKING
仙 六

1903–04 ***Perf. 14x13½*** **Unwmkd.**

No.	Type	Description	Unused	Used
1	A3	1c *lil bl*	1.75	1.75
2	A3	2c brn, *buff*	1.75	1.75
3	A3	4c cl, *lav*	1.75	1.75
4	A3	5c yel grn	1.75	1.75
5	A3	10c red	1.75	1.75
6	A3	15c gray	1.75	1.75
7	A3	20c red, *grn*	1.75	1.75
8	A3	25c blue	23.50	23.50
9	A3	25c *rose* ('04)	3.00	3.00
10	A3	30c brn, *bis*	3.75	3.75
11	A3	40c red, *straw*	25.00	25.00
12	A3	50c car, *rose*	130.00	130.00
13	A3	50c brn, *az* ('04)	75.00	75.00
14	A3	75c vio, *org*	23.50	23.50
15	A3	1fr brnz grn, *straw*	25.00	25.00
16	A3	5fr red lil, *lav*	45.00	45.00
		Nos. 1-16 (16)	366.00	366.00

Many varieties of the surcharge exist on Nos. 1–14.

Stamps of Indo-China and French China, issued in 1902 with similar overprint, but without Chinese characters, were not officially authorized.

Stamps of Indo-China, 1892–1906, Surcharged in Red or Black

Tch'ong K'ing
花銀八厘

1906

No.	Type	Description	Unused	Used
17	A4	1c ol grn (R)	1.00	1.00
18	A4	2c vio brn, *buff*	1.00	1.00
19	A4	4c cl, *bluish* (R)	1.00	1.00
20	A4	5c dp grn (R)	1.00	1.00
21	A4	10c carmine	1.00	1.00
22	A4	15c org brn, *bl*	3.00	3.00
23	A4	20c red, *grn*	1.00	1.00
24	A4	25c dp bl	2.00	2.00
25	A4	30c pale brn	1.50	1.50
26	A4	35c *yellow*(R)	1.50	1.50
27	A4	40c *bluish* (R)	3.00	3.00
28	A4	50c bis brn	3.00	3.00
29	A3	75c dp vio, *org* (R)	18.50	18.50
30	A4	1fr pale grn	14.00	14.00
31	A4	2fr brn, *org*(R)	14.00	14.00
32	A3	5fr red lil, *lav*	62.50	62.50
33	A4	10fr org brn, *grn*	70.00	70.00
		Nos. 17-33 (17)	199.00	199.00

Variety "T" omitted in surcharge occurs once in each sheet of Nos. 17–33. Other surcharge varieties exist, such as inverted surcharge on 1c and 2c.

Stamps of Indo-China, 1907, Surcharged "TCHONGKING" and Value in Chinese in Red or Blue.

1908

No.	Type	Description	Unused	Used
34	A5	1c ol brn & blk	15	15
35	A5	2c brn & blk	30	30
36	A5	4c bl & blk	40	40
37	A5	5c grn & blk	75	75
38	A5	10c red & blk (Bl)	1.00	1.00
39	A5	15c vio & blk	1.40	1.40
40	A6	20c vio & blk	1.40	1.40
41	A6	25c bl & blk	1.40	1.40
42	A6	30c brn & blk	1.40	1.40
43	A6	35c ol grn & blk	3.00	3.00
44	A6	40c brn & blk	7.00	7.00
45	A6	50c car & blk (Bl)	4.50	4.50
46	A7	75c ver & blk (Bl)	4.50	4.50
47	A8	1fr car & blk (Bl)	5.00	5.00
48	A9	2fr grn & blk	45.00	45.00
49	A10	5fr bl & blk	15.00	15.00
50	A11	10fr pur & blk	150.00	150.00
		Nos. 34-50 (17)	242.20	242.20

The Chinese characters overprinted on Nos. 1 to 50 repeat the denomination of the basic stamp.

Issue of 1908 Surcharged with New Values in Cents or Piastres in Black, Red or Blue.

1919

No.	Type	Description	Unused	Used
51	A5	⅖c on 1c ol brn & blk	30	30
52	A5	⅘c on 2c yel brn & blk	45	45
53	A5	1⅗c on 4c bl & blk (R)	65	60
54	A5	2c on 5c grn & blk	45	40
55	A5	4c on 10c red & blk (Bl)	40	35
56	A5	6c on 15c vio & blk	40	30
57	A6	8c on 20c vio & blk	40	30
58	A6	10c on 25c bl & blk	70	55
59	A6	12c on 30c brn & blk	75	50

No.	Type	Description	Unused	Used
60	A6	14c on 35c ol grn & blk	75	40
a.		Closed "4"	7.50	6.25
61	A6	16c on 40c yel brn & blk	1.00	75
a.		"16 CENTS" dbl.	50.00	45.00
62	A6	20c on 50c car & blk (Bl)	5.00	4.50
63	A7	30c on 75c ver & blk (Bl)	1.00	70
64	A8	40c on 1fr car & blk (Bl)	1.40	1.00
65	A9	80c on 2fr grn & blk (R)	2.75	2.00
66	A10	2pi on 5fr bl & blk (R)	3.75	3.00
67	A11	4pi on 10fr pur & blk (R)	4.00	3.25
		Nos. 51-67 (17)	24.15	19.35

YUNNAN FOU
(Formerly Yunnan Sen, later known as Kunming)

YUNNANSEN

Stamps of Indo-China Surcharged in Black 仙六

1903-04 ***Perf. 14x13½.*** **Unwmkd.**

No.	Type	Description	Unused	Used
1	A3	1c *lil bl*	3.75	3.25
2	A3	2c brn, *buff*	3.00	3.00
3	A3	4c cl, *lav*	3.00	3.00
4	A3	5c yel grn	3.00	2.50
5	A3	10c red	3.00	2.50
6	A3	15c gray	3.75	3.00
7	A3	20c red, *grn*	4.50	3.50
8	A3	25c blue	3.75	3.50
9	A3	30c brn, *bis*	5.00	3.50
10	A3	40c red, *straw*	40.00	27.50
11	A3	50c car, *rose*	225.00	210.00
12	A3	50c brn, *az* ('04)	100.00	100.00
13	A3	75c dp vio, *org*	28.50	25.00
a.		"INDO-CHINE" inverted	18,500.	
14	A3	1fr brnz grn, *straw*	28.50	25.00
15	A3	5fr red lil, *lav*	55.00	55.00
		Nos. 1-15 (15)	509.75	470.25

The Chinese characters overprinted on Nos. 1 to 15 repeat the denomination of the basic stamp.

Many varieties of the surcharge exist on Nos. 1–15.

Stamps of Indo-China, 1892–1906, Surcharged in Red or Black

Yunnan-Fou

1906 ***Perf. 14x13½.*** **Unwmkd.**

No.	Type	Description	Unused	Used
17	A4	1c ol grn (R)	1.50	1.50
18	A4	2c vio brn, *buff*	1.75	1.75
19	A4	4c cl, *bluish* (R)	2.00	2.00
20	A4	5c dp grn (R)	2.00	2.00
21	A4	10c carmine	2.00	2.00
22	A4	15c org brn, *bl*	3.00	3.00
23	A4	20c red, *grn*	2.50	2.50
24	A4	25c dp bl	2.50	2.50
25	A4	30c pale brn	2.50	2.50
26	A4	35c *yel* (R)	3.50	3.50
27	A4	40c *bluish* (R)	3.00	3.00
28	A4	50c bis brn	3.00	3.00
29	A3	75c dp vio, *org* (R)	24.00	24.00
30	A4	1fr pale grn	12.00	12.00
31	A4	2fr brn, *org* (R)	12.00	12.00
32	A3	5fr red lil, *lav*	35.00	35.00
33	A4	10fr org brn, *grn*	40.00	40.00
		Nos. 17-33 (17)	152.25	152.25

Various varieties of the surcharge exist on Nos. 18, 20, 21 and 27.

Stamps of Indo-China, 1907, Surcharged "YUNNANFOU", and Value in Chinese in Red or Blue.

1908

No.	Type	Description	Unused	Used
34	A5	1c ol brn & blk	45	45
35	A5	2c brn & blk	45	45
36	A5	4c bl & blk	45	45
37	A5	5c grn & blk	95	95
38	A5	10c red & blk (Bl)	50	50
39	A5	15c vio & blk	2.50	2.00
40	A6	20c vio & blk	2.75	2.25
41	A6	25c bl & blk	2.75	2.25
42	A6	30c brn & blk	3.00	2.75
43	A6	35c ol grn & blk	3.00	2.75
44	A6	40c brn & blk	4.00	4.00
45	A6	50c car & blk (Bl)	4.00	4.00
46	A7	75c ver & blk (Bl)	5.00	4.25
47	A8	1fr car & blk (Bl)	7.50	7.00
48	A9	2fr grn & blk	12.50	12.50
a.		"YUNANNFOU"	1,250.	1,250.
49	A10	5fr bl & blk	25.00	22.50
a.		"YUNANNFOU"	1,250.	1,250.
50	A11	10fr pur & blk	50.00	50.00
a.		"YUNANNFOU"	1,250.	1,250.
		Nos. 34-50 (17)	124.80	119.05

The Chinese characters overprinted on Nos. 17 to 50 repeat the denomination of the basic stamp.

1919

Issue of 1908 Surcharged with New Values in Cents or Piastres in Black, Red or Blue.

No.	Type	Description	Unused	Used
51	A5	2/5c on 1c ol brn & blk	45	40
a.		New value double	62.50	
52	A5	4/5c on 2c yel brn & blk	70	60
53	A5	1 3/5c on 4c bl & blk (R)	80	75
54	A5	2c on 5c grn & blk	70	60
a.		Triple surcharge	100.00	
55	A5	4c on 10c red & blk (Bl)	70	60
56	A5	6c on 15c vio & blk	70	60
57	A6	8c on 20c vio & blk	1.00	90
58	A6	10c on 25c bl & blk	1.40	1.25
59	A6	12c on 30c brn & blk	1.10	1.00
60	A6	14c on 35c ol grn & blk	2.25	2.10
a.		Closed "4"	55.00	55.00
61	A6	16c on 40c yel brn & blk	2.50	2.25
62	A6	20c on 50c car & blk (Bl)	1.40	1.40
63	A7	30c on 75c ver & blk (Bl)	2.50	2.25
64	A8	40c on 1fr car & blk (Bl)	2.75	2.50
65	A9	80c on 2fr grn & blk (R)	4.00	4.00
a.		Triple surch., one inverted	125.00	
66	A10	2pi on 5fr bl & blk (R)	22.50	22.50
67	A11	4pi on 10fr pur & blk (R)	7.00	6.50
		Nos. 51-67 (17)	52.45	50.20

OFFICES IN CRETE

Austria, France, Italy and Great Britain maintained their own post offices in Crete during the period when that country was an autonomous state.

100 CENTIMES=1 FRANC

Liberty, Equality and Fraternity

A1

"Rights of Man"

A2

Liberty and Peace (Symbolized by Olive Branch)

A3

Typographed.

1902-03 ***Perf. 14x13½.*** **Unwmkd.**

No.	Type	Description	Unused	Used
1	A1	1c gray	75	75
2	A1	2c vio brn	80	75
3	A1	3c red org	80	75
4	A1	4c yel brn	80	75
5	A1	5c green	60	45
6	A2	10c rose red	1.00	60
7	A2	15c pale red ('03)	1.00	80
8	A2	20c brn vio ('03)	1.25	1.10
9	A2	25c bl ('03)	1.50	1.25
10	A2	30c lil ('03)	2.75	2.25
11	A3	40c red & pale bl	4.50	3.50
12	A3	50c bis brn & lav	6.75	5.00
13	A3	1fr cl & ol grn	9.50	8.50
14	A3	2fr gray vio & yel	14.50	12.50
15	A3	5fr dk bl & buff	21.50	18.50
		Nos. 1-15 (15)	68.00	57.45

A4

A5

Black Surcharge.

1903

No.	Type	Description	Unused	Used
16	A4	1pi on 25c bl	16.00	14.00
17	A5	2pi on 50c bis brn & lav	27.50	25.00
18	A5	4pi on 1fr cl & ol grn	45.00	37.50
19	A5	8pi on 2fr gray vio & yel	57.50	55.00
20	A5	20pi on 5fr dk bl & buff	90.00	67.50
		Nos. 16-20 (5)	236.00	199.00

OFFICES IN EGYPT

French post offices formerly maintained in Alexandria and Port Said.

100 CENTIMES=1 FRANC

ALEXANDRIA

A1

French Stamps Overprinted in Red, Blue or Black.

Perf. 14x13½

1899–1900 **Unwmkd.**

No.	Type	Description	Unused	Used
1	A1	1c *lil bl* (R)	55	55
a.		Double overprint	55.00	
b.		Triple overprint	55.00	
2	A1	2c brn, *buff* (Bl)	90	90
3	A1	3c gray, *grysh* (Bl)	1.10	80
4	A1	4c cl, *lav*(Bl)	90	80
5	A1	5c yel grn, (I) (R)	1.75	1.25
a.		Type II (R)	62.50	47.50
6	A1	10c *lav*, (I) (R)	3.75	3.00
a.		Type II (R)	25.00	15.00
7	A1	15c bl (R)	3.00	2.50
8	A1	20c red, *grn*	6.00	3.25
a.		Double ovpt.		
9	A1	25c *rose* (R)	2.75	1.75
a.		Inverted overprint	32.50	
b.		Double overprint, one inverted	55.00	
10	A1	30c brn, *bis*	8.00	4.00
11	A1	40c red, *straw*	6.00	5.50
12	A1	50c car, *rose* (II)	10.00	8.00
a.		Type I	65.00	8.00
13	A1	1fr brnz grn, *straw*	10.00	8.00
14	A1	2fr brn, *az* ('00)	45.00	37.50
15	A1	5fr red lil, *lav*	60.00	55.00
		Nos. 1-15 (15)	159.70	132.80

A2

A3

A4

1902-03

No.	Type	Description	Unused	Used
16	A2	1c gray	20	15
17	A2	2c vio brn	20	18
18	A2	3c red org	20	15
19	A2	4c yel brn	35	25
20	A2	5c green	55	30
21	A3	10c rose red	75	25
22	A3	15c orange	55	35
a.		15c pale red ('03)	90	55
23	A3	20c brn vio ('03)	85	55
24	A3	25c bl ('03)	40	15
25	A3	30c vio ('03)	2.50	1.50
26	A4	40c red & pale bl	2.50	1.10
27	A4	50c bis brn & lav	3.00	1.25
28	A4	1fr cl & ol grn	3.50	1.50
29	A4	2fr gray vio & yel	7.25	5.50
30	A4	5fr dk bl & buff	9.00	8.00
		Nos. 16-30 (15)	31.80	21.18

The 2c, 5c, 10c, 20c and 25c exist imperf. Price, each $15.

See also Nos. 77–86.

Stamps of 1902-03 Surcharged Locally in Black **4 Mill.**

1921

No.	Type	Description	Unused	Used
31	A2	2m on 5c grn	2.50	2.00
32	A2	3m on 3c red org	2.75	2.25
a.		Larger numeral	35.00	32.50
33	A3	4m on 10c rose	2.25	2.00
34	A2	5m on 1c dk gray	2.75	2.25
35	A2	5m on 4c yel brn	2.75	2.50
36	A3	6m on 15c org	1.50	1.50
a.		Larger numeral	32.50	32.50
37	A3	8m on 20c brn vio	2.25	2.00
a.		Larger numeral	16.00	15.00
38	A3	10m on 25c bl	1.10	1.00
a.		Inverted surcharge	17.50	17.50
b.		Double surcharge	17.50	17.50
39	A3	12m on 30c vio	6.75	6.25
40	A2	15m on 2c vio brn	2.75	2.75

Surcharged **15 Mill.**

No.	Type	Description	Unused	Used
41	A4	15m on 40c red & pale bl	7.25	6.25
42	A4	15m on 50c bis brn & lav	2.75	2.75
43	A4	30m on 1fr cl & ol grn	85.00	75.00

4	A4	60m on 2fr gray vio & yel	110.00	110.00
a.		Larger numeral	275.00	275.00
5	A4	150m on 5fr dk bl & buff	170.00	170.00

Port Said Nos. 20 and 19 Surcharged like Nos. 32 and 40.

5A	A2	3m on 3c red org	47.50	50.00
6	A2	15m on 2c vio brn	47.50	50.00

Alexandria No. 28 Surcharged with Two New Values.

1921

46A	A4	30m on 15m on 1fr cl & ol grn	550.00	550.00

The surcharge "15 Mill." was made in error and is cancelled by a bar.

The surcharges were lithographed on Nos. 31, 33, 38, 39 and 42 and typographed on the other stamps of the 1921 issue. Nos. 34, 36 and 37 were surcharged by both methods.

Alexandria Stamps of 1902-03 Surcharged in Paris — 2 MILLIEMES

1921–23

47	A2	1m on 1c gray	85	85
48	A2	2m on 5c grn	60	60
49	A3	4m on 10c rose	1.25	1.10
50	A3	4m on 10c grn ('23)	90	75
51	A2	5m on 3c red org ('23)	2.75	2.25
52	A3	6m on 15c org	70	65
53	A3	8m on 20c brn vio	55	40
54	A3	10m on 25c bl	50	40
55	A3	10m on 30c vio	1.75	1.50
56	A3	15m on 50c bl ('23)	1.10	75

Surcharged — 15 MILLIÈMES

57	A4	15m on 50c bis brn & lav	1.60	1.35
58	A4	30m on 1fr cl & ol grn	1.00	80
59	A4	60m on 2fr gray vio & yel	*1,000.*	*1,000.*
60	A4	60m on 2fr org & pale bl ('23)	5.50	3.75
61	A4	150m on 5fr bl & buff	5.25	3.25
		Nos. 47-58, 60-61 (14)	24.30	18.40

Stamps and Types of 1902-03 Surcharged with New Values and Bars in Black.

1925

62	A2	1m on 1c gray	40	40
63	A2	2m on 5c org	35	35
64	A2	2m on 5c grn	75	75
65	A3	4m on 10c grn	45	35
66	A2	5m on 3c red org	35	35
67	A3	6m on 15c org	45	45
68	A3	8m on 20c brn vio	35	35
69	A3	10m on 25c bl	30	30
70	A3	15m on 50c bl	60	60
71	A4	30m on 1fr cl & ol grn	80	65
72	A4	60m on 2fr org & pale bl	1.75	1.35
73	A4	150m on 5fr dk bl & buff	2.25	1.75
		Nos. 62-73 (12)	8.80	7.65

Types of 1902-03 Issue.

1927-28

77	A2	3m org ('28)	70	60
81	A3	15m sl bl	70	60
82	A3	20m rose lil ('28)	2.25	1.50
84	A4	50m org & bl	4.50	3.75
85	A4	100m sl bl & buff	5.50	4.50
86	A4	250m gray grn & red	11.00	7.25
		Nos. 77-86 (6)	24.65	18.20

SEMI-POSTAL STAMPS.

Regular Issue of 1902–03 Surcharged in Carmine — ✚5c

1915 *Perf. 14x13½.* **Unwmkd.**

B1	A3	10c +5c rose	35	35

Sinking Fund Issue.

Type of 1902-03 Issue Surcharged in Blue or Black — +5 Mm Caisse d'Amortissement

1927-30

B2	A3	15m +5m dp org	90	90
B3	A3	15m +5m red vio ('28)	1.75	1.75
a.		15m +5m vio ('30)	3.75	3.75

Type of 1902-03 Issue Surcharged as in 1927-28.

1929

B4	A3	15m +5m fawn	2.75	2.75

POSTAGE DUE STAMPS.

Postage Due Stamps of France, 1893-1920, Surcharged in Paris in Black — 2 MILLIEMES

1922 *Perf. 14x13½.* **Unwmkd.**

J1	D2	2m on 5c bl	1.00	1.00
J2	D2	4m on 10c brn	1.00	1.00
J3	D2	10m on 30c rose red	1.10	1.10
J4	D2	15m on 50c brn vio	1.45	1.45
J5	D2	30m on 1fr red brn, *straw*	2.25	2.25
		Nos. J1-J5 (5)	6.80	6.80

D3

1928 Typographed.

J6	D3	1m slate	85	85
J7	D3	2m lt bl	60	60
J8	D3	4m lil rose	75	75
J9	D3	5m gray grn	65	65
J10	D3	10m lt red	75	75
J11	D3	20m vio brn	60	60
J12	D3	30m green	1.75	1.75
J13	D3	40m lt vio	1.75	1.75
		Nos. J6-J13 (8)	7.70	7.70

Nos. J6 to J13 were also available for use in Port Said.

PORT SAID

A1

Stamps of France Overprinted in Red, Blue or Black.

Perf. 14x13½.

1899-1900 **Unwmkd.**

1	A1	1c *lil bl* (R)	65	55
2	A1	2c brn, *buff* (bl)	75	65
3	A1	3c gray, *grysh* (Bl)	95	70
4	A1	4c cl, *lav* (Bl)	95	65
5	A1	5c yel grn (I) (R)	3.75	2.00
a.		Type II (R)	25.00	6.25
6	A1	10c *lav* (I) (R)	5.50	5.50
a.		Type II (R)	32.50	22.50
7	A1	15c bl (R)	5.50	3.00
8	A1	20c red, *grn*	6.25	3.00
9	A1	25c *rose*(R)	5.50	1.00
a.		Double overprint	72.50	
10	A1	30c brn, *bis*	5.50	3.50
a.		Inverted overprint	67.50	
11	A1	40c red, *straw*	6.25	3.75
12	A1	50c car, *rose*(II)	9.00	5.50
a.		Type I	150.00	45.00
b.		Dbl. ovpt. (II)	110.00	
13	A1	1fr brnz grn, *straw*	12.00	6.25
14	A1	2fr brn, *az* ('00)	35.00	27.50
15	A1	5fr red lil, *lav*	55.00	35.00
		Nos. 1-15 (15)	152.55	98.55

Regular Issue Surcharged in Red — PORT SAID VINGT CINQ

1899

16	A1	25c on 10c *lav*	67.50	14.00

With Additional Surcharge "25."

17	A1	25c on 10c *lav*	225.00	85.00

A2 A3

A4

1902-03 Typographed.

18	A2	1c gray	30	25
19	A2	2c vio brn	30	25
20	A2	3c red org	35	25
21	A2	4c yel brn	45	30
22	A2	5c bl grn	45	35
a.		5c yel grn	1.40	1.10
23	A3	10c rose red	60	35
24	A3	15c pale red ('03)	80	70
a.		15c org	80	70
25	A3	20c brn vio ('03)	75	40
26	A3	25c bl ('03)	85	50
27	A3	30c vio ('03)	2.25	1.75
28	A4	40c red & pale bl	2.25	1.75
29	A4	50c bis brn & lav	2.75	2.25
30	A4	1fr cl & ol grn	4.00	3.00
31	A4	2fr gray vio & yel	6.25	5.50
32	A4	5fr dk bl & buff	14.00	12.00
		Nos. 18-32 (15)	36.35	29.60

See Nos. 83–92.

Stamps of 1902-03 Surcharged Locally — 2 Milliemes

1921

33	A2	2m on 5c grn	3.25	3.25
a.		Inverted surcharge	17.50	17.50
34	A3	4m on 10c rose	3.25	3.25
a.		Inverted surcharge	17.50	17.50
35	A2	5m on 1c gray	3.25	3.25
a.		Inverted surcharge	27.50	27.50
c.		Surcharged "2 Milliemes"	22.50	22.50
36	A2	5m on 2c vio brn	5.50	5.50
a.		Surcharged "2 Milliemes"	27.50	27.50
b.		Sames as "a," inverted	45.00	45.00
37	A2	5m on 3c red org	4.50	4.50
a.		Inverted surcharge	18.50	18.50
b.		On Alexandria #18	150.00	150.00
38	A2	5m on 4c yel brn	4.00	4.00
a.		Inverted surcharge	27.50	27.50
39	A2	10m on 2c vio brn	4.50	4.50
40	A2	10m on 4c yel brn	8.50	8.50
a.		Inverted surcharge	27.50	27.50
41	A3	10m on 25c bl	2.75	2.75
a.		Inverted surcharge	27.50	27.50
42	A3	12m on 30c vio	18.00	18.00
43	A2	15m on 4c yel brn	3.50	3.50
a.		Inverted surcharge	30.00	30.00
44	A3	15m on 15c pale red	20.00	20.00
a.		Inverted surcharge	40.00	40.00
45	A3	15m on 20c brn vio	20.00	20.00
a.		Inverted surcharge	42.50	42.50
46	A4	30m on 50c bis brn & lav	160.00	160.00
47	A4	60m on 50c bis brn & lav	170.00	170.00
48	A4	150m on 50c bis brn & lav	200.00	200.00

Nos. 46, 47 and 48 have a bar between the numerals and "Millièmes", which is in capital letters.

Same Surcharge on Stamps of French Offices in Turkey, 1902-03.

49	A2	2m on 2c vio brn	40.00	40.00
50	A2	5m on 1c gray	40.00	40.00
a.		"5" inverted	350.00	350.00

Stamps of 1902-03 Surcharged — 15 MILLIEMES

51	A4	15m on 40c red & pale bl	25.00	25.00
a.		"MILLtEMES"	50.00	50.00
52	A4	15m on 50c bis brn & lav	32.50	32.50
a.		"MILLtEMES"	120.00	120.00
b.		Bar below 15	27.50	27.50
53	A4	30m on 1fr cl & ol grn	110.00	110.00
a.		"MILLtEMES"	350.00	350.00
54	A4	60m on 2fr gray vio & yel	35.00	35.00
a.		"MILLtEMES"	140.00	140.00
55	A4	150m on 5fr dk bl & buff	135.00	135.00
a.		"MILLtEMES"	375.00	375.00

Stamps of 1902–03 Surcharged in Paris — 2 MILLIÈMES

1921–23

56	A2	1m on 1c gray	50	50
57	A2	2m on 5c grn	50	50
58	A3	4m on 10c rose	90	90
59	A2	5m on 3c red org	3.50	3.50
60	A3	6m on 15c org	1.10	1.10
a.		6m on 15c pale red	5.00	5.00
61	A3	8m on 20c brn vio	80	80
62	A3	10m on 25c bl	1.50	1.50
63	A3	10m on 30c vio	2.75	2.75
64	A3	15m on 50c bl	2.25	2.25

Surcharged — 15 MILLIÈMES

65	A4	15m on 50c bis brn & lav	2.25	2.25
66	A4	30m on 1fr cl & ol grn	3.00	3.00
67	A4	60m on 2fr gray vio & yel	50.00	50.00
68	A4	60m on 2fr org & pale bl	4.00	4.00
69	A4	150m on 5fr bl & buff	3.25	3.25
		Nos. 56-69 (14)	76.30	76.30

Stamps and Types of 1902–03 Surcharged with New Values and Bars

1925

70	A2	1m on 1c gray	25	25
71	A2	2m on 5c grn	30	30
72	A3	4m on 10c rose red	30	30
73	A2	5m on 3c red org	30	30
74	A3	6m on 15c org	35	35
75	A3	8m on 20c brn vio	30	30
76	A3	10m on 25c bl	35	35
77	A3	15m on 50c bl	35	35
78	A4	30m on 1fr cl & ol grn	55	55
79	A4	60m on 2fr org & pale bl	75	75
80	A4	150m on 5fr dk bl & buff	1.00	1.00
		Nos. 70-80 (11)	4.80	4.80

Types of 1902-03 Issue.

1927-28

83	A2	3m org ('28)	55	55
87	A3	15m sl bl	60	60
88	A3	20m rose lil ('28)	65	65
90	A4	50m org & bl	1.40	1.40
91	A4	100m sl bl & buff	1.75	1.75
92	A4	250m gray grn & red	3.00	3.00
		Nos. 83-92 (6)	7.95	7.95

SEMI-POSTAL STAMPS.

Regular Issue of 1902-03 Surcharged in Carmine **+5c**

1915 *Perf. 14x13½.* **Unwmkd.**

B1	A3	10c +5c rose	80	80

Sinking Fund Issue.

Type of 1902-03 Issue Surcharged in Blue or Black **+5 Mm Caisse d'Amortissement**

1927-30				
B2	A3	15m +5m dp org (Bl)	80	80
B3	A3	15m +5m red vio ('28)	80	80
a.		15m+5m vio ('30)	1.75	1.75
B4	A3	15m +5m fawn ('29)	1.00	1.00

POSTAGE DUE STAMPS.

Postage Due Stamps of France, 1893–1906, Surcharged Locally in Black **15 Millièmes**

1921 *Perf. 14x13½.* **Unwmkd.**

J1	D2	12m on 10c brn	25.00	25.00
J2	D2	15m on 5c bl	27.50	27.50
J3	D2	30m on 20c ol grn	30.00	30.00
a.		Invtd. surch.	250.00	250.00
J4	D2	30m on 50c red vio	*1,800.*	*1,800.*

Same Surcharged in Red or Blue **4 MILLIEMES**

1921				
J5	D2	2m on 5c bl (R)	25.00	25.00
a.		Blue surcharge	150.00	150.00
J6	D2	4m on 10c brn (Bl)	25.00	25.00
a.		Surcharged "15 Milliemes"	325.00	325.00
J7	D2	10m on 30c red (Bl)	25.00	25.00
a.		Inverted surcharge	55.00	55.00
J8	D2	15m on 50c brn vio (Bl)	32.50	32.50
a.		Inverted surcharge	60.00	60.00

Nos. J5–J8 exist with second "M" in "Milliemes" inverted, also with final "S" omitted.

Alexandria Nos. J6–J13 were also available for use in Port Said.

French Offices In Morocco

See French Morocco.

FRENCH OFFICES IN TURKISH EMPIRE

(Levant)

Various powers maintained post offices in the Turkish Empire before World War I by authority of treaties which ended with the signing of the Treaty of Lausanne in 1923. The foreign post offices were closed Oct. 27, 1923.

100 CENTIMES=1 FRANC
25 CENTIMES=40 PARAS=1 PIASTRE

A1

Stamps of France Surcharged in Black or Red.
Perf. 14x13½.

1885–1901 **Unwmkd.**

1	A1	1pi on 25c yel, *straw* ('85)	225.00	5.25
a.		Inverted surch.	1,100.	1,100.
2	A1	1pi on 25c *rose* (R) ('86)	75	35
a.		Inverted surch.	110.00	85.00
3	A1	2pi on 50c car, *rose* (II) ('90)	6.25	75
a.		Type I ('01)	130.00	15.00
4	A1	3pi on 75c car, *rose* ('85)	11.00	4.50
5	A1	4pi on 1fr brnz grn, *straw* ('85)	7.50	3.75
6	A1	8pi on 2fr brn, *az* ('00)	15.00	9.00
7	A1	20pi on 5fr red lil, *lav* ('90)	37.50	17.50

A2

A3

A4

A5

A6

Typographed.

1902–07 *Perf. 14x13½.*

21	A2	1c gray	20	15
22	A2	2c vio brn	30	25
23	A2	3c red org	30	25
24	A2	4c yel brn	60	55
a.		Imperf., pair	32.50	
25	A2	5c grn ('06)	30	20
26	A3	10c rose red	35	15
27	A3	15c pale red ('03)	75	60
28	A3	20c brn vio ('03)	80	60
29	A3	25c bl ('07)	22.50	18.00
a.		Imperf., pair	200.00	
30	A3	30c lil ('03)	1.50	1.10
31	A4	40c red & pale bl	1.50	1.10
32	A4	50c bis brn & lav ('07)	72.50	67.50
a.		Imperf., pair	500.00	
33	A4	1fr cl & ol grn ('07)	175.00	175.00
a.		Imperf., pair	550.00	

Black Surcharge.

34	A5	1pi on 25c bl ('03)	40	10
a.		Second "I" omitted	10.00	9.00
b.		Double surch.	22.50	20.00
35	A6	2pi on 50c bis brn & lav	90	35
36	A6	4pi on 1fr cl & ol grn	1.10	55
a.		Imperf., pair	325.00	
37	A6	8pi on 2fr gray vio & yel	7.25	4.00
38	A6	20pi on 5fr dk bl & buff	2.25	1.40
		Nos. 21-38 (18)	288.50	271.85

Nos. 29, 32–33 were used during the early part of 1907 in the French Offices at Harrar and Diredawa, Ethiopia. Djibouti and Port Said stamps were also used.

No. 27 Surcharged in Green **1 Piastre Beyrouth**

1905				
39	A3	1pi on 15c pale red	800.00	125.00
a.		"Piastte"	*2,500.*	450.00

Stamps of France 1900-21 Surcharged:

30 PARAS (a) **1 PIASTRE 20 PARAS** (b) **15 PIASTRES** (c)

1921-22				
40	A22 (a)	30pa on 5c grn	35	25
41	A22 (a)	30pa on 5c org	35	25
42	A22 (b)	1pi 20pa on 10c red	35	25
43	A22 (b)	1pi 20pa on 10c grn	35	25
44	A22 (b)	3pi 30pa on 25c bl	35	25
45	A22 (b)	4pi 20pa on 30c org	35	25
a.		"4" omitted	450.00	
46	A20 (b)	7pi 20pa on 50c bl	35	25
47	A18 (c)	15pi on 1fr car & ol grn	60	40
48	A18 (c)	30pi on 2fr org & pale bl	5.00	3.25
49	A18 (c)	75pi on 5fr dk bl & buff	3.25	2.00
		Nos. 40-49 (10)	11.30	7.40

Stamps of France, 1903-07, Handstamped **3 PIASTRES 30 PARAS**

1923				
52	A22	1pi 20pa on 10c red	22.50	22.50
54	A20	3pi 30pa on 15c gray grn	8.50	8.50
55	A22	7pi 20pa on 35c vio	9.00	9.00
a.		1pi 20pa on 35c vio	375.00	375.00
b.		Double surch.	40.00	

CAVALLE
(Cavalla)

A1

A2

Stamps of France Overprinted or Surcharged in Red, Blue or Black
Perf. 14x13½.

1893–1900 **Unwmkd.**

1	A1	5c grn, *grnsh* (R)	8.00	6.25
a.		Double overprint		
2	A1	5c yel grn (I) ('00) (R)	9.00	6.25
3	A1	10c *lav* (II) (Bl)	11.00	7.25
a.		10c *lav* (I)	80.00	67.50
4	A1	15c bl (R)	12.50	9.00
5	A2	1pi on 25c *rose* (Bl)	14.00	10.00
6	A2	2pi on 50c car, *rose* (Bl)	40.00	27.50
7	A2	4pi on 1fr brnz grn, *straw* (R)	40.00	32.50
8	A2	8pi on 2fr brn, *az* ('00) (Bk)	47.50	45.00
		Nos. 1-8 (8)	182.00	143.75

A3

A4

A5

A6

1902-03				
9	A3	5c green	60	6
10	A4	10c rose red ('03)	70	6
11	A4	15c orange	90	7
a.		15c pale red ('03)	3.50	3.5

Surcharged in Black.

12	A5	1pi on 25c bl	1.40	1.1
13	A6	2pi on 50c bis brn & lav	3.25	2.50
14	A6	4pi on 1fr cl & ol grn	4.50	4.00
15	A6	8pi on 2fr gray vio & yel	6.75	6.25
		Nos. 9-15 (7)	18.10	15.80

DEDEAGH
(Dedeagatch)

A1

A2

Stamps of France Overprinted or Surcharged in Red, Blue or Black.
Perf. 14x13½.

1893-1900 **Unwmkd.**

1	A1	5c grn, *grnsh* (II) (R)	6.00	5.00
2	A1	5c yel grn (I) ('00) (R)	6.00	5.50
3	A1	10c *lav* (II) (Bl)	9.00	8.00
a.		Type I	18.50	11.00
4	A1	15c bl (R)	11.50	8.50
5	A2	1pi on 25c *rose* (Bl)	14.00	11.50
6	A2	2pi on 50c car, *rose* (Bl)	25.00	22.50
7	A2	4pi on 1fr brnz grn, *straw* (R)	30.00	25.00
8	A2	8pi on 2fr brn, *az* ('00) (Bk)	45.00	37.50
		Nos. 1-8 (8)	146.50	123.50

A3

A4

A5

A6

1902–03				
9	A3	5c green	50	45
10	A4	10c rose red ('03)	60	45
11	A4	15c orange	1.10	60

Black Surcharge.

	A5	1pi on 25c bl ('03)	1.25	70
	A6	2pi on 50c bis brn & lav	3.00	2.75
a.		Double surcharge	67.50	
	A6	4pi on 1fr cl & ol grn	5.50	5.00
	A6	8pi on 2fr gray vio & yel	9.00	6.75
		Nos. 9-18 (7)	20.95	16.70

PORT LAGOS

A1 A2

Stamps of France Overprinted or Surcharged in Red or Blue.

1893 ***Perf. 14x13½*** **Unwmkd.**

	A1	5c grn, *grnsh* (R)	12.00	8.00
	A1	10c *lav* (Bl)	25.00	17.50
	A1	15c bl (R)	47.50	35.00
	A2	1pi on 25c *rose*	32.50	27.50
	A2	2pi on 50c car, *rose* (Bl)	80.00	47.50
	A2	4pi on 1fr brnz grn, *straw* (R)	50.00	50.00

VATHY
(Samos)

A1 A2

Stamps of France Overprinted or Surcharged in Red, Blue or Black.

Perf. 14x13½

1894-1900 **Unwmkd.**

1	A1	5c grn, *grnsh* (R)	4.50	4.00
2	A1	5c yel grn (I) ('00) (R)	4.50	4.00
a.		Type II	40.00	32.50
3	A1	10c *lav* (I) (Bl)	7.25	6.25
a.		Type II	22.50	15.00
4	A1	15c bl (R)	7.25	7.25
5	A2	1pi on 25c *rose* (Bl)	9.00	6.25
6	A2	2pi on 50c car, *rose* (Bl)	16.00	16.00
7	A2	4pi on 1fr brnz grn, *straw* (R)	16.00	16.00
8	A2	8pi on 2fr brn, *az* ('00) (Bk)	40.00	37.50
9	A2	20pi on 5fr lil, *lav* ('00) (Bk)	60.00	55.00
		Nos. 1-9 (9)	164.50	152.25

OFFICES IN ZANZIBAR

Until 1906 France maintained post offices in the Sultanate of Zanzibar, but in that year Great Britain assumed direct control over this protectorate and the French withdrew their postal system.

16 ANNAS=1 RUPEE

A1

A2

A4

A5

Stamps of France Surcharged in Red, Blue or Black.

1894-96 ***Perf. 14x13½*** **Unwmkd.**

1	A1	½a on 5c grn, *grnsh* (R)	2.75	2.25
2	A1	1a on 10c *lav* (Bl)	5.50	4.00
3	A1	1½a on 15c bl ('96) (R)	9.50	8.50
a.		"ANNAS"	45.00	45.00
4	A1	2a on 20c red, *grn* ('96) (Bk)	5.50	4.50
5	A1	2½a on 25c *rose* (Bl)	4.00	3.25
a.		Double surcharge	75.00	
6	A1	3a on 30c brn, *bis* ('96) (Bk)	9.50	8.50
7	A1	4a on 40c red, *straw* ('96) (Bk)	9.50	8.50
8	A1	5a on 50c car, *rose* (Bl)	14.00	12.00
9	A1	7½a on 75c vio, *org* ('96) (R)	200.00	175.00
10	A1	10a on 1fr brnz grn, *straw* (R)	22.50	18.50
11	A1	50a on 5fr red lil, *lav* ('96) (Bk)	150.00	140.00

1894

12	A2	½a & 5c on 1c *lil bl* (R)	85.00	85.00
13	A2	1a & 10c on 3c gray, *grysh* (R)	85.00	85.00
14	A2	2½a & 25c on 4c cl, *lav* (Bk)	125.00	125.00
15	A2	5a & 50c on 20c red, *grn* (Bk)	125.00	125.00
16	A2	10a & 1fr on 40c red, *straw* (Bk)	250.00	250.00

There are two distinct types of the figures 5c, four of the 25c and three of each of the others of this series.

A3

Surcharged in Red, Blue or Black.

1896-1900

17	A3	½a on 5c grn, *grnsh* (R)	2.75	2.65
18	A3	½a on 5c yel grn (I) (R)	2.75	2.50
a.		Type II	2.75	2.75
19	A3	1a on 10c *lav* (II) (Bl)	3.25	3.00
a.		Type I	5.50	5.50
20	A3	1½a on 15c bl (R)	2.75	2.50
21	A3	2a on 20c red, *grn* (Bk)	2.75	2.75
a.		"ZANZIBAR" double	45.00	45.00
b.		"ZANZIBAR" triple	55.00	
22	A3	2½a on 25c *rose* (Bl)	3.00	2.75
23	A3	3a on 30c brn, *bis* (Bk)	3.00	3.00
24	A3	4a on 40c red, *straw* (Bk)	3.00	3.00
25	A3	5a on 50c rose, *rose* (II) (Bl)	15.00	11.50
a.		Type I	42.50	40.00
26	A3	10a on 1fr brnz grn, *straw* (R)	7.75	6.25
27	A3	20a on 2fr brn, *az* (Bk)	10.00	8.00
a.		"ZANZIBAS"	375.00	375.00
28	A3	50a on 5fr lil, *lav* (Bk)	20.00	18.00
a.		"ZANZIBAS"	1,350.	1,350.
		Nos. 17-28 (12)	76.00	65.90

1897

29	A4	2½a & 25c on ½a on 5c grn, *grnsh*	550.00	90.00
30	A4	2½a & 25c on 1a on 10c *lav*	2,250.	550.00
31	A4	2½a & 25c on 1½a on 15c bl	2,250.	450.00
32	A5	5a & 50c on 3a on 30c brn, *bis*	2,250.	450.00
33	A5	5a & 50c on 4a on 40c red, *straw*	2,250.	450.00

A6

A7

Printed on the Margins of Sheets of French Stamps.

1897

34	A6	2½a & 25c grn, *grnsh*	625.00
35	A6	2½a & 25c *lav*	1,500.
36	A6	2½a & 25c bl	1,500.
37	A7	5a & 50c brn, *bis*	1,200.
38	A7	5a & 50c red, *straw*	1,500.

There are several varieties of figures in the above surcharges.

A8 A9

A10

Surcharged in Red or Black.

1902-03

39	A8	½a on 5c grn (R)	2.25	1.75
40	A9	1a on 10c rose red ('03)	2.75	2.50
41	A9	1½a on 15c pale red ('03)	6.00	5.50
42	A9	2a on 20c brn vio ('03)	7.25	6.00
43	A9	2½a on 25c bl ('03)	6.75	6.00
44	A9	3a on 30c lil ('03)	6.00	4.75
a.		5a on 30c (error)	150.00	150.00
45	A10	4a on 40c red & pale bl	10.00	9.00
46	A10	5a on 50c bis brn & lav	7.25	6.50
47	A10	10a on 1fr cl & ol grn	11.50	11.00
48	A10	20a on 2fr gray vio & yel	27.50	25.00
49	A10	50a on 5fr dk bl & buff	40.00	40.00
		Nos. 39-49 (11)	127.25	118.00

Nos. 23–24 Surcharged in Black:

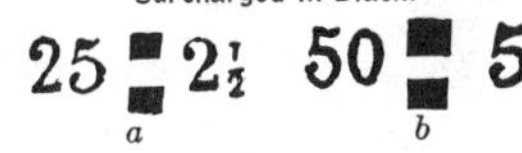

1fr 10

c

1904

50	A3	25(c) & 2½(a) on 4a on 40c red, *straw*	550.00
51	A3	50(c) & 5(a) on 3a on 30c brn, *bis*	625.00
52	A3	50(c) & 5(a) on 4a on 40c red, *straw*	625.00
53	A3	1fr & 10(a) on 3a on 30c brn, *bis*	1,000.
54	A3	1fr & 10(a) on 4a on 40c red, *straw*	1,050.

Stamps of 1902-03 Issue Surcharged in Red or Black:

2 25 (d) 25c 2½ (e) 50c (f) 1fr (g) cinq dix

55	A8 (d)	25(c) & 2(a) on ½a on 5c grn (R)	1,200.	55.00
56	A9 (e)	25c & 2½(a) on 1a on 10c rose red	2,500.	60.00
a.		Inverted surcharge		600.00
57	A9 (e)	25c & 2½(a) on 3c on 30c lil		1,150.
a.		Inverted surcharge		1,000.
b.		Double surchare, both inverted		1,600.
58	A9 (f)	50c & 5(a) on 3a on 30c lil		625.00
59	A9 (g)	1fr & 10(a) on 3a on 30c lil		750.00

Postage Due Stamps of 1897 Issue With Various Surcharges.

Overprinted "Timbre" in Red.

60	D1	½a on 5c bl	225.00

Overprinted "Affrancht" in Black.

61	D1	1a on 10c brn	225.00

With Red Bars Across "CHIFFRE" and "TAXE"

62	D1	1½a on 15c grn	450.00

The illustrations are not exact reproductions of the new surcharges but are merely intended to show their relative positions and general styles.

POSTAGE DUE STAMPS.

D1

Stamps of France Surcharged in Red, Blue or Black.

1897 ***Perf. 14x13½.*** **Unwmkd.**

J1	D1	½a on 5c bl (R)	7.25	4.50
J2	D1	1a on 10c brn (Bl)	7.25	4.50
a.		Inverted surcharge	55.00	55.00
J3	D1	1½a on 15c grn (R)	9.00	5.00
J4	D1	3a on 30c car (Bk)	11.00	8.00
J5	D1	5a on 50c lil (Bl)	11.00	7.75
a.		2½a on 50c lil (Bl)	450.00	450.00
		Nos. J1-J5 (5)	45.50	29.75

Methods and style of listing are detailed in "Special Notices" at the front of this volume.

FRENCH COLONIES

From 1859 to 1906 and in 1944 and 1945 special stamps were issued for use in all French Colonies which did not have stamps of their own.

100 CENTIMES=1 FRANC

Perforations: Nos. 1–45 are known variously perforated unofficially.

Gum: Many of Nos. 1-45 were issued without gum. Some were gummed locally.

Reprints: Nos. 1–7, 9–12, 24, 26–42, 44 and 45 were reprinted officially in 1887. These reprints are ungummed and the colors of both design and paper are deeper or brighter than the originals. Price for Nos. 1–6, $30 each.

> **Prices of early French Colonies stamps vary according to condition. Quotations for Nos. 1–23 are for fine copies. Very fine to superb specimens sell at much higher prices, and inferior or poor copies sell at reduced prices, depending on the condition of the individual specimen.**

Eagle and Crown
A1

Typographed.

1859–65 *Imperf.* **Unwmkd.**

1	A1	1c ol grn, *pale bl* ('62)	12.50	15.00
2	A1	5c yel grn, *grnsh* ('62)	14.00	11.00
3	A1	10c bis, *yel*	17.50	6.25
a.		Pair, one sideways	725.00	350.00
4	A1	20c bl, *bluish* ('65)	22.50	11.00
5	A1	40c org, *yelsh*	14.00	7.25
6	A1	80c car rose, *pnksh* ('65)	55.00	45.00

Napoleon III
A2 A3

Ceres A4 Napoleon III A5

1871–72 *Imperf.*

7	A2	1c ol grn, *pale bl* ('72)	55.00	55.00
8	A3	5c yel grn, *grnsh* ('72)	625.00	400.00
9	A4	10c bis, *yelsh*	250.00	115.00
a.		Tête bêche pair	*22,500.*	*17,500.*
10	A4	15c bis, *yelsh*('72)	200.00	11.00
11	A4	20c bl, *bluish*	400.00	115.00
a.		Tête bêche pair		*12,000.*
12	A4	25c bl, *bluish* ('72)	120.00	11.00
13	A5	30c brn, *yelsh*	110.00	32.50
14	A4	40c org, *yelsh* (I)	200.00	12.50
a.		Type II	*2,750.*	500.00
b.		Pair, types I & II	*5,500.*	*1,350.*
15	A5	80c rose, *pnksh*	675.00	90.00

For types I and II of 40c see illustrations over No. 1 of France.

Ceres
A6 A7

1872–77 *Imperf.*

16	A6	1c ol grn, *pale bl* ('73)	12.50	14.00
17	A6	2c red brn, *yelsh* ('76)	400.00	575.00
18	A6	4c gray ('76)	*7,250.*	500.00
19	A6	5c grn, *pale bl*	12.50	9.00
20	A7	10c bis, *rose* ('76)	150.00	11.00
21	A7	15c bis ('77)	450.00	95.00
22	A7	30c brn, *yelsh*	75.00	17.50
23	A7	80c rose, *pnksh* ('73)	325.00	115.00

No. 17 was used only in Cochin China, 1876-77. Excellent forgeries of Nos. 17 and 18 exist.

With reference to the stamps of France and French Colonies in the same designs and colors see the note after France No. 9.

Peace and Commerce A8 Commerce A9

1877–78 **Type I.** *Imperf.*

24	A8	1c grn, *grnsh*	25.00	30.00
25	A8	4c grn, *grnsh*	15.00	11.50
26	A8	30c brn, *yelsh*('78)	32.50	32.50
27	A8	40c ver, *straw*	21.00	19.00
28	A8	75c car, *rose* ('78)	62.50	55.00
29	A8	1fr brnz grn, *straw*	27.50	16.00

Type II.

30	A8	2c grn, *grnsh*	11.50	10.00
31	A8	5c grn, *grnsh*	15.00	5.00
32	A8	10c grn, *grnsh*	80.00	11.00
33	A8	15c gray, *grysh*	225.00	67.50
34	A8	20c red brn, *straw*	55.00	6.25
35	A8	25c ultra *bluish*	32.50	9.00
a.		25c bl, *bluish* ('78)	*4,500.*	175.00
36	A8	35c vio blk, *org*('78)	40.00	27.50

1878–80 **Type II.**

38	A8	1c *lil bl*	16.00	16.00
39	A8	2c brn, *buff*	14.00	11.50
40	A8	4c cl, *lav*	20.00	20.00
41	A8	10c *lav* ('79)	90.00	17.50
42	A8	15c bl ('79)	27.50	11.50
43	A8	20c red, *grn* ('79)	72.50	11.50
44	A8	25c *red*('79)	475.00	300.00
45	A8	25c yel, *straw*('80)	525.00	27.50

No. 44 was used only in Mayotte, Nossi-Bé and New Caledonia. Forgeries exist.

The 3c yellow, 3c gray, 15c yellow, 20c blue, 25c rose and 5fr lilac were printed together with the reprints, and were never issued.

1881-86 *Perf. 14x13½.*

46	A9	1c *lil bl*	1.75	1.75
47	A9	2c brn, *buff*	2.25	2.25
48	A9	4c cl, *lav*	2.25	2.25
49	A9	5c grn, *grnsh*	2.25	1.50
50	A9	10c *lavender*	4.50	2.50
51	A9	15c blue	8.00	1.50
52	A9	20c red, *yel grn*	20.00	9.00
53	A9	25c yel, *straw*	6.50	2.50
54	A9	25c *rose* ('86)	6.50	1.50
55	A9	30c brn, *bis*	18.50	12.00
56	A9	35c vio blk, *yel org*	20.00	15.00
a.		35c vio blk, *yel*	32.50	18.50
57	A9	40c ver, *straw*	22.50	16.00
58	A9	75c car, *rose*	52.50	27.50
59	A9	1fr brnz grn, *straw*	35.00	20.00

Nos. 46–59 exist imperforate. They are proofs and were not used for postage, except the 10c.

For stamps of type A9 surcharged with numerals see: Cochin China, Diego Suarez, Gabon, Madagascar, Nossi Be, New Caledonia, Reunion, Senegal, Tahiti.

SEMI-POSTAL STAMPS.

Resistance Fighters
SP1

Lithographed.

1943 *Rouletted* **Unwmkd.**

B1	SP1	1.50fr +98.50fr ind & gray	12.50	15.00

The surtax was for the benefit of patriots and the French Committee of Liberation.

No. B1 was printed in sheets of 10 (5x2) with adjoining labels for each stamp. The label shows the Lorraine cross in indigo in a gray frame.

Colonies Offering Aid to France
SP2

1943 *Perf. 12*

B2	SP2	9fr +41fr red vio	60	75

The surtax was for the benefit of French Patriots.

Patriots and Map of France
SP3

1943

B3	SP3	50c +4.50fr yel grn	45	55
B4	SP3	1.50fr +8.50fr cer	45	55
B5	SP3	3fr +12fr grnsh bl	45	55
B6	SP3	5fr +15fr ol gray	45	55

The surtax was for the aid of combatants and patriots.

Refugee Family
SP4

1943

B7	SP4	10fr +40fr dl bl	2.00	2.50

The surtax was for refugee relief work.

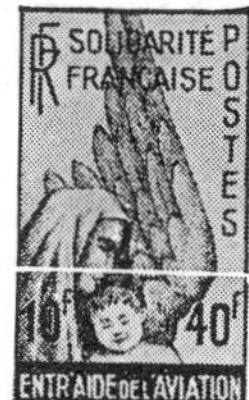

Woman and Child with Wing
SP5

1944

B8	SP5	10fr +40fr grnsh blk	2.50	2.[illegible]

The surtax was for the general benefit of aviation.

Nos. B1–B8 were originally prepared for use in the French Colonies, but after the landing of Free French troops in Corsica they were used there and later also in Southern France. They became valid throughout France in November 1944.

POSTAGE DUE STAMPS.

D1

Typographed.

1884-85 *Imperf.* **Unwmkd.**

J1	D1	1c black	1.75	1.75
J2	D1	2c black	1.75	1.75
J3	D1	3c black	1.75	1.75
J4	D1	4c black	2.00	1.75
J5	D1	5c black	2.75	2.00
J6	D1	10c black	4.00	2.75
J7	D1	15c black	7.25	4.50
J8	D1	20c black	7.25	6.00
J9	D1	30c black	9.00	4.50
J10	D1	40c black	11.50	4.50
J11	D1	60c black	18.50	11.00
J12	D1	1fr brown	15.00	11.50
a.		1fr blk	175.00	
J13	D1	2fr brown	14.00	10.00
a.		2fr blk	175.00	
J14	D1	5fr brown	50.00	32.50
a.		5fr blk	225.00	

Nos. J12a, J13a and J14a were not regularly issued.

1894-1906

J15	D1	5c pale bl	45	45
J16	D1	10c gray brn	45	45
J17	D1	15c pale grn	45	45
J18	D1	20c ol grn ('06)	45	45
J19	D1	30c carmine	75	60
J20	D1	50c lilac	75	60
J21	D1	60c brn, *buff*	2.00	1.25
a.		60c dk vio, *buff*	2.00	1.25
J22	D1	1fr red, *buff*	2.75	1.75
a.		1fr rose, *buff*	10.00	9.00
		Nos. J15-J22 (8)	8.05	6.00

D2

1945 **Lithographed** *Perf. 12*

J23	D2	10c sl bl	5	5
J24	D2	15c yel grn	5	5
J25	D2	25c dp org	6	6
J26	D2	50c grnsh blk	35	35
J27	D2	60c cop brn	35	35
J28	D2	1fr dp red lil	15	15
J29	D2	2fr red	35	35
J30	D2	4fr sl gray	90	90
J31	D2	5fr brt ultra	90	90
J32	D2	10fr purple	5.50	3.75
J33	D2	20fr dl brn	1.60	1.60
J34	D2	50fr dp grn	2.50	2.50
		Nos. J23-J34 (12)	12.76	11.01

FRENCH CONGO

(frĕnch kŏng'gō)

LOCATION—Central Africa.

GOVT.—French possession.

French Congo was originally a separate colony, but was joined in 1888 to Gabon and placed under one commissioner-general with a lieutenant-governor presiding in Gabon and another in French Congo. In 1894 the military holdings in Ubangi were attached to French Congo, and in 1900 the Chad military protectorate was added. Postal service was not established in Ubangi or Chad, however, at that time. In 1906 Gabon and Middle Congo were separated and French Congo ceased to exist as such. Chad and Ubangi remained attached to Middle Congo as the joint dependency of "Ubangi—Chari—Chad," and Middle Congo stamps were used there.

Issues of the Republic of the Congo are listed under Congo Republic (ex-French).

100 Centimes = 1 Franc

Stamps of French Colonies Surcharged Horizontally in Red or Black

Congo français

5c.

1891 ***Perf. 14x13½.*** **Unwmkd.**

1	A9	5c on 1c *lil bl*(R)	*3,750.*	*2,500.*
2	A9	5c on 1c *lil bl*	90.00	45.00
a.		Double surcharge	375.00	185.00
3	A9	5c on 15c bl	150.00	62.50
a.		Double surcharge	375.00	185.00
5	A9	5c on 25c *rose*	62.50	27.50
a.		inverted surcharge	135.00	40.00

1891–92

First "O" of "Congo" is a Capital, "Francais" with Capital "F".

6	A9	5c on 20c red, *grn*	600.00	225.00
7	A9	5c on 25c *rose*	50.00	15.00
a.		Surch. vert.	120.00	50.00
8	A9	10c on 25c *rose*	85.00	22.50
a.		Inverted surcharge	150.00	45.00
b.		Surch. vert.	100.00	37.50
c.		First "o" of "Congo" small	100.00	30.00
d.		Double surcharge	225.00	67.50
9	A9	10c on 40c red, *straw*	1,350.	225.00
10	A9	15c on 25c *rose*	75.00	16.50
a.		Surch. vert.	110.00	35.00
b.		Inverted surcharge	100.00	35.00
c.		Double surch.	185.00	60.00

First "O" of Congo small. Surcharge Vertical, Reading Down or Up. No period.

11	A9	5c on 25c *rose*
12	A9	10c on 25c *rose*
13	A9	15c on 25c *rose*

Postage Due Stamps
of French Colonies
Surcharged in Red
or Black
Reading Down
or Up
Congo français
Timbres poste
10 c

1892 ***Imperf.***

14	D1	5c on 5c blk (R)	60.00	50.00
15	D1	5c on 20c blk (R)	60.00	50.00
16	D1	5c on 30c blk (R)	85.00	72.50
17	D1	10c on 1fr brn	75.00	55.00
a.		Double surcharge		
b.		Surch. horiz.		*750.00*

Excellent counterfeits of Nos. 1–17 exist.

Navigation and Commerce
A3

1892–1900 **Typo.** ***Perf. 14x13½***

Colony Name in Blue or Carmine

18	A3	1c *lil bl*	75	60
19	A3	2c brn, *buff*	90	80
a.		Name double	55.00	40.00
20	A3	4c cl, *lav*	1.00	90
a.		Name in blk and in bl	55.00	40.00
21	A3	5c grn, *grnsh*	2.25	2.00
22	A3	10c *lavender*	7.50	5.25
a.		Name double	210.00	200.00
23	A3	10c red ('00)	1.00	60
24	A3	15c bl, quadrille paper	18.50	5.75
25	A3	15c gray ('00)	3.25	2.75
26	A3	20c red, *grn*	9.50	5.75
27	A3	25c *rose*	8.50	6.25
28	A3	25c bl ('00)	4.00	3.50
29	A3	30c brn, *bis*	9.50	6.00
30	A3	40c red, *straw*	18.50	11.00
31	A3	50c car, *rose*	20.00	11.00
32	A3	50c brn, *az* ('00)	3.75	3.50
a.		Name double	275.00	275.00
33	A3	75c dp vio, *org*	15.00	11.00
34	A3	1fr brnz grn, *straw*	22.50	12.00
		Nos. 18-34 (17)	146.40	88.65

Leopard
A4

Bakalois Woman
A5

Coconut Grove
A6

Wmk. 122

Wmkd. Thistle Branch. (122)

1900 ***Perf. 11***

35	A4	1c brn vio & gray lil	30	30
a.		Background inverted	18.50	18.50
36	A4	2c brn & org	30	30
a.		2c dk red & red	67.50	
b.		Imperf., pair	27.50	27.50
37	A4	4c scar & gray bl	45	30
a.		4c dk red & red	350.00	
b.		Background inverted	21.00	21.00
38	A4	5c grn & gray grn	70	30
a.		Imperf., pair	57.50	57.50
39	A4	10c dk red & red	2.00	80
a.		Imperf., pair	57.50	57.50
40	A4	15c dl vio & ol grn	70	30
a.		Imperf. pair	40.00	40.00

Wmk. 123

Wmkd. Rose Branch. (123)

41	A5	20c yel grn & org	65	38
42	A5	25c bl & pale bl	1.10	55
43	A5	30c car rose & org	1.15	60
44	A5	40c org brn & brt grn	2.00	75
a.		Imperf., pair	37.50	37.50
b.		Center inverted	50.00	50.00
45	A5	50c gray vio & lil	2.25	1.75
46	A5	75c red vio & org	4.75	3.25
a.		Imperf., pair	37.50	37.50

Wmk. 124

Wmkd. Olive Branch. (124)

47	A6	1fr gray lil & ol	9.00	5.75
a.		Center inverted	135.00	135.00
b.		Imperf., pair	52.50	52.50
48	A6	2fr car & brn	14.00	8.75
a.		Imperf., pair	90.00	90.00
49	A6	5fr brn org & gray	32.50	27.50
a.		5fr ocher & gray	300.00	300.00
b.		Center inverted	185.00	185.00
c.		Wmk. 123	100.00	
d.		Imperf., pair	210.00	210.00
		Nos. 35-49 (15)	71.85	51.58

Nos. 26 and 29 Surcharged in Black

Valeur
15

1900 ***Perf. 14x13½*** **Unwmkd.**

50	A3	5c on 20c red, *grn*	*11,000.*	*3,750.*
a.		Dbl. surch.		*7,500.*
51	A3	15c on 30c brn, *bis*	*6,750.*	*1,500.*
a.		Dbl. surch.		*3,250.*

Nos. 43 and 48 Surcharged in Black:

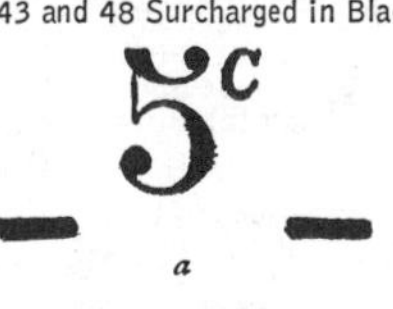

1903 ***Perf. 11*** **Wmk. 123**

52	A5	5c on 30c car rose & org	150.00	67.50
a.		Inverted surcharge	1,000.	

Wmk. 124

53	A6	10c on 2fr car & brn	210.00	72.50
a.		Inverted surcharge	*1,000.*	
b.		Double surcharge	*1,250.*	

Counterfeits of the preceding surcharges are known.

FRENCH EQUATORIAL AFRICA

(frĕnch ē'kwȧ·tō'rĭ·ăl ăf'rĭ·kȧ)

LOCATION—North of Belgian Congo and south of Libya.

GOVT.—Former French Colony.

AREA—959,256 square miles.

POP.—4,491,785.

CAPITAL—Brazzaville.

In 1910 Gabon and Middle Congo, with its military dependencies, were politically united as French Equatorial Africa. The component colonies were granted administrative autonomy. In 1915 Ubangi-Chari-Chad was made an autonomous civilian colony and in 1920 Chad was made a civil colony. In 1934 the four colonies were administratively united as one colony, but this federation was not completed until 1936. Each colony had its own postal administration until 1936 when they were united. The postal issues of the former colonial subdivisions are listed under the names of those colonies.

In 1958, French Equatorial Africa was divided into four republics: Chad, Congo, Gabon and Central African Republic (formerly Ubangi-Chari).

100 Centimes = 1 Franc

Stamps of Gabon, 1932, Overprinted "Afrique Equatoriale Francaise" and Bars Similar to "a" and "b" in Black

Perf. 13x13½, 13½x13.

1936 **Unwmkd.**

1	A16	1c brn vio	6	6
2	A16	2c blk, *rose*	6	6
3	A16	4c green	35	22
4	A16	5c grnsh bl	32	22
5	A16	10c red, *yel*	32	27
6	A17	40c brn vio	65	55
7	A17	50c red brn	60	38
8	A17	1fr yel grn, *bl*	15.00	6.75
9	A18	1.50fr dl bl	1.10	50
10	A18	2fr brn red	8.50	4.50
		Nos. 1-10 (10)	26.96	13.51

Stamps of Middle Congo, 1933 Overprinted in Black:

AFRIQUE
ÉQUATORIALE
FRANÇAISE

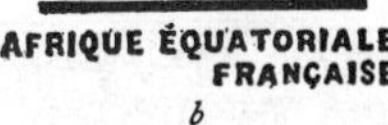

a

AFRIQUE ÉQUATORIALE
FRANÇAISE

b

AFRIQUE EQUATORIALE
FRANÇAISE

c

1936

11	A4 (b)	1c lt brn	7	7
12	A4 (b)	2c dl bl	8	8
13	A4 (b)	4c ol grn	22	18
14	A4 (b)	5c red vio	28	22
15	A4 (b)	10c slate	55	45
16	A4 (b)	15c dk vio	60	45
17	A4 (b)	20c red, *pink*	50	35
18	A4 (b)	25c orange	1.35	1.10

19	A5 (a)	40c org brn	1.35	1.10
20	A5 (c)	50c blk vio	1.10	85
21	A5 (c)	75c blk, *pink*	2.00	1.50
22	A5 (a)	90c carmine	1.25	1.10
23	A5 (c)	1.50fr dk bl	80	55
24	A6 (a)	5fr sl bl	25.00	15.00
25	A6 (a)	10fr black	14.00	11.00
26	A6 (a)	20fr dk brn	15.00	11.00
		Nos. 11-26 (16)	64.15	45.00

Paris International Exposition Issue.

Common Design Types

1937, Apr. 15 Engraved. *Perf. 13.*

27	CD74	20c dk vio	1.10	1.10
28	CD75	30c dk grn	1.10	1.10
29	CD76	40c car rose	1.10	1.10
30	CD77	50c dk brn & bl	90	90
31	CD78	90c red	1.10	1.10
32	CD79	1.50fr ultra	1.10	1.10
		Nos. 27-32 (6)	6.40	6.40

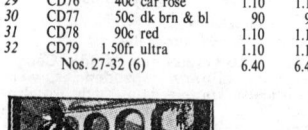

Logging on Loéme River
A1

People of Chad
A2

Pierre Savorgnan de Brazza
A3

Emile Gentil
A4

Paul Crampel
A5

Governor Victor Liotard
A6

Two types of 25c:
I. Wide numerals (4mm.).
II. Narrow numerals (3½mm.).

1937-40 Photo. *Perf. 13½x13*

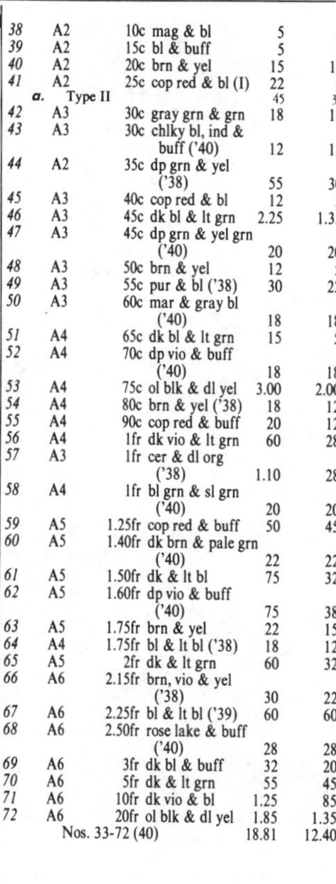

33	A1	1c brn & yel	5	4
34	A1	2c vio & grn	6	6
35	A1	3c bl & yel ('40)	12	12
36	A1	4c mag & bl	6	6
37	A1	5c dk & lt grn	5	5
38	A2	10c mag & bl	5	5
39	A2	15c bl & buff	5	5
40	A2	20c brn & yel	15	12
41	A2	25c cop red & bl (I)	22	6
a.		Type II	45	32
42	A3	30c gray grn & grn	18	18
43	A3	30c chlky bl, ind & buff ('40)	12	12
44	A2	35c dp grn & yel ('38)	55	30
45	A3	40c cop red & bl	12	5
46	A3	45c dk bl & lt grn	2.25	1.35
47	A3	45c dp grn & yel grn ('40)	20	20
48	A3	50c brn & yel	12	5
49	A3	55c pur & bl ('38)	30	22
50	A3	60c mar & gray bl ('40)	18	18
51	A4	65c dk bl & lt grn	15	5
52	A4	70c dp vio & buff ('40)	18	18
53	A4	75c ol blk & dl yel	3.00	2.00
54	A4	80c brn & yel ('38)	18	12
55	A4	90c cop red & buff	20	12
56	A4	1fr dk vio & lt grn	60	28
57	A3	1fr cer & dl org ('38)	1.10	28
58	A4	1fr bl grn & sl grn ('40)	20	20
59	A5	1.25fr cop red & buff	50	45
60	A5	1.40fr dk brn & pale grn ('40)	22	22
61	A5	1.50fr dk & lt bl	75	32
62	A5	1.60fr dp vio & buff ('40)	75	38
63	A5	1.75fr brn & yel	22	15
64	A4	1.75fr bl & lt bl ('38)	18	12
65	A5	2fr dk & lt grn	60	32
66	A6	2.15fr brn, vio & yel ('38)	30	22
67	A6	2.25fr bl & lt bl ('39)	60	60
68	A6	2.50fr rose lake & buff ('40)	28	28
69	A6	3fr dk bl & buff	32	20
70	A6	5fr dk & lt grn	55	45
71	A6	10fr dk vio & bl	1.25	85
72	A6	20fr ol blk & dl yel	1.85	1.35
		Nos. 33-72 (40)	18.81	12.40

Colonial Arts Exhibition Issue

Souvenir Sheet.

Common Design Type

1937 *Imperf.*

73	CD79	3fr red brn	3.25	3.25

Sheet size: 111x99mm.

Count Louis Edouard Bouet-Willaumez and His Ship "La Malouine"—A7

1938, Dec. 5 *Perf. 13½.*

74	A7	65c gray brn	55	55
75	A7	1fr dp rose	55	55
76	A7	1.75fr blue	85	85
77	A7	2fr dl vio	90	90

Issued in commemoration of the centenary of Gabon.

New York World's Fair Issue.

Common Design Type

1939, May 10 Engr. *Perf. 12½x12*

78	CD82	1.25fr car lake	80	80
79	CD82	2.25fr ultra	80	80

Common Design Types

pictured in section at front of book.

Libreville View and Marshal Petain
A7a

1941 Engraved *Perf. 12½x12*

79A	A7a	1fr bluish grn	75	
79B	A7a	2.50fr blue	75	

Nos. 79A-79B were issued by the Vichy government, and were not placed on sale in the colony. This is also true of four stamps of types A2, A3 and A5 without "RF" monogram released in 1943-44.

Stamps of 1936-40, Overprinted in Carmine or Black:

AFRIQUE FRANÇAISE LIBRE
a

LIBRE
b

1940-41 *Perf. 13½x13*

80	A1 (a)	1c brn & yel (C)	45	45
81	A1 (a)	2c vio & grn (C)	55	55
82	A1 (a)	3c bl & yel (C)	55	55
83	A4 (b)	4c ol grn (Bk) (No. 13)	5.50	5.50
84	A1 (a)	5c dk grn & lt grn (C)	60	60
85	A2 (a)	10c mag & bl (Bk)	80	80
86	A2 (a)	15c bl & buff (C)	80	80
87	A2 (a)	20c brn & yel (C)	90	90
88	A2 (a)	25c cop red & bl (Bk)	3.00	3.00
89	A3 (b)	30c gray grn & grn (C)	6.50	6.00
90	A3 (b)	30c gray grn & grn (Bk) ('41)	75	65
91	A3 (b)	30c chlky bl, ind & buff (C) ('41)	5.50	5.00
92	A3 (b)	30c chlky bl, ind & buff (Bk) ('41)	3.25	3.25
93	A2 (a)	35c dp grn & yel (C)	80	80
94	A3 (b)	40c cop red & bl (Bk)	32	28
a.		Double overprint	20.00	
95	A3 (b)	45c dp grn & yel grn (C)	55	35
96	A3 (b)	45c dp grn & yel grn (Bk) ('41)	32	30
a.		Double overprint	5.00	5.00
97	A3 (b)	50c brn & yel (C)	2.50	2.25
98	A3 (b)	50c brn & yel (Bk) ('41)	1.50	1.50
a.		Double overprint	35.00	
99	A3 (b)	55c pur & bl (C)	55	35
100	A3 (b)	55c pur & bl (Bk) ('41)	35	30
a.		Double overprint	6.00	6.00
b.		Double, one inverted	20.00	
101	A3 (b)	60c mar & gray bl (Bk)	35	30
102	A4 (b)	65c dk bl & lt grn (Bk)	30	30
a.		Double overprint	20.00	
103	A4 (b)	70c dp vio & buff (Bk)	30	[illegible]
a.		Double overprint	5.00	[illegible]
104	A4 (b)	75c ol blk & dl yel (Bk)	20.00	[illegible]
105	A4 (b)	80c brn & yel (Bk)	28	
a.		Double overprint	20.00	
106	A4 (b)	90c cop red & buff (Bk)	45	
a.		Double overprint	20.00	
b.		Double, one inverted	20.00	
107	A4 (b)	1fr bl grn & sl grn (Bk)	3.25	[illegible]
108	A4 (b)	1fr bl grn & sl grn (C) ('41)	2.50	[illegible]
109	A3 (b)	1fr cer & dl org (Bk)	65	[illegible]
110	A5 (b)	1.40fr dk brn & pale grn (Bk)	22	[illegible]
a.		Double overprint	4.00	[illegible]
111	A5 (b)	1.50fr dk bl & lt bl (Bk)	30	[illegible]
a.		Double overprint	6.00	[illegible]
112	A5 (b)	1.60fr dp vio & buff (Bk)	30	[illegible]
113	A5 (b)	1.75fr brn & yel (Bk)	55	[illegible]
114	A6 (b)	2.15fr brn, vio & yel (Bk)	38	[illegible]
a.		Double overprint	4.00	[illegible]
115	A6 (b)	2.25fr bl & lt bl (C)	55	[illegible]
a.		Double overprint	6.00	[illegible]
116	A6 (b)	2.25fr bl & lt bl (Bk) ('41)	90	[illegible]
a.		Double overprint	20.00	
117	A6 (b)	2.50fr rose lake & buff (Bk)	38	[illegible]
a.		Double overprint	20.00	
118	A6 (b)	3fr dk bl & buff (C)	55	[illegible]
119	A6 (b)	3fr dk bl & buff (Bk) ('41)	90	[illegible]
a.		Double overprint	5.50	[illegible]
120	A6 (b)	5fr dk grn & lt grn (C)	2.00	[illegible]
121	A6 (b)	5fr dk grn & lt grn (Bk) ('41)	57.50	[illegible]
122	A6 (b)	10fr dk vio & bl (C)	1.00	[illegible]
123	A6 (b)	10fr dk vio & bl (Bk) ('41)	37.50	[illegible]
a.		Double overprint		
124	A6 (b)	20fr ol blk & dl yel (C)	1.00	[illegible]
125	A6 (b)	20fr ol blk & dl yel (Bk) ('41)	5.00	[illegible]
		Nos. 80-125 (46)	173.15	[illegible]

Nos. 48, 51 Surcharged in Black or Carmine

LIBRE 75c

1940

126	A3	75c on 50c brn & yel (Bk)	22	22
a.		Double surcharge		
127	A4	1fr on 65c dk bl & lt grn (C)	22	22
a.		Double surcharge	3.50	

Middle Congo No. 67
Overprinted in Carmine:

AFRIQUE FRANÇAISE LIBRE

Perf. 13½

128	A4	4c ol grn	21.00	20.00

Stamps of 1940
With Additional Overprint in Black **24-10-40**

1940 **Perf. 13½x13**

129	A4	80c brn & yel	8.50	6.25
a.		Overprint without "2"	20.00	
130	A4	1fr bl grn & sl grn	8.50	6.25
131	A3	1fr cer & dl org	8.50	6.25
132	A5	1.50fr dk bl & lt bl	8.50	6.25

These stamps were sold affixed to post cards and at a slight increase over face value to cover the cost of the cards.

Issued to commemorate the arrival of General de Gaulle in Brazzaville, capital of Free France, October 24, 1940.

Stamps of 1937-40
Overprinted in Black **Afrique Française Libre**

1941

133	A1	1c brn & yel	60	60
134	A1	2c vio & grn	60	60
135	A1	3c bl & yel	60	60
136	A1	5c dk & lt grn	60	60
137	A2	10c mag & bl	60	60
138	A2	15c bl & buff	60	60
139	A2	20c brn & yel	60	60
140	A2	25c cop red & bl	2.00	2.00
141	A2	35c dp grn & yel	1.50	1.50
a.		Double overprint	10.00	
		Nos. 133-141 (9)	7.70	7.70

There are two settings of the overprint on Nos. 133 to 141 and C10. The first has a space of 1 mm. between lines of the overprint, the second has space of 2 mm.

Phoenix
A8

1941 **Photogravure** **Perf. 14x14½**

142	A8	5c brown	4	4
143	A8	10c dk bl	5	5
144	A8	25c emerald	5	5
145	A8	30c dp org	8	10
146	A8	40c dk sl grn	15	12
147	A8	80c red brn	10	8
148	A8	1fr dp red lil	12	8
149	A8	1.50fr brt red	8	8
150	A8	2fr gray	12	12
151	A8	2.50fr brt ultra	32	25
152	A8	4fr dl vio	28	22
153	A8	5fr yel bis	28	22
154	A8	10fr dp brn	38	38
155	A8	20fr dp grn	60	40
		Nos. 142-155 (14)	2.65	2.19

Eboue Issue.
Common Design Type
Engraved.

1945 **Perf. 13.** **Unwmkd.**

156	CD91	2fr black	18	18
157	CD91	25fr Prus grn	90	90

Nos. 156 and 157 exist imperforate.

Nos. 142, 144 and 151
Surcharged with New Values and Bars in Red, Carmine or Black.

1946 **Perf. 14x14½**

158	A8	50c on 5c brn (R)	28	28
159	A8	60c on 5c brn (R)	28	28
160	A8	70c on 5c brn (R)	22	22
161	A8	1.20fr on 5c brn (C)	22	22
162	A8	2.40fr on 25c emer	35	35
163	A8	3fr on 25c emer	60	60
164	A8	4.50fr on 25c emer	60	60
165	A8	15fr on 2.50fr brt ultra (C)	60	60
		Nos. 158-165 (8)	3.15	3.15

Black Rhinoceros and Rock Python
A9

Jungle Scene
A10

Mountainous Shore Line
A11

Gabon Forest
A12

Niger Boatman
A13

Young Bacongo Woman
A14

Engraved.

1946 **Perf. 12½** **Unwmkd.**

166	A9	10c dp bl	4	4
167	A9	30c vio blk	5	5
168	A9	40c dp org	5	5
169	A10	50c vio bl	5	5
170	A10	60c dk car	22	15
171	A10	80c dk ol grn	22	15
172	A11	1fr dp org	28	18
173	A11	1.20fr dp cl	32	30
174	A11	1.50fr dk grn	55	45
175	A12	2fr dk vio brn	10	6
176	A12	3fr rose car	10	5
177	A12	3.60fr red brn	1.00	90
178	A12	4fr dp bl	22	12
179	A13	5fr dk brn	30	6
180	A13	6fr dp bl	30	12
181	A13	10fr black	32	8
182	A14	15fr brown	75	10
183	A14	20fr dp cl	60	15
184	A14	25fr black	90	18
		Nos. 166-184 (19)	6.37	3.24

Imperforates

Most French Equatorial Africa stamps from 1951 onward exist imperforate in issued and trial colors, and also in small presentation sheets in issued colors.

Pierre Savorgnan de Brazza
A15

1951, Nov. 5 **Perf. 13**

185	A15	10fr ind & dk grn	50	15

Issued to commemorate the centenary of the birth of Pierre Savorgnan de Brazza, explorer.

Military Medal Issue.
Common Design Type
Engraved and Typographed.

1952, Dec. 1 **Perf. 13**

186	CD101	15fr multi	2.75	2.25

Lt. Gov. Adolphe L. Cureau—A16

1954, Sept. 20 **Engraved**

187	A16	15fr ol grn & red brn	80	30

Savannah Monitor—A17

1955, May 2 **Unwmkd.**

188	A17	8fr dk grn & cl	80	30

Issued in connection with the International Exhibition for Wildlife Protection, Paris, May 1955.

FIDES Issue.

Boali Waterfall and Power Plant, Ubangi-Chari
A18

Designs: 10fr, Cotton, Chad. 15fr, Brazzaville Hospital, Middle Congo. 20fr, Libreville Harbor, Gabon.

1956, Apr. 25 **Perf. 13x12½**

189	A18	5fr dk brn & cl	22	12
190	A18	10fr blk & bluish grn	30	18
191	A18	15fr ind & gray vio	30	10
192	A18	20fr dk red & red org	38	15

See note after Common Design Type CD103.

Coffee Issue.

Coffee
A19

1956, Oct. **Engraved** **Perf. 13**

193	A19	10fr brn vio & vio bl	40	12

Leprosarium at Mayumba and Maltese Cross—A20

1957, Mar. 11

194	A20	15fr grn, bl grn & red	75	32

Issued in honor of the Knights of Malta.

Giant Eland
A21

Animals: 2fr, Lions. 3fr, Elephant. 4fr, Greater kudu. (3fr and 4fr vertical.)

1957, Nov. 4

195	A21	1fr grn & brn	12	10
196	A21	2fr Prus grn & ol grn	12	10
197	A21	3fr grn, gray & bl	15	12
198	A21	4fr mar & gray	18	15

WHO Building, Brazzaville
A22

1958, May 19 **Engraved.** **Perf. 13**

199	A22	20fr dk grn & org brn	55	40

Issued to commemorate the 10th anniversary of the World Health Organization.

Flower Issue
Common Design Type

Design: 10fr, Euadania. 25fr, Spathodea.

1958, July 7 **Photo.** **Perf. 12x12½**

200	CD104	10fr dk vio, yel & grn	35	22
201	CD104	25fr grn, yel & red	60	30

Human Rights Issue
Common Design Type

1958, Dec. 10 **Engraved.** **Perf. 13**

202	CD105	20fr Prus grn & dk bl	90	65

SEMI-POSTAL STAMPS.

Common Design Type

1938, Oct. 24 **Engraved.**

B1	CD80	1.75fr +50c brt ultra	10.00	10.00

Stamps of 1937-38
Surcharged in Black or Red **+35c**

1938, Nov. 7 **Perf. 13x13½**

B2	A4	65c +35c dk bl & lt grn (R)	1.10	80

B3	A4	1.75fr +50c bl & lt bl (Bk)	1.10	80

The surtax was for welfare.

French Revolution Issue
Common Design Type
Name and Value Typo. in Black.

1939, July 5 Photogravure.

B4	CD83	45(c) +25(c) grn	7.25	7.25
B5	CD83	70(c) +30(c) brn	7.25	7.25
B6	CD83	90(c) +35(c) red org	7.25	7.25
B7	CD83	1.25fr +1fr rose pink	7.25	7.25
B8	CD83	2.25fr +2fr bl	7.25	7.25
		Nos. B4-B8 (5)	36.25	36.25

Issued to commemorate the 150th anniversary of the French Revolution. The surtax was used for the defense of the colonies.

Common Design Type and

Native Artilleryman
SP1

Gabon Infantryman
SP2

1941 Photogravure *Perf. 13½*

B8A	SP1	1fr +1fr red	1.50
B8B	CD86	1.50fr +3fr mar	1.50
B8C	SP2	2.50fr +1fr bl	1.50

Nos. B8A-B8C were issued by the Vichy government and not placed on sale in the colony.

Nos. 79A-79B were surcharged "OEUVRES COLONIALES" and surtax (including change of denomination of the 2.50fr to 50c). These were issued in 1944 by the Vichy government and not placed on sale in the colony.

Brazza and Stanley Pool
SP3

1941 Photogravure. *Perf. 14½x14.*

B9	SP3	1fr +2fr dk brn & red	35	35

The surtax was for a monument to Pierre Savorgnan de Brazza.

Regular Stamps of 1937-39 Surcharged in Red

Afrique
Française
Combattante

+ 50 fr.

1943, June 28 *Perf. 13½x13*

B10	A6	2.25fr +50fr bl & lt bl	6.25	6.25
B11	A6	10fr +100fr dk vio & bl	17.50	17.50

Nos. 129 and 132 with additional Surcharge in Carmine

LIBÉRATION

+ 10 fr.

1944

B12	A4	80c +10fr brn & yel	7.50	7.50
B13	A5	1.50fr +15fr dk bl & lt bl	7.50	7.50

Same Surcharge printed Vertically on Stamps of 1941.

Perf. 14x14½.

B14	A8	5c +10fr brn	3.25	3.25
B15	A8	10c +10fr dk bl	3.25	3.25
B16	A8	25c +10fr emer	3.25	3.25
B17	A8	30c +10fr dp org	3.25	3.25
B18	A8	40c +10fr dk sl grn	3.25	3.25
B19	A8	1fr +10fr dp red lil	3.25	3.25
B20	A8	2fr +20fr gray	3.25	3.25
B21	A8	2.50fr +25fr brt ultra	3.25	3.25
		Nos. B12-B21 (10)	41.00	41.00

Nos. 129 and 132 with additional Surcharge in Carmine

RÉSISTANCE

+ 10 fr.

1944 *Perf. 13½x13*

B22	A4	80c +10fr brn & yel	8.50	8.50
B23	A5	1.50fr +15fr dk bl & lt bl	8.50	8.50

Same Surcharge printed Vertically on Stamps of 1941.

Perf. 14x14½

B24	A8	5c +10fr brn	3.75	3.75
B25	A8	10c +10fr dk bl	3.75	3.75
B26	A8	25c +10fr emer	3.75	3.75
B27	A8	30c +10fr dp org	3.75	3.75
B28	A8	40c +10fr dk sl grn	3.75	3.75
B29	A8	1fr +10fr dp red lil	3.75	3.75
B30	A8	2fr +20fr gray	3.75	3.75
B31	A8	2.50fr +25fr brt ultra	3.75	3.75
B32	A8	4fr +40fr dl vio	3.75	3.75
B33	A8	5fr +50fr yel bis	3.75	3.75
B34	A8	10fr +100fr dp brn	3.75	3.75
B35	A8	20fr +200fr dp grn	3.75	3.75
		Nos. B22-B35 (14)	62.00	62.00

Nos. B12 to B35 were issued to raise funds for the Committee to Aid the Fighting Men and Patriots of France.

Red Cross Issue
Common Design Type

1944 Photogravure. *Perf. 14½x14*

B38	CD90	5fr +20fr ryl bl	55	55

The surtax was for the French Red Cross and national relief.

Tropical Medicine Issue
Common Design Type

1950, May 15 Engraved. *Perf. 13*

B39	CD100	10fr +2fr dk bl grn & vio brn	2.75	2.75

The surtax was for charitable work.

AIR POST STAMPS.

Hydroplane over Pointe-Noire
AP1

Trimotor over Stanley Pool
AP2

Photogravure.

1937 *Perf. 13½* **Unwmkd.**

C1	AP1	1.50fr ol blk & yel	15	15
C2	AP1	2fr mag & bl	22	22
C3	AP1	2.50fr grn & buff	22	22
C4	AP1	3.75fr brn & lt grn	30	30
C5	AP2	4.50fr cop red & bl	30	30
C6	AP2	6.50fr bl & lt grn	60	60
C7	AP2	8.50fr red brn & yel	60	60
C8	AP2	10.75fr vio & lt grn	60	60
		Nos. C1-C8 (8)	2.99	2.99

V4

Stamps of types AP1 and AP2 without "R F" and stamp of the design shown above were issued in 1943 and 1944 by the Vichy Government, but were not placed on sale in the colony.

Nos. C1, C3-C7 Overprinted in Black

Afrique Française
Libre

1940-41

C9	AP1	1.50fr ('41)	125.00	125.00
a.		Double overprint		
C10	AP1	2.50fr	60	60
a.		Double overprint	50.00	
C11	AP1	3.75fr ('41)	120.00	120.00
C12	AP2	4.50fr	60	60
a.		Double overprint	50.00	50.00
C13	AP2	6.50fr	1.00	1.00
C14	AP2	8.50fr	60	60

No. C8 Surcharged in Carmine

Afrique Française
Libre
50 fr.

C15	AP2	50fr on 10.75fr	4.50	4.50

No. C3 Surcharged in Black

Afrique Française
Libre
10F

C16	AP1	10fr on 2.50fr ('41)	57.50	52.50
		Nos. C9-C16 (8)	309.80	304.80

Counterfeits of Nos. C9 and C11 exist. See note following No. 141.

Common Design Type

1941 Photogravure *Perf. 14½x14*

C17	CD87	1fr dk org	30	22
C18	CD87	1.50fr brt red	30	22
C19	CD87	5fr brn red	75	40
C20	CD87	10fr black	75	50
C21	CD87	25fr ultra	60	50
C22	CD87	50fr dk grn	40	40
C23	CD87	100fr plum	70	60
		Nos. C17-C23 (7)	3.80	2.84

Victory Issue
Common Design Type
Engraved.

1946, May 8 *Perf. 12½* **Unwmkd.**

C24	CD92	8fr lil rose	55	55

Chad to Rhine Issue
Common Design Types

1946, June 6

C25	CD93	5fr dk vio	35	[illegible]
C26	CD94	10fr sl grn	35	[illegible]
C27	CD95	15fr dp bl	60	[illegible]
C28	CD96	20fr red org	75	[illegible]
C29	CD97	25fr sepia	90	[illegible]
C30	CD98	50fr brn car	1.10	[illegible]
		Nos. C25-C30 (6)	4.05	[illegible]

Palms and Village—AP3

Village and Waterfront—AP4

Bearers in Jungle—AP5

1946 Engraved. *Perf. 13.*

C31	AP3	50fr red brn	1.25	30
C32	AP4	100fr grnsh blk	1.80	45
C33	AP5	200fr dp bl	3.50	80

UPU Issue
Common Design Type

1949, July 4

C34	CD99	25fr green	5.25	5.25

Brazza Holding Map—AP6

1951, Nov. 5

C35	AP6	15fr brn, ind & red	75	25

Issued to commemorate the centenary of the birth of Pierre Savorgnan de Brazza, explorer.

Archbishop Augouard and St. Anne Cathedral, Brazzaville
AP7

1952, Dec. 1

C36	AP7	15fr ol grn, dk brn & vio brn	2.00	1.10

Issued to commemorate the centenary of the birth of Archbishop Philippe-Prosper Augouard.

Anhingas—AP8

1953, Feb. 16

C37	AP8	500fr grnsh blk, blk & sl	17.50	2.25

Liberation Issue
Common Design Type

1954, June 6

C38	CD102	15fr vio & vio brn	2.25	2.25

Log Rafts—AP9

Designs: 100fr, Fishing boats and nets, Lake Chad. 200fr, Age of mechanization.

1955, Jan. 24 **Engraved**

C39	AP9	50fr ind, brn & dk grn	80	22
C40	AP9	100fr aqua, dk grn & blk brn	2.25	28
C41	AP9	200fr red & dp plum	3.25	75

Gov. Gen. Félix Eboué, View of Brazzaville and the Pantheon
AP10

1955, Apr. 30 ***Perf. 13*** **Unwmkd.**

C42	AP10	15fr sep, brn & sl bl	1.50	90

Gen. Louis Faidherbé and African Sharpshooter—AP11

1957, July 20

C43	AP11	15fr sep & org ver	1.10	85

Centenary of French African Troops.

AIR POST SEMI-POSTAL STAMPS.

French Revolution Issue
Common Design Type
Photogravure.

1939 ***Perf. 13.*** **Unwmkd.**

Name and Value Typo. in Orange.

CB1	CD83	4.50fr +4fr brn blk	14.00	14.00

V5

V6

V7

Stamps of the designs shown above and stamp of Cameroun type V10 inscribed "Afrique Equatoriale Frcaise" were issued in 1942 by the Vichy Government, but were not placed on sale in the colony.

No. C8 Surcharged in Red

Afrique
Française
Combattante
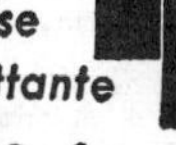
+200 fr.

1943, June 28 ***Perf. 13½***

CB2	AP2	10.75fr +200fr vio & lt grn	85.00	85.00

Counterfeits exist.

POSTAGE DUE STAMPS.

Numeral of Value on Equatorial Butterfly
D1 D2

Photogravure.

1937 ***Perf. 13*** **Unwmkd.**

J1	D1	5c redsh pur & lt bl	4	4
J2	D1	10c cop red & buff	6	6
J3	D1	20c dk grn & grn	6	6
J4	D1	25c red brn & buff	8	8
J5	D1	30c cop red & lt bl	12	12
J6	D1	45c mag & yel grn	25	25
J7	D1	50c dk ol grn & buff	20	20
J8	D1	60c redsh pur & yel	35	35
J9	D1	1fr brn & yel	40	40
J10	D1	2fr dk bl & buff	60	60
J11	D1	3fr red brn & lt grn	60	60
		Nos. J1-J11 (11)	2.76	2.76

1947 **Engraved.**

J12	D2	10c red	8	8
J13	D2	30c dp org	8	8
J14	D2	50c grnsh bl	8	8
J15	D2	1fr carmine	12	12
J16	D2	2fr emerald	12	12
J17	D2	3fr dp red lil	15	15
J18	D2	4fr dp ultra	18	18
J19	D2	5fr red brn	30	30
J20	D2	10fr pck bl	55	55
J21	D2	20fr sepia	65	65
		Nos. J12-J21 (10)	2.23	2.23

FRENCH GUIANA

(frĕnch gē-ä'nȧ)

LOCATION — On the northeast coast of South America bordering on the Atlantic Ocean.

GOVT.—Former French colony.

AREA—34,740 sq. mi.

POP.—28,537 (1946).

CAPITAL—Cayenne.

Formerly a colony, French Guiana became an overseas department of France in 1946.

100 Centimes = 1 Franc

Stamps of French Colonies Surcharged in Black

Déc. 1886.
GUY. FRANÇ.
0f 05

a

1886, Dec. ***Imperf.*** **Unwmkd.**

1	A8	5c on 2c grn, *grnsh*	275.00	275.00
b.		No "f" after "O"	325.00	325.00

Perf. 14x13½.

2	A9	5c on 2c brn, *buff*	285.00	275.00
b.		No "f" after "O"	215.00	200.00

Two types of No. 1: Surcharge 12mm. high, and surcharge 10½mm. high.

Avril 1887.
GUY FRANÇ
0f 20

b

Avril 1887.
GUY FRANÇ.
0f 25

c

Date Line Reads "^Vril 1887"

1887, Apr. ***Imperf.***

4	A8	20c on 35c *org*	22.50	21.00

Date Line Reads "Avril 1887"

5	A8	5c on 2c grn, *grnsh*	55.00	52.50
6	A8	20c on 35c *org*	150.00	120.00
7	A7	25c on 30c brn, *yelsh*	16.50	15.00

Variety "small 'f' omitted" occurs on Nos. 5–7.

French Colonies Nos. 22 and 26 Surcharged:

DÉC. 1887.
GUY. FRANÇ.
5c

d

8	A7	5c on 30c brn, *yelsh*	62.50	60.00
a.		Double surcharge	350.00	350.00
b.		Inverted surcharge	450.00	450.00
c.		Pair, one without surcharge	625.00	625.00
9	A8	5c on 30c brn, *yelsh*	725.00	725.00

French Colonies Nos. 22 and 28 Surcharged:

Février 1888
GUY. FRANÇ
5

e

Février 1888
GUY. FRANÇ
10

f

1888

10	A7	5c on 30c brn, *yelsh*	62.50	62.50
b.		Double surcharge	210.00	210.00
c.		Inverted surcharge	210.00	210.00
11	A8	10c on 75c car, *rose*	110.00	110.00

Stamps of French Colonies Overprinted in Black

GUYANE.

1892, Feb. 20 ***Imperf.***

12	A8	2c grn, *grnsh*	425.00	425.00
13	A7	30c brn, *yelsh*	62.50	62.50
14	A8	35c *orange*	1,250.	1,000.
15	A8	40c red, *straw*	50.00	45.00
16	A8	75c car, *rose*	55.00	45.00
a.		Inverted overprint	185.00	185.00
17	A8	1fr brnz grn, *straw*	75.00	62.50
a.		Inverted overprint	250.00	250.00

1892 ***Perf. 14x13½***

18	A9	1c *lil bl*	21.00	14.00
19	A9	2c brn, *buff*	16.50	14.00
20	A9	4c cl, *lav*	16.50	14.00
21	A9	5c grn, *grnsh*	16.50	14.00
a.		Inverted overprint	45.00	45.00
b.		Double overprint	45.00	
22	A9	10c *lavender*	25.00	18.50
a.		Inverted overprint	25.00	18.50
23	A9	15c blue	24.00	18.50
24	A9	20c red, *grn*	22.50	18.50
25	A9	25c *rose*	32.50	16.50
26	A9	30c brn, *bis*	18.50	16.50
27	A9	35c *orange*	85.00	85.00
28	A9	40c red, *straw*	60.00	55.00
a.		Inverted overprint	65.00	60.00
29	A9	75c car, *rose*	55.00	50.00
30	A9	1fr brnz grn, *straw*	90.00	90.00

French Colonies No. 51 Surcharged

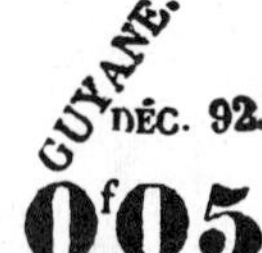

1892, Dec.

31	A9	5c on 15c bl	11.00	9.00

Navigation and Commerce
A12

1892–1904 **Typographed**

Name of Colony in Blue or Carmine.

32	A12	1c *lil bl*	60	60
33	A12	2c brn, *buff*	45	45
34	A12	4c cl, *lav*	60	45
a.		"GUYANE" double	75.00	75.00
35	A12	5c grn, *grnsh*	4.50	3.25
36	A12	5c yel grn ('04)	45	30
37	A12	10c *lavender*	3.75	1.75
38	A12	10c red ('00)	1.50	50
39	A12	15c bl, quadrille paper	11.00	1.10

No.	Type	Description	Unused	Used
40	A12	15c gray, *lt gray* ('00)	45.00	35.00
41	A12	20c red, *grn*	8.00	5.50
42	A12	25c *rose*	6.00	1.20
43	A12	25c bl ('00)	7.25	6.50
44	A12	30c brn, *bis*	7.50	5.50
45	A12	40c red, *straw*	7.50	5.50
46	A12	50c car, *rose*	11.00	5.50
47	A12	50c brn, *az* ('00)	9.00	7.25
48	A12	75c dp vio, *org*	15.00	8.00
49	A12	1fr brn grn, *straw*	6.25	5.25
50	A12	2fr vio, *rose* ('02)	85.00	3.75
		Nos. 32-50 (19)	230.35	97.35

Great Anteater
A13

Washing Gold
A14

Palm Grove at Cayenne—A15

1905–28

No.	Type	Description	Unused	Used
51	A13	1c black	5	5
52	A13	2c blue	6	6
53	A13	4c red brn	8	8
54	A13	5c green	32	22
55	A13	5c org ('22)	5	5
56	A13	10c rose	12	5
57	A13	10c grn ('22)	12	12
58	A13	10c red, *bluish* ('25)	12	6
59	A13	15c violet	45	38
60	A14	20c red brn	12	6
61	A14	25c blue	55	30
62	A14	25c vio ('22)	28	15
63	A14	30c black	45	30
64	A14	30c rose ('22)	12	12
65	A14	30c red org ('25)	12	8
66	A14	30c dk grn, *grnsh* ('28)	38	38
67	A14	35c *yel* ('06)	12	5
68	A14	40c rose	12	6
69	A14	40c blk ('22)	22	15
70	A14	45c ol ('07)	35	12
71	A14	50c violet	90	80
72	A14	50c bl ('22)	15	15
73	A14	50c gray ('25)	28	15
74	A14	60c lil, *rose* ('25)	15	12
75	A14	65c myr grn ('26)	15	12
76	A14	75c green	38	30
77	A14	85c mag ('26)	28	12
78	A15	1fr rose	30	12
79	A15	1fr bl, *bluish* ('25)	28	15
80	A15	1fr bl, *yel grn* ('28)	85	85
81	A15	1.10fr lt red ('28)	55	55
82	A15	2fr blue	35	30
83	A15	2fr org red, *yel* ('26)	60	45
84	A15	5fr black	2.10	1.85
85	A15	10fr grn, *yel* ('24)	5.00	5.00
a.		Printed on both sides	21.00	21.00
86	A15	20fr brn lake ('24)	7.25	6.75
		Nos. 51-86 (36)	23.77	20.62

Issue of 1892 Surcharged in Black or Carmine

05 *j* 10 *k*

1912

No.	Type	Description	Unused	Used
87	A12	5c on 2c brn, *buff*	35	35
88	A12	5c on 4c cl, *lav* (C)	30	30
89	A12	5c on 20c red, *grn*	35	35
90	A12	5c on 25c *rose* (C)	90	90
91	A12	5c on 30c brn, *bis* (C)	55	55
92	A12	10c on 40c red, *straw*	30	30
93	A12	10c on 50c car, *rose*	75	75
a.		Double surcharge	150.00	
		Nos. 87-93 (7)	3.50	3.50

Two spacings between the surcharged numerals are found on Nos. 87 to 93.

No. 59 Surcharged in Various Colors **0,01 =**

1922

No.	Type	Description	Unused	Used
94	A13	1c on 15c vio (Bk)	12	12
95	A13	2c on 15c vio (Bl)	12	12
a.		Inverted surch.	30.00	
96	A13	4c on 15c vio (G)	12	12
a.		Double surch.	32.50	
97	A13	5c on 15c vio (R)	12	12

Type of 1905–28 Surcharged in Blue

VINGT FRANCS — VINGT FRANCS

1923

No.	Type	Description	Unused	Used
98	A15	10fr on 1fr grn, *yel*	5.50	5.50
99	A15	20fr on 5fr lil, *rose*	5.50	5.50

Stamps and Types of 1905-28 Surcharged with New Value and Bars in Black or Red.

1924-27

No.	Type	Description	Unused	Used
100	A13	25c on 15c vio ('25)	12	12
101	A15	25c on 2fr bl ('24)	12	12
a.		Double surcharge	37.50	
b.		Triple surcharge	47.50	
102	A14	65c on 45c ol (R) ('25)	38	38
103	A14	85c on 45c ol (R) ('25)	38	38
104	A14	90c on 75c red ('27)	38	38
105	A15	1.05fr on 2fr lt yel brn ('27)	38	38
106	A15	1.25fr on 1fr ultra (R) ('26)	38	38
107	A15	1.50fr on 1fr lt bl ('27)	55	55
108	A15	3fr on 5fr vio ('27)	55	55
a.		No period after "F"	3.50	3.50
		Nos. 100-108 (9)	3.24	3.24

Carib Archer
A16

Shooting Rapids, Maroni River
A17

Government Building, Cayenne
A18

1929-40 *Perf. 13½x14.*

No.	Type	Description	Unused	Used
109	A16	1c gray lil & grnsh bl	6	6
110	A16	2c dk red & bl grn	4	4
111	A16	3c gray lil & grnsh bl ('40)	5	5
112	A16	4c ol brn & red vio	12	12
113	A16	5c Prus bl & red org	6	6
114	A16	10c mag & brn	6	6
115	A16	15c yel brn & red org	6	6
116	A16	20c dk bl & ol grn	12	12
117	A16	25c dk red & dk brn	12	12

Perf. 14x13½.

No.	Type	Description	Unused	Used
118	A17	30c dl & lt grn	22	15
119	A17	30c grn & brn ('40)	5	5
120	A17	35c Prus grn & ol grn ('38)	30	30
121	A17	40c org brn & ol gray	5	5
122	A17	45c grn & dk brn	32	32
123	A17	45c ol grn & lt grn ('40)	12	12
124	A17	50c dk bl & ol gray	12	12
125	A17	55c vio bl & car ('38)	45	45
126	A17	60c sal & grn ('40)	12	12
127	A17	65c sal & grn	30	30
128	A17	70c ind & sl bl ('40)	28	28
129	A17	75c ind & sl bl	50	50
130	A17	80c blk & vio bl ('38)	22	22
131	A17	90c dk red & ver	30	30
132	A17	90c red vio & brn ('39)	28	28
133	A17	1fr lt vio & brn	30	30
134	A17	1fr car & lt red ('38)	95	90
135	A17	1fr blk & vio bl ('40)	12	12
136	A18	1.05fr ver & olvn	2.00	1.50
137	A18	1.10fr ol brn & red vio	2.00	1.50
138	A18	1.25fr blk brn & bl grn ('33)	30	30
139	A18	1.25fr rose & lt red ('39)	15	15
140	A18	1.40fr ol brn & red vio ('40)	28	28
141	A18	1.50fr dk bl & lt bl	10	10
142	A18	1.60fr ol brn & bl grn ('40)	15	15
143	A18	1.75fr brn red & blk brn ('33)	75	75
144	A18	1.75fr vio bl ('38)	30	30
145	A18	2fr dk grn & rose red	12	12
146	A18	2.25fr vio bl ('39)	28	28
147	A18	2.50fr cop red & brn ('40)	28	28
148	A18	3fr brn red & red vio	30	30
149	A18	5fr dl vio & yel grn	30	30
150	A18	10fr ol gray & dp ultra	45	40
151	A18	20fr ind & ver	70	55
		Nos. 109-151 (43)	14.15	12.83

Colonial Exposition Issue.
Common Design Types
Name of Country Printed in Black.

1931 Engraved. *Perf. 12½.*

No.	Type	Description	Unused	Used
152	CD70	40c dp grn	2.00	2.00
153	CD71	50c violet	2.00	2.00
154	CD72	90c red org	2.00	2.00
155	CD73	1.50fr dl bl	2.00	2.00

Recapture of Cayenne by d'Estrées, 1676
A19

Products of French Guiana
A20

1935, Oct. 21 *Perf. 13*

No.	Type	Description	Unused	Used
156	A19	40c gray brn	2.25	2.25
157	A19	50c dl red	4.50	3.00
158	A19	1.50fr ultra	2.25	2.25
159	A20	1.75fr lil rose	6.25	5.50
160	A20	5fr brown	4.50	4.00
161	A20	10fr bl grn	4.50	4.00
		Nos. 156-161 (6)	24.25	21.00

Issued to commemorate the tercentenary of the founding of French possessions in the West Indies.

Paris International Exposition Issue.
Common Design Types

1937, Apr. 15

No.	Type	Description	Unused	Used
162	CD74	20c dp vio	45	45
163	CD75	30c dk grn	45	45
164	CD76	40c car rose	45	45
165	CD77	50c dk brn	45	45
166	CD78	90c red	45	45
167	CD79	1.50fr ultra	45	45
		Nos. 162-167 (6)	2.70	2.70

Colonial Arts Exhibition Issue
Souvenir Sheet.
Common Design Type

1937 *Imperf.*

No.	Type	Description	Unused	Used
168	CD75	3fr violet	2.25	2.25

Sheet size: 118x99mm.

New York World's Fair Issue
Common Design Type
Engraved.

1939, May 10 *Perf. 12½x12*

No.	Type	Description	Unused	Used
169	CD82	1.25fr car lake	45	45
170	CD82	2.25fr ultra	45	45

View of Cayenne and Marshal Petain
A21a

1941 Engraved *Perf. 12½x12*

No.	Type	Description	Unused	Used
170A	A21a	1fr dp lil	30	
170B	A21a	2.50fr blue	30	

Nos. 170A–170B were issued by the Vichy government and were not placed on sale in the colony. This is also true of three stamps of types A16–A18 without "RF" released in 1944.

Common Design Types
pictured in section at front of book.

Eboue Issue.
Common Design Type

1945	Engraved.	Perf. 13.		
171	CD91	2fr black	30	30
172	CD91	25fr Prus grn	45	45

This issue exists imperforate.

Arms of Cayenne
A22

1945		Lithographed	Perf. 12	
173	A22	10c dp gray vio	6	6
174	A22	30c brn org	6	6
175	A22	40c lt bl	6	6
176	A22	50c vio brn	6	6
177	A22	60c org yel	6	6
178	A22	70c pale brn	12	12
179	A22	80c lt grn	12	12
180	A22	1fr blue	10	10
181	A22	1.20fr brt vio	12	12
182	A22	1.50fr dp org	30	30
183	A22	2fr black	30	30
184	A22	2.40fr red	28	28
185	A22	3fr pink	30	30
186	A22	4fr dp ultra	30	30
187	A22	4.50fr dp yel grn	30	30
188	A22	5fr org brn	30	30
189	A22	10fr dk vio	30	30
190	A22	15fr rose car	30	30
191	A22	20fr ol grn	40	40
		Nos. 173-191 (19)	3.84	3.84

Hammock
A23

Guiana Girl
A26

Maroni River Bank
A24

Inini Scene
A25

Toucans
A27

Parrots—A28

Engraved

1947, June 2		Perf. 13.	Unwmkd.	
192	A23	10c dk bl grn	6	6
193	A23	30c brt red	6	6
194	A23	50c dk vio brn	6	6
195	A24	60c grnsh blk	8	6
196	A24	1fr red brn	12	12
197	A24	1.50fr blk brn	12	12
198	A25	2fr dp yel grn	12	12
199	A25	2.50fr dp ultra	22	18
200	A25	3fr red brn	30	28
201	A26	4fr blk brn	60	45
202	A26	5fr dp bl	45	38
203	A26	6fr red brn	45	38
204	A27	10fr dp ultra	1.75	1.50
205	A27	15fr blk brn	2.00	1.75
206	A27	20fr red brn	2.50	2.25
207	A28	25fr brt bl grn	3.25	2.50
208	A28	40fr blk brn	3.25	2.75
		Nos. 192-208 (17)	15.39	13.02

SEMI-POSTAL STAMPS.

Regular Issue of 1905–28
Surcharged in Red

1915		Perf. 13½x14.	Unwmkd.	
B1	A13	10c +5c rose	6.25	6.25
a.		Inverted surcharge	52.50	45.00
b.		Double surcharge	37.50	35.00

Regular Issue of 1905–28
Surcharged in Rose

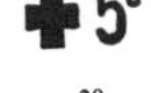

B2	A13	10c +5c rose	28	28

Curie Issue
Common Design Type

1938		Perf. 13.		
B3	CD80	1.75fr +50c brt ultra	4.50	4.50

French Revolution Issue
Common Design Type

1939 Photogravure
Name and Value in Black.

B4	CD83	45c +25c grn	3.75	3.75
B5	CD83	70c +30c brn	3.75	3.75
B6	CD83	90c +35c red org	3.75	3.75
B7	CD83	1.25fr +1fr rose pink	3.75	3.75
B8	CD83	2.25fr +2fr bl	3.75	3.75
		Nos. B4-B8 (5)	18.75	18.75

Common Design Type and

Colonial Infantryman
SP1

Colonial Policeman
SP2

1941	Photogravure	Perf. 13½	
B9	SP1	1fr +1fr red	45
B10	CD86	1.50fr +3fr mar	60
B11	SP2	2.50fr +1fr bl	45

Nos. B9–B11 were issued by the Vichy government, and were not placed on sale in the colony.

Nos. 170A–170B were surcharged "OEUVRES COLONIALES" and surtax (including change of denomination of the 2.50fr to 50c). These were issued in 1944 by the Vichy government, and not placed on sale in the colony.

Red Cross Issue
Common Design Type

1944		Perf. 14½x14.		
B12	CD90	5fr +20fr dk cop brn	45	45

The surtax was for the French Red Cross and national relief.

AIR POST STAMPS.

Cayenne—AP1

Photogravure.

1933, Nov. 20		Perf. 13½	Unwmkd.	
C1	AP1	50c org brn	12	12
C2	AP1	1fr yel grn	12	12
C3	AP1	1.50fr dk bl	12	12
C4	AP1	2fr orange	12	12
C5	AP1	3fr black	30	30
C6	AP1	5fr violet	12	12
C7	AP1	10fr ol grn	28	28
C8	AP1	20fr scarlet	35	35
		Nos. C1-C8 (8)	1.53	1.53

V4

V5

Stamp of type AP1 without "RF" and stamps of the designs shown above were issued in 1942 and 1944 by the Vichy Government, but were not placed on sale in the colony.

Common Design Type

1945	Photo.	Perf. 14½x14		
C9	CD87	50fr dk grn	55	55
C10	CD87	100fr plum	75	75

Victory Issue
Common Design Type

1946, May 8	Engraved.	Perf. 12½.		
C11	CD92	8fr black	60	60

Issued to commemorate the European victory of the Allied Nations in World War II.

Chad to Rhine Issue
Common Design Types

1946, June 6

C12	CD93	5fr dk sl bl	38	38
C13	CD94	10fr lil rose	38	38
C14	CD95	15fr dk vio brn	42	42
C15	CD96	20fr dk sl grn	50	50
C16	CD97	25fr vio brn	50	50
C17	CD98	50fr brt lil	65	65
		Nos. C12-C17 (6)	2.83	2.83

Eagles—AP2

Tapir
AP3

Toucans—AP4

1947, June 2	Engraved.	Perf. 13		
C18	AP2	50fr dp grn	6.25	6.25
C19	AP3	100fr red brn	6.25	6.25
C20	AP4	200fr dk gray bl	11.00	11.00

AIR POST SEMI-POSTAL STAMP

French Revolution Issue
Common Design Type
Photogravure

1939, July 5 Perf. 13 Unwmkd.
Name & Value Typo. in Orange

CB1	CD83	5fr +4fr brn blk	7.25	7.25

V6

Stamps of the design shown above and stamp of Cameroun type V10 inscribed "Guyane Francaise" were issued in 1942 by the Vichy Government, but were not placed on sale in the colony.

POSTAGE DUE STAMPS.

Postage Due Stamps of France, 1893–1926, Overprinted **GUYANE FRANÇAISE**

1925-27		Perf. 14x13½.	Unwmkd.	
J1	D2	5c lt bl	5	5
J2	D2	10c brown	15	15
J3	D2	20c ol grn	15	15
J4	D2	50c vio brn	30	28
J5	D2	3fr mag ('27)	3.50	3.25

Surcharged in Black

GUYANE FRANÇAISE 25 centimes à percevoir

J6	D2	15c on 20c ol grn	15	15
a.		Blue surcharge	17.50	
J7	D2	25c on 5c lt bl	28	22
J8	D2	30c on 20c ol grn	35	28
J9	D2	45c on 10c brn	22	18
J10	D2	60c on 5c lt bl	30	30
J11	D2	1fr on 20c ol grn	55	50
J12	D2	2fr on 50c vio brn	55	60
		Nos. J1-J12 (12)	6.55	6.11

Royal Palms
D3

Guiana Girl
D4

1929, Oct. 14 Typo. *Perf. 13½x14*

J13	D3	5c ind & Prus bl	8	8
J14	D3	10c bis brn & Prus grn	6	6
J15	D3	20c grn & rose red	5	5
J16	D3	30c ol brn & rose red	25	25
J17	D3	50c vio & ol brn	28	28
J18	D3	60c brn red & ol brn	35	35
J19	D4	1fr dp bl & org brn	45	45
J20	D4	2fr brn red & bluish grn	70	70
J21	D4	3fr vio & blk	1.10	1.10
		Nos. J13-J21 (9)	3.32	3.32

D5

1947, June 2 Engr. *Perf. 14x13*

J22	D5	10c dk car rose	5	5
J23	D5	30c dl grn	5	5
J24	D5	50c black	7	7
J25	D5	1fr brt ultra	15	15
J26	D5	2fr dk brn red	15	15
J27	D5	3fr dp vio	18	18
J28	D5	4fr red	30	30
J29	D5	5fr brn vio	38	38
J30	D5	10fr bl grn	65	65
J31	D5	20fr lil rose	75	75
		Nos. J22-J31 (10)	2.73	2.73

FRENCH GUINEA

(frĕnch gĭn'ĭ)

LOCATION—On the coast of West Africa, between Portuguese Guinea and Sierra Leone.

GOVT.—Former French colony.

AREA—89,436 sq. mi.

POP.—2,058,442 (est. 1941).

CAPITAL—Conakry.

French Guinea stamps were replaced by those of French West Africa around 1944–45. French Guinea became the Republic of Guinea Oct. 2, 1958. See "Guinea" for issues of the republic.

100 Centimes = 1 Franc.

Navigation and Commerce
A1

Fulah Shepherd
A2

Perf. 14x13½.

1892-1900 Typographed. Unwmkd.

Name of Colony in Blue or Carmine

1	A1	1c *lil bl*	50	50
2	A1	2c brn, *buff*	60	60
3	A1	4c cl, *lav*	85	85
4	A1	5c grn, *grnsh*	2.85	2.40
5	A1	10c *lavender*	2.85	1.75
6	A1	10c red ('00)	17.50	13.50
7	A1	15c bl, quadrille paper	3.00	2.25
8	A1	15c gray, *lt gray* ('00)	50.00	42.50
9	A1	20c red, *grn*	6.75	5.50
10	A1	25c *rose*	4.50	3.75
11	A1	25c bl ('00)	8.50	7.25
12	A1	30c brn, *bis*	14.00	11.00
13	A1	40c red, *straw*	14.00	11.00
a.		"GUINEE FRANCAISE" double	200.00	185.00
14	A1	50c car, *rose*	18.50	10.00
15	A1	50c brn, *az* ('00)	11.50	9.00
16	A1	75c dp vio, *org*	25.00	19.00
17	A1	1fr brnz grn, *straw*	19.00	13.50
		Nos. 1-17 (17)	199.90	154.35

1904

18	A2	1c *yel grn*	38	22
19	A2	2c vio brn, *buff*	38	32
20	A2	4c car, *bl*	60	45
21	A2	5c grn, *grnsh*	60	45
22	A2	10c carmine	1.10	55
23	A2	15c vio, *rose*	3.25	1.75
24	A2	20c car, *grn*	5.00	4.00
25	A2	25c blue	5.50	4.00
26	A2	30c brown	9.00	7.25
27	A2	40c red, *straw*	11.50	9.00
28	A2	50c brn, *az*	11.50	9.00
29	A2	75c grn, *org*	13.50	12.50
30	A2	1fr brnz grn, *straw*	18.00	14.00
31	A2	2fr red, *org*	37.50	35.00
32	A2	5fr grn, *yel grn*	55.00	50.00
		Nos. 18-32 (15)	172.81	148.49

Gen. Louis Faidherbé
A3

Oil Palm
A4

Dr. Noel Eugène Ballay
A5

1906–07

Name of Colony in Red or Blue.

33	A3	1c gray	35	35
34	A3	2c brown	40	35
35	A3	4c brn, *bl*	55	45
36	A3	5c green	1.20	75
37	A3	10c car (B)	7.25	80
38	A4	20c *blue*	2.00	1.25
39	A4	25c bl, *pnksh*	2.85	2.50
40	A4	30c brn, *pnksh*	2.25	1.50
41	A4	35c *yellow*	1.00	75
42	A4	45c choc, *grnsh gray*	2.00	1.75
43	A4	50c dp vio	4.50	3.75
44	A4	75c bl, *org*	2.25	1.75
45	A5	1fr blk, *az*	8.50	7.50
46	A5	2fr bl, *pink*	17.50	16.50
47	A5	5fr car, *straw* (B)	25.00	24.00
		Nos. 33-47 (15)	77.60	63.95

Regular Issues Surcharged in Black or Carmine

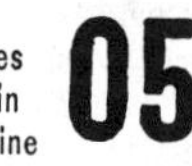

05 *a* 10 *b*

1912

On Issue of 1892–1900

Surcharged Type *a*

48	A1	5c on 2c brn, *buff*	55	55
49	A1	5c on 4c cl, *lav* (C)	35	35
50	A1	5c on 15c bl (C)	35	35
51	A1	5c on 20c red, *grn*	1.75	1.75
52	A1	5c on 30c brn, *bis* (C)	2.00	2.00

Surcharged Type *b*

53	A1	10c on 40c red, *straw*	75	75
54	A1	10c on 75c dp vio, *org*	2.75	2.75
a.		Double surcharge, inverted	100.00	

On Issue of 1904.

Surcharged Type *a*

55	A2	5c on 2c vio brn, *buff*	35	35
a.		Pair, one without surcharge	250.00	
56	A2	5c on 4c car, *bl*	35	35
57	A2	5c on 15c vio, *rose*	35	35
58	A2	5c on 20c car, *grn*	35	35
59	A2	5c on 25c bl (C)	35	35
60	A2	5c on 30c brn (C)	50	50

Surcharged Type *b*

61	A2	10c on 40c red, *straw*	60	60
62	A2	10c on 50c brn, *az* (C)	1.40	1.40
		Nos. 48-62 (15)	12.75	12.75

Two spacings between the surcharged numerals are found on Nos. 48 to 62.

Ford at Kitim
A6

1913–33 *Perf. 13½x14*

63	A6	1c vio & bl	4	4
64	A6	2c brn & vio brn	4	4
65	A6	4c gray & blk	5	5
66	A6	5c yel grn & bl grn	12	12
a.		Booklet pane of 4		
67	A6	5c brn vio & grn ('22)	5	5
68	A6	10c red org & rose	12	12
a.		Booklet pane of 4		
69	A6	10c yel grn & bl grn ('22)	5	5
70	A6	10c vio & ver ('25)	6	5
71	A6	15c vio brn & rose ('16)	5	5
72	A6	15c gray grn & yel grn ('25)	5	5
73	A6	15c red brn & rose lil ('27)	15	7
74	A6	20c brn & vio	5	5
75	A6	20c grn & bl grn ('26)	35	28
76	A6	20c brn red & brn ('27)	12	6
77	A6	25c ultra & bl	38	35
78	A6	25c blk & vio ('22)	30	22
79	A6	30c vio brn & grn	30	28
80	A6	30c red org & rose ('22)	12	12
81	A6	30c rose red & grn ('25)	5	5
82	A6	30c dl grn & bl grn ('28)	60	25
83	A6	35c bl & rose	12	12
84	A6	40c grn & gray	35	30
85	A6	45c brn & red	45	35
86	A6	50c ultra & blk	2.25	1.35
87	A6	50c ultra & bl ('22)	30	18
88	A6	50c yel brn & ol ('25)	6	5
89	A6	60c vio, *pnksh* ('25)	12	12
90	A6	65c yel brn & sl bl ('26)	60	50
91	A6	75c red & ultra	60	45
92	A6	75c ind & dl bl ('25)	30	22
93	A6	75c mag & yel grn ('27)	60	45
94	A6	85c ol grn & red brn ('26)	35	30
95	A6	90c brn red & rose ('30)	2.25	2.00
96	A6	1fr vio & blk	45	30
97	A6	1.10fr vio & ol brn ('28)	2.50	2.25
98	A6	1.25fr vio & yel brn ('33)	65	45
99	A6	1.50fr dk bl & lt bl ('30)	2.00	1.10
100	A6	1.75fr ol brn & vio ('33)	75	60
101	A6	2fr org & vio brn	1.10	45
102	A6	3fr red vio ('30)	3.00	2.40
103	A6	5fr blk & vio	4.25	4.00
104	A6	5fr dl bl & blk ('22)	75	70
		Nos. 63-104 (42)		

Nos. 66 and 68 exist on both ordinary and chalky paper, No. 71 on chalky paper only.

Type of 1913–33 Surcharged

60 = 60

1922

105	A6	60c on 75c vio, *pnksh*	30	30

Stamps and Type of 1913-33 Surcharged with New Value and Bars.

1924-27

106	A6	25c on 2fr org & brn (R)	7	7
107	A6	25c on 5fr dl bl & blk ('24)	8	8
108	A6	65c on 75c rose & ultra ('25)	45	45
109	A6	85c on 75c rose & ultra ('25)	45	45
110	A6	90c on 75c brn red & cer ('27)	75	75
111	A6	1.25fr on 1fr dk bl & ultra ('26)	30	30
112	A6	1.50fr on 1fr dp bl & lt bl ('27)	75	75
113	A6	3fr on 5fr mag & sl ('27)	1.75	1.75
114	A6	10fr on 5fr bl & bl grn, *bluish* ('27)	3.25	3.25
115	A6	20fr on 5fr rose lil & brn ol, *pnksh* ('27)	7.50	7.50
		Nos. 106-115 (10)	15.35	15.35

Colonial Exposition Issue.
Common Design Types

1931 Engraved. *Perf. 12½.*

Name of Country in Black.

116	CD70	40c dp grn	2.00	1.75
117	CD71	50c violet	2.00	1.75
118	CD72	90c red org	2.00	1.75
119	CD73	1.50fr dl bl	1.50	1.40

Paris International Exposition Issue.
Common Design Types

1937 *Perf. 13.*

120	CD74	20c dp vio	60	60
121	CD75	30c dk grn	60	60
122	CD76	40c car rose	75	75
123	CD77	50c dk brn	75	75
124	CD78	90c red	75	75
125	CD79	1.50fr ultra	75	75
		Nos. 120-125 (6)	4.20	4.20

Colonial Arts Exhibition Issue.
Souvenir Sheet.
Common Design Type

1937 *Imperf.*

126	CD76	3fr Prus grn	2.25	2.25

Sheet size: 118x99mm.

Guinea Village—A7

Hausa Basket Workers—A8

Forest Waterfall—A9

Guinea Women
A10

1938-40 *Perf. 13*

128	A7	2c vermilion	3	3
129	A7	3c ultra	4	4
130	A7	4c green	5	5
131	A7	5c rose car	5	5
132	A7	10c pck bl	5	5
133	A7	15c vio brn	5	5
134	A8	20c dk car	5	5
135	A8	25c pck bl	12	7
136	A8	30c ultra	10	7
137	A8	35c green	22	22
138	A8	40c blk brn ('40)	10	6
139	A8	45c dk grn ('40)	12	12
140	A8	50c red brn	12	7
141	A9	55c dk ultra	28	22
142	A9	60c dk ultra ('40)	35	35
143	A9	65c green	32	22
144	A9	70c grn ('40)	35	35
145	A9	80c rose vio	22	22
146	A9	90c rose vio ('39)	38	38
147	A9	1fr org red	75	60
148	A9	1fr brn blk ('40)	25	25
149	A9	1.25fr org red ('39)	40	40
150	A9	1.40fr brn ('40)	45	45
151	A9	1.50fr brown	75	60
152	A10	1.60fr org red ('40)	38	38
153	A10	1.75fr ultra	30	25
154	A10	2fr magenta	45	28
155	A10	2.25fr brt ultra ('39)	60	60
156	A10	2.50fr brn blk ('40)	45	45
157	A10	3fr pck bl	28	22
158	A10	5fr rose vio	32	28
159	A10	10fr sl grn	55	40
160	A10	20fr chocolate	85	70
		Nos. 128-160 (33)	9.78	8.53

Caillié Issue
Common Design Type

1939 Engraved *Perf. 12½x12*

161	CD81	90c org brn & org	45	45
162	CD81	2fr brt vio	45	45
163	CD81	2.25fr ultra & dk bl	45	45

Issued to commemorate the centenary of the death of René Caillié, French explorer.

New York World's Fair Issue.
Common Design Type

1939

164	CD82	1.25fr car lake	45	45
165	CD82	2.25fr ultra	45	45

Ford at Kitim and Marshal Petain
A11

1941 *Perf. 12x12½.*

166	A11	1fr green	22	28
167	A11	2.50fr dp bl	22	28

Nos. 166-167 were issued by the Vichy government. Seven stamps of types A7-A10 without "RF" are also Vichy issues (1943-44), but are believed not to have been placed on sale in the colony.

Stamps of French Guinea were followed by those of French West Africa.

Common Design Types

pictured in section at front of book.

SEMI-POSTAL STAMPS.

Regular Issue of 1913 Surcharged in Red ✚ 5c

1915 *Perf. 13½x14.* **Unwmkd.**

B1	A6	10c +5c org & rose	45	30

No. B1 exists on both ordinary and chalky paper.

Curie Issue
Common Design Type

1938 Engraved. *Perf. 13.*

B2	CD80	1.75fr +50c brt ultra	4.00	4.00

French Revolution Issue
Common Design Type

1939 Photogravure.

Name and Value Typo. in Black.

B3	CD83	45(c) +25(c) grn	2.50	2.50
B4	CD83	70(c) +30(c) brn	2.50	2.50
B5	CD83	90(c) +35(c) red org	2.50	2.50
B6	CD83	1.25fr +1fr rose pink	2.50	2.50
B7	CD83	2.25fr +2fr bl	2.50	2.50
		Nos. B3-B7 (5)	12.50	12.50

Stamps of 1938, Surcharged in Black

SECOURS
+ 1 fr.
NATIONAL

1941 *Perf. 13.* **Unwmkd.**

B8	A8	50c +1fr red brn	60	60
B9	A9	80c +2fr rose vio	2.25	2.00
B10	A9	1.50fr +2fr brn	2.25	2.00
B11	A10	2fr +3fr mag	2.25	2.00

Common Design Type and

Senegalese Soldier
SP1

Colonial Infantryman
SP2

1941 *Perf. 13* **Unwmkd.**

B12	SP1	1fr +1fr red	45
B13	CD86	1.50fr +3fr mar	45
B14	SP2	2.50fr +1fr bl	45

Nos. B12-B14 were issued by the Vichy government, and were not placed on sale in the colony.

Nos. 166-167 were surcharged "OEUVRES COLONIALES" and surtax (including change of denomination of the 2.50fr to 50c). These were issued in 1944 by the Vichy government and not placed on sale in the colony.

AIR POST STAMPS.

Common Design Type
Engraved.

1940 *Perf. 12½x12.* **Unwmkd.**

C1	CD85	1.90fr ultra	18	18
C2	CD85	2.90fr dk red	22	22
C3	CD85	4.50fr dk gray grn	30	30
C4	CD85	4.90fr yel bis	38	38
C5	CD85	6.90fr dp org	40	40
		Nos. C1-C5 (5)	1.48	1.48

Common Design Types

1942 Engraved.

C6	CD88	50c car & bl	5	
C7	CD88	1fr brn & blk	12	
C8	CD88	2fr dk grn & red brn	15	
C9	CD88	3fr dk bl & scar	22	
C10	CD88	5fr vio & brn red	22	

Frame Engraved, Center Typographed.

C11	CD89	10fr ultra, ind & vio	30	
C12	CD89	20fr rose car, mag & gray bl	32	
C13	CD89	50fr yel grn, dl grn & gray blk	55	1.10
		Nos. C6-C13 (8)	1.93	

There is doubt whether Nos. C6-C12 were officially placed in use.

AIR POST SEMI-POSTAL STAMPS.

Stamps of types of Dahomey V1, V2 and V3, and of Cameroun V10, inscribed "Guinée", "Guinée Frcaise" or "Guinée Francaise," were issued in 1942 by the Vichy Government, but were not placed on sale in the colony.

POSTAGE DUE STAMPS.

Fulah Woman
D1

Heads and Coast
D2

Typographed.

1905 *Perf. 14x13½* **Unwmkd.**

J1	D1	5c blue	60	60
J2	D1	10c brown	65	65
J3	D1	15c green	2.00	1.75
J4	D1	30c rose	2.25	1.25
J5	D1	50c black	3.75	3.00
J6	D1	60c dl org	5.25	3.75
J7	D1	1fr violet	17.50	15.00
		Nos. J1-J7 (7)	32.00	26.00

1906-08

J8	D2	5c grn, *grnsh* ('08)	7.50	5.75
J9	D2	10c vio brn ('08)	3.25	2.75
J10	D2	15c dk bl ('08)	2.25	2.00
J11	D2	20c *yellow*	2.25	2.00
J12	D2	30c red, *straw* ('08)	12.00	10.00
J13	D2	50c vio ('08)	11.00	10.00
J14	D2	60c blk, *buff* ('08)	10.00	9.00
J15	D2	1fr *pnksh* ('08)	6.25	5.50
		Nos. J8-J15 (8)	51.25	44.25

D3

D4

1914

J16	D3	5c green	6	6
J17	D3	10c rose	8	8
J18	D3	15c gray	15	15
J19	D3	20c brown	15	15
J20	D3	30c blue	15	15
J21	D3	50c black	32	32
J22	D3	60c orange	70	70
J23	D3	1fr violet	70	70
		Nos. J16-J23 (8)	2.31	2.31

Type of 1914 Issue Surcharged **2F.**

1927

J24	D3	2fr on 1fr lil rose	2.25	2.25
J25	D3	3fr on 1fr org brn	2.75	2.75

1938 Engraved.

J26	D4	5c dk vio	4	4
J27	D4	10c carmine	4	4
J28	D4	15c green	5	5
J29	D4	20c red brn	5	5
J30	D4	30c rose vio	15	15
J31	D4	50c chocolate	25	25
J32	D4	60c pck bl	35	35
J33	D4	1fr vermilion	35	35
J34	D4	2fr ultra	40	40
J35	D4	3fr black	45	45
		Nos. J26-J35 (10)	2.13	2.13

A 10c of type D4 without "RF" was issued in 1944 by the Vichy Government, but was not placed on sale in the colony.

FRENCH INDIA

(frĕnch ĭn'dĭ-ȧ)

LOCATION—East coast of India bordering on Bay of Bengal.
GOVT.—Former French Territory.
AREA—196 sq. mi.
POP.—323,295 (1941).
CAPITAL—Pondichéry.

French India was an administrative unit comprising the five settlements of Chandernagor, Karikal, Mahé, Pondichéry and Yanaon. These united with India in 1949 and 1954.

100 Centimes = 1 Franc
24 Caches = 1 Fanon (1923)
8 Fanons = 1 Rupie

Navigation and Commerce
A1

A2

Perf. 14x13½.

1892-1907 Typographed. Unwmkd.

Colony Name in Blue or Carmine

No.	Type	Description	Unused	Used
1	A1	1c *lil bl*	45	45
2	A1	2c brn, *buff*	60	60
3	A1	4c cl, *lav*	75	75
4	A1	5c grn, *grnsh*	2.00	1.50
5	A1	10c *lavender*	3.25	1.50
6	A1	10c red ('00)	1.25	90
7	A1	15c bl, quadrille paper	3.25	2.10
8	A1	15c gray, *lt gray* ('00)	11.50	11.50
9	A1	20c red, *grn*	2.75	1.75
10	A1	25c *rose*	1.25	90
11	A1	25c bl ('00)	4.50	4.00
12	A1	30c brn, *bis*	21.00	17.50
13	A1	35c *yel* ('06)	4.50	4.00
14	A1	40c red, *straw*	2.40	1.75
15	A1	45c *gray grn* ('07)	1.75	1.40
16	A1	50c car, *rose*	2.50	1.75
17	A1	50c brn, *az* ('00)	4.00	3.50
18	A1	75c dp vio, *org*	3.50	3.50
19	A1	1fr brnz grn, *straw*	4.50	4.50
		Nos. 1-19 (19)	75.70	63.85

Nos. 10 and 16 Surcharged in Carmine or Black — 0,05

1903

No.	Type	Description	Unused	Used
20	A1	5c on 25c *rose*	160.00	90.00
21	A1	10c on 25c *rose*	160.00	90.00
22	A1	15c on 25c *rose*	52.50	52.50
23	A1	40c on 50c car, *rose* (Bk)	250.00	210.00

Counterfeits of Nos. 20–23 abound.

1903

No.	Type	Description	Unused	Used
24	A2	5c gray bl & blk	9.00	9.00

Brahma
A5

Kali Temple near Pondichéry
A6

1914–22 *Perf. 13½x14, 14x13½*

No.	Type	Description	Unused	Used
25	A5	1c gray & blk	6	6
26	A5	2c brn vio & blk	8	8
27	A5	2c grn & brn vio ('22)	12	12
28	A5	3c brn & blk	12	12
29	A5	4c org & blk	15	15
30	A5	5c bl grn & blk	22	22
31	A5	5c vio brn & blk ('22)	12	12
32	A5	10c dp rose & blk	28	28
33	A5	10c grn & blk ('22)	20	20
34	A5	15c vio & blk	30	30
35	A5	20c org red & blk	45	45
36	A5	25c bl & blk	45	45
37	A5	25c ultra & fawn ('22)	28	28
38	A5	30c ultra & blk	55	55
39	A5	30c rose & blk ('22)	35	35
40	A6	35c choc & blk	55	55
41	A6	40c org red & blk	55	55
42	A6	45c bl grn & blk	55	55
43	A6	50c dp rose & blk	45	45
44	A6	50c ultra & bl ('22)	35	35
45	A6	75c bl & blk	90	90
46	A6	1fr yel & blk	90	90
47	A6	2fr vio & blk	2.00	2.00
48	A6	5fr ultra & blk	70	70
49	A6	5fr rose & blk ('22)	1.00	1.00
		Nos. 25-49 (25)	11.68	11.68

No. 34 Surcharged — 0,01 — in Various Colors.

1922

No.	Type	Description	Unused	Used
50	A5	1c on 15c (Bk)	30	30
51	A5	2c on 15c (Bl)	30	30
53	A5	5c on 15c (R)	30	30

Stamps and Types of 1914-22 Surcharged with New Values in Caches, Fanons and Rupies in Black, Red or Blue:

1 FANON

2 CACHES

12 CACHES

3

ROUPIES

1923-28

No.	Type	Description	Unused	Used
54	A5	1ca on 1c gray & blk (R)	9	8
55	A5	2ca on 5c vio brn & blk	13	13
a.		Horizontal pair, imperf. between		
56	A5	3ca on 3c brn & blk	18	18
57	A5	4ca on 4c org & blk	30	22
58	A5	6ca on 10c grn & blk	35	35
59	A6	6ca on 45c bl grn & blk (R)	28	28
60	A5	10ca on 20c dp red & bl grn ('28)	80	80
61	A5	12ca on 15c vio & blk	38	38
62	A5	15ca on 20c org & blk	45	45
63	A6	16ca on 35c lt bl & yel brn ('28)	90	90
64	A5	18ca on 30c rose & blk	45	45
65	A6	20ca on 45c grn & dl red ('28)	55	55
66	A5	1fa on 25c dp grn & rose red ('28)	1.10	1.10
67	A6	1fa3ca on 35c choc & blk (Bl)	45	45
68	A6	1fa6ca on 40c org & blk (R)	55	40
69	A6	1fa12ca on 50c ultra & bl (Bl)	45	45
70	A6	1fa12ca on 75c bl & blk (Bl)	45	45
a.		Double surch.	55.00	
71	A6	1fa16ca on 75c brn red & grn ('28)	1.10	1.00
72	A5	2fa9ca on 25c ultra & fawn (Bl)	60	45
73	A6	2fa12ca on 1fr vio & dk brn ('28)	90	90
74	A6	3fa3ca on 1fr yel & blk (R)	60	60
a.		Double surch.	55.00	
75	A6	6fa6ca on 2fr vio & blk (Bl)	2.10	1.75
76	A6	1r on 1fr grn & dp bl (R) ('26)	2.65	2.50
77	A6	2r on 5fr rose & blk (R)	2.65	2.50
a.		Double surch.	55.00	
78	A6	3r on 2fr gray & bl vio (R) ('26)	5.75	5.00
79	A6	5r on 5fr rose & blk, *grnsh* ('26)	7.25	6.25
		Nos. 54-79 (26)	31.46	28.57

Nos. 60, 63, 66 and 73 have the original value obliterated by bars.

A7

A8

1929

No.	Type	Description	Unused	Used
80	A7	1ca dk gray & blk	8	8
81	A7	2ca vio brn & blk	8	8
82	A7	3ca brn & blk	8	8
83	A7	4ca org & blk	8	8
84	A7	6ca gray grn & grn	15	15
85	A7	10ca brn, red & grn	18	18
86	A8	12ca grn & lt grn	25	22
87	A7	16ca brt bl & blk	32	28
88	A7	18ca brn red & ver	32	28
89	A7	20ca dk bl & grn, *bluish*	28	28
90	A8	1fa gray grn & rose red	22	18
91	A8	1fa6ca red org & blk	22	18
92	A8	1fa12ca dp bl & ultra	22	18
93	A8	1fa16ca rose red & grn	35	35
94	A8	2fa12ca brt vio & brn	45	32
95	A8	6fa6ca dl vio & blk	45	32
96	A8	1r gray grn & dp bl	35	28
97	A8	2r rose & blk	55	28
98	A8	3r lt gray & gray lil	85	55
99	A8	5r rose & blk, *grnsh*	1.20	75
		Nos. 80-99 (20)	6.68	5.10

Colonial Exposition Issue.

Common Design Types

1931 Engraved. *Perf. 12½*

No.	Type	Description	Unused	Used
100	CD70	10ca dp grn	1.25	
101	DC71	12ca violet	1.25	
102	CD72	18ca red org	1.25	
103	CD73	1fa12ca dl bl	1.25	

Paris International Exposition Issue.

Common Design Types

1937 *Perf. 1*

No.	Type	Description	Unused	Used
104	CD74	8ca dp vio	55	
105	CD75	12ca dk grn	55	
106	CD76	16ca car rose	55	
107	CD77	20ca dk brn	55	
108	CD78	1fa12ca red	55	
109	CD79	2fa12ca ultra	55	
		Nos. 104-109 (6)	3.30	3.

Colonial Arts Exhibition Issue.

Souvenir Sheet.

Common Design Type

1937 *Imperf*

No.	Type	Description	Unused	Used
110	CD79	5fa red vio	2.25	2.

Sheet size: 118x99mm.

New York World's Fair Issue.

Common Design Type

1939 Engraved *Perf. 12½x12*

No.	Type	Description	Unused	Used
111	CD82	1fa12ca car lake	60	
112	CD82	2fa12ca ultra	75	

Temple near Pondichéry and Marshal Petain—A9

1941 Engraved *Perf. 12½x12*

No.	Type	Description	Unused	Used
112A	A9	1fa16ca car & red	28	
112B	A9	4fa4ca blue	28	

Nos. 112A–112B were issued by the Vichy government, and were not placed on sale in French India.

Stamps of 1923 Overprinted in Carmine or Blue:

FRANCE LIBRE

a b

Perf. 13½x14, 14x13½.

1941 Unwmkd.

No.	Type	Description	Unused	Used
113	A5 (a)	15ca on 20c org & blk (C)	28.50	28.50
114	A5 (a)	18ca on 30c rose & blk (C)	90	90
115	A6 (a)	1fa3ca on 35c choc & blk (C)	37.50	37.50
a.		Horiz. ovpt.	32.50	32.50
116	A5 (b)	2fa9ca on 25c ultra & fawn (Bl)	550.00	450.00
a.		Ovpt. "a" (Bl)	575.00	450.00
b.		Ovpt. "b" (C)	800.00	

Common Design Types pictured in section at front of book.

Stamps of 1929 Overprinted in Carmine or Blue.

117 A7 (a) 2ca vio brn & blk (C) 3.25 3.25
118 A7 (a) 3ca brn & blk (C) 90 90
119 A7 (a) 4ca org & blk (C) 2.75 2.50
120 A7 (a) 6ca gray grn & grn (C) 60 60
121 A7 (a) 10ca brn red & grn (Bl) 80 70
122 A8 (a) 12ca grn & lt grn (C) 80 70
123 A7 (a) 16ca brt bl & blk (C) 1.00 80
123A A7 (a) 18ca brn red & ver (Bl) 375.00 325.00
124 A7 (a) 20ca dk bl & grn, *bluish* (C) 80 70
125 A8 (a) 1fa gray grn & rose red (Bl) 70 70
126 A8 (a) 1fa6ca red org & blk (C) 90 75
127 A8 (a) 1fa12ca dp bl & ultra (C) 2.00 1.75
128 A8 (a) 1fa16ca rose red & grn (C) 80 60
129 A8 (a) 2fa12ca brt vio & brn (C) 80 60
130 A8 (a) 6fa6ca dl vio & blk (C) 85 75
131 A8 (a) 1r gray grn & dp bl (C) 85 75
132 A8 (a) 2r rose & blk (C) 85 75
133 A8 (a) 3r lt gray & gray lil (C) 90 80
134 A8 (a) 5r rose & blk, *grnsh* (C) 3.50 2.50
Nos. 113-115, 117-123, 124-134 (21) 89.95 87.00

Same Overprints on Paris Exposition Issue of 1937.

Perf. 13.

135 CD74 (b) 8ca dp vio (C) 2.50 2.50
135A CD74 (b) 8ca dp vio (Bl) 100.00 100.00
135B CD74 (a) 8ca dp vio (C) 72.50 72.50
135C CD74 (a) 8ca dp vio (Bl) 100.00 100.00
136 CD75 (a) 12ca dk grn (C) 1.75 1.75
137 CD76 (a) 16ca car rose (Bl) 1.75 1.75
138 CD78 (a) 1fa12ca red (Bl) 1.75 1.75
139 CD79 (a) 2fa12ca ultra (C) 1.75 1.75
Nos. 135-139 (8) 282.00 282.00

Inverted overprints exist.

Souvenir Sheet

No. 110 Overprinted "FRANCE LIBRE" Diagonally in Blue Violet

Two types of overprint:
I. Overprint 37mm. With serifs.
II. Overprint 24mm., as type "a" shown above No. 113. No serifs.

1941 ***Imperf.*** **Unwmkd.**

140 CD79 5fa red vio (I) 325.00 300.00
a. Type II 450.00 350.00

Overprinted on New York World's Fair Issue, 1939.

Perf. 12½x12.

141 CD82 (a) 1fa12ca car lake (Bl) 1.10 1.10
142 CD82 (a) 2fa12ca ultra (C) 1.10 1.10

Lotus Flowers
A10

Photogravure

1942 ***Perf. 14x14½*** **Unwmkd.**

143 A10 2ca brown 15 15
144 A10 3ca dk bl 15 15
145 A10 4ca emerald 15 15
146 A10 6ca dk org 15 15
147 A10 12ca grnsh blk 15 15
148 A10 16ca rose vio 15 15
149 A10 20ca dk red brn 35 35
150 A10 1fa brt red 35 28
151 A10 1fa18ca sl blk 45 28
152 A10 6fa6ca brt ultra 45 38
153 A10 1r dl vio 35 38
154 A10 2r bister 55 45
155 A10 3r chocolate 60 55
156 A10 5r dk grn 80 70
Nos. 143-156 (14) 4.80 4.27

Stamps of 1923–39 Overprinted in Blue or Carmine

FRANCE LIBRE
c

FRANCE LIBRE
d

Perf. 13½x14, 14x13½.

1942–43

Overprinted on No. 64

156A A5 (c) 18ca on 30c rose & blk (B) 135.00 90.00

Overprinted on Stamps of 1929

157 A7 (c) 2ca vio brn & blk (C) 45 45
a. Black overprint 15.00 15.00
158 A7 (c) 3ca brn & blk (C) 55 55
159 A7 (c) 6ca gray grn & grn (Bl) 60 60
160 A8 (d) 12ca grn & lt grn (Bl) 90 90
161 A7 (c) 16ca brt bl & blk (C) 60 60
162 A7 (c) 18ca brn red & ver (Bl) 60 60
163 A7 (c) 20ca dk bl & grn, *bluish* (Bl) ('43) 2.25 1.75
164 A7 (c) 20ca dk bl & grn, *bluish* (C) 60 60
165 A8 (d) 1fa gray grn & rose red (Bl) 45 45
166 A8 (d) 1fa6ca red org & blk (C) 70 70
167 A8 (d) 1fa12ca dp bl & ultra (C) 60 60
168 A8 (d) 1fa16ca rose red & grn (Bl) 45 45
169 A8 (d) 2fa12ca brt vio & brn (Bl) 22.50 22.50
170 A8 (d) 2fa12ca brt vio & brn (C) 65 65
171 A8 (d) 6fa6ca dl vio & blk (C) 1.00 1.00
172 A8 (d) 1r gray grn & dp bl (C) 2.10 2.10
173 A8 (d) 2r rose & blk (C) 2.00 2.00
174 A8 (d) 3r lt gray & gray lil (C) 2.10 2.10
175 A8 (d) 3r lt gray & gray lil (Bl) ('43) 62.50 57.50
176 A8 (d) 5r rose & blk, *grnsh* (C) 2.50 2.50
Nos. 156A-176 (21) 239.10 188.60

Same Overprints on Paris International Exposition Issue of 1937.

Perf. 13.

177 CD74 (c) 8ca dp vio (Bl) 2.75 2.25
178 CD75 (d) 12ca dk grn (Bl) 2.50 2.50
179 CD76 (d) 16ca car rose (Bl) 700.00 550.00
180 CD78 (d) 1fa12ca red (Bl) 45 45
181 CD79 (d) 2fa12ca ultra (C) 1.40 1.40

Same Overprint on New York World's Fair Issue, 1939.

Perf. 12½x12.

182 CD82 (d) 1fa12ca car lake (Bl) 75 75
183 CD82 (d) 2fa12ca ultra (C) 1.50 1.50

No. 87 Surcharged in Carmine

FRANCE LIBRE
2 fa 9 ca

1942–43 ***Perf. 13½x14***

184 A7 1ca on 16ca 32.50 18.50
185 A7 4ca on 16ca ('43) 32.50 18.50
186 A7 10ca on 16ca 21.00 7.50
187 A7 15ca on 16ca 18.50 7.50
188 A7 1fa3ca on 16ca ('43) 32.50 15.00
189 A7 2fa9ca on 16ca ('43) 27.50 27.50
190 A7 3fa3ca on 16ca ('43) 21.00 11.50
Nos. 184-190 (7) 185.50 106.00

Nos. 95–99 Surcharged in Carmine

FRANCE LIBRE
1 cache

1943 ***Perf. 14x13½.***

191 A8 1ca on 6fa6ca dl vio & blk 5.00 4.00
192 A8 4ca on 6fa6ca dl vio & blk 5.50 4.50
193 A8 10ca on 6fa6ca dl vio & blk 1.10 75
194 A8 15ca on 6fa6ca dl vio & blk 2.25 85
195 A8 1fa3ca on 6fa6ca dl vio & blk 3.25 1.50
196 A8 2fa9ca on 6fa6ca dl vio & blk 2.75 2.25
197 A8 3fa3ca on 6fa6ca dl vio & blk 4.00 2.50
198 A8 1ca on 1r gray grn & dp bl 2.25 2.25
199 A8 2ca on 1r gray grn & dp bl 60 60
200 A8 4ca on 1r gray grn & dp bl 60 55
201 A8 6ca on 2r rose & blk 50 45
202 A8 10ca on 2r rose & blk 75 75
203 A8 12ca on 2r rose & blk 55 45
204 A8 15ca on 3r lt gray & gray lil 45 45
205 A8 16ca on 3r lt gray & gray lil 45 45
206 A8 1fa3ca on 3r lt gray & gray lil 55 55
207 A8 1fa6ca on 5r rose & blk, *grnsh* 75 75
208 A8 1fa12ca on 5r rose & blk, *grnsh* 75 60
209 A8 1fa16ca on 5r rose & blk, *grnsh* 75 60
Nos. 191-209 (19) 32.80 24.80

In 1943, twenty-seven stamps were overprinted in red or dark blue, "FRANCE TOUJOURS" and a Lorraine Cross within a circle measuring 17½mm. in diameter. The stamps overprinted were 19 denominations of the regular 1929 postage series, plus Nos. 104 to 109 and Nos. 111 and 112. Of each stamp, 200 were overprinted.

No. 95 Surcharged in Carmine with New Value and Bars.

1943 ***Perf. 14x13½.*** **Unwmkd.**

209A A8 1ca on 6fa6ca 12.50 7.50
209B A8 4ca on 6fa6ca 12.50 7.50
209C A8 10ca on 6fa6ca 4.00 2.75
209D A8 15ca on 6fa6ca 4.00 2.75
209E A8 1fa3ca on 6fa6ca 9.00 7.50
209F A8 2fa9ca on 6fa6ca 10.00 7.50
209G A8 3fa3ca on 6fa6ca 10.00 7.50
Nos. 209A-209G (7) 62.00 43.00

Eboue Issue.

Common Design Type

1945 **Engraved.** ***Perf. 13.***

210 CD91 3fa8ca black 22 22
211 CD91 5r 1fa 16ca Prus grn 40 40

Nos. 210 and 211 exist imperforate.

Apsaras
A11

Brahman Ascetic
A12

Designs: 6ca, 8ca, 10ca, Dvarabalagar. 12ca, 15ca, 1fa, Vishnu. 1fa 6ca, 2fa, 2fa 2ca, Dvarabalagar (foot raised). 2fa 12ca, 3fa, 5fa, Temple Guardian. 7fa 12ca, 1r 2fa, 1r 4fa 12ca, Tigoupalagar.

1948 Photogravure ***Perf. 13x13½***

212 A11 1ca dk ol grn 4 4
213 A11 2ca org brn 6 6
214 A11 4ca vio, *cr* 6 6
215 A11 6ca yel org 38 22
216 A11 8ca gray blk 45 38
217 A11 10ca dl yel grn, *pale grn* 45 38
218 A11 12ca vio brn 22 18
219 A11 15ca Prus grn 22 18
220 A11 1fa vio, *pale rose* 45 30
221 A11 1fa6ca brn red 38 38
222 A11 2fa dk grn 38 27
223 A11 2fa 2ca bl, *cr* 60 45
224 A11 2fa12ca brown 60 55
225 A11 3fa dp org 1.00 60
226 A11 5fa red vio, *rose* 80 60
227 A11 7fa12ca dk brn 70 60
228 A11 1r2fa brn blk 2.00 1.75
229 A11 1r 4fa 12ca ol grn 2.25 2.00
Nos. 212-229 (18) 11.04 9.00

1952

230 A12 18ca rose red 45 45
231 A12 1fa15ca vio bl 80 80
232 A12 4fa ol grn 1.00 1.00

Military Medal Issue.
Common Design Type

1952 Engr. and Typo. *Perf. 13*

233	CD101	1fa multi	1.25	1.25

SEMI-POSTAL STAMPS.

Regular Issue of 1914 Surcharged in Red ✚ 5c

1915 *Perf. 14x13½* **Unwmkd.**

B1	A5	10c +5c rose & blk	45	45
a.		Inverted surch.	32.50	32.50

There were two printings of this surcharge; in the first it was placed at the bottom of the stamp, in the second it was near the top.

Regular Issue of 1914 Surcharged in Red 5 ✠

1916

B2	A5	10c +5c rose & blk	5.50	5.50
a.		Inverted surch.	32.50	32.50
b.		Double surch.	30.00	30.00

Surcharged 5 C

B3	A5	10c +5c rose & blk	90	90

Surcharged

5 c

B4	A5	10c +5c rose & blk	45	45

Surcharged ✚ 5c

B5	A5	10c +5c rose & blk	55	55

Curie Issue
Common Design Type

1938 Engraved. *Perf. 13.*

B6	CD80	2fa12ca +20ca brt ultra	4.50	4.50

French Revolution Issue
Common Design Type

1939 Photogravure.

Name and Value Typo. in Black.

B7	CD83	18ca +10ca grn	2.75	2.75
B8	CD83	1fa6ca +12ca brn	2.75	2.75
B9	CD83	1fa12ca +16ca red org	2.75	2.75
B10	CD83	1fa16ca +1fa16ca rose pink	2.75	2.75
B11	CD83	2fa12ca +3fa bl	2.75	2.75
		Nos. B7-B11 (5)	13.75	13.75

Common Design Type and

Non-Commissioned Officer, Native Guard
SP1

Sepoy
SP2

1941 Photogravure *Perf. 13½*

B12	SP1	1fa16ca +1fa16ca red	45
B13	CD86	2fa12ca +5fa mar	45
B13A	SP2	4fa4ca +1fa16ca bl	45

Nos. B12–B13A were issued by the Vichy government, and were not placed on sale in French India.

Nos. 112A–112B were surcharged "OEUVRES COLONIALES" and surtax (including change of denomination of the 4fa 4ca to 20ca). These were issued in 1944 by the Vichy government and were not placed on sale in French India.

Red Cross Issue
Common Design Type

1944 Photogravure. *Perf. 14½x14.*

B14	CD90	3fa +1r 4fa dk ol brn	38	38

The surtax was for the French Red Cross and national relief.

Tropical Medicine Issue
Common Design Type

1950 Engraved. *Perf. 13.*

B15	CD100	1fa +10ca ind & dp bl	90	90

The surtax was for charitable work.

AIR POST STAMPS.
Common Design Type
Photogravure.

1942 *Perf. 14½x14.* **Unwmkd.**

C1	CD87	4fa dk org	32	28
C2	CD87	1r brt red	32	32
C3	CD87	2r brn red	45	40
C4	CD87	5r black	55	55
C5	CD87	8r ultra	80	70
C6	CD87	10r dk grn	95	85
		Nos. C1-C6 (6)	3.39	3.10

Victory Issue
Common Design Type

1946 Engraved. *Perf. 12½*

C7	CD92	4fa dk bl grn	45	45

Issued to commemorate the European Victory of the Allied Nations in World War II.

Chad to Rhine Issue
Common Design Types

1946, June 6

C8	CD93	2fa12ca ol bis	40	40
C9	CD94	5fa dk bl	40	40
C10	CD95	7fa12ca dk pur	55	55
C11	CD96	1r2fa green	55	55
C12	CD97	1r4fa12ca dk car	60	60
C13	CD98	3r1fa vio brn	60	60
		Nos. C8-C13 (6)	3.10	3.10

A 3r ultramarine and red, picturing the Temple of Chindambaram, was sold at Paris June 7 to July 8, 1948, but not placed on sale in the colony.

Bas-relief Figure of Goddess
AP1

Wing and Temple
AP2

Bird over Palms
AP3

Perf. 12x13, 13x12.

1949 Photogravure **Unwmkd.**

C14	AP1	1r yel & plum	2.25	1.75
C15	AP2	2r grn & dk grn	3.25	2.75
C16	AP3	5r lt bl & vio brn	8.00	7.50

UPU Issue
Common Design Type

1949 Engraved *Perf. 13*

C17	CD99	6fa lil rose	3.25	3.25

Issued to commemorate the 75th anniversary of the formation of the Universal Postal Union.

Liberation Issue
Common Design Type

1954, June 6

C18	CD102	1fa sep & vio brn	2.50	2.50

AIR POST SEMI-POSTAL STAMPS.

V4

Stamps of the above design and of Cameroun type V10 inscribed "Etabts Frcais dans l'Inde" were issued in 1942 by the Vichy Government, but were not placed on sale in French India.

POSTAGE DUE STAMPS.

Postage Due Stamps of France, 1893–1941.

Surcharged **6 CACHES** like Regular Issue in Black, Blue or Red.

1923 *Perf. 14x13½.* **Unwmkd.**

J1	D2	6ca on 10c brn (Bl)	40	40
J2	D2	12ca on 25c rose (Bk)	40	40
J3	D2	15ca on 20c ol grn (R)	45	45
J4	D2	1fa6ca on 30c red (Bl)	55	55
J5	D2	1fa12a on 50c brn vio (Bl)	60	60
J6	D2	1fa15ca on 5c bl (Bk)	75	75
J7	D2	3fa3ca on 1fr red brn, *straw* (Bl)	1.10	1.10
		Nos. J1-J7 (7)	4.25	4.25

Types of Postage Due Stamps of French Colonies, 1884-85, Surcharged with New Values as in 1923 in Red or Black. Bars over Original Values.

1928

J8	D1	4ca on 20c gray lil	45	45
J9	D1	1fa on 30c org	60	
J10	D1	1fa16ca on 5c bl blk (R)	65	
J11	D1	3fa on 1 fr lt grn	1.00	1.

D3

D4

1929 Typographed

J12	D3	4ca dp red	22	2
J13	D3	6ca blue	28	2
J14	D3	12ca green	28	2
J15	D3	1fa brown	50	5
J16	D3	1fa12ca lil gray	45	4
J17	D3	1fa16ca buff	45	4
J18	D3	3fa lilac	70	7
		Nos. J12-J18 (7)	2.88	2.8

Photogravure.

1948 *Perf. 13x13½.* **Unwmkd.**

J19	D4	1ca dk vio	5	
J20	D4	2ca dk brn	5	5
J21	D4	6ca bl grn	12	12
J22	D4	12ca dp org	18	18
J23	D4	1fa dk car rose	22	22
J24	D4	1fa12ca brown	30	30
J25	D4	2fa dk sl bl	35	35
J26	D4	2fa12ca hn brn	45	45
J27	D4	5fa dk ol grn	70	70
J28	D4	1r dk bl vio	90	90
		Nos. J19-J28 (10)	3.32	3.32

FRENCH MOROCCO
(frĕnch mô·rŏk'ō)

LOCATION—Northwest coast of Africa.

GOVT.—Former French Protectorate.

AREA—153,870 sq. mi.

POP.—8,340,000 (estimated 1954).

CAPITAL—Rabat.

French Morocco was a French Protectorate from 1912 until 1956 when it, along with the Spanish and Tangier zones of Morocco, became the independent country, Morocco.

Stamps inscribed "Tanger" were for use in the international zone of Tangier in northern Morocco.

100 Centimos = 1 Peseta
100 Centimes = 1 franc (1917)

French Offices in Morocco

A1

A2

Stamps of France Surcharged in Red or Black.
Perf. 14x13½.

1891–1900 **Unwmkd.**

1	A1	5c on 5c grn, *grnsh* (R)	4.00	1.75
a.		Imperf., pair	50.00	
2	A1	5c on 5c yel grn (I) (R) ('99)	15.00	14.00
a.		Type II	15.00	13.00
3	A1	10c on 10c *lav* (II) (R)	16.00	1.75
a.		Type I	18.00	8.00
b.		10c on 25c *rose*	550.00	
4	A1	20c on 20c red, *grn*	18.00	13.50
5	A1	25c on 25c *rose* (R)	13.00	60
a.		Double surcharge	90.00	
b.		Imperf., pair	60.00	
6	A1	50c on 50c car, *rose* (II)	45.00	16.00
a.		Type I	225.00	140.00

7	A1	1p on 1fr brnz grn, *straw*	50.00	32.50
8	A1	2p on 2fr brn, *az* (Bk) ('00)	140.00	125.00
		Nos. 1-8 (8)	301.00	205.10

No. 3b was never sent to Morocco.

France Nos. J15–J16
Overprinted in Carmine.

1893

9	A2	5c black	1,150.	550.00
10	A2	10c black	1,000.	350.00

Counterfeits exist.

A3

A4

A5

Surcharged in Red or Black.

1902–10

11	A3	1c on 1c gray (R)('08)	38	30
a.		Surcharge omitted		
12	A3	2c on 2c vio brn ('08)	55	45
13	A3	3c on 3c red org ('08)	60	45
14	A3	4c on 4c yel brn ('08)	5.00	3.25
15	A3	5c on 5c grn (R)	2.25	60
a.		Double surch.		75.00
16	A4	10c on 10c rose red ('03)	1.75	60
a.		Surcharge omitted		
17	A4	20c on 20c brn vio ('03)	12.00	7.25
18	A4	25c on 25c bl ('03)	12.00	90
19	A4	35c vio ('10)	18.00	11.00
20	A5	50c on 50c bis brn & lav ('03)	20.00	5.00
21	A5	1p on 1fr cl & ol grn ('03)	52.50	35.00
22	A5	2p on 2fr gray vio & yel ('03)	60.00	35.00
		Nos. 11-22 (12)	185.03	99.80

Nos. 11–14 exist spelled CFNTIMOS or GENTIMOS.
The 25c on 25c with surcharge omitted is listed as No. 81a.

Postage Due Stamps
Nos. J1–J2
Handstamped

1903

24	D2	5c on 5c lt bl	625.00
25	D2	10c on 10c choc	1,100.

Nos. 24 and 25 were used only on Oct. 10, 1903. Used copies were not canceled, the overprint serving as a cancelation.
Counterfeits exist.

Types of 1902–10 Issue
Surcharged in
Red or Blue

1
سنتيم

1911-17

26	A3	1c on 1c gray (R)	22	12
27	A3	2c on 2c vio brn	30	18
28	A3	3c on 3c org	30	18
29	A3	5c on 5c grn (R)	35	12
30	A4	10c on 10c rose	12	6
a.		Imperf. pair	110.00	
31	A4	15c on 15c org ('17)	1.00	90
32	A4	20c on 20c brn vio	2.25	1.40
33	A4	25c on 25c bl (R)	1.10	45
34	A4	35c on 35c vio (R)	3.75	1.40
35	A5	40c on 40c red & pale bl ('17)	3.25	2.50
36	A5	50c on 50c bis brn & lav (R)	12.50	6.75
37	A5	1p on 1fr cl & ol grn	8.50	3.00
		Nos. 26-37 (12)	33.64	17.06

Stamps of this design were issued by the Cherifien posts in 1912–13. The Administration Cherifienne des Postes, Telegraphes et Telephones was formed in 1911 under French guidance.

French Protectorate

A6

A7

A8

Issue of 1911-17
Overprinted "Protectorat Francais"

1914–21

38	A6	1c on 1c gray	22	18
39	A6	2c on 2c vio brn	22	18
40	A6	3c on 3c org	45	35
41	A6	5c on 5c grn	12	5
a.		New value omitted	125.00	125.00
42	A7	10c on 10c rose	12	5
a.		New value omitted	210.00	210.00
43	A7	15c on 15c org ('17)	15	5
a.		New value omitted	45.00	45.00
44	A7	20c on 20c brn vio	2.25	1.40
a.		"Protectorat Francais" double	125.00	125.00
45	A7	25c on 25c bl	55	5
a.		New value omitted	150.00	150.00
46	A7	25c on 25c vio ('21)	45	6
a.		"Protectorat Francais" omitted	22.50	22.50
b.		"Protectorat Francais" double	75.00	75.00
c.		"Protectorat Francais" double (R + Bk)	67.50	67.50
47	A7	30c on 30c vio ('21)	6.25	5.00
48	A7	35c on 35c vio	2.25	80
49	A8	40c on 40c red & pale bl	6.50	4.00
a.		New value omitted	150.00	150.00
50	A8	45c on 45c grn & bl ('21)	20.00	18.00
51	A8	50c on 50c bis brn & lav	38	18
a.		"Protectorat Francais" inverted	60.00	50.00
b.		"Protectorat Francais" double		
52	A8	1p on 1fr cl & ol grn	90	18
a.		"Protectorat Francais" inverted	150.00	150.00
b.		New value double	75.00	75.00
c.		New value double, one inverted	75.00	75.00
53	A8	2p on 2fr gray vio & yel	1.75	80
a.		New value omitted	75.00	75.00
b.		"Protectorat Francais" omitted	45.00	45.00
c.		New value double		
d.		New value double, one inverted		
54	A8	5p on 5fr dk bl & buff	5.50	2.00
		Nos. 38-54 (17)	48.06	33.33

Tower of Hassan, Rabat
A9

Mosque of the Andalusians, Fez
A10

City Gate, Chella
A11

Koutoubiah, Marrakesh
A12

Bab Mansour, Meknés
A13

Remains of Hadrian's Temple
A14

Engraved.

1917 ***Perf. 13½x14, 14x13½***

55	A9	1c grnsh gray	15	15
56	A9	2c brn lil	28	22
57	A9	3c org brn	22	18
a.		Imperf., pair	30.00	30.00
58	A10	5c yel grn	18	6
59	A10	10c rose red	18	6
60	A10	15c dk gray	18	12
a.		Imperf., pair	25.00	25.00
61	A11	20c red brn	1.60	1.25
62	A11	25c dl bl	1.40	30
63	A11	30c gray vio	1.75	1.25
64	A12	35c orange	1.50	1.10
65	A12	40c ultra	60	35
66	A12	45c gray grn	8.50	4.50
67	A13	50c dk brn	3.00	1.50
a.		Imperf., pair	27.50	27.50
68	A13	1fr slate	3.50	2.00
a.		Imperf., pair	20.00	20.00
69	A14	2fr blk brn	110.00	55.00
70	A14	5fr dk gray grn	22.50	20.00
71	A14	10fr black	22.50	21.00
		Nos. 55-71 (17)	178.04	109.04

See note following No. 115.
See Nos. 93–105.

Types of the 1902-10 Issue Overprinted **TANGER**

1918-24 ***Perf. 14x13½.***

72	A3	1c gray	15	15
73	A3	2c vio brn	15	15
74	A3	3c red org	22	22
75	A3	5c green	28	22
76	A3	5c org ('23)	55	50
77	A4	10c rose	28	28
78	A4	10c grn ('24)	28	22
79	A4	15c orange	60	45
80	A4	20c vio brn	90	80
81	A4	25c blue	1.10	70
a.		"TANGER" omitted	200.00	150.00
82	A4	30c red org ('24)	1.25	90
83	A4	35c violet	1.25	85
84	A5	40c red & pale bl	1.25	85
85	A5	50c bis brn & lav	12.50	7.25
86	A4	50c blue	10.00	5.00
87	A5	1fr cl & ol grn	5.00	2.25
88	A5	2fr org & pale bl ('24)	40.00	35.00
89	A5	5fr dk bl & buff ('24)	35.00	30.00
		Nos. 72-89 (18)	110.76	85.79

Types of 1917 and

Tower of Hassan, Rabat
A15

Bab Mansour, Meknès
A16

Scene in Volubilis
A17

1923–27 **Photo.** ***Perf. 13½***

90	A15	1c ol grn	5	5
91	A15	2c brn vio	5	5
92	A15	3c yel brn	5	5
93	A10	5c orange	6	6
94	A10	10c yel grn	6	5
95	A10	15c dk gray	6	5
96	A11	20c red brn	6	5
97	A11	20c red vio ('27)	30	30
98	A11	25c ultra	6	6
99	A11	30c dp red	6	6
100	A11	30c turq bl ('27)	45	30
101	A12	35c violet	30	30
102	A12	40c org red	5	5
103	A12	45c dp grn	6	6
104	A16	50c dl turq	12	12
105	A12	50c dk ol grn ('27)	32	12
106	A16	60c lilac	28	18
107	A16	75c red vio ('27)	28	28
108	A16	1fr dp brn	32	22
109	A16	1.05fr red brn ('27)	60	55
110	A16	1.40fr dl rose ('27)	30	30
111	A16	1.50fr turq bl ('27)	45	12
112	A17	2fr ol brn	55	45
113	A17	3fr dp red ('27)	55	55
114	A17	5fr dk gray grn	1.75	1.25

115	A17	10fr black	4.50	2.75
		Nos. 90-115 (26)	11.69	8.38

Nos. 90–110, 112–115 exist imperf.

The stamps of 1917 were line engraved. Those of 1923–27 were printed by photogravure and have in the margin at lower right the imprint "Helio Vaugirard".

No. 102 Surcharged in Black

15c 15c

1930

120	A12	15c on 40c org red	60	60

Nos. 100, 106 and 110 Surcharged in Blue Similarly to No. 176.

1931

121	A11	25c on 30c turq bl	90	90
a.		Inverted surch.	40.00	32.50
122	A16	50c on 60c lil	38	15
a.		Inverted surch.	45.00	40.00
123	A16	1fr on 1.40fr rose	1.40	70
a.		Inverted surch.	45.00	40.00

Old Treasure House and Tribunal, Tangier
A18

Roadstead at Agadir
A19

Post Office at Casablanca
A20

Moulay Idriss of the Zehroun
A21

Kasbah of the Oudayas, Rabat
A22

Court of the Medersa el Attarine at Fez
A23

Saadiens' Tombs at Marrakesh
A25

Kasbah of Si Madani el Glaoui at Ouarzazat—A24

1933–34 Engraved *Perf. 13*

124	A18	1c ol blk	8	4
125	A18	2c red vio	8	6
126	A19	3c dk brn	8	6
127	A19	5c brn red	8	6
128	A20	10c bl grn	12	6
129	A20	15c black	8	6
130	A20	20c red brn	12	12
131	A21	25c dk bl	12	6
132	A21	30c emerald	22	5
133	A21	40c blk brn	22	12
134	A22	45c brn vio	28	28
135	A22	50c dk bl grn	18	4
a.		Booklet pane of 10		
136	A22	65c brn red	6	6
a.		Booklet pane of 10		
137	A23	75c red vio	22	6
138	A23	90c org red	22	5
139	A23	1fr dp brn	45	7
140	A23	1.25fr blk ('34)	60	30
141	A24	1.50fr ultra	28	5
142	A24	1.75fr myr grn ('34)	22	7
143	A24	2fr yel brn	1.25	5
144	A24	3fr car rose	25.00	3.25
145	A25	5fr red brn	3.25	65
146	A25	10fr black	4.00	3.00
147	A25	20fr bluish gray	4.50	3.00
		Nos. 124-147 (24)	41.71	11.62

No. 135 Surcharged in Red

40c

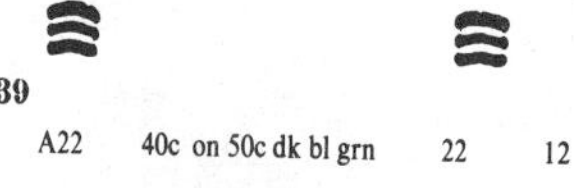

1939

148	A22	40c on 50c dk bl grn	22	12

Mosque of Salé
A26

Sefrou
A27

Cedars
A28

Goatherd
A29

Ramparts of Salé
A30

Scimitar-horned Oryxes
A31

Fez
A33

Valley of Draa
A32

1939–42

149	A26	1c rose vio	5	3
150	A27	2c emerald	5	5
151	A27	3c ultra	5	5
152	A26	5c dk bl grn	8	5
153	A27	10c brt red vio	8	6
154	A28	15c dk grn	8	5
155	A28	20c blk brn	8	5
156	A29	30c dp bl	8	5
157	A29	40c chocolate	8	6
158	A29	45c Prus grn	22	22
159	A30	50c rose red	60	45
159A	A30	50C Prus grn ('40)	12	6
160	A30	60c turq bl	60	45
160A	A30	60c choc ('40)	12	5
161	A31	70c dk vio	8	5
162	A32	75c grnsh blk	22	22
163	A32	80c pck bl ('40)	12	5
163A	A32	80c dk grn ('42)	12	5
164	A30	90c ultra	12	5
165	A28	1fr chocolate	12	5
165A	A32	1.20fr rose vio ('42)	22	12
166	A32	1.25fr hn brn	45	28
167	A32	1.40fr rose vio	22	12
168	A30	1.50fr cop red ('40)	8	6
168A	A30	1.50fr rose ('42)	8	6
169	A33	2fr Prus grn	8	6
170	A33	2.25fr dk bl	22	22
170A	A26	2.40fr red ('42)	12	5
171	A26	2.50fr scarlet	45	30
171A	A26	2.50fr dp bl ('40)	40	30
172	A33	3fr blk brn	12	12
172A	A26	4fr dp ultra ('42)	12	5
172B	A32	4.50fr grnsh blk ('42)	28	12
173	A31	5fr dk bl	28	18
174	A31	10fr red	45	35
174A	A31	15fr Prus grn ('42)	2.00	1.75
175	A31	20fr dk vio brn	75	75
		Nos. 149-175 (37)	9.61	7.16

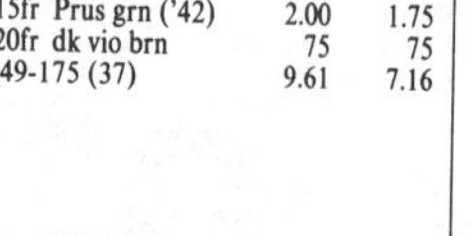

See also Nos. 197–219.

No. 136 Surcharged in Black

35c

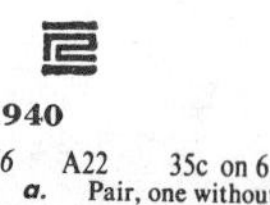

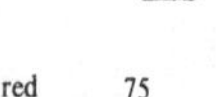

1940

176	A22	35c on 65c brn red	75	45
a.		Pair, one without surcharge	1.25	90

The surcharge was applied on alternate rows in the sheet, making pairs, one stamp with a surcharge and one without. This was done to make a pair equal 1 franc, the new rate.

One Aim Alone —Victory
A34

Tower of Hassan, Rabat
A35

1943 Lithographed *Perf. 12.*

177	A34	1.50fr dp bl	4	4

1943

178	A35	10c rose lil	4	4
179	A35	30c blue	4	4
180	A35	40c lake	4	4
181	A35	50c bl grn	4	4
182	A35	60c dk vio brn	4	4
183	A35	70c rose vio	4	4
184	A35	80c gray grn	4	4
185	A35	1fr car lake	4	4
186	A35	1.20fr violet	4	4
187	A35	1.50fr red	4	4
188	A35	2fr lt bl grn	18	5
189	A35	2.40fr car rose	8	5
190	A35	3fr ol brn	12	5
191	A35	4fr dk ultra	15	5
192	A35	4.50fr sl blk	8	5
193	A35	5fr dl bl	15	15
194	A35	10fr org brn	22	6
195	A35	15fr sl grn	60	18
196	A35	20fr dp plum	75	22
		Nos. 178-196 (19)	2.73	1.26

Types of 1939-42.
Perf. 13½x14, 14x13½.

1945-47 Typographed. Unwmkd.

197	A27	10c red vio	6	6
199	A29	40c chocolate	10	6
200	A30	50c Prus grn	8	6
203	A28	1fr choc ('46)	8	6
204	A32	1.20fr vio brn ('46)	8	6
205	A27	1.30fr bl ('47)	20	18
206	A30	1.50fr dp red	6	6
207	A33	2fr Prus grn	8	6
209	A33	3fr blk brn	8	6
210	A29	3.50fr dk red ('47)	30	28
212	A31	4.50fr mag ('47)	7	6
214	A31	5fr indigo	35	22
215	A32	6fr chlky bl ('46)	12	6
216	A31	10fr red	55	45
217	A31	15fr Prus grn	65	38
218	A31	20fr dk vio brn	80	70
219	A31	25fr blk brn	90	90
		Nos. 197-219 (17)	4.56	3.71

The Terraces
A37

Mountain District
A39

Fortress
A38

Marrakesh
A40

Gardens of Fez—A41

Ouarzazat District
A42

Engraved.

1947-48 ***Perf. 13*** **Unwmkd.**

221	A37	10c blk brn	5	4
222	A37	30c brt red	12	6
223	A37	50c brt grnsh bl	6	4
224	A37	60c brt red vio	6	5
225	A38	1fr black	6	5
226	A38	1.50fr blue	6	5
227	A39	2fr brt grn	18	18
228	A39	3fr brn red	6	6
229	A40	4fr dk bl vio	7	6
230	A41	5fr dk grn	28	22
231	A40	6fr crimson	10	5
232	A41	10fr dp bl ('47)	18	6
233	A42	15fr dk grn ('47)	40	35
234	A42	20fr hn brn ('47)	30	6
235	A42	25fr pur ('47)	80	40
		Nos. 221-235 (15)	2.78	1.73

1948-49

236	A37	30c purple	4	4
237	A38	2fr vio brn ('49)	6	5
238	A40	4fr green	7	5
239	A41	8fr org ('49)	28	15
240	A41	10fr blue	30	25
241	A42	10fr car rose	25	6
242	A38	12fr red	35	22
243	A42	18fr dp bl	55	45
		Nos. 236-243 (8)	1.90	1.27

No. 175 Surcharged with New Value and Wavy Lines in Carmine.

1948

244	A31	8fr on 20fr dk vio brn	38	28

Fortified Oasis—A43

Walled City—A44

1949

245	A43	5fr bl grn	15	5
246	A44	15fr red	45	5
247	A44	25fr ultra	60	12

See also No. 300.

Detail, Gate of Oudayas, Rabat
A45

Nejjarine Fountain, Fez
A46

Garden, Meknes
A47

1949 ***Perf. 14x13***

248	A45	10c black	6	4
249	A45	50c rose brn	15	13
250	A45	1fr bl vio	8	6
251	A46	2fr dk car rose	8	6
252	A46	3fr dk bl	8	5
253	A46	5fr brt grn	17	5
254	A47	8fr dk bl grn	35	4
255	A47	10fr brt red	45	15
		Nos. 248-255 (8)	1.42	58

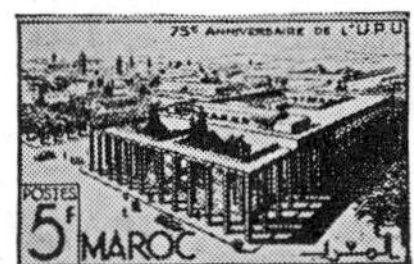

Postal Administration Building, Meknes
A48

1949, Oct. ***Perf. 13***

256	A48	5fr dk grn	90	90
257	A48	15fr dp car	1.10	1.10
258	A48	25fr dp bl	1.25	1.25

Issued to commemorate the 75th anniversary of the formation of the Universal Postal Union.

Todra Valley
A49

1950

259	A49	35fr red brn	60	15
260	A49	50fr indigo	60	5

See also No. 270.

Nos. 204 and 205 Surcharged in Black or Blue

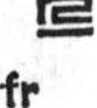

1fr

1950 ***Perf. 14x13½, 13½x14***

261	A32	1fr on 1.20fr vio brn (Bk)	10	6
262	A27	1fr on 1.30fr bl (Bl)	10	6

The surcharge is transposed and spaced to fit the design on No. 262.

No. 231 Surcharged with New Value and Wavy Lines in Black.

1951 ***Perf. 13***

263	A40	5fr on 6fr crim	12	12

Statue of Gen. Jacques Leclerc
A50

1951, Apr. 28 **Engraved**

264	A50	10fr bl grn	80	80
265	A50	15fr dp car	80	80
266	A50	25fr indigo	80	80

Issued to commemorate the unveiling of a monument to Gen. Leclerc at Casablanca, April 28, 1951. See No. C39.

Loustau Hospital, Oujda
A51

Designs: 15fr, New Hospital, Meknes. 25fr, New Hospital, Rabat.

1951

267	A51	10fr ind & pur	60	60
268	A51	15fr Prus grn & red brn	60	60
269	A51	25fr dk brn & ind	75	75

Todra Valley Type of 1950.

1951

270	A49	30fr ultra	55	22

Pigeons at Fountain
A52

Karaouine Mosque, Fez
A53

Patio, Oudayas
A54

Oudayas Point, Rabat
A55

Patio of Old House
A56

Type I (No. 275) Type II (No. 276)

Perf. 14x13, 13.

1951-53 **Engraved.** **Unwmkd.**

271	A52	5fr mag ('52)	8	4
272	A53	6fr bl grn ('52)	18	18
273	A52	8fr brn ('52)	15	15
273A	A53	10fr rose red ('53)	20	5
274	A53	12fr dp ultra ('52)	30	6
275	A54	15fr red brn (I)	1.20	6
276	A54	15fr red brn (II)	30	5
277	A55	15fr pur ('52)	40	5
278	A55	18fr red ('52)	60	45
279	A56	20fr dp grnsh bl ('52)	45	30
		Nos. 271-279 (10)	3.86	1.39

See also Nos. 297-299.

8th-10th Century Capital
A57

Casablanca Monument
A58

Capitals: 20fr, XIIth Century. 25fr, XIIth–XVIth Century. 50fr, XVIIth Century.

1952, Apr. 5 ***Perf. 13***

280	A57	15fr dp bl	1.40	1.40
281	A57	20fr red	1.40	1.40
282	A57	25fr purple	1.40	1.40
283	A57	50fr dp grn	1.40	1.40

1952, Sept. 22 **Engr. & Typo.**

284	A57	15fr multi	1.25	1.00

Issued to commemorate the centenary of the creation of the French Military Medal.

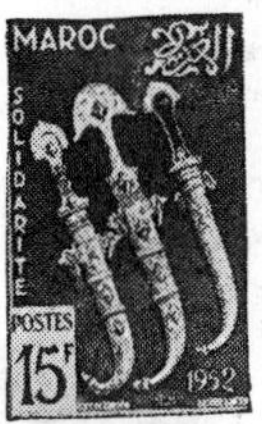

Daggers of South Morocco
A59

Post Rider and Public Letter-writer
A60

Designs: 20fr and 25fr, Antique brooches.

1953, Mar. 27 **Engraved.**

285	A59	15fr dk car rose	1.40	1.40
286	A59	20fr vio brn	1.40	1.40
287	A59	25fr dk bl	1.40	1.40

See No. C46.

1953, May 16

288	A60	15fr vio brn	75	75

Stamp Day, May 16, 1953.

Bine el Ouidane Dam
A61

1953, Nov. 3 ***Perf. 13***

290	A61	15fr indigo	75	75

See also No. 295.

Mogador Fortress
A62

Design: 30fr, Moorish knights.

1953, Dec. 4

291	A62	15fr green	75	75
292	A62	30fr red brn	75	75

Issued to aid Army Welfare Work.

Nos. 226 and 243 Surcharged with New Value and Wavy Lines in Black.

1954

293	A38	1fr on 1.50fr bl	8	8
294	A42	15fr on 18fr dp bl	30	30

Dam Type of 1953.

1954, Mar. 8

295	A61	15fr red brn & ind	45	18

Station of Rural Automobile Post
A63

1954, Apr. 10

296	A63	15fr dk bl grn	55	55

Stamp Day, April 10, 1954.

Types of 1951-53

1954 Engraved. *Perf. 14x13*

297	A52	15fr dk bl grn	30	5

Typographed.

298	A52	5fr magenta	25	18
299	A55	15fr rose vio	45	28

Walled City Type of 1949

1954 Engraved. *Perf. 13*

300	A44	25fr purple	50	28

Marshal Lyautey at Rabat
A64

Lyautey, Builder of Cities
A65

Designs: 15fr, Marshal Lyautey at Khenifra. 50fr, Hubert Lyautey, Marshal of France.

1954, Nov. 17

301	A64	5fr indigo	1.40	1.40
302	A64	15fr dk grn	1.40	1.40
303	A65	30fr rose brn	1.75	1.75
304	A65	50fr dk red brn	1.75	1.75

Issued to commemorate the centenary of the birth of Marshal Hubert Lyautey.

Franco-Moslem Education
A66

Moslem Student at Blackboard
A67

Designs: 30fr, Moslem school at Camp Boulhaut. 50fr, Moulay Idriss College at Fez.

1955, Apr. 16 *Perf. 13* Unwmkd.

305	A66	5fr indigo	80	80
306	A67	15fr rose lake	80	80
307	A66	30fr chocolate	1.10	1.10
308	A67	50fr dk bl grn	1.10	1.10

Issued to publicize Franco-Moslem solidarity.

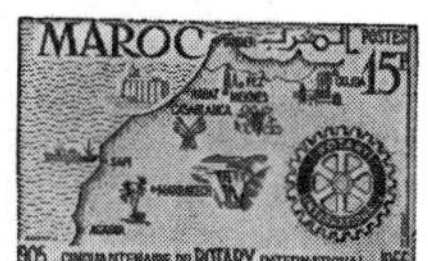

Map and Rotary Emblem
A68

1955, June 11

309	A68	15fr bl & org brn	75	60

Issued to commemorate the 50th anniversary of the founding of Rotary International.

Post Office, Mazagan
A69

1955, May 24

310	A69	15fr red	38	38

Stamp Day.

Bab el Chorfa, Fez
A70

Mahakma (Courthouse), Casablanca
A71

Fortress, Safi
A72

Designs: 50c, 1fr, 2fr, Mrissa Gate, Salé. 10fr, 12fr, 15fr, Minaret at Rabat. 30fr, Menara Garden, Marrakesh. 40fr, Tafraout Village. 50fr, Portuguese cistern, Mazagan. 75fr, Garden of Oudaya, Rabat.

1955 *Perf. 13½x13, 13x13½, 13*

311	A70	50c brn vio	6	3
312	A70	1fr blue	6	4
313	A70	2fr red lil	6	4
314	A70	3fr bluish blk	8	4
315	A70	5fr vermilion	38	22
316	A70	6fr green	18	18
317	A70	8fr org brn	35	32
318	A70	10fr vio brn	60	18
319	A70	12fr grnsh bl	22	5
320	A70	15fr magenta	55	4
321	A71	18fr dk grn	75	55
322	A71	20fr brn lake	30	5
323	A72	25fr brt ultra	1.10	15
324	A72	30fr green	1.10	35
325	A72	40fr org red	55	12
326	A72	50fr blk brn	3.00	22
327	A71	75fr grnsh bl	75	60
		Nos. 311-327 (17)	10.09	3.18

Succeeding issues, released under the Kingdom, are listed under Morocco in Vol. III.

SEMI-POSTAL STAMPS.

French Protectorate

No. 30 Surcharged in Red ✚ 5c

1914 *Perf. 14x13½* Unwmkd.

B1	A4	10c +5c on 10c rose	*12,500.*	*11,500.*

No. B1 is known only with inverted surcharge.

Same Surcharge on No. 42 with "Protectorat Francais".

B2	A7	10c +5c on 10c rose	1.75	1.75
a.		Double surcharge	50.00	50.00
b.		Inverted surcharge	67.50	67.50
c.		"c" omitted	30.00	30.00

On Nos. B1 and B2 the cross is set up from pieces of metal (quads), the horizontal bar being made from two long pieces, the vertical bar from two short pieces. Each cross in the setting of twenty-five differs from the others.

No. 30 Handstamp Surcharged in Red ✚ 5c

B3	A4	10c +5c on 10c rose	*1,000.*	*850.00*

No. B3 was issued at Oujda. The surcharge ink is water-soluble.

No. 42 Surcharged in Vermilion or Carmine ✚ 5c

B4	A7	10c +5c on 10c rose (V)	10.00	10.00
a.		Double surcharge	65.00	60.00
b.		Inverted surcharge	75.00	65.00
c.		Double surcharge, one inverted	70.00	65.00
B5	A7	10c +5c on 10c rose (C)	160.00	160.00

On Nos. B4 and B5 the horizontal bar of the cross is single and not as thick as on Nos. B1 and B2.

No. B5 was sold largely at Casablanca.

SP1

SP2

1915 Carmine Surcharge.

B6	SP1	5c +5c grn	1.10	90
a.		Inverted surcharge	100.00	100.00

No. B6 was not issued without the Red Cross surcharge.

B7	SP2	10c +5c rose	1.25	1.25

No. B7 was used in Tangier.

SP3

SP4

France No. B2 Overprinted in Black.

B8	SP3	10c +5c red	2.75	2.75

1917 Carmine Surcharge.

B9	SP4	10c +5c on 10c rose	1.25	1.25

On No. B9 the horizontal bar of the cross is made from a single, thick piece of metal.

Marshal Hubert Lyautey
SP5

1935, May 15 Photo. *Perf. 13x13½*

B10	SP5	50c +50c red	5.50	5.50
B11	SP5	1fr +1fr dk grn	5.50	5.50
B12	SP5	5fr +1fr blk brn	25.00	25.00

Stamps of 1933-34 Surcharged in Blue or Red

O.S.E.
+3 c

1938 *Perf. 13.*

B13	A18	2c +2c red vio (Bl)	2.75	2.75
B14	A19	3c +3c dk brn (Bl)	2.75	2.75
B15	A20	20c +20c red brn (Bl)	2.75	2.75
B16	A21	40c +40c blk brn (R)	2.75	2.75
B17	A22	65c +65c brn red (Bl)	2.75	2.75
B18	A23	1.25fr +1.25fr blk (R)	2.75	2.75
B19	A24	2fr +2fr yel brn (Bl)	2.75	2.75
B20	A25	5fr +5fr red brn (Bl)	2.75	2.75
		Nos. B13-B20 (8)	22.00	22.00

Stamps of 1939 Surcharged in Black

+2f

Enfants de France au Maroc

1942

B21	A29	45c +2fr Prus grn	2.10	2.10
B22	A30	90c +4fr ultra	2.10	2.10
B23	A32	1.25fr +6fr hn brn	2.10	2.10
B24	A26	2.50fr +8fr scar	2.10	2.10

The arrangement of the surcharge differs slightly on each denomination.

No. 207 Surcharged in Black

AIDEZ
LES
TUBERCULEUX

+ 1f

1945 *Perf. 13½x14* Unwmkd.

B26	A33	2fr +1fr Prus grn	12	12

Mausoleum of Marshal Lyautey
SP7

Statue of Marshal Lyautey
SP8

1945 Lithographed *Perf. 11½*

B27	SP7	2fr +3fr dk bl	15	15

The surtax was for French works of solidarity.

3f

No. B26 Surcharged in Red

1946 *Perf. 13½x14*

B28	A33	3fr (+1fr) on 2fr+1fr Prus grn	6	6

Engraved.

1946, Dec. 16 *Perf. 13½x14, 13*

B29	SP8	2fr +10fr blk	60	60
B30	SP8	3fr +15fr cop red	75	75
B31	SP8	10fr +20fr brt bl	1.25	1.25

The surtax was for works of solidarity.

JOURNÉE
DU
TIMBRE
1947

No. 212
Surcharged in
Rose Violet

+5F50

1947, Mar. 15 *Perf. 13½x14*

B32	A31	4.50fr +5.50fr mag	60	60

Stamp Day, 1947.

Map and Symbols of Prosperity from Phosphates
SP9

1947 *Perf. 13*

B33	SP9	4.50fr +5.50fr grn	38	38

Issued to commemorate the 25th anniversary of the exploitations of the Cherifien Office of Phosphates.

Power
SP10

Health
SP11

1948, Feb. 9

B34	SP10	6fr +9fr red brn	1.10	1.10
B35	SP11	10fr +20fr dp ultra	1.10	1.10

The surtax was for combined works of Franco-Moroccan solidarity.

Type of Regular Issue of 1923, Inscribed: "Journée du Timbre 1948."

1948, Mar. 6

B36	A16	6fr +4fr red brn	45	45

Stamp Day, Mar. 6, 1948.

Battleship off Moroccan Coast
SP12

1948, Aug.

B37	SP12	6fr +9fr pur	80	80

The surtax was for naval charities

Wheat Field near Meknès
SP13

Designs: 2fr+5fr, Olive grove, Taroudant. 3fr+7fr, Net and coastal view. 5fr+10fr, Aguedal Gardens, Marrakesh.

1949, Apr. 12 Engraved Unwmkd.

Inscribed: "SOLIDARITÉ 1948."

B38	SP13	1fr +2fr org	60	60
B39	SP13	2fr +5fr car	60	60
B40	SP13	3fr +7fr pck bl	60	60
B41	SP13	5fr +10fr dk brn vio	60	60
a.		Sheet of four	8.00	8.00
		Nos. B38-B41, CB31-CB34 (8)	5.60	5.60

No. B41a contains one each of Nos. B38-B41. Size: 120x96mm.

Gazelle Hunter, from 1899 Local Stamp—SP14

1949, May 1

B42	SP14	10fr +5fr choc & car rose	75	75

Stamp Day and 50th anniversary of Mazagan-Marrakesh local postage stamp.

Moroccan Soldiers and Flag
SP15

Rug Weaving
SP16

1949

B43	SP15	10fr +10fr brt red	60	60

The surtax was for Army Welfare Work.

1950, Apr. 11

Designs: 2fr+5fr, Pottery making. 3fr+7fr, Bookbinding. 5fr+10fr, Copper work.

Inscribed: "SOLIDARITE 1949."

B44	SP16	1fr +2fr dp car	1.10	1.10
B45	SP16	2fr +5fr dk grnsh bl	1.10	1.10
B46	SP16	3fr +7fr dk pur	1.10	1.10
B47	SP16	5fr +10fr red brn	1.10	1.10
a.		Sheet of four	8.00	8.00
		Nos. B44-B47, CB36-CB39 (8)	7.60	7.60

No. B47a contains one each of Nos. B44-B47. Size: 95½x120½mm.

Ruins of Sala Colonia at Chella
SP17

1950, Sept. 25 Engraved. *Perf. 13*

B48	SP17	10fr +10fr dp mag	60	60
B49	SP17	15fr +15fr ind	60	60

The surtax was for Army Welfare Work.

AIR POST STAMPS.
French Protectorate

Biplane over Casablanca
AP1

Photogravure.

1922-27 *Perf. 13½* Unwmkd.

C1	AP1	5c dp org ('27)	12	12
a.		Imperf., pair	35.00	
C2	AP1	25c dp ultra	35	18
a.		Imperf., pair	47.50	
C3	AP1	50c grnsh bl	12	12
a.		Imperf., pair	37.50	
C4	AP1	75c dp bl	37.50	6.50
a.		Imperf., pair	400.00	
C5	AP1	75c dp grn	12	5
a.		Imperf., pair	47.50	
C6	AP1	80c vio brn ('27)	60	18
a.		Imperf., pair	35.00	
C7	AP1	1fr vermilion	12	5
a.		Imperf., pair	45.00	
C8	AP1	1.40fr brn lake ('27)	75	50
C9	AP1	1.90fr dp bl ('27)	1.00	70
C10	AP1	2fr blk vio	60	45
a.		2fr dp vio	75	45
b.		Imperf., pair	125.00	
C11	AP1	3fr gray blk ('27)	90	50
		Nos. C1-C11 (11)	42.18	9.35

The 25c, 50c, 75c deep green and 1fr each were printed in two or three types, differing in frameline thickness, or hyphen in "Helio-Vaugirard" imprint.

Nos. C8-C9 Surcharged in Blue or Black

1fr

1931, Apr. 10

C12	AP1	1fr on 1.40fr (B)	75	75
a.		Inverted surcharge	160.00	160.00
C13	AP1	1.50fr om 1.90fr (Bk)	75	75

Rabat and Tower of Hassan
AP2

Casablanca—AP3

1933, Jan. Engraved

C14	AP2	50c dk bl	38	22
C15	AP2	80c org brn	22	18
C16	AP2	1.50fr brn red	30	15
C17	AP3	2.50fr car rose	2.00	28
C18	AP3	5fr violet	1.00	65
C19	AP3	10fr bl grn	45	45
		Nos. C14-C19 (6)	4.35	1.93

Storks and Minaret, Chella
AP4

Plane and Map of Morocco
AP5

1939-40 *Perf. 13*

C20	AP4	80c Prus grn	5	5
C21	AP4	1fr dk red	5	5
C22	AP5	1.90fr ultra	5	6
C23	AP5	2fr red vio ('40)	6	5
C24	AP5	3fr chocolate	6	6
C25	AP4	5fr violet	45	40
C26	AP5	10fr turq bl	38	30
		Nos. C20-C26 (7)	1.10	97

Plane over Oasis
AP6

1944 Lithographed *Perf. 11½*

C27	AP6	50c Prus grn	6	4
C28	AP6	2fr ultra	12	12
C29	AP6	5fr scarlet	12	12
C30	AP6	10fr violet	30	30
C31	AP6	50fr black	55	55
C32	AP6	100fr dp bl & red	1.50	1.50
		Nos. C27-C32 (6)	2.65	2.63

Plane—AP7

1945 Engraved *Perf. 13*

C33	AP7	50fr sepia	40	40

Moulay Idriss
AP8

La Medina—AP9

1947-48

C34	AP8	9fr dk rose car	18	15
C35	AP8	40fr dk bl	45	18
C36	AP8	50fr dp cl ('47)	45	12
C37	AP9	100fr dp grnsh bl	1.25	45
C38	AP9	200fr hn brn	2.25	90
		Nos. C34-C38 (5)	4.58	1.80

Leclerc Type of Regular Issue

1951, Apr. 28

C39	A50	50fr purple	90	90

Issued to commemorate the unveiling of a monument to Gen. Leclerc at Casablanca, April 28, 1951.

Kasbah of the Oudayas, Rabat
AP11

1951, May 22

C40	AP11	300fr purple	11.50	6.25

Ben Smine Sanatorium
AP12

1951, June 4

C41	AP12	50fr pur & Prus grn	1.40	1.40

Fortifications, Chella
AP13

Plane Near Marrakesh
AP14

Fort, Anti-Atlas Mountains
AP15

View of Fez
AP16

1952, Apr. 19 *Perf. 13* **Unwmkd.**

C42	AP13	10fr bl grn	45	15
C43	AP14	40fr red	60	30
C44	AP15	100fr brown	1.75	32
C45	AP16	200fr purple	5.00	2.50

Antique Brooches
AP17

1953, Mar. 27

C46	AP17	50fr dk grn	1.40	1.40

"City" of the Agdal, Meknes
AP18

Designs: 20fr, Yakoub el Mansour, Rabat. 40fr, Ainchock, Casablanca. 50fr, El Aliya, Fedala.

1954, Mar. 8

C47	AP18	10fr ol brn	1.25	1.25
C48	AP18	20fr purple	1.25	1.25
C49	AP18	40fr red brn	1.25	1.25
C50	AP18	50fr dp grn	1.40	1.40

Franco-Moroccan solidarity.

Naval Vessel and Sailboat
AP19

Village in the Anti-Atlas
AP20

"Ksar es Souk," Rabat and Plane
AP21

1954, Oct. 18

C51	AP19	15fr dk bl grn	80	80
C52	AP19	30fr vio bl	90	90

1955, July 25 Engraved. *Perf. 13*

Designs: 200fr, Estuary of Bou Regreg, Rabat and Plane.

C53	AP20	100fr brt vio	1.35	22
C54	AP20	200fr brt car	2.25	60
C55	AP21	500fr grnsh bl	6.00	2.75

AIR POST SEMI-POSTAL STAMPS.

French Protectorate

Moorish Tribesmen
SPAP1

Designs: 25c, Moor plowing with camel and burro. 50c, Caravan nearing Saffi. 75c, Walls, Marrakesh. 80c, Sheep grazing at Azrou. 1fr, Gate at Fez. 1.50fr, Aerial view of Tangier. 2fr, Aerial view of Casablanca. 3fr, Storks on old wall, Rabat. 5fr, Moorish fete.

Perf. 13½

1928, July 26 Photo. **Unwmkd.**

CB1	SPAP1	5c dp bl	2.25	2.25
CB2	SPAP1	25c brn org	2.25	2.25
CB3	SPAP1	50c red	2.25	2.25
CB4	SPAP1	75c org brn	2.25	2.25
CB5	SPAP1	80c ol grn	2.25	2.25
CB6	SPAP1	1fr orange	2.25	2.25
CB7	SPAP1	1.50fr Prus bl	2.25	2.25
CB8	SPAP1	2fr dp brn	2.25	2.25
CB9	SPAP1	3fr dp vio	2.25	2.25
CB10	SPAP1	5fr brn blk	2.25	2.25
		Nos. CB1-CB10 (10)	22.50	22.50

These stamps were sold in sets only and at double their face value. The money received for the surtax was divided among charitable and social organizations. The stamps were not sold at post offices but solely by subscription to the Moroccan Postal Administration.

Stamps of 1928 Overprinted **Tanger** in Red or Blue.

1929, Feb. 1

CB11	SPAP1	5c dp bl (R)	2.25	2.25
CB12	SPAP1	25c brn org (Bl)	2.25	2.25
CB13	SPAP1	50c red (Bl)	2.25	2.25
CB14	SPAP1	75c org brn (Bl)	2.25	2.25
CB15	SPAP1	80c ol grn (R)	2.25	2.25
CB16	SPAP1	1fr org (Bl)	2.25	2.25
CB17	SPAP1	1.50fr Prus bl (R)	2.25	2.25
CB18	SPAP1	2fr dp brn (R)	2.25	2.25
CB19	SPAP1	3fr dp vio (R)	2.25	2.25
CB20	SPAP1	5fr brn blk (R)	2.25	2.25
		Nos. CB11-CB20 (10)	22.50	22.50

These stamps were sold at double their face values and only in Tangier. The surtax benefited various charities.

Marshal Hubert Lyautey
SPAP10

1935, May 15 *Perf. 13½*

CB21	SPAP10	1.50fr +1.50fr bl	14.00	12.00

Nos. C14, C19 Surcharged in Red **O.S.E. +50 c**

1938 *Perf. 13*

CB22	AP2	50c +50c dk bl	2.75	2.75
CB23	AP3	10fr +10fr bl grn	2.75	2.75

Plane over Oasis
SPAP11

Statue of Marshal Lyautey
SPAP12

1944 Lithographed *Perf. 11½*

CB23A	SPAP11	1.50fr +98.50fr red, dp bl & blk	75	75

The surtax was for charity among the liberated French.

No. C29 Surcharged in Black **+ 5F 18 Juin 1940 ‡ 18 Juin 1946**

1946, June 18 *Perf. 11*

CB24	AP6	5fr +5fr scar	40	40

Issued to commemorate the 6th anniversary of the appeal made by Gen. Charles de Gaulle, June 18, 1940. The surtax was for the Free French Association of Morocco.

1946, Dec. Engraved. *Perf. 13*

CB25	SPAP12	10fr +30fr dk grn	90	90

The surtax was for works of solidarity.

Replenishing Stocks of Food
SPAP13

Agriculture
SPAP14

1948, Feb. 9 **Unwmkd.**

CB26	SPAP13	9fr +16fr dp grn	90	90
CB27	SPAP14	20fr +35fr brn	90	90

The surtax was for combined works of Franco-Moroccan solidarity.

Tomb of Marshal Hubert Lyautey
SPAP15

1948, May 18 *Perf. 13*

CB28	SPAP15	10fr +25fr dk grn	60	60

Lyautey Exposition, Paris, June, 1948.

P. T. T. Clubhouse
SPAP16

1948, June 7 **Engraved**

CB29	SPAP16	6fr +34fr dk grn	90	90
CB30	SPAP16	9fr +51fr red brn	90	90

The surtax was used for the Moroccan P. T. T. employees vacation colony at Ifrane.

View of Agadir
SPAP17

Plane over Globe
SPAP18

Designs: 6fr+9fr, Fez. 9fr+16fr, Atlas Mountains. 15fr+25fr, Valley of Draa.

1949, Apr. 12 *Perf. 13*

Inscribed: "SOLIDARITÉ 1948."

CB31	SPAP17	5fr +5fr dk grn	80	80
CB32	SPAP17	6fr +9fr org red	80	80
CB33	SPAP17	9fr +16fr blk brn	80	80

CB34	SPAP17	15fr +25fr ind	80	80
a.		Sheet of four	8.00	8.00

No. CB34a contains one each of Nos. CB31–CB34. Size: 96x120mm.

1950, Mar. 11 **Engr. and Typo.**

CB35	SPAP18	15fr +10fr bl grn & car	60	60

Issued to commemorate the "Day of the Stamp," March 11–12, 1950, and to mark the 25th anniversary of the first air post link between Casablanca and Dakar.

Scenes and Map: Northwest Corner
SPAP19

Designs (quarters of map): 6fr+9fr, Northeast. 9fr+16fr, Southwest. 15fr+25fr, Southeast.

1950, Apr. 11 **Engraved**

Inscribed: "SOLIDARITÉ 1949."

CB36	SPAP19	5fr +5fr dp ultra	80	80
CB37	SPAP19	6fr +9fr Prus grn	80	80
CB38	SPAP19	9fr +16fr dk brn	80	80
CB39	SPAP19	15fr +25fr brn red	80	80
a.		Sheet of four	8.00	8.00

No. CB39a contains one each of Nos. CB36–CB39. Size: 120½x95½mm.

Arch of Triumph of Caracalla at Volubilis
SPAP20

1950, Sept. 25 **Unwmkd.**

CB40	SPAP20	10fr +10fr sep	60	60
CB41	SPAP20	15fr +15fr bl grn	60	60

The surtax was for Army Welfare Work.

Casablanca Post Office and First Air Post Stamp—SPAP21

1952, Mar. 8 ***Perf. 13***

CB42	SPAP21	15fr +5fr red brn & dp grn	1.75	1.75

Issued to publicize the "Day of the Stamp," March 8, 1952, and to commemorate the 30th anniversary of French Morocco's first air post stamp.

POSTAGE DUE STAMPS.

French Offices in Morocco

Postage Due Stamps and Types of France Surcharged in Red or Black — 5 CENTIMOS

1896 ***Perf. 14x13½.*** **Unwmkd.**

On Stamps of 1891-93.

J1	D2	5c on 5c lt bl (R)	2.25	1.40
J2	D2	10c on 10c choc (R)	4.00	1.40
J3	D2	30c on 30c car	9.00	6.50
a.		Pair, one without surcharge		
J4	D2	50c on 50c lil	9.00	5.50
a.		"S" of "CENTIMOS" omitted		13.00
J5	D2	1p on 1fr lil brn	175.00	140.00

1909-10

On Stamps of 1908-10.

J6	D3	1c on 1c ol grn (R)	75	75
J7	D3	10c on 10c vio	16.00	14.00
J8	D3	30c on 30c bis	19.00	18.00
J9	D3	50c on 50c red	25.00	25.00

Postage Due Stamps of France Surcharged in Red or Blue — 5

1911

On Stamps of 1893-96.

J10	D2	5c on 5c bl (R)	1.40	1.40
J11	D2	10c on 10c choc (R)	4.00	4.00
a.		Double surch.	45.00	45.00
J12	D2	50c on 50c lil (Bl)	5.50	5.50

On Stamps of 1908-10.

J13	D3	1c on 1c ol grn (R)	60	60
J14	D3	10c on 10c vio (R)	2.25	2.25
J15	D3	30c on 30c bis (R)	2.75	2.75
J16	D3	50c on 50c red (Bl)	5.50	5.50
		Nos. J10-J16 (7)	22.00	22.00

French Protectorate

D4

D5

1915–17

Type of 1911 Issue Overprinted "Protectorat Francais".

J17	D4	1c on 1c blk	7	5
a.		New value double	57.50	
J18	D4	5c on 5c bl	45	45
J19	D4	10c on 10c choc	75	70
J20	D4	20c on 20c ol grn	75	70
J21	D4	30c on 30c rose red	2.25	2.00
J22	D4	50c on 50c vio brn	3.50	2.00
		Nos. J17-J22 (6)	7.77	5.90

Nos. J13 to J16 With Additional Overprint "Protectorat Francais".

1915

J23	D3	1c on 1c ol grn	45	45
J24	D3	10c on 10c vio	80	70
J25	D3	30c on 30c bis	1.10	95
J26	D3	50c on 50c red	1.10	1.00

1917–26 **Typographed**

J27	D5	1c black	5	5
J28	D5	5c dp bl	12	5
J29	D5	10c brown	18	12
J30	D5	20c ol grn	60	45
J31	D5	30c rose	12	7
J32	D5	50c lil brn	15	12
J33	D5	1fr red brn, *straw* ('26)	45	22
J34	D5	2fr vio ('26)	60	32
		Nos. J27-J34 (8)	2.27	1.40

Postage Due Stamps of France, 1882-1906 Overprinted **TANGER**

1918

J35	D2	1c black	25	25
J36	D2	5c blue	38	38
J37	D2	10c chocolate	60	60
J38	D2	15c green	2.00	2.00
J39	D2	20c ol grn	2.00	2.00
J40	D2	30c rose red	5.00	5.00
J41	D2	50c vio brn	7.00	7.00
		Nos. J35-J41 (7)	17.23	17.23

Postage Due Stamps of France, 1908-19 Overprinted **TANGER**

1918

J42	D3	1c ol grn	30	30
J43	D3	10c violet	45	45
J44	D3	20c bister	2.75	2.75
J45	D3	40c red	6.00	6.00

Nos. J31 and J29 Surcharged — 50c

1944 ***Perf. 14x13½*** **Unwmkd.**

J46	D5	50c on 30c rose	1.40	1.40
J47	D5	1fr on 10c brn	2.00	1.75
J48	D5	3fr on 10c brn	5.00	3.25

Type of 1917–1926

1945-52 **Typographed.**

J49	D5	1fr brn lake ('47)	35	35
J50	D5	2fr rose lake ('47)	50	38
J51	D5	3fr ultra	22	15
J52	D5	4fr red org	22	18
J53	D5	5fr green	45	12
J54	D5	10fr yel brn	45	15
J55	D5	20fr car ('50)	60	45
J56	D5	30fr dl brn ('52)	1.25	90
		Nos. J49-J56 (8)	4.04	2.68

PARCEL POST STAMPS.

French Protectorate

PP1

1917 ***Perf. 13½x14*** **Unwmkd.**

Q1	PP1	5c green	28	18
Q2	PP1	10c carmine	32	22
Q3	PP1	20c lil brn	32	28
Q4	PP1	25c blue	55	32
Q5	PP1	40c dk brn	1.00	35
Q6	PP1	50c red org	1.10	32
Q7	PP1	75c pale sl	1.40	90
Q8	PP1	1f ultra	2.00	28
Q9	PP1	2f gray	2.75	40
Q10	PP1	5f violet	4.00	40
Q11	PP1	10f black	6.25	40
		Nos. Q1-Q11 (11)	19.97	4.05

FRENCH POLYNESIA

(French Oceania)

LOCATION—South Pacific Ocean.
GOVT.—French Overseas Territory.
AREA—1,544 sq. mi.
POP.—137,382 (1977).
CAPITAL—Papeete.

In 1903 various French Establishments in the South Pacific were united to form a single colony. Most important of the island groups are the Society Islands, Marquesas Islands, the Tuamotu group and the Gambier, Austral and Rapa Islands. Tahiti, largest of the Society group, ranks first in importance.

100 Centimes = 1 Franc

Navigation and Commerce
A1

Perf. 14x13½.

1892–1907 **Typographed** **Unwmkd.**

Name of Colony in Blue or Carmine.

1	A1	1c *lil bl*	55	55
2	A1	2c brn, *buff*	75	75
3	A1	4c cl, *lav*	1.25	1.10
4	A1	5c grn, *grnsh*	3.25	2.75
5	A1	5c yel grn ('06)	60	45
6	A1	10c *lavender*	8.50	3.75
7	A1	10c red ('00)	60	45
8	A1	15c bl, quadrille paper	6.25	3.25
9	A1	15c gray, *lt gray* ('00)	1.25	1.10
10	A1	20c red, *grn*	5.75	2.50
11	A1	25c *rose*	15.00	9.00
12	A1	25c bl ('00)	3.75	2.50
13	A1	30c brn, *bis*	4.50	3.75
14	A1	35c *yel* ('06)	2.00	1.40
15	A1	40c red, *straw*	37.50	24.00
16	A1	45c *gray grn* ('07)	1.25	1.25
17	A1	50c car, *rose*	3.50	2.25
18	A1	50c brn, *az* ('00)	80.00	62.50
19	A1	75c dp vio, *org*	4.00	2.75
20	A1	1fr brnz grn, *straw*	5.50	4.00
		Nos. 1-20 (20)	185.75	130.05

Tahitian Girl
A2

Kanakas
A3

Fautaua Valley
A4

1913-30

21	A2	1c vio & brn	12	12
22	A2	2c brn & blk	12	12
23	A2	4c org & bl	15	15
24	A2	5c grn & yel grn	15	15
25	A2	5c bl & blk ('22)	15	15
26	A2	10c rose & org	32	28
27	A2	10c bl grn & yel grn ('22)	18	18
28	A2	10c org red & brn red, *bluish* ('26)	38	38
29	A2	15c org & blk ('15)	15	15
a.		Imperf., pair	17.50	
30	A2	20c blk & vio	12	12
a.		Imperf., pair	27.50	
31	A2	20c grn & bl grn ('26)	15	15
32	A2	20c brn red & dk brn ('27)	38	38
33	A3	25c ultra & bl	22	12
34	A3	25c vio & rose ('22)	12	12
35	A3	30c gray & brn	1.00	90
a.		Imperf., pair	62.50	
36	A3	30c rose & red org ('22)	30	30
37	A3	30c blk & red org ('26)	12	12
38	A3	30c sl bl & bl grn ('27)	45	45
39	A3	35c grn & rose	22	12
40	A3	40c blk & grn	22	18
41	A3	45c org & red	28	28
42	A3	50c dk brn & blk	3.25	2.75
43	A3	50c ultra & bl ('22)	22	22
44	A3	50c gray & bl vio ('26)	22	22
45	A3	60c grn & blk ('26)	22	22

46	A3	65c ol brn & red vio ('27)	75	75
47	A3	75c vio brn & vio	60	45
48	A3	90c brn red & rose ('30)	4.75	4.75
49	A4	1fr rose & blk	65	50
50	A4	1.10fr vio & dk brn ('28)	60	55
51	A4	1.40fr bis brn & vio ('29)	1.25	1.25
52	A4	1.50fr ind & bl ('30)	5.00	5.00
53	A4	2fr dk brn & grn	1.25	1.00
54	A4	5fr vio & bl	3.00	2.50
		Nos. 21-54 (34)	27.06	25.08

No. 7 Overprinted

EFO
1915

1915

55	A1	10c red	75	60
a.		Inverted overprint	25.00	25.00

No. 29 Surcharged

10

1916

56	A2	10c on 15c org & blk	45	45

Nos. 22, 41 and 29 Surcharged

05
1921

1921

57	A2	5c on 2c brn & blk	8.50	8.50
58	A3	10c on 45c org & red	7.50	7.50
59	A2	25c on 15c org & blk	2.00	2.00

On No. 58 the new value and date are set wide apart and without bar.

Types of 1913-30 Issue Surcharged

60

1923-27

60	A3	60c on 75c bl & brn	12	12
61	A4	65c on 1fr dk bl & ol (R) ('25)	45	45
62	A4	85c on 1fr dk bl & ol (R) ('25)	45	45
63	A3	90c on 75c brn red & cer ('27)	32	32

No. 26 Surcharged

45 c.
1924

1924

64	A2	45c on 10c rose & org	50	50
a.		Inverted surch.	110.00	110.00

Stamps and Type of 1913-30 Surcharged with New Value and Bars

1924-27

65	A4	25c on 2fr dk brn & grn	28	28
66	A4	25c on 5fr vio & bl	35	35
67	A4	1.25fr on 1fr dk bl & ultra (R) ('26)	35	35
68	A4	1.50fr on 1fr dk bl & lt bl ('27)	45	45
69	A4	20fr on 5fr org & brt vio ('27)	7.00	5.50
		Nos. 65-69 (5)	8.43	6.93

Surcharged TROIS FRANCS

1926

70	A4	3fr on 5fr gray & bl (Bk)	45	45
71	A4	10fr on 5fr grn & blk (R)	1.50	1.40

Papetoai Bay, Moorea
A5

1929, Mar. 25

72	A5	3fr grn & dk brn	2.75	2.75
73	A5	5fr lt bl & dk brn	5.00	5.00
74	A5	10fr lt red & dk brn	11.50	11.50
75	A5	20fr lil & dk brn	15.00	15.00

Colonial Exposition Issue.
Common Design Types

1931, Apr. 13 Engr. *Perf. 12½*

Name of Country Printed in Black.

76	CD70	40c dp grn	1.50	1.50
77	CD71	50c violet	1.50	1.50
78	CD72	90c red org	1.50	1.50
79	CD73	1.50fr dl bl	2.00	2.00

Spear Fishing
A12

Tahitian Girl
A13

Idols
A14

Photogravure.

1934-39 *Perf. 13½, 13½x13*

80	A12	1c gray blk	6	6
81	A12	2c claret	7	7
82	A12	3c lt bl ('39)	7	7
83	A12	4c orange	15	15
84	A12	5c violet	25	25
85	A12	10c dk brn	7	7
86	A12	15c green	12	12
87	A12	20c red	8	8
88	A13	25c gray bl	15	15
89	A13	30c yel grn	38	38
90	A13	30c org brn ('39)	12	12
91	A14	35c dp grn ('38)	1.00	1.00
92	A13	40c red vio	12	12
93	A13	45c brn org	2.25	2.25
94	A13	45c dk grn ('39)	35	35
95	A13	50c violet	6	6
96	A13	55c bl ('38)	1.35	1.35
97	A13	60c blk ('39)	12	12
98	A13	65c brown	85	85
99	A13	70c brt pink ('39)	22	22
100	A13	75c ol grn	1.50	1.50
101	A13	80c vio brn ('38)	35	35
102	A13	90c rose red	22	22
103	A14	1fr red brn	12	12
104	A14	1.25fr brn vio	2.25	2.25
105	A14	1.25fr rose red ('39)	22	22
106	A14	1.40fr org yel ('39)	22	22
107	A14	1.50fr blue	22	22
108	A14	1.60fr dl vio ('39)	22	22
109	A14	1.75fr olive	1.50	1.50
110	A14	2fr red	22	22
111	A14	2.25fr dp bl ('39)	20	20
112	A14	2.50fr blk ('39)	30	30
113	A14	3fr brn org ('39)	30	30
114	A14	5fr red vio ('39)	30	30
115	A14	10fr dk grn ('39)	70	70
116	A14	20fr dk brn ('39)	1.00	1.00
		Nos. 80-116 (37)	17.68	17.68

Common Design Types pictured in section at front of book.

Paris International Exposition Issue.
Common Design Types

1937 Engraved. *Perf. 13.*

117	CD74	20c dp vio	60	60
118	CD75	30c dk grn	60	60
119	CD76	40c car rose	60	60
120	CD77	50c dk brn & bl	60	60
121	CD78	90c red	70	70
122	CD79	1.50fr ultra	75	75
		Nos. 117-122 (6)	3.85	3.85

Colonial Arts Exhibition Issue.
Souvenir Sheet.
Common Design Type

1937 *Imperf.*

123	CD78	3fr emerald	2.50	2.50

Sheet size: 118x99mm.

New York World's Fair Issue.
Common Design Type

1939, May 10 Engr. *Perf. 12½x12*

124	CD82	1.25fr car lake	60	60
125	CD82	2.25fr ultra	60	60

Fautaua Valley and Marshal Petain
A15

1941 Engraved *Perf. 12½x12*

125A	A15	1fr bluish grn	22
125B	A15	2.50fr dp bl	22

Nos. 125A-125B were issued by the Vichy government, and were not placed on sale in the colony. This is also true of five stamps of types A12-A14 without "RF" released in 1942-44.

Stamps of 1929-39 Overprinted in Black or Red

FRANCE LIBRE

1941 *Perf. 14x13½, 13½x13*

126	A14	1fr red brn (Bk)	1.25	1.40
127	A14	2.50fr blk (R)	1.40	1.00
128	A5	3fr grn & dk brn (R)	1.75	1.75
129	A14	3fr brn org (Bk)	1.75	1.75
130	A5	5fr lt bl & dk brn (R)	2.25	2.25
131	A14	5fr red vio (Bk)	2.25	2.25
132	A5	10fr lt red & dk brn (R)	3.25	3.25
133	A14	10fr dk grn (R)	14.00	14.00
134	A5	20fr lil & dk brn (R)	27.50	27.50
135	A14	20fr dk brn (R)	11.50	11.50
		Nos. 126-135 (10)	66.90	66.65

Ancient Double Canoe
A16

1942 Photo. *Perf. 14½x14*

136	A16	5c dk brn	7	7
137	A16	10c dk gray bl	10	6
138	A16	25c emerald	10	6
139	A16	30c red org	10	6
140	A16	40c dk sl grn	10	6
141	A16	80c red brn	10	12
142	A16	1fr rose vio	12	8
143	A16	1.50fr brt red	22	18
144	A16	2fr gray blk	22	22
145	A16	2.50fr brt ultra	55	55
146	A16	4fr dl vio	32	28
147	A16	5fr bister	32	28
148	A16	10fr dp brn	38	32
149	A16	20fr dp grn	50	38
		Nos. 136-149 (14)	3.20	2.72

Eboue Issue.
Common Design Type

1945 Engraved *Perf. 13*

150	CD91	2fr black	22	[illegible]
151	CD91	25fr Prus grn	55	[illegible]

Nos. 150 and 151 exist imperforate.

Nos. 136, 138 and 145 Surcharged with New Values and Bars in Carmine or Black.

1946 *Perf. 14½x14.*

152	A16	50c on 5c (C)	15	[illegible]
153	A16	60c on 5c (C)	15	[illegible]
154	A16	70c on 5c (C)	15	[illegible]
155	A16	1.20fr on 5c (C)	15	[illegible]
156	A16	2.40fr on 25c (Bk)	30	[illegible]
157	A16	3fr on 25c (Bk)	22	22
158	A16	4.50fr on 25c (Bk)	45	45
159	A16	15fr on 2.50fr (C)	55	55
		Nos. 152-159 (8)	2.12	2.12

Coast of Mooréa
A17

Fisherman and Catch
A18

Tahitian Girl
A20

House at Faa
A19

Island of Borabora
A21

Island Women
A22

Engraved.

1948 *Perf. 13* **Unwmkd.**

160	A17	10c brown	6	6
161	A17	30c bl grn	6	6
162	A17	40c dp bl	6	6
163	A18	50c red brn	12	12
164	A18	60c dk brn ol	12	12
165	A18	80c brt bl	12	12
166	A19	1fr red brn	15	10
167	A19	1.20fr slate	18	15
168	A19	1.50fr dp ultra	22	18
169	A20	2fr sepia	35	28
170	A20	2.40fr red brn	45	45

171	A20	3fr purple	2.75	60
172	A20	4fr bl blk	35	35
173	A21	5fr sepia	50	42
174	A21	6fr stl bl	55	42
175	A21	10fr dk brn ol	80	35
176	A22	15fr vermilion	1.50	1.00
177	A22	20fr slate	1.75	85
178	A22	25fr sepia	2.00	1.00
		Nos. 160-178 (19)	12.09	6.69

Imperforates

Most French Polynesia stamps from 1948 onward exist imperforate in issued and trial colors, and also in small presentation sheets in issued colors.

Military Medal Issue.

Common Design Type

Engraved and Typographed.

1952, Dec. 1

179	CD101	3fr blk, grn, yel & pur	2.50	2.50

Girl of Borabora
A23

Girl Playing Guitar
A24

1955, Sept. 26 **Engraved**

180	A23	9fr dk brn, blk & red	5.50	4.00

FIDES Issue.

Common Design Type

Design: 3fr, Dry dock at Papeete.

1956, Oct. 22 Engr. *Perf. 13x12½*

181	CD103	3fr grnsh bl	65	60

1958, Nov. 3 *Perf. 13* Unwmkd.

Design: 4fr, 7fr, 9fr, Man with headdress. 10fr, 20fr, Girl with shells on beach.

182	A24	10c grn & redsh brn	30	30
183	A24	25c sl grn, cl & car	35	35
184	A24	1fr brt bl, brn & red org	45	45
185	A24	2fr brn, vio brn & vio	45	45
186	A24	4fr sl grn & org yel	60	60
187	A24	7fr red brn, grn & org	1.35	1.00
188	A24	9fr vio brn, grn & org	1.75	1.35
189	A24	10fr dk bl, brn & car	2.10	1.25
190	A24	20fr pur, rose red & brn	3.50	2.75
		Nos. 182-190 (9)	10.85	8.50

See Nos. 302–304.

Human Rights Issue

Common Design Type

1958, Dec. 10

191	CD105	7fr dk gray & dk bl	8.50	7.25

Flower Issue

Common Design Type

Design: 4fr, Breadfruit.

1959, Jan. Photo. *Perf. 12½x12*

192	CD104	4fr multi	3.00	2.50

Spear Fishing
A25

Tahitian Dancers
A26

1960, May 16 Engraved *Perf. 13*

193	A25	5fr grn, brn & lil	70	60
194	A26	17fr ultra, brt grn & red brn	3.00	1.85

Post Office, Papeete
A27

1960, Dec. 15 *Perf. 13* Unwmkd.

195	A27	16fr grn, bl & cl	3.25	2.25

Saraca Indica
A28

Design: 25fr, Hibiscus.

1962, July 12 Photo. *Perf. 13*

196	A28	15fr multi	5.00	3.50
197	A28	25fr multi	6.00	4.50

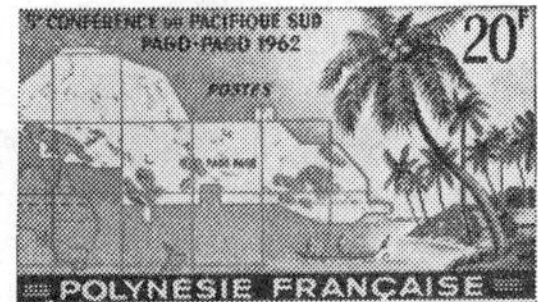

Map of Australia and South Pacific—A29

1962, July 18 *Perf. 13x12*

198	A29	20fr multi	6.00	4.00

Issued to commemorate the Fifth South Pacific Conference, Pago Pago, July 1962.

Spined Squirrelfish—A30

Fish: 10fr, One-spot butterflyfish. 30fr, Radiate lionfish. 40fr, Horned boxfish.

1962, Dec. 15 Engraved *Perf. 13*

199	A30	5fr blk, mag & bis	1.75	80
200	A30	10fr multi	2.75	1.10
201	A30	30fr multi	4.50	3.00
202	A30	40fr multi	7.25	5.50

South Pacific Games Issue

Soccer
A30a

Design: 50fr, Throwing the javelin.

1963, Aug. 29 Photo. *Perf. 12½*

203	A30a	20fr brt ultra & brn	4.50	3.00
204	A30a	50fr brt car rose & ultra	6.25	4.50

Issued to publicize the South Pacific Games, Suva, Aug. 29–Sept. 7.

Red Cross Centenary Issue

Common Design Type

1963, Sept. 2 Engraved *Perf. 13*

205	CD113	15fr vio brn, gray & car	9.00	7.00

International Red Cross centenary.

Human Rights Issue

Common Design Type

1963, Dec. 10 *Perf. 13* Unwmkd.

206	CD117	7fr grn & vio bl	7.25	6.25

Philatec Issue

Common Design Type

1964, Apr. 9 *Perf. 13* Unwmkd.

207	CD118	25fr grn, dk sl grn & red	7.25	6.25

Tahitian Dancer
A31

1964, May 14 Engraved *Perf. 13*

208	A31	1fr multi	45	45
209	A31	3fr dp cl, blk & org	65	65

Soldiers, Truck and Battle Flag
A32

1964, July 10 Photo. *Perf. 12½*

210	A32	5fr multi	3.25	1.50

Issued to honor the Tahitian Volunteers of the Pacific Battalion. See No. C31.

Tuamotu Scene
A33

Views: 4fr, Borabora. 7fr, Papeete Harbor. 8fr, Paul Gauguin's tomb, Marquesas. 20fr, Mangareva, Gambier Islands.

1964, Dec. 1 Litho. *Perf. 12½x13*

211	A33	2fr multi	40	40
212	A33	4fr multi	60	40
213	A33	7fr multi	1.25	90
214	A33	8fr multi	1.50	90
215	A33	20fr multi	3.50	2.50
		Nos. 211-215, C32 (6)	11.25	7.35

Painting from a School Dining Room
A34

1965, Nov. 29 Engraved *Perf. 13*

216	A34	20fr dk brn, sl grn & dk car	8.00	3.75

Issued to publicize the School Canteen Program. See No. C38.

Outrigger Canoe on Lagoon
A35

Ships: 11fr, Large cruising yacht (vert.). 12fr, Motorboat for sport fishing. 14fr, Outrigger canoes with sails. 19fr, Schooner (vert.). 22fr, Modern coaster "Oiseau des Isles II."

1966, Aug. 30 Engraved *Perf. 13*

217	A35	10fr brt ultra, emer & mar	1.10	50
218	A35	11fr mar, dk bl & sl grn	1.25	1.00
219	A35	12fr emer, dk bl & red lil	1.60	1.25
220	A35	14fr brn, bl & sl grn	2.25	1.40
221	A35	19fr scar, sl grn & dp bl	2.50	1.40
222	A35	22fr multi	3.50	2.25
		Nos. 217-222 (6)	12.20	7.80

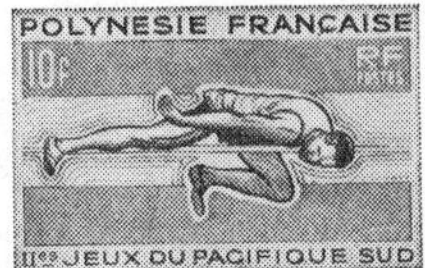

High Jump
A36

Designs: 20fr, Pole vault (vert.). 40fr, Women's basketball (vert.). 60fr, Hurdling.

1966, Dec. 15 Engraved *Perf. 13*

223	A36	10fr dk red, lem & blk	85	60
224	A36	20fr bl, emer & blk	2.00	1.10
225	A36	40fr emer, brt pink & blk	3.50	2.25
226	A36	60fr dl yel, bl & blk	5.50	4.50

Issued to commemorate the Second South Pacific Games, Nouméa, New Caledonia, Dec. 8–18.

Poi Pounder
A37

Javelin Throwing
A38

1967, June 15 Engraved *Perf. 13*

227	A37	50fr org & blk	6.75	5.00

Issued to commemorate the 50th anniversary of the Society for Oceanic Studies.

1967, July 11

Designs: 5fr, Spring dance (horiz.). 15fr, Horse race (horiz.). 16fr, Fruit carriers' race. 21fr, Canoe race (horiz.).

228	A38	5fr multi	80	50
229	A38	13fr multi	1.40	70
230	A38	15fr multi	1.50	90
231	A38	16fr multi	2.00	1.40
232	A38	21fr multi	3.50	2.00
		Nos. 228-232 (5)	9.20	5.50

Issued to publicize the July Festival.

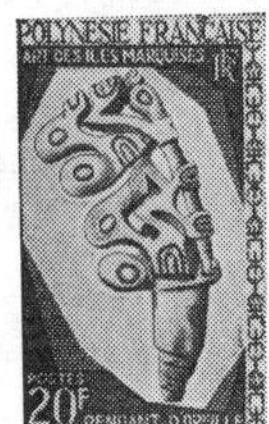

Earring
A39

Art of the Marquesas Islands: 10fr, Carved mother-of-pearl. 15fr, Decorated canoe paddle. 23fr, Oil vessel. 25fr, Carved stilt stirrups. 30fr, Fan handles. 35fr, Tattooed man. 50fr, Tikis.

1967–68 Engraved *Perf. 13*

233	A39	10fr dp cl, dl red & ultra ('68)	1.00	60
234	A39	15fr blk & emer ('68)	1.40	90
235	A39	20fr ol gray, dk car & lt bl	1.75	1.25
236	A39	23fr dk brn, ocher & bl ('68)	2.25	1.50
237	A39	25fr dk brn, dk bl & lil	2.50	1.50
238	A39	30fr brn & red lil	3.25	1.75
239	A39	35fr ultra & dk brn ('68)	4.75	2.50
240	A39	50fr brn, sl grn & lt bl	6.00	3.50
		Nos. 233-240 (8)	22.90	13.50

Issue dates: 20fr, 25fr, 30fr, 50fr, Dec. 19, 1967; others Feb. 28, 1968.

WHO Anniversary Issue
Common Design Type

1968, May 4 Engraved *Perf. 13*

241	CD126 15fr bl grn, mar & dp vio	2.25	1.10
242	CD126 16fr org, lil & bl grn	3.25	1.20

Issued for the 20th anniversary of the World Health Organization.

Human Rights Year Issue
Common Design Type

1968, Aug. 10 Engraved *Perf. 13*

243	CD127 15fr bl, red & brn	2.25	1.50
244	CD127 16fr brn, brt pink & ultra	3.25	2.25

Tiare Apetahi
A40

Flower: 17fr, Tiare Tahiti.

1969, Mar. 27 Photo. *Perf. 12½x13*

245	A40	9fr multi	1.40	70
246	A40	17fr multi	2.25	1.10

Runner
A41

Designs: 9fr, Boxer (horiz.). 17fr, High jump. 22fr, Long jump.

1969, Aug. 13 Engraved *Perf. 13*

247	A41	9fr bl, vio & sep	1.40	70
248	A41	17fr red, sep & cl	1.75	1.10
249	A41	18fr bl, brn ol & cl	2.25	1.40
250	A41	22fr brt grn & choc	3.25	2.25

Issued to publicize the 3rd South Pacific Games, Port Moresby, Papua and New Guinea, Aug. 13–23.

ILO Issue
Common Design Type

1969, Nov. 24 Engraved *Perf. 13*

251	CD131 17fr org, emer & ol	2.25	1.10
252	CD131 18fr org, dk brn & vio bl	2.75	1.40

Territorial Assembly
A42

Buildings: 14fr, Governor's Residence. 17fr, House of Tourism. 18fr, Maeva Hotel. 24fr, Taharaa Hotel.

1969, Dec. 22 Photo. *Perf. 12½x12*

253	A42	13fr blk & multi	1.10	60
254	A42	14fr blk & multi	1.50	70
255	A42	17fr blk & multi	1.85	1.00
256	A42	18fr blk & multi	2.50	1.10
257	A42	24fr blk & multi	2.75	1.75
		Nos. 253-257 (5)	9.70	5.15

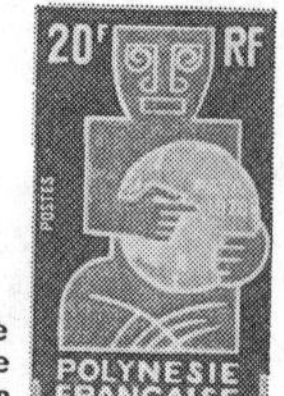

Stone Figure with Globe
A43

Designs: 40fr, Globe, plane, map of Polynesia and men holding "PATA" sign (horiz.). 60fr, Polynesian carrying globe.

1970, Apr. 7 Engraved *Perf. 13*

258	A43	20fr dp plum, gray & bl	2.25	1.20
259	A43	40fr emer, rose lil & ultra	4.50	2.50
260	A43	60fr red brn, bl & dk brn	5.75	3.75

Issued to publicize the 1970 Pacific Area Travel Association Congress (PATA).

U.P.U. Headquarters Issue
Common Design Type

1970, May 20 Engraved *Perf. 13*

261	CD133 18fr mar, pur & brn	2.75	1.40
262	CD133 20fr lil rose, ol & ind	3.50	2.00

Night Fishing—A44

1971, May 11 Photo. *Perf. 13*

263	A44	10fr multi	3.25	1.50

See Nos. C71–C73.

Flowers
A45

Designs: Various flowers. 12fr is horiz.

Perf. 12½x13, 13x12½

1971, Aug. 27

264	A45	8fr multi	1.00	70
265	A45	12fr multi	2.00	1.00
266	A45	22fr multi	3.00	1.75

Day of a Thousand Flowers.

Water-skiing Slalom—A46

Designs: 20fr, Water-skiing, jump (vert.). 40fr, Figure water-skiing.

1971, Oct. 11 Engraved *Perf. 13*

267	A46	10fr grnsh bl, dk red & brn	1.40	75
268	A46	20fr car, emer & brn	2.85	1.50
269	A46	40fr brn, grn & lil	5.00	3.25

World water-skiing championships, Oct. 1971.

De Gaulle Issue
Common Design Type

Designs: 30fr, Gen. de Gaulle, 1940. 50fr, Pres. de Gaulle, 1970.

1971, Nov. 9 Engraved *Perf. 13*

270	CD134 30fr red lil & blk	3.50	2.75
271	CD134 50fr red lil & blk	5.50	3.50

First anniversary of the death of Charles de Gaulle (1890–1970), president of France.

Map of Tahiti and Jerusalem Cross
A47

1971, Dec. 18 Photo. *Perf. 13x12½*

272	A47	28fr lt bl & multi	5.00	2.25

2nd rally of French Boy Scouts and Guides, Taravao, French Polynesia.

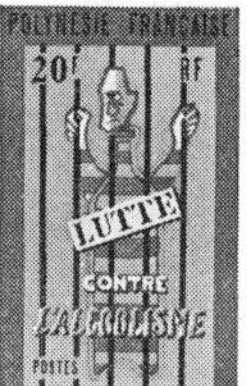

"Alcoholism"
A48

Mother and Child
A49

1972, Mar. 24 Photo. *Perf. 13*

273	A48	20fr brn & multi	2.75	1.75

Fight against alcoholism.

1973, Sept. 26 Photo. *Perf. 12½x13*

274	A49	28fr pale yel & multi	4.00	2.25

Day nursery.

Polynesian Golfer
A50

Design: 24fr, Atimaono Golf Course.

1974, Feb. 27 Photogravure *Perf. 13*

275	A50	16fr multi	2.25	1.40
276	A50	24fr multi	3.25	2.25

Atimaono Golf Course.

Hand Throwing Life Preserver to Puppy—A51

1974, May 9 Photo. *Perf. 13*

277	A51	21fr brt bl & multi	3.25	1.50

Society for the Protection of Animals.

Around a Fire, on the Beach
A52

Polynesian Views: 2fr, Lagoons and mountains. 6fr, Pebble divers. 10fr, Lonely Mountain and flowers (vert.). 15fr, Sailing ship at sunset. 20fr, Lagoon and mountain.

1974, May 22

278	A52	2fr multi	40	30
279	A52	5fr multi	65	50
280	A52	6fr multi	70	55
281	A52	10fr multi	90	65
282	A52	15fr multi	1.50	85
283	A52	20fr multi	2.25	1.40
		Nos. 278-283 (6)	6.40	4.25

Polynesian Woman and UPU Emblem
A53

Lion, Sun and Emblem
A54

1974, Oct. 9 Engraved *Perf. 13*

284	A53	65fr multi	4.50	3.25

Centenary of Universal Postal Union.

1975, June 17 Photogravure

285	A54	26fr multi	3.50	1.75

15th anniversary of Lions International in Tahiti.

Fish and Leaf—A55

1975, July 9 Litho. *Perf. 12*

286	A55	19fr dp ultra & grn	3.25	1.75

Polynesian Association for the Protection of Nature.

Pompidou Type of France 1975

1976, Feb. 16 Engr. *Perf. 13*

287	A668	49fr dk vio & blk	4.00	2.00

Georges Pompidou (1911–74), President of France (1965–74).

Alain Gerbault and Sailboat
A56

1976, May 25 Photo. *Perf. 13*

288	A56	90fr multi	5.00	3.50

50th anniversary of Alain Gerbault's arrival in Bora Bora.

Turtle
A57

Design: 42fr, Hand protecting bird.

1976, June 24 Litho. *Perf. 12½*

289	A57	18fr multi	1.50	75
290	A57	42fr multi	3.25	1.50

World Ecology Day.

A. G. Bell, Telephone, Radar and Satellite—A58

1976, Sept. 15 Engr. *Perf. 13*

291	A58	37fr multi	3.25	1.50

Centenary of first telephone call by Alexander Graham Bell, Mar. 10, 1876.

Marquesas Dugout Canoe—A59

Dugout Canoes from: 30fr, Raiatea. 75fr, Tahiti. 100fr, Tuamotu.

1976, Dec. 16 Litho. *Perf. 13x12½*

292	A59	25fr multi	1.40	85
293	A59	30fr multi	2.00	1.25
294	A59	75fr multi	3.50	2.25
295	A59	100fr multi	4.50	3.25

Sailing Ship—A60

Designs: Various sailing vessels.

1977, Dec. 22 Litho. *Perf. 13*

296	A60	20fr multi	1.25	70
297	A60	50fr multi	2.50	1.10
298	A60	85fr multi	3.25	1.75
299	A60	120fr multi	5.00	3.25

Hibiscus
A61

Girl with Shells on Beach
A62

Designs: 10fr, Vanda orchids. 16fr, Pua (fagraea berteriana). 22fr, Gardenia.

1978–79 Photo. *Perf. 12½x13*

300	A61	10fr multi	45	35
301	A61	13fr multi	75	38
302	A61	16fr multi	1.10	40
303	A61	22fr multi	75	55

Issue dates: Nos. 301–302, Aug. 23, 1978; Nos. 300, 303, Jan. 25, 1979.

1978, Nov. 3 Engr. *Perf. 13*

Designs (as type A24 with "1958 1978" added): 28fr, Man with headdress. 36fr, Girl playing guitar.

304	A62	20fr multi	90	40
305	A62	28fr multi	1.10	50
306	A62	36fr multi	1.50	1.00
a.		Souvenir sheet of 3	4.50	4.50

20th anniversary of stamps inscribed: Polynesie Francaise. No. 306a contains Nos. 304–306; dark brown marginal inscription and design. Size: 130x100mm.

Tahiti—A63

Ships: 30fr, Monowai. 75fr, Tahitien. 100fr, Mariposa.

1978, Dec. 29 Litho. *Perf. 13x12½*

307	A63	15fr multi	90	60
308	A63	30fr multi	1.40	90
309	A63	75fr multi	3.25	1.75
310	A63	100fr multi	4.00	2.75

Porites Coral
A64

Design: 37fr, Montipora coral.

1979, Feb. 15 *Perf. 13x12½*

311	A64	32fr multi	1.10	70
312	A64	37fr multi	1.35	85

Raiatea
A65

Landscapes: 1fr, Moon over Bora Bora. 2fr, Mountain peaks, Ua Pu. 3fr, Sunset over Motu Tapu. 5fr, Motu Beach. 6fr, Palm and hut, Tuamotu.

1979, Mar. 8 *Perf. 13x13½*

313	A65	1fr multi	6	6
314	A65	2fr multi	6	6
315	A65	3fr multi	12	5
316	A65	4fr multi	18	6
317	A65	5fr multi	32	12
318	A65	6fr multi	32	28
		Nos. 313-318 (6)	1.06	63

Dance Costumes, Fetia
A66

Dance Costumes: 51fr, Teanuanua. 74fr, Temaeva.

1979, July 14 Litho. *Perf. 12½*

319	A66	45fr multi	1.35	75
320	A66	51fr multi	1.50	90
321	A66	74fr multi	2.75	1.50

Hill, Great Britain No. 53, Tahiti No. 28—A67

1979, Aug. 1 Engraved *Perf. 13*

322	A67	100fr multi	3.25	2.25

Sir Rowland Hill (1795–1879), originator of penny postage.

Hastula Strigilata
A68

Shells: 28fr, Scabricola variegata. 35fr, Fusinus undatus.

1979, Aug. 21 Litho. *Perf. 12½*

323	A68	20fr multi	60	45
324	A68	28fr multi	75	45
325	A68	35fr multi	1.00	65

Statue Holding Rotary Emblem—A69

1979, Nov. 30 Litho. *Perf. 13*

326	A69	47fr multi	1.50	80

Rotary International, 75th anniversary; Papeete Rotary Club, 20th anniversary.

Myripristis Murdjan—A70

Fish: 8fr, Napoleon fish. 12fr, Emperor fish.

1980, Jan. 21 Litho. *Perf. 12½*

327	A70	7fr multi	35	18
328	A70	8fr multi	35	18
329	A70	12fr multi	55	35

No. 326 Overprinted and Surcharged in Gold:
"75eme / ANNIVERSAIRE / 1905-1980"

1980, Feb. 23 Litho. *Perf. 13*
330 A69 77fr on 47fr multi 2.25 1.35

Rotary International, 75th anniversary.

CNEXO Fish Hatchery—A71

1980, Mar. 17 Photo. *Perf. 13x13½*
331 A70 15fr *shown* 55 32
332 A70 22fr *Crayfish* 65 40

Papeete Post Office Building Opening—A72

1980, May 5 Photo. *Perf. 13x12½*
333 A71 50fr multi 1.40 80

Tiki and Festival Emblem
A73

1980, June 30 Photo. *Perf. 13½*
334 A73 34fr *shown* 70 55
335 A73 39fr *Drum (pahu)* 80 55
336 A73 49fr *Ax (to'i)* 1.00 70
a. Souvenir sheet of 3 3.00 3.00

South Pacific Arts Festival, Port Moresby, Papua New Guinea. No. 336a contains Nos. 334-336; multicolored margin shows festival emblem. Size: 136x100mm.

Titmouse henparrot
A74

Charles de Gaulle
A75

Photogravure

1980, Oct. 20 *Perf. 13x12½, 12½x13*
337 A74 25fr *White sea-swallow, horiz.* 55 35
338 A74 35fr *shown* 70 50
339 A74 45fr *Minor frigate bird, horiz.* 90 55

1980, Nov. 9 Engr. *Perf. 12½x13*
340 A75 100fr multi 2.25 1.40

Naso Vlamingi (Karaua)—A76

1981, Feb. 5 Litho. *Perf. 12½*
341 A76 13fr shown 25 16
342 A76 16fr Lutjanus vaigensis toau 32 25
343 A76 24fr Plectropomus leopardus tonu 50 30

Indoor Fish Breeding Tanks, Cnexo Hatchery—A77

1981, May 14 Photo. *Perf. 13x13½*
344 A77 23fr shown 48 28
345 A77 41fr Mussels 85 60

Folk Dancers—A78

1981, July 10 Litho. *Perf. 13x13½, 13½x13*
346 A78 26fr shown 55 32
347 A78 28fr Dancer 58 35
348 A78 44fr Dancers, vert. 90 65

Sterna Bergii—A79

1981, Sept. 24 Litho. *Perf. 13*
349 A79 47fr shown 95 75
350 A79 53fr Ptilinopus purpuratus, vert. 1.10 65
351 A79 65fr Estrilda astrild, vert. 1.30 90

Huahine Island—A80

1981, Oct. 22 Litho. *Perf. 12½*
352 A80 34fr shown 72 40
353 A80 134fr Maupiti 2.80 1.50
354 A80 136fr Bora-Bora 2.85 1.50

Parrot Fish—A81

1982, Feb. 4 Photo. *Perf. 13x13½*
355 A81 30fr shown 60 40
356 A81 31fr Regal angel 65 42
357 A81 45fr Spotted bass 90 70

Pearl Industry—A82

1982, Apr. 22 Photo. *Perf. 13x13½*
358 A82 7fr Pearl beds 14 8
359 A82 8fr Extracting pearls 16 10
360 A82 10fr Pearls 20 14

Tahiti "No. 1A," Emblem—A83

1982, May 12 Engr. *Perf. 13*
361 A83 150fr multi 3.00 1.75
a. Souvenir sheet 3.00 1.75

PHILEXFRANCE Stamp Exhibition, Paris, June 11-21. No. 361a contains No. 361 in changed colors; blue marginal inscription. Size: 122x95mm.

King Holding Carved Scepter—A84

Designs: Coronation ceremony.

1982, July 14 Photo. *Perf. 13½x13*
362 A84 12fr shown 25 14
363 A84 13fr King, priest 26 14
364 A84 17fr Procession 35 18

Championship Emblem—A85

1982, Aug. 13 *Perf. 13*
365 A85 90fr multi 1.80 1.00

4th Hobie-Cat 16 World Catamaran Sailing Championship, Tahiti, Aug. 15-21.

First Colloquium on New Energy Sources—A86

1982, Sept. 29 Litho.
366 A86 46fr multi 92 65

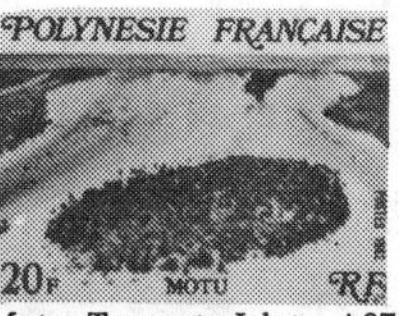

Motu, Tuamotu Islet—A87

1982, Oct. 12 Litho. *Perf. 13*
367 A87 20fr shown 40 25
368 A87 33fr Tupai Atoll 65 35
369 A87 35fr Gambier Islds. 70 40

Bird Type of 1981

1982, Nov. 17 Litho. *Perf. 13*
370 A79 37fr Sacred egret 75 60
371 A79 39fr Pluvialis dominica, vert. 80 65
372 A79 42fr Lonchura castaneothorax 85 68

Fish—A88

1983, Feb. 9 Litho. *Perf. 13x13½*
373 A88 8fr Acanthurus lineatus 16 10
374 A88 10fr Caranx melampygus 20 12
375 A88 12fr Carcharhinus melanopterus 24 15

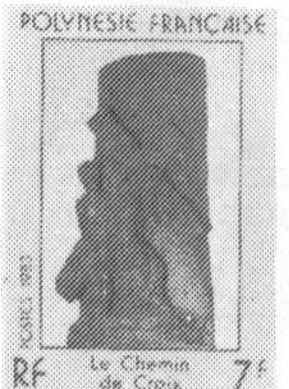

The Way of the Cross, Sculpture by Damien Haturau—A89

1983, Mar. 9 Litho. *Perf. 13*
376 A89 7fr shown 14 8
377 A89 21fr Virgin and Child 42 25
378 A89 23fr Christ 46 26

SEMI-POSTAL STAMPS.

Nos. 55 and 26 Surcharged in Red + 5c

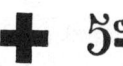

1915 *Perf. 14x13½* **Unwmkd.**

B1	A1	10c +5c red	6.25	6.25
a.		"e" instead of "c"	15.00	15.00
b.		Inverted surcharge	40.00	40.00
B2	A2	10c +5c rose & org	2.25	2.25
a.		"e" instead of "c"	11.50	11.50
b.		"c" inverted	11.50	11.50
c.		Inverted surcharge	35.00	35.00

Surcharged in Carmine + 5c

B3	A2	10c +5c rose & org	70	70
a.		"e" instead of "c"	6.25	6.25
b.		Inverted surcharge	37.50	37.50

Surcharged in Carmine + 5c

1916

B4	A2	10c +5c rose & org	70	70

Curie Issue
Common Design Type

1938 **Engraved.** *Perf. 13*

B5	CD80	1.75fr +50c brt ultra	5.00	5.00

French Revolution Issue
Common Design Type

1939 Photogravure

Name and Value Typo. in Black.

B6	CD83	45(c) +25(c) grn	3.75	3.75
B7	CD83	70(c) +30(c) brn	3.75	3.75
B8	CD83	90(c) +35(c) red org	3.75	3.75
B9	CD83	1.25fr +1fr rose pink	3.75	3.75
B10	CD83	2.25fr +2fr bl	3.75	3.75
		Nos. B6-B10 (5)	18.75	18.75

Common Design Type and

Marine Officer
SP1

"L'Astrolabe"
SP2

1941 Photogravure *Perf. 13½*

B11	SP1	1fr +1fr red	60
B12	CD86	1.50fr +3fr mar	60
B12A	SP2	2.50fr +1fr bl	60

Nos. B11–B12A were issued by the Vichy government, and were not placed on sale in the colony.

Nos. 125A–125B were surcharged "OEUVRES COLONIALES" and surtax (including change of denomination of the 2.50fr to 50c). These were issued in 1944 by the Vichy government and not placed on sale in the colony.

Red Cross Issue
Common Design Type

1944 Photogravure. *Perf. 14½x14.*

B13	CD90	5fr +20fr pck bl	42	42

The surtax was for the French Red Cross and national relief.

Tropical Medicine Issue
Common Design Type

1950 Engraved. *Perf. 13.*

B14	CD100	10fr +2fr dk bl grn & dk grn	1.25	1.25

The surtax was for charitable work.

AIR POST STAMPS.

Seaplane in Flight
AP1

Photogravure.

1934, Nov. 5 *Perf. 13½* **Unwmkd.**

C1	AP1	5fr green	18	18

V4

Stamps of type AP1 without "RF" monogram and stamp of the above design were issued in 1944 by the Vichy Government, but were not placed on sale in the colony.

No. C1 Overprinted in Red

FRANCE LIBRE

1941

C2	AP1	5fr green	1.10	1.10

Common Design Type

1942 *Perf. 14½x14.*

C3	CD87	1fr dk org	22	22
C4	CD87	1.50fr brt red	22	22
C5	CD87	5fr brn red	35	35
C6	CD87	10fr black	55	55
C7	CD87	25fr ultra	75	75
C8	CD87	50fr dk grn	55	55
C9	CD87	100fr plum	75	75
		Nos. C3-C9 (7)	3.39	3.39

Victory Issue
Common Design Type

1946, May 8 Engr. *Perf. 12½*

C10	CD92	8fr dk grn	60	60

Issued to commemorate the European Victory of the Allied Nations in World War II.

Chad to Rhine Issue
Common Design Types

1946, June 6

C11	CD93	5fr red org	70	70
C12	CD94	10fr dk ol bis	70	70
C13	CD95	15fr dk yel grn	70	70
C14	CD96	20fr carmine	80	80
C15	CD97	25fr dk rose vio	80	80
C16	CD98	50fr black	1.40	1.40
		Nos. C11-C16 (6)	5.10	5.10

Shearwater and Moorea Landscape
AP2

Fishermen—AP3

Shearwater over Maupiti Shoreline
AP4

1948, Mar. 1 *Perf. 13* **Unwmkd.**

C17	AP2	50fr red brn	7.25	6.75
C18	AP3	100fr purple	6.25	5.75
C19	AP4	200fr bl grn	15.00	11.50

UPU Issue
Common Design Type

1949

C20	CD99	10fr dp bl	5.00	5.00

Gauguin's "Nafea faaipoipo"
AP5

1953, Sept. 24

C21	AP5	14fr dk brn, dk gray grn & red	45.00	45.00

Issued to commemorate the 50th anniversary of the death of Paul Gauguin.

Liberation Issue
Common Design Type

1954, June 6

C22	CD102	3fr dk grnsh bl & bl grn	1.35	1.35

Bahia Peak, Borabora—AP6

1955, Sept. 26 *Perf. 13* **Unwmkd.**

C23	AP6	13fr ind & bl	3.25	2.75

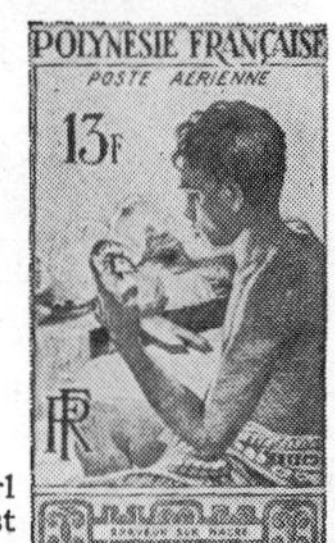

Mother-of-Pearl Artist
AP7

Designs: 50fr, "Women of Tahiti," Gauguin (horiz.). 100fr, "The White Horse," Gauguin. 200fr, Night fishing at Moorea (horiz.).

1958, Nov. 3 **Engr.** *Perf. 13*

C24	AP7	13fr multi	2.75	1.35
C25	AP7	50fr multi	7.25	3.25
C26	AP7	100fr multi	12.50	5.75
C27	AP7	200fr lil & sl	18.50	7.50

Airport, Papeete—AP8

1960, Dec. 15

C28	AP8	13fr rose lil, vio, & yel grn	2.25	1.20

Telstar Issue
Common Design Type

1962, Dec. 5 *Perf. 13*

C29	CD111	50fr red lil, mar & vio bl	7.00	5.50

Tahitian Dancer
AP10

1964, May 14 Photo. *Perf. 13*

C30	AP10	15fr multi	2.75	1.40

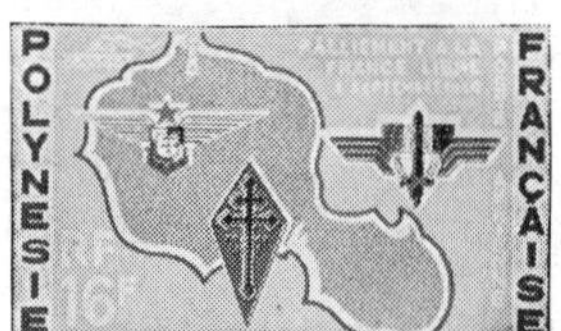

Map of Tahiti and Free French Emblems—AP11

1964, July 10 **Unwmkd.**

C31	AP11	16fr multi	7.25	3.50

Issued to commemorate the rallying of French Polynesia to the Free French cause.

Moorea Scene—AP12

1964, Dec. 1 Litho. *Perf. 13*

C32	AP12	23fr multi	4.00	2.25

ITU Issue
Common Design Type

1965, May 17 Engraved *Perf. 13*

C33	CD120	50fr vio, red brn & bl	55.00	22.50

Issued to commemorate the centenary of the International Telecommunication Union.

Paul Gauguin—AP13

Design: 25fr, Gauguin Museum (stylized). 40fr, Primitive statues at Gauguin Museum.

1965 Engraved *Perf. 13*

C34	AP13	25fr ol grn	4.50	2.25
C35	AP13	40fr bl grn	6.25	3.25
C36	AP13	75fr brt red brn	11.50	7.25

Opening of Gauguin Museum, Papeete.

Skin Diver with Spear Gun—AP14

1965, Sept. 1 Engraved *Perf. 13*

C37	AP14	50fr red brn, dl bl & dk grn	45.00	35.00

World Championships in Underwater Fishing, Tuamotu Archipelago, Sept. 1965.

Painting from a School Dining Room — AP15

Radio Tower, Globe and Palm — AP16

1965, Nov. 29

C38	AP15	80fr brn, bl, dl bl & red	11.00	7.25

School Canteen Program.

1965, Dec. 29 Engraved *Perf. 13*

C39	AP16	60fr org, grn & dk brn	9.50	5.75

50th anniversary of the first radio link between Tahiti and France.

French Satellite A-1 Issue

Common Design Type

Designs: 7fr, Diamant Rocket and launching installations. 10fr, A-1 satellite.

1966, Feb. 7

C40	CD121	7fr choc, dp grn & lil	3.50	3.50
C41	CD121	10fr lil, dp grn & dk brn	4.50	4.50
a.		Strip of 2 + label	8.50	8.50

Issued to commemorate the launching of France's first satellite, Nov. 26, 1965. No. C41a contains one each of Nos. C40–C41 and dark brown label with commemorative inscription. Each sheet contains 16 triptychs (2x8).

French Satellite D-1 Issue

Common Design Type

1966, May 10 Engraved *Perf. 13*

C42	CD122	20fr brn, brt grn & cl	5.00	2.75

Papeete Harbor—AP17

1966, June 30 Photo. *Perf. 13*

C43	AP17	50fr multi	8.50	5.00

"Vive Tahiti" by A. Benichou

AP18

1966, Nov. 28 Photo. *Perf. 13*

C44	AP18	13fr multi	4.50	2.25

Explorer's Ship and Canoe—AP19

Designs: 60fr, Polynesian costume and ship. 80fr, Louis Antoine de Bougainville (vert.).

1968 Engraved *Perf. 13*

C45	AP19	40fr grn, bl & ocher	4.50	2.00
C46	AP19	60fr brt bl, org & blk	5.75	2.75
C47	AP19	80fr red lil, sal & lake	6.75	5.00
a.		Souv. sheet of 3	20.00	20.00

Issued to commemorate the 200th anniversary of the discovery of Tahiti by Louis Antoine de Bougainville. No. C47a contains one each of Nos. C45–C47. Ocher marginal inscription. Size: 174x99mm.

The Meal, by Paul Gauguin—AP20

1968, July 30 Photo. *Perf. 12x12½*

C48	AP20	200fr multi	27.50	21.00

See also Nos. C63–C67, C78–C82, C89–C93, C98.

Shot Put — AP21

PATA 1970 Poster — AP22

1968, Oct. 12 Engraved *Perf. 13*

C49	AP21	35fr dk car rose & brt grn	6.25	3.25

Issued to commemorate the 19th Olympic Games, Mexico City, Oct. 12–27.

Concorde Issue

Common Design Type

1969, Apr. 17

C50	CD129	40fr red brn & car rose	32.50	18.50

1969, July 9 Photo. *Perf. 12½x13*

C51	AP22	25fr bl & multi	5.50	2.25

Issued to publicize PATA 1970 (Pacific Area Travel Association Congress), Tahiti.

Underwater Fishing

AP23

Design: 52fr, Hand holding fish made up of flags (vert.).

1969, Aug. 5 Photo. *Perf. 13*

C52	AP23	48fr blk, grnsh bl & red lil	5.50	3.25
C53	AP23	52fr bl, blk & red	8.00	5.00

Issued to publicize the World Underwater Fishing Championships.

Gen. Bonaparte as Commander of the Army in Italy, by Jean Sebastien Rouillard

AP24

1969, Oct. 15 Photo. *Perf. 12½x12*

C54	AP24	100fr car & multi	62.50	50.00

Bicentenary of the birth of Napoleon Bonaparte (1769–1821).

Eiffel Tower, Torii and EXPO Emblem — AP25

Pearl Diver Descending, and Basket — AP26

Design: 30fr, Mount Fuji, Tower of the Sun and EXPO emblem (horiz.).

1970, Sept. 15 Photo. *Perf. 13*

C55	AP25	30fr multi	4.50	2.7
C56	AP25	50fr multi	8.00	5.0

EXPO '70 International Exposition, Osaka, Japan, Mar. 15–Sept. 13.

1970, Sept. 30 Engraved *Perf. 13*

Designs: 5fr, Diver collecting oysters. 18fr, Implantation into oyster (horiz.). 27fr, Open oyster with pearl. 50fr, Woman with mother of pearl jewelry.

C57	AP26	2fr sl, grnsh bl & red brn	90	4
C58	AP26	5fr grnsh bl, ultra & org	1.25	7
C59	AP26	18fr sl, mag & org	2.25	1.2
C60	AP26	27fr brt pink, brn & dl lil	3.25	2.2
C61	AP26	50fr gray, red brn & org	5.00	3.5
		Nos. C57-C61(5)	12.65	8.1

Pearl industry of French Polynesia.

The Thinker, by Auguste Rodin and Education Year Emblem—AP27

1970, Oct. 15 Engraved *Perf. 13*

C62	AP27	50fr bl, ind & fawn	6.25	4.0

International Education Year.

Painting Type of 1968

Paintings by Artists Living in Polynesia: 20fr, Woman on the Beach, by Yves de Saint-Front. 40fr, Abstract, by Frank Fay. 60fr, Woman and Shells, by Jean Guillois. 80fr, Hut under Palms, by Jean Masson. 100fr, Polynesian Girl, by Jean-Charles Bouloc (vert.).

Perf. 12x12½, 12½x12

1970, Dec. 14 Photogravure

C63	AP20	20fr brn & multi	3.75	2.25
C64	AP20	40fr brn & multi	6.75	4.50
C65	AP20	60fr brn & multi	10.00	6.00
C66	AP20	80fr brn & multi	12.50	8.50
C67	AP20	100fr brn & multi	20.00	12.50
		Nos. C63-C67 (5)	53.00	33.75

South Pacific Games Emblem

AP28

1971, Jan. 26 *Perf. 12½*

C68 AP28 20fr ultra & multi 2.75 1.40

Publicity for 4th South Pacific Games, held in Papeete, Sept. 8–19, 1971.

Memorial Flame
AP29

1971, March 19 Photo. *Perf. 12½*

C69 AP29 5fr multi 2.75 1.50

In memory of Charles de Gaulle.

Soldier and Badge—AP30

1971, Apr. 21

C70 AP30 25fr multi 6.25 4.50

30th anniversary of departure of Tahitian volunteers to serve in World War II.

Water Sports Type of Regular Issue

Designs: 15fr, Surfing (vert.). 16fr, Skin diving (vert.). 20fr, Water-skiing with kite.

1971, May 11 Photo. *Perf. 13*

C71 A44 15fr multi 2.25 1.10
C72 A44 16fr multi 2.75 1.50
C73 A44 20fr multi 3.25 1.75

Sailing
AP31

Designs: 18fr, Golf. 27fr, Archery. 53fr, Tennis.

1971, Sept. 8 *Perf. 12½*

C74 AP31 15fr multi 1.75 90
C75 AP31 18fr multi 2.75 1.50
C76 AP31 27fr multi 3.25 2.00
C77 AP31 53fr multi 5.00 2.85
a. Souvenir sheet of 4 15.00 15.00

4th South Pacific Games, Papeete, Sept. 8–19. No. C77a contains one each of Nos. C74–C77. Black marginal inscription. Size: 136x169mm.

Painting Type of 1968

Paintings by Artists Living in Polynesia: 20fr, Hut and Palms, by Isabelle Wolf. 40fr, Palms on Shore, by André Dobrowolski. 60fr, Polynesian Woman, by Françoise Séli (vert.). 80fr, Holy Family, by Pierre Heymann (vert.). 100fr, Crowd, by Nicolai Michoutouchkine.

1971, Dec. 15 Photo. *Perf. 13*

C78 AP20 20fr multi 3.25 2.00
C79 AP20 40fr multi 4.50 3.00
C80 AP20 60fr multi 7.50 5.00
C81 AP20 80fr multi 10.00 6.00
C82 AP20 100fr multi 17.50 12.00
Nos. C78-C82 (5) 42.75 28.00

Papeete Harbor—AP32

1972, Jan. 13

C83 AP32 28fr vio & multi 4.50 2.75

Free port of Papeete, 10th anniversary.

Figure Skating and Dragon
AP33

1972, Jan. 25 Engraved *Perf. 13*

C84 AP33 20fr ultra, lake & brt grn 5.00 2.25

11th Winter Olympic Games, Sapporo, Japan, Feb. 3–13.

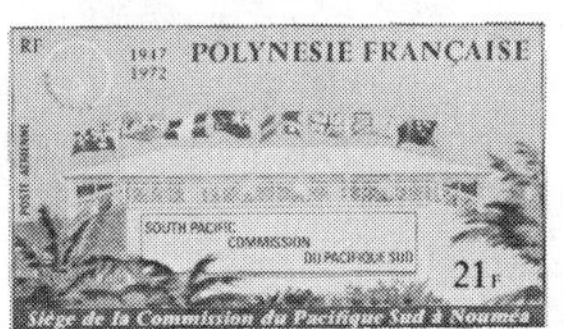

South Pacific Commission
Headquarters, Noumea—AP34

1972, Feb. 5 Photogravure *Perf. 13*

C85 AP34 21fr bl & multi 3.50 1.50

South Pacific Commission, 25th anniversary.

Festival Emblem
AP35

1972, May 9 Engr. *Perf. 13*

C86 AP35 36fr org, bl & grn 3.75 2.75

South Pacific Festival of Arts, Fiji, May 6–20.

Kon Tiki and Route, Callao to
Tahiti—AP36

1972, Aug. 18 Photo. *Perf. 13*

C87 AP36 16fr dk & lt bl, blk & org 3.75 2.00

25th anniversary of the arrival of the raft Kon Tiki in Tahiti.

Charles de Gaulle and Memorial
AP37

1972, Dec. 9 Engraved *Perf. 13*

C88 AP37 100fr slate 15.00 11.00

Gen. Charles de Gaulle (1890–1970), president of France.

Painting Type of 1968

Paintings by Artists Living in Polynesia; 20fr, Horses, by Georges Bovy. 40fr, Sailboats, by Ruy Juventin (vert.). 60fr, Harbor, by André Brooke. 80fr, Farmers, by Daniel Adam (vert.). 100fr, Dancers, by Aloysius Pilioko (vert.).

1972, Dec. 14 Photogravure

C89 AP20 20fr gold & multi 3.50 2.00
C90 AP20 40fr gold & multi 5.00 2.75
C91 AP20 60fr gold & multi 7.50 4.50
C92 AP20 80fr dk grn, buff & dk brn 12.00 6.00
C93 AP20 100fr gold & multi 13.00 11.00
Nos. C89-C93 (5) 41.00 26.25

St. Teresa and Lisieux Basilica
AP38

1973, Jan. 23 Engraved *Perf. 13*

C94 AP38 85fr multi 11.50 6.00

Centenary of the birth of St. Teresa of Lisieux (1873–1897), Carmelite nun.

Nicolaus Copernicus—AP39

1973, Mar. 7 Engraved *Perf. 13*

C95 AP39 100fr brn, vio bl & red lil 11.50 7.25

500th anniversary of the birth of Nicolaus Copernicus (1473–1543), Polish astronomer.

Plane over Tahiti—AP40

1973, Apr. 3 Photo. *Perf. 13*

C96 AP40 80fr ultra, gold & lt grn 9.00 5.50

Air France's World Tour via Tahiti.

DC-10 at Papeete Airport—AP41

1973, May 18 Engraved *Perf. 13*

C97 AP41 20fr bl, ultra & sl grn 4.50 2.00

Start of DC-10 service.

Painting Type of 1968

Design: 200fr, "Ta Matete" (seated women), by Paul Gauguin.

1973, June 7 Photo. *Perf. 13*

C98 AP20 200fr multi 20.00 14.00

70th anniversary of the death of Paul Gauguin (1848–1903), painter.

Pierre Loti and Characters from his
Books—AP42

1973, July 4 Engraved *Perf. 13*

C99 AP42 60fr multi 6.75 3.75

50th anniversary of the death of Pierre Loti (1850–1923), French naval officer and writer.

"Sun,"
by Jean
Francois
Favre
AP43

Paintings by Artists Living in Polynesia: 40fr, Woman with Flowers, by Eliane de Gennes. 60fr, Seascape, by Alain Sidet. 80fr, Crowded Bus, by Francois Ravello. 100fr, Stylized Boats, by Jackie Bourdin (horiz.).

1973, Dec. 13 Photo. *Perf. 13*

C100 AP43 20fr gold & multi 2.25 1.50
C101 AP43 40fr gold & multi 3.50 2.25
C102 AP43 60fr gold & multi 5.25 4.50
C103 AP43 80fr gold & multi 7.50 6.50
C104 AP43 100fr gold & multi 12.00 8.50
Nos. C100-C104 (5) 30.50 23.25

Bird, Fish, Flower
and Water
AP44

1974, June 12 Photo. *Perf. 13*

C105	AP44	12fr bl & multi	3.25	1.50

Nature protection.

Catamaran under Sail
AP45

1974, July 22 Engraved *Perf. 13*

C106	AP45	100fr multi	8.50	5.00

2nd Catamaran World Championships.

Still-life, by Rosine Temarui-Masson
AP46

Paintings by Artists Living in Polynesia: 40fr, Palms and House on Beach, by Marcel Chardon. 60fr, Man, by Marie-Françoise Avril. 80fr, Polynesian Woman, by Henriette Robin. 100fr, Lagoon by Moonlight, by David Farsi (horiz.).

1974, Dec. 12 Photogravure *Perf. 13*

C107	AP46	20fr gold & multi	2.25	1.40
C108	AP46	40fr gold & multi	3.25	2.00
C109	AP46	60fr gold & multi	4.50	2.75
C110	AP46	80fr gold & multi	6.25	3.50
C111	AP46	100fr gold & multi	11.00	5.00
		Nos. C107-C111 (5)	27.25	14.65

See also Nos. C122–C126.

Polynesian Gods of Travel—AP47

Designs: 75fr, Tourville hydroplane, 1929. 100fr, Passengers leaving plane.

1975, Feb. 7 Engraved *Perf. 13*

C112	AP47	50fr sep, pur & brn	3.50	2.00
C113	AP47	75fr grn, bl & red	5.50	3.50
C114	AP47	100fr grn, sep & car	7.25	4.75

Fifty years of Tahitian aviation.

French Ceres Stamp and Woman
AP48

1975, May 29 Engr. *Perf. 13*

C115	AP48	32fr ver, brn & blk	3.25	1.50

ARPHILA 75 International Philatelic Exhibition, Paris, June 6–16.

Shot Put and Games' Emblem
AP50

Designs: 30fr, Volleyball. 40fr, Women's swimming.

1975, Aug. 1 Photo. *Perf. 13*

C117	AP50	25fr dk red & multi	2.25	1.50
C118	AP50	30fr emer & multi	2.75	1.50
C119	AP50	40fr vio bl & multi	3.25	1.85

5th South Pacific Games, Guam, Aug. 1–10.

Flowers, Athlete, View of Montreal
AP51

1975, Oct. 15 Engr. *Perf. 13*

C120	AP51	44fr brt bl, ver & blk	3.25	2.00

Pre-Olympic Year 1975.

U.P.U. Emblem, Jet and Letters—AP52

1975, Nov. 5 Engr. *Perf. 13*

C121	AP52	100fr brn, bl & ol	7.25	4.50

World Universal Postal Union Day.

Paintings Type of 1974

Paintings by Artists Living in Polynesia: 20fr, Beach Scene, by R. Marcel Marius (horiz.). 40fr, Roofs with TV antennas, by M. Anglade (horiz.). 60fr, Street scene with bus, by J. Day (horiz.). 80fr, Tropical waters (fish), by J. Steimetz. 100fr, Women, by A. van der Heyde.

1975, Dec. 17 Litho. *Perf. 13*

C122	AP46	20fr gold & multi	1.85	1.50
C123	AP46	40fr gold & multi	2.25	2.00
C124	AP46	60fr gold & multi	5.00	3.50
C125	AP46	80fr gold & multi	7.50	5.25
C126	AP46	100fr gold & multi	10.00	6.75
		Nos. C122-C126 (5)	26.60	19.00

Concorde—AP53

1976, Jan. 21 Engr. *Perf. 13*

C127	AP53	100fr car, bl & ind	8.00	5.50

First commercial flight of supersonic jet Concorde from Paris to Rio de Janeiro, Jan. 21.

Adm. Rodney, Count de la Perouse, "Barfleur" and "Triomphant" in Battle—AP54

Design: 31fr, Count de Grasse and Lord Graves, "Ville de Paris" and "Le Terible" in Chesapeake Bay Battle.

1976, Apr. 15 Engr. *Perf. 13*

C128	AP54	24fr grnsh bl, lt brn & blk	2.00	1.40
C129	AP54	31fr mag, red & lt brn	2.75	1.75

American Bicentennial.

King Pomaré I
AP55

Portraits: 21fr, King Pomaré II. 26fr, Queen Pomaré IV. 30fr, King Pomaré V.

1976, Apr. 28 Litho. *Perf. 12½*

C130	AP55	18fr ol & multi	90	60
C131	AP55	21fr multi	1.40	80
C132	AP55	26fr gray & multi	1.50	80
C133	AP55	30fr plum & multi	1.75	1.20

Pomaré Dynasty. See Nos. C141–C144.

Running and Maple Leaf—AP56

Designs: 34fr, Long jump (vert.). 50fr, Olympic flame and flowers.

1976, July 19 Engr. *Perf. 13*

C134	AP56	26fr ultra & multi	1.50	6
C135	AP56	34fr ultra & multi	2.00	9
C136	AP56	50fr ultra & multi	2.75	1.5
a.		Miniature sheet of 3	8.50	8.5

21st Olympic Games, Montreal, Canada, July 17–Aug. 1. No. C136a contains one each of Nos. C134–C136. Size: 180x100 mm.

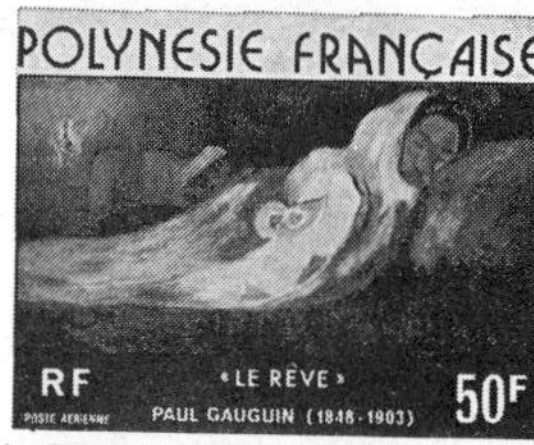

The Dream, by Paul Gauguin—AP57

1976, Oct. 17 Photo. *Perf. 13*

C137	AP57	50fr multi	3.75	2.00

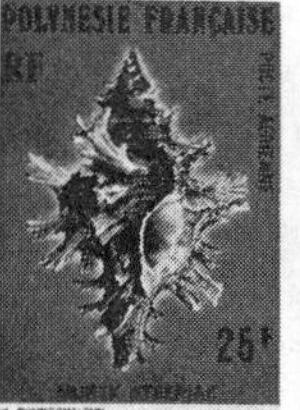

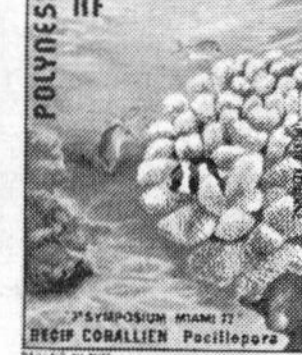

Murex Steeriae AP58 Pocillopora AP59

Sea Shells: 27fr, Conus Gauguini. 35fr, Conus marchionatus.

1977, Mar. 14 Photo. *Perf. 12½x13*

C138	AP58	25fr vio bl & multi	1.10	60
C139	AP58	27fr ultra & multi	1.40	80
C140	AP58	35fr bl & multi	2.00	1.00

See Nos. C156–C158.

Royalty Type of 1976

Portraits: 19fr, King Maputeoa, Mangareva. 33fr, King Camatoa V, Raiatea. 39fr, Queen Vaekehu, Marquesas. 43fr, King Teurarii III, Rurutu.

1977, Apr. 19 Litho. *Perf. 12½*

C141	AP55	19fr dl red & multi	90	65
C142	AP55	33fr dk bl & multi	1.25	90
C143	AP55	39fr ultra & multi	1.40	1.00
C144	AP55	43fr grn & multi	1.50	1.10

Polynesian rulers.

Perf. 13x12½, 12½x13

1977, May 23 Photogravure

Design: 25fr, Acropora (horiz.).

C145	AP59	25fr multi	1.10	60
C146	AP59	33fr multi	1.75	80

3rd Symposium on Coral Reefs, Miami, Fla. See Nos. C162–C163.

De Gaulle Memorial AP60 Tahitian Dancer AP61

Photogravure and Embossed

1977, June 18 *Perf. 13*

C147	AP60	40fr gold & multi	2.00	1.25

5th anniversary of dedication of De Gaulle memorial at Colombey-les-Deux-Eglises.

1977, July 14 Litho. *Perf. 12½*

C148	AP61	27fr multi	1.40	70

Charles A. Lindbergh and Spirit of St. Louis—AP62

1977, Aug. 18 Litho. *Perf. 12½*

C149	AP62	28fr multi	1.50	90

Charles A. Lindbergh's solo transatlantic flight from New York to Paris, 50th anniversary.

Mahoe AP63 — Palms on Shore AP64

Design: 12fr, Frangipani.

1977, Sept. 15 Photo. *Perf. 12½x13*

C150	AP63	8fr multi	45	35
C151	AP63	12fr multi	65	50

1977, Nov. 8 Photo. *Perf. 12½x13*

C152	AP64	32fr multi	1.75	1.00

Ecology, protection of trees.

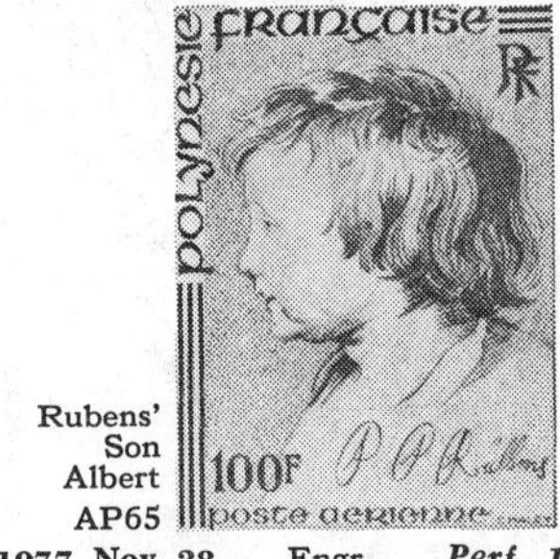

Rubens' Son Albert AP65

1977, Nov. 28 Engr. *Perf. 13*

C153	AP65	100fr grnsh blk & rose cl	4.50	4.00

Peter Paul Rubens (1577–1640), painter, 400th birth anniversary.

Capt. Cook and "Discovery"—AP66

Design: 39fr, Capt. Cook and "Resolution."

1978, Jan. 20 Engr. *Perf. 13*

C154	AP66	33fr multi	1.50	1.10
C155	AP66	39fr multi	2.00	1.25

Bicentenary of Capt. James Cook's arrival in Hawaii.

Shell Type of 1977

Sea Shells: 22fr, Erosaria obvelata. 24fr, Cypraea ventriculus. 31fr, Lambis robusta.

1978, Apr. 13 Photo. *Perf. 13½x13*

C156	AP58	22fr brt bl & multi	90	60
C157	AP58	24fr brt bl & multi	1.10	70
C158	AP58	31fr brt bl & multi	1.40	80

Tahitian Woman and Boy, by Gauguin AP67

1978, May 7 *Perf. 13*

C159	AP67	50fr multi	3.25	2.25

Paul Gauguin (1848–1903), 75th death anniversary.

Antenna and ITU Emblem AP68

1978, May 17 Litho. *Perf. 13*

C160	AP68	80fr gray & multi	3.50	2.25

10th World Telecommunications Day.

Soccer and Argentina '78 Emblem AP69

1978, June 1

C161	AP69	28fr multi	1.25	80

11th World Cup Soccer Championship, Argentina, June 1–25.

Coral Type of 1977

Designs: 26fr, Fungia (horiz.). 34fr, Millepora.

Perf. 13x12½, 12½x13

1978, July 13 Photogravure

C162	AP59	26fr multi	90	65
C163	AP59	34fr multi	1.40	85

Radar Antenna, Polynesian Woman AP70

1978, Sept. 5 Engr. *Perf. 13*

C164	AP70	50fr bl & blk	2.25	1.50

Papenoo earth station.

Bird and Rainbow over Island—AP71

1978, Oct. 5 Photogravure

C165	AP71	23fr multi	90	55

Nature protection.

Nos. C154–C155 Overprinted in Black or Violet Blue: ' "1779–1979" / BICENTENAIRE / DE LA / MORT DE'

1979, Feb. 14 Engr. *Perf. 13*

C166	AP66	33fr multi	1.35	70
C167	AP66	39fr multi (VBl)	1.75	1.10

Bicentenary of Capt. Cook's death. On No. C167 date is last line of overprint.

Children, Toys and IYC Emblem AP72

1979, May 3 Engr. *Perf. 13*

C168	AP72	150fr multi	5.50	4.00

International Year of the Child.

"Do you expect a letter?" by Paul Gauguin—AP73

1979, May 20 Photo. *Perf. 13*

C169	AP73	200fr multi	7.25	4.50

Shell and Carved Head—AP74

1979, June 30 Engr. *Perf. 13*

C170	AP74	44fr multi	1.40	90

Museum of Tahiti and the Islands.

See "Special Notices" at the front of this volume for data on the listing methods of this Catalogue, abbreviations, condition, prices and examination.

Conference Emblem over Island AP75

1979, Oct. 6 Photo. *Perf. 13*

C171	AP75	23fr multi	80	45

19th South Pacific Conference, Tahiti, Oct. 6–12.

Flying Boat "Bermuda"—AP76

Planes Used in Polynesia: 40fr, DC-4 over Papeete. 60fr, Britten-Norman "Islander." 80fr, Fairchild F-27A. 120fr, DC-8 over Tahiti.

1979, Dec. 19 Litho. *Perf. 13*

C172	AP76	24fr multi	70	45
C173	AP76	40fr multi	1.10	60
C174	AP76	60fr multi	1.75	90
C175	AP76	80fr multi	2.25	1.40
C176	AP76	120fr multi	3.25	2.25
		Nos. C172-C176 (5)	9.05	5.60

See Nos. C180-C183.

Window on Tahiti, by Henri Matisse AP77

1980, Feb. 18 Photo.

C177	AP77	150fr multi	4.00	2.75

Marshi Metua No Tehamana, by Gauguin—AP78

1980, Aug. 18 Photo. *Perf. 13*

C178	AP78	500fr multi	10.00	6.25

Sydpex '80, Philatelic Exhibition, Sydney Town Hall—AP79

1980, Sept. 29 **Photo.** ***Perf. 13***

C179	AP79	70fr multi	1.50	90

Aviation Type of 1979

1980, Dec. 15 **Litho.** ***Perf. 13***

C180	AP76	15fr *Catalina*	32	28
C181	AP76	26fr *Twin Otter*	55	32
C182	AP76	30fr *CAMS 55*	60	38
C183	AP76	50fr *DC-6*	1.10	55

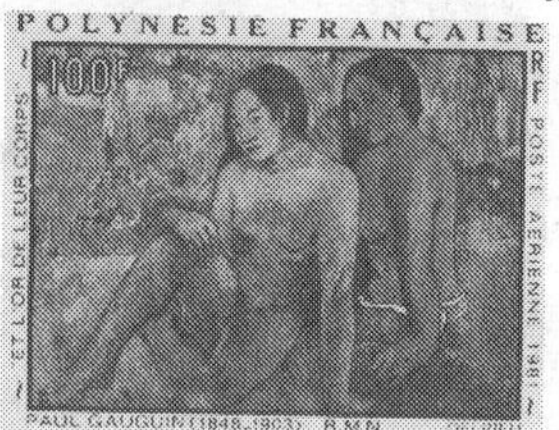

And The Gold of their Bodies, by Gauguin—AP80

1981, Mar. 15 **Photo.** ***Perf. 13***

C184	AP80	100fr multi	2.25	1.50

20th Anniv. of Manned Space Flight—AP81

1981, June 13 **Litho.** ***Perf. 12½***

C185	AP81	300fr multi	6.00	4.50

First Intl. Pirogue (6-man Canoe) Championship—AP82

1981, July 25 **Litho.** ***Perf. 13x12½***

C186	AP82	200fr multi	4.00	2.50

Matavai Bay, by William Hodges—AP83

Paintings: 60fr, Poedea, by John Weber (vert.). 80fr, Omai, by Joshua Reynolds (vert.). 120fr, Point Venus, by George Tobin.

1981, Dec. 10 **Photo.** ***Perf. 13***

C187	AP83	40fr multi	80	50
C188	AP83	60fr multi	1.20	70
C189	AP83	80fr multi	1.60	1.10
C190	AP83	120fr multi	2.40	1.50

TB Bacillus Centenary—AP84

1982, Mar. 24 **Engr.** ***Perf. 13***

C191	AP84	200fr multi	4.00	3.00

1982 World Cup—AP85

1982, May 18 **Litho.** ***Perf. 13***

C192	AP85	250fr multi	5.00	3.75

French Overseas Possessions' Week, Sept. 18-25—AP86

1982, Sept. 17 **Engr.**

C193	AP86	110fr multi	2.25	1.50

Painting Type of 1981

Designs: 50fr, The Tahitian, by M. Radiguet (vert.). 70fr, Souvenir of Tahiti, by C. Giraud. 100fr, Beating Cloth Lengths, by Atlas JL the Younger. 160fr, Papeete Harbor, by C.F. Gordon Cumming.

1982, Dec. 15 **Photo.** ***Perf. 13***

C194	AP83	50fr multi	1.00	75
C195	AP83	70fr multi	1.40	1.05
C196	AP83	100fr multi	2.00	1.40
C197	AP83	160fr multi	3.25	2.25

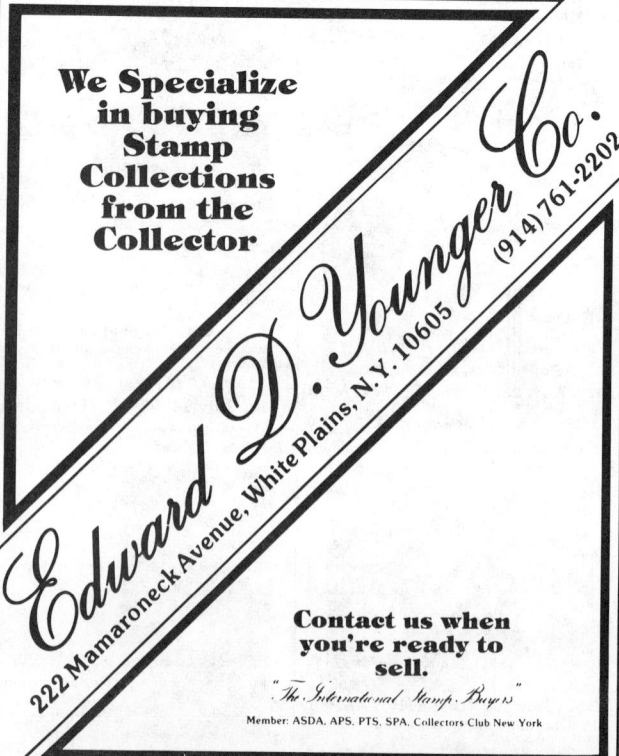

AIR POST SEMI-POSTAL STAMP.

French Revolution Issue
Common Design Type
Photogravure.

1939, July 5 ***Perf. 13*** **Unwmkd.**
Name and Value Typo. in Orange.

CB1	CD83	5fr +4fr brn blk	7.50	7.50

V5

Stamps of the above design and of Cameroun type V10 inscribed "Etabts Frcais de l'Océanie" were issued in 1942 by the Vichy Government, but were not placed on sale in the colony.

POSTAGE DUE STAMPS.

Postage Due Stamps of French Colonies, 1894-1906, Overprinted **Établissements Français de l'Océanie**

1926-27 ***Perf. 14x13½*** **Unwmkd.**

J1	D1	5c lt bl	15	15
J2	D1	10c brown	28	28
J3	D1	20c ol grn	32	32
J4	D1	30c dl red	28	28
J5	D1	40c rose	45	45
J6	D1	60c bl grn	38	38
J7	D1	1fr red brn, *straw*	55	55
J8	D1	3fr mag ('27)	2.25	2.25

With Additional Surcharge of New Value

J9	D1	2fr on 1fr org red	85	85
		Nos. J1-J9 (9)	5.51	5.51

Fautaua Falls, Tahiti
D2

Tahitian Youth
D3

1929 **Typographed** ***Perf. 13½x14***

J10	D2	5c lt bl & dk brn	18	18
J11	D2	10c ver & grn	18	18
J12	D2	30c dk brn & dk red	32	32
J13	D2	50c yel grn & dk brn	22	22
J14	D2	60c dl vio & yel grn	65	65
J15	D3	1fr Prus bl & red vio	38	38
J16	D3	2fr brn red & dk brn	28	28
J17	D3	3fr bl vio & bl grn	40	40
		Nos. J10-J17 (8)	2.61	2.61

D4

Polynesian Club
D5

1948 **Engraved.** ***Perf. 14x13.***

J18	D4	10c brt bl grn	6	6
J19	D4	30c blk brn	8	8
J20	D4	50c dk car rose	8	8
J21	D4	1fr ultra	18	18
J22	D4	2fr dk bl grn	25	25
J23	D4	3fr red	32	32
J24	D4	4fr violet	40	40
J25	D4	5fr lil rose	50	50
J26	D4	10fr slate	1.00	1.00
J27	D4	20fr red brn	1.35	1.35
		Nos. J18-J27 (10)	4.22	4.22

1958 ***Perf. 14x13*** **Unwmkd.**

J28	D5	1fr dk brn & grn	25	25
J29	D5	3fr bluish blk & hn brn	38	38
J30	D5	5fr brn & ultra	50	50

OFFICIAL STAMPS

Bread-fruit
O1

Polynesian Fruits: 2fr, 3fr, 5fr, like 1fr. 7fr, 8fr, 10fr, 15fr, "Vi Tahiti." 19fr, 20fr, 25fr, 35fr, Avocados. 50fr, 100fr, 200fr, Mangos.

1977, June 9 **Litho.** ***Perf. 12½***

O1	O1	1fr ultra & multi	5	5
O2	O1	2fr ultra & multi	6	4
O3	O1	3fr ultra & multi	8	4
O4	O1	5fr ultra & multi	10	10
O5	O1	7fr red & multi	20	18
O6	O1	8fr red & multi	25	22
O7	O1	10fr red & multi	30	28
O8	O1	15fr red & multi	42	35
O9	O1	19fr blk & multi	50	38
O10	O1	20fr blk & multi	55	45
O11	O1	25fr blk & multi	65	55
O12	O1	35fr blk & multi	85	65
O13	O1	50fr blk & multi	1.35	1.10
O14	O1	100fr red & multi	2.25	2.00
O15	O1	200fr ultra & multi	4.50	4.25
		Nos. O1-O15 (15)	12.11	10.64

Unused Prices
Catalogue prices for unused stamps through 1960 are for hinged copies in fine condition.

See "Special Notices" at the front of this volume for data on the listing methods of this Catalogue, abbreviations, condition, prices and examination.

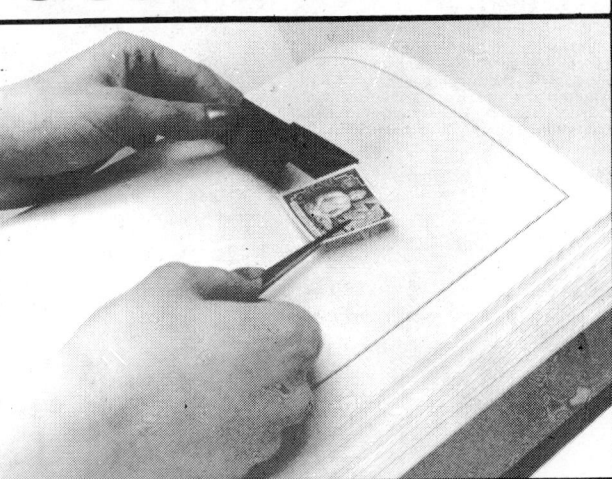

FRENCH SOUTHERN and ANTARCTIC TERRITORIES

AREA—9,000 sq. mi.
POP.—191 (1978).

Formerly dependencies of Madagascar, these areas, comprising the Kerguelen Archipelago; St. Paul, Amsterdam and Crozet Islands and Adelie Land in Antarctica, achieved territorial status on Aug. 6, 1955.

100 Centimes = 1 Franc

Madagascar No. 289 Overprinted in Red:

TERRES AUSTRALES ET ANTARCTIQUES FRANÇAISES

Engraved.

1955, Oct. 28 *Perf. 13* Unwmkd.

1	A25	15f dk grn & dp ultra	25.00	25.00

Rockhopper Penguins, Crozet Archipelago—A1

New Amsterdam A2

Design: 10fr, 15fr, Elephant seal.

1956, Apr. 25 Engr. *Perf. 13*

2	A1	50c dk bl, sep & yel	60	65
3	A1	1fr ultra, org & gray	60	65
4	A2	5fr bl & dp ultra	1.60	1.75
5	A2	8fr gray vio & dk brn	13.00	13.50
6	A2	10fr indigo	2.25	2.50
7	A2	15fr ind & brn vio	2.85	3.00
		Nos. 2-7 (6)	20.90	22.05

Polar Observation A3

1957, Oct. 11

8	A3	5fr blk & vio	4.25	4.25
9	A3	10fr rose red	5.00	5.00
10	A3	15fr dk bl	5.00	5.00

International Geophysical Year, 1957–58.

Imperforates

Most stamps of this French possession exist imperforate in issued and trial colors, and also in small presentation sheets in issued colors.

Flower Issue

Common Design Type

Design: Pringlea (horiz.).

1959 Photogravure. *Perf. 12½x12*

11	CD104	10fr sal, grn & yel	3.75	3.75

Common Design Types

pictured in section at front of book.

Light-mantled Sooty Albatross A4

Coat of Arms A5

Designs: 40c, Skua (horiz.). 12fr, King shag.

1959, Sept. 14 Engraved. *Perf. 13*

12	A4	30c bl, grn & red brn	60	60
13	A4	40c blk, dl red brn & bl	60	60
14	A4	12fr lt bl & blk	5.00	5.00

Typographed

Perf. 13x14

15	A5	20fr ultra, lt bl & yel	17.50	17.50

Sheathbills A6

Designs: 4fr, Sea leopard (horiz.). 25fr, Weddell seal at Kerguélen (horiz.). 85fr, King penguin.

1960, Dec. 15 Engraved *Perf. 13*

16	A6	2fr grnsh bl, gray & choc	1.00	1.00
17	A6	4fr bl, dk brn & dk grn	2.50	2.50
18	A6	25fr sl grn, bis brn & blk	11.00	11.00
19	A6	85fr grnsh bl, org & blk	18.50	18.50

Yves-Joseph de Kerguélen-Trémarec—A7

1960, Nov. 22

20	A7	25fr red org, dk bl & brn	17.50	17.50

Issued to honor Yves-Joseph de Kerguélen-Trémarec, discoverer of the Kerguélen Archipelago.

Charcot, Compass Rose and "Pourquoi-pas?" A8

1961, Dec. 26 *Perf. 13* Unwmkd.

21	A8	25fr brn, grn & red	15.00	15.00

Issued to commemorate the 25th anniversary of the death of Commander Jean Charcot, Antarctic explorer.

Elephant Seals Fighting A9

1963, Feb. 11 Engraved *Perf. 13*

22	A9	8fr dk bl, blk & cl	5.00	5.00

See No. C4.

Penguins and Camp on Crozet Island A10

Design: 20fr, Research station and IQSY emblem.

1963, Dec. 16 *Perf. 13* Unwmkd.

23	A10	5fr blk, red brn & Prus bl	12.50	12.50
24	A10	20fr vio, sl & red brn	52.50	52.50

Issued to publicize the International Quiet Sun Year, 1964–65. See No. C6.

Great Blue Whale A11

Black-browed Albatross A12

Aurora Australis, Map of Antarctica and Rocket A13

Designs: 10fr, Cape pigeons. 12fr, Phylica trees, Amsterdam Island. 15fr, Killer whale (orca).

1966-69 Engraved *Perf. 13*

25	A11	5fr brt bl & ind	4.25	4.25
26	A12	10fr sl, ind & ol brn ('69)	22.50	22.50
27	A11	12fr brt bl, sl grn & lem ('69)	11.50	11.50
27A	A11	15fr ol, dk bl & ind ('69)	6.00	6.00
28	A12	20fr sl, ol & org ('68)	275.00	275.00
		Nos. 25-28 (5)	319.25	319.25

Issue dates: 5fr, Dec. 12, 1966; 20fr, Jan. 31, 1968; 10fr, 12fr, Jan. 6, 1969; 15fr, Dec. 21, 1969.

1967, March 4 Engraved *Perf. 13*

29	A13	20fr mag, bl & blk	22.50	22.50

Issued to commemorate the launching of the first space rocket from Adelie Land, January, 1967.

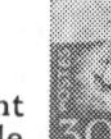

Dumont D'Urville A14

1968, Jan. 20

30	A14	30fr lt ultra, dk bl & dk brn	100.00	100.00

Jules Sébastien César Dumont D'Urville (1790–1842), French naval commander and South Seas explorer.

WHO Anniversary Issue

Common Design Type

1968, May 4 Engraved *Perf. 13*

31	CD126	30fr red, yel & bl	45.00	45.00

Issued for the 20th anniversary of the World Health Organization.

Human Rights Year Issue

Common Design Type

1968, Aug. 10 Engraved *Perf. 13*

32	CD127	30fr grnsh bl, red & brn	45.00	45.00

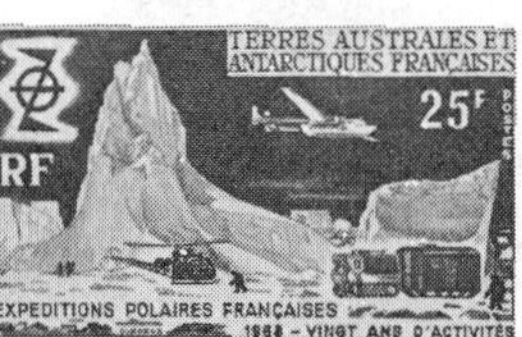

Polar Camp with Helicopter, Plane and Snocat Tractor A15

1969, Mar. 17 Engraved *Perf. 13*

33	A15	25fr Prus bl, lt grnsh bl & brn red	11.50	11.50

20 years of French Polar expeditions.

ILO Issue

Common Design Type

1970, Jan. 1 Engraved *Perf. 13*

35	CD131	20fr org, dk bl & brn	9.00	9.00

U.P.U. Headquarters Issue

Common Design Type

1970, May 20 Engraved *Perf. 13*

36	CD133	50fr bl, plum & ol bis	22.50	22.50

Ice Fish—A16

Fish: Nos. 38–43, Antarctic cods, various species. 135fr, Zanchlorhynchus spinifer.

1971 Engraved *Perf. 13*

37	A16	5fr brt grn, ind & org	65	65
38	A16	10fr redsh brn & dp vio	90	90
39	A16	20fr dp cl, brt grn & org	1.50	1.50
40	A16	22fr pur, brn ol & mag	1.15	1.15
41	A16	25fr grn, ind & org	1.75	1.75
42	A16	30fr sep, gray & bl vio	3.00	3.00
43	A16	35fr sl grn, dk brn & ocher	2.25	2.25
44	A16	135fr Prus bl, dp org & ol grn	4.50	4.50
		Nos. 37-44 (8)	15.70	15.70

Issue dates: Nos. 37–39, 41–42, Jan. 1; Nos. 40, 43–44, Dec. 22.

Map of Antarctica
A17

Microzetia Mirabilis
A18

1971, Dec. 22

45	A17	75fr red	32.50	32.50

Tenth anniversary of the Antarctic Treaty pledging peaceful uses of and scientific co-operation in Antarctica.

1972

Insects: 15fr, Christiansenia dreuxi. 22f, Phtirocoris antarcticus. 30fr, Antarctophytosus atriceps. 40fr, Paractora drenxi. 140fr, Pringleophaga Kerguelenensis.

46	A18	15fr cl, org & brn	1.10	1.10
47	A18	22fr vio bl, sl grn & yel	1.40	1.40
48	A18	25fr grn, rose lil & pur	3.00	3.00
49	A18	30fr bl & multi	2.25	2.25
50	A18	40fr dk brn, ocher & blk	2.50	2.50
51	A18	140fr bl, emer & brn	6.25	6.25
		Nos. 46-51 (6)	16.50	16.50

Issue dates: Nos. 48, 50–51, Jan. 3; Nos. 46–47, 49, Dec. 16.

De Gaulle Issue
Common Design Type

Designs: 50fr, Gen. de Gaulle, 1940. 100fr, Pres. de Gaulle, 1970.

1972, Feb. 1 Engraved *Perf. 13*

52	CD134	50fr brt grn & blk	9.00	9.00
53	CD134	100fr brt grn & blk	13.00	13.00

First anniversary of death of Charles de Gaulle (1890–1970), president of France.

Kerguelen Cabbage
A19

Designs: 61fr, Azorella selago (horiz.). 87fr, Acaena ascendens (horiz.).

1972–73

54	A19	45fr dl red, ultra & sl grn	2.75	2.75
55	A19	61fr multi ('73)	1.85	1.85
56	A19	87fr multi ('73)	2.25	2.25

Issue dates: 45fr, Dec. 18, 1972; others, Dec. 13, 1973.

Mailship Sapmer and Map of Amsterdam Island—A20

1974, Dec. 31 Engraved *Perf. 13*

57	A20	75fr bl, blk & dk brn	3.75	3.75

25th anniversary of postal service.

Antarctic Tern
A21

Designs: 50c, Antarctic petrel. 90c, Sea lioness. 1fr, Weddell seal. 1.20fr, Kerguelen cormorant (vert.). 1.40fr, Gentoo penguin (vert.).

1976, Jan. Engraved *Perf. 13*

58	A21	40c multi	75	75
59	A21	50c multi	1.00	1.00
60	A21	90c multi	2.00	2.00
61	A21	1fr multi	3.75	3.75
62	A21	1.20fr multi	4.50	4.50
63	A21	1.40fr multi	6.75	6.75
		Nos. 58-63 (6)	18.75	18.75

James Clark Ross
A22

James Cook
A23

Design: 30c, Climbing Mount Ross.

1976, Dec. 16 Engr. *Perf. 13*

64	A22	30c multi	2.25	2.25
65	A22	3fr multi	4.50	4.50

First climbing of Mount Ross, Kerguelen Island, by James Clark Ross, Jan. 5, 1875.

1976, Dec. 16

66	A23	70c multi	12.50	12.50

Bicentenary of Capt. Cook's voyage past Kerguelen Island. See No. C46.

Commerson's Dolphins
A24

Design: 1.10fr, Blue whale.

1977, Feb. 1 Engraved *Perf. 13*

67	A24	1.10fr bl & ind	1.75	1.75
68	A24	1.50fr multi	3.50	3.50

Macrocystis Algae—A25

Salmon Hatchery—A26

Magga Dan—A27

Designs: 70c, Durvillea algae. 90c, Albatross. 1fr, Underwater sampling and scientists (vert.). 1.40fr, Thala Dan and penguins.

1977, Dec. 20 Engr. *Perf. 13*

69	A25	40c ol brn & bis	35	35
70	A26	50c dk bl & pur	40	40
71	A25	70c blk, grn & brn	60	60
72	A26	90c grn, brt bl & brn	55	55
73	A27	1fr slate	70	70
74	A27	1.20fr multi	1.00	1.00
75	A27	1.40fr multi	1.20	1.20
		Nos. 69-75 (7)	4.80	4.80

See Nos. 77–79.

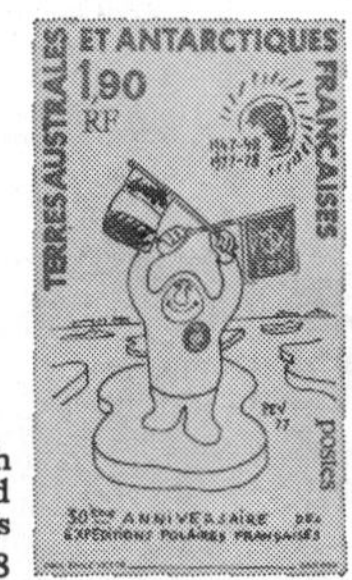

Explorer with French and Expedition Flags
A28

1977, Dec. 24

76	A28	1.90fr multi	2.50	2.50

French Polar expeditions, 1947–48, 30th anniversary.

Types of 1977

Designs: 40c, Forbin, destroyer. 50c Jeanne d'Arc, helicopter carrier. 1.40fr, Kerguelen cormorant.

1979, Jan. 1 Engr. *Perf. 13*

77	A27	40c blk & bl	1.25	1.25
78	A27	50c blk & bl	1.40	1.40
79	A26	1.40fr multi	90	90

R. Rallier du Baty
A29

1979, Jan. 1

80	A29	1.20fr cit & ind	1.35	1.35

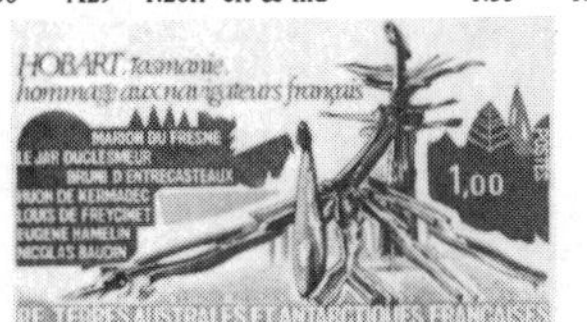

French Navigators Monument, Hobart—A30

1979, Jan. 1

81	A30	1fr multi	70	70

French navigators and explorers.

Petrel—A31

1979 Engraved *Perf. 13*

82	A31	70c *Rockhopper penguins*, vert.		
83	A31	1fr *shown*	55	55

Commandant Bourdais—A32

1979

84	A32	1.10fr *Doudart de Lagree*, vert.	72	72
85	A32	1.50fr *shown*	85	85

Admiral Antoine d'Entrecasteaux
A33

Sebastian de el Cano
A34

1979

86	A33	1.20fr multi	70	70

1979

Discovery of Amsterdam Island, 1522: 4fr, Victoria, horiz.

87	A34	1.40fr multi	90	90
88	A34	4fr multi	2.50	2.50

Adelie Penguins—A35

Adelie Penguin—A36

Sea Leopard—A37

1980, Dec. 15 **Engraved** ***Perf. 13***

89	A35	50c	rose vio	1.25	1.25
90	A36	60c	multi	90	90
91	A35	1.20fr	multi	1.25	1.25
92	A37	1.30fr	multi	65	65
93	A37	1.80fr	multi	90	90

20th Anniv. of Antarctic Treaty—A38

1981, June 23 **Engr.** ***Perf. 13***

94	A38	1.80fr	multi	*3.00*	*3.00*

Alouette II—A39

1981-82 **Engr.** ***Perf. 13***

95	A39	55c	brn & multi	30	30
96	A39	65c	bl & multi	32	32

Jean Loranchet—A40

1981

97	A40	1.40fr	multi	70	70

Landing Ship Le Gros Ventre, Kerguelen—A41

1883, Jan. 3 **Engr.** ***Perf. 13***

98	A41	55c	multi	30	30

Our Lady of the Winds Statue and Church, Kerguelen
A42

Martinde Vivies, Navigator
A43

1983, Jan. 3

99	A42	1.40fr	multi	70	70
100	A43	1.60fr	multi	80	80

Eaton's Ducks—A44

1983, Jan. 3

101	A44	1.50fr	multi	75	75
102	A44	1.80fr	multi	90	90

Trawler Austral—A45

1983, Jan. 3

103	A45	2.30fr	multi	1.15	1.15

AIR POST STAMPS

Emperor Penguins and Map of Antarctica—AP1

Engraved

1956, April 25 ***Perf. 13*** **Unwmkd.**

C1 AP1 50fr lt ol grn & dk grn 35.00 35.00
C2 AP1 100fr dl bl & ind 35.00 35.00

Wandering Albatross—AP2

1959, Sept. 14

C3 AP2 200fr brn red, bl & blk 25.00 25.00

Adélie Penguins—AP3

1963, Feb. 11 ***Perf. 13*** **Unwmkd.**

C4 AP3 50fr blk, dk bl & dp cl 42.50 42.50

Telstar Issue

Common Design Type

1963, Feb. 11

C5 CD111 50fr dp bl, ol & grn 27.50 27.50

Radio Towers, Adelie Penguins and IQSY Emblem AP4

1963, Dec. 16 **Engraved**

C6 AP4 100fr bl, ver & blk 120.00 120.00

International Quiet Sun Year, 1964–65.

Discovery of Adelie Land—AP5

1965, Jan. 20 **Engraved** ***Perf. 13***

C7 AP5 50fr bl & ind 120.00 120.00

125th anniversary of the discovery of Adelie Land by Dumont d'Urville.

ITU Issue

Common Design Type

1965, May 17 ***Perf. 13*** **Unwmkd.**

C8 CD120 30fr Prus bl, sep & dk car rose 225.00 225.00

Issued to commemorate the centenary of the International Telecommunication Union.

French Satellite A-1 Issue

Common Design Type

Designs: 25fr, Diamant rocket and launching installations. 30fr, A-1 satellite.

1966, Mar. 2 **Engraved** ***Perf. 13***

C9 CD121 25fr dk grn, choc & sl 16.50 16.50
C10 CD121 30fr choc, sl & dk grn 16.50 16.50
a. Strip of 2 + label 35.00 35.00

Issued to commemorate the launching of France's first satellite, Nov. 26, 1965. No. C10a contains one each of Nos. C9–C10 and label with dark green commemorative inscription. Each sheet contains 16 triptychs (2x8).

French Satellite D-1 Issue

Common Design Type

1966, Mar. 27

C11 CD122 50fr dk pur, lil & org 35.00 35.00

Issued to commemorate the launching of the D-1 satellite at Hammaguir, Algeria, Feb. 17, 1966.

Ionospheric Research Pylon, Adelie Land AP6

1966, Dec. 12

C12 AP6 25fr plum, bl & dk brn 16.50 16.50

Port aux Français, Emperor Penguin and Explorer—AP7

Design: 40fr, Aerial view of Saint Paul Island.

1968–69 **Engraved** ***Perf. 13***

C13 AP7 40fr brt bl & dk gray ('69) 30.00 30.00
C14 AP7 50fr lt ultra, dk grn & blk 115.00 115.00

Kerguelen Island and Rocket AP8

Design: 30fr, Adelie Land.

1968, Apr. 22 **Engraved** ***Perf. 13***

C15 AP8 25fr sl grn, dk brn & Prus bl 14.00 14.00
C16 AP8 30fr dk brn, sl grn & Prus bl 14.00 14.00
a. Strip of 2 + label 30.00 30.00

Issued to commemorate space explorations with Dragon rockets, 1967–68. No. C16a contains one each of Nos. C15–C16 and label with slate green and dark brown commemorative inscription.

Eiffel Tower, Antarctic Research Station, Ship from Paris Arms and Albatross AP9

1969, Jan. 13

C17 AP9 50fr brt bl 35.00 35.00

Issued to commemorate the 5th Consultative Meeting of the Antarctic Treaty Powers, Paris, Nov. 18, 1968.

Concorde Issue

Common Design Type

1969, Apr. 17

C18 CD129 85fr ind & bl 37.50 37.50

Map of Amsterdam Island AP10

Map of Kerguelen Island—AP11

Coat of Arms AP12

Designs: 50fr, Possession Island. 200fr, Point Geology Archipelago.

1969–71 **Engraved** ***Perf. 13***

C19 AP10 30fr brn ('70) 5.00 5.00
C20 AP11 50fr sl grn, bl & dk red ('70) 11.00 11.00
C21 AP11 100fr bl & blk 10.00 10.00
C22 AP10 200fr sl grn, brn & Prus bl ('71) 20.00 20.00
C23 AP12 500fr pck bl 15.00 15.00
Nos. C19-C23 (5) 61.00 61.00

The 30fr commemorates the 20th anniversary of the Amsterdam Island Meteorological Station.

Issue dates: 30fr , Mar. 27, 1970; 50fr, Dec. 22, 1970; 100fr, 500fr, Dec. 21, 1969; 200fr, Jan. 1, 1971.

Port-aux-Français, 1970—AP13

Design: 40fr, Port-aux-Français, 1950.

1971, Mar. 9 **Engraved** ***Perf. 13***

C24 AP13 40fr bl, ocher & sl grn 5.50 5.50
C25 AP13 50fr bl, grn ol & sl grn 6.50 6.50
a. Strip of 2 + label 12.50 12.50

20th anniversary of Port-aux-Françai_ on Kerguelen Island. No. C25a contains one each of Nos. C24–C25 and label with blue and brown olive commemorative inscription.

Marquis de Castries Taking Possession of Crozet Island, 1772—AP14

Design: 250fr, Fleur-de-lis flag raising on Kerguelen Island.

1972 **Engraved** ***Perf. 13***

C26 AP14 100fr black 9.50 9.50
C27 AP14 250fr blk & dk brn 13.00 13.00

Bicentenary of the discovery of the Crozet and Kerguelen Islands. Issue dates: 100fr, Jan. 24; 250fr, Feb. 23.

M. S. Galliéni—AP15

1973, Jan. 25 **Engr.** ***Perf. 13***

C28 AP15 100fr blk & bl 13.00 13.00

Exploration voyages of the Galliéni.

"Le Mascarin," 1772—AP16

Sailing Ships: 145fr, "L'Astrolabe," 1840. 150fr, "Le Rolland," 1774. 185fr, "La Victoire," 1522.

1973, Dec. 13 Engraved *Perf. 13*

C29	AP16	120fr brn ol	3.00	3.00
C30	AP16	145fr brt ultra	3.50	3.50
C31	AP16	150fr slate	4.00	4.00
C32	AP16	185fr ocher	4.50	4.50

Ships used in exploring Antarctica.
See Nos. C37–C38.

Alfred Faure Base—AP17

Design: Nos. C33–C35 show panoramic view of Alfred Faure Base.

1974, Jan. 7 Engraved *Perf. 13*

C33	AP17	75fr Prus bl, ultra & brn	2.75	2.75
C34	AP17	110fr Prus bl, ultra & brn	3.25	3.25
C35	AP17	150fr Prus bl, ultra & brn	4.75	4.75
		Triptych (Nos. C33-C35)	12.50	12.50

10th anniversary of the Alfred Faure Antarctic Base. Nos. C33–C35 printed se-tenant.

Penguin, Map of Antarctica, Letters AP18

1974, Oct. 9 Engraved *Perf. 13*

C36	AP18	150fr multi	4.50	4.50

Centenary of Universal Postal Union.

Ship Type of 1973

Designs: 100fr, "Le Français." 200fr, "Pourquoi-pas?"

1974, Dec. 16 Engraved *Perf. 13*

C37	AP16	100fr brt bl	2.50	2.50
C38	AP16	200fr dk car rose	4.00	4.00

Ships used in exploring Antarctica.

Rockets over Kerguelen Islands—AP19

Design: 90fr, Northern lights over map of northern coast of Russia.

1975, Jan. 26 Engraved *Perf. 13*

C39	AP19	45fr pur & multi	1.75	1.75
C40	AP19	90fr pur & multi	1.75	1.75
a.		Strip of 2 + label	3.50	3.50

Franco-Soviet magnetosphere research. No. C40a contains one each of Nos. C39–C40, and label with red inscription and indigo design. Sheets contain 5 No. C40a.

"La Curieuse"—AP20

Ships: 2.70fr, Commandant Charcot. 4fr, Marion-Dufresne.

1976, Jan. Engraved *Perf. 13*

C41	AP20	1.90fr multi	1.50	1.50
C42	AP20	2.70fr multi	2.50	2.50
C43	AP20	4fr red & multi	3.00	3.00

Dumont D'Urville Base, 1956—AP21

Design: 4fr, Dumont D'Urville Base, 1976, Adelie Land.

1976, Jan.

C44	AP21	1.20fr multi	1.25	1.25
C45	AP21	4fr multi	3.75	3.75
a.		Strip of 2 + label	5.50	5.50

20th anniversary of the Dumont D'Urville Antarctic Base. No. C45a contains one each of Nos. C44–C45 and label with map of Antarctica and penguins.

Capt. Cook's Ships Passing Kerguelen Island—AP22

1976, Dec. 31 Engr. *Perf. 13*

C46	AP22	3.50fr sl & bl	8.00	8.00

Bicentenary of Capt. Cook's voyage past Kerguelen Island.

Sea Lion and Cub AP23

1977–79 Engr. *Perf. 13*

C47	AP23	4fr dk bl & grn ('79)	2.50	2.50
C48	AP23	10fr multi	11.50	11.50

Satellite Survey, Kerguelen—AP24

Designs: 70c, Geophysical laboratory. 1.90fr, Satellite and Kerguelen tracking station. 3fr, Satellites, Adelie Land.

1977–79 Engr. *Perf. 13*

C49	AP24	50c multi ('79)	45	45
C50	AP24	70c multi ('79)	60	60
C51	AP24	1.90fr multi ('79)	1.25	1.25
C52	AP24	2.70fr multi ('78)	2.50	2.50
C53	AP24	3fr multi	3.50	3.50
		Nos. C49-C53 (5)	8.30	8.30

Elephant Seals AP25

1979, Jan. 1

C54	AP25	10fr blk & bl	5.50	5.50

Challenger—AP26

1979, Jan. 1

C55	AP26	2.70fr blk & bl	2.00	2.00

Antarctic expeditions to Crozet and Kerguelen Islands, 1972–1976.

La Recherche and L'Esperance—AP27

1979

C56	AP27	1.90fr dp bl	90	90

Arrival of d'Entrecasteaux and Kermadec at Amsterdam Island, Mar. 28, 1792.

Lion Rock—AP28

1979

C57	AP28	90c multi	58	58

Natural Arch, Kerguelen Island, 1840—AP29

1979

C58	AP29	2.70fr multi	1.40	1.40

Phylica Nitida, Amsterdam Island—AP30

1979

C59	AP30	10fr multi	4.50	4.50

Charles de Gaulle, 10th Anniversary of Death—AP31

1980, Nov. 9 Engraved *Perf. 13*

C60	AP31	5.40fr multi	10.00	10.00

HB-40 Castor Truck and Trailer—AP32

1980, Dec. 15

C61	AP32	2.40fr multi	1.10	1.10

Supply Ship Saint Marcouf—AP33

1980, Dec. 15

C62	AP33	3.50fr *shown*	1.25	1.25
C63	AP33	7.30fr *Icebreaker Norsel*	3.25	3.25

Glacial Landscape, Dumont D'Urville Sea—AP34

Chionis—AP35

Adele Dumont D'Urville (1798-1842)—AP36

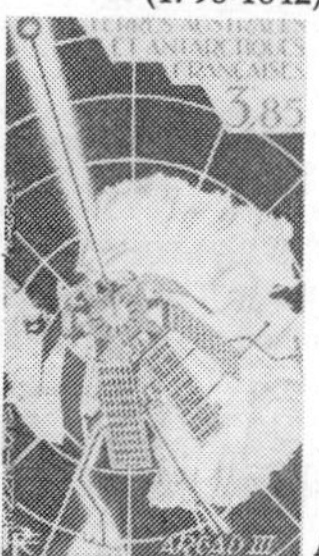

Arcad III—AP37

25th Anniv. of Charcot Station—AP38

Antares—AP39

1981-82 Engr. *Perf. 13, 12½x13 (2fr)*

C64	AP34	1.30fr multi	65	65
C65	AP35	1.50fr black	75	75
C66	AP36	2fr blk & lt brn	1.00	1.00
C67	AP37	3.85fr multi	2.00	2.00
C68	AP38	5fr multi	2.50	2.50
C69	AP39	8.40fr multi	4.25	4.25
		Nos. C64-C69 (6)	11.15	11.15

PHILEXFRANCE '82 Stamp Exhibition, Paris, June 11-21—AP40

1982, June 11 Engr. *Perf. 13*

C70	AP40	8fr multi	4.00	4.00

French Overseas Possessions Week, Sept. 18-25—AP41

1982, Sept. 17 Engr. *Perf. 13*

C71	AP41	5fr Commandant Charcot	2.50	2.50

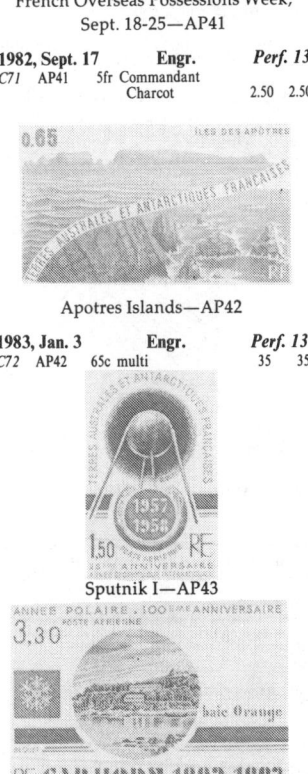

Apotres Islands—AP42

1983, Jan. 3 Engr. *Perf. 13*

C72	AP42	65c multi	35	35

Sputnik I—AP43

Orange Bay Base, Cape Horn, 1883—AP44

Intl. Polar Year Centenary and 24th Anniv. of Intl. Geophysical Year: 5.20fr, Scoresby Sound Base, Greenland, 1983. Nos. C73-C75 se-tenant.

1983, Jan. 3

C73	AP43	1.50fr multi	75	75
C74	AP44	3.30fr multi	1.65	1.65
C75	AP44	5.20fr multi	2.60	2.60

AP45

1983, Jan. 3

C76	AP45	4.55fr dk bl	2.30	2.30

Abstract, by G. Mathieu—AP46

1983, Jan. 3 Photo. *Perf. 13x13½*

C77	AP46	25fr multi	12.50	12.50

FRENCH SUDAN

(frĕnch sōō·dăn'; -dän')

LOCATION—In northwest Africa, north of French Guinea and Ivory Coast.

GOVT.—Former French Colony.

AREA—590,966 sq. mi.

POP.—3,794,270 (1941).

CAPITAL—Bamako.

In 1899 French Sudan was abolished as a separate colony and was divided among Dahomey, French Guinea, Ivory Coast, Senegal and Senegambia and Niger. Issues for French Sudan were resumed in 1921.

From 1906 to 1921 a part of this territory was known as Upper Senegal and Niger. A part of Upper Volta was added in 1933. See Mali.

100 Centimes = 1 Franc

Navigation and Commerce
A1 A2

Stamps of French Colonies, Surcharged in Black.

1894 *Perf. 14x13½* Unwmkd.

1	A1	15c on 75c car, *rose*	*1,850.*	*1,350.*
2	A1	25c on 1fr brnz grn, *straw*	*2,250.*	*1,000.*

The imperforate stamp like No. 1 was made privately in Paris from a fragment of the lithographic stone which had been used in the Colony for surcharging No. 1.
Counterfeit surcharges exist.

1894-1900 Typographed

Name of colony in Blue or Carmine.

3	A2	1c *lil bl*	80	80
4	A2	2c brn, *buff*	90	90
5	A2	4c cl, *lav*	2.25	2.25
6	A2	5c grn, *grnsh*	3.25	3.00
7	A2	10c *lavender*	7.25	7.25
8	A2	10c red ('00)	1.50	1.50
9	A2	15c bl, quadrille paper	2.25	2.00
10	A2	15c gray, *lt gray* ('00)	3.25	3.25
11	A2	20c red, *grn*	12.00	11.00
12	A2	25c *rose*	12.00	11.00
13	A2	25c bl ('00)	2.75	2.75
14	A2	30c brn, *bis*	21.00	16.00
15	A2	40c red, *straw*	13.00	11.00
16	A2	50c car, *rose*	22.50	21.00
17	A2	50c brn, *az* ('00)	4.50	4.50
18	A2	75c dp vio, *org*	17.50	17.50
19	A2	1fr brnz grn, *straw*	3.75	3.75
		Nos. 3-19 (17)	130.45	119.45

Camel and Rider
A3

Stamps of Upper Senegal and Niger Overprinted in Black.

1921-30 *Perf. 13½x14*

21	A3	1c brn vio & vio	6	6
22	A3	2c dk gray & dl vio	6	6

23	A3	4c blk & bl	6	6
24	A3	5c ol brn & dk brn	10	10
25	A3	10c yel grn & bl grn	10	10
26	A3	10c red vio & bl ('25)	10	10
27	A3	15c red brn & org	8	8
28	A3	15c yel grn & dp grn ('25)	10	10
29	A3	15c org brn & vio ('27)	45	45
30	A3	20c brn vio & blk	10	10
31	A3	25c blk & bl grn	22	22
a.		Booklet pane of 4		
32	A3	30c red org & rose	22	22
33	A3	30c bl grn & blk ('26)	12	12
34	A3	30c dl grn & bl grn ('28)	60	60
35	A3	35c rose & vio	10	10
36	A3	40c gray & rose	30	22
37	A3	45c bl & ol brn	22	18
38	A3	50c ultra & bl	30	25
39	A3	50c red org & bl ('26)	32	18
40	A3	60c vio, *pnksh* ('26)	15	12
41	A3	65c bis & pale bl ('28)	45	45
42	A3	75c org & ol brn	28	28
43	A3	90c brn red & pink ('30)	2.25	2.25
44	A3	1fr dk brn & dl vio	45	40
45	A3	1.10fr gray lil & red vio ('28)	80	80
46	A3	1.50fr dp bl & bl ('30)	2.25	2.25
47	A3	2fr grn & bl	75	70
48	A3	3fr red vio ('30)	4.00	4.00
a.		Double overprint	65.00	
49	A3	5fr vio & blk	2.25	2.25
		Nos. 21-49 (29)	17.24	16.80

Type of 1921 Surcharged **60 = 60**

1922

50	A3	60c on 75c vio, *pnksh*	22	22

Stamps and Type of 1921-30 Surcharged with New Values and Bars.

1925–27

51	A3	25c on 45c bl & ol brn ('25)	22	22
52	A3	65c on 75c org & ol brn ('25)	45	40
53	A3	85c on 2fr grn & bl ('25)	60	55
54	A3	85c on 5fr vio & blk ('25)	60	55
55	A3	90c on 75c brn red & sal pink ('27)	80	70
56	A3	1.25fr on 1fr dp bl & lt bl (R) ('26)	45	40
57	A3	1.50fr on 1fr dp bl & ultra ('27)	45	40
58	A3	3fr on 5fr dl red & brn org ('27)	1.50	90
59	A3	10fr on 5fr brn red & bl grn ('27)	8.00	6.25
60	A3	20fr on 5fr vio & ver ('27)	11.00	9.00
		Nos. 51-60 (10)	24.07	19.37

Sudanese Woman A4

Entrance to the Residency at Djenné A5

Sudanese Boatman A6

1931–40 Typo. *Perf. 13x14.*

61	A4	1c dk red & blk	5	5
62	A4	2c dp bl & org	6	6
63	A4	3c dk red & blk ('40)	6	6
64	A4	4c gray lil & rose	6	6
65	A4	5c ind & grn	10	10
66	A4	10c ol grn & rose	6	6
67	A4	15c blk & brt vio	10	10
68	A4	20c hn brn & lt bl	10	10
69	A4	25c red vio & lt red	10	6
70	A5	30c grn & lt grn	22	10
71	A5	30c dk bl & red org ('40)	12	12
72	A5	35c ol grn & grn ('38)	10	8
73	A5	40c ol grn & pink	10	10
74	A5	45c dk bl & red org	30	28
75	A5	45c ol grn & grn ('40)	15	15
76	A5	50c red & blk	6	6
77	A5	55c ultra & car ('38)	22	22
78	A5	60c brt bl & brn ('40)	32	32
79	A5	65c brt vio & blk	10	10
80	A5	70c vio bl & car rose ('40)	12	12
81	A5	75c brt bl & ol brn	75	60
82	A5	80c car & brn ('38)	10	10
83	A5	90c dp red & red org	30	28
84	A5	90c brt vio & sl blk ('39)	18	18
85	A5	1fr ind & grn	3.00	50
86	A5	1fr rose red ('38)	1.50	32
87	A5	1fr car & brn ('40)	12	12
88	A6	1.25fr vio & dl vio ('33)	30	18
89	A6	1.25fr red ('39)	18	18
90	A6	1.40fr brt vio & blk ('40)	18	18
91	A6	1.50fr dk bl & ultra	22	10
92	A6	1.60fr brn & dp bl ('40)	18	18
93	A6	1.75fr dk brn & dp bl ('33)	22	22
94	A6	1.75fr vio bl ('38)	22	22
95	A6	2fr org brn & grn	30	10
96	A6	2.25fr vio bl & ultra ('39)	30	30
97	A6	2.50fr lt brn ('40)	38	38
98	A6	3fr Prus grn & brn	30	10
99	A6	5fr red & blk	60	38
100	A6	10fr dl bl & grn	80	65
101	A6	20fr red vio & brn	1.00	80
		Nos. 61-101 (41)	13.63	8.37

Colonial Exposition Issue.

Common Design Types

1931 Engraved *Perf. 12½*

Name of Country Printed in Black.

102	CD70	40c dp grn	1.00	1.00
103	CD71	50c violet	1.00	1.00
104	CD72	90c red org	1.00	1.00
105	CD73	1.50fr dl bl	1.00	1.00

Paris International Exposition Issue.

Common Design Types

1937 *Perf. 13.*

106	CD74	20c dp vio	55	55
107	CD75	30c dk grn	55	55
108	CD76	40c car rose	55	55
109	CD77	50c dk brn	55	55
110	CD78	90c red	55	55
111	CD79	1.50fr ultra	55	55
		Nos. 106-111 (6)	3.30	3.30

Colonial Arts Exhibition Issue.

Souvenir Sheet.

Common Design Type

1937 Engraved *Imperf.*

112	CD77	3fr mag & blk	2.00	2.00

Sheet size: 118x99mm.

Caillie Issue

Common Design Type

1939 *Perf. 12½x12.*

113	CD81	90c org brn & org	35	35
114	CD81	2fr brt vio	35	35
115	CD81	2.25fr ultra & dk bl	35	35

Centenary of the death of René Caillié (1799–1838), French explorer.

New York World's Fair Issue.

Common Design Type

1939, May 10

116	CD82	1.25fr car lake	45	45
117	CD82	2.25fr ultra	45	45

Entrance to the Residency at Djenné and Marshal Pétain
A7

1941 Engraved *Perf. 12x12½.*

118	A7	1fr green	22	22
119	A7	2.50fr blue	22	22

Stamps of types A4 and A5 without "RF" were issued in 1943 and 1944 by the Vichy Government, but were not placed on sale in the colony.

Stamps of French Sudan were superseded by those of French West Africa.

SEMI-POSTAL STAMPS.

Curie Issue

Common Design Type

Engraved.

1938 *Perf. 13* Unwmkd.

B1	CD80	1.75fr +50c brt ultra	5.00	5.00

French Revolution Issue

Common Design Type

1939 Photogravure.

Name and Value Typo. in Black.

B2	CD83	45(c) +25(c) grn	3.00	3.00
B3	CD83	70(c) +30(c) brn	3.00	3.00
B4	CD83	90(c) +35(c) red org	3.00	3.00
B5	CD83	1.25fr +1fr rose pink	3.00	3.00
B6	CD83	2.25fr +2fr bl	3.00	3.00
		Nos. B2-B6 (5)	15.00	15.00

Stamps of 1931–40, Surcharged in Black or Red **SECOURS + 1 fr. NATIONAL**

1941 *Perf. 13x14*

B7	A5	50c +1fr red & blk (R)	75	75
B8	A5	80c +2fr car & brn (Bk)	3.25	3.25
B9	A6	1.50fr +2fr dk bl & ultra (Bk)	3.25	3.25
B10	A6	2fr +3fr org brn & grn (Bk)	3.25	3.25

Common Design Type and

Native Officer SP1

Aviation Officer SP2

1941 Photogravure *Perf. 13½*

B11	SP1	1fr +1fr red	45	
B12	CD86	1.50fr +3fr cl	45	
B13	SP2	2.50fr +1fr bl	45	

The surtax was for the defense of the colonies.

Nos. B11–B13 were issued by the Vichy government and were not placed on sale in the colony.

Stamps of type A7, surcharged "OEUVRES COLONIALES" and new values, were issued in 1944 by the Vichy Government, but were not placed on sale in the colony.

AIR POST STAMPS.

Common Design Type

Engraved.

1940 *Perf. 12½x12.* Unwmkd.

C1	CD85	1.90fr ultra	18	18
C2	CD85	2.90fr dk red	18	18
C3	CD85	4.50fr dk gray grn	38	38
C4	CD85	4.90fr yel bis	38	38
C5	CD85	6.90fr dp org	38	38
		Nos. C1-C5 (5)	1.50	1.50

Common Design Types

1942

C6	CD88	50c car & bl	8	30
C7	CD88	1fr brn & blk	12	
C8	CD88	2fr dk grn & red brn	15	
C9	CD88	3fr dk bl & scar	22	
C10	CD88	5fr vio & brn red	22	

Frame Engraved, Center Typographed.

C11	CD89	10fr ultra, ind & gray blk	22	
C12	CD89	20fr rose car, mag & lt vio	22	
C13	CD89	50fr yel grn, dl grn & dl bl	60	90
		Nos. C6-C13 (8)	1.83	

There is doubt whether Nos. C7–C12 were officially placed in use.

AIR POST SEMI-POSTAL STAMPS.

Stamps of type of Dahomey V1, V2, V3 and V4 inscribed "Soudan Frcais", "Soudan" or "Soudan Francais" were issued in 1942 by the Vichy Government, but were not placed on sale in the colony.

POSTAGE DUE STAMPS.

D1

D2

Postage Due Stamps of
Upper Senegal and Niger
Overprinted in Black.

Typographed.

.921	*Perf. 14x13½*		Unwmkd.	
	D1	5c green	18	18
	D1	10c rose	25	25
	D1	15c gray	25	25
	D1	20c brown	32	32
	D1	30c blue	30	30
	D1	50c black	50	50
	D1	60c orange	60	60
	D1	1fr violet	75	75
		Nos. J1-J8 (8)	3.15	3.15

Type of 1921 Issue Surcharged **2F.**

1927				
	D1	2fr on 1fr lil rose	2.40	2.40
0	D1	3fr on 1fr org brn	2.40	2.40

1931				
1	D2	5c green	6	6
2	D2	10c rose	6	6
3	D2	15c gray	7	7
4	D2	20c dk brn	8	8
5	D2	30c dk bl	10	10
6	D2	50c black	12	12
7	D2	60c dp org	22	22
8	D2	1fr violet	40	40
9	D2	2fr lil rose	50	50
20	D2	3fr red brn	50	50
		Nos. J11-J20 (10)	2.11	2.11

FRENCH WEST AFRICA

(frĕnch wĕst′ ăf′rĭ-kȧ)

LOCATION—Northwestern Africa.

GOVT.—Former French colonial administrative unit.

AREA—1,821,768 sq. mi.

POP.—18,777,163 (est.).

CAPITAL—Dakar.

French West Africa comprised the former colonies of Senegal, French Guinea, Ivory Coast, Dahomey, French Sudan, Mauritania, Niger and Upper Volta.

In 1958, these former colonies became republics, eventually issuing their own stamps. Until the republic issues appeared, stamps of French West Africa continued in use. The Senegal and Sudanese Republics issued stamps jointly as the Federation of Mali, starting in 1959.

50 fr.

Senegal No. 156
Surcharged in Red

1943	*Perf. 12½x12.*		Unwmkd.	
	A30	1.50fr on 65c dk vio	22	22
	A30	5.50fr on 65c dk vio	30	30
	A30	50fr on 65c dk vio	1.10	65

Mauritania No. 91 Surcharged in Red

5 fr.

1944			*Perf. 13*	
	A7	3.50fr on 65c dp grn	12	12
	A7	4fr on 65c dp grn	22	15
	A7	5fr on 65c dp grn	38	30
	A7	10fr on 65c dp grn	40	28
		Nos. 1-7 (7)	2.74	2.02

Common Design Types

pictured in section at front of book.

Senegal Nos. 143, 148 and 188
Surcharged with New Values
in Black or Orange.

1944	*Perf. 12½x12*			
8	A29	1.50fr on 15c blk (O)	22	22
9	A29	4.50fr on 15c blk (O)	30	30
10	A29	5.50fr on 2c brn	60	45
11	A29	10fr on 15c blk (O)	75	60
12	CD81	20fr on 90c org brn & org	60	38
13	CD81	50fr on 90c org brn & org	1.10	60

Mauritania No. 109
Surcharged in Black.

14	A6	15fr on 90c org brn & org	38	30
		Nos. 8-14 (7)	3.95	2.85

Eboue Issue.

Common Design Type

1945		Engraved	*Perf. 13*	
15	CD91	2fr black	32	32
16	CD91	25fr Prus grn	80	80

Nos. 15 and 16 exist imperforate.

Colonial Soldiers
A1

1945		Lithographed	*Perf. 12*	
17	A1	10c ind & buff	6	4
18	A1	30c ol & yel	6	5
19	A1	40c bl & buff	15	15
20	A1	50c red org & gray	6	6
21	A1	60c ol brn & bl	6	6
22	A1	70c mag & cit	20	20
23	A1	80c bl grn & pale lem	12	12
24	A1	1fr brn vio & cit	5	5
25	A1	1.20fr gray brn & cit	1.50	1.10
26	A1	1.50fr choc & pink	5	5
27	A1	2fr ocher & gray	30	18
28	A1	2.40fr red & gray	45	40
29	A1	3fr brn red & yelsh	12	5
30	A1	4fr ultra & pink	12	8
31	A1	4.50fr org brn & yelsh	12	12
32	A1	5fr dk pur & yelsh	12	8
33	A1	10fr ol grn & pink	70	12
34	A1	15fr org & yel	90	45
35	A1	20fr sl grn & grnsh	90	60
		Nos. 17-35 (19)	6.04	3.96

Rifle Dance, Mauritania
A2

Shelling Coconuts, Togo
A6

Bamako Dike, French Sudan
A3

Trading Canoe, Niger River
A4

Oasis of Bilma, Niger
A5

Kouandé Weaving, Dahomey
A7

Donkey Caravan, Senegal
A8

Crocodile and Hippopotamus, Ivory Coast
A9

Bamako Fountain, French Sudan
A11

Gathering Coconuts, French Guinea
A10

Peul Woman of Djenné
A12

Bamako Market
A13

Dahomey Laborer
A14

Woman of Mauritania
A15

Fula Woman, French Guinea
A16

Djenné Mosque, French Sudan
A17

Monorail Train, Senegal
A18

Agni Woman, Ivory Coast
A19

Azwa Women at Niger River
A20

Engraved.

1947	*Perf. 12½*		Unwmkd.	
36	A2	10c blue	3	3
37	A3	30c red brn	4	4
38	A4	40c gray grn	4	4
39	A5	50c red brn	4	4
40	A6	60c gray blk	28	28
41	A7	80c brn vio	35	30
42	A8	1fr maroon	6	6
43	A9	1.20fr dk bl grn	45	30
44	A10	1.50fr ultra	60	50
45	A11	2fr red org	6	6
46	A12	3fr chocolate	28	15
47	A13	3.60fr brn red	60	45
48	A14	4fr dp bl	12	12
49	A15	5fr dk gray grn	12	12
50	A16	6fr dk bl	22	12
51	A17	10fr brn red	45	12
52	A18	15fr sepia	50	5
53	A19	20fr chocolate	50	5
54	A20	25fr grnsh blk	90	15
		Nos. 36-54 (19)	5.64	2.98

Types of 1947.

1948 Re-engraved.

55	A6	60c brn ol	35	18
56	A12	3fr chocolate	18	12

Nos. 40 and 46 are inscribed "TOGO" in lower margin. Inscription omitted on Nos. 55 and 56.

Imperforates

Most stamps of French West Africa from 1949 onward exist imperforate in issued and trial colors, and also in small presentation sheets in issued colors.

Military Medal Issue.

Common Design Type

Engraved and Typographed.

1952, Dec. 1 *Perf. 13*

57	CD101	15fr blk, grn, yel & blk brn	2.75	2.75

Treich Laplène and Map
A21

1952, Dec. 1 Engraved

58	A21	40fr brn lake	70	12

Issued to honor Marcel Treich Laplene, a leading contributor to the development of Ivory Coast.

Medical Laboratory
A22

1953, Nov. 18

59	A22	15fr brn, dk bl grn & blk brn	50	5

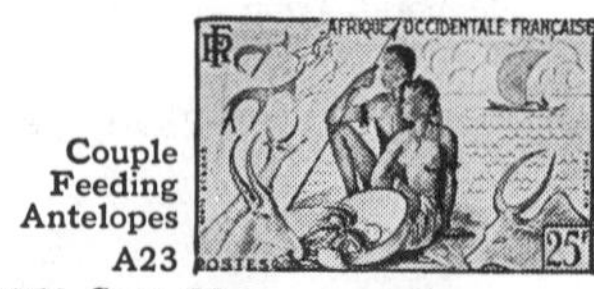

Couple Feeding Antelopes
A23

1954, Sept. 20

60	A23	25fr multi	60	8

Gov. Noel Eugène Ballay
A24

1954, Nov. 29

61	A24	8fr ind & brn	60	32

Chimpanzee
A25

Giant Pangolin
A26

1955, May 2 *Perf. 13* **Unwmkd.**

62	A25	5fr dk gray & dk brn	60	32
63	A26	8fr dk brn & bl grn	60	32

Issued in connection with the International Exhibition for Wildlife Protection, Paris, May 1955.

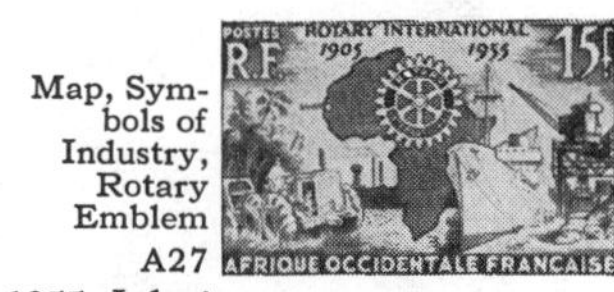

Map, Symbols of Industry, Rotary Emblem
A27

1955, July 4

64	A27	15fr dk bl	60	35

Issued to commemorate the 50th anniversary of the founding of Rotary International.

FIDES Issue

Mossi Railroad Upper Volta
A28

Designs: 1fr, Date grove, Mauritania. 2fr, Milo Bridge, French Guinea. 4fr, Cattle raising, Niger. 15fr, Farm machinery and landscape, Senegal. 17fr, Woman and Sansanding River, French Sudan. 20fr, Palm oil production, Dahomey. 30fr, Road construction, Ivory Coast.

1956 Engraved *Perf. 13x12½*

65	A28	1fr dk grn & dk bl grn	30	28
66	A28	2fr dk bl grn & bl	30	28
67	A28	3fr dk brn & red brn	45	40
68	A28	4fr dk car rose	60	22
69	A28	15fr ind & ultra	60	35
70	A28	17fr dk bl & ind	60	35
71	A28	20fr rose lake	90	38
72	A28	30fr dk pur & cl	90	45
		Nos. 65-72 (8)	4.65	2.71

See note after Cameroun No. 329.

Coffee Issue.

Coffee
A28a

1956, Oct. 22 *Perf. 13*

73	A28a	15fr dk bl grn	30	10

Mobile Leprosy Clinic and Maltese Cross
A29

1957, Mar. 11

74	A29	15fr dl red brn, pur & red	60	35

Issued in honor of the Knights of Malta.

Map of Africa
A30

1958, Feb. *Perf. 13* **Unwmkd.**

75	A30	20fr grnsh bl, blk & dl red brn	60	35

Issued to publicize the sixth International Congress for African Tourism at Dakar.

"Africa" and Communications Symbols
A31

1958, Mar. 15 Engraved

76	A31	15fr org, ultra & choc	60	35

Stamp Day. See No. 86.

Abidjan Bridge
A32

1958, Mar. 15

77	A32	20fr dk sl grn & grnsh bl	60	28

Bananas
A33

1958, May 19 *Perf. 13*

78	A33	20fr rose lil, dk grn & ol	55	15

Flower Issue

Common Design Type

Designs: 10fr, Gloriosa. 25fr, Adenopus. 30fr, Cyrtosperma. 40fr, Cistanche. 65fr, Crinum Moorei.

1958–59 Photogravure. *Perf. 12x12½*

79	CD104	10fr multi	35	15
80	CD104	25fr red, yel & grn ('59)	45	22
81	CD104	30fr multi	50	40
82	CD104	40fr blk brn, grn & yel ('59)	75	60
83	CD104	65fr multi	1.00	60
		Nos. 79-83 (5)	3.05	1.97

Moro Naba Sagha and Map
A34

1958, Nov. 1 Engraved *Perf. 13*

84	A34	20fr ol brn, car & vio	45	35

Issued to commemorate the 10th anniversary of the reestablishment of the Upper Volta territory.

Human Rights Issue

Common Design Type

1958, Dec. 10

85	CD105	20fr mar & dk bl	90	9

Type of 1958 Redrawn.

1959, Mar. 21 Engraved *Perf. 13*

86	A31	20fr red, grnsh bl & sl grn	90	7

Name of country omitted on No. 86; "RF" replaced by "CF," inscribed "Dakar-Abidjan."

Stamp Day.

SEMI-POSTAL STAMPS.

Red Cross Issue

Common Design Type

Photogravure.

1944 *Perf. 14½x14.* **Unwmkd.**

B1	CD90	5fr +20fr plum	2.75	2.7

The surtax was for the French Red Cross and national relief.

Type of France, 1945, Overprinted in Black **A O F**

1945 Engraved. *Perf. 13.*

B2	SP150	2fr +3fr org red	35	3

Tropical Medicine Issue

Common Design Type

1950, May 15 *Perf. 13*

B3	CD100	10fr +2fr red brn & sep	3.25	3.2

The surtax was for charitable work.

AIR POST STAMPS.

Common Design Type

Photogravure.

1945 *Perf. 14½x14* **Unwmkd.**

C1	CD87	5.50fr ultra	38	35
C2	CD87	50fr dk grn	1.40	35
C3	CD87	100fr plum	1.40	45

Victory Issue

Common Design Type

1946, May 8 Engr. *Perf. 12½*

C4	CD92	8fr violet	55	55

Chad to Rhine Issue

Common Design Types

1946, June 6

C5	CD93	5fr brn car	60	60
C6	CD94	10fr dp bl	60	60
C7	CD95	15fr brt vio	75	75
C8	CD96	20fr dk sl grn	90	90
C9	CD97	25fr ol brn	1.40	1.40
C10	CD98	50fr brown	1.75	1.75
		Nos. C5-C10 (6)	6.00	6.00

Antoine de Saint-Exupéry, Map and Natives
AP1

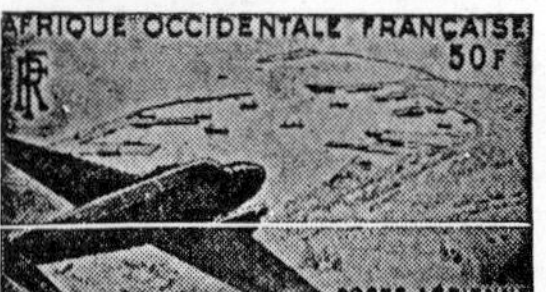

Plane over Dakar—AP2

Great White Egrets in Flight—AP3

Natives and Phantom Plane—AP4

1947, Mar. 24 Engraved

C11	AP1	8fr red brn	30	28
C12	AP2	50fr rose vio	1.25	28
C13	AP3	100fr ultra	4.50	2.00
C14	AP4	200fr sl gray	5.00	2.00

UPU Issue

Common Design Type

1949, July 4 *Perf. 13*

C15	CD99	25fr multi	4.25	4.25

Vridi Canal, Abidjan—AP5

1951, Nov. 5 *Perf. 13* **Unwmkd.**

C16	AP5	500fr red org, bl grn & dp ultra	12.50	2.25

Liberation Issue

Common Design Type

1954, June 6

C17	CD102	15fr ind & ultra	2.00	2.00

Logging—AP6

Designs: 100fr, Radiotelephone exchange. 200fr, Baobab trees.

1954, Sept. 20

C18	AP6	50fr ol grn & org brn	1.25	28
C19	AP6	100fr ind, dk brn & dk grn	1.75	45
C20	AP6	200fr bl grn, grnsh blk & brn lake	5.75	1.50

Gen. Louis Faidherbé and African Sharpshooter AP7

1957, July 20 *Perf. 13* **Unwmkd.**

C21	AP7	15fr ind & bl	1.00	1.00

Centenary of French African troops.

Gorée Island and Woman—AP8

Designs: 20fr, Map with planes and ships. 25fr, Village and modern city. 40fr, Seat of Council of French West Africa. 50fr, Worker, ship and peanut plant. 100fr, Bay of N'Gor.

1958, March 15 Engraved

C22	AP8	15fr blk brn, grn & vio	50	38
C23	AP8	20fr blk brn, dk bl & red brn	50	38
C24	AP8	25fr blk vio, bis & grn	50	38
C25	AP8	40fr dk bl, brn & grn	50	38
C26	AP8	50fr vio, brn & grn	90	55
C27	AP8	100fr brn, bl & grn	2.00	70
a.		Souvenir sheet	5.75	5.75
		Nos. C22-C27 (6)	4.90	2.77

Issued to commemorate the centenary of Dakar.

No. C27a measures 185x125mm. and contains one each of Nos. C22–C27, with picture of old Dakar in center and inscribed: "Centenaire de Dakar."

Woman Playing Native Harp AP9

1958, Dec. 1 *Perf. 13* **Unwmkd.**

C28	AP9	20fr red brn, blk & gray	60	40

Issued in connection with the inauguration of Nouakchot as capital of Mauritania.

POSTAGE DUE STAMPS.

D1

Engraved.

1947 *Perf. 13* **Unwmkd.**

J1	D1	10c red	8	8
J2	D1	30c dp org	8	8
J3	D1	50c grnsh blk	15	15
J4	D1	1fr carmine	15	15
J5	D1	2fr emerald	15	15
J6	D1	3fr red lil	18	18
J7	D1	4fr dp ultra	28	28
J8	D1	5fr red brn	75	75
J9	D1	10fr pck bl	1.10	1.10
J10	D1	20fr sepia	2.00	2.00
		Nos. J1-J10 (10)	4.92	4.92

OFFICIAL STAMPS

Mask

O1

Typographed.

1958 *Perf. 14x13* **Unwmkd.**

Various Masks.

O1	O1	1fr dk brn red	30	28
O2	O1	3fr brt grn	30	28
O3	O1	5fr crim rose	22	6
O4	O1	10fr lt ultra	30	6
O5	O1	20fr brt red	38	6
O6	O1	25fr purple	38	6
O7	O1	30fr green	45	40
O8	O1	45fr gray blk	60	45
O9	O1	50fr dk red	85	30
O10	O1	65fr brt ultra	1.10	45
O11	O1	100fr ol bis	1.90	35
O12	O1	200fr dp grn	4.50	1.00
		Nos. O1-O12 (12)	11.28	3.75

FUNCHAL

(fōōn·shäl')

LOCATION—A city and administrative district in the Madeira island group in the Atlantic Ocean northwest of Africa.

GOVT.—A part of the Republic of Portugal.

POP.—150,574 (1900).

Postage stamps of Funchal were superseded by those of Madeira. These, in turn, were displaced by the stamps of Portugal.

1000 Reis=1 Milreis

King Carlos

A1 A2

Perf. 11½, 12½, 13½

1892–93 Typographed **Unwmkd.**

1	A1	5r yellow	1.25	1.00
a.		Half used as 2½r on cover		25.00
b.		Perf. 11½	5.50	4.00
2	A1	10r red vio	1.20	1.10
3	A1	15r chocolate	2.50	1.50
4	A1	20r lavender	3.25	1.75
a.		Perf. 13½	6.50	4.50
5	A1	25r dk grn	2.50	1.25
6	A1	50r ultra	3.25	1.00
a.		Perf. 13½	7.50	2.00
7	A1	75r carmine	6.50	5.00
8	A1	80r yel grn	8.50	7.00
a.		Perf. 13½	12.50	10.00
9	A1	100r brn, *yel* ('93)	5.00	3.75
a.		Diagonal half used as 50r on cover		
10	A1	150r car, *rose* ('93)	27.50	20.00
11	A1	200r dk bl, *bl* ('93)	32.50	25.00
12	A1	300r dk bl, *sal* ('93)	37.50	25.00

The reprints of this issue have shiny white gum and clean-cut perforation 13½. The shades differ from those of the originals and the uncolored paper is thin. Price $1.50 each.

1897–1905 *Perf. 12*

Name and Value in Black except Nos. 25 and 34.

13	A2	2½r gray	20	20
14	A2	5r orange	25	22
15	A2	10r lt grn	25	22
16	A2	15r brown	3.50	2.50
17	A2	15r gray grn ('99)	2.00	1.75
18	A2	20r gray vio	60	40
19	A2	25r sea grn	1.75	50
20	A2	25r car rose ('99)	75	25
a.		Booklet pane of 6		
21	A2	50r dk bl	2.75	1.10
a.		Perf. 12½	10.00	4.00
22	A2	50r ultra ('05)	60	40
23	A2	65r sl bl ('98)	60	40
24	A2	75r rose	90	70
25	A2	75r brn & red, *yel* ('05)	1.00	1.50
26	A2	80r violet	75	50
27	A2	100r dk bl, *bl*	75	50
a.		Diagonal half used as 50r on cover		
28	A2	115r org brn, *pink* ('98)	1.25	1.25
29	A2	130r gray brn, *buff* ('98)	1.25	1.25
30	A2	150r lt brn, *buff*	1.25	75
31	A2	180r sl, *pnksh* ('98)	1.25	1.25
32	A2	200r red vio, *pale lil*	2.25	2.25
33	A2	300r bl, *rose*	2.25	2.00
34	A2	500r blk & red, *bl*	2.25	1.75
a.		Perf. 12½	7.00	5.50
		Nos. 13-34 (22)	28.40	21.64

NUMBER CHANGES

in Scott's 1984 Standard Catalogue, Vol. II

No. in 1983 Cat.	No. in 1984 Cat.
ARGENTINA	
1206	1204
1208-1210	1205-1207
1212	1208
1214-1219	1209-1214
1219A	1218
1294	1215
1297	1216
1299	1217
BULGARIA	
2467	C129
2771	deleted
C129-C131	C130-C132
CHINA (People's Republic)	
648a	deleted
650a	deleted
651	651a
651b	651
653a	deleted
1046a	deleted
COLOMBIA	
3a	deleted
CUBA	
177c	deleted
183B	deleted
225b	deleted
DANZIG	
25d	deleted
30d	deleted
DENMARK	
280a	deleted
281a	deleted
285a	deleted
306b	deleted
318a	deleted
318b	deleted
318c	deleted
319a	deleted
417a	deleted
438a	deleted
439b	deleted
439c	deleted
DOMINICAN REPUBLIC	
RA8B-RA8E	265B-265E
RA91	deleted
EGYPT	
C60a	deleted
C61a	deleted
FRANCE Offices in Egypt, Port Said	
35b	deleted

ADDENDA

These stamps were received too late for inclusion in their proper places in the Catalogue. Later issues will be found listed in Scott's Chronicle of New Issues.

ALGERIA

AIR POST STAMP

Storks and Plane AP7

1979, Mar. 24 **Photo.** ***Perf. 11½***

C19	AP7	10d multicolored	5.00	2.50

ANDORRA, FRENCH

Wild Cat—A143

1982, Oct. 9 **Engr.** ***Perf.***

300	A143	1.80fr shown	85	60
301	A143	2.60fr Pine trees	1.25	80

TB Bacillus Centenary A144

St. Thomas Aquinas (1225-1274) A145

1982, Nov. 13

302	A144	2.10fr Koch, lungs	1.10	72

1982, Dec. 4

303	A145	2fr multi	1.00	70

Manned Flight Bicentenary—A146

1983, Feb. 26 **Engr.** ***Perf. 13***

304	A146	2fr multi	1.00	70

AUSTRIA

Landscape Type of 1973

Design: 9s, Asten, Carthinia.

1983, Feb. 9 **Photo. & Engr.** ***Perf. 14***
Size: 23x29mm.

1107	A395	9s red	1.35	90

25th Anniv. of Austrian Airlines—A632

1983, Mar. 31 **Photo.** ***Perf. 13½x14***

1236	A632	6s multi	90	60

Work Inspection Centenary—A633

1983, Apr. 8 **Photo.** ***Perf. 13½***

1237	A633	4s multi	60	40

Gottweig Monastery, 900th Anniv. A635

7th World Pacemakers' Symposium A636

1983, Apr. 29 **Photo. & Engr.** ***Perf. 13½***

1239	A635	3s multi	45	30

1983, Apr. 29 **Photo.** ***Perf. 14x13½***

1240	A636	4s multi	60	40

BELGIUM

SEMI-POSTAL STAMPS

50th Anniv. of Catholic Charities—SP465

1983, Jan. 22 **Photo.** ***Perf. 11½***

B1022	SP465	10 +2fr multi	60	60

Mountain Climbing—SP466

1983, Mar. 7 **Photo.** ***Perf.***

B1023	SP466	12 +3fr shown	1.05	1.05
B1024	SP466	20 +5fr Hiking	1.75	1.75

Surtax was for Red Cross.

BULGARIA

AIR POST STAMPS

Clock Tower, Byalla Cherkva AP60

Clock Towers: 23s, Botevgrad. 25s, Pazardgick. 35s, Grabovo. 53s, Tryavna.

1979, June 5 **Litho.** ***Perf. 12x12½***

C133	AP60	13s multicolored	22	10
C134	"	23s "	40	18
C135	"	25s "	45	20
C136	"	35s "	60	28
C137	"	53s "	95	45

CENTRAL AFRICA

UN Decade for African Transportation and Communication, 1978-88—A160

1983, Jan. 31 **Litho.** ***Perf. 13½x13***

572	A160	5fr Modes of communication	4	3
573	A160	60fr like 5fr	50	25
574	A160	120fr Map, jet	1.00	50
575	A160	175fr like 120fr	1.60	80

CHINA

AIR POST STAMPS

Presidental Palace and Tzu-Ch'iang Squadron—AP15

1980, June 18 **Litho.** ***Perf. 13½***

C81	AP15	$5 *shown*	25	20
C82	AP15	$7 *China Airlines jet*	35	32
C83	AP15	$12 *China flag, jet*	60	50

CONGO REPUBLIC

SEMI-POSTAL STAMPS

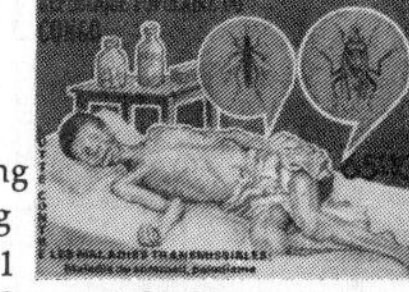

Boy Suffering from Sleeping Sickness—SP1

Fight Against Communicable Diseases; 40fr+5fr, Examination, treatment (vert.).

1981, June 6 **Litho.** ***Perf. 13***

B5	SP1	40 + 5fr multi	36	18
B6	SP1	65 + 10fr multi	60	30

IYD Type of 1981

1981, June 29 ***Perf. 12½***

B7	A192	75 + 5fr multi	65	32

DENMARK

SEMI-POSTAL STAMPS

Intl. Year of the Disabled—SP36

1981, Sept. 10 **Engr.** ***Perf. 12½x13***

B61	SP36	2k +20o dk bl	50	50

Stem and Broken Line—SP37

1982, May 3 **Engr.** ***Perf. 13***

B62	SP37	2k +40o dl red	75	75

Surtax was for Danish Multiple Sclerosis Society.

Nurse with Patient—SP38

1983, Jan. 27 **Engr.** ***Perf.***

B63	SP38	2k +40o multi	75	75

EGYPT

SEMI-POSTAL STAMP

Afghan Solidarity—SP33

Wmk. 342

1981, July 15 **Photo.** *Perf. 11½*

B48	SP33	20m + 10m multi	15	15

ETHIOPIA

25th Anniv. of Economic Commission for Africa—A218

1983, Apr. 29 **Photo.** *Perf. 14*

1065	A218	80c multi	80	80
1066	A218	1b multi	1.00	1.00

FINLAND

Hame Castle Type of 1982

Coil Stamp

1982, Sept. 1 **Engr.** *Perf. 11½ Vert.*

642	A316	90p brn red	45	30

FRANCE

POSTAGE DUE STAMPS

Ampedus Cinnabarinus—D8

1982, Jan. 4 **Engr.** *Perf. 13*

J106	D8	10c shown	5	3
J107	D8	20c Dorcadion fuliginator	5	3
J108	D8	50c Pyrochroa coccinea	15	8
J109	D8	1fr Scarites laevigatus	30	10
J110	D8	2fr Trichius gallicus	60	15
J111	D8	4fr Apoderus coryli	1.20	30

1983, Jan. 3 **Engr.** *Perf. 13*

J112	D8	30c Leptura cordigera	10	3
J113	D8	40c Paederus littoralis	12	5
J114	D8	3fr Adalia alpina	90	20
J115	D8	5fr Trichodes alvearius	1.50	40

OFFICIAL STAMPS

For the Council of Europe.

New Council Headquarters, Strasbourg—O3

1981, Nov. 21 **Engr.**

1027	O3	1.40fr multi	45	45
1028	O3	1.60fr multi	50	50
1029	O3	2.30fr multi	70	70

1982, Nov. 13 **Engr.**

1030	O3	1.80fr multi	55	55
1031	O3	2.60fr multi	80	80

For the United Nations Educational, Scientific and Cultural Organization

Fort St. Elmo, Malta—O6

Designs: 1.40fr, Building, Fez, Morocco (vert.). 1.60fr, Seated deity, Sukhotai, Thailand (vert.).

1981, Dec. 12

2024	O6	1.40fr multi	45	45
2025	O6	1.60fr multi	50	50
2026	O6	2.30fr multi	70	70

Hue, Vietnam—O7

1982, Oct. 23 **Engr.**

2027	O7	1.80fr shown	55	55
2028	O7	2.60fr St. Michael Church ruins, Brazil	80	80

BULGARIA

Balloon Over Plovdiv AP57a

1977, Sept. 3

C129	AP57a	25s yel, brn & red	45	30

INDEX and IDENTIFIER

See also Addenda and For the Record

NUMERICAL INDEX OF WATERMARKS

(VOL. II)

Wmk.	Country	Page*
a-g	Chile	463
84-90	Argentina	94-98
91	Austria	140
	Bosnia and Herzegovina	261
96	Belgium	188
97-101	Brazil	271-273
103	China	484
104-105	Cuba	673-674
106	Cuba	667
107	Czechoslovakia	694
108-110	Danzig	761-763
111-114	Danish West Indies	760-761
	Denmark	766-767
115-116	Dominican Republic	785, 787
116	Colombia	591
117	Ecuador	817
118-120	Egypt	850-851
121	Finland	920
122-124	French Congo	1017
125	Albania	57
	Cameroun	400
	Caroline Islands	428
	Danzig	763
127	Colombia	591
140	Eritrea	891
	Ethiopia	913
145	Bulgaria	326
168	Bulgaria	323
	Finland	919
171	Armenia	137
	Far Eastern Republic	913
193	Brazil	273
194	Colombia	578
195	Egypt	851
205	Argentina	99
206	Brazil	273
207	Estonia	896
208	Finland	920
215	Chile	465
	Costa Rica	653
218	Brazil	273
220	Albania	32
221-222	Brazil	274
229	Colombia	578
	Costa Rica	652
	Cuba	677
232	Angola	87
233	Ecaudor	848
236	Brazil	275
237	Danzig	479
245	Brazil	275
249	Brazil	276
255	Colombia	579
256	Brazil	277
261	China	489
263	Slovakia	745
264	Brazil	277
267-268	Brazil	279
270-271	Brazil	319
273	Finland	921
275	Bulgaria	329
278	Croatia	671
281	Brazil	279
	China	497
282	Ethiopia	901
287	Argentina	103
288	Argentina	100
315	Egypt	856
318	Egypt	856
321	Cuba	684
323	China	498
328	Egypt	858
331	Colombia	584
340	Ecuador	839
341	Czechoslovakia	710
342	Egypt	860
346	Colombia	586
363	Finland	927
365	Argentina	112
367	Ecuador	829
368	China	510
370	China	510

*Page indicates where illustration may be found.

Scott Catalogue Philatelic Marketplace

2

This "Yellow Pages" section of your Scott Catalogue contains advertisements to help you find what you need, when you need it .... conveniently.

APPROVALS

100 MINT GRENADA $1.00

Incredibly beautiful pictorial collection of 100 different unused Grenada sent for just $1.00 to introduce our delightful approvals. A truly great value from the popular British West Indies. Write today.

D.M. Darling & Co. P.O. Box 1157 Rockville, MD 20850

AUCTIONS

barry rieger, ltd. *prop. noun:* 1.Reliable, courteous service 2. Public auctions of the highest caliber held on a regular basis 3. Catalogs sent free upon request 4. A knowledgeable staff ready to assist you should you wish to sell your collection outright or through our auction. 5. Consignors given liberal advances for larger holdings.

Barry J. Rieger, Ltd. The very definition of a fine auction house.

Barry J. Rieger, Ltd.

Auctioneers

312-693-3370 5725 N.E. River Rd. Chicago, IL 60631

JACQUES C. SCHIFF, JR., INC
195 Main Street, Ridgefield Park, NJ 07660
U.S., Worldwide Stamps & Postal History
A brochure of our services is available

Send For Your Free Catalog

Quality Auctions

Quality Auctions, Ltd.

Box 3116, Middletown, N.Y. 10940
Telephone: (914) 343-2174

Consign all or part of your collection to a *Quality* auction and you'll receive professional service and . . . .

$ the Highest Realization

SOUTHEASTERN STAMP CO. INC.
See Display Ad in Vol. I & US Specialized
1720 Harrison St., Suite 1815, Hollywood, Fl 33020

AUSTRIA

DR. MARTERBAUER & CO. (ASDA, APS)
Ask for free list; want lists welcome
Lobkowitzplatz 1, A 1010 Vienna, Austria

BUYING & SELLING

MICHAEL ROGERS

- MEMBER: ASDA, APS, GPS, BIA, AAMS
- U.S. & Foreign stamps and covers
- Our Specialties; U.S., European, British and Zeppelin Flights
- Each price list sent for 40¢ postage.

ALWAYS BUYING

The Winter Park Stamp & Coin Shop	Florida Stamp & Coin Co. Inc.
340 Park Avenue, North	2507-A E. Colonial Dr.
Winter Park, Florida 32789	Orlando, Florida 32803
(305) 628-1120	(305) 894-3021

METRO STAMP CO. INC.
See Our Display Ad in This Section
75-20 Metropolitan Ave., Middle Village, NY 11379

EDWARD D. YOUNGER CO.
See Our Display Ad in Color Section
222 Mamaroneck Ave., White Plains, NY 10605

CZECHOSLOVAKIA

SVATIK.
Offer 1-Send $10 for $60 worth of Czech stamps.
Offer 2-Send $25 for $100 worth of choice used Czech stamps.
Offer 3-Send $35 for $100 worth of choice Czech mint stamps.
Include $3 for shipping—want list filled.
SVATIK
PO Box 53, Ingleside, IL 60041
312-866-3435 office
312-587-5609 home

COVERS

WE BUY W-EUROPE before 1960
Iradj Zarnegin, P.O. Box 4650
Leemen Str. 46, 4051 Basle Switzerland.
Phone 22.78.49

NEW ISSUES

PHILATELIC SERVICES

JAMES H. CRUM (APS, ASDA, ANS) (Est. 1929)
Thousands of Stamps plus Personal Helpful Advice
2720 E. Gage Ave., Huntington Park, CA 90255 213-588-4467

PHILATELIC SOCIETIES

AMERICAN PHILATELIC SOCIETY
America's foremost stamp collector's society
P.O. Box 8000, State College, PA 16801

PRINTING

COSMOS PRESS
"Typesetting, Printing, Binding, Mailing"
141 East 25th Street, N.Y.C., NY 10010

SPECIAL OFFERS

American Stamp Dealers' Assoc., Inc.
5 Dakota Dr., Suite 102
Lake Success, N.Y. 11042
(516) 775-3600
It took strategy to make the right moves in creating a code, that assures you of professional ethics!
ASDA DEALERS OFFER...
Honesty
Integrity
Dedication
Expertise
Reliability
Hobby Builders
ASDA
NOW IT'S YOUR MOVE!
Look for the ASDA symbol before you buy or sell!

SUBWAY SELLS LINDNER-T HINGELESS ALBUMS AT DISCOUNT PRICES

The LINDNER*T album houses your stamps in a special glass-clear foil which will not scratch or dull ... even with continued use. Now your stamps will be completely protected — inside a sleeve — not on top of the page. And you'll never need to buy mounts again. With the unique LINDNER*T sleeve you can see both sides of your stamps. Inserting the stamps is simple ... just position them and forget them. They won't slide. They always lie flat. And they are always safe from damage. The new LINDNER*T system is the most modern and simple to use, hingeless country album of the world. • Stamps can be inserted and removed, without the danger of damaging them • The entire stamp, including the top perforation, is fully protected • Additional stamps may be kept in the acetate pockets • The stamps will never slide from their places • Stamps can be examined from the back — without removing the stamps from the album • Matching hingeless blank pages are available • Full 10" x 12" page size.

THE SYMBOL OF QUALITY IN PHILATELY

LINDNER-T COUNTRY-ALBUMS

Sold PAGES ONLY by country and sections. Binders sold separately. 1982 Supplements included. Write for 1982 Supplement List.

	List	Sale
EUROPE		
Andorra (Fr.)		
1931-1971	43.70	34.95
1972-1982	23.00	18.40
Andorra (Sp.)		
1928-1982	28.70	22.95
Argentina		
1970-1977	51.30	41.05
1978-1982	53.90	43.15
Austria		
1850-1918	41.80	33.45
1918-1921	22.80	18.25
1922-1937	49.40	39.50
1938-1945	36.10	28.90
1945-1967	93.10	74.50
1968-1974	51.30	41.05
1975-1982	51.60	41.30
Lombardy	39.90	31.90
Bosnia-Her	22.80	18.25
Azores	8.95	7.15
Belgium		
1849-1939	89.30	71.45
1940-1944	41.80	33.45
1944-1956	64.60	51.70
1957-1964	62.70	50.15
1965-1971	60.80	48.65
1972-1980	77.80	62.30
1982	18.95	15.15
Railways	53.20	42.55
Brazil		
1967-1974	76.00	60.80
1975-1981	74.10	59.30
1982	—	16.95
Bulgaria		
1971-1975	96.90	77.50
1976-1979	96.90	77.50
1980-1982	75.50	60.40
Czechoslovakia		
1965-1967	51.30	41.05
1968-1971	60.80	48.65
1972-1979	108.30	86.60
1980-1982	54.60	43.70
Denmark		
1851-1959	66.50	53.20
1960-1971	28.50	22.80
1972-1982	42.00	33.60
Egypt		
1971-1981	76.00	60.80
1982	—	8.95
Faroe Is.	12.95	10.35
Mini Shts	105.40	84.30
Finland		
1856-1962	77.90	62.30
1963-1981	57.00	45.60
1982	—	6.95
France		
1849-1940	89.30	71.45
1940-1944	32.30	25.85
1945-1956	91.20	72.95
1960-1971	81.70	65.35
1972-1976	45.60	36.50
1977-1982	63.30	50.65
French Antarctic		
1948-1981	34.40	27.55
French Polynesia		
1958-1982	76.40	61.15

T-BLANK-SYSTEM

The blank page system is a custom-made format. No measuring; no cutting, no messy glueing.

The blank system is available in 60 different formats. The system allows individual layouts of singles, blocks, souvenir sheets, cover or combinations.

Write for your list of all 60 formats.

	List	Sale
30 most popular pages	44.00	35.20
One each of all 60 sizes	81.00	64.80
Individual pages	1.70 ea.	1.60
(Specify Sizes)	10 or more ea.	$1.45
Black or White Backing	5.80	4.65

BINDERS AND DUSTCASES

BINDER CAPACITIES T-Pages (55-60)
Blank Pages (80-90) Omnia Pages (40)
Cover Pages (55)

All binders are 18 ring mechanism and come complete with matching fly leaves and page lifters.

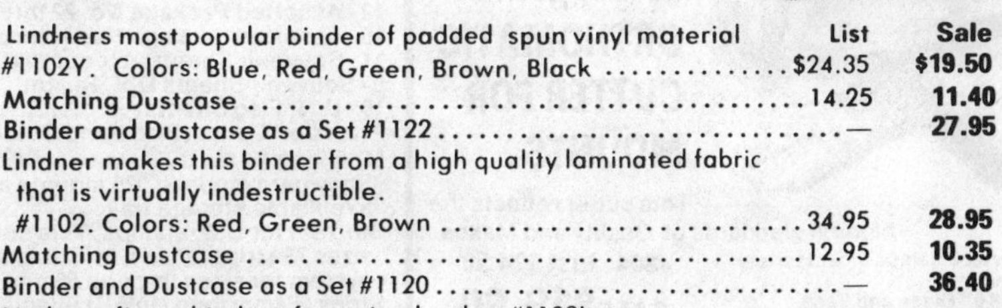

	List	Sale
Lindners most popular binder of padded spun vinyl material #1102Y. Colors: Blue, Red, Green, Brown, Black	$24.35	$19.50
Matching Dustcase	14.25	11.40
Binder and Dustcase as a Set #1122	—	27.95
Lindner makes this binder from a high quality laminated fabric that is virtually indestructible. #1102. Colors: Red, Green, Brown	34.95	28.95
Matching Dustcase	12.95	10.35
Binder and Dustcase as a Set #1120	—	36.40
Lindners finest binder of genuine leather #1102L. Colors: Wine, Green, Blue, Black, Tan.	59.95	47.95
Matching Dustcase	12.95	10.35
Binder and Dustcase as a Set #1121	—	55.50

SHIPPING CHARGES: Orders up to $20 add $1.20 (in Canada add $1.60). Orders over $20, add 6%. NY residents add tax. VISA or Master Card welcome.

For easy ordering CALL TOLL FREE: 1 (800) 221-9960
Except NY Call: 212-227-8637 CALL TODAY!
111 Nassau St., Dept. SV2, New York, NY 10038

SUBWAY SELLS SHOWGARD MOUNTS AT DISCOUNT PRICES

• Showgard mounts are available in cut style of strip form • Showgard mounts design prevents stamps from falling out but permits the full flow of air • The insertion and removal system is simple and efficient • Showgard foil does not shrink or discolor, and is 100% waterproof.

1. Turn stamp over direction of arrow.

2. Place stamp into the free half as far as it will go.

3. Allow mount to flap back into place. The stamp is now securely centered but can be removed without damage to stamp or mount.

NOTE: SHOWGARD mounts are pre-gummed on the entire back. Moisten top half lightly. The bottom half remains free. Available in dark black or all clear, please specify.
Strips 215mm long (8½'') - Sizes 20-33, 22 strips per pkg., 36-61, 15 strips per package.

Description	Size	Description	Size	Description	Size
U.S. Mini's	20mm	U.S. Jamestown	30mm	U.S. Hatteras	44mm
Narrow Airs	22mm	Semi Jumbos	31mm	Blocks of 4	48mm
Early U.S. Can	24mm	U.S. Clark, Misc.	33mm	Comm. Blks.	50mm
U.S. Commems	25mm	Foreign Issues	36mm	Plain Blks. of 4	52mm
U.S. Fam. Amer.	27mm	Foreign Issues	39mm	Plate Blks. of 6	57mm
Foreign Issues	28mm	U.S. Comm	41mm	Souvenir Sheets	61mm

LIST $2.75 PER PKG **SALE $2.20** PER PKG, EA. SIZE

STRIPS 240mm LONG (9¾'')
SIZES 63-89, 10 STRIPS PER PKG - 100, 120, 7 STRIPS PER PKG

Overrun Flag Blks	63mm	Souvenir Shts.	80mm	Israel Tab Blks.	84mm
Israel Pl. Blks.	66mm	U.N. Chagall SS	82mm	U.N. IB-6	89mm
Souvenir Shts.	68mm	Miniature Shts.	120mm	U.N. IB-6	100mm
U.N. IB-4	74mm				

LIST $3.25 PER PKG **SALE $2.60** PER PKG, EA. SIZE

STRIPS 264mm LONG (10½'') - 10 STRIPS PER PKG (Except 265/231)

		List	Sale			List	Sale
Moon Landing P.B.	70mm	$4.75	**$3.80**	Gravure Strip of 20	111mm	5.75	**$4.60**
Brit. Souv. Sheet	91mm	4.75	**3.80**	UPU Plate Bl.	127mm	6.95	**5.55**
Plate Strip of 20	105mm	4.75	**3.80**	U.N. Mini Sheets	137mm	7.50	**6.00**
Same-Wide Selvage	107mm	4.75	**3.80**	Apollo Soyuz P.B.	158mm	8.25	**6.60**

5-FULL PANES COMMEM. & REG. ISSUE.....265/231 LIST $7.25 **SALE 5.80**

STRIPS 260mm LONG (10¼'') - 10 STRIPS PER PKG

Postal People Strip of 10	260/40	Gravure-Reg. Issue - Strip 20	260/59
13c Eagle-Plate - Strip of 20	260/55		

LIST $3.25 PER PKG **SALE $2.60** PER PKG, EA. SIZE

PLATE BLOCKS AND COVERS, PRE-CUT

25 - Reg. Issue Plate Blocks	57/55	10 - Jumbo Plate Blocks	127.70
20 - Rotary Press Comm. Pl. Blks.	106/55	10 - First Day Covers	165/94
20 - Giori Press. Comm. Pl. Blks.	105/57		

LIST $2.25 PER PKG **SALE $1.80** PER PKG, EA. SIZE

PRE-CUT SIZES FOR SINGLES 40 PIECES PER PKG

Description	Size	#	Description	Size	#	Description	Size	#
U.S. Jumbo	50/31	C	Semi Jumbo	41/31	AH	Famous Amer	25/27	T
Same — Vertical	31/50	CV	U.S. Reg. Issues	22/25	E	United Nations	33/27	V
U.S. Commem.	40/25	J	Same — Horiz.	25/22	EH	United Nations	40/27	N
Same — Vertical	25/40	JV						

LIST $1.25 PER PKG **SALE $1.00** PER PKG, EA. SIZE

MISCELLANEOUS ASSORTMENT PACKS

		List	Sale
12 - Assorted Package No. 22 thru No. 41	MPK	$2.50	**$2.00**
15 - Assorted Package No. 76 thru No. 171 (Black Only)	MPK2	11.50	**9.20**
11 - Souvenir Sheets, except 204/153	AB	2.25	**1.80**
5 - Souvenir Sheets U.S. Bicent.	204/153	3.50	**2.80**
10 - U.N. Flag Sheets	187/144	6.50	**5.20**
Precision Cutter (Blade and Guide)	601	6.50	**5.20**

Mounting kit for U.S. stamps. Contains 8 packets of pre-cut Showgard mounts, 320 mounts in the most used U.S. sizes in a refillable storage tray .... U.S. 2 List $9.90 **SALE $7.90**

Strip set for U.S. stamps. This set contains the 15 most used sizes 75 strips, all in a refillable storage tray and index system for sizes through 55mm .... U.S. 3 List $15.95 **SALE $12.75**

Strips 264mm long (10½'') Special Sizes from MPK-11 Pkg. (Black Only) 76, 109, 115, 117, 121, 131, 135, 139, 143mm .... ea. size 10 - $8.00, 25 - $16.00
147, 151, 163, 167, 171mm .... ea. size 10 - $10.00, 25 - $20.00

SHOWGARD AT HOME STORAGE SYSTEM

keeps your accessories accessible! This is the modular SHOWGARD AT HOME STORAGE SYSTEM with 2 Basic Units (No. 790) on top of the stacking 3 drawer set (No. 793). Introducing a unique way to organize your philatelic accessories.

The basic unit #790 fits snugly on the stacking drawer set #793 with a gliding interlock connection.
New "Showgard At Home" desk top organizer for Showgard mounts and other philatelic accessories. The unit has an organizing table, four sectional dividers, a mount measuring gauge, and a dust cover.
#790 List $13.95 .... **$11.15**
AT HOME drawers. Three deep drawers provide ample storage for stamp collectors essentials like tongs, magnifiers, guillotines, gauges, and even 8½'' x 11'' album pages.
#793 List $14.95 .... **$11.95**

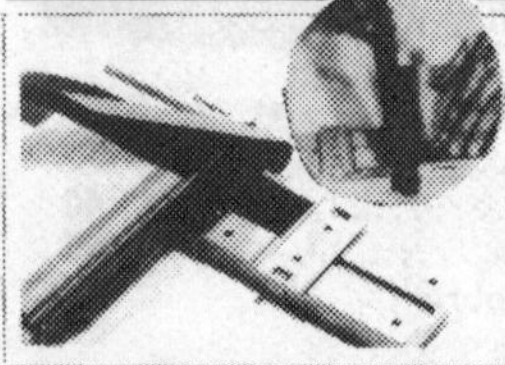

SHOWGARD ORTHOMATIC CUTTER FOR MOUNTS

This cutter reflects the highest standards of Quality and Makes.

- Perfect stamps mounts every time
- Full 6'' Blade and Base
- Extension Gauge for Repeating Sizes
- Constant Border
- Cutting Blade and Plate of Finest Solingen Steel

#604 List $24.50
SALE $19.60

Excal Mini Cutter
#602 List $12.95
SALE $10.35

SHIPPING CHARGES:

Orders up to $20 add $1.20 (in Canada add $1.60).
Orders over $20, add 6%. NY residents add tax.
VISA or Master Card welcome.

For easy ordering CALL TOLL FREE: 1 (800) 221-9960
Except NY Call: 212-227-8637 CALL TODAY!
111 Nassau St., Dept. SV2, New York, NY 10038

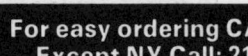

SUBWAY SELLS HAGNER STOCK SHEETS AT DISCOUNT PRICES

HAGNER STOCK SHEETS

All 1st Quality, No 2nds!
ONE AND TWO SIDED STOCK SHEETS FITS ALL STANDARD 3-RING, 4-RING BINDERS

Private collectors and government philatelic departments throughout the world have found the Hagner stock sheets the most functional and the safest method of preserving or displaying stamps and stamp collections. No hinges ... no mounts ... no time wasted cutting and measuring ... no sticking. The Hagner system eliminates all such problems, yet brings total page protection for your stamps at reasonable cost. Hagner stock sheets are available for containing any size stamps or blocks, singles, souvenir sheets or FDCs all in one album! The heavy, glass-clear spring action polyester film pockets provide an instant protection in every respect. No interleaving required. Just lift the edges, bend the strip backwards, place the stamps in the required position and let snap back the polyester film pocket. Guaranteed no falling out, no sliding or shifting! Specify # rows when ordering.

Black or white pockets on one side.
List $1.00 ea. .... **Sale 10 for $7.95 100 for $73.50**
2-sided black only
List $1.50 each .... **Sale 6 for $7.95 100 for $109.25**

CHECK THIS HANDY ORDER FORM

	Enter Quantity		
	Black One Side	White One Side	Black Two Sides
1 Row			
2 Rows			
3 Rows			
3 Rows-Diff.			
4 Rows			
5 Rows			
6 Rows			
7 Rows			
8 Rows			

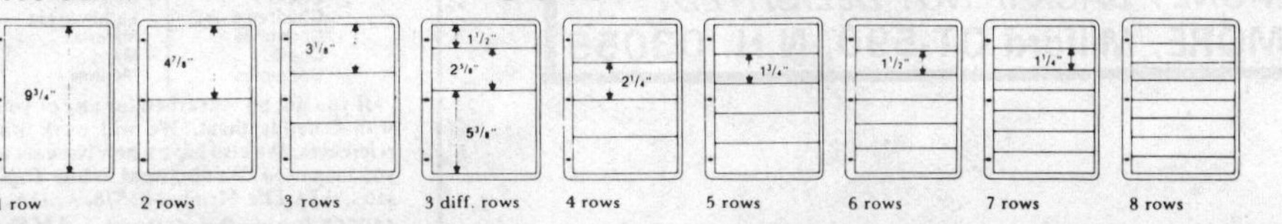

Imported from Germany. Made of finest quality material, quality so high they look handmade. Better binding than comparably priced stockbooks.

GLASSINE POCKETS
White Pages

	List	Sale
K2/8 16-7"x9" Pgs	$7.95	**$6.35**
K4/8 16-9"x12" Pgs	9.95	**7.95**
K4/16 32-9"x12" Pgs	15.95	**12.75**
K4/24 48-9"x12" Pgs	24.95	**19.95**
KT4/32 64-9"x12" Pgs with Leatherette Cover	38.75	**31.00**

ACETATE POCKETS
Black Pages

	List	Sale
KB4/8 16-9"x12" Pgs	$13.25	**$10.60**
KB4/16 32-9"x12" Pgs	21.95	**17.55**
KB4/24 48-9"x12" Pgs	38.50	**30.80**

ACETATE POCKETS
Deluxe Covers, Acetate Interleaving Black pages

	List	Sale
KZBO/8 16-7¼"x9½" Pgs	$13.00	**$10.40**
KZB4/8 16-9"x12" Pgs	18.00	**14.40**
KZB4/16 32-9"x12" Pgs	36.50	**29.20**
KB3D 32-9"x12" Pgs with 5 small, 2 lg. strips on Each Page	29.95	**23.95**
KB-BAZ 32-9"x12" Pgs 4 Pockets on Each page for Blocks	39.95	**31.95**

MORLEY-BRIGHT WATERMARK DETECTOR

The only Watermark Detector that can even find the watermark of a stamp on cover, and in just a few easy steps. Detects watermarks without eyestrain. No chemicals ever come into contact with your valuable stamps. Designed by a philatelist to give maximum efficiency. Provides the opportunity to make a permanent printed copy of the watermark.

1 .... **List 39.95 Sale $29.95**
REFILL SACHET Thick Paste R1 or Thin R2 .... **$4.00**

SHIPPING CHARGES: Orders up to $20 add $1.20 (in Canada add $1.60). Orders over $20, add 6%. NY residents add tax. VISA or Master Card welcome.

for easy ordering CALL TOLL FREE 1 (800) 221-9960
Except NY Call: 212-227-8637 CALL TODAY!
111 Nassau St., Dept. SV2 New York, NY 10038

AMERICA'S 1 DISCOUNT DEALER
Save On Your Stamps & Stamp Supplies

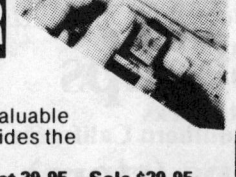